The
Wadsworth
Anthology
of

drama

FIFTH EDITION

The Wadsworth Anthology of

drama

W. B. WORTHEN
University of California, Berkeley

THOMSON
WADSWORTH

Australia • Brazil • Canada • Mexico • Singapore • Spain • United Kingdom • United States

THOMSON
™
WADSWORTH

The Wadsworth Anthology of Drama
Fifth Edition
W. B. Worthen

Publisher: *Michael Rosenberg*
Acquisitions Editor: *Aron Keesbury*
Development Editor: *Mary Beth Walden*
Editorial Assistant: *Cheryl Forman*
Technology Project Manager: *Tim Smith*
Managing Marketing Manager: *Mandee Eckersley*
Marketing Assistant: *Dawn Giovanniello*
Associate Marketing Communications Manager: *Patrick Rooney*
Senior Project Manager, Editorial Production: *Samantha Ross*
Senior Art Director: *Bruce Bond*

Senior Print Buyer: *Mary Beth Hennebury*
Senior Permissions Editor: *Isabel Alves*
Permissions Editor: *Marcy Lunetta*
Production Service/Compositor: *Graphic World Inc.*
Photo Manager: *Sheri Blaney*
Photo Researcher: *Lili Weiner*
Cover Designer: *Lucille Tenazas*
Cover Printer: *Coral Graphics*
Printer: *QuebecorWorld-Taunton*
Cover Art: © *Mike Powell/Getty Images*

Printed in the United States of America
2 3 4 5 6 7 09 08 07 06

Library of Congress Control Number: 2005935618

ISBN 1-4130-1767-3

Thomson Higher Education
25 Thomson Place
Boston, MA 02210-1202
USA

For more information about our products, contact us at:
Thomson Learning Academic Resource Center
1-800-423-0563

For permission to use material from this text or product, submit a request online at **http://www.thomsonrights.com**. Any additional questions about permissions can be submitted by e-mail to **thomsonrights@thomson.com**.

Contents

UNIT IV

Early Modern Europe 371

UNIT V

Modern Europe 523

UNIT VI

The United States   969

UNIT VII

World Stages 1313

Preface

Studying drama is more than reading plays. It requires us to study the theaters where the plays were produced, the cultures that framed those theaters, and the critical and performance history that has framed the meanings of drama over time. *The Wadsworth Anthology of Drama* presents drama in these two important contexts: in the play's original theater and the society that sustained it, and in *our* culture, where the play continues to live both as literature and as theatrical performance.

The Wadsworth Anthology of Drama offers a comprehensive collection of classic and contemporary plays from Europe, the Americas, Africa, and Asia. Designed to be used in a variety of drama and theater courses, in general surveys of drama and theater, in courses on tragedy and/or comedy, or in classes on modern theater, *The Wadsworth Anthology of Drama* offers an unusually comprehensive collection of classic theater and an unrivaled selection of contemporary drama drawn from around the world.

The fifth edition of *The Wadsworth Anthology of Drama* builds on the strengths and success of previous editions. It is divided into seven units, each focused on a significant period in the history of drama and theater: Athens in the fifth century BCE (six plays); feudal Japan (two plays); England in the late Middle Ages and Renaissance (five plays); England, France, Spain, and colonial Mexico in the seventeenth and eighteenth centuries (five plays); Europe from 1850 through the twentieth century (fourteen plays); the United States (thirteen plays); and contemporary stages around the world (eleven plays). As in previous editions, each unit of the fifth edition begins with an extensive introduction, placing drama in the context of a specific historical era and using illustrations of theater design to develop a precise sense of stage practice. The unit introductions end with a section, "Reading the Material Theater," which presents original documents from the history of the theater for students' consideration. Each play is accompanied by a brief biography of the playwright and a short introduction to the play. Each unit concludes with a selection of critical readings organized by the headings "Critical Contexts" and "Critical Perspectives." *The Wadsworth Anthology of Drama* emphasizes the diversity of drama and theater throughout history, both in its selection of plays and essays and in the issues and ideas raised for discussion as well.

The fifth edition of *The Wadsworth Anthology of Drama* has been extensively revised and while it continues to be a comprehensive text, it has been updated to be the most topical and useful volume for contemporary students of dramatic literature and of theater history. The fifth edition retains plays by Aeschylus, Sophocles, Euripides, Aristophanes, Marlowe, Shakespeare, Calderón, Molière, Racine, Ibsen, Chekhov, Shaw, Pirandello, Brecht, Beckett, Pinter, Churchill, Boucicault, Glaspell, O'Neill, Baraka/Jones, Shepard, Wilson, Hwang, Kushner, Soyinka, Friel, and Highway. In addition, the text offers several distinctive features:

- A revision of the last unit, "World Stages," focusing on postcolonial drama and theater, which now includes a new play from Australia (Louis Nowra's *The Golden Age*), Athol Fugard's *"Master Harold" . . . and the boys,* Václav Havel's *Temptation,* and Vassily Sigarev's *Black Milk,* among plays from China, India, Martinique, Argentina, Nigeria, Northern Ireland, South Africa, and Canada
- Streamlined collection of critical essays in each unit
- A greater emphasis on the history of theatrical production and contemporary production practices
- A large selection of plays by women (ten)
- A large selection of comedies (eleven)

- Expanded treatment of the drama of Eastern Europe, including a play by Václav Havel, and by the brilliant Russian playwright Vassily Sigarev
- An example of Britain's "New Brutalism," Sarah Kane's *Blasted*
- David Hare's brilliant dramatization of the events leading up to the Unites States' invasion of Iraq, *Stuff Happens*
- A significant commitment to the unit on American drama, which continues to include a nineteenth-century melodrama—Boucicault's *Octoroon,* Arthur Miller's *Death of a Salesman,* and other cornerstones of the American stage
- Inclusion of Luis Valdez's masterwork, *Zoot Suit,* to accompany plays from Latin America (Gambaro's *Information for Foreigners*), a Spanish Golden Age classic (Calderón's *Life Is a Dream*) and a brilliant play from colonial Mexico, Sor Juana's *loa* to *The Divine Narcissus*
- A significant focus on "race" in American theater, including plays by Amiri Baraka/LeRoi Jones (*Dutchman*), Luis Valdez (*Zoot Suit*), August Wilson (*Fences*), David Henry Hwang (*M. Butterfly*), Anna Deavere Smith (*Fires in the Mirror*), and Suzan-Lori Parks's Pulitzer Prize-winning play *Topdog/Underdog*
- A significant expansion of the unit on modern European theater, to include a greater emphasis on women's playwriting throughout the period (Minna Canth's *Anna-Liisa,* Caryl Churchill's *Cloud Nine,* and Sarah Kane's *Blasted*)
- First Nations Native playwright Tomson Highway's *Dry Lips Oughta Move to Kapuskasing*
- "Aside" sections in each unit—an opening essay devoted to topics of special importance: Roman drama and theater, Sanskrit drama and theater, the masque, the new Shakespeare's Globe Theatre in London, *commedia dell' arte,* melodrama, the Federal Theater Project, performance art, and intercultural performance
- Two student essays in the online "Writing about Drama and Theater" section, focusing on different approaches to Caryl Churchill's *Cloud Nine*

The fifth edition retains many of the critical essays of the fourth edition, such as selections by Aristotle, Nietzsche, Sue-Ellen Case, Zeami, Sir Philip Sidney, John Dryden, Katharine Eisaman Maus, Émile Zola, Martin Esslin, Fredric Jameson, Bertolt Brecht, Antonin Artaud, Arthur Miller, Amiri Baraka/LeRoi Jones, Frantz Fanon, Homi Bhabha, and Helen Gilbert and Joanne Tompkins, adding an important essay from Augusto Boal's *Theater of the Oppressed.* The fifth edition retains other important essays as well, including Graham Ley on the relationship between Aristotle, Bharatamuni, and Zeami; Phyllis Rackin on "misogyny" in early modern culture and contemporary scholarship; Una Chaudhuri on the geography of modern drama; and the debate between August Wilson and Robert Brustein on race in American theater. *The Wadsworth Anthology of Drama* continues its effort to enable students and teachers to explore the issues of representation in the theater and the ways that culture shapes identity, gender and sexuality, power, and race.

The Wadsworth Anthology of Drama is designed for both beginning and advanced students. An introduction to writing about drama and theater furnishes beginning students with an outline of the formal and rhetorical practices used in writing about plays; this essay complements the documentary essays on "Reading the Material Theater" in each unit. The book also includes a useful glossary of dramatic, theatrical, and literary terms and an extensive bibliography of drama, of theater history, and of works about plays and playwrights is available online. *The Wadsworth Anthology of Drama* provides a wide-ranging survey of drama and theater, one that presents both traditional issues and the materials to interrogate those traditions.

Acknowledgments

This edition of *The Wadsworth Anthology of Drama* has faced many unique challenges, and I am grateful to the editorial staff of Thomson Wadsworth for bringing this fifth edition to fruition. I'm especially grateful to Michael Rosenberg, Aron Keesbury, and Mary Beth

Walden for their involvement in the project, and to Samantha Ross, Lili Weiner, Sheri Blaney, Marcy Lunetta, and Mike Ederer.

I would also like to thank the many instructors and scholars who commented on the fourth edition, suggesting ways we might improve this edition:

Gwendolyn Alker, *New York University*
Joe Allen, *Dutchess Community College*
Lisa Bernd, *Case Western Reserve University*
Cynthia Bowers, *Kennesaw State University*
Barry Brunetti, *DePaul University*
Paul Buczkowski, *Eastern Michigan University*
Lon Bumgarner, *University of North Carolina–Charlotte*
Steven Burch, *University of Alabama*
Sydney Chalfa, *Macon State College*
David Charles, *Rollins College*
Una Chaudhuri, *New York University*
Greg A. Chavez, *DePaul University*
Teresa Choate, *Kean University*
Gail Ciociola, *Villanova University*
Linda Nell Cooper, *Liberty University*
Michael Cooper, *Texarkana College*
Mark Cosdon, *Allegheny College*
Sergio Costola, *Southwestern University*
Thomas DeFrantz, *Massachusetts Institute of Technology*
Kathleen Dimmick, *Bennington College*
Bill Dynes, *University of Indianapolis*
Jay Edelnant, *University of Northern Iowa*
D. Layne Ehlers, *Bacone College*
Brenda Eppley, *Harrisburg Area Community College*
David S. Escoffery, *Southwest Missouri State University*
Anne Megan Evans, *Reed College*
Patsy Fowler, *Gonzaga University*
Jeffrey Frame, *Trevecca Nazarene University*
Dave Hartley, *Central Florida Community College*
Anne-Charlotte Harvey, *San Diego State University*
Ann Haugo, *Illinois State University*
Charles L. Hayes, *Radford University*
Graley Herren, *Xavier University*
Robin Huber, *Cerritos College*
Amy Hughes, *Baruch College*
Melissa Hurt, *Dodge City Community College*
David Jortner, *Allegheny College*
Hilary Justice, *Illinois State University*
Jonathan Kalb, *Hunter College, City University of New York*
Douglas Lanier, *University of New Hampshire*
Dawn Larsen, *Volunteer State College*
Ralph Leary, *Clarion University*
David E. Majewski, *Richard Bland College*
Joan McAfee, *Southern Connecticut State University*
Janet E. McLean, *Viterbo University*
Lee E. Neibert, *St. Gregory's University*

Wendy C. Nielsen, *Montclair State University*
Karen O'Brien, *University of California, Irvine*
Keith O'Neill, *Dutchess Community College*
Elinor L. Parker, *Westfield State College*
Jennifer Parker, *Florida State University*
Leslie Pasternack, *Northeastern University*
Katricia G. Pierson, *William Woods University*
Mark Pizzato, *University of North Carolina–Charlotte*
Marthe Reed, *University of Louisiana at Lafayette*
Joan E. Robbins, *Ohio Northern University*
R. Gary Rogers, *Lake-Sumter Community College*
Jeff Skillings, *Dean College*
James Symons, *University of Colorado, Boulder*
C. Patrick Tyndall, *University of Arkansas–Fayetteville*
Jef Vowell, *University of California, Irvine*
Chris Wixson, *Eastern Illinois University*
Boyd H. Wolz, *University of Louisiana at Monroe*
Leigh Woods, *University of Michigan*
Robert L. Yowell, *Northern Arizona University*

I would also like to thank the instructors and scholars who commented on the third edition, suggesting ways we might improve the fourth edition:

Sherri Dienstfrey (Idaho State University), Oliver Gerland (University of Colorado at Boulder), Sue Hagedorn (Virginia Tech), Michael Harrawood (Florida Atlantic University), Gregory Kable (University of North Carolina at Chapel Hill), Margaret Knapp (Arizona State University), Kim Marra (University of Iowa), Jenna Moskowitz (New York University), Scott Phillips (Auburn University), Gary Rogers (Lake Sumter Community College), Susan Speers (University of Akron), Wanda Strukus (Boston College), Stephani Etheridge Woodson (Arizona State University).

I would also like to thank those who responded to our survey on the second edition, suggesting ways we might improve the third edition:

David Adamson (University of North Carolina, Chapel Hill), Gilbert L. Bloom (Ball State University), Brian Boney (University of Texas), Cynthia Bowers (Loyola University), Karen Buckley (University of Wisconsin, Whitewater), Susan Carlson (Iowa State University), Allen Chesler (Northern Illinois University), Barbara Clayton (University of Wisconsin, Madison), Kathleen Colligan Cleary (Clark State Community College), Jill Dolan (City University of New York), David S. Escoffery (University of Pittsburgh), Anthony Graham-White (University of Illinois at Chicago), John E. Hallwas (Western Illinois University), L.W. Harrison (Santa Rosa Junior College), Anne-Charlotte Harvey (San Diego State University), Gregory Kable (University of North Carolina, Chapel Hill), Lawrence Kinsman (New Hampshire College), Ann Klautsch (Boise State University), Margaret Knapp (Arizona State University), Josephine Lee (University of Minnesota), Michael J. Longrie (University of Wisconsin, Whitewater), Kim Marra (University of Iowa), Carla McDonough (Eastern Illinois University), John F. O'Malley (DePaul University), Michael Peterson (Millikin University), Carol Rocamora (NYU Tisch School of the Arts), Hans Rudnick (Southern Illinois University), Terry Donovan Smith (University of Washington), Tramble Turner (Penn State University), Jon W. Tuttle (Francis Marion University), Timothy Wiles (Indiana University), Barry Yzereef (University of Calgary).

I would also like to thank those who responded to the survey for the third edition: George Adams (University of Wisconsin, Whitewater), Ruth Anderson (San Diego State University), Cynthia Bowers (Loyola University), Ruth Contrell (New Mexico State University), Kenneth Cox (Oklahoma State University), Mary Emery (University of Wisconsin, Whitewater), Tom Empy (Casper College), Lawrence Fink (Ohio State University), James Fisher (Wabash College), Kay Forston (Phillips University), Melissa Gibson (University of Pittsburgh), Marsha Morrison (Genesee Community College), Chris Mullen (University of North Carolina, Chapel Hill), Lurana O'Malley (University of Hawai'i), Gwendolyn Orel (University of Pittsburgh), Eva Patton (Fordham University), Richard Schauer (University of Wisconsin, Whitewater), John Terhes (Chemeketa Community College), Charles Trainer (Siena College), Tramble Turner (Penn State University).

I am also indebted to Stanton Garner, Jr. (University of Tennessee), Josephine Lee (University of Minnesota), Sarah Bryant-Bertail (University of Washington), Jorge Huerta (University of California, San Diego), Kristin Pauka (Univerrsity of Hawai'i), and Barbara Sellars-Young (University of California, Davis) for their help and advice on the third edition. My special thanks to Lurana Donnels O'Malley, of the University of Hawai'i, for her assistance with Units 2 and 7; to James Brandon, again of the University of Hawai'i, for graciously providing photographs and other materials related to the University's productions of *Matsukaze* and *Chuushingura;* and to Octavio Rivera, of la Universidad de las Américas, for his help in providing photographs of his excellent production of Sor Juana's *loa* to *The Divine Narcissus.*

I would also like to thank reviewers for the second edition: George R. Adams (University of Wisconsin, Whitewater), Bonnie M. Anderson (San Diego State University), Karen Buckley (University of Wisconsin, Whitewater), Kathleen Colligan Cleary (Clark State Community College), Mary Ann Emery (University of Wisconsin, Whitewater), Lawrence E. Fink (Ohio State University), Melissa Gibson (University of Pittsburgh), Kiki Gounaridou (University of Pittsburgh), Anne-Charlotte Harvey (San Diego State University), Dennis Kennedy (Trinity College, Dublin), Chris Mullen (University of North Carolina, Chapel Hill), Lurana O'Malley (University of Hawai'i), Gwen Orel (University of Pittsburgh), Angela Peckenpaugh (University of Wisconsin, Whitewater), Ruth Schauer (University of Wisconsin, Whitewater). In addition, I am grateful to the following reviewers of the manuscript of the second edition for their valuable revision suggestions: Bradley Boney (University of Texas, Austin), Anne Brannen (Duquesne University), Susan Carlson (Iowa State University), S. Alan Chesler (Northern Illinois University), Cyndia Susan Clegg (Pepperdine University), Jill Dolan (City University of New York), Anthony J. Fichera (University of North Carolina, Chapel Hill), L. W. Harrison (Santa Rosa Junior College), Margaret Knapp (Arizona State University), Josephine Lee (University of Minnesota), Michael Longrie (University of Wisconsin, Whitewater), Michael Peterson (University of Wisconsin, Madison), Eula Thompson (Jefferson State Community College), Jon Tuttle (Francis Marion University).

My thanks to the people who read and commented on the manuscript of the first edition, making it more accurate and useful for instructors: Stanton B. Garner, Jr. (University of Tennessee), Josephine Lee (University of Minnesota), Don Moore (Louisiana State University).

I remain grateful to Sharon Mazer, of the University of Canterbury (New Zealand), for her superb work on the Instructor's Manual to previous editions. I would also like to thank Kathleen M. Gough for her superb work on the new edition of the Instructor's Manual. And my sincere thanks to Stephen T. Jordan for originally proposing this project, to Oscar

G. Brockett of the University of Texas at Austin for allowing me to think out loud about what a book like this one might accomplish. I am grateful to my wife, Hana Worthen, for everything she has done for me, and for her great help with this edition.

Finally, I would like to encourage anyone using this book to feel free to drop me a line with ideas and suggestions for later editions. To the many students and colleagues who have called, sent me a note to correct my oversights and omissions, or have graciously spoken to me about the book at professional meetings and conferences, my sincere thanks for your attention and kindness. The flaws and faults that remain are, of course, entirely my own doing.

—W. B. W.

The
Wadsworth
Anthology
of

drama

Introduction: Drama, Theater, and Culture

Of the many kinds of literature, drama is perhaps the most immediately involved in the life of its community. Drama shares with such other literary modes as lyric poetry, the novel, the epic, and romance the ability to represent and challenge social, political, philosophical, and esthetic attitudes. But unlike most literature, drama has generally been composed for performance, confronting the audience in the public, sociable confines of a theater.

To understand **DRAMA,** we need to understand **THEATER,** because the theater forges the active interplay between drama and its community.[1] On a practical level, for instance, the community must determine where drama will take place, and it is in the theater that a space is carved out for dramatic performance. Not surprisingly, the place of the theater in a city's social and physical geography often symbolizes drama's place in the culture at large. In classical Athens, the theater adjoined a sacred precinct, and plays were part of an extensive religious and civic festival. Greek drama accordingly engages questions of moral, political, and religious authority. In seventeenth-century Paris, the close affiliation between the theater and the court of Louis XIV is embodied in drama's concern with power, authority, and the regulation of rebellious passions. In the United States today, most live theater takes place either in the privileged setting of colleges and universities or in the "theater districts" of major cities, competing for an audience alongside movie theaters, nightclubs, and other entertainments. Drama also seems to be struggling to define itself as part of an established cultural tradition reaching back to Aeschylus and as part of the lively diversity of contemporary popular culture. Social attitudes are reflected in the theater in other ways, too; during performance, the theater constructs its own "society" of performers and spectators. Staging a play puts it immediately into a dynamic social exchange: the interaction between dramatic characters, between characters and the actors who play them, between the performers and the audience, between the drama onstage and the drama of life outside the theater.

READING DRAMA AND SEEING THEATER

The Greek word for theater, *THEATRON,* means "seeing place," and plays performed in the theater engage their audiences largely through visual means. Less than a century ago, live plays could be seen only on the stage; today, most of us see drama in a variety of media: on film and television as well as in the theater. Yet for the past 500 years or so we have also had access to plays in another, nontheatrical venue: by reading them in books. To see a play performed and to read it in a book are two very different activities, but these distinct experiences of drama can be made to enrich one another in a number of ways.

In the theater, a dramatic text is fashioned into an event, something existing in space and time. The space of the stage, with whatever setting is devised, becomes the place of the drama. The characters are embodied by specific individuals. How a given actor interprets a role tends to shape the audience's sense of that dramatic character; for the duration of the play, it is difficult to imagine another kind of performance—a different Oedipus, Lear, or Nora Helmer than the one standing before us in the flesh. The drama onstage is also bound by the temporal exigencies of performance. The process of performance is irreversible; for the duration of the performance, each moment becomes significant and yet unrecoverable—we can't flip back a few pages to an earlier scene, or rewind the videotape. When a company puts a play into stage production, it inevitably confronts these material facts of the theater: a specific cast of actors, a given theatrical space, a certain amount of money to spend, and the necessity of transforming the rich possibilities offered by the play into a clear and meaningful performance. To make the drama active and concrete, theatrical production puts a specific interpretation of the play on the stage. Whether or

---

[1]Terms in boldface small capital letters are defined in the Glossary; italicized terms are non-English terms.

not to play Caliban in Shakespeare's *The Tempest* as a native of the West Indies; whether to play Torvald Helmer in Ibsen's *A Doll House* as a patriarchal autocrat or as someone bewildered by a changing world; whether to set *Phaedra* in a classical, neoclassical, or a modern setting; whether to use cross-gender or intercultural casting in *The Homecoming*—these are some of the kinds of questions that a production must face, and how the production decides such issues inevitably leads the audience toward a particular sense of the play. Everything that happens onstage becomes meaningful for an audience, something to interpret. Even apparently irrelevant facts—a short actor cast to play Hamlet in Shakespeare's play, or a beautiful actress playing Brecht's Mother Courage—become part of the audience's experience of the play, particularizing the play, lending it a definite flavor and meaning.

Reading a play presents us with a different experience of the drama. Reading plays is, first of all, a relatively recent phenomenon. In early theaters, such as those of classical Athens and Rome, medieval Europe, and even Renaissance Europe of the sixteenth century, drama was almost entirely a theatrical mode, rather than a mode of literature. Although the texts of plays were written down, by and large, audiences came into contact with drama primarily through theatrical performance. By the late sixteenth century, though, the status of drama began to change. The recovery and prestige of Greek and Latin literature led to pervasive familiarity with classical texts, including plays. Throughout Europe, schooling was conducted mainly in Latin, and the plays of Roman playwrights such as Plautus, Terence, and Seneca were frequently used to teach Latin grammar and rhetoric. These plays were widely imitated by playwrights writing drama in vernacular languages for emerging secular, commercial theaters. Printing made it possible to disseminate texts more widely, and plays slowly came to be regarded as worthy of publication and preservation in book form. By the late nineteenth century, widespread literacy created a large reading public and a great demand for books; continued improvements in printing technology provided the means to meet the demand. Playwrights often published their plays as books before they could be produced onstage, with some profound effects. The detailed narrative stage directions in plays by Bernard Shaw, Eugene O'Neill, or Henrik Ibsen, for instance, are useful to a stage director and set designer, but they principally fill in a kind of novelistic background for the reading audience who will experience the play only on the page.

Theater audiences are bound to the temporality and specificity of the stage, but readers have the freedom to compose the play in much more varied ways. A reader can pause over a line, teasing out possible meanings, in effect stopping the progress of the play. Readers are not bound by the linear progress of the play's action, in that they can flip back and forth in the play, looking for clues, confirmations, or connections. Nor are readers bound by the stringent physical economy of the stage, the need to embody the characters with individual actors, to specify the dramatic locale as a three-dimensional space. While actors and directors must decide on a specific interpretation of each moment and every character in the play, readers can keep several competing interpretations alive in the imagination at the same time.

Both ways of thinking about drama are demanding, and students of drama should try to develop a sensitivity to both approaches. Treating the play like a novel or poem, decomposing and recomposing it critically, leads to a much fuller sense of the play's potential meanings, its gaps and inconsistencies; it allows us to question the text without the need to come to definite conclusions. Treating the play as a design for the stage forces us to make commitments, to articulate and defend a particular version of the play, and to find ways of making those meanings active onstage, visible in performance. As readers, one way to develop a sense of the reciprocity between stage and page is to think of the play as constructed mainly of actions, not of words. Think of seeing a play in an unknown language: the *action* of the play would still emerge in its larger outlines, carried by the deeds of the characters. Not knowing the words would not prevent the audience from understanding what a character is doing onstage—threatening, lying, persuading, boasting.

When reading a play, it is easy to be seduced by the text, to think of the play's language as mainly narrative, describing the attitudes of the character. For performers onstage, however, speech—language in action—is always a way of doing something. One way for readers to attune themselves to this active quality of dramatic writing is to ask questions of the text from the point of view of performers or characters. What do I—Lysistrata, Everyman, Miranda—want in this speech? How can I use this speech to help me get it? What am I trying to do by speaking in this way? Although questions like these are still removed from the actual practice of performance, they can help readers unfamiliar with drama begin to read plays in theatrical terms.

Another way to enrich the reading experience of drama is to imagine staging the play: how could the design of the set, the movements of the actors, the pacing of the scenes affect the play's meaning, make the play mean something in particular? Questions of this kind can help to make the play seem more concrete, but they have one important limitation. When asking questions like these, it is tempting to imagine the play being performed in today's theaters, according to our conventions of acting and stagecraft, and within the social and cultural context that frames the theater now. To imagine the play on our stage is, of course, to produce it in our contemporary idiom, informed by our notions both of theater and of the world our theater represents. However, while envisioning performance, we should also imagine the play in the circumstances of its original theater, a theater located in a different culture and possibly sharing few practices of stagecraft with the modern theater. How would Hamlet's advice to the players have appeared on the Globe theater's empty platform stage in 1601? Are there ways in which the text capitalizes on this likeness between Shakespeare's company of actors and those Hamlet addresses fictively in the play? In a theater where a complete, "realistic" illusion was not possible (and, possibly, not even desirable), how does Shakespeare's play turn the conditions of theatrical performance to dramatic advantage? Both reading drama and staging drama involve a complex double-consciousness, inviting us to see the plays with contemporary questions in mind, while at the same time imagining them on their original stages. In this doubleness lies an important dramatic principle: plays can speak to us in our theater but perhaps always retain something of their original accents.

DRAMA AND THEATER IN HISTORY

Throughout its development, dramatic art has changed as the theater's place in the surrounding society has changed. The categories that we apply to drama and theater today—art versus entertainment, popular versus classic, literary versus theatrical—are of relatively recent vintage. They imply ways of thinking about drama and theater that are foreign to the function of theater in many other cultures. Much as drama and theater today emerge in relation to other media of dramatic performance like film and television, so in earlier eras the theater defined itself in relation to other artistic, social, and religious institutions. Placed in a different sphere of culture, drama and theater gained a different kind of significance than they have in the United States today.

Drama and theater often arise in relation to religious observance. In ancient Egypt, for instance, religious rituals involved the imitation of events in a god's or goddess's life. In Greece, drama may have had similar origins; by the sixth century BCE, the performance of plays had become part of a massive religious festival celebrating the god Dionysus. The plays performed in this theater—including those of Aeschylus, Sophocles, Euripides, and Aristophanes gathered here—were highly wrought and intellectually, morally, and esthetically complex and demanding works. Aristotle classes drama among other forms of poetry, but in classical Athens these plays occupied a very different position in the spectrum of culture than do drama or "art" today, precisely because of their central role in the City Dionysia. The Roman theater set drama in the context of a much greater variety of performance—chariot racing, juggling, gladiatorial shows—and while plays were performed on religious holidays, drama was more clearly related to secular entertainments than it had been in Athens. Theater waned in Europe with the decline of the Roman Empire and the systematic efforts of the Catholic church to prevent theatrical performance. Yet when theater was revived in the late Middle Ages, it emerged with the support of the church itself. By the year 1000, brief dramatizations illustrated the liturgy of the Catholic Mass; by the fourteenth century, a full range of dramatic forms—plays dramatizing the lives of saints, morality plays, narrative plays on Christian history—was used to illustrate Christian doctrine and to celebrate important days in the Christian year. Like plays in classical Athens, these plays were produced through community effort rather than by specialized "theaters" in the modern sense. Although we now regard medieval drama as extraordinarily rich and complex "literature," in its own era it was part of a different strand of culture, sharing space with other forms of pageantry and religious celebration, rather than being read with the poetry of Chaucer or Dante.

Similarly, in feudal Japan, the Buddhists developed a form of theater to illustrate the central concepts of their faith. Throughout the twelfth and thirteenth centuries, an increasing number of professional players came to imitate these dramatic performances on secular occasions, and for secular audiences. By the fourteenth century, it became conventional for the great samurai lords, or *SHOGUNS,* to patronize a theatrical company, giving rise to the classical era of the Noh theater. The social history of theater in Japan was complicated by other factors as well. The aristocratic **NOH** theater was rivaled by the popular, often quite contemporary, **KABUKI** theater. Government restrictions on the professions (which tended to make acting a family business, passed on through generations), and Japan's militant isolationism (coming to an end only in the mid-nineteenth century), have contributed to making Japan's classical theater survive in many ways unchanged. Moreover, in many parts of Asia, including China and India, theater was understood as a mixed medium, more centrally emphasizing song and dance as a way of developing the narrative, and many forms of performance—the wide variety of Indian folk theater forms, and of Chinese traditional forms, including **BEIJING OPERA**—developed extremely disciplined and highly stylized performance conventions. These traditional theaters, sometimes tied to aristocratic privilege, sometimes to religious ritual, sometimes to civic celebration, were sharply challenged by the influence of Western dramatic and theatrical practices—spoken drama, dramatic realism, and the notion of a secular, profit-making entertainment-theater—beginning in the eighteenth and nineteenth centuries. The rise of *SHINGEKI* or modern theater in the early twentieth century in Japan, of "spoken drama" at the same time in China, and of Western theatrical methods in India are closely tied to the characteristic forms of globalization of that period, economic imperialism and political colonialism; anticolonial, nationalist, and independence movements throughout Asia have tended both to revive classical forms of traditional theater, and to force a rapprochement with the imported forms of Western theater.

Secular performance did, of course, also take place in classical and medieval Europe, including improvised farces on contemporary life, fairground shows, puppetry, mimes, and other quasi-dramatic events. Many plays were performed only on religious occasions, though, and their performers were usually itinerant, lacking the social and institutional support that would provide them with lasting and continuous existence. Only in the Renaissance of the fifteenth and sixteenth centuries did the Western theater begin to assume the function it has today: a fully secular, profit-making, commercial enterprise. Although Renaissance theaters continually vied with religious and state officials for the freedom to practice their trade, by the sixteenth century, the European theater was part of a secular entertainment market, competing with bear-baiting, animal shows, athletic contests, public executions, royal and civic pageants, public preaching, and many other attractions to draw a paying public. The theater emerged in this period as a distinct institution, supported by its own income; the theater became a trade, a profession, a business, rather than a necessary function of the state or of religious worship. Indeed, if drama in classical Athens was conceived more as religious ritual than as "art" in a modern sense, drama in Renaissance London was classed mainly as popular "entertainment." The theater only gradually became recognized as an arena for "literary" accomplishment, for literary status in this period was reserved mainly for skill demonstrated in forms like the sonnet, the prose romance, or the epic—forms that could win the authors a measure of aristocratic prestige and patronage. As part of the motley, vulgar world of the public theater, plays were not considered serious, permanent literature.

However, the desire to transform drama from ephemeral theatrical "entertainment" into permanent literary "art" begins to be registered in the Renaissance. The poet and playwright Ben Jonson included plays in the 1616 edition of his *Works,* insisting on the literary importance of the volume by publishing it in the large, **FOLIO** format generally reserved for classical authors. In 1623, seven years after his death, William Shakespeare's friends and colleagues published a similar, folio-sized collection of his plays, a book that was reprinted several times throughout the seventeenth century. By the 1660s and 1670s, writers at the court of Louis XIV in Paris could achieve both literary and social distinction as dramatists; Jean Racine's reputation as a playwright, in part at least, helped to win his appointment as Louis's royal historiographer. Yet, despite many notable exceptions, the theatrical origins of drama prevented contemporary plays from being regarded as "literature"—although plays from earlier eras were increasingly republished and gradually seen to have "literary" merit. Indeed, by the nineteenth century, contemporary plays often achieved "literary" recognition by avoiding the theater altogether. English poets like Lord Byron and Percy Bysshe Shelley, for instance, wrote plays that were in many ways unstageable, and so preserved them from degrading contact with the tawdry stage. The English critic Charles Lamb remarked in a famous essay that he preferred reading Shakespeare's plays to seeing them in the theater; for Lamb, the practical mechanics of acting and the stage intruded on the experience of the drama's poetic dimension. In fact, the great playwrights of the late nineteenth century— Henrik Ibsen, Anton Chekhov, August Strindberg, and even the young Bernard Shaw—carved a space for themselves as dramatists by writing plays *in opposition* to the values of their contemporary audiences and to the practice of their contemporary theater—a strategy that would have seemed unimaginable to Aeschylus, Shakespeare, or even Molière. To bring their plays successfully to the stage, new theaters and new theater practices had to be devised, and a new audience had to be found, or made.

This split between the "literary drama" and the "popular theater" has become the condition of twentieth-century drama and theater: plays of the artistic **AVANT-GARDE** are more readily absorbed into the **CANON** of literature, while more conventional entertainments—television screenplays, for instance—remain outside it. The major modern playwrights from Ibsen to Luigi Pirandello to Samuel Beckett first wrote for small theaters and were produced by experimental companies playing to coterie audiences on the fringes of the theatrical "mainstream." This sense of modernist "art" as opposed to the values of bourgeois culture was not confined to drama and theater. Modernist fiction and poetry, cubist and abstract painting and sculpture, modern dance, and modern music all developed a new formal complexity, thematic abstraction, and critical self-consciousness in opposition to the sentimental superficiality they found in conventional art forms. This modernist tendency has itself produced a kind of reaction, a desire to bring the devices of popular culture and mass culture into drama, as a way of altering the place of the theater in society and changing the relationship between the spectators and the stage. Bertolt Brecht's **ALIENATION EFFECT,** Samuel Beckett's importation of circus and film clowns to absurdist theater, Heiner Müller's **PASTICHE** of *Hamlet* in his **POSTMODERN** *Hamletmachine,* or Wole Soyinka's interweaving of African ritual and fourth-wall realism in *Death and the King's Horseman* are all examples of this reaction. For the theater has been challenged by film and television to define its space in contemporary culture, and, given the pervasive availability of other media, theater has increasingly seemed to occupy a place akin to that of opera, among the privileged, elite forms of "high culture." As a result, innovation in today's theater often takes place on the margins or fringes of mainstream theater and mainstream culture: in smaller companies experimenting with new performance forms, in subversive theaters confronting political oppression in many parts of the world, and in theaters working to form a new audience and a new sense of theater by conceiving new forms of drama.

DRAMATIC GENRES

Perhaps because its meaning must emerge rapidly and clearly in performance, drama tends to be compressed and condensed; its characters tend toward types, and its action tends toward certain general patterns as well. It is conventional to speak of these kinds of drama as **GENRES,** each with its own identifying formal structure and typical themes. In the Western theater, following Aristotle's *The Poetics,* **TRAGEDY** is usually considered to concern the fate of an individual hero, singled out from the community through circumstances and through his or her own actions. In the course of the drama, the hero's course of action entwines with events and circumstances beyond his or her control. As a result, the hero's final downfall—usually, but not always, involving death—seems at once both chosen and inevitable. **COMEDY** on the other hand, focuses on the fortunes of the community itself. While the hero of tragedy is usually unique, the heroes of comedy often come in pairs—the lovers who triumph over their parents in romantic comedies, the dupe and the trickster at the center of more ironic or satirical comic modes. While tragedy points toward the hero's downfall or death, comedy generally points toward some kind of broader reform or remaking of society, usually signaled by a wedding or other celebration at the end of the play.

To speak of genre in this way, though, is to suggest that these ideal critical abstractions actually exist in some form, exemplified more or less adequately by particular plays. Yet, as the very different genres of Japanese or Indian theater suggest, terms like *tragedy* and *comedy,* or **MELO-DRAMA, TRAGOCOMEDY, FARCE,** and others, arise from our efforts to find continuities between extraordinarily different kinds of drama: between plays written in different theaters, for different purposes, to please different audiences, under different historical pressures. When we impose these terms in a prescriptive way, we usually find that the drama eludes them or even calls them into question. Aristotle's brilliant sense of Greek tragedy in *The Poetics,* for instance, hardly "applies" with equal force to Greek plays as different as *Agamemnon, Oedipus the King,* and *Medea,* or Kan'ami's elegant Noh drama, *Matsukaze,* let alone later plays like *Hamlet* or *Endgame.* In his essay, "Tragedy and the Common Man," Arthur Miller tries to preserve "tragedy" for modern drama by redefining Aristotle's description of the hero of tragedy. Instead of Aristotle's hero, a man (not a woman) of an elevated social station, Miller argues that the modern hero should be an average, "common" man (not a woman), precisely because the "best families" do not seem normative to us or representative of our basic values, a goal he pursued in his classic American tragedy, *Death of a Salesman.* Our exemplary characters are taken from the middle classes. Yet to redefine the hero in this way calls Aristotle's other qualifications—the idea of the hero's character and actions, the meaning of the tragic "fall"—into question as well, forcing us to redefine Aristotelian tragedy in ways that make it something entirely new, something evocative in modern terms.

In approaching the question of genre, then, it is often useful to avoid asking how a play exemplifies the universal and unchanging features of tragedy or comedy. Instead, one could ask how a play or a theater *invents* tragedy or comedy for its contemporary audience. What terms does the drama present, what formal features does it use, to represent human experience? How do historically "local" genres—Renaissance **REVENGE TRAGEDY,** French **NEOCLASSICAL DRAMA,** modern **THEATER OF THE ABSURD, KABUKI,** or even the **KATHAKALI** of southern India—challenge, preserve, or redefine broader notions of genre?

DRAMATIC FORM

In about 335 BCE, Aristotle's *The Poetics* set down the formal elements of drama, and the influence of Aristotle's description has been massive: today we still speak of dramatic form in terms of its **PLOT, CHARACTERS, LANGUAGE, THEME,** and its performative elements, what Aristotle called **MUSIC** and **SPECTACLE.** Any student of drama can profit by thinking about how these formal elements function in a given play. How are the incidents of the play—its plot—arranged? What effects are achieved by *this* ordering, rather than by another? How does the plot relate to the play's narrative story, which includes events dating from before the play begins? How does the plot, the structure of the events—for instance, Nora Helmer's first act in *A Doll House* is to enter the house, and her last act is to leave it—develop the play's themes? We might then ask how the play defines its characters. What elements of human experience—family history, psychological motivation, public action—seem to be most prominent in a play's conception of "character"? How do the formal conventions of characterization, such as blank verse in Shakespeare's plays and the densely poetic language of Noh theater, affect our reading of the characters and our understanding of them as representations of human beings?

Although Aristotle presents these elements of drama as distinct, in practice they are mutually defining, making it very difficult to speak of them separately. A play's language, for example, can be analyzed purely for its verbal and rhetorical features, but it is more interesting to ask how the language affects our understanding of the characters or invests the play with certain thematic possibilities. Similarly, while we may regard a play's themes as inside the play, they actually arise only in our interpretation of the play. The themes are something we create by asking certain questions about the play's plotting, its characterization, its use of language. The artificiality of separating these features becomes especially clear when we turn to a play's theatrical dimension. Although Aristotle suggests that a play's literary and theatrical dimensions are independent, to get a real sense of drama we must see the play both as literature and as theater. We must assess how an audience's sense of the play's plot, characters, and themes are shaped by the kinds of spectacle demanded by the play and provided by the theater. The "meaning" of Greek drama cannot be separated from its conditions of performance: the religious festival, the huge amphitheater, the masked actors, the singing, dancing chorus. The barren "sterile promontory" of *Hamlet,* Phaedra's claustral chamber, cross-dressed performance in Churchill's *Cloud Nine:* these elements of the theatrical spectacle are not outside the meaning of the drama; they are its means, the vehicle for achieving that meaning on the stage.

In a book like this one—indeed, in any book—it is difficult to convey a real sense of the power of theater. It is possible, though, to imagine this experience and to discuss it through the materials collected here: dramatic texts, descriptions of stage practice, illustrations of theaters, photographs, essays. However, an obstacle to understanding arises from a split between the disciplines we use to understand drama and theater. At many colleges and universities, this split is represented in the geography of the campus itself, where the English or Literature departments, which teach dramatic literature, are housed in one building, and the Theater or Drama department, which teaches acting, directing, design, and which actually stages the plays, is housed in another. "Literary" approaches to drama focus our attention initially, sometimes exclusively, on the text of a play and train the complex strategies of poetics and poetic interpretation on it. Such interpretation regards the dramatic text as incomplete and specifies the text's range of possible meanings by placing it in various textual and cultural contexts; in a sense, the negotiation between the text and these contexts determines what we can say the play *means*.

"Theatrical" approaches to drama tend to see a play in terms of stage practice, both in the terms of the play's original production and in the light of performance practice today. This approach interrogates the play's staging: how it can be set, what obstacles it presents to acting and casting, what the dramatic effects of costume and design will be. "Theatrical" interpretation regards the dramatic text as an incomplete design for performance and trains the complex machinery of stage representation—directing, acting, design, costuming on the task of fleshing the script out as performed action. The meaning of the play in this regard emerges from what we can make the play *do*.

The literary and theatrical approaches to drama and theater share the assumption that plays are not fully meaningful in themselves; they share the sense that the meaning of drama emerges from the kinds of questions we ask of it, the contexts—literary, historical, theoretical, theatrical—in which we can make it perform, and make it mean something in particular. Although each approach can seem needlessly mysterious, involving its own specialized language and critical practice, its own set of "right" questions and "right" answers, this book has been assembled with the belief that the literary and the theatrical approaches are necessary complements to each other.

In the units that follow, each introductory essay attempts to provide an overview of the dense implication of drama and theater in its culture, and, often, how dramatic literature and theatrical practices have been revived, engaged, or transformed by succeeding generations. Each essay, in other words, introduces the social, political, and cultural milieu of the theater; the theater's physical and symbolic position in the landscape of its culture; the theater's representation of gendered, sexual, and racial identities; the physical design of theaters, and the practices of acting and staging; and the dynamic impact of dramatic—literary—innovation on the work of performance. Although these issues are treated differently, given different prominence in each essay, this constellation of questions stems from a single conviction: that thinking about drama requires that we think about how plays perform as literature, in culture and history, and on the stage.

One of the greatest challenges, for professional scholars and students alike, to understanding the history of drama and theater has to do with the nature of evidence. As any detective drama illustrates—think of Sherlock Holmes—"facts" only become "evidence" when they are subjected to a coherent interpretation, an explanatory narrative. So, too, understanding the "facts" of the theatrical past means transforming them into "evidence," evidence that materializes a certain understanding, interpretation, or explanation of the meaning of drama and theater in history. The difficulties of historiography—the writing of history—with regard to early drama and theater are self-evident. Most of the plays of classical Athens, for example, have been lost; those that survive represent only a small percentage of the "evidence" for the practice of Greek playwrights. Much of the evidence for theatrical practice—how actors worked, the movements of the chorus, the function of music, the behavior of audiences, even the composition of audiences—has had to be adduced from written documents and visual images often far-removed from the theater itself, for these practices (much like the teaching of acting today) were part of an ongoing tradition that was handed directly from performer to performer, or citizen to citizen. Many theatrical traditions around the world originated in nonliterate oral cultures, which successfully preserved the developing forms and practices of performance over centuries, as long as the communities who sustained them continued to flourish. Often regarded as "primitive," "uncivilized," or simply subversive by invading colonial powers, even traditional practices that survived well into the historical period have sometimes been eradicated (Wole Soyinka's *Death and the King's Horseman* provides a striking image of the ways the English governors of Nigeria regarded several centuries-old traditional performance practices). Nonetheless, some of these traditions survive: though they date from about the sixteenth century, *kathakali* performances in southern India seem to preserve some of the dramatic and performance traditions of ancient Sanskrit performance, as it was described in Bharatamuni's *Natyasastra*. Of course, the rise of print not only forged a fissure between literary drama and theatrical performance: it also provided the means to document a wide variety of theatrical practice and—since the purpose of print is to multiply texts in great numbers—to provide a greater chance that such documents would survive. For this reason, beginning in the sixteenth century, the print-record provides a massive archive of information about the practices of performance: in the publication of plays; in the efflorescence of diaries and memoirs containing information about the stage; in the rise of theatrical journalism in the eighteenth century; in playbills, posters, programs; and in a wide variety of theatrical illustrations—pictures of actors, plays, theaters. In combination with the increasing likelihood that theatrical buildings, sets, costumes, and the records of theater companies have survived, the history of the modern theater is, comparatively speaking, an embarrassment of riches. Needless to say, it has recently become possible even to record performance, on still photographs and film, videotape, and digital media. While it is important to recognize that such recordings are themselves only partial "evidence" for the work of a given production—What is the camera leaving out of the picture? How is close-up distorting what an audience might see? How did the production change in order to be filmed? How did the live production change after it was filmed?—they do provide an invaluable resource for future generations of students.

In each unit, this edition of *The Wadsworth Anthology of Drama* provides a piece of that material past, a document or an image that provides some insight into theatrical practice. Some of these records are visual, and indeed may have had no direct relation to performance in their day: scholars now use them to attempt to reconstruct elements of lost theaters. Several of these records are written documents, often chestnuts in the history of drama and theater. The purpose of including these records here is experimental: how can you use such records to interrogate some aspect of a past performance? What kind of story does the document tell, and what stories does it conceal? What kind of interpretation of theater history does the document enable? What kinds of evidentiary problems does it pose? Reading the documents of the theater's material past is one way to engage in the challenging work of imagining the power of dramatic performance.

Classical Athens

Greek amphitheater at the site of the ancient city of Morgantina, Sicily.

Great drama arises where the theater occupies an important place in the life of the community. In many respects, Western understanding of drama originated in fifth-century (500–400) BCE classical Athens, where the theater played a central role in politics, religion, and society. The Athenians invented forms of **TRAGEDY** and **COMEDY** that persist to the present day. In tragedy, the Greeks dramatized climactic events in the lives of legendary heroes from prehistory and myth, bringing ethical problems of motive and action to the stage. In comedy, the theater staged satiric portraits of the life of the ***POLIS*** (the city-state), vividly depicting the energetic conflicts of contemporary Athens in matters of politics, war, education—even the arts of drama. Playwrights through the long history of the theater have continued to find in Greek drama both a model and a point of resistance against which to practice their own craft (see, for example, Jean Racine's *Phaedra* or Bernard Shaw's *Major Barbara* in this book). And we need only recall Sigmund Freud's understanding of the "Oedipus complex" to sense the influence of models of action derived from the Greek theater on later Western culture.

Athens and Sparta were dominant rival powers in fifth-century Greece, which comprised many small independent city-states, each with its own political and cultural institutions, form of government, and alliances. Dramatic performances took place under a variety of circumstances in all Greek cities, but drama as we know it developed in Athens. Dramatic performance in Athens was part of citywide religious festivals honoring the god Dionysus, the most important being the **CITY DIONYSIA.** Plays were produced for contests in which playwrights, actors, and choruses competed for prizes and for distinction among their fellow citizens. These contests, held in an outdoor amphitheater adjoining the sacred temple of the god, followed several days of religious parades and sacrifices. This connection between early drama and religion suggests that the essential nature of Greek drama lies in its supposed "origins" in religious ritual. But the City Dionysia was also a massive civic spectacle that went far beyond religious worship, emphasizing the theater's implication in other areas of public life. Dramatic performance contributed to this celebration of Athens' economic power, cultural accomplishment, and military might. The City Dionysia united religion and politics, enabling Athenians to celebrate both Dionysus and the achievements of their *polis*.

THE CITY DIONYSIA

The City Dionysia was the most prominent of four religious festivals held in Athens and the surrounding province of Attica between December and April; it took place in the month of Elaphebolion (March–April), one month after the previous festival. Although its purpose was primarily a religious one, the City Dionysia was structured around a series of contests between individual citizens and between major Athenian social groups—the ten (later twelve to fifteen) "tribes" that formed the city's basic political and military units. Dramatic performance was introduced to the City Dionysia during the sixth century BCE and became the centerpiece of the elaborate festival. Each year a city magistrate, or ***ARCHON,*** honored selected wealthy citizens by choosing them to finance one of the three principal tragic dramatists competing for a prize at the festival. Each sponsor, called a ***CHOREGOS,*** was responsible for hiring the **CHORUS** of young men who sang and danced in the plays. The *choregos* hired musicians and provided costumes and other support for the playwright to whom he was assigned. Later in the period, the state assigned the leading actor to the *choregos* as well, and this actor also competed for a prize. The playwright was responsible for training the chorus and the actors, and for some of the acting himself, and he shared his prize with the *choregos*. Serving as a *choregos* was both a civic duty and an important honor, equivalent to other tasks imposed on the wealthy—maintaining a battleship for a year or training athletes for the Olympic games.

Taking place over several days, the City Dionysia opened with a display of actors and choruses to the city; on the next day there was a lavish parade of religious officials through the city, followed by religious observances and sacrifices held in the theater. Athens also received its annual tribute of goods, money, and slaves from subject and allied states at this time, and war orphans raised at state expense were displayed to the audience. After this display of religious worship and civic pride, two days were devoted to contests of **DITHYRAMBS,** hymns sung and danced by a large chorus. Each of Athens' tribes sponsored two choruses: one consisting of fifty men, another consisting of fifty boys. The city's politics revolved around the tribes, and their contribution to the festival was prominent in this contest. The dithyrambic contest involved a thousand Athenian citizens directly in the performance, a significant portion of the adult male citizens. (It is estimated that Athens in the fifth century had a total population of about 300,000: 100,000 slaves, 30,000 noncitizen foreigners, and 30,000 to 40,000 adult male citizens; women and children were not citizens.) Following the dithyrambs, the main dramatic contest began. The competing playwrights each produced a **TRILOGY** of tragedies, staged over three days. A trilogy could take a single theme or series of events as its subject (like the three plays of Aeschylus' *Oresteia,* 458 BCE), or present three distinct, unrelated dramas. A rugged farce called a **SATYR PLAY** followed the performance of each complete trilogy and was considered part of it; these plays parodied a god's activities, with actors dressed as satyrs—half-man, half-goat. After 486 BCE, comedies were also awarded prizes, but it is unclear whether the comedies were performed on a single day or spread over several days. Prominent citizens representing each of the tribes served as judges and awarded prizes to the playwrights, their *choregoi,* and the actors.

THE THEATER OF DIONYSUS

The Greek theater was a public spectacle, a kind of combination of Inauguration Day, the Super Bowl, the Academy Awards, Memorial Day, and a major religious holiday. Plays were first produced in the **AGORA** (marketplace), which often served as a performance place for festivals in Athens and in the surrounding **DEMES** of Attica, which also staged dramatic performances. However, the size and importance of the City Dionysia required a separate site, and a theater was built on the slope of the Acropolis, near the precinct of Dionysus. The original theater, a ring of wooden seats facing a circular floor, was later refined, enlarged, and constructed of stone. By the time of Aeschylus, Euripides, Sophocles, and Aristophanes, the Athenian theater had achieved its basic design: a circular floor for dancing and acting, ringed by a hillside **AMPHITHEATER** and backed by a low, rectangular building.

The focus of the classical amphitheater, which seated about 14,000 people, was the round **ORCHESTRA** ("dancing place") containing the central altar of Dionysus, at which the festival sacrifices were performed. The dithyrambic choruses performed their ecstatic dances in the orchestra, and most of the action of the plays took place there as well. Facing the orchestra, the hillside was divided into wedge-shaped seating areas. The citizens sat on wooden benches with their tribes: leaders and priests in the front of the sections, women perhaps toward the rear or possibly in a separate section. *Metics* (resident aliens) and visitors were probably seated in a separate area. Special front and center seats, called *prohedria,* were reserved for the judges and the priests of Dionysus.

Behind the *orchestra,* a low building called the **SKENE** faced the audience. Although the *skene* became a permanent stone structure in the fourth century BCE, in the fifth century it was a temporary wooden building, used for changing masks and possibly also for changing costumes. Playwrights quickly found the theatrical potential latent in the *skene's* facade and

EARLY AMPHITHEATER

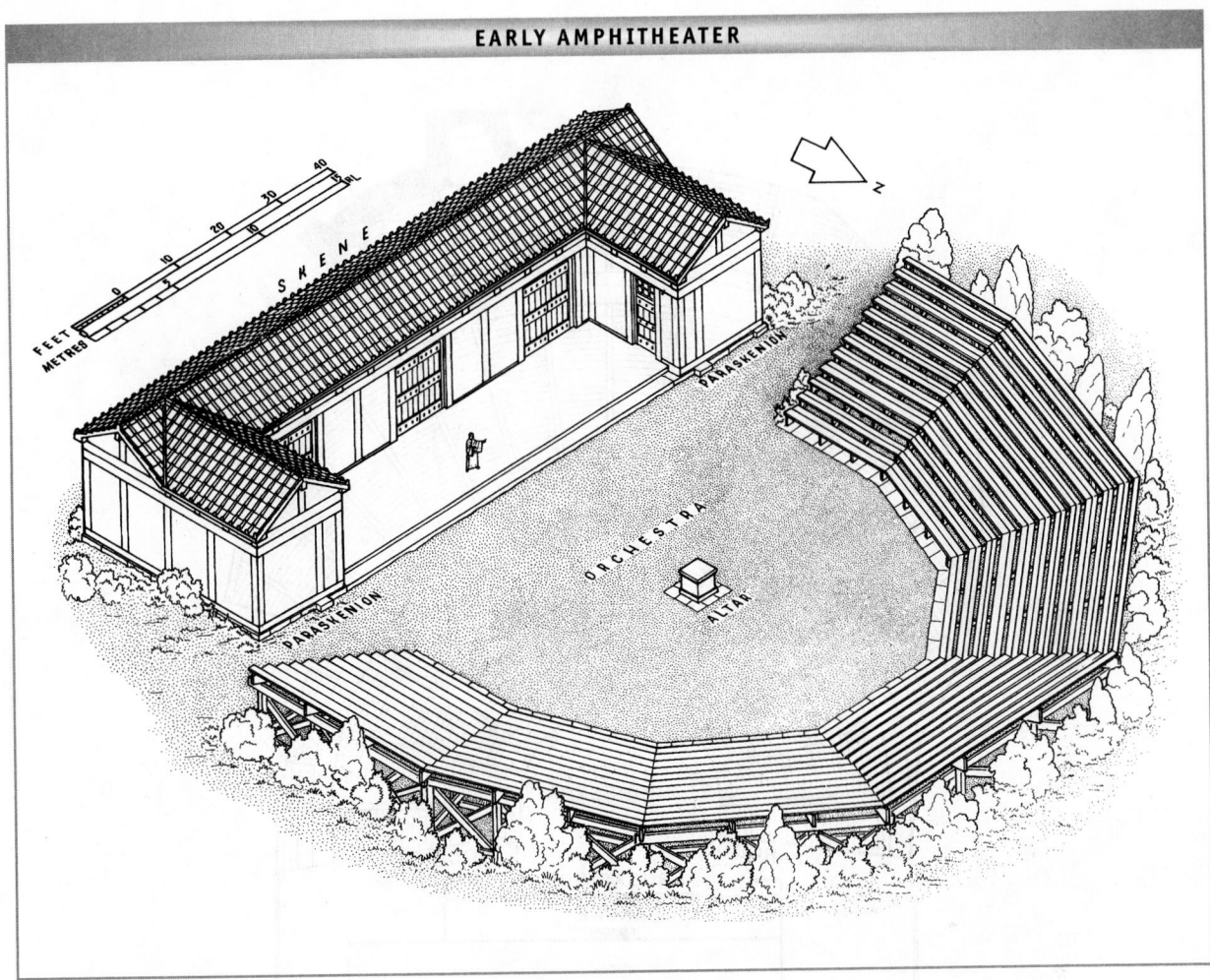

This is an artist's reconstruction of an early theater in Eretria, Greece. Notice that the seating is constructed of wooden benches and the *skene* is a temporary structure.

set of doors; through these doors the audience heard Agamemnon being murdered in his bath, or saw eyeless Oedipus return to confront the Chorus and his future in exile. In Aeschylus' *Agamemnon,* the Watchman awaits the signal fires on the palace roof, and in performance he may have waited on the roof of the *skene.* The theater also used some machinery for scenic effects: a rolling platform (the **EKKYKLEMA**) used to bring objects or bodies from the *skene* into the orchestra; a crane (**MACHINA**) to raise or lower characters—the gods, for instance—from the orchestra over the roof of the *skene;* later, in the fourth century, painted panels were used to indicate the play's setting or location.

THEATER AND SOCIAL LIFE

The experience of theater in classical Athens was in some ways akin to participation in other institutions of civic life. Athens was a participatory democracy for its citizens, although citizenship was restricted to adult male Athenians: women, foreigners, slaves, freed slaves, and children were not citizens. Citizens sat in the assembly to discuss and vote on matters of state policy, and they were eligible to serve in all public and military offices as well. Attendance at the City Dionysia was, then, like other aspects of Athenian public life, a privilege and an

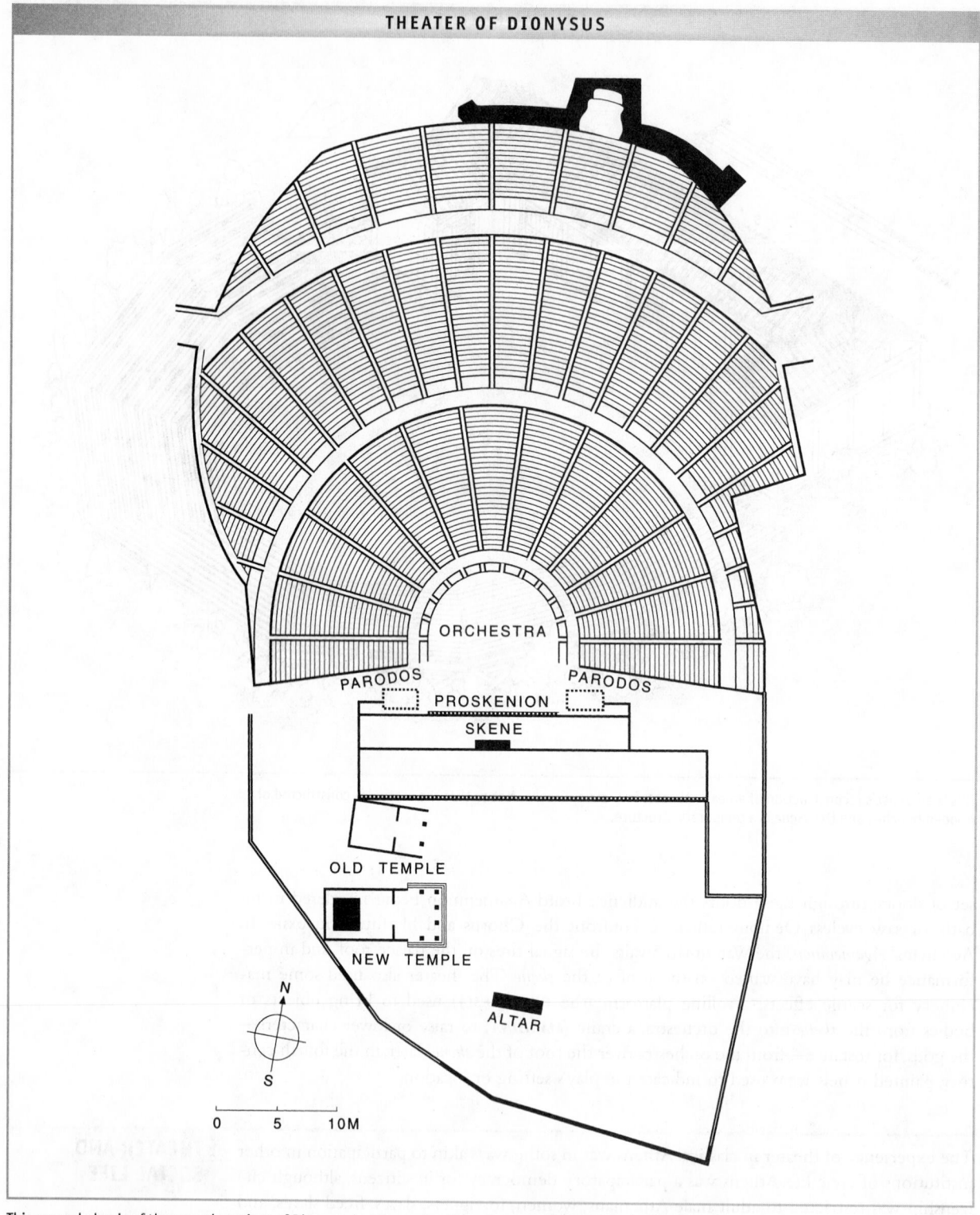

THEATER OF DIONYSUS

ORCHESTRA

PARODOS

PARODOS

PROSKENION

SKENE

OLD TEMPLE

NEW TEMPLE

ALTAR

N

S

0   5   10M

This ground plan is of the sacred precinct of Dionysus in Athens, fourth century BCE. Notice that the theater is much larger than the earlier theater at provincial Eretria. The large and permanent *skene* was constructed after the fifth century BCE.

obligation mainly reserved for citizens. Citizens received tickets to the festival from officials in their neighborhood, or **DEME;** tickets may have been awarded on the basis of participation in other civic obligations—serving in the courts, the assembly, the army. At the theater, citizens sat together with members of their tribe. In a sense, the theater offered a visual map of the organization of Athenian society, for the tribes formed the basis of political participation outside the theater: The Athenian Assembly and the army were similarly arranged by tribe. Organized by tribes, with precedence given to religious officials and with inferior status or nonparticipation accorded to noncitizens such as women, slaves, and foreigners, the theater of Dionysus mirrored the structure of Athenian society.

The fifth century BCE was the era of Athens' greatest political power and cultural vitality and an era of intense reciprocity between Athenian theater and society. Yet the tension manifest in Greek drama perhaps points to the precarious stability of the Athenian *polis.* The Athenian maritime empire, forged after the defeat of massive Persian forces in 479, was resisted by the smaller Greek states and opposed by Athens' chief rival, the military state of Sparta. Following a long period of hostility and skirmishing, Athens and Sparta declared war against each other in 431 BCE, resulting in Athens' utter defeat in 404. Athenian democracy was replaced by an oppressive oligarchy, the Thirty Tyrants. Although the tyrants were rapidly overthrown and democracy restored, Athens never regained the dynamic cultural life and political power it enjoyed during the fifth century. And although dramatic performance continued after the restoration of democracy, the theater's central role in the *polis* seems to have declined after the Spartan victory. Yet, the theater became one of Greece's most widely disseminated cultural products. When Alexander the Great conquered Greece, the Near East, and northern Africa, he took Greek culture—including theater and drama—with him throughout his empire. And when the Roman Empire later absorbed Alexander's former dominions, it also appropriated Greek dramatic traditions, the design of Greek theaters, and the arts and religion of Greece, as well.

DRAMA AND PERFORMANCE

In his *Poetics,* Aristotle suggests that drama originated in the singing of the dithyrambic choruses; a masked actor was first used to respond to the chorus as an individualized "character" in the mid–sixth century BCE, an innovation attributed to the playwright Thespis, about whom little else is known. Aeschylus was the first to use two actors, probably taking one of the parts himself; in the 460s, Sophocles introduced a third actor and was successfully imitated by Aeschylus in his *Oresteia* in 458 BCE. In general, classical tragedy can be performed with three actors and comedy with four, although each actor may play several parts. All of the performers in the Greek theater—the dramatists, actors, musicians, and chorus members—were male citizens of Athens, as was most of the audience. The dramatic choruses were perhaps composed of young men between the ages of seventeen, when military training began, and twenty-one, when Athenian men entered into adulthood.

The chorus of tragedy both sang and danced, and it was expected to perform with grace and precision. Actors and choruses wore full-head masks made of painted linen or lightweight wood. The main characters' masks were individualized, but the members of the chorus all wore identical masks, giving a special force to the conflict between the unique claims of the protagonist and the more diffuse claims of his society. Costuming in comedy was somewhat more complex. Aristophanes' plays suggest that the chorus at times wore animal masks. The comic protagonists' masks, though, were again individualized; since Aristophanes often put his contemporaries in his plays—Socrates in *Clouds,* for instance, or Euripides in *Frogs*—the masks probably resembled these citizens quite closely. Comic actors often sported a leather **PHALLUS,** clearly visible in statues depicting comic actors and of much dramatic use in plays like *Lysistrata.*

In reading Greek drama, we should remember that its leading parts—both the leading character and the chorus—were designed for competition, as instruments for the actor and chorus to win prizes. The literary brilliance of the plays is, in this sense, a means to enable a particular virtuosity in performance.

WOMEN IN THE ATHENIAN THEATER

In Athenian tragedy and comedy, female characters were played by men. Not only did men sponsor and write the plays, but the "women" onstage were literally men in disguise. Yet, many plays throw the theatrical convention of men playing women into relief. In Euripides' play *The Bacchae,* Pentheus is possessed by Dionysus when he dresses up as a woman and Dionysus admires his good looks; in *Lysistrata,* the Spartan woman Lampito is closely and physically examined by Lysistrata and the other women in ways that focus the audience's attention precisely on the fact that the woman is being played by a man. Drama, then, participated fully in Athens' denial of equality to women. Athena says as much in Aeschylus' *The Eumenides* when she judges Orestes' murder of his mother as a lesser crime than Clytaemnestra's murder of her husband. Looking closely at both the drama and its performance can help us to see how justice, power, and gender came to be arranged in Athenian society.

Although the theater—like Athenian society—was a male-dominated institution, Greek drama repeatedly inquires into the nature of gendered behavior and uses female characters to focus some of its most challenging questions. Given the absence of women from the stage and their marginal status in the theater and in the state, it is fascinating to note how many plays turn on the action of female characters. Women were not themselves citizens of Athens, and their prerogatives, which were considerable, in the *polis* were defined only through marriage to a citizen. Yet many of the plays raise critical moral, ethical, and political problems through the actions of women: Clytaemnestra and Cassandra in Aeschylus' *Agamemnon,* Medea in Euripides' *Medea,* and the women of Aristophanes' *Lysistrata* and *Assembly of Women.* Although Aristotle probably voices his contemporaries' views when he remarks in his *Poetics* that "a woman can be good, or a slave, although one of these classes [women] is inferior and the other, as a class, worthless," the theater stages women in ways that implicitly challenge the authority of this "natural" connection between the good, the legitimate, and the masculine. As a category that troubles the "natural" linkage between masculinity and humanity itself, women in Greek drama often appear to stage a crisis in how the state imagines and justifies itself.

FORMS OF GREEK DRAMA

Formally, the organization of Greek tragedy is somewhat different from that of modern plays, because Greek drama is based on the singing and dancing of the chorus, for whom many of the plays were named. Most plays begin with a **PROLOGUE,** such as the Watchman's speech at the opening of *Agamemnon,* followed by the **PARODOS** (entrance) of the singing and dancing chorus. Several **EPISODES** follow, in which the central characters engage one another and the chorus; the chorus itself often sings (and dances) several **ODES,** which are used to enunciate and enlarge on the play's pivotal issues, and the chorus often becomes a decisive character in the play, as it does in Aeschylus' *Agamemnon* or Euripides' *The Bacchae.* The choral odes are written in lyric meters different from the meters used for the characters' speeches. The play's **CATASTROPHE,** literally its "down turn," marks some change in the hero's status and is followed by the departure of the characters from the stage and the **EXODOS,** or final song, dance, and departure of the chorus. Comedy—at least for Aristophanes, whose plays are the only surviving comedies from the period—is structured similarly, although Aristophanes' plays usually include a long **PARABASIS,** a choral ode delivered to the audience discussing political issues, and a final **KOMOS,** a scene of choral dancing and revelry.

This formal description, however, hardly accounts for the real and continued power of Greek drama, which arises from an intense and economical relationship between (1) a situation, usually at the point of climax as the play opens, (2) a complex of characters, each with distinctive goals and motives, (3) a chorus used both as a character and as a commentator on the action, and (4) a series of incidents that precipitates a crisis and brings the meaning of the **PROTAGONIST**'s actions into focus. Aristotle called this crisis the ***PERIPETEIA,*** or "reversal," in the external situation or fortunes of the main character, and he argued that it should be accompanied by an act of ***ANAGNORISIS,*** or "recognition," in which the character responds to this change. Indeed, Aristotle argued that when the pressure of the tragic action produces a close relationship between reversal and recognition, it instills in the audience intense feelings of fear and pity and then effects ***CATHARSIS,*** a purgation of these emotions.

Because the plays were written for a contest, it is not surprising that their language and construction provide opportunity for powerful acting, particularly since the plays were judged only in performance. Yet the stage action of Greek drama is hardly spectacular in the modern sense. Although the visual dimension of Agamemnon's descent from the chariot onto the blood-red tapestry, or Medea's appearance in the dragon-drawn chariot, or even the aching gait of the men in *Lysistrata* is critical to any understanding of these plays, scenes of murder, suicide, or battle usually take place offstage, to be vividly reported by messengers— as in the reports of Jocasta's death and Oedipus' blinding, or of the death of Jason's young bride in *Medea*. Cassandra's graphic prophecy of Agamemnon's murder likewise provides a brutal counterpoint to the slaughter taking place offstage.

The scenic simplicity of the Greek theater enabled playwrights to achieve a special kind of concentration, one that capitalized on the special circumstances of the open-air, festival theater. Greek comedy has come down to us in the work of only two playwrights, Aristophanes and Menander (c. 342–c. 291 BCE). While Aristophanes' plays—usually called **OLD COMEDY**— are energetic and sometimes ribald comedies lampooning the Athenian *polis* and its leading citizens, Menander's comedies—called **NEW COMEDY**—are more generally concerned with mores and manners. Menander wrote more than 100 plays, but only one of his comedies— *The Grouch*—survives in its entirety. Menander's plays were often focused on a comic conflict between parents and children, devising situations and characters that forged an important link between the Greek and Roman theaters, and helped to establish the enduring traditions of stage comedy.

While the comedies center on the life of the community, the stage action of Greek tragedy focuses on the relation between the hero's intention, action, and consequence in ways that typically pit the hero's greatest talents against his unavoidable destiny, his society, his family, and himself. This recipe has provided—in plays from the era of Aeschylus, Sophocles, and Euripides to our own—the substance of tragic drama. The characteristic concerns of Greek drama speak undeniably of classical Athens, but the plays also represent trials of decision, suffering, and desperation with a power and purpose that continue to speak to us in accents very much our own.

GREEK DRAMA IN PERFORMANCE HISTORY

The forms of Greek drama and theater remained in use after the fall of Athens to Sparta; indeed, they were both exported to Rome, Egypt, and the Middle East by Alexander. Yet while tragedy and comedy continued to be written and performed throughout the Greek Mediterranean throughout the Hellenistic period (fourth and third centuries BCE) and beyond, and theater design continued to develop and refine the classical amphitheater, in an important sense the tradition of dramatic writing and performance inaugurated in fifth-century Athens was confined to the Greek provinces. The modes of Greek drama and (to a lesser extent) performance survived somewhat longer in the eastern reaches of the Roman Empire, but in the west they gradually disappeared under the influence of Roman culture. Moreover, although the manuscripts of Greek drama—and of important collateral texts, such as Aristotle's *Poetics*—continued

ROMAN DRAMA AND THEATER

Although many of their traditions were absorbed from Greece, the Romans developed a distinctive theater, quite different from the Athenian stage. From its beginnings, Roman theater was more varied than the Greek stage, including acrobatics, juggling, athletic events, gladiatorial combats, and skits. In the sixth and seventh centuries BCE, Rome was a relatively unimportant town, ruled by the Etruscan kingdoms of northern Italy. In 509 the Romans drove out the Etruscans and founded a republic; the republic expanded its influence throughout the fourth century BCE and eventually came to control many territories once governed by the Greeks and by Alexander. Much as the Romans absorbed other Greek cultural institutions, they also absorbed Greek theater and drama, which were first performed in Rome in the mid–third century, in 240 BCE. As Rome's political influence expanded, particularly under the Roman Empire (27 BCE–476 CE), the Romans disseminated their characteristic cultural institutions—including theater and drama—throughout Europe, North Africa, and the Middle East.

Like the Greeks, the Romans associated the drama with festivals, but the Romans not only produced plays on festival occasions throughout the year, they also developed a much wider variety of theatrical entertainments, of which drama was only a small part. Some of the Roman entertainments descended from the sixth-century BCE *ludi Romani,* which included chariot racing, boxing, and other athletic contests, and Greek drama was first performed in Rome at these games. Moreover, Greek drama not only competed with other nondramatic entertainment, it also was rivaled by an indigenous dramatic form known as **ATELLAN FARCE.** Associated with the town of Atella (near present-day Naples), these farces were probably improvised comic skits, involving stock characters and played by masked actors.

After the introduction of tragedy and comedy to the *ludi Romani* in 240 BCE, dramatic performances were introduced to several other festivals, and by 179 BCE, drama was being performed at major religious festivals throughout the year: at the *ludi Romani* honoring Jupiter in September, at a second festival consecrated to Jupiter in November, at festivals honoring Flora and the Great Mother in April, and at a festival honoring Apollo in July. Dramatic performances, though still associated with festivals, were much more common in Rome than in fifth-century Athens, not only because special celebrations sometimes included theatrical performance, but also because any disruption in the rituals connected with the festivals required that the entire festival be repeated, including the dramatic performances.

Given the variety of entertainments offered in Rome—including the chariot races and gladiatorial combats that became increasingly popular in the later Empire, especially after 300 CE—it is not surprising that the Romans built several different kinds of entertainment buildings, stadiums and racecourses as well as theaters. Yet until 55 BCE, theaters in Rome were temporary, built and taken down for each festival. In the first century BCE, the Romans began to build permanent theaters with some regularity. Like their Greek predecessors, the Roman theaters were outdoor amphitheaters, but the Romans built their theaters on level ground, and their superior engineering—particularly the Romans' use of arches in construction—enabled them to build much more massive buildings. Roman theaters were generally three stories in height. A rectangular stage house, or **SCAENA,** stood like the Greek *skene* behind the semicircular orchestra and faced a steeply tiered semicircular auditorium. The facade of the *scaena* was elaborately ornamented with columns and porticos. The Romans built theaters of stone throughout the Empire; many of the Greek theaters that remain today were refurbished and redesigned by the Romans.

Although the Romans continued to perform plays from the Greek theater, they also developed a native strain of drama—represented in the plays of Plautus, Terence, and Seneca. Titus Maccius Plautus (c. 254–c. 184 BCE) is

to be copied for students and readers, they fell out of public circulation. The few texts that have survived of the plays of Aeschylus, Sophocles, Euripides, and Aristophanes are based on copies made for teachers and scholars in Byzantium, dating from the third and fourth centuries CE. Not only have most of their plays been lost (Sophocles is said to have written 123 plays, of which we have seven; Aeschylus is thought to have written more than seventy, of which seven remain; Euripides' nineteen plays are all that remain of more than ninety), but the entire dramatic output of 700 years of theater was lost as well—the names of Agathon, Thespis, Chairemon, Theodektes, Philokles, Ariastas, and others are all that remain of their work. Moreover, since these manuscripts were collected in scholarly or monastic libraries, they have been subject to the destructive forces of history. Many Greek plays were lost in the burning of the library at Alexandria during Caesar's invasion of Egypt; the crusaders sacked Constantinople (previously known as Byzantium) in 1204, and in the process destroyed a city that had joined eastern and western cultures for centuries.

probably the most influential Roman comic playwright. His earliest surviving plays date from 205 BCE, or about thirty-five years after Greek drama was first introduced to Rome; Plautus is thought to have based many of his comedies on Greek New Comedy, but none of these prototypes survives. Plautus is thought to have written more than 100 comedies, many of which—*Amphitryon, The Braggart Warrior, The Rope,* and *The Menaechmus Twins,* for example—established the formal conventions of later comedy. Publius Terentius Afer (c. 195–159 BCE), usually called Terence, was probably born in Carthage and brought to Rome as a slave. Unlike the prolific Plautus, Terence wrote only six comedies, all of which survive, and strove throughout his career to adapt Greek originals to the Roman stage: *The Woman of Andros, Mother-in-Law, Self-Tormentor, Eunuch, Phormio,* and *The Brothers.* The plays of Plautus and Terence have been particularly influential on the form and structure of later European comedy; not only did they establish many of the forms and character types developed by later playwrights, but in the late Middle Ages and Renaissance, their plays were often used to teach Latin in the schools, giving rise to generations of playwrights—including William Shakespeare, Christopher Marlowe, and Molière—who found in Roman drama a form for their own contemporary plays.

The only surviving Roman tragedies were written by Lucius Annaeus

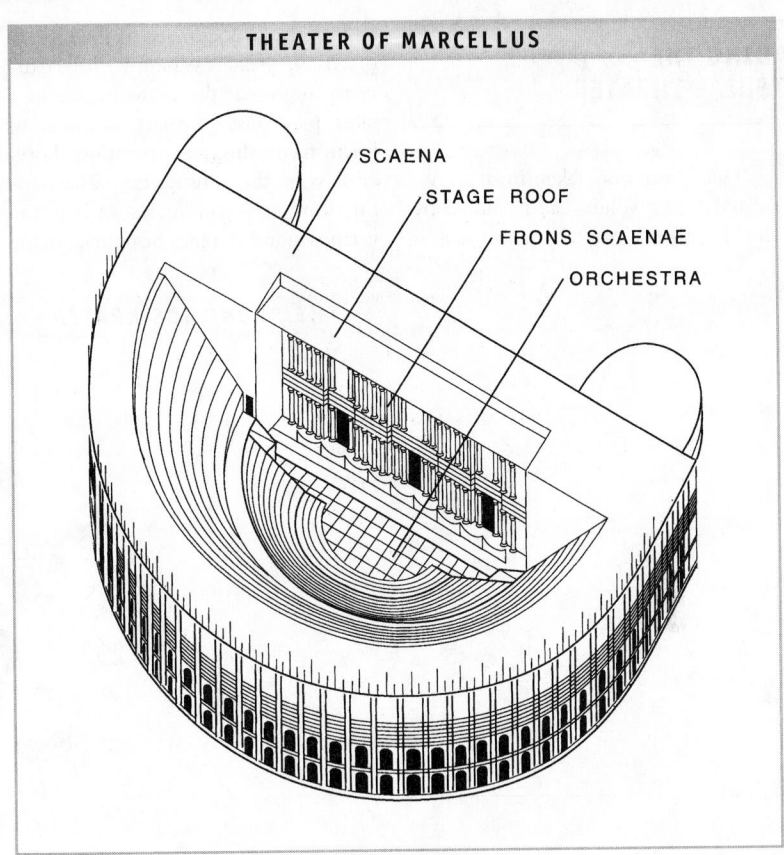

THEATER OF MARCELLUS

SCAENA
STAGE ROOF
FRONS SCAENAE
ORCHESTRA

The Theater of Marcellus was built in Rome, 13–11 BCE.

Seneca (5 BCE–65 CE). Seneca's tragedies were adapted from Greek plays but tend to be more sensational and violent; indeed, it is doubtful that they were performed in the theater. Although only nine of Seneca's plays survive—*The Trojan Women, Medea, Oedipus, Phaedra, Thyestes, Hercules on Oeta, Hercules Mad, The Phoenecian Women, Agamemnon*—Senecan tragedy also exerted an important influence on later drama, especially in the English Renaissance, where Senecan tragedy provided a prototype for the nascent English drama of the sixteenth century.

However, for all their violence, the Crusades also reopened cultural contact with the Islamic Middle East; many of the texts of Greek and Roman culture had been translated into Arabic or had been preserved by Islamic scholars and libraries. With the reopening of European trading and military contacts in the fourteenth, fifteenth, and sixteenth centuries, Europe was able to rediscover the literature of classical Greece, sometimes in Latin translations, sometimes only through commentaries on still-lost texts (such as Aristotle's *Poetics*). In many respects, though, this recovery was principally of Roman theater and drama. The prestige and availability of texts by Latin authors like Plautus, Terence, and Seneca meant that these playwrights were widely taught in schools, convents (such as Gandersheim, where the canoness Hrosvitha [953–973 CE] wrote six comedies modeled on Terence's plays), and universities, where their plays were often performed; the influence of these playwrights can be felt everywhere in European drama of the sixteenth century, most familiarly in Shakespeare's early comedies (like *A Comedy of Errors,* based on Plautus' *The Menaechmus Twins*) and in the

READING THE MATERIAL THEATER

This illustration, taken from an Attic red-figure volute *krater* painted by the "Pronomos painter" c. 450 BCE, is an important document in the history of Greek theater. While it doesn't directly represent the performance of a satyr play onstage, there is much to learn from this vase painting. Look closely at the illustration: What distinctions can you make among the various figures? First, of course, many of the figures seem to be holding their theatrical masks, and several seem to be gazing at them. But among the male figures, several are bearded adult men, while a larger number are beardless, suggesting that they are younger, adolescents. What role do you think they play in the performance? One

THE PRONOMOS *KRATER*

These actors, apparently in a satyr play, appear on a vase painting by the Pronomos painter. Notice that the central seated figure of Dionysus (holding the polelike *thyrsus*) is surrounded by actors holding their masks. The older, bearded actor to the right of Dionysus, wearing the lionskin over his shoulder, is apparently playing Hercules, the

vogue for violent tragedies reminiscent of Seneca's unstaged dramas, plays like Shakespeare's *Titus Andronicus*. The rediscovery of Vitruvius' first-century book on Roman architecture, *De Architectura,* in 1414 (it was printed—a new technology—in 1486) also led a generation of fifteenth- and sixteenth-century architects to design and build theaters on what they took to be a Roman model.

In many respects, though, Greek drama only became widely known in Europe in the later seventeenth and eighteenth centuries, where Greek plays often provided the models for contemporary playwrights, such as Jean Racine (see Unit IV), as well as for the first operas. And it was only in the nineteenth and twentieth centuries that the restoration of classical amphitheaters and the historical and archaeological recovery of the theatrical practices of classical Athens began to make possible experiments in staging classical Greek drama in ways that attempted to approximate the circumstances of classical theater or that attempted to translate those circumstances into a more effective modern idiom. Since the late nineteenth century, for example, the amphitheater at Epidaurus has often been used to stage classical Greek plays in ways that attempt to approximate the traditions of fifth-century Athenian performance.

hint here may be the figure dancing in the bottom row of figures: He has put on his mask, is wearing the *phallos,* and seems to have a satyr's tail. The central figure seated on the throne, with the *thyrsus* in his hand and vines growing just to the left, is labeled "Dionysus," as though the god were seated among the players (he shares the seat with his wife, Ariadne), but there are several other characters who seem to be in costume; the most identifiable is looking at his mask, wearing a full-body costume and carrying the lion-skin of Heracles. Although the illustration seems to provide some fascinating clues to the nature of theatrical performance, it is also misleading in some obvious ways: Just to the right of Ariadne is a seated female figure holding a mask.

protagonist of the play. The other, younger and beardless figures may compose the chorus. While Hercules holds an individualized mask, the chorus members all hold masks similar to each other, and they wear costumes suggestive of satyrs.

Clearly, of course, much has changed in the last 2,500 years, and performing classical drama poses a series of challenges to modern performers. First, the chorus—both its singing and dancing performance style and its function in the drama—has posed a critical problem for modern companies and audiences: German director Max Reinhardt staged a production of *The Oresteia* in 1919 that was among the first of his productions to experiment with large crowds onstage; later productions have tended to make the chorus smaller and more energetic in an attempt to recapture the exciting movement of the classical chorus. Beyond that, the use of masks in classical theater is no longer conventional on the modern stage, although many modern playwrights—Eugene O'Neill, for example, in *Strange Interlude* (1928)—have experimented with masks in an attempt to render psychological complexity with what they take to be "classical" decorum. The 1981 National Theatre (London) production of *The Oresteia,* directed by Sir Peter Hall, used an entirely male cast and performed the play in masks; this production was the first English-language production of a Greek tragedy to be performed in the classical theater at Epidaurus. Although this effort to "recover" the initial circumstances and flavor of Greek performance has driven many performances, Greek drama has also provided the framework for a number of important **AVANT-GARDE** theatrical experiments in the modern era. Of course, Racine's adaptation of Euripides in *Phaedra* might be considered an "updating" of this kind, but in the modern era, stage practices have often been used not so much to recover the classical past as to restage the plays in a modern idiom. Josef Svoboda's brilliant 1963 production of *Oedipus the King* in Prague, for example, took place on a thirty-foot-wide staircase that rose from the bottom of the orchestra pit to beyond the top of the proscenium. The French director Ariane Mnouchkine staged a production of Euripides' *Iphigeneia at Aulis* as an introduction to her staging of *The Oresteia* in 1990 (under the overall title *Les Atrides*); this brilliant production used makeup, costume, movement, and dance idioms from classical Indian and Indonesian theater, implying that a contemporary staging of the Greek classics might well turn to another tradition of "classical" performance to find a still-living stage language. Both for directors—Peter Sellars' 1993 staging of Aeschylus' *The Persians* framed the play with allusions to the Gulf War—and for writers, such as Heiner Müller (*Medeamaterial*), Charles Mee, Jr. (*Orestes*), Caryl Churchill (*A Mouthful of Birds,* based on Euripides' *The Bacchae,* and written with David Lan), Timberlake Wertenbaker (who has translated several Greek plays), Wole Soyinka (*The Bacchae of Euripides*), and others, the theater and drama of classical Athens continue to provide a way to see and understand ourselves.

Framed by a masked member of the Chorus and Jocasta, Oedipus—played here by Laurence Olivier in the landmark 1945 production of *Oedipus the King*—seems finally to recognize the "truth" that he has been seeking.

Framed in a doorway and lit in profile, Diana Rigg embodies the isolation and abandonment of Euripides' *Medea.*

Aeschylus

Aeschylus (c. 523–456 BCE), whose life spanned the first half of the Athenian fifth century, witnessed Athens' chief political and military conflicts and became its preeminent dramatist. His epitaph suggests that he fought at the battle of Marathon against the Persians, and the detailed description of the naval battle at Salamis in his play *The Persians* implies that he may have fought there as well. Aeschylus added the second actor to dramatic performance, only one of his many achievements in the theater. He won his first victory as a playwright at the City Dionysia in 484 BCE, and in 472 BCE produced *The Persians,* for which Pericles served as his sponsoring *choregos.* In 468 BCE he was defeated by Sophocles, but was again victorious with his trilogy *The Oresteia* and the accompanying satyr play *Proteus* (now lost) in 458. Aeschylus died in Sicily in 456 BCE. Of about seventy plays that he is said to have written, seven survive: *The Suppliants, The Persians, Seven Against Thebes, Prometheus Bound,* and *The Oresteia* trilogy—*Agamemnon, The Libation Bearers,* and *The Eumenides.*

THE ORESTEIA

Aeschylus was already an accomplished playwright when he wrote *The Oresteia* in 458 BCE, and his mastery is evident everywhere in the trilogy. Working from the model of Homer's *Odyssey,* Aeschylus fashioned a complex and original narrative of injustice and retribution, relying on events and characters well-known to his Athenian audience. Indeed, *The Oresteia* depends on the audience's understanding of events that took place a generation before the opening of the first play, *Agamemnon.* In the previous generation, the two sons of Pelops—Atreus and Thyestes—began a bitter feud for control of Argos. Thyestes disputed his brother's claim to the throne and seduced his wife; for this he was exiled, but later returned to Argos with his children to ask Atreus' forgiveness. Atreus received his brother, but had the children secretly murdered and baked into a dish that he served to Thyestes. When the truth was revealed to him, Thyestes fled with his one remaining child, Aegisthus, leaving a terrible curse on Atreus, his family, and his descendants.

This curse gives rise to the action of *The Oresteia,* for Aeschylus shows how murder and revenge are played out across the next two generations of the house of Atreus, involving

In this production of *Agamemnon* by the American Repertory Theater, the imagery of the "net" used throughout Aeschylus' play is realized in the scenic design of the play.

Thyestes' son, Aegisthus; Atreus' two sons, Menelaus and Agamemnon; and Agamemnon's wife, Clytaemnestra, and their children, Iphigeneia, Electra, and Orestes. Although most trilogies in the Greek theater were not interconnected in this way, Aeschylus' *Oresteia* uses the trilogy form to shape an epic drama.

Agamemnon

Agamemnon is the first of three plays—including *The Libation Bearers* and *The Eumenides*—collectively called *The Oresteia.* The force of much of Aeschylus' drama lies in a powerful economy of action and character, everywhere visible in *Agamemnon.* *Agamemnon* opens with a watchman awaiting the signal fire that will announce the end of the war on Troy and the return of Agamemnon. This nighttime scene immediately invests the play with a dark sense of foreboding. The opening lyrics of the Chorus provide the context for Agamemnon's arrival by recounting the events of ten years before, when Agamemnon, to secure favorable winds for sailing against Troy, sacrificed his own daughter Iphigeneia. Clytaemnestra, eager to punish Agamemnon for his brutal murder of their daughter, is recognized at once as a deceptive and powerful queen, feared by the Argive elders of the Chorus. Cassandra's curse—that her prophecies will never be believed—is appallingly enacted before us at the moment of Agamemnon's murder, and Aegisthus appears as a kind of thug, dehumanized by his cruel and vengeful mission. For a modern audience, the most problematic character is Agamemnon himself, seen onstage in only one scene. Yet this brief scene testifies to the intricate knotting of history and temperament in the design of Aeschylus' tragedy, and in the design of *The Oresteia* as a whole. We see Agamemnon's lordly ambition for success and glory, his malleability, his insensitivity to his own wrongdoing. Treading on the crimson tapestries, Agamemnon follows a trail of blood leading him into the house of Atreus, to his accounting for the murder of Iphigeneia, to Aegisthus' fulfillment of Thyestes' curse, and to his own death. The cycle of retribution continues in the remaining plays of the trilogy.

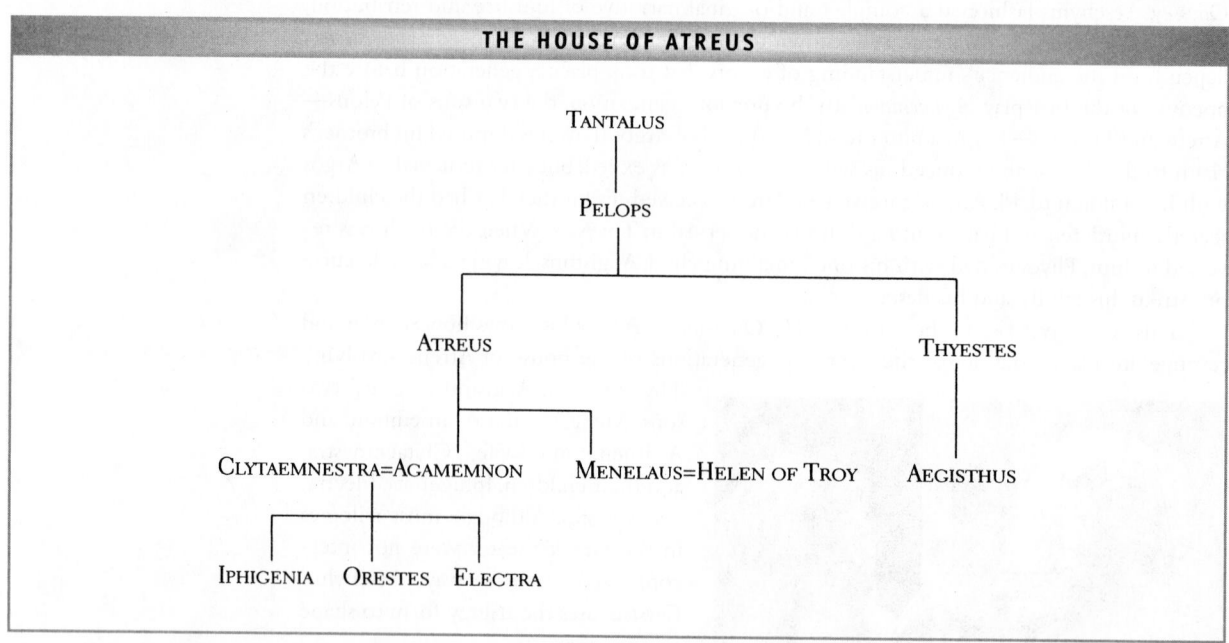

THE HOUSE OF ATREUS

TANTALUS

PELOPS

ATREUS   THYESTES

CLYTAEMNESTRA=AGAMEMNON   MENELAUS=HELEN OF TROY   AEGISTHUS

IPHIGENIA   ORESTES   ELECTRA

The family of Atreus, King of Mycenae and father of Agamemnon and Menelaus, is the focus of powerfully tragic myths and dramas.

AGAMEMNON

Aeschylus

TRANSLATED BY ROBERT FAGLES

CHARACTERS

WATCHMAN   CHORUS, THE OLD MEN OF
CLYTAEMNESTRA   ARGOS *and their* LEADER
HERALD   ATTENDANTS *of Clytaemnestra*
AGAMEMNON   *and of Agamemnon*
CASSANDRA   BODYGUARD *of Aegisthus*
AEGISTHUS

TIME AND SCENE: *A night in the tenth and final autumn of the Trojan War. The house of Atreus in Argos. Before it, an altar stands unlit; a watchman on the high roof fights to stay awake.*

WATCHMAN: Dear gods, set me free from all the pain,
    the long watch I keep, one whole year awake . . .
    propped on my arms, crouched on the roofs of Atreus
    like a dog.
          I know the stars by heart,
5   the armies of the night, and there in the lead
    the ones that bring us snow or the crops of summer,
    bring us all we have—
    our great blazing kings of the sky,
    I know them, when they rise and when they fall . . .
10   and now I watch for the light, the signal-fire
    breaking out of Troy, shouting Troy is taken.
    So she commands, full of her high hopes.
    That woman—she manoeuvres like a man.

    And when I keep to my bed, soaked in dew,
15   and the thoughts go groping through the night
    and the good dreams that used to guard my sleep . . .
    not here, it's the old comrade, terror, at my neck.
    I mustn't sleep, no—

(Shaking himself awake.)

          Look alive, sentry.
    And I try to pick out tunes, I hum a little,
20   a good cure for sleep, and the tears start,
    I cry for the hard times come to the house,
    no longer run like the great place of old.

    Oh for a blessed end to all our pain,
    some godsend burning through the dark—

(Light appears slowly in the east; he struggles to his feet and scans it.)

          I salute you!
25   You dawn of the darkness, you turn night to day—
    I see the light at last.
    They'll be dancing in the streets of Argos
    thanks to you, thanks to this new stroke of—
          Aieeeeee!
    There's your signal clear and true, my queen!
30   Rise up from bed—hurry, lift a cry of triumph

through the house, praise the gods for the beacon,
    if they've taken Troy . . .
          But there it burns,
    fire all the way. I'm for the morning dances.
    Master's luck is mine. A throw of the torch
    has brought us triple-sixes—we have won!   35
    My move now—

(Beginning to dance, then breaking off, lost in thought.)

          Just bring him home. My king.
    I'll take your loving hand in mine and then . . .
    the rest is silence. The ox is on my tongue.
    Aye, but the house and these old stones,
    give them a voice and what a tale they'd tell.   40
    And so would I, gladly . . .
    I speak to those who know; to those who don't
    my mind's a blank. I never say a word.

(He climbs down from the roof and disappears into the palace through a side entrance. A CHORUS, *the old men of Argos who have not learned the news of victory, enters and marches round the altar.)*

CHORUS: Ten years gone, ten to the day
    our great avenger went for Priam—   45
      Menelaus and lord Agamemnon,
    two kings with the power of Zeus,
    the twin throne, twin sceptre,
    Atreus' sturdy yoke of sons
    launched Greece in a thousand ships,   50
    armadas cutting loose from the land,
    armies massed for the cause, the rescue—

(From within the palace CLYTAEMNESTRA *raises a cry of triumph.)*

    the heart within them screamed for all-out war!
    Like vultures robbed of their young,
      the agony sends them frenzied,   55
    soaring high from the nest, round and
    round they wheel, they row their wings,
    stroke upon churning thrashing stroke,
    but all the labour, the bed of pain,
      the young are lost forever.   60
    Yet someone hears on high—Apollo,

---

8 **our great blazing kings** major constellations that demarcate
the seasons

35 **triple-sixes** a winning throw of dice

Pan or Zeus—the piercing wail
these guests of heaven raise,
and drives at the outlaws, late
65   but true to revenge, a stabbing Fury!

(CLYTAEMNESTRA *appears at the doors and pauses with her entourage.*)

So towering Zeus the god of guests
drives Atreus' sons at Paris,
all for a woman manned by many
the generations wrestle, knees
70   grinding the dust, the manhood drains,
the spear snaps in the first blood rites
        that marry Greece and Troy.
And now it goes as it goes
and where it ends is Fate.
75   And neither by singeing flesh
nor tipping cups of wine
nor shedding burning tears can you
enchant away the rigid Fury.

(CLYTAEMNESTRA *lights the altar-fires.*)

We are the old, dishonoured ones,
80   the broken husks of men.
Even then they cast us off,
the rescue mission left us here
to prop a child's strength upon a stick.
What if the new sap rises in his chest?
85   He has no soldiery in him,
        no more than we,
and we are aged past ageing,
gloss of the leaf shrivelled,
three legs at a time we falter on.
90   Old men are children once again,
        a dream that sways and wavers
into the hard light of day.
                            But you,
daughter of Leda, queen Clytaemnestra,
what now, what news, what message
95   drives you through the citadel
        burning victims? Look,
the city gods, the gods of Olympus,
gods of the earth and public markets—
all the altars blazing with your gifts!
100   Argos blazes! Torches
race the sunrise up her skies—
drugged by the lulling holy oils,
        unadulterated,
run from the dark vaults of kings.
105   Tell us the news!
What you can, what is right—
Heal us, soothe our fears!
Now the darkness comes to the fore,
now the hope glows through your victims,
110   beating back this raw, relentless anguish
        gnawing at the heart.

(CLYTAEMNESTRA *ignores them and pursues her rituals; they assemble for the opening chorus.*)

O but I still have power to sound the god's command at
        the roads
that launched the kings. The gods breathe power through
        my song,
        my fighting strength. Persuasion grows with the years—
I sing how the flight of fury hurled the twin command,   115
        one will that hurled young Greece
and winged the spear of vengeance straight for Troy!
The kings of birds to kings of the beaking prows, one black,
        one with a blaze of silver
        skimmed the palace spearhand right   120
        and swooping lower, all could see,
            plunged their claws in a hare, a mother
        bursting with unborn young—the babies spilling,
quick spurts of blood—cut off the race just dashing
        into life!
    Cry, cry for death, but good win out in glory in the end.   125
But the loyal seer of the armies studied Atreus' sons,
two sons with warring hearts—he saw two eagle-kings
        devour the hare and spoke the things to come,
"Years pass, and the long hunt nets the city of Priam,
        the flocks beyond the walls,   130
a kingdom's life and soul—Fate stamps them out.
Just let no curse of the gods lour on us first,
        shatter our giant armour
            forged to strangle Troy. I see
                pure Artemis bristle in pity—   135
                yes, the flying hounds of the Father
            slaughter for armies . . . their own victim . . . a
                woman
trembling young, all born to die—She loathes the eagles'
        feast!"
Cry, cry for death, but good win out in glory in the end.
    "Artemis, lovely Artemis, so kind   140
to the ravening lion's tender, helpless cubs,
the suckling young of beasts that stalk the wilds—
        bring this sign for all its fortune,
            all its brutal torment home to birth!
I beg you, Healing Apollo, soothe her before   145
her crosswinds hold us down and moor the ships too long,
pressing us on to another victim . . .
        nothing sacred, no,
            no feast to be eaten
                the architect of vengeance   150

(*Turning to the palace.*)

            growing strong in the house
            with no fear of the husband
here she waits
the terror raging back and back in the future
        the stealth, the law of the hearth, the mother—   155
            Memory womb of Fury child-avenging
                Fury!"
    So as the eagles wheeled at the crossroads,

---

89 **three legs** a reference to the use of a walking stick as a third
leg in old age

126 **the loyal seer** Calchas, who foretold much hardship at the
outset of the Trojan War

Calchas clashed out the great good blessings mixed with doom
for the halls of kings, and singing with our fate
160   we cry, cry for death, but good win out in glory in the end.

Zeus, great nameless all in all,
if that name will gain his favour,
I will call him Zeus.
I have no words to do him justice,
165   weighing all in the balance,
all I have is Zeus, Zeus—
lift this weight, this torment from my spirit,
cast it once for all.

He who was so mighty once,
170   storming for the wars of heaven,
he has had his day.
And then his son who came to power
met his match in the third fall
and he is gone. Zeus, Zeus—
175   raise your cries and sing him Zeus the Victor!
You will reach the truth:

Zeus has led us on to know,
the Helmsman lays it down as law
that we must suffer, suffer into truth.
180   We cannot sleep, and drop by drop at the heart
the pain of pain remembered comes again,
and we resist, but ripeness comes as well.
From the gods enthroned on the awesome rowing-bench
there comes a violent love.

185   So it was that day the king,
the steersman at the helm of Greece,
would never blame a word the prophet said—
swept away by the wrenching winds of fortune
he conspired! Weatherbound we could not sail,
190   our stores exhausted, fighting strength hard-pressed,
and the squadrons rode in the shallows off Chalkis
where the riptide crashes, drags,

and winds from the north pinned down our hulls at Aulis,
port of anguish . . . head winds starving,
195   sheets and the cables snapped
and the men's minds strayed,
the pride, the bloom of Greece
was raked as time ground on,
ground down, and then the cure for the storm
200   and it was harsher—Calchas cried,
"My captains, Artemis must have blood!"—
so harsh the sons of Atreus
dashed their sceptres on the rocks,
could not hold back the tears,

205   and I still can hear the older warlord saying,
"Obey, obey, or a heavy doom will crush me!—
Oh but doom will crush me
once I rend my child,
the glory of my house—
210   a father's hands are stained,
blood of a young girl streaks the altar.
Pain both ways and what is worse?
Desert the fleets, fail the alliance?
No, but stop the winds with a virgin's blood,
215   feed their lust, their fury?—feed their fury!—

Law is law!—
   Let all go well."

And once he slipped his neck in the strap of Fate,
his spirit veering black, impure, unholy,
once he turned he stopped at nothing,   220
seized with the frenzy
blinding driving to outrage—
wretched frenzy, cause of all our grief!
Yes, he had the heart
to sacrifice his daughter,
to bless the war that avenged a woman's loss,   225
a bridal rite that sped the men-of-war.
"My father, father!"—she might pray to the winds;
no innocence moves her judges mad for war.
Her father called his henchmen on,
on with a prayer,   230
"Hoist her over the altar
like a yearling, give it all your strength!
She's fainting—lift her,
sweep her robes around her,
but slip this strap in her gentle curving lips . . .   235
here, gag her hard, a sound will curse the house"—

and the bridle chokes her voice . . . her saffron robes
pouring over the sand
   her glance like arrows showering
wounding every murderer through with pity
clear as a picture, live,   240
she strains to call their names . . .
I remember often the days with father's guests
when over the feast her voice unbroken,
pure as the hymn her loving father
bearing third libations, sang to Saving Zeus—   245
transfixed with joy, Atreus' offspring
throbbing out their love.

What comes next? I cannot see it, cannot say.
The strong techniques of Calchas do their work.
But Justice turns the balance scales,   250
sees that we suffer
and we suffer and we learn.
And we will know the future when it comes.
Greet it too early, weep too soon.
It all comes clear in the light of day.   255
Let all go well today, well as she could want,

(*Turning to* CLYTAEMNESTRA.)

our midnight watch, our lone defender,
single-minded queen.
LEADER: We've come,
Clytaemnestra. We respect your power.
Right it is to honour the warlord's woman   260
once he leaves the throne.
        But why these fires?
Good news, or more good hopes? We're loyal,
we want to hear, but never blame your silence.

---

245 **third libations** offered to Zeus, following libations to the gods of Olympus and the spirits of the dead

CLYTAEMNESTRA: Let the new day shine—as the proverb says—
265   glorious from the womb of Mother Night.

(Lost in prayer, then turning to the CHORUS.*)*

    You will hear a joy beyond your hopes.
    Priam's citadel—the Greeks have taken Troy!
LEADER: No, what do you mean? I can't believe it.
CLYTAEMNESTRA: Troy is ours. Is that clear enough?
LEADER: The joy of it,
270   stealing over me, calling up my tears—
CLYTAEMNESTRA: Yes, your eyes expose your loyal hearts.
LEADER: And you have proof?
CLYTAEMNESTRA: I do,
    I must. Unless the god is lying.
LEADER: That,
    or a phantom spirit sends you into raptures.
275 CLYTAEMNESTRA: No one takes me in with visions—senseless
    dreams.
LEADER: Or giddy rumour, you haven't indulged yourself—
CLYTAEMNESTRA: You treat me like a child, you mock me?
LEADER: Then when did they storm the city?
CLYTAEMNESTRA: Last night, I say, the mother of this
    morning.
280 LEADER: And who on earth could run the news so fast?
CLYTAEMNESTRA: The god of fire—rushing fire from Ida!
    And beacon to beacon rushed it on to me,
    my couriers riding home the torch.
                From Troy
    to the bare rock of Lemnos, Hermes' Spur,
285   and the Escort winged the great light west
    to the Saving Father's face, Mount Athos hurled it
    third in the chain and leaping Ocean's back
    the blaze went dancing on to ecstasy—pitch-pine
    streaming gold like a new-born sun—and brought
290   the word in flame to Mount Makistos' brow.
    No time to waste, straining, fighting sleep,
    that lookout heaved a torch glowing over
    the murderous straits of Euripos to reach
    Messapion's watchmen craning for the signal.
295   Fire for word of fire! tense with the heather
    withered gray, they stack it, set it ablaze—
    the hot force of the beacon never flags,
    it springs the Plain of Asôpos, rears
    like a harvest moon to hit Kithairon's crest
300   and drives new men to drive the fire on.
    That relay pants for the far-flung torch,
    they swell its strength outstripping my commands
    and the light inflames the marsh, the Gorgon's Eye,
    it strikes the peak where the wild goats range—
305   my laws, my fire whips that camp!
    They spare nothing, eager to build its heat,
    and a huge beard of flame overcomes the headland
    beetling down the Saronic Gulf, and flaring south
    it brings the dawn to the Black Widow's face—
310   the watch that looms above your heads—and now
    the true son of the burning flanks of Ida

---

281 **Ida** mountain near Troy   286 **Saving Father's face** Mount
Athos, a seat of Zeus the Savior in northern Greece   309 **Black
Widow's face** "Spider Mountain," perhaps the citadel of Mycenae

    crashes on the roofs of Atreus' sons!
    And I ordained it all.
    Torch to torch, running for their lives,
    one long succession racing home my fire.   315
                One,
    first in the laps and last, wins out in triumph.
    There you have my proof, my burning sign, I tell you—
    the power my lord passed on from Troy to me!
LEADER: We'll thank the gods, my lady—first this story,
    let me lose myself in the wonder of it all!   320
    Tell it start to finish, tell us all.
CLYTAEMNESTRA: The city's ours—in our hands this very day!
    I can hear the cries in crossfire rock the walls.
    Pour oil and wine in the same bowl,
    what have you, friendship? A struggle to the end.   325
    So with the victors and the victims—the outcries,
    you can hear them clashing like their fates.

    They are kneeling by the bodies of the dead,
    embracing men and brothers, infants over
    the aged loins that gave them life, and sobbing,   330
    as the yoke constricts their last free breath,
    for every dear one lost.
                And the others,
    there, plunging breakneck through the night—
    the labour of battle sets them down, ravenous,
    to breakfast on the last remains of Troy.   335
    Not by rank but chance, by the lots they draw,
    they lodge in the houses captured by the spear,
    settling in so soon, released from the open sky,
    the frost and dew. Lucky men, off guard at last,
    they sleep away their first good night in years.   340
    If only they are revering the city's gods,
    the shrines of the gods who love the conquered land,
    no plunderer will be plundered in return.
    Just let no lust, no mad desire seize the armies
    to ravish what they must not touch—   345
    overwhelmed by all they've won!
                The run for home
    and safety waits, the swerve at the post,
    the final lap of the gruelling two-lap race.
    And even if the men come back with no offence
    to the gods, the avenging dead may never rest—   350
    Oh let no new disaster strike! And here
    you have it, what a woman has to say.
    Let the best win out, clear to see.
    A small desire but all that I could want.
LEADER: Spoken like a man, my lady, loyal,   355
    full of self-command. I've heard your sign
    and now your vision.

(Reaching towards her as she turns and re-enters the palace.)

             Now to praise the gods.
    The joy is worth the labour.
CHORUS: O Zeus my king and Night, dear Night,
    queen of the house who covers us with glories,   360
    you slung your net on the towers of Troy,
    neither young nor strong could leap
    the giant dredge net of slavery,
        all-embracing ruin.
    I adore you, iron Zeus of the guests   365

and your revenge—you drew your longbow
year by year to a taut full draw
till one bolt, not falling short
or arching over the stars,
370   could split the mark of Paris!
The sky stroke of god!—it is all Troy's to tell,
but even I can trace it to its cause:
god does as god decrees.
        And still some say
375   that heaven would never stoop to punish men
who trample the lovely grace of things
untouchable. How wrong they are!
        A curse burns bright on crime—
            full-blown, the father's crimes will blossom,
380   burst into the son's.
Let there be less suffering . . .
give us the sense to live on what we need.

            Bastions of wealth
            are no defence for the man
385   who treads the grand altar of Justice
                down and out of sight.

Persuasion, maddening child of Ruin
overpowers him—Ruin plans it all.
And the wound will smoulder on,
390   there is no cure,
a terrible brilliance kindles on the night.
He is bad bronze scraped on a touchstone:
put to the test, the man goes black.
        Like the boy who chases
395   a bird on the wing, brands his city,
            brings it down and prays,
but the gods are deaf
to the one who turns to crime, they tear him down.

        So Paris learned:
400   he came to Atreus' house
        and shamed the tables spread for guests,
            he stole away the queen.

And she left her land chaos, clanging shields,
companions tramping, bronze prows, men in bronze,
405   and she came to Troy with a dowry, death,
strode through the gates
        defiant in every stride,
as prophets of the house looked on and wept,
"Oh the halls and the lords of war,
410   the bed and the fresh prints of love.
I *see* him, unavenging, unavenged,
the stun of his desolation is so clear—
        he longs for the one who lies across the sea
until her phantom seems to sway the house.

415   Her curving images,
            her beauty hurts her lord,
            the eyes starve and the touch
                of love is gone,

"and radiant dreams are passing in the night,
420   the memories throb with sorrow, joy with pain . . .
        it is pain to dream and see desires
slip through the arms,
        a vision lost for ever

winging down the moving drifts of sleep."
So he grieves at the royal hearth   425
yet others' grief is worse, far worse.
All through Greece for those who flocked to war
they are holding back the anguish now,
    you can feel it rising now in every house;
I tell you there is much to tear the heart.   430

            They knew the men they sent,
            but now in place of men
            ashes and urns come back
                to every hearth.

War, War, the great gold-broker of corpses   435
holds the balance of the battle on his spear!
Home from the pyres he sends them,
    home from Troy to the loved ones,
heavy with tears, the urns brimmed full,
    the heroes return in gold-dust,   440
dear, light ash for men; and they weep,
they praise them, "He had skill in the swordplay,"
        "He went down so tall in the onslaught,"
"All for another's woman." So they mutter
in secret and the rancour steals   445
towards our staunch defenders, Atreus' sons.

            And there they ring the walls, the young,
            the lithe, the handsome hold the graves
            they won in Troy; the enemy earth
                rides over those who conquered.   450

The people's voice is heavy with hatred,
now the curses of the people must be paid,
and now I wait, I listen . . .
    there—there is something breathing
under the night's shroud. God takes aim   455
    at the ones who murder many;
the swarthy Furies stalk the man
gone rich beyond all rights—with a twist
        of fortune grind him down, dissolve him
into the blurring dead—there is no help.   460
The reach for power can recoil,
the bolt of god can strike you at a glance.

            Make me rich with no man's envy,
            neither a raider of cities, no,
            nor slave come face to face with life   465
                overpowered by another.

(Speaking singly.)

—Fire comes and the news is good,
    it races through the streets
but is it true? Who knows?
Or just another lie from heaven?   470

—Show us the man so childish, wonderstruck,
    he's fired up with the first torch,
then when the message shifts
he's sick at heart.
            —Just like a woman
to fill with thanks before the truth is clear.   475

—So gullible. Their stories spread like wildfire,
    they fly fast and die faster;
rumours voiced by women coming to nothing.

LEADER: Soon we'll know her fires for what they are,
480 her relay race of torches hand-to-hand—
know if they're real or just a dream,
the hope of a morning here to take our senses.
I see a herald running from the beach
and a victor's spray of olive shades his eyes
485 and the dust he kicks, twin to the mud of Troy,
shows he has a voice—no kindling timber
on the cliffs, no signal-fires for him.
He can shout the news and give us joy,
or else . . . please, not that.
                                   Bring it on,
490 good fuel to build the first good fires.
And if anyone calls down the worst on Argos
let him reap the rotten harvest of his mind.

(*The* HERALD *rushes in and kneels on the ground.*)

HERALD: Good Greek earth, the soil of my fathers!
Ten years out, and a morning brings me back.
495 All hopes snapped but one—I'm home at last.
Never dreamed I'd die in Greece, assigned
the narrow plot I love the best.
                                   And now
I salute the land, the light of the sun,
our high lord Zeus and the king of Pytho—
500 no more arrows, master, raining on our heads!
At Scamander's banks we took our share,
your longbow brought us down like plague.
Now come, deliver us, heal us—lord Apollo!
Gods of the market, here, take my salute.
505 And you, my Hermes, Escort,
loving Herald, the herald's shield and prayer!—
And the shining dead of the land who launched the armies,
warm us home . . . we're all the spear has left.
You halls of the kings, you roofs I cherish,
510 sacred seats—you gods that catch the sun,
if your glances ever shone on him in the old days,
greet him well—so many years are lost.
He comes, he brings us light in the darkness,
free for every comrade, Agamemnon lord of men.

515 Give him the royal welcome he deserves!
He hoisted the pickaxe of Zeus who brings revenge,
he dug Troy down, he worked her soil down,
the shrines of her gods and the high altars, gone!—
and the seed of her wide earth he ground to bits.
520 That's the yoke he claps on Troy. The king,
the son of Atreus comes. The man is blest,
the one man alive to merit such rewards.

Neither Paris nor Troy, partners to the end,
can say their work outweighs their wages now.
525 Convicted of rapine, stripped of all his spoils,
and his father's house and the land that gave it life—
he's scythed them to the roots. The sons of Priam
pay the price twice over.

499–502 **the king of Pytho . . . plague** at Troy, when Agamemnon refused to release a daughter of Apollo's priest, Apollo ("king
of Pytho") visited a plague upon the Greeks by shooting his arrows among them 528 **pay the price twice over** in ancient
Greek law, double damages were the penalty for theft

LEADER: Welcome home
from the wars, herald, long live your joy.
HERALD: Our joy—
now I could die gladly. Say the word, dear gods. 530
LEADER: Longing for your country left you raw?
HERALD: The tears fill my eyes, for joy.
LEADER: You too,
down the sweet disease that kills a man
with kindness . . .
HERALD: Go on, I don't see what you—
LEADER: Love
for the ones who love you—that's what took you. 535
HERALD: You mean
the land and the armies hungered for each other?
LEADER: There were times I thought I'd faint with longing.
HERALD: So anxious for the armies, why?
LEADER: For years now,
only my silence kept me free from harm.
HERALD: What,
with the kings gone did someone threaten you? 540
LEADER: So much . . .
now as you say, it would be good to die.
HERALD: True, we *have* done well.
Think back in the years and what have you?
A few runs of luck, a lot that's bad.
Who but a god can go through life unmarked? 545
A long, hard pull we had, if I would tell it all.
The iron rations, penned in the gangways
hock by jowl like sheep. Whatever miseries
break a man, our quota, every sun-starved day.

Then on the beaches it was worse. Dug in 550
under the enemy ramparts—deadly going.
Out of the sky, out of the marshy flats
the dews soaked us, turned the ruts we fought from
into gullies, made our gear, our scalps
crawl with lice. 555
              And talk of the cold,
the sleet to freeze the gulls, and the big snows
come avalanching down from Ida. Oh but the heat,
the sea and the windless noons, the swells asleep,
dropped to a dead calm . . .

But why weep now? 560
It's over for us, over for them.
The dead can rest and never rise again;
no need to call their muster. We're alive,
do we have to go on raking up old wounds?
Good-bye to all that. Glad I am to say it. 565

For us, the remains of the Greek contingents,
the good wins out, no pain can tip the scales,
not now. So shout this boast to the bright sun—
fitting it is—wing it over the seas and rolling earth:

"Once when an Argive expedition captured Troy 570
they hauled these spoils back to the gods of Greece,
they bolted them high across the temple doors,
the glory of the past!"
              And hearing that,
men will applaud our city and our chiefs,
and Zeus will have the hero's share of fame— 575
he did the work.

That's all I have to say.
LEADER: I'm convinced, glad that I was wrong.
    Never too old to learn; it keeps me young.

(CLYTAEMNESTRA *enters with her women.*)

        First the house and the queen, it's their affair,
580   but I can taste the riches.
CLYTAEMNESTRA: I cried out long ago!—
    for joy, when the first herald came burning
    through the night and told the city's fall.
    And there were some who smiled and said,
    "A few fires persuade you Troy's in ashes.
585   Women, women, elated over nothing."

    You made me seem deranged.
    For all that I sacrificed—a woman's way,
    you'll say—station to station on the walls
    we lifted cries of triumph that resounded
590   in the temples of the gods. We lulled and blessed
    the fires with myrrh and they consumed our victims.

(*Turning to the* HERALD.)

    But enough. Why prolong the story?
    From the king himself I'll gather all I need.
    Now for the best way to welcome home
595   my lord, my good lord . . .
                    No time to lose!
    What dawn can feast a woman's eyes like this?
    I can see the light, the husband plucked from war
    by the Saving God and open wide the gates.

    Tell him that, and have him come with speed,
600   the people's darling—how they long for him.
    And for his wife,
    may he return and find her true at hall,
    just as the day he left her, faithful to the last.
    A watchdog gentle to him alone,

(*Glancing towards the palace.*)

                            savage
605   to those who cross his path. I have not changed.
    The strains of time can never break our seal.
    In love with a new lord, in ill repute I am
    as practised as I am in dyeing bronze.

    That is my boast, teeming with the truth.
610   I am proud, a woman of my nobility—
    I'd hurl it from the roofs!

(*She turns sharply, enters the palace.*)

LEADER: She speaks well, but it takes no seer to know
    she only says what's right.

(*The* HERALD *attempts to leave; the* LEADER *takes him by the arm.*)

                    Wait, one thing.
    Menelaus, is he home too, safe with the men?
615   The power of the land—dear king.
HERALD: I doubt that lies will help my friends,
    in the lean months to come.

---

580 **I can taste the riches** according to custom, the bearer of
good news was rewarded

LEADER: Help us somehow, tell the truth as well.
    But when the two conflict it's hard to hide—
    out with it.   620
HERALD: He's lost, gone from the fleets!
    He and his ship, it's true.
LEADER: After you watched him
    pull away from Troy? Or did some storm
    attack you all and tear him off the line?
HERALD: There,
    like a marksman, the whole disaster cut to a word.
LEADER: How do the escorts give him out—dead or alive?   625
HERALD: No clear report. No one knows . . .
    only the wheeling sun that heats the earth to life.
LEADER: But then the storm—how did it reach the ships?
    How did it end? Were the angry gods on hand?
HERALD: This blessed day, ruin it with *them?*   630
    Better to keep their trophies far apart.

    When a runner comes, his face in tears,
    saddled with what his city dreaded most,
    the armies routed, two wounds in one,
    one to the city, one to hearth and home . . .   635
    our best men, droves of them, victims
    herded from every house by the two-barb whip
    that Ares likes to crack,
                    that charioteer
    who packs destruction shaft by shaft,
    careering on with his brace of bloody mares—   640
    When he comes in, I tell you, dragging that much pain,
    wail your battle-hymn to the Furies, and high time!
    But when he brings salvation home to a city
    singing out her heart—
    how can I mix the good with so much bad   645
    and blurt out this?—
                    "Storms swept the Greeks,
    and not without the anger of the gods!"
    Those enemies for ages, fire and water,
    sealed a pact and showed it to the world—
    they crushed our wretched squadrons.   650
                    Night looming,
    breakers lunging in for the kill
    and the black gales come brawling out of the north—
    ships ramming, prow into hooking prow, gored
    by the rush-and-buck of hurricane pounding rain
    by the cloudburst—   655
                    ships stampeding into the darkness,
    lashed and spun by the savage shepherd's hand!

    But when the sun comes up to light the skies
    I see the Aegean heaving into a great bloom
    of corpses . . . Greeks, the pick of a generation
    scattered through the wrecks and broken spars.   660

    But not us, not our ship, our hull untouched.
    Someone stole us away or begged us off.
    No mortal—a god, death grip on the tiller,
    or lady luck herself, perched on the helm,
    she pulled us through, she saved us. Aye,   665
    we'll never battle the heavy surf at anchor,
    never shipwreck up some rocky coast.

---

648 **fire and water** lightning and the sea

But once we cleared that sea-hell, not even
trusting luck in the cold light of day,
670 we battened on our troubles, they were fresh—
the armada punished, bludgeoned into nothing.
And now if one of them still has the breath
he's saying *we* are lost. Why not?
We say the same of him. Well,
675 here's to the best.
                    And Menelaus?
Look to it, he's come back, and yet . . .
if a shaft of the sun can track him down,
alive, and his eyes full of the old fire—
thanks to the strategies of Zeus, Zeus
680 would never tear the house out by the roots—
then there's hope our man will make it home.

You've heard it all. Now you have the truth.

(*Rushing out.*)

CHORUS: Who—what power named the name that drove your
          fate?—
what hidden brain could divine your future,
685 steer that word to the mark,
to the bride of spears,
     the whirlpool churning armies,
          Oh for all the world a Helen!
Hell at the prows, hell at the gates
690 hell on the men-of-war,
from her lair's sheer veils she drifted
     launched by the giant western wind,
          and the long tall waves of men in armour,
huntsmen trailing the oar-blades' dying spoor
695 slipped into her moorings,
     Simois' mouth that chokes with foliage,
               bayed for bloody strife,
for Troy's Blood Wedding Day—she drives her word,
her burning will to the birth, the Fury
700 late but true to the cause,
to the tables shamed
     and Zeus who guards the hearth—
          the Fury makes the Trojans pay!
Shouting their hymns, hymns for the bride
705 hymns for the kinsmen doomed
to the wedding march of Fate.
     Troy changed her tune in her late age,
          and I think I hear the dirges mourning
"Paris, born and groomed for the bed of Fate!"
710 They mourn with their life breath,
     they sing their last, the sons of Priam
               born for bloody slaughter.
     So a man once reared
a lion cub at hall, snatched
715 from the breast, still craving milk
     in the first flush of life.
A captivating pet for the young,
and the old men adored it, pampered it
     in their arms, day in, day out,
720 like an infant just born.
Its eyes on fire, little beggar,
fawning for its belly, slave to food.

But it came of age
and the parent strain broke out
and it paid its breeders back.   725
     Grateful it was, it went
through the flock to prepare a feast,
an illicit orgy—the house swam with blood,
     none could resist that agony—
          massacre vast and raw!   730
From god there came a priest of ruin,
adopted by the house to lend it warmth.
And the first sensation Helen brought to Troy . . .
call it a spirit
     shimmer of winds dying   735
          glory light as gold
          shaft of the eyes dissolving, open bloom
     that wounds the heart with love.
But veering wild in mid-flight
she whirled her wedding on to a stabbing end,   740
slashed at the sons of Priam—hearthmate, friend to the
     death,
          sped by Zeus who speeds the guest,
a bride of tears, a Fury.

There's an ancient saying, old as man himself:
men's prosperity   745
     never will die childless,
          once full-grown it breeds.
          Sprung from the great good fortune in the race
     comes bloom on bloom of pain—
insatiable wealth! But not I,   750
I alone say this. Only the reckless act
can breed impiety, multiplying crime on crime,
     while the house kept straight and just
is blessed with radiant children.

          But ancient Violence longs to breed,   755
               new Violence comes
     when its fatal hour comes, the demon comes
     to take her toll—no war, no force, no prayer
          can hinder the midnight Fury stamped
     with parent Fury moving through the house.   760

          But Justice shines in sooty hovels,
               loves the decent life.
     From proud halls crusted with gilt by filthy hands
          she turns her eyes to find the pure in spirit—
     spurning the wealth stamped counterfeit with praise,   765
          she steers all things towards their destined end.

(AGAMEMNON *enters in his chariot, his plunder borne before him by
his entourage; behind him, half hidden, stands* CASSANDRA. *The*
OLD MEN *press towards him.*)

Come, my king, the scourge of Troy,
     the true son of Atreus—
How to salute you, how to praise you
neither too high nor low, but hit   770
the note of praise that suits the hour?
So many prize some brave display,

---

725 **it paid its breeders back** on reaching maturity, children
customarily made thank offerings to their parents

775 they prefer some flaunt of honour
        once they break the bounds.
    When a man fails they share his grief,
    but the pain can never cut them to the quick.
    When a man succeeds they share his glory,
    torturing their faces into smiles.
    But the good shepherd knows his flock.
780 When the eyes seem to brim with love
        and it is only unction, fawning,
    he will know, better than we can know.
    That day you marshalled the armies
    all for Helen—no hiding it now—
785 I drew you in my mind in black;
    you seemed a menace at the helm,
        sending men to the grave
    to bring her home, that hell on earth.
    But now from the depths of trust and love
790 I say Well fought, well won—
        the end is worth the labour!
    Search, my king, and learn at last
    who stayed at home and kept their faith
        and who betrayed the city.

AGAMEMNON: First,
795 with justice I salute my Argos and my gods,
    my accomplices who brought me home and won
    my rights from Priam's Troy—the just gods.
    No need to hear our pleas. Once for all
    they consigned their lots to the urn of blood,
800 they pitched on death for men, annihilation
    for the city. Hope's hand, hovering
    over the urn of mercy, left it empty.
    Look for the smoke—it is the city's seamark,
    building even now.
                            The storms of ruin live!
805 Her last dying breath, rising up from the ashes
    sends us gales of incense rich in gold.

    For that we must thank the gods with a sacrifice
    our sons will long remember. For their mad outrage
    of a queen we raped their city—we were right.
810 The beast of Argos, foals of the wild mare,
    thousands massed in armour rose on the night
    the Pleiades went down, and crashing through
    their walls our bloody lion lapped its fill,
    gorging on the blood of kings.
                            Our thanks to the gods,
815 long drawn out, but it is just the prelude.

(CLYTAEMNESTRA *approaches with her* ATTENDANTS; *they are carrying dark red tapestries.* AGAMEMNON *turns to the leader.*)

    And your concern, old man, is on my mind.
    I hear you and agree, I will support you.
    How rare, men with the character to praise
820 a friend's success without a trace of envy,
    poison to the heart—it deals a double blow.
    Your own losses weigh you down but then,

799–802 **they consigned . . . empty** Athenian citizens voted in law cases by placing one hand over each of two urns and dropping a voting-pebble into either the urn for acquittal or the urn for condemnation   810 **the wild mare** the Trojan Horse

---

    look at your neighbour's fortune and you weep.
    Well I know. I understand society,
    the flattering mirror of the proud.
                            My comrades . . .
825 they're shadows, I tell you, ghosts of men
    who swore they'd die for me. Only Odysseus:
    I dragged that man to the wars but once in harness
    he was a trace-horse, he gave his all for me.
    Dead or alive, no matter, I can praise him.

830 And now this cause involving men and gods.
    We must summon the city for a trial,
    found a national tribunal. Whatever's healthy,
    shore it up with law and help it flourish.
    Wherever something calls for drastic cures
835 we make our noblest effort: amputate or wield
    the healing iron, burn the cancer at the roots.

    Now I go to my father's house—
    I give the gods my right hand, my first salute.
    The ones who sent me forth have brought me home.

(*He starts down from the chariot, looks at* CLYTAEMNESTRA, *stops, and offers up a prayer.*)

840 Victory, you have sped my way before,
    now speed me to the last.

(CLYTAEMNESTRA *turns from the king to the* CHORUS.)

CLYTAEMNESTRA: Old nobility of Argos
    gathered here, I am not ashamed to tell you
    how I love the man. I am older,
    and the fear dies away . . . I am human.
845 Nothing I say was learned from others.
    This is my life, my ordeal, long as the siege
    he laid at Troy and more demanding.
                                      First,
    when a woman sits at home and the man is gone,
    the loneliness is terrible,
850 unconscionable . . .
    and the rumours spread and fester,
    a runner comes with something dreadful,
    close on his heels the next and his news worse,
    and they shout it out and the whole house can hear:
855 and wounds—if he took one wound for each report
    to penetrate these walls, he's gashed like a dragnet,
    more, if he had only died . . .
    for each death that swelled his record, he could boast
    like a triple-bodied Geryon risen from the grave,
860 "Three shrouds I dug from the earth, one for every body
    that went down!"
                            The rumours broke like fever,
    broke and then rose higher. There were times
    they cut me down and eased my throat from the noose.
    I wavered between the living and the dead.

(*Turning to* AGAMEMNON.)

                                      And so
865 our child is gone, not standing by our side,

826–828 **Only Odysseus . . . trace-horse** to try to evade conscription for the Trojan War, Odysseus feigned madness, but performed loyally once at war   859 **Geryon** a three-bodied giant killed by Heracles

the bond of our dearest pledges, mine and yours;
by all rights our child should be here . . .
Orestes. You seem startled.
You needn't be. Our loyal brother-in-arms
870   will take good care of him, Strophios the Phocian.
He warned from the start we court two griefs in one.
You risk all on the wars—and what if the people
rise up howling for the king, and anarchy
should dash our plans?
                        Men, it is their nature,
875   trampling on the fighter once he's down.
Our child is gone. That is my self-defence
and it is true.
      For me, the tears that welled
like springs are dry. I have no tears to spare.
I'd watch till late at night, my eyes still burn,
880   I sobbed by the torch I lit for you alone.

(*Glancing towards the palace.*)

I never let it die . . . but in my dreams
the high thin wail of a gnat would rouse me,
piercing like a trumpet—I could see you
suffer more than all
885   the hours that slept with me could ever bear.

I endured it all. And now, free of grief,
I would salute that man the watchdog of the fold,
the mainroyal, saving stay of the vessel,
rooted oak that thrusts the roof sky-high,
890   the father's one true heir.
Land at dawn to the shipwrecked past all hope,
light of the morning burning off the night of storm,
the cold clear spring to the parched horseman—
O the ecstasy, to flee the yoke of Fate!
895   It is right to use the titles he deserves.
Let envy keep her distance. We have suffered
long enough.

(*Reaching towards* AGAMEMNON.)

                     Come to me now, my dearest,
down from the car of war, but never set the foot
that stamped out Troy on earth again, my great one.

900   Women, why delay? You have your orders.
Pave his way with tapestries.

(*They begin to spread the crimson tapestries between the king and the palace doors.*)

                        Quickly.
Let the red stream flow and bear him home
to the home he never hoped to see—Justice,
lead him in!
              Leave all the rest to me.
905   The spirit within me never yields to sleep.
We will set things right, with the god's help.
We will do whatever Fate requires.
AGAMEMNON: There
is Leda's daughter, the keeper of my house.

---

908 **Leda** visited by Zeus in the form of a swan, Leda conceived both Clytaemnestra and Helen

And the speech to suit my absence, much too long.
But the praise that does us justice,   910
let it come from others, then we prize it.
                              This—
you treat me like a woman. Grovelling, gaping up at me—
what am I, some barbarian peacocking out of Asia?
Never cross my path with robes and draw the lightning.
Never—only the gods deserve the pomps of honour   915
and the stiff brocades of fame. To walk on them . . .
I am human, and it makes my pulses stir
with dread.
              Give me the tributes of a man
and not a god, a little earth to walk on,
not this gorgeous work.   920
There is no need to sound my reputation.
I have a sense of right and wrong, what's more—
heaven's proudest gift. Call no man blest
until he ends his life in peace, fulfilled.
If I can live by what I say, I have no fear.   925
CLYTAEMNESTRA: One thing more. Be true to your ideals and
      tell me—
AGAMEMNON: True to my ideals? Once I violate them I am
      lost.
CLYTAEMNESTRA: Would you have sworn this act to god in a
      time of terror?
AGAMEMNON: Yes, if a prophet called for a last, drastic rite.
CLYTAEMNESTRA: But Priam—can you see him if he had your   930
      success?
AGAMEMNON: Striding on the tapestries of god, I see him
      now.
CLYTAEMNESTRA: And *you* fear the reproach of common
      men?
AGAMEMNON: The voice of the people—aye, they have
      enormous power.
CLYTAEMNESTRA: Perhaps, but where's the glory without a
      little gall?
AGAMEMNON: And where's the woman in all this lust for   935
      glory?
CLYTAEMNESTRA: But the great victor—it becomes him to
      give way.
AGAMEMNON: Victory in this . . . war of ours, it means so
      much to you?
CLYTAEMNESTRA: O give way! The power is yours if you
      surrender,
all of your own free will, to me!
AGAMEMNON: Enough.
If you are so determined—   940

(*Turning to the* ATTENDANTS, *pointing to his boots.*)

Let someone help me off with these at least.
Old slaves, they've stood me well.
                              Hurry,
and while I tread his splendours dyed red in the sea,
may no god watch and strike me down with envy
from on high. I feel such shame—   945
to tread the life of the house, a kingdom's worth
of silver in the weaving.

(*He steps down from the chariot to the tapestries and reveals* CASSANDRA, *dressed in the sacred regalia, the fillets, robes, and sceptre of Apollo.*)

Done is done.
Escort this stranger in, be gentle.
Conquer with compassion. Then the gods
950   shine down upon you, gently. No one chooses
the yoke of slavery, not of one's free will—
and she least of all. The gift of the armies,
flower and pride of all the wealth we won,
she follows me from Troy.
                                           And now,
955   since you have brought me down with your insistence,
just this once I enter my father's house,
trampling royal crimson as I go.

(*He takes his first steps and pauses.*)

CLYTAEMNESTRA: There is the sea
and who will drain it dry? Precious as silver,
inexhaustible, ever-new, it breeds the more we reap it—
960   tides on tides of crimson dye our robes blood-red.
Our lives are based on wealth, my king,
the gods have seen to that.
Destitution, our house has never heard the word.
I would have sworn to tread on legacies of robes,
965   at one command from an oracle, deplete the house—
suffer the worst to bring that dear life back!

(*Encouraged,* AGAMEMNON *strides to the entrance.*)

When the root lives on, the new leaves come back,
spreading a dense shroud of shade across the house
to thwart the Dog Star's fury. So you return
970   to the father's hearth, you bring us warmth in winter
like the sun—
                        And you are Zeus when Zeus
tramples the bitter virgin grape for new wine
and the welcome chill steals through the halls, at last
the master moves among the shadows of his house,
fulfilled.

(AGAMEMNON *goes over the threshold; the* ATTENDANTS *gather up
the tapestries while* CLYTAEMNESTRA *prays.*)

975   Zeus, Zeus, master of all fulfilment, now fulfil our
prayers—
speed our rites to their fulfilment once for all!

(*She enters the palace, the doors close, the* OLD MEN *huddle in terror.*)

CHORUS: Why, why does it rock me, never stops,
this terror beating down my heart,
                        this seer that sees it all—
980   it beats its wings, uncalled unpaid
thrust on the lungs
the mercenary song beats on and on
singing a prophet's strain—
                        and I can't throw it off
985   like dreams that make no sense,
and the strength drains
that filled the mind with trust,
and the years drift by and the driven sand
                        has buried the mooring lines

---

969 **Dog Star** Sirius, whose rising commonly marks the hot
"dog days" of summer

---

that churned when the armoured squadrons cut for Troy ...   990
and now I believe it, I can prove he's home,
                        my own clear eyes for witness—
                                                      Agamemnon!
Still it's chanting, beating deep so deep in the heart
this dirge of the Furies, oh dear god,
not fit for the lyre, its own master   995
                it kills our spirit
kills our hopes
and it's real, true, no fantasy—
                stark terror whirls the brain
                        and the end is coming   1000
                Justice comes to birth—
I pray my fears prove false and fall
and die and never come to birth!
Even exultant health, well we know,
                exceeds its limits, comes so near disease   1005
it can breach the wall between them.

Even a man's fate, held true on course,
                in a blinding flash rams some hidden reef;
but if caution only casts the pick of the cargo—
one well-balanced cast—   1010
the house will not go down, not outright;
labouring under its wealth of grief
the ship of state rides on.

Yes, and the great green bounty of god,
sown in the furrows year by year and reaped each fall   1015
can end the plague of famine.

But a man's life-blood
                is dark and mortal.
Once it wets the earth
what song can sing it back?   1020
Not even the master-healer
                who brought the dead to life—
Zeus stopped the man before he did more harm.

Oh, if only the gods had never forged
the chain that curbs our excess,   1025
                one man's fate curbing the next man's fate,
my heart would outrace my song, I'd pour out all I feel—
                but no, I choke with anguish,
                        mutter through the nights.
Never to ravel out a hope in time   1030
and the brain is swarming, burning—

(CLYTAEMNESTRA *emerges from the palace and goes to* CASSAN-
DRA, *impassive in the chariot.*)

CLYTAEMNESTRA: Won't you come inside? I mean you,
                Cassandra.
Zeus in all his mercy wants you to share
some victory libations with the house.
The slaves are flocking. Come, lead them   1035
up to the altar of the god who guards
our dearest treasures.

---

995 **not fit for the lyre** the lyre-god, Apollo, required songs of
joy, not mourning   1021 **the master-healer** the physician As-
clepius, who restored a dead man to life and was struck dead in
consequence by Zeus

Down from the chariot,
this is no time for pride. Why even Heracles,
they say, was sold into bondage long ago,
1040 he had to endure the bitter bread of slaves.
But if the yoke descends on you, be grateful
for a master born and reared in ancient wealth.
Those who reap a harvest past their hopes
are merciless to their slaves.
                                    From us
1045 you will receive what custom says is right.

(CASSANDRA *remains impassive.*)

LEADER: It's *you* she is speaking to, it's all too clear.
You're caught in the nets of doom—obey
if you can obey, unless you cannot bear to.
CLYTAEMNESTRA: Unless she's like a swallow, possessed
1050 of her own barbaric song, strange, dark.
I speak directly as I can—she must obey.
LEADER: Go with her. Make the best of it, she's right.
Step down from the seat, obey her.
CLYTAEMNESTRA: Do it now—
I have no time to spend outside. Already
1055 the victims crowd the hearth, the Navelstone,
to bless this day of joy I never hoped to see!—
our victims waiting for the fire and the knife,
and you,
if you want to taste our mystic rites, come now.
1060 If my words can't reach you—

(*Turning to the* LEADER.)

                                    Give her a sign,
one of her exotic handsigns.
LEADER: I think
the stranger needs an interpreter, someone clear.
She's like a wild creature, fresh caught.
CLYTAEMNESTRA: She's mad,
her evil genius murmuring in her ears.
1065 She comes from a *city* fresh caught.
She must learn to take the cutting bridle
before she foams her spirit off in blood—
and that's the last I waste on her contempt!

(*Wheeling, re-entering the palace. The* LEADER *turns to* CASSAN-
DRA, *who remains transfixed.*)

LEADER: Not I, I pity her. I will be gentle.
1070 Come, poor thing. Leave the empty chariot—
Of your own free will try on the yoke of Fate.
CASSANDRA: Aieeeeee! Earth—Mother—
                          Curse of the Earth—Apollo Apollo!
LEADER: Why cry to Apollo?
He's not the god to call with sounds of mourning.
1075 CASSANDRA: Aieeeeee! Earth—Mother—
                          Rape of the Earth—Apollo Apollo!
LEADER: Again, it's a bad omen.
She cries for the god who wants no part of grief.

(CASSANDRA *steps from the chariot, looks slowly towards the
rooftops of the palace.*)

1038–1040 **Why even Heracles . . . slaves** as punishment,
Heracles was sold in bondage by Hermes to Omphale, queen of
Lydia 1055 **the Navelstone** an allusion to Apollo's "World
Navel," a stone erected at Delphi

CASSANDRA: God of the long road,
                          Apollo *Apollo* my destroyer—
you destroy me once, destroy me twice—   1080
LEADER: She's about to sense her own ordeal, I think.
Slave that she is, the god lives on inside her.
CASSANDRA: God of the iron marches,
                          Apollo *Apollo* my destroyer—
where, where have you led me now? what house—   1085
LEADER: The house of Atreus and his sons. Really—
don't you know? It's true, see for yourself.
CASSANDRA: No . . . the house that hates god,
an echoing womb of guilt, kinsmen
        torturing kinsmen, severed heads,   1090
slaughterhouse of heroes, soil streaming blood—
LEADER: A keen hound, this stranger.
Trailing murder, and murder she will find.
CASSANDRA: See, my witnesses—
I trust to them, to the babies   1095
        wailing, skewered on the sword,
their flesh charred, the father gorging on their parts—
LEADER: We'd heard your fame as a seer,
but no one looks for seers in Argos.
CASSANDRA: Oh no, what horror, what new plot,   1100
new agony this?—
it's growing, massing, deep in the house,
        a plot, a monstrous—*thing*
        to crush the loved ones, no,
there is no cure, and rescue's far away and—   1105
LEADER: I can't read these signs; I knew the first,
the city rings with them.
CASSANDRA: You, you godforsaken—you'd do *this?*
The lord of your bed,
you bathe him . . . his body glistens, then—   1110
        how to tell the climax?—
        comes so quickly, see,
hand over hand shoots out, hauling ropes—
                          then lunge!
LEADER: Still lost. Her riddles, her dark words of god—
I'm groping, helpless.   1115
CASSANDRA: No no, look *there!*—
what's that? some net flung out of hell—
        No, she is the snare,
the bedmate, deathmate, murder's strong right arm!
        Let the insatiate discord in the race
rear up and shriek "Avenge the victim—stone them dead!" 1120
LEADER: What Fury is this? Why rouse it, lift its wailing
through the house? I hear you and lose hope.
CHORUS: Drop by drop at the heart, the gold of life ebbs out.
        We are the old soldiers . . . wounds will come
with the crushing sunset of our lives.   1125
Death is close, and quick.
CASSANDRA: Look out! *look out!*—
Ai, drag the great bull from the mate!—
        a thrash of robes, she traps him—
writhing—
        black horn glints, twists—
                          she gores him through!
And now he buckles, look, the bath swirls red—   1130
There's stealth and murder in the cauldron, do you hear?
LEADER: I'm no judge, I've little skill with the oracles,
but even I know danger when I hear it.

CHORUS: What good are the oracles to men? Words, more
    words,
1135   and the hurt comes on us, endless words
and a seer's techniques have brought us
terror and the truth.
CASSANDRA: The agony—O I am breaking!—Fate's so hard,
    and the pain that floods my voice is mine alone.
1140   Why have you brought me here, tormented as I am?
Why, unless to die with him, why else?
LEADER AND CHORUS: Mad with the rapture—god speeds
    you on
        to the song, the deathsong,
like the nightingale that broods on sorrow,
1145   mourns her son, her son,
her life inspired with grief for him,
she lilts and shrills, dark bird that lives for night.
CASSANDRA: The nightingale—O for a song, a fate like hers!
    The gods gave her a life of ease, swathed her in wings,
1150   no tears, no wailing. The knife waits for me.
They'll splay me on the iron's double edge.
LEADER AND CHORUS: Why?—what god hurls you on, stroke
    on stroke
        to the long dying fall?
Why the horror clashing through your music,
1155   terror struck to song?—
why the anguish, the wild dance?
Where do your words of god and grief begin?
CASSANDRA: Ai, the wedding, wedding of Paris,
    death to the loved ones. Oh Scamander,
1160   you nursed my father . . . once at your banks
I nursed and grew, and now at the banks
of Acheron, the stream that carries sorrow,
it seems I'll chant my prophecies too soon.
LEADER AND CHORUS: What are you saying? Wait, it's clear,
1165   a child could see the truth, it wounds within,
                  like a bloody fang it tears—
I hear your destiny—breaking sobs,
             cries that stab the ears.
CASSANDRA: Oh the grief, the grief of the city
1170   ripped to oblivion. Oh the victims,
the flocks my father burned at the wall,
    rich herds in flames . . . no cure for the doom
that took the city after all, and I,
her last ember, I go down with her.
1175 LEADER AND CHORUS: You cannot stop, your song goes on—
some spirit drops from the heights and treads you down
             and the brutal strain grows—
your death-throes come and come and
        I cannot see the end!
1180 CASSANDRA: Then off with the veils that hid the fresh
    young bride—
we will see the truth.
Flare up once more, my oracle! Clear and sharp
as the wind that blows towards the rising sun,
I can feel a deeper swell now, gathering head
1185   to break at last and bring the dawn of grief.

1145 **her son** Itys, son of Philomela, the mother was transformed into a nightingale after she inadvertently tricked her
husband, Tereus, into eating their son's flesh

No more riddles. I will teach you.
Come, bear witness, run and hunt with me.
We trail the old barbaric works of slaughter.

These roofs—look up—there is a dancing troupe
that never leaves. And they have their harmony   1190
but it is harsh, their words are harsh, they drink
beyond the limit. Flushed on the blood of men
their spirit grows and none can turn away
their revel breeding in the veins—the Furies!
They cling to the house for life. They sing,   1195
sing of the frenzy that began it all,
strain rising on strain, showering curses
on the man who tramples on his brother's bed.

There. Have I hit the mark or not? Am I a fraud,
a fortune-teller babbling lies from door to door?   1200
Swear how well I know the ancient crimes
that live within this house.
LEADER: And if I did?
Would an oath bind the wounds and heal us?
But you amaze me. Bred across the sea,
your language strange, and still you sense the truth   1205
as if you had been here.
CASSANDRA: Apollo the Prophet
introduced me to his gift.
LEADER: A *god*—and moved with love?
CASSANDRA: I was ashamed to tell this once,
but now . . .   1210
LEADER: We spoil ourselves with scruples,
long as things go well.
CASSANDRA: He came like a wrestler,
magnificent, took me down and breathed his fire
through me and—
LEADER: You bore him a child?
CASSANDRA: I yielded,
then at the climax I recoiled—I deceived Apollo!
LEADER:
But the god's skills—they seized you even then?   1215
CASSANDRA: Even then I told my people all the grief to come.
LEADER: And Apollo's anger never touched you?—is it
    possible?
CASSANDRA: Once I betrayed him I could never be believed.
LEADER: We believe you. Your visions seem so true.
CASSANDRA: Aieeeee!—
the pain, the terror! the birth-pang of the seer   1220
who tells the truth—
                it whirls me, oh,
the storm comes again, the crashing chords!
Look, you see them nestling at the threshold?
Young, young in the darkness like a dream,
like children really, yes, and their loved ones   1225
brought them down . . .
             their hands, they fill their hands
with their own flesh, they are serving it like food,
holding out their entrails . . . now it's clear,
I can see the armfuls of compassion, see the father
reach to taste and—   1230
            For so much suffering,
I tell you, someone plots revenge.
A lion who lacks a lion's heart,
he sprawled at home in the royal lair

and set a trap for the lord on his return.
1235 My lord . . . I must wear his yoke, I am his slave.
The lord of the men-of-war, he obliterated Troy—
he is so blind, so lost to that detestable hellhound
who pricks her ears and fawns and her tongue draws out
her glittering words of welcome—
                  No, he cannot see
1240 the stroke that Fury's hiding, stealth, and murder.
What outrage—the woman kills the man!
                  What to call
that . . . monster of Greece, and bring my quarry down?
Viper coiling back and forth?
                Some sea-witch?—
Scylla crouched in her rocky nest—nightmare of sailors?
1245 Raging mother of death, storming deathless war against
the ones she loves!
             And how she howled in triumph,
boundless outrage. Just as the tide of battle
broke her way, she seems to rejoice that he
is safe at home from war, saved for her.
1250 Believe me if you will. What will it matter
if you won't? It comes when it comes,
and soon you'll see it face to face
and say the seer was all too true.
You will be moved with pity.
LEADER: Thyestes' feast,
1255 the children's flesh—that I know,
and the fear shudders through me. It's true,
real, no dark signs about it. I hear the rest
but it throws me off the scent.
CASSANDRA: Agamemnon.
You will see him dead.
LEADER: Peace, poor girl!
1260 Put those words to sleep.
CASSANDRA: No use,
the Healer has no hand in this affair.
LEADER: Not if it's true—but god forbid it is!
CASSANDRA: You pray, and they close in to kill!
LEADER: What man prepares this, this dreadful—
CASSANDRA: Man?
1265 You *are* lost, to every word I've said.
LEADER: Yes—
I don't see who can bring the evil off.
CASSANDRA: And yet I know my Greek, too well.
LEADER: So does the Delphic oracle,
but he's hard to understand.
CASSANDRA: His *fire!*—
1270 sears me, sweeps me again—the torture!
Apollo Lord of the Light, you burn,
you blind me—
        Agony!
           She is the lioness,
she rears on her hind legs, she beds with the wolf
when her lion king goes ranging—
                she will kill me—
1275 Ai, the torture!
         She is mixing her drugs,
adding a measure more of hate for me.

1244 **Scylla** a many-headed monster who terrorized sailors

She gloats as she whets the sword for him.
He brought me home and we will pay in carnage.

Why mock yourself with these—trappings, the rod,
the god's wreath, his yoke around my throat?   1280
Before I die I'll tread you—

(*Ripping off her regalia, stamping it into the ground.*)

                Down, out,
die die die!
Now you're down. I've paid you back.
Look for another victim—I am free at last—
make her rich in all your curse and doom.   1285

(*Staggering backwards as if wrestling with a spirit tearing at her robes.*)

                    See,
Apollo himself, his fiery hands—I feel him again,
he's stripping off my robes, the Seer's robes!
And after he looked down and saw me mocked,
even in these, his glories, mortified by friends
I loved, and they hated me, they were so blind   1290
to their own demise—
             I went from door to door,
I was wild with the god, I heard them call me
"Beggar! Wretch! Starve for bread in hell!"

And I endured it all, and now he will
extort me as his due. A seer for the Seer.   1295
He brings me here to die like this,
not to serve at my father's altar. No,
the block is waiting. The cleaver steams
with my life blood, the first blood drawn
for the king's last rites.   1300

(*Regaining her composure and moving to the altar.*)

             We will die,
but not without some honour from the gods.
There will come another to avenge us,
born to kill his mother, born
his father's champion. A wanderer, a fugitive
driven off his native land, he will come home   1305
to cope the stones of hate that menace all he loves.
The gods have sworn a monumental oath: as his father lies
upon the ground he draws him home with power like a
    prayer.

Then why so pitiful, why so many tears?
I have seen my city faring as she fared,   1310
and those who took her, judged by the gods,
faring as they fare. I must be brave.
It is my turn to die.

(*Approaching the doors.*)

I address you as the Gates of Death.
I pray it comes with one clear stroke,   1315
no convulsions, the pulses ebbing out
in gentle death. I'll close my eyes and sleep.
LEADER: So much pain, poor girl, and so much truth,
you've told so much. But if you *see* it coming,
clearly—how can you go to your own death,   1320
like a beast to the altar driven on by god,
and hold your head so high?

CASSANDRA: No escape, my friends,
not now.
LEADER: But the last hour should be savoured.
CASSANDRA: My time has come. Little to gain from flight.
1325 LEADER: You're brave, believe me, full of gallant heart.
CASSANDRA: Only the wretched go with praise like that.
LEADER: But to go nobly lends a man some grace.
CASSANDRA: My noble father—you and your noble children.

(She nears the threshold and recoils, groaning in revulsion.)

LEADER: What now? what terror flings you back?
1330   Why? Unless some horror in the brain—
CASSANDRA: Murder.
    The house breathes with murder—bloody shambles!
LEADER: No, no, only the victims at the hearth.
CASSANDRA: I know that odour. I smell the open grave.
LEADER: But the Syrian myrrh, it fills the halls with
        splendour,
1335   can't you sense it?
CASSANDRA: Well, I must go in now,
    mourning Agamemnon's death and mine.
    Enough of life!

(Approaching the doors again and crying out.)

                    Friends—I cried out,
    not from fear like a bird fresh caught,
    but that you will testify to how I died.
1340 When the queen, woman for woman, dies for me,
    and a man falls for the man who married grief.
    That's all I ask, my friends. A stranger's gift
    for one about to die.
LEADER: Poor creature, you
    and the end you see so clearly. I pity you.
1345 CASSANDRA: I'd like a few words more, a kind of dirge,
    it is my own. I pray to the sun,
    the last light I'll see,
    that when the avengers cut the assassins down
    they will avenge me too, a slave who died,
1350 an easy conquest.
                    Oh men, your destiny.
    When all is well a shadow can overturn it.
    When trouble comes a stroke of the wet sponge,
    and the picture's blotted out. And that,
    I think that breaks the heart.

(She goes through the doors.)

1355 CHORUS: But the lust for power never dies—
        men cannot have enough.
    No one will lift a hand to send it
    from his door, to give it warning,
    "Power, never come again!"
1360   Take this man: the gods in glory
    gave him Priam's city to plunder,
    brought him home in splendour like a god.
    But now if he must pay for the blood
        his fathers shed, and die for the deaths
1365   he brought to pass, and bring more death
    to avenge his dying, show us one
        who boasts himself born free
    of the raging angel, once he hears—

(Cries break out within the palace.)

AGAMEMNON: Aagh!
Struck deep—the death-blow, deep—
LEADER: Quiet. Cries,
    but who? Someone's stabbed—   1370
AGAMEMNON: Aaagh, again . . .
second blow—struck home.
LEADER: The work is done,
    you can feel it. The king, and the great cries—
    Close ranks now, find the right way out.

(But the OLD MEN scatter, each speaks singly.)

CHORUS: —I say send out heralds, muster the guard,
        they'll save the house.   1375
                        —And I say rush in now,
        catch them red-handed—butchery running on their
        blades.
    —Right with you, do something—now or never!
    —Look at them, beating the drum for insurrection.
                                            —Yes,
        we're wasting time. They rape the name of caution,
        their hands will never sleep.   1380
                        —Not a plan in sight.
    Let men of action do the planning, too.
    —I'm helpless. Who can raise the dead with words?
    —What, drag out our lives? bow down to the tyrants,
        the ruin of the house?
                        —Never, better to die
        on your feet than live on your knees.   1385
                            —Wait,
        do we take the cries for signs, prophesy like seers
        and give him up for dead?
                    —No more suspicions,
        not another word till we have proof.
                        —Confusion
        on all sides—one thing to do. See how it stands
        with Agamemnon, once and for all we'll see—   1390

*(He rushes at the doors. They open and reveal a silver cauldron that
holds the body of AGAMEMNON shrouded in bloody robes, with the
body of CASSANDRA to his left and CLYTAEMNESTRA standing to
his right, sword in hand. She strides towards the CHORUS.)*

CLYTAEMNESTRA: Words, endless words I've said to serve the
        moment—
    now it makes me proud to tell the truth.
    How else to prepare a death for deadly men
    who seem to love you? How to rig the nets
    of pain so high no man can overleap them?   1395
    I brooded on this trial, this ancient blood feud
    year by year. At last my hour came.
    Here I stand and here I struck
    and here my work is done.
    I did it all. I don't deny it, no.   1400
    He had no way to flee or fight his destiny—

*(Unwinding the robes from AGAMEMNON's body, spreading them
before the altar where the OLD MEN cluster around them, unified as
a chorus once again.)*

our never-ending, all embracing net, I cast it
wide for the royal haul, I coil him round and round
in the wealth, the robes of doom, and then I strike him
1405 once, twice, and at each stroke he cries in agony—
he buckles at the knees and crashes here!
And when he's down I add the third, last blow,
to the Zeus who saves the dead beneath the ground
I send that third blow home in homage like a prayer.

1410 So he goes down, and the life is bursting out of him—
great sprays of blood, and the murderous shower
wounds me, dyes me black and I, I revel
like the Earth when the spring rains come down,
the blessed gifts of god, and the new green spear
1415 splits the sheath and rips to birth in glory!

So it stands, elders of Argos gathered here.
Rejoice if you can rejoice—I glory.
And if I'd pour upon his body the libation
it deserves, what wine could match my words?
1420 It is right and more than right. He flooded
the vessel of our proud house with misery,
with the vintage of the curse and now
he drains the dregs. My lord is home at last.
LEADER: You appal me, you, your brazen words—
1425 exulting over your fallen king.
CLYTAEMNESTRA: And you,
you try me like some desperate woman.
My heart is steel, well you know. Praise me,
blame me as you choose. It's all one.
Here is Agamemnon, my husband made a corpse
1430 by this right hand—a masterpiece of Justice.
Done is done.
CHORUS: Woman!—what poison cropped from the soil
or strained from the heaving sea, what nursed you,
drove you insane? You brave the curse of Greece.
    You have cut away and flung away and now
1435 the people cast you off to exile,
broken with our hate.
CLYTAEMNESTRA: And now you sentence me?—
you banish *me* from the city, curses breathing
down my neck? But *he*—
name one charge you brought against him then.
1440 He thought no more of it than killing a beast,
and his flocks were rich, teeming in their fleece,
but he sacrificed his own child, our daughter,
the agony I laboured into love
to charm away the savage winds of Thrace.
1445 Didn't the law demand you banish him?—
hunt him from the land for all his guilt?
But now you witness what I've done
and you are ruthless judges.
                    Threaten away!
I'll meet you blow for blow. And if I fall
1450 the throne is yours. If god decrees the reverse,
late as it is, old men, you'll learn your place.
CHORUS: Mad with ambition,
                shrilling pride!—some Fury
crazed with the carnage rages through your brain—
1455   I can see the flecks of blood inflame your eyes!
But vengeance comes—you'll lose your loved ones,
stroke for painful stroke.

CLYTAEMNESTRA: Then learn this, too, the power of my
    oaths.
By the child's Rights I brought to birth,
by Ruin, by Fury—the three gods to whom   1460
I sacrificed this man—I swear my hopes
will never walk the halls of fear so long
as Aegisthus lights the fire on my hearth.
Loyal to me as always, no small shield
to buttress my defiance.   1465
                    Here he lies.
He brutalized me. The darling of all
the golden girls who spread the gates of Troy.
And here his spear-prize . . . what wonders she beheld!—
the seer of Apollo shared my husband's bed,
his faithful mate who knelt at the rowing-benches,   1470
worked by every hand.
                    They have their rewards.
He as you know. And she, the swan of the gods
who lived to sing her latest, dying song—
his lover lies beside him.
She brings a fresh, voluptuous relish to my bed!   1475
CHORUS: Oh quickly, let me die—
no bed of labour, no, no wasting illness . . .
bear me off in the sleep that never ends,
            now that he has fallen,
now that our dearest shield lies battered—   1480
        Woman made him suffer,
                woman struck him down.

Helen the wild, maddening Helen,
one for the many, the thousand lives
you murdered under Troy. Now you are crowned   1485
with this consummate wreath, the blood
that lives in memory, glistens age to age.
Once in the halls she walked and she was war,
angel of war, angel of agony, lighting men to death.
CLYTAEMNESTRA: Pray no more for death, broken   1490
as you are. And never turn
    your wrath on her, call her
the scourge of men, the one alone
who destroyed a myriad Greek lives—
Helen the grief that never heals.   1495
CHORUS: The *spirit!*—you who tread
the house and the twinborn sons of Tantalus—
you empower the sisters, Fury's twins
        whose power tears the heart!
Perched on the corpse your carrion raven   1500
    glories in her hymn,
            her screaming hymn of pride.
CLYTAEMNESTRA: Now you set your judgement straight,
    you summon *him!* Three generations
        feed the spirit in the race.   1505
Deep in the veins he feeds our bloodlust—
aye, before the old wound dies
it ripens in another flow of blood.
CHORUS: The great curse of the house, the spirit,
dead weight wrath—and you can praise it!   1510

1472 **the swan** the bird of Apollo, reputed to sing only when about to die   1497 **the twinborn sons of Tantalus** here, Agamemnon and Menelaus

Praise the insatiate doom that feeds
relentless on our future and our sons.
Oh all through the will of Zeus,
the cause of all, the one who works it all.
1515   What comes to birth that is not Zeus?
Our lives are pain, what part not come from god?

Oh my king, my captain,
how to salute you, how to mourn you?
What can I say with all my warmth and love?
1520   Here in the black widow's web you lie,
gasping out your life
in a sacrilegious death, dear god,
reduced to a slave's bed,
my king of men, yoked by stealth and Fate,
1525   by the wife's hand that thrust the two-edged sword.
CLYTAEMNESTRA: You claim the work is mine, call me
Agamemnon's wife—you are so wrong.
Fleshed in the wife of this dead man,
the spirit lives within me,
1530   our savage ancient spirit of revenge.
In return for Atreus' brutal feast
he kills his perfect son—for every
murdered child, a crowning sacrifice.
CHORUS: And *you,* innocent of his murder?
1535   And who could swear to that? and how? . . .
and still an avenger could arise,
bred by the fathers' crimes, and lend a hand.
He wades in the blood of brothers,
stream on mounting stream—black war erupts
1540   and where he strides revenge will stride,
clots will mass for the young who were devoured.

Oh my king, my captain,
how to salute you, how to mourn you?
What can I say with all my warmth and love?
1545   Here in the black widow's web you lie,
gasping out your life
in a sacrilegious death, dear god,
reduced to a slave's bed,
my king of men, yoked by stealth and Fate,
1550   by the wife's hand that thrust the two-edged sword.
CLYTAEMNESTRA: No slave's death, I think—
no stealthier than the death he dealt
our house and the offspring of our loins,
Iphigeneia, girl of tears.
1555   Act for act, wound for wound!
Never exult in Hades, swordsman,
here you are repaid. By the sword
you did your work and by the sword you die.
CHORUS: The mind reels—where to turn?
1560   All plans dashed, all hope! I cannot think . . .
the roofs are toppling, I dread the drumbeat thunder
the heavy rains of blood will crush the house
the first light rains are over—
Justice brings new acts of agony, yes,
1565   on new grindstones Fate is grinding sharp the sword of
Justice.
Earth, dear Earth,
if only you'd drawn me under
long before I saw him huddled
in the beaten silver bath.

Who will bury him, lift his dirge?   1570

(*Turning to* CLYTAEMNESTRA.)

You, can you dare *this?*
To kill your lord with your own hand
then mourn his soul with tributes, terrible tributes—
do his enormous works a great dishonour.
This god-like man, this hero. Who at the grave   1575
will sing his praises, pour the wine of tears?
Who will labour there with truth of heart?
CLYTAEMNESTRA: This is no concern of yours.
The hand that bore and cut him down
will hand him down to Mother Earth.   1580
This house will never mourn for him.
Only our daughter Iphigeneia,
by all rights, will rush to meet him
first at the churning straits,
the ferry over tears—   1585
she'll fling her arms around her father,
pierce him with her love.
CHORUS: Each charge meets counter-charge.
None can judge between them. Justice.
The plunderer plundered, the killer pays the price.   1590
The truth still holds while Zeus still holds the throne:
the one who acts must suffer—
that is law. Who can tear from the veins
the bad seed, the curse? The race is welded to its ruin.
CLYTAEMNESTRA: At last you see the future and the truth!   1595
But I will swear a pact with the spirit
born within us. I embrace his works,
cruel as they are but done at last,
if he will leave our house
in the future, bleed another line   1600
with kinsmen murdering kinsmen.
Whatever he may ask. A few things
are all I need, once I have purged
our fury to destroy each other—
purged it from our halls.   1605

(AEGISTHUS *has emerged from the palace with his* BODYGUARD
and stands triumphant over the body of AGAMEMNON.)

AEGISTHUS: O what a brilliant day
it is for vengeance! Now I can say once more
there are gods in heaven avenging men,
blazing down on all the crimes of earth.
Now at last I see this man brought down
in the Furies' tangling robes. It feasts my eyes—   1610
he pays for the plot his father's hand contrived.

Atreus, this man's father, was king of Argos.
My father, Thyestes—let me make this clear—
Atreus' brother challenged him for the crown,
and Atreus drove him out of house and home   1615
then lured him back, and home Thyestes came,
poor man, a suppliant to his own hearth,
to pray that Fate might save him.
                    So it did.

1585 **the ferry** Charon's ferry across the River Styx into the underworld

1620 There was no dying, no staining our native ground
with his blood. Thyestes was the guest,
and this man's godless father—

(*Pointing to* AGAMEMNON.)

The zeal of the host outstripping a brother's love,
made my father a feast that seemed a feast for gods,
a love feast of his children's flesh.
                                        He cuts
1625 the extremities, feet and delicate hands
into small pieces, scatters them over the dish
and serves it to Thyestes throned on high.
He picks at the flesh he cannot recognize,
the soul of innocence eating the food of ruin—
1630 look,

(*Pointing to the bodies at his feet.*)

         that feeds upon the house! And then,
when he sees the monstrous thing he's done, he shrieks,
he reels back head first and vomits up that butchery,
tramples the feast—brings down the curse of Justice:
"Crash to ruin, all the race of Pleisthenes, crash down!"

1635 So you see him, down. And I, the weaver of Justice,
plotted out the kill. Atreus drove us into exile,
my struggling father and I, a babe-in-arms,
his last son, but I became a man
and Justice brought me home. I was abroad
1640 but I reached out and seized my man,
link by link I clamped the fatal scheme
together. Now I could die gladly, even I—
now I see this monster in the nets of Justice.
LEADER: Aegisthus, you revel in pain—you sicken me.
1645 You say you killed the king in cold blood,
single-handed planned his pitiful death?
I say there's no escape. In the hour of judgement,
trust to this, your head will meet the people's
rocks and curses.
AEGISTHUS: You say! you slaves at the oars—
1650 while the master on the benches cracks the whip?
You'll learn, in your late age, how much it hurts
to teach old bones their place. We have techniques—
chains and the pangs of hunger,
two effective teachers, excellent healers.
1655 They can even cure old men of pride and gall.
Look—can't you see? The more you kick
against the pricks, the more you suffer.
LEADER: You, pathetic—
the king had just returned from battle.
1660 You waited out the war and fouled his lair,
you planned my great commander's fall.
AEGISTHUS: Talk on—
you'll scream for every word, my little Orpheus.
We'll see if the world comes dancing to your song,
your absurd barking—snarl your breath away!
1665 I'll make you dance, I'll bring you all to heel.
LEADER: *You* rule Argos? You who schemed his death
but cringed to cut him down with your own hand?

1634 **Pleisthenes** an unidentified ancestral figure, perhaps
Atreus or Pelops   1662 **Orpheus** a musician who enchanted
even rocks and trees with his lyre

AEGISTHUS: The treachery was the woman's work, clearly.
I was a marked man, his enemy for ages.
But I will use his riches, stop at nothing   1670
to civilize his people. All but the rebel:
him I'll yoke and break—
no cornfed colt, running free in the traces.
Hunger, ruthless mate of the dark torture-chamber,
trains her eyes upon him till he drops!   1675
LEADER: Coward, why not kill the man yourself?
Why did the woman, the corruption of Greece
and the gods of Greece, have to bring him down?
Orestes—
         If he still sees the light of day,
bring him home, good Fates, home to kill   1680
this pair at last. Our champion in slaughter!
AEGISTHUS: Bent on insolence? Well, you'll learn, quickly.
At them, men—you have your work at hand!

(*His men draw swords: the* OLD MEN *take up their sticks.*)

LEADER: At them, first at the hilt, to the last man—
AEGISTHUS: First at the hilt, I'm not afraid to die.   1685
LEADER: It's death you want and death you'll have—
we'll make that word your last.

(CLYTAEMNESTRA *moves between them, restraining* AEGISTHUS.)

CLYTAEMNESTRA: No more, my dearest,
no more grief. We have too much to reap
right here, our mighty harvest of despair.   1690
Our lives are based on pain. No bloodshed now.

Fathers of Argos, turn for home before you act
and suffer for it. What we did was destiny.
If we could end the suffering, how we would rejoice.
The spirit's brutal hoof has struck our heart.   1695
And that is what a woman has to say.
Can you accept the truth?

(CLYTAEMNESTRA *turns to leave.*)

AEGISTHUS: But these . . . mouths
that bloom in filth—spitting insults in my teeth.
You tempt your fates, you insubordinate dogs—
to hurl abuse at me, your master!   1700
LEADER: No Greek
worth his salt would grovel at your feet.
AEGISTHUS: I—I'll stalk you all your days!
LEADER: Not if the spirit brings Orestes home.
AEGISTHUS: Exiles feed on hope—well I know.
LEADER: More,   1705
gorge yourself to bursting—soil justice, while you can.
AEGISTHUS: I promise you, you'll pay, old fools—in good
time, too!
LEADER: Strut on your own dunghill, you cock beside your
mate.
CLYTAEMNESTRA: Let them howl—they're impotent. You and
I have power now.
We will set the house in order once for all.

(*They enter the palace; the great doors close behind them; the* OLD
MEN *disband and wander off.*)

The cycle of retribution continues in the remaining plays of the trilogy. In *The Libation Bearers,* Agamemnon's son, Orestes, returns to Argos from exile, where he had been sent by Aegisthus and Clytaemnestra, to avenge the murder of his father. He arrives in secret and watches while his sister, Electra (and the chorus of slavewomen bearing libations), pours libations at Agamemnon's grave. As in *Agamemnon,* much of Aeschylus' dramatic power is achieved through a striking sense of the verbal and visual economy of theater. Electra finds the locks of hair that Orestes has left on the grave, and longing for her brother's return, carefully steps into the footprints he has made in the sand: "The heel, the curve of the arch / like twins." Much as Agamemnon's downfall seems inevitable the moment he steps on the crimson tapestries, so the retribution for his murder begins when Electra measures the print of her brother, who then steps out from his hiding place.

Indeed, the image of Agamemnon bound and slaughtered echoes everywhere in *The Libation Bearers,* not only in the way Orestes describes his vengeful murder of Aegisthus and Clytaemnestra, but in the way these acts entwine Orestes in a complex moral history as well. For while Orestes' execution of Aegisthus—an adulterer, a murderer, and (most importantly) a kinsman—seems simple justice, murdering his mother, Clytaemnestra, is a more appalling and ambiguous crime, not as readily excused as righteous revenge. The cycle of crime and retribution enacted in *The Oresteia* takes another turn, then, at the close of *The Libation Bearers,* as Orestes is caught in the snare of his own crimes and beset by those monstrous figures of guilt, the Furies.

The Libation Bearers

THE LIBATION BEARERS

Aeschylus

TRANSLATED BY ROBERT FAGLES

CHARACTERS

ORESTES, *son of Agamemnon and Clytaemnestra*
PYLADES, *his companion*
ELECTRA, *his sister*
CHORUS OF SLAVEWOMEN *and their* LEADER
CLYTAEMNESTRA
CILISSA, *Orestes' old nurse*
AEGISTHUS
A SERVANT *of Aegisthus*
ATTENDANTS *of Orestes*
BODYGUARD *of Aegisthus*
A PORTER

TIME AND SCENE: *Several years have passed since Agamemnon's death. At Argos, before the tomb of the king and his fathers, stands an altar; behind it looms the house of Atreus.*

ORESTES *and* PYLADES *enter, dressed as travellers.* ORESTES *kneels and prays.*

ORESTES: Hermes, lord of the dead, look down and guard
   the fathers' power. Be my saviour, I beg you,
   be my comrade now.
                      I have come home
   to my own soil, an exile home at last.
5 Here at the mounded grave I call my father,
   Hear me—I am crying out to you . . .

(*He cuts two locks of hair and lays them on the grave.*)

   There is a lock for Inachos who nursed me
   into manhood, there is one for death.

   I was not here to mourn you when you died,
10 my father, never gave the last salute
   when they bore your corpse away.

(ELECTRA *and a* CHORUS OF SLAVEWOMEN *enter in procession. They are dressed in black and bear libations, moving towards* ORESTES *at the grave.*)

                              What's this?
   Look, a company moving towards us. Women,
   robed in black . . . so clear in the early light.

I wonder what they mean, what turn of fate?—
some new wound to the house?   15
Or perhaps they come to honour you, my father,
bearing cups to soothe and still the dead.
That's right, it must be . . .
Electra, I think I see *her* coming, there,
my own sister, worn, radiant in her grief—   20
Dear god, let me avenge my father's murder—
fight beside me now with all your might!
Out of their way, Pylades. I must know
what they mean, these women turning towards us,
what their prayers call forth.   25

(*They withdraw behind the tomb.*)

CHORUS: Rushed from the house we come
   escorting cups for the dead,
   in step with the hands' hard beat,
               our cheeks glistening,
   flushed where the nails have raked new furrows running 30
      blood;
   and life beats on, and
   we nurse our lives with tears,
   to the sound of ripping linen beat our robes in sorrow,
      close to the breast the beats throb
   and laughter's gone and fortune throbs and throbs.   35

   Aie!—bristling Terror struck—
      the seer of the house,
   the nightmare ringing clear
               breathed its wrath in sleep,

---

7 **Inachos** the chief river of Argos. Young men in ancient Greece customarily on reaching manhood dedicated a lock of their long, youthful hair to the local river-god. Here Orestes combines this ceremony with another rite of offering a lock to a dearly loved dead person   11ff. **What's this? . . .** the one manuscript in which this play has survived begins here. The previous lines are restored from scattered quotations preserved in the works of other Greek writers. The full speech may have been much longer (like the prologue to Eumenides)

23 **Pylades** son of Strophios, prince of Phokis, where Orestes had been in exile since before his father's death. In the legends Pylades plays a variety of roles, from Orestes' host to the future husband of Electra, but here he appears as the spokesman of Apollo, as the austerity of his single utterance (887ff.) will suggest

40 in the midnight watch a cry!—the voice of Terror
deep in the house, bursting down
on the women's darkened chambers, yes,
and the old ones, skilled at dreams, swore oaths to god
and called,
'The proud dead stir under earth,
45 they rage against the ones who took their lives.'

But the gifts, the empty gifts
she hopes will ward them off—
good Mother Earth!—that godless woman sends me
here . . .
I dread to say her prayer.
50 What can redeem the blood that wets the soil?
Oh for the hearthfire banked with grief,
the rampart's down, a fine house down—
dark, dark, and the sun, the life is curst,
and mist enshrouds the halls
55 where the lords of war went down.
And the ancient pride no war,
no storm, no force could tame,
ringing in all men's ears, in all men's hearts is gone.
They are afraid. Success,
60 they bow to success, more god than god himself.
But Justice waits and turns the scales:
a sudden blow for some at dawn,
for some in the no man's land of dusk
her torments grow with time,
65 and the lethal night takes others.

And the blood that Mother Earth consumes
clots hard, it won't seep through, it breeds revenge
and frenzy goes through the guilty,
seething like infection, swarming through the brain.
70 For the one who treads a virgin's bed
there is no cure. All the streams of the world,
all channels run into one
to cleanse a man's red hands will swell the bloody tide.

And I . . . Fate and the gods brought down their yoke,
75 they ringed our city, out of our fathers' halls
they led us here as slaves.
And the will breaks, we kneel at their command—
our masters right or wrong!
And we beat the tearing hatred down,
80 behind our veils we weep for her,

(*Turning to* ELECTRA.)

her senseless fate.
Sorrow turns the secret heart to ice.
ELECTRA: Dear women,
you keep the house in order, best you can;
and now you've come to the grave to say a prayer
85 with me, my escorts. I'll need your help with this.
What to say when I pour the cup of sorrow?

(*Lifting her libation cup.*)

What kindness, what prayer can touch my father?
Shall I say I bring him love for love, a woman's
love for husband? My mother, love from her?
90 I've no taste for that, no words to say
as I run the honeyed oil on father's tomb.

Or try the salute we often use at graves?
'A wreath for a wreath. Now bring the givers
gifts to match' . . . no, give them pain for pain.
Or silent, dishonoured, just as father died, 95
empty it out for the soil to drink and then
retrace my steps, like a slave sent out with scourings
left from the purging of the halls, and throw
the cup behind me, looking straight ahead.
Help me decide, my friends. Join me here. 100
We nurse a common hatred in the house.
Don't hide your feelings—no, fear no one.
Destiny waits us all,

(*Looking towards the tomb.*)

born free,
or slaves who labour under another's hand.
Speak to me, please. Perhaps you've had 105
a glimpse of something better.
LEADER: I revere
your father's death-mound like an altar.
I'll say a word, now that you ask,
that comes from deep within me.
ELECTRA: Speak on,
with everything you feel for father's grave. 110
LEADER: Say a blessing as you pour, for those who love you.
ELECTRA: And of the loved ones, whom to call my friends?
leader: First yourself, then all who hate Aegisthus.
ELECTRA: I and you. I can say a prayer for us
and then for—
LEADER: You know, try to say it. 115
ELECTRA: There is someone else to rally to our side?
LEADER: Remember Orestes, even abroad and gone.
ELECTRA: Well said, the best advice I've had.
LEADER: Now for the murderers. Remember them and—
ELECTRA: What?
I'm so unseasoned, teach me what to say. 120
leader: Let some god or man come down upon them.
ELECTRA: Judge or avenger, which?
LEADER: Just say 'the one who murders in return!'
ELECTRA: How can I ask the gods for that
and keep my conscience clear? 125
LEADER: How not,
and pay the enemy back in kind?

(ELECTRA *kneels at the grave in prayer.*)

ELECTRA: —Herald king
of the world above and the quiet world below,
lord of the dead, my Hermes, help me now.
Tell the spirits underground to hear my prayers,
and the high watch hovering over father's roofs, 130
and have her listen too, the Earth herself
who brings all things to life and makes them strong,
then gathers in the rising tide once more.

And I will tip libations to the dead.
I call out to my father. Pity me, 135
dear Orestes too.
Rekindle the light that saves our house!
We're auctioned off, drift like vagrants now.
Mother has pawned us for a husband, Aegisthus,

140   her partner in her murdering.
                        I go like a slave,
and Orestes driven from his estates while they,
they roll in the fruits of all your labours,
magnificent and sleek. O bring Orestes home,
with a happy twist of fate, my father. Hear me,
145   make me far more self-possessed than mother,
make this hand more pure.

These prayers for us. For our enemies I say,
Raise up your avenger, into the light, my father—
kill the killers in return, with justice!
150   So in the midst of prayers for good I place
this curse for them.
                  Bring up your blessings,
up into the air, led by the gods and Earth
and all the rights that bring us triumph.

(Pouring libations on the tomb and turning to the women.)

These are my prayers. Over them I pour libations.
155   Yours to adorn them with laments, to make them bloom,
so custom says—sing out and praise the dead.
CHORUS: Let the tears fall, ring out and die,
              die with the warlord at this bank,
this bulwark of the good, defence against the bad,
160   the guilt, the curse we ward away
with prayer and all we pour. Hear me, majesty, hear me,
       lord of glory, from the darkness of your heart.
                         Ohhhhhh!—
       Dear god, let him come! Some man
with a strong spear, born to free the house,
165   with the torsion bow of Scythia bent for slaughter,
splattering shafts like a god of war—sword in fist
          for the slash-and-hack of battle!

(ELECTRA remains at the grave, staring at the ground.)

ELECTRA: Father,
you have it now, the earth has drunk your wine.
Wait, friends, here's news. Come share it.
LEADER: Speak on,
170   my heart's a dance of fear.
ELECTRA: A lock of hair,
    here on the grave . . .
LEADER: Whose? A man's?
    A growing girl's?
ELECTRA: And it has the marks,
    and anyone would think—
LEADER: What?
    We're old. You're young, now you teach us.

---

165 **bow of Scythia** named after the people of South Russia who originated it, was shaped with a double curve, like a Cupid's bow, to give it extra torsion. As Heracles regularly used one, the chorus may be thinking of him here, invoking him in his aspect of the liberator, which he shared with Perseus; see n. 818. Imagery of athletics seems to have an optimistic effect—each sport seems to bring Orestes closer to victory, but his charioteering and his archery will bring him failure in the end. Wrestling seems to predominate in this play about engagement and embrace; see 343, 378, 485f., 676, 853, 1019ff., 1031

ELECTRA: No one could have cut this lock but I and—   175
LEADER: Callous they are, the ones who ought to shear
    the hair and mourn.
ELECTRA: Look at the texture, just like—
LEADER: Whose? I want to know.
ELECTRA: Like mine, identical,
    can't you see?
LEADER: Orestes . . . he brought a gift in secret?
ELECTRA: It's *his*—I can see his curls.   180
LEADER: And how could he risk the journey here?
ELECTRA: He sent it, true, a lock to honour father.
LEADER: All the more cause for tears. You mean
    he'll never set foot on native ground again.

ELECTRA: Yes!
It's sweeping over me too—anguish like a breaker—   185
a sword ripping through my heart!
Tears come like the winter rains that flood the gates—
can't hold them back, when I see this lock of hair.

How could I think another Greek could play
the prince with this?   190
           She'd never cut it,
the murderess, my mother. She insults the name,
she and her godless spirit preying on her children.

But how, how can I come right out and say it *is*
the glory of the dearest man I know—Orestes?
Stop, I'm fawning on hope.   195
            Oh, if only
it had a herald's voice, kind and human—
I'm so shaken, torn—and told me clearly
to throw it away, they severed it from a head
that I detest. Or it could sorrow with me
like a brother, aye,   200
this splendour come to honour father's grave.

We call on the gods, and the gods well know
what storms torment us, sailors whirled to nothing.
But if we are to live and reach the haven,
one small seed could grow a mighty tree—   205
Look, tracks.
         A new sign to tell us more.
Footmarks . . . pairs of them, like mine.
Two outlines, two prints, his own, and there,
a fellow traveller's.

(Putting her foot into ORESTES' print.)

           The heel, the curve of the arch
like twins.   210

(While ORESTES emerges from behind the grave, she follows cautiously in his steps until they come together.)

206ff. **tracks . . .** the thick dust around Agamemnon's tomb, where no wise Argive would go for fear of Clytaemnestra's wrath, would take a clear impression. The recognition of special characteristics in a footprint, which Euripides found ludicrous (*Electra*, 503ff.), might have been common practice in an epoch of skilled hunters and trackers. Moreover, Electra finds a resemblance in the contours of her brother's print, not its size

Step by step, my step in his . . .
                                    we meet—
Oh the pain, like pangs of labour—this is madness!
ORESTES: Pray for the future. Tell the gods they've brought
   your prayers to birth, and pray that we succeed.

(ELECTRA *draws back, struggling for composure.*)

ELECTRA: The gods—why now? What have I ever won
   from them?
215 ORESTES: The sight you prayed to see for many years.
ELECTRA: And you know the one I call?
ORESTES: I know Orestes,
   know he moves you deeply.
ELECTRA: Yes,
   but now what's come to fill my prayers?
ORESTES: Here I am. Look no further.
220 No one loves you more than I.
ELECTRA: No,
   it's a trap, stranger . . . a net you tie around me?
ORESTES: Then I tie myself as well.
ELECTRA: But the pain,
   you're laughing at all—
ORESTES: Your pain is mine.
   If I laugh at yours, I only laugh at mine.
ELECTRA: *Orestes*—
225 can I call you?—are you really—
ORESTES: I am!
   Open your eyes. So slow to learn.
   You saw the lock of hair I cut in mourning.
   You scanned my tracks, you could see my marks,
230 your breath leapt, you all but saw me in the flesh—
   Look—

(*Holding the lock to his temple, then to* ELECTRA*'s.*)

   put it where I cut it.
   It's your brother's. Try, it matches yours.

(*Removing a strip of weaving from his clothing.*)

   Work of your own hand, you tamped the loom,
   look, there are wild creatures in the weaving.

(*She kneels beside him, weeping; he lifts her to her feet and they embrace.*)

235 No, no, control yourself—don't lose yourself in joy!
   Our loved ones, well I know, would slit our throats.
LEADER: Dearest, the darling of your father's house,
   hope of the seed we nursed with tears—you save us.
   Trust to your power, win your father's house once more!
240

233 **Work . . . hand** presumably what Orestes now displays as proof of his identity is a garment woven by Electra with a distinctive design of wild animals, sent to him as a gift during his exile or given to him at birth as a swaddling band. Images of crafts and artistry may have a constructive effect in *The Libation Bearers*—the smith of Fate may counteract his work in Agamemnon (*Agamemnon* 1564f., *The Libation Bearers* 628ff.); Clytaemnestra's masterwork, the robes, will stimulate Orestes' conscience even as they drive him mad; see *The Libation Bearers* 975ff.

ELECTRA: You light to my eyes, four loves in one!
   I have to call you father, it is fate;
   and I turn to you the love I gave my mother—
   I despise her, she deserves it, yes,
   and the love I gave my sister, sacrificed
   on the cruel sword, I turn to you.   245
   You were my faith, my brother—
   you alone restore my self-respect.

(*Praying.*)

   Power and Justice, Saving Zeus, Third Zeus,
   almighty all in all, be with us now.
ORESTES: Zeus, Zeus, watch over all we do,   250
   fledglings reft of the noble eagle father.
   He died in the coils, the viper's dark embrace.
   We are his orphans worn down with hunger,
   weak, too young to haul the father's quarry
   home to shelter.   255
                    Look down on us!
   I and Electra, too, I tell you, children
   robbed of our father, both of us bound
   in exile from our house.
                    And what a father—
   a priest at sacrifice, he showered you
   with honours. Put an end to his nestlings now   260
   and who will serve you banquets rich as his?
   Destroy the eagle's brood, you can never
   send a sign that wins all men's belief.
   Rot the stock of a proud dynastic tree—
   it can never shore your altar steaming   265
   with the oxen in the mornings. Tend us—
   we seem in ruins now, I know. Up from nothing
   rear a house to greatness.
LEADER: Softly, children,
   white hopes of your father's hearth. Someone
   might hear you, children, charmed with his own voice 270
   blurt all this out to the masters. Oh, just once
   to see them—live bones crackling in the fire
   spitting pitch!
ORESTES: Apollo will never fail me, no,
   his tremendous power, his oracle charges me
   to see this trial through.   275
                    I can still hear the god—
   a high voice ringing with winters of disaster,
   piercing the heart within me, warm and strong,
   unless I hunt my father's murderers, cut them down
   in their own style—they destroyed my birthright.
   'Gore them like a bull!' he called, 'or pay their debt 280
   with your own life, one long career of grief.'

244 **my sister** Iphigeneia, sacrificed by Agamemnon. In other accounts Electra has a living sister, Chrysothemis, who is often seen as her foil, weak, conventional. Here, as Sidgwick says, 'Iphigeneia dead, Electra is alone.' **282ff. He . . .** this vividly phrased passage describes the two main punishments for those who become polluted by refusing to exact vengeance for a kinsman's murder (a relic of a primitive state of society before the community as a whole punished murderers according to a legal process). The first punishment consists of foul and maddening sicknesses (including a kind of leprosy), and the second, forcible ejection from the community

He revealed so much about us,
told how the dead take root beneath the soil,
they grow with hate and plague the lives of men.
285 He told of the leprous boils that ride the flesh,
their wild teeth gnawing the mother tissue, aye,
and a white scurf spreads like cancer over these,
and worse, he told how assaults of Furies spring
to life on the father's blood . . .
                                You can *see* them—
290 the eyes burning, grim brows working over you in the
        dark—
the dark sword of the dead!—your murdered kinsmen
pleading for revenge. And the madness haunts
the midnight watch, the empty terror shakes you,
harries, drives you on—an exile from your city—
295 a brazen whip will mutilate your back.

For such as us, no share in the wine-bowl,
no libations poured in love. You never see
your father's wrath but it pulls you from the altars.
There is no refuge, none to take you in.
300 A pariah, reviled, at long last you die,
withered in the grip of all this dying.

Such oracles are persuasive, don't you think?
And even if I am not convinced,
the rough work of the world is still to do.
305 So many yearnings meet and urge me on.
The god's commands. Mounting sorrow for father.
Besides, the lack of patrimony presses hard;
and my compatriots, the glory of men
who toppled Troy with nerves of singing steel,
310 go at the beck and call of a brace of women.
Womanhearted he is—if not, we'll soon see.

(*The* LEADER *lights the altar fires.* ORESTES, ELECTRA, *and the*
CHORUS *gather for the invocation at the grave.*)

CHORUS: Powers of destiny, mighty queens of Fate!—
by the will of Zeus your will be done,
press on to the end now,
315   Justice turns the wheel.
'Word for word, curse for curse
be born now,' Justice thunders,
    hungry for retribution,
'stroke for bloody stroke be paid.
320   The one who acts must suffer.'
Three generations strong the word resounds.
ORESTES: Dear father, father of dread,
what can I do or say to reach you now?
    What breath can reach from here
325 to the bank where you lie moored at anchor?
What light can match your darkness? None,
but there is a kind of grace that comes
    when the tears revive a proud old house
and Atreus' sons, the warlords lost and gone.
330 LEADER: The ruthless jaws of the fire,
my child, can never tame the dead,
        his rage inflames his sons.
Men die and the voices rise, they light the guilty, true—
cries raised for the fathers, clear and just,
335   will hunt their killers harried to the end.

ELECTRA: Then hear me now, my father,
it is my turn, my tears are welling now,
    as child by child we come
to the tomb and raise the dirge, my father
Your grave receives a girl in prayer   340
and a man in flight, and we are one,
    and the pain is equal, whose is worse?
And who outwrestles death—what third last fall?
CHORUS: But still some god, if he desires,
may work our strains to a song of joy,   345
from the dirges chanted over the grave
        may lift a hymn in the kings' halls
and warm the loving cup you stir this morning.
ORESTES: If only at Troy
a Lycian cut you down, my father—   350
gone, with an aura left at home behind you,
    children to go their ways
and the eyes look on them bright with awe,
and the tomb you win on headlands seas away
    would buoy up the house . . .   355
LEADER: And loved by the men you loved
who died in glory, there you'd rule
                beneath the earth—lord, prince,
stern aide to the giant kings who judge the shadows there.
You were a king of kings when you drew breath;   360
the mace you held could make men kneel or die.
ELECTRA: No, not under Troy!—
not dead and gone with them, my father,
hordes pierced by the spear Scamander washes down.
Sooner the killers die   365
as they killed you—at the hands of friends,
and the news of death would come from far away,
we'd never know this grief.
CHORUS: You are dreaming, children,
dreams dearer than gold, more blest   370
than the Blest beyond the North Wind's raging.
    Dreams are easy, oh,
but the double lash is striking home.
Now our comrades group underground.
Our masters' reeking hands are doomed—   375
    the children take the day!
ORESTES: That thrills his ear,
        that arrow lands!
            Zeus, Zeus, force up from the earth
destruction, late but true to the mark,   380
to the reckless heart, the killing hand—
    for parents of revenge revenge be done.
LEADER: And the ripping cries of triumph mine
to sing when the man is stabbed,
        the woman dies—   385
    why hide what's deep inside me,
black wings beating, storming the spirit's prow—
            hurricane, slashing hatred!
ELECTRA: Both fists at once
        come down, come down—
            Zeus, crush their skulls! Kill! kill!   390

384f. **man . . . woman** the man and the woman here are
Aegisthus and Clytaemnestra

Now give the land some faith, I beg you,
from these ancient wrongs bring forth our rights.
Hear me, Earth, and all you lords of death.
CHORUS: It is the law: when the blood of slaughter
395   wets the ground it wants more blood.
Slaughter cries for the Fury
of those long dead to bring destruction
on destruction churning in its wake!
ORESTES: Sweet Earth, how long?—great lords of death, look on,
400   you mighty curses of the dead. Look on
the last of Atreus' children, here, the remnant
helpless, cast from home . . . god, where to turn?
LEADER: And again my pulses race and leap,
I can feel your sobs, and hope
405   becomes despair
and the heart goes dark to hear you—
then the anguish ebbs, I see you stronger,
hope and the light come on me.
ELECTRA: *What* hope?—what force to summon, what can
help?
410   What but the pain we suffer, bred by her?
So let her fawn. She can never soothe her young wolves—
Mother dear, you bred our wolves' raw fury.
LEADER AND CHORUS: I beat and beat the dirge like a
Persian mourner,
hands clenched tight and the blows are coming thick
and fast,
415   you can see the hands shoot out,
now hand over hand and down—the head pulsates,
blood at the temples pounding to explode!
ELECTRA: Reckless, brutal mother—oh dear god!—
The brutal, cruel cortège,
420   the warlord stripped of his honour guard
and stripped of mourning rites—
you dared entomb your lord unwept, unsung.
ORESTES: Shamed for all the world, you mean—
dear god, my father degraded so!
425   Oh she'll pay,
she'll pay, by the gods and these bare hands—
just let me take her life and *die!*
LEADER AND CHORUS: Shamed? *Butchered,* I tell you—
hands lopped,
strung to shackle his neck and arms!
430   So she worked,
she buried him, made your life a hell.
Your father mutilated—do you hear?
ELECTRA: You tell him of father's death, but I was an outcast,
worthless, leashed like a vicious dog in a dark cell.
435   I wept—laughter died that day . . .
I wept, pouring out the tears behind my veils.
Hear *that,* my brother, carve it on your heart!

413ff. **Persian mourner** Persian professional mourners were
renowned for the violence of their lamentations. The women
here accomplish the rites which were denied the king at the time
of his death   428f. **hands lopped . . .** a reference to the practice of mutilation—cutting off the hands and feet of a dead enemy and tying them on a rope around his neck and under his
armpits, to prevent his ghost from pursuing the killer

LEADER AND CHORUS: Let it ring in your ears
but let your heart stand firm.
The outrage stands as it stands,   440
you burn to know the end,
but first be strong, be steel, then down and fight.
ORESTES: I am calling you, my father—be with all you love!
ELECTRA: I am with you, calling through my tears.
LEADER AND CHORUS: We band together now, the call   445
resounds—
hear us now, come back into the light.
Be with us, battle all you hate.
ORESTES: Now force *clash* with force—right with right!
ELECTRA: Dear gods, be just—win back our rights.
LEADER AND CHORUS: The flesh crawls to hear them pray.   450
The hour of doom has waited long . . .
pray for it once, and oh my god, it comes.
CHORUS: Oh, the torment bred in the race,
the grinding scream of death
and the stroke that hits the vein,   455
the haemorrhage none can staunch, the grief,
the curse no man can bear.

But there is a cure in the house
and not outside it, no,
not from others but from *them,*   460
their bloody strife. We sing to you,
dark gods beneath the earth.

Now hear, you blissful powers underground—
answer the call, send help.
Bless the children, give them triumph now.   465

(*They withdraw, while* ELECTRA *and* ORESTES *come to the altar.*)

ORESTES: Father, king, no royal death you died—
give me the power now to rule our house.
ELECTRA: I need you too, my father.
Help me kill her lover, then go free.
ORESTES: Then men will extend the sacred feast to you.   470
Or else, when the steam and the rich savour burn
for Mother Earth, you will starve for honour.
ELECTRA: And I will pour my birthright out to you—
the wine of the fathers' house, my bridal wine,
and first of all the shrines revere your tomb.   475
ORESTES: O Earth, bring father up to watch me fight.
ELECTRA: O Persephone, give us power—lovely, gorgeous
power!
ORESTES: Remember the bath—they stripped away your
life, my father.
ELECTRA: Remember the all-embracing net—they made it
first for you.
ORESTES: Chained like a beast—chains of hate, not bronze,   480
my father!
ELECTRA: Shamed in the schemes, the hoods they slung
around you!
ORESTES: Does our taunting wake you, oh my father?
ELECTRA: Do you lift your beloved head?
ORESTES: Send us justice, fight for all you love,
or help us pin them grip for grip. They threw you—   485
don't you long to throw them down in turn?
ELECTRA: One last cry, father. Look at your nestlings
stationed at your tomb—pity
your son and daughter. We are all you have.

490 ORESTES: Never blot out the seed of Pelops here.
  Then in the face of death you cannot die.

(*The* LEADER *comes forward again.*)

  LEADER: The voices of children—salvation to the dead!
    Corks to the net, they rescue the linen meshes
    from the depths. This line will never drown!
495 ELECTRA: Hear us—the long wail we raise is all for you!
    Honour our call and you will save yourself.
  LEADER: And a fine thing it is to lengthen out the dirge;
    you adore a grave and fate they never mourned.
    But now for action—now you're set on action,
500 put your stars to proof.
  ORESTES: So we will.
    One thing first, I think it's on the track.
    Why did she send libations? What possessed her,
    so late, to salve a wound past healing?
    To the unforgiving dead she sends this sop,
505 this . . . who am I to appreciate her gifts?
    They fall so short of all her failings. True,
    'pour out your all to atone an act of blood,
    you work for nothing'. So the saying goes.
    I'm ready. Tell me what you know.
  LEADER: I know, my boy,
510 I was there. She had bad dreams. Some terror
    came groping through the night, it shook her,
    and she sent these cups, unholy woman.
  ORESTES: And you know the dream, you can tell it clearly?
  LEADER: She dreamed she bore a snake, said so herself and . . .
515 ORESTES: Come to the point—where does the story end?
  LEADER: . . . she swaddled it like a baby, laid it to rest.
  ORESTES: And food, what did the little monster want?
  LEADER: She gave it her breast to suck—she was dreaming.
  ORESTES: And didn't it tear her nipple, the brute inhuman—
520 LEADER: Blood curdled the milk with each sharp tug . . .
  ORESTES: No empty dream. The vision of a man.
  LEADER: . . . and she woke with a scream, appalled,
    and rows of torches, burning out of the blind dark,
    flared across the halls to soothe the queen,
525 and then she sent the libations for the dead,
    an easy cure she hopes will cut the pain.
  ORESTES: No,
    I pray to the Earth and father's grave to bring
    that dream to life in me. I'll play the seer—
    it all fits together, watch!
530 If the serpent came from the same place as I,
    and slept in the bands that swaddled me, and its jaws
    spread wide for the breast that nursed me into life
    and clots stained the milk, mother's milk,
    and she cried in fear and agony—so be it.
535 As she bred this sign, this violent prodigy
    so she dies by violence. I turn serpent,
    I kill her. So the vision says.
  LEADER: You are the seer for me, I like your reading.
    Let it come! But now rehearse your friends.
540 Say do this, or don't do that—
  ORESTES: The plan is simple. My sister goes inside.
    And I'd have her keep the bond with me a secret.
    They killed an honoured man by cunning, so
    they die by cunning, caught in the same noose.
545 So he commands,
    Apollo the Seer who's never lied before.

And I like a stranger, equipped for all events,
  go to the outer gates with this man here,
  Pylades, a friend, the house's friend-in-arms.
  And we both will speak Parnassian, both try   550
  for the native tones of Delphi.
                    Now, say none
  at the doors will give us a royal welcome
  (after all the house is ridden by a curse),
  well then we wait . . . till a passer-by will stop
  and puzzle and make insinuations at the house,   555
  'Aegisthus shuts his door on the man who needs him.
  Why, I wonder—does he know? Is he home?'

But once through the gates, across the threshold,
  once I find that man on my father's throne,
  or returning late to meet me face to face,   560
  and his eyes shift and fall—
                    I promise you,
  before he can ask me, 'Stranger, who are you?'—
  I drop him dead, a thrust of the sword, and twist!
  Our Fury never wants for blood. His she drinks unmixed,
  our third libation poured to Saving Zeus.   565

(*Turning to* ELECTRA.)

Keep a close watch inside, dear, be careful.
  We must work together step by step.

(*To the* CHORUS.)

                    And you,
  better hold your tongues, religiously.
  Silence, friends, or speak when it will help.

(*Looking towards* PYLADES *and the death-mound and beyond.*)

For the rest, watch over me, I need you—   570
  guide my sword through struggle, guide me home!

(*As* ORESTES, PYLADES, *and* ELECTRA *leave, the women reassemble for the* CHORUS.)

CHORUS: Marvels, the Earth breeds many marvels,
          terrible marvels overwhelm us.
    The heaving arms of the sea embrace and swarm
  with savage life. And high in the no man's land of night   575
    torches hang like swords. The hawk on the wing,
          the beast astride the fields
      can tell of the whirlwind's fury roaring strong.

    Oh but a man's high daring spirit,
          who can account for that? Or woman's   580
  desperate passion daring past all bounds?
  She couples with every form of ruin known to mortals.

---

565 **our third . . . Zeus** third after Thyestes' feast and Agamemnon's assassination (1064ff.), or third after Agamemnon's murder of Iphigeneia and Clytaemnestra's murder of the king. That a murder should be a libation is a savage irony, of course, though like a third libation poured to Zeus, it will ultimately mitigate the sufferings of the house

Woman, frenzied, driven wild with lust,
    twists the dark, warm harness
585   of wedded love—tortures man and beast!

Well you know, you with a sense of truth
    recall Althaia,
the heartless mother
who killed her son,
590   ai! what a scheme she had—
     she rushed his destiny,
      lit the bloody torch
preserved from the day he left her loins with a cry—
     the life of the torch paced his,
595   burning on till Fate burned out his life.

There is one more in the tales of hate:
    remember Scylla,
the girl of slaughter
seduced by foes
600   to take her father's life.
    The gift of Minos,
     a choker forged in gold
turned her head and Nisos' immortal lock she cut
     as he slept away his breath . . .
605   ruthless bitch, now Hermes takes her down.

Now that I call to mind old wounds that never heal—
    Stop, it's time for the wedded love-in-hate,
for the curse of the halls,
    the woman's brazen cunning
610   bent on her lord in arms,
    her warlord's power—
     Do you respect such things?
I prize the hearthstone warmed by faith,
a woman's temper nothing bends to outrage.

First at the head of legendary crime stands Lemnos.
615   People shudder and moan, and can't forget—
each new horror that comes
    we call the hells of Lemnos.
    Loathed by the gods for guilt,
    cast off by men, disgraced, their line dies out.
620   Who could respect what god detests?
What of these tales have I not picked with justice?

The sword's at the lungs!—it stabs deep,
    the edge cuts through and through
and Justice drives it—Outrage still lives on,
    not trodden to pieces underfoot, not yet,   625
    though the laws lie trampled down,
     the majesty of Zeus.

The anvil of Justice stands fast
    and Fate beats out her sword.
Tempered for glory, a child will wipe clean   630
the inveterate stain of blood shed long ago—
    Fury brings him home at last,
    the brooding mother Fury!

(*The women leave.* ORESTES *and* PYLADES *approach the house of Atreus.*)

ORESTES: Slave, the slave!—
    where is he? Hear me pounding the gates?
    Is there a man inside the house?   635
    For the third time, come out of the halls!
    If Aegisthus has them welcome friendly guests.

(*A voice from inside.*)

PORTER: All right, I hear you . . .
    Where do you come from, stranger? Who are you?
ORESTES: Announce me to the masters of the house.   640
    I've come for them, I bring them news.
                Hurry,
    the chariot of the night is rushing on the dark!
    The hour falls, the traveller casts his anchor
    in an inn where every stranger feels at home.
                Come out!
    Whoever rules the house. The woman in charge.   645
    No, the man, better that way.
    No scruples then. Say what you mean,
    man to man launch in and prove your point,
    make it clear, strong.

(CLYTAEMNESTRA *emerges from the palace, attended by* ELECTRA.)

CLYTAEMNESTRA: Strangers, please,
    tell me what you would like and it is yours.   650
    We've all you might expect in a house like ours.
    We have warm baths and beds to charm away your pains
    and the eyes of Justice look on all we do.
    But if you come for higher things, affairs
    that touch the state, that is the men's concern   655
    and I will stir them on.
ORESTES: I am a stranger,
    from Daulis, close to Delphi, I'd just set out,
    packing my own burden bound for Argos
    (here I'd put my burden down and rest),
    when I met a perfect stranger, out of the blue,   660
    who asks about my way and tells me his.
               Strophios,
    a Phocian, so I gathered in conversation.
    'Well, my friend,' he says, 'out for Argos
    in any case? Remember to tell the parents
    he is dead, Orestes . . .   665
            promise me please

---

587 **Althaia** daughter of Thestios and Eurythemis, was a notorious example of an unloving mother: in anger at the death of one of her brothers she caused the death of her son Meleager by burning a log on which his life was magically dependent 597 **Scylla** of Megara (not the monster with the same name in the *Odyssey*) betrayed her father, Nisos (whose life depended on a magical lock of hair on his head), to Minos, king of Crete, when he was besieging their city. Her motive was love, according to legend, and her crime betrayed her people. Aeschylus, however, makes Scylla the object of a bribe, and her crime remains quite private, in contrast to Clytaemnestra's greater guilt and destructiveness that follow 614 **Lemnos** as a third example of feminine ruthlessness and treachery, the Chorus cites the abominable massacre of husbands by the women of Lemnos

(it's only right), it will not slip your mind.
Then whatever his people want, to bring him home
or bury him here, an alien, all outcast here
forever, won't you ferry back their wishes?
670 As it is, a bronze urn is armour to his embers.
The man's been mourned so well . . .'
                                        I only tell you
what I heard. And am I speaking now
with guardians, kinsmen who will care?
It's hard to say. But a parent ought to know.
  CLYTAEMNESTRA: I, I—
675 your words, you storm us, raze us to the roots,
you curse of the house so hard to wrestle down!
How you range—targets at peace, miles away,
and a shaft from your lookout brings them down.
You strip me bare of all I love, destroy me,
680 now—Orestes.
And he was trained so well, we'd been so careful,
kept his footsteps clear of the quicksand of death.
Just now, the hope of the halls, the surgeon to cure
our Furies' lovely revel—he seemed so close,
685 he's written off the rolls.
  ORESTES: If only I were . . .
my friends, with hosts as fortunate as you
if only I could be known for better news
and welcomed like a brother. The tie between
the host and stranger, what is kinder?
690 But what an impiety, so it seemed to me,
not to bring this to a head for loved ones.
I was bound by honour, bound by the rights
of hospitality.
  CLYTAEMNESTRA: Nothing has changed.
For all that you receive what you deserve,
695 as welcome in these halls as one of us.
Wouldn't another bear the message just as well?
But you must be worn from the long day's journey—
time for your rewards.

(*To* ELECTRA.)

                        Escort him in,
where the men who come are made to feel at home.
700 He and his retinue, and fellow travellers.
Let them taste the bounty of our house.
Do it, as if you depended on his welfare.

And we will rouse the powers in the house
and share the news. We never lack for loved ones,
705 we will probe this turn of fortune every way.

(ELECTRA *leads* ORESTES, PYLADES, *and their retinue into the
halls;* CLYTAEMNESTRA *follows, while the* CHORUS *reassembles.*)

  LEADER: Oh dear friends who serve the house,
            when can we speak out, when
        can the vigour of our voices serve Orestes?
  CHORUS: Queen of the Earth, rich mounded Earth,
710   breasting over the lord of ships,
        the king's corpse at rest,
        hear us now, now help us,
            now the time is ripe—

Down to the pit Persuasion goes
with all her cunning. Hermes of Death,   715
the great shade patrols the ring
to guide the struggles, drive the tearing sword.
  LEADER: And I think our new friend is at his mischief.
  Look, Orestes' nurse in tears.

(*Enter* CILISSA.)

Where now, old-timer, padding along the gates?   720
With pain a volunteer to go your way.
  CILISSA: 'Aegisthus,'
  your mistress calling, 'hurry and meet your guests.
  There's news. It's clearer man to man, you'll see.'

And she looks at the maids and pulls that long face
and down deep her eyes are laughing over the work   725
that's done. Well and good for her. For the house
it's the curse all over—the strangers make that plain.
But let him hear, he'll revel once he knows.
                        Oh god,
the life is hard. The old griefs, the memories
mixing, cups of pain, so much pain in the halls,   730
the house of Atreus . . . I suffered, the heart within me
always breaking, oh, but I never shouldered
misery like this. So many blows, good slave,
I took my blows.
                Now dear Orestes—
the sweetest, dearest plague of all our lives!   735
Red from your mother's womb I took you, reared you . . .
nights, the endless nights I paced, your wailing
kept me moving—led me a life of labour,
all for what?
            And such care I gave it . . .
baby can't think for itself, poor creature.   740
You have to nurse it, don't you? Read its mind,
little devil's got no words, it's still swaddled.
Maybe it wants a bite or a sip of something,
or its bladder pinches—a baby's soft insides
have a will of their own. I had to be a prophet.   745
Oh I tried, and missed, believe you me, I missed,
and I'd scrub its pretty things until they sparkled.
Washerwoman and wet-nurse shared the shop.
A jack of two trades, that's me,
and an old hand at both . . .   750
                        and so I nursed Orestes,
yes, from his father's arms I took him once,
and now they say he's dead,
I've suffered it all, and now I'll fetch that man,
the ruination of the house—give him the news,
he'll relish every word.   755
  LEADER: She tells him to come,
  but how, prepared?
  CILISSA: Prepared, how else?
  I don't see . . .
  LEADER: With his men, I mean, or all alone?
  CILISSA: Oh, she says to bring his bodyguard, his cut-throats.
  LEADER: No, not now, not if you hate our master—
  tell him to come alone.   760
  Nothing for him to fear then, when he hears.

Have him come quickly, too, rejoicing all the way!
The teller sets the crooked message straight.
CILISSA: What,
    you're glad for the news that's come?
LEADER: Why not,
765   if Zeus will turn the evil wind to good?
CILISSA: But how? Orestes, the hope of the house is gone.
LEADER: Not yet. It's a poor seer who'd say so.
CILISSA: What are you saying?—something I don't know?
LEADER: Go in with your message. Do as you're told.
770   May the gods take care of cares that come from them.
CILISSA: Well, I'm off. Do as I'm told.
    And here's to the best . . .
    some help, dear gods, some help.

(*Exit.*)

CHORUS: O now bend to my prayer, Father Zeus,
775   lord of the gods astride the sky—
        grant them all good fortune,
        the lords of the house who strain to see
                strict discipline return.
        Our cry is the cry of Justice,
780   Zeus, safeguard it well.

                                        Zeus, Zeus,
        set him against his enemies in the halls!
        Do it, rear him to greatness—two, threefold
            he will repay you freely, gladly.

        Look now—watch the colt of a man you loved,
785   yoked to the chariot of pain.
        Now the orphan needs you—
        harness his racing, rein him in,
                preserve his stride so we
        can watch him surge at the last turn,
790   storming for the goal.

        And you who haunt the vaults
        where the gold glows in the darkness,
        hear us now, good spirits of the house,
            conspire with us—come,
795   and wash old works of blood
        in the fresh-drawn blood of Justice.
        Let the grey retainer, murder, breed no more.

        And you, Apollo, lord of the glorious masoned cavern,
            grant that this man's house lift up its head,
800   that we may see with loving eyes
            the light of freedom burst from its dark veil!

        And lend a hand and scheme
        for the rights, my Hermes, help us,
        sail the action on with all your breath.
805   Reveal what's hidden, please,
            or say a baffling word
        in the night and blind men's eyes—
        when the morning comes your word is just as dark.

Soon, at last, in the dawn that frees the house,
    we sea-widows wed to the winds   810
        will beat our mourning looms of song
                and sing, 'Our ship's come in!
    Mine, mine is the wealth that swells her holds—
    those I love are home and free of death.'

But you, when your turn in the action comes, be strong.   815
    When she cries 'Son!' cry out 'My *father's* son!'
        Go through with the murder—innocent at last.

Raise up the heart of Perseus in your breast!
    And for all you love under earth
        and all above its rim, now scarf your eyes   820
            against the Gorgon's fury—
        In, go in for the slaughter now!

(*Enter* AEGISTHUS, *alone*.)

The butcher comes. Wipe out death with death.
AEGISTHUS: Coming, coming. Yes, I have my summons.
    There's news, I gather, travellers here to tell it.   825
    No joy in the telling, though—Orestes dead.
    Saddle the house with a bloody thing like that
    and it might just collapse. It's still raw
    from the last murders, galled and raw.
    But how to take the story, for living truth?   830
    Or work of a woman's panic, gossip starting up
    in the night to flicker out and die?

(*Turning to the* LEADER.)

                                        Do you know?
    Tell me, clear my mind.
LEADER: We've heard a little.
    But get it from the strangers, go inside.
    Messengers have no power. Nothing like   835
    a face-to-face encounter with the source.
AEGISTHUS: —Must see him, test the messenger. Where was he
    when the boy died, standing on the spot?
    Or is he dazed with rumour, mouthing hearsay?
    No, he'll never trap me open-eyed!   840

(*Striding through the doors.*)

CHORUS: Zeus, Zeus, what can I say?—
    how to begin this prayer, call down
        the gods for help? what words
    can reach the depth of all I feel?
    Now they swing to the work,   845
    the red edge of the cleaver
    hacks at flesh and men go down.
    Agamemnon's house goes down—
        all-out disaster now,

---

798 **cavern** the temple of Apollo at Delphi, in particular the chasm in the ground over which his sacred tripod stood, drawing up prophetic vapours from the earth   803 **Hermes** here the god of stratagems, especially deceptive messages

818 **Perseus** according to tradition, the grandson of an earlier, pre-Pelopid king of Argos. He killed the Gorgon, Medusa, whose serpentine hair and lethal glance could petrify a man, by shielding his eyes and using Athena's help. His country, his enemy, his patron goddess, and his role as a liberator all suggest a parallel with Orestes

850   or a son ignites the torch of freedom,
       wins the throne, the citadel,
         the fathers' realms of gold.
       The last man on the bench, a challenger
       must come to grips with two. Up,
855   like a young god, Orestes, wrestle—
         let it be to win.

(A scream inside the palace.)

     —Listen!
         —What's happening?
                   —The house,
     what have they done to the house?
LEADER: Back,
     till the work is over! Stand back—
860   they'll count us clean of the dreadful business.

(The women scatter; a wounded SERVANT *of Aegisthus enters.)*

     Look, the die is cast, the battle's done.
SERVANT: Ai,
     Ai, all over, master's dead—Aie,
     a third, last salute. Aegisthus is no more.

(Rushing at a side door, struggling to work it open.)

     Open up, wrench the bolts on the women's doors.
865   Faster! A strong young arm it takes,
     but not to save him now, he's finished.
     What's the use?
            Look—wake up!
                 No good,
     I call to the deaf, to sleepers . . . a waste of breath.
     Where are you, Clytaemnestra? What are you doing?
870 LEADER: Her head is ripe for lopping on the block.
     She's next, and justice wields the axe.

(The door opens, and CLYTAEMNESTRA *comes forth.)*

CLYTAEMNESTRA: What now?
     Why this shouting up and down the halls?
SERVANT: The dead are cutting down the quick, I tell you!
CLYTAEMNESTRA: Ah, a riddle. I do well at riddles.
875   By cunning we die, precisely as we killed.
     Hand me the man-axe, someone, hurry!

(The SERVANT *dashes out.)*

     Now we will see. Win all or lose all,
     we have come to this—the crisis of our lives.

(The main doors open; ORESTES, *sword in hand, is standing over the body of* AEGISTHUS, *with* PYLADES *close behind him.)*

ORESTES: It's you I want. This one's had enough.
880 CLYTAEMNESTRA: Gone, my violent one—Aegisthus, very dear.
ORESTES: You love your man? Then lie in the same grave.
     You can never be unfaithful to the dead.

(Pulling her towards AEGISTHUS' *body.)*

CLYTAEMNESTRA: Wait, my son—no respect for this, my child?
     The breast you held, drowsing away the hours,
     soft gums tugging the milk that made you grow?   885

*(*ORESTES *turns to* PYLADES.)*

ORESTES: What will I do, Pylades?—I dread to kill my mother!
PYLADES: What of the future? What of the Prophet God Apollo,
     the Delphic voice, the faith and oaths we swear?
     Make all mankind your enemy, not the gods.
ORESTES: O you win me over—good advice.   890

(Wheeling on CLYTAEMNESTRA, *thrusting her towards* AEGISTHUS.)*

                     This way—
     I want to butcher you—right across his body!
     In life you thought he dwarfed my father—Die!—
     go down with him forever!
                 You love this man,
     the man you should have loved you hated.
CLYTAEMNESTRA: I gave you life. Let me grow old with you.   895
ORESTES: What—kill my father, then you'd live with me?
CLYTAEMNESTRA: Destiny had a hand in that, my child.
ORESTES: This too: destiny is handing you your death.
CLYTAEMNESTRA: You have no fear of a mother's curse, my son?
ORESTES: Mother? You flung me to a life of pain.   900
CLYTAEMNESTRA: Never flung you, placed you in a comrade's house.
ORESTES: —Disgraced me, sold me, a freeborn father's son.
CLYTAEMNESTRA: Oh? then name the price I took for you.
ORESTES: I am ashamed to mention it in public.
CLYTAEMNESTRA: Please, and tell your father's failings, too.   905
ORESTES: Never judge him—he suffered, you sat here at home.
CLYTAEMNESTRA: It hurts women, being kept from men, my son.
ORESTES: Perhaps . . . but the man slaves to keep them safe at home.
CLYTAEMNESTRA: —I see murder in your eyes, my child— mother's murder!
ORESTES: You are the murderer, not I—and you will kill   910 yourself.
CLYTAEMNESTRA: Watch out—the hounds of a mother's curse will hunt you down.
ORESTES: But how to escape a father's if I fail?
CLYTAEMNESTRA: I must be spilling live tears on a tomb of stone.
ORESTES: Yes, my father's destiny—it decrees your death.
CLYTAEMNESTRA: Ai—you are the snake I bore—I gave you life!
ORESTES: Yes! 915
     That was the great seer, that terror in your dreams.
     You killed and it was outrage—suffer outrage now.

(He draws her over the threshold; the doors close behind them, and the CHORUS *gathers at the altar.)*

LEADER: I even mourn the victims' double fates.
     But Orestes fought, he reached the summit
     of bloodshed here—we'd rather have it so.   920
     The bright eye of the halls must never die.

CHORUS: Justice came at last to the sons of Priam,
    late but crushing vengeance, yes,
    but to Agamemnon's house returned
925   the double lion,
        the double onslaught
      drove to the hilt—the exile sped by god,
    by Delphi's just command that drove him home.

    Lift the cry of triumph O! the master's house
930   wins free of grief, free of the ones
    who bled its wealth, the couple stained with murder,
        free of Fate's rough path.

    He came back with a lust for secret combat,
    stealthy, cunning vengeance, yes,
935   but his hand was steered in open fight
    by god's true daughter,
        Right, Right we call her,
    we and our mortal voices aiming well—
    she breathes her fury, shatters all she hates.

940   Lift the cry of triumph O! the master's house
      wins free of grief, free of the ones
    who bled its wealth, the couple stained with murder,
        free of Fate's rough path.

    Apollo wills it so!—
945 Apollo, clear from the Earth's deep cleft
    his voice came shrill, 'Now stealth will master stealth!'
    And the pure god came down and healed our ancient
      wounds,
    the heavens come, somehow, to lift our yoke of grief—
    Now to praise the heavens' just command.

950   Look, the light is breaking!
    The huge chain that curbed the halls gives way.
      Rise up, proud house, long, too long
    your walls lay fallen, strewn along the earth.

    Time brings all to birth—
955 soon Time will stride through the gates with blessings,
    once the hearth burns off corruption, once
    the house drives off the Furies. Look, the dice of Fate
    fall well for all to see. We sing how fortune smiles—
    the aliens in the house are routed out at last!

960   Look, the light is breaking!
    The huge chain that curbed the halls gives way.
      Rise up, proud house, long, too long
    your walls lay fallen, strewn along the earth.

(*The doors open. Torches light* PYLADES *and* ORESTES, *sword in hand, standing over the bodies of* CLYTAEMNESTRA *and* AEGISTHUS, *as* CLYTAEMNESTRA *stood over the bodies of* AGAMEMNON *and* CASSANDRA.)

ORESTES: Behold the double tyranny of our land!
965   They killed my father, stormed my father's house.
    They had their power when they held the throne.
    Great lovers still, as you may read their fate.
    True to their oath, hand in hand they swore
    to kill my father, hand in hand to die.
970   Now they keep their word.

(*Unwinding from the bodies on the bier the robes that entangled* AGAMEMNON, *he displays them, as* CLYTAEMNESTRA *had displayed them, to the* CHORUS *at the altar.*)

        Look once more on this,
    you who gather here to attend our crimes—
    the master-plot that bound my wretched father,
    shackled his ankles, manacled his hands.
    Spread it out! Stand in a ring around it,
    a grand shroud for a man.   975
            Here, unfurl it
    so the Father—no, not mine but the One
    who watches over all, the Sun can behold
    my mother's godless work. So he may come,
    my witness when the day of judgement comes,
    that I pursued this bloody death with justice,   980
    mother's death.
            Aegisthus, why mention him?
    The adulterer dies. An old custom, justice.
    But she who plotted this horror against her husband,
    she carried his children, growing in her womb
    and she—I loved her once   985
    and now I loathe, I have to loathe—
               what is she?

(*Kneeling by the body of his mother.*)

    Some moray eel, some viper born to rot her mate
    with a single touch, no fang to strike him,
    just the wrong, the reckless fury in her heart!

(*Glancing back and forth from* CLYTAEMNESTRA *to the robes.*)

    This—how can I dignify this . . . snare for a beast?—   990
    sheath for a corpse's feet?
            This winding-sheet,
    this tent for the bath of death!
            No, a hunting net,
    a coiling—what to call—?
            Foot-trap—
    woven of robes . . .
    why, this is perfect gear for the highwayman   995
    who entices guests and robs them blind and plies
    the trade of thieves. With a sweet lure like this
    he'd hoist a hundred lives and warm his heart.

    Live with such a woman, marry *her*? Sooner
    the gods destroy me—die without an heir!   1000
CHORUS: Oh the dreadful work . . .
    Death calls and she is gone.
      But oh, for you, the survivor,
    suffering is just about to bloom.
ORESTES: Did she do the work or not?—Here, come close—   1005
    This shroud's my witness, dyed with Aegisthus' blade—
    Look, the blood ran here, conspired with time to blot
    the swirling dyes, the handsome old brocade.

(*Clutching* AGAMEMNON's *robes, burying his face in them and weeping.*)

    Now I can praise you, now I am here to mourn.
    You were my father's death, great robe, I hail you!   1010
    Even if I must suffer the work and the agony

and all the race of man—
                                        I embrace you . . . you,
my victory, are my guilt, my curse, and still—
CHORUS: No man can go through life
1015   and reach the end unharmed.
                    Aye, trouble is now,
            and trouble still to come.
ORESTES: But *still,*
        that you may know—
                                        I see no end in sight,
I am a charioteer—the reins are flying, look,
1020   the mares plunge off the track—
                                        my bolting heart,
        it beats me down and terror beats the drum,
        my dance-and-singing master pitched to fury—

And still, while I still have some self-control,
I say to my friends in public: I killed my mother,
1025   not with a little justice. She was stained
        with father's murder, she was cursed by god.
        And the magic spells that fired up my daring?
        One comes first. The Seer of Delphi who declared,
        'Go through with this and you go free of guilt.
1030   Fail and—'
                    I can't repeat the punishment.
        What bow could hit the crest of so much pain?

(PYLADES *gives* ORESTES *a branch of olive and invests him in the robes of* APOLLO, *the wreath and insignia of suppliants to Delphi.*)

Now look on me, armed with the branch and wreath,
a suppliant bound for the Navelstone of Earth,
Apollo's sacred heights
1035   where they say the fire of heaven can never die.

(*Looking at his hand that still retains the sword.*)

I must escape this blood . . . it is my own.
—Must turn towards his hearth,
none but his, the Prophet God decreed.

I ask you, Argos and all my generations,
1040   remember how these brutal things were done.
        Be my witness to Menelaus when he comes.
        And now I go, an outcast driven off the land,
        in life, in death, I leave behind a name for—

LEADER: But you've done well. Don't burden yourself
        with bad omens, lash yourself with guilt.   1045
        You've set us free, the whole city of Argos,
        lopped the heads of these two serpents once for all.

(*Staring at the women and beyond,* ORESTES *screams in terror.*)

ORESTES: No, no! Women—look—like Gorgons,
        shrouded in black, their heads wreathed,
        swarming serpents!—   1050
                        Cannot stay, I must move on.
LEADER: What dreams can whirl you so? You of all men,
        you have your father's love. Steady, nothing
        to fear with all you've won.
ORESTES: No dreams, these torments,
        not to me, they're clear, real—the hounds
        of mother's hate.   1055
LEADER: The blood's still wet on your hands.
        It puts a kind of frenzy in you . . .
ORESTES: *God Apollo!*
        Here they come, thick and fast,
        their eyes dripping hate—
LEADER: One thing
        will purge you. Apollo's touch will set you free
        from all your . . . torments.   1060
ORESTES: You can't see them
        I can, they drive me on! I must move on—

(*He rushes out;* PYLADES *follows close behind.*)

LEADER: Farewell then. God look down on you with kindness,
        guard you, grant you fortune.
CHORUS: Here once more, for the third time,
        the tempest in the race has struck   1065
        the house of kings and run its course.
            First the children eaten,
        the cause of all our pain, the curse.
        And next the kingly man's ordeal,
        the bath where the proud commander,   1070
        lord of Achaea's armies lost his life.
        And now a third has come, but who?
            A third like Saving Zeus?
        Or should we call him death?
        Where will it end?—   1075
        where will it sink to sleep and rest,
            this murderous hate, this Fury?

The Eumenides opens with what is surely one of the most striking images in all of Greek theater. The priestess of Apollo's shrine at Delphi opens the doors of the skene to reveal Orestes—the olive branch of the suppliant in one hand, a bloody sword in the other at prayer, surrounded by the sleeping Chorus of the Furies: "they are black and utterly / repulsive, and they snore with breath that drives one back. / From their eyes drips the foul ooze." Orestes has come to Delphi to seek relief from the Furies; he prays to Apollo the Lawgiver that his act, murderous though it was, was ultimately a form of just retribution for the crimes that Aegisthus and Clytaemnestra had enacted on his father. The Eumenides raises the framing question of The Oresteia as a whole: How can a civil society survive when its code of justice is an endless cycle of retribution?

The final scene of The Eumenides is a trial, a scene that both enacts and betrays the founding ideology of Athens. Athene is summoned to conduct a trial, and constitutes a jury of Athenian citizens to adjudicate between Orestes and the Furies. Much of the debate between the Chorus and Apollo (who represents Orestes) concerns the relationship between justice and gender. For while the Chorus argues that Orestes' crime, spilling his mother's blood and then assuming the throne of Argos, is at least as horrific as Clytaemnestra's murder of Agamemnon, Apollo argues that killing a woman, even one's mother, is a lesser crime than killing a man, not least because it is the man, and not the woman, who is the bearer of life into the world:

> The mother is no parent of that which is called
> her child, but only nurse of the new-planted seed
> that grows. The parent is he who mounts.

Athene, who, of course, sprang fully conceived from the head of Zeus is called to witness, and saying, "I am always for the male," casts her tie-breaking vote for Orestes: "And if the other votes are even, Orestes wins." The lots are counted, and Orestes is exonerated. Aeschylus' play enacts the triumph of Athenian democracy over a merely retributive justice, at the same time that it encodes that justice with the politics of gender. The sense that the masculine is the generative gender reveals the contradictory strains at the core of Athenian democracy itself: Like the justice the jury delivers, Athenian democracy depends on the subordination of "others" (women, slaves, foreigners) within the perspective of masculine "equality."

Yet while the terrible curse of the house of Atreus is finally resolved, the vengeful Furies remain unsatisfied. Throughout The Eumenides, the Furies' dynamic singing and dancing drive the energy of the play's performance. In a theatrical sense, the justice of the court will be persuasive only if the Furies themselves are transformed as well. Much as the ghastly crimes of the house of Atreus have been resolved by the Athenian jury, so Athene transforms the Furies from evil scourges into ministers of grace, bringing them into the symbolic order of Athenian democracy. Indeed, while The Oresteia exemplifies Athenian tragedy, we might think that the cycle as a whole has a fundamentally comic structure, bringing its audience from the nighttime fear and isolation of the Watchman who opens Agamemnon to the final festivities of The Eumenides, for at the play's close, Athene summons the women of Athens, who invest the Furies in their new "purple stained robes," and in their new role as well; no longer will they be figures of chastening punishment, but figures of fortune and prosperity, bringing "blessings" to the citizens of Athens. In the symbolic structure of The Oresteia, the dark crimes of the past give way to a vision of social order, as Athene leads the procession from the theater.

This third play of The Oresteia is translated by Richmond Lattimore. Readers of the trilogy will note that Lattimore's style is slightly more imagistic than Robert Fagles's style in the preceding plays. Also, since the Greek alphabet does not correspond exactly to the Ro-

The Eumenides

man alphabet, modern English translations are sometimes inconsistent in their spelling of Greek names—Jocasta or Iokaste, for instance, or Athene or Athena.

NOTE: Various editions of Greek drama divide the lines of lyric passages in various ways, but editors regularly follow the traditional line numbers whether their own line divisions tally with these numbers or not. This accounts for what may appear to be erratic line numbering in our translations, for instance, *The Eumenides* 360 and following. The line numbering in the translations in this volume is that of [H. W.] Smyth's text ["Loeb Classical Library," London and New York: William Heinemann, Ltd., and G. P. Putnam's Sons, 1926].

Richmond Lattimore

THE EUMENIDES

Aeschylus

TRANSLATED BY RICHMOND LATTIMORE

CHARACTERS

PRIESTESS OF APOLLO, *the* PYTHIA
APOLLO
HERMES *(silent)*
GHOST OF CLYTAEMNESTRA
ORESTES
ATHENE
CHORUS OF EUMENIDES (FURIES)
SECOND CHORUS OF WOMEN OF ATHENS
JURORS, HERALD, CITIZENS OF ATHENS *(all silent parts)*

SCENE: *For the first part of the play (1–234) the scene is Delphi, before the sanctuary of Pythian Apollo. The action of the rest of the play (235 to the end) takes place at Athens, on the Acropolis before the temple of Athene. A simple change in the backdrop will indicate the shift.*

Enter, alone, the PYTHIA.

PYTHIA: I give first place of honor in my prayer to her
who of the gods first prophesied, the Earth; and next
to Themis, who succeeded to her mother's place
of prophecy; so runs the legend; and in third
5   succession, given by free consent, not won by force,
another Titan daughter of Earth was seated here.
This was Phoebe. She gave it as a birthday gift
to Phoebus, who is called still after Phoebe's name.
And he, leaving the pond of Delos and the reef,
10   grounded his ship at the roadstead of Pallas, then
made his way to this land and a Parnassian home.
Deep in respect for his degree Hephaestus' sons
conveyed him here, for these are builders of roads, and
     changed
the wilderness to a land that was no wilderness.
15   He came so, and the people highly honored him,
with Delphus, lord and helmsman of the country. Zeus
made his mind full with godship and prophetic craft
and placed him, fourth in a line of seers, upon this throne.
So, Loxias is the spokesman of his father, Zeus.
20   These are the gods I set in the proem of my prayer.
But Pallas-before-the-temple has her right in all
I say. I worship the nymphs where the Corycian rock
is hollowed inward, haunt of birds and paced by gods.
Bromius, whom I forget not, sways this place. From here
25   in divine form he led his Bacchanals in arms
to hunt down Pentheus like a hare in the deathtrap.
I call upon the springs of Pleistus, on the power
of Poseidon, and on final loftiest Zeus,
then go to sit in prophecy on the throne. May all
30   grant me that this of all my entrances shall be
the best by far. If there are any Hellenes here
let them draw lots, so enter, as the custom is.
My prophecy is only as the god may guide.

(She enters the temple and almost immediately comes out again.)

     Things terrible to tell and for the eyes to see
35   terrible drove me out again from Loxias' house
so that I have no strength and cannot stand on springing
feet, but run with hands' help and my legs have no speed.

An old woman afraid is nothing: a child, no more.
     See, I am on my way to the wreath-hung recess
and on the centrestone I see a man with god's   40
defilement on him postured in the suppliant's seat
with blood dripping from his hands and from a new-
     drawn sword,
holding too a branch that had grown high on an olive
tree, decorously wrapped in a great tuft of wool,
and the fleece shone. So far, at least, I can speak clear.   45
     In front of this man slept a startling company
of women lying all upon the chairs. Or not
women, I think I call them rather gorgons, only
not gorgons either, since their shape is not the same.
I saw some creatures painted in a picture once,   50
who tore the food from Phineus, only these had no
wings, that could be seen; they are black and utterly
repulsive, and they snore with breath that drives one back.
From their eyes drips the foul ooze, and their dress is such
as is not right to wear in the presence of the gods'   55
statues, nor even into any human house.
I have never seen the tribe that owns this company
nor know what piece of earth can claim with pride it bore
such brood, and without hurt and tears for labor given.
     Now after this the master of the house must take   60
his own measures: Apollo Loxias, who is very strong
and heals by divination; reads portentous signs,
and so clears out the houses others hold as well.

(Exit. The doors of the temple open and show ORESTES *surrounded by the sleeping* FURIES, APOLLO *and* HERMES *beside him.)*

APOLLO: I will not give you up. Through to the end standing
     your guardian, whether by your side or far away,   65
I shall not weaken toward your enemies. See now
how I have caught and overpowered these lewd creatures.
The repulsive maidens have been stilled to sleep, those gray
and aged children, they with whom no mortal man,
no god, nor even any beast, will have to do.   70
It was because of evil they were born, because
they hold the evil darkness of the Pit below
Earth, loathed alike by men and by the heavenly gods.
Nevertheless, run from them, never weaken. They
will track you down as you stride on across the long   75

land, and your driven feet forever pound the earth,
on across the main water and the circle-washed
cities. Be herdsman to this hard march. Never fail
until you come at last to Pallas' citadel.
80   Kneel there, and clasp the ancient idol in your arms,
and there we shall find those who will judge this case,
   and words
to say that will have magic in their figures. Thus
you will be rid of your afflictions, one for all.
For it was I who made you strike your mother down.
85 ORESTES: My lord Apollo, you understand what it means to do
no wrong. Learn also what it is not to neglect.
None can mistrust your power to do good, if you will.
   APOLLO: Remember: the fear must not give you a beaten heart.
Hermes, you are my brother from a single sire.
90   Look after him, and as you are named the god who guides,
be such in strong fact. He is my suppliant. Shepherd him
with fortunate escort on his journeys among men.
The wanderer has rights which Zeus acknowledges.

(*Exit* APOLLO, *then* ORESTES *guided by* HERMES. *Enter the*
GHOST OF CLYTAEMNESTRA.)

CLYTAEMNESTRA: You would sleep, then? And what use are
   you, if you sleep?
95   It is because of you I go dishonored thus
among the rest of the dead. Because of those I killed
my bad name among the perished suffers no eclipse
but I am driven in disgrace. I say to you
that I am charged with guilt most grave by these. And yet
100   I suffered too, horribly, and from those most dear,
yet none among the powers is angered for my sake
that I was slaughtered, and by matricidal hands.
Look at these gashes in my heart, think where they came
from. Eyes illuminate the sleeping brain,
105   but in the daylight man's future cannot be seen.
   Yet I have given you much to lap up, outpourings
without wine, sober propitiations, sacrificed
in secrecy of night and on a hearth of fire
for you, at an hour given to no other god.
110   Now I watch all these honors trampled into the ground,
and he is out and gone away like any fawn
so lightly, from the very middle of your nets,
sprung clear, and laughing merrily at you. Hear me.
It is my life depends upon this spoken plea.
115   Think then, O goddesses beneath the ground. For I,
the dream of Clytaemnestra, call upon your name.

(*The* FURIES *stir in their sleep and whimper.*)

CLYTAEMNESTRA: Oh, whimper, then, but your man has got
   away and gone far. He has friends to help him, who are
   not like mine.

(*They whimper again.*)

120 CLYTAEMNESTRA: Too much sleep and no pity for my
   plight. I stand,
   his mother, here, killed by Orestes. He is gone.

(*They moan in their sleep.*)

CLYTAEMNESTRA: You moan, you sleep. Get on your feet
   quickly, will you?
   What have you yet got done, except to do evil?   125

(*They moan again.*)

CLYTAEMNESTRA: Sleep and fatigue, two masterful conspirators,
   have dimmed the deadly anger of the mother-snake.

(*The* CHORUS *start violently, then speak in their sleep.*)

CHORUS: Get him, get him, get him, get him. Make sure.   130
CLYTAEMNESTRA: The beast you are after is a dream, but
   like the hound
   whose thought of hunting has no lapse, you bay him on.
   What are you about? Up, let not work's weariness
   beat you, nor slacken with sleep so you forget my pain.
   Scold your own heart and hurt it, as it well deserves,   135
   for this is discipline's spur upon her own. Let go
   upon this man the stormblasts of your bloodshot breath,
   wither him in your wind, after him, hunt him down
   once more, and shrivel him in your vitals' heat and flame.

(*The* GHOST *disappears, and the* CHORUS *waken and, as they
waken, speak severally.*)

CHORUS: Waken. You are awake, wake her, as I did you.   140
   You dream still? On your feet and kick your sleep aside.
   Let us see whether this morning-song means vanity.

(*Here they begin to howl.*)

Sisters, we have had wrong done us.
When I have undergone so much and all in vain.
Suffering, suffering, bitter, oh shame shame,   145
unendurable wrong.
The hunted beast has slipped clean from our nets and gone.
Sleep won me, and I lost my capture.

Shame, son of Zeus! Robber is all you are.
A young god, you have ridden down powers gray with age,   150
taken the suppliant, though a godless man, who hurt
the mother who gave him birth.
Yourself a god, you stole the matricide away.
Where in this act shall any man say there is right?

The accusation came upon me from my dreams,   155
and hit me, as with goad in the mid-grip of his fist
the charioteer strikes,
but deep, beneath lobe and heart.
The executioner's cutting whip is mine to feel   160
and the weight of pain is big, heavy to bear.

Such are the actions of the younger gods. These hold
by unconditional force, beyond all right, a throne
that runs reeking blood,
blood at the feet, blood at the head.   165
The very stone centre of earth here in our eyes horrible
with blood and curse stands plain to see.

Himself divine, he has spoiled his secret shrine's
hearth with the stain, driven and hallooed the action on. 170

He made man's way cross the place of the ways of god
and blighted age-old distributions of power.

175 He has wounded me, but he shall not get this man away.
Let him hide under the ground, he shall never go free.
Cursed suppliant, he shall feel against his head
another murderer rising out of the same seed.

(APOLLO *enters again from his sanctuary.*)

APOLLO: Get out, I tell you, go and leave this house. Away
180 in haste, from your presence set the mantic chamber free,
else you may feel the flash and bite of a flying snake
launched from the twisted thong of gold that spans my bow
to make you in your pain spew out the black and foaming
blood of men, vomit the clots sucked from their veins.
185 This house is no right place for such as you to cling
upon; but where, by judgment given, heads are lopped
and eyes gouged out, throats cut, and by the spoil of sex
the glory of young boys is defeated, where mutilation
lives, and stoning, and the long moan of tortured men
190 spiked underneath the spine and stuck on pales. Listen
to how the gods spit out the manner of that feast
your loves lean to. The whole cast of your shape is guide
to what you are, the like of whom should hole in the cave
of the blood-reeking lion, not in oracular
195 interiors, like mine nearby, wipe off your filth.
Out then, you flock of goats without a herdsman, since
no god has such affection as to tend this brood.
CHORUS: My lord Apollo, it is your turn to listen now.
Your own part in this is more than accessory.
200 You are the one who did it; all the guilt is yours.
APOLLO: So? How? Continue speaking, until I understand.
CHORUS: You gave this outlander the word to kill his mother.
APOLLO: The word to exact price for his father. What of that?
CHORUS: You then dared take him in, fresh from his
bloodletting.
205 APOLLO: Yes, and I told him to take refuge in this house.
CHORUS: You are abusive then to those who sped him here?
APOLLO: Yes. It was not for you to come near this house;
CHORUS: and yet
we have our duty. It was to do what we have done.
APOLLO: An office? You? Sound forth your glorious privilege.
210 CHORUS: This: to drive matricides out of their houses.
APOLLO: Then
what if it be the woman and she kills her man?
CHORUS: Such murder would not be the shedding of kindred
blood.
APOLLO: You have made into a thing of no account, no place,
the sworn faith of Zeus and of Hera, lady
215 of consummations, and Cypris by such argument
is thrown away, outlawed, and yet the sweetest things
in man's life come from her, for married love between
man and woman is bigger than oaths, guarded by right
of nature. If when such kill each other you relent
220 so as not to take vengeance nor eye them in wrath,
then I deny your manhunt of Orestes goes
with right. I see that one cause moves you to strong rage
but on the other clearly you are unmoved to act.
Pallas divine shall review the pleadings of this case.
225 CHORUS: Nothing will ever make me let that man go free.

APOLLO: Keep after him then, and make more trouble for
yourselves.
CHORUS: Do not try to dock my privilege by argument.
APOLLO: I would not take your privilege if you gave it me.
CHORUS: No, for you are called great beside the throne of
Zeus
already, but the motherblood drives me, and I go   230
to win my right upon this man and hunt him down.
APOLLO: But I shall give the suppliant help and rescue, for
if I willingly fail him who turns to me for aid,
his wrath, before gods and men, is a fearful thing.

(*They go out, separately. The scene is now Athens, on the Acropolis
before the temple and statue of Athene.* ORESTES *enters and takes
suppliant posture at the feet of the statue.*)

ORESTES: My lady Athene, it is at Loxias' behest   235
I come. Then take in of your grace the wanderer
who comes, no suppliant, not unwashed of hand, but one
blunted at last, and worn and battered on the outland
habitations and the beaten ways of men.
Crossing the dry land and the sea alike, keeping   240
the ordinances of Apollo's oracle
I come, goddess, before your statue and your house
to keep watch here and wait the issue of my trial.

(*The* CHORUS *enter severally, looking for* ORESTES.)

CHORUS: So. Here the man has left a clear trail behind; keep on, 245
keep on, as the unspeaking accuser tells us, by
whose sense, like hounds after a bleeding fawn, we trail
our quarry by the splash and drip of blood. And now
my lungs are blown with abundant and with wearisome
work, mankilling. My range has been the entire extent
of land, and, flown unwinged across the open water,   250
I am here, and give way to no ship in my pursuit.
Our man has gone to cover somewhere in this place.
The welcome smell of human blood has told me so.

Look again, look again,
search everywhere, let   255
not the matricide
steal away and escape.

(*They see* ORESTES.)

See there! He clings to defence
again, his arms winding the immortal goddess'
image, so tries to be quit out of our hands.   260
It shall not be. His mother's blood spilled on the ground
can not come back again.
It is all soaked and drained into the ground and gone.

You must give back for her blood from the living man
red blood of your body to suck, and from your own   265
I could feed, with bitter-swallowed drench,
turn your strength limp while yet you live and drag
you down
where you must pay for the pain of the murdered mother,
and watch the rest of the mortals stained with violence
against god or guest   270
or hurt parents who were close and dear,

each with the pain upon him that his crime deserves.
Hades is great, Hades calls men to reckoning
there under the ground,
275   sees all, and cuts it deep in his recording mind.
ORESTES: I have been beaten and been taught, I understand
the many rules of absolution, where it is right
to speak and where be silent. In this action now
speech has been ordered by my teacher, who is wise.
280   The stain of blood dulls now and fades upon my hand.
My blot of matricide is being washed away.
When it was fresh still, at the hearth of the god, Phoebus,
this was absolved and driven out by sacrifice
of swine, and the list were long if I went back to tell
285   of all I met who were not hurt by being with me.
Time in his aging overtakes all things alike.
Now it is from pure mouth and with good auspices
I call upon Athene, queen of this land, to come
and rescue me. She, without work of her spear, shall win
290   myself and all my land and all the Argive host
to stand her staunch companion for the rest of time.
Whether now ranging somewhere in the Libyan land
beside her father's crossing and by Triton's run
of waters she sets upright or enshrouded foot
295   rescuing there her friends, or on the Phlegraean flat
like some bold man of armies sweeps with eyes the scene,
let her come! She is a god and hears me far away.
So may she set me free from what is at my back.
CHORUS: Neither Apollo nor Athene's strength must win
300   you free, save you from going down forgotten, without
knowing where joy lies anywhere inside your heart,
blood drained, chewed dry by the powers of death, a
    wraith, a shell.
You will not speak to answer, spew my challenge away?
You are consecrate to me and fattened for my feast,
305   and you shall feed me while you live, not cut down first
at the altar. Hear the spell I sing to bind you in.

Come then, link we our choral. Ours
to show forth the power
and terror of our music, declare
310   our rights of office, how we conspire
to steer men's lives.
We hold we are straight and just. If a man
can spread his hands and show they are clean,
no wrath of ours shall lurk for him.
315   Unscathed he walks through his life time.
But one like this man before us, with stained
hidden hands, and the guilt upon him,
shall find us beside him, as witnesses
of the truth, and we show clear in the end
320   to avenge the blood of the murdered.

Mother, O my mother night, who gave me
birth, to be a vengeance on the seeing
and the blind, hear me. For Leto's
youngling takes my right away,
325   stealing from my clutch the prey
that crouches, whose blood would wipe
at last the motherblood away.

Over the beast doomed to the fire
this is the chant, scatter of wits,
frenzy and fear, hurting the heart,   330
song of the Furies
binding brain and blighting blood
in its stringless melody.
This the purpose that the all-involving
destiny spun, to be ours and to be shaken   335
never: when mortals assume outrage
of own hand in violence,
these we dog, till one goes
under earth. Nor does death
set them altogether free.   340

Over the beast doomed to the fire
this is the chant, scatter of wits,
frenzy and fear, hurting the heart,
song of the Furies
binding brain and blighting blood   345
in its stringless melody.

When we were born such lots were assigned for our
    keeping.
So the immortals must hold hands off, nor is there   350
one who shall sit at our feasting.
For sheer white robes I have no right and no portion.

I have chosen overthrow
of houses, where the Battlegod   355
grown within strikes near and dear
down. So we swoop upon this man
here. He is strong, but we wear him down
for the blood that is still wet on him.

Here we stand in our haste to wrench from all others 360
these devisings, make the gods clear of our counsels
so that even appeal comes
not to them, since Zeus has ruled our blood dripping 365
    company
outcast, nor will deal with us.

I have chosen overthrow
of houses, where the Battlegod
grown within strikes near and dear
down. So we swoop upon this man
here. He is strong, but we wear him down
for the blood that is still wet on him.

Men's illusions in their pride under the sky melt
down, and are diminished into the ground, gone
before the onset of our black robes, pulsing   370
of our vindictive feet against them.

For with a long leap from high
above and dead drop of weight
I bring foot's force crashing down
to cut the legs from under even   375
the runner, and spill him to ruin.

He falls, and does not know in the daze of his folly.
Such in the dark of man is the mist of infection
that hovers, and moaning rumor tells how his house lies
380 under fog that glooms above.

For with a long leap from high
above, and dead drop of weight,
I bring foot's force crashing down
to cut the legs from under even
the runner, and spill him to ruin.
All holds. For we are strong and skilled;
we have authority; we hold
memory of evil; we are stern
385 nor can men's pleadings bend us. We
drive through our duties, spurned, outcast
from gods, driven apart to stand in light
not of the sun. So sheer with rock are ways
for those who see, as upon those whose eyes are lost.

Is there a man who does not fear
390 this, does not shrink to hear
how my place has been ordained,
granted and given by destiny
and god, absolute? Privilege
primeval yet is mine, nor am I without place
395 though it be underneath the ground
and in no sunlight and in gloom that I must stand.

(ATHENE *enters, in full armor.*)

ATHENE: From far away I heard the outcry of your call.
It was beside Scamandrus. I was taking seisin
of land, for there the Achaean lords of war and first
400 fighters gave me large portion of all their spears
had won, the land root and stock to be mine for all
eternity, for the sons of Theseus a choice gift.
From there, sped on my weariless feet, I came, wingless
but in the rush and speed of the aegis fold. And now
405 I see upon this land a novel company
which, though it brings no terror to my eyes, brings still
wonder. Who are you? I address you all alike,
both you, the stranger kneeling at my image here,
410 and you, who are like no seed ever begotten, not
seen ever by the gods as goddesses, nor yet
stamped in the likenesses of any human form.
But no. This is the place of the just. Its rights forbid
even the innocent to speak evil of his mates.
415 CHORUS: Daughter of Zeus, you shall hear all compressed
to brief
measure. We are the gloomy children of the night.
Curses they call us in our homes beneath the ground.
ATHENE: I know your race, then, and the names by which
you are called.
CHORUS: You shall be told of our position presently.
420 ATHENE: I can know that, if one will give me a clear account.
CHORUS: We drive from home those who have shed the
blood of men.
ASTHENE: Where is the place, then, where the killer's flight
shall end?
CHORUS: A place where happiness is nevermore allowed.
ATHENE: Is he one? Do you blast him to this kind of flight?
425 CHORUS: Yes. He murdered his mother by deliberate choice.

ATHENE: By random force, or was it fear of someone's wrath?
CHORUS: Where is the spur to justify man's matricide?
ATHENE: Here are two sides, and only half the argument.
CHORUS: He is unwilling to give or to accept an oath.
ATHENE: You wish to be called righteous rather than act right. 430
CHORUS: No. How so? Out of the riches of your wit, explain.
ATHENE: I say, wrong must not win by technicalities.
CHORUS: Examine him then yourself. Decide it, and be fair.
ATHENE: You would turn over authority in this case to me?
CHORUS: By all means. Your father's degree, and yours, 435
deserve as much.
ATHENE: Your turn, stranger. What will you say in answer?
Speak,
tell me your country and your birth, what has befallen
you, then defend yourself against the anger of these;
if it was confidence in the right that made you sit
to keep this image near my hearth, a supplicant 440
in the tradition of Ixion, sacrosanct.
Give me an answer which is plain to understand.
ORESTES: Lady Athene, first I will take the difficult thought
away that lies in these last words you spoke. I am
no supplicant, nor was it because I had a stain 445
upon my hand that I sat at your image. I
will give you a strong proof that what I say is true.
It is the law that the man of the bloody hand must speak
no word until, by action of one who can cleanse,
blood from a young victim has washed his blood away. 450
Long since, at the homes of others, I have been absolved
thus, both by running waters and by victims slain.
I count this scruple now out of the way. Learn next
with no delay where I am from. I am of Argos
and it is to my honor that you ask the name 455
of my father, Agamemnon, lord of seafarers,
and your companion when you made the Trojan city
of Ilium no city any more. He died
without honor when he came home. It was my mother
of the dark heart, who entangled him in subtle gyves 460
and cut him down. The bath is witness to his death.
I was an exile in the time before this. I came back
and killed the woman who gave me birth. I plead guilty.
My father was dear, and this was vengeance for his blood.
Apollo shares responsibility for this. 465
He counterspurred my heart and told me of pains to come
if I should fail to act against the guilty ones.
This is my case. Decide if it be right or wrong.
I am in your hands. Where my fate falls, I shall accept.
ATHENE: The matter is too big for any mortal man 470
who thinks he can judge it. Even I have not the right
to analyse cases of murder where wrath's edge
is sharp, and all the more since you have come, and clung
a clean and innocent supplicant, against my doors.
You bring no harm to my city. I respect your rights. 475

Yet these, too, have their work. We cannot brush them aside,
and if this action so runs that they fail to win,
the venom of their resolution will return
to infect the soil, and sicken all my land to death.
Here is dilemma. Whether I let them stay or drive 480
them off, it is a hard course and will hurt. Then, since
the burden of the case is here, and rests on me,
I shall select judges of manslaughter, and swear

them in, establish a court into all time to come.
485   Litigants, call your witnesses, have ready your proofs
      as evidence under bond to keep this case secure.
      I will pick the finest of my citizens, and come
      back. They shall swear to make no judgment that is not
      just, and make clear where in this action the truth lies.

(Exit.)

490   CHORUS: Here is overthrow of all
        the young laws, if the claim
        of this matricide shall stand
        good, his crime be sustained.
        Should this be, every man will find a way
495   to act at his own caprice;
        over and over again in time
        to come, parents shall await
        the deathstroke at their children's hands.

        We are the Angry Ones. But we
500   shall watch no more over works
        of men, and so act. We shall
        let loose indiscriminate death.
        Man shall learn from man's lot, forejudge
        the evils of his neighbor's case,
        see respite and windfall in storm:
505   pathetic prophet who consoles
        with strengthless cures, in vain.

        Nevermore let one who feels
        the stroke of accident, uplift
510   his voice and make outcry, thus:
        "Oh Justice!
        Throned powers of the Furies, help!"
        Such might be the pitiful cry
        of some father, of the stricken
515   mother, their appeal. Now
        the House of Justice has collapsed.

        There are times when fear is good.
        It must keep its watchful place
        at the heart's controls. There is
520   advantage
        in the wisdom won from pain.
        Should the city, should the man
        rear a heart that nowhere goes
        in fear, how shall such a one
525   any more respect the right?

        Refuse the life of anarchy;
        refuse the life devoted to
        one master.
        The in-between has the power
530   by God's grant always, though
        his ordinances vary.
        I will speak in defence
        of reason: for the very child
        of vanity is violence;
535   but out of health
        in the heart issues the beloved
        and the longed-for, prosperity.

All for all I say to you:
bow before the altar of right.
You shall not   540
eye advantage, and heel
it over with foot of force.
Vengeance will be upon you.
The all is bigger than you.
Let man see this and take   545
care, to mother and father,
and to the guest
in the gates welcomed, give all rights
that befall their position.

The man who does right, free-willed, without constraint   550
shall not lose happiness
nor be wiped out with all his generation.
But the transgressor, I tell you, the bold man
who brings in confusion of goods unrightly won,
at long last and perforce, when ship toils   555
under tempest must strike his sail
in the wreck of his rigging.

He calls on those who hear not, caught inside
the hard wrestle of water.
The spirit laughs at the hot hearted man,   560
the man who said "never to me," watches him
pinned in distress, unable to run free of the crests.
He had good luck in his life. Now
he smashes it on the reef of Right
and drowns, unwept and forgotten.   565

(ATHENE re-enters, guiding twelve citizens chosen as JURORS and attended by a HERALD. Other CITIZENS follow.)

ATHENE: Herald, make proclamation and hold in the host
  assembled. Let the stabbing voice of the Etruscan
  trumpet, blown to the full with mortal wind, crash out
  its high call to all the assembled populace
  For in the filling of this senatorial ground   570
  it is best for all the city to be silent and learn
  the measures I have laid down into the rest of time.
  So too these litigants, that their case be fairly tried.

(Trumpet call. All take their places. Enter APOLLO.)

CHORUS: My lord Apollo, rule within your own domain.
  What in this matter has to do with you? Declare.   575
APOLLO: I come to testify. This man, by observed law,
  came to me as suppliant, took his place by hearth and hall,
  and it was I who cleaned him of the stain of blood.
  I have also come to help him win his case. I bear
  responsibility for his mother's murder.   580

(To ATHENE.)

                                      You
  who know the rules, initiate the trial. Preside.
ATHENE: *(To the FURIES.)* I declare the trial opened. Yours is
    the first word.
  For it must justly be the pursuer who speaks first
  and opens the case, and makes plain what the action is.

585 CHORUS: We are many, but we shall cut it short. You, then,
    word against word answer our charges one by one.
    Say first, did you kill your mother or did you not?
ORESTES: Yes, I killed her. There shall be no denial of that.
CHORUS: There are three falls in the match and one has
    gone to us.
590 ORESTES: So you say. But you have not even thrown your man.
CHORUS: So. Then how did you kill her? You are bound to say.
ORESTES: I do. With drawn sword in my hand I cut her throat.
CHORUS: By whose persuasion and advice did you do this?
ORESTES: By order of this god, here. So he testifies.
595 CHORUS: The Prophet guided you into this matricide?
ORESTES: Yes. I have never complained of this. I do not now.
CHORUS: When sentence seizes you, you will talk a different
    way.
ORESTES: I have no fear. My father will aid me from the grave.
CHORUS: Kill your mother, then put trust in a corpse! Trust on.
600 ORESTES: Yes. She was dirtied twice over with disgrace.
CHORUS: Tell me how, and explain it to the judges here.
ORESTES: She murdered her husband, and thereby my father
    too.
CHORUS: Of this stain, death has set her free. But you still live.
ORESTES: When she lived, why did you not descend and
    drive her out?
605 CHORUS: The man she killed was not of blood congenital.
ORESTES: But am I then involved with my mother by
    blood-bond?
CHORUS: Murderer, yes. How else could she have nursed
    you beneath
    her heart? Do you forswear your mother's intimate blood?
ORESTES: Yours to bear witness now, Apollo, and expound
610   the case for me, if I was right to cut her down.
    I will not deny I did this thing, because I did
    do it. But was the bloodshed right or not? Decide
    and answer. As you answer, I shall state my case.
APOLLO: To you, established by Athene in your power,
615   I shall speak justly. I am a prophet, I shall not
    lie. Never, for man, woman, nor city, from my throne
    of prophecy have I spoken a word, except
    that which Zeus, father of Olympians, might command.
    This is justice. Recognize then how great its strength.
620   I tell you, follow our father's will. For not even
    the oath that binds you is more strong than Zeus is strong.
CHORUS: Then Zeus, as you say, authorized the oracle
    to this Orestes, stating he could wreak the death
    of his father on his mother, and it would have no force?
625 APOLLO: It is not the same thing for a man of blood to die
    honored with the king's staff given by the hand of god,
    and that by means of a woman, not with the far cast
    of fierce arrows, as an Amazon might have done,
    but in a way that you shall hear, O Pallas and you
630   who sit in state to judge this action by your vote.

    He had come home from his campaigning. He had done
    better than worse, in the eyes of a fair judge. She lay
    in wait for him. It was the bath. When he was at
    its edge, she hooded the robe on him, and in the blind
635   and complex toils tangled her man, and chopped him down.

    There is the story of the death of a great man,
    solemn in all men's sight, lord of the host of ships.

    I have called the woman what she was, so that the people
    whose duty it is to try this case may be inflamed.
CHORUS: Zeus, by your story, gives first place to the father's 640
    death.
    Yet Zeus himself shackled elder Cronus, his own
    father. Is this not contradiction? I testify,
    judges, that this is being said in your hearing.
APOLLO: You foul animals, from whom the gods turn in
    disgust,
    Zeus could undo shackles, such hurt can be made good, 645
    and there is every kind of way to get out. But once
    the dust has drained down all a man's blood, once the man
    has died, there is no raising of him up again.
    This is a thing for which my father never made
    curative spells. All other states, without effort 650
    of hard breath, he can completely rearrange.
CHORUS: See what it means to force acquittal of this man.
    He has spilled his mother's blood upon the ground. Shall he
    then be at home in Argos in his father's house?
    What altars of the community shall he use? Is there 655
    a brotherhood's lustration that will let him in?
APOLLO: I will tell you, and I will answer correctly. Watch.
    The mother is no parent of that which is called
    her child, but only nurse of the new-planted seed
    that grows. The parent is he who mounts. A stranger she 660
    preserves a stranger's seed, if no god interfere.
    I will show you proof of what I have explained. There can
    be a father without any mother. There she stands,
    the living witness, daughter of Olympian Zeus,
    she who was never fostered in the dark of the womb 665
    yet such a child as no goddess could bring to birth.
    In all else, Pallas, as I best may understand,
    I shall make great your city and its populace.
    So I have brought this man to sit beside the hearth
    of your house, to be your true friend for the rest of time, 670
    so you shall win him, goddess, to fight by your side,
    and among men to come this shall stand a strong bond
    that his and your own people's children shall be friends.
ATHENE: Shall I assume that enough has now been said, and tell
    the judges to render what they believe a true verdict? 675
CHORUS: Every arrow we had has been shot now. We wait
    on their decision, to see how the case has gone.
ATHENE: So then. How shall I act correctly in your eyes?
APOLLO: You have heard what you have heard, and as you
    cast your votes,
    good friends, respect in your hearts the oath that you 680
    have sworn.
ATHENE: If it please you, men of Attica, hear my decree
    now, on this first case of bloodletting I have judged.
    For Aegeus' population, this forevermore
    shall be the ground where justices deliberate.
    Here is the Hill of Ares, here the Amazons 685
    encamped and built their shelters when they came in arms
    for spite of Theseus, here they piled their rival towers
    to rise, new city, and dare his city long ago,
    and slew their beasts for Ares. So this rock is named
    from then the Hill of Ares. Here the reverence 690
    of citizens, their fear and kindred do-no-wrong
    shall hold by day and in the blessing of night alike
    all while the people do not muddy their own laws
    with foul infusions. But if bright water you stain

695 with mud, you nevermore will find it fit to drink.
No anarchy, no rule of a single master. Thus
I advise my citizens to govern and to grace,
and not to cast fear utterly from your city. What
man who fears nothing at all is ever righteous? Such
700 be your just terrors, and you may deserve and have
salvation for your citadel, your land's defence,
such as is nowhere else found among men, neither
among the Scythians, nor the land that Pelops held.
I establish this tribunal. It shall be untouched
705 by money-making, grave but quick to wrath, watchful
to protect those who sleep, a sentry on the land.

These words I have unreeled are for my citizens,
advice into the future. All must stand upright
now, take each man his ballot in his hand, think on
710 his oath, and make his judgment. For my word is said.
CHORUS: I give you counsel by no means to disregard
this company. We can be a weight to crush your land.
APOLLO: I speak too. I command you to fear, and not
make void the yield of oracles from Zeus and me.
715 CHORUS: You honor bloody actions where you have no right.
The oracles you give shall be no longer clean.
APOLLO: My father's purposes are twisted then. For he
was appealed to by Ixion, the first murderer.
CHORUS: Talk! But for my part, if I do not win the case,
720 I shall come back to this land and it will feel my weight.
APOLLO: Neither among the elder nor the younger gods
have you consideration. I shall win this suit.
CHORUS: Such was your action in the house of Pheres. Then
you beguiled the Fates to let mortals go free from death.
725 APOLLO: Is it not right to do well by the man who shows
you worship, and above all when he stands in need?
CHORUS: You won the ancient goddesses over with wine
and so destroyed the orders of an elder time.
APOLLO: You shall not win the issue of this suit, but shall
730 be made to void your poison to no enemy's hurt.
CHORUS: Since you, a young god, would ride down my
elder age,
I must stay here and listen to how the trial goes,
being yet uncertain to loose my anger on the state.
ATHENE: It is my task to render final judgment here.
735 This is a ballot for Orestes I shall cast.
There is no mother anywhere who gave me birth,
and, but for marriage, I am always for the male
with all my heart, and strongly on my father's side.
So, in a case where the wife has killed her husband, lord
740 of the house, her death shall not mean most to me. And if
the other votes are even, then Orestes wins.
You of the jurymen who have this duty assigned,
shake out the ballots from the vessels, with all speed.
ORESTES: Phoebus Apollo, what will the decision be?
745 CHORUS: Darkness of night, our mother, are you here to watch?
ORESTES: This is the end for me. The noose, or else the light.
CHORUS: Here our destruction, or our high duties confirmed.
APOLLO: Shake out the votes accurately, Athenian friends.
Be careful as you pick them up. Make no mistake.
750 In the lapse of judgment great disaster comes. The cast
of a single ballot has restored a house entire.
ATHENE: The man before us has escaped the charge of blood.
The ballots are in equal number for each side.

ORESTES: Pallas Athene, you have kept my house alive.
When I had lost the land of my fathers you gave me 755
a place to live. Among the Hellenes they shall say:
"A man of Argos lives again in the estates
of his father, all by grace of Pallas Athene, and
Apollo, and with them the all-ordaining god
the Savior"—who remembers my father's death, who looked 760
upon my mother's advocates, and rescues me.
I shall go home now, but before I go I swear
to this your country and to this your multitude
of people into all the bigness of time to be,
that never man who holds the helm of my state shall come 765
against your country in the ordered strength of spears,
but though I lie then in my grave, I still shall wreak
helpless bad luck and misadventure upon all
who stride across the oath that I have sworn: their ways
disconsolate make, their crossings full of evil 770
augury, so they shall be sorry that they moved.
But while they keep the upright way, and hold in high
regard the city of Pallas, and align their spears
to fight beside her, I shall be their gracious spirit.
And so farewell, you and your city's populace. 775
May you outwrestle and overthrow all those who come
against you, to your safety and your spears' success.

(*Exit. Exit also* APOLLO.)

CHORUS: Gods of the younger generation, you have ridden
down
the laws of the elder time, torn them out of my hands.
I, disinherited, suffering, heavy with anger 780
shall let loose on the land
the vindictive poison
dripping deadly out of my heart upon the ground;
this from itself shall breed
cancer, the leafless, the barren 785
to strike, for the right, their low lands
and drag its smear of mortal infection on the ground.
What shall I do? Afflicted
I am mocked by these people.
I have borne what can not 790
be borne. Great the sorrows and the dishonor upon
the sad daughters of night.
ATHENE: Listen to me. I would not have you be so grieved.
For you have not been beaten. This was the result 795
of a fair ballot which was even. You were not
dishonored, but the luminous evidence of Zeus
was there, and he who spoke the oracle was he
who ordered Orestes so to act and not be hurt.
Do not be angry any longer with this land 800
nor bring the bulk of your hatred down on it, do not
render it barren of fruit, nor spill the dripping rain
of death in fierce and jagged lines to eat the seeds.
In complete honesty I promise you a place
of your own, deep hidden under ground that is yours by 805
right
where you shall sit on shining chairs beside the hearth
to accept devotions offered by your citizens.
CHORUS: Gods of the younger generation, you have ridden
down
the laws of the elder time, torn them out of my hands.
I, disinherited, suffering, heavy with anger 810

shall let loose on the land
the vindictive poison
dripping deadly out of my heart upon the ground;
this from itself shall breed
815 cancer, the leafless, the barren
to strike, for the right, their low lands
and drag its smear of mortal infection on the ground.
What shall I do? Afflicted
I am mocked by these people.
820 I have borne what can not
be borne. Great the sorrow and the dishonor upon
the sad daughters of night.
ATHENE: No, not dishonored. You are goddesses. Do not
825 in too much anger make this place of mortal men
uninhabitable. I have Zeus behind me. Do
we need to speak of that? I am the only god
who know the keys to where his thunderbolts are locked.
We do not need such, do we? Be reasonable
830 and do not from a reckless mouth cast on the land
spells that will ruin every thing which might bear fruit.
No. Put to sleep the bitter strength in the black wave
and live with me and share my pride of worship. Here
is a big land, and from it you shall win first fruits
835 in offerings for children and the marriage rite
for always. Then you will say my argument was good.
CHORUS: That they could treat me so!
I, the mind of the past, to be driven under the ground
out cast, like dirt!
840 The wind I breathe is fury and utter hate.
Earth, ah, earth
what is this agony that crawls under my ribs?
Night, hear me, O Night,
845 mother. They have wiped me out
and the hard hands of the gods
and their treacheries have taken my old rights away.
ATHENE: I will bear your angers. You are elder born than I
and in that you are wiser far than I. Yet still
850 Zeus gave me too intelligence not to be despised.
If you go away into some land of foreigners,
I warn you, you will come to love this country. Time
in his forward flood shall ever grow more dignified
for the people of this city. And you, in your place
855 of eminence beside Erechtheus in his house
shall win from female and from male processionals
more than all lands of men beside could ever give.
Only in this place that I haunt do not inflict
your bloody stimulus to twist the inward hearts
860 of young men, raging in a fury not of wine,
nor, as if plucking the heart from fighting cocks,
engraft among my citizens that spirit of war
that turns their battle fury inward on themselves.
No, let our wars range outward hard against the man
865 who has fallen horribly in love with high renown.
No true fighter I call the bird that fights at home.
Such life I offer you, and it is yours to take.
Do good, receive good, and be honored as the good
are honored. Share our country, the beloved of god.
870 CHORUS: That they could treat me so!
I, the mind of the past, to be driven under the ground
out cast, like dirt!
The wind I breathe is fury and utter hate.

Earth, ah, earth
what is this agony that crawls under my ribs? 875
Night, hear me, O Night,
mother. They have wiped me out
and the hard hands of the gods
and their treacheries have taken my old rights away. 880
ATHENE: I will not weary of telling you all the good things
I offer, so that you can never say that you,
an elder god, were driven unfriended from the land
by me in my youth, and by my mortal citizens.
But if you hold Persuasion has her sacred place 885
of worship, in the sweet beguilement of my voice,
then you might stay with us. But if you wish to stay
then it would not be justice to inflict your rage
upon this city, your resentment or bad luck
to armies. Yours the baron's portion in this land 890
if you will, in all justice, with full privilege.
CHORUS: Lady Athene, what is this place you say is mine?
ATHENE: A place free of all grief and pain. Take it for yours.
CHORUS: If I do take it, shall I have some definite powers?
ATHENE: No household shall be prosperous without your will. 895
CHORUS: You will do this? You will really let me be so strong?
ATHENE: So we shall straighten the lives of all who worship us.
CHORUS: You guarantee such honor for the rest of time?
ATHENE: I have no need to promise what I can not do.
CHORUS: I think you will have your way with me. My hate 900
is going.
ATHENE: Stay here, then. You will win the hearts of others, too.
CHORUS: I will put a spell upon the land. What shall it be?
ATHENE: Something that has no traffic with evil success.
Let it come out of the ground, out of the sea's water,
and from the high air make the waft of gentle gales 905
wash over the country in full sunlight, and the seed
and stream of the soil's yield and of the grazing beasts
be strong and never fail our people as time goes,
and make the human seed be kept alive. Make more
the issue of those who worship more your ways, for as 910
the gardener works in love, so love I best of all
the unblighted generation of these upright men.
All such is yours for granting. In the speech and show
and pride of battle, I myself shall not endure
this city's eclipse in the estimation of mankind. 915
CHORUS: I accept this home at Athene's side.
I shall not forget the cause
of this city, which Zeus all powerful and Ares
rule, stronghold of divinities,
glory of Hellene gods, their guarded altar. 920
So with forecast of good
I speak this prayer for them
that the sun's bright magnificence shall break out wave
on wave of all the happiness 925
life can give, across their land.
ATHENE: Here are my actions. In all good will
toward these citizens I establish in power
spirits who are large, difficult to soften.
To them is given the handling entire 930
of men's lives. That man
who has not felt the weight of their hands
takes the strokes of life, knows not whence, not why,
for crimes wreaked in past generations
drag him before these powers. Loud his voice 935

but the silent doom
hates hard, and breaks him to dust.
CHORUS: Let there blow no wind that wrecks the trees.
I pronounce words of grace.
940   Nor blaze of heat blind the blossoms of grown plants, nor
cross the circles of its right
place. Let no barren deadly sickness creep and kill.
Flocks fatten. Earth be kind
945   to them, with double fold of fruit
in time appointed for its yielding. Secret child
of earth, her hidden wealth, bestow
blessing and surprise of gods.
ATHENE: Strong guard of our city, hear you these
950   and what they portend? Fury is a high queen
of strength even among the immortal gods
and the undergods, and for humankind
their work is accomplished, absolute, clear:
for some, singing; for some, life dimmed
955   in tears; theirs the disposition.
CHORUS: Death of manhood cut down
before its prime I forbid:
girls' grace and glory find
men to live life with them.
960   Grant, you who have the power.
And O, steering spirits of law,
goddesses of destiny,
sisters from my mother, hear;
in all houses implicate,
965   in all time heavy of hand
on whom your just arrest befalls,
august among goddesses, bestow.
ATHENE: It is my glory to hear how these
generosities
970   are given my land. I admire the eyes
of Persuasion, who guided the speech of my mouth
toward these, when they were reluctant and wild.
Zeus, who guides men's speech in councils, was too
strong; and my ambition
975   for good wins out in the whole issue.
CHORUS: This my prayer: Civil War
fattening on men's ruin shall
not thunder in our city. Let
not the dry dust that drinks
980   the black blood of citizens
through passion for revenge
and bloodshed for bloodshed
be given our state to prey upon.
Let them render grace for grace.
985   Let love be their common will;
let them hate with single heart.
Much wrong in the world thereby is healed.
ATHENE: Are they taking thought to discover that road
where speech goes straight?
990   In the terror upon the faces of these
I see great good for our citizens.
While with good will you hold in high honor
these spirits, their will shall be good, as you steer

your city, your land
on an upright course clear through to the end.   995
CHORUS: Farewell, farewell. High destiny shall be yours
by right. Farewell, citizens
seated near the throne of Zeus,
beloved by the maiden he loves,
civilized as years go by,   1000
sheltered under Athene's wings,
grand even in her father's sight.
ATHENE: Goddesses, farewell. Mine to lead, as these
attend us, to where
by the sacred light new chambers are given.   1005
Go then. Sped by majestic sacrifice
from these, plunge beneath the ground. There hold
off what might hurt the land; pour in
the city's advantage, success in the end.
You, children of Cranaus, you who keep   1010
the citadel, guide these guests of the state.
For good things given,
your hearts' desire be for good to return.
CHORUS: Farewell and again farewell, words spoken twice over,
all who by this citadel,   1015
mortal men, spirits divine,
hold the city of Pallas, grace
this my guestship in your land.
Life will give you no regrets.   1020
ATHENE: Well said. I assent to all the burden of your prayers,
and by the light of flaring torches now attend
your passage to the deep and subterranean hold,
as by us walk those women whose high privilege
it is to guard my image. Flower of all the land   1025
of Theseus, let them issue now, grave companies,
maidens, wives, elder women, in processional.
In the investiture of purple stained robes
dignify them, and let the torchlight go before
so that the kindly company of these within   1030
our ground may shine in the future of strong men to come.
CHORUS: (*Of women who have been forming for
processional.*) Home, home, O high, O aspiring
Daughters of Night, aged children, in blithe processional.
Bless them, all here, with silence.   1035

In the primeval dark of earth-hollows
held in high veneration with rights sacrificial
bless them, all people, with silence.

Gracious be, wish what the land wishes,   1040
follow, grave goddesses, flushed in the flamesprung
torchlight gay on your journey.
Singing all follow our footsteps.

There shall be peace forever between these people
of Pallas and their guests. Zeus the all seeing   1045
met with Destiny to confirm it.
Singing all follow our footsteps.

(*Exeunt omnes, in procession.*)

Sophocles

Like Aeschylus, Sophocles (c. 496–406 BCE) had an important career in the civic life of Athens as well as in the theater. He was treasurer for the Athenian imperial league, and served as one of ten generals who led a campaign against Samos, an island threatening to secede from the Athenian alliance. In 411 BCE, he was appointed to a committee called to examine Athens' disastrous military campaign in Sicily. Sophocles' greatest achievements, though, were in the theater. Sophocles was responsible for introducing a third actor into dramatic performance, an innovation rapidly imitated by other playwrights, including Aeschylus and Euripides. He also enlarged the size of the chorus from twelve to fifteen men. Sophocles won his first victory, against Aeschylus, in 468 BCE; he was victorious twenty-four times in his career and never finished lower than second in the dramatic competition. Of the 120 plays attributed to Sophocles, only seven survive: *Ajax, Trachiniae, Antigone, Oedipus the King, Electra, Philoctetes,* and *Oedipus at Colonus.* Fragments of a satyr play, *The Trackers,* also remain. The three "Theban" plays—*Antigone, Oedipus the King,* and *Oedipus at Colonus*—are thematically related, but, unlike *The Oresteia* of Aeschylus, were not composed as a trilogy. *Antigone,* a play about Oedipus' daughters after his banishment from Thebes, was composed about 441 BCE; *Oedipus the King* was first produced sometime shortly after the declaration of war with Sparta in 431 BCE; and *Oedipus at Colonus* was first produced after Sophocles' death and Athens' defeat.

Oedipus the King is framed by two acts of identification, recognition, and acknowledgment. The action of the play is about the deepening and horrible understanding of what it means for the hero to recognize who he is—what it means to *be* Oedipus.

OEDIPUS THE KING

This production of Sophocles' *Oedipus the King* adapts the ritualized elements of Greek theater to a modern African setting.

In *The Poetics,* written nearly a century later (about 335 BCE), Aristotle frequently refers to *Oedipus the King* as a definitive example of the form and purpose of tragedy. Modern audiences, though, sometimes find the play baffling, in part because the prophecy delivered to Oedipus' parents, Laius and Jocasta—that their son will murder his father and marry his mother—seems to rob Oedipus of the ability to act, to decide his fate through his own deeds. The tension between destiny and discovery is central to the play; to understand it, we should pay attention to the function of the oracle at Delphi both in the Greek world and in Oedipus the King. The Greeks consulted the oracle at Delphi on a variety of matters, ranging from personal decisions to problems of state. For example, in the play, Laius and Jocasta have consulted the oracle to learn the future of their child, and Oedipus turns to Delphi to find out whether Polybus is actually his father. At the same time, the oracle also speaks on important public issues—about the cause of the plague afflicting Thebes and about what should be done with Oedipus after his blinding. Sophocles lived in an era of increasing skepticism, when political conflict and the rise of rhetorical training raised questions about the nature and significance of truth—even the truth of oracular revelation. It is not surprising that characters in *Oedipus the King* frequently question such prophecy or have difficulty learning how to accept and interpret it, as when Oedipus flees Corinth to avoid murdering his father.

Critical as the prophecy is to Oedipus' life, Oedipus' deeds are really at issue in *Oedipus the King.* Sophocles chose to begin and end his drama on the day of Oedipus' discovery of his own identity. The play focuses less on the prophecy than on the course and meaning of Oedipus' actions, on *how* he comes to recognize himself as the criminal he seeks. Oedipus arrives at this recognition only through an extraordinary effort of action and decision: Oedipus calls for the exile of Laius' murderer; he insults Tiresias when the prophet tries to evade his questions; he accuses Creon; he threatens the old shepherd with torture in order to learn the truth of his birth. The oracle says that Oedipus will commit his terrible crimes of murder and incest, but Oedipus *chooses* the relentless, brutal pursuit of the truth himself, even to the point of his own incrimination and destruction. The tragedy of *Oedipus the King* lies in the fearsome turn of events caused by Oedipus' inflexible compulsion to discover the truth.

Aristotle considers the hero of tragedy at some length, in terms that are at once compelling and confusing, particularly in the case of Oedipus. Aristotle suggests in *The Poetics* that the hero of tragedy should be "a man who is neither a paragon of virtue and justice nor undergoes the change to misfortune through any real badness or wickedness but because of some mistake," a description that leads some to look for the cause of this error within Oedipus' character, in a so-called tragic flaw. But, in fact, when he says that the character's "mistake"—or *HAMARTIA*—is not the result of "any real badness or wickedness," Aristotle seems to deny that the hero's downfall is the effect of any moral "flaw" at all. It might help us to remember that to his audience, Oedipus may have seemed to share some typically "Athenian" characteristics. Oedipus' passion for inquiry, his abrupt decisiveness, and his impulsive desire to act were seen as the stereotypical traits of Athenian citizens and of Athens as a city. Far from being "flaws," these are just the qualities that made Oedipus (and Athens) successful. What is "tragic" about Oedipus' fate in *Oedipus the King* is the way that his own surest strengths—the aggressive, pragmatic qualities that enabled him to outwit the Sphinx—lead, on this one occasion, to his destruction. Oedipus' "mistake" is neither a moral failing nor a deed that he might have avoided; it is simply that he is Oedipus and acts like Oedipus—intelligent, masterful, assertive, impatient, impulsive. The tragedy lies in the way that acting like Oedipus leads him, as it has always led him in the past, to the discovery of the truth he seeks, this time with ruinous consequences.

OEDIPUS THE KING

Sophocles

TRANSLATED BY ROBERT FAGLES

CHARACTERS

OEDIPUS, *king of Thebes*
A PRIEST *of Zeus*
CREON, *brother of Jocasta*
A CHORUS *of Theban citizens
and their* LEADER
TIRESIAS, *a blind prophet*
JOCASTA, *the queen, wife of
Oedipus*

A MESSENGER *from Corinth*
A SHEPHERD
A MESSENGER *from inside the
palace*
ANTIGONE, ISMENE, *daughters
of Oedipus and Jocasta*
GUARDS *and* ATTENDANTS
PRIESTS *of Thebes*

TIME AND SCENE: *The royal house of Thebes. Double doors
dominate the façade; a stone altar stands at the center of the stage.*

Many years have passed since OEDIPUS *solved the riddle of the Sphinx
and ascended the throne of Thebes, and now a plague has struck the
city. A procession of* PRIESTS *enters; suppliants, broken and despondent, they carry branches wound in wool and lay them on the altar.*

The doors open. GUARDS *assemble.* OEDIPUS *comes forward, majestic
but for a telltale limp, and slowly views the condition of his people.*

OEDIPUS: Oh my children, the new blood of ancient Thebes,
    why are you here? Huddling at my altar,
    praying before me, your branches wound in wool.
    Our city reeks with the smoke of burning incense,
5   rings with cries for the Healer and wailing for the dead.
    I thought it wrong, my children, to hear the truth
    from others, messengers. Here I am myself—
    you all know me, the world knows my fame:
    I am Oedipus.

(Helping a PRIEST *to his feet.)*

              Speak up, old man. Your years,
10   your dignity—you should speak for the others.
    Why here and kneeling, what preys upon you so?
    Some sudden fear? some strong desire?
    You can trust me. I am ready to help,
    I'll do anything. I would be blind to misery
15   not to pity my people kneeling at my feet.
PRIEST: O Oedipus, king of the land, our greatest power!
    You see us before you now, men of all ages
    clinging to your altars. Here are boys,
    still too weak to fly from the nest,
20   and here the old, bowed down with the years,
    the holy ones—a priest of Zeus myself—and here
    the picked, unmarried men, the young hope of Thebes.
    And all the rest, your great family gathers now,
    branches wreathed, massing in the squares,
25   kneeling before the two temples of queen Athena
    or the river-shrine where the embers glow and die
    and Apollo sees the future in the ashes.
                 Our city—
    look around you, see with your own eyes
    our ship pitches wildly, cannot lift her head
30   from the depths, the red waves of death . . .
    Thebes is dying. A blight on the fresh crops
    and the rich pastures, cattle sicken and die,

and the women die in labor, children stillborn,
and the plague, the fiery god of fever hurls down
on the city, his lightning slashing through us—   35
raging plague in all its vengeance, devastating
the house of Cadmus! And black Death luxuriates
in the raw, wailing miseries of Thebes.

Now we pray to you. You cannot equal the gods,
your children know that, bending at your altar.   40
But we do rate you first of men,
both in the common crises of our lives
and face-to-face encounters with the gods.
You freed us from the Sphinx, you came to Thebes
and cut us loose from the bloody tribute we had paid   45
that harsh, brutal singer. We taught you nothing,
no skill, no extra knowledge, still you triumphed.
A god was with you, so they say, and we believe it—
you lifted up our lives.
              So now again,
Oedipus, king, we bend to you, your power—   50
we implore you, all of us on our knees:
find us strength, rescue! Perhaps you've heard
the voice of a god or something from other men,
Oedipus . . . what do you know?
The man of experience—you see it every day—   55
his plans will work in a crisis, his first of all.

Act now—we beg you, best of men, raise up our city!
Act, defend yourself, your former glory!
Your country calls you savior now
for your zeal, your action years ago.   60
Never let us remember of your reign:
you helped us stand, only to fall once more.
Oh raise up our city, set us on our feet.
The omens were good that day you brought us joy—
be the same man today!   65
Rule our land, you know you have the power,
but rule a land of the living, not a wasteland.
Ship and towered city are nothing, stripped of men
alive within it, living all as one.
OEDIPUS: My children,
I pity you. I see—how could I fail to see   70
what longings bring you here? Well I know
you are sick to death, all of you,
but sick as you are, not one is sick as I.

Your pain strikes each of you alone, each
75 in the confines of himself, no other. But my spirit
grieves for the city, for myself and all of you.
I wasn't asleep, dreaming. You haven't wakened me—
I have wept through the nights, you must know that,
groping, laboring over many paths of thought.
80 After a painful search I found one cure:
I acted at once. I sent Creon,
my wife's own brother, to Delphi—
Apollo the Prophet's oracle—to learn
what I might do or say to save our city.

85 Today's the day. When I count the days gone by
it torments me . . . what is he doing?
Strange, he's late, he's gone too long.
But once he returns, then, then I'll be a traitor
if I do not do all the god makes clear.
90 PRIEST: Timely words. The men over there
are signaling—Creon's just arriving.
OEDIPUS: (*Sighting* CREON, *then turning to the altar.*) Lord Apollo,
let him come with a lucky word of rescue,
shining like his eyes!
PRIEST: Welcome news, I think—he's crowned, look,
95 and the laurel wreath is bright with berries.
OEDIPUS: We'll soon see. He's close enough to hear

(*Enter* CREON *from the side; his face is shaded with a wreath.*)

Creon, prince, my kinsman, what do you bring us?
What message from the god?
CREON: Good news.
I tell you even the hardest things to bear,
100 if they should turn out well, all would be well.
OEDIPUS: Of course, but what were the god's *words*? There's
no hope
and nothing to fear in what you've said so far.
CREON: If you want my report in the presence of these
people . . .

(*Pointing to the* PRIESTS *while drawing* OEDIPUS *toward the palace.*)

I'm ready now, or we might go inside.
OEDIPUS: Speak out,
105 speak to us all. I grieve for these, my people,
far more than I fear for my own life.
CREON: Very well,
I will tell you what I heard from the god.
Apollo commands us—he was quite clear—
"Drive the corruption from the land,
110 don't harbor it any longer, past all cure,
don't nurse it in your soil—root it out!"
OEDIPUS: How can we cleanse ourselves—what rites?
What's the source of the trouble?
CREON: Banish the man, or pay back blood with blood.
115 Murder sets the plague-storm on the city.
OEDIPUS: Whose murder?
Whose fate does Apollo bring to light?
CREON: Our leader,
my lord, was once a man named Laius,
before you came and put us straight on course.
OEDIPUS: I know—
or so I've heard. I never saw the man myself.

CREON: Well, he was killed, and Apollo commands us now— 120
he could not be more clear,
"Pay the killers back—whoever is responsible."
OEDIPUS: Where on earth are they? Where to find it now,
the trail of the ancient guilt so hard to trace?
CREON: "Here in Thebes," he said. 125
Whatever is sought for can be caught, you know,
whatever is neglected slips away.
OEDIPUS: But where,
in the palace, the fields or foreign soil,
where did Laius meet his bloody death?
CREON: He went to consult an oracle, Apollo said, 130
and he set out and never came home again.
OEDIPUS: No messenger, no fellow-traveler saw what
happened?
Someone to cross-examine?
CREON: No,
they were all killed but one. He escaped,
terrified, he could tell us nothing clearly, 135
nothing of what he saw—just one thing.
OEDIPUS: What's that?
One thing could hold the key to it all,
a small beginning give us grounds for hope.
CREON: He said thieves attacked them—a whole band,
not single-handed, cut King Laius down. 140
OEDIPUS: A thief,
so daring, so wild, he'd kill a king? Impossible,
unless conspirators paid him off in Thebes.
CREON: We suspected as much. But with Laius dead
no leader appeared to help us in our troubles.
OEDIPUS: Trouble? Your *king* was murdered—royal blood! 145
What stopped you from tracking down the killer
then and there?
CREON: The singing, riddling Sphinx.
She . . . persuaded us to let the mystery go
and concentrate on what lay at our feet.
OEDIPUS: No,
I'll start again—I'll bring it all to light myself! 150
Apollo is right, and so are you, Creon,
to turn our attention back to the murdered man.
Now you have *me* to fight for you, you'll see:
I am the land's avenger by all rights,
and Apollo's champion too. 155
But not to assist some distant kinsman, no,
for my own sake I'll rid us of this corruption.
Whoever killed the king may decide to kill me too,
with the same violent hand—by avenging Laius
I defend myself. 160

(*To the* PRIESTS.)

Quickly, my children.
Up from the steps, take up your branches now.

(*To the* GUARDS.)

One of you summon the city here before us,
tell them I'll do everything. God help us,
we will see our triumph—or our fall.

(OEDIPUS *and* CREON *enter the palace, followed by the* GUARDS.)

165 PRIEST: Rise, my sons. The kindness we came for
        Oedipus volunteers himself.
        Apollo has sent his word, his oracle—
        Come down, Apollo, save us, stop the plague.

(*The* PRIESTS *rise, remove their branches, and exit to the side. Enter a* CHORUS, *the citizens of Thebes, who have not heard the news that* CREON *brings. They march around the altar, chanting.*)

CHORUS: Zeus!
        Great welcome voice of Zeus, what do you bring?
170   What word from the gold vaults of Delphi
        comes to brilliant Thebes? Racked with terror—
                                        terror shakes my heart
        and I cry your wild cries, Apollo, Healer of Delos
        I worship you in dread . . . what now, what is your price?
175   some new sacrifice? some ancient rite from the past
        come round again each spring?—
                        what will you bring to birth?
        Tell me, child of golden Hope
                warm voice that never dies!

180   You are the first I call, daughter of Zeus
        deathless Athena—I call your sister Artemis,
        heart of the market place enthroned in glory,
                                guardian of our earth—
        I call Apollo, Archer astride the thunderheads of heaven—
185   O triple shield against death, shine before me now!
        If ever, once in the past, you stopped some ruin
        launched against our walls
                you hurled the flame of pain
        far, far from Thebes—you gods
190   come now, come down once more!
                                        No, no
        the miseries numberless, grief on grief, no end—
        too much to bear, we are all dying
        O my people . . .
                Thebes like a great army dying
195   and there is no sword of thought to save us, no
        and the fruits of our famous earth, they will not ripen
        no and the women cannot scream their pangs to birth—
        screams for the Healer, children dead in the womb
                and life on life goes down
200   you can watch them go
                like seabirds winging west, outracing the day's fire
        down the horizon, irresistibly
                streaking on to the shores of Evening
                                                Death
        so many deaths, numberless deaths on deaths, no end—
205   Thebes is dying, look, her children
        stripped of pity . . .
                generations strewn on the ground
        unburied, unwept, the dead spreading death
        and the young wives and gray-haired mothers with them
210   cling to the altars, trailing in from all over the city—
        Thebes, city of death, one long cortege
                and the suffering rises
                        wails for mercy rise
        and the wild hymn for the Healer blazes out
215   clashing with our sobs our cries of mourning—
                O golden daughter of god, send rescue
        radiant as the kindness in your eyes!

Drive him back!—the fever, the god of death
                        that raging god of war
not armored in bronze, not shielded now, he burns me,   220
battle cries in the onslaught burning on—
O rout him from our borders!
Sail him, blast him out to the Sea-queen's chamber
                        the black Atlantic gulfs
        or the northern harbor, death to all   225
where the Thracian surf comes crashing.
Now what the night spares he comes by day and kills—
the god of death.
                O lord of the stormcloud,
you who twirl the lightning, Zeus, Father,
thunder Death to nothing!   230

Apollo, lord of the light, I beg you—
        whip your longbow's golden cord
showering arrows on our enemies—shafts of power
champions strong before us rushing on!

Artemis, Huntress,   235
torches flaring over the eastern ridges—
                ride Death down in pain!

God of the headdress gleaming gold, I cry to you—
your name and ours are one, Dionysus—
        come with your face aflame with wine   240
                your raving women's cries
        your army on the march! Come with the lightning
come with torches blazing, eyes ablaze with glory!
Burn that god of death that all gods hate!

(OEDIPUS *enters from the palace to address the* CHORUS, *as if addressing the entire city of Thebes.*)

OEDIPUS: You pray to the gods? Let me grant your prayers.   245
        Come, listen to me—do what the plague demands:
        you'll find relief and lift your head from the depths.

        I will speak out now as a stranger to the story,
        a stranger to the crime. If I'd been present then,
        there would have been no mystery, no long hunt   250
        without a clue in hand. So now, counted
        a native Theban years after the murder,
        to all of Thebes I make this proclamation:
        if any one of you knows who murdered Laius,
        the son of Labdacus, I order him to reveal   255
        the whole truth to me. Nothing to fear,
        even if he must denounce himself,
        let him speak up
        and so escape the brunt of the charge—
        he will suffer no unbearable punishment,   260
        nothing worse than exile, totally unharmed.

(OEDIPUS *pauses, waiting for a reply.*)

                                            Next,
        if anyone knows the murderer is a stranger,
        a man from alien soil, come, speak up.
        I will give him a handsome reward, and lay up
        gratitude in my heart for him besides.   265

(*Silence again, no reply.*)

But if you keep silent, if anyone panicking,
trying to shield himself or friend or kin,
rejects my offer, then hear what I will do.
I order you, every citizen of the state
270 where I hold throne and power: banish this man—
whoever he may be—never shelter him, never
speak a word to him, never make him partner
to your prayers, your victims burned to the gods.
Never let the holy water touch his hands.
275 Drive him out, each of you, from every home.
He is the plague, the heart of our corruption,
as Apollo's oracle has just revealed to me.
So I honor my obligations:
I fight for the god and for the murdered man.

280 Now my curse on the murderer. Whoever he is,
a lone man unknown in his crime
or one among many, let that man drag out
his life in agony, step by painful step—
I curse myself as well . . . if by any chance
285 he proves to be an intimate of our house,
here at my hearth, with my full knowledge,
may the curse I just called down on him strike me!

These are your orders: perform them to the last.
I command you, for my sake, for Apollo's, for this
country
290 blasted root and branch by the angry heavens.
Even if god had never urged you on to act,
how could you leave the crime uncleansed so long?
A man so noble—your king, brought down in blood—
you should have searched. But I am the king now,
295 I hold the throne that he held then, possess his bed
and a wife who shares our seed . . . why, our seed
might be the same, children born of the same mother
might have created blood-bonds between us
if his hope of offspring had not met disaster—
300 but fate swooped at his head and cut him short.
So I will fight for him as if he were my father,
stop at nothing, search the world
to lay my hands on the man who shed his blood,
the son of Labdacus descended of Polydorus,
305 Cadmus of old and Agenor, founder of the line:
their power and mine are one.
                              Oh dear gods,
my curse on those who disobey these orders!
Let no crops grow out of the earth for them—
shrivel their women, kill their sons,
310 burn them to nothing in this plague
that hits us now, or something even worse.
But you, loyal men of Thebes who approve my actions,
may our champion, Justice, may all the gods
be with us, fight beside us to the end!
315 LEADER: In the grip of your curse, my king, I swear
I'm not the murderer, I cannot point him out.
As for the search, Apollo pressed it on us—
he should name the killer.
OEDIPUS: Quite right,
but to force the gods to act against their will
320 no man has the power.
LEADER: Then if I might mention
the next best thing . . .

OEDIPUS: The third best too—
don't hold back, say it.
LEADER: I still believe . . .
Lord Tiresias sees with the eyes of Lord Apollo.
Anyone searching for the truth, my king,
might learn it from the prophet, clear as day.   325
OEDIPUS: I've not been slow with that. On Creon's cue
I sent the escorts, twice, within the hour.
I'm surprised he isn't here.
LEADER: We need him—
without him we have nothing but old, useless rumors.
OEDIPUS: Which rumors? I'll search out every word.   330
LEADER: Laius was killed, they say, by certain travelers.
OEDIPUS: I know—but no one can find the murderer.
LEADER: If the man has a trace of fear in him
he won't stay silent long,
not with your curses ringing in his ears.   335
OEDIPUS: He didn't flinch at murder,
he'll never flinch at words.

(*Enter* TIRESIAS, *the blind prophet, led by a boy with escorts in attendance. He remains at a distance.*)

LEADER: Here is the one who will convict him, look,
they bring him on at last, the seer, the man of god.
The truth lives inside him, him alone.   340
OEDIPUS: O Tiresias,
master of all the mysteries of our life,
all you teach and all you dare not tell,
signs in the heavens, signs that walk the earth!
Blind as you are, you can feel all the more
what sickness haunts our city. You, my lord,   345
are the one shield, the one savior we can find.

We asked Apollo—perhaps the messengers
haven't told you—he sent his answer back:
"Relief from the plague can only come one way.
Uncover the murderers of Laius,   350
put them to death or drive them into exile."
So I beg you, grudge us nothing now, no voice,
no message plucked from the birds, the embers
or the other mantic ways within your grasp.
Rescue yourself, your city, rescue me—   355
rescue everything infected by the dead.
We are in your hands. For a man to help others
with all his gifts and native strength:
that is the noblest work.
TIRESIAS: How terrible—to see the truth
when the truth is only pain to him who sees!   360
I knew it well, but I put it from my mind,
else I never would have come.
OEDIPUS: What's this? Why so grim, so dire?
TIRESIAS: Just send me home. You bear your burdens,
I'll bear mine. It's better that way,   365
please believe me.
OEDIPUS: Strange response . . . unlawful,
unfriendly too to the state that bred and reared you—
you withhold the word of god.
TIRESIAS: I fail to see
that your own words are so well-timed.
I'd rather not have the same thing said of me . . .   370

OEDIPUS: For the love of god, don't turn away,
 not if you know something. We beg you,
 all of us on our knees.
  TIRESIAS: None of you knows—
 and I will never reveal my dreadful secrets,
375 not to say your own.
  OEDIPUS: What? You know and you won't tell?
 You're bent on betraying us, destroying Thebes?
  TIRESIAS: I'd rather not cause pain for you or me.
 So why this . . . useless interrogation?
380 You'll get nothing from me.
  OEDIPUS: Nothing! You,
 you scum of the earth, you'd enrage a heart of stone!
 You won't talk? Nothing moves you?
 Out with it, once and for all!
  TIRESIAS: You criticize my temper . . . unaware
385 of the one *you* live with, you revile me.
  OEDIPUS: Who could restrain his anger hearing you?
 What outrage—you spurn the city!
  TIRESIAS: What will come will come.
 Even if I shroud it all in silence.
390 OEDIPUS: What will come? You're bound to *tell* me that.
  TIRESIAS: I will say no more. Do as you like, build your anger
 to whatever pitch you please, rage your worst—
  OEDIPUS: Oh I'll let loose, I have such fury in me—
 now I see it all. You helped hatch the plot,
395 you did the work, yes, short of killing him
 with your own hands—and given eyes I'd say
 you did the killing single-handed!
  TIRESIAS: Is that so!
 I charge you, then, submit to that decree
 you just laid down: from this day onward
400 speak to no one, not these citizens, not myself.
 You are the curse, the corruption of the land!
  OEDIPUS: You, shameless—
 aren't you appalled to start up such a story?
 You think you can get away with this?
  TIRESIAS: I have already.
405 The truth with all its power lives inside me.
  OEDIPUS: Who primed you for this? Not your prophet's trade.
  TIRESIAS: You did, you forced me, twisted it out of me.
  OEDIPUS: What? Say it again—I'll understand it better.
  TIRESIAS: Didn't you understand, just now?
410 Or are you tempting me to talk?
  OEDIPUS: No, I can't say I grasped your meaning.
 Out with it, again!
  TIRESIAS: I say you are the murderer you hunt.
  OEDIPUS: That obscenity, twice—by god, you'll pay.
415 TIRESIAS: Shall I say more, so you can really rage?
  OEDIPUS: Much as you want. Your words are nothing—
 futile.
  TIRESIAS: You cannot imagine . . . I tell you,
 you and your loved ones live together in infamy,
 you cannot see how far you've gone in guilt.
420 OEDIPUS: You think you can keep this up and never suffer?
  TIRESIAS: Indeed, if the truth has any power.
  OEDIPUS: It does
 but not for you, old man. You've lost your power,
 stone-blind, stone-deaf—senses, eyes blind as stone!
  TIRESIAS: I pity you, flinging at me the very insults
425 each man here will fling at you so soon.

OEDIPUS: Blind,
 lost in the night, endless night that nursed you!
 You can't hurt me or anyone else who sees the light—
 you can never touch me.
  TIRESIAS: True, it is not your fate
 to fall at my hands. Apollo is quite enough,
 and he will take some pains to work this out. 430
  OEDIPUS: Creon! Is this conspiracy his or yours?
  TIRESIAS: Creon is not your downfall, no, you are your own.
  OEDIPUS: O power—
 wealth and empire, skill outstripping skill
 in the heady rivalries of life,
 what envy lurks inside you! Just for this, 435
 the crown the city gave me—I never sought it,
 they laid it in my hands—for this alone, Creon,
 the soul of trust, my loyal friend from the start
 steals against me . . . so hungry to overthrow me
 he sets this wizard on me, this scheming quack, 440
 this fortune-teller peddling lies, eyes peeled
 for his own profit—seer blind in his craft!

 Come here, you pious fraud. Tell me,
 when did you ever prove yourself a prophet?
 When the Sphinx, that chanting Fury kept her 445
  deathwatch here,
 why silent then, not a word to set our people free?
 There was a riddle, not for some passer-by to solve—
 it cried out for a prophet. Where were you?
 Did you rise to the crisis? Not a word,
 you and your birds, your gods—nothing. 450
 No, but I came by, Oedipus the ignorant,
 I stopped the Sphinx! With no help from the birds,
 the flight of my own intelligence hit the mark.

 And this is the man you'd try to overthrow?
 You think you'll stand by Creon when he's king? 455
 You and the great mastermind—
 you'll pay in tears, I promise you, for this,
 this witch-hunt. If you didn't look so senile
 the lash would teach you what your scheming means!
  LEADER: I would suggest his words were spoken in anger, 460
 Oedipus . . . yours too, and it isn't what we need.
 The best solution to the oracle, the riddle
 posed by god—we should look for that.
  TIRESIAS: You are the king no doubt, but in one respect,
 at least, I am your equal: the right to reply. 465
 I claim that privilege too.
 I am not your slave. I serve Apollo.
 I don't need Creon to speak for me in public.
          So,
 you mock my blindness? Let me tell you this.
 You with your precious eyes, 470
 you're blind to the corruption of your life,
 to the house you live in, those you live with—
 who *are* your parents? Do you know? All unknowing
 you are the scourge of your own flesh and blood,
 the dead below the earth and the living here above, 475
 and the double lash of your mother and your father's
  curse
 will whip you from this land one day, their footfall
 treading you down in terror, darkness shrouding
 your eyes that now can see the light!

Soon, soon
480   you'll scream aloud—what haven won't reverberate?
What rock of Cithaeron won't scream back in echo?
That day you learn the truth about your marriage,
the wedding-march that sang you into your halls,
the lusty voyage home to the fatal harbor!
485   And a crowd of other horrors you'd never dream
will level you with yourself and all your children.

There. Now smear us with insults—Creon, myself
and every word I've said. No man will ever
be rooted from the earth as brutally as you.

490   OEDIPUS: Enough! Such filth from him? Insufferable—
what, still alive? Get out—
faster, back where you came from—vanish!
TIRESIAS: I would never have come if you hadn't called me here.
OEDIPUS: If I thought you would blurt out such absurdities,
495   you'd have died waiting before I'd had you summoned.
TIRESIAS: Absurd, am I! To you, not to your parents:
the ones who bore me found me sane enough.
OEDIPUS: Parents—who? Wait . . . who is my father?
TIRESIAS: This day will bring your birth and your destruction.
500   OEDIPUS: Riddles—all you can say are riddles, murk and
darkness.
TIRESIAS: Ah, but aren't you the best man alive at solving
riddles?
OEDIPUS: Mock me for that, go on, and you'll reveal my
greatness.
TIRESIAS: Your great good fortune, true, it was your ruin.
OEDIPUS: Not if I saved the city—what do I care?
505   TIRESIAS: Well then, I'll be going.

(*To his* ATTENDANT.)

Take me home, boy.
OEDIPUS: Yes, take him away. You're a nuisance here.
Out of the way, the irritation's gone.

(*Turning his back on* TIRESIAS, *moving toward the palace.*)

TIRESIAS: I will go,
once I have said what I came here to say.
I will never shrink from the anger in your eyes—
510   you can't destroy me. Listen to me closely:
the man you've sought so long, proclaiming,
cursing up and down, the murderer of Laius—
he is here. A stranger,
you may think, who lives among you,
515   he soon will be revealed a native Theban
but he will take no joy in the revelation.
Blind who now has eyes, beggar who now is rich,
he will grope his way toward a foreign soil,
a stick tapping before him step by step.

(OEDIPUS *enters the palace.*)

520   Revealed at last, brother and father both
to the children he embraces, to his mother
son and husband both—he sowed the loins
his father sowed, he spilled his father's blood!

Go in and reflect on that, solve that.
525   And if you find I've lied
from this day onward call the prophet blind.

(TIRESIAS *and the boy exit to the side.*)

CHORUS: Who—
who is the man the voice of god denounces
resounding out of the rocky gorge of Delphi?
The horror too dark to tell,
whose ruthless bloody hands have done the work?   530
His time has come to fly
to outrace the stallions of the storm
his feet a streak of speed—
Cased in armor, Apollo son of the Father
lunges on him, lightning-bolts afire!   535
And the grim unerring Furies
closing for the kill.
Look,
the word of god has just come blazing
flashing off Parnassus' snowy heights!
That man who left no trace—   540
after him, hunt him down with all our strength!
Now under bristling timber
up through rocks and caves he stalks
like the wild mountain bull—
cut off from men, each step an agony, frenzied, racing blind   545
but he cannot outrace the dread voices of Delphi
ringing out of the heart of Earth,
the dark wings beating around him shrieking doom
the doom that never dies, the terror—
The skilled prophet scans the birds and shatters me with   550
terror!
I can't accept him, can't deny him, don't know what to say,
I'm lost, and the wings of dark foreboding beating—
I cannot see what's come, what's still to come . . .
and what could breed a blood feud between
Laius' house and the son of Polybus?   555
I know of nothing, not in the past and not now,
no charge to bring against our king, no cause
to attack his fame that rings throughout Thebes—
not without proof—not for the ghost of Laius,
not to avenge a murder gone without a trace.   560

Zeus and Apollo know, they know, the great masters
of all the dark and depth of human life.
But whether a mere man can know the truth,
whether a seer can fathom more than I—
there is no test, no certain proof   565
though matching skill for skill
a man can outstrip a rival. No, not till I see
these charges proved will I side with his accusers.
We saw him then, when the she-hawk swept against him,
saw with our own eyes his skill, his brilliant triumph—   570
there was the test—he was the joy of Thebes!
Never will I convict my king, never in my heart.

(Enter CREON *from the side.*)

CREON: My fellow-citizens, I hear King Oedipus
levels terrible charges at me. I had to come.
I resent it deeply. If, in the present crisis,   575
he thinks he suffers any abuse from me,
anything I've done or said that offers him
the slightest injury, why, I've no desire
to linger out this life, my reputation in ruins.

580 The damage I'd face from such an accusation
is nothing simple. No, there's nothing worse:
branded a traitor in the city, a traitor
to all of you and my good friends.
LEADER: True,
but a slur might have been forced out of him,
585 by anger perhaps, not any firm conviction.
CREON: The charge was made in public, wasn't it?
I put the prophet up to spreading lies?
LEADER: Such things were said . . .
I don't know with what intent, if any.
590 CREON: Was his glance steady, his mind right
when the charge was brought against me?
LEADER: I really couldn't say, I never look
to judge the ones in power.

(*The doors open.* OEDIPUS *enters.*)

Wait,
here's Oedipus now.
OEDIPUS: You—here? You have the gall
595 to show your face before the palace gates?
You, plotting to kill me, kill the king—
I see it all, the marauding thief himself
scheming to steal my crown and power!
Tell me,
in god's name, what did you take me for,
600 coward or fool, when you spun out your plot?
Your treachery—you think I'd never detect it
creeping against me in the dark? Or sensing it,
not defend myself? Aren't you the fool,
you and your high adventure. Lacking numbers,
605 powerful friends, out for the big game of empire—
you need riches, armies to bring that quarry down!
CREON: Are you quite finished? It's your turn to listen
for just as long as you've . . . instructed me.
Hear me out, then judge me on the facts.
610 OEDIPUS: You've a wicked way with words, Creon,
but I'll be slow to learn—from you.
I find you a menace, a great burden to me.
CREON: Just one thing, hear me out in this.
OEDIPUS: Just one thing,
don't tell *me* you're not the enemy, the traitor.
615 CREON: Look, if you think crude, mindless stubbornness
such a gift, you've lost your sense of balance.
OEDIPUS: If you think you can abuse a kinsman,
then escape the penalty, you're insane.
CREON: Fair enough, I grant you. But this injury
620 you say I've done you, what is it?
OEDIPUS: Did you induce me, yes or no,
to send for that sanctimonious prophet?
CREON: I did. And I'd do the same again.
OEDIPUS: All right then, tell me, how long is it now
625 since Laius . . .
CREON: Laius—what did *he* do?
OEDIPUS: Vanished,
swept from sight, murdered in his tracks.
CREON: The count of the years would run you far back . . .
OEDIPUS: And that far back, was the prophet at his trade?
CREON: Skilled as he is today, and just as honored.

OEDIPUS: Did he ever refer to me then, at that time?   630
CREON: No,
never, at least, when I was in his presence.
OEDIPUS: But you did investigate the murder, didn't you?
CREON: We did our best, of course, discovered nothing.
OEDIPUS: But the great seer never accused me then—why not?
CREON: I don't know. And when I don't, *I* keep quiet.   635
OEDIPUS: You do know this, you'd tell it too—
if you had a shred of decency.
CREON: What?
If I know, I won't hold back.
OEDIPUS: Simply this:
if the two of you had never put heads together,
we would never have heard about *my* killing Laius.   640
CREON: If that's what he says . . . well, you know best.
But now I have a right to learn from you
as you just learned from me.
OEDIPUS: Learn your fill,
you never will convict me of the murder.
CREON: Tell me, you're married to my sister, aren't you?   645
OEDIPUS: A genuine discovery—there's no denying that.
CREON: And you rule the land with her, with equal power?
OEDIPUS: She receives from me whatever she desires.
CREON: And I am the third, all of us are equals?
OEDIPUS: Yes, and it's there you show your stripes—   650
you betray a kinsman.
CREON: Not at all.
Not if you see things calmly, rationally,
as I do. Look at it this way first:
who in his right mind would rather rule
and live in anxiety than sleep in peace?   655
Particularly if he enjoys the same authority.
Not I, I'm not the man to yearn for kingship,
not with a king's power in my hands. Who would?
No one with any sense of self-control.
Now, as it is, you offer me all I need,   660
not a fear in the world. But if I wore the crown . . .
there'd be many painful duties to perform,
hardly to my taste.
How could kingship
please me more than influence, power
without a qualm? I'm not that deluded yet,   665
to reach for anything but privilege outright,
profit free and clear.
Now all men sing my praises, all salute me,
now all who request your favors curry mine.
I am their best hope: success rests in me.   670
Why give up that, I ask you, and borrow trouble?
A man of sense, someone who sees things clearly
would never resort to treason.
No, I have no lust for conspiracy in me,
nor could I ever suffer one who does.   675

Do you want proof? Go to Delphi yourself,
examine the oracle and see if I've reported
the message word-for-word. This too:
if you detect that I and the clairvoyant
have plotted anything in common, arrest me,   680
execute me. Not on the strength of one vote,
two in this case, mine as well as yours.

But don't convict me on sheer unverified surmise.
How wrong it is to take the good for bad,
685 purely at random, or take the bad for good.
But reject a friend, a kinsman? I would as soon
tear out the life within us, priceless life itself.
You'll learn this well, without fail, in time.
Time alone can bring the just man to light—
690 the criminal you can spot in one short day.
LEADER: Good advice,
my lord, for anyone who wants to avoid disaster.
Those who jump to conclusions may go wrong.
OEDIPUS: When my enemy moves against me quickly,
plots in secret, I move quickly too, I must,
695 I plot and pay him back. Relax my guard a moment,
waiting his next move—he wins his objective,
I lose mine.
CREON: What do you want?
You want me banished?
OEDIPUS: No, I want you dead.
CREON: Just to show how ugly a grudge can . . .
OEDIPUS: So,
700 still stubborn? you don't think I'm serious?
CREON: I think you're insane.
OEDIPUS: Quite sane—in my behalf.
CREON: Not just as much in mine?
OEDIPUS: You—my mortal enemy?
CREON: What if you're wholly wrong?
OEDIPUS: No matter—I must rule.
CREON: Not if you rule unjustly.
OEDIPUS: Hear him, Thebes, my city!
705 CREON: My city too, not yours alone!
LEADER: Please, my lords.

(*Enter* JOCASTA *from the palace.*)

                           Look, Jocasta's coming,
and just in time too. With her help
you must put this fighting of yours to rest.
JOCASTA: Have you no sense? Poor misguided men,
710 such shouting—why this public outburst?
Aren't you ashamed, with the land so sick,
to stir up private quarrels?

(*To* OEDIPUS.)

Into the palace now. And Creon, you go home.
Why make such a furor over nothing?
715 CREON: My sister, it's dreadful . . . Oedipus, your husband,
he's bent on a choice of punishments for me,
banishment from the fatherland or death.
OEDIPUS: Precisely. I caught him in the act, Jocasta,
plotting, about to stab me in the back.
720 CREON: Never—curse me, let me die and be damned
if I've done you any wrong you charge me with.
JOCASTA: Oh god, believe it, Oedipus,
honor the solemn oath he swears to heaven.
Do it for me, for the sake of all your people.

(*The* CHORUS *begins to chant.*)

725 CHORUS: Believe it, be sensible
give way, my king, I beg you!

OEDIPUS: What do you want from me, concessions?
CHORUS: Respect him—he's been no fool in the past
and now he's strong with the oath he swears to god.
OEDIPUS: You know what you're asking?   730
CHORUS: I do.
OEDIPUS: Then out with it!
CHORUS: The man's your friend, your kin, he's under oath—
don't cast him out, disgraced,
branded with guilt on the strength of hearsay only.
OEDIPUS: Know full well, if that is what you want
you want me dead or banished from the land.   735
CHORUS: Never—
no, by the blazing Sun, first god of the heavens!
Stripped of the gods, stripped of loved ones,
let me die by inches if that ever crossed my mind.
But the heart inside me sickens, dies as the land dies
and now on top of the old griefs you pile this,   740
your fury—both of you!
OEDIPUS: Then let him go,
even if it does lead to my ruin, my death
or my disgrace, driven from Thebes for life.
It's you, not him I pity—your words move me.
He, wherever he goes, my hate goes with him.   745
CREON: Look at you, sullen in yielding, brutal in your rage—
you will go too far. It's perfect justice:
natures like yours are hardest on themselves.
OEDIPUS: Then leave me alone—get out!
CREON: I'm going.
You're wrong, so wrong. These men know I'm right. 750

(*Exit to the side. The* CHORUS *turns to* JOCASTA.)

CHORUS: Why do you hesitate, my lady
why not help him in?
JOCASTA: Tell me what's happened first.
CHORUS: Loose, ignorant talk started dark suspicions
and a sense of injustice cut deeply too.   755
JOCASTA: On both sides?
CHORUS: Oh yes.
JOCASTA: What did they say?
CHORUS: Enough, please, enough! The land's so racked already
or so it seems to me . . .
End the trouble here, just where they left it.
OEDIPUS: You see what comes of your good intentions now? 760
And all because you tried to blunt my anger.
CHORUS: My king,
I've said it once, I'll say it time and again—
I'd be insane, you know it,
senseless, ever to turn my back on you.
You who set our beloved land—storm-tossed, shattered— 765
straight on course. Now again, good helmsman,
steer us through the storm!

(*The* CHORUS *draws away, leaving* OEDIPUS *and* JOCASTA *side by side.*)

JOCASTA: For the love of god,
Oedipus, tell me too, what is it?
Why this rage? You're so unbending.
OEDIPUS: I will tell you. I respect you, Jocasta,   770
much more than these men here . . .

(*Glancing at the* CHORUS.)

Creon's to blame, Creon schemes against me.
JOCASTA: Tell me clearly, how did the quarrel start?
OEDIPUS: He says I murdered Laius—I am guilty.
775 JOCASTA: How does he know? Some secret knowledge
or simple hearsay?
OEDIPUS: Oh, he sent his prophet in
to do his dirty work. You know Creon,
Creon keeps his own lips clean.
JOCASTA: A prophet?
Well then, free yourself of every charge!
780 Listen to me and learn some peace of mind:
no skill in the world,
nothing human can penetrate the future.
Here is proof, quick and to the point.

An oracle came to Laius one fine day
785 (I won't say from Apollo himself
but his underlings, his priests) and it declared
that doom would strike him down at the hands of a son,
our son, to be born of our own flesh and blood. But Laius,
so the report goes at least, was killed by strangers,
790 thieves, at a place where three roads meet . . . my son—
he wasn't three days old and the boy's father
fastened his ankles, had a henchman fling him away
on a barren, trackless mountain.
                                There, you see?
Apollo brought neither thing to pass. My baby
795 no more murdered his father than Laius suffered—
his wildest fear—death at his own son's hands.
That's how the seers and all their revelations
mapped out the future. Brush them from your mind.
Whatever the god needs and seeks
800 he'll bring to light himself, with ease.
OEDIPUS: Strange,
hearing you just now . . . my mind wandered,
my thoughts racing back and forth.
JOCASTA: What do you mean? Why so anxious, startled?
OEDIPUS: I thought I heard you say that Laius
805 was cut down at a place where three roads meet.
JOCASTA: That was the story. It hasn't died out yet.
OEDIPUS: Where did this thing happen? Be precise.
JOCASTA: A place called Phocis, where two branching roads,
one from Daulia, one from Delphi,
810 come together—a crossroads.
OEDIPUS: When? How long ago?
JOCASTA: The heralds no sooner reported Laius dead
than you appeared and they hailed you king of Thebes.
OEDIPUS: My god, my god—what have you planned to do to me?
815 JOCASTA: What, Oedipus? What haunts you so?
OEDIPUS: Not yet.
Laius—how did he look? Describe him.
Had he reached his prime?
JOCASTA: He was swarthy,
and the gray had just begun to streak his temples,
and his build . . . wasn't far from yours.
OEDIPUS: Oh no no,
820 I think I've just called down a dreadful curse
upon myself—I simply didn't know!

JOCASTA: What are you saying? I shudder to look at you.
OEDIPUS: I have a terrible fear the blind seer can see.
I'll know in a moment. One thing more—
JOCASTA: Anything,
afraid as I am—ask, I'll answer, all I can.   825
OEDIPUS: Did he go with a light or heavy escort,
several men-at-arms, like a lord, a king?
JOCASTA: There were five in the party, a herald among them,
and a single wagon carrying Laius.
OEDIPUS: Ai—
now I can see it all, clear as day.   830
Who told you all this at the time, Jocasta?
JOCASTA: A servant who reached home, the lone survivor.
OEDIPUS: So, could he still be in the palace—even now?
JOCASTA: No indeed. Soon as he returned from the scene
and saw you on the throne with Laius dead and gone,   835
he knelt and clutched my hand, pleading with me
to send him into the hinterlands, to pasture,
far as possible, out of sight of Thebes.
I sent him away. Slave though he was,
he'd earned that favor—and much more.   840
OEDIPUS: Can we bring him back, quickly?
JOCASTA: Easily. Why do you want him so?
OEDIPUS: I am afraid,
Jocasta, I have said too much already.
That man—I've got to see him.
JOCASTA: Then he'll come.
But even I have a right, I'd like to think,   845
to know what's torturing you, my lord.
OEDIPUS: And so you shall—I can hold nothing back from you,
now I've reached this pitch of dark foreboding.
Who means more to me than you? Tell me,
whom would I turn toward but you   850
as I go through all this?

My father was Polybus, king of Corinth.
My mother, a Dorian, Merope. And I was held
the prince of the realm among the people there,
till something struck me out of nowhere,   855
something strange . . . worth remarking perhaps,
hardly worth the anxiety I gave it.
Some man at a banquet who had drunk too much
shouted out—he was far gone, mind you—
that I am not my father's son. Fighting words!   860
I barely restrained myself that day
but early the next I went to mother and father,
questioned them closely, and they were enraged
at the accusation and the fool who let it fly.
So as for my parents I was satisfied,   865
but still this thing kept gnawing at me,
the slander spread—I had to make my move.
                                And so,
unknown to mother and father I set out for Delphi,
and the god Apollo spurned me, sent me away
denied the facts I came for,   870
but first he flashed before my eyes a future
great with pain, terror, disaster—I can hear him cry,
"You are fated to couple with your mother, you will bring
a breed of children into the light no man can bear to see—
you will kill your father, the one who gave you life!"   875

I heard all that and ran. I abandoned Corinth,
from that day on I gauged its landfall only
by the stars, running, always running
toward some place where I would never see
880 the shame of all those oracles come true.
And as I fled I reached that very spot
where the great king, you say, met his death.

Now, Jocasta, I will tell you all.
Making my way toward this triple crossroad
885 I began to see a herald, then a brace of colts
drawing a wagon, and mounted on the bench . . . a man,
just as you've described him, coming face-to-face,
and the one in the lead and the old man himself
were about to thrust me off the road—brute force—
890 and the one shouldering me aside, the driver,
I strike him in anger!—and the old man, watching me
coming up along his wheels—he brings down
his prod, two prongs straight at my head!
I paid him back with interest!
895 Short work, by god—with one blow of the staff
in this right hand I knock him out of his high seat,
roll him out of the wagon, sprawling headlong—
I killed them all—every mother's son!

Oh, but if there is any blood-tie
900 between Laius and this stranger . . .
what man alive more miserable than I?
More hated by the gods? *I* am the man
no alien, no citizen welcomes to his house,
law forbids it—not a word to me in public,
905 driven out of every hearth and home.
And all these curses I—no one but I
brought down these piling curses on myself!
And you, his wife, I've touched your body with these,
the hands that killed your husband cover you with blood.

910 Wasn't I born for torment? Look me in the eyes!
I am abomination—heart and soul!
I must be exiled, and even in exile
never see my parents, never set foot
on native ground again. Else I am doomed
915 to couple with my mother and cut my father down . . .
Polybus who reared me, gave me life.
                              But why, why?
Wouldn't a man of judgment say—and wouldn't he be
   right—
some savage power has brought this down upon my head?

Oh no, not that, you pure and awesome gods,
920 never let me see that day! Let me slip
from the world of men, vanish without a trace
before I see myself stained with such corruption,
stained to the heart.
LEADER: My lord, you fill our hearts with fear.
925 But at least until you question the witness,
do take hope.
OEDIPUS: Exactly. He is my last hope—
I am waiting for the shepherd. He is crucial.
JOCASTA: And once he appears, what then? Why so urgent?
OEDIPUS: I will tell you. If it turns out that his story
930 matches yours, I've escaped the worst.

JOCASTA: What did I say? What struck you so?
OEDIPUS: You said
   thieves—
he told you a whole band of them murdered Laius.
So, if he still holds to the same number,
I cannot be the killer. One can't equal many.
But if he refers to one man, one alone,   935
clearly the scales come down on me:
I am guilty.
JOCASTA: Impossible. Trust me,
I told you precisely what he said,
and he can't retract it now;
the whole city heard it, not just I.   940
And even if he should vary his first report
by one man more or less, still, my lord,
he could never make the murder of Laius
truly fit the prophecy. Apollo was explicit:
my son was doomed to kill my husband . . . my son,   945
poor defenseless thing, he never had a chance
to kill his father. They destroyed him first.

So much for prophecy. It's neither here nor there.
From this day on. I wouldn't look right or left.
OEDIPUS: True, true. Still, that shepherd,   950
someone fetch him—now!
JOCASTA: I'll send at once. But do let's go inside.
I'd never displease you, least of all in this.

(OEDIPUS *and* JOCASTA *enter the palace.*)

CHORUS: Destiny guide me always
Destiny find me filled with reverence   955
   pure in word and deed.
Great laws tower above us, reared on high
born for the brilliant vault of heaven—
   Olympian Sky their only father,
nothing mortal, no man gave them birth,   960
their memory deathless, never lost in sleep:
within them lives a mighty god, the god does not
   grow old.

Pride breeds the tyrant
violent pride, gorging, crammed to bursting
   with all that is overripe and rich with ruin—   965
clawing up to the heights, headlong pride
crashes down the abyss—sheer doom!
   No footing helps, all foothold lost and gone.
But the healthy strife that makes the city strong—
I pray that god will never end that wrestling: 970
god, my champion, I will never let you go.

But if any man comes striding, high and mighty
   in all he says and does,
no fear of justice, no reverence
for the temples of the gods—   975
   let a rough doom tear him down,
repay his pride, breakneck, ruinous pride!
If he cannot reap his profits fairly
   cannot restrain himself from outrage—
mad, laying hands on the holy things untouchable!   980

Can such a man, so desperate, still boast
he can save his life from the flashing bolts of god?

If all such violence goes with honor now
    why join the sacred dance?

985   Never again will I go reverent to Delphi,
      the inviolate heart of Earth
    or Apollo's ancient oracle at Abae
    or Olympia of the fires—
      unless these prophecies all come true
990   for all mankind to point toward in wonder.
    King of kings, if you deserve your titles
      Zeus, remember, never forget!
    You and your deathless, everlasting reign.

    They are dying, the old oracles sent to Laius,
995   now our masters strike them off the rolls.
      Nowhere Apollo's golden glory now—
      the gods, the gods go down.

(*Enter* JOCASTA *from the palace, carrying a suppliant's branch wound in wool.*)

JOCASTA: Lords of the realm, it occurred to me,
    just now, to visit the temples of the gods,
1000   so I have my branch in hand and incense too.

    Oedipus is beside himself. Racked with anguish,
    no longer a man of sense, he won't admit
    the latest prophecies are hollow as the old—
    he's at the mercy of every passing voice
1005   if the voice tells of terror.
    I urge him gently, nothing seems to help,
    so I turn to you, Apollo, you are nearest.

(*Placing her branch on the altar, while an old herdsman enters from the side, not the one just summoned by the King but an unexpected* MESSENGER *from Corinth.*)

    I come with prayers and offerings . . . I beg you,
    cleanse us, set us free of defilement!
1010   Look at us, passengers in the grip of fear,
    watching the pilot of the vessel go to pieces.
MESSENGER: (*Approaching* JOCASTA *and the* CHORUS.) Strangers,
    please, I wonder if you could lead us
    to the palace of the king . . . I think it's Oedipus.
    Better, the man himself—you know where he is?
1015 LEADER: This is his palace, stranger. He's inside.
    But here is his queen, his wife and mother
    of his children.
MESSENGER: Blessings on you, noble queen,
    queen of Oedipus crowned with all your family—
    blessings on you always!
1020 JOCASTA: And the same to you, stranger, you deserve it . . .
    such a greeting. But what have you come for?
    Have you brought us news?
MESSENGER: Wonderful news—
    for the house, my lady, for your husband too.
JOCASTA: Really, what? Who sent you?
MESSENGER: Corinth.
1025 I'll give you the message in a moment.
    You'll be glad of it—how could you help it?—
    though it costs a little sorrow in the bargain.
JOCASTA: What can it be, with such a double edge?

MESSENGER: The people there, they want to make your Oedipus
    king of Corinth, so they're saying now.   1030
JOCASTA: Why? Isn't old Polybus still in power?
MESSENGER: No more. Death has got him in the tomb.
JOCASTA: What are you saying? Polybus, dead?—dead?
MESSENGER: If not,
    if I'm not telling the truth, strike me dead too.
JOCASTA: (*To a* SERVANT.) Quickly, go to your master, tell him
    this!   1035

    You prophecies of the gods, where are you now?
    This is the man that Oedipus feared for years,
    he fled him, not to kill him—and now he's dead,
    quite by chance, a normal, natural death,
    not murdered by his son.   1040
OEDIPUS: (*Emerging from the palace.*)
          Dearest,
    what now? Why call me from the palace?
JOCASTA: (*Bringing the* MESSENGER *closer.*) Listen to *him,* see for
    yourself what all
    those awful prophecies of god have come to.
OEDIPUS: And who is he? What can he have for me?
JOCASTA: He's from Corinth, he's come to tell you   1045
    your father is no more—Polybus—he's dead!
OEDIPUS: (*Wheeling on the* MESSENGER.) What? Let me have it
    from your lips.
MESSENGER: Well,
    if that's what you want first, then here it is:
    make no mistake, Polybus is dead and gone.
OEDIPUS: How—murder? sickness?—what? what killed him?   1050
MESSENGER: A light tip of the scales can put old bones to rest.
OEDIPUS: Sickness then—poor man, it wore him down.
MESSENGER: That,
    and the long count of years he'd measured out.
OEDIPUS: So!
    Jocasta, why, why look to the Prophet's hearth,
    the fires of the future? Why scan the birds   1055
    that scream above our heads? They winged me on
    to the murder of my father, did they? That was my doom?
    Well look, he's dead and buried, hidden under the earth,
    and here I am in Thebes, I never put hand to sword—
    unless some longing for me wasted him away,   1060
    then in a sense you'd say I caused his death.
    But now, all those prophecies I feared—Polybus
    packs them off to sleep with him in hell!
    They're nothing, worthless.
JOCASTA: There.
    Didn't I tell you from the start?   1065
OEDIPUS: So you did. I was lost in fear.
JOCASTA: No more, sweep it from your mind forever.
OEDIPUS: But my mother's bed, surely I must fear—
JOCASTA: Fear?
    What should a man fear? It's all chance,
    chance rules our lives. Not a man on earth   1070
    can see a day ahead, groping through the dark.
    Better to live at random, best we can.
    And as for this marriage with your mother—
    have no fear. Many a man before you,
    in his dreams, has shared his mother's bed.   1075
    Take such things for shadows, nothing at all—

Live, Oedipus,
as if there's no tomorrow!

OEDIPUS: Brave words,
and you'd persuade me if mother weren't alive.
1080 But mother lives, so for all your reassurances
I live in fear, I must.

JOCASTA: But your father's death,
that, at least, is a great blessing, joy to the eyes!

OEDIPUS: Great, I know . . . but I fear *her*—she's still alive.

MESSENGER: Wait, who is this woman, makes you so afraid?

1085 OEDIPUS: Merope, old man. The wife of Polybus.

MESSENGER: The queen? What's there to fear in her?

OEDIPUS: A dreadful prophecy, stranger, sent by the gods.

MESSENGER: Tell me, could you? Unless it's forbidden
other ears to hear.

OEDIPUS: Not at all.
1090 Apollo told me once—it is my fate—
I must make love with my own mother,
shed my father's blood with my own hands.
So for years I've given Corinth a wide berth,
and it's been my good fortune too. But still,
1095 to see one's parents and look into their eyes
is the greatest joy I know.

MESSENGER: You're afraid of that?
That kept you out of Corinth?

OEDIPUS: My *father*, old man—
so I wouldn't kill my father.

MESSENGER: So that's it.
Well then, seeing I came with such good will, my king,
1100 why don't I rid you of that old worry now?

OEDIPUS: What a rich reward you'd have for that!

MESSENGER: What do you think I came for, majesty?
So you'd come home and I'd be better off.

OEDIPUS: Never, I will never go near my parents.

1105 MESSENGER: My boy, it's clear, you don't know what you're
doing.

OEDIPUS: What do you mean, old man? For god's sake, explain.

MESSENGER: If you ran from *them,* always dodging home . . .

OEDIPUS: Always, terrified Apollo's oracle might come true—

MESSENGER: And you'd be covered with guilt, from both your
parents.

1110 OEDIPUS: That's right, old man, that fear is always
with me.

MESSENGER: Don't you know? You've really nothing to fear.

OEDIPUS: But why? If I'm their son—Merope, Polybus?

MESSENGER: Polybus was nothing to you, that's why, not in
blood.

OEDIPUS: What are you saying—Polybus was not my father?

1115 MESSENGER: No more than I am. He and I are equals.

OEDIPUS: My father—
how can my father equal nothing? You're nothing to me!

MESSENGER: Neither was he, no more your father than I am.

OEDIPUS: Then why did he call me his son?

MESSENGER: You were a gift,
years ago—know for a fact he took you
1120 from my hands.

OEDIPUS: No, from another's hands?
Then how could he love me so? He loved me, deeply . . .

MESSENGER: True, and his early years without a child
made him love you all the more.

OEDIPUS: And you, did you . . .
buy me? find me by accident?

MESSENGER: I stumbled on you,
down the woody flanks of Mount Cithaeron.   1125

OEDIPUS: So close,
what were you doing here, just passing through?

MESSENGER: Watching over my flocks, grazing them on the
slopes.

OEDIPUS: A herdsman, were you? A vagabond, scraping for
wages?

MESSENGER: Your savior too, my son, in your worst hour.

OEDIPUS: Oh—
when you picked me up, was I in pain? What exactly?   1130

MESSENGER: Your ankles . . . they tell the story. Look at
them.

OEDIPUS: Why remind me of that, that old affliction?

MESSENGER: Your ankles were pinned together. I set you free.

OEDIPUS: That dreadful mark—I've had it from the cradle.

MESSENGER: And you got your name from that misfortune   1135
too,
the name's still with you.

OEDIPUS: Dear god, who did it?—
mother? father? Tell me.

MESSENGER: I don't know.
The one who gave you to me, he'd know more.

OEDIPUS: What? You took me from someone else?
You didn't find me yourself?   1140

MESSENGER: No sir,
another shepherd passed you on to me.

OEDIPUS: Who? Do you know? Describe him.

MESSENGER: He called himself a servant of . . .
if I remember rightly—Laius.

(JOCASTA *turns sharply.*)

OEDIPUS: The king of the land who ruled here long ago?   1145

MESSENGER: That's the one. That herdsman was *his* man.

OEDIPUS: Is he still alive? Can I see him?

MESSENGER: They'd know best, the people of these parts.

(OEDIPUS *and the* MESSENGER *turn to the* CHORUS.)

OEDIPUS: Does anyone know that herdsman,
the one he mentioned? Anyone seen him   1150
in the fields, here in the city? Out with it!
The time has come to reveal this once for all.

LEADER: I think he's the very shepherd you wanted to see,
a moment ago. But the queen, Jocasta,
she's the one to say.   1155

OEDIPUS: Jocasta,
you remember the man we just sent for?
Is *that* the one he means?

JOCASTA: That man . . .
why ask? Old shepherd, talk, empty nonsense,
don't give it another thought, don't even think—

OEDIPUS: What—give up now, with a clue like this?   1160
Fail to solve the mystery of my birth?
Not for all the world!

JOCASTA: Stop—in the name of god,
if you love your own life, call off this search!
My suffering is enough.

OEDIPUS: Courage!
1165   Even if my mother turns out to be a slave,
        and I a slave, three generations back,
        you would not seem common.
JOCASTA: Oh no,
        listen to me, I beg you, don't do this.
OEDIPUS: Listen to you? No more. I must know it all,
1170   must see the truth at last.
JOCASTA: No, please—
        for your sake—I want the best for you!
OEDIPUS: Your best is more than I can bear.
JOCASTA: You're doomed—
        may you never fathom who you are!
OEDIPUS: (*To a servant.*) Hurry, fetch me the herdsman, now!
1175   Leave her to glory in her royal birth.
JOCASTA: Aieeeeee—
                    man of agony—
        that is the only name I have for you,
        that, no other—ever, ever, ever!

(*Flinging through the palace doors. A long, tense silence follows.*)

LEADER: Where's she gone, Oedipus?
1180   Rushing off, such wild grief . . .
        I'm afraid that from this silence
        something monstrous may come bursting forth.
OEDIPUS: Let it burst! Whatever will, whatever must!
        I must know my birth, no matter how common
1185   it may be—I must see my origins face-to-face.
        She perhaps, she with her woman's pride
        may well be mortified by my birth,
        but I, I count myself the son of Chance,
        the great goddess, giver of all good things—
1190   I'll never see myself disgraced. She is my mother!
        And the moons have marked me out, my blood-brothers,
        one moon on the wane, the next moon great with power.
        That is my blood, my nature—I will never betray it,
        never fail to search and learn my birth!
1195 CHORUS: Yes—if I am a true prophet
            if I can grasp the truth,
            by the boundless skies of Olympus,
            at the full moon of tomorrow, Mount Cithaeron
            you will know how Oedipus glories in you—
1200   you, his birthplace, nurse, his mountain-mother!
        And we will sing you, dancing out your praise—
        you lift our monarch's heart!
            Apollo, Apollo, god of the wild cry
                may our dancing please you!
                                Oedipus—
1205   son, dear child, who bore you?
        Who of the nymphs who seem to live forever
        mated with Pan, the mountain-striding Father?
        Who was your mother? who, some bride of Apollo
        the god who loves the pastures spreading toward the sun?
1210   Or was it Hermes, king of the lightning ridges?
        Or Dionysus, lord of frenzy, lord of the barren peaks—
        did he seize you in his hands, dearest of all his lucky
            finds?—
            found by the nymphs, their warm eyes dancing, gift
        to the lord who loves them dancing out his joy!

(OEDIPUS *strains to see a figure coming from the distance. Attended by palace* GUARDS, *an old* SHEPHERD *enters slowly, reluctant to approach the king.*)

OEDIPUS: I never met the man, my friends . . . still,   1215
        if I had to guess, I'd say that's the shepherd,
        the very one we've looked for all along.
        Brothers in old age, two of a kind,
        he and our guest here. At any rate
        the ones who bring him in are my own men,   1220
        I recognize them.

(*Turning to the* LEADER.)

                But you know more than I,
        you should, you've seen the man before.
LEADER: I know him, definitely. One of Laius' men,
        a trusty shepherd, if there ever was one.
OEDIPUS: You, I ask you first, stranger,   1225
        you from Corinth—is this the one you mean?
MESSENGER: You're looking at him. He's your man.
OEDIPUS: (*To the* SHEPHERD.) You, old man, come over here—
        look at me. Answer all my questions.
        Did you ever serve King Laius?   1230
SHEPHERD: So I did . . .
        a slave, not bought on the block though,
        born and reared in the palace.
OEDIPUS: Your duties, your kind of work?
SHEPHERD: Herding the flocks, the better part of my life.
OEDIPUS: Where, mostly? Where did you do your grazing?   1235
SHEPHERD: Well,
        Cithaeron sometimes, or the foothills round about.
OEDIPUS: This man—you know him? ever see him there?
SHEPHERD: (*Confused, glancing from the* MESSENGER *to the king.*)
        Doing what? What man do you mean?
OEDIPUS: (*Pointing to the* MESSENGER.) This one here—ever
        have dealings with him?
SHEPHERD: Not so I could say, but give me a chance,   1240
        my memory's bad . . .
MESSENGER: No wonder he doesn't know me, master.
        But let me refresh his memory for him.
        I'm sure he recalls old times we had
        on the slopes of Mount Cithaeron;   1245
        he and I, grazing our flocks, he with two
        and I with one—we both struck up together,
        three whole seasons, six months at a stretch
        from spring to the rising of Arcturus in the fall,
        then with winter coming on I'd drive my herds   1250
        to my own pens, and back he'd go with his
        to Laius' folds.

(*To the* SHEPHERD.)

                Now that's how it was,
        wasn't it—yes or no?
SHEPHERD: Yes, I suppose . . .
        it's all so long ago.
MESSENGER: Come, tell me,
        you gave me a child back then, a boy, remember?   1255
        A little fellow to rear, my very own.
SHEPHERD: What? Why rake up that again?

MESSENGER: Look, here he is, my fine old friend—
    the same man who was just a baby then.
1260 SHEPHERD: Damn you, shut your mouth—quiet!
OEDIPUS: Don't lash out at him, old man—
    you need lashing more than he does.
SHEPHERD: Why,
    master, majesty—what have I done wrong?
OEDIPUS: You won't answer his question about the boy.
1265 SHEPHERD: He's talking nonsense, wasting his breath.
OEDIPUS: So, you won't talk willingly—
    then you'll talk with pain.

(The GUARDS seize the SHEPHERD.)

SHEPHERD: No, dear god, don't torture an old man!
OEDIPUS: Twist his arms back, quickly!
SHEPHERD: God help us, why?—
1270   what more do you need to know?
OEDIPUS: Did you give him that child? He's asking.
SHEPHERD: I did . . . I wish to god I'd died that day.
OEDIPUS: You've got your wish if you don't tell the truth.
SHEPHERD: The more I tell, the worse the death I'll die.
1275 OEDIPUS: Our friend here wants to stretch things out,
    does he?

(Motioning to his men for torture.)

SHEPHERD: No, no, I gave it to him—I just said so.
OEDIPUS: Where did you get it? Your house? Someone else's?
SHEPHERD: It wasn't mine, no, I got it from . . . someone.
OEDIPUS: Which one of them?

(Looking at the citizens.)

               Whose house?
SHEPHERD: No—
1280   god's sake, master, no more questions!
OEDIPUS: You're a dead man if I have to ask again.
SHEPHERD: Then—the child came from the house . . .
    of Laius.
OEDIPUS: A slave? or born of his own blood?
SHEPHERD: Oh no,
1285   I'm right at the edge, the horrible truth—I've got to say it!
OEDIPUS: And I'm at the edge of hearing horrors, yes, but I
    must hear!
SHEPHERD: All right! His son, they said it was—his son!
    But the one inside, your wife,
    she'd tell it best.
OEDIPUS: My wife—
1290   *she* gave it to you?
SHEPHERD: Yes, yes, my king.
OEDIPUS: Why, what for?
SHEPHERD: To kill it.
OEDIPUS: Her own child,
1295   how could she?
SHEPHERD: She was afraid—
    frightening prophecies.
OEDIPUS: What?
SHEPHERD: They said—
    he'd kill his parents.
1300 OEDIPUS: But you gave him to this old man—why?

SHEPHERD: I pitied the little baby, master,
    hoped he'd take him off to his own country,
    far away, but he saved him for this, this fate.
    If you are the man he says you are, believe me,
    you were born for pain.   1305
OEDIPUS: O god—
    all come true, all burst to light!
    O light—now let me look my last on you!
    I stand revealed at last—
    cursed in my birth, cursed in marriage,
    cursed in the lives I cut down with these hands!   1310

(Rushing through the doors with a great cry. The Corinthian MESSEN-
GER, the SHEPHERD, and ATTENDANTS exit slowly to the side.)

CHORUS: O the generations of men
    the dying generations—adding the total
    of all your lives I find they come to nothing . . .
           does there exist, is there a man on earth
    who seizes more joy than just a dream, a vision?   1315
    And the vision no sooner dawns than dies
    blazing into oblivion.

    You are my great example, you, your life
    your destiny, Oedipus, man of misery—
    I count no man blest.   1320

           You outranged all men!
      Bending your bow to the breaking-point
    you captured priceless glory, O dear god,
    and the Sphinx came crashing down,
           the virgin, claws hooked
    like a bird of omen singing, shrieking death—   1325
    like a fortress reared in the face of death
    you rose and saved our land.

    From that day on we called you king
    we crowned you with honors, Oedipus, towering over all—
    mighty king of the seven gates of Thebes.   1330
    But now to hear your story—is there a man more agonized?
    More wed to pain and frenzy? Not a man on earth,
    the joy of your life ground down to nothing
    O Oedipus, name for the ages—
        one and the same wide harbor served you   1335
              son and father both
    son and father came to rest in the same bridal chamber.
    How, how could the furrows your father plowed
    bear you, your agony, harrowing on
    in silence O so long?   1340

           But now for all your power
    Time, all-seeing Time has dragged you to the light,
    judged your marriage monstrous from the start—
    the son and the father tangling, both one—
    O child of Laius, would to god
        I'd never seen you, never never!   1345
      Now I weep like a man who wails the dead
    and the dirge comes pouring forth with all my heart!
    I tell you the truth, you gave me life
    my breath leapt up in you
    and now you bring down night upon my eyes.   1350

(Enter a MESSENGER from the palace.)

MESSENGER: Men of Thebes, always first in honor,
   what horrors you will hear, what you will see,
   what a heavy weight of sorrow you will shoulder . . .
   if you are true to your birth, if you still have
1355   some feeling for the royal house of Thebes.
   I tell you neither the waters of the Danube
   nor the Nile can wash this palace clean.
   Such things it hides, it soon will bring to light—
   terrible things, and none done blindly now,
1360   all done with a will. The pains
   we inflict upon ourselves hurt most of all.
LEADER: God knows we have pains enough already.
   What can you add to them?
MESSENGER: The queen is dead.
LEADER: Poor lady—how?
1365 MESSENGER: By her own hand. But you are spared the worst,
   you never had to watch . . . I saw it all,
   and with all the memory that's in me
   you will learn what that poor woman suffered.

   Once she'd broken in through the gates,
1370   dashing past us, frantic, whipped to fury,
   ripping her hair out with both hands—
   straight to her rooms she rushed, flinging herself
   across the bridal-bed, doors slamming behind her—
   once inside, she wailed for Laius, dead so long,
1375   remembering how she bore his child long ago,
   the life that rose up to destroy him, leaving
   its mother to mother living creatures
   with the very son she'd borne.
   Oh how she wept, mourning the marriage-bed
1380   where she let loose that double brood—monsters—
   husband by her husband, children by her child.
                                  And then—
   but how she died is more than I can say. Suddenly
   Oedipus burst in, screaming, he stunned us so
   we couldn't watch her agony to the end,
1385   our eyes were fixed on him. Circling
   like a maddened beast, stalking, here, there,
   crying out to us—
                  Give him a sword! His wife,
   no wife, his mother, where can he find the mother earth
   that cropped two crops at once, himself and all his
      children?
1390   He was raging—one of the dark powers pointing the way,
   none of us mortals crowding around him, no,
   with a great shattering cry—someone, something leading
      him on—
   he hurled at the twin doors and bending the bolts back
   out of their sockets, crashed through the chamber.
1395   And there we saw the woman hanging by the neck,
   cradled high in a woven noose, spinning,
   swinging back and forth. And when he saw her,
   giving a low, wrenching sob that broke our hearts,
   slipping the halter from her throat, he eased her down,
1400   in a slow embrace he laid her down, poor thing . . .
   then, what came next, what horror we beheld!

   He rips off her brooches, the long gold pins
   holding her robes—and lifting them high,
   looking straight up into the points,

he digs them down the sockets of his eyes, crying, "You,   1405
   you'll see no more the pain I suffered, all the pain I caused!
   Too long you looked on the ones you never should have seen,
   blind to the ones you longed to see, to know! Blind
   from this hour on! Blind in the darkness—blind!"
   His voice like a dirge, rising, over and over   1410
   raising the pins, raking them down his eyes.
   And at each stroke blood spurts from the roots,
   splashing his beard, a swirl of it, nerves and clots—
   black hail of blood pulsing, gushing down.

   These are the griefs that burst upon them both,   1415
   coupling man and woman. The joy they had so lately,
   the fortune of their old ancestral house
   was deep joy indeed. Now, in this one day,
   wailing, madness and doom, death, disgrace,
   all the griefs in the world that you can name,   1420
   all are theirs forever.
LEADER: Oh poor man, the misery—
   has he any rest from pain now?

(A voice within, in torment.)

MESSENGER: He's shouting,
   "Loose the bolts, someone, show me to all of Thebes!
   My father's murderer, my mother's—"
   No, I can't repeat it, it's unholy.   1425
   Now he'll tear himself from his native earth,
   not linger, curse the house with his own curse.
   But he needs strength, and a guide to lead him on.
   This is sickness more than he can bear.

(The palace doors open.)

                                  Look,
   he'll show you himself. The great doors are opening—   1430
   you are about to see a sight, a horror
   even his mortal enemy would pity.

(Enter OEDIPUS, blinded, led by a boy. He stands at the palace steps,
as if surveying his people once again.)

CHORUS: Oh, the terror—
   the suffering, for all the world to see,
   the worst terror that ever met my eyes.
   What madness swept over you? What god,   1435
   what dark power leapt beyond all bounds,
   beyond belief, to crush your wretched life?—
   godforsaken, cursed by the gods!
   I pity you but I can't bear to look.
   I've much to ask, so much to learn,   1440
   so much fascinates my eyes,
   but you . . . I shudder at the sight.
OEDIPUS: Oh, Ohh—
   the agony! I am agony—
   where am I going? where on earth?
         where does all this agony hurl me?   1445
   where's my voice?—
            winging, swept away on a dark tide—
   My destiny, my dark power, what a leap you made!
CHORUS: To the depths of terror, too dark to hear, to see.
OEDIPUS: Dark, horror of darkness   1450

my darkness, drowning, swirling around me
crashing wave on wave—unspeakable, irresistible
    headwind, fatal harbor! Oh again,
the misery, all at once, over and over
1455   the stabbing daggers, stab of memory
raking me insane.
CHORUS: No wonder you suffer
twice over, the pain of your wounds,
the lasting grief of pain.
OEDIPUS: Dear friend, still here?
Standing by me, still with a care for me,
1460   the blind man? Such compassion,
        loyal to the last. Oh it's you,
I know you're here, dark as it is
I'd know you anywhere, your voice—
it's yours, clearly yours.
CHORUS: Dreadful, what you've done . . .
1465 how could you bear it, gouging out your eyes?
What superhuman power drove you on?
OEDIPUS: Apollo, friends, Apollo—
he ordained my agonies—these, my pains on pains!
But the hand that struck my eyes was mine,
1470   mine alone—no one else—
        I did it all myself!
What good were eyes to me?
Nothing I could see could bring me joy.
CHORUS: No, no, exactly as you say.
OEDIPUS: What can I ever see?
1475   What love, what call of the heart
can touch my ears with joy? Nothing, friends.
Take me away, far, far from Thebes,
    quickly, cast me away, my friends—
this great murderous ruin, this man cursed to heaven,
1480   the man the deathless gods hate most of all!
CHORUS: Pitiful, you suffer so, you understand so much . . .
I wish you had never known.
OEDIPUS: Die, die—
whoever he was that day in the wilds
who cut my ankles free of the ruthless pins,
1485 he pulled me clear of death, he saved my life
for this, this kindness—
        Curse him, kill him!
If I'd died then, I'd never have dragged myself,
my loved ones through such hell.
CHORUS: Oh if only . . . would to god.
1490 OEDIPUS: I'd never have come to
  this,
    my father's murderer—never been branded
mother's husband, all men see me now! Now,
    loathed by the gods, son of the mother I defiled
    coupling in my father's bed, spawning lives in the loins
1495 that spawned my wretched life. What grief can crown this
  grief?
        It's mine alone, my destiny—I am Oedipus!
CHORUS: How can I say you've chosen for the best?
Better to die than be alive and blind.
OEDIPUS: What I did was best—don't lecture me,
1500 no more advice. I, with *my* eyes,
how could I look my father in the eyes
when I go down to death? Or mother, so abused . . .

I have done such things to the two of them,
crimes too huge for hanging.
        Worse yet,
the sight of my children, born as they were born,   1505
how could I long to look into their eyes?
No, not with these eyes of mine, never.
Not this city either, her high towers,
the sacred glittering images of her gods—
I am misery! I, her best son, reared   1510
as no other son of Thebes was ever reared,
I've stripped myself, I gave the command myself.
All men must cast away the great blasphemer,
the curse now brought to light by the gods,
the son of Laius—I, my father's son!   1515

Now I've exposed my guilt, horrendous guilt,
could I train a level glance on you, my countrymen?
Impossible! No, if I could just block off my ears,
the springs of hearing, I would stop at nothing—
I'd wall up my loathsome body like a prison,   1520
blind to the sound of life, not just the sight.
Oblivion—what a blessing . . .
for the mind to dwell a world away from pain.

O Cithaeron, why did you give me shelter?
Why didn't you take me, crush my life out on the spot?   1525
I'd never have revealed my birth to all mankind.

O Polybus, Corinth, the old house of my fathers,
so I believed—what a handsome prince you raised—
under the skin, what sickness to the core.
Look at me! Born of outrage, outrage to the core.   1530
O triple roads—it all comes back, the secret,
dark ravine, and the oaks closing in
where the three roads join . . .
You drank my father's blood, my own blood
spilled by my own hands—you still remember me?   1535
What things you saw me do? Then I came here
and did them all once more!
        Marriages! O marriage,
you gave me birth, and once you brought me into the
  world
you brought my sperm rising back, springing to light,
fathers, brothers, sons—one murderous breed—   1540
brides, wives, mothers. The blackest things
a man can do, I have done them all!
        No more—
it's wrong to name what's wrong to do. Quickly,
for the love of god, hide me somewhere,
kill me, hurl me into the sea   1545
where you can never look on me again.

(*Beckoning to the* CHORUS *as they shrink away.*)

        Closer,
it's all right. Touch the man of grief.
Do. Don't be afraid. My troubles are mine
and I am the only man alive who can sustain them.

(*Enter* CREON *from the palace, attended by palace* GUARDS.)

LEADER: Put your requests to Creon. Here he is,   1550
just when we need him. He'll have a plan, he'll act.

Now that he's the sole defense of the country
in your place.
OEDIPUS: Oh no, what can I say to him?
How can I ever hope to win his trust?
1555 I wronged him so, just now, in every way.
You must see that—I was so wrong, so wrong.
CREON: I haven't come to mock you, Oedipus,
or to criticize your former failings.

(*Turning to the* GUARDS.)

                                    You there,
have you lost all respect for human feelings?
1560 At least revere the Sun, the holy fire
that keeps us all alive. Never expose a thing
of guilt and holy dread so great it appalls
the earth, the rain from heaven, the light of day!
Get him into the halls—quickly as you can.
1565 Piety demands no less. Kindred alone
should see a kinsman's shame. This is obscene.
OEDIPUS: Please, in god's name . . . you wipe my fears away,
coming so generously to me, the worst of men.
Do one thing more, for your sake, not mine.
1570 CREON: What do you want? Why so insistent?
OEDIPUS: Drive me out of the land at once, far from sight,
where I can never hear a human voice.
CREON: I'd have done that already, I promise you.
First I wanted the god to clarify my duties.
1575 OEDIPUS: The god? His command was clear, every word:
death for the father-killer, the curse—
he said destroy me!
CREON: So he did. Still. In such a crisis
it's better to ask precisely what to do.
OEDIPUS: So miserable—
1580 you would consult the god about a man like me?
CREON: By all means. And this time, I assume,
even you will obey the god's decrees.
OEDIPUS: I will,
I will. And you, I command you—I beg you . . .
the woman inside, bury her as you see fit.
1585 It's the only decent thing,
to give your own the last rites. As for me,
never condemn the city of my fathers
to house my body, not while I'm alive, no,
let me live on the mountains, on Cithaeron,
1590 my favorite haunt, I have made it famous.
Mother and father marked out that rock
to be my everlasting tomb—buried alive.
Let me die there, where they tried to kill me.

Oh but this I know: no sickness can destroy me,
1595 nothing can. I would never have been saved
from death—I have been saved
for something great and terrible, something strange.
Well let my destiny come and take me on its way!
About my children, Creon, the boys at least,
1600 don't burden yourself. They're men,
wherever they go, they'll find the means to live.
But my two daughters, my poor helpless girls,
clustering at our table, never without me
hovering near them . . . whatever I touched,

they always had their share. Take care of them,   1605
I beg you. Wait, better—permit me, would you?
Just to touch them with my hands and take
our fill of tears. Please . . . my king.
Grant it, with all your noble heart.
If I could hold them, just once, I'd think   1610
I had them with me, like the early days
when I could see their eyes.

(ANTIGONE *and* ISMENE, *two small children, are led in from the
palace by a nurse.*)

                                    What's that?
O god! Do I really hear you sobbing?—
my two children. Creon, you've pitied me?
Sent me my darling girls, my own flesh and blood!   1615
Am I right?
CREON: Yes, it's my doing.
I know the joy they gave you all these years,
the joy you must feel now.
OEDIPUS: Bless you, Creon!
May god watch over you for this kindness,
better than he ever guarded me.   1620
                                    Children, where are you?
Here, come quickly—

(*Groping for* ANTIGONE *and* ISMENE, *who approach their father cautiously, then embrace him.*)

                                    Come to these hands of mine,
your brother's hands, your own father's hands
that served his once bright eyes so well—
that made them blind. Seeing nothing, children,
knowing nothing, I became your father,   1625
I fathered you in the soil that gave me life.

How I weep for you—I cannot see you now . . .
just thinking of all your days to come, the bitterness,
the life that rough mankind will thrust upon you.
Where are the public gatherings you can join,   1630
the banquets of the clans? Home you'll come,
in tears, cut off from the sight of it all,
the brilliant rites unfinished.
And when you reach perfection, ripe for marriage,
who will he be, my dear ones? Risking all   1635
to shoulder the curse that weighs down my parents,
yes and you too—that wounds us all together.
What more misery could you want?
Your father killed his father, sowed his mother,
one, one and the selfsame womb sprang you—   1640
he cropped the very roots of his existence.

Such disgrace, and you must bear it all!
Who will marry you then? Not a man on earth.
Your doom is clear: you'll wither away to nothing,
single, without a child.   1645

(*Turning to* CREON.)

                                    Oh Creon,
you are the only father they have now . . .
we who brought them into the world
are gone, both gone at a stroke—

1650 Don't let them go begging, abandoned,
women without men. Your own flesh and blood!
Never bring them down to the level of my pains.
Pity them. Look at them, so young, so vulnerable,
shorn of everything—you're their only hope.
Promise me, noble Creon, touch my hand!

(*Reaching toward* CREON, *who draws back.*)

1655 You, little ones, if you were old enough
to understand, there is much I'd tell you.
Now, as it is, I'd have you say a prayer.
Pray for life, my children,
live where you are free to grow and season.
1660 Pray god you find a better life than mine,
the father who begot you.
CREON: Enough.
You've wept enough. Into the palace now.
OEDIPUS: I must, but I find it very hard.
CREON: Time is the great healer, you will see.
1665 OEDIPUS: I am going—you know on what condition?
CREON: Tell me. I'm listening.
OEDIPUS: Drive me out of Thebes, in exile.
CREON: Not I. Only the gods can give you that.
OEDIPUS: Surely the gods hate me so much—
1670 CREON: You'll get your wish at once.

OEDIPUS: You consent?
CREON: I try to say what I mean; it's my habit.
OEDIPUS: Then take me away. It's time.
CREON: Come along, let go of the children.
OEDIPUS: No—
don't take them away from me, not now! No no no!

(*Clutching his daughters as the* GUARDS *wrench them loose and take them through the palace doors.*)

CREON: Still the king, the master of all things?   1675
No more: here your power ends.
None of your power follows you through life.

(*Exit* OEDIPUS *and* CREON *to the palace. The* CHORUS *comes forward to address the audience directly.*)

CHORUS: People of Thebes, my countrymen, look on Oedipus.
He solved the famous riddle with his brilliance,
he rose to power, a man beyond all power.   1680
Who could behold his greatness without envy?
Now what a black sea of terror has overwhelmed him.
Now as we keep our watch and wait the final day,
count no man happy till he dies, free of pain at last.

(*Exit in procession.*)

Euripides

Euripides (c. 484–406 BCE) was the youngest of the three tragic playwrights whose plays remain today. Although he first competed in the City Dionysia in 455 BCE and won his first victory in 441 BCE, Euripides won only four victories in his lifetime and left Athens about 408 BCE for the court of King Archileus of Macedon, where he died. We do not know why Euripides won so infrequently, but his tragedies are much more bitter and ironic than those of Aeschylus or Sophocles, brilliantly unfolding the selfish capriciousness of gods and heroes alike. Of the roughly ninety plays Euripides is thought to have written, eighteen survive, and most of these were written and produced during the war with Sparta: *Alcestis, Medea, Heracleidae, Hippolytus, Cyclops* (a satyr play), *Heracles, Iphigeneia in Tauris, Helen, Hecuba, Andromache, The Trojan Women, Ion, The Suppliant Women, Orestes, Electra, The Phoenician Women.* Three additional plays—*Iphigeneia at Aulis, The Bacchae,* and *Alcmaeon at Corinth* (now lost)—were written in Macedon and brought to Athens by the playwright's son, Euripides the Younger. This trilogy, produced after Euripides' death, won him his final prize at the City Dionysia.

Although many Greek tragedies center on female characters—think of Clytaemnestra in Aeschylus' *Agamemnon,* for example, or Sophocles' *Antigone*—Euripides was famous in Athens for centering his tragedies so frequently on women. Euripides was hardly a feminist in any modern sense, yet more than his contemporaries, he used his tragic heroines to explore the relationship between gender and the other conceptual, political, social, and esthetic categories organizing Athenian life.

As in all roles in the Athenian theater, the role of Medea was played by a male actor; nonetheless, in many ways *Medea* illustrates Euripides' skeptical and ironic regard for conventional attitudes and his tendency toward a more sensational form of tragic action. Like Shakespeare's *Hamlet, Medea* is a tragedy of revenge, in which Medea poisons her husband Jason's newly married wife and her father, Creon, and in the play's climactic moment executes

MEDEA

In this modernized production of Euripides' *Medea* by the Abbey Theatre of Dublin, Fiona Shaw's Medea enacts the slaughter of the children behind an illuminated Plexiglas screen.

her own children from her marriage with Jason. What sometimes seems most monstrous to modern readers and audiences is that Medea herself—in one of Euripides' most striking uses of the *machina*—flees Corinth alive at the end of the play, rising above the *skene* in a dragon-drawn chariot, draped in the bodies of her dead children, taunting and reviling the impotent Jason. That is, modern audiences sometimes feel that Medea herself should die at the play's close if *Medea* is to be a truly tragic drama, as though by dying Medea would be "punished" for her revenge in some appalling vision of tragic "justice." But Euripides seems uninterested in such a moralized version of tragedy. Indeed, as Aristotle implies in *The Poetics,* tragedy is a deeply dialectical, contradictory way of representing human experience: tragedy arises from the unresolvable tension between pity and fear, from the relationship between the hero's actions (remembering that the tragic hero is neither a paragon of virtue nor inherently wicked) and their terrible, somehow fitting consequences. Although Aristotle praises Sophocles' *Oedipus the King* as the best-constructed tragedy, he also remarks that Euripides "is felt by the audience to be the most tragic, at least, of the poets." To grasp Euripides' sense of tragedy means placing Medea's execution of the children within the context of the action as a whole—an act that brings her history to bear in one exacting deed; an act like Agamemnon's treading on the carpet or Oedipus' blistering interrogation of the ancient shepherd.

At the play's opening, Medea is an outcast, a foreign exile in Corinth, and the play repeatedly stresses Medea's otherness—she is an Eastern exotic, she has little respect for Greek culture and its institutions, and she is a sorceress as well. Medea is consistently shown to be a figure of willful passion, brought into exile through her love for Jason. Falling in love with Jason when he went to Colchis in search of the Golden Fleece, Medea used her sorcery to help Jason gain the Fleece, betraying her father and killing her brother in the bargain. When the play opens, Jason has returned to Greece with Medea and their children; in Corinth, however, Jason decides to marry the daughter of King Creon. Creon, no doubt recognizing that Medea and her children will pose a constant threat to his own line of succession, has ruled that Medea and her children must again be sent into exile.

Yet as Medea suggests to the Chorus, the indignity that Jason has thrust upon her—being doubly exiled, from her country and from her marriage—is in an important sense merely an extension of the state of all women in Greek culture. For once women "Buy a husband and take for our bodies / A master," they are exiled from their own homes, and from the mastery of their own lives. Inasmuch as women are represented as creatures of passion, they are "exiled" as well from the organizing principles of the Greek state: Reason, the law, and legitimate society are identified in the play as the preserve of men. Euripides makes Jason the spokesman for these values. When Jason first confronts Medea, he takes pride in his talents as a speaker, listing his arguments in support of taking a new wife almost as though he were arguing in the courtroom or conducting a philosophical demonstration. But while Oedipus, for instance, uses the strategies of philosophic inquiry to discover the truth, Jason's arguments seem to conceal the truth—he is betraying Medea and their children, after all—behind a smokescreen of sophistic rhetoric. Having brought Medea into exile, Jason argues that she is fortunate merely to "inhabit a Greek land and understand our ways / How to live by law instead of the sweet will of force." Yet the law that Jason praises seems designed to enable him to act out his own "sweet will"—taking a second wife—while it prevents Medea from acting on hers. The more Jason insists that he is acting reasonably, the more unreasonable his arguments become; he grows increasingly irritable, and finally insulting: "You women have got into such a state of mind / That, if your life at night is good, you think you have / Everything." Euripides' treatment of Jason is typical of his tendency to present an ironic view of the heroes of Greek mythology. Here, in making Jason the representative of Greek values—reason, law, justice—Euripides suggests the limits of those values. For the Chorus clearly sees Jason's "reason" as a self-indulgent pretense: "Though you have made this speech of yours look well, / . . . / You have betrayed your wife and are acting badly."

As Medea comes to recognize, both Jason and the masculine laws of Corinth are willing to betray her, to call her fidelity and love merely irrational, to force her again into exile. Having poisoned Creon and his daughter, Medea first claims to kill the children in order that they not be slain "by another hand less kindly to them." But it is also clear that in killing the children, Medea revenges herself on Jason in the only way open to her; he has little regard for her love for him, but the children are his property, an extension of himself, of his identity. What is more important, the children are his successors, representing his continued presence in the world. For as Jason laments, Medea has contrived a punishment for him that no Greek woman would have dared: In leaving him childless, Medea transforms Jason into an exile like herself, prophesying that he will die "without distinction."

Medea's acts epitomize the ethical ambiguity that drives Greek tragedy. Agamemnon strides on the blood-red carpet, magisterially desecrating the honor of his family as he had once done in sacrificing Iphigeneia; Oedipus sentences the hidden criminal to exile, only to discover that he is the criminal he seeks. To force Jason into a childless exile, Medea commits the kind of crime that Jason has repeatedly drawn her to enact: She murders what she loves in order to insist on the priority and power of her love for him. As in other classical tragedies, the hero chooses to act in a way that is not only consistent with her past, but a self-conscious reenactment of it. The *peripeteia,* the reversal that defines the tragic action, seems in many ways to be a kind of restoration as well, revealing destructive consequences that have been latent in the action from the beginning.

It should be clear that while Euripides interrogates the relationship between reason and passion, culture and nature, the rational and the irrational, science and magic, *Medea* does not finally disrupt or overturn this relationship. Nor does the play finally question the way that Greek culture gendered these categories as masculine and feminine, expressing the conceptual and political hierarchies of its own making as the "natural" outgrowth of some essential gender difference. Euripides exposes the destructive tension lurking in Greek conceptions of gender, power, and identity, but the language of tragedy is not the language of revolution, because although tragedy frequently exposes the values of its world as contradictory and destructive, it also accepts those values as somehow inevitable, unavoidable. Medea flees Corinth and the abusive Jason, but only by destroying herself in the same way she destroys Jason; Medea triumphs over Jason, but only by destroying her family and becoming an exile yet again. The only alternative that *Medea* offers to the way that Medea— and, she argues, all women—is positioned as an outsider, an "exile" to the governing categories of Greek life, is a deeper, more permanent isolation.

MEDEA

Euripides

TRANSLATED BY REX WARNER

CHARACTERS

MEDEA, *princess of Colchis and wife of*
JASON, *son of Aeson, king of Iolcus*
TWO CHILDREN *of Medea and Jason*
CREON, *king of Corinth*

AEGEUS, *king of Athens*
NURSE *to Medea*
TUTOR *to Medea's children*
MESSENGER
CHORUS *of Corinthian women*
ATTENDANTS

SCENE: *In front of* MEDEA'*s house in Corinth.*

Enter from the house Medea's NURSE.

NURSE: How I wish the Argo never had reached the land
Of Colchis, skimming through the blue Symplegades,
Nor ever had fallen in the glades of Pelion
The smitten fir-tree to furnish oars for the hands
5 Of heroes who in Pelias' name attempted
The Golden Fleece! For then my mistress Medea
Would not have sailed for the towers of the land of Iolcus,
Her heart on fire with passionate love for Jason;
Nor would she have persuaded the daughters of Pelias
10 To kill their father, and now be living here
In Corinth with her husband and children. She gave
Pleasure to the people of her land of exile,
And she herself helped Jason in every way.
This is indeed the greatest salvation of all—
15 For the wife not to stand apart from the husband.
But now there's hatred everywhere, Love is diseased.
For, deserting his own children and my mistress,
Jason has taken a royal wife to his bed,
The daughter of the ruler of this land, Creon.
20 And poor Medea is slighted, and cries aloud on the
Vows they made to each other, the right hands clasped
In eternal promise. She calls upon the gods to witness
What sort of return Jason has made to her love.
She lies without food and gives herself up to suffering,
25 Wasting away every moment of the day in tears.
So it has gone since she knew herself slighted by him.
Not stirring an eye, not moving her face from the ground,
No more than either a rock or surging sea water
She listens when she is given friendly advice.
30 Except that sometimes she twists back her white neck and
Moans to herself, calling out on her father's name,
And her land, and her home betrayed when she came away
with
A man who now is determined to dishonor her.
Poor creature, she has discovered by her sufferings
35 What it means to one not to have lost one's own country.

----

1 **Argo** Jason's ship on the expedition of the Argonauts, sent by
Pelias, king of Iolcus in Thessaly (Jason's uncle, who had usurped
the throne), to Colchis on the Black Sea. The Symplegades were
clashing rocks, one of the obstacles along the way. Pelion is a
mountain in Thessaly. Medea was a princess of Colchis who fell
in love with Jason and followed him back to Greece

She has turned from the children and does not like to see
them.
I am afraid she may think of some dreadful thing,
For her heart is violent. She will never put up with
The treatment she is getting. I know and fear her
Lest she may sharpen a sword and thrust to the heart,   40
Stealing into the palace where the bed is made,
Or even kill the king and the new-wedded groom,
And thus bring a greater misfortune on herself.
She's a strange woman. I know it won't be easy
To make an enemy of her and come off best.   45
But here the children come. They have finished playing.
They have no thought at all of their mother's trouble.
Indeed it is not usual for the young to grieve.

(Enter from the right the slave who is the TUTOR *to Medea's two small children. The* CHILDREN *follow him.)*

TUTOR: You old retainer of my mistress' household,
Why are you standing here all alone in front of the   50
Gates and moaning to yourself over your misfortune?
Medea could not wish you to leave her alone.
NURSE: Old man, and guardian of the children of Jason,
If one is a good servant, it's a terrible thing
When one's master's luck is out; it goes to one's heart.   55
So I myself have got into such a state of grief
That a longing stole over me to come outside here
And tell the earth and air of my mistress' sorrows.
TUTOR: Has the poor lady not yet given up her crying?
NURSE: Given up? She's at the start, not halfway through her   60
tears.
TUTOR: Poor fool—if I may call my mistress such a name—
How ignorant she is of trouble more to come.
NURSE: What do you mean, old man? You needn't fear to
speak.
TUTOR: Nothing. I take back the words which I used just now.
NURSE: Don't, by your beard, hide this from me, your   65
fellow-servant.
If need be, I'll keep quiet about what you tell me.
TUTOR: I heard a person saying, while I myself seemed
Not to be paying attention, when I was at the place
Where the old draught-players sit, by the holy fountain,
That Creon, ruler of the land, intends to drive   70
These children and their mother in exile from Corinth.
But whether what he said is really true or not
I do not know. I pray that it may not be true.

NURSE: And will Jason put up with it that his children
75   Should suffer so, though he's no friend to their mother?
TUTOR: Old ties give place to new ones. As for Jason, he
    No longer has a feeling for this house of ours.
NURSE: It's black indeed for us, when we add new to old
    Sorrows before even the present sky has cleared.
80 TUTOR: But you be silent, and keep all this to yourself.
    It is not the right time to tell our mistress of it.
NURSE: Do you hear, children, what a father he is to you?
    I wish he were dead—but no, he is still my master.
    Yet certainly he has proved unkind to his dear ones.
85 TUTOR: What's strange in that? Have you only just discovered
    That everyone loves himself more than his neighbor?
    Some have good reason, others get something out of it.
    So Jason neglects his children for the new bride.
NURSE: Go indoors, children. That will be the best thing.
90   And you, keep them to themselves as much as possible.
    Don't bring them near their mother in her angry mood.
    For I've seen her already blazing her eyes at them
    As though she meant some mischief and I am sure that
    She'll not stop raging until she has struck at someone.
95   May it be an enemy and not a friend she hurts!

(MEDEA *is heard inside the house.*)

MEDIA: Ah, wretch! Ah, lost in my sufferings,
    I wish, I wish I might die.
NURSE: What did I say, dear children? Your mother
    Frets her heart and frets it to anger.
100   Run away quickly into the house.
    And keep well out of her sight.
    Don't go anywhere near, but be careful
    Of the wildness and bitter nature
    Of that proud mind.
105   Go now! Run quickly indoors.
    It is clear that she soon will put lightning
    In that cloud of her cries that is rising
    With a passion increasing. O, what will she do,
    Proud-hearted and not to be checked on her course,
110   A soul bitten into with wrong?

(*The* TUTOR *takes the* CHILDREN *into the house.*)

MEDEA: Ah, I have suffered
    What should be wept for bitterly. I hate you,
    Children of a hateful mother. I curse you
    And your father. Let the whole house crash.
115 NURSE: Ah, I pity you, you poor creature.
    How can your children share in their father's
    Wickedness? Why do you hate them? Oh children,
    How much I fear that something may happen!
    Great people's tempers are terrible, always
120   Having their own way, seldom checked.
    Dangerous they shift from mood to mood.
    How much better to have been accustomed
    To live on equal terms with one's neighbors.
    I would like to be safe and grow old in a
125   Humble way. What is moderate sounds best,
    Also in practice is best for everyone.
    Greatness brings no profit to people.
    God indeed, when in anger, brings
    Greater ruin to great men's houses.

(*Enter, on the right, a* CHORUS *of Corinthian women. They have come
to inquire about* MEDEA *and to attempt to console her.*)

CHORUS: I heard the voice, I heard the cry   130
    Of Colchis' wretched daughter.
    Tell me, mother, is she not yet
    At rest? Within the double gates
    Of the court I heard her cry. I am sorry
    For the sorrow of this home. O, say, what has happened?   135
NURSE: There is no home. It's over and done with.
    Her husband holds fast to his royal wedding,
    While she, my mistress, cries out her eyes
    There in her room, and takes no warmth from
    Any word of any friend.   140
MEDEA: O, I wish
    That lightning from heaven would split my head open.
    Oh, what use have I now for life?
    I would find my release in death
    And leave hateful existence behind me.   145
CHORUS: O God and Earth and Heaven!
    Did you hear what a cry was that
    Which the sad wife sings?
    Poor foolish one, why should you long.
    For that appalling rest?   150
    The final end of death comes fast.
    No need to pray for that.
    Suppose your man gives honor
    To another woman's bed.
    It often happens. Don't be hurt.   155
    God will be your friend in this.
    You must not waste away
    Grieving too much for him who shared your bed.
MEDEA: Great Themis, lady Artemis, behold
    The things I suffer, though I made him promise,   160
    My hateful husband. I pray that I may see him,
    Him and his bride and all their palace shattered
    For the wrong they dare to do me without cause.
    Oh, my father! Oh, my country! In what dishonor
    I left you, killing my own brother for it.   165
NURSE: Do you hear what she says, and how she cries
    On Themis, the goddess of Promises, and on Zeus,
    Whom we believe to be the Keeper of Oaths?
    Of this I am sure, that no small thing
    Will appease my mistress' anger.   170
CHORUS: Will she come into our presence?
    Will she listen when we are speaking
    To the words we say?
    I wish she might relax her rage
    And temper of her heart.   175
    My willingness to help will never
    Be wanting to my friends.
    But go inside and bring her
    Out of the house to us,
    And speak kindly to her: hurry,   180
    Before she wrongs her own.
    This passion of hers moves to something great.

---

159 **Themis . . . Artemis** goddesses: Themis was the goddess of
justice; the virgin Artemis would be sensitive to the plight of
women   165 **brother** during the escape from Colchis, to delay
her father's pursuit

NURSE: I will, but I doubt if I'll manage
　　To win my mistress over.
185　But still I'll attempt it to please you.
　　Such a look she will flash on her servants
　　If any comes near with a message.
　　Like a lioness guarding her cubs,
　　It is right, I think, to consider
190　Both stupid and lacking in foresight
　　Those poets of old who wrote songs
　　For revels and dinners and banquets,
　　Pleasant sounds for men living at ease;
　　But none of them all has discovered
195　How to put to an end with their singing
　　Or musical instruments grief,
　　Bitter grief, from which death and disaster
　　Cheat the hopes of a house. Yet how good
　　If music could cure men of this! But why raise
200　To no purpose the voice at a banquet? For *there* is
　　Already abundance of pleasure for men
　　With a joy of its own.

(*The* NURSE *goes into the house.*)

CHORUS: I heard a shriek that is laden with sorrow,
　　Shrilling out her hard grief she cries out
205　Upon him who betrayed both her bed and her marriage.
　　Wronged, she calls on the gods,
　　On the justice of Zeus, the oath sworn,
　　Which brought her away
　　To the opposite shore of the Greeks
210　Through the gloomy salt straits to the gateway
　　Of the salty unlimited sea.

(MEDEA, *attended by servants, comes out of the house.*)

MEDEA: Women of Corinth, I have come outside to you
　　Lest you should be indignant with me; for I know
　　That many people are overproud, some when alone,
215　And others when in company. And those who live
　　Quietly, as I do, get a bad reputation.
　　For a just judgment is not evident in the eyes
　　When a man at first sight hates another, before
　　Learning his character, being in no way injured;
220　And a foreigner especially must adapt himself.
　　I'd not approve of even a fellow-countryman
　　Who by pride and want of manners offends his neighbors.
　　But on me this thing has fallen so unexpectedly.
　　It has broken my heart. I am finished. I let go
225　All my life's joy. My friends, I only want to die.
　　It was everything to me to think well of one man,
　　And he, my own husband, has turned out wholly vile.
　　Of all things which are living and can form a judgment
　　We women are the most unfortunate creatures.
230　Firstly, with an excess of wealth it is required
　　For us to buy a husband and take for our bodies
　　A master; for not to take one is even worse.
　　And now the question is serious whether we take
　　A good or bad one; for there is no easy escape
235　For a woman, nor can she say no to her marriage.
　　She arrives among new modes of behavior and manners.
　　And needs prophetic power, unless she has learned at home,
　　How best to manage him who shares the bed with her.

And if we work out all this well and carefully.
And the husband lives with us and lightly bears his yoke.　240
Then life is enviable. If not, I'd rather die.
A man, when he's tired of the company in his home,
Goes out of the house and puts an end to his boredom
And turns to a friend or companion of his own age.
But we are forced to keep our eyes on one alone.　245
What they say of us is that we have a peaceful time
Living at home, while they do the fighting in war.
How wrong they are! I would very much rather stand
Three times in the front of battle than bear one child.
Yet what applies to me does not apply to you.　250
You have a country. Your family home is here.
You enjoy life and the company of your friends.
But I am deserted, a refugee, thought nothing of
By my husband—something he won in a foreign land.
I have no mother or brother, nor any relation　255
With whom I can take refuge in this sea of woe.
This much then is the service I would beg from you:
If I can find the means or devise any scheme
To pay my husband back for what he has done to me—
Him and his father-in-law and the girl who married him—　260
Just to keep silent. For in other ways a woman
Is full of fear, defenseless, dreads the sight of cold
Steel; but, when once she is wronged in the matter of love,
No other soul can hold so many thoughts of blood.
CHORUS: This I will promise. You are in the right, Medea,　265
　　In paying your husband back. I am not surprised at you
　　For being sad.
　　　　　　　　　But look! I see our King Creon
　　Approaching. He will tell us of some new plan.

(*Enter, from the right,* CREON, *with attendants.*)

CREON: You, with that angry look, so set against your husband.
　　Medea, I order you to leave my territories　270
　　An exile, and take along with you your two children,
　　And not to waste time doing it. It is my decree,
　　And I will see it done. I will not return home
　　Until you are cast from the boundaries of my land.
MEDEA: Oh, this is the end for me. I am utterly lost.　275
　　Now I am in the full force of the storm of hate
　　And have no harbor from ruin to reach easily.
　　Yet still, in spite of it all, I'll ask the question:
　　What is your reason, Creon, for banishing me?
CREON: I am afraid of you—why should I dissemble it?—　280
　　Afraid that you may injure my daughter mortally.
　　Many things accumulate to support my feeling.
　　You are a clever woman, versed in evil arts.
　　And are angry at having lost your husband's love.
　　I hear that you are threatening, so they tell me,　285
　　To do something against my daughter and Jason
　　And me, too. I shall take my precautions first.
　　I tell you, I prefer to earn your hatred now
　　Than to be soft-hearted and afterward regret it.
MEDEA: This is not the first time, Creon. Often previously　290
　　Through being considered clever I have suffered much.
　　A person of sense ought never to have his children
　　Brought up to be more clever than the average.
　　For, apart from cleverness bringing them no profit,
　　It will make them objects of envy and ill-will.　295
　　If you put new ideas before the eyes of fools

They'll think you foolish and worthless into the bargain;
And if you are thought superior to those who have
Some reputation for learning, you will become hated.
300 I have some knowledge myself of how this happens;
For being clever, I find that some will envy me,
Others object to me. Yet all my cleverness
Is not so much.
              Well, then, are you frightened, Creon,
That I should harm you? There is no need. It is not
305 My way to transgress the authority of a king.
How have you injured me? You gave your daughter away
To the man you wanted. Oh, certainly I hate
My husband, but you, I think, have acted wisely;
Nor do I grudge it you that your affairs go well.
310 May the marriage be a lucky one! Only let me
Live in this land. For even though I have been wronged,
I will not raise my voice, but submit to my betters.
CREON: What you say sounds gentle enough. Still in my heart
I greatly dread that you are plotting some evil,
315 And therefore I trust you even less than before.
A sharp-tempered woman, or, for that matter, a man,
Is easier to deal with than the clever type
Who holds her tongue. No. You must go. No need for more
Speeches. The thing is fixed. By no manner of means
320 Shall you, an enemy of mine, stay in my country.
MEDEA: I beg you. By your knees, by your new-wedded girl.
CREON: Your words are wasted. You will never persuade me.
MEDEA: Will you drive me out, and give no heed to my prayers?
CREON: I will, for I love my family more than you.
325 MEDEA: O my country! How bitterly now I remember you!
CREON: I love my country too—next after my children.
MEDEA: O what an evil to men is passionate love!
CREON: That would depend on the luck that goes along with it.
MEDEA: O God, do not forget who is the cause of this!
330 CREON: Go. It is no use. Spare me the pain of forcing you.
MEDEA: I'm spared no pain. I lack no pain to be spared me.
CREON: Then you'll be removed by force by one of my men.
MEDEA: No. Creon, not that! But do listen, I beg you.
CREON: Woman, you seem to want to create a disturbance.
335 MEDEA: I *will* go into exile. *This* is not what I beg for.
CREON: Why then this violence and clinging to my hand?
MEDEA: Allow me to remain here just for this one day,
So I may consider where to live in my exile.
And look for support for my children, since their father
340 Chooses to make no kind of provision for them.
Have pity on them! You have children of your own.
It is natural for you to look kindly on them.
For myself I do not mind if I go into exile.
It is the children being in trouble that I mind.
345 CREON: There is nothing tyrannical about my nature,
And by showing mercy I have often been the loser.
Even now I know that I am making a mistake.
All the same you shall have your will. But this I tell you,
That if the light of heaven tomorrow shall see you,
350 You and your children in the confines of my land,
You die. This word I have spoken is firmly fixed.
But now, if you must stay, stay for this day alone.
For in it you can do none of the things I fear.

(*Exit* CREON, *with his attendants.*)

CHORUS: Oh, unfortunate one! Oh, cruel!
Where will you turn? Who will help you?   355
What house or what land to preserve you
From ill can you find?
Medea, a god has thrown suffering
Upon you in waves of despair.
MEDEA: Things have gone badly every way. No doubt of that 360
But not these things this far, and don't imagine so.
There are still trials to come for the new-wedded pair,
And for their relations pain that will mean something.
Do you think that I would ever have fawned on that man
Unless I had some end to gain or profit in it?   365
I would not even have spoken or touched him with my hands.
But he has got to such a pitch of foolishness
That, though he could have made nothing of all my plans
By exiling me, he has given me this one day
To stay here, and in this I will make dead bodies   370
Of three of my enemies—father, the girl, and my husband.
I have many ways of death which I might suit to them,
And do not know, friends, which one to take in hand;
Whether to set fire underneath their bridal mansion,
Or sharpen a sword and thrust it to the heart,   375
Stealing into the palace where the bed is made.
There is just one obstacle to this. If I am caught
Breaking into the house and scheming against it,
I shall die, and give my enemies cause for laughter.
It is best to go by the straight road, the one in which 380
I am most skilled, and make away with them by poison.
So be it then.
And now suppose them dead. What town will receive me?
What friend will offer me a refuge in his land,
Or the guaranty of his house and save my own life? 385
There is none. So I must wait a little time yet,
And if some sure defense should then appear for me,
In craft and silence I will set about this murder.
But if my fate should drive me on without help,
Even though death is certain, I will take the sword 390
Myself and kill, and steadfastly advance to crime.
It shall not be—I swear it by her, my mistress,
Whom most I honor and have chosen as partner,
Hecate, who dwells in the recesses of my hearth—
That any man shall be glad to have injured me.   395
Bitter I will make their marriage for them and mournful,
Bitter the alliance and the driving me out of the land.
Ah, come, Medea, in your plotting and scheming
Leave nothing untried of all those things which you know.
Go forward to the dreadful act. The test has come 400
For resolution. You see how you are treated. Never
Shall you be mocked by Jason's Corinthian wedding,
Whose father was noble, whose grandfather Helius.
You have the skill. What is more, you were born a woman,
And women, though most helpless in doing good deeds, 405
Are of every evil the cleverest of contrivers.
CHORUS: Flow backward to your sources, sacred rivers,
And let the world's great order be reversed.
It is the thoughts of *men* that are deceitful,
Their pledges that are loose.   410

---

394 **Hecate** a goddess of the night   403 **Helius** sun god

Story shall now turn my condition to a fair one,
Women are paid their due.
No more shall evil-sounding fame be theirs.

Cease now, you muses of the ancient singers,
415 To tell the tale of my unfaithfulness;
For not on us did Phoebus, lord of music,
Bestow the lyre's divine
Power, for otherwise I should have sung an answer
To the other sex. Long time
420 Has much to tell of us, and much of them.

You sailed away from your father's home,
With a heart on fire you passed
The double rocks of the sea.
And now in a foreign country
425 You have lost your rest in a widowed bed,
And are driven forth, a refugee
In dishonor from the land.

Good faith has gone, and no more remains
In great Greece a sense of shame.
430 It has flown away to the sky.
No father's house for a haven
Is at hand for you now, and another queen
Of your bed has dispossessed you and
Is mistress of your home.

(*Enter* JASON, *with attendants.*)

435 JASON: This is not the first occasion that I have noticed
How hopeless it is to deal with a stubborn temper.
For, with reasonable submission to our ruler's will,
You might have lived in this land and kept your home.
As it is you are going to be exiled for your loose speaking.
440 Not that I mind myself. You are free to continue
Telling everyone that Jason is a worthless man.
But as to your talk about the king, consider
Yourself most lucky that exile is your punishment.
I, for my part, have always tried to calm down
445 The anger of the king, and wished you to remain.
But you will not give up your folly, continually
Speaking ill of him, and so you are going to be banished.
All the same, and in spite of your conduct, I'll not desert
My friends, but have come to make some provision for you,
450 So that you and the children may not be penniless
Or in need of anything in exile. Certainly
Exile brings many troubles with it. And even
If you hate me, I cannot think badly of you.
MEDEA: O coward in every way—that is what I call you,
455 With bitterest reproach for your lack of manliness,
You have come, you, my worst enemy, have come to me!
It is not an example of overconfidence
Or of boldness thus to look your friends in the face,
Friends you have injured—no, it is the worst of all
460 Human diseases, shamelessness. But you did well
To come, for I can speak ill of you and lighten
My heart, and you will suffer while you are listening.
And first I will begin from what happened first.
I saved your life, and every Greek knows I saved it.
465 Who was a shipmate of yours aboard the Argo.

When you were sent to control the bulls that breathed fire
And yoke them, and when you would sow that deadly field.
Also that snake, who encircled with his many folds
The Golden Fleece and guarded it and never slept,
I killed, and so gave you the safety of the light. 470
And I myself betrayed my father and my home,
And came with you to Pelias' land of Iolcus.
And then, showing more willingness to help than wisdom,
I killed him, Pelias, with a most dreadful death
At his own daughters' hands, and took away your fear. 475
This is how I behaved to you, you wretched man,
And you forsook me, took another bride to bed,
Though you had children; for, if that had not been,
You would have had an excuse for another wedding.
Faith in your word has gone. Indeed, I cannot tell 480
Whether you think the gods whose names you swore by then
Have ceased to rule and that new standards are set up,
Since you must know you have broken your word to me.
O my right hand, and the knees which you often clasped
In supplication, how senselessly I am treated 485
By this bad man, and how my hopes have missed their mark!
Come, I will share my thoughts as though you were a
    friend—
You! Can I think that you would ever treat me well?
But I will do it, and these questions will make you
Appear the baser. Where am I to go? To my father's? 490
Him I betrayed and his land when I came with you.
To Pelias' wretched daughters? What a fine welcome
They would prepare for me who murdered their father!
For this is my position—hated by my friends
At home, I have, in kindness to you, made enemies 495
Of others whom there was no need to have injured.
And how happy among Greek women you have made me
On your side for all this! A distinguished husband
I have—for breaking promises. When in misery
I am cast out of the land and go into exile, 500
Quite without friends and all alone with my children,
That will be a fine shame for the new-wedded groom,
For his children to wander as beggars and she who saved
    him.
O God, you have given to mortals a sure method
Of telling the gold that is pure from the counterfeit; 505
Why is there no mark engraved upon men's bodies,
By which we could know the true ones from the false ones?
CHORUS: It is a strange form of anger, difficult to cure,
When two friends turn upon each other in hatred.
JASON: As for me, it seems I must be no bad speaker. 510
But, like a man who has a good grip of the tiller,
Reef up his sail, and so run away from under
This mouthing tempest, woman, of your bitter tongue.
Since you insist on building up your kindness to me.
My view is that Cypris was alone responsible 515
Of men and gods for the preserving of my life.
You are clever enough—but really I need not enter
Into the story of how it was love's inescapable
Power that compelled you to keep my person safe.
On this I will not go into too much detail. 520

---

416 **Phoebus** Apollo

515 **Cypris** Aphrodite, *goddess of love*

In so far as you helped me, you did well enough.
But on this question of saving me, I can prove
You have certainly got from me more than you gave.
Firstly, instead of living among barbarians,
525 You inhabit a Greek land and understand our ways,
How to live by law instead of the sweet will of force.
And all the Greeks considered you a clever woman.
You were honored for it; while, if you were living at
The ends of the earth, nobody would have heard of you.
530 For my part, rather than stores of gold in my house
Or power to sing even sweeter songs than Orpheus,
I'd choose the fate that made me a distinguished man.
There is my reply to your story of my labors.
Remember it was you who started the argument.
535 Next for your attack on my wedding with the princess:
Here I will prove that, first, it was a clever move,
Secondly, a wise one, and, finally, that I made it
In your best interests and the children's. Please keep calm.
When I arrived here from the land of Iolcus,
540 Involved, as I was, in every kind of difficulty,
What luckier chance could I have come across than this,
An exile to marry the daughter of the king?
It was not—the point that seems to upset you—that I
Grew tired of your bed and felt the need of a new bride;
545 Nor with any wish to outdo your number of children.
We have enough already. I am quite content.
But—this was the main reason—that we might live well,
And not be short of anything. I know that all
A man's friends leave him stone-cold if he becomes poor.
550 Also that I might bring my children up worthily
Of my position, and, by producing more of them
To be brothers of yours, we would draw the families
Together and all be happy. You need no children.
And it pays me to do good to those I have now
555 By having others. Do you think this a bad plan?
You wouldn't if the love question hadn't upset you.
But you women have got into such a state of mind
That, if your life at night is good, you think you have
Everything; but, if in that quarter things go wrong,
560 You will consider your best and truest interests
Most hateful. It would have been better far for men
To have got their children in some other way, and women
Not to have existed. Then life would have been good.
CHORUS: Jason, though you have made this speech of yours
look well,
565 Still I think, even though others do not agree,
You have betrayed your wife and are acting badly.
MEDEA: Surely in many ways I hold different views
From others, for I think that the plausible speaker
Who is a villain deserves the greatest punishment.
570 Confident in his tongue's power to adorn evil,
He stops at nothing. Yet he is not really wise.
As in your case. There is no need to put on the airs
Of a clever speaker, for one word will lay you flat.
If you were not a coward, you would not have married
575 Behind my back, but discussed it with me first.
JASON: And you, no doubt, would have furthered the proposal,
If I had told you of it, you who even now
Are incapable of controlling your bitter temper.
MEDEA: It was not that. No, you thought it was not respectable
580 As you got on in years to have a foreign wife.

JASON: Make sure of this: it was not because of a woman
I made the royal alliance in which I now live.
But, as I said before, I wished to preserve you
And breed a royal progeny to be brothers
To the children I have now, a sure defense to us. 585
MEDEA: Let me have no happy fortune that brings pain with it,
Or prosperity which is upsetting to the mind!
JASON: Change your ideas of what you want, and show more
sense.
Do not consider painful what is good for you.
Nor, when you are lucky, think yourself unfortunate. 590
MEDEA: You can insult me. You have somewhere to turn to.
But I shall go from this land into exile, friendless.
JASON: It was what you chose yourself. Don't blame others for it.
MEDEA: And how did I choose it? Did I betray my husband?
JASON: You called down wicked curses on the king's family. 595
MEDEA: A curse, that is what I am become to your house too.
JASON: I do not propose to go into all the rest of it;
But, if you wish for the children or for yourself
In exile to have some of my money to help you,
Say so, for I am prepared to give with open hand, 600
Or to provide you with introductions to my friends
Who will treat you well. You are a fool if you do not
Accept this. Cease your anger and you will profit.
MEDEA: I shall never accept the favors of friends of yours,
Nor take a thing from you, so you need not offer it. 605
There is no benefit in the gifts of a bad man.
JASON: Then, in any case, I call the gods to witness that
I wish to help you and the children in every way,
But you refuse what is good for you. Obstinately
You push away your friends. You are sure to suffer for it. 610
MEDEA: Go! No doubt you hanker for your virginal bride,
And are guilty of lingering too long out of her house.
Enjoy your wedding. But perhaps—with the help of God—
You will make the kind of marriage that you will regret.

(JASON *goes out with his attendants.*)

CHORUS: When love is in excess
It brings a man no honor 615
Nor any worthiness.
But if in moderation Cypris comes,
There is no other power at all so gracious.
O goddess, never on me let loose the unerring
Shaft of your bow in the poison of desire. 620

Let my heart be wise.
It is the gods' best gift.
On me let mighty Cypris
Inflict no wordy wars or restless anger 625
To urge my passion to a different love.
But with discernment may she guide women's weddings,
Honoring most what is peaceful in the bed.

O country and home,
Never, never may I be without you, 630
Living the hopeless life,
Hard to pass through and painful,
Most pitiable of all.
Let death first lay me low and death
Free me from this daylight, 635
There is no sorrow above
The loss of a native land.

I have seen it myself,
Do not tell of a secondhand story.
640   Neither city nor friend
Pitied you when you suffered
The worst of sufferings.
O let him die ungraced whose heart
Will not reward his friends,
645   Who cannot open an honest mind
No friend will he be of mine.

(Enter AEGEUS, *king of Athens, an old friend of* MEDEA.)

AEGEUS: Medea, greeting! This is the best introduction
Of which men know for conversation between friends.
MEDEA: Greeting to you too, Aegeus, son of King Pandion.
650   Where have you come from to visit this country's soil?
AEGEUS: I have just left the ancient oracle of Phoebus.
MEDEA: And why did you go to earth's prophetic center?
AEGEUS: I went to inquire how children might be born to me.
MEDEA: Is it so? Your life still up to this point is childless?
655   AEGEUS: Yes. By the fate of some power we have no children.
MEDEA: Have you a wife, or is there none to share your bed?
AEGEUS: There is. Yes, I am joined to my wife in marriage.
MEDEA: And what did Phoebus say to you about children?
AEGEUS: Words too wise for a mere man to guess their
meaning.
660   MEDEA: It is proper for me to be told the god's reply?
AEGEUS: It is. For sure what is needed is cleverness.
MEDEA: Then what was his message? Tell me, if I may hear.
AEGEUS: I am not to loosen the hanging foot of the wineskin …
MEDEA: Until you have done something, or reached some
country?
665   AEGEUS: Until I return again to my hearth and house.
MEDEA: And for what purpose have you journeyed to this
land?
AEGEUS: There is a man called Pittheus, king of Troezen.
MEDEA: A son of Pelops, they say, a most righteous man.
AEGEUS: With him I wish to discuss the reply of the god.
670   MEDEA: Yes. He is wise and experienced in such matters.
AEGEUS: And to me also the dearest of all my spear-friends.
MEDEA: Well, I hope you have good luck, and achieve your
will.
AEGEUS: But why this downcast eye of yours, and this pale
cheek?
MEDEA: O Aegeus, my husband has been the worst of all to me.
675   AEGEUS: What do you mean? Say clearly what has caused this
grief.
MEDEA: Jason wrongs me, though I have never injured him.
AEGEUS: What has he done? Tell me about it in clearer words.
MEDEA: He has taken a wife to his house, supplanting me.
AEGEUS: Surely he would not dare to do a thing like that.
680   MEDEA: Be sure he has. Once dear, I now am slighted by him.
AEGEUS: Did he fall in love? Or is he tired of your love?
MEDEA: He was greatly in love, this traitor to his friends.
AEGEUS: Then let him go, if, as you say, he is so bad.
MEDEA: A passionate love—for an alliance with the king.
685   AEGEUS: And who gave him his wife? Tell me the rest of it.
MEDEA: It was Creon, he who rules this land of Corinth.
AEGEUS: Indeed, Medea, your grief was understandable.
MEDEA: I am ruined. And there is more to come: I am
banished.

AEGEUS: Banished? By whom? Here you tell me of a new
wrong.
MEDEA: Creon drives me an exile from the land of Corinth.   690
AEGEUS: Does Jason consent? I cannot approve of this.
MEDEA: He pretends not to, but he will put up with it.
Ah, Aegeus, I beg and beseech you, by your beard
And by your knees I am making myself your suppliant,
Have pity on me, have pity on your poor friend,   695
And do not let me go into exile desolate,
But receive me in your land and at your very hearth.
So may your love, with God's help, lead to the bearing
Of children, and so may you yourself die happy.
You do not know what a chance you have come on here.   700
I will end your childlessness, and I will make you able
To beget children. The drugs I know can do this.
AEGEUS: For many reasons, woman, I am anxious to do
This favor for you. First, for the sake of the gods,
And then for the birth of children which you promise,   705
For in that respect I am entirely at my wits' end.
But this is my position: if you reach my land,
I, being in my rights, will try to befriend you.
But this much I must warn you of beforehand:
I shall not agree to take you out of this country;   710
But if you by yourself can reach my house, then you
Shall stay there safely. To none will I give you up
But from this land you must make your escape yourself,
For I do not wish to incur blame from my friends.
MEDEA: It shall be so. But, if I might have a pledge from you 715
For this, then I would have from you all I desire.
AEGEUS: Do you not trust me? What is it rankles with you?
MEDEA: I trust you, yes. But the house of Pelias hates me,
And so does Creon. If you are bound by this oath,
When they try to drag me from your land, you will not   720
Abandon me; but if our pact is only words,
With no oath to the gods, you will be lightly armed,
Unable to resist their summons. I am weak,
While they have wealth to help them and a royal house.
AEGEUS: You show much foresight for such negotiations.   725
Well, if you will have it so, I will not refuse.
For, both on my side this will be the safest way
To have some excuse to put forward to your enemies,
And for you it is more certain. You may name the gods.
MEDEA: Swear by the plain of Earth, and Helius, father   730
Of my father, and name together all the gods …
AEGEUS: That I will act or not act in what way? Speak.
MEDEA: That you yourself will never cast me from your land,
Nor, if any of my enemies should demand me,
Will you, in your life, willingly hand me over.   735
AEGEUS: I swear by the Earth, by the holy light of Helius,
By all the gods, I will abide by this you say.
MEDEA: Enough. And, if you fail, what shall happen to you?
AEGEUS: What comes to those who have no regard for heaven.
MEDEA: Go on your way. Farewell. For I am satisfied.   740
And I will reach your city as soon as I can,
Having done the deed I have to do and gained my end.

(AEGEUS *goes out.*)

CHORUS: May Hermes, god of travelers,
Escort you, Aegeus, to your home!
And may you have the things you wish   745
So eagerly; for you

Appear to me to be a generous man.

MEDEA: God, and God's daughter, justice, and light of Helius!
Now, friends, has come the time of my triumph over

750 My enemies, and now my foot is on the road.
Now I am confident they will pay the penalty.
For this man, Aegeus, has been like a harbor to me
In all my plans just where I was most distressed.
To him I can fasten the cable of my safety

755 When I have reached the town and fortress of Pallas.
And now I shall tell to you the whole of my plan.
Listen to these words that are not spoken idly.
I shall send one of my servants to find Jason
And request him to come once more into my sight.

760 And when he comes, the words I'll say will be soft ones.
I'll say that I agree with him, that I approve
The royal wedding he has made, betraying me.
I'll say it was profitable, an excellent idea.
But I shall beg that my children may remain here:

765 Not that I would live in a country that hates me
Children of mine to feel their enemies' insults,
But that by a trick I may kill the king's daughter.
For I will send the children with gifts in their hands
To carry to the bride, so as not to be banished—

770 A finely woven dress and a golden diadem.
And if she takes them and wears them upon her skin
She and all who touch the girl will die in agony;
Such poison will I lay upon the gifts I send.
But there, however, I must leave that account paid.

775 I weep to think of what a deed I have to do
Next after that; for I shall kill my own children.
My children, there is none who can give them safety.
And when I have ruined the whole of Jason's house,
I shall leave the land and flee from the murder of my

780 Dear children, and I shall have done a dreadful deed.
For it is not bearable to be mocked by enemies.
So it must happen. What profit have I in life?
I have no land, no home, no refuge from my pain.
My mistake was made the time I left behind me

785 My father's house, and trusted the words of a Greek,
Who, with heaven's help, will pay me the price for that.
For those children he had from me he will never
See alive again, nor will he on his new bride
Beget another child, for she is to be forced

790 To die a most terrible death by these my poisons.
Let no one think me a weak one, feeble-spirited,
A stay-at-home, but rather just the opposite,
One who can hurt my enemies and help my friends;
For the lives of such persons are most remembered.

795 CHORUS: Since you have shared the knowledge of your plan
with us,
I both wish to help you and support the normal
Ways of mankind, and tell you not to do this thing.

MEDEA: I can do no other thing. It is understandable
For you to speak thus. You have not suffered as I have.

800 CHORUS: But can you have the heart to kill your flesh and
blood?

MEDEA: Yes, for this is the best way to wound my husband.

CHORUS: And you, too. Of women you will be most unhappy.

MEDEA: So it must be. No compromise is possible.

(*She turns to the* NURSE.)

Go, you, at once, and tell Jason to come to me.
You I employ on all affairs of greatest trust.   805
Say nothing of these decisions which I have made.
If you love your mistress, if you were born a woman.

CHORUS: From of old the children of Erechtheus are
Splendid, the sons of blessed gods. They dwell
In Athens' holy and unconquered land,   810
Where famous Wisdom feeds them and they pass gaily
Always through that most brilliant air where once, they say,
That golden Harmony gave birth to the nine
Pure Muses of Pieria.

And beside the sweet flow of Cephisus' stream,   815
Where Cypris sailed, they say, to draw the water,
And mild soft breezes breathed along her path,
And on her hair were flung the sweet-smelling garlands
Of flowers of roses by the Lovers, the companions
Of Wisdom, her escort, the helpers of men   820
In every kind of excellence.

How then can these holy rivers
Or this holy land love you,
Or the city find you a home,
You, who will kill your children,   825
You, not pure with the rest?
O think of the blow at your children
And think of the blood that you shed.
O, over and over I beg you,
By your knees I beg you do not   830
Be the murderess of your babes!

O where will you find the courage
Or the skill of hand and heart,
When you set yourself to attempt
A deed so dreadful to do?   835
How, when you look upon them,
Can you tearlessly hold the decision
For murder? You will not be able,
When your children fall down and implore you,
You will not be able to dip   840
Steadfast your hand in their blood.

(*Enter* JASON, *with attendants.*)

JASON: I have come at your request. Indeed, although you are
Bitter against me, this you shall have: I will listen
To what new thing you want, woman, to get from me.

MEDEA: Jason, I beg you to be forgiving toward me   845
For what I said. It is natural for you to bear with
My temper, since we have had much love together.
I have talked with myself about this and I have
Reproached myself. "Fool" I said, "why am I so mad?
Why am I set against those who have planned wisely?   850
Why make myself an enemy of the authorities
And of my husband, who does the best thing for me
By marrying royalty and having children who
Will be as brothers to my own? What is wrong with me?

---

755 **fortress of Pallas** Athens, the town of Athena

808 **children of Erechtheus** the Athenians   815 **beside . . .
stream** at Athens

855 Let me give up anger, for the gods are kind to me.
Have I not children, and do I not know that we
In exile from our country must be short of friends?"
When I considered this I saw that I had shown
Great lack of sense, and that my anger was foolish.
860 Now I agree with you. I think that you are wise
In having this other wife as well as me, and I
Was mad. I should have helped you in these plans of yours,
Have joined in the wedding, stood by the marriage bed,
Have taken pleasure in attendance on your bride.
865 But we women are what we are—perhaps a little
Worthless; and you men must not be like us in this,
Nor be foolish in return when we are foolish.
Now, I give in, and admit that then I was wrong.
I have come to a better understanding now.

(She turns toward the house.)

870 Children, come here, my children, come outdoors to us!
Welcome your father with me, and say goodbye to him,
And with your mother, who just now was his enemy,
Join again in making friends with him who loves us.

(Enter the CHILDREN, *attended by the* TUTOR.*)*

We have made peace, and all our anger is over.
875 Take hold of his right hand—O God, I am thinking
Of something which may happen in the secret future.
O children, will you just so, after a long life,
Hold out your loving arms at the grave? O children,
How ready to cry I am, how full of foreboding!
880 I am ending at last this quarrel with your father,
And, look my soft eyes have suddenly filled with tears.
CHORUS: And the pale tears have started also in my eyes.
O may the trouble not grow worse than now it is!
JASON: I approve of what you say. And I cannot blame you
Even for what you said before. It is natural
885 For a woman to be wild with her husband when he
Goes in for secret love. But now your mind has turned
To better reasoning. In the end you have come to
The right decision, like the clever woman you are.
And of you, children, your father is taking care.
890 He has made, with God's help, ample provision for you.
For I think that a time will come when you will be
The leading people in Corinth with your brothers.
You must grow up. As to the future, your father
And those of the gods who love him will deal with that.
895 I want to see you, when you have become young men,
Healthy and strong, better men than my enemies.
Medea, why are your eyes all wet with pale tears?
Why is your cheek so white and turned away from me?
Are not these words of mine pleasing for you to hear?
900 MEDEA: It is nothing. I was thinking about these children.
JASON: You must be cheerful. I shall look after them well.
MEDEA: I will be. It is not that I distrust your words,
But a woman is a frail thing, prone to crying.
JASON: But why then should you grieve so much for these
children?
905 MEDEA: I am their mother. When you prayed that they
might live
I felt unhappy to think that these things will be.
But come, I have said something of the things I meant
To say to you, and now I will tell you the rest.

Since it is the king's will to banish me from here— 910
And for me, too, I know that this is the best thing,
Not to be in your way by living here or in
The king's way, since they think me ill-disposed to them—
I then am going into exile from this land;
But do you, so that you may have the care of them, 915
Beg Creon that the children may not be banished.
JASON: I doubt if I'll succeed, but still I'll attempt it.
MEDEA: Then you must tell your wife to beg from her father
That the children may be reprieved from banishment.
JASON: I will, and with her I shall certainly succeed. 920
MEDEA: If she is like the rest of us women, you will.
And I, too, will take a hand with you in this business,
For I will send her some gifts which are far fairer,
I am sure of it, than those which now are in fashion,
A finely woven dress and a golden diadem, 925
And the children shall present them. Quick, let one of you
Servants bring here to me that beautiful dress.

(One of her attendants goes into the house.)

She will be happy not in one way, but in a hundred,
Having so fine a man as you to share her bed,
And with this beautiful dress which Helius of old, 930
My father's father, bestowed on his descendants.

(Enter attendant carrying the poisoned dress and diadem.)

There, children, take these wedding presents in your hands.
Take them to the royal princess, the happy bride,
And give them to her. She will not think little of them.
JASON: No, don't be foolish, and empty your hands of these. 935
Do you think the palace is short of dresses to wear?
Do you think there is no gold there? Keep them, don't
give them
Away. If my wife considers me of any value,
She will think more of me than money, I am sure of it.
MEDEA: No, let me have my way. They say the gods themselves 940
Are moved by gifts, and gold does more with men than words.
Hers is the luck, her fortune that which god blesses;
She is young and a princess; but for my children's reprieve
I would give my very life, and not gold only.
Go children, go together to that rich palace, 945
Be suppliants to the new wife of your father,
My lady, beg her not to let you be banished.
And give her the dress—for this is of great importance,
That she should take the gift into her hand from yours.
Go, quick as you can. And bring your mother good news 950
By your success of those things which she longs to gain.

*(*JASON *goes out with his attendants, followed by the* TUTOR *and the* CHILDREN *carrying the poisoned gifts.)*

CHORUS: Now there is no hope left for the children's lives.
Now there is none. They are walking already to murder.
The bride, poor bride, will accept the curse of the gold,
Will accept the bright diadem. 955
Around her yellow hair she will set that dress
Of death with her own hands.

The grace and the perfume and glow of the golden robe
Will charm her to put them upon her and wear the wreath,
And now her wedding will be with the dead below, 960
Into such a trap she will fall,

Poor thing, into such a fate of death and never
Escape from under that curse.

You, too, O wretched bridegroom, making your match
    with kings,
965   You do not see that you bring
Destruction on your children and on her,
Your wife, a fearful death.
Poor soul, what a fall is yours!

In your grief, too, I weep, mother of little children,
970   You who will murder your own,
In vengeance for the loss of married love
Which Jason has betrayed
As he lives with another wife.

(*Enter the* TUTOR *with the* CHILDREN.)

TUTOR: Mistress, I tell you that these children are reprieved,
975   And the royal bride has been pleased to take in her hands
Your gifts. In that quarter the children are secure.
    But come,
Why do you stand confused when you are fortunate?
Why have you turned round with your cheek away from me?
980   Are not these words of mine pleasing for you to hear?
MEDEA: Oh! I am lost!
TUTOR: That word is not in harmony with my tidings.
MEDEA: I am lost, I am lost!
TUTOR: Am I in ignorance telling you
Of some disaster, and not the good news I thought?
985   MEDEA: You have told what you have told. I do not blame you.
TUTOR: Why then this downcast eye, and this weeping of tears?
MEDEA: Oh, I am forced to weep, old man. The gods and I,
    I in a kind of madness, have contrived all this.
TUTOR: Courage! You, too, will be brought home by your
    children.
990   MEDEA: Ah, before that happens I shall bring others home.
TUTOR: Others before you have been parted from their
    children.
Mortals must bear in resignation their ill luck.
MEDEA: That is what I shall do. But go inside the house,
And do for the children your usual daily work.

(*The* TUTOR *goes into the house.* MEDEA *turns to her* CHILDREN.)

995   O children, O my children, you have a city,
You have a home, and you can leave me behind you,
And without your mother you may live there forever.
But I am going in exile to another land
1000   Before I have seen you happy and taken pleasure in you,
Before I have dressed your brides and made your marriage
    beds
And held up the torch at the ceremony of wedding.
Oh, what a wretch I am in this my self-willed thought!
What was the purpose, children, for which I reared you?
For all my travail and wearing myself away?
1005   They were sterile, those pains I had in the bearing of you.
Oh surely once the hopes in you I had, poor me,
Were high ones: you would look after me in old age,
And when I died would deck me well with your own
    hands;
A thing which all would have done. Oh but now it is gone,
1010   That lovely thought. For, once I am left without you,

Sad will be the life I'll lead and sorrowful for me.
And you will never see your mother again with
Your dear eyes, gone to another mode of living.
Why, children, do you look upon me with your eyes?
Why do you smile so sweetly that last smile of all?   1015
Oh, Oh, what can I do? My spirit has gone from me,
Friends, when I saw that bright look in the children's eyes.
I cannot bear to do it. I renounce my plans
I had before. I'll take my children away from
This land. Why should I hurt their father with the pain   1020
They feel, and suffer twice as much of pain myself?
No, no, I will not do it. I renounce my plans.
Ah, what is wrong with me? Do I want to let go
My enemies unhurt and be laughed at for it?
I must face this thing. Oh, but what a weak woman   1025
Even to admit to my mind these soft arguments.
Children, go into the house. And he whom law forbids
To stand in attendance at my sacrifices,
Let him see to it. I shall not mar my handiwork.
Oh! Oh!   1030
Do not, O my heart, you must not do these things!
Poor heart, let them go, have pity upon the children.
If they live with you in Athens they will cheer you.
No! By Hell's avenging furies it shall not be—
This shall never be, that I should suffer my children   1035
To be the prey of my enemies' insolence.
Every way is it fixed. The bride will not escape.
No, the diadem is now upon her head, and she,
The royal princess, is dying in the dress, I know it.
But—for it is the most dreadful of roads for me   1040
To tread, and them I shall send on a more dreadful still—
I wish to speak to the children.

(*She calls the* CHILDREN *to her.*)

                        Come, children, give
Me your hands, give your mother your hands to kiss them.
Oh the dear hands, and O how dear are these lips to me,
And the generous eyes and the bearing of my children!   1045
I wish you happiness, but not here in this world.
What is here your father took. Oh how good to hold you!
How delicate the skin, how sweet the breath of children!
Go, go! I am no longer able, no longer
To look upon you. I am overcome by sorrow.   1050

(*The* CHILDREN *go into the house.*)

I know indeed what evil I intend to do,
But stronger than all my afterthoughts is my fury,
Fury that brings upon mortals the greatest evils.

(*She goes out to the right, toward the royal palace.*)

CHORUS: Often before
I have gone through more subtle reasons,   1055
And have come upon questionings greater
Than a woman should strive to search out.
But we too have a goddess to help us
And accompany us into wisdom.
Not all of us. Still you will find   1060
Among many women a few,
And our sex is not without learning.
This I say, that those who have never
Had children, who know nothing of it,

1065 In happiness have the advantage
Over those who are parents.
The childless, who never discover
Whether children turn out as a good thing
Or as something to cause pain, are spared
1070 Many troubles in lacking this knowledge.
And those who have in their homes
The sweet presence of children, I see that their lives
Are all wasted away by their worries.
First they must think how to bring them up well and
1075 How to leave them something to live on.
And then after this whether all their toil
Is for those who will turn out good or bad,
Is still an unanswered question.
And of one more trouble, the last of all,
1080 That is common to mortals I tell.
For suppose you have found them enough for their living,
Suppose that the children have grown into youth
And have turned out good, still, if God so wills it,
Death will away with your children's bodies,
1085 And carry them off into Hades.
What is our profit, then, that for the sake of
Children the gods should pile upon mortals
After all else
This most terrible grief of all?

(Enter MEDEA, *from the spectators' right.*)

1090 MEDEA: Friends, I can tell you that for long I have waited
For the event. I stare toward the place from where
The news will come. And now, see one of Jason's servants
Is on his way here, and that labored breath of his
Shows he has tidings for us, and evil tidings.

(Enter, *also from the right, the* MESSENGER.)

1095 MESSENGER: Medea, you who have done such a dreadful thing,
So outrageous, run for your life, take what you can,
A ship to bear you hence or chariot on land.
MEDEA: And what is the reason deserves such flight as this?
MESSENGER: She is dead, only just now, the royal princess,
1100 And Creon dead, too, her father, by your poisons.
MEDEA: The finest words you have spoken. Now and hereafter
I shall count you among my benefactors and friends.
MESSENGER: What! Are you right in the mind? Are you not mad,
Woman? The house of the king is outraged by you.
1105 Do you enjoy it? Not afraid of such doings?
MEDEA: To what you say I on my side have something too
To say in answer. Do not be in a hurry, friend,
But speak. How did they die? You will delight me twice
As much again if you say they died in agony.
1110 MESSENGER: When those two children, born of you, had
    entered in,
Their father with them, and passed into the bride's house,
We were pleased, we slaves who were distressed by your
    wrongs.
All through the house we were talking of but one thing,
How you and your husband had made up your quarrel.
1115 Some kissed the children's hands and some their yellow
    hair,
And I myself was so full of my joy that I
Followed the children into the women's quarters.

Our mistress, whom we honor now instead of you,
Before she noticed that your two children were there,
Was keeping her eye fixed eagerly on Jason. 1120
Afterwards, however, she covered up her eyes,
Her cheek paled, and she turned herself away from him,
So disgusted was she at the children's coming there.
But your husband tried to end the girl's bad temper,
And said "You must not look unkindly on your friends. 1125
Cease to be angry. Turn your head to me again.
Have as your friends the same ones as your husband has.
And take these gifts, and beg your father to reprieve
These children from their exile. Do it for my sake."
She, when she saw the dress, could not restrain herself. 1130
She agreed with all her husband said, and before
He and the children had gone far from the palace,
She took the gorgeous robe and dressed herself in it,
And put the golden crown around her curly locks,
And arranged the set of the hair in a shining mirror, 1135
And smiled at the lifeless image of herself in it.
Then she rose from her chair and walked about the room,
With her gleaming feet stepping most soft and delicate,
All overjoyed with the present. Often and often
She would stretch her foot out straight and look along it. 1140
But after that it was a fearful thing to see.
The color of her face changed, and she staggered back,
She ran, and her legs trembled, and she only just
Managed to reach a chair without falling flat down.
An aged woman servant who, I take it, thought 1145
This was some seizure of Pan or another god,
Cried out "God bless us," but that was before she saw
The white foam breaking through her lips and her rolling
The pupils of her eyes and her face all bloodless.
Then she raised a different cry from that "God bless us," 1150
A huge shriek, and the women ran, one to the king,
One to the newly wedded husband to tell him
What had happened to his bride; and with frequent sound
The whole of the palace rang as they went running.
One walking quickly round the course of a race-track 1155
Would now have turned the bend and be close to the goal,
When she, poor girl, opened her shut and speechless eye,
And with a terrible groan she came to herself.
For a twofold pain was moving up against her.
The wreath of gold that was resting around her head 1160
Let forth a fearful stream of all-devouring fire,
And the finely woven dress your children gave to her,
Was fastening on the unhappy girl's fine flesh.
She leapt up from the chair, and all on fire she ran,
Shaking her hair this way and now that, trying 1165
To hurl the diadem away; but fixedly
The gold preserved its grip, and, when she shook her hair,
Then more and twice as fiercely the fire blazed out.
Till, beaten by her fate, she fell down to the ground,
Hard to be recognized except by a parent. 1170
Neither the setting of her eyes was plain to see,
Nor the shapeliness of her face. From the top of
Her head there oozed out blood and fire mixed together.
Like the drops on pine-bark, so the flesh from her bones
Dropped away, torn by the hidden fang of the poison. 1175
It was a fearful sight; and terror held us all
From touching the corpse. We had learned from what had
    happened.
But her wretched father, knowing nothing of the event,

Came suddenly to the house, and fell upon the corpse,
1180 And at once cried out and folded his arms about her,
And kissed her and spoke to her, saying, "O my poor child,
What heavenly power has so shamefully destroyed you?
And who has set me here like an ancient sepulcher,
Deprived of you? O let me die with you, my child!"
1185 And when he had made an end of his wailing and crying,
Then the old man wished to raise himself to his feet;
But, as the ivy clings to the twigs of the laurel,
So he stuck to the fine dress, and he struggled fearfully.
For he was trying to lift himself to his knee,
1190 And she was pulling him down, and when he tugged hard
He would be ripping his aged flesh from his bones.
At last his life was quenched, and the unhappy man
Gave up the ghost, no longer could hold up his head.
There they lie close, the daughter and the old father,
1195 Dead bodies, an event he prayed for in his tears.
As for your interests, I will say nothing of them,
For you will find your own escape from punishment.
Our human life I think and have thought a shadow,
And I do not fear to say that those who are held
1200 Wise among men and who search the reasons of things
Are those who bring the most sorrow on themselves.
For of mortals there is no one who is happy.
If wealth flows in upon one, one may be perhaps
Luckier than one's neighbor, but still not happy.

(Exit.)

1205 CHORUS: Heaven, it seems, on this day has fastened many
Evils on Jason, and Jason has deserved them.
Poor girl, the daughter of Creon, how I pity you
And your misfortunes, you who have gone quite away
To the house of Hades because of marrying Jason.
1210 MEDEA: Women, my task is fixed: as quickly as I may
To kill my children, and start away from this land,
And not, by wasting time, to suffer my children
To be slain by another hand less kindly to them.
Force every way will have it they must die, and since
1215 This must be so, then I, their mother, shall kill them.
Oh, arm yourself in steel, my heart! Do not hang back
From doing this fearful and necessary wrong.
Oh, come, my hand, poor wretched hand, and take the
sword.
Take it, step forward to this bitter starting point,
1220 And do not be a coward, do not think of them,
How sweet they are, and how you are their mother. Just for
This one short day be forgetful of your children,
Afterward weep; for even though you will kill them,
They were very dear—Oh, I am an unhappy woman!

(With a cry she rushes into the house.)

1225 CHORUS: O Earth, and the far shining
Ray of the Sun, look down, look down upon
This poor lost woman, look, before she raises
The hand of murder against her flesh and blood.
Yours was the golden birth from which
1230 She sprang, and now I fear divine
Blood may be shed by men.
O heavenly light, hold back her hand,
Check her, and drive from out the house
The bloody Fury raised by fiends of Hell.

Vain waste, your care of children; 1235
Was it in vain you bore the babes you loved,
After you passed the inhospitable strait
Between the dark blue rocks, Symplegades?
O wretched one, how has it come,
This heavy anger on your heart, 1240
This cruel bloody mind?
For God from mortals asks a stern
Price for the stain of kindred blood
In like disaster falling on their homes.

(A cry from ONE OF THE CHILDREN *is heard.)*

CHORUS: Do you hear the cry, do you hear the children's cry? 1245
O you hard heart, O woman fated for evil!
ONE OF THE CHILDREN: *(From within.)* What can I do and how
escape my mother's hands?
ANOTHER CHILD: *(From within.)* O my dear brother, I cannot tell.
We are lost.
CHORUS: Shall I enter the house? Oh, surely I should
Defend the children from murder. 1250
A CHILD: *(From within.)* O help us, in God's name, for now we
need your help.
Now, now we are close to it. We are trapped by the sword.
CHORUS: O your heart must have been made of rock or steel,
You who can kill
With your own hand the fruit of your own womb. 1255
Of one alone I have heard, one woman alone
Of those of old who laid her hands on her children,
Ino, sent mad by heaven when the wife of Zeus
Drove her out from her home and made her wander;
And because of the wicked shedding of blood 1260
Of her own children she threw
Herself, poor wretch, into the sea and stepped away
Over the sea-cliff to die with her two children.
What horror more can be? O women's love,
So full of trouble, 1265
How many evils have you caused already!

(Enter JASON, *with attendants.)*

JASON: You women, standing close in front of this dwelling,
Is she, Medea, she who did this dreadful deed,
Still in the house, or has she run away in flight?
For she will have to hide herself beneath the earth, 1270
Or raise herself on wings into the height of air,
If she wishes to escape the royal vengeance.
Does she imagine that, having killed our rulers,
She will herself escape uninjured from this house?
But I am thinking not so much of her as for 1275
The children—her the king's friends will make to suffer
For what she did. So I have come to save the lives
Of my boys, in case the royal house should harm them
While taking vengeance for their mother's wicked deed.
CHORUS: O Jason, if you but knew how deeply you are 1280
Involved in sorrow, you would not have spoken so.
JASON: What is it? That she is planning to kill me also?
CHORUS: Your children are dead, and by their own mother's
hand.
JASON: What! That is it? O woman, you have destroyed me!
CHORUS: You must make up your mind your children are no 1285
more.
JASON: Where did she kill them? Was it here or in the house?

CHORUS: Open the gates and there you will see them murdered.
JASON: Quick as you can unlock the doors, men, and undo
    The fastenings and let me see this double evil,
1290   My children dead and her—Oh her I will repay.

(*His attendants rush to the door.* MEDEA *appears above the house in a chariot drawn by dragons. She has the dead bodies of the* CHILDREN *with her.*)

MEDEA: Why do you batter these gates and try to unbar them,
    Seeking the corpses and for me who did the deed?
    You may cease your trouble, and, if you have need of me,
    Speak, if you wish. You will never touch me with your hand,
1295   Such a chariot has Helius, my father's father,
    Given me to defend me from my enemies.
JASON: You hateful thing, you woman most utterly loathed
    By the gods and me and by all the race of mankind,
    You who have had the heart to raise a sword against
1300   Your children, you, their mother, and left me childless—
    You have done this, and do you still look at the sun
    And at the earth, after these most fearful doings?
    I wish you dead. Now I see it plain, though at that time
    I did not, when I took you from your foreign home
1305   And brought you to a Greek house, you, an evil thing,
    A traitress to your father and your native land.
    The gods hurled the avenging curse of yours on me.
    For your own brother you slew at your own hearthside,
    And then came aboard that beautiful ship, the Argo.
1310   And that was your beginning. When you were married
    To me, your husband, and had borne children to me,
    For the sake of pleasure in the bed you killed them.
    There is no Greek woman who would have dared such
        deeds,
    Out of all those whom I passed over and chose you
1315   To marry instead, a bitter destructive match,
    A monster, not a woman, having a nature
    Wilder than that of Scylla in the Tuscan sea.
    Ah! no, not if I had ten thousand words of shame
    Could I sting you. You are naturally so brazen.
1320   Go, worker in evil, stained with your children's blood.
    For me remains to cry aloud upon my fate,
    Who will get no pleasure from my newly wedded love,
    And the boys whom I begot and brought up, never
    Shall I speak to them alive. Oh, my life is over!
1325 MEDEA: Long would be the answer which I might have made to
    These words of yours, if Zeus the father did not know
    How I have treated you and what you did to me.
    No, it was not to be that you should scorn my love,
    And pleasantly live your life through, laughing at me;
1330   Nor would the princess, nor he who offered the match,
    Creon, drive me away without paying for it.
    So now you may call me a monster, if you wish,
    A Scylla housed in the caves of the Tuscan sea.
    I too, as I had to, have taken hold of your heart.
1335 JASON: You feel the pain yourself. You share in my sorrow.
MEDEA: Yes, and my grief is gain when you cannot mock it.
JASON: O children, what a wicked mother she was to you!
MEDEA: They died from a disease they caught from their
    father.

1317 **Scylla** a monster in the *Odyssey*

JASON: I tell you it was not my hand that destroyed them.
MEDEA: But it was your insolence, and your virgin wedding. 1340
JASON: And just for the sake of that you chose to kill them.
MEDEA: Is love so small a pain, do you think, for a woman?
JASON: For a wise one, certainly. But you are wholly evil.
MEDEA: The children are dead. I say this to make you suffer.
JASON: The children, I think, will bring down curses on you. 1345
MEDEA: The gods know who was the author of this sorrow.
JASON: Yes, the gods know indeed, they know your loathsome
    heart.
MEDEA: Hate me. But I tire of your barking bitterness.
JASON: And I of yours. It is easier to leave you.
MEDEA: How then? What shall I do? I long to leave you too. 1350
JASON: Give me the bodies to bury and to mourn them.
MEDEA: No, that I will not. I will bury them myself,
    Bearing them to Hera's temple on the promontory;
    So that no enemy may evilly treat them
    By tearing up their grave. In this land of Corinth   1355
    I shall establish a holy feast and sacrifice
    Each year for ever to atone for the blood guilt.
    And I myself go to the land of Erechtheus
    To dwell in Aegeus' house, the son of Pandion.
    While you, as is right, will die without distinction, 1360
    Struck on the head by a piece of the Argo's timber,
    And you will have seen the bitter end of my love.
JASON: May a Fury for the children's sake destroy you,
    And justice, Requitor of blood.
MEDEA: What heavenly power lends an ear   1365
    To a breaker of oaths, a deceiver?
JASON: Oh, I hate you, murderess of children.
MEDEA: Go to your palace. Bury your bride.
JASON: I go, with two children to mourn for.
MEDEA: Not yet do you feel it. Wait for the future.   1370
JASON: Oh, children I loved!
MEDEA: I loved them, you did not.
JASON: You loved them, and killed them.
MEDEA: To make you feel
    pain.
JASON: Oh, wretch that I am, how I long
    To kiss the dear lips of my children!
MEDEA: Now you would speak to them, now you would kiss 1375
    them.
    Then you rejected them.
JASON: Let me, I beg you,
    Touch my boys delicate flesh.
MEDEA: I will not. Your words are all wasted.
JASON: O God, do you hear it, this persecution,
    These my sufferings from this hateful   1380
    Woman, this monster, murderess of children?
    Still what I can do that I will do:
    I will lament and cry upon heaven,
    Calling the gods to bear me witness,
    How you have killed my boys and prevent me from 1385
    Touching their bodies or giving them burial.
    I wish I had never begot them to see them
    Afterward slaughtered by you.
CHORUS: Zeus in Olympus is the overseer
    Of many doings. Many things the gods   1390
    Achieve beyond our judgment. What we thought
    Is not confirmed and what we thought not god
    Contrives. And so it happens in this story.

Aristophanes

Aristophanes (c. 450–c. 388 BCE) pursued his career as a playwright throughout the Peloponnesian War. As he observed the decline and defeat of Athens, his comedies relentlessly attacked the war and the individuals and attitudes that supported it. Aristophanes first entered the City Dionysia in 427 BCE and first won in 426 BCE with a now-lost play that satirized the policies and character of the military leader Cleon. Many of Aristophanes' plays—*Birds, Lysistrata, Assembly of Women*—use a utopian premise to criticize the war, but in other plays, Aristophanes lampoons other aspects of city life. In *Frogs,* for instance, a pompous Aeschylus and an embittered Euripides come from Hades to vie with one another once again; in *Clouds,* Aristophanes ridicules the sophists—professional teachers of rhetoric—for their ability to argue any side of an issue, and he particularly singles out Socrates for blame. The impact of Aristophanes' comedy on Athens should not be underestimated. In Plato's *Apology,* Socrates cites Aristophanes' portrayal of him in *Clouds* as one of the factors that turned Athenian sentiment against him, resulting in his trial and sentence of execution. Aristophanes' plays include *Acharnians, Knights, Clouds, Wasps, Peace, Birds, Lysistrata, Women Celebrating the Thesmophoria, Frogs, Assembly of Women,* and *Plutus.*

LYSISTRATA

Lysistrata is one of several plays critical of Athens' war with Sparta. Produced in 411 BCE, the play follows shortly on a disastrous phase of the war for Athens. Two years earlier, the Athenian raid on Sicily had failed, and the navy was decimated, leaving Athens vulnerable to attack by Sparta. Although the navy was rebuilt before Sparta mounted its final assault, Athens fell to Sparta in 404 BCE.

Lysistrata explores the premise that the women of Greece—drawn from all the major city-states and regions—could unite to oppose the war. Led by the Athenian Lysistrata (her name means "disband the army"), the women barricade themselves on the Acropolis, withholding sex from the men until peace can be declared. Aristophanes provides each of his

Displaying an "eclectic" design combining classical and modern costume elements, this production of Aristophanes' *Lysistrata* also displays an updated version of the Greek costume *phallus* as well.

women with the physical attributes and accent typical of her region. The large and power-ful Spartan woman Lampito, for example, is both an expert in the Spartan rump-kicking dance and speaks in what was—to an Athenian audience—an outlandish accent (to make this clear for English-speaking readers, this translation gives Lampito an exaggerated South-ern drawl).

Lysistrata addresses the politics of its era in a variety of ways. It is, of course, a passion-ate plea for peace, concluding with a scene of comic feasting and dancing enjoyed by all the characters in the play, Athenians and Spartans, men and women. For modern audiences, though, the play's connection between gender and politics may seem more immediate. On one hand, the play implies an equality between men and women. The women claim that the morality of their domestic sphere is superior to the military morality pursued by the men, and to get the women back, the men are forced to compromise with them. On the other hand, although *Lysistrata* seems to provide women with political power, their power resides wholly in their sexuality; they can interrupt, but not change, the fact that they are the prop-erty of men. The Theater of Dionysus could not, of course, put women on the stage, and Lysistrata, Lampito, Kalonike, and the rest—even the naked girl Harmony—were all played by men in padded costumes. In the play and in the *polis,* women were defined principally through their relation to men. The limited influence women could exert was subordinate to the civil power that Aristophanes and his audience took to be the "natural" preserve of the male audience. Despite the play's earthy humor and apparent feminism, *Lysistrata* documents the actual status of women in classical Athens; their power is restricted to the sphere of the *oikos,* or home, and can be practiced only through their subservience to men, who, as citi-zens, finally can command women's bodies, the home, and the state as well.

LYSISTRATA

Aristophanes

TRANSLATED BY DONALD SUTHERLAND

CHARACTERS

LYSISTRATA ⎫
KALONIKE ⎬ *Athenian women*
MYRRHINA ⎭
LAMPITO, *a Spartan woman*
CHORUS OF OLD MEN
CHORUS OF OLD WOMEN
ATHENIAN COMMISSIONER

OLD MARKET WOMAN
CINESIAS, *an Athenian,*
    husband of Myrrhina
SPARTAN HERALD
SCYTHIAN POLICEMEN
PORTER
ATHENIAN OFFICIAL

ATHENIANS
SPARTAN AMBASSADORS
ATHENIAN AMBASSADORS
HARMONY
LADY COP

A street in Athens before daylight.

LYSISTRATA: If anyone had asked them to a festival
    of Aphrodite or of Bacchus or of Pan,
    you couldn't get through Athens for the tambourines,
    but now there's not one solitary woman here.
5   Except my next-door neighbor. Here she's coming out.
    Hello, Kalonike.
KALONIKE: Hello, Lysistrata.
    What are you so upset about? Don't scowl so, dear.
    You're less attractive when you knit your brows and glare.
LYSISTRATA: I know, Kalonike, but I am smoldering
10   with indignation at the way we women act.
    Men think we are so gifted for all sorts of crime
    that we will stop at nothing—
KALONIKE: Well, we are, by Zeus!
LYSISTRATA: —but when it comes to an appointment here
    with me
    to plot and plan for something really serious
15   they lie in bed and do not come.
KALONIKE: They'll come, my dear.
    You know what trouble women have in going out:
    one of us will be wrapped up in her husband still,
    another waking up the maid, or with a child
    to put to sleep, or give its bath, or feed its pap.
20 LYSISTRATA: But they had other more important things to do
    than those.
KALONIKE: What ever is it, dear Lysistrata?
    What have you called us women all together for?
    How much of a thing is it?
LYSISTRATA: Very big.
KALONIKE: And thick?
LYSISTRATA: Oh very thick indeed.
KALONIKE: Then *how* can we be late?
25 LYSISTRATA: That's not the way it is. Or we would all be here.
    But it is something I have figured out myself
    and turned and tossed upon for many a sleepless night.
KALONIKE: It must be something slick you've turned and
    tossed upon!
30 LYSISTRATA: So slick that the survival of all Greece depends
    upon the women.
KALONIKE: On the women? In that case
    poor Greece has next to nothing to depend upon.
LYSISTRATA: Since now it's we who must decide affairs of state:
    either there is to be no Spartan left alive—
KALONIKE: A very good thing too, if none were left,
    by Zeus!

LYSISTRATA: —and every living soul in Thebes to be destroyed— 35
KALONIKE: Except the eels! Spare the delicious eels of Thebes!
LYSISTRATA: —and as for Athens—I can't bring myself to say
    the like of that for us. But just think what I mean!
    Yet if the women meet here as I told them to
    from Sparta, Thebes, and all of their allies, 40
    and we of Athens, all together we'll save Greece.
KALONIKE: What reasonable thing could women ever do,
    or glorious, we who sit around all prettied up
    in flowers and scandalous saffron-yellow gowns,
    groomed and draped to the ground in oriental stuffs 45
    and fancy pumps?
LYSISTRATA: And those are just the very things
    I count upon to save us—wicked saffron gowns,
    perfumes and pumps and rouge and sheer transparent
    frocks.
KALONIKE: But what use can they be?
LYSISTRATA: So no man in our time
    will raise a spear against another man again— 50
KALONIKE: I'll get a dress dyed saffron-yellow, come what may!
LYSISTRATA: —nor touch a shield—
KALONIKE: I'll slip into the sheerest gown!
LYSISTRATA: —nor so much as a dagger—
KALONIKE: I'll buy a pair of pumps!
LYSISTRATA: So don't you think the women should be here
    by now?
KALONIKE: I don't. They should have *flown* and got here 55
    long ago.
LYSISTRATA: You'll see, my dear. They will, like good Athenians,
    do everything too late. But from the coastal towns
    no woman is here either, nor from Salamis.
KALONIKE: I'm certain those from Salamis have crossed the
    strait:
    they're always straddling *something* at this time of night. 60
LYSISTRATA: Not even those I was expecting would be first
    to get here, from Acharnae, from so close to town,
    not even they are here.
KALONIKE: But one of them, I know,
    is under way, and three sheets to the wind, by now.
    But look—some women are approaching over there. 65
LYSISTRATA: And over here are some, coming this way—
KALONIKE: Phew! Phew!
    Where are they from?
LYSISTRATA: Down by the marshes.
KALONIKE: Yes, by Zeus!
    It smells as if the bottoms had been all churned up!

(*Enter* MYRRHINA, *and others.*)

MYRRHINA: Hello Lysistrata. Are we a little late?
70   What's that? Why don't you speak?
LYSISTRATA: I don't think much of you,
   Myrrhina, coming to this business only now.
MYRRHINA: Well, I could hardly find my girdle in the dark.
   If it's so urgent, tell us what it is. We're here.
KALONIKE: Oh no. Let's wait for just a little while until
75   the delegates from Sparta and from Thebes arrive.
LYSISTRATA: You show much better judgment.

(*Enter* LAMPITO, *and others.*)

                       Here comes Lampito!
LYSISTRATA: Well, darling Lampito! My dearest Spartan friend!
   How very sweet, how beautiful you look! That fresh
   complexion! How magnificent your figure is!
80   Enough to crush a bull!
LAMPITO: Ah shorely think Ah could.
   Ah take mah exacise. Ah jump and thump mah butt.
KALONIKE: And really, what a handsome set of tits you have!
LAMPITO: You feel me ovah lahk a cow fo sacrafahce!
LYSISTRATA: And this other young thing—where ever is *she* from?
85 LAMPITO: She's prominent, Ah sweah, in Thebes—a delegate
   ample enough.
LYSISTRATA: By Zeus, she represents Thebes well,
   having so trim a ploughland.
KALONIKE: Yes, by Zeus, she does!
   There's not a weed of all her field she hasn't plucked.
LYSISTRATA: And who's the other girl?
LAMPITO: Theah's nothing small, Ah sweah,
90   or tahght about her folks in Corinth.
KALONIKE: No, by Zeus!—
   to judge by this side of her, nothing small or tight.
LAMPITO: But who has called togethah such a regiment
   of all us women?
LYSISTRATA: Here I am. I did.
LAMPITO: Speak up,
   just tell us what you want.
KALONIKE: Oh yes, by Zeus, my dear,
95   do let us know what the important business is!
LYSISTRATA: Let me explain it, then. And yet . . . before I do . . .
   I have one little question.
KALONIKE: Anything you like.
LYSISTRATA: Don't you all miss the fathers of your little ones,
   your husbands who have gone away to war? I'm sure
100   you all have husbands in the armies far from home.
KALONIKE: Mine's been away five months in Thrace—
   a general's guard,
   posted to see his general does not desert.
MYRRHINA: And mine has been away in Pylos seven whole
   months.
LAMPITO: And mahn, though he does get back home on leave
   sometahms,
105   no soonah has he come than he is gone again.
LYSISTRATA: No lovers either. Not a sign of one is left.
   For since our eastern allies have deserted us
   they haven't sent a single six-inch substitute
   to serve as leatherware replacement for our men.
110   Would you be willing, then, if I thought out a scheme,
   to join with me to end the war?

KALONIKE: Indeed I would,
   even if I had to pawn this very wrap-around
   and drink up all the money in one day, I would!
MYRRHINA: And so would I, even if I had to see myself
   split like a flounder, and give half of me away!   115
LAMPITO: And so would Ah! Ah'd climb up Mount
   Taÿgetos
   if Ah just had a chance of seeing peace from theah!
LYSISTRATA: Then I will tell you. I may now divulge my
   plan.
   Women of Greece!—if we intend to force the men
   to make a peace, we must abstain . . .   120
KALONIKE: From what? Speak out!
LYSISTRATA: But will you do it?
KALONIKE: We will, though death should be the price!
LYSISTRATA: Well then, we must abstain utterly from the prick.
   Why do you turn your backs? Where are you off to now?
   And you—why pout and make such faces, shake your heads?
   Why has your color changed? Why do you shed those tears?   125
   Will you do it or will you not? Why hesitate?
KALONIKE: I will not do it. Never. Let the war go on!
MYRRHINA: Neither will I. By Zeus, no! Let the war go on!
LYSISTRATA: How can you say so, Madam Flounder, when just
   now
   you were declaiming you would split yourself in half?   130
KALONIKE: Anything else you like, anything! If I must
   I'll gladly walk through fire. That, rather than the prick!
   Because there's nothing like it, dear Lysistrata.
LYSISTRATA: How about you?
MYRRHINA: I too would gladly walk through fire.
LYSISTRATA: Oh the complete depravity of our whole sex!   135
   It is no wonder tragedies are made of us,
   we have such unrelenting unity of mind!
   But you, my friend from Sparta, dear, if you alone
   stand by me, only you, we still might save the cause.
   Vote on my side!   140
LAMPITO: They'ah hahd conditions, mahty hahd,
   to sleep without so much as the fo'skin of one . . .
   but all the same . . . well . . . yes. We need peace just as
   bad.
LYSISTRATA: Oh dearest friend!—the one real woman of them all!
KALONIKE: And if we really should abstain from what you say—
   which Heaven forbid!—do you suppose on that account   145
   that peace might come to be?
LYSISTRATA: I'm absolutely sure.
   If we should sit around, rouged and with skins well
   creamed,
   with nothing on but a transparent negligé,
   and come up to them with our deltas plucked quite smooth,
   and, once our men get stiff and want to come to grips,   150
   we do not yield to them at all but just hold off,
   they'll make a truce in no time. There's no doubt of that.
LAMPITO: We say in Spahta that when Menelaos saw
   Helen's ba'e apples he just tossed away his swo'd.
KALONIKE: And what, please, if our husbands just toss *us* away?   155
LYSISTRATA: Well, you have heard the good old saying: Know
   Thyself.
KALONIKE: It isn't worth the candle. I hate cheap substitutes.
   But what if they should seize and drag us by brute force
   into the bedroom?
LYSISTRATA: Hang onto the doors!
KALONIKE: And if—
   they beat us?
                       160

LYSISTRATA: Then you must give in, but nastily,
and do it badly. There's no fun in it by force.
And then, just keep them straining. They will give it up
in no time—don't you worry. For never will a man
enjoy himself unless the woman coincides.

165 KALONIKE: If both of you are for this plan, then so are we.

LAMPITO: And we of Spahta shall persuade ouah men to keep
the peace sinceahly and with honah in all ways,
but how could anyone pe'suade the vulgah mob
of Athens not to deviate from discipline?

170 LYSISTRATA: Don't worry, we'll persuade our men. They'll keep
the peace.

LAMPITO: They won't, so long as they have battleships afloat
and endless money sto'ed up in the Pahthenon.

LYSISTRATA: But that too has been carefully provided for:
we shall take over the Acropolis today.

175 The oldest women have their orders to do that:
while *we* meet here, *they* go as if to sacrifice
up there, but really seizing the Acropolis.

LAMPITO: All should go well. What you say theah is very
smaht.

LYSISTRATA: In that case, Lampito, what are we waiting for?

180 Let's take an oath, to bind us indissolubly.

LAMPITO: Well, just you show us what the oath is. Then we'll
sweah.

LYSISTRATA: You're right. Where is that lady cop?

(*To the armed* LADY COP *looking around for a* LADY COP.)

What do you think
you're looking for? Put down your shield in front of us,
there, on its back, and someone get some scraps of gut.

185 KALONIKE: Lysistrata, what in the world do you intend
to make us take an oath on?

LYSISTRATA: What? Why, on a shield,
just as they tell me some insurgents in a play
by Aeschylus once did, with a sheep's blood and guts.

KALONIKE: Oh *don't*, Lysistrata, don't swear upon a *shield,*
190 not if the oath has anything to do with peace!

LYSISTRATA: Well then, what *will* we swear on? Maybe we
should get
a white horse somewhere, like the Amazons, and cut
some bits of gut from it.

KALONIKE: *Where* would we get a horse?

LYSISTRATA: But what kind of an oath *is* suitable for us?

195 KALONIKE: By Zeus, I'll tell you if you like. First we put down
a big black drinking-cup, face up, and then we let
the neck of a good jug of wine bleed into it,
and take a solemn oath to—add no water in.

LAMPITO: Bah Zeus, Ah jest can't tell you how Ah lahk that
oath!

200 LYSISTRATA: Someone go get a cup and winejug from inside.

(KALONIKE *goes and is back in a flash.*)

KALONIKE: My dears, my dearest dears—how's *this* for pottery?
You feel good right away, just laying hold of it.

LYSISTRATA: Well, set it down, and lay your right hand on
this pig.
O goddess of Persuasion, and O Loving-cup,
205 accept this victim's blood! Be gracious unto us.

KALONIKE: It's not anaemic, and flows clear. Those are good signs.

LAMPITO: What an aroma, too! Bah Castah it *is* sweet!

KALONIKE: My dears, if you don't mind—I'll be the first to
swear.

LYSISTRATA: By Aphrodite, no! If you had drawn first place
by lot—but now let all lay hands upon the cup.   210
Yes, Lampito—and now, let one of you repeat
for all of you what I shall say. You will be sworn
by every word she says, and bound to keep this oath:
No lover and no husband and no man on earth—

KALONIKE: No lover and no husband and no man on earth—   215

LYSISTRATA: *shall e'er approach me with his penis up.* Repeat.

KALONIKE: shall e'er approach me with his penis up. Oh dear,
my knees are buckling under me, Lysistrata!

LYSISTRATA: *and I shall lead an unlaid life alone at home,*

KALONIKE: and I shall lead an unlaid life alone at home,   220

LYSISTRATA: *wearing a saffron gown and groomed and beautified*

KALONIKE: wearing a saffron gown and groomed and beautified

LYSISTRATA: *so that my husband will be all on fire for me*

KALONIKE: so that my husband will be all on fire for me

LYSISTRATA: *but I will never willingly give in to him*   225

KALONIKE: but I will never willingly give in to him

LYSISTRATA: *and if he tries to force me to against my will*

KALONIKE: and if he tries to force me to against my will

LYSISTRATA: *I'll do it badly and not wiggle in response*

KALONIKE: I'll do it badly and not wiggle in response   230

LYSISTRATA: *nor toward the ceiling will I lift my Persian pumps*

KALONIKE: nor toward the ceiling will I lift my Persian pumps

LYSISTRATA: *nor crouch down as the lions on cheese-graters do*

KALONIKE: nor crouch down as the lions on cheese-graters do

LYSISTRATA: *and if I keep my promise, may I drink of this*—   235

KALONIKE: and if I keep my promise, may I drink of this—

LYSISTRATA: *but if I break it, then may water fill the cup!*

KALONIKE: but if I break it, then may water fill the cup!

LYSISTRATA: Do you all swear to this with her?

ALL: We do, by Zeus!

LYSISTRATA: I'll consecrate our oath now.   240

KALONIKE: Share alike, my dear,
so we'll be friendly to each other from the start.

LAMPITO: What was that screaming?

LYSISTRATA: That's what I was telling you:
the women have already seized the Parthenon
and the Acropolis. But now, dear Lampito,
return to Sparta and set things in order there—   245
but leave these friends of yours as hostages with us—
And let *us* join the others in the citadel
and help them bar the gates.

KALONIKE: But don't you think the men
will rally to the rescue of the citadel,
attacking us at once?   250

LYSISTRATA: They don't worry me much:
they'll never bring against us threats or fire enough
to force open the gates, except upon our terms.

KALONIKE: Never by Aphrodite! Or we'd lose our name
for being battle-axes and unbearable!

(*Exeunt. The scene changes to the Propylaea of the Acropolis. A*
CHORUS OF VERY OLD MEN *struggles slowly in, carrying logs and
firepots.*)

ONE OLD MAN: Lead on! O Drakës, step by step, although your   255
shoulder's aching
and under this green olive log's great weight
your back be breaking!

ANOTHER: Eh, life is long but always has
260   more surprises for us!
     Now who'd have thought we'd live to hear
          this, O Strymodorus?—

     The wives we fed and looked upon
     as helpless liabilities
265   now dare to occupy the Parthenon,
     our whole Acropolis, for once they seize
     the Propylaea, straightway
     they lock and bar the gateway.

CHORUS: Let's rush to the Acropolis with due precipitation
270   and lay these logs down circlewise, till presently we turn them
     into one mighty pyre to make a general cremation
     of all the women up there—eh! with our own hands we'll
       burn them,
     the leaders and the followers, without discrimination!

AN OLD MAN: They'll never have the laugh on me!
275   Though I may not look it,
      I rescued the Acropolis
         when the Spartans took it
     about a hundred years ago.
     We laid a siege that kept their king
280   six years unwashed, so when I made him throw
     his armor off, for all his blustering,
     in nothing but his shirt he
     looked very very dirty.

CHORUS: How strictly I besieged the man! These gates were
     all invested
285   with seventeen ranks of armored men all equally ferocious!
     Shall women—by Euripides and all the gods detested—
     not be restrained—with me on hand—from something so
     atrocious?
     They shall!—or may our trophies won at Marathon be bested!
290   But we must go a long way yet
      up that steep and winding road
     before we reach the fortress where we want to get.
       How shall we ever drag this load,
       lacking pack-mules, way up there?
      I can tell you that my shoulder has caved in
     beyond repair!
295   Yet we must trudge ever higher,
        ever blowing on the fire,
      so its coals will still be glowing when we get
     where we are going
          Fooh! Fooh!
          Whoo! I choke!
300   What a smoke!

       Lord Heracles! How fierce it flies
        out against me from the pot!
     and like a rabid bitch it bites me in the eyes!
        It's female fire, or it would not
305   scratch my poor old eyes like this.
      Yet undaunted we must onward, up the high
     Acropolis
        where Athena's temple stands
        fallen into hostile hands.
      O my comrades! shall we ever have a greater
     need to save her?
310   Fooh! Fooh!
          Whoo! I choke!
          What a smoke!

FIRST OLD MAN: Well, thank the gods, I see the fire is yet
     alive and waking!
SECOND OLD MAN: Why don't we set our lumber down right
     here in handy batches,
     then stick a branch of grape-vine in the pot until it catches   315
THIRD OLD MAN: and hurl ourselves against the gate with
     battering and shaking?
FIRST OLD MAN: and if the women won't unbar at such an
     ultimatum
     we'll set the gate on fire and then the smoke will suffocate
     'em.
SECOND OLD MAN: Well, let's put down our load. Fooh fooh,
     what smoke! But blow as needed!
THIRD OLD MAN: Your ablest generals *these* days would not carry   320
     wood like *we* did.
SECOND OLD MAN: At last the lumber ceases grinding my poor
     back to pieces!
THIRD OLD MAN: These are your orders, Colonel Pot: wake up
     the coals and bid them
     report here and present to me a torch lit up and flaring.
FIRST OLD MAN: O Victory, be with us! If you quell the
     women's daring
     we'll raise a splendid trophy of how you and we undid   325
     them!

(*A* CHORUS OF MIDDLE-AGED WOMEN *appears in the offing.*)

A WOMAN: I think that I perceive a smoke in which appears a
     flurry
     of sparks as of a lighted fire. Women, we'll have to hurry!
CHORUS OF WOMEN: Oh fleetly fly, oh swiftly flit,
       my dears, e'er Kalykë be lit
       and with Kritylla swallowed up alive   330
         in flames which the gales dreadfully drive
         and deadly old men fiercely inflate!
     Yet one thing I'm afraid of: will I not arrive too late?
     for filling up my water-jug has been no easy matter
     what with the crowd at the spring in the dusk and the   335
         clamor and pottery clatter.
        Pushed as I was, jostled by slave-
        women and sluts marked with a brand
        yet with my jug firmly in hand
        here I have come, hoping to save   340
         my burning friends and brave,

        for certain windy, witless, old,
        and wheezy fools, so I was told,
     with wood some tons in weight crept up this path,
        not having in mind heating a bath   345
        but uttering threats, vowing they will
     consume those nasty women into cinders on grill!
     But O Athena! never may I see my friends igniting!
     Nay!—let them save all the cities of Greece and their
        people from folly and fighting!   350
       Goddess whose crest flashes with gold,
       they were so bold taking your shrine
       only for this—Goddess who holds
       Athens—for *this* noble design,
       braving the flames, calling on you   355
        to carry water too!

(ONE OF THE OLD MEN *urinates noisily.*)

CHORUS OF WOMEN: Be still! What was that noise? Aha! Oh, wicked and degraded!
Would any good religious men have ever done what *they* did?

CHORUS OF MEN: Just look! It's a surprise-attack! Oh, dear, we're being raided

360   by swarms of them below us when we've got a swarm above us!

CHORUS OF WOMEN: Why panic at the sight of us? This is not many of us.
We number tens of thousands but you've hardly seen a fraction.

CHORUS OF MEN: O Phaidrias, shall they talk so big and we not take some action?
Oh, should we not be bashing them and splintering our lumber?

(*The* OLD MEN *begin to strip for combat.*)

365 CHORUS OF WOMEN: Let us, too, set our pitchers down, so they will not encumber
our movements if these gentlemen should care to offer battle.

CHORUS OF MEN: Oh someone should have clipped their jaws—twice, thrice, until they rattle—
(as once the poet put it)—then we wouldn't hear their prating.

CHORUS OF WOMEN: Well, here's your chance. Won't someone hit me? Here I stand, just waiting!

370   No other bitch will ever grab your balls, the way I'll treat you!

CHORUS OF MEN: Shut up—or I will drub you so old age will never reach you!

CHORUS OF WOMEN: Won't anyone step and lay one finger on Stratyllis?

CHORUS OF MEN: And if we pulverize her with our knuckles, will you kill us?

CHORUS OF WOMEN: No, only chew your lungs out and your innards and your eyes, sir.

375 CHORUS OF MEN: How clever is Euripides! There is no poet wiser:
he says indeed that women are the worst of living creatures.

CHORUS OF WOMEN: Now is the time, Rhodippe: let us raise our brimming pitchers.

CHORUS OF MEN: Why come up here with water, you, the gods' abomination?

CHORUS OF WOMEN: And why come here with fire, you tomb? To give yourself cremation?

380 CHORUS OF MEN: To set your friends alight upon a pyre erected for them.

CHORUS OF WOMEN: And so we brought our water-jugs. Upon your pyre we'll pour them.

CHORUS OF MEN: *You'll* put my fire out?

CHORUS OF WOMEN: Any time! You'll see there's nothing to it.

CHORUS OF MEN: I think I'll grill you right away, with just this torch to do it!

CHORUS OF WOMEN: Have you some dusting-powder? Here's your wedding-bath all ready.

385 CHORUS OF MEN: *You'll* bathe me, garbage that you are?

CHORUS OF WOMEN: Yes, bridegroom, just hold steady!

CHORUS OF MEN: Friends, you have heard her insolence—

CHORUS OF WOMEN: I'm free-born, not your slave, sir.

CHORUS OF MEN: I'll have this noise of yours restrained—

CHORUS OF WOMEN: Court's out—so be less grave, sir.

CHORUS OF MEN: Why don't you set her hair on fire?

CHORUS OF WOMEN: Oh, Water, be of service!

CHORUS OF MEN: Oh woe is me!

CHORUS OF WOMEN: Was it too hot?

CHORUS OF MEN: Oh, stop! What *is* this? Hot? Oh no!   390

CHORUS OF WOMEN: I'm watering you to make you grow.

CHORUS OF MEN: I'm withered from this chill I got!

CHORUS OF WOMEN: You've got a fire, so warm yourself.
You're trembling: are you nervous?

(*Enter* ATHENIAN COMMISSIONER, *escorted by four* SCYTHIAN POLICEMEN *with bows and quivers slung on their backs.*)

COMMISSIONER: Has the extravagance of women broken out
into full fury, with their banging tambourines   395
and constant wailings for their oriental gods,
and on the roof-tops their Adonis festival,
which I could hear myself from the Assembly once?
For while Demostratos—that numbskull—had the floor,
urging an expedition against Sicily,   400
his wife was dancing and we heard her crying out
"Weep for Adonis!"—so the expedition failed
with such an omen. When the same Demostratos
was urging that we levy troops from our allies
his wife was on the roof again, a little drunk: 405
"Weep for Adonis! Beat your breast!" says she. At that,
he gets more bellicose, that god-Damn-ox-tratos.
To this has the incontinence of women come!

CHORUS OF MEN: You haven't *yet* heard how outrageous they can be!
With other acts of violence, these women here   410
have showered us from their jugs, so now we are reduced
to shaking out our shirts as if we'd pissed in them.

COMMISSIONER: Well, by the God of Waters, what do you expect?
When we ourselves conspire with them in waywardness
and give them good examples of perversity   415
such wicked notions naturally sprout in them.
We go into a shop and say something like this:
"Goldsmith, about that necklace you repaired: last night
my wife was dancing, when the peg that bolts the catch
fell from its hole. I have to sail for Salamis,   420
but if you have the time, by all means try to come
towards evening, and put in the peg she needs."
Another man says to a cobbler who is young
and has no child's-play of a prick, "Cobbler," he says,
"her sandal-strap is pinching my wife's little toe,   425
which is quite delicate. So please come by at noon
and stretch it for her so it has a wider play."
Such things as that result of course in things like this:
when I, as a Commissioner, have made a deal
to fit the fleet with oars and need the money now,   430
I'm locked out by these women from the very gates.
But it's no use just standing here. Bring on the bars,
so I can keep these women in their proper place.
What are *you* gaping at, you poor unfortunate?
Where are *you* looking? Only seeing if a bar   435
is open yet downtown? Come, drive these crowbars in
under the gates on that side, pry away, and I
will pry away on this.

(LYSISTRATA *comes out.*)

LYSISTRATA: No need to pry at all.
I'm coming out, of my own will. What use are bars?
440   It isn't bolts and bars we need so much as brains.
COMMISSIONER: Really, you dirty slut? Where is that officer?
Arrest her, and tie both her hands behind her back.
LYSISTRATA: By Artemis, just let him lift a hand at me
and, public officer or not, you'll hear him howl.
445 COMMISSIONER: You let her scare you? Grab her round the
middle, you.
Then *you* go help him and between you get her tied.

(KALONIKE *comes out.*)

KALONIKE: By Artemis, if you just lay one hand on her
I have a mind to trample the shit out of you.
COMMISSIONER: It's out already! Look! Now where's the other
one?
450   Tie up *that* woman first. She babbles, with it all.

(MYRRHINA *comes out.*)

MYRRHINA: By Hecatë, if you just lay a hand on her
you'll soon ask for a cup—to get your swellings down!

(*The* POLICEMAN *dashes behind the* COMMISSIONER *and clings to
him for protection.*)

COMMISSIONER: What happened? Where's that bowman, now?
Hold onto *her!*

(*He moves quickly away downhill.*)

I'll see that none of you can get away through here!
455 LYSISTRATA: By Artemis, you come near her and I'll bereave
your head of every hair! You'll weep for each one, too.
COMMISSIONER: What a calamity! This one has failed me too.
But never must we let ourselves be overcome
by women. All together now, O Scythians—
460   let's march against them in formation!
LYSISTRATA: You'll find out
that inside there we have four companies
of fighting women perfectly equipped for war.
COMMISSIONER: Charge! Turn their flanks, O Scythians! and tie
their hands!
LYSISTRATA: O allies—comrades—women! Sally forth and fight!
465   O vegetable vendors, O green-grocery-
grain-garlic-bread-bean-dealers and inn-keepers all!

(*A group of fierce* OLD MARKET-WOMEN, *carrying baskets of vegetables, spindles, etc., emerges. There is a volley of vegetables. The*
SCYTHIANS *are soon routed.*)

Come pull them, push them, smite them, smash them
into bits!
Rail and abuse them in the strongest words you know!
Halt, Halt! Retire in order! We'll forego the spoils!
470 COMMISSIONER: (*Tragically, like say Xerxes.*) Oh what reverses
have my bowmen undergone!
LYSISTRATA: But what did you imagine? Did you think you came
against a pack of slaves? Perhaps you didn't know
that women can be resolute?
COMMISSIONER: I know they can—
above all when they spot a bar across the way.

CHORUS OF MEN: Commissioner of Athens, you are spending 475
words unduly,
to argue with these animals, who only roar the louder,
or don't you know they showered us so coldly and so
cruelly,
and in our undershirts at that, and furnished us no powder?
CHORUS OF WOMEN: But beating up your neighbor is
inevitably bringing
a beating on yourself, sir, with your own eyes black and   480
bloody.
I'd rather sit securely like a little girl demurely
not stirring up a single straw nor harming anybody,
So long as no one robs my hive and rouses me to stinging.
CHORUS OF MEN: How shall we ever tame these brutes? We
cannot tolerate
the situation further, so we must investigate   485
this occurrence and find
with what purpose in mind
they profane the Acropolis, seize it, and lock
the approach to this huge and prohibited rock,
to our holiest ground!   490
Cross-examine them! Never believe one word
they tell you—refute them, confound them!
We must get to the bottom of things like this
and the circumstances around them.
COMMISSIONER: Yes indeed! and I want to know first one   495
thing:
just *why* you committed this treason,
barricading the fortress with locks and bars—
I insist on knowing the reason.
LYSISTRATA: To protect all the money up there from you—
you'll have nothing to fight for without it.   500
COMMISSIONER: You think it is *money* we're fighting for?
LYSISTRATA: All the troubles we have are about it.
It was so Peisander and those in power
of his kind could embezzle the treasure
that they cooked up emergencies all the time.   505
Well, let them, if such is their pleasure,
but they'll never get into this money again,
though you men should elect them to spend it.
COMMISSIONER: And just what will *you* do with it?
LYSISTRATA: Can you ask?
Of course we shall superintend it.   510
COMMISSIONER: You will superintend the treasury, *you!?*
LYSISTRATA: And why should it strike you so funny?
when we manage our houses in everything
and it's we who look after your money.
COMMISSIONER: But it's not the same thing!   515
LYSISTRATA: Why not?
COMMISSIONER: It's war,
and *this* money must pay the expenses.
LYSISTRATA: To begin with, you needn't be waging war.
COMMISSIONER: To survive, we don't need our defenses?
LYSISTRATA: You'll survive: we shall save you.
COMMISSIONER: Who? You?
LYSISTRATA: Yes, we.
COMMISSIONER: You absolutely disgust me.   520
LYSISTRATA: You may like it or not, but you *shall* be saved.
COMMISSIONER: I protest!
LYSISTRATA: If you care to, but, trust me,
this has got to be done all the same.

COMMISSIONER: It has?
      It's illegal, unjust, and outrageous!
525 LYSISTRATA: We must save you, sir.
      COMMISSIONER: Yes? And if I refuse?
      LYSISTRATA: You will much the more grimly engage us.
      COMMISSIONER: And whence does it happen that war and peace
            are fit matters for women to mention?
      LYSISTRATA: I will gladly explain—
      COMMISSIONER: And be quick, or else
530   you'll be howling!
      LYSISTRATA: Now, just pay attention
            and keep your hands to yourself, if you can!
      COMMISSIONER: But I can't. You can't think how I suffer
            from holding them back in my anger!
      AN OLD WOMAN: Sir—
            if you don't you will have it much rougher.
535 COMMISSIONER: You may croak that remark to yourself, you hag!
            Will *you* do the explaining?
      LYSISTRATA: I'll do it.
            Heretofore we women in time of war
                  have endured very patiently through it,
            putting up with whatever you men might do,
540   for never a peep would you let us
            deliver on your unstatesmanly acts
                  no matter how much they upset us,
            but we knew very well, while we sat at home,
                  when you'd handled a big issue poorly,
545   and we'd ask you then, with a pretty smile
                  though our heart would be grieving us sorely,
            "And what were the terms for a truce, my dear,
                  you drew up in assembly this morning?"
            "And what's it to you?" says our husband, "Shut up!"
550   —so, as ever, at this gentle warning
            I of course would discreetly shut up.
      KALONIKE: Not me!
            You can bet I would never be quiet!
      COMMISSIONER: I'll bet, if you weren't, you were beaten up.
      LYSISTRATA: *I'd* shut up, and I do not deny it,
555   but when plan after plan was decided on,
                  so bad we could scarcely believe it,
            I would say "This last is so mindless, dear,
                  I cannot think how you achieve it!"
            And then he would say, with a dirty look,
560   "Just you think what your spindle is for, dear,
            or your head will be spinning for days on end—
                  let the *men* attend to the war, dear."
      COMMISSIONER: By Zeus, *he* had the right idea!
      LYSISTRATA: You fool!
            Right ideas were quite out of the question,
565   when your reckless policies failed, and yet
                  we never could make a suggestion.
            And lately we heard you say so yourselves:
                  in the streets there'd be someone lamenting:
            "There's not one man in the country now!"
570   —and we heard many others assenting.
            After that, we conferred through our deputies
                  and agreed, having briefly debated,
            to act in common to save all Greece
                  at once—for why should we have waited?
575 So now, when we women are talking sense,
            if you'll only agree to be quiet

and to listen to us as we did to you,
            you'll be very much edified by it.
COMMISSIONER: *You* will edify *us!* I protest!
LYSISTRATA: Shut up!
COMMISSIONER: *I'm* to shut up and listen, you scum, you?!   580
      Sooner death! And a veil on your head at that!
LYSISTRATA: We'll fix that. It may really become you:
      do accept this veil as a present from me.
      Drape it modestly—so—round your head, do you see?
      And now—*not* a word more, sir.   585
KALONIKE: Do accept this dear little wool-basket, too!
      Hitch your girdle and card! Here are beans you may
            chew
      the way all of the nicest Athenians do—
      and the *women* will see to the war, sir!
CHORUS OF WOMEN: Oh women, set your jugs aside and keep   590
      a closer distance:
      our friends may need from us as well some resolute
      assistance.

      Since never shall I weary of the stepping of the dance
nor will my knees of treading, for these ladies I'll advance
            anywhere they may lead,
            and they're daring indeed,   595
      they have wit, a fine figure, and boldness of heart,
      they are prudent and charming, efficient and smart,
            patriotic and brave!

But, O manliest grandmothers, onward now!   600
      And you matronly nettles, don't waver!
but continue to bristle and rage, my dears,
      for you've still got the wind in your favor!

(*The* CHORUS OF WOMEN *and the* OLD MARKET-WOMEN *join.*)

LYSISTRATA: But if only the spirit of tender Love
      and the power of sweet Aphrodite
were to breathe down over our breasts and thighs   605
      an attraction both melting and mighty,
and infuse a pleasanter rigor in men,
      raising only their cudgels of passion,
then I think we'd be known throughout all of Greece
      as makers of peace and good fashion.   610
COMMISSIONER: Having done just what?
LYSISTRATA: Well, first of all
      we shall certainly make it unlawful
      to go madly to market in armor.
AN OLD MARKET-WOMAN: Yes!
      By dear Aphrodite, it's awful!
LYSISTRATA: For now, in the midst of the pottery-stalls   615
      and the greens and the beans and the garlic,
      men go charging all over the market-place
      in full armor and beetling and warlike.
COMMISSIONER: They must do as their valor impels them to!
LYSISTRATA: But it makes a man only look funny   620
      to be wearing a shield with a Gorgon's head
      and be wanting sardines for less money.
OLD MARKET-WOMAN: Well, I saw a huge cavalry-captain once
      on a stallion that scarcely could hold him,
      pouring into his helmet of bronze a pint   625
      of pea-soup an old women had sold him,
      and a Thracian who, brandishing shield and spear
      like some savage Euripides staged once,

630   when he'd frightened a vendor of figs to death,
        gobbled up all her ripest and aged ones.
COMMISSIONER: And how, on the international scale,
    can you straighten out the enormous
    confusion among all the states of Greece?
LYSISTRATA: Very easily.
COMMISSIONER: How? Do inform us.
635 LYSISTRATA: When our skein's in a tangle we take it thus
    on our spindles, or haven't you seen us?—
    one on this side and one on the other side,
    and we work out the tangles between us.
    And that is the way we'll undo this war,
640   by exchanging ambassadors, whether
    you like it or not, one from either side,
    and we'll work out the tangles together.
COMMISSIONER: Do you really think that with wools and skeins
    and just being able to spin you
645 can end these momentous affairs, you fools?
LYSISTRATA: With any intelligence in you
    you statesmen would govern as we work wool,
    and in everything Athens would profit.
COMMISSIONER: How so? Do tell.
LYSISTRATA: First, you take raw fleece
650   and you wash the beshittedness off it:
just so, you should first lay the city out
    on a washboard and beat out the rotters
and pluck out the sharpers like burrs, and when
    you find tight knots of schemers and plotters
655 who are out for key offices, card them loose,
    but best tear off their heads in addition.
Then into one basket together card
    all those of a good disposition
be they citizens, resident aliens, friends,
660   an ally or an absolute stranger,
even people in debt to the commonwealth,
    you can mix them all in with no danger.
And the cities which Athens has colonized—
    by Zeus, you should try to conceive them
665 as so many shreddings and tufts of wool
    that are scattered about and not leave them
to lie around loose, but from all of them
    draw the threads in here, and collect them
into one big ball and then weave a coat
670   for the people, to warm and protect them.
COMMISSIONER: Now, isn't this awful? They treat the state
    like wool to be beaten and carded,
who have nothing at all to do with war!
LYSISTRATA: Yes we do, you damnable hard-head!
675 We have none of your honors but we have more
    than double your sufferings by it.
First of all, we bear sons whom you send to war.
COMMISSIONER: Don't bring up our old sorrows! Be quiet!
LYSISTRATA: And now, when we ought to enjoy ourselves,
680   making much of our prime and our beauty,
we are sleeping alone because all the men
    are away on their soldierly duty.
But never mind *us*—when young girls grow old
    in their bedrooms with no men to share them.
685 COMMISSIONER: You seem to forget that men, too, grow old.
LYSISTRATA: By Zeus, but you cannot compare them!

When a man gets back, though he be quite gray,
    he can wed a young girl in a minute,
but the season of woman is very short:
    she must take what she can while she's in it.   690
And you know she must, for when it's past,
    although you're not awfully astute, you're
aware that no man will marry her then
    and she sits staring into the future.
COMMISSIONER: But he who can raise an erection still—   695
LYSISTRATA: Is there some good reason you don't drop dead?
    We'll sell you a coffin if you but will.
    Here's a string of onions to crown your head
    and I'll make a honey-cake large and round
    you can feed to Cerberus underground!   700
FIRST OLD MARKET-WOMAN: Accept these few fillets of leek
    from me!
SECOND OLD MARKET-WOMAN: Let me offer you these for your
    garland, sir!
LYSISTRATA: What now? Do you want something else you see?
    Listen! Charon's calling his passenger—
    will you catch the ferry or still delay   705
    when his other dead want to sail away?
COMMISSIONER: Is it not downright monstrous to treat *me* like
    this?
    By Zeus, I'll go right now to the Commissioners
    and show myself in evidence, just as I am!

(He begins to withdraw with dignity and his four Scythian policemen.)

LYSISTRATA: Will you accuse us of not giving you a wake?   710
    But your departed spirit will receive from us
    burnt offerings in due form, two days from now at dawn!

*(LYSISTRATA with the other women goes into the Acropolis. The
COMMISSIONER, etc., have left. The MALE CHORUS and the mixed
FEMALE CHORUS are alone.)*

CHORUS OF MEN: No man now dare fall to drowsing, if he
    wishes to stay free!
Men, let's strip and gird ourselves for this eventuality!

To me this all begins to have a smell   715
of bigger things and larger things as well:
most of all I sniff a tyranny afoot. I'm much afraid
certain secret agents of the Spartans may have come,
meeting under cover here, in Cleisthenes' home,
instigating those damned women by deceit to make a raid   720
upon our treasury and that great sum
the city paid my pension from.

Sinister events already!—think of lecturing the state,
women as they are, and prattling on of things like shields
    of bronze,
even trying hard to get us reconciled to those we hate—   725
those of Sparta, to be trusted like a lean wolf when it
    yawns!
All of this is just a pretext, men, for a dictatorship—
but to me they shall not dictate! Watch and ward! A
    sword I'll hide
underneath a branch of myrtle; through the agora I'll slip,
following Aristogeiton, backing the tyrannicide!   730

(*The* OLD MEN *pair off to imitate the gestures of the famous group statue of the tyrannicides Harmodius and Aristogeiton.*)

Thus I'll take my stand beside him! Now my rage is
  goaded raw
I'm as like as not to clip this damned old woman on the jaw!
CHORUS OF WOMEN: Your own mother will not know you when
  you come home, if you do!
Let us first, though, lay our things down, O my dear old
  friends
and true.

735   For now, O fellow-citizens, we would
      consider what will do our city good.
Well I may, because it bred me up in wealth and elegance:
  letting me at seven help with the embroidering
  of Athena's mantle, and at ten with offering
740   cakes and flowers. When I was grown and beautiful I had
      my chance
      to bear her baskets, at my neck a string
      of figs, and proud as anything.

Must I not, then, give my city any good advice I can?
Need you hold the fact against me that I was not born a man,
745   when I offer better methods than the present ones, and when
  I've a share in this economy, for I contribute men?
But, you sad old codgers, *yours* is forfeited on many scores:
  you have drawn upon our treasure dating from the Persian
  wars,
  what they call grampatrimony, and you've paid no taxes back.
750   Worse, you've run it nearly bankrupt, and the prospect's
      pretty black.
Have you anything to answer? Say you were within the law
and I'll take this rawhide boot and clip you one across the
  jaw!

CHORUS OF MEN: Greater insolence than ever!—
                      that's the method that she calls
755   "better"—if you would believe her.
But this threat must be prevented! Every man with both
  his balls
must make ready—take our shirts off, for a man must reek
  of male
outright—not wrapped up in leafage like an omelet for sale!

760   Forward and barefoot: we'll do it again
      to the death, just as when we resisted
      tyranny out at Leipsydrion, when
      we really existed!

765   Now or never we must grow
      young again and, sprouting wings
      over all our bodies, throw
      off this heaviness age brings!

For if any of us give them even just a little hold
nothing will be safe from their tenacious grasp. They are
  so bold
they will soon build ships of war and, with exorbitant intent,
770   send such navies out against us as Queen Artemisia sent.
But if they attack with horse, our knights we might as
  well delete:
nothing rides so well as woman, with so marvelous a seat,
never slipping at the gallop. Just look at those Amazons

in that picture in the Stoa, from their horses bringing bronze
axes down on men. We'd better grab *these* members of the   775
  sex
one and all, arrest them, get some wooden collars on their
  necks!
CHORUS OF WOMEN: By the gods, if you chagrin me
                        or annoy me, if you dare,
                        I'll turn loose the sow that's in me
till you rouse the town to help you with the way I've done   780
  your hair!
Let us too make ready, women, and our garments quickly
  doff
so we'll smell like women angered fit to bite our fingers off!

      Now I am ready: let one of the men
      come against me, and *he'll* never hanker
      after a black bean or garlic again: 785
      no woman smells ranker!

      Say a single unkind word,
      I'll pursue you till you drop,
      as the beetle did the bird.
      My revenge will never stop!   790

Yet you will not worry me so long as Lampito's alive
and my noble friends in Thebes and other cities still
  survive.
You'll not overpower us, even passing seven decrees or eight,
you, poor brutes, whom everyone and everybody's
  neighbors hate.
Only yesterday I gave a party, honoring Hecatë,   795
but when I invited in the neighbor's child to come and play,
such a pretty thing from Thebes, as nice and quiet as you
  please,
just an eel, they said she couldn't, on account of your
  decrees.
You'll go on forever passing such decrees without a check
till somebody takes you firmly by the leg and breaks your   800
  neck!

(LYSISTRATA *comes out. The* CHORUS OF WOMEN *addresses her in the manner of tragedy.*)

Oh Queen of this our enterprise and all our hopes,
  wherefore in baleful brooding hast thou issued forth?
LYSISTRATA: The deeds of wicked women and the female mind
  discourage me and set me pacing up and down.
CHORUS OF WOMEN: What's that? What's that you say?   805
LYSISTRATA: The truth, alas, the truth!
CHORUS OF WOMEN: What is it that's so dreadful? Tell it to
  your friends.
LYSISTRATA: A shameful thing to tell and heavy not to tell.
CHORUS OF WOMEN: Oh, never hide from me misfortune that is
  ours!
LYSISTRATA: To put it briefly as I can, we are in heat.   810
CHORUS OF WOMEN: Oh Zeus!
LYSISTRATA: Why call on Zeus? This is the
  way things are.
At least it seems I am no longer capable
of keeping them from men. They are deserting me.
This morning I caught one of them digging away
to make a tunnel to Pan's grotto down the slope,   815

another letting herself down the parapet
with rope and pulley, and another climbing down
its sheerest face, and yesterday was one I found
sitting upon a sparrow with a mind to fly
820   down to some well-equipped whoremaster's place in town.
Just as she swooped I pulled her backward by the hair.
They think of every far-fetched excuse they can
for going home. And here comes one deserter now.
You there, where are you running?

FIRST WOMAN: I want to go home,
825   because I left some fine Milesian wools at home
that must be riddled now with moths.

LYSISTRATA: Oh, damn your moths!
Go back inside.

FIRST WOMAN: But I shall come back right away,
just time enough to stretch them out upon my bed.

LYSISTRATA: Stretch nothing out, and don't you go away at all.

830   FIRST WOMAN: But shall I let my wools be ruined?

LYSISTRATA: If you must.

SECOND WOMAN: Oh miserable me! I sorrow for the flax
I left at home unbeaten and unstripped!

LYSISTRATA: One more—
wanting to leave for stalks of flax she hasn't stripped.
Come back here!

SECOND WOMAN: But, by Artemis, I only want
835   to strip my flax. Then I'll come right back here again.

LYSISTRATA: Strip me no strippings! If you start this kind of
thing
some other woman soon will want to do the same.

THIRD WOMAN: O lady Artemis, hold back this birth until
I can get safe to some unconsecrated place!

840   LYSISTRATA: What is this raving?

THIRD WOMAN: I'm about to have a child.

LYSISTRATA: But you weren't pregnant yesterday.

THIRD WOMAN: I am today.
Oh, send me home this instant, dear Lysistrata,
so I can find a midwife.

LYSISTRATA: What strange tale is this?
What is this hard thing you have here?

THIRD WOMAN: The child is male.

845   LYSISTRATA: By Aphrodite, no! You obviously have
some hollow thing of bronze. I'll find out what it is.
You silly thing!—you have Athena's helmet here—
and claiming to be pregnant!

THIRD WOMAN: So I am, by Zeus!

LYSISTRATA: In that case, what's the helmet for?

THIRD WOMAN: So if the pains
850   came on me while I'm still up here, I might give birth
inside the helmet, as I've seen the pigeons do.

LYSISTRATA: What an excuse! The case is obvious. Wait here.
I want to show this bouncing baby helmet off.

(*She passes the huge helmet around the* CHORUS OF WOMEN.)

SECOND WOMAN: But I can't even sleep in the Acropolis,
855   not for an instant since I saw the sacred snake!

FOURTH WOMAN: The owls are what are killing *me*. How can I
sleep
with their eternal whit-to-whoo-to-whit-to-whoo?

LYSISTRATA: You're crazy! Will you stop this hocus-pocus now?

No doubt you miss your husbands: don't you think that they
are missing us as much? I'm sure the nights they pass   860
are just as hard. But, gallant comrades, do bear up,
and face these gruelling hardships yet a little while.
There is an oracle that says we'll win, if we
only will stick together. Here's the oracle.

CHORUS OF WOMAN: Oh, read us what it says!   865

LYSISTRATA: Keep silence, then and hear:
"*Now when to one high place are gathered the fluttering
swallows,
Fleeing the Hawk and the Cock however hotly it follows.
Then will their miseries end, and that which is over be under:
Thundering Zeus will decide.*

A WOMAN: Will *we* lie on top now, I wonder?

LYSISTRATA: *But if the Swallows go fighting each other and   870
springing and winging
Out of the holy and high sanctuary, then people will never
Say there was any more dissolute bitch of a bird whatsoever.*"

A WOMAN: The oracle is clear, by Zeus!

LYSISTRATA: By *all* the gods!
So let us not renounce the hardships we endure.
But let us go back in. Indeed, my dearest friends,   875
it would be shameful to betray the oracle.

(*Exeunt into the Acropolis.*)

CHORUS OF MEN: Let me tell you a story I heard one day
when I was a child:
There was once a young fellow Melanion by name
who refused to get married and ran away   880
to the wild.
To the mountains he came
and inhabited there
in a grove
and hunted the hare   885
both early and late
with nets that he wove
and also a hound
and he never came home again, such was his hate,
all women he found   890
so nasty, and we
quite wisely agree.

Let us kiss you, dear old dears!

CHORUS OF WOMEN: With no onions, you'll shed tears!

CHORUS OF MEN: I mean, lift my leg and *kick*.   895

CHORUS OF WOMEN: My, you wear your thicket thick!

CHORUS OF MEN: Great Myronides was rough
at the front and black enough
in the ass to scare his foes.
Just ask anyone who knows: 900
it's with hair that wars are won—
take for instance Phormion.

CHORUS OF WOMEN: Let me tell you a story in answer to
Melanion's case.
There is now a man, Timon, who wanders around   905
in the wilderness, hiding his face from view
in a place
where the brambles abound
so he looks like a chip
off a Fury,   910

curling his lip.
Now Timon retired
in hatred and pure
contempt of all men

915 and he cursed them in words that were truly inspired
again and again
but women he found
delightful and sound.

Would you like your jaw repaired?

920 CHORUS OF MEN: Thank you, no. You've got me scared.
CHORUS OF WOMEN: Let me jump and kick it though.
CHORUS OF MEN: You will let your man-sack show.
CHORUS OF WOMEN: All the same you wouldn't see,
old and gray as I may be,

925 any superfluity
of unbarbered hair on me;
it is plucked and more, you scamp,
since I singe it with a lamp!

(*Enter* LYSISTRATA *on the wall.*)

LYSISTRATA: Women, O women, come here quickly, here to me!
930 WOMAN: Whatever is it? Tell me! What's the shouting for?
LYSISTRATA: I see a man approaching, shaken and possessed,
seized and inspired by Aphrodite's power.
O thou, of Cyprus, Paphos, and Cythera, queen!
continue straight along this way you have begun!
935 A WOMAN: Whoever he is, where is he?
LYSISTRATA: Near Demeter's shrine.
A WOMAN: Why yes, by Zeus, he is. Whoever can he be?
LYSISTRATA: Well, look at him. Do any of you know him?
MYRRHINA: Yes.
I do. He's my own husband, too, Cinesias.
LYSISTRATA: Then it's your duty now to turn him on a spit,
940 cajole him and make love to him and not make love,
to offer everything, short of those things of which
the wine-cup knows.
MYRRHINA: I'll do it, don't you fear.
LYSISTRATA: And I
will help you tantalize him. I will stay up here
and help you roast him slowly. But now, disappear!

(*Enter* CINESIAS.)

945 CINESIAS: Oh how unfortunate I am, gripped by what spasms,
stretched tight like being tortured on a wheel!
LYSISTRATA: Who's there? Who has got this far past the
sentries?
CINESIAS: I.
LYSISTRATA: A man?
CINESIAS: A man, for sure.
LYSISTRATA: Then clear away from here.
CINESIAS: Who're you, to throw me out?
LYSISTRATA: The look-out for the day.
950 CINESIAS: Then, for the gods' sake, call Myrrhina out for me.
LYSISTRATA: You don't say! Call Myrrhina out! And who are you?
CINESIAS: Her husband. I'm Cinesias Paionides.
LYSISTRATA: Well, my dear man, hello! Your name is not
unknown
among us here and not without a certain fame,
955 because your wife has it forever on her lips.

She can't pick up an egg or quince but she must say:
Cinesias would enjoy it so!
CINESIAS: How wonderful!
LYSISTRATA: By Aphrodite, yes. And if we chance to talk
of husbands, your wife interrupts and says the rest
are nothing much compared to her Cinesias.   960
CINESIAS: Go call her.
LYSISTRATA: Will you give me something if I do?
CINESIAS: Indeed I will, by Zeus, if it is what you want.
I can but offer what I have, and I have this.
LYSISTRATA: Wait there. I will go down and call her.
CINESIAS: Hurry up!
because I find no charm whatever left in life   965
since she departed from the house. I get depressed
whenever I go into it, and everything
seems lonely to me now, and when I eat my food
I find no taste in it at all because I'm stiff.
MYRRHINA: (*offstage*) I love him, how I love him! But he   970
doesn't want
my love! (*on wall*) So what's the use of calling me to him?
CINESIAS: My sweet little Myrrhina, why do you act like that?
Come down here.
MYRRHINA: There? By Zeus, I certainly will not.
CINESIAS: Won't you come down, Myrrhina, when I'm calling
you?
MYRRHINA: Not when you call me without needing   975
anything.
CINESIAS: Not needing anything? I'm desperate with need.
MYRRHINA: I'm going now.
CINESIAS: Oh no! No, don't go yet! At least
you'll listen to the baby. Call your mammy, you.
BABY: Mammy mammy mammy!
CINESIAS: What's wrong with you? Have you no pity on your 980
child
when it is six days now since he was washed or nursed?
MYRRHINA: Oh, I have pity. But his father takes no care of him.
CINESIAS: Come down, you flighty creature, for the child.
MYRRHINA: Oh, what it is to be a mother! I'll come down,
for what else can I do?   985

(MYRRHINA *exits to reenter below.*)

CINESIAS: It seems to me she's grown
much younger, and her eyes have a more tender look.
Even her being angry with me and her scorn
are just the things that pain me with the more desire.
MYRRHINA: Come let me kiss you, dear sweet little baby mine,
with such a horrid father. Mammy loves you, though.   990
CINESIAS: But why are you so mean? Why do you listen to
those other women, giving me such pain?—And you,
you're suffering yourself.
MYRRHINA: Take your hands off of me!
CINESIAS: But everything we have at home, my things and yours,
you're letting go to pieces.   995
MYRRHINA: Little do I care!
CINESIAS: Little you care even if your weaving's pecked apart
and carried off by chickens?
MYRRHINA: (*Bravely.*)   Little I care, by Zeus!
CINESIAS: You have neglected Aphrodite's rituals
for such a long time now. Won't you come back again?

1000 MYRRHINA: Not I, unless you men negotiate a truce
    and make an end of war.
CINESIAS: Well, if it's so decreed,
    we will do even that.
MYRRHINA: Well, if it's so decreed,
    I will come home again. Not now. I've sworn I won't.
CINESIAS: All right, all right. But now lie down with me once
    more.
1005 MYRRHINA: No! No!—yet I don't say I'm not in love with you.
CINESIAS: You love me? Then why not lie down, Myrrhina dear?
MYRRHINA: Don't be ridiculous! Not right before the child!
CINESIAS: By Zeus, of course not. Manes, carry him back home.
    There now. You see the baby isn't in your way.
1010   Won't you lie down?
MYRRHINA: But *where,* you rogue, just where
    is one to do it?
CINESIAS: Where? Pan's grotto's a fine place.
MYRRHINA: But how could I come back to the Acropolis
    in proper purity?
CINESIAS: Well, there's a spring below
    the grotto—you can very nicely bathe in that.

(Ekkyklema or inset-scene with grotto.)

1015 MYRRHINA: And then I'm under oath. What if I break my vows?
CINESIAS: Let me bear all the blame. Don't worry about your
    oath.
MYRRHINA: Wait here, and I'll go get a cot for us.
CINESIAS: No no,
    the ground will do.
MYRRHINA: No, by Apollo! Though you *are*
    so horrid, I can't have you lying on the ground.

(Leaves.)

1020 CINESIAS: You know, the woman loves me—*that's* as plain as day.
MYRRHINA: There. Get yourself in bed and I'll take off my
    clothes.
    Oh, what a nuisance! I must go and get a mat.
CINESIAS: What for? I don't need one.
MYRRHINA: Oh yes, by Artemis!
    On the bare cords? How ghastly!
CINESIAS: Let me kiss you now.
1025 MYRRHINA: Oh, very well.
CINESIAS: Wow! Hurry, hurry and come back.

(MYRRHINA leaves. A long wait.)

MYRRHINA: Here is the mat. Lie down now, while I get
    undressed.
    Oh, what a nuisance! You don't have a pillow, dear.
CINESIAS: But I don't need one, not one bit!
MYRRHINA: By Zeus, *I* do!

(Leaves.)

CINESIAS: Poor prick, the service around here is terrible!
1030 MYRRHINA: Sit up, my dear, jump up! Now I've got
    everything.
CINESIAS: Indeed you have. And now, my golden girl, come
    here.

MYRRHINA: I'm just untying my brassiere. Now don't forget:
    about that treaty—you won't disappoint me, dear?
CINESIAS: By Zeus, no! On my life!
MYRRHINA: You have no blanket, dear.
CINESIAS: By Zeus, I do not need one. I just want to screw. 1035
MYRRHINA: Don't worry, dear, you will. I'll be back right away.

(Leaves.)

CINESIAS: This number, with her bedding, means to murder me.
MYRRHINA: Now raise yourself upright.
CINESIAS: But *this* is upright now!
MYRRHINA: Wouldn't you like some perfume?
CINESIAS: By Apollo, no!
MYRRHINA: By Aphrodite, yes! You must—like it or not. 1040

(Leaves.)

CINESIAS: Lord Zeus! Just let the perfume spill! That's all I ask!
MYRRHINA: Hold out your hand. Take some of this and rub it on.
CINESIAS: This perfume, by Apollo, isn't sweet at all.
    It smells a bit of stalling—not of wedding nights!
MYRRHINA: I brought the *Rhodian* perfume! How absurd of me! 1045
CINESIAS: It's fine! Let's keep it.
MYRRHINA: You *will* have your little joke.

(Leaves.)

CINESIAS: Just let me at the man who first distilled perfumes!
MYRRHINA: Try this, in the long vial.
CINESIAS: I've got one like it, dear.
    But don't be tedious. Lie down. And please don't bring
    anything more. 1050
MYRRHINA: *(Going.)* That's what I'll do, by Artemis!
    I'm taking off my shoes. But dearest, don't forget
    you're going to vote for peace.
CINESIAS: I will consider it.
    She has destroyed me, murdered me, that woman has!
    On top of which she's got me skinned and gone away!

    What shall I do? Oh, whom shall I screw, 1055
    cheated of dear Myrrhina, the first
    beauty of all, a creature divine?
    How shall I tend this infant of mine?
    Find me a pimp: it has to be nursed!
CHORUS OF MEN: *(In tragic style, as if to Prometheus or
    Andromeda bound.)*
    In what dire woe, how heavy-hearted 1060
    I see thee languishing, outsmarted!
      I pity thee, alas I do.
    What kidney could endure such pain,
    what spirit could, what balls, what back,
    what loins, what sacroiliac, 1065
    if they came under such a strain
    and never had a morning screw?
CINESIAS: O Zeus! the twinges! Oh, the twitches!
CHORUS OF MEN: And this is what she did to you,
    that vilest, hatefullest of bitches! 1070
CINESIAS: Oh nay, by Zeus, she's dear and sweet!
CHORUS OF MEN: How can she be? She's vile, O Zeus, she's vile!
    Oh treat her, Zeus, like so much wheat—
    O God of Weather, hear my prayer—

1075 and raise a whirlwind's mighty blast
to roll her up into a pile
and carry her into the sky
far up and up and then at last
drop her and land her suddenly
1080 astride that pointed penis there!

(*The ekkyklema turns, closing the inset-scene. Enter, from opposite sides, a* SPARTAN HERALD *and an* ATHENIAN OFFICIAL.)

SPARTAN: Wheah is the Senate-house of the Athenians?
Ah wish to see the chaihman. Ah have news fo him.
ATHENIAN: And who are you? Are you a Satyr or a man?
SPARTAN: Ah am a herald, mah young friend, yes, by the gods,
1085 and Ah have come from Sparta to negotiate.
ATHENIAN: And yet you come here with a spear under your
arm?
SPARTAN: Not Ah, bah Zeus, not Ah!
ATHENIAN: Why do you turn around?
Why throw your cloak out so in front? Has the long trip
given you a swelling?
SPARTAN: Ah do think the man is queah!
1090 ATHENIAN: But you have an erection, oh you reprobate!
SPARTAN: Bah Zeus, Ah've no sech thing! And don't you fool
around!
ATHENIAN: And what have you got there?
SPARTAN: A Spahtan scroll-stick, suh.
ATHENIAN: Well, if it is, *this* is a Spartan scroll-stick, too.
But look, I know what's up: you can tell *me* the truth.
1095 Just how are things with you in Sparta: tell me that.
SPARTAN: Theah is uprising in all Spahta. Ouah allies
are all erect as well. We need ouah milkin'-pails.
ATHENIAN: From where has this great scourge of frenzy fallen
on you?
From Pan?
SPARTAN: No, Ah think Lampito began it all,
1100 and then, the othah women throughout Spahta joined
togethah, just lahk at a signal fo a race,
and fought theah husbands off and drove them from theah
cunts.
ATHENIAN: So, how're you getting on?
SPARTAN: We suffah. Through the town
we walk bent ovah as if we were carrying
1105 lamps in the wind. The women will not let us touch
even theah berries, till we all with one acco'd
have made a peace among the cities of all Greece.
ATHENIAN: This is an international conspiracy
launched by the women! Now I comprehend it all!
1110 Return at once to Sparta. Tell them they must send
ambassadors fully empowered to make peace.
And our Assembly will elect ambassadors
from our side, when I say so, showing them this prick.
SPARTAN: Ah'll run! Ah'll flah! Fo all you say is excellent!
1115 CHORUS OF MEN: No wild beast is more impossible than
woman is to fight,
nor is fire, nor has the panther such unbridled appetite!
CHORUS OF WOMEN: Well you know it, yet you go on warring
with me without end,
when you might, you cross-grained creature, have me as a
trusty friend.

CHORUS OF MEN: Listen: I will never cease from hating women
till I die!
CHORUS OF WOMEN: Any time you like. But meanwhile is   1120
there any reason why
I should let you stand there naked, looking so ridiculous?
I am only coming near you, now, to slip your coat on, thus.
CHORUS OF MEN: That was very civil of you, very kind to treat
me so,
when in such uncivil rage I took it off a while ago.
CHORUS OF WOMEN: Now you're looking like a man again,   1125
and not ridiculous.
If you hadn't hurt my feelings, I would not have made a fuss,
I would even have removed that little beast that's in your eye.
CHORUS OF MEN: *That* is what was hurting me! Well, won't
you take my ring to pry
back my eyelid? Rake the beast out. When you have it, let
me see,
for some time now it's been at my eye and irritating me.   1130
CHORUS OF WOMEN: Very well, I will—though you were *born*
an irritable man.
What a monster of a gnat, by Zeus! Look at it if you can.
Don't you see it? It's a native of great marshes, can't you tell?
CHORUS OF MEN: Much obliged, by Zeus! The brute's been
digging at me like a well!
So that now you have removed it, streams of tears come   1135
welling out.
CHORUS OF WOMEN: I will dry them. You're the meanest man
alive, beyond a doubt,
yet I will, and kiss you, too.
CHORUS OF MEN: Don't kiss me!
CHORUS OF WOMEN: If you will or not!
CHORUS OF MEN: Damn you! Oh, what wheedling flatterers
you all are, born and bred!
That old proverb is quite right and not inelegantly said:
"There's no living *with* the bitches and, without them,   1140
even *less*"—
so I might as well make peace with you, and from now on,
I guess,
I'll do nothing mean to you and, from you, suffer nothing
wrong.
So let's draw our ranks together now and start a little song:

For a change, we're not preparing
any mean remark or daring   1145
aimed at any man in town,
but the very opposite: we plan to do and say
only good to everyone,
when the ills we have already are sufficient anyway.
Any man or woman who   1150
wants a little money, oh
say three minas, maybe two,
kindly let us know.
What we have is right in here.
(Notice we have purses, too!)   1155
And if ever peace appear,
he who takes our loan today
never need repay.

We are having guests for supper,
allies asked in by our upper   1160
classes to improve the town.

There's pea-soup, and I had killed a sucking-pig of mine:
I shall see it is well done,
so you will be tasting something very succulent and fine.

1165   Come to see us, then, tonight
early, just as soon as you
have a bath and dress up right:
bring your children, too.
Enter boldly, never mind
1170   asking anyone in sight.
Go straight in and you will find
you are quite at home there, but
all the doors are shut.

And here come the Spartan ambassadors,
1175   dragging beards that are really the biggest I
have ever beheld, and around their thighs
they are wearing some sort of a pig-sty.

Oh men of Sparta, let me bid you welcome first,
and then you tell us how you are and why you come.
1180   SP. AMB.: What need is theah to speak to you in many words?
Fo you may see youahself in what a fix we come.
CHORUS OF MEN: Too bad! Your situation has become
terribly hard and seems to be at fever-pitch.
SP. AMB.: Unutterably so! And what is theah to say?
1185   Let someone bring us peace on any tuhms he will!
CHORUS OF MEN: And here I see some natives of Athenian soil,
holding their cloaks far off their bellies, like the best
wrestlers, who sicken at the touch of cloth. It seems
that overtraining may bring on this strange disease.
1190   ATH. AMB.: Will someone tell us where to find Lysistrata?
We're men, and here we are, in this capacity.
CHORUS OF MEN: This symptom and that other one sound
much alike.
Toward morning I expect convulsions do occur?
ATH. AMB.: By Zeus, we are exhausted with just doing that,
1195   so, if somebody doesn't reconcile us quick,
there's nothing for it: we'll be screwing Cleisthenes.
CHORUS OF MEN: Be carefulput your cloaks on, or you might
be seen
by some young blade who knocks the phalluses off herms.
ATH. AMB.: By Zeus, an excellent idea!
SP. AMB.: (Having overheard.)   Yes, bah the gods!
1200   It altogethah is. Quick, let's put on our cloaks.

(Both groups cover quick and then recognize each other with full
diplomatic pomp.)

ATH. AMB.: Greetings, O men of Sparta! (To his group.) We have
been disgraced!
SP. AMB.: (To one of his group.) Mah dearest fellah, what a
dreadful thing fo us,
if these Athenians had seen ouah wo'st defeat!
ATH. AMB.: Come now, O Spartans: one must specify each point.
1205   Why have you come here?
SP. AMB.:   To negotiate a peace.
We ah ambassadahs.
ATH. AMB.:   Well put. And so are we.
Therefore, why do we not call in Lysistrata,
she who alone might get us to agree on terms?
SP. AMB.: Call her or any man, even a Lysistratus!

CHORUS OF MEN: But you will have no need, it seems, to call   1210
her now,
for here she is. She heard you and is coming out.
CHORUS OF MEN and CHORUS OF WOMEN: All hail, O manliest
woman of all!
It is time for you now to be turning
into something still better, more dreadful, mean,
unapproachable, charming, discerning,   1215
for here are the foremost nations of Greece,
bewitched by your spells like a lover,
who have come to you, bringing you all their claims,
and to you turning everything over.
LYSISTRATA: The work's not difficult, if one can catch them now   1220
while they're excited and not making passes at
each other. I will soon find out. Where's HARMONY?

(A naked maid, perhaps wearing a large ribbon reading HARMONY,
appears from inside.)

Go take the Spartans first, and lead them over here,
not with a rough hand nor an overbearing one,
nor, as our husbands used to do this, clumsily,   1225
but like a woman, in our most familiar style:
If he won't give his hand, then lead him by the prick.
And now, go bring me those Athenians as well,
leading them by whatever they will offer you.
O men of Sparta, stand right here, close by my side,   1230
and you stand over there, and listen to my words.
I am a woman, yes, but there is mind in me.
In native judgment I am not so badly off,
and, having heard my father and my elders talk
often enough, I have some cultivation, too.   1235
And so, I want to take and scold you, on both sides,
as you deserve, for though you use a lustral urn
in common at the altars, like blood-relatives,
when at Olympia, Delphi, or Thermopylae—
how many others I might name if I took time!—   1240
yet, with barbarian hordes of enemies at hand,
it is Greek men, it is Greek cities, you destroy.
That is one argument so far, and it is done.
ATH. AMB.: My prick is skinned alive—that's what's destroying me.
LYSISTRATA: Now, men of Sparta—for I shall address you first—   1245
do you not know that once one of your kings came here
and as a suppliant of the Athenians
sat by our altars, death-pale in his purple robe,
and begged us for an army? For Messenē then
oppressed you, and an earthquake from the gods as well.   1250
Then Cimon went, taking four thousand infantry,
and saved the whole of Lacedaemon for your state.
That is the way Athenians once treated you;
you ravage their land now, which once received you well.
ATH. AMB.: By Zeus, these men are in the wrong, Lysistrata!   1255
SP. AMB.: (With his eyes on HARMONY.) We'ah wrong . . .
What an unutterably lovely ass!
LYSISTRATA: Do you suppose I'm letting you Athenians off?
Do you not know that once the Spartans in their turn,
when you were wearing the hide-skirts of slavery,
came with their spears and slew many Thessalians,   1260
many companions and allies of Hippias?

They were the only ones who fought for you that day,
freed you from tyranny and, for the skirt of hide,
gave back your people the wool mantle of free men.
1265 SP. AMB.: Ah nevah saw a woman broadahin her views.
ATH. AMB.: And I have never seen a lovelier little nook.
LYSISTRATA: So why, when you have done each other so much
good,
go on fighting with no end of malevolence?
Why don't you make a peace? Tell me, what's in your way?
1270 SP. AMB.: Whah, *we* ah willin', if *they* will give up to us
that very temptin' cuhve. (*Of* HARMONY, *as hereafter.*)
LYSISTRATA: What curve, my friend?
SP. AMB.:   The bay
of Pylos, which we've wanted and felt out so long.
ATH. AMB.: No, by Poseidon, you will not get into that!
LYSISTRATA: Good friend, do let them have it.
ATH. AMB.:   No! What other town
1275 can we manipulate so well?
LYSISTRATA: Ask them for one.
ATH. AMB.: Damn, let me think! Now first suppose you cede
to us
that bristling tip of land, Echinos, behind which
the gulf of Malia recedes, and those long walls,
the legs on which Megara reaches to the sea.
1280 SP. AMB.: No, mah deah man, not *everything,* bah Castah, no!
LYSISTRATA: Oh, give them up. Why quarrel for a pair of legs?
ATH. AMB.: I'd like to strip and get to plowing right away.
SP. AMB.: And *Ah* would lahk to push manuah, still earliah.
LYSISTRATA: When you have made a peace, then you will do
all that.
1285 But if you want to do it, first deliberate,
go and inform your allies and consult with them.
ATH. AMB.: Oh, damn our allies, my good woman! We are stiff.
Will all of our allies not stand resolved with us—
namely, to screw?
SP. AMB.:   And so will ouahs, Ah'll guarantee.
1290 ATH. AMB.: Our mercenaries, even, will agree with us.
LYSISTRATA: Excellent. Now to get you washed and purified
so you may enter the Acropolis, where we
women will entertain you out of our supplies.
You will exchange your pledges there and vows for peace.
1295 And after that each one of you will take his wife,
departing then for home.
ATH. AMB.:   Let's go in right away.
SP. AMB.: Lead on, ma'am, anywheah you lahk.
ATH. AMB.:   Yes, and be quick.

(*Exeunt into Acropolis.*)

CHORUS OF MEN *and* CHORUS OF WOMEN:
All the rich embroideries, the
scarves, the gold accessories, the
1300 trailing gowns, the robes I own
I begrudge to no man: let him take what things he will
for his children or a grown
daughter who must dress for the procession up Athena's
hill.
Freely of my present stocks
1305 I invite you all to take.
There are here no seals nor locks

very hard to break.
Search through every bag and box,
Look—you will find nothing there   1310
if your eyesight isn't fine—
sharper far than mine!

Are there any of you needing
food for all the slaves you're feeding,
all your little children, too?
I have wheat in tiny grains for you, the finest sort,   1315
and I also offer you
plenty of the handsome strapping grains that slaves get by the
quart.

So let any of the poor
visit me with bag or sack
which my slave will fill with more   1320
wheat than they can pack,
giving each his ample share.
Might I add that at my door
I have watch-dogs? So beware.
Come too close by day or night,   1325
you will find they bite.

(*Voice of drunken* ATHENIANS *from inside.*)

FIRST ATHENIAN: Open the door! (*Shoves the* PORTER *aside.*)
                                        And will you get out of my way?

(*A second drunken* ATHENIAN *follows. The first sees the* CHORUS.)

What are you sitting there for? Shall I, with this torch,
burn you alive? (*Drops character.*)
                              How vulgar! Oh, how commonplace!
I can not do it!   1330

(*Starts back in. The second* ATHENIAN *stops him and remonstrates
with him in a whisper. The first turns and addresses the audience.*)

                              Well, if it really must be done
to please you, we shall face it and go through with it.
CHORUS OF MEN *and* CHORUS OF WOMEN:
And we shall face it and go through with it with you.
FIRST ATHENIAN: (*In character again, extravagantly.*)
Clear out of here! Or you'll be wailing for your hair!

(CHORUS OF WOMEN *scours away in mock terror.*)

Clear out of here! so that the Spartans can come out
and have no trouble leaving, after they have dined.   1335

(CHORUS OF MEN *scours away in mock terror.*)

SECOND ATHENIAN: I never saw a drinking-party like this
one:
even the Spartans were quite charming, and of course
we make the cleverest company, when in our cups.
FIRST ATHENIAN: You're right, because when sober we are not
quite sane.
If I can only talk the Athenians into it,   1340
we'll always go on any embassy quite drunk,
for now, going to Sparta sober, we're so quick
to look around and see what trouble we can make
that we don't listen to a single word they say—

1345   instead we think we hear them say what they do not—
and none of our reports on anything agree.
But just now everything was pleasant. If a man
got singing words belonging to another song,
we all applauded and swore falsely it was fine!

1350   But here are those same people coming back again
to the same spot! Go and be damned, the pack of you!

(The CHORUS OF MEN AND WOMEN, *having thrown off their
masks, put on other cloaks, and rushed back on stage, stays put.)*

SECOND ATHENIAN: Yes, damn them, Zeus! Just when the
    party's coming out!

(The party comes rolling out.)

A SPARTAN: *(To another.)* Mah very chahmin friend, will you
    take up youah flutes?
1355   Ah'll dance the dipody and sing a lovely song
of us and the Athenians, of both at once!
FIRST ATHENIAN: *(As pleasantly as he can.)*
Oh yes, take up your little reeds, by all the gods:
I very much enjoy seeing you people dance.

SPARTAN: Memory, come,
1360   come inspiah thah young
           votaries to song,
           come inspiah theah dance!

(Other SPARTANS *join.)*

        Bring thah daughtah, bring the sweet
          Muse, fo well she knows
1365   us and the Athenians,
          how at Ahtemisium
        they in godlike onslaught rose
        hahd against the Puhsian fleet,
          drove it to defeat!
1370   Well she knows the Spartan waws,
          how Leonidas
          in the deadly pass
          led us on lahk baws
        whettin' shahp theah tusks, how sweat
1375   on ouah cheeks in thick foam flowahed,
        off ouah legs how thick it showahed,
          fo the Puhsian men were mo'
          than the sands along the sho'.
        Goddess, huntress, Ahtemis,
1380   slayeh of the beasts, descend:
        vuhgin goddess, come to this
        feast of truce to bind us fast
        so ouah peace may nevah end.
        Now let friendship, love, and wealth
1385   come with ouah acco'd at last.
        May we stop ouah villainous
        wahly foxy stealth!
          Come, O huntress, heah to us,
          heah, O vuhgin, neah to us!

LYSISTRATA: Come, now that all the rest has been so well
    arranged,
you Spartans take these women home; these others, you. 1390
Let husband stand beside his wife, and let each wife
stand by her husband: then, when we have danced a dance
to thank the gods for our good fortune, let's take care
hereafter not to make the same mistakes again.
ATHENIAN: Bring on the chorus! Invite the three Graces to 1395
    follow,
and then call on Artemis, call her twin brother,
the leader of choruses, healer Apollo!
CHORUS OF MEN AND WOMEN: *(Joins.)* Pray for their friendliest
    favor, the one and the other.
    Call Dionysus, his tender eyes casting
    flame in the midst of his Maenads ecstatic with dancing. 1400
    Call upon Zeus, the resplendent in fire,
    call on his wife, rich in honor and ire,
    call on the powers who possess everlasting
    memory, call them to aid,
    call them to witness the kindly, entrancing 1405
    peace Aphrodite has made!
        Alalai!
          Bound, and leap high! Alalai!
          Cry, as for victory, cry
          Alalai! 1410
LYSISTRATA: Sing us a new song, Spartans, capping our new song.
SPARTANS: Leave thah favohed mountain's height,
    Spahtan Muse, come celebrate
    Amyclae's lord with us and great
    Athena housed in bronze; 1415
    praise Tyndareus' paih of sons,
    gods who pass the days in spoht
    wheah the cold Eurotas runs.

(General dancing.)

    Now to tread the dance,
    now to tread it light, 1420
    praising Spahta, wheah you find
        love of singing quickened bah the pounding beat
        of dancing feet,
    when ouah guhls lahk foals cavoht
    wheah the cold Eurotas runs, 1425
    when they fleetly bound and prance
        till theah haih unfilleted shakes in the wind,
    as of Maenads brandishin'
    ahvied wands and revelin',
        Leda's daughtah, puah and faiah, 1430
        leads the holy dances theah.
FULL CHORUS: *(As everyone leaves dancing.)*
    So come bind up youah haih with youah hand,
        with youah feet make a bound
    lahk a deeah; fo the chorus clap out
        an encouragin' sound, 1435
        singin' praise of the temple of bronze
        housin' her we adaw:
    sing the praise of Athena: the goddess unvanquished in
    waw!

CRITICAL CONTEXTS

ARISTOTLE (384–322 BCE)

from *The Poetics* (c. 335 BCE)

TRANSLATED BY GERALD F. ELSE

Born near Macedonia, Aristotle entered the Academy in Athens at the age of seventeen to study with Plato. After Plato's death, Aristotle conducted research in natural history, mainly botany and zoology, throughout the Aegean region and served as the tutor of the young Alexander the Great in Macedon before returning to Athens to found the Lyceum in 355 BCE.

Aristotle wrote extensively on topics ranging from ethics, rhetoric, and metaphysics to physics and natural history. In The Poetics, *he analyzes the field of poetry into different "species" or genres (epic, tragedy, comedy, dithyramb) and attempts to discover the basic features of each. The Poetics* demonstrates Aristotle's extensive knowledge of drama, which he uses to refine a keen sense of the form and purpose of tragedy. We should remember that *The Poetics* was written sometime after 335 BCE, roughly a century after the height of the Athenian theater. And although* The Poetics *is the cornerstone of Western dramatic criticism, the meaning of several of Aristotle's key terms—**MIMESIS** (imitation), **CATHARSIS** (purgation), and **HAMARTIA** (error)—remain controversial.*

Students approaching The Poetics *for the first time often have difficulty with the compressed logic of Aristotle's text, which may have formed something akin to notes for a lecture—a basis for expansion and discussion. Given Aristotle's representation of poetry according to natural "species," one way into his thinking may be to attempt to relate the functions of the various parts of tragedy: What is the relationship between Aristotle's conception of plot and of character? What is the logic that sustains his claim that plot is the principal element of tragedy, more important than character, language, or spectacle? What is the nature of "imitation," as Aristotle expresses it here? Given Aristotle's sense of just and unjust imitation, should we take imitation as a straightforward synonym for realism?*

BASIC CONSIDERATIONS

The art of poetic composition in general and its various species, the function and effect of each of them; how the plots should be constructed if the composition is to be an artistic success; how many other component elements are involved in the process, and of what kind; and similarly all the other questions that fall under this same branch of inquiry— these are the problems we shall discuss; let us begin in the right and natural way, with basic principles.

Epic composition, then; the writing of tragedy, and of comedy also; the composing of dithyrambs; and the greater part of the making of music with flute and lyre: these are all in point of fact, taken collectively, imitative processes. They differ from each other, however, in three ways, namely by virtue of having (1) different means, (2) different objects, and (3) different methods of imitation.

THE DIFFERENTIATION ACCORDING TO MEDIUM

First, in the same way that certain people imitate a variety of things by means of shapes and colors, making visible replicas of them (some doing this on the basis of art, others out of habit), while another group produces its mimicry with the voice, so in the case of the arts we just mentioned: they all carry on their imitation through the media of rhythm, speech, and melody, but with the latter two used separately or together. Thus the arts of flute and lyre music, and any others of similar nature and effect, such as the art of the pan-pipe, produce their imitation using melody and rhythm alone, while there is another which does so using speeches or verses alone, bare of music, and either mixing the verses with one another or employing just one certain kind—an art which is, as it happens, nameless up to the present time. In fact, we could not even assign a common name to the mimes of Sophron and Xenarchus and the Socratic discourses: nor again if somebody should compose his imitation in trimeters or elegiac couplets or certain other verses of that kind. (Except people do link up poetic composition with verse and speak of "elegiac poets," "epic poets," not treating them as poets by virtue of their imitation, but employing the term as a common appellation going along with the use of verse. And in fact the name is also applied to anyone who treats a medical or scientific topic in verses, yet Homer and Empedocles actually have nothing in common except their verse; hence the proper term for the one is "poet," for the other, "science-writer" rather than "poet.") and likewise if someone should mix all the kinds of verse together in composing his imitation, as Chaeremon composed a *Centaur* using all the verses.

Such is the disjunction we feel is called for in these cases. There are on the other hand certain arts which use all the aforesaid media, I mean such as rhythm, song, and verse. The composition of dithyrambs and of nomes does so, and both tragedy and comedy. But there is a difference in that some of these arts use all the media at once while others use them in different parts of the work.

These then are the differentiations of the poetic arts with respect to the media in which the poets carry on their imitation.

THE OBJECTS OF IMITATION

Since those who imitate men in action, and these must necessarily be either worthwhile or worthless people (for definite characters tend pretty much to develop in men of action), it follows that they imitate men either better or worse than the average, as the painters do—for Polygnotus used to portray superior and Pauson inferior men; and it is evident that each of the forms of imitation aforementioned will include these differentiations, that is, will differ by virtue of imitating objects which are different in this sense. Indeed, it is possible for these dissimilarities to turn up in flute and lyre playing, and also in prose dialogues and bare verses: Thus Homer imitated superior men and Hegemon of Thasos, the inventor of parody, and Nicochares, the author of the *Deiliad,* inferior ones, likewise in connection with dithyrambs and nomes, for one can make the imitation the way Timotheus and Philoxenus did their *Cyclopes.* Finally, the difference between tragedy and comedy coincides exactly with the master-difference: Namely the one tends to imitate people better, the other one people worse, than the average.

THE MODES OF IMITATION

The third way of differentiating these arts is by the mode of imitation. For it is possible to imitate the same objects, and in the same media, (1) by narrating part of the time and dramatizing the rest of the time, which is the way Homer composes (mixed mode), or (2) with the same person continuing without change (straight narrative), or (3) with all the persons who are performing the imitation acting, that is, carrying on for themselves (straight dramatic mode).

JOTTINGS, CHIEFLY ON COMEDY

Poetic imitation, then, shows these three *differentiae,* as we said at the beginning: in the media, objects, and modes of imitation. So in one way Sophocles would be the same (kind of) imitator as Homer, since they both imitate worthwhile people, and in another way the same as Aristophanes, for they both imitate people engaged in action, doing things. In fact some authorities maintain that that is why plays are called dramas, because the imitation is of men acting (*drôntas,* from *drân,* "do, act"). It is also the reason why both tragedy and comedy are claimed by the Dorians: comedy by

the Megarians, both those from hereabouts, who say that it came into being during the period of their democracy, and those in Sicily, and tragedy by some of those in the Peloponnese. They use the names "comedy" and "drama" as evidence; for *they* say that they call their outlying villages *kômai* while the Athenians call theirs "demes" (*dêmoi*)—the assumption being that the participants in comedy were called *kômôidoi* not from their being revelers but because they wandered from one village to another, being degraded and excluded from the city—and that they call "doing" or "acting" *drân* while the Athenians designate it by *prattein.*

THE ORIGIN AND DEVELOPMENT OF POETRY

So much, then, for the *differentiae* of imitation, their number and identity. As to the origin of the poetic art as a whole, it stands to reason that two operative causes brought it into being, both of them rooted in human nature. Namely (1) the habit of imitating is congenital to human beings from childhood (actually man differs from the other animals in that he is the most imitative and learns his first lessons through imitation), and so is (2) the pleasure that all men take in works of imitation. A proof of this is what happens in our experience. There are things which we see with pain so far as they themselves are concerned but whose images, even when executed in very great detail, we view with pleasure. Such is the case for example with renderings of the least favored animals, or of cadavers. The cause of this also is that learning is eminently pleasurable not only to philosophers but to the rest of mankind in the same way, although their share in the pleasure is restricted. For the reason they take pleasure in seeing the images is that in the process of viewing they find themselves learning, that is, reckoning what kind a given thing belongs to: "This individual is a So-and-so." Because if the viewer happens not to have seen such a thing before, the reproduction will not produce the pleasure *qua* reproduction but through its workmanship or color or something else of that sort.

Since, then, imitation comes naturally to us, and melody and rhythm too (it is obvious that verses are segments of the respective rhythms), in the beginning it was those who were most gifted in these respects who, developing them little by little, brought the making of poetry into being out of improvisations. And the poetic enterprise split into two branches, in accordance with the two kinds of character. Namely, the soberer spirits were imitating noble actions and the actions of noble persons, while the cheaper ones were imitating those of the worthless, producing lampoons and invectives at first just as the other sort were producing hymns and encomia. . . . In them (that is, the invectives), in accordance with what is suitable and fitting, iambic verse also put in its appearance; indeed that is why it is called "iambic" now, because it is the verse in which they used to "iambize," that is, lampoon each other. And so some of the early poets became composers of epic, the others of iambic, verses.

Now it happens that we cannot name anyone before Homer as the author of that kind of poem (that is, an iambic poem), though it stands to reason that there were many who were; but from Homer on we can do so: thus his *Margites* and other poems of that sort. However, just as on the serious side Homer was most truly a poet, since he was the only one who not only composed well but constructed dramatic imitations, so too he was the first to adumbrate the forms of comedy by producing a (1) dramatic presentation, and not of invective but of (2) the ludicrous. For as the *Iliad* stands in relation to our tragedies, so the *Margites* stands in relation to our comedies.

Once tragedy and comedy had been partially brought to light, those who were out in pursuit of the two kinds of poetic activity, in accordance with their own respective natures, became in the one case comic poets instead of iambic poets, in the other case producers of tragedies instead of epics, because these genres were higher and more esteemed than the others. Now to review the question whether even tragedy is adequate to the basic forms or not—a question which is (can be) judged both by itself, in the abstract, and in relationship to our theater audiences—that is another story. However that may be, it did spring from an improvisational beginning (both it and comedy: the one from those who led off the dithyramb, the other from those who did so for the phallic performances [?] which still remain on the program in many of our cities); it did expand gradually, each feature being further developed as it appeared; and after it had gone through a number of phases it stopped upon attaining its full natural growth. Thus Aeschylus was the first to expand the troupe of assisting actors from one to two, shorten the choral parts, and see to it that the dialogue takes first place; (. . .) at the same time the verse became iambic trimeter instead of trochaic tetrameter. For in the beginning they used the tetrameter because the form of composition was "satyr-like," that is, more given over to dancing, but when speech came along the very nature of the case turned up the appropriate verse. For iambic is the most speech-like of verses. An indication of this is that we speak more iambics than any other kind of verse in our conversation with each other, whereas we utter hexameters rarely, and when we do we abandon the characteristic tone-pattern of ordinary speech.

Further, as to plurality of episodes and the other additions which are recorded as having been made to tragedy, let our account stop here; for no doubt it would be burdensome to record them in detail.

COMEDY

Comedy is as we said it was, an imitation of persons who are inferior; not, however, going all the way to full villainy, but imitating the ugly, of which the ludicrous is one part. The ludicrous, that is, is a failing or a piece of ugliness which causes no pain or destruction; thus, to go no farther, the comic mask is something ugly and distorted but painless.

Now the stages of development of tragedy, and the men who were responsible for them, have not escaped notice, but comedy did escape notice in the beginning because it was not taken seriously. (In fact it was late in its history that the presiding magistrate officially "granted a chorus" to the comic poets; until then they were volunteers.) Thus comedy already possessed certain defining characteristics when the first "comic poets," so-called, appear in the record. Who gave it masks, or prologues, or troupes of actors and all that sort of thing, is not known. The composing of plots came originally from Sicily; of the Athenian poets, Crates was the first to abandon the lampooning mode and compose arguments, that is, plots, of a general nature.

EPIC AND TRAGEDY

Well then, epic poetry followed in the wake of tragedy up to the point of being a (1) good-sized (2) imitation (3) in verse (4) of people who are to be taken seriously; but in its having its verse unmixed with any other and being narrative in character, there they differ. Further, so far as its length is concerned tragedy tries as hard as it can to exist during a single daylight period, or to vary but little, while the epic is not limited in its time and so differs in that respect. Yet originally they used to do this in tragedies just as much as they did in epic poems.

The constituent elements are partly identical and partly limited to tragedy. Hence anybody who knows about good and bad tragedy knows about epic also; for the elements that the epic possesses appertain to tragedy as well, but those of tragedy are not all found in the epic.

TRAGEDY AND ITS SIX CONSTITUENT ELEMENTS

Our discussions of imitative poetry in hexameters, and of comedy, will come later; at present let us deal with tragedy, recovering from what has been said so far the definition of its essential nature, as it was in development. Tragedy, then, is a process of imitating an action which has serious implications, is complete, and possesses magnitude; by means of language which has been made sensuously attractive, with each of its varieties found separately in the parts; enacted by the persons themselves and not presented through narrative; through a course of pity and fear completing the purification of tragic acts which have those emotional characteristics. By "language made sensuously attractive" I mean language that has rhythm and melody, and by "its varieties found separately" I mean the fact that certain parts of the play are carried on through spoken verses alone and others the other way round, through song.

Now first of all, since they perform the imitation through action (by acting it), the adornment of their visual appearance will perforce constitute some part of the making of tragedy; and song-composition and verbal expression also, for those are the media in which they perform the imitation. By "verbal expression" I mean the actual composition of the verses, and by "song-composition" something whose meaning is entirely clear.

Next, since it is an imitation of an action and is enacted by certain people who are performing the action, and since those people must necessarily have certain traits both of character and thought (for it is thanks to these two factors that we speak of people's actions also as having a defined character, and it is in accordance with their actions that all either succeed or fail); and since the imitation of the action is the plot, for by "plot" I mean here the structuring of the events, and by the "characters" that in accordance with which we say that the persons who are acting have a defined moral character, and by "thought" all the passages in which they attempt to prove some thesis or set forth an opinion—it follows of necessity, then, that tragedy as a whole has just six constituent elements, in relation to the essence that makes it a distinct species; and they are plot, characters, verbal expression, thought, visual adornment, and song-composition. For the elements by which they imitate are two (i.e., verbal expression and song-composition), the manner in which they imitate is one (visual adornment), the things they imitate are three (plot, characters, thought), and there is nothing more beyond these. These then are the constituent forms they use.

THE RELATIVE IMPORTANCE OF THE SIX ELEMENTS

The greatest of these elements is the structuring of the incidents. For tragedy is an imitation not of men but of a life, an action, and they have moral quality in accordance with their characters but are happy or unhappy in accordance with their actions; hence they are not active in order to imitate their characters, but they include the characters along with the actions for the sake of the latter. Thus the structure of events, the plot, is the goal of tragedy, and the goal is the greatest thing of all.

Again: a tragedy cannot exist without a plot, but it can without characters: thus the tragedies of most of our modern poets are devoid of character, and in general many poets are like that; so also with the relationship between Zeuxis and Polygnotus, among the painters: Polygnotus is a good portrayer of character, while Zeuxis' painting has no dimension of character at all.

Again: if one strings end to end speeches that are expressive of character and carefully worked in thought and expression, he still will not achieve the result which we said was the aim of tragedy; the job will be done much better by a tragedy that is more deficient in these other respects but has a plot, a structure of events. It is much the same case as with painting: the most beautiful pigments smeared on at random will not give as much pleasure as a black-and-white outline picture. Besides, the most powerful means tragedy has for swaying our feelings, namely the peripeties and recognitions, are elements of the plot.

Again: an indicative sign is that those who are beginning a poetic career manage to hit the mark in verbal expression and character portrayal sooner than they do in plot construction; and the same is true of practically all the earliest poets.

So plot is the basic principle, the heart and soul, as it were, of tragedy, and the characters come second: . . . it is the imitation of an action and imitates the persons primarily for the sake of their action.

Third in rank is thought. This is the ability to state the issues and appropriate points pertaining to a given topic, an ability which springs from the arts of politics and rhetoric; in fact the earlier poets made their characters talk "politically," the present-day poets rhetorically. But "character" is that kind of utterance which clearly reveals the bent of a man's moral choice (hence there is no character in that class of utterances in which there is nothing at all that the speaker is choosing or rejecting), while "thought" is the passages in which they try to prove that something is so or not so, or state some general principle.

Fourth is the verbal expression of the speeches. I mean by this the same thing that was said earlier, that the "verbal expression" is the conveyance of thought through language: a statement which has the same meaning whether one says "verses" or "speeches."

The song-composition of the remaining parts is the greatest of the sensuous attractions, and the visual adornment of the dramatic persons can have a strong emotional effect but is the least artistic element, the least connected with the poetic art; in fact the force of tragedy can be felt even without benefit of public performance and actors, while for the production of the visual effect the property man's art is even more decisive than that of the poets.

GENERAL PRINCIPLES OF THE TRAGIC PLOT

With these distinctions out of the way, let us next discuss what the structuring of the events should be like, since this is both the basic and the most important element in the tragic art. We have established, then, that tragedy is an imitation of an action which is complete and whole and has some magnitude (for there is also such a thing as a whole that has no magnitude). "Whole" is that which has beginning, middle, and end. "Beginning" is that which does not necessarily follow on something else, but after it something else naturally is or happens; "end," the other way round, is that which naturally follows on something else, either necessarily or for the most part, but nothing else after it; and "middle" that which naturally follows on something else and something else on it. So, then, well-constructed plots should neither begin nor end at any chance point but follow the guidelines just laid down.

Furthermore, since the beautiful, whether a living creature or anything that is composed of parts, should not only have these in a fixed order to one another but also possess a definite size which does not depend on chance—for beauty depends on size and order; hence neither can a very tiny creature turn out to be beautiful (since our perception of it grows blurred as it approaches the period of imperceptibility) nor an excessively huge one (for then it cannot all be perceived at once and so its unity and wholeness are lost), if for example there were a creature a thousand miles long—so, just as in the case of living creatures they must have some size, but one that can be taken in in a single view, so with plots: they should have length, but such that they are easy to remember. As to a limit of the length, the one is determined by the tragic competitions and the ordinary span of attention. (If they had to compete with a hundred tragedies they would compete by the water clock, as they say used to be done [?].) But the limit fixed by the very nature of the case is: the longer the plot, up to the point of still being perspicuous as a whole, the finer it is so far as size is concerned; or to put it in general terms, the length in which, with things happening in unbroken sequence, a shift takes place either probably or necessarily from bad to good fortune or from good to bad—that is an acceptable norm of length.

But a plot is not unified, as some people think, simply because it has to do with a single person. A large, indeed an indefinite number of things can happen to a given individual, some of which go to constitute no unified event; and in the same way there can be many acts of a given individual from which no single action emerges. Hence it seems clear that those poets are wrong who have composed Heracleïds, Theseïds, and the like. They think that since Heracles was a single person it follows that the plot will be single too. But Homer, superior as he is in all other respects, appears to have grasped this point well also, thanks either to art or nature, for in composing an Odyssey he did not incorporate into it everything that happened to the hero, for example how he was wounded on Mt. Parnassus or how he feigned madness at the muster, neither of which events, by happening, made it at all necessary or probable that the other should happen. Instead, he composed the Odyssey—and the Iliad similarly—around a unified action of the kind we have been talking about.

A poetic imitation, then, ought to be unified in the same way as a single imitation in any other mimetic field, by having a single object: since the plot is an imitation of an action, the latter ought to be both unified and complete, and the component events ought to be so firmly compacted that if any one of them is shifted to another place, or removed, the whole is loosened up and dislocated; for an element whose addition or subtraction makes no perceptible extra difference is not really a part of the whole.

From what has been said it is also clear that the poet's job is not to report what has happened but what is likely to happen: that is, what is capable of happening according to the rule of probability or necessity. Thus the difference between the historian and the poet is not in their utterances being in verse or prose (it would be quite possible for Herodotus' work to be translated into verse, and it would not be any the less a history with verse than it is without it); the difference lies in the fact that the historian speaks of what has happened, the poet of the kind of thing that *can* happen. Hence also poetry is a more philosophical and serious business than history; for poetry speaks more of universals, history of particulars. "Universal" in this case is what kind of person is likely to do or say certain kinds of things, according to probability or necessity; that is what poetry aims at, although it gives its persons particular names afterward; while the "particular" is what Alcibiades did or what happened to him.

In the field of comedy this point has been grasped: our comic poets construct their plots on the basis of general probabilities and then assign names to the persons quite arbitrarily, instead of dealing with individuals as the old iambic poets did. But in tragedy they still cling to the historically given names. The reason is that what is possible is persuasive; so what has not happened we are not yet ready to believe is possible, while what has happened is, we feel, obviously possible: for it would not have happened if it were impossible. Nevertheless, it is a fact that even in our tragedies, in some cases only one or two of the names are traditional, the rest being invented, and in some others none at all. It is so, for example, in Agathon's Antheus—the names in it are as fictional as the events—and it gives no less pleasure because of that. Hence the poets ought not to cling at all costs to the traditional plots, around which our tragedies are constructed. And in fact it is absurd to go searching for this kind of authentication, since even the familiar names are familiar to only a few in the audience and yet give the same kind of pleasure to all.

So from these considerations it is evident that the poet should be a maker of his plots more than of his verses, insofar as he is a poet by virtue of his imitations and what he imitates is actions. Hence even if it happens that he puts something that has actually taken place into poetry, he is none the less a poet; for there is nothing to prevent some of the things that have happened from being the kind of things that can happen, and that is the sense in which he is their maker.

SIMPLE AND COMPLEX PLOTS

Among simple plots and actions the episodic are the worst. By "episodic" plot I mean one in which there is no probability or necessity for the order in which the episodes follow one another. Such structures are composed by the bad poets because they are bad poets, but by the good poets because of the actors: in composing contest pieces for them, and stretching out the plot beyond its capacity, they are forced frequently to dislocate the sequence.

Furthermore, since the tragic imitation is not only of a complete action but also of events that are fearful and pathetic, and these come about best when they come about contrary to one's expectation yet logically, one following from the other; that way they will be more productive of wonder than if they happen merely at random, by chance—because even among chance occurrences the ones people consider most marvelous are those that seem to have come about as if on purpose: for example the way the statue of Mitys at Argos killed the man who had been the cause of Mitys' death, by falling on him while he was attending the festival; it stands to reason, people think, that such things don't happen by chance—so plots of that sort cannot fail to be artistically superior.

Some plots are simple, others are complex; indeed the actions of which the plots are imitations already fall into these two categories. By "simple" action I mean one the development of which being continuous and unified in the manner stated above, the reversal comes without peripety or recognition, and by "complex" action one in which the reversal is continuous but with recognition or peripety or both. And these developments must grow out of the very structure of the plot itself, in such a way that on the basis of what has happened previously this particular outcome follows either by necessity or in accordance with probability; for there is a great difference in whether these events happen because of those or merely after them.

"Peripety" is a shift of what is being undertaken to the opposite in the way previously stated, and that in accordance with probability or necessity as we have just been saying; as

for example in the *Oedipus* the man who has come, thinking that he will reassure Oedipus, that is, relieve him of his fear with respect to his mother, by revealing who he once was, brings about the opposite; and in the *Lynceus,* as he (Lynceus) is being led away with every prospect of being executed, and Danaus pursuing him with every prospect of doing the executing, it comes about as a result of the other things that have happened in the play that he is executed and Lynceus is saved. And "recognition" is, as indeed the name indicates, a shift from ignorance to awareness, pointing in the direction either of close blood ties or of hostility, of people who have previously been in a clearly marked state of happiness or unhappiness.

The finest recognition is one that happens at the same time as a peripety, as is the case with the one in the *Oedipus.* Naturally, there are also other kinds of recognition: it is possible for one to take place in the prescribed manner in relation to inanimate objects and chance occurrences, and it is possible to recognize whether a person has acted or not acted. But the form that is most integrally a part of the plot, the action, is the one aforesaid; for that kind of recognition combined with peripety will excite either pity or fear (and these are the kinds of action of which tragedy is an imitation according to our definition), because both good and bad fortune will also be most likely to follow that kind of event. Since, further, the recognition is a recognition of persons, some are of one person by the other one only (when it is already known who the "other one" is), but sometimes it is necessary for both persons to go through a recognition, as for example Iphigenia is recognized by her brother through the sending of the letter, but of him by Iphigenia another recognition is required.

These then are two elements of plot: peripety and recognition; third is the *pathos.* Of these, peripety and recognition have been discussed; a *pathos* is a destructive or painful act, such as deaths on stage, paroxysms of pain, woundings, and all that sort of thing.

THE TRAGIC SIDE OF TRAGEDY: PITY AND FEAR AND THE PATTERNS OF THE COMPLEX PLOT

The "parts" of tragedy which should be used as constituent elements were mentioned earlier; . . . but what one should aim at and what one should avoid in composing one's plots, and whence the effect of tragedy is to come, remains to be discussed now, following immediately upon what has just been said.

Since, then, the construction of the finest tragedy should be not simple but complex, and at the same time imitative of fearful and pitiable happenings (that being the special character of this kind of poetry), it is clear first of all that

(1) neither should virtuous men appear undergoing a change from good to bad fortune, for that is not fearful, nor pitiable either, but morally repugnant; nor (2) the wicked from bad fortune to good—that is the most untragic form of all, it has none of the qualities that one wants: it is productive neither of ordinary sympathy nor of pity nor of fear—nor again (3) the really wicked man changing from good fortune to bad, for that kind of structure will excite sympathy but neither pity nor fear, since the one (pity) is directed towards the man who does not deserve his misfortune and the other (fear) towards the one who is like the rest of mankind—what is left is the man who falls between these extremes. Such is a man who is neither a paragon of virtue and justice nor undergoes the change to misfortune through any real badness or wickedness but because of some mistake; one of those who stand in great repute and prosperity, like Oedipus and Thyestes: conspicuous men from families of that kind.

So, then, the artistically made plot must necessarily be single rather than double, as some maintain, and involve a change not from bad fortune to good fortune but the other way round, from good fortune to bad, and not thanks to wickedness but because of some mistake of great weight and consequence, by a man such as we have described or else on the good rather than the bad side. An indication comes from what has been happening in tragedy: at the beginning the poets used to "tick off" whatever plots came their way, but nowadays the finest tragedies are composed about a few houses: they deal with Alcmeon, Oedipus, Orestes, Meleager, Thyestes, Telephus, and whichever others have had the misfortune to do or undergo fearful things.

Thus the technically finest tragedy is based on this structure. Hence those who bring charges against Euripides for doing this in his tragedies are making the same mistake. His practice is correct in the way that has been shown. There is a very significant indication: on our stages and in the competitions, plays of this structure are accepted as the most tragic, *if* they are handled successfully, and Euripides, though he may not make his other arrangements effectively, still is felt by the audience to be the most tragic, at least, of the poets.

Second comes the kind which is rated first by certain people, having its structure double like the *Odyssey* and with opposite endings for the good and bad. Its being put first is due to the weakness of the audiences; for the poets follow along, catering to their wishes. But this particular pleasure is not the one that springs from tragedy but is more characteristic of comedy.

PITY AND FEAR AND THE TRAGIC ACT

Now it is possible for the fearful or pathetic effect to come from the actors' appearance, but it is also possible for it to arise from the very structure of the events, and this is closer to the mark and characteristic of a better poet. Namely, the plot must be so structured, even without benefit of any visual effect, that the one who is hearing the events unroll shudders with fear and feels pity at what happens: which is what one would experience on hearing the plot of the *Oedipus*. To set out to achieve this by means of the masks and costumes is less artistic, and requires technical support in the staging. As for those who do not set out to achieve the fearful through the masks and costumes, but only the monstrous, they have nothing to do with tragedy at all; for one should not seek any and every pleasure from tragedy, but the one that is appropriate to it.

Since it is the pleasure derived from pity and fear by means of imitation that the poet should seek to produce, it is clear that these qualities must be built into the constituent events. Let us determine, then, which kinds of happening are felt by the spectator to be fearful, and which pitiable. Now such acts are necessarily the work of persons who are near and dear (close blood kin) to one another, or enemies, or neither. But when an enemy attacks an enemy there is nothing pathetic about either the intention or the deed, except in the actual pain suffered by the victim; nor when the act is done by "neutrals"; but when the tragic acts come within the limits of close blood relationship, as when brother kills or intends to kill brother or do something else of that kind to him, or son to father or mother to son or son to mother—those are the situations one should look for.

Now although it is not admissible to break up the transmitted stories—I mean for instance that Clytemestra was killed by Orestes, or Eriphyle by Alcmeon—one should be artistic both in inventing stories and in managing the ones that have been handed down. But what we mean by "artistic" requires some explanation.

It is possible, then, (1) for the act to be performed as the older poets presented it, knowingly and wittingly; Euripides did it that way also, in Medea's murder of her children. It is possible (2) to refrain from performing the deed, with knowledge. Or it is possible (3) to perform the fearful act, but unwittingly, then recognize the blood relationship later, as Sophocles' Oedipus does; in that case the act is outside the play, but it can be in the tragedy itself, as with Astydamas' Alcmeon, or Telegonus in the *Wounding of Odysseus*. A further mode, in addition to these, is (4) while intending because of ignorance to perform some black crime, to discover the relationship before one does it. And there is no other mode besides these; for one must necessarily either do the deed or not, and with or without knowledge of what it is.

Of these modes, to know what one is doing but hold off and not perform the act (No. 2) is worst: it has the morally repulsive character and at the same time is not tragic; for there is no tragic act. Hence nobody composes that way, or only rarely, as, for example, Haemon threatens Creon in the *Antigone*. Performing the act (with knowledge) (No. 1) is second (poorest). Better is to perform it in ignorance and recognize what one has done afterward (No. 3); for the repulsive quality does not attach to the act, and the recognition has a shattering emotional effect. But the best is the last (No. 4): I mean a case like the one in the *Cresphontes* where Merope is about to kill her son but does not do so because she recognizes him first; or in *Iphigenia in Tauris* the same happens with sister and brother; or in the *Helle* the son recognizes his mother just as he is about to hand her over to the enemy.

The reason for what was mentioned a while ago, namely that our tragedies have to do with only a few families, is this: It was because the poets, when they discovered how to produce this kind of effect in their plots, were conducting their search on the basis of chance, not art; hence they have been forced to focus upon those families which happen to have suffered tragic happenings of this kind.

THE TRAGIC CHARACTERS

Enough, then, concerning the structure of events and what traits the tragic plots should have. As for the characters, there are four things to be aimed at. First and foremost, that they be good. The persons will have character if in the way previously stated their speech or their action reveals the moral quality of some choice, and good character if a good choice. Good character exists, moreover, in each category of persons; a woman can be good, or a slave, although one of these classes (to wit, women) is inferior and the other, as a class, worthless. Second, that they be appropriate; for it is possible for a character to be brave, but inappropriately to a woman. Third is likeness to human nature in general; for this is different from making the character good and appropriate according to the criteria previously mentioned. And fourth is consistency. For even if the person being imitated is inconsistent, and that kind of character has been taken as the theme, he should be inconsistent in a consistent fashion.

An example of moral depravity that accomplishes no necessary purpose is the Menelaus in Euripides' *Orestes;* of an unsuitable and inappropriate character, the lamentation of Odysseus in the *Scylla* and the speech of Melanippe; and of the inconsistent, *Iphigenia at Aulis,* for the girl who pleads for her life is in no way like the later one.

In character portrayal also, as in plot construction, one should always strive for either the necessary or the probable, so that it is either necessary or probable for that kind of person to do or say that kind of thing, just as it is for one event

to follow the other. It is evident, then, that the dénouements of plots also should come out of the character itself, and not from the "machine" as in the *Medea* or with the sailing of the fleet in the *Aulis*. Rather the machine should be used for things that lie outside the drama proper, either previous events that a human being cannot know, or subsequent events which require advance prophecy and exposition; for we grant the gods the ability to foresee everything. But let there be no illogicality in the web of events, or if there is, let it be outside the play like the one in Sophocles' *Oedipus*.

Since tragedy is an imitation of persons who are better than average, one should imitate the good portrait painters, for in fact, while rendering likenesses of their sitters by reproducing their individual appearance, they also make them better-looking; so the poet, in imitating men who are irascible or easygoing or have other traits of that kind, should make them, while still plausibly drawn, morally good, as Homer portrayed Achilles as good yet like other men.

TECHNIQUES OF RECOGNITION

What recognition is generically, was stated earlier; now as to its varieties: First comes the one that is least artistic and is most used, merely out of lack of imagination, that by means of tokens. Of these some are inherited, like "the lance that all the Earth-born wear," or "stars" such as Carcinus employs in his *Thyestes;* some are acquired, and of those some are on the body, such as scars, others are external, like the well-known amulets or the recognition in the *Tyro* by means of the little ark. There are better and poorer ways of using these; for example, Odysseus was recognized in different ways by means of his scar, once by the nurse and again by the swineherds. Those that are deliberately cited for the sake of establishing an identity, and all that kind, are less artistic, while those that develop naturally but unexpectedly, like the one in the foot-washing scene, are better.

Second poorest are those that are contrived by the poet and hence are inartistic; for example the way, in the *Iphigenia*, she recognizes that it is Orestes: *she* was recognized by means of the letter, but *he* goes out of his way to say what the poet, rather than the plot, wants him to say. Thus this mode is close kin to the error mentioned above: he might as well have actually worn some tokens. Similarly, in Sophocles' *Tereus*, the "voice of the shuttle."

Third poorest is that through recollection, by means of a certain awareness that follows on seeing or hearing something, like the one in the *Cypriotes* of Dicaeogenes where the hero bursts into tears on seeing the picture, and the one in Book 8 of the *Odyssey:* Odysseus weeps when he hears the lyre-player and is reminded of the War; in both cases the recognition follows.

Fourth in ascending order is the recognition based on reasoning; for example in the *Libation-Bearers:* "Somebody like me has come; nobody is like me but Orestes; therefore he has come." And the one suggested by the sophist Polyidus in speaking of the *Iphigenia:* it would have been natural, he said, for Orestes to draw the conclusion (aloud): "My sister was executed as a sacrifice, and now it is my turn." Also in the *Tydeus* of Theodectes: "I came expecting to find my son, and instead I am being destroyed myself." Or the one in the *Daughters of Phineus:* when they see the spot they reflect that it was indeed their fate to die here; for they had been exposed here as babies also. There is also one based on mistaken inference on the part of the audience, as in *Odysseus the False Messenger.* In that play, that he and no one else can

string the bow is an assumption, a premise invented by the poet, and also his saying that he would recognize the bow when in fact he had not seen it; whereas the notion that he (the poet) has made his invention for the sake of the other person who would make the recognition, that is a mistaken inference.

The best recognition of all is the one that arises from the events themselves; the emotional shock of surprise is then based on probabilities, as in Sophocles' *Oedipus* and in the *Iphigenia;* for it was only natural that she should wish to send a letter. Such recognitions are the only ones that dispense with artificial inventions and visible tokens. And second-best are those based on reasoning. . . .

CRITICAL PERSPECTIVES

SUE-ELLEN CASE
from "Classic Drag: The Greek Creation of Female Parts" (1985)

A prominent scholar and theoretician of feminism and theater, Sue-Ellen Case examines the complicity of traditional theatrical practices—cross-dressing in the Greek theater, for example—in the patriarchal structure of Western culture. Professor Case has written many influential studies of gender, sexuality, and theater and is the author of Feminism and Theatre *(1988) and of* The Domain-Matrix *(1997).*

In this essay, Case sets the action of classical Greek theater—notably The Oresteia *and* Medea—*in the context of contemporary feminist theory. Given this orientation to the drama, what elements of the plays emerge as most significant in Case's argument? In what ways does this "reading against the grain" open perspectives on the value and belief-system of classical Athens? How are terms like "justice" or "nature" interrogated by this interpretive strategy?*

From a feminist perspective, the initial observations about the history of theatre noted the absences of women within the tradition. Since traditional scholarship has focused on evidence related to written texts, the absence of women playwrights became central to early feminist investigations. The fact that there was no significant number of extant texts written by women for the stage until the seventeenth century produced a rather astounding sense of absence in the classical traditions of the theatre. The silence of women's voices in these traditions led feminist historians who were interested in women playwrights to concentrate on periods in which they did emerge: primarily the seventeenth century in England, the nineteenth century in America, and the twentieth century in Europe and America. These studies produced a number of new anthologies of plays by women and biographies of women playwrights that began to appear in the early seventies.

Work on the classical periods became possible by studying the image of women within plays written by men. Many scholars attribute the beginning of this type of textual discovery to the popular book by Kate Millett entitled *Sexual Politics* (1970). Millett's book illustrated a way to recognize and interpret the images of women in male literature as misogynistic. *Sexual Politics* offered a way to read against texts by becoming aware of their gendered bias and, as the title suggests, to foreground the notion that art is not distinct from politics. While Millett's book concentrated on describing the images of women, other early works such as Judith Fetterly's *The Resisting Reader* articulated a posture for resisting reading texts by men as they were conventionally read. Fetterly outlined ways to read against texts to discover the feminist subtext latent in such subversions. Works on images of women still predominate in the feminist criticism of historical texts. Numerous re-visions of Aeschylus and Shakespeare are currently being produced. The images are commonly identified as being one of two basic

types: positive roles, which depict women as independent, intelligent, and even heroic and a surplus of misogynistic roles commonly identified as the Bitch, the Witch, the Vamp, or the Virgin/Goddess. These roles reflect the perspective of the playwright or of the theatrical tradition on women. Originally, feminist historians used these theatrical images of women as evidence of the kind of lives actual women might have lived in the period. For example, what the characters and situations of Medea or Phaedra might tell us about the lives of powerful women in Greece. This approach was useful because traditional socio-economic histories tend to exhibit the same absence of women as does the literature. In the seventies, groundbreaking work on women in history was done in both realms: the socio-historical evidence identified in theatrical texts, and the publication of newly-collated documents on laws, social practices, and economic restrictions on women in history. This work enabled feminist critics and historians to produce a new kind of cultural analysis, which is based on the interplay of cultural phenomena, such as plays, theatre practice, and socio-economic evidence, to discover the nature of women's lives in the classical periods.

Yet, the discovery of the complicity of art with political projects, as well as the complicity of traditional history with the patriarchy led to new discoveries which reverse the original interpretations of these documents. The feminist critic may no longer believe that the portrayal of women in classical plays by men relates to the lives of actual women. Instead, the feminist critic may assume that the images of women in these plays represent a fiction of women constructed by the patriarchy. This assumption originates in a central practice within classical cultures: the division between private and public life. The public life becomes privileged in the classical plays and histories, while the private life remains relatively invisible. The new feminist analyses prove that this division is gender-specific, i.e., the public life is the property of men and women are relegated to the invisible private sphere. The result of the suppression of actual women in the classical world created the invention of a representation of the gender "Woman" within the culture. This "Woman" appeared on the stage, in the myths, and in the plastic arts, representing the patriarchal values attached to the gender of "Woman" while suppressing the experiences, stories, feelings, and fantasies of actual women.[1] The new feminist approach to these cultural fictions divides this "Woman" as a male-produced fiction from historical women, insisting that there is little connection between the two categories. Within theatre practice, the clearest illustration of this division is in the tradition of the all-male stage. "Woman" was played by male actors in drag, while actual women were banned from the stage. The classical acting practice reveals the construction of the fictional gender created by the patriarchy. The classical plays and theatrical conventions can now be regarded as allies in the project of suppressing actual women and replacing them with the masks of patriarchal production.

The beginning of the activity and literature known as theatre is traditionally assigned to the plays and practices of the Athenian festivals of Dionysos in sixth and fifth century BCE. Our notions of plays, acting, physical theatre space, costume, mask, and relation of play to audience begin with these Athenian festivals. In the sixth century, both women and men participated in these ceremonies, but by the fifth century, when the ceremonies were becoming what is known as theatre, women disappeared from the practice. Scholars do not record any evidence for specific laws or codes forbidding women to appear in the songs and dances, nor is there any evidence for the specific date or occasion of the beginning of their omission. Margarete Bieber, a recognized authority on this history, merely notes that it was part of "Attic morality" which "banished women from public life."[2] This implies, then, that the reason for this practice must be sought in the emerging cultural codes of Athens, rather than in specific political or theatrical practices. Three elements of Athenian culture help to understand the emerging theatrical practice: the new economic practices, the new cultural project and the new genealogy of the gods. The intersection of all of these elements will be theatrically legitimatized in the text of *The Oresteia*.

Among the new economic practices, the rise of the family unit radically altered the role of women in Greek public life. Ironically, the important role women began to assume within the family unit was the cause of their removal from public life. The family unit became the new site for the creation and transmission of personal wealth. With the rise of the *polis,* the large network inherent in aristocracies gave way to single families. The rise of metals as commodities and the small-scale cultivation of land made it possible for individuals to control their own wealth. Yet while ownership became more individual and located within the family unit, it was limited to the male gender. Women were restricted to limited conditions of ownership and exchange. For example, women could only enter into inheritance transactions in the absence of a male and women were not allowed to barter for property over one *medimnos* (bushel). Within this new economy, women became a medium of exchange and marriage became an institution of ownership.[3] In fact, the word for marriage, *ekdosis,* meant loan—women were loaned to their husbands by their fathers, and in the case of a divorce, they were returned to their fathers.

With this change in the organization of wealth came a concomitant change in the organization of political units. The *oikos,* or household, became the basic unit for citizenship.[4] Citizenship was dependent upon family lines—a son was granted citizenship only if his parents were citizens, but without a son the parents could not retain their citizenship. This new condition for citizenship led to the strict definition and regulation of the sex life of the woman. The mother/wife assumed a new moral/legal dimension for the legitimacy and security of heirs and, by extension, political membership in the *polis.* Clear lines of reproduction were vital to the *polis,* making adultery a crime against society, rather than a sign of personal transgression. At the same time that the household became controlled by needs of the state, its activities became totally separate from those which were considered the business of the state, the mark of the citizen, or the activities of public life. Nancy Hartsock, in her book *Money, Sex, and Power,* describes it this way: The Greeks defined the household as a private, apolitical space from the public, political space of the *polis.* "The result was a theorization of

[1]See Teresa de Lauretis, *Alice Doesn't: Feminism, Semiotics, Cinema* (Bloomington: Indiana University Press, 1984), for a thorough development of the concept of "Woman."

[2]Margarete Bieber, *The History of the Greek and Roman Theatre* (Princeton: Princeton University Press, 1939), p. 9.

[3]See Gayle Rubin, "The Traffic in Women: Notes on the 'Political Economy' of Sex," in *Toward an Anthropology of Women,* ed. Rayna R. Reiter (New York: Monthly Review Press, 1975), for a discussion of women as a medium of exchange through the institution of marriage and kinship laws.

[4]Marilyn Arthur, "'Liberated' Women: The Classical Era," in *Becoming Visible: Women in European History,* eds. Renate Bridenthal and Claudia Koonz (Boston: Houghton Mifflin, 1977), pp. 67–68.

politics and political power as activities that occurred in a masculine arena characterized by freedom from necessary labor, dominance of intellect or soul," while the domestic space was defined by necessary labor and as a place where bodily needs were dominant.[5] Since Athenian women were confined to the house (explicitly in the laws of Solon), they were removed from the public life of the intellect and the soul and confined to the world of domestic labor, childbearing, and concomitant sexual activities. Actual women disappeared from the public life of the *polis*, lost their economic and legal powers and became objects of exchange. Within the socio-economic life of the *polis*, it is not surprising that their participation in the Dionysian festivals was restricted to private practices, resulting in their eventual exclusion from the stage.

Alongside these new legal and economic practices came new cultural institutions. Athens created new architecture, new religions, new myths, and the practice of theatre. These cultural institutions became allied with the suppression of women by creating the new gender role of "Woman" that would privilege the masculine gender and oppress the feminine one. At base, the new cultural categories of gender were constructed as categories of difference and polarity.[6] "Woman" appeared as the opposite of man. This move can best be seen in the new myths and architectural depictions of the amazons. The image of amazons is central to the female gender conflated with the outsider and with polar differences from the Greek male citizen. The amazons, dangerous but defeated, reverse the "natural" gender roles. They are warriors who force men to do "women's" work, such as child rearing, while the women go off to war.[7] The amazons also embody other myths of gender reversal—they keep female babies and dispose of the male ones, while the custom was to dispose of female babies.[8] Moreover, the word "amazon" (no breast) ties such practices to a biological, secondary sex characteristic specific to the female. The new architecture of the Acropolis, the civic center of Athens, displays the downfall of the amazons and the rise of Athena. Central to the new political order, then, is the demise of these women who would defy correct gender associations and the rise of a woman who would enforce the new image of "Woman" in the *polis*. This demise of the old images of women and the rise of Athena are central themes in *The Oresteia*.

The genealogy of the gods provides the mytho-historical context for this creation of the new "Woman." The history of the gods explains why genders are opposite, locked in conflict, and why the male gender must defeat the former female one. The myth of the first earth-mother-goddess, Gaia, is a story of the dangers of her womb—the story of her children is one of murders and castrations. It concludes with the final conquest by Zeus, who swallows his wife Metis in order to gain her power of reproduction and then gives birth to Athena. Athena represents the end of the dangers of the womb, for she has no mother (breaking with matriarchal and female-identification), has no sexuality (she remains a virgin), defeats the amazons, allies herself with the reign of Zeus and Apollo, and thereby brings order to Athens. About this same time, Dionysos, a new god, appears in Athens and usurps the role of fertility and sexuality which the earlier female goddesses had retained. This male usurpation of female fertility will later be idealized by Plato in his famous midwife metaphor, while the assimilation of female sexuality will be usurped by boys in the social practice of male homosexuality (also later idealized by Plato). The genealogy of the gods thus divides female sexuality from power, assimilating female sexuality in the figure of Dionysos and isolating power in the image of the motherless virgin, Athena.

The rise of drama, within the Athenian state festivals dedicated to the celebration of Dionysos, places theatre securely within this new patriarchal institution of gender wars. Theatre must be gender-specific to the male and enact the suppression of actual women as well as the representation of the new "Woman." The maenads (the female celebrants of the Dionysian festivals) must dance into oblivion, while the satyrs (the male celebrants) must become the first choruses of the drama. "The singer Arion is said to have given to the singers of the dithyramb . . . the costume of the satyrs. The practice of representing someone other than oneself grew out of this ecstasy and led to the mimic art of the actors."[9] In other words, the power of representation was given only to the male celebrants. The invention of acting was gender-specific—the actor was the satyr. The gender-specific quality of the actor in the satyr play was even underscored by his wearing of the leather phallus. Yet in order to dramatize the battle of the genders, the female must somehow be represented: the male actor would need to perform the female role. Though scholars and theatre historians never mention this strange phenomenon in more than passing remarks, Bieber does note one specific problem for male actors in their representations of women: on the vases, the maenads seem to be in a state of ecstasy—to play maenads, the male actors needed the comprehension of the religious emotion felt by these women.[10] Yet a more central problem emerges: how

---

[5] Nancy Hartsock, *Money, Sex and Power: Toward a Feminist Historical Materialism* (New York: Longman, 1983), p. 187.

[6] Page duBois, *Centaurs and Amazons* (Ann Arbor: University of Michigan Press, 1982), p. 2.

[7] William Blake Tyrell, *Amazons: A Study in Athenian Mythmaking* (Baltimore: Johns Hopkins University Press, 1984), p. 47.

[8] Tyrell, p. 55.

---

[9] Bieber, p. 1.

[10] Bieber, p. 9.

does one depict a woman? How does the male actor signal to the audience that he is a woman? Along with the female costume of the shorter tunic and the female mask with longer hair, he might have indicated through gesture, movement, and vocal intonation that the character was female. In considering this portrayal, it is important to remember that the notion of the female derived from the male point of view, which remained alien to female experience and reflected the perspective of her gendered opposite. This vocabulary of gestures initiated the image of "Woman" as she is seen on the stage—institutionalized through patriarchal culture and represented by male-originated signs of her appropriate gender behavior. Moreover, the practice of male actors playing women probably encouraged the creation of female roles which lent themselves to generalization and stereotype. The depiction and development of female characters in the written texts must have accommodated the practice of their representation onstage. Though all characters were formalized and masked, the cross-gender casting for female characters distinguished them in kind from the male characters. A subtextual message was delivered about the nature of the female gender, its behavior, appearance, and formal distance from the representation of the male.

The Athenian theatre practice created a political and aesthetic arena for ritualized and codified gender behavior, linking it to civic privileges and restrictions. The elevation of this gender principle to the term "classic" canonizes it as a paradigmatic element of the history of theatre, connoting the expulsion of women from the canon and the ideal. The etymology of "classic," connoting class, indicates that this expulsion is also related to the economic and legal privileges of the "first class"—a class to which women were denied admittance. The consonance of aesthetic criteria with economic ones becomes clear in the term itself. In each of the cultures which has produced "classics" for the stage (not only the Athenian, but the Roman and the Elizabethan) women were denied access to the stage and to legal and economic enfranchisement. These same production values are embedded in the texts of these periods. Female characters are derived from the absence of actual women on the stage and from the reasons for their absence. Each culture which valorizes the reproduction of those "classic" texts actively participates in the same patriarchal subtext which created those female characters as "Woman." Though we cannot examine a production of the Greek classics, we can examine one of the "classic" texts produced for the Dionysian festivals and reproduced in the history of theatrical productions, history, and criticism within our own contemporary culture. The trilogy *of The Oresteia* exhibits all of the themes and practices discussed above. Moreover, its elevated position in the canon illustrates its lasting value. A feminist reading of *The Oresteia*

illustrates the defeat of the old matriarchal genealogy, the nature of "Woman" as portrayed on the stage, the rise of Athena, and the legacy of the suppression of actual women.

THE ORESTEIA

Many feminist critics and historians have analyzed *The Oresteia* as a text central to the formalization of misogyny. Simone de Beauvoir and Kate Millett describe it as the mythical rendering of a patriarchal takeover. Nancy Hartsock argues that it associates the female gender with sexuality and nature, those forces that must be tamed in outside activities and within the inner person for the survival of the *polis*.[11] Hartsock describes *The Oresteia* within the dramatic festivals that are themselves associated with male gender activities. The drama, like the four-horse chariot race, is a contest. It formalizes *agons* (contests) and the notion of winners and losers. The festivals associate the heroic ideal of valor in battle with the peacetime ideal of rhetorical and dramatic competition.[12] The subject of the drama is the subject of war—the male warrior hero. When this *agon* is inscribed with the conflicts of gender, the dramatic dice are loaded for the same gender-specific hero to win. *The Oresteia* enacts the "battle of the sexes," using Athenian cultural and political codes to prescribe that women must lose the battle.

Early in the first play of the trilogy, *Agamemnon*, the chorus of old men explicates the dramatic situation within the perspective of male-female problems. The old men describe a promiscuous woman (Helen) as the cause of the Trojan war in which Agamemnon is presently engaged and they tell of the war fleet launched by Agamemnon's sacrifice of his virgin-daughter Iphigenia. The Trojan war and the relationship of Agamemnon and Clytemnestra are already fraught with conflicts embedded in gender roles. Then the chorus prepares the audience for the entrance of Clytemnestra by linking gender with certain attributes of character. They suggest that steady resolve and intensity of purpose are gender-specific when they refer to the male (inner) strength of Clytemnestra (line 13).[13] Within this context Clytemnestra enters, played by a man. After s/he speaks, the chorus congratulates her for thinking like a man and dismisses her announcement of the end of the war as just "like a woman to take rapture before fact" (line 475). These lines presume certain gender roles regarding the judgment of evidence and decision-making. Within the theatre practice, they also play with a certain level of irony since a man

[11] Hartsock, p. 192.

[12] Hartsock, p. 198.

[13] All citations of *The Oresteia* are from *Complete Greek Tragedies*, Vol. 1, *Aeschylus*, eds. David Grene, Richmond Lattimore (Chicago: Chicago University Press, 1960).

in drag plays a woman who "thinks like a man." Clearly, the primary referent is the male. The notion of female, like the notion of the amazon, disrupts the male order. Clytemnestra is introduced as a figure of that disruption. The absence of the male king has provided her with "unnatural" political power. In his absence, she has taken a male lover. By this act, she disrupts the gender code of female sexuality, for the tradition was that women were to remain monogamous even during ten year wars. The chorus treats Clytemnestra's liaison as dangerous. Yet when Agamemnon enters with his sexual war booty, Cassandra, the implication of social disruption is not in the text. In fact, the dramatic pathos of the drama favors Agamemnon, despite his treatment of women as evidenced by his rape of Cassandra or his murder of Iphigenia.

Cassandra provides the Athenian image of the woman in the public arena (even though she is played by a man). She has certain privileges of belonging (she is the priestess of Apollo which assures her of sexual liaisons with citizens of rank such as Agamemnon), but she does not have the privilege of effective public speech because of her prior refusal to be violated by Apollo. Cassandra's entrance, as an outsider, as Agamemnon's booty, mute to Clytemnestra and expelled from effective dialogue, even portrayed by a male actor, projects the strength of the misogyny embedded in the Athenian patriarchal order. What remains in the play is only Clytemnestra's murder of Agamemnon and her complete vilification. At the end, the chorus mourns Agamemnon as one who had to fight a war for a woman and then be killed by one (lines 1481–1482).

The third play, *The Eumenides,* decides the winner of the battle of the sexes within the play, within Athens, and within the genealogy of the gods. From a feminist perspective, it is ironic that this play dramatizes the so-called beginnings of democracy. Moreover, within theatre history, *The Eumenides* is often marked as the play of the new order of civilization which created our western tradition of reason and fair play. This may be an accurate description, for it does make the deciding gender judgments of Athenian culture and condemns women to their subservient role in Western civilization. The play rests upon a new genealogy of the gods. It opens with the old order, the vile goddesses, the Eumenides. They create an ugly, frightening characterization of the earlier chthonic female religions. The masks created for them were famous for their disgusting appearance. An extant remark about them states that "Aeschylus' Eumenides horrified women into miscarriages,"[14] an interesting anecdote for its gender and sexual connotations. The Eumenides have arrived in Athens, while pursuing Orestes to revenge his murder of his mother. They describe their role as the punishment of matricide (line 210).

Orestes appeals to Apollo for help and Athena appears to solve the problem. She institutes a trial, exhibiting Athenian methods of justice, to try Orestes for his murder. The decision is to set Orestes free. This conclusion is damning evidence for the public rationalization of misogyny, for it rests upon establishing the parental line as male. The mother is not the parent, but the nurse of the child. The parent is defined as he who mounts (lines 658–661). Athena is the supreme proof of this fact because she had no mother and was begat by the male god Zeus (lines 734–738). The Eumenides are confined to a cave and their function is no longer to revenge matricide, but to preside over marriages. Thus, the trilogy which began with the end of the Trojan war and proceeded through the house of Agamemnon ends with the institution of democracy deciding the role of gender and the definition of procreation. This ending can be seen as paradigmatic of future plot structures in the Western playwriting tradition. A majority of plays will conclude various kinds of civic, historical, and psychological problems with the institution of marriage. The proper gender role for women is inscribed in this conclusion.

The feminist reader of *The Oresteia* discovers that she must read against the text, resisting not only its internal sense of pathos and conclusion, but also the historical and cultural codes which surround it, including its treatment within theatre history. The pathos the feminist reader feels may be for Iphigenia and Clytemnestra rather than for Agamemnon. She may perceive Athena as a male-identified woman in alliance with the male network of power rather than as a hero of Athens. She definitely feels excluded from the conventions of the stage, bewildered by the conviction of cross-gender casting which is only practiced in terms of female characters. Mimesis is not possible for her. Perhaps the feminist reader will decide that the female roles have nothing to do with women, that these roles should be played by men, as fantasies of "Woman" as "Other" than men, disruptions of a patriarchal society which illustrates its fear and loathing of the female parts. In fact, the feminist reader might become persuaded that the Athenian roles of Medea, Clytemnestra, Cassandra, or Phaedra are properly played as drag roles. The feminist reader might conclude that women need not relate to these roles or even attempt to identify with them. Moreover, the feminist historian might conclude that these roles contain no information about the experience of real women in the classical world. Nevertheless, the feminist scholars must recognize that theatre originated in this kind of cultural climate and that the Athenian experience will continue to provide a certain paradigm of theatrical practice for the rest of Western theatrical/cultural history. By linking practice, text, and cultural practice in this new way, she may enhance her understanding of how the hegemonic structure of patriarchal practice was instituted in Athens. . . .

[14]Sir Arthur Pickard-Cambridge, *The Dramatic Festivals of Athens* (Oxford: Clarendon Press, 1968), p. 265.

Classical Japan

Acting in the Noh theater.

The drama and theater of the Asian world has a history as complex and multifaceted as the histories of the many civilizations, peoples, and nations that have been said—by the West—to compose the "Asian world." India, for example, has a literature—in SANSKRIT—more than 3,000 years old. Although the golden age of Sanskrit theater took place in the fourth and fifth centuries, theater of various kinds—folk, classical, and modern—thrives in India today. The conventions of Indian theater have pervasively influenced the theater of southeast Asia; the Sanskrit epic poems *Mahabharata* and *Ramayana* provide the characters and settings, for example, for the beautiful shadow-puppet theater of Java in Indonesia—the *WAYANG KULIT*—and related forms of performance using dolls or live actors.

The masked dance drama of Korea—called *KAMYONGUK*—is related both to Chinese and Japanese theater, and Korea, like other Asian countries, has developed an important modern theater as well.

European knowledge of China's theater probably dates from Marco Polo's visits (1254–1324); we know of more than 550 playwrights who wrote after the Mongol invasion during China's Yüan dynasty (1279–1368), part of a theatrical tradition that is recorded as early as 1000 BCE and that developed throughout the Han (206 BCE–221 CE), Hui (589–614), T'ang (618–904), and Sung (960–1279) periods. Several plays from the Yüan theater have been adapted by European playwrights; Voltaire's *The Orphan of China* (1755), an adaptation of Chi Chunhsiang's *The House of Chao,* was the first Chinese play to become widely known in Europe, and Li Hsing's *The Story of the Chalk Circle* has been adapted several times, notably by Bertolt Brecht in *The Caucasian Chalk Circle* (1944). After the Mongols were expelled during the Ming dynasty (1368–1644), the center of theatrical activity shifted from northern China toward southern cities such as Hangchow. It was only during the eighteenth and nineteenth centuries, under the Ch'ing dynasty (1644–1912), that the most characteristic form of modern Chinese theater, the *BEIJING OPERA,* began to take the shape that it has today, sharing the stage with both Western and Western-style plays, and with a vigorous experimental theater working in a more distinctly Chinese dramatic idiom.

Although no one theater can be said to represent these rich and diverse theatrical traditions, the classical theater of Japan shares many features common to other Asian theaters: it blends aristocratic and popular affiliations; it descends from social and religious ritual traditions; it coordinates acting, dance, music, and spectacle; many of its plots and characters are derived from familiar literary and historical narratives and legends; its performance conventions are elaborately stylized and refined; and its performers are often trained with a level of formality not found in Western theater. This is hardly surprising, in that the introduction of Buddhism into Japan during the sixth century coincided with an important period of Japanese cultural and political expansion; for the next two centuries, Japan was actively in contact with the vital cultures of India, China, and Korea. Although the period of "classical" Japanese theater—roughly the twelfth through the eighteenth centuries—coincides with an extended period of cultural isolation, the expansion of Japan's military, political, and economic power in the nineteenth and twentieth centuries has again brought Japanese culture into dialogue with Asia and the West. Indeed, while Japan's imperial ambitions—the invasion of China and much of the Pacific Rim before and during World War II—were extinguished with the atomic bombing of Hiroshima and Nagasaki, Japanese theater and drama have continued to develop both in response to Western culture and through the experimental innovation of its own traditions.

The classical Japanese theater is a product of a distinctive period in the history of Japan, extending from 1192, when the emperor gave all civil and secular power to a **SHOGUN**, a hereditary military leader, to 1868, when the emperor regained state as well as religious authority. For better than 750 years the Japanese emperors lived in Kyoto, engaged in largely ceremonial duties, while the *shoguns,* based in Edo, exercised all political and judicial authority. The Genroku period (1680–1730) saw an extraordinary flowering of Japanese art and culture supported by the shogunate; this was the period of Basho, the famous *haiku* poet; of Ihara Saikaku, the novelist; and of Chikamatsu Monzaemon, Japan's greatest playwright. Although the Noh theater was in decline by the Genroku period, the three principal modes of Japanese classical theater—**NOH, DOLL THEATER,** and **KABUKI**—are in different ways the product of the elaborately hierarchical culture of feudal Japan, and of the increasing tension between the class of warriors who ruled Japan and a class of artisans and merchants—sometimes called simply **CHONIN,** or townsmen—whose economic power was centered in Japan's cities. With the rise of the shogunate, Japanese society assumed a feudal character that represented the interests and values of its ruling class of **SAMURAI** warriors. Owing their allegiance to the *shogun,* the ranks of the *samurai* comprised various warrior lords, or **DAIMYO,** and their attendant warriors. As in other feudal societies, in Japan it was both a right and an obligation to display the signs and behavior of one's caste. The *samurai,* for example, were expected to obey a stringent honor code, one that required their absolute loyalty to the *shogun,* to the *samurai* caste, and to its military ethos. If a *samurai* betrayed his lord, he and his followers risked becoming outcasts, called **RŌNIN** or "men adrift." The most famous Kabuki drama, *Chūshingura* (1748), takes the fortunes of such a *samurai* lord and his forty-seven followers as its subject, and *rōnin* are common figures in the Japanese theater. This organization extended throughout Japanese society; not only was Japanese society divided into major castes, but its professions—including theater and prostitution, often closely associated in the popular imagination—were strictly controlled through an elaborate guild system. In the major cities, theaters were built in specifically licensed quarters, and actors were generally required to live in or near those districts. Much as tradespeople had to make their trade known through conventions of dress (a practice common in Europe at this time as well), so actors were required in 1709 to shave their forelocks as a public sign of their profession.

Under the Ashikaga shogunate, which began in 1338 and ended in a civil war in the late sixteenth century, not only were the values of the *samurai* dominant, but the privileges of the *samurai* relative to other castes—such as the many ranks of merchants, artisans, farmers, and peasants—were rigidly observed. The principal forms of theatrical entertainment, especially Noh (or Nō) theater, were both sponsored by and largely reserved for the elite *samurai* castes and represented the literary and cultural values of their patrons. In 1603, Tokugawa Ieyasu (1542–1616) became the Emperor's *shogun,* and in the Tokugawa period (1603–1867; sometimes called the Edo period, after the city that was his seat, present-day Tokyo), Japan entered a period of extended peace and increasing cultural isolation. In the seventeenth century, the *shoguns* began to expel all foreigners from Japan, reserving specific enclaves in port cities like Nagasaki as protected zones where foreign trade might be undertaken. As cities such as Osaka, Tokyo, and Kyoto became significant urban centers, the merchant classes became wealthier and more powerful. Although their status was lower than that of the *samurai,* many of the merchants amassed huge fortunes that far exceeded the wealth of many *samurai.* The *samurai* still exerted political authority—in 1705 the *samurai* confiscated the fortune of a merchant to whom many of them were indebted—but the merchant classes came to dominate the cultural sphere as they became the principal audience for poetry, fiction, and theater. Although all three forms of classical Japanese theater are preserved and performed today, they first became popular in different eras of Japan's history: The Noh, as it is now known, was developed largely between the fourteenth and early seventeenth centuries; the doll theater's greatest popularity was in the late seventeenth century; Kabuki, which is said to have originated when Okuni, a dancer from the Izumo Shrine in Kyoto, began to perform satirical skits in Kyoto in 1603, developed largely between the late seventeenth and mid-eighteenth centuries.

Although Noh theater achieved its highly literary and ceremonial form in the fourteenth century, it is usually said to have developed from performance modes popular throughout the tenth and eleventh centuries, the **SARUGAKU-NO,** and a related form, **DENGAKU-NO.** "Noh" means "accomplishment" or "performance," and both forms of entertainment contributed elements to the development of Noh theater and drama. *Dengaku-no* may have had more explicit ritual elements, and was initially associated with the native Japanese religion of Shinto, but both forms involved acrobatics, comic role-playing, and dance. *Sarugaku* means "monkey music," which may give some idea of the exuberance of these performances. In the twelfth century, however, *sarugaku-no* was adapted by Buddhist priests to illustrate tenets of Buddhist thought and belief, and performances were given to large audiences at major temples, acted by lower-ranking priests. In time, professional players both imitated these performances outside the temples and were hired to replace the priests in temple performances; by the mid-twelfth century, guilds of performers were attached to major temples. In return for free performances during religious ceremonies and festivals, the professional guilds were given a monopoly on performing in the region of the temple.

Although the *sarugaku-no* and *dengaku-no* seem to have been energetic and spirited forms of entertainment, it was the association with the contemplative and literary elements of Buddhism that were to have the greatest effect on the formation of Noh theater. In 1374, Kan'ami Kiyotsugu (1333–1384)—a leader of one of the four main *sarugaku-no* troupes—performed before the *shogun* Yoshimitsu Ashikaga (1358–1408). Kan'ami was one of the great innovators of his era and is thought to have contributed to giving the Noh its current form. He emphasized the rhythmic nature of the musical accompaniment, developed a greater use of mime in acting, and correlated dance and musical elements more closely with a dramatic plot. These innovations might well have been lost, however, had the *shogun* not been so impressed that he took Kan'ami and his son, Zeami Motokiyo (1363–1444), under his patronage. Kan'ami's troupe became the most influential in Japan, and after his father's death Zeami assumed control of the company, until he was exiled from the court in 1434 by one of Yoshimitsu's sons. Together, Kan'ami and Zeami gave the Noh drama its now-traditional ethos and shape. Kan'ami's innovations were explored and formalized by Zeami, who wrote or revised more than 100 of the 241 plays that make up the Noh repertoire and described the philosophical, esthetic, and practical goals of Noh performance in several theoretical essays. In time, the *daimyo,* emulating the *shogun,* came to sponsor their own Noh performers. Because the performers and performances were so closely bound to the status of the *samurai* caste, however, Noh never became a popular or even very public form of theater. Although *samurai* occasionally sponsored "subscription" performances of Noh for the "townsmen," these highly refined, intensely literary dramas were definitively the entertainment of the elite.

The esthetics of Noh derive from the Buddhist emphasis on **ZEN,** or contemplation, an attitude of repose and withdrawal from worldly desire and distraction. Noh performance aims to induce a similar kind of attentive repose in its audience, to evoke what is called **YUGEN** (often translated as "grace," although for Western readers this may have irrelevant Christian connotations), a mood or state of mind responsive to the mysterious, graceful, and impermanent beauty of the performance. For this reason, perhaps, Noh drama is not really driven by the cause-and-effect narrative logic of Western drama. Noh plays are typically

THE DEVELOPMENT OF NOH THEATER

centered on scenes of revelation that climax in the main actor's principal dance. Rather than imitating life, a Noh play should evoke the "flower," as Zeami termed the fusion of esthetic, spiritual, and moral beauty arising from the performance.

Noh Dramatic Form

A "typical" Noh play might begin with the **WAKI,** or secondary actor, meeting the **SHITE,** or principal actor, at a site of historical, legendary, or mythological importance. The *waki* enters first, and in his opening song—sometimes called the **TRAVELING SONG,** because he sings it while making his entrance—announces who he is (often a priest) and where he is going. The *shite* then enters, taking the role of an ordinary person. They discuss the significance of the place, perhaps where a legendary warrior was killed in battle. The characters speak a densely literary language, for part of the Noh dramatist's skill is shown in his cunning ability to borrow allusions and quotations from Japanese literature; the actors repeat and emphasize a network of phrases and images that convey the play's central theme. The chorus—kneeling stage left—also contributes to this "literary" texture, narrating some of the action and singing or reciting some of the dialogue. The *shite* then leaves the stage, and in some Noh productions a **KYŌGEN** (a brief farce also descended from *sarugaku*) is performed. When the *shite* returns, however, he reveals who he really is, usually a god, hero, or demon connected with the place whose destiny is troubled; he might, for example, be the ghost of the legendary warrior. In a manner of speaking, the character continues to haunt this place because he or she is unable to let go of the world, of the "character" and its investment in the world that are the essence of his or her being. The ghost is haunted by the tortuous attitude or emotion that keeps him or her connected to the world. Unlike a Greek or Shakespearean tragedy, a Noh play does not conclude with a speech of recognition or response; instead, Noh drama concludes with an intricate dance, a beautiful interplay of dialogue, dance, narration, and music for the audience's contemplation.

Since the active repertoire of Noh drama has remained more or less the same for over 400 years, it is perhaps not surprising that other elements of Noh theater and performance have become highly systematic and conventionalized. There are five types of Noh drama—plays praising the gods, plays about warriors, plays about women, plays about madness or

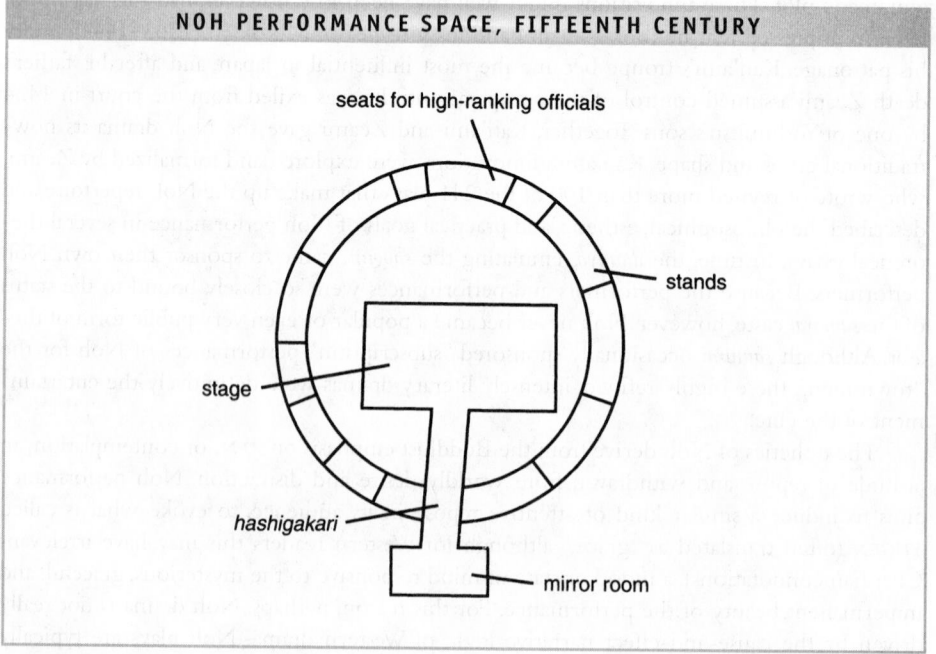

NOH PERFORMANCE SPACE, FIFTEENTH CENTURY

seats for high-ranking officials

stands

stage

hashigakari

mirror room

This is the ground plan of the performance space in the time of Zeami.

spirits, and plays about demons—and in classical Japan, a program of Noh performance included one play from each of these categories, performed in this order, with a *kyōgen* between each Noh play. In modern Japan it has become more common to perform only two or three plays followed by a *kyōgen,* in part because the pace of performance is much slower today. Although women at one time performed in Noh theater, in 1629 women were banned from the Japanese stage; while women do perform in the modern Japanese theater, Noh companies are now traditionally all male. Plays are performed by the *shite* who is masked, an unmasked *waki,* and actors who play the *shite*'s companions (TSURE). A chorus of six to ten men both sings and narrates from a position to the side of the stage, and musicians—a flute and two or three drums—are positioned at the rear of the stage. The drums beat rhythmically, punctuating and accentuating the actors' delivery, while the flute plays in a kind of counterpoint to their speech. The *shite*'s mask is drawn from one of five categories—old person, male, female, gods, monsters—and the clothing of the performers is similarly stylized: The actors sometimes wear elaborate headdresses, and sumptuous silk clothing, arranged and layered in particular ways for certain roles. The members of the chorus wear the traditional dress of the *samurai.* Attendants clothed in black are present onstage throughout the performance, helping the actors with costumes and masks and placing and removing properties when needed; they are always senior actors of the company, because they may also need to step in to finish a performance if an actor is unable to continue. The stage is bare of sets, and hand properties are few and conventional; a bundle of firewood might be represented by a few sticks bound with flowers. Similarly, many of the properties are purely symbolic: A twig carried by a grieving woman is the sign of her madness. Throughout the performance, the actors move slowly and ceremonially; indeed, many of their actions must take place at a prescribed area of the stage.

Although the Noh stage was shaped somewhat differently in Kan'ami's and Zeami's era, by 1615 it had assumed the shape it retains to this day. A stage (*BUTAI*), roughly eighteen feet square, extends into the audience area; the stage is roofed like the early shrines from which

The Noh Stage

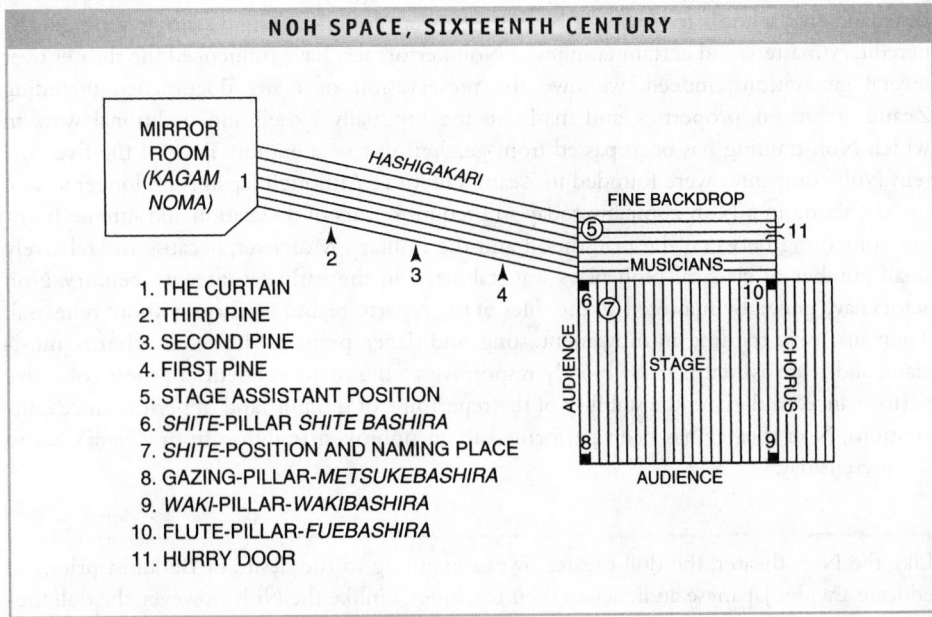

NOH SPACE, SIXTEENTH CENTURY

MIRROR ROOM (KAGAM NOMA)   1
HASHIGAKARI
FINE BACKDROP
⑤ ——— 11
MUSICIANS
6 ⑦   10
AUDIENCE   STAGE   CHORUS
8   9
AUDIENCE

1. THE CURTAIN
2. THIRD PINE
3. SECOND PINE
4. FIRST PINE
5. STAGE ASSISTANT POSITION
6. *SHITE*-PILLAR *SHITE BASHIRA*
7. *SHITE*-POSITION AND NAMING PLACE
8. GAZING-PILLAR-*METSUKEBASHIRA*
9. *WAKI*-PILLAR-*WAKIBASHIRA*
10. FLUTE-PILLAR-*FUEBASHIRA*
11. HURRY DOOR

This ground plan shows the stage with the mirror room, the *hashigakari,* the *shitebashira,* the *wakibashira,* the *metsukebashira,* and the *fuebashira,* as well as the locations for the musicians and the chorus.

it derives, and the audience is seated in front and on the stage-right side. A painted backdrop behind the stage always pictures the Yogo Pine at the Kasuga Shrine in Nara. The stage is always of highly polished wood, with sounding jars concealed beneath it to resonate with the emphatic stamping that is part of the actors' performance. The musicians are seated directly behind the main stage area on a second, narrow stage (*ATOZA*); they are in full view of the audience and are able to see the actors and adjust their playing to the actors' performance throughout the play. A small entrance, called the **HURRY DOOR,** leads off the stage-left side of the *atoza,* which is used by the stage assistants, the chorus, and for the exit of dead characters. A second narrow stage runs along the stage-left side of the stage, the *WAKI-ZA,* where the chorus is seated, again in view of the audience and able to adjust their narration and singing to the pace of the actors. Finally, a long bridge, the *HASHIGAKARI,* leads from the upstage right corner of the stage out to the **MIRROR ROOM,** where the costumed actors have been studying themselves to get into the character. The *hashigakari* is six feet wide by thirty-three to fifty-two feet long; it is bordered by a narrow strip of white pebbles, on which stand three pine trees, representing heaven, earth, and man.

The four pillars that support the roof over the stage also have specific functions in the performance and provide a sense of the ceremonial formality of Noh theater. The upstage right pillar closest to the *hashigakari* is called the **SHITEBASHIRA,** or *shite's* pillar. When the *shite* enters the *hashigakari,* he slides his feet (which are bound in cotton cloth) slowly along the floor; reaching the *shitebashira,* he pauses to announce who he is, where he is coming from, and where he is going (sometimes the *waki* will make this announcement when the *shite* reaches the *shitebashira*). The pillar downstage right is called the **METSUKEBASHIRA,** the gazing or eye-fixing pillar. It is the place where the *shite* looks while delivering his speech and which he watches through the slits in his mask to help orient his performance; given the tiny eye-openings in Noh masks, the *metsukebashira* is nearly all the *shite* can see. Downstage left, diagonally across from the *shitebashira,* is the *WAKIBASHIRA,* where the *waki* is often stationed when the *shite* enters. Upstage left is the **FUEBASHIRA,** the flute-player's pillar, where the flute-player is positioned.

As Zeami suggests in "Teachings on Style and the Flower", the training of a Noh actor in the fourteenth century was presumed to be lifelong, more a vocation than an occupation. Under the shogunate, Noh performers were given the privileges of the *samurai* caste, and five schools for training Noh actors were founded. These schools were run by hereditary masters, and certain families of Noh performers have influenced the theater over several generations; indeed, we owe the preservation of many documents (including Zeami's treatises), properties, and masks to the unusually closed and traditional ways in which Noh training has been passed from generation to generation. Four of the five current Noh companies were founded in Zeami's lifetime. Although Japan is no longer a caste society, acting in a Noh company today still requires years of dedication and intense training, something between the priesthood and the military. Moreover, because the relatively small number of classical Noh plays was stabilized in the early seventeenth century, Noh actors have generally mastered all the roles of the repertoire and perform without rehearsal. Their intensive training in movement, song, and dance prepares the actors, chorus, musicians, and stage assistants to be closely responsive to the many subtleties of their collective performance. And given the stability of the repertoire, of training, and of performance conventions, Noh theater has been performed in an unbroken tradition from Zeami's era to the present day.

THE DEVELOPMENT OF DOLL THEATER

Like the Noh theater, the doll theater owes something to the desire of Buddhist priests to educate a wider Japanese audience in their teachings. Unlike the Noh, however, the doll theater was not supported or protected directly by the shogunate, and it came to enjoy a more popular audience. The doll theater arose from the confluence of two kinds of performance: puppet shows and storytelling to music. Much like the itinerant performers of *sarugaku-no,* wandering puppeteers became associated with shrines and temples in the twelfth century. At the same time, a form of live storytelling also became popular, the singing and recitation of legends and stories to the accompaniment of the *BIWA,* a four-stringed, plucked instrument. One of the most popular of these narratives was *The Tale of Jōruri,* a love story about a wealthy girl named Jōruri; although the story dates from the fifteenth century, it became popular when it was performed to a musical instrument imported from the Ryukyu Islands between 1558 and 1569, the *SAMISEN.* The *samisen,* a three-stringed instrument that is both plucked and struck, has a much wider tonal and dynamic range than the *biwa.* Samisen-accompanied dialogue and narrative became so popular that this kind of performance was termed simply *JŌRURI.* In effect, the doll theater is a form of *jōruri* in which the song and spoken narrative are accompanied by puppet performance.

Although puppets had been used in Japan for several centuries, puppets were first used in conjunction with *jōruri* performances in the sixteenth century; puppet-*jōruri* performances have been recorded in Kyoto as early as 1596, and by the late seventeenth century there were important doll theaters in both Tokyo and Osaka. As in the Noh, the plays performed in the doll theaters used narrative, dialogue, music, and acting to convey the dramatic action, and in the seventeenth century playwrights writing for the doll theaters adapted plots and characters directly from Noh models. In part, however, because of their derivation from the romantic *jōruri* narratives, in part because their audiences were well-to-do merchants and citizens rather than the aristocratic *samurai,* and in part because they were competing with the more salacious Kabuki theaters for that audience, the doll theaters came to dramatize events more closely approaching contemporary life. Although the earliest doll theater plays were on historical and legendary subjects (like the Noh plays), by the late seventeenth and early eighteenth centuries, doll drama concerned stagings of current events, and romanticized portrayals of contemporary life, called "domestic plays" or *SEWAMONO.* Although the shogunate forbade the staging of current events in 1703, the shoguns were more concerned about the satirical portrayals of *samurai* common in Kabuki; playwrights continued to write about contemporary events.

The doll theater played a major role in the development of Japanese theater generally. When Gidayu Takemoto (1651–1714), a famous performer of *jōruri,* opened the Takemoto Theater in Osaka in 1684, he began a collaboration with Chikamatsu Monzaemon (1653–1725), now generally recognized as Japan's greatest dramatist. Chikamatsu wrote an important body of plays for the doll theater, on historical subjects as well as on contemporary life. His play *Love Suicides at Sonezaki* (1703) concerns the double suicide of a young merchant and a prostitute in 1703 and was renowned for the beauty of its language and the power of its performance. The genre became so popular that in 1722 the shogunate banned plays about double suicide, which were common in both the doll theater and the Kabuki theater, perhaps fearing that Chikamatsu's play would be imitated by romantic young Japanese. Not only did Chikamatsu and other playwrights—notably Chikamatsu Hanji (1725–1783) and Uemura Bunrakuken (1737–1810), for whom the current puppet theater of Japan, *BUNRAKU,* is named—produce an extraordinarily rich body of plays, but also these plays were immediately mined by the Kabuki theaters, providing a source of material for living actors as well as the doll theater's elaborate puppets.

The Doll Theater Stage

The stage of the doll theater is thirty-six feet wide by twenty-six feet deep and is divided into three sections, each separated by a low screen. The three puppeteers who operate each puppet are visible throughout the performance. They are costumed in elegant traditional clothes and are seated behind the screens. The puppeteers and their dolls share the stage with several other performers: the stage assistants, dressed in black as in the Noh theater; the announcer; the narrator; and the *samisen* player. The announcer begins the performance by announcing the title of the play and introducing the narrator and the *samisen* player. The narrator is responsible for the verbal art of the play in a direct development of his role in the *jōruri*: he narrates the story of the play, speaks the dialogue of the characters and expresses their emotions as well, smiling, laughing, weeping, and so on. Later in the eighteenth century several narrators were used, one for each of the major characters in the drama. The *samisen* is played to augment, clarify, and deepen the narrator's performance, lending it a special plangency.

As in the Noh theater, performance in the doll theater is extremely ceremonial and precise, and performers undergo years of training to achieve their craft. Although marionettes were used in the seventeenth century, hand-operated puppets became increasingly popular and by 1736 had supplanted earlier forms. The typical doll is three or four feet tall and is operated by three puppeteers. The most senior operator, dressed in a formal nineteenth-century costume, stands behind the doll and holds it up; he works a system of strings and pulleys within the head that control the doll's head, eyebrows, and eyelids, and he also operates the doll's right arm and right hand by means of hidden strings. His two assistants are clothed in black like the stage assistants, and their faces are covered; one assistant operates the left arm and hand, and the other assistant operates the legs and feet. Much as training in the Noh theater resembles that of a traditional art, so learning to operate the puppets of the doll theater entails a lifetime of commitment. Puppeteers take an apprenticeship of ten years to learn to operate the legs and feet of the dolls with sufficient grace; they then take another ten years to learn the correct operation of the left arm and hand before spending the final ten years on mastering the subtleties of the right arm, right hand, and head.

Doll theater contributed extensively to the dramatic repertoire of the Kabuki theater, and the fixed poses of the puppets are sometimes thought to contribute to the exaggerated expressive stance of the Kabuki actors, the **MIE**. But the doll theater contributed other innovations to Japanese theater and to world theater generally. Much as the dolls increased in complexity throughout the late seventeenth century and early eighteenth century—gaining eye movement in 1730, finger joints and movements in 1733, and so on—so the stage itself became increasingly mechanized. By 1715 the doll theaters were using movable settings, and by 1727 elevator traps were used to raise and lower scenery visibly through the floor of the stage. This machinery not only was put to use in the more spectacular Kabuki theater, but also was adapted and imitated by theaters around the world. Although the doll theater was surpassed in popularity by the Kabuki in the nineteenth century, it continues to be sponsored by the Japanese government and performed regularly in Osaka and Tokyo.

THE DEVELOPMENT OF KABUKI THEATER

Kabuki is in many ways the most energetic and spectacular mode of classical Japanese theater, using live actors to stage intense and passionate dramas whose effect is heightened by a range of powerful performance conventions and by an elaborately mechanized stage. As in the doll theater, Kabuki arose as a popular form of entertainment, supported by audiences outside the aristocratic sphere of Noh performance. Although Kabuki drama, as in the drama of the doll theaters, was initially derived from the plays of the Noh theater, Kabuki theater rapidly developed its own dramatic style and performance esthetics.

Unlike Noh and doll theater, Kabuki did not originate in medieval performance forms like the *sarugaku-no* and the *biwa*-accompanied narratives that became *jōruri*. Instead, Kabuki began in 1603, when Okuni, who claimed to be a priestess from the Izumo Grand Shrine, set up an impromptu stage in the Kyoto riverbed, where she performed dances and satirical skits. Okuni's company was largely composed of women, and within a short time a number of companies—some involving prostitutes, who offered performances as entertainment—were established in Kyoto and elsewhere. Although comic roles—called *SARUWAKA*—were always performed by men, the earliest troupes were composed mainly of women, called either *ONNA KABUKI* (women's Kabuki) or *YŪGO KABUKI* (prostitutes' Kabuki). At the same time, however, other Kabuki companies, composed mainly of adolescent boys, became popular.

Throughout the early period of Kabuki, its performers—both women and boys—were frequently associated with prostitution, which extended in various ways to a variety of leisure activities: to bathhouses, dances, and to the practice of *GEISHA,* which has its origins at this time. All of these activities, however, were distinct from the work of the *YŪGO,* or professional prostitute. As in other respects, the shogunate treated Kabuki like prostitution, beginning in 1624 to license companies and theater districts.

The boundary between theater and prostitution—by men, women, and boys—was difficult to police, though, and in 1652 authorities finally banned the boys' Kabuki—*WAKASHU KABUKI*—outright. Thereafter, the only Kabuki companies that were licensed to perform were the *YARO KABUKI,* or adult male Kabuki companies, which are now traditional.

The repertoire of Kabuki theater contains two kinds of plays, one based on historical or legendary incidents, and *sewamono* or "domestic plays," based on contemporary events. Okuni had once acted the role of a young *samurai* soliciting a prostitute, and plays based on the visit of a wealthy and powerful young man to the "licensed quarter" became a popular Kabuki genre, particularly in Kyoto and Osaka. Many of these plays, including *Love Letter from the Licensed Quarter* (1780), concern the fortunes of Yūgiri, a well-known courtesan of the Osaka Shinmachi quarter who died in 1678. Chikamatsu—whose *Love Suicides at Sonezaki* (1703) adapted the conventions of Kabuki to the doll stage—played a central role in this regard as well: he worked as the house playwright to a famous Kabuki company for more than twenty years. Although plays that dramatize love suicides and plays staging the scandals of the *samurai* caste were banned after 1722, playwrights continued to write about contemporary life under the guise of one of the other major genres of Kabuki theater, the history play. It quickly became apparent that by changing names and setting the drama in the past, playwrights were able to write domestic plays thinly veiled as history. For example, in 1703 the forty-seven retainers of Lord Asano took revenge on their master's disgrace at the hands of a shogunate official by killing the official and then committing *seppuku,* or ritual disembowelment. Within two weeks, a Kabuki play alluding to the incident was staged, and then was rapidly closed by the government. When Chikamatsu turned to these events in 1710, he set the play in the fourteenth century to sidestep the ban, and one of the most famous Kabuki plays—*Chūshingura* (1748)—concerns these events as well.

The Kabuki Stage

Kabuki is very much a performance genre, and its plays were organized around the abilities of its actors rather than around a literary script. For this reason, even the plays written by the most influential Kabuki playwrights—Chikamatsu Monzaemon, Takedo Izumo (1691–1756), and Kawatake Mokuami (1816–1893)—began as outlines of scenes to be elaborated by a cadre of assistant playwrights. A Kabuki company contained forty to sixty actors, each of whom specialized in a certain kind of role and expected the playwright to devise scenes that would allow him to display his talents. Companies generally included a leading-man actor, or *TACHIYAKU,* and specialists in villainous men (*KATAKIYAKU*), in young men and boys (*WAKASHUGATA*), in comic roles (*DOKEKATA*), and in women's roles (*ONNAGATA*), which were also divided according to age and type.

Finally, the unusual duration of a Kabuki performance also demanded the talents of the playwright's staff of assistants. Kabuki performances originally began about three o'clock in the morning and did not conclude until dusk; the fourteen- to fifteen-hour production was composed of a series of scenes arranged around a common theme or mood. The production usually began with a dance play, followed by a familiar play from the company's repertoire. Because the play was familiar to the company, it required little preparation. Then the

KABUKI STAGE, NINETEENTH CENTURY

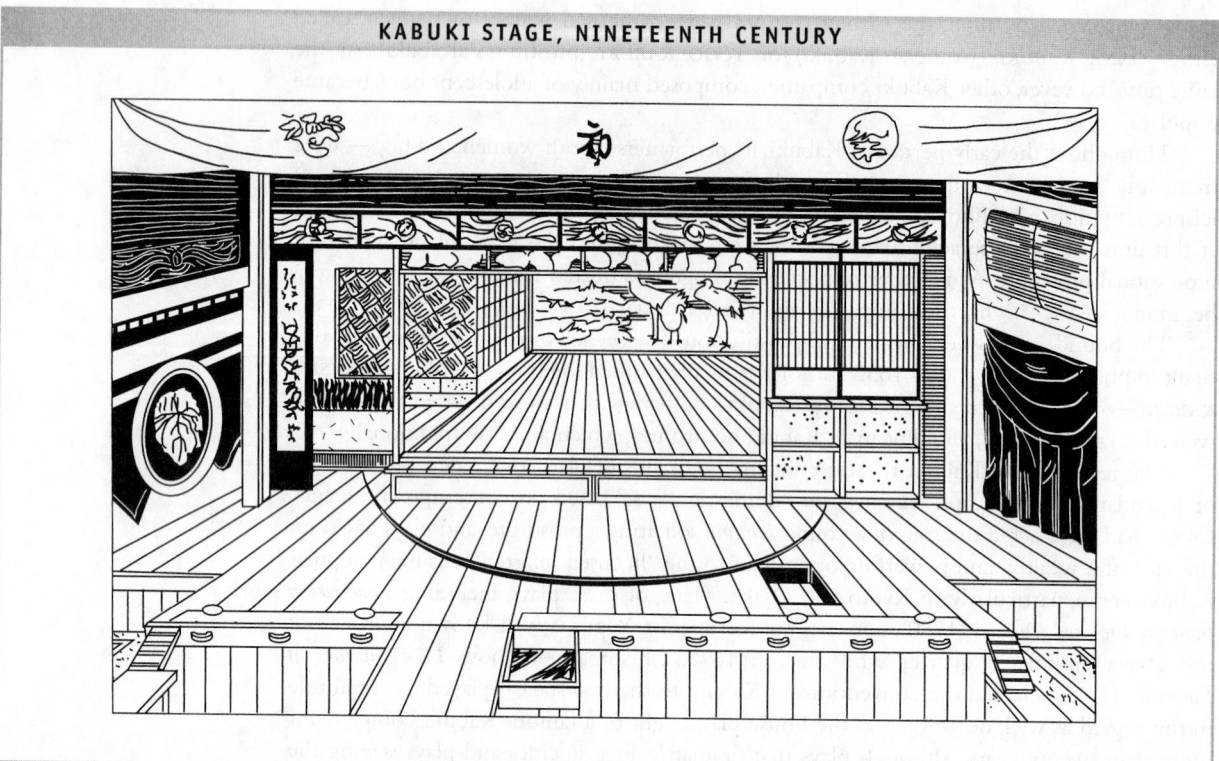

Notice the screens to the side of the stage, the *hanamichi* (which attaches to the front of the stage in the lower left-center of the picture), and a revolving platform in the center of the stage. (From Brockett, Oscar G. *History of the Theatre,* 7ᵗʰ Edition. Published by Allyn and Bacon, Boston, MA. Copyright © 1995 by Pearson Education. Reprinted by permission of the publisher.)

company would perform one or two short practice plays, written by apprentice playwrights and performed by actors-in-training as part of their education. The main play—the **HON KYŌGEN**—would be performed at about seven o'clock in the morning and lasted until dusk. This play was outlined by the house playwright in collaboration with the company's leading actor and manager, and he would write the most important sections himself; the company's second and third rank playwrights would elaborate dialogue for the rest of the play. The play was customarily divided into four sections: a history section in four to six acts (**JIDAIMONO**) concerning the exploits of the *samurai;* a dance; a *sewamono* (contemporary) section in one to three acts, set in the milieu of artisans, traders, and merchants; and a concluding dance drama. Kabuki performances today are generally given in two programs, lasting from eleven to four o'clock and from four-thirty until nine-thirty in the evening. Although it is rare to see a full-length Kabuki play performed today, the four-part sequence is still followed.

Kabuki is very much an actor's theater. The actors undergo a long period of training, and as in Noh theater, certain families of actors have dominated the history of Kabuki. Indeed, Kabuki actors often wear their family crest in performance, and audiences frequently compare an actor's performance in a given role with his father's or his uncle's. Originating as a form of dance, Kabuki places a premium on choreography, which accompanies gesture and speech as a means of realizing the character's essential tone or feeling in a precise and elegant image. Yet the actors play directly to the audience, and the most striking moments in the performance—the *mie,* a highly conventionalized posed performance of passion—are underscored as performance when the stage assistants clap two pieces of wood loudly and rhythmically together. The actors play conventional roles, and each role in the Kabuki repertoire has a conventional costume associated with it. The costumes are extremely cumbersome, so the actors are often helped by stage assistants clothed in black who position properties and move pieces of the set. The actors are not masked, but wear an elaborate and conventionalized makeup, usually of red and black lines and patterns ranged over a white base; *onnagata* actors generally add only eyebrow lines and rouged cheeks and lips to an otherwise white face. Given its close relationship to *jōruri* and doll theater, it is not surprising that Kabuki usually requires a narrator onstage as well who not only sets the scene, but comments on the action throughout; he also occasionally speaks dialogue. Kabuki actors never sing, so their songs are sung by the narrator and by an onstage chorus. Moreover, each play is accompanied by traditional music, played by musicians wearing the traditional *samurai* costume. The orchestra for Kabuki is considerably larger than that for Noh and makes use of flutes, bells, drums, cymbals, and gongs, as well as the *samisen*.

Although the first Kabuki companies played on impromptu stages, they soon were allowed to use Noh theaters; given their raffish character, however, Kabuki companies were not allowed to have roofed theaters until 1724. Like the doll theater, Kabuki theater quickly made use of scenic technology; the elevator stage was in use by 1736, and by the late eighteenth century it was common for Kabuki theaters to have a revolving stage, sometimes two independent turntables with one turning inside the other. Kabuki makes extensive use of scenery, though much of it is of a symbolic or ornamental nature. Like properties in this theater, which tend to be suggestive of the objects they represent, the scenery of a Kabuki performance is openly theatrical in character: the scenery is changed in view of the audience by visible assistants (who help the actors as well) and aims to suggest the locale of the scene rather than put it on the stage in a realistic way. It is a measure, though, of the relationship between the extroverted Kabuki performance and its audience that its most distinguishing feature involves the audience more directly in the production. In the early eighteenth century, Kabuki theaters added a **HANAMICHI,** or elevated bridge, extending from the rear of the auditorium to the stage. Actors made their exits and entrances here, and scenes could be played on the *hanamichi* as well. By the 1770s, a second *hanamichi* was added, and the area between the two *hanamichi* was divided into floor boxes, while other rows of seating ran along the sides of the auditorium. Although the second *hanamichi* is still required for some plays, it is generally no longer in use.

The restoration of the emperor in 1868 not only brought about the collapse of the shogunate, but also ended Japan's isolation. It also dramatized the economic weakness of the *samurai* relative to the merchant class. In many respects, Japan's theater was vulnerable to extinction, especially the Noh and doll theaters, which had no truly popular audience; Kabuki was the only theater which continued to attract new plays, playwrights, and audiences in the nineteenth and twentieth centuries. But the Japanese worked to preserve their classical theater, and it is still possible today to see plays from the Noh, doll theater, and Kabuki repertoire in excellent, traditional productions.

After 1868, Japan became open to cultural influence from the West, and a variety of dramatic and theatrical forms came to rival the traditional genres of Noh, *jōruri,* and Kabuki. **SHIMPA,** a theatrical movement originating in Osaka in the 1880s, responded to the Western theater's use of more colloquial language and contemporary dramatic settings. However, because many of the *shimpa* actors were drawn from Kabuki, *shimpa* gradually came to resemble Kabuki in performance, even though its dramas were more evidently based on recent news events, crimes, and political controversies. Although *shimpa* and its successor, **SHINGEKI**—a "realistic" dramatic movement that both imported and imitated the plays of Ibsen, Chekhov, Shaw, and others—marked an important move away from the classical genres, they continued to be performed in the twentieth century.

CLASSICAL JAPANESE DRAMA IN PERFORMANCE HISTORY

(ASIDE)
SANSKRIT DRAMA AND THEATER

The cultures, languages, and theater of the Indian subcontinent have been transformed by three massive invasions: by the Aryans sometime between 3000 and 2000 BCE; by the Moslems, who brought both the Persian language and the Koran, in the tenth and eleventh centuries; and by the British, beginning in the seventeenth century. The Aryan language—Sanskrit (literally, "the perfected tongue")—became the foundation of ancient Indian culture. Sanskrit was a spoken language until early in the first millennium, when Prakit became the vernacular. Something like Latin in medieval Europe, Sanskrit was reserved for ritual, religious, and academic uses, and for India's rich literature and theater. Sanskrit is the language of the *Rgveda*, a collection of prayers and hymns composed between 1500 and 1000 BCE that is the oldest work in any Indo-European language. The two major epics of Indian culture—the *Mahabharata* and the *Ramayana*—date from around 1000 BCE, but took their current form during India's golden age, which lasted from the second century CE into the ninth century. Although it had long been thought in the West that Sanskrit theater gradually disappeared after the Moslem invasions of the tenth and eleventh centuries, Sanskrit plays were still performed in Kerala—a state in the southwest of India—by performers who were part of a hereditary caste connected to religious temples.

Hindu belief and the caste structure of ancient Indian society inform the esthetics of Sanskrit theater and drama. Ancient India was a rigidly stratified society composed of four hereditary castes, each of which was subdivided: the *Brahmins* (priests and intellectuals), *Kshatriyas* (aristocrats, warriors), *Vaisyas* (craftsmen, farmers), and *Sudras* (unskilled workers, peasants). Although these castes were devised and perpetuated along racial and economic lines, they also translated Hindu religious beliefs into the organizing structure of society. Hindu is based on a belief in Brahman, or "world-soul." Although different aspects of Brahman are often represented as distinct gods—Brahma the creator, Siva the destroyer, Vishnu the preserver, for example—these gods are really aspects of Brahman, the only whole, perfect, and unchanging being. The created universe is arrayed hierarchically, according to the degree that each being is able to contemplate or participate in this sense of wholeness or perfection.

In performance, Sanskrit drama emblematizes this dichotomy between the distracting diversity of lived experience and the contemplation of wholeness and perfection; Sanskrit theater offers its audience a richly varied performance while inducing the audience to adopt a unifying and impersonal, even contemplative mood. Most of our understanding of Sanskrit drama derives from the second-century *Natyasastra,* or *Art of the Theater,* usually attributed to the playwright Bharata, from several other treatises, and from the twenty-five plays that remain. Much as ancient Greek plays were based on myth and legend mainly drawn from the *Iliad* and the *Odyssey,* Sanskrit plays were generally based on heroic stories taken from the *Mahabharata* and the *Ramayana* and were divided into two groups: *RUPAKA* (major drama) and *UPA-RUPAKA* (minor drama). *Rupaka* are of various lengths and include the plays of Bharata; Bhasa's second-century plays *The Vision of Vasavadatta* and *Carudatta;* King Sudraka's *The Clay Cart* (written sometime between the fourth and eighth centuries); Kalidasa's fifth-century *Sakuntala;* and the seventh-century plays of King Harsa and Bhavabhuti. As in the Japanese Noh, the narrative of the play is less critical than the attitude it produces: the impersonal and contemplative mood of wholeness called *RASA.* According to the *Natyasastra,* there are eight basic *rasas* or moods that a play should strive to produce—erotic, comic, pathetic, furious, heroic, terrible, odious, and marvelous—and while a given play may include several *rasas,* it should be designed so that one mood dominates. Moreover, these *rasas* are related to the *BHAVA,* the emotions or feelings displayed in the play by the characters. The eight *bhavas*—desire, comic or sympathetic laughter, sadness, anger, vigor or power, fear, loathing, and wonder—are the organizing, "stable" emotions staged in the play, and are complicated by thirty-three "unsta-

Indeed, the Japanese classical theater was perhaps most keenly threatened by Japan's defeat in World War II and the subsequent occupation. As part of the postwar occupation of Japan, the United States established a Civil Information and Education Section, which had as part of its duties both the protection of traditional Japanese culture and the importation of "progressive," democratic culture, including American literature and drama. This office often came into conflict with the occupation's censorship office, concerned as it was to prevent the spread of imperial Japanese political ideas. Although neither Noh nor *jōruri* seemed to pose much of a political threat, the popular Kabuki theater had long been associated with the feudal ideology of Japanese nationalism, and the censors were much more careful in their approval of Kabuki theater. The first Kabuki play to be produced after the end of occupable" emotions. The subtle balance and interplay of the *bhavas* should evoke a sense of harmony and perfection, the dominant *rasa* of the play.

As in Hindu philosophy, Sanskrit drama aims to produce a sense of oneness from the diversity of experience; *rasa* arises from each play's cunning interplay of the range of *bhavas,* of dialogue written in both verse and prose, of Sanskrit and Prakit, and of character types ranging from gods, kings, and heroes to servants, peasants, and children. Yet despite this diversity, Sanskrit plays have several common characteristics. Each play not only produces its main mood or *rasa,* it also illustrates the workings of *karma* or cosmic justice. For this reason, Sanskrit drama falls outside the Western understanding of tragedy, and Sanskrit playwrights are urged by the *Natyasastra* not to represent death onstage. Sanskrit is spoken by all the male Brahmin and Kshatriya characters in the play, whereas women, peasants, and children speak Prakit, as does the jester character who appears in most plays, often as the hero's sidekick. Although plays vary in length from one act to ten acts, each act generally takes place within a single day; the action usually takes place in several earthly and heavenly locations.

Plays were performed on a variety of occasions in ancient India—at festivals, weddings, coronations, and at other public events—and the play's *rasa* was appropriate to the occasion. The *Natyasastra* describes three kinds of theater structure—square, rectangular, and triangular—each in three different sizes. The rectangular theaters

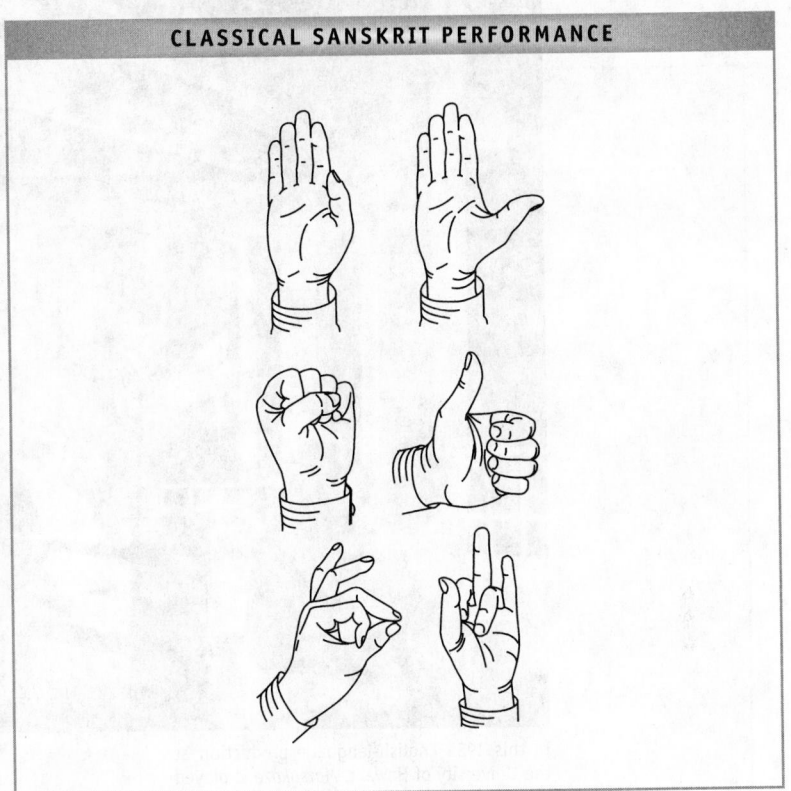

CLASSICAL SANSKRIT PERFORMANCE

These six hand positions are used in a classical Sanskrit performance.

were divided into two equal areas. The audience area was supported by four pillars, representing both the four compass points and the four principal castes. The stage area was divided into two parts—a relatively shallow performing space divided from a backstage area by a wall.

Performances were accompanied by a variety of musical instruments and were elaborately ceremonial in character; actors used an elaborate system of movement, gesture, and speech. Because the performers were to represent codified *bhavas,* the *Natyasastra* described the gestures appropriate to them: for instance, thirty-two different eye movements, thirty-two positions for the feet, twenty-four gestures for one hand. Both the Sanskrit drama and texts like the *Natyasastra* document the extraordinary theatrical vitality of the golden age of classical Indian culture.

tion censorship in 1948 was, in fact, the great *samurai* revenge play, *Chūshingura,* often known in English as *The Loyal Forty-Seven Samurai.*

Since the war, the traditional modes of Japanese theater have become popular not only in Japan, but throughout the world. Several modern playwrights—notably Mishima Yukio—have either written new Noh or Kabuki plays or have adapted earlier dramas to modern settings. Moreover, the revival of Japanese classical theater has been part of an important resurgence of interest in traditional modes of artistic expression in Japan, which has taken place alongside Japan's emergence as a leading political, economic, and cultural power in the late twentieth century.

In this 1989 English-language production at the University of Hawai'i, *Matsukaze* is played on a traditional Noh stage.

Exemplifying the elegant movement of Kabuki theater, this scene from the University of Hawai'i production of *Chūshingura* shows Kampei protecting Okaru from attackers, who threaten them with cherry-blossom weapons.

This view of the *Matsukaze* shows the musicians and chorus, as well as the *hashigakari*.

In the University of Hawai'i production of *Chūshingura* (1979), Lord Enya Hangan commits *seppuku*, watched by the shogun's messengers.

READING THE MATERIAL THEATER

One of the great traditions of Japan is the art of portraiture, and many of Japan's greatest artists made portraits of celebrated actors. As historical records, however, these portraits are somewhat difficult to use: like Japanese theater, Japanese painting was itself a highly conventionalized activity. Nonetheless, these illustrations provide a striking insight into the power of performance on Japan's classical stage. Here is a portrait of the actor Seki Sanjūrō II (1805–1870) in the role of Kyōgoku Takumi, by the great artist Kunisada (1786–1865). Kunisada lived toward the end of the Edo period; shortly after his death, in 1867, the last of the Tokugawa shoguns resigned, leading to the increasing openness to the West characteristic of the Meiji period. In this sense, Kunisada's printmaking—which covers natural subjects, as well as the circumscribed life of the court, the brothels, and the theaters—documents the final phases of traditional Japanese culture before the massive impact of European and American modernity.

In his long career, Kunisada made a large number of theatrical portraits which were engraved and printed; he also occasionally illustrated scenes of backstage life. (See the excellent overview of Kunisada's work provided by Sebastian Izzard, J. Thomas Rimer, and John T. Carpenter in *Kunisada's World,* a catalogue of the exhibition "Kunisada's World" shown at the Japan Society Gallery in New York in 1993 [New York: Japan Society, 1993] from which this portrait and descriptive information are taken.) This portrait is part of a series of 150 portraits of Kabuki actors that Kunisada planned to print late in his life; he completed seventy-two. The cartouches—the small bars with en-graved Japanese characters—list the actor's name and the role he is playing in the illustration, as well as Kunisada's signature. In many respects these portraits seem heavily conventionalized, even idealized, and we know that Kunisada based many of them on earlier portraits; some portraits—of actors whose careers were over before Kunisada began his work—are based on portraits executed by other artists. Nonetheless, the portraits capture a number of significant features of Kabuki theater. In most of the portraits, Kunisada shows the actor in the *mie*—a moment of intense passion, in which the actor freezes and moves his eyes rapidly, as a way of demonstrating the intensity of his feelings; this action is usually sustained by the musicians' drumming and often prompts shouts of encouragement and applause from the audience.

Beyond that, what features of the portrait seem prominent? What kind of roles do you think were his speciality? Given the conventionality of the portrait, how do you interpret the strong and energetic sense of line in the image, evident especially around his nose and chin?

Seki Sanjūrō II as Kyōgoku Takumi, in a portrait by Kunisada.

Kan'ami Kiyotsugu

Kan'ami Kiyotsugu (1333–1384) was one of the principal performers of *sarugaku-no* and the leader of a prominent company. When he appeared before the *shogun* Yoshimitsu Ashikiga in 1374, the *shogun* was so impressed with the company that he retained them as his players. Kan'ami is generally credited with refining and systematizing the Noh for his aristocratic audience and with writing many of the plays that became part of the standard Noh repertoire. Kan'ami's son, Zeami Motokiyo (1363–1444), succeeded his father as the leader of the company and had a massive influence on the development of the Noh. Zeami both reworked older plays and wrote many new plays of his own; of the 241 plays in the Noh repertoire, more than 100 are connected to Zeami. Zeami influenced the development of Noh in other respects as well, mainly in writing sixteen essays on Noh esthetics. These essays cover a range of topics, including the training of actors, the proper style of dramatic writing, and the goals of performance. Although Zeami enjoyed the favor of Yoshimitsu until the *shogun's* death in 1408, he fared less well under the rule of Yoshimitsu's son, Yoshimochi (1386–1428) and was banished to the remote island of Sado in 1434 when Yoshimochi's younger brother Yoshinori (1394–1441) became *shogun*. The reasons for Yoshinori's hostility to Zeami are not clear but may involve Yoshinori's preference for another playwright, On'ami. Zeami did succeed in passing his essays on to his son-in-law, Komparu Zenchiku (1405–1468), who became an important Noh playwright and theoretician. Not much is known about the end of Zeami's life; legend has it that he was able to return to the mainland after Yoshinori was assassinated in 1441.

MATSUKAZE

Matsukaze was originally written by Kan'ami and extensively reworked by Zeami; it has remained in the Noh repertoire since the fifteenth century and is performed by all Noh companies.

This elegant drama, like most Noh plays, takes place in a setting familiar from the classic literature of Japan, the Bay of Suma. Suma is principally associated with the famous poet, courtier, and scholar Ariwaka no Yukihira (818–893), whose exile at Suma was recounted in his own poetry and formed the basis for many stories and legends. It also inspired the narrative of Genji's exile at Suma in the Japanese epic *Tale of Genji*. The narrative of the play, though, seems to have been invented by Kan'ami. The play opens when the *waki*—playing a priest—enters the stage, singing a traveling song about his arrival at Suma. He asks the *kyōgen* (playing a villager) about the significance of the pine tree, and he is informed that it memorializes two fisher girls, Murasame and Matsukaze, who have long since died. Shortly thereafter, Murasame—played by the *tsure*—enters, followed by the *shite*, Matsukaze. The two girls elaborately mime dipping brine into their cart with their fans, and in speeches that quote from Yukihira and from other poets, they describe their desolation. Their language here is rich with imagery, particularly of the changing sea, the hard lives of the fishermen, and of the moon, a Buddhist symbol of enlightenment. As is typical of the Noh, many of their lines are spoken by the Chorus.

Although the *shite* and his *tsure* do not leave the stage, they retire to the *shitebashira*, where they mime sitting in their small hut. The *waki*—who has observed them throughout the first scene—approaches the hut and asks for shelter, quoting one of Yukihira's poems in passing. The girls then reveal that they are the ghosts of Matsukaze and Murasame, still "steeped in longing" for the exiled poet, even in death. They had fallen in love with Yukihira during his exile at Suma, and he had given them their names, "Wind in the Pines" (*matsukaze*) and "Autumn Rain" (*murasame*), names redolent of the imagery of classical Japanese poetry. The girls were not able to follow Yukihira when he returned to court after his exile;

This production of Kan'ami's *Matsukaze* emphasizes the traditional spatial, costume, and performance elements of Noh theater.

all they have in his memory is his hunting cloak and court hat. Driven nearly to madness with her eternal grief, Matsukaze puts on Yukihira's cloak and hat for her final dance.

Matsukaze is an evocative example of the way Noh theater attempts to capture a particular mood through the collaborative interplay between each of its highly wrought arts. The beauty of the language, the delicacy of characterization, the succinct action, the music of the flute and drums, the chanting of the Chorus, and the refinement of the acting combine to capture the subtle intensity of feeling for which Noh theater is famous.

MATSUKAZE

Kan'ami Kiyotsugu

TRANSLATED BY ROYALL TYLER

CHARACTERS

AN ITINERANT PRIEST *(waki)*   MATSUKAZE *(shite)*
A VILLAGER *(kyōgen)*   MURASAME *(tsure)*

PLACE: *Suma Bay in Settsu Province*
TIME: *Autumn, the Ninth Month*

(The stage assistant places a stand with a pine sapling set into it at the front of the stage. The PRIEST *enters and stands at the naming-place. He carries a rosary.)*

PRIEST: I am a priest who travels from province to province.
Lately I have been in the Capital. I visited the famous sites
and ancient ruins, not missing a one. Now I intend to
make a pilgrimage to the western provinces. *(He faces for-*
5 *ward.)* I have hurried, and here I am already at the Bay of
Suma in Settsu Province. *(His attention is caught by the pine
tree.)* How strange! That pine on the beach has a curious
look. There must be a story connected with it. I'll ask
someone in the neighborhood. *(He faces the bridgeway.)* Do
10 you live in Suma?

(The VILLAGER *comes down the bridgeway to the first pine. He
wears a short sword.)*

VILLAGER: Perhaps I am from Suma; but first tell me what
you want.
PRIEST: I am a priest and I travel through the provinces. Here
on the beach I see a solitary pine tree with a wooden
15 tablet fixed to it, and a poem slip hanging from the tablet.
Is there a story connected with the tree? Please tell me
what you know.
VILLAGER: The pine is linked with the memory of two fisher
girls, Matsukaze and Murasame. Please say a prayer for
20 them as you pass.
PRIEST: Thank you. I know nothing about them, but I will
stop at the tree and say a prayer for them before I move on.
VILLAGER: If I can be of further service, don't hesitate to ask.
PRIEST: Thank you for your kindness.
25 VILLAGER: At your command, sir.

(The VILLAGER *exits. The* PRIEST *goes to stage center and turns
toward the pine tree.)*

PRIEST: So, this pine tree is linked with the memory of two
fisher girls, Matsukaze and Murasame. It is sad! Though
their bodies are buried in the ground, their names linger
on. This lonely pine tree lingers on also, ever green and
30 untouched by autumn, their only memorial. Ah! While I
have been chanting sutras and invoking Amida Buddha for
their repose, the sun, as always on autumn days, has
quickly set. That village at the foot of the mountain is a
long way. Perhaps I can spend the night in this fisherman's
35 salt shed.

*(He kneels at the waki-position. The stage assistant brings out the
prop, a cart for carrying pails of brine, and sets it by the gazing-pillar.
He places a pail on the cart.)*

*(*MURASAME *enters and comes down the bridgeway as far as the first
pine. She wears the tsure mask.* MATSUKAZE *follows her and stops
at the third pine. She wears the wakaonna mask. Each carries a
water pail. They face each other.)*

MATSUKAZE AND MURASAME: A brine cart wheeled along
the beach
Provides a meager livelihood:
The sad world rolls
Life by quickly and in misery!
MURASAME: Here at Suma Bay   40
The waves shatter at our feet,
And even the moonlight wets our sleeves
With its tears of loneliness.

*(*MURASAME *goes to stage center while* MATSUKAZE *moves to the*
shite *position.)*

MATSUKAZE: The autumn winds are sad.
When the Middle Counselor Yukihira   45
Lived here back a little from the sea,
They inspired his poem,
"Salt winds blowing from the mountain pass...."
On the beach, night after night,
Waves thunder at our door;   50
And on our long walks to the village
We've no companion but the moon.
Our toil, like all of life, is dreary,
But none could be more bleak than ours.
A skiff cannot cross the sea,   55
Nor we this dream world.
Do we exist, even?
Like foam on the salt sea,
We draw a cart, friendless and alone,
Poor fisher girls whose sleeves are wet   60
With endless spray, and tears
From our hearts' unanswered longing.
CHORUS: Our life is so hard to bear
That we envy the pure moon

---

48 **"Salt . . . pass"** from the poem by Yukihira, No. 876 in the
Shinkokinshū: "The sleeves of the traveler have turned cold; the
wind from Suma Bay blows through the pass."   52 **We've . . .
moon** a modified quotation from the poem by Hōkyō Chūmei,
No. 187 in the *Kin'yōshū*: "Pillow of grass—as I sleep on my journey I realize I have no companion but the moon."   58–59 **salt sea**
the words "salt sea," which can also be translated "brine," lead to
mention of the brine cart even though the cart does not logically
belong in the context   64 **That . . . moon** from the poem by
Fujiwara Takamitsu, No. 435 in the *Shūishū*: "In this world which
seems difficult to pass through, how I envy the pure moon!"

65   Now rising with the tide.
       But come, let us dip brine,
       Dip brine from the rising tide!
       Our reflections seem to shame us!

*(They look down as if catching a glimpse of their reflections in the
water. The movement of their heads "clouds" the expression on their
masks, making it seem sad.)*

       Yes, they shame us!
70   Here, where we shrink from men's eyes,
       Drawing our timorous cart;
       The withdrawing tide
       Leaves stranded pools behind.
       How long do they remain?
75   If we were the dew on grassy fields,
       We would vanish with the sun.
       But we are sea tangle,
       Washed up on the shore,
       Raked into heaps by the fishermen,
80   Fated to be discarded, useless,
       Withered and rotting,
       Like our trailing sleeves,
       Like our trailing sleeves.

(They look down again.)

       Endlessly familiar, still how lovely
85   The twilight at Suma!
       The fishermen call out in muffled voices;
       At sea, the small boats loom dimly,
       Across the faintly glowing face of the moon
       Flights of wild geese streak,
90   And plovers flock below along the shore.
       Fall gales and stiff sea winds:
       These are things, in such a place,
       That truly belong to autumn.
       But oh, the terrible, lonely nights!

(They hide their faces.)

95 MATSUKAZE: Come, dip the brine.
  MURASAME: Where the seas flood and fall,
       Let us tie our sleeves back to our shoulders.
  MATSUKAZE: Think only, "Dip the brine."
  MURUSAME: We ready ourselves for the task,
100 MATSUKAZE: But for women, this cart is too hard.
  CHORUS: While the rough breakers surge and fall,

(MURASAME moves upstage to stand beside MATSUKAZE.)

       While the rough breakers surge and fall,
       And cranes among the reeds
       Fly up with sharp cries.
105   The four winds add their wailing.
       How shall we pass the cold night?

(They look up.)

       The late moon is so brilliant—
       What we dip is its reflection!
       Smoke from the salt fires
110   May cloud the moon—take care!

---

85 **The twilight** the following description is generally inspired
by the "Exile at Suma" chapter of *The Tale of Genji*

       Are we always to spend only
       The sad autumns of fishermen?
       At Ojima in Matsushima

*(MATSUKAZE half-kneels by the brine cart and mimes dipping with
her fan.)*

       The fisherfolk, like us,
       Delight less in the moon   115
       Than in the dipping of its reflection;
       There they take delight in dipping
       Reflections of the moon.

(MATSUKAZE returns to the shite *position.)*

       We haul our brine from afar,
       As in far-famed Michinoku   120
       And at the salt kilns of Chika—
       Chika, whose name means "close by."
MATSUKAZE: Humble folk hauled wood for salt fires
       At the ebb tide on Akogi Shore.
CHORUS: On Ise Bay there's Twice-See Beach—   125
       Oh, could I live my life again!

(MATSUKAZE looks off into the distance.)

MATSUKAZE: On days when pine groves stand hazy,
       And the sea lanes draw back
       From the coast at Narumi—
CHORUS: You speak of Narumi; this is Naruo,   130
       Where pines cut off the moonlight
       From the reed-thatched roofs of Ashinoya.
MATSUKAZE: Who is to tell of our unhappiness
       Dipping brine at Nada?
       With boxwood combs set in our hair,   135
       From rushing seas we draw the brine,
       Oh look! I have the moon in my pail!

---

113 **Ojima** is one of the islands at Matsushima, a place renowned
for its scenic beauty. Both names are conventionally associated in
poetry with *ama,* fisherwomen   120 **As in far-famed** the following passage is a *tsukushi,* or "exhaustive enumeration," of place-
names associated with the sea, including allusions and plays on
words. This passage was apparently borrowed from an older work,
a play called *Tōei* that was set by Ashinoya Bay. Michinoku is a
general name for the northern end of the island of Honshu. Chika
was another name for Shiogama ("Salt Kiln"), and sounds like the
word meaning "near"   124 **Akogi** the name of a stretch of
shore on Ise Bay. The pulling in of the nets and the hauling of the
wood for the salt kilns at Akogi were frequently mentioned in poetry   125 **Twice-See Beach** (*Futami-ga-ura*) is a word evocative
of Ise and often used in poetry for the meaning of its name
129 **Narumi** often mentioned in poetry because of its dry flats that
appeared at low tide   132 **Ashinoya** (modern Ashiya) and
Naruo are two places near Suma. Ashinoya means literally "reed
house"   134 **Dipping . . . Nada** derived from the poem in the
eighty-seventh episode of the *Ise Monogatari:* "At Nada by
Ashinoya, I have no respite from boiling brine for salt; I have
come without even putting a boxwood comb in my hair." 135 **With
boxwood** the line recalls the poem quoted in the previous note,
but it is used because of the pivot-word *tsuge no,* "of boxwood," and
tsuge, "to inform." Similarly, *kushi sashi,* "Setting a comb (in the
hair)," leads into *sashi-kuru nami,* "in-rushing waves"

(MURASAME *kneels before the brine cart and places her pail on it.* MATSUKAZE, *still standing, looks into her pail.*)

MATSUKAZE: In my pail too I hold the moon!
CHORUS: How lovely! A moon here too!

(MURASAME *picks up the rope tied to the cart and gives it to* MAT-SUKAZE, *then moves to the* shite *position.* MATSUKAZE *looks up.*)

140 MATSUKAZE: The moon above is one;
    Below it has two, no, three reflections

(*She looks into both pails.*)

    Which shine in the flood tide tonight,

(*She pulls the cart to a spot before the musicians.*)

    And on our cart we load the moon!
    No, life is not all misery
145 Here by the sea lanes.

(*She drops the rope. The stage assistant removes the cart.* MAT-SUKAZE *sits on a low stool and* MURASAME *kneels beside her, a sign that the two women are resting inside their hut. The* PRIEST *rises.*)

PRIEST: The owner of the salt shed has returned. I shall ask for
    a night's lodging. (*To* MATSUKAZE *and* MURASAME.) I beg
    your pardon. Might I come inside?
MURASAME: (*Standing and coming forward a little.*) Who might
150 you be?
PRIEST: A traveler, overtaken by night on my journey. I should
    like to ask lodging for the night.
MURASAME: Wait here. I must ask the owner. (*She kneels before*
    MATSUKAZE.) A traveler outside asks to come in and spend
155 the night.
MATSUKAZE: That is little enough, but our hut is so wretched
    we cannot ask him in. Please tell him so.
MURASAME: (*Standing, to the* PRIEST.) I have spoken to the
    owner. She says the house is too wretched to put anyone up.
160 PRIEST: I understand those feelings
    Perfectly, but poverty makes
    No difference at all to me.
    I am only a priest. Please
    Say I beg her to let
165 Me spend the night.
MURASAME: No, we really cannot put you up.
MATSUKAZE: (*To* MURASAME.) Wait!
    I see in the moonlight
    One who has renounced the world.
170 He will not mind a fisherman's hut,
    With its rough pine pillars and bamboo fence;
    I believe it is very cold tonight,
    So let him come in and warm himself
    At our sad fire of rushes.
175 You may tell him that.
MURASAME: Please come in.
PRIEST: Thank you very much. Forgive me for intruding.

(*He takes a few steps forward and kneels.* MURASAME *goes back beside* MATSUKAZE.)

MATSUKAZE: I wished from the beginning to invite you in,
    but this place is so poor I felt I must refuse.

PRIEST: You are very kind. I am a priest and a traveler, and   180
    never stay anywhere very long. Why prefer one lodging to
    another? In any case, what sensitive person would not pre-
    fer to live here at Suma, in the quiet solitude. Yukihira
    wrote,
    "If ever anyone   185
    Chances to ask for me,
    Say I live alone,
    Soaked by the dripping seaweed
    On the shore of Suma Bay."
    (*He looks at the pine tree.*) A while ago I asked someone the   190
    meaning of that solitary pine on the beach. I was told it
    grows there in memory of two fisher girls, Matsukaze and
    Murasame. There is no connection between them and me,
    but I went to the pine anyway and said a prayer for them.
    (MATSUKAZE *and* MURASAME *weep. The* PRIEST *stares at*   195
    them.) This is strange! They seem distressed at the mention
    of Matsukaze and Murasame. Why?
MATSUKAZE AND MURASAME: Truly, when a grief is hidden,
    Still, signs of it will show.
    His poem, "If ever anyone   200
    Chances to ask for me,"
    Filled us with memories which are far too fond.
    Tears of attachment to the world
    Wet our sleeves once again.
PRIEST: Tears of attachment to the world? You speak as   205
    though you are no longer of the world. Yukihira's poem
    overcame you with memories. More and more bewilder-
    ing! Please, both of you, tell me who you are.
MATSUKAZE AND MURASAME: We would tell you our names,
    But we are too ashamed!   210
    No one, ever,
    Has chanced to ask for us,
    Long dead as we are,
    And so steeped in longing
    For the world by Suma Bay   215
    That pain has taught us nothing.
    Ah, the sting of regret!
    But having said this,
    Why should we hide our names any longer?
    At twilight you said a prayer   220
    By a mossy grave under the pine
    For two fisher girls,
    Matsukaze and Murasame.
    We are their ghosts, come to you.
    When Yukihira was here he whiled away   225
    Three years of weary exile
    Aboard his pleasure boat,
    His heart refreshed
    By the moon of Suma Bay.
    There were, among the fisher girls   230
    Who hauled brine each evening,
    Two sisters whom he chose for his favors.
    "Names to fit the season!"
    He said, calling us
    Pine Wind and Autumn Rain.   235
    We had been Suma fisher girls,
    Accustomed to the moon,

185–189 **"If ever . . . Bay"** poem No. 962 in the *Kokinshū*

But he changed our salt makers' clothing
To damask robes,
240   Burnt with the scent of faint perfumes.
MATSUKAZE: Then, three years later, Yukihira
Returned to the Capital.
MURASAME: Soon, we heard he had died, oh so young!
MATSUKAZE: How we both loved him!
245   Now the message we pined for
Would never, never come.
CHORUS: Pine Wind and Autumn Rain
Both drenched their sleeves with the tears
Of hopeless love beyond their station,
250   Fisher girls of Suma.
Our sin is deep, O priest.
Pray for us, we beg of you!

(*They press their palms together in supplication.*)

Our love grew rank as wild grasses;
Tears and love ran wild.
255   It was madness that touched us.
Despite spring purification,
Performed in our old robes,
Despite prayers inscribed on paper streamers,
The gods refused us their help.
260   We were left to melt away
Like foam on the waves,
And, in misery, we died.

(MATSUKAZE *looks down, shading her mask.*)

Alas! How the past evokes our longing!
Yukihira, the Middle Counselor,

(*The stage assistant puts a man's cloak and court hat in* MAT-
SUKAZE'*s left hand.*)

265   Lived three years here by Suma Bay.
Before he returned to the Capital,
He left us these keepsakes of his stay:
A court hat and a hunting cloak.
Each time we see them,

(*She looks at the cloak.*)

270   Our love grows again,
And gathers like dew
On the tip of a leaf
So that there's no forgetting,
Not for an instant.
275   Oh endless misery!

(*She places the cloak in her lap.*)

"This keepsake
Is my enemy now;
For without it

(*She lifts the cloak.*)

I might forget."

(*She stares at the cloak.*)

The poem says that   280
And it's true:
My anguish only deepens.

(*She weeps.*)

MATSUKAZE: "Each night before I go to sleep,
I take off the hunting cloak
CHORUS: And hang it up . . ."   285

(*The keepsakes in her hand, she stands and, as in a trance, takes a
few steps toward the gazing-pillar.*)

I hung all my hopes
On living in the same world with him,
But being here makes no sense at all
And these keepsakes are nothing.

(*She starts to drop the cloak, only to cradle it in her arms and press
it to her.*)

I drop it, but I cannot let it lie;   290
So I take it up again
To see his face before me yet once more.

(*She turns to her right and goes toward the naming-place, then stares
down the bridgeway as though something were coming after her.*)

"Awake or asleep,
From my pillow, from the foot of my bed,
Love rushes in upon me."   295
Helplessly I sink down,
Weeping in agony.

(*She sits at the* shite *position, weeping. The stage assistant helps her
take off her outer robe and replace it with the cloak. He also helps tie
on the court hat.*)

MATSUKAZE: The River of Three Fords
Has gloomy shallows
Of never-ending tears;   300
I found, even there,
An abyss of wildest love.

---

240 **Burnt . . .** derived from a poem by Fujiwara Tameuji, No. 361 in the *Shingo-senshū*: "The fishermen of Suma are accustomed to the moon, spending the autumn in clothes wet with waves blown by the salt wind."   258 **Despite prayers . . .** literally, "purification on the day of the serpent." The ceremony was performed on the first day of the serpent in the third month. Genji had the ceremony performed while he was at Suma. The streamers were conventional Shinto offerings

276–279 **"This keepsake . . . forget"** a slightly modified quotation of the anonymous poem, No. 746 in the *Kokinshū*. It is also quoted in *Lady Han*   283–285 **"Each night . . . up"** the first part of a poem by Ki no Tomonori, No. 593 in the *Kokinshū*. The last two lines run: "When I wear it there is no instant when I do not long for him."   293–295 **"Awake . . . me"** the first part of an anonymous poem, No. 1023 in the *Kokinshū*. The last part runs: "Helpless, I stay in the middle of the bed."   298 **River of Three Fords** the river of the afterworld

Oh joy! Look! Over there!
Yukihira has returned!

(*She rises, staring at the pine tree.*)

305   He calls me by my name, Pine Wind!
       I am coming!

(*She goes to the tree.* MURASAME *hurriedly rises and follows. She catches* MATSUKAZE's *sleeve.*)

MURASAME: For shame! For such thoughts as these
       You are lost in the sin of passion.
       All the delusions that held you in life—
310   None forgotten!

(*Both step back from the tree.*)

       That is a pine tree.
       And Yukihira is not here.
MATSUKAZE: You are talking nonsense!

(*She looks at the pine tree.*)

315   This pine is Yukihira!
       "Though we may part for a time,
       If I hear you are pining for me,
       I'll hurry back."
       Have you forgotten those words he wrote?
MURASAME: Yes, I had forgotten!
320   He said, "Though we may part for a time,
       If you pine, I will return to you."
MATSUKAZE: I have not forgotten.
       And I wait for the pine wind
       To whisper word of his coming.
325 MURASAME: If that word should ever come,
       My sleeves for a while
       Would be wet with autumn rain.
MATSUKAZE: So we await him. He will come,
       Constant ever, green as a pine.
330 MURASAME: Yes, we can trust
MATSUKAZE: his poem:
CHORUS: "I have gone away

315–317 **"Though . . . back"** paraphrase of the poem by Yukihira, No. 365 in the *Kokinshū*. Another paraphrase is given in the following speech by Murasame, and the poem is given in its correct form below. In Japanese *matsu* means both "pine tree" and "to wait."

(MURASAME, *weeping, kneels before the flute player.* MATSUKAZE *goes to the first pine on the bridgeway, then returns to the stage and dances.*)

MATSUKAZE: Into the mountains of Inaba,
       Covered with pines,
       But if I hear you pine,   335
       I shall come back at once."
       Those are the mountain pines
       Of distant Inaba,

(*She looks up the bridgeway.*)

       And these are the pines
       On the curving Suma shore.   340
       Here our dear prince once lived.
       If Yukihira comes again,
       I shall go stand under the tree

(*She approaches the tree.*)

       Bent by the sea-wind,
       And, tenderly, tell him   345

(*She stands next to the tree.*)

       I love him still!

(*She steps back a little and weeps. Then she circles the tree, her dancing suggesting madness.*)

CHORUS: Madly the gale howls through the pines,
       And breakers crash in Suma Bay;
       Through the frenzied night
       We have come to you   350
       In a dream of deluded passion.
       Pray for us! Pray for our rest!

(*At stage center,* MATSUKAZE *presses her palms together in supplication.*)

       Now we take our leave. The retreating waves
       Hiss far away, and a wind sweeps down
       From the mountain to Suma Bay.   355
       The cocks are crowing on the barrier road.
       Your dream is over. Day has come.
       Last night you heard the autumn rain;
       This morning all that is left
       Is the wind in the pines,   360
       The wind in the pines.

---

336 **"I . . . once"** the poem by Yukihira mentioned in the previous note

Chūshingura: The Forty-Seven Samurai

In 1701, at the court of the *shogun* in Edo, the *daimyo* of *Akō,* Lord Asano, drew his sword and slightly wounded Lord Kira, one of the *shogun's* officials; as a consequence of drawing his sword at the court—a capital crime—Lord Asano was sentenced to *seppuku,* or ritual suicide. In the following months, Asano's *rōnin,* or retainers, felt themselves to have been dishonored and humiliated by the ruling against their lord, and plotted to take revenge. In January of 1703 they made a bold nighttime raid on Lord Kira's mansion. When they found Kira, they beheaded him, and ceremoniously marched with his head to Lord Asano's tomb. The raid on Lord Kira was, not surprisingly, a major scandal, and posed the shogunate with a difficult legal and political problem: on the one hand, Lord Asano's *rōnin* had acted with superb loyalty, risking their lives to avenge the honor of their feudal lord, upholding the values of the *samurai*; on the other hand, they had formed an illegal secret conspiracy and had carried out murder. Two months after taking revenge on Lord Kira, the *rōnin* were ordered by the *shogun* to commit *seppuku* themselves.

These are the historical events standing behind one of the *jōruri* and Kabuki theaters' most famous and enduring narratives, the tale of *The Forty-Seven Samurai.* Within weeks of the verdict, a host of plays were written and performed, mainly in the *jōruri* theaters; in most cases, however, the Tokagawa edict against staging contemporary events forced playwrights to alter the characters' names, and to set the story in an earlier historical period. In 1710, the great playwright Chikamatsu Monzaemon (1623–1725) wrote a play for the puppet theater entitled *Goban Taiheiki,* which relocated the events of contemporary Edo to the four-

This scene from the University of Hawai'i production of *Chūshingura* emphasizes the formal energy of Kabuki theater.

teenth century. Probably the first professional playwright in Japanese history, Chikamatsu (born Sugimori Nobumori) was the second son of the Sugimori *samurai* family. He moved with his family to Kyoto in his teens, and took the stage name Chikamatsu in his thirties, becoming a celebrated playwright for the *jōruri* theater, and collaborating with the most famous Kabuki actor of his era, Tojuro Sakata (1647–1709). A member of the *rōnin* himself, Chikamatsu was sympathetic with the dishonor done to Asano's retainers, and in his staging of their dramatic revenge established many of the dramatic conventions that would become standard in later versions of the story. In the next thirty years, Chikamatsu's play was one of hundreds of plays on the subject performed before the opening of the classic version of the story—*Kanadehon Chūshingura*—at the Takemoto puppet theater in 1748. Within the year, four Kabuki theaters (three in Edo and one in Kyoto) staged versions of *Chūshingura* which rapidly became part of the standard Kabuki repertory. The story of the forty-seven samurai has been one of the most enduring and popular of all Kabuki plays.

Although the Kabuki versions of *Chūshingura* are based on *jōruri* narratives, the genesis of plays in the Kabuki theater was quite different from that in the puppet theater. While the *jōruri* theaters closely followed the elaborately crafted dramatic text supplied by the playwright, in the Kabuki theater, the performers tended to take existing stories and refashion them in order to showcase their talents. While *Chūshingura* is one of the few plays still occasionally performed in the all-day form of *jōruri*, Kabuki performance tends to concentrate on several scenes from the narrative that have now become standard, which enables the play to be performed within the shorter duration of contemporary Kabuki theater. In this sense, the version of *Chūshingura: The Forty-Seven Samurai* printed here follows traditional Kabuki practice: it is a version of *Kanadehon Chūshingura* prepared by the professional Kabuki actor Nakamura Matagorō II, for a three-hour, English-language production at the University of Hawai'i in 1979. Readers who wish to consult the entire *jōruri* text should consult Donald Keene's *Chūshingura: The Treasury of Loyal Retainers*.

CHŪSHINGURA: THE FORTY-SEVEN SAMURAI

Adaptation by Nakamura Matagorō II and James R. Brandon

TRANSLATED BY JAMES R. BRANDON, JUNKO BERBERICH, AND MICHAEL FELDMAN

CHARACTERS

TADAYOSHI, *younger brother of the shogun*

KŌNO MORONAO, *chief councilor of the shogun and governor of Kamakura*

MOMONOI WAKASANOSUKE, *a young samurai*

ENYA HANGAN, *a young provincial lord*

KAOYO, *wife of Enya Hangan*

KAKOGAWA HONZŌ, *chief retainer of Wakasanosuke*

SAGISAKA BANNAI, *retainer of Moronao*

OKARU, *in love with Kampei, and later his wife*

KAMPEI, *retainer of Enya Hangan*

ISHIDŌ, *the shogun's representative at Hangan's death*

YAKUSHIJI, *envoy from the shogun*

GOEMON, *elderly retainer of Enya Hangan*

RIKIYA, *son of Yuranosuke*

ŌBOSHI YURANOSUKE, *chief retainer of Enya Hangan*

KUDAYŪ, *former retainer of Enya Hangan, now Moronao's spy*

HEIEMON, *older brother of Okaru*

SHIMIZU ICHIGAKU, *Moronao's bodyguard*

TAKEMORI KITAHACHI, *retainer to Enya Hangan*

PROVINCIAL LORDS
FOOTMEN
RETAINERS
LADIES-IN-WAITING
MAIDS
MALE GEISHA
FIGHTING CHORUS
SOLDIERS
STAGE ASSISTANTS
SAMISEN PLAYER
NARRATOR

STAGE MANAGER
SECOND STAGE MANAGER
KIYOMOTO SINGER
JESTER

TIME AND PLACE OF ACTION

Act I   SCENE 1: Hachiman Shrine in Kamakura, 1338.

SCENE 2: Outside the gate of the shogunal mansion in Kamakura, the next evening.

SCENE 3: The Pine Room of the shogunal mansion in Kamakura, a few minutes later.

Act II   SCENE 1: Along the road, near Mt. Fuji, the following morning.

SCENE 2: A reception room in Enya Hangan's mansion, the same day.

SCENE 3: The rear gate of Enya Hangan's mansion, immediately following.

Act III   SCENE 1: The Ichiriki Brothel in Kyoto, eighteen months later.

SCENE 2: The garden of Moronao's mansion in Kamakura, several days later.

ACT ONE

SCENE I

Hachiman Shrine

Two sharp clacks of the hardwood ki signal offstage musicians to begin slow and regular drum and flute music, "Kata Shagiri" ("Half-Shagiri"). The deliberate pace of the music gradually accelerates. The lights in the auditorium dim slightly; the audience watches the kabuki curtain of broad rust, black, and green stripes. Very slowly, the curtain is pushed open by a STAGE ASSISTANT walking from stage right to left. Ki clacks intersperse every eighth, every fourth, then every second drum beat. Drumming and ki intermingle as the tempo rapidly increases during the last few feet of the curtain opening. The scene is a ceremonial audience before Hachiman Shrine in Kamakura. The shogun's brother, TADAYOSHI, is seated on the center of a broad stone platform running across the back of the stage. He wears a subdued Chinese-style court robe with bloused trousers and a gold lacquered hat. On his left sits the highest local official of the government, KŌNO MORONAO. A voluminous black robe with large sleeves and trailing trousers encase his body and a high black hat increases his height. Six PROVINCIAL LORDS kneel behind them on the platform. Kneeling on the ground before them are two samurai officials, MOMONOI WAKASANOSUKE and ENYA HANGAN dressed, respectively, in powder blue and yellow robes of the same exaggerated cut as MORONAO's, and HANGAN's wife, KAOYO. She wears a silk embroidered kimono and outer robe of deep blue. Two FOOTMEN sit on the ground cross-legged to the right. The heads of all the charac-

ters are dropped forward limply on their chests, in imitation of puppets before they have been brought to life. Two ki clacks signal the music to stop and the action of the scene to begin.

STAGE MANAGER: (*Rhythmic, prolonged calls from offstage right.*) Hear ye, hear ye, hear ye, hear ye, hear ye, hear ye . . . hear ye!

(Deep, thick chords of a jōruri, or puppet-style, samisen are heard from the small room above the set stage left. The team of jōruri SAMISEN PLAYER and NARRATOR are not seen, but they can see the action on stage through the thin bamboo blind that hangs in front of them. The NARRATOR constantly shifts his vocal style between a kind of half-spoken chanting and singing. His tones are rich and full and unabashedly project the extremes of human emotion. Each syllable is precisely uttered. Sharp samisen chords punctuate the end of a chanted phrase; they become melodic under sung passages. A syllable can be clipped or staccato, or it can be prolonged into a lengthy obligato, spread over many samisen chords, so that the narrative line compresses or expands in time in order to best project the theatrical needs of the moment.)

NARRATOR: (*Chants.*) "A banquet laid out before your eyes! Without eating of its food, never will you be able to know its taste!" Likewise, a country in peace . . . its able retainers will hide their gallantry and chivalry. (*Sings.*) Take our story as an example . . . witness here and now . . .

SECOND STAGE MANAGER: (*Calling from offstage left.*) Hear ye, hear ye, hear ye, hear ye . . . hear ye!

5

10 STAGE MANAGER: (*Calling from offstage center.*) Hear ye, hear
    ye . . . hear ye!
    NARRATOR: (*Chants.*) Ashikaga government chief Takauji has
    Kyoto as the headquarters of his reign, his power expand-
    ing far. The time is the closing of February, thirteen thirty-
15 eight. The place is Kamakura in the east, at Hachiman
    Shrine, now completed in its awesome grandeur. (*Sings.*)
    Gathered here to celebrate a battle fought and won are
    lords of distinction, in their solemn moments. (*Chants.*)
    Acting as government proxy, Ashikaga Tadayoshi has just
20 arrived from the capital . . . of Kyoto!

    (*At the mention of his name,* TADAYOSHI *raises his head, opens his
    eyes, and elegantly flicks open his sleeves: puppetlike, he has been
    "brought to life."*)

    Here in Kamakura, he is received by the shogun's official,
    Kōno Moronao! The officers of the reception are:
    Momonoi Wakasanosuke Yasuchika, Moronao's target of
    displeasure for his rough manners, and Hakushu's castle
25 lord, Enya Hangan Takasada. (*Sings.*) Among these men, a
    single flower, Lady Kaoyo, wife of Hangan.

    (*Each character, as named, comes to life, showing his or her person-
    ality through the simple actions of lifting the head, opening the eyes,
    and adjusting the trailing kimono sleeves:* MORONAO's *evil
    nature—seven abrupt head jerks ending in a fierce* mie *pose with
    eyes crossed, arms extending aggressively forward as two loud beats
    of the wooden* tsuke *call attention to the pose;* WAKASANOSUKE's
    *impetuosity—five strong movements of the head, sudden opening
    of the eyes, each arm flicked out independently;* HANGAN's
    *composure—three smooth head movements, gentle eye opening, and
    both sleeves elegantly adjusted;* KAOYO's *modesty—no movement at
    all except for the slow raising of the head. Narrative shifts to song.*)

    Moronao casts amorous eyes at this rare beauty. Loyal
    men, bowing low. . .

    (MORONAO *leers openly at* KAOYO. *Then everyone places their
    hands on the floor and they make a ceremonious, deep bow to*
    TADAYOSHI. *Narrative returns to chanting.*)

    As Tadayoshi speaks, all listen in reverence!

    (*All lift their heads and listen respectfully.*)

30 TADAYOSHI: (*Clear, unaffected voice, looking straight ahead.*) At-
    tend, Lady Kaoyo!
    KAOYO: (*Bowing.*) My lord.
    TADAYOSHI: It is the shogun, not I, who has summoned you
    here. You served the emperor Godaigo when he bestowed
35 upon the warrior Yoshisada the imperial battle crown.
    Now, with prayers commemorating our victory in battle,
    my brother the shogun wills that this battle crown be ded-
    icated to the shrine of Hachiman, god of war. If you can,
    confirm that this, and no other, is the one! Come, come!
40 Answer me, answer me!
    KAOYO: (*Bowing.*) My lord.
    NARRATOR: (*Chants.*) Attendants carry forth the precious bat-
    tle crown, bending down to open up the heavy wooden
    chest. Lifting up the battle crown . . . is it the one of fame?
45 (*Sings.*) Though gazing closely at the battle crown held
    high, she will only speak when she is certain . . . and then,
    floating famous fragrance of the crown well known . . .

    (*The two* FOOTMEN *place a large wooden chest center and remove
    its lid. They bring out a samurai helmet. Its golden fittings gleam in
    the light.* KAOYO *moves forward the better to observe it, kneels, and
    noticing its special perfume, nods decisively.*)

    KAOYO: This is the very crown Yoshisada wore in battle, I can
    say with certainty.
    NARRATOR: (*Chants.*) Saying these words, Kaoyo bows deep 50
    in reverence.

    (*She bows. A* FOOTMAN *places the helmet at* TADAYOSHI's *feet.
    With the second* FOOTMAN, *he carries off the chest.*)

    TADAYOSHI: Enya Hangan! Momonoi Wakasanosuke! In con-
    junction with the dedication, all ceremonies are placed in
    your care. Consult Lord Moronao. Kaoyo, you may go!
    KAOYO: (*Bowing.*) My lord.   55
    NARRATOR: (*Chants.*) Kaoyo has now been freed of her de-
    manding task, waiting as his lordship . . . into the palace goes!

    (TADAYOSHI *rises; a* STAGE ASSISTANT *takes off the stool he has
    been sitting on. Without looking to the right or left, he walks with a
    dignified gait down the steps. He stops and poses. Drum and flute
    play stately exit music.* TADAYOSHI *flicks open his sleeves, turns, and
    moves slowly off left.* PROVINCIAL LORDS *rise and follow, their for-
    mal court trousers trailing behind them.* FOOTMEN *bring up the rear.
    They exit. The music continues in the background as* HANGAN,
    WAKASANOSUKE, *and* KAOYO *play out in silence their petitions to*
    MORONAO *for permission to depart. To* HANGAN's *polite bow of re-
    quest* MORONAO *nods condescendingly.* HANGAN *rises, and with
    unruffled composure, goes off left, carrying the helmet with him, to be
    deposited in the shrine.* WAKASANOSUKE *bows brusquely, scarcely
    bothering to conceal his contempt for* MORONAO. *In response,*
    MORONAO *deliberately and disdainfully averts his gaze. Moving to
    where he is in* MORONAO's *line of sight again,* WAKASANOSUKE
    bows a second time, more brusquely still. Again MORONAO *ignores
    him and looks away. Trembling with fury,* WAKASANOSUKE *moves
    directly in front of* MORONAO *and bows a third time.* MORONAO
    looks over his head as if the young samurai were not there.
    WAKASANOSUKE *leaps up in rage, strikes back his sleeve, and rushes
    off left. Music stops.* MORONAO *laughs soundlessly, then looks ex-
    pectantly to* KAOYO, *who bows politely, rises, and starts to move
    away.* MORONAO *rises, a* STAGE ASSISTANT *removing the stool on
    which he has been sitting. He stops* KAOYO *with an unctuous, but
    clearly threatening, command.*)

    MORONAO: One moment, Lady Kaoyo! I wish to have a
    word with you. I believe that you and I share in common
    an unspoken passion, for the art of writing poetry. Will 60
    you accept from me this poem, composed with loving
    care, your reply to which I will not be displeased to re-
    ceive from your own lips, Kaoyo, my lady.
    NARRATOR: (*Chants.*) From his sleeve to her sleeve, a love let-
    ter from Moronao! (*Sings.*) Saying not a single word, she 65
    throws it aside.

    (*Crossing to her,* MORONAO *looks around to see that no one is
    watching. He passes a love letter into* KAOYO's *sleeve. She takes it
    out, and looking at the salutation, knows immediately what it is.
    Coldly she drops it to the ground.* MORONAO *scoops it up and tucks
    it away in the breast of his kimono.*)

MORONAO: (*Insinuatingly.*) Casually you cast my letter to the ground, but you will not cast down my intentions that easily. Until you accept my love, I will track you, chase you, wear you down. In the palace your husband is my puppet, to rise or to fall in his duties, solely on Moronao's will. Kaoyo, my lady . . . well? Do you not agree?

(*He glances about again, then moves behind her and enfolds her in a rough embrace. She discreetly tries to free herself: their bodies sway back and forth.*)

NARRATOR: (*Sings.*) In her heart are angry words but Kaoyo refrains. Dear Lady Kaoyo, tears in her eyes.

(*Without warning* WAKASANOSUKE *strides on. Taking in the situation at a glance, he turns his back.*)

WAKASANOSUKE: Ahem! Ahem! (*Furious,* MORONAO *breaks away.* WAKASANOSUKE *moves beside* KAOYO.) Lady Kaoyo, Lord Tadayoshi dismissed you long ago. If you linger, you are risking his displeasure. Go! Do not stay a moment longer!

KAOYO: Yes, good Lord Wakasanosuke, with your permission, I shall take my leave.

NARRATOR: (*Sings.*) Burdened with care, to her mansion . . . Kaoyo returns.

(KAOYO *bows and moves quickly onto the* hanamichi, *the rampway which extends from the stage, through the audience, to the rear of the auditorium. She stops at the "seven-three" position, that is, the position seven-tenths of the distance from the back of the auditorium and three-tenths from the stage. She poses, puts her hands inside her kimono sleeves, then regally moves down the* hanamichi. *She passes out of sight as the narration ends.*)

MORONAO: (*Snarling.*) No one summoned you! You are insolent, Wakasanosuke! Kaoyo was entreating me, in private audience, to guide Hangan in his palace duties. That is how even the mighty must grovel before the shogun's chief councilor. And who are you? A country rustic, a nobody. So low a single word from Moronao would send you tumbling into the streets to beg for your food! And you call yourself a samurai? A samurai? (MORONAO *strikes* WAKASANOSUKE's *chest with his heavy fan.*) You . . . a sa-mu-rai? (*On the last three syllables,* MORONAO *strikes* WAKASANOSUKE's *chest, sword hilt, and chest again.* WAKASANOSUKE *falls back.*) B–b–blockhead country bumpkin!

NARRATOR: (*Chants.*) You dare to meddle, little man? Moronao's revenge! Bursting in hot anger, Wakasanosuke . . . here in the sacred shrine before his Majesty, a moment of patience is all I need! One more word decides my life, death may be my fate! Wakasanosuke now holds himself in!

(*To the narration:* WAKASANOSUKE *poses with hand on the hilt of his sword; he notices he is in a sacred shrine and falls back; his hand trembles; he nods with determination, throws his fan into the air, and lunges forward as if to draw his sword.* MORONAO *slaps his fan against* WAKASANOSUKE's *sword arm and glares at his young opponent in alarm and rage. At that moment a cry is heard from off-stage announcing the return of* TADAYOSHI.)

VOICES OFF: (*In unison.*) Bow down!
MORONAO: (*Snarling.*) Bow down, I say!

(MORONAO *strikes* WAKASANOSUKE's *sword arm viciously with his closed fan.* WAKASANOSUKE *drops to one knee, glares at* MORONAO, *and poses with his hand on his sword.* MORONAO *rushes up the platform steps, suddenly pivots back to face* WAKASANOSUKE, *flips open his sleeves, and poses in a fierce* mie. MORONAO *crosses his eyes and glares to two loud beats of the* tsuke. WAKASANOSUKE *restrains himself; his chest heaves. The curtain is run closed to accelerating* ki *clacks. A single* ki *clack marks the end of the scene and signals the offstage drum and flute to play "Sagariha" ["Departure"] as the scene is changed.*)

SCENE II
Bribery and Rendezvous

Two ki *clacks: the curtain is run open. Ki clacks accelerate, then fade away. The scene is the rear gate of the shogunal mansion in Kamakura where the state ceremonies are to be held. It is night. Pale blue light floods the stage. One ki clack signals action to begin.*

NARRATOR: (*Chants.*) Chief retainer of Wakasanosuke, (*Sings.*) Kakogawa Honzō comes in with a tray full of gifts, a self-assigned task.

(HONZŌ, *carrying a tray of silks as a bribe for* MORONAO, *comes onto the* hanamichi. *He stops at the seven-three position, looks toward the gate, and poses.*)

HONZŌ: Bannai. Master Bannai.

(BANNAI, *a comic villain, enters from inside the gate.* HONZŌ *moves quickly onto the stage, places the gifts on the ground, and kneels respectfully before* BANNAI.)

BANNAI: (*Officiously.*) Someone calls me. Who is it, who is it? (*Notices* HONZŌ. *Starts.*) State your business, I am a busy man!
HONZŌ: (*Bowing obsequiously.*) I am Kakogawa Honzō, chief retainer of Momonoi Wakasanosuke.
BANNAI: (*Chuckles delightedly.*) The bluebird Wakasanosuke and his friend, the yellow canary Enya Hangan, are country chickens. What a cackling they will make in the palace. Oh, my master, Lord Moronao, will pluck them clean!
HONZŌ: (*Carefully watching* BANNAI's *expression.*) That is the matter on which I have come, good Bannai. My master is young and untutored in the intricacies of palace etiquette. Only with Lord Moronao's generous guidance will he be able to carry out his important duties. Taking this opportunity, I express my gratitude for your master's favor.

(HONZŌ *bows low.* BANNAI *turns front with a self-satisfied smirk on his face.*)

BANNAI: Everyone needs a chief councilor's favors. But your Wakasanosuke was rude to my master. Go back where you came from, go back, go away! (BANNAI *strikes a pose: feet together, head up, right fist extended toward* HONZŌ.)
HONZŌ: What you say is true, still please accept these gifts on behalf of Wakasanosuke and his grateful followers.

(HONZŌ *bows toward the gifts of silk. He looks about, to be sure they are unseen, then takes out a wrapped package of gold coins. Moving forward on his knees to* BANNAI's *side, he drops the package into the open kimono sleeve.*)

Carry my message to Lord Moronao. Do what is necessary, good Bannai. Will you do so, Bannai? Bannai?

(HONZŌ *tugs lightly on* BANNAI'*s sleeve.*)

NARRATOR: (*Chants.*) Wondering, Bannai takes it in his hand!

(BANNAI *flicks* HONZŌ'*s hand away and in doing so strikes the heavy
coins. He clutches his fingers in pain, then wonders what his hand hit.
He sneaks a look at the coins. He reacts with delighted surprise.*)

NARRATOR: (*Sings.*) Money talks words of power!

30 BANNAI: (*Effusive, his attitude completely changed.*) Well, well,
Kakogawa Honzō, how nice of you to come. (*He squats
and bows to* HONZŌ.) You have come at the right moment:
the ceremonial rooms are being prepared. Come, come!

(BANNAI *picks up the tray of gifts, rises, and gestures for* HONZŌ *to
follow him.*)

HONZŌ: (*Bowing carefully.*) I am a person of no importance, I
35   do not dare enter the palace.
BANNAI: (*Proudly.*) If Lord Moronao is with you, who would
dare object? Come, I will show you the rooms.
HONZŌ: I will enter then, most gratefully.
BANNAI: Then come along. Come along!

(BANNAI *poses.* HONZŌ *bows. They cross toward the gate: three
times* BANNAI *turns back, chuckling and bowing, to beckon* HONZŌ
forward. At the gate BANNAI *stops short.*)

40 Master Honzō, the threshold is high.
NARRATOR: (*Sings.*) Moronao is happy. Honzō bought the
life of Wakasanosuke. His scheme now is accomplished.
Together they go.

(BANNAI *steps carefully over the foot-high threshold of the gate and
goes inside, followed by* HONZŌ.)

NARRATOR: (*A nō song, as if part of the entertainment inside the
mansion.*)
        "At the end of the journey we have reached Takasago Bay;
45   At the end of the journey we have reached Takasago Bay."

(OKARU, *a beautiful young girl in her late teens, enters on the
hanamichi. She wears a maiden's trailing kimono with long sleeves,
in a purple arrow pattern. She holds a lacquered letter box in her
right hand. She stops at the seven-three position, looks toward the
gate, and poses.*)

OKARU: My Lady Kaoyo urgently sends this letter to her husband, Lord Enya Hangan. How fortunate that I, her favorite, was allowed to bring it. Dearest Kampei, I cannot
bear to be apart from you a single moment.

(*Offstage musicians play nō-style drum and flute music in the background.* KAMPEI, *a young samurai, enters from the gate followed by
a* RETAINER. *They wear black kimono under stiff vests; their divided
skirts are folded up to their knees, showing that they are on guard
duty.* KAMPEI *is in the service of* HANGAN *and is* OKARU'*s lover.*
OKARU *sees him and runs to meet him.*)

50 KAMPEI: Okaru, is it you?
OKARU: (*Coquettishly.*) Dearest Kampei, I missed you so.

KAMPEI: (*Flustered and worried about meeting her while he is on a
But why are you here at the palace gate, at night, and a
alone?
OKARU: I've come for Lady Kaoyo. "Meet Kampei and tell   55
him he is to ask my husband to deliver this letter to Lord
Moronao"—those were her very words.

(OKARU *passes him the letter box.*)

KAMPEI: (*Unsure.*) I am to deliver this directly to Lord
Hangan?
HOKARU: Yes, dearest Kampei.

(*She smiles invitingly at him.*)

KAMPEI: Wait for me, Okaru.   60

(*He turns to go.*)

OKARU: (*She holds his sleeve.*) Kampei!
KAMPEI: I should take it to our master myself. I should be
with him. It is my duty not to leave his side in the palace.
I . . .

(*He is irresolute. He tries to leave; she tugs gently, persuasively at his
sleeve. He looks into her pleading eyes. He decides. He turns to the
RETAINER.*)

    Take this immediately to Lord Hangan.   65
RETAINER: I will.

(*The* RETAINER *takes the letter box, bows, and crosses into the gate.*)

OKARU: I want to be with you so. Now that we are here,
together . . .
KAMPEI: You are flushed with excitement, Okaru!
OKARU: (*Taking his hand in hers.*) Please come. I don't care!   70
NARRATOR: (*Sings.*) Seizing fast her lover's hand . . . she leads
him away!

(*She presses against him boldly, folding her arm over his. They pose:
a sharp ki clack emphasizes the moment. Offstage drum and samisen
resume in the background. They look excitedly into each other's eyes
and then hurriedly cross into the darkness of the trees beyond the gate.
The curtain is run quickly closed to accelerating ki clacks. Music ends.
Soft, intermittent ki clacks mark time while the scene is changed.*)

SCENE III
Pine Room

*Two ki clacks: the curtain opens. The scene is a large reception room
of the shogunal mansion called the Pine Room because of the designs
painted on the gold sliding doors extending across the full stage. A
single ki clack: action begins.*

NARRATOR: (*Chants.*) Utter indignation, for Moronao is late!
Impatiently waiting in the palace . . . Wakasanosuke!

(WAKASANOSUKE *rushes onto the hanamichi. He drops to one knee
at the seven-three position, resolutely slaps his thigh, and poses, waiting for the arrival of* MORONAO. *A sliding door left opens. Rapid
drum and flute music.* BANNAI *ushers* MORONAO *on stage, bowing
obsequiously. He carries a small paper lantern to light the room. Without a word,* WAKASANOSUKE *leaps to his feet, slips his sword arm*

free of the restricting formal vest, and rushes to attack MORONAO. BANNAI *momentarily is able to block* WAKASANOSUKE's *path, but then is hurled to the floor as* WAKASANOSUKE *pushes past.* MORONAO *falls to his knees. He clasps his hands together pleadingly.* BANNAI *throws his arms around* WAKASANOSUKE's *lower leg, holding him fast. Music stops.*)

MORONAO: There you are, there you are, Lord Wakasanosuke, good Wakasanosuke. Your early arrival makes me ashamed,
5 ashamed, so very ashamed. I was rude to you at Hachiman Shrine. I was. (WAKASANOSUKE *edges forward as if to draw.*) Now, now, now, you have every right to be angry. But have pity on a foolish old samurai. I throw my sword at your feet. I clasp my hands and apologize. Bannai, Bannai,
10 you too, bow, apologize to Lord Wakasanosuke.
NARRATOR: (*Sings.*) Flattering, and what is more, detestable words so sweet. Taken aback completely, Wakasanosuke wonders what has happened. There is nothing he can do . . .

(MORONAO *bows his head low to the floor.* WAKASANOSUKE *cannot believe his eyes, seeing the proud councilor abasing himself. He kicks* BANNAI *away, slips his sword arm inside his vest, and strides past* MORONAO. MORONAO *circles to avoid him, crawling on his hands and knees indecorously.* WAKASANOSUKE *turns back, spitting out his words.*)

WAKASANOSUKE: Contemptible samurai!

(*He strides off stage left.*)

15 MORONAO: I was wrong, I was wrong, I apologize, I apologize, I . . .

(*Eyes fearfully on the ground,* MORONAO *continues.* BANNAI *registers comic shock, seeing his master bowing and speaking to no one. He scurries forward on his hands and knees. He pulls* MORONAO's *sleeve. Music stops. Their eyes meet.* BANNAI *nods in the direction of* WAKASANOSUKE's *exit.* MORONAO *sees that he is alone and sighs with relief. Recovering his dignity, he sits up.*)

MORONAO: Bannai, that stupid young puppy meant, I think, to kill me. "A sword in a fool's hand makes the wise man cautious."
20 BANNAI: (*Bowing.*) Oh yes, my lord, how true.
NARRATOR: (*Chants "Jo no Mai" ["Slow Dance"] drum and flute music.*) Who has planned this mischievous fate? (*Sings.*) Enya Hangan . . . innocent of this all, proceeds to Moronao. (*Chants.*) Moronao . . . seeing his victim!

(*Simultaneously,* BANNAI *arranges his master's sword and the lantern and exits stage left while* HANGAN *appears on the hanamichi, carrying in his left hand the letter box given by* KAMPEI's *retainer. Noh-style "Jo no Mai" drum and flute music continues in the background.*)

MORONAO: (*Ominously.*) Late, late, late! You're late, Hangan!

(HANGAN *bows slightly and hurries on stage. He kneels, bowing again.*)

25 HANGAN: I humbly beg your pardon for being a few moments late. I come ready for your instructions. First, however, I have been asked by my wife to place this letter in your hands.

(*He moves forward on his knees, places the letter box on the floor beside* MORONAO, *moves back, and bows respectfully.*)

MORONAO: (*Feigning ignorance.*) Hmm, hmm. A letter from Lady Kaoyo? To me? (*Opens the box and removes the letter card.*) Ah, I understand. My poetic skill is renowned. No 30 doubt she wishes me to place the touch of my pen upon her heartfelt words, to correct any blemishes. There is time before the ceremonies. Sit and be at ease. (*He reads.*) "A woman's love does, not lie in the hopeful eye, of her beholder; not beholden to lie I, aver never to lie with you." 35 (*Music stops.* MORONAO *again.*) "Not beholden to lie I, aver never to lie . . . with you."
NARRATOR: (*Chanting rapidly.*) After weighing the words . . . Kaoyo has rejected my love and this is the proof! This must mean that Hangan has found out my intention! (*Sings.*) 40 Anger and humiliation . . . but pretending ignorance.

(MORONAO *looks straight forward, his face frozen in humiliated rage, his right hand slowly closing into a rigid fist that crushes his brocade silk robe. Masking his emotions he turns toward* HANGAN. *Drum and flute music resume.*)

MORONAO: Hangan, was this poem shown to you?
HANGAN: (*Bows politely.*) I have not seen it until this moment, your Excellency.

(*Reassured that* HANGAN *is not party to* KAOYO's *insult,* MORONAO *proceeds to deliberately humiliate him.*)

MORONAO: Is that so? Well, the lord of little Hakushu castle 45 has a clever wife. She can dash off a subtle poem like this. A woman so talented and famous for her beauty must be a source of great husbandly pride. Such a superlative creature in fact, that her infatuated husband, not bearing to be separated from her, finds his sacred duties at the palace . . . 50 wearisome!

(MORONAO *casually turns his back to* HANGAN, *idly playing with his fan.*)

NARRATOR: (*Chants.*) Moronao is filled with spiteful words of insinuation. Riding on his frustration . . . any may be his prey. Hangan is perplexed at the burst of displeasure. (*Sings.*) Gushing anger, he holds it down, holds it in! 55

(HANGAN *starts. He almost turns to confront* MORONAO, *but then suppresses his anger. He pretends to smile, as if sharing* MORONAO's *joke. Ominous drum beats continue in the background.*)

HANGAN: Ha, ha, ha, ha. I see my lordship is in a playful mood. He has, perhaps, been drinking and is feeling in good humor. Yes, surely my lord has been drinking. Ha, ha, ha, ha.
MORONAO: (*Dangerously, facing* HANGAN.) What is that? When 60 have you seen me drinking? You, who have never offered me as much as a cup of wine? Whether I, Moronao, choose to drink or not, nothing keeps me from *my* duty! The one who's been drinking is you, Hangan. You've come from a drinking party with your charming wife, she 65 pouring for you, and you pouring for her! Isn't that why you come to the palace late?

(HANGAN's *face tightens.* MORONAO *notices and turns away with a malicious look in his eye.*)

70 Isn't there a story about a stay-at-home like you, helpless beyond his front door? I seem to recall . . . ah, yes, the "Tadpole in the Puddle." There once was a young tadpole that lived in a tiny puddle. He knew no other place between heaven and earth, and so he thought his puddle the most wonderful home in the world. One day a compassionate person passed by, just like Moronao, who, taking 75 pity, lifted him from his stagnant pool and released him in the waters of a broad river. (*Arms out,* MORONAO *deliberately strikes* HANGAN's *chest with his heavy fan.*) Well, the tadpole was out of his depth, dropped suddenly into the great world from his shallow one. Completely at a loss, willy-80 nilly he went this way, and willy-nilly he went that way. (*Pointing with fan.*) And in the end he ran headfirst smack into a bridgepost. (*Strikes* HANGAN *full in the chest with his fan.*) And shivering and quivering, and shivering and quivering, the little tadpole expired. (*Twirling his fan in limp fin-*85 *gers.*) The tadpole is . . . you! (*Looks full into* HANGAN's *straining face.*) Oh? I do believe the young tadpole has lost his tail and is turning into a toad. (HANGAN *turns and glares furiously at* MORONAO.) Yes, with your eyes bulging out, Hangan, you look exactly like a toad. Ha, ha, ha, ha! This 90 Moronao has lived many years, but this is the first time I've seen in the palace a toad wearing clothes. Oh, come here, come here, Bannai, Hangan's turning into a toad. Hangan *is* a toad, a sa-mu-rai toad! (*Drum beats stop. Silence.* MORONAO *deliberately strikes* HANGAN's *chest, sword* 95 *hilt, and chest with his fan.*) Ha, ha, ha, ha, ha!

NARRATOR: (*Chants.*) Toad! Devil talk! Demon words!

(MORONAO *rears back, points contemptuously at* HANGAN *with his fan, rotates his head, and poses in a* mie *to two loud* tsuke *beats. Music stops.*)

Hangan can no more take the vile old man!

HANGAN: (*Slowly, with dangerous, suppressed fury.*) Do you dare compare Enya Hangan Takasada, castle lord of Hakushu . . . 100 to a toad? You cannot possibly mean the words you have said! Have you gone out of your mind . . . Councilor Moronao!

(HANGAN *pivots to face* MORONAO, *slapping his thigh for emphasis.*)

MORONAO: (*Darkly.*) Watch yourself, Hangan! Remember I am councilor of the shogun. No one calls me insane. You 105 are ludicrous!

HANGAN: You have been deliberately insulting me? Do you dare tell me that!

MORONAO: (*Insinuating.*) Indeed, I dare. And if I dare, who are you to complain?

110 HANGAN: (*Drawn out.*) If you dare . . .

MORONAO: (*Leaning in insolently.*) If I dare . . . ?

HANGAN: Hmm!

(HANGAN's *patience snaps. He rises on one knee, his hand on his sword.* MORONAO *instantly parries* HANGAN's *sword arm with his closed fan.*)

MORONAO: (*Commandingly.*) The palace! (MORONAO *slaps* HANGAN's *sword arm away and the two men pull back:* MORONAO *fearfully,* HANGAN *furious.*) The palace! The 115 palace! It is the palace! Don't you know the law? Draw your sword in the palace and your house will be destroyed! Don't you know that! (*Drum beats resume.* MORONAO *slaps his fan commandingly on the floor.* HANGAN, *anguished that he must restrain his rage, folds his arms tightly over the hilts of his* 120 *swords and slowly sinks back onto his haunches.* MORONAO *notes this and is emboldened to continue his provocation.*) Hm, since you know . . . then go ahead, kill me. Well . . . draw . . . draw . . . draw your sword. Come, kill me! Kill me . . . Hangan!

(MORONAO *forces himself bodily against* HANGAN *and leans against* HANGAN's *swords. They pose. Burning with humiliation,* HANGAN *abases himself in order to fulfill his ceremonial duties. He backs away and bows low.*)

HANGAN: A moment, a moment, Lord Moronao, I beg your 125 indulgence. Without thinking I spoke out of turn. I implore you, instruct me in my duties for the ceremony. I will do as you say. Humbly, I beseech you, your Excellency.

(*Music stops.* HANGAN *looks up from his bow.* MORONAO *smugly turns away, avoiding his gaze.* HANGAN's *patience snaps a second time: his hand leaps for his sword. Instantly* MORONAO *reacts.*)

MORONAO: Your hand!
HANGAN: My hand?   130
MORONAO: (*With all his authority.*) Yes, your hand!
HANGAN: This hand . . .

(*He hesitates, looks at his trembling hand, then drops his hands to the floor and bows in defeat.*)

. . . humbly begs your forgiveness.

MORONAO: (*Savoring his victory.*) So, you apologize, do you? Very well, very well. Soon instructions in great detail for 135 today's ceremony.

HANGAN: (*Looks up hopefully.*) . . . will be given to me?

MORONAO: (*Viciously.*) No, not to you! To Wakasanosuke! (HANGAN *is stunned, motionless. In silence* MORONAO *casually rises, tears* KAOYO's *letter card in two, and throws the pieces in* 140 HANGAN's *face.*) There is no educating a provincial barbarian.

(MORONAO *deliberately turns his back and kicks his left and right trailing trouser legs in* HANGAN's *face.* HANGAN *rears back. Chuckling,* MORONAO *starts to leave.*)

HANGAN: Moronao! Wait!

(HANGAN *steps on* MORONAO's *trailing trouser leg.* MORONAO *is brought up short. He tugs at the trouser; it is held fast.*)

MORONAO: (*Deadly calm.*) Be careful. You'll soil my trousers. Hop. Hop, hop, hop. (MORONAO *turns to leave, but cannot* 145 *move.*) So, you won't hop away, little toad? Can there be something else you want?

HANGAN: What I want is . . .

MORONAO: What you want is . . . ?

(HANGAN *quietly slips his sword arm free of the stiff vest.* MO-RONAO *turns and thrusts his sneering face toward* HANGAN.)

150 HANGAN: (*A scream.*) You!

(HANGAN's *short sword flashes out of its sheath and gashes* MORONAO's *forehead. Drum and flute play furious "Haya Mai" ("Fast Dance").* MORONAO *staggers and falls.* BANNAI *rushes on to help his master flee.* HANGAN *leaps to his feet and is about to finish* MORONAO *with a second blow when* HONZŌ, *who has been hiding behind a decorative screen stage right, rushes out and seizes* HANGAN *from behind.*)

NARRATOR: "Hold me not! My foe is there!"

(*Six* PROVINCIAL LORDS *run on from right.* HANGAN *struggles to get free, but he is encircled and held fast. In desperation he hurls his sword after the disappearing enemy. A single sharp clack of the* ki. *The sword falls short. He reaches out with both hands after* MORONAO *and poses: his fingers curl into fists and his chest heaves with sobs of mortification. But* HONZŌ *and the* PROVINCIAL LORDS *hold him fast. To gradually accelerating* ki *clacks the curtain is run closed. Offstage musicians play "Shagiri." A single* ki *clack concludes the act.*)

ACT TWO

SCENE I
Fugitive Travel

The large drum beats melancholy "Yama Oto" ("Mountain Pattern"). To accelerating ki *clacks the curtain is slowly pushed open. A sky-blue curtain fills the stage. A single* ki *clack: the blue curtain drops and is whisked away by black-robed* STAGE ASSISTANTS *to reveal a colorful springtime scene in the country. Snow-covered Mt. Fuji is seen in the background, pink cherry blossoms bloom everywhere.* OKARU *and* KAMPEI *stand center, their faces hidden behind a straw hat. A temple bell tolls in the distance. Kiyomoto music begins from offstage.* KAMPEI *lowers the hat and we see the lovers dressed for traveling: kimono skirts raised and a bundle over* KAMPEI's *shoulder. They mime in slow dance movements to the kiyomoto lyrics the story of their disgrace and flight.*

KIYOMOTO SINGER: Oh, you who flee, do you not see yon green field, a veil of new green?

(*They look at the flowers at their feet, to the left and the right. They look into each other's eyes, then pose gazing into the distance. Singing ends;* samisen *continues in the background. Facing upstage, they pass their sandals and* KAMPEI's *hat and bundle to two* STAGE ASSISTANTS. *They turn front and kneel center stage.* KAMPEI *places his long sword on the ground beside him.*)

KAMPEI: (*Melancholy.*) Giving myself over in love to you, I failed
5 our master when he needed me, and now we are fugitives fleeing in the dead of night I know not where. When I think of it, I no longer have the heart to live. Say prayers over the grave of this dishonored samurai. Okaru . . . farewell.

(KAMPEI *takes his short sword from his sash and is about to draw the blade. Gently she seizes it and prevents him.*)

OKARU: No, I won't have you saying that again. I am to blame
10 that you were not beside Lord Hangan. I cannot live with-

out you. If you die then so must I. But rather than praising your spirit, people will say we died as lovers frequently do. Please, live, dearest Kampei. Live . . . in love . . . for me.

(KAMPEI *tries to draw the sword again. She pulls one way, he the other.* KAMPEI, *irresolute, allows her to take the short sword. She places it beside her, away from his reach.*)

KIYOMOTO SINGER: " 'Twas then my heart went astray. It was when you, yes, you made me love, oh, so imprudently. 15 Blame my imprudent heart that spoke to me thus: 'So easy it is to die, but you must live, live on.' "

(KAMPEI *takes up the long sword to kill himself. Again, she gently holds the scabbard so that he cannot draw. They rise and move left, then right, in a delicate struggle for the sword. Allowing himself to be persuaded, they pose with the sword held firmly in her hands. He looks away, wiping his falling tears. She takes the sword and places it out of his reach. They kneel side-by-side.*)

KAMPEI: Your tenderness overwhelms me. (*Nods with resolution.*) We will flee across the mountains to your father's home.
OKARU: (*Smiling, relieved.*) You make me so happy. 20
KAMPEI: In time I know I can find a way to atone for deserting my master. Come, let us go.
OKARU: (*Meekly.*) Yes, Kampei.
KIYOMOTO SINGER: Now for travel they prepare, but who should confront them! 25

(KAMPEI *rises and poses facing front.*)

BANNAI: (*Off, at the rear of the* hanamichi.) Hey, hey! Here we go!
FIGHTING CHORUS: (*Also off.*) Haaa!

(*Loud beats of the big drum. Strong accelerating* tsuke *pattern as* BANNAI *runs onto the* hanamichi *followed by eight of his men, the* FIGHTING CHORUS. BANNAI *has his kimono tucked up to his knees, and a cord holds back his sleeves. His makeup has become ludicrous: bat-shaped eyebrows, drooping eyes, and a tiny blue-gray mustache. The* FIGHTING CHORUS *is dressed identically in red leggings and arm coverings and red and white patterned kimono that stop at their knees. Each carries a branch of cherry blossoms as a weapon.* BANNAI *stops at the seven-three position.* KAMPEI *escorts* OKARU *to the left, out of harm's way, and stands calmly.*)

BANNAI: (*A comic challenge.*) Hey, hey! Kampei!

(*He stamps forward with two steps, each accented by two* tsuke *beats. He and his men march on stage. The men, alert for their master's call, kneel upstage in two rows.* BANNAI *faces front, with a supercilious look. He speaks in a special rhythmical pattern,* nori, *in which each dialogue phrase fits into an eight-beat* samisen *musical phrase. He accompanies the tale with comic gestures.*)

Your stupid master, Enya Hangan, Takasada and my honored master, Councilor Moronao, met in the palace while, 30 chittering chattering, chittering chattering, your master Hangan, flew into a snit. Taking a teensy sword, he whipped it out, he made a slash. He is a traitor, locked up in his residence, boxed up like a criminal. Ha ha ha . . . ha ha ha . . . haha haha hahaha! Hangan has been hauled 35 away! I'll catch you like a chick! I'll pluck you like a duck! I am claiming Okaru! Well? Well? Well, well? (*Accelerating.*)

Well, well, well, well, well! Kampei! Your goose is cooked! Give her . . . to me!

(BANNAI *stands on tiptoe, holds his sword hilts threateningly, and cocks his head in comic* mie *to two beats of the* tsuke.)

40   KIYOMOTO SINGER: "Give her to me," yells Sagisaka Bannai. Kampei bursts out with mocking laughter.
KAMPEI: (*Laughs, then speaks in rhythmic* nori *phrases.*) You are a funny bird, Sagisaka Bannai, a little chirping sparrow, I could swallow in a bite. (*Rapidly.*) Kampei's fiery gaze
45   could fry you to a crisp! But instead of eating you, I will make you eat crow!

(KAMPEI *slips his fists out of the breast of his kimono, allowing the black outer kimono to drop. An inner kimono of brilliant crimson color is revealed. He stamps aggressively forward, then poses with arms outstretched, head cocked in a* mie *to two* tsuke *beats.* BANNAI *tumbles to the ground terrified.*)

KIYOMOTO SINGER: Glaring and with arms outstretched, Kampei stands before him!
BANNAI: (*Weakly.*) Help!

(KIYOMOTO *samisen and drums play instrumental music as the eight members of the* FIGHTING CHORUS *attack* KAMPEI. KAMPEI *waves half of them past him until he stands center in a* mie *position. Four men face him from either side, holding their cherry branches as if they were swords. They strike at him right, left, right. He forces them back. They fall away. They pose in a* mie *to two* tsuke *beats.* KAMPEI *now fights his opponents in a series of group combats that are executed in delicate, controlled dance patterns. Rhythmic drums and* samisen *support the action.*)

50   KIYOMOTO SINGER: Cherry, cherry blossoms! A name, oh, so beloved.

(*One man on each side strikes at* KAMPEI *with the cherry branch. Three times* KAMPEI *avoids, then seizing the tips of the branches, he whirls them in a circle and presses them to their knees. He poses in a* mie. *Flicking the branches away, the men are hit on the forehead; they retreat.* KAMPEI *nonchalantly dusts off his hands.*)

"No, no, you can't have her," and why should that be?

(*One man on each side seizes* KAMPEI's *arms. They struggle right, left, right.* KAMPEI *flicks them forward onto their knees. They try to seize his feet, he backs up. They rush in to encircle him. He avoids, then casually taps them on the back. They do a cartwheel and fall prostrate on the ground.* KAMPEI *poses in a* mie.)

So tender, so fine, so frail, never to be won by you!

(*Four men form a square around* KAMPEI. *Two-by-two they attack, but he pivots to avoid them. Six men strike with their cherry branches.* KAMPEI *drops to his knees, deftly knocks the wind out of them with an open-hand blow, and, with a sweeping gesture, knocks them off their feet. They fall on their bottoms in unison.*)

Delightful, though she's only to be seen. How can you
55   ever feel true love, if she won't play with you!

(*The* FIGHTING CHORUS *retires upstage.* BANNAI *pulls* OKARU *by the sleeve. Foolishly flirting, he touches his cheek to her hand.* KAMPEI

pushes him away, and when BANNAI *tries to get past to* OKARU, *blocks his way.* BANNAI *slips under* KAMPEI's *sleeve, but is caught and held by the nape of the neck.* BANNAI *struggles free, strikes at* KAMPEI, *is kicked to his knees, and finally is grasped by the ear, lifted, and spun around.* BANNAI *is near tears in frustration and humiliation. Trying once again, he raises his fist, but* KAMPEI *turns and casually pushes* BANNAI *to the ground.* KAMPEI *stamps forward and poses in a strong* mie *to two* tsuke *beats.*)

BANNAI: (*Plaintively.*) Take him!

(*Large drum and* tsuke *beats. The* FIGHTING CHORUS *attacks in unison:* KAMPEI *passes them off right and left as he strides from stage left to right; he turns and passes unharmed between them as they strike at him with their cherry branches. One man, coming from hiding, strikes at* KAMPEI *from behind.* KAMPEI *kicks him to the ground, places his foot on his back, and poses in a strong* mie *to two beats of the* tsuke. KAMPEI *kicks the man away and attacks. Booming drum accelerates. The* FIGHTING CHORUS *retreats. They run pell-mell down the* hanamichi *and out of sight.* KAMPEI *poses in a powerful "stone-throwing"* mie *to two beats of the* tsuke. BANNAI *sneaks up.*)

BANNAI: Kampei, here I come!

(BANNAI *raises his sword to strike.* KAMPEI *catches his wrist, spins him around, forces him to his knees, and raises the sword.*)

KAMPEI: (*Bantering.*) Shall I cut your ears off? (*Terrified,* BANNAI *covers his ears with wildly trembling hands.*) Shall I cut off your nose? (BANNAI *covers his nose.*) Or shall I simply kill you?   60
OKARU: Killing him would bring more trouble. So, please, just let him go.
BANNAI: (*Foolishly, imitating* OKARU's *inflections.*) So, please, just let him go!

(BANNAI *clasps his trembling hands together in prayer.*)

KIYOMOTO SINGER: Oh, how he prattles on, that bird, Sag-   65
isaka! Smoothing his ruffled feathers, slowly, then faster, flirts with death, and yet to live, away he flies!

(KAMPEI *nods agreement. He casually rolls* BANNAI *across the stage away from* OKARU. *He poses facing front.* BANNAI *rubs his throat, then noticing* KAMPEI *is holding his sword, meekly gestures a request that it be returned. Contemptuously,* KAMPEI *tosses the sword on the ground.* BANNAI *leaps back in terror. Gathering his courage, he snares the sword with his foot, then suddenly turns and raises the sword as if to strike. A fierce glance from* KAMPEI *deflates him completely. He turns and escapes off right, lifting his legs high in the air in a "stork walk."*)

KAMPEI: He deserved to die. But his death would be a crime to add to my disloyalty.

(*A cock crows in the distance. They both look up into the sky. They speak in melancholy, poetic tones.*)

Already it is dawning . . .   70
OKARU: . . . on the peaks of the mountains . . .
KAMPEI: . . . the eastern light glows . . .
OKARU and KAMPEI: (*In unison.*) . . . lighting trailing clouds.

(*They pose together center stage, absorbed in their own melancholy.*)

KIYOMOTO SINGER: They fly away at daybreak, like the crows
75　　that cry, "caw, caw." So dear to each other, in love, in love.

(*A* STAGE ASSISTANT *passes to* OKARU *the hat, bundle, and swords.
Dutifully,* OKARU *helps* KAMPEI *adjust the bundle and slide the
swords into his sash. They put on their sandals. A temple bell tolls.
They move apart, pose, then move back-to-back.*)

　　Though they must hasten to depart, their minds are filled
　　with woe. Who would doubt their loyalty if they proved
　　the guilt they feel? Away they go.

(*They look into each other's eyes. Restraining tears,* KAMPEI *puts on
a manly bearing, takes* OKARU *by the hand, and turns to begin their
long journey.* BANNAI *sneaks up behind them. He holds* OKARU *by
the waist.*)

BANNAI: Okaru is mine, all mine!

(KAMPEI *moves to block* BANNAI, *passing* OKARU *to safety on the
hanamichi. He pushes* BANNAI *away and turns to join* OKARU.)

80　BANNAI: Kampei, wait!
　　KAMPEI: (*Turning back at the seven-three position.*) Bannai, you
　　　　want. . . . ?
　　BANNAI: (*Posing.*) Kampei, I want . . .
　　KAMPEI: Hmm?
85　BANNAI: (*Deflated.*) Nothing.
　　KAMPEI: Simpleton!

(*A loud ki clack:* BANNAI *collapses to the ground. Drum booms
loudly.* KAMPEI *takes* OKARU's *hand and slowly they exit down the
hanamichi. Kiyomoto samisen plays plaintive chords and ki clacks
accelerate as the curtain begins to close.* BANNAI *is in the path of
the curtain. He retreats before it, then, realizing it is hopeless, seizes
the curtain with both hands and, grinning happily, prances across the
stage, closing the curtain and disappearing from sight. A single ki
clack: drum and flute play lively "Shagiri" to close the scene.*)

SCENE II

Hangan's Suicide

*Two ki clacks: the curtain is slowly opened to the rachetlike sound of
an old-fashioned clock. The scene is a large, formal room in* HANGAN's
*mansion. Sliding doors that make up the rear wall are painted powder
blue and covered with silver crests of* HANGAN's *clan. Tatami matting
covers the floor.* HANGAN, *dressed in a simple kimono and vest so pale
a blue-gray that it verges on white, kneels center. He faces two envoys
from the shogun,* ISHIDŌ *and* YAKUSHIJI, *who are sitting stage left on
high stools. They wear dark kimono, vests, and trousers.* ISHIDŌ's *sympathetic manner contrasts sharply with* YAKUSHIJI's *derisive attitude.*
GOEMON, *a senior retainer of* HANGAN, *kneels upstage. Silence.*
ISHIDŌ *rises and faces* HANGAN. *He takes from the breast of his kimono a large folded letter. He holds it reverently to his forehead.*

ISHIDŌ: Hear the shogun's command. (*Removing the letter from
　　its envelope, he reads.*) "Whereas, Enya Hangan Takasada,
　　you have willfully committed an act of bloodshed against
　　our chief councilor, Moronao, and thereby have defiled
5　　the palace, know that your estates, large and small, are
　　hereby confiscated and you are ordered to end your life by
　　seppuku."

(ISHIDŌ *gravely holds the open letter in front of him, so* HANGAN
can read the order with his own eyes. After glancing at it, HANGAN
bows respectfully.)

HANGAN: (*With perfect control.*) In all respects I accept the
　　shogun's command.
NARRATOR: (*Chants.*) From the adjoining room, knocking　10
　　on the door . . .

(*A* RETAINER *knocks on the sliding door. He speaks in a faint, muffled voice, suggesting tears.*)

RETAINER: (*Off.*) Goemon, Goemon. We, Lord Hangan's re-
　　tainers, beg permission to see our master . . .
RETAINERS: (*Off, quietly in unison.*) . . . one last time.
GOEMON: (*Bowing to* HANGAN.) My lord, your retainers wish　15
　　to see you.
HANGAN: Tell them not until Chief Retainer Yuranosuke has
　　arrived from our province.
GOEMON: (*Facing the door.*) You heard our lord. You may enter
　　when Yuranosuke arrives, not before.　　　　　　　　　　20
RETAINERS: (*Scarcely audible.*) Ahhh.
NARRATOR: (*Sings.*) Their plea, not granted . . . no one dares
　　utter a single word. In the room, silence prevails.

(HANGAN *rises and retires upstage, where he kneels with his back to
the audience.*)

GOEMON: (*Quietly, facing offstage right.*) Proceed.
RETAINER: (*Faintly, off.*) Yes.　　　　　　　　　　　　　　25

(*In complete silence arrangements are made for* HANGAN's *death by
ritual disembowelment.* RETAINERS, *dressed in somber blue and gray
kimono, vests, and split trousers, swiftly and unobtrusively enter. They
place two tatami mats center to make a six-foot square platform. They
cover it with a pure white cloth. Sprigs of green, in small bamboo hold-
ers, are placed at the four corners. With downcast eyes, the* RETAINERS
slip quietly away. GOEMON *bows to* HANGAN *indicating that the place
of suicide is ready.* HANGAN *rises, slowly pivots front, and crosses down
to the cloth seat. Unconsciously his gaze drifts to the* hanamichi: *he
is waiting for the arrival of his chief retainer,* YURANOSUKE, *and does
not want to die before passing to him his last instructions. His right foot
touches the cloth. He remembers it is obligatory to step into the place
of suicide with the left foot. He glances at the envoys to see if they have
noticed: they are gazing straight ahead. He deliberately steps onto the
cloth and slowly kneels.*)

NARRATOR: (*Chants.*) Rikiya proceeds with the saddest or-
　　der. (*Sings.*) The master's suicide blade weighing heavy on
　　his heart . . .

(YURANOSUKE's *son,* RIKIYA, *enters from up left. He carries a plain
wooden tray bearing the short dagger with which* HANGAN *will kill
himself. The long sleeves of his black kimono and a delicate forelock
of hair indicate he is a youth, not yet grown to manhood. He places
the tray on the floor before the envoys for their verification. He bows.*
ISHIDŌ *and* YAKUSHIJI *look at the blade, then nod to each other that
it is satisfactory.* ISHIDŌ *nods gravely to* RIKIYA.)

NARRATOR: Before Lord Hangan he lays the blade.

(RIKIYA *places the tray on the cloth before* HANGAN, *bows low, and
then looks up for instructions.* HANGAN *looks gently into* RIKIYA's

eyes and with a single head movement indicates that RIKIYA *is to leave: a boy so young should not have to witness* seppuku. RIKIYA *politely shakes his head: until his father arrives, he must fulfill his father's duties.* HANGAN *repeats the order to leave; again* RIKIYA *shakes his head. Impressed by the boy's loyalty,* HANGAN *nods that he may stay.* RIKIYA *bows gratefully, rises, backs away, and takes a place beside* GOEMON.)

30 NARRATOR: (*Sings.*) Taking off, in hushed silence, his outer clothes to expose his death robe . . . securing the seat of death.

(HANGAN *prepares himself for death with calm deliberation. He slips off the vest, letting it drop to his waist. He tucks the ends under his legs so as to hold his body in place after he has died. He drops the outer kimono to his waist and tucks it in as well. Beneath he is wearing a pure white kimono appropriate for death, an indication to the envoys that he was prepared to die even before they brought the shogun's command. He places his hands firmly on his thighs and looks intently down the* hanamichi.)

HANGAN: (*Softly but urgently.*) Rikiya.
RIKIYA: (*Bowing.*) Yes.
35 HANGAN: Yuranosuke . . . ?
RIKIYA: Yuranosuke . . . (*He looks down the* hanamichi *for a sign that his father has arrived.*) . . . has not as yet arrived.
NARRATOR: (*Sings.*) Proper steps for suicide, he lifts the tray and bows. (*Chants.*) Waiting no longer, the blade in his
40 hand.

(HANGAN *prepares the dagger. He lifts the tray to his forehead respectfully. He ceremoniously takes the dagger in his right hand and a sheet of white paper in his left. He wraps the paper around the blade until only its tip is bare. He is now able to grasp the blade low for extra leverage. He holds the blade at ready on his thigh. The tip points to his stomach. Outwardly calm, his voice betrays his anxiety.*)

HANGAN: Rikiya, Rikiya!
RIKIYA: (*Bowing.*) Yes.
HANGAN: Yuranosuke . . . ?
RIKIYA: Yes! (RIKIYA *bows and rushes to the end of the* hanamichi.
45   *He falls to his knees, looks to the right, the left, then straight ahead, searching for sight of his father. His lip trembles, he is close to tears.*) Yuranosuke . . . (*He rushes back and throws himself on the floor before* HANGAN.) . . . has not as yet arrived!
HANGAN: (*Calmly.*) Tell him that I regret . . . not seeing him
50   one last time. (HANGAN *nods that* RIKIYA *may retire and pivots slightly toward* ISHIDŌ.) Lord Ishidō, I ask that you witness and report my death.
NARRATOR: (*Sings.*) Here at last the time has come, the blade is aimed. Hangan . . . thrusts it in . . . thrusts it deep!

(HANGAN *places the tray behind him. He rises slightly on his knees, looking one last time down the* hanamichi *for* YURANOSUKE. *He holds the dagger under the ribs on his left side. With a sudden jerk he thrusts the blade into his stomach. Involuntarily his body drops forward and his head falls. Rapid narrative shifts to chanting.*)

55   Running at a desperate speed, the awaited person comes! Here at last is Ōboshi Yuranosuke! A frantic gaze at his master: "Is he still alive?" Overcome by the sight, he falls on his knees!

(YURANOSUKE *bursts onto the* hanamichi, *running frantically, all decorum cast aside. He wears a formal gray kimono, vest, and trousers pulled up for travel. Reaching the seven-three position, he sees his master in the midst of suicide. He reels, falls back, then slowly sinks to his knees.*)

ISHIDŌ: (*Rising.*) Is it Ōboshi Yuranosuke?   60
YURANOSUKE: It is.
ISHIDŌ: (*Urgently.*) Approach, approach quickly!

(YURANOSUKE *attempts to rise, but his legs will not function. He weeps unashamedly. To gain control of himself, he reaches inside the breast of his kimono to pull tight the inner cloth binding his waist. With great effort he pushes himself up from the floor and moves unsteadily to* HANGAN's *side. He falls to his knees and bows deeply.*)

NARRATOR: (*Chants.*) The men of Hangan, all, till now forbidden . . . but no longer! They come rushing in!

(*Ten* RETAINERS *enter swiftly from up right. They are barefooted and carry no swords. They fall to their knees in a row upstage and, following* YURANOSUKE's *lead, bow deeply to their master* HANGAN. YURANOSUKE's *eyes remain downcast and* HANGAN, *in pain, does not yet look up.*)

YURANOSUKE: Ōboshi Yuranosuke kneels before my lord.
HANGAN: (*Weakly.*) Yuranosuke?   65
YURANOSUKE: I am here.
HANGAN: At last you've come.
YURANOSUKE: All that I could ever ask is to be at your side in these last moments . . .
HANGAN: Ah, it makes me content as well. (*Slowly their gazes* 70
    meet.) You have heard, have you not . . . everything . . . everything . . . ?

(*His voice trails off in pain.* YURANOSUKE *edges closer, looking meaningfully at* HANGAN.)

YURANOSUKE: Yes!
HANGAN: (*Rousing himself.*) I am humiliated . . . !
YURANOSUKE: (*Interrupting.*) No words can express such feel- 75
    ings as I hold. Nothing remains now but for me to assure you a just end.
HANGAN: (*Meaningfully.*) One thing remains.
NARRATOR: (*Chants.*) Gripping tight the blade, cutting straight across in disembowelment. (*Sings.*) Such moments 80
    of agony . . . exhaling his breath . . .

(HANGAN *cuts his stomach across from left to right. Although the pain is excruciating and his lips tremble and his breathing grows labored,* HANGAN *maintains the stoic decorum expected of a samurai until the blade reaches its final point just under the right ribs. Then breath seems to leave him. His body sags. He braces his left hand on his thigh.*)

HANGAN: (*Faintly.*) Yuranosuke . . . Yuranosuke . . . come close . . .
YURANOSUKE: Yes.

(HANGAN *is near death.* YURANOSUKE *slides forward urgently. Knowing* HANGAN *cannot speak openly because the shogun's envoys are present, he searches his master's face for some command.*)

85 HANGAN: Take this blade . . . to remind you . . . do not forget. Re-ve-n . . . (YURANOSUKE *starts.* HANGAN *must not say "revenge" out loud.* HANGAN *catches himself.*) . . . remember me.

(*Weakly* HANGAN *looks into* YURANOSUKE'S *face, then down the* hanamichi. YURANOSUKE *follows* HANGAN'S *gaze. Master and retainer look deeply into each other's eyes.* YURANOSUKE *understands that in spite of his master's seeming calm acceptance of the death sentence,* HANGAN *passionately desires vengeance against the enemy outside the mansion, that is,* MORONAO.)

YURANOSUKE: (*Passionately.*) I swear!

(YURANOSUKE *slaps his chest for emphasis and bows deeply.* HANGAN *knows that* YURANOSUKE *understands. He is now free to die. He smiles.*)

HANGAN: Ha ha. Ha ha. Ha, ha, ha, ha . . .

(*The laugh fades. With ebbing strength,* HANGAN *pulls the blade from his stomach. He gasps.*)

90 NARRATOR: (*Chants.*) Aiming the blade at his throat . . . one slash across. Breathing his last breath, lifeless he crumples.

(*Weakened hands, trembling violently, lift the blade upward. He tilts his head. His neck is exposed. A quick slash and the jugular vein is cut. His body rises upward in three spasms of breath. His eyes flutter closed. He falls limply forward, dead. Silently* ISHIDŌ *rises. A* STAGE ASSISTANT *whisks his stool offstage.* ISHIDŌ *places the shogun's letter on his open fan and places them on* HANGAN'S *body. He moves stage right and kneels beside* YURANOSUKE.)

ISHIDŌ: (*Quietly.*) Yuranosuke, Yakushiji now assumes authority over Hangan's estates. Hangan's retainers are hereby denied the rank of samurai and are disbanded. I will report 95 to the shogun that the death of Hangan is accomplished. You have my deepest sympathy, Yuranosuke.

NARRATOR: (*Sings.*) Ishidō, the envoy, expresses sympathy. His sad assignment is over.

(ISHIDŌ *rises facing the line of* RETAINERS. *He raises his arms in a gesture of condolence. The* RETAINERS *look up, then bow respectfully. Slowly* ISHIDŌ *walks to the seven-three position on the* hanamichi. *At a signal from* YURANOSUKE, RIKIYA *moves forward to see him out.* ISHIDŌ *turns back.*)

ISHIDŌ: There is no need. There is no need.

100 NARRATOR: He prays silently.

(ISHIDŌ *folds his hands and, with downcast eyes, walks slowly down the* hanamichi *and out of sight.*)

NARRATOR: (*Chants.*) Yakushiji holds them in contempt!

(YAKUSHIJI *rises brusquely. The* STAGE ASSISTANT *takes away his stool.*)

YAKUSHIJI: Now that he's dead, I'm master here! Cart the corpse away, while I settle in. Show me the way! (*He starts to go, then turns back.*) It's a sad time, isn't it! Ha, ha, ha, ha!

(YAKUSHIJI *strides off left, shown out by a* RETAINER. *Complete silence.* YURANOSUKE *moves in to attend to his master's body. He*

straightens the legs and brings kimono and vest up over the torso. He moves closer and tries to take the dagger from HANGAN's hand. In death HANGAN's fingers hold it tightly. YURANOSUKE falls back weeping. He gently massages his master's hand until the fingers are warmed, softened, and the dagger slips from their grasp. YURANOSUKE places the dagger carefully into the breast of his kimono. He backs away. He and the RETAINERS bow expectantly.)

NARRATOR: (*Singing plaintively.*) Lady Kaoyo enters from an- 105 other room. Her hair so long and black, oh, so beautiful, now pitiful, it is no more. She will pray as a nun, till her end.

(KAOYO *and four* LADIES-IN-WAITING *enter from the left, walking with downcast eyes. They are dressed in pure white kimono and hold Buddhist rosaries. The last* LADY-IN-WAITING *carries a small tray on which rests the cloth-wrapped remains of* KAOYO's *long hair. They kneel left. The* MAIDS *bow deeply.*)

KAOYO: (*Quietly.*) Yuranosuke. When I think of why my husband had to die, and that I was the cause . . .

YURANOSUKE: (*Firmly.*) My lady, please understand our 110 heartfelt feelings. All of us, each retainer offers his deepest condolence.

(YURANOSUKE *bows to* KAOYO, *then nods to* GOEMON. GOEMON *and the* RETAINERS *rise and move in a circle around their master. Silently, they take up the white cloth, the tatami mats, tray, and sprigs of green. They exit upstage right.* HANGAN *moves off behind the cloth. In an instant all sign of the suicide is removed.*)

KAOYO: Yuranosuke.

YURANOSUKE: Yes, my lady.

KAOYO: I offer my lock of hair.

(*The* LADY-IN-WAITING *places the tray with the hair center stage.* YURANOSUKE *sees it and weeps.* KAOYO *turns to show her close-cropped head.*)

NARRATOR: (*Prolonged, melancholy singing.*) Kaoyo is left be- 115 hind, her grief is so . . . o . . . o . . . She yearns to go to the temple . . .

(*She rises, as if to follow her husband, but* YURANOSUKE *stops her with a commanding gesture.*)

YURANOSUKE: My lady!

(*She falls back weakly. A single* ki *clack. They move into a pose:* YURANOSUKE *picks up the tray with one hand and forces her back with the other;* KAOYO *faces front, lifts the rosary to her eyes, and sobs silently.* Ki *clacks accelerate as the curtain is slowly walked closed.*)

SCENE III
Outer Gate

Two ki *clacks signal drum and flute to play "Toki no Taiko" ("Time Drum"). The curtain is pushed quickly open. The scene is outside the massive outer gate of* HANGAN's *mansion. No one is on stage.*

NARRATOR: (*Chanting rapidly.*) Farewell to Hangan. Now his body lies alone. The young retainers run back from the temple! They no longer can hold the shame inside!

(*To loud, accelerating* tsuke *beats,* RIKIYA *leads a band of* RETAINERS *onto the* hanamichi. *They urge each other on with shouts of "Kill* them!" "They won't have our lord's mansion!" "We'll fight them!" "Lord Hangan was unjustly killed!" At the same time YURANOSUKE and GOEMON come out of a small door in the gate. GOEMON rushes up to the RETAINERS with outstretched arms, shouting, "Stop, stop!" YURANOSUKE roughly pushes RIKIYA to the ground.)

YURANOSUKE: (*Furious.*) What, you too, Rikiya? What are
5   you thinking of, trying to attack the mansion? We are no longer samurai. We cannot fight Yakushiji's men. (*Drops to one knee, hand on the hilt of his short sword.*) If you do not stop, I shall commit seppuku on this very spot! Do you want to be my seconds, all of you?
10   RETAINERS: No, but master . . .
YURANOSUKE: (*Implacably.*) Then will you stop when I tell you?
RETAINERS: Yes, but . . .
YURANOSUKE: It will achieve nothing to die now!

(*The* RETAINERS *cannot disobey. Grumbling and rebellious, they begin to fall back.*)

NARRATOR: (*Chants.*) Behind the gate is heard . . . Yakushiji's
15   voice!
YAKUSHIJI: (*Off.*) Hey, men, there's a sight. Newly hatched ex-samurai, milling around like chickens with their heads cut off! It's enough to make you laugh!
YAKUSHIJI'S MEN: (*Off.*) Ha, ha, ha, ha, ha!
20   FIRST RETAINER: Do you . . .
RETAINERS: . . . hear that?

(*Furious, they turn to storm the gate, hands on the hilts of their swords.* YURANOSUKE *springs into their path and blocks the way.*)

YURANOSUKE: Have you forgotten our late lord?
RETAINERS: No, but . . .
YURANOSUKE: Not now! Go back, go back! Go back I tell you!

(YURANOSUKE *draws himself up commandingly. He runs his hand up the edge of his vest and poses in a furious* mie. *Two* tsuke *beats.*)

25   NARRATOR: (*Sings.*) "Go back," he commands!
YURANOSUKE: (*Almost in a scolding tone now.*) Back, back, back.

(YURANOSUKE *waves them away. They fall back grudgingly, then turn and stride off down the* hanamichi. YURANOSUKE *watches them leave. He is alone. Silence. He sighs with relief. The hand at his breast slides down until it accidentally touches the dagger. He slowly drops to his knees and takes it out. He unwraps the covering purple cloth. The blade tip is red with* HANGAN's *blood.*)

NARRATOR: (*Sings.*) The suicide blade, red with blood, cries out for revenge . . . cries out for revenge! Burning tears rake his heart, tears . . . falling . . . falling . . . falling . . . falling . . .

(*Gazing at the blade,* YURANOSUKE's *chest heaves. He covers his eyes to hide the tears.*)

30   Hangan's last words of vengeance imbedded deep in Yuranosuke. (*Chanting.*) We know indeed the motive of Yuranosuke, his revenge to be noted for many ages . . . forty-seven loyal men immortalized!

(*He wipes blood from the blade onto his palm and then deliberately brings his hand up to his mouth. He licks the blood as an oath of*

vengeance. *Music stops. Silence.* YURANOSUKE *begins his long pantomime of departure. He carefully wraps the dagger in the purple cloth. He holds it to his forehead respectfully. He places it in the breast of his kimono. He rises and stands. He slaps the dust from his knees. He adjusts his trousers. He folds both hands inside his kimono sleeves. He rests his hands on the hilts of his swords. He half-closes his eyes, regretting deeply that he must abandon his master's mansion. A temple bell tolls in the distance. Pensively, he begins to walk away from the gate. The gate recedes, indicating* YURANOSUKE *has covered a long distance. He turns back. A crow caws in the distance. He resumes the painful separation. A crow caws a second time. A second bell tolls. He stops, stricken with the finality of parting. Then, he moves onto the* hanamichi. *Once more he turns back and, as if he has no heart to continue, slides to his knees. A temple bell tolls. Plaintive, tentative chords of the samisen begin. He rises, begins to walk away, looks sadly over his shoulder for one last glimpse, then resolutely turns and strides down the* hanamichi *and out of sight. Music crescendoes and* ki *clacks accelerate: the curtain is run closed. Drum and flute play rapid "Shagiri" to end the scene.*)

ACT THREE

SCENE I
Ichiriki Brothel

Two ki *clacks: the curtain is pushed open to offstage singing of "Hana ni Asobaba" ("If You Play in the Flowers"). The scene is the Ichiriki Brothel in the Gion licensed quarter in Kyoto. Two pavilions are set in a garden. Lying on his side in the larger room, stage center, is* YURANOSUKE. *He is feigning sleep, his face covered with a half-open fan. He wears an elegant purple kimono and matching cloak. Curtains are at the back and a stone water basin is left. Three steps lead down into the garden. Paper-covered sliding doors conceal the interior of the smaller pavilion, stage left. It is several feet higher off the ground than the center pavilion.*

NARRATOR: (*Singing briskly.*) The mountains and the moon. From the eastern mountains, just a few miles, breathless from running fast, the young man . . . Rikiya.

(RIKIYA *enters on the* hanamichi. *A purple scarf covers his head and serves as a partial disguise. His black kimono is hiked up at the sides, to free his legs for running. He stops at a garden gate set on the* hanamichi *at the seven-three position. He looks back to see if he is being observed, then swiftly passes through the gate, closing it.*)

Entering the brothel garden . . . there lies Yuranosuke, pretending to be drunk. Taking caution to wake his father in   5 secrecy, he walks softly in, stepping close to him. The sword guard speaks!

(RIKIYA *sees his father. He mounts the steps, kneels, and makes a ringing sound by striking sword guard against sheath.* YURANOSUKE *gestures* RIKIYA *away with a sleepy movement of the fan.* RIKIYA *crosses swiftly back through the gate, closes it, looks around to be certain they are not being observed, and kneels to wait for his father. Offstage* samisen *play tentative chords.* YURANOSUKE *rises. He staggers as if drunk, ad-libbing, "That was heady wine. I need some air. Don't go away, girls. I'll be in the garden." He looks through the curtains to see if anyone is watching. He crosses to the gate, stumbling several times in order to have the chance to look carefully in all directions. He stands swaying, fan before his face. He speaks guardedly.*)

YURANOSUKE: Rikiya, do I hear the sound of urgency in the echo of your sword?

10 RIKIYA: Yes, Father. I bring a secret message from Lady Kaoyo. (RIKIYA *brings out a letter from his right sleeve and passes it to* YURANOSUKE, *who puts it immediately into the breast of his kimono without examining it.*)

YURANOSUKE: (*Carefully.*) Did she say anything to you?

15 RIKIYA: (*Rising on his knees urgently.*) Soon, soon our enemy . . .

YURANOSUKE: Rikiya! "Soon at night our enemy, flees like plovers o'er the sea. . . ."

(*Music swells. To cover the slip of his son's tongue,* YURANOSUKE *sings a well-known passage from a now play. He staggers in a circle looking to see if anyone has heard* RIKIYA's *remark. Simultaneously,* RIKIYA *pivots in the opposite direction, looking for eavesdroppers.* YURANOSUKE *gestures for* RIKIYA *to come closer;* RIKIYA *whispers* KAOYO's *message in his father's ear. The curtains in the room center part.* KUDAYŪ *peeks out. He is a gray-haired former retainer of* HANGAN, *now secretly working for* MORONAO. *He wears a plain brown kimono and cloak. He watches for a moment, then slips away.*)

YURANOSUKE: Send a palanquin for me tonight. Tell the others to be ready. Go, go!

20 NARRATOR: (*Sings.*) No time left for hesitation . . . to the eastern hills, homeward now . . .

(YURANOSUKE *sharply gestures with the fan.* RIKIYA *bows, rises, and holding firmly onto the hilts of his swords, begins to leave.*)

YURANOSUKE: Rikiya!

RIKIYA: (*Returning and bowing.*) Yes.

YURANOSUKE: Be careful while passing through the quarter.
25 Then hurry! Go now!

RIKIYA: Yes!

NARRATOR: Rikiya returns home.

(RIKIYA *realizes his mistake; he is holding his swords ready to draw, thus calling attention to himself. He hides the hilts with his sleeves. Swiftly, carefully, he hurries down the* hanamichi *out of sight. Offstage* samisen *play "Odoriji Aikata" ("Dance Melody"). Four* MAIDS *and a male* JESTER *enter through the curtain, ad-libbing, "Yura, where are you?" "Come drink with us." "Don't leave us, Yura."* YURANOSUKE *pretends drunkenness again.*)

FIRST MAID: Yura, Yura, are you here?

YURANOSUKE: Hmm. You've come to get me? I'm a lucky
30 man. Come close all of you, let's amuse ourselves. Come, sing and dance for me.

(YURANOSUKE *sits on the steps. The* MAIDS *and the* JESTER *kneel in the garden in a semicircle around him.*)

SECOND MAID: Very well . . .

ALL: . . . let's begin, let's begin!

(*Lilting music of offstage* samisen, *drum, and bell accompanies various dances and songs. These are extemporized by the performers from production to production.* MAIDS *and* JESTER *ad-lib comic banter throughout.*)

MAIDS: (*Clapping as they sing.*) "What will it be like, what will
35 it be like? If you don't be careful, we will make you drink. Ah, what will it be like, what will it be like?"

(JESTER *and* THIRD MAID *rise and move center. They do a game of jan-ken-po, "scissors-paper-stone." He loses. She laughingly pushes him. He falls in a heap on the ground. The* MAIDS *rise and form pairs.*)

FOURTH MAID: Come, let's dance!

ALL: "First your left foot, then your right, tap, tap, tap;
Around we go, back again;
Are you ready, one, two, three!"   40

(*They circle left, then right, touching palms of their outstretched hands. They turn their backs to each other and bump bottoms on the count of three. With peals of laughter they recover their balance. The* JESTER *and* YURANOSUKE *laugh and applaud.*)

YURANOSUKE: Very good, very good!

FIRST MAID: How about a game, Yura dear?

JESTER: Blind man's bluff!

SECOND MAID: You be It!

ALL: Yes, yes!   45

(YURANOSUKE *tries to wave them away, but they playfully surround him and put a cloth over his eyes. They twirl him around in the center of the garden, and move left, laughing and clapping in time to their song.*)

ALL: "Yura, Yura, over here;
Listen to our clapping hands."

YURANOSUKE: (*Sings.*) "I'll catch you all, soon enough you'll see."

(*He stumbles in their direction. They easily avoid his outstretched arms and flee to the other side of the garden.*)

ALL: "Yura, Yura over here;
Come and catch us if you can."   50

YURANOSUKE: "I'll catch you all, and make you drink with me."

(*They duck under his arms. When he turns back to continue pursuit, they take him by the hands and, still singing and clapping, lead him off to the inner room with his blindfold still in place. They are no sooner off than* KUDAYŪ's *head pops through the curtain on the other side of the stage. Samisen* music stops. KUDAYŪ *peers about intently. He slips into the room.*)

KUDAYŪ: That letter Rikiya gave to Yuranosuke . . . the rumor of a vendetta must be true! He has not forgotten; they are plotting, just as I thought. When I tell Moronao, what will be my great reward? If, of course, it's true. I'll spy him out! 55
Here's a perfect place to hide.

(*He sees a hiding place. He removes a board under the veranda, opening a space for him to crawl in. He hides behind the steps.* YURANOSUKE *enters alone from upstage, pretending to be drunk.*)

YURANOSUKE: I'll be back . . . don't wait, girls . . . in a minute, I'll be back.

(*Samisen* music resumes. He looks around. Seeing he is alone, he drops his pretense. He rinses his mouth with water from the stone basin. He spits it out. It falls on the unsuspecting* KUDAYŪ. *He takes out the letter from* KAOYO *and holds it respectfully to his forehead. He begins to read, slowly unrolling the letter until it reaches the ground. At the same time the paper doors slide open to reveal* OKARU *in the small room left. She wears the elaborate hairstyle and clinging kimono of a courtesan.*)

NARRATOR: (*Sings.*) Evening breeze, brings a courtesan, Kam-
60   pei's wife Okaru, away from her love. Someone has sent a
       love letter, "I wish it were for me." Okaru from a room
       above, tries to see the words. Too far in the evening dusk, the
       letters are not clear to read. Thinking of a way out, a mirror
       in her hand, she leans back . . . mirror held up high, reflec-
65   tion of the letter. Under the floor a spy, Kudayū waits . . . the
       trailing letter glows in the moonlight. (*Chants.*) Who could
       know someone is reading words of confidence?

(*The three form a tableau:* YURANOSUKE *is engrossed in reading the secret letter;* OKARU *views the letter backwards in a mirror; and* KU-DAYŪ, *spectacles on his nose, reads the bottom portion, line-by-line, as it comes down to him. Narrative shifts to singing.*)

       Okaru, unaware that her hairpin has loosened! (*Chants.*) It
       drops to the floor! Surprised by the sound above, he
70   quickly hides the letter . . . Yuranosuke! Underneath Ku-
       dayū smirking at his game. (*Sings.*) Okaru pretends noth-
       ing has happened here.

(YURANOSUKE *quickly resumes his drunken role. He begins to roll up the letter, but not before* KUDAYŪ *rips off the part he has been reading.* OKARU *puts down the mirror, picks up a fan, and turns to* YURANOSUKE.)

OKARU: (*Languidly.*) Yura dear, is it you?
YURANOSUKE: Hmm, Okaru? So close at hand, what are you
75   doing?
OKARU: (*In poetic form of seven and five syllables.*) Yura dear, it's
       all your fault, I drank too much wine; my head is whirling
       round and I can scarcely see; I have come to sober up,
       wafted by the evening breeze.

(YURANOSUKE *reaches the end of the letter. He feels the ragged edge. Startled, he looks quickly at the letter, then puts it away in the breast of his kimono. He takes out a piece of tissue paper and wads it up, covering his action by improvising conversation with* OKARU.)

80 YURANOSUKE: Hmm. Wafted by the evening breeze, you say?
       Wafted by the evening breeze? Ah!

(*He drops the wad of paper to the ground.* KUDAYŪ, *thinking it is part of the letter, snatches it and stuffs it into his kimono breast.* YURANOSUKE *falls back, supposedly in a drunken stupor, but actually wanting to ponder what to do next. He decides. Soft samisen plays "Odoriji Aikata" in the background.*)

       Hm. Okaru, there is something I want to talk to you
       about. Come over here.
OKARU: (*Rises as if to leave her room.*) Very well, I'll come
85   around and visit you.
YURANOSUKE: (*Coming down into the garden.*) No, Okaru, if
       you go that way the maids will catch you. They will force
       on you more wine. Ah, a ladder. Fortune smiles. Climb
       down this way and you won't be seen. (*Places a ladder against*
       OKARU's *pavilion. Bantering.*) Descend for me, Okaru!
90 OKARU: (*Coquettishly on the ladder.*) I've never climbed a lad-
       der before.
YURANOSUKE: You've climbed other things.

OKARU: I'm not used to this strange position. It frightens me.
YURANOSUKE: You're past the age to be afraid of a new po-   95
       sition. Straddle it, open your legs, it'll all go smoothly.
OKARU: Don't be naughty, Yura. I tell you it frightens me. It's
       swaying like a boat.
YURANOSUKE: Never mind, I'll throw in my anchor. That
       will hold you down. Where shall I put it? (*He tries to lift*   100
       her skirt with his fan. She brushes his hand away.)
OKARU: You mustn't peek, Yura.
YURANOSUKE: (*Singing.*) "I adore your crescent moon, glis-
       tening in its secret grotto." Ha, ha, ha.
OKARU: (*Pouting.*) If you talk that way, I won't come down.   105
YURANOSUKE: Don't prattle like a virgin. You're a courtesan
       in the Gion brothel. I'll take you from behind. (YURA-
       NOSUKE *embraces her from behind.*)
OKARU: Oh, stop it.
YURANOSUKE: Then come, come.   110
OKARU: I am, I am!

(*Laughing, she slips off the final rung of the ladder and moves away from* YURANOSUKE. *She kneels right, fanning herself.* YURA-NOSUKE *glances at her sharply, then resumes the drunken pose. He stoops to retrieve the dropped hairpin and crosses to give it to her.*)

YURANOSUKE: (*Casually.*) Just now, Okaru, did something
       catch your eye?
OKARU: I . . . nothing.
YURANOSUKE: (*Coaxing.*) Come now, didn't you see, didn't   115
       you see . . .
OKARU: . . . your interesting letter . . .
YURANOSUKE: . . . from up above?
OKARU: (*Lightly.*) Hmm, yes.
YURANOSUKE: And you read it all?   120
OKARU: Oh, you do go on.

(*Covering his concern, he pretends to stumble. He recovers his bal-ance, singing a now song which both hides and expresses his feelings.*)

YURANOSUKE: "Fate conspires to bring, my life to this crisis. . . ."
       (*Mimes striking a nō drum.*) Ya, tum, tum, tum! Ha, ha, ha!
OKARU: (*Turns to him, laughing.*) What in the world do you
       mean?   125
YURANOSUKE: It means that of all the women in the world, I
       have become enamored of you. Come live with me, Okaru.
OKARU: Stop it. You're such a tease!
YURANOSUKE: (*Grandiloquently.*) I will redeem your contract
       with the master of the brothel and take you away.   130
OKARU: I don't believe it. You're making fun of me.
YURANOSUKE: I'll prove it's not a lie. Be my mistress for just
       three days, and after that, Okaru, your spirit will be free to
       go where it will.
OKARU: (*Taking him seriously for the first time.*) For three days? 135
YURANOSUKE: On my sacred oath as a samurai. Live with me
       for three days. I'll find the master and buy your contract
       now. Well, is it agreed?

(OKARU *looks carefully at him to see if it possibly can be true. They pose. She bows low.*)

OKARU: I am grateful, Yuranosuke.
YURANOSUKE: Can it make you happy to be redeemed . . .   140
       by this Yuranosuke?

OKARU: Oh, yes!

YURANOSUKE: Such radiance shines in that happy face.

(*They pose: she looks at him with gratitude; flicking open his fan, he covers his face to hide his stricken expression.*)

YURANOSUKE: Don't go away now. I'll be right back.

145 OKARU: Three days? Yes, Yuranosuke. I'll be here.

(*Offstage, sad "Yo ni mo Inga" ["Nighttime Fate"] is sung quietly. They lightly ad-lib to cover his exit. Still pretending to be drunk, he staggers up the steps. He turns back several times. He passes through the curtains in search of the master of the house. When he is gone she kneels center stage, trembling with excitement.*)

OKARU: How happy I am! I must write to dearest Kampei that I am coming home! And to Mother and Father, to tell the wonderful news!

(*She hurries up the steps into the center room, brings out a writing box and roll of letter paper, kneels, and begins to write a letter home. Song ends.*)

NARRATOR: (*Chants.*) Now appears . . . Heiemon!

(*Offstage samisen briskly play "Odoriji Aikata." A young samurai strides on from the right into the garden. His hair is severely drawn back and his plain kimono suggests poverty. It is HEIEMON, OKARU's older brother, in search of both YURANOSUKE and OKARU. He looks around, then seeing a woman in the room, enters and sits behind her. He speaks brusquely, almost rudely.*)

150 HEIEMON: Sorry to trouble you, Miss, but I am looking for a young woman, from my hometown of Yamazaki, by the name of Okaru, brought here a year ago . . .

(*Hearing her name OKARU turns. They recognize each other.*)

Sister!

OKARU: Heiemon! Oh! I feel ashamed for you to see me here!

(*OKARU's demeanor completely changes: in the presence of a male family member who is her elder, she becomes submissive, gentle, a little girl seeking approbation. She hides her face. She rushes down the steps, and falls to her knees. HEIEMON, though stern, acts protectively toward her. He rises and poses on the steps.*)

155 HEIEMON: What is there to feel ashamed of? When I returned home Mother told me you had sold yourself to this brothel, hoping that with your contract price Kampei could contribute to the vendetta against Lord Hangan's enemy. You have willingly sacrificed yourself for your hus-
160 band and for Lord Hangan. I am proud of you, Okaru! (*He poses at the top of the steps: right foot forward, right arm extended protectively in her direction.*)

OKARU: (*Hesitantly, looks up at him.*) Then you're not going to scold me?

165 HEIEMON: Scold you? I am filled with admiration, filled with admiration!

(*He crosses down the steps and kneels. He sits proudly, sword placed on the ground beside him.*)

OKARU: I'm happy that you think kindly of me. (*Becoming excited.*) Oh, there are so many things I want to ask my dear big brother. I don't know where to begin . . . how is Kam . . .

HEIEMON: (*Uneasy.*) Kam . . . ? 170

(OKARU *is embarrassed to have asked about her husband first. She changes the subject.*)

OKARU: Come . . . tell me, how is Mother?

HEIEMON: Set your mind at ease. Mother is well.

OKARU: And Father? Nothing troubles him, I hope?

HEIEMON: (*Uncomfortably.*) Hm . . . Father . . . he is at rest . . . he is at rest. 175

OKARU: (*Modestly.*) And what of Kampei?

HEIEMON: Kampei? Ah . . . well . . . he is as well as can be.

OKARU: You set my heart at ease. (*Bubbling.*) Oh, I forgot. . . be happy for me, Brother. Tonight, without warning, Yuranosuke offered to buy out my contract. 180

HEIEMON: Yuranosuke did that? (*Trying to understand how such a thing could be.*) Ah, then he's become your patron?

OKARU: Nonsense. We have only drunk together two or three times. And Heiemon, it's almost too good to be true. After three days he will let me come home. 185

HEIEMON: Hm? Then you told him you are Kampei's wife?

OKARU: How could I, a prostitute, tell him that and bring disgrace to Kampei and to my parents?

HEIEMON: (*Facing front.*) Hm! Then he is no more than a whoremaster! (*He slaps his thigh in anger.*) He has no intention of avenging Hangan, our lord and master! 190

OKARU: Oh, no, Brother, he has. He has. Listen . . .

NARRATOR: (*Sings.*) In whispers, the content of the letter is revealed.

(OKARU *and* HEIEMON *rise. He leans forward. She whispers in his ear. They pose for a moment, then break apart and kneel.*)

OKARU: . . . so you see? 195

HEIEMON: (*Shocked.*) Then you read it all?

OKARU: Yes, and after reading it, his eye met mine, and flirting, he looked me up and down, up and down, and then began to talk of taking me away.

(OKARU *mimes his flirting by pressing the backs of her index fingers together, right on top of left, then left on top of right.* HEIEMON *is puzzled. He tries to understand her words, miming as she did.*)

HEIEMON: What? After reading it, flirting, he looked you up 200 and down, up and down . . . (*He slaps his thigh for emphasis.*) Ah! Now I understand!

OKARU: (*Laughing.*) You startled me.

HEIEMON: (*Facing the inner room, he bows low.*) Forgive me, Master Yuranosuke, I misjudged you! I was wrong, forgive me! 205

OKARU: Dearest Brother, what in the world are you doing?

HEIEMON: (*Turns and looks into* OKARU's *eyes.*) Dear Sister. There is something I must ask of you. Okaru, do now exactly as I say.

OKARU: You sound so very stiff and formal. What must you 210 ask of me?

HEIEMON: What I must ask of you is . . .

OKARU: What you must ask of me is . . . ?

HEIEMON: Okaru, let your brother take your life!

(*He springs to his feet and whips out his long sword. She falls back. Rapid "Odoriji Aikata." To double beats of the* tsuke, *he slashes at her right, left, right. She avoids. She rises and pushes him away. He turns to strike; she distracts him with a shower of tissue paper drawn from her breast and thrown in the air. She runs to the* hanamichi; *he follows. She closes the gate between them. They pose in a* mie *to two loud* tsuke *beats: on the ground, she holds up her hands imploringly; he stands with legs together, the sword directly overhead as if to strike. Music stops.*)

215 OKARU: (*Appealing to him.*) What am I supposed to have done wrong? You have no right to just do as you please. I have my husband and both my parents to care for. Forgive me if I have spoken out of turn. I clasp my hands and beg you to spare me!

220 NARRATOR: (*Sings.*) Seeing his sister's clasped hands . . . a brother's love overwhelms the dutiful heart. He can only cry.

(*He tries to but cannot strike his sister. He falls back distraught, turns upstage to face away from her, holds the sword behind his back, and weeps unashamedly. When the narration is finished, he turns to face* OKARU. *He is contrite. Slow offstage "Odoriji Aikata" resumes in the background.*)

HEIEMON: I was wrong, Okaru, not to explain. Come, come over here.

(*He waves her to him. She flounces.*)

OKARU: No, I will not come near you.

225 HEIEMON: (*Sternly.*) When your elder brother calls, why don't you come?

OKARU: (*Sweetly.*) If you want to know, I'll tell you why: I think you still intend to kill me, and I don't like that at all!

(HEIEMON *notices the long sword in his hand. He puts it on the ground and pushes it toward her.*)

HEIEMON: Ah, this. There is nothing to stop you now. So
230 come, come!

OKARU: Yes, there is. Something else.

(*She points at the short sword in his sash. Annoyed, he pushes it toward her.*)

HEIEMON: There, now. Come over here!

(*She rises and is about to cross through the gate. She looks at him and stops.*)

OKARU: Your face is so frightening.

HEIEMON: I can't help that. This is the face I was born with.
235 OKARU: Well then, please turn around.

HEIEMON: What a nuisance. Like this? Like this?

(*Grumbling, he turns his back. He poses with arms stretched out to either side.*)

OKARU: Now, don't look. Keep your face turned away. (*She cautiously goes through the gate, picks up the swords, and puts them out of his reach. She kneels behind him, placing her hands
240 on his sash. Music stops. She poses.*) All right, here I am.

Brother dear, what is it you want? (*He turns to face her. He places his hands protectively on her shoulders. They pose.*)

HEIEMON: (*Voice filled with emotion, he speaks in poetic form of seven and five syllables.*) Once you were a samurai, now a courtesan; combing out your silken hair, while the world 245 has changed; precious Sister how pitiful, totally unaware of the life you left behind!

(HEIEMON *breaks away and kneels left.* OKARU *moves close.*)

OKARU: Totally unaware . . . of what, Heiemon?

HEIEMON: Soon after you left home last year, one rainy night, Father was . . . 250

OKARU: (*Frightened.*) Father was . . . ?

HEIEMON: (*Choked scream.*) . . . struck down by a robber and slain by his sword!

OKARU: (*Falls back slackly.*) That cannot be true.

HEIEMON: You must be strong, Okaru. You look forward to 255 leaving here and being with your husband . . .

OKARU: Yes . . . Kampei . . . what about Kampei?

HEIEMON: Kampei . . .

OKARU: Kampei . . . ?

HEIEMON: (*A terrible scream.*) Cut open his stomach and is dead! 260

(*He mimes the suicide and collapses, weeping.* OKARU *falls back, shocked, hardly able to breathe.*)

OKARU: Kampei . . . oh . . . no. What shall I do? What shall I do?

HEIEMON: I know, I know, I know . . .

(*They speak alternately, then faster and faster, until they are speaking at the same time. Then their grief-stricken voices fade away.* OKARU *crawls to her older brother and puts her head on his lap. She weeps pitiably. At last* HEIEMON *gains control of himself. He gently disengages himself.*)

HEIEMON: Don't you see? Yuranosuke is not a man to be infatuated, and he did not know you were Kampei's wife. 265 Okaru, you were wrong to have read that secret letter. Yuranosuke's loyalty is clear. He cannot risk letting you live and he intends to buy your contract . . . just to kill you! Rather than dying at someone else's hand, let me be the one to take your life. Let me prove to Yuranosuke and his 270 followers that though I am a mere foot soldier, my spirit is as loyal as theirs. Let me serve our late master. Give me your life, dear Sister!

NARRATOR: (*Sings.*) The tragedy is disclosed! Okaru is prepared!

(HEIEMON *is agonized by the conflict between his duty to* HANGAN *and his love for* OKARU. *He beseeches her with clasped hands.* OKARU *willingly prepares to sacrifice herself. Gently she opens his hands.*)

OKARU: It is my karma not to meet my beloved husband and 275 father again. There is no reason for me to live.

(*She crosses to get the swords, returns, and places them before him.*)

Brother dear, please end my life now.

(*She turns her back, clasps her hands in prayer, and drops her head forward, exposing her neck to his sword.*)

HEIEMON: Admirable resolve. Namu Amida Butsu. Praise Buddha the Merciful.

(*He stands. He unsheaths the sword. He raises it to strike.* YURA-NOSUKE'*s voice is heard from behind the curtain.*)

280 YURANOSUKE: (*Off.*) Wait, wait! Stop at once! (*He enters.*) Your behavior is admirable, both of you. I acknowledge your loyalty. Heiemon, I hereby permit you to accompany us on our journey to the east.

(HEIEMON *and* OKARU *move right and kneel respectfully.* HEIEMON *is excited by* YURANOSUKE'*s acceptance of him into the vendetta group.*)

HEIEMON: Then you are ready? And I may go with you?
285   Okaru, Sister, do you hear? I am forever grateful.

(HEIEMON *bows to* YURANOSUKE. YURANOSUKE *comes down the steps.*)

YURANOSUKE: Okaru, for your loyalty, your husband, Kampei, will be admitted to our league. And since he was unable during his life to kill even a single enemy, let your action, Okaru, serve as his apology to Lord Hangan in the
290   afterlife . . . here and now . . .

(YURANOSUKE *takes* HEIEMON'*s long sword and places it in* OKARU'*s hands. He guides her to the veranda. They pose.*)

NARRATOR: (*Chants.*) Thrusting deep through the dark of the hiding place. The hateful spy, Kudayū, a fatal blow in his shoulder, rolls and turns in deadly pain!

(*They thrust the sword under the veranda. Double* tsuke *beats.* KU-DAYŪ *cries out.* HEIEMON *drags the mortally wounded* KUDAYŪ *into the garden and throws him to the ground.* YURANOSUKE *kneels, and holding* KUDAYŪ *by the scruff of the neck, strikes furiously with closed fan.*)

YURANOSUKE: Kudayū, you wretch! Traitor! More than forty
295   of us day and night have shed tears of agony. We have parted from our children, deserted our parents, and sold our wives into prostitution all in order to avenge our Lord Hangan's death. And you, who enjoyed wealth and honor in his service, have betrayed your master and become Mo-
300   ronao's spy! Fiend! Demon! You are a monster!

NARRATOR: (*Sings.*) As if to grind him into the ground, Yuranosuke . . . his burst of anger cannot be gratified!

(*He strikes him five times to sharp* tsuke *beats. Then contemptuously he pushes him away. Bringing his hand to his eyes,* YURANOSUKE *openly weeps. Just then the* MAIDS *cry out offstage. Rapid "Odoriji Aikata." Instantly* YURANOSUKE *reverts to his pose as a drunken brothel patron. He rises, staggering. The* MAIDS *enter and kneel in a semicircle in the center room.*)

FIRST MAID: Master Yuranosuke, Master Yuranosuke . . .
SECOND MAID: . . . your palanquin has arrived.
305 YURANOSUKE: You've come for me?
ALL: We will see you out.

(YURANOSUKE *crosses up the steps and stands at the top. He gestures for* OKARU *to join him there and for* HEIEMON *to pick up the nearly dead* KUDAYŪ. *Music stops.*)

YURANOSUKE: Heiemon. Take our drunken friend to the Kamo River. Let him drown his sorrows . . . in the waters there!

(YURANOSUKE *flicks open his fan and raises it overhead.* OKARU *kneels beside* YURANOSUKE, *placing her hands on his sash.* HEIEMON *drapes* KUDAYŪ'*s limp body over his shoulder. A single sharp clack of the ki. They freeze in a group* mie *pose. Ki clacks accelerate, drum beats speed up, and offstage "Odoriji Aikata" crescendoes as the curtain is slowly pushed closed.*)

SCENE II

Vendetta

Two sharp ki *clacks: large drum softly beats "Yuki Oto" ("Snow Sound"). The ki clacks accelerate to accompany the opening of the curtain. The scene is the garden of* MORONAO'*s mansion in Edo. It is night. Snow is falling. Rocks, trees, ground, and small bridge across a pond are covered with a mantle of white. Soft, rapid* tsuke *beats. Several* WOMEN *from* MORONAO'*s household rush on from the left. They are wearing nightclothes. Frightened and confused they urge each other to flee. They disappear. Drum and* tsuke *beats crescendo. Two* RETAINERS *with drawn swords rush on from the right. They pose.*

MORONAO'S RETAINER: I am Riku Handayū, retainer of Moronao. Name yourself!
HANGAN'S RETAINER: Akagaki Genzō, loyal to Enya Hangan. Let me pass!

(*They pose. Another two* RETAINERS *run on from the left.*)

MORONAO'S RETAINER: You will burn in hell before you 5 touch Lord Moronao!
HANGAN'S RETAINER: I, Katayama Genta, will take his head for Lord Hangan! Stand aside!

(*Large drum pattern of triple beats, "Mitsudaiko," and loud continuous* tsuke *beats. The paired opponents fight: they slash and parry with their long swords. In the end* HANGAN'*s men gain the upper hand;* MORONAO'*s men turn and are pursued off stage. Drumming changes to quiet "Snow Sound."* SHIMIZU *enters on the* hanamichi. *He is a famous swordsman hired by* MORONAO *as a bodyguard. A woman's kimono is draped over his head as a disguise, to allow him to reach the side of his master without being detained by* HANGAN'*s men. He stops at the seven-three position.*)

SHIMIZU: The war drum. Yuranosuke has come at last. But he will not succeed. The moon shall see the severed heads of 10 forty-seven rōnin before it witnesses the death of Lord Moronao!

(SHIMIZU *rushes on stage. He meets* TAKEMORI, *one of* HANGAN'*s men. They circle each other warily.* SHIMIZU'*s swords are seen.*)

TAKEMORI: Stop! Who are you?
SHIMIZU: (*Dropping the kimono to his waist.*) I am Shimizu Ichigaku, protector of Lord Moronao. 15
TAKEMORI: And I am Takemori Kitahachi! I've come for Moronao's head!
SHIMIZU: Then you must take mine first.
TAKEMORI: Come, fight! Fight!

(*"Mitsudaiko" drumming, loud* tsuke *beats, and "Chuwya Aikata"* samisen *music accompany the battle.* TAKEMORI *attacks, rushing past*

SHIMIZU. SHIMIZU *throws tiny daggers at* TAKEMORI, *who falls to the ground to evade. One of* HANGAN's *spearmen rushes on from the right, forcing* SHIMIZU *away from* TAKEMORI. SHIMIZU *is attacked from both sides. He slips free and runs onto the bridge over the pond. He is attacked by spear and sword simultaneously.* TAKEMORI *reaches under his guard and stabs* SHIMIZU *in the chest. A second slash, down his back, sends* SHIMIZU *toppling into the water of the pond and out of sight. Drum crescendoes. A loud whistle is heard off left. It signals* MORONAO's *capture.* MORONAO *is dragged on by several of* HANGAN's *men. He is thrown to the ground. He wears nothing except a white sleeping kimono. He is unarmed.* YURANOSUKE, RIKIYA, GOEMON, HEIEMON, *and other* RETAINERS *enter. They surround* MORONAO, *watching him carefully.* YURANOSUKE *kneels beside* MORONAO *politely.*)

20 YURANOSUKE: We allow you to die, Moronao, by your own hand . . . with this blade.

(*He unwraps* HANGAN's *suicide dagger and respectfully places it before* MORONAO, *offering him the opportunity to die with honor, instead of being killed.* MORONAO *is shaking with fright. He picks up the dagger as if to kill himself, then lunges at* YURANOSUKE. *Seizing* MORONAO's *wrist,* YURANOSUKE *turns the dagger against* MORONAO *and plunges it into his breast.* MORONAO *cries out once, then falls back dead. The* RETAINERS *form a ring around* MORONAO, *hiding him from view.* TAKEMORI *raises his sword and with a single stroke cuts off* MORONAO's *head. Two loud tsuke beats. It is wrapped in a white cloth and held high at the end of a spear.* MORONAO *moves offstage unseen behind a black cloth held by a* STAGE ASSISTANT. *The* RETAINERS *rise triumphantly.*)

YURANOSUKE: You have fought bravely, all of you. Your years of hardship, endured without thought of self, have brought success to our cherished plan. What joy Lord Hangan's spirit must feel for your deeds. On his behalf I thank you. 25
GOEMON: And now, let us bring Moronao's head to our master!

(*Spoken lightly, the lines are in poetic phrases of seven and five syllables.*)

YURANOSUKE: Deep concerns like drifted snow, melt in the clear of day . . .
RIKIYA: . . . at last our long awaited, vengeance is achieved . . . 30
GOEMON: . . . together with the clearing, of the morning clouds . . .
AGAKI: . . . at the cock's crow announcing, dawn of a new day . . .
TAKEMORI: . . . our hearts filled to overflowing, rise with the 35
rising sun . . .
GOEMON: . . . as we go together to . . .
ALL: . . . our Lord Hangan's grave.
YURANOSUKE: Shout victory together! Victory!

(*Single ki clack: offstage drum and samisen play "Taka no Hara" ("Hawk Plain") slowly, gradually accelerating until the scene is over. Each person turns to those next to him, nods, wipes tears of gratitude, grips an elbow, or places a hand on a shoulder. Then their thoughts return to their master,* HANGAN, *and all of them stand silent, posed in mingled happiness and grief. The curtain closes to rapidly accelerating ki clacks. The offstage musicians play "Shagiri" indicating the play is over.*)

CRITICAL CONTEXTS

ZEAMI MOTOKIYO (1363–1444)

from "A Mirror Held to the Flower" (1424)

TRANSLATED BY J. THOMAS RIMER AND YAMAZAKI MASAKAZU

Although Zeami's treatises describe the practical and esthetic foundations of the Noh (Nō) theater, they were not well known until the twentieth century. Since the Noh was organized around prominent families of actors, Zeami's texts were passed on in private and shown only to those who had been properly initiated. The first definitive edition of the treatises was published in 1940.

In "A Mirror Held to the Flower," Zeami discusses the training of Noh performers, emphasizing the interplay between physical training, spiritual development, and acting style in the production of the "flower"—beauty—in Noh performance. In this translation, the central term yugen *has been translated as "Grace." Although Zeami's language can seem remote to modern students, it is important to pay attention to the ways his understanding of acting relates to the process of Noh drama. How would you relate the kind of skills and attention that Zeami describes here to the demands of Noh drama?*

An actor must not only rehearse thoroughly with his teachers but he must learn through practice to imitate their peerless performances. Indeed, it is precisely because the art of these great performers has been brought to the highest levels of training that they can present in their acting an appearance of total mastery and ease, thus fascinating their audiences. If a beginner wishes merely to imitate this level of accomplishment, he may seem to achieve its semblance, yet there will be nothing moving in his performance. A truly great artist has for many years succeeded in training both his body and his spirit; he can hold back much of his potential in reserve and perform in an easy fashion, so that only seven-tenths of his art is visible. If a beginner tries to perform in this fashion, without the proper practice, he will only imitate what he can observe, and so his spirit and his performance can not reach beyond that seven-tenths he can grasp. What is more, his own progress will be blocked.

Therefore, when a student is learning his craft, the teacher should show not his own high level of ability [in which there is a reserve of artistry], but, as he did when he too was a beginner, indicate to his pupils how to use fully both their minds and bodies. After such lessons have been absorbed the students will gradually reach a level of mastery and attain a level of ease in their own performances, understand how to hold in reserve a certain amount of their own physical energy, and grasp of themselves the principle that "what is felt by the heart is ten, what appears in movement seven."

UNDERSTANDING THE PROPER MEANING OF LEARNING OUR ART

In general, a performance of Perfect Fluency cannot be imitated. And if an actor makes an attempt to imitate it, the very effort involved in the attempt will produce a tension that cannot be a part of Perfect Fluency. Only something that is meant to appear difficult can actually be imitated. "The truth and what looks like it are two different things,"[1] it is said. Thus, could there be any way to imitate the truth of the master actor's easy performance? Indeed, ease and difficulty are two aspects of the same thing. There is a separate teaching on this matter. The means by which a student learns from a teacher are well known, and so no special comment is needed here. However, the teacher's official certification of the student must be based on a thorough examination of his capacities and devotion; otherwise, certification should not be given. If the student's basic abilities are insufficient, no certification is possible. Should certification be given when talent is lacking, a level of accomplishment is suggested that cannot actually be matched. The certification will be fraudulent and the results meaningless; therefore, it should not be given. In the *Book of Changes* it is written that "if suitable teachings are given to those who are not suitable, the hatred of Heaven will be aroused."[2] In order that such a suitable person can be created, three conditions must be present. First, he must possess himself the requisite talent. Secondly, he must adore his art and show a total dedication to the path of *Nō*. Thirdly, he must have a teacher capable of showing him the proper way. If these three conditions cannot be met, the candidate will not be suitable. A suitable person is one who has the capacity to achieve the highest reaches of his art, to be recognized himself as a teacher.

---

[1] A popular saying found in many texts circulated in this period.

[2] The quotation as recorded here does not appear in the *Book of Changes* (*I ching*).

When I observe the artistic abilities of young performers now, it appears that "skipping"[3] has become commonplace. This situation comes about because they imitate without study. An actor must begin by studying the Two Basic Arts and the Three Role Types, continue to practice all that is appropriate for his age, and carry on his studies in the proper sequence, so that he will reach a stage of mastery in all the arts of the *Nō* that can permit him to perform in any artistic style. To learn only by imitation and so only manage a temporary resolution seems indeed to represent a kind of "skipping." For example, when studying the Two Basic Arts, one must not study the Three Role Types. When the time comes to study the Three Role Types, one must put off for a certain time the study of military roles [as they demand intense physical effort]. When an actor does come to study the military roles, then the demon roles in both the Delicacy within Strength and Rough styles of movement should be put off for a certain time, since there is an appropriate moment to learn them as well. To attempt to learn all these roles at once—what a terribly difficult thing it would be. And the degree of difficulty would be unexpectedly high. Therefore, even if by "skipping" a young performer manages to fool the public into thinking that he is a master, he will achieve a momentary Flower. And as such an artist grows older, his art will decline. And even should his art not decline, it would be impossible for him to achieve true renown. This point must be firmly kept in mind.

Concerning "skipping," there is another matter to consider. If an actor is inordinately fond of new plays, and should he come step by step to abandon the older repertory he performed in the past, he can never master the art of *Nō* and will only be "skipping." Rather, the actor must fix a repertory of standard plays at which he excels and then mix new plays in with them. If he plays only fresh pieces and neglects the plays to which he is accustomed, the results, in terms of the art of the *Nō*, will be a disgraceful "skipping" indeed. Besides, if only unusual pieces are performed, then that procedure of itself loses its novelty. If a mixture of old and new is achieved, then both the old and the new alike will seem novel. Such becomes the undying flower. As Confucius said, "He who by reanimating the Old can gain knowledge of the New is fit to be a teacher."[4]

HAVING A REAL UNDERSTANDING OF SKILL

If an actor has become fully proficient at music and dance, he may be called skillful. If he has not become fully accomplished, there will be no denying his shortcomings. On the other hand, there is a kind of real skill based on still different considerations. For example, there are actors whose abilities in dance and chant show no shortcomings, yet who have not achieved a high reputation. Then again, there are actors whose voices are not attractive and whose mastery of dancing and singing show defects, yet who are widely thought of as accomplished performers. The reason for this is that both dancing and gesture are external skills. The essentials of our art lie in the spirit. They represent a true enlightenment established through art. Thus, if an actor knows how to create interest and can perform from an understanding of this spirit, he will gain a reputation as a fine actor even if he has not mastered every aspect of his craft. Such being the case, if an actor really wants to become a master, he cannot simply depend on his skill in dance and gesture. Rather, mastery seems to depend on the actor's own state of self-understanding and the sense of style with which he has been blessed. Real discernment of the nature of the differences between external skill and interior understanding forms the basis of true mastery. Thus it is that an actor who has merely perfected his technique will have little of interest to show. Other actors, from the beginning of their careers, can fascinate their audiences. So it is that an actor, from the time he is young until he masters seven-tenths, eight-tenths, even all of his technique and reaches the level of a master, will continue to interest others for quite separate considerations.

Still higher than the level of interest, there is a level of skill that will simply make the audience gasp, without reflection, in surprise and pleasure. This level will be termed one of a pure Feeling that Transcends Cognition. The response to such a performance is such that there is no occasion for reflection, no time for a spectator to realize how well the performance is contrived. Such a state might be referred to as "purity unmixed."[5] In the *Book of Changes,* when the Chinese character for "feeling" (*kan*) is written, the element that stands for "mind" (*kokoro*) is eliminated [and the character is written as] in order to illustrate the fact that when true feeling is involved, there is no room in the concept for reflection as a function of the mind.[6]

[3]"Skipping" (*tendoku*) was a term originally used to mean "turning the *sutras*," chanting the first few lines and then skipping the rest to save time, as a kind of devotional exercise. Zeami of course uses the term ironically.

[4]See Arthur Waley, *The Analects of Confucius,* Book II, No. 11, page 90.

[5]A term sometimes used to indicate the high level of excellence in *waka* poetry. The term is probably of Zen origin.

[6]For a translation into English of this section of the *I ching*, see Richard Wilhelm, tr., *The I Ching or Book of Changes,* pages 122–125. The interpretation of the passage is evidently Zeami's.

Thus it is that the actor comes to possess various levels of artistic skill. If a beginning actor continues on through all the various stages of his training, he will be called a good actor, but not necessarily anything more. Yet there is still a higher level where real mastery is possible. If the spectators are truly fascinated with an actor's performance, he can be said to have reached the level of a master. If, in addition, he possesses the ability to create for his audience an intensity of pure feeling that goes beyond the workings of the mind, he will have achieved the level of greatest reputation. Thus an actor should pursue his study of Nō through these various levels, develop his skills, and through his own spiritual understanding, bring his art to the highest possible level of fulfillment.

SHALLOW AND DEEP

Concerning Nō performance, there is one matter that must be given particularly serious consideration. If a performance is given without sufficient attention to detail, it will be without interest. On the other hand, if too much attention is given by the performer to details, the whole performance risks to shrink in scale. Then again, if the actor thinks to play his part as liberally as possible, the opportunities for the audience to witness his skill will be fewer, and there will be a tendency for his performance to become slow and monotonous. An understanding of this distinction is of the greatest importance. An actor might, on first reflection, think that the parts of the play requiring intricate skills should be played in as complex a fashion as possible, while those moments requiring a more general approach should be played as broadly as possible. Yet in fact this kind of distinction cannot be made unless an actor knows the art of Nō very well indeed. A student must question his teacher closely on such matters, so that these distinctions become clear. There is, however, one general principle that can be kept in mind. For the chant, the dance, and the various sorts of gestures that will be employed, the actor's spirit should be as delicately attuned as possible, but, at the same time, his physical stance should be as relaxed and broad as possible. An actor must comprehend these principles and stick to them.

In general, it can be said that, in the case of the Nō, an art that is based on general and flexible principles can be made subtle and detailed. But a Nō that is merely meticulous in conception cannot easily develop on a large and relaxed scale. After all, the small can be contained in the large, but not the large in the small. A great deal of skill needs to be given over to this matter. A Nō that possesses both these qualities will truly be full and rich. Indeed, when ice formed during the deep cold melts, the ice formed during a brief chilly spell will melt as well.

ENTERING THE REALM OF GRACE

The aesthetic quality of Grace is considered the highest ideal of perfection in many arts. Particularly in the Nō, Grace can be regarded as the highest principle. However, although the quality of Grace is manifested in performance and audiences give it high appreciation, there are very few actors who in fact possess that quality. This is because they have never had a taste of the real Grace themselves. So it is that few actors have entered this world.

What kind of realm is represented by what is termed Grace? For example, if we take the general appearance of the world and observe the various sorts of people who live there, it might be said that Grace is best represented in the character of the nobility, whose deportment is of such a high quality and who receive the affection and respect not given to others in society. If such is the case, then their dignified and mild appearance represents the essence of Grace. Therefore, the stage appearance of Grace is best indicated by their refined and elegant carriage. If an actor examines closely the nobility's beautiful way of speaking and studies the words and habitual means of expression that such elevated persons use, even to observing their tasteful choice of language when saying the smallest things, such can be taken to represent the Grace of speech. In the case of the chant, when the melody flows smoothly and naturally on the ear and sounds suitably mild and calm, this quality can be said to represent the Grace of music. In the case of the dance, if the actor studies until he is truly fluent, so that his appearance on stage will be sympathetic and his carriage both unostentatious and moving to those who observe him, he will surely manifest the Grace of the dance. When he is acting a part, if he makes his appearance beautiful in the Three Role Types, he will have achieved Grace in his performance. Again, when presenting a role of fearsome appearance, a demon's role for example, even should the actor use a rough manner to a certain extent, he must not forget to preserve a graceful appearance, and he must remember the principles of "what is felt in the heart is ten," and "violent body movements, gentle foot movements," so that his stage appearance will remain elegant. Thus he may manifest the Grace of a demon's role.

An actor must come to grasp those various types of Grace and absorb them within himself; for no matter what kind of role he may assume, he must never separate himself from the virtue of Grace. No matter what the role—whether the character be of high or low rank, a man, a woman, a priest or lay person, a farmer or country person, even a beggar or an outcast—it should seem as though each were holding a branch of flowers in his hand. In this one respect they exhibit the same appeal, despite whatever differences they may show in their social positions. This Flower represents the beauty of their stance in the *nō*, and the ability to reveal this kind of stance in performance represents, of course, its spirit. In order to study the Grace of words, the actor must study the art of composing poetry; and to study the Grace of physical appearance, he must study the aesthetic qualities of elegant costume, so that, in every aspect of his art, no matter how the role may change that the actor is playing, he will always maintain one aspect in his performance that shows Grace. Such it is to know the seed of Grace.

However, it may well happen that an actor will put such an importance on his impersonation of the particulars of his role, regarding this aspect of his performance as the highest of his art, that he will neglect to maintain the beauty of the stance he has properly assumed. Thus he will fail to enter the world of Grace. And if he does not enter into the world of Grace, he cannot approach the level of Highest Fruition. And unless he reaches this highest level of accomplishment, he will never be recognized as a great actor. There are indeed few masters who have attained those heights. Thus an actor must rehearse with the utmost diligence on this critical point of the representation of Grace.

This Highest Fruition of an actor represents precisely the appearance of this deeply beautiful posture. I cannot repeat too often that an actor must rehearse with the need for the proper preparation of his body always in mind. Thus it is of crucial importance that, beginning with the Two Basic Arts down to the specifics of any role that may be played, the stance of the actor be attractive so as to represent this Highest Fruition in every circumstance. If the actor's posture is unattractive, his art will invariably appear vulgar. In any case, whatever gestures may be seen or music may be heard, however great the variety, the fact that the actor's stance is beautifully assumed represents the true attainment of Grace. An actor may be said to have entered the world of Grace when he has of his own accord studied these principles and made himself master of them. If an actor does not work to fulfill them and thinks that, without mastering every aspect of his art, he can still try to attain this Grace, he will, in fact, never know it during his entire lifetime.

PAYING HEED TO THE ACCUMULATION OF SKILLS

Studying the art of the *Nō*, having the reputation of a superior actor, and rising in merit as the years pass by depends on a proper accumulation of skills. Yet the nature of such an accumulation will differ depending on where the actor lives and performs. Even if he earns a reputation as a fine actor, if the praise he earns is not from those who live in the capital, it can have little significance for him. Even an actor who has earned genuine praise in the capital, should he return to his native place and continue to perform in the countryside, will merely expend his energies in attempting not to forget those means of expression that he learned in the capital, and because of his false sense that he still remembers how to perform properly, he will little by little slacken in his persistence in maintaining his beauty of performance. The result will be an accumulation of bad experiences. Such a stagnation of experience must be shunned.

In the capital, on the other hand, the actor will be performing before discerning spectators so that, should he become careless concerning any element in his art and so fail to progress, he will soon notice a response from his audience; then too, as criticism and comment come to him, he will eventually disregard the unsatisfactory elements in his art, accumulate only positive artistic experiences, and discover that his art has become polished. Of its own accord his skill will become as burnished as a jewel. There is a saying that "sagebrush, which has the ability to bend, even should it grow up among flax plants, will come out straight, without correction, while white sand, when mixed with earth, will become black like the rest."[7] Thus by living in the capital, an actor is in the proper environment, and the insufficiencies in his art will naturally disappear. This gradual lessening of error is in itself the accumulation of good experience. There is no way that an artist can simply set out to pile up these experiences of his own accord. Rather, let me repeat again and again a warning that, if an actor does not take cognizance of his good experiences, they will stagnate and turn into an accumulation of bad experiences.

So it is that even a skilled performer as he grows older will come to depend on his increasingly old-fashioned art, which has become so through an accumulation caused by his own stagnation. Although audiences may dislike his performances, he thinks only that he has been recognized as an artist of great merit for a long time. Thus he does not recognize the real feelings of his audiences. He therefore loses the chance to make his final appearances on the stage successful—such an important opportunity in an actor's career.

All of this is the result of piling up of such bad experiences. The greatest caution must be taken against this.

CONNECTING ALL THE ARTS THROUGH ONE INTENSITY OF MIND

It is often commented on by audiences that "many times a performance is effective when the actor does nothing." Such an accomplishment results from the actor's greatest, most

---

[7] An expression widely circulated during the medieval period in various forms, probably originating in the writings of Tseng Ts'an, one of the most important disciples of Confucius.

secret skill. From the techniques involved in the Two Basic Arts down to all the gestures and the various kinds of Role Playing, all such skills are based on the abilities found in the actor's body. Thus to speak of an actor "doing nothing" actually signifies that interval which exists between two physical actions. When one examines why this interval "when nothing happens" may seem so fascinating, it is surely because of the fact that, at the bottom, the artist never relaxes his inner tension. At the moment when the dance has stopped, or the chant has ceased, or indeed at any of those intervals that can occur during the performance of a role, or, indeed, during any pause or interval, the actor must never abandon his concentration but must keep his consciousness of that inner tension. It is this sense of inner concentration that manifests itself to the audience and makes the moment enjoyable.

However, it is wrong to allow an audience to observe the actor's inner state of control directly. If the spectators manage to witness this, such concentration will merely become another ordinary skill or action, and the feeling in the audience that "nothing is happening" will disappear.

The actor must rise to a selfless level of art, imbued with a concentration that transcends his own consciousness, so that he can bind together the moments before and after that instant when "nothing happens." Such a process constitutes that inner force that can be termed "connecting all the arts through one intensity of mind."

"Indeed, when we come to face death, our life might be likened to a puppet on a cart (decorated for a great festival). As soon as one string is cut, the creature crumbles and fades."[8] Such is the image given of the existence of man, caught in the perpetual flow of life and death. This constructed puppet, on a cart, shows various aspects of himself but cannot come to life of itself. It represents a deed performed by moving strings. At the moment when the strings are cut, the figure falls and crumbles. *Sarugaku* too is an art that makes use of just such artifice. What supports these illusions and gives them life is the intensity of mind of the actor. Yet the existence of this intensity must not be shown directly to the audience. Should they see it, it would be as though they could see the strings of a puppet. Let me repeat again: the actor must make his spirit the strings, and without letting his audience become aware of them, he will draw together the forces of his art. In that way, true life will reside in his *Nō*.

In general, such attitudes need not be limited to the moments involved in actual performance. Morning and night alike, and in all the activities of daily life, an actor must never abandon his concentration, and he must retain his resolve.

Thus, if without ever slackening, he manages to increase his skills, his art of the *Nō* will grow ever greater. This particular point represents one of the most secret of all the teachings concerning our art. However, in actual rehearsal, there must be within this concentration some variations of tension and relaxation.

THE MOMENT OF PEERLESS CHARM

The character *myō* in the term *myōsho* [Peerless Charm] means "exquisite" or "delicate." But it also has the meaning of an appearance that transcends any specific form. Such a transcendence of form represents an expression of this Peerless Charm.

When one speaks of such moments in terms of the *Nō*, this Charm should exist in every aspect of our art, from the Two Basic Arts to gesture. Yet precisely where can it be located? It seems to be found nowhere. If an actor can possess this arresting power, he must be a performer of surpassing skill. However, if an actor is truly blessed with great talent, he will show from his beginnings some shadow of this Charm. The actor will not himself be conscious of it, but spectators of discernment will always find this quality within him. Ordinary spectators, on the other hand, will merely find that his performances are enjoyable in some mysterious fashion. And indeed even in the case of an actor of the highest skill, he will at best have come only to the realization that he somehow does possess this skill. Still, he will have no consciousness that he is practicing it at any given moment. An actor will possess this quality precisely because he does not recognize it; if such a moment could in any way be put into words, this Charm could no longer exist.

When one ponders carefully the substance of this Peerless Charm, can it not be said that an artist may approach it when he has truly learned his craft and attained Perfect Fluency, when he has transcended all stages of his art to the point where he performs everything with ease and exhibits every skill without care, thus achieving a selfless art that rises above any artifice? When an actor manages to ascend to the aesthetic level of Grace, will he indeed not be somewhat closer to this power of beauty? These matters must be pondered deeply.

JUDGING THE *NŌ*

When it comes to making crucial judgments concerning the *Nō*, people invariably have different ideas. It is difficult indeed for any particular *Nō* to match the tastes of everyone. Thus the basis of judgment should be made on the strength of the performances of accomplished actors who enjoy a wide reputation.

First of all, one should look and listen with great care during actual performances so as to understand why some

---

[8]A saying attributed to a priest of the Rinzai sect of Zen Buddhism in Japan, Gettan Sowkow (1316?–1389).

plays succeed and why others do not. Plays that succeed possess three qualities: Sight, Sound, and Heart.

As for the *Nō* that succeeds through Sight, the stage atmosphere will be colorful from the beginning, the dancing and music will have an attractive air, the spectators, noblemen and commoners alike, will be spontaneous in their praise, the atmosphere brilliant. Such is the *Nō* that is effective to the eye. It goes without saying that such a performance will please the discriminating; even those who know nothing of the *Nō* will find such a performance enjoyable. However, concerning such performances, there is one point that an actor must keep in mind. If the performance passes by altogether too well and with too much appeal, and if every aspect seems enjoyable, then the feelings of the audience will tend to become over-stimulated, and their sensibilities in appreciating the details of the acting will be coarsened. For this part, an actor may be impetuous and, since he wants to exhaust every aspect of his art, will make no allowance for a slackening of pace, either for himself or for the audience. In an attempt to make every aspect of the performance successful, a surface brilliance is achieved, but the end results may be unsatisfactory. This kind of abuse arises when the play goes too well. On such an occasion, the play should be performed in a more restrained manner, all the artistic appearances made more moderate, and the eyes and ears of the spectators given some surcease, so that they can have an occasion to rest and breathe easily and the audience can be given the quiet necessary to observe the really skillful elements in the performance. Then, if the results are successful, the plays that follow will seem stronger, so that, whatever the number of plays that may be staged, their fascination for the audience will never be exhausted. So it is that an effective *Nō* performance can be said to succeed through the art of Sight.

Nō that can be said to succeed through Sound shows from the very beginning a serious atmosphere. The music and text are chosen in accord with the season [and the time of day], thus creating a gentle, relaxed, and enjoyable effect. Above all, it is the chant that should create the main impression. Only a peerless artist of highest experience can achieve this effect during a performance. However, the kind of sober flavor engendered by such a performance cannot be understood by country audiences and the like.

This kind of *Nō,* when performed by a peerless actor, can give rise through his spiritual resources to various aesthetic qualities that make the play become more and more enjoyable as it goes along. In the case of an artist of the second rank, however, whose art has not fully matured, he will cause the day's performance to lag if he decides to follow such a presentation by a famous actor with one of his own in a *Nō* that is also of this particular variety. When such a player follows the kind of performance that has successfully created a cool and quiet atmosphere, as he continues on he will only create a gloomy mood in the succeeding plays. An actor must be aware of this difficulty and put his energies into his performance in order to begin to increase the number of stimulating moments in the play, so as to bring an element of surprise to his audience. Of course, as a truly peerless player has naturally a wide repertory and is highly trained in body and mind, his art will be effectively manifested in his dance and chant, so that his performance will naturally progress in an enjoyable manner. A player of the second rank, however, must take great care so that, as the performance continues, the atmosphere does not go dead. Concerning this point, when thinking to keep up the atmosphere of his performance, the actor must not reveal his methods to the audience. The spectators must merely feel that the performance is enjoyable. Such is the actor's secret, based on long-mastered precedents as to how to perform successfully. All I have written above can explain how a *Nō* can succeed through Sound.

When it comes to the *Nō* that succeeds through the Heart, a truly gifted actor of *sarugaku,* after he has mastered the whole repertory, will have the ability even when performing a play of no particular distinction in terms of chant, dance, gesture, or plot, to create even in the midst of a certain dullness a particular poetic quality that can move the hearts of his audience. This level of attainment is not usually grasped even by connoisseurs; how much more beyond any imaginings of a country audience must be such an art. Indeed, such a quality must seem to represent the propitious manifestation of an actor of the highest abilities. Such a performance can be termed a *Nō* that succeeds through the Heart, a *Nō* that surpasses technique, a *Nō* that transcends outward manifestation.

An actor must learn to discriminate between the kinds of artistic qualities that display those various differences. There are spectators of discernment who do not really understand the art of the *Nō.* On the other hand, there are those spectators who possess a true grasp of the essential nature of the *Nō* but who cannot observe subtle differences. Those who have both a practical and a theoretical understanding of *Nō* represent the highest level of spectator. For example, there are occasions when a fine performance does not meet with success, and times when an unskilled performance pleases, but no one must use these exceptions as a basis for one's general judgments. For example, truly gifted players customarily have success with outdoor and other large-scale performances, while lesser actors perform profitably at smaller playing areas at country fairs or on other such occasions.

An actor who understands how to make his performance attractive to his audience brings good fortune to the *Nō.*

Then too, a spectator who understands the heart of the actor as he watches a performance is a gifted spectator. The following might be said concerning making judgments: forget the specifics of a performance and examine the whole. Then forget the performance and examine the actor. Then forget the actor and examine his inner spirit. Then, forget that spirit, and you will grasp the nature of the Nō.

THE MATTER OF MASTERING THE CHANT

There are two aspects to the study of the chant. The person who composes the text should know the principles of music and how to make the words flow together in a euphonious fashion. For his part, the performer who sings must know how to fit the melody to the words and to chant the syllables and words in a clear and correct manner. Since the beauty of the chant derives from the syllables and the words performed, the melodies must be composed in such a way that the pronunciation is always correctly represented, and the linking between the phrases smooth and flexible. When the chant is performed, if the singer has mastered these principles and really knows them well, both the composition and the performance will reinforce each other and produce an enjoyable effect. As this is true, a standard should be established by which the melody is attached to the chant. The flow of the phrases must be attractive, and the sound characteristics of the text must be in harmony with the melody, so that the results will of themselves be musical. That is, the melody provides the basic frame for the musical composition, and the artistic effect derives from the spirit of the performer, who shades the melody in terms of the flow of the phrases. Thus an actor has various elements of music that he must master—the physical problems of using the breath, the development of his own emotional concentration in order to direct it properly, and the understanding of the melody, as well as the music that lies behind the melody. In terms of practicing the musical aspects of Nō, the following should be taken to heart: forget the voice and understand the shading of the melody. Forget the melody and understand the pitch. Forget the pitch and understand the rhythm.

In learning the art of musical performance, there is a proper order to be followed: first, the words of the text must be learned thoroughly; then the melody must be mastered; then the actor must learn how to color the melody; finally, he must learn how to apply the proper pitch accent. After all these steps are taken, the actor must concentrate on how to bring his performances to flower. At every stage, an emphasis must be placed on the rhythm. When practicing the voice, miss no occasion to obtain this kind of training, so beneficial to personal development.

Then there is the matter of accent in musical performance. In the case of auxiliary words or particles, the prob-

lem is not a serious one. However, mistaken accents on such substantive words as nouns, verbs, and adjectives[9] are harmful. Understanding the importance of this distinction is crucial. Serious study must be given to this point. When speaking of mistaken accents on these substantive words, I refer to pronunciations with improper pitch accent, which affect the meaning of the words. In the case of particles and auxiliary words, the problem has to do with the voicing of such sounds as te, ni, ha, and the like. Concerning correct pronunciation for these sounds, when the flow of words in the course of the singing moves effectively, even if the pronunciation becomes altered to some extent, so long as the rhythm is correct, the problem is not a serious one. It is said that words that make a heavy or a light effect, that are clear or complex in sound, depend on the forward flow of the text. In addition, there are various customs and rules concerning sound changes when words are juxtaposed together. Study the transmitted teachings carefully on this matter. As concerns particles that come at the end of phrases, such as ha, ni, no, o, ka, te, mo, shi, and so forth, even if there should be some deviation in their pronunciation, there will be nothing disagreeable in the sound as long as the melody is tasteful. In other words, the movement of the melody should be supported by these various particles. In the chanting, every syllable must not simply be pronounced in a flat manner, with an equal length and emphasis given to all of them. Those sounds which represent substantive words should be pronounced briskly, so that their meaning remains clear, while the sound of the auxiliary syllables can be rather freely regulated—slow or fast—in order to make the melody more colorful.

[Remember that] the principle of using four basic tones is used [in Chinese].[10]

In The History of the Former Han by Pan Ku,[11] it is written [concerning the legendary origin of the melody] that "as for the origins of the twelve-pitch gamut, a man [named Ling

---

[9]That is, independent, uninflected words usually written with Chinese characters.

[10]Zeami doubtless wished to stress the importance of proper pitch accent for substantive words in Japanese, usually written in Chinese characters, by this reference to the Chinese language. For a concise description of the function of tones in classical Chinese, see James J.Y. Liu, The Art of Chinese Poetry, pages 21–22.

[11]Pan Ku's history was the first of the so-called dynastic histories of China. For a general description of the text and its subject matter, see Burton Watson, Early Chinese Literature, pages 103–109. Zeami's quotation contains minor errors. For an explanation of the significance of the passage in the history of Chinese music, see Kenneth J. DeWoskin, A Song for One or Two, pages 59–61.

Lun] climbed Mount Kun-lun and, hearing the voice of the male and female phoenix, created the six *ryo* pitches and six *ritsu* pitches of the twelve-pitch gamut." *Ritsu,* since it is derived from the voice of the male phoenix, represents the principle of *yang. Ryo,* which imitates the voice of the female phoenix, represents *yin. Ritsu* represents the kind of sound that goes from high to low, and the breath is inhaled. *Ryo* represents a sound that goes from low to high, and the breath is exhaled. Breathing appropriate to *ritsu* is produced through a state of tension; *ryo* is produced in a state of ease. Then too, *ritsu* can be considered as appropriate to Non-Being, *ryo* appropriate to Being. Thus, a thin, high voice [a "vertical" voice] is appropriate for *ritsu,* while a thick, low voice [a "horizontal" voice] is appropriate for *ryo.*

In the *Analects,*[12] it is written that "the hides of the bear, the tiger, and the panther are used as targets [for the hunter's] arrow. The tiger is the prince's target, the panther the nobleman's target, and the bear the target of the officers of state." If this sequence is followed, it would doubtless be correct to write "tiger, panther, bear." But for the sake of euphony, the order is changed to "bear, tiger, and panther."

THE ULTIMATE KEYS OF OUR ART

The contents of this work have now all been set forth. There is nothing to learn in addition to what has been set down here. Indeed, there is nothing else involved but to "understand the *Nō*" with one's very being. If this fundamental principle is not observed, the various matters discussed here will serve no purpose. If an actor really wishes to master the *Nō,* he must set aside all other pursuits and truly give his whole soul to our art; then, as his learning increases and his experience grows, he will gradually of himself reach a level of awareness and so come to understand the *Nō.*

First of all, an actor must deeply believe what his teacher tells him and take those instructions to heart. The numerous teachings involved are contained in the various points discussed in this book, but the actor must truly master them and engrave them on his heart, so that, when he is actually in a performance, he can try out in practice the various things that he has learned. Then, as a result, he will value those principles, and, as he comes to revere the art of *Nō,* he will as time passes come to understand the real secret of success in our art. In whatever artistic pursuit, one studies and then understands, so that he will know how to carry out his art in ac-

tual practice. In *sarugaku* as well, one must study and learn, so that these various principles can be put into practice.

All these secret teachings can be summed up by saying that an actor must continually earn mastery through constant practice, from his apprenticeship through his old age. When I speak of studying through old age, I refer to the fact that from the time of an actor's apprenticeship until the peak of his maturity there are various arts that must be mastered. It is only from the time that an actor passes forty that he can slowly begin to make use of restraint in his physical performance. In other words, he must learn the means of artistic expression appropriate for an actor of his age. When the actor passes fifty, then he can begin to use the technique of "doing nothing." This represents a crucial stage in an actor's career. The first thing to learn at this point is the necessity to limit the kinds of plays in the actor's repertory. His musical performance now becomes the center of his style of performance, his acting style becomes simpler, and his dancing and gestures grow more restrained. He should only give a hint of his former colorful appearance. In fact, the art of music remains the one area in which an actor at this age can excel. This is true because an older voice will have exhausted its natural and untrained qualities, and the voice that remains will be highly polished, in whatever style of vocal production the actor may wish to use; thus whatever music is chanted, the results will always be enjoyable. This is a sure means to achieve a successful performance. Thus an older actor should learn carefully to make his age serve his own artistic purposes and work all the harder to train himself appropriately.

Concerning roles that can be played by older actors, old men and women are doubtless the most appropriate. However, depending on the strong points of a particular actor, he may not necessarily be limited to these two. Still, an actor who wishes to create an atmosphere of serenity in his performance will find the roles of older characters best suited to him. If his special strength lies in roles demanding energetic movement, however, those will not be suitable for the aesthetic qualities appropriate to the art of older actors. In any case, within these limits, he should perform his dances and gestures while limiting himself to six-tenths or seven-tenths of "what is felt by the heart is ten," so as to perform in a manner appropriate to his age. Such is the means to master the art suitable for the older actor.

In our Kanze school, there is one phrase that is of infinite value concerning the fundamentals of any artistic accomplishment: an actor must never forget the experiences he has undergone as a beginning artist. In the transmitted teaching, there are three explanations provided for this. Accordingly:

—He must never forget the fresh experiences he first went through as a young performer.

---

[12]No such passage appears in the *Analects,* but a somewhat similar one does appear in the *Chou li* or *Rites of Chou.* Both this passage and the preceding section on *The History of the Former Han* were added to Zeami's text in the form of notes, and may not be by his hand.

—At each level of accomplishment, there are new levels of fresh experience that the actor must encounter for the first time, as though he were a beginner, and then never forget.

—After the actor becomes older, there are still new stages of fresh experience that must never be forgotten.

Here are the teachings contained in these maxims in more detail.

Concerning the maxim that "he must never forget the fresh experiences he first went through as a young performer," it can be said that, if the actor retains the feelings he had at that time, he will profit from them in many ways as he grows older. As the expression has it, "an understanding of errors in the past will turn them into advantages in the future." Or, "seeing the cart in front turn over serves as a warning to the cart that follows." Forgetting the arts one has learned as a beginner amounts in fact to forgetting the skills an actor may possess at a later point in his career. The fact that his art has been perfected and his reputation has been made can only be the result of the development of his own skill. But if he does not take cognizance of how his skills have improved, he will unknowingly revert to the level he possessed as a beginner. Such a reversal means that his art is actually degenerating. His ability to maintain a sense of his present level of accomplishment shows that he has not forgotten the skills learned as a young performer. I cannot stress this principle too strongly: if an actor loses his memory of his unmatured skills, he will be forced to revert to them. On the other hand, if he does not forget them, his later accomplishments will be genuine. And, if they are genuine, his abilities, as they increase, will insure that his art can never retrogress. Thus, this truth can serve as a distinction between truth and error.

Young actors must therefore take cognizance of the current level of their accomplishment, realize that they are still only beginners, and understand that they must not lose sight of their own skills that still remain to be developed. In this way, they can truly work to lift the level of their art. To lose consciousness of the level of one's ability is to forget how to advance in the art; under such circumstances, an artist's skill will not increase. Therefore, young artists must never lose their perceptions of their actual level of ability.

Secondly, there is the principle that "at each level of accomplishment, there are new levels of fresh experience that the actor must encounter for the first time, as though he were a beginner, and then never forget." This means that, for the actor, from his beginnings through the height of his career and into his old age, there are always various suitable means of expression he must practice and learn. On all these occasions he can be seen as a beginner. Therefore, if at each stage he abandons and forgets what has come before, he will only possess the artistic ability that matches what he is doing at that particular moment in his career. If, on the other hand, he has managed to maintain in himself all the skills that he has previously mastered, so that he can still make use of them, then he can perform in an ever-increasing variety of styles. These "new skills" refer to those he has learned for the first time at every successive stage in his career. Maintaining them all and combining them together at one time means that he has forgotten none of them. It is just through such efforts that a *shite* becomes an artist of wide-ranging abilities. Thus one must never forget what he has learned at each stage of his career.

Finally, "after the actor becomes older, there are still new stages of fresh experience that must never be forgotten." Truly, although there are limits on a human life, the *Nō* never comes to an end. If an actor has mastered every technique appropriate to each stage in his career, then when it comes time to learn what is correct for an older actor, he will still be able to enjoy a new experience even at this late stage in his career. If an actor still possesses this attitude when he reaches this high level, his art will still contain everything about the *Nō* that he has managed to learn before. When he passes the age of fifty, as I have said, an actor need have no other plan than to "do nothing special." To face the challenge of having no other technique than to "do nothing special"—is the art of an older actor really so different than that of a beginner?

So it is that if an actor manages to live his whole life without forgetting how and what he has learned at any one time in his career, the level of his art will steadily increase during his last years, and his abilities will never degenerate. To live one's life without ever exhausting the depths of the *Nō* represents the most profound principle of our school, a principle that must be passed on from child to grandchild, generation to generation as a secret teaching of our house. Passing on the importance of these attitudes I have described above will serve as a means to develop the artistry of all generations to come. On the other hand, if an actor forgets this "experience of a beginner," he will surely not be able to pass the conception along to others in later generations. An artist must not forget this "experience of a beginner," but must convey it to those who follow, for countless generations.

In addition to what I have written here, another who studies the *Nō* may, depending on his own abilities and discernment, be able to discover still other truths.

All of the *Teachings on Style and the Flower* (Zeami's treatise on Noh theater), beginning with the chapter called "The Practice of the *Nō* in Relation to the Age of the Actor" down to the "Separate Secret Teaching," is a secret document that makes clear the *Nō* by using the metaphor of the flower. That text represents an account of various elements in the art of my father Kan'ami, set down twenty years after his death, and serves as a record of what I learned from him. The present treatise, on the other hand, represents discoveries that have occurred to me from time to time concerning the *Nō* over a period of forty years, down to the time of my own advanced age. Summing them up, I have written out my observations in six sections and twenty parts,[13] which I leave behind as a memento of my art.

Ōe 31 [1424], 1st day of the 6th month

Zeami

---

[13]The indication of twenty parts suggests that the manuscript was originally arranged in some different fashion.

This teaching was passed on by Zeami himself for the succeeding generations of his house and should not be shown to actors from other troupes. Luckily, thanks to the Will of Heaven, which knows that my heart reveres the art of the *Nō*, this manuscript has come into my hands. This secret teaching forms the very core of the art of our school, and it has been written down to guide the art of our family. It is a text of fearsome power. Thus it must not be shown carelessly to others.

Eikyō 9 [1437], 8th month, 8th day

Komparu Zenchiku[14]

---

[14]Komparu's signature is an attribution; the identity of the writer is not altogether certain.

CRITICAL PERSPECTIVES

GRAHAM LEY

"Aristotle's *Poetics*, Bharatamuni's *Natyasastra*, and Zeami's Treatises: Theory as Discourse" (2000)

Graham Ley has written widely about Greek and Renaissance culture and performance, and is the author of From Mimesis to Interculturalism: Readings of Theatrical Theory Before and After Modernism. *In this essay, he compares the understandings of theater and performance expressed by three of the world's major classical theater traditions, as they are expressed by Aristotle, Bharatamuni, and Zeami. Students often find these essays challenging, and Ley offers a number of ways not only to address each author, but to compare between them.*

Comparisons between the Greek and *nō* theatres, and between the Greek and Sanskrit theatres and the theoretical writings associated with them, have their own traditions in modern scholarship and take a variety of forms.[1] Inevitably insights about the qualities of the original theatrical experience are a major objective of such comparisons. The theoretical writings can be seen credibly as repositories of information capable, to a degree, of being recomposed into understanding and appreciation. In addition, certain leading concepts, such as those that gather round the English word "imitation" (Greek *mimesis,* Sanskrit *anukarana,* Japanese *monomane*) predictably attract major critical attention.

Treating all three bodies of writing as forms of composition or discourses in their own right is an alternative approach that can yield different results and illuminate different aspects of theory and its relationship to practice. The material is complex, of course, and any initial treatment is bound to have its limitations. Here I want to consider various characteristics of the *Poetics,* the *Natyasastra,* and Zeami's treatises under two provisional headings. The first, context and status, is documentary in tone. The second, the discourse of theory, includes critical analysis of writings.

CONTEXT AND STATUS

The *Poetics* of Aristotle has a wide and discernible context that embraces texts now known only by name or inference. It begins in the work itself, which almost certainly included a second part on comedy and may well have contained an excursus on katharsis that amplified the minimal mention of the concept in what survives of the text.[2] In addition, Aristotle is known to have written a work, *On Poets,* in dialogue form and in three books, as well as books on *Victories in the Festivals of Dionysos* and on *Records of Production (Didaskaliai).* The last of these were certainly documentary rather than critical or theoretical. These works should be placed alongside six books of *Homeric Problems*—which may have been related to the kind of treatment epic receives in the later part of the surviving text of the *Poetics*—and a work *On Music.*

The surviving *Poetics* is an esoteric work, which means that it was closely associated with Aristotle's oral teaching in his school, the Lykaion (Lyceum). This status contrasts with the lost *On Poets,* which belonged to the exoteric works designed to be reproduced in manuscript and read outside the school. One should note that the written dialogue form had been thoroughly established by Plato as a mode of promulgating the advantages of the pursuit of spoken, philosophical dialectic. There is, of course, a remarkable irony here: Aristotle's *On Poets* has disappeared into minimal fragments, while his *Poetics* has had a massive influence as writing in the public domain. But further questions remain: what exactly was retained for oral teaching, and why was it retained? Aristotle's intentions cannot be known, nor is it clear how the esoteric writings (all of the works we have by Aristotle) came to replace the exoteric writings in circulation. One possible answer is that this kind of retention within the teaching system might relate to a sense of an exclusive audience (plausibly his pupils) and transmission within the school (of ideas to successive teachers).[3]

Certain aspects of context and status are perhaps less problematic. Aristotle in his documentary works on the dramatic festivals is clearly concerned with the record—and hence with the formation of what we might call a classic sense of achievement in drama. This is plainly a characteristic of the *Poetics,* which is not by any means a manifesto for initiative or change. This consolidation of a classic sense is also apparent in the contemporary activities associated with Lykourgos in Athens, where Aristotle was repeatedly resident. The theatre of Dionysos received a lavish reinstatement in stone, which must have fixed the form in which dramas might be played; Lykourgos also assured a definitive collection of past playscripts and secured finance for statues of playwrights. We can also be reasonably clear about the existence of a kind of writing called a *techne,* or an "art." What these treatises exactly contained is unknown, but they were written on a specific skill often by a practitioner. Sophocles wrote a treatise *On the Chorus;* the sculptor and bronze-caster Polykleitos wrote a *Canon* (his famous statue *Spear-Carrier* or *Doryphoros* was also called "The Canon"); and other specialist works are also testified. The absence of a *techne* on dramaturgy permits Aristotle to write one.

Quite why he should is another matter, and in this respect the evidence of his *Rhetoric* is interesting. The *Rhetoric* is itself a *techne,* of what could be considered an unrespectable art, and Aristotle is clearly aiming to provide rhetoric with a respectable and indeed a philosophically sound status as a public activity. Public speaking, in the political or legal spheres, was a major constituent of Athenian public life, but Aristotle was of the opinion that many of its more serious aspects had not been considered in any previous written treatment (*techne*) of the art. In book 3 of the *Rhetoric,* in writing of the importance of "delivery" or "performance" by the orator or the actor, Aristotle incidentally notes that "in the case of tragedy actors now have more effect than the poets," and it is clear that he is thinking of success in the dramatic competitions (Aristotle 1991, 216).[4] A theory of the emotions related to that in the *Poetics;* a consideration of "style" or *lexis,* also prominent in the *Poetics;* the importance of argument, rhythm, and the arrangement of the parts of a speech—all suggest that the rehabilitation of rhetoric as a serious and social art in the *Rhetoric* offers us a helpful context for understanding the discursive context of the *Poetics.*

The final and overwhelming part of the context is the formulation of the status of philosophy, and I shall return to this issue in the following section. Inherited concepts are of great importance, and much of our understanding of the *Poetics* and its influence depends on appreciating the significance of the Platonic term "mimesis." Platonic philosophy, like that of Aristotle, is deeply political, concerned with the values and practices of the polis and its inhabitants, and the principal claim of Platonic philosophy was to a close relationship with truth. These two characteristics combine to make philosophical discourse supposedly the most powerful and secure discourse, capable of subjecting social practice to a controlling analysis. The *Poetics* is supported by a web of such philosophical analyses and arguments having to do with cognition, ethics, and psychology. Drama is something to be known, not merely practiced, and to be knowable it needs to be identified or fixed in best practice.[5]

The *Natyasastra* is undoubtedly a compendium, and as such it is open to interesting or frustrating questions about authorship and to what one might call the analytic or unitarian tendencies—namely, the inclination to believe that

the compilation is (respectively) the work of many or substantially of one.[6] As a consequence, its date is open to debate, as well, and arguments exist for placing it between about the fourth century B.C. and a millennium later. The situation is not helped by uncertainty about the dates or eras of other significant Sanskrit writings. The mythical figure of Bharata as a sage with disciples, one who is capable of cursing an aberrant performer, is prominent in one of the plays of Kalidasa, *Vikramorvasiya,* and the ironic mythology of the playwright accords perfectly well—in a minimal way—with what is found in the *Natyasastra.* But even a fixed or nearly certain date for the activity of Kalidasa would not in principle inform us greatly about the relationship between theory and practice.[7]

But there are more substantial indicators of a context that is bound up closely with status. The claim of the treatise as it stands is that of a fifth Veda, a position that might otherwise be accorded to *itihasa,* or mythical learning, as represented by epic poetry, notably the *Mahabharata;*[8] I shall return to this issue later. But the status of the theatre itself is far more dubious. The performers of drama are cursed with a position in the lowest caste of Sudras, while the theory and the mythical status of its compiler Bharata are clearly raised above that demeaning level. This dilemma advertises a problematic role for the compendium in its first principles—and in particular for the status of the *natyacarya* and the *sutradhara* who control and direct the activities of a company of players.

There are further aspects of context that present themselves immediately. The compilation of a *sastra* on the theatre plainly invites comparison with the status of other *sastra* writings, such as the *Manu Smrti* on *dharma* (duty, religious and social obligation), the *Arthasastra* (ascribed to Kautilya) on *artha,* worldly good, and hence politics, and the *Kamasutra* (of Vatsyayana) on *kama,* or pleasure, specifically sexual satisfaction. The generally discursive *sastra* literature of treatises follows the esoteric sutra literature of condensed aphorisms, originally associated with cult and the rituals observed in the Veda literature.[9] The *Natyasastra* itself insists (in chapter 35) that knowledge of the other *sastra* writings is essential for the *sutradhara* (usually translated as the "director" of the company); the three varieties of the stage building are originally conceived, it is claimed, in accordance with the *sastra* literature. As a text, the *Natyasastra* is plainly writing itself into a complex intertextuality.

Religious sanction is thoroughly apparent, not only in the founding or charter myth of the opening section (and in chapters 22 and 36), but in the subsequent and precise instructions for preparing a playhouse and for the preliminaries of performance. Bharata is a sage who is invited by the gods to assume the implementation of the fifth Veda invented by Brahma, compiled from elements of the other four, but unlike them open to those of the Sudra caste. Despite this last provision, theatrical performance initially pertains to the gods as audience, and even to the demons, and the gods are installed all over the stage. A further performance concerned with dharma, *kama,* and *artha* is then shown to Siva, who provides the religious sanction for dance in drama. But the extent to which the activity is placed in the ritual world by this fifth Veda is apparent in the roles prescribed for the *natyacarya* in the worship of the stage, where he takes over from the opening prayers of the Brahmins (chapter 3), and for the *sutradhara* in the preliminaries to performance, in which he is succeeded by the *sthapaka* (introducer), who should resemble the *sutradhara* and is himself a Brahmin. The distinction between *natyacarya* and *sutradhara* in the *Natyasastra* is by no means clear, but the treatise affords them the role of priests in ritual observation consonant with the Vedas, and comprehensive in its scope.[10] From conception to the moment of performance the *Natyasastra* ensures an unbroken thread of religious engagement for the theatre.

The ritual is not, however, the only form of status assured to the theatre by the *sastra.* Appropriate conduct, as described and prescribed in the *sastra* literature, will not only be religious in its orientation. The categorization with which the *Natyasastra* abounds is part of a scheme of order, of appropriateness, which may be applied as much to character as to gesture. The discipline of the allocation of Sanskrit and Prakrit speech to characters (in chapter 18) acknowledges the distinctions of caste and the demeaning circumstances that may qualify caste status, while the modes of address to be followed in drama (chapter 19) secure conformity with the established order. In this respect the compilation of rules in the *sastra* is an assurance to authority of respectability for the practice of theatre. Hence what may appear as no more than an established formulaic opening to chapter 19, addressed to the best of the Brahmins who have questioned Bharata from the beginning of the treatise, actually presents order to those at its apex. The creation of a *sastra,* not the creation of drama, is the continuing subject of the *Natyasastra,* and that creation offers both context and status to a theatre practice, which is all the more likely to wish to conform to its precepts for just those reasons.

In the *Natyasastra,* it is the "sons of Bharata" who are to carry on and perform the tradition established by their father and received from Brahma and Siva. In the coda to *Shūgyoku tokka,* Takeda Komparu Hachemon records in 1656 that as a result of the unlucky death of his elder brother, Ujikatsu Shichirō, his father had felt it necessary to pass on the "secret book" to him (Rimer and Yamazaki 1984, 147).[11] He himself is now passing it on to his successor, since "the

line of transmission must not be allowed to be interrupted." This short statement reflects, somewhat pathetically, what had happened at the death of Zeami's older son, Motomasa, in 1432, an event that confirmed the transmission of Zeami's written teachings out of the male succession to his son-in-law Komparu Zenchiku.[12] For Takeda Komparu Hachemon the possession of texts is a signal of the right to succeed: "Since the beginning, these secrets were given to the head of the house alone and it has never been permitted for other children or other descendants to make inquiries concerning these profound secrets" (Rimer and Yamazaki 1984, 147). For Zeami, writing the original treatise on the *nō* (*Fūshikaden;* 1402 with later additions) had been an initiative undertaken explicitly to record the teachings of his father Kan'ami, who had died in 1384. The testament was to serve the "house" of his family, and perhaps the most explicit occasion for its composition was Zeami's sense of a decline in the *nō.* This is first expressed as a fear in *Fūshikaden* (from 1400) but quickly turns into a statement in the same work (from 1402) and reappears later in *Shikadō* of 1420 as a constant if theoretical conviction (pp. 30, 37, and 72 respectively). The motif of decline is not hard to trace in Aristotle's attitude to the art of tragedy, and the threat of decadence is a minor mythical theme in the *Natyasastra* as well. Like success, it is a prominent motive for the creation of theoretical texts, and it is inevitably used to affirm a normative code.

The motif of decline, in alliance with the transmission of a secretive authority, not only issues the strongest imperative to the succession but also presupposes a history of achievement. In his coda to *Shūgyoku tokka,* Takeda Komparu Hachemon takes the line of transmission back to "our ancestor Hata no Kōkatsu." In doing so he reiterates and affirms the genealogy of *nō* constructed for his successors, and in honor of his father, by Zeami at the start of his first treatise, *Fūshikaden.* In this genealogy, Hata no Kōkatsu was commissioned by Prince Shōtokuto provide entertainments called *sarugaku* for the sake of peace, and this art was inherited by his descendants, to be performed at the shrines of Kasuga and Hie. A religious sanction for the ancestral *nō,* performed for the public good, is allied to imperial patronage, in a prefiguring of the patronage extended by the shogun to Kan'ami and his son Zeami. The mythology is elaborated later in *Fūshikaden,* when the actions of Shōtuku are doubled by those of the Emperor Murakami, who revives the patronage by extending it to a successor of Kōkatsu named Hata no Ujiyasu. His descendant is identified as the head of the Komparu company by Zeami (pp. 34–36).

Sarugaku is dignified in its history by these associations. There exists a description of a *sarugaku* entertainment from the eleventh century by Fujiwara no Akihira, which includes mimetic pieces alongside juggling and acrobatics, featuring such figures as an aged local magistrate, a frightened monk, "a respected nun who . . . seeks the gift of swaddling clothes for the baby shortly to be born," and "the official . . . believed to be a serious man [who] one day whistles unintentionally the tune of a flute" (Inoura 1971, 43–44). Chinese *san-yueh*, "which included comic mime, singing and dancing, as well as acrobatics and conjuring tricks," was "transmitted to Japan in the eighth century, both from China itself and from Korea" (Konishi 1991, 520). The performers of *sarugaku* were originally "exempted from taxes and labor levies," and when this exemption was withdrawn in 782 many chose to remain outside the census and hence were considered and effectively classed as outcasts: *semmin* (ibid.). The continuing fragility of social status for the performer even in the later period is reflected in the disapproval of the aristocrat Go-oshikōji Kintada for the favor shown by the shogun to the boy Zeami: "*Sarugaku* like this is the occupation of beggars, and such favor for a *sarugaku* player indicates disorder in the nation" (Hare 1986, 16). Indeed, as modern biographical studies have disclosed, patronage was to desert Zeami later.

But *Sarugaku nō* is given more than a recurrent myth of high patronage to enhance its functional discipline of self-respect. Although he seemingly dismisses an origin in India and a time scale that stretches back to the gods at the opening of *Fūshikaden*, Zeami returns to both themes with greater conviction and to greater effect later in the treatise. The story of the dance of Uzume drawing the sun goddess Amaterasu from the cave, which may be found in the cosmogony of the eighth-century *Nihongi*, becomes a foundation myth for *sarugaku* (Rimer and Yamazaki 1984, 31–32).[13] This initiative by Zeami parallels the divine myths for the origin of poetry proposed in the famous preface by Tsurayuki to the first imperial anthology, *Kokin Waka Shū*, of the ninth century. India assumes significance because it permits Zeami to ascribe a Buddhist origin to *sarugaku* and claims precedence over China, the true historical source of *san-yueh*, which is nonetheless permitted to enter the multiple frame as the spiritual nationality of Hatano Kōkatsu (pp. 32–33).

The relationship of the creation and composition of the treatises to the poetics of *waka* and linked verse is most apparent in the adoption of the value term *"yugen"* (often translated as "grace"), but the centrality of the flower imagery cannot be ignored.[14] It is found in Tsurayuki and Yoshimoto, a contemporary of Zeami's father, whose influence on Zeami has been alleged, and Zeami's appropriation of *yugen* and the flower to the actor's performance represents his most profound theoretical elevation of the disciplined art of the *nō*.[15] In *Fūshikaden*, Zeami admitted that *yugen* was traditionally identified with a rival style of *sarugaku*, the *Omi*, in

contrast to the traditional identification of Zeami's own Yamato style with role playing or "imitation," *monomane* (Rimer and Yamazaki 1984, 38). A mediation of these two concepts, under the presiding aspirational imagery of the flower, occupies much of the labor of the treatises, one that is rendered fraught by the elusiveness of taste in the dominant patrons.[16]

In *Fūshikaden*, an outstanding performer is "one whose speech lacks no refinement and whose appearance creates a feeling of grace." In Kakyō (1424), "grace is best represented in the character of the nobility," their appearance, and their way of speaking (pp. 3 and 93 respectively). Those from the lower orders who are represented in *nō* must "exhibit the same appeal, despite whatever differences they may show in their social positions." By "living in the capital, an actor is in the proper environment." And "if the praise he earns is not from those who live in the capital, it can have little significance for him" (pp. 94, 96, and 95 respectively). *Yugen* is a certain sign of acceptance and status for Zeami: it is considered "the highest ideal of perfection in many arts" and thus can be regarded as "the highest principle" of the *nō* (p. 92, again from Kakyō). Creating a composed performance that accords with the taste of the nobility—and maintains it with the continuity afforded to poetry—is the intricate and paradoxical aspiration of these written treatises for an ephemeral art.

THE DISCOURSE OF THEORY

European poetics is significantly lacking in a myth of origin, although modernity has often made use of the Greek experience to create one. Epic poetry, of course, alluded to the muse or the Muses, though the Homeric poems are modest on the subject. (The muse is no more than *thea*, "goddess," in the first line of Homer's *Iliad*.) Only Hesiod is expansive in his *Theogony*. In the opening of that poem, Hesiod is approached by these daughters of Zeus on Mount Helicon and more or less compelled to sing of the gods and the Muses. But this seems little more than an elaborate conceit founded on the formulaic, invocatory appeal to a muse found in the opening lines of the Homeric epics. Their specializations were established far later, and for Aristotle they are of no importance whatsoever. Nor, indeed, is the imposing figure of Dionysos, whose ecstatic divinity presided over the theatrical festivals of Athens. The historical or social beginnings of tragedy and comedy do find a place in his introductory discussions in the *Poetics*, but they enter (in chapter 3) as rival claims based on etymology and dialect, or as the barest of developmental schemes, which takes two existing forms of celebration (dithyramb and phallic songs) and posits them cursorily as antecedents.

The lack of a divine charter for both epic and tragedy—or even for comedy and satyric drama, which were nothing if not explicitly Dionysiac—is striking, and its absence must direct us to a substitute. There is, certainly, some possibility of finding one in the briefly stated theory of katharsis, which is perhaps the most fascinating and enigmatic of all the theoretical topics in the *Poetics*.[17] Katharsis has a remarkable resonance in Greek culture, because it combines connotations of medical purging with those of religious purification, allowing Aristotle to claim for tragedy a function that had the widest possible implications for personal and public good.[18] The ceremonies introducing the dramatic festivals included a purification of the theatre, and much of modern criticism and theory has inclined to understand tragedy and comedy as religious drama, often with an emphasis on the ritual scapegoat and the sacrifice.[19] It would not be an exaggeration to state that the lack of a divine charter in the leading theoretical source of antiquity has prompted modern criticism to concentrate at least some of its energies on supplying one—whether in Nietzsche's heady combination of Apollo and Dionysos (Nietzsche 1967) or in Girard's immensely influential sacrificial theory, an anthropological substitute for ancient religious belief (Girard 1977).

Aristotle first defines tragedy at the opening of chapter 6 of the *Poetics* in the famous formulation beginning: "Tragedy, then, is a representation of an action that is worth serious attention, complete in itself, and of some amplitude" (Aristotle 1965, 38–39). The representation is of human beings performing actions, and the definition, like the central concerns of the analysis that follows it, is quite plainly indebted to Plato, who provided his own working definition in his ruthless critique of tragedy in book 10 of the *Republic*: "Drama represents human beings in action, either voluntarily or under compulsion; in that action they fare, as they think, well or ill, and experience joy or sorrow" (Plato 1974, 371). It is interesting that in these typical modern translations the general term "representation" is projected onto antiquity. "Mimesis" and its cognates are used by both Plato and Aristotle. Here Plato actually proposes that "the mimetic [art or skill, *techne*] imitates" (for "drama represents" in the preceding translation). For Plato, the implied reference to a *techne* recalls its fixed place in a descending valuation of "skills": from the user who alone really understands use, to the maker who attempts to provide it, to the artistic imitator. This order parallels an order of truth: from the ideal but intangible "forms" of things, to the skillful manifestation of them in creation, and, at the lowest level, to the realm of their imitation in art.[20] For Plato, the skills of the user and those of the maker (or artisan) are superior to those of the mimic artist.

In stating that Aristotle's definition of tragedy is delayed until chapter 6 of the *Poetics* I am drawing attention to the fact that the presiding definition is present from the beginning and is inherited from Plato. The *Poetics* assumes the challenge posed by Plato in book 10 for "men who are not poets themselves but who love poetry" to mount a defense of poetry in prose, "proving that she doesn't only give pleasure but brings lasting benefit to human life and human society" (Plato 1974, 376). Aristotle's approach to this task is to leave the descriptive definition of mimesis firmly in place for poetry but to alter it significantly—which he does most effectively by identifying it with "nature," or *phusis,* in chapter 4 of the *Poetics*. Mimesis is a natural activity and fundamental to learning. This is a complete contradiction of Plato's censure, which had lack of truth or an extremely remote access to the truth as its negative criterion for poetry and art. Aristotle also deftly plays with one of those Platonic triads mentioned earlier by emphasizing the terms *"poiesis"* and *"poietike"* in relation to the art (*techne*) of poetry. This picks up the second of Plato's levels in skills, that of the maker or artisan (the *techne* of *poiesis*)—and identifies it with the third or lower level of *mimetike*. By implication, both making and imitating are natural, and Plato's presiding skill of the user or consumer is picked up in the second "natural" aspect of mimesis for Aristotle, which is the pleasure derived from looking at or listening to imitations (again in chapter 4 of the *Poetics*). Thus all three Platonic skills are, in this synthesis, rendered natural and functional in learning by Aristotle. It is an immensely subtle resolution of apparent distinctions and difficulties, achieved without rejecting the primary definition established by the master.

Both mimesis and the concept of action entailed by it result in the domination of plot (*muthos*), action, and incident in the theoretical analysis of tragedy as a *poiesis,* and these matters are in the control of the *poietes,* the playwright, who directs his own composition. The beneficial effects to be felt by the community from the proper creation and execution of tragedy depend on the understanding of the playwright, and Aristotle's *Poetics* is almost exclusively a dramaturgical theory. It is conceived from first principles as a contribution to the discourse of philosophy and is addressed—as an esoteric discourse—to that elite which might attend to discussions in the Lykaion. But it is the philosophical discourse and the philosophical *logos* that preside over the foundation of European poetics, and this has had a slightly bizarre result: namely, the ultimate subordination of almost all attempted theories or disciplines of the art to concepts of nature and truth. In this respect, it is interesting to note that there is no evidence whatsoever to suggest that tragedy ever regarded itself as a mimesis or that the concept had any serious artistic viability before its dubious place in the Platonic order of illusion.[21]

The question of authorship in the *Natyasastra* is bound up with the narrative strategies of the compendium. Explicitly there are three gods who provide an impetus: Brahma, who responds to a request from the gods to create a fifth Veda for all the castes; Siva, who responds to an early performance with the categorization of dance (chapter 4); and Visnu, who provides the inspiration for the *vrtti* (styles or modes) of performance by his struggle with the two demons Madhu and Kaitabha (chapter 22). In fact, struggle lies at the heart of the creation of drama, since the demons are insulted by the first play, which takes the form of a fight between the gods and demons, who are defeated. Their anger leads them to paralyze the performers and prompts Indra to thrash the demons with his flagpole, which becomes a symbol of the gods 'protection for the stage. Brahma's resolution of the conflict is to reassure the demons that they are included in a total representation of existence, which pays close attention to *dharma, artha,* and *kama* (chapter 1). In this respect the *Natyasastra* in itself lays claim to the status of *itihasa,* as an instructive account of the affairs of gods, demons, and human beings, at the same time as it claims a comparable status for the products of its guidance as a *sastra*—namely, theatrical plays. This comprehensive scope entails an ambitious concept of *anukarana,* or mimicry, which must include the actions of all creation and by so doing can include the competence of the other *sastras,* as Brahma is made to claim in chapter 1.

The narrative frame of the *Natyasastra* is apparent in the opening and closing chapters, and the form it takes is a result of the foundation myth's emphasis on a divine origin. Drama is conceived as a performance for the gods, with the demons initially a disruptive component of the audience, and the subsequent involvement of Siva as lord of the dance leaves the foundation of a theatre and the establishment of the preliminary rites of performance firmly in that context. The priestly role assigned to the *natyacarya* and the *sutradhara,* and even the *sidhaka,* conforms to this vital charter for the fifth Veda. This divine context is ideal for the presentation of the ordering of an art which is the *sastra,* but it leaves unanswered the inevitable translation of a divinely conceived art to a human level. In chapter 36, the myth of Urvasi, one of the *apsara*s or heavenly dancers created by Brahma to dance gracefully in the original performance, offers a traditional vehicle for a descent from heaven to earth, since she is drawn to the king Pururavas.[22] But since Urvasi herself is withdrawn again to heaven, this myth is itself framed in chapter 36 by a further account, which has the king's grandson, Nahusa, requesting substitutes for Urvasi, who are provided by the sons of Bharata. They are then able to unite with the women of the harem of the king, who had been taught by

Urvasi, and provide a lineage of performers. On the condition of their fulfillment of the prescriptions of the *sastra,* the sons of Bharata are permitted to return to heaven.

The complexity of this translation from heaven to earth, and its narrative postponement in the *sastra,* are the result of the conflict between the aspirational claims of the "art" in its treatise and the low status accorded to performers. In chapter 36 the sons of Bharata became drunk with knowledge of the *Natyaveda* and produced a lampoon of the sages—who cursed them by expelling them from the caste of Brahmins and placing them among the Sudras, the lowest caste. It is Bharata who acts as a mediator and directs them to accept the opportunity presented by the request of the king Nahusa. The effect of this narrative subtlety is to reconcile the existence of a *sastra* and a fifth Veda with the performance of drama for all the classes, including the Sudras, prescribed in the opening chapter of the compendium.[23] But the *sastra* itself must not be compromised, and the concluding sections of chapter 36 reiterate its divine origins as a discourse, promising those who follow it comprehension of all the other *sastra*s and the achievement of a merit that accords with those who practice sacrifice and study the Vedas with divine approval.

The complex charter and justification of the concluding chapter of the *Natyasastra* is, like the treatise as a whole, a narrative recounted to the sages who question Bharata himself. The framework of question and extended answer is made explicit repeatedly in the opening of the treatise (chapters 1, 2, 5, and 6), prompting responses on the origins, on the playhouse, on the preliminaries, and on the *rasa*s, and is understood to cover the categorizing narrative until its renewal at the opening of the final chapter. But this concluding chapter, with its reference to the amplifications made to the *sastra* by Kohala and the sons of Bharata, returns to the subject of the composition of the treatise, which extends beyond the personage of Bharata. In this respect, it exhibits the same embracing knowledge of itself that we find in the very first chapter, where Bharata is initially introduced in the third person in his dialogue with the sages. The narrative and authoritative persona of Bharata is distanced in the frame from absolute ownership of the text as a document.

The text itself contains one further aspect that complicates our understanding of it as a discourse. In the opening to chapter six the sages request of Bharata an explanation of the "digest" or "thesis" (*samgraha*) alongside those of the "memorial verses" (*karika*) and "etymology" (*nirukta*). It is clear from Bharata's response (6.8–11) that the core element of these three terms is the aphoristic sutra, typically expressed in the (memorial) verse or verses that offer a rule or meaning, possibly reliant on etymology; when accompanied by a commentary, these form the digest, or *samgraha*. Chapters 6 and 7, which contain the discussion of the emotional theory of *bhava*s and *rasa*s, with the audience prominent in consideration, are indeed composed as a commentary surrounding and amplifying a set of these memorial verses, which are quoted directly. This format is particularly prominent in chapter 7, where the first memorial verses announce a relatively plain aesthetic order dependent on etymology: a *bhava* is an instrument of causation, which makes something "pervade," and so words and gestures illustrating the *bhava*s permit the meaning of the playwright to "pervade" the audience. In the traditional verse of 7.6, the determinants and consequents that control the *bhava*s are themselves "things which are created by human nature and are in accordance with the ways of human nature and with the ways of the world" (Ghosh 1967, 120). Most noticeably, the traditional verse of 7.7 in referring to *rasa* uses the metaphor of fire, the *rasa* spreading over the body as fire consumes a dry stick. This image seems to be completely detached from the more familiar metaphor of "taste" (itself expressed in other verses in 6.31–33), and apparently is designed to describe an effect rather than analyze a process.

The subsequent account of the *bhava*s, which forms the substance of chapter 7, is heavily based on memorial verses related to each state, with the treatise adding a commentary that is in many respects no more than a recapitulation of what is contained in the verses. Thus love, laughter, sorrow, and so forth are to be shown by an engagingly simple form of physical mimicry, or *anukarana*, appropriate to each state. In its most appealing form, this kind of precept offers observations such as "death . . . should be represented by the absence of any further movement of the body" (7.89; Ghosh 1967, 144). It is noticeable that the concluding *sattvika* states of the chapter, which are themselves perhaps the extreme of physical representation by the actor (sweating and goose pimples are two of them), are accompanied by no memorial verses (7.93–106). Since physicality is the express concern of the imitation already prescribed in the verses for the preceding *bhava*s, this is perhaps not surprising. There is only one reference in the memorial verses quoted in the chapter to the other *sastra*s, and that is descriptive, when the state of "assurance" is to be portrayed in the theatre by an actor instructing pupils and explaining the *sastra*s (7.82). The aesthetics of these verses of chapter 7, as observations on the art of performance, encode a relatively simple if detailed form of imitation, mimicry, or *anukarana*, which is far from carrying the conceptual connotations of the cosmic and universal "representation" determined by Brahma. But that is because the *Natyasastra* is very far from being just a handbook for performance, even for the play-

wright or the *natyacarya* or *sutradhara* to whom it is often implicitly addressed.

Both etymology and memorial verses play their part in Zeami's discourse, who has one complete treatise (*Kyūi*) composed as a commentary upon mystical aphorisms. But the intertextuality of the treatises is by no means confined to the influence of Zen Buddhism, as might be concluded from Zeami's later life and the tenor of *Kyūi*, including as it does quotations from Mencius, Confucius' *Analects,* and *waka* poetry. Also important in Zeami is a principle of *monomane,* or imitation, a term that modulates in the treatises from the relative simplicity of mimicry—such as that found in chapter 7 of the *Natyasastra*—to an imposing problematic of an art. As role playing is seen to be essential to the characteristics of Zeami's inheritance of Yamato *sarugaku,* so mimicry is essential to role playing, and it features early in *Fūshikaden.* Movement, gesture, and manner of speaking are clearly components of *monomane,* but costume may carry a great deal (emphasized in relation to women, mad persons, and warriors), as may the handling of defining properties (a fan, a sword); facial expression must not be an object of *monomane.* But the presiding prescription is emphatic: "Role playing involves an imitation, in every particular, with nothing left out" (Rimer and Yamazaki 1984, 10).

The governing principle seems simple enough, and in its ideal form would be dependent on observation, but the simplicity is from the beginning subject to qualifications. So "playing the part of a ruler or a high official" will confront the actor with his inevitable ignorance of the manners of the court nobility (ibid.). Similar problems affect the portrayal of women of high rank, but the deficiencies may be made up by feedback from appropriate members of the audience (noble males) and tactful inquiry and investigation (noble women). These comments apply explicitly to compensation for the difficulties of direct observation in given cases, and with regard to "an ordinary woman" or to "persons of high profession" *monomane* can apparently operate directly (pp. 11 and 10 respectively). Yet this apparent simplicity of mimicry may be misleading. The commonplace actions of laborers and rustics must not be "copied too realistically," and a general principle is asserted that "men of lowly occupation should not be imitated in any meticulous fashion, nor shown to men of refined taste." Yet those who "have traditionally been found congenial as poetic subjects" (woodcutters, grass cutters, charcoal burners, salt workers) may be imitated in detail. This leads to the formulation of a second general principle: "The degree of imitation must vary, depending on the kind of role being performed" (p. 10). It is a principle that appears later in *Kakyō* in close association with *yugen* and the governing metaphor of the flower, which is introduced to provide a resolution of the inherent problem:

> No matter what the role—whether the character be of high or low rank, a man, a woman, a priest or lay person, a farmer or country person, even a beggar or an outcast—it should seem as though each were holding a branch of flowers in his hand. In this one respect they exhibit the same appeal, despite whatever differences they may show in their social positions. [p. 94]

As a discursive term of the treatises, *monomane* charts the intense and subtle transition from the overt, satirical mimicry of early *sangaku* to the delicate compromises that reflect the presiding taste of the nobility. But *monomane* also has different operations to perform within the texts. It may, for example, express the relationship between teacher and pupil. Here again the apparent simplicity of *monomane* (representing a sound tradition of in-body learning) contains the problematic of the relationship. A pupil must imitate, but superficial imitation is not the art (*Shikadō*); and the teacher must not expose his highest levels of attainment to imitation by the pupil but should offer only what the pupil can follow (*Kakyō*, pp. 66 and 87 respectively). In this respect, *monomane* in the treatises operates as a control on the effectiveness and possible errors of *monomane* in the tradition of oral teaching: as *Shikadō* states plainly at its conclusion, the treatises are written because not just any training will do (pp. 72–73).[24] A similar operation for the term is found in discussions of the relationships between actors, where *monomane* must not be restricted to the exclusive imitation of what is superior, as might be assumed (*Fūshikaden*, pp. 24–25). It may also introduce the distinction between "function" and "substance," or "externalization" and "internalization," in the imitation of acting, which may follow the surface of excellence rather than the spirit (*Shikadō*, pp. 71 and 66 respectively). In this respect, *monomane* introduces the hidden—much as it does in the discussion of the portrayal of the mad or possessed, where the mimicry of their external state is nothing without the imitation of the dominant feeling or the possessing spirit (*Fūshikaden*, pp. 13–14).

In its ultimate expression, *monomane* will cancel itself completely—as it does in the portrayal of the old man by the "truly gifted player" who becomes the role and has "assumed the personality of an old man." Although the illusion persists for the audience, the actor will actually play the part like the youth the old man would like to be. This inversion is a paradox of imitation, and once again the problematics of *monomane* resolve themselves in the metaphor of the flower: such an outstanding portrayal is like "a flower blooming on an ancient tree" (*Fūshikaden*, pp. 55–56). The instability ascribed to *monomane* by Zeami leads inevitably to the flower as the

governing metaphor of aspiration in the treatises—much as the mastery of the problems of role playing is the absolute preliminary to an understanding of "the flower that does not fade" in *Fūshikaden* (p. 30). The goal of success lies in the image of the flower, but success itself may be illusory if it is only temporary (pp. 37 and 39). While *monomane* may be adjusted to the demands of *yugen*, in the compromise between the Yamato and Omi styles of performance that inspires the composition of the treatises, the metaphorical range of the flower offers a far more impressive set of resolutions. Thus the flower is a mediating principle between styles, even including *dengaku*, which "represents quite a different form of art from our own." *Fūshikaden* contends: "Styles of acting and the basic forms of art may differ variously, but what is effective about each is common to all. This moving quality is the Flower. It is recognised as crucial to Yamato and Omi *sarugaku* and to *dengaku* as well" (p. 39).

"This moving quality" readily expresses the range and capability of metaphor, which may conjoin what is apparently different in the conviction of a resolution. As a consequence, it can mediate between a country audience and the nobility, in the person of the player who possesses it (p. 50), and can cover the appeal of different levels of attainment to such audiences: "Now, as concerns the Nine Levels, it goes without saying that the flower is manifested in the upper three levels, yet in the middle three and lower three levels of our art as well, insofar as they possess elements of interest, there are appropriate flowers for them as well" (*Shūgyoku tokka*, p. 130). The upper three are for the "highly cultivated"; the middle and lower, it seems, are for "farmers and rural people."

The ambition represented by the image of the flower summarizes Zeami's aspirations for the transcendence of cultural obstacles facing the ideal *nō* performer. The ambition is present in the image, which is one of attainment and manifestation (and so of consummate approval from an audience) whenever it is applied. But the aspirations apply to what may appear to be irreconcilable. Thus in chapter 5 of *Fūshikaden*, the actor who has mastered "the real secrets of his art" and has "achieved his Flower" will be respected everywhere and will "perform ably in the style of Yamato and Omi *sarugaku*, and even in the style of *dengaku*, depending on the wishes of his audience" (p. 40). The image contains and transcends a serious paradox, since the claim to universal respect is deeply problematic if an audience without discrimination cannot appreciate a good player. But the flower does not wither in such circumstances: "Thus, while it is true that an untutored audience may not be able to grasp the elements that make a performer good, and thereby appreciate him, nevertheless a truly gifted player, if he really makes use of all his artistic skill, should be able to move even an undiscriminating audience" (pp. 39–40).

The tasks set for the image by aspiration are daunting. Not only must the actor know all the styles, but he must also master his own. And unless he does so he will "not only fail to grasp the fundamentals of his own proper art but will certainly fail to understand any of the others," or the flower will elude him (ibid.). The problem of different flowers and different audiences and their levels of appreciation leads to a variety of evasions. Hence Zeami suggests that in order to please a provincial audience the actor may need to draw on "the easy style of performance he used when a beginner"; yet when a good actor faces a withdrawal of favor "because of some situation over which he has no control," he may retain his flower by performing in the provinces (pp. 41 and 42 respectively).

It is, of course, the image that must be retained by theoretical aspiration, even at the cost of a temporary loss of conviction. And if metaphor is to be retained, it must be allowed to collapse under the strain into something more potent. It cannot hold in all circumstances. A good play may be performed in front of a discerning audience by a good player, but it still may not succeed: although the balance of yin and yang may be to blame, Zeami is obliged to admit that, contradictory as it may seem to the terms in which he has framed the example, one of the only answers is to assume that the actor has actually failed to "achieve the proper flower" (p. 45). It is in the secret teaching of chapter 7 of *Fūshikaden* that Zeami finally acknowledges that the range of metaphor is in fact banal and something further is required for the image. If "the flower can be used . . . as a metaphor for all things in the *nō*," and mostly describes what "seems novel to the imagination of the spectator," then its attempted application to all discursive circumstances will result in its degradation, prompted by an eventual failure to resolve or to reconcile successfully (pp. 52–53). The antidote to this debasement of a vital currency is the discovery, or the invention, of the gold standard—namely, the meta-metaphor, the collapse of the metaphor into itself to emerge as a symbol: "The player who has studied his art to its furthest reaches will come to know the Flower that lies within the Flower" (p. 55).

This extremity of remote aspiration can be located in the "Flower drawn from past and future," a symbol that is introduced toward the close of *Fūshikaden* only to be apparently withdrawn, since "no one has ever heard of such a supremely gifted artist from the beginnings of our art down to the present day" (p. 57). But the composition of the treatises as a compelling charter for the Kanze house ensures that there must be one exemplar, as writing enshrines the founding father of achievement, Kan'ami. Ultimately the treatises are the secret, and the secret lies in the treatises, from which it can never be fully extracted, because once recognized actual achievement vanishes: "Where there are secrets, the Flower exists; without secrets, the Flower does not exist" (p. 60).

CONCLUDING COMMENTS

After opening out a discussion of all three bodies of writing, I do not wish to offer a misrepresentative closure in the form of summarizing conclusions. I have considered related questions of status and discourse, but there are many other issues of equal importance that one might add to a discussion of this kind. Plainly a consideration of the theoretical discourses from the point of the addressees is bound to be intriguing—to different degrees in relation to each—but we should probably resist the temptation to ascribe the composition of theory to a kind of humanist pragmatism. So, with Aristotle, we can assume a manifest address in the *Poetics* to the potential playwright (in contrast to the actor) or poet, but the address to Plato and the continuing discourse of philosophy in the Greek schools is even more pronounced. The *Natyasastra* codifies procedure and possibility most explicitly for the director or supervisor of a company, at times shifting its address to the playwright, but its immediate addressees, the sages who question Bharata, are part of a far more imposing fiction that is essential to the work. With Zeami, the picture is complex in a different way. The head of the school, and the succession, are an overt concern, and the accent lies heavily on excellence by the actor in performance. But there is an accompanying expectation in the dialogic portion of *Fūshikaden* (chapter 3) that figures of this sort should expect to compose their own scripts (pp. 21–22) in a more satisfactory alternative to the task of selection and interpretation; and instruction and ultimately models are given in the later *Sandō* (pp. 148–162). The composition of scripts, as in Aristotle and the *Natyasastra,* is brought firmly under theoretical control and, like performance, is subject to the potentially transcendent model established by the theorist Zeami.[25] If there is an invitation to apparent addressees in all three bodies of material, it is by no means an invitation to the kinds of artistic initiative that created the form.

That theory has its own dynamic of continuity is quite clear, not just from the example of the *Poetics* in Western thought, but from works in the Sanskrit and Japanese traditions that have not entered into this discussion. The *Natyasastra* inspired both commentary and digest, and its modern interpretation would not take the form it has without the vision of Abhinavagupta and his reading in the *Abhinavabharati*.[26] The composition and compilation of *Sarugaku Dangi* by his son Motoyoshi redefined Zeami in the role he had assigned to his own father, and recent publication has explored the quality and significance of Zeami's immediate theoretical successor, Komparu Zenchiku.[27] In Zenchiku's vision of Six Circles and One Dewdrop, the sense of attainment he received from his teacher Zeami is rendered into a symbolism relatively devoid of pragmatic instruction or reference to dramaturgy. In its turn, it is itself then susceptible to commentary from Buddhist and Confucian sources, as Thornhill has closely examined; in fact, the text contains these commentaries and renders them into a further synthesis (Thornhill 1993; Nearman 1995). For Zenchiku, therefore, the first sphere of his symbolic order represents "the spirit that circulates, flowing without ceasing even for a moment," to which Nearman adds the following commentary:

> That is, even though the first sphere is presented by a static, two-dimensional circle, this diagram is intended to convey the idea of ceaseless movement, a circulation of undifferentiated energy that is omnidirectional, and like a bird's egg, it contains all that is necessary for the ultimate production of a vital phenomenal manifestation. [Nearman 1995, 249]

This is theory in its most transcendent mode—and as striking a confirmation of its existence as discourse as one might expect to find.

NOTES

I am grateful to the University of Exeter for a research grant in support of this study and, as well, to the staffs of the Library of the Indian Institute and the Japanese Library in the Nissan Institute in Oxford for their help. My thanks are also due to Samuel L. Leiter and Marvin Carlson.

1. For examples see Megumi (1989), Sukla (1977), Gupt (1994), and Smethurst (1989), who cites Japanese comparative scholarship. Gopalakrishnan (1991) and Rajakaruna (1993) offer short, comparative studies of Indian and *nō* theatre. The reader should note that my bibliography, for reasons of space and proportion, is indicative only.

2. Janko (1984) discusses the evidence for the contents of a second book of the *Poetics* and presents a tentative reconstruction.

3. The ancient Greek tradition holds that Aristotle's esoteric works were transmitted by successive heads of the Peripatetic school of philosophy; see the introduction to Lucas (1968, x).

4. These early chapters of book 3 also refer to the existence of a *techne* literature on the "art" of style and delivery (performative speaking) in rhetoric.

5. Translations and studies of Aristotle's *Poetics* abound. Here I mention one commentary (Halliwell 1986), one collection of essays (Rorty 1992), and one monograph (Belfiore 1992).

6. The debate goes back as far as the earliest major commentator, Abhinavagupta. For discussions see, among others, Gupt (1994, 29ff.) and Dasgupta and De (1962).

7. See the essay by Gerow, "Sanskrit Dramatic Theory and Kalidasa's Plays," in Miller (1984, 42–64). This volume includes a translation of Kalidasa's Vikramorvasiya (Urvasi Won by Valor) by D. Gitomer.

8. See Keith (1924, 12–13) and MacDonell (1900, 284, 288–289, and 294) on Vyasa, the mythical compiler of the epic, who had supposedly arranged the four Vedas.

9. On the sutras see MacDonell (1900, chaps. 2 and 9); part 3 of Keith (1920) is devoted to what he terms the "Scientific Literature," namely the *sastra* writings. The reader should note that the date of Keith's edition is as given on the title page; but his preface indicates (pp. viii and xxviii) that the book was actually published in 1928 and certainly after the publication of Keith (1924).

10. One division of the sutra literature had dealt with the rites that might be performed by the householder and his wife in accordance with the Vedas; see MacDonell (1900, 37). But this should not, in principle, affect our understanding of the status afforded to the *natyacarya* and *sutradhara* by the *Natyasastra* in the context of the ritual dedication of the theatre.

11. All quotations from the treatises of Zeami are taken from this volume of translations, which has become a standard textbook. For comparison, Nearman (1984) gives details in his bibliography of his annotated translations of selected treatises (including *Kakyō*) for *Monumenta Nipponica*, while dePoorter (1986) provides an annotated translation of the *Sarugaku Dangi*, a compilation to which I do not refer in this discussion. De Poorter's "Appendix 1" (1986, 242–249) usefully lists all the writings of Zeami with indications of date and subject, and cites translations in English, French, and German.

12. For the biography of Zeami see Hare (1986, chap. 1).

13. For the myth of Amaterasu in the *Nihongi* see Aston (1896, 41–45).

14. On *yugen* as a criterion in poetic theory see Putzar (1973, 63–64) and de Poorter: "From the twelfth century this word was used in Japan for the judgement of poems" (1986, 55). Compare Ueda Makoto (1991, 40), who declares of the fourteenth-century usage by the poet Yoshimoto that "the term seems to designate a certain idea roughly equivalent to elegance, gracefulness, or polished beauty." On the problems of translation for the term in Zeami see Hare (1986, 300), who seems to prefer "elegance"; compare Rimer and Yamazaki (1984, 260), who opt for the use of "grace" throughout.

15. On the imagery of blossoms and flower in Tsurayuki and Yoshimoto see the examples given by Ueda (1991, 8 and 41).

16. Most biographical and critical accounts attach great importance to the issue of taste in the successive *shoguns* and the audience. See, for example, Raz (1983, 70–122), Hare (1986, 11–38), and Konishi (1991, 520–560).

17. The famous formulation of katharsis occurs at the beginning of chapter 6 of the *Poetics*.

18. For a wide variety of interpretations of katharsis in the *Poetics* see the essays collected by Rorty (1992).

19. On the celebration of the dramatic festivals see the essay by Goldhill, "The City Dionysia and Civic Ideology," in Winkler and Zeitlin (1990); see also the essay by Cole, "Procession and Celebration at the Dionysia," in Scodel (1993).

20. See Plato (1974) on the three skills (pp. 367–369) and on the descending order of knowledge (pp. 359–364).

21. On *mimesis* and related terms before Plato see Else (1958).

22. The myth of Urvasi is found in the most ancient of the four Vedas, the Rig Veda, book 10, number 95; for a translation with notes and a short commentary see O'Flaherty (1981, 252–256).

23. The claim that drama allows for the instruction of all castes, including the Sudras who were excluded from listening to the Vedas, was also made on behalf of the *Mahabharata*; see MacDonell (1900, 289).

24. The control exercised by the treatises on the oral or in-body teaching is also made apparent in the *Kakyō's* concern that proper principles should be followed in the certification of pupils (p. 88).

25. Quinn (1993) observes that Zeami's assumption in *Sandō* that performers were "capable of composing both the lines and the music of their own plays" was "unprecedented" but came to be the norm: "Collaboration was the more common practice, *sarugaku* professionals composing the music and poets composing the lines" (p. 55). It is interesting, here, to compare the situation in relation to the substantially untheorized (and later) *kabuki*; see Dunn and Torigoe (1969, 20–21 and 118).

26. On the value of Abhinavagupta see the short summary by Ghosh (1961, xlvii–xlix). Gupt (1994) makes extensive use of the commentary and provides a summary of *rasa* criticism up to and including the *Abhinavabharati* in the eleventh century (pp. 260–271); the analysis on pp. 236–247, which reproduces his own argument in Gupt (1990), is a good example of its weight in the interpretation of significant concepts. There is a translation of the immensely influential part of the *Abhinavabharati* that refers to chapter 6 of the *Natyasastra* in Gnoli (1956); see also Chari (1990).

27. For the *Sarugaku Dangi,* in addition to the translation in Rimer and Yamazaki (1984, 172–256), see de Poorter (1986). On the transmission from Zeami to Komparu Zenchiku see Pinnington (1997). Zenchiku's treatises, and the commentaries upon them from Buddhist and Confucian sources, are the subject of Thornhill (1993); Nearman has provided a series of annotated translations, comparable to those he executed for Zeami, of the *Rokurin Ichiro* treatises of Zenchiku in four successive issues of *Monumenta Nipponica* (beginning with Nearman 1995).

REFERENCES

Aristotle. 1965. *On the Art of Poetry*. Translated by T. S. Dorsch. In *Aristotle, Horace, Longinus: Classical Literary Criticism*. Harmondsworth: Penguin.

———. 1991. *The Art of Rhetoric*. Translated by H. C. Lawson-Tancred. Harmondsworth: Penguin.

Aston, William G., trans. 1896. *Nihongi: Chronicles of Japan from the Earliest Times to A.D. 697*. London: Kegan Paul.

Belfiore, Elizabeth. 1992. *Tragic Pleasures: Aristotle on Plot and Emotion*. Princeton: Princeton University Press.

Chari, V. K. 1990. *Sanskrit Criticism*. Honolulu: University of Hawai'i Press.

Dasgupta, S. N., and S. K. De. 1962. *A History of Sanskrit Literature, Classical Period*. 2nd ed. Calcutta: University of Calcutta Press.

de Poorter, E. 1986. *Zeami's Talks on Sarugaku: An Annotated Translation of the* Sarugaku Dangi. Amsterdam: Gieben.

Dunn, Charles J., and Torigoe Bunzo, eds. and trans. 1969. *The Actors' Analects*. New York: Columbia University Press.

Else, Gerald F. 1958. "Imitation in the Fifth Century." *Classical Philology* 53:73–90.

Ghosh, Manomohan, trans. 1961. *Natyasastra*. Vol. 2. Calcutta: Asiatic Society.

———. 1967. *Natyasastra*. Vol. 1. 2nd ed. Calcutta: Manisha Granthalaya.

Girard, René. 1977. *Violence and the Sacred*. Translated by P. Gregory. Baltimore: Johns Hopkins University Press.

Gnoli, R. 1956. *The Aesthetic Experience According to Abhinavagupta*. Rome: Istituto Italiano per il Medio e Estremo Oriente.

Gopalakrishnan, S. 1991. "Kutiyattam and Noh: Commonalities and Divergences." *Sangeet Natak* 99:35–42.

Gupt, Bharat. 1990. "Clarification on *Lokodharmi* and *Natyadharmi*." *Sangeet Natak* 95:35–44.

———. 1994. *Dramatic Concepts, Greek and Indian: A Study of the* Poetics *and the* Natyasastra. New Delhi: D. K. Printworld.

Halliwell, Stephen. 1986. *Aristotle's* Poetics. Chapel Hill: University of North Carolina Press.

Hare, Thomas B. 1986. *Zeami's Style: The Noh Plays of Zeami Motokiyo*. Stanford: Stanford University Press.

Inoura Yoshinobo. 1971. *A History of Japanese Theatre*. Vol. 1: *Noh and Kyogen*. Tokyo: Kokusai Bunka Shinkokai.

Janko, Richard. 1984. *Aristotle on Comedy: Towards a Reconstruction of Poetics II*. Berkeley: University of California Press.

Keith, Arthur B. 1920. *A History of Sanskrit Literature*. London: Oxford University Press.

———. 1924. *The Sanskrit Drama*. London: Oxford University Press.

Konishi Jin'ichi. 1991. *A History of Japanese Literature*. Vol. 3: *The High Middle Ages*. Translated by A. Gatten and M. Harrison. Edited by E. Miner. Princeton: Princeton University Press.

Lucas, Donald W., ed. 1968. *Aristotle* Poetics. Oxford: Clarendon Press.

MacDonell, Arthur A. 1900. *A History of Sanskrit Literature*. London: Heinemann.

Megumi Sata. 1989. "Aristotle's *Poetics* and Zeami's Teachings on Style and the Flower." *Asian Theatre Journal* 6(1):47–56.

Miller, Barbara S., ed. 1984. *Theater of Memory: The Plays of Kalidasa*. New York: Columbia University Press.

Nearman, Mark J. 1984. "Feeling in Relation to Acting: An Outline of Zeami's Views." *Asian Theatre Journal* 1(1): 40–51.

———. 1995. "The Visions of a Creative Artist: Zenchiku's *Rokurin Ichiro* Treatises." *Monumenta Nipponica* 50(2): 235–261.

Nietzsche, Friedrich. 1967. *The Birth of Tragedy and The Case of Wagner*. Translated by W. Kaufmann. New York: Vintage.

O'Flaherty, Wendy D. 1981. *The Rig Veda: An Anthology*. Harmondsworth: Penguin.

Pinnington, N. J. 1997. "Crossed Paths: Zeami's Transmission to Zenchiku." *Monumenta Nipponica* 52(2):201–234.

Plato. 1974. *The Republic*. Translated by D. Lee. Harmondsworth: Penguin.

Putzar, E. 1973. *Japanese Literature: A Historical Outline*. Tucson: University of Arizona Press.

Quinn, S. F. 1993. "How to Write a Noh Play: Zeami's *Sandō*." *Monumenta Nipponica* 48(1):53–88.

Rajakaruna, D. A. 1993. "The Classical Noh Theatre of Japan: An Indian Approach." *Sangeet Natak* 108–109:17–22.

Raz, Jacob. 1983. *Audience and Actors: A Study of Their Interaction in the Japanese Traditional Theatre*. Leiden: Brill.

Rimer, J. Thomas, and Yamazaki Masakazu. 1984. *On the Art of the Noh Drama: The Major Treatises of Zeami*. Princeton: Princeton University Press.

Rorty, Amélie O., ed. 1992. *Essays on Aristotle's Poetics*. Princeton: Princeton University Press.

Scodel, Ruth, ed. 1993. *Theater and Society in the Classical World*. Ann Arbor: University of Michigan Press.

Smethurst, Mae. 1989. *The Art of Aeschylus and Zeami*. Princeton: Princeton University Press.

Sukla, A. C. 1977. *The Concept of Imitation in Greek and Indian Aesthetics*. Calcutta: Rupa.

Thornhill, A. H. 1993. *Six Circles, One Dewdrop: The Religio-Aesthetic World of Komparu Zenchiku*. Princeton: Princeton University Press.

Ueda Makoto. 1991. *Literary and Art Theories in Japan*. Ann Arbor: University of Michigan Press.

Winkler, John J., and Froma I. Zeitlin, eds. 1990. *Nothing to Do with Dionysos?: Athenian Drama in Its Social Context*. Princeton: Princeton University Press.

Medieval and Renaissance England

A performance of *The Tempest* at the new Shakespeare's Globe Theatre, on the Bankside in London. The theater is a meticulous reconstruction of the Globe Theatre of 1613.

The fifteenth, sixteenth, and seventeenth centuries saw Europe transformed by the extraordinary cultural revolution we now call the European Renaissance. Fueled by new technology such as printing and by new scientific, political, and religious ideas, explosive change transformed European culture. The known world expanded beyond the sea to embrace the New World; the recovery of Greek and Latin literature spurred a sweeping intellectual revolution; strong centralized monarchies in Spain, Portugal, France, and England created new empires abroad and fought to control an increasingly restive populace at home; the Protestant Reformation undermined the religious and political authority of the Catholic church, beginning a period of violent religious conflict; and the "new philosophy"—modern science—of Copernicus, Bacon, and Galileo seemed to put even the physical world of heaven and earth in doubt. "'Tis all in pieces, all coherence gone," the poet John Donne wrote in 1611, voicing the profound anxiety and exhilaration of many of his contemporaries: "Prince, subject, father, son are things forgot. / For every man alone thinks that he hath got / To be a Phoenix." The changing tides of thought swept away the crumbling edifice of the medieval world—the feudal state, the universal church, scholastic philosophy, an ordered heaven, and revealed truth—and opened the way for the modern world.

This revolution also infused the theater; the Renaissance, especially in Italy, France, Spain, and England, is one of the great ages of theatrical and dramatic achievement. In England, the professional theater as we know it originated at this time: the history of the secular, profit-making, commercial theater is conventionally dated from the opening of the first theater building, The Theatre, in London in 1576. Licensed and protected as an aristocratic entertainment, the theater was also a popular institution in which commoners such as William Shakespeare, Richard Burbage, Edward Alleyn, Inigo Jones, and others, could indeed rise like the phoenix. However, to understand the revolutionary impact of theater and drama in Shakespeare's era, we need to understand their conservative inheritance, their deep indebtedness to the medieval stage that preceded them.

DRAMA AND THEATER IN MEDIEVAL ENGLAND

Dramatic performance in medieval Europe was thoroughly conditioned by the Catholic church's central role in the life of the community. Having closed the Roman theaters in the sixth century, the church maintained a vigilant opposition to the secular theater and the vices associated with it. Yet the revival of theater in Europe, beginning in the tenth century, was inspired and sponsored by the church itself. The four major dramatic forms in the late Middle Ages were connected with the church, its rituals, and its calendar of religious observances: LITURGICAL DRAMA enacted as part of the liturgy of the Catholic Mass; CYCLE PLAYS, illustrating scriptural history and performed by craft guilds on the feast of Corpus Christi; MORALITY DRAMA, enacting the symbolic structure of Christian life; and plays written and performed in schools and universities, sometimes imitating classical plays. In England, cycle and morality plays particularly influenced the later, secular drama of the sixteenth century.

Liturgical Drama

The earliest dramatic records, dating from the ninth century, are musical TROPES, brief elaborations of the authorized liturgy, written to amplify the scriptural text and enhance its impact and appeal. These compositions were set to music and sung in ANTIPHONAL

207

PERFORMANCE (back and forth, in dialogue) between monks or boy choristers to accompany the liturgy of the Mass. In England, Ethelwold, Bishop of Winchester, wrote a series of lessons concerning the conduct of the Mass, the *Regularis Concordia* (965–975), including instructions for such performances. What follows are his instructions to the priests for representing the visit of the three Marys to the tomb of Christ after the Crucifixion (translated from Latin). This trope is often called the *Quem Quaeritis,* after the Latin text spoken by the "angel": "Whom seek you?":

> While the third lesson is being chanted, let four brethren vest themselves; of whom, let one, vested in an alb, enter as if to take part in the service, and let him without being observed approach the place of the sepulchre [i.e., near the altar], and there, holding a palm in his hand, let him sit down quietly. While the third responsory is being sung, let the remaining three follow, all of them vested in copes, and carrying in their hands censers filled with incense; and slowly, in the manner of seeking something, let them come before the place of the sepulchre. These things are done in imitation of the angel seated in the monument, and of the women coming with spices to anoint the body of Jesus. When therefore that one seated shall see the three, as if straying about and seeking something, approach him, let him begin in a dulcet voice of medium pitch to sing:

> *Whom seek ye in the sepulchre, O followers of Christ?*

> When he has sung this to the end, let the three respond in unison:

> *Jesus of Nazareth, which was crucified, O celestial one.*

> To whom that one:

> *He is not here; he is risen; just as he foretold.*
> *Go, announce that he is risen from the dead.*

> At the word of this command let those three turn themselves to the choir, saying:

> *Alleluia! The Lord is risen to-day.*
> *The strong lion, the Christ, the Son of God. Give thanks to God.*

> This said, let the former, again seating himself, as if recalling them, sing the anthem:

> *Come, and see the place where the Lord was laid. Alleluia! Alleluia!*

> And saying this, let him rise and let him lift the veil and show them the place bare of the cross, but only the cloths laid there with which the cross was wrapped. Seeing which, let them set down the censers which they carried into the same sepulchre, and let them take up the cloth and spread it out before the eyes of the clergy; and as if making known that the Lord had risen and was not now therein wrapped, let them sing this anthem:

> *The Lord is risen from the sepulchre.*
> *Who for us hung upon the cross.*

> And let them place the cloth upon the altar. The anthem being ended, let the Prior, rejoicing with them at the triumph of our King, in that, having conquered death, he arose, begin the hymn:

> *We praise thee, O God.*

> This begun, all the bells chime out together.[1]

Despite its brevity and the limitations imposed by the liturgy itself, this trope has the elements of drama: a progressive plot, the involvement of specific characters, conflict and resolution. Ethelwold's "stage directions" convey a subtle sense of how character can be created by performance and a fine sense of visual spectacle as well, all within the narrow scope allowed by the Mass.

---

[1]*Regularis Concordia,* in *Chief Pre-Shakespearean Dramas,* ed. Joseph Quincy Adams (Boston: Houghton Mifflin, 1924), 9–10.

Throughout the Middle Ages and beyond, liturgical plays of this kind became increasingly common and complex. Enacted in different locations within the church, called **MANSIONS,** liturgical drama provided a model for the forms of religious drama that came to be performed outside the church and outside the framework of the liturgy. In the tenth and eleventh centuries, the church sponsored dramatized scenes from the life of Christ or the lives of the saints, staged on important Christian holidays. For example, a town might commemorate the entrance of Christ into Jerusalem on Palm Sunday with a procession to the cathedral in which townspeople enacted various roles. In addition, the church oversaw the production of cycles of plays, which became a principal mode of theatrical and dramatic innovation. These cycles were performed sixty days after Easter as part of the feast of Corpus Christi, a holiday inaugurated in the fourteenth century to celebrate the doctrine of the Eucharist. The Corpus Christi festival frequently featured the performance of a series of plays dramatizing scriptural history: the Creation, Old Testament events (Noah and the Flood, Abraham and Isaac), scenes from the New Testament (the Annunciation, Herod and the Slaughter of the Innocents), and prophetic plays concerning the Harrowing of Hell and the Last Judgment. The production of these plays could last several days or weeks and called on the services of the entire town. Each craft guild (or *mystery,* as the guilds were called; the cycles are sometimes called **MYSTERY CYCLES**) financed and produced a different play, often on a subject appropriate to the guild. The shipwrights' guild might undertake the Noah play, the Three Kings play might be assigned to the goldsmiths, and so on. The plays were the property of the guilds and passed through generations of guild members. In major towns with many craft guilds, the cycles often included a large number of plays. Of the English cycles, the York cycle is the longest, containing forty-eight plays; the Wakefield cycle has thirty-two; and the Chester cycle has twenty-four.

Although they were produced for a popular, largely illiterate audience, the cycle dramas are extremely sophisticated and required the talents of trained performers. One of the cycles' most powerful and typical features is their use of **ANACHRONISM**—the blending of the historical past with contemporary events and characters. Many of the characters who appear in the plays are medieval English peasants, who often display an ironic, even theatrical sense of their involvement in the scriptural events of the past. One of the most telling uses of this technique occurs in the York *Crucifixion;* the York playwright conveys the Roman soldiers' hardness to the message of Christ by making them jest with him about the crucifixion they are performing:

> **1 SOLDIER:** (*To* CHRIST.) Say, Sir, how likes you now
>   This work that we have wrought?
> **2 SOLDIER:** We pray you say us how
>   Ye feel, or faint ye aught.
> **JESUS:** . . . My Father, that all bales [evils] may beet [abate].
>   Forgive these men that do me pine [pain].
>   What they work wot [know] they nought;
>   Therefore, my Father, I crave,
>   Let never their sins be sought,
>   But see their souls to save.
> **1 SOLDIER:** We! Hark! he jangles like a jay.

By characterizing the jesting Roman soldiers as, in effect, contemporaries of the medieval audience, the play implies that biblical events are part of the audience's contemporary history. Seeing their neighbors enacting the biblical scenes and seeing contemporary characters share the stage with biblical figures must have emphasized the immediacy of the ongoing Christian story.

Cycle Drama

Morality Drama   Like the cycle plays, morality plays dramatized elements of Christian life. Instead of staging events from scriptural history, morality drama stages a symbolic **ALLEGORY** of the Christian's spiritual journey through life. Increasingly popular throughout the fourteenth and fifteenth centuries, plays like *The Castle of Perseverance* (c. 1425), *Mankind* (c. 1470), and *Everyman* (c. 1500) emphasized the individual's struggle with sin, while the cycle plays emphasized the larger patterns of Christian history. Later playwrights, including Shakespeare, found both models useful. The cycles provided a pattern for staging the epic sweep of secular English history, and morality drama provided a supple device for representing psychological and moral conflict. Morality plays often provided the structure for the secular plays written at schools and universities as well, and for the **INTERLUDES** performed at court as a break from holiday feasting. They also provided a staple technique for characterization in the later secular drama. Christopher Marlowe's *Doctor Faustus* (1590) uses the Good and Evil Angels to externalize Faustus's moral conflict, and other playwrights frequently used the devices of morality drama to dramatize the difficulties of political choice. In John Skelton's interlude, *Magnificence* (1516), written for Henry VIII or Thomas Sackville, and Thomas Norton's *Gorboduc* (1561), the monarch is shown to make his decisions framed by a host of allegorized counselors, good and bad advisers who approximate the role played in morality drama by angels and demons.

STAGING MEDIEVAL DRAMA   Medieval plays were often acted on or near **PAGEANT WAGONS.** In some towns the audience seems to have remained stationary at various locations while the wagons and their plays proceeded past them; in other towns, the wagons were drawn in a procession of **TABLEAUX VIVANTS** (posed scenes) through the town and then arranged in an open area for the performance, allowing the audience to move from play to play. In Chester, for example, a list survives of the stations where the plays were performed, and for York it is possible to trace the route of the pageant wagons through the city. Given the size and complexity of these performances, it's not surprising to find that they were not easily performed on one day: the procession took three days at Chester, and began at 4:30 A.M. in York, lasting until past midnight. The plays combined historical and contemporary elements; in performance, the staging produced a close and powerful relationship between the dramatic characters and the audience. In the Coventry play of the Magi, for example, Herod raves when he discovers that the three kings have escaped him:

> I Stamp! I Stare! I look all about!
> Might I them take, I should them burn at a glede [fire]!
> I rant! I run! and now run I wode [mad]
> A! That these villain traitors hath marred this my mood!
> They shall be hanged, if I may come them to!
>
> (*Here Herod rages in the pagond* [pageant wagon] *and in the street also.*)[2]

Herod's rage was certainly one of the highlights of the medieval cycles. Shakespeare, at least, seems to refer to it in *Hamlet* (1600), when he has Hamlet remind his actors that they should be restrained and natural in their performance, because overacting "out-Herods Herod." The stage direction also suggests that Herod's frenzy carried him from the wagon and into the street, into a closer and more effective relationship to his audience. This interaction between actor and audience is characteristic of popular theater and is a feature of medieval performance carried into Renaissance acting. It also suggests that the "place" of

---

[2]The Coventry *Magi, Herod, and the Slaughter of the Innocents,* in *Chief Pre-Shakespearean Dramas,* ed. Joseph Quincy Adams (Boston: Houghton Mifflin, 1924), 163.

medieval drama, the fictitious locale of the play, was not firmly localized onstage; the actors/characters could move easily back and forth between Herod's Jerusalem and the medieval audience, and even onstage places could be rapidly and easily transformed. This flexibility also allowed medieval playwrights to treat stage space symbolically. The ground plot for *The Castle of Perseverance,* for instance—with its scaffolds for various evils, its moat, and its central castle—clearly offers us a symbolic locale rather than an actual geography. The

MEDIEVAL PAGEANT WAGON

One actor is playing in the street in front of the wagon.

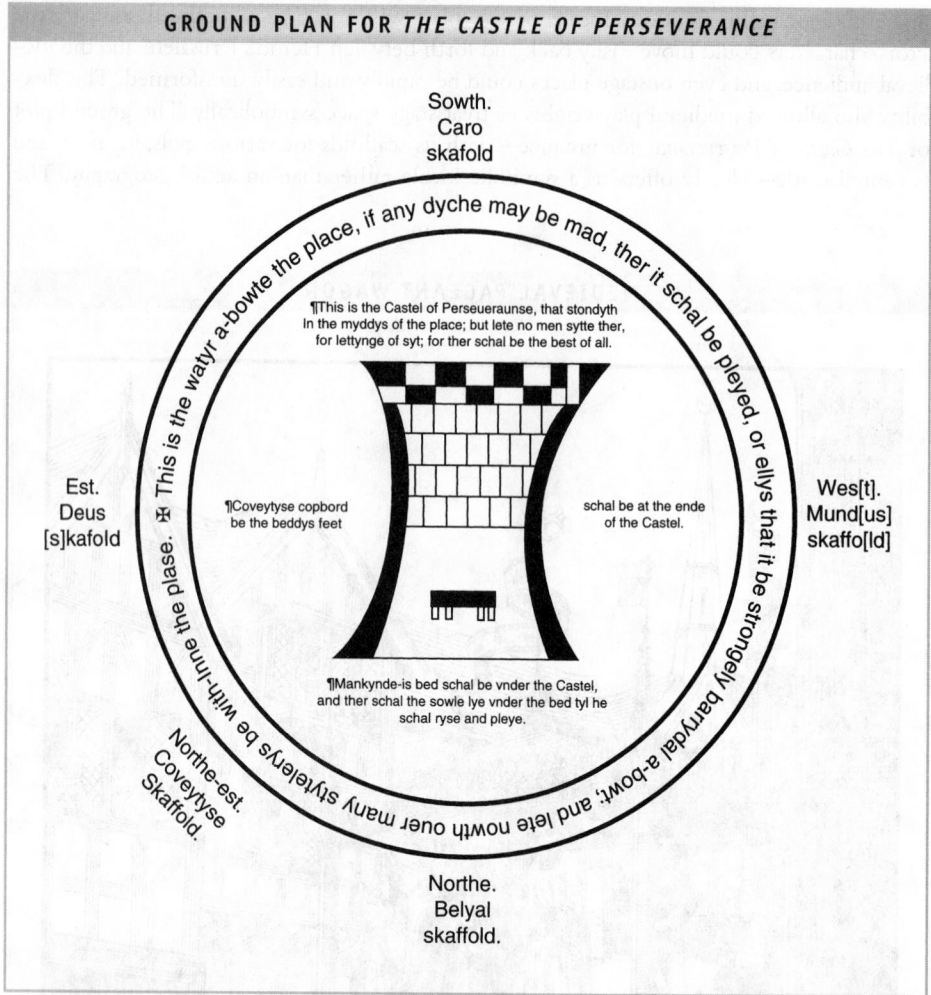

GROUND PLAN FOR *THE CASTLE OF PERSEVERANCE*

Sowth.
Caro
skafold

This is the watyr a-bowte the place, if any dyche may be mad, ther it schal be pleyed, or ellys that it be strongly barryd al a-bowt; and lete nowth ouer many stytelerys be with-inne the plase. ✠ This is the watyr a-bowte the plase.

¶This is the Castel of Perseueraunse, that stondyth In the myddys of the place; but lete no men sytte ther, for lettynge of syt; for ther schal be the best of all.

Est.
Deus
[s]kafold

¶Coveytyse copbord be the beddys feet

schal be at the ende of the Castel.

Wes[t].
Mund[us]
skaffo[ld]

¶Mankynde-is bed schal be vnder the Castel, and ther schal the sowle lye vnder the bed tyl he schal ryse and pleye.

Northe-est.
Coveytyse
Skaffold.

Northe.
Belyal
skaffold.

The ground-plot for the medieval morality play shows five scaffolds (North, Northeast, South, East, and West) arranged around a playing area, with a castle in the center. A ditch enclosed the castle to keep spectators at a distance. In the manuscript, a note beneath the drawing describes the costumes and special effects: "He that shall play Belial (a devil), look that he have gunpowder burning in pipes in his hands and in his ears, and in his arse, when he goes to battle. The four daughters should be clad in mantles; Mercy in white, Ruthwiseness in red, all together, Truth in sad green, and Peace all in black; and they shall play in the place all together until they bring up the soul."

various demons on their scaffolds stand at a symbolic distance, not an actual distance, from the central castle.

This complex of dramatic conventions, staging practices, and audience attitudes is a legacy of the medieval theater passed on to later theater. Although the medieval stage was only one of many influences on it, the drama of the sixteenth and seventeenth centuries is reminiscent of medieval drama in many ways. Renaissance drama frequently treats secular history according to a providential design similar to that of the cycles; it often treats its characters in the symbolic terms of the medieval morality dramas; and it uses both acting and stage space to create an immediacy between the fictive play and its audience. These habits take on very different meanings in Renaissance London, in a city and in a state in which the Anglican Protestant church is the state religion and where signs of Catholicism—or, in fact, of any religious subject matter—in the theater could be read as an act of sedition. The medieval theater provided the forms of drama and the practices of theater that were refashioned by the political, social, and theatrical pressures of the new era.

The explosion of theatrical and dramatic activity in London can be marked by two dates: 1567, when John Brayne built the Red Lion, London's first purpose-built theater (his brother-in-law, James Burbage, built The Theatre in 1576); and 1642, when plays were suspended and theaters were closed at the outbreak of the Civil War. The theater underwent profound changes from the reign of Elizabeth I (ruled 1558–1603) to the reigns of her successors James I (1603–1625) and Charles I (1625–1642, executed 1649), yet at the same time it endured the intense social and cultural upheavals of the period with remarkable consistency. As an institution, the new professional theater witnessed the emergence of England as a modern state; the rise of England as an important mercantile and naval power, aided by the defeat of the Spanish Armada in 1588; the expansion of English interests in the New World; the growth of the city of London to roughly 250,000 inhabitants; and the ascendance of the Puritan faction that closed the theaters and deposed and executed the king.

The professional theater—a new institution in England, though already established on the continent—necessarily reflected the political and social strains of the time. These strains are most readily visible in the many laws regulating theatrical performance. The location of theater buildings, the structure and organization of theater companies, and the entire scene of theatrical activity in Renaissance London epitomized the fundamental tensions of English society as it moved from the medieval to the modern world.

The sixteenth century witnessed intense religious and civil controversy, dating in part from Henry VIII's divorce from Catherine of Aragon in 1532 and his consequent excommunication from the Catholic church in 1533. Once Henry established the Protestant Church of England as the religion of the realm in 1535, English politics were often dictated by England's vulnerability to the massive, hostile powers of the Catholic church in Rome and Catholic states such as France and Spain. Within England, a variety of Protestant sects competed with each other, with the government, and with the Church of England for power. This was also a period of profound changes in the ordering of society, a period of growing mercantile power, of aristocratic discontent with the power of the monarchy, and of the rise of new merchants and other social groups into prominence and power. As a result, the Crown was eternally on guard to suppress civil unrest or religious nonconformity.

Given this volatile political climate, it is not surprising that the Crown sought to limit and control public assembly, including theatrical performances. Laws were frequently directed against the theater, particularly against productions identified with England's Catholic past. In 1548, for example, the English church cancelled the Feast of Corpus Christi, and the production of the cycle plays was systematically suppressed. In 1569, the York cycle was performed for the last time, and in 1575, the mayor of Chester was arrested for allowing cycle plays to be performed. The last cycle performance took place in Coventry in 1576, and the last record of any Corpus Christi play being performed in England (before the modern era) dates from 1605, in Kendal. Morality plays may have seemed less sectarian in the kind of instruction they offered; features of morality drama were more readily absorbed by the secular theater.

Yet while the Crown limited and censored the stage, it also maintained its traditional patronage of the theater. The population of London nearly tripled in Shakespeare's lifetime, from roughly 80,000 in 1564 to more than 200,000 at his death in 1616. The Elizabethan era was characterized by several large crop failures, a deflation in the value of currency, repeated bouts of the plague, and persistent threats of invasion from without and sedition from within. Not surprisingly, both the queen and her Privy Council, and the local city magistrates throughout England, were fearful both of itinerant travelers and of large—potentially riotous—assemblies. The famous "Act for the punishment of Vagabonds" of 1572 is a case in point. The law prohibited itinerant players and entertainers from wandering throughout the realm, but its ultimate effect was to establish permanent theatrical companies under the protection of noble patrons. The law ordered that "all Fencers, Bearwards, Common Players in Interludes, and Minstrels, not belonging to any Baron of this Realm, or towards any other honorable Personage of greater Degree . . . [who] wander abroad and have not License of two Justices of the Peace at the least . . . shall be taken adjudged and deemed Rogues Vagabonds and Sturdy Beggars." Unless they belonged to the retinue of a nobleman, players were classed with common vagrants and could be arrested and fined. Protected as servants, a company of players could receive a license to perform in public.

The statute points to the strong bond between the theater and the aristocracy, and patents granted by Elizabeth entitled noblemen to retain companies of actors as servants. These patents—granted for the Lord Chamberlain's Men (Shakespeare's company), the Lord Admiral's Men (who produced Marlowe's plays), and others—shaped the professional theater of Renaissance London. Elizabeth authorized such companies to perform "Comedies, Tragedies, Interludes, and stage plays" in public, in London and elsewhere. Yet, in granting these privileges, the Crown made significant qualifications. Elizabeth expanded the powers of her Master of Revels, Edmund Tilney, requiring "all and every plaier or plaiers with their playmakers, either belonging to any noble man or otherwise" to "appear before him with all such plaies, Tragedies, Comedies or showes as they shall in readiness or meane to sett forth," and to receive his approval before their performance. Censorship in the period was extensive, and Elizabeth also stipulated that plays "be not published or shown in the time of common prayer, or in the time of great and common plague in our said City of London." Religious and civic officials exerted considerable authority over when and where plays could actually be performed and where theaters could legally be built, and they often closed theaters for months at a time because of plague or civil strife. In 1594, the Privy Council restricted London to two companies (the Lord Chamberlain's Men and the Lord Admiral's Men) and restricted them to public performance at the Globe and Rose theaters when in London.

Professional Companies

The City of London, as in many towns, had its own ordinances prohibiting plays within the city limits, and for this reason James Burbage—a member of the Earl of Leicester's company—built The Theatre to the north of the city. Within a decade theaters had been built to the north of the city and to the south, across the Thames River.

Although they were technically "servants," the major acting companies—the most famous being the Lord Chamberlain's Men, patented in 1593 and then given royal sponsorship as the King's Men when King James I succeeded Elizabeth in 1603—were organized as stockholding, profit-making corporations; that is, as business enterprises in the modern sense. Their economic survival depended on their public performances, because their patron might command and finance only a few productions per year. Several investors, or **SHARERS,** put up the capital to finance the company and took a percentage of its profits. The sharers were not just investors; they were involved in all aspects of the theater. In 1603, for instance, the sharers of the King's Men included Shakespeare (playwright and actor), Richard Burbage (James Burbage's son and the company's principal actor, who was the first to play Shakespeare's King Lear, Hamlet, and Macbeth), the actors John Heminges and Henry Condell (who later published Shakespeare's plays), and the comic actors William Sly (see *The Taming of the Shrew*) and Robert Armin (who played the Fool in *King Lear*), among others. The sharers were responsible for building or leasing a theater, for purchasing plays, for taking on boy actors as apprentices, and for hiring other actors for each production. They also were liable when legal proceedings were brought against the company.

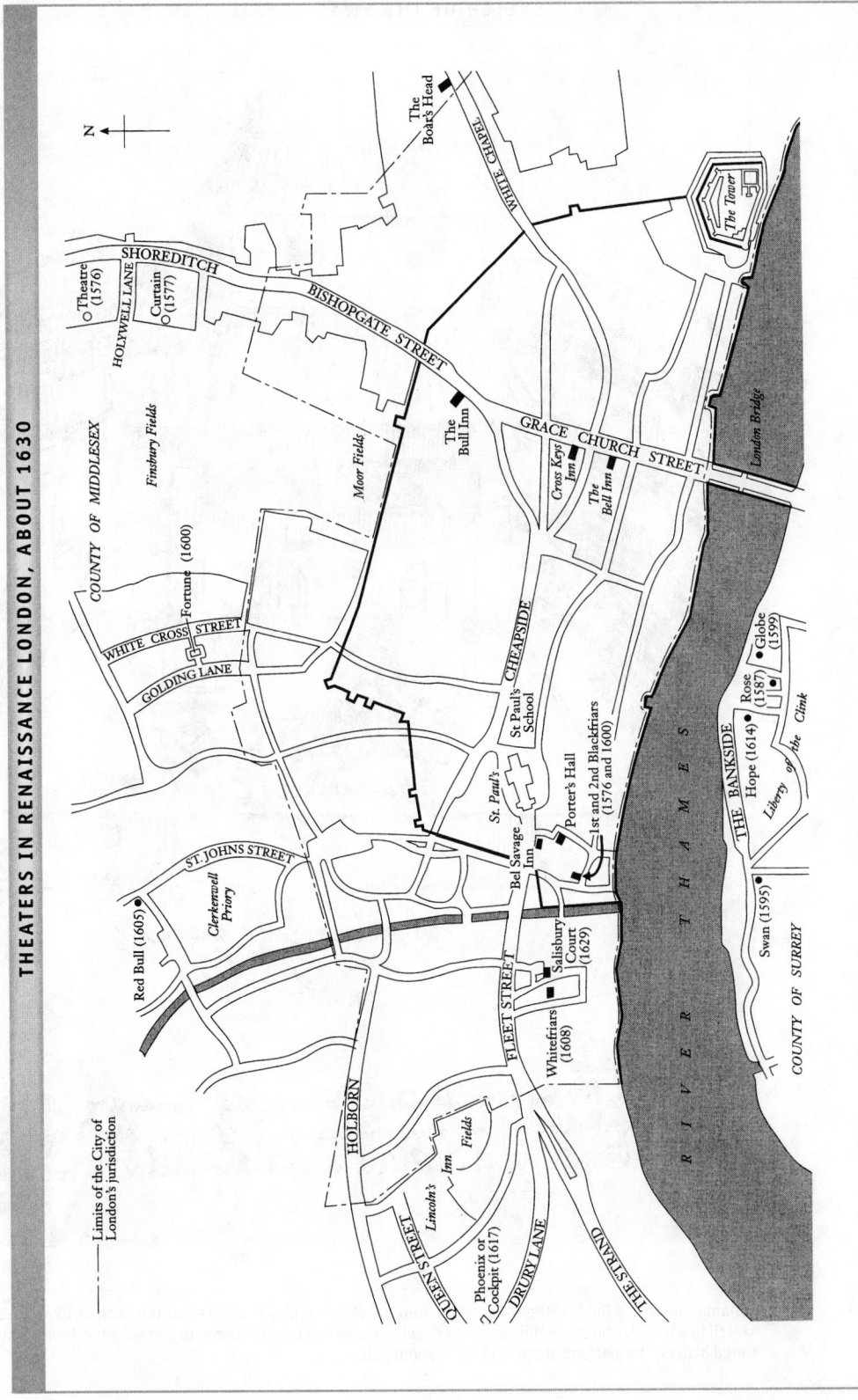

THEATERS IN RENAISSANCE LONDON, ABOUT 1630

A number of theaters were constructed in London after 1574. The dark line extending from The Tower (lower right) to Blackfriars in the west is the old city wall. Note that, with the exception of the first and second Blackfriars theaters, the theaters are either north of the city (the Fortune, The Theatre, the Curtain, the Red Bull) or south of the Thames River (the Swan, the Hope, the Rose, the Globe).

SKETCH OF THE SWAN THEATER, 1596

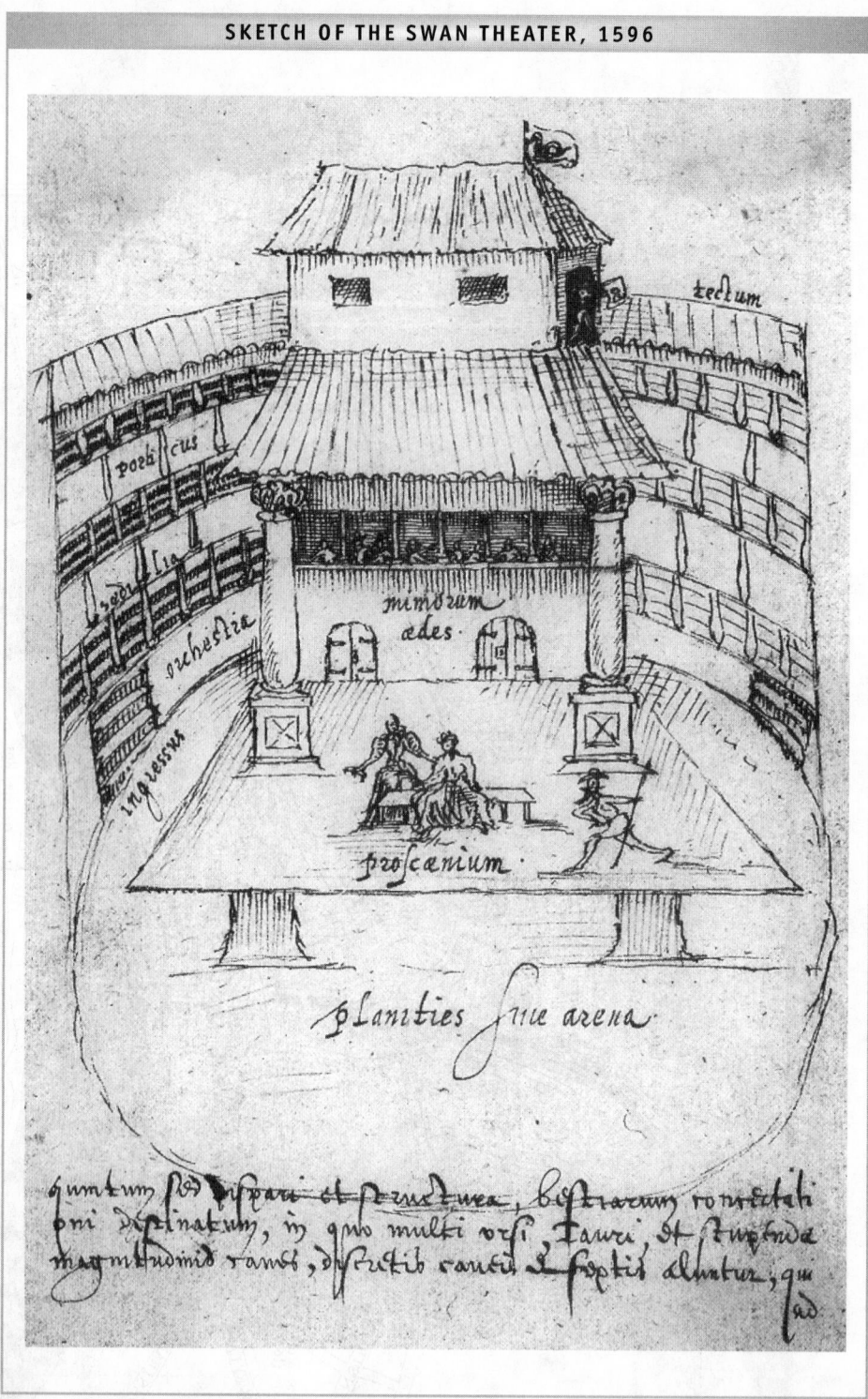

Johannes de Witt, a Dutch visitor to London, drew a sketch of a play in progress at the Swan in 1596. He sent the sketch to a friend, who made this copy. The drawing shows the tiring house with its two stage doors, a three-tiered gallery, the platform stage, and the standing pit.

MODERN RECONSTRUCTION OF THE SWAN THEATER

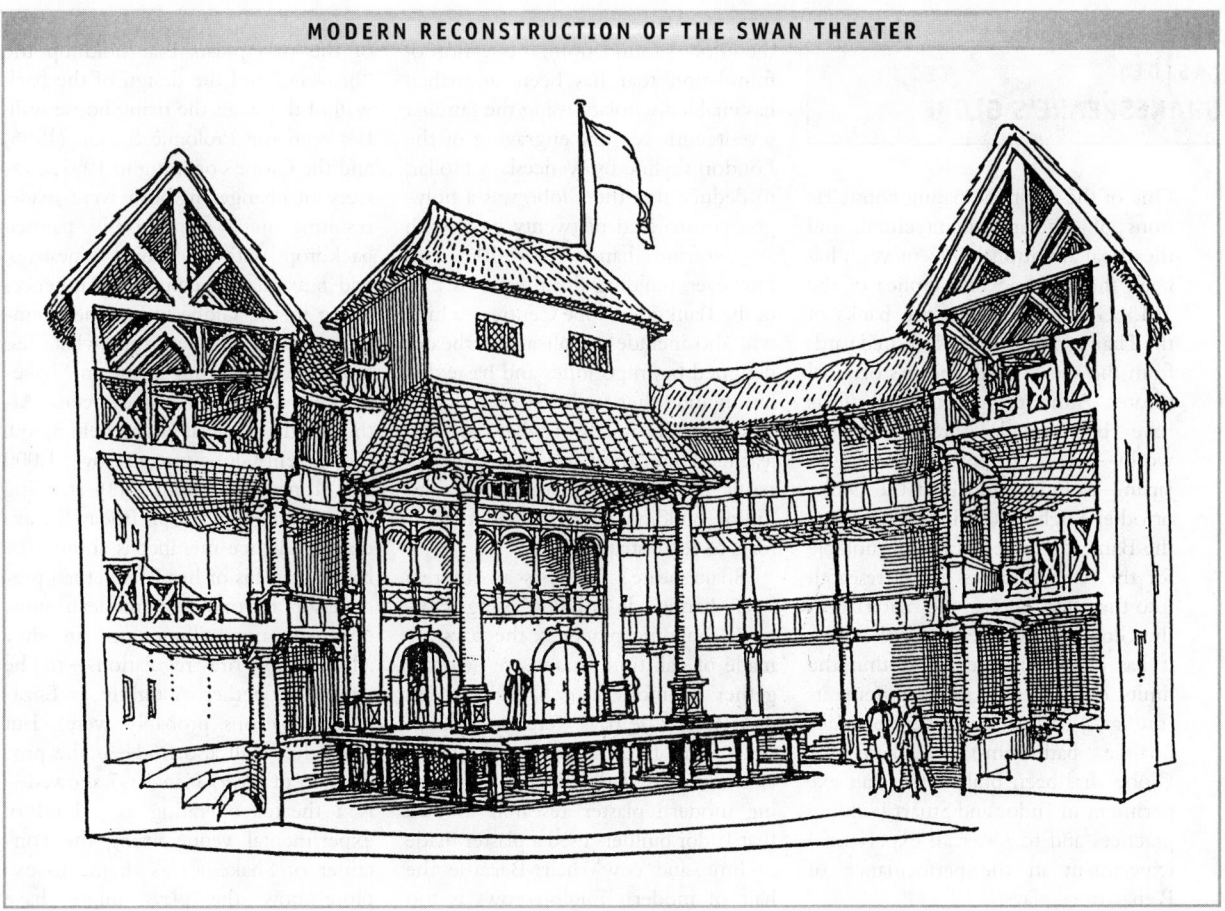

C. Walter Hodges based this reconstruction on the de Witt sketch.

Although several companies flourished during the theater's heyday, life for actors and playwrights was hard. Until 1594, all professional playing companies were forced to perform in a variety of places, in London's various theaters and on tour. Although the scene with the players in *Hamlet* implies that touring was an occasional hardship of the London companies, recent research demonstrates that touring had been commonplace before the building of London's theaters and remained an important aspect of a theater company's vitality throughout the period. Playwrights, who were paid a flat fee by the company for the script of a play, hustled to scrape together a living: Thomas Dekker spent time in debtors' prison, and Ben Jonson died in penury. On the other hand, the theater also provided an opportunity for advancement as well. Several actors, including Richard Burbage and Edward Alleyn, were able to amass considerable fortunes. Shakespeare used the money he received as sharer to invest in property both in London and in his home, Stratford-upon-Avon, where he purchased a large house and land. Such careers were the exception rather than the rule, however, in an era when the theater was widely regarded as illicit and was frequently declared illegal.

English companies performed on three kinds of stage—large, open, outdoor buildings called **PUBLIC THEATERS** that held as many as 3,000 people; smaller, indoor, more elite **PRIVATE THEATERS** holding perhaps 700; and private performances at court or at the home of the patron. Public theaters, inspired both by the innyard booths where companies performed on

The Theaters

(ASIDE)
SHAKESPEARE'S GLOBE

One of the most fascinating constellations of scholarly, architectural, and theatrical ambition in recent years has been the building of a replica of the 1613 Globe theater on the banks of the Thames River, a few hundred yards from the site of Shakespeare's original theater. Although a variety of efforts have been made throughout the world—one is currently under way in Japan—to build models of the Globe or other English Renaissance theaters, the Bankside project has been notable for the scrupulousness of its research into the location, size, and materials of the Globe and for the care with which it has been constructed. Within the limits of modern legal requirements (fire laws) and social conventions (accessible bathrooms), "Shakespeare's Globe" has been built both as an experiment in Tudor and Stuart building practices and to foster an experiential experiment in the performance of Renaissance plays.

The American actor Sam Wanamaker instigated the project and remained its guiding force until his death in 1993. Part of Wanamaker's vision was that the theater should be both a theatrical and a scholarly endeavor, and much of the success of the final project is due to the team he assembled, including the scholar Andrew Gurr, architect Theo Crosby (who died in 1994), and artistic director Mark Rylance. The accuracy of the building was immeasurably helped by the discovery in 1989 of a section of the Globe's foundation beneath a nineteenth-century building adjacent to the Southwark bridge; although Anchor Terrace is protected as a landmark (preventing much excavation of

the Globe's foundation), the section of foundation that has been unearthed has enabled scholars, using the familiar seventeenth-century engraving of the London skyline by Wenceslaus Hollar, to deduce that the Globe was a polygon constructed of twenty bays, with an exterior diameter of 100 feet. However, building the theater as part of the Bankside Globe Centre—which will also include a replica of a theater designed by Inigo Jones and has exhibition and other facilities—was not an easy task, and much of what has been learned about the Globe has been the result of scholarly investigation into Tudor building practices and the efforts to reconstruct them.

Shakespeare's Globe is an impressively handmade building, using traditional building practices: the bays are made of oak timbers and are held together by more than 6,000 wooden pegs. Once the bays were erected, the walls were filled in with oak staves, lath, and then plastered: rather than using modern plaster, research showed that Tudor builders used a plaster made of lime and cow's hair. Because the hair of modern English cows is too short, the Globe builders used a lime plaster mixed with goat hair. A fire sheet was put between each wall, and tests on the resulting lath-and-plaster showed that it could resist 1,000 degrees Fahrenheit for three hours— long enough to empty the theater in an emergency (when the Globe burned in 1613, no injuries were reported, either). The building is also the first wood-framed building to be built in London since the great fire of 1666: its thatched roof is applied in the traditional manner and has been treated with a fire-retardant chemical, and a sprinkler system is installed just under the roofline.

By far the most controversial aspect of the building has been the location

of the two pillars that hold up the "heavens," and the design of the back wall of the stage, the tiring house wall. Between the Prologue Season (1996) and the Globe's opening in 1997, a variety of changes in both were made, resulting in a sumptuously painted backdrop with additional tapestries, and faux-marble columns. Audiences going to the Globe today find themselves in a theater somewhat less crowded than a full house in Shakespeare's day might have been. Although the original Globe held 3,000, the current Globe seats just over 1,000 and can hold about 500 standing "groundlings" in the pit (today, the average audience member is about 10% larger than his or her Elizabethan predecessor; beyond that, modern audiences are not willing—nor are they allowed by fire regulations—to be jammed together as tightly as Elizabethan patrons probably were). But what they will also find—as the production of *Henry V* in 1997 showed— is a theater operating as a kind of experimental venue, using the container of Shakespeare's drama to explore how the plays might have worked in their original conditions. At the present time, the company intends to do some productions in period dress (the costumes often themselves made with Tudor cloth-making and dye techniques), but to do others in modern dress. The result of a massive and energetic combination of talents, Shakespeare's Globe is finally meant to work as a living theater.[1]

---

[1]The building of the Globe was recorded in a variety of newspaper and scholarly accounts throughout the early 1990s; students interested in learning more about Shakespeare's Globe should consult Shakespeare's Globe Education Centre, Bankside, London SE1 9DT, United Kingdom.

THE GLOBE THEATER FOUNDATION

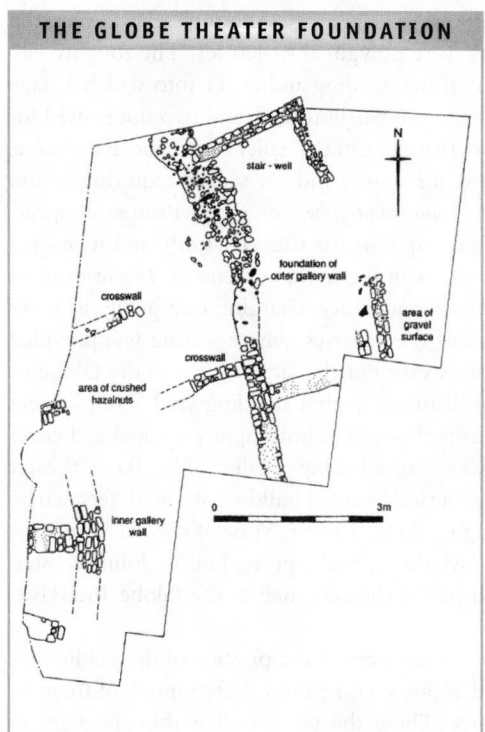

In 1989, part of the foundation of the Globe theater was discovered. This portion of the Globe foundation extends from beneath a landmark nineteenth-century building; the remainder of the Globe foundation is beneath the building and therefore cannot be excavated. Nonetheless, this section of the inner and outer wall of the theater, and of the exterior stairwell which led to the galleries, has enabled scholars to gauge with much greater accuracy both the size and configuration of Shakespeare's theater.

DESIGNING SHAKESPEARE'S GLOBE

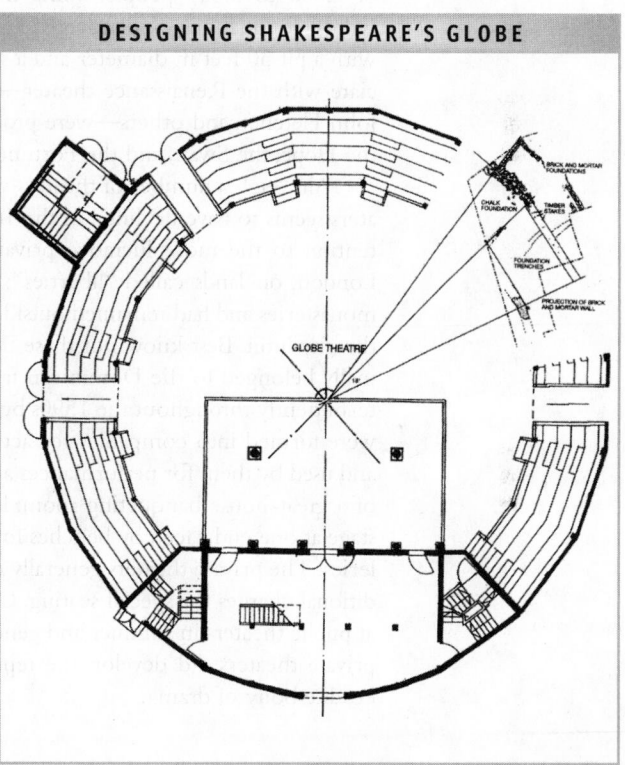

This illustration shows how the archaeological evidence of the Globe theater foundations has been used, along with other evidence, to develop a new understanding of the theater's size and shape. The foundations, which comprise two "bays" or sections of the Globe's exterior structure, enabled Theo Crosby, the architect of the reconstructed Shakespeare's Globe in London, to estimate the overall dimensions of the building (about ninety-nine feet in diameter) and also to determine that the Globe was a twenty-sided polygon.

tour and by the circular arenas used for animal baiting, were outdoor buildings accommodating a large and diverse audience for afternoon performances. Although one theater, the Fortune, was rectangular, most public theaters were polygonal structures. The roughly circular, three-story gallery surrounded an open pit for standing audiences, into which a stage extended at a height of about five feet. The stage was partly roofed, and two doors used for entrances were set into the rear wall, or **TIRING HOUSE.** On the gallery level above the stage, small rooms were used for aristocratic seating, for music, and for scenes requiring action above the stage—as in the balcony scene in *Romeo and Juliet,* or when Prospero appears "aloft" in *The Tempest.* The stage had a central trapdoor (or **GRAVE TRAP**), and its roofed area held a pulley for raising or lowering actors (as in the masque scene in *The Tempest*) or properties. The public theaters catered to a paying audience, charging one penny to enter the pit and an additional penny to enter each of the galleries, where seating was provided on benches. Estimates on the size of the theaters vary, but the largest, such as the Globe or the Fortune, were about 100 feet in external diameter, with a standing yard about 70 feet across, and a stage 45 feet wide and 27 feet deep; they could hold tightly-packed audiences of 2,000 to 3,000 people. Some theaters were considerably smaller. The Rose theater (whose foundation was discovered in 1989) was a twelve-sided building about 70 feet across, with a pit 50 feet in diameter and a stage roughly 25 by 15 feet. Most of the plays we associate with the Renaissance theater—those of Marlowe, Shakespeare, Jonson, John Webster, John Fletcher, and others—were produced in public theaters such as the Globe, the Rose, the Hope, the Swan, and the Fortune.

Although a number of theaters were built in this period, the prestige of the public theaters seems to have declined in the 1620s and 1630s as companies shifted much of their attention to the more lucrative private theaters. These theaters stood within the City of London, on lands called "liberties"; a liberty was a property that had once belonged to monasteries and had remained outside the city's legal jurisdiction, even though it was within the city limit. Best known of these theaters is the Blackfriars playhouse (the property originally belonged to the Dominican friars, who wore black gowns). Blackfriars was used intermittently throughout the 1590s by boys' companies, troupes of boy chapel choristers who were formed into companies for acting plays. Blackfriars was acquired by the King's Men and used by them for performances after 1608. These theaters were modeled along the lines of a great-house banqueting room: long indoor rooms illuminated by candles, with a low stage at one end, faced by benches for seating and flanked by additional seats along side galleries. The private theaters generally charged sixpence or more for basic admission, with additional charges for special seating. Companies performed at private theaters in winter and at public theaters in summer and generally brought the same repertoire to both venues. The private theaters did develop the reputation, however, for originating a more satirical and erudite body of drama.

DRAMA AND PERFORMANCE

Performing plays in **REPERTORY** over perhaps as many as 200 days a year, the London companies competed with each other for their audiences and generated an enormous demand for new plays. The plays that they bought and performed are among the greatest works of English literature. English drama in this period comprises plays on English history (such as Shakespeare's *Henry V* and *Richard III,* or Marlowe's *Edward II*); on classical history (Shakespeare's *Julius Caesar* and *Coriolanus,* Ben Jonson's *Sejanus*); romantic comedies (such as Shakespeare's *A Midsummer Night's Dream*); city comedies (Shakespeare's *Measure for Measure*); heroic tragedies (Shakespeare's *Hamlet* and *King Lear,* John Webster's *The Duchess of Malfi*); and plays of intrigue or satire (John Marston's *The Malcontent,* Thomas Middleton's *The Changeling*). Later in the period, audiences seemed to develop a taste for plays they called **TRAGICOMEDIES,** usually romantic plays that begin in the tragic vein but proceed to a happy resolution. Several of John Fletcher's plays are tragicomedies of this kind, and Shakespeare's *Cymbeline* and *The Tempest* resemble tragicomedy as well.

This list of genres suggests both the fertile range of innovation in the Renaissance theater and the drama's dependence on models drawn from the classical and medieval theaters. Roman drama—the comedies of Plautus and Terence and the tragedies of Seneca—was widely used in schools and universities as part of the teaching of Latin, and university students often staged these plays in Latin. It is not surprising, then, that some features of classical drama made their way into the Renaissance theater. The model of Shakespearean romantic comedy—mistaken identities, separated lovers, an irascible old man or father, a wily servant— derives directly from Plautus's plays; indeed, Shakespeare's *Comedy of Errors* directly adapts Plautus's *The Menaechmus Twins.* In a similar fashion, the violence of Seneca's tragedies makes its way directly into the action of Elizabethan drama. Formally and thematically, however, Renaissance drama also differs sharply from its classical ancestors. Renaissance plays tend to be more diffuse, involving a greater variety of characters and multiple plots; in tragedy, the action is often not quite as closely focused on the fortunes of a single hero as it is in classical tragedy. In these and other ways—in the Christian providence that seems to stand behind the action of many plays, in its variety of contemporary characters, in its use of symbolic anachronism, and in the complex relationship between the dramatic world and the world of the audience—Renaissance drama bears the signs of its medieval inheritance.

Playwrights generally wrote in **BLANK VERSE,** an unrhymed **IAMBIC PENTAMETER** line (ten syllables with alternating stress), and occasionally used other verse forms as well. They often used prose, sometimes for emphasis, sometimes to develop the qualities of a particular character. Although modern editors divided the plays into five acts, in most cases Renaissance playwrights probably did not compose their plays in this form. Performance on the public theater stage was rapid and continuous. The theaters used an open stage, few large properties, and had little or no scenery onstage, so that scenes could follow one another without interruption.

Despite the absence of elaborate stage sets, performance in the Renaissance theater was nonetheless spectacular. Actors used costumes, properties, and language to transform the midafternoon stage into a dramatic locale—Prospero's desert island, Lear's heath, Faustus's study. Some larger properties could be wheeled out from the rear doors, or perhaps raised from the trap: a throne, for instance, or a bed for Desdemona in *Othello,* or the hell-mouth used at the end of *Doctor Faustus.* A cannon fired during a production of Shakespeare's *Henry VIII* in 1613 unfortunately set fire to the Globe and burned it to the ground.

The unlocalized stage of medieval drama can be seen as the forerunner of the Renaissance theater's fluid use of stage space. The open stage made for an almost cinematic flexibility in performance, as the play could range rapidly from scene to scene, place to place. Costuming was eclectic and anachronistic: the actors wore mainly Elizabethan clothing, adding armor, royal finery, motley, or some "classical" style of gowns when needed. The actors—Burbage, Alleyn, Will Kemp, among many others—were widely praised for their power and effectiveness. Their acting style was oratorical in tragedy and extemporaneous in comedy, but there is no doubt that many were consummate performers, in command of dozens of roles that could be put into play at short notice.

WOMEN IN DRAMA AND PERFORMANCE

Boy actors played a significant part in the experience of English theater, for boy actors played the parts of women and girls onstage, including major roles like Lady Macbeth, Ophelia, and Cleopatra. Much as they did in classical Athens, "women" emerged onstage in Renaissance London only as a side-effect of masculine attitudes and performances. In the English theater, this **CROSS-DRESSING** came into special prominence, though, because the romantic, sexual, and political intrigue so popular in Renaissance plays was often focused on

THE JACOBEAN COURT MASQUE

One of the principal obligations of the professional companies was to perform at court or for their patron. Performances at court often took place during holidays and were commanded with increasing frequency by James I and Charles I. The companies performed many of their staple plays at court, but they also performed special entertainments called MASQUES, plays written in verse, usually on mythological subjects, that involved dancing, fanciful costumes, music, and special scenic machinery and effects. While the actors spoke the lines in these plays, they shared the stage with members of the court, who performed in the elaborate dances that began, punctuated, and ended the masques. The little play that Prospero puts on for Ferdinand and Miranda in Shakespeare's *The Tempest* resembles court masques in many ways, with its cast of goddesses, its formal singing and dancing, and the ceremonial quality of the occasion it celebrates.

Masques were an elaborate and expensive entertainment; some were performed on special state occasions. Jonson's *Hymenaei* (1605) celebrated the marriage of Lady Essex and *The Masque of Oberon* (1610) was written to celebrate Prince Henry's investiture as Prince of Wales, and all had important implications for the mythology of the Stuart dynasty. Because members of the royal and aristocratic families performed in the masques, the poet was challenged to devise a setting and dramatic narrative that were elevated enough for the courtly audience and to dignify the aristocratic performers. Each masque included several "grand masquing dances," which were performed by members of the court, often costumed as "characters" in the masque.

Jonson was by far the most renowned writer of masques, though the playwrights James Shirley, William Davenant (who became a critically important theater manager after the restoration of the monarchy in 1660), and others also wrote masques. Jonson wrote more than a dozen masques, and in the course of his long career innovated the genre in several ways. While the earlier Stuart masques tend to have a relatively simple narrative, later masques, beginning with *The Masque of Queens* (1609), adopted a more complicated structure. *The Masque of Queens* begins with an ANTIMASQUE, a scene involving witches, goblins, or demons who are magically transformed into goddesses or allegorical virtues in the course of the action.

His majesty, then, being set, and the whole company in full expectation, the part of the scene which first presented itself was an ugly hell, which flaming beneath, smoked unto the top of the roof. And in respect all evils are, morally said to come from hell, . . . these witches, with a kind of hollow and infernal music, came forth from thence. First one, then two, and three, and more, till their number increased to eleven, all differently attired: some with rats on their head, some on their shoulders; others with ointment pots at their girdles; all with spindles, timbrels, rattles or other venefical [having to do with witchcraft] instruments, making a confused noise, with strange gestures.

The witches dance and pronounce a series of charms until, suddenly, "with a strange and sudden music,"

they fell into a magical dance full of preposterous change and gesticulation. . . . In the heat of their dance on the sudden was heard a sound of loud music, as if many instruments had made one blast; with which not only the hags themselves but the hell into which they ran quite vanished, and the whole face of the scene altered, scarce suffering the memory of such a thing. But in the place of it appeared a glorious and magnificent building figuring the House of Fame, in the top of which were discovered the twelve masquers sitting upon a throne triumphal erected in form of a pyramid and circled with all store of light. From whom a person, by this time descended, in the furniture of Perseus, and expressing heroic and masculine virtue began to speak.[1]

The antimasque establishes a world of demonic disorder, which suddenly vanishes when the members of the court appear in the House of Fame, among classical heroes and virtues. We can get a sense of the delicacy of Jonson's situation when we recognize that the performers of the masque included the queen herself, as well as the countesses of Arundel, Derby, Huntington, Bedford, Essex, and Montgomery, Viscountess Cranborne, and several ladies in waiting. Members of the court were both performers and the audience of this self-enclosed spectacle, which almost of necessity reflected back on its audience an idealized vision of courtly perfection. Indeed, in the last Stuart masque, *Salmacida Spolia,* written by Davenant, both the king and the queen were among the dancers.

As an ambitious writer, Jonson thought the masques were essentially a vehicle for his splendid poetry. But as even this brief description suggests, the masques were highly dependent on the development of new scenic technology and on the skills of the architect and designer Inigo Jones (1573–1652). The masques were unusually expensive: one of King James's masques cost more than £4,000, and one of King Charles's cost £21,000. Much of

_____

[1] From *Ben Jonson: Selected Masques,* ed. Stephen Orgel (New Haven, CT: Yale University Press, 1970).

this money was spent on the elaborate, changeable scenery that accompanied the masques, the first changeable scenery in the English theater. Inigo Jones designed the theater space where masques were performed, the banqueting hall of Whitehall Palace. Jones had visited Italy in 1600; he may have visited again during 1607–1608, and he is known to have been in Italy from 1613 to 1615. In Italy he came into contact with the theater designs of Andrea Palladio (1518–1580), who adapted the design of classical Roman theaters for indoor stages: Palladio's Teatro Olimpico had a curved amphitheater-like auditorium and a proscenium stage. As court architect and designer, Jones had the opportunity both to import Palladio's understanding of theatrical design, and to develop his own interest in elaborate spectacle. The stage at Whitehall was about forty feet wide by twenty-eight feet deep, and gently raked. Although Jones's theater at Whitehall changed during his long tenure at court, it eventually consisted of staggered wings and a backdrop to convey a sense of perspective. Unlike both the public and private theaters of Renaissance London, Jones's theater was the first to use changeable scenery, and when the theaters reopened in 1660, the English companies brought this aristocratic inheritance with them: Jones's **WINGS-AND-BACKDROP** designs became the basic model for changeable scenery throughout the eighteenth century.

Jones's interest in spectacle was far reaching, and he devised the instruments to execute many of Jonson's most elaborate poetic images: flying machines, a globe that opened to reveal several aristocratic dancers, and brilliant costumes to dress the masques' allegorical characters. But it was Jones's development of a perspective in the theater that was most deeply implicated in the rhetoric of court life. At Whitehall performances, the King sat on a raised, central dais directly in front of the stage; since none of the other courtiers could be seated with their backs to the King,

FIERY SPIRIT

Inigo Jones created this costume for a fiery spirit in 1635.

those closer to the stage were seated along the side walls of the room, while others were seated behind the royal spectator. It has been argued that the king was positioned in a complex relation to the stage and to the rest of the audience: not only was he the only spectator for whom the illusion of perspective was complete (the other spectators could probably see between the wings, for example), but the rest of the audience could *see* that only the king had a perfect vision of the world onstage. The closer one sat to the royal seat, the more one's view of the illusion onstage approximated the king's ideal vantage. Spectators and performers, in other words, engaged in a richly hierarchical sense of illusion in which the King's centrality—and, in a sense, his omniscience—was constantly displayed, and each spectator's distance from that sense of illusion was constantly experienced. Like Jonson, whose texts frequently betray his intense

awareness of his royal audience and aristocratic performers, Jones's perspective theater reflects the increasingly absolutist ideology of the Stuart monarchy.

The banqueting hall at Whitehall played one more ironic role in the history of performance. Charles I became increasingly hostile to Parliament—he refused to call Parliament from 1629 to 1640—and when civil war broke out in 1642, Charles fled London. The Royalist forces were concentrated in Oxford, and in 1647 Charles was defeated and captured by the Parliamentary army. In 1649, he was sentenced to death by Parliament, and he visited the Whitehall banquet hall on his way to his execution. The executioner's block was set on a large public stage outside a window of the banquet hall; Charles was led through the room where the masques' brilliant fantasies had been staged for him to his own last performance—the public stage where he was beheaded.

COSTUMES FOR SHAKESPEARE'S *TITUS ANDRONICUS*

Dating from about 1595, this drawing appears to show a scene from *Titus Andronicus,* by William Shakespeare.
Two of the actors wear pseudoclassical Roman costumes; the others are dressed in Elizabethan clothing.

female characters and therefore on the performance of the boy actors. Indeed, the drama frequently uses cross-dressing as a way of interrogating the power and perquisites of gender, in ways that sometimes confirm and sometimes question the role of gender in English society. English society was an overtly hierarchical one, and despite the power of the "Virgin Queen," women had little access to education, most could not hold property, and they were generally subject to discrimination of many kinds. In this social economy and in a theater in which Puritan opposition to the stage frequently criticized the theater's "effeminacy," the absence of women from the stage became a powerful sign of their absence from other scenes of power. Much as sumptuary laws prevented individuals from wearing jewels and clothing above their social station, so too was cross-dressing a legal offense in sixteenth-century England, punishable by whipping and a prison sentence. The license of the theater, the freedom to create magical new worlds on the stage, was, like other forms of power in the period, the prerogative of men, and the images that men created for the stage are in important ways imprinted with the signs of a specifically masculine imagination. As with all stage conventions, cross-dressing was deeply implicated in the values of the culture outside the theater, so much so that when women did perform onstage in England—a French company used actresses at Blackfriars in 1629—they met with hostility, ridicule, and rejection.

Nonetheless, women not only attended the theater, but a few—aristocratic women, who often patronized poets and other artists—also wrote plays, and sometimes performed in them at court. Queen Elizabeth is thought to have translated a passage from Seneca's *Hercules on Mount Oeta,* and other women similarly adapted or wrote plays. Mary Sidney, Countess of Pembroke and sister of Sir Philip Sidney, translated Robert Garnier's play *The Tragedy of Antonie* in the 1590s. Her niece, Lady Mary Wroth (daughter of Mary Sidney's brother, Robert, and a frequent participant in Jacobean court masques), wrote a mythological play,

Love's Victory, probably in the early 1620s. Perhaps the best-known plays today are Elizabeth Cary, Viscountess of Falkland's *Tragedy of Miriam* (published in 1613) and the plays published by Margaret Cavendish, Marchioness of Newcastle, in 1662 and 1668. Although these plays were not staged—aristocratic women did not traffic in theater business—they have since become a critical part of our understanding of English Renaissance drama.

The theater had an extraordinary hold on the English imagination. In their many progresses, pageants, and allegorical entertainments, the English monarchs revealed a keen sense of the power of fictive images to represent reality, or a version of it, and so to shape their subjects' understanding of royal power. Playwrights and audiences also found in the theater a magical image of human possibility. Think of Prospero summoning the storm, Ariel, and other spirits with his stagey magic; or of the playwright John Webster's description of "an excellent actor": "All men have been of his occupation, and indeed what he doth feignedly, that do others essentially: this day one plays a Monarch, the next a private person. Here one acts a Tyrant, on the morrow an Exile; a Parasite [sponger] this man tonight, tomorrow a Precisian [Puritan], and so of divers others." Acting and the theater provided a liberating image of human—or, at least, masculine—power: the power to transform oneself and the world. However, the rich, strange, transforming freedom of the theater could also seem empty and terrifying, even demonic. Rather than an image of human potential, the theater could seem to offer an image of the poverty of human action, the sterile and deceptive emptiness of the world we make and inhabit. As King Lear preaches to blinded Gloucester, "When we are born, we cry that we are come / To this great stage of fools." Puritan critics of the theater insistently reminded audiences that the stage's methods—to seduce with the vain and showy image of a false reality—were also Satan's, and that the theater subversively invited audiences to "unman, unChristian, uncreate themselves." Yet it is precisely this transforming power that lies at the heart of the Renaissance theater's fascination for its audience. Although the theater sometimes seemed to depict a world threatened with constant change and loss, it also presented the power of illusion to recreate the real.

Although the banning of the cycle dramas in England in the sixteenth century marked an ending of the traditions of medieval drama and theater there, the same was not true on the continent, where both cycle dramas and morality dramas continued to be performed. In Spain, for example, the **AUTOS SACRAMENTALES**—morality plays on Christian themes— were produced in major cities such as Madrid, and had an important influence on dramatic writing as well (see Unit IV). Similarly, staging short pageants—like the shepherd plays or *pastorelas* performed today throughout Latin America, and in many Latino communities in the United States, before Christmas—has remained a part of religious festivities in many places; perhaps the most striking of these is the processional staging of the Passion held in Oberammergau, Germany.

In many respects, though, the vivid and popular style of the cycle plays had to wait until the late nineteenth and early twentieth centuries to find an audience; when the manuscripts of the four English cycles first began to be studied seriously in the nineteenth century, their plays were seen merely as primitive precursors to the more finished, literary achievement of English Renaissance dramatists. However, this model of the "evolution" of dramatic forms, from "simple" to "complex," is not really borne out by a close examination of the plays themselves, which use a popular literary and theatrical medium to undertake a drama of enormous subtlety, scope, and power. Beginning in the twentieth century, a number of efforts were made to stage medieval drama—both the cycle plays and morality plays, such as *Everyman*—and the force and theatrical vitality of the plays became immediately apparent. In recent years, the cycle plays have been staged frequently, both in their traditional

MEDIEVAL AND RENAISSANCE DRAMA IN PERFORMANCE AND HISTORY

locations (at York, for instance), and elsewhere: the University of Toronto and the Court Theater at the University of Chicago have mounted very well received versions.

Although the English theaters were closed in 1642, interrupting the practices both of playwriting and of theatrical performance, the secular drama of Renaissance England has had in many respects a more sustained tradition. When the theaters reopened in 1660, they reopened in a very different form—indoor theaters, using lights and stage machinery, replaced the outdoor public theaters of the Jacobean and Caroline periods—and to a much more narrowly circumscribed audience (see Unit IV). And while there was considerable demand for new plays, for many years some plays of the Renaissance period held the stage, and indeed provided the dramatic conventions on which new plays were mapped. While today we tend to think of Shakespeare as the preeminent writer of his era, in the Restoration period, Shakespeare's plays were revived less frequently than those of other playwrights, notably Ben Jonson, James Shirley, and Francis Beaumont and John Fletcher; it was only in the eighteenth century that Shakespeare's plays began to have something approaching their current popularity.

The history of Shakespeare in the theater, however, is a history of adaptation: the concept that Shakespeare's plays have an inner logic and should be performed "as they were written" is a purely modern idea. Shakespeare's plays were, of course, altered in the practice of his own company, and playwrights in the later seventeenth and eighteenth centuries adapted the plays to the taste of their era. John Dryden, for example, transformed Shakespeare's erotically supercharged Antony and Cleopatra into an honorable Roman and his staid matron in his version of *Antony and Cleopatra,* called *All for Love* (1677). Nahum Tate's version of Shakespeare's *King Lear* (1681) concludes with Edgar marrying Cordelia (yes, she lives) and retiring happily offstage with Lear (he lives, too) and Kent; this version of *Lear* held the stage well into the nineteenth century. Rather than regarding these revisions as quaintly misguided, we should recognize that theatrical production always rewrites the drama in the idiom of the day; to their audiences, these productions were fully "Shakespearean," just as recent films—Kenneth Branagh's setting of *Hamlet* in the nineteenth century, Baz Luhrmann's framing *Romeo and Juliet* as a gang war in a Latin American Verona, or Michael Almereyda's use of Ethan Hawke as an alienated, technologically adept modern New Yorker in his *Hamlet*—are efforts to make Shakespeare speak in ways that will be powerful to audiences today.

Indeed, today we tend to think of Shakespeare across a variety of media: in film and television and advertising as well as in a range of theatrical venues. But for the seventeenth, eighteenth, and nineteenth centuries, Shakespeare was the property of the theater, and many actors and actresses became famous for their portrayals of Shakespearean roles: Thomas Betterton (1635–1710), Charles Macklin (1700–1797), Sarah Siddons (1755–1831), Edmund Kean (1789–1833), Sir Henry Irving (1838–1905), the first English actor to be knighted, and Ellen Terry (1847–1928) are just a few. In many respects, though, David Garrick (1717–1779) had the greatest impact as a Shakespearean actor. In part through his celebrated performances—he was renowned as Hamlet, Macbeth, and Richard III—Garrick helped to create a new interest in Shakespeare in the theater: he had his portrait painted frequently in Shakespearean roles (Hogarth's painting of Garrick as Richard III is a famous example), and he used his popularity to advance Shakespeare's reputation, not least by staging a Shakespeare Jubilee in Stratford. Garrick was a friend of the great literary critic Samuel Johnson, and Garrick's efforts in the theater coincided with a series of attempts to produce better, more accurate editions of Shakespeare's plays. But although Garrick had the reputation of restoring "Shakespeare's" original texts to the stage, he could hardly hope to succeed in the face of a century of popular stage adaptations. Although Garrick did introduce some Shakespearean material that had previously been cut from performances, his King Lear survived the play just as Nahum Tate's did, and his Richard III bawled out—as he had ever since Colley Cibber revised the play in 1700—"Off with his head!" (Indeed, Cibber's version of *Richard III* cuts several characters and persisted on-stage well into the twentieth century; it also partly informs Laurence Olivier's film of the play.)

The stage production of Shakespearean drama has always responded to the beliefs and values of its contemporary audiences. Tate's adaptation of *King Lear* was praised by Johnson, for example, for its happy ending seemed to restore justice in the theater; Johnson thought Shakespeare's original ending fine for readers, but too bleak and destructive for the stage. Shakespeare's plays were adapted to the more melodramatic and sentimental tastes of the eighteenth century; in the nineteenth century, a vogue for historical accuracy and stage realism led to a series of splendid efforts to reconstruct the historical setting of the plays: medieval Scotland in Charles Kean's 1853 *Macbeth* or Christian-era England in Henry Irving's *Cymbeline* (1896). These changes in taste are reflected in acting style as well: Betterton's portrayal of Hamlet was renowned in the late seventeenth century for its gravity and grace; Betterton is said never to have raised his arms above his waist, an illustration of neoclassical decorum in performance. By the early decades of the nineteenth century, Samuel Taylor Coleridge remarked that watching Edmund Kean in performance was akin to reading Shakespeare "by flashes of lightning"; Kean's performance impressed his audiences precisely through his well-crafted *lack* of decorum, in accord with Romantic beliefs about emotional expressivity. Irving is in many ways the first modern actor in what we would recognize as a psychological tradition of acting; although his career preceded the Russian director Constantin Stanislavski's pioneering work on the style of realistic performance (see Unit V), Irving's penchant for subtle physical details of characterization—his enemies called them mannerisms—gave his work a psychological concreteness and complexity that was powerful to an audience whose understanding of dramatic character was trained on the novels of Charles Dickens and George Eliot.

The theater also registers its culture's changing social attitudes in its portrayal of Shakespearean roles. Charles Macklin, for example, was probably the first actor to take a more sympathetic portrayal of the Jewish moneylender Shylock in *The Merchant of Venice;* the role had traditionally been performed as a satiric stereotype. Yet even Macklin retained the comic red wig and beard with which Shylock had always been performed; Edmund Kean was the first actor to get rid of them. Henry Irving's production of the play ended after the Act IV trial scene: in his version, *The Merchant of Venice* becomes something more like "The Tragedy of Shylock." In 1994, Peter Sellars set the play in a version of Los Angeles and drew explicit parallels to the police beating of Rodney King and the uprising that followed the acquittal of the officers involved. In Sellars's production the play's Jews were all played as African Americans; the Venetians were all played as Latinos and Latinas; and Portia and her retinue were all played as Asian Americans. Although Sellars's production was deservedly controversial, it illustrates a sense that Shakespeare's drama is capable of entering into new situations unimagined by Shakespeare, and of saying new things as well.

In the twentieth century, the pictorial style favored by Victorian theaters has largely been replaced in an effort to stage the plays in the simpler style of Shakespeare's theater. The first experiments of this kind were undertaken by William Poel (1852–1934), who used his Elizabethan Stage Society to produce versions of *Twelfth Night* and other plays on an open stage, and using a text more closely approximating Shakespeare's. Poel made it possible to see Shakespeare's plays as lively and fast-moving (all those scene changes in Victorian productions had made a Shakespeare play a very long evening, requiring many cuts to compensate for all the time it took to raise and lower sets), and regardless of whether directors (a new role in the theater also dating to this period) have chosen to stage the plays in Elizabethan or other settings, the sense of a rapidly changing series of scenes, localized not by extensive sets onstage but by the language and action, informs most twentieth-century Shakespeare. Indeed, it is often said that filmic techniques—quick cutting between scenes made possible by camera work and editing—provided a means to understand how Shakespearean drama might be played differently onstage.

It is now possible to see a range of Shakespeares on the contemporary stage—not only Shakespeare performed in languages other than English, but through the eclectic range of theatrical styles characteristic of the modern stage. Some productions—the "restored" versions, such as the 1997 *Henry V,* at Shakespeare's Globe in London—work hard to use Elizabethan costumes to produce the flavor of Shakespeare's theater. Other productions set the plays in a different historical era (there have been several recent *Henry V* productions set in the American Civil War, for example) to make the workings of the play's society visible to us in more familiar circumstances. Still others use eclectic staging, combining set and costume elements from a variety of periods to take Shakespeare out of history—in the Royal Shakespeare Company's 1991 *Troilus and Cressida,* for example, Agamemnon appeared in a breastplate and a ratty old cardigan sweater: a kind of timeless image of the doddering old general.

Of course, the ability of the modern stage to bring a great technological flexibility to Shakespeare is matched by the possibilities of film. Shakespeare plays were among the first subjects of silent filmmakers, and many of the most distinguished films of the twentieth century are versions of Shakespearean drama. Indeed, contemporary students of Shakespeare are often much more likely to see a Shakespeare film than a live Shakespeare performance, especially with the number of exciting Shakespeare films produced in the 1990s: Kenneth Branagh in *Henry V, Much Ado About Nothing,* and *Hamlet;* Ian McKellan in *Richard III;* Mel Gibson in *Hamlet;* Leonardo Di Caprio and Claire Danes in *Romeo + Juliet.* As a part of the common cultural inheritance of the West—and indeed, frequently challenged as such by resistant, postcolonial productions in India, Canada, Africa, and elsewhere—Shakespeare is produced today across the spectrum of performance.

Michael Pennington appears as Hamlet in the Royal Shakespeare Company production, 1980.

In this scene from an American Shakespeare Theater production of *The Tempest,* Ariel describes how he has performed Prospero's commands.

As the "cavalier" costumes suggest, John Gielgud's acclaimed 1934 production of *Hamlet* was set in the later seventeenth century, rather than in the Elizabethan era; here, Hamlet and Laertes duel in the play's final scene.

READING THE MATERIAL THEATER

One of the most chastening facts concerning the early modern theater is that most of the drama performed on its stages has been lost: plays were given to the theater companies in handwritten manuscript; they were copied out by hand into parts—scrolls containing each actor's part, with cues for each of his speeches—and the copy of the play maintained by the company was, likewise, a handwritten copy. Needless to say, nearly all such manuscripts have been lost.

Although by the later sixteenth century typesetting was a familiar technology in Renaissance England, the proliferation of printed documents —volumes of classical Latin texts, broadsides, ballads, religious pamphlets, guides to domestic work, conduct books for courtiers—presented Shakespeare's audiences with an information explosion much akin to the one we face in the digital age. At the same time, print was not understood to be an appropriate vehicle for all forms of writing. Poets, for example, saw print—associated with declassé mercantile world—as an inferior mode for circulating their poems: to gain the kind of aristocratic prestige (and patronage) they most desired, poets typically circulated their poems in manuscript among the aristocrats at court.

Beyond that, printing was a relatively expensive endeavor, and theater companies—who owned the text of the play, having purchased it from the playwright—had little incentive to publish a successful play. Yet plays were published, frequently in a small, inexpensive format; because the sheet of paper on which the text is printed is folded twice (into four) before the book is bound, these small books are known bibliographically as **QUARTOS.** Because of their size, the sometimes slipshod character of their presswork, and their association with the theater, quarto volumes of plays were also stigmatized; Sir Thomas Bodley—whose library, the Bodleian, remains the Oxford University library—famously refused to purchase such "idle riffe-raffes" for his collection. Since quarto-sized volumes of individual plays were usually published in very small quantities, they are today quite rare.

Many of Shakespeare's plays were published in quarto form during his lifetime (*Hamlet,* for example, was published in two very different quarto versions), but nearly half of his plays— including *Macbeth, Antony and Cleopatra, The Tempest* and others—would be unknown to us without the efforts of two of his fellow-sharers, John Heminges and Henry Condell, who published a nearly complete collection of Shakespeare's plays (in the large-size **FOLIO** format) in 1623, seven years after the playwright's death. This was a signal event in the history of dramatic publishing—in 1623, only one other English dramatist, Ben Jonson, had published a collected *Works* on this scale.

We can learn a lot about the condition of the theater and about the relationship between theater practice and the emerging norms of print culture by closely examining the printed texts of Shakespeare's plays in both quarto and folio versions. Here, for example, is the title page of *Titus Andronicus,* one of Shakespeare's earliest successes, a play that has been adapted for film by the director and designer Julie Taymor, and a play that testifies to the fascination that Senecan drama held for playwrights and audiences in the 1580s and 1590s. It is a violent, rhetorically rich play. What can we learn about the theater, and about Renaissance attitudes toward theater, drama, and literature, from this title page? Some aspects to consider: How is the page designed? What are its most prominent visual features? How are different typefaces used to highlight different kinds of information? How is the book designed to appeal to a potential purchaser? What elements are visually prominent and which are less prominent? Is there information missing that might seem necessary to a modern purchaser? How can we read the information presented here as an index of the relation between two newly emerging industries—professional theater and literary publishing—in the period?

THE MOST LA mentable Romaine Tragedie of Titus Andronicus:

As it was Plaide by the Right Honourable the Earle of *Darbie*, Earle of *Pembrooke*, and Earle of *Suffex* their Seruants,

LONDON,
Printed by Iohn Danter, and are to be sold by *Edward White* & *Thomas Millington*, at the little North doore of Paules at the figne of the Gunne.
1594.

THE WAKEFIELD SECOND SHEPHERDS' PAGEANT

The cycle of Corpus Christi plays performed in the Yorkshire town of Wakefield is one of the best known of the cycles, not least due to the influence of an unknown writer known now as "the Wakefield Master." But while there is considerable information about the performance of the cycles in Chester and in York, much less is known about performance at Wakefield. In York, for example, each play in the Corpus Christi cycle was probably performed on a separate pageant wagon; the wagons were arranged in the order of the plays—from the first play, *The Fall of the Angels,* to the last, *The Last Judgment*—and proceeded through the city, stopping at each of twelve stations. Although we know that this procession began at 4:30 in the morning and proceeded until past midnight, scholars are still not entirely clear on the logistics of the entire cycle's performance.

The data recording productions at Wakefield are much sketchier than for York; Martial Rose suggests in his book, *The Wakefield Mystery Plays,* that the plays might have been staged at Wakefield in a different way. After a procession through the city, the wagons might have been brought to a single location—a square, or perhaps before the cathedral—where all the plays could be performed in sequence for a single audience. As in other towns, however, each pageant could have been performed by a different guild, and the guild would have had the responsibility both for developing the text of the play, and for maintaining appropriate costumes and properties, as well as the pageant wagon. However, the single surviving manuscript of the plays from Wakefield (usually called the Towneley manuscript) is somewhat less complete than the records of other towns: only three of the pageants are specifically assigned to individual guilds.

But the Wakefield cycle is interesting for many other reasons, though, not least for the work of the "Wakefield Master," who probably wrote in the early part of the fifteenth century. Although many of the pageants in the Wakefield cycle are similar to those in York—Wakefield had once been a part of York—six of the pageants in the manuscript use an unusual nine-line stanza. Although it's not clear whether these pageants were originally composed by the same individual or merely revised by the same hand, they share similar stylistic elements and are usually attributed to a single author. As is the case in *The Second Shepherds' Pageant,* these plays are distinctive in their hard-nosed portrayal of the tough conditions of rural life in medieval England and are written in a pungent south Yorkshire dialect. The Wakefield Master is usually said to have written, revised, or contributed to the Wakefield *Killing of Abel* play (possibly produced by the Glovers' guild), its *Noah* play, two plays on the subject of the shepherds, and a brilliant version of *The Buffeting of Christ.*

The Second Shepherds' Pageant is typical of the medieval cycle plays in its insis-

In this scene from *The Second Shepherds' Pageant,* Mak confronts one of the Shepherds.

tent counterpoint between the human world and the promise of eternal salvation, and this counterpoint is handled with the Wakefield Master's typical energy and subtlety. The first half of the play is a comedy, involving Mak's unsuccessful—and hilarious—attempt to pass off the lamb he has stolen from a group of local shepherds as his child; the second portion of the play begins with the Angel's appearance and summoning of the shepherds to Bethlehem. On one level, of course, the play's explicit parallel between Mak's lamb/child and the annunciation of the birth of Jesus, the Lamb of God, suggests a discontinuity between the tricky, trivial, and ultimately deceptive human world and the salvation that is to come. Indeed, it's a measure of the Wakefield Master's sure grasp of the sensibilities of his audience that this potentially blasphemous parody of the Nativity (Mak's wife swaddling the lamb to disguise it as their newborn baby) works not to undermine the miracle of the Christian narrative, but to distinguish the distractions of the fallen, human world from the powerful promise of salvation incarnated in the Nativity itself. The Angel appears to the shepherds at the moment they toss Mak in a blanket, and it should be noted that he does not accompany them to Bethlehem.

While *The Second Shepherds' Pageant* makes a searching formal comparison between human and divine events, it also uses anachronism in particularly effective ways: the Wakefield Master portrays the shepherds at the outset of the play not as long-ago characters in the faraway Holy Land; they are vividly characterized as the contemporaries of their medieval audience. We can hear the accents of a hard-working, overtaxed rural population irritated by their landed, supercilious masters throughout the opening moments of the play: when the First Shepherd complains of being "Fortaxed and rammed / We are made hand-tamed / With these gentlery-men" or when the Third Shepherd says that we "that sweats and swinks, / Eat our bread full dry, and that me forthinks. / We are oft wet and weary when mastermen winks." The plot of the play, in other words, enforces a formal contrast between the world of Mak and the promised deliverance of the Savior; in its insistent staging of the Christian narrative as something happening now, among us in its audience, the play forges a likeness between the past and the present, linking them together in a common Christian time. Like many cycle plays, the Wakefield *Second Shepherds' Pageant* asks its audience to contemplate the relationship between the eternal and the temporal by staging the Christian narrative in the everyday terms of medieval life.

THE WAKEFIELD SECOND SHEPHERDS' PAGEANT

Anonymous

CHARACTERS

FIRST SHEPHERD, *Coll*　　　WIFE OF MAK, *Gill*
SECOND SHEPHERD, *Gib*　　ANGEL
THIRD SHEPHERD, *Daw*　　　MARY, *with the Christ-child*
MAK, *the Sheep-stealer*

SCENE ONE

The open fields.

1 SHEPHERD: Lord, what these weathers are cold! And I am
　　　ill happed.
　　I am near-hand dold, so long have I napped;
　　My legs they fold, my fingers are chapped,
　　It is not as I would, for I am all lapped
5　　In sorrow.
　　In storms and tempest,
　　Now in the east, now in the west,
　　Woe is him has never rest
　　Mid-day nor morrow!

10　But we sely husbands that walk on the moor,
　　In faith, we are near-hands out of the door.
　　No wonder, as it stands, if we be poor,
　　For the tilth of our lands lies fallow as the floor,
　　As ye ken.
15　We are so hammed,
　　Fortaxed and rammed,
　　We are made hand-tamed
　　With these gentlery-men.

　　Thus they reave us our rest, our Lady them wary!
20　These men that are lord-fast, they cause the plough tarry.
　　That, men say, is for the best; we find it contrary.
　　Thus are husbands oppressed, in point to miscarry
　　On live.
　　Thus hold they us under,
25　Thus they bring us in blunder;
　　It were great wonder
　　And ever should we thrive.

　　For may he get a paint sleeve or a brooch, nowadays,
　　Woe is him that him grieve, or once again-says!

Dare no man him repreve, what mastery he mays;　　30
And yet may no man lieve one word that he says—
No letter.
He can make purveyance
With boast and braggance,
And all is through maintenance　　35
Of men that are greater.

There shall come a swain as proud as a po;
He must borrow my wain, my plough also;
Then I am full fain to grant ere he go.
Thus live we in pain, anger, and woe　　40
By night and day.
He must have, if he langed,
If I should forgang it;
I were better be hanged
Than once say him nay.　　45

It does me good, as I walk thus by mine own,
Of this world for to talk in manner of moan.
To my sheep will I stalk and harken anon,
There abide on a balk, or sit on a stone
Full soon;　　50
For I trow, pardie,
True men if they be,
We get more company
Ere it be noon.

(*Enter* SECOND SHEPHERD.)

2 SHEPHERD: Benste and Dominus, what may this bemean?　55
Why fares this world thus? Oft have we not seen.
Lord, these weathers are spitous, and the winds full keen,
And the frosts so hideous they water mine een—
No lie.
Now in dry, now in wet,　　60
Now in snow, now in sleet,
When my shoon freeze to my feet
It is not all easy.

---

1 **what . . . happed** how cold this weather is! And I am poorly clad　2 **near-hand dold** nearly numb　3 **they fold** give way　4 **lapped** wrapped　10 **But . . . husbands** but we poor husbandmen　11 **we . . . door** we are nearly homeless　13 **tilth** arable part　15 **hammed** crippled　16 **fortaxed and rammed** overtaxed and crushed　17–18 **We . . . gentlerymen** we are reduced to submission by these gentry　19 **They . . . wary** they rob us of our rest, our Lady curse them!　20 **lord–fast** bound to a lord　22–23 **in . . . live** in danger of coming to mortal harm　25 **blunder** trouble　27 **ever** if　28 **For . . . brooch** if he is able to get an embroidered sleeve, i.e., a lord's livery　29 **again–says** gainsays

30 **Dare . . . mays** no man dare reprove him, no matter what force he uses　31 **lieve** believe　33 **He . . . purveyance** he can requisition [our belongings]　34 **braggance** bragging　35 **maintenance** support　37 **po** peacock　42–43 **He . . . it** he must have what he wants, even if I have to go without it　46 **mine own** myself　47 **moan** grumble　49 **balk** a strip of rough grassland dividing two ploughed portions of a common field　51 **pardie** by God　55 **Benste** benedicite (bless us); **bemean** mean　56 **oft . . . seen** we have not often seen the like　57 **spitous** cruel　58 **een** eyes

But as far as I ken, or yet as I go,
65 We sely wedmen dree mickle woe:
We have sorrow then and then; it falls oft so.
Silly Copple, our hen, both to and fro
She cackles;
But begin she to croak,
70 To groan or to cluck,
Woe is him our cock,
For he is in the shackles.

These men that are wed have not all their will;
When they are full hard sted, they sigh full still.
75 God wot they are led full hard and full ill;
In bower nor in bed they say nought theretill.
This tide
My part have I fun,
I know my lesson:
80 Woe is him that is bun,
For he must abide.

But now late in our lives—a marvel to me,
That I think my heart rives such wonders to see;
What that destiny drives it should so be—
85 Some men will have two wives, and some men three
In store;
Some are woe that have any.
But so far can I:
Woe is him that has many,
90 For he feels sore.

But, young men, of wooing, for God that you bought,
Be well ware of wedding, and think in your thought:
'Had I wist' is a thing that serveth of nought.
Mickle still mourning has wedding home brought,
95 And griefs,
With many a sharp shower;
For thou mayst catch in an hour
That shall sow thee full sour
As long as thou lives.

100 For, as ever read I epistle, I have one to my fere
As sharp as thistle, as rough as a briar.
She is browed like a bristle, with a sour-loten cheer;
Had she once wet her whistle, she could sing full clear
Her paternoster.

She is as great as a whale,   105
She has a gallon of gall;
By him that died for us all,
I would I had run to I had lost her!
1 SHEPHERD: God look over the raw! Full deafly ye stand,
2 SHEPHERD: Yea, the devil in thy maw, so tariand!   110
Saw'st thou awre of Daw?
1 SHEPHERD: Yea, on a lea-land
Heard I him blow. He comes here at hand,
Not far.
Stand still.
2 SHEPHERD: Why?
1 SHEPHERD: For he comes, hope I.   115
2 SHEPHERD: He will make us both a lie,
But if we beware.

(*Enter* THIRD SHEPHERD.)

3 SHEPHERD: Christ's cross me speed, and Saint Nicholas!
Thereof had I need; it is worse than it was.
Whoso could take heed and let the world pass,   120
It is ever in dread and brickle as glass,
And slithes.
This world fared never so,
With marvels mo and mo—
Now in weal, now in woe,   125
And all thing writhes.

Was never since Noah's flood such floods seen,
Winds and rains so rude, and storms so keen:
Some stammered, some stood in doubt, as I ween.
Now God turn all to good! I say as I mean,   130
For ponder:
These floods so they drown,
Both in fields and in town,
And bear all down;
And that is a wonder.   135

We that walk on the nights our cattle to keep,
We see sudden sights when other men sleep.
Yet methink my heart lights; I see shrews peep.
Ye are two all-wights—I will give my sheep
A turn.   140
But full ill have I meant;
As I walk on this bent,
I may lightly repent,
My toes if I spurn.

64–66 **But . . . then** but as far as I know or as my experience
goes, we poor married men suffer much woe: we have sorrow
time and again   71 **Woe . . . cock** unhappy is our cock   74
When . . . still when they are hard put to it they sigh unceasingly   76–79 **they . . . lesson** they never answer back. Now I've
found out what I have to do   80 **bun** bound (in marriage)   81
abide remain so   83 **rives** breaks   84 **What . . . be** whatever
destiny compels must come to pass   87 **woe** miserable   88 **can**
know   90 **sore** pain   91 **But . . . bought** but young men, as
for wooing, by God who redeemed you   92 **well ware** very
wary   93 **Had . . . nought** 'If only I had known' is something
that doesn't help you   94 **mickle** constant   96 **shower** pang
98 **That . . . sour** what shall grieve you most bitterly   100 **I
. . . fere** I have one for my mate   102 **She . . . cheer** she has
bristly brows and a sour-looking face

---

108 **to** till   109 **God . . . stand** God save the audience! You stand
there as deaf as a post (the First Shepherd has evidently been trying
to attract the other's attention)   110–112 **Yea . . . blow** the devil
in your belly for tarrying so long! Have you seen Daw anywhere?
. . . Yea, in a fallow field I heard him blow [his horn]   115 **hope**
think   116 **make** tell   117 **if** unless   119 **it** i.e., the world
120–23 **Whose . . . so** anyone who could look on and let the
world go by [would see that] it is always fearful and as brittle as
glass, and slides away (that is, is transitory). But the world never behaved in this way before   124 **mo** more   126 **writhes** changes
129 **ween** fear   131 **ponder** consider   138 **lights** grows light;
shrews rogues   139 **all-wights** monsters   139–144 **I . . . spurn**
I will turn my sheep away. But I have been ill disposed [to the shep-
herds], as I walk on this field, I may stub my toes in easy penance

145   Ah, sir, God you save, and master mine!
    A drink fain would I have, and somewhat to dine.
1 SHEPHERD: Christ's curse, my knave, thou art a lither hine!
2 SHEPHERD: What, the boy list rave! Abide unto syne;
    We have made it.
150   Ill thrift on thy pate!
    Though the shrew came late,
    Yet is he, in state
    To dine—if he had it.

3 SHEPHERD: Such servants as I, that sweat and swinks,
155   Eat our bread full dry, and that me forthinks.
    We are oft wet and weary when master-men winks;
    Yet come full lately both dinners and drinks.
    But nately
    Both our dame and our sire,
160   When we have run in the mire,
    They can nip at our hire,
    And pay us full lately.

    But hear my truth, master: for the fare that ye make,
    I shall do thereafter—work as I take.
165   I shall do a little, sir, and among ever lake,
    For yet lay my supper never on my stomach
    In fields.
    Whereto should I threap?
    With my staff can I leap;
170   And men say 'Light cheap
    Litherly foryields.'

1 SHEPHERD: Thou wert an ill lad to ride on wooing
    With a man that had but little of spending.
2 SHEPHERD: Peace, boy, I bade. No more jangling,
175   Or I shall make thee full rad, by the heaven's king!
    With thy gauds—
    Where are our sheep, boy?—we scorn.
3 SHEPHERD: Sir, this same day at morn
    I them left in the corn,
180   When they rang Lauds.

    They have pasture good, they cannot go wrong.
1 SHEPHERD: That is right. By the rood, these nights are long!
    Yet I would, ere we yode, one gave us a song.
2 SHEPHERD: So I thought as I stood, to mirth us among.
185 **3 SHEPHERD:** I grant.

---

147 **lither hine** lazy hind   148–149 **What . . . it** what, the boy is pleased to rave! Wait till later; we have finished it (i.e., our meal) 150 **thrift** luck   152 **in state** ready   154 **swinks** toil   155 **forthinks** displeases   156 **winks** sleep   157 **full lately** tardily 158 **nately** thoroughly   161 **They . . . hire** they can stint our wages   163–167 **But . . . fields** but hear my promise, master: in return for the food you provide, I shall do accordingly work as I'm paid. I shall do but little, sir, and betweenwhiles play all the time   168 **threap** haggle   170–173 **Light . . . spending** 'A cheap bargain repays badly.' . . . You'd be the wrong lad for anyone that's hard up to take a-wooing with him (cf. *Othello* 3.3.71)   174–177 **Peace . . . boy** stop your wrangling, or I'll quickly make you, by the king of heaven. We scorn your pranks—where are our sheep, boy?   180 **Lauds** the first of the seven canonical offices, usually sung at daybreak   182 **rood** cross 183 **yode** went   184 **to . . . among** to gladden us meanwhile

1 SHEPHERD: Let me sing the tenory.
2 SHEPHERD: And I the treble so high.
3 SHEPHERD: Then the mean falls to me.
    Let see how ye chant.

(They sing. Then MAK *enters with a cloak covering his tunic.)*

MAK: Now, Lord, for thy names seven, that made both moon 190
    and starns
    Well more than I can neven, thy will, Lord, of me tharns.
    I am all uneven; that moves oft my harns.
    Now would God I were in heaven, for there weep no bairns
    So still.
1 SHEPHERD: Who is that pipes so poor?   195
MAK: Would God ye wist how I foor!
    Lo, a man that walks on the moor,
    And has not all his will.
2 SHEPHERD: Mak, where hast thou gone? Tell us tiding.
3 SHEPHERD: Is he come? Then ilkone take heed to his thing.   200

(He takes MAK's *cloak from him.)*

MAK: What! I be a yeoman, I tell you, of the king,
    The self and the same, sond from a great lording,
    And sich.
    Fie on you! Go hence
    Out of my presence!   205
    I must have reverence.
    Why, who be ich?
1 SHEPHERD: Why make ye it so quaint? Mak, ye do wrong.
2 SHEPHERD: But, Mak, list ye saint? I trow that ye long.
3 SHEPHERD: I trow the shrew can paint, the devil might him 210
    hang!
MAK: I shall make complaint, and make you all to thwang
    At a word,
    And tell even how ye doth.
1 SHEPHERD: But, Mak, is that sooth?
    Now take out that Southern tooth,   215
    And set in a turd!
2 SHEPHERD: Mak, the devil in your eye! A stroke would I
    lene you.
3 SHEPHERD: Mak, know ye not me? By God, I could teen you.
MAK: God look you all three! Methought I had seen you.
    Ye are a fair company.   220
1 SHEPHERD: Can ye now mean you?
2 SHEPHERD: Shrew, peep!

---

186 **tenory** tenor   190–192 **Now . . . harns** now, Lord, by thy seven names, who made both moon and stars far more than I can name, thy will concerning me, Lord, is lacking. I am all at sixes and sevens; that often unsettles my brain   194 **still** incessantly 195 **Who . . . poor** who is it that cries so piteously?   196 **wist** knew; **foor** fared   199 **tiding** news   200 **ilkone** everyone 202 **sond** messenger   203 **sich** such like   208 **Why . . . quaint** why are you so uppish?   209 **But . . . long** but, Mak, do you want to play saint? I believe you do   210 **paint** deceive 211 **and . . . thwang** and have you all flogged   213 **doth** do 215 **Now . . . tooth** southern speech. (Mak has been trying to talk southern English)   216 **set** put   217 **lene** give   218 **teen** hurt   219 **look** save   220 **Can . . . you** can you remember now?   221 **peep** pry about

Thus late as thou goes,
What will men suppose?
And thou hast an ill noise
225 Of stealing of sheep.
MAK: And I am true as steel, all men wot;
But a sickness I feel that holds me full hot:
My belly fares not well, it is out of estate.
3 SHEPHERD: Seldom lies the devil dead by the gate.
230 MAK: Therefore
Full sore am I and ill;
If I stand stone-still,
I eat not a needle
This month and more.
235 1 SHEPHERD: How fares thy wife? By my hood, how fares she?
MAK: Lies waltering—by the rood—by the fire, lo!
And a house full of brood. She drinks well, too;
Ill speed other good that she will do!
But she
240 Eats as fast as she can,
And ilk year that comes to man
She brings forth a lakan—
And, some years, two.

But were I now more gracious, and richer by far,
245 I were eaten out of house and of harbour.
Yet is she a foul dowse, if ye come near;
There is none that trows nor knows a war
Than ken I.
Now will ye see what I proffer?
250 To give all in my coffer
To-morn at next to offer
Her head-masspenny.

2 SHEPHERD: I wot so forwaked is none in this shire;
I would sleep if I taked less to my hire.
255 3 SHEPHERD: I am cold and naked, and would have a fire.
1 SHEPHERD: I am weary, forraked, and run in the mire—
Wake thou!
2 SHEPHERD: Nay, I will lie down by.
For I must sleep, truly.
260 3 SHEPHERD: As good a man's son was I
As any of you.

But, Mak, come hither! Between shalt thou lie down.
MAK: Then might I let you bedene of that ye would rown,
No dread.

From my top to my toe, (*He recites a night-spell.*) 265
Manus tuas commendo,
Pontio Pilato.
Christ's cross me speed!

Now were time for a man that lacks what he would
To stalk privily then unto a fold, 270
And nimbly to work then, and be not too bold,
For he might abuy the bargain, if it were told
At the ending.
Now were time for to reel;
But he needs good counsel 275
That fain would fare well,
And has but little spending.

But about you a circle, as round as a moon,
To I have done what I will, till that it be noon,
That ye lie stone-still to that I have done; 280
And I shall say theretill of good words a fone:
'On height,
Over your heads, my hand I lift.
Out go your eyes! Fordo your sight!'
But yet I must make better shift, 285
And it be right.

Lord, what they sleep hard!—that may ye all hear.
Was I never a shepherd, but now will I lere.
If the flock be scared, yet shall I nip near.
How! draw hitherward! Now mends our cheer 290
From sorrow
A fat sheep, I dare say,
A good fleece, dare I lay.
Eft-quit when I may,
But this will I borrow. 295

(*He goes home with the sheep.*)

SCENE TWO

Mak's cottage.

MAK: How, Gill, art thou in? Get us some light.
WIFE: Who makes such din this time of the night?
I am set for to spin; I hope not I might
Rise a penny to win, I shrew them on height!
So fares 5
A housewife that has been,
To be raised thus between.
Here may no note be seen
For such small chares.

---

223 **suppose** suspect   224 **noise** reputation   225 **Of** for
227 **full hot** severely   228 **estate** condition   229 **Seldom . . .
gate** seldom lies the devil dead by the roadside, i.e., appearances
may be deceptive   232–233 **If . . . needle** may I be turned to stone
if I have eaten a morsel   236 **waltering** sprawling   237 **brood**
children   238 **Ill speed** i.e., there is no hope of her doing much
else   241 **ilk** every   242 **lakan** baby   244 **gracious** prosperous
245 **harbour** home   246 **dowse** wench   247 **There . . . war**
there is none who believes [he knows] or [really] knows a worse
one   250–252 **To give . . . head-masspenny** tomorrow at the
latest to give all in my coffer as an offering for her soul   253 **forwaked** wearied with waking   254 **if . . . hire** even if I should get
less wages   256 **forraked** worn out with walking   258 **by** near
by   262 **between** between us   263–264 **Then . . . dread** then
I might keep you from whispering what you want, no doubt

272–273 **For . . . ending** for he might pay dearly for it, if it
came to a final reckoning   274 **reel** move quickly   277
spending money   278 **circle** (magic) circle   279 **To** till   281
And . . . fone and I shall also say a few good words   282 **On
height** high   284–287 **Out . . . hard** 'Lose your power of
sight.' But yet I must make better efforts, if things are to come
right. Lord, how soundly they sleep!   288 **lere** learn   289 **yet
. . . near** yet I shall grab [a sheep] tightly   290–292 **Now . . .
sheep** now a fat sheep shall comfort us   294 **Eft-quit** repay
ii. 3–9 I . . . chares I don't think I can earn a penny by getting
up [from my spinning], curse them! Any woman who has been
a housewife knows what it means to be got up from her work
continually. I have no work to show because of such small chores

10 MAK: Good wife, open the heck! See'st thou not what I
      bring?
   WIFE: I may thole thee draw the sneck. Ah, come in, my
      sweeting!
   MAK: Yea, thou thar not reck of my long standing.
   WIFE: By the naked neck art thou like for to hang.
   MAK: Do way!
15   I am worthy my meat,
      For in a strait can I get
      More than they that swink and sweat
      All the long day.

      Thus it fell to my lot, Gill; I had such grace.
20 WIFE: It were a foul blot to be hanged for the case.
   MAK: I have scaped, Jelott, oft as hard a glase.
   WIFE: 'But so long goes the pot to the water,' men says,
      'At last
      Comes it home broken.'
25 MAK: Well know I the token,
      But let it never be spoken!
      But come and help fast.
      I would he were flain; I list well eat.
      This twelvemonth was I not so fain of one sheep-meat.
30 WIFE: Come they ere he be slain, and hear the sheep bleat—
   MAK: Then might I be ta'en: that were a cold sweat!
      Go spar
      The gate-door.
   WIFE: Yes, Mak,
      For and they come at thy back—
35 MAK: Then might I buy, for all the pack,
      The devil of the war.

   WIFE: A good bourd have I spied, since thou canst none:
      Here shall we him hide, till they be gone,
      In my cradle. Abide! Let me alone,
40   And I shall lie beside in childbed and groan.
   MAK: Thou red,
      And I shall say thou wast light
      Of a knave-child this night.
   WIFE: Now well is me day bright
45   That ever was I bred!

      This is a good guise and a far cast;
      Yet a woman's advice helps at the last.
      I wot never who spies; again go thou fast.
   MAK: But I come ere they rise, else blows a cold blast!

---

10 **heck** inner door   11 **I . . . sneck** I will let you draw the
latch   12 **Yea . . . standing** you needn't mind about my standing [outside] so long   14 **Do way!** enough!   15 **meat** food
16 **strait** fix   17 **swink** toil   20 **blot** deed   21 **glase** blow
25 **token** portent   28–29 **I . . . meat** I wish he were skinned;
I am eager to eat. At no time this year have I been so glad of a
meal of mutton   32 **spar** fasten   33 **gate-door** enter door
34 **and** if   35–36 **Then . . . war** then I may get the devil of a
bad time from the whole pack of them   37 **bourd** jest; **canst**
knowest   41 **red** ready   42 **light** delivered   43 **knave-child**
boy   44–46 **Now . . . cast** I'm happy when I think of the
bright day I was born! This is a good method and a cunning trick
48 **again . . . fast** return again quickly [to the others]   49 **else**
unless

I will go sleep.   50
Yet sleep all this meny;
And I shall go stalk privily,
As it had never been I
That carried their sheep.

SCENE THREE

The open fields.

1 SHEPHERD: *Resurrex a mortuus!* have hold my hand!
      Judas carnas dominus! I may not well stand:
      My foot sleeps, by Jesus, and I walter fastand.
      I thought that we laid us full near England.
2 SHEPHERD: Ah, yea?   5
      Lord, what I have slept well!
      As fresh as an eel,
      As light I me feel
      As leaf on a tree.

3 SHEPHERD: Benste be herein! So me quakes,   10
      My heart is out of skin, what-so it makes.
      Who makes all this din? So my brow blakes,
      To the door will I win. Hark, fellows, wakes!
      We were four:
      See ye awre of Mak now?   15
1 SHEPHERD: We were up ere thou.
2 SHEPHERD: Man, I give God avow
      Yet yede he nawre.

3 SHEPHERD: Methought he was lapped in a wolf-skin.
1 SHEPHERD: So are many happed now—namely within.   20
3 SHEPHERD: When we had long napped, methought with a
      gin
      A fat sheep he trapped; but he made no din.
2 SHEPHERD: Be still!
      Thy dream makes thee wood;
      It is but phantom, by the rood.   25
1 SHEPHERD: Now God turn all to good,
      If it be his will.

2 SHEPHERD: Rise, Mak, for shame! Thou liest right long.
   MAK: Now Christ's holy name be us among!
      What is this? For Saint Jame, I may not well gang!   30
      I trow I be the same. Ah, my neck has lain wrong
      Enough. (*They help him to get up.*)
      Mickle thank! Since yester-even,
      Now by Saint Stephen,
      I was flayed with a sweven—   35
      My heart out of slough.

---

51 **meny** company
iii. 3 **I . . . fastand** I'm tottering with hunger   5 **Ah, yea?** Oh,
really?   6 **Lord . . . well** how well I have slept!   10 **Benste** blessing   10–11 **So . . . makes** I tremble so much, my heart is in my
mouth, whatever the reason for it   12 **blakes** darkens   13 **win**
go; **wakes** wake up   15 **See . . . now?** have you seen Mak anywhere?   17–18 **Man . . . nawre** I vow to God he's gone nowhere
yet   20 **So . . . within** many are covered like that nowadays, especially underneath   21 **gin** snare   24 **wood** mad   30 **For
. . . Jame** by Saint James; **gang** walk   31–32 **Ah . . . Enough**
my neck has been lying very crookedly   35–36 **I . . . slough** I
was terrified by a dream—I nearly jumped out of my skin

I thought Gill began to croak and travail full sad,
Well-night at the first cock, of a young lad
For to mend our flock. Then be I never glad;
40   I have tow on my rock more than ever I had.
Ah, my head!
A house full of young tharms,
The devil knock out their harns!
Woe is him has many bairns,
45   And thereto little bread.

I must go home, by your leave, to Gill, as I thought.
I pray you look my sleeve, that I steal nought;
I am loath you to grieve or from you take aught.
3 SHEPHERD: Go forth, ill might thou chieve! Now would I
          we sought,
50   This morn,
That we had all our store.
1 SHEPHERD: But I will go before.
Let us meet.
2 SHEPHERD: Where?
3 SHEPHERD: At the crooked thorn.

SCENE FOUR

Mak's cottage.

MAK: Undo this door! Who is here? How long shall I stand?
WIFE: Who makes such a bere? Now walk in the wenyand!
MAK: Ah, Gill, what cheer? It is I, Mak, your husband.
WIFE: Then may we see here the devil in a band,
5   Sir Guile!
Lo, he comes with a lote,
As he were holden in the throat.
I may not sit at my note
A hand-long while.
10 MAK: Will ye hear what fare she makes to get her a glose?
And does naught but lakes, and claws her toes.
WIFE: Why, who wanders, who wakes? Who comes, who
          goes?
Who brews, who bakes? What makes me thus hoarse?
And then
15   It is ruth to behold—
Now in hot, now in cold,
Full woeful is the household
That wants a woman.

But what end hast thou made with the herds, Mak?
20 MAK: The last word that they said when I turned my back,
They would look that they had their sheep, all the pack.

I hope they will not be well paid when they their sheep
          lack,
Pardie!
But how-so the game goes,
To me they will suppose,   25
And make a foul noise,
And cry out upon me.

But thou must do as thou hight.
WIFE: I accord me theretill;
I shall swaddle him right in my cradle.
If it were a greater sleight, yet could I help till.   30
I will lie down straight. Come hap me.
MAK: I will.
WIFE: Behind!
Come Coll and his marrow,
They will nip us full narrow.
MAK: But I may cry 'Out, harrow!'   35
The sheep if they find.

WIFE: Harken ay when they call; they will come anon.
Come and make ready all, and sing by thine own;
Sing lullay thou shall, for I must groan,
And cry out by the wall on Mary and John,   40
For sore.
Sing lullay on fast,
When thou hearest at the last;
And but I play a false cast,
Trust me no more.   45

SCENE FIVE

The crooked thorn.

3 SHEPHERD: Ah, Coll, good morn! Why sleepest thou not?
1 SHEPHERD: Alas, that ever was I born! We have a foul blot—
A fat wether have we lorn.
3 SHEPHERD: Marry, God's forbot!
2 SHEPHERD: Who should do us that scorn? That were a foul
          spot.
1 SHEPHERD: Some shrew.   5
I have sought with my dogs
All Horbury shrogs,
And, of fifteen hogs,
Found I but one ewe.

3 SHEPHERD: Now trow me, if ye will—by Saint Thomas of 10
          Kent,
Either Mak or Gill was at that assent.

---

37 **full sad** hard   39 **mend** increase   40 **I . . . had** I have more
tow on my distaff (i.e., more trouble in store) than ever I had
42 **tharms** bellies   43 **harns** brains   46 **thought** intended
47 **look** examine   49 **chieve** prosper   49–51 **Now . . . store**
now I want us this morning to see that we have all our stock
iv. 2 **bere** din; **Now . . . wenyand** walk in the waning moon,
i.e., at an unlucky time   4 **band** noose   6 **lote** noise   7 **holden**
held my   8 **note** work   9 **hand-long** brief   10 **Will . . . glose**
will you listen to the fuss she makes in the hope of excusing herself?   11 **lakes** play   15 **ruth** a pity   16 **Now . . . cold** i.e., at
all times   18 **wants** lacks   19 **herds** shepherds

22 **hope** think; **well paid** pleased   24 **how-so** however   25
To . . . suppose they will suspect me   28 **hight** promised; **I .
. . theretill** I agree to that   30 **sleight** trick; **Yet . . . till** I could
still help with it   31 **straight** straightway; **hap** cover   33 **marrow** make   34 **narrow** hard   35 **Out, harrow!** a cry for help
39 **lullay** lullaby   41 **sore** pain   42 **on fast** quickly   44 **And
. . . cast** and if I don't play a false trick
v. 3 **lorn** lost; **God's forbot!** God forbid!   4 **scorn** insult; **spot**
disgrace   7 **Horbury** Horbury, near Wakefield; **shrogs** thickets
8–9 **And . . . ewe** among fifteen hogs (or young sheep) I found
only a ewe, i.e., the wether was missing   10 **Saint Thomas of
Kent** St. Thomas of Canterbury   11 **Either . . . assent** either
Mak or Gill was a party to it

1 SHEPHERD: Peace, man, be still! I saw when he went.
  Thou slander'st him ill; thou ought to repent
  Good speed.
15 2 SHEPHERD: Now as ever might I thee,
  If I should even here die,
  I would say it were he
  That did that same deed.

3 SHEPHERD: Go we thither, I rede, and run on our feet.
20 Shall I never eat bread, the sooth to I wit.
1 SHEPHERD: Nor drink in my head, with him till I meet.
2 SHEPHERD: I will rest in no stead till that I him greet,
  My brother.
  One I will hight:
25 Till I see him in sight,
  Shall I never sleep one night
  There I do another.

SCENE SIX

Mak's cottage.

3 SHEPHERD: Will ye hear how they hack? Our sire list croon.
1 SHEPHERD: Heard I never none crack so clear out of tone.
  Call on him.
2 SHEPHERD: Mak, undo your door soon!
MAK: Who is it that spake, as it were noon,
5 On loft?
  Who is that, I say?
3 SHEPHERD: Good fellows, were it day.
MAK: As far as ye may,
  Good, speak soft,
10 Over a sick woman's head, that is at maleese;
  I had liefer be dead ere she had any disease.
WIFE: Go to another stead! I may not well quease;
  Each foot that ye tread goes thorough my nose
  So high.
15 1 SHEPHERD: Tell us, Mak, if ye may,
  How fare ye, I say?
MAK: But are ye in this town to-day?
  Now how fare ye?

  Ye have run in the mire, and are wet yet;
20 I shall make you a fire, if ye will sit.
  A nurse would I hire. Think ye on yet?

---

14 **Good speed** quickly   15 **Now . . . thee** as I hope to prosper
19 **rede** advise   20 **the . . . wit** Till I know the truth   22 **stead**
place   23 **My brother** a friendly form of address   24 **One . . .**
hight one thing I will promise   27 **There** where
vi. 1 **Will . . . croon** do you hear them trilling? Our gentleman is
pleased to croon   2 **crack** bawl; **tone** tune   3 **soon** immediately
4–5 **Who . . . loft?** who is it that spoke aloud, as though it were
noon?   7 **were it** if only it were   9 **Good** good sirs   10–11 **Over**
. . . disease because of a sick woman who is in distress; I had rather
die than she should suffer any discomfort   12 **quease** breathe
13–14 **Each . . . high** every step you tread goes through my nose
so strongly, i.e., goes right through my head   21–23 **A nurse . . .**
season I would like to hire a nurse. Do you still remember [my
dream about a new addition to the family]? I've been paid my wages
in full for a while—this is my dream come true

Well quit is my hire—my dream, this is it—
A season.
I have bairns, if ye knew,
Well more than enew;   25
But we must drink as we brew,
And that is but reason.

I would ye dined ere ye yode. Methink that ye sweat.
2 SHEPHERD: Nay, neither mends our mood drink nor
  meat.
MAK: Why, sir, ails you aught but good?   30
3 SHEPHERD: Yea, our sheep that we gete
  Are stolen as they yode. Our loss is great.
MAK: Sirs, drink!
  Had I been there,
  Some should have bought it full sore.
1 SHEPHERD: Marry, some men trow that ye were,   35
  And that us forthinks.
2 SHEPHERD: Mak, some men trows that it should be ye.
3 SHEPHERD: Either ye or your spouse, so say we.
MAK: Now if ye have suspouse to Gill or to me,
  Come and rip our house, and then may ye see   40
  Who had her.
  If I any sheep fot,
  Either cow or stot—
  And Gill, my wife, rose not
  Here since she laid her—   45
  As I am true and leal, to God here I pray
  That this be the first meal that I shall eat this day.
1 SHEPHERD: Mak, as have I sele, advise thee, I say:
  He learned timely to steal that could not say nay.
WIFE: I swelt!   50
  Out, thieves, from my wones!
  Ye come to rob us for the nonce.
MAK: Hear ye not how she groans?
  Your hearts should melt.

WIFE: Out, thieves, from my bairn! Nigh him not there. 55
MAK: Wist ye how she had farn, your hearts would be sore.
  Ye do wrong, I you warn, that thus come before
  To a woman that has farn; but I say no more.
WIFE: Ah, my middle!
  I pray to God so mild,   60
  If ever I you beguiled,
  That I eat this child
  That lies in this cradle.

MAK: Peace, woman, for God's pain, and cry not so!
  Thou spillest thy brain, and makest me full woe.   65

---

25 **enew** enough   28 **yode** went   30 **Why . . . good** why, sir,
is anything wrong with you?; **gete** tend   34 **bought** paid for
36 **forthinks** displeases   37 **trows** believe   39 **suspouse** suspicion   40 **rip** ransack   42 **fot** fetched   43 **stot** heifer   46 **leal**
honest   48–49 **Mak . . . nay** Mak, as I hope for happiness, take
thought I say: he learned early to steal who could not say no [to
another's property]   50 **swelt** feel faint   51 **wones** house
52 **Ye . . . nonce** you come on purpose to rob us   55 **Nigh . . .**
there do not go near him there   56 **Wist . . . farn** if you knew
what she had been through   58 **To . . . farn** to a woman who
has been in labour   62 **eat** may eat   65 **spillest** injurest

2 SHEPHERD: I trow our sheep be slain. What find ye two?

3 SHEPHERD: All work we in vain; as well may we go.
But hatters!
I can find no flesh,
70   Hard nor nesh,
Salt nor fresh,
But two tome platters.

Quick cattle but this, tame nor wild,
None, as have I bliss, as loud as he smelled.

75 WIFE: No, so God me bless, and give me joy of my child!

1 SHEPHERD: We have marked amiss; I hold us beguiled.

2 SHEPHERD: Sir, don.
Sir—our Lady him save!—
Is your child a knave?

80 MAK: Any lord might him have,
This child, to his son.

When he wakens he kips, that joy is to see.

3 SHEPHERD: In good time to his hips, and in sely.
But who were his gossips so soon ready?

85 MAK: So fair fall their lips!

1 SHEPHERD: (*Aside.*)   Hark now, a lie!

MAK: So God them thank,
Parkin, and Gibbon Waller, I say,
And gentle John Horne, in good fay—
He made all the garray—
90   With the great shank.

2 SHEPHERD: Mak, friends will we be, for we are all one.

MAK: We? Now I hold for me, for mends get I none.
Farewell all three!—all glad were ye gone.

3 SHEPHERD: Fair words may there be, but love is there none
95   This year. (*They leave the cottage.*)

1 SHEPHERD: Gave ye the child anything?

2 SHEPHERD: I trow not one farthing.

3 SHEPHERD: Fast again will I fling;
Abide ye me there. (*He returns to the cottage.*)

100   Mak, take it to no grief, if I come to thy bairn.

MAK: Nay, thou dost me great reprief, and foul hast thou farn.

3 SHEPHERD: The child will it not grieve, that little day-starn
Mak, with your leave, let me give your bairn
But sixpence.

MAK: Nay, do way! He sleeps.   105

3 SHEPHERD: Methink he peeps.

MAK: When he wakens he weeps.
I pray you go hence.

3 SHEPHERD: Give me leave him to kiss, and lift up the clout.

(*He glimpses the sheep.*)

What the devil is this? He has a long snout!   110

1 SHEPHERD: He is marked amiss. We wait ill about.

2 SHEPHERD: Ill-spun weft, iwis, ay comes foul out.
Aye, so! (*He recognizes the sheep.*)
He is like to our sheep!

3 SHEPHERD: How, Gib, may I peep?   115

1 SHEPHERD: I trow kind will creep
Where it may not go.

2 SHEPHERD: This was a quaint gaud and a far cast;
It was a high fraud.

3 SHEPHERD: Yea, sirs, was't.
Let burn this bawd and bind her fast.   120
A false scold hangs at the last;
So shalt thou.
Will ye see how they swaddle
His four feet in the middle?
Saw I never in a cradle.   125
A horned lad ere now.

MAK: Peace, bid I. What, let be your fare!
I am he that him begat, and yond woman him bare.

1 SHEPHERD: What devil shall he hat, Mak? Lo, God, Mak's heir!

2 SHEPHERD: Let be all that. Now God give him care,   130
I sagh.

WIFE: A pretty child is he
As sits on a woman's knee;
A dillydown, pardie,
To gar a man laugh.   135

3 SHEPHERD: I know him by the ear-mark; that is a good token.

MAK: I tell you, sirs, hark! his nose was broken.
Since told me a clerk that he was forspoken.

1 SHEPHERD: This is a false work; I would fain be wroken.
Get weapon!   140

WIFE: He was taken with an elf,
I saw it myself;
When the clock struck twelve,
Was he forshapen.

2 SHEPHERD: Ye two are well feft sam in a stead.   145

---

68 **hatters** confound it   70 **nesh** soft   72 **But** only; **tome** empty   73–74 **Quick . . . smelled** live stock but this (i.e., the 'baby' in the cradle), tame or wild, none [have I found], as I hope to be happy, that smelled as loud as he (i.e., the missing sheep)   76 **We . . . amiss** aimed wrongly, i.e., made a mistake   77 **don** completely   79 **knave** boy   82 **kips** snatches   83 **In . . . sely** a good and happy future to him   84 **gossips** godparents   85 **So . . . lips** good luck to them   88 **John Horne** the shepherd in the *First Shepherds' Pageant* who quarrels with Gib about the pasturing of an imaginary flock of sheep; **fay** good faith   89 **garray** commotion   90 **shank** long legs   91 **all one** agreed   92 **Now . . . none** for my own part, I'm holding back, for I get no amends   93 **all . . . gone** [I should be] very glad if you were gone (probably an aside)   98 **Fast . . . fling** I will dash back   100 **take . . . grief** don't take offence   101 **Nay . . . farn** nay, you do me great shame, and you have behaved badly   102 **day-starn** star

109 **clout** cloth   111–112 **He . . . out** he is misshapen. We do wrong to pry about . . . Ill-spun weft, indeed, always comes out badly, i.e., what is bred in the bone will come out in the flesh   116–118 **I . . . cast** nature will creep where it cannot walk, i.e., assert itself in one way or another . . . This was a clever dodge and a cunning trick   127 **fare** uproar   129 **he hat** be called   130 **care** sorrow   131 **I sagh** I saw [the sheep myself]   134 **dilly-down** darling   135 **gar** make   138 **forspoken** bewitched   139 **wroken** avenged   141 **with** by   144 **forshapen** transformed   145 **Ye . . . stead** you two are well endowed together in one place, i.e., are as clever a pair of rascals as ever lived under one roof

1 SHEPHERD: Since they maintain their theft, let do them to
    dead.
MAK: If I trespass eft, gird off my head.
    With you will I be left.
3 SHEPHERD: Sirs, do my rede:
    For this trespass
150   We will neither ban ne flite,
    Fight nor chide,
    But have done as tite,
    And cast him in canvas.

(*They toss* MAK *in a blanket.*)

SCENE SEVEN

The open fields.

1 SHEPHERD: Lord, what I am sore, in point for to burst!
    In faith, I may no more; therefore will I rest.
2 SHEPHERD: As a sheep of seven score he weighed in my fist.
    For to sleep aywhere methink that I list.
5 3 SHEPHERD: Now I pray you
    Lie down on this green.
1 SHEPHERD: On these thieves yet I mean.
3 SHEPHERD: Whereto should ye teen?
    Do as I say you.

(*An* ANGEL *sings 'Gloria in excelsis,' and then says:*)

10 ANGEL: Rise, herdmen hend, for now is he born
    That shall take from the fiend that Adam had lorn;
    That warlock to shend, this night is he born.
    God is made your friend now at this morn,
    He behests.
15   At Bedlem go see
    There lies that free
    In a crib full poorly,
    Betwixt two beasts.
1 SHEPHERD: This was a quaint steven that ever yet I heard.
20   It is a marvel to neven, thus to be scared.
2 SHEPHERD: Of God's son of heaven he spoke upward.
    All the wood on a leven methought that he gard
    Appear.
3 SHEPHERD: He spake of a bairn
25   In Bedlem, I you warn.
1 SHEPHERD: That betokens yond starn;
    Let us seek him there.
2 SHEPHERD: Say, what was his song? Heard ye not how he
    cracked it,

    Three breves to a long?
3 SHEPHERD: Yea, marry, he hacked it:
    Was no crochet wrong, nor no thing that lacked it. 30
1 SHEPHERD: For to sing us among, right as he knacked it,
    I can.
2 SHEPHERD: Let see how ye croon.
    Can ye bark at the moon?
3 SHEPHERD: Hold your tongues! Have done! 35
1 SHEPHERD: Hark after, then.

(*Sings.*)

2 SHEPHERD: To Bedlem he bade that we should gang;
    I am full adrad that we tarry too long.
3 SHEPHERD: Be merry and not sad—of mirth is our song!
    Everlasting glad to meed may we fang 40
    Without noise.
1 SHEPHERD: Hie we thither forthy,
    If we be wet and weary,
    To that child and that lady;
    We have it not to lose. 45
2 SHEPHERD: We find by the prophecy—let be your din!—
    Of David and Isay, and more than I min—
    They prophesied by clergy—that in a virgin
    Should he light and lie, to sloken our sin,
    And slake it, 50
    Our kind, from woe;
    For Isay said so:
    Ecce virgo
    Concipiet a child that is naked.

3 SHEPHERD: Full glad may we be, and abide that day 55
    That lovely to see, that all mights may.
    Lord, well were me for once and for ay,
    Might I kneel on my knee, some word for to say
    To that child.
    But the angel said 60
    In a crib was he laid;
    He was poorly arrayed,
    Both meek and mild.

1 SHEPHERD: Patriarchs that have been, and prophets beforn,
    They desired to have seen this child that is born. 65
    They are gone full clean; that have they lorn.
    We shall see him, I ween, ere it be morn,
    To token.
    When I see him and feel,
    Then wot I full well 70
    It is true as steel

---

146 **dead** death   147 **eft** again; **gird** strike   148 **With . . .
rede** I throw myself on your mercy. . . . Take my advice
150 **ban** curse; **flite** quarrel   152 **as tite** at once
vii. 4 For . . . list I think I would be glad to sleep anywhere
7 **mean** think   8 **teen** vex yourself   10 **hend** gentle   12 **warlock** the devil; **shend** destroy   14 **behests** promises
15 **Bedlem** Bethlehem   16 **There** where; **free** noble one
19 **quaint steven** elegant voice   20 **neven** tell of   21 **upward**
on high   22–23 **All . . . Appear** I thought he made the whole
wood appear as if lit up by lightning   28 **cracked** sang

29 **hacked** trilled   30 **Was . . . it** No crochet was wrong, and
there was nothing it lacked   31 **knacked** sang   37 **gang** go
38 **adrad** afraid   40–41 **Everlasting . . . noise** we can get
everlasting joy as our reward without any fuss   42 **Hie** therefore
43 **If** even if   45 **We . . . lose** we must not forget it   47 **Isay**
Isaiah; **min** remember   48 **clergy** learning   49 **light** alight;
sloken quench   50 **slake** relieve   51 **kind** race   53–54 *Ecce
. . . Concipiet* behold, a virgin shall conceive   56–57 **That . . .
ay** to see that lovely one who is almighty. Lord, I would be happy
for once and all   64 **beforn** in the past   66 **They . . . lorn** that
chance have they lost   68 **token** as a sign

That prophets have spoken:
To so poor as we are that he would appear,
First find and declare by his messenger.
75 2 SHEPHERD: Go we now, let us fare; the place is us near.
3 SHEPHERD: I am ready and yare; go we in fere
To that bright.
Lord, if thy will be—
We are lewd all three—
80   Thou grant us some kins glee
To comfort thy wight.

SCENE EIGHT

The stable in Bethlehem.

1 SHEPHERD: Hail, comely and clean; hail, young child!
Hail, maker, as I mean, of a maiden so mild!
Thou hast waried, I ween, the warlock so wild:
The false guiler of teen, now goes he beguiled.
5   Lo, he merries,
Lo, he laughs, my sweeting!
A well fare meeting!
I have holden my heting:
Have a bob of cherries.
10 2 SHEPHERD: Hail, sovereign saviour, for thou hast us
sought!
Hail, freely food and flower, that all thing hast
wrought!
Hail, full of favour, that made all of nought!
Hail! I kneel and I cower. A bird have I brought
To my bairn.
15   Hail, little tiny mop!

Of our creed thou art crop;
I would drink on thy cop,
Little daystarn.
3 SHEPHERD: Hail, darling dear, full of Godhead!
I pray thee be near when that I have need.   20
Hail, sweet is thy cheer! My heart would bleed
To see thee sit here in so poor weed,
With no pennies.
Hail! Put forth thy dall!
I bring thee but a ball: 25
Have and play thee withal,
And go to the tennis.
MARY: The Father of heaven, God omnipotent,
That set all on seven, his Son has he sent.
My name could he neven, and light ere he went.   30
I conceived him full even through might, as he meant;
And now is he born.
He keep you from woe!—
I shall pray him so.
Tell forth as ye go,   35
And min on this morn.
1 SHEPHERD: Farewell, lady, so fair to behold,
With thy child on thy knee.
2 SHEPHERD: But he lies full cold.
Lord, well is me! Now we go, thou behold.
3 SHEPHERD: Forsooth, already it seems to be told   40
Full oft.
1 SHEPHERD: What grace we have fun!
2 SHEPHERD: Come forth; now are we won!
3 SHEPHERD: To sing are we bun:
Let take on loft.   45

---

74 **First . . . messenger** find [us] first of all, and make known
[his birth] through his messenger   76 **yare** eager; **in fere** together   77 **bright** bright one   79 **lewd** simple   80–81 **Thou
. . . wight** grant us some joyful way of comforting thy child
viii. 1 **clean** pure   2 **of** born of   3 **waried** cursed; **warlock**
the false and malicious deceiver i.e., the devil   5 **merries** is
merry   7 **well fare** very fine   8 **I . . . heting** I have kept my
promise   9 **bob** bunch   11 **flower** noble child   15 **mop**
moppet

16–17 **Of . . . cop** you are the head of our faith; I would drink
in your cup (i.e., the cup of the eucharist)   22 **weed** clothing
24 **dall** hand   29 **That . . . seven** that made all the world in
seven days   30–31 **My . . . meant** he named my name and
alighted in me before He went. I conceived him indeed through
God's might, as His purpose was   36 **min** remember   43 **won**
redeemed   44 **bun** bound   45 **Let . . . loft** let us begin loudly

EVERYMAN

Everyman was written late in the fifteenth century and strongly resembles a Flemish play, *Elckerlijc* ("Everyman"), which was printed in 1495. It seems likely that one of the two plays is a translation of the other, but scholars are uncertain about which is the original. Given the play's subtle treatment of the Catholic doctrine of salvation, it has sometimes been argued that *Everyman* was written by a monk or cleric. Yet *Everyman* is hardly a theological treatise; it brims with a vitality that brings the reality of impending death vividly to the stage.

In the play, God orders Death to seek out Everyman and prepare him to die. Like most people, though, Everyman is not ready to meet his end. He first tries to bribe Death and then pleads unsuccessfully for mercy. When Death does not relent, Everyman begins a kind of spiritual journey, confronting several allegorical figures and asking them to accompany him to the grave. Medieval allegory often involved the personification of moral or psychological abstractions, much like the characters that Everyman meets: Fellowship, Kindred, Goods, Good Deeds, Knowledge, and so on. In performance, however, these abstractions become vividly fleshed-out, for the playwright gives these characters traits and behaviors that make them powerfully "real" and recognizable as individuals on the stage rather than as abstract moral emblems. As Everyman proceeds toward death, he is deserted by most of his worldly attributes, but Good Deeds remains faithful to him, especially once he has repented. Although the playwright concludes *Everyman* with a moralizing sermon by the Doctor, we may well feel that the theatrical lesson of the play has at least as much to do with the humanizing of Everyman and his poignant confrontation with our common mortality.

This production of *Everyman* transforms what may at first seem a statically "allegorical" drama into a visceral, choreographed spectacle.

EVERYMAN

Anonymous

TRANSLATED BY A. C. CAWLEY

CHARACTERS

GOD	COUSIN	STRENGTH
MESSENGER	GOODS	DISCRETION
DEATH	GOOD DEEDS	FIVE WITS
EVERYMAN	KNOWLEDGE	ANGEL
FELLOWSHIP	CONFESSION	DOCTOR
KINDRED	BEAUTY	

Here beginneth a treatise how the High Father of Heaven sendeth death to summon every creature to come and give account of their lives in this world, and is in manner of a moral play.

MESSENGER: I pray you all give your audience,
    And hear this matter with reverence,
    By figure a moral play:
    The *Summoning of Everyman* called it is,
5   That of our lives and ending shows
    How transitory we be all day.
    This matter is wondrous precious,
    But the intent of it is more gracious,
    And sweet to bear away.
10   The story saith: Man, in the beginning
    Look well, and take good heed to the ending,
    Be you never so gay!
    Ye think sin in the beginning full sweet,
    Which in the end causeth the soul to weep,
15   When the body lieth in clay.
    Here shall you see how Fellowship and Jollity,
    Both Strength, Pleasure, and Beauty,
    Will fade from thee as flower in May;
    For ye shall hear how our Heaven King
20   Calleth Everyman to a general reckoning:
    Give audience, and hear what he doth say.   (*Exit.*)

(GOD *speaketh:*)

GOD: I perceive, here in my majesty,
    How that all creatures be to me unkind,
    Living without dread in worldly prosperity:
25   Of ghostly sight the people be so blind,
    Drowned in sin, they know me not for their God;
    In worldly riches is all their mind,
    They fear not my righteousness, the sharp rod.
    My law that I showed, when I for them died,
30   They forget clean, and shedding of my blood red;
    I hanged between two, it cannot be denied;
    To get them life I suffered to be dead;
    I healed their feet, with thorns hurt was my head.
    I could do no more than I did, truly;
35   And now I see the people do clean forsake me:
    They use the seven deadly sins damnable,
    As pride, covetise, wrath, and lechery
    Now in the world be made commendable;

    And thus they leave of angels the heavenly company.
    Every man liveth so after his own pleasure,   40
    And yet of their life they be nothing sure:
    I see the more that I them forbear
    The worse they be from year to year.
    All that liveth appaireth fast;
    Therefore I will, in all the haste,   45
    Have a reckoning of every man's person;
    For, and I leave the people thus alone
    In their life and wicked tempests,
    Verily they will become much worse than beasts;
    For now one would by envy another up eat;   50
    Charity they do all clean forget.
    I hoped well that every man
    In my glory should make his mansion,
    And thereto I had them all elect;
    But now I see, like traitors deject,   55
    They thank me not for the pleasure that I to them meant,
    Nor yet for their being that I them have lent,
    I proffered the people great multitude of mercy,
    And few there be that asketh it heartily.
    They be so cumbered with worldly riches   60
    That needs on them I must do justice,
    On every man living without fear.
    Where art thou, Death, thou mighty messenger?

(*Enter* DEATH.)

DEATH: Almighty God, I am here at your will,
    Your commandment to fulfill.   65
GOD: Go thou to Everyman,
    And show him, in my name,
    A pilgrimage he must on him take,
    Which he in no wise may escape;
    And that he bring with him a sure reckoning   70
    Without delay or any tarrying.

(GOD *withdraws.*)

DEATH: Lord, I will in the world go run overall,
    And cruelly outsearch both great and small;
    Every man will I beset that liveth beastly
    Out of God's laws, and dreadeth not folly.   75

---

3 **By figure** in form   6 **all day** always   8 **But . . . gracious** but the purpose of it is more devout   23 **unkind** ungrateful   25 **Of ghostly sight** in spiritual vision   32 **I . . . dead** I consented to die   37 **covetise** covetousness

41 **And . . . sure** and yet their lives are by no means obscure   44 **appaireth** degenerates   47 **and** if   48 **tempests** tumults   55 **deject** abject   59 **heartily** earnestly   72 **overall** everywhere

He that loveth riches I will strike with my dart,
His sight to blind, and from heaven to depart—
Except that alms be his good friend—
In hell for to dwell, world without end.
80   Lo, yonder I see Everyman walking.
Full little he thinketh on my coming;
His mind is on fleshly lusts and his treasure,
And great pain it shall cause him to endure
Before the Lord, Heaven King.

(*Enter* EVERYMAN.)

85   Everyman, stand still! Whither art thou going
Thus gaily? Hast thou thy Maker forget?
EVERYMAN: Why askest thou?
Wouldest thou wit?
DEATH: Yea, sir; I will show you:
90   In great haste I am sent to thee
From God out of his majesty.
EVERYMAN: What, sent to me?
DEATH: Yea, certainly.
Though thou have forget him here,
95   He thinketh on thee in the heavenly sphere,
As, ere we depart, thou shalt know.
EVERYMAN: What desireth God of me?
DEATH: That shall I show thee:
A reckoning he will needs have
100 Without any longer respite.
EVERYMAN: To give a reckoning longer leisure I crave;
This blind matter troubleth my wit.
DEATH: On thee thou must take a long journey;
Therefore thy book of count with thee thou bring,
105 For turn again thou cannot by no way.
And look thou be sure of thy reckoning,
For before God thou shalt answer, and show
Thy many bad deeds, and good but a few;
How thou hast spent thy life, and in what wise,
110 Before the chief Lord of paradise.
Have ado that we were in that way,
For, wit thou well, thou shalt make none attorney.
EVERYMAN: Full unready I am such reckoning to give.
I know thee not. What messenger art thou?
115 DEATH: I am Death, that no man dreadeth,
For every man I rest, and no man spareth;
For it is God's commandment
That all to me should be obedient.
EVERYMAN: O Death, thou comest when I had thee least in
mind!
120 In thy power it lieth me to save;
Yet of my good will I give thee, if thou will be kind:
Yea, a thousand pound shalt thou have,
And defer this matter till another day.
DEATH: Everyman, it may not be, by no way.
125 I set not by gold, silver, nor riches,

Ne by pope, emperor, king, duke, ne princes;
For, and I would receive gifts great,
All the world I might get;
But my custom is clean contrary.
I give thee no respite. Come hence, and not tarry.   130
EVERYMAN: Alas, shall I have no longer respite?
I may say Death giveth no warning!
To think on thee, it maketh my heart sick,
For all unready is my book of reckoning.
But twelve year and I might have abiding,   135
My counting-book I would make so clear
That my reckoning I should not need to fear.
Wherefore, Death, I pray thee, for God's mercy,
Spare me till I be provided of remedy.
DEATH: Thee availeth not to cry, weep, and pray;   140
But haste thee lightly that thou were gone that journey,
And prove thy friends if thou can;
For, wit thou well, the tide abideth no man,
And in the world each living creature
For Adam's sin must die of nature.   145
EVERYMAN: Death, if I should this pilgrimage take,
And my reckoning surely make,
Show me, for saint charity,
Should I not come again shortly?
DEATH: No, Everyman; and thou be once there,   150
Thou mayst never more come here,
Trust me verily.
EVERYMAN: O gracious God in the high seat celestial,
Have mercy on me in this most need!
Shall I have no company from this vale terrestrial   155
Of mine acquaintance, that way me to lead?
DEATH: Yea, if any be so hardy
That would go with thee and bear thee company.
Hie thee that thou were gone to God's magnificence,
Thy reckoning to give before his presence.   160
What, weenest thou thy life is given thee,
And thy worldly goods also?
EVERYMAN: I had wend so, verily.
DEATH: Nay, nay; it was but lent thee;
For as soon as thou art go,   165
Another a while shall have it, and then go therefro,
Even as thou hast done.
Everyman, thou art mad! Thou hast thy wits five,
And here on earth will not amend thy life;
For suddenly I do come.   170
EVERYMAN: O wretched caitiff, whither shall I flee,
That I might scape this endless sorrow?
Now, gentle Death, spare me till to-morrow,
That I may amend me
With good advisement.   175
DEATH: Nay, thereto I will not consent,
Nor no man will I respite;
But to the heart suddenly I shall smite
Without any advisement.
And now out of thy sight I will me hie;   180
See thou make thee ready shortly,

---

77 **depart** separate   88 **wit** know   102 **blind** obscure   104
count account   105 **turn again** return   111 **Have . . . way**
i.e., let's see about making that journey   112 **none attorney** no
one [your] advocate   115 **that . . . dreadeth** who fears no man
116 **rest** arrest   121 **good** goods   123 **And defer** if you defer
125 **set not by** care not for

---

143 **tide** time   161 **weenest** suppose   163 **wend** supposed
165 **go** gone   166 **therefro** from it   175 **advisement** reflection

For thou mayst say this is the day
That no man living may scape away.

(*Exit* DEATH.)

EVERYMAN: Alas, I may well weep with sighs deep!
185   Now have I no manner of company
To help me in my journey, and me to keep;
And also my writing is full unready.
How shall I do now for to excuse me?
I would to God I had never be get!
190   To my soul a full great profit it had be;
For now I fear pains huge and great.
The time passeth, Lord, help, that all wrought!
For though I mourn it availeth nought.
The day passeth. and is almost ago;
195   I wot not well what for to do.
To whom were I best my complaint to make?
What and I to Fellowship thereof spake,
And showed him of this sudden chance?
For in him is all mine affiance;
200   We have in the world so many a day
Be good friends in sport and play.
I see him yonder, certainly.
I trust that he will bear me company;
Therefore to him will I speak to ease my sorrow.
205   Well met, good Fellowship, and good morrow!

(FELLOWSHIP *speaketh:*)

FELLOWSHIP: Everyman, good morrow, by this day!
Sir, why lookest thou so piteously?
If any thing be amiss, I pray thee me say,
That I may help to remedy.
210 EVERYMAN: Yea, good Fellowship, yea;
I am in great jeopardy.
FELLOWSHIP: My true friend, show to me your mind;
I will not forsake thee to my life's end,
In the way of good company.
215 EVERYMAN: That was well spoken, and lovingly.
FELLOWSHIP: Sir, I must needs know your heaviness;
I have pity to see you in any distress.
If any have you wronged, ye shall revenged be,
Though I on the ground be slain for thee—
220   Though that I know before that I should die.
EVERYMAN: Verily, Fellowship, gramercy.
FELLOWSHIP: Tush! by thy thanks I set not a straw.
Show me your grief, and say no more.
EVERYMAN: If I my heart should to you break,
225   And then you to turn your mind from me,
And would not me comfort when ye hear me speak,
Then should I ten times sorrier be.
FELLOWSHIP: Sir, I say as I will do indeed.
EVERYMAN: Then be you a good friend at need:
230   I have found you true herebefore.
FELLOWSHIP: And so ye shall evermore;
For, in faith; and thou go to hell,

I will not forsake thee by the way.
EVERYMAN: Ye speak like a good friend; I believe you well.
I shall deserve it, and I may.   235
FELLOWSHIP: I speak of no deserving, by this day!
For he that will say, and nothing do,
Is not worthy with good company to go;
Therefore show me the grief of your mind,
As to your friend most loving and kind.   240
EVERYMAN: I shall show you how it is:
Commanded I am to go a journey,
A long way, hard and dangerous,
And give a strait count, without delay,
Before the high Judge, Adonai.   245
Wherefore, I pray you, bear me company,
As ye have promised, in this journey.
FELLOWSHIP: That is matter indeed. Promise is duty;
But, and I should take such a voyage on me,
I know it well, it should be to my pain;   250
Also it maketh me afeard, certain.
But let us take counsel here as well as we can,
For your words would fear a strong man.
EVERYMAN: Why, ye said if I had need
Ye would me never forsake, quick ne dead,   255
Though it were to hell, truly.
FELLOWSHIP: So I said, certainly,
But such pleasures be set aside, the sooth to say;
And also, if we took such a journey,
When should we come again?   260
EVERYMAN: Nay, never again, till the day of doom.
FELLOWSHIP: In faith, then will not I come there!
Who hath you these tidings brought?
EVERYMAN: Indeed, Death was with me here.
FELLOWSHIP: Now, by God that all hath bought,   265
If Death were the messenger,
For no man that is living to-day
I will not go that loath journey—
Not for the father that begat me!
EVERYMAN: Ye promised, otherwise, pardie.   270
FELLOWSHIP: I wot well I said so, truly;
And yet if thou wilt eat, and drink, and make good cheer,
Or haunt to women the lusty company,
I would not forsake you while the day is clear,
Trust me verily.   275
EVERYMAN: Yea, thereto ye would be ready!
To go to mirth, solace, and play,
Your mind will sooner apply,
Than to bear me company in my long journey.
FELLOWSHIP: Now, in good faith, I will not that way.   280
But and thou will murder, or any man kill,
In that I will help thee with a good will.
EVERYMAN: O, that is a simple advice indeed.
Gentle fellow, help me in my necessity!
We have loved long, and now I need;   285
And now, gentle Fellowship, remember me.

185 **keep** guard   187 **writing** the writing of Everyman's accounts   189 **be get** been born   194 **ago** gone   197 **and if** 199 **affiance** trust   206 **by this day** an asseveration   216 **heaviness** sorrow   224 **break** open

235 **deserve** repay   244 **strait count** strict account 245 **Adonai** a Hebrew name for God   248 **That . . . indeed** that is a good reason indeed [for asking me]   253 **fear** frighten 265 **bought** redeemed   268 **loath** loathsome   270 **pardie** by God   273 **Or . . . company** or frequent the pleasant company of women   274 **while . . . clear** until daybreak   278 **apply** attend

FELLOWSHIP: Whether ye have loved me or no,
    By Saint John, I will not with thee go.
EVERYMAN: Yet, I pray thee, take the labour, and do so much
    for me
290   To bring me forward, for saint charity,
    And comfort me till I come without the town.
FELLOWSHIP: Nay, and thou would give me a new gown,
    I will not a foot with thee go;
    But, and thou had tarried, I would not have left thee so.
295   And as now God speed thee in thy journey,
    For from thee I will depart as fast as I may.
EVERYMAN: Whither away, Fellowship? Will thou forsake me?
FELLOWSHIP: Yea, by my fay! To God I betake thee.
EVERYMAN: Farewell, good Fellowship; for thee my heart is
    sore.
300   Adieu for ever! I shall see thee no more.
FELLOWSHIP: In faith, Everyman, farewell now at the ending;
    For you I will remember that parting is mourning.

(*Exit* FELLOWSHIP.)

EVERYMAN: Alack! shall we thus depart indeed—
    Ah, Lady, help!—without any more comfort?
305 Lo, Fellowship forsaketh me in my most need.
    For help in this world whither shall I resort?
    Fellowship herebefore with me would merry make,
    And now little sorrow for me doth he take.
    It is said, 'In prosperity men friends may find,
310   Which in adversity be full unkind.'
    Now whither for succour shall I flee,
    Sith that Fellowship hath forsaken me?
    To my kinsmen I will, truly,
    Praying them to help me in my necessity;
315 I believe that they will do so,
    For kind will creep where it may not go.
    I will go say, for yonder I see them.
    Where be ye now, my friends and kinsmen?

(*Enter* KINDRED *and* COUSIN.)

KINDRED: Here be we now at your commandment.
320   Cousin, I pray you show us your intent
    In any wise, and do not spare.
COUSIN: Yea, Everyman, and to us declare
    If ye be disposed to go anywhither;
    For, wit you well, we will live and die together.
325 KINDRED: In wealth and woe we will with you hold,
    For over his kin a man may be bold.
EVERYMAN: Gramercy, my friends and kinsmen kind.
    Now shall I show you the grief of my mind:
    I was commanded by a messenger,
330   That is a high king's chief officer;
    He bade me go a pilgrimage, to my pain,

    And I know well I shall never come again;
    Also I must give a reckoning strait,
    For I have a great enemy that hath me in wait,
    Which intendeth me for to hinder.   335
KINDRED: What account is that which ye must render?
    That would I know.
EVERYMAN: Of all my works I must show
    How I have lived and my days spent;
    Also of ill deeds that I have used   340
    In my time, sith life was me lent;
    And of all virtues that I have refused.
    Therefore, I pray you, go thither with me
    To help to make mine account, for saint charity.
COUSIN: What, to go thither? Is that the matter?   345
    Nay, Everyman, I had liefer fast bread and water
    All this five year and more.
EVERYMAN: Alas, that ever I was bore!
    For now shall I never be merry,
    If that you forsake me.   350
KINDRED: Ah, sir, what ye be a merry man!
    Take good heart to you, and make no moan.
    But one thing I warn you, by Saint Anne—
    As for me, ye shall go alone.
EVERYMAN: My Cousin, will you not with me go?   355
COUSIN: No, by our Lady! I have the cramp in my toe.
    Trust not to me, for, so God me speed,
    I will deceive you in your most need.
KINDRED: It availeth not us to tice.
    Ye shall have my maid with all my heart;   360
    She loveth to go to feasts, there to be nice,
    And to dance, and abroad to start:
    I will give her leave to help you in that journey,
    If that you and she may agree.
EVERYMAN: Now show me the very effect of your mind: 365
    Will you go with me, or abide behind?
KINDRED: Abide behind? Yea, that will I, and I may!
    Therefore farewell till another day.

(*Exit* KINDRED.)

EVERYMAN: How should I be merry or glad?
    For fair promises men to me make,   370
    But when I have most need they me forsake.
    I am deceived; that maketh me sad.
COUSIN: Cousin Everyman, farewell now,
    For verily I will not go with you.
    Also of mine own an unready reckoning   375
    I have to account; therefore I make tarrying.
    Now God keep thee, for now I go.

(*Exit* COUSIN.)

---

290 **bring me forward** escort me   298 **fay** faith; **betake** commend   303 **depart** part   312 **Sith** since   316 **For . . . go** For kinship will creep where it cannot walk, that is, blood is thicker than water   317 **go say** essay, try   321 **In . . . spare** without fail, and do not hold back   323 **anywhither** anywhere   325 **hold** side   326 **For . . . bold** for a man may be sure of his kinsfolk

334 **For . . . wait** a great enemy (the devil) who has me under observation   340 **used** practised   346 **I . . . water** I had rather fast on bread and water   348 **bore** born   351 **what . . . man** what a merry man you are   359 **It . . . tice** it is no use trying to entice us   361 **nice** wanton   362 **abroad to start** go out and about   365 **effect** tenor

EVERYMAN: Ah, Jesus, is all come hereto?
Lo, fair words maketh fools fain;
380 They promise, and nothing will do, certain.
My kinsmen promised me faithfully
For to abide with me steadfastly,
And now fast away do they flee:
Even so Fellowship promised me.
385 What friend were best me of to provide?
I lose my time here longer to abide.
Yet in my mind a thing there is:
All my life I have loved riches;
If that my Good now help me might,
390 He would make my heart full light.
I will speak to him in this distress—
Where art thou, my Goods and riches?

(GOODS *speaks from a corner.*)

GOODS: Who calleth me? Everyman? What! hast thou haste?
I lie here in corners, trussed and piled so high,
395 And in chests I am locked so fast,
Also sacked in bags. Thou mayst see with thine eye
I cannot stir; in packs low I lie.
What would ye have? Lightly me say.
EVERYMAN: Come hither, Goods, in all the haste thou may,
400 For of counsel I must desire thee.
GOODS: Sir, and ye in the world have sorrow or adversity,
That can I help you to remedy shortly.
EVERYMAN: It is another disease that grieveth me;
In this world it is not, I tell thee so.
405 I am sent for, another way to go,
To give a strait count general
Before the highest Jupiter of all;
And all my life I have had joy and pleasure in thee,
Therefore, I pray thee, go with me,
410 For, peradventure, thou mayst before God Almighty
My reckoning help to clean and purify;
For it is said ever among
That money maketh all right that is wrong.
GOODS: Nay, Everyman, I sing another song.
415 I follow no man in such voyages;
For, and I went with thee,
Thou shouldst fare much the worse for me;
For because on me thou did set thy mind,
Thy reckoning I have made blotted and blind,
420 That thine account thou cannot make truly;
And that hast thou for the love of me.
EVERYMAN: That would grieve me full sore,
When I should come to that fearful answer.
Up, let us go thither together.
425 GOODS: Nay, not so! I am too brittle, I may not endure;
I will follow no man one foot, be ye sure.
EVERYMAN: Alas, I have thee loved, and had great pleasure
All my life-days on good and treasure.

GOODS: That is to thy damnation, without leasing,
For my love is contrary to the love everlasting;   430
But if thou had me loved moderately during,
As to the poor to give part of me,
Then shouldst thou not in this dolour be,
Nor in this great sorrow and care.
EVERYMAN: Lo, now was I deceived ere I was ware,   435
And all I may wite misspending of time.
GOODS: What, weenest thou that I am thine?
EVERYMAN: I had wend so.
GOODS: Nay, Everyman, I say no.
As for a while I was lent thee;   440
A season thou hast had me in prosperity.
My condition is man's soul to kill;
If I save one, a thousand I do spill.
Weenest thou that I will follow thee?
Nay, not from this world, verily.   445
EVERYMAN: I had wend otherwise.
GOODS: Therefore to thy soul Goods is a thief;
For when thou art dead, this is my guise—
Another to deceive in this same wise
As I have done thee, and all to his soul's reprief.   450
EVERYMAN: O false Goods, cursed may thou be.
Thou traitor to God, that hast deceived me
And caught me in thy snare!
GOODS: Marry, thou brought thyself in care,
Whereof I am glad;   455
I must needs laugh, I cannot be sad.
EVERYMAN: Ah, Goods, thou hast had long my heartly love;
I gave thee that which should be the Lord's above.
But wilt thou not go with me indeed?
I pray thee truth to say.   460
GOODS: No, so God me speed!
Therefore farewell, and have good day.

(*Exit* GOODS.)

EVERYMAN: O, to whom shall I make my moan
For to go with me in that heavy journey?
First Fellowship said he would with me gone;   465
His words were very pleasant and gay,
But afterward he left me alone.
Then spake I to my kinsmen, all in despair,
And also they gave me words fair;
They lacked no fair speaking,   470
But all forsook me in the ending.
Then went I to my Goods, that I loved best,
In hope to have comfort, but there had I least;
For my Goods sharply did me tell
That he bringeth many into hell.   475
Then of myself I was ashamed,

---

385 **me . . . provide** to provide myself with   389 **Good** Goods
398 **Lightly** quickly   400 **For . . . thee** for I must entreat your
advice   403 **disease** trouble   412 **For . . . among** for it is
sometimes said   419 **blind** obscure

---

429 **without leasing** without a lie, that is, truly   431–432 **But
. . . me** but if you had loved me moderately during your lifetime,
so as to give part of me to the poor   433 **dolour** distress
435 **ware** aware   436 **And . . . time** and I may blame it all on
the bad use I have made of time   438 **wend** supposed   442 **condition** nature   443 **spill** ruin   448 **guise** practice   450 **reprief** shame   457 **heartly** heartfelt

And so I am worthy to be blamed;
Thus may I well myself hate.
Of whom shall I now counsel take?
480 I think that I shall never speed
Till that I go to my Good Deed.
But, alas, she is so weak
That she can neither go nor speak;
Yet will I venture on her now.
485 My Good Deeds, where be you?

(GOOD DEEDS *speaks from the ground*.)

GOOD DEEDS: Here I lie, cold in the ground;
Thy sins hath me sore bound,
That I cannot stir.
EVERYMAN: O Good Deeds, I stand in fear!
490 I must you pray of counsel,
For help now should come right well.
GOOD DEEDS: Everyman, I have understanding
That ye be summoned account to make
Before Messias, of Jerusalem King;
495 And you do by me, that journey with you will I take.
EVERYMAN: Therefore I come to you, my moan to make;
I pray you that ye will go with me,
GOOD DEEDS: I would full fain, but I cannot stand, verily.
EVERYMAN: Why, is there anything on you fall?
500 GOOD DEEDS: Yea, sir, I may thank you of all;
If ye had perfectly cheered me,
Your book of count full ready had be.
Look, the books of your works and deeds eke!
Behold how they lie under the feet,
505 To your soul's heaviness.
EVERYMAN: Our Lord Jesus help me!
For one letter here I cannot see.
GOOD DEEDS: There is a blind reckoning in time of distress.
EVERYMAN: Good Deeds, I pray you help me in this need,
510 Or else I am for ever damned indeed;
Therefore help me to make reckoning
Before the Redeemer of all thing,
That King is, and was, and ever shall.
GOOD DEEDS: Everyman, I am sorry of your fall,
515 And fain would I help you, and I were able.
EVERYMAN: Good Deeds, your counsel I pray you give me.
GOOD DEEDS: That shall I do verily;
Though that on my feet I may not go,
I have a sister that shall with you also,
520 Called Knowledge, which shall with you abide,
To help you to make that dreadful reckoning.

(*Enter* KNOWLEDGE.)

---

483 **go** walk   484 **venture** gamble   491 **For . . . well** for help
would now be very welcome   495 **And . . . me** if you do as I
advise   499 **fall** befallen   500 **of** for   501 **If . . . me** if you had
encouraged me fully   503 **eke** also   508 **There . . . distress** a
sinful person in this hour of need finds that the account of his
good deeds is dimly written and difficult to read   520 **Knowledge** the meaning of Knowledge here is acknowledgment or
recognition of sins

KNOWLEDGE: Everyman, I will go with thee, and be thy guide,
In thy most need to go by thy side.
EVERYMAN: In good condition I am now in every thing,
And am wholly content with this good thing,   525
Thanked be God my creator.
GOOD DEEDS: And when she hath brought you there
Where thou shalt heal thee of thy smart,
Then go you with your reckoning and your Good Deeds
together,
For to make you joyful at heart   530
Before the blessed Trinity.
EVERYMAN: My Good Deeds, gramercy!
I am well content, certainly,
With your words sweet.
KNOWLEDGE: Now go we together lovingly   535
To Confession, that cleansing river.
EVERYMAN: For joy I weep; I would we were there!
But, I pray you, give me cognition
Where dwelleth that holy man, Confession.
KNOWLEDGE: In the house of salvation: 540
We shall find him in that place,
That shall us comfort, by God's grace.

(KNOWLEDGE *takes* EVERYMAN *to* CONFESSION.)

Lo, this is Confession. Kneel down and ask mercy,
For he is in good conceit with God Almighty.
EVERYMAN: O glorious fountain, that all uncleanness doth clarify,   545
Wash from me the spots of vice unclean,
That on me no sin may be seen.
I come with Knowledge for my redemption,
Redempt with heart and full contrition;
For I am commanded a pilgrimage to take,   550
And great accounts before God to make.
Now I pray you, Shrift, mother of salvation,
Help my Good Deeds for my piteous exclamation.
CONFESSION: I know your sorrow well, Everyman.
Because with Knowledge ye come to me,   555
I will you comfort as well as I can,
And a precious jewel I will give thee,
Called penance, voider of adversity;
Therewith shall your body chastised be,
With abstinence and perseverance in God's service.   560
Here shall you receive that scourge of me,
Which is penance strong that ye must endure,
To remember thy Saviour was scourged for thee
With sharp scourges, and suffered it patiently;
So must thou, ere thou scape that painful pilgrimage.   565
Knowledge, keep him in this voyage,
And by that time Good Deeds will be with thee.
But in any wise be siker of mercy,
For your time draweth fast; and ye will saved be,
Ask God mercy, and he will grant truly.   570

---

528 **smart** pain   538 **cognition** knowledge   540 **In . . . salvation** in the church   544 **conceit** esteem   549 **Redempt . . .
contrition** redeemed by heartfelt and full contrition   552 **Shrift**
confession   553 **for . . . exclamation** in answer to my piteous
cry   558 **voider** expeller   568 **siker** sure   569 **draweth fast**
draws quickly to an end; **and** if

When with the scourge of penance man doth him bind,
The oil of forgiveness then shall he find.
EVERYMAN: Thanked be God for his gracious work!
    For now I will my penance begin;
575   This hath rejoiced and lighted my heart,
    Though the knots be painful and hard within.
KNOWLEDGE: Everyman, look your penance that ye fulfil,
    What pain that ever it to you be;
    And Knowledge shall give you counsel at will
580   How your account ye shall make clearly.
EVERYMAN: O eternal God, O heavenly figure,
    O way of righteousness, O goodly vision,
    Which descended down in a virgin pure
    Because he would every man redeem,
585   Which Adam forfeited by his disobedience:
    O blessed Godhead, elect and high divine,
    Forgive my grievous offence;
    Here I cry thee mercy in this presence.
    O ghostly treasure, O ransomer and redeemer,
590   Of all the world hope and conductor,
    Mirror of joy, and founder of mercy,
    Which enlumineth heaven and earth thereby,
    Hear my clamorous complaint, though it late be;
    Receive my prayers, of thy benignity;
595   Though I be a sinner most abominable,
    Yet let my name be written in Moses' table.
    O Mary, pray to the Maker of all thing,
    Me for to help at my ending;
    And save me from the power of my enemy,
600   For Death assaileth me strongly.
    And, Lady, that I may by mean of thy prayer
    Of your Son's glory to be partner,
    By the means of his passion, I it crave;
    I beseech you help my soul to save.
605   Knowledge, give me the scourge of penance;
    My flesh therewith shall give acquittance:
    I will now begin, if God give me grace.
KNOWLEDGE: Everyman, God give you time and space!
    Thus I bequeath you in the hands of our Saviour;
610   Now may you make your reckoning sure.
EVERYMAN: In the name of the Holy Trinity,
    My body sore punished shall be:
    Take this, body, for the sin of the flesh!

(*Scourges himself.*)

571 **him** himself 575 **lighted** lightened 576 **Though . . . within** though the knots [of the scourge] be painful and hard to my body 586 **divine** divinity 588 **in this presence** in the presence of this company 592 **thereby** besides 596 **Yet . . . table** medieval theologians regarded the two tables given on Sinai as symbols of baptism and penance, respectively. Thus Everyman is asking to be numbered among those who have escaped damnation by doing penance for their sins 599 **my enemy** the devil 601–603 **And . . . crave** and, Lady, I beg that through the mediation of thy prayer I may share in your Son's glory, in consequence of His passion 606 **acquittance** satisfaction (as a part of the sacrament of penance) 608 **space** opportunity

Also thou delightest to go gay and fresh,
And in the way of damnation thou did me bring, 615
Therefore suffer now strokes and punishing.
Now of penance I will wade the water clear,
To save me from purgatory, that sharp fire.

(GOOD DEEDS *rises from the ground.*)

GOOD DEEDS: I thank God, now I can walk and go,
    And am delivered of my sickness and woe. 620
    Therefore with Everyman I will go, and not spare;
    His good works I will help him to declare.
KNOWLEDGE: Now, Everyman, be merry and glad!
    Your Good Deeds cometh now; ye may not be sad.
    Now is your Good Deeds whole and sound, 625
    Going upright upon the ground.
EVERYMAN: My heart is light, and shall be evermore;
    Now will I smite faster than I did before.
GOOD DEEDS: Everyman, pilgrim, my special friend,
    Blessed be thou without end; 630
    For thee is preparate the eternal glory.
    Ye have me made whole and sound,
    Therefore I will bide by thee in every stound.
EVERYMAN: Welcome, my Good Deeds; now I hear thy voice,
    I weep for very sweetness of love. 635
KNOWLEDGE: Be no more sad, but ever rejoice;
    God seeth thy living in his throne above.
    Put on this garment to thy behoof,
    Which is wet with your tears,
    Or else before God you may it miss, 640
    When ye to your journey's end come shall.
EVERYMAN: Gentle Knowledge, what do ye it call?
KNOWLEDGE: It is a garment of sorrow:
    From pain it will you borrow;
    Contrition it is, 645
    That geteth forgiveness;
    It pleaseth God passing well.
GOOD DEEDS: Everyman, will you wear it for your heal?
EVERYMAN: Now blessed be Jesu, Mary's Son,
    For now have I on true contrition. 650
    And let us go now without tarrying;
    Good Deeds, have we clear our reckoning?
GOOD DEEDS: Yea, indeed, I have it here.
EVERYMAN: Then I trust we need not fear;
    Now, friends, let us not part in twain. 655
KNOWLEDGE: Nay, Everyman, that will we not, certain.
GOOD DEEDS: Yet must thou lead with thee
    Three persons of great might.
EVERYMAN: Who should they be?
GOOD DEEDS: Discretion and Strength they hight, 660
    And thy Beauty may not abide behind.
KNOWLEDGE: Also ye must call to mind
    Your Five Wits as for your counsellors.
GOOD DEEDS: You must have them ready at all hours.
EVERYMAN: How shall I get them hither? 665

631 **preparate** prepared 633 **stound** trial 638 **behoof** advantage 644 **borrow** release 647 **passing** exceedingly 648 **heal** salvation 660 **hight** are called 663 **Wits** senses

KNOWLEDGE: You must call them all together,
   And they will hear you incontinent.
EVERYMAN: My friends, come hither and be present,
   Discretion, Strength, my Five Wits, and Beauty.

(*Enter* BEAUTY, STRENGTH, DISCRETION, *and* FIVE WITS.)

670   BEAUTY: Here at your will we be all ready.
   What will ye that we should do?
   GOOD DEEDS: That ye would with Everyman go,
   And help him in his pilgrimage.
   Advise you, will ye with him or not in that voyage?
675   STRENGTH: We will bring him all thither,
   To his help and comfort, ye may believe me.
   DISCRETION: So will we go with him all together.
   EVERYMAN: Almighty God, lofed may thou be!
   I give thee laud that I have hither brought
680   Strength, Discretion, Beauty, and Five Wits. Lack
      I nought.
   And my Good Deeds, with Knowledge clear,
   All be in my company at my will here;
   I desire no more to my business.
   STRENGTH: And I, Strength, will by you stand in distress,
685   Though thou would be in battle fight on the ground.
   FIVE WITS: And though it were through the world round,
   We will not depart for sweet ne sour.
   BEAUTY: No more will I unto death's hour
   Whatsoever thereof befall.
690   DISCRETION: Everyman, advise you first of all;
   Go with a good advisement and deliberation.
   We all give you virtuous monition
   That all shall be well.
   EVERYMAN: My friends, harken what I will tell:
695   I pray God reward you in his heavenly sphere.
   Now harken, all that be here,
   For I will make my testament
   Here before you all present:
   In alms half my good I will give with my hands twain
700   In the way of charity, with good intent,
   And the other half still shall remain
   In queth, to be returned there it ought to be.
   This I do in despite of the fiend of hell,
   To go quit out of his peril
705   Ever after and this day.
   KNOWLEDGE: Everyman, harken what I say:
   Go to priesthood, I you advise,
   And receive of him in any wise
   The holy sacrament and ointment together.
710   Then shortly see ye turn again hither;
   We will all abide you here.
   FIVE WITS: Yea, Everyman, hie you that ye ready were.

There is no emperor, king, duke, ne baron,
That of God hath commission
As hath the least priest in the world being;   715
For of the blessed sacraments pure and benign
He beareth the keys, and thereof hath the cure
For man's redemption—it is ever sure—
Which God for our soul's medicine
Gave us out of his heart with great pine.   720
Here in this transitory life, for thee and me,
The blessed sacraments seven there be:
Baptism, confirmation, with priesthood good,
And the sacrament of God's precious flesh and blood,
Marriage, the holy extreme unction, and penance;   725
These seven be good to have in remembrance,
Gracious sacraments of high divinity.
EVERYMAN: Fain would I receive that holy body,
   And meekly to my ghostly father I will go.
FIVE WITS: Everyman, that is the best that ye can do.   730
   God will you to salvation bring,
   For priesthood exceedeth all other thing:
   To us Holy Scripture they do teach,
   And converteth man from sin heaven to reach;
   God hath to them more power given   735
   Than to any angel that is in heaven.
   With five words he may consecrate,
   God's body in flesh and blood to make,
   And handleth his Maker between his hands.
   The priest bindeth and unbindeth all bands,   740
   Both in earth and in heaven.
   Thou ministers all the sacraments seven;
   Though we kissed thy feet, thou were worthy;
   Thou art surgeon that cureth sin deadly:
   No remedy we find under God   745
   But all only priesthood.
   Everyman, God gave priests that dignity,
   And setteth them in his stead among us to be;
   Thus be they above angels in degree.

(EVERYMAN *goes to the priest to receive the last sacraments.*)

KNOWLEDGE: If priests be good, it is so, surely.   750
   But when Jesus hanged on the cross with great smart,
   There he gave out of his blessed heart
   The same sacrament in great torment:
   He sold them not to us, that Lord omnipotent.
   Therefore Saint Peter the apostle doth say   755
   That Jesu's curse hath all they
   Which God their Saviour do buy or sell,
   Or they for any money do take or tell.
   Sinful priests giveth the sinners example bad;
   Their children sitteth by other men's fires, I have heard; 760

---

667 **incontinent** immediately 674 **Advise** consider 678 **lofed** praised 683 **to** for 687 **for . . . sour** that is, in happiness or adversity 688 **unto** until 691 **advisement** reflection 692 **monition** forewarning 701–702 **And . . . be** the meaning seems to be that Everyman's immovable property (his body) will lie at rest in the earth 704–705 **To . . . day** to go free out of his power today and ever after 708 **in any wise** without fail 712 **hie . . . were** hurry and prepare yourself

714 **commission** authority 715 **being** living 720 **pine** suffering 728 **that holy body** the sacrament 729 **ghostly** spiritual 737 **five words** *Hoc est enim corpus meum* ("This is my body") 742 **ministers** administer 746 **But . . . priesthood** except only from the priesthood 750 **it is so** that they are above the angels 755–757 **Therefore . . . sell** the reference here is to the sin of simony (Acts 8:18 ff.) 760 **Their . . . fires** their children are illegitimate

And some haunteth women's company
With unclean life, as lusts of lechery:
These be with sin made blind.
FIVE WITS: I trust to God no such may we find;
765 Therefore let us priesthood honour,
And follow their doctrine for our souls' succour.
We be their sheep, and they shepherds be
By whom we all be kept in surety.
Peace, for yonder I see Everyman come,
770 Which hath made true satisfaction.
GOOD DEEDS: Methink it is he indeed.

(*Re-enter* EVERYMAN.)

EVERYMAN: Now Jesu be your alder speed!
I have received the sacrament for my redemption,
And then mine extreme unction:
775 Blessed be all they that counselled me to take it!
And now, friends, let us go without longer respite;
I thank God that ye have tarried so long.
Now set each of you on this rood your hand,
And shortly follow me:
780 I go before there I would be; God be our guide!
STRENGTH: Everyman, we will not from you go
Till ye have done this voyage long.
DISCRETION: I, Discretion, will bide by you also.
KNOWLEDGE: And though this pilgrimage be never so strong,
785 I will never part you fro.
STRENGTH: Everyman, I will be as sure by thee
As ever I did by Judas Maccabee.

(EVERYMAN *comes to his grave.*)

EVERYMAN: Alas, I am so faint I may not stand;
My limbs under me doth fold.
790 Friends, let us not turn again to this land,
Not for all the world's gold;
For into this cave must I creep
And turn to earth, and there to sleep.
BEAUTY: What, into this grave? Alas!
795 EVERYMAN: Yea, there shall ye consume, more and less.
BEAUTY: And what, should I smother here?
EVERYMAN: Yea, by my faith, and never more appear.
In this world live no more we shall,
But in heaven before the highest Lord of all.
800 BEAUTY: I cross out all this; adieu, by Saint John!
I take my cap in my lap, and am gone.
EVERYMAN: What, Beauty, whither will ye?
BEAUTY: Peace, I am deaf; I look not behind me,
Not and thou wouldest give me all the gold in thy chest.

(*Exit* BEAUTY.)

772 **be . . . speed** be the helper of you all   778 **rood** cross
784 **strong** grievous   785 **you fro** from you   786–787 **Every-man . . . Maccabee** I will stand by you as steadfastly as ever I did by Judas Maccabaeus (I Macc. 3)   795 **consume . . . less** decay, all of you   800 **I . . . this** I cancel all this, that is, my promise to stay with you   801 **I . . . lap** I doff my cap (so low that it comes) into my lap

EVERYMAN: Alas, whereto may I trust? 805
Beauty goeth fast away from me;
She promised with me to live and die.
STRENGTH: Everyman, I will thee also forsake and deny;
Thy game liketh me not at all.
EVERYMAN: Why, then, ye will forsake me all? 810
Sweet Strength, tarry a little space.
STRENGTH: Nay, sir, by the rood of grace!
I will hie me from thee fast,
Though thou weep till thy heart to-brast.
EVERYMAN: Ye would ever bide by me, ye said. 815
STRENGTH: Yea, I have you far enough conveyed.
Ye be old enough, I understand,
Your pilgrimage to take on hand;
I repent me that I hither came.
EVERYMAN: Strength, you to displease I am to blame; 820
Yet promise is debt, this ye well wot.
STRENGTH: In faith, I care not.
Thou art but a fool to complain;
You spend your speech and waste your brain.
Go thrust thee into the ground! 825

(*Exit* STRENGTH.)

EVERYMAN: I had wend surer I should you have found.
He that trusteth in his Strength
She him deceiveth at the length.
Both Strength and Beauty forsaketh me;
Yet they promised me fair and lovingly. 830
DISCRETION: Everyman, I will after Strength be gone;
As for me, I will leave you alone.
EVERYMAN: Why, Discretion, will you forsake me?
DISCRETION: Yea, in faith, I will go from thee,
For when Strength goeth before 835
I follow after evermore.
EVERYMAN: Yet, I pray thee, for the love of the Trinity,
Look in my grave once piteously.
DISCRETION: Nay, so nigh will I not come;
Farewell, every one! 840

(*Exit* DISCRETION.)

EVERYMAN: O, all thing faileth, save God alone—
Beauty, Strength, and Discretion;
For when Death bloweth his blast,
They all run from me full fast.
FIVE WITS: Everyman, my leave now of thee I take; 845
I will follow the other, for here I thee forsake.
EVERYMAN: Alas, then may I wail and weep,
For I took you for my best friend.
FIVE WITS: I will no longer thee keep;
Now farewell, and there an end. 850

(*Exit* FIVE WITS.)

EVERYMAN: O Jesu, help! All hath forsaken me.
GOOD DEEDS: Nay, Everyman; I will bide with thee.
I will not forsake thee indeed;

809 **liketh** pleases   811 **space** while   814 **to-brast** break
820 **you . . . blame** I am to blame for displeasing you

Thou shalt find me a good friend at need.

855 EVERYMAN: Gramercy, Good Deeds! Now may I true friends
    see.
    They have forsaken me, every one;
    I loved them better than my Good Deeds alone.
    Knowledge, will ye forsake me also?

KNOWLEDGE: Yea, Everyman, when ye to Death shall go;
860   But not yet, for no manner of danger.

EVERYMAN: Gramercy, Knowledge, with all my heart.

KNOWLEDGE: Nay, yet I will not from hence depart
    Till I see where ye shall become.

EVERYMAN: Methink, alas, that I must be gone
865   To make my reckoning and my debts pay,
    For I see my time is nigh spent away.
    Take example, all ye that this do hear or see,
    How they that I loved best do forsake me,
    Except my Good Deeds that bideth truly.

870 GOOD DEEDS: All earthly things is but vanity:
    Beauty, Strength, and Discretion do man forsake,
    Foolish friends, and kinsmen, that fair spake—
    All fleeth save Good Deeds, and that am I.

EVERYMAN: Have mercy on me, God most mighty;
875   And stand by me, thou mother and maid, holy Mary.

GOOD DEEDS: Fear not; I will speak for thee.

EVERYMAN: Here I cry God mercy.

GOOD DEEDS: Short our end, and minish our pain;
    Let us go and never come again.

880 EVERYMAN: Into thy hands, Lord, my soul I commend;
    Receive it, Lord, that it be not lost,
    As thou me boughtest, so me defend,
    And save me from the fiend's boast,
    That I may appear with that blessed host
885   That shall be saved at the day of doom.
    In manus tuas, of mights most
    For ever, *commendo spiritum meum.*

(*He sinks into his grave.*)

KNOWLEDGE: Now hath he suffered that we all shall endure;
    The Good Deeds shall make all sure.
    Now hath he made ending;   890
    Methinketh that I hear angels sing,
    And make great joy and melody
    Where Everyman's soul received shall be.

ANGEL: Come, excellent elect spouse, to Jesu!
    Hereabove thou shalt go   895
    Because of thy singular virtue.
    Now the soul is taken the body fro,
    Thy reckoning is crystal-clear.
    Now shalt thou into the heavenly sphere,
    Unto the which all ye shall come   900
    That liveth well before the day of doom.

(*Enter* DOCTOR.)

DOCTOR: This moral men may have in mind.
    Ye hearers, take it of worth, old and young,
    And forsake Pride, for he deceiveth you in the end;
    And remember Beauty, Five Wits, Strength, and   905
        Discretion,
    They all at the last do every man forsake,
    Save his Good Deeds there doth he take.
    But beware, for and they be small
    Before God, he hath no help at all;
    None excuse may be there for every man.   910
    Alas, how shall he do then?
    For after death amends may no man make,
    For then mercy and pity doth him forsake.
    If his reckoning be not clear when he doth come,
    God will say: '*Ite, maledicti, in ignem eternum.*'   915
    And he that hath his account whole and sound,
    High in heaven he shall be crowned;
    Unto which place God bring us all thither,
    That we may live body and soul together.
    Thereto help the Trinity!   920
    Amen, say ye, for saint charity.

THUS ENDETH THIS MORAL PLAY OF EVERYMAN

863 **where . . . become** what shall become of you   878 **Short
. . . pain** shorten our end, and diminish our pain   886–887 *In
. . . meum* Into thy hands, most mighty One for ever, I commend
my spirit

894 **spouse** bride of Jesus [a common medieval metaphor to express the idea of the soul's union with God]   903 **take . . .
worth** value it   907 **Save** unless   915 *Ite . . . eternum* depart,
ye cursed, into everlasting fire (Matthew xxv.41)

Christopher Marlowe

Born in the same year as Shakespeare, Christopher Marlowe (1564–1593) pursued a very different kind of life than his famous contemporary. Unlike Shakespeare, Marlowe had a university education; schooled at the King's School in Canterbury, Marlowe then attended Corpus Christi College, Cambridge. Marlowe left Cambridge in 1587, and his first play—*Tamburlaine,* in two full-length parts—was produced later that year. He wrote several important plays in the course of the next six years: *Doctor Faustus* (c. 1589), *The Jew of Malta* (c. 1590), and *Edward II* (c. 1591). Marlowe also wrote *Dido, Queen of Carthage,* possibly while still at Cambridge, and a play about the St. Bartholomew massacre of Huguenots in Paris, *The Massacre at Paris* (1593). Marlowe was an accomplished poet and wrote the narrative poem *Hero and Leander* (published in 1598), among many others. He was known at court and to influential advisers to Queen Elizabeth, such as Sir Walter Raleigh and Sir Francis Walsingham. It is not surprising that Marlowe's life has been much romanticized, especially given his reputation for iconoclasm, his association with occultists, and his service as one of Elizabeth's spies in Europe. Marlowe was arrested on several occasions for fighting and died from injuries he received in a tavern fight in 1593; there is some speculation that he may have been assassinated. He was twenty-nine years old.

Despite the brevity of his career, Marlowe is deservedly ranked among the greatest of English playwrights. The rhetorical flourish of what Ben Jonson called his "mighty line" and the brilliance of his language are unsurpassed in their majesty and power. His plays were popular in part no doubt because they starred Edward Alleyn, the major actor of the 1580s and early 1590s. Alleyn was the son-in-law of Philip Henslowe, a theatrical entrepreneur who built several theaters in London; their efforts, and Marlowe's plays, made them rich men. Indeed, Marlowe's plays remain alive today through the depth and force of their principal roles. In Faustus and Tamburlaine, Marlowe created roles of a rich and involved subjectivity, characters of the psychological complexity that would become one of the hallmarks of English drama.

DOCTOR FAUSTUS

Marlowe based his play on a popular German narrative, the *History of Doctor Johann Faust,* published in 1587. Audiences might also have seen in Faustus some resemblance to John Dee, Queen Elizabeth's royal astrologer. *Doctor Faustus* was celebrated in its day and would certainly have made a spectacular impression on audiences in the public theater. We know from Henslowe's accounts that his theater had a "hell mouth for Doctor Faustus," some kind of grotesque opening from which the devils could leap to snare Faustus and haul him off to damnation. The devils themselves were covered with flames, fireworks, and firecrackers. Tradition has it that Alleyn—clearly a real showman—wore a cross prominently displayed around his neck as a way of "defending" himself should real devils be summoned by his performance of Faustus.

The magic of the play, however, arises from the attraction exerted by Faustus himself. Like many of Marlowe's heroes, Faustus is an "overreacher," a man who magnificently and self-destructively tries to go beyond his own limitations, perhaps even beyond the limits of human nature itself. We can see this magnificent energy at the play's opening, when Faustus turns away from Aristotle and philosophy, from medicine, from the law, and from theology to the seductive arts of magic, striking the bargain with the devil that gives him the power to gratify his insatiable curiosity in exchange for his mortal soul.

Modern readers are sometimes confused by *Doctor Faustus*'s morality play elements, the pageant of the Seven Deadly Sins, and the Good and Bad angels who frame Faustus's temptation. Marlowe brings a medieval vision of the tragic "fall of those who stood in high degree" into collision with the more psychologically oriented vision of tragedy that is characteristic of the modern secular world. Certainly the Good and Bad angels point to what is right and wrong about Faustus's temptation. What is fascinating about the play is the way that Faustus's desire to be ravished by new experiences not only overcomes his scruples, but ours as well. Marlowe's play relies on the fact that despite the angels' warnings, we will want to see where Faustus's overreaching will take him.

Faustus—like Prospero in Shakespeare's *The Tempest*—could be taken as a figure for the Renaissance sense of human potential, here realized in its negative or self-destructive dimension. Faustus also seems to provide a figure for the morality of the theater itself, because the power that Faustus exercises in the play increasingly seems to be illusory, merely theatrical. The spectacles that Faustus conjures are finally only shows—Mephostophilis and Helen are just devils in disguise—and the power he wields has increasingly trivial results: tricking the Pope degenerates into hoodwinking the horse-courser and setting antlers on Benvolio's head. Faustus is damned for bargaining away his soul, but what finally seems to turn the play toward tragedy is what he sells his soul for: not for the world, but for the illusion of a world, a kind of endless and impoverished theater. We might well recall that the illusions that damn Faustus are, in many ways, the same illusions we have come to the theater to see. The theater makes Faustus's temptation real to its audience by tempting it with many of the same arts.

Mephostophilis confronts Faustus in Marlowe's *Doctor Faustus*.

DOCTOR FAUSTUS

Christopher Marlowe
EDITED BY SYLVAN BARNET

CHARACTERS

CHORUS
DOCTOR FAUSTUS
WAGNER, *his student and servant*
GOOD ANGEL
BAD ANGEL
VALDES } *magicians*
CORNELIUS }
THREE SCHOLARS
LUCIFER, *prince of devils*
MEPHOSTOPHILIS, *a devil*
ROBIN, *a clown*
BELZEBUB, *a devil*
PRIDE
COVETOUSNESS
ENVY
WRATH } *the Seven Deadly Sins*
GLUTTONY
SLOTH
LECHERY
DICK, *a clown*
POPE ADRIAN
RAYMOND, *King of Hungary*

BRUNO, *rival Pope appointed by the Emperor*
TWO CARDINALS
ARCHBISHOP OF RHEIMS
FRIARS
VINTNER
MARTINO }
FREDERICK } *gentlemen at the Emperor's court*
BENVOLIO }
THE GERMAN EMPEROR, CHARLES THE FIFTH
DUKE OF SAXONY
TWO SOLDIERS
HORSE-COURSER, *a clown*
CARTER, *a clown*
HOSTESS OF A TAVERN
DUKE OF VANHOLT
DUCHESS OF VANHOLT
SERVANT
OLD MAN
DARIUS OF PERSIA, ALEXANDER THE GREAT, ALEXANDER'S
  PARAMOUR, HELEN OF TROY, DEVILS, PIPER, CARDINALS,
  MONKS, FRIARS, ATTENDANTS, SOLDIERS, SERVANTS, TWO
  CUPIDS

PROLOGUE

Enter CHORUS.

Not marching in the fields of Trasimene
Where Mars did mate the warlike Carthagens,
Nor sporting in the dalliance of love
In courts of kings where state is overturned,
5 Nor in the pomp of proud audacious deeds
Intends our muse to vaunt his heavenly verse.
Only this, gentles—We must now perform
The form of Faustus' fortunes, good or bad:
And now to patient judgments we appeal
10 And speak for Faustus in his infancy.
Now is he born of parents base of stock
In Germany within a town called Rhode;
At riper years to Wittenberg he went
Whereas his kinsmen chiefly brought him up.

So much he profits in divinity   15
That shortly he was graced with doctor's name,
Excelling all, and sweetly can dispute
In th' heavenly matters of theology;
Till swoll'n with cunning, of a self-conceit,
His waxen wings did mount above his reach   20
And melting, heavens conspired his overthrow!
For falling to a devilish exercise
And glutted now with learning's golden gifts
He surfeits upon cursèd necromancy:
Nothing so sweet as magic is to him   25
Which he prefers before his chiefest bliss—
And this the man that in his study sits.

(*Exit.*)

Prologue s.d. **Chorus** a single actor (here, perhaps, Wagner, Faustus' servant-student)   1 **Trasimene** Lake Trasimene, site of one of Hannibal's victories over the Romans, 217 BCE (Marlowe is not known to have written on this subject, though lines 3–4 may refer to his Edward II, and line 5 to his Tamburlaine) 2 **Mars did mate** i.e., the Roman army encountered   4 **state** government   6 **muse** poet; **vaunt** proudly display   12 **Rhode** Roda   14 **Whereas** where

16 **graced** alluding to the official "grace" permitting the student to take his degree   19 **cunning, of a self-conceit** ingenuity, born of arrogance   20 **waxen wings** alluding to Icarus, who flew by means of wings made of feathers waxed to a framework; despite the warning of his father, Icarus soared too near the sun, the wax melted, and he plunged to his death   24 **necromancy** literally, divination by means of the spirits of the dead, but here probably equivalent to black magic   26 **prefers before his chiefest bliss** sets above his hope of salvation

ACT ONE

SCENE I

FAUSTUS *in his study.*

FAUSTUS: Settle thy studies Faustus, and begin
    To sound the depth of that thou wilt profess.
    Having commenced, be a divine in show—
    Yet level at the end of every art
5   And live and die in Aristotle's works.
    Sweet *Analytics,* 'tis thou hast ravished me.
    Bene disserere est finis logices.
    Is to dispute well logic's chiefest end?
    Affords this art no greater miracle?
10   Then read no more, thou has attained that end.
    A greater subject fitteth Faustus' wit:
    Bid *on kai me on* farewell, and Galen come:
    Be a physician Faustus, heap up gold,
    And be eternized for some wondrous cure.
15   *Summum bonum medicinae sanitas,*
    The end of physic is our body's health.
    Why Faustus hast thou not attained that end?
    Are not thy bills hung up as monuments
    Whereby whole cities have escaped the plague
20   And thousand desperate maladies been cured?
    Yet art thou still but Faustus and a man.
    Could'st thou make men to live eternally
    Or being dead raise them to life again,
    Then this profession were to be esteemed.
25   Physic farewell! Where is Justinian?
    Si una eademque res legatur duobus, alter rem, alter
        valorem rei, et cetera.
    A petty case of paltry legacies.
    Exhereditare filium non potest pater, nisi—
30   Such is the subject of the *Institute*
    And universal body of the law!
    This study fits a mercenary drudge
    Who aims at nothing but external trash,
    Too servile and illiberal for me.
35   When all is done, divinity is best.
    Jerome's Bible, Faustus, view it well.

Stipendium peccati mors est. Ha! *Stipendium et cetera.* The re-
ward of sin is death? That's hard: *Si peccasse negamus, fal-
limur, et nulla est in nobis veritas.* If we say that we have no
sin, we deceive ourselves, and there is no truth in us. Why,   40
then belike, we must sin, and so consequently die.
Ay, we must die an everlasting death.
What doctrine call you this? *Che serà, serà:*
What will be, shall be! Divinity, adieu!
These metaphysics of magicians   45
And negromantic books are heavenly;
Lines, circles, letters, characters—
Ay, these are those that Faustus most desires.
O, what a world of profit and delight,
Of power, of honor, and omnipotence   50
Is promised to the studious artisan!
All things that move between the quiet poles
Shall be at my command: emperors and kings
Are but obeyed in their several provinces
But his dominion that exceeds in this   55
Stretcheth as far as doth the mind of man:
A sound magician is a demi-god!
Here tire my brains to get a deity!

(*Enter* WAGNER.)

Wagner, commend me to my dearest friends.
The German Valdes and Cornelius.   60
Request them earnestly to visit me.
WAGNER: I will, sir.

(*Exit.*)

FAUSTUS: Their conference will be a greater help to me
    Than all my labors, plod I ne'er so fast.

(*Enter the* [GOOD] ANGEL *and the* [EVIL] SPIRIT.)

GOOD ANGEL: O Faustus, lay that damnèd book aside   65
    And gaze not on it lest it tempt thy soul
    And heap God's heavy wrath upon thy head!
    Read, read the Scriptures—that is blasphemy!
BAD ANGEL: Go forward Faustus, in that famous art
    Wherein all nature's treasure is contained.   70
    Be thou on earth as Jove is in the sky,
    Lord and commander of these elements!

I.i. s.d. **Faustus in his study** probably at his last line the Chorus drew back a curtain at the rear of the stage, disclosing
Faustus   2 **profess** study and teach   3 **commenced** taken a
degree   4 **level** aim   6 **Analytics** title of two treatises by Aristotle on logic   7 **Bene . . . logices** the end (i.e., purpose) of logic
is to argue well (Latin)   11 **wit** intelligence   12 *on kai me on*
being and not being (Greek); **Galen** Greek authority on medicine, second century CE   15 *Summum . . . sanitas* health is the
greatest good of medicine (Latin, translated from Aristotle's
Nichomachean Ethics)   16 **physic** medicine   18 **bills** prescriptions   25 **Justinian** Roman emperor and authority on law
(483–565) who ordered the compilation of the *Institutes*   26–27
Si . . . et cetera if one thing is willed to two persons, one of them
shall have the thing itself, the other the value of the thing, and so
forth (Latin)   29 *Exhereditare . . . nisi* a father cannot disinherit
his son unless (Latin)   36 **Jerome's Bible** the Latin translation
made by St. Jerome (c. 340–420)

37 *Stipendium . . . est* the wages of sin is death (Romans vi.23; if
Faustus had gone on to read the rest of the verse, he would have
found that "the gift of God is eternal life through Jesus Christ our
Lord")   38–39 *Si . . . veritas* from 1 John 1:8, translated in the
next two lines: Faustus neglects the following verse: "If we confess our sins, He is faithful and just to forgive us our sins, and to
cleanse us from all unrighteousness"   43 *Che serà, serà* (Italian,
translated in the first half of the next line)   45 **metaphysics**
subjects lying beyond (or studied after) physics   46 **negromantic** black magical (though probably here also associated with
"necromantic," i.e., concerned with raising the spirits of the dead)
51 **artisan** i.e., expert   52 **quiet** motionless   55 **this** i.e., magic
58 **get** beget   63 **conference** conversation.   64 s.d. **Spirit** Bad
Angel, devil (the two angels probably enter the stage from separate doors)   68 **that** i.e., the book of magic

(*Exeunt* ANGELS.)

FAUSTUS: How am I glutted with conceit of this!
    Shall I make spirits fetch me what I please?
75   Resolve me of all ambiguities?
    Perform what desperate enterprise I will?
    I'll have them fly to India for gold,
    Ransack the ocean for orient pearl,
    And search all corners of the new-found world
80   For pleasant fruits and princely delicates;
    I'll have them read me strange philosophy
    And tell the secrets of all foreign kings;
    I'll have them wall all Germany with brass
    And make swift Rhine circle fair Wittenberg;
85   I'll have them fill the public schools with silk
    Wherewith the students shall be bravely clad.
    I'll levy soldiers with the coin they bring
    And chase the Prince of Parma from our land
    And reign sole king of all the provinces!
90   Yea, stranger engines for the brunt of war
    Than was the fiery keel at Antwerp bridge
    I'll make my servile spirits to invent.

(*Enter* VALDES *and* CORNELIUS.)

    Come German Valdes and Cornelius
    And make me blest with your sage conference.
95   Valdes, sweet Valdes, and Cornelius,
    Know that your words have won me at the last
    To practice magic and concealèd arts.
    Philosophy is odious and obscure,
    Both law and physic are for petty wits,
100   Divinity is basest of the three—
    Unpleasant, harsh, contemptible, and vile.
    'Tis magic, magic, that hath ravished me!
    Then, gentle friends, aid me in this attempt
    And I, that have with subtle syllogisms
105   Graveled the pastors of the German church
    And made the flow'ring pride of Wittenberg
    Swarm to my problems as th' infernal spirits
    On sweet Musaeus when he came to hell,
    Will be as cunning as Agrippa was,
110   Whose shadows made all Europe honor him.
VALDES: Faustus, these books, thy wit, and our experience
    Shall make all nations to canonize us.

As Indian Moors obey their Spanish lords,
So shall the spirits of every element
Be always serviceable to us three: 115
Like lions shall they guard us when we please,
Like Almain rutters with their horsemen's staves
Or Lapland giants trotting by our sides;
Sometimes like women or unwedded maids
Shadowing more beauty in their airy brows   120
Than has the white breasts of the queen of love;
From Venice shall they drag huge argosies
And from America the golden fleece
That yearly stuffs old Philip's treasury,
If learnèd Faustus will be resolute.   125
FAUSTUS: Valdes, as resolute am I in this
    As thou to live; therefore object it not.
CORNELIUS: The miracles that magic will perform
    Will make thee vow to study nothing else.
    He that is grounded in astrology,   130
    Enriched with tongues, well seen in minerals,
    Hath all the principles magic doth require.
    Then doubt not Faustus but to be renowned
    And more frequented for this mystery
    Than heretofore the Delphian oracle.   135
    The spirits tell me they can dry the sea
    And fetch the treasure of all foreign wracks,
    Yea, all the wealth that our forefathers hid
    Within the massy entrails of the earth.
    Then tell me Faustus, what shall we three want?   140
FAUSTUS: Nothing, Cornelius. O, this cheers my soul!
    Come, show me some demonstrations magical
    That I may conjure in some bushy grove
    And have these joys in full possession.
VALDES: Then haste thee to some solitary grove,   145
    And bear wise Bacon's and Albanus' works,
    The Hebrew Psalter, and New Testament;
    And whatsoever else is requisite
    We will inform thee ere our conference cease.
CORNELIUS: Valdes, first let him know the words of art,   150
    And then, all other ceremonies learned,
    Faustus may try his cunning by himself.
VALDES: First I'll instruct thee in the rudiments,
    And then wilt thou be perfecter than I.
FAUSTUS: Then come and dine with me, and after meat   155
    We'll canvass every quiddity thereof,
    For ere I sleep I'll try what I can do:
    This night I'll conjure though I die therefor!

(*Exeunt omnes.*)

---

73 **conceit of this** i.e., the conception of being a magician
75 **Resolve me of** explain to me   77 **India** either the West Indies (America) or the East Indies   78 **orient** lustrous and precious   85 **public schools** universities   86 **bravely** splendidly
88 **Prince of Parma** Spanish governor-general of the Low Countries during 1579–1592   90 **brunt** assault   91 **fiery keel** burning ship sent by the Netherlanders in 1585 against a bridge erected by Parma to blockade Antwerp (Antwerp here is adjectival, not genitive)   105 **Graveled** confounded   107 **problems** questions proposed for disputation   108 **Musaeus** legendary Greek poet   109 **Agrippa** Cornelius Agrippa of Nettesheim (1486–1535), German author of *De occulta philosophia,* a survey of Renaissance magic; Agrippa was believed to have raised spirits ("shadows") from the dead

113 **Indian Moors** American Indians   117 **Almain rutters** German cavalrymen   120 **Shadowing** sheltering   124 **Philip** King Philip II of Spain (1527–1598)   131 **well seen** skilled
134 **frequented for this mystery** resorted to for this art
135 **Delphian oracle** oracle of Apollo at Delphi   139 **massy** massive   140 **want** lack   143 **conjure** raise spirits   146 **Bacon** Roger Bacon, medieval friar and scientist; **Albanus** perhaps Pietro d'Abano, medieval writer on medicine and philosophy
156 **canvass every quiddity** discuss every essential detail
158 s.d. *omnes* all (Latin)

SCENE II

Enter two SCHOLARS.

1 SCHOLAR: I wonder what's become of Faustus that was wont
to make our schools ring with *sic probo*.

(*Enter* WAGNER.)

2 SCHOLAR: That shall we presently know. Here comes his boy.
1 SCHOLAR: How now sirrah, where's thy master?
5 WAGNER: God in heaven knows.
1 SCHOLAR: Why, dost not thou know then?
WAGNER: Yes, I know, but that follows not.
1 SCHOLAR: Go to sirrah, leave your jesting and tell us where
he is.
10 WAGNER: That follows not by force of argument, which you,
being licentiates, should stand upon; therefore, acknowledge your error and be attentive.
2 SCHOLAR: Then you will not tell us?
WAGNER: You are deceived, for I will tell you. Yet if you were
15 not dunces, you would never ask me such a question. For is
he not corpus naturale? And is not that mobile? Then wherefore should you ask me such a question? But that I am by nature phlegmatic, slow to wrath, and prone to lechery—to
love. I would say—it were not for you to come within forty
20 foot of the place of execution—although I do not doubt but
to see you both hanged the next sessions. Thus, having triumphed over you, I will set my countenance like a precisian
and begin to speak thus: Truly, my dear brethren, my master
is within at dinner, with Valdes and Cornelius, as this wine, if
25 it could speak, would inform your worships; and so, the Lord
bless you, preserve you, and keep you, my dear brethren.

(*Exit.*)

1 SCHOLAR: O Faustus, then I fear that which I have long
suspected,
That thou art fall'n into that damnèd art
For which they two are infamous through the world.
30 2 SCHOLAR: Were he a stranger, not allied to me,
The danger of his soul would make me mourn.
But come, let us go and inform the rector.
It may be his grave counsel may reclaim him.
1 SCHOLAR: I fear me nothing will reclaim him now.
35 2 SCHOLAR: Yet let us see what we can do.

(*Exeunt.*)

I.ii. 2 *sic probo* thus I prove it (Latin) 3 **presently** at once;
boy servant (an impoverished student) 4 **sirrah** term of address used to an inferior 8 **Go to** exclamation of impatience
11 **licentiates** possessors of a degree preceding the master's degree; **stand upon** make much of 15 **dunces** (1) fools (2) hair-
splitters 16 **corpus naturale . . . mobile** natural matter . . .
movable (Latin, scholastic definition of the subject-matter of
physics) 18 **phlegmatic** sluggish 20 **the place of execution** the place of action, i.e., the dining room (with quibble on
gallows) 21 **sessions** sittings of a court 22 **precisian** Puritan
(Wagner goes on to parody the style of the Puritans) 32 **rector**
head of the university

SCENE III

Thunder. Enter LUCIFER *and four* DEVILS. FAUSTUS *to them with
this speech.*

FAUSTUS: Now that the gloomy shadow of the night,
Longing to view Orion's drizzling look,
Leaps from th' antarctic world unto the sky
And dims the welkin with her pitchy breath,
Faustus, begin thine incantations   5
And try if devils will obey thy hest,
Seeing thou hast prayed and sacrificed to them.
Within this circle is Jehovah's name
Forward and backward anagrammatized,
Th' abbreviated names of holy saints,   10
Figures of every adjunct to the heavens,
And characters of signs and erring stars,
By which the spirits are enforced to rise:
Then fear not, Faustus, to be resolute
And try the utmost magic can perform.   15

(*Thunder.*)

*Sint mihi dei Acherontis propitii! Valeat numen triplex Iehovae!
Ignei, aerii, aquatici, spiritus, salvete! Orientis princeps, Belzebub
inferni ardentis monarcha, et Demogorgon, propitiamus vos ut
appareat et surgat Mephostophilis! Quid tu moraris? Per Ieho-
vam, Gehennam, et consecratam aquam quam nunc spargo,*   20
*signumque crucis quod nunc facio, et per vota nostra, ipse nunc
surgat nobis dicatus Mephostophilis!*

(*Enter a* DEVIL.)

I charge thee to return and change thy shape,
Thou art too ugly to attend on me.
Go, and return an old Franciscan friar: 25
That holy shape becomes a devil best.

(*Exit* DEVIL.)

I.iii. s.d. **Enter . . . Devils** (they are invisible to Faustus; perhaps they enter through a trapdoor and climb to the upper playing area, as implied in 5.2 s.d.) 2 **Orion** constellation
appearing at the beginning of winter, associated with rain 4
welkin sky 8 **circle** circle the conjuror draws around him on
the ground, to call the spirits and to protect himself from them
11 **adjunct to** heavenly body fixed to 12 **signs and erring
stars** signs of the Zodiac and planets 16–22 *Sint . . .
Mephostophilis* may the gods of the lower region be favorable to
me. Away with the trinity of Jehovah. Hail, spirits of fire, air, water. Prince of the east, Belzebub monarch of burning hell, and
Demogorgon, we pray to you that Mephostophilis may appear
and rise. Why do you delay? By Jehovah, Gehenna, and the holy
water which now I sprinkle, and the sign of the cross which now
I make, and by our vows, may Mephostophilis himself now rise
to serve us (Latin) 22 s.d. **Devil** the word "dragon" oddly appears, after "surgat Mephostophilis," in the preceding conjuration. It makes no sense in the sentence, and it has therefore been
omitted from the present text, but perhaps it indicates that a
dragon briefly appears at that point, or perhaps the devil referred
to in the present stage direction is disguised as a dragon

I see there's virtue in my heavenly words.
Who would not be proficient in this art?
How pliant is this Mephostophilis,
30   Full of obedience and humility,
Such is the force of magic and my spells.

(*Enter* MEPHOSTOPHILIS.)

MEPHOSTOPHILIS: Now Faustus, what wouldst thou have me do?
FAUSTUS: I charge thee wait upon me whilst I live
To do whatever Faustus shall command,
35   Be it to make the moon drop from her sphere
Or the ocean to overwhelm the world.
MEPHOSTOPHILIS: I am a servant to great Lucifer
And may not follow thee without his leave.
No more than he commands must we perform.
40   FAUSTUS: Did not he charge thee to appear to me?
MEPHOSTOPHILIS: No, I came now hither of mine own accord.
FAUSTUS: Did not my conjuring raise thee? Speak.
MEPHOSTOPHILIS: That was the cause, but yet *per accidens:*
For when we hear one rack the name of God,
45   Abjure the Scriptures and his savior Christ.
We fly in hope to get his glorious soul.
Nor will we come unless he use such means
Whereby he is in danger to be damned.
Therefore the shortest cut for conjuring
50   Is stoutly to abjure the Trinity
And pray devoutly to the prince of hell.
FAUSTUS: So Faustus hath already done, and holds this principle,
There is no chief but only Belzebub:
To whom Faustus doth dedicate himself.
55   This word "damnation" terrifies not me
For I confound hell in Elysium:
My ghost be with the old philosophers!
But leaving these vain trifles of men's souls,
Tell me, what is that Lucifer thy Lord?
60   MEPHOSTOPHILIS: Arch-regent and commander of all spirits.
FAUSTUS: Was not that Lucifer an angel once?
MEPHOSTOPHILIS: Yes Faustus, and most dearly loved of God.
FAUSTUS: How comes it then that he is prince of devils?
MEPHOSTOPHILIS: O, by aspiring pride and insolence.
65   For which God threw him from the face of heaven.
FAUSTUS: And what are you that live with Lucifer?
MEPHOSTOPHILIS: Unhappy spirits that fell with Lucifer,
Conspired against our God with Lucifer,
And are forever damned with Lucifer.
70   FAUSTUS: Where are you damned?
MEPHOSTOPHILIS: In hell.
FAUSTUS: How comes it then that thou art out of hell?
MEPHOSTOPHILIS: Why this is hell, nor am I out of it.
Think'st thou that I who saw the face of God
75   And tasted the eternal joys of heaven
Am not tormented with ten thousand hells
In being deprived of everlasting bliss?

O Faustus, leave these frivolous demands
Which strikes a terror to my fainting soul!
FAUSTUS: What, is great Mephostophilis so passionate   80
For being deprivèd of the joys of heaven?
Learn thou of Faustus manly fortitude
And scorn those joys thou never shalt possess.
Go bear these tidings to great Lucifer:
Seeing Faustus hath incurred eternal death   85
By desperate thoughts against Jove's deity,
Say he surrenders up to him his soul
So he will spare him four and twenty years,
Letting him live in all voluptuousness,
Having thee ever to attend on me,   90
To give me whatsoever I shall ask,
To tell me whatsoever I demand,
To slay mine enemies and to aid my friends
And always be obedient to my will.
Go and return to mighty Lucifer   95
And meet me in my study at midnight,
And then resolve me of thy master's mind.
MEPHOSTOPHILIS: I will, Faustus.
FAUSTUS: Had I as many souls as there be stars
I'd give them all for Mephostophilis.   100
By him I'll be great emperor of the world,
And make a bridge through the moving air
To pass the ocean with a band of men;
I'll join the hills that bind the Afric shore
And make that country continent to Spain,   105
And both contributary to my crown;
The Emperor shall not live but by my leave,
Nor any potentate of Germany.
Now that I have obtained what I desired
I'll live in speculation of this art   110
Till Mephostophilis return again.

(*Exit.*)

(*Exeunt* LUCIFER *and* DEVILS.)

SCENE IV

Enter WAGNER *and* [ROBIN] *the clown.*

WAGNER: Come hither, sirrah boy.
ROBIN: Boy! O, disgrace to my person! Zounds, boy in your
face! You have seen many boys with such pickadevants, I
am sure.
WAGNER: Sirrah, hast thou no comings in?   5
ROBIN: Yes, and goings out too, you may see sir.

---

79 **strikes** it is not unusual to have a plural subject—especially
when it has a collective force—take a verb ending in *-s*   80 **passionate** emotional   97 **resolve** inform   102 **through** pronounced "thorough"   105 **continent to** continuous with
110 **speculation** contemplation

I.iv. s.d. **Clown** buffoon   2 **Zounds** by God's wounds   3
pickadevants pointed beards   5 **comings in** income (the
Clown then quibbles on "goings out," i.e., expenses and also
holes in his clothes through which his body pokes

---

43 *per accidens* the immediate (but not ultimate) cause (Latin)
44 **rack** torture   46 **glorious** (1) splendid (2) presumptuous
56 **confound hell in Elysium** do not distinguish between hell
and Elysium   57 **ghost** spirit; **old** i.e., pre-Christian   60 **spirits** devils

WAGNER: Alas, poor slave! See how poverty jests in his naked-
ness. I know the villain's out of service, and so hungry that
I know he would give his soul to the devil for a shoulder
10 of mutton, though it were blood-raw.
ROBIN: Not so, neither! I had need to have it well roasted, and
good sauce to it, if I pay so dear, I can tell you.
WAGNER: Sirrah, wilt thou be my man and wait on me? And
I will make thee go like *Qui mihi discipulus*.
15 ROBIN: What, in verse?
WAGNER: No, slave, in beaten silk and stavesacre.
ROBIN: Stavesacre? That's good to kill vermin! Then, belike,
if I serve you I shall be lousy.
WAGNER: Why, so thou shalt be, whether thou dost it or no;
20 for sirrah, if thou dost not presently bind thyself to me for
seven years, I'll turn all the lice about thee into familiars
and make them tear thee in pieces.
ROBIN: Nay sir, you may save yourself a labor, for they are as
familiar with me as if they paid for their meat and drink,
25 I can tell you.
WAGNER: Well sirrah, leave your jesting and take these guilders.
ROBIN: Yes marry sir, and I thank you too.
WAGNER: So, now thou art to be at an hour's warning whensoever and wheresoever the devil shall fetch thee.
30 ROBIN: Here, take your guilders, I'll none of 'em!
WAGNER: Not I, thou art pressed. Prepare thyself, for I will
presently raise up two devils to carry thee away. Banio!
Belcher!
ROBIN: Belcher! And Belcher come here I'll belch him. I am
35 not afraid of a devil!

(*Enter two* DEVILS.)

WAGNER: How now sir, will you serve me now?
ROBIN: Ay, good Wagner, take away the devil then.
WAGNER: Spirits, away! (*Exeunt* DEVILS.) Now sirrah, follow me.
ROBIN: I will sir! But hark you master, will you teach me this
40 conjuring occupation?
WAGNER: Ay sirrah, I'll teach thee to turn thyself to a dog or
a cat or a mouse or a rat or anything.
ROBIN: A dog or a cat or a mouse or a rat? O brave Wagner!
WAGNER: Villain, call me Master Wagner. And see that you
45 walk attentively, and let your right eye be always diame-
trally fixed upon my left heel, that thou mayst *quasi vesti-
giis nostris insistere*.
ROBIN: Well sir, I warrant you.

(*Exeunt.*)

---

14 ***Qui mihi discipulus*** one who is my disciple, i.e., like the
servant of a learned man (the Latin is the beginning of a
poem, familiar to Renaissance schoolboys, on proper behavior)
16 **beaten** embroidered (leading to the quibble on the sense
"hit"); **stavesacre** preparation from seeds of delphinium, used to
kill vermin 21 **familiars attendant** demons 26 **guilders**
Dutch coins 27 **marry** indeed (a mild oath, from "by the Virgin
Mary") 31 **pressed** enlisted into service 34 **And** if 43 **brave**
splendid 45 **diametrally** directly 46–47 ***quasi vestigiis nostris
insistere*** as if to step in our footsteps

ACT TWO

SCENE I

Enter FAUSTUS *in his study.*

FAUSTUS: Now, Faustus, must thou needs be damned;
Canst thou not be saved!
What boots it then to think on God or heaven?
Away with such vain fancies, and despair—
Despair in God and trust in Belzebub!   5
Now go not backward, Faustus, be resolute!
Why waverst thou? O something soundeth in mine ear,
"Abjure this magic, turn to God again."
Ay, and Faustus will turn to God again.
To God? He loves thee not;   10
The god thou serv'st is thine own appetite
Wherein is fixed the love of Belzebub!
To him I'll build an altar and a church
And offer lukewarm blood of newborn babies!

(*Enter the two* ANGELS.)

BAD ANGEL: Go forward, Faustus, in that famous art.   15
GOOD ANGEL: Sweet Faustus, leave that execrable art.
FAUSTUS: Contrition, prayer, repentance, what of these?
GOOD ANGEL: O, they are means to bring thee unto heaven.
BAD ANGEL: Rather illusions, fruits of lunacy,
That make men foolish that do use them most.   20
GOOD ANGEL: Sweet Faustus, think of heaven and heavenly
things.
BAD ANGEL: No Faustus, think of honor and of wealth.

(*Exeunt* ANGELS.)

FAUSTUS: Wealth!
Why, the signory of Emden shall be mine!
When Mephostophilis shall stand by me   25
What power can hurt me? Faustus, thou art safe.
Cast no more doubts! Mephostophilis, come,
And bring glad tidings from great Lucifer.
Is't not midnight? Come Mephostophilis,
Veni, veni, Mephostophile!   30

(*Enter* MEPHOSTOPHILIS.)

Now tell me, what saith Lucifer thy Lord?
MEPHOSTOPHILIS: That I shall wait on Faustus whilst he lives,
So he will buy my service with his soul.
FAUSTUS: Already Faustus hath hazarded that for thee.
MEPHOSTOPHILIS: But now thou must bequeath it solemnly   35
And write a deed of gift with thine own blood,
For that security craves Lucifer.
If thou deny it I must back to hell.
FAUSTUS: Stay Mephostophilis and tell me
What good will my soul do thy lord?   40
MEPHOSTOPHILIS: Enlarge his kingdom.

II.i. 3 boots avails 24 **signory of Emden** lordship of the
rich German port at the mouth of the Ems 30 ***Veni, veni,
Mephostophile*** come, come, Mephostophilis (Latin)

FAUSTUS: Is that the reason why he tempts us thus?
MEPHOSTOPHILIS: *Solamen miseris socios habuisse doloris.*
FAUSTUS: Why, have you any pain that torture other?
45 MEPHOSTOPHILIS: As great as have the human souls of men.
     But tell me, Faustus, shall I have thy soul—
     And I will be thy slave and wait on thee
     And give thee more than thou hast wit to ask?
FAUSTUS: Ay Mephostophilis. I'll give it him.
50 MEPHOSTOPHILIS: Then, Faustus, stab thy arm courageously
     And bind thy soul that at some certain day
     Great Lucifer may claim it as his own.
     And then be thou as great as Lucifer!
FAUSTUS: Lo, Mephostophilis, for love of thee
55 Faustus hath cut his arm and with his proper blood
     Assures his soul to be great Lucifer's,
     Chief lord and regent of perpetual night.
     View here this blood that trickles from mine arm
     And let it be propitious for my wish.
60 MEPHOSTOPHILIS: But Faustus,
     Write it in manner of a deed of gift.
FAUSTUS: Ay so I do—But Mephostophilis,
     My blood congeals and I can write no more.
MEPHOSTOPHILIS: I'll fetch thee fire to dissolve it straight.

(*Exit.*)

65 FAUSTUS: What might the staying of my blood portend?
     Is it unwilling I should write this bill?
     Why streams it not that I may write afresh:
     "Faustus gives to thee his soul"? O there it stayed.
     Why shouldst thou not? Is not thy soul thine own?
70   Then write again: "Faustus gives to thee his soul."

(*Enter* MEPHOSTOPHILIS *with the chafer of fire.*)

MEPHOSTOPHILIS: See Faustus, here is fire. Set it on.
FAUSTUS: So, now the blood begins to clear again.
     Now will I make an end immediately.
MEPHOSTOPHILIS: (*Aside.*) What will not I do to obtain his soul!
75 FAUSTUS: *Consummatum est!* This bill is ended:
     And Faustus hath bequeathed his soul to Lucifer.
     —But what is this inscription on mine arm?
     Homo fuge! Whither should I fly?
     If unto God, He'll throw me down to hell.
80   My senses are deceived, here's nothing writ.
     O yes, I see it plain! Even here is writ.
     Homo fuge! Yet shall not Faustus fly!
MEPHOSTOPHILIS: (*Aside.*) I'll fetch him somewhat to delight
     his mind.

(*Exit.*)

(*Enter* DEVILS *giving crowns and rich apparel to* FAUSTUS. *They dance and then depart.*)

---

43 *Solamen . . . doloris* misery loves company (Latin) 44 **other** others 49 **him** i.e., to Lucifer 55 **proper** own 56 **Assures** conveys by contract 66 **bill** contract s.d. **chafer** portable grate 71 **it** i.e., the receptacle containing the congealed blood 75 *Consummatum est* it is finished (Latin: a blasphemous repetition of Christ's words on the cross; see John xix.30) 78 *Homo fuge* fly, man (Latin)

(*Enter* MEPHOSTOPHILIS.)

FAUSTUS: What means this show? Speak. Mephostophilis.
MEPHOSTOPHILIS: Nothing Faustus, but to delight thy mind 85
     And let thee see what magic can perform.
FAUSTUS: But may I raise such spirits when I please?
MEPHOSTOPHILIS: Ay Faustus, and do greater things than
     these.
FAUSTUS: Then, Mephostophilis, receive this scroll,
     A deed of gift of body and of soul: 90
     But yet conditionally that thou perform
     All covenants and articles between us both.
MEPHOSTOPHILIS: Faustus, I swear by hell and Lucifer
     To effect all promises between us both.
FAUSTUS: Then hear me read it, Mephostophilis: 95

     "On these conditions following:
         First, that Faustus may be a spirit in form and substance.
         Secondly, that Mephostophilis shall be his servant and
     be by him commanded.
         Thirdly, that Mephostophilis shall do for him and bring 100
     him whatsoever.
         Fourthly, that he shall be in his chamber or house in-
     visible.
         Lastly, that he shall appear to the said John Faustus at all
     times in what form or shape soever he please:
         I, John Faustus of Wittenberg, Doctor, by these pre- 105
     sents, do give both body and soul to Lucifer, prince of the
     east, and his minister Mephostophilis, and furthermore
     grant unto them that, four and twenty years being expired,
     and these articles above written being inviolate, full power
     to fetch or carry the said John Faustus, body and soul, flesh, 110
     blood, or goods, into their habitation wheresoever.
                                        By me John Faustus."

MEPHOSTOPHILIS: Speak Faustus, do you deliver this as your
     deed?
FAUSTUS: Ay, take it, and the devil give thee good of it!
MEPHOSTOPHILIS: So now Faustus, ask me what thou wilt. 115
FAUSTUS: First will I question with thee about hell.
     Tell me, where is the place that men call hell?
MEPHOSTOPHILIS: Under the heavens.
FAUSTUS: Ay, so are all things else, but whereabouts?
MEPHOSTOPHILIS: Within the bowels of these elements 120
     Where we are tortured and remain forever.
     Hell hath no limits nor is circumscribed
     In one self place, but where we are is hell,
     And where hell is there must we ever be.
     And to be short, when all the world dissolves 125
     And every creature shall be purified
     All places shall be hell that is not heaven!
FAUSTUS: I think hell's a fable.
MEPHOSTOPHILIS: Ay, think so still—till experience change
     thy mind!

---

97 **spirit** evil spirit, devil (but to see Faustus as transformed now into a devil deprived of freedom to repent is to deprive the remainder of the play of much of its meaning) 109 **inviolate** unviolated

130 FAUSTUS: Why, dost thou think that Faustus shall be damned?
MEPHOSTOPHILIS: Ay, of necessity, for here's the scroll
    In which thou hast given thy soul to Lucifer.
FAUSTUS: Ay, and body too; but what of that?
    Think'st thou that Faustus is so fond to imagine
135   That after this life there is any pain?
    No, these are trifles and mere old wives' tales.
MEPHOSTOPHILIS: But I am an instance to prove the contrary,
    For I tell thee I am damned and now in hell!
FAUSTUS: Nay, and this be hell, I'll willingly be damned—
140   What, sleeping, eating, walking, and disputing?
    But leaving this, let me have a wife, the fairest maid in
        Germany, for I am wanton and lascivious and cannot
        live without a wife.
MEPHOSTOPHILIS: Well Faustus, thou shalt have a wife.

(*He fetches in a woman* DEVIL [*with fireworks*].)

145 FAUSTUS: What sight is this?
MEPHOSTOPHILIS: Now Faustus, will thou have a wife?
FAUSTUS: Here's a hot whore indeed! No, I'll no wife.
MEPHOSTOPHILIS: Marriage is but a ceremonial toy, (*Exit*
    SHE-DEVIL.)
    And if thou lovest me, think no more of it.
150   I'll cull thee out the fairest courtesans
    And bring them every morning to thy bed.
    She whom thine eye shall like thy heart shall have,
    Were she as chaste as was Penelope,
    As wise as Saba, or as beautiful
155   As was bright Lucifer before his fall.
    Here, take this book and peruse it well.
    The iterating of these lines brings gold;
    The framing of this circle on the ground
    Brings thunder, whirlwinds, storm, and lightning;
160   Pronounce this thrice devoutly to thyself,
    And men in harness shall appear to thee,
    Ready to execute what thou command'st.
FAUSTUS: Thanks Mephostophilis for this sweet book.
    This will I keep as chary as my life.

(*Exeunt.*)

SCENE II

Enter FAUSTUS *in his study and* MEPHOSTOPHILIS.

FAUSTUS: When I behold the heavens, then I repent
    And curse thee, wicked Mephostophilis,
    Because thou has deprived me of those joys.
MEPHOSTOPHILIS: 'Twas thine own seeking Faustus, thank
    thyself.

---

134 **fond** foolish   148 **toy** trifle   150 **cull thee out** select for
you   153 **Penelope** wife of Ulysses, famed for her fidelity
154 **Saba** the Queen of Sheba   157 **iterating** repetition
158 **framing** drawing   161 **harness** armor   164 s.d. **Exeunt** a
scene following this stage direction has probably been lost. Earlier
Wagner hired the Clown; later the Clown is an ostler possessed of
one of Faustus' conjuring books. Possibly, then, the lost scene was
a comic one, showing the Clown stealing a book and departing

But think'st thou heaven is such a glorious thing?   5
    I tell thee, Faustus, it is not half so fair
    As thou or any man that breathe on earth.
FAUSTUS: How prov'st thou that?
MEPHOSTOPHILIS: 'Twas made for man; then he's more excellent.
FAUSTUS: If heaven was made for man, 'twas made for me!   10
    I will renounce this magic and repent.

(*Enter the two* ANGELS.)

GOOD ANGEL: Faustus, repent: yet God will pity thee!
BAD ANGEL: Thou art a spirit: God cannot pity thee!
FAUSTUS: Who buzzeth in mine ears I am a spirit?
    Be I a devil, yet God may pity me—   15
    Yea, God will pity me if I repent.
BAD ANGEL: Ay, but Faustus never shall repent.

(*Exit* ANGELS.)

FAUSTUS: My heart is hardened, I cannot repent.
    Scarce can I name salvation, faith, or heaven,
    Swords, poison, halters, and envenomed steel   20
    Are laid before me to dispatch myself.
    And long ere this I should have done the deed
    Had not sweet pleasure conquered deep despair.
    Have not I made blind Homer sing to me
    Of Alexander's love and Oenon's death?   25
    And hath not he that built the walls of Thebes
    With ravishing sound of his melodious harp
    Made music with my Mephostophilis?
    Why should I die then or basely despair?
    I am resolved, Faustus shall not repent!   30
    Come Mephostophilis, let us dispute again
    And reason of divine astrology.
    Speak, are there many spheres above the moon?
    Are all celestial bodies but one globe
    As is the substance of this centric earth?   35
MEPHOSTOPHILIS: As are the elements, such are the heavens,
    Even from the moon unto the empyreal orb
    Mutually folded in each others' spheres,
    And jointly move upon one axle-tree,
    Whose terminé is termed the world's wide pole.   40
    Nor are the names of Saturn, Mars, or Jupiter
    Feigned but are erring stars.
FAUSTUS: But have they all one motion,
    Both *situ et tempore?*
MEPHOSTOPHILIS: All move from east to west in four and   45
    twenty hours upon the poles of the world but differ in
    their motions upon the poles of the zodiac.

II.ii.   12 yet still, even now   **25 Alexander . . . Oenon's** Paris,
also called Alexander, was Oenone's lover, but he later deserted
her for Helen of Troy, causing the Trojan War, the subject of
Homer's Iliad   **26 he** Amphion, whose music charmed stones to
form the walls of Thebes   **35 centric** central   **36 such** i.e.,
separate but combined; the idea is that the heavenly bodies are
separate but their spheres are concentric ("folded"), and all—
from the nearest (the moon) to the farthest ("the empyreal orb"
or empyrean)—move on one axletree   **40 terminé** end, extremity   **42 erring stars** planets   **44 situ et tempore** in place
and in time

FAUSTUS: These slender questions Wagner can decide.
    Hath Mephostophilis no greater skill?
50   Who knows not the double motion of the planets?
    That the first is finished in a natural day.
    The second thus: Saturn in thirty years;
    Jupiter in twelve; Mars in four; the sun, Venus, and Mer-
    cury in a year; the moon in twenty-eight days. These are
55   fresh-men's suppositions. But tell me, hath every sphere a
    dominion or *intelligentia*?
MEPHOSTOPHILIS: Ay.
FAUSTUS: How many heavens or spheres are there?
MEPHOSTOPHILIS: Nine: the seven planets, the firmament, and
60   the empyreal heaven.
FAUSTUS: But is there not *coelum igneum et crystallinum*?
MEPHOSTOPHILIS: No Faustus, they be but fables.
FAUSTUS: Resolve me then in this one question. Why are not
    conjunctions, oppositions, aspects, eclipses all at one time,
65   but in some years we have more, in some less?
MEPHOSTOPHILIS: *Per inaqualem motum respectu totius.*
FAUSTUS: Well, I am answered. Now tell me, who made the
    world?
MEPHOSTOPHILIS: I will not.
70 FAUSTUS: Sweet Mephostophilis, tell me.
MEPHOSTOPHILIS: Move me not, Faustus!
FAUSTUS: Villain, have not I bound thee to tell me any-
    thing?
MEPHOSTOPHILIS: Ay, that is not against our kingdom. This is.
    Thou art damned. Think thou of hell!
75 FAUSTUS: Think, Faustus, upon God, that made the world.
MEPHOSTOPHILIS: Remember this!

(*Exit.*)

FAUSTUS: Ay, go accursèd spirit to ugly hell!
    'Tis thou hast damned distressèd Faustus' soul—
    Is't not too late?

(*Enter the two* ANGELS.)

80 BAD ANGEL: Too late.
GOOD ANGEL: Never too late, if Faustus will repent.
BAD ANGEL: If thou repent, devils will tear thee in pieces.
GOOD ANGEL: Repent, and they shall never raze thy skin.

(*Exeunt* ANGELS.)

FAUSTUS: O Christ, my savior, my savior!
85   Help to save distressèd Faustus' soul.

(*Enter* LUCIFER, BELZEBUB, *and* MEPHOSTOPHILIS.)

LUCIFER: Christ cannot save thy soul, for He is just.
    There's none but I have interest in the same.
FAUSTUS: O, what art thou that look'st so terribly?

LUCIFER: I am Lucifer
    And this is my companion prince in hell.   90
FAUSTUS: O Faustus, they are come to fetch thy soul!
BELZEBUB: We are come to tell thee thou dost injure us.
LUCIFER: Thou call'st on Christ contrary to thy promise.
BELZEBUB: Thou should'st not think on God.
LUCIFER: Think on the Devil.
BELZEBUB: And his dam too.   95
FAUSTUS: Nor will Faustus henceforth. Pardon him for this,
    And Faustus vows never to look to heaven!
    Never to name God or to pray to Him,
    To burn His Scriptures, slay His ministers,
    And make my spirits pull His churches down.   100
LUCIFER: So shalt thou show thyself an obedient servant,
    And we will highly gratify thee for it.
BELZEBUB: Faustus, we are come from hell in person to show
    thee some pastime. Sit down and thou shalt behold the
    Seven Deadly Sins appear to thee in their own proper 105
    shapes and likeness.
FAUSTUS: That sight will be as pleasant to me as Paradise was
    to Adam the first day of his creation.
LUCIFER: Talk not of Paradise or creation but mark the show.
    Go Mephostophilis, fetch them in.   110

(*Enter the* SEVEN DEADLY SINS [*led by a* PIPER].)

BELZEBUB: Now Faustus, question them of their names and
    dispositions.
FAUSTUS: That shall I soon. What art thou, the first?
PRIDE: I am Pride. I disdain to have any parents. I am like to
    Ovid's flea, I can creep into every corner of a wench: 115
    sometimes, like a periwig I sit upon her brow; next, like a
    necklace I hang about her neck; then, like a fan of feath-
    ers I kiss her; and then, turning myself to a wrought
    smock, do what I list—But fie, what a smell is here! I'll
    not speak a word more for a king's ransom unless the 120
    ground be perfumed and covered with cloth of arras.
FAUSTUS: Thou art a proud knave indeed. What art thou, the
    second?
COVETOUSNESS: I am Covetousness, begotten of an old churl
    in a leather bag; and might I now obtain my wish, this 125
    house, you and all, should turn to gold that I might lock
    you safe into my chest. O my sweet gold!
FAUSTUS: And what art thou, the third?
ENVY: I am Envy, begotten of a chimney-sweeper and an oys-
    terwife. I cannot read and therefore wish all books burned. 130
    I am lean with seeing others eat. O, that there would come
    a famine over all the world that all might die and I live
    alone! Then thou shouldst see how fat I'd be. But must
    thou sit and I stand? Come down, with a vengeance!
FAUSTUS: Out, envious wretch! But what art thou, the fourth? 135

---

51 **natural day** twenty-four hours   55 **suppositions** premises
55–56 **dominion or *intelligentia*** governing angel or intelligence
(believed to impart motion to the sphere)   61 ***coelum igneum et
crystallinum*** a heaven of fire and a crystaline sphere (Latin)
64 **at one time** i.e., at regular intervals   66 **Per . . . totius** because of unequal speed within the system (Latin)   71 **Move**
anger   83 **raze** scratch   87 **interest in** legal claim on

95 **dam** mother   105 **Seven Deadly Sins** so called because
they cause spiritual death; they are Pride, Covetousness, Envy,
Wrath, Gluttony, Sloth, Lechery   115 **Ovid's flea** flea in
Carmen de pulce, a lewd poem mistakenly attributed to Ovid
118 **wrought smock** decorated petticoat   121 **cloth of arras**
Flemish cloth used for tapestries   125 **leather bag** moneybag (?)
129–130 **chimney-sweeper . . . oysterwife** i.e., dirty and smelly

WRATH: I am Wrath. I had neither father nor mother. I leapt out of a lion's mouth when I was scarce an hour old and ever since have run up and down the world with these case of rapiers, wounding myself when I could get none
140 to fight withal. I was born in hell! And look to it, for some of you shall be my father.

FAUSTUS: And what art thou, the fifth?

GLUTTONY: I am Gluttony. My parents are all dead, and the devil a penny they have left me, but a small pension: and
145 that buys me thirty meals a day and ten bevers, a small tri-fle to suffice nature. I come of a royal pedigree. My father was a gammon of bacon, and my mother was a hogshead of claret wine. My godfathers were these: Peter Pickled-herring and Martin Martlemas-beef. But my godmother.
150 O, she was an ancient gentlewoman: her name was Margery March-beer. Now Faustus, thou hast heard all my progeny, wilt thou bid me to supper?

FAUSTUS: Not I.

GLUTTONY: Then the devil choke thee!

155 FAUSTUS: Choke thyself, glutton! What art thou, the sixth?

SLOTH: Heigh-ho! I am Sloth. I was begotten on a sunny bank. Heigh-ho, I'll not speak a word more for a king's ransom.

FAUSTUS: And what are you, Mistress Minx, the seventh and last?

LECHERY: Who, I, I sir? I am one that loves an inch of raw
160 mutton better than an ell of fried stockfish, and the first letter of my name begins with Lechery.

LUCIFER: Away to hell, away! On, piper!

(*Exeunt the* SEVEN SINS.)

FAUSTUS: O, how this sight doth delight my soul!

LUCIFER: But Faustus, in hell is all manner of delight.

165 FAUSTUS: O, might I see hell and return again safe, how happy were I then!

LUCIFER: Faustus, thou shalt. At midnight I will send for thee. Meanwhile peruse this book and view it thoroughly, And thou shalt turn thyself into what shape thou wilt.

170 FAUSTUS: Thanks mighty Lucifer. This will I keep as chary as my life.

LUCIFER: Now Faustus, farewell.

FAUSTUS: Farewell great Lucifer. Come Mephostophilis.

(*Exeunt omnes several ways.*)

SCENE III

Enter [ROBIN] *the clown.*

ROBIN: What, Dick, look to the horses there till I come again! I have gotten one of Doctor Faustus' conjuring books, and now we'll have such knavery as't passes.

(*Enter* DICK.)

DICK: What, Robin, you must come away and walk the horses.

ROBIN: I walk the horses? I scorn't, faith. I have other matters 5
in hand. Let the horses walk themselves an they will. (*Reading.*) A *per se*—a; t, h, e—the; o *per se*—o; deny orgon—gor-gon. Keep further from me, O thou illiterate and unlearned hostler!

DICK: 'Snails, what hast thou got there, a book? Why, thou 10
canst not tell ne'er a word on't.

ROBIN: That thou shalt see presently. Keep out of the circle, I say, lest I send you into the hostry with a vengeance.

DICK: That's like, 'faith! You had best leave your foolery, for an my master come, he'll conjure you, 'faith. 15

ROBIN: My master conjure me? I'll tell thee what. An my master come here, I'll clap as fair a pair of horns on's head as e'er thou sawest in thy life.

DICK: Thou need'st not do that, for my mistress hath done it.

ROBIN: Ay, there be of us here that have waded as deep into 20
matters as other men—if they were disposed to talk.

DICK: A plague take you! I thought you did not sneak up and down after her for nothing. But I prithee tell me in good sadness Robin, is that a conjuring book?

ROBIN: Do but speak what thou't have me to do, and I'll do't. 25
If thou't dance naked, put off thy clothes, and I'll conjure thee about presently. Or if thou't go but to the tavern with me, I'll give thee white wine, red wine, claret wine, sack, muscadine, malmsey, and whippin—crusthold-belly-hold. And we'll not pay one penny for it. 30

DICK: O brave! Prithee let's to it presently, for I am as dry as a dog.

ROBIN: Come then, let's away.

(*Exeunt.*)

ACT THREE

Enter the CHORUS.

Learnèd Faustus,
To find the secrets of astronomy
Graven in the book of Jove's high firmament,
Did mount him up to scale Olympus' top:
Where, sitting in a chariot burning bright 5
Drawn by the strength of yokèd dragons' necks,
He views the clouds, the planets, and the stars,
The tropics, zones, and quarters of the sky,
From the bright circle of the hornèd moon
Even to the height of *primum mobile*: 10

---

138 **these case** this pair   145 **bevers** snacks (literally drinks) 147 **gammon** haunch   149 **Martlemas-beef** cattle slaugh-tered at Martinmas (11 November) and salted for winter con-sumption   151 **March-beer** strong beer brewed in March; **progeny** ancestry   156 **Heigh-ho** a yawn or tired greeting 159 **inch of raw mutton** i.e., penis ("mutton" in a bawdy sense commonly alludes to a prostitute, but since here the speaker is a woman, the allusion must be to a male)   160 **an ell of . . . stockfish** forty-five inches of dried cod   171 **chary** carefully 178 s.d. **several** various

---

II.iii. 6 **an** if   7 *per se* by itself (Latin; the idea is, "A by itself spells A")   7–8 **deny orgon—gorgon** Robin is trying to read the name "Demogorgon"   10 **'Snails** by God's nails   13 **hostry** hostelry inn   17 **horns** as the next speech indicates, horns were said to adorn the head of a man whose wife was unfaithful   23 **in good sadness** seriously   28 **sack** sherry   29 **whippincrust** illiterate pronunciation of "hippocras," a spiced wine

III Chorus 8 **zones** segments of the sky   9 **circle** orbit 10 **primum mobile** the outermost sphere, the empyrean

And whirling round with this circumference
Within the concave compass of the pole,
From east to west his dragons swiftly glide
And in eight days did bring him home again.
15   Not long he stayed within his quiet house
To rest his bones after his weary toil
But new exploits do hale him out again.
And mounted then upon a dragon's back,
That with his wings did part the subtle air,
20   He now is gone to prove cosmography,
That measures coasts and kingdoms of the earth,
And as I guess will first arrive at Rome
To see the Pope and manner of his court
And take some part of holy Peter's feast,
25   The which this day is highly solemnized.

(*Exit.*)

SCENE I

Enter FAUSTUS *and* MEPHOSTOPHILIS.

FAUSTUS: Having now, my good Mephostophilis,
Passed with delight the stately town of Trier,
Environed round with airy mountain tops,
With walls of flint, and deep-entrenchèd lakes,
5   Not to be won by any conquering prince:
From Paris next, coasting the realm of France,
We saw the river Main fall into Rhine,
Whose banks are set with groves of fruitful vines:
Then up to Naples, rich Campania,
10   Whose buildings fair and gorgeous to the eye,
The streets straight forth and paved with finest brick,
Quarters the town in four equivalents.
There saw we learnèd Maro's golden tomb,
The way he cut an English mile in length
15   Through a rock of stone in one night's space.
From thence to Venice, Padua, and the rest,
In one of which a sumptuous temple stands
That threats the stars with her aspiring top,
Whose frame is paved with sundry colored stones
20   And roofed aloft with curious work in gold.
Thus hitherto hath Faustus spent his time.
But tell me now, what resting-palace is this?
Hast thou, as erst I did command,
Conducted me within the walls of Rome?
25   MEPHOSTOPHILIS: I have, my Faustus, and for proof thereof
This is the goodly palace of the Pope,
And cause we are no common guests
I choose his privy chamber for our use.
FAUSTUS: I hope his Holiness will bid us welcome.
30   MEPHOSTOPHILIS: All's one, for we'll be bold with his venison.
But now my Faustus, that thou may'st perceive
What Rome contains for to delight thine eyes,

Know that this city stands upon seven hills
That underprop the groundwork of the same:
Just through the midst runs flowing Tiber's stream   35
With winding banks that cut it in two parts,
Over the which four stately bridges lean
That make safe passage to each part of Rome.
Upon the bridge called Ponte Angelo
Erected is a castle passing strong   40
Where thou shalt see such store of ordinance
As that the double cannons forged of brass
Do match the number of the days contained
Within the compass of one complete year,
Beside the gates and high pyramides   45
That Julius Caesar brought from Africa.
FAUSTUS: Now, by the kingdoms of infernal rule,
Of Styx, of Acheron, and the fiery lake
Of ever-burning Phlegethon, I swear
That I do long to see the monuments   50
And situation of bright-splendent Rome.
Come therefore, let's away.
MEPHOSTOPHILIS: Nay stay my Faustus. I know you'd see the
Pope
And take some part of holy Peter's feast,
The which this day with high solemnity,   55
This day, is held through Rome and Italy
In honor of the Pope's triumphant victory.
FAUSTUS: Sweet Mephostophilis, thou pleasest me.
Whilst I am here on earth let me be cloyed
With all things that delight the heart of man.   60
My four and twenty years of liberty
I'll spend in pleasure and in dalliance,
That Faustus' name, whilst this bright frame doth stand,
May be admirèd through the furthest land.
MEPHOSTOPHILIS: 'Tis well said, Faustus, come then, stand   65
by me
And thou shalt see them come immediately.
FAUSTUS: Nay stay, my gentle Mephostophilis,
And grant me my request, and then I go.
Thou know'st, within the compass of eight days
We viewed the face of heaven, of earth, and hell.   70
So high our dragons soared into the air
That looking down the earth appeared to me
No bigger than my hand in quantity—
There did we view the kingdoms of the world,
And what might please mine eye I there beheld.   75
Then in this show let me an actor be
That this proud Pope may Faustus' cunning see!
MEPHOSTOPHILIS: Let it be so, my Faustus, but first stay
And view their triumphs as they pass this way.
And then devise what best contents thy mind   80
By cunning in thine art to cross the Pope
Or dash the pride of this solemnity—
To make his monks and abbots stand like apes
And point like antics at his triple crown,

---

20 **prove cosmography** test maps, i.e., explore the universe

III.i. 2 **Trier** German city on the Moselle, also known as Trèves   4 **deep-entrenchèd lakes** moats   13 **Maro** Vergil (Publius Vergilius Maro, 70–19 BCE)   15 **Through** pronounced "thorough"

---

37 **lean** bend   45 **pyramides** obelisk (pronounced py-ràm-i-des)   48–49 **Styx, Acheron, Phlegethon** rivers of the underworld   79 **triumphs** spectacular displays   84 **antics** grotesque figures, buffoons

85   To beat the beads about the friars' pates,
      Or clap huge horns upon the cardinals' heads,
      Or any villainy thou canst devise—
      And I'll perform it, Faustus. Hark, they come!
      This day shall make thee be admired in Rome!

(*Enter the* CARDINALS *and* BISHOPS, *some bearing crosiers, some the pillars;* MONKS *and* FRIARS *singing their procession; then the* POPE *and* RAYMOND *King of Hungary, with* BRUNO *led in chains.*)

90   POPE: Cast down our footstool.
      RAYMOND: Saxon Bruno, stoop,
          Whilst on thy back his Holiness ascends
          Saint Peter's chair and state pontifical.
      BRUNO: Proud Lucifer, that state belongs to me—
          But thus I fall to Peter, not to thee.
95   POPE: To me and Peter shalt thou grov'lling lie
          And crouch before the papal dignity!
          Sound triumpets then, for thus Saint Peter's heir
          From Bruno's back ascends Saint Peter's chair!

(*A flourish while he ascends.*)

      Thus as the gods creep on with feet of wool
100   Long ere with iron hands they punish men,
      So shall our sleeping vengeance now arise
      And smite with death thy hated enterprise.
      Lord Cardinals of France and Padua,
      Go forthwith to our holy consistory
105   And read amongst the statutes decretal
      What by the holy council held at Trent
      The sacred synod hath decreed for him
      That doth assume the papal government
      Without election and a true consent.
110   Away, and bring us word with speed!
      1 CARDINAL: We go my lord.

(*Exeunt* [*two*] CARDINALS.)

      POPE: Lord Raymond—

(*Talks to him apart.*)

      FAUSTUS: Go haste thee, gentle Mephostophilis,
          Follow the cardinals to the consistory
115   And as they turn their superstitious books
          Strike them with sloth and drowsy idleness
          And make them sleep so sound that in their shapes
          Thyself and I may parley with this Pope,
          This proud confronter of the Emperor!
120   —And in despite of all his holiness
          Restore this Bruno to his liberty
          And bear him to the states of Germany!

---

89 **admired** wondered at; s.d. **Raymond King of Hungary . . . Bruno** unhistorical figures; Bruno is the emperor's nominee for the papal throne   92 **state** throne   98 s.d. **flourish** trumpet fanfare   104 **consistory** i.e., meeting-place of the papal consistory or senate   105 **statutes decretal** i.e., ecclesiastical laws   106 **council held at Trent** intermittently from 1545 to 1563   107 **synod** council

MEPHOSTOPHILIS: Faustus, I go.
FAUSTUS: Dispatch it soon.
      The Pope shall curse that Faustus came to Rome.   125

(*Exit* FAUSTUS *and* MEPHOSTOPHILIS.)

BRUNO: Pope Adrian, let me have some right of law:
    I was elected by the Emperor.
POPE: We will depose the Emperor for that deed
    And curse the people that submit to him.
    Both he and thou shalt stand excommunicate   130
    And interdict from church's privilege
    And all society of holy men.
    He grows too proud in his authority,
    Lifting his lofty head above the clouds,
    And like a steeple overpeers the church.   135
    But we'll pull down his haughty insolence.
    And as Pope Alexander, our progenitor,
    Trod on the neck of German Frederick,
    Adding this golden sentence to our praise:
    "That Peter's heirs should tread on emperors   140
    And walk upon the dreadful adder's back,
    Treading the lion and the dragon down,
    And fearless spurn the killing basilisk"—
    So will we quell that haughty schismatic
    And by authority apostolical   145
    Depose him from his regal government.
BRUNO: Pope Julius swore to princely Sigismond,
    For him and the succeeding Popes of Rome,
    To hold the emperors their lawful lords.
POPE: Pope Julius did abuse the church's rites   150
    And therefore none of his decrees can stand.
    Is not all power on earth bestowed on us?
    And therefore though we would, we cannot err.
    Behold this silver belt whereto is fixed
    Seven golden keys fast sealed with seven seals   155
    In token of our sevenfold power from heaven
    To bind or loose, lock fast, condemn, or judge,
    Resign or seal, or whatso pleaseth us.
    Then he and thou and all the world shall stoop—
    Or be assurèd of our dreadful curse   160
    To light as heavy as the pains of hell.

(*Enter* FAUSTUS *and* MEPHOSTOPHILIS *like the* CARDINALS.)

MEPHOSTOPHILIS: (*Aside.*) Now tell me Faustus, are we not
    fitted well?
FAUSTUS: (*Aside.*) Yes Mephostophilis, and two such cardinals
    Ne'er served a holy Pope as we shall do.
    But whilst they sleep within the consistory   165
    Let us salute his reverend Fatherhood.
RAYMOND: Behold my lord, the cardinals are returned.
POPE: Welcome grave fathers, answer presently,
    What have our holy council there decreed
    Concerning Bruno and the Emperor   170

---

137 **Pope Alexander** Pope Alexander III (d. 1181) compelled the Emperor Frederick Barbarossa to kneel before him; **progenitor** predecessor   143 **basilisk** fabulous monster said to kill with a glance   158 **Resign** unseal   168 **presently** immediately

In quittance of their late conspiracy
Against our state and papal dignity?
FAUSTUS: Most sacred patron of the church of Rome,
By full consent of all the synod
175   Of priests and prelates it is thus decreed:
That Bruno and the German Emperor
Be held as lollards and bold schismatics
And proud disturbers of the church's peace.
And if that Bruno by his own assent,
180   Without enforcement of the German peers,
Did seek to wear the triple diadem
And by your death to climb Saint Peter's chair,
The statutes decretal have thus decreed:
He shall be straight condemned of heresy
185   And on a pile of fagots burnt to death.
POPE: It is enough. Here, take him to your charge
And bear him straight to Ponte Angelo
And in the strongest tower enclose him fast.
Tomorrow, sitting in our consistory
190   With all our college of grave cardinals
We will determine of his life or death.
Here, take his triple crown along with you
And leave it in the church's treasury.
Make haste again, my good lord cardinals,
195   And take our blessing apostolical.
MEPHOSTOPHILIS: (*Aside.*) So, so! Was never devil thus
blessed before.
FAUSTUS: (*Aside.*) Away sweet Mephostophilis, be gone!
The cardinals will be plagued for this anon.

(*Exeunt* FAUSTUS *and* MEPHOSTOPHILIS [*with* BRUNO].)

POPE: Go presently and bring a banquet forth,
200   That we may solemnize Saint Peter's feast
And with Lord Raymond, King of Hungary,
Drink to our late and happy victory.

(*Exeunt.*)

SCENE II

A sennet while the banquet is brought in, and then enter FAUSTUS
and MEPHOSTOPHILIS *in their own shapes.*

MEPHOSTOPHILIS: Now Faustus, come prepare thyself for
mirth.
The sleepy cardinals are hard at hand
To censure Bruno, that is posted hence,
And on a proud-paced steed as swift as thought
5   Flies o'er the Alps to fruitful Germany,
There to salute the woeful Emperor.
FAUSTUS: The Pope will curse them for their sloth today
That slept both Bruno and his crown away.
But now, that Faustus may delight his mind
10   And by their folly make some merriment,

Sweet Mephostophilis, so charm me here
That I may walk invisible to all
And do whate'er I please unseen of any.
MEPHOSTOPHILIS: Faustus, thou shalt. Then kneel down
presently,
Whilst on thy head I lay my hand   15
And charm thee with this magic wand.
First wear this girdle, then appear
Invisible to all are here:
The planets seven, the gloomy air,
Hell, and the Furies' forkèd hair,   20
Pluto's blue fire, and Hecat's tree
With magic spells so compass thee
That no eye may thy body see.
So Faustus, now for all their holiness,
Do what thou wilt, thou shalt not be discerned.   25
FAUSTUS: Thanks Mephostophilis. Now friars, take heed
Lest Faustus make your shaven crowns to bleed.
MEPHOSTOPHILIS: Faustus, no more. See where the cardinals
come.

(*Enter* POPE [*and* FRIARS] *and all the* LORDS [*with* KING RAY-
MOND *and the* ARCHBISHOP OF RHEIMS]. *Enter the* [*two*] CAR-
DINALS *with a book.*)

POPE: Welcome lord cardinals. Come, sit down.
Lord Raymond, take your seat. Friars, attend,   30
And see that all things be in readiness
As best beseems this solemn festival.
1 CARDINAL: First may it please your sacred Holiness
To view the sentence of the reverend synod
Concerning Bruno and the Emperor.   35
POPE: What needs this question? Did I not tell you
Tomorrow we would sit i' th' consistory
And there determine of his punishment?
You brought us word, even now, it was decreed
That Bruno and the cursèd Emperor   40
Were by the holy council both condemned
For loathèd lollards and base schismatics.
Then wherefore would you have me view that book?
1 CARDINAL: Your Grace mistakes. You gave us no such charge.
RAYMOND: Deny it not; we all are witnesses   45
That Bruno here was late delivered you
With his rich triple crown to be reserved
And put into the church's treasury.
BOTH CARDINALS: By holy Paul we saw them not.
POPE: By Peter you shall die   50
Unless you bring them forth immediately.
Hale them to prison, lade their limbs with gyves.
False prelates, for this hateful treachery
Cursed be your souls to hellish misery.

(*Exeunt* ATTENDANTS *with two* CARDINALS.)

---

171 **quittance of** requital for   177 **lollards** heretics   194 **again**
i.e., to return

III.ii. s.d. **sennet** set of notes played on a trumpet signaling an
approach or a departure

20 **Furies' forkèd hair** the hair of the Furies consisted of
snakes, whose forked tongues may be implied here   21 **Hecat**
Hecate, goddess of magic (possibly her "tree" is the gallows-tree,
but possibly "tree" is a slip for "three," Hecate being the triple
goddess of heaven, earth, and hell)   52 **gyves** fetters

55 FAUSTUS: So, they are safe. Now Faustus, to the feast.
    The Pope had never such a frolic guest.
POPE: Lord Archbishop of Rheims, sit down with us.
ARCHBISHOP: I thank your Holiness.
FAUSTUS: Fall to, the devil choke you an you spare!
60 POPE: Who's that spoke? Friars, look about.
    Lord Raymond, pray fall to. I am beholding
    To the Bishop of Milan for this so rare a present.
FAUSTUS: (*Aside.*) I thank you, sir!

(*Snatches the dish.*)

POPE: How now! Who snatched the meat from me?
65   Villains, why speak you not?
    My good Lord Archbishop, here's a most dainty dish
    Was sent me from a cardinal in France.
FAUSTUS: (*Aside.*) I'll have that too!

(*Snatches the dish.*)

POPE: What lollards do attend our Holiness
70   That we receive such great indignity!
    Fetch me some wine.
FAUSTUS: (*Aside.*) Ay, pray do, for Faustus is adry.
POPE: Lord Raymond, I drink unto your Grace.
FAUSTUS: (*Aside.*) I pledge your Grace.

(*Snatches the goblet.*)

75 POPE: My wine gone too? Ye lubbers, look about
    And find the man that doth this villainy,
    Or by our sanctitude you all shall die.
    I pray, my lords, have patience at this troublesome banquet.
ARCHBISHOP: Please it your Holiness, I think it be some
80   ghost crept out of purgatory, and now is come unto your
    Holiness for his pardon.
POPE: It may be so:
    Go then, command our priests to sing a dirge
    To lay the fury of this same troublesome ghost.

(*Exit* ATTENDANT.)

(*The* POPE *crosses himself before eating.*)

85 FAUSTUS: How now! Must every bit be spicèd with a cross?
    Nay then, take that!

(*Strikes the* POPE.)

POPE: O, I am slain! Help me my lords!
    O come and help to bear my body hence.
    Damned be this soul forever for this deed.

(*Exeunt the* POPE *and his train.*)

90 MEPHOSTOPHILIS: Now Faustus, what will you do now?
    For I can tell you, you'll be cursed with bell, book, and
    candle.

FAUSTUS: Bell, book, and candle. Candle, book, and bell.
    Forward and backward, to curse Faustus to hell!

(*Enter the* FRIARS, *with bell, book, and candle for the dirge.*)

1 FRIAR: Come brethren, let's about our business with good 95
    devotion.
    Cursèd be he that stole his Holiness' meat from the table.
    Maledicat Dominus!
    Cursèd be he that struck his Holiness a blow on the face.
    Maledicat Dominus!

(FAUSTUS *strikes a* FRIAR.)

    Cursèd be he that took Friar Sandelo a blow on the pate. 100
    Maledicat Dominus!
    Cursèd be he that disturbeth our holy dirge.
    Maledicat Dominus!
    Cursèd be he that took away his Holiness' wine.
    Maledicat Dominus! 105

([FAUSTUS *and* MEPHOSTOPHILIS] *beat the* FRIARS, *fling fireworks among them and exeunt.*)

SCENE III

Enter [ROBIN] *the clown and* DICK *with a cup.*

DICK: Sirrah Robin, we were best look that your devil can
    answer the stealing of this same cup, for the vintner's boy
    follows us at the hard heels.
ROBIN: 'Tis no matter, let him come! An he follow us I'll so
    conjure him as he was never conjured in his life, I warrant 5
    him. Let me see the cup.

(*Enter* VINTNER.)

DICK: Here 'tis. Yonder he comes. Now Robin, now or never
    show thy cunning.
VINTNER: O, are you here? I am glad I have found you. You
    are a couple of fine companions! Pray, where's the cup you 10
    stole from the tavern?
ROBIN: How, how! We steal a cup? Take heed what you say.
    We look not like cup-stealers, I can tell you.
VINTNER: Never deny't, for I know you have it, and I'll search
    you. 15
ROBIN: Search me? Ay, and spare not! (*Aside.*) Hold the cup,
    Dick. Come, come. Search me, search me.

(VINTNER *searches him.*)

VINTNER: Come on sirrah, let me search you now.
DICK: Ay ay, do do. (*Aside.*) Hold the cup, Robin. I fear not
    your searching. We scorn to steal your cups, I can tell you. 20

(VINTNER *searches him.*)

---

59 **Fall to** set to work (here, as commonly, "start eating")
91–92 **bell, book, and candle** implements used in excommunicating (the bell was tolled, the book closed, the candle extinguished)

---

97 *Maledicat Dominus* may the Lord curse him (Latin)

III.iii. 3 **at the hard heels** hard at heel, closely   10 **companions** fellows (contemptuous)

VINTNER: Never outface me for the matter, for sure the cup
 is between you two.
ROBIN: Nay, there you lie! 'Tis beyond us both.
VINTNER: A plague take you. I thought 'twas your knavery to
25 take it away. Come, give it me again.
ROBIN: Ay, much! When, can you tell? (*Aside.*) Dick, make
 me a circle and stand close at my back and stir not for thy
 life. Vintner, you shall have your cup anon. (*Aside.*) Say
 nothing, Dick! O *per se,* o; Demogorgon, Belcher, and
30 Mephostophilis!

(*Enter* MEPHOSTOPHILIS. *Exit* VINTNER.)

MEPHOSTOPHILIS: You princely legions of infernal rule,
 How am I vexèd by these villains' charms!
 From Constantinople have they brought me now
 Only for pleasure of these damnèd slaves.
35 ROBIN: By lady sir, you have had a shrewd journey of it. Will
 it please you to take a shoulder of mutton to supper and
 a tester in your purse and go back again?
DICK: Ay, I pray you heartily, sir. For we called you but in jest,
 I promise you.
40 MEPHOSTOPHILIS: To purge the rashness of this cursèd deed,
 First be thou turnèd to this ugly shape,
 For apish deeds transformèd to an ape.
ROBIN: O brave! An ape! I pray sir, let me have the carrying
 of him about to show some tricks.
45 MEPHOSTOPHILIS: And so thou shalt. Be thou transformed to
 a dog and carry him upon thy back. Away, be gone!
ROBIN: A dog! That's excellent. Let the maids look well to
 their porridge-pots, for I'll into the kitchen presently.
 Come Dick, come.

(*Exeunt the two* CLOWNS.)

50 MEPHOSTOPHILIS: Now with the flames of ever-burning fire
 I'll wing myself and forthwith fly amain
 Unto my Faustus, to the Great Turk's count.

(*Exit.*)

ACT FOUR

Enter CHORUS.

 When Faustus had with pleasure ta'en the view
 Of rarest things and royal courts of kings,
 He stayed his course and so returnèd home,
 Where such as bare his absence but with grief,
5 I mean his friends and nearest companions,
 Did gratulate his safety with kind words.
 And in their conference of what befell
 Touching his journey through the world and air
 They put forth questions of astrology
10 Which Faustus answered with such learnèd skill

 As they admired and wondered at his wit
 Now is his fame spread forth in every land.
 Amongst the rest the Emperor is one,
 Carolus the Fifth, at whose palace now
 Faustus is feasted 'mongst his noblemen.   15
 What there he did in trial of his art
 I leave untold, your eyes shall see performed.

(*Exit.*)

SCENE I

Enter MARTINO *and* FREDERICK *at several doors.*

MARTINO: What ho, officers, gentlemen!
 Hie to the presence to attend the Emperor.
 Good Frederick, see the rooms be voided straight,
 His Majesty is coming to the hall.
 Go back and see the state in readiness.   5
FREDERICK: But where is Bruno, our elected Pope,
 That on a fury's back came post from Rome?
 Will not his Grace consort the Emperor?
MARTINO: O yes, and with him comes the German conjurer,
 The learnèd Faustus, fame of Wittenberg,   10
 The wonder of the world for magic art:
 And he intends to show great Carolus
 The race of all his stout progenitors
 And bring in presence of his Majesty
 The royal shapes and warlike semblances   15
 Of Alexander and his beauteous paramour.
FREDERICK: Where is Benvolio?
MARTINO: Fast asleep, I warrant you.
 He took his rouse with stoups of Rhenish wine
 So kindly yesternight to Bruno's health
 That all this day the sluggard keeps his bed.   20
FREDERICK: See, see, his window's ope. We'll call to him.
MARTINO: What ho, Benvolio!

(*Enter* BENVOLIO *above at a window, in his nightcap, buttoning.*)

BENVOLIO: What a devil ail you two?
MARTINO: Speak softly sir, lest the devil hear you,
 For Faustus at the court is late arrived   25
 At his heels a thousand furies wait
 To accomplish whatsoever the doctor please.
BENVOLIO: What of this?
MARTINO: Come, leave thy chamber first, and thou shalt see
 This conjurer perform such rare exploits   30
 Before the Pope and royal Emperor
 As never yet was seen in Germany.
BENVOLIO: Has not the Pope enough of conjuring yet?
 He was upon the devil's back late enough!

---

23 **beyond us both** apparently Robin has managed to place the
cup at some distance from where he now stands   26 **When,
can you tell** a scornful reply   35 **shrewd** bad   37 **tester** sixpence   42 **apish** (1) foolish (2) imitative
IV Chorus   6 gratulate express joy in   7 **conference** discussion

---

14 **Carolus the Fifth** Charles V (1500–1558), Holy Roman
Emperor

IV.i. s.d. **several** separate   2 **presence** presence-chamber
3 **voided straight** emptied immediately   5 **state** chair of state,
throne   8 **consort** attend   16 **Alexander and his beauteous
paramour** Alexander the Great and his mistress, Thaïs   18 **took
his rouse with stoups** had drinking bouts with full goblets
31 **the Pope** i.e., Bruno

35 And if he be so far in love with him
  I would he would post with him to Rome again.
  FREDERICK: Speak, wilt thou come and see this sport?
  BENVOLIO: Not I.
  MARTINO: Wilt thou stand in thy window and see it then?
  BENVOLIO: Ay, and I fall not asleep i'th' meantime.
40 MARTINO: The Emperor is at hand, who comes to see
  What wonders by black spells may compassed be.
  BENVOLIO: Well, go you attend the Emperor. I am content for
  this once to thrust my head out at a window, for they say
  if a man be drunk overnight the devil cannot hurt him in
45 the morning. If that be true, I have a charm in my head
  shall control him as well as the conjurer, I warrant you.

(*Exit* [MARTINO *with* FREDERICK. BENVOLIO *remains at window*].)

SCENE II

A sennet. CHARLES *the German Emperor,* BRUNO, [DUKE OF]
SAXONY, FAUSTUS, MEPHOSTOPHILIS, FREDERICK, MARTINO,
and ATTENDANTS.

  EMPEROR: Wonder of men, renownèd magician,
  Thrice-learnèd Faustus, welcome to our court,
  This deed of thine in setting Bruno free
  From his and our professèd enemy,
5 Shall add more excellence unto thine art
  Than if by powerful necromantic spells
  Thou could'st command the world's obedience.
  For ever be beloved of Carolus!
  And if this Bruno thou hast late redeemed
10 In peace possess the triple diadem
  And sit in Peter's chair despite of chance,
  Thou shalt be famous through all Italy
  And honored of the German Emperor.
  FAUSTUS: These gracious words, most royal Carolus
15 Shall make poor Faustus to his utmost power
  Both love and serve the German Emperor
  And lay his life at holy Bruno's feet.
  For proof whereof, if so your Grace be pleased,
  The doctor stands prepared by power of art
20 To cast his magic charms that shall pierce through
  The ebon gates of ever-burning hell,
  And hale the stubborn furies from their caves
  To compass whatsoe'er your Grace commands.
  BENVOLIO: Blood! He speaks terribly. But for all that I do not
25 greatly believe him. He looks as like a conjurer as the
  Pope to a costermonger.
  EMPEROR: Then Faustus, as thou late didst promise us,
  We would behold that famous conqueror

Great Alexander and his paramour
In their true shapes and state majestical,   30
That we may wonder at their excellence.
FAUSTUS: Your Majesty shall see them presently.—
  Mephostophilis away,
  And with a solemn noise of trumpets' sound
  Present before this royal Emperor   35
  Great Alexander and his beauteous paramour.
MEPHOSTOPHILIS: Faustus, I will.

(*Exit.*)

BENVOLIO: Well master doctor, an your devils come not away
  quickly, you shall have me asleep presently. Zounds, I
  could eat myself for anger to think I have been such an ass   40
  all this while to stand gaping after the devils' governor and
  can see nothing.
FAUSTUS: I'll make you feel something anon if my art fail me
    not!
  My lord, I must forewarn your Majesty
  That when my spirits present the royal shapes   45
  Of Alexander and his paramour,
  Your Grace demand no questions of the King
  But in dumb silence let them come and go.
EMPEROR: Be it as Faustus please; we are content.
BENVOLIO: Ay ay, and I am content too. And thou bring   50
  Alexander and his paramour before the Emperor, I'll be
  Actaeon and turn myself to a stag.
FAUSTUS: (*Aside.*) And I'll play Diana and send you the horns
  presently.

(*Sennet. Enter at one [door] the* EMPEROR ALEXANDER, *at the
other* DARIUS. *They meet.* DARIUS *is thrown down.* ALEXANDER
kills him, takes off his crown, and offering to go out, his PARAMOUR
meets him. He embraceth her and sets DARIUS' *crown upon her
head, and coming back both salute the* EMPEROR; *who leaving his
state offers to embrace them, which* FAUSTUS *seeing suddenly stays
him. Then trumpets cease and music sounds.*)

  My gracious lord, you do forget yourself.   55
  These are but shadows, not substantial.
EMPEROR: O pardon me, my thoughts are so ravished
  With sight of this renownèd Emperor,
  That in mine arms I would have compassed him.
  But Faustus, since I may not speak to them,   60
  To satisfy my longing thoughts at full,
  Let me this tell thee: I have heard it said
  That this fair lady whilst she lived on earth,
  Had on her neck a little wart or mole.
  How may I prove that saying to be true?   65
FAUSTUS: Your Majesty may boldly go and see.
EMPEROR: Faustus, I see it plain!
  And in this sight thou better pleasest me
  Than if I gained another monarchy.

---

46 s.d. **Benvolio remains at window** because Benvolio does
not leave the stage, this scene cannot properly be said to be
ended. But the present edition, following its predecessors for
convenience of reference, begins a new scene

IV.ii. s.d. **sennet** trumpet fanfare (the absence of a verb in the rest
of the stage direction perhaps indicates that the Emperor and his
party do not enter but rather are "discovered," as Faustus may have
been discovered at the beginning of 1.1, if the Chorus drew back
a curtain)   9 **redeemed** freed   26 **costermonger** fruit-seller

---

39 **Zounds** by God's wounds   52 **Actaeon** legendary hunter
who saw the naked goddess Diana bathing. She transformed him
into a stag, and he was torn to pieces by his own hounds
54 s.d. **Darius** King of Persia, defeated by Alexander in 334 BCE
59 **compassed** encompassed, embraced

70 FAUSTUS: Away, be gone! (*Exit show.*)
      See, see my gracious lord, what strange beast is yon that
      thrusts his head out at the window!
    EMPEROR: O wondrous sight! See, Duke of Saxony,
      Two spreading horns most strangely fastened
75   Upon the head of young Benvolio.
    SAXONY: What, is he asleep or dead?
    FAUSTUS: He sleeps my lord, but dreams not of his horns.
    EMPEROR: This sport is excellent. We'll call and wake him.
      What ho, Benvolio!
80 BENVOLIO: A plague upon you! Let me sleep awhile.
    EMPEROR: I blame thee not to sleep much, having such a head
      of thine own.
    SAXONY: Look up Benvolio! 'Tis the Emperor calls.
    BENVOLIO: The Emperor! Where? O zounds, my head!
85 EMPEROR: Nay, and thy horns hold, 'tis no matter for thy head,
      for that's armed sufficiently.
    FAUSTUS: Why, how now Sir Knight? What, hanged by the
      horns? This is most horrible! Fie fie, pull in your head for
      shame! Let not all the world wonder at you.
90 BENVOLIO: Zounds doctor, is this your villainy?
    FAUSTUS: Oh, say not so sir: The doctor has no skill,
      No art, no cunning to present these lords
      Or bring before this royal Emperor
      The mighty monarch, warlike Alexander.
95   If Faustus do it, you are straight resolved
      In bold Actaeon's shape to turn a stag.
      And therefore my lord, so please your Majesty,
      I'll raise a kennel of hounds shall hunt him so
      As all his footmanship shall scarce prevail
100   To keep his carcass from their bloody fangs.
      Ho, Belimote, Argiron, Asterote!
    BENVOLIO: Hold, hold! Zounds, he'll raise up a kennel of dev-
      ils I think, anon. Good my lord, entreat for me. 'Sblood, I
      am never able to endure these torments.
105 EMPEROR: Then good master doctor,
      Let me entreat you to remove his horns.
      He has done penance now sufficiently.
    FAUSTUS: My gracious lord, not so much for injury done to
      me, as to delight your Majesty with some mirth, hath
110   Faustus justly requited this injurious knight; which being all
      I desire, I am content to remove his horns. Mephostophilis,
      transform him. And hereafter sir, look you speak well of
      scholars.
    BENVOLIO: (*Aside.*) Speak well of ye! 'Sblood, and scholars be
115   such cuckold-makers to clap horns on honest men's heads
      o' this order, I'll ne'er trust smooth faces and small ruffs
      more. But an I be not revenged for this, would I might be
      turned to a gaping oyster and drink nothing but salt water.

    (*Exit.*)

    EMPEROR: Come Faustus, while the Emperor lives,
120   In recompense of this thy high desert,

87–88 **hanged by the horns** the spreading horns prevent Benvolio from pulling his head inside of the window   103 **'Sblood**
by God's blood   110 **injurious** insulting   116 **small ruffs**
(worn by scholars, in contrast to the large ruffs worn by
courtiers)

      Thou shalt command the state of Germany
      And live beloved of mighty Carolus.

(*Exeunt omnes.*)

SCENE III

Enter BENVOLIO, MARTINO, FREDERICK, *and* SOLDIERS.

    MARTINO: Nay, sweet Benvolio, let us sway thy thoughts
      From this attempt against the conjurer.
    BENVOLIO: Away! You love me not to urge me thus.
      Shall I let slip so great an injury
      When every servile groom jests at my wrongs   5
      And in their rustic gambols proudly say,
      "Benvolio's head was graced with horns today"?
      O, may these eyelids never close again
      Till with my sword I have that conjurer slain!
      If you will aid me in this enterprise,   10
      Then draw your weapons and be resolute;
      If not, depart. Here will Benvolio die
      But Faustus' death shall quit my infamy.
    FREDERICK: Nay, we will stay with thee, betide what may,
      And kill that doctor if he come this way.   15
    BENVOLIO: Then, gentle Frederick, hie thee to the grove
      And place our servants and our followers
      Close in an ambush there behind the trees.
      By this, I know, the conjurer is near.
      I saw him kneel and kiss the Emperor's hand   20
      And take his leave laden with rich rewards.
      Then soldiers, boldly fight. If Faustus die,
      Take you the wealth, leave us the victory.
    FREDERICK: Come soldiers, follow me unto the grove.
      Who kills him shall have gold and endless love.   25

(*Exit* FREDERICK *with the* SOLDIERS.)

    BENVOLIO: My head is lighter than it was by th' horns—
      But yet my heart more ponderous than my head,
      And pants until I see that conjurer dead.
    MARTINO: Where shall we place ourselves, Benvolio?
    BENVOLIO: Here will we stay to bide the first assault.   30
      O, were that damnèd hell-hound but in place
      Thou soon should'st see me quit my foul disgrace.

(*Enter* FREDERICK.)

    FREDERICK: Close, close! The conjurer is at hand
      And all alone comes walking in his gown.
      Be ready then and strike the peasant down!   35
    BENVOLIO: Mine be that honor then! Now sword, strike home!
      For horns he gave I'll have his head anon.

(*Enter* FAUSTUS *with the false head.*)

    MARTINO: See see, he comes.
    BENVOLIO: No words. This blow ends all!

(*Strikes* FAUSTUS.)

IV.iii. let slip ignore   13 **But** unless; **quit** avenge   35 **peasant**
low fellow

FAUSTUS: O!

40 FREDERICK: Groan you, master doctor?

BENVOLIO: Break may his heart with groans! Dear Frederick, see,
    Thus will I end his griefs immediately.

(*Cuts off* FAUSTUS' *false head.*)

MARTINO: Strike with a willing hand! His head is off.

BENVOLIO: The devil's dead, the furies now may laugh.

45 FREDERICK: Was this that stern aspect, that awful frown,
    Made the grim monarch of infernal spirits
    Tremble and quake at his commanding charms?

MARTINO: Was this that damnèd head whose heart conspired
    Benvolio's shame before the Emperor?

50 BENVOLIO: Ay, that's the head, and here the body lies
    Justly rewarded for his villainies.

FREDERICK: Come let's devise how we may add more shame
    To the black scandal of his hated name.

BENVOLIO: First, on his head in quittance of my wrongs

55   I'll nail huge forkèd horns and let them hang
    Within the window where he yoked me first
    That all the world may see my just revenge.

MARTINO: What use shall we put his beard to?

BENVOLIO: We'll sell it to a chimney-sweeper. It will wear out
60   ten birchen brooms, I warrant you.

FREDERICK: What shall eyes do?

BENVOLIO: We'll put out his eyes, and they shall serve for
    buttons to his lips to keep his tongue from catching
    cold.

65 MARTINO: An excellent policy! And now sirs, having divided
    him, what shall the body do?

(FAUSTUS *rises.*)

BENVOLIO: Zounds, the devil's alive again!

FREDERICK: Give him his head for God's sake!

FAUSTUS: Nay keep it. Faustus will have heads and hands,
70   Ay, all your hearts, to recompense this deed.
    Knew you not, traitors, I was limited
    For four and twenty years to breathe on earth?
    And had you cut my body with your swords
    Or hewed this flesh and bones as small as sand,
75   Yet in a minute had my spirit returned
    And I had breathed a man made free from harm.
    But wherefore do I dally my revenge?
    Asteroth, Belimoth, Mephostophilis!

(*Enter* MEPHOSTOPHILIS *and other* DEVILS.)

    Go horse these traitors on your fiery backs
80   And mount aloft with them as high as heaven,
    Thence pitch them headlong to the lowest hell.
    Yet stay, the world shall see their misery,
    And hell shall after plague their treachery.
    Go Belimoth, and take this caitiff hence
85   And hurl him in some lake of mud and dirt:

---

84 **caitiff** wretch

    Take thou this other, drag him through the woods
    Amongst the pricking thorns and sharpest briars:
    Whilst with my gentle Mephostophilis
    This traitor flies unto some steepy rock
90   That rolling down may break the villain's bones
    As he intended to dismember me.
    Fly hence, dispatch my charge immediately!

FREDERICK: Pity us, gentle Faustus, save our lives!

FAUSTUS: Away!

FREDERICK: He must needs go that the devil drives.

(*Exeunt* SPIRITS *with the* KNIGHTS.)

(*Enter the ambushed* SOLDIERS.)

1 SOLDIER: Come sirs, prepare yourselves in readiness. 95
    Make haste to help these noble gentlemen.
    I heard them parley with the conjurer.

2 SOLDIER: See where he comes, dispatch, and kill the slave!

FAUSTUS: What's here, an ambush to betray my life?
    Then Faustus, try thy skill. Base peasants, stand! 100
    For lo, these trees remove at my command
    And stand as bulwarks 'twixt yourselves and me
    To shield me from your hated treachery!
    Yet to encounter this your weak attempt
    Behold an army comes incontinent. 105

(FAUSTUS *strikes the door, and enter a* DEVIL *playing on a drum, after him another bearing an ensign, and divers with weapons:* MEPHOSTOPHILIS *with fireworks: they set upon the* SOLDIERS *and drive them out.* [*Exeunt all.*])

SCENE IV

Enter at several doors BENVOLIO, FREDERICK, *and* MARTINO, *their heads and faces bloody and besmeared with mud and dirt, all having horns on their heads.*

MARTINO: What ho, Benvolio!

BENVOLIO: Here! What, Frederick, ho!

FREDERICK: O, help me gentle friend. Where is Martino?

MARTINO: Dear Frederick, here,
    Half smothered in a lake of mud and dirt,
    Through which the furies dragged me by the heels. 5

FREDERICK: Martino, see, Benvolio's horns again.

MARTINO: O misery! How now Benvolio?

BENVOLIO: Defend me, heaven! Shall I be haunted still?

MARTINO: Nay fear not man, we have no power to kill.

BENVOLIO: My friends transformed thus! O hellish spite, 10
    Your heads are all set with horns.

FREDERICK: You hit it right:
    It is your own you mean. Feel on your head.

BENVOLIO: Zounds, horns again!

MARTINO: Nay chafe not man, we all are sped.

BENVOLIO: What devil attends this damned magician,
    That spite of spite our wrongs are doubled? 15

---

101 **remove** move   105 **incontinent** immediately

IV.iv. 8 **haunted** the following line suggests that there is a quibble on "hunted," Benvolio now resembling a stag   13 **chafe** fret; **sped** done for, ruined (because of the horns)

FREDERICK: What may we do that we may hide our shames?
BENVOLIO: If we should follow him to work revenge
    He'd join long asses' ears to these huge horns
    And make us laughing-stocks to all the world.
20 MARTINO: What shall we then do, dear Benvolio?
BENVOLIO: I have a castle joining near these woods,
    And thither we'll repair and live obscure
    Till time shall alter this our brutish shapes.
    Sith black disgrace hath thus eclipsed our fame,
25   We'll rather die with grief than live with shame.

(*Exeunt omnes.*)

SCENE V

Enter FAUSTUS *and the* HORSE-COURSER.

HORSE-COURSER: I beseech your worship, accept of these
    forty dollars.
FAUSTUS: Friend, thou canst not buy so good a horse for so
    small a price. I have no great need to sell him, but if thou
5   likest him for ten dollars more, take him, because I see
    thou hast a good mind to him.
HORSE-COURSER: I beseech you sir, accept of this. I am a
    very poor man and have lost very much of late by horse-
    flesh, and this bargain will set me up again.
10 FAUSTUS: Well, I will not stand with thee. Give me the
    money. Now sirrah, I must tell you that you may ride him
    o'er hedge and ditch and spare him not. But, do you hear,
    in any case ride him not into the water.
HORSE-COURSER: How sir, not into the water! Why, will he
15   not drink of all waters?
FAUSTUS: Yes, he will drink of all waters, but ride him not
    into the water: o'er hedge and ditch or where thou wilt,
    but not into the water. Go bid the hostler deliver him
    unto you, and remember what I say.
20 HORSE-COURSER: I warrant you sir. O joyful day! Now am I
    a made man forever.

(*Exit.*)

FAUSTUS: What art thou, Faustus, but a man condemned to die?
    Thy fatal time draws to a final end;
    Despair doth drive distrust into my thoughts.
25   Confound these passions with a quiet sleep.
    Tush, Christ did call the thief upon the cross!
    Then rest thee Faustus, quiet in conceit.

(*He sits to sleep.*)

(*Enter the* HORSE-COURSER *wet.*)

HORSE-COURSER: O what a cozening doctor was this! I riding my horse into the water, thinking some hidden mystery had been in the horse, I had nothing under me but a   30
little straw and had much ado to escape drowning. Well,
I'll go rouse him and make him give me my forty dollars
again. Ho, sirrah doctor, you cozening scab! Master doctor, awake and rise, and give me my money again, for your
horse is turned to a bottle of hay. Master doctor!   35

(*He pulls off his leg.*)

    Alas, I am undone! What shall I do? I have pulled off his leg.
FAUSTUS: O help, help! The villain hath murdered me!
HORSE-COURSER: Murder or not murder, now he has but
    one leg I'll outrun him, and cast this leg into some ditch
    or other.
FAUSTUS: Stop him, stop him, stop him!—Ha, ha, ha! Faustus   40
    hath his leg again, and the horse-courser a bundle of hay
    for his forty dollars.

(*Enter* WAGNER.)

    How now, Wagner? What news with thee?
WAGNER: If it please you, the Duke of Vanholt doth earnestly
    entreat your company, and hath sent some of his men to   45
    attend you with provision fit for your journey.
FAUSTUS: The Duke of Vanholt's an honorable gentleman,
    and one to whom I must be no niggard of my cunning.
    Come, away!

(*Exeunt.*)

SCENE VI

Enter [ROBIN] *the clown,* DICK, HORSE-COURSER, *and a* CARTER.

CARTER: Come my masters, I'll bring you to the best beer in
    Europe. What ho, hostess! Where be these whores?

(*Enter* HOSTESS.)

HOSTESS: How now? What lack you? What, my old guests,
    welcome.
ROBIN: (*Aside.*) Sirrah Dick, dost thou know why I stand so   5
    mute?
DICK: (*Aside.*) No Robin, why is't?
ROBIN: (*Aside.*) I am eighteen pence on the score. But say
    nothing. See if she have forgotten me.
HOSTESS: Who's this that stands so solemnly by himself?   10
    What, my old guest!
ROBIN: O, hostess, how do you? I hope my score stands still.
HOSTESS: Ay, there's no doubt of that, for methinks you make
    no haste to wipe it out.
DICK: Why hostess, I say, fetch us some beer!   15
HOSTESS: You shall, presently.—Look up into th' hall there, ho!

(*Exit.*)

---

24 **Sith** since

IV.v. s.d. **Horse-courser** horse trader   2 **dollars** German
coins   8 **horse-flesh** the possibility of a quibble on "whores
flesh" is increased by "set me up" and "stand" in the ensuing dialogue   10 **stand** haggle   16 **drink of all waters** i.e., go anywhere   23 **fatal time** life span   26 **Christ . . . cross** in Luke
xxiii.39–43 Christ promised one of the thieves that he would be
with Christ in paradise   27 **quiet in conceit** with a quiet mind

---

28 **cozening** deceiving   35 **bottle** bundle

IV.vi. 8 **on the score** in debt

DICK: Comes sirs, what shall we do now till mine hostess comes?

CARTER: Marry sir, I'll tell you the bravest tale how a con-
20 jurer served me. You know Doctor Faustus?

HORSE-COURSER: Ay, a plague take him! Here's some on's have cause to know him. Did he conjure thee too?

CARTER: I'll tell you how he served me. As I was going to Wittenberg t'other day with a load of hay, he met me and
25 asked me what he should give me for as much hay as he could eat. Now sir, I thinking that a little would serve his turn, bad him take as much as he would for three far-things. So he presently gave me my money and fell to eat-ing; and as I am a cursen man, he never left eating till he
30 had eat up all my load of hay.

ALL: O monstrous, eat a whole load of hay!

ROBIN: Yes yes, that may be, for I have heard of one that has eat a load of logs.

HORSE-COURSER: Now sirs, you shall hear how villainously
35 he served me. I went to him yesterday to buy a horse of him, and he would by no means sell him under forty dol-lars. So sir, because I knew him to be such a horse as would run over hedge and ditch and never tire, I gave him his money. So, when I had my horse, Doctor Faustus bade
40 me ride him night and day and spare him no time. "But," quoth he, "in any case ride him not into the water." Now sir, I thinking the horse had had some quality that he would not have me know of, what did I but rid him into a great river—and when I came just in the midst, my horse
45 vanished away and I sate straddling upon a bottle of hay.

ALL: O brave doctor!

HORSE-COURSER: But you shall hear how bravely I served him for it. I went me home to his house, and there I found him asleep. I kept ahallowing and whooping in his ears,
50 but all could not wake him. I seeing that, took him by the leg and never rested pulling till I had pulled me his leg quite off, and now 'tis at home in mine hostry.

DICK: And has the doctor but one leg then? That's excellent, for one of his devils turned me into the likeness of an ape's face.

55 CARTER: Some more drink, hostess!

ROBIN: Hark you, we'll into another room and drink awhile, and then we'll go seek out the doctor.

(*Exeunt omnes.*)

SCENE VII

Enter the DUKE OF VANHOLT, *his* [SERVANTS,] DUCHESS, FAUS-TUS, *and* MEPHOSTOPHILIS.

DUKE: Thanks master doctor, for these pleasant sights. Nor know I how sufficiently to recompense your great deserts in erecting that enchanted castle in the air, the sight whereof so delighted me,
5 As nothing in the world could please me more.

FAUSTUS: I do think myself, my good lord, highly recompensed in that it pleaseth your Grace to think but well of that which Faustus hath performed.—But gracious lady, it may be that you have taken no pleasure in those sights. There-

fore I pray you tell me what is the thing you most desire to 10
have: be it in the world it shall be yours. I have heard that great-bellied women do long for things are rare and dainty.

DUCHESS: True master doctor, and since I find you so kind, I will make known unto you what my heart desires to have: and were it now summer, as it is January, a dead time of 15
the winter, I would request no better meat than a dish of ripe grapes.

FAUSTUS: This is but a small matter. Go Mephostophilis, away!

(*Exit* MEPHOSTOPHILIS.)

Madam, I will do more than this for your content.

(*Enter* MEPHOSTOPHILIS *again with the grapes.*)

Here, now taste ye these. They should be good, 20
For they come from a far country, I can tell you.

DUKE: This makes me wonder more than all the rest, that at this time of the year when every tree is barren of his fruit, from whence you had these ripe grapes.

FAUSTUS: Please it your Grace, the year is divided into two 25
circles over the whole world, so that when it is winter with us, in the contrary circle it is likewise summer with them, as in India, Saba, and such countries that lie far east, where they have fruit twice a year. From whence, by means of a swift spirit that I have, I had these grapes 30
brought as you see.

DUCHESS: And trust me, they are the sweetest grapes that e'er I tasted.

(*The* CLOWNS [ROBIN, DICK, CARTER, *and* HORSE-COURSER] *bounce at the gate within.*)

DUKE: What rude disturbers have we at the gate?
Go pacify their fury, set it ope, 35
And then demand of them what they would have.

(*They knock again and call out to talk with* FAUSTUS.)

A SERVANT: Why, how now masters, what a coil is there! What is the reason you disturb the Duke?

DICK: We have no reason for it, therefore a fig for him!

SERVANT: Why saucy varlets, dare you be so bold! 40

HORSE-COURSER: I hope sir, we have wit enough to be more bold than welcome.

SERVANT: It appears so. Pray be bold elsewhere And trouble not the Duke.

DUKE: What would they have? 45

SERVANT: They all cry out to speak with Doctor Faustus.

CARTER: Ay, and we will speak with him.

DUKE: Will you sir? Commit the rascals.

DICK: Commit with us! He were as good commit with his father as commit with us! 50

---

29 **cursen** i.e., Christian (dialect form)   32–33 **eat a load of logs** been drunk   52 **hostry** inn

---

IV.vii.   12 **great-bellied** i.e., pregnant   16 **meat** food   25 **two circles** i.e., the northern and the southern hemispheres (though later in the speech he talks of east and west rather than of north and south)   s.d. **bounce** knock   37 **coil** turmoil   38 **reason** pro-nounced like "raisin," leading to the quibble on "fig"; a "fig" here is an obscene contemptuous gesture in which the hand is clenched and the thumb is thrust between the first and second fingers, making the thumb resemble the stem of a fig, or a penis   48 **Commit** imprison (Dick proceeds to quibble on the idea of committing adultery)

FAUSTUS: I do beseech your Grace, let them come in.
 They are good subject for a merriment.
DUKE: Do as thou wilt, Faustus, I give thee leave.
FAUSTUS: I thank your Grace.

(*Enter* [ROBIN] *the clown,* DICK, CARTER, *and* HORSE-COURSER.)

                          Why, how now my good friends?
55   'Faith, you are too outrageous; but come near,
 I have procured your pardons. Welcome all.
ROBIN: Nay sir, we will be welcome for our money, and we
 will pay for what we take. What ho, give's half a dozen of
 beer here, and be hanged!
60 FAUSTUS: Nay, hark you, can you tell me where you are?
CARTER: Ay, marry can I, we are under heaven.
SERVANT: Ay, but Sir Sauce-box, know you in what place?
HORSE-COURSER: Ay ay, the house is good enough to drink
 in. Zounds, fill us some beer, or we'll break all the barrels
65   in the house and dash out all your brains with your bottles.
FAUSTUS: Be not so furious. Come, you shall have beer.
 My lord, beseech you give me leave awhile;
 I'll gage my credit 'twill content your Grace.
DUKE: With all my heart, kind doctor, please thyself.
70   Our servants and our court's at thy command.
FAUSTUS: I humbly thank your Grace.—Then fetch some beer.
HORSE-COURSER: Ay marry, there spake a doctor indeed! And
 'faith, I'll drink a health to thy wooden leg for that word.
FAUSTUS: My wooden leg? What dost thou mean by that?
75 CARTER: Ha, ha, ha, dost hear him Dick? He has forgot his leg.
HORSE-COURSER: Ay ay, he does not stand much upon that.
FAUSTUS: No, 'faith, not much upon a wooden leg.
CARTER: Good lord, that flesh and blood should be so frail
 with your worship! Do not you remember a horse-
80   courser you sold a horse to?
FAUSTUS: Yes, I remember I sold one a horse.
CARTER: And do you remember you bid he should not ride
 into the water?
FAUSTUS: Yes, I do very well remember that.
85 CARTER: And do you remember nothing of your leg?
FAUSTUS: No, in good sooth.
CARTER: Then I pray remember your curtsy.
FAUSTUS: I thank you sir.
CARTER: 'Tis not so much worth. I pray you tell me one thing.
90 FAUSTUS: What's that?
CARTER: Be both your legs bedfellows every night together?
FAUSTUS: Would'st thou make a colossus of me that thou ask-
 est me such questions?
CARTER: No, truly sir, I would make nothing of you, but I
95   would fain know that.

(*Enter* HOSTESS *with drink.*)

FAUSTUS: Then I assure thee certainly they are.
CARTER: I thank you, I am fully satisfied.
FAUSTUS: But wherefore dost thou ask?

CARTER: For nothing, sir, but methinks you should have a
 wooden bedfellow of one of 'em.   100
HORSE-COURSER: Why, do you hear sir, did not I pull off one
 of your legs when you were asleep?
FAUSTUS: But I have it again now I am awake. Look you here sir.
ALL: O horrible! Had the doctor three legs?
CARTER: Do you remember sir, how you cozened me and eat 105
 up my load of—

(FAUSTUS *charms him dumb.*)

DICK: Do you remember how you made me wear an ape's—

(FAUSTUS *charms him.*)

HORSE-COURSER: You whoreson conjuring scab! Do you remember how you cozened me with a ho—

(FAUSTUS *charms him.*)

ROBIN: Ha' you forgotten me? You think to carry it away 110
 with your "hey-pass" and "re-pass"? Do you remember
 the dog's fa—

([FAUSTUS *charms him.*] *Exeunt* CLOWNS.)

HOSTESS: Who pays for the ale? Hear you master doctor, now
 you have sent away my guests, I pray who shall pay me for
 my a—   115

([FAUSTUS *charms her.*] *Exit* HOSTESS.)

DUCHESS: My Lord,
 We are much beholding to this learnèd man.
DUKE: So are we madam, which we will recompense
 With all the love and kindness that we may:
 His artful sport drives all sad thoughts away.   120

(*Exeunt.*)

ACT FIVE

SCENE I

Thunder and lightning. Enter DEVILS *with covered dishes:*
MEPHOSTOPHILIS *leads them into* FAUSTUS' *study. Then enter*
WAGNER.

WAGNER: I think my master means to die shortly. He has
 made his will and given me his wealth: his house, his
 goods, and store of golden plate—besides two thousand
 ducats ready coined. I wonder what he means. If death
 were nigh, he would not frolic thus. He's now at supper   5
 with the scholars, where there's such belly-cheer as Wagner in his life ne'er saw the like! And see where they
 come. Belike the feast is done.

(*Exit.*)

---

68 **gage** pledge   76 **stand much upon** quibble on "attach
much importance to"   87 **curtsy** also called "a leg," hence
there is a quibble on the Carter's previous speech   92 **colossus**
huge statue in the harbor at Rhodes, between whose legs ships
were said to have sailed

111 **hey-pass, re-pass** conjuring expressions

V.i. 7 **Belike** most likely   1–7 **I think . . . done** though
printed as prose in the quarto, as here, perhaps this speech should
be verse, the lines ending *shortly, wealth, plate, coined, nigh, supper,
belly-cheer, like, done*

(*Enter* FAUSTUS, MEPHOSTOPHILIS, *and two or three* SCHOLARS.)

1 SCHOLAR: Master Doctor Faustus, since our conference
about fair ladies, which was the beautifulest in all the
10 world, we have determined with ourselves that Helen of
Greece was the admirablest lady that ever lived. Therefore
master doctor, if you will do us so much favor as to let us
see that peerless dame of Greece, whom all the world admires for majesty, we should think ourselves much be-
15 holding unto you.

FAUSTUS: Gentlemen,
For that I know your friendship is unfeigned,
It is not Faustus' custom to deny
The just request of those that wish him well:
20 You shall behold that peerless dame of Greece
No otherwise for pomp or majesty
Than when Sir Paris crossed the seas with her
And brought the spoils to rich Dardania.
Be silent then, for danger is in words.

(*Music sounds.* MEPHOSTOPHILIS *brings in* HELEN: *she passeth over
the stage.*)

25 2 SCHOLAR: Was this fair Helen, whose admired worth
Made Greece with ten years' wars afflict poor Troy?
3 SCHOLAR: Too simple is my wit to tell her worth,
Whom all the world admires for majesty.
1 SCHOLAR: Now we have seen the pride of nature's work,
30 We'll take our leaves, and for this blessèd sight
Happy and blest be Faustus evermore.
FAUSTUS: Gentlemen, farewell, the same wish I to you.

(*Exeunt* SCHOLARS.)

(*Enter an* OLD MAN.)

OLD MAN: O gentle Faustus, leave this damnèd art,
This magic that will charm thy soul to hell
35 And quite bereave thee of salvation.
Though thou hast now offended like man,
Do not persever in it like a devil.
Yet, yet, thou hast an amiable soul
If sin by custom grow not into nature.
40 Then, Faustus, will repentance come too late!
Then, thou are banished from the sight of heaven!
No mortal can express the pains of hell!
It may be this my exhortation
Seems harsh and all unpleasant. Let it not.
45 For gentle son, I speak it not in wrath
Or envy of thee but in tender love
And pity of thy future misery:
And so have hope that this my kind rebuke,
Checking thy body, may amend thy soul.
50 FAUSTUS: Where art thou, Faustus? Wretch, what hast thou
done!

(MEPHOSTOPHILIS *gives him a dagger.*)

Hell claims his right and with a roaring voice
Says "Faustus, come, thine hour is almost come!"
And Faustus now will come to do thee right!
OLD MAN: O stay, good Faustus, stay thy desperate steps!
I see an angel hover o'er thy head,   55
And with a vial full of precious grace
Offers to pour the same into thy soul:
Then call for mercy and avoid despair.
FAUSTUS: O friend,
I feel thy words to comfort my distressèd soul: 60
Leave me awhile to ponder on my sins.
OLD MAN: Faustus, I leave thee, but with grief of heart,
Fearing the enemy of thy hapless soul.

(*Exit.*)

FAUSTUS: Accursèd Faustus! Wretch, what hast thou done!
I do repent, and yet I do despair: 65
Hell strives with grace for conquest in my breast!
What shall I do to shun the snares of death?
MEPHOSTOPHILIS: Thou traitor Faustus, I arrest thy soul
For disobedience to my sovereign lord.
Revolt, or I'll in piecemeal tear thy flesh.   70
FAUSTUS: I do repent I e'er offended him.
Sweet Mephostophilis, entreat thy lord
To pardon my unjust presumption,
And with my blood again I will confirm
The former vow I made to Lucifer.   75
MEPHOSTOPHILIS: Do it then, Faustus, with unfeignèd heart
Lest greater dangers do attend thy drift.
FAUSTUS: Torment, sweet friend, that base and agèd man
That durst dissuade me from thy Lucifer,
With greatest torment that our hell affords.   80
MEPHOSTOPHILIS: His faith is great. I cannot touch his soul.
But what I may afflict his body with
I will attempt, which is but little worth.
FAUSTUS: One thing, good servant, let me crave of thee
To glut the longing of my heart's desire: 85
That I may have unto my paramour
That heavenly Helen which I saw of late,
Whose sweet embraces may extinguish clear
Those thoughts that do dissuade me from my vow,
And keep mine oath I made to Lucifer.   90
MEPHOSTOPHILIS: This or what else my Faustus shall desire
Shall be performed in twinkling of an eye.

(*Enter* HELEN *again, passing over between two* CUPIDS.)

FAUSTUS: Was this the face that launched a thousand ships
And burnt the topless towers of Ilium?
Sweet Helen, make me immortal with a kiss.   95
Her lips suck forth my soul. See where it flies!
Come Helen, come, give me my soul again.
Here will I dwell, for heaven is in these lips
And all is dross that is not Helena.

---

23 **spoils** booty (including Helen); **Dardania** Troy   35 **bereave** deprive   37 **persever** accent on second syllable   38 **an
amiable soul** a soul worthy of love   49 **Checking** rebuking

---

70 **Revolt** return (to your allegiance)   94 **topless** i.e., so tall
their tops are beyond sight; **Ilium** Troy

100 I will be Paris, and for love of thee
    Instead of Troy shall Wittenberg be sacked:
    And I will combat with weak Menelaus
    And wear thy colors on my plumèd crest.
    Yea, I will wound Achilles in the heel
105 And then return to Helen for a kiss.
    O, thou art fairer than the evening's air
    Clad in the beauty of a thousand stars,
    Brighter art thou than flaming Jupiter
    When he appeared to hapless Semele,
110 More lovely than the monarch of the sky
    In wanton Arethusa's azure arms,
    And none but thou shalt be my paramour.

(*Exeunt.*)

SCENE II

Thunder. Enter LUCIFER, BELZEBUB, *and* MEPHOSTOPHILIS.

LUCIFER: Thus from infernal Dis do we ascend
    To view the subjects of our monarchy,
    Those souls which sin seals the black sons of hell.
    'Mong which as chief, Faustus, we come to thee,
5   Bringing with us lasting damnation
    To wait upon thy soul. The time is come
    Which makes it forfeit.
MEPHOSTOPHILIS: And this gloomy night
    Here in this room will wretched Faustus be.
BELZEBUB: And here we'll stay
10 To mark him how he doth demean himself.
MEPHOSTOPHILIS: How should he but in desperate lunacy?
    Fond worldling, now his heart blood dries with grief.
    His conscience kills it, and his laboring brain
    Begets a world of idle fantasies
15 To overreach the devil; but all in vain:
    His store of pleasures must be sauced with pain!
    He and his servant Wagner are at hand.
    Both come from drawing Faustus' lastest will.
    See where they come.

(*Enter* FAUSTUS *and* WAGNER.)

20 FAUSTUS: Say Wagner, thou hast perused my will;
    How dost thou like it?
WAGNER: Sir, so wondrous well
    As in all humble duty I do yield
    My life and lasting service for your love.

(*Enter the* SCHOLARS.)

---

102 **Menelaus** Greek king, deserted by Helen for Paris
104 **Achilles** greatest of the Greek warriors   109 **Semele**
beloved by Jupiter, who promised to do whatever she wished; she
asked to see him in his full splendor, and the sight incinerated her
111 **Arethusa** a nymph, here apparently loved by Jupiter, "the
monarch of the sky"

V.ii. s.d. **Enter Lucifer, Belzebub, and Mephostophilis** probably they rise out of a trapdoor and ascend to the upper stage,
Mephostophilis descending to the main stage at line 86   1 **infernal Dis** the underworld (named for its ruler)   12 **Fond** foolish

FAUSTUS: Gramercies, Wagner—Welcome gentlemen.

(*Exit* WAGNER.)

1 SCHOLAR: Now worthy Faustus, methinks your looks are   25
    changed.
FAUSTUS: O gentlemen!
2 SCHOLAR: What ails Faustus?
FAUSTUS: Ah my sweet chamber-fellow, had I lived with thee,
    then had I lived still!—But now must die eternally. Look
    sirs, comes he not, comes he not?   30
1 SCHOLAR: O my dear Faustus, what imports this fear?
2 SCHOLAR: Is all our pleasure turned to melancholy?
3 SCHOLAR: He is not well with being over-solitary.
2 SCHOLAR: If it be so, we'll have physicians and Faustus shall
    be cured.   35
3 SCHOLAR: 'Tis but a surfeit sir, fear nothing.
FAUSTUS: A surfeit of deadly sin that hath damned both body
    and soul!
2 SCHOLAR: Yet Faustus, look up to heaven and remember
    mercy is infinite.   40
FAUSTUS: But Faustus' offense can ne'er be pardoned. The
    serpent that tempted Eve may be saved, but not Faustus!
    O gentlemen, hear with patience and tremble not at my
    speeches. Though my heart pant and quiver to remember
    that I have been a student here these thirty years. O, would 45
    I had never seen Wittenberg, never read book.—And
    what wonders I have done all Germany can witness, yea
    all the world, for which Faustus hath lost both Germany
    and the world, yea heaven itself—heaven, the seat of God,
    the throne of the blessed, the kingdom of joy—and must 50
    remain in hell for ever! hell, O hell forever! Sweet friends,
    what shall become of Faustus being in hell forever?
2 SCHOLAR: Yet Faustus, call on God.
FAUSTUS: On God, whom Faustus hath abjured? On God,
    whom Faustus hath blasphemed? O my God, I would weep, 55
    but the devil draws in my tears! Gush forth blood instead of
    tears, yea life and soul! O, he stays my tongue! I would lift
    up my hands, but see, they hold 'em, they hold 'em!
ALL: Who, Faustus?
FAUSTUS: Why, Lucifer and Mephostophilis. O gentlemen, I   60
    gave them my soul for my cunning.
ALL: O, God forbid!
FAUSTUS: God forbade it indeed, but Faustus hath done it.
    For the vain pleasure of four and twenty years hath Faus-
    tus lost eternal joy and felicity, I writ them a bill with   65
    mine own blood. The date is expired. This is the time.
    And he will fetch me.
1 SCHOLAR: Why did not Faustus tell us of this before, that
    divines might have prayed for thee?
FAUSTUS: Oft have I thought to have done so, but the devil   70
    threatened to tear me in pieces if I named God—to fetch
    me body and soul if I once gave ear to divinity; and now
    'tis too late! Gentlemen, away, lest you perish with me.
2 SCHOLAR: O, what may we do to save Faustus?
FAUSTUS: Talk not of me but save yourselves and depart.   75
3 SCHOLAR: God will strengthen me. I will stay with Faustus.

---

24 **Gramercies** thank you   36 **a surfeit** indigestion

1 SCHOLAR: Tempt not God, sweet friend, but let us into the
next room and pray for him.

FAUSTUS: Ay, pray for me, pray for me. And what noise soever
80   you hear come not unto me, for nothing can rescue me.

2 SCHOLAR: Pray thou, and we will pray that God may have
mercy upon thee.

FAUSTUS: Gentlemen, farewell! If I live till morning, I'll visit
you. If not, Faustus is gone to hell.

85 ALL: Faustus, farewell.

(*Exeunt* SCHOLARS.)

MEPHOSTOPHILIS: Ay, Faustus, now thou hast no hope of
heaven.
Therefore, despair! Think only upon hell,
For that must be thy mansion, there to dwell.

FAUSTUS: O thou bewitching fiend, 'twas thy temptation
90   Hath robbed me of eternal happiness.

MEPHOSTOPHILIS: I do confess it Faustus, and rejoice.
'Twas I, that when thou wert i'the way to heaven
Damned up thy passage. When thou took'st the book
To view the Scriptures, then I turned the leaves
95   And led thine eye.
What, weep'st thou! 'Tis too late, despair, farewell!
Fools that will laugh on earth, most weep in hell.

(*Exit.*)

(*Enter the* GOOD ANGEL *and the* BAD ANGEL *at several doors.*)

GOOD ANGEL: O Faustus, if thou hadst given ear to me
Innumerable joys had followèd thee.
100 But thou did'st love the world.

BAD ANGEL: Gave ear to me,
And now must taste hell's pains perpetually.

GOOD ANGEL: O, what will all thy riches, pleasures, pomps
Avail thee now?

BAD ANGEL: Nothing but vex thee more,
To want in hell, that had on earth such store.

(*Music while the throne descends.*)

105 GOOD ANGEL: O, thou hast lost celestial happiness,
Pleasures unspeakable, bliss without end.
Had'st thou affected sweet divinity,
Hell or the devil had had no power on thee.
Had'st thou kept on that way, Faustus behold
110 In what resplendent glory thou had'st sat
In yonder throne, like those bright shining saints,
And triumphed over hell! That hast thou lost.

(*Throne ascends.*)

And now, poor soul, must thy good angel leave thee,
The jaws of hell are open to receive thee.

(*Exit.*)

(*Hell is discovered.*)

BAD ANGEL: Now Faustus, let thine eyes with horror stare   115
Into that vast perpetual torture-house.
There are the furies, tossing damnèd souls
On burning forks. Their bodies boil in lead.
There are live quarters broiling on the coals,
That ne'er can die: this ever-burning chair   120
Is for o'er-tortured souls to rest them in.
These that are fed with sops of flaming fire
Were gluttons and loved only delicates
And laughed to see the poor starve at their gates.
But yet all these are nothing. Thou shalt see   125
Ten thousand tortures that more horrid be.

FAUSTUS: O, I have seen enough to torture me.

BAD ANGEL: Nay, thou must feel them, taste the smart of all:
He that loves pleasure must for pleasure fall.
And so I leave thee Faustus, till anon: 130
Then wilt thou tumble in confusion.

(*Exit.*)

(*The clock strikes eleven.*)

FAUSTUS: O Faustus!
Now hast thou but one bare hour to live
And then thou must be damned perpetually.
Stand still, you ever-moving spheres of Heaven   135
That time may cease and midnight never come:
Fair nature's eye, rise, rise again and make
Perpetual day, or let this hour be but a year,
A month, a week, a natural day—
That Faustus may repent and save his soul.   140
O lente lente currite noctis equi!
The stars move still, time runs, the clock will strike:
The devil will come, and Faustus must be damned!
O, I'll leap up to my God! Who pulls me down?
See, see where Christ's blood streams in the firmament! 145
One drop of blood will save me. O my Christ!—
Rend not my heart for naming of my Christ!
Yet will I call on Him! O spare me, Lucifer!—
Where is it now? 'Tis gone: and see where God
Stretcheth out His arm and bends His ireful brows! 150
Mountains and hills, come, come and fall on me
And hide me from the heavy wrath of God!
No?
Then will I headlong run into the earth.
Gape earth! O no, it will not harbor me.   155
You stars that reigned at my nativity,
Whose influence hath allotted death and hell,
Now draw up Faustus like a foggy mist
Into the entrails of yon laboring cloud
That when you vomit forth into the air,   160
My limbs may issue from your smoky mouths—
But let my soul mount and ascend to heaven!

(*The watch strikes.*)

---

104 s.d. **throne** symbolic of heaven   107 **affected** preferred

119 **quarters** bodies   131 **confusion** destruction   141 **O . . .
*equi*** slowly, slowly run, O horses of the night (Latin, adapted
from Ovid's *Amores*, I.xiii.40, where a lover regretfully thinks of
the coming of the dawn)

O half the hour is passed! 'Twill all be passed anon!
O God,
165   If thou wilt not have mercy on my soul
Yet for Christ's sake, whose blood hath ransomed me,
Impose some end to my incessant pain!
Let Faustus live in hell a thousand years,
A hundred thousand, and at last be saved!
170   No end is limited to damnèd souls!
Why wert thou not a creature wanting soul?
Or why is this immortal that thou hast?
O, Pythagoras' metempsychosis, were that true
This soul should fly from me and I be changed
175   Into some brutish beast.
All beasts are happy, for when they die
Their souls are soon dissolved in elements.
But mine must live still to be plagued in hell!
Cursed be the parents that engendered me!
180   No Faustus, curse thyself, curse Lucifer
That hath deprived thee of the joys of heaven.

(*The clock strikes twelve.*)

It strikes, it strikes! Now body, turn to air,
Or Lucifer will bear thee quick to hell!
O soul, be changed into small water-drops
185   And fall into the ocean, ne'er be found.

(*Thunder, and enter the* DEVILS.)

My God, my God! Look not so fierce on me!
Adders and serpents, let me breathe awhile!
Ugly Hell, gape not! Come not Lucifer!
I'll burn my books!—O Mephostophilis!

(*Exeunt* [DEVILS *with* FAUSTUS].)

SCENE III

Enter the SCHOLARS.

1 SCHOLAR: Come gentlemen, let us go visit Faustus,
    For such a dreadful night was never seen
    Since first the world's creation did begin!
    Such fearful shrieks and cries were never heard!
    Pray heaven, the doctor have escaped the danger.   5
2 SCHOLAR: O, help us heaven, see, here are Faustus' limbs
    All torn asunder by the hand of death!
3 SCHOLAR: The devils whom Faustus served have torn him
        thus:
    For 'twixt the hours of twelve and one, methought
    I heard him shriek and call aloud for help,   10
    At which self time the house seemed all on fire
    With dreadful horror of these damnèd fiends.
2 SCHOLAR: Well gentlemen, though Faustus' end be such
    As every Christian heart laments to think on,
    Yet for he was a scholar once admired   15
    For wondrous knowledge in our German schools,
    We'll give his mangled limbs due burial;
    And all the students, clothed in mourning black,
    Shall wait upon his heavy funeral.

(*Exeunt.*)

(*Enter* CHORUS.)

Cut is the branch that might have grown full straight   20
And burnèd is Apollo's laurel bough
That sometime grew within this learnèd man.
Faustus is gone: regard his hellish fall,
Whose fiendful fortune may exhort the wise
Only to wonder at unlawful things,   25
Whose deepness doth entice such forward wits
To practice more than heavenly power permits.

(*Exit.*)

(*Terminat hora diem; terminat Author opus.*)

---

170 **limited to** set for   173 **metempsychosis** transmigration
of souls (a doctrine held by Pythagoras, philosopher of the sixth
century BCE)   178 **still** always   183 **quick** alive   189 s.d.
Exeunt [Devils with Faustus] possibly the devils drag Faustus
into the "hell" that was "discovered" at 5.2.114, and then toss his
limbs onto the stage, or possibly the limbs are revealed in 5.3.6
by withdrawing a curtain at the rear of the stage

V.iii. 11 **self** same   19 **wait upon** attend; **heavy** sad   21 **laurel
bough** symbol of wisdom, here associated with Apollo, god of divination   25 **Only to wonder at** i.e., merely to observe at a distance, with awe   27 s.d. **Terminat . . . opus** the hour ends the day;
the author ends his work (this Latin tag probably is not Marlowe's
but the printer's, though it is engaging to believe Marlowe wrote
it, ending his play at midnight, the hour of Faustus' death)

William Shakespeare

Given the fact that William Shakespeare (1564–1616) was a commoner and that he worked in the ephemeral trades of the theater, what we know about his life is extraordinarily rich and revealing, especially in comparison to the lives of other playwrights of the period, such as Christopher Marlowe or John Webster. William Shakespeare was born in Stratford-upon-Avon, a town to the northwest of London in Warwickshire. He was baptized on April 26, 1564, and was probably born a few days earlier—his birth date is conventionally given as April 23, the feast day of St. George, the patron saint of England, and the day on which Shakespeare died fifty-two years later in 1616, again at his home in Stratford. One of eight children, Shakespeare was the son of a glover—a tradesman who worked with a variety of leather goods. It is not known whether Shakespeare attended the local school, the King's New School, but like other schools of the period, it would have provided him with an extensive grounding in Latin grammar, rhetoric, and literature. Later in his career, Shakespeare often drew on works he could have read at such a school: plays by Terence and Plautus, the poetry of Virgil and Ovid, the writings of Caesar.

He married Anne Hathaway in November 1582; she was twenty-six and he was eighteen. In May 1583 they had their first daughter, Susannah, followed by twins, Hamnet and Judith, born in 1585. Although his wife and children remained in Stratford throughout his career, Shakespeare went to London sometime in the late 1580s, possibly joining one of the theater companies that passed through Stratford.

By the 1590s, Shakespeare was established in London as an up-and-coming playwright; he was associated with the Lord Chamberlain's Men; he had written several plays on English history; and he was at work on several comedies and tragedies. When plague closed the theaters in London from the summer of 1592 through the spring of 1594, Shakespeare wrote two narrative poems, *Venus and Adonis* and *The Rape of Lucrece,* which he dedicated to Henry Wriothesley, the third Earl of Southampton, in a bid for patronage. He later wrote *The Phoenix and the Turtle* and circulated a brilliant and ambitious sequence of sonnets in manuscript before publishing it in 1609. As a shareholder of the Lord Chamberlain's Men, Shakespeare would have had many duties; no doubt he acted many parts, and we know he

In the celebrated 1954 production of Shakespeare's *Hamlet,* Richard Burton takes leave of Claire Bloom as Ophelia.

appeared in two plays by his contemporary, Ben Jonson—*Every Man in His Humour* and *Sejanus*. In 1598, the Lord Chamberlain's men tore down The Theatre, brought the timbers south of the city, and used them to build a new theater, the Globe. The Globe would remain the principal public-theater venue for the rest of Shakespeare's career, complemented by court and private-theater performances.

Shakespeare became the most popular playwright in London. He profited handsomely from his efforts at the Globe and from the patronage of the court, particularly after James I came to the throne in 1603 and took on the Lord Chamberlain's company as his own King's Men. Shakespeare used his income to buy a large house, called New Place, in Stratford, and throughout his career added to his property there; he retired and returned to Stratford in 1613. He drew up a will shortly before he died in 1616, leaving property to his family and mentioning gifts for several of his friends, including members of the King's Men: Richard Burbage, John Heminges, and Henry Condell. Heminges and Condell proved true to Shakespeare, for in 1623 they took Shakespeare's plays and published them in a single large volume. In an era when plays were not regarded as "literature," this was an important event. Although many of Shakespeare's plays had been published individually during his lifetime, roughly half of Shakespeare's plays (*Macbeth, Antony and Cleopatra,* and *The Tempest,* for instance) existed only in manuscript form at Shakespeare's death and certainly would not have survived without the efforts of Heminges and Condell. This complete volume is now usually called the "First Folio," because it is printed in a large, **FOLIO**-sized format (about twice the dimensions of this book). The First Folio contains thirty-six of Shakespeare's plays; two more plays all or partly by Shakespeare and published in his lifetime (*Pericles* and *The Two Noble Kinsmen*) were left out of the Folio, and it is generally thought that Shakespeare contributed to a thirty-ninth play, *Sir Thomas More,* of which only a short manuscript section survives. More recently, several scholars have argued that Shakespeare collaborated on a history play, *Edward III.* Finally, although many people have advanced the thesis that someone else actually wrote the "Shakespeare" plays—Sir Francis Bacon, Francis Walsingham, the Earl of Oxford, among others—these claims belong to the realm of myth, not to the realm of history.

The range of Shakespeare's accomplishment as a playwright is astonishing. Early in his career, Shakespeare wrote two cycles of plays on English history—*Henry VI* (Parts 1, 2, and 3) and *Richard III;* and *Richard II, Henry IV* (Parts 1 and 2), and *Henry V*—that not only established a vogue for history plays but gave the English audience an epic version of the struggles that founded the Tudor and Stuart dynasties. Shakespeare's early comedies—*The Comedy of Errors, Two Gentlemen of Verona*—are very much in the vein of Plautus. Later comedies—*A Midsummer Night's Dream, As You Like It, Twelfth Night, The Merchant of Venice*—explore a variety of complex relations between love, sexuality, adulthood, ethnic discrimination, power, politics, and money. To many audiences today, Shakespeare is most remembered for *Hamlet* and the magisterial series of tragedies that followed, including *Othello, King Lear,* and *Macbeth.* Shakespeare's achievements often began with experimentation. The major tragedies benefitted from his earlier efforts in the mode of the Roman playwright Seneca in *Titus Andronicus,* in morality drama in *Richard III,* in romantic tragedy in *Romeo and Juliet,* and political intrigue–drama in *Julius Caesar.* In his final years as a playwright, Shakespeare seems to have collaborated with John Fletcher on a few occasions and to have turned his hand to plays in the vein of "tragicomedy," now generally called **RO-MANCE:** *Pericles, Cymbeline, The Winter's Tale,* and *The Tempest.*

HAMLET

In his landmark study, *The Idea of a Theater,* actor/scholar Francis Fergusson characterized *Hamlet* as one of the "sphinxes of literature," a play that has repeatedly drawn actors, audiences, and scholars into its labyrinthine mystery. Yet while *Hamlet,* like the brooding young

prince of Denmark, may now seem like a difficult and philosophical problem, to its original audiences the play was a version of a popular genre on the Elizabethan stage, the revenge
tragedy. As in many of his other plays, Shakespeare adapted his tragedy from a variety of
known materials. The story of Amlethus, a disinherited Danish prince who uses feigned
madness and cunning to avenge his father's murder and regain the throne from his villainous uncle, dates from the twelfth-century *Historia Danica* of the Danish historian Saxo
Grammaticus; it was later adapted as a tragic narrative by François de Belleforest and included in his *Histoires tragiques* in 1576. Although Shakespeare may have known these versions, it is more certain that he knew a now-lost play on the subject of Hamlet's revenge
that was staged in the 1580s. This play—usually called the *Ur-Hamlet* by scholars—was possibly written by Thomas Kyd, the author of another popular revenge tragedy, *The Spanish
Tragedy.* While little is known about this play, we do know that it had at least one element
of Shakespeare's play; in 1596, the playwright and novelist Thomas Lodge remarked on a
play in which a pale ghost "cried so miserably at the Theater, like an oyster-wife, 'Hamlet,
revenge!'"

A ghost, a sinister and deceptive family, a court full of busybodies and spies, a broken
romance, an elaborate play-within-the-play, a command, sometimes from beyond the grave,
to take revenge, an elaborate finale in which the stage is littered with corpses—these devices
were common in revenge tragedies preceding Shakespeare's play, such as *The Spanish Tragedy,*
and common also in those which capitalized on *Hamlet's* success in 1601, plays like John
Marston's *The Malcontent* and Cyril Tourneur's *The Revenger's Tragedy* (which opens with a
man speaking to a skull) and John Webster's *The White Devil. Hamlet* avails itself of all these
devices, but it also reflects and refracts them; the play seems to question what it means to
take action, simply to act, let alone take revenge, in a world of such complete duplicity that
any behavior might seem the treacherous "actions that a man might play." In his famous essay, "The World of *Hamlet,*" Maynard Mack suggests that the play is in the "interrogative
mood": not only does Hamlet repeatedly ask questions of himself and others ("To be or not
to be . . . ," "Is it not monstrous . . . ," and so on), but much of the action of the play involves, as Polonius suggests, using theatrical "indirections" to "find directions out": Polonius
sends Reynaldo to spread dishonorable rumors about Laertes, to see whether Laertes is being virtuous in Paris; Claudius and Polonius "stage" Ophelia for Hamlet, hoping to discover
whether he's mad for revenge or madly in love; Hamlet hopes that the players' *The Murder
of Gonzago* will reveal Claudius's guilt; Polonius hides fatally behind the arras while Hamlet
interrogates Gertrude; Claudius stages a "duel" between Hamlet and Laertes that is really a
design for murder.

The world of *Hamlet* is a world in which appearances sometimes deceive and sometimes speak the truth: not being able to read the signs—as Ophelia, Rosencrantz and
Guildenstern, and Polonius all discover—can be fatal. Indeed, the play's obsession with
seeming ("Seems, madam? Nay, it is. I know not 'seems,'" Hamlet declares in his first scene
in the play) perhaps explains its obsession with the arts of seeming, with acting, performance, theater. In *Hamlet,* Shakespeare undertakes an extended meditation on the purpose
and limits of theater. Hamlet, of course, is quite familiar with the theater, and Shakespeare
clearly characterizes the troupe of players as his audience's contemporaries; not only is the
company all male, but they seem to have left the city—as many professional companies did
in the late 1590s—as a result of the "war of the theaters," the contemporary vogue for companies of boy-actors performing satirical plays. Moreover, Hamlet's famous advice to the
players (3.2) suggests that he has a keen eye for performance. He chastens the actors not to
"mouth it, as many of our players do," not to "saw the air too much with your hand," but
to "Suit the action to the word, the word to the action." Yet in *Hamlet,* words and actions
are more often than not suited to deception, to the extent that to Hamlet "this goodly
frame, the earth, seems . . . a sterile promontory." Hamlet's blatant reference to the Globe

itself—an actor, surrounded by the circular frame of the Globe, standing on the bare plat-form of the stage—suggests a skeptical regard for the theater's creation. While plays like *A Midsummer Night's Dream* or perhaps *The Tempest* suggest the theater's ability to present heal-ing fictions, the theater in *Hamlet* is presented from a more ironic, even disaffected perspec-tive: to be trapped in a theatrical world, a world where performance outruns truth, is to be trapped in a world of empty and sterile pretending.

Shakespeare was clearly captivated by the character of Hamlet, which is often described as the richest acting role in the theatrical repertoire. But the theatricality that besets Hamlet in the shady world of Elsinore also poses problems for Hamlet's many interpreters, not only for Polonius and Claudius—who spend much of the play trying to "read" Hamlet, figure him out—but for the generations of actors, audiences, and scholars who have attempted to "pluck out the heart of [his] mystery." The difficulties of sounding Hamlet, how-ever, are also part of the play's elaborate design. From his opening scene in the play, in which Hamlet both wears the conventional black of mourning and chides his mother for presuming that he is seeming to be in mourning, Hamlet's performance challenges his audiences (both onstage and off) to "read" him, to interpret his character through the signs and signals of his behavior. That is, Hamlet presents the audience with the same challenges that any actor does, inviting us to interpret "that within" from the various behaviors that pass "show." And, con-trary to Laurence Olivier—whose brilliant film of the play opens with a voice intoning that *Hamlet* is the story "of a man who could not make up his mind"—Hamlet seems to act deci-sively throughout the play; what's difficult about reading Hamlet is that it's hard to tell when he's *acting* and when he's "acting in earnest." Hamlet feigns madness in some scenes, but seems madly out of control in others, such as the "nunnery" scene with Ophelia or the scene in Gertrude's closet. He asks the player to act the part of vengeful Pyrrhus, then seems to adopt the murderous swagger of the stage revenger, and then to question his performance ("Why, what an ass am I"). He directs the players to insert a scene into *The Murder of Gonzago* to trick Claudius into revealing his guilt, and then can't seem to keep himself off the stage, interrupt-ing and interpreting the play as they play it. He's so offended when Laertes stagily leaps into Ophelia's grave that he outperforms Laertes's overacting: "Nay, an thou'lt mouth, / I'll rant as well as thou." Even Hamlet's soliloquies are problematic in this regard. For although we might think that we hear the "true" Hamlet when he speaks alone onstage, how can we know that Hamlet isn't trying on another role, either for his own benefit or ours—as he seems to do when he plays the revenger in the "O what a rogue and peasant slave am I" speech? And as the play proceeds, Hamlet's soliloquies become less frequent, and less revealing: when he re-turns from England in Act 5—having sent his friends Rosencrantz and Guildenstern to their death—the play provides him with no more solo speeches; like the court, we have only Hamlet's abrupt and irritable actions to go on.

Hamlet was evidently a success when it was first performed in 1600 or 1601; a pirated version of the play (the so-called bad quarto, Q1) was published in 1603, presumably be-cause the play's popularity suggested that a published text could make some money. A ver-sion of the play authorized by the King's Men was published in 1604 (the second quarto, Q2), and the play was later included in the 1623 Folio (F); although Q1 is the most corrupt version of the play, Q2 and F are by no means identical, and most modern texts collate elements of both versions.

From its inception, *Hamlet* has been a popular play with actors and audiences, and from Richard Burbage's creation of the role, Hamlet has been a mark of distinction in the history of English acting: the Restoration actor Thomas Betterton and the great eighteenth-century actor David Garrick were both admired in the part (Henry Fielding's novel *Tom Jones* contains a memorable parody of Garrick's performance). In the late nine-teenth century Sir Henry Irving, the first actor to be knighted in England, gave a cele-brated performance in which Hamlet never left the stage, but several other characters

(Rosencrantz and Guildenstern, for instance) were cut entirely. In the twentieth century, the play has, if anything, confirmed its reputation as an obligatory test for great actors, who have given a host of brilliant performances: Sir John Gielgud and Sir Laurence Olivier both produced fine stage versions of the play, and Olivier later won a Best Film Academy Award for his film version. Since World War II, Richard Burton, Jonathan Pryce, Derek Jacobi, and Michael Pennington are among the many actors to have given distinguished performances of this demanding play. The complexity of the play is something that faces actors even more immediately than readers of the play, because they will have to find a way to suit their acting to Hamlet's wild and whirling character. As Michael Pennington remarks in an essay on playing Hamlet, "To pull it off will take the actor further down into his psyche, memory and imagination, and further outwards to the limits of his technical knowledge and equipment, than he has probably been before."[1]

---

[1] Philip Brockbank, ed., *Players of Shakespeare: Essays in Shakespearean Performance by Twelve Players with the Royal Shakespeare Company* (Cambridge: Cambridge University Press, 1985), 117.

HAMLET

William Shakespeare

EDITED BY CYRUS HOY

CHARACTERS

CLAUDIUS, *King of Denmark*
HAMLET, *son to the late, and nephew to the present king*
POLONIUS, *Lord Chamberlain*
HORATIO, *friend to Hamlet*
LAERTES, *son to Polonius*
VOLTEMAND
CORNELIUS
ROSENCRANTZ *courtiers*
GUILDENSTERN
OSRIC
A GENTLEMAN
A PRIEST
MARCELLUS *officers*
BERNARDO

FRANCISCO, *a soldier*
REYNALDO, *servant to Polonius*
PLAYERS
TWO CLOWNS, *grave-diggers*
FORTINBRAS, *Prince of Norway*
A NORWEGIAN CAPTAIN
ENGLISH AMBASSADORS
GERTRUDE, *Queen of Denmark, and mother of Hamlet*
OPHELIA, *daughter to Polonius*
GHOST OF HAMLET'S FATHER
LORDS, LADIES, OFFICERS, SOLDIERS, SAILORS, MESSENGERS, *and* ATTENDANTS

SCENE: *Denmark.*

ACT ONE

SCENE I

Enter BERNARDO *and* FRANCISCO, *two sentinels.*

BERNARDO: Who's there?
FRANCISCO: Nay, answer me. Stand, and unfold yourself.
BERNARDO: Long live the king!
FRANCISCO: Bernardo?
5 BERNARDO: He.
FRANCISCO: You come most carefully upon your hour.
BERNARDO: 'Tis now struck twelve. Get thee to bed, Francisco.
FRANCISCO: For this relief much thanks. 'Tis bitter cold,
    And I am sick at heart.
10 BERNARDO: Have you had quiet guard?
FRANCISCO: Not a mouse stirring.
BERNARDO: Well, good night.
    If you do meet Horatio and Marcellus,
    The rivals of my watch, bid them make haste.

(*Enter* HORATIO *and* MARCELLUS.)

FRANCISCO: I think I hear them. Stand, ho! Who is there?
15 HORATIO: Friends to this ground.
MARCELLUS: And liegemen to the Dane.
FRANCISCO: Give you good night.
MARCELLUS: O, farewell, honest soldier!
    Who hath relieved you?
FRANCISCO: Bernardo hath my place.
    Give you good night.

(*Exit* FRANCISCO.)

MARCELLUS: Holla, Bernardo!
BERNARDO: Say—
    What, is Horatio there?

HORATIO: A piece of him.
BERNARDO: Welcome, Horatio. Welcome, good Marcellus.   20
HORATIO: What, has this thing appeared again to-night?
BERNARDO: I have seen nothing.
MARCELLUS: Horatio says 'tis but our fantasy,
    And will not let belief take hold of him
    Touching this dreaded sight twice seen of us.   25
    Therefore I have entreated him along
    With us to watch the minutes of this night,
    That if again this apparition come,
    He may approve our eyes and speak to it.
HORATIO: Tush, tush, 'twill not appear.   30
BERNARDO: Sit down awhile,
    And let us once again assail your ears,
    That are so fortified against our story,
    What we have two nights seen.
HORATIO: Well, sit we down,
    And let us hear Bernardo speak of this.
BERNARDO: Last night of all,   35
    When yond same star that's westward from the pole
    Had made his course t' illume that part of heaven
    Where now it burns, Marcellus and myself,
    The bell then beating one—

(*Enter* GHOST.)

MARCELLUS: Peace, break thee off. Look where it comes again.   40
BERNARDO: In the same figure like the king that's dead.
MARCELLUS: Thou art a scholar; speak to it, Horatio.
BERNARDO: Looks 'a not like the king? Mark it, Horatio.
HORATIO: Most like. It harrows me with fear and wonder.
BERNARDO: It would be spoke to.   45
MARCELLUS: Question it, Horatio.
HORATIO: What art thou that usurp'st this time of night
    Together with that fair and warlike form

I.i. 13 **rivals** partners   15 **Dane** King of Denmark

29 **approve** confirm   36 **pole** polestar   44 **harrows** afflicts, distresses

In which the majesty of buried Denmark
Did sometimes march? By heaven I charge thee, speak.

50 MARCELLUS: It is offended.

BERNARDO: See, it stalks away.

HORATIO: Stay. Speak, speak. I charge thee, speak.

(*Exit* GHOST.)

MARCELLUS: 'Tis gone and will not answer.

BERNARDO: How now, Horatio! You tremble and look pale.
Is not this something more than fantasy?

55 What think you on't?

HORATIO: Before my God, I might not this believe
Without the sensible and true avouch
Of mine own eyes.

MARCELLUS: Is it not like the king?

HORATIO: As thou art to thyself.

60 Such was the very armour he had on
When he the ambitious Norway combated.
So frowned he once when, in an angry parle,
He smote the sledded Polacks on the ice.
'Tis strange.

65 MARCELLUS: Thus twice before, and jump at this dead hour,
With martial stalk hath he gone by our watch.

HORATIO: In what particular thought to work I know not,
But in the gross and scope of mine opinion,
This bodes some strange eruption to our state.

70 MARCELLUS: Good now, sit down, and tell me he that knows,
Why this same strict and most observant watch
So nightly toils the subject of the land,
And why such daily cast of brazen cannon
And foreign mart for implements of war;

75 Why such impress of shipwrights, whose sore task
Does not divide the Sunday from the week.
What might be toward that this sweaty haste
Doth make the night joint-laborer with the day?
Who is't that can inform me?

HORATIO: That can I.

80 At least, the whisper goes so. Our last king,
Whose image even but now appeared to us,
Was as you know by Fortinbras of Norway,
Thereto pricked on by a most emulate pride,
Dared to the combat; in which our valiant Hamlet

85 (For so this side of our known world esteemed him)
Did slay this Fortinbras; who by a sealed compact
Well ratified by law and heraldry,
Did forfeit, with his life, all those his lands
Which he stood seized of, to the conqueror;

90 Against the which a moiety competent

Was gagèd by our king; which had returned
To the inheritance of Fortinbras,
Had he been vanquisher; as, by the same comart
And carriage of the article designed,
His fell to Hamlet. Now, sir, young Fortinbras,   95
Of unimprovèd mettle hot and full,
Hath in the skirts of Norway here and there
Sharked up a list of lawless resolutes
For food and diet to some enterprise
That hath a stomach in't; which is no other,   100
As it doth well appear unto our state,
But to recover of us by strong hand
And terms compulsatory, those foresaid lands
So by his father lost; and this, I take it,
Is the main motive of our preparations,   105
The source of this our watch, and the chief head
Of this post-haste and romage in the land.

BERNARDO: I think it be no other but e'en so.
Well may it sort that this portentous figure
Comes armèd through our watch; so like the king   110
That was and is the question of these wars.

HORATIO: A mote it is to trouble the mind's eye.
In the most high and palmy state of Rome,
A little ere the mightiest Julius fell,
The graves stood tenantless and the sheeted dead   115
Did squeak and gibber in the Roman streets;
As stars with trains of fire, and dews of blood,
Disasters in the sun; and the moist star,
Upon whose influence Neptune's empire stands,
Was sick almost to doomsday with eclipse.   120
And even the like precurse of feared events,
As harbingers preceding still the fates
And prologue to the omen coming on,
Have heaven and earth together demonstrated
Unto our climatures and countrymen.   125

(*Enter* GHOST.)

But soft, behold, lo where it comes again!
I'll cross it though it blast me.—Stay, illusion.

([GHOST] *spreads his arms.*)

If thou hast any sound or use of voice,
Speak to me.
If there be any good thing to be done,   130
That may to thee do ease, and grace to me,
Speak to me.
If thou art privy to thy country's fate,
Which happily foreknowing may avoid,

---

48 **buried Denmark** the buried King of Denmark   49 **sometimes** formerly   57 **sensible** confirmed by one of the senses   61 **Norway** King of Norway   62 **parle** parley   63 **sledded Polacks** the Poles mounted on sleds or sledges   65 **jump** just, exactly   68 **gross and scope** general drift   72 **toils** causes to toil; **subject** people   74 **mart** traffic, bargaining   75 **impress** conscription   77 **toward** imminent, impending   83 **emulate** ambitious   87 **heraldry** the law of arms, regulating tournaments and state combats   89 **seized** possessed   90 **moiety competent** sufficient portion

91 **gagèd** pledged   93 **comart** joint bargain   94 **carriage** import   96 **unimprovèd** unrestrained   98 **Sharked up** picked up indiscriminately   100 **stomach** spice of adventure   106 **head** fountainhead   107 **romage** turmoil   109 **sort** suit, be in accordance   112 **mote** particle of dust   113 **palmy** flourishing   115 **sheeted** in shrouds   118 **Disasters** ominous signs; **moist star** the moon   121 **precurse** heralding, foreshadowing   122 **harbingers** forerunners; **still** ever   123 **omen** ominous event   125 **climatures** regions   127 **cross it** cross its path   134 **happily** haply, perchance

135 O, speak!
Or if thou hast uphoarded in thy life
Extorted treasure in the womb of earth,
For which, they say, you spirits oft walk in death,

(*The cock crows.*)

Speak of it. Stay, and speak. Stop it, Marcellus.
140 MARCELLUS: Shall I strike at it with my partisan?
HORATIO: Do, if it will not stand.
BERNARDO: 'Tis here.
HORATIO: 'Tis here!

(*Exit* GHOST.)

MARCELLUS: 'Tis gone!
We do it wrong, being so majestical,
To offer it the show of violence;
145 For it is as the air, invulnerable,
And our vain blows malicious mockery.
BERNARDO: It was about to speak when the cock crew.
HORATIO: And then it started like a guilty thing
Upon a fearful summons. I have heard
150 The cock, that is the trumpet to the morn,
Doth with his lofty and shrill-sounding throat
Awake the god of day and at his warning,
Whether in sea or fire, in earth or air,
Th' extravagant and erring spirit hies
155 To his confine; and of the truth herein
This present object made probation.
MARCELLUS: It faded on the crowing of the cock.
Some say that ever 'gainst that season comes
Wherein our Saviour's birth is celebrated,
160 The bird of dawning singeth all night long,
And then, they say, no spirit dare stir abroad.
The nights are wholesome, then no planets strike,
No fairy takes, nor witch hath power to charm,
So hallowed and so gracious is that time.
165 HORATIO: So have I heard and do in part believe it.
But look, the morn in russet mantle clad
Walks o'er the dew of yon high eastward hill.
Break we our watch up, and by my advice
Let us impart what we have seen to-night
170 Unto young Hamlet, for, upon my life
This spirit, dumb to us, will speak to him.
Do you consent we shall acquaint him with it,
As needful in our loves, fitting our duty?
MARCELLUS: Let's do't, I pray, and I this morning know
175 Where we shall find him most convenient.

(*Exeunt.*)

SCENE II

Flourish. Enter CLAUDIUS, KING OF DENMARK, GERTRUDE THE
QUEEN, COUNCILLORS, [*including*] POLONIUS *and his son* LAERTES,
HAMLET, *cum aliis* [*including* VOLTEMAND *and* CORNELIUS.]

---

140 **partisan** pike   154 **extravagant** straying, vagrant; **erring**
wandering   156 **probation** proof   158 **'gainst** just before
162 **strike** blast, destroy by malign influence   163 **takes** be-
witches

I.ii. s.d. **cum aliis** with others

KING: Though yet of Hamlet our dear brother's death
The memory be green, and that it us befitted
To bear our hearts in grief, and our whole kingdom
To be contracted in one brow of woe,
Yet so far hath discretion fought with nature   5
That we with wisest sorrow think on him,
Together with remembrance of ourselves.
Therefore our sometime sister, now our queen,
Th' imperial jointress to this warlike state,
Have we, as 'twere with a defeated joy,   10
With an auspicious and a dropping eye,
With mirth in funeral and with dirge in marriage,
In equal scale weighing delight and dole,
Taken to wife; nor have we herein barred
Your better wisdoms, which have freely gone   15
With this affair along. For all, our thanks.
Now follows that you know young Fortinbras,
Holding a weak supposal of our worth,
Or thinking by our late dear brother's death
Our state to be disjoint and out of frame,   20
Colleaguèd with this dream of his advantage,
He hath not failed to pester us with message
Importing the surrender of those lands
Lost by his father, with all bands of law,
To our most valiant brother. So much for him.   25
Now for ourself, and for this time of meeting,
Thus much the business is: we have here writ
To Norway, uncle of young Fortinbras—
Who, impotent and bedrid, scarcely hears
Of this his nephew's purpose—to suppress   30
His further gait herein, in that the levies,
The lists, and full proportions are all made
Out of his subject; and we here dispatch
You, good Cornelius, and you, Voltemand,
For bearers of this greeting to old Norway,   35
Giving to you no further personal power
To business with the king, more than the scope
Of these delated articles allow.
Farewell, and let your haste commend your duty.
CORNELIUS: ⎫ In that and all things will we show our duty 40
VOLTEMAND: ⎭
KING: We doubt it nothing, heartily farewell.

(*Exeunt* VOLTEMAND *and* CORNELIUS.)

And now, Laertes, what's the news with you?
You told us of some suit. What is't, Laertes?
You cannot speak of reason to the Dane
And lose your voice. What wouldst thou beg, Laertes, 45
That shall not be my offer, not thy asking?
The head is not more native to the heart,
The hand more instrumental to the mouth,
Than is the throne of Denmark to thy father.
What wouldst thou have, Laertes?   50

---

9 **jointress** a widow who holds a jointure or life interest in an
estate   14 **barred** excluded   21 **Colleaguèd** united   31 **gait**
proceeding   32 **proportions** forces or supplies for war   38
delated expressly stated   44 **Dane** King of Denmark   45 **lose**
your voice speak in vain   47 **native** joined by nature   48 **in-**
strumental serviceable

LAERTES: My dread lord,
   Your leave and favour to return to France,
   From whence, though willingly, I came to Denmark
   To show my duty in your coronation,
   Yet now I must confess, that duty done,
55   My thoughts and wishes bend again toward France,
   And bow them to your gracious leave and pardon.
KING: Have you your father's leave? What says Polonius?
POLONIUS: He hath, my lord, wrung from me my slow leave
   By laborsome petition, and at last
60   Upon his will I sealed my hard consent.
   I do beseech you give him leave to go.
KING: Take thy fair hour, Laertes. Time be thine,
   And thy best graces spend it at thy will.
   But now, my cousin Hamlet, and my son—
65 HAMLET: (Aside.) A little more than kin, and less than kind.
KING: How is it that the clouds still hang on you?
HAMLET: Not so, my lord. I am too much in the sun.
QUEEN: Good Hamlet, cast thy nighted color off,
   And let thine eye look like a friend on Denmark.
70   Do not for ever with thy vailèd lids
   Seek for thy noble father in the dust.
   Thou know'st 'tis common—all that lives must die,
   Passing through nature to eternity.
HAMLET: Ay, madam, it is common.
QUEEN: If it be,
75   Why seems it so particular with thee?
HAMLET: Seems, madam? Nay, it is. I know not 'seems.'
   'Tis not alone my inky cloak, good mother,
   Nor customary suits of solemn black,
   Nor windy suspiration of forced breath,
80   No, nor the fruitful river in the eye,
   Nor the dejected haviour of the visage,
   Together with all forms, moods, shapes of grief,
   That can denote me truly. These indeed seem,
   For they are actions that a man might play,
85   But I have that within which passeth show—
   These but the trappings and the suits of woe.
KING: 'Tis sweet and commendable in your nature, Hamlet,
   To give these mourning duties to your father,
   But you must know your father lost a father,
90   That father lost, lost his, and the survivor bound
   In filial obligation for some term
   To do obsequious sorrow. But to persever
   In obstinate condolement is a course
   Of impious stubbornness. 'Tis unmanly grief.
95   It shows a will most incorrect to heaven,
   A heart unfortified, a mind impatient,
   An understanding simple and unschooled.
   For what we know must be, and is as common
   As any the most vulgar thing to sense,
100   Why should we in our peevish opposition
   Take it to heart? Fie, 'tis a fault to heaven,
   A fault against the dead, a fault to nature,

To reason most absurd, whose common theme
Is death of fathers, and who still hath cried,
From the first corse till he that died to-day,   105
'This must be so.' We pray you throw to earth
This unprevailing woe, and think of us
As of a father, for let the world take note
You are the most immediate to our throne,
And with no less nobility of love   110
Than that which dearest father bears his son
Do I impart toward you. For your intent
In going back to school in Wittenberg,
It is most retrograde to our desire,
And we beseech you, bend you to remain   115
Here in the cheer and comfort of our eye,
Our chiefest courtier, cousin, and our son.
QUEEN: Let not thy mother lose her prayers, Hamlet.
   I pray thee stay with us, go not to Wittenberg.
HAMLET: I shall in all my best obey you, madam.   120
KING: Why, 'tis a loving and a fair reply.
   Be as ourself in Denmark. Madam, come.
   This gentle and unforced accord of Hamlet
   Sits smiling to my heart, in grace whereof,
   No jocund health that Denmark drinks to-day   125
   But the great cannon to the clouds shall tell,
   And the king's rouse the heaven shall bruit again,
   Respeaking earthly thunder. Come away.

(Flourish. Exeunt all but HAMLET.)

HAMLET: O, that this too too sallied flesh would melt,
   Thaw and resolve itself into a dew,   130
   Or that the Everlasting had not fixed
   His canon 'gainst self-slaughter. O God, God,
   How weary, stale, flat, and unprofitable
   Seem to me all the uses of this world!
   Fie on't, ah, fie, 'tis an unweeded garden   135
   That grows to seed. Things rank and gross in nature
   Possess it merely. That it should come to this,
   But two months dead, nay, not so much, not two.
   So excellent a king, that was to this
   Hyperion to a satyr, so loving to my mother,   140
   That he might not beteem the winds of heaven
   Visit her face too roughly. Heaven and earth,
   Must I remember? Why, she would hang on him
   As if increase of appetite had grown
   By what it fed on, and yet, within a month—   145
   Let me not think on't. Frailty, thy name is woman—
   A little month, or ere those shoes were old
   With which she followed my poor father's body

---

56 **pardon** indulgence 60 **hard** reluctant 64 **cousin** kinsman of any kind except parent, child, brother, or sister 65 **kin** related as nephew; **kind** (1) affectionate (2) natural, lawful 70 **vailèd** lowered 75 **particular** personal, individual 92 **obsequious** dutiful in performing funeral obsequies or manifesting regard for the dead; **persever** persevere

105 **corse** corpse 114 **retrograde** contrary 127 **rouse** full draught of liquor; **bruit** echo 129 **sallied** sullied. "Sallied" is the reading of *Quarto 2 (Q2, also Q1). Folio (F)* reads "solid." Since Hamlet's primary concern is with the fact of the flesh's impurity, not with its corporeality, the choice as between Q and F clearly lies with Q. "Sally" is a legitimate sixteenth-century form of "sully"; it occurs in Dekker's *Patient Grissil* (1.1.12), printed in 1603, as F.T. Bowers has pointed out (in "Hamlet's 'Sullied' or 'Solid' Flesh. A Bibliographical Case-History," *Shakespeare Survey* 9 [1956]: p. 44); and it occurs as a noun at 2.1.39 of *Hamlet* 132 **canon** law 137 **merely** entirely 140 **Hyperion** the sun god 141 **beteem** allowed

Like Niobe, all tears, why she—
150 O God, a beast that wants discourse of reason
Would have mourned longer—married with my uncle,
My father's brother, but no more like my father
Than I to Hercules. Within a month,
Ere yet the salt of most unrighteous tears
155 Had left the flushing in her gallèd eyes,
She married. O, most wicked speed, to post
With such dexterity to incestuous sheets!
It is not, nor it cannot come to good.
But break my heart, for I must hold my tongue.

(*Enter* HORATIO, MARCELLUS, *and* BERNARDO.)

160 HORATIO: Hail to your lordship!
HAMLET: I am glad to see you well.
Horatio—or I do forget myself.
HORATIO: The same, my lord, and your poor servant ever.
HAMLET: Sir, my good friend, I'll change that name with you.
And what make you from Wittenberg, Horatio?
165 Marcellus?
MARCELLUS: My good lord!
HAMLET: I am very glad to see you. (*To* BERNARDO.) Good
even, sir.—
But what, in faith, make you from Wittenberg?
HORATIO: A truant disposition, good my lord.
170 HAMLET: I would not hear your enemy say so,
Nor shall you do my ear that violence
To make it truster of your own report
Against yourself. I know you are no truant.
But what is your affair in Elsinore?
175 We'll teach you to drink deep ere you depart.
HORATIO: My lord, I came to see your father's funeral.
HAMLET: I prithee, do not mock me, fellow-student,
I think it was to see my mother's wedding.
HORATIO: Indeed, my lord, it followed hard upon.
180 HAMLET: Thrift, thrift, Horatio. The funeral baked meats
Did coldly furnish forth the marriage tables.
Would I had met my dearest foe in heaven
Or ever I had seen that day, Horatio!
My father—methinks I see my father.
185 HORATIO: Where, my lord?
HAMLET: In my mind's eye, Horatio.
HORATIO: I saw him once, 'a was a goodly king.
HAMLET: 'A was a man, take him for all in all,
I shall not look upon his like again.
HORATIO: My lord, I think I saw him yesternight.
190 HAMLET: Saw who?
HORATIO: My lord, the king your father.
HAMLET: The king my father?
HORATIO: Season your admiration for a while
With an attent ear, till I may deliver

Upon the witness of these gentlemen
This marvel to you.   195
HAMLET: For God's love, let me hear!
HORATIO: Two nights together had these gentlemen,
Marcellus and Bernardo, on their watch
In the dead waste and middle of the night
Been thus encountered. A figure like your father,
Armed at point exactly, cap-a-pe,   200
Appears before them, and with solemn march
Goes slow and stately by them. Thrice he walked
By their oppressed and fear-surprisèd eyes
Within his truncheon's length, whilst they, distilled
Almost to jelly with the act of fear,   205
Stand dumb and speak not to him. This to me
In dreadful secrecy impart they did,
And I with them the third night kept the watch,
Where, as they had delivered, both in time,
Form of the thing, each word made true and good,   210
The apparition comes. I knew your father.
These hands are not more like.
HAMLET: But where was this?
MARCELLUS: My lord, upon the platform where we watch.
HAMLET: Did you not speak to it?
HORATIO: My lord, I did,
But answer made it none. Yet once methought   215
It lifted up it head and did address
Itself to motion, like as it would speak;
But even then the morning cock crew loud,
And at the sound it shrunk in haste away
And vanished from our sight.   220
HAMLET: 'Tis very strange.
HORATIO: As I do live, my honoured lord, 'tis true,
And we did think it writ down in our duty
To let you know of it.
HAMLET: Indeed, sirs, but
This troubles me. Hold you the watch to-night?
ALL: We do, my lord.   225
HAMLET: Armed, say you?
ALL: Armed, my lord.
HAMLET: From top to toe?
ALL: My lord, from head to foot.
HAMLET: Then saw you not his face.
HORATIO: O yes, my lord, he wore his beaver up.
HAMLET: What, looked he frowningly?
HORATIO: A countenance more in sorrow than in anger.   230
HAMLET: Pale or red?
HORATIO: Nay, very pale.
HAMLET: And fixed his eyes upon you?
HORATIO: Most constantly.
HAMLET: I would I had been there.
HORATIO: It would have much amazed you.
HAMLET: Very like.
Stayed it long?   235
HORATIO: While one with moderate haste might tell
a hundred.
BOTH: Longer, longer.

---

149 **Niobe** wife of Amphion, King of Thebes, she boasted of
having more children than Leto and was punished when her
seven sons and seven daughters were slain by Apollo and
Artemis, children of Leto; in her grief she was changed by Zeus
into a stone, which continually dropped tears   150 **wants** lacks;
discourse of reason the reasoning faculty   155 **gallèd** sore
from rubbing or chafing   163 **change** exchange   164 **make**
do   182 **dearest** direst   192 **Season** temper, moderate; **admiration** wonder, astonishment

---

200 **at point** exactly in every particular; **cap-a-pe** from head to
foot   204 **truncheon** military leader's baton   216 **it** its   228
beaver the part of the helmet that was drawn down to cover the
face   235 **tell** count

HORATIO: Not when I saw't.

HAMLET: His beard was grizzled, no?

HORATIO: It was as I have seen it in his life,
    A sable silvered.

HAMLET: I will watch to-night.
240   Perchance 'twill walk again.

HORATIO: I warr'nt it will.

HAMLET: If it assume my noble father's person,
    I'll speak to it though hell itself should gape
    And bid me hold my peace. I pray you all,
    If you have hitherto concealed this sight,
245   Let it be tenable in your silence still,
    And whatsomever else shall hap to-night,
    Give it an understanding but no tongue.
    I will requite your loves. So fare you well.
    Upon the platform 'twixt eleven and twelve
250   I'll visit you.

ALL: Our duty to your honor.

HAMLET: Your loves, as mine to you. Farewell.

(*Exeunt* [*all but* HAMLET].)

    My father's spirit in arms? All is not well.
    I doubt some foul play. Would the night were come!
    Till then sit still, my soul. Foul deeds will rise,
255   Though all the earth o'erwhelm them, to men's eyes.

(*Exit*.)

SCENE III

Enter LAERTES *and* OPHELIA *his sister.*

LAERTES: My necessaries are embarked. Farewell.
    And, sister, as the winds give benefit
    And convoy is assistant, do not sleep,
    But let me hear from you.

OPHELIA: Do you doubt that?

5 LAERTES: For Hamlet, and the trifling of his favor,
    Hold it a fashion and a toy in blood,
    A violet in the youth of primy nature,
    Forward, not permanent, sweet, not lasting,
    The perfume and suppliance of a minute,
10 No more.

OPHELIA: No more but so?

LAERTES: Think it no more.
    For nature crescent does not grow alone
    In thews and bulk, but as this temple waxes
    The inward service of the mind and soul
    Grows wide withal. Perhaps he loves you now,
15   And now no soil nor cautel doth besmirch
    The virtue of his will, but you must fear,
    His greatness weighed, his will is not his own,
    For he himself is subject to his birth.

He may not, as unvalued persons do,
Carve for himself, for on his choice depends   20
The safety and health of this whole state,
And therefore must his choice be circumscribed
Unto the voice and yielding of that body
Whereof he is the head. Then if he says he loves you,
It fits your wisdom so far to believe it   25
As he in his particular act and place
May give his saying deed, which is no further
Than the main voice of Denmark goes withal.
Then weigh what loss your honor may sustain
If with too credent ear you list his songs,   30
Or lose your heart, or your chaste treasure open
To his unmastered importunity.
Fear it, Ophelia, fear it, my dear sister,
And keep you in the rear of your affection,
Out of the shot and danger of desire.   35
The chariest maid is prodigal enough
If she unmask her beauty to the moon.
Virtue itself scapes not calumnious strokes.
The canker galls the infants of the spring
Too oft before their buttons be disclosed,   40
And in the morn and liquid dew of youth
Contagious blastments are most imminent.
Be wary then; best safety lies in fear.
Youth to itself rebels, though none else near.

OPHELIA: I shall the effect of this good lesson keep   45
    As watchman to my heart. But, good my brother,
    Do not as some ungracious pastors do,
    Show me the steep and thorny way to heaven,
    Whiles like a puffed and reckless libertine
    Himself the primrose path of dalliance treads   50
    And recks not his own rede.

LAERTES: O, fear me not.

(*Enter* POLONIUS.)

    I stay too long. But here my father comes.
    A double blessing is a double grace;
    Occasion smiles upon a second leave.

POLONIUS: Yet here, Laertes? Aboard, aboard, for shame!   55
    The wind sits in the shoulder of your sail,
    And you are stayed for. There, my blessing with thee,
    And these few precepts in thy memory
    Look thou character. Give thy thoughts no tongue,
    Nor any unproportioned thought his act.   60
    Be thou familiar, but by no means vulgar.
    Those friends thou hast, and their adoption tried,
    Grapple them to thy soul with hoops of steel,
    But do not dull thy palm with entertainment
    Of each new-hatched, unfledged courage. Beware   65
    Of entrance to a quarrel, but being in,

---

237 **grizzled** grayish   239 **sable silvered** black mixed with white   245 **tenable** retained   246 **whatsomever** whatsover 253 **doubt** suspect

I.iii. 6 **fashion** the creation of a season only; **toy in blood** passing fancy 7 **primy** of the springtime 11 **crescent** growing 12 **thews** sinews, strength; **this temple** the body 15 **cautel** deceit 16 **will** desire 17 **greatness weighed** high position considered

19 **unvalued persons** persons of no social importance 20 **Carve for himself** act according to his own inclination 23 **yielding** assent 30 **credent** trusting 34 **affection** feeling 39 **canker** canker-worm (which feeds on roses); **galls** injures 40 **buttons** buds 42 **blastments** blights 51 **recks** regards; **rede** counsel 59 **character** engrave 60 **unproportioned** inordinate 61 **vulgar** common 65 **courage** young blood, man of spirit

Bear't that th' opposèd may beware of thee.
Give every man thy ear, but few thy voice;
Take each man's censure, but reserve thy judgement.
70 Costly thy habit as thy purse can buy,
But not expressed in fancy; rich not gaudy,
For the apparel oft proclaims the man,
And they in France of the best rank and station
Are of a most select and generous chief in that.
75 Neither a borrower nor a lender be,
For loan oft loses both itself and friend,
And borrowing dulls th' edge of husbandry.
This above all, to thine own self be true,
And it must follow as the night the day
80 Thou canst not then be false to any man.
Farewell. My blessing season this in thee!
LAERTES: Most humbly do I take my leave, my lord.
POLONIUS: The time invites you. Go, your servants tend.
LAERTES: Farewell, Ophelia, and remember well
85 What I have said to you.
OPHELIA: 'Tis in my memory locked,
And you yourself shall keep the key of it.
LAERTES: Farewell.

(*Exit* LAERTES.)

POLONIUS: What is 't, Ophelia, he hath said to you?
OPHELIA: So please you, something touching the Lord
       Hamlet.
90 POLONIUS: Marry, well bethought.
'Tis told me he hath very oft of late
Given private time to you, and you yourself
Have of your audience been most free and bounteous.
If it be so—as so 'tis put on me,
95 And that in way of caution—I must tell you,
You do not understand yourself so clearly
As it behooves my daughter and your honor.
What is between you? Give me up the truth.
OPHELIA: He hath, my lord, of late made many tenders
100 Of his affection to me.
POLONIUS: Affection? Pooh! You speak like a green girl,
Unsifted in such perilous circumstance.
Do you believe his tenders, as you call them?
OPHELIA: I do not know, my lord, what I should think.
105 POLONIUS: Marry, I will teach you. Think yourself a baby
That you have ta'en these tenders for true pay
Which are not sterling. Tender yourself more dearly,
Or (not to crack the wind of the poor phrase,
Running it thus) you'll tender me a fool.
110 OPHELIA: My lord, he hath importuned me with love
In honorable fashion.
POLONIUS: Ay, fashion you may call it. Go to, go to.
OPHELIA: And hath given countenance to his speech, my lord,
With almost all the holy vows of heaven.
115 POLONIUS: Ay, springes to catch woodcocks. I do know,
When the blood burns, how prodigal the soul
Lends the tongue vows. These blazes, daughter,
Giving more light than heat, extinct in both

Even in their promise, as it is a-making,
You must not take for fire. From this time   120
Be something scanter of your maiden presence.
Set your entreatments at a higher rate
Than a command to parle. For Lord Hamlet,
Believe so much in him that he is young,
And with a larger tether may he walk   125
Than may be given you. In few, Ophelia,
Do not believe his vows, for they are brokers,
Not of that dye which their investments show,
But mere implorators of unholy suits,
Breathing like sanctified and pious bawds,   130
The better to beguile. This is for all:
I would not, in plain terms, from this time forth
Have you so slander any moment leisure
As to give words or talk with the Lord Hamlet.
Look to't, I charge you. Come your ways.   135
OPHELIA: I shall obey, my lord.

(*Exeunt.*)

SCENE IV

Enter HAMLET, HORATIO, *and* MARCELLUS.

HAMLET: The air bites shrewdly; it is very cold.
HORATIO: It is a nipping and an eager air.
HAMLET: What hour now?
HORATIO: I think it lacks of twelve.
MARCELLUS: No, it is struck.
HORATIO: Indeed? I heard it not. It then draws near the season 5
Wherein the spirit held his wont to walk.

(*A flourish of trumpets, and two pieces go off.*)

What does this mean, my lord?
HAMLET: The king doth wake to-night and takes his rouse,
Keeps wassail, and the swagg'ring up-spring reels,
And as he drains his draughts of Rhenish down,   10
The kettledrum and trumpet thus bray out
The triumph of his pledge.
HORATIO: Is it a custom?
HAMLET: Ay, marry, is't,
But to my mind, though I am native here
And to the manner born, it is a custom   15
More honored in the breach than the observance.
This heavy-headed revel east and west
Makes us traduced and taxed of other nations.
They clepe us drunkards, and with swinish phrase
Soil our addition, and indeed it takes   20
From our achievements, though performed at height,
The pith and marrow of our attribute.
So oft it chances in particular men,
That for some vicious mole of nature in them,

---

122 **entreatments** military negotiations for surrender   127
brokers go-betweens   128 **investments** clothes   129 **implorators** solicitors

I.iv. 2 **eager** sharp   9 **wassail** carousal; **up-spring** a German
dance   18 **taxed of** censured by   19 **clepe** call   20 **addition**
title added to a man's name to denote his rank   22 **attribute**
reputation

---

74 **chief** eminence   77 **husbandry** thriftiness   81 **season**
ripen   83 **tend** attend, wait   90 **Marry** by Mary   99 **tenders**
offers   102 **Unsifted** untried   115 **springes** snares

25   As, in their birth, wherein they are not guilty
    (Since nature cannot choose his origin),
    By the o'ergrowth of some complexion,
    Oft breaking down the pales and forts of reason,
    Or by some habit that too much o'er-leavens
30   The form of plausive manners—that these men,
    Carrying, I say, the stamp of one defect,
    Being nature's livery or fortune's star,
    His virtues else, be they as pure as grace,
    As infinite as man may undergo,
35   Shall in the general censure take corruption
    From that particular fault. The dram of evil
    Doth all the noble substance often doubt
    To his own scandal.

(Enter GHOST.)

HORATIO: Look, my lord, it comes.
HAMLET: Angels and ministers of grace defend us!
40   Be thou a spirit of health or goblin damned,
    Bring with thee airs from heaven or blasts from hell,
    Be thy intents wicked or charitable,
    Thou com'st in such a questionable shape
    That I will speak to thee. I'll call thee Hamlet,
45   King, father, royal Dane. O, answer me!
    Let me not burst in ignorance, but tell
    Why thy canonized bones, hearsèd in death,
    Have burst their cerements; why the sepulchre
    Wherein we saw thee quietly interred,
50   Hath oped his ponderous and marble jaws
    To cast thee up again. What may this mean
    That thou, dead corse, again in complete steel
    Revisits thus the glimpses of the moon,
    Making night hideous, and we fools of nature
55   So horridly to shake our disposition
    With thoughts beyond the reaches of our souls?
    Say, why is this? wherefore? What should we do?

([GHOST] *beckons.)*

HORATIO: It beckons you to go away with it,
    As if it some impartment did desire
60   To you alone.
MARCELLUS: Look, with what courteous action
    It waves you to a more removèd ground.
    But do not go with it.
HORATIO: No, by no means.
HAMLET: It will not speak; then I will follow it.
HORATIO: Do not, my lord.
HAMLET: Why, what should be the fear?
65   I do not set my life at a pin's fee,
    And for my soul, what can it do to that,
    Being a thing immortal as itself?
    It waves me forth again. I'll follow it.

---

26 **his** its 27 **complexion** one of the four temperaments (sanguine, melancholy, choleric, and phlegmatic) 29 **o'er-leavens** works change throughout 30 **plausive** pleasing 32 **livery** badge; **star** a person's fortune, rank, or destiny, viewed as determined by the stars 37 **doubt** put out, obliterate 38 **his** its 47 **canonized** buried according to the church's rule; **hearsèd** coffined, buried 59 **impartment** communication

HORATIO: What if it tempt you toward the flood, my lord,
    Or to the dreadful summit of the cliff   70
    That beetles o'er his base into the sea,
    And there assume some other horrible form,
    Which might deprive your sovereignty of reason
    And draw you into madness? Think of it.
    The very place puts toys of desperation,   75
    Without more motive, into every brain
    That looks so many fathoms to the sea
    And hears it roar beneath.
HAMLET: It waves me still.
    Go on. I'll follow thee.
MARCELLUS: You shall not go, my lord.   80
HAMLET: Hold off your hands.
HORATIO: Be ruled; You shall not go.
HAMLET: My fate cries out,
    And makes each petty artere in this body
    As hardy as the Nemean lion's nerve.
    Still am I called. Unhand me, gentlemen.
    By heaven, I'll make a ghost of him that lets me.   85
    I say, away—Go on. I'll follow thee.

([*Exeunt*] GHOST *and* HAMLET.)

HORATIO: He waxes desperate with imagination.
MARCELLUS: Let's follow. 'Tis not fit thus to obey him.
HORATIO: Have after. To what issue will this come?
MARCELLUS: Something is rotten in the state of Denmark.   90
HORATIO: Heaven will direct it.
MARCELLUS: Nay, let's follow him.

(Exeunt.)

SCENE V

Enter GHOST *and* HAMLET.

HAMLET: Whither wilt thou lead me? Speak. I'll go no further.
GHOST: Mark me.
HAMLET: I will.
GHOST: My hour is almost come
    When I to sulph'rous and tormenting flames
    Must render up myself.
HAMLET: Alas, poor ghost!
GHOST: Pity me not, but lend thy serious hearing   5
    To what I shall unfold.
HAMLET: Speak. I am bound to hear.
GHOST: So art thou to revenge, when thou shalt hear.
HAMLET: What?
GHOST: I am thy father's spirit,
    Doomed for a certain term to walk the night,   10
    And for the day confined to fast in fires,
    Till the foul crimes done in my days of nature
    Are burnt and purged away. But that I am forbid
    To tell the secrets of my prison house,
    I could a tale unfold whose lightest word   15
    Would harrow up thy soul, freeze thy young blood,

---

71 **beetles** juts out 73 **sovereignty of reason** state of being ruled by reason 75 **toys** fancies, impules 82 **artere** artery 83 **Nemean lion** slain by Hercules in the performance of one of his twelve labors 85 **lets** hinders

Make thy two eyes like stars start from their spheres,
Thy knotted and combinèd locks to part,
And each particular hair to stand an end,
20   Like quills upon the fretful porpentine.
But this eternal blazon must not be
To ears of flesh and blood. List, list, O, list!
If thou didst ever thy dear father love—
HAMLET: O God!
25 GHOST: Revenge his foul and most unnatural murder.
HAMLET: Murder!
GHOST: Murder most foul, as in the best it is,
But this most foul, strange, and unnatural.
HAMLET: Haste me to know't, that I, with wings as swift
30   As meditation or the thoughts of love,
May sweep to my revenge.
GHOST: I find thee apt,
And duller shouldst thou be than the fat weed
That roots itself in ease on Lethe wharf,
Wouldst thou not stir in this. Now, Hamlet, hear.
35 'Tis given out that, sleeping in my orchard,
A serpent stung me. So the whole ear of Denmark
Is by a forgèd process of my death
Rankly abused. But know, thou noble youth,
The serpent that did sting thy father's life
40   Now wears his crown.
HAMLET: O my prophetic soul!
My uncle!
GHOST: Ay, that incestuous, that adulterate beast,
With witchcraft of his wits, with traitorous gifts—
O wicked wit and gifts that have the power
45   So to seduce!—won to his shameful lust
The will of my most seeming virtuous queen.
O Hamlet, what a falling off was there,
From me, whose love was of that dignity
That it went hand in hand even with the vow
50   I made to her in marriage, and to decline
Upon a wretch whose natural gifts were poor
To those of mine!
But virtue, as it never will be moved,
Though lewdness court it in a shape of heaven,
55   So lust, though to a radiant angel linked,
Will sate itself in a celestial bed
And prey on garbage.
But soft, methinks I scent the morning air.
Brief let me be. Sleeping within my orchard,
60   My custom always of the afternoon,
Upon my secure hour thy uncle stole,
With juice of cursed hebona in a vial,
And in the porches of my ears did pour
The leperous distilment, whose effect
65   Holds such an enmity with blood of man
That swift as quicksilver it courses through
The natural gates and alleys of the body,
And with a sudden vigor it doth posset
And curd, like eager droppings into milk,

The thin and wholesome blood. So did it mine,   70
And a most instant tetter barked about
Most lazar-like with vile and loathsome crust
All my smooth body.
Thus was I sleeping by a brother's hand
Of life, of crown, of queen, at once dispatched,   75
Cut off even in the blossoms of my sin,
Unhouseled, disappointed, unaneled,
No reck'ning made, but sent to my account
With all my imperfections on my head.
O, horrible! O, horrible! most horrible!   80
If thou hast nature in thee, bear it not,
Let not the royal bed of Denmark be
A couch for luxury and damnèd incest.
But howsomever thou pursues this act,
Taint not thy mind, nor let thy soul contrive   85
Against thy mother aught. Leave her to heaven,
And to those thorns that in her bosom lodge
To prick and sting her. Fare thee well at once.
The glowworm shows the matin to be near,
And gins to pale his uneffectual fire.   90
Adieu, adieu, adieu. Remember me.

(*Exit.*)

HAMLET: O all you host of heaven! O earth! What else?
And shall I couple hell? O, fie! Hold, hold, my heart,
And you, my sinews, grow not instant old,
But bear me stiffly up. Remember thee?   95
Ay, thou poor ghost, whiles memory holds a seat
In this distracted globe. Remember thee?
Yea, from the table of my memory
I'll wipe away all trivial fond records,
All saws of books, all forms, all pressures past   100
That youth and observation copied there,
And thy commandment all alone shall live
Within the book and volume of my brain,
Unmixed with baser matter. Yes, by heaven!
O most pernicious woman!   105
O villain, villain, smiling, damnèd villain!
My tables—meet it is I set it down
That one may smile, and smile, and be a villain
At least I am sure it may be so in Denmark.   (*Writing.*)
So, uncle, there you are. Now to my word: 110
It is 'Adieu, adieu! Remember me,'
I have sworn't.

(*Enter* HORATIO *and* MARCELLUS.)

HORATIO: My lord, my lord!
MARCELLUS: Lord Hamlet!
HORATIO: Heavens secure him!
HAMLET: So be it!

---

71 **tetter** a skin eruption; **barked** covered as with bark   77 **Unhouseled** without having received the sacrament; **disappointed** unprepared; **unaneled** without extreme unction   83 **luxury** lust   89 **matin** morning   97 **globe** head   98 **table** writing tablet, memorandum book (as at line 107, below; here metaphorically of the mind)   99 **fond** foolish   100 **saws** sayings; **forms** concepts; **pressures** impressions

---

I.v. 19 **an** on   20 **porpentine** porcupine   21 **eternal blazon** proclamation of the secrets of eternity   33 **Lethe** the river in Hades that brings forgetfulness   37 **process** account   61 **secure** free from suspicion   62 **hebona** an imaginary poison, associated with henbane   68 **posset** curdle   69 **eager** acid

115 MARCELLUS: Illo, ho, ho, my lord!
   HAMLET: Hillo, ho, ho, boy! Come, bird, come.
   MARCELLUS: How is't, my noble lord?
   HORATIO: What news, my lord?
   HAMLET: O, wonderful!
   HORATIO: Good my lord, tell it.
   HAMLET: No, you will reveal it.
120 HORATIO: Not I, my lord, by heaven.
   MARCELLUS: Nor I, my lord.
   HAMLET: How say you then, would heart of man once think it?
      But you'll be secret?
   BOTH: Ay, by heaven, my lord.
   HAMLET: There's never a villain dwelling in all Denmark
      But he's an arrant knave.
125 HORATIO: There needs no ghost, my lord, come from the grave
      To tell us this.
   HAMLET: Why, right, you are in the right,
      And so without more circumstance at all
      I hold it fit that we shake hands and part,
      You, as your business and desire shall point you,
130   For every man has business and desire
      Such as it is, and for my own poor part,
      I will go pray.
   HORATIO: These are but wild and whirling words, my lord.
   HAMLET: I am sorry they offend you, heartily;
135   Yes, faith, heartily.
   HORATIO: There's no offence, my lord.
   HAMLET: Yes, by Saint Patrick, but there is, Horatio,
      And much offence too. Touching this vision here,
      It is an honest ghost, that let me tell you
      For your desire to know what is between us,
140   O'ermaster't as you may. And now, good friends,
      As you are friends, scholars, and soldiers,
      Give me one poor request.
   HORATIO: What is't, my lord? We will.
   HAMLET: Never make known what you have seen to-night.
145 BOTH: My lord, we will not.
   HAMLET: Nay, but swear't.
   HORATIO: In faith,
      My lord, not I.
   MARCELLUS: Nor I, my lord, in faith.
   HAMLET: Upon my sword.
   MARCELLUS: We have sworn, my lord, already.
   HAMLET: Indeed, upon my sword, indeed.

(GHOST *cries under the stage.*)

   GHOST: Swear.
   HAMLET: Ha, ha, boy, say'st thou so? Art thou there, truepenny?
150   Come on. You hear this fellow in the cellarage.
      Consent to swear.
   HORATIO: Propose the oath, my lord.
   HAMLET: Never to speak of this that you have seen,
      Swear by my sword.
   GHOST: (*Beneath.*) Swear.
155 HAMLET: Hic et ubique? Then we'll shift our ground.

---

115 **Illo, ho, ho** cry of the falconer to summon his hawk   136
Saint Patrick associated, in the late middle ages, with purgatory,
whence the ghost has presumably come   149 **truepenny** honest fellow   155 **Hic et ubique** here and everywhere

---

      Come hither, gentlemen,
      And lay your hands again upon my sword.
      Swear by my sword
      Never to speak of this that you have heard.
   GHOST: (*Beneath.*) Swear by his sword.   180
   HAMLET: Well said, old mole! Canst work i' th' earth so fast?
      A worthy pioneer! Once more remove, good friends.
   HORATIO: O day and night, but this is wondrous strange!
   HAMLET: And therefore as a stranger give it welcome.
      There are more things in heaven and earth, Horatio,   165
      Than are dreamt of in your philosophy.
      But come.
      Here as before, never, so help you mercy,
      How strange or odd some'er I bear myself
      (As I perchance hereafter shall think meet   170
      To put an antic disposition on),
      That you, at such times, seeing me, never shall,
      With arms encumbered thus, or this head-shake,
      Or by pronouncing of some doubtful phrase,
      As 'Well, well, we know,' or 'We could, and if we would' 175
      Or 'If we list to speak,' or 'There be, and if they might'
      Or such ambiguous giving out, to note
      That you know aught of me—this do swear,
      So grace and mercy at your most need help you.
   GHOST: (*Beneath.*) Swear.   180
   HAMLET: Rest, rest, perturbèd spirit! So, gentlemen,
      With all my love I do commend me to you,
      And what so poor a man as Hamlet is
      May do t' express his love and friending to you,
      God willing, shall not lack. Let us go in together,   185
      And still your fingers on your lips, I pray.
      The time is out of joint. O cursèd spite
      That ever I was born to set it right!
      Nay, come, let's go together.

(*Exeunt.*)

ACT TWO

SCENE I

Enter old POLONIUS *with his man* [REYNALDO].

POLONIUS: Give him this money and these notes. Reynaldo.
REYNALDO: I will, my lord.
POLONIUS: You shall do marvellous wisely, good Reynaldo,
   Before you visit him, to make inquire
   Of his behavior.   5
REYNALDO: My lord, I did intend it.
POLONIUS: Marry, well said, very well said. Look you, sir,
   Enquire me first what Danskers are in Paris,
   And how, and who, what means, and where they keep,
   What company, at what expense; and finding
   By this encompassment and drift of question   10
   That they do know my son, come you more nearer
   Than your particular demands will touch it.
   Take you as 'twere some distant knowledge of him,

---

162 **pioneer** miner   171 **antic** mad   173 **encumbered** folded

II.i. 7 **Danskers** Danes   8 **means** wealth   10 **encompassment** talking round the matter

As thus, 'I know his father and his friends,
15 And in part him,' do you mark this, Reynaldo?
REYNALDO: Ay, very well, my lord.
POLONIUS: 'And in part him, but,' you may say, 'not well,
     But if't be he I mean, he's very wild,
     Addicted so and so.' And there put on him
20 What forgeries you please; marry, none so rank
     As may dishonour him. Take heed of that.
     But, sir, such wanton, wild, and usual slips
     As are companions noted and most known
     To youth and liberty.
REYNALDO: As gaming, my lord?
25 POLONIUS: Ay, or drinking, fencing, swearing, quarrelling,
     Drabbing—you may go so far.
REYNALDO: My lord, that would dishonour him.
POLONIUS: Faith, no, as you may season it in the charge.
     You must not put another scandal on him,
30   That he is open to incontinency.
     That's not my meaning. But breathe his faults so quaintly
     That they may seem the taints of liberty,
     The flash and outbreak of a fiery mind,
     A savageness in unreclaimèd blood,
35   Of general assault.
REYNALDO: But, my good lord—
POLONIUS: Wherefore should you do this?
REYNALDO: Ay, my lord,
     I would know that.
POLONIUS: Marry, sir, here's my drift,
     And I believe it is a fetch of warrant.
     You laying these slight sullies on my son,
40   As 'twere a thing a little soiled i' th' working,
     Mark you,
     Your party in converse, him you would sound,
     Having ever seen in the prenominate crimes
     The youth you breathe of guilty, be assured
45   He closes with you in this consequence,
     'Good sir', or so, or 'friend', or 'gentleman',
     According to the phrase or the addition
     Of man and country.
REYNALDO: Very good, my lord.
POLONIUS: And then, sir, does 'a this—'a does—What was I
     about to say?
50   By the mass, I was about to say something.
     Where did I leave?
REYNALDO: At 'closes in the consequence.'
POLONIUS: At 'closes in the consequence'—ay, marry,
     He closes thus: 'I know the gentleman.
55   I saw him yesterday, or th' other day,
     Or then, or then, with such, and such, and as you say,
     There was 'a gaming, there o'ertook in 's rouse;
     There falling out at tennis', or perchance
     'I saw him enter such a house of sale',
60   Videlicet, a brothel, or so forth.

See you, now—
     Your bait of falsehood takes this carp of truth,
     And thus do we of wisdom and of reach,
     With windlasses and with assays of bias,
     By indirections find directions out;   65
     So by my former lecture and advice
     Shall you my son. You have me, have you not?
REYNALDO: My lord, I have.
POLONIUS: God bye ye; fare ye well.
REYNALDO: Good my lord.
POLONIUS: Observe his inclination in yourself.   70
REYNALDO: I shall, my lord.
POLONIUS: And let him ply his music.
REYNALDO: Well, my lord.
POLONIUS: Farewell.

(*Exit* REYNALDO.)

(*Enter* OPHELIA.)

                       How now, Ophelia! what's the matter?
OPHELIA: O my lord, my lord, I have been so affrighted!
POLONIUS: With what, i' th' name of God?   75
OPHELIA: My lord, as I was sewing in my closet,
     Lord Hamlet, with his doublet all unbraced,
     No hat upon his head, his stockings fouled,
     Ungartered, and down-gyvèd to his ankle,
     Pale as his shirt, his knees knocking each other,   80
     And with a look so piteous in purport
     As if he had been loosèd out of hell
     To speak of horrors—he comes before me.
POLONIUS: Mad for thy love?
OPHELIA: My lord, I do not know,
     But truly I do fear it.   85
POLONIUS: What said he?
OPHELIA: He took me by the wrist, and held me hard,
     Then goes he to the length of all his arm,
     And with his other hand thus o'er his brow,
     He falls to such perusal of my face
     As 'a would draw it. Long stayed he so.   90
     At last, a little shaking of mine arm
     And thrice his head thus waving up and down,
     He raised a sigh so piteous and profound
     As it did seem to shatter all his bulk
     And end his being. That done, he lets me go,   95
     And with his head over his shoulder turned,
     He seemed to find his way without his eyes,
     For out adoors he went without their helps,
     And to the last bended their light on me.
POLONIUS: Come, go with me. I will go seek the king.   100
     This is the very ecstasy of love,
     Whose violent property fordoes itself,
     And leads the will to desperate undertakings
     As oft as any passion under heaven
     That does afflict our natures. I am sorry.   105
     What, have you given him any hard words of late?

---

20 **forgeries** invented wrongdoings 24 **liberty** license 26
Drabbing whoring 28 **season** moderate 31 **quaintly** delicately 34 **unreclaimèd** untamed 35 **Of general assault** assailing all 38 **fetch of warrant** allowable device 43
prenominate before-named 45 **closes** agrees; **in this consequence** as follows 47 **addition** title 60 **Videlicet** namely

---

63 **reach** ability 64 **windlasses** roundabout approaches; **as-
says of bias** indirect attempts 68 **God buy ye** God be with
you 76 **closet** private room 77 **unbraced** unlaced 79
down-gyvèd hanging down, like gyves or fetters on a prisoner's
ankles 101 **ecstasy** madness 102 **fordoes** destroys

OPHELIA: No, my good lord, but as you did command
 I did repel his letters, and denied
 His access to me.
POLONIUS: That hath made him mad.
110 I am sorry that with better heed and judgement
 I had not quoted him. I feared he did but trifle,
 And meant to wrack thee; but beshrew my jealousy.
 By heaven, it is as proper to our age
 To cast beyond ourselves in our opinions
115 As it is common for the younger sort
 To lack discretion. Come, go we to the king.
 This must be known, which being kept close, might move
 More grief to hide than hate to utter love.
 Come.

(*Exeunt.*)

SCENE II

Flourish. Enter KING *and* QUEEN, ROSENCRANTZ, *and*
GUILDENSTERN [*and* ATTENDANTS].

KING: Welcome, dear Rosencrantz and Guildenstern.
 Moreover that we much did long to see you,
 The need we have to use you did provoke
 Our hasty sending. Something have you heard
5 Of Hamlet's transformation—so call it,
 Sith nor th' exterior nor the inward man
 Resembles that it was. What it should be,
 More than his father's death, that thus hath put him
 So much from th' understanding of himself,
10 I cannot dream of. I entreat you both
 That, being of so young days brought up with him,
 And sith so neighboured to his youth and havior,
 That you vouchsafe your rest here in our court
 Some little time, so by your companies
15 To draw him on to pleasures, and to gather
 So much as from occasion you may glean,
 Whether aught to us unknown afflicts him thus,
 That opened, lies within our remedy.
QUEEN: Good gentlemen, he hath much talked of you,
20 And sure I am two men there is not living
 To whom he more adheres. If it will please you
 To show us so much gentry and good will
 As to expend your time with us awhile
 For the supply and profit of our hope,
25 Your visitation shall receive such thanks
 As fits a king's remembrance.
ROSENCRANTZ: Both your majesties
 Might, by the sovereign power you have of us,
 Put your dread pleasures more into command
 Than to entreaty.
GUILDENSTERN: But we both obey,
30 And here give up ourselves in the full bent
 To lay our service freely at your feet,
 To be commanded.
KING: Thanks, Rosencrantz and gentle Guildenstern.

QUEEN: Thanks, Guildenstern and gentle Rosencrantz.
 And I beseech you instantly to visit   35
 My too much changed son. Go, some of you,
 And bring these gentlemen where Hamlet is.
GUILDENSTERN: Heavens make our presence and our practices
 Pleasant and helpful to him!
QUEEN: Ay, amen!

(*Exeunt* ROSENCRANTZ *and* GUILDENSTERN [*with some* AT-
TENDANTS].)

(*Enter* POLONIUS.)

POLONIUS: Th' ambassadors from Norway, my good lord, 40
 Are joyfully returned.
KING: Thou still hast been the father of good news.
POLONIUS: Have I, my lord? I assure my good liege,
 I hold my duty as I hold my soul,
 Both to my God and to my gracious king;   45
 And I do think—or else this brain of mine
 Hunts not the trail of policy so sure
 As it hath used to do—that I have found
 The very cause of Hamlet's lunacy.
KING: O, speak of that, that do I long to hear.   50
POLONIUS: Give first admittance to th' ambassadors.
 My news shall be the fruit to that great feast.
KING: Thyself do grace to them, and bring them in.

(*Exit* POLONIUS.)

 He tells me, my dear Gertrude, he hath found
 The head and source of all your son's distemper. 55
QUEEN: I doubt it is no other but the main,
 His father's death and our o'erhasty marriage.
KING: Well, we shall sift him.

(*Enter* AMBASSADORS [VOLTEMAND *and* CORNELIUS], *with*
POLONIUS.)

       Welcome, my good friends,
 Say, Voltemand, what from our brother Norway?
VOLTEMAND: Most fair return of greetings and desires. 60
 Upon our first, he sent out to suppress
 His nephew's levies, which to him appeared
 To be a preparation 'gainst the Polack,
 But better looked into, he truly found
 It was against your highness, whereat grieved, 65
 That so his sickness, age, and impotence
 Was falsely borne in hand, sends out arrests
 On Fortinbras, which he in brief obeys,
 Receives rebuke from Norway, and in fine,
 Makes vow before his uncle never more 70
 To give th' assay of arms against your majesty.
 Whereon old Norway, overcome with joy,
 Gives him three score thousand crowns in annual fee,
 And his commission to employ those soldiers,
 So levied as before, against the Polack, 75
 With an entreaty, herein further shown, (*Gives a paper.*)
 That it might please you to give quiet pass
 Through your dominions for this enterprise,

---

111 **quoted** observed 112 **wrack** ruin 113 **proper to** characteristic of 117 **close** secret; **move** cause

II.ii. 6 Sith **since** 18 **opened** disclosed 22 **gentry** courtesy

42 **still** ever 56 **doubt** suspect 63 **the Polack** the Polish
nation 67 **borne in hand** deceived 69 **in fine** in the end
71 **assay** trial

On such regards of safety and allowance
80   As therein are set down.
KING: It likes us well,
   And at our more considered time we'll read,
   Answer, and think upon this business.
   Meantime we thank you for your well-took labor.
   Go to your rest; at night we'll feast together.
85   Most welcome home!

(*Exeunt* AMBASSADORS.)

POLONIUS: This business is well ended.
   My liege and madam, to expostulate
   What majesty should be, what duty is,
   Why day is day, night night, and time is time,
   Were nothing but to waste night, day and time.
90   Therefore, since brevity is the soul of wit,
   And tediousness the limbs and outward flourishes,
   I will be brief. Your noble son is mad.
   Mad call I it, for to define true madness,
   What is't but to be nothing else but mad?
95   But let that go.
QUEEN: More matter with less art.
POLONIUS: Madam, I swear I use no art at all.
   That he is mad, 'tis true: 'tis true 'tis pity.
   And pity 'tis 'tis true. A foolish figure,
   But farewell it, for I will use no art.
100   Mad let us grant him, then, and now remains
   That we find out the cause of this effect,
   Or rather say the cause of this defect,
   For this effect defective comes by cause.
   Thus it remains, and the remainder thus.
105   Perpend.
   I have a daughter—have while she is mine—
   Who in her duty and obedience, mark,
   Hath given me this. Now gather, and surmise.   (*Reads.*)
      'To the celestial, and my soul's idol, the most beautified
110   Ophelia'—That's an ill phrase, a vile phrase, 'beautified' is
   a vile phrase. But you shall hear. Thus: (*Reads.*)
      'In her excellent white bosom, these, etc.'
QUEEN: Came this from Hamlet to her?
POLONIUS: Good madam, stay awhile. I will be faithful.
(*Reads letter.*)

115   'Doubt thou the stars are fire,
               Doubt that the sun doth move;
               Doubt truth to be a liar;
               But never doubt I love.

      'O dear Ophelia, I am ill at these numbers. I have not
120   art to reckon my groans, but that I love thee best, O most
   best, believe it. Adieu.
                  'Thine evermore, most dear lady, whilst
                        this machine is to him, Hamlet.'
   This in obedience hath my daughter shown me,
125   And more above, hath his solicitings,
   As they fell out by time, by means and place,
   All given to mine ear.

KING: But how hath she
   Received his love?
POLONIUS: What do you think of me?
KING: As of a man faithful and honourable.
POLONIUS: I would fain prove so. But what might you think,   130
   When I had seen this hot love on the wing,
   (As I perceived it, I must tell you that,
   Before my daughter told me), what might you,
   Or my dear majesty your queen here, think,
   If I had played the desk or table-book,   135
   Or given my heart a winking, mute and dumb,
   Or looked upon this love with idle sight,
   What might you think? No, I went round to work,
   And my young mistress thus I did bespeak:
   'Lord Hamlet is a prince out of thy star.   140
   This must not be'. and then I prescripts gave her,
   That she should lock herself from his resort,
   Admit no messengers, receive no tokens.
   Which done, she took the fruits of my advice;
   And he repelled, a short tale to make,   145
   Fell into a sadness, then into a fast,
   Thence to a watch, thence into a weakness,
   Thence to a lightness, and, by this declension,
   Into the madness wherein now he raves,
   And all we mourn for.   150
KING: Do you think 'tis this?
QUEEN: It may be, very like.
POLONIUS: Hath there been such a time—I would fain
         know that—
   That I have positively said ''Tis so,'
   When it proved otherwise?
KING: Not that I know.
POLONIUS: (*Pointing to his head and shoulder.*) Take this from   155
         this, if this be otherwise:
   If circumstances lead me, I will find
   Where truth is hid, though it were hid indeed
   Within the centre.
KING: How may we try it further?
POLONIUS: You know, sometimes he walks four hours together
   Here in the lobby.   160
QUEEN: So he does, indeed.
POLONIUS: At such a time I'll loose my daughter to him.
   Be you and I behind an arras then.
   Mark the encounter. If he love her not,
   And be not from his reason fall'n thereon,
   Let me be no assistant for a state,   165
   But keep a farm and carters.
KING: We will try it.

(*Enter* HAMLET [*reading on a book*].)

QUEEN: But look where sadly the poor wretch comes reading.
POLONIUS: Away, I do beseech you both away,
   I'll board him presently.

([*Exeunt*] king and queen [*with attendants*].)

                  O, give me leave.

---

79 **regards** considerations   90 **wit** understanding   95 **matter**
meaning, sense   105 **Perpend** consider   119 **numbers** verses
123 **machine** body

135 **played . . . table-book** acted as silent go-between   138
round directly   147 **watch** sleeplessness   148 **lightness** light-
headedness   158 **centre** centre of the earth and of the Ptole-
maic universe   169 **board** accost; **presently** immediately

170 How does my good Lord Hamlet?
HAMLET: Well, God-a-mercy.
POLONIUS: Do you know me, my lord?
HAMLET: Excellent well, you are a fishmonger.
POLONIUS: Not I, my lord.
175 HAMLET: Then I would you were so honest a man.
POLONIUS: Honest, my lord?
HAMLET: Ay, sir, to be honest as this world goes, is to be one
man picked out of ten thousand.
POLONIUS: That's very true, my lord.
180 HAMLET: For if the sun breed maggots in a dead dog, being a
good kissing carrion—Have you a daughter?
POLONIUS: I have, my lord.
HAMLET: Let her not walk i' th' sun. Conception is a blessing,
but as your daughter may conceive—friend, look to 't.
185 POLONIUS: (Aside.) How say you by that? Still harping on my
daughter. Yet he knew me not at first. 'A said I was a fishmonger. 'A is far gone. And truly in my youth I suffered
much extremity for love, very near this. I'll speak to him
again.—What do you read, my lord?
190 HAMLET: Words, words, words.
POLONIUS: What is the matter, my lord?
HAMLET: Between who?
POLONIUS: I mean the matter that you read, my lord.
HAMLET: Slanders, sir; for the satirical rogue says here that old
195 men have grey beards, that their faces are wrinkled, their
eyes purging thick amber and plum-tree gum, and that
they have a plentiful lack of wit, together with most weak
hams—all which, sir, though I most powerfully and po-
tently believe, yet I hold it not honesty to have it thus set
200 down, for yourself, sir, shall grow old as I am, if like a crab
you could go backward.
POLONIUS: (Aside.) Though this be madness, yet there is
method in 't.—Will you walk out of the air, my lord?
HAMLET: Into my grave?
205 POLONIUS: (Aside.) Indeed, that's out of the air. How pregnant sometimes his replies are! a happiness that often madness hits on, which reason and sanity could not so
prosperously be delivered of. I will leave him, and suddenly contrive the means of meeting between him and
210 my daughter.—My lord, I will take my leave of you.
HAMLET: You cannot take from me anything that I will not
more willingly part withal—except my life, except my
life, except my life.

(*Enter* GUILDENSTERN *and* ROSENCRANTZ.)

POLONIUS: Fare you well, my lord.
215 HAMLET: These tedious old fools!
POLONIUS: You go to seek the Lord Hamlet. There he is.
ROSENCRANTZ: (*To* POLONIUS.) *God save you, sir!*

(*Exit* POLONIUS.)

GUILDENSTERN: My honored lord!
ROSENCRANTZ: My most dear lord!
220 HAMLET: My excellent good friends! How dost thou,
Guildenstern?
Ah, Rosencrantz! Good lads, how do ye both?

ROSENCRANTZ: As the indifferent children of the earth.
GUILDENSTERN: Happy in that we are not over-happy;
On Fortune's cap we are not the very button.   225
HAMLET: Nor the soles of her shoe?
ROSENCRANTZ: Neither, my lord.
HAMLET: Then you live about her waist, or in the middle of
her favors?
GUILDENSTERN: Faith, her privates we.   230
HAMLET: In the secret parts of Fortune? O, most true, she is a
strumpet. What news?
ROSENCRANTZ: None, my lord, but that the world's grown
honest.
HAMLET: Then is doomsday near. But your news is not true. 235
Let me question more in particular. What have you, my
good friends, deserved at the hands of Fortune, that she
sends you to prison hither?
GUILDENSTERN: Prison, my lord!
HAMLET: Denmark's a prison.   240
ROSENCRANTZ: Then is the world one.
HAMLET: A goodly one, in which there are many confines,
wards, and dungeons, Denmark being one o' th' worst.
ROSENCRANTZ: We think not so, my lord.
HAMLET: Why then 'tis none to you; for there is nothing either 245
good or bad, but thinking makes it so. To me it is a prison.
ROSENCRANTZ: Why then your ambition makes it one. 'Tis
too narrow for your mind.
HAMLET: O God, I could be bounded in a nutshell and count
myself a king of infinite space, were it not that I have bad 250
dreams.
GUILDENSTERN: Which dreams indeed are ambition; for the
very substance of the ambitious is merely the shadow of a
dream.
HAMLET: A dream itself is but a shadow.   255
ROSENCRANTZ: Truly, and I hold ambition of so airy and
light a quality that it is but a shadow's shadow.
HAMLET: Then are our beggars bodies, and, our monarchs and
outstretched heroes the beggars' shadows. Shall we to th'
court? for, by my fay, I cannot reason.   260
BOTH: We'll wait upon you.
HAMLET: No such matter. I will not sort you with the rest of
my servants; for to speak to you like an honest man, I am
most dreadfully attended. But in the beaten way of friendship, what make you at Elsinore?   265
ROSENCRANTZ: To visit you, my lord; no other occasion.
HAMLET: Beggar that I am, I am ever poor in thanks, but I
thank you; and sure, dear friends, my thanks are too dear
a halfpenny. Were you not sent for? Is it your own inclin-
ing? Is it a free visitation? Come, come, deal justly with 270
me. Come, come, nay speak.
GUILDENSTERN: What should we say, my lord?
HAMLET: Anything but to the purpose. You were sent for, and
there is a kind of confession in your looks, which your
modesties have not craft enough to color. I know the 275
good king and queen have sent for you.
ROSENCRANTZ: To what end, my lord?
HAMLET: That you must teach me. But let me conjure you by
the rights of our fellowship, by the consonancy of our

---

205 **pregnant** full of meaning   206 **happiness** aptness

223 **indifferent** average   225 **button** knob on the top of the
cap   260 **fay** faith   262 **sort you with** put you in the same
class with

280 youth, by the obligation of our ever-preserved love, and by
what more dear a better proposer can charge you withal be
even and direct with me whether you were sent for or no.

ROSENCRANTZ: (*Aside to* GUILDENSTERN.) What say you?

HAMLET: (*Aside.*) Nay, then, I have an eye of you.—If you
285 love me, hold not off.

GUILDENSTERN: My lord, we were sent for.

HAMLET: I will tell you why; so shall my anticipation prevent
your discovery, and your secrecy to the king and queen
moult no feather. I have of late—but wherefore I know
290 not—lost all my mirth, forgone all custom of exercises; and
indeed it goes so heavily with my disposition, that this
goodly frame the earth seems to me a sterile promontory,
this most excellent canopy the air, look you, this brave
o'er-hanging firmament, this majestical roof fretted with
295 golden fire, why it appeareth nothing to me but a foul and
pestilent congregation of vapors. What a piece of work is a
man, how noble in reason, how infinite in faculties, in form
and moving, how express and admirable in action, how like
an angel in apprehension, how like a god: the beauty of the
300 world, the paragon of animals. And yet to me, what is this
quintessence of dust? Man delights not me, nor woman
neither, though by your smiling you seem to say so.

ROSENCRANTZ: My lord, there was no such stuff in my
thoughts.

305 HAMLET: Why did ye laugh, then, when I said 'Man delights
not me'?

ROSENCRANTZ: To think, my lord, if you delight not in man,
what lenten entertainment the players shall receive from
you. We coted them on the way, and hither are they com-
310 ing to offer you service.

HAMLET: He that plays the king shall be welcome—his
majesty shall have tribute on me; the adventurous knight
shall use his foil and target; the lover shall not sigh gratis;
the humorous man shall end his part in peace; the clown
315 shall make those laugh whose lungs are tickle o' th' sere;
and the lady shall say her mind freely, or the blank verse
shall halt for 't. What players are they?

ROSENCRANTZ: Even those you were wont to take such delight in, the tragedians of the city.

320 HAMLET: How chances it they travel? Their residence, both in
reputation and profit, was better both ways.

ROSENCRANTZ: I think their inhibition comes by the means
of the late innovation.

HAMLET: Do they hold the same estimation they did when I
was in the city? Are they so followed?   325

ROSENCRANTZ: No, indeed, are they not.

HAMLET: How comes it? Do they grow rusty?

ROSENCRANTZ: Nay, their endeavour keeps in the wonted pace;
but there is, sir, an eyrie of children, little eyases, that cry out
on the top of question, and are most tyrannically clapped   330
for't. These are now the fashion, and so berattle the common
stages (so they call them) that many wearing rapiers are afraid
of goose quills and dare scarce come thither.

HAMLET: What, are they children? Who maintains 'em? How
are they escoted? Will they pursue the quality no longer   335
than they can sing? Will they not say afterwards, if they
should grow themselves to common players (as it is most
like, if their means are no better), their writers do them
wrong to make them exclaim against their own succession?

ROSENCRANTZ: 'Faith, there has been much to do on both   340
sides; and the nation holds it no sin to tarre them to controversy. There was for a while no money bid for argument,
unless the poet and the player went to cuffs in the question.

HAMLET: Is't possible?

GUILDENSTERN: O, there has been much throwing about of   345
brains.

HAMLET: Do the boys carry it away?

ROSENCRANTZ: Ay, that they do, my lord, Hercules and his
load too.

HAMLET: It is not very strange, for my uncle is King of Den-   350
mark, and those that would make mouths at him while
my father lived give twenty, forty, fifty, a hundred ducats
apiece for his picture in little. 'Sblood, there is something
in this more than natural, if philosophy could find it out.

(*A flourish.*)

GUILDENSTERN: There are the players.   355

HAMLET: Gentlemen, you are welcome to Elsinore. Your
hands. Come then th' appurtenance of welcome is fashion
and ceremony. Let me comply with you in this garb, lest
my ex-tent to the players, which I tell you must show
fairly outwards, should more appear like entertainment   360
than yours. You are welcome. But my uncle-father and
aunt-mother are deceived.

GUILDENSTERN: In what, my dear lord?

HAMLET: I am but mad north-north-west; when the wind is
southerly I know a hawk from a handsaw.   365

---

287 **prevent** forestall   288 **discovery** disclosure   294 **fretted**
decorated with fretwork   308 **lenten** scanty   309 **coted** passed
313 **foil and target** spear and shield   313–314 **humorous
man** the actor who plays the eccentric character dominated by
one of the four humors   315 **tickle o' th' sere** easily set off
(**sere** is that part of a gunlock which keeps the hammer at full or
half cock)   316 **halt** limp   322 **inhibition** prohibition of plays
by authority (possibly with reference to decree of the Privy
Council of 22 June 1600, limiting the number of London theater
companies to two, and stipulating that the two were to perform
only twice a week)   323 **innovation** meaning uncertain (sometimes taken to refer to the reintroduction, ca. 1600, on the London theatrical scene of companies of boy actors performing in
private theaters; sometimes interpreted as "political upheaval,"
with special reference to Essex's rebellion, February, 1601)

329 **eyrie** nest; **eyases** nestling hawks (here, the boys in the children's companies training as actors)   330 **on the top of question** louder than all others on matter of dispute   331–332
common stages public theaters of the **common players** (below, line 337), organized in companies composed mainly of adult
actors   333 **goose quills** pens (of the satiric dramatists writing
for the private theaters)   335 **escoted** maintained; **pursue the
quality** continue in the profession of acting   336 **sing** i.e., until their voices change   341 **tarre** incite   342 **argument** plot
of a play   349 **load** i.e., the world (the sign of the Globe theater represented Hercules bearing the world on his shoulders)
351 **mouths** grimaces   353 **in little** in miniature   357 **appurtenance** adjuncts   358–359 **extent** welcome   365 **hawk**
mattock or pickaxe (also called "hack," here used with a play on
hawk as a bird); **handsaw** a saw managed with one hand (here
used with a play on some corrupt form of *hernshaw*, "heron")

(*Enter* POLONIUS.)

POLONIUS: Well be with you, gentlemen.

HAMLET: Hark you, Guildenstern—and you too—at each ear a hearer. That great baby you see there is not yet out of his swaddling clouts.

370 ROSENCRANTZ: Happily he is the second time come to them, for they say an old man is twice a child.

HAMLET: I will prophesy he comes to tell me of the players. Mark it.—You say right, sir, a Monday morning, 'twas then indeed.

375 POLONIUS: My lord, I have news to tell you.

HAMLET: My lord, I have news to tell you. When Roscius was an actor in Rome—

POLONIUS: The actors are come hither, my lord.

HAMLET: Buzz, buzz.

380 POLONIUS: Upon my honor—

HAMLET: Then came each actor on his ass—

POLONIUS: The best actors in the world, either for tragedy, comedy, history, pastoral, pastoral-comical, historical-pastoral, tragical-historical, tragical-comical-historical-

385 pastoral, scene individable, or poem unlimited. Seneca cannot be too heavy nor Plautus too light. For the law of writ and the liberty, these are the only men.

HAMLET: O Jephthah, judge of Israel, what a treasure hadst thou!

390 POLONIUS: What a treasure had he, my lord?

HAMLET: Why—

> 'One fair daughter, and no more,
> The which he loved passing well.'

POLONIUS: (*Aside.*) Still on my daughter.

395 HAMLET: Am I not i' th' right, old Jephthah?

POLONIUS: If you call me Jephthah, my lord, I have a daughter that I love passing well.

HAMLET: Nay, that follows not.

POLONIUS: What follows then, my lord?

400 HAMLET: Why—

> 'As by lot, God wot,'

and then, you know,

> 'It came to pass, as most like it was.'

The first row of the pious chanson will show you more,
405 for look where my abridgement comes.

(*Enter the* PLAYERS.)

You are welcome, masters; welcome, all.—I am glad to see thee well.—Welcome, good friends. O, old friend! Why thy face is valanced since I saw thee last. Come'st thou to beard me in Denmark?—What, my young lady and mistress? By'r lady, your ladyship is nearer to heaven than 410 when I saw you last by the altitude of a chopine. Pray God, your voice, like a piece of uncurrent gold, be not cracked within the ring.—Masters, you are all welcome. We'll e'en to't like French falconers, fly at any thing we see. We'll have a speech straight. Come give us a taste of 415 your quality, come a passionate speech.

1 PLAYER: What speech, my good lord?

HAMLET: I heard thee speak me a speech once, but it was never acted, or if it was, not above once, for the play, I remember, pleased not the million; 'twas caviary to the general. But it 420 was—as I received it, and others whose judgements in such matters cried in the top of mine—an excellent play, well digested in the scenes, set down with as much modesty as cunning. I remember one said there were no sallets in the lines to make the matter savory, nor no matter in the phrase 425 that might indict the author of affectation, but called it an honest method, as wholesome as sweet, and by very much more handsome than fine. One speech in't I chiefly loved. 'Twas Æneas' tale to Dido and thereabout of it especially when he speaks of Priam's slaughter. If it live in your mem- 430 ory, begin at this line—let me see, let me see:

> 'The rugged Pyrrhus, like th' Hyrcanian beast'—

'tis not so;—it begins with Pyrrhus—

> 'The rugged Pyrrhus, he whose sable arms,
> Black as his purpose, did the night resemble 435
> When he lay couchèd in the ominous horse,
> Hath now this dread and black complexion smeared
> With heraldry more dismal; head to foot
> Now is he total gules, horridly tricked
> With blood of fathers, mothers, daughters, sons, 440
> Baked and impasted with the parching streets,
> That lend a tyrannous and a damnèd light
> To their lord's murder. Roasted in wrath and fire,
> And thus o'er-sizèd with coagulate gore,
> With eyes like carbuncles, the hellish Pyrrhus 445
> Old grandsire Priam seeks.'

So, proceed you.

POLONIUS: Fore God, my lord, well spoken, with good accent and good discretion.

1 PLAYER: 'Anon he finds him 450
> Striking too short at Greeks. His antique sword,
> Rebellious to his arm, lies where it falls,

---

370 **Happily** perhaps   376 **Roscius** the greatest of Roman comic actors, though regarded by the Elizabethans as a tragic one   384–385 **scene individable** i.e., a play that observes the unities of time and place   385 **poem unlimited** a play that does not observe the unities; **Seneca** Roman writer of tragedies   386 **Plautus** Roman comic dramatist; **law of writ and the liberty** i.e., plays according to strict classical rules, and those that ignored the unities of time and place   388 **Jephthah** was compelled to sacrifice a beloved daughter (Judges 2). Hamlet quotes from a contemporary ballad titled *Jephthah, Judge of Israel* at lines 392–393, 401, and 403   404 **row** stanza

408 **valanced** bearded   409 **young lady** i.e., the boy who plays female roles   411 **chopine** a shoe with high cork heel and sole   412–413 **cracked within the ring** a coin cracked within the circle surrounding the head of the sovereign was no longer legal tender and so *uncurrent*   415 **straight** immediately   420 **caviary** caviare; **general** multitude   422–423 **digested** arranged   424 **sallets** salads, highly seasoned passages   428 **more handsome than fine** admirable rather than appealing by mere cleverness   432 **Hyrcanian beast** tiger   436 **horse** i.e., the Trojan horse   439 **gules** heraldic term for red; **tricked** delineated   444 **o'er-sizèd** covered as with size; **coagulate** clotted

Repugnant to command. Unequal matched,
Pyrrhus at Priam drives, in rage strikes wide.
455 But with the whiff and wind of his fell sword
Th' unnervèd father falls. Then senseless Ilium,
Seeming to feel this blow, with flaming top
Stoops to his base, and with a hideous crash
Takes prisoner Pyrrhus' ear. For, lo! his sword,
460 Which was declining on the milky head
Of reverend Priam, seemed i' th' air to stick.
So as a painted tyrant Pyrrhus stood,
And like a neutral to his will and matter,
Did nothing.
465 But as we often see, against some storm,
A silence in the heavens, the rack stand still,
The bold winds speechless, and the orb below
As hush as death, anon the dreadful thunder
Doth rend the region; so, after Pyrrhus' pause,
470 A rousèd vengeance sets him new awork,
And never did the Cyclops' hammers fall
On Mars's armor, forged for proof eterne
With less remorse than Pyrrhus' bleeding sword
Now falls on Priam.
475 Out, out, thou strumpet, Fortune! All you gods,
In general synod take away her power,
Break all the spokes and fellies from her wheel,
And bowl the round nave down the hill of heaven
As low as to the fiends.'
480 POLONIUS: This is too long.
HAMLET: It shall to the barber's with your beard.—Prithee,
say on. He's for a jig, or a tale of bawdry, or he sleeps. Say
on, come to Hecuba.
1 PLAYER: 'But who, ah woe! had seen the mobled queen—'
485 HAMLET: 'The mobled queen'?
POLONIUS: That's good.
1 PLAYER: 'Run barefoot up and down, threat'ning the flames
With bisson rheum; a clout upon that head
Where late the diadem stood, and for a robe,
490 About her lank and all o'er-teemèd loins,
A blanket, in the alarm of fear caught up—
Who this had seen, with tongue in venom steeped,
'Gainst Fortune's state would treason have pronounced.
But if the gods themselves did see her then,
495 When she saw Pyrrhus make malicious sport
In mincing with his sword her husband's limbs,
The instant burst of clamor that she made,
Unless things mortal move them not at all,
Would have made milch the burning eyes of heaven,
500 And passion in the gods.'
POLONIUS: Look whe'r he has not turned his color, and has
tears in's eyes. Prithee no more.

---

453 **Repugnant** refractory   455 **fell** fierce, cruel   465 **against**
just before   466 **rack** mass of cloud   469 **region** air   471
Cyclops giant workmen who made armor in the smithy of Vulcan   472 **proof eterne** to be forever impenetrable   477 **fellies**
the curved pieces forming the rim of a wheel   478 **nave** hub of
a wheel   484 **mobled** muffled   488 **bisson rheum** blinding
tears   490 **o'er-teemed** exhausted by many births   493 **state**
government   499 **milch** moist, tearful (lit., milk, giving)

HAMLET: 'Tis well. I'll have thee speak out the rest of this
soon.—Good my lord, will you see the players well bestowed? Do you hear, let them be well used, for they are   505
the abstract and brief chronicles of the time; after your
death you were better have a bad epitaph than their ill report while you live.
POLONIUS: My lord, I will use them according to their desert.
HAMLET: God's bodkin, man, much better. Use every man af-   510
ter his desert, and who shall 'scape whipping? Use them
after your own honor and dignity. The less they deserve,
the more merit is in your bounty. Take them in.
POLONIUS: Come, sirs.
HAMLET: Follow him, friends. We'll hear a play tomorrow.   515
(*Aside to* 1 PLAYER.) Dost thou hear me, old friend, can
you play the 'Murder of Gonzago'?
1 PLAYER: Ay, my lord.
HAMLET: We'll ha't tomorrow night. You could for a need
study a speech of some dozen or sixteen lines which I   520
would set down and insert in't, could you not?
1 PLAYER: Ay, my lord.
HAMLET: Very well. Follow that lord, and look you mock him
not.

(*Exeunt* POLONIUS *and* PLAYERS.)

My good friends, I'll leave you till night. You are welcome   525
to Elsinore.
ROSENCRANTZ: Good my lord!

(*Exeunt* [ROSENCRANTZ *and* GUILDENSTERN].)

HAMLET: Ay, so God by to you. Now I am alone.
O, what a rogue and peasant slave am I!
Is it not monstrous that this player here,   530
But in a fiction, in a dream of passion,
Could force his soul so to his own conceit
That from her working all his visage wanned;
Tears in his eyes, distraction in his aspect,
A broken voice, and his whole function suiting   535
With forms to his conceit? And all for nothing,
For Hecuba!
What's Hecuba to him or he to Hecuba,
That he should weep for her? What would he do
Had he the motive and the cue for passion   540
That I have? He would drown the stage with tears,
And cleave the general ear with horrid speech,
Make mad the guilty, and appal the free,
Confound the ignorant, and amaze indeed
The very faculties of eyes and ears.   545
Yet I,
A dull and muddy-mettled rascal, peak
Like John-a-dreams, unpregnant of my cause,
And can say nothing; no, not for a king
Upon whose property and most dear life   550
A damned defeat was made. Am I a coward?
Who calls me villain, breaks my pate across,

---

506 **abstract** summary account   510 **God's bodkin** by God's
dear body   532 **conceit** imagination   542 **general** public
547 **muddy-mettled** dull-spirited; **peak** mope   548 **unpregnant** not quickened to action

Plucks off my beard and blows it in my face,
Tweaks me by the nose, gives me the lie i' th' throat
555 As deep as to the lungs? Who does me this?
Ha, 'swounds, I should take it; for it cannot be
But I am pigeon-livered and lack gall
To make oppression bitter, or ere this
I should 'a fatted all the region kites
560 With this slave's offal. Bloody, bawdy villain!
Remorseless, treacherous, lecherous, kindless villain!
Why, what an ass am I! This is most brave,
That I, the son of a dear father murdered,
Prompted to my revenge by heaven and hell,
565 Must like a whore unpack my heart with words,
And fall a-cursing like a very drab,
A scullion! Fie upon 't! foh!
About, my brains! Hum—I have heard
That guilty creatures sitting at a play,
570 Have by the very cunning of the scene
Been struck so to the soul that presently
They have proclaimed their malefactions:
For murder, though it have no tongue, will speak
With most miraculous organ. I'll have these players
575 Play something like the murder of my father
Before mine uncle. I'll observe his looks.
I'll tent him to the quick. If 'a do blench,
I know my course. The spirit that I have seen
May be the devil, and the devil hath power
580 T' assume a pleasing shape, yea, and perhaps
Out of my weakness and my melancholy,
As he is very potent with such spirits,
Abuses me to damn me. I'll have grounds
More relative than this. The play's the thing
585 Wherein I'll catch the conscience of the king.

(*Exit.*)

ACT THREE

SCENE I

Enter KING, QUEEN, POLONIUS, OPHELIA, ROSENCRANTZ,
GUILDENSTERN, LORDS.

KING: And can you by no drift of conference
   Get from him why he puts on this confusion,
   Grating so harshly all his days of quiet
   With turbulent and dangerous lunacy?
5 ROSENCRANTZ: He does confess he feels himself distracted,
   But from what cause 'a will by no means speak.

---

559 **region kites** kites of the air   561 **kindless** unnatural. Following this line, *F* adds the words "Oh Vengeance!" Their inappropriateness to the occasion is noted by Professor Harold Jenkins (in his "Playhouse Interpolations in the Folio Text of Hamlet," *Studies in Bibliography* 13 [1960]: 37). Professor Jenkins remarks that the folio text, by introducing Hamlet's "call for vengeance while he is still absorbed in self-reproaches, both anticipates and misconstrues" the crisis of his passion and of the speech, which comes in fact at line 568 ("**About, my brains**"), when "he abandons his self-reproaches and plans action"   567 **scullion** kitchen wench   571 **presently** immediately   577 **tent** probe; **blench** flinch   583 **Abuses** deludes   584 **relative** relevant

GUILDENSTERN: Nor do we find him forward to be sounded,
   But with a crafty madness keeps aloof
   When we would bring him on to some confession
   Of his true state.   10
QUEEN: Did he receive you well?
ROSENCRANTZ: Most like a gentleman.
GUILDENSTERN: But with much forcing of his disposition.
ROSENCRANTZ: Niggard of question, but of our demands
   Most free in his reply.
QUEEN: Did you assay him
   To any pastime?   15
ROSENCRANTZ: Madam, it so fell out that certain players
   We o'er-raught on the way. Of these we told him,
   And there did seem in him a kind of joy
   To hear of it. They are here about the court,
   And as I think, they have already order   20
   This night to play before him.
POLONIUS: 'Tis most true,
   And he beseeched me to entreat your majesties
   To hear and see the matter.
KING: With all my heart, and it doth much content me
   To hear him so inclined.   25
   Good gentlemen, give him a further edge,
   And drive his purpose into these delights.
ROSENCRANTZ: We shall, my lord.

(*Exeunt* ROSENCRANTZ *and* GUILDENSTERN.)

KING: Sweet Gertrude, leave us too;
   For we have closely sent for Hamlet hither,
   That he, as 'twere by accident, may here   30
   Affront Ophelia.
   Her father and myself (lawful espials)
   We'll so bestow ourselves that, seeing unseen,
   We may of their encounter frankly judge,
   And gather by him, as he is behaved,   35
   If 't be th' affliction of his love or no
   That thus he suffers for.
QUEEN: I shall obey you.—
   And for your part, Ophelia, I do wish
   That your good beauties be the happy cause
   Of Hamlet's wildness. So shall I hope your virtues   40
   Will bring him to his wonted way again,
   To both your honors.
OPHELIA: Madam, I wish it may.

(*Exit* QUEEN *with* LORDS.)

POLONIUS: Ophelia, walk you here.—Gracious, so please you,
   We will bestow ourselves.—(*To* OPHELIA.) Read on this book,
   That show of such an exercise may color   45
   Your loneliness.—We are oft to blame in this,
   'Tis too much proved, that with devotion's visage
   And pious action we do sugar o'er
   The devil himself.

III.i. 7 **forward** willing   14 **assay** try to win   17 **o'er-raught** overtook   26 **give him a further edge** sharpen his inclination   29 **closely** privately   31 **Affront** meet face to face   32 **espials** spies   45 **exercise** act of devotion; **color** give an appearance of naturalness to

KING: (*Aside*.)   O, 'tis too true.
50 How smart a lash that speech doth give my conscience!
    The harlot's cheek, beautied with plast'ring art,
    Is not more ugly to the thing that helps it
    Then is my deed to my most painted word.
    O heavy burden!
55 POLONIUS: I hear him coming. Let's withdraw, my lord.

(*Exeunt* KING *and* POLONIUS.)

(*Enter* HAMLET.)

HAMLET: To be, or not to be, that is the question:
    Whether 'tis nobler in the mind to suffer
    The slings and arrows of outrageous fortune,
    Or to take arms against a sea of troubles,
60 And by opposing end them. To die, to sleep—
    No more; and by a sleep to say we end
    The heartache, and the thousand natural shocks
    That flesh is heir to: 'tis a consummation
    Devoutly to be wished. To die, to sleep—
65 To sleep, perchance to dream, ay there's the rub;
    For in that sleep of death what dreams may come
    When we have shuffled off this mortal coil
    Must give us pause. There's the respect
    That makes calamity of so long life:
70 For who would bear the whips and scorns of time,
    Th' oppressor's wrong, the proud man's contumely,
    The pangs of despised love, the law's delay,
    The insolence of office, and the spurns
    That patient merit of th' unworthy takes,
75 When he himself might his quietus make
    With a bare bodkin? Who would fardels bear,
    To grunt and sweat under a weary life,
    But that the dread of something after death,
    The undiscovered country, from whose bourn
80 No traveller returns, puzzles the will,
    And makes us rather bear those ills we have
    Than fly to others that we know not of?
    Thus conscience does make cowards of us all,
    And thus the native hue of resolution
85 Is sicklied o'er with the pale cast of thought,
    And enterprises of great pitch and moment
    With this regard their currents turn awry
    And lose the name of action. Soft you now,
    The fair Ophelia.—Nymph, in thy orisons
90 Be all my sins remembered.
    OPHELIA: Good my lord,
    How does your honor for this many a day?
    HAMLET: I humbly thank you, well.
    OPHELIA: My lord, I have remembrances of yours
    That I have longed long to re-deliver.
95 I pray you now receive them.
    HAMLET: No, not I,
    I never gave you aught.

OPHELIA: My honored lord, you know right well you did,
    And with them words of so sweet breath composed
    As made the things more rich. Their perfume lost,
100 Take these again, for to the noble mind
    Rich gifts wax poor when givers prove unkind.
    There, my lord.
HAMLET: Ha, ha! are you honest?
OPHELIA: My lord?
105 HAMLET: Are you fair?
OPHELIA: What means your lordship?
HAMLET: That if you be honest and fair, your honesty should
    admit no discourse to your beauty.
OPHELIA: Could beauty, my lord, have better commerce than
    with honesty? 110
HAMLET: Ay, truly, for the power of beauty will sooner trans-
    form honesty from what it is to a bawd than the force of
    honesty can translate beauty into his likeness. This was
    sometime a paradox, but now the time gives it proof. I did
    love you once. 115
OPHELIA: Indeed, my lord, you made me believe so.
HAMLET: You should not have believed me, for virtue cannot
    so inoculate our old stock but we shall relish of it. I loved
    you not.
OPHELIA: I was the more deceived. 120
HAMLET: Get thee to a nunnery. Why wouldst thou be a
    breeder of sinners? I am myself indifferent honest, but yet I
    could accuse me of such things that it were better my
    mother had not borne me: I am very proud, revengeful, am-
    bitious, with more offences at my beck than I have thoughts 125
    to put them in, imagination to give them shape, or time to
    act them in. What should such fellows as I do crawling be-
    tween earth and heaven? We are arrant knaves all; believe
    none of us. Go thy ways to a nunnery. Where's your father?
OPHELIA: At home, my lord. 130
HAMLET: Let the doors be shut upon him, that he may play
    the fool nowhere but in's own house. Farewell.
OPHELIA: O, help him, you sweet heavens!
HAMLET: If thou dost marry, I'll give thee this plague for thy
    dowry: be thou as chaste as ice, as pure as snow, thou shalt 135
    not escape calumny. Get thee to a nunnery, farewell. Or if
    thou wilt needs marry, marry a fool, for wise men know
    well enough what monsters you make of them. To a nun-
    nery, go, and quickly too. Farewell.
OPHELIA: Heavenly powers, restore him! 140
HAMLET: I have heard of your paintings well enough. God
    hath given you one face, and you make yourselves another.
    You jig and amble, and you lisp; you nickname God's crea-
    tures, and make your wantonness your ignorance. Go to, I'll
    no more on't, it hath made me mad. I say we will have no 145
    moe marriage. Those that are married already, all but one,
    shall live. The rest shall keep as they are. To a nunnery, go.

(*Exit*.)

OPHELIA: O, what a noble mind is here o'erthrown!
    The courtier's, soldier's, scholar's, eye, tongue, sword,

---

52 **to** compared to   65 **rub** obstacle (lit., obstruction encountered by bowler's ball)   67 **coil** bustle, turmoil   75 **quietus** settlement   76 **bodkin** dagger; **fardels** burdens   79 **bourn** realm
86 **pitch** height   87 **regard** consideration   89 **orisons** prayers

103 **honest** chaste   118 **inoculate** graft   122 **indifferent**
honest moderately respectable   144 **make your wantonness**
your ignorance excuse your wanton behavior with the plea
that you don't know any better   145 **moe** more

150 Th' expectancy and rose of the fair state,
The glass of fashion and the mould of form,
Th' observed of all observers, quite quite down!
And I of ladies most deject and wretched,
That sucked the honey of his musiced vows,
155 Now see that noble and most sovereign reason
Like sweet bells jangled, out of time and harsh;
That unmatched form and feature of blown youth
Blasted with ecstasy. O, woe is me
T' have seen what I have seen, see what I see!

(*Enter* KING *and* POLONIUS.)

160 KING: Love? His affections do not that way tend,
Nor what he spake, though it lacked form a little,
Was not like madness. There's something in his soul,
O'er which his melancholy sits on brood,
And I do doubt the hatch and the disclose
165 Will be some danger; which for to prevent,
I have in quick determination
Thus set it down: he shall with speed to England
For the demand of our neglected tribute.
Haply the seas and countries different,
170 With variable objects, shall expel
This something-settled matter in his heart
Whereon his brains still beating puts him thus
From fashion of himself. What think you on't?
POLONIUS: It shall do well. But yet do I believe
175 The origin and commencement of his grief
Sprung from neglected love.—How now, Ophelia?
You need not tell us what Lord Hamlet said;
We heard it all.—My lord, do as you please,
But if you hold it fit, after the play
180 Let his queen-mother all alone entreat him
To show his grief. Let her be round with him,
And I'll be placed, so please you, in the ear
Of all their conference. If she find him not,
To England send him; or confine him where
185 Your wisdom best shall think.
KING: It shall be so.
Madness in great ones must not unwatched go.

(*Exeunt.*)

SCENE II

Enter HAMLET *and three of the* PLAYERS.

HAMLET: Speak the speech, I pray you, as I pronounced it to
you, trippingly on the tongue; but if you mouth it as many
of our players do, I had as lief the town-crier spoke my
lines. Nor do not saw the air too much with your hand
5 thus, but use all gently, for in the very torrent, tempest, and
as I may say, whirlwind of your passion, you must acquire
and beget a temperance that may give it smoothness. O, it
offends me to the soul to hear a robustious periwig-pated
fellow tear a passion to tatters, to very rags, to split the ears

of the groundlings, who for the most part are capable of 10
nothing but inexplicable dumb shows and noise. I would
have such a fellow whipped for o'erdoing Termagant. It
out-Herods Herod. Pray you avoid it.
1 PLAYER: I warrant your honour.
HAMLET: Be not too tame neither, but let your own discre- 15
tion be your tutor. Suit the action to the word, the word
to the action, with this special observance, that you o'er-
step not the modesty of nature; for any thing so o'erdone
is from the purpose of playing, whose end both at the first,
and now, was and is, to hold as 'twere the mirror up to na- 20
ture, to show virtue her own feature, scorn her own image, and the very age and body of the time his form and
pressure. Now this overdone, or come tardy off, though it
make the unskilful laugh, cannot but make the judicious
grieve, the censure of the which one must in your al- 25
lowance o'erweigh a whole theatre of others. O, there be
players that I have seen play—and heard others praise, and
that highly—not to speak it profanely, that neither having
th' accent of Christians, nor the gait of Christian, pagan,
nor man, have so strutted and bellowed that I have thought 30
some of nature's journeymen had made men, and not
made them well, they imitated humanity so abominably.
1 PLAYER: I hope we have reformed that indifferently with us.
HAMLET: O, reform it altogether. And let those that play your
clowns speak no more than is set down for them, for there 35
be of them that will themselves laugh, to set on some
quantity of barren spectators to laugh too, though in the
meantime some necessary question of the play be then to
be considered. That's villanous, and shows a most pitiful
ambition in the fool that uses it. Go, make you ready. 40

(*Exeunt* PLAYERS.)

(*Enter* POLONIUS, GUILDENSTERN, *and* ROSENCRANTZ.)

How now, my lord? Will the king hear this piece of work?
POLONIUS: And the queen too, and that presently.
HAMLET: Bid the players make haste. (*Exit* POLONIUS.)
Will you two help to hasten them?
ROSENCRANTZ: Ay, my lord. 45

(*Exeunt they two.*)

HAMLET: What, ho! Horatio!

(*Enter* HORATIO.)

HORATIO: Here, sweet lord, at your service.
HAMLET: Horatio, thou art e'en as just a man
As e'er my conversation coped withal.
HORATIO: O my dear lord! 50
HAMLET: Nay, do not think I flatter,
For what advancement may I hope from thee,
That no revenue hast but thy good spirits

---

150 **expectancy** hope   151 **glass** mirror   157 **blown** blooming   158 **ecstasy** madness   160 **affections** emotions   164
doubt fear   181 **round** plain-spoken

III.ii. 10 **groundlings** spectators who paid least and stood on
the ground   12 **Termagant** thought to be a Mohammedan deity, and represented in medieval mystery plays as a violent and
ranting personage; **Herod** represented in the mystery plays as a
blustering tyrant   25 **censure** judgment, opinion   33 **indifferently** fairly well   49 **coped** encountered

To feed and clothe thee? Why should the poor be flattered?
No, let the candied tongue lick absurd pomp,
55 And crook the pregnant hinges of the knee
Where thrift may follow fawning. Dost thou hear?
Since my dear soul was mistress of her choice
And could of men distinguish her election,
S'hath sealed thee for herself, for thou hast been
60 As one in suff'ring all that suffers nothing,
A man that Fortune's buffets and rewards
Hast ta'en with equal thanks; and blest are those
Whose blood and judgment are so well comeddled
That they are not a pipe for Fortune's finger
65 To sound what stop she please. Give me that man
That is not passion's slave, and I will wear him
In my heart's core, ay, in my heart of heart,
As I do thee. Something too much of this.
There is a play to-night before the king.
70 One scene of it comes near the circumstance
Which I have told thee of my father's death.
I prithee, when thou seest that act afoot,
Even with the very comment of thy soul
Observe my uncle. If his occulted guilt
75 Do not itself unkennel in one speech,
It is a damnèd ghost that we have seen,
And my imaginations are as foul
As Vulcan's stithy. Give him heedful note,
For I mine eyes will rivet to his face,
80 And after we will both our judgements join
In censure of his seeming.
HORATIO: Well, my lord.
If 'a steal aught the whilst this play is playing,
And 'scape detecting, I will pay the theft.

(*Enter Trumpets and Kettledrums,* KING, QUEEN, POLONIUS,
OPHELIA, [ROSENCRANTZ, GUILDENSTERN, *and other* LORDS
attendant].)

HAMLET: They are coming to the play. I must be idle.
85   Get you a place.
KING: How fares our cousin Hamlet?
HAMLET: Excellent, i' faith, of the chameleon's dish. I eat the
    air, promise-crammed. You cannot feed capons so.
KING: I have nothing with this answer, Hamlet. These words
90   are not mine.
HAMLET: No, nor mine now. (*To* POLONIUS.) My lord, you
    played once i' th' university, you say?
POLONIUS: That did I, my lord; and was accounted a good
    actor.
95 HAMLET: What did you enact?
POLONIUS: I did enact Julius Caesar. I was killed i' th' Capi-
    tol; Brutus killed me.
HAMLET: It was a brute part of him to kill so capital a calf
    there. Be the players ready?
100 ROSENCRANTZ: Ay, my lord, they stay upon your patience.

---

55 **pregnant** ready   56 **thrift** profit   58 **election** choice   63
co-meddled mingled   73 **the very comment of thy soul**
with a keenness of observation that penetrates to the very being
74 **occulted** hidden   75 **unkennel** reveal   78 **stithy** forge
81 **censure** opinion   84 **idle** crazy   87 **chameleon's dish** the
air, on which the chameleon was supposed to feed

QUEEN: Come hither, my dear Hamlet, sit by me.
HAMLET: No, good mother, here's metal more attractive.
POLONIUS: (*To the* KING.) O, ho! do you mark that?
HAMLET: Lady, shall I lie in your lap?

(*Lying down at* OPHELIA's *feet.*)

OPHELIA: No, my lord.   105
HAMLET: I mean, my head upon your lap?
OPHELIA: Ay, my lord.
HAMLET: Do you think I meant country matters?
OPHELIA: I think nothing, my lord.
HAMLET: That's a fair thought to lie between maids' legs.   110
OPHELIA: What is, my lord?
HAMLET: Nothing.
OPHELIA: You are merry, my lord.
HAMLET: Who, I?
OPHELIA: Ay, my lord.   115
HAMLET: O God, your only jig-maker! What should a man
    do but be merry? For look you how cheerfully my
    mother looks, and my father died within's two hours.
OPHELIA: Nay, 'tis twice two months, my lord.
HAMLET: So long? Nay then, let the devil wear black, for I'll   120
    have a suit of sables. O heavens! die two months ago, and
    not forgotten yet? Then there's hope a great man's mem-
    ory may outlive his life half a year, but, by'r lady 'a must
    build churches then, or else shall 'a suffer not thinking on,
    with the hobby-horse, whose epitaph is   125

        'For O, for O, the hobby-horse is forgot!'

(*The trumpets sound. Dumb Show follows.*)

(*Enter a* KING *and a* QUEEN [*very lovingly*]; *the* QUEEN *embracing
him and he her.* [*She kneels, and makes show of protestation unto
him.*] *He takes her up, and declines his head upon her neck. He lies
him down upon a bank of flowers; she, seeing him asleep, leaves him.
Anon comes in another man, takes off his crown, kisses it, pours poison in the sleeper's ears, and leaves him. The* QUEEN *returns, finds
the* KING *dead, makes passionate action. The* POISONER *with some
three or four come in again, seem to condole with her. The dead body
is carried away. The* POISONER *woos the* QUEEN *with gifts; she
seems harsh awhile, but in the end accepts love.*)

(*Exeunt.*)

OPHELIA: What means this, my lord?
HAMLET: Marry, this is miching mallecho; it means mischief.
OPHELIA: Belike this show imports the argument of the play.

(*Enter* PROLOGUE.)

HAMLET: We shall know by this fellow. The players cannot   130
    keep counsel; they'll tell all.
OPHELIA: Will 'a tell us what this show meant?
HAMLET: Ay, or any show that you will show him. Be not you
    ashamed to show, he'll not shame to tell you what it means.

---

125 **hobby-horse** the figure of a horse fastened round the waist
of a morris dancer. Puritan efforts to suppress the country sports
in which the hobby-horse figured led to a popular ballad
lamenting the fact that "the hobby-horse is forgot"   128 **miching mallecho** skulking or crafty crime

135 OPHELIA: You are naught, you are naught. I'll mark the play.
PROLOGUE:

> For us, and for our tragedy,
> Here stooping to your clemency,
> We beg your hearing patiently.

(*Exit.*)

HAMLET: Is this a prologue, or the posy of a ring?
140 OPHELIA: 'Tis brief, my lord.
HAMLET: As woman's love.

(*Enter [the* PLAYER] KING *and* QUEEN.)

PLAYER KING: Full thirty times hath Phoebus' cart gone round
    Neptune's salt wash and Tellus' orbèd ground,
    And thirty dozen moons with borrowed sheen
145   About the world have times twelve thirties been,
    Since love our hearts and Hymen did our hands
    Unite comutual in most sacred bands.
PLAYER QUEEN: So many journeys may the sun and moon
    Make us again count o'er ere love be done!
150   But woe is me, you are so sick of late,
    So far from cheer and from your former state,
    That I distrust you. Yet though I distrust,
    Discomfort you, my lord, it nothing must.
    For women's fear and love hold quantity,
155   In neither aught, or in extremity.
    Now what my love is proof hath made you know,
    And as my love is sized, my fear is so.
    Where love is great, the littlest doubts are fear;
    Where little fears grow great, great love grows there.
160 PLAYER KING: Faith, I must leave thee, love, and shortly too;
    My operant powers their functions leave to do.
    And thou shalt live in this fair world behind,
    Honored, beloved; and haply one as kind
    For husband shalt thou—
PLAYER QUEEN: O, confound the rest!
165   Such love must needs be treason in my breast.
    In second husband let me be accurst!
    None wed the second but who killed the first.
HAMLET: That's wormwood.
PLAYER QUEEN: The instances that second marriage move
170   Are base respects of thrift, but none of love.
    A second time I kill my husband dead,
    When second husband kisses me in bed.
PLAYER KING: I do believe you think what now you speak,
    But what we do determine oft we break.
175   Purpose is but the slave to memory,
    Of violent birth, but poor validity;
    Which now, like fruit unripe, sticks on the tree,
    But fall unshaken when they mellow be.
    Most necessary 'tis that we forget
180   To pay ourselves what to ourselves is debt.

---

135 **naught** naughty, lewd   139 **posy** brief motto engraved on a fingerring   142 **Phoebus' cart** the sun's chariot   143 **Tellus' orbed ground** the earth (Tellus was the Roman goddess of the earth)   146 **Hymen** god of marriage   152 **distrust** fear for   154 **hold quantity** are proportional, weigh alike   157 **as my love is sized** according to the greatness of my love   161 **operant** vital   169 **instances** motives   176 **validity** endurance

    What to ourselves in passion we propose,
    The passion ending, doth the purpose lose.
    The violence of either grief or joy
    Their own enactures with themselves destroy.
    Where joy most revels, grief doth most lament;   185
    Grief joys, joy grieves, on slender accident.
    This world is not for aye, nor 'tis not strange
    That even our loves should with our fortunes change;
    For 'tis a question left us yet to prove,
    Whether love lead fortune, or else fortune love.   190
    The great man down, you mark his favorite flies;
    The poor advanced makes friends of enemies;
    And hitherto doth love on fortune tend,
    For who not needs shall never lack a friend,
    And who in want a hollow friend doth try,   195
    Directly seasons him his enemy.
    But orderly to end where I begun,
    Our wills and fates do so contrary run
    That our devices still are overthrown;
    Our thoughts are ours, their ends none of our own.   200
    So think thou wilt no second husband wed,
    But die thy thoughts when thy first lord is dead.
PLAYER QUEEN: Nor earth to me give food, nor heaven light,
    Sport and repose lock from me day and night.
    To desperation turn my trust and hope,   205
    An anchor's cheer in prison be my scope,
    Each opposite that blanks the face of joy
    Meet what I would have well, and it destroy,
    Both here and hence pursue me lasting strife,
    If once a widow, ever I be wife!   210
HAMLET: If she should break it now!
PLAYER KING: 'Tis deeply sworn. Sweet, leave me here awhile.
    My spirits grow dull, and fain I would beguile
    The tedious day with sleep.

(*Sleeps.*)

PLAYER QUEEN: Sleep rock thy brain.
    And never come mischance between us twain!   215

(*Exit.*)

HAMLET: Madam, how like you this play?
QUEEN: The lady doth protest too much, methinks.
HAMLET: O, but she'll keep her word.
KING: Have you heard the argument? Is there no offence in't?
HAMLET: No, no, they do but jest, poison in jest; no offence   220
    i' th' world.
KING: What do you call the play?
HAMLET: 'The Mouse-trap.' Marry, how? Tropically. This play
    is the image of a murder done in Vienna. Gonzago is the
    duke's name; his wife, Baptista. You shall see anon. 'Tis a   225
    knavish piece of work, but what of that? Your majesty, and
    we that have free souls, it touches us not. Let the galled
    jade winch, our withers are unwrung.

(*Enter* LUCIANUS.)

---

184 **enactures** enactments   187 **aye** ever   196 **seasons him** ripens him into   206 **anchor's** anchorite's   227 **galled jade** sorebacked horse

This is one Lucianus, nephew to the king.

230 OPHELIA: You are as good as a chorus, my lord.

HAMLET: I could interpret between you and your love, if I could see the puppets dallying.

OPHELIA: You are keen, my lord, you are keen.

HAMLET: It would cost you a groaning to take off mine edge.

235 OPHELIA: Still better, and worse.

HAMLET: So you mis-take your husbands.—Begin, murderer. Leave thy damnable faces and begin. Come, the croaking raven doth bellow for revenge.

LUCIANUS: Thoughts black, hands apt, drugs fit, and time

240   agreeing,

  Confederate season, else no creature seeing.

  Thou mixture rank, of midnight weeds collected,

  With Hecate's ban thrice blasted, thrice infected,

  Thy natural magic and dire property

  On wholesome life usurp immediately.

(Pours the poison in his ears.)

245 HAMLET: 'A poisons him i' th' garden for his estate. His name's Gonzago. The story is extant, and written in very choice Italian. You shall see anon how the murderer gets the love of Gonzago's wife.

OPHELIA: The king rises.

250 HAMLET: What, frighted with false fire?

QUEEN: How fares my lord?

POLONIUS: Give o'er the play.

KING: Give me some light. Away!

POLONIUS: Lights, lights, lights!

(Exeunt all but HAMLET and HORATIO.)

255 HAMLET: Why, let the strucken deer go weep,

  The hart ungallèd play.

  For some must watch, while some must sleep;

  Thus runs the world away.

  Would not this, sir, and a forest of feathers—if the rest of

260 my fortunes turn Turk with me—with two Provincial roses on my razed shoes, get me a fellowship in a cry of players?

HORATIO: Half a share.

HAMLET: A whole one, I.

  For thou dost know, O Damon dear,

265   This realm dismantled was

  Of Jove himself, and now reigns here

  A very, very—pajock.

HORATIO: You might have rhymed.

HAMLET: O good Horatio, I'll take the ghost's word for a

270 thousand pound. Didst perceive?

HORATIO: Very well, my lord.

HAMLET: Upon the talk of the poisoning.

HORATIO: I did very well note him.

HAMLET: Ah, ha! Come, some music. Come, the recorders.

For if the king like not the comedy,   275

  Why then, belike, he likes it not, perdy.

Come, some music.

(Enter ROSENCRANTZ *and* GUILDENSTERN.*)*

GUILDENSTERN: Good my lord, vouchsafe me a word with you.

HAMLET: Sir, a whole history.

GUILDENSTERN: The king, sir—   280

HAMLET: Ay, sir what of him?

GUILDENSTERN: Is in his retirement marvellous distempered.

HAMLET: With drink, sir?

GUILDENSTERN: No, my lord, with choler.

HAMLET: Your wisdom should show itself more richer to sig-   285 nify this to the doctor, for for me to put him to his purgation would perhaps plunge him into more choler.

GUILDENSTERN: Good my lord, put your discourse into some frame, and start not so wildly from my affair.

HAMLET: I am tame, sir. Pronounce.   290

GUILDENSTERN: The queen, your mother, in most great affliction of spirit, hath sent me to you.

HAMLET: You are welcome.

GUILDENSTERN: Nay, good my lord, this courtesy is not of the right breed. If it shall please you to make me a wholesome   295 answer, I will do your mother's commandment. If not, your pardon and my return shall be the end of my business.

HAMLET: Sir, I cannot.

GUILDENSTERN: What, my lord?

HAMLET: Make you a wholesome answer; my wit's diseased.   300 But, sir, such answer as I can make, you shall command, or rather, as you say, my mother. Therefore no more, but to the matter. My mother, you say—

ROSENCRANTZ: Then thus she says: your behaviour hath struck her into amazement and admiration.   305

HAMLET: O wonderful son, that can so stonish a mother! But is there no sequel at the heels of this mother's admiration? Impart.

ROSENCRANTZ: She desires to speak with you in her closet ere you go to bed.   310

HAMLET: We shall obey, were she ten times our mother. Have you any further trade with us?

ROSENCRANTZ: My lord, you once did love me.

HAMLET: And do still, by these pickers and stealers.

ROSENCRANTZ: Good my lord, what is your cause of distem-   315 per? You do surely bar the door upon your own liberty, if you deny your griefs to your friend.

HAMLET: Sir, I lack advancement.

ROSENCRANTZ: How can that be, when you have the voice of the king himself for your succession in Denmark?   320

HAMLET: Ay, sir, but 'While the grass grows'—the proverb is something musty.

---

242 **Hecate** goddess of witchcraft; **blasted** fallen under a blight 259 **feathers** plumes for actors' costumes 260 **Provincial roses** i.e., Provençal roses. Ribbon rosettes resembling these French roses were used to decorate shoes 261 **razed** with ornamental slashing; **cry** company 267 **pajock** presumably a variant form of "patch-cock," a despicable person. Cf. 3.4.104

275 **For if . . . comedy** a seeming parody of *The Spanish Tragedy,* 4.1.197–98 ("And if the world like not this tragedy, / Hard is the hap of old Hieronimo"), where another revenger's dramatic entertainment is referred to 287 **choler** one of the four bodily humors, an excess of which gave rise to anger 295 **wholesome** reasonable 307 **admiration** wonder 314 **pickers and stealers** hands 321 **'while the grass grows'** a proverb ending 'the horse starves'

(*Enter the* PLAYERS *with recorders.*)

O, the recorders! Let me see one. To withdraw with
you—why do you go about to recover the wind of me, as
325   if you would drive me into a toil?
GUILDENSTERN: O, my lord, if my duty be too bold, my love
   is too unmannerly.
HAMLET: I do not well understand that. Will you play upon
   this pipe?
330 GUILDENSTERN: My lord, I cannot.
HAMLET: I pray you.
GUILDENSTERN: Believe me, I cannot.
HAMLET: I beseech you.
GUILDENSTERN: I know no touch of it, my lord.
335 HAMLET: It is easy as lying. Govern these ventages with your
   fingers and thumb, give it breath with your mouth, and it
   will discourse most eloquent music. Look you, these are
   the stops.
GUILDENSTERN: But these cannot I command to any ut-
340   t'rance of harmony. I have not the skill.
HAMLET: Why look you now, how unworthy a thing you make
   of me! You would play upon me, you would seem to know
   my stops, you would pluck out the heart of my mystery, you
   would sound me from my lowest note to the top of my com-
345   pass; and there is music, excellent voice, in this little organ,
   yet cannot you make it speak. 'Sblood, do you think I am easier to be played on than a pipe? Call me what instrument you
   will, though you can fret me, you cannot play upon me.

(*Enter* POLONIUS.)

350   God bless you, sir!
POLONIUS: My lord, the queen would speak with you, and
   presently.
HAMLET: Do you see yonder cloud that's almost in shape of a
   camel?
355 POLONIUS: By th' mass and 'tis, like a camel indeed.
HAMLET: Methinks it is like a weasel.
POLONIUS: It is backed like a weasel.
HAMLET: Or like a whale.
POLONIUS: Very like a whale.
360 HAMLET: Then I will come to my mother by and by. (*Aside.*)
   They fool me to the top of my bent.—I will come by and by.
POLONIUS: I will say so.

(*Exit* POLONIUS.)

HAMLET: 'By and by' is easily said. Leave me, friends.

(*Exeunt all but* HAMLET.)

   'Tis now the very witching time of night,
365   When churchyards yawn and hell itself breathes out
   Contagion to this world. Now could I drink hot blood,
   And do such bitter business as the day
   Would quake to look on. Soft, now to my mother.
   O heart, lose not thy nature; let not ever
370   The soul of Nero enter this firm bosom.

Let me be cruel, not unnatural;
I will speak daggers to her, but use none.
My tongue and soul in this be hypocrites:
How in my words somever she be shent,
To give them seals never my soul consent!   375

(*Exit.*)

SCENE III

Enter KING, ROSENCRANTZ, *and* GUILDENSTERN.

KING: I like him not, nor stands it safe with us
   To let his madness range. Therefore prepare you.
   I your commission will forthwith dispatch,
   And he to England shall along with you.
   The terms of our estate may not endure   5
   Hazard so near's as doth hourly grow
   Out of his brows.
GUILDENSTERN: We will ourselves provide,
   Most holy and religious fear it is
   To keep those many many bodies safe
   That live and feed upon your majesty.   10
ROSENCRANTZ: The single and peculiar life is bound
   With all the strength and armor of the mind
   To keep itself from noyance, but much more
   That spirit upon whose weal depends and rests
   The lives of many. The cess of majesty   15
   Dies not alone, but like a gulf doth draw
   What's near it with it. It is a massy wheel
   Fixed on the summit of the highest mount,
   To whose huge spokes ten thousand lesser things
   Are mortised and adjoined, which when it falls,   20
   Each small annexment, petty consequence,
   Attends the boist'rous ruin. Never alone
   Did the king sigh, but with a general groan.
KING: Arm you, I pray you, to this speedy voyage,
   For we will fetters put about this fear,   25
   Which now goes too free-footed.
ROSENCRANTZ: We will haste us.

(*Exeunt Gentlemen* [ROSENCRANTZ *and* GUILDENSTERN].)

(*Enter* POLONIUS.)

POLONIUS: My lord, he's going to his mother's closet.
   Behind the arras I'll convey myself
   To hear the process. I'll warrant she'll tax him home,
   And as you said, and wisely was it said,   30
   'Tis meet that some more audience than a mother,
   Since nature makes them partial, should o'erhear
   The speech of vantage. Fare you well, my liege.
   I'll call upon you ere you go to bed,
   And tell you what I know.   35

---

374 **somever,** soever; **shent** reproved, abused

III.iii. 5 **terms of our estate** conditions required for our rule
as king   7 **brows** threatening looks that suggest the dangerous
plots Hamlet's brain is hatching   11 **peculiar** private   13 **noyance** harm   15 **cess** cessation, extinction   20 **mortised**
jointed (as with mortise and tenon)   33 **of vantage** (1) in addition; (2) from a convenient place for listening

---

323 **withdraw** step aside for private conversation   325 **toil** net,
snare   335 **ventages** holes or stops in the recorder   348 **fret**
(1) a stop on the fingerboard of a guitar (2) annoy   370 **Nero**
Roman emperor who murdered his mother

KING: Thanks, dear my lord. (*Exit* POLONIUS.)
　　O, my offence is rank, it smells to heaven;
　　It hath the primal eldest curse upon't,
　　A brother's murder. Pray can I not,
　　Though inclination be as sharp as will.
40　My stronger guilt defeats my strong intent,
　　And like a man to double business bound,
　　I stand in pause where I shall first begin,
　　And both neglect. What if this cursèd hand
　　Were thicker than itself with brother's blood,
45　Is there not rain enough in the sweet heavens
　　To wash it white as snow? Whereto serves mercy
　　But to confront the visage of offence?
　　And what's in prayer but this twofold force,
　　To be forestallèd ere we come to fall,
50　Or pardoned being down? Then I'll look up.
　　My fault is past. But, O, what form of prayer
　　Can serve my turn? 'Forgive me my foul murder'?
　　That cannot be, since I am still possessed
　　Of those effects for which I did the murder—
55　My crown, mine own ambition, and my queen.
　　May one be pardoned and retain th' offence?
　　In the corrupted currents of this world
　　Offence's gilded hand may shove by justice,
　　And oft 'tis seen the wicked prize itself
60　Buys out the law. But 'tis not so above
　　There is no shuffling: there the action lies
　　In his true nature, and we ourselves compelled,
　　Even to the teeth and forehead of our faults,
　　To give in evidence. What then? What rests?
65　Try what repentance can. What can it not?
　　Yet what can it when one can not repent?
　　O wretched state! O bosom black as death!
　　O limèd soul, that struggling to be free
　　Art more engaged! Help, angels! Make assay.
70　Bow, stubborn knees, and heart with strings of steel,
　　Be soft as sinews of the new-born babe.
　　All may be well.

(*He kneels.*)

(*Enter* HAMLET.)

HAMLET: Now might I do it pat, now 'a is a-praying,
　　And now I'll do't—and so 'a goes to heaven,
75　And so am I revenged. That would be scanned.
　　A villain kills my father, and for that,
　　I, his sole son, do this same villain send
　　To heaven.
　　Why, this is hire and salary, not revenge.
80　'A took my father grossly, full of bread,
　　With all his crimes broad blown, as flush as May;
　　And how his audit stands who knows save heaven?
　　But in our circumstance and course of thought
　　'Tis heavy with him; and am I then revenged

　　To take him in the purging of his soul,   85
　　When he is fit and seasoned for his passage?
　　No.
　　Up, sword, and know thou a more horrid hent.
　　When he is drunk asleep, or in his rage,
　　Or in th' incestuous pleasure of his bed,   90
　　At game a-swearing, or about some act
　　That has no relish of salvation in't—
　　Then trip him, that his heels may kick at heaven,
　　And that his soul may be as damned and black
　　As hell, whereto it goes. My mother stays.   95
　　This physic but prolongs thy sickly days.

(*Exit.*)

KING: (*Rising.*) My words fly up, my thoughts remain below.
　　Words without thoughts never to heaven go.

(*Exit.*)

SCENE IV

Enter [QUEEN] GERTRUDE *and* POLONIUS.

POLONIUS: 'A will come straight. Look you lay home to him.
　　Tell him his pranks have been too broad to bear with,
　　And that your grace hath screened and stood between
　　Much heat and him. I'll silence me even here.
　　Pray you be round.   5
QUEEN: I'll warrant you. Fear me not.
　　Withdraw, I hear him coming.

(POLONIUS *goes behind the arras.*)

(*Enter* HAMLET.)

HAMLET: Now, mother, what's the matter?
QUEEN: Hamlet, thou hast thy father much offended.
HAMLET: Mother, you have my father much offended.
QUEEN: Come, come, you answer with an idle tongue.   10
HAMLET: Go, go, you question with a wicked tongue.
QUEEN: Why, how, now, Hamlet?
HAMLET: What's the matter now?
QUEEN: Have you forgot me?
HAMLET: No, by the rood, not so:
　　You are the queen, your husband's brother's wife,
　　And would it were not so, you are my mother.   15
QUEEN: Nay, then I'll set those to you that can speak.
HAMLET: Come, come, and sit you down. You shall not budge.
　　You go not till I set you up a glass
　　Where you may see the inmost part of you.
QUEEN: What will thou do? Thou wilt not murder me?   20
　　Help, ho!
POLONIUS: (*Behind.*) What, ho! help!
HAMLET: (*Draws.*) How now! a rat?
　　Dead for a ducat, dead!

(*Thrusts his sword through the arras and kills* POLONIUS.)

---

39 **will** carnal desire　61 **shuffling** doubledealing; **action** legal
action　68 **limèd** soul caught by sin as the bird by lime　69 **assay** an effort　80 **grossly** unprepared spiritually　81 **as flush
as May** in full flower　83 **in our circumstance** considering all
evidence; **course** beaten way, habit

---

88 **hent** occasion, opportunity

III.iv. 5 Following Polonius's "Pray you be round" (which in *F*
reads "Pray you be round with him"), *F* adds the line: "*Hamlet
within.* Mother, mother, mother"　13 **rood** cross

25 POLONIUS: (*Behind.*) O, I am slain!
    QUEEN: O me, what hast thou done?
    HAMLET: Nay, I know not.
      Is it the king?
    QUEEN: O, what a rash and bloody deed is this!
    HAMLET: A bloody deed? Almost as bad, good mother,
30   As kill a king and marry with his brother.
    QUEEN: As kill a king?
    HAMLET: Ay, lady, it was my word.

(*Lifts up the arras and sees the body of* POLONIUS.)

    Thou wretched, rash, intruding fool, farewell!
    I took thee for thy better. Take thy fortune.
    Thou find'st to be too busy is some danger.—
35   Leave wringing of your hands. Peace, sit you down
    And let me wring your heart, for so I shall
    If it be made of penetrable stuff,
    If damnèd custom have not brazed it so
    That it be proof and bulwark against sense.
40 QUEEN: What have I done that thou dar'st wag thy tongue
    In noise so rude against me?
    HAMLET: Such an act
    That blurs the grace and blush of modesty,
    Calls virtue hypocrite, takes off the rose
    From the fair forehead of an innocent love,
45   And sets a blister there, makes marriage-vows
    As false as dicers' oaths. O, such a deed
    As from the body of contraction plucks
    The very soul, and sweet religion makes
    A rhapsody of words. Heaven's face does glow
50   O'er this solidity and compound mass
    With heated visage, as against the doom—
    Is thought-sick at the act.
    QUEEN: Ay me, what act,
    That roars so loud, and thunders in the index?
    HAMLET: Look here, upon this picture and on this.
55   The counterfeit presentment of two brothers.
    See what a grace was seated on this brow:
    Hyperion's curls, the front of Jove himself,
    An eye like Mars, to threaten and command,
    A station like the herald Mercury
60   New lighted on a heaven-kissing hill—
    A combination and a form indeed
    Where every god did seem to set his seal
    To give the world assurance of a man.
    This was your husband. Look you now what follows.
65   Here is your husband, like a mildewed ear
    Blasting his wholesome brother. Have you eyes?
    Could you on this fair mountain leave to feed,
    And batten on this moor? Ha! have you eyes?
    You cannot call it love, for at your age
70   The heyday in the blood is tame, it's humble,

And waits upon the judgement, and what judgement
Would step from this to this? Sense sure you have,
Else could you not have motion, but sure that sense
Is apoplexed, for madness would not err
Nor sense to ecstasy was ne'er so thralled   75
But it reserved some quantity of choice
To serve in such a difference. What devil was't
That thus hath cozened you at hoodman-blind?
Eyes without feeling, feeling without sight,
Ears without hands or eyes, smelling sans all,   80
Or but a sickly part of one true sense
Could not so mope. O shame! where is thy blush?
Rebellious hell,
If thou canst mutine in a matron's bones,
To flaming youth let virtue be as wax   85
And melt in her own fire. Proclaim no shame
When the compulsive ardor gives the charge,
Since frost itself as actively doth burn,
And reason pandars will.
QUEEN: O Hamlet, speak no more!
    Thou turn'st mine eyes into my very soul,   90
    And there I see such black and grainèd spots
    As will not leave their tinct.
HAMLET: Nay, but to live
    In the rank sweat of an enseamèd bed,
    Stewed in corruption, honeying and making love
    Over the nasty sty—   95
QUEEN: O, speak to me no more!
    These words like daggers enter in mine ears.
    No more, sweet Hamlet.
HAMLET: A murderer and a villain,
    A slave that is not twentieth part the tithe
    Of your precedent lord, a vice of kings,
    A cutpurse of the empire and the rule,   100
    That from a shelf the precious diadem stole
    And put it in his pocket—
QUEEN: No more.

(*Enter* GHOST.)

HAMLET: A king of shreds and patches—
    Save me and hover o'er me with your wings,   105
    You heavenly guards! What would your gracious figure?
QUEEN: Alas, he's mad.
HAMLET: Do you not come your tardy son to chide,
    That lapsed in time and passion lets go by
    Th' important acting of your dread command?   110
    O, say!
GHOST: Do not forget. This visitation
    Is but to whet thy almost blunted purpose.
    But look, amazement on thy mother sits.
    O, step between her and her fighting soul!   115

---

38 **brazed** plated it as with brass   39 **proof** impenetrable, as of armor   47 **contraction** the contract of marriage   50 **this solidity and compound mass** the earth, as compounded of the four elements   51 **doom** Judgment Day   53 **index** table of contents; thus, indication of what is to follow   55 **counterfeit presentment** portrait   57 **front** forehead   59 **station** bearing figure   68 **batten** feed like an animal   70 **heyday** ardor

---

72 **Sense** the senses collectively, which according to Aristotelian tradition are found in all creatures that have the power of locomotion   75 **ecstasy** madness   78 **hoodman-blind** blindman's bluff   80 **sans** without   82 **mope** act without full use of one's wits   89 **will** desire   91 **grainèd spots** indelible stains   92 **tinct** color   93 **enseamèd** greasy   99 **vice** a character in the morality plays, presented often as a buffoon (here, a caricature)

Conceit in weakest bodies strongest works.
Speak to her, Hamlet.
HAMLET: How is it with you, lady?
QUEEN: Alas, how is't with you,
That you do bend your eye on vacancy,
120   And with th' incorporal air do hold discourse?
Forth at your eyes your spirits wildly peep,
And as the sleeping soldiers in th' alarm,
Your bedded hair like life in excrements
Start up and stand an end. O gentle son,
125   Upon the heat and flame of thy distemper
Sprinkle cool patience. Whereon do you look?
HAMLET: On him, on him! Look you how pale he glares.
His form and cause conjoined, preaching to stones,
Would make them capable.—Do not look upon me,
130   Lest with this piteous action you convert
My stern effects. Then what I have to do
Will want true color—tears perchance for blood.
QUEEN: To whom do you speak this?
HAMLET: Do you see nothing there?
135   QUEEN: Nothing at all, yet all that is I see.
HAMLET: Nor did you nothing hear?
QUEEN: No, nothing but ourselves.
HAMLET: Why, look you there. Look, how it steals away.
My father, in his habit as he lived!
140   Look where he goes even now out at the portal.

(*Exit* GHOST.)

QUEEN: This is the very coinage of your brain.
This bodiless creation ecstasy
Is very cunning in.
HAMLET: My pulse as yours doth temperately keep time,
145   And makes us healthful music. It is not madness
That I have uttered. Bring me to the test,
And I the matter will re-word, which madness
Would gambol from. Mother, for love of grace,
Lay not that flattering unction to your soul,
150   That not your trespass but my madness speaks.
It will but skin and film the ulcerous place
Whiles rank corruption, mining all within,
Infects unseen. Confess yourself to heaven,
Repent what's past, avoid what is to come,
155   And do not spread the compost on the weeds,
To make them ranker. Forgive me this my virtue,
For in the fatness of these pursy times
Virtue itself of vice must pardon beg,
Yea, curb and woo for leave to do him good.
160   QUEEN: O Hamlet, thou hast cleft my heart in twain.
HAMLET: O, throw away the worser part of it,
And live the purer with the other half.
Good night—but go not to my uncle's bed.
Assume a virtue, if you have it not.
165   That monster custom, who all sense doth eat,

---

116 **Conceit** imagination   123 **excrements** nails, hair (whatever grows out of the body)   124 **an** on   129 **capable** able to respond   132 **want** lack   148 **gambol** leap or start, as a shying horse   149 **unction** ointment; hence, soothing notion   152 **mining** undermining   157 **fatness** grossness, slackness; **pursy** corpulent   165 **who all sense doth eat** who consumes all human sense, both bodily and spiritual

Of habits devil, is angel yet in this,
That to the use of actions fair and good
He likewise gives a frock or livery
That aptly is put on. Refrain to-night,
And that shall lend a kind of easiness   170
To the next abstinence; the next more easy;
For use almost can change the stamp of nature,
And either curb the devil, or throw him out
With wondrous potency. Once more, good night,
And when you are desirous to be blest,   175
I'll blessing beg of you. For this same lord,
I do repent; but heaven hath pleased it so,
To punish me with this, and this with me,
That I must be their scourge and minister.
I will bestow him and will answer well   180
The death I gave him. So, again, good night.
I must be cruel only to be kind.
This bad begins and worse remains behind.
One word more, good lady.
QUEEN: What shall I do?
HAMLET: Not this, by no means, that I bid you do: 185
Let the bloat king tempt you again to bed,
Pinch wanton on your cheek, call you his mouse,
And let him, for a pair of reechy kisses,
Or paddling in your neck with his damned fingers,
Make you to ravel all this matter out,   190
That I essentially am not in madness,
But mad in craft. 'Twere good you let him know,
For who that's but a queen, fair, sober, wise,
Would from a paddock, from a bat, a gib,
Such dear concernings hide? Who would so do?   195
No, in despite of sense and secrecy,
Unpeg the basket on the house's top,
Let the birds fly, and like the famous ape,
To try conclusions, in the basket creep
And break your own neck down.   200
QUEEN: Be thou assured, if words be made of breath
And breath of life, I have no life to breathe
What thou hast said to me.
HAMLET: I must to England; you know that?
QUEEN: Alack,
I had forgot. 'Tis so concluded on.   205
HAMLET: There's letters sealed, and my two school-fellows,
Whom I will trust as I will adders fanged,
They bear the mandate; they must sweep my way
And marshal me to knavery. Let it work,

---

166 **Of habits devil** being a devil in, or in respect of, habits (with a play on "habits," as meaning both settled practices and garments, whereby devilish practices contrast with "actions fair and good," line 167, and devilish garments contrast with the "frock or livery" of line 168, which custom in its angelic aspect provides)   183 **This** i.e., the death of Polonius (cf. line 178); **remains behind** is yet to come   188 **reechy** dirty   191 **essentially** in fact   194 **paddock** toad; **gib** tom-cat   197–200 **Unpeg the basket . . . neck down** the story is lost (in it, apparently, the ape carries a cage of birds to the top of a house, releases them by accident, and, surprised at their flight, imagines he can imitate it by first creeping into the basket and then leaping out. The moral of the story, for the queen, is not to expose herself to destruction by making public what good sense decrees should be kept secret.)

210 For 'tis the sport to have the engineer
Hoist with his own petar; and 't shall go hard
But I will delve one yard below their mines
And blow them at the moon. O, 'tis most sweet
When in one line two crafts directly meet.
215 This man shall set me packing.
I'll lug the guts into the neighbour room.
Mother, good night indeed. This counsellor
Is now most still, most secret and most grave,
Who was in life a foolish prating knave.
220 Come sir, to draw toward an end with you.
Good night, mother.

(*Exit* [HAMLET *tugging in* POLONIUS].)

ACT FOUR

SCENE I

Enter KING [*to the*] QUEEN, *with* ROSENCRANTZ *and* GUILDEN-STERN.

KING: There's matter in these sighs, these profound heaves,
You must translate, 'tis fit we understand them.
Where is your son?
QUEEN: Bestow this place on us a little while.

(*Exeunt* ROSENCRANTZ *and* GUILDENSTERN.)

5   Ah, mine own lord, what have I seen to-night!
KING: What, Gertrude, how does Hamlet?
QUEEN: Mad as the sea and wind when both contend
Which is the mightier. In his lawless fit,
Behind the arras hearing something stir,
10   Whips out his rapier, cries 'A rat, a rat!'
And in this brainish apprehension kills
The unseen good old man.
KING: O heavy deed!
It had been so with us had we been there.
His liberty is full of threats to all—
15   To you yourself, to us, to every one.
Alas, how shall this bloody deed be answered?
It will be laid to us, whose providence
Should have kept short, restrained, and out of haunt,
This mad young man. But so much was our love,
20   We would not understand what was most fit,
But like the owner of a foul disease,
To keep it from divulging, let it feed
Even on the pith of life. Where is he gone?
QUEEN: To draw apart the body he hath killed,
25   O'er whom his very madness, like some ore
Among a mineral of metals base,
Shows itself pure: 'a weeps for what is done.
KING: O Gertrude, come away!
The sun no sooner shall the mountains touch
30   But we will ship him hence, and this vile deed

We must with all our majesty and skill,
Both countenance and excuse. Ho, Guildenstern!

(*Enter* ROSENCRANTZ *and* GUILDENSTERN.)

Friends both, go join you with some further aid.
Hamlet in madness hath Polonius slain,
And from his mother's closet hath he dragged him.   35
Go seek him out; speak fair, and bring the body
Into the chapel. I pray you haste in this.

(*Exeunt* ROSENCRANTZ *and* GUILDENSTERN.)

Come, Gertrude, we'll call up our wisest friends
And let them know both what we mean to do
And what's untimely done; so haply slander—   40
Whose whisper o'er the world's diameter,
As level as the cannon to his blank,
Transports his poisoned shot—may miss our name,
And hit the woundless air. O, come away!
My soul is full of discord and dismay.   45

(*Exeunt.*)

SCENE II

Enter HAMLET.

HAMLET: Safely stowed.—But soft, what noise? who calls on
Hamlet? O, here they come.

([*Enter*] ROSENCRANTZ, [GUILDENSTERN,] *and* OTHERS.)

ROSENCRANTZ: What have you done, my lord, with the dead
body?
HAMLET: Compounded it with dust, whereto 'tis kin.   5
ROSENCRANTZ: Tell us where 'tis, that we may take it thence
And bear it to the chapel.
HAMLET: Do not believe it.
ROSENCRANTZ: Believe what?
HAMLET: That I can keep your counsel and not mine own.   10
Besides, to be demanded of a sponge—what replication
should be made by the son of a king?
ROSENCRANTZ: Take you me for a sponge, my lord?
HAMLET: Ay, sir, that soaks up the king's countenance, his re-
wards, his authorities. But such officers do the king best   15
service in the end. He keeps them, like an apple in the
corner of his jaw, first mouthed to be last swallowed.
When he needs what you have gleaned, it is but squeez-
ing you and, sponge, you shall be dry again.
ROSENCRANTZ: I understand you not, my lord.   20
HAMLET: I am glad of it. A knavish speech sleeps in a foolish
ear.
ROSENCRANTZ: My lord, you must tell us where the body is,
and go with us to the king.
HAMLET: The body is with the king, but the king is not with   25
the body.
The king is a thing—

---

211 **petar** a bomb or charge for blowing in gates   217 **indeed**
in earnest (cf. lines 163, 174, 181)

IV.i. The action is continuous with that of the preceding scene.
The Queen does not leave the stage.   2 **translate** explain   11
brainish apprehension frenzied delusion   18 **out of haunt**
away from society   26 **mineral** mine

---

42 **As level as** sure of aim; **blank** target

IV.ii. 1 After the words "Safely stowed," *F* adds the line: "*Gentlemen within. Hamlet,* Lord *Hamlet.*" Here, as at 3.4.5 "when a
character speaks of hearing someone coming, *F* provides, though
Q does not, for the audience to hear it too" (Jenkins, *SB*, 13.35)
11 **replication** reply

GUILDENSTERN: A thing, my lord!

HAMLET: Of nothing. Bring me to him. Hide fox, and all after.

(*Exeunt.*)

SCENE III

Enter KING, *and two or three.*

KING: I have sent to seek him, and to find the body.
How dangerous is it that this man goes loose!
Yet must not we put the strong law on him.
He's loved of the distracted multitude,
5   Who like not in their judgement but their eyes,
And where 'tis so, th' offender's scourge is weighed,
But never the offence. To bear all smooth and even,
This sudden sending him away must seem
Deliberate pause. Diseases desperate grown
10   By desperate appliance are relieved,
Or not at all.

(*Enter* ROSENCRANTZ, [GUILDENSTERN,] *and all the rest.*)

How now! what hath befall'n?

ROSENCRANTZ: Where the dead body is bestowed, my lord,
We cannot get from him.

KING: But where is he?

ROSENCRANTZ: Without, my lord; guarded, to know your
pleasure.

15   KING: Bring him before us.

ROSENCRANTZ: Ho! bring in the lord.

(*They enter* [*with* HAMLET].)

KING: Now, Hamlet, where's Polonius?

HAMLET: At supper.

KING: At supper? Where?

HAMLET: Not where he eats, but where 'a is eaten. A certain
20   convocation of politic worms are e'en at him. Your worm
is your only emperor for diet. We fat all creatures else to
fat us, and we fat ourselves for maggots. Your fat king and
your lean beggar is but variable service—two dishes, but
to one table. That's the end.

25   KING: Alas, alas!

HAMLET: A man may fish with the worm that hath eat of a
king, and eat of the fish that hath fed of that worm.

KING: What dost thou mean by this?

HAMLET: Nothing but to show you how a king may go a
30   progress through the guts of a beggar.

KING: Where is Polonius?

HAMLET: In heaven. Send thither to see. If your messenger
find him not there, seek him i' th' other place yourself. But
if, indeed, you find him not within this month, you shall
35   nose him as you go up the stairs into the lobby.

KING: (*To* ATTENDANTS.) Go seek him there.

HAMLET: 'A will stay till you come.

---

29 **Hide fox, and all after** presumably a cry in some game such
as hide-and-seek. The words, which do not occur in *Q2,* may
be an actor's addition

IV.iii. 9 **Deliberate pause** carefully considered   30 **progress**
the state journey of a ruler

(*Exeunt* ATTENDANTS.)

KING: Hamlet, this deed, for thine especial safety—
Which we do tender, as we dearly grieve
For that which thou hast done—must send thee hence   40
With fiery quickness. Therefore prepare thyself.
The bark is ready, and the wind at help,
Th' associates tend, and everything is bent
For England.

HAMLET: For England?

KING: Ay, Hamlet.

HAMLET: Good.

KING: So is it, if thou knew'st our purposes.   45

HAMLET: I see a cherub that sees them. But come, for England!
Farewell, dear mother.

KING: Thy loving father, Hamlet.

HAMLET: My mother. Father and mother is man and wife, man
and wife is one flesh. So, my mother. Come, for England.   50

(*Exit.*)

KING: Follow him at foot: tempt him with speed aboard.
Delay it not: I'll have him hence to-night.
Away! for every thing is sealed and done
That else leans on th' affair. Pray you make haste.

(*Exeunt all but the* KING.)

And, England, if my love thou hold'st at aught—   55
As my great power thereof may give thee sense,
Since yet thy cicatrice looks raw and red
After the Danish sword, and thy free awe
Pays homage to us—thou mayst not coldly set
Our sovereign process, which imports at full   60
By letters congruing to that effect
The present death of Hamlet. Do it, England.
For like the hectic in my blood he rages,
And thou must cure me. Till I know 'tis done,
Howe'er my haps, my joys were ne'er begun.   65

(*Exit.*)

SCENE IV

Enter FORTINBRAS *with his* ARMY *over the stage.*

FORTINBRAS: Go, captain, from me greet the Danish king.
Tell him that by his license Fortinbras
Craves the conveyance of a promised march
Over his kingdom. You know the rendezvous.
If that his majesty would aught with us,   5
We shall express our duty in his eye,
And let him know so.

CAPTAIN: I will do't, my lord.

---

39 **tender** value   46 **cherub** one of the cherubim, the watchmen or sentinels of heaven, and thus endowed with the keenest
vision   57 **cicatrice** scar, used here of memory of a defeat   59
coldly set regard with indifference   60 **process** mandate   61
congruing to in accordance with   63 **hectic** consumptive
fever   65 **haps** fortunes

IV.iv. 3 **conveyance** conduct   6 **eye** presence

FORTINBRAS: Go softly on.

(*Exeunt all but the* CAPTAIN.)

(*Enter* HAMLET, ROSENCRANTZ, [GUILDENSTERN,] *and* OTHERS.)

HAMLET: Good sir, whose powers are these?

10 CAPTAIN: They are of Norway, sir.

HAMLET: How purposed, sir, I pray you?

CAPTAIN: Against some part of Poland.

HAMLET: Who commands them, sir?

CAPTAIN: The nephew to old Norway, Fortinbras.

15 HAMLET: Goes it against the main of Poland, sir,
    Or for some frontier?

CAPTAIN: Truly to speak, and with no addition,
    We go to gain a little patch of ground
    That hath in it no profit but the name.

20   To pay five ducats, five, I would not farm it;
    Nor will it yield to Norway or the Pole
    A ranker rate should it be sold in fee.

HAMLET: Why, then the Polack never will defend it.

CAPTAIN: Yes, it is already garrisoned.

25 HAMLET: Two thousand souls and twenty thousand ducats
    Will not debate the question of this straw.
    This is th' imposthume of much wealth and peace,
    That inward breaks, and shows no cause without
    Why the man dies. I humbly thank you, sir.

30 CAPTAIN: God buy you, sir.

(*Exit.*)

ROSENCRANTZ: Will 't please you go, my lord?

HAMLET: I'll be with you straight. Go a little before.

(*Exeunt all but* HAMLET.)

    How all occasions do inform against me,
    And spur my dull revenge! What is a man,
    If his chief good and market of his time
35   Be but to sleep and feed? A beast, no more.
    Sure he that made us with such large discourse,
    Looking before and after, gave us not
    That capability and godlike reason
    To fust in us unused. Now, whether it be
40   Bestial oblivion, or some craven scruple
    Of thinking too precisely on th' event—
    A thought which, quartered, hath but one part wisdom
    And ever three parts coward—I do not know
    Why yet I live to say 'This thing's to do',
45   Sith I have cause, and will, and strength, and means,
    To do 't. Examples gross as earth exhort me:
    Witness this army of such mass and charge,
    Led by a delicate and tender prince,
    Whose spirit, with divine ambition puffed,
50   Makes mouths at the invisible event,
    Exposing what is mortal and unsure
    To all that fortune, death, and danger dare,

    Even for an eggshell. Rightly to be great
    Is not to stir without great argument,
    But greatly to find quarrel in a straw   55
    When honor's at the stake. How stand I then,
    That have a father killed, a mother stained,
    Excitements of my reason and my blood,
    And let all sleep, while to my shame I see
    The imminent death of twenty thousand men   60
    That for a fantasy and trick of fame
    Go to their graves like beds, fight for a plot
    Whereon the numbers cannot try the cause,
    Which is not tomb enough and continent
    To hide the slain? O, from this time forth,   65
    My thoughts be bloody, or be nothing worth!

(*Exit.*)

SCENE V

Enter HORATIO, [QUEEN] GERTRUDE, *and a* GENTLEMAN.

QUEEN: I will not speak with her.

GENTLEMAN: She is importunate, indeed distract.
    Her mood will needs be pitied.

QUEEN: What would she have?

GENTLEMAN: She speaks much of her father, says she hears
    There's tricks i' th' world, and hems, and beats her heart,   5
    Spurns enviously at straws, speaks things in doubt
    That carry but half sense. Her speech is nothing,
    Yet the unshaped use of it doth move
    The hearers to collection; they aim at it,
    And botch the words up fit to their own thoughts,   10
    Which, as her winks and nods and gestures yield them,
    Indeed would make one think there might be thought,
    Though nothing sure, yet much unhappily.

HORATIO: 'Twere good she were spoken with, for she may strew
    Dangerous conjectures in ill-breeding minds.   15

QUEEN: Let her come in. (*Exit* GENTLEMAN.)
    (*Aside.*) To my sick soul, as sin's true nature is,
    Each toy seems prologue to some great amiss.
    So full of artless jealousy is guilt,
    It spills itself in fearing to be spilt.   20

(*Enter* OPHELIA [*distracted*].)

OPHELIA: Where is the beauteous majesty of Denmark?

QUEEN: How now, Ophelia!

OPHELIA: (*She sings.*)

53–56 **Rightly to be great . . . honor's at the stake** i.e., to be rightly great is *not* to refuse to act ("stir") in a dispute ("argument") because the grounds are insufficient, but to be moved to action even in trivial circumstances where a question of honor is involved   63 **try the cause** settle by combat   64 **continent** receptacle

IV.v. 6 **Spurns enviously at straws** takes exception, spitefully, to trifles   7 **nothing** nonsense   8 **unshaped use** disordered manner   9 **collection** attempts at shaping meaning; **aim** guess   13 **sure** certain   18 **toy** trifle   19 **artless jealousy** ill-concealed suspicion   20 **spills** destroys

---

15 **main** chief part   17 **addition** exaggeration   20 **To pay** i.e., for a yearly rental   22 **a ranker rate** a greater price; **sold in fee** sold with absolute and perpetual possession   27 **imposthume** abscess   32 **inform** take shape   34 **market** profit   36 **discourse** power of reasoning   39 **fust** grow musty   50 **Makes mouths at** makes scornful faces at, derides

How should I your true love know
From another one?
25 By his cockle hat and staff,
And his sandal shoon.

QUEEN: Alas, sweet lady, what imports this song?
OPHELIA: Say you? Nay, pray you mark. (*Song.*)

He is dead and gone, lady,
30 He is dead and gone;
At his head a grass-green turf,
At his heels a stone.

O, ho!

QUEEN: Nay, but Ophelia—
OPHELIA: Pray you mark.

(*Sings.*)

35   White his shroud as the mountain snow—

(*Enter* KING.)

QUEEN: Alas, look here, my lord.
OPHELIA: (*Song.*)

Larded all with sweet flowers;
Which bewept to the grave did not go
With true-love showers.

40 KING: How do you, pretty lady?
OPHELIA: Well, good dild you! They say the owl was a baker's
daughter. Lord, we know what we are, but know not what
we may be. God be at your table!
KING: Conceit upon her father.
45 OPHELIA: Pray let's have no words of this, but when they ask
you what it means, say you this:

(*Song.*)

To-morrow is Saint Valentine's day,
All in the morning betime,
And I a maid at your window,
50 To be your Valentine.
Then up he rose, and donned his clo'es,
And dupped the chamber-door,
Let in the maid, that out a maid
Never departed more.

55 KING: Pretty Ophelia—
OPHELIA: Indeed, without an oath, I'll make an end on't:

(*Sings.*)

By Gis and by Saint Charity,
Alack, and fie for shame!
Young men will do't, if they come to't;

By cock, they are to blame.   60
Quoth she 'Before you tumbled me,
You promised me to wed.'

He answers:

'So would I a' done, by yonder sun,
An thou hadst not come to my bed.'   65

KING: How long hath she been thus?
OPHELIA: I hope all will be well. We must be patient, but I
cannot choose but weep, to think they would lay him i' th'
cold ground. My brother shall know of it, and so I thank
you for your good counsel. Come, my coach! Good night, 70
ladies, good night. Sweet ladies, good night, good night.

(*Exit.*)

KING: Follow her close; give her good watch, I pray you.

(*Exeunt* HORATIO *and* GENTLEMEN.)

O, this is the poison of deep grief; it springs
All from her father's death, and now behold!
O Gertrude, Gertrude,   75
When sorrows come, they come not single spies,
But in battalions: first, her father slain;
Next, your son gone, and he most violent author
Of his own just remove; the people muddied,
Thick and unwholesome in their thoughts and whispers 80
For good Polonius' death; and we have done but greenly
In hugger-mugger to inter him; poor Ophelia
Divided from herself and her fair judgement,
Without the which we are pictures, or mere beasts;
Last, and as much containing as all these,   85
Her brother is in secret come from France,
Feeds on his wonder, keeps himself in clouds,
And wants not buzzers to infect his ear
With pestilent speeches of his father's death.
Wherein necessity, of matter beggared,   90
Will nothing stick our person to arraign
In ear and ear, O my dear Gertrude, this,
Like to a murd'ring piece, in many places
Gives me superfluous death. Attend,   (*A noise within.*)

(*Enter a* MESSENGER.)

Where are my Switzers? Let them guard the door.   95
What is the matter?
MESSENGER: Save yourself, my lord.
The ocean, overpeering of his list,
Eats not the flats with more impiteous haste
Then young Laertes, in a riotous head,
O'erbears your officers. The rabble call him lord,   100
And as the world were now but to begin,

---

25 **cockle hat** hat bearing a cockle shell, worn by a pilgrim who
had been to the shrine of St. James of Compostella, in Spain   26
shoon shoes   37 **Larded** garnished, strewn   41 **good dild you**
God yield (requite) you   41–42 **They say the owl was a baker's
daughter** allusion to a folktale in which a baker's daughter was
transformed into an owl because of her ungenerous behavior (giving short measure) when Christ asked for bread in the baker's shop
44 **Conceit upon her father** i.e., obsessed with her father's death
48 **betime** early   52 **dupped** opened   57 **Gis** Jesus

60 **cock** corruption of God   79 **remove** banishment, departure; **muddied** stirred up and confused   81 **greenly** without
judgment   82 **hugger-mugger** secrecy and disorder   87 **in
clouds** i.e., of suspicion and rumor   88 **wants** lacks   90 **of
matter beggared** lacking facts   91 **nothing stick** in no way
hesitate   93 **murd'ring piece** cannon loaded with shot meant
to scatter   94 *F* omits the King's 'Attend,' but substitutes, by way
of drawing attention to the "noise within"   95 **Switzers** Swiss
bodyguard   97 **list** boundary   99 **riotous head** turbulent mob

Antiquity forgot, custom not known,
The ratifiers and props of every word,
They cry 'Choose we, Laertes shall be king'.
105 Caps, hands, and tongues, applaud it to the clouds,
'Laertes shall be king, Laertes king!'
QUEEN: How cheerfully on the false trail they cry!

(*A noise within.*)

O, this is counter, you false Danish dogs!
KING: The doors are broke.

(*Enter* LAERTES *with* OTHERS.)

110 LAERTES: Where is this king?—Sirs, stand you all without.
ALL: No, let's come in.
LAERTES: I pray you give me leave.
ALL: We will, we will.

(*Exeunt his followers.*)

LAERTES: I thank you. Keep the door.—O thou vile king,
    Give me my father!
QUEEN: Calmly, good Laertes,
115 LAERTES: That drop of blood that's calm proclaims me bastard,
    Cries cuckold to my father, brands the harlot
    Even here between the chaste unsmirchèd brow
    Of my true mother.
KING: What is the cause, Laertes,
    That thy rebellion looks so giant-like?
120 Let him go, Gertrude. Do not fear our person.
    There's such divinity doth hedge a king
    That treason can but peep to what it would,
    Acts little of his will. Tell me, Laertes.
    Why thou art thus incensed. Let him go, Gertrude.
125 Speak, man.
LAERTES: Where is my father?
KING: Dead.
QUEEN: But not by him.
KING: Let him demand his fill.
LAERTES: How came he dead? I'll not be juggled with.
    To hell allegiance, vows to the blackest devil,
130 Conscience and grace to the profoundest pit!
    I dare damnation. To this point I stand,
    That both the worlds I give to negligence,
    Let come what comes, only I'll be revenged
    Most throughly for my father.
135 KING: Who shall stay you?
LAERTES: My will, not all the world's.
    And for my means, I'll husband them so well
    They shall go far with little.
KING: Good Laertes,
    If you desire to know the certainty
    Of your dear father, is't writ in your revenge
140 That, swoopstake, you will draw both friend and foe,
    Winner and loser?
LAERTES: None but his enemies.

---

108 **counter** hunting backward on the trail   120 **fear** fear for
134 **throughly** thoroughly   140 **swoopstake** sweepstake, taking all the stakes on the gambling table

KING: Will you know them, then?
LAERTES: To his good friends thus wide I'll ope my arms,
    And like the kind life-rend'ring pelican,
    Repast them with my blood.   145
KING: Why, now you speak
    Like a good child and a true gentleman.
    That I am guiltless of your father's death,
    And am most sensibly in grief for it,
    It shall as level to your judgement 'pear
    As day does to your eye.   150

(*A noise within:* 'Let her come in.')

LAERTES: How now! what noise is that?

(*Enter* OPHELIA.)

O heat, dry up my brains! tears seven times salt
Burn out the sense and virtue of mine eye!
By heaven, thy madness shall be paid with weight
Till our scale turn the beam. O rose of May,   155
Dear maid, kind sister, sweet Ophelia!
O heavens! is 't possible a young maid's wits
Should be as mortal as an old man's life?
Nature is fine in love, and where 'tis fine
It sends some precious instance of itself   160
After the thing it loves.
OPHELIA: (*Song.*)

        They bore him barefac'd on the bier;
        Hey non nonny, nonny, hey nonny;
        And in his grave rain'd many a tear—

Fare you well, my dove!   165
LAERTES: Hadst thou thy wits, and didst persuade revenge,
    It could not move thus.
OPHELIA: You must sing 'A-down, a-down,' and you 'Call him
    a-down-a.' O, how the wheel becomes it! It is the false
    stew ard, that stole his master's daughter.   170
LAERTES: This nothing's more than matter.
OPHELIA: There's rosemary, that's for remembrance. Pray you,
    love, remember. And there is pansies, that's for thoughts.
LAERTES: A document in madness, thoughts and remem-
    brance fitted.   175

---

144 **pelican** supposed to feed her young with her own blood
149 **level** plain   153 **virtue** power   159 **fine** refined to purity
169 **wheel** burden, refrain   172–180 Harold Jenkins, in his Ar-
den edition of *Hamlet* (London and New York, 1982) 536–542,
suggests that Ophelia gives rosemary (emblematic of remembrance) and pansies (of thoughts) to Laertes; that she gives fennel
and columbines (both signifying marital infidelity) to the queen;
she gives rue (for repentance) to the king (keeping some for herself as a sign of her sorrow, but noting that the king is to wear his
rue with a **difference,** an heraldic term designating a mark for
distinguishing one branch of a family from another in a coat-of-
arms). The daisy, an emblem of love's victims, is given to the king
as substitute for the absent Hamlet, whose absence he has caused.
The king would also be given the violets (emblems of faithfulness,
associated both with Ophelia's love for Hamlet, and Polonius's
service to the state, both now lost) were these still available. Each
gift of flowers represents a symbolic reproach to the recipient

OPHELIA: There's fennel for you, and columbines. There's rue
for you, and here's some for me. We may call it herb of grace
a Sundays. O, you must wear your rue with a difference.
There's a daisy. I would give you some violets, but they with
180 ered all when my father died. They say 'a made a good end,

(*Sings.*)   For bonny sweet Robin is all my joy.

LAERTES: Thought and affliction, passion, hell itself,
She turns to favor and to prettiness.
OPHELIA: (*Song.*)

185   And will 'a not come again?
           And will 'a not come again?
           No, no, he is dead:
           Go to thy death-bed:
           He never will come again.

190   His beard was as white as snow,
           All flaxen was his poll:
           He is gone, he is gone,
           And we cast away moan:
           God ha' mercy on his soul!

And of all Christian souls, I pray God. God buy you. (*Exit.*)
195 LAERTES: Do you see this, O God?
KING: Laertes, I must commune with your grief,
Or you deny me right. Go but apart,
Make choice of whom your wisest friends you will,
And they shall hear and judge 'twixt you and me.
200 If by direct or by collateral hand
They find us touched, we will our kingdom give,
Our crown, our life, and all that we call ours,
To you in satisfaction; but if not,
Be you content to lend your patience to us,
205 And we shall jointly labour with your soul
To give it due content.
LAERTES: Let this be so.
His means of death, his obscure funeral—
No trophy, sword, nor hatchment, o'er his bones,
No noble rite nor formal ostentation—
210 Cry to be heard, as 'twere from heaven to earth,
That I must call't in question.
KING: So you shall;
And where th' offence is let the great axe fall.
I pray you go with me.

(*Exeunt.*)

SCENE VI

Enter HORATIO *and* OTHERS.

HORATIO: What are they that would speak with me?
GENTLEMAN: Sea-faring men, sir. They say they have letters
for you.
HORATIO: Let them come in. (*Exit* GENTLEMAN.)
I do not know from what part of the world
5 I should be greeted, if not from Lord Hamlet.

(*Enter* SAILORS.)

SAILOR: God bless you, sir.
HORATIO: Let him bless thee too.
SAILOR: 'A shall sir, an't please him. There's a letter for you,
sir—it comes from th' ambassador that was bound for England—if your name be Horatio, as I am let to know it is. 10
HORATIO: (*Reads.*) 'Horatio, when thou shalt have overlooked this, give these fellows some means to the king.
They have letters for him. Ere we were two days old at
sea, a pirate of very warlike appointment gave us chase.
Finding ourselves too slow of sail, we put on a compelled 15
valor, and in the grapple I boarded them. On the instant
they got clear of our ship, so I alone became their prisoner. They have dealt with me like thieves of mercy, but
they knew what they did; I am to do a good turn for
them. Let the king have the letters I have sent, and repair 20
thou to me with as much speed as thou wouldest fly
death. I have words to speak in thine ear will make thee
dumb; yet are they much too light for the bore of the
matter. These good fellows will bring thee where I am.
Rosencrantz and Guildenstern hold their course for En- 25
gland. Of them I have much to tell thee, Farewell.
              'He that thou knowest thine, Hamlet.'
Come, I will give you way for these your letters,
And do't the speedier that you may direct me
To him from whom you brought them.

(*Exeunt.*)

SCENE VII

Enter KING *and* LAERTES.

KING: Now must your conscience my acquittance seal,
And you must put me in your heart for friend,
Sith you have heard, and with a knowing ear,
That he which hath your noble father slain
Pursued my life.   5
LAERTES: It well appears. But tell me
Why you proceeded not against these feats,
So criminal and so capital in nature,
As by your safety, wisdom, all things else,
You mainly were stirred up.
KING: O, for two special reasons,
Which may to you, perhaps, seem much unsinewed, 10
But yet to me th' are strong. The queen his mother
Lives almost by his looks, and for myself—
My virtue or my plague, be it either which—
She's so conjunctive to my life and soul
That, as the star moves not but in his sphere, 15
I could not but by her. The other motive,
Why to a public count I might not go,
Is the great love the general gender bear him,
Who, dipping all his faults in their affection,
Work, like the spring that turneth wood to stone, 20
Convert his gyves to graces; so that my arrows,
Too slightly timbered for so loud a wind,

---

190 **poll** head   208 **hatchment** coat of arms

IV.vi.   23 **bore** literally, caliber of a gun; hence, size, importance

IV.vii.   7 **capital** punishable by death   10 **unsinewed** weak
14 **conjunctive** closely joined   17 **count** reckoning   18 **general gender** common people   21 **gyves** fetters

Would have reverted to my bow again,
And not where I had aimed them.
25 LAERTES: And so have I a noble father lost,
A sister driven into desp'rate terms,
Whose worth, if praises may go back again,
Stood challenger on mount of all the age
For her perfections. But my revenge will come.
30 KING: Break not your sleeps for that. You must not think
That we are made of stuff so flat and dull
That we can let our beard be shook with danger,
And think it pastime. You shortly shall hear more.
I loved your father, and we love our self,
35 And that, I hope, will teach you to imagine—

(*Enter a* MESSENGER *with letters.*)

MESSENGER: These to your majesty; this to the queen.
KING: From Hamlet! Who brought them?
MESSENGER: Sailors, my lord, they say. I saw them not.
They were given me by Claudio; he received them
40 Of him that brought them.
KING: Laertes, you shall hear them.—
Leave us. (*Exit* MESSENGER.)
(*Reads.*) 'High and mighty, you shall know I am set naked
on your kingdom. To-morrow shall I beg leave to see
your kingly eyes, when I shall, first asking your pardon,
45 thereunto recount the occasion of my sudden and more
strange return. Hamlet.'
What should this mean? Are all the rest come back?
Or is it some abuse, and no such thing?
LAERTES: Know you the hand?
50 KING: 'Tis Hamlet's character. 'Naked!'
And in a postscript here, he says 'alone.'
Can you devise me?
LAERTES: I am lost in it, my lord. But let him come.
It warms the very sickness in my heart
55 That I shall live and tell him to his teeth
'Thus didst thou.'
KING: If it be so, Laertes—
As how should it be so, how otherwise?—
Will you be ruled by me?
LAERTES: Ay, my lord,
So you will not o'errule me to a peace.
60 KING: To thine own peace. If he be now returned,
As checking at his voyage, and that he means

---

35 Following the entrance of the Messenger, the King says in *F*
"How now? What Newes?" and the Messenger replies, "Letters
my Lord from *Hamlet*." Jenkins comments (*SB* 13.36): "In Q the
King is not told the letters come from Hamlet; he is left to find
this out as he reads, and his cry 'From *Hamlet*' betokens his astonishment on doing so. I think Hamlet would not have approved of the *F* messenger who robs his bomb of the full force
of its explosion. Shakespeare's messenger did not even know he
carried such a bomb, for the letters had reached him via sailors
who were ignorant of their sender. They took him for 'th' Em-
bassador that was bound for *England*' (4.4.9). *F*, with its too
knowledgeable messenger, by seeking to enhance the effect, destroys it." 52 **devise** explain to 61 **checking at** turning aside
from (like a falcon turning from its quarry for other prey)

No more to undertake it, I will work him
To an exploit now ripe in my device,
Under the which he shall not choose but fall;
And for his death no wind of blame shall breathe 65
But even his mother shall uncharge the practice
And call it accident.
LAERTES: My lord, I will be ruled;
The rather if you could devise it so
That I might be the organ.
KING: It falls right.
You have been talked of since your travel much, 70
And that in Hamlet's hearing, for a quality
Wherein they say you shine. Your sum of parts
Did not together pluck such envy from him
As did that one, and that, in my regard,
Of the unworthiest siege. 75
LAERTES: What part is that, my lord?
KING: A very riband in the cap of youth,
Yet needful too, for youth no less becomes
The light and careless livery that it wears
Than settled age his sables and his weeds,
Importing health and graveness. Two months since 80
Here was a gentleman of Normandy.
I have seen myself, and served against, the French,
And they can well on horseback, but this gallant
Had witchcraft in't. He grew unto his seat,
And to such wondrous doing brought his horse, 85
As had he been incorpsed and demi-natured
With the brave beast. So far he topped my thought
That I, in forgery of shapes and tricks,
Come short of what he did.
LAERTES: A Norman was't?
KING: A Norman. 90
LAERTES: Upon my life, Lamord.
KING: The very same.
LAERTES: I know him well. He is the brooch indeed
And gem of all the nation.
KING: He made confession of you,
And gave you such a masterly report 95
For art and exercise in your defence,
And for your rapier most especial,
That he cried out 'twould be a sight indeed
If one could match you. The scrimers of their nation,
He swore had neither motion, guard, nor eye, 100
If you opposed them. Sir, this report of his
Did Hamlet so envenom with his envy
That he could nothing do but wish and beg
Your sudden coming o'er, to play with you.
Now out of this— 105
LAERTES: What out of this, my lord?
KING: Laertes, was your father dear to you?
Or are you like the painting of a sorrow,
A face without a heart?
LAERTES: Why ask you this?

---

66 **uncharge the practice** regard the deed as free from villainy
69 **organ** instrument 75 **siege** rank 79 **weeds** garments
86 **incorpsed** made one body; **demi-natured** like a centaur,
half man half horse 87 **topped** excelled 88 **forgery** invention 99 **scrimers** fencers (French *escrimeurs*)

KING: Not that I think you did not love your father,
110 But that I know love is begun by time,
And that I see, in passages of proof,
Time qualifies the spark and fire of it.
There lives within the very flame of love
A kind of wick or snuff that will abate it,
115 And nothing is at a like goodness still,
For goodness, growing to a plurisy,
Dies in his own too much. That we would do,
We should do when we would; for this 'would' changes,
And hath abatements and delays as many
120 As there are tongues, are hands, are accidents,
And then this 'should' is like a spendthrift's sigh,
That hurts by easing. But to the quick of th' ulcer—
Hamlet comes back; what would you undertake
To show yourself in deed your father's son
125 More than in words?
LAERTES: To cut his throat i' th' church.
KING: No place, indeed, should murder sanctuarize;
Revenge should have no bounds. But good Laertes,
Will you do this, keep close within your chamber;
Hamlet returned shall know you are come home;
130 We'll put on those shall praise your excellence,
And set a double varnish on the fame
The Frenchman gave you, bring you in fine together,
And wager on your heads. He, being remiss,
Most generous, and free from all contriving,
135 Will not peruse the foils, so that with ease,
Or with a little shuffling, you may choose
A sword unbated, and in a pass of practice
Requite him for your father.
LAERTES: I will do't,
And for that purpose I'll anoint my sword.
140 I bought an unction of a mountebank
So mortal that but dip a knife in it,
Where it draws blood no cataplasm so rare,
Collected from all simples that have virtue
Under the moon, can save the thing from death
145 That is but scratched withal. I'll touch my point
With this contagion, that if I gall him slightly,
It may be death.
KING: Let's further think of this,
Weigh what convenience both of time and means
May fit us to our shape. If this should fail,
150 And that our drift look through our bad performance,
'Twere better not assayed. Therefore this project
Should have a back or second that might hold
If this should blast in proof. Soft! let me see.
We'll make a solemn wager on your cunnings—
155 I ha't.
When in your motion you are hot and dry—

As make your bouts more violent to that end—
And that he calls for drink, I'll have preferred him
A chalice for the nonce, whereon but sipping,
If he by chance escape your venomed stuck, 160
Our purpose may hold there.—But stay, what noise?

(*Enter* QUEEN.)

QUEEN: One woe doth tread upon another's heel,
So fast they follow. Your sister's drowned, Laertes.
LAERTES: Drowned! O, where?
QUEEN: There is a willow grows askant the brook 165
That shows his hoar leaves in the glassy stream.
Therewith fantastic garlands did she make
Of crowflowers, nettles, daisies, and long purples
That liberal shepherds give a grosser name,
But our cold maids do dead men's fingers call them. 170
There on the pendent boughs her crownet weeds
Clamb'ring to hang, an envious sliver broke,
When down her weedy trophies and herself
Fell in the weeping brook. Her clothes spread wide,
And mermaid-like awhile they bore her up, 175
Which time she chanted snatches of old lauds,
As one incapable of her own distress,
Or like a creature native and indued
Unto that element. But long it could not be
Till that her garments, heavy with their drink, 180
Pulled the poor wretch from her melodious lay
To muddy death.
LAERTES: Alas, then, she is drowned?
QUEEN: Drowned, drowned.
LAERTES: Too much of water hast thou, poor Ophelia,
And therefore I forbid my tears; but yet 185
It is our trick; nature her custom holds,
Let shame say what it will. When these are gone,
The woman will be out. Adieu, my lord.
I have a speech o' fire that fain would blaze
But that this folly drowns it. 190

(*Exit.*)

KING: Let's follow, Gertrude.
How much I had to do to calm his rage!
Now fear I this will give it start again;
Therefore let's follow.

(*Exeunt.*)

ACT FIVE

SCENE I

Enter two CLOWNS.

---

111 **passages of proof** incidents of experience   112 **qualifies**
weakens   116 **plurisy** excess   122 **quick** sensitive flesh   126
sanctuarize give sanctuary to   133 **remiss** careless   135 **peruse** inspect   137 **unbated** not blunted; **pass of practice**
treacherous thrust   142 **cataplasm** poultice   143 **simples**
medicinal herbs   149 **shape** plan   150 **drift** scheme   152
back or second something in support   153 **blast in proof**
burst during trial (like a faulty cannon)   156 **motion** exertion

---

158 **preferred** offered to   159 **nonce** occasion   160 **stuck**
thrust   165 **askant** alongside   166 **hoar** gray   169 **liberal**
free-spoken, licentious   170 **cold** chaste   171 **crownet** coronet   172 **envious** malicious   176 **lauds** hymns   177 **incapable of** insensible to   178 **indued** endowed   188 **woman**
unmanly part of nature

V.i. s.d. **clowns** rustics

CLOWN: Is she to be buried in Christian burial when she wilfully seeks her own salvation?

OTHER: I tell thee she is, therefore make her grave straight. The crowner hath sat on her, and finds it Christian burial.

5 CLOWN: How can that be, unless she drowned herself in her own defence?

OTHER: Why, 'tis found so.

CLOWN: It must be 'se offendendo', it cannot be else. For here lies the point: if I drown myself wittingly, it argues an act,

10 and an act hath three branches—it is to act, to do, and to perform; argal, she drowned herself wittingly.

OTHER: Nay, but hear you, Goodman Delver.

CLOWN: Give me leave. Here lies the water; good. Here stands the man; good. If the man go to this water and

15 drown himself, it is, will he, nill he, he goes—mark you that. But if the water come to him and drown him, he drowns not himself. Argal, he that is not guilty of his own death shortens not his own life.

OTHER: But is this law?

20 CLOWN: Ay, marry, is't; crowner's quest law.

OTHER: Will you ha' the truth on 't? If this had not been a gentlewoman, she should have been buried out o' Christian burial.

CLOWN: Why, there thou say'st. And the more pity that great

25 folk should have count'nance in this world to drown or hang themselves more than their even-Christen. Come, my spade. There is no ancient gentlemen but gard'ners, ditchers, and grave-makers. They hold up Adam's profession.

OTHER: Was he a gentleman?

30 CLOWN: 'A was the first that ever bore arms.

OTHER: Why, he had none.

CLOWN: What, art a heathen? How dost thou understand the Scripture? The Scripture says Adam digged. Could he dig without arms? I'll put another question to thee. If thou

35 answerest me not to the purpose, confess thyself—

OTHER: Go to.

CLOWN: What is he that builds stronger than either the mason, the shipwright, or the carpenter?

OTHER: The gallows-maker for that frame outlives a thousand

40 tenants.

CLOWN: I like thy wit well, in good faith. The gallows does well. But how does it well? It does well to those that do ill. Now thou dost ill to say the gallows is built stronger than the church. Argal, the gallows may do well to thee.

45 To't again, come.

OTHER: 'Who builds stronger than a mason, a shipwright, or a carpenter?'

CLOWN: Ay tell me that, and unyoke.

OTHER: Marry, now I can tell.

50 CLOWN: To't.

OTHER: Mass, I cannot tell.

(Enter HAMLET and HORATIO afar off.)

CLOWN: Cudgel thy brains no more about it, for your dull ass will not mend his pace with beating. And when you are asked this question next, say 'a grave-maker.' The houses he makes lasts till doomsday. Go, get thee in, and fetch me 55 a stoup of liquor. (Exit OTHER CLOWN.)

(HAMLET and HORATIO come forward as CLOWN digs and sings.)

(Song.)

In youth, when I did love, did love,
    Methought it was very sweet,
To contract-O-the time, for-a-my behove,
    O, methought, there-a-was nothing-a-meet. 60

HAMLET: Has this fellow no feeling of his business, that 'a sings at gravemaking?

HORATIO: Custom hath made it in him a property of easiness.

HAMLET: 'Tis e'en so. The hand of little employment hath the daintier sense. 65

CLOWN: (Song.)

But age, with his stealing steps,
    Hath clawed me in his clutch,
And hath shipped me into the land,
    As if I had never been such.

(Throws up a skull.)

HAMLET: That skull had a tongue in it, and could sing once. 70 How the knave jowls it to the ground, as if 'twere Cain's jawbone, that did the first murder! This might be the pate of a politician, which this ass now o'erreaches; one that would circumvent God, might it not?

HORATIO: It might, my lord. 75

HAMLET: Or of a courtier, which could say 'Good morrow, sweet lord! How dost thou, sweet lord?' This might be my Lord Such-a-one, that praised my Lord Such-a-one's horse, when 'a went to beg it, might it not?

HORANTIO: Ay, my lord. 80

HAMLET: Why, e'en so, and now my Lady Worm's, chopless, and knock'd about the mazzard with a sexton's spade. Here's fine revolution, an we had the trick to see't. Did these bones cost no more the breeding but to play at loggats with them? Mine ache to think on't. 85

CLOWN: (Song.)

A pick-axe and a spade, a spade,
    For and a shrouding sheet:
O, a pit of clay for to be made
    For such a guest is meet.

(Throws up another skull.)

HAMLET: There's another. Why may not that be the skull of 90 a lawyer? Where be his quiddities now, his quillets, his

---

4 **crowner** coroner   8 **se offendendo** the Clown's blunder for **se defendendo** ("in self-defense")   11 **argal** therefore (corrupt form of *ergo*)   20 **quest** inquest   26 **even-Christen** fellow Christian   48 **tell me that, and unyoke** answer the question and then you can relax

56 **stoup** tankard   59 **behove** benefit   59–60 The repeated *a* and *o* may represent the Clown's vocal embellishments, but more probably they represent his grunting as he takes breath in the course of his digging   63 **a property of easiness** a habit that comes easily to him   71 **jowls** hurls   74 **circumvent** cheat   81 **chopless** with lower jaw missing   82 **mazzard** head   84–85 **loggats** small logs of wood for throwing at a mark   91 **quiddities** subtle distinctions; **quillets** quibbles

cases, his tenures, and his tricks? Why does he suffer this mad knave now to knock him about the sconce with a dirty shovel, and will not tell him of his action of battery? 95 Hum! This fellow might be in's time a great buyer of land, with his statutes, his recognizances, his fines, his double vouchers, his recoveries. Is this the fine of his fines, and the recovery of his recoveries, to have his fine pate full of fine dirt? Will his vouchers vouch him no more of his pur- 100 chases, and double ones too, than the length and breadth of a pair of indentures? The very conveyances of his lands will scarcely lie in this box, and must th' inheritor himself have no more, ha?

HORATIO: Not a jot more, my lord.

105 HAMLET: Is not parchment made of sheepskins?

HORANTIO: Ay, my lord, and of calves' skins too.

HAMLET: They are sheep and calves which seek out assurance in that. I will speak to this fellow. Whose grave's this, sirrah?

CLOWN: Mine, sir. (*Sings.*)

110   O, a pit of clay for to be made—

HAMLET: I think it be thine indeed, for thou liest in't.

CLOWN: You lie out on't, sir, and therefore 'tis not yours. For my part, I do not lie in't, yet it is mine.

HAMLET: Thou dost lie in't, to be in't and say it is thine. 'Tis 115 for the dead, not for the quick; therefore thou liest.

CLOWN: 'Tis a quick lie, sir; 'twill away again from me to you.

HAMLET: What man dost thou dig it for?

CLOWN: For no man, sir.

HAMLET: What woman, then?

120 CLOWN: For none neither.

HAMLET: Who is to be buried in't?

CLOWN: One that was a woman, sir; but, rest her soul, she's dead.

HAMLET: How absolute the knave is! We must speak by the 125 card, or equivocation will undo us. By the Lord, Horatio, this three years I have took note of it, the age is grown so picked that the toe of the peasant comes so near the heel of the courtier, he galls his kibe. How long hast thou been a grave-maker?

130 CLOWN: Of all the day i' th' year, I came to't that day that our last King Hamlet overcame Fortinbras.

HAMLET: How long is that since?

CLOWN: Cannot you tell that? Every fool can tell that. It was that very day that young Hamlet was born—he that is 135 mad, and sent into England.

HAMLET: Ay, marry, why was he sent into England?

CLOWN: Why, because 'a was mad. 'A shall recover his wits there; or, if a do not, 'tis no great matter there.

HAMLET: Why?

140 CLOWN: 'Twill not be seen in him there. There the men are as mad as he.

---

96 **recognizances** legal bonds, defining debts; vouchers persons vouched or called on to warrant a title   97 **recoveries** legal processes to break an entail   100–101 **pair of indentures** deed or legal agreement in duplicate   101 **conveyances** deeds by which property is transferred   124 **absolute** positive   125 **card** card on which the points of the mariner's compass are marked (i.e., absolutely to the point)   127 **picked** fastidious 128 **kibe** chilblain

HAMLET: How came he mad?

CLOWN: Very strangely, they say.

HAMLET: How strangely?

CLOWN: Faith, e'en with losing his wits.   145

HAMLET: Upon what ground?

CLOWN: Why, here in Denmark. I have been sexton here, man and boy, thirty years.

HAMLET: How long will a man lie i' th' earth ere he rot?

CLOWN: Faith, if 'a be not rotten before 'a die—as we have 150 many pocky corses now-a-days that will scarce hold the laying in—'a will last you some eight year or nine year. A tanner will last you nine year.

HAMLET: Why he more than another?

CLOWN: Why, sir, his hide is so tanned with his trade that 'a 155 will keep out water a great while and your water is a sore decayer of your whoreson dead body. Here's a skull now hath lain you i' th' earth three and twenty years.

HAMLET: Whose was it?

CLOWN: A whoreson mad fellow's it was. Whose do you 160 think it was?

HAMLET: Nay, I know not.

CLOWN: A pestilence on him for a mad rogue! 'a poured a flagon of Rhenish on my head once. This same skull, sir, was, sir, Yorick's skull, the king's jester.   165

HAMLET: (*Takes the skull.*) This?

CLOWN: E'en That.

HAMLET: Alas, poor Yorick! I knew him, Horatio—a fellow of infinite jest, of most excellent fancy. He hath bore me on his back a thousand times, and now how abhorred in my 170 imagination it is! My gorge rises at it. Here hung those lips that I have kissed I know not how oft. Where be your gibes now, your gambols, your songs, your flashes of mer- riment that were wont to set the table on a roar? Not one now to mock your own grinning? Quite chop-fall'n? 175 Now get you to my lady's chamber, and tell her, let her paint an inch thick, to this favour she must come. Make her laugh at that. Prithee, Horatio, tell me one thing.

HORATIO: What's that, my lord?

HAMLET: Dost thou think Alexander looked o' this fashion i' 180 th' earth?

HORATIO: E'en so.

HAMLET: And smelt so? Pah!

(*Throws down the skull.*)

HORATIO: E'en so, my lord.

HAMLET: To what base uses we may return, Horatio! Why 185 may not imagination trace the noble dust of Alexander till 'a find it stopping a bung-hole?

HORATIO: 'Twere to consider too curiously to consider so.

HAMLET: No, faith, not a jot, but to follow him thither with modesty enough, and likelihood to lead it. Alexander died, 190 Alexander was buried, Alexander returneth to dust; the dust is earth; of earth we make loam; and why of that loam whereto he was converted might they not stop a beer-barrel?

    Imperious Caesar, dead and turned to clay,
    Might stop a hole to keep the wind away.   195

---

151 **pocky** infected with pox (syphilis)   164 **Rhenish** Rhine wine   188 **too curiously** over ingeniously

O, that that earth which kept the world in awe
Should patch a wall t'expel the winter's flaw!

But soft, but soft awhile! Here comes the king,
The queen, the courtiers.

(*Enter* KING, QUEEN, LAERTES, *and the Corse* [*with a Doctor of Divinity as* PRIEST *and* LORDS *attendant*].)

                             Who is this they follow?
200   And with such maimèd rites? This doth betoken
The corse they follow did with desperate hand
Fordo it own life. 'Twas of some estate.
Couch we awhile and mark.

(*Retires with* HORATIO.)

LAERTES: What ceremony else?
205 HAMLET: That is Laertes, a very noble youth. Mark.
LAERTES: What ceremony else?
DOCTOR: Her obsequies have been as far enlarged
    As we have warranty. Her death was doubtful,
    And but that great command o'ersways the order,
210   She should in ground unsanctified been lodged
    Till the last trumpet. For charitable prayers,
    Shards, flints and pebbles should be thrown on her.
    Yet here she is allowed her virgin crants,
    Her maiden strewments and the bringing home
215   Of bell and burial.
LAERTES: Must there no more be done?
DOCTOR: No more be done.
    We should profane the service of the dead
    To sing a requiem and such rest to her
    As to peace-parted souls.
LAERTES: Lay her i' th' earth,
220   And from her fair and unpolluted flesh
    May violets spring! I tell thee, churlish priest,
    A minist'ring angel shall my sister be
    When thou liest howling.
HAMLET: What, the fair Ophelia!
QUEEN: Sweets to the sweet. Farewell!

(*Scatters flowers.*)

225   I hoped thou shouldst have been my Hamlet's wife.
    I thought thy bride-bed to have decked, sweet maid,
    And not have strewed thy grave.
LAERTES: O treble woe
    Fall ten times treble on that cursèd head,
    Whose wicked deed thy most ingenious sense
230   Deprived thee of! Hold off the earth awhile,
    Till I have caught her once more in mine arms.

(*Leaps into the grave.*)

    Now pile your dust upon the quick and dead,
    Till of this flat a mountain you have made

T' o'er-top old Pelion or the skyish head
Of blue Olympus.   235
HAMLET: (*Coming forward.*) What is he whose grief
    Bears such an emphasis, whose phrase of sorrow
    Conjures the wand'ring stars, and makes them stand
    Like wonder-wounded hearers? This is I,
    Hamlet the Dane.

(LAERTES *climbs out of the grave.*)
                                                240

LAERTES: The devil take thy soul!

(*Grappling with him.*)

HAMLET: Thou pray'st not well.
    I prithee take thy fingers from my throat,
    For though I am not splenitive and rash,
    Yet have I in me something dangerous,
    Which let thy wisdom fear. Hold off thy hand.
KING: Pluck them asunder.   245
QUEEN: Hamlet! Hamlet!
ALL: Gentlemen!
HORATIO: Good my lord, be quiet.

(*The* ATTENDANTS *part them.*)

HAMLET: Why, I will fight with him upon this theme
    Until my eyelids will no longer wag.   250
QUEEN: O my son, what theme?
HAMLET: I loved Ophelia. Forty thousand brothers
    Could not with all their quantity of love
    Make up my sum. What wilt thou do for her?
KING: O, he is mad, Laertes.   255
QUEEN: For love of God, forbear him.
HAMLET: 'Swounds, show me what thou't do.
    Woo't weep, woo't fight, woo't fast, woo't tear thyself,
    Woo't drink up eisel, eat a crocodile?
    I'll do't. Dost come here to whine?   260
    To outface me with leaping in her grave?
    Be buried quick with her, and so will I,
    And if thou prate of mountains, let them throw
    Millions of acres on us, till our ground,
    Singeing his pate against the burning zone,   265
    Make Ossa like a wart! Nay, an thou'lt mouth,
    I'll rant as well as thou.
QUEEN: This is mere madness;
    And thus awhile the fit will work on him.
    Anon, as patient as the female dove
    When that her golden couplets are disclosed,   270
    His silence will sit drooping.
HAMLET: Hear you, sir.
    What is the reason that you use me thus?

---

234 **Pelion** a mountain in Thessaly, like Olympus, line 235, and Ossa, line 266 (the allusion is to the war in which the Titans fought the gods and, in their attempt to scale heaven, heaped Ossa and Olympus on Pelion, or Pelion and Ossa on Olympus) 237 **such an emphasis** so vehement an expression or display 242 **splenitive** fiery-tempered (from the spleen, seat of anger) 258 **Woo't** wilt (thou) 259 **eisel** vinegar 270 **couplets** newly hatched pair

---

197 **flaw** gust   202 **Fordo** destroy; **it** its   212 **Shards** bits of broken pottery   213 **crants** garland   229 **most ingenious** of quickest apprehension

I loved you ever. But it is no matter.
Let Hercules himself do what he may,
275   The cat will mew, and dog will have his day.
  KING: I pray thee, good Horatio, wait upon him.

(*Exit* HAMLET *and* HORATIO.)

  (*To* LAERTES.) Strengthen your patience in our last night's
    speech.
  We'll put the matter to the present push.—
  Good Gertrude, set some watch over your son.—
280   This grave shall have a living monument.
  An hour of quiet shortly shall we see;
  Till then in patience our proceeding be.

(*Exeunt.*)

SCENE II

Enter HAMLET *and* HORATIO.

  HAMLET: So much for this, sir; now shall you see the other.
    You do remember all the circumstance?
  HORATIO: Remember it, my lord!
  HAMLET: Sir, in my heart there was a kind of fighting
5   That would not let me sleep. Methought I lay
    Worse than the mutines in the bilboes. Rashly,
    And praised be rashness for it—let us know,
    Our indiscretion sometime serves us well,
    When our deep plots do pall; and that should learn us
10   There's a divinity that shapes our ends,
    Rough-hew them how we will—
  HORATIO: That is most certain.
  HAMLET: Up from my cabin,
    My sea-gown scarfed about me, in the dark
    Groped I to find out them, had my desire,
15   Fingered their packet, and in fine withdrew
    To mine own room again, making so bold,
    My fears forgetting manners, to unseal
    Their grand commission; where I found, Horatio—
    Ah, royal knavery!—an exact command,
20   Larded with many several sorts of reasons
    Importing Denmark's health and England's too,
    With, ho! such bugs and goblins in my life,
    That on the supervise, no leisure bated,
    No, not to stay the grinding of the axe,
25   My head should be struck off.
  HORATIO: Is't possible?
  HAMLET: Here's the commission; read it at more leisure.
    But will thou hear me how I did proceed?
  HORATIO: I beseech you.
  HAMLET: Being thus benetted round with villainies,
30   Or I could make a prologue to my brains,
    They had begun the play. I sat me down,
    Devised a new commission, wrote it fair.

V.ii. 6 **mutines** mutineers; **bilboes** fetters   9 **pall** fail   15
Fingered filched   20 **Larded** garnished   22 **bugs and goblins** imaginary horrors (here, horrendous crimes attributed to
Hamlet, and represented as dangers should he be allowed to live)
23 **supervise** perusal; **bated** deducted, allowed   24 **stay** await
30 **Or** ere

I once did hold it, as our statists do,
A baseness to write fair, and laboured much
How to forget that learning; but sir, now   35
It did me yeoman's service. Wilt thou know
Th' effect of what I wrote?
  HORATIO: Ay, good my lord.
  HAMLET: An earnest conjuration from the king,
    As England was his faithful tributary,
    As love between them like the palm might flourish,   40
    As peace should still her wheaten garland wear
    And stand a comma 'tween their amities,
    And many such like as's of great charge,
    That on the view and knowing of these contents,
    Without debatement further more or less,   45
    He should the bearers put to sudden death,
    Not shriving-time allowed.
  HORATIO: How was this sealed?
  HAMLET: Why, even in that was heaven ordinant,
    I had my father's signet in my pursue,
    Which was the model of that Danish seal,   50
    Folded the writ up the form of th' other,
    Subscribed it, gave't th' impression, placed it safely,
    The changeling never known. Now the next day
    Was our sea-fight, and what to this was sequent
    Thou knowest already.   55
  HORATIO: So Guildenstern and Rosencrantz go to't.
  HAMLET: Why, man, they did make love to this employment.
    They are not near my conscience; their defeat
    Does by their own insinuation grow.
    'Tis dangerous when the baser nature comes   60
    Between the pass and fell incensèd points
    Of mighty opposites.
  HORATIO: Why, what a king is this!
  HAMLET: Does it not, think thee, stand me now upon—
    He that hath killed my king and whored my mother,
    Popped in between th' election and my hopes,   65
    Thrown out his angle for my proper life,
    And with such coz'nage—is't not perfect conscience,
    To quit him with this arm? And is't not to be damned
    To let this canker of our nature come
    In further evil?   70
  HORATIO: It must be shortly known to him from England
    What is the issue of the business there.
  HAMLET: It will be short; the interim is mine.
    And a man's life's no more than to say 'one.'
    But I am very sorry, good Horatio,   75
    That to Laertes I forgot myself;
    For by the image of my cause I see
    The portraiture of his. I'll court his favours.

---

33 **statists** statesmen   42 **comma** a connective that also acknowledges separateness   43 **charge** (1) importance (2) burden
(the double meaning fits the play that makes "as's" into "asses")
48 **ordinant** guiding   52 **Subscribed** signed   59 **insinuation**
intrusion   61 **pass** thrust; **fell** fierce   63 **Does it not . . .
stand me now upon** is it not incumbent upon me   65 **election** i.e., to the kingship. Denmark being an elective monarchy
66 **angle** fishing line; **proper** own   68 **quit** repay

But sure the bravery of his grief did put me
80　Into a tow'ring passion.

HORATIO:　　　　　　Peace; who comes here?

(*Enter* [OSRIC] *a courtier.*)

OSRIC: Your lordship is right welcome back to Denmark.

HAMLET: I humbly thank you, sir. (*Aside to* HORATIO.) Dost know this water-fly?

HORATIO: (*Aside to* HAMLET.) No, my good lord.

85　HAMLET: (*Aside to* HORATIO.) Thy state is the more gracious, for 'tis a vice to know him. He hath much land, and fertile. Let a beast be lord of beasts, and his crib shall stand at the king's mess. 'Tis a chough, but as I say, spacious in the possession of dirt.

90　OSRIC: Sweet lord, if your lordship were at leisure, I should impart a thing to you from his majesty.

HAMLET: I will receive it, sir, with all diligence of spirit. Put your bonnet to his right use. 'Tis for the head.

OSRIC: I thank you lordship, it is very hot.

95　HAMLET: No, believe me, 'tis very cold; the wind is northerly.

OSRIC: It is indifferent cold, my lord, indeed.

HAMLET: But yet methinks it is very sultry and hot for my complexion.

OSRIC: Exceedingly, my lord; it is very sultry, as 'twere—I can
100　not tell how. My lord, his majesty bade me signify to you that 'a has laid a great wager on your head. Sir, this is the matter—

HAMLET: I beseech you, remember.

(HAMLET *moves him to put on his hat.*)

OSRIC: Nay, good my lord; for my ease, in good faith. Sir, here
105　is newly come to court Laertes; believe me, an absolute gentleman, full of most excellent differences, of very soft society and great showing. Indeed, to speak feelingly of him, he is the card or calendar of gentry, for you shall find in him the continent of what part a gentleman would see.

110　HAMLET: Sir, his definement suffers, no perdition in you, though I know to divide him inventorially would dozy th' arithmetic of memory, and yet but yaw neither in respect of his quick sail. But in the verity of extolment, I take him to be a soul of great article, and his infusion of such dearth
115　and rareness as, to make true diction of him, his semblable is his mirror, and who else would trace him, his umbrage, nothing more.

OSRIC: Your lordship speaks most infallibly of him.

HAMLET: The concernancy, sir? Why do we wrap the gentle-
120　man in our more rawer breath?

OSRIC: Sir?

HORATIO: It's not possible to understand in another tongue? You will to't, sir, really.

HAMLET: What imports the nomination of this gentleman?

OSRIC: Of Laertes?　　　　　　　　　　　　　　　125

HORATIO: (*Aside.*) His purse is empty already. All's golden words are spent.

HAMLET: Of him, sir.

OSRIC: I know you are not ignorant—

HAMLET: I would you did, sir; yet, in faith, if you did, it would　130
not much approve me. Well, sir.

OSRIC: You are not ignorant of what excellence Laertes is—

HAMLET: I dare not confess that, lest I should compare with him in excellence; but to know a man well were to know himself.　　　　　　　　　　　　　　　　　　135

OSRIC: I mean, sir, for his weapon; but in the imputation laid on him by them in his meed, he's unfellowed.

HAMLET: What's his weapon?

OSRIC: Rapier and dagger.

HAMLET: That's two of his weapons—but well.　　140

OSRIC: The king, sir, hath wagered with him six Barbary horses, against the which he has impawned, as I take it, six French rapiers and poniards, with their assigns, as girdle, hangers, and so. Three of the carriages, in faith, are very dear to fancy, very responsive to the hilts, most delicate　145
carriages, and of very liberal conceit.

HAMLET: What call you the carriages?

HORATIO: (*Aside to* HAMLET.) I knew you must be edified by the margent ere you had done.

OSRIC: The carriages, sir, are the hangers.　　　150

HAMLET: The phrase would be more germane to the matter if we could carry cannon by our sides. I would it might be hangers till then. But on! Six Barbary horses against six French swords, their assigns, and three liberal conceited carriages; that's the French bet against the Danish. Why is　155
this all impawned, as you call it?

OSRIC: The king, sir, hath laid, sir, that in a dozen passes between yourself and him he shall not exceed you three hits; he hath laid on twelve for nine, and it would come to immediate trial if your lordship would vouchsafe the answer.　160

HAMLET: How if I answer no?

OSRIC: I mean, my lord, the opposition of your person in trial.

HAMLET: Sir, I will walk here in the hall. If it please his majesty, it is the breathing time of day with me. Let the foils be brought, the gentleman willing, and the king hold　165
his purpose; I will win for him an I can. If not, I will gain nothing but my shame and the odd hits.

---

79 **bravery** ostentatious display　88 **mess** table; **chough** jackdaw; thus, a chatterer　96 **indifferent** somewhat　98 **complexion** temperament　106 **differences** distinguishing qualities　107 **great showing** distinguished appearance　108 **card** map　109 **continent** all-containing embodiment　110 **definement** definition　111 **divide him inventorially** classify him in detail; **dozy** dizzy　112 **yaw** hold to a course unsteadily, like a ship that steers wild　114 **article** scope, importance; **infusion** essence; **dearth** scarcity　115 **semblable** likeness　116 **trace** (1) draw, (2) follow; **umbrage** shadow　119 **concernancy** import, relevance

---

123 **to't** i.e., to get an understanding　124 **nomination** mention　131 **approve** commend　133 **compare** compete　137 **meed** pay; **unfellowed** unequaled　142 **impawned** staked　143 **assigns** appendages　144 **carriages** an affected word for hangers, i.e., straps from which the weapon was hung　146 **liberal conceit** elaborate design　149 **margent** margin (where explanatory notes were printed)　157–158 **in a dozen passes . . . he shall not exceed you three hits** the odds the King proposes seem to be that in a match of twelve bouts, Hamlet will win at least five. Laertes would need to win by at least eight to four　159 **he hath laid on twelve for nine** "he" apparently is Laertes, who has seemingly raised the odds against himself by wagering that out of twelve bouts he will win nine　164 **breathing time** time for taking exercise　166 **an** if

OSRIC: Shall I deliver you so?

HAMLET: To this effect, sir, after what flourish your nature will.

170 OSRIC: I commend my duty to your lordship.

HAMLET: Yours. (*Exit* OSRIC.) He does well to commend it himself; there are no tongues else for's turn.

HORATIO: This lapwing runs away with the shell on his head.

HAMLET: 'A did comply, sir, with his dug, before 'a sucked it.
175 Thus has he, and many more of the same bevy that I know the drossy age dotes on, only got the tune of the time; and out of an habit of encounter, a kind of yesty collection which carries them through and through the most fanned and winnowed opinions; and do but blow them to their
180 trial, the bubbles are out.

(*Enter a* LORD.)

LORD: My lord, his majesty commended him to you by young Osric, who brings back to him that you attend him in the hall. He sends to know if your pleasure hold to play with Laertes, or that you will take longer time.

185 HAMLET: I am constant to my purposes: they follow the king's pleasure. If his fitness speaks, mine is ready; now or whensoever, provided I be so able as now.

LORD: The king and queen and all are coming down.

HAMLET: In happy time.

190 LORD: The queen desires you to use some gentle entertainment to Laertes before you fall to play.

HAMLET: She well instructs me.

(*Exit* LORD.)

HORATIO: You will lose, my lord.

HAMLET: I do not think so. Since he went into France, I have
195 been in continual practice. I shall win at the odds. But thou wouldst not think how ill all's here about my heart. But it is no matter.

HORATIO: Nay, good my lord—

HAMLET: It is but foolery, but it is such a kind of gaingiving
200 as would perhaps trouble a woman.

HORATIO: If your mind dislike any thing, obey it. I will forestall their repair hither, and say you are not fit.

HAMLET: Not a whit, we defy augury. There is a special providence in the fall of a sparrow. If it be now, 'tis not to
205 come; if it be not to come, it will be now; if it be not now, yet it will come. The readiness is all. Since no man of aught he leaves knows, what is't to leave betimes? Let be.

(*A table prepared. [Enter] trumpets, drums, and* OFFICERS *with cushions;* KING, QUEEN, [OSRIC,] *and all the* STATE, [with] *foils, daggers, and* LAERTES.)

KING: Come, Hamlet, come, and take this hand from me.

(*The* KING *puts* LAERTES' *hand into* HAMLET'*s.*)

210 HAMLET: Give me your pardon, sir. I have done you wrong,
But pardon 't as you are a gentleman.
This presence knows, and you must needs have heard,
How I am punished with a sore distraction.
What I have done   215
That might your nature, honour, and exception,
Roughly awake, I here proclaim was madness.
Was 't Hamlet wronged Laertes? Never Hamlet.
If Hamlet from himself be ta'en away,
And when he's not himself does wrong Laertes,   220
Then Hamlet does it not. Hamlet denies it.
Who does it then? His madness. If't be so,
Hamlet is of the faction that is wronged;
His madness is poor Hamlet's enemy.
Sir, in this audience,   225
Let my disclaiming from a purposed evil
Free me so far in your most generous thoughts
That I have shot mine arrow o'er the house,
And hurt my brother.

LAERTES: I am satisfied in nature,
Whose motive in this case should stir me most   230
To my revenge. But in my terms of honor
I stand aloof, and will no reconcilement
Till by some elder masters of known honor,
I have a voice and precedent of peace
To keep my name ungored. But till that time   235
I do receive your offered love like love,
And will not wrong it.

HAMLET: I embrace if freely,
And will this brother's wager frankly play.
Give us the foils.

LAERTES: Come, one for me.

HAMLET: I'll be your foil, Laertes. In mine ignorance   240
Your skill shall, like a star i' th' darkest night,
Stick fiery off indeed.

LAERTES: You mock me, sir.

HAMLET: No, by this hand.

KING: Give them the foils, young Osric. Cousin Hamlet,
You know the wager?

HAMLET: Very well, my lord;   245
Your Grace has laid the odds o'th' weaker side.

KING: I do not fear it, I have seen you both;
But since he is bettered, we have therefore odds.

LAERTES: This is too heavy; let me see another.

HAMLET: This likes me well. These foils have all a length?

(*They prepare to play.*)

250

OSRIC: Ay, my good lord.

KING: Set me the stoups of wine upon that table.
If Hamlet give the first or second hit,

---

173 **lapwing** a bird reputedly so precocious as to run as soon as hatched   174 **comply** observe the formalities of courtesy; **dug** mother's nipple   175 **bevy** a covey of quails or lapwings   176 **drossy** frivolous   177 **encounter** manner of address or accosting; **yesty collection** a frothy and superficial patchwork of terms from the conversation of others   179 **winnowed** tested, freed from inferior elements   186 **fitness** convenience, inclination   199 **gaingiving** misgiving

232 **voice and precedent** authoritative statement justified by precedent   238 **foil** (1) setting for gem (2) weapon   246 **bettered** perfected through training   248 **have all a length** are all of the same length   252 **quit in answer** literally, give as good as he gets (i.e., if the third bout is a draw)

Or quit in answer of the third exchange,
255   Let all the battlements their ordnance fire.
The king shall drink to Hamlet's better breath,
And in the cup an union shall he throw,
Richer than that which four successive kings
In Denmark's crown have worn. Give me the cups,
260   And let the kettle to the trumpet speak,
The trumpet to the cannoneer without,
The cannons to the heavens, the heaven to earth,
'Now the king drinks to Hamlet.' Come begin—

(*Trumpets the while.*)

And you, the judges, bear a wary eye.
HAMLET: Come on, sir.
LAERTES: Come, my lord.

(*They play.*)

HAMLET: One.
LAERTES: No.
HAMLET: Judgment.
OSRIC: A hit, a very palpable hit.

265   (*Drums, trumpets, and shot. Flourish; a piece goes off.*)

LAERTES: Well, again.
KING: Stay, give me drink. Hamlet, this pearl is thine.
Here's to thy health. Give him the cup.
HAMLET: I'll play this bout first; set it by awhile.
Come.

270   (*They play.*)

Another hit; what say you?
LAERTES: I do confess't.
KING: Our son shall win.
QUEEN: He's fat, and scant of breath.
275   Here, Hamlet, take my napkin, rub thy brows.
The queen carouses to thy fortune, Hamlet.
HAMLET: Good madam!
KING: Gertrude, do not drink.
QUEEN: I will, my lord; I pray you pardon me.
280   KING: (*Aside.*) It is the poisoned cup; it is too late.
HAMLET: I dare not drink yet, madam; by and by.
QUEEN: Come, let me wipe thy face.
LAERTES: My lord, I'll hit him now.
KING: I do not think't.
LAERTES: (*Aside.*) And yet it is almost against my conscience.
285   HAMLET: Come, for the third, Laertes. You but dally.
I pray you pass with your best violence;
I am afeard you make a wanton of me.
LAERTES: Say you so? come on.

(*They play.*)

OSRIC: Nothing, neither way.
LAERTES: Have at you now!

(LAERTES *wounds* HAMLET; *then, in scuffling, they change rapiers.*)

290   KING: Part them. They are incensed.
HAMLET: Nay, come again.

(HAMLET *wounds* LAERTES. *The* QUEEN *falls.*)

OSRIC: Look to the queen there, ho!
HORATIO: They bleed on both sides. How is it, my lord?
OSRIC: How is't Laertes?   295
LAERTES: Why, as a woodcock to mine own springe, Osric.
I am justly killed with mine own treachery.
HAMLET: How does the queen?
KING: She swoons to see them bleed.
QUEEN: No, no, the drink, the drink! O my dear Hamlet!
The drink, the drink! I am poisoned.

(*Dies.*)
                                                300
HAMLET: O villany! Ho! let the door be locked.
Treachery! Seek it out.

(LAERTES *falls. Exit* OSRIC.)

LAERTES: It is here, Hamlet. Hamlet, thou art slain;
No med'cine in the world can do thee good.
In thee there is not half an hour's life.   305
The treacherous instrument is in thy hand,
Unbated and envenomed. The foul practice
Hath turned itself on me. Lo, here I lie,
Never to rise again. Thy mother's poisoned.
I can no more. The king, the king's to blame.   310
HAMLET: The point envenomed too!
Then, venom, to thy work.

(*Wounds the* KING.)

ALL: Treason! treason!
KING: O, yet defend me, friends. I am but hurt.
HAMLET: Here, thou incestuous, murd'rous, damnèd Dane, 315
Drink off this potion. Is thy union here?
Follow my mother.

(KING *dies.*)

LAERTES: He is justly served.
It is a poison tempered by himself.
Exchange forgiveness with me, noble Hamlet.
Mine and my father's death come not upon thee,
Nor thine on me!

(*Dies.*)   320

HAMLET: Heaven make thee free of it! I follow thee.
I am dead, Horatio. Wretched queen, adieu!
You that look pale and tremble at this chance,
That are but mutes or audience to this act,   325
Had I but time, as this fell sergeant Death

---

255 **union** pearl   272 **fat** out of training   285 **make a wanton of me** trifle with me

294 **springe** trap   305 **Unbated** unblunted; practice plot   324 **fell** cruel; **sergeant** an officer whose duty is to summon persons to appear before a court

Is strict in his arrest, O, I could tell you—
But let it be. Horatio, I am dead:
Thou livest; report me and my cause aright
To the unsatisfied.

330 HORATIO: Never believe it:
I am more an antique Roman than a Dane.
Here's yet some liquor left.

HAMLET: As th'art a man,
Give me the cup. Let go. By heaven, I'll ha't.
O God, Horatio, what a wounded name,
335 Things standing thus unknown, shall live behind me!
If thou didst ever hold me in thy heart,
Absent thee from felicity awhile,
And in this harsh world draw thy breath in pain,
To tell my story.

(*A march afar off.*)

What warlike noise is this?

(*Enter* OSRIC.)

340 OSRIC: Young Fortinbras, with conquest come from Poland,
To th' ambassadors of England gives
This warlike volley.

HAMLET: O, I die, Horatio!
The potent poison quite o'er-crows my spirit.
I cannot live to hear the news from England,
345 But I do prophesy th' election lights
On Fortinbras. He has my dying voice.
So tell him, with th' occurrents, more and less,
Which have solicited—the rest is silence.

(*Dies.*)

HORATIO: Now cracks a noble heart. Good night, sweet
prince, And flights of angels sing thee to thy rest!

(*March within.*)

Why does the drum come hither?

(*Enter* FORTINBRAS, *with the* AMBASSADORS [*and with drum, col-*
350 *ors, and* ATTENDANTS].)

FORTINBRAS: Where is this sight?
HORATIO: What is it you would see?
If aught of woe or wonder, cease your search.

FORTINBRAS: This quarry cries on havoc. O proud Death,
What feast is toward in thine eternal cell   355
That thou so many princes at a shot
So bloodily hast struck?
AMBASSADORS: The sight is dismal;
And our affairs from England come too late.
The ears are senseless that should give us hearing
To tell him his commandment is fulfilled,   360
That Rosencrantz and Guildenstern are dead.
Where should we have our thanks?
HORATIO: Not from his mouth,
Had it th' ability of life to thank you.
He never gave commandment for their death.
But since, so jump upon this bloody question,   365
You from the Polack wars, and you from England,
Are here arrived, give order that these bodies
High on a stage be placèd to the view,
And let me speak to th' yet unknowing world
How these things came about. So shall you hear   370
Of carnal, bloody, and unnatural acts;
Of accidental judgements, casual slaughters;
Of deaths put on by cunning and forced cause;
And, in this upshot, purposes mistook
Fall'n on th' inventors' heads. All this can I
Truly deliver.   375
FORTINBRAS: Let us haste to hear it.
And call the noblest to the audience.
For me, with sorrow I embrace my fortune.
I have some rights of memory in this kingdom,
Which now to claim my vantage doth invite me.   380
HORATIO: Of that I shall have also cause to speak,
And from his mouth whose voice will draw on more.
But let this same be presently performed,
Even while men's minds are wild, lest more mischance
On plots and errors happen.
FORTINBRAS: Let four captains   385
Bear Hamlet like a soldier to the stage,
For he was likely, had he been put on,
To have proved most royal; and for his passage
The soldier's music and the rite of war
Speak loudly for him.   390
Take up the bodies. Such a sight as this
Becomes the field, but here shows much amiss.
Go, bid the soldiers shoot.

---

352 **quarry** pile of dead   353 **toward** impending   363 **jump**
exactly   371 **put on** instigated; **forced cause** by reason of
compulsion   385 **put on** set to perform in office   386 **passage** death

---

341 **o'er-crows** triumphs over   344 **voice** vote   345 **more
and less** great and small   346 **solicited** incited, prompted

THE TEMPEST

The Tempest was staged at court in 1611. It is probably the last play that Shakespeare wrote without a collaborator, and generations of readers and audiences have taken Prospero as an image of Shakespeare himself: when Prospero puts aside his powerful, theatrical magic, Shakespeare may in a sense be making his farewell to the stage.

Renaissance audiences might have taken *The Tempest* as an example of a new kind of play becoming increasingly popular in the early seventeenth century: tragicomedy. Renaissance tragicomedy generally opens in the severe, disturbing mood of tragedy and builds to a moment of crisis; it then resolves into a comic finale of festivity, marriage, and harmony. That is, this version of "tragicomedy" concerns the play's plot structure, rather than its tone or mood. Shakespeare's company, the King's Men, had staged several plays by John Fletcher, one of the premier writers of tragicomedy, and it is inviting to see Shakespeare trying out his hand at the new genre late in his career in plays such as *Pericles, Cymbeline, The Winter's Tale,* and *The Tempest. The Tempest* begins as something like a revenge tragedy: Prospero plots to revenge himself on his usurping brother Antonio, and Sebastian's plot to murder Alonso also smacks of tragic intrigue. However, The Tempest, while raising the problems of tragedy, resolves them in the mode of comedy. Instead of murdering his brother, Prospero marries his daughter, Miranda, to Alonso's son, Ferdinand. The spirit Ariel prompts Prospero to discover that "The rarer action is / In virtue than in vengeance."

In other respects, *The Tempest* shares the forms and moods of Shakespearean comedy. In a plot reminiscent of many of Shakespeare's earlier comedies, Prospero's daughter, Miranda, falls instantly in love with Alonso's son, Ferdinand, for in *The Tempest,* virtue "naturally" recognizes virtue in others. The marriage also promises to heal the political rifts between Milan and Naples, and Prospero devises an elegant entertainment to lend the engagement an aura of sanctity. In its mythological characters, verse, song, and dance, Prospero's play resembles the masques frequently performed at court on such occasions. The romantic comedy of Ferdinand and Miranda is balanced by the play's more ironic treatment of Caliban, Stephano, and Trinculo. If the magical meeting of the lovers urges us to believe that the virtuous are drawn naturally together, the fact that Caliban takes the boozy Stephano and Trinculo for gods, and that the three of them try to over-

Patrick Stewart as Prospero conjures the storm in the Joseph Papp Public Theater production of Shakespeare's *The Tempest.*

throw Prospero from his second kingdom, suggests a parallel recognition—that bad nature also seeks itself out in others.

Although Prospero and Doctor Faustus may practice different kinds of magic, both are figures of the common desire to transcend nature through art. But much as Faustus is finally damned for his bargain with Mephostophilis, so Prospero learns that his own nature, and human nature generally, cannot be overcome. Prospero must learn to forgive to return to the world from his magic island-prison. Indeed, if the power of Prospero's artful magic is symbolized by the capable spirit Ariel, its limitations are suggested by Caliban. In some ways, Caliban represents a European imagination of human nature in its elemental form, an image of human nature that in the sixteenth and seventeenth centuries was often reinforced by European contacts with the indigenous peoples of the Americas and Africa. For although Prospero's island is located in the Mediterranean, many of its features—and the shipwreck motif—seem to be drawn from pamphlets describing the exploration of the New World. In 1609, a fleet of English ships bound for Virginia was wrecked by a storm in the Bermudas; and while many of the ships eventually reached Jamestown, one, the Sea Adventure, remained lost for nearly a year. When the ship finally reached Virginia in May of 1610, the Englishmen's story of survival and their encounters with the natives of the "still-vexed Bermoothes" was widely published in pamphlets that Shakespeare seems to have read while writing the play.

The play's setting and sources have led critics to see *The Tempest* as a play not only about the state of human nature, but also about the conquest and subjection of the native peoples represented by Caliban. Caliban is clearly seen from the point of view of the European settlers: Prospero calls him a devil and a slave and uses him as a beast of burden; his language is simple; and instead of using the arts of romance on Miranda, as Ferdinand does, he tries to rape Miranda in an effort to people the island with Calibans. Caliban was the master of the island's nature, its "fresh springs, brine pits, barren place and fertile," but in attempting to civilize Caliban, Prospero has succeeded only in deforming him. Caliban is now neither "natural" nor civilized, but a parody of European "humanity": "You taught me language, and my profit on't / Is, I know how to curse."

Prospero's stagey magic, his ability to conjure storms and spectacles, is a glorious image of Renaissance "overreaching." As in *A Midsummer Night's Dream* or *Hamlet,* Shakespeare uses *The Tempest* to frame his final, most subtle imaging of the extraordinary powers of art— the arts of magic, of civilization, of the theater. At the same time, *The Tempest* also expresses the limitations of that art: neither Sebastian nor Antonio seems fundamentally changed by Prospero's magic. And much as Caliban has been changed, the play finally can find no voice, no language for Caliban to speak. In recent years, stage productions have sometimes taken the play as an opportunity to investigate the dynamics of colonialism. Lewis Baumander's production (Toronto, 1987) set the play on the Queen Charlotte Islands, off the coast of British Columbia, Canada, during the late eighteenth century, when these islands were being explored and settled by British seamen. Not only have other productions (Jonathan Miller's 1988 *Tempest*) more generally interrogated the questions of cultural and racial domination posed in Shakespeare's play, but many writers—Roberto Fernández Retamar, for example, in *Caliban* (1989)—have seen in Shakespeare's play an allegory of the West's continued representational power over its colonial and postcolonial subjects. Aimé Césaire's play *A Tempest* is perhaps the best-known dramatic response to *The Tempest,* and it is included in Unit VII.

The Tempest is also the subject of one of the most famous and experimental Shakespeare films of the 1990s, Peter Greenaway's *Prospero's Books* (1991).

THE TEMPEST

William Shakespeare

EDITED BY DAVID BEVINGTON

CHARACTERS

ALONSO, *King of Naples*
SEBASTIAN, *his brother*
PROSPERO, *the right Duke of Milan*
ANTONIO, *his brother, the usurping Duke of Milan*
FERDINAND, *son to the King of Naples*
GONZALO, *an honest old Counselor*
ADRIAN *and*
FRANCISCO } *Lords*
CALIBAN, *a savage and deformed Slave*
TRINCULO, *a Jester*
STEPHANO, *a drunken Butler*

MASTER *of a Ship*
BOATSWAIN
MARINERS
MIRANDA, *daughter to Prospero*
ARIEL, *an airy Spirit*
IRIS
CERES
JUNO } *[presented by]* SPIRITS
NYMPHS
REAPERS
[*Other* SPIRITS *attending on Prospero.*]

ACT ONE

SCENE I

An uninhabited island.

A tempestuous noise of thunder and lightning heard. Enter a SHIP-
MASTER *and a* BOATSWAIN.

MASTER: Boatswain!
BOATSWAIN: Here, master. What cheer?
MASTER: Good speak to th' mariners. Fall to 't, yarely, or we
run ourselves aground. Bestir, bestir.

(*Exit.*)

(*Enter* MARINERS.)

5 BOATSWAIN: Heigh, my hearts! Cheerly, cheerly, my hearts!
Yare, yare! Take in the topsail. Tend to th' master's whistle.— Blow till thou burst thy wind, if room enough!

(*Enter* ALONSO, SEBASTIAN, ANTONIO, FERDINAND, GONZALO,
and others.)

ALONSO: Good boatswain, have care. Where's the master?
Play the men.
10 BOATSWAIN: I pray now, keep below.
ANTONIO: Where is the master, bos'n?
BOATSWAIN: Do you not hear him? You mar our labor. Keep
your cabins; you do assist the storm.
GONZALO: Nay, good, be patient.
15 BOATSWAIN: When the sea is. Hence! What cares these roarers for the name of king? To cabin! Silence! Trouble us not.
GONZALO: Good, yet remember whom thou hast aboard.
BOATSWAIN: None that I more love than myself. You are a
counselor; if you can command these elements to silence,
20 and work the peace of the present, we will not hand a

rope more. Use your authority. If you cannot, give thanks
you have liv'd so long, and make yourself ready in your
cabin for the mischance of the hour, if it so hap.—
Cheerly, good hearts!—Out of our way, I say.

(*Exit.*)

GONZALO: I have great comfort from this fellow. Methinks he   25
hath no drowning mark upon him; his complexion is perfect gallows. Stand fast, good Fate, to his hanging! Make the
rope of his destiny our cable, for our own doth little advantage. If he be not born to be hang'd, our case is miserable.

(*Exeunt.*)

(*Enter* BOATSWAIN.)

BOATSWAIN: Down with the topmast! Yare! Lower, lower!   30
Bring her to try with main-course. (*A cry within.*) A
plague upon this howling! They are louder than the
weather or our office.

(*Enter* SEBASTIAN, ANTONIO, *and* GONZALO.)

Yet again? What do you here? Shall we give o'er and
drown? Have you a mind to sink?   35
SEBASTIAN: A pox o' your throat, you bawling, blasphemous,
incharitable dog!
BOATSWAIN: Work you then.
ANTONIO: Hang, cur! Hang, you whoreson, insolent noisemaker! We are less afraid to be drown'd than thou art.   40
GONZALO: I'll warrant him for drowning, though the ship
were no stronger than a nutshell and as leaky as an unstanch'd wench.

I.i. Location: On a ship at sea.   3 **Good** i.e., it's good you've
come; or, my good fellow; *yarely* nimbly   6 **Tend** attend   7 **Blow**
(addressed to the wind); **if room enough** as long as we have sea-
room enough   8–9 **Play the men** act like men (?) ply, urge the men
to exert themselves (?)   15 **roarers** waves or winds, or both; spoken
to as though they were "bullies" or "blusterers"   20 **hand** handle

26–27 **complexion . . . gallows** appearance shows he was born
to be hanged (and therefore, according to the proverb, in no danger of drowning)   28 **our . . . advantage** i.e., our own cable is
of little benefit   31 **Bring . . . course** sail her close to the wind
by means of the mainsail   32 **our office** i.e., the noise we make
at our work   41 **warrant him for drowning** guarantee that
he will never be drowned   42 **unstanch'd** insatiable, loose, unrestrained

BOATSWAIN: Lay her a-hold, a-hold! Set her two courses off
45   to sea again! Lay her off!

(*Enter* MARINERS *wet.*)

MARINERS: All lost! To prayers, to prayers! All lost!

(*Exeunt.*)

BOATSWAIN: What, must our mouths be cold?
GONZALO: The King and Prince at prayers! Let's assist them,
    For our case is as theirs.
SEBASTIAN: I am out of patience.
50 ANTONIO: We are merely cheated of our lives by drunkards.
    This wide-chopp'd rascal! Would thou mightst lie drowning
    The washing of ten tides!
GONZALO: He'll be hang'd yet,
    Though every drop of water swear against it
    And gape at wid'st to glut him.

(*A confused noise within:*)

                   "Mercy on us!"—
55 "We split, we split!"—"Farewell my wife and children!"–
"Farewell, brother!"—"We split, we split, we split!"

(*Exit* BOATSWAIN.)

ANTONIO: Let's all sink wi' th' King.
SEBASTIAN: Let's take leave of him.

(*Exit* [*with* ANTONIO].)

GONZALO: Now would I give a thousand furlongs of sea for an
60   acre of barren ground, long heath, brown furze, anything.
    The wills above be done! But I would fain die a dry death.

(*Exit.*)

SCENE II

Enter PROSPERO [*in his magic robes*] *and* MIRANDA.

MIRANDA: If by your art, my dearest father, you have
    Put the wild waters in this roar, allay them.
    The sky, it seems, would pour down stinking pitch,
    But that the sea, mounting to th' welkin's cheek,
5   Dashes the fire out. O, I have suffered
    With those that I saw suffer! A brave vessel,
    Who had, no doubt, some noble creature in her,
    Dash'd all to pieces. O, the cry did knock
    Against my very heart! Poor souls, they perish'd.

---

44 **a-hold** a-hull, close to the wind; **courses** sails, i.e., foresail as
well as mainsail, set in an attempt to get the ship back out into
open water   47 **must . . . cold** i.e., let us heat up our mouths
with liquor   50 **merely** quite   51 **wide-chopp'd** with mouth
wide open   51–52 **lie . . . tides** (Pirates were hanged on the
shore and left until three tides had come in.)   54 **glut** swallow
60 **heath** uncultivated ground; heather; **furze** a weed growing
on waste land

I.ii. Location: The island. Before Prospero's cell.   4 **welkin's
cheek** sky's face   6 **brave** gallant, splendid

Had I been any god of power, I would   10
    Have sunk the sea within the earth or ere
    It should the good ship so have swallow'd and
    The fraughting souls within her.
PROSPERO: Be collected.
    No more amazement. Tell your piteous heart
    There's no harm done.   15
MIRANDA: O, woe the day!
PROSPERO: No harm.
    I have done nothing but in care of thee,
    Of thee, my dear one, thee, my daughter, who
    Art ignorant of what thou art, nought knowing
    Of whence I am, nor that I am more better
    Than Prospero, master of a full poor cell,   20
    And thy no greater father.
MIRANDA: More to know
    Did never meddle with my thoughts.
PROSPERO: 'Tis time
    I should inform thee farther. Lend thy hand,
    And pluck my magic garment from me. So,

(*Lays down his magic robe and staff.*)

    Lie there, my art. Wipe thou thine eyes; have comfort.   25
    The direful spectacle of the wrack, which touch'd
    The very virtue of compassion in thee,
    I have with such provision in mine art
    So safely ordered that there is no soul—
    No, not so much perdition as an hair   30
    Betid to any creature in the vessel
    Which thou heard'st cry, which thou saw'st sink. Sit
        down;
    For thou must now know farther.
MIRANDA: You have often
    Begun to tell me what I am, but stopp'd
    And left me to a bootless inquisition,   35
    Concluding, "Stay, not yet."
PROSPERO: The hour's now come;
    The very minute bids thee ope thine ear.
    Obey and be attentive. Canst thou remember
    A time before we came unto this cell?
    I do not think thou canst, for then thou wast not   40
    Out three years old.
MIRANDA: Certainly, sir, I can.
PROSPERO: By what? By any other house or person?
    Of anything the image, tell me, that
    Hath kept with thy remembrance.
MIRANDA: 'Tis far off,
    And rather like a dream than an assurance   45
    That my remembrance warrants. Had I not
    Four or five women once that tended me?
PROSPERO: Thou hadst, and more, Miranda. But how is it
    That this lives in thy mind? What seest thou else
    In the dark backward and abysm of time?   50

---

11 **or ere** before   13 **fraughting** forming the cargo; **collected**
calm, composed   14 **amazement** consternation   20 **full** very
30 **perdition** loss   31 **Betid** happened   35 **bootless inquisition** profitless inquiry   41 **Out** fully   45–46 **assurance . . .
warrants** certainty that my memory guarantees

If thou rememb'rest aught ere thou cam'st here,
How thou cam'st here thou mayst.

MIRANDA: But that I do not.

PROSPERO: Twelve year since, Miranda, twelve year since,
Thy father was the Duke of Milan and
55 A prince of power.

MIRANDA: Sir, are not you my father?

PROSPERO: Thy mother was a piece of virtue, and
She said thou wast my daughter; and thy father
Was Duke of Milan; and thou his only heir
And princess no worse issued.

MIRANDA: O the heavens!
60 What foul play had we, that we came from thence?
Or blessed was 't we did?

PROSPERO: Both, both, my girl.
By foul play, as thou say'st, were we heav'd thence,
But blessedly holp hither.

MIRANDA: O, my heart bleeds
To think o' th' teen that I have turn'd you to,
65 Which is from my remembrance! Please you, farther.

PROSPERO: My brother and thy uncle, call'd Antonio—
I pray thee mark me—that a brother should
Be so perfidious!—he whom next thyself
Of all the world I lov'd, and to him put
70 The manage of my state, as at that time
Through all the signories it was the first
And Prospero the prime duke, being so reputed
In dignity, and for the liberal arts
Without a parallel; those being all my study,
75 The government I cast upon my brother
And to my state grew stranger, being transported
And rapt in secret studies. Thy false uncle—
Dost thou attend me?

MIRANDA: Sir, most heedfully.

PROSPERO: Being once perfected how to grant suits,
80 How to deny them, who t' advance and who
To trash for overtopping, new created
The creatures that were mine, I say, or chang'd 'em,
Or else new form'd 'em; having both the key
Of officer and office, set all hearts i' th' state
85 To what tune pleas'd his ear, that now he was
The ivy which had hid my princely trunk,
And suck'd my verdure out on 't. Thou attend'st not.

MIRANDA: O, good sir, I do.

PROSPERO: I pray thee mark me.
I, thus neglecting worldly ends, all dedicated
90 To closeness and the bettering of my mind
With that which, but by being so retir'd,
O'er-priz'd all popular rate, in my false brother
Awak'd an evil nature; and my trust,

Like a good parent, did beget of him
A falsehood in its contrary as great   95
As my trust was, which had indeed no limit,
A confidence sans bound. He being thus lorded,
Not only with what my revenue yielded,
But what my power might else exact—like one
Who having into truth, by telling of it,   100
Made such a sinner of his memory
To credit his own lie—he did believe
He was indeed the Duke, out o' th' substitution,
And executing th' outward face of royalty,
With all prerogative. Hence his ambition growing—   105
Dost thou hear?

MIRANDA: Your tale, sir, would cure deafness.

PROSPERO: To have no screen between this part he play'd
And him he play'd it for, he needs will be
Absolute Milan. Me, poor man, my library
Was dukedom large enough. Of temporal royalties   110
He thinks me now incapable; confederates—
So dry he was for sway—wi' th' King of Naples
To give him annual tribute, do him homage,
Subject his coronet to his crown, and bend
The dukedom yet unbow'd—alas, poor Milan!—   115
To most ignoble stooping.

MIRANDA: O the heavens!

PROSPERO: Mark his condition and th' event, then tell me
If this might be a brother.

MIRANDA: I should sin
To think but nobly of my grandmother.
Good wombs have borne bad sons.   120

PROSPERO: Now the condition.
This King of Naples, being an enemy
To me inveterate, hearkens my brother's suit,
Which was that he, in lieu o' th' premises
Of homage and I know not how much tribute,
Should presently extirpate me and mine   125
Out of the dukedom and confer fair Milan
With all the honors on my brother. Whereon,
A treacherous army levied, one midnight
Fated to th' purpose, did Antonio open
The gates of Milan, and, i' th' dead of darkness,   130
The ministers for th' purpose hurried thence
Me and thy crying self.

MIRANDA: Alack, for pity!
I, not rememb'ring how I cried out then,

---

94 **good parent** alludes to the proverb that good parents often bear bad children; see also line 120 97 **sans** without; lorded raised to lordship, with power and wealth 100–102 **Who . . . lie** i.e., who, by repeatedly telling the lie (that he was indeed Duke of Milan), made his memory such a confirmed sinner against truth that he began to believe his own lie 103 **out o'** as a result of 104 **And . . . royalty** and (as a result) his carrying out all the ceremonial functions of royalty 108 **him** i.e., himself 109 **Absolute Milan** unconditional Duke of Milan 110 **temporal royalties** practical prerogatives and responsibilities of a sovereign 111 **confederates** conspires, allies himself 112 **dry** thirsty 113 **him** i.e., the King of Naples 114 **his . . . his** Antonio's . . . the King of Naples' 117 **condition** pact; **event** outcome 123 **in . . . premises** in return for the stipulation 125 **presently extirpate** at once remove

---

56 **piece** masterpiece, exemplar 59 **issued** born, descended 63 **holp** helped 64 **teen . . . to** trouble I've caused you to remember, or put you to 65 **from** out of 71 **signories** i.e., city-states of northern Italy 79 **perfected** grown skillful 81 **trash** check a hound by tying a weight to its neck; **overtopping** running too far ahead of the pack; or, growing too tall 82 **creatures** dependents; **or** either 83 **key** (1) key for unlocking (2) tool for tuning stringed instruments 90 **closeness** retirement, seclusion 91–92 **but . . . rate** except that it was done in retirement, (would have) surpassed in value all popular estimate

Will cry it o'er again. It is a hint
135 That wrings mine eyes to 't.
PROSPERO: Hear a little further,
And then I'll bring thee to the present business
Which now's upon 's, without the which this story
Were most impertinent.
MIRANDA: Wherefore did they not
That hour destroy us?
PROSPERO: Well demanded, wench.
140 My tale provokes that question. Dear, they durst not,
So dear the love my people bore me, nor set
A mark so bloody on the business, but
With colors fairer painted their foul ends.
In few, they hurried us aboard a bark,
145 Bore us some leagues to sea, where they prepar'd
A rotten carcass of a butt, not rigg'd,
Nor tackle, sail, nor mast; the very rats
Instinctively have quit it. There they hoist us,
To cry to th' sea that roar'd to us, to sigh
150 To th' winds whose pity, sighing back again,
Did us but loving wrong.
MIRANDA: Alack, what trouble
Was I then to you!
PROSPERO: O, a cherubin
Thou wast that did preserve me. Thou didst smile,
Infused with a fortitude from heaven,
155 When I have deck'd the sea with drops full salt,
Under my burden groan'd, which rais'd in me
An undergoing stomach, to bear up
Against what should ensue.
MIRANDA: How came we ashore?
PROSPERO: By Providence divine.
160 Some food we had, and some fresh water, that
A noble Neapolitan, Gonzalo,
Out of his charity, who being then appointed
Master of this design, did give us, with
Rich garments, linens, stuffs, and necessaries,
165 Which since have steaded much. So, of his gentleness,
Knowing I lov'd my books, he furnish'd me
From mine own library with volumes that
I prize above my dukedom.
MIRANDA: Would I might
But ever see that man!
PROSPERO: Now I arise.

(*Resumes his magic robes.*)

170 Sit still, and hear the last of our sea-sorrow.
Here in this island we arriv'd; and here
Have I, thy schoolmaster, made thee more profit
Than other princess' can that have more time
For vainer hours and tutors not so careful.

MIRANDA: Heavens thank you for 't! And now, I pray you, sir,   175
For still 'tis beating in my mind, your reason
For raising this sea-storm?
PROSPERO: Know thus far forth.
By accident most strange, bountiful Fortune,
Now my dear lady, hath mine enemies
Brought to this shore; and by my prescience   180
I find my zenith doth depend upon
A most auspicious star, whose influence
If now I court not but omit, my fortunes
Will ever after droop. Here cease more questions.
Thou art inclin'd to sleep; 'tis a good dullness,   185
And give it way. I know thou canst not choose.

(MIRANDA *sleeps.*)

Come away, servant, come! I am ready now.
Approach, my Ariel, come.

(*Enter* ARIEL.)

ARIEL: All hail, great master! Grave sir, hail! I come
To answer thy best pleasure; be 't to fly,   190
To swim, to dive into the fire, to ride
On the curl'd clouds. To thy strong bidding, task
Ariel and all his quality.
PROSPERO: Hast thou, spirit,
Perform'd to point the tempest that I bade thee?
ARIEL: To every article.   195
I boarded the King's ship; now on the beak,
Now in the waist, the deck, in every cabin,
I flam'd amazement. Sometime I'd divide,
And burn in many places; on the topmast,
The yards, and boresprit, would I flame distinctly,   200
Then meet and join. Jove's lightnings, the precursors
O' th' dreadful thunder-claps, more momentary
And sight-outrunning were not; the fire and cracks
Of sulphurous roaring the most mighty Neptune
Seem to besiege and make his bold waves tremble,   205
Yea, his dread trident shake.
PROSPERO: My brave spirit!
Who was so firm, so constant, that this coil
Would not infect his reason?
ARIEL: Not a soul
But felt a fever of the mad and play'd
Some tricks of desperation. All but mariners   210
Plung'd in the foaming brine and quit the vessel;
Then all afire with me, the King's son, Ferdinand,
With hair up-staring—then like reeds, not hair—
Was the first man that leapt; cried, "Hell is empty,
And all the devils are here."   215

---

134 **hint** occasion   138 **impertinent** irrelevant   144 **few** few
words   146 **butt** cask, tub   151 **loving wrong** i.e., the winds
pitied Prospero and Miranda though of necessity they blew them
from shore   155 **deck'd** covered (with salt tears); adorned   156
which i.e., the smile   157 **undergoing stomach** courage to
go on   165 **steaded much** been of much use   172 **more
profit** profit more   173 **princess'** princesses

---

181 **zenith** height of fortune (astrological term)   182 **influence** astrological power   187 **Come away** come   192 **task**
make demands upon   193 **quality** (1) fellow-spirits (2) abilities
194 **to point** to the smallest detail   196 **beak** prow   197
waist midships; **deck** poopdeck at the stern   198 **flam'd
amazement** struck terror in the guise of fire, i.e., St. Elmo's fire
200 **boresprit** bowsprit; distinctly in different places   207 **coil**
tumult   209 **of the mad** i.e., such as madmen feel   213 **up-
staring** standing on end

PROSPERO: Why, that's my spirit!
    But was not this nigh shore?
ARIEL: Close by, my master.
PROSPERO: But are they, Ariel, safe?
ARIEL: Not a hair perish'd.
    On their sustaining garments not a blemish,
    But fresher than before; and, as thou bad'st me,
220   In troops I have dispers'd them 'bout the isle.
    The King's son have I landed by himself,
    Whom I left cooling of the air with sighs
    In an odd angle of the isle and sitting,
    His arms in this sad knot.

(Folds his arms.)

PROSPERO: Of the King's ship,
225   The mariners, say how thou hast dispos'd,
    And all the rest o' th' fleet.
ARIEL: Safely in harbor
    Is the King's ship; in the deep nook, where once
    Thou call'dst me up at midnight to fetch dew
    From the still-vex'd Bermoothes, there she's hid;
230   The mariners all under hatches stow'd,
    Who, with a charm join'd to their suff'red labor,
    I have left asleep; and for the rest o' th' fleet,
    Which I dispers'd, they all have met again
    And are upon the Mediterranean flote
235   Bound sadly home for Naples,
    Supposing that they saw the King's ship wrack'd
    And his great person perish.
PROSPERO: Ariel, thy charge
    Exactly is perform'd. But there's more work.
    What is the time o' th' day?
ARIEL: Past the mid season.
240 PROSPERO: At least two glasses. The time 'twixt six and now
    Must by us both be spent most preciously.
ARIEL: Is there more toil? Since thou dost give me pains,
    Let me remember thee what thou hast promis'd,
    Which is not yet perform'd me.
PROSPERO: How now? Moody?
245   What is 't thou canst demand?
ARIEL: My liberty.
PROSPERO: Before the time be out? No more!
ARIEL: I prithee,
    Remember I have done thee worthy service,
    Told thee no lies, made thee no mistakings, serv'd
    Without or grudge or grumblings. Thou didst promise
250   To bate me a full year.
PROSPERO: Dost thou forget
    From what a torment I did free thee?
ARIEL: No.

PROSPERO: Thou dost, and think'st it much to tread the ooze
    Of the salt deep,
    To run upon the sharp wind of the north,
    To do me business in the veins o' th' earth   255
    When it is bak'd with frost.
ARIEL: I do not, sir.
PROSPERO: Thou liest, malignant thing! Hast thou forgot
    The foul witch Sycorax, who with age and envy
    Was grown into a hoop? Hast thou forgot her?
ARIEL: No, sir.   260
PROSPERO: Thou hast. Where was she born? Speak. Tell me.
ARIEL: Sir, in Argier.
PROSPERO: O, was she so? I must
    Once in a month recount what thou hast been,
    Which thou forget'st. This damn'd witch Sycorax,
    For mischiefs manifold and sorceries terrible   265
    To enter human hearing, from Argier,
    Thou know'st, was banish'd; for one thing she did
    They would not take her life. Is not this true?
ARIEL: Ay, sir.
PROSPERO: This blue-ey'd hag was hither brought with child   270
    And here was left by th' sailors. Thou, my slave,
    As thou report'st thyself, was then her servant;
    And, for thou wast a spirit too delicate
    To act her earthy and abhorr'd commands,
    Refusing her grand hests, she did confine thee,   275
    By help of her more potent ministers,
    And in her most unmitigable rage,
    Into a cloven pine, within which rift
    Imprison'd thou didst painfully remain
    A dozen years; within which space she died   280
    And left thee there, where thou did'st vent thy groans
    As fast as mill-wheels strike. Then was this island—
    Save for the son that she did litter here,
    A freckled whelp hag-born—not honor'd with
    A human shape.   285
ARIEL: Yes, Caliban her son.
PROSPERO: Dull thing, I say so; he, that Caliban
    Whom now I keep in service. Thou best know'st
    What torment I did find thee in; thy groans
    Did make wolves howl and penetrate the breasts
    Of ever angry bears. It was a torment   290
    To lay upon the damn'd, which Sycorax
    Could not again undo. It was mine art,
    When I arriv'd and heard thee, that made gape
    The pine and let thee out.
ARIEL: I thank thee, master.
PROSPERO: If thou more murmur'st, I will rend an oak   295
    And peg thee in his knotty entrails till
    Thou hast howl'd away twelve winters.
ARIEL: Pardon, master;
    I will be correspondent to command
    And do my spriting gently.

---

218 **sustaining garments** garments that buoyed them up in the sea   223 **angle** corner   224 **sad knot** folded arms are indicative of melancholy   227 **nook** bay   229 **still-vex'd Bermoothes** ever stormy Bermudas. Perhaps refers to the then-recent Bermuda shipwreck; see Play Introduction   231 **with . . . labor** by means of a spell added to all the labor they have undergone   234 **flote** sea   239 **mid season** noon   240 **glasses** i.e., hourglasses   243 **remember** remind   250 **bate** remit, deduct

---

258 **envy** malice   262 **Argier** Algiers   267 **one . . . did** perhaps a reference to her pregnancy, for which her life would be spared   270 **blue-ey'd** with dark circles under the eyes   273 **for** because   275 **hests** commands   296 **his** its   298 **correspondent** responsive, submissive

300 PROSPERO: Do so, and after two days
   I will discharge thee.
   ARIEL: That's my noble master!
   What shall I do? Say what? What shall I do?
   PROSPERO: Go make thyself like a nymph o' th' sea.
      Be subject
305   To no sight but thine and mine, invisible
   To every eyeball else. Go take this shape
   And hither come in 't. Go, hence with diligence!

   (*Exit* [ARIEL].)

   Awake, dear heart, awake! Thou hast slept well;
   Awake!
   MIRANDA: The strangeness of your story put
310   Heaviness in me.
   PROSPERO: Shake it off. Come on;
   We'll visit Caliban my slave, who never
   Yields us kind answer.
   MIRANDA: 'Tis a villain, sir,
   I do not love to look on.
   PROSPERO: But, as 'tis,
   We cannot miss him. He does make our fire,
315   Fetch in our wood, and serves in offices
   That profit us. What, ho! Slave! Caliban!
   Thou earth, thou! Speak.
   CALIBAN: (*Within.*)   There's wood enough within.
   PROSPERO: Come forth, I say! There's other business for thee.
   Come, thou tortoise! When?

   (*Enter* ARIEL *like a water-nymph.*)

320   Fine apparition! My quaint Ariel,
   Hark in thine ear.

   (*Whispers.*)

   ARIEL: My lord, it shall be done.

   (*Exit.*)

   PROSPERO: Thou poisonous slave, got by the devil himself
   Upon thy wicked dam, come forth!

   (*Enter* CALIBAN.)

   CALIBAN: As wicked dew as e'er my mother brush'd
325   With raven's feather from unwholesome fen
   Drop on you both! A south-west blow on ye
   And blister you all o'er!
   PROSPERO: For this, be sure, tonight thou shalt have cramps,
   Side-stitches that shall pen thy breath up; urchins
330   Shall, for that vast of night that they may work,
   All exercise on thee. Thou shalt be pinch'd

As thick as honeycomb, each pinch more stinging
   Than bees that made 'em.
CALIBAN: I must eat my dinner.
   This island's mine, by Sycorax my mother,
   Which thou tak'st from me. When thou cam'st first,   335
   Thou strok'st me and made much of me, wouldst
      give me
   Water with berries in 't, and teach me how
   To name the bigger light, and how the less,
   That burn by day and night; and then I lov'd thee
   And show'd thee all the qualities o' th' isle,   340
   The fresh springs, brine-pits, barren place and fertile.
   Curs'd be I that did so! All the charms
   Of Sycorax, toads, beetles, bats, light on you!
   For I am all the subjects that you have,
   Which first was mine own king; and here you sty me   345
   In this hard rock, whiles you do keep from me
   The rest o' th' island.
PROSPERO: Thou most lying slave,
   Whom stripes may move, not kindness! I have us'd thee,
   Filth as thou art, with humane care, and lodg'd thee
   In mine own cell, till thou didst seek to violate   350
   The honor of my child.
CALIBAN: O ho, O ho! Would't had been done!
   Thou didst prevent me; I had peopled else
   This isle with Calibans.
MIRANDA: Abhorred slave,
   Which any print of goodness wilt not take,   355
   Being capable of all ill! I pitied thee,
   Took pains to make thee speak, taught thee each hour
   One thing or other. When thou didst not, savage,
   Know thine own meaning, but wouldst gabble like
   A thing most brutish, I endow'd thy purposes   360
   With words that made them known. But thy vile race,
   Though thou didst learn, had that in 't which good
      natures
   Could not abide to be with; therefore wast thou
   Deservedly confin'd into this rock,
   Who hadst deserv'd more than a prison.   365
CALIBAN: You taught me language, and my profit on 't
   Is, I know how to curse. The red plague rid you
   For learning me your language!
PROSPERO: Hag-seed, hence!
   Fetch us in fuel; and be quick, thou'rt best,
   To answer other business. Shrug'st thou, malice?   370
   If thou neglect'st or dost unwillingly
   What I command, I'll rack thee with old cramps,
   Fill all thy bones with aches, make thee roar
   That beasts shall tremble at thy din.
CALIBAN: No, pray thee.
   (*Aside.*) I must obey. His art is of such pow'r,   375

---

314 **miss** do without   320 **quaint** ingenious   323 **wicked** mischievous, harmful   326 **south-west** i.e., wind thought to bring disease   329 **urchins** hedgehogs; here, suggesting goblins in the guise of hedgehogs   330 **vast** lengthy, desolate time; **that . . . work** malignant spirits were thought to be restricted to the hours of darkness

348 **stripes** lashes   354–365 **Abhorred . . . prison** sometimes assigned by editors to Prospero   360 **purposes** meanings, desires   361 **race** natural disposition; species, nature   367 **red plague** bubonic plague; **rid** destroy   368 **learning** teaching; **Hag-seed** offspring of a female demon   369 **thou'rt best** you'd be well advised   372 **old** such as old people suffer; or, plenty of   373 **aches** pronounced "aitches"

It would control my dam's god, Setebos,
And make a vassal of him.
PROSPERO: So, slave, hence!

(*Exit* CALIBAN.)

(*Enter* FERDINAND; *and* ARIEL, *invisible, playing and singing.*
[FERDINAND *does not see* PROSPERO *and* MIRANDA.])

(ARIEL's *song.*)

        Come unto these yellow sands,
          And then take hands.
380   Curtsied when you have and kiss'd,
          The wild waves whist,
        Foot it featly here and there;
        And, sweet sprites, the burden bear.
          Hark, hark!

(*Burden, dispersedly* [*within*].)

385   Bow-wow.
        The watch-dogs bark.

(*Burden, dispersedly* [*within*].)

        Bow-wow.
        Hark, hark! I hear
        The strain of strutting chanticleer
390   Cry, Cock-a-diddle-dow.

FERDINAND: Where should this music be? I' th' air or th'
    earth?
    It sounds no more; and, sure, it waits upon
    Some god o' th' island. Sitting on a bank,
    Weeping again the King my father's wrack,
395 This music crept by me upon the waters,
    Allaying both their fury and my passion
    With its sweet air. Thence I have follow'd it,
    Or it hath drawn me rather. But 'tis gone.
    No, it begins again.

(ARIEL's *song.*)

400   Full fathom five thy father lies;
          Of his bones are coral made;
        Those are pearls that were his eyes.
          Nothing of him that doth fade
        But doth suffer a sea-change
405   Into something rich and strange.
        Sea-nymphs hourly ring his knell:

(*Burden* [*within*].)

        Ding-dong.
        Hark, now I hear them—Ding-dong,
        bell.

410 FERDINAND: The ditty does remember my drown'd father.
    This is no mortal business, nor no sound
    That the earth owes. I hear it now above me.

PROSPERO: The fringed curtains of thine eye advance
    And say what thou seest yond.
MIRANDA: What is 't! A spirit!
    Lord, how it looks about! Believe me, sir,
    It carries a brave form. But 'tis a spirit.   415
PROSPERO: No, wench, it eats and sleeps and hath such
    senses
    As we have, such. This gallant which thou seest
    Was in the wrack; and, but he's something stain'd
    With grief, that's beauty's canker, thou mightst call him
    A goodly person. He hath lost his fellows   420
    And strays about to find 'em.
MIRANDA: I might call him
    A thing divine, for nothing natural
    I ever saw so noble.
PROSPERO: (*Aside.*)   It goes on, I see,
    As my soul prompts it. Spirit, fine spirit, I'll free thee
    Within two days for this.   425
FERDINAND: (*Seeing* MIRANDA.) Most sure, the goddess
    On whom these airs attend!—Vouchsafe my pray'r
    May know if you remain upon this island,
    And that you will some good instruction give
    How I may bear me here. My prime request,
    Which I do last pronounce, is, O you wonder!   430
    If you be maid or no?
MIRANDA: No wonder, sir,
    But certainly a maid.
FERDINAND: My language? Heavens!
    I am the best of them that speak this speech,
    Were I but where 'tis spoken.
PROSPERO: (*Coming forward.*)   How? The best?
    What wert thou, if the King of Naples heard thee?   435
FERDINAND: A single thing, as I am now, that wonders
    To hear thee speak of Naples. He does hear me;
    And that he does I weep. Myself am Naples,
    Who with mine eyes, never since at ebb, beheld
    The King my father wrack'd.   440
MIRANDA: Alack, for mercy!
FERDINAND: Yes, faith, and all his lords, the Duke of Milan
    And his brave son being twain.
PROSPERO: (*Aside.*)   The Duke of Milan
    And his more braver daughter could control thee,
    If now 'twere fit to do 't. At the first sight
    They have chang'd eyes. Delicate Ariel,   445
    I'll set thee free for this. (*To* FERDINAND.) A word, good sir.
    I fear you have done yourself some wrong. A word!

---

413 **advance** raise   415 **brave** excellent   418 **but** except that; **something stain'd** somewhat disfigured   419 **canker** cankerworm (feeding on buds and leaves)   423 **It goes on** i.e., my plan works   427 **remain** dwell   429 **bear me** conduct myself; **prime** chief   433 **best** i.e., in birth   436 **single** (1) solitary (2) feeble   437–438 **He . . . weep** i.e., this man to whom I speak (Prospero) hears me as I hear him, proving to me I am indeed alive, not dreaming, and am in the sad plight I imagined (?)   438 **Naples** the King of Naples (also in line 437)   442 **son** the only reference in the play to a son of Antonio   443 **control** confute   445 **chang'd eyes** exchanged amorous glances   447 **done . . . wrong** i.e., spoken falsely

---

381 **whist** being hushed   382 **featly** nimbly   383 **burden** refrain, undersong   384 s.d. **dispersedly** i.e., from all directions   410 **remember** commemorate   412 **owes** owns

MIRANDA: (*Aside.*) Why speaks my father so ungently? This
    Is the third man that e'er I saw, the first
450   That e'er I sigh'd for. Pity move my father
    To be inclin'd my way!
FERDINAND: O, if a virgin,
    And your affection not gone forth, I'll make you
    The Queen of Naples.
PROSPERO: Soft, sir! One word more.
    (*Aside.*) They are both in either's pow'rs; but this swift
      business
455   I must uneasy make, lest too light winning
    Make the prize light. (*To* FERDINAND.) One word more:
      I charge thee
    That thou attend me. Thou dost here usurp
    The name thou ow'st not, and hast put thyself
    Upon this island as a spy, to win it
460   From me, the lord on 't.
FERDINAND: No, as I am a man.
MIRANDA: There's nothing ill can dwell in such a temple.
    If the ill spirit have so fair a house,
    Good things will strive to dwell with 't.
PROSPERO: Follow me.—
    Speak not you for him; he's a traitor.—Come,
465   I'll manacle thy neck and feet together.
    Sea-water shalt thou drink; thy food shall be
    The fresh-brook mussels, wither'd roots, and husks
    Wherein the acorn cradled. Follow.
FERDINAND: No.
    I will resist such entertainment till
470   Mine enemy has more pow'r.

    (*He draws, and is charmed from moving.*)

MIRANDA: O dear father,
    Make not too rash a trial of him, for
    He's gentle, and not fearful.
PROSPERO: What, I say,
    My foot my tutor?—Put thy sword up, traitor,
    Who mak'st a show but dar'st not strike, thy conscience
475   Is so possess'd with guilt. Come, from thy ward,
    For I can here disarm thee with this stick
    And make thy weapon drop.

    (*Brandishes his staff.*)

MIRANDA: (*Trying to hinder him.*)   Beseech you, father.
PROSPERO: Hence! Hang not on my garments.
MIRANDA: Sir, have pity!
    I'll be his surety.
PROSPERO: Silence! One word more
480   Shall make me chide thee, if not hate thee. What,
    An advocate for an imposter? Hush!
    Thou think'st there is no more such shapes as he,
    Having seen but him and Caliban. Foolish wench,

    To th' most of men this is a Caliban
    And they to him are angels.   485
MIRANDA: My affections
    Are then most humble; I have no ambition
    To see a goodlier man.
PROSPERO: (*To* FERDINAND.) Come on, obey.
    Thy nerves are in their infancy again
    And have no vigor in them.
FERDINAND: So they are.
    My spirits, as in a dream, are all bound up.   490
    My father's loss, the weakness which I feel,
    The wrack of all my friends, nor this man's threats
    To whom I am subdu'd, are but light to me,
    Might I put through my prison once a day
    Behold this maid. All corners else o' th' earth   495
    Let liberty make use of; space enough
    Have I in such a prison.
PROSPERO: (*Aside.*) It works. (*To* FERDINAND.) Come on.—
    Thou hast done well, fine Ariel! (*To* FERDINAND.) Follow
      me.
    (*To* ARIEL.) Hark what thou else shalt do me.
MIRANDA: (*To* FERDINAND.)   Be of comfort.
    My father's of a better nature, sir,   500
    Than he appears by speech. This is unwonted
    Which now came from him.
PROSPERO: (*To* ARIEL.)   Thou shalt be as free
    As mountain winds, but then exactly do
    All points of my command.
ARIEL: To th' syllable.
PROSPERO: (*To* FERDINAND.) Come, follow. (*To* MIRANDA.)   505
    Speak not for him.

    (*Exeunt.*)

ACT TWO

SCENE I

Enter ALONSO, SEBASTIAN, ANTONIO, GONZALO, ADRIAN, FRANCISCO, *and others.*

GONZALO: Beseech you, sir, be merry. You have cause,
    So have we all, of joy, for our escape
    Is much beyond our loss. Our hint of woe
    Is common; every day some sailor's wife,
    The masters of some merchant, and the merchant,   5
    Have just our theme of woe; but for the miracle,
    I mean our preservation, few in millions
    Can speak like us. Then wisely, good sir, weigh
    Our sorrow with our comfort.
ALONSO: Prithee, peace.
SEBASTIAN: (*To* ANTONIO.) He receives comfort like cold   10
    porridge.

---

455 **uneasy** difficult   455–456 **light . . . light** easy . . . cheap
458 **ow'st** ownest   469 **entertainment** treatment   472 **gentle** wellborn; **fearful** cowardly   473 **foot** subordinate (Miranda, the foot, presumes to instruct Prospero, the head)   475 **ward** defensive posture (in fencing)

---

484 **To** compared to   488 **nerves** sinews   499 **me** for me

II.i. Location: Another part of the island.   3 **hint of** occasion for   5 **masters . . . the merchant** officers of some merchant vessel and the merchant himself, the owner   11 **porridge** with a pun on *peace* and *pease,* a usual ingredient of porridge

ANTONIO: (*To* SEBASTIAN.) The visitor will not give him o'er so.

SEBASTIAN: Look, he's winding up the watch of his wit; by and by it will strike.

GONZALO: Sir—

SEBASTIAN: (*To* ANTONIO.) One. Tell.

GONZALO: When every grief is entertain'd that's offer'd, Comes to th' entertainer—

SEBASTIAN: A dollar.

GONZALO: Dolor comes to him, indeed. You have spoken truer than you purpos'd.

SEBASTIAN: You have taken it wiselier than I meant you should.

GONZALO: Therefore, my lord—

ANTONIO: Fie, what a spendthrift is he of his tongue!

ALONSO: I prithee, spare.

GONZALO: Well, I have done. But yet—

SEBASTIAN: He will be talking.

ANTONIO: Which, of he or Adrian, for a good wager, first begins to crow?

SEBASTIAN: The old cock.

ANTONIO: The cock'rel.

SEBASTIAN: Done. The wager?

ANTONIO: A laughter.

SEBASTIAN: A match!

ADRIAN: Though this island seem to be desert—

SEBASTIAN: Ha, ha, ha!

ANTONIO: So, you're paid.

ADRIAN: Uninhabitable and almost inaccessible—

SEBASTIAN: Yet—

ADRIAN: Yet—

ANTONIO: He could not miss 't.

ADRIAN: It must needs be of subtle, tender, and delicate temperance.

ANTONIO: Temperance was a delicate wench.

SEBASTIAN: Ay, and a subtle, as he most learnedly deliver'd.

ADRIAN: The air breathes upon us here most sweetly.

SEBASTIAN: As if it had lungs, and rotten ones.

ANTONIO: Or as 'twere perfum'd by a fen.

GONZALO: Here is everything advantageous to life.

ANTONIO: True, save means to live.

SEBASTIAN: Of that there's none, or little.

GONZALO: How lush and lusty the grass looks! How green!

ANTONIO: The ground indeed is tawny.

SEBASTIAN: With an eye of green in 't.

ANTONIO: He misses not much.

SEBASTIAN: No; he doth but mistake the truth totally.

GONZALO: But the rarity of it is—which is indeed almost beyond credit—

SEBASTIAN: As many vouch'd rarities are.

GONZALO: That our garments, being, as they were, drench'd in the sea, hold notwithstanding their freshness and glosses, being rather new-dyed than stain'd with salt water.

ANTONIO: If but one of his pockets could speak, would it not say he lies?

SEBASTIAN: Ay, or very falsely pocket up his report.

GONZALO: Methinks our garments are now as fresh as when we put them on first in Afric, at the marriage of the King's fair daughter Claribel to the King of Tunis.

SEBASTIAN: 'Twas a sweet marriage, and we prosper well in our return.

ADRIAN: Tunis was never grac'd before with such a paragon to their queen.

GONZALO: Not since widow Dido's time.

ANTONIO: Widow! A pox o' that! How came that widow in? Widow Dido!

SEBASTIAN: What if he had said "widower Aeneas" too? Good Lord, how you take it!

ADRIAN: "Widow Dido" said you? You make me study of that. She was of Carthage, not of Tunis.

GONZALO: This Tunis, sir, was Carthage.

ADRIAN: Carthage?

GONZALO: A assure you, Carthage.

ANTONIO: His word is more than the miraculous harp.

SEBASTIAN: He hath rais'd the wall and houses too.

ANTONIO: What impossible matter will he make easy next?

SEBASTIAN: I think he will carry this island home in his pocket and give it his son for an apple.

ANTONIO: And, sowing the kernels of it in the sea, bring forth more islands.

GONZALO: Ay.

---

12 **visitor** one taking nourishment and comfort to the sick, i.e., Gonzalo; **give him o'er** abandon him 17 **Tell** keep count 18–19 **When . . . entertainer** when every sorrow that presents itself is accepted without resistance, there comes to the recipient 20 **dollar** widely circulated coin, the German *Thaler* and the Spanish *piece of eight*. Sebastian puns on *entertainer* in the sense of *innkeeper*; to Gonzalo, *dollar* suggests *dolor*, grief. 29–30 **Which . . . crow** which of the two, Gonzalo or Adrian, do you bet will speak (crow) first 31 **old cock** i.e., Gonzalo 32 **cock'rel** i.e., Adrian 34 **laughter** (1) burst of laughter (2) sitting of eggs. When Adrian, the *cock'rel*, begins to speak two lines later, Sebastian loses the bet. Some editors alter the speech prefixes in lines 37–38 so that Antonio enjoys his laugh as the prize for winning, but possibly Sebastian pays for losing with a laugh 35 **A match** a bargain; agreed 42 **miss 't** (1) avoid saying "Yet" (2) miss the island 44 **temperance** climate 45 **Temperance** a girl's name; **delicate** here it means *given to pleasure, voluptuous;* in line 43, *pleasant.* Antonio is evidently suggesting that "tender, and delicate temperance" sounds like a Puritan phrase, which Antonio then mocks by applying the words to a woman rather than an island. He began this bawdy comparison with a double entendre on *inaccessible*, line 39 46 **subtle** here it means *tricky;* in line 43, *delicate;* **deliver'd** uttered. Sebastian joins in the Puritan baiting of Antonio with his use of the pious cant phrase "learnedly deliver'd"

53 **lusty** healthy 54 **tawny** dull brown, yellowish 55 **eye** tinge, or spot (perhaps with reference to Gonzalo's eye or judgment) 60 **vouch'd** certified 64 **pockets** i.e., because they are muddy 66 **pocket up** receive unprotestingly, fail to respond to a challenge 72 **to** for 74 **widow Dido** Queen of Carthage, deserted by Aeneas. She was in fact a widow when Aeneas, a widower, met her, but Antonio may be amused at the term "widow" to describe a woman deserted by her lover 84 **miraculous harp** alludes to Amphion's harp with which he raised the walls of Thebes; Gonzalo has exceeded that deed by creating a modern Carthage—walls *and* houses—mistakenly on the site of Tunis 91 **Ay** Gonzalo may be reasserting his point about Carthage, or he may be responding ironically to Antonio who in turn answers sarcastically

ANTONIO: Why, in good time.

GONZALO: (*To* ALONSO.) Sir, we were talking that our garments seem now as fresh as when we were at Tunis at the
95   marriage of your daughter, who is now queen.

ANTONIO: And the rarest that e'er came there.

SEBASTIAN: Bate, I beseech you, widow Dido.

ANTONIO: O, widow Dido? Ay, widow Dido.

GONZALO: Is not, sir, my doublet as fresh as the first day I
100   wore it? I mean, in a sort.

ANTONIO: That "sort" was well fish'd for.

GONZALO: When I wore it at your daughter's marriage?

ALONSO: You cram these words into mine ears against
The stomach of my sense. Would I had never
105   Married my daughter there! For, coming thence,
My son is lost and, in my rate, she too,
Who is so far from Italy removed
I ne'er again shall see her. O thou mine heir
Of Naples and of Milan, what strange fish
110   Hath made his meal on thee?

FRANCISCO: Sir, he may live.
I saw him beat the surges under him,
And ride upon their backs. He trod the water,
Whose enmity he flung aside, and breasted
The surge most swoll'n that met him. His bold head
115   'Bove the contentious waves he kept, and oared
Himself with his good arms in lusty stroke
To th' shore, that o'er his wave-worn basis bowed,
As stooping to relieve him. I not doubt
He came alive to land.

ALONSO: No, no, he's gone.

120   SEBASTIAN: Sir, you may thank yourself for this great loss,
That would not bless our Europe with your daughter,
But rather loose her to an African,
Where she at least is banish'd from your eye,
Who hath cause to wet the grief on 't.

ALONSO: Prithee, peace.

125   SEBASTIAN: You were kneel'd to and importun'd otherwise
By all of us, and the fair soul herself
Weigh'd between loathness and obedience, at
Which end o' th' beam should bow. We have lost your son,
I fear, for ever. Milan and Naples have
130   Moe widows in them of their business' making
Than we bring men to comfort them.
The fault's your own.

ALONSO: So is the dear'st o' th' loss.

GONZALO: My lord Sebastian,
The truth you speak doth lack some gentleness,

And time to speak it in. You rub the sore,   135
When you should bring the plaster.

SEBASTIAN: Very well.

ANTONIO: And most chirurgeonly.

GONZALO: It is foul weather in us all, good sir,
When you are cloudy.

SEBASTIAN: (*To* ANTONIO.) Foul weather?

ANTONIO: (*To* SEBASTIAN.)   Very foul.

GONZALO: Had I plantation of this isle, my lord—   140

ANTONIO: He'd sow 't with nettle-seed.

SEBASTIAN: Or docks, or mallows.

GONZALO: And were the king on 't, what would I do?

SEBASTIAN: Scape being drunk for want of wine.

GONZALO: I' th' commonwealth I would by contraries
Execute all things; for no kind of traffic   145
Would I admit; no name of magistrate;
Letters should not be known; riches, poverty,
And use of service, none; contract, succession,
Bourn, bound of land, tilth, vineyard, none;
No use of metal, corn, or wine, or oil;   150
No occupation; all men idle, all,
And women too, but innocent and pure;
No sovereignty—

SEBASTIAN: Yet he would be king on 't.

ANTONIO: The latter end of his commonwealth forgets the
beginning.

GONZALO: All things in common nature should produce   155
Without sweat or endeavor. Treason, felony,
Sword, pike, knife, gun, or need of any engine,
Would I not have; but nature should bring forth,
Of it own kind, all foison, all abundance,
To feed my innocent people.   160

SEBASTIAN: No marrying 'mong his subjects?

ANTONIO: None, man; all idle—whores and knaves.

GONZALO: I would with such perfection govern, sir,
T' excel the golden age.

SEBASTIAN: Save his Majesty!

ANTONIO: Long live Gonzalo!   165

GONZALO: And—do you mark me, sir?

ALONSO: Prithee, no more. Thou dost talk nothing to me.

GONZALO: I do well believe your Highness, and did it to minister occasion to these gentlemen, who are of such sensible
and nimble lungs that they always use to laugh at nothing.

ANTONIO: 'Twas you we laugh'd at.   170

GONZALO: Who in this kind of merry fooling am nothing to
you; so you may continue and laugh at nothing still.

---

92 **in good time** an expression of ironical acquiescence or
amazement; i.e., *sure, right away*   96 **rarest** most remarkable,
beautiful   97 **Bate** abate, except, leave out (i.e., don't forget
Dido; or, let's have no more talk of Dido)   100 **in a sort** in a
way   104 **stomach** appetite   105 **Married** given in marriage
106 **rate** estimation, consideration   116 **lusty** vigorous   117
that . . . bowed that hung out over its wave-worn foot   118
As as if   124 **Who** which, i.e., the eye   126–128 **the fair . . .
bow** i.e., Claribel herself was poised uncertain between unwillingness to marry and obedience to her father as to which end of
the scale should sink, which should prevail   130 **Moe** more
133 **dear'st** heaviest, most costly

135 **time** appropriate time   137 **chirurgeonly** like a skilled
surgeon. Antonio mocks Gonzalo's medical analogy of a *plaster*
applied curatively to a wound   140 **plantation** colonization
(with subsequent wordplay on the literal meaning)   141 **docks,
mallows** various weeds   144 **by contraries** by what is directly
opposite to usual custom   145 **traffic** trade   147 **Letters**
learning   148 **use of service** custom of employing servants;
succession holding of property by right of inheritance   149
Bourn boundaries; bound of land landmarks; **tilth** tillage of soil
150 **corn** grain   157 **engine** instrument of warfare   159 **it** its;
foison plenty   164 **Save** God save   167–168 **minister occasion** furnish opportunity   168 **sensible** sensitive

ANTONIO: What a blow was there given!

SEBASTIAN: An it had not fall'n flat-long.

175 GONZALO: You are gentlemen of brave mettle; you would lift the moon out of her sphere, if she would continue in it five weeks without changing.

(*Enter* ARIEL [*invisible*] *playing solemn music.*)

SEBASTIAN: We would so, and then go a-batfowling.

ANTONIO: Nay, good my lord, be not angry.

180 GONZALO: No, I warrant, you, I will not adventure my discretion so weakly. Will you laugh me asleep? For I am very heavy.

ANTONIO: Go sleep, and hear us.

(*All sleep except* ALONSO, SEBASTIAN, *and* ANTONIO.)

ALONSO: What, all so soon asleep? I wish mine eyes

185 Would, with themselves, shut up my thoughts. I find They are inclin'd to do so.

SEBASTIAN: Please you, sir,
Do not omit the heavy offer of it.
It seldom visits sorrow; when it doth,
It is a comforter.

ANTONIO: We two, my lord,

190 Will guard your person while you take your rest,
And watch your safety.

ALONSO: Thank you. Wondrous heavy.

(ALONSO *sleeps. Exit* ARIEL.)

SEBASTIAN: What a strange drowsiness possesses them!

ANTONIO: It is the quality o' th' climate.

SEBASTIAN: Why
Doth it not then our eyelids sink? I find not

195 Myself dispos'd to sleep.

ANTONIO: Nor I; my spirits are nimble.
They fell together all, as by consent;
They dropp'd, as by a thunder-stroke. What might,
Worthy Sebastian? O, what might—? No more—
And yet methinks I see it in thy face,

200 What thou shouldst be. Th' occasion speaks thee, and
My strong imagination sees a crown
Dropping upon thy head.

SEBASTIAN: What, art thou waking?

ANTONIO: Do you not hear me speak?

SEBASTIAN: I do; and surely
It is a sleepy language and thou speak'st

205 Out of thy sleep. What is it thou didst say?

This is a strange repose, to be asleep
With eyes wide open—standing, speaking, moving—
And yet so fast asleep.

ANTONIO: Noble Sebastian,
Thou let'st thy fortune sleep—die, rather; wink'st
Whiles thou art waking.   210

SEBASTIAN: Thou dost snore distinctly;
There's meaning in thy snores.

ANTONIO: I am more serious than my custom. You
Must be so too, if heed me; which to do
Trebles thee o'er.

SEBASTIAN: Well, I am standing water.

ANTONIO: I'll teach you how to flow.   215

SEBASTIAN: Do so. To ebb
Hereditary sloth instructs me.

ANTONIO: O,
If you but knew how you the purpose cherish
Whiles thus you mock it! How, in stripping it,
You more invest it! Ebbing men, indeed,
Most often do so near the bottom run   220
By their own fear or sloth.

SEBASTIAN: Prithee say on.
The setting of thine eye and cheek proclaim
A matter from thee, and a birth indeed
Which throes thee much to yield.

ANTONIO: Thus, sir:
Although this lord of weak remembrance, this,   225
Who shall be of as little memory
When he is earth'd, hath here almost persuaded—
For he's a spirit of persuasion, only
Professes to persuade—the King his son's alive,
'Tis as impossible that he's undrown'd   230
As he that sleeps here swims.

SEBASTIAN: I have no hope
That he's undrown'd.

ANTONIO: O, out of that "no hope"
What great hope have you! No hope that way is
Another way so high a hope that even
Ambition cannot pierce a wink beyond,   235

---

174 **An** if; **flat-long** with the flat of the sword, i.e., ineffectually. (Cf. *fallen flat.*)   178 **a-batfowling** hunting birds at night with lantern and stick; also, gulling a simpleton. Gonzalo is the simpleton, or fowl, and Sebastian will use the moon as his lantern 180–81 **adventure . . . weakly** risk my reputation for discretion for so trivial a cause (by getting angry at these sarcastic fellows)   182 **heavy** sleep   183 **Go . . . us** let our laughing send you to sleep, or, go to sleep and hear us laugh at you   187 **omit** neglect; **heavy** drowsy   200 **speaks** calls upon; or, pronounces, proclaims. Sebastian as usurper of Alonso's crown

209 **wink'st** shut your eyes   214 **Trebles thee o'er** makes you three times as great and rich; **standing water** water which neither ebbs nor flows, at a standstill, indecisive   216 **Hereditary sloth** natural laziness   217 **purpose** i.e., of being king; **cherish** i.e., make dear, enrich   219 **invest** clothe. Antonio's paradox is that by skeptically stripping away illusions Sebastian can see the essence of a situation and the opportunity it presents, or that by disclaiming and deriding his purpose Sebastian shows how he values it   220 **the bottom** i.e., on which unadventurous men may go aground and miss the tide of fortune   222 **setting** set expression (of earnestness)   223 **matter** matter of importance   224 **throes** causes pain, as in giving birth   225 **this lord** i.e., Gonzalo; **remembrance** (1) power of remembering (2) being remembered after his death   227 **earth'd** buried   228–229 **only . . . persuade** i.e., whose whole function (as a privy councilor) is to persuade   233 **that way** i.e., in regard to Ferdinand's being saved   235–236 **Ambition . . . there** ambition itself cannot see any further than that hope (of the crown), but is unsure of itself in seeing even so far, is dazzled by daring to think so high

But doubt discovery there. Will you grant with me
That Ferdinand is drown'd?

SEBASTIAN: He's gone.

ANTONIO: Then, tell me,
Who's the next heir of Naples?

SEBASTIAN: Claribel.

ANTONIO: She that is Queen of Tunis; she that dwells
240   Ten leagues beyond man's life; she that from Naples
Can have no note, unless the sun were post—
The man i' th' moon's too slow—till new-born chins
Be rough and razorable; she that from whom
We all were sea-swallow'd, though some cast again,
245   And by that destiny to perform an act
Whereof what's past is prologue, what to come
In yours and my discharge.

SEBASTIAN: What stuff is this? How say you?
'Tis true, my brother's daughter's Queen of Tunis;
250   So is she heir of Naples; 'twixt which regions
There is some space.

ANTONIO: A space whose ev'ry cubit
Seems to cry out, "How shall that Claribel
Measure us back to Naples? Keep in Tunis,
And let Sebastian wake." Say this were death
255   That now hath seiz'd them; why, they were no worse
Than now they are. There be that can rule Naples
As well as he that sleeps; lords that can prate
As amply and unnecessarily
As this Gonzalo; I myself could make
260   A chough of as deep chat. O, that you bore
The mind that I do! What a sleep were this
For your advancement! Do you understand me?

SEBASTIAN: Methinks I do.

ANTONIO: And how does your content
Tender your own good fortune?

SEBASTIAN: I remember
265   You did supplant your brother Prospero.

ANTONIO: True.
And look how well my garments sit upon me,
Much feater than before. My brother's servants
Were then my fellows; now they are my men.

SEBASTIAN: But, for your conscience?

270   ANTONIO: Ay, sir, where lies that? If 'twere a kibe,
'Twould put me to my slipper; but I feel not
This deity in my bosom. Twenty consciences,
That stand 'twixt me and Milan, candied be they
And melt ere they molest! Here lies your brother,
275   No better than the earth he lies upon,

---

240 **Ten . . . life** i.e., it would take more than a lifetime to get
there   241 **note** news, intimation; **post** messenger   243 **from**
on our voyage from   244 **cast** were disgorged (with a pun on
casting of parts for a play)   247 **discharge** performance   253
Measure us i.e., traverse the cubits, find her way   254 **wake**
i.e., to his good fortune   259–260 **I . . . chat** I could teach a
jackdaw to talk as wisely, or, be such a garrulous talker myself
263 **content** desire, inclination   264 **Tender** regard, look after
267 **feater** more becomingly, fittingly   270 **kibe** chilblain, sore
on the heel   271 **put me to** oblige me to wear   273 **Milan**
the dukedom of Milan; **candied** frozen, congealed in crystalline
form

If he were that which now he's like—that's dead,
Whom I, with this obedient steel, three inches of it,
Can lay to bed forever; whiles you, doing thus,
To the perpetual wink for aye might put
This ancient morsel, this Sir Prudence, who   280
Should not upbraid our course. For all the rest,
They'll take suggestion as a cat laps milk;
They'll tell the clock to any business that
We say befits the hour.

SEBASTIAN: Thy case, dear friend,
Shall be my precedent. As thou got'st Milan,   285
I'll come by Naples. Draw thy sword. One stroke
Shall free thee from the tribute which thou payest,
And I the king shall love thee.

ANTONIO: Draw together;
And when I rear my hand, do you the like,
To fall it on Gonzalo.   290

(*They draw.*)

SEBASTIAN: O, but one word.

(*They talk apart.*)

(*Enter* ARIEL [*invisible*], *with music and song.*)

ARIEL: My master through his art foresees the danger
That you, his friend, are in, and sends me forth—
For else his project dies—to keep them living.

(*Sings in* GONZALO's *ear.*)

While you here do snoring lie,
Open-ey'd conspiracy
His time doth take.   295
If of life you keep a care,
Shake off slumber, and beware.
Awake, awake!

ANTONIO: Then let us both be sudden.   300

GONZALO: (*Waking.*) Now, good angels preserve the King!

(*The others wake.*)

ALONSO: Why, how now, ho, awake? Why are you drawn?
Wherefore this ghastly looking?

GONZALO: What's the matter?

SEBASTIAN: Whiles we stood here securing your repose,
Even now, we heard a hollow burst of bellowing   305
Like bulls, or rather lions. Did 't not wake you?
It struck mine ear most terribly.

ALONSO: I heard nothing.

ANTONIO: O, 'twas a din to fright a monster's ear,
To make an earthquake! Sure it was the roar
Of a whole herd of lions.   310

ALONSO: Heard you this, Gonzalo?

GONZALO: Upon mine honor, sir, I heard a humming,
And that a strange one too, which did awake me.

---

279 **wink** sleep, closing of eyes   283 **tell the clock** i.e., answer
appropriately, chime   287 **tribute** (See 1.2.113–24)   296 **time**
opportunity   304 **securing** standing guard over

I shak'd you, sir, and cried. As mine eyes open'd,
315   I saw their weapons drawn. There was a noise,
That's verily. 'Tis best we stand upon our guard,
Or that we quit this place. Let's draw our weapons.

ALONSO: Lead off this ground, and let's make further search
For my poor son.

320   GONZALO: Heavens keep him from these beasts!
For he is, sure, i' th' island.

ALONSO: Lead away.

ARIEL: (*Aside.*) Prospero my lord shall know what I have done.
So, King, go safely on to seek thy son.

(*Exeunt [severally].*)

SCENE II

Enter CALIBAN *with a burden of wood. A noise of thunder heard.*

CALIBAN: All the infections that the sun sucks up
From bogs, fens, flats, on Prosper fall and make him
By inch-meal a disease! His spirits hear me,
And yet I needs must curse. But they'll nor pinch,
5   Fright me with urchin-shows, pitch me i' th' mire,
Nor lead me, like a firebrand, in the dark
Out of my way, unless he bid 'em; but
For every trifle are they set upon me;
Sometime like apes that mow and chatter at me
10   And after bite me, then like hedgehogs which
Lie tumbling in my barefoot way and mount
Their pricks at my footfall; sometime am I
All wound with adders who with cloven tongues
Do hiss me into madness.

(*Enter* TRINCULO.)

                    Lo, now, lo!
15   Here comes a spirit of his, and to torment me
For bringing wood in slowly. I'll fall flat;
Perchance he will not mind me.

(*Lies down.*)

TRINCULO: Here's neither bush nor shrub, to bear off any
weather at all, and another storm brewing; I hear it sing i'
20   th' wind. Yond same black cloud, yond huge one, looks like
a foul bombard that would shed his liquor. If it should
thunder as it did before, I know not where to hide my
head. Yond same cloud cannot choose but fall by pailfuls.
(*Sees* CALIBAN.) What have we here? A man or a fish? Dead
25   or alive? A fish, he smells like a fish; a very ancient and fish-
like smell; a kind of not of the newest Poor-John. A strange
fish! Were I in England now, as once I was, and had but this
fish painted, not a holiday fool there but would give a piece

of silver. There would this monster make a man; any strange
beast there makes a man. When they will not give a doit to   30
relieve a lame beggar, they will lay out ten to see a dead Indian. Legg'd like a man! And his fins like arms! Warm, o' my
troth! I do now let loose my opinion, hold it no longer: this
is no fish, but an islander, that hath lately suffer'd by a thunderbolt. (*Thunder.*) Alas, the storm is come again! My best   35
way is to creep under his gaberdine; there is no other shelter hereabout. Misery acquaints a man with strange bedfellows. I will here shroud till the dregs of the storm be past.

(*Creeps under* CALIBAN's *garment.*)

(*Enter* STEPHANO, *singing, [a bottle in his hand].*)

STEPHANO: "I shall no more to sea, to sea,   40
              Here shall I die ashore—"

This is a very scurvy tune to sing at a man's funeral.
Well, here's my comfort.

(*Drinks.*)

(*Sings.*)

        "The master, the swabber, the boatswain and I,
            The gunner and his mate
        Lov'd Mall, Meg, and Marian, and Margery,   45
            But none of us car'd for Kate;
            For she had a tongue with a tang,
            Would cry to a sailor, 'Go hang!'
        She lov'd not the savor of tar nor of pitch,
            Yet a tailor might scratch her where'er she did itch.   50
            Then to sea, boys, and let her go hang!"

This is a scurvy tune too; but here's my comfort.

(*Drinks.*)

CALIBAN: Do not torment me! Oh!

STEPHANO: What's the matter? Have we devils here? Do you
put tricks upon 's with savages and men of Ind, ha? I have   55
not scap'd drowning to be afeard now of your four legs;
for it hath been said, "As proper a man as ever went on
four legs cannot make him give ground"; and it shall be
said so again while Stephano breathes at' nostrils.

CALIBAN: This spirit torments me! Oh!   60

STEPHANO: This is some monster of the isle with four legs,
who hath got, as I take it, an ague. Where the devil should
he learn our language? I will give him some relief, if it be
but for that. If I can recover him and keep him tame and
get to Naples with him, he's a present for any emperor   65
that ever trod on neat's-leather.

CALIBAN: Do not torment me, prithee. I'll bring my wood
home faster.

**II.ii. Location: Another part of the island.   3 By inch-
meal** inch by inch   **4 nor** neither   **5 urchin-shows** apparitions shaped like hedgehogs   **6 like a firebrand** in the guise of
a will-o'-the-wisp   **9 mow** make faces   **17 mind** notice   **18
bear off** keep off   **21 foul bombard** dirty leathern bottle; his
its   **26 Poor-John** salted hake, type of poor fare   **28 painted**
i.e., painted on a sign set up outside a booth or tent at a fair

---

29 make a man make one's fortune   **30 doit** small coin   **36
gaberdine** cloak, loose upper garment   **38 shroud** take shelter;
dregs i.e., last remains   **55 Ind** India   **57 proper** handsome;
four legs the conventional phrase would supply *two legs*   **59 at'**
at the   **64 for that** i.e., for knowing our language; recover restore   **66 neat's-leather** cowhide

STEPHANO: He's in his fit now and does not talk after the wis-
70 est. He shall taste of my bottle; if he have never drunk
wine afore, it will go near to remove his fit. If I can recover
him and keep him tame, I will not take too much for him;
he shall pay for him that hath him, and that soundly.

CALIBAN: Thou dost me yet but little hurt;
75 Thou wilt anon, I know it by thy trembling.
Now Prosper works upon thee.

STEPHANO: Come on your ways; open your mouth; here is
that which will give language to you, cat. Open your
mouth; this will shake your shaking, I can tell you, and
80 that soundly. (*Gives* CALIBAN *drink*.) You cannot tell who's
your friend. Open your chaps again.

TRINCULO: I should know that voice. It should be—but he is
drown'd; and these are devils. O defend me!

STEPHANO: Four legs and two voices; a most delicate mon-
85 ster! His forward voice now is to speak well of his friend;
his backward voice is to utter foul speeches and to detract.
If all the wine in my bottle will recover him, I will help
his ague. Come. (*Gives drink*.) Amen! I will pour some in
thy other mouth.

90 TRINCULO: Stephano!

STEPHANO: Doth thy other mouth call me? Mercy, mercy!
This is a devil, and no monster. I will leave him; I have no
long spoon.

TRINCULO: Stephano! If thou beest Stephano, touch me and
95 speak to me; for I am Trinculo—be not afeard—thy good
friend Trinculo.

STEPHANO: If thou beest Trinculo, come forth. I'll pull thee by
the lesser legs. If any be Trinculo's legs, these are they. (*Pulls
him out*.) Thou art very Trinculo indeed! How cam'st thou
100 to be the siege of this moon-calf? Can he vent Trinculos?

TRINCULO: I took him to be kill'd with a thunder-stroke. But
art thou not drown'd, Stephano? I hope now thou art not
drown'd. Is the storm overblown? I hid me under the dead
moon-calf's gaberdine for fear of the storm. And art thou
105 living, Stephano? O Stephano, two Neapolitans scap'd!

STEPHANO: Prithee, do not turn me about; my stomach is not
constant.

CALIBAN: These be fine things, an if they be not sprites.
That's a brave god and bears celestial liquor.
110 I will kneel to him.

STEPHANO: How didst thou scape? How cam'st thou hither?
Swear by this bottle how thou cam'st hither. I escap'd
upon a butt of sack which the sailors heav'd o'erboard—
by this bottle, which I made of the bark of a tree with
115 mine own hands since I was cast ashore.

CALIBAN: (*Kneeling*.) I'll swear upon that bottle to be thy true
subject, for the liquor is not earthly.

STEPHANO: Here; swear then how thou escap'dst.

TRINCULO: Swum ashore, man, like a duck. I can swim like a
duck, I'll be sworn.   120

STEPHANO: Here, kiss the book. Though thou canst swim like
a duck, thou art made like a goose.

(*Gives drink*.)

TRINCULO: O Stephano, hast any more of this?

STEPHANO: The whole butt, man. My cellar is in a rock by
the sea-side where my wine is hid. How now, moon-calf? 125
How does thine ague?

CALIBAN: Hast thou not dropp'd from heaven?

STEPHANO: Out o' th' moon, I do assure thee. I was the man
i' th' moon when time was.

CALIBAN: I have seen thee in her and I do adore thee.   130
My mistress show'd me thee and thy dog and thy bush.

STEPHANO: Come, swear to that; kiss the book. I will furnish
it anon with new contents. Swear.

(*Gives drink*.)

TRINCULO: By this good light, this is a very shallow monster!
I afeard of him? A very weak monster! The man i' th' 135
moon? A most poor credulous monster! Well drawn, monster, in good sooth!

CALIBAN: I'll show thee every fertile inch o' th' island;
And I will kiss thy foot. I prithee, by my god.

TRINCULO: By this light, a most perfidious and drunken 140
monster! When's god's asleep, he'll rob his bottle.

CALIBAN: I'll kiss thy foot. I'll swear myself thy subject.

STEPHANO: Come on then; down, and swear.

(CALIBAN *swears*.)

TRINCULO: I shall laugh myself to death at this puppy-headed
monster. A most scurvy monster! I could find in my heart 145
to beat him—

STEPHANO: Come, kiss.

TRINCULO: But that the poor monster's in drink. An abominable monster!

CALIBAN: I'll show thee the best springs; I'll pluck thee berries; 150
I'll fish for thee and get thee wood enough.
A plague upon the tyrant that I serve!
I'll bear him no more sticks, but follow thee,
Thou wondrous man.

TRINCULO: A most ridiculous monster, to make a wonder of 155
a poor drunkard!

CALIBAN: I prithee, let me bring thee where crabs grow;
And I with my long nails will dig thee pig-nuts,
Show thee a jay's nest, and instruct thee how
To snare the nimble marmoset. I'll bring thee   160

---

72 **I will . . . much** i.e., no sum can be too much 73 **hath**
possesses, receives 78 **cat . . . mouth** allusion to the proverb,
"Good liquor will make a cat speak" 81 **chaps** jaws 92–93
long spoon allusion to the proverb, "He that sups with the devil
has need of a long spoon" 100 **siege** excrement; **moon-calf**
monster, abortion. Supposed to be caused by the influence of the
moon; **vent** emit 106–107 not constant unsteady 108 **an if**
if 109 **brave** fine, magnificent 113 **butt of sack** barrel of
Canary wine

121 **book** i.e., bottle 129 **when time was** once upon a time
131 **dog . . . bush** the man in the moon was popularly imagined to have with him a dog and a bush of thorn 134 **By . . .
light** by God's light, by this good light from heaven 136 **Well
drawn** well pulled (on the bottle) 157 **crabs** crab apples 158
pig-nuts peanuts 160 **marmoset** small monkey

To clust'ring filberts, and sometimes I'll get thee
Young scamels from the rock. Wilt thou go with me?

STEPHANO: I prithee now, lead the way without any more
talking. Trinculo, the King and all our company else being
drown'd, we will inherit here. Here! Bear my bottle. Fellow Trinculo, we'll fill him by and by again.

CALIBAN: (*Sings drunkenly.*)

          Farewell, master; farewell, farewell!

TRINCULO: A howling monster; a drunken monster!

CALIBAN: No more dams I'll make for fish,
        Nor fetch in firing
     At requiring,
    Nor scrape trenchering, nor wash dish.
       'Ban, 'Ban, Ca-Caliban
     Has a new master, get a new man.
    Freedom, high-day! High-day, freedom!
      Freedom, high-day, freedom!

STEPHANO: O brave monster! Lead the way.

(*Exeunt.*)

ACT THREE

SCENE I

Enter FERDINAND, *bearing a log.*

FERDINAND: There be some sports are painful, and their labor
Delight in them sets off; some kinds of baseness
Are nobly undergone; and most poor matters
Point to rich ends. This my mean task
Would be as heavy to me as odious, but
The mistress which I serve quickens what's dead
And makes my labors pleasures. O, she is
Ten times more gentle than her father's crabbed,
And he's compos'd of harshness. I must remove
Some thousands of these logs and pile them up,
Upon a sore injunction. My sweet mistress
Weeps when she sees me work, and says such baseness
Had never like executor. I forget;
But these sweet thoughts do even refresh my labors,
Most busy lest, when I do it.

(*Enter* MIRANDA; *and* PROSPERO [*at a distance, unseen*].)

MIRANDA: Alas, now, pray you,
Work not so hard. I would the lightning had
Burnt up those logs that you are enjoin'd to pile!
Pray, set it down and rest you. When this burns,

'Twill weep for having wearied you. My father
Is hard at study; pray now, rest yourself.
He's safe for these three hours.

FERDINAND: O most dear mistress,
The sun will set before I shall discharge
What I must strive to do.

MIRANDA: If you'll sit down,
I'll bear your logs the while. Pray give me that.
I'll carry it to the pile.

FERDINAND: No, precious creature,
I had rather crack my sinews, break my back,
Than you should such dishonor undergo
While I sit lazy by.

MIRANDA: It would become me
As well as it does you; and I should do it
With much more ease, for my good will is to it,
And yours it is against.

PROSPERO: (*Aside.*)   Poor worm, thou art infected!
This visitation shows it.

MIRANDA: You look wearily.

FERDINAND: No, noble mistress, 'tis fresh morning with me
When you are by at night. I do beseech you—
Chiefly that I might set it in my prayers—
What is your name?

MIRANDA: Miranda.—O my father,
I have broke your hest to say so.

FERDINAND: Admir'd Miranda!
Indeed the top of admiration! Worth
What's dearest to the world! Full many a lady
I have ey'd with best regard, and many a time
Th' harmony of their tongues hath into bondage
Brought my too diligent ear. For several virtues
Have I lik'd several women, never any
With so full soul but some defect in her
Did quarrel with the noblest grace she ow'd
And put it to the foil. But you, O you,
So perfect and so peerless, are created
Of every creature's best!

MIRANDA: I do not know
One of my sex; no woman's face remember,
Save, from my glass, mine own. Nor have I seen
More that I may call men than you, good friend,
And my dear father. How features are abroad,
I am skilless of; but, by my modesty,
The jewel in my dower, I would not wish
Any companion in the world but you,
Nor can imagination form a shape,
Besides yourself, to like of. But I prattle
Something too wildly, and my father's precepts
I therein do forget.

FERDINAND: I am in my condition
A prince, Miranda; I do think, a king—
I would, not so!—and would no more endure
This wooden slavery than to suffer
The flesh-fly blow my mouth. Hear my soul speak:

---

162 **scamels** possibly "seamews," mentioned in Strachey's letter, or
shellfish; or perhaps from *squamelle*, furnished with little scales.
Contemporary French and Italian travel accounts report that the
natives of Patagonia in South America ate small fish described as
fort scameux and *squame*   165 **inherit** take possession   172
trenchering trenchers, wooden plates   175 **high-day** holiday (?)

III.i. Location: Before Prospero's cell.   2 **sets off** makes seem
greater by contrast   6 **quickens** gives life to   11 **sore injunction**
severe command   15 **Most . . . it** i.e., least troubled by my labor
when I think of her (?) The line may be in need of emendation

---

32 **visitation** (1) visit (2) visitation of the plague, i.e., infection
of love   37 **hest** command   45 **ow'd** owned   46 **put . . . foil**
(1) overthrew it (as in wrestling) (2) served as a "foil" or contrast
to set it off   53 **skilless** ignorant   63 **blow** befoul with fly-eggs

The very instant that I saw you, did
65 My heart fly to your service; there resides,
To make me slave to it; and for your sake
Am I this patient log-man.
MIRANDA: Do you love me?
FERDINAND: O heaven, O earth, bear witness to this sound,
And crown what I profess with kind event
70 If I speak true! If hollowly, invert
What best is boded me to mischief! I
Beyond all limit of what else i' th' world
Do love, prize, honor you.
MIRANDA: (*Weeping.*)   I am a fool
To weep at what I am glad of.
PROSPERO: (*Aside.*)   Fair encounter
75 Of two most rare affections! Heavens rain grace
On that which breeds between 'em!
FERDINAND: Wherefore weep you?
MIRANDA: At mine unworthiness, that dare offer
What I desire to give, and much less take
What I shall die to want. But this is trifling,
80 And all the more it seeks to hide itself
The bigger bulk it shows. Hence, bashful cunning,
And prompt me, plain and holy innocence!
I am your wife, if you will marry me;
If not, I'll die your maid. To be your fellow
85 You may deny me, but I'll be your servant,
Whether you will or no.
FERDINAND: My mistress, dearest,
And I thus humble ever.
MIRANDA: My husband, then?
FERDINAND: Ay, with a heart as willing
As bondage e'er of freedom. Here's my hand.
90 MIRANDA: And mine, with my heart in 't. And now farewell
Till half an hour hence.
FERDINAND: A thousand thousand!

(*Exeunt* [FERDINAND *and* MIRANDA *severally*].)

PROSPERO: So glad of this as they I cannot be,
Who are surpris'd with all; but my rejoicing
At nothing can be more. I'll to my book,
95 For yet ere supper-time must I perform
Much business appertaining.

SCENE II

Enter CALIBAN, STEPHANO, *and* TRINCULO.

STEPHANO: Tell not me. When the butt is out, we will drink
water, not a drop before. Therefore bear up, and board
'em. Servant-monster, drink to me.
TRINCULO: Servant-monster? The folly of this island! They
5 say there's but five upon this isle; we are three of them. If
th' other two be brain'd like us, the state totters.

---

69 **kind event** favorable outcome   70 **hollowly** insincerely,
falsely   71 **boded** destined for   79 **want** lack   84 **fellow**
mate, equal

III.ii. Location: Another part of the island.   1 **out** empty
2 **bear . . . 'em** Stephano uses the terminology of maneuvering
at sea and boarding a vessel under attack as a way of urging an
assault on the liquor supply

STEPHANO: Drink, servant-monster, when I bid thee. Thy
eyes are almost set in thy head.

(*Gives drink.*)

TRINCULO: Where should they be set else? He were a brave
monster indeed if they were set in his tail.   10
STEPHANO: My man-monster hath drown'd his tongue in sack.
For my part, the sea cannot drown me; I swam, ere I could
recover the shore, five and thirty leagues off and on. By this
light, thou shalt be my lieutenant, monster, or my standard.
TRINCULO: Your lieutenant, if you list; he's no standard.   15
STEPHANO: We'll not run, Monsieur Monster.
TRINCULO: Nor go neither, but you'll lie like dogs and yet
say nothing neither.
STEPHANO: Moon-calf, speak once in thy life, if thou beest a
good moon-calf.   20
CALIBAN: How does thy honor? Let me lick thy shoe.
I'll not serve him; he is not valiant.
TRINCULO: Thou liest, most ignorant monster, I am in case to
justle a constable. Why, thou debosh'd fish thou, was there
ever man a coward that hath drunk so much sack as I to-   25
day? Wilt thou tell a monstrous lie, being but half a fish
and half a monster?
CALIBAN: Lo, how he mocks me! Wilt thou let him, my lord?
TRINCULO: "Lord," quoth he? That a monster should be such
a natural!   30
CALIBAN: Lo, lo, again! Bite him to death, I prithee.
STEPHANO: Trinculo, keep a good tongue in your head. If you
prove a mutineer—the next tree! The poor monster's my
subject and he shall not suffer indignity.
CALIBAN: I thank my noble lord. Wilt thou be pleas'd   35
To hearken once again to the suit I made to thee?
STEPHANO: Marry, will I. Kneel and repeat it; I will stand, and
so shall Trinculo.

(CALIBAN *kneels.*)

(*Enter* ARIEL, *invisible.*)

CALIBAN: As I told thee before, I am subject to a tyrant,
A sorcerer, that by his cunning hath   40
Cheated me of the island.
ARIEL: Thou liest.
CALIBAN: Thou liest, thou jesting monkey, thou!
I would my valiant master would destroy thee.
I do not lie.
STEPHANO: Trinculo, if you trouble him any more in 's tale,   45
by this hand, I will supplant some of your teeth.

---

8 **set** fixed in a drunken stare; or sunk, like the sun   9 **brave**
fine, splendid   13 **recover** arrive at   14 **standard** standard-
bearer, ancient, i.e., ensign (as distinguished from *lieutenant,* line
15)   15 **list** prefer; **no standard** i.e., not able to stand up   16
run (1) retreat (2) urinate (taking Trinculo's *standard* line 15, in
the old sense of *conduit*)   17 **go** walk; **lie** (1) tell lies (2) lie prostrate (3) excret   23–24 **case . . . constable** i.e., in fit condition,
made valiant by drink, to taunt or challenge the police; **debosh'd**
i.e., debauched   30 **natural** (1) idiot (2) natural as opposed to
unnatural, monster-like   33 **the next tree** i.e., you'll hang   37
Marry i.e., indeed (originally an oath by the Virgin Mary)

TRINCULO: Why, I said nothing.

STEPHANO: Mum, then, and no more.—Proceed.

CALIBAN: I say, by sorcery he got this isle;

50 From me he got it. If thy greatness will
    Revenge it on him—for I know thou dar'st,
    But this thing dare not—

STEPHANO: That's most certain.

CALIBAN: Thou shalt be lord of it, and I'll serve thee.

55 STEPHANO: How now shall this be compass'd? Canst thou
    bring me to the party?

CALIBAN: Yea, yea, my lord. I'll yield him thee asleep,
    Where thou mayst knock a nail into his head.

ARIEL: Thou liest; thou canst not.

60 CALIBAN: What a pied ninny's this! Thou scurvy patch!
    I do beseech thy greatness, give him blows
    And take his bottle from him. When that's gone
    He shall drink nought but brine, for I'll now show him
    Where the quick freshes are.

65 STEPHANO: Trinculo, run into no further danger. Interrupt
    the monster one word further, and, by this hand, I'll turn
    my mercy out o' doors and make a stock-fish of thee.

TRINCULO: Why, what did? I did nothing. I'll go farther off.

STEPHANO: Didst thou not say he lied?

70 ARIEL: Thou liest.

STEPHANO: Do I so? Take thou that. (Beats TRINCULO.) As
    you like this, give me the lie another time.

TRINCULO: I did not give the lie. Out o' your wits and hearing
    too? A pox o' your bottle! This can sack and drinking do. A
75 murrain on your monster, and the devil take your fingers!

CALIBAN: Ha, ha, ha!

STEPHANO: Now, forward with your tale.

(To TRINCULO.)

    Prithee, stand further off.

CALIBAN: Beat him enough. After a little time
80 I'll beat him too.

STEPHANO: Stand farther.—Come, proceed.

CALIBAN: Why, as I told thee, 'tis a custom with him
    I' th' afternoon to sleep. There thou mayst brain him,
    Having first seiz'd his books, or with a log
85 Batter his skull, or paunch him with a stake,
    Or cut his wezand with thy knife. Remember
    First to possess his books; for without them
    He's but a sot, as I am, nor hath not
    One spirit to command. They all do hate him
90 As rootedly as I. Burn but his books.
    He has brave utensils—for so he calls them—
    Which, when he has a house, he'll deck withal.
    And that most deeply to consider is
    The beauty of his daughter. He himself
95 Calls her a nonpareil. I never saw a woman,
    But only Sycorax my dam and she;

    But she as far surpasseth Sycorax
    As great'st does least.

STEPHANO: Is it so brave a lass?

CALIBAN: Ay, lord; she will become thy bed, I warrant,   100
    And bring thee forth brave brood.

STEPHANO: Monster, I will kill this man. His daughter and I will
    be king and queen—save our Graces!—and Trinculo and
    thyself shall be viceroys. Dost thou like the plot, Trinculo?

TRINCULO: Excellent.   105

STEPHANO: Give me thy hand. I am sorry I beat thee; but,
    while thou liv'st, keep a good tongue in thy head.

CALIBAN: Within this half hour will he be asleep.
    Wilt thou destroy him then?

STEPHANO: Ay, on mine honor.   110

ARIEL: (Aside.) This will I tell my master.

CALIBAN: Thou mak'st me merry; I am full of pleasure.
    Let us be jocund. Will you troll the catch
    You taught me but while-ere?

STEPHANO: At thy request, monster, I will do reason, any rea-   115
    son. Come on, Trinculo, let us sing.

(Sings.)

        "Flout 'em and scout 'em
        And scout 'em and flout 'em!
            Thought is free."

CALIBAN: That's not the tune.   120

(ARIEL plays the tune on a tabor and pipe.)

STEPHANO: What is this same?

TRINCULO: This is the tune of our catch, play'd by the pic-
    ture of Nobody.

STEPHANO: If thou beest a man, show thyself in thy likeness.
    If thou beest a devil, take 't as thou list.   125

TRINCULO: O, forgive me my sins!

STEPHANO: He that dies pays all debts. I defy thee. Mercy
    upon us!

CALIBAN: Art thou afeard?

STEPHANO: No, monster, not I.   130

CALIBAN: Be not afeard. This isle is full of noises,
    Sounds and sweet airs, that give delight and hurt not.
    Sometimes a thousand twangling instruments
    Will hum about mine ears, and sometimes voices
    That, if I then had wak'd after long sleep,   135
    Will make me sleep again; and then, in dreaming,
    The clouds methought would open and show riches
    Ready to drop upon me, that, when I wak'd,
    I cried to dream again.

STEPHANO: This will prove a brave kingdom to me, where I   140
    shall have my music for nothing.

CALIBAN: When Prospero is destroy'd.

STEPHANO: That shall be by and by. I remember the story.

---

52 **this thing** i.e., Trinculo   60 **pied ninny** fool in motley;
patch fool   64 **quick freshes** running springs   67 **stock-fish**
dried cod beaten before cooking   72 **give me the lie** call me
a liar to my face   75 **murrain** plague (literally, a cattle disease)
85 **paunch** stab in the belly   86 **wezand** windpipe   88 **sot**
fool   91 **brave utensils** fine furnishings

---

113 **troll the catch** sing the round   114 **while-ere** a short
time ago   118 **scout** deride s.d. **tabor** small drum   122–123
picture of Nobody refers to a familiar figure with head, arms,
and legs, but no trunk   125 **take 't . . . list** i.e., take my defiance as you please, as best you can

TRINCULO: The sound is going away. Let's follow it, and after
145   do our work.
STEPHANO: Lead, monster; we'll follow. I would I could see
   this taborer; he lays it on.
TRINCULO: Wilt come? I'll follow, Stephano.

(*Exeunt [following* ARIEL'*s music*]*.*)

SCENE III

Enter ALONSO, SEBASTIAN, ANTONIO, GONZALO, ADRIAN,
FRANCISCO, *etc.*

GONZALO: By 'r lakin, I can go no further, sir;
   My old bones aches. Here's a maze trod indeed
   Through forth-rights and meanders! By your patience,
   I needs must rest me.
ALONSO: Old lord, I cannot blame thee,
5   Who am myself attach'd with weariness,
   To th' dulling of my spirits. Sit down, and rest.
   Even here I will put off my hope and keep it
   No longer for my flatterer. He is drown'd
   Whom thus we stray to find, and the sea mocks
10   Our frustrate search on land. Well, let him go.

(ALONSO *and* GONZALO *sit.*)

ANTONIO: (*Aside to* SEBASTIAN.) I am right glad that he's so
   out of hope.
   Do not, for one repulse, forego the purpose
   That you resolv'd t' effect.
SEBASTIAN: (*To* ANTONIO.)   The next advantage
   Will we take throughly.
15 ANTONIO: (*To* SEBASTIAN.) Let it be tonight,
   For, now they are oppress'd with travail, they
   Will not, nor cannot, use such vigilance
   As when they are fresh.
SEBASTIAN: (*To* ANTONIO.) I say tonight. No more.

(*Solemn and strange music; and* PROSPERO *on the top, invisible.*)

ALONSO: What harmony is this? My good friends, hark!
GONZALO: Marvelous sweet music!

(*Enter several strange shapes, bringing in a banquet, and dance about
it with gentle actions of salutations; and, inviting* [ALONSO], *etc., to
eat, they depart.*)

20 ALONSO: Give us kind keepers, heavens! What were these?
SEBASTIAN: A living drollery. Now I will believe
   That there are unicorns, that in Arabia
   There is one tree, the phoenix' throne, one phoenix
   At this hour reigning there.

III.iii. Location: Another part of the island.   1 **By 'r lakin**
by our Ladykin, by our Lady   3 **forth-rights and meanders**
paths straight and crooked   5 **attach'd** seized   12 **for** because
of   14 **throughly** thoroughly   17 s.d. **on the top** at some
high point of the tiring-house or the theatre   20 **kind keepers**
guardian angels   21 **drollery** puppet show

ANTONIO: I'll believe both;
   And what does else want credit, come to me,   25
   And I'll be sworn 'tis true. Travelers ne'er did lie,
   Though fools at home condemn 'em.
GONZALO: If in Naples
   I should report this now, would they believe me
   If I should say I saw such islanders?
   For, certes, these are people of the island,   30
   Who, though they are of monstrous shape, yet, note,
   Their manners are more gentle, kind, than of
   Our human generation you shall find
   Many, nay, almost any.
PROSPERO: (*Aside.*)   Honest lord,
   Thou hast said well; for some of you there present   35
   Are worse than devils.
ALONSO: I cannot too much muse
   Such shapes, such gesture, and such sound, expressing,
   Although they want the use of tongue, a kind
   Of excellent dumb discourse.
PROSPERO: (*Aside.*)   Praise in departing.
FRANCISCO: They vanish'd strangely.   40
SEBASTIAN: No matter, since
   They have left their viands behind; for we have stomachs.
   Will 't please you taste of what is here?
ALONSO: Not I.
GONZALO: Faith, sir, you need not fear. When we were boys,
   Who would believe that there were mountaineers
   Dew-lapp'd like bulls, whose throats had hanging at 'em   45
   Wallets of flesh? Or that there were such men
   Whose heads stood in their breasts? Which now we find
   Each putter-out of five for one will bring us
   Good warrant of.
ALONSO: I will stand to and feed,
   Although my last—no matter, since I feel   50
   The best is past. Brother, my lord the Duke,
   Stand to and do as we.

(*They approach the table.*)

(*Thunder and lightning. Enter* ARIEL, *like a harpy; claps his wings
upon the table; and, with a quaint device, the banquet vanishes.*)

ARIEL: You are three men of sin, whom Destiny,
   That hath to instrument this lower world
   And what is in 't, the never-surfeited sea   55

---

25 **want credit** lack credence   30 **certes** certainly   36 **muse**
wonder at   39 **Praise in departing** i.e., save your praise until
the end of the performance   45 **Dew-lapp'd** having a dewlap,
or fold of skin hanging from the neck, like cattle   47 **in their
breasts** i.e., like the Anthropophagi described in Othello   48
putter-out . . . one one who invests money, or gambles on the
risks of travel on the condition that, if he returns safely, he is to
receive five times the amount deposited; hence, any traveler   49
stand to fall to; take the risk   52 s.d. **harpy** a fabulous monster
with a woman's face and vulture's body, supposed to be a minister of divine vengeance; **quaint device** ingenious stage contrivance; **banquet vanishes** i.e., the food vanishes; the table
remains until line 82   54 **to** i.e., as its

Hath caus'd to belch up you, and on this island
Where man doth not inhabit—you 'mongst men
Being most unfit to live. I have made you mad;
And even with such-like valor men hang and drown
60 Their proper selves.

(ALONSO, SEBASTIAN, *and* ANTONIO *draw their swords.*)

You fools! I and my fellows
Are ministers of Fate. The elements,
Of whom your swords are temper'd, may as well
Wound the loud winds, or with bemock'd-at stabs
Kill the still-closing waters, as diminish
65 One dowle that's in my plume. My fellow-ministers
Are like invulnerable. If you could hurt,
Your swords are now too massy for your strengths
And will not be uplifted. But remember—
For that's my business to you—that you three
70 From Milan did supplant good Prospero;
Expos'd unto the sea, which hath requit it,
Him and his innocent child; for which foul deed
The pow'rs, delaying, not forgetting, have
Incens'd the seas and shores, yea, all the creatures,
75 Against your peace. Thee of thy son, Alonso,
They have bereft; and do pronounce by me
Ling'ring perdition, worse than any death
Can be at once, shall step by step attend
You and your ways; whose wraths to guard you from—
80 Which here, in this most desolate isle, else falls
Upon your heads—is nothing but heart's sorrow
And a clear life ensuing.

(*He vanishes in thunder; then, to soft music, enter the shapes again,
and dance, with mocks and mows, and carrying out the table.*)

PROSPERO: Bravely the figure of this harpy hast thou
Perform'd, my Ariel; a grace it had devouring.
85 Of my instruction hast thou nothing bated
In what thou hadst to say. So, with good life
And observation strange, my meaner ministers
Their several kinds have done. My high charms work,
And these mine enemies are all knit up
90 In their distractions. They now are in my pow'r;
And in these fits I leave them, while I visit
Young Ferdinand, whom they suppose is drown'd,
And his and mine lov'd darling.

(*Exit above.*)

GONZALO: I' th' name of something holy, sir, why stand you
In this strange stare? 95
ALONSO: O, it is monstrous, monstrous!
Methought the billows spoke and told me of it;
The winds did sing it to me, and the thunder,
That deep and dreadful organ-pipe, pronounc'd
The name of Prosper; it did bass my trespass.
Therefore my son i' th' ooze is bedded, and 100
I'll seek him deeper than e'er plummet sounded
And with him there lie mudded.

(*Exit.*)

SEBASTIAN: But one fiend at a time,
I'll fight their legions o'er.
ANTONIO: I'll be thy second.

(*Exeunt* [SEBASTIAN *and* ANTONIO].)

GONZALO: All three of them are desperate. Their great guilt, 105
Like poison given to work a great time after,
Now 'gins to bite the spirits. I do beseech you,
That are of suppler joints, follow them swiftly
And hinder them from what this ecstasy
May now provoke them to. 110
ADRIAN: Follow, I pray you.

(*Exeunt omnes.*)

ACT FOUR

SCENE I

Enter PROSPERO, FERDINAND, *and* MIRANDA.

PROSPERO: If I have too austerely punish'd you,
Your compensation makes amends, for I
Have given you here a third of mine own life,
Or that for which I live; who once again
I tender to thy hand. All thy vexations 5
Were but my trials of thy love, and thou
Hast strangely stood the test. Here, afore Heaven,
I ratify this my rich gift. O Ferdinand,
Do not smile at me that I boast her off,
For thou shalt find she will outstrip all praise 10
And make it halt behind her.
FERDINAND: I do believe it
Against an oracle.

---

59 **such-like valor** i.e., the reckless valor derived from madness   60 **proper** own   62 **whom** which   64 **still-closing** always closing again when parted   65 **dowle** soft, fine feather   66 **like** likewise, similarly; **If** even if   71 **requit** requited, avenged   79 **whose** refers to the heavenly powers s.d. **mocks and mows** mocking gestures and grimaces   83 **Bravely** finely, dashing   84 **a grace . . . devouring** i.e., you gracefully caused the banquet to disappear as if you had consumed it (with puns on *grace* meaning "gracefulness" and "a blessing on the meal," and on *devouring* meaning "a literal eating" and "an all-consuming or ravishing grace")   85 **bated** abated, diminished   86 **good life** faithful reproduction   87 **observation strange** exceptional attention to detail; **meaner** i.e., subordinate to Ariel   88 **several kinds** individual parts

94 **why** Gonzalo was not addressed in Ariel's speech to the "three men of sin," line 53, and is not as they are in a maddened state; see lines 105–107   95 **it** i.e., my sin   99 **bass my trespass** proclaim my trespass like a bass note in music   104 **o'er one** after another

IV.i. Location: Before Prospero's cell.   3 **a third** i.e., Miranda, into whose education Prospero has put a third of his life (?) or who represents a large part of what he cares about, along with his dukedom and his learned study (?)   7 **strangely** extraordinarily   9 **boast her off** i.e., praise her so   11 **halt** limp   12 **Against an oracle** i.e., even if an oracle should declare otherwise

PROSPERO: Then, as my gift and thine own acquisition
   Worthily purchas'd, take my daughter. But
15 If thou dost break her virgin-knot before
   All sanctimonious ceremonies may
   With full and holy rite be minist'red,
   No sweet aspersion shall the heavens let fall
   To make this contract grow; but barren hate,
20 Sour-ey'd disdain, and discord shall bestrew
   The union of your bed with weeds so loathly
   That you shall hate it both. Therefore take heed,
   As Hymen's lamps shall light you.
FERDINAND: As I hope
   For quiet days, fair issue, and long life,
25 With such love as 'tis now, the murkiest den,
   The most opportune place, the strong'st suggestion
   Our worser genius can, shall never melt
   Mine honor into lust, to take away
   The edge of that day's celebration
30 When I shall think or Phoebus' steeds are founder'd
   Or Night kept chain'd below.
PROSPERO: Fairly spoke.
   Sit then and talk with her; she is thine own.

(FERDINAND *and* MIRANDA *sit.*)

   What, Ariel! My industrious servant, Ariel!

(*Enter* ARIEL.)

   ARIEL: What would my potent master? Here I am.
35 PROSPERO: Thou and thy meaner fellows your last service
   Did worthily perform; and I must use you
   In such another trick. Go bring the rabble,
   O'er whom I give thee pow'r, here to this place.
   Incite them to quick motion, for I must
40 Bestow upon the eyes of this young couple
   Some vanity of mine art. It is my promise,
   And they expect it from me.
ARIEL: Presently?
PROSPERO: Ay, with a twink.
ARIEL: Before you can say "come" and "go,"
45   And breathe twice and cry "so, so,"
   Each one, tripping on his toe,
   Will be here with mop and mow.
   Do you love me, master? No?
50 PROSPERO: Dearly, my delicate Ariel. Do not approach
   Till thou dost hear me call.
ARIEL: Well, I conceive.

(*Exit.*)

_____

16 **sanctimonious** sacred   18 **aspersion** dew, shower   23
Hymen's Hymen was the Greek and Roman god of marriage
27 **worser genius** evil genius, or evil attendant spirit   30 **or** either;
founder'd broken down, made lame (i.e., Ferdinand will
wait impatiently for the bridal night)   37 **rabble** band, i.e., the
meaner fellows of line 35   41 **vanity** illusion   47 **mop and
mow** gestures and grimaces   50 **conceive** understand

PROSPERO: Look thou be true; do not give dalliance
   Too much the rein. The strongest oaths are straw
   To th' fire i' th' blood. Be more abstemious,
   Or else good night your vow!
FERDINAND: I warrant you, sir;
   The white cold virgin snow upon my heart   55
   Abates the ardor of my liver.
PROSPERO: Well.
   Now come, my Ariel! Bring a corollary,
   Rather than want a spirit. Appear, and pertly!
   No tongue! All eyes! Be silent.

(*Soft music.*)

(*Enter* IRIS.)

IRIS: Ceres, most bounteous lady, thy rich leas   60
   Of wheat, rye, barley, vetches, oats, and pease;
   Thy turfy mountains, where live nibbling sheep,
   And flat meads thatch'd with stover, them to keep;
   Thy banks with pioned and twilled brims,
   Which spongy April at thy hest betrims,   65
   To make cold nymphs chaste crowns; and thy broom-
     groves,
   Whose shadow the dismissed bachelor loves,
   Being lass-lorn; thy pole-clipt vineyard;
   And thy sea-marge, sterile and rocky-hard,
   Where thou thyself dost air—the queen o' th' sky, 70
   Whose wat'ry arch and messenger am I,
   Bids thee leave these, and with her sovereign grace.

(JUNO *descends* [*slowly in her car*].)

   Here on this grass-plot, in this very place,
   To come and sport. Her peacocks fly amain.
   Approach, rich Ceres, her to entertain.   75

(*Enter* CERES.)

CERES: Hail, many-color'd messenger, that ne'er
   Dost disobey the wife of Jupiter,
   Who with thy saffron wings upon my flow'rs
   Diffusest honey-drops, refreshing show'rs,
   And with each end of thy blue bow dost crown   80
   My bosky acres and my unshrubb'd down,

_____

56 **liver** as the presumed seat of the passions   57 **corollary** surplus,
extra supply   58 **want** lack; **pertly** briskly s.d. **Iris** goddess
of the rainbow, and Juno's messenger   60 **Ceres** goddess
of the generative power of nature; **leas** meadows   61 **vetches** plants
for forage, fodder   63 **stover** winter fodder for cattle   64 **pioned
and twilled** undercut by the swift current and protected by
roots and branches woven into a mat (?)   66 **broom-groves**
clumps of broom, gorse, yellow-flowered shrub   67 **dismissed
bachelor** rejected male lover   68 **pole-clipt** hedged in with
poles; or pruned   70 **queen o' th' sky** i.e., Juno   71 **wat'ry
arch** rainbow   72 s.d. **Juno descends** i.e., starts her descent
from the "heavens" above the stage (?)   74 **peacocks** birds sacred
to Juno, and used to pull her chariot; **amain** with full speed
75 **entertain** receive   81 **bosky** wooded; **down** upland

Rich scarf to my proud earth; why hath thy Queen
Summon'd me hither, to this short-grass'd green?
IRIS: A contract of true love to celebrate,
85 And some donation freely to estate
On the bless'd lovers.
CERES: Tell me, heavenly bow,
If Venus or her son, as thou dost know,
Do now attend the Queen? Since they did plot
The means that dusky Dis my daughter got,
90 Her and her blind boy's scandal'd company
I have forsworn.
IRIS: Of her society
Be not afraid. I met her deity
Cutting the clouds towards Paphos, and her son
Dove-drawn with her. Here thought they to have done
95 Some wanton charm upon this man and maid,
Whose vows are, that no bed-right shall be paid
Till Hymen's torch be lighted; but in vain;
Mars's hot minion is return'd again;
Her waspish-headed son has broke his arrows,
100 Swears he will shoot no more, but play with sparrows
And be a boy right out.

(JUNO *alights.*)

CERES: Highest Queen of state,
Great Juno, comes; I know her by her gait.
JUNO: How does my bounteous sister? Go with me
To bless this twain, that they may prosperous be
105 And honor'd in their issue.

(*They sing.*)

JUNO: Honor, riches, marriage-blessing,
Long continuance, and increasing,
Hourly joys be still upon you!
Juno sings her blessings on you.
110 CERES: Earth's increase, foison plenty,
Barns and garners never empty,
Vines with clust'ring bunches growing,
Plants with goodly burden bowing;
Spring come to you at the farthest
115 In the very end of harvest!
Scarcity and want shall shun you;
Ceres' blessing so is on you.

FERDINAND: This is a most majestic vision, and
Harmonious charmingly. May I be bold
120 To think these spirits?
PROSPERO: Spirits, which by mine art
I have from their confines call'd to enact
My present fancies.

FERDINAND: Let me live here ever;
So rare a wond'red father and a wife
Makes this place Paradise.

(JUNO *and* CERES *whisper, and send* IRIS *on employment.*)

PROSPERO: Sweet now, silence!
Juno and Ceres whisper seriously; 125
There's something else to do. Hush and be mute,
Or else our spell is marr'd.
IRIS: You nymphs, call'd Naiads, of the windring brooks,
With your sedg'd crowns and ever-harmless looks,
Leave your crisp channels, and on this green land 130
Answer your summons; Juno does command.
Come, temperate nymphs, and help to celebrate
A contract of true love; be not too late.

(*Enter certain* NYMPHS.)

You sunburnt sicklemen, of August weary,
Come hither from the furrow and be merry. 135
Make holiday; your rye-straw hats put on
And these fresh nymphs encounter every one
In country footing.

(*Enter certain* REAPERS, *properly habited. They join with the* NYMPHS *in a graceful dance, towards the end whereof* PROSPERO *starts suddenly, and speaks; after which, to a strange, hollow, and confused noise, they heavily vanish.*)

PROSPERO: (*Aside.*) I had forgot that foul conspiracy
Of the beast Caliban and his confederates 140
Against my life. The minute of their plot
Is almost come. (*To the* SPIRITS.) Well done! Avoid; no
more!
FERDINAND: This is strange. Your father's in some passion
That works him strongly.
MIRANDA: Never till this day
Saw I him touch'd with anger so distemper'd. 145
PROSPERO: You do look, my son, in a mov'd sort,
As if you were dismay'd. Be cheerful, sir.
Our revels now are ended. These our actors,
As I foretold you, were all spirits and
Are melted into air, into thin air; 150
And, like the baseless fabric of this vision,
The cloud-capp'd tow'rs, the gorgeous palaces,
The solemn temples, the great globe itself,
Yea, all which it inherit, shall dissolve
And, like this insubstantial pageant faded, 155
Leave not a rack behind. We are such stuff
As dreams are made on, and our little life
Is rounded with a sleep. Sir, I am vex'd.
Bear with my weakness; my old brain is troubled.

---

85 **estate** bestow 87 **son** i.e., Cupid 89 **Dis . . . got** Pluto, or Dis, god of the infernal regions, carried off Persephone, daughter of Ceres, to be his bride in Hades 90 **Her** i.e., Venus; **scandal'd** scandalous 92 **her deity** i.e., her highness 93 **Paphos** place on the island of Cyprus, sacred to Venus 98 **Mars' hot minion** i.e., Venus, the beloved of Mars 99 **waspish-headed** fiery, hotheaded, peevish 100 **sparrows** supposed lustful, and sacred to Venus 101 **right out** outright 110 **foison plenty** plentiful harvest 111 **garners** granaries

---

123 **wond'red** wonder-performing, wondrous; **wife** sometimes emended to *wise* 128 **windring** wandering, winding (?) 130 **crisp** curled, rippled 132 **temperate** chaste 138 **country footing** country dancing; s.d. **heavily** slowly, dejectedly 142 **Avoid** depart, withdraw 146 **mov'd sort** troubled state, condition 148 **revels** entertainments, pageants 151 **baseless** without substance 154 **which it inherit** who occupy it 156 **rack** wisp of cloud 157 **on** of

160 Be not disturb'd with my infirmity.
    If you be pleas'd, retire into my cell
    And there repose. A turn or two I'll walk
    To still my beating mind.
    FERDINAND, MIRANDA: We wish your peace.

(*Exeunt.*)

PROSPERO: Come with a thought! I thank thee, Ariel. Come.

(*Enter* ARIEL.)

165 ARIEL: Thy thoughts I cleave to. What's thy pleasure?
    PROSPERO: Spirit,
    We must prepare to meet with Caliban.
    ARIEL: Ay, my commander. When I presented Ceres,
    I thought to have told thee of it, but I fear'd
    Lest I might anger thee.
170 PROSPERO: Say again, where didst thou leave these varlets?
    ARIEL: I told you, sir, they were red-hot with drinking,
    So full of valor that they smote the air
    For breathing in their faces; beat the ground
    For kissing of their feet; yet always bending
175 Towards their project. Then I beat my tabor,
    At which, like unback'd colts, they prick'd their ears,
    Advanc'd their eyelids, lifted up their noses
    As they smelt music. So I charm'd their ears
    That calf-like they my lowing follow'd through
180 Tooth'd briers, sharp furzes, pricking goss, and thorns,
    Which ent'red their frail shins. At last I left them
    I' th' filthy-mantled pool beyond your cell,
    There dancing up to th' chins, that the foul lake
    O'erstunk their feet.
    PROSPERO: This was well done, my bird.
185 Thy shape invisible retain thou still.
    The trumpery in my house, go bring it hither,
    For stale to catch these thieves.
    ARIEL: I go, I go.

(*Exit.*)

PROSPERO: A devil, a born devil, on whose nature
    Nurture can never stick; on whom my pains,
190 Humanely taken, all, all lost, quite lost!
    And as with age his body uglier grows,
    So his mind cankers. I will plague them all,
    Even to roaring.

(*Enter* ARIEL, *loaden with glistering apparel, etc.*)

    Come, hang them on this line.

([ARIEL *hangs up the showy finery;* PROSPERO *and* ARIEL *remain, invisible.*] *Enter* CALIBAN, STEPHANO, *and* TRINCULO, *all wet.*)

CALIBAN: Pray you, tread softly, that the blind mole may not
    Hear a foot fall. We now are near his cell.   195
STEPHANO: Monster, your fairy, which you say is a harmless
    fairy, has done little better than play'd the Jack with us.
TRINCULO: Monster, I do smell all horse-piss, at which my
    nose is in great indignation.
STEPHANO: So is mine. Do you hear, monster? If I should take   200
    a displeasure against you, look you—
TRINCULO: Thou wert but a lost monster.
CALIBAN: Good my lord, give me thy favor still.
    Be patient, for the prize I'll bring thee to
    Shall hoodwink this mischance. Therefore speak softly.   205
    All's hush'd as midnight yet.
TRINCULO: Ay, but to lose our bottles in the pool—
STEPHANO: There is not only disgrace and dishonor in that,
    monster, but an infinite loss.
TRINCULO: That's more to me than my wetting. Yet this is   210
    your harmless fairy, monster!
STEPHANO: I will fetch off my bottle, though I be o'er ears
    for my labor.
CALIBAN: Prithee, my King, be quiet. See'st thou here,
    This is the mouth o' th' cell. No noise, and enter.   215
    Do that good mischief which may make this island
    Thine own for ever, and I, thy Caliban,
    For aye thy foot-licker.
STEPHANO: Give me thy hand. I do begin to have bloody
    thoughts.   220
TRINCULO: (*Seeing the finery.*) O King Stephano! O peer! O
    worthy Stephano! Look what a wardrobe here is for thee!
CALIBAN: Let it alone, thou fool! It is but trash.
TRINCULO: O, ho, monster! We know what belongs to a frip-
    pery. O King Stephano! (*Takes a gown.*)   225
STEPHANO: Put off that gown, Trinculo. By this hand, I'll have
    that gown.
TRINCULO: Thy Grace shall have it.
CALIBAN: The dropsy drown this fool! What do you mean
    To dote thus on such luggage? Let's alone   230
    And do the murder first. If he awake,
    From toe to crown he'll fill our skins with pinches,
    Make us strange stuff.
STEPHANO: Be you quiet, monster. Mistress line, is not this
    my jerkin? (*Takes it down.*) Now is the jerkin under the 235
    line. Now, jerkin, you are like to lose your hair and prove
    a bald jerkin.
TRINCULO: Do, do! We steal by line and level, an 't like your
    Grace.

---

164 **with a thought** i.e., on the instant, or summoned by my thought, no sooner thought on than here   167 **presented** acted the part of, or introduced   176 **unback'd** unbroken, unridden   177 **Advanc'd** lifted up   180 **goss** gorse, a prickly shrub   182 **filthy-mantled** covered with a slimy coating   186 **trumpery** cheap goods, the *glistering apparel* mentioned in the following stage direction   187 **stale** (1) decoy (2) out of fashion garments (with possible further suggestions of *fit for a stale* or prostitute, *stale* meaning "horse-piss," line 198, and *steal*, pronounced like *stale*)   192 **cankers** festers, grows malignant   193 **line** lime tree or linden

197 **Jack** (1) Knave (2) will-o-the-wisp   205 **hoodwink** cover up, make you not see (a hawking term)   221 **King . . . peer** alludes to the old ballad beginning, "King Stephen was a worthy peer"   224 **frippery** place where cast-off clothes are sold   230 **luggage** cumbersome trash   235 **jerkin** jacket make of leather; **under the line** under the lime tree (with punning sense of being south of the equinoctial line or equator; sailors to the southern regions were popularly supposed to lose their hair from scurvy or other diseases. Stephano also quibbles bawdily on losing hair through syphilis, and in *Mistress* and *jerkin*)   238 **by line and level** i.e., by means of plumb-line and carpenter's level, methodically (with pun on *line*, "lime tree," line 235, and *steal* pronounced *stale*, i.e., prostitute, continuing Stephano's bawdy quibble); **an 't like** if it please

240 STEPHANO: I thank thee for that jest. Here's a garment for 't.
(*Gives a garment.*) Wit shall not go unrewarded while I am
king of this country. "Steal by line and level" is an excellent pass of pate. There's another garment for 't.

TRINCULO: Monster, come, put some lime upon your fingers,
245 and away with the rest.

CALIBAN: I have none on 't. We shall lose our time,
And all be turn'd to barnacles, or to apes
With foreheads villainous low.

STEPHANO: Monster, lay to your fingers. Help to bear this
250 away where my hogshead of wine is, or I'll turn you out
of my kingdom. Go to, carry this.

TRINCULO: And this.

STEPHANO: Ay, and this.

(*They collect more and more garments.*)

(*A noise of hunters heard. Enter divers* SPIRITS, *in shape of dogs and
hounds, hunting them about,* PROSPERO *and* ARIEL *setting them on.*)

PROSPERO: Hey, Mountain, hey!
255 ARIEL: Silver! There it goes, Silver!
PROSPERO: Fury, Fury! There, Tyrant, there! Hark! Hark!

(CALIBAN, STEPHANO, *and* TRINCULO *are driven out.*)

Go charge my goblins that they grind their joints
With dry convulsions, shorten up their sinews
With aged cramps, and more pitch-spotted make them
260 Than pard or cat o' mountain.
ARIEL: Hark, they roar!
PROSPERO: Let them be hunted soundly. At this hour
Lies at my mercy all mine enemies.
Shortly shall all my labors end, and thou
Shalt have the air at freedom. For a little
265 Follow, and do me service.

(*Exeunt.*)

ACT FIVE

SCENE I

Enter PROSPERO *in his magic robes,* [*with his staff,*] *and* ARIEL.

PROSPERO: Now does my project gather to a head.
My charms crack not, my spirits obey, and Time
Goes upright with his carriage. How's the day?
ARIEL: On the sixth hour; at which time, my lord,
5   You said our work should cease.

---

243 **pass of pate** sally of wit   244 **lime** birdlime, sticky substance (to give Caliban sticky fingers)   247 **barnacles** barnacle
geese, formerly supposed to be hatched from seashells attached
to trees and to fall thence into the water; here evidently used, like
apes, as types of simpletons   248 **villainous** miserably   258
dry associated with age, arthritic (?); **convulsions** cramps   259
aged characteristic of old age   260 **pard** panther or leopard;
cat o' mountain wildcat

V.i. Location: Before Prospero's cell.   3 **his carriage** its
burden (i.e., Time is unstopped, runs smoothly)

PROSPERO: I did say so,
When first I rais'd the tempest. Say, my spirit,
How fares the King and 's followers?
ARIEL: Confin'd together
In the same fashion as you gave in charge,
Just as you left them; all prisoners, sir,
In the line-grove which weather-fends your cell.   10
They cannot budge till your release. The King,
His brother, and yours, abide all three distracted,
And the remainder mourning over them,
Brimful of sorrow and dismay; but chiefly
Him that you term'd, sir, "The good old lord, Gonzalo."   15
His tears runs down his beard like winter's drops
From eaves of reeds. Your charm so strongly works 'em
That if you now beheld them, your affections
Would become tender.
PROSPERO: Dost thou think so, spirit?
ARIEL: Mine would, sir, were I human.   20
PROSPERO: And mine shall.
Hast thou, which art but air, a touch, a feeling
Of their afflictions, and shall not myself,
One of their kind, that relish all as sharply,
Passion as they, be kindlier mov'd than thou art?
Though with their high wrongs I am struck to th' quick,   25
Yet with my nobler reason 'gainst my fury
Do I take part. The rarer action is
In virtue than in vengeance. They being penitent,
The sole drift of my purpose doth extend
Not a frown further. Go release them, Ariel.   30
My charms I'll break, their senses I'll restore,
And they shall be themselves.
ARIEL: I'll fetch them, sir.

(*Exit.*)

(PROSPERO *traces a charmed circle with his staff.*)

PROSPERO: Ye elves of hills, brooks, standing lakes, and groves,
And ye that on the sands with printless foot
Do chase the ebbing Neptune, and do fly him   35
When he comes back; you demi-puppets that
By moonshine do the green sour ringlets make,
Whereof the ewe not bites; and you whose pastime
Is to make midnight mushrooms, that rejoice
To hear the solemn curfew; by whose aid,   40
Weak masters though ye be, I have bedimm'd
The noontide sun, call'd forth the mutinous winds,
And 'twixt the green sea and the azur'd vault
Set roaring war; to the dread rattling thunder
Have I given fire, and rifted Jove's stout oak   45

---

10 **line-grove** grove of lime trees; **weather-fends** protects from
the weather   11 **your release** you release them   17 **eaves of
reeds** thatched roofs   23 **relish all** experience quite   24 **Passion** experience deep feeling   27 **rarer** nobler   33–50 **Ye . . .
art** this famous passage is an embellished paraphrase of Golding's
translation of Ovid's *Metamorphoses,* 7.197–219   36 **demi-
puppets** puppets of half-size, i.e., elves and fairies   37 **green
sour ringlets** fairy rings, circles in grass (actually produced by
mushrooms)   44–45 **to . . . fire** I have discharged the dread rattling thunderbolt   45 **rifted** riven, split

With his own bolt; the strong-bas'd promontory
Have I made shake, and by the spurs pluck'd up
The pine and cedar; graves at my command
Have wak'd their sleepers, op'd, and let 'em forth
50   By my so potent art. But this rough magic
I here abjure, and, when I have requir'd
Some heavenly music, which even now I do,
To work mine end upon their senses that
This airy charm is for, I'll break my staff,
55   Bury it certain fathoms in the earth,
And deeper than did ever plummet sound
I'll drown my book.

(*Solemn music.*)

(*Here enters* ARIEL *before; then* ALONSO, *with a frantic gesture, attended by* GONZALO; SEBASTIAN *and* ANTONIO *in like manner, attended by* ADRIAN *and* FRANCISCO. *They all enter the circle which* PROSPERO *had made, and there stand charm'd; which* PROSPERO *observing, speaks:*)

A solemn air, and the best comforter
To an unsettled fancy, cure thy brains,
60   Now useless, boil'd within thy skull! There stand,
For you are spell-stopp'd.
Holy Gonzalo, honorable man,
Mine eyes, ev'n sociable to the show of thine,
Fall fellowly drops. The charm dissolves apace,
65   And as the morning steals upon the night,
Melting the darkness, so their rising senses
Begin to chase the ignorant fumes that mantle
Their clearer reason. O good Gonzalo,
My true preserver, and a loyal sir
70   To him thou follow'st! I will pay thy graces
Home both in word and deed. Most cruelly
Didst thou, Alonso, use me and my daughter.
Thy brother was a furtherer in the act.
Thou art pinch'd for 't now, Sebastian. Flesh and blood,
75   You, brother mine, that entertain'd ambition,
Expell'd remorse and nature, who, with Sebastian,
Whose inward pinches therefore are most strong,
Would here have kill'd your king, I do forgive thee,
Unnatural though thou art.—Their understanding
80   Begins to swell, and the approaching tide
Will shortly fill the reasonable shore
That now lies foul and muddy. Not one of them
That yet looks on me, or would know me. Ariel,
Fetch me the hat and rapier in my cell.

(ARIEL *goes to the cell and returns immediately.*)

85   I will discase me, and myself present
As I was sometime Milan. Quickly, spirit;
Thou shalt ere long be free.

(ARIEL *sings and helps to attire him.*)

ARIEL: Where the bee sucks, there suck I;
In a cowslip's bell I lie;
There I couch when owls do cry.   90
On the bat's back I do fly
After summer merrily.
Merrily, merrily shall I live now
Under the blossom that hangs on the bough.

PROSPERO: Why, that's my dainty Ariel! I shall miss thee;   95
But yet thou shalt have freedom. So, so, so.
To the King's ship, invisible as thou art!
There shalt thou find the mariners asleep
Under the hatches. The master and the boatswain
Being awake, enforce them to this place,   100
And presently, I prithee.
ARIEL: I drink the air before me, and return
Or ere your pulse twice beat. (*Exit.*)
GONZALO: All torment, trouble, wonder, and amazement
Inhabits here. Some heavenly power guide us   105
Out of this fearful country!
PROSPERO: Behold, sir King,
The wronged Duke of Milan, Prospero.
For more assurance that a living prince
Does now speak to thee, I embrace thy body;
And to thee and thy company I bid   110
A hearty welcome.

(*Embraces him.*)

ALONSO: Whe'er thou be'st he or no,
Or some enchanted trifle to abuse me,
As late I have been, I not know. Thy pulse
Beats as of flesh and blood; and, since I saw thee,
Th' affliction of my mind amends, with which,   115
I fear, a madness held me. This must crave,
An if this be at all, a most strange story.
Thy dukedom I resign, and do entreat
Thou pardon me my wrongs. But how should Prospero
Be living and be here?   120
PROSPERO: (*To* GONZALO.)   First, noble friend,
Let me embrace thine age, whose honor cannot
Be measur'd or confin'd.

(*Embraces him.*)

GONZALO: Whether this be
Or be not, I'll not swear.
PROSPERO: Yet do yet taste
Some subtleties o' th' isle, that will not let you
Believe things certain. Welcome, my friends all!   125
(*Aside to* SEBASTIAN *and* ANTONIO.) But you, my brace of
lords, were I so minded,

---

47 **spurs** roots   51 **requir'd** requested   58 **and** i.e., which is
63 **sociable** sympathetic; **show** appearance   64 **Fall** let fall   70
pay thy graces reward your favors   71 **Home** fully   76 **remorse** pity; **nature** natural feeling   85 **discase** disrobe   86 **As
. . . Milan** in my former appearance as Duke of Milan

96 **So, so, so** expresses approval of Ariel's help as valet   112 **trifle** trick of magic; **abuse** deceive   116 **crave** require   117 **An
. . . all** if this is actually happening   118 **Thy . . . resign** Alonso
made arrangement with Antonio at the time of Prospero's banishment for Milan to pay tribute to Naples; see 1.2.113–127
124 **subtleties** illusions, magical powers

I here could pluck his Highness' frown upon you
And justify you traitors. At this time
I will tell no tales.

SEBASTIAN: The devil speaks in him.

PROSPERO: No.

130   For you, most wicked sir, whom to call brother
Would even infect my mouth, I do forgive
Thy rankest fault—all of them; and require
My dukedom of thee, which perforce I know
Thou must restore.

ALONSO: If thou be'st Prospero,

135   Give us particulars of thy preservation,
How thou hast met us here, who three hours since
Were wrack'd upon this shore; where I have lost—
How sharp the point of this remembrance is!—
My dear son Ferdinand.

PROSPERO: I am woe for 't, sir.

140   ALONSO: Irreparable is the loss, and Patience
Says it is past her cure.

PROSPERO: I rather think
You have not sought her help, of whose soft grace
For the like loss I have her sovereign aid
And rest myself content.

ALONSO: You the like loss?

145   PROSPERO: As great to me as late; and, supportable
To make the dear loss, have I means much weaker
Than you may call to comfort you, for I
Have lost my daughter.

ALONSO: A daughter?

150   O heavens, that they were living both in Naples,
The king and queen there! That they were, I wish
Myself were mudded in that oozy bed
Where my son lies. When did you lose your daughter?

PROSPERO: In this last tempest. I perceive these lords

155   At this encounter do so much admire
That they devour their reason and scarce think
Their eyes do offices of truth, their words
Are natural breath. But, howsoev'r you have
Been justled from your senses, know for certain

160   That I am Prospero and that very duke
Which was thrust forth of Milan, who most strangely
Upon this shore, where you were wrack'd, was landed,
To be the lord on 't. No more yet of this,
For 'tis a chronicle of day by day,

165   Not a relation for a breakfast nor
Befitting this first meeting. Welcome, sir;
This cell's my court. Here have I few attendants
And subjects none abroad. Pray you look in.
My dukedom since you have given me again,

170   I will requite you with as good a thing,
At least bring forth a wonder, to content ye
As much as me my dukedom.

(*Here* PROSPERO *discovers* FERDINAND *and* MIRANDA, *playing at chess.*)

MIRANDA: Sweet lord, you play me false.

FERDINAND: No, my dearest love,
I would not for the world.   175

MIRANDA: Yes, for a score of kingdoms you should wrangle,
And I would call it fair play.

ALONSO: If this prove
A vision of the island, one dear son
Shall I twice lose.

SEBASTIAN: A most high miracle!

FERDINAND: Though the seas threaten, they are merciful;   180
I have curs'd them without cause. (*Kneels.*)

ALONSO: Now all the blessings
Of a glad father compass thee about!
Arise, and say how thou cam'st here.

MIRANDA: O, wonder!
How many goodly creatures are there here!
How beauteous mankind is! O brave new world,   185
That has such people in 't!

PROSPERO: 'Tis new to thee.

ALONSO: What is this maid with whom thou wast at play?
Your eld'st acquaintance cannot be three hours.
Is she the goddess that hath sever'd us,
And brought us thus together?   190

FERDINAND: Sir, she is mortal;
But by immortal Providence she's mine.
I chose her when I could not ask my father
For his advice, nor thought I had one. She
Is daughter to this famous Duke of Milan,
Of whom so often I have heard renown,   195
But never saw before; of whom I have
Receiv'd a second life; and second father
This lady makes him to me.

ALONSO: I am hers.
But, O, how oddly will it sound that I
Must ask my child forgiveness!   200

PROSPERO: There, sir, stop.
Let us not burden our remembrances with
A heaviness that's gone.

GONZALO: I have inly wept
Or should have spoke ere this. Look down, you gods,
And on this couple drop a blessed crown!
For it is you that have chalk'd forth the way   205
Which brought us hither.

ALONSO: I say Amen, Gonzalo!

GONZALO: Was Milan thrust from Milan, that his issue
Should become kings of Naples? O, rejoice
Beyond a common joy, and set it down
With gold on lasting pillars: In one voyage   210
Did Claribel her husband find at Tunis,
And Ferdinand, her brother, found a wife

---

128 **justify you** prove you to be   139 **woe** sorry   145 **late** recent   155 **admire** wonder   156–158 **scarce . . . breath** scarcely believe that their eyes inform them accurately what they see or that their words are naturally spoken   172 s.d. **discovers** i.e., by opening a curtain, presumably rear-stage

176–177 **Yes . . . play** i.e., yes, even if we were playing for twenty kingdoms, something less than the whole world, you would still contend mightily against me and play me false, and I would let you do it as though it were fair play; or, if you were to play not just for stakes but literally for kingdoms, my accusation of false play would be out of order in that your "wrangling" would be proper   185 **brave** splendid, gorgeously appareled, handsome   188 **eld'st** longest   207 **Was Milan** was the Duke of Milan

Where he himself was lost; Prospero his dukedom
In a poor isle; and all of us ourselves
215 When no man was his own.
ALONSO: (*To* FERDINAND *and* MIRANDA.) Give me your hands.
Let grief and sorrow still embrace his heart
That doth not wish you joy!
GONZALO: Be it so! Amen!

(*Enter* ARIEL, *with the* MASTER *and* BOATSWAIN *amazedly
following.*)

O, look, sir, look, sir! Here is more of us.
I prophesied, if a gallows were on land,
220 This fellow could not drown. Now, blasphemy,
That swear'st grace o'erboard, not an oath on shore?
Hast thou no mouth by land? What is the news?
BOATSWAIN: The best news is that we have safely found
Our King and company; the next, our ship—
225 Which, but three glasses since, we gave out split—
Is tight and yare and bravely rigg'd as when
We first put out to sea.
ARIEL: (*Aside to* PROSPERO.) Sir, all this service
Have I done since I went.
PROSPERO: (*Aside to* ARIEL.) My tricksy spirit!
ALONSO: These are not natural events; they strengthen
230 From strange to stranger. Say, how came you hither?
BOATSWAIN: If I did think, sir, I were well awake,
I'd strive to tell you. We were dead of sleep,
And—how we know not—all clapp'd under hatches;
Where but even now with strange and several noises
235 Of roaring, shrieking, howling, jingling chains,
And moe diversity of sounds, all horrible,
We were awak'd; straightway, at liberty;
Where we, in all her trim, freshly beheld
Our royal, good, and gallant ship, our master
240 Cap'ring to eye her. On a trice, so please you,
Even in a dream, were we divided from them
And were brought moping hither.
ARIEL: (*Aside to* PROSPERO.)   Was 't well done?
PROSPERO: (*Aside to* ARIEL.) Bravely, my diligence. Thou
shalt be free.
ALONSO: This is as strange a maze as e'er men trod,
245 And there is in this business more than nature
Was ever conduct of. Some oracle
Must rectify our knowledge.
PROSPERO: Sir, my liege,
Do not infest your mind with beating on
The strangeness of this business. At pick'd leisure,
250 Which shall be shortly, single I'll resolve you,
Which to you shall seem probable, of every
These happen'd accidents; till when, be cheerful
And think of each thing well. (*Aside to* ARIEL.) Come
hither, spirit.
Set Caliban and his companions free;

Untie the spell. (*Exit* ARIEL.) How fares my gracious sir? 255
There are yet missing of your company
Some few odd lads that you remember not.

(*Enter* ARIEL, *driving in* CALIBAN, STEPHANO, *and* TRINCULO, *in
their stol'n apparel.*)

STEPHANO: Every man shift for all the rest, and let no man
take care of himself; for all is but fortune. Coragio, bully-
monster, coragio!   260
TRINCULO: If these be true spies which I wear in my head,
here's a goodly sight.
CALIBAN: O Setebos, these be brave spirits indeed!
How fine my master is! I am afraid
He will chastise me.   265
SEBASTIAN: Ha, ha!
What things are these, my lord, Antonio?
Will money buy 'em?
ANTONIO: Very like. One of them
Is a plain fish, and no doubt marketable.
PROSPERO: Mark but the badges of these men, my lords, 270
Then say if they be true. This misshapen knave,
His mother was a witch, and one so strong
That could control the moon, make flows and ebbs,
And deal in her command without her power.
These three have robb'd me; and this demi-devil— 275
For he's a bastard one—had plotted with them
To take my life. Two of these fellows you
Must know and own; this thing of darkness I
Acknowledge mine.
CALIBAN: I shall be pinch'd to death.
ALONSO: Is not this Stephano, my drunken butler? 280
SEBASTIAN: He is drunk now. Where had he wine?
ALONSO: And Trinculo is reeling ripe. Where should they
Find this grand liquor that hath gilded 'em?
How cam'st thou in this pickle?
TRINCULO: I have been in such a pickle since I saw you last 285
that, I fear me, will never out of my bones. I shall not fear
flyblowing.
SEBASTIAN: Why, how now, Stephano?
STEPHANO: O, touch me not! I am not Stephano, but a cramp. 290
PROSPERO: You'd be king o' the isle, sirrah?
STEPHANO: I should have been a sore one then.
ALONSO: (*Pointing to* CALIBAN.) This is a strange thing as e'er
I look'd on.

---

216 **still** always; **his** that man's   217 **That** who   225 **glasses**
i.e., hours; **gave** out reported   226 **yare** ready   240 **Cap'ring
to eye** dancing for joy to see   242 **moping** in a daze   246
conduct guide, leader   248 **infest** harass, disturb   249 **pick'd**
chosen, convenient   250 **single** i.e., by my own human powers
252 **accidents** occurrences

259 **Coragio** courage; bully-monster gallant monster (ironical)
264 **fine** splendidly attired   270 **badges** emblems of cloth or
silver worn on the arms of retainers. Prospero refers here to the
stolen clothes as emblems of their villainy   271 **true** honest
274 **deal . . . power** wield the moon's power, either without
her authority or beyond her influence   278 **own** recognize, admit as belonging to you   283 **gilded** (1) flushed, made drunk
(2) covered with gilt (suggesting the horse-urine)   284 **pickle**
(1) fix, predicament (2) pickling brine (in this case, horse urine)
286–287 **fly-blowing** i.e., being fouled by fly-eggs (from which
he is saved by being pickled)   291 **sirrah** Standard form of address to an inferior   292 **sore** (1) tyrannical (2) wracked by
pain

PROSPERO: He is as disproportion'd in his manners
295   As in his shape. Go, sirrah, to my cell;
         Take with you your companions. As you look
         To have my pardon, trim it handsomely.
CALIBAN: Ay, that I will; and I'll be wise hereafter
         And seek for grace. What a thrice-double ass
300   Was I to take this drunkard for a god
         And worship this dull fool!
PROSPERO: Go to; away!
ALONSO: Hence, and bestow your luggage where you found it.
SEBASTIAN: Or stole it, rather.

(*Exeunt* CALIBAN, STEPHANO, *and* TRINCULO.)

PROSPERO: Sir, I invite your Highness and your train
305   To my poor cell, where you shall take your rest
         For this one night; which, part of it, I'll waste
         With such discourse as, I not doubt, shall make it
         Go quick away—the story of my life,
         And the particular accidents gone by
310   Since I came to this isle. And in the morn
         I'll bring you to your ship, and so to Naples,
         Where I have hope to see the nuptial
         Of these our dear-belov'd solemnized;
         And thence retire me to my Milan, where
315   Every third thought shall be my grave.
ALONSO: I long
         To hear the story of your life, which must
         Take the ear strangely.
PROSPERO: I'll deliver all;
         And promise you calm seas, auspicious gales,
         And sail so expeditious that shall catch
320   Your royal fleet far off. (*Aside to* ARIEL.) My Ariel, chick,

---

306 **waste** spend   309 **accidents** occurrences   317 **Take** take
effect upon, enchant; **deliver** declare, relate

That is thy charge. Then to the elements
Be free, and fare thou well!—Please you, draw near.

(*Exeunt omnes.*)

EPILOGUE

Spoken by PROSPERO.

Now my charms are all o'erthrown,
And what strength I have 's mine own,
Which is most faint. Now, 'tis true,
I must be here confin'd by you,
Or sent to Naples. Let me not,   5
Since I have my dukedom got
And pardon'd the deceiver, dwell
In this bare island by your spell,
But release me from my bands
With the help of your good hands.   10
Gentle breath of yours my sails
Must fill, or else my project fails,
Which was to please. Now I want
Spirits to enforce, art to enchant,
And my ending is despair,   15
Unless I be reliev'd by prayer,
Which pierces so that it assaults
Mercy itself and frees all faults.
As you from crimes would pardon'd be,
Let your indulgence set me free.   20

(*Exit.*)

---

322 **draw near** i.e., enter my cell

Epilogue   9 bands bonds   **10 hands** i.e., applause (the noise
of which would break the spell of silence)   **13 want** lack   **16
prayer** i.e., Prospero's petition to the audience   **17 assaults**
rightfully gains the attention of   **18 frees** obtains forgiveness of
19 crimes sins

CRITICAL CONTEXTS

SIR PHILIP SIDNEY (1554–1586)

from *Apology for Poetry* (1598)

EDITED BY FORREST G. ROBINSON

Philip Sidney was one of the preeminent courtiers of his day. He was a familiar figure at the court of Queen Elizabeth I, led an ill-fated military expedition to the Netherlands (where he was fatally wounded), wrote an important sonnet sequence, Astrophil and Stella, *and a prose romance,* Arcadia. *His* Apology for Poetry *develops a defense of poets and poetry based on their ability to offer a fictive "golden world," an idealized image of reality that can edify, entertain, and instruct.*

Reading Sidney's Apology, *it is useful to bear several questions in mind: What is the problem that Sidney is attempting to address here? Is there a moral or ethical problem posed by poetry, particularly by the fact that poetry is a form of fiction, of lying? Why is it important to Sidney to compare the poet with the historian and the philosopher? What are the underlying problems that Sidney is attempting to address in his assessment of contemporary dramatic genres?*

. . . There is no art delivered to mankind that hath not the works of nature for his principal object, without which they could not consist, and on which they so depend, as they become actors and players, as it were, of what nature will have set forth. So doth the astronomer look upon the stars, and by that he seeth, setteth down what order nature hath taken therein. So do the geometrician and arithmetician in their diverse sorts of quantities. So doth the musician in times tell you which by nature agree, which not. The natural philosopher thereon hath his name, and the moral philosopher standeth upon the natural virtues, vices, and passions of man; and follow nature (saith he) therein, and thou shalt not err. The lawyer saith what men have determined; the historian what men have done. The grammarian speaketh only of the rules of speech, and the rhetorician and logician, considering what in nature will soonest prove and persuade, thereon give artificial[1] rules, which still are compassed within the circle of a question, according to the proposed matter. The physician weigheth the nature of a man's body, and the nature of things helpful or hurtful unto it. And the metaphysic, though it be in the second and abstract notions, and therefore be counted supernatural, yet doth he indeed build upon the depth of nature. Only the poet, disdaining to be tied to any such subjection, lifted up with the vigor of his own invention, doth grow in effect another nature, in making things either better than nature bringeth forth, or quite anew, forms such as never were in nature, as the Heroes, Demigods, Cyclops, Chimeras, Furies, and such like; so as he goeth hand in hand with nature, not enclosed within the narrow warrant of her gifts, but freely ranging only within the zodiac of his own wit.

Nature never set forth the earth in so rich tapestry as divers poets have done, neither with pleasant rivers, fruitful trees, sweet smelling flowers, nor whatsoever else may make the too much loved earth more lovely. Her world is brazen, the poets only deliver a golden. . . .

Our tragedies and comedies (not without cause cried out against), observing rules neither of honest civility nor of skillful poetry, excepting *Gorboduc*[2] (again I say, of those that I have seen), which notwithstanding, as it is full of stately speeches and well sounding phrases, climbing to the height of Seneca his[3] style, and as full of notable morality, which it doth most delightfully teach, and so obtain the very end of poesy; yet in troth it is very defectious in the circumstances, which grieveth me, because it might not remain as an exact model of all tragedies. For it is faulty both in place and time, the two necessary companions of all corporal actions. For where the stage should always represent but one place, and the uttermost time presupposed in it should be, both by Aristotle's precept and common reason, but one day, there is both many days and many places inartificially[4] imagined.

But if it be so in *Gorboduc,* how much more in all the rest? where you shall have Asia of the one side, and Afric of the other, and so many other under-kingdoms, that the player, when he cometh in, must ever begin with telling where he is, or else the tale will not be conceived. Now ye shall have three ladies walk to gather flowers, and then we must believe the stage to be a garden. By and by we hear news of shipwreck in

---

[1]**artificial** humanly contrived, rather than natural

[2]**Gorboduc** an early English play (first performed in 1562), modeled on the tragedies of Seneca

[3]**Seneca his** Seneca's

[4]**inartificially** artlessly

360 UNIT III · MEDIEVAL AND RENAISSANCE ENGLAND

the same place, and then we are to blame if we accept it not for a rock. Upon the back of that comes out a hideous monster with fire and smoke, and then the miserable beholders are bound to take it for a cave. While in the meantime two armies fly in, represented with four swords and bucklers, and then what hard heart will not receive it for a pitched field?

Now of time they are much more liberal, for ordinary it is that two young princes fall in love. After many traverses, she is got with child, delivered of a fair boy, he is lost, groweth a man, falls in love, and is ready to get another child, and all this in two hours' space: which, how absurd it is in sense, even sense may imagine, and art hath taught, and all ancient examples justified, and at this day, the ordinary players in Italy will not err in. Yet will some bring in an example of Eunuchus in Terence, that containeth matter of two days, yet far short of twenty years. True it is, and so was it to be played in two days, and so fitted to the time it set forth. And though Plautus hath in one place done amiss, let us hit with him, and not miss with him. But they will say, how then shall we set forth a story which containeth both many places and many times? And do they not know that a tragedy is tied to the laws of poesy, and not of history, not bound to follow the story, but having liberty, either to feign a quite new matter, or to frame the history to the most tragical conveniency? Again, many things may be told which cannot be showed, if they know the difference betwixt reporting and representing. . . .

CRITICAL PERSPECTIVES

PHYLLIS RACKIN
"Misogyny Is Everywhere" (2000)

Phyllis Rackin is an important American scholar of Shakespeare and Renaissance drama and culture, whose books include Stages of History: Shakespeare's English Chronicles *and (with Jean E. Howard)* Engendering a Nation: A Feminist Account of Shakespeare's English Histories. *In this essay, Rackin undertakes a double-barreled argument: she at once attempts to assess the treatment of women in contemporary Renaissance scholarship, and the actual place of women in Renaissance society. How does she go about these two complementary tasks? What do you take to be the purpose of her effort to throw light on the day-to-day working lives of women in Shakespeare's era? Are there ways in which the silence of women in the literature of Shakespeare's era is prolonged by the critical discourse of today?*

> Misogyny presents an interpretive embarrassment of riches: it is everywhere, unabashed in its articulation and so overdetermined in its cultural roots that individual instances sometimes seem emotionally underdetermined, rote and uninflected expressions of what would go without saying if it weren't said so often.
> Mullaney (1994: 141)

This description of late sixteenth-century English culture is likely to ring true for readers of current feminist/historicist Shakespeare criticism. "In historical research," as a wise old teacher once warned me, "you're likely to find what you are looking for"; and what most of us have been looking for in recent years is a history of men's anxiety in the face of female power, of women's disempowerment, and of outright misogyny. I want to interrogate that history, not because it is necessarily incorrect but because it is incomplete. It constitutes only one of many stories that could be told about women's place in Shakespeare's world, and I think we need to consider the implications of its current hegemony. Why does the evidence for misogyny in Shakespeare's world strike the writer as "an interpretive embarrassment of riches"? Who is enriched by the many "rote and uninflected expressions of what would go without saying if it weren't said so often" in recent feminist criticism?

One reason the story of patriarchal oppression has become so influential is that it has been disseminated in recent textbooks. The editor of a reader designed to illustrate *The Cultural Identity of Seventeenth-Century Woman*, for instance, states flatly that

> Woman's place was within doors, her business domestic. . . . Women of evident intelligence themselves accepted this divorce between the private (feminine) and public (masculine) spheres

---

From *A Feminist Companion to Shakespeare*, ed. Dympna Callaghan (Oxford: Blackwell, 2000), 43–55.

and, despite the recent precedents of Mary Queen of Scots, Mary Tudor and Elizabeth, they shared the age's "distaste . . . for the notion of women's involvement in politics." (Keeble 1994: 186)

However, even the most sophisticated scholarship often includes similar claims. For example, in what is likely to become a standard history of gender in early modern England, Anthony Fletcher writes,

> It was conventional, as we have seen, to assume men and women had clearly defined gender roles indoors and out of doors. . . . Femininity, as we have seen, was presented as no more than a set of negatives. The requirement of chastity was, as we have seen, the overriding measure of female gender. Woman not only had to be chaste but had to be seen to be chaste: silence, humility and modesty were the signifiers that she was so. (1995: 120–2)

Some of the most important recent feminist/historicist literary scholarship includes reminders that "the period was fraught with anxiety about rebellious women and particularly their rebellion through language" (Newman 1991: 40); that "women's reading was policed and their writing prohibited or marked as transgressive even when they were not engaged in other criminal activities" (Dolan 1996: 159); and that "an obsessive energy was invested in exerting control over the unruly woman—the woman who was exercising either her sexuality or her tongue under her own control rather than under the rule of a man" (Boose 1991: 195). In a sense, of course, these quotations are misleading because they are taken out of context, and they belie the subtlety and complexity of the arguments from which they were taken. Nonetheless, I believe the excerpts are significant because they indicate how often even the best feminist scholarship feels the need to situate itself within a patriarchal master narrative.

Feminist scholars found a brilliant explication of that narrative in Peter Stallybrass's essay, "Patriarchal Territories: The Body Enclosed," which argued that women's bodies were assumed to be "*naturally* 'grotesque'" and that women were therefore "subjected to constant surveillance . . . because, as Bakhtin says of the grotesque body, it is 'unfinished, outgrows itself, transgresses its own limits.'" This constant surveillance, Stallybrass continued, focused on "three specific areas: the mouth, chastity, the threshold of the house," which "were frequently collapsed into each other." "Silence, the closed mouth, is made a sign of chastity. And silence and chastity are, in turn, homologous to woman's enclosure within the house" (Stallybrass 1986: 126–7). Published in 1986, "Patriarchal Territories" theorized the relationships between sexual loathing, the silencing of women's voices, and the constriction of women's activities in a beautifully articulated analysis that has proved to have remarkable influence and explanatory power in subsequent feminist criticism. It is significant, I believe, that the conclusion of Stallybrass's article, where he suggests that the figure of the unruly woman was also valorized as a rallying point for protest against social injustice, was often ignored.

The pervasive scholarly investment in Renaissance misogyny has lead to a massive rereading of Shakespeare's plays. As Valerie Traub observes, "It is by now a commonplace that Shakespeare was preoccupied with the uncontrollability of women's sexuality; witness the many plots concerning the need to prove female chastity, the threat of adultery, and, even when female fidelity is not a major theme of the play, the many references to cuckoldry in songs, jokes, and passing remarks" (1995: 121). Reminders that women were expected to be chaste, silent, and obedient probably occur more frequently in recent scholarship than they did in the literature of Shakespeare's time; the connections between female speech and female sexual transgression are retraced and the anxieties evoked by the possibility of female power are discovered in play after play. "Female sexuality in Shakespeare's plays," we are told, "is invariably articulated as linguistic transgression—that is, a verbal replication of female obliquity" (Carroll 1995: 184). If speech is transgressive, reading and writing are even more dangerous. Lavinia's gruesome fate in *Titus Andronicus,* for instance, is "expressive of the anxieties she generates as an educated, and hence potentially unruly, woman" (Eaton, cited by Garner and Sprengnether 1996: 12–13).

Plays with overtly repressive and misogynist themes have proved increasingly popular, and the stories they tell are held up as historically accurate expressions of beliefs generally endorsed in Shakespeare's time. *The Taming of the Shrew,* for instance, is the subject of 105 listings for the years 1985–97 in the online *MLA Bibliography,* far more than any of the other early comedies (for those same years, the *Bibliography* lists twenty-eight for *Two Gentlemen of Verona,* forty-seven for *Comedy of Errors,* and sixty-one for *Love's Labour's Lost*). Other plays are reinterpreted. *The Merchant of Venice,* for example, "instructs its audience that daughters who submit, who know their place, will ultimately fare better than daughters who rebel" (Leventen 1991: 75). The heroines of Shakespeare's middle comedies were especially attractive to the feminist critics of the 1970s, when it seemed important to mobilize Shakespeare's authority in the service of our own political goals. In the 1980s, however, a more pessimistic picture emerged as scholars marshaled historical evidence to demonstrate the pervasiveness of patriarchal beliefs and practices and discredit the optimistic feminist readings of the 1970s as unhistorical.

One of the characteristics that traditionally made the heroines of Shakespeare's middle comedies attractive is their erotic appeal, but influential critics associated that attraction with the fact that they were portrayed by male actors. Stephen Greenblatt's widely cited article on "Fiction and Friction" used Thomas Laqueur's arguments about the conception of a single-sexed body in Renaissance anatomical theory to argue that "the open secret of identity—that within differentiated individuals is a single structure, identifiably male—is presented literally in the all-male cast." "Men," Greenblatt wrote, "love women precisely as *representations,* a love the original performances of these plays literalized in the person of the boy actor" (1988: 93). For Lisa Jardine, the heroines of these plays were "sexually enticing *qua* transvestied boys, and the plays encourage the audience to view them as such" (1991: 61). Moreover, at the same time that criticism like Greenblatt's and Jardine's taught us to recognize that cross-dressed boys may have been objects of desire for Shakespeare's original audience, we were also taught that sexualized women were not: female sexual desire, we are repeatedly told, was regarded as threatening. In *Antony and Cleopatra,* for instance, "Egypt's queen . . . resembles other Jacobean females who in desiring or being desired become a source of pollution" (Tennenhouse 1986: 144). In *II Henry VI,* depicting "Margaret as a figure of open and unrestrained sexual passion is one way of demonizing her and representing the dangers of a femininity not firmly under the control of a father or husband" (Howard and Rackin 1997: 74).

Sexual passion is not the only characteristic that makes women threatening in recent feminist Shakespeare criticism, where it seems that virtually any manifestation of female strength or ability, even if it is admired by other characters on stage, would have had to evoke anxiety in the original audiences. Helena in *All's Well That Ends Well* is a good example. In the playtext her virtues are celebrated and her aspirations endorsed by the King and the Countess. The Introduction to the play in the Riverside Shakespeare summed up the traditional view of the character: "Helena is prized by the older generation not only because they recognize her intrinsic worth, but because she is a living example of the attitudes of the past" (Evans et al. 1997: 535). She is also the center of dramatic interest, with the longest part in the play. According to the Spevack *Concordance* (1968), she speaks 15.858 percent of the words in the script; Bertram speaks only 9.042 percent, a total that is exceeded not only by Helena, but also by his mother, who has 9.618 percent. Nonetheless, according to a leading male feminist critic,

> Helena's gender makes impossible any one-sided identification with Helena against Bertram. . . . Reacting against Helena's triumph, Shakespeare remains in part sympathetically bound to the besieged male positions of both Bertram and the king; the play thereby gives voice not only to the two male characters' discomfiture but also to Shakespeare's. The authorial division that blocks a convincing resolution is significant because it dramatizes a much larger cultural quandary: the society's inability to accommodate, without deep disturbance, decisive female control. (Erickson 1991: 73–4)

The last two sentences are carefully worded, attributing ambivalence about Helena's achievement and anxiety about the spectacle of "decisive female control" to Shakespeare and to the culture in which he wrote, thus authorizing ambivalence and anxiety as the historically appropriate responses to Helena's triumph. But the first sentence I quoted—"Helena's gender makes impossible any one-sided identification with Helena against Bertram"—seems to claim even more. The present tense of the verb seems to universalize Erickson's reading and deny its historical specificity, implying that ambivalence and anxiety are the only possible responses to the character for any reader or viewer in any time or place.

It may be unfair to make too much of Erickson's use of the present tense, but it points to a larger problem for historicist literary criticism, which has pressing implications for feminist/historicist scholarship. The conventions of scholarly writing have been to write about literary texts in the present tense, thus expressing their imaginative presence, and about historical events in the past tense to mark their temporal distance from the writer who recounts them. This distinction is breaking down, both in popularized history, where the present tense is increasingly used to describe past events, and in postmodern historical theory, which is shaped by the recognition that history, no less than fiction, is constantly updated to fit the shapes of present interests and assumptions. The question of grammatical tense poses an especially pressing problem for new historicist literary criticism. The present tense effaces historical distance, the past

denies literary presence, and the distinction between past tense for history and present tense for fiction implicitly denies the imbrication of the literary text in its historical context that animates the entire new historicist project. If the text and its historical context are components of a seamless discursive web, it is difficult to sustain the grammatical distinction between present and past tenses that marks the separation of literary text from its historical context. But if that distinction is elided, where does the new historicist scholar situate herself in relation to the literary/historical objects of her analysis? Using the present tense, as Erickson does in the passage I quoted, seems to claim universal validity for a historically situated response. At the same time, however, it implicitly acknowledges that the version of past experience being constructed is a projection of current interests and anxieties.

The present tense is also the conventional form for references to the work of other scholars, as if it too existed in a timeless, ahistorical space. As we all know, however, scholarly texts, no less than the texts scholars study, are imbricated in the historical contexts in which they were produced and shaped by the social locations and personal interests and desires of their writers, even though the conventions of academic civility make those factors difficult to discuss. Nonetheless, I believe it is important to note, not only that the feminist/historicist Shakespeare criticism of the 1980s often tended to privilege male experience, emphasizing masculine anxiety in the face of powerful women, but also that some of the most influential work of that period was, in fact, the work of male critics.

One of the most influential modern readings of *As You Like It,* for instance, Louis Adrian Montrose's 1981 article, "'The Place of a Brother,'" proposed to reverse the then prevailing view of the play by arguing that "what happens to Orlando at home is not Shakespeare's contrivance to get him into the forest; what happens to Orlando in the forest is Shakespeare's contrivance to remedy what has happened to him at home" (Montrose 1981: 29). Just as Oliver has displaced Orlando from his rightful place in the patriarchy, Montrose's reading displaces Rosalind from her place as the play's protagonist, focusing instead upon the relationships among brothers, fathers, and sons. Although Oliver appears only briefly on stage and the brothers' reconciliation is narrated, not shown, the main issue in the play is said to be Orlando's troubled relationship with his brother and consequent loss of his rightful place in society; Rosalind is reduced to a vehicle for its restoration: marrying her enables Orlando to become "heir apparent to the reinstated Duke" (Montrose 1981: 38). Montrose does not cite Gayle Rubin's 1975 article on "the traffic in women," but this is the paradigm that seems to lie behind his argument.[1] The power of Rubin's paradigm is so great that it supersedes the textual evidence that the marriage satisfies Rosalind's own long-standing desire (see, e.g., I.iii.9) and that it is she, not her father, who tells Orlando "To you I give myself" (V.iv.106). In fact, none of the marriages in the play is arranged by a father. The only marriage that can be said to be arranged is that of Silvius and Phoebe, which Rosalind herself arranges. Rosalind dominates the action of the play (she has the longest part in the script, speaking, according to the Spevack *Concordance* (1968), 26.744 percent of the words in the playscript). Nonetheless, Montrose's argument that the play "is a structure for her containment" (1981: 52) has been widely influential in subsequent criticism.

With the turn to history in literary studies generally, and especially in the field of the Renaissance, feminist Shakespeare criticism has been almost completely shaped by the scholarly consensus about the pervasiveness of masculine anxiety and women's disempowerment in Shakespeare's world. Much of this criticism is sympathetic to women's plights, exposing women's oppression and describing the sociological, psychological, and ideological mechanisms that produced it, but it poses problems which are simultaneously intellectual and political. Feminist scholarship needs history, and it needs the analytic instruments the new historicism provides. The problem is that the conceptual categories that shape contemporary scholarly discourse, no less than the historical records of the past, are often man-made and shaped by men's anxieties, desires, and interests. As such, they constitute instruments of women's exclusion, and often of women's oppression. What Kathleen McLuskie wrote about *Measure for Measure* in 1985 seems increasingly applicable to the entire Shakespearean canon and to historical accounts of the world in which he wrote: "Feminist criticism," she argued, "is restricted to exposing its own exclusion from the text. It has no point of entry into it, for the dilemmas of the narrative and the sexuality under discussion are constructed in completely male terms" (McLuskie 1994: 97). How then can we enter the discourse of current feminist/historicist Shakespeare criticism without becoming so thoroughly inscribed within its categories that we are forced to imagine both the plays and the culture in which they were produced from a male point of view?

It is important to remember that feminist criticism began with a political agenda, although—especially in the United States—it has increasingly entered the mainstream of academic discourse. The current interest in issues of sex and gender has provided increased academic visibility for feminist concerns and increased professional visibility for academic feminists, but it has not come without costs. Adopted as

a conceptual tool by women and men without a serious political commitment to feminist political agendas, criticism designated as "feminist" has provided arguments that can just as easily be used to naturalize women's oppression as to oppose it. Among the consequences of this selective history for feminist students of Shakespeare's plays is the fact that we are being taught to read from the subject position of a man, and a misogynist man at that. The cultural prestige of Shakespeare makes his plays a model for contemporary values and the privileged site where past history is reconstructed. Even academic historians often turn to Shakespeare for evidence of past practices and attitudes (the index to Anthony Fletcher's *Gender, Sex and Subordination in England 1500-1800*, for instance, lists fifty-four references to Shakespeare's plays). For the feminist political project, there are obvious dangers in contemplating our past from the point of view of late twentieth-century academic men who may—consciously or not—be anxious or ambivalent about the progress women have made in the wake of the contemporary women's movement. The stories we tell about the past have consequences for the present and future, and if the story of misogyny and oppression is the only story we tell about the past, we risk a dangerous complacency in the present. Like the Virginia Slims ads that tell us, "You've come a long way, baby" because we can now smoke openly rather than hiding our habits from our menfolk, an oversimplified history that emphasizes past oppression is likely to encourage an equally oversimplified optimism about our present situation. As Lena Cowen Orlin observes, "if we have enjoyed this construction of women, perhaps it is because it offers us the comforting reassurance that history has made progress and that we have come a long way (baby) from our early modern predecessors."[2]

This is not to deny that there is ample evidence for a history of misogyny and of women's oppression in Shakespeare's world and that there are good reasons why it needed to be told. All the statements I have cited are documented with quotations from early modern texts and citations of early modern cultural practice; and, as Linda Boose has eloquently written in her brilliant study of *The Taming of the Shrew*, it is essential to "assert an intertextuality that binds the obscured records of a painful women's history" to the Shakespearean text because "that history has paid for the right to speak itself"; and "the impulse to rewrite the more oppressively patriarchal material in this play serves the very ideologies about gender that it makes less visible by making less offensive" (1991: 181–2). However, as Boose also makes clear, although the history of male misogyny is inextricably entangled with the history of women's oppression, those histories had strikingly different consequences for women and men. In considering the evidence for Renaissance misogyny and the oppressive practices it produced, it is essential to remember an essential axiom of postmodern historical study—the fact that, as Sandra Harding has wittily remarked, there is no such thing as a "view from nowhere." We need to view the textual evidence for misogyny and oppression more critically, considering both the social locations of the original writers and those of the contemporary scholars who have put those texts back into circulation.

As Deborah Payne has argued in another context, certain anecdotes, texts, and passages from texts are repeatedly cited and assumed "to represent dominant social views: for positivists, a historical transparency; for poststructuralists, a sign within a culturally determined system of signification. This 'short-circuit fallacy' . . . can occur only by ignoring [the writer of the text's or the recorder of the anecdote's] vexed position within the social space" from which he writes (1995: 22). Payne adopts the phrase "short-circuit fallacy" from Pierre Bourdieu, who defines it as ignoring "the crucial mediation provided by . . . the field of cultural production . . . a social space with its own logic, within which agents struggle over stakes of a particular kind." "The most essential bias," he goes on to warn, is the "'ethnocentrism of the scientist,' which consists in ignoring everything that the analyst injects into his perception of the object by virtue of the fact that he is placed outside of the object, that he observes it from afar and from above" (Bourdieu and Wacquant 1992: 69–70). Carol Thomas Neely makes a similar point in a recent study of madness and gender in Shakespeare's tragedies and early modern culture:

> The complexities of reading the discourse of madness in Shakespeare and his culture reveal the difficulty and necessity of historicizing: examining one's own position and that of one's subject(s) in contemporary culture in relation to the construction of those subject(s) which emerged in early modern culture, working to tease out disjunctions and connections. This project reveals that the shape of gender difference cannot be assumed but must always be reformulated in specific historical contexts. (1996: 96)

The lesson, in the words of Jean E. Howard's famous essay on the new historicism, is that "there is no transcendent space from which one can perceive the past 'objectively.'" "Our view," she continues, "is always informed by our present position" (Howard 1986: 22). It follows from this that "objectivity is not in any pure form a possibility," that "interpretive and even descriptive acts" are inevitably political, and that "any move into history is [therefore] an intervention" (Howard 1986: 43).

One strategy for intervention adopted by feminist scholars in the 1980s and 1990s has been to look for places for fe-

male agency within patriarchal scripts. In 1981, for instance, Coppélia Kahn argued in *Man's Estate* that the power over women given to men by patriarchy made men paradoxically "vulnerable to women" because "a woman's subjugation to her husband's will was the measure of his patriarchal authority and thus of his manliness" (Kahn 1981: 15–17). In 1985, Catherine Belsey pointed out in *The Subject of Tragedy* that women convicted of witchcraft were empowered at the moment of their execution by the "requirement for confessions from the scaffold," which, "paradoxically . . . offered women a place from which to speak in public with a hitherto unimagined authority which was not diminished by the fact that it was demonic" (Belsey 1985: 190–1). In 1994, Frances E. Dolan focused in *Dangerous Familiars* on early modern representations of domestic crimes perpetrated by women in an effort "to uncover the possibilities, however contingent and circumscribed, for human agency in historical process" because "accounts of domestic violence" are "one set of scripts in which women could be cast as agents, albeit in problematic terms" (Dolan 1994: 5).

Increasingly, however, feminist scholars are challenging the patriarchal narrative itself, recovering the materials for alternative narratives and emphasizing that repressive prescriptions should not be regarded as descriptions of actual behavior. In her 1993 study of *Women and Property in Early Modern England,* Amy Louise Erickson points out that

> it is one thing to observe that early modern male writers invariably described women's place in the social hierarchy, the "great chain of being", entirely in terms of marriage. It is quite another to remember that they did so in a society in which most adult women in the population at any given time were not married—they were either widowed or they had never married. (Erickson 1993: 8–9)

Similarly, in a 1997 essay, Diana E. Henderson reminds us that

> Some aristocratic women, in fact, managed to avoid being confined to any of their numerous homes, much less "the" home; those at the other end of the social scale might have no home at all, and they could hardly afford to create gendered space. . . . Texts (especially literary ones) tend to preserve the voices and perspectives of those who dominated within society; we must supplement them with both historical data and our scholarly imaginations if we wish to hear more of the conversation. Female-headed households in *Gammer Gurton's Needle* may be only a schoolmaster's source of comedy or deflected anxiety, but it is also true that there were many female-headed households in town and city alike; historical study of Southwark, the theater district itself, reveals that at least 16 percent of households were headed by a woman. The type of historical evidence we bring to bear when interpreting plays undoubtedly informs what types of domesticity we see represented, what gaps we notice, how we value them. (Henderson 1997: 192)

Thus, while *As You Like It* is a fantasy, the female household that Rosalind and Celia establish in the forest had precedents in the very district where the theater was located. Moreover, Rosalind's role in arranging her own marriage and Phoebe's as well also had ample precedents in the real world. As Margaret Ezell has demonstrated, early modern women played central roles in arranging marriages, not only their own, but those of their daughters, nieces, and granddaughters as well. Far more fathers than mothers had died by the time their children reached marriageable age (Ezell 1987: 18). Moreover, even when both parents were alive, great numbers of women lived away from their parents' homes, often supporting themselves independently and negotiating their own marriages. Vivien Brodsky Elliott's study of single women in the London marriage market during the years 1598 to 1619 shows that women who had migrated from the country to work in London tended to marry later than London-born women and to marry men who were closer to their own age, statistics which, Elliott concludes, suggest "a greater freedom of choice of spouse and a more active role for women in the courtship and marriage process" (Elliott 1982: 89): "without the control or influence of their parents the marriage process for them was one in which they had an active role in initiating their own relationships, in finding suitable partners, and in conducting courtships" (Elliott 1982: 97). Among the upper levels of society where there was more property involved and parents were more likely to take an active role in arranging their children's marriages, Ezell's study of women's correspondence with other women reveals that mothers, grandmothers, and aunts played central roles in negotiating marriages for their children (Ezell 1987: 20–34).

Women's power and authority extended beyond the limits of their families. The example of the Tudor queens Mary and Elizabeth is well known, and the "anomaly" of Elizabeth's position has been endlessly noted; but they were not the only women who exercised political authority. Patricia Crawford's examination of voting registers reveals that in some parts of England, "women had been regularly voting in parliamentary elections during the seventeenth century into the 1650s at least" (Orgel 1996: 74). Women also possessed considerable economic power, not only through inheritance from fathers and husbands (and from mothers and other female relatives as well), but also by virtue of their own gainful employment. Widows were usually named executrix in their husband's wills, and when a husband died intestate, the widow was legally entitled to administer the estate (Erickson 1993: 19, 61–78, 175). Bess of Hardwick began with a marriage portion of forty marks, but ended, after inheriting the property of four successive husbands, as the Countess of Shrewsbury and one of the wealthiest women in England (Hogrefe 1977).

Women lower on the social scale earned their livings, not only as servants, but also in a variety of trades that took them outside the household. Itinerant chapwomen peddled a variety of goods, and Amy Louise Erickson has noted that "prohibitions upon girls and women appearing in public places like markets and fairs are entirely absent from early modern ballads and broadsides" (Erickson 1993: 10). Women's prominence in the marketplace is also attested by the drawings of thirteen London food markets produced by Hugh Alley in 1598, which include numerous images of women, both alone and with other women or men, both buying and selling. These images are particularly significant, because Alley's text is not specifically concerned with the activities of women in the markets; the women are simply there, apparently as a matter of course.

Even the guilds, generally believed to be bastions of male privilege, included women. The Statute of Artificers referred to apprentices as "persons"; and individual acts mentioned girls as well as boys and mistresses as well as masters: women were legally entitled, not only to enter apprenticeship, but also to take on apprentices of their own (Snell 1985: 177). As Stephen Orgel points out,

> until late in the seventeenth century women in one place or another, were admitted into practically every English trade or guild. Women did not, moreover, limit their efforts to ladylike pursuits: in Chester, in 1575, there were five women blacksmiths. Elsewhere, women were armourers, bootmakers, printers, pewterers, goldsmiths, farriers, and so forth . . . and they pursued these trades not as wives, widows, or surrogates, but as fully independent, legally responsible craftspersons. This point needs especially to be stressed, since a common modern way of ignoring the presence of women in the Renaissance workforce is to claim that they were there only as emanations of absent or dead husbands: this is not the case. The *percentage* of female apprentices is especially notable, for a practice that Lawrence Stone and E. P. Thompson believe did not exist. In Southampton, for example, at the beginning of the seventeenth century, 48 percent—almost half—the apprentices were women. (Orgel 1996: 73; see also Clark 1992; Snell 1985)

The historical evidence I have sampled undermines the current scholarly consensus that respectable women were expected to stay at home, that they were economically dependent on fathers and husbands, and that they were subjected to constant surveillance by jealous men, obsessively anxious about their sexual fidelity. I found it because I was looking for it. Historical evidence, as my old teacher reminded me, is subject to selective citation and motivated interpretation. The same, of course, is true of literary texts. In a 1985 study of *King John,* I easily discovered that

> Lady Faulconbridge's infidelity has created the nightmare situation that haunts the patriarchal imagination—a son not of her husband's getting destined to inherit her husband's lands and ti-

tle. Like Shakespeare's ubiquitous cuckold jokes, the Faulcon-
bridge episode bespeaks the anxiety that motivates the stri-
dency of patriarchal claims and repressions. (Rackin 1985: 341)

That reading seemed valid to me because it confirmed the
paradigmatic view of women's place in Shakespeare's world.
Looking at it now, I realize that it elided a number of features
of the text: the facts that the revelation of Lady Faulcon-
bridge's adultery is depicted in humorous terms, that the
Bastard it produced is a sympathetic character, that he welcomes the revelation of his bastardy, and that it results in his
acceptance as the son of Richard Cordelion and consequent
social elevation. Of course, the lady's husband, who might indeed have been jealous, is no longer alive when the revelation occurs.

Nonetheless, if we reexamine the representations of male
sexual jealousy in Shakespeare's other plays, it is difficult to
sustain the assumption that it expresses a normative view.
Othello's jealousy of Desdemona is the source of tragedy,
Leontes's jealousy of Hermione is the source of near-tragedy,
Ford's jealousy of his wife is the subject of comic debunking.
And all are mistaken. To be sure, Shakespeare does depict unfaithful wives. Goneril and Margaret are obvious examples.
But it is worth noting that in neither case is the woman's infidelity her only, or even her chief, offense; and neither husband is wracked by jealousy. In other plays of the period,
unfaithful wives are forgiven. Sometimes, in fact, their infidelity goes undetected. Consider, for instance, the case of
Winnifride in *The Witch of Edmonton,* who is pregnant by another man when she marries Frank Thorney, who believes the
baby is his. Never punished for her transgression, she is depicted throughout in sympathetic terms and, at the end of the
play, is welcomed into the home of the supremely virtuous
Carters. Sir Arthur Clarington, the coldhearted aristocrat who
seduced Winnifride when she was his maidservant, is denounced as "the instrument that wrought all" the "misfortunes" of the other characters. According to Old Carter, he is
"worthier to be hang'd" than Frank Thorney, who murdered
Carter's daughter (V.ii).

In attempting to interpret plays historically, probably
the best starting place for a feminist critic is Jean E.
Howard's reminder that women were paying customers in
early modern theaters (Howard 1988: 439–40; see also Gurr
1996: 61–5 and appendices 1 and 2; Levin 1989). According
to the records of early English playgoers compiled by Andrew
Gurr, these included respectable women, such as the wife of
John Overall, who was Regius Professor of Theology at Cambridge from 1596 to 1607 and Dean of St. Paul's from 1602 to
1618 (Gurr 1996: 207). In fact, Gurr found far more references to citizens' wives and ladies than to whores (1996: 62),
even though references to prostitutes seeking customers are

more familiar to modern readers whose assumptions about
the women in the playhouses have been shaped by scholarly
citations of anti-theatrical literature. Those assumptions
were not, apparently, shared by the players, who explicitly
defer to female playgoers in prologues and epilogues and express the players' awareness that the women in the audience,
as well as the men, had to be pleased. The Epilogue to *As You
Like It* is a good case in point. Spoken by the actor who played
Rosalind, it addresses female and male playgoers separately,
beginning with the women, whom it charges "to like as much
of this play as please you," thus suggesting that the "you" in
the play's title refers primarily to them. The Epilogue to
Shakespeare's *Henry VIII* expects to hear "good" about the
play "only in / The merciful construction of good women, /
For such a one we showed 'em," acknowledging that positive
representations of female characters were likely to appeal to
female playgoers. In *The Knight of the Burning Pestle,* a citizen and his wife repeatedly interrupt the players to demand
changes in the represented action, and although both are
the subjects of satire, there is no suggestion that her interruptions are more inappropriate than his because she is a
woman or that her husband's wishes are more to be honored
than hers. Ben Jonson, whom it would be difficult to accuse
of excessive deference to women, dedicated *The Alchemist* to
Lady Mary Wroth, and declared in the Prologue to *Epicoene*
his intention to provide a dramatic feast "fit for ladies . . .
lords, knights, squires, . . . your waiting-wench and city-
wires [i.e., citizens' wives who wore fashionable ruffs supported by wires], . . . your men, and daughters of
Whitefriars." Jonson's assumption that women's interests
might be different from men's and that both needed to be
pleased is supported by no less a personage than Queen
Anne, who not only patronized two companies of players (The
Children of the Queen's Revels and Queen Anne's Men), but
also, according to the French ambassador, attended plays in
which "the comedians of the metropolis bring [King James]
upon the stage." The Queen, the ambassador reported, "attends these representations in order to enjoy the laugh
against her husband" (Chambers 1951: I, 325).

It is generally assumed that private playhouse audiences were more homogeneous than those in the large public amphitheaters like Shakespeare's Globe, but even the
private playhouses catered to women as well as men, and, as
these examples show, those women came into the playhouses with tastes, interests, and allegiances which were
not necessarily the same as men's. Moreover, it is difficult to
imagine a totalizing master narrative that would account for
the varied experience, tastes, interests, and allegiances of
all the women who enjoyed playgoing in Shakespeare's England. They included applewives and fishwives, doxies and

respectable citizens, queens and great ladies (Gurr 1996: 60–4). Because playing was a commercial enterprise, it was in the players' interests to please as many of the paying customers as they could, the women no less than the men. The female playgoers in Shakespeare's London brought their own perspectives to the action. Perhaps we should try harder to emulate their example. *Women* were everywhere in Shakespeare's England, but the variety of their roles in life and in the scripts of plays too often "goes without saying." If we wanted to look for it, I think we could find "an interpretive embarrassment of riches" for a revitalized feminist criticism.[3]

NOTES

1. "The Traffic in Women" is a core text for contemporary feminist/historicist criticism, but, as Stephen Orgel observes, this "brilliant, classic essay" illustrates how "even the most powerful feminist analyses are often in collusion with precisely the patriarchal assumptions they undertake to displace." "To define Renaissance culture simply as a patriarchy," he explains, is "to limit one's view to the view the dominant culture took of itself; to assert that within it women were domestic creatures and a medium of exchange is to take Renaissance ideology at its word, and thereby to elide and suppress the large number of women who operated outside the family system, and the explicit social and legal structures that enabled them, in this patriarchy, to do so" (Orgel 1996: 125).

2. I am grateful to Lena Cowen Orlin for sharing with me her brilliant unpublished essay, "The Witness Who Spoke When the Cock Crowed," and allowing me to quote from it. Here is the context of her comment: "Here [in second-wave feminism], the female victim has been an object of our scholarly desires. Literary historians have so often repeated the mantra that women were enjoined to be chaste, silent, and obedient; have so often described the spatial restrictions on women; have so often 'explained' playtexts in terms taken from the most conservative literatures of their time, that the reigning orthodoxy of historiography has become that of patriarchal philosophy. I have myself been oppressed by the sheer weight of the homiletic record, by the sermons and conduct books that are so readily available, so generically familiar, so textually congenial. I and perhaps others have been seduced by the efforts of our own research into thinking these prescriptions were culturally operative in a way that they cannot have been in many women's daily lives. Even though we have reminded ourselves that such admonitions would not have been necessary had their strictures been more generally observed, we have nonetheless persisted in depicting women as victims of unrelenting misogyny, patriarchy, and oppression. If we have enjoyed this construction of women, perhaps it is because it offers us the comforting reassurance that history has made progress and that we have come a long way (baby) from our early modern predecessors" (Orlin 1998).

3. I wish to thank Rebecca Bushnell, Jean E. Howard, Lena Cowen Orlin, and Donald Rackin for helpful critical readings of drafts of this essay.

REFERENCES AND FURTHER READING

Archer, I., Barron, C., and Harding, V. (eds.) 1988: *Hugh Alley's Caveat: The Markets of London in 1598*. London: London Topographical Society Publication No. 137.

Belsey, C. 1985: *The Subject of Tragedy: Identity and Difference in Renaissance Drama*. London: Methuen.

Boose, L. E. 1991: "Scolding Brides and Bridling Scolds: Taming the Woman's Unruly Member." *Shakespeare Quarterly*, 42, 179–213.

Bourdieu, P. and Wacquant, L. J. D. 1992: *An Invitation to Reflexive Sociology*. Chicago: University of Chicago Press.

Carroll, W. C. 1995: "The Virgin Not: Language and Sexuality in Shakespeare." In Deborah E. Barker and Ivo Kamps (eds.), *Shakespeare and Gender: A History*. London and New York: Verso, 283–301.

Chambers, E. K. 1951: *The Elizabethan Stage*. Oxford: Clarendon Press. Reprinted with corrections. (Original work published 1923.)

Clark, A. 1992: *Working Life of Women in the Seventeenth Century*. Third edition. London and New York: Routledge.

Dolan, F. E. 1994: *Dangerous Familiars: Representations of Domestic Crime in England 1550–1700*. Ithaca and London: Cornell University Press.

——1996: "Reading, Writing, and Other Crimes." In Valerie Traub, M. Lindsay Kaplan, and Dympna Callaghan (eds.), *Feminist Readings of Early Modern Culture: Emerging Subjects*. Cambridge: Cambridge University Press, 142–67.

Eaton, S. 1996: "A Woman of Letters: Lavinia in *Titus Andronicus*." In Shirley Nelson Carner and Madelon Sprengnether (eds.), *Shakespearean Tragedy and Gender*. Bloomington: Indiana University Press, 54–74.

Elliott, V. B. 1982: "Single Women in the London Marriage Market: Age, Status and Mobility, 1598–1619." In R. B. Outhwaite (ed.), *Marriage and Society: Studies in the Social History of Marriage*. New York: St. Martin's Press, 81–100.

Erickson, A. L. 1993: *Women and Property in Early Modern England*. London and New York: Routledge.

Erickson, P. 1991: *Rewriting Shakespeare, Rewriting Ourselves*. Berkeley: University of California Press.

Evans, G. B. et al. 1997: *The Riverside Shakespeare*. Second edition. Boston and New York: Houghton Mifflin.

Ezell, M. 1987: *The Patriarch's Wife: Literary Evidence and the History of the Family*. Chapel Hill and London: University of North Carolina Press.

Fletcher, A. 1995: *Gender, Sex and Subordination in England 1500–1800*. New Haven and London: Yale University Press.

Garner, S. N. and Sprengnether, M. (eds.) 1996: *Shakespearean Tragedy and Gender*. Bloomington: Indiana University Press.

Greenblatt, S. 1988: "Fiction and Friction." In *Shakespearean Negotiations: The Circulation of Social Energy in Renaissance England*. Berkeley: University of California Press, 66–93.

Gurr, A. 1996: *Playgoing in Shakespeare's London*. Second edition. Cambridge: Cambridge University Press.

Henderson, D. E. 1997: "The Theater and Domestic Culture." In John D. Cox and David Scott Kastan (eds.), *A New History of Early English Drama*. New York: Columbia University Press, 173–94.

Hogrefe, P. 1977: *Women of Action in Tudor England*. Ames, IA: Iowa State University Press.

Howard, J. E. 1986: "The New Historicism in Renaissance Studies." *English Literary Renaissance*, 16, 13–43.

——1988: "Crossdressing, the Theatre, and Gender Struggle in Early Modern England." *Shakespeare Quarterly*, 39, 418–40.

——and Rackin, P. 1997: *Engendering a Nation: A Feminist Account of Shakespeare's English Histories*. London and New York: Routledge.

Jardine, L. 1991: "Boy Actors, Female Roles, and Elizabethan Eroticism." In David Scott Kastan and Peter Stallybrass (eds.), *Staging the Renaissance: Reinterpretations of Elizabethan and Jacobean Drama*. New York and London: Routledge, 57–67.

Kahn, C. 1981: *Man's Estate: Masculine Identity in Shakespeare*. Berkeley: University of California Press.

Keeble, N. H. (ed.) 1994: *The Cultural Identity of Seventeenth-Century Woman: A Reader*. London: Routledge.

Leventen, C. 1991: "Patrimony and Patriarchy in *The Merchant of Venice*." In Valerie Wayne (ed.), *The Matter of Difference: Materialist Feminist Criticism of Shakespeare*. Ithaca: Cornell University Press, 59–79.

Levin, R. 1989: "Women in the Renaissance Theatre Audience." *Shakespeare Quarterly*, 40, 165–74.

McLuskie, K. 1994: "The Patriarchal Bard: Feminist Criticism and Shakespeare: *King Lear* and *Measure for Measure*." In Jonathan Dollimore and Alan Sinfield (eds.), *Political Shakespeare: Essays in Cultural Materialism*. Second edition. Ithaca: Cornell University Press, 88–108.

Montrose, L. A. 1981: "'The Place of a Brother' in *As You Like It*: Social Process and Comic Form." *Shakespeare Quarterly*, 32, 28–54.

Mullaney, S. 1994: "Mourning and Misogyny: *Hamlet, The Revenger's Tragedy,* and the Final Progress of Elizabeth I, 1600–1607." *Shakespeare Quarterly*, 45, 139–62.

Neely, C. T. 1996: "'Documents in Madness': Reading Madness and Gender in Shakespeare's Tragedies and Early Modern Culture." In Shirley Nelson Garner and Madelon Sprengnether (eds.), *Shakespearean Tragedy and Gender*. Bloomington: Indiana University Press, 75–104.

Newman, K. 1991: *Fashioning Femininity and English Renaissance Drama*. Chicago: University of Chicago Press.

Orgel, S. 1996: *Impersonations: The Performance of Gender in Shakespeare's England*. Cambridge: Cambridge University Press.

Orlin, L. C. 1998: "The Witness Who Spoke When the Cock Crowed." Unpublished essay.

Payne, D. C. 1995: "Reified Object or Emergent Professional? Retheorizing the Restoration Actress." In J. Douglas Canfield and Deborah C. Payne (eds.), *Cultural Readings of Restoration and Eighteenth-Century English Theater*. Athens and London: University of Georgia Press, 13–38.

Rackin, P. 1985: "Anti-Historians: Women's Roles in Shakespeare's Histories." *Theatre Journal*, 37, 329–44.

Rubin, G. 1975: "The Traffic in Women: Notes on the 'Political Economy' of Sex." In Reina Reiter (ed.), *Towards an Anthropology of Women*. New York: Monthly Review Press, 157–210.

Snell, K. D. M. 1985: "The Apprenticeship of Women." In *Annals of the Labouring Poor: Social Change and Agrarian England, 1660–1900*. Cambridge: Cambridge University Press, 270–319.

Spevack, M. 1968: *A Complete and Systematic Concordance to the Works of Shakespeare*. Hildesheim: Georg Olms.

Stallybrass, P. 1986: "Patriarchal Territories: The Body Enclosed." In Margaret W. Ferguson, Maureen Quilligan, and Nancy J. Vickers (eds.), *Rewriting the Renaissance: The Discourses of Sexual Difference in Early Modern Europe*. Chicago: University of Chicago Press, 123–42.

Tennenhouse, L. 1986: *Power on Display: The Politics of Shakespeare's Genres*. New York and London: Methuen.

Traub, V. 1995: "Jewels, Statues, and Corpses: Containment of Female Erotic Power." In Deborah E. Barker and Ivo Kamps (eds.), *Shakespeare and Gender: A History*. London and New York: Verso, 120–41.

IV

Early Modern Europe

The 1993 Willamette College production of Aphra Behn's *The Rover*.

I n London, Paris, and Madrid, theater and drama experienced a second "renaissance" in the later seventeenth century. In these cities, the theater came under the influence and protection of the king and his court, and the theaters of both London and Paris adapted Italian staging practices, as did the theaters of the Spanish court. As scenic technology became increasingly complex and spectacular, theater buildings achieved the form they would hold well into the nineteenth century, and the work of new playwrights and new dramatic designs invigorated the dramatic repertoire.

Yet for all their similarities, the theaters of Restoration England, of Louis XIV's France, and of the Spanish "Golden Age" were sustained by very different social and political climates. In France, Louis XIV declared *"L'état, c'est moi"*—"I am the state"—in 1660, confidently drawing all state authority into the person of the king and his magnificent court. The later seventeenth century in France was a period of royal absolutism, as the throne worked to consolidate its power. In England, conditions were very different, for 1660 brought the restoration of the monarchy. The Restoration period saw an ongoing negotiation between newly installed Charles II and Parliament for power, in which Parliament gradually gained control of many royal prerogatives. In both countries, the theater became associated with the throne and reflected the tensions animating social and political life.

In France, a character in Molière's play *Tartuffe* drew the official portrait of the absolute monarch: "A Prince who sees into our inmost hearts, / And can't be fooled by any trickster's arts." Yet the authoritarian policies of the French government, the internecine competition among members of the court, and even the fortunes of the theater suggest that the king's claim of absolute power was challenged in a variety of ways. Under Louis XIII (reigned 1610–1643) and Louis XIV (reigned 1643–1715), the Crown strove to centralize its power by crushing the claims of the landed nobility and by expanding French rule in a series of costly wars. Since Louis XIII came to the throne at the age of nine, when his father—Henry IV—was assassinated, much of this expansion was carried on by his chief minister, Cardinal Richelieu (1585–1642), and Richelieu's successor, Cardinal Mazarin (1602–1661). The suppression of the traditional nobility was achieved largely through Richelieu's formation of a new bureaucracy loyal to the Crown, partly composed of politically active clergy and partly of commoners promoted over the heads of the nobility to critical positions in the government. Allowing these "new men" to buy aristocratic titles, the Crown raised money and further diluted the power of the nobility. The Crown's ravenous appetite for cash to pay for the lavish life of the court and for expensive building projects, such as the palace of Versailles (built by Louis XIV in 1673), further weakened the nobility and alienated the peasantry. Using tax-farmers, who paid a fixed sum to the government in exchange for the authority to collect taxes and pocket the excess as profit, the Crown squeezed the nobles' wealth directly into the royal coffers, impoverishing their lands and making the peasantry increasingly rebellious.

A poor and disaffected peasantry, a jealous aristocracy, an upstart bourgeoisie, and an increasingly authoritarian and isolated monarchy: this became the recipe for revolution. Although the French Revolution did not erupt until 1789, France suffered civil convulsions throughout the seventeenth century that dramatize the tension between Louis' absolutist rhetoric and the political realities of his reign. The nobles led a series of rebellions called

THE POLITICAL CLIMATE

the Fronde throughout the 1640s and 1650s, in an effort to unseat Louis and his powerful ministers. Louis defeated these uprisings and finally sealed the fate of his enemies when he required the nobility to attend him at Versailles, so he could keep his eye on their activities. However, the Fronde was part of a more pervasive unrest. Relentless taxation, economic stagnation, and repeated famines throughout the seventeenth century made the peasants angry as well, and peasant riots and rebellions took place in nearly every province of France in nearly every decade of the century. Finally, Louis XIV also had difficulty with the most volatile issue of seventeenth-century Europe—religious dissent. The close ties between the Crown and the church often resulted in the suppression of Protestant sects, particularly the Calvinist French Huguenots. Protestant rebellion had forced the enactment of the Edict of Nantes in 1598, granting the Huguenots considerable religious freedom. Louis XIV revoked the Edict in 1685, giving the government wider latitude to suppress increasingly energetic religious protest. Louis XIV carefully crafted the image of the "Le Roi Soleil"—the Sun King—whose absolute authority seemed almost a force of nature, not a fact of politics. Throughout his reign, though, Louis had to contend with recalcitrant factions who refused to accept completely his characterization of the king's power.

In England, resistance to royal authority had been much more successful. Between 1603 and 1642, the Stuart kings James I (reigned 1603–1625) and his son, Charles I (reigned 1625–1649), worked to limit the power of Parliament and to enforce increasingly strict religious laws that suppressed the Protestant Puritan sects and demanded conformity with the Church of England. In 1642, Parliament passed legislation limiting the powers of the throne, and Civil War between Parliamentary and Royalist forces erupted. Charles I was executed in 1649; his wife and children (including the future king, Charles II) escaped to France. From 1653 to 1658, Oliver Cromwell served as Lord Protector of the realm, but Royalist sentiments eventually prevailed and established Charles II (reigned 1660–1685) on the throne.

Although the monarchy was restored—the term *Restoration* refers generally to the period of Charles II's reign and the remainder of the seventeenth century—Charles II was in no position to command the nation, and English politics in the later seventeenth century mainly concerned the negotiation of power between the Crown and Parliament. Charles' death in 1685 spurred a crisis in that his son James II (reigned 1685–1688) was Catholic and threatened to compromise English religious and civil autonomy from the Catholic church and the Catholic states of Europe. In 1689, Parliament effectively deposed James, inviting his Protestant daughter Mary (reigned as Mary II, 1689–1694) and her husband, William of Orange (reigned as William III, 1689–1702), to return to England and assume the throne. While Louis XIV increasingly insisted on the autonomous power of the throne in France, the Parliament in England finally achieved a lasting compromise with the Crown in the form of a constitutional monarchy. In bringing William and Mary into power, Parliament gained the authority of consent over royal succession, a power it confirmed in 1702 in naming James II's daughter Anne as successor (reigned as Queen Anne, 1702–1714).

While in an important sense the gulf separating French and English culture has always been narrow and deep, like the English Channel, Spanish culture in the Renaissance arises from a very different history. Spain was occupied by the Moors in 711 and is still marked by its five centuries of Islamic culture. In 1479, Ferdinand of Aragon and Isabella of Castile were married, forming the alliance that gave rise to modern Spain. In 1480 they joined forces with the Catholic Inquisition, expelling Jews from the country. At the Conquest of Granada in 1492, the Moors were finally driven out of Spain.

Having formed a single state, the Spanish monarchy successfully expanded its reach into a global empire during the sixteenth century. Under Charles V, Spain's territory included its many New World colonies as well as the Netherlands and the Holy Roman Empire of central Europe, and the culture of the Spanish court was unrivaled in Europe; this was the era of Velásquez and El Greco. During the reign of Philip II (1556–1598), however, Spain's domination of Europe began to wane. Spain became involved in a brutal and expensive effort to retain control of the Netherlands, a hotbed of Protestant resistance. English soldiers—Sir Philip Sidney and Ben Jonson, among others—fought the Spanish in the Netherlands, and Philip tried in several ways to outmaneuver the English. He proposed marriage to Queen Elizabeth, but as with other suitors, she strung him along for political purposes and finally refused him. He also mounted a massive naval invasion of England, the Spanish Armada of 1588, which was surprisingly defeated. Spain continued to wane in the seventeenth century, eventually losing the Netherlands and losing Portugal in 1657. By 1665, Spain was ruled by the last of the Hapsburg kings, the deformed imbecile Charles II (1665–1700). The death of Charles II drew all of Europe into the Wars of the Spanish Succession.

THEATER IN FRANCE, 1660–1700

Louis XIV's familiar sobriquet, "Le Roi Soleil," derives from a role he played in a court ballet devised for him in 1653. A fine dancer, Louis sponsored and took part in a wide variety of entertainments. Moreover, the centralization of power in the king and the court paralleled the increasing institutionalization of the arts under Louis XIV, as a means of advancing his own prestige and of keeping control over potentially seditious activities. The most famous of these institutions—the **ACADÉMIE FRANÇAISE**—was chartered in 1637 and used by Cardinal Richelieu to evaluate a critical controversy surrounding Pierre Corneille's play *The Cid*. Corneille's detractors had sharply attacked the play, and Richelieu urged the Académie to resolve whether *The Cid* could legitimately be described as effective tragedy in neoclassical terms (on *neoclassicism,* see p. 384). In return, Richelieu promoted the Académie and its aims, the purification of French language and literature, and the advancement of official French culture. Louis XIV assumed the role of official protector of the Académie Française in 1672 and sponsored other institutions as ornaments to his reign: the Académie Royale de Musique (1672), the Académie Royale de Peinture et de Sculpture (1648), the Académie des Inscriptions (1663), the Académie des Sciences (1666), and the Académie de l'Architecture (1671). The institution of the stage was no exception. Theatrical companies had always needed the king's license to play in Paris, and Louis licensed several companies and named Molière's company as the *Troupe du roi.* After Molière's death in 1673, the leading tragic actress in Paris, Mademoiselle Champmeslé, joined with Molière's troupe and gained the king's patronage. The new company—the **COMÉDIE FRANÇAISE**—opened in August of 1680. It held a **MONOPOLY** on the production of all spoken drama in French, and although this monopoly has long since vanished, the Comédie Française remains the principal company performing the French classical repertoire.

In Louis XIV's Paris, the institutions of art—including the theater—were identified with the prerogatives of the king and his court, though the structure of the theater had its roots in practices dating back to the Middle Ages. Throughout the later Middle Ages and into the sixteenth century, stage production in Paris was controlled by the Confrérie de la Passion, a guildlike corporation initially formed to stage religious drama. In 1545 the Confrérie purchased land in Paris from the Duke of Burgundy and erected the Hôtel de Bourgogne, at the time probably the only permanent theater building in Europe (*hôtel* in this case means "hall" or "large building"). Extensively remodeled in 1647, the Hôtel de Bourgogne served as the model for other theaters built in the seventeenth century: the Théâtre du Marais (built in a tennis court in 1629, rebuilt in 1644); the Palais-Cardinal (built by Richelieu in 1640; later renamed the Palais-Royal); the Salle des Machines (1642), and the Comédie Française (1689).

The shape of these theaters owes something to the Hôtel de Bourgogne, and something to tennis courts as well, for tennis courts were often used as theaters. (In the sixteenth and seventeenth centuries, tennis courts were long indoor rooms with side galleries.) These

GROUND PLAN OF THE COMÉDIE FRANÇAISE THEATER

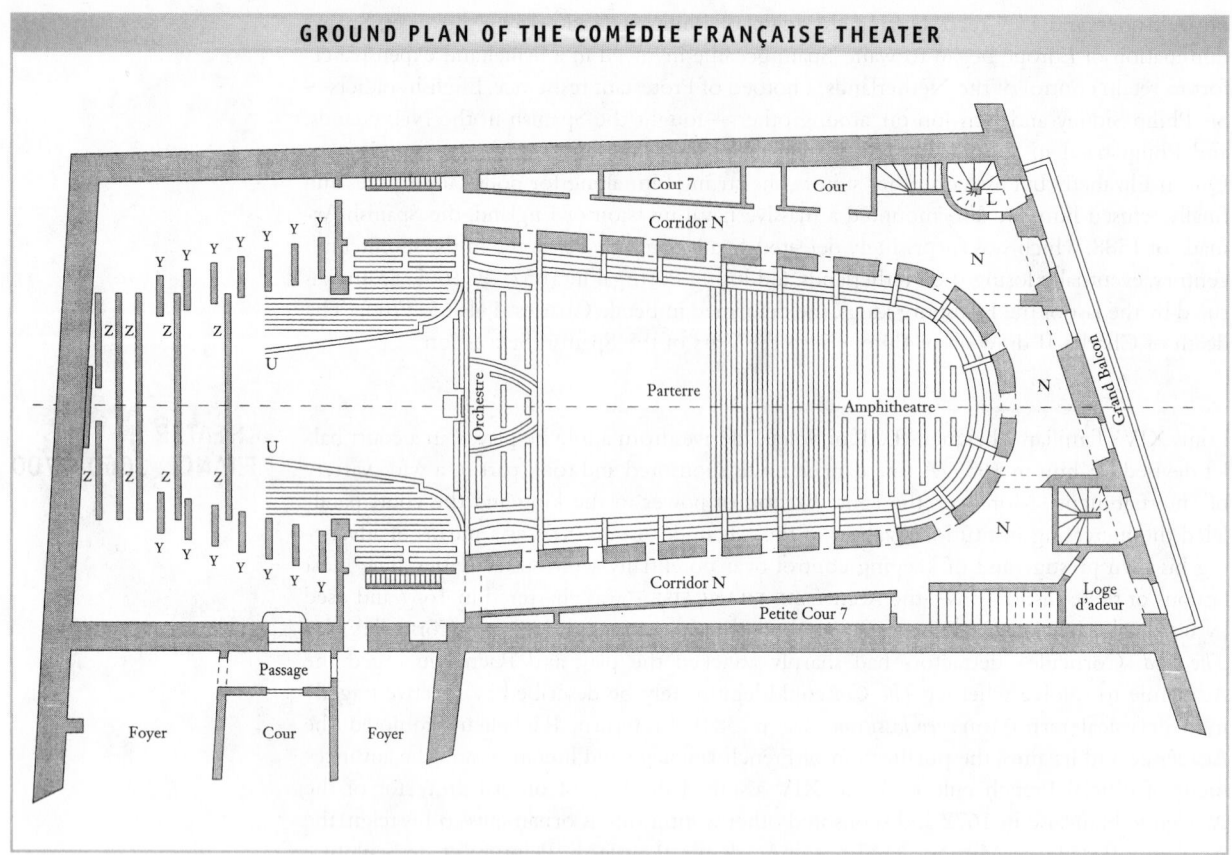

The Comédie Française had this basic design from 1689 to 1770. Note the open *parterre,* the wings (marked Y), and the backdrops (Z). The benches on the stage were added during the eighteenth century.

theaters generally had deep, **RAKED STAGES** (40 feet deep, 45 feet wide at the Hôtel de Bourgogne) that faced an open **PIT** called the **PARTERRE** (literally, "on the ground") which was used for standing spectators. The auditorium had **BOXES** on three sides; **GALLERY** seating rose above the boxes opposite the stage; some patrons were also seated on the stage itself. The theaters were large—the Hôtel de Bourgogne initially held 1,600 spectators, the Comédie Française held 2,000—and many theaters made extensive use of stage scenery, sometimes concocting extraordinary spectacles. In a fantasy celebrating Louis XIV's wedding in 1662, the entire royal family and its entourage were "flown" by machines in the Salle des Machines; in a production in 1671, 300 deities were lifted aloft. The dramatic theaters—the Hôtel de Bourgogne, the Palais-Royal, the Comédie Française—tended to avoid such effects, using instead a single setting for each play, depending on the genre of the play. The theaters generally used a series of staggered **WINGS AND BACKDROP** to create the effect of perspective, adapting both scenic practices and scene-changing technology from Italian theaters.

Acting companies in Paris were organized as investment corporations requiring the patronage of the Crown and had long included women in their ranks. Louis XIV's reign saw a series of great actresses take the stage, Mademoiselle DuParc and Mademoiselle Champmeslé among them. Companies were comprised of twelve members (eight men, four women), who shared the company's profits. The company hired additional actors when necessary. The Comédie Française standardized this practice: its twelve main actors—called

SOCIÉTAIRES—ran the company for twenty years, and new *sociétaires* could be recruited only after the retirement of current members. Actors in the Comédie Française received an annual subsidy from the Crown and a retirement pension if they completed their twenty years with the company. The company purchased plays, which were cast by the author. Throughout the 1650s and 1660s the major companies kept about 70 plays in repertoire and generally played three or four times per week. After the 1680s, the Comédie Française began daily performances, beginning at 5 P.M.

We should recall that life at court was itself a kind of performance, and that attending the theater provided ample opportunity for aristocrats, courtiers, and aspiring courtiers to display and preen themselves. In a milieu so dependent on the king's preference, we can easily imagine how stage seating and side boxes emphasized that the evening's entertainment included the audience's performances as well as the actors'. This sense of the reciprocity between court and stage is signaled more concretely by the fortunes of the Parisian theaters after Louis XIV moved the court to Versailles. Although five companies flourished in Paris while Louis kept court in the city, by 1700 only two remained.

THEATER IN ENGLAND, 1660–1737

At the outbreak of the English Civil War in 1642, Parliament closed the London theaters, putting a stop to dramatic performance. Some companies managed to mount secret productions between 1642 and 1660, but Parliament and city officials moved quickly to suppress them, sometimes by destroying the theater buildings. In the 1650s, however, William Davenant (1606–1668), a Royalist supporter of Charles I and successor to Ben Jonson as writer of court masques, attempted to mount operas. In 1656 he succeeded in staging a production of *The Siege of Rhodes* at Rutland House, performing it again in 1658 and 1659 at the Cockpit theater and elsewhere in London.

The restoration of Charles II to the throne in 1660 inaugurated a period of renewed theatrical vitality. As in France—where Charles developed a taste for theater during his exile—the theater was closely associated with royal prerogatives. Upon his return, Charles rewarded **PATENTS** to William Davenant and Thomas Killegrew (1612–1683) to open theaters under royal authority. These **PATENT THEATERS** (also called "theaters royal")—Davenant's Duke's company, and Killigrew's King's company—thus held a royal monopoly on the production of spoken English drama. Although they underwent huge modifications, the patent theaters dominated the legitimate theater until the mid-nineteenth century, when legislation was passed that finally broke their monopoly. Yet monopoly could not guarantee support. The two companies, unable to turn a profit, were united into a single company from 1682 to 1695.

When the theaters reopened in 1660, theatrical taste had changed significantly. Although a few of the older, pre-1642 theater buildings were still standing, they could not handle the new theater technology. For, as in the French theater, the English theater rapidly encouraged the development of scenic practices already well-known in Italy—a **PROSCENIUM** stage and moveable painted wings and backdrop used to create a visual setting for the play. Onstage, theaters used stock sets—one for classical tragedy, one for romantic comedy, and so on—that conformed to the dramatic genre of the play. In 1661, Davenant converted Lisle's Tennis Court to the Lincoln's Inn Fields Theater, which measured 30 by 70 feet; he replaced this theater with the Dorset Garden Theater in 1671. Killegrew erected his Theatre Royal in Bridges Street in 1663. When it burned in 1672, he built a new Theatre Royal in Drury Lane, which opened in 1674; a theater has occupied this site down to the present time.

The new English theaters were much smaller than the French theaters. The Drury Lane theater, for example, held 650 to 700 people, though it was expanded throughout the late seventeenth and eighteenth centuries and eventually held more than 2,000. Nonetheless,

CHRISTOPHER WREN'S THEATRE ROYAL, DRURY LANE

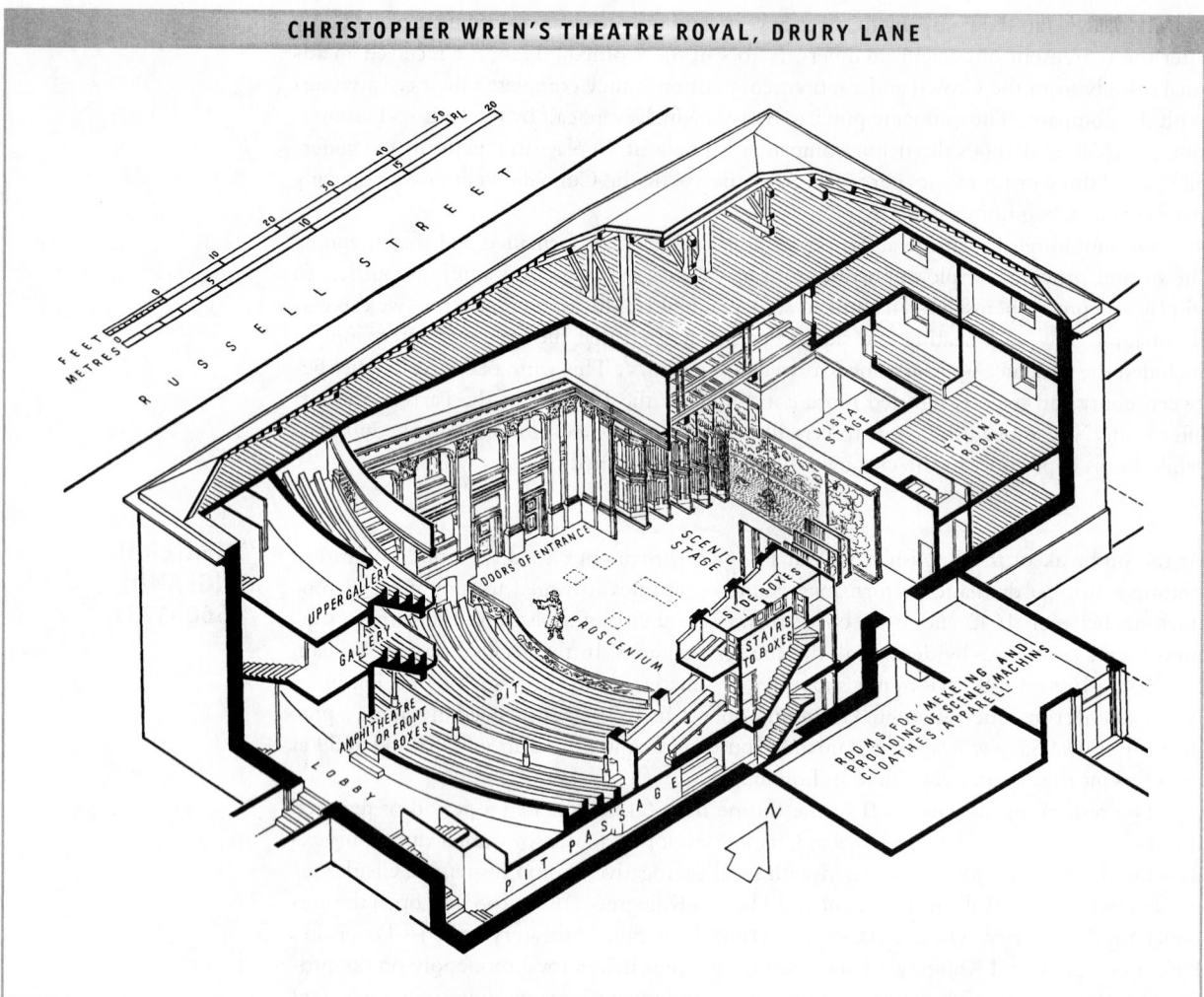

In 1674, Christopher Wren designed a new Theatre Royal, Drury Lane. Note that the acting area extends to the apron, in front of the wing and backdrop stage scenery. Pit seating, side boxes, and two galleries also are visible.

like the French theaters, the English houses also introduced new design and staging practices: a proscenium stage flanked by a large **APRON,** footlights to illuminate the stage, a raked pit with benches (the French *parterre* was flat and had no seats), side and rear box seats, and a rear gallery. This division of the house accorded with social and class distinctions in the audience, which was in any event a narrow selection of the English public, in part because the theater was recognized as the ornament of the privileged, and—not incidentally—because plays were produced in the afternoon, when working people could not easily attend. The entire auditorium was lighted by chandeliers, making the audience itself very much a part of the show: in an important sense the performance did not stop at the edge of the stage. Although the theaters were not at the court itself, they were frequently patronized by courtiers and the nobility, who preened and displayed themselves to the audience—sometimes from seats onstage. Charles II—who numbered the well-known actress Nell Gwynn (1650–1687) among his many mistresses—was also frequently in the audience.

Companies were generally managed by one of the actors, and they avoided the need for lengthy casting and rehearsal by developing **LINES OF BUSINESS,** in which each actor would specialize in a particular type of character: heroic lead, comic lead, male heavy, female heavy, utility player, and so on. Acting style was relatively formal, and actors often played downstage on the apron directly to the audience; a famous speech—one of Hamlet's soliloquies, for example—would be delivered directly to the audience, something like an operatic aria today, a practice called **POINTING.** As the theater developed in the later seventeenth century, sharing companies were replaced by companies financed by outside investors, who paid the actors salaries and took a percentage of the profits. Companies were large and salaries low; actors were compensated by **BENEFIT** performances, in which the actor (on his or her benefit night) received the entire profit from a given evening's performance, minus the operating expenses of the house. The practice of supplementing salaries with benefit performances continued well into the nineteenth century, and although most benefit nights—after the house expenses were deducted—left the actors with little additional pay, benefits provided an excuse to keep actors' salaries low.

By far the greatest innovation in the English theater, though, was the introduction of actresses onstage. English comedies in this period were often frankly concerned with sexual intrigue, and the actresses who played in them—and in the new heroic tragedies, and in the plays by Shakespeare, Jonson, Fletcher, and other Renaissance playwrights who continued to hold the stage—also had a reputation for sexual licentiousness. Yet, while several actresses, like Nell Gwynne, were mistresses of the famous and powerful, the phenomenon of regarding actresses as sexual objects, of classing them with prostitutes, has more to do with the status and vulnerability of working women in a highly stratified and patriarchal society than it does with the immorality of the stage or its performers. Indeed, actresses' ongoing struggle to assert themselves as legitimate performers was born at this time as well, epitomized in the careers of Elizabeth Barry (1658–1713), Anne Bracegirdle (1663–1748), and many others.

THEATER IN SPAIN'S GOLDEN AGE, 1580–1680

As in medieval England and France, medieval Spanish theater was strongly influenced by the church, which saw in the drama a source of instruction and inspiration. Although there is some evidence for liturgical drama as early as the twelfth century, the principal form of medieval theater was the *AUTO SACRAMENTALE,* a form of allegorical religious drama initially devised to celebrate the feast of Corpus Christi. But while the mystery cycles were suppressed in Protestant England, the Spanish *autos* continued to be performed alongside the secular theater until they were banned in 1765. Like the English cycles, the *autos* were in civic hands, and by the late sixteenth century major cities would perform *autos* as many as three times per year, usually in the central city plaza before a gathering of citizens and civic officials. Professional actors were hired for the *autos* and were drawn through the city on wagons (*CARROS*); the *carros* were heavily decorated, and a prize was given for the most spectacular *carro.* Despite their abstract themes, the *autos* remained extremely popular and drew on the talents of the best playwrights of the era—between 1647 and 1681, for instance, all the *autos* performed in Madrid were written by Pedro Calderón de la Barca.

Philip II, Philip III, and Philip IV were all interested in theater and commissioned playwrights to devise entertainments; during the reign of Philip III, Spain developed an impressive court theater. Early in the seventeenth century, this court theater merely occupied a hall at the Alcázar palace, as Ben Jonson and Inigo Jones had done at Whitehall palace in England, and it produced a similar kind of entertainment: mythological dramas that required spectacular scenery, effects, and costumes. But by the 1630s, the center of court theater shifted to the new palace of Buen Retiro. Here, in 1640 Cosme Lotti (d. 1643) was retained to build a permanent theater that could perform the scenic effects of the Italian theater. This theater was roofed, but in its basic design resembled the most influential of Spanish theaters in the Golden Age, the public theater or *CORRAL.*

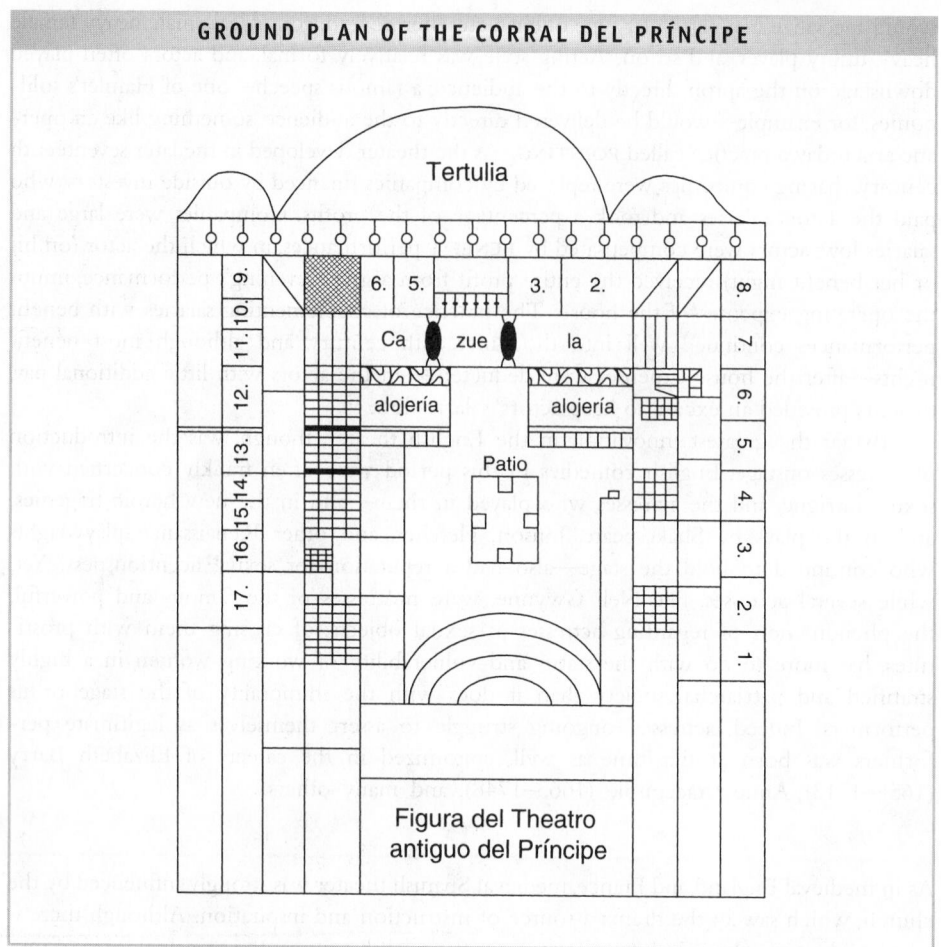

GROUND PLAN OF THE CORRAL DEL PRÍNCIPE

Tertulia

Ca zue la

alojería   alojería

Patio

Figura del Theatro
antiguo del Príncipe

Made in 1730, this drawing of the Corral del Príncipe shows the important features of the theater: the *patio,* the *alojería,* the *gradas* (unmarked), and the *cazuela.*

Although the Spanish public theater resembled the public theaters of Elizabethan London, it stood in a much different relationship to city life. While the English theaters were banned from the city proper and were erected across the Thames in Southwark, the Spanish theaters were public institutions. Since the medieval church held the rights to theatrical production, the public theaters were licensed by religious confraternities in the sixteenth century, which used the funds for various charitable purposes, including maintaining the general hospital of Madrid. By the early seventeenth century, these funds were paid directly to the city, and theaters continued to subsidize charities well into the nineteenth century. Companies of actors were licensed to play in the city, and took a lease on a *corral* for a stated period of time. In general, Spanish companies toured major cities and towns, and only Seville and Madrid allowed two companies to perform at the same time. While playwrights were initially associated with individual companies, by the seventeenth century playwrights would sell their plays to the company: they were paid very well for an *auto,* and adequately for a regular play—about 500 reales, or about 10 times the daily wage of a laborer. Although companies were composed of men and boys until 1587, when women were allowed to appear onstage, the church issued a decree banning women from performing onstage in 1596. By 1599, however, a royal council ruled that actresses could be permitted, providing they were married to a member of the company; it also ruled against cross-dressing, so that when

VIEW OF THE CORRAL DEL PRÍNCIPE

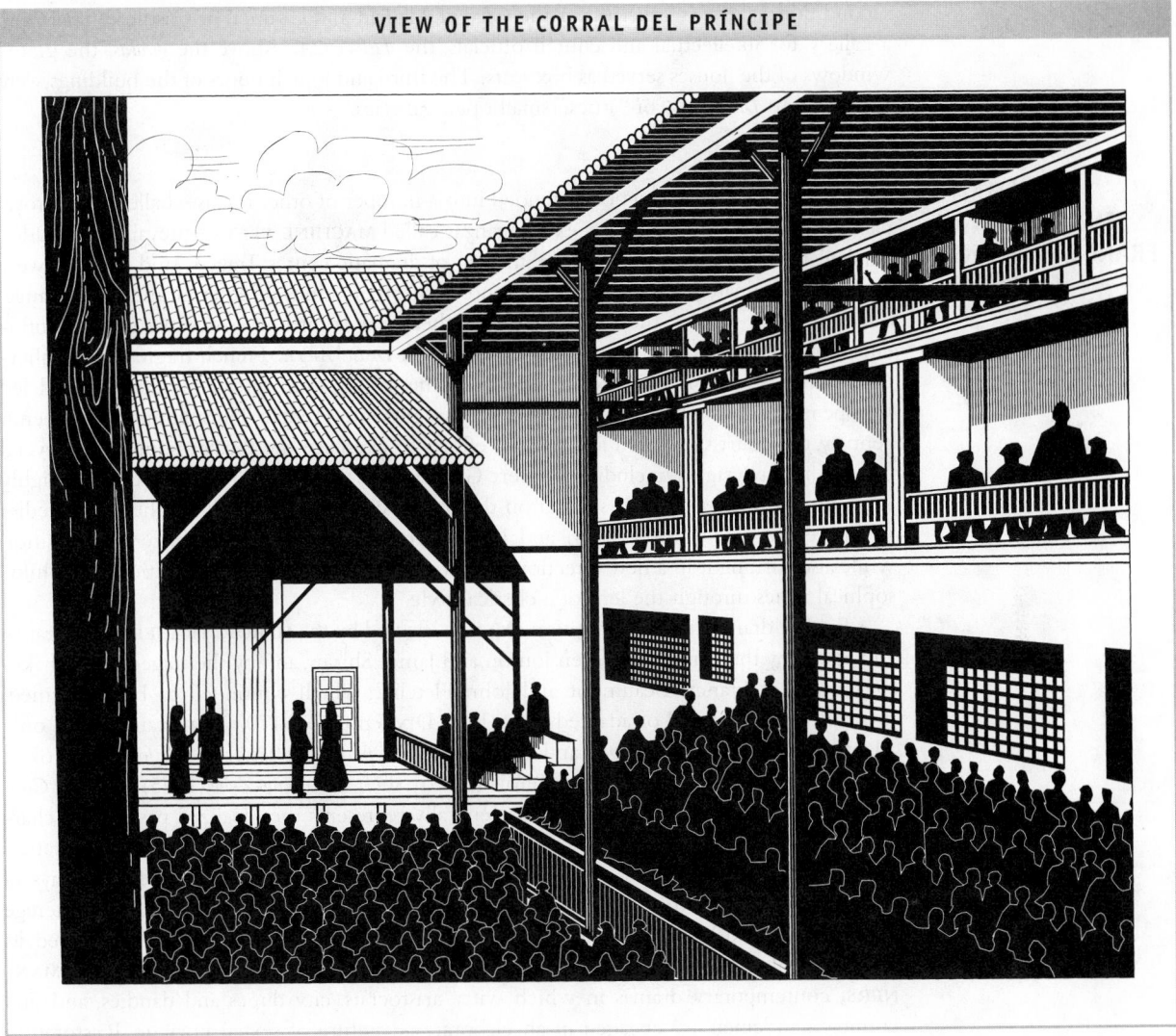

This illustration provides a view of the Corral del Príncipe from the rear of the *patio,* perhaps from the *cazuela.*

Rosaura appeared dressed as a man in Calderón's *Life Is a Dream,* the actress wore a man's costume only down to the waist with a skirt below.

The reciprocity between the city and the theater is also revealed in the design of public theaters of the golden age, particularly the two principal theaters of Madrid, the Corral de la Cruz, opened in 1579 as Spain's first theater, and the Corral del Príncipe, opened in 1583. The theaters were originally merely stages placed in a courtyard enclosed on three or four sides by four-story buildings; over time the theaters gradually acquired possession of these structures, but in the meantime the buildings' galleries and windows could be sold to spectators separately. The central courtyard or *PATIO* was unroofed, and like the pit of English theaters was occupied by standing spectators. In the seventeenth century, a few rows of benches (called *TABURETES*) were erected near the stage, on a raised and fenced dais. Along the sides of the *patio* rose the *GRADAS,* steeply raked rows of seats that rose to the second floor. The *ALOJERÍA,* a tavern, served refreshments, and was located at the rear of the *patio;* above the *alojería* were several stories of galleries: the *CAZUELA,* or women's gallery, on the second floor; above it galleries for the City of Madrid and Council of Castile officials; and a gallery for intellectual and church officials, the *TERTULIA*. Above the *gradas,* the grated windows of the houses served as box seats. The third and fourth floors of the buildings were converted to *DESVANES* or "attics," small open galleries.

DRAMATIC INNOVATION IN FRANCE, ENGLAND, AND SPAIN

Although theatrical production extended into a number of other forms—ballet, opera, royal pageants, and the special-effects extravaganzas called **MACHINE PLAYS**—prevailing attitudes, particularly in France, prohibited the mixing of dramatic genres: Tragedy and comedy were firmly discriminated from one another and from others kinds of entertainment. In France, comedy—and, indeed, the organization of theatrical companies—was particularly influenced by the techniques of the Italian *COMMEDIA DELL'ARTE*. French tragic drama inherited a taste for classical subject matter from the schools and universities, which had led Europe in translating Greek and Roman playwrights into French. Throughout the sixteenth century, the court sponsored a variety of efforts to classicize the theater, supporting several important playwrights, including Robert Garnier and Étienne Jodelle, who created highly wrought and refined tragedies based on the model of classical drama. The heroic tragedies of Pierre Corneille (1606–1684) and Jean Racine (1639–1699) epitomize this tradition while also turning it in a new direction, refracting contemporary moral, political, and philosophical issues through the lens of a classical style.

English drama in the Restoration also was affected by the **HEROIC TRAGEDIES** of France and Spain, by the comedies of Ben Jonson and James Shirley, and by the tragedies of Shakespeare and of Francis Beaumont and John Fletcher, which continued to be performed, though often in revised or adapted form. John Dryden (1631–1700), for example, not only adapted versions of *The Tempest* and *Antony and Cleopatra* (the latter as *All for Love,* 1677), but also wrote plays in the mode of heroic tragedy, such as *Aureng-Zebe* (1675) and *The Conquest of Granada* (1669). Heroic tragedy generally represents the idealized passions of characters forced to choose between love and personal honor. Comic drama took its inspiration both from European models—Molière's plays, for example—and from the earlier plays of Ben Jonson, but in the plays of William Wycherly (1640–1716), Sir George Etherege (1635–1692), and William Congreve (1670–1729), English comedy rapidly developed its own original style. Restoration comedies are most often in the vein of **COMEDY OF MANNERS,** contemporary dramas in which witty aristocrats, city dupes and dandies, and dull country gentlemen are engaged in an elaborate adventure of sexual intrigue. Restoration comedy is often elegant and verbally polished, and obsessed with issues of class, privilege, manners, and sex. In addition, much as the Restoration theater witnessed the rise of actresses onstage, it also saw the first women to achieve success as playwrights: Aphra Behn (1640–1689), Catharine Trotter (1679–1749), and Susanna Centlivre (1670–1723).

After the turn of the century, the risqué character of many plays spurred one of the perennial movements to restrain the theater as an immoral institution. Partly as a result of Jeremy Collier's diatribe *A Short View of the Immorality and Profaneness of the English Stage* (1698), and partly as a result of changing attitudes and social mores, English comedy after 1700—the plays of Sir Richard Steele (1672–1729), Colley Cibber (1671–1757), George Farquhar (1678–1707), Oliver Goldsmith (1728–1774), and Richard Brinsley Sheridan (1751–1816), for instance—became more romantic and sentimental. Moreover, political satire in English theater was also sharply limited with the passing of the Stage Licensing Act of 1737. After 1737, all plays produced for public entertainment had to be submitted for censorship prior to production. The censor could require changes, delete words, passages, or scenes, or refuse to grant permission entirely. Confronting the Act by producing a nonlicensed play was to risk the fining and imprisonment of everyone involved in the production. While theaters found a variety of ways to subvert or sidestep the law, the censorship remained in effect—with some modifications—until 1968, inhibiting the possibility of dramatic innovation.

The term *commedia dell' arte* means the "comedy of the professional players," and *commedia* became popular throughout Europe in the sixteenth century. *Commedia* companies were itinerant (though one was established in Paris for part of Louis XIV's reign), organized around ten or twelve actors, men and women, each of whom played a stock character who could be easily recognized by typical and routine behavior. Although the characters were fixed, the plots that *commedia* companies played were generally improvised; the actor relied on the traits of his or her character and a core of stage business from which to invent action and dialogue. The cast usually included one or two pairs of young lovers (the **INNAMORATO** and **INNAMORATA**), good-looking, aristocratic, or fashionable characters played without masks. The rest of the cast was masked and played more stereotypical roles: the **CAPITANO,** a military braggart and coward, played with sword and cape; the **PANTALONE,** an elderly dupe, often in love, played in stockings, breeches, and slippers; the **DOTTORE,** sometimes actually a doctor, but otherwise a pedantic friend of the Pantalone; and a variety of comic parts called **ZANNI,** usually sly servants. The most familiar of these parts is *Arlecchino,* or **HARLEQUIN,** a cunning character who is usually an acrobat, wearing a patched costume (later refined to a diamond-shaped pattern), a black cap, and carrying his slapstick—the origin of our term "slapstick," which gives some idea of what *commedia* humor was like. *Commedia* was also popular in England, but it had fewer long-term effects on the comic drama than on the rise of English **PANTOMIME.** In England, plays were often followed by a short **AFTERPIECE,** which frequently led Harlequin into adventures with mythological characters. John Rich (1692–1761), taking the name Lun, was the most famous Harlequin of the early eighteenth-century English stage.

PANTALONE AND HARLEQUIN

Note the mask and breeches of the Pantalone (left), and the mask, slapstick, and diamond-shaped patches of the Harlequin (right).

In the early sixteenth century, a Spanish theatrical manager may well have written his own plays and acted in them himself. Lope de Rueda (1510–1565), for example, was a touring performer and the author of both *autos* and secular plays. But by the late sixteenth century, companies would pay a playwright for the play, and the theaters had made several genres popular: the *CAPA Y ESPADA* or heroic/romantic "cape and sword" play was very popular, as was the *RUIDO* or "noise" play. But the forms of Golden Age drama were in many ways determined by the extraordinary and prolific career of Lope Félix de Vega Carpio (1562–1635). Lope de Vega is frequently said to have written more than 1,500 plays—which points to the immense popularity of the theater and its constant need for new material—and more than 450 of his plays have survived. He is particularly associated with *COMEDIA NUEVA,* a genre mixing the tragic and the comic, high and low characters (including the *GRACIOSO,* a comic fool), and usually having a romantic plot. In the intervals between the acts of his plays, short interludes (*ENTREMESES*) were performed, which were coherent plays in themselves. Like other playwrights in this period, Lope de Vega also wrote *autos,* but his best-known work is *Fuente Ovejuna* (1614), a play about a vicious tyrant that critics have seen as an allegory on Portuguese independence.

Lope shared the stage with several equally brilliant playwrights, principally with Pedro Calderón de la Barca (1600–1681), who succeeded Lope de Vega as Spain's most influential dramatist. Miguel de Cervantes (1547–1616), the author of *Don Quixote,* wrote about thirty plays, of which sixteen remain. Tirso de Molina (1584–1648) was a friar who had written more than 400 plays—eighty survive—before he was reprimanded by the Council of Castile; his best-known play, *El Burlador de Seville* (*The Trickster of Seville*) is the earliest play on the subject of Don Juan. The playwright Guillén de Castro (1569–1631) was a friend of Lope de Vega; his influence on the French theater is perhaps as marked as it was in Spain. Guillén de Castro wrote *Las Mocedades del Cid* (*The Youthful Adventures of the Cid*), which was adapted by Corneille as *Le Cid* and ignited a furious controversy about neoclassical esthetics.

NEOCLASSICISM, DRAMA, AND THEATER

In both France and England, the arts in general and drama in particular were closely regulated by the state, a state of affairs sustained by the rise of **NEOCLASSICISM.** Neoclassicism is, in the simplest sense, the revival of what was taken to be a "classical" ordering of the arts. The literature of classical Greece and Rome began to be recovered in the fourteenth and fifteenth centuries, first through the dissemination of texts preserved in monasteries and later through expanded contact with the Islamic world in the sixteenth and seventeenth centuries. Translating, imitating, and adapting classical texts, European writers in the later seventeenth century appeared to "revive" the principles of classical art. In practice, however, neoclassicism offered an *interpretation* of the classics, emphasizing order, control, decorum, reason, and harmony.

In many respects, neoclassicism relied on the authority of Aristotle's *Poetics,* published first in Latin translation in 1498 and then in Italian in 1549, and on the series of critical commentaries written on Aristotle throughout the sixteenth century. Aristotle's *Poetics* is something of a naturalist's description of the several species of poetry and their characteristics, but readers in the sixteenth and seventeenth centuries fell under the influence of Aristotle's enormous authority (see *Doctor Faustus,* Act 1) and quickly transformed the *Poetics* into a prescription, a series of rules, for producing the most perfect and effective tragedies. Two central precepts of the *Poetics* regard the tragic hero's actions: Those acts must seem both necessary and probable, and they should not entirely violate moral expectations. Neoclassical critics and playwrights schematized Aristotle's descriptions as necessary features of dramatic composition, arguing that a tragedy should be rigorously and causally plotted and should reveal the workings of providential justice through the actions of universalized or typical characters. These goals were transformed into the famous "unities" of neoclassicism: A play should take place within a single day (unity of time), in one location (unity of place), and consist of a single line of action, a single plot (unity of action). The action of neoclassical tragedy, therefore, is concentrated, maintaining a uniformity of tone and style called **DECORUM.** Plays in this mode maintain a single, narrow range of language and behavior; the action is either idealized (rather than realistic) in tragedy, or commonplace in comedy: tragic characters are classic and heroic, while comic characters are contemporary, even bourgeois; tragedy undertakes the conflict between the ideal passions of love and honor, while comedy takes its cue from more earthly desires—lust, greed, hypocrisy, and so on. Following the recovery of Vitruvius' *De Architectura* (15 BCE) in 1414, this neoclassical sensibility urged the modern stage to imitate Vitruvius' distinction between the proper stage settings of tragedy and comedy: classical architecture for tragedy, urban architecture for comedy. Especially in seventeenth-century Paris, theaters adjusted their stagecraft to these ideals of regularity and decorum, assigning a generalized palace setting to the elevated world of tragedy, and the *chambre à quatre portes*—the room with four doors—to the lower, contemporary world of comedy.

Writing later in the eighteenth century, the Englishman Thomas Davies characterized the differences between French and English audiences and suggests that neoclassical ideals did not take root as deeply in the English theater as they did in France:

> The Frenchman, when he goes to a play, seems to make his entertainment a matter of importance. The long speeches in the plays of Corneille, Racine, Crébillon, and Voltaire, which would disgust an English ear, are extremely pleasing to our light neighbours: they sit in silence, and enjoy the beauty of sentiment, and energy of language; and are taught habitually to cry at scenes of distress. The Englishman looks upon the theatre as a place of amusement; he does not expect to be alarmed with terror, or wrought upon by scenes of commiseration; but he is surprised into the feeling of those passions, and sheds tears because he cannot avoid it. The theatre, to most Englishmen, becomes a place of instruction by chance.

Davies, of course, betrays a common chauvinism of the English toward the French: while the French are pedantic and calculating, the English are spontaneous. But this distinction between English and French theaters—one for "art," one for "entertainment"; one tragic, one comic—conceals the fundamental likenesses between the two institutions and the plays they put on the stage. As the plays of Corneille, Racine, and Dryden suggest, neoclassical tragedy imposes severe and artificial forms on the irrepressible forces of the passions, which inevitably break through the formal speech and decorous behavior of the characters to destroy them and sometimes the state as well. Comedy of the period in England and in France reveals a cognate tension, as the formal acting styles and stereotyped characters common in Restoration comedy seem barely able to contain the bottomless appetites of the plays' heroes. To this extent, neoclassical decorum embodies a barely contained anxiety about the power of forms—forms of conduct, forms of art, forms of state—to prevent a revolution of unreason and disorder.

EARLY MODERN DRAMA IN PERFORMANCE AND HISTORY

In many respects, the theater of seventeenth-century Europe is continuous with our own. Given the fact that the European monarchies were rapidly expanding their political and mercantile influence around the globe, it's not surprising to find that their culture became exported as well, often to the cultivated elites of their new colonies. In Mexico, for example, the seventeenth-century nun Sor Juana Inés de la Cruz (1651–1695) composed both *autos* and full-length dramas that echo—and, indeed, rival—the plays of the Spanish playwrights Calderón and Lope de Vega. The English drama of this period was exported as well; Farquhar's *The Recruiting Officer* was the first play to be performed in the penal colony of Australia. Moreover, the seventeenth century saw the institutionalization of theater as a commercial activity: in its architecture (indoor theaters, proscenium stages), in its greater appeal to a bourgeois audience, even in institutions like the Comédie Française (which, of course, continues to produce the plays of Molière and Racine), this theater is the direct forebear of the modern European theater, and in many ways the progenitor of its colonial theaters as well.

While the plays in this unit are all still in the classical repertory of modern theaters, these plays tend to pose particular problems to modern directors and actors. Although many

READING THE MATERIAL THEATER

One of the most challenging elements of theater history is the interpretation of the documentary record. Indeed, with the rise of print, the theater spawned its own information explosion, as newspaper descriptions, reviews, memoirs, and even published letters provide accounts of the practices of the stage. Yet these documents themselves often require a skeptical eye. Anthony Aston's *A Brief Supplement to Colley Cibber, Exq: His Lives of the Late Famous Actors and Actresses* (published in London in 1748) provides what seems to be an eyewitness account of the acting style of Thomas Betterton (1635–1710). What features of Betterton's physique and style emerge most strongly to Aston? Are there class or cultural implications in the various terms Aston uses to praise Betterton? How does Aston distinguish between Betterton's success in comic and tragic roles? How does he distinguish between Betterton's style in comedy and that of Estcourt and Harper?

Mr. Betterton (although a superlative good Actor) labour'd under ill Figure, being clumsily made, having a great Head, a short thick Neck, stoop'd in the Shoulders, and had fat short Arms, which he rarely lifted higher than his Stomach. –His Left Hand frequently lodg'd in his Breast, between his Coat and Waistcoat, while, with his Right, he prepar'd his Speech. –His Actions were few, but just. –He had little Eyes, and a broad Face, a little Pock-fretten, a corpulent Body, and thick Legs, with large Feet. –He was better to meet, than to follow; for his Aspect was serious, venerable, and majestic; in his latter Time a little Paralytic. –His Voice was low and grumbling; yet he could Time it by an artificial *Climax,* which enforc'd universal Attention, even from the *Fops* and *Orange-girls.* –He was incapable of dancing, even in a Country-Dance; as was MRS. BARRY: But their good Qualities were more than equal to their Deficiencies. –While MRS. BRACEGIRDLE sung very agreeably in the LOVES of *Mars and Venus,* and danced in a Country-Dance, as well as MR. WILKS, though not with so much Art and Foppery, but like a well-bred Gentleman. –Mr. BETTERTON was the most extensive Actor, from *Alexander* to *Sir John Falstaff;* but in that last Character, he wanted the Waggery of ESTCOURT, the Drollery of HARPER, and Sallaciousness of JACK EVANS. –But, then *Estcourt* was too trifling; *Harper* had too much of the *Bartholomew-Fair;* and *Evans* misplac'd his Humour. –Thus, you see what *Flaws* are in *bright Diamonds;* –And I have often wish'd that Mr. *Betterton* would have resign'd the Part of HAMLET to some young Actor, (who might have Personated, though not have Acted, it better) for, when he threw himself at *Ophelia's* Feet, he appear'd a little too grave for a young Student, lately come from the University of *Wirtemberg;* and his *Repartees* seem'd rather as *Apophthegms* from a *sage Philosopher,* than the *sporting Flashes* of a young HAMLET; and no one else could have pleas'd the Town, he was so rooted in their Opinion. His younger Contemporary (*Betterton* 63, *Powell* 40 Years old), POWELL attempted several of *Betterton's* Parts, as *Alexander, Jaffeir, &c,* but lost his Credit; as, in *Alexander,* he maintain'd not the Dignity of a King, but Out-Heroded HEROD; and in his poison'd mad Scene, *outrav'd all Probability;* while *Betterton* kept his Passion under, and shew'd it most (as Fame smoaks most, when stifled). *Betterton,* from the Time he was dress'd to the End of the Play, kept his Mind in the same Temperament and Adaptness, as the present Character required.

plays of this period—*Tartuffe* or *The Rover*—are given a contemporary setting, and concern themselves with relatively familiar characters, their language and characterization tends to be quite formal. Molière, for example, writes in a rich and fluid verse, even for the part of Tartuffe; Behn's cavaliers speak in prose, but their language is nonetheless dynamic and rhetorically complex. For modern actors, the elegance of this language often provides a point of entry to these characters, a way of seizing on the carefully discriminated social hierarchies at work in the cultures of these plays. Indeed, this verbal formality often becomes a kind of keynote to other aspects of performance as well, leading to a certain stateliness of physical movement and gesture, and an elegant balance of design elements as well. And yet in part because they are part of a classical repertoire, these plays have also inspired experiment and adaptation, a challenge to directors, designers, and actors to make it new.

PEDRO CALDERÓN DE LA BARCA

Like many of his contemporaries, Pedro Calderón de la Barca (1600–1681) was a prolific playwright; he is thought to have written more than 200 plays, of which about 100 survive. Calderón was born in Madrid on January 17, 1600, the son of a minor court official. He was educated at a Jesuit "college," or preparatory school, before attending the University of Alcalá de Henares and the University of Salamanca. In 1620 he entered and won a poetry competition in honor of St. Isidore, which brought his writing to the attention of Lope de Vega, one of the judges of the contest. His first play, *Love, Honor, and Power,* was performed at court in 1623, but Calderón—who served intermittently in the military in the early 1620s—did not become established as a playwright until some time after 1626, when his plays were popular both at court and in the public theaters. With the death of Lope in 1635, Calderón became the most important playwright in Spain; he was knighted by Philip IV and became the principal court playwright in 1636.

Many of Calderón's plays in this period are either *capa y espada* plays, like *The Phantom Lady* (1629), or "love and honor" plays. *El alcalde de Zalamea* (*The Mayor of Zalamea,* 1642) is typical of the "love and honor" genre. In the play, a peasant's daughter is raped by a soldier; through a series of coincidents, the peasant becomes the mayor just as the soldier is apprehended, and he is torn between his desire for revenge, his obligation to enforce the process of law, and Christian charity. Calderón's most important play, *La vida es sueño* (*Life Is a Dream*) was produced in 1636. Throughout his career, Calderón also wrote *autos sacramentales,* but these became more significant later in his life. Calderón's mistress died in 1648, and Calderón entered the priesthood in 1651, possibly in grief over her loss; he also adopted and raised her child, who may have been his natural son. He was appointed priest of a Toledo parish, but the bishop objected to his playwriting, and Calderón devoted himself to *autos* thereafter; his *autos* were so popular that between 1647 and 1681 the only *autos* performed in Madrid were by Calderón. Calderón was made chaplain to the king in 1663 and died in retirement in 1681.

LIFE IS A DREAM

Life Is a Dream typifies the concerns of Calderón's mature drama: It is a play that tests the relationship between love and honor and conducts a searching meditation on human nature itself. The play is set in a mythological Poland, ruled by King Basil. Several years before the current action, it was predicted that if Basil's son, Segismund, were to succeed to the throne, he "would be the most outrageous / Of all men, the most cruel of all princes, / And impious of all monarchs, by whose acts / The kingdom would be torn up and divided." Basil, not willing to murder his son to save his country, has had Segismund removed from court and imprisoned in a cave, where he is attended only by the old courtier Clotaldo. This is where Rosaura—a well-born woman, also forsaken by her father—finds Segismund at the opening of the play.

Calderón begins his interrogation of human nature in the characterization of Segismund. Raised like a beast, Segismund is impulsive and untamed; though he opens the play complaining about his life of constant punishment, when he sees Rosaura (disguised as a man) watching him, he seizes and threatens to kill her. Yet when Rosaura kneels to him and begs for mercy, Segismund feels a strange sensation:

> Your voice has softened me, your presence halted me,
> And now, confusingly, I feel respect
> For you.

In the opening of Pedro Calderon de la Barca's *Life Is a Dream,* Rosaura defends herself against Segismund, who is clothed in animal hides.

Living in captivity and isolation, Segismund is a "human monster": his behavior is ruled neither by reason nor by the conventions of polite society. Yet Segismund responds to Rosaura's plea for mercy as though some element of human sympathy were native to him. At the outset of the play, Calderón presents two contrasting views of human nature. In one perspective, human beings—like other animals—are ruled by their passions, which can only be governed by the civilizing force of law and reason; since Segismund has been raised without benefit of culture, he represents humanity in this unadorned state. Yet at the same time, Segismund's innate response to Rosaura suggests a second view of human nature, one in which sympathy, kindness, and morality are not imposed on human nature by education and society, but are somehow innate to humanity itself.

Just as Segismund relents toward Rosaura, Clotaldo suddenly bursts in and arrests her; Basil has decreed that even the existence of his son must remain a secret. But in arresting Rosaura, Clotaldo takes her sword, which he immediately recognizes as the sword he had left "fair Violante" years before: Rosaura—who has traveled to Poland disguised as a man for protection—must be Clotaldo's "son." Clotaldo is now caught in the classic "love-and-honor" bind. His duty to his king requires him to arrest and eventually execute anyone who spies Basil's secret son; yet to honor his bond to the king, he must betray the natural love he should show to his own child.

As the play proceeds, Clotaldo's effort to reclaim his son is paralleled by Basil's guilty desire to restore his own son to society. Basil hits on an experiment: He will put Segismund to sleep and awaken him at court; when he awakens, Segismund will be told that he is now the king. If his behavior is civilized and restrained, then Basil will know that the prophecy was wrong and will acknowledge Segismund as his heir; if his behavior is threatening, he will be sent back to prison. But Basil's plan has one flaw: Having been raised in solitude, Segismund has no understanding of the elaborate conventions of courtly behavior. When he awakens as "king," he is rude to Prince Astolfo, offensively forward to Stella, and murderously impulsive to the servants who try to restrain and control his behavior. His behavior is so outrageous that he is again knocked unconscious and sent back to his prison.

Returned to captivity, Segismund can only understand his sojourn at court as a beautiful dream, a dream that becomes an image for the fleeting and illusory joys of life itself. But this recognition reforms Segismund, enables him to recognize that he can only assume his full humanity by governing his passions. In the play's final moments, Segismund is released from prison by a rebellious mob, who have come to release Segismund in order to overthrow Basil. When Segismund and his army confront Basil, the old king not only assumes that he has lost his kingdom, but that Segismund will kill him, in part to repay Basil for stealing the better part of his life. But Segismund now understands that although Basil's treatment has made him "savage" in his passions—an "inhuman monster"—the only way to regain his humanity is to govern his desire for revenge. So Segismund submits himself to Basil, who recognizes that his son has been reformed and gives him the kingdom: in conquering himself, Segismund wins the throne as well.

Calderón's drama is a deeply philosophical play, and the characters meditate extensively on the nature and meaning of their behavior. But *Life Is a Dream* is in some sense also a political play; its rich examination of "human nature" is conducted from a deeply aristocratic perspective. The only way that Segismund can demonstrate his humanity, after all, is to recognize and accept the conventions of courtly behavior as "natural." It is a sign of Segismund's acceptance of those values that his first act as king is to sentence the soldier who liberated him from prison to a life imprisonment of his own.

LIFE IS A DREAM

Pedro Calderón de la Barca

TRANSLATED BY ROY CAMPBELL

CHARACTERS

BASIL, *King of Poland*
SEGISMUND, *Prince*
ASTOLFO, *Duke of Muscovy*
CLOTALDO, *old man*
CLARION, *a comical servant*
ROSAURA, *a lady*

STELLA, *a princess*
SOLDIERS, GUARDS, MUSICIANS, SERVANTS, RETINUES, WOMEN

The scene is laid in the court of Poland, a nearby fortress, and the open country

ACT ONE

On one side a craggy mountain: on the other a rude tower whose base serves as a prison for SEGISMUND. *The door facing the spectators is open. The action begins at nightfall.*

ROSAURA, *dressed as a man, appears on the rocks climbing down to the plain: behind her comes* CLARION.

ROSAURA: You headlong hippogriff who match the gale
    In rushing to and fro, you lightning-flicker
    Who give no light, you scaleless fish, you bird
    Who have no coloured plumes, you animal
5   Who have no natural instinct, tell me whither
    You lead me stumbling through this labyrinth
    Of naked crags! Stay here upon this peak
    And be a Phaëthon to the brute-creation!
    For I, pathless save only for the track
10   The laws of destiny dictate for me,
    Shall, blind and desperate, descend this height
    Whose furrowed brows are frowning at the sun.
    How rudely, Poland, you receive a stranger
    (Hardly arrived, but to be treated hardly)
15   And write her entry down in blood with thorns.
    My plight attests this well, but after all,
    Where did the wretchèd ever pity find?

CLARION: Say *two* so wretchèd. Don't you leave me out
    When you complain! If we two sallied out
20   From our own country, questing high adventure,
    And after so much madness and misfortune
    Are still two here, and were two when we fell
    Down those rough crags—shall I not be offended
    To share the trouble yet forego the credit?

25 ROSAURA: I did not give you shares in my complaint
    So as not to rob you of the right to sorrow
    Upon your own account. There's such relief
    In venting grief that a philosopher
    Once said that sorrows should not be bemoaned
30   But sought for pleasure.

CLARION: Philosopher?
    I call him a long-bearded, drunken sot
    And would they'd cudgelled him a thousand blows
    To give him something worth his while lamenting!
    But, madam, what should we do, by ourselves,
35   On foot and lost at this late hour of day,
    Here on this desert mountain far away—
    The sun departing after fresh horizons?

ROSAURA: Clarion, how can I answer, being both
    The partner of your plight and your dilemma?

CLARION: Would anyone believe such strange events?   40

ROSAURA: If there my sight is not deceived by fancy,
    In the last timid light that yet remains
    I seem to see a building.

CLARION: Either my hopes
    Are lying or I see the signs myself.

ROSAURA: Between the towering crags, there stands so small   45
    A royal palace that the lynx-eyed sun
    Could scarce perceive it at midday, so rude
    In architecture that it seems but one
    Rock more down-toppled from the sun-kissed crags
    That form the jaggèd crest.   50

CLARION: Let's go closer,
    For we have stared enough: it would be better
    To let the inmates makes us welcome.

ROSAURA: See:
    The door, or, rather, that funereal gap,
    Is yawning wide—whence night itself seems born,
    Flowing out from its black, rugged centre.   55

(A sound of chains is heard.)

CLARION: Heavens! What's that I hear?

ROSAURA: I have become
    A block immovable of ice and fire.

CLARION: Was that a little chain? Why, I'll be hanged
    If that is not the clanking ghost of some
    Past galley-slave—my terror proves it is!   60

SEGISMUND: Oh, miserable me! Unhappy me!

ROSAURA: How sad a cry that is! I fear new trials
    And torments.

CLARION: It's a fearful sound.

ROSAURA: Oh, come,
    My Clarion, let us fly from suffering!

CLARION: I'm in such sorry trim, I've not the spirit   65
    Even to run away.

ROSAURA: And if you had,
    You'd not have seen that door, not known of it.
    When one's in doubt, the common saying goes
    One walks between two lights.

CLARION: I'm the reverse.

70   It's not that way with me.
    ROSAURA: What then disturbs you?
    CLARION: I walk in doubt between two darknesses.
    ROSAURA: Is not that feeble exhalation there
        A light? That pallid star whose fainting tremors,
        Pulsing a doubtful warmth of glimmering rays,
75   Make even darker with its spectral glow
        That gloomy habitation? Yes! because
        By its reflection (though so far away)
        I recognise a prison, grim and sombre,
        The sepulchre of some poor living carcase.
80   And, more to wonder at, a man lies there
        Clothed in the hides of savage beasts, with limbs
        Loaded with fetters, and a single lamp
        For company. So, since we cannot flee,
        Let us stay here and listen to his plaint
85   And what his sorrows are.
    SEGISMUND: Unhappy me!
        Oh, miserable me! You heavens above,
        I try to think what crime I've done against you
        By being born. Although to have been born,
        I know, is an offence, and with just cause
90   I bear the rigours of your punishment:
        Since to be born is man's worst crime. But yet
        I long to know (to clarify my doubts)
        What greater crime, apart from being born,
        Can thus have earned my greater chastisement.
95   Aren't others born like me? And yet they seem
        To boast a freedom that I've never known.
        The bird is born, and in the hues of beauty
        Clothed with its plumes, yet scarce has it become
        A feathered posy—or a flower with wings—
100   When through ethereal halls it cuts its way,
        Refusing the kind shelter of its nest.
        And I, who have more soul than any bird,
        Must have less liberty?
        The beast is born, and with its hide bright-painted,
105   In lovely tints, has scarce become a spangled
        And starry constellation (thanks to the skilful
        Brush of the Painter) than its earthly needs
        Teach it the cruelty to prowl and kill,
        The monster of its labyrinth of flowers.
110   Yet I, with better instincts than a beast,
        Must have less liberty?
        The fish is born, the birth of spawn and slime,
        That does not even live by breathing air.
        No sooner does it feel itself a skiff
115   Of silver scales upon the wave than swiftly
        It roves about in all directions taking
        The measure of immensity as far
        As its cold blood's capacity allows.
        Yet I, with greater freedom of the will,
120   Must have less liberty?
        The brook is born, and like a snake unwinds
        Among the flowers. No sooner, silver serpent,
        Does it break through the blooms than it regales
        And thanks them with its music for their kindness,
125   Which opens to its course the majesty
        Of the wide plain. Yet I, with far more life,
        Must have less liberty?

        This fills me with such passion, I become
        Like the volcano Etna, and could tear
        Pieces of my own heart out of my breast!   130
        What law, justice, or reason can decree
        That man alone should never know the joys
        And be alone excepted from the rights
        God grants a fish, a bird, a beast, a brook?
    ROSAURA: His words have filled me full of fear and pity.   135
    SEGISMUND: Who is it overheard my speech? Clotaldo?
    CLARION: Say "yes!"
    ROSAURA: It's only a poor wretch, alas,
        Who in these cold ravines has overheard
        Your sorrows.
    SEGISMUND: Then I'll kill you

(*Seizes her.*)

        So as to leave no witness of my frailty.   140
        I'll tear you into bits with these strong arms!
    CLARION: I'm deaf. I wasn't able to hear that.
    ROSAURA: If you were human born, it is enough
        That I should kneel to you for you to spare me.
    SEGISMUND: Your voice has softened me, your presence   145
        halted me,
        And now, confusingly, I feel respect
        For you. Who are you? Though here I have learned
        So little of the world, since this grim tower
        Has been my cradle and my sepulchre;
        And though since I was born (if you can say   150
        I really have been born) I've only seen
        This rustic desert where in misery
        I dwell alone, a living skeleton,
        An animated corpse; and though till now,
        I never spoke, save to one man who hears   155
        My griefs and through whose converse I have heard
        News of the earth and of the sky; and though,
        To astound you more, and make you call me
        A human monster, I dwell here, and am
        A man of the wild animals, a beast   160
        Among the race of men; and though in such
        Misfortune, I have studied human laws,
        Instructed by the birds, and learned to measure
        The circles of the gentle stars, you only
        Have curbed my furious rage, amazed my vision,   165
        And filled with wonderment my sense of hearing.
        Each time I look at you, I feel new wonder!
        The more I see of you, the more I long
        To go on seeing more of you. I think
        My eyes are dropsical, to go on drinking   170
        What it is death for them to drink, because
        They go on drinking that which I am dying
        To see and that which, seen, will deal me death.
        Yet let me gaze on you and die, since I
        Am so bewitched I can no longer think   175
        What not seeing you would do to me—the sight
        Itself being fatal! that would be more hard
        Than dying, madness, rage, and fiercest grief:
        It would be life—worst fate of all because
        The gift of life to such a wretchèd man   180
        Would be the gift of death to happiness!

ROSAURA: Astonished as I look, amazed to hear,
    I know not what to say nor what to ask.
    All I can say is that heaven guided me
185   Here to be comforted, if it is comfort
    To see another sadder than oneself.
    They say a sage philosopher of old,
    Being so poor and miserable that he
    Lived on the few plain herbs he could collect,
190   One day exclaimed: "Could any man be poorer
    Or sadder than myself?"—when, turning round,
    He saw the very answer to his words.
    For there another sage philosopher
    Was picking up the scraps he'd thrown away.
195   I lived cursing my fortune in this world
    And asked within me: "Is there any other
    Suffers so hard a fate?" Now out of pity
    You've given me the answer. For within me
    I find upon reflection that my griefs
200   Would be as joys to you and you'd receive them
    To give you pleasure. So if they perchance
    In any measure may afford relief,
    Listen attentively to my misfortune
    And take what is left over for yourself.
205   I am . . .
    CLOTALDO: (*Within.*) Guards of the tower! You sluggards
    Or cowards, you have let two people pass
    Into the prison bounds . . .
    ROSAURA: Here's more confusion!
    SEGISMUND: That is Clotaldo, keeper of my prison.
    Are my misfortunes still not at an end?
210 CLOTALDO: Come. Be alert, and either seize or slay them
    Before they can resist!
    VOICES: (*Within.*)   Treason! Betrayal!
    CLARION: Guards of the tower who let us pass unhindered,
    Since there's a choice, to seize us would be simpler.

(*Enter* CLOTALDO *with* SOLDIERS. *He holds a pistol and they all wear masks.*)

    CLOTALDO: (*Aside to the* SOLDIERS.) Cover your faces, all! It's
    a precaution
215   Imperative that nobody should know us
    While we are here.
    CLARION: What's this? A masquerade?
    CLOTALDO: O you, who ignorantly passed the bounds
    And limits of this region, banned to all—
    Against the king's decree which has forbidden
220   That any should find out the prodigy
    Hidden in these ravines—yield up your weapons
    Or else this pistol, like a snake of metal,
    Will spit the piercing venom of two shots
    With scandalous assault upon the air.
225 SEGISMUND: Tyrannic master, ere you harm these people
    Let my life be the spoil of these sad bonds
    In which (I swear it by Almighty God)
    I'll sooner rend myself with hands and teeth
    Amid these rocks than see them harmed and mourn
230   Their suffering.
    CLOTALDO: Since you know, Segismund,
    That your misfortunes are so huge that, even

Before your birth, you died by heaven's decree,
    And since you know these walls and binding chains
    Are but the brakes and curbs to your proud frenzies,
    What use is it to bluster?   235

(*To the* GUARDS.)

                  Shut the door
    Of this close prison! Hide him in its depths!
SEGISMUND: Ah, heavens, how justly you denied me freedom!
    For like a Titan I would rise against you,
    Pile jasper mountains high on stone foundations
    And climb to burst the windows of the sun!   240
CLOTALDO: Perhaps you suffer so much pain today
    Just to forestall that feat.
ROSAURA: Now that I see
    How angry pride offends you, I'd be foolish
    Not to plead humbly at your feet for life.
    Be moved by me to pity. It would be   245
    Notoriously harsh that neither pride
    Nor humbleness found favour in your eyes!
CLARION: And if neither Humility nor Pride
    Impress you (characters of note who act
    And motivate a thousand mystery plays)   250
    Let me, here, who am neither proud nor humble,
    But merely something halfway in between,
    Plead to you both for shelter and for aid.
CLOTALDO: Ho, there!
SOLDIER: Sir?
CLOTALDO: Take their weapons. Bind their eyes
    So that they cannot see the way they're led.   255
ROSAURA: This is my sword. To nobody but you
    I yield it, since you're, after all, the chief.
    I cannot yield to one of meaner rank.
CLARION: My sword is such that I will freely give it
    To the most mean and wretched.   260

(*To one* SOLDIER.)

                  Take it, you!
ROSAURA: And if I have to die, I'll leave it to you
    In witness of your mercy. It's a pledge
    Of great worth and may justly be esteemed
    For someone's sake who wore it long ago.
CLOTALDO: (*Apart.*) Each moment seems to bring me new   265
    misfortune!
ROSAURA: Because of that, I ask you to preserve
    This sword with care. Since if inconstant Fate
    Consents to the remission of my sentence,
    It has to win me honour. Though I know not
    The secret that it carries, I do know   270
    It has got one—unless I trick myself—
    And prize it just as the sole legacy
    My father left me.
CLOTALDO: Who then was your father?
ROSAURA: I never knew.
CLOTALDO: And why have you come here?
ROSAURA: I came to Poland to avenge a wrong.   275
CLOTALDO: (*Apart.*) Sacred heavens!

(*On taking the sword he becomes very perturbed.*)

What's this? Still worse and worse.
I am perplexed and troubled with more fears.

(*Aloud.*)

Tell me: who gave that sword to you?
ROSAURA: A woman.
CLOTALDO: Her name?
ROSAURA: A secret I am forced to keep.
280 CLOTALDO: What makes you think this sword contains a
                    secret?
        ROSAURA: That she who gave it to me said: "Depart
                To Poland. There with subtlety and art
                Display it so that all the leading people
                And noblemen can see you wearing it,
285   And I know well that there's a lord among them
                Who will both shelter you and grant you favour."
                But, lest he should be dead, she did not name him.
        CLOTALDO: (*Aside.*) Protect me, heavens! What is this I hear?
                I cannot say if real or imagined
290   But here's the sword I gave fair Violante
                In token that, whoever in the future
                Should come from her to me wearing this sword,
                Would find in me a tender father's love.
                Alas, what can I do in such a pass,
295   When he who brings the sword to win my favour
                Brings it to find his own red death instead
                Arriving at my feet condemned already?
                What strange perplexity! How hard a fate!
                What an inconstant fortune to be plagued with!
300   This is my son not only by all signs
                But also by the promptings of my heart,
                Since, seeing him, my heart seems to cry out
                To him, and beat its wings, and, though unable
                To break the locks, behaves as one shut in,
305   Who, hearing noises in the street outside,
                Cranes from the window-ledge. Just so, not knowing
                What's really happening, but hearing sounds,
                My heart runs to my eyes which are its windows
                And out of them flows into bitter tears.
310   Protect me, heaven! What am I to do?
                To take him to the king is certain death.
                To hide him is to break my sacred oath
                And the strong law of homage. From one side
                Love of one's own, and from the other loyalty—
315   Call me to yield. Loyalty to my king
                (Why do I doubt?) comes before life and honour.
                Then live my loyalty, and let him die!
                When I remember, furthermore, he came
                To avenge an injury—a man insulted
320   And unavenged is in disgrace. My son
                Therefore he is not, nor of noble blood.
                But if some danger has mischanced, from which
                No one escapes, since honour is so fragile
                That any act can smash it, and it takes
325   A stain from any breath of air, what more
                Could any nobleman have done than he,
                Who, at the cost of so much risk and danger,
                Comes to avenge his honour? Since he's so brave
                He is my son, and my blood's in his veins.

And so betwixt the one doubt and the other,   330
The most important mean between extremes
Is to go to the king and tell the truth—
That he's my son, to kill, if so he wishes.
Perhaps my loyalty thus will move his mercy
And if I thus can merit a live son   335
I'll help him to avenge his injury.
But if the king prove constant in his rigour
And deal him death, he'll die in ignorance
That I'm his father.

(*Aloud to* ROSAURA *and* CLARION.)

                          Come then, strangers, come!
And do not fear that you have no companions   340
In your misfortunes, since, in equal doubt,
Tossed between life and death, I cannot guess
Which is the greater evil or the less.

A hall at the royal palace, in court

Enter ASTOLFO *and* SOLDIERS *at one side: from the other side*
PRINCESS STELLA *and* [WOMEN]. *Military music and salvos.*

ASTOLFO: To greet your excellent bright beams
        As brilliant as a comet's rays,   345
        The drums and brasses mix their praise
        With those of fountains, birds, and streams.
        With sounds alike, in like amaze,
        Your heavenly face each voice salutes,
        Which puts them in such lively fettle,   350
        The trumpets sound like birds of metal,
        The songbirds play like feathered flutes.
        And thus they greet you, fair señora—
        The salvos, as their queen, the brasses,
        As to Minerva when she passes,   355
        The songbirds to the bright Aurora,
        And all the flowers and leaves and grasses
        As doing homage unto Flora,
        Because you come to cheat the day
        Which now the night has covered o'er—   360
        Aurora in your spruce array,
        Flora in peace, Pallas in war,
        But in my heart the queen of May.
STELLA: If human voice could match with acts
        You would have been unwise to say   365
        Hyperboles that a few facts
        May well refute some other day
        Confounding all this martial fuss
        With which I struggle daringly,
        Since flatteries you proffer thus   370
        Do not accord with what I see.
        Take heed that it's an evil thing
        And worthy of a brute accursed,
        Loud praises with your mouth to sing
        When in your heart you wish the worst.   375
ASTOLFO: Stella, you have been badly misinformed
        If you doubt my good faith. Here let me beg you
        To listen to my plea and hear me out.
        The third Eugtorgius died, the King of Poland.

380   Basil, his heir, had two fair sisters who
    Bore you, my cousin, and myself. I would not
    Tire you with all that happened here. You know
    Clorilene was your mother who enjoys,
    Under a better reign, her starry throne.
385   She was the elder. Lovely Recisunda
    (Whom may God cherish for a thousand years!)
    The younger one, my mother and your aunt,
    Was wed in Muscovy. Now to return:
    Basil has yielded to the feebleness
390   Of age, loves learnèd study more than women,
    Has lost his wife, is childless, will not marry.
    And so it comes that you and I both claim
    The heirdom of the realm. You claim that you
    Were daughter to the elder daughter. I
395   Say that my being born a man, although
    Son of the younger daughter, gives me title
    To be preferred. We've told the king, our uncle,
    Of both of our intentions. And he answered
    That he would judge between our rival claims,
400   For which the time and place appointed was
    Today and here. For the same reason I
    Have left my native Muscovy. With that
    Intent I come—not seeking to wage war
    But so that you might thus wage war on me!
405   May Love, wise god, make true what people say
    (Your "people" is a wise astrologer)
    By settling this through your being chosen queen—
    Queen and my consort, sovereign of my will;
    My uncle crowning you, for greater honour;
410   Your courage conquering, as it deserves;
    My love applauding you, its emperor!
STELLA: To such chivalrous gallantry, my breast
    Cannot hold out. The imperial monarchy
    I wish were mine only to make it yours—
415   Although my love is not quite satisfied
    That you are to be trusted since your speech
    Is somewhat contradicted by that portrait
    You carry in the locket round your neck.
ASTOLFO: I'll give you satisfaction as to that.

(*Drums.*)

420   But these loud instruments will not permit it
    That sound the arrival of the king and council.

(*Enter* KING BASIL *with his following.*)

STELLA: Wise Thales . . .
ASTOLFO: Learned Euclid . . .
STELLA: Among the signs . . .
ASTOLFO: Among the stars . . .
STELLA: Where you preside in power . . .
ASTOLFO: Where you reside . . .
STELLA: And plot their paths . . .
425 ASTOLFO: And trace their fiery trails . . .
STELLA: Describing . . .
ASTOLFO: . . . Measuring and judging them . . .
STELLA: Please read my stars that I, in humble bonds . . .
ASTOLFO: Please read them, so that I in soft embraces . . .
STELLA: May twine as ivy to this tree!

ASTOLFO: May find
    Myself upon my knees before these feet!   430
BASIL: Come and embrace me, niece and nephew. Trust me,
    Since you're both loyal to my loving precepts,
    And come here so affectionately both—
    In nothing shall I leave you cause to cavil,
    And both of you as equals will be treated.   435
    The gravity of what I have to tell
    Oppresses me, and all I ask of you
    Is silence: the event itself will claim
    Your wonderment. So be attentive now,
    Belovèd niece and nephew, illustrious courtiers,   440
    Relatives, friends, and subjects! You all know
    That for my learning I have merited
    The surname of The Learnèd, since the brush
    Of great Timanthes, and Lisippus' marbles—
    Stemming oblivion (consequence of time)—   445
    Proclaimed me to mankind Basil the Great.
    You know the science that I most affect
    And most esteem is subtle mathematics
    (By which I forestall time, cheat fame itself)
    Whose office is to show things gradually.   450
    For when I look my tables up and see,
    Present before me, all the news and actions
    Of centuries to come, I gain on Time—
    Since Time recounts whatever I have said
    After I say it. Those snowflaking haloes,   455
    Those canopies of crystal spread on high,
    Lit by the sun, cut by the circling moon,
    Those diamond orbs, those globes of radiant crystal
    Which the bright stars adorn, on which the signs
    Parade in blazing excellence, have been   460
    My chiefest study all through my long years.
    They are the volumes on whose adamantine
    Pages, bound up in sapphire, heaven writes,
    In lines of burnished gold and vivid letters,
    All that is due to happen, whether adverse   465
    Or else benign. I read them in a flash,
    So quickly that my spirit tracks their movements—
    Whatever road they take, whatever goal
    They aim at. Would to heaven that before
    My genius had been the commentary   470
    Writ in their margins, or the index to
    Their pages, that my life had been the rubble,
    The ruin, and destruction of their wrath,
    And that my tragedy in them had ended,
    Because, to the unlucky, even their merit   475
    Is like a hostile knife, and he whom knowledge
    Injures is but a murderer to himself.
    And this I say myself, though my misfortunes
    Say it far better, which, to marvel at,
    I beg once more for silence from you all.   480
    With my late wife, the queen, I had a son,
    Unhappy son, to greet whose birth the heavens
    Wore themselves out in prodigies and portents.
    Ere the sun's light brought him live burial
    Out of the womb (for birth resembles death)   485
    His mother many times, in the delirium
    And fancies of her sleep, saw a fierce monster
    Bursting her entrails in a human form,

490 Born spattered with her lifeblood, dealing death,
     The human viper of this century!
     The day came for his birth, and every presage
     Was then fulfilled, for tardily or never
     Do the more cruel ones prove false. At birth
     His horoscope was such that the bright sun,
495 Stained in its blood, entered ferociously
     Into a duel with the moon above.
     The whole earth seemed a rampart for the strife
     Of heaven's two lights, who—though not hand-to-hand—
     Fought light-to-light to gain the mastery!
500 The worst eclipse the sun has ever suffered
     Since Christ's own death horrified earth and sky.
     The whole earth overflowed with conflagrations
     So that it seemed the final paroxysm
     Of existence. The skies grew dark. Buildings shook.
505 The clouds rained stones. The rivers ran with blood.
     In this delirious frenzy of the sun,
     Thus, Segismund was born into the world,
     Giving a foretaste of his character
     By killing his own mother, seeming to speak thus
510 By his ferocity: "I am a man,
     Because I have begun now to repay
     All kindnesses with evil." To my studies
     I went forthwith, and saw in all I studied
     That Segismund would be the most outrageous
515 Of all men, the most cruel of all princes,
     And impious of all monarchs, by whose acts
     The kingdom would be torn up and divided
     So as to be a school of treachery
     And an academy of vices. He,
520 Risen in fury, amidst crimes and horrors,
     Was born to trample me (with shame I say it)
     And make of my grey hairs his very carpet.
     Who is there but believes an evil Fate?
     And more if he discovers it himself,
525 For self-love lends its credit to our studies.
     So I, believing in the Fates, and in
     The havoc that their prophecies predestined,
     Determined to cage up this newborn tiger
     To see if on the stars we sages have
530 Some power. I gave out that the prince had died
     Stillborn, and, well-forewarned, I built a tower
     Amidst the cliffs and boulders of yon mountains
     Over whose tops the light scarce finds its way,
     So stubbornly their obelisks and crags
535 Defend the entry to them. The strict laws
     And edicts that I published then (declaring
     That nobody might enter the forbidden
     Part of the range) were passed on that account.
     There Segismund lives to this day, a captive,
540 Poor and in misery, where, save Clotaldo,
     His guardian, none have seen or talked to him.
     The latter has instructed him in all
     Branches of knowledge and in the Catholic faith,
     Alone the witness of his misery.
545 There are three things to be considered now:
     Firstly, Poland, that I love you greatly,
     So much that I would free you from the oppression
     And servitude of such a tyrant king.

     He would not be a kindly ruler who
     Would put his realm and homeland in such danger.   550
     The second fact that I must bear in mind
     Is this: that to deny my flesh and blood
     The rights which law, both human and divine,
     Concedes, would not accord with Christian charity,
     For no law says that, to prevent another   555
     Being a tyrant, I may be one myself,
     And if my son's a tyrant, to prevent him
     From doing outrage, I myself should do it.
     Now here's the third and last point I would speak of,
     Namely, how great an error it has been   560
     To give too much belief to things predicted,
     Because, even if his inclination should
     Dictate some headlong, rash precipitancies,
     They may perhaps not conquer him entirely,
     For the most accursèd destiny, the most   565
     Violent inclination, the most impious
     Planet—all can but influence, not force,
     The free will which man holds direct from God.
     And so, between one motive and another
     Vacillating discursively, I hit   570
     On a solution that will stun you all.
     I shall tomorrow, but without his knowing
     He is my son—your king—place Segismund
     (For that's the name with which he was baptised)
     Here on my throne, beneath my canopy,   575
     Yes, in my very place, that he may govern you
     And take command. And you must all be here
     To swear him fealty as his loyal subjects.
     Three things may follow from this test, and these
     I'll set against the three which I proposed.   580
     The first is that should the prince prove prudent,
     Stable, and benign—thus giving the lie
     To all that prophecy reports of him—
     Then you'll enjoy in him your rightful ruler
     Who was so long a courtier of the mountains   585
     And neighbour to the beasts. Here is the second:
     If he prove proud, rash, cruel, and outrageous,
     And with a loosened rein gallop unheeding
     Across the plains of vice, I shall have done
     My duty, and fulfilled my obligation   590
     Of mercy. If I then re-imprison him,
     That's incontestably a kingly deed—
     Not cruelty but merited chastisement.
     The third thing's this: that if the prince should be
     As I've described him, then—by the love I feel   595
     For you, my vassals—I shall give you worthier
     Rulers to wear the sceptre and the crown;
     Because your king and queen will be my nephew
     And niece, each with an equal right to rule,
     Each gaining the inheritance he merits,   600
     And joined in faith of holy matrimony.
     This I command you as a king, I ask you
     As a kind father, as a sage I pray you,
     As an experienced old man I tell you,
     And (if it's true, as Spanish Seneca   605
     Says, that the king is slave unto his nation)
     This, as a humble slave, I beg of you.
ASTOLFO: If it behoves me to reply (being

The person most involved in this affair)
610   Then, in the name of all, let Segismund
Appear! It is enough that he's your son!
ALL: Give us our prince: we want him for our king!
BASIL: Subjects, I thank you for your kindly favour.
Accompany these, my two Atlases,
615   Back to their rooms. Tomorrow you shall see him.
ALL: Long live the great King Basil! Long live Basil!

(*Exeunt all, accompanying* STELLA *and* ASTOLFO. *The king remains.*)

(*Enter* CLOTALDO *with* ROSAURA *and* CLARION.)

CLOTALDO: May I have leave to speak, sire?
BASIL: Oh, Clotaldo!
You're very welcome.
CLOTALDO: Thus to kneel before you
Is always welcome, sire—yet not today
620   When sad and evil Fate destroys the joy
Your presence normally concedes.
BASIL: What's wrong?
CLOTALDO: A great misfortune, sire, has come upon me
Just when I should have met it with rejoicing.
BASIL: Continue.
CLOTALDO: Sire, this beautiful young man
625   Who inadvertently and daringly
Came to the tower, wherein he saw the prince,
Is my . . .
BASIL: Do not afflict yourself, Clotaldo.
Had it not been just now, I should have minded,
I must confess. But I've revealed the secret,
630   And now it does not matter if he knows it.
Attend me afterwards. I've many things
To tell you. You in turn have many things
To do for me. You'll be my minister,
I warn you, in the most momentous action
635   The world has ever seen. These prisoners, lest you
Should think I blame your oversight, I'll pardon.

(*Exit.*)

CLOTALDO: Long may you live, great sire! A thousand years!

(*Aside.*)

Heaven improves our fates. I shall not tell him
Now that he is my son, since it's not needed
640   Till he's avenged.

(*Aloud.*)

Strangers, you may go free.
ROSAURA: Humbly I kiss your feet.
CLARION: Whilst I'll just *miss* them—
Old friends will hardly quibble at one letter.
ROSAURA: You've granted me my life, sir. I remain
645   Your servant and eternally your debtor.
CLOTALDO: No! It was not your life I gave you. No!
Since any wellborn man who, unavenged,
Nurses an insult does not live at all.
And seeing you have told me that you came

For that sole reason, it was not life I spared—   650
Life in disgrace is not a life at all.

(*Aside.*)

I see this spurs him.
ROSAURA: Freely I confess it—
Although you spared my life, it was no life.
But I will wipe my honour's stain so spotless
That after I have vanquished all my dangers   655
Life well may seem a shining gift from you.
CLOTALDO: Take here your burnished steel: 'twill be enough,
Bathed in your enemies' red blood, to right you.
For steel that once was mine (I mean of course
Just for the time I've had it in my keeping)   660
Should know how to avenge you.
ROSAURA: Now, in your name I gird it on once more
And on it I will swear to take revenge
Although my foe were even mightier.
CLOTALDO: Is he so powerful?   665
ROSAURA: So much so that . . .
Although I have no doubt in your discretion . . .
I say no more because I'd not estrange
Your clemency.
CLOTALDO: You would have won me had you told me, since
That would prevent me helping him.   670

(*Aside.*)

If only I could discover who he is!
ROSAURA: So that you'll not think that I value lightly
Such confidence, know that my adversary
Is no less than Astolfo, Duke of Muscovy.
CLOTALDO: (*Aside.*) (I hardly can withstand the grief it   675
gives me
For it is worse than aught I could imagine!
Let us inquire of him some further facts.)

(*Aloud.*)

If you were born a Muscovite, your ruler
Could never have affronted you. Go back
Home to your country. Leave this headstrong valour.   680
It will destroy you.
ROSAURA: Though he's been my prince,
I know that he has done me an affront.
CLOTALDO: Even though he slapped your face, that's no
affront.

(*Aside.*)

O heavens!
ROSAURA: My insult was far deeper!
CLOTALDO: Tell it:
Since nothing I imagine could be deeper.   685
ROSAURA: Yes. I will tell it, yet, I know not why,
With such respect I look upon your face,
I venerate you with such true affection,
With such high estimation do I weigh you,
That I scarce dare to tell you—these men's clothes   690
Are an enigma, not what they appear.
So now you know. Judge if it's no affront

695   That here Astolfo comes to wed with Stella
        Although betrothed to me. I've said enough.

(*Exeunt* ROSAURA *and* CLARION.)

CLOTALDO: Here! Listen! Wait! What mazed confusion!
        It is a labyrinth wherein the reason
        Can find no clue. My family honour's injured.
        The enemy's all powerful. I'm a vassal
        And she's a woman. Heavens! Show a path
700   Although I don't believe there is a way!
        There's nought but evil bodings in the sky.
        The whole world is a prodigy, say I.

ACT TWO

A hall in the royal palace.

Enter BASIL *and* CLOTALDO.

CLOTALDO: All has been done according to your orders.
BASIL: Tell me, Clotaldo, how it went?
CLOTALDO: Why, thus:
        I took to Segismund a calming drug
        Wherein are mixed herbs of especial virtue,
5   Tyrannous in their overpowering strength
        Which seize and steal and alienate man's gift
        Of reasoning, thus making a live corpse
        Of him. His violence evaporated
        With all his faculties and senses too.
10   There is no need to prove it's possible
        Because experience teaches us that medicine
        Is full of natural secrets, that there is no
        Animal, plant, or stone that has not got
        Appointed properties. If human malice
15   Explores a thousand poisons which deal death,
        Who then can doubt, that being so, that other
        Poisons, less violent, cause only sleep?
        But (leaving that doubt aside, as proven false
        By every evidence) hear then the sequel:
20   I went down into Segismund's close prison
        Bearing the drink wherein, with opium,
        Henbane and poppies had been mixed. With him
        I talked a little while of the humanities,
        In which dumb Nature has instructed him,
25   The mountains and the heavens and the stars,
        In whose divine academies he learned
        Rhetoric from the birds and the wild creatures.
        To lift his spirit to the enterprise
        Which you require of him, I chose for subject
30   The swiftness of a stalwart eagle, who,
        Deriding the base region of the wind,
        Rises into the sphere reserved for fire,
        A feathered lightning, an untethered comet.
        Then I extolled such lofty flight and said:
35   "After all, he's the king of birds, and so
        Takes precedence, by right, over the rest."
        No more was needful for, in taking up
        Majesty for his subject, he discoursed
        With pride and high ambition, as his blood

40   Naturally moves, incites, and spurs him on
        To grand and lofty things, and so he said
        That in the restless kingdom of the birds
        There should be those who swear obedience, too!
        "In this, my miseries console me greatly,
45   Because if I'm a vassal here, it's only
        By force, and not by choice. Of my own will
        I would not yield in rank to any man."
        Seeing that he grew furious—since this touched
        The theme of his own griefs—I gave the potion
50   And scarcely had it passed from cup to breast
        Before he yielded all his strength to slumber.
        A chill sweat ran through all his limbs and veins.
        Had I not known that this was mere feigned death
        I would have thought him dead. Then came the men
55   To whom you've trusted this experiment,
        Who placed him in a coach and brought him here
        To your own rooms, where all things were prepared
        In royalty and grandeur as befitting
        His person. In your own bed they have laid him
60   Where, when the torpor wanes, they'll do him service
        As if he were Your Majesty himself.
        All has been done as you have ordered it,
        And if I have obeyed you well, my lord,
        I'd beg a favour (pardon me this freedom)—
65   To know what your intention is in thus
        Transporting Segismund here to the palace.
BASIL: Your curiosity is just, Clotaldo,
        And yours alone I'll satisfy. The star
        Which governs Segismund, my son, in life,
70   Threatens a thousand tragedies and woes.
        And now I wish to see whether the stars
        (Which never lie—and having shown to us
        So many cruel signs seem yet more certain)
        May yet be brought to moderate their sentence,
75   Whether by prudence charmed or valour won,
        For man does have the power to rule his stars.
        I would examine this, bringing him here
        Where he may know he is my son, and make
        Trial of his talent. If magnanimously
80   He conquers and controls himself, he'll reign,
        But if he proves a tyrant and is cruel,
        Back to his chains he'll go. Now, you will ask,
        Why did we bring him sleeping in this manner
        For the experiment? I'll satisfy you,
85   Down to the smallest detail, with my answer.
        If he knows that he is my son today,
        And if tomorrow he should find himself
        Once more reduced to prison, to misery,
        He would despair entirely, knowing truly
90   Who, and whose son, he is. What consolation
        Could he derive, then, from his lot? So I
        Contrive to leave an exit for such grief,
        By making him believe it was a dream.
        By these means we may learn two things at once:
95   First, his character—for he will really be
        Awake in all he thinks and all his actions;
        Second, his consolation—which would be
        (If he should wake in prison on the morrow,
        Although he saw himself obeyed today)
100   That he might understand he had been dreaming,

And he will not be wrong, for in this world,
Clotaldo, all who live are only dreaming.
CLOTALDO: I've proofs enough to doubt of your success,
But now it is too late to remedy it.
105 From what I can make out, I think he's awakened
And that he's coming this way, by the sound.
BASIL: I shall withdraw. You, as his tutor, go
And guide him through his new bewilderments
By answering his queries with the truth.
110 CLOTALDO: You give me leave to tell the truth of it?
BASIL: Yes, because knowing all things, he may find
Known perils are the easiest to conquer.

(*Exit* BASIL. *Enter* CLARION.)

CLARION: It cost me four whacks to get here so quickly.
I caught them from a red-haired halberdier
115 Sprouting a ginger beard over his livery,
And I've come to see what's going on.
No windows give a better view than those
A man brings with him in his head, not asking
For tickets of admission or paid seats,
120 Since at all functions, festivals, or feasts
He looks out with the same nice self-composure.
CLOTALDO: (*Aside.*) Here's Clarion who's the servant of that
person—
That trader in woes, importer from Poland
Of my disgrace.

(*Aloud.*)

Come, Clarion, what news?
125 CLARION: Item the first: encouraged by the fact
Your clemency's disposed to venge her insult,
Rosaura has resumed her proper clothing.
CLOTALDO: That's right: it's less indecorous and bold.
CLARION: Item: she's changed her name, and given out
130 That she's your niece. And now they've made so much
Of her that she's been raised to maid of honour
To the unique and only princess, Stella.
CLOTALDO: That's right: her honour stands to my account.
CLARION: Indeed she merely bides the time till you
135 Will settle all accounts about her honour.
CLOTALDO: Biding the time is wise, for in the end
It's Time that's going to settle all accounts!
CLARION: Item: that she's attended like a queen,
Because they take her for your niece. Item:
140 That I, who trudged along with her, am dying
Of hunger. Nobody remembers me,
Nor yet remembers that I'm like my name
And (should I sound my Clarion) could tell
All to the king and Stella and Astolfo.
145 For I am both a Clarion and a servant—
Two things which ill-accord with secrecy.
If silence should, by chance, let slip my hand,
Then there's a chorus which would fit me well:
"Dawn-breaking Clarion plays no better tune!"
150 CLOTALDO: You've reason for complaint. I'll satisfy it
If you'll but serve me . . .
CLARION: Hush, here's Segismund!

(*Enter* MUSICIANS, *singing, and* SERVANTS *arraying* SEGISMUND,
who seems amazed.)

SEGISMUND: Heavens above! What's this that I am seeing?
I wonder at it all, with naught of fear!
But with a mighty doubt, I disbelieve it!
I?—in a sumptuous palace? I—encircled   155
With rich brocades and silks? I—overwhelmed
With servants in such brilliant liveries?
I—to awake in such a gorgeous bed?
I—in the middle of so many footmen
Who clothe me in rich garments? I'm awake: 160
It would be false to take this for a dream.
Am I not Segismund? Heavens! disabuse me
If I'm mistaken. Say, what could have happened
In my imagination while I slept—
That I should find myself in such a place?   165
But why should I worry, whatever it was?
I'll let myself be served and entertained—
Befall what may.
FIRST SERVANT: (*Aside to* SECOND SERVANT *and* CLARION.)
                He's very melancholy!
SECOND SERVANT: Who would not be, considering all that's
happened
To him?   170
CLARION: I would not be!
SECOND SERVANT: You, speak to him.
FIRST SERVANT: Shall they begin to sing again?
SEGISMUND: Why, no,
I would not have them sing.
SECOND SERVANT: You're so distraught,
I wish you entertained.
SEGISMUND: My griefs are such
That no mere voices can amuse me now—
Only the martial music pleased my mind.   175
CLOTALDO: Your Highness, mighty prince, give me your hand
To kiss. I'm glad to be the first to offer
Obedience at your feet.
SEGISMUND: (*Aside.*)   This is Clotaldo.
How is it he, that tyrannised my thralldom,
Should now be treating me with such respect?   180

(*Aloud.*)

Tell me what's happening all round me here.
CLOTALDO: With the perplexities of your new state,
Your reason will encounter many doubts,
But I shall try to free you from them all
(If that may be) because you now must know   185
You are hereditary Prince of Poland.
If you have been withdrawn from public sight
Under restraint, it was in strict obedience
To Fate's inclemency, which will permit
A thousand woes to fall upon this empire   190
The moment that you wear the sovereign's crown.
But trusting that you'll prudently defeat
Your own malignant stars (since they can be
Controlled by magnanimity) you've been
Brought to this palace from the tower you knew   195
Even while your soul was yielded up to sleep.
My lord the king, your father, will be coming
To see you, and from him you'll learn the rest.
SEGISMUND: Then, vile, infamous traitor, what have I
To know more than this fact of who I am,   200
To show my pride and power from this day onward?

How have you played your country such a treason
As to deny me, against law and right,
The rank which is my own?
CLOTALDO: Unhappy me!
205 SEGISMUND: You were a traitor to the law, a flattering liar
To your own king, and cruel to myself.
And so the king, the law, and I condemn you,
After such fierce misfortunes as I've borne,
To die here by my hands.
SECOND SERVANT: My lord!
SEGISMUND: Let none
210 Get in the way. It is in vain. By God!
If you intrude, I'll throw you through the window.
SECOND SERVANT: Clotaldo, fly!
CLOTALDO: Alas, poor Segismund!
That you should show such pride, all unaware
That you are dreaming this.

(*Exit.*)

SECOND SERVANT: Take care! Take care!
215 SEGISMUND: Get out!
SECOND SERVANT: He was obeying the king's orders.
SEGISMUND: In an injustice, no one should obey
The king, and I'm his prince.
SECOND SERVANT: He had no right
To look into the rights and wrongs of it.
SEGISMUND: You must be mad to answer back at me.
220 CLARION: The prince is right. It's you who're in the
wrong!
SECOND SERVANT: Who gave you right to speak?
CLARION: I simply took it.
SEGISMUND: And who are you?
CLARION: I am the go-between,
And in this art I think I am a master—
Since I'm the greatest jackanapes alive.
225 SEGISMUND: (*To* CLARION.) In all this new world, you're the
only one
Of the whole crowd who pleases me.
CLARION: Why, my lord,
I am the best pleaser of Segismunds
That ever was: ask anybody here!

(*Enter* ASTOLFO.)

ASTOLFO: Blessèd the day, a thousand times, my prince,
230 On which you landed here on Polish soil
To fill with so much splendour and delight
Our wide horizons, like the break of day!
For you arise as does the rising sun
Out of the rugged mountains, far away.
235 Shine forth then! And although so tardily
You bind the glittering laurels on your brows,
The longer may they last you still unwithered.
SEGISMUND: God save you.
ASTOLFO: That you do not know me, sir,
Is some excuse for greeting me without
240 The honour due to me. I am Astolfo
The Duke of Muscovy. You are my cousin.
We are of equal rank.
SEGISMUND: Then if I say,
"God save you," do I not display good feeling?

But since you take such note of who you are,
The next time that I see you, I shall say   245
"God save you *not*," if you would like that better.
SECOND SERVANT: (*To* ASTOLFO.) Your Highness, make
allowance for his breeding
Amongst the mountains. So he deals with all.

(*To* SEGISMUND.)

Astolfo does take precedence, Your Highness—
SEGISMUND: I have no patience with the way he came   250
To make his solemn speech, then put his hat on!
SECOND SERVANT: He's a grandee!
SEGISMUND: I'm grander than grandees!
SECOND SERVANT: For all that, there should be respect
between you,
More than among the rest.
SEGISMUND: And who told you
To mix in my affairs?   255

(*Enter* STELLA.)

STELLA: Many times welcome to Your Royal Highness,
Now come to grace the dais that receives him
With gratitude and love. Long may you live
August and eminent, despite all snares,
And count your life by centuries, not years!   260
SEGISMUND: (*Aside to* CLARION.) Now tell me, who's this
sovereign deity
At whose divinest feet Heaven lays down
The fleece of its aurora in the east?
CLARION: Sir, it's your cousin Stella.
SEGISMUND: She were better
Named "sun" than "star"!   265

(*To* STELLA.)

                               Though your speech was fair,
Just to have seen you and been conquered by you
Suffices for a welcome in itself.
To find myself so blessed beyond my merit
What can I do but thank you, lovely Stella,
For you could add more brilliance and delight   270
To the most blazing star? When you get up
What work is left the sun to do? O give me
Your hand to kiss, from out whose cup of snow
The solar horses drink the fires of day!
STELLA: Be a more gentle courtier.   275
ASTOLFO: I am lost.
SECOND SERVANT: I know Astolfo's hurt. I must divert him.

(*To* SEGISMUND.)

Sir, you should know that thus to woo so boldly
Is most improper. And, besides, Astolfo . . .
SEGISMUND: Did I not tell you not to meddle with me?
SECOND SERVANT: I only say what's just.   280
SEGISMUND: All this annoys me.
Nothing seems just to me but what I want.
SECOND SERVANT: Why, sir, I heard you say that no obedience
Or service should be lent to what's unjust.
SEGISMUND: You also heard me say that I would throw
Anyone who annoys me from that balcony.   285

SECOND SERVANT: With men like me you cannot do such
    things.
SEGISMUND: No? Well, by God, I'll have to prove it then!

(*He takes him in his arms and rushes out, followed by many, to return soon after.*)

ASTOLFO: What on earth have I seen? Can it be true?
STELLA: Go, all, and stop him!
SEGISMUND: (*Returning.*)   From the balcony
290   He's fallen in the sea. How strange it seems!
ASTOLFO: Measure your acts of violence, my lord:
    From crags to palaces, the distance is
    As great as that between man and the beasts.
SEGISMUND: Well, since you are for speaking out so boldly,
295   Perhaps one day you'll find that on your shoulders
    You have no head to place your hat upon.

(*Exit* ASTOLFO. *Enter* BASIL.)

BASIL: What's happened here?
SEGISMUND: Nothing at all. A man
    Wearied me, so I threw him in the sea.
CLARION: (*To* SEGISMUND.) Be warned. That is the king.
BASIL: On the first day,
300   So soon, your coming here has cost a life?
SEGISMUND: He said I couldn't: so I won the bet.
BASIL: It grieves me, Prince, that, when I hoped to see you
    Forewarned, and overriding Fate, in triumph
    Over your stars, the first thing I should see
305   Should be such rigour—that your first deed here
    Should be a grievous homicide. Alas!
    With what love, now, can I offer my arms,
    Knowing your own have learned to kill already?
    Who sees a dirk, red from a mortal wound,
310   But does not fear it? Who can see the place
    Soaking in blood, where late a man was murdered,
    But even the strongest must respond to nature?
    So in your arms seeing the instrument
    Of death, and looking on a blood-soaked place,
315   I must withdraw myself from your embrace,
    And though I thought in loving bonds to bind
    Your neck, yet fear withholds me from your arms.
SEGISMUND: Without your loving arms I can sustain
    Myself as usual. That such a loving father
320   Could treat me with such cruelty, could thrust me
    From his side ungratefully, could rear me
    As a wild beast, could hold me for a monster,
    And pray that I were dead, that such a father
    Withholds his arms from winding round my neck,
325   Seems unimportant, seeing that he deprives
    Me of my very being as a man.
BASIL: Would to heaven I had never granted it,
    For then I never would have heard your voice,
    Nor seen your outrages.
SEGISMUND: Had you denied
330   Me being, then I would not have complained,
    But that you took it from me when you gave it—
    That is my quarrel with you. Though to give
    Is the most singular and noble action,
    It is the basest action if one gives

Only to take away.   335
BASIL: How well you thank me
    For being raised from pauper to a prince!
SEGISMUND: In this what is there I should thank you for?
    You tyrant of my will! If you are old
    And feeble, and you die, what can you give me
    More than what is my own by right of birth?   340
    You are my father and my king, therefore
    This grandeur comes to me by natural law.
    Therefore, despite my present state, I'm not
    Indebted to you, rather can I claim
    Account of all those years in which you robbed me   345
    Of life and being, liberty, and honour.
    You ought to thank me that I press no claim
    Since you're my debtor, even to bankruptcy.
BASIL: Barbarous and outrageous brute! The heavens
    Have now fulfilled their prophecy: I call   350
    Them to bear witness to your pride. Although
    You know now, disillusioned, who you are,
    And see yourself where you take precedence,
    Take heed of this I say: be kind and humble
    Since it may be that you are only dreaming,   355
    Although it seems to you you're wide-awake.

(*Exit* BASIL.)

SEGISMUND: Can I perhaps be dreaming, though I seem
    So wide-awake? No: I am not asleep,
    Since I can touch, and realise what I
    Have been before, and what I am today.   360
    And if you even now relented, Father,
    There'd be no cure since I know who I am
    And you cannot, for all your sighs and groans,
    Cheat me of my hereditary crown.
    And if I was submissive in my chains   365
    Before, then I was ignorant of what I am,
    Which I now know (and likewise know that I
    Am partly man but partly beast as well).

(*Enter* ROSAURA *in woman's clothing.*)

ROSAURA: (*Aside.*) I came in Stella's train. I am afraid
    Of meeting with Astolfo, since Clotaldo   370
    Says he must not know who I am, not see me,
    Because (he says) it touches on my honour.
    And well I trust Clotaldo since I owe him
    The safety of my life and honour both.
CLARION: What pleases you, and what do you admire   375
    Most, of the things you've seen here in the world?
SEGISMUND: Why, nothing that I could not have foreseen—
    Except the loveliness of women! Once,
    I read among the books I had out there
    That who owes God most grateful contemplation   380
    Is Man: who is himself a tiny world.
    But I think who owes God more grateful study
    Is Woman—since she is a tiny heaven,
    Having as much more beauty than a man
    As heaven than earth. And even more, I say,   385
    If she's the one that I am looking at.
ROSAURA: (*Aside.*) That is the prince. I'll go.
SEGISMUND: Stop! Woman! Wait!

Don't join the sunset with the breaking day
By fading out so fast. If east and west
390   Should clash like that, the day would surely suffer
A syncope. But what is this I see?
ROSAURA: What I am looking at I doubt, and yet
    Believe.
SEGISMUND: (*Aside.*) This beauty I have seen before.
ROSAURA: (*Aside.*) This pomp and grandeur I have seen before
395   Cooped in a narrow dungeon.
SEGISMUND: (*Aside.*)   I have found
    My life at last.

(*Aloud.*)

        Woman (for that sole word
Outsoars all wooing flattery of speech
From one that is a man), woman, who are you?
If even long before I ever saw you
400   You owed me adoration as your prince,
How much the more should you be conquered by me
Now I recall I've seen you once before!
Who are you, beauteous woman?
ROSAURA: (*Aside.*)   I'll pretend.

(*Aloud.*)

    In Stella's train, I am a luckless lady.
405 SEGISMUND: Say no such thing. You are the sun from which
The minor star that's Stella draws its life,
Since she receives the splendour of your rays.
I've seen how in the kingdom of sweet odours,
Commander of the squadrons of the flowers,
410   The rose's deity presides, and is
Their empress by divine right of her beauty.
Among the precious stones which can be listed
In the academy of mines, I've seen
The diamond much preferred above the rest,
415   And crowned their emperor, for shining brightest.
In the revolving empire of the stars
The morning star takes pride among the others.
In their perfected spheres, when the sun calls
The planets to his council, he presides
420   And is the very oracle of day.
Then if among stars, gems, planet, and flowers
The fairest are exalted, why do you
Wait on a lesser beauty than yourself
Who are, in greater excellence and beauty,
425   The sun, the morning star, the diamond, and the rose!

(*Enter* CLOTALDO, *who remains by the stage-curtain.*)

CLOTALDO: (*Aside.*) I wish to curb him, since I brought
    him up.
    But, what is this?
ROSAURA: I reverence your favour,
And yet reply, rhetorical, with silence,
For when one's mind is clumsy and untaught,
430   He answers best who does not speak at all.
SEGISMUND: Stay! Do not go! How can you wish to go
And leave me darkened by my doubts?
ROSAURA: Your Highness,

I beg your leave to go.
SEGISMUND: To go so rudely
Is not to beg my leave but just to take it.
ROSAURA: But if you will not grant it, I must take it.   435
SEGISMUND: That were to change my courtesy to rudeness.
Resistance is like venom to my patience.
ROSAURA: But even if this deadly, raging venom
Should overcome your patience, yet you dare not
And could not treat me with dishonour, sir.   440
SEGISMUND: Why, just to see then if I can, and dare to—
You'll make me lose the fear I bear your beauty,
Since the impossible is always tempting
To me. Why, only now I threw a man
Over this balcony who said I couldn't: 445
And so to find out if I can or not
I'll throw your honour through the window too.
CLOTALDO: (*Aside.*) He seems determined in this course.
    Oh, heavens!
What's to be done that for a second time
My honour's threatened by a mad desire?   450
ROSAURA: Then with good reason it was prophesied
Your tyranny would wreak this kingdom
Outrageous scandals, treasons, crimes, and deaths.
But what can such a creature do as you
Who are not even a man, save in the name—   455
Inhuman, barbarous, cruel, and unbending
As the wild beasts amongst whom you were nursed?
SEGISMUND: That you should not insult me in this way
I spoke to you most courteously, and thought
I'd thereby get my way; but if you curse me thus   460
Even when I am speaking gently, why,
By the living God, I'll really give you cause.
Ho there! Clear out, the lot of you, at once!
Leave her to me! Close all the doors upon us.
Let no one enter!   465

(*Exeunt* CLARION *and other* ATTENDANTS.)

ROSAURA: I am lost . . . I warn you . . .
SEGISMUND: I am a tyrant and you plead in vain.
CLOTALDO: (*Aside.*) Oh, what a monstrous thing! I must
    restrain him
    Even if I die for it.

(*Aloud.*)

        Sir! Wait! Look here!
SEGISMUND: A second time you have provoked my anger,
You feeble, mad old man! Do you prize lightly   470
My wrath and rigour that you've gone so far?
CLOTALDO: Brought by the accents of her voice, I came
To tell you you must be more peaceful
If still you hope to reign, and warn you that
You should not be so cruel, though you rule—   475
Since this, perhaps, is nothing but a dream.
SEGISMUND: When you refer to disillusionment
You rouse me near to madness. Now you'll see,
Here as I kill you, if it's truth or dreaming!

(*As he tries to pull out his dagger,* CLOTALDO *restrains him and
throws himself on his knees before him.*)

480 CLOTALDO: It's thus I'd save my life: and hope to do so—
 SEGISMUND: Take your presumptuous hand from off this steel.
 CLOTALDO: Till people come to hold your rage and fury
  I shall not let you go.
 ROSAURA: O heavens!
 SEGISMUND: Loose it,

(They struggle.)

  I say, or else—you interfering fool—
485 I'll crush you to your death in my strong arms!
 ROSAURA: Come quickly! Here's Clotaldo being killed!

(Exit.)

(ASTOLFO appears as CLOTALDO falls on the floor, and the former stands between SEGISMUND and CLOTALDO.)

 ASTOLFO: Why, what is this, most valiant prince? What?
   Staining
  Your doughty steel in such old, frozen blood?
  For shame! For shame! Sheathe your illustrious weapon!
490 SEGISMUND: When it is stained in his infamous blood!
 ASTOLFO: At my feet here he has found sanctuary
  And there he's safe, for it will serve him well.
 SEGISMUND: Then serve me well by dying, for like this
  I will avenge myself for your behaviour
495 In trying to annoy me first of all.
 ASTOLFO: To draw in self-defence offends no king,
  Though in his palace.

(ASTOLFO draws his sword and they fight.)

 CLOTALDO: *(To* ASTOLFO.) Do not anger him!

(Enter BASIL, STELLA, and ATTENDANTS.)

 BASIL: Hold! Hold! What's this? Fighting with naked swords?
 STELLA: *(Aside.)* It is Astolfo! How my heart misgives me!
500 BASIL: Why, what has happened here?
 ASTOLFO: Nothing, my Lord,
  Since you've arrived.

(Both sheathe their swords.)

 SEGISMUND: Much, though you *have* arrived.
  I tried to kill the old man.
 BASIL: Had you no
  Respect for those white hairs?
 CLOTALDO: Sire, since they're only
  Mine, as you well can see, it does not matter!
505 SEGISMUND: It is in vain you'd have me hold white hairs
  In such respect, since one day you may find
  Your own white locks prostrated at my feet
  For still I have not taken vengeance on you
  For the foul way in which you had me reared.

(Exit.)

510 BASIL: Before that happens you will sleep once more
  Where you were reared, and where what's happened may
  Seem just a dream (being mere earthly glory).

(All save ASTOLFO and STELLA leave.)

 ASTOLFO: How seldom does prediction fail, when evil!
  How oft, foretelling good! Exact in harm,
  Doubtful in benefit! Oh, what a great   515
  Astrologer would be one who foretold
  Nothing but harms, since there's no doubt at all
  That they are always due! In Segismund
  And me the case is illustrated clearly.
  In him, crimes, cruelties, deaths, and disasters   520
  Were well predicted, since they all came true.
  But in my own case, to predict for me
  (As I foresaw beholding rays which cast
  The sun into the shade and outface heaven)
  Triumphs and trophies, happiness and praise,   525
  Was false—and yet was true: it's only just
  That when predictions start with promised favours
  They should end in disdain.
 STELLA: I do not doubt
  Your protestations are most heartfelt; only
  They're not for me, but for another lady   530
  Whose portrait you were wearing round your neck
  Slung in a locket when you first arrived.
  Since it is so, she only can deserve
  These wooing flatteries. Let her repay you
  For in affairs of love, flatteries and vows   535
  Made for another are mere forged credentials.

(ROSAURA enters but waits by the curtain.)

 ROSAURA: *(Aside.)* Thanks be to God, my troubles are near
   ended!
  To judge from what I see, I've naught to fear.
 ASTOLFO: I will expel that portrait from my breast
  To make room for the image of your beauty   540
  And keep it there. For there where Stella is
  Can be no room for shade, and where the sun is
  No place for any star. I'll fetch the portrait.

(Aside.)

  Forgive me, beautiful Rosaura, that,
  When absent, men and women seldom keep   545
  More faith than this.

(Exit.)

(ROSAURA comes forward.)

 ROSAURA: *(Aside.)*   I could not hear a word. I was afraid
  That they would see me.
 STELLA: Oh, Astrea!
 ROSAURA: My lady!
 STELLA: I am delighted that you came. Because
  To you alone would I confide a secret.
 ROSAURA: Thereby you greatly honour me, your servant.   550
 STELLA: Astrea, in the brief time I have known you
  I've given you the latchkey of my will.
  For that, and being who you are, I'll tell you
  A secret which I've very often hidden
  Even from myself.   555

ROSAURA: I am your slave.
STELLA: Then, briefly:
    Astolfo, who's my cousin (the word cousin
    Suffices, since some things are plainly said
    Even by thinking them), is to wed me
    If Fortune thus can wipe so many cares
560   Away with one great joy. But I am troubled
    In that, the day he first came here, he carried
    A portrait of a lady round his neck.
    I spoke to him about it courteously.
    He was most amiable, he loves me well,
565   And now he's gone for it. I am embarrassed
    That he should give it me himself. Wait here,
    And tell him to deliver it to you.
    Do not say more. Since you're discreet and fair:
    You'll surely know just what love is.

(Exit.)

ROSAURA: Great heavens!
570   How I wish that I did not! For who could be
    So prudent or so skilful as would know
    What to advise herself in such a case?
    Lives there a person on this earth today
    Who's more beset by the inclement stars,
575   Who has more cares besieging him, or fights
    So many dire calamities at once?
    What can I do in such bewilderment
    Wherein it seems impossible to find
    Relief or comfort? Since my first misfortune
580   No other thing has chanced or happened to me
    But was a new misfortune. In succession
    Inheritors and heirs of their own selves
    (Just like the Phoenix, his own son and father)
    Misfortunes reproduce themselves, are born,
585   And live by dying. In their sepulchre
    The ashes they consume are hot forever.
    A sage once said misfortunes must be cowards
    Because they never dare to walk alone
    But come in crowds. I say they are most valiant
590   Because they always charge so bravely on
    And never turn their backs. Who charges with them
    May dare all things because there is no fear
    That they'll ever desert him; and I say it
    Because in all my life I never once
595   Knew them to leave me, nor will they grow tired
    Of me till, wounded and shot through and through
    By Fate, I fall into the arms of death.
    Alas, what can I do in this dilemma?
    If I reveal myself, then old Clotaldo,
600   To whom I owe my life, may take offence,
    Because he told me to await the cure
    And mending of my honour in concealment.
    If I don't tell Astolfo who I am
    And he detects me, how can I dissimulate?
605   Since even if I say I am not I,
    The voice, the language, and the eyes will falter,
    Because the soul will tell them that they lie.
    What shall I do? It is in vain to study
    What I should do, when I know very well

    That, whatsoever way I choose to act,   610
    When the time comes I'll do as sorrow bids,
    For no one has control over his sorrows.
    Then since my soul dares not decide its actions
    Let sorrow fill my cup and let my grief
    Reach its extremity and, out of doubts   615
    And vain appearances, once and for all
    Come out into the light—and Heaven shield me!

(Enter ASTOLFO.)

ASTOLFO: Here, lady, is the portrait . . . but . . . great God!
ROSAURA: Why does Your Highness halt, and stare
    astonished?
ASTOLFO: Rosaura! Why, to see you here!   620
ROSAURA: Rosaura?
    Sir, you mistake me for some other lady.
    I am Astrea, and my humble station
    Deserves no perturbation such as yours.
ASTOLFO: Enough of this pretence, Rosaura, since
    The soul can never lie. Though as Astrea   625
    I see you now, I love you as Rosaura.
ROSAURA: Not having understood Your Highness' meaning
    I can make no reply except to say
    That Stella (who might be the star of Venus)
    Told me to wait here and to tell you from her   630
    To give to me the portrait you were fetching
    (Which seems a very logical request)
    And I myself will take it to my lady.
    Thus Stella bids: even the slightest things
    Which do me harm are governed by some star.   635
ASTOLFO: Even if you could make a greater effort
    How poorly you dissimulate, Rosaura!
    Tell your poor eyes they do not harmonise
    With your own voice, because they needs must jangle
    When the whole instrument is out of time.   640
    You cannot match the falsehood of your words
    With the sincerity of what you're feeling.
ROSAURA: All I can say is—that I want the portrait.
ASTOLFO: As you require a fiction, with a fiction
    I shall reply. Go and tell Stella this: 645
    That I esteem her so, it seems unworthy
    Only to send the counterfeit to her
    And that I'm sending her the original.
    And you, take the original along with you,
    Taking yourself to her.   650
ROSAURA: When a man starts
    Forth on a definite task, resolved and valiant,
    Though he be offered a far greater prize
    Than what he seeks, yet he returns with failure
    If he returns without his task performed.
    I came to get that portrait. Though I bear   655
    The original with me, of greater value,
    I would return in failure and contempt
    Without the copy. Give it me, Your Highness,
    Since I cannot return without it.
ASTOLFO: But
    If I don't give it you, how can you do so?   660
ROSAURA: Like this, ungrateful man! I'll take it from you.

(She tries to wrest it from him.)

ASTOLFO: It is in vain.
ROSAURA: By God, it shall not come
    Into another woman's hands!
ASTOLFO: You're terrifying!
ROSAURA: And you're perfidious!
ASTOLFO: Enough, my dear
665   Rosaura!
ROSAURA: I, your dear? You lie, you villain!

(They are both clutching the portrait.)

(Enter STELLA.)

STELLA: Astrea and Astolfo, what does this mean?
ASTOLFO: *(Aside.)* Here's Stella.
ROSAURA: *(Aside.)*   Love, grant me the strength to win
    My portrait.

(To STELLA.)

        If you want to know, my lady,
    What this is all about, I will explain.
670 ASTOLFO: *(To ROSAURA, aside.)* What do you mean?
ROSAURA: You told me to await
    Astolfo here and ask him for a portrait
    On your behalf. I waited here alone
    And as one thought suggests another thought,
    Thinking of portraits, I recalled my own
675   Was here inside my sleeve. When one's alone,
    One is diverted by a foolish trifle
    And so I took it out to look at it.
    It slipped and fell, just as Astolfo here,
    Bringing the portrait of the other lady,
680   Came to deliver it to you as promised.
    He picked my portrait up, and so unwilling
    Is he to give away the one you asked for,
    Instead of doing so, he seized upon
    The other portrait which is mine alone
685   And will not give it back though I entreated
    And begged him to return it. I was angry
    And tried to snatch it back. That's it he's holding,
    And you can see yourself if it's not mine.
STELLA: Let go the portrait.

(She snatches it from him.)

ASTOLFO: Madam!
STELLA: The draughtsman
690   Was not unkind to truth.
ROSAURA: Is it not mine?
STELLA: Why, who could doubt it?
ROSAURA: Ask him for the other.
STELLA: Here, take your own, Astrea. You may leave us.
ROSAURA: *(Aside.)* Now I have got my portrait, come what
    will.

(Exit.)

STELLA: Now give me up the portrait that I asked for
695   Although I'll see and speak to you no more.
    I do not wish to leave it in your power
    Having been once so foolish as to beg it.

ASTOLFO: *(Aside.)* Now how can I get out of this foul trap?

(To STELLA.)

    Beautiful Stella, though I would obey you,
    And serve you in all ways, I cannot give you   700
    The portrait, since . . .
STELLA: You are a crude, coarse villain
    And ruffian of a wooer. For the portrait—
    I do not want it now, since, if I had it,
    It would remind me I had asked you for it.

(Exit.)

ASTOLFO: Listen! Look! Wait! Let me explain!   705

(Aside.)

                          Oh, damn
    Rosaura! How the devil did she get
    To Poland for my ruin and her own?

The prison of SEGISMUND *in the tower.*

SEGISMUND *lying on the ground loaded with fetters and clothed in skins as before.* CLOTALDO, *two* ATTENDANTS, *and* CLARION.

CLOTALDO: Here you must leave him—since his reckless pride
    Ends here today where it began.
ATTENDANT: His chain
    I'll rivet as it used to be before.   710
CLARION: O Prince, you'd better not awake too soon
    To find how lost you are, how changed your fate,
    And that your fancied glory of an hour
    Was but a shade of life, a flame of death!
CLOTALDO: For one who knows so well to wield his tongue   715
    It's fit a worthy place should be provided
    With lots of room and lots of time to argue.
    This is the fellow that you have to seize

(To the ATTENDANTS.*)*

    And that's the room in which you are to lock him.

(Points to the nearest cell.)

CLARION: Why me?   720
CLOTALDO: Because a Clarion who knows
    Too many secrets must be kept in gaol—
    A place where even clarions are silent.
CLARION: Have I, by chance, wanted to kill my father
    Or thrown an Icarus from a balcony?
    Am I asleep or dreaming? To what end   725
    Do you imprison me?
CLOTALDO: You're Clarion.
CLARION: Well, say I swear to be a cornet now,
    A silent one, a wretched instrument . . . ?

(They hustle him off. CLOTALDO *remains.)*

(Enter BASIL, *wearing a mask.)*

BASIL: Clotaldo.

CLOTALDO: Sire . . . and is it thus alone
730   Your Majesty has come?
      BASIL: Vain curiosity
      To see what happens here to Segismund.
      CLOTALDO: See where he lies, reduced to misery!
      BASIL: Unhappy prince! Born at a fatal moment!
            Come waken him, now he has lost his strength
735   With all the opium he's drunk.
      CLOTALDO: He's stirring
      And talking to himself.
      BASIL: What is he dreaming?
      Let's listen now.
      SEGISMUND: He who chastises tyrants
            Is a most pious prince . . . Now let Clotaldo
            Die by my hand . . . my father kiss my feet . . .
740   CLOTALDO: He threatens me with death!
      BASIL: And me with insult
      And cruelty.
      CLOTALDO: He'd take my life away.
      BASIL: And he'd humiliate me at his feet.
      SEGISMUND: (*Still in a dream.*) Throughout the expanse of
            this world's theatre
            I'll show my peerless valour, let my vengeance
745   Be wreaked, and the Prince Segismund be seen
            To triumph—over his father . . . but, alas!

      (*Awakening.*)

            Where am I?
      BASIL: (*To* CLOTALDO.) Since he must not see me here,
            I'll listen further off. You know your cue.

      (*Retires to one side.*)

      SEGISMUND: Can this be I? Am I the same who, chained
750   And long imprisoned, rose to such a state?
            Are you not still my sepulchre and grave,
            You dismal tower? God! What things I have dreamed!
      CLOTALDO: (*Aside.*) Now I must go to him to disenchant him.

      (*Aloud.*)

            Awake already?
      SEGISMUND: Yes: it was high time.
755   CLOTALDO: What? Do you have to spend all day asleep?
            Since I was following the eagle's flight
            With tardy discourse, have you still lain here
            Without awaking?
      SEGISMUND: No. Nor even now
            Am I awake. It seems I've always slept,
760   Since, if I've dreamed what I've just seen and heard
            Palpably and for certain, then I am dreaming
            What I see now—nor is it strange I'm tired,
            Since what I, sleeping, see, tells me that I
            Was dreaming when I thought I was awake.
765   CLOTALDO: Tell me your dream.
      SEGISMUND: That's if it *was* a dream!
            No, I'll not tell you what I dreamed; but what
            I lived and saw, Clotaldo, I *will* tell you.
            I woke up in a bed that might have been
            The cradle of the flowers, woven by Spring.
770   A thousand nobles, bowing, called me Prince,

Attiring me in jewels, pomp, and splendour.
My equanimity you turned to rapture
Telling me that I was the Prince of Poland.
CLOTALDO: I must have got a fine reward!
SEGISMUND: Not so:
      For as a traitor, twice, with rage and fury,   775
      I tried to kill you.
CLOTALDO: Such cruelty to me?
SEGISMUND: I was the lord of all, on all I took revenge,
      Except I loved one woman . . . I believe
      That *that* was true, though all the rest has faded.

(*Exit* BASIL.)

CLOTALDO: (*Aside.*) I see the king was moved, to hear him   780
      speak.

(*Aloud.*)

      Talking of eagles made you dream of empires,
      But even in your dreams it's good to honour
      Those who have cared for you and brought you up.
      For Segismund, even in dreams, I warn you
      Nothing is lost by trying to do good.   785

(*Exit.*)

SEGISMUND: That's true, and therefore let us subjugate
      The bestial side, this fury and ambition,
      Against the time when we may dream once more,
      As certainly we shall, for this strange world
      Is such that but to live here is to dream.   790
      And now experience shows me that each man
      Dreams what he is until he is awakened.
      The king dreams he's a king and in this fiction
      Lives, rules, administers with royal pomp.
      Yet all the borrowed praises that he earns   795
      Are written in the wind, and he is changed
      (How sad a fate!) by death to dust and ashes.
      What man is there alive who'd seek to reign
      Since he must wake into the dream that's death.
      The rich man dreams his wealth which is his care   800
      And woe. The poor man dreams his sufferings.
      He dreams who thrives and prospers in this life.
      He dreams who toils and strives. He dreams who injures,
      Offends, and insults. So that in this world
      Everyone dreams the thing he is, though no one   805
      Can understand it. I dream I am here,
      Chained in these fetters. Yet I dreamed just now
      I was in a more flattering, lofty station.
      What is this life? A frenzy, an illusion,
      A shadow, a delirium, a fiction.   810
      The greatest good's but little, and this life
      Is but a dream, and dreams are only dreams.

ACT THREE

The tower.

Enter CLARION.

CLARION: I'm held in an enchanted tower, because
      Of all I know. What would they do to me
      For all I don't know, since—for all I know—
      They're killing me by starving me to death.

5   O that a man so hungry as myself
       Should live to die of hunger while alive!
       I am so sorry for myself that others
       May well say "I can well believe it," since
       This silence ill accords with my name "Clarion,"
10   And I just can't shut up. My fellows here?
       Spiders and rats—fine feathered songsters those!
       My head's still ringing with a dream of fifes
       And trumpets and a lot of noisy humbug
       And long processions as of penitents
15   With crosses, winding up and down, while some
       Faint at the sight of blood besmirching others.
       But now to tell the truth, I am in prison.
       For knowing secrets, I am kept shut in,
       Strictly observed as if I were a Sunday,
20   And feeling sadder than a Tuesday, where
       I neither eat nor drink. They say a secret
       Is sacred and should be as strictly kept
       As any saint's day on the calendar.
       Saint Secret's Day for me's a working day
25   Because I'm never idle then. The penance
       I suffer here is merited, I say:
       Because being a lackey, I was silent,
       Which, in a servant, is a sacrilege.

(*A noise of drums and trumpets.*)

FIRST SOLDIER: (*Within.*) Here is the tower in which he is
          imprisoned.
30   Smash in the door and enter, everybody!
       CLARION: Great God! They've come to seek me. That is
          certain
       Because they say I'm here. What can they want?

(*Enter several* SOLDIERS.)

FIRST SOLDIER: Go in.
SECOND SOLDIER: He's here!
CLARION: No, he's not here!
ALL THE SOLDIERS: Our lord!
CLARION: What, are they drunk?
FIRST SOLDIER: You are our rightful prince.
35   We do not want and never shall allow
       A stranger to supplant our trueborn prince.
       Give us your feet to kiss!
ALL THE SOLDIERS: Long live the prince!
CLARION: Bless me, if it's not real! In this strange kingdom
       It seems the custom, everyday, to take
40   Some fellow and to make him prince and then
       Shut him back in this tower. That *must* be it!
       So I must play my role.
ALL THE SOLDIERS: Give us your feet.
CLARION: I can't. They're necessary. After all
       What sort of use would be a footless prince?
45 SECOND SOLDIER: All of us told your father, as one man,
       We want no prince of Muscovy but you!
CLARION: You weren't respectful to my father? Shame!
FIRST SOLDIER: It was our loyalty that made us tell him.
CLARION: If it was loyalty, you have my pardon.
50 SECOND SOLDIER: Restore your empire. Long live Segismund!

CLARION: (*Aside.*) That is the name they seem to give to all
       These counterfeited princes.

(*Enter* SEGISMUND.)

SEGISMUND: Who called Segismund?
CLARION: (*Aside.*) I seem to be a hollow sort of prince.
FIRST SOLDIER: Which of you's Segismund?
SEGISMUND: I am.
SECOND SOLDIER: (*To* CLARION.)   Then why,
       Rash fool, did you impersonate the prince   55
       Segismund?
CLARION: What? I, Segismund? Yourselves
       Be-Segismunded me without request.
       All yours was both the rashness and the folly.
FIRST SOLDIER: Prince Segismund, whom we acclaim our lord,
       Your father, great King Basil, in his fear   60
       That heaven would fulfil a prophecy
       That one day he would kneel before your feet
       Wishes now to deprive you of the throne
       And give it to the Duke of Muscovy.
       For this he called a council, but the people   65
       Discovered his design and knowing, now,
       They have a native king, will have no stranger.
       So scorning the fierce threats of destiny,
       We've come to seek you in your very prison,
       That aided by the arms of the whole people,   70
       We may restore you to the crown and sceptre,
       Taking them from the tyrant's grasp. Come, then:
       Assembling here, in this wide desert region,
       Hosts of plebeians, bandits, and freebooters,
       Acclaim you king. Your liberty awaits you!   75
       Hark to its voice!

(*Shouts within.*)

                Long life to Segismund!
SEGISMUND: Once more, you heavens will that I should dream
       Of grandeur, once again, 'twixt doubts and shades,
       Behold the majesty of pomp and power
       Vanish into the wind, once more you wish   80
       That I should taste the disillusion and
       The risk by which all human power is humbled,
       Of which all human power should live aware.
       It must not be. I'll not be once again
       Put through my paces by my fortune's stars.   85
       And since I know this life is all a dream,
       Depart, vain shades, who feign, to my dead senses,
       That you have voice and body, having neither!
       I want no more feigned majesty, fantastic
       Display, nor void illusions, that one gust   90
       Can scatter like the almond tree in flower,
       Whose rosy buds, without advice or warning,
       Dawn in the air too soon and then, as one,
       Are all extinguished, fade, and fall, and wither
       In the first gust of wind that comes along!   95
       I know you well. I know you well by now.
       I know that all that happens in yourselves
       Happens as in a sleeping man. For me
       There are no more delusions and deceptions
       Since I well know this life is all a dream.   100

SECOND SOLDIER: If you think we are cheating, just sweep
    Your gaze along these towering peaks, and see
    The hosts that wait to welcome and obey you.
SEGISMUND: Already once before I've seen such crowds
105   Distinctly, quite as vividly as these:
    And yet it was a dream.
SECOND SOLDIER: No great event
    Can come without forerunners to announce it
    And this is the real meaning of your dream.
SEGISMUND: Yes, you say well. It was the fore-announcement
110   And just in case it was correct, my soul,
    (Since life's so short) let's dream the dream anew!
    But it must be attentively, aware
    That we'll awake from pleasure in the end.
    Forewarned of that, the shock's not so abrupt,
115   The disillusion's less. Evils anticipated
    Lose half their sting. And armed with this precaution—
    That power, even when we're sure of it, is borrowed
    And must be given back to its true owner—
    We can risk anything and dare the worst.
120   Subjects, I thank you for your loyalty.
    In me you have a leader who will free you,
    Bravely and skilfully, from foreign rule.
    Sound now to arms, you'll soon behold my valour.
    Against my father I must march and bring
125   Truth from the stars. Yes: he must kneel to me.

(*Aside.*)

    But yet, since I may wake before he kneels,
    Perhaps I'd better not proclaim what may not happen.
ALL: Long live Segismund!

(*Enter* CLOTALDO.)

CLOTALDO: Gracious heavens! What is
    This riot here?
SEGISMUND: Clotaldo!
CLOTALDO: Sir!

(*Aside.*)

                    He'll prove
130   His cruelty on me.
CLARION: I bet he throws him
    Over the mountain.
CLOTALDO: At your royal feet
    I kneel, knowing my penalty is death.
SEGISMUND: Rise, rise, my foster father, from the ground,
    For you must be the compass and the guide
135   In which I trust. You brought me up, and I
    Know what I owe your loyalty. Embrace me!
CLOTALDO: What's that you say?
SEGISMUND: I know I'm in a dream,
    But I would like to act well, since good actions,
    Even in a dream, are not entirely lost.
140 CLOTALDO: Since doing good is now to be your glory,
    You will not be offended that I too
    Should do what's right. You march against your father!
    I cannot give you help against my king.
    Here at your feet, my lord, I plead for death.

SEGISMUND: (*Aloud.*) Villain!   145

(*Aside.*)

                    But let us suffer this annoyance.
    Though my rage would slay him, yet he's loyal.
    A man does not deserve to die for that.
    How many angry passions does this leash
    Restrain in me, this curb of knowing well
    That I must wake and find myself alone!   150
SECOND SOLDIER: All this fine talk, Clotaldo, is a cruel
    Spurn of the public welfare. We are loyal
    Who wish our own prince to reign over us.
CLOTALDO: Such loyalty, after the king were dead,
    Would honour you. But while the king is living   155
    He is our absolute, unquestioned lord.
    There's no excuse for subjects who oppose
    His sovereignty in arms.
FIRST SOLDIER: We'll soon see well
    Enough, Clotaldo, what this loyalty
    Is worth.   160
CLOTALDO: You would be better if you had some.
    It is the greatest prize.
SEGISMUND: Peace, peace, I pray you.
CLOTALDO: My lord!
SEGISMUND: Clotaldo, if your feelings
    Are truly thus, go you, and serve the king;
    That's prudence, loyalty, and common sense.
    But do not argue here with anyone   165
    Whether it's right or wrong, for every man
    Has his own honour.

CLOTALDO: Humbly I take my leave.

(*Exit.*)

SEGISMUND: Now sound the drums and march in rank and
    order
    Straight to the palace.
ALL: Long live Segismund!
SEGISMUND: Fortune, we go to reign! Do not awake me   170
    If I am dreaming! Do not let me fall
    Asleep if it is true! To act with virtue
    Is what matters, since if this proves true,
    That truth's sufficient reason in itself;
    If not, we win us friends against the time   175
    When we at last awake.

A room in the royal palace.

Enter BASIL *and* ASTOLFO.

BASIL: Whose prudence can rein in a bolting horse?
    Who can restrain a river's pride, in spate?
    Whose valour can withstand a crag dislodged
    And hurtling downwards from a mountain peak?   180
    All these are easier by far than to hold back
    A crowd's proud fury, once it has been roused.
    It has two voices, both proclaiming war,
    And you can hear them echoing through the mountains,

185   Some shouting "Segismund," others "Astolfo."
        The scene I set for swearing of allegiance
        Lends but an added horror to this strife:
        It has become the back cloth to a stage
        Where Fortune plays out tragedies in blood.

190 ASTOLFO: My lord, forget the happiness and wealth
        You promised me from your most blessèd hand.
        If Poland, which I hope to rule, refuses
        Obedience to my right, grudging me honour,
        It is because I've got to earn it first.

195   Give me a horse, that I with angry pride
        May match the thunder in my voice and ride
        To strike, like lightning, terror far and wide.

(*Exit* ASTOLFO.)

BASIL: No remedy for what's infallible!
        What is foreseen is perilous indeed!

200   If something has to be, there's no way out;
        In trying to evade it, you but court it.
        This law is pitiless and horrible.
        Thinking one can evade the risk, one meets it:
        My own precautions have been my undoing,

205   And I myself have quite destroyed my kingdom.

(*Enter* STELLA.)

STELLA: If you, my lord, in person do not try
        To curb the vast commotion that has started
        In all the streets between the rival factions,
        You'll see your kingdom, swamped in waves of crimson,

210   Swimming in its own blood, with nothing left
        But havoc, dire calamity, and woe.
        So frightful is the damage to your empire
        That, seen, it strikes amazement; heard, despair.
        The sun's obscured, the very winds are hindered.

215   Each stone is a memorial to the dead.
        Each flower springs from a grave while every building
        Appears a mausoleum, and each soldier
        A premature and walking skeleton.

(*Enter* CLOTALDO.)

CLOTALDO: Praise be to God, I reach your feet alive!
220 BASIL: Clotaldo! What's the news of Segismund?
CLOTALDO: The crowd, a headstrong monster blind with rage,
        Entered his dungeon tower and set him free.
        He, now exalted for the second time,
        Conducts himself with valour, boasting how

225   He will bring down the truth out of the stars.
BASIL: Give me a horse, that I myself, in person,
        May vanquish such a base, ungrateful son!
        For I, in the defence of my own crown,
        Shall do by steel what science failed to do.

(*Exit.*)

230 STELLA: I'll be Bellona to your Sun, and try
        To write my name next yours in history.
        I'll ride as though I flew on outstretched wings
        That I may vie with Pallas.

(*Exit.*)

(*Enter* ROSAURA, *holding back* CLOTALDO.)

ROSAURA: I know that all is war, Clotaldo, yet
        Although your valour calls you to the front,   235
        First hear me out. You know quite well that I
        Arrived in Poland poor and miserable,
        Where, shielded by your valour, I found mercy.
        You told me to conceal myself, and stay
        Here in the palace, hiding from Astolfo.   240
        He saw me in the end, and so insulted
        My honour that (although he saw me clearly)
        He nightly speaks with Stella in the garden.
        I have the key to it and I will show you
        How you can enter there and end my cares.   245
        Thus bold, resolved, and strong, you can recover
        My honour, since you're ready to avenge me
        By killing him.
CLOTALDO: It's true that I intended,
        Since first I saw you (having heard your tale)
        With my own life to rectify your wrongs.   250
        The first step that I took was bid you dress
        According to your sex, for fear Astolfo
        Might see you as you were, and deem you wanton.
        I was devising how we could recover
        Your honour (so much did it weigh on me)   255
        Even though we had to kill him. (A wild plan—
        Though since he's not my king, I would not flinch
        From killing him.) But then, when suddenly
        Segismund tried to kill me, it was he
        Who saved my life with his surpassing valour.   260
        Consider: how can I requite Astolfo
        With death for giving me my life so bravely,
        And when my soul is full of gratitude?
        So torn between the two of you I stand—
        Rosaura, whose life I saved, and Astolfo,   265
        Who saved my life. What's to be done? Which side
        To take, and whom to help, I cannot judge.
        What I owe you in that I gave you life
        I owe to him in that he gave me life.
        And so there is no course that I can take   270
        To satisfy my love. I am a person
        Who has to act, yet suffer either way.
ROSAURA: I should not have to tell so brave a man
        That if it is nobility to give,
        It's baseness to receive. That being so   275
        You owe no gratitude to him, admitting
        That it was he who gave you life, and you
        Who gave me life, since he forced you to take
        A meaner role, and through me you assumed
        A generous role. So you should side with me: 280
        My cause is so far worthier than his own
        As giving is than taking.
CLOTALDO: Though nobility
        Is with the giver, it is gratitude
        That dwells with the receiver. As a giver
        I have the name of being generous: 285
        Then grant me that of being grateful too
        And let me earn the title and be grateful,
        As I am liberal, giving or receiving.
ROSAURA: You granted me my life, at the same time
        Telling me it was worthless, since dishonoured,   290

And therefore was no life. Therefore from you
I have received no life at all. And since
You should be liberal first and grateful after
(Since so you said yourself) I now entreat you
295 Give me the life, the life you never gave me!
As giving magnifies the most, give first
And then be grateful after, if you will!
CLOTALDO: Won by your argument, I will be liberal.
Rosaura, I shall give you my estate
300 And you shall seek a convent, there to live.
This measure is a happy thought, for, see,
Fleeing a crime, you find a sanctuary.
For when the empire's threatened with disasters
And is divided thus, I, born a noble,
305 Am not the man who would augment its woes.
So with this remedy which I have chosen
I remain loyal to the kingdom, generous
To you, and also grateful to Astolfo.
And thus I choose the course that suits you best.
310 Were I your father, what could I do more?
ROSAURA: Were you my father, then I would accept
The insult. Since you are not, I refuse.
CLOTALDO: What do you hope to do then?
ROSAURA: Kill the duke!
CLOTALDO: A girl who never even knew her father
315 Armed with such courage?
ROSAURA: Yes.
CLOTALDO: What spurs you on?
ROSAURA: My good name.
CLOTALDO: In Astolfo you will find . . .
ROSAURA: My honour rides on him and strikes him
down!
CLOTALDO: Your king, too, Stella's husband!
ROSAURA: Never, never
Shall that be, by almighty God, I swear!
320 CLOTALDO: Why, this is madness!
ROSAURA: Yes it is!
CLOTALDO: Restrain it.
ROSAURA: That I cannot.
CLOTALDO: Then you are lost forever!
ROSAURA: I know it!
CLOTALDO: Life and honour both together!
ROSAURA: I well believe it!
CLOTALDO: What do you intend?
ROSAURA: My death.
CLOTALDO: This is despair and desperation.
325 ROSAURA: It's honour.
CLOTALDO: It is nonsense.
ROSAURA: It is valour.
CLOTALDO: It's frenzy.
ROSAURA: Yes, it's anger! Yes, it's fury!
CLOTALDO: In short you cannot moderate your passion?
ROSAURA: No.
CLOTALDO: Who is there to help you?
ROSAURA: I, myself.
CLOTALDO: There is no cure?
ROSAURA: There is no cure!
CLOTALDO: Think well
330 If there's not some way out . . .
ROSAURA: Some other way
To do away with me . . .

(*Exit.*)

CLOTALDO: If you are lost,
My daughter, let us both be lost together!

In the country.

Enter SEGISMUND *clothed in skins.* SOLDIERS *marching.* CLARION.
Drums beating.

SEGISMUND: If Rome, today, could see me here, renewing
Her olden triumphs, she might laugh to see
A wild beast in command of mighty armies,   335
A wild beast, to whose fiery aspirations
The firmament were all too slight a conquest!
But stoop your flight, my spirit. Do not thus
Be puffed to pride by these uncertain plaudits
Which, when I wake, will turn to bitterness   340
In that I won them only to be lost.
The less I value them, the less I'll miss them.

(*A trumpet sounds.*)

CLARION: Upon a rapid courser (pray excuse me,
Since if it comes to mind I must describe it)
In which it seems an atlas was designed   345
Since if its body is earth, its soul is fire
Within its breast, its foam appears the sea,
The wind its breath, and chaos its condition,
Since in its soul, its foam, its breath and flesh,
It seems a monster of fire, earth, sea, and wind,   350
Upon the horse, all of a patchwork colour,
Dappled, and rushing forward at the will
Of one who plies the spur, so that it flies
Rather than runs—see how a woman rides
Boldly into your presence.   355
SEGISMUND: Her light blinds me.
CLARION: Good God! Why, here's Rosaura!
SEGISMUND: It is heaven
That has restored her to my sight once more.

(*Enter* ROSAURA *with sword and dagger in riding costume.*)

ROSAURA: Generous Segismund, whose majesty
Heroically rises in the lustre
Of his great deeds out of his night of shadows,   360
And as the greatest planet, in the arms
Of his aurora, lustrously returns
To plants and roses, over hills and seas,
When, crowned with gold, he looks abroad, dispersing
Radiance, flashing his rays, bathing the summits,   365
And broidering the fringes of the foam,
So may you dawn upon the world, bright sun
Of Poland, that a poor unhappy woman
May fall before your feet and beg protection
Both as a woman and unfortunate—   370
Two things that must oblige you, sire, as one
Who prizes yourself as valiant, each of them
More than suffices for your chivalry.

343–355 **Upon a . . . presence** Clarion's speech is a parody of
exaggerated style including Calderón's [R.C.]

Three times you have beheld me now, three times
375 Been ignorant of who I am, because
Three times you saw me in a different clothing.
The first time you mistook me for a man,
Within that rigorous prison, where your hardships
Made mine seem pleasure. Next time, as a woman,
380 You saw me, when your pomp and majesty
Were as a dream, a phantasm, a shade.
The third time is today when, as a monster
Of both the sexes, in a woman's costume
I bear a soldier's arms. But to dispose you
385 The better to compassion, hear my story.
My mother was a noble in the court
Of Moscow, who, since most unfortunate,
Must have been beautiful. Then came a traitor
And cast his eyes on her (I do not name him,
390 Not knowing who he is). Yet I deduce
That he was valiant too from my own valour,
Since he gave form to me—and I could wish
I had been born in pagan times, that I might
Persuade myself he was some god of those
395 Who rain in showers of gold, turn into swans
Or bulls, for Danaës, Ledas, or Europas.
That's strange: I thought I was just rambling on
By telling old perfidious myths, yet find
I've told you how my mother was cajoled.
400 Oh, she was beautiful as no one else
Has been, but was unfortunate like all.
He swore to wed her (that's an old excuse)
And this trick reached so nearly to her heart
That thought must weep, recalling it today.
405 The tyrant left her only with his sword
As Aeneas left Troy. I sheathed its blade here
Upon my thigh, and I will bare it too
Before the ending of this history.
Out of this union, this poor link which neither
410 Could bind the marriage nor handcuff the crime,
Myself was born, her image and her portrait,
Not in her beauty, but in her misfortune,
For mine's the same. That's all I need to say.
The most that I can tell you of myself
415 Is that the man who robbed me of the spoils
And trophies of my honour is Astolfo.
Alas! to name him my heart rages so
(As hearts will do when men name enemies).
Astolfo was my faithless and ungrateful
420 Lord, who (quite forgetful of our happiness,
Since of a past love even the memory fades)
Came here to claim the throne and marry Stella
For she's the star who rises as I set.
It's hard to credit that a star should sunder
425 Lovers the stars had made conformable!
So hurt was I, so villainously cheated,
That I became mad, brokenhearted, sick,
Half wild with grief, and like to die, with all
Hell's own confusion ciphered on my mind
430 Like Babel's incoherence. Mutely I told
My griefs (since woes and griefs declare themselves
Better than can the mouth, by their effects),
When, with my mother (we were by ourselves),

She broke the prison of my pent-up sorrows
And from my breast they all rushed forth in troops. 435
I felt no shyness, for in knowing surely
That one to whom one's errors are recounted
Has also been an ally in her own,
One finds relief and rest, since bad example
Can sometimes serve for a good purpose too. 440
She heard my plaint with pity, and she tried
To palliate my sorrows with her own.
How easily do judges pardon error
When they've offended too! An example,
A warning, in herself, she did not trust 445
To idleness, or the slow cure of time,
Nor try to find a remedy for her honour
In my misfortunes, but, with better counsel,
She bade me follow him to Poland here
And with prodigious gallantry persuade him 450
To pay the debt to honour that he owes me.
So that it would be easier to travel,
She bade me don male clothing, and took down
This ancient sword which I am wearing now.
Now it is time that I unsheathe the blade 455
As I was bid, for, trusting in its sign,
She said: "Depart to Poland, show this sword
That all the nobles may behold it well,
And it may be that one of them will take
Pity on you, and counsel you, and shield you." 460
I came to Poland and, you will remember,
Entered your cave. You looked at me in wonder.
Clotaldo passionately took my part
To plead for mercy to the king, who spared me,
Then, when he heard my story, bade me change 465
Into my own clothes and attend on Stella,
There to disturb Astolfo's love and stop
Their marriage. Again you saw me in woman's dress
And were confused by the discrepancy.
But let's pass to what's new: Clotaldo, now 470
Persuaded that Astolfo must, with Stella,
Come to the throne, dissuades me from my purpose,
Against the interests of my name and honour.
But seeing you, O valiant Segismund,
Are claiming your revenge, now that the heavens 475
Have burst the prison of your rustic tower,
(Wherein you were the tiger of your sorrows,
The rock of sufferings and direful pains)
And sent you forth against your sire and country,
I come to aid you, mingling Dian's silks 480
With the hard steel of Pallas. Now, strong Captain,
It well behoves us both to stop this marriage—
Me, lest my promised husband should be wed,
You, lest, when their estates are joined, they weigh
More powerfully against your victory. 485
I come, as a mere woman, to persuade you
To right my shame; but, as a man, I come
To help you battle for your crown. As woman,
To melt your heart, here at your feet I fall;
But, as a man, I come to serve you bravely 490
Both with my person and my steel, and thus,
If you today should woo me as a woman,
Then I should have to kill you as a man would

In honourable service of my honour;
495　Since I must be three things today at once—
Passionate, to persuade you: womanly,
To ply you with my woes: manly, to gain
Honour in battle.
SEGISMUND:　　　　Heavens! If it is true I'm dreaming,
Suspend my memory, for in a dream
500　So many things could not occur. Great heavens!
If I could only come free of them all!
Or never think of any! Who ever felt
Such grievous doubts? If I but dreamed that triumph
In which I found myself, how can this woman
505　Refer me to such sure and certain facts?
Then all of it was true and not a dream.
But if it be the truth, why does my past life
Call it a dream? This breeds the same confusion.
Are dreams and glories so alike, that fictions
510　Are held for truths, realities for lies?
Is there so little difference in them both
That one should question whether what one sees
And tastes is true or false? What? Is the copy
So near to the original that doubt
515　Exists between them? Then if that is so,
And grandeur, power, majesty, and pomp,
Must all evaporate like shades at morning,
Let's profit by it, this time, to enjoy
That which we only can enjoy in dreams.
520　Rosaura's in my power: my soul adores her beauty.
Let's take the chance. Let love break every law
On which she has relied in coming here
And kneeling, trustful, prostrate at my feet.
This is a dream. If so, dream pleasures now
525　Since they must turn to sorrows in the end!
But with my own opinions, I begin
Once again to convince myself. Let's think.
If it is but vainglory and a dream,
Who for mere human vainglory would lose
530　True glory? What past blessing is not merely
A dream? Who has known heroic glories,
That deep within himself, as he recalls them
Has never doubted that they might be dreams?
But if this all should end in disenchantment,
535　Seeing that pleasure is a lovely flame
That's soon converted into dust and ashes
By any wind that blows, then let us seek
That which endures in thrifty, lasting fame
In which no pleasures sleep, nor grandeurs dream.
540　Rosaura's without honour. In a prince
It's worthier to restore it than to steal it.
I shall restore it, by the living God,
Before I win my throne! Let's shun the danger
And fly from the temptation which is strong!
545　Then sound to arms!

(*To a* SOLDIER.)

Today I must give battle before darkness
Buries the rays of gold in green-black waves!
ROSAURA: My lord! Alas, you stand apart, and offer
No word of pity for my plight. How is it

You neither hear nor see me nor even yet　　550
Have turned your face on me?
SEGISMUND:　　　　　　Rosaura, for your honour's sake
I must be cruel to you, to be kind.
My voice must not reply to you because
My honour must reply to you. I am silent
Because my deeds must speak to you alone.　　555
I do not look at you since, in such straits,
Having to see your honour is requited,
I must not see your beauty.

(*Exit with* SOLDIERS.)

ROSAURA: What strange enigma's this? After such trouble
Still to be treated with more doubtful riddles!　　560

(*Enter* CLARION.)

CLARION: Madam, may you be visited just now?
ROSAURA: Why, Clarion, where have you been all this time?
CLARION: Shut in the tower, consulting cards
About my death: "to be or not to be."
And it was a near thing.　　565
ROSAURA:　　　　Why?
CLARION:　　　　　　Because I know
The secret who you are: in fact, Clotaldo . . .

(*Drums.*)

But hush what noise is that?
ROSAURA:　　　　　　What can it be?
CLARION: From the beleaguered palace a whole squadron
Is charging forth to harry and defeat
That of fierce Segismund.　　570
ROSAURA:　　　　　　Why, what a coward
Am I, not to be at his side, the terror
And scandal of the world, while such fierce strife
Presses all round in lawless anarchy.

(*Exit.*)

VOICES OF SOME: Long live our king!
VOICES OF OTHERS:　　　　Long live our liberty!
CLARION: Long live both king and liberty. Yes, live!　　575
And welcome to them both! I do not worry.
In all this pother, I behave like Nero
Who never grieved at what was going on.
If I had anything to grieve about
It would be me, myself. Well hidden here　　580
Now, I can watch the sport that's going on.
This place is safe and hidden between crags,
And since death cannot find me here, two figs for death!

(*He hides. Drums and the clash of arms are heard.*)

(*Enter* BASIL, CLOTALDO, *and* ASTOLFO, *fleeing.*)

BASIL: Was ever king so hapless as myself
Or father more ill used?　　585
CLOTALDO:　　　　　Your beaten army
Rush down, in all directions, in disorder.
ASTOLFO: The traitors win!

BASIL: In battles such as these
      Those on the winning side are ever "loyal,"
      And traitors the defeated. Come, Clotaldo,
590   Let's flee from the inhuman cruelty
      Of my fierce son!

(*Shots are fired within.* CLARION *falls wounded.*)

CLARION: Heavens, save me!
ASTOLFO: Who is this
      Unhappy soldier bleeding at our feet?
CLARION: I am a most unlucky man who, wishing
      To guard myself from death, have sought it out
595   By fleeing from it. Shunning it, I found it,
      Because, to death, no hiding-place is secret.
      So you can argue that whoever shuns it
      Most carefully runs into it the quickest.
      Turn, then, once more into the thick of battle:
600   There is more safety there amidst the fire
      And clash of arms than here on this secluded
      Mountain, because no hidden path is safe
      From the inclemency of Fate; and so,
      Although you flee from death, yet you may find it
605   Quicker than you expect, if God so wills.

(*He falls dead.*)

BASIL: "If God so wills" . . . With what strange eloquence
      This corpse persuades our ignorance and error
      To better knowledge, speaking from the mouth
      Of its fell wound, where the red liquid flowing
610   Seems like a bloody tongue which teaches us
      That the activities of man are vain
      When they are pitted against higher powers.
      For I, who wished to liberate my country
      From murder and sedition, gave it up
615   To the same ills from which I would have saved it.
CLOTALDO: Though Fate, my lord, knows every path, and finds
      Him whom it seeks even in the midst of crags
      And thickets, it is not a Christian judgment
      To say there is no refuge from its fury.
620   A prudent man can conquer Fate itself.
      Though you are not exempted from misfortune,
      Take action to escape it while you can!
ASTOLFO: Clotaldo speaks as one mature in prudence,
      And I as one in valour's youthful prime.
625   Among the thickets of this mount is hidden
      A horse, the very birth of the swift wind.
      Flee on him, and I'll guard you in the rear.
BASIL: If it is God's will I should die, or if
      Death waits here for my coming, I will seek
630   Him out today, and meet him face to face.

(*Enter* SEGISMUND, STELLA, ROSAURA, SOLDIERS, *and their* TRAIN.)

A SOLDIER: Amongst the thickets of this mountain
635   The king is hiding.
SEGISMUND: Seek him out at once!
      Leave no foot of the summit unexplored
      But search from stem to stem and branch to branch!
CLOTALDO: Fly, sir!

BASIL: What for?
ASTOLFO: What do you mean to do?
BASIL: Astolfo, stand aside!
CLOTALDO: What is your wish?
BASIL: To take a cure I've needed for sometime.

(*To* SEGISMUND.)

      If you have come to seek me, here I am.

(*Kneeling.*)

      Your father, prince, kneels humbly at your feet.
      The white snow of my hair is now your carpet.   640
      Tread on my neck and trample on my crown!
      Lay low and drag my dignity in dust!
      Take vengeance on my honour! Make a slave
      Of me and, after all I've done to thwart them,
      Let Fate fulfil its edict and claim homage   645
      And Heaven fulfil its oracles at last!
SEGISMUND: Illustrious court of Poland, who have been
      The witnesses of such unwonted wonders,
      Attend to me, and hear your prince speak out.
      What Heaven decrees and God writes with his finger 650
      (Whose prints and ciphers are the azure leaves
      Adorned with golden lettering of the stars)
      Never deceives nor lies. They only lie
      Who seek to penetrate the mystery
      And, having reached it, use it to ill purpose.   655
      My father, who is here to evade the fury
      Of my proud nature, made me a wild beast:
      So, when I, by my birth of gallant stock,
      My generous blood, and inbred grace and valour,
      Might well have proved both gentle and forbearing, 660
      The very mode of life to which he forced me,
      The sort of bringing up I had to bear
      Sufficed to make me savage in my passions.
      What a strange method of restraining them!
      If one were to tell any man: "One day   665
      You will be killed by an inhuman monster,"
      Would it be the best method he could choose
      To wake that monster when it was asleep?
      Or if they told him: "That sword which you're wearing
      Will be your death," what sort of cure were it   670
      To draw it forth and aim it at his breast?
      Or if they told him: "Deep blue gulfs of water
      Will one day be your sepulchre and grave
      Beneath a silver monument of foam,"
      He would be mad to hurl himself in headlong   675
      When the sea highest heaved its showy mountains
      And crystalline sierras plumed with spray.
      The same has happened to the king as to him
      Who wakes a beast which threatens death, to him
      Who draws a naked sword because he fears it,   680
      To him who dives into the stormy breakers.
      Though my ferocious nature (hear me now)
      Was like a sleeping beast, my inborn rage
      A sheathèd sword, my wrath a quiet ripple,
      Fate should not be coerced by man's injustice—   685
      This rouses more resentment. So it is
      That he who seeks to tame his fortune must

Resort to moderation and to measure.
He who foresees an evil cannot conquer it
690   Thus in advance, for though humility
Can overcome it, this it can do only
When the occasion's there, for there's no way
To dodge one's fate and thus evade the issue.
Let this strange spectacle serve as example—
695   This prodigy, this horror, and this wonder,
Because it is no less than one, to see,
After such measures and precautions taken
To thwart it, that a father thus should kneel
At his son's feet, a kingdom thus be shattered.
700   This was the sentence of the heavens above,
Which he could not evade, much though he tried.
Can I, younger in age, less brave, and less
In science than the king, conquer that fate?

(*To the* KING.)

Sire, rise, give me your hand, now that the heavens
705   Have shown you that you erred as to the method
To vanquish them. Humbly I kneel before you
And offer you my neck to tread upon.
BASIL: Son, such a great and noble act restores you
Straight to my heart. Oh, true and worthy prince!
710   You have won both the laurel and the palm.
Crown yourself with your deeds! For you *have* conquered!
ALL: Long live Segismund! Long live Segismund!
SEGISMUND: Since I have other victories to win,
The greatest of them all awaits me now:
715   To conquer my own self. Astolfo, give
Your hand here to Rosaura, for you know
It is a debt of honour and must be paid.
ASTOLFO: Although, it's true, I owe some obligations—
She does not know her name or who she is,
720   It would be base to wed a woman who . . .
CLOTALDO: Hold! Wait! Rosaura's of as noble stock
As yours, Astolfo. In the open field
I'll prove it with my sword. She is my daughter

And that should be enough.
ASTOLFO: What do you say?
CLOTALDO: Until I saw her married, righted, honoured,   725
I did not wish for it to be discovered.
It's a long story but she is my daughter.
ASTOLFO: That being so, I'm glad to keep my word.
SEGISMUND: And now, so that the princess Stella here
Will not remain disconsolate to lose   730
A prince of so much valour, here I offer
My hand to her, no less in birth and rank.
Give me your hand.
STELLA: I gain by meriting
So great a happiness.
SEGISMUND: And now, Clotaldo,
So long so loyal to my father, come   735
To my arms. Ask me anything you wish.
FIRST SOLDIER: If thus you treat a man who never served you,
What about me who led the revolution
And brought you from your dungeon in the tower?
What will you give me?   740
SEGISMUND: That same tower and dungeon
From which you never shall emerge till death.
No traitor is of use after his treason.
BASIL: All wonder at your wisdom!
ASTOLFO: What a change
Of character!
ROSAURA: How wise and prudent!
SEGISMUND: Why
Do you wonder? Why do you marvel, since   745
It was a dream that taught me and I still
Fear to wake up once more in my close dungeon?
Though that may never happen, it's enough
To dream it might, for thus I came to learn
That all our human happiness must pass   750
Away like any dream, and I would here
Enjoy it fully ere it glide away,
Asking (for noble hearts are prone to pardon)
Pardon for faults in the actors or the play.

Molière

Jean-Baptiste Poquelin (1622–1673) was born into a prosperous mercantile family with connections at court; his father, Jean Poquelin, secured the honor of *tapissier ordinaire du roi,* the upholsterer to the court, which carried an annual pension. Jean Poquelin also educated his son in the traditional disciplines of the humanities, philosophy, and the classics and must have intended a life at court for him. In 1643, Jean-Baptiste joined with the Illustre Théâtre, a theatrical company run by the Béjart family, took the stage name Molière, and after a brief period performing in Parisian tennis courts, left with the company to play in the provinces. In 1658, after several hard and impoverished years of touring, when Molière is thought to have mastered the techniques of *commedia dell' arte,* the company was invited to perform in Paris.

Molière's career was closely tied to the court. When his brother died in 1660, he received the position of court upholsterer and the income it provided. More important, Molière became a significant playwright and both wrote and acted in a splendid series of plays that satirized the manners and morals of elegant society: *Les Précieuses Ridicules* (1659), *Sganarelle* (1660), *School for Husbands* (1661), *School for Wives* (1662), *Dom Juan* (1665), *The Misanthrope* (1666), *The Doctor in Spite of Himself* (1666), *The Miser* (1668), *The Learned Ladies* (1672), and *The Imaginary Invalid* (1673). Molière also prepared other entertainments at court, including many royal pageants, ballets, and machine plays devised by and for Louis XIV. In addition to being a great dramatist, Molière was a fine comic actor as well and performed in his own plays; he died shortly after playing the title role in the fourth performance of *The Imaginary Invalid.*

The fortunes of *Tartuffe* suggest Molière's importance at court. When Molière initially produced the first three acts of the play in 1664, the clergy protested and banned the play from production in Paris. Many of Molière's plays had excited controversy, and in this case Molière appealed to the king and proceeded to revise the play. Louis's attitude is perhaps revealed by the fact that he made Molière's company the *Troupe du roi* ("King's Company") in 1665, but even the throne could not prevent the clergy from censoring Molière's second version of the play in 1667, newly titled *The Impostor.* Molière finally produced the play to acclaim in 1669, and the record of his efforts is preserved in the series of letters and prefaces included here.

Molière's theatrical company was the most influential of its day. After his death, his young wife Amanda Béjart and the actress Mademoiselle Champmeslé—newly defected from the rival company at the Hôtel de Bourgogne—established a new company, the Comédie Française. Yet although Molière achieved extraordinary status at court, because he was an actor he remained stigmatized in ways that playwrights like Racine and Corneille were not. Following its standard practice, and perhaps because of *Tartuffe*'s notoriety, the church refused to bury Molière in sacred ground. Louis XIV intervened, but was only able to persuade the Archbishop of Paris to bury Molière in a parish cemetery. The burial was conducted at night, by two priests, with no funeral ceremony.

TARTUFFE

The Catholic church criticized *Tartuffe* for its portrait of hypocritical piety, but the fact that Molière played the part of Orgon may suggest that the play is as much about Tartuffe's effect on that benighted householder as it is about the title character. For if Tartuffe is hypocritical, Orgon is obsessed, less with piety than with his own desire to achieve a kind of total power and authority in his household, a kind of domestic absolutism; he is, in a sense, a comic, bourgeois Louis XIV in miniature. Moreover, Tartuffe dupes Orgon not by tricking him, but by inviting Orgon to fulfill his own fantasy of autonomy and authority. As he brags

Tartuffe seduces Elmire while Orgon hides beneath the table in Molière's *Tartuffe*.

to the sensible Cléante, under Tartuffe's teaching, "my soul's been freed / From earthly loves, and every human tie: / My mother, children, brother, and wife could die, / And I'd not feel a single moment's pain." Helping Orgon to realize this fantasy, Tartuffe transforms him into a kind of monster: Orgon comes near to selling his daughter, disinheriting his son, allowing his wife to be raped, and losing his family's property and fortune.

Tartuffe is very much a play of the world, a satiric comedy. Set in an urban landscape, the play insistently translates the idealized passions of tragedy and romantic comedy—love, honor, loyalty—into their ironic counterparts—lust, hypocrisy, betrayal. Molière peoples the play with individualized versions of the unchanging types of *commedia dell' arte* and the Roman comedy that inspired it: the reasonable and attractive heroes; an old, pedantic, self-absorbed dupe; a wily and conniving villain; a clever and witty servant. Yet Molière reinvents this range of stock characters, brilliantly turning his play toward an exploration of the folly of self-deception. For while we might take the neoclassical conflict between reason and the passions to be the hallmark of tragedy, it surges through this play as well. Orgon's passionate solipsism is, for all its ridiculousness, no less profound, troubling, or destructive than the obsessed affections of Racine's Phaedra and Hippolytus. Also, Orgon's redemption, by fiat of the king, seems no less arbitrary than the vengeful caprice of Venus or Neptune in Racine's tragedy.

Since the characters cannot change in Molière's comedy, change must happen to them. Molière's most brilliant device here arises in the person of the king's officer, who appears to apprehend Tartuffe and to restore Orgon and his family to their property: property is what establishes the position, the place, the social and individual identity of these characters. Although Molière's DEUS EX MACHINA might be regarded as an elegant (though somewhat clumsy) compliment to the king—and, perhaps, as a sly jab at the clerical critics who attacked *Tartuffe*—this device plays a subtle role in dramatizing the nature of royal authority. For in *Tartuffe,* the king has the power to assign every person to his or her proper place, to see into our inmost hearts, to structure the moral and social order of the world as the reflection of his own will and judgment: *"L'état, c'est moi."* In this sense, even though *Tartuffe* unleashes the uncontrollable power of self-delusion and the power and destructive fantasies of absolute authority, the play concludes by asserting the legitimacy of that absolute power. Molière's *deus ex machina* testifies both to the power and to the arbitrariness of the king's authority.

PREFACE[1]

TRANSLATED BY RICHARD WILBUR

Here is a comedy that has excited a good deal of discussion and that has been under attack for a long time; and the persons who are mocked by it have made it plain that they are more powerful in France than all whom my plays have satirized up to this time. Noblemen, ladies of fashion, cuckolds, and doctors all kindly consented to their presentation, which they themselves seemed to enjoy along with everyone else; but hypocrites do not understand banter: they became angry at once, and found it strange that I was bold enough to represent their actions and to care to describe a profession shared by so many good men. This is a crime for which they cannot forgive me, and they have taken up arms against my comedy in a terrible rage. They were careful not to attack it at the point that had wounded them: they are too crafty for that and too clever to reveal their true character. In keeping with their lofty custom, they have used the cause of God to mask their private interests; and *Tartuffe,* they say, is a play that offends piety: It is filled with abominations from beginning to end, and nowhere is there a line that does not deserve to be burned. Every syllable is wicked, the very gestures are criminal, and the slightest glance, turn of the head, or step from right to left conceals mysteries that they are able to explain to my disadvantage. In vain did I submit the play to the criticism of my friends and the scrutiny of the public: all the corrections I could make, the judgment of the king and queen who saw the play,[2] the approval of great princes and ministers of state who honored it with their presence, the opinion of good men who found it worthwhile; all this did not help. They will not let go of their prey, and every day of the week they have pious zealots abusing me in public and damning me out of charity.

I would care very little about all they might say except that their devices make enemies of men whom I respect and gain the support of genuinely good men, whose faith they know and who, because of the warmth of their piety, readily accept the impressions that others present to them. And it is this which forces me to defend myself. Especially to the truly devout do I wish to vindicate my play, and I beg of them with all my heart not to condemn it before seeing it, to rid themselves of preconceptions, and not aid the cause of men dishonored by their actions.

If one takes the trouble to examine my comedy in good faith, he will surely see that my intentions are innocent throughout, and tend in no way to make fun of what men revere; that I have presented the subject with all the precautions that its delicacy imposes; and that I have used all the art and skill that I could to distinguish clearly the character of the hypocrite from that of the truly devout man. For that purpose I used two whole acts to prepare the appearance of my scoundrel. Never is there a moment's doubt about his character; he is known at once from the qualities I have given him; and from one end of the play to the other, he does not say a word, he does not perform an action which does not depict to

---

[1]Molière added his three petitions to Louis XIV; they follow the preface.
[2]Louis XIV was married to Marie Thérèse of Austria.

the audience the character of a wicked man, and which does not bring out in sharp relief the character of the truly good man which I oppose to it.

I know full well that by way of reply, these gentlemen try to insinuate that it is not the role of the theater to speak of these matters; but with their permission, I ask them on what do they base this fine doctrine. It is a proposition they advance as no more than a supposition, for which they offer not a shred of proof; and surely it would not be difficult to show them that comedy, for the ancients, had its origin in religion and constituted a part of its ceremonies; that our neighbors, the Spaniards, have hardly a single holiday celebration in which a comedy is not a part; and that even here in France, it owes its birth to the efforts of a religious brotherhood who still own the Hôtel de Bourgogne, where the most important mystery plays of our faith were presented[3]; that you can still find comedies printed in gothic letters under the name of a learned doctor of the Sorbonne[4]; and without going so far, in our own day the religious dramas of Pierre Corneille[5] have been performed to the admiration of all France.

If the function of comedy is to correct men's vices, I do not see why any should be exempt. Such a condition in our society would be much more dangerous than the thing itself; and we have seen that the theater is admirably suited to provide correction. The most forceful lines of a serious moral statement are usually less powerful than those of satire; and nothing will reform most men better than the depiction of their faults. It is a vigorous blow to vices to expose them to public laughter. Criticism is taken lightly, but men will not tolerate satire. They are quite willing to be mean, but they never like to be ridiculed.

I have been attacked for having placed words of piety in the mouth of my impostor. Could I avoid doing so in order to represent properly the character of a hypocrite? It seemed to me sufficient to reveal the criminal motives which make him speak as he does, and I have eliminated all ceremonial phrases, which nonetheless he would not have been found using incorrectly. Yet some say that in the fourth act he sets forth a vicious morality; but is not this a morality which everyone has heard again and again? Does my comedy say anything new here? And is there any fear that ideas so thoroughly detested by everyone can make an impression on men's minds; that I make them dangerous by presenting them in the theater; that they acquire authority from the lips of a scoundrel? There is not the slightest suggestion of any of this; and one must either approve the comedy of *Tartuffe* or condemn all comedies in general.

This has indeed been done in a furious way for some time now, and never was the theater so much abused.[6] I cannot deny that there were Church Fathers who condemned comedy; but neither will it be denied me that there were some who looked on it somewhat more favorably. Thus authority, on which censure is supposed to depend, is destroyed by this disagreement; and the only conclusion that can be drawn from this difference of opinion among men enlightened by the same wisdom is that they viewed comedy in different ways, and that some considered it in its purity, while others regarded it in its corruption and confused it with all those wretched performances which have been rightly called performances of filth.

---

[3]A reference to the *Confrérie de la Passion et Résurrection de Notre-Seigneur* (the Fraternity of the Passion and Resurrection of Our Saviour), founded in 1402. The Hôtel de Bourgogne was a rival theater of Molière.

[4]Probably Maitre Jehán Michel, a medical doctor who wrote mystery plays.

[5]Pierre Corneille (1606–1684) and Racine were France's two greatest writers of classic tragedy. The two dramas Molière doubtlessly had in mind were *Polyeucte* (1643) and *Théodore, vierge et martyre* (1645).

[6]Molière had in mind Nicole's two attacks on the theater: *Visionnaries* (1666) and *Traité de Comédie*, and the Prince de Condé's *Traité de Comédie* (1666).

And in fact, since we should talk about things rather than words, and since most misunderstanding comes from including contrary notions in the same word, we need only to remove the veil of ambiguity and look at comedy in itself to see if it warrants condemnation. It will surely be recognized that as it is nothing more than a clever poem which corrects men's faults by means of agreeable lessons, it cannot be condemned without injustice. And if we listened to the voice of ancient times on this matter, it would tell us that its most famous philosophers have praised comedy—they who professed so austere a wisdom and who ceaselessly denounced the vices of their times. It would tell us that Aristotle spent his evenings at the theater[7] and took the trouble to reduce the art of making comedies to rules. It would tell us that some of its greatest and most honored men took pride in writing comedies themselves,[8] and that others did not disdain to recite them in public; that Greece expressed its admiration for this art by means of handsome prizes and magnificent theaters to honor it; and finally, that in Rome this same art also received extraordinary honors; I do not speak of Rome run riot under the license of the emperors, but of disciplined Rome, governed by the wisdom of the consuls, and in the age of the full vigor of Roman dignity.

I admit that there have been times when comedy became corrupt. And what do men not corrupt every day? There is nothing so innocent that men cannot turn it to crime; nothing so beneficial that its values cannot be reversed; nothing so good in itself that it cannot be put to bad uses. Medical knowledge benefits mankind and is revered as one of our most wonderful possessions; and yet there was a time when it fell into discredit, and was often used to poison men. Philosophy is a gift of Heaven; it has been given to us to bring us to the knowledge of a God by contemplating the wonders of nature; and yet we know that often it has been turned away from its function and has been used openly in support of impiety. Even the holiest of things are not immune from human corruption, and every day we see scoundrels who use and abuse piety, and wickedly make it serve the greatest of crimes. But this does not prevent one from making the necessary distinctions. We do not confuse in the same false inference the goodness of things that are corrupted with the wickedness of the corrupt. The function of an art is always distinguished from its misuse; and as medicine is not forbidden because it was banned in Rome,[9] nor philosophy because it was publicly condemned in Athens,[10] we should not suppress comedy simply because it has been condemned at certain times. This censure was justified then for reasons which no longer apply today; it was limited to what was then seen; and we should not seize on these limits, apply them more rigidly than is necessary, and include in our condemnation the innocent along with the guilty. The comedy that this censure attacked is in no way the comedy that we want to defend. We must be careful not to confuse the one with the other. There may be two persons whose morals may be completely different. They may have no resemblance to one another except in their names, and it would be a terrible injustice to want to condemn Olympia, who is a good woman, because there is also an Olympia who is lewd. Such procedures would make for great confusion everywhere. Everything under the sun would be condemned; now since this rigor is not applied to the countless instances of abuse we see every day, the same should hold for comedy, and those plays should be approved in which instruction and virtue reign supreme.

---

[7]A reference to Aristotle's *The Poetics* (composed between 335 and 322 BCE, the year of his death).

[8]The Roman consul and general responsible for the final destruction of Carthage in 146 BCE, Scipio Africanus Minor (c. 185–129 BCE), collaborated with the writer of comedies, Terence (Publius Terentius Afer, c. 195 or 185–c. 159 BCE).

[9]Pliny the Elder says that the Romans expelled their doctors at the same time that the Greeks did theirs.

[10]An allusion to Socrates' condemnation to death.

I know there are some so delicate that they cannot tolerate a comedy, who say that the most decent are the most dangerous, that the passions they present are all the more moving because they are virtuous, and that men's feelings are stirred by these presentations. I do not see what great crime it is to be affected by the sight of a generous passion; and this utter insensitivity to which they would lead us is indeed a high degree of virtue! I wonder if so great a perfection resides within the strength of human nature, and I wonder if it is not better to try to correct and moderate men's passions than to try to suppress them altogether. I grant that there are places better to visit than the theater; and if we want to condemn every single thing that does not bear directly on God and our salvation, it is right that comedy be included, and I should willingly grant that it be condemned along with everything else. But if we admit, as is in fact true, that the exercise of piety will permit interruptions, and that men need amusement, I maintain that there is none more innocent than comedy. I have dwelled too long on this matter. Let me finish with the words of a great prince on the comedy, *Tartuffe*.[11]

Eight days after it had been banned, a play called *Scaramouche the Hermit*[12] was performed before the court; and the king, on his way out, said to this great prince: "I should really like to know why the persons who make so much noise about Molière's comedy do not say a word about *Scaramouche*." To which the prince replied, "It is because the comedy of *Scaramouche* makes fun of Heaven and religion, which these gentlemen do not care about at all, but that of Molière makes fun of *them,* and that is what they cannot bear."

Molière

First Petition[13]
(PRESENTED TO THE KING ON THE COMEDY OF TARTUFFE)

Sire,

As the duty of comedy is to correct men by amusing them, I believed that in my occupation I could do nothing better than attack the vices of my age by making them ridiculous; and as hypocrisy is undoubtedly one of the most common, most improper, and most dangerous, I thought, Sire, that I would perform a service for all good men of your kingdom if I wrote a comedy which denounced hypocrites and placed in proper view all of the contrived poses of these incredibly virtuous men, all of the concealed villainies of these counterfeit believers who would trap others with a fraudulent piety and a pretended virtue.

I have written this comedy, Sire, with all the care and caution that the delicacy of the subject demands; and so as to maintain all the more properly the admiration and respect due to truly devout men, I have delineated my character as sharply as I could; I have left no room for doubt; I have removed all that might confuse good with evil, and have used for this painting only the specific colors and essential lines that make one instantly recognize a true and brazen hypocrite.

Nevertheless, all my precautions have been to no avail. Others have taken advantage of the delicacy of your feelings on religious matters, and they have been able to deceive you

---

[11]One of Molière's benefactors who liked the play was the Prince de Condé; the Prince had *Tartuffe* read to him and also privately performed for him.

[12]A troupe of Italian comedians had just performed the licentious farce, where a hermit dressed as a monk makes love to a married woman, announcing that *questo e per mortificar la carne* ("this is to mortify the flesh").

[13]The first of the three *petitions* or *placets* to Louis XIV concerning the play. On May 12, 1664, *Tartuffe*—or at least the first three acts roughly as they now stand—was performed at Versailles. A cabal unfavorable to Molière, including the Archbishop of Paris, Hardouin de Péréfixe, Queen-Mother Anne of Austria, certain influential courtiers, and the Brotherhood or Company of the Holy Sacrament (formed in 1627 to enforce morality), arranged that the play be banned and Molière censured.

on the only side of your character which lies open to deception: your respect for holy things. By underhanded means, the Tartuffes have skillfully gained Your Majesty's favor, and the models have succeeded in eliminating the copy, no matter how innocent it may have been and no matter what resemblance was found between them.

Although the suppression of this work was a serious blow for me, my misfortune was nonetheless softened by the way in which Your Majesty explained his attitude on the matter; and I believed, Sire, that Your Majesty removed any cause I had for complaint, as you were kind enough to declare that you found nothing in this comedy that you would forbid me to present in public.

Yet, despite this glorious declaration of the greatest and most enlightened king in the world, despite the approval of the Papal Legate[14] and of most of our churchmen, all of whom, at private readings of my work, agreed with the views of Your Majesty, despite all this, a book has appeared by a certain priest[15] which boldly contradicts all of these noble judgments. Your Majesty expressed himself in vain, and the Papal Legate and churchmen gave their opinion to no avail: Sight unseen, my comedy is diabolical, and so is my brain; I am a devil garbed in flesh and disguised as a man,[16] a libertine, a disbeliever who deserves a punishment that will set an example. It is not enough that fire expiate my crime in public, for that would be letting me off too easily: The generous piety of this good man will not stop there; he will not allow me to find any mercy in the sight of God; he demands that I be damned, and that will settle the matter.

This book, Sire, was presented to Your Majesty; and I am sure that you see for yourself how unpleasant it is for me to be exposed daily to the insults of these gentlemen, what harm these abuses will do my reputation if they must be tolerated, and finally, how important it is for me to clear myself of these false charges and let the public know that my comedy is nothing more than what they want it to be. I will not ask, Sire, for what I need for the sake of my reputation and the innocence of my work: enlightened kings such as you do not need to be told what is wished of them; like God, they see what we need and know better than we what they should give us. It is enough for me to place my interests in Your Majesty's hands, and I respectfully await whatever you may care to command.

(August, 1664)

Second Petition[17]

(PRESENTED TO THE KING IN HIS CAMP BEFORE THE CITY OF LILLE, IN FLANDERS)

Sire,

It is bold indeed for me to ask a favor of a great monarch in the midst of his glorious victories; but in my present situation, Sire, where will I find protection anywhere but where I seek it, and to whom can I appeal against the authority of the power that crushes me,[18] if not to the source of power and authority, the just dispenser of absolute law, the sovereign judge and master of all?

---

[14]Cardinal Legate Chigi, nephew to Pope Alexander VII, heard a reading of *Tartuffe* at Fontainebleau on August 4, 1664.

[15]Pierre Roullé, the curate of St. Barthélémy, who wrote a scathing attack on the play and sent his book to the king.

[16]Molière took some of these phrases from Roullé.

[17]On August 5, 1667, *Tartuffe* was performed at the Palais-Royal. The opposition—headed by the First President of Parliament—brought in the police, and the play was stopped. Since Louis was campaigning in Flanders, friends of Molière brought the second *placet* to Lille. Louis had always been favorable toward the playwright; in August 1665, Molière's company, the *Troupe de Monsieur* (nominally sponsored by Louis's brother Philippe, Duc d'Orléans) had become the *Troupe du Roi*.

[18]President de Lanvignon, in charge of the Paris police.

My comedy, Sire, has not enjoyed the kindnesses of Your Majesty. All to no avail, I produced it under the title of *The Hypocrite* and disguised the principal character as a man of the world; in vain I gave him a little hat, long hair, a wide collar, a sword, and lace clothing,[19] softened the action and carefully eliminated all that I thought might provide even the shadow of grounds for discontent on the part of the famous models of the portrait I wished to present; nothing did any good. The conspiracy of opposition revived even at mere conjecture of what the play would be like. They found a way of persuading those who in all other matters plainly insist that they are not to be deceived. No sooner did my comedy appear than it was struck down by the very power which should impose respect; and all that I could do to save myself from the fury of this tempest was to say that Your Majesty had given me permission to present the play and I did not think it was necessary to ask this permission of others, since only Your Majesty could have refused it.

I have no doubt, Sire, that the men whom I depict in my comedy will employ every means possible to influence Your Majesty, and will use, as they have used already, those truly good men who are all the more easily deceived because they judge of others by themselves.[20] They know how to display all of their aims in the most favorable light; yet, no matter how pious they may seem, it is surely not the interests of God which stir them; they have proven this often enough in the comedies they have allowed to be performed hundreds of times without making the least objection. Those plays attacked only piety and religion, for which they care very little; but this play attacks and makes fun of them, and that is what they cannot bear. They will never forgive me for unmasking their hypocrisy in the eyes of everyone. And I am sure that they will not neglect to tell Your Majesty that people are shocked by my comedy. But the simple truth, Sire, is that all Paris is shocked only by its ban, that the most scrupulous persons have found its presentation worthwhile, and men are astounded that individuals of such known integrity should show so great a deference to people whom everyone should abominate and who are so clearly opposed to the true piety which they profess.

I respectfully await the judgment that Your Majesty will deign to pronounce: But it's certain, Sire, that I need not think of writing comedies if the Tartuffes are triumphant, if they thereby seize the right to persecute me more than ever, and find fault with even the most innocent lines that flow from my pen.

Let your goodness, Sire, give me protection against their envenomed rage, and allow me, at your return from so glorious a campaign, to relieve Your Majesty from the fatigue of his conquests, give him innocent pleasures after such noble accomplishments, and make the monarch laugh who makes all Europe tremble!

(August, 1667)

Third Petition
(PRESENTED TO THE KING)

Sire,

A very honest doctor[21] whose patient I have the honor to be, promises and will legally contract to make me live another thirty years if I can obtain a favor for him from Your Majesty. I told him of his promise that I do not deserve so much, and that I should be glad to help him if he will merely agree not to kill me. This favor, Sire, is a post of canon at your royal chapel of Vincennes, made vacant by death.

---

[19]There is evidence that in 1664 Tartuffe played his role dressed in a cassock, thus allying him more directly to the clergy.

[20]Molière apparently did not know that de Lanvignon had been affiliated with the Company of the Holy Sacrament for the previous ten years.

[21]A physician friend, M. de Mauvillain, who helped Molière with some of the medical details of *Le Malade imaginaire*.

May I dare to ask for this favor from Your Majesty on the very day of the glorious resurrection of *Tartuffe,* brought back to life by your goodness? By this first favor I have been reconciled with the devout, and the second will reconcile me with the doctors.[22] Undoubtedly this would be too much grace for me at one time, but perhaps it would not be too much for Your Majesty, and I await your answer to my petition with respectful hope.

(February, 1669)

---

[22]Doctors are ridiculed to varying degrees in earlier plays of Molière: *Dom Juan, L'Amour médecin,* and *Le Médecin malgré lui.*

TARTUFFE

Molière

TRANSLATED BY RICHARD WILBUR

CHARACTERS

MADAME PERNELLE, *Orgon's mother*
ORGON, *Elmire's husband*
ELMIRE, *Orgon's wife*
DAMIS, *Orgon's son, Elmire's stepson*
MARIANE, *Orgon's daughter, Elmire's stepdaughter, in love with Valère*
VALÈRE, *in love with Mariane*
CLÉANTE, *Orgon's brother-in-law*

TARTUFFE, *a hypocrite*
DORINE, *Mariane's lady's-maid*
M. LOYAL, *a bailiff*
A POLICE OFFICER
FLIPOTE, *Madame Pernelle's maid*

The scene throughout: Orgon's house in Paris

ACT ONE

SCENE I

MADAME PERNELLE *and* FLIPOTE, *her maid,* ELMIRE, MARIANE, DORINE, DAMIS, CLÉANTE

MADAME PERNELLE: Come, come, Flipote; it's time I left this place.
ELMIRE: I can't keep up, you walk at such a pace.
MADAME PERNELLE: Don't trouble, child; no need to show me out.
It's not your manners I'm concerned about.
5 ELMIRE: We merely pay you the respect we owe.
But, Mother, why this hurry? Must you go?
MADAME PERNELLE: I must. This house appals me. No one in it
Will pay attention for a single minute.
Children, I take my leave much vexed in spirit.
10 I offer good advice, but you won't hear it.
You all break in and chatter on and on.
It's like a madhouse with the keeper gone.
DORINE: If . . .
MADAME PERNELLE: Girl, you talk too much, and I'm afraid
You're far too saucy for a lady's-maid.
15 You push in everywhere and have your say.
DAMIS: But . . .
MADAME PERNELLE: You, boy, grow more foolish every day.
To think my grandson should be such a dunce!
I've said a hundred times, if I've said it once,
That if you keep the course on which you've started,
20 You'll leave your worthy father broken-hearted.
MARIANE: I think . . .
MADAME PERNELLE: And you, his sister, seem so pure,
So shy, so innocent, and so demure.
But you know what they say about still waters.
I pity parents with secretive daughters.
25 ELMIRE: Now, Mother . . .
MADAME PERNELLE   And as for you, child, let me add
That your behavior is extremely bad,
And a poor example for these children, too.
Their dear, dead mother did far better than you.
You're much too free with money, and I'm distressed
30 To see you so elaborately dressed.
When it's one's husband that one aims to please,
One has no need of costly fripperies.

CLÉANTE: Oh, Madam, really . . .
MADAME PERNELLE: You are her brother, Sir,
And I respect and love you; yet if I were
My son, this lady's good and pious spouse,   35
I wouldn't make you welcome in my house.
You're full of worldly counsels which, I fear,
Aren't suitable for decent folk to hear.
I've spoken bluntly, Sir; but it behooves us
Not to mince words when righteous fervor moves us.   40
DAMIS: Your man Tartuffe is full of holy speeches . . .
MADAME PERNELLE: And practises precisely what he preaches.
He's a fine man, and should be listened to.
I will not hear him mocked by fools like you.
DAMIS: Good God! Do you expect me to submit   45
To the tyranny of that carping hypocrite?
Must we forgo all joys and satisfactions
Because that bigot censures all our actions?
DORINE: To hear him talk—and he talks all the time—
There's nothing one can do that's not a crime.   50
He rails at everything, your dear Tartuffe.
MADAME PERNELLE: Whatever he reproves deserves reproof.
He's out to save your souls, and all of you
Must love him, as my son would have you do.
DAMIS: Ah no, Grandmother, I could never take   55
To such a rascal, even for my father's sake.
That's how I feel, and I shall not dissemble.
His every action makes me seethe and tremble
With helpless anger, and I have no doubt
That he and I will shortly have it out.   60
DORINE: Surely it is a shame and a disgrace
To see this man usurp the master's place—
To see this beggar who, when first he came,
Had not a shoe or shoestring to his name
So far forget himself that he behaves   65
As if the house were his, and we his slaves.
MADAME PERNELLE: Well, mark my words, your souls would fare far better
If you obeyed his precepts to the letter.
DORINE: You see him as a saint. I'm far less awed;
In fact, I see right through him. He's a fraud.   70
MADAME PERNELLE: Nonsense!
DORINE: His man Laurent's the same, or worse;
I'd not trust either with a penny purse.
MADAME PERNELLE: I can't say what his servant's morals may be;

His own great goodness I can guarantee.
75 You all regard him with distaste and fear
Because he tells you what you're loath to hear,
Condemns your sins, points out your moral flaws,
And humbly strives to further Heaven's cause.
DORINE: If sin is all that bothers him, why is it
80 He's so upset when folk drop in to visit?
Is Heaven so outraged by a social call
That he must prophesy against us all?
I'll tell you what I think: if you ask me,
He's jealous of my mistress' company.
85 MADAME PERNELLE: Rubbish! (*To* ELMIRE.) He's not alone,
child, in complaining
Of all of your promiscuous entertaining.
Why, the whole neighborhood's upset, I know,
By all these carriages that come and go,
With crowds of guests parading in and out
90 And noisy servants loitering about.
In all of this, I'm sure there's nothing vicious;
But why give people cause to be suspicious?
CLÉANTE: They need no cause; they'll talk in any case.
Madam, this world would be a joyless place
95 If, fearing what malicious tongues might say,
We locked our doors and turned our friends away.
And even if one did so dreary a thing,
D'you think those tongues would cease their chattering?
One can't fight slander; it's a losing battle;
100 Let us instead ignore their tittle-tattle.
Let's strive to live by conscience' clear decrees,
And let the gossips gossip as they please.
DORINE: If there is talk against us, I know the source:
It's Daphne and her little husband, of course.
105 Those who have greatest cause for guilt and shame
Are quickest to besmirch a neighbor's name.
When there's a chance for libel, they never miss it;
When something can be made to seem illicit
They're off at once to spread the joyous news,
110 Adding to fact what fantasies they choose.
By talking up their neighbor's indiscretions
They seek to camouflage their own transgressions,
Hoping that others' innocent affairs
Will lend a hue of innocence to theirs,
115 Or that their own black guilt will come to seem
Part of a general shady color-scheme.
MADAME PERNELLE: All that is quite irrelevant. I doubt
That anyone's more virtuous and devout
Than dear Orante; and I'm informed that she
120 Condemns your mode of life most vehemently.
DORINE: Oh, yes, she's strict, devout, and has no taint
Of worldliness; in short, she seems a saint.
But it was time which taught her that disguise;
She's thus because she can't be otherwise.
125 So long as her attractions could enthrall,
She flounced and flirted and enjoyed it all,
But now that they're no longer what they were
She quits a world which fast is quitting her,
And wears a veil of virtue to conceal
130 Her bankrupt beauty and her lost appeal.
That's what becomes of old coquettes today:
Distressed when all their lovers fall away,
They see no recourse but to play the prude,

And so confer a style on solitude.
Thereafter, they're severe with everyone, 135
Condemning all our actions, pardoning none,
And claiming to be pure, austere, and zealous
When, if the truth were known, they're merely jealous,
And cannot bear to see another know
The pleasures time has forced them to forgo. 140
MADAME PERNELLE: (*Initially to* ELMIRE.) That sort of talk is
what you like to hear;
Therefore you'd have us all keep still, my dear,
While Madam rattles on the livelong day.
Nevertheless, I mean to have my say.
I tell you that you're blest to have Tartuffe 145
Dwelling, as my son's guest, beneath this roof;
That Heaven has sent him to forestall its wrath
By leading you, once more, to the true path;
That all he reprehends is reprehensible,
And that you'd better heed him, and be sensible. 150
These visits, balls, and parties in which you revel
Are nothing but inventions of the Devil.
One never hears a word that's edifying:
Nothing but chaff and foolishness and lying,
As well as vicious gossip in which one's neighbor 155
Is cut to bits with épée, foil, and saber.
People of sense are driven half-insane
At such affairs, where noise and folly reign
And reputations perish thick and fast.
As a wise preacher said on Sunday last, 160
Parties are Towers of Babylon, because
The guests all babble on with never a pause;
And then he told a story which, I think . . .

(*To* CLÉANTE.)

I heard that laugh, Sir, and I saw that wink!
Go find your silly friends and laugh some more! 165
Enough; I'm going; don't show me to the door.
I leave this household much dismayed and vexed;
I cannot say when I shall see you next.

(*Slapping* FLIPOTE.)

Wake up, don't stand there gaping into space!
I'll slap some sense into that stupid face. 170
Move, move, you slut.

SCENE II

CLÉANTE, DORINE

CLÉANTE: I think I'll stay behind;
I want no further pieces of her mind.
How that old lady . . .
DORINE: Oh, what wouldn't she say
If she could hear you speak of her that way!
She'd thank you for the *lady*, but I'm sure 5
She'd find the *old* a little premature.
CLÉANTE: My, what a scene she made, and what a din!
And how this man Tartuffe has taken her in!
DORINE: Yes, but her son is even worse deceived;
His folly must be seen to be believed. 10

In the late troubles, he played an able part
And served his king with wise and loyal heart,
But he's quite lost his senses since he fell
Beneath Tartuffe's infatuating spell.
15 He calls him brother, and loves him as his life,
Preferring him to mother, child, or wife.
In him and him alone will he confide;
He's made him his confessor and his guide;
He pets and pampers him with love more tender
20 Than any pretty mistress could engender,
Gives him the place of honor when they dine,
Delights to see him gorging like a swine,
Stuffs him with dainties till his guts distend,
And when he belches, cries "God bless you, friend!"
25 In short, he's mad; he worships him; he dotes;
His deeds he marvels at, his words he quotes,
Thinking each act a miracle, each word
Oracular as those that Moses heard.
Tartuffe, much pleased to find so easy a victim,
30 Has in a hundred ways beguiled and tricked him,
Milked him of money, and with his permission
Established here a sort of Inquisition.
Even Laurent, his lackey, dares to give
Us arrogant advice on how to live;
35 He sermonizes us in thundering tones
And confiscates our ribbons and colognes.
Last week he tore a kerchief into pieces
Because he found it pressed in a *Life of Jesus*:
He said it was a sin to juxtapose
40 Unholy vanities and holy prose.

SCENE III

ELMIRE, MARIANE, DAMIS, CLÉANTE, DORINE

ELMIRE: (*To* CLÉANTE.) You did well not to follow; she stood
    in the door
  And said *verbatim* all she'd said before.
  I saw my husband coming. I think I'd best
  Go upstairs now, and take a little rest.
5 CLÉANTE: I'll wait and greet him here; then I must go.
  I've really only time to say hello.
DAMIS: Sound him about my sister's wedding, please.
  I think Tartuffe's against it, and that he's
  Been urging Father to withdraw his blessing.
10 As you well know, I'd find that most distressing.
  Unless my sister and Valère can marry,
  My hopes to wed *his* sister will miscarry,
  And I'm determined . . .
DORINE: He's coming.

SCENE IV

ORGON, CLÉANTE, DORINE

ORGON: Ah, Brother, good-day.
CLÉANTE: Well, welcome back. I'm sorry I can't stay.
  How was the country? Blooming, I trust, and green?
ORGON: Excuse me, Brother; just one moment.

(*To* DORINE.)

                                Dorine . . .

(*To* CLÉANTE.)

  To put my mind at rest, I always learn   5
  The household news the moment I return.

(*To* DORINE.)

  Has all been well, these two days I've been gone?
  How are the family? What's been going on?
DORINE: Your wife, two days ago, had a bad fever,
  And a fierce headache which refused to leave her.   10
ORGON: Ah. And Tartuffe?
DORINE: Tartuffe? Why, he's round and red,
  Bursting with health, and excellently fed.
ORGON: Poor fellow!
DORINE: That night, the mistress was unable
  To take a single bite at the dinner-table.
  Her headache-pains, she said, were simply hellish.   15
ORGON: Ah. And Tartuffe?
DORINE: He ate his meal with relish,
  And zealously devoured in her presence
  A leg of mutton and a brace of pheasants.
ORGON: Poor fellow!
DORINE: Well, the pains continued strong,
  And so she tossed and tossed the whole night long,   20
  Now icy-cold, now burning like a flame.
  We sat beside her bed till morning came.
ORGON: Ah. And Tartuffe?
DORINE: Why, having eaten, he rose
  And sought his room, already in a doze,
  Got into his warm bed, and snored away   25
  In perfect peace until the break of day.
ORGON: Poor fellow!
DORINE: After much ado, we talked her
  Into dispatching someone for the doctor.
  He bled her, and the fever quickly fell.
ORGON: Ah. And Tartuffe?   30
DORINE: He bore it very well.
  To keep his cheerfulness at any cost,
  And make up for the blood *Madame* had lost,
  He drank, at lunch, four beakers full of port.
ORGON: Poor fellow!
DORINE: Both are doing well, in short.
  I'll go and tell *Madame* that you've expressed   35
  Keen sympathy and anxious interest.

SCENE V

ORGON, CLÉANTE

CLÉANTE: That girl was laughing in your face, and though
  I've no wish to offend you, even so
  I'm bound to say that she had some excuse.
  How can you possibly be such a goose?
  Are you so dazed by this man's hocus-pocus   5
  That all the world, save him, is out of focus?
  You've given him clothing, shelter, food, and care;
  Why must you also . . .
ORGON: Brother, stop right there.
  You do not know the man of whom you speak.
CLÉANTE: I grant you that. But my judgment's not so weak   10
  That I can't tell, by his effect on others . . .

ORGON: Ah, when you meet him, you two will be like brothers!
There's been no loftier soul since time began.
He is a man who . . . a man who . . . an excellent man.
15 To keep his precepts is to be reborn,
And view this dunghill of a world with scorn.
Yes, thanks to him I'm a changed man indeed.
Under his tutelage my soul's been freed
From earthly loves, and every human tie:
20 My mother, children, brother, and wife could die,
And I'd not feel a single moment's pain.

CLÉANTE: That's a fine sentiment, Brother; most humane.

ORGON: Oh, had you seen Tartuffe as I first knew him,
Your heart, like mine, would have surrendered to him.
25 He used to come into our church each day
And humbly kneel nearby, and start to pray.
He'd draw the eyes of everybody there
By the deep fervor of his heartfelt prayer;
He'd sigh and weep, and sometimes with a sound
30 Of rapture he would bend and kiss the ground;
And when I rose to go, he'd run before
To offer me holy-water at the door.
His serving-man, no less devout than he,
Informed me of his master's poverty;
35 I gave him gifts, but in his humbleness
He'd beg me every time to give him less.
"Oh, that's too much," he'd cry, "too much by twice!
I don't deserve it. The half, Sir, would suffice."
And when I wouldn't take it back, he'd share
40 Half of it with the poor, right then and there.
At length, Heaven prompted me to take him in
To dwell with us, and free our souls from sin.
He guides our lives, and to protect my honor
Stays by my wife, and keeps an eye upon her;
45 He tells me whom she sees, and all she does,
And seems more jealous than I ever was!
And how austere he is! Why, he can detect
A mortal sin where you would least suspect;
In smallest trifles, he's extremely strict.
50 Last week, his conscience was severely pricked
Because, while praying, he had caught a flea
And killed it, so he felt, too wrathfully.

CLÉANTE: Good God, man! Have you lost your common sense—
Or is this all some joke at my expense?
55 How can you stand there and in all sobriety . . .

ORGON: Brother, your language savors of impiety.
Too much free-thinking's made your faith unsteady,
And as I've warned you many times already,
'Twill get you into trouble before you're through.

60 CLÉANTE: So I've been told before by dupes like you:
Being blind, you'd have all others blind as well;
The clear-eyed man you call an infidel,
And he who sees through humbug and pretense
Is charged, by you, with want of reverence.
65 Spare me your warnings, Brother; I have no fear
Of speaking out, for you and Heaven to hear,
Against affected zeal and pious knavery.
There's true and false in piety, as in bravery,
And just as those whose courage shines the most
70 In battle, are the least inclined to boast,
So those whose hearts are truly pure and lowly
Don't make a flashy show of being holy.
There's a vast difference, so it seems to me,

Between true piety and hypocrisy:
How do you fail to see it, may I ask? 75
Is not a face quite different from a mask?
Cannot sincerity and cunning art,
Reality and semblance, be told apart?
Are scarecrows just like men, and do you hold
That a false coin is just as good as gold? 80
Ah, Brother, man's a strangely fashioned creature
Who seldom is content to follow Nature,
But recklessly pursues his inclination
Beyond the narrow bounds of moderation,
And often, by transgressing Reason's laws, 85
Perverts a lofty aim or noble cause.
A passing observation, but it applies.

ORGON: I see, dear Brother, that you're profoundly wise;
You harbor all the insight of the age.
You are our one clear mind, our only sage, 90
The .era's oracle, its Cato too,
And all mankind are fools compared to you.

CLÉANTE: Brother, I don't pretend to be a sage,
Nor have I all the wisdom of the age.
There's just one insight I would dare to claim: 95
I know that true and false are not the same;
And just as there is nothing I more revere
Than a soul whose faith is steadfast and sincere,
Nothing that I more cherish and admire
Than honest zeal and true religious fire, 100
So there is nothing that I find more base
Than specious piety's dishonest face—
Than these bold mountebanks, these histrios
Whose impious mummeries and hollow shows
Exploit our love of Heaven, and make a jest 105
Of all that men think holiest and best;
These calculating souls who offer prayers
Not to their Maker, but as public wares,
And seek to buy respect and reputation
With lifted eyes and sighs of exaltation; 110
These charlatans, I say, whose pilgrim souls
Proceed, by way of Heaven, toward earthly goals,
Who weep and pray and swindle and extort,
Who preach the monkish life, but haunt the court,
Who make their zeal the partner of their vice— 115
Such men are vengeful, sly, and cold as ice,
And when there is an enemy to defame
They cloak their spite in fair religion's name,
Their private spleen and malice being made
To seem a high and virtuous crusade, 120
Until, to mankind's reverent applause,
They crucify their foe in Heaven's cause.
Such knaves are all too common; yet, for the wise,
True piety isn't hard to recognize,
And, happily, these present times provide us 125
With bright examples to instruct and guide us.
Consider Ariston and Périandre;
Look at Oronte, Alcidamas, Clitandre;
Their virtue is acknowledged; who could doubt it?
But you won't hear them beat the drum about it. 130
They're never ostentatious, never vain,
And their religion's moderate and humane;
It's not their way to criticize and chide:
They think censoriousness a mark of pride,
And therefore, letting others preach and rave, 135

They show, by deeds, how Christians should behave.
They think no evil of their fellow man,
But judge of him as kindly as they can.
They don't intrigue and wangle and conspire;
140   To lead a good life is their one desire;
The sinner wakes no rancorous hate in them;
It is the sin alone which they condemn;
Nor do they try to show a fiercer zeal
For Heaven's cause than Heaven itself could feel.
145   These men I honor, these men I advocate
As models for us all to emulate.
Your man is not their sort at all, I fear:
And, while your praise of him is quite sincere,
I think that you've been dreadfully deluded.
150   ORGON: Now then, dear Brother, is your speech concluded?
CLÉANTE: Why, yes.
ORGON: Your servant, Sir.

(He turns to go.)

CLÉANTE: No, Brother; wait.
There's one more matter. You agreed of late
That young Valère might have your daughter's hand.
ORGON: I did.   And set the date, I understand.
CLÉANTE:
155   ORGON: Quite so.
CLÉANTE: You've now postponed it; is that true?
ORGON: No doubt.
CLÉANTE: The match no longer pleases you?
ORGON: Who knows?
CLÉANTE: D'you mean to go back on your word?
ORGON: I won't say that.
CLÉANTE: Has anything occurred
Which might entitle you to break your pledge?
160   ORGON: Perhaps.
CLÉANTE: Why must you hem, and haw, and hedge?
The boy asked me to sound you in this affair . . .
ORGON: It's been a pleasure.
CLÉANTE: But what shall I tell Valère?
ORGON: Whatever you like.
CLÉANTE: But what have you decided?
What are your plans?
ORGON: I plan, Sir, to be guided
165   By Heaven's will.
CLÉANTE: Come, Brother, don't talk rot.
You've given Valère your word; will you keep it, or not?
ORGON: Good day.
CLÉANTE: This looks like poor Valère's undoing;
I'll go and warn him that there's trouble brewing.

ACT TWO

SCENE I

ORGON, MARIANE

ORGON: Mariane.
MARIANE: Yes, Father?
ORGON: A word with you; come here.
MARIANE: What are you looking for?
ORGON: *(Peering into a small closet.)*
                              Eavesdroppers, dear.

I'm making sure we shan't be overheard.
Someone in there could catch our every word.
Ah, good, we're safe. Now, Mariane, my child,   5
You're a sweet girl who's tractable and mild,
Whom I hold dear, and think most highly of.
MARIANE: I'm deeply grateful, Father, for your love.
ORGON: That's well said, Daughter; and you can repay me
If, in all things, you'll cheerfully obey me.   10
MARIANE: To please you, Sir, is what delights me best.
ORGON: Good, good. Now, what d'you think of Tartuffe, our
    guest?
MARIANE: I, Sir?
ORGON: Yes. Weigh your answer; think it through.
MARIANE: Oh, dear. I'll say whatever you wish me to.
ORGON: That's wisely said, my Daughter. Say of him, then,   15
That he's the very worthiest of men,
And that you're fond of him, and would rejoice
In being his wife, if that should be my choice.
Well?
MARIANE: What?
ORGON: What's that?
MARIANE: I . . .
ORGON: Well?
MARIANE: Forgive me, pray.
ORGON: Did you not hear me?   20
MARIANE: Of *whom,* Sir, must I say
That I am fond of him, and would rejoice
In being his wife, if that should be your choice?
ORGON: Why, of Tartuffe.
MARIANE: But, Father, that's false, you know.
Why would you have me say what isn't so?
ORGON: Because I am resolved it shall be true.   25
That it's my wish should be enough for you.
MARIANE: You can't mean, Father . . .
ORGON: Yes, Tartuffe shall be
Allied by marriage to this family,
And he's to be your husband, is that clear?
It's a father's privilege . . .   30

SCENE II

DORINE, ORGON, MARIANE

ORGON: *(To* DORINE.)   What are you doing in here?
Is curiosity so fierce a passion
With you, that you must eavesdrop in this fashion?
DORINE: There's lately been a rumor going about—
Based on some hunch or chance remark, no doubt—   5
That you mean Mariane to wed Tartuffe.
I've laughed it off, of course, as just a spoof.
ORGON: You find it so incredible?
DORINE: Yes, I do.
I won't accept that story, even from you.
ORGON: Well, you'll believe it when the thing is done.   10
DORINE: Yes, yes, of course. Go on and have your fun.
ORGON: I've never been more serious in my life.
DORINE: Ha!
ORGON: Daughter, I mean it; you're to be his wife.
DORINE: No, don't believe your father; it's all a hoax.
ORGON: See here, young woman . . .   15
DORINE: Come, Sir, no more jokes;

You can't fool us.

ORGON: How dare you talk that way?

DORINE: All right, then: we believe you, sad to say.
       But how a man like you, who looks so wise
       And wears a moustache of such splendid size,
20   Can be so foolish as to . . .

ORGON: Silence, please!
       My girl, you take too many liberties.
       I'm master here, as you must not forget.

DORINE: Do let's discuss this calmly; don't be upset.
       You can't be serious, Sir, about this plan.
25   What should that bigot want with Mariane?
       Praying and fasting ought to keep him busy.
       And then, in terms of wealth and rank, what is he?
       Why should a man of property like you
       Pick out a beggar son-in-law?

ORGON: That will do.
30   Speak of his poverty with reverence.
       His is a pure and saintly indigence
       Which far transcends all worldly pride and pelf.
       He lost his fortune, as he says himself,
       Because he cared for Heaven alone, and so
35   Was careless of his interests here below.
       I mean to get him out of his present straits
       And help him to recover his estates—
       Which, in his part of the world, have no small fame.
       Poor though he is, he's a gentleman just the same.

40 DORINE: Yes, so he tells us; and, Sir, it seems to me
       Such pride goes very ill with piety.
       A man whose spirit spurns this dungy earth
       Ought not to brag of lands and noble birth;
       Such worldly arrogance will hardly square
45   With meek devotion and the life of prayer.
       . . . But this approach, I see, has drawn a blank;
       Let's speak, then, of his person, not his rank.
       Doesn't it seem to you a trifle grim
       To give a girl like her to a man like him?
50   When two are so ill-suited, can't you see
       What the sad consequences is bound to be?
       A young girl's virtue is imperilled, Sir,
       When such a marriage is imposed on her;
       For if one's bridegroom isn't to one's taste,
55   It's hardly an inducement to be chaste,
       And many a man with horns upon his brow
       Has made his wife the thing that she is now.
       It's hard to be a faithful wife, in short,
       To certain husbands of a certain sort,
60   And he who gives his daughter to a man she hates
       Must answer for her sins at Heaven's gates.
       Think, Sir, before you play so risky a role.

ORGON: This servant-girl presumes to save my soul!

DORINE: You would do well to ponder what I've said.

65 ORGON: Daughter, we'll disregard this dunderhead.
       Just trust your father's judgment. Oh, I'm aware
       That I once promised you to young Valère;
       But now I hear he gambles, which greatly shocks me;
       What's more, I've doubts about his orthodoxy.
70   His visits to church, I note, are very few.

DORINE: Would you have him go at the same hours as you,
       And kneel nearby, to be sure of being seen?

ORGON: I can dispense with such remarks, Dorine.

(*To* MARIANE.)

       Tartuffe, however, is sure of Heaven's blessing,
       And that's the only treasure worth possessing.   75
       This match will bring you joys beyond all measure;
       Your cup will overflow with every pleasure;
       You two will interchange your faithful loves
       Like two sweet cherubs, or two turtle-doves.
       No harsh word shall be heard, no frown be seen,   80
       And he shall make you happy as a queen.

DORINE: And she'll make him a cuckold, just wait and see.

ORGON: What language!

DORINE: Oh, he's a man of destiny;
       He's *made* for horns, and what the stars demand
       Your daughter's virtue surely can't withstand.   85

ORGON: Don't interrupt me further. Why can't you learn
       That certain things are none of your concern?

DORINE: It's for your own sake that I interfere.

(*She repeatedly interrupts* ORGON *just as he is turning to speak to
his daughter.*)

ORGON: Most kind of you. Now, hold your tongue, d'you
          hear?

DORINE: If I didn't love you . . .   90

ORGON: Spare me your affection.

DORINE: I'll love you, Sir, in spite of your objection.

ORGON: Blast!

DORINE: I can't bear, Sir, for your honor's sake,
       To let you make this ludicrous mistake.

ORGON: You mean to go on talking?

DORINE: If I didn't protest
       This sinful marriage, my conscience couldn't rest. 95

ORGON: If you don't hold your tongue, you little shrew . . .

DORINE: What, lost your temper? A pious man like you?

ORGON: Yes! Yes! You talk and talk. I'm maddened by it.
       Once and for all, I tell you to be quiet.

DORINE: Well, I'll be quiet. But I'll be thinking hard.   100

ORGON: Think all you like, but you had better guard
       That saucy tongue of yours, or I'll . . .

(*Turning back to* MARIANE.)

                                   Now, child,
       I've weighed this matter fully.

DORINE: (*Aside.*)   It drives me wild
       That I can't speak.

(ORGON *turns his head, and she is silent.*)

ORGON: Tartuffe is no young dandy,
       But, still, his person . . .   105

DORINE: (*Aside.*)   Is as sweet as candy.

ORGON: Is such that, even if you shouldn't care
       For his other merits . . .

(*He turns and stands facing* DORINE, *arms crossed.*)

DORINE: (*Aside.*)   They'll make a lovely pair.
       If I were she, no man would marry me
       Against my inclination, and go scot-free.
       He'd learn, before the wedding-day was over,   110
       How readily a wife can find a lover.

ORGON: (*To* DORINE.) It seems you treat my orders as a joke.
DORINE: Why, what's the matter? 'Twas not to you I spoke.
ORGON: What *were* you doing?
DORINE: Talking to myself, that's all.
115   ORGON: Ah! (*Aside.*) One more bit of impudence and gall,
        And I shall give her a good slap in the face.

(*He puts himself in position to slap her;* DORINE, *whenever he glances at her, stands immobile and silent.*)

        Daughter, you shall accept, and with good grace,
        The husband I've selected . . .Your wedding-day . . .

(*To* DORINE.)

        Why don't you talk to yourself?
DORINE: I've nothing to say.
120   ORGON: Come, just one word.
DORINE: No thank you, Sir. I pass.
ORGON: Come, speak; I'm waiting.
DORINE: I'd not be such an ass.
ORGON: (*Turning to* MARIANE.) In short, dear Daughter, I
        mean to be obeyed,
        And you must bow to the sound choice I've made.
DORINE: (*Moving away.*) I'd not wed such a monster, even in jest.

(ORGON *attempts to slap her, but misses.*)

125   ORGON: Daughter, that maid of yours is a thorough pest;
        She makes me sinfully annoyed and nettled.
        I can't speak further; my nerves are too unsettled.
        She's so upset me by her insolent talk,
        I'll calm myself by going for a walk.

SCENE III

DORINE, MARIANE

DORINE: (*Returning.*) Well, have you lost your tongue, girl?
        Must I play
        Your part, and say the lines you ought to say?
        Faced with a fate so hideous and absurd,
        Can you not utter one dissenting word?
5   MARIANE: What good would it do? A father's power is great.
DORINE: Resist him now, or it will be too late.
MARIANE: But . . .
DORINE: Tell him one cannot love at a father's whim;
        That you shall marry for yourself, not him;
        That since it's you who are to be the bride,
10   It's you, not he, who must be satisfied;
        And that if his Tartuffe is so sublime,
        He's free to marry him at any time.
MARIANE: I've bowed so long to Father's strict control,
        I couldn't oppose him now, to save my soul.
15   DORINE: Come, come, Mariane. Do listen to reason, won't you?
        Valère has asked your hand. Do you love him, or don't you?
MARIANE: Oh, how unjust of you! What can you mean
        By asking such a question, dear Dorine?
        You know the depth of my affection for him;
20   I've told you a hundred times how I adore him.
DORINE: I don't believe in everything I hear;
        Who knows if your professions were sincere?

MARIANE: They were, Dorine, and you do me wrong to
        doubt it;
        Heaven knows that I've been all too frank about it.
DORINE: You love him, then?   25
MARIANE: Oh, more than I can express.
DORINE: And he, I take it, cares for you no less?
MARIANE: I think so.
DORINE: And you both, with equal fire,
        Burn to be married?
MARIANE: That is our one desire.
DORINE: What of Tartuffe, then? What of your father's plan?
MARIANE: I'll kill myself, if I'm forced to wed that man.   30
DORINE: I hadn't thought of that recourse. How splendid!
        Just die, and all your troubles will be ended!
        A fine solution. Oh, it maddens me
        To hear you talk in that self-pitying key.
MARIANE: Dorine, how harsh you are! It's most unfair.   35
        You have no sympathy for my despair.
DORINE: I've none at all for people who talk drivel
        And, faced with difficulties, whine and snivel.
MARIANE: No doubt I'm timid, but it would be wrong . . .
DORINE: True love requires a heart that's firm and strong.   40
MARIANE: I'm strong in my affection for Valère,
        But coping with my father is his affair.
DORINE: But if your father's brain has grown so cracked
        Over his dear Tartuffe that he can retract
        His blessing, though your wedding-day was named,   45
        It's surely not Valère who's to be blamed.
MARIANE: If I defied my father, as you suggest,
        Would it not seem unmaidenly, at best?
        Shall I defend my love at the expense
        Of brazeness and disobedience?   50
        Shall I parade my heart's desires, and flaunt . . .
DORINE: No, I ask nothing of you. Clearly you want
        To be Madame Tartuffe, and I feel bound
        Not to oppose a wish so very sound.
        What right have I to criticize the match?   55
        Indeed, my dear, the man's a brilliant catch.
        Monsieur Tartuffe! Now, there's a man of weight!
        Yes, yes, Monsieur Tartuffe, I'm bound to state,
        Is quite a person; that's not to be denied;
        'Twill be no little thing to be his bride.   60
        The world already rings with his renown;
        He's a great noble—in his native town;
        His ears are red, he has a pink complexion,
        And all in all, he'll suit you to perfection.
MARIANE: Dear God!   65
DORINE: Oh, how triumphant you will feel
        At having caught a husband so ideal!
MARIANE: Oh, do stop teasing, and use your cleverness
        To get me out of this appalling mess.
        Advise me, and I'll do whatever you say.
DORINE: Ah no, a dutiful daughter must obey   70
        Her father, even if he weds her to an ape.
        You've a bright future; why struggle to escape?
        Tartuffe will take you back where his family lives,
        To a small town aswarm with relatives—
        Uncles and cousins whom you'll be charmed to meet.   75
        You'll be received at once by the elite,
        Calling upon the bailiff's wife, no less—
        Even, perhaps, upon the mayoress,

Who'll sit you down in the *best* kitchen chair.
80   Then, once a year, you'll dance at the village fair
  To the drone of bagpipes—two of them, in fact—
  And see a puppet-show, or an animal act.
  Your husband . . .
MARIANE: Oh, you turn my blood to ice!
  Stop torturing me, and give me your advice.
DORINE: (*Threatening to go.*)
85   Your servant, Madam.
MARIANE: Dorine, I beg of you . . .
DORINE: No, you deserve it; this marriage must go through.
MARIANE: Dorine!
DORINE: No.
MARIANE: Not Tartuffe! You know I think him . . .
DORINE: Tartuffe's your cup of tea, and you shall drink him.
MARIANE: I've always told you everything, and relied . . .
90   DORINE: No. You deserve to be tartuffified.
MARIANE: Well, since you mock me and refuse to care,
  I'll henceforth seek my solace in despair:
  Despair shall be my counsellor and friend,
  And help me bring my sorrows to an end.

  (*She starts to leave.*)

95   DORINE: There now, come back; my anger has subsided.
  You do deserve some pity, I've decided.
MARIANE: Dorine, if Father makes me undergo
  This dreadful martyrdom, I'll die, I know.
DORINE: Don't fret; it won't be difficult to discover
100 Some plan of action . . . But here's Valère, your lover.

SCENE IV

VALÈRE, MARIANE, DORINE

VALÈRE: Madam, I've just received some wondrous news
  Regarding which I'd like to hear your views.
MARIANE: What news?
VALÈRE: You're marrying Tartuffe.
MARIANE: I find
  That Father does have such a match in mind.
5   VALÈRE: Your father, Madam . . .
MARIANE: . . . has just this minute said
  That it's Tartuffe he wishes me to wed.
VALÈRE: Can he be serious?
MARIANE: Oh, indeed he can;
  He's clearly set his heart upon the plan.
VALÈRE: And what position do you propose to take,
10   Madam?
MARIANE: Why—I don't know.
VALÈRE: For heaven's sake—
  You don't know?
MARIANE: No.
VALÈRE: Well, well!
MARIANE: Advise me, do.
VALÈRE: Marry the man. That's my advice to you.
MARIANE: That's your advice?
VALÈRE: Yes.
MARIANE: Truly?
VALÈRE: Oh, absolutely.
  You couldn't choose more wisely, more astutely.
15   MARIANE: Thanks for this counsel; I'll follow it, of course.

VALÈRE: Do, do; I'm sure 'twill cost you no remorse.
MARIANE: To give it didn't cause your heart to break.
VALÈRE: I gave it, Madam, only for your sake.
MARIANE: And it's for your sake that I take it, Sir.
DORINE: (*Withdrawing to the rear of the stage.*) Let's see which   20
  fool will prove the stubborner.
VALÈRE: So! I am nothing to you, and it was flat
  Deception when you . . .
MARIANE: Please, enough of that.
  You've told me plainly that I should agree
  To wed the man my father's chosen for me,
  And since you've deigned to counsel me so wisely,   25
  I promise, Sir, to do as you advise me.
VALÈRE: Ah, no, 'twas not by me that you were swayed.
  No, your decision was already made;
  Though now, to save appearances, you protest
  That you're betraying me at my behest.   30
MARIANE: Just as you say.
VALÈRE: Quite so. And I now see
  That you were never truly in love with me.
MARIANE: Alas, you're free to think so if you choose.
VALÈRE: I choose to think so, and here's a bit of news:
  You've spurned my hand, but I know where to turn   35
  For kinder treatment, as you shall quickly learn.
MARIANE: I'm sure you do. Your noble qualities
  Inspire affection . . .
VALÈRE: Forget my qualities, please.
  They don't inspire you overmuch, I find.
  But there's another lady I have in mind   40
  Whose sweet and generous nature will not scorn
  To compensate me for the loss I've borne.
MARIANE: I'm no great loss, and I'm sure that you'll transfer
  Your heart quite painlessly from me to her.
VALÈRE: I'll do my best to take it in my stride.   45
  The pain I feel at being cast aside.
  Time and forgetfulness may put an end to.
  Or if I can't forget, I shall pretend to.
  No self-respecting person is expected
  To go on loving once he's been rejected.   50
MARIANE: Now, that's a fine, high-minded sentiment.
VALÈRE: One to which any sane man would assent.
  Would you prefer it if I pined away
  In hopeless passion till my dying day?
  Am I to yield you to a rival's arms   55
  And not console myself with other charms?
MARIANE: Go then: console yourself; don't hesitate.
  I wish you to; indeed, I cannot wait.
VALÈRE: You wish me to?
MARIANE: Yes.
VALÈRE: That's the final straw.
  Madam, farewell. Your wish shall be my law.   60

(*He starts to leave, and then returns: this repeatedly.*)

MARIANE: Splendid.
VALÈRE: (*Coming back again.*)
            This breach, remember, is of your making;
  It's you who've driven me to the step I'm taking.
MARIANE: Of course.
VALÈRE: (*Coming back again.*)
            Remember, too, that I am merely
  Following your example.

MARIANE: I see that clearly.
65 VALÈRE: Enough. I'll go and do your bidding, then.
MARIANE: Good.
VALÈRE: (*Coming back again.*)
                         You shall never see my face again.
MARIANE: Excellent.
VALÈRE: (*Walking to the door, then turning about.*)
                         Yes?
MARIANE: What?
VALÈRE: What's that? What did you say?
MARIANE: Nothing. You're dreaming.
VALÈRE: Ah. Well, I'm on my way.
    Farewell, *Madame.*

(*He moves slowly away.*)

MARIANE: Farewell.
DORINE: (*To* MARIANE.)   If you ask me,
70   Both of you are as mad as mad can be.
    Do stop this nonsense, now. I've only let you
    Squabble so long to see where it would get you.
    Whoa there, Monsieure Valère!

(*She goes and seizes* VALÈRE *by the arm; he makes a great show of resistance.*)

VALÈRE: What's this, Dorine?
DORINE: Come here.
VALÈRE: No, no, my heart's too full of spleen.
75   Don't hold me back; her wish must be obeyed.
DORINE: Stop!
VALÈRE: It's too late now; my decision's made.
DORINE: Oh, pooh!
MARIANE: (*Aside.*)
                    He hates the sight of me, that's plain.
    I'll go, and so deliver him from pain.
DORINE: (*Leaving* VALÈRE, *running after* MARIANE.) And now
    you run away! Come back.
MARIANE: No, no.
80   Nothing you say will keep me here. Let go!
VALÈRE: (*Aside.*) She cannot bear my presence, I perceive.
    To spare her further torment, I shall leave.
DORINE: (*Leaving* MARIANE, *running after* VALÈRE.) Again!
    You'll not escape, Sir; don't you try it.
    Come here, you two. Stop fussing, and be quiet.

(*She takes* VALÈRE *by the hand, then* MARIANE, *and draws them together.*)

VALÈRE: (*To* DORINE.)
85   What do you want of me?
MARIANE: (*To* DORINE.)
                              What is the point of this?
DORINE: We're going to have a little armistice.

(*To* VALÈRE.)

    Now, weren't you silly to get so overheated?
VALÈRE: Didn't you see how badly I was treated?
DORINE: (*To* MARIANE.) Aren't you a simpleton, to have lost
    your head?
90 MARIANE: Didn't you hear the hateful things he said?

DORINE: (*To* VALÈRE.) You're both great fools. Her sole
    desire, Valère,
    Is to be yours in marriage. To that I'll swear.

(*To* MARIANE.)

    He loves you only, and he wants no wife
    But you, Mariane. On that I'll stake my life.
MARIANE: (*To* VALÈRE.) Then why you advised me so, I
    cannot see.   95
VALÈRE: (*To* MARIANE.) On such a question, why ask advice
    of *me?*
DORINE: Oh, you're impossible. Give me your hands, you two.

(*To* VALÈRE.)

    Yours first.
VALÈRE: (*Giving* DORINE *his hand.*)
                    But why?
DORINE: (*To* MARIANE.)
                              And now a hand from you.
MARIANE: (*Also giving* DORINE *her hand.*)
    What are you doing?
DORINE: There: a perfect fit.
    You suit each other better than you'll admit.   100

(VALÈRE *and* MARIANE *hold hands for some time without looking at each other.*)

VALÈRE: (*Turning toward* MARIANE.) Ah, come, don't be so
    haughty. Give a man
    A look of kindness, won't you, Mariane?

(MARIANE *turns toward* VALÈRE *and smiles.*)

DORINE: I tell you, lovers are completely mad!
VALÈRE: (*To* MARIANE.) Now come, confess that you were
    very bad
    To hurt my feelings as you did just now.   105
    I have a just complaint, you must allow.
MARIANE: *You* must allow that you were most unpleasant . . .
DORINE: Let's table that discussion for the present;
    Your father has a plan which must be stopped.
MARIANE: Advise us, then; what means must we adopt?   110
DORINE: We'll use all manner of means, and all at once.

(*To* MARIANE.)

    Your father's addled; he's acting like a dunce.
    Therefore you'd better humor the old fossil.
    Pretend to yield to him, be sweet and docile,
    And then postpone, as often as necessary,   115
    The day on which you have agreed to marry.
    You'll thus gain time, and time will turn the trick.
    Sometimes, for instance, you'll be taken sick,
    And that will seem good reason for delay;
    Or some bad omen will make you change the day—   120
    You'll dream of muddy water, or you'll pass
    A dead man's hearse, or break a looking-glass.
    If all else fails, no man can marry you
    Unless you take his ring and say "I do."
    But now, let's separate. If they should find   125
    Us talking here, our plot might be divined.

(*To* VALÈRE.)

Go to your friends, and tell them what's occurred,
And have them urge her father to keep his word.
Meanwhile, we'll stir her brother into action,
130   And get Elmire, as well, to join our faction.
Good-bye.
VALÈRE: (*To* MARIANE.)
          Though each of us will do his best,
It's your true heart on which my hopes shall rest.
MARIANE: (*To* VALÈRE.) Regardless of what Father may decide,
None but Valère shall claim me as his bride.
135   VALÈRE: Oh, how those words content me! Come what will ...
DORINE: Oh, lover, lovers! Their tongues are never still.
Be off, now.
VALÈRE: (*Turning to go, then turning back.*)
          One last word ...
DORINE: No time to chat:
You leave by this door; and *you* leave by that.

(DORINE *pushes them, by the shoulders, toward opposing doors.*)

ACT THREE

SCENE I

DAMIS, DORINE

DAMIS: May lightning strike me even as I speak,
May all men call me cowardly and weak,
If any fear or scruple holds me back
From settling things, at once, with that great quack!
5   DORINE: Now, don't give way to violent emotion.
Your father's merely talked about this notion,
And words and deeds are far from being one.
Much that is talked about is left undone.
DAMIS: No, I must stop that scoundrel's machinations;
10   I'll go and tell him off; I'm out of patience.
DORINE: Do calm down and be practical. I had rather
My mistress dealt with him—and with your father.
She has some influence with Tartuffe, I've noted.
He hangs upon her words, seems most devoted,
15   And may, indeed, be smitten by her charm.
Pray Heaven it's true! 'Twould do our cause no harm.
She sent for him, just now, to sound him out
On this affair you're so incensed about;
She'll find out where he stands, and tell him, too,
20   What dreadful strife and trouble will ensue
If he lends countenance to your father's plan.
I couldn't get in to see him, but his man
Says that he's almost finished with his prayers.
Go, now. I'll catch him when he comes downstairs.
25   DAMIS: I want to hear this conference, and I will.
DORINE: No, they must be alone.
DAMIS: Oh, I'll keep still.
DORINE: Not you. I know your temper. You'd start a brawl,
And shout and stamp your foot and spoil it all.
Go on.
DAMIS: I won't; I have a perfect right ...
30   DORINE: Lord, you're a nuisance! He's coming; get out of
          sight.

(DAMIS *conceals himself in a closet at the rear of the stage.*)

SCENE II

TARTUFFE, DORINE

TARTUFFE: (*Observing* DORINE, *and calling to his manservant
          offstage.*)
Hang up my hair-shirt, put my scourge in place,
And pray, Laurent, for Heaven's perpetual grace.
I'm going to the prison now, to share
My last few coins with the poor wretches there.
DORINE: (*Aside.*) Dear God, what affectation! What a fake!   5
TARTUFFE: You wished to see me?
DORINE: Yes ...
TARTUFFE: (*Taking a handkerchief from his pocket.*)
                For mercy's sake,
Please take this handkerchief, before you speak.
DORINE: What?
TARTUFFE: Cover that bosom, girl. The flesh is weak,
And unclean thoughts are difficult to control.
Such sights as that can undermine the soul.   10
DORINE: Your soul, it seems, has very poor defenses,
And flesh makes quite an impact on your senses.
It's strange that you're so easily excited;
My own desires are not so soon ignited,
And if I saw you naked as a beast,   15
Not all your hide would tempt me in the least.
TARTUFFE: Girl, speak more modestly; unless you do,
I shall be forced to take my leave of you.
DORINE: Oh, no, it's I who must be on my way;
I've just one little message to convey.   20
Madame is coming down, and begs you, Sir,
To wait and have a word or two with her.
TARTUFFE: Gladly.
DORINE: (*Aside.*) *That* had a softening effect!
I think my guess about him was correct.
TARTUFFE: Will she be long?   25
DORINE: No: that's her step I hear.
Ah, here she is, and I shall disappear.

SCENE III

ELMIRE, TARTUFFE

TARTUFFE: May Heaven, whose infinite goodness we adore,
Preserve your body and soul forevermore,
And bless your days, and answer thus the plea
Of one who is its humblest votary.
ELMIRE: I thank you for that pious wish. But please,   5
Do take a chair and let's be more at ease.

(*They sit down.*)

TARTUFFE: I trust that you are once more well and strong?
ELMIRE: Oh, yes: the fever didn't last for long.
TARTUFFE: My prayers are too unworthy, I am sure,
To have gained from Heaven this most gracious cure;   10
But lately, Madam, my every supplication
Has had for object your recuperation.
ELMIRE: You shouldn't have troubled so. I don't deserve it.

TARTUFFE: Your health is priceless, Madam, and to preserve it
15   I'd gladly give my own, in all sincerity.
  ELMIRE: Sir, you outdo us all in Christian charity.
    You've been most kind. I count myself your debtor.
  TARTUFFE: 'Twas nothing, Madam. I long to serve you better.
  ELMIRE: There's a private matter I'm anxious to discuss.
20   I'm glad there's no one here to hinder us.
  TARTUFFE: I too am glad; it floods my heart with bliss
    To find myself alone with you like this.
    For just this chance I've prayed with all my power—
    But prayed in vain, until this happy hour.
25 ELMIRE: This won't take long, Sir, and I hope you'll be
    Entirely frank and unconstrained with me.
  TARTUFFE: Indeed, there's nothing I had rather do
    Than bare my inmost heart and soul to you.
    First, let me say that what remarks I've made
30   About the constant visits you are paid
    Were prompted not by any mean emotion,
    But rather by a pure and deep devotion,
    A fervent zeal . . .
  ELMIRE: No need for explanation.
    Your sole concern, I'm sure, was my salvation.
  TARTUFFE: (*Taking* ELMIRE*'s hand and pressing her fingertips.*)
35   Quite so; and such great fervor do I feel . . .
  ELMIRE: Ooh! Please! You're pinching!
  TARTUFFE: 'Twas from excess of zeal.
    I never meant to cause you pain, I swear.
    I'd rather . . .

(*He places his hand on* ELMIRE*'s knee.*)

  ELMIRE: What can your hand be doing there?
  TARTUFFE: Feeling your gown; what soft, fine-woven stuff!
40 ELMIRE: Please, I'm extremely ticklish. That's enough.

(*She draws her chair away;* TARTUFFE *pulls his after her.*)

  TARTUFFE: (*Fondling the lace collar of her gown.*) My, my, what
      lovely lacework on your dress!
    The workmanship's miraculous, no less.
    I've not seen anything to equal it.
  ELMIRE: Yes, quite. But let's talk business for a bit.
45   They say my husband means to break his word
    And give his daughter to you, Sir. Had you heard?
  TARTUFFE: He did once mention it. But I confess
    I dream of quite a different happiness.
    It's elsewhere, Madam, that my eyes discern
50   The promise of that bliss for which I yearn.
  ELMIRE: I see: you care for nothing here below.
  TARTUFFE: Ah, well—my heart's not made of stone, you know.
  ELMIRE: All your desires mount heavenward, I'm sure,
    In scorn of all that's earthly and impure.
55 TARTUFFE: A love of heavenly beauty does not preclude
    A proper love for earthly pulchritude;
    Our senses are quite rightly captivated
    By perfect works our Maker has created.
    Some glory clings to all that Heaven has made;
60   In you, all Heaven's marvels are displayed.
    On that fair face, such beauties have been lavished,
    The eyes are dazzled and the heart is ravished;
    How could I look on you, O flawless creature,

And not adore the Author of all Nature,
Feeling a love both passionate and pure   65
For you, his triumph of self-portraiture?
At first, I trembled lest that love should be
A subtle snare that Hell had laid for me;
I vowed to flee the sight of you, eschewing
A rapture that might prove my soul's undoing;   70
But soon, fair being, I became aware
That my deep passion could be made to square
With rectitude, and with my bounden duty.
I thereupon surrendered to your beauty.
It is, I know, presumptuous on my part   75
To bring you this poor offering of my heart,
And it is not my merit, Heaven knows,
But your compassion on which my hopes repose.
You are my peace, my solace, my salvation;
On you depends my bliss—or desolation;   80
I bide your judgment and, as you think best,
I shall be either miserable or blest.
ELMIRE: Your declaration is most gallant, Sir,
    But don't you think it's out of character?
    You'd have done better to restrain your passion   85
    And think before you spoke in such a fashion.
    It ill becomes a pious man like you . . .
TARTUFFE: I may be pious, but I'm human too:
    With your celestial charms before his eyes,
    A man has not the power to be wise.   90
    I know such words sound strangely, coming from me,
    But I'm no angel, nor was meant to be,
    And if you blame my passion, you must needs
    Reproach as well the charms on which it feeds.
    Your loveliness I had no sooner seen   95
    Than you became my soul's unrivalled queen;
    Before your seraph glance, divinely sweet,
    My heart's defenses crumbled in defeat,
    And nothing fasting, prayer, or tears might do
    Could stay my spirit from adoring you.   100
    My eyes, my sighs have told you in the past
    What now my lips make bold to say at last,
    And if, in your great goodness, you will deign
    To look upon your slave, and ease his pain,—
    If, in compassion for my soul's distress,   105
    You'll stoop to comfort my unworthiness,
    I'll raise to you, in thanks for that sweet manna,
    An endless hymn, an infinite hosanna.
    With me, of course, there need be no anxiety.
    No fear of scandal or of notoriety.   110
    These young court gallants, whom all the ladies fancy,
    Are vain in speech, in action rash and chancy;
    When they succeed in love, the world soon knows it;
    No favor's granted them but they disclose it
    And by the looseness of their tongues profane   115
    The very altar where their hearts have lain.
    Men of my sort, however, love discreetly,
    And one may trust our reticence completely.
    My keen concern for my good name insures
    The absolute security of yours;   120
    In short, I offer you, my dear Elmire,
    Love without scandal, pleasure without fear.
ELMIRE: I've heard your well-turned speeches to the end,

And what you urge I clearly apprehend.
125 Aren't you afraid that I may take a notion
To tell my husband of your warm devotion,
And that, supposing he were duly told,
His feelings toward you might grow rather cold?

TARTUFFE: I know, dear lady, that your exceeding charity
130 Will lead your heart to pardon my temerity;
That you'll excuse my violent affection
As human weakness, human imperfection;
And that—O fairest!—you will bear in mind
That I'm but flesh and blood, and am not blind.

135 ELMIRE: Some women might do otherwise, perhaps,
But I shall be discreet about your lapse;
I'll tell my husband nothing of what's occurred
If, in return, you'll give your solemn word
To advocate as forcefully as you can
140 The marriage of Valère and Mariane,
Renouncing all desire to dispossess
Another of his rightful happiness,
And . . .

SCENE IV

DAMIS, ELMIRE, TARTUFFE

DAMIS: (*Emerging from the closet where he has been hiding.*)
    No! We'll not hush up this vile affair;
I heard it all inside that closet there,
Where Heaven, in order to confound the pride
Of this great rascal, prompted me to hide.
5 Ah, now I have my long-awaited chance
To punish his deceit and arrogance,
And give my father clear and shocking proof
Of the black character of his dear Tartuffe.

ELMIRE: Ah no, Damis; I'll be content if he
10 Will study to deserve my leniency.
I've promised silence—don't make me break my word;
To make a scandal would be too absurd.
Good wives laugh off such trifles, and forget them;
Why should they tell their husbands, and upset them?

15 DAMIS: You have your reasons for taking such a course,
And I have reasons, too, of equal force.
To spare him now would be insanely wrong.
I've swallowed my just wrath for far too long
And watched this insolent bigot bringing strife
20 And bitterness into our family life.
Too long he's meddled in my father's affairs,
Thwarting my marriage-hopes, and poor Valère's.
It's high time that my father was undeceived,
And now I've proof that can't be disbelieved—
25 Proof that was furnished me by Heaven above.
It's too good not to take advantage of.
This is my chance, and I deserve to lose it
If, for one moment, I hesitate to use it.

ELMIRE: Damis . . .

DAMIS: No, I must do what I think right.
30 Madam, my heart is bursting with delight,
And, say whatever you will, I'll not consent
To lose the sweet revenge on which I'm bent.
I'll settle matters without more ado;
And here, most opportunely, is my cue.

SCENE V

ORGON, DAMIS, TARTUFFE, ELMIRE

DAMIS: Father, I'm glad you've joined us. Let us advise you
Of some fresh news which doubtless will surprise you.
You've just now been repaid with interest
For all your loving-kindness to our guest.
He's proved his warm and grateful feelings toward you;   5
It's with a pair of horns he would reward you.
Yes, I surprised him with your wife, and heard
His whole adulterous offer, every word.
She, with her all too gentle disposition,
Would not have told you of his proposition;   10
But I shall not make terms with brazen lechery,
And feel that not to tell you would be treachery.

ELMIRE: And I hold that one's husband's peace of mind
Should not be spoilt by tattle of this kind.
One's honor doesn't require it: to be proficient   15
In keeping men at bay is quite sufficient.
These are my sentiments, and I wish, Damis,
That you had heeded me and held your peace.

SCENE VI

ORGON, DAMIS, TARTUFFE

ORGON: Can it be true, this dreadful thing I hear?
TARTUFFE: Yes, Brother, I'm a wicked man, I fear:
A wretched sinner, all depraved and twisted,
The greatest villain that has ever existed.
My life's one heap of crimes, which grows each minute;   5
There's naught but foulness and corruption in it;
And I perceive that Heaven, outraged by me,
Has chosen this occasion to mortify me.
Charge me with any deed you wish to name;
I'll not defend myself, but take the blame.   10
Believe what you are told, and drive Tartuffe
Like some base criminal from beneath your roof;
Yes, drive me hence, and with a parting curse:
I shan't protest, for I deserve far worse.
ORGON: (*To* DAMIS.) Ah, you deceitful boy, how dare you try   15
To stain his purity with so foul a lie?
DAMIS: What! Are you taken in by such a bluff?
Did you not hear . . . ?
ORGON: Enough, you rogue, enough!
TARTUFFE: Ah, Brother, let him speak: you're being unjust.
Believe his story; the boy deserves your trust.   20
Why, after all, should you have faith in me?
How can you know what I might do, or be?
Is it on my good actions that you base
Your favor? Do you trust my pious face?
Ah, no, don't be deceived by hollow shows;   25
I'm far, alas, from being what men suppose;
Though the world takes me for a man of worth,
I'm truly the most worthless man on earth.

(*To* DAMIS.)

Yes, my dear son, speak out now: call me the chief
Of sinners, a wretch, a murderer, a thief;   30

Load me with all the names men most abhor;
I'll not complain; I've earned them all, and more;
I'll kneel here while you pour them on my head
As a just punishment for the life I've led.
ORGON: (*To* TARTUFFE.)
35   This is too much, dear Brother.

(*To* DAMIS.)

                                        Have you no heart?
DAMIS: Are you so hoodwinked by this rascal's art. . . ?
ORGON: Be still, you monster.

(*To* TARTUFFE.)

                           Brother, I pray you, rise.

(*To* DAMIS.)

    Villain!
DAMIS: But . . .
ORGON: Silence!
DAMIS: Can't you realize. . . ?
ORGON: Just one word more, and I'll tear you limb from limb.
40 TARTUFFE: In God's name, Brother, don't be harsh with him.
    I'd rather far be tortured at the stake
    Than see him bear one scratch for my poor sake.
ORGON: (*To* DAMIS.)
    Ingrate!
TARTUFFE: If I must beg you, on bended knee,
    To pardon him . . .
ORGON: (*Falling to his knees, addressing* TARTUFFE.)
                       Such goodness cannot be!

(*To* DAMIS.)

45   Now, *there's* true charity!
DAMIS: What, you. . . ?
ORGON: Villain, be still!
    I know your motives; I know you wish him ill:
    Yes, all of you—wife, children, servants, all—
    Conspire against him and desire his fall,
    Employing every shameful trick you can
50 To alienate me from this saintly man.
    Ah, but the more you seek to drive him away,
    The more I'll do to keep him. Without delay,
    I'll spite this household and confound its pride
    By giving him my daughter as his bride.
55 DAMIS: You're going to force her to accept his hand?
ORGON: Yes, and this very night, d'you understand?
    I shall defy you all, and make it clear
    That I'm the one who gives the orders here.
    Come, wretch, kneel down and clasp his blessed feet,
60   And ask his pardon for your black deceit.
DAMIS: I ask that swindler's pardon? Why, I'd rather . . .
ORGON: So! You insult him, and defy your father!
    A stick! A stick! (*To* TARTUFFE.) No, no—release me, do.

(*To* DAMIS.)

    Out of my house this minute! Be off with you,
65   And never dare set foot in it again.
DAMIS: Well, I shall go, but . . .

ORGON: Well, go quickly, then.
    I disinherit you; an empty purse
    Is all you'll get from me—except my curse!

SCENE VII

ORGON, TARTUFFE

ORGON: How he blasphemed your goodness! What a son!
TARTUFFE: Forgive him, Lord, as I've already done.

(*To* ORGON.)

    You can't know how it hurts when someone tries
    To blacken me in my dear Brother's eyes.
ORGON: Ahh!   5
TARTUFFE: The mere thought of such ingratitude
    Plunges my soul into so dark a mood . . .
    Such horror grips my heart . . . I gasp for breath,
    And cannot speak, and feel myself near death.
ORGON:

(*He runs, in tears, to the door through which he has just driven his son.*)

    You blackguard! Why did I spare you? Why did I not
    Break you in little pieces on the spot?   10
    Compose yourself, and don't be hurt, dear friend.
TARTUFFE: These scenes, these dreadful quarrels, have got to end.
    I've much upset your household, and I perceive
    That the best thing will be for me to leave.
ORGON: What are you saying!   15
TARTUFFE: They're all against me here;
    They'd have you think me false and insincere.
ORGON: Ah, what of that? Have I ceased believing in you?
TARTUFFE: Their adverse talk will certainly continue,
    And charges which you now repudiate
    You may find credible at a later date.   20
ORGON: No, Brother, never.
TARTUFFE: Brother, a wife can sway
    Her husband's mind in many a subtle way.
ORGON: No, no.
TARTUFFE: To leave at once is the solution;
    Thus only can I end their persecution.
ORGON: No, no, I'll not allow it; you shall remain.   25
TARTUFFE: Ah, well; 'twill mean much martyrdom and pain,
    But if you wish it . . .
ORGON: Ah!
TARTUFFE: Enough; so be it.
    But one thing must be settled, as I see it.
    For your dear honor, and for our friendship's sake,
    There's one precaution I feel bound to take.   30
    I shall avoid your wife, and keep away . . .
ORGON: No, you shall not, whatever they may say.
    It pleases me to vex them, and for spite
    I'd have them see you with her day and night.
    What's more, I'm going to drive them to despair   35
    By making you my only son and heir;
    This very day, I'll give to you alone
    Clear deed and title to everything I own.
    A dear, good friend and son-in-law-to-be

40   Is more than wife, or child, or kin to me.
      Will you accept my offer, dearest son?
TARTUFFE: In all things, let the will of Heaven be done.
ORGON: Poor fellow! Come, we'll go draw up the deed.
      Then let them burst with disappointed greed!

ACT FOUR

SCENE I

CLÉANTE, TARTUFFE

CLÉANTE: Yes, all the town's discussing it, and truly,
      Their comments do not flatter you unduly.
      I'm glad we've met, Sir, and I'll give my view
      Of this sad matter in a word or two.
5   As for who's guilty, that I shan't discuss;
      Let's say it was Damis who caused the fuss;
      Assuming, then, that you have been ill-used
      By young Damis, and groundlessly accused,
      Ought not a Christian to forgive, and ought
10   He not to stifle every vengeful thought?
      Should you stand by and watch a father make
      His only son an exile for your sake?
      Again I tell you frankly, be advised:
      The whole town, high and low, is scandalized;
15   This quarrel must be mended, and my advice is
      Not to push matters to a further crisis.
      No, sacrifice your wrath to God above,
      And help Damis regain his father's love.
TARTUFFE: Alas, for my part I should take great joy
20   In doing so. I've nothing against the boy.
      I pardon all, I harbor no resentment;
      To serve him would afford me much contentment.
      But Heaven's interest will not have it so:
      If he comes back, then I shall have to go.
25   After his conduct—so extreme, so vicious—
      Our further intercourse would look suspicious.
      God knows what people would think! Why, they'd describe
      My goodness to him as a sort of bribe;
      They'd say that out of guilt I made pretense
30   Of loving-kindness and benevolence—
      That, fearing my accuser's tongue, I strove
      To buy his silence with a show of love.
CLÉANTE: Your reasoning is badly warped and stretched,
      And these excuses, Sir, are most far-fetched.
35   Why put yourself in charge of Heaven's cause?
      Does Heaven need our help to enforce its laws?
      Leave vengeance to the Lord, Sir; while we live,
      Our duty's not to punish, but forgive;
      And what the Lord commands, we should obey
40   Without regard to what the world may say.
      What! Shall the fear of being misunderstood
      Prevent our doing what is right and good?
      No, no; let's simply do what Heaven ordains,
      And let no other thoughts perplex our brains.
45 TARTUFFE: Again, Sir, let me say that I've forgiven
      DAMIS, and thus obeyed the laws of Heaven;
      But I am not commanded by the Bible
      To live with one who smears my name with libel.
CLÉANTE: Were you commanded, Sir, to indulge the whim

Of poor Orgon, and to encourage him   50
In suddenly transferring to your name
A large estate to which you have no claim?
TARTUFFE: 'Twould never occur to those who know me best
      To think I acted from self-interest.
      The treasures of this world I quite despise;   55
      Their specious glitter does not charm my eyes;
      And if I have resigned myself to taking
      The gift which my dear Brother insists on making,
      I do so only, as he well understands,
      Lest so much wealth fall into wicked hands,   60
      Lest those to whom it might descend in time
      Turn it to purposes of sin and crime,
      And not, as I shall do, make use of it.
      For Heaven's glory and mankind's benefit.
CLÉANTE: Forget these trumped-up fears. Your argument 65
      Is one the rightful heir might well resent;
      It is a moral burden to inherit
      Such wealth, but give Damis a chance to bear it.
      And would it not be worse to be accused
      Of swindling, than to see that wealth misused?   70
      I'm shocked that you allowed Orgon to broach
      This matter, and that you feel no self-reproach;
      Does true religion teach that lawful heirs
      May freely be deprived of what is theirs?
      And if the Lord has told you in your heart   75
      That you and young Damis must dwell apart,
      Would it not be the decent thing to beat
      A generous and honorable retreat,
      Rather than let the son of the house be sent,
      For your convenience, into banishment?   80
      Sir, if you wish to prove the honesty
      Of your intentions . . .
TARTUFFE: Sir, it is half-past three.
      I've certain pious duties to attend to,
      And hope my prompt departure won't offend you.
CLÉANTE: (Alone.) Damn.   85

SCENE II

ELMIRE, MARIANE, CLÉANTE, DORINE

DORINE: Stay, Sir, and help Mariane, for Heaven's sake!
      She's suffering so, I fear her heart will break.
      Her father's plan to marry her off tonight
      Has put the poor child in a desperate plight.
      I hear him coming. Let's stand together, now,   5
      And see if we can't change his mind, somehow,
      About this match we all deplore and fear.

SCENE III

ORGON, ELMIRE, MARIANE, CLÉANTE, DORINE

ORGON: Hah! Glad to find you all assembled here.

(*To* MARIANE.)

      This contract, child, contains your happiness,
      And what it says I think your heart can guess.
MARIANE: (*Falling to her knees.*) Sir, by that Heaven which
      sees me here distressed,

5   And by whatever else can move your breast,
    Do not employ a father's power, I pray you,
    To crush my heart and force it to obey you,
    Nor by your harsh commands oppress me so
    That I'll begrudge the duty which I owe—
10 And do not so embitter and enslave me
    That I shall hate the very life you gave me.
    If my sweet hopes must perish, if you refuse
    To give me to the one I've dared to choose,
    Spare me at least—I beg you, I implore—
15 The pain of wedding one whom I abhor;
    And do not, by a heartless use of force,
    Drive me to contemplate some desperate course.
    ORGON: (*Feeling himself touched by her.*) Be firm, my soul.
        No human weakness, now.
    MARIANE: I don't resent your love for him. Allow
20 Your heart free rein, Sir; give him your property,
    And if that's not enough, take mine from me;
    He's welcome to my money; take it, do,
    But don't, I pray, include my person too.
    Spare me, I beg you; and let me end the tale
25 Of my sad days behind a convent veil.
    ORGON: A convent! Hah! When crossed in their amours,
    All lovesick girls have the same thought as yours.
    Get up! The more you loathe the man, and dread him,
    The more ennobling it will be to wed him.
30 Marry Tartuffe, and mortify your flesh!
    Enough; don't start that whimpering afresh.
    DORINE: But why. . . ?
    ORGON: Be still, there. Speak when you're
        spoken to.
    Not one more bit of impudence out of you.
    CLÉANTE: If I may offer a word of counsel here . . .
35 ORGON: Brother, in counseling you have no peer;
    All your advice is forceful, sound, and clever;
    I don't propose to follow it, however.
    ELMIRE: (*To* ORGON.) I am amazed, and don't know what
        to say;
    Your blindness simply takes my breath away.
40 You are indeed bewitched, to take no warning
    From our account of what occurred this morning.
    ORGON: Madam, I know a few plain facts, and one
    Is that you're partial to my rascal son;
    Hence, when he sought to make Tartuffe the victim
45 Of a base lie, you dared not contradict him.
    Ah, but you underplayed your part, my pet;
    You should have looked more angry, more upset.
    ELMIRE: When men make overtures, must we reply
    With righteous anger and a battle-cry?
50 Must we turn back their amorous advances
    With sharp reproaches and with fiery glances?
    Myself, I find such offers merely amusing,
    And make no scenes and fusses in refusing;
    My taste is for good-natured rectitude,
55 And I dislike the savage sort of prude
    Who guards her virtue with her teeth and claws,
    And tears men's eyes out for the slightest cause;
    The Lord preserve me from such honor as that,
    Which bites and scratches like an alley-cat!
60 I've found that a polite and cool rebuff
    Discourages a lover quite enough.

ORGON: I know the facts, and I shall not be shaken.
ELMIRE: I marvel at your power to be mistaken.
    Would it, I wonder, carry weight with you
    If I could *show* you that our tale was true?   65
ORGON: Show me?
ELMIRE: Yes.
ORGON: Rot.
ELMIRE: Come, what if I found a way
    To make you see the facts as plain as day?
ORGON: Nonsense.
ELMIRE: Do answer me; don't be absurd.
    I'm not now asking you to trust our word.
    Suppose that from some hiding-place in here   70
    You learned the whole sad truth by eye and ear—
    What would you say of your good friend, after that?
ORGON: Why, I'd say . . . nothing, by Jehoshaphat!
    It can't be true.
ELMIRE: You've been too long deceived,
    And I'm quite tired of being disbelieved.   75
    Come now: let's put my statements to the test,
    And you shall see the truth made manifest.
ORGON: I'll take that challenge. Now do your uttermost.
    We'll see how you make good your empty boast.
ELMIRE: (*To* DORINE.)
    Send him to me.   80
DORINE: He's crafty; it may be hard
    To catch the cunning scoundrel off his guard.
ELMIRE: No, amorous men are gullible. Their conceit
    So blinds them that they're never hard to cheat.
    Have him come down. (*To* CLÉANTE *and* MARIANE.)
        Please leave us, for a bit.

SCENE IV

ELMIRE, ORGON

ELMIRE: Pull up this table, and get under it.
ORGON: What?
ELMIRE: It's essential that you be well-hidden.
ORGON: Why there?
ELMIRE: Oh, Heavens! Just do as you are bidden
    I have my plans; we'll soon see how they fare.
    Under the table, now; and once you're there,   5
    Take care that you are neither seen nor heard.
ORGON: Well, I'll indulge you, since I gave my word
    To see you through this infantile charade.
ELMIRE: Once it is over, you'll be glad we played.

(*To her husband, who is now under the table.*)

    I'm going to act quite strangely, now, and you   10
    Must not be shocked at anything I do.
    Whatever I may say, you must excuse
    As part of that deceit I'm forced to use.
    I shall employ sweet speeches in the task
    Of making that impostor drop his mask;   15
    I'll give encouragement to his bold desires,
    And furnish fuel to his amorous fires.
    Since it's for your sake, and for his destruction,
    That I shall seem to yield to his seduction,
    I'll gladly stop whenever you decide   20

That all your doubts are fully satisfied.
I'll count on you, as soon as you have seen
What sort of man he is, to intervene,
And not expose me to his odious lust
25 One moment longer than you feel you must.
Remember: you're to save me from my plight
Whenever . . . He's coming! Hush! Keep out of sight!

SCENE V

TARTUFFE, ELMIRE, ORGON

TARTUFFE: You wish to have a word with me, I'm told.
ELMIRE: Yes. I've a little secret to unfold.
Before I speak, however, it would be wise
To close that door, and look about for spies.

(TARTUFFE *goes to the door, closes it, and returns.*)

5 The very last thing that must happen now
Is a repetition of this morning's row.
I've never been so badly caught off guard.
Oh, how I feared for you! You saw how hard
I tried to make that troublesome Damis
10 Control his dreadful temper, and hold his peace.
In my confusion, I didn't have the sense
Simply to contradict his evidence;
But as it happened, that was for the best,
And all has worked out in our interest.
15 This storm has only bettered your position;
My husband doesn't have the least suspicion,
And now, in mockery of those who do,
He bids me be continually with you.
And that is why, quite fearless of reproof,
20 I now can be alone with my Tartuffe,
And why my heart—perhaps too quick to yield—
Feels free to let its passion be revealed.
TARTUFFE: Madam, your words confuse me. Not long ago,
You spoke in quite a different style, you know.
25 ELMIRE: Ah, Sir, if that refusal made you smart,
It's little that you know of woman's heart,
Or what that heart is trying to convey
When it resists in such a feeble way!
Always, at first, our modesty prevents
30 The frank avowal of tender sentiments;
However high the passion which inflames us,
Still, to confess its power somehow shames us.
Thus we reluct, at first, yet in a tone
Which tells you that our heart is overthrown,
35 That what our lips deny, our pulse confesses,
And that, in time, all noes will turn to yesses.
I fear my words are all too frank and free,
And a poor proof of woman's modesty;
But since I'm started, tell me, if you will—
40 Would I have tried to make Damis be still,
Would I have listened, calm and unoffended,
Until your lengthy offer of love was ended,
And been so very mild in my reaction,
Had your sweet words not given me satisfaction?
45 And when I tried to force you to undo

The marriage-plans my husband has in view,
What did my urgent pleading signify
If not that I admired you, and that I
Deplored the thought that someone else might own
Part of a heart I wished for mine alone? 50
TARTUFFE: Madam, no happiness is so complete
As when, from lips we love, come words so sweet;
Their nectar floods my every sense, and drains
In honeyed rivulets through all my veins.
To please you is my joy, my only goal; 55
Your love is the restorer of my soul;
And yet I must beg leave, now, to confess
Some lingering doubts as to my happiness
Might this not be a trick? Might not the catch
Be that you wish me to break off the match 60
With Mariane, and so have feigned to love me?
I shan't quite trust your fond opinion of me
Until the feelings you've expressed so sweetly
Are demonstrated somewhat more concretely,
And you have shown, by certain kind concessions, 65
That I may put my faith in your professions.
ELMIRE:

(*She coughs, to warn her husband.*)

Why be in such a hurry? Must my heart
Exhaust its bounty at the very start?
To make that sweet admission cost me dear,
But you'll not be content, it would appear, 70
Unless my store of favors is disbursed
To the last farthing, and at the very first.
TARTUFFE: The less we merit, the less we dare to hope,
And with our doubts, mere words can never cope.
We trust no promised bliss till we receive it; 75
Not till a joy is ours can we believe it.
I, who so little merit your esteem,
Can't credit this fulfillment of my dream,
And shan't believe it, Madam, until I savor
Some palpable assurance of your favor. 80
ELMIRE: My, how tyrannical your love can be,
And how it flusters and perplexes me!
How furiously you take one's heart in hand,
And make your every wish a fierce command!
Come, must you hound and harry me to death? 85
Will you not give me time to catch my breath?
Can it be right to press me with such force,
Give me no quarter, show me no remorse,
And take advantage, by your stern insistence,
Of the fond feelings which weaken my resistance? 90
TARTUFFE: Well, if you look with favor upon my love,
Why, then, begrudge me some clear proof thereof?
ELMIRE: But how can I consent without offense
To Heaven, toward which you feel such reverence?
TARTUFFE: If Heaven is all that holds you back, don't worry. 95
I can remove that hindrance in a hurry.
Nothing of that sort need obstruct our path.
ELMIRE: Must one not be afraid of Heaven's wrath?
TARTUFFE: Madam, forget such fears, and be my pupil,
And I shall teach you how to conquer scruple. 100
Some joys, it's true, are wrong in Heaven's eyes;

Yet Heaven is not averse to compromise;
There is a science, lately formulated,
Whereby one's conscience may be liberated,
105   And any wrongful act you care to mention
May be redeemed by purity of intention.
I'll teach you, Madam, the secrets of that science;
Meanwhile, just place on me your full reliance.
Assuage my keen desires, and feel no dread:
110   The sin, if any, shall be on my head.

(ELMIRE *coughs, this time more loudly.*)

You've a bad cough.
ELMIRE: Yes, yes. It's bad indeed.
TARTUFFE: (*Producing a little paper bag.*) A bit of licorice may
be what you need.
ELMIRE: No, I've a stubborn cold, it seems. I'm sure it
Will take much more than licorice to cure it.
115   TARTUFFE: How aggravating.
ELMIRE: Oh, more than I can say.
TARTUFFE: If you're still troubled, think of things this way:
No one shall know our joys, save us alone,
And there's no evil till the act is known;
It's scandal, Madam, which makes it an offense,
120   And it's no sin to sin in confidence.
ELMIRE: (*Having coughed once more.*) Well, clearly I must do as
you require,
And yield to your importunate desire.
It is apparent, now, that nothing less
Will satisfy you, and so I acquiesce.
125   To go so far is much against my will;
I'm vexed that it should come to this; but still,
Since you are so determined on it, since you
Will not allow mere language to convince you,
And since you ask for concrete evidence, I
130   See nothing for it, now, but to comply.
If this is sinful, if I'm wrong to do it,
So much the worse for him who drove me to it.
The fault can surely not be charged to me.
TARTUFFE: Madam, the fault is mine, if fault there be,
135   And . . .
ELMIRE: Open the door a little, and peek out;
I wouldn't want my husband poking about.
TARTUFFE: Why worry about the man? Each day he grows
More gullible; one can lead him by the nose.
To find us here would fill him with delight,
140   And if he saw the worst, he'd doubt his sight.
ELMIRE: Nevertheless, do step out for a minute
Into the hall, and see that no one's in it.

SCENE VI

ORGON, ELMIRE

ORGON: (*Coming out from under the table.*) That man's a
perfect monster, I must admit!
I'm simply stunned. I can't get over it.
ELMIRE: What, coming out so soon? How premature!
Get back in hiding, and wait until you're sure.
5   Stay till the end, and be convinced completely;

We mustn't stop till things are proved concretely.
ORGON: Hell never harbored anything so vicious!
ELMIRE: Tut, don't be hasty. Try to be judicious.
Wait, and be certain that there's no mistake.
No jumping to conclusions, for Heaven's sake!   10

(*She places* ORGON *behind her, as* TARTUFFE *re-enters.*)

SCENE VII

TARTUFFE, ELMIRE, ORGON

TARTUFFE: (*Not seeing* ORGON.) Madam, all things have
worked out to perfection;
I've given the neighboring rooms a full inspection;
No one's about; and now I may at last . . .
ORGON: (*Intercepting him.*) Hold on, my passionate fellow,
not so fast!
I should advise a little more restraint.   5
Well, so you thought you'd fool me, my dear saint!
How soon you wearied of the saintly life—
Wedding my daughter, and coveting my wife!
I've long suspected you, and had a feeling
That soon I'd catch you at your double-dealing.   10
Just now, you've given me evidence galore;
It's quite enough; I have no wish for more.
ELMIRE: (*To* TARTUFFE.) I'm sorry to have treated you so
slyly.
But circumstances forced me to be wily.
TARTUFFE: Brother, you can't think . . .   15
ORGON: No more talk from you;
Just leave this household, without more ado.
TARTUFFE: What I intended . . .
ORGON: That seems fairly clear.
Spare me your falsehoods and get out of here.
TARTUFFE: No, I'm the master, and you're the one to go!
This house belongs to me, I'll have you know,   20
And I shall show you that you can't hurt *me*
By this contemptible conspiracy,
That those who cross me know not what they do,
And that I've means to expose and punish you,
Avenge offended Heaven, and make you grieve   25
That ever you dared order me to leave.

SCENE VIII

ELMIRE, ORGON

ELMIRE: What was the point of all that angry chatter?
ORGON: Dear God, I'm worried. This is no laughing
matter.
ELMIRE: How so?
ORGON: I fear I understood his drift.
I'm much disturbed about that deed of gift.
ELMIRE: You gave him . . . ?   5
ORGON: Yes, it's all been drawn and signed.
But one thing more is weighing on my mind.
ELMIRE: What's that?
ORGON: I'll tell you; but first let's see if there's
A certain strong-box in his room upstairs.

ACT FIVE

SCENE I

ORGON, CLÉANTE

CLÉANTE: Where are you going so fast?
ORGON: God knows!
CLÉANTE: Then wait;
    Let's have a conference, and deliberate
    On how this situation's to be met.
ORGON: That strong-box has me utterly upset;
5   This is the worst of many, many shocks.
CLÉANTE: Is there some fearful mystery in that box?
ORGON: My poor friend Argas brought that box to me
    With his own hands, in utmost secrecy;
    'Twas on the very morning of his flight.
10   It's full of papers which, if they came to light,
    Would ruin him—or such is my impression.
CLÉANTE: Then why did you let it out of your possession?
ORGON: Those papers vexed my conscience, and it seemed
    best
    To ask the counsel of my pious guest.
15   The cunning scoundrel got me to agree
    To leave the strong-box in his custody,
    So that, in case of an investigation,
    I could employ a slight equivocation
    And swear I didn't have it, and thereby,
20   At no expense to conscience, tell a lie.
CLÉANTE: It looks to me as if you're out on a limb.
    Trusting him with that box, and offering him
    That deed of gift, were actions of a kind
    Which scarcely indicate a prudent mind.
25   With two such weapons, he has the upper hand,
    And since you're vulnerable, as matters stand,
    You erred once more in bringing him to bay.
    You should have acted in some subtler way.
ORGON: Just think of it: behind that fervent face,
30   A heart so wicked, and a soul so base!
    I took him in, a hungry beggar, and then . . .
    Enough, by God! I'm through with pious men:
    Henceforth I'll hate the whole false brotherhood,
    And persecute them worse than Satan could.
35 CLÉANTE: Ah, there you go—extravagant as ever.
    Why can you not be rational? You never
    Manage to take the middle course, it seems,
    But jump, instead, between absurd extremes.
    You've recognized your recent grave mistake
40   In falling victim to a pious fake;
    Now, to correct that error, must you embrace
    An even greater error in its place,
    And judge our worthy neighbors as a whole
    By what you've learned of one corrupted soul?
45   Come, just because one rascal made you swallow
    A show of zeal which turned out to be hollow,
    Shall you conclude that all men are deceivers,
    And that, today, there are no true believers?
    Let atheists make that foolish inference;
50   Learn to distinguish virtue from pretense,
    Be cautious in bestowing admiration,
    And cultivate a sober moderation.

    Don't humor fraud, but also don't asperse
    True piety; the latter fault is worse,
    And it is best to err, if err one must,   55
    As you have done, upon the side of trust.

SCENE II

DAMIS, ORGON, CLÉANTE

DAMIS: Father, I hear that scoundrel's uttered threats
    Against you; that he pridefully forgets
    How, in his need, he was befriended by you,
    And means to use your gifts to crucify you.
ORGON: It's true, my boy. I'm too distressed for tears.   5
DAMIS: Leave it to me, Sir; let me trim his ears.
    Faced with such insolence, we must not waver.
    I shall rejoice in doing you the favor
    Of cutting short his life, and your distress.
CLÉANTE: What a display of young hotheadedness!   10
    Do learn to moderate your fits of rage.
    In this just kingdom, this enlightened age,
    One does not settle things by violence.

SCENE III

MADAME PERNELLE, MARIANE, ELMIRE, DORINE, DAMIS, OR-
GON, CLÉANTE

MADAME PERNELLE: I hear strange tales of very strange
    events.
ORGON: Yes, strange events which these two eyes beheld.
    The man's ingratitude is unparalleled.
    I save a wretched pauper from starvation.
    House him, and treat him like a blood relation,   5
    Shower him every day with my largesse,
    Give him my daughter, and all that I possess;
    And meanwhile the unconscionable knave
    Tries to induce my wife to misbehave;
    And not content with such extreme rascality,   10
    Now threatens me with my own liberality,
    And aims, by taking base advantage of
    The gifts I gave him out of Christian love,
    To drive me from my house, a ruined man,
    And make me end a pauper, as he began.   15
DORINE: Poor fellow!
MADAME PERNELLE: No, my son, I'll never bring
    Myself to think him guilty of such a thing.
ORGON: How's that?
MADAME PERNELLE: The righteous always were maligned.
ORGON: Speak clearly, Mother. Say what's on your mind.
MADAME PERNELLE: I mean that I can smell a rat, my dear.   20
    You know how everybody hates him, here.
ORGON: That has no bearing on the case at all.
MADAME PERNELLE: I told you a hundred times, when you
    were small,
    That virtue in this world is hated ever;
    Malicious men may die, but malice never.   25
ORGON: No doubt that's true, but how does it apply?
MADAME PERNELLE: They've turned you against him by a
    clever lie.
ORGON: I've told you, I was there and saw it done.

MADAME PERNELLE: Ah, slanderers will stop at nothing, Son.

30 ORGON: Mother, I'll lose my temper . . . For the last time,
   I tell you I was witness to the crime.

MADAME PERNELLE: The tongues of spite are busy night and
      noon
   And to their venom no man is immune.

ORGON: You're talking nonsense. Can't you realize

35   I saw it; saw it; saw it with my eyes?
   Saw, do you understand me? Must I shout it
   Into your ears before you'll cease to doubt it?

MADAME PERNELLE: Appearances can deceive, my son.
      Dear me,
   We cannot always judge by what we see.

40 ORGON: Drat! Drat!

MADAME PERNELLE: One often interprets things awry;
   Good can seem evil to a suspicious eye.

ORGON: Was I to see his pawing at Elmire
   As an act of charity?

MADAME PERNELLE: Till his guilt is clear,
   A man deserves the benefit of the doubt.

45   You should have waited, to see how things turned out.

ORGON: Great God in Heaven, what more proof did I need?
   Was I to sit there, watching, until he'd . . .
   You drive me to the brink of impropriety.

MADAME PERNELLE: No, no, a man of such surpassing piety

50   Could not do such a thing. You cannot shake me.
   I don't believe it, and you shall not make me.

ORGON: You vex me so that, if you weren't my mother,
   I'd say to you . . . some dreadful thing or other.

DORINE: It's your turn now, Sir, not to be listened to;

55   You'd not trust us, and now she won't trust you.

CLÉANTE: My friends, we're wasting time which should be
      spent
   In facing up to our predicament.
   I fear that scoundrel's threats weren't made in sport.

DAMIS: Do you think he'd have the nerve to go to court?

60 ELMIRE: I'm sure he won't: they'd find it all too crude
   A case of swindling and ingratitude.

CLÉANTE: Don't be too sure. He won't be at a loss
   To give his claims a high and righteous gloss;
   And clever rogues with far less valid cause

65   Have trapped their victims in a web of laws.
   I say again that to antagonize
   A man so strongly armed was most unwise.

ORGON: I know it; but the man's appalling cheek
   Outraged me so, I couldn't control my pique.

70 CLÉANTE: I wish to Heaven that we could devise
   Some truce between you, or some compromise.

ELMIRE: If I had known what cards he held, I'd not
   Have roused his anger by my little plot.

ORGON: (To DORINE, as M. LOYAL enters.) What is that fellow
      looking for? Who is he?

75   Go talk to him—and tell him that I'm busy.

SCENE IV

MONSIEUR LOYAL, MADAME PERNELLE, ORGON, DAMIS, MARI-
ANE, DORINE, ELMIRE, CLÉANTE

MONSIEUR LOYAL: Good day, dear sister. Kindly let me see
   Your master.

DORINE: He's involved with company,
   And cannot be disturbed just now, I fear.

MONSIEUR LOYAL: I hate to intrude; but what has brought
      me here
   Will not disturb your master, in any event.   5
   Indeed, my news will make him most content.

DORINE: Your name?

MONSIEUR LOYAL: Just say that I bring greetings from
   Monsieur Tartuffe, on whose behalf I've come.

DORINE: (To ORGON.) Sir, he's a very gracious man, and bears
   A message from Tartuffe, which, he declares,   10
   Will make you most content.

CLÉANTE: Upon my word,
   I think this man had best be seen, and heard.

ORGON: Perhaps he has some settlement to suggest.
   How shall I treat him? What manner would be best?

CLÉANTE: Control your anger, and if he should mention   15
   Some fair adjustment, give him your full attention.

MONSIEUR LOYAL: Good health to you, good Sir. May
      Heaven confound
   Your enemies, and may your joys abound.

ORGON: (Aside, to CLÉANTE.) A gentle salutation: it confirms
   My guess that he is here to offer terms.   20

MONSIEUR LOYAL: I've always held your family most dear;
   I served your father, Sir, for many a year.

ORGON: Sir, I must ask your pardon; to my shame,
   I cannot now recall your face or name.

MONSIEUR LOYAL: Loyal's my name; I come from   25
      Normandy,
   And I'm a bailiff, in all modesty.
   For forty years, praise God, it's been my boast
   To serve with honor in that vital post,
   And I am here, Sir, if you will permit
   The liberty, to serve you with this writ . . .   30

ORGON: To—what?

MONSIEUR LOYAL: Now, please, Sir, let us have no friction:
   It's nothing but an order of eviction.
   You are to move your goods and family out
   And make way for new occupants, without
   Deferment or delay, and give the keys . . .   35

ORGON: I? Leave this house?

MONSIEUR LOYAL: Why yes, Sir, if you please.
   This house, Sir, from the cellar to the roof,
   Belongs now to the good Monsieur Tartuffe,
   And he is lord and master of your estate
   By virtue of a deed of present date,   40
   Drawn in due form, with clearest legal phrasing . . .

DAMIS: Your insolence is utterly amazing!

MONSIEUR LOYAL: Young man, my business here is not with
      you,
   But with your wise and temperate father, who,
   Like every worthy citizen, stands in awe   45
   Of justice, and would never obstruct the law.

ORGON: But . . .

MONSIEUR LOYAL: Not for a million, Sir, would you rebel
   Against authority; I know that well.
   You'll not make trouble, Sir, or interfere
   With the execution of my duties here.   50

DAMIS: Someone may execute a smart tattoo
   On that black jacket of yours, before you're through.

MONSIEUR LOYAL: Sir, bid your son be silent. I'd much regret

55   Having to mention such a nasty threat
          Of violence, in writing my report.
DORINE: (*Aside.*) This man Loyal's a most disloyal sort!
MONSIEUR LOYAL: I love all men of upright character,
          And when I agreed to serve these papers, Sir,
          It was your feelings that I had in mind.
60   I couldn't bear to see the case assigned
          To someone else, who might esteem you less
          And so subject you to unpleasantness.
ORGON: What's more unpleasant than telling a man to leave
          His house and home?
MONSIEUR LOYAL: You'd like a short reprieve?
65   If you desire, Sir, I shall not press you,
          But wait until tomorrow to dispossess you.
          Splendid. I'll come and spend the night here, then,
          Most quietly, with half a score of men.
          For form's sake, you might bring me, just before
70   You go to bed, the keys to the front door.
          My men, I promise, will be on their best
          Behavior, and will not disturb your rest.
          But bright and early, Sir, you must be quick
          And move out all your furniture, every stick;
75   The men I've chosen are both young and strong,
          And with their help it shouldn't take you long.
          In short, I'll make things pleasant and convenient,
          And since I'm being so extremely lenient,
          Please show me, Sir, a like consideration,
80   And give me your entire cooperation.
ORGON: (*Aside.*) I may be all but bankrupt, but I vow
          I'd give a hundred louis, here and now,
          Just for the pleasure of landing one good clout
          Right on the end of that complacent snout.
85 CLÉANTE: Careful; don't make things worse.
DAMIS: My bootsole itches
          To give that beggar a good kick in the breeches.
DORINE: Monsieur Loyal, I'd love to hear the whack
          Of a stout stick across your fine broad back.
MONSIEUR LOYAL: Take care: a woman too may go to jail if
90   She uses threatening language to a bailiff.
CLÉANTE: Enough, enough, Sir. This must not go on.
          Give me that paper, please, and then begone.
MONSIEUR LOYAL: Well, *au revoir.* God give you all good cheer!
ORGON: May God confound you, and him who sent you
          here!

SCENE V

ORGON, CLÉANTE, MARIANE, ELMIRE, MADAME PERNELLE,
DORINE, DAMIS

ORGON: Now, Mother, was I right or not? This writ
          Should change your notion of Tartuffe a bit.
          Do you perceive his villainy at last?
MADAME PERNELLE: I'm thunderstruck. I'm utterly aghast.
5 DORINE: Oh, come, be fair. You mustn't take offense
          At this new proof of his benevolence.
          He's acting out of selfless love, I know.
          Material things enslave the soul, and so
          He kindly has arranged your liberation
10   From all that might endanger your salvation.
ORGON: Will you not ever hold your tongue, you dunce?

CLÉANTE: Come, you must take some action, and at once.
ELMIRE: Go tell the world of the low trick he's tried.
          The deed of gift is surely nullified
          By such behavior, and public rage will not   15
          Permit the wretch to carry out his plot.

SCENE VI

VALÈRE, ORGON, CLÉANTE, ELMIRE, MARIANE, MADAME PER-
NELLE, DAMIS, DORINE

VALÈRE: Sir, though I hate to bring you more bad news,
          Such is the danger that I cannot choose.
          A friend who is extremely close to me
          And knows my interest in your family
          Has, for my sake, presumed to violate   5
          The secrecy that's due to things of state,
          And sends me word that you are in a plight
          From which your one salvation lies in flight.
          That scoundrel who's imposed upon you so
          Denounced you to the King an hour ago   10
          And, as supporting evidence, displayed
          The strong-box of a certain renegade
          Whose secret papers, so he testified,
          You had disloyally agreed to hide.
          I don't know just what charges may be pressed,   15
          But there's a warrant out for your arrest;
          Tartuffe has been instructed, furthermore,
          To guide the arresting officer to your door.
CLÉANTE: He's clearly done this to facilitate
          His seizure of your house and your estate.   20
ORGON: That man, I must say, is a vicious beast!
VALÈRE: Quick, Sir; you mustn't tarry in the least.
          My carriage is outside, to take you hence;
          This thousand louis should cover all expense.
          Let's lose no time, or you shall be undone;   25
          The sole defense, in this case, is to run.
          I shall go with you all the way, and place you
          In a safe refuge to which they'll never trace you.
ORGON: Alas, dear boy, I wish that I could show you
          My gratitude for everything I owe you.   30
          But now is not the time; I pray the Lord
          That I may live to give you your reward.
          Farewell, my dears; be careful . . .
CLÉANTE: Brother, hurry.
          We shall take care of things; you needn't worry.

SCENE VII

The OFFICER, TARTUFFE, VALÈRE, ORGON, ELMIRE, MARIANE,
MADAME PERNELLE, DORINE, CLÉANTE, DAMIS

TARTUFFE: Gently, Sir, gently; stay right where you are.
          No need for haste; your lodging isn't far.
          You're off to prison, by order of the Prince.
ORGON: This is the crowning blow, you wretch; and since
          It means my total ruin and defeat,   5
          Your villainy is now at last complete.
TARTUFFE: You needn't try to provoke me; it's no use.
          Those who serve Heaven must expect abuse.
CLÉANTE: You are indeed most patient, sweet, and blameless.

10 DORINE: How he exploits the name of Heaven! It's shameless.
   TARTUFFE: Your taunts and mockeries are all for naught;
      To do my duty is my only thought.
   MARIANE: Your love of duty is more meritorious,
      And what you've done is little short of glorious.
15 TARTUFFE: All deeds are glorious, Madam, which obey
      The sovereign prince who sent me here today.
   ORGON: I rescued you when you were destitute,
      Have you forgotten that, you thankless brute?
   TARTUFFE: No, no, I well remember everything;
20   But my first duty is to serve my King.
      That obligation is so paramount
      That other claims, beside it, do not count;
      And for it I would sacrifice my wife,
      My family, my friend, or my own life.
25 ELMIRE: Hypocrite!
   DORINE: All that we most revere, he uses
      To cloak his plots and camouflage his ruses.
   CLÉANTE: If it is true that you are animated
      By pure and loyal zeal, as you have stated,
      Why was this zeal not roused until you'd sought
30   To make Orgon a cuckold, and been caught?
      Why weren't you moved to give your evidence
      Until your outraged host had driven you hence?
      I shan't say that the gift of all his treasure
      Ought to have damped your zeal in any measure;
35   But if he is a traitor, as you declare,
      How could you condescend to be his heir?
   TARTUFFE: (*To the* OFFICER.) Sir, spare me all this clamor; it's
      growing shrill.
      Please carry out your orders, if you will.
   OFFICER: Yes, I've delayed too long, Sir. Thank you kindly.
40   You're just the proper person to remind me.
      Come, you are off to join the other boarders
      In the King's prison, according to his orders.
   TARTUFFE: Who? I, Sir?
   OFFICER: Yes.
   TARTUFFE: To prison? This can't be true!
   OFFICER: I owe an explanation, but not to you.

   (*To* ORGON.)

45   Sir, all is well; rest easy, and be grateful.
      We serve a Prince to whom all sham is hateful,
      A Prince who sees into our inmost hearts,
      And can't be fooled by any trickster's arts.
      His royal soul, though generous and human,
50   Views all things with discernment and acumen;
      His sovereign reason is not lightly swayed,
      And all his judgments are discreetly weighed.
      He honors righteous men of every kind,
      And yet his zeal for virtue is not blind,

      Nor does his love of piety numb his wits   55
      And make him tolerant of hypocrites.
      'Twas hardly likely that this man could cozen
      A King who's foiled such liars by the dozen.
      With one keen glance, the King perceived the whole
      Perverseness and corruption of his soul,   60
      And thus high Heaven's justice was displayed:
      Betraying you, the rogue stood self-betrayed.
      The King soon recognized Tartuffe as one
      Notorious by another name, who'd done
      So many vicious crimes that one could fill   65
      Ten volumes with them, and be writing still.
      But to be brief: our sovereign was appalled
      By this man's treachery toward you, which he called
      The last, worst villainy of a vile career,
      And bade me follow the impostor here   70
      To see how gross his impudence could be,
      And force him to restore your property.
      Your private papers, by the King's command,
      I hereby seize and give into your hand.
      The King, by royal order, invalidates   75
      The deed which gave this rascal your estates,
      And pardons, furthermore, your grave offense
      In harboring an exile's documents.
      By these decrees, our Prince rewards you for
      Your loyal deeds in the late civil war,   80
      And shows how heartfelt is his satisfaction
      In recompensing any worthy action,
      How much he prizes merit, and how he makes
      More of men's virtues than of their mistakes.
   DORINE: Heaven be praised!   85
   MADAME PERNELLE: I breathe again, at last.
   ELMIRE: We're safe.
   MARIANE: I can't believe the danger's past.
   ORGON: (*To* TARTUFFE.)
      Well, traitor, now you see . . .
   CLÉANTE: Ah, Brother, please,
      Let's not descend to such indignities.
      Leave the poor wretch to his unhappy fate,
      And don't say anything to aggravate   90
      His present woes; but rather hope that he
      Will soon embrace an honest piety,
      And mend his ways, and by a true repentance
      Move our just King to moderate his sentence.
      Meanwhile, go kneel before your sovereign's throne   95
      And thank him for the mercies he has shown.
   ORGON: Well said: let's go at once and, gladly kneeling,
      Express the gratitude which all are feeling.
      Then, when that first great duty has been done,
      We'll turn with pleasure to a second one,   100
      And give Valère, whose love has proven so true,
      The wedded happiness which is his due.

Jean Racine

Jean Racine (1639–1699) pursued a career closely connected with the dominant institutions of Parisian culture: the court, the church, and the stage. Racine's parents both died in his early childhood, and he was raised by his grandfather and enrolled at the school of the famous and controversial abbey at Port-Royal. Port-Royal was associated with an emphatically unworldly Catholic sect, the Jansenists, that was brutally suppressed in the seventeenth century. Racine's education at Port-Royal played a decisive role in his intellectual life and in the course of his career as a dramatist.

At Port-Royal, Racine perfected his study of Greek and Latin, considered a career in the church, and became ambitious for public success and for a life at court. By the early 1660s he had written several courtly poems—on Louis XIV's marriage, on his illness—that brought him to the attention of the established writers at court: Jean La Fontaine, Nicholas Boileau-Despréaux, and Molière. His first surviving play, *La Thebaïde,* was performed by Molière's company in 1664. In 1665, he gave *Alexandre* to Molière's company as well, but he was dissatisfied with Molière's production. He then gave the play to the rival company at the Hôtel de Bourgogne, where it played opposite Molière's production. Molière withdrew the play, and the hostilities between the two playwrights intensified in 1667 when Mademoiselle DuParc, Molière's leading lady—and possibly Racine's mistress—defected from Molière's company to create the title role in Racine's *Andromaque.* This play initiates the stunning series of Racine's major plays, *Britannicus* (1669), *Bérénice* (1670), *Bajazet* (1672), *Mithridate* (1673), *Iphigénie* (1674), and *Phèdre* (1677).

Phaedra (as it is known in English) is Racine's most celebrated play—and his most controversial. The play, originally entitled *Phèdre et Hippolyte,* opened in January 1677 at the Hôtel de Bourgogne, but Racine's enemies at court persuaded Jacques Pradon (1632–1698), a minor playwright, to open his own play about Phaedra at the Palais-Royal theater. The plays ran against one another, inviting comparison and criticism. After *Phaedra,* Racine married and retired from Paris to Port-Royal. He was also appointed to the coveted position of court historiographer and in 1684 wrote a history of Louis XIV's wars. Racine's two last plays, *Esther* (1688) and *Athalie* (1690), are religious dramas, written at the request of Louis's second wife, Madame de Maintenon, to be performed privately at St. Cyr, a girls' academy. Racine was buried at Port-Royal in 1699, and his remains were moved when the abbey was subsequently destroyed.

Throughout his career, Racine maintained contact with Port-Royal, responding to its criticism of his work in the theater, defending Port-Royal in ecclesiastical matters, and writing a history of the abbey. However, Port-Royal's most pervasive influence on Racine's drama has to do with the Jansenist sense of sin, of the impossibility of redeeming human action. Inspired by the writing of Cornelius Otto Jansen (1558–1638), the Jansenists held that mankind lives in a state of essential sin and corruption and summoned their followers to retire from the world in order to contemplate the moral abyss dividing mankind from God's mercy. What made Jansenism particularly threatening to the church in the seventeenth century was its resistance to the authority of Rome and its call for a solitary and contemplative clergy, which challenged the massive public and political role played by the church in the affairs of the French state. Racine's plays touch only metaphorically on the strictly religious issues surrounding the Jansenist debate, but they are directly concerned with the philosophical themes of Jansenist belief: the sense of unavoidable guilt, the tortuous process of introspection, and the desire to escape the world of action.

PHAEDRA

If René Descartes' famous *cogito ergo sum* ("I think, therefore I am") can be taken to represent a neoclassical concern for rational order, *Phaedra* might be said to illustrate a similar

One of Phaedra's celebrated tirades from Racine's *Phaedra,* produced by the American Repertory Theatre.

principle in terms of tragedy: "I feel, therefore I suffer." The play's main characters, particularly Hippolytus and Phaedra, feel and suffer precisely because reason fails to control the massive passions welling up within them, passions that deepen the rift between the corruption they feel and the uncorrupted ideals they never can achieve.

Racine's Jansenist beliefs have an indirect but profound impact in *Phaedra.* The world of the play is a world of unavoidable sin in which action leads inevitably to wrongdoing and catastrophe and in which flight is impossible. The characters define themselves according to fixed and unattainable ideals that are subverted by their irresistible, even criminal passions. Hippolytus pursues an ideal of heroic innocence and self-containment, violated in his own eyes by his love for Aricia. Theseus is consumed by his passion for power, conquest, and authority and feels betrayed when he believes that he has been usurped by his son. Phaedra's honor, and even her humanity, are shattered by her adulterous, incestuous desire for her stepson. The play's elegant compression concentrates the action exclusively on these characters; their confidants—Theramenes and Oenone—function largely as screens on which Racine projects the tempestuous passions of the main characters. Although the characters blame the gods for the desire they suffer, the destructive force of the characters' passions really rises from within. In the world of *Phaedra,* action is impossible and sin is inevitable. The characters are each destroyed by the monsters they become.

PREFACE
TRANSLATED BY R.C. KNIGHT

Here is another tragedy on a subject taken from Euripides. The action follows a somewhat different course, but I have enriched my play with everything in his that I considered most strikingly beautiful. Had I borrowed no more than the conception of Phaedra's character, I might say I owe him the most reasonable thing, perhaps, that I have given to the theatre. I am not surprised that this character was so successful in Euripides' time, and now again in our own, considering that it has every quality required by Aristotle in the tragic hero, and proper to arouse compassion and terror. For Phaedra is not altogether guilty, and not altogether innocent. She is drawn by her destiny, and the anger of the Gods, into an unlawful passion which she is the first to hold in horror. She makes every endeavour to overcome it. She chooses death rather than disclose it to anyone. And when forced to reveal it, she speaks of it with such shame and confusion as leave no doubt that her crime is rather a punishment from the Gods, than an impulse of her own will.

I have even taken pains to make her a little less odious than she is in the tragedies of antiquity, where she brings herself, unprompted, to accuse Hippolytus. I felt that a false testimony was something too base, too black, to put into the mouth of a Princess possessed otherwise of sentiments so noble and virtuous. Such baseness seemed to me more fitting to a Nurse, who might have more slave-like propensities; though even she only enters upon the lying accusation to save the life and honour of her mistress. If Phaedra acquiesces, it is because she is beside herself in the agitation of her thoughts, and the next moment she comes on with the intention of vindicating the guiltless and publishing the truth.

Hippolytus is accused, in Euripides and in Seneca, of actually raping his step-mother—*vim corpus tulit;* here, of no more than the intention. I desired to spare Theseus a sense of shame which might have made him less acceptable to my audience.

As for the figure of Hippolytus, I had read in ancient authors that Euripides was blamed for depicting him as a philosopher free of all imperfection—so that the death of the youthful Prince gave rise to far more indignation than pity. I felt I should give him a failing that might render him somewhat guilty towards his father, without detracting at all from that magnanimity which makes him spare Phaedra's honour and go to his doom without accusing her. By failing I mean his involuntary passion for Aricia, the daughter and the sister of his father's mortal enemies.

This Aricia is not a child of my invention. Virgil relates that Hippolytus married her, and she bore him a son, after Aesculapius had brought him back to life. And I have read too, in certain authors, that Hippolytus had married and brought into Italy an Athenian maiden of high birth, named Aricia, who had given her name to an Italian township.

I adduce these authorities, because I have most scrupulously endeavoured to keep close to the legend. I have even taken the history of Theseus just as it is in Plutarch.

It is this historian who mentions that the belief in Theseus' descent to the underworld to abduct Proserpine was occasioned by a journey he made into Epirus towards the source of the Acheron, where a King, whose wife Pirithous sought to carry off, held Theseus prisoner after putting Pirithous to death. Thus I have tried to retain the verisimilitude of history, and yet to lose none of the embellishments of fable, so rich in the stuff of poetry. And the rumour of Theseus' death, based on the legendary journey, gives rise to that declaration of Phaedra's love which proves one of the principal causes of her unhappy plight, and which she would never have dared utter while she believed her husband to be alive.

For the rest, I dare not yet assert this play to be in truth the best of my tragedies. I leave my readers, and time, to set its rightful price upon it. What I can assert is that I have composed none where virtue is shown to more advantage than here. The slightest faults are severely punished. The bare thought of crime is regarded with no less horror than crime itself. The failings of love are treated as real failings. The passions are offered to view only to show all the ravage they create. And vice is everywhere painted in such hues, that its hideous face may be recognised and loathed. Here is the proper aim for every man to keep in sight who works for the public. And this, above all, was the purpose of the earliest tragic poets. Their stage was a school where virtue was taught no less well than in the schools of the philosophers. Thus Aristotle consented to draw up the rules of the dramatic poem; Socrates, the sagest of the philosophers, thought it no shame to set his hand to the tragedies of Euripides. It were much to be desired that our works should be found as serious and as full of useful instruction as the pages of those poets. It might bring about a reconciliation between the tragic art and a number of persons, noted for their religion and learning, who have denounced it of late, but might well look upon it with less disfavour if authors cared as much to instruct as to entertain their audience, and carried out thereby the true purpose of tragedy.

Jean Racine
(1677)

PHAEDRA

Jean Racine

TRANSLATED BY R.C. KNIGHT

CHARACTERS

THESEUS, *son of Aegeus, King of Athens*
PHAEDRA, *wife of Theseus, daughter of Minos and Pasiphaë*
HIPPOLYTUS, *son of Theseus by Antiope, Queen of the Amazons*
ARICIA, *daughter of Pallas, descended from the ancient kings of Athens*
OENONE, *nurse and confidant of Phaedra*

THERAMENES, *tutor of Hippolytus*
ISMENE, *confidant to Aricia*
PANOPE, *one of Phaedra's women*
GUARDS

The scene is in Trozen, a town in the Peloponnese

ACT ONE

HIPPOLYTUS, THERAMENES

HIPPOLYTUS: My mind's made up: I sail, Theramenes.
No more for me the tranquil days of Trozen,
For in the mortal tempest of my doubts
I am dishonoured if I linger here.
5 Six months ago my father sailed and left me
Ignorant what befalls a head so cherished,
Ignorant even where he may be hidden—
THERAMENES: So where will you go to look for him, my lord?
Already, to relieve a fear I shared,
10 I have scoured the two seas that Corinth holds asunder.
Demanded Theseus of the tribes that live
Where Acheron drives down headlong into Hell,
Searched Elis, skirted Taenarum, and even
Traversed the waves where Icarus fell and perished.
15 What hope new-risen or what happier skies
Will light you to his footsteps? Why, perhaps,
Who knows, perhaps the King your father wishes
Not to unveil the mystery of his venture,
And while his peril fills your thought and ours,
20 Serene, weaving the latest of his loves,
The hero waits to seize the unguarded moment—
HIPPOLYTUS: Stop, good Theramenes. You slander Theseus;
There is a nobler cause for these delays;
After the follies of forgotten youth
25 The wanderings of his inconstant heart
Are fixed at length, and Phaedra fears no rival.
So once more—I shall go where duty points
And fly a land I cannot bear to see.
THERAMENES: But my lord, how long have you despised the presence
30 Of these calm fields, the pleasure of your childhood
Whose solitude was dearer to you than
The splendid stir of Athens and the court?
What fear has banished you, or else what heartache?
HIPPOLYTUS: Those days are past. Pleasure and peace have vanished
35 Since first the Gods directed to our shore
The child of Minos and Pasiphaë.
THERAMENES: I see: there is the cause, the hated presence—
Phaedra, who came, your father's dangerous bride,
Looked on you once, and by your prompt exile
40 Gave the first measure of her new-won power.

But all that dogged hate and old aversion
Has passed with time, passed or at least abated;
And after all what danger lies in her,
A woman dying, crying out for death?
45 Stricken by ills that none can make her utter,
Tired of her life, tired of the day that lights her,
What can she do to you?
HIPPOLYTUS: I do not fear
Anything her aversion could devise.
I sail to fly another enemy,
50 I do admit: I fly Aricia,
The youngest and the last of all that house
In fatal league against ours.
THERAMENES: You, my lord,
Are turned against her too? But Pallas' daughter
Surely had no part in her brothers' treason,
55 And must you hate that unoffending grace?
HIPPOLYTUS: I would not fly her if I hated her.
THERAMENES: My lord, have I permission to interpret
Your flight? Must I suppose that you are not
The old implacable Hippolytus,
60 The outlaw of Love's empire, he that vowed
Never to wear the yoke his father wore?
Can it be that a slighted and a smarting Goddess
Will press you to the service of her shrine,
Reduce you to the rank of common men
65 And vindicate that father by your fate?
Can it be love, my lord?
HIPPOLYTUS: How can you say it,
My friend, that knew the childhood of my heart
And all its growth in pride and fierce resolve?
Shall I dishonour it, disown myself?
70 First, as a babe, at an Amazonian breast
I drank the resolution that astounds you,
But once of age to look upon myself
I wished to be no other than I was.
Then, in the faithful service of your kindness
75 As you rehearsed for me my father's story,
Do you remember how my soul blazed up
At each particular in the noble toils
Of the intrepid hero, as we showed him
Turning the world from thoughts of lost Alcides
80 By monsters strangled and by brigands slain—
Procrustes, Sinnis, Sciro, Cercyon
And Epidaurus scattered with the limbs
Of her gigantic tyrant, and the gore

Reeking from all Crete, of the Minotaur?
85 But when you told other ignobler feats—
A faith so cheaply pledged, and ever new,
Helen torn from a mother's arms in Sparta,
In Salamis the sighs of Periboea,
So many more than he can even name,
90 Victims too credulous of a lover's tongue;
What barren rocks heard Ariadne's sorrows;
How Phaedra, last and under happier auspice,
Followed him—then I wished the tale untold;
Often I urged you hasten and be done;
95 And would my wishes had redeemed from fame
That darker half of such a fair renown!
And now, by the spite of Heaven, shall I be
Degraded to the same indignity?
—Baseness beyond excuse, for those were frailties
100 Unseen amid a multitude of honours,
While not one trophy of a monster slain
Entitles me to fail as he has failed.
Even if I lost my freedom and my pride
How could I yield them to Aricia?
105 How could my disobedient sense forget
That which divides us irremovably?
The King denies her, denies her fallen brothers,
By violent laws, continuance of their line;
Their name must die for ever in her death,
110 Their guilty branch must bear no other fruit,
And till the tomb, submissive and sequestered,
The torch of wedlock must not burn for her.
Am I to oppose my father and his wrath?
Embrace her claims? and give a precedent
115 To treason? and embark my youth—

THERAMENES: My lord,
If the marked hour draws on, our arguments
Escape the notice of the incurious Heavens.
No. Theseus wished you blind, and gave you eyes;
His hate inflames the passion he forbids you,
120 And adds enchantment to his prisoner's charms.
But come, why look askance at honest love?
Why not make trial where its sweetness lies?
Why be enchained by vain and foolish scruples?
Who fears to stray that follows Hercules?
125 Many a stubborn heart has Venus bent—
Where would you be yourself and your defiance
Had chaste Antiope been as chaste as you
And never warmed to Theseus' flame? But why
Face out a falsehood with the pride of words?
130 Confess how things have changed: not now as once,
Aloof, intractable, we see you guide
A skimming chariot along the beaches
Or, adept in the mystery Neptune taught,
Break an unmastered courser to the curb;
135 Less often our halloos awake the forests;
Your eyes droop, weighted with a secret fire . . .
The case is clear—you are in love, in flame,
In torment, and you will not show your wound.
Is it Aricia?

HIPPOLYTUS: Theramenes,
140 I sail today, and go to find my father.
THERAMENES: Without an audience of Phaedra?
HIPPOLYTUS: No.

I will see her; I cannot well do less.
You may send word.—But what is the fresh misfortune
Disturbs her favorite Oenone so?

(*Enter* OENONE.)

OENONE: Alas, my lord, what grief can equal mine?   145
The Queen is near her utmost bourne of fate;
She that I watch by night and day unsleeping
Dies in my arms, and will not tell her sickness.
Her thought is all at variance with itself;
Her sick disquiet drives her from her bed   150
To see the light of day. But by her orders
No eye of man may see her suffering.
—Here she is.
HIPPOLYTUS: Very well; then I retire
Not to offend with this unwelcome face.

(*Exeunt* HIPPOLYTUS *and* THERAMENES.)

(*Enter* PHAEDRA.)

PHAEDRA: No more, for I can move no more, Oenone.   155
Let me rest; I am faint, my strength has left me.
My darkened eyes are dazzled by the light,
My wavering knees are weak beneath my weight.
Ah me!

(*Sits.*)

OENONE: High Gods, relent and see our tears!
PHAEDRA: These fripperies, these veils, they hang so heavy!   160
Whose was the unkind hand that piled and bound
These clustering locks that weigh upon my brow?
So feeble and so weary, all these things
Grieve me and weary me.
OENONE: How can we please you?
Yourself, repentant of your wicked thoughts,   165
You called in haste for clothes and ornaments;
Yourself you rallied your forgotten vigour,
You wanted to be out and see the sunlight.
Now you are here, my lady, and it seems
You loathe the very light that you desired.   170
PHAEDRA: Splendid begetter of a seed afflicted,
Father from whom my mother claimed her birth,
O blushing Sun ashamed of my despair,
Now, for the last time, I salute thy face.
OENONE: What, still possessed of such a fearful purpose?   175
Shall I for ever see you, turned from life,
Enact the mournful ritual of your death?
PHAEDRA: Oh give me the shadow of the forest glades!
Or let my eye piercing the glorious dust
Follow the wheeling chariot in the course!   180
OENONE: My lady?
PHAEDRA: Oh, I am mad. What have I said?
Where am I, where are my thoughts, my wandering mind?
Lost, for the Gods have taken it away.
My face is hot, Oenone, with my shame;
I cannot hide my guilty sufferings   185
And tears descend that I cannot restrain.
OENONE: Blush if you must, but blush to keep a silence

That doubles all the misery you suffer.
Rebellious to all tending, deaf to all pleas,
190 Will you unpitying allow your life
To flow away? What madness cuts it short?
What spell, what poison stanches up its course?
Thrice has the sky been muffled up in shade
And still is sleep a stranger to your eyes;
195 Thrice has the day displaced the gloom of night
And still you fast, and still your body wastes.
What dark temptation leads you on? What right
Invests you with the power to take your life—
Wronging the Gods from whom you draw your being,
200 Failing the husband who received your promise,
Failing still more your helpless children, doomed
To bitter lives of bondage; for reflect,
The very day that takes their mother from them
Rebuilds the hope of that Barbarian's child,
205 That arrogant enemy of you and yours,
The boy the Amazonian stranger bore,
Hippolytus—
PHAEDRA: O Gods!
OENONE: That charge strikes home!
PHAEDRA: Woman, how dare you name that name to me?
OENONE: Why, now your anger is most justly roused.
210 It heartens me that you should shrink to hear
That fatal name. Then live. For love, for duty,
Live; if you would not have the Scythian's son,
Bending your children to his hated yoke,
Lord it over the fairest blood of Greece
215 And of the Gods. But do not wait, each moment
You die. Rally, betimes, your prostrate vigour
While yet your almost spent and guttering life
Still glows, and may be kindled once again.
PHAEDRA: I have outlived the right to live already.
220 OENONE: Why, is there some remorse that feeds upon you?
What have you done that drives you so distraught?
Your hands have never dipped in guiltless blood?
PHAEDRA: I thank the Gods my hands are free of evil.
Would that my heart were innocent as they!
225 OENONE: What resolution, then, have you conceived
To terrify your heart before the time?
PHAEDRA: I have said enough. Ask me no more, have pity;
For if I die it is to keep within me
This dreadful secret.
OENONE: Keep it then, and die;
230 But other hands, not mine, will close your eyes.
Yours is a weak and flickering fire, but I
Will lose my spirit first among the dead;
There are many avenues and all unbarred;
An injured heart will soon perceive the best.—
235 Ungrateful mistress, when did I betray you?
Have you forgotten that these hands received you
When you were born? My children and my home,
I have left all for you: and all for this.
PHAEDRA: What do you think to gain by this beseeching?
240 You will shrink with horror if I break my silence.
OENONE: What can you tell me then more horrible
Than thus to see you die before my face?
PHAEDRA: And when you know my destiny and my weakness
Still I shall die, and only die more guilty.

OENONE: My lady, by the tears I shed for you, 245
By these your trembling knees I hold entwined,
Deliver me from deadly fear and doubt.
PHAEDRA: You wish it. Rise.
OENONE: Speak on, and I will listen.
PHAEDRA: How shall I tell, ye Gods, or where begin?
OENONE: Your fears are insults to my loyalty. 250
PHAEDRA: O deathless hate of Venus, fatal vengeance!
O heavy doom of love upon my mother!
OENONE: Forget, my lady. Hide that memory
And keep it from the ears of later times.
PHAEDRA: Love left thee dying, sweet sister Ariadne, 255
Lying forsaken by the alien waters.
OENONE: Let by, my lady. Must your mortal grief
Be vented on the dearest of your blood?
PHAEDRA: Of this doomed blood, I, by the will of Venus,
I perish now the last and most accursed. 260
OENONE: You love!
PHAEDRA: To madness and to ecstasy.
OENONE: Who?
PHAEDRA: There's the horror that surpasses horror:
I love . . . at the fatal name I blench and tremble—
I love . . .
OENONE: But who?
PHAEDRA: You know the Amazon's son,
The young Prince who endured so much, through me . . . 265
OENONE: O Gods! Hippolytus!
PHAEDRA: You spoke the name!
OENONE: Sweet Heavens! You have chilled my very blood.
O race polluted, hopeless, lamentable!
Woe worth the day that brought us to these shores!
Why did we venture? 270
PHAEDRA: It was long ago
And far from here. When first the rite of Hymen
Bound my obedience to the son of Aegeus—
My happiness, my peace then seemed so plain—
Careless in Athens stood my conqueror.
I saw and gazed, I blushed and paled again, 275
A blind amazement rose and blurred my mind;
My eyes were dim, my lips forgot to speak,
This, I knew, was the awful flame of Venus,
The fated torment of her chosen victims.
I tried to ward it off with prayers, with vows 280
And offerings, a temple built and decked,
And in the midst of endless sacrifices
I searched the entrails for my erring wisdom.
Weak drugs for irremediable love!
Even as my hand spilt incense at the shrine, 285
Even as my lips invoked the name of Venus
I prayed Hippolytus, my eyes beheld
Hippolytus, and while the altars steamed
I offered all to him I dared not name.
I fled him everywhere. O bitterness, 290
He looked upon me in his father's features.
At last, I turned upon myself. I forced
Myself to play the torturer against
The dreaded enemy I loved too well,
Put on the bride's abhorrence of the stepson, 295
Pleaded and pressed until I banished him
Out of his father's arms, his father's heart.

Once more I breathed; and after this, Oenone,
My life, serener, flowed in blameless ways,
300 Pleasing my husband, covering my pain,
Tending the fruits of his unhappy bed:
Foolish expedients! and inexorable
Hardness of destiny!—My lord himself
Brought me to Trozen and my banished foe.
305 The ancient wound gaped deep, and bled again.
No longer is it a secret flame that flickers
About my veins: headlong in onset Venus
Hangs on her quarry! I abhorred my guilt,
Life was a curse, my love a misery;
310 I looked for death to save my name, and bury
Far from the day the darkness of these fires.
I could not face your strivings and your tears.
Now you know all; and it is well, if you
Stand but aside from my advancing death.
315 Abstain at last from undeserved reproaches,
And leave your useless effort to revive
The embers of a fast-expiring fire.

(*Enter* PANOPE.)

PANOPE: I wish that I could hide the news, my lady,
That I am forced to bring you. Death has taken
320 Your lord, our most indomitable King;
And you alone are ignorant of your loss.
OENONE: What is this, Panope?
                                      My lady's prayers
Will never now bring Theseus back to Athens,
And mariners that landed here today
325 Have told Hippolytus that he is dead.
PHAEDRA: Gods!
PANOPE: Athens wavers in the choice of masters.
One boasts allegiance to the Prince your son;
One, reckless of the statutes of the land,
Presumes to favour the Barbarian's child,
330 My lady; and they say a rank sedition
Proclaims Aricia and the blood of Pallas.
I knew it was my duty to report
Such perils. Hippolytus is ready now
To sail, and many fear if he arrives
335 In this tempestuous season, he will sway
A fickle multitude.
OENONE: Panope, thank you:
Your news was precious, and the Queen has heard.

(*Exit* PANOPE.)

OENONE: My lady, I had thrown away all pleadings,
All hope to move you, and my only thought
340 Was to attend you past the gates of the tomb,
But new disaster points new purposes,
An altered fortune, and an altered duty.
     Theseus is dead, and you are his successor,
My lady, with a son that looks to you—
345 A slave alone, and if you live a king.
No other will uphold his friendless quarrel,
No other wipe away his orphan tears;
Only in Heaven will his hearers be

The Gods, your judges and his ancestors.
Live then, in liberty from all misgiving;   350
Your love is now as unremarkable
As any love, for death disjoins the bond
That made its foulness and its infamy.
Henceforth the image of Hippolytus
Is not so terrible, and you may see him   355
With perfect guiltlessness. But what if now,
Despairing of a better understanding,
He takes command of these rebellious throngs?
Open his eyes, soften that stubborn heart.
Prince of these smiling coasts, his patrimony   360
Is here in Trozen, but he knows the laws;
He knows that they deliver to your son
The queenly ramparts that Minerva reared.
Your rightful enemy is also his:
Unite your forces to defeat Aricia.   365
PHAEDRA: So be it. I commit my way to you.
I will live, if I still have strength to live
And if a mother's love can even now
Revive in my wasted flesh the seeds of life.

ACT TWO

ARICIA, ISMENE

ARICIA: He asked to see me here? Hippolytus
Wanted to see me and to say farewell?
Are you quite certain? Is this true, Ismene?
ISMENE: Much more than this, now that the King is dead.
Prepare yourself, my lady; all the hearts   5
He kept at bay will cluster at your feet.
All Greece will bring its tributes to Aricia,
Enfranchised now and sovereign of her fortunes.
ARICIA: So then, Ismene, it is no idle talk.
And I have no oppressor and no foe?   10
ISMENE: My lady, none. The Heavens have relented
And Theseus walks among your fathers' shades.
ARICIA: What enterprise has brought him to his death?
Do they say?
ISMENE: Rumours wild and past belief;
Some say that in a lover's last adventure   15
The seas have claimed this ever-wandering husband;
Some say, and everywhere the news is sown,
That with Pirithous he went down to Hell,
Saw the Cocytus and the coasts of darkness
And stood alive amid a world of shadows,   20
But could not scale the gloomy track again
Nor pass the bourne men never pass but once.
ARICIA: Shall mortal men, before the last leave-taking,
Fathom those sullen deeps of the Departed?
What sorcery lured him to their awful shore?   25
ISMENE: My lady, he is dead, and you alone
Doubt it. All Athens grieves for him, all Trozen
Knows, and salutes Hippolytus for Prince.
And in these walls, despairing for her son,
Phaedra takes counsel of her trembling friends.   30
ARICIA: And you suppose that, kinder than his father,
Hippolytus will make my bondage sweeter
And pity me?

ISMENE: My lady, yes, I do.

ARICIA: But do you know the hard Hippolytus?

35   What makes you fancy he could feel compassion
     For me alone, who never felt for woman?
     He never joins our customary paths
     And hides himself wherever we are not.

ISMENE: Oh, I know all the legend of his coldness;

40   But when you met the proud Hippolytus
     I own the strangeness of his reputation
     Sharpened the edge of my curiosity.
     I saw a face at variance with the fable;
     At once your eyes disturbed that hard assurance

45   And his, avoiding you but all in vain,
     Melted at once, and could not turn away.
     His pride may yet refuse the name of lover
     But I'll believe his looks, and not his tongue.

ARICIA: Ah, sweet Ismene, how my heart devours

50   The unhoped-for comfort of a mere perhaps!
     You that have known me, did you once imagine
     This heart, the plaything of unpitying Fortune,
     Starved of all sustenance except despair,
     Would learn of love and the wild woes of love?

55   Child of Earth's child, last of a royal lineage,
     Sole remnant spared by battlefield and hatred,
     I lost the last proud blossoms of our tree,
     Six brothers, in the springtime of their year.
     The steel reaped all, and Earth's unwilling furrows

60   Drank her own blood, the blood of her Erechtheus.
     Since then you know what rigorous decree
     Defies all Greeks to lift their eyes to mine—
     For a mutinous ardour in the sister's breast
     Might wake the embers in her brothers' urns—

65   And you remember how I laughed to scorn
     Those calculations of the victor's fear;
     I held that love itself was slavery
     And even thanked the King for a constraint
     So fit and favourable to my distaste—

70   Then, yes; but then I had not seen his son.
     Not that subservient to the eye's seduction
     I love him for that beauty, that demeanour,
     Graces of partial Nature, gifts that he
     Ignores, if ever he has noticed them;

75   I see richer and dearer treasures in him—
     His father's parts, and not his father's failings;
     For I confess I love the manly pride
     That never bent under the yoke of Love.
     Phaedra was flattered by the doubtful glory

80   Of Theseus' courtly sighs: but I am prouder
     And will not stoop to share an easy prize
     Or occupy an undefended heart.
     No, but to shape a will as yet unbending,
     To waken pain in a proof-armoured bosom,

85   To lead a slave that never thought to serve,
     Vainly at war against the pleasing chain—
     There's a reward worthy of my ambition;
     Hercules was an easier adversary
     Who readily disarmed and quick to yield

90   Lent no such lustre to his overthrow.
     But dear Ismene, these are reckless dreams:
     Resistance there will be, and all too stubborn,
     And you shall hear me soon in humbler strain

     Lament the coldness that I praise today.
     He love, Hippolytus? What heights of fortune   95
     Could ever bring him—

ISMENE: Only let him speak;
     He is coming now.

(*Enter* HIPPOLYTUS.)

HIPPOLYTUS: My lady, before I sail
     I owe you some account of my intentions.
     My father's dead: and well enough my fears
     Foretold the causes of his late homecoming—   100
     Death only, and the closure of his toils
     Could hold him from the world so long. The Gods
     At last abandon to the fatal Spinners
     Alcides' friend, his fellow, his successor.
     —I know your enmity will not forbid   105
     His son to assert these titles he has earned.—
     One hope alleviates my deepest sorrow,
     For I can end a harsh and long subjection:
     I here revoke laws that have caused me grief—
     The full bestowal of your life and hand   110
     Is yours alone, and in my patrimony,
     This Trozen, seat of Pittheus my grandfather,
     Which willingly defers his crown to me
     I leave you free and freer than its Prince.

ARICIA: Show me less kindness, I could bear it better.   115
     So much regard for me in my abjection
     Binds me, my lord, more even than you know,
     To that constraint you would have put away.

HIPPOLYTUS: Doubtful who stands the next in title, Athens
     Canvasses you, and me, and Phaedra's son.   120

ARICIA: Me, my lord?

HIPPOLYTUS: I have never shut my eyes
     To arrogant laws that seem to bar my claim:
     The Greeks reject me for my mother's race.
     But if my brother were my only rival
     I could appeal to certain natural laws   125
     And make them good against the law's caprice.
     I have a better reason to refrain:
     To you I yield, say rather I restore
     The seat, the sceptre, that your fathers held
     Of the illustrious mortal, son of Earth.   130
     It only passed to Aegeus by adoption;
     And next my father, Athens' second founder,
     Was hailed and crowned for all his benefits
     While your unhappy brothers lay forgotten.
     Now, Athens calls you home within her ramparts,   135
     Too long the ancient quarrel lives in pain,
     Too long your blood, that flowed along her fields,
     Reeks from the furrows where it found its birth.—
     Trozen I hold. As for the son of Phaedra
     The Cretan acres yield him rich retirement.   140
     Attica falls to you. I sail, to join
     My partisans with yours, in your support.

ARICIA: At every word more troubled and bewildered,
     Can I, or dare I, think I heard you rightly?
     Have I my senses, is this your intent?   145
     What God, my lord, what God inspired your mind?
     Rightly your glory sounds in every climate
     But reputation falls behind the truth.

150   What, will you cheat yourself on my behalf?
      It was enough indeed to think that you
      Hated me not, and held a mind untainted
      By this long enmity—
HIPPOLYTUS: How could I hate you?
      Men may deride this proud unconquered heart
      But do they think a monster gave me birth?
155   What brutishness or what inveterate malice
      Could see your face and not forget its fury?
      And how should I withstand this subtle spell—
ARICIA: My lord! . . .
HIPPOLYTUS: My tongue has carried me too far;
      But wisdom fails and yields to the compulsion . . .
160   Now that my silence has been partly broken,
      My lady, I must needs go on, and speak
      The secret that my soul cannot contain.—
      Here stands a Prince of all men most unhappy,
      A monument of overthrown presumption;
165   I, long a truant from the law of love
      And long a mocker of its votaries,
      That stayed ashore watching the luckless sailor
      And never thought myself to fight the tempest,
      Levelled at last beneath the common fate
170   By strange tides I am borne far from myself.
      My wanton liberty has learnt to yield
      And in an instant this bold heart was tamed.
      Six months or nearly, in despair and shame,
      I've borne the arrow burning in my side;
175   Vainly I pit my strength against myself
      And you. I fly you where you are, and find you
      Where you are not; deep in the forest glade
      Your picture chases me; sunlight and shade
      Alike retrace your features and alike
180   Betray the fugitive that would be free,
      And I, for all my fruitless pains, look round
      To find Hippolytus, and know him not.
      My bow, my bounds, my spear, my chariot,
      Weary me. Neptune's lessons are forgotten;
185   Only my lamentations fill the groves,
      My stabled coursers know my voice no more.
              Perhaps this tale I tell of uncouth passion
      Will make you blush to own your handiwork:
      Wild terms, indeed, to offer up a heart!
190   And chains too fair for such a slave to claim!
      And yet my tribute therefore ranks the higher;
      Consider that I speak an unknown language
      And do not spurn these faltered words of love
      That you alone could teach Hippolytus.

(*Enter* THERAMENES.)

195   THERAMENES: Close on my heels, my lord, the Queen
              approaches
      Asking for you.
HIPPOLYTUS: For me?
THERAMENES: In what intention
      I do not know, but messengers have come
      Bidding you wait on her before you sail.
HIPPOLYTUS: The Queen? What should I say to her? Or she . . .
200   ARICIA: You cannot disappoint her wish, my lord.
      Even to such an enemy is due

Some sign of formal pity for her grief.
HIPPOLYTUS: So you go. And I sail. And still I know not
      Whether my worship has incensed my goddess,
      Whether this heart I leave in your two hands . . .   205
ARICIA: Sail, Prince. Pursue your noble purposes;
      Bring me the realm of Athens for dominion;
      Whatever gift you make shall be accepted,
      But that imperial, that unhoped-for state
      Is not the dearest of your offerings.   210

(*Exeunt* ARICIA *and* ISMENE.)

HIPPOLYTUS: Good friend, are all things ready?—But I hear
      The Queen.—Have all things ordered for our sailing.
      Send out the signal. Haste, command, return
      And free me from the burden of this meeting.

(*Exit* THERAMENES.)

(*Enter* PHAEDRA *and* OENONE.)

PHAEDRA: He is here. My blood retreats toward my heart.   215
      I see him, and forget what I should speak.
OENONE: Be mindful of the son that trusts in you!
PHAEDRA: They say that you are taking ship at once,
      My lord. I came to join my grief with yours,
      And with the story of a mother's terrors—   220
      My child is fatherless, and soon the day
      Will dawn that brings him to another deathbed;
      So fiercely even now assailed and threatened,
      Your strength alone can champion his weakness.—
      But deep within me throbs the preying thought   225
      That his complaint will never reach your ear,
      That through my child your angry justice soon
      Will strike a hated memory.
HIPPOLYTUS: My lady,
      So infamous a wish was never mine.
PHAEDRA: But you have seen me unremittingly   230
      Pursue your hate, my lord; and how could you
      Explore the bottom of my soul and read
      My secret there? I threw myself upon
      Your just resentment; I would not suffer you
      Within the self-same frontiers; privily   235
      And openly I waged my war, and set
      The width of seas between your path and mine.
      I even gave explicit orders not
      To breathe your name before my presence. Yet,
      If by the wrong the penalty were measured,   240
      If only hatred could achieve your hatred,
      Never did woman more deserve your tears,
      My lord, and less your enmity.
HIPPOLYTUS: No mother
      That watches for her children's interest
      Forgives the other children of her house;   245
      I know, my lady. Untoward mistrust
      Is always near when men have married twice.
      Another in your place would have conceived
      No less suspicion, and I might have suffered
      Deeper indignities.   250
PHAEDRA: Ah but, my lord,

The Gods—as now they stand my witnesses—
Deigned to release me from this general law.
How different are the thoughts that ravage me!
HIPPOLYTUS: It is too soon, my lady, for such thoughts;
255   The sunshine may still light your husband's eye,
And Heaven still may yield him to our prayers;
Neptune's his friend, and that high patronage
Will not in vain be canvassed by my father.
PHAEDRA: No man has twice explored the coasts of Death,
260   My lord. If Theseus touched the sullen shores
Vainly we look for Gods to send him home:
Harsh Acheron is grasping and holds fast
His prey. But did I say that he is dead?
He breathes again in you; I see the King,
265   See him, speak to him, thrill . . . My mind is wandering,
My lord, my madness speaks the thing it should not.
HIPPOLYTUS: This is a prodigy of loyal love:
Theseus is gone, yet lives within your mind
And fires the ardour of your loving heart.
270   PHAEDRA: Yes, Prince, for him indeed I yearn, I languish;
I love him—not the man that Hell has claimed,
The butterfly that every beauty lured,
The adulterous ravisher that would have stained
The God of Hell's own bed; but faithful, fine,
275   Sometimes aloof, and pure, gallant and gay,
Young, stealing every heart upon his road—
So do they character our Gods, and so
I see you now; those eyes, that voice, were his,
That generous red of virtue in your cheek,
280   When first he drove across the Cretan foam,
Meet meditation for the virgin dreams
Of Minos' daughters. You, where were you then
Among the flower and chivalry of Greece?
Where was Hippolytus—alas, too young—
285   The day his vessel grounded on our shore?
You would have slain the terror of the island,
The monster lapped in labyrinthine wiles;
Into your hand my sister would have thrust,
To unweave those riddling and deceitful ways,
290   The thread of life and death. But no, she would not—
Love would have found a readier wit in me,
And I, Prince, I, devoted and assured,
Could have resolved the devious Labyrinth;
What would I not have done for that sweet head?
295   How should a thread content your fearful lover?
Half-claimant in the peril that you claimed
I would have walked before you in the way,
And Phaedra, steadfast in the Labyrinth,
Would have returned again with you, or else
300   With you remained.
HIPPOLYTUS: Great Gods, what have you said?
My lady, can it be that you forget
That Theseus is my father, and your husband?
PHAEDRA: And why do you suppose I had forgotten,
Prince? Do I appear so careless of my honour?
305   HIPPOLYTUS: Forgive, my lady. I own, I blush to own
How blameless are the words that I reproved.
My shame can face it out no more before you,
So let me go . . .
PHAEDRA: Ah, leave your heartless lying.
You understand and you have heard enough.

Very well then, you shall learn what Phaedra is   310
And all her frenzy. Yes; I am in love.
But never think that even while I love you
I can absolve myself, or hide my face
From my own guiltiness. And never think
The wanton love that blurs my better mind   315
Grew with the treachery of my consent.
I, singled out for a celestial vengeance,
Unpitied victim, I abhor myself
More than you hate me. Let the Gods bear witness,
Those Gods that set the fire within my breast,   320
The fatal fire of my accursed line;
Those Gods whose majesty and might exulted
In the beguiling of a mortal's weakness.
Turn back the past yourself; how I have laboured
To seem malignant, savage, how I fostered   325
Your hatred as my ally in the fight.
Did I escape you? No, I banished you.
What fruit repaid these unavailing cares?
You loathed me more, I could not love you less;
Your suffering doubled the spell that binds me,   330
The withering ravage of my flames, my tears.
Your eyes can testify that this is true—
If for one moment they could bear my sight.
Why, this confession of my bitter secret,
My shameful secret, do you think that I   335
Have made it willingly? I came in fear
For one defenceless that I dare not fail:
I came to pray you not to hate my child.
Precarious resolution of a mind
Too full of what it loves! I came, and spoke   340
Of nothing else but you. So now, do justice.
Punish me for this execrable passion.
Approve yourself a hero's son indeed
And sweep this monster from the universe.
Dare Theseus' widow love Hippolytus?   345
Truly so vile a monster must not live.
My heart is here, and here is where you strike.
Eager to make atonement for its fault
I feel it swell and bound to meet your hand:
Strike. Or am I unworthy of your steel,   350
Or will your hate refuse so sweet a doom,
Or would ignoble blood sully your fingers?
Then hold your hand and let me have your sword.
Give it me.
OENONE: Stop, my lady. Heavenly powers!
What would you do? But somebody is coming: 355
Escape their sight, be quick, come back, or face
Inevitable shame.

(*Exeunt* PHAEDRA *and* OENONE. *Enter* THERAMENES.)

THERAMENES: Was that the Queen
Half dragged, half rushing out? What, my lord, what
Are all these marks of grief? You stand disarmed,
Dumb, pale . . .   360
HIPPOLYTUS: Come, let us go, Theramenes.
I cannot think of what I have heard and witnessed;
I cannot see myself without disgust.
Phaedra . . . No more, great Gods! Oblivion
Must shroud away the secret and the shame.

365 THERAMENES: If you would leave, my lord, the sail hangs
   ready;
  But Athens is beforehand with her answer:
  Her chiefs have counted votes among the tribes;
  Your brother has their suffrage, Phaedra wins.
HIPPOLYTUS: Phaedra!
THERAMENES: A herald of the will of Athens
370   Will bring the reins of state into her hands.
  Her son is King.
HIPPOLYTUS: Ye Gods that know her heart,
  Is it her righteousness you would repay?
THERAMENES: And now dark rumours speak again of
  Theseus:
  Some tell that men have seen him in Epirus
375   Alive; though, I, who went to seek him there,
  I know full well, my lord . . .
HIPPOLYTUS: It may be so.
  But I would hear whatever rumour tells,
  Consult this public cry, divine its sources.
  If it be worthless to delay our journey
380   We sail; and cost the venture what it will
  I'll save the sceptre for a worthy hand.

ACT THREE

PHAEDRA, OENONE

PHAEDRA: Send them away, these heralds and these honours.
  Have they a balm to ease a tortured mind?
  Unkind, is Phaedra fit for public show?
  Rather conceal me, for my secret's out:
5   Intemperate desire has seen the light,
  And what these lips had never thought to utter
  He heard. Immortal Gods! and how he listened,
  How long he parried, how deviously he turned
  To baffle the approaches of my speech!
10   How visibly he yearned to leave my presence!
  How painfully his blush revived my shame!
  Why did you disappoint me of my death?
  Ah, when his weapon pointed at my breast
  Did he blench? Did he stir to snatch it back?
15   Enough for him my fingers at the hilt
  And in his heartless reckoning it was vile,
  Profaned, a blade that would defile his hand.
OENONE: And so complaining, dwelling on your sorrow,
  You feed a fire that wisdom would have quenched.
20   Should not a worthy child of Minos' blood
  Look for serenity in nobler tasks,
  Fly from a struggle that you cannot win,
  Learn to assume the guidance of a kingdom
  And be a Queen?
PHAEDRA: Queen, I? And hold command,
25   While my own senses rage in mutiny,
  While in my soul wisdom has lost dominion,
  While shame and slavery has bowed my head,
  And death is waiting?
OENONE: Fly.
PHAEDRA: I cannot leave him.
OENONE: You drove him away, and cannot go from him?
30 PHAEDRA: I cannot now. He has seen my raging soul,
  Seen me transgress the rigid pale of virtue;

Before those stony eyes I have poured out
My shame, and now, unbidden, secret hope
Has slipped into my breast. Ay, you yourself,
Rallying the wasted forces of my life,   35
The parting spirit ready on my lips,
Wooed me from death with false and soothing words;
You half persuaded me that I might love.
OENONE: Ah, call me guilty, or call me innocent,
  I would do worse if anything could save you. 40
  But, if resentment ever stung your mind,
  Can you forget the blow of his rebuff,
  The insolence, the icy cruelty
  That eyed you all but prostrate at his feet,
  The arrogant disdain?—how odious 45
  Had Phaedra only seen him as I saw!
PHAEDRA: What if he lost this arrogance, Oenone?
  He has the harshness of his forest ways,
  And in his arduous life Hippolytus
  Has never heard of love until today. 50
  What if surprise had robbed him of his speech?
  What if we blamed him more than he deserved?
OENONE: He was conceived in a Barbarian's womb.
PHAEDRA: Barbarian, Scythian, still she learned to love.
OENONE: He hates our sex with firm and deadly hate. 55
PHAEDRA: So I shall never fear another woman.
  Enough: such counsels had their season once;
  My passion now commands you, and not my reason.
  Though hard and inaccessible to love,
  Another side lies weaker to attack— 60
  The sweets of empire tempted him, I think;
  Athens allured him more than he could hide.
  His ships already turned their prows to sea
  With canvas rigged and offered to the breeze.
  Find him, Oenone, find the ambitious boy, 65
  Show him the glitter of the Athenian crown,
  Bid him assume the diadem and the glory;
  I only ask to lay it on his brow,
  Into his hand descends authority
  I cannot grasp, and he shall teach my son 70
  The science of command—even he might
  Look as a father on him. In his power
  I now resign the orphan and the mother.
  Incline his heart by any means you know,
  Use—do not blush—the voice of supplication, 75
  I sanction all. I have no other hope;
  Go, till you come again I cannot tell
  What else I have to do.

(*Exit* OENONE.)

PHAEDRA: (*Alone.*) O Thou, that knowest
  How deep in shame my soul is overwhelmed,
  Venus, O Venus unappeasable, 80
  This is the consummation of thy hatred.
  These must be the limits of thy cruelty.
  Thy triumph is entire, each shot has told.
  Art thou not sated yet with victory?
  Find tougher quarry then: Hippolytus 85
  Rejects thy deity, derides thy wrath,
  He never bent the knee before thy altar;
  Thy name seems hideous in his stubborn ears,

90   Goddess, avenge; our grievances are one!
        Teach him to love . . . Oenone, here so soon?
        I am rejected then, you were not heard.

(*Enter* OENONE.)

OENONE: Stifle the memory of a hopeless passion,
        My lady; summon up your earlier virtue.
        The King's not dead, and you will see him soon.
95   Theseus has landed. He is coming here.
        The populace are rushing to salute him,
        And as I passed obedient to your mission
        Unending cheers rose up on every hand—
PHAEDRA: He is not dead. Nothing else signifies,
100   Oenone. I revealed a lawless love
        That wounds him in his honour. And he lives.
        What needs there more?
OENONE: But yet—
PHAEDRA: I told you so;
        And you would not. Foreboding and remorse
        Have yielded to your tears. Only this morning
105   My death was not unworthy to be pitied:
        I took your counsel, and I die disgraced.
OENONE: Die?
PHAEDRA: Righteous Gods! The things this day has seen!
        And now, as I meet my husband and his son
        I know this witness of adulterous passion
110   Studies my countenance before his father—
        My heart heavy with sighs he would not hear,
        My eyelids drenched with tears that he despised.
        Do you think his tenderness for Theseus' honour
        Would hide away the memory of my falsehood,
115   My treason to a father and a King?
        Will he repress the loathing I inspire?
        What if he did? I know my treachery,
        Oenone. And if there are intrepid women
        Who taste a flawless quietude in crime
120   And force their countenance to show no shame,
        I am not such. My misdeeds rise before me;
        And even now these over-arching walls
        Seem full of tongues, impatient to accuse me
        Before my husband, and proclaim his wrong.
125   Oh for a death, and surcease from this anguish!
        Is life so precious and so hard to leave?
        Need the tormented hesitate to die?
        Only I fear the name I leave behind—
        The legacy of horror for my children,
130   Whose blood, the very blood of Jupiter,
        Should swell their hearts with pride: now they must lift
        The burden of a mother's infamy.
        My soul foretells that malice, soon or late,
        Will throw my black reproach into their faces,
135   And crushed so cruelly they may never dare
        To look with level eyes upon their kind.
OENONE: It is most true. They both are to be pitied,
        And never sorrow was foretold more surely.
        But why abandon them to the ordeal?
140   Why be the witness that betrays your cause?
        For all is lost; and all the world will judge
        That Phaedra knows her guilt, and dare not wait

        The awful presence of an outraged husband.
        Hippolytus should thank you for a deed
        Stronger than all his words on his behalf;   145
        And what can I respond to your accuser?
        Confounded, tongue-tied, I must live to see
        Him taste a hideous triumph undisturbed
        And chronicle your shame to all mankind.
        May fire from Heaven fall upon me sooner!   150
        But tell me this, and tell without dissembling:
        Do you still love him, this presumptuous Prince?
        How does he now appear . . . ?
PHAEDRA: I see him now
        Grim as a monster and as terrible.
OENONE: Then why concede him victory unresisted?   155
        Do you fear him? Attack before he strikes
        And use the imputation he prepares
        For you. What can refute you? Every sign
        Informs against him—first his sword that Fortune
        Leaves in your hands, and then this day's distress,   160
        And those disconsolate months of misery,
        And long ago his father's mind prepared
        When long ago you claimed his banishment.
PHAEDRA: Shall I defame and murder innocence?
OENONE: Lend me but silence and my zeal suffices.   165
        Like you I shudder at my remedy
        And dread it deeper than a thousand deaths.
        But either this, or else I lose my mistress,
        And in your loss all other values fade.
        So I will speak. Theseus will rage, but still   170
        He'll take no more revenge than banishment.
        A father punishing is still a father
        Whose love is louder than the voice of justice;
        But guiltless blood is nothing in the scales
        Against the imperilled honour of your name.   175
        That is a jewel far too dear to hazard;
        It is a law we dare not disobey;
        And when our honour stands at such a cost
        Virtue itself must go for sacrifice.
        —Here they are. I see Theseus.   180
PHAEDRA: And I see
        Hippolytus, and his unflinching eyes
        Spell my dishonour. Do what you will, Oenone.
        I am in your hands. In this tormented hour
        To save myself is more than I can do.

(*Enter* THESEUS, HIPPOLYTUS, *and* THERAMENES.)

THESEUS: Fortune has smiled again, my dearest lady,   185
        And now your sweet embrace—
PHAEDRA: No, Theseus; stop,
        Do not pollute this love and this delight.
        No longer I deserve this tenderness.
        You have been wronged. The jealousy of Fortune
        Has not respected her you left behind you;   190
        And now, unworthy to approach your love,
        My sole desire must be for solitude.

(*Exit* PHAEDRA.)

THESEUS: What is this cheerless welcome that I find here,
        My son?

HIPPOLYTUS: A riddle Phaedra must interpret,
195   No one else can. But now if prayers can move
         I ask but this, my lord, never to see
         Her face again, but to live out my life
         Safe, far away, forgotten by the Queen.
      THESEUS: Now you, my son, forsake me!
      HIPPOLYTUS: For you know
200   I never sought her, but you brought her here
         At your departure; and the coasts of Trozen
         Became the dwelling of Aricia
         And of the Queen. I was to be their guardian.
         But now what duty keeps me from my life?
205   Inglorious victories among the forests
         Weary my idle youth, my wasted skill.
         I long to waken from obscurity
         And tip my hunter's spear in a nobler red.
         Before you had spent the years that I have counted
210   What robbers, what oppressors, and what monsters
         Had known the weight of that revengeful arm,
         Victor and scourge of wanton insolence!
         While on the quiet shore of either sea
         The traveller learnt to take his road in peace;
215   Hercules heard your prowess and drew breath,
         Leaving his triumphs and his toils to you—
         And I, the unknown son of such a father,
         Have much to do to reach my mother's footsteps.
         Now let my unfledged valour learn to dare;
220   Let me, if anywhere some monster yet
         Escapes you, drag its trophy to your feet,
         Or by the record of a glorious failure
         Find life for ever in a fitting death
         And show posterity I was your son.
225   THESEUS: What is it, what invading blast of fear
         Empties my very home at my approach?
         Why, O ye Gods, to face these shrinking looks,
         This lack of love, did ye deliver me?
         I had one friend. His unregarding passion
230   Conspired to carry back from far Epirus
         The tyrant's Queen. I helped, against my will,
         But Fate was pitiless, and we were blind.
         The villain caught me all unarmed, unwatching,
         And these two eyes—that weep him yet—beheld
235   Pirithous under the fangs of beasts
         Fatted on human slaughter; and I spent
         Deep in the sightless silence of his dungeons
         Down near the horrible empire of the Dead,
         Six months. Then Heaven thought on me again.
240   I tricked the watchful eyes. I purged creation
         Of one perfidious enemy, and his blood
         Glutted his own fell monsters. Now at length
         Free, and restored to all that's left to love,
         Now that my soul aspires to nothing more
245   Than the enjoyment of their blessed sight,
         Grief and lament is all my salutation,
         None will abide to suffer my embraces;
         And, chilled by the contagion of the fears
         That breathe about my path, I'd rather be
250   A prisoner again and in Epirus.
            Speak out. Phaedra declares I've been betrayed.
         Who wronged me? Why is not the wrong avenged?

Has Greece, so long beholden to this arm,
Offered a refuge to the criminal?
—You will not answer? Is my son, my son,   255
A shield and ally of my enemies?
I will go in, for this suspense unmans me.
I will find out the culprit and the offence.
Phaedra must tell me what her sorrow is.

(*Exit* THESEUS.)

HIPPOLYTUS: What did her words portend? They froze my   260
      blood:
   Would Phaedra in her ecstasy of frenzy
   Denounce her guilt and give her case away?
   Gods, when the King is told! Death-dealing Love,
   What blighting mists thou hast wrapped around his
      house!
   And I with my secret of disloyal passion,   265
   What was I once, what will he think me now!
   My mind is dark with unaccomplished shapes
   Of evil: but need innocence be afraid?
   I must look for better times and better ways
   To move my father's heart, and then reveal   270
   Love he may doom to parting and to tears
   But fixed beyond his force to overthrow.

ACT FOUR

THESEUS, OENONE

THESEUS: Ah! What have you said? The rebel, the betrayer
   Conceived this outrage on his father's honour?
   How unrelenting is thy hand upon me,
   O Destiny! I know not where I go,
   I know not what I do. All my long kindness   5
   Wasted, paid with this hideous wanton plot!
   And with the argument and threat of steel
   To enforce his dark design! I know that sword,
   I gave it him, I strapped it to his side—
   For nobler work than this. Not all the bonds   10
   Of blood itself could hold him back; and she
   Could hesitate to punish, and her silence
   Showed mercy to the wrongdoer!
OENONE: Say rather
   Showed mercy to a father's suffering.
   Shamed by a lover's frenzy, and ashamed   15
   That her chaste eyes could kindle such a fire,
   She would have died, my lord, and dimmed for ever
   Herself the innocent lustre of those eyes.
   The arm was raised. I hastened, I preserved
   Her life for the embraces of her lord,   20
   And pitying your fears and her confusion
   Became the unwilling spokesman of her tears.
THESEUS: The perfidy! Yes, for all his craft, he paled;
   He quaked with fear, I saw it as he came;
   I marvelled then to feel his joylessness   25
   And froze against the chill of his embrace.
   —Did you not say, the love that burns in him
   Had shown itself in Athens long before?
OENONE: My lord, remember how the Queen abhorred him;

30   It was unhallowed love that caused her hatred.
        THESEUS: And now, in Trozen, it has flared again?
        OENONE: I have told you all, my lord; but I have left
            My lady too long now with her deadly sorrow,
            And, by your leave, my place is at her side.

        (*Exit* OENONE. *Enter* HIPPOLYTUS.)

35   THESEUS: So, here he comes. Great Gods, that noble carriage
            Would it not blind another's eye, as mine?
            Then sacrilegious and adulterous heads
            May flaunt the sacred emblem of the pure?
            Why is there no infallible badge to blazon
40   The minds of our dissembling race of men?
        HIPPOLYTUS: May I not know, my lord, why such a weight
            Of cloud darkens the majesty of your brow?
            Must this be secret from my loyalty?
        THESEUS: Dissembler! Dare you come so near to me?
45   Monster the thunderbolts reprieve too long,
            Corrupted straggler of the brigand race
            I cleansed the earth of once, how dare you still
            Parade that odious face, here where your frenzy
            Clutched at a father's bed? How dare you pace
50   These halls where all things tell of your dishonour?
            Why are you not far hence, where skies unknown
            Illumine coasts that never knew my name?
            Away, you traitor. Do not stand and tempt
            A hate, an anger hardly to be stayed.
55   Enough for me the indelible reproach
            Of fathering you, without the soil of murder
            To smother my bright deeds from memory.
            —Away. And if you would not share the sentence
            Of all the villains that this hand has felled
60   Take care that never again the sun that lights us
            Finds your rebellious feet upon this shore.
            Away, I tell you, out of my dominions
            And cleanse them for ever of your loathsome presence.
                And now hear, Neptune, hear. If once my courage
65   Scoured off a scum of bandits from thy coasts
            Remember thou hast sworn in recompense
            To grant one prayer. In long and stern confinement
            I called not thy undying power; I saved thee
            Thrifty of all the aid I hoped for, till
70   A greater need. Today I pray: avenge
            A mourning father. To thy wrath I leave
            This profligate. Still his lust in his blood.
            Let Theseus read thy kindness in thy rage.
        HIPPOLYTUS: With such a love Hippolytus is charged
75   By Phaedra! Weight of horror crushes me;
            So many assaults unlooked-for, stroke on stroke,
            Leave me no words.
        THESEUS: And so you judged that Phaedra's
            Compliant silence would have muffled up
            Your savage insolence. You might have waited
80   To gather up the sword that now, in her hands,
            Helps to convict you. Or why not, better still,
            Heap up the measure of your infamy
            With one good blow to finish breath and life?
        HIPPOLYTUS: After a calumny so infamous
            I should let truth be heard—but for a secret
85   That touches you, my lord. I beg you sanction

        Respect that silences what I might say;
        Labour no more to probe into your pain,
        Look on my life, consider what I am:
        The greatest crimes have lesser crimes before them;   90
        The rest is easy when the way is known;
        Like virtue, vice is gradual. No one day
        Made any good man vile, murderous, incestuous,
        And innocence is slow to dare, and slow
        To push beyond the boundaries of law.   95
        I had a mother, as chaste as she was valiant,
        Nor have I derogated from my blood;
        Pittheus, wise among men, took up my nurture
        After her hands. I would not praise myself,
        But, if one virtue was allotted mine,   100
        May I not claim, my lord, to loathe that act
        My enemies presume to speak of? This
        Has made Hippolytus his name in Greece—
        Unstudied honour rude in its excess,
        Rugged, intractable austerity.   105
        The daylight is no cleaner than the deeps
        Of this my heart. What, sacrilegious lust
        Could stain Hippolytus?
    THESEUS: And this condemns you:
        That was the foul source fed your vaunted coldness—
        No one but Phaedra could bewitch your eyes;   110
        No other woman's love was worth your interest
        Unless it offered pleasures more than lawful.
    HIPPOLYTUS: No, father, you shall hear the truth. This heart
        Has not refused an honourable yoke.
        Here at your feet I will confess—I love,   115
        And love in disobedience to your will.
        Aricia's beauty holds my heart enslaved
        And Pallas' daughter has subdued your son.
        I worship her, forgetful of my duty
        And have no room to feel another passion.   120
    THESEUS: You love her! No—a pitiful pretence;
        You feign that crime to clear yourself of this.
    HIPPOLYTUS: These six months I have hid from love, and
            loved,
        My lord; I came here to confess to you
        In trembling. But is it so? Will nothing move you?   125
        What fearful oath will win you to believe?
        Witness the Earth, the Heavens, and all Nature . . .
    THESEUS: What felon ever feared a perjury?
        Peace, peace. Waste no more time on idle stories
        If that fine virtue rests on aids like these.   130
    HIPPOLYTUS: You see it as a mockery, a lie:
        But Phaedra in her heart of hearts knows better.
    THESEUS: Shall I endure so much effrontery?
    HIPPOLYTUS: What place of exile, and how long a time
        Do you appoint?   135
    THESEUS: Past the Pillars of Hercules
        A traitor's presence is too close for me.
    HIPPOLYTUS: What friendship shall I find to comfort me
        When you have cast me out, dishonoured thus?
    THESEUS: Find yourself friends whose dangerous regard
        Goes to adultery and honours incest,   140
        Deceivers, ingrates, free of law and shame,
        Fit to protect a criminal like you.
    HIPPOLYTUS: And still you taunt me with adultery
        And incest. How can I reply? But Phaedra

145   Came of a mother, Phaedra's is a blood,
      My lord, you do not need me to recall it,
      More laden with their awful taint than mine.
    THESEUS: How dare you go so far before my face?
      For the last time, villain, avoid my sight,
150   Leave me; or force a father in his rage
      To have you flung with infamy from the place.

(*Exit* HIPPOLYTUS.)

    And now you go towards your waiting doom
    Irrevocably. For by that River's name
    Terrible even to the immortal Gods,
155   Neptune has sworn his oath, and will perform it.
    Yes, and I loved you, and in spite of all,
    Before the hour is come, my bowels yearn
    For pity of you. But I have too much cause—
    Did ever a deeper injury wound a father?
160   Ye righteous Gods, that see me thus prostrated,
    Did I give being to a son like this?

(*Enter* PHAEDRA.)

    PHAEDRA: My lord, you see me here impelled by terror:
      Just now, when that terrible voice assailed my ears,
      I thought the threat might come to a fulfilment.
165   Let me beg you, if there still is time, have pity
      On your own race, your own blood; do not force me,
      My lord, to hear it crying from the earth.
      Spare me the endless misery of laying
      That fearful stain on a paternal hand.
170 THESEUS: My lady, I have kept my hand unstained
      And still the unnatural boy has not escaped;
      Immortal hands will undertake his doom,
      Neptune's my debtor; you shall be avenged.
    PHAEDRA: Your debtor, Neptune! Then your prayer of hate . . .
175 THESEUS: Are you afraid it might be heard too soon?
      No, join your own entreaty with my curses,
      Paint me his crimes once more in all their blackness
      Inflame my faint and still-too-sluggish rage—
      He has added guilt more than the guilt you knew;
180   His frenzy spends itself in railing on you,
      He swears that all your words are perjuries,
      He says Aricia claims his heart, his love,
      His loyalty.
    PHAEDRA: No, my lord!
    THESEUS: That is what he told me;
      Not that a flimsy lie could impose on me.
185   I hope to hear that Neptune's justice falls
      Swiftly, and till that hour I'll ply his altars
      And keep him mindful of his undying word.

(*Exit* THESEUS.)

    PHAEDRA: He leaves me, with this dreadful news, alone.
      Ah Gods, the fire that I dreamed was safely stifled
190   To wake no more! Dreadful, unlooked-for news!
      All trepidation and remorse, all speed
      Out of Oenone's clinging arms of fear
      I came to save his son. And who can tell
      What might have been had conscience had its way?
195   Whether I might have spoken of my guilt,

Might have let slip, had he but left me time,
The entire and awful truth?—He has felt love,
Hippolytus, who never felt for me;
Aricia claims his loyalty, his heart . . .
Gods! while I pleaded, while my prayer beat   200
On those rigid eyes, that unrelenting brow,
I thought he bore impenetrable armour
Always the same and closed to all alike.
And now another has overthrown his pride,
Another finds favour in the tyrant's eyes;   205
Perhaps his heart is easy to entreat
And condescends to any plea but mine.
And I am fool enough to be his friend!

(*Enter* OENONE.)

—Oenone, do you know what I have heard?
OENONE: No; I have tried to find you in alarm,   210
    Wondering what sudden impulse drove you here
    And how it may imperil you . . .
PHAEDRA: Oenone,
    Who would have thought there was another woman?
OENONE: You say—
PHAEDRA: Hippolytus, I tell you, loves—
    The adversary I could never shake,   215
    Vexed by submission, impatient of complaining,
    The ogre that I never could encounter
    Undaunted; he is tamed and brought to heel,
    Aricia has forced the access to his heart.
OENONE: Aricia!   220
PHAEDRA: Oh, I never thought of these,
    These newest tortures that I live to taste:
    All the old despairs, the ecstasies, the broodings,
    Raging of flame, and horror of remorse,
    And that slight of unendurable denial
    Were barely foretastes of my torment here.   225
    They, lovers! Did they bewitch these watchful eyes?
    What time did they find to meet? Since when? What
      place?
    What furtive means? You knew. Why was I left
    To treasure foolish dreams? You might have told me
    Of their stolen pleasure. Were they often seen   230
    Speaking, or lingering? Was it the forest shades
    That sheltered them? Ah, but they had liberty
    To see the face they sought. The Heavens smiled
    On the innocence of their embrace, no fear
    Restrained their eager steps, and each fair day   235
    Rose clear and candid on their love. And I
    Disowned, dishonoured in the whole creation
    I fled the sun, I could not face the daylight,
    Death was the only godhead I could pray;
    Gall on my tongue, and tears my only drink;   240
    Happy, if any privacy of grief
    Had left me this one pitiable solace,
    To taste a last precarious luxury;
    But the forced travesty of a smiling face
    Deprived me even of the right to weep.   245
OENONE: They reap no harvest of their vain desires:
    They'll meet no more.
PHAEDRA: They'll love for evermore.
    Now as I speak—the poison of the thought!—

Mocking the fury of a rival wronged,
250 Forgetful of the exile that divides them,
They swear a thousand times never to part.
No, I will not yield to the insult of their joy,
Oenone. Help me, pity my jealousy.
Aricia must be crushed. I must stir up
255 My husband's wrath against that hated house—
No feeble sentence serves, the sister's crime
Is more than all her brothers'. I'll entreat him
In rage and jealousy.
                                    What am I doing?
Where is reason in my wandering mind? I, jealous?
260 I, entreat Theseus? He, my husband, lives
And still I burn—for whom? Still yearn—for whom?
At every word each separate hair lifts up
Upon my head. My guilt has filled the measure—
I crave for incest, dream of calumny,
265 My murderous hands, avid of vengeance, burn
To bathe in the blood of innocence. Misery!
And dare I live, and dare I face the sight
Of that sacred Sun, the giver of my life,
I, grandchild of the high Father of the Gods,
270 My forebears crowding Heaven and all creation?
Where may I hide? Flee to the night of Hell?
No, no, not there; for there my father's hands
Inexorable lift the doomsday urn,
They say, and Minos stands in deathly justice
275 Over the pallid multitudes of men.
Will that great shade not start in ghastly anger
When I in shame before his awful gaze,
His daughter, plead my guilt, and deeds perhaps
Unheard in all the calendar of Hell?
280 Father, what will you say to these? I see
The tremendous urn roll thundering at your feet;
I see you ponder unknown penalties
To execute yourself upon your own . . .
Forgive. A cruel God detests your seed,
285 A heavenly vengeance breathed in me the frenzy
You see. Alas, and still of all the guilt
And all the shame that never will release me
My fearful heart has never reaped the sweets.
Pursued while yet I breathe by ceaseless evils
290 I wait to yield a bruised and broken life.
OENONE: My lady, come, dismiss a causeless terror,
Be more indulgent to a venial failing—
You love; but driven by a fatal charm.
It is not ours to challenge Destiny.
295 Was this a wonder never seen till now?
Were you the first that Love has overthrown?
Weakness was ever part of man's condition;
So, mortal, bow to a mortal's destiny.
You struggle against an immemorial yoke:
300 Even the Gods that live in high Olympus
Whose judgements hold a guilty world in dread
Have loved, and sometimes loved against the law.
PHAEDRA: Still you dare speak? And this is your advice,
And till the end you mean to drug my mind?
305 I hate you. All your help has been my downfall.
You dragged me back to the unbearable sunshine;
Your prayers were louder than the voice of right;
The man that I shunned, you made me see.

Was it your business? And now have all the lies
Of those false lips dared blacken such a life?   310
You may have killed him. His father's impious vows
And blind revenge perhaps are gratified
Already. I'll hear no more. Leave me alone,
Loathly inhuman monster; leave my sight,
Leave me alone to shape my bitter future.   315
On you I pray the justice of the Gods;
And may they make you the eternal warning
Of all cringing cunning sycophants that nourish
Their masters' dearest weakness, urge the way
Their cravings tend, and smooth the slope of crime;   320
Accursed flatterers, deadliest gift of all
That angry Heaven inflicts upon a King! (*Exit.*)
OENONE: (*Alone.*) O ye Gods! To have borne so much for
        her, forgone
So much!—This is my pay. And it is just.

ACT FIVE

HIPPOLYTUS, ARICIA, ISMENE

ARICIA: And in this extremity you will not speak
And will not undeceive a loving father?
Cruel, if you can disregard my tears
And lightly say goodbye to me for ever,
Then sail, and leave Aricia with her grief;   5
But do not go in certainty of death.
Fight the foul imputation on your honour,
Constrain your father to unsay his curses.
There is time yet. What reason, or what folly
Makes you leave all the advantage to the accuser?   10
Tell Theseus what you know.
HIPPOLYTUS: Have I not told
What may be told? Would you have me reveal
To light the shameful mystery of his bed
Or by too scrupulous report bring down
Confusion on a father's honoured head?   15
Alone you know this horror. You, and the Gods,
Alone receive the outpouring of my heart.
See if I love you: I have shown to you
What I would fain have veiled from my own thoughts.
But under what a seal, you know. Forget,   20
My lady, if you can, that I have spoken;
Let me believe this hideous affair
Will never be breathed between those blameless lips.
We set our trust upon the righteous Heavens.
My cause is theirs; and Phaedra, whether soon   25
Or in the slow procedure of their justice,
Will not escape disgrace. This deference
I ask of you; and all the rest I sweep
Before the liberty of my wrath. I bid you
No longer be a slave. I bid you dare   30
To come with me, dare to be banned with me.
Break from a poisoned house where Virtue breathes
A deathly and a desecrated air;
Turn into profit for a headlong flight
All the disorder following on my fall.   35
The means I offer: you have still no guard
But my own men. Most powerful patrons wait us—
Argos extends her arms, and Sparta welcomes;

Let common friends receive our just laments,
40   Otherwise Phaedra rakes our wreckage up,
Evicts us both from a throne our fathers left us,
And strips us both for spoils to deck her son.
The moment beckons, grasp it. But what fear
Restrains you? What suspends your doubtful mind?
45   Only for your sake have I dared so far.
When I am all on fire, why are you ice?
Are you unwilling to adventure on
An outlaw's path?
   ARICIA: Oh, but how happily,
My lord, I'd taste of exile so; how eagerly
50   Embrace a life forgotten of all beside
And linked with yours! But lacking that sweet bond
Can I in honour join your wanderings?
I know the sternest laws do not forbid me
To fly your father's power: he is not mine,
55   I owe him no obedience; and to fly
From an oppressor is the right of all.
But you, my lord, love me. And anxious honour . . .
HIPPOLYTUS: And can you think I rate that honour cheaply?
No, no. I came with worthier designs—
60   Escape your foes, and follow as my bride.
Free in adversity, since Heaven has freed us,
Our pledges need no words but ours, and Hymen
Robbed of his torchlit rites is Hymen still.
     By Trozen's gates, among those sepulchres,
65   Antique memorials of my father's pride,
A wayside temple holy and renowned
Stands grim protector of the plighted word;
There falsehood dare not raise her voice, or falls
Blasted at once, and certitude of death
70   Lays chains invincible on perjury.
May we not there with solemn mutual oath
Give and receive our hearts' enduring faith
Before the shrine, and pray the Deity
For his protection and paternal love?
75   I will invoke each mighty God to hear me—
Maiden Diana, Juno's majesty,
And every name whose present patronage
Shall seal and sanctify my true intent.
  ARICIA: The King is here. Fly, Prince, depart at once.
80   I shall remain awhile to hide my purpose.
Away—but send me back a trusty servant
To guide my footsteps safely to your side.

(*Exit* HIPPOLYTUS.)

(*Enter* THESEUS.)

THESEUS: Lighten the mists, ye Gods, and show my eyes
The truth they seek for here!
                  Now, sweet Ismene,
85   See everything is done. Be ready quickly.

(*Exit* ISMENE.)

THESEUS: You seem disturbed, your colour fails, my lady.
What was Hippolytus doing in this place?
ARICIA: Taking an everlasting leave, my lord.
THESEUS: And so your eyes have tamed that rebel heart
90   And brought him to his earliest thoughts of love.

ARICIA: I must not hide the truth from you, my lord.
He has not learnt your unjust hate from you;
He did not treat me like a criminal.
THESEUS: You mean he vowed you everlasting passion.
I should not build on that unsettled heart.   95
He swore as deep to others.
ARICIA: He, my lord?
THESEUS: I wish you could have taught him constancy.
How could you bear that loathsome competition?
ARICIA: And how can you bear loathsome calumnies
To blacken all the lustre of his fame?   100
Have you so little knowledge of his nature?
Can you not tell the guiltless from the guilty?
Only your eyes are darkened by a cloud
That lets his goodness gleam on all the world.
Oh stop, relent. He must not be the victim   105
Of false accusers. Repent your murderous curses.
Tremble, my lord, tremble, lest frowning Heaven
Hate you enough to take you at your word—
Gods may accept our offerings in anger
And punish with the presents we entreated.   110
THESEUS: No, blind as you are with ill-requited love
You will not blind me to his villainy;
For I have witnesses, beyond reproach,
Beyond suspicion—I have seen tears flow,
Tears that were true.   115
ARICIA: Look to yourself, my lord:
Your matchless weight of arm redeemed mankind
From monsters past all counting—but not all,
The breed is not destroyed, and you have saved
One . . . I must say no more; your son forbids me.
Knowing what deference his heart still holds   120
I should increase his suffering too much
Dared I continue. Let me imitate
His generous scruple, and excuse myself
While nothing forces me to break my silence.

(*Exit* ARICIA.)

THESEUS: (*Alone.*) But what is in her mind? What lurks   125
below
A tale so often broached, and never told?
Is it a stratagem without a meaning?
Is it conspiracy to bind me on
A rack of doubt? And secret in my heart
Steeled to be cruel, what is the small voice   130
That pleads for mercy, and unmans my wrath,
Perplexes me and tears me?—I must see
Her woman once again; I know too little.
—Guard! Fetch Oenone, and send her in alone.

(*Enter* PANOPE.)

PANOPE: I cannot say what thoughts are in her heart,   135
But the distraction motions of the Queen
Fill me with fear, my lord. Death and despair
Are painted on her face, and the deathly tint
Sits even now upon her cheeks. Already
Pursued with scorn and chiding from her side,   140
Oenone has plunged to death among the waves.
None knows what wild will drove her, and her voice
Is covered in the murmur of the tide.

THESEUS: What have you said?

PANOPE: Her going gave no peace;
145   Confusion gains in the Queen's divided soul:
       One moment, soothing her mysterious grief,
       She takes her children, bathes them in her tears;
       And suddenly, her motherhood dismissed,
       She drives them from her with a look of loathing.
150   Her restless steps come and go purposeless
       And we are strangers in her fevered eyes.
       Thrice she has written, only to repent,
       And thrice destroyed the message uncompleted.
       My lord, be gracious: see her, comfort her.
155 THESEUS: Is it so? Oenone's dead, and Phaedra waits
       For death? Call for my son, let him plead his cause,
       Let him speak to me, and I will listen.

       (*Exit* PANOPE.)

                                     Neptune,
       Delay thy deadly gift, be not too sudden,
       Rather refuse it utterly. What if
160   I was seduced too soon by worthless words?
       What if my cruel hands were raised too rashly?
       What wretchedness would follow from that vow!

       (*Enter* THERAMENES.)

THESEUS: Is it you, Theramenes? Where is my son?
       What have you done with him? His careful tending
165   Has been your charge from earliest infancy.
       But why the tears I see upon your cheeks?
       What of my son?
THERAMENES: O late, O vain regret,
       O useless love! Hippolytus is no more.
THESEUS: Oh Gods!
THERAMENES: I saw him die, the best and sweetest
170   Of human kind—and, let me say, my lord,
       The purest also.
THESEUS: Is my son dead? Now,
       Now that these arms reached out for him, the Gods
       Impatient urged his execution on?
       How did I lose him? What immortal stroke . . . ?
175 THERAMENES: Still close behind us lay the gates of Trozen.
       He drove his chariot, his grieving guard
       Matching his silence, marched on either hand.
       Sunk in his thought, the loose reins lying free,
       He brought us on the causeway to Mycenae;
180   And the noble beasts, so eager once to leap
       At the least inflexion of a master's voice,
       Now bent dull eyes to earth and drooping crests
       As if communing with his bitter mood.
       —Suddenly from the sea an awful cry
185   Shattered the silence of the air. And then
       A second voice wailed answer from the landward.
       Our blood was frozen in our inmost hearts.
       Stiffly rose up the listening horses' manes.
       And now from the level deep immense there heaves
190   A boiling mount of brine, and still it swells,
       Rears wavelike foaming down on us and breaks
       To belch a ravening monster at our feet
       Whose threatening brow is broadened with huge horns,
       Whose body, cased in golden glint of scales,

Thrashes a train of sinuous writing whorls.   195
Indomitable bull, malignant dragon,
Its long-drawn bellows rumble down the shore;
Heaven quails, earth shudders at the portent, air
Reeks with its pestilential breath. The wave
Withdraws again, aghast at what it bore.   200
We fly to the nearby temple; not one lingers
Or wraps himself in unavailing valour.
Hippolytus, honouring his hero blood,
Hippolytus alone checks, wheels his team,
Snatches the spears, charges upon the creature,   205
Aims, and unerring flings. A gaping slash
Fair in the monster's flank drives it in bounds
Of pain and fury to the horses' feet
To roar and wallow and from flaming jaws
To spatter them with blood and cloud and fire.   210
Reckless, they plunge aside. They hear no more,
Answer no more to bridle or to voice.
The charioteer spends all his strength in vain
While they redden the bits with spume that is bright
       with blood.
Even, men say, some more than mortal shape   215
Borne on the horrible confusion plied
Their dusty flanks with goads. Where terror leads them
Stand rocks. The axle screeches, snaps. The car
Crashes in fragments; and my fearless master
Drops tangled in the reins . . .—Forgive my weakness. 220
In that tormenting image lives a source
Of quenchless tears.—I watched, my lord, I watched
Your helpless son dragging behind the steeds
His hands had fed. He tried to call to them:
Instead, his cries startle them. So they gallop   225
And make one wound of all his living flesh.
       Now as the plain is pealing with our grief
The violent fit is spent. They slacken speed,
And stop, where close at hand his father's tombs
And ancient sculptures hold the chill remains   230
And memories of Kings. I run, behind me
Run all his guard, reading the traces painted
By his gallant blood, past the empurpled crags,
Past dripping brambles hung about with spoils
Of bloody hair. I reach him, I speak; he gives me   235
A hand and greets me with a dying gaze
That quickly closes. And I hear these words:
       'My guiltless days are forfeit to the Gods.
Do you after my death be watchful over
The sad Aricia; and, sweet friend, if ever   240
My father undeceived should come to mourn
The misadventure of a slandered son,
To lay in peace my blood and wailing shade
Bid him be gentle to the captive maiden,
Render her . . .' On the word the lifeless youth   245
Fell back into my arms a ravaged corpse,
The dreadful triumph of an angry Heaven,
Where not a father's eye could undertake
To know his child.
THESEUS: O child! O dearest hope
I cast away! Gods, ye unswerving Gods,   250
Too faithfully ye served me! Now must life
Henceforward be a death of long-drawn sorrow.
THERAMENES: And now in fear and haste Aricia,

Stealing, my lord, from your captivity
255 To hear his nuptial vow before the Gods,
Approached. There are the red and steaming grasses,
And there—what welcome for a bride's regard!—
There is Hippolytus, but motionless,
Featureless, bloodless. First she seeks to question
260 Her misery, and, seeing, still demands
Hippolytus. Then, too pitifully assured,
After one glance reproachful to the skies
Cold, with one cry, lifeless upon the dead
She falls. Ismene, weeping, is beside her
265 And draws her back to life and life's despair;
And I, still subject to the hostile daylight,
Return to speak a hero's last desires
And so fulfil the grievous ministry
His dying heart committed to my love.
270 —But here I see the deadliest of his foes.

(*Enter* PHAEDRA, PANOPE, *and* GUARDS.)

THESEUS: Well, victory is yours: my son is gone.
Much, much I could suspect; deep rankling doubt
Acquits him in my heart and troubled mind—
But he is dead: your sacrifice, my lady;
275 Take it, find satisfaction in the forfeit
Unmerited or just. It matters little
That evermore my eyes be blindfolded;
Let him be criminal if you accuse.
His loss alone is theme enough for sorrow,
280 No need to look for new and fearful knowledge
That, impotent to bring the dead again,
Could pile at most new suffering on the old.
Let me escape, leave you and leave these shores,
Flying the bloody image of a son
285 Mangled—before that harrying memory
I could long for exile from the world of men.
All things upbraid me, all increase my anguish—
My very name (for nameless, I could hide),
The very honours that the Gods bestowed,
290 Whose murderous grace I'll mourn, and not again
Importune them with fruitless prayers of mine;
Do what they might, their fatal condescension

Could not console for what they took away.
PHAEDRA: Theseus, I have repented of my silence.
Your son requires his innocence from my lips;   295
Yes, he was guiltless.
THESEUS: This to me, his father!
And on your solemn faith I sentenced him.
Can any pretext for an act so vile—
PHAEDRA: My time is measured. Listen to me, Theseus.
I, on your dutiful and temperate son,   300
Looked with profaning and incestuous eyes—
The flame of Heaven lighted in my bosom
A fatal fire. Oenone did the rest;
She feared Hippolytus, my passion known,
Would publish all the madness that he loathed;   305
Presuming on my feebleness, she came
With that base story of my victim's guilt.
Self-chosen, easy death among the waves
Punished her perfidy and foiled my anger,
And by now the knife would have cleft my destiny,   310
But goodness still cried out for vindication.
I chose the slower path. I chose to pour
Into your ears before I joined the dead
The chronicle of my remorse. I have drained
And mingled with my burning blood a draught   315
Medea left in Athens. Now already
Her poison makes it progress toward my heart
Striking that heart with cold it never knew;
Faintly already I perceive the daylight
And you I wrong by my unworthy presence;   320
And death, blurring the sunbeams from these eyes
Whose glance polluted them, restores the light
To perfect purity.
PANOPE: My lord, she is dying.
THESEUS: And would the dark remembrance too might die
Of what she has done! Come, all is now too plain.   325
I must enfold what still remains to touch
Of my dear son, and expiate in tears
The blind curse I shall evermore bewail
With dear-bought honours rendered at his tomb;
And, better to placate his injured spirit,   330
I will forget the voice of ancient vengeance
And look upon his lover as my child.

Aphra Behn

Little is known about the early life of England's first female professional playwright, Aphra Behn (1640–1689), who may have been born Eaffrey Johnson in Kent. She left England just after the restoration of Charles II for the South American colony of Surinam, where she lived from 1663 to 1664. Again, many of the details about her life there are unknown, though Surinam provided the setting for her great novel, *Oroonoko: or, The Royal Slave,* published in 1688. Returning to England, she appears to have married someone named Behn; in *The Passionate Shepherdess: Aphra Behn 1640–89* (London: Jonathan Cape, 1977; p. 48), Maureen Duffy accounts for several possible candidates, but also suggests that Aphra Behn's marriage may have been a legitimating fiction: "Mr. Behn, her putative husband, has less substance than any character she invented." By the mid-1660s, however, Aphra Behn was serving Charles II as a spy in Antwerp and seems to have been caught up in the politics surrounding the Dutch invasion of Surinam. When she returned to England penniless in 1667, she was sent to debtors' prison and appealed to the government for her wages. Between 1670 and her death in 1689, however, Behn emerged as a famous and influential writer; in addition to her novel *Oroonoko,* Behn had a successful career as a poet and celebrated playwright. She wrote fifteen plays, beginning with *The Forced Marriage: or, The Jealous Bridegroom* (1668), a tragicomedy produced by Thomas Betterton at Lincoln's Inn Fields. Behn's major plays are mainly in the mode of Restoration comedy and were successful both in their day and well into the eighteenth century: her best-known plays today are *The Rover* (1677), *The Feigned Courtesans* (1679), which was dedicated to her friend and supporter (and the King's mistress), the actress Nell Gwynn, *The Second Part of The Rover* (1681), and *The City Heiress* (1682). Her novel *Oroonoko* was dramatized by Thomas Southerne in 1695 and was popular onstage throughout the eighteenth century. Aphra Behn was part of the elite milieu of intellectual culture of her day, the friend of courtiers such as Buckingham and Rochester, and of writers like Otway and Dryden. Although her work was, in a sense, recovered for modern readers by Virginia Woolf's famous essay *A Room of One's Own,* Behn's plays have been increasingly popular and successful in the theater. Aphra Behn is buried in Westminster Abbey.

THE ROVER

The Rover is a comedy of intrigue, set in Naples during the Carnival. The play concerns the sexual adventures of a band of Englishmen—Belvile, Willmore (the Rover), and Blunt—and their efforts to seduce the heroine Florinda and her sister Hellena. As in many Restoration comedies, *The Rover* takes a frank attitude toward sexual and financial negotiations, which are often paired in the play. The play opens with Hellena's rejection of a life in the convent and her decision to "provide my self this Carnival, if there be e'er a handsome proper fellow." In the course of the play, Hellena flirts with Willmore; Willmore wins the services (and, unfortunately, the love) of the courtesan Angelica, who eventually tries to murder him; Willmore and Blunt nearly rape Florinda on several occasions; and Blunt is tricked by a prostitute and turned out into the street in his shirt and underwear, "before consummation."

Yet despite the licentiousness of its action, the play clearly depends on a deeply ingrained sense of propriety, much of which operates through class distinctions. While it "would anger us vilely to be trussed up for a rape upon a maid of quality," one of the gentlemen declares, it seems otherwise acceptable to "ruffle a harlot." Morality, in *The Rover,* is in many ways determined by class and wealth. These distinctions are both troubled and confirmed by the important function of disguise and masking in the play. Since the action of *The Rover* takes place during Carnival, the main characters meet only in disguise. Masking enables the characters both to flirt without dishonoring themselves and to discover the truth

The Williamstown Theatre Festival production of *The Rover*, featuring Edward Hermann, Harry Groener, Christopher Reeve, and Stephen Collins.

about one another. In fact, masking in the play empowers the women, in that the temporary masking of the Carnival allows the women to escape their enforced lives at home and to meet men in public. Florinda and Hellena, for instance, can marry only with their brother Pedro's permission. He wants to marry his sisters to the wealthiest—and oldest—suitors, who will be able to settle large fortunes on them. However, the young Englishmen who attract the two sisters are Royalist supporters of Charles II, currently exiled from Cromwell's Protectorate because they support the Crown. As a result, although they are well-born, they are currently without funds and so are a poor match for Florinda and Hellena, at least in Pedro's eyes.

Masking also enables the women to escape Pedro's control, to act on their own behalf. Indeed, although the women are more modest than the Rover, they are equally devious in their pursuit of a lover—though the women insist on marriage as the price of their virginity. In Behn's brilliant comedy, the women emerge as the agents—as well as the objects—of the play's erotic intrigue.

In recent years, *The Rover* has received a number of excellent stage productions—at Minneapolis's Guthrie Theater, the Royal Shakespeare Company, and on many university campuses.

THE ROVER
OR THE BANISH'D CAVALIERS
Aphra Behn
EDITED BY MONTAGUE SUMMERS

CHARACTERS

Don ANTONIO, *the Vice-Roy's Son*
Don PEDRO, *a Noble Spaniard, his Friend*
BELVILE, *an English Colonel in love with Florinda*
WILLMORE, *the Rover*
FREDERICK, *an English Gentleman, and Friend to Belvile and Blunt*
BLUNT, *an English Country Gentleman*
STEPHANO, *Servant to Don Pedro*
PHILIPPO, *Lucetta's Gallant*
SANCHO, *Pimp to Lucetta*
BISKEY *and* SEBASTIAN, *two Bravoes to Angelica*
DIEGO, *Page to Don Antonio*
PAGE *to Hellena*
BOY, *Page to Belvile*

Blunt's MAN
OFFICERS *and* SOLDIERS
FLORINDA, *Sister to Don Pedro*
HELLENA, *a gay young Woman design'd for a Nun, and Sister to Florinda*
VALERIA, *a Kinswoman to Florinda*
ANGELICA BIANCA, *a famous Curtezan*
MORETTA, *her Woman*
CALLIS, *Governess to Florinda and Hellena*
LUCETTA, *a jilting Wench*
SERVANTS, *other* MASQUERADERS, MEN *and* WOMEN

SCENE: *Naples, in Carnival-time.*

PROLOGUE
Written by a Person of Quality

WITS, like Physicians, never can agree,
When of a different Society;
And Rabel's Drops were never more cry'd down
By all the Learned Doctors of the Town,
5 Than a new Play, whose Author is unknown:
Nor can those Doctors with more Malice sue
(And powerful Purses) the dissenting Few,
Than those with an insulting Pride do rail
At all who are not of their own Cabal.
10   If a Young Poet hit your Humour right,
You judge him then out of Revenge and Spite;
So amongst Men there are ridiculous Elves,
Who Monkeys hate for being too like themselves:
So that the Reason of the Grand Debate,
15 Why Wit so oft is damn'd, when good Plays take,
Is, that you censure as you love or hate.
Thus, like a learned Conclave, Poets sit
Catholick Judges both of Sense and Wit,
And damn or save, as they themselves think fit.
20 Yet those who to others Faults are so severe,
Are not so perfect, but themselves may err.
Some write correct indeed, but then the whole
(Bating their own dull Stuff i'th' Play) is stole:
As Bees do suck from Flowers their Honey-dew,
25 So they rob others, striving to please you.
   Some write their Characters genteel and fine,
But then they do so toil for every Line,
That what to you does easy seem, and plain,
Is the hard issue of their labouring Brain.
30 And some th' Effects of all their Pains we see,
Is but to mimick good Extempore.
Others by long Converse about the Town,
Have Wit enough to write a leud Lampoon,

But their chief Skill lies in a Baudy Song.
In short, the only Wit that's now in Fashion 35
Is but the Gleanings of good Conversation.
As for the Author of this coming Play,
I ask'd him what he thought fit I should say,
In thanks for your good Company to day:
He call'd me Fool, and said it was well known, 40
You came not here for our sakes, but your own.
New Plays are stuff'd with Wits, and with Debauches,
That croud and sweat like Cits in *May*-day Coaches.

ACT ONE

SCENE I

A Chamber.

Enter FLORINDA *and* HELLENA.

FLORINDA: What an impertient thing is a young Girl bred in a Nunnery! How full of Questions! Prithee no more, Hellena; I have told thee more than thou understand'st already.

HELLENA: The more's my Grief; I wou'd fain know as much as you, which makes me so inquisitive; nor is't enough to know 5 you're a Lover, unless you tell me too, who 'tis you sigh for.

FLORINDA: When you are a Lover, I'll think you fit for a Secret of that nature.

HELLENA: 'Tis true, I was never a Lover yet—but I begin to have a shreud Guess, what 'tis to be so, and fancy it very 10 pretty to sigh, and sing, and blush and wish, and dream and wish, and long and wish to see the Man; and when I do, look pale and tremble; just as you did when my Brother brought home the fine *English* Colonel to see you—what do you call him? Don *Belvile.* 15

FLORINDA: Fie, *Hellena.*

HELLENA: That Blush betrays you—I am sure 'tis so—or is it Don *Antonio* the Vice-Roy's Son?—or perhaps the rich

old Don *Vincentio,* whom my father designs for your Hus-
20   band?—Why do you blush again?
FLORINDA: With Indignation; and how near soever my Father
       thinks I am to marrying that hated Object, I shall let him
       see I understand better what's due to my Beauty, Birth and
       Fortune, and more to my Soul, than to obey those unjust
25   Commands.
HELLENA: Now hang me, if I don't love thee for that dear
       Disobedience. I love Mischief strangely, as most of our Sex
       do, who are come to love nothing else—But tell me, dear
       Florinda, don't you love that fine *Anglese?*—for I vow next
30   to loving him my self, 'twill please me most that you do
       so, for he is so gay and so handsom.
FLORINDA: *Hellena,* a Maid design'd for a Nun ought not to
       be so curious in a Discourse of Love.
HELLENA: And dost thou think that ever I'll be a Nun? Or at
35   least till I'm so old, I'm fit for nothing else. Faith no, Sis-
       ter; and that which makes me long to know whether you
       love *Belvile,* is because I hope he has some mad Compan-
       ion or other, that will spoil my Devotion; nay I'm resolv'd
       to provide my self this Carnival, if there be e'er a hand-
40   som Fellow of my Humour above Ground, tho I ask first.
FLORINDA: Prithee be not so wild.
HELLENA: Now you have provided your self with a Man, you
       take no Care for poor me—Prithee tell me, what dost thou
       see about me that is unfit for Love—have not I a world of
45   Youth? a Humour gay? a Beauty passable? a Vigour desir-
       able? well shap'd? clean limb'd? sweet breath'd? and Sense
       enough to know how all these ought to be employ'd to the
       best Advantage: yes, I do and will. Therefore lay aside your
       Hopes of my Fortune, by my being a Devotee, and tell me
50   how you came acquainted with this *Belvile;* for I perceive
       you knew him before he came to *Naples.*
FLORINDA: Yes, I knew him at the Siege of *Pampelona,* he was
       then a Colonel of *French* Horse, who when the Town was
       ransack'd, nobly treated my Brother and my self, preserv-
55   ing us from all Insolencies; and I must own, (besides great
       Obligations) I have I know not what, that pleads kindly
       for him about my Heart, and will suffer no other to en-
       ter—But see my Brother.

(*Enter Don* PEDRO, STEPHANO, *with a Masquing Habit, and* CALLIS.)

PEDRO: Good morrow, Sister. Pray, when saw you your Lover
60   Don *Vincentio?*
FLORINDA: I know not, Sir—*Callis,* when was he here? for I
       consider it so little, I know not when it was.
PEDRO: I have a Command from my Father here to tell you,
       you ought not to despise him, a Man of so vast a Fortune,
65   and such a Passion for you—*Stephano,* my things—

(*Puts on his Masquing Habit.*)

FLORINDA: A Passion for me! 'tis more than e'er I saw, or had
       a desire should be known—I hate *Vincentio,* and I would
       not have a Man so dear to me as my Brother follow the
       ill Customs of our Country, and make a Slave of his Sis-
70   ter—And Sir, my Father's Will, I'm sure, you may divert.

---

52 Siege of *Pampelona* Pampluna, the strongly fortified capital
of Navarra and very frequently a center of military operations

PEDRO: I know not how dear I am to you, but I wish only to
       be rank'd in your Esteem, equal with the *English* Colonel
       Belvile—Why do you frown and blush? Is there any Guilt
       belongs to the Name of that Cavalier?
FLORINDA: I'll not deny I value *Belvile:* when I was expos'd to such   75
       Dangers as the licens'd Lust of common Soldiers threatened,
       when Rage and Conquest flew thro the City—then *Belvile,*
       this Criminal for my sake, threw himself into all Dangers to
       save my Honour, and will you not allow him my Esteem?
PEDRO: Yes, pay him what you will in Honour—but you must   80
       consider Don *Vincentio's* Fortune, and the Jointure he'll
       make you.
FLORINDA: Let him consider my Youth, Beauty and Fortune;
       which ought not to be thrown away on his Age and Jointure.
PEDRO: 'Tis true, he's not so young and fine a Gentleman as   85
       that *Belvile*—but what Jewels will that Cavalier present
       you with? those of his Eyes and Heart?
HELLENA: And are not those better than any Don *Vincentio*
       has brought from the *Indies?*
PEDRO: Why how now! Has your Nunnery-breeding taught   90
       you to understand the Value of Hearts and Eyes?
HELLENA: Better than to believe *Vincentio* deserves Value from
       any woman—He may perhaps encrease her Bags, but not
       her Family.
PEDRO: This is fine—Go up to your Devotion, you are not   95
       design'd for the Conversation of Lovers.
HELLENA: (*Aside.*) Nor Saints yet a while I hope.
       Is't not enough you make a Nun of me, but you must cast
       my Sister away too, exposing her to a worse confinement
       than a religious Life?   100
PEDRO: The Girl's mad—Is it a Confinement to be carry'd
       into the Country, to an antient Villa belonging to the
       Family of the *Vincentio's* these five hundred Years, and have
       no other Prospect than that pleasing one of seeing all her
       own that meets her Eyes—a fine Air, large Fields and Gar-   105
       dens, where she may walk and gather Flowers?
HELLENA: When? By Moon-Light? For I'm sure she dares not
       encounter with the heat of the Sun; that were a Task only
       for Don *Vincentio* and his *Indian* Breeding, who loves it in
       the Dog-days—And if these be her daily Divertisements,   110
       what are those of the Night? to lie in a wide Moth-eaten
       Bed-Chamber with Furniture in Fashion in the Reign of
       King *Sancho* the First; the Bed that which his Forefathers
       liv'd and dy'd in.
PEDRO: Very well.   115
HELLENA: This Apartment (new furbisht and fitted out for the
       young Wife) he (out of Freedom) makes his Dressing-
       room; and being a frugal and a jealous Coxcomb, instead of
       a Valet to uncase his feeble Carcase, he desires you to do that
       Office—Signs of Favour, I'll assure you, and such as you   120
       must not hope for, unless your Woman be out of the way.
PEDRO: Have you done yet?
HELLENA: That Honour being past, the Giant stretches it self,
       yawns and sighs a Belch or two as loud as a Musket, throws

---

113 King *Sancho* the First Sancho I, 'the Fat,' of Castile and
Leon, reigned 955–967: Sancho I of Aragon 1067–1094. But the
phrase is here only in a vague general sense to denote some
musty and immemorial antiquity without any exact reference

125 himself into Bed, and expects you in his foul Sheets, and e'er you can get your self undrest, calls you with a Snore or two—And are not these fine Blessings to a young Lady?

PEDRO: Have you done yet?

130 HELLENA: And this man you must kiss, nay, you must kiss none but him too—and nuzle thro his Beard to find his Lips—and this you must submit to for threescore Years, and all for a Jointure.

PEDRO: For all your Character of Don *Vincentio*, she is as like to marry him as she was before.

135 HELLENA: Marry Don *Vincentio!* hang me, such a Wedlock would be worse than Adultery with another Man: I had rather see her in the *Hostel de Dieu,* to waste her Youth there in Vows, and be a Handmaid to Lazers and Cripples, than to lose it in such a Marriage.

140 PEDRO: You have consider'd, Sister, that *Belvile* has no Fortune to bring you to, is banisht his Country, despis'd at home, and pity'd abroad.

HELLENA: What then? the Vice-Roy's Son is better than that Old Sir Fisty. Don *Vincentio!* Don *Indian!* he thinks he's 145 trading to *Gambo* still, and wou'd barter himself (that Bell and Bawble) for your Youth and Fortune.

PEDRO: *Callis,* take her hence, and lock her up all this Carnival, and at Lent she shall begin her everlasting Penance in a Monastery.

150 HELLENA: I care not, I had rather be a Nun, than be oblig'd to marry as you wou'd have me, if I were design'd for't.

PEDRO: Do not fear the Blessing of that Choice—you shall be a Nun.

HELLENA: Shall I so? you may chance to be mistaken in my 155 way of Devotion—(*Aside.*) A Nun! yes I am like to make a fine Nun! I have an excellent Humour for a Grate: No, I'll have a Saint of my own to pray to shortly, if I like any that dares venture on me.

PEDRO: *Callis,* make it your Business to watch this wild Cat. 160 As for you, *Florinda,* I've only try'd you all this while, and urg'd my Father's Will; but mine is, that you would love *Antonio,* he is brave and young, and all that can compleat the Happiness of a gallant Maid—This Absence of my Father will give us opportunity to free you from *Vincentio,* 165 by marrying here, which you must do to morrow.

FLORINDA: To morrow!

PEDRO: To morrow, or 'twill be too late—'tis not my Friendship to *Antonio,* which makes me urge this, but Love to thee, and Hatred to *Vincentio*—therefore resolve upon't to morrow.

170 FLORINDA: Sir, I shall strive to do, as shall become your Sister.

PEDRO: I'll both believe and trust you—Adieu.

(*Exeunt* PEDRO *and* STEPHANO.)

HELLENA: As become his Sister!—That is, to be as resolved your way, as he is his—

(HELLENA *goes to* CALLIS.)

FLORINDA: I ne'er till now perceiv'd my Ruin near, 175 I've no Defence against *Antonio's* Love,

---

137 **Hostel de Dieu** the first Spanish hospital was erected at Granada by St. Juan de Dios before 1550   145 **Gambo** the Gambia in West Africa has been a British Colony since 1664, when a fort, now Fort James, was founded at the mouth of the river

For he has all the Advantages of Nature,
The moving Arguments of Youth and Fortune.

HELLENA: But hark you, *Callis,* you will not be so cruel to lock me up indeed: will you?

CALLIS: I must obey the Commands I hate—besides, do you 180 consider what a Life you are going to lead?

HELLENA: Yes, *Callis,* that of a Nun: and till then I'll be indebted a World of Prayers to you, if you let me now see, what I never did, the Divertisements of a Carnival.

CALLIS: What, go in Masquerade? 'twill be a fine farewell to 185 the World I take it—pray what wou'd you do there?

HELLENA: That which all the World does, as I am told, be as mad as the rest, and take all innocent Freedom—Sister, you'll go too, will you not? come prithee be not sad— We'll out-wit twenty Brothers, if you'll be ruled by me— 190 Come put off this dull Humour with your Clothes, and assume one as gay, and as fantastick as the Dress my Cousin *Valeria* and I have provided, and let's ramble.

FLORINDA: *Callis,* will you give us leave to go?

CALLIS: (*Aside.*) I have a youthful Itch of going my self. 195 —Madam, if I thought your Brother might not know it, and I might wait on you, for by my troth I'll not trust young Girls alone.

FLORINDA: Thou see'st my Brother's gone already, and thou shalt attend and watch us. 200

(*Enter* STEPHANO.)

STEPHANO: Madam, the Habits are come, and your Cousin *Valeria* is drest, and stays for you.

FLORINDA: 'Tis well—I'll write a Note, and if I chance to see *Belvile,* and want an opportunity to speak to him, that shall let him know what I've resolv'd in favour of him. 205

HELLENA: Come, let's in and dress us.

(*Exeunt.*)

SCENE II

A Long Street.

Enter BELVILE, MELANCHOLY, BLUNT, *and* FREDERICK.

FREDERICK: Why, what the Devil ails the Colonel, in a time when all the World is gay, to look like mere Lent thus? Hadst thou been long enough in *Naples* to have been in love, I should have sworn some such Judgment had befall'n thee.

BELVILE: No, I have made no new Amours since I came to 5 Naples.

FREDERICK: You have left none behind you in Paris.

BELVILE: Neither.

FREDERICK: I can't divine the Cause then; unless the old Cause, the want of Mony. 10

BLUNT: And another old Cause, the want of a Wench— Wou'd not that revive you?

BELVILE: You're mistaken, *Ned.*

BLUNT: Nay, 'Sheartlikins, then thou art past Cure.

FREDERICK: I have found it out; thou hast renew'd thy Ac- 15 quaintance with the Lady that cost thee so many Sighs at the Siege of *Pampelona*—pox on't, what d'ye call her—her Brother's a noble *Spaniard*—Nephew to the dead General—

---

14 **'Sheartlikins** by God's heart

Florinda—ay, *Florinda*—And will nothing serve thy turn but
20 that damn'd virtuous Woman, whom on my Consicience
thou lov'st in spite too, because thou seest little or no possibility of gaining her?

BELVILE: Thou art mistaken, I have Interest enough in that
lovely Virgin's Heart, to make me proud and vain, were it
25 not abated by the Severity of a Brother, who perceiving
my Happiness—

FREDERICK: Has civilly forbid thee the House?

BELVILE: 'Tis so, to make way for a powerful Rival, the Vice-
Roy's Son, who has the advantage of me, in being a Man of
30 Fortune, a *Spaniard,* and her Brother's Friend; which gives
him liberty to make his Court, whilst I have recourse only to
Letters, and distant Looks from her Window, which are as soft
and kind as those which Heav'n sends down on Penitents.

BLUNT: Hey day! 'Sheartlikins, Simile! by this Light the Man
35 is quite spoil'd—*Frederick,* what the Devil are we made of,
that we cannot be thus concern'd for a Wench?—'Sheartlikins, our *Cupids* are like the Cooks of the Camp, they
can roast or boil a Woman, but they have none of the fine
Tricks to set 'em off, no Hogoes to make the Sauce pleas-
40 ant, and the Stomach sharp.

FREDERICK: I dare swear I have had a hundred as young, kind
and handsom as this *Florinda;* and Dogs eat me, if they
were not as troublesom to me i'th' Morning as they were
welcome o'er night.

45 BLUNT: And yet, I warrant, he wou'd not touch another
Woman, if he might have her for nothing.

BELVILE: That's thy Joy, a cheap Whore.

BLUNT: Why, 'dsheartlikins, I Love a frank Soul—When did
you ever hear of an honest Woman that took a Man's
50 Mony? I warrant 'em good ones—But, Gentlemen, you
may be free, you have been kept so poor with Parliaments
and Protectors, that the little Stock you have is not worth
preserving—but I thank my Stars, I have more Grace than
to forfeit my Estate by Cavaliering.

55 BELVILE: Methinks only following the Court should be sufficient to entitle 'em to that.

BLUNT: 'Sheartlikins, they know I follow it to do it no good,
unless they pick a hole in my Coat for lending you Mony
now and then; which is a greater Crime to my Con-
60 science, Gentlemen, than to the Common-wealth.

(*Enter* WILLMORE.)

WILLMORE: Ha! dear *Belvile!* noble Colonel!

BELVILE: *Willmore!* welcome ashore, my dear Rover!—what
happy Wind blew us this good Fortune?

WILLMORE: Let me salute you my dear *Fred,* and then com-
65 mand me—How is't honest Lad?

FREDERICK: Faith, Sir, the old Complement, infinitely the
better to see my dear mad *Willmore* again—Prithee why
camest thou ashore? and where's the Prince?

WILLMORE: He's well, and reigns still Lord of the watery El-
70 ement—I must aboard again within a Day or two, and my
Business ashore was only to enjoy my self a little this Carnival.

BELVILE: Pray know our new Friend, Sir, he's but bashful, a
raw Traveller, but honest, stout, and one of us.

---

39 **Hogoes** Haut-goût, a relish

(*Embraces* BLUNT.)

WILLMORE: That you esteem him, gives him an Interest here.

BLUNT: Your Servant, Sir.   75

WILLMORE: But well—Faith I'm glad to meet you again in a
warm Climate, where the kind Sun has its god-like Power
still over the Wine and Woman.—Love and Mirth are my
Business in *Naples*; and if I mistake not the Place, here's an
excellent Market for Chapmen of my Humour.   80

BELVILE: See here be those kind Merchants of Love you look
for.

(*Enter several* MEN *in masquing Habits, some playing on Musick,
others dancing after;* WOMEN *drest like Curtezans, with Papers pin-
n'd to their Breasts, and Baskets of Flowers in their Hands.*)

BLUNT: 'Sheartlikins, what have we here!

FREDERICK: Now the Game begins.

WILLMORE: Fine pretty Creatures! may a stranger have leave 85
to look and love?—What's here—(*Reads the Paper.*): *Roses
for every Month!*

BLUNT: Roses for every Month! what means that?

BELVILE: They are, or wou'd have you think they're Curtezans,
who here in *Naples* are to be hir'd by the Month.   90

WILLMORE: Kind and obliging to inform us—Pray where do
these Roses grow? I would fain plant some of 'em in a
Bed of mine.

WOMAN: Beware such Roses, Sir.

WILLMORE: A Pox of fear: I'll be bak'd with thee between a 95
pair of Sheets, and that's thy proper Still, so I might but
strow such Roses over me and under me—Fair one,
wou'd you wou'd give me leave to gather at your Bush
this idle Month, I wou'd go near to make some Body
smell of it all the Year after.   100

BELVILE: And thou hast need of such a Remedy, for thou
stinkest of Tar and Rope-ends, like a Dock or Pesthouse.

(*The* WOMAN *puts her self into the Hands of a* MAN, *and Exit.*)

WILLMORE: Nay, nay, you shall not leave me so.

BELVILE: By all means use no Violence here.

WILLMORE: Death! just as I was going to be damnably in 105
love, to have her led off! I could pluck that Rose out of
his Hand, and even kiss the Bed, the Bush it grew in.

FREDERICK: No Friend to Love like a long Voyage at Sea.

BLUNT: Except a Nunnery, *Frederick.*

WILLMORE: Death! but will they not be kind, quickly be 110
kind? Thou know'st I'm no tame Sigher, but a rampant
Lion of the Forest.

(*Two* MEN *drest all over with Horns of several sorts, making Grimaces at one another, with Papers pinn'd on their Backs, advance
from the farther end of the Scene.*)

BELVILE: Oh the fantastical Rogues, how they are dress'd! 'tis
a Satir against the whole Sex.

WILLMORE: Is this a Fruit that grows in this warm Country? 115

BELVILE: Yes: 'Tis pretty to see these *Italian* start, swell, and stab
at the Word *Cuckold,* and yet stumble at Horns on every
Threshold.

WILLMORE: See what's on their Back—(*Reads.*) *Flowers for
every Night.*—Ah Rogue! And more sweet than Roses of 120
ev'ry Month! This is a Gardiner of *Adam's* own breeding.

(*They dance.*)

BELVILE: What think you of those grave People?—is a Wake in *Essex* half so mad or extravagant?

WILLMORE: I like their sober grave way, 'tis a kind of legal authoriz'd Fornication, where the Men are not chid for 't, nor the Women despis'd, as amongst our dull *English;* even the Monsieurs want that part of good Manners.

BELVILE: But here in *Italy* a Monsieur is the humblest best-bred Gentleman—Duels are so baffled by Bravos that an age shews not one, but between a *Frenchman* and a Hang-man, who is as much too hard for him on the Piazza, as they are for a *Dutchman* on the new Bridge—But see another Crew.

(*Enter* FLORINDA, HELLENA, *and* VALERIA, *drest like Gipsies;* CALLIS *and* STEPHANO, LUCETTA, PHILIPPO, *and* SANCHO *in Masquerade.*)

HELLENA: Sister, there's your *Englishman,* and with him a handsome proper Fellow—I'll to him, and instead of telling him his Fortune, try my own.

WILLMORE: Gipsies, on my Life—Sure these will prattle if a Man cross their Hands. (*Goes to* HELLENA.)—Dear pretty (and I hope) young Devil, will you tell an amorous Stranger what Luck he's like to have?

HELLENA: Have a care how you venture with me, Sir, lest I pick your Pocket, which will more vex your *English* Humour, than an *Italian* Fortune will please you.

WILLMORE: How the Devil cam'st thou to know my Country and Humour?

HELLENA: The first I guess by a certain forward Impudence, which does not displease me at this time; and the Loss of your Money will vex you, because I hope you have but very little to lose.

WILLMORE: Egad Child, thou'rt i'th' right; it is so little, I dare not offer it thee for a Kindness—But cannot you divine what other things of more value I have about me, that I would more willingly part with?

HELLENA: Indeed no, that's the Business of a Witch, and I am but a Gipsy yet—Yet, without looking in your Hand, I have a parlous Guess, 'tis some foolish Heart you mean, an inconstant *English* Heart, as little worth stealing as your Purse.

WILLMORE: Nay, then thou dost deal with the Devil, that's certain—Thou hast guess'd as right as if thou hadst been one of that Number it has languisht for—I find you'll be better acquainted with it; nor can you take it in a better time, for I am come from Sea, Child; and *Venus* not being propitious to me in her own Element, I have a world of Love in store—Wou'd you would be good-natur'd, and take some on't off my Hands.

HELLENA: Why—I could be inclin'd that way—but for a fool-ish Vow I am going to make—to die a Maid.

WILLMORE: Then thou art damn'd without Redemption; and as I am a good Christian, I ought to charity to divert so wicked a Design—therefore prithee, dear Creature, let me know quickly when and where I shall begin to set a help-ing hand to so good a Work.

HELLENA: If you should prevail with my tender Heart (as I begin to fear you will, for you have horrible loving Eyes) there will be difficulty in't that you'll hardly undergo for my sake.

WILLMORE: Faith, Child, I have been bred in Dangers, and wear a Sword that has been employ'd in a worse Cause, than for a handsom kind Woman—Name the Danger—let it be any thing but a long Siege, and I'll undertake it.

HELLENA: Can you storm?

WILLMORE: Oh, most furiously.

HELLENA: What think you of a Nunnery-wall? for he that wins me, must gain that first.

WILLMORE: A Nun! Oh how I love thee for't! there's no Sin-ner like a young Saint—Nay, now there's no denying me: the old Law had no Curse (to a Woman) like dying a Maid; witness *Jephtha's* Daughter.

HELLENA: A very good Text this, if well handled; and I perceive, Father Captain, you would impose no severe Penance on her who was inclin'd to console her self before she took Orders.

WILLMORE: If she be young and handsom.

HELLENA: Ay, there's it—but if she be not—

WILLMORE: By this Hand, Child, I have an implicit Faith, and dare venture on thee with all Faults—besides, 'tis more meritorious to leave the World when thou hast tasted and prov'd the Pleasure on't; then 'twill be a Virtue in thee, which now will be pure Ignorance.

HELLENA: I perceive, good Father Captain, you design only to make me fit for Heaven—but if on the contrary you should quite divert me from it, and bring me back to the World again, I should have a new Man to seek I find; and what a grief that will be—for when I begin, I fancy I shall love like any thing: I never try'd yet.

WILLMORE: Egad, and that's kind—Prithee, dear Creature, give me Credit for a Heart, for faith, I'm a very honest Fel-low—Oh, I long to come first to the Banquet of Love; and such a swinging Appetite I bring—Oh, I'm impatient. Thy Lodging, Sweetheart, thy Lodging, or I'm a dead man.

HELLENA: Why must we be either guilty of Fornication or Mur-der, if we converse with you Men?—And is there no differ-ence between leave to love me, and leave to lie with me?

WILLMORE: Faith, Child, they were made to go together.

LUCETTA: (*Pointing to* BLUNT.) Are you sure this is the Man?

SANCHO: When did I mistake your Game?

LUCETTA: This is a stranger, I know by his gazing; if he be brisk he'll venture to follow me; and then, if I understand my Trade, he's mine: he's *English* too, and they say that's a sort of good natur'd loving People, and have generally so kind an opinion of themselves, that a Woman with any Wit may flatter 'em into any sort of Fool she pleases.

BLUNT: 'Tis so—she is taken—I have Beauties which my false Glass at home did not discover.

(*She often passes by* BLUNT *and gazes on him; he struts, and cocks, and walks, and gazes on her.*)

FLORINDA: This Woman watches me so, I shall get no Op-portunity to discover my self to him, and so miss the in-tent of my coming—But as I was saying, Sir—(*Looking in his Hand.*) by this Line you should be a Lover.

BELVILE: I thought how right you guess'd, all Men are in love, or pretend to be so—Come, let me go, I'm weary of this fooling.

(*Walks away.*)

FLORINDA: I will not, till you have confess'd whether the Passion that you have vow'd *Florinda* be true or false.

(*She holds him, he strives to get from her.*)

BELVILE: *Florinda!*

(*Turns quick towards her.*)

235 FLORINDA: Softly.
BELVILE: Thou hast nam'd one will fix me here for ever.
FLORINDA: She'll be disappointed then, who expects you this Night at the Garden-gate, and if you'll fail not—as let me
240 see the other Hand—you will go near to do—she vows to die or make you happy.

(*Looks on* CALLIS, *who observes 'em.*)

BELVILE: What canst thou mean?
FLORINDA: That which I say—Farewell.

(*Offers to go.*)

BELVILE: Oh charming Sybil, stay, complete that Joy, which, as it is, will turn into Distraction!—Where must I be? at the
245 Garden-gate? I know it—at night you say—I'll sooner forfeit Heaven than disobey.

(*Enter* DON PEDRO *and other Masquers, and pass over the Stage.*)

CALLIS: Madam, your Brother's here.
FLORINDA: Take this to instruct you farther.

(*Gives him a Letter, and goes off.*)

FREDERICK: Have a care, Sir, what you promise; this may be
250 a Trap laid by her Brother to ruin you.
BELVILE: Do not disturb my Happiness with Doubts.

(*Opens the Letter.*)

WILLMORE: My dear pretty Creature, a Thousand Blessings on thee; still in this Habit, you say, and after Dinner at this Place.
HELLENA: Yes, if you will swear to keep your Heart, and not
255 bestow it between this time and that.
WILLMORE: By all the little Gods of Love I swear, I'll leave it with you; and if you run away with it, those Deities of Justice will revenge me.

(*Exeunt all the* WOMEN *except* LUCETTA.)

FREDERICK: Do you know the Hand?
260 BELVILE: 'Tis *Florinda's.*
    All Blessings fall upon the virtuous Maid.
FREDERICK: Nay, no Idolatry, a sober Sacrifice I'll allow you.
BELVILE: Oh Friends! the welcom'st News, the softest Letter!—nay, you shall see it; and could you now be serious,
265 I might be made the happiest Man the Sun shines on.
WILLMORE: The Reason of this mighty Joy.
BELVILE: See how kindly she invites me to deliver her from the threaten'd Violence of her Brother—will you not assist me?
WILLMORE: I know not what thou mean'st, but I'll make one
270 at any Mischief where a Woman's concern'd—but she'll be grateful to us for the Favour, will she not?
BELVILE: How mean you?
WILLMORE: How should I mean? Thou know'st there's but one way for a Woman to oblige me.
275 BELVILE: Don't prophane—the Maid is nicely virtuous.

WILLMORE: Who pox, then she's fit for nothing but a Husband; let her e'en go, Colonel.
FREDERICK: Peace, she's the Colonel's Mistress, Sir.
WILLMORE: Let her be the Devil; if she be thy Mistress, I'll
serve her—name the way.   280
BELVILE: Read here this Postcript.

(*Gives him a Letter.*)

WILLMORE: (*Reads.*) *At Ten at night—at the Garden-Gate—of which, if I cannot get the Key, I will contrive a way over the Wall—come attended with a Friend or two.*—Kind heart, if
we three cannot weave a String to let her down a Garden-   285
Wall, 'twere pity but the Hangman wove one for us all.
FREDERICK: Let her alone for that: your Woman's Wit, your fair kind Woman, will not out-trick a Brother or a Jew, and contrive like a Jesuit in Chains—but see, *Ned Blunt* is
stoln out after the Lure of a Damsel.   290

(*Exit* BLUNT *and* LUCETTA.)

BELVILE: So he'll scarce find his way home again, unless we get him cry'd by the Bell-man in the Market-place, and 'twou'd sound prettily—a lost *English* Boy of Thirty.
FREDERICK: I hope 'tis some common crafty Sinner, one that
will fit him; it may be she'll sell him for *Peru,* the Rogue's   295
sturdy and would work well in a Mine; at least I hope she'll dress him for our Mirth; cheat him of all, then have him well-favour'dly bang'd, and turn'd out naked at Midnight.
WILLMORE: Prithee what Humour is he of, that you wish
him so well?   300
BELVILE: Why, of an *English* Elder Brother's Humour, educated in a Nursery, with a Maid to tend him till Fifteen, and lies with his Grand-mother till he's of Age; one that knows no Pleasure beyond riding to the next Fair, or going up to *London* with his right Worshipful Father in Par-   305
liament-time; wearing gay Clothes, or making honourable Love to his Lady Mother's Landry-Maid; gets drunk at a Hunting-Match, and ten to one then gives some Proofs of his Prowess—A pox upon him, he's our Banker, and has
all our Cash about him, and if he fail we are all broke.   310
FREDERICK: Oh let him alone for that matter, he's of a damn'd stingy Quality, that will secure our Stock. I know not in what Danger it were indeed, if the Jilt should pretend she's in love with him, for 'tis a kind believing Cox-
comb; otherwise if he part with more than a Piece of   315
Eight—geld him: for which offer he may chance to be beaten, if she be a Whore of the first Rank.
BELVILE: Nay the Rogue will not be easily beaten, he's stout enough; perhaps if they talk beyond his Capacity, he may
chance to exercise his Courage upon some of them; else   320
I'm sure they'll find it as difficult to beat as to please him.
WILLMORE: 'Tis a lucky Devil to light upon so kind a Wench!
FREDERICK: Thou hadst a great deal of talk with thy little Gipsy, coud'st thou do no good upon her? for mine was
hard-hearted.   325
WILLMORE: Hang her, she was some damn'd honest Person of Quality, I'm sure, she was so very free and witty. If her Face

---

315 **a Piece of Eight** a piastre, a coin of varying values in different countries

be but answerable to her Wit and Humour, I would be bound to Constancy this Month to gain her. In the mean time, have you made no kind Acquaintance since you came to Town?—You do not use to be honest so long, Gentlemen.

FREDERICK: Faith Love has kept us honest, we have been all fir'd with a Beauty newly come to Town, the famous *Pad-uana Angelica Bianca.*

WILLMORE: What, the Mistress of the dead *Spanish* General?

BELVILE: Yes, she's now the only ador'd Beauty of all the Youth in *Naples,* who put on all their charms to appear lovely in her sight, their Coaches, Liveries, and themselves, all gay, as on a Monarch's Birth-Day, to attract the Eyes of this fair Charmer, while she has the Pleasure to behold all languish for her that see her.

FREDERICK: 'Tis pretty to see with how much Love the Men regard her, and how much Envy the Women.

WILLMORE: What Gallant has she?

BELVILE: None, she's exposed to Sale, and four Days in the Week she's yours—for so much a Month.

WILLMORE: The very Thought of it quenches all manner of Fire in me—yet prithee let's see her.

BELVILE: Let's first to Dinner, and after that we'll pass the Day as you please—but at Night ye must all be at my Devotion.

WILLMORE: I will not fail you.

(Exeunt.)

ACT TWO

SCENE I

The Long Street.

Enter BELVILE *and* FREDERICK *in Masquing-Habits, and* WILL-MORE *in his own Clothes, with a Vizard in his Hand.*

WILLMORE: But why thus disguis'd and muzzl'd?

BELVILE: Because whatever Extravagances we commit in these Faces, our own may not be oblig'd to answer 'em.

WILLMORE: I should have chang'd my Eternal Buff too: but no matter, my little Gipsy wou'd not have found me out then: for if she should change hers, it is impossible I should know her, unless I should hear her prattle—A Pox on't, I cannot get her out of my Head: Pray Heaven, if ever I do see her again, she prove damnable ugly, that I may fortify my self against her Tongue.

BELVILE: Have a care of Love, for o' my conscience she was not of a Quality to give thee any hopes.

WILLMORE: Pox on 'em, why do they draw a Man in then? She has play'd with my Heart so, that 'twill never lie still till I have met with some kind Wench, that will play the Game out with me—Oh for my Arms full of soft, white, kind—Woman! such as I fancy *Angelica.*

BELVILE: This is her House, if you were but in stock to get admittance; they have not din'd yet; I perceive the Picture is not out.

(Enter BLUNT.*)*

WILLMORE: I long to see the Shadow of the fair Substance, a Man may gaze on that for nothing.

BLUNT: Colonel, thy Hand—and thine, *Frederick.* I have been an Ass, a deluded Fool, a very Coxcomb from my Birth till this Hour, and heartily repent my little Faith.

BELVILE: What the Devil's the matter with thee *Ned?*

BLUNT: Oh such a Mistress, *Frederick,* such a Girl!

WILLMORE: Ha! where? *Frederick.* Ay where!

BLUNT: So fond, so amorous, so toying and fine! and all for sheer Love, ye Rogue! Oh how she lookt and kiss'd! and sooth'd my Heart from my Bosom. I cannot think I was awake, and yet methinks I see and feel her Charms still— *Frederick.*—Try if she have not left the Taste of her balmy Kisses upon my Lips—

(Kisses him.)

BELVILE: Ha, ha, ha! *Willmore.* Death Man, where is she?

BLUNT: What a Dog was I to stay in dull *England* so long— How have I laught at the Colonel when he sigh'd for Love! but now the little Archer has reveng'd him, and by his own Dart, I can guess at all his Joys, which then I took for Fancies, mere Dreams and Fables—Well, I'm resolved to sell all in Essex, and plant here for ever.

BELVILE: What a Blessing 'tis, thou hast a Mistress thou dar'st boast of; for I know thy Humour is rather to have a pro-claim'd Clap, than a secret Amour.

WILLMORE: Dost know her Name?

BLUNT: Her Name? No, 'sheartlikins: what care I for Names?— She's fair, young, brisk and kind, even to ravishment: and what a Pox care I for knowing her by another Title?

WILLMORE: Didst give her anything?

BLUNT: Give her!—Ha, ha, ha! why, she's a Person of Quality —That's a good one, give her! 'sheartlikins dost think such Creatures are to be bought? Or are we provided for such a Purchase? Give her, quoth ye? Why she presented me with this Bracelet, for the Toy of a Diamond I us'd to wear: No, Gentlemen, *Ned Blunt* is not every Body—She expects me again to night.

WILLMORE: Egad that's well; we'll all go.

BLUNT: Not a Soul: No, Gentlemen, you are Wits; I am a dull Country Rogue, I.

FREDERICK: Well, Sir, for all your Person of Quality, I shall be very glad to understand your Purse be secure; 'tis our whole Estate at present, which we are loth to hazard in one Bottom: come, Sir, unload.

BLUNT: Take the necessary Trifle, useless now to me, that am belov'd by such a Gentlewoman—'sheartlikins Money! Here take mine too.

FREDERICK: No, keep that to be cozen'd, that we may laugh.

WILLMORE: Cozen'd!—Death! wou'd I cou'd meet with one, that wou'd cozen me of all the Love I cou'd spare to night.

FREDERICK: Pox 'tis some common Whore upon my Life.

BLUNT: A Whore! yes with such Clothes! such Jewels! such a House! such Furniture, and so attended! a Whore!

BELVILE: Why yes, Sir, they are Whores, tho they'll neither entertain you with Drinking, Swearing, or Baudy; are Whores in all those gay Clothes, and right Jewels; are Whores with great Houses richly furnisht with Velvet Beds, Store of Plate, handsome Attendance, and fine Coaches, are Whores and errant ones.

WILLMORE: Pox on't, where do these fine Whores live?

80 BELVILE: Where no Rogue in Office yclep'd Constables dare give 'em laws, nor the Wine-inspired Bullies of the Town break their Windows; yet they are Whores, tho this *Essex* Calf believe them Persons of Quality.

BLUNT: 'Sheartlikins, y'are all Fools, there are things about
85 this *Essex* Calf, that shall take with the Ladies, beyond all your Wits and Parts—This Shape and Size, Gentlemen, are not to be despis'd; my Waste tolerably long, with other inviting Signs, that shall be nameless.

WILLMORE: Egad I believe he may have met with some Per-
90 son of Quality that may be kind to him.

BELVILE: Dost thou perceive any such tempting things about him, should make a fine Woman, and of Quality, pick him out from all Mankind, to throw away her Youth and Beauty upon, nay, and her dear Heart too?—no, no, *An-*
95 *gelica* has rais'd the Price too high.

WILLMORE: May she languish for Mankind till she die, and be damn'd for that one Sin alone.

(*Enter two* BRAVOES, *and hang up a great Picture of* ANGELICA'S *against the Balcony, and two little ones at each side of the Door.*)

BELVILE: See there the fair Sign to the Inn, where a Man may lodge that's Fool enough to give her Price.

(WILLMORE *gazes on the Picture.*)

100 BLUNT: 'Sheartlikins, Gentlemen, what's this?

BELVILE: A famous Curtezan that's to be sold.

BLUNT: How! to be sold! nay then I have nothing to say to her—sold! what Impudence is practis'd in this Coun-try?—With Order and Decency Whoring's established
105 here by virtue of the Inquisition—Come let's be gone, I'm sure we're no Chapmen for this Commodity.

FREDERICK: Thou art none, I'm sure, unless thou could'st have her in thy Bed at the Price of a Coach in the Street.

WILLMORE: How wondrous fair she is—a Thousand Crowns
110 a Month—by Heaven as many Kingdoms were too little. A plague of this Poverty—of which I ne'er complain, but when it hinders my Approach to Beauty, which Virtue ne'er could purchase.

(*Turns from the Picture.*)

BLUNT: What's this?—(*Reads.*) *A Thousand Crowns a Month!*—
115 'Sheartlikins, here's a Sum! sure 'tis a mistake.—Hark you, Friend, does she take or give so much by the Month!

FREDERICK: A Thousand Crowns! Why, 'tis a Portion for the *Infanta.*

BLUNT: Hark ye, Friends, won't she trust?
120 BRAVO: This is a Trade, Sir, that cannot live by Credit.

(*Enter* DON PEDRO *in Masquerade, follow'd by* STEPHANO.)

BELVILE: See, here's more Company, let's walk off a while.

(PEDRO *reads. Exeunt* ENGLISH. *Enter* ANGELICA *and* MORETTA *in the Balcony, and draw a Silk Curtain.*)

PEDRO: Fetch me a Thousand Crowns, I never wish to buy this Beauty at an easier Rate.

(*Passes off.*)

ANGELICA: Prithee what said those Fellows to thee?

BRAVO: Madam, the first were Admirers of Beauty only, but 125 no purchasers; they were merry with your Price and Pic-ture, laught at the Sum, and so past off.

ANGELICA: No matter, I'm not displeas'd with their rallying; their Wonder feeds my Vanity, and he that wishes to buy, gives me more Pride, than he that gives my Price can 130 make me Pleasure.

BRAVO: Madam, the last I knew thro all his disguises to be Don *Pedro*, Nephew to the General, and who was with him in *Pampelona.*

ANGELICA: Don *Pedro*! my old Gallant's Nephew! When his 135 Uncle dy'd, he left him a vast Sum of Money; it is he who was so in love with me at *Padua*, and who us'd to make the General so jealous.

MORETTA: Is this he that us'd to prance before our Window and take such care to shew himself an amorous Ass? if I am 140 not mistaken, he is the likeliest Man to give your Price.

ANGELICA: The Man is brave and generous, but of an Hu-mour so uneasy and inconstant, that the victory over his Heart is as soon lost as won; a Slave that can add little to the Triumph of the Conqueror; but inconstancy's the Sin 145 of all Mankind, therefore I'm resolv'd that nothing but Gold shall charm my Heart.

MORETTA: I'm glad on't; 'tis only interest that Women of our Profession ought to consider: tho I wonder what has kept you from that general Disease of our Sex so long, I mean 150 that of being in love.

ANGELICA: A kind, but sullen Star, under which I had the Happiness to be born; yet I have had no time for Love; the bravest and noblest of Mankind have purchas'd my Favours at so dear a Rate, as if no Coin but Gold were 155 current with our Trade—But here's Don *Pedro* again, fetch me my Lute—for 'tis for him or Don *Antonio* the Vice-Roy's Son, that I have spread my Nets.

(*Enter at one Door Don* PEDRO, *and* STEPHANO; *Don* ANTONIO *and* DIEGO [*his page*], *at the other Door, with people following him in Masquerade, antickly attir'd, some with Musick: they both go up to the Picture.*)

ANTONIO: A thousand Crowns! had not the Painter flatter'd her, I should not think it dear. 160

PEDRO: Flatter'd her! by Heaven he cannot. I have seen the Original, nor is there one Charm here more than adorns her Face and Eyes; all this soft and sweet, with a certain languishing Air, that no Artist can represent.

ANTONIO: What I heard of her Beauty before had fir'd my 165 Soul, but this confirmation of it has blown it into a flame.

PEDRO: Ha!

PAGE: Sir, I have known you throw away a Thousand Crowns on a worse Face, and tho y' are near your Marriage, you may venture a little Love here; *Florinda*—will not miss it. 170

PEDRO: (*Aside.*) Ha! *Florinda*! Sure 'tis *Antonio.*

ANTONIO: *Florinda*! name not those distant Joys, there's not one thought of her will check my Passion here.

PEDRO: Florinda scorn'd! and all my Hopes defeated of the Possession of Angelica! (*A noise of a Lute above. Antonio* 175 *gazes up.*) Her Injuries by Heaven he shall not boast of.

(Song to a Lute above.)

Song

When *Damon* first began to love,
He languisht in a soft Desire,
And knew not how the Gods to move,
180   To lessen or increase his Fire,
For *Caelia* in her charming Eyes
   Wore all Love's Sweet, and all his Cruelties.

II

But as beneath a Shade he lay,
Weaving of Flow'rs for *Caelia's* Hair,
185   She chanc'd to lead her Flock that way,
And saw the am'rous Shepherd there.
She gaz'd around upon the Place,
And saw the Grove (resembling Night)
To all the Joys of Love invite,
190   Whilst guilty Smiles and Blushes drest her Face.
At this the bashful Youth all Transport grew,
And with kind Force he taught the Virgin how
To yield what all his Sighs cou'd never do.

ANTONIO: By Heav'n she's charming fair!

(ANGELICA throws open the Curtains, and bows to ANTONIO, who pulls off his Vizard, and bows and blows up Kisses. PEDRO unseen looks in his Face.)

195   PEDRO: 'Tis he, the false *Antonio!*
ANTONIO: Friend, where must I pay my offering of Love?

(To the bravo.)

   My Thousand Crowns I mean.
PEDRO: That offering I have design'd to make,
   And yours will come too late.
200   ANTONIO: Prithee be gone, I shall grow angry else,
   And then thou art not safe.
PEDRO: My Anger may be fatal, Sir, as yours;
   And he that enters here may prove this Truth.
ANTONIO: I know not who thou art, but I am sure thou'rt
205   worth my killing, and aiming at *Angelica.*

(They draw and fight.)

(Enter WILLMORE and BLUNT, who draw and part 'em.)

BLUNT: 'Sheartlikins, here's fine doings.
WILLMORE: Tilting for the Wench I'm sure—nay gad, if that
   wou'd win her, I have as good a Sword as the best of ye—
   Put up—put up, and take another time and place, for this
210   is design'd for Lovers only.

(They all put up.)

PEDRO: We are prevented; dare you meet me to morrow on
   the *Molo?*
For I've a Title to a better quarrel,
That of *Florinda,* in whose credulous Heart
Thou'st made an Int'rest, and destroy'd my Hopes.
215   ANTONIO: Dare?
I'll meet thee there as early as the Day.

PEDRO: We will come thus disguis'd, that whosoever chance
   to get the better, he may escape unknown.
ANTONIO: It shall be so.

(Exit PEDRO and STEPHANO.)

Who shou'd this Rival be? unless the *English* Colonel, of   220
whom I've often heard Don Pedro speak; it must be he, and
time he were removed, who lays a Claim to all my Happiness.

(WILLMORE having gaz'd all this while on the Picture, pulls down a little one.)

WILLMORE: This posture's loose and negligent,
   The sight on't wou'd beget a warm desire
   In Souls, whom Impotence and Age had chill'd.   225
   —This must along with me.
BRAVO: What means this rudeness, Sir?—restore the Picture.
ANTONIO: Ha! Rudeness committed to the fair *Angelica!*—
   Restore the Picture, Sir.
WILLMORE: Indeed I will not, Sir.   230
ANTONIO: By Heav'n but you shall.
WILLMORE: Nay, do not shew your Sword; if you do, by this
   dear Beauty—I will shew mine too.
ANTONIO: What right can you pretend to't?
WILLMORE: That of Possession which I will maintain—you   235
   perhaps have 1000 Crowns to give for the Original.
ANTONIO: No matter, Sir, you shall restore the Picture.
ANGELICA: Oh, *Moretta!* what's the matter?

(ANGELICA and MORETTA above.)

ANTONIO: Or leave your Life behind.
WILLMORE: Death! you lye—I will do neither.   240
ANGELICA: Hold, I command you, if for me you fight.

(They fight, the Spaniards join with ANTONIO, BLUNT laying on like mad. They leave off and bow.)

WILLMORE: How heavenly fair she is!—ah Plague of her Price.
ANGELICA: You Sir in Buff, you that appear a Soldier, that first
   began this Insolence.
WILLMORE: 'Tis true, I did so, if you call it Insolence for a   245
   Man to preserve himself; I saw your charming Picture, and
   was wounded: quite thro my Soul each pointed Beauty
   ran; and wanting a Thousand Crowns to procure my
   Remedy, I laid this little Picture to my Bosom—which if
   you cannot allow me, I'll resign.   250
ANGELICA: No, you may keep the Trifle.
ANTONIO: You shall first ask my leave, and this.

(Fight again as before.)

(Enter BELVILE and FREDERICK who join with the English.)

ANGELICA: Hold; will you ruin me?—*Biskey, Sebastian,* part them.

(The SPANIARDS are beaten off.)

MORETTA: Oh Madam, we're undone, a pox upon that rude
   Fellow, he's set on to ruin us: we shall never see good days,   255
   till all these fighting poor Rogues are sent to the Gallies.

(Enter BELVILE, BLUNT and WILLMORE, with his shirt bloody.)

BLUNT: 'Sheartlikins, beat me at this Sport, and I'll ne'er wear Sword more.

BELVILE: The Devil's in thee for a mad Fellow, thou art always one at an unlucky Adventure.—Come, let's be gone whilst we're safe, and remember these are *Spaniards,* a sort of People that know how to revenge an Affront.

FREDERICK: (*To* WILLMORE.) You bleed; I hope you are not wounded.

WILLMORE: Not much:—a plague upon your Dons, if they fight no better they'll ne'er recover *Flanders.*—What the Devil was't to them that I took down the Picture?

BLUNT: Took it! 'Sheartlikins, we'll have the great one too; 'tis ours by Conquest.—Prithee, help me up, and I'll pull it down.—

ANGELICA: Stay, Sir, and e'er you affront me further, let me know how you durst commit this Outrage—To you I speak, Sir, for you appear like a Gentleman.

WILLMORE: To me, Madam?—Gentlemen, your Servant.

(BELVILE *stays him.*)

BELVILE: Is the Devil in thee? Do'st know the danger of en-tring the house of an incens'd Curtezan?

WILLMORE: I thank you for your care—but there are other matters in hand, there are, tho we have no great Tempta-tion.—Death! let me go.

FREDERICK: Yes, to your Lodging, if you will, but not in here.—Damn these gay Harlots—by this Hand I'll have as sound and hansome a Whore for a Patacoone.—Death, Man, she'll murder thee.

WILLMORE: Oh! fear me not, shall I not venture where a Beauty calls? a lovely charming Beauty? for fear of dan-ger! when by Heaven there's none so great as to long for her, whilst I want Money to purchase her.

FREDERICK: Therefore 'tis loss of time, unless you had the thousand Crowns to pay.

WILLMORE: It may be she may give a Favour, at least I shall have the pleasure of saluting her when I enter, and when I depart.

BELVILE: Pox, she'll as soon lie with thee, as kiss thee, and sooner stab than do either—you shall not go.

ANGELICA: Fear not, Sir, all I have to wound with, is my Eyes.

BLUNT: Let him go, 'Sheartlikins, I believe the Gentlewoman means well.

BELVILE: Well, take thy Fortune, we'll expect you in the next Street.—Farewell Fool,—farewell—

WILLMORE: B'ye Colonel—

(*Goes in.*)

FREDERICK: The Rogue's stark mad for a Wench.

(*Exeunt.*)

SCENE II

A Fine Chamber.

Enter WILLMORE, ANGELICA, *and* MORETTA.

ANGELICA: Insolent, Sir, how durst you pull down my Picture?

WILLMORE: Rather, how durst you set it up, to tempt poor amorous Mortals with so much Excellence? which I find you have but too well consulted by the unmerciful price you set upon't.—Is all this Heaven of Beauty shewn to move Despair in those that cannot buy? and can you think the effects of that Despair shou'd be less extravagant than I have shewn?

ANGELICA: I sent for you to ask my Pardon, Sir, not to aggra-vate your Crime.—I thought I shou'd have seen you at my Feet imploring it.

WILLMORE: You are deceived, I came to rail at you, and talk such Truths, too, as shall let you see the Vanity of that Pride, which taught you how to set such a Price on Sin. For such it is, whilst that which is Love's due is meanly barter'd for.

ANGELICA: Ha, ha, ha, alas, good Captain, what pity 'tis your edifying Doctrine will do no good upon me—*Moretta,* fetch the Gentleman a Glass, and let him survey himself, to see what Charms he has,—(*Aside in a soft tone.*) and guess my Business.

MORETTA: He knows himself of old, I believe those Breeches and he have been acquainted ever since he was beaten at *Worcester.*

ANGELICA: Nay, do not abuse the poor Creature.—

MORETTA: Good Weather-beaten Corporal, will you march off? we have no need of your Doctrine, tho you have of our Charity; but at present we have no Scraps, we can af-ford no kindness for God's sake; in fine, Sirrah, the Price is too high i'th' Mouth for you, therefore troop, I say.

WILLMORE: Here, good Fore-Woman of the Shop, serve me, and I'll be gone.

MORETTA: Keep it to pay your Landress, your Linen stinks of the Gun-Room; for here's no selling by Retail.

WILLMORE: Thou hast sold plenty of thy stale Ware at a cheap Rate.

MORETTA: Ay, the more silly kind Heart I, but this is an Age wherein Beauty is at higher Rates.—In fine, you know the price of this.

WILLMORE: I grant you 'tis here set down a thousand Crowns a Month—Baud, take your black Lead and sum it up, that I may have a Pistole-worth of these vain gay things, and I'll trouble you no more.

MORETTA: Pox on him, he'll fret me to Death:—abominable Fellow, I tell thee, we only sell by the whole Piece.

WILLMORE: 'Tis very hard, the whole Cargo or nothing—Faith, Madam, my Stock will not reach it, I cannot be your Chapman.—Yet I have Countrymen in Town, Mer-chants of Love, like me; I'll see if they'll put for a share, we cannot lose much by it, and what we have no use for, we'll sell upon the *Friday's* Mart, at—*Who gives more?* I am studying, Madam, how to purchase you, tho at present I am unprovided of Money.

ANGELICA: Sure, this from any other Man would anger me—nor shall he know the Conquest he has made—Poor an-gry Man, how I despise this railing.

WILLMORE: Yes, I am poor—but I'm a Gentleman,
And one that scorns this Baseness which you practise.
Poor as I am, I would not sell my self,
No, not to gain your charming high-priz'd Person.

---

282 **Patacoone** a Spanish coin

41 **Pistole** a gold coin

60   Tho I admire you strangely for your Beauty,
      Yet I contemn your Mind.
      —And yet I wou'd at any rate enjoy you;
      At your own rate—but cannot—See here
      The only Sum I can command on Earth;
65   I know not where to eat when this is gone:
      Yet such a Slave I am to Love and Beauty,
      This last reserve I'll sacrifice to enjoy you.
      —Nay, do not frown, I know you are to be bought,
      And wou'd be bought by me, by me,
70   For a mean trifling Sum, if I could pay it down.
      Which happy knowledge I will still repeat,
      And lay it to my Heart, it has a Virtue in't,
      And soon will cure those Wounds your Eyes have made.
      —And yet—there's something so divinely powerful there—
75   Nay, I will gaze—to let you see my Strength.

(*Holds her, looks on her, and pauses and sighs.*)

      By Heaven, bright Creature—I would not for the World
      Thy Fame were half so fair as thy Face.

(*Turns her away from him.*)

ANGELICA: (*Aside.*) His words go thro me to the very Soul.
      —If you have nothing else to say to me.
80   WILLMORE: Yes, you shall hear how infamous you are—
      For which I do not hate thee:
      But that secures my Heart, and all the Flames it feels
      Are but so many Lusts,
      I know it by their sudden bold intrusion.
85   The Fire's impatient and betrays, 'tis false—
      For had it been the purer Flame of Love,
      I should have pin'd and languish'd at your Feet,
      E'er found the Impudence to have discover'd it.
      I now dare stand your Scorn, and your Denial.
90   MORETTA: Sure she's bewitcht, that you can stand thus tamely,
      and hear his saucy railing.—Sirrah, will you be gone?
      ANGELICA: How dare you take this liberty?—(*To* MORETTA.)
      Withdraw.—Pray, tell me, Sir, are not you guilty of the
      same mercenary Crime? When a Lady is proposed to you
95   for a Wife, you never ask, how fair, discreet, or virtuous she
      is; but what's her Fortune—which if but small, you cry—
      She will not do my business—and basely leave her, tho she
      languish for you.—Say, is not this as poor?
      WILLMORE: It is a barbarous Custom, which I will scorn to
100   defend in our Sex, and do despise in yours.
      ANGELICA: Thou art a brave Fellow! put up thy Gold, and know
      That were thy Fortune large, as is thy Soul,
      Thou shouldst not buy my Love,
      Couldst thou forget those mean Effects of Vanity,
105   Which set me out to sale; and as a Lover, prize
      My yielding Joys.
      Canst thou believe they'l be entirely thine,
      Without considering they were mercenary?
      WILLMORE: (*Aside.*) I cannot tell, I must bethink me first—
110   ha, Death, I'm going to believe her.
      ANGELICA: Prithee, confirm that Faith—or if thou canst
      not—flatter me a little, 'twill please me from thy Mouth.
      WILLMORE: Curse on thy charming Tongue! dost thou return
      My feign'd Contempt with so much subtilty?

(*Aside.*)

      Thou'st found the easiest way into my Heart,   115
      Tho I yet know that all thou say'st is false.

(*Turning from her in a Rage.*)

ANGELICA: By all that's good 'tis real,
      I never lov'd before, tho oft a Mistress.
      —Shall my first Vows be slighted?
      WILLMORE: (*Aside.*) What can she mean?   120
      ANGELICA: (*In an angry tone.*) I find you cannot credit me.
      WILLMORE: I know you take me for an errant Ass,
      An Ass that may be sooth'd into Belief,
      And then be us'd at pleasure.
      —But, Madam, I have been so often cheated   125
      By perjur'd, soft, deluding Hypocrites,
      That I've no Faith left for the cozening Sex,
      Especially for Women of your Trade.
      ANGELICA: The low esteem you have of me, perhaps
      May bring my Heart again: 130
      For I have Pride that yet surmounts my Love.

(*She turns with Pride, he holds her.*)

WILLMORE: Throw off this Pride, this Enemy to Bliss,
      And shew the Power of Love: 'tis with those Arms
      I can be only vanquisht, made a Slave.
      ANGELICA: Is all my mighty Expectation vanisht?   135
      —No, I will not hear thee talk,—thou hast a Charm
      In every word, that draws my Heart away.
      And all the thousand Trophies I design'd,
      Thou hast undone—Why are thou soft?
      Thy Looks are bravely rough, and meant for War.   140
      Could thou not storm on still?
      I then perhaps had been as free as thou.
      WILLMORE: (*Aside.*) Death! how she throws her Fire about
           my Soul!
      —Take heed, fair Creature, how you raise my Hopes,
      Which once assum'd pretend to all Dominion.   145
      There's not a Joy thou hast in store
      I shall not then command:
      For which I'll pay thee back my Soul, my Life.
      Come, let's begin th' account this happy minute.
      ANGELICA: And will you pay me then the Price I ask?   150
      WILLMORE: Oh, why dost thou draw me from an awful
           Worship,
      By shewing thou art no Divinity?
      Conceal the Fiend, and shew me all the Angel;
      Keep me but ignorant, and I'll be devout,
      And pay my Vows for ever at this Shrine.   155

(*Kneels, and kisses her Hand.*)

ANGELICA: The Pay I mean is but thy Love for mine.—Can
      you give that?
      WILLMORE: Intirely—come, let's withdraw: where I'll renew
      my vows,—and breathe 'em with such Ardour, thou shalt
      not doubt my Zeal.   160
      ANGELICA: Thou hast a Power too strong to be resisted.

(*Exit* WILLMORE *and* ANGELICA.)

MORETTA: Now my Curse go with you—Is all our Project
fallen to this? to love the only Enemy to our Trade? Nay,
to love such a Shameroon, a very Beggar; nay, a Pirate-
165 Beggar, whose Business is to rifle and be gone, a No-Pur-
chase, No-Pay Tatterdemalion, an English Piccaroon; a
Rogue that fights for daily Drink, and takes a Pride in being loyally lousy—Oh, I could curse now, if I durst—This
is the Fate of most Whores.

170 *Trophies, which from believing Fops we win,*
Are Spoils to those who cozen us again.

ACT THREE

SCENE I

A Street.

Enter FLORINDA, VALERIA, HELLENA, *in Antick different Dresses
from what they were in before,* CALLIS *attending.*

FLORINDA: I wonder what should make my Brother in so ill
a Humour: I hope he has not found out our Ramble this
Morning.
HELLENA: No, if he had, we should have heard on't at both
5 Ears, and have been mew'd up this Afternoon; which I
would not for the World should have happen'd—Hey ho!
I'm sad as a Lover's Lute.
VALERIA: Well, methinks we have learnt this Trade of Gipsies
as readily as if we had been bred upon the Road to *Loretto:*
10 and yes I did so fumble, when I told the Stranger his Fortune, that I was afraid I should have told my own and
yours by mistake—But methinks *Hellena* has been very serious ever since.
FLORINDA: I would give my Garters she were in love, to be
15 reveng'd upon her, for abusing me—How is't, *Hellena?*
HELLENA: Ah!—would I had never seen my mad Monsieur—and
yet for all your laughing I am not in love—and yet this small
Acquaintance, o'my Conscience, will never out of my Head.
VALERIA: Ha, ha, ha—I laugh to think how thou art fitted with a
20 Lover, a Fellow that, I warrant, loves every new Face he sees.
HELLENA: Hum—he has not kept his Word with me here—
and may be taken up—that thought is not very pleasant to
me—what the Duce should this be now that I feel?
VALERIA: What is't like?
25 HELLENA: Nay, the Lord knows—but if I should be hanged, I
cannot chuse but be angry and afraid, when I think that mad
Fellow should be in love with any Body but me—What to
think of my self I know not—Would I could meet with
some true damn'd Gipsy, that I might know my Fortune.
30 VALERIA: Know it! why there's nothing so easy; thou wilt love
this wandering Inconstant till thou find'st thy self hanged
about his Neck, and then be as mad to get free again.
FLORINDA: Yes, *Valeria;* we shall see her bestride his Baggage-
horse, and follow him to the Campaign.
35 HELLENA: So, so; now you are provided for, there's no care
taken of poor me—But since you have set my Heart a
wishing, I am resolv'd to know for what. I will not die of
the Pip, so I will not.

---

164 **shameroon** a trickster, a cozening rascal

FLORINDA: Art thou mad to talk so? Who will like thee well
enough to have thee, that hears what a mad Wench thou art? 40
HELLENA: Like me! I don't intend every he that likes me shall
have me, but he that I like: I shou'd have staid in the Nunnery still, if I had lik'd my Lady Abbess as well as she lik'd
me. No, I came thence, not (as my wise Brother imagines)
to take an eternal Farewel of the World, but to love and to 45
be belov'd; and I will be belov'd, or I'll get one of your
Men, so I will.
VALERIA: Am I put into the Number of Lovers?
HELLENA: You! my Couz, I know thou art too good natur'd to
leave us in any Design: Thou wou't venture a Cast, tho thou 50
comest off a Loser, especially with such a Gamester—I ob-
serv'd your Man, and your willing ears incline that way; and
if you are not a Lover, 'tis an Art soon learnt—that I find.

(Sighs.)

FLORINDA: I wonder how you learnt to love so easily, I had a
thousand Charms to meet my Eyes and Ears, e'er I cou'd 55
yield; and 'twas the knowledge of *Belvile's* Merit, not the
surprising Person, took my Soul—Thou art too rash to
give a Heart at first sight.
HELLENA: Hang your considering Lover; I ne'er thought beyond the Fancy, that 'twas a very pretty, idle, silly kind of 60
Pleasure to pass ones time with, to write little, soft, non-
sensical Billets, and with great difficulty and danger receive Answers; in which I shall have my Beauty prais'd, my
Wit admir'd (tho little or none) and have the Vanity and
Power to know I am desirable; then I have the more In- 65
clination that way, because I am to be a Nun, and so shall
not be suspected to have any such earthly Thoughts about
me—But when I walk thus—and sigh thus—they'll think
my Mind's upon my Monastery, and cry, how happy 'tis
she's so resolv'd!—But not a Word of Man. 70
FLORINDA: What a mad Creature's this!
HELLENA: I'll warrant, if my Brother hears either of you sigh,
he cries (gravely)—I fear you have the Indiscretion to be in
love, but take heed of the Honour of our House, and your
own unspotted Fame; and so he conjures on till he has laid 75
the soft-wing'd God in your Hearts, or broke the
Birdsnest—But see here comes your Lover: but where's my
inconstant? let's stop aside, and we may learn something.

(Go aside.)

(Enter BELVILE, FREDERICK, *and* BLUNT.*)*

BELVILE: What means this? the Picture's taken in.
BLUNT: It may be the Wench is good-natur'd, and will be 80
kind *gratis.* Your Friend's a proper handsom Fellow.
BELVILE: I rather think she has cut his Throat and is fled: I am
mad he should throw himself into Dangers—Pox on't, I
shall want him to night—let's knock and ask for him.
HELLENA: My heart goes a-pit a-pat, for fear 'tis my Man they 85
talk of.

(Knock, MORETTA *above.)*

MORETTA: What would you have?
BELVILE: Tell the Stranger that enter'd here about two Hours
ago, that his Friends stay here for him.

90 MORETTA: A Curse upon him for *Moretta,* would he were at the Devil—but he's coming to you.

(*Enter* WILLMORE.)

HELLENA: I, I, 'tis he. Oh how this vexes me.

BELVILE: And how, and how, dear Lad, has Fortune smil'd? Are we to break her Windows, or raise up Altars to her! hah!

95 WILLMORE: Does not my Fortune sit triumphant on my Brow? dost not see the little wanton God there all gay and smiling? have I not an Air about my Face and Eyes, that distinguish me from the Croud of common Lovers? By Heav'n, *Cupid*'s Quiver has not half so many Darts as her

100 Eyes—Oh such a Bona Roba, to sleep in her Arms is lying in Fresco, all perfum'd Air about me.

HELLENA: (*Aside.*) Here's fine encouragement for me to fool on.

WILLMORE: Hark ye, where didst thou purchase that rich Canary we drank to-day? Tell me, that I may adore the

105 Spigot, and sacrifice to the Butt: the Juice was divine, into which I must dip my Rosary, and then bless all things that I would have bold or fortunate.

BELVILE: Well, Sir, let's go take a Bottle, and hear the Story of your Success.

110 FREDERICK: Would not *French* Wine do better?

WILLMORE: Damn the hungry Balderdash; cheerful Sack has a generous Virtue in't, inspiring a successful Confidence, gives Eloquence to the Tongue, and Vigour to the Soul; and has in a few Hours compleated all my Hopes and Wishes. There's

115 nothing left to raise a new Desire in me—Come let's be gay and wanton—and, Gentlemen, study, study what you want, for here are Friends,—that will supply, Gentlemen,—hark! what a charming sound they make—'tis he and she Gold whilst here, shall beget new Pleasures every moment.

120 BLUNT: But hark ye, Sir, you are not married, are you?

WILLMORE: All the Honey of Matrimony, but none of the Sting, Friend.

BLUNT: 'Sheartlikins, thou'rt a fortunate Rogue.

WILLMORE: I am so, Sir, let these inform you.—Ha, how

125 sweetly they chime! Pox of Poverty, it makes a Man a Slave, makes Wit and Honour sneak, my Soul grew lean and rusty for want of Credit.

BLUNT: 'Sheartlikins, this I like well, it looks like my lucky Bargain! Oh how I long for the Approach of my Squire,

130 that is to conduct me to her House again. Why! here's two provided for.

FREDERICK: By this light y're happy Men.

BLUNT: Fortune is pleased to smile on us, Gentlemen,—to smile on us.

(*Enter* SANCHO, *and pulls* BLUNT *by the Sleeve. They go aside.*)

135 SANCHO: Sir, my Lady expects you—she has remov'd all that might oppose your Will and Pleasure—and is impatient till you come.

BLUNT: Sir, I'll attend you—Oh the happiest Rogue! I'll take no leave, lest they either dog me, or stay me.

(*Exit with* SANCHO.)

140 BELVILE: But then the little Gipsy is forgot?

WILLMORE: A Mischief on thee for putting her into my thoughts; I had quite forgot her else, and this Night's Debauch had drunk her quite down.

HELLENA: Had it so, good Captain?

(*Claps him on the Back.*)

WILLMORE: Ha! I hope she did not hear.   145

HELLENA: What, afraid of such a Champion!

WILLMORE: Oh! you're a fine Lady of your word, are you not? to make a Man languish a whole day—

HELLENA: In tedious search of me.

WILLMORE: Egad, Child, thou'rt in the right, hadst thou seen   150
what a melancholy Dog I have been ever since I was a Lover, how I have walkt the Streets like a *Capuchin,* with my Hands in my Sleeves—Faith, Sweetheart, thou wouldst pity me.

HELLENA: Now, if I should be hang'd, I can't be angry with him, he dissembles so heartily—Alas, good Captain, what   155
pains you have taken—Now were I ungrateful not to reward so true a Servant.

WILLMORE: Poor Soul! that's kindly said, I see thou bearest a Conscience—come then for a beginning shew me thy dear Face.   160

HELLENA: I'm afraid, my small Acquaintance, you have been staying that swinging stomach you boasted of this morning; I remember then my little Collation would have gone down with you, without the Sauce of a handsom Face—Is your Stomach so quesy now?   165

WILLMORE: Faith long fasting, Child, spoils a Man's Appetite—yet if you durst treat, I could so lay about me still.

HELLENA: And would you fall to, before a Priest says Grace?

WILLMORE: Oh fie, fie, what an old out-of-fashion'd thing hast thou nam'd? Thou could'st not dash me more out of   170
Countenance, shouldst thou shew me an ugly Face.

(*Whilst he is seemingly courting* HELLENA, *enter* ANGELICA, MORETTA, BISKEY, *and* SEBASTIAN, *all in Masquerade:* ANGELICA *sees* WILLMORE *and starts.*)

ANGELICA: Heavens, is't he? and passionately fond to see another Woman?

MORETTA: What cou'd you expect less from such a Swaggerer?

ANGELICA: Expect! as much as I paid him, a Heart intire,   175
Which I had pride enough to think when e'er I gave
It would have rais'd the Man above the Vulgar,
Made him all Soul, and that all soft and constant.

HELLENA: You see, Captain, how willing I am to be Friends with you, till Time and Ill-luck make us Lovers; and ask   180
you the Question first, rather than put your Modesty to the blush, by asking me: for alas, I know you Captains are such strict Men, severe Observers of your Vows to Chastity, that 'twill be hard to prevail with your tender Conscience to marry a young willing Maid.   185

WILLMORE: Do not abuse me, for fear I should take thee at thy word, and marry thee indeed, which I'm sure will be Revenge sufficient.

HELLENA: O' my Conscience, that will be our Destiny, because we are both of one humour; I am as inconstant as you, for   190
I have considered, Captain, that a handsom Woman has a great deal to do whilst her Face is good, for then is our Harvest-time to gather Friends; and should I in these days of my Youth, catch a fit of foolish Constancy, I were undone; 'tis loitering by day-light in our great Journey: therefore declare, I'll allow but one year for Love, one year for   195
Indifference, and one year for Hate—and then—go hang

your self—for I profess myself the gay, the kind, and the inconstant—the Devil's in't if this won't please you.

200 WILLMORE: Oh most damnably!—I have a Heart with a hole
quite thro it too, no Prison like mine to keep a Mistress in.

ANGELICA: (*Aside.*) Purjur'd Man! how I believe thee now!

HELLENA: Well, I see our Business as well as Humours are
alike, yours to cozen as many Maids as will trust you, and
205 I as many Men as have Faith—See if I have not as desperate a lying look, as you can have for the heart of you.

(*Pulls off her Vizard; he starts.*)

—How do you like it, Captain?

WILLMORE: Like it! by Heav'n, I never saw so much Beauty.
Oh the Charms of those sprightly black Eyes, that strangely
210 fair Face, full of Smiles and Dimples! those soft round melting cherry Lips! and small even white Teeth! not to be ex-
prest, but silently adored!—Oh one Look more, and strike
me dumb, or I shall repeat nothing else till I am mad.

(*He seems to court her to pull off her Vizard: she refuses.*)

ANGELICA: I can endure no more—nor is it fit to interrupt
215 him; for if I do, my Jealousy has so destroy'd my Reason,—I shall undo him—Therefore I'll retire. And you *Sebastian* (*To one of her bravoes.*) follow that Woman, and learn
who 'tis; (*To the other bravo.*) while you tell the Fugitive, I
would speak to him instantly.

(*Exit.*)

(*This while* FLORINDA *is talking to* BELVILE, *who stands sullenly.*
FREDERICK *courting* VALERIA.)

220 VALERIA: Prithee, dear Stranger, be not so sullen; for tho you
have lost your Love, you see my Friend frankly offers you
hers, to play with in the mean time.

BELVILE: Faith, Madam, I am sorry I can't play at her Game.

FREDERICK: Pray leave your Intercession, and mind your own
225 Affair, they'll better agree apart; he's a model Sigher in
Company, but alone no Woman escapes him.

FLORINDA: Sure he does but rally—yet if it should be true—
I'll tempt him farther—Believe me, noble Stranger, I'm no
common Mistress—and for a little proof on't—wear this
230 Jewel—nay, take it, Sir, 'tis right, and Bills of Exchange
may sometimes miscarry.

BELVILE: Madam, why am I chose out of all Mankind to be
the Object of your Bounty?

VALERIA: There's another civil Question askt.

235 FREDERICK: Pox of's Modesty, it spoils his own Markets, and
hinders mine.

FLORINDA: Sir, from my Window I have often seen you; and
Women of Quality have so few opportunities for Love,
that we ought to lose none.

240 FREDERICK: Ay, this is something! here's a Woman!—When
shall I be blest with so much kindness from your fair
Mouth? (*Aside to* BELVILE.) Take the Jewel, Fool.

BELVILE: You tempt me strangely, Madam, every way.

FLORINDA: (*Aside.*) So, if I find him false, my whole Repose
245 is gone.

BELVILE: And but for a Vow I've made to a very fine Lady, this
Goodness had subdu'd me.

FREDERICK: Pox on't be kind, in pity to me be kind, for I am
to thrive here but as you treat her Friend.

HELLENA: Tell me what did you in yonder House, and I'll 250
unmasque.

WILLMORE: Yonder House—oh—I went to—a—to—why,
there's a Friend of mine lives there.

HELLENA: What a she, or a he Friend?

WILLMORE: A Man upon my Honour! a Man—A she Friend! 255
no, no, Madam, you have done my Business, I thank you.

HELLENA: And was't your Man Friend, that had more Darts
in's Eyes than *Cupid* carries in a whole Budget of Arrows?

WILLMORE: So—

HELLENA: Ah such a *Bona Roba:* to be in her Arms is lying in 260
Fresco, all perfumed Air about me—Was this your Man
Friend too?

WILLMORE: So—

HELLENA: That gave you the He, and the She—Gold, that
begets young Pleasures. 265

WILLMORE: Well, well, Madam, then you see there are Ladies
in the World, that will not be cruel—there are, Madam,
there are—

HELLENA: And there be Men too as fine, wild, inconstant Fellows as your self, there be, Captain, there be, if you go to 270
that now—therefore I'm resolv'd—

WILLMORE: Oh!

HELLENA: To see your Face no more—

WILLMORE: Oh!

HELLENA: Till to morrow. 275

WILLMORE: Egad you frighted me.

HELLENA: Nor then neither, unless you'l swear never to see
that Lady more.

WILLMORE: See her!—why! never to think of Womankind
again? 280

HELLENA: Kneel, and swear.

(*Kneels, she gives him her Hand.*)

WILLMORE: I do, never to think—to see—to love—nor lie
with any but thy self.

HELLENA: Kiss the Book.

WILLMORE: Oh, most religiously. 285

(*Kisses her Hand.*)

HELLENA: Now what a wicked Creature am I, to damn a
proper Fellow.

CALLIS: (*To* FLORINDA.) Madam, I'll stay no longer, 'tis e'en dark.

FLORINDA: However, Sir, I'll leave this with you—that when
I'm gone, you may repent the opportunity you have lost 290
by your modesty.

(*Gives him the Jewel, which is her Picture, and Exits. He gazes after her.*)

WILLMORE: 'Twill be an Age till to morrow,—and till then I
will most impatiently expect you—Adieu, my dear pretty
Angel.

(*Exeunt all the* WOMEN.)

BELVILE: Ha! *Florinda's* Picture! 'twas she her self—what a dull 295
Dog was I? I would have given the World for one minute's
discourse with her.—

FREDERICK: This comes of your Modesty,—ah pox on your
Vow, 'twas ten to one but we had lost the Jewel by't.

300 BELVILE: *Willmore! the blessed'st Opportunity lost!—Florinda, Friends, Florinda!*

WILLMORE: Ah Rogue! such black Eyes, such a Face, such a Mouth, such Teeth,—and so much Wit!

BELVILE: All, all, and a thousand Charms besides.

305 WILLMORE: Why, dost thou know her?

BELVILE: Know her! ay, ay, and a Pox take me with all my Heart for being modest.

WILLMORE: But hark ye, Friend of mine, are you my Rival? and have I been only beating the Bush all this while?

310 BELVILE: I understand thee not—I'm mad—see here—

(Shews the Picture.)

WILLMORE: Ha! whose Picture is this?—'tis a fine Wench.

FREDERICK: The Colonel's Mistress, Sir.

WILLMORE: Oh, oh, here—I thought it had been another Prize—come, come, a Bottle will set thee right again.

(Gives the Picture back.)

315 BELVILE: I am content to try, and by that time 'twill be late enough for our Design.

WILLMORE: Agreed.

Love does all day the Soul's great Empire keep,
But Wine at night lulls the soft God asleep.

(Exeunt.)

SCENE II

LUCETTA's *House.*

Enter BLUNT *and* LUCETTA *with a Light.*

LUCETTA: Now we are safe and free, no fears of the coming home of my old jealous Husband, which made me a little thoughtful when you came in first—but now Love is all the business of my Soul.

5 BLUNT: *(Aside.)* I am transported—Pox on't, that I had but some fine things to say to her, such as Lovers use—I was a Fool not to learn of *Frederick* a little by Heart before I came—something I must say.—'Sheartlikins, sweet Soul, I am not us'd to complement, but I'm an honest Gentle-

10 man, and thy humble Servant.

LUCETTA: I have nothing to pay for so great a Favour, but such a Love as cannot but be great, since at first sight of that sweet Face and Shape it made me your absolute Captive.

BLUNT: *(Aside.)* Kind heart, how prettily she talks! Egad I'll

15 show her Husband a *Spanish* Trick; send him out of the World, and marry her: she's damnably in love with me, and will ne'er mind Settlements, and so there's that sav'd.

LUCETTA: Well, Sir, I'll go and undress me, and be with you instantly.

20 BLUNT: Make haste then, for 'dsheartlikins, dear Soul, thou canst not guess at the pain of a longing Lover, when his Joys are drawn within the compass of a few minutes.

LUCETTA: You speak my Sense, and I'll make haste to pro-vide it.

(Exit.)

BLUNT: 'Tis a rare Girl, and this one night's enjoyment with 25 her will be worth all the days I ever past in Essex.—Would she'd go with me into *England,* tho to say truth, there's plenty of Whores there already.—But a pox on 'em they are such mercenary prodigal Whores, that they want such a one as this, that's free and generous, to give 'em good Ex- 30 amples:—Why, what a House she has! how rich and fine!

(Enter SANCHO.*)*

SANCHO: Sir, my Lady has sent me to conduct you to her Chamber.

BLUNT: Sir, I shall be proud to follow—Here's one of her Ser-vants too: 'dsheartlikins, by his Garb and Gravity he might 35 be a Justice of Peace in *Essex,* and is but a Pimp here.

(Exeunt.)

(The Scene changes to a Chamber with an Alcove-Bed in it, a Table, &c. LUCETTA *in Bed. Enter* SANCHO *and* BLUNT, *who takes the Candle of* SANCHO *at the Door.)*

SANCHO: Sir, my Commission reaches no farther.

BLUNT: Sir, I'll excuse your Complement:—what, in Bed, my sweet Mistress?

LUCETTA: You see, I still out-do you in kindness. 40

BLUNT: And thou shalt see what haste I'll make to quit scores—oh the luckiest Rogue!

(Undresses himself.)

LUCETTA: Shou'd you be false or cruel now!

BLUNT: False, 'Sheartlikins, what dost thou take me for a *Jew?* an insensible Heathen,—A Pox of thy old jealous Hus- 45 band: and he were dead, egad, sweet Soul, it shou'd be none of my fault, if I did not marry thee.

LUCETTA: It never shou'd be mine.

BLUNT: Good Soul, I'm the fortunatest Dog!

LUCETTA: Are you not undrest yet? 50

BLUNT: As much as my Impatience will permit.

(Goes towards the Bed in his Shirt and Drawers.)

LUCETTA: Hold, Sir, put out the Light, it may betray us else.

BLUNT: Any thing, I need no other Light but that of thine Eyes!—*(Aside.)* 'sheartlikins, there I think I had it.

(Puts out the Candle, the Bed descends, he gropes about to find it.)

—Why—why—where am I got? what, not yet?—where 55 are your sweetest?—ah, the Rogue's silent now—a pretty Love-trick this—how she'll laugh at me anon!—you need not, my dear Rogue! you need not! I'm all on a fire al-ready—come, come, now call me in for pity—Sure I'm enchanted! I have been round the Chamber, and can find 60 neither Woman, nor Bed—I lockt the Door, I'm sure she cannot go that way; or if she cou'd, the Bed cou'd not—Enough, enough, my pretty Wanton, do not carry the Jest too far—Ha, betray'd! Dogs! Rogues! Pimps! help! help!

(Lights on a Trap, and is let down. Enter LUCETTA, PHILIPPO, *and* SANCHO *with a Light.)*

65 PHILIPPO: Ha, ha, ha, he's dispatcht finely.

LUCETTA: Now, Sir, had I been coy, we had mist of this Booty.

PHILIPPO: Nay when I saw 'twas a substantial Fool, I was mollified; but when you doat upon a Serenading Coxcomb, upon a Face, fine Clothes, and a Lute, it makes me rage.

70 LUCETTA: You know I never was guilty of that Folly, my dear *Philippo,* but with your self—But come let's see what we have got by this.

PHILIPPO: A rich Coat!—Sword and Hat!—these Breeches too—are well lin'd!—see here a Gold Watch!—a Purse—

75 ha! Gold!—at least two hundred Pistoles! a bunch of Diamond Rings; and one with the Family Arms!—a Gold Box!—with a Medal of his King! and his Lady Mother's Picture!—these were sacred Reliques, believe me!—see, the Wasteband of his Breeches have a Mine of Gold!—

80 Old Queen *Bess's.* We have a Quarrel to her ever since Eighty Eight, and may therefore justify the Theft, the Inquisition might have committed it.

LUCETTA: See, a Bracelet of bow'd Gold, these his Sister ty'd about his Arm at parting—but well—for all this, I fear his

85 being a Stranger may make a noise, and hinder our Trade with them hereafter.

PHILIPPO: That's our security; he is not only a Stranger to us, but to the Country too—the Common-Shore into which he is descended, thou know'st, conducts him into another

90 Street, which this Light will hinder him from ever finding again—he knows neither your Name, nor the Street where your House is, nay, nor the way to his own Lodgings.

LUCETTA: And art not thou an unmerciful Rogue, not to afford him one Night for all this?—I should not have been

95 such a *Jew.*

PHILIPPO: Blame me not, *Lucetta,* to keep as much of thee as I can to my self—come, that thought makes me wanton,—let's to Bed,—*Sancho,* lock up these.

This is the Fleece which Fools do bear,
100 *Design'd for witty Men to sheer.*

(*Exeunt.*)

(*The Scene changes, and discovers* BLUNT*, creeping out of a Common Shore, his Face, &c., all dirty.*)

BLUNT: Oh Lord!

(*Climbing up.*)

I am got out at last, and (which is a Miracle) without a Clue—and now to Damning and Cursing—but if that would ease me, where shall I begin? with my Fortune, my

105 self, or the Quean that cozen'd me—What a dog was I to believe in Women! Oh Coxcomb—ignorant conceited Coxcomb! to fancy she cou'd be enamour'd with my Person, at the first sight enamour'd—Oh, I'm a cursed Puppy, 'tis plain, Fool was writ upon my Forehead, she perceiv'd it,—saw the

110 *Essex* Calf there—for what Allurements could there be in this Countenance? which I can indure, because I'm acquainted with it—Oh, dull silly Dog! to be thus sooth'd into a Cozening! Had I been drunk, I might fondly have credited the young Quean! but as I was in my right Wits, to be thus cheated, confirms I am a dull believing *English* Country 115 Fop.—But my Comrades! Death and the Devil, there's the worst of all—then a Ballad will be sung to Morrow on the *Prado,* to a lousy Tune of the enchanted Squire, and the annihilated Damsel—But *Frederick* that Rogue, and the Colonel, will abuse me beyond all Christian patience—had she left 120 me my Clothes, I have a Bill of Exchange at home wou'd have sav'd my Credit—but now all hope is taken from me— Well, I'll home (if I can find the way) with this Consolation, that I am not the first kind believing Coxcomb; but there are, Gallants, many such good Natures amongst ye.   125

And tho you've better Arts to hide your Follies,
Adsheartlikins y'are all as errant Cullies.

SCENE III

The Garden, in the Night.

Enter FLORINDA*, undress'd, with a Key, and a little Box.*

FLORINDA: Well, thus far I'm in my way to Happiness; I have got my self free from *Callis;* my Brother too, I find by yonder light, is gone into his Cabinet, and thinks not of me: I have by good Fortune got the Key of the Garden Back-door,— I'll open it, to prevent *Belvile's* knocking,—a little noise will 5 now alarm my Brother. Now am I as fearful as a young Thief. (*Unlocks the Door.*)—Hark,—what noise is that?— Oh, 'twas the Wind that plaid amongst the Boughs.—*Belvile* stays long, methinks—it's time—stay—for fear of a surprize, I'll hide these Jewels in yonder Jessamin.   10

(*She goes to lay down the Box.*)

(*Enter* WILLMORE *drunk.*)

WILLMORE: What the Devil is become of these Fellows, *Belvile* and *Frederick?* They promis'd to stay at the next corner for me, but who the Devil knows the corner of a full Moon?— Now—whereabouts am I?—hah—what have we here? a Garden!—a very convenient place to sleep in—hah—what 15 has God sent us here?—a Female—by this light, a Woman; I'm a Dog if it be not a very Wench.—

FLORINDA: He's come!—hah—who's there?

WILLMORE: Sweet Soul, let me salute thy Shoe-string.

FLORINDA: 'Tis not my *Belvile*—good Heavens, I know him 20 not.—Who are you, and from whence come you!

WILLMORE: Prithee—prithee, Child—not so many hard Questions—let it suffice I am here, Child—Come, come kiss me.

FLORINDA: Good Gods! what luck is mine?

WILLMORE: Only good luck, Child, parlous good luck.—Come 25 hither,—'tis a delicate shining Wench,—by this Hand she's perfum'd, and smells like any Nosegay.—Prithee, dear Soul, let's not play the Fool, and lose time,—precious time—for as Gad shall save me, I'm as honest a Fellow as breathes,—tho I am a little disguis'd at present.—Come, I say,—why, thou may'st 30 be free with me, I'll be very secret. I'll not boast who 'twas oblig'd me, not I—for hang me if I know thy Name.

---

83 **bow'd Gold** *bowed* is still used in the North of England for bent: 'a bowed pin'

30 **disguis'd** a common phrase for drunk

FLORINDA: Heavens! what a filthy beast is this!

WILLMORE: I am so, and thou oughtst the sooner to lie with
35   me for that reason,—for look you, Child, there will be no
        Sin in't, because 'twas neither design'd nor premeditated;
        'tis pure Accident on both sides—that's a certain thing
        now—Indeed should I make love to you, and you vow Fi-
        delity—and swear and lye till you believ'd and yielded—
40   Thou art therefore (as thou art a good Christian) oblig'd
        in Conscience to deny me nothing. Now—come, be
        kind, without any more idle prating.

FLORINDA: Oh, I am ruin'd—wicked Man, unhand me.

WILLMORE: Wicked! Egad, Child, a Judge, were he young and
45   vigorous, and saw those Eyes of thine, would know 'twas
        they gave the first blow—the first provocation.—Come,
        prithee let's lose no time, I say—this is a fine convenient
        place.

FLORINDA: Sir, let me go, I conjure you, or I'll call out.

50 WILLMORE: Ay, ay, you were best to call Witness to see how
        finely you treat me—do.—

FLORINDA: I'll cry Murder, Rape, or any thing, if you do not
        instantly let me go.

WILLMORE: A Rape! Come, come, you lye, you Baggage, you
55   lye: What, I'll warrant you would fain have the World be-
        lieve now that you are not so forward as I. No, not you,—
        why at this time of Night was your Cobweb-door set
        open, dear Spider—but to catch Flies?—Hah come—or I
        shall be damnably angry.—Why what a Coil is here.—

60 FLORINDA: Sir, can you think—

WILLMORE: That you'd do it for nothing? oh, oh, I find what
        you'd be at—look here, here's a Pistole for you—here's a
        work indeed—here—take it, I say.—

FLORINDA: For Heaven's sake, Sir, as you're a Gentleman—

65 WILLMORE: So—now—she would be wheedling me for
        more—what, you will not take it then—you're resolv'd
        you will not.—Come, come, take it, or I'll put it up again;
        for, look ye, I never give more.—Why, how now, Mistress,
        are you so high i'th' Mouth, a Pistole won't down with
70   you?—hah—why, what a work's here—in good time—
        come, no struggling, be gone—But an y'are good at a
        dumb Wrestle, I'm for ye,—look ye,—I'm for ye.—

(*She struggles with him.*)

(*Enter* BELVILE *and* FREDERICK.)

BELVILE: The Door is open, a Pox of this mad Fellow, I'm angry
        that we've lost him, I durst have sworn he had follow'd us.

75 FREDERICK: But you were so hasty, Colonel, to be gone.

FLORINDA: Help, help,—Murder!—help—oh, I'm ruin'd.

BELVILE: Ha, sure that's *Florinda's* Voice.

(*Comes up to them.*)

—A Man! Villain, let go that Lady.

(*A noise.*)

(WILLMORE *turns and draws,* FREDERICK *interposes.*)

FLORINDA: *Belvile!* Heavens! my Brother too is coming, and
80   'twill be impossible to escape.—*Belvile,* I conjure you to
        walk under my Chamber-window, from whence I'll give

you some instructions what to do—This rude Man has
undone us.

(*Exit.*)

WILLMORE: *Belvile!*

(*Enter* PEDRO, STEPHANO, *and other Servants with Lights.*)

PEDRO: I'm betray'd; run, *Stephano,* and see if *Florinda* be safe. 85

(*Exit* STEPHANO.)

So who'er they be, all is not well, I'll to *Florinda's* Chamber.

(*They fight, and* PEDRO's *Party beats 'em out; going out, meets*
STEPHANO.)

STEPHANO: You need not, Sir, the poor Lady's fast asleep, and
        thinks no harm: I wou'd not wake her, Sir, for fear of
        frightning her with your danger.

PEDRO: I'm glad she's there—Rascals, how came the Garden- 90
        Door open?

STEPHANO: That Question comes too late, Sir: some of my
        Fellow-Servants Masquerading I'll warrant.

PEDRO: Masquerading! a leud Custom to debauch our
        Youth—there's something more in this than I imagine. 95

(*Exeunt.*)

SCENE IV

Changes to the Street.

Enter BELVILE *in Rage,* FREDERICK *holding him, and* WILLMORE
melancholy.

WILLMORE: Why, how the Devil shou'd I know *Florinda?*

BELVILE: Ah plague of your ignorance! if it had not been
        Florinda, must you be a Beast?—a Brute, a senseless
        Swine?

WILLMORE: Well, Sir, you see I am endu'd with Patience—I   5
        can bear—tho egad y're very free with me methinks,—I
        was in good hopes the Quarrel wou'd have been on my
        side, for so uncivilly interrupting me.

BELVILE: Peace, Brute, whilst thou'rt safe—oh, I'm distracted.

WILLMORE: Nay, nay, I'm an unlucky Dog, that's certain.   10

BELVILE: Ah curse upon the Star that rul'd my Birth! or what-
        soever other Influence that makes me still so wretched.

WILLMORE: Thou break'st my Heart with these Complaints;
        there is no Star in fault, no Influence but Sack, the cursed
        Sack I drank.   15

FREDERICK: Why, how the Devil came you so drunk?

WILLMORE: Why, how the Devil came you so sober?

BELVILE: A curse upon his thin Skull, he was always before-
        hand that way.

FREDERICK: Prithee, dear Colonel, forgive him, he's sorry for 20
        his fault.

BELVILE: He's always so after he has done a mischief—a
        plague on all such Brutes.

WILLMORE: By this Light I took her for an errant Harlot.

BELVILE: Damn your debaucht Opinion: tell me, Sot, hadst thou 25
        so much sense and light about thee to distinguish her to be

a Woman, and could'st not see something about her Face
and Person, to strike an awful Reverence into thy Soul?

WILLMORE: Faith no, I consider'd her as mere a Woman as I
30   could wish.

BELVILE: 'Sdeath I have no patience—draw, or I'll kill you.

WILLMORE: Let that alone till to morrow, and if I set not all
right again, use your Pleasure.

BELVILE: To morrow, damn it.
35   The spiteful Light will lead me to no happiness.
To morrow is *Antonio*'s, and perhaps
Guides him to my undoing;—oh that I could meet
This Rival, this powerful Fortunate.

WILLMORE: What then?

40 BELVILE: Let thy own Reason, or my Rage instruct thee.

WILLMORE: I shall be finely inform'd then, no doubt; hear
me, Colonel—hear me—shew me the Man and I'll do his
Business.

BELVILE: I know him no more than thou, or if I did, I should
45   not need thy aid.

WILLMORE: This you say is *Angelica*'s House, I promis'd the
kind Baggage to lie with her to Night.

(*Offers to go in.*)

(*Enter* ANTONIO *and his Page.* ANTONIO *knocks on the Hilt of his
Sword.*)

ANTONIO: You paid the thousand Crowns I directed?

PAGE: To the Lady's old Woman, Sir, I did.

50 WILLMORE: Who the Devil have we here?

BELVILE: I'll now plant my self under *Florinda*'s Window, and
if I find no comfort there, I'll die.

(*Exit* BELVILE *and* FREDERICK. *Enter* MORETTA.)

MORETTA: Page!

PAGE: Here's my Lord.

55 WILLMORE: How is this, a Piccaroon going to board my
Frigate! here's one Chase-Gun for you.

(*Drawing his Sword, justles* ANTONIO *who turns and draws. They
fight,* ANTONIO *falls.*)

MORETTA: Oh, bless us, we are all undone!

(*Runs in, and shuts the Door.*)

PAGE: Help, Murder!

(BELVILE *returns at the noise of fighting.*)

BELVILE: Ha, the mad Rogue's engag'd in some unlucky Ad-
60   venture again.

(*Enter two or three* MASQUERADERS.)

MASQUERADER: Ha, a Man kill'd!

WILLMORE: How! a Man kill'd! then I'll go home to sleep.

(*Puts up, and reels out. Exeunt* MASQUERADERS *another way.*)

BELVILE: Who shou'd it be! pray Heaven the Rogue is safe, for
all my Quarrel to him.

(*As* BELVILE *is groping about, enter an* OFFICER *and six* SOL-
DIERS.)

SOLDIER: Who's there?   65

OFFICER: So, here's one dispatcht—secure the Murderer.

BELVILE: Do not mistake my Charity for Murder: I came to
his Assistance.

(SOLDIERS *sieze on* BELVILE.)

OFFICER: That shall be tried, Sir.—St. *Jago*, Swords drawn in
the Carnival time!   70

(*Goes to* ANTONIO.)

ANTONIO: Thy Hand prithee.

OFFICER: Ha, Don *Antonio*! look well to the Villain there.—
How is't, Sir?

ANTONIO: I'm hurt.

BELVILE: Has my Humanity made me a Criminal?   75

OFFICER: Away with him.

BELVILE: What a curst Chance is this!

(*Exeunt* SOLDIERS *with* BELVILE.)

ANTONIO: (*To the* OFFICER.) This is the Man that has set upon
me twice—carry him to my Apartment till you have fur-
ther Orders from me.   80

(*Exit.* ANTONIO *led.*)

ACT FOUR

SCENE I

A fine Room.

Discovers BELVILE, *as by Dark alone.*

BELVILE: When shall I be weary of railing on Fortune, who is
resolv'd never to turn with Smiles upon me?—Two such
Defeats in one Night—none but the Devil and that mad
Rogue could have contriv'd to have plagued me with—I
am here a Prisoner—but where?—Heaven knows—and if   5
there be Murder done, I can soon decide the Fate of a
Stranger in a Nation without Mercy—Yet this is nothing
to the Torture my Soul bows with, when I think of losing
my fair, my dear *Florinda*.—Hark—my Door opens—a
Light—a Man—and seems of Quality—arm'd too.—   10
Now shall I die like a Dog without defence.

(*Enter* ANTONIO *in a Night-Gown, with a Light; his Arm in a
Scarf, and a Sword under his Arm: He sets the Candle on the Table.*)

ANTONIO: Sir, I come to know what Injuries I have done
you, that could provoke you to so mean an Action, as to
attack me basely, without allowing time for my Defence.

BELVILE: Sir, for a Man in my Circumstances to plead Inno-   15
cence, would look like Fear—but view me well, and you
will find no marks of a Coward on me, nor any thing that
betrays that Brutality you accuse me of.

ANTONIO: In vain, Sir, you impose upon my Sense,
You are not only he who drew on me last Night,   20

But yesterday before the same House, that of *Angelica*.
Yet there is something in your Face and Mein—

BELVILE: I own I fought to day in the defence of a Friend of
mine, with whom you (if you're the same) and your
25   Party were first engag'd.
Perhaps you think this Crime enough to kill me,
But if you do, I cannot fear you'll do it basely.

ANTONIO: No, Sir, I'll make you fit for a Defence with this.

(*Gives him the Sword.*)

BELVILE: This Gallantry surprizes me—nor know I how to
30   use this Present, Sir, against a Man so brave.

ANTONIO: You shall not need;
For know, I come to snatch you from a Danger
That is decreed against you;
Perhaps your Life, or long Imprisonment:
35   And 'twas with so much Courage you offended,
I cannot see you punisht.

BELVILE: How shall I pay this Generosity?

ANTONIO: It had been safer to have kill'd another,
Than have attempted me:
40   To shew your Danger, Sir, I'll let you know my Quality;
And 'tis the Vice-Roy's Son whom you have wounded.

BELVILE: (*Aside.*) The Vice-Roy's Son!
Death and Confusion! was this Plague reserved
To compleat all the rest?—oblig'd by him!
45   The Man of all the World I would destroy.

ANTONIO: You seem disorder'd, Sir.

BELVILE: Yes, trust me, Sir, I am, and 'tis with pain
That Man receives such Bounties,
Who wants the pow'r to pay 'em back again.

50 ANTONIO: To gallant Spirits 'tis indeed uneasy;
—But you may quickly over-pay me, Sir.

BELVILE: Then I am well—(*Aside.*) kind Heaven! but set us
even,
That I may fight with him, and keep my Honour safe.
—Oh, I'm impatient, Sir, to be discounting
55   The mighty Debt I owe you; command me quickly—

ANTONIO: I have a Quarrel with a Rival, Sir,
About the Maid we love.

BELVILE: (*Aside.*) Death, 'tis *Florinda* he means—
That Thought destroys my Reason, and I shall kill him—
60 ANTONIO: My Rival, Sir.
Is one has all the Virtues Man can boast of.

BELVILE: Death! who shou'd this be?

ANTONIO: He challeng'd me to meet him on the *Molo*,
As soon as Day appear'd; but last Night's quarrel
65   Has made my Arm unfit to guide a Sword.

BELVILE: I apprehend you, Sir, you'd have me kill the Man
That lays a claim to the Maid you speak of.
—I'll do't—I'll fly to do it.

ANTONIO: Sir, do you know her?
70 BELVILE: —No, Sir, but 'tis enough she is admired by you.

ANTONIO: Sir, I shall rob you of the Glory on't,
For you must fight under my Name and Dress.

BELVILE: That Opinion must be strangely obliging that makes
You think I can personate the brave *Antonio*,
75   Whom I can but strive to imitate.

ANTONIO: You say too much to my Advantage.

Come, Sir, the Day appears that calls you forth.
Within, Sir, is the Habit.

(*Exit* ANTONIO.)

BELVILE: Fantastick Fortune, thou deceitful Light,
That cheats the wearied Traveller by Night,   80
Tho on a Precipice each step you tread,
I am resolv'd to follow where you lead.

(*Exit.*)

SCENE II

The Molo.

Enter FLORINDA *and* CALLIS *in Masques, with* STEPHANO.

FLORINDA: (*Aside.*) I'm dying with my fears; *Belvile's* not coming,
As I expected, underneath my Window,
Makes me believe that all those Fears are true.
—Canst thou not tell with whom my Brother fights?

STEPHANO: No, Madam, they were both in Masquerade, I was   5
by when they challeng'd one another, and they had decided the Quarrel then, but were prevented by some Cavaliers; which made 'em put it off till now—but I am sure
'tis about you they fight.

FLORINDA: (*Aside.*) Nay then 'tis with *Belvile*, for what other   10
Lover have I that dares fight for me, except *Antonio*? and
he is too much in favour with my Brother—If it be he, for
whom shall I direct my Prayers to Heaven?

STEPHANO: Madam, I must leave you; for if my Master see me,
I shall be hang'd for being your Conductor.—I escap'd nar-   15
rowly for the Excuse I made for you last night i'th' Garden.

FLORINDA: And I'll reward thee for't—prithee no more.

(*Exit* STEPHANO.)

(*Enter Don* PEDRO *in his Masquing Habit.*)

PEDRO: *Antonio's* late to day, the place will fill, and we may be
prevented.

(*Walks about.*)

FLORINDA: (*Aside.*) Antonio! sure I heard amiss.   20

PEDRO: But who would not excuse a happy Lover.
When soft fair Arms comfine the yielding Neck;
And the kind Whisper languishingly breathes,
Must you be gone so soon?
Sure I had dwelt for ever on her Bosom.   25
—But stay, he's here.

(*Enter* BELVILE *drest in* ANTONIO'*s Clothes.*)

FLORINDA: 'Tis not *Belvile*, half my Fears are vanisht.

PEDRO: *Antonio!*—

BELVILE: (*Aside.*) This must be he.
You're early, Sir,—I do not use to be out-done this way.   30

PEDRO: The wretched, Sir, are watchful, and 'tis enough
You have the advantage of me in *Angelica*.

BELVILE: (*Aside.*) Angelica!
Or I've mistook my Man! Or else *Antonio*,

35   Can he forget his Interest in *Florinda,*
       And fight for common Prize?
PEDRO: Come, Sir, you know our terms—
BELVILE: (*Aside.*) Be Heaven, not I.
       —No talking, I am ready, Sir.

(*Offers to fight.* FLORINDA *runs in.*)

40 FLORINDA: (*To* BELVILE.) Oh, hold! who'er you be, I do con-
       jure you hold. If you strike here—I die—
PEDRO: *Florinda!*
BELVILE: *Florinda* imploring for my Rival!
PEDRO: Away, this Kindness is unseasonable.

(*Puts her by, they fight; she runs in just as* BELVILE *disarms* PEDRO.)

45 FLORINDA: Who are you, Sir, that dare deny my Prayers?
BELVILE: Thy Prayers destroy him; if thou wouldst preserve him.
       Do that thou'rt unacquainted with, and curse him.

(*She holds him.*)

FLORINDA: By all you hold most dear, by her you love,
       I do conjure you, touch him not.
50 BELVILE: By her I love!
       See—I obey—and at your Feet resign
       The useless Trophy of my Victory.

(*Lays his sword at her Feet.*)

PEDRO: *Antonio,* you've done enough to prove you love *Florinda.*
BELVILE: Love *Florinda!*
55   Does Heaven love Adoration, Pray'r, or Penitence?
       Love her! here Sir,—your Sword again.

(*Snatches up the Sword, and gives it him.*)

       Upon this Truth I'll fight my Life away.
PEDRO: No, you've redeem'd my Sister, and my Friendship.
BELVILE: Don *Pedro!*

(*He gives him* FLORINDA *and pulls off his Vizard to shew his Face,
and puts it on again.*)

60 PEDRO: Can you resign your Claims to other Women,
       And give your Heart intirely to *Florinda?*
BELVILE: Intire, as dying Saints Confessions are.
       I can delay my happiness no longer.
       This minute let me make *Florinda* mine:
65 PEDRO: This minute let it be—no time so proper,
       This Night my Father will arrive from *Rome,*
       And possibly may hinder what we propose.
FLORINDA: Oh Heavens! this Minute!

(*Enter* MASQUERADERS, *and pass over.*)

BELVILE: Oh, do not ruin me!
70 PEDRO: The place begins to fill; and that we may not be ob-
       serv'd, do you walk off to St. *Peter*'s Church, where I will
       meet you, and conclude your Happiness.
BELVILE: I'll meet you there—(*Aside.*) if there be no more
       Saints Churches in *Naples.*

FLORINDA: Oh stay, Sir, and recall your hasty Doom: 75
       Alas I have not yet prepar'd my Heart
       To entertain so strange a Guest.
PEDRO: Away, this silly Modesty is assum'd too late.
BELVILE: Heaven, Madam! what do you do?
FLORINDA: Do! despise the Man that lays a Tyrant's Claim   80
       To what he ought to conquer by Submission.
BELVILE: You do not know me—move a little this way.

(*Draws her aside.*)

FLORINDA: Yes, you may even force me to the Altar,
       But not the holy Man that offers there
       Shall force me to be thine.   85

(PEDRO *talks to* CALLIS *this while.*)

BELVILE: Oh do not lose so blest an opportunity!
       See—'tis your *Belvile*—not *Antonio,*
       Whom your mistaken Scorn and Anger ruins.

(*Pulls off his Vizard.*)

FLORINDA: *Belvile!*
       Where was my Soul it cou'd not meet thy Voice,   90
       And take this knowledge in?

(*As they are talking, enter* WILLMORE *finely drest, and* FREDERICK.)

WILLMORE: No Intelligence! no News of *Belvile* yet—well I am
       the most unlucky Rascal in Nature—ha!—am I deceiv'd—
       or is it he—look, *Frederick*—'tis he—my dear *Belvile.*

(*Runs and embraces him.* BELVILE's *Vizard falls out on's Hand.*)

BELVILE: Hell and Confusion seize thee!   95
PEDRO: Ha! *Belvile!* I beg your Pardon, Sir.

(*Takes* FLORINDA *from him.*)

BELVILE: Nay, touch her not, she's mine by Conquest, Sir.
       I won her by my Sword.
WILLMORE: Did'st thou so—and egad, Child, we'll keep her
       by the Sword.   100

(*Draws on* PEDRO, BELVILE *goes between.*)

BELVILE: Stand off.
       Thou'rt so profanely leud, so curst by Heaven,
       All Quarrels thou espousest must be fatal.
WILLMORE: Nay, an you be so hot, my Valour's coy,
       And shall be courted when you want it next.   105

(*Puts up his Sword.*)

BELVILE: You know I ought to claim a Victor's Right,

(*To* PEDRO.)

       But you're the Brother to divine *Florinda,*
       To whom I'm such a Slave—to purchase her,
       I durst not hurt the Man she holds so dear.
PEDRO: 'Twas by *Antonio*'s, not by *Belvile*'s Sword,   110
       This Question should have been decided, Sir:

I must confess much to your Bravery's due,
Both now, and when I met you last in Arms.
But I am nicely punctual in my word,
115   As Men of Honour ought, and beg your Pardon.

(*Aside to* FLORINDA *as they are going out.*)

—For this Mistake another Time shall clear.
—This was some Plot between you and *Belvile*:
But I'll prevent you.

(BELVILE *looks after her, and begins to walk up and down in a Rage.*)

WILLMORE: Do not be modest now, and lose the Woman: but
120   if we shall fetch her back, so—
BELVILE: Do not speak to me.
WILLMORE: Not speak to you!—Egad, I'll speak to you, and
    will be answered too.
BELVILE: Will you, Sir?
125   WILLMORE: I know I've done some mischief, but I'm so dull
    a Puppy, that I am the Son of a Whore, if I know how, or
    where—prithee inform my Understanding.—
BELVILE: Leave me I say, and leave me instantly.
WILLMORE: I will not leave you in this humour, nor till I
130   know my Crime.
BELVILE: Death, I'll tell you, Sir—

(*Draws and runs at* WILLMORE; *he runs out;* BELVILE *after him,*
FREDERICK *interposes.*)

(*Enter* ANGELICA, MORETTA, *and* SEBASTIAN.)

ANGELICA: Ha—*Sebastian*—Is not that *Willmore?* haste, haste,
    and bring him back.
FREDERICK: The Colonel's mad—I never saw him thus be-
135   fore; I'll after 'em, lest he do some mischief, for I am sure
    Willmore will not draw on him.

(*Exit.*)

ANGELICA: I am all Rage! my first desires defeated
    For one, for ought he knows, that has no
    Other Merit than her Quality,—
140   Her being Don *Pedro*'s Sister—He loves her:
    I know 'tis so—dull, dull, insensible—
    He will not see me now tho oft invited;
    And broke his Word last night—false perjur'd Man!
    —He that but yesterday fought for my Favours,
145   And would have made his Life a Sacrifice
    To've gain'd one Night with me,
    Must now be hired and courted to my Arms.
MORETTA: I told you what wou'd come on't, but *Moretta*'s an
    old doating Fool—Why did you give him five hundred
150   Crowns, but to set himself out for other Lovers? You
    shou'd have kept him poor, if you had meant to have had
    any good from him.
ANGELICA: Oh, name not such mean Trifles.—Had I given him all
    My Youth has earn'd from Sin,
155   I had not lost a Thought nor Sigh upon't.
    But I have given him my eternal Rest,
    My whole Repose, my future Joys, my Heart;
    My Virgin Heart. *Moretta!* oh 'tis gone!

MORETTA: Curse on him, here he comes;
    How fine she has made him too!   160

(*Enter* WILLMORE *and* SEBASTIAN. ANGELICA *turns and walks away.*)

WILLMORE: How now, turn'd Shadow?
    Fly when I pursue, and follow when I fly!

(*Sings.*)

    Stay gentle Shadow of my Dove,
        And tell me e'er I go,
    Whether the Substance may not prove   165
        A fleeting Thing like you.

There's a soft kind Look remaining yet.

(*As she turns she looks on him.*)

ANGELICA: Well, Sir, you may be gay; all Happiness, all Joys
    pursue you still, Fortune's your Slave, and gives you every
    hour choice of new Hearts and Beauties, till you are cloy'd   170
    with the repeated Bliss, which others vainly languish
    for—But know, false Man, that I shall be reveng'd.

(*Turns away in a Rage.*)

WILLMORE: So, 'gad, there are of those faint-hearted Lovers,
    whom such a sharp Lesson next their Hearts would make
    as impotent as Fourscore—pox o' this whining—my   175
    Bus'ness is to laugh and love—a pox on't; I hate your
    sullen Lover, a Man shall lose as much time to put you in
    Humour now, as would serve to gain a new Woman.
ANGELICA: I scorn to cool that Fire I cannot raise,
    Or do the Drudgery of your virtuous Mistress.   180
WILLMORE: A virtuous Mistress! Death, what a thing thou
    hast found out for me! why what the Devil should I do
    with a virtuous Woman?—a fort of ill'natur'd Creatures,
    that take a Pride to torment a Lover. Virtue is but an In-
    firmity in Women, a Disease that renders even the hand-   185
    som ungrateful; whilst the ill-favour'd, for want of
    Sollicitations and Address, only fancy themselves so.—I
    have lain with a Woman of Quality, who has all the while
    been railing at Whores.
ANGELICA: I will not answer for your Mistress's Virtue,   190
    Tho she be young enough to know no Guilt:
    And I could wish you would persuade my Heart,
    'Twas the two hundred thousand Crowns you courted.
WILLMORE: Two hundred thousand Crowns! what Story's
    this?—what Trick?—what Woman?—ha.   195
ANGELICA: How strange you make it! have you forgot the
    Creature you entertain'd on the Piazza last night?
WILLMORE: Ha, my Gipsy worth two hundred thousand
    Crowns!—oh how I long to be with her—pox, I knew
    she was of Quality.   200
ANGELICA: False Man, I see my Ruin in thy Face.
    How many vows you breath'd upon my Bosom,
    Never to be unjust—have you forgot so soon?
WILLMORE: Faith no, I was just coming to repeat 'em—but
    here's a Humour indeed—would make a Man a Saint—   205
    (*Aside.*) Wou'd she'd be angry enough to leave me, and
    command me not to wait on her.

(*Enter* HELLENA, *drest in Man's Clothes.*)

HELLENA: This must be *Angelica,* I know it by her mumping
Matron here—Ay, ay, 'tis she: my mad Captain's with her
210 too, for all his swearing—how this unconstant Humour
makes me love him:—pray, good grave Gentlewoman, is
not this *Angelica?*
MORETTA: My too young Sir, it is—I hope 'tis one from Don
Antonio.

(*Goes to* ANGELICA.)

215 HELLENA: (*Aside.*) Well, something I'll do to vex him for this.
ANGELICA: I will not speak with him; am I in humour to receive a Lover?
WILLMORE: Not speak with him! why I'll be gone—and wait
your idler minutes—Can I shew less Obedience to the
220 thing I love so fondly?

(*Offers to go.*)

ANGELICA: A fine Excuse this—stay—
WILLMORE: And hinder your Advantage: should I repay your
Bounties so ungratefully?
ANGELICA: Come, hither, Boy,—that I may let you see
225 How much above the Advantages you name
I prize one Minute's Joy with you.
WILLMORE: Oh, you destroy me with this Endearment.

(*Impatient to be gone.*)

—Death, how shall I get away!—Madam, 'twill not be fit
I should be seen with you—besides, it will not be conve-
230 nient—and I've a Friend—that's dangerously sick.
ANGELICA: I see you're impatient—yet you shall stay.
WILLMORE: And miss my Assignation with my Gipsy.

(*Aside, and walks about impatiently.* MORETTA *brings* HELLENA,
who addresses her self to ANGELICA.)

HELLENA: Madam, You'l hardly pardon my Intrusion,
When you shall know my Business;
235 And I'm too young to tell my Tale with Art:
But there must be a wondrous store of Goodness
Where so much Beauty dwells.
ANGELICA: A pretty Advocate, whoever sent thee,
—Prithee proceed—Nay, Sir, you shall not go.

(*To* WILLMORE, *who is stealing off.*)

240 WILLMORE: Then shall I lose my dear Gipsy for ever.
(*Aside.*)—Pox on't, she stays me out of spite.
HELLENA: I am related to a Lady, Madam,
Young, rich, and nobly born, but has the fate
To be in love with a young *English* Gentleman.
245 Strangely she loves him, at first sight she lov'd him,
But did adore him when she heard him speak;
For he, she said, had Charms in every word,
That fail'd not to surprize, to wound, and conquer—
WILLMORE: (*Aside.*) Ha, Egad I hope this concerns me.
250 ANGELICA: 'Tis my false Man, he means—wou'd he were gone.
This Praise will raise his Pride and ruin me—(*To*
WILLMORE.) Well,

Since you are so impatient to be gone.
I will release you, Sir.
WILLMORE: (*Aside.*) Nay, then I'm sure 'twas me he spoke of,
this cannot be the Effects of Kindness in her.   255
—No, Madam, I've consider'd better on't,
And will not give you cause of Jealousy.
ANGELICA: But, Sir, I've—business, that—
WILLMORE: This shall not do, I know 'tis but to try me.
ANGELICA: (*Aside.*) Well, to your Story, Boy,—tho 'twill undo me. 260
HELLENA: With this Addition to his other Beauties,
He won her unresisting tender Heart,
He vow'd and sigh'd, and swore he lov'd her dearly;
And she believ'd the cunning Flatterer,
And thought her self the happiest Maid alive: 265
To day was the appointed time by both,
To consummate their Bliss;
The Virgin, Altar, and the Priest were drest,
And whilst she languisht for the expected Bridegroom,
She heard, he paid his broken Vows to you.   270
WILLMORE: (*Aside.*) So, this is some dear Rogue that's in love
with me, and this way lets me know it; or if it be not me,
she means some one whose place I may supply.
ANGELICA: Now I perceive
The cause of thy Impatience to be gone,   275
And all the business of this glorious Dress.
WILLMORE: Damn the young Prater, I know not what he means.
HELLENA: Madam,
In your fair Eyes I read too much concern
To tell my farther Business.   280
ANGELICA: Prithee, sweet Youth, talk on, thou may'st perhaps
Raise here a Storm that may undo my Passion,
And then I'll grant thee any thing.
HELLENA: Madam, 'tis to intreat you, (oh unreasonable!)
You wou'd not see this Stranger;   285
For if you do, she vows you are undone,
Tho Nature never made a Man so excellent;
And sure he'ad been a God, but for Inconstancy.
WILLMORE: (*Aside.*) Ah, Rogue, how finely he's instructed!
—'Tis plain some Woman that has seen me *en passant.*   290
ANGELICA: Oh, I shall burst with Jealousy! do you know the
Man you speak of?—
HELLENA: Yes, Madam, he us'd to be in Buff and Scarlet.
ANGELICA: (*To* WILLMORE.) Thou, false as Hell, what canst
thou say to this?   295
WILLMORE: By Heaven—
ANGELICA: Hold, do not damn thy self—
HELLENA: Nor hope to be believ'd.

(*He walks about, they follow.*)

ANGELICA: Oh, perjur'd Man!
Is't thus you pay my generous Passion back?   300
HELLENA: Why wou'd you, Sir, abuse my Lady's Faith?
ANGELICA: And use me so unhumanly?
HELLENA: A Maid so young, so innocent—
WILLMORE: Ah, young Devil!
ANGELICA: Dost thou not know thy Life is in my Power?   305
HELLENA: Or think my Lady cannot be reveng'd?
WILLMORE: (*Aside.*) So, so, the Storm comes finely on.
ANGELICA: Now thou art silent, Guilt has struck thee dumb.

Oh, hadst thou still been so, I'd liv'd in safety.

(*She turns away and weeps.*)

310 WILLMORE: (*Aside to* HELLENA, *looks towards* ANGELICA *to watch her turning; and as she comes towards them, he meets her.*) Sweetheart, the Lady's Name and House—quickly: I'm impatient to be with her.—

HELLENA: (*Aside.*) So now is he for another Woman.

315 WILLMORE: The impudent'st young thing in Nature! I cannot persuade him out of his Error, Madam.

ANGELICA: I know he's in the right,—yet thou'st a Tongue That wou'd persuade him to deny his Faith.

(*In Rage walks away.*)

WILLMORE: (*Said softly to* HELLENA.) Her Name, her Name, dear Boy—

320 HELLENA: Have you forgot it, Sir?

WILLMORE: (*Aside.*) Oh, I perceive he's not to know I am a Stranger to his Lady.
—Yes, yes, I do know—but—I have forgot the—

(ANGELICA *turns.*)

—By Heaven, such early confidence I never saw.

ANGELICA: Did I not charge you with this Mistress, Sir?
325 Which you denied, tho I beheld your Perjury.
This little Generosity of thine has render'd back my Heart.

(*Walks away.*)

WILLMORE: So, you have made sweet work here, my little mischief;
Look your Lady be kind and good-natur'd now, or I shall have but a cursed Bargain on't.

(ANGELICA *turns towards them.*)

330 —The Rogue's bred up to Mischief,
Art thou so great a Fool to credit him?

ANGELICA: Yes, I do; and you in vain impose upon me.
—Come hither, Boy—Is not this he you speak of?

HELLENA: (HELLENA *looks in his Face, he gazes on her.*) I think—
335 it is; I cannot swear, but I vow he has just such another lying Lover's look.

WILLMORE: (*Aside.*) Hah! do not I know that Face?—
By Heaven, my little Gipsy! what a dull Dog was I? Had I but lookt that way, I'd known her.
340 Are all my hopes of a new Woman banisht?
—Egad, if I don't fit thee for this, hang me.
—Madam, I have found out the Plot.

HELLENA: Oh Lord, what does he say? am I discover'd now?

WILLMORE: Do you see this young Spark here?

345 HELLENA: He'll tell her who I am.

WILLMORE: Who do you think this is?

HELLENA: Ay, ay, he does know me.—Nay, dear Captain, I'm undone if you discover me.

WILLMORE: Nay, nay, no cogging; she shall know what a pre-
350 cious Mistress I have.

---

349 **cogging** to cog = to trick, wheedle, or cajole

HELLENA: Will you be such a Devil?

WILLMORE: Nay, nay, I'll teach you to spoil sport you will not make.—This small Ambassador comes not from a Person of Quality, as you imagine, and he says; but from a very er-
355 rant Gipsy, the talkingst, pratingst, cantingst little Animal thou ever saw'st.

ANGELICA: What news you tell me! that's the thing I mean.

HELLENA: (*Aside.*) Wou'd I were well off the place.—If ever I go a Captain-hunting again.—

WILLMORE: Mean that thing? that Gipsy thing? thou may'st 360 as well be jealous of thy Monkey, or Parrot as her: a *German* Motion were worth a dozen of her, and a Dream were a better Enjoyment, a Creature of Constitution fitter for Heaven than Man.

HELLENA: (*Aside.*) Tho I'm sure he lyes, yet this vexes me. 365

ANGELICA: You are mistaken, she's a *Spanish* Woman Made up of no such dull Materials.

WILLMORE: Materials! Egad, and she be made of any that will either dispense, or admit of Love, I'll be bound to conti-
370 nence.

HELLENA: (*Aside to him.*) Unreasonable Man, do you think so?

WILLMORE: You may Return, my little Brazen Head, and tell your Lady, that till she be handsom enough to be belov'd, or I dull enough to be religious, there will be small hopes of me.

ANGELICA: Did you not promise then to marry her? 375

WILLMORE: Not I, by Heaven.

ANGELICA: You cannot undeceive my fears and torments, till you have vow'd you will not marry her.

HELLENA: If he swears that, he'll be reveng'd on me indeed for all my Rogueries. 380

ANGELICA: I know what Arguments you'll bring against me, Fortune and Honour.

WILLMORE: Honour! I tell you, I hate it in your Sex; and those that fancy themselves possest of that Foppery, are the most impertinently troublesom of all Woman-kind, and 385 will transgress nine Commandments to keep one: and to satisfy your Jealousy I swear—

HELLENA: (*Aside to him.*) Oh, no swearing, dear Captain—

WILLMORE: If it were possible I should ever be inclin'd to marry, it should be some kind young Sinner, one that has 390 Generosity enough to give a favour handsomely to one that can ask it discreetly, one that has Wit enough to man-age an Intrigue of Love—oh, how civil such a Wench is, to a Man than does her the Honour to marry her.

ANGELICA: By Heaven, there's no Faith in any thing he says. 395

(*Enter* SEBASTIAN.)

SEBASTIAN: Madam, *Don Antonio*—

ANGELICA: Come hither.

HELLENA: Ha, *Antonio!* he may be coming hither, and he'll cer-tainly discover me, I'll therefore retire without a Ceremony.

(*Exit* HELLENA.)

ANGELICA: I'll see him, get my Coach ready. 400

SEBASTIAN: It waits you, Madam.

WILLMORE: This is lucky: what, Madam, now I may be gone and leave you to the enjoyment of my Rival?

ANGELICA: Dull Man, that canst not see how ill, how poor That false dissimulation looks—Be gone, 405 And never let me see thy cozening Face again,

Lest I relapse and kill thee.
WILLMORE: Yes, you can spare me now,—farewell till you are
in a better Humour—I'm glad of this release—
410   Now for my Gipsy:
For tho to worse we change, yet still we find
New Joys, New Charms, in a new Miss that's kind.

(*Exit* WILLMORE.)

ANGELICA: He's gone, and in this Ague of My Soul
The shivering Fit returns;
415   Oh with what willing haste he took his leave,
As if the long'd for Minute were arriv'd,
Of some blest Assignation.
In vain I have consulted all my Charms,
In vain this Beauty priz'd, in vain believ'd
420   My eyes cou'd kindle any lasting Fires.
I had forgot my Name, my Infamy,
And the Reproach that Honour lays on those
That dare pretend a sober passion here.
Nice Reputation, tho it leave behind
425   More Virtues than inhabit where that dwells,
Yet that once gone, those virtues shine no more.
—Then since I am not fit to belov'd,
I am resolv'd to think on a Revenge
On him that sooth'd me thus to my undoing.

(*Exeunt.*)

SCENE III

A Street.

Enter FLORINDA *and* VALERIA *in Habits different from what they
have been seen in.*

FLORINDA: We're happily escap'd, yet I tremble still.
VALERIA: A Lover and fear! why, I am but half a one, and yet
I have Courage for any Attempt. Would *Hellena* were here.
I wou'd fain have had her as deep in this Mischief as we,
5   she'll fare but ill else I doubt.
FLORINDA: She pretended a Visit to the *Augustine* Nuns, but
I believe some other design carried her out, pray Heavens
we light on her.
VALERIA: When I saw no reason wou'd go good on her, I fol-
10   low'd her into the Wardrobe, and as she was looking for
something in a great Chest, I tumbled her in by the Heels,
snatcht the Key of the Apartment where you were confin'd, lockt her in, and left her bauling for help.
FLORINDA: 'Tis well you resolve to follow my Fortunes, for
15   thou darest never appear at home again after such an Action.
VALERIA: That's according as the young Stranger and I shall
agree—But to our business—I deliver'd your Letter, your
Note to *Belvile,* when I got out under pretence of going
to Mass, I found him at his Lodging, and believe me it
20   came seasonably; for never was Man in so desperate a
Condition. I told him of your Resolution of making your
escape to day, if your Brother would be absent long
enough to permit you; if not, die rather than be *Antonio's.*
FLORINDA: Thou shou'dst have told him I was confin'd to my
25   Chamber upon my Brother's suspicion, that the Business
on the *Molo* was a Plot laid between him and I.

VALERIA: I said all this, and told him your Brother was now
gone to his Devotion, and he resolves to visit every
Church till he find him; and not only undeceive him in
that, but caress him so as shall delay his return home.   30
FLORINDA: Oh Heavens! he's here, and *Belvile* with him too.

(*They put on their Vizards.*)

(*Enter Don* PEDRO, BELVILE, WILLMORE; BELVILE, *and Don* PE-
DRO *seeming in serious Discourse.*)

VALERIA: Walk boldly by them, I'll come at a distance, lest he
suspect us.

(*She walks by them, and looks back on them.*)

WILLMORE: Ha! A Woman! and of an excellent Mien!
PEDRO: She throws a kind look back on you.   35
WILLMORE: Death, tis a likely Wench, and that kind look shall
not be cast away—I'll follow her.
BELVILE: Prithee do not.
WILLMORE: Do not! By Heavens to the Antipodes, with such
an Invitation.   40

(*She goes out, and* WILLMORE *follows her.*)

BELVILE: 'Tis a mad Fellow for a Wench.

(*Enter* FREDERICK.)

FREDERICK: Oh Colonel, such News.
BELVILE: Prithee what?
FREDERICK: News that will make you laugh in spite of Fortune.
BELVILE: What, *Blunt* has had some damn'd Trick put upon   45
him, cheated, bang'd, or clapt?
FREDERICK: Cheated, Sir, rarely cheated of all but his Shirt
and Drawers; the unconscionable Whore too turn'd him
out before Consummation, so that traversing the Streets at
Midnight, the Watch found him in this *Fresco,* and con-   50
ducted him home: By Heaven 'tis such a slight, and yet I
durst as well have been hang'd as laugh at him, or pity
him; he beats all that do but ask him a Question, and is in
such an Humour—
PEDRO: Who is't has met with this ill usage, Sir?   55
BELVILE: (*Aside.*) A Friend of ours, whom you must see for
Mirth's sake. I'll imploy him to give *Florinda* time for an
escape.
PEDRO: Who is he?
BELVILE: A young Countryman of ours, one that has been ed-   60
ucated at so plentiful a rate, he yet ne'er knew the want of
Money, and 'twill be a great Jest to see how simply he'll
look without it. For my part I'll lend him none, and the
Rogue knows not how to put on a borrowing Face, and
ask first. I'll let him see how good 'tis to play our parts   65
whilst I play his—Prithee, *Frederick* do go home and keep
him in that posture till we come.

(*Exeunt.*)

(*Enter* FLORINDA *from the farther end of the Scene, looking behind her.*)

FLORINDA: I am follow'd still—hah—my Brother too advancing this way, good Heavens defend me from being
seen by him.   70

(She goes off.)

(Enter WILLMORE, *and after him* VALERIA, *at a little distance.)*

WILLMORE: Ah! There she sails, she looks back as she were willing to be boarded, I'll warrant her Prize.

(He goes out, VALERIA *following.)*

(Enter HELLENA, *just as he goes out, with a* PAGE.*)*

HELLENA: Hah, is not that my Captain that has a Woman in chase?—'tis not *Angelica.* Boy, follow those People at a dis-
75 tance, and bring me an Account where they go in.—I'll find his Haunts, and plague him every where.—ha—my Brother!

(Exit PAGE. BELVILE, WILLMORE, *and* PEDRO *cross the Stage:* HEL-
LENA *runs off.)*

(Scene changes to another Street. Enter FLORINDA.*)*

FLORINDA: What shall I do, my Brother now pursues me. Will no kind Power protect me from his Tyranny?—Hah, here's
80 a Door open, I'll venture in, since nothing can be worse than to fall into his Hands, my Life and Honour are at stake, and my Necessity has no choice.

(She goes in. Enter VALERIA, *and* HELLENA'S PAGE *peeping after* FLORINDA.*)*

PAGE: Here she went in, I shall remember this House.

(Exit PAGE.*)*

VALERIA: This is *Belvile's* Lodgings; she's gone in as readily as
85 if she knew it—hah—here's that mad Fellow again, I dare not venture in—I'll watch my Opportunity.

(Goes aside. Enter WILLMORE, *gazing about him.)*

WILLMORE: I have lost her hereabouts—Pox on't she must not scape me so.

(Goes out.)

(Scene changes to BLUNT'S *chamber, discovers him sitting on a couch in his shirt and drawers, reading.)*

BLUNT: So, now my Mind's a little at Peace, since I have re-
90 solv'd Revenge—A Pox on this Taylor tho, for not bring-
ing home the Clothes I bespoke; and a Pox of all poor Cavaliers, a Man can never keep a spare Suit for 'em; and I shall have these Rogues come in and find me naked; and then I'm undone; but I'm resolv'd to arm my self—the
95 Rascals shall not insult over me too much.

(Puts on an old rusty Sword and Buff-Belt.)

—Now, how like a Morrice-Dancer I am equipt—a fine Lady-like Whore to cheat me thus, without affording me a Kindness for my Money, a Pox light on her, I shall never be reconciled to the Sex more, she has made me as faithless as
100 a Physician, as uncharitable as a Churchman, and as ill-
natur'd as a Poet. O how I'll use all Womenkind hereafter! what wou'd I give to have one of 'em within my reach now!

any Mortal thing in Petticoats, kind Fortune, send me; and I'll forgive thy last Night's Malice—Here's a cursed Book too, (a Warning to all young Travellers) that can instruct me 105 how to prevent such Mischiefs now 'tis too late. Well 'tis a rare convenient thing to read a little now and then, as well as hawk and hunt.

(Sits down again and reads.)

(Enter to him FLORINDA.*)*

FLORINDA: This House is haunted sure, 'tis well furnisht and no living thing inhabits it—hah—a Man! Heavens how 110 he's attir'd! sure 'tis some Rope-dancer, or Fencing-Master; I tremble now for fear, and yet I must venture now to speak to him—Sir, if I may not interrupt your Meditations—

(He starts up and gazes.)

BLUNT: Hah—what's here? Are my wishes granted? and is not that a she Creature? Adsheartlikins 'tis! what wretched 115 thing art thou—hah!
FLORINDA: Charitable Sir, you've told your self already what I am; a very wretched Maid, forc'd by a strange unlucky Accident, to seek a safety here, and must be ruin'd, if you do not grant it. 120
BLUNT: Ruin'd! Is there any Ruin so inevitable as that which now threatens thee? Dost thou know, miserable Woman, into what Den of Mischiefs thou art fall'n? what a Bliss of Confusion?—hah—dost not see something in my looks that frights thy guilty Soul, and makes thee wish to change 125 that Shape of Woman for any humble Animal, or Devil? for those were safer for thee, and less mischievous.
FLORINDA: Alas, what mean you, Sir? I must confess your Looks have something in 'em makes me fear; but I be-
seech you, as you seem a Gentleman, pity a harmless Vir- 130
gin, that takes your House for Sanctuary.
BLUNT: Talk on, talk on, and weep too, till my faith return. Do, flatter me out of my Senses again—a harmless Virgin with a Pox, as much one as t'other, adsheartlikins. Why, what the Devil can I not be safe in my House for you? not 135 in my Chamber? nay, even being naked too cannot secure me. This is an Impudence greater than has invaded me yet.—Come, no Resistance.

(Pulls her rudely.)

FLORINDA: Dare you be so cruel?
BLUNT: Cruel, adsheartlikins as a Gally-slave, or a *Spanish* 140 Whore: Cruel, yes, I will kiss and beat thee all over; kiss, and see thee all over; thou shalt lie with me too, not that I care for the Injoyment, but to let you see I have ta'en de-
liberated Malice to thee, and will be revenged on one Whore for the Sins of another; I will smile and deceive 145 thee, flatter thee, and beat thee, kiss and swear, and lye to thee, imbrace thee and rob thee, as she did me, fawn on thee, and strip thee stark naked, then hang thee out at my Window by the Heels, with a Paper of scurvey Verses fasten'd to thy Breast, in praise of damnable Women—Come, 150 come along.
FLORINDA: Alas, Sir, must I be sacrific'd for the Crimes of the most infamous of my Sex? I never understood the Sins you name.

BLUNT: Do, persuade the Fool you love him, or that one of you
155   can be just or honest; tell me I was not an easy Coxcomb, or
any strange impossible Tale: it will be believ'd sooner than
thy false Showers or Protestations. A Generation of damn'd
Hypocrites, to flatter my very Clothes from my back! dissembling Witches! are these the Returns you make an hon-
160   est Gentleman that trusts, believes, and loves you?—But if I
be not even with you—Come along, or I shall—

(*Pulls her again.*)

(*Enter* FREDERICK.)

FREDERICK: Hah, what's here to do?
BLUNT: Adsheartlikins, *Frederick* I am glad thou art come, to
be a Witness of my dire Revenge.
165   FREDERICK: What's this, a Person of Quality too, who is upon
the Ramble to supply the Defects of some grave impotent
Husband?
BLUNT: No, this has another Pretence, some very unfortunate
Accident brought her hither, to save a Life pursued by I
170   know not who, or why, and forc'd to take Sanctuary here
at Fools Haven. Adsheartlikins to me of all Mankind for
Protection? Is the Ass to be cajol'd again, think ye? No,
young one, no Prayers or Tears shall mitigate my Rage;
therefore prepare for both my Pleasure of Enjoyment and
175   Revenge, for I am resolved to make up my Loss here on
thy Body, I'll take it out in kindness and in beating.
FREDERICK: Now, Mistress of mine, what do you think of this?
FLORINDA: I think he will not—dares not be so barbarous.
FREDERICK: Have a care, *Blunt,* she fetch'd a deep Sigh, she is
180   inamour'd with thy Shirt and Drawers, she'll strip thee
even of that. There are of her Calling such unconscionable
Baggages, and such dexterous Thieves, they'll flea a Man,
and he shall ne'er miss his Skin, till he feels the Cold.
There was a Country-man of ours robb'd of a Row of
185   Teeth whilst he was sleeping, which the Jilt made him buy
again when he wak'd—You see, Lady, how little Reason
we have to trust you.
BLUNT: 'Dsheartlikins, why, this is most abominable.
FLORINDA: Some such Devils there may be, but by all that's
190   holy I am none such, I entered here to save a Life in danger.
BLUNT: For no goodness I'll warrant her.
FREDERICK: Faith, Damsel, you had e'en confess the plain
Truth, for we are Fellows not to be caught twice in the
same Trap: Look on that Wreck, a tight Vessel when he set
195   out of Haven, well trim'd and laden, and see how a Female
Piccaroon of this Island of Rogues has shatter'd him, and
canst thou hope for any Mercy?
BLUNT: No, no, Gentlewoman, come along, adsheartlikins we
must be better acquainted—we'll both lie with her, and
200   then let me alone to bang her.
FREDERICK: I am ready to serve you in matters of Revenge,
that has a double Pleasure in't.
BLUNT: Well said. You hear, little one, how you are condem-
n'd by publick Vote to the Bed within, there's no resisting
205   your Destiny, Sweetheart.

(*Pulls her.*)

FLORINDA: Stay, Sir, I have seen you with *Belvile,* an *English*
Cavalier, for his sake use me kindly; you know how, Sir.

BLUNT: *Belvile!* why, yes, Sweeting, we do know *Belvile,* and
wish he were with us now, he's a Cormorant at Whore and
Bacon, he'd have a Limb or two of thee, my Virgin Pullet: 210
but 'tis no matter, we'll leave him the Bones to pick.
FLORINDA: Sir, if you have any Esteem for that *Belvile,* I conjure you to treat me with more Gentleness; he'll thank
you for the Justice.
FREDERICK: Hark ye, *Blunt,* I doubt we are mistaken in this   215
matter.
FLORINDA: Sir, If you find me not worth *Belvile's* Care, use
me as you please; and that you may think I merit better
treatment than you threaten—pray take this Present—

(*Gives him a Ring: He looks on it.*)

BLUNT: Hum—A Diamond! why, 'tis a wonderful Virtue now   220
that lies in this Ring, a mollifying Virtue; adsheartlikins
there's more persuasive Rhetorick in't, than all her Sex
can utter.
FREDERICK: I begin to suspect something; and 'twou'd anger
us vilely to be truss'd up for a Rape upon a Maid of Qual-   225
ity, when we only believe we ruffle a Harlot.
BLUNT: Thou art a credulous Fellow, but adsheartlikins I have
no Faith yet; why, my Saint prattled as parlously as this
does, she gave me a Bracelet too, a Devil on her: but I sent
my Man to sell it to day for Necessaries, and it prov'd as   230
counterfeit as her Vows of Love.
FREDERICK: However let it reprieve her till we see *Belvile.*
BLUNT: That's hard, yet I will grant it.

(*Enter a* SERVANT.)

SERVANT: Oh, Sir, the Colonel is just come with his new
Friend and a *Spaniard* of Quality, and talks of having you   235
to Dinner with 'em.
BLUNT: 'Dsheartlikins, I'm undone—I would not see 'em for
the World: Harkye, *Frederick* lock up the Wench in your
Chamber.
FREDERICK: Fear nothing, Madam, whate'er he threatens,   240
you're safe whilst in my Hands.

(*Exit* FREDERICK *and* FLORINDA.)

BLUNT: And, Sirrah—upon your Life, say—I am not at
home—or that I am asleep—or—or any thing—away—
I'll prevent them coming this way.

(*Locks the Door and Exeunt.*)

ACT FIVE

SCENE I

BLUNT'*s Chamber.*

After a great knocking as at his Chamber-door, enter BLUNT *softly,
crossing the Stage in his Shirt and Drawers, as before.*

(*Call within.*) Ned, Ned Blunt, Ned Blunt.

BLUNT: The Rogues are up in Arms, 'dsheartlikins, this villainous *Frederick* has betray'd me, they have heard of my
blessed Fortune.

(*And knocking within.*) Ned Blunt, Ned, Ned—   5

BELVILE: Why, he's dead, sir, without dispute dead, he has not been seen to day; let's break open the Door—here—Boy—

BLUNT: Ha, break open the Door! 'dsheartlikins that mad Fellow will be as good as his word.

10 BELVILE: Boy, bring something to force the Door.

(*A great noise within at the Door again.*)

BLUNT: So, now must I speak in my own Defence, I'll try what Rhetorick will do—hold—hold, what do you mean, Gentlemen, what do you mean?

BELVILE: Oh Rogue, art alive? prithee open the Door, and

15 convince us.

BLUNT: Yes, I am alive, Gentlemen—but at present a little busy.

BELVILE: (*Within.*) How! *Blunt* grown a man of Business! come, come, open, and let's see this Miracle.

BLUNT: No, no, no, no, Gentlemen, 'tis no great Business—

20 but—I am—at—my Devotion,—'dsheartlikins, will you not allow a man time to pray?

BELVILE: (*Within.*) Turn'd religious! a greater Wonder than the first, therefore open quickly, or we shall unhinge, we shall.

BLUNT: This won't do—Why, hark ye, Colonel; to tell you

25 the plain Truth, I am about a necessary Affair of Life.—I have a Wench with me—you apprehend me? the Devil's in't if they be so uncivil as to disturb me now.

WILLMORE: How, a Wench! Nay, then we must enter and partake; no Resistance,—unless it be your Lady of Quality,

30 and then we'll keep our distance.

BLUNT: So, the Business is out.

WILLMORE: Come, come, lend more hands to the Door,—now heave altogether—so, well done, my Boys—

(*Breaks open the Door. Enter* BELVILE, WILLMORE, FREDERICK, PEDRO, *and* BELVILE's *page:* BLUNT *looks simply, they all laugh at him, he lays his hand on his Sword, and comes up to* WILLMORE.)

BLUNT: Hark ye, Sir, laugh out your laugh quickly, d'ye hear,

35 and be gone, I shall spoil your sport else; 'dsheartlikins, Sir, I shall—the Jest has been carried on too long,—(*Aside.*) a Plague upon my Taylor—

WILLMORE: 'Sdeath, how the Whore has drest him! Faith, Sir, I'm sorry.

40 BLUNT: Are you so, Sir? keep't to your self then, Sir, I advise you, d'ye hear? for I can as little endure your Pity as his Mirth.

(*Lays his Hand on's Sword.*)

BELVILE: Indeed, *Willmore,* thou wert a little too rough with *Ned Blunt's* Mistress; call a Person of Quality Whore, and one so young, so handsome, and so eloquent!—ha, ha, ha.

45 BLUNT: Hark ye, Sir, you know me, and know I can be angry; have a care—for 'dsheartlikins I can fight too—I can, Sir,—do you mark me—no more.

BELVILE: Why so peevish, good *Ned?* some Disappointments, I'll warrant—What! did the jealous Count her Husband

50 return just in the nick?

(*They laugh.*)

BLUNT: Or the Devil, Sir,—d'ye laugh? Look ye, settle me a good sober Countenance, and that quickly too, or you shall know *Ned Blunt* is not—

BELVILE: Not every Body, we know that.

55 BLUNT: Not an Ass, to be laught at, Sir.

WILLMORE: Unconscionable Sinner, to bring a Lover so near his Happiness, a vigorous passionate Lover, and then not only cheat him of his Moveables, but his Desires too.

BELVILE: Ah, Sir, a Mistress is a Trifle with *Blunt,* he'll have a

60 dozen the next time he looks abroad; his Eyes have Charms not to be resisted: There needs no more than to expose that taking Person to the view of the Fair, and he leads 'em all in Triumph.

PEDRO: Sir, tho I'm a stranger to you, I'm ashamed at the

65 rudeness of my Nation; and could you learn who did it, would assist you to make an Example of 'em.

BLUNT: Why, ay, there's one speaks sense now, and handsomly; and let me tell you Gentlemen, I should not have shew'd my self like a Jack-Pudding, thus to have made you Mirth, but that

70 I have revenge within my power; for know, I have got into my possession a Female, who had better have fallen under any Curse, than the Ruin I design her: 'dsheartlikins, she assaulted me here in my own Lodgings, and had doubtless committed a Rape upon me, had not this Sword defended me.

75 FREDERICK: I knew not that, but o' my Conscience thou hadst ravisht her, had she not redeem'd her self with a Ring—let's see't, *Blunt.*

(BLUNT *shews the Ring.*)

BELVILE: (*Goes to whisper to him.*) Hah!—the Ring I gave *Florinda* when we exchang'd our Vows!—hark ye, *Blunt*—

80 WILLMORE: No whispering, good Colonel, there's a Woman in the case, no whispering.

BELVILE: Hark ye, Fool, be advis'd, and conceal both the Ring and the Story, for your Reputation's sake; don't let People know what despis'd Cullies we *English* are: to be cheated

85 and abus'd by one Whore, and another rather bribe thee than be kind to thee, is an Infamy to our Nation.

WILLMORE: Come, come, where's the Wench! we'll see her, let her be what she will, we'll see her.

PEDRO: Ay, ay, let us see her, I can soon discover whether she

90 be of Quality, or for your Diversion.

BLUNT: She's in *Frederick's* Custody.

WILLMORE: Come, come, the Key.

(*To* FREDERICK *who gives him the Key, they are going.*)

BELVILE: Death! what shall I do?—stay, Gentlemen—yet if I hinder 'em, I shall discover all—hold, let's go one at

95 once—give me the Key.

WILLMORE: Nay, hold there, Colonel, I'll go first.

FREDERICK: Nay, no Dispute, *Ned* and I have the property of her.

WILLMORE: Damn Property—then we'll draw Cuts.

(BELVILE *goes to whisper* WILLMORE.)

Nay, no Corruption, good Colonel: come, the longest Sword carries her.—

100 (*They all draw, forgetting Don* PEDRO, *being a Spaniard, had the longest.*)

BLUNT: I yield up my Interest to you Gentlemen, and that will be Revenge sufficient.

WILLMORE: The Wench is yours—(*To* PEDRO.) Pox of his *Toledo,* I had forgot that.

105 FREDERICK: Come, Sir, I'll conduct you to the Lady.

(*Exit* FREDERICK *and* PEDRO.)

BELVILE: (*Aside.*) To hinder him will certainly discover—
Dost know, dull Beast, what Mischief thou hast done?

(WILLMORE *walking up and down out of Humour.*)

WILLMORE: Ay, ay, to trust our Fortune to Lots, a Devil on't,
'twas madness, that's the Truth on't.

110 BELVILE: Oh intolerable Sot!

(*Enter* FLORINDA, *running masqu'd,* PEDRO *after her,* WILLMORE *gazing round her.*)

FLORINDA: (*Aside.*) Good Heaven, defend me from discovery.
PEDRO: 'Tis but in vain to fly me, you are fallen to my Lot.
BELVILE: Sure she is undiscover'd yet, but now I fear there is
no way to bring her off.

115 WILLMORE: Why, what a Pox is not this my Woman, the same
I follow'd but now?

(PEDRO *talking to* FLORINDA, *who walks up and down.*)

PEDRO: As if I did not know ye, and your Business here.
FLORINDA: (*Aside.*) Good Heaven! I fear he does indeed—
PEDRO: Come, pray be kind, I know you meant to be so
120   when you enter'd here, for these are proper Gentlemen.
WILLMORE: But, Sir—perhaps the Lady will not be impos'd
upon, she'll chuse her Man.
PEDRO: I am better bred, than not to leave her Choice free.

(*Enter* VALERIA, *and is surpriz'd at the Sight of Don* PEDRO.)

VALERIA: (*Aside.*) Don *Pedro* here! there's no avoiding him.
125 FLORINDA: (*Aside.*) *Valeria!* then I'm undone—
VALERIA: (*To* PEDRO, *running to him.*) Oh! have I found you,
Sir—
—The strangest Accident—if I had breath—to tell it.
PEDRO: Speak—is *Florinda* safe? *Hellena* well?
130 VALERIA: Ay, ay, Sir—*Florinda*—is safe—from any fears of you.
PEDRO: Why, where's *Florinda?*—speak.
VALERIA: Ay, where indeed, Sir? I wish I could inform you,—
But to hold you no longer in doubt—
FLORINDA: (*Aside.*) Oh, what will she say!
135 VALERIA: She's fled away in the Habit of one of her Pages,
Sir—but *Callis* thinks you may retrieve her yet, if you
make haste away; she'll tell you, Sir, the rest—(*Aside.*) if
you can find her out.
PEDRO: Dishonourable Girl, she has undone my Aim—Sir—
140   you see my necessity of leaving you, and I hope you'll pardon it: my Sister, I know, will make her flight to you; and
if she do, I shall expect she should be render'd back.
BELVILE: I shall consult my Love and Honour, Sir.

(*Exit* PEDRO.)

FLORINDA: (*To* VALERIA.) My dear Preserver, let me imbrace
145   thee.
WILLMORE: What the Devil's all this?

BLUNT: Mystery by this Light.
VALERIA: Come, come, make haste and get your selves married quickly, for your Brother will return again.
BELVILE: I am so surpriz'd with Fears and Joys, so amaz'd to   150
find you here in safety, I can scarce persuade my Heart
into a Faith of what I see—
WILLMORE: Harkye, Colonel, is this that Mistress who has cost
you so many Sighs, and me so many Quarrels with you?
BELVILE: It is—(*To* FLORINDA.) Pray give him the Honour of   155
your Hand.
WILLMORE: Thus it must be receiv'd then.

(*Kneels and kisses her Hand.*)

And with it give your Pardon too.
FLORINDA: The Friend to *Belvile* may command me anything.
WILLMORE: (*Aside.*) Death, wou'd I might, 'tis a surprizing   160
Beauty.
BELVILE: Boy, run and fetch a Father instantly.

(*Exit* PAGE.)

FREDERICK: So, now do I stand like a Dog, and have not a
Syllable to plead my own Cause with: by this Hand,
Madam, I was never thorowly confounded before, nor   165
shall I ever more dare look up with Confidence, till you
are pleased to pardon me.
FLORINDA: Sir, I'll be reconcil'd to you on one Condition,
that you'll follow the Example of your Friend, in marry-
ing a Maid that does not hate you, and whose Fortune (I   170
believe) will not be unwelcome to you.
FREDERICK: Madam, had I no Inclinations that way, I shou'd
obey your kind Commands.
BELVILE: Who, *Frederick* marry; he has so few Inclinations for
Womankind, that had he been possest of Paradise, he   175
might have continu'd there to this Day, if no Crime but
Love cou'd have disinherited him.
FREDERICK: Oh, I do not use to boast of my Intrigues.
BELVILE: Boast! why thou do'st nothing but boast; and I dare
swear, wer't thou as innocent from the Sin of the Grape, as   180
thou art from the Apple, thou might'st yet claim that right
in *Eden* which our first Parents lost by too much loving.
FREDERICK: I wish this Lady would think me so modest a Man.
VALERIA: She shou'd be sorry then, and not like you half so
well, and I shou'd be loth to break my Word with you;   185
which was, That if your Friend and mine are agreed, it
shou'd be a Match between you and I.

(*She gives him her Hand.*)

FREDERICK: Bear witness, Colonel, 'tis a Bargain.

(*Kisses her Hand.*)

BLUNT: (*To* FLORINDA.) I have a Pardon to beg too; but adsheartlikins I am so out of Countenance, that I am a Dog   190
if I can say any thing to purpose.
FLORINDA: Sir, I heartily forgive you all.
BLUNT: That's nobly said, sweet Lady—*Belvile,* prithee present her her Ring again, for I find I have not Courage to
approach her my self.   195

(*Gives him the Ring, he gives it to* FLORINDA. *Enter* BOY.)

BOY: Sir, I have brought the Father that you sent for.

BELVILE: 'Tis well, and now my dear *Florinda*, let's fly to compleat that mighty Joy we have so long wish'd and sigh'd for. Come, *Frederick* you'll follow?

200 FREDERICK: Your Example, Sir, 'twas ever my Ambition in War, and must be so in Love.

WILLMORE: And must not I see this juggling Knot ty'd?

BELVILE: No, thou shalt do us better Service, and be our Guard, lest Don *Pedro's* sudden Return interrupt the Ceremony.

205 WILLMORE: Content; I'll secure this Pass.

(*Exit* BELVILE, FLORINDA, FREDERICK, *and* VALERIA. *Enter page.*)

BOY: (*To* WILLMORE.) Sir, there's a Lady without wou'd speak to you.

WILLMORE: Conduct her in, I dare not quit my Post.

BOY: And, Sir, your Taylor waits you in your Chamber.

210 BLUNT: Some comfort yet, I shall not dance naked at the Wedding.

(*Exit* BLUNT *and* BOY.)

(*Enter again the* BOY, *conducting in* ANGELICA *in a masquing Habit and a Vizard*, WILLMORE *runs to her.*)

WILLMORE: This can be none but my pretty Gipsy—Oh, I see you can follow as well as fly—Come, confess thy self the most malicious Devil in Nature, you think you have done

215 my Bus'ness with *Angelica*—

ANGELICA: Stand off, base Villain—

(*She draws a Pistol and holds to his Breast.*)

WILLMORE: Hah, 'tis not she: who art thou? and what's thy Business?

ANGELICA: One thou hast injur'd, and who comes to kill thee

220 for't.

WILLMORE: What the Devil canst thou mean?

ANGELICA: By all my Hopes to kill thee—

(*Holds still the Pistol to his Breast, he going back, she following still.*)

WILLMORE: Prithee on what Acquaintance? for I know thee not.

ANGELICA: Behold this Face!—so lost to thy Remembrance!

225 And then call all thy Sins about thy Soul,

(*Pulls off her Vizard.*)

And let them die with thee.

WILLMORE: *Angelica!*

ANGELICA: Yes, Traitor.

Does not thy guilty Blood run shivering thro thy Veins?

230 Hast thou no Horrour at this Sight, that tells thee,

Thou hast not long to boast thy shameful Conquest?

WILLMORE: Faith, no Child, my Blood keeps its old Ebbs and Flows still, and that usual Heat too, that cou'd oblige thee with a Kindness, had I but opportunity.

235 ANGELICA: Devil! dost wanton with my Pain—have at thy Heart.

WILLMORE: Hold, dear Virago! hold thy Hand a little,

I am not now at leisure to be kill'd—hold and hear me—

(*Aside.*) Death, I think she's in earnest.

ANGELICA: (*Aside, turning from him.*) Oh if I take not heed,

My coward Heart will leave me to his Mercy.   240

—What have you, Sir, to say?—but should I hear thee,

Thoud'st talk away all that is brave about me:

(*Follows him with the Pistol to his Breast.*)

And I have vow'd thy Death, by all that's sacred.

WILLMORE: Why, then, there's an end of a proper handsom

Fellow, that might have liv'd to have done good Service 245

yet:—That's all I can say to't.

ANGELICA: (*Pausingly.*) Yet—I wou'd give thee—time for Penitence.

WILLMORE: Faith, Child, I thank God, I have ever took care

to lead a good, sober, hopeful Life, and am of a Religion

that teaches me to believe, I shall depart in Peace.   250

ANGELICA: So will the Devil: tell me

How many poor believing Fools thou hast undone;

How many Hearts thou hast betray'd to ruin!

—Yet, these are little Mischiefs to the Ills

Thou'st taught mine to commit: thou'st taught it Love.   255

WILLMORE: Egad, 'twas shrewdly hurt the while.

ANGELICA: —Love, that has robb'd it of its Unconcern,

Of all that Pride that taught me how to value it,

And in its room a mean submissive Passion was convey'd,

That made me humbly bow, which I ne'er did   260

To any thing but Heaven.

—Thou, perjur'd Man, didst this, and with thy Oaths,

Which on thy Knees thou didst devoutly make,

Soften'd my yielding Heart—And then, I was a Slave—

Yet still had been content to've worn my Chains,   265

Worn 'em with Vanity and Joy for ever,

Hadst thou not broke those Vows that put them on.

—'Twas then I was undone.

(*All this while follows him with a Pistol to his Breast.*)

WILLMORE: Broke my Vows! why, where hast thou lived?

Amongst the Gods! For I never heard of mortal Man,   270

That has not broke a thousand Vows.

ANGELICA: Oh, Impudence!

WILLMORE: *Angelica!* that Beauty has been too long tempting,

Not to have made a thousand Lovers languish,

Who in the amorous Favour, no doubt have sworn   275

Like me; did they all die in that Faith? still adoring?

I do not think they did.

ANGELICA: No, faithless Man: had I repaid their Vows, as I did

thine, I wou'd have kill'd the ungrateful that had aban-

don'd me.   280

WILLMORE: This old General has quite spoil'd thee, nothing

makes a Woman so vain, as being flatter'd; your old Lover

ever supplies the Defects of Age, with intolerable Dotage,

vast Charge, and that which you call Constancy; and at-

tributing all this to your own Merits, you domineer, and 285

throw your Favours in's Teeth, upbraiding him still with

the Defects of Age, and cuckold him as often as he de-

ceives your Expectations. But the gay, young, brisk Lover,

that brings his equal Fires, and can give you Dart for Dart,

he'll be as nice as you sometimes.   290

ANGELICA: All this thou'st made me know, for which I hate thee.

Had I remain'd in innocent Security,
I shou'd have thought all Men were born my Slaves;
And worn my Pow'r like Lightning in my Eyes,
295   To have destroy'd at Pleasure when offended.
—But when Love held the Mirror, the undeceiving Glass
Reflected all the Weakness of my Soul, and made me
      know,
My richest Treasure being lost, my Honour,
All the remaining Spoil cou'd not be worth
300   The Conqueror's Care or Value.
—Oh how I fell like a long worship'd Idol,
Discovering all the Cheat!
Wou'd not the Incense and rich Sacrifice,
Which blind Devotion offer'd at my Altars,
305   Have fall'n to thee?
Why woud'st thou then destroy my fancy'd Power?
WILLMORE: By Heaven thou art brave, and I admire thee
      strangely.
I wish I were that dull, that constant thing,
Which thou woud'st have, and Nature never meant me:
310   I must, like chearful Birds, sing in all Groves,
And perch on every Bough,
Billing the next kind She that flies to meet me;
Yet after all cou'd build my Nest with thee,
Thither repairing when I'd lov'd my round,
315   And still reserve a tributary Flame.

(*Offers her a Purse of Gold.*)

—To gain your Credit, I'll pay you back your Charity,
And be oblig'd for nothing but for Love.
ANGELICA: Oh that thou wert in earnest!
So mean a Thought of me,
320   Wou'd turn my Rage to Scorn, and I shou'd pity thee,
And give thee leave to live;
Which for the publick Safety of our Sex,
And my own private Injuries, I dare not do.
Prepare—

(*Follows still, as before.*)

325   —I will no more be tempted with Replies.
WILLMORE: Sure—
ANGELICA: Another Word will damn thee! I've heard thee talk
      too long.

(*She follows him with a Pistol ready to shoot: he retires still amaz'd.*)

(*Enter Don* ANTONIO, *his Arm in a Scarf, and lays hold on the Pistol.*)

ANTONIO: Hah! *Angelica!*
ANGELICA: *Antonio!* What Devil brought thee hither?
330   ANTONIO: Love and Curiosity, seeing your Coach at Door.
Let me disarm you of this unbecoming Instrument of
Death.—

(*Takes away the Pistol.*)

Amongst the Number of your Slaves, was there not one
      worthy the Honour to have fought your Quarrel?
335   —Who are you, Sir, that are so very wretched

To merit Death from her?
WILLMORE: One, sir, that cou'd have made a better End of an
amorous Quarrel without you, than with you.
ANTONIO: Sure 'tis some Rival—hah—the very Man took
down her Picture yesterday—the very same that set on me   340
last night—Blest opportunity—

(*Offers to shoot him.*)

ANGELICA: Hold, you're mistaken, Sir.
ANTONIO: By Heaven the very same!
—Sir, what pretensions have you to this Lady?
WILLMORE: Sir, I don't use to be examin'd, and am ill at all   345
      Disputes but this—

(*Draws,* ANTONIO *offers to shoot.*)

ANGELICA: (*To* WILLMORE.) Oh, hold! you see he's arm'd
      with certain Death:
—And you, *Antonio,* I command you hold,
By all the Passion you've so lately vow'd me.

(*Enter Don* PEDRO, *sees* ANTONIO, *and stays.*)

PEDRO: (*Aside.*) Hah, *Antonio!* and *Angelica!*   350
ANTONIO: When I refuse Obedience to your Will,
May you destroy me with your mortal Hate.
By all that's Holy I adore you so,
That even my Rival, who has Charms enough
To make him fall a Victim to my Jealousy,   355
Shall live, nay, and have leave to love on still.
PEDRO: (*Aside.*) What's this I hear?
ANGELICA: (*Pointing to* WILLMORE.) Ah thus, 'twas thus he
      talk'd, and I believ'd.
—*Antonio,* yesterday,
I'd not have sold my Interest in his Heart,   360
For all the Sword has won and lost in Battle.
—But now to show my utmost of Contempt,
I give thee Life—which if thou would'st preserve,
Live where my Eyes may never see thee more,
Live to undo some one, whose Soul may prove   365
So bravely constant to revenge my Love.

(*Goes out,* ANTONIO *follows, but* PEDRO *pulls him back.*)

PEDRO: *Antonio*—stay.
ANTONIO: Don *Pedro*—
PEDRO: What Coward Fear was that prevented thee
From meeting me this Morning on the *Molo*?   370
ANTONIO: Meet you?
PEDRO: Yes me; I was the Man that dar'd thee to't.
ANTONIO: Hast thou so often seen me fight in War,
To find no better Cause to excuse my Absence?
—I sent my Sword and one to do thee Right,   375
Finding my self uncapable to use a Sword.
PEDRO: But 'twas *Florinda's* Quarrel that we fought,
And you to shew how little you esteem'd her,
Sent me your Rival, giving him your Interest.
—But I have found the Cause of this Affront,   380
But when I meet you fit for the Dispute,
—I'll tell you my Resentment.

ANTONIO: I shall be ready, Sir, e'er long to do your Reason.

(*Exit* ANTONIO.)

385 PEDRO: If I cou'd find *Florinda,* now whilst my Anger's high, I think I shou'd be kind, and give her to *Belvile* in Revenge.

WILLMORE: Faith, Sir, I know not what you wou'd do, but I be-lieve the Priest within has been so kind.

PEDRO: How! my Sister married?

390 WILLMORE: I hope by this time she is, and bedded too, or he has not my longings about him.

PEDRO: Dares he do thus? Does he not fear my Pow'r?

WILLMORE: Faith not at all. If you will go in, and thank him for the Favour he has done your Sister, so; if not, Sir, my Power's greater in this House than yours; I have a damn'd 395 surly Crew here, that will keep you till the next Tide, and then clap you an board my Prize; my Ship lies but a League off the *Molo,* and we shall show your Donship a damn'd *Tramontana* Rover's Trick.

(*Enter* BELVILE.)

BELVILE: This Rogue's in some new Mischief—hah, *Pedro* re-400 turn'd!

PEDRO: Colonel *Belvile,* I hear you have married my Sister.

BELVILE: You have heard truth then, Sir.

PEDRO: Have I so? then, Sir, I wish you Joy.

BELVILE: How!

405 PEDRO: By this Embrace I do, and I glad on't.

BELVILE: Are you in earnest?

PEDRO: By our long Friendship and my Obligations to thee, I am. The sudden Change I'll give you Reasons for anon. Come lead me into my Sister, that she may know I now 410 approve her Choice.

(*Exit* BELVILE *with* PEDRO. WILLMORE *goes to follow them. Enter* HELLENA *as before in Boy's Clothes, and pulls him back.*)

WILLMORE: Ha! my Gipsy—Now a thousand Blessings on thee for this Kindness. Egad, Child, I was e'en in despair of ever seeing thee again; my Friends are all provided for within, each Man his kind Woman.

415 HELLENA: Hah! I thought they had serv'd me some such Trick.

WILLMORE: And I was e'en resolv'd to go aboard, condemn my self to my lone Cabin, and the Thoughts of thee.

HELLENA: And cou'd you have left me behind? wou'd you have been so ill-natur'd?

420 WILLMORE: Why, 'twou'd have broke my Heart, Child—but since we are met again, I defy foul Weather to part us.

HELLENA: And wou'd you be a faithful Friend now, if a Maid shou'd trust you?

WILLMORE: For a Friend I cannot promise, thou art of a 425 Form so excellent, a Face and Humour too good for cold dull Friendship; I am parlously afraid of being in love, Child, and you have not forgot how severely you have us'd me.

HELLENA: That's all one, such Usage you must still look for, to find out all your Haunts, to rail at you to all that love

you, till I have made you love only me in your own De- 430 fence, because no body else will love.

WILLMORE: But hast thou no better Quality to recommend thy self by?

HELLENA: Faith none, Captain—Why, 'twill be the greater Charity to take me for thy Mistress, I am a lone Child, a 435 kind of Orphan Lover; and why I shou'd die a Maid, and in a Captain's Hands too, I do not understand.

WILLMORE: Egad, I was never claw'd away with Broad-Sides from any Female before, thou hast one Virtue I adore, good-Nature; I hate a coy demure Mistress, she's as trou- 440 blesom as a Colt, I'll break none; no, give me a mad Mis-tress when mew'd, and in flying on[e] I dare trust upon the Wing, that whilst she's kind will come to the Lure.

HELLENA: Nay, as kind as you will, good Captain, whilst it lasts, but let's lose no time. 445

WILLMORE: My time's as precious to me, as thine can be; therefore, dear Creature, since we are so well agreed, let's retire to my Chamber, and if ever thou were treated with such savory Love—Come—My Bed's prepar'd for such a Guest, all clean and sweet as thy fair self; I love to steal a 450 Dish and a Bottle with a Friend, and hate long Graces—Come, let's re-tire and fall to.

HELLENA: 'Tis but getting my Consent, and the Business is soon done; let but old Gaffer *Hymen* and his Priest say Amen to't, and I dare lay my Mother's Daughter by as proper a Fel- 455 low as your Father's Son, without fear or blushing.

WILLMORE: Hold, hold, no Bugg Words, Child, Priest and *Hymen:* prithee add Hangman to 'em to make up the Consort—No, no, we'll have no Vows but Love, Child, nor Witness but the Lover; the kind Diety injoins naught but 460 love and enjoy. *Hymen* and Priest wait still upon Portion, and Joynture; Love and Beauty have their own Cere-monies. Marriage is as certain a Bane to Love, as lending Money is to Friendship: I'll neither ask nor give a Vow, tho I could be content to turn Gipsy, and become a Left-hand 465 Bridegroom, to have the Pleasure of working that great Miracle of making a Maid a Mother, if you durst venture; 'tis upse Gipsy that, and if I miss, I'll lose my Labour.

HELLENA: And if you do not lose, what shall I get? A Cradle full of Noise and Mischief, with a Pack of Repentance at 470 my Back? Can you teach me to weave Incle to pass my time with? 'Tis upse Gipsy that too.

WILLMORE: I can teach thee to weave a true Love's Knot better.

HELLENA: So can my Dog.

WILLMORE: Well, I see we are both upon our Guard, and I see 475 there's no way to conquer good Nature, but by yielding—here—give me thy Hand—one Kiss and I am thine—

HELLENA: One Kiss! How like my Page he speaks; I am resolv'd you shall have none, for asking such a sneaking Sum—He that will be satisfied with one Kiss, will never die of that 480 Longing; good Friend single-Kiss, is all your talking come to this? A Kiss, a Caudle! farewel, Captain single-Kiss.

(*Going out he stays her.*)

---

398 *Tramontana* Italian and Spanish *tramontano* = from beyond the mountains

468 **upse** *Op zijn* (Dutch) = in the fashion or manner of, *Upse Gipsy* = like a gipsy   471 **Incle** linen thread or yarn which was woven into a tape once very much in use

WILLMORE: Nay, if we part so, let me die like a Bird upon a
    Bough, at the Sheriff's Charge. By Heaven, both the *Indies*
485 shall not buy thee from me. I adore thy Humour and will
    marry thee, and we are so of one Humour, it must be a
    Bargain—give me thy Hand—

(*Kisses her hand.*)

    And now let the blind ones (Love and Fortune) do their worst.
HELLENA: Why, God-a-mercy, Captain!
490 WILLMORE: But harkye—The Bargain is now made; but is it
    not fit we should know each other's Names? That when
    we have Reason to curse one another hereafter, and Peo-
    ple ask me who 'tis I give to the Devil, I may at least be
    able to tell what Family you came of.
495 HELLENA: Good reason, Captain; and where I have cause, (as I
    doubt not but I shall have plentiful) that I may know at
    whom to throw my—Blessings—I beseech ye your Name.
WILLMORE: I am call'd *Robert the Constant*.
HELLENA: A very fine Name! pray was it your Faulkner or
500 Butler that christen'd you? Do they not use to whistle
    when then call you?
WILLMORE: I hope you have a better, that a Man may name
    without crossing himself, you are so merry with mine.
HELLENA: I am call'd *Hellena the Inconstant*.

(*Enter* PEDRO, BELVILE, FLORINDA, FREDERICK, *and* VALERIA.)

505 PEDRO: Hah! *Hellena*!
FLORINDA: *Hellena*!
HELLENA: The very same—hah my Brother! now, Captain,
    shew your Love and Courage; stand to your Arms, and de-
    fend me bravely, or I am lost for ever.
510 PEDRO: What's this I hear? false Girl, how came you hither,
    and what's your Business? Speak.

(*Goes roughly to her.*)

WILLMORE: Hold off, Sir, you have leave to parly only.

(*Puts himself between.*)

HELLENA: I had e'en as good tell it, as you guess it. Faith,
    Brother, my Business is the same with all living Creatures
515 of my Age, to love, and be loved, and here's the Man.
PEDRO: Perfidious Maid, hast thou deceiv'd me too, deceiv'd
    thy self and Heaven?
HELLENA: 'Tis time enough to make my Peace with that: Be
    you but kind, let me alone with Heaven.
520 PEDRO: *Belvile*, I did not expect this false Play from you; was't
    not enough you'd gain *Florinda* (which I pardon'd) but
    your leud Friends too must be inrich'd with the Spoils of
    a noble Family?
BELVILE: Faith, Sir, I am as much surpriz'd at this as you can be:
525 Yet, Sir, my Friends are Gentlemen, and ought to be es-
    teem'd for their Misfortunes, since they have the Glory to
    suffer with the best of Men and Kings; 'tis true, he's a Rover
    of Fortune, yet a Prince aboard his little wooden World.
PEDRO: What's this to the maintenance of a Woman or her
530 Birth and Quality?
WILLMORE: Faith, Sir, I can boast of nothing but a Sword
    which does me Right where-e'er I come, and has de-

fended a worse Cause than a Woman's: and since I lov'd
    her before I either knew her Birth or Name, I must pur-
    sue my Resolution, and marry her.   535
PEDRO: And is all your holy Intent of becoming a Nun de-
    bauch'd into a Desire of Man?
HELLENA: Why—I have consider'd the matter, Brother, and
    find the Three hundred thousand Crowns my Uncle left
    me (and you cannot keep from me) will be better laid out 540
    in Love than in Religion, and turn to as good an Ac-
    count—let most Voices carry it, for Heaven or the Captain?
ALL CRY: Captain, a Captain.
HELLENA: Look ye, Sir, 'tis a clear Case.
PEDRO: (*Aside.*) Oh I am mad—if I refuse, my Life's in Dan- 545
    ger—Come—There's one motive induces me—take
    her—I shall now be free from the fear of her Honour;
    guard it you now, if you can, I have been a Slave to't long
    enough.

(*Gives her to him.*)

WILLMORE: Faith, Sir, I am of a Nation, that are of opinion a
    Woman's Honour is not worth guarding when she has a   550
    mind to part with it.
HELLENA: Well said, Captain.
PEDRO: (*To* VALERIA.) This was your Plot, Mistress, but I hope
    you have married one that will revenge my Quarrel to
    you—   555
VALERIA: There's no altering Destiny, Sir.
PEDRO: Sooner than a Woman's Will, therefore I forgive you
    all—and wish you may get my Father's Pardon as easily;
    which I fear.

(*Enter* BLUNT *drest in a Spanish Habit, looking very ridiculously;
his* MAN *adjusting his Band.*)

MAN: 'Tis very well, Sir.   560
BLUNT: Well, Sir, 'dsheartlikins I tell you 'tis damnable ill,
    Sir—a Spanish Habit, good Lord! cou'd the Devil and my
    Taylor devise no other Punishment for me, but the Mode
    of a Nation I abominate?
BELVILE: What's the matter, *Ned*?   565
BLUNT: Pray view me round, and judge—

(*Turns round.*)

BELVILE: I must confess thou art a kind of an odd Figure.
BLUNT: In a Spanish Habit with a Vengeance! I had rather be
    in the Inquisition for Judaism, than in this Doublet and
    Breeches; a Pillory were an easy Collar to this, three   570
    Hand-fuls high; and these Shoes too are worse than the
    Stocks, with the Sole an Inch shorter than my Foot: In
    fine, Gentlemen, methinks I look altogether like a Bag of
    Bays stuff'd full of Fools Flesh.
BELVILE: Methinks 'tis well, and makes the look *en Cavalier*:   575
    Come, Sir, settle your Face, and salute our Friends, Lady—
BLUNT: Hah! Say'st thou so, my little Rover?

(*To* HELLENA.)

    Lady—(if you be one) give me leave to kiss your Hand,
    and tell you, adsheartlikins, for all I look so, I am your
    humble Servant—A Pox of my *Spanish* Habit.   580

WILLMORE: Hark—what's this?

(*Musick is heard to Play. Enter* BOY.)

BOY: Sir, as the Custom is, the gay People in Masquerade, who make every Man's House their own, are coming up.

(*Enter several* MEN *and* WOMEN *in masquing Habits, with Musick, they put themselves in order and dance.*)

585 BLUNT: Adsheartlikins, wou'd 'twere lawful to pull off their false Faces, that I might see if my Doxy were not amongst 'em.

BELVILE: Ladies and Gentlemen, since you are come so *a propos,* you must take a small Collation with us.

(*To the* MASQUERADERS.)

590 WILLMORE: Whilst we'll to the Good Man within, who stays to give us a Cast of his Office.

(*To* HELLENA.)

—Have you no trembling at the near approach?

HELLENA: No more than you have in an Engagement or a Tempest.

595 WILLMORE: Egad, thou'rt a brave Girl, and I admire thy
    Love and Courage.
    Lead on, no other Dangers they can dread,
    Who venture in the Storms o'th' Marriage-Bed.

(*Exeunt.*)

EPILOGUE

THE banisht Cavaliers! a Roving Blade!
A popish Carnival! a Masquerade!
The Devil's in't if this will please the Nation,
In these our blessed Times of Reformation,
5 When Conventicling is so much in Fashion.
And yet—
That mutinous Tribe less Factions do beget,
Than your continual differing in Wit;

Your Judgment's (as your Passions) a Disease:
Nor Muse nor Miss your Appetite can please;   10
You're grown as nice as queasy Consciences,
Whose each Convulsion, when the Spirit moves,
Damns every thing that Maggot disapproves.
    With canting Rule you wou'd the Stage refine,
And to dull Method all our Sense confine.   15
With th' Insolence of Common-wealths you rule,
Where each gay Fop, and politick brave Fool
On Monarch Wit impose without controul.
As for the last who seldom sees a Play,
Unless it be the old Black-Fryers way,   20
Shaking his empty Noodle o'er *Bamboo,*
He crys—Good Faith, these Plays will never do.
—Ah, Sir, in my young days, what lofty Wit,
What high-strain'd Scenes of Fighting there were writ:
These are slight airy Toys. But tell me, pray,   25
What has the *House of Commons* done to day?
Then shews his Politicks, to let you see
Of State Affairs he'll judge as notably,
As he can do of Wit and Poetry.
The younger Sparks, who hither do resort,   30
Cry—
Pox o' your gentle things, give us more Sport;
—Damn me, I'm sure 'twill never please the Court.
    Such Fops are never pleas'd, unless the Play
Be stuff'd with Fools, as brisk and dull as they: 35
Such might the Half-Crown spare, and in a Glass
At home behold a more accomplisht Ass,
Where they may set their Cravats, Wigs and Faces,
And practice all their Buffoonry Grimaces;
See how this—Huff becomes—this Dammy—flare—   40
Which they at home may act, because they dare,
But—must with prudent Caution do elsewhere.
Oh that our *Nokes,* or *Tony Lee* could show
A Fop but half so much to th' Life as you.

---

43 **Nokes, or Tony Lee** James Nokes and Antony Leigh, the two famous actors, were the leading low comedians of the day

Sor Juana Inés de la Cruz

Juana Inés de Asbaje y Ramírez de Santillana (1648/1651–1695) was probably born in late November or early December of 1648 to the daughter of a wealthy landowner (Isabel Ramírez de
Santillana) and an army officer (Pedro Manuel de Asbaje y Vargas Manchucha) serving in the
Spanish New World colony of New Spain—present-day Mexico. Although her parents had two
other children (Isabel Ramírez had three additional children with another officer), they were
not married, and Juana Inés was born an illegitimate "daughter of the church." Raised in the
provincial town of Panoyan, Juana had access to her grandfather's library and, by her own account, was a voracious reader, as she later wrote in her *Answer to Sor Filotea* (written 1691):

> When I was six or seven years old and already knew how to read and write, along with all the other
> skills like embroidery and sewing that women learn, I heard that in Mexico City there were a Uni-
> versity and Schools where they studied sciences. As soon as I heard this I began to slay my poor
> mother with insistent and annoying pleas, begging her to dress me in men's clothes and send me
> to the capital, to the home of some relatives she had there, so that I could enter the University and
> study. She refused, and was right in doing so; but I quenched my desire by reading a great variety
> of books that belonged to my grandfather, and neither punishments nor scoldings could prevent
> me. And so when I did go to Mexico City, people marveled not so much at my intelligence as at
> my memory and the facts I knew at an age when it seemed I had scarcely had time to speak.[1]

Juana was sent to live with her mother's relatives in Mexico City in 1659. She lived with
them for five years until she moved into the home of the viceroy, where she served in the
court of the vicereine, Doña Leonor Carreto, Marquisa de Mancera.

Although she began to write on both religious and secular subjects while at court,
Juana's career was closely tied to the church. In 1666, she joined the Carmelite convent of
San José, but the penitential strictness of the order seems to have caused her health to suffer, and she left the convent after three months. Still eager to join a convent, she agreed to
sit for an examination by the viceroy and forty scholars assembled to test the range of her
knowledge, as a means to confirm her suitability for religious life. According to Diego Cal-
lega, a priest who wrote the first biography of Sor Juana, she performed like a "royal galleon
attacked by canoes," and was admitted to the convent of Santa Paula in 1669, where she took
the name Sor Juana Inés de la Cruz. (Illegitimate children were not admissible to convent
life; at this time, Juana claimed that her parents had been married, and that her birth date
was November 12, 1651; a baptismal record for 1648—listing Juana's aunt and uncle as godparents of an infant "Inés"—is now usually taken as evidence for her birth in that year.)

Although the convent was cloistered, Sor Juana received money to support her servants
and was able to receive guests, to study, and to write; she was also closely connected to the
social life of New Spain's capital city. The Aztec city of Tenochtitlán had supported some
250,000 inhabitants before the conquest in 1520, but Mexico City was a much smaller city
in the seventeenth century. While war, disease, and enslavement drastically reduced the native population, the general population was augmented not only by the annual arrival of
peninsulares (new inhabitants from Spain), but by an increasing population of *criollos* (people
of European descent born in Mexico, like Sor Juana) and *mestizos,* as well as by a growing
number of African slaves and immigrants from other Spanish colonies. In the 1800 census,
for example, the population of Mexico City was 137,000, making it the largest city in the
Americas. The church wielded extensive political power in Mexico (there were sixteen convents in Mexico City alone), and—as in Europe—the leaders of the church and of the state
were often drawn from the same aristocratic families. In this sense, it's not surprising that

---

[1]See *The Answer/La Respuesta, Including a Selection of Poems,* ed. and trans. Electa Arenal and Amanda
Powell (New York: Feminist Press, 1994).

Religion, costumed as a Spanish nobleman, surveys the fallen Aztec men and women after the battle between Zeal and Occident, in the 1997 Universidad de las Americas production of the *loa* to *The Divine Narcissus* by Sor Juana Inés de la Cruz.

throughout her life, Sor Juana was an intimate acquaintance of aristocratic circles in Mexico City, particularly of the viceroys and vicereines.

One vicereine, Maria Luisa Manrique de Lara y Gonzaga (whose husband was viceroy 1680–1686), was the inspiration of several of Sor Juana's poems and had her first volume, *Inundación Castálida,* published in Madrid in 1689 (the title refers to the nymph Castálida, who drowned herself rather than be seduced by Apollo); the title-page described Sor Juana as "the Tenth Muse." By 1690, Sor Juana was arguably the most accomplished secular and philosophical writer in the Americas: She mastered the baroque forms of secular Spanish poetry, writing not only sixty-five sonnets and many ballads and occasional poems, but two well-known comedies (including *Los empeños de una casa*) that were staged. She also wrote sixteen sets of **VILLANCICOS,** carols performed at the Mass; these often incorporate her understanding both of African dialects and of the indigenous Nahua language and were performed at cathedrals throughout Mexico during her lifetime. She wrote three *auto sacramentales,* two of which were performed; thirty-two **LOAS;** a brilliant philosophical treatise *The First Dream* (1685); and a defense of women's claim to an intellectual and spiritual life, *Answer to Sor Filotea.*

Yet despite her fame, Sor Juana was under continual pressure from the church to conform to the more "feminine" role of quiet devotion and service. Early in her career she struggled with her confessor, Antonio Núñez de Miranda, who regarded writing as improper for women, especially for women of the church. Although Sor Juana succeeded in dismissing him as her confessor, he continued to agitate for her silence with higher church officials, including the misogynist archbishop Francisco Aguian y Seijas. In 1690—shortly after her second volume of poetry had been published in Madrid, and her brilliant *auto The Divine Narcissus,* had been published in Mexico—the church's opposition came to a head. During that year, Sor Juana wrote a theological critique of a sermon written forty years earlier, an essay clearly not intended for publication; her friend, the bishop of Puebla, Manuel

Fernández de Santa Cruz, asked her to send it to him. Without her permission, he published Sor Juana's essay under the title *Carta atenagórica*—"Letter Worthy of Athena." Despite the praise implied in the title, the bishop was in fact eager to expose Sor Juana to censure and appended his own corrective letter to her treatise—from "Sor Filotea," "lover of God." This public rebuke spurred Sor Juana's brilliant *Answer to Sor Filotea de la Cruz,* a passionate defense of both her intellectual life and its contribution to her faith, written in 1691 but published only after her death in 1700. Despite her defense, however, Sor Juana acceded to the will of the church in 1692. Her last set of *villancicos* was performed at the cathedral in Oaxaca; she sold both her musical instruments and her extensive library (among the largest private libraries in the Americas at the time), and in 1694 she signed—in blood—a new declaration of faith, vowing to give up secular studies as well. She died during an epidemic that swept Mexico City in April 1695.

Sor Juana's poetry, plays, and philosophical writings are well known in Spanish, and many have been published in English translations; the Mexican poet Octavio Paz has written a celebrated biography of Sor Juana: *Sor Juana, or, The Traps of Faith,* trans. Margaret Sayers Peden (Cambridge: Harvard University Press, 1988).

LOA TO THE DIVINE NARCISSUS

The Divine Narcissus is a full-length *auto sacramental,* an allegorical drama on the subject of the Eucharist that Sor Juana wrote in 1687. She intended to submit it to be performed in Madrid as part of a competition for new *autos* following the death of Calderón, who had been the sole author of *autos* performed in the Spanish capital before his death in 1681. Although the death of the queen in 1689 forced the cancellation of the festival, Sor Juana's *The Divine Narcissus* and its introductory *loa* remain among the most accomplished examples of this important genre of Spanish-language drama.

Although the *loa* can be used for either secular or sacred purposes, Sor Juana uses it here specifically to introduce the themes of the *auto,* which uses the Greek story of Echo and Narcissus to allegorize the theological doctrine of the Eucharist. However, to modern readers and audiences, the *loa* is perhaps more interesting for its staging of colonial conflict; through an allegorical conversation between Zeal (a *conquistador*), Religion (a Spanish lady), and the Aztec rulers (Occident and America), the short play also stages an allegory of the conquest of Mexico and its consequences. Although there is no record of the play being performed in Sor Juana's lifetime, it clearly records aspects of Aztec life—the opening dance and ritual worship of the God of the Seeds—that were legally prohibited in seventeenth-century New Spain, while staging a debate between the Aztec leaders and the Spanish invaders who insist on replacing the native religion with the practice of Christianity. While the bullheaded *conquistador,* Zeal, is on the point of murdering the defeated Aztecs, they are spared by Religion, who hears in their account of their religious rituals a profane version of the miracle of the Eucharist:

> What images,
> what dark designs, what shadowings
> of truths most sacred to our Faith
> do these lies seek to imitate?

Religion works to bring Christian salvation to Occident and America by pointing out the similarities between their religion and the mysteries of the Eucharist:

> a God composed
> of human blood, an offering
> of sacrifice, and in himself
> does He combine with bloody death
> the life-sustaining seeds of earth?

To instruct Occident and America, Religion decides to

> make for you a metaphor
> a concept clothed in rhetoric
> so colorful that what I show
> to you, your eyes will clearly see.

The *auto* that follows, *The Divine Narcissus,* is Religion's illustrative "metaphor," her way of explaining the Eucharist to the inhabitants of the New World.

Written by a *criolla,* as part of a competition to take place in Madrid, Sor Juana's play is in many ways a barometer of the situation of colonial writing; the final dialogue between Zeal and Religion considers whether such a play, written in the colony about colonial subjects, will be received in "the crown city of Madrid, / which is the center of the Faith, / the seat of Catholic majesty" as an act of "impropriety." Although written at the height of Spain's imperial expansion, and indeed in many ways written to celebrate that expansion, Sor Juana's *loa* to *The Divine Narcissus* deftly registers many of the tensions that typically inform colonial writing: between the colony and the capital, between the native population and their invaders, for instance. But particularly in the brittle relationship between Zeal and Religion and the more charitable relationship between Religion and America, Sor Juana seems to open another kind of critique as well; Religion refuses, for example, to sanction the extermination, or even the subjugation, of Occident and America. While the *loa* testifies unambigiously to Sor Juana's confidence in the universality of her faith, it also seems to question some of the ways religion is used to advance Spain's political and economic mission in this new and distinct society.

LOA TO THE DIVINE NARCISSUS

Sor Juana Inés de la Cruz

TRANSLATED BY PATRICIA A. PETERS AND RENÉE DOMEIER, O.S.B.

CHARACTERS

OCCIDENT	RELIGION	AZTECS
AMERICA	MUSIC	DANCERS
ZEAL	SOLDIERS	

SCENE ONE

Enter OCCIDENT, *a gallant-looking Aztec, wearing a crown. By his side is* AMERICA, *an Aztec woman of poised self-possession. They are dressed in the mantas and huipiles worn for singing a tocotín. They seat themselves on two chairs. On each side, Aztec men and women dance with feathers and rattles in their hands, as is customary for those doing this dance. While they dance,* MUSIC *sings.*

MUSIC: O, Noble Mexicans,
whose ancient ancestry
comes forth from the clear light
and brilliance of the Sun,
5 since this, of all the year,
is your most happy feast
in which you venerate
your greatest deity,
come and adorn yourselves
10 with vestments of your rank;
let your holy fervor be
made one with jubilation;
and celebrate in festive pomp
the great God of the Seeds!

15 MUSIC: Since the abundance of
our native fields and farms
is owed to him alone
who gives fertility,
then offer him your thanks,
20 for it is right and just
to give from what has grown,
the first of the new fruits.
From your own veins, draw out
and give, without reserve,
25 the best blood, mixed with seed,
so that his cult be served,
and celebrate in festive pomp,
the great God of the Seeds!

(OCCIDENT *and* AMERICA *sit, and* MUSIC *ceases.*)

OCCIDENT: Of all the deities to whom
30 our rites demand I bend my knee—
among two thousand gods or more
who dwell within this royal city
and who require the sacrifice
of human victims still entreating
35 for life until their blood is drawn
and gushes forth from hearts still beating
and bowels still pulsing—I declare,
among all these, (it bears repeating),

whose ceremonies we observe,
the greatest is, surpassing all   40
this pantheon's immensity
the great God of the Seeds.

AMERICA: And you are right, since he alone
daily sustains our monarchy
because our lives depend on his   45
providing crops abundantly;
and since he gives us graciously
the gift from which all gifts proceed,
our fields rich with golden maize,
the source of life through daily bread, 50
we render him our highest praise.
Then how will it improve our lives
if rich America abounds
in gold from mines whose smoke deprives
the fields of their fertility   55
and with their clouds of filthy soot
will not allow the crops to grow
which blossom now so fruitfully
from seeded earth? Moreover, his
protection of our people far   60
exceeds our daily food and drink,
the body's sustenance. Indeed,
he feeds us with his very flesh
(first purified of every stain).
We eat his body, drink his blood,   65
and by this sacred meal are freed
and cleansed from all that is profane,
and thus, he purifies our soul.
And now, attentive to his rites,
together let us all proclaim: 70

OCCIDENT, AMERICA, DANCERS and MUSIC: We celebrate in
festive pomp,
the great God of the Seeds!

SCENE TWO

They exit dancing. Enter Christian RELIGION *as a Spanish lady,* ZEAL *as a Captain General in armor, and Spanish* SOLDIERS.

RELIGION: How, being Zeal, can you suppress
the flames of righteous Christian wrath
when here before your very eyes
idolatry, so blind with pride,   5
adores, with superstitious rites
an idol, leaving your own bride,
the holy faith of Christ disgraced?

ZEAL: Religion, trouble not your mind
or grieve my failure to attack,

10   complaining that my love is slack,
for now the sword I wear is bared,
its hilt in hand, clasped ready and
my arm raised high to take revenge.
Please stand aside and deign to wait
15   till I requite your grievances.

(*Enter* OCCIDENT *and* AMERICA *dancing, and accompanied by*
MUSIC, *who enters from the other side.*)

MUSIC: And celebrate in festive pomp,
the great God of the Seeds!
ZEAL: Here they come! I will confront them.
RELIGION: And I, in peace, will also go
20   (before your fury lays them low)
for justice must with mercy kiss;
I shall invite them to arise
from superstitious depths to faith.
ZEAL: Let us approach while they are still
25   absorbed in their lewd rituals.
MUSIC: And celebrate in festive pomp,
the great God of the Seeds!

(ZEAL *and* RELIGION *cross the stage.*)

RELIGION: Great Occident, most powerful;
America, so beautiful
30   and rich; you live in poverty
amid the treasures of your land.
Abandon this irreverent cult
with which the demon has waylaid you.
Open your eyes! Follow the path
35   that leads straightforwardly to truth,
to which my love yearns to persuade you.
OCCIDENT: Who are these unknown people, so
intrusive in my sight, who dare
to stop us in our ecstasy?
40   Heaven forbid such infamy!
AMERICA: Who are these nations, never seen,
that wish, by force, to pit themselves
against my ancient power supreme?
OCCIDENT: Oh, you alien beauty fair;
45   oh, pilgrim woman from afar,
who comes to interrupt my prayer,
please speak and tell me who you are.
RELIGION: Christian Religion is my name,
and I intend that all this realm
50   will make obeisance unto me.
OCCIDENT: An impossible concession!
AMERICA: Yours is but a mad obsession!
OCCIDENT: You will meet with swift repression.
AMERICA: Pay no attention; she is mad!
55   Let us go on with our procession.
MUSIC and AZTECS: And celebrate in festive pomp,
the great God of the Seeds!
ZEAL: How is this, barbarous Occident?
Can it be, sightless Idolatry,
60   that you insult Religion,
the spouse I cherish tenderly?
Abomination fills your cup
and overruns the brim, but see
that God will not permit you to

continue drinking down delight,   65
and I am sent to deal your doom.
OCCIDENT: And who are you who frightens all
who only look upon your face?
ZEAL: I am Zeal. Does that surprise you?
Take heed! for when your excesses   70
bring disgrace to fair Religion,
then will Zeal arise to vengeance;
for insolence I will chastise you.
I am the minister of God,
Who growing weary with the sight   75
of overreaching tyrannies
so sinful that they reach the height
of error, practiced many years,
has sent me forth to penalize you.
And thus, these military hosts   80
with flashing thunderbolts of steel,
the ministers of His great wrath
are sent, His anger to reveal.
OCCIDENT: What god? What sin? What tyranny?
What punishment do you foresee?   85
Your reasons make no sense to me,
nor can I make the slightest guess
who you might be with your insistence
on tolerating no resistance,
impeding us with rash persistence   90
from lawful worship as we sing.
MUSIC: And celebrate with festive pomp,
the great God of the Seeds!
AMERICA: Madman, blind, and barbarous,
with mystifying messages   95
you try to mar our calm and peace,
destroying the tranquility
that we enjoy. Your plots must cease,
unless, of course, you wish to be
reduced to ashes, whose existence   100
even the winds will never sense.
(*To* OCCIDENT.) And you, my spouse, and your cohort,
close off your hearing and your sight
to all their words; refuse to heed
their fantasies of zealous might;   105
proceed to carry out your rite.
Do not concede to insolence
from foreigners intent to dull
our ritual's magnificence.
MUSIC: And celebrate with festive pomp,   110
the great God of the Seeds!
ZEAL: Since our initial offering
of peaceful terms, you held so cheap,
the dire alternative of war,
I guarantee you'll count more dear.   115
Take up your arms! To war! To war!

(*Drums and trumpets sound.*)

OCCIDENT: What miscarriages of justice
has heaven sent against me?
What are these weapons, blazing fire,
before my unbelieving eyes?   120
Get ready, guards! Aim well, my troops,
Your arrows at this enemy!

AMERICA: What lightening bolts does heaven send
    to lay me low? What molten balls
125 of burning lead so fiercely rain?
    What centaurs crush with monstrous force
    and cause my people such great pain?
    (*Within.*) To arms! To arms! War! War!

([*Drums and trumpets*] *sound.*)

(*Within.*) Long life to Spain! Long live her king!

(*The battle begins. Indians enter through one door and flee through another with the Spanish pursuing at their heels. From back stage,* OCCIDENT *backs away from* RELIGION *and* AMERICA *retreats before* ZEAL's *onslaught.*)

SCENE THREE

RELIGION: Give up, arrogant Occident!
OCCIDENT: I must bow to your aggression,
    but not before your arguments.
ZEAL: Die, impudent America!
5 RELIGION: Desist! Do not give her to Death;
    her life is of some worth to us.
ZEAL: How can you now defend this maid
    who has so much offended you?
RELIGION: America has been subdued
10   because your valor won the strife,
    but now my mercy intervenes
    in order to preserve her life.
    It was your part to conquer her
    by force with military might;
15   mine is to gently make her yield,
    persuading her by reason's light.
ZEAL: But you have seen the stubbornness
    with which these blind ones still abhor
    your creed; is it not better far
20   that they all die?
RELIGION: Good Zeal, restrain
    your justice, and do not kill them.
    My gentle disposition deigns
    to forbear vengeance and forgive.
    I want them to convert and live.
25 AMERICA: If your petition for my life
    and show of Christian charity
    are motivated by the hope
    that you, at last, will conquer me,
    defeating my integrity
30   with verbal steel where bullets failed,
    then you are sadly self-deceived.
    A weeping captive, I may mourn
    for liberty, yet my will grows
    beyond these bonds; my heart is free,
35   and I will worship my own gods!
OCCIDENT: Forced to surrender to your power,
    I have admitted my defeat,
    but still it must be clearly said
    that violence cannot devour
40   my will, nor force constrain its right.
    Although in grief, I now lament,
    a prisoner, your cruel might

has limits. You cannot prevent
my saying here within my heart
I worship the great God of Seeds!   45

SCENE FOUR

RELIGION: Wait! What you perceive as force
    is not coercion, but affection.
    What god is this that you adore?
OCCIDENT: The great God of the Seeds
    who causes fields to bring forth fruit.   5
    To him the lofty heavens bow;
    to him the rains obedience give;
    and when, at last, he cleanses us
    from stains of sin, then he invites
    us to the meal that he prepares.   10
    Consider whether you could find
    a god more generous and good
    who blesses more abundantly
    than he whom I describe to you.
RELIGION: (*Aside.*) O God, help me! What images,   15
    what dark designs, what shadowings
    of truths most sacred to our Faith
    do these lies seek to imitate?
    O false, sly, and deceitful snake!
    O asp, with sting so venomous!   20
    O hydra, that from seven mouths
    pours noxious poisons, every one
    a passage to oblivion!
    To what extent, with this facade
    do you intend maliciously   25
    to mock the mysteries of God?
    Mock on! for with your own deceit,
    if God empowers my mind and tongue,
    I'll argue and impose defeat.
AMERICA: Why do you find yourself perplexed?   30
    Do you not see there is no god
    other than ours who verifies
    with countless blessings his great works?
RELIGION: In doctrinal disputes, I hold
    with the apostle Paul, for when   35
    he preached to the Athenians
    and found they had a harsh decree
    imposing death on anyone
    who tried to introduce new gods,
    since he had noticed they were free   40
    to worship at a certain shrine,
    an altar to "the Unknown God,"
    he said to them, "This Lord of mine
    is no new god, but one unknown
    that you have worshipped in this place,   45
    and it is He, my voice proclaims."
    And thus I—

(OCCIDENT *and* AMERICA *whisper to each other.*)

        Listen, Occident!
and hear me, blind Idolatry!
for all your happiness depends
on listening attentively.   50
These miracles that you recount,

these prodigies that you suggest,
these apparitions and these rays
of light in superstition dressed
55 are glimpsed but darkly through a veil.
These portents you exaggerate,
attributing to your false gods
effects that you insinuate,
but wrongly so, for all these works
60 proceed from our true God alone,
and of His Wisdom come to birth.
Then if the soil richly yields,
and if the fields bud and bloom,
if fruits increase and multiply,
65 if seeds mature in earth's dark womb,
if rains pour forth from leaden sky,
all is the work of His right hand;
for neither the arm that tills the soil
nor rains that fertilize the land
70 nor warmth that calls life from the tomb
of winter's death can make plants grow;
for they lack reproductive power
if Providence does not concur,
by breathing into each of them
75 a vegetative soul.
AMERICA: That might be so;
then tell me, is this God so kind—
this deity whom you describe—
that I might touch Him with my hands,
these very hands that carefully
80 create the idol, here before you,
an image made from seeds of earth
and innocent, pure human blood
shed only for this sacred rite?
RELIGION: Although the Essence of Divinity
85 is boundless and invisible,
because already It has been
eternally united with
our nature, He resembles us
so much in our humanity
90 that He permits unworthy priests
to take Him in their humble hands.
AMERICA: In this, at least, we are agreed,
for to my god no human hands
are so unstained that they deserve
95 to touch him; nonetheless, he gives
this honor graciously to those
who serve him with their priestly lives.
No others dare to touch the god,
nor in the sanctuary stand.
100 ZEAL: A reverence most worthily
directed to the one true God!
OCCIDENT: Whatever else you claim, now tell
me this: Is yours a God composed
of human blood, an offering
105 of sacrifice, and in Himself
does He combine with bloody death
the life-sustaining seeds of earth?
RELIGION: As I have said, His boundless
Majesty is insubstantial,
110 but in the Holy Sacrifice

of Mass, His blessed humanity
is placed unbloody under the
appearances of bread, which comes
from seeds of wheat and is transformed
into His Body and His Blood;   115
and this most holy Blood of Christ,
contained within a sacred cup,
is verily the offering
most innocent, unstained, and pure
that on the altar of the cross   120
was the redemption of the world.
AMERICA: Such miracles, unknown to us,
make me desire to believe;
but would the God that you reveal
offer Himself so lovingly   125
transformed for me into a meal
as does the god that I adore?
RELIGION: In truth, He does. For this alone
His Wisdom came upon the earth
to dwell among all humankind.   130
AMERICA: And so that I can be convinced,
may I not see this Deity?
OCCIDENT: And so that I can be made free
of old beliefs that shackle me?
RELIGION: Yes, you will see when you are bathed   135
in crystal waters from the font
of baptism.
OCCIDENT: And well I know,
in preparation to attend
a banquet, I must bathe, or else
our ancient custom I offend.   140
ZEAL: Your vain ablutions will not do
the cleansing that your stains require.
OCCIDENT: Then what?
RELIGION: There is a sacrament
of living waters, which can cleanse
and purify you of your sins.   145
AMERICA: Because you deluge my poor mind
with concepts of theology,
I've just begun to understand;
there is much more I want to see,
and my desire to know is now   150
by holy inspiration led.
OCCIDENT: And I desire more keenly still
to know about the life and death
of the God you say is in the bread.
RELIGION: Then come along with me, and I   155
shall make for you a metaphor,
a concept clothed in rhetoric
so colorful that what I show
to you, your eyes will clearly see;
for now I know that you require   160
objects of sight instead of words,
by which faith whispers in your ears
too deaf to hear; I understand,
for you necessity demands
that through the eyes, faith find her way   165
to her reception in your hearts.
OCCIDENT: Exactly so. I do prefer
to see the things you would impart.

SCENE FIVE

RELIGION: Then come.

ZEAL: Religion, answer me:
  what metaphor will you employ
  to represent these mysteries?

RELIGION: An *auto* will make visible
5   through allegory images
  of what America must learn
  and Occident implores to know
  about the questions that now burn
  within him so.

ZEAL: What will you call
10   this play in allegory cast?

RELIGION: *Divine Narcissus*, let it be,
  because if that unhappy maid
  adored an idol which disguised
  in such strange symbols the attempt
15   the demon made to counterfeit
  the great and lofty mystery
  of the most Blessed Eucharist,
  then there were also, I surmise,
  among more ancient pagans hints
20   of such high marvels symbolized.

ZEAL: Where will your drama be performed?

RELIGION: In the crown city of Madrid,
  which is the center of the Faith,
  the seat of Catholic majesty,
25   to whom the Indies owe their best
  beneficence, the blessed gift
  of Holy Writ, the Gospel light
  illuminating all the West.

ZEAL: That you should write in Mexico
30   for royal patrons don't you see
  to be an impropriety?

RELIGION: Is it beyond imagination
  that something made in one location
  can in another be of use?
35   Furthermore, my writing it
  comes, not of whimsical caprice,
  but from my vowed obedience
  to do what seems beyond my reach.
  Well, then, this work, however rough
40   and little polished it might be,
  results from my obedience,
  and not from any arrogance.

ZEAL: Then answer me, Religion, how
  (before you leave the matter now),
45   will you respond when you are chid
  for loading the whole Indies on

a stage to transport to Madrid?

RELIGION: The purpose of my play can be
  none other than to glorify
  the Eucharistic Mystery;   50
  and since the cast of characters
  are no more than abstractions which
  depict the theme with clarity,
  then surely no one should object
  if they are taken to Madrid;   55
  distance can never hinder thought
  with persons of intelligence,
  nor seas impede exchange of sense.

ZEAL: Then, prostrate at his royal feet,
  beneath whose strength two worlds are joined   60
  we beg for pardon of the King;

RELIGION: and from her eminence, the Queen;

AMERICA: whose sovereign and anointed feet
  the humble Indies bow to kiss;

ZEAL: and from the Royal High Council;   65

RELIGION: and from the ladies, who bring light
  into their hemisphere;

AMERICA: and from
  their poets, I most humbly beg
  forgiveness for my crude attempt,
  desiring with these awkward lines   70
  to represent the Mystery.

OCCIDENT: Let's go, for anxiously I long to see
  exactly how this God of yours
  will give Himself as food to me.

(AMERICA, OCCIDENT, *and* ZEAL *sing:*)

  The Indies know   75
  and do concede
  who is the true
  God of the Seeds.
  In loving tears
  which joy prolongs   80
  we gladly sing
  our happy songs.

ALL: Blest be the day
  when I could see
  and worship the   85
  great God of Seeds.

(*They all exit, dancing and singing.*)

CRITICAL CONTEXTS

JOHN DRYDEN (1631–1700)

"Preface to *Troilus and Cressida*, Containing the Grounds of Criticism in Tragedy" (1679)

EDITED BY ARTHUR C. KIRSCH

John Dryden is the most important English critic and poet of the late seventeenth century; he was appointed poet laureate and royal historiographer in 1668 and was also the author of many plays, both comedies and heroic tragedies. In 1679, he wrote an adaptation of Shakespeare's Troilus and Cressida, *and in his "Preface" to the play Dryden argues for neoclassical principles of unity and decorum.*

In the "Preface," Dryden frames a specifically neoclassical sense of the purpose and function of tragedy. One way into this essay is through a comparison with Aristotle, and indeed, with Greek tragedy. How do Dryden's criteria at once invoke and revise the sense of tragic construction in Aristotle's The Poetics? *Beyond that, what are the features of Shakespearean drama that seem to require Dryden's attention as a reviser? What is the sense of decorum that Dryden wishes to urge, and that Shakespeare's original play seems to violate?*

The poet Aeschylus was held in the same veneration by the Athenians of after ages as Shakespeare is by us; and Longinus has judged, in favor of him, that he had a noble boldness of expression, and that his imaginations were lofty and heroic; but, on the other side, Quintilian affirms that he was daring to extravagance. 'Tis certain that he affected pompous words, and that his sense too often was obscured by figures. Notwithstanding these imperfections, the value of his writings after his decease was such that his countrymen ordained an equal reward to those poets who could alter his plays to be acted on the theater, with those whose productions were wholly new, and of their own. The case is not the same in England; though the difficulties of altering are greater, and our reverence for Shakespeare much more just, than that of the Grecians for Aeschylus. In the age of that poet, the Greek tongue was arrived to its full perfection; they had then amongst them an exact standard of writing and of speaking. The English language is not capable of such a certainty; and we are at present so far from it that we are wanting in the very foundation of it, a perfect grammar. Yet it must be allowed to the present age that the tongue in general is so much refined since Shakespeare's time that many of his words, and more of his phrases, are scarce intelligible. And of those which we understand, some are ungrammatical, others coarse; and his whole style is so pestered with figurative expressions, that it is as affected as it is obscure. 'Tis true, that in his later plays he had worn off somewhat of the rust; but the tragedy which I have undertaken to correct was, in all probability, one of his first endeavors on the stage.[1]

---

[1] Actually, *Troilus and Cressida*, which was probably written around 1602, came at the midpoint of Shakespeare's career.

The original story was written by one Lollius, a Lombard, in Latin verse, and translated by Chaucer into English; intended, I suppose, a satire on the inconstancy of women: I find nothing of it among the Ancients; not so much as the name Cressida once mentioned. Shakespeare (as I hinted), in the apprenticeship of his writing, modeled it into that play which is now called by the name of *Troilus and Cressida*; but so lamely is it left to us, that it is not divided into acts; which fault I ascribe to the actors who printed it after Shakespeare's death; and that too so carelessly, that a more uncorrect copy I never saw. For the play itself, the author seems to have begun it with some fire; the characters of Pandarus and Thersites are promising enough; but as if he grew weary of his task, after an entrance or two, he lets 'em fall: and the later part of the tragedy is nothing but a confusion of drums and trumpets, excursions and alarms. The chief persons, who give name to the tragedy, are left alive; Cressida is false, and is not punished. Yet after all, because the play was Shakespeare's, and that there appeared in some places of it the admirable genius of the author, I undertook to remove that heap of rubbish under which many excellent thoughts lay wholly buried. Accordingly, I new modeled the plot; threw out many unnecessary persons; improved those characters which were begun and left unfinished: as Hector, Troilus, Pandarus, and Thersites; and added that of Andromache. After this I made, with no small trouble, an order and connection of all the scenes; removing them from the places where they were inartificially set; and though it was impossible to keep 'em all unbroken, because the scene must be sometimes in the city and sometimes in the camp, yet I have so ordered them that there is a coherence of 'em with one another, and a dependence on the main design: no leaping from Troy to the Grecian tents, and thence back again in the same act; but a due proportion of time allowed for every motion. I need not say that I have refined his language, which before was obsolete; but I am willing to acknowledge that as I have often drawn his English nearer to our times, so I have sometimes conformed my own to his; and consequently, the language is not altogether so pure as it is significant. The scenes of Pandarus and Cressida, of Troilus and Pandarus, of Andromache with Hector and the Trojans, in the second act, are wholly new; together with that of Nestor and Ulysses with Thersites, and that of Thersites with Ajax and Achilles. I will not weary my reader with the scenes which are added of Pandarus and the lovers, in the third; and those of Thersites, which are wholly altered; but I cannot omit the last scene in it, which is almost half the act, betwixt Troilus and Hector. The occasion of raising it was hinted to me by Mr. Betterton: the contrivance and working of it was my own. They who think to do me an injury by saying that it is an imitation of the scene betwixt Brutus and Cassius, do me an honor by supposing I could imitate the incomparable Shakespeare; but let me add that if Shakespeare's scene, or that faulty copy of it in *Amintor and Melantius*, had never been, yet Euripides had furnished me with an excellent example in his *Iphigenia*, between Agamemnon and Menelaus; and from thence, indeed, the last turn of it is borrowed.[2] The occasion which Shakespeare, Euripides, and Fletcher have all taken is the same; grounded upon friendship: and the quarrel of two virtuous men, raised by natural degrees to the extremity of passion, is conducted in all three to the declination of the same passion, and concludes with a warm renewing of their friendship. But the particular groundwork which Shakespeare has taken is incomparably the best; because he has not only chosen two of the greatest heroes of their age, but has likewise interested the liberty of Rome, and their own honors who were the redeemers of it, in this debate. And if he has made Brutus, who was naturally a patient man, to fly into excess at first, let it be remembered in his defense that, just before, he has received the news of Portia's death; whom the poet, on purpose neglecting a little chronology, supposes to have died before Brutus, only to give him an occasion of being more easily exasperated. Add to this that the injury he had received from Cassius had long been brooding in his mind; and that a melancholy man, upon consideration of an affront, es-

pecially from a friend, would be more eager in his passion than he who had given it, though naturally more choleric.

Euripides, whom I have followed, has raised the quarrel betwixt two brothers who were friends. The foundation of the scene was this: the Grecians were windbound at the port of Aulis, and the oracle had said that they could not sail, unless Agamemnon delivered up his daughter to be sacrificed: he refuses; his brother Menelaus urges the public safety; the father defends himself by arguments of natural affection, and hereupon they quarrel. Agamemnon is at last convinced, and promises to deliver up Iphigenia, but so passionately laments his loss that Menelaus is grieved to have been the occasion of it and, by a return of kindness, offers to intercede for him with the Grecians, that his daughter might not be sacrificed. But my friend Mr. Rymer has so largely, and with so much judgment, described this scene, in comparing it with that of Melantius and Amintor, that it is superfluous to say more of it; I only named the heads of it, that any reasonable man might judge it was from thence I modeled my scene betwixt Troilus and Hector. I will conclude my reflections on it with a passage of Longinus, concerning Plato's imitation of Homer: "We ought not to regard a good imitation as a theft, but as a beautiful idea of him who undertakes to imitate, by forming himself on the invention and the work of another man; for he enters into the lists like a new wrestler, to dispute the prize with the former champion. This sort of emulation, says Hesiod, is honorable, 'this strife is wholesome to man,'[3] when we combat for victory with a hero, and are not without glory even in our overthrow. Those great men whom we propose to ourselves as patterns of our imitation serve us as a torch, which is lifted up before us to enlighten our passage; and often elevate our thoughts as high as the conception we have of our author's genius."[4]

I have been so tedious in three acts that I shall contract myself in the two last. The beginning scenes of the fourth act are either added or changed wholly by me; the middle of it is Shakespeare altered, and mingled with my own; three or four of the last scenes are altogether new. And the whole fifth act, both the plot and the writing, are my own additions.

But having written so much for imitation of what is excellent, in that part of the preface which related only to myself, methinks it would neither be unprofitable nor unpleasant to inquire how far we ought to imitate our own poets, Shakespeare and Fletcher, in their tragedies: and this will occasion another inquiry, how those two writers differ between themselves. But since neither of these questions

---

[2]The comparison of the quarrels between Amintor and Melantius in Beaumont and Fletcher's *Maid's Tragedy* and Agamemnon and Menelaus in Euripides's *Iphigenia in Aulis* had already been made by Rymer in his *Tragedies of the Last Age* (1678), as Dryden acknowledges in the following paragraph.

---

[3]ἀγαθὴ δ᾽ ἔρις ἐστὶ βροτοῖσιν (*Works and Days*, 1.24).

[4]*On the Sublime*, 13.4.

can be solved unless some measures be first taken by which we may be enabled to judge truly of their writings, I shall endeavor, as briefly as I can, to discover the grounds and reason of all criticism, applying them in this place only to tragedy. Aristotle with his interpreters, and Horace, and Longinus, are the authors to whom I owe my lights; and what part soever of my own plans, or of this, which no mending could make regular, shall fall under the condemnation of such judges, it would be impudence in me to defend. . . .

THE GROUNDS OF CRITICISM IN TRAGEDY

Tragedy is thus defined by Aristotle (omitting what I thought unnecessary in his definition). 'Tis an imitation of one entire, great, and probable action; not told, but represented; which, by moving in us fear and pity, is conducive to the purging of those two passions in our minds. More largely thus, tragedy describes or paints an action, which action must have all the proprieties above named. First, it must be one or single, that is, it must not be a history of one man's life; suppose of Alexander the Great, or Julius Caesar, but one single action of theirs. This condemns all Shakespeare's historical plays, which are rather chronicles represented than tragedies, and all double action of plays. As to avoid a satire upon others, I will make bold with my own *Marriage à-la-Mode,* where there are manifestly two actions, not depending on one another: but in *Oedipus* there cannot properly be said to be two actions, because the love of Adrastus and Eurydice has a necessary dependence on the principal design, into which it is woven. The natural reason of rule is plain; for two different independent actions distract the attention and concernment of the audience, and consequently destroy the intention of the poet: if his business be to move terror and pity, and one of his actions be comical, the other tragical, the former will divert the people, and utterly make void his greater purpose. Therefore, as in perspective, so in tragedy, there must be a point of sight in which all the lines terminate; otherwise the eye wanders, and the work is false. This was the practice of the Grecian stage. But Terence made an innovation in the Roman: all his plays have double actions; for it was his custom to translate two Greek comedies, and to weave them into one of his, yet so that both the actions were comical, and one was principal, the other but secondary or subservient. And this has obtained on the English stage, to give us the pleasure of variety.

As the action ought to be one, it ought, as such, to have order in it, that is, to have a natural beginning, a middle, and an end. A natural beginning, says Aristotle, is that which could not necessarily have been placed after another thing, and so of the rest. This consideration will arraign all plays after the new model of Spanish plots, where accident is heaped upon accident, and that which is first might as reasonably be

last: an inconvenience not to be remedied but by making one accident naturally produce another, otherwise 'tis a farce and not a play. Of this nature is the *Slighted Maid,*[5] where there is no scene in the first act which might not by as good reason be in the fifth. And if the action ought to be one, the tragedy ought likewise to conclude with the action of it. Thus in *Mustapha,*[6] the play should naturally have ended with the death of Zanger, and not have given us the grace cup after dinner of Solyman's divorce from Roxolana.

The following properties of the action are so easy that they need not my explaining. It ought to be great, and to consist of great persons, to distinguish it from comedy, where the action is trivial, and the persons of inferior rank. The last quality of the action is that it ought to be *probable,* as well as admirable and great. 'Tis not necessary that there should be historical truth in it; but always necessary that there should be a likeness of truth, something that is more than barely possible, *probable* being that which succeeds or happens oftener than it misses. To invent therefore a probability, and to make it wonderful, is the most difficult undertaking in the art of poetry; for that which is not wonderful is not great; and that which is not probable will not delight a reasonable audience. This action, thus described, must be represented and not told, to distinguish dramatic poetry from epic: but I hasten to the end or scope of tragedy, which is to rectify or purge our passions, fear and pity.

To instruct delightfully is the general end of all poetry. Philosophy instructs, but it performs its work by precept: which is not delightful, or not so delightful as example. To purge the passions by example is therefore the particular instruction which belongs to tragedy. Rapin, a judicious critic, has observed from Aristotle that pride and want of commiseration are the most predominant vices in mankind: therefore, to cure us of these two, the inventors of tragedy have chosen to work upon two other passions, which are fear and pity. We are wrought to fear by their setting before our eyes some terrible example of misfortune, which happened to persons of the highest quality; for such an action demonstrates to us that no condition is privileged from the turns of fortune; this must of necessity cause terror in us, and consequently abate our pride. But when we see that the most virtuous, as well as the greatest, are not exempt from such misfortunes, that consideration moves pity in us, and insensibly works us to be helpful to, and tender over, the distressed, which is the noblest and most god-like of moral virtues. Here 'tis observable that it is absolutely necessary to make a man virtuous, if we desire he should be pitied: we

---

[5]By Sir Robert Stapylton (1663).

[6]By Roger Boyle, Earl of Orrery (first performed in 1665).

lament not, but detest, a wicked man; we are glad when we behold his crimes are punished, and that poetical justice[7] is done upon him. Euripides was censured by the critics of his time for making his chief characters too wicked: for example, Phaedra, though she loved her son-in-law with reluctancy, and that it was a curse upon her family for offending Venus, yet was thought too ill a pattern for the stage. Shall we therefore banish all characters of villainy? I confess I am not of that opinion; but it is necessary that the hero of the play be not a villain; that is, the characters which should move our pity ought to have virtuous inclinations, and degrees of moral goodness in them. As for a perfect character of virtue, it never was in nature, and therefore there can be no imitation of it; but there are allays of frailty to be allowed for the chief persons, yet so that the good which is in them shall outweigh the bad, and consequently leave room for punishment on the one side, and pity on the other.

After all, if anyone will ask me whether a tragedy cannot be made upon any other grounds than those of exciting pity and terror in us, Bossu,[8] the best of modern critics, answers thus in general: that all excellent arts, and particularly that of poetry, have been invented and brought to perfection by men of a transcendent genius; and that therefore they who practice afterwards the same arts are obliged to tread in their footsteps, and to search in their writings the foundation of them; for it is not just that new rules should destroy the authority of the old. But Rapin writes more particularly thus[9]: that no passions in a story are so proper to move our concernment as fear and pity; and that it is from our concernment we receive our pleasure, is undoubted; when the soul becomes agitated with fear for one character, or hope for another, then it is that we are pleased in tragedy by the interest which we take in their adventures.

Here, therefore, the general answer may be given to the first question, how far we ought to imitate Shakespeare and Fletcher in their plots: namely, that we ought to follow them so far only as they have copied the excellencies of those who invented and brought to perfection dramatic poetry: those things only excepted which religion, customs of countries, idioms of languages, etc., have altered in the superstructures, but not in the foundation of the design.

How defective Shakespeare and Fletcher have been in all their plots, Mr. Rymer has discovered in his criticisms: neither can we who follow them be excused from the same or greater errors; which are the more unpardonable in us, be-

cause we want their beauties to countervail our faults. The best of their designs, the most approaching to antiquity, and the most conducing to move pity, is the *King and No King*; which, if the farce of Bessus were thrown away, is of that inferior sort of tragedies which end with a prosperous event. 'Tis probably derived from the story of Oedipus, with the character of Alexander the Great, in his extravagancies, given to Arbaces. The taking of this play, amongst many others, I cannot wholly ascribe to the excellency of the action; for I find it moving when it is read: 'tis true, the faults of the plot are so evidently proved that they can no longer be denied. The beauties of it must therefore lie either in the lively touches of the passion: or we must conclude, as I think we may, that even in imperfect plots there are less degrees of nature, by which some faint emotions of pity and terror are raised in us: as a less engine will raise a less proportion of weight, though not so much as one of Archimedes' making; for nothing can move our nature, but by some natural reason, which works upon passions. And since we acknowledge the effect, there must be something in the cause.

The difference between Shakespeare and Fletcher in their plotting seems to be this: that Shakespeare generally moves more terror, and Fletcher more compassion. For the first had a more masculine, a bolder and more fiery genius; the second, a more soft and womanish. In the mechanic beauties of the plot, which are the observation of the three unities, time, place, and action, they are both deficient; but Shakespeare most. Ben Jonson reformed those errors in his comedies, yet one of Shakespeare's was regular before him; which is, *The Merry Wives of Windsor*. For what remains concerning the design, you are to be referred to our English critic. That method which he has prescribed to raise it from mistake, or ignorance of the crime, is certainly the best, though 'tis not the only: for amongst all the tragedies of Sophocles, there is but one, *Oedipus*, which is wholly built after that model.

After the plot, which is the foundation of the play, the next thing to which we ought to apply our judgment is the manners, for now the poet comes to work above ground: the ground-work indeed is that which is most necessary, as that upon which depends the firmness of the whole fabric; yet it strikes not the eye so much as the beauties or imperfections of the manners, the thoughts, and the expressions.

The first rule which Bossu prescribes to the writer of an heroic poem, and which holds too by the same reason in all dramatic poetry, is to make the moral of the work, that is, to lay down to yourself what that precept of morality shall be, which you would insinuate into the people; as namely, Homer's (which I have copied in my *Conquest of Granada*) was, that union preserves a commonwealth, and discord

---

[7]A phrase first coined by Rymer in *The Tragedies of the Last Age.*

[8]Le Bossu, author of *Traité du poème épique* (1675).

[9]In *Réflexions sur la poétique d'Aristote* (1674).

destroys it; Sophocles, in his *Oedipus,* that no man is to be accounted happy before his death. 'Tis the moral that directs the whole action of the play to one center; and that action or fable is the example built upon the moral, which confirms the truth of it to our experience: when the fable is designed, then and not before, the persons are to be introduced with their manners, characters, and passions.

The manners in a poem are understood to be those inclinations, whether natural or acquired, which move and carry us to actions, good, bad, or indifferent, in a play; or which incline the persons to such or such actions. I have anticipated part of this discourse already, in declaring that a poet ought not to make the manners perfectly good in his best persons; but neither are they to be more wicked in any of his characters than necessity requires. To produce a villain, without other reason than a natural inclination to villainy is, in poetry, to produce an effect without a cause; and to make him more a villain than he has just reason to be, is to make an effect which is stronger than the cause.

The manners arise from many causes; and are either distinguished by complexion, as choleric and phlegmatic, or by the differences of age or sex, of climates, or quality of the persons, or their present condition. They are likewise to be gathered from the several virtues, vices, or passions, and many other commonplaces which a poet must be supposed to have learned from natural philosophy, ethics, and history; of all which whosoever is ignorant, does not deserve the name of poet.

But as the manners are useful in this art, they may be all comprised under these general heads: first, they must be apparent; that is, in every character of the play, some inclinations of the person must appear: and these are shown in the actions and discourse. Secondly, the manners must be suitable, or agreeing to the persons; that is, to the age, sex, dignity, and the other general heads of manners: thus, when a poet has given the dignity of a king to one of his persons, in all his actions and speeches, that person must discover majesty, magnanimity, and jealousy of power, because these are suitable to the general manners of a king. The third property of manners is resemblance; and this is founded upon the particular characters of men, as we have them delivered to us by relation or history; that is, when a poet has the known character of this or that man before him, he is bound to represent him such, at least not contrary to that which fame has reported him to have been. Thus, it is not a poet's choice to make Ulysses choleric, or Achilles patient, because Homer has described 'em quite otherwise. Yet this is a rock on which ignorant writers daily split; and the absurdity is as monstrous as if a painter should draw a coward running from a battle, and tell us it was the picture of Alexander the Great.

The last property of manners is that they be constant and equal, that is, maintained the same through the whole design: thus, when Virgil had once given the name of *pious* to Aeneas, he was bound to show him such, in all his words and actions through the whole poem. All these properties Horace has hinted to a judicious observer: "1. you must mark the manners of each age; 2. or follow tradition; 3. or create your own convention; 4. let each character remain constant and consistent with itself."[10]

From the manners, the characters of persons are derived; for indeed the characters are no other than the inclinations, as they appear in the several persons of the poem; a character being thus defined, that which distinguishes one man from another. Not to repeat the same things over again which have been said of the manners, I will only add what is necessary here. A character, or that which distinguishes one man from all others, cannot be supposed to consist of one particular virtue, or vice, or passion only; but 'tis a composition of qualities which are not contrary to one another in the same person; thus the same man may be liberal and valiant, but not liberal and covetous; so in a comical character, or humour (which is an inclination to this or that particular folly), Falstaff is a liar, and a coward, a glutton, and a buffoon, because all these qualities may agree in the same man; yet it is still to be observed that one virtue, vice, and passion ought to be shown in every man, as predominant over all the rest; as covetousness in Crassus, love of his country in Brutus; and the same in characters which are feigned.

The chief character or hero in a tragedy, as I have already shown, ought in prudence to be such a man who has so much more in him of virtue than of vice, that he may be left amiable to the audience, which otherwise cannot have any concernment for his sufferings; and 'tis on this one character that the pity and terror must be principally, if not wholly, founded—a rule which is extremely necessary, and which none of the critics that I know have fully enough discovered to us. For terror and compassion work but weakly when they are divided into many persons. If Creon had been the chief character in *Oedipus,* there had neither been terror nor compassion moved; but only detestation of the man and joy for his punishment; if Adrastus and Eurydice had been made more appealing characters, then the pity had been divided, and lessened on the part of Oedipus: but making Oedipus the best and bravest person, and even Jocasta but an underpart to him, his virtues and the punishment of his fatal crime drew both the pity and the terror to himself.

---

[10] *1. notandi sunt tibi mores; 2. aut famam sequere; 3. aut sibi convenientia finge; 4. servetur ad imum, qualis ab incepto processerit, et sibi constet (Ars poetica,* 11.156, 119, 126–127).

By what had been said of the manners, it will be easy for a reasonable man to judge whether the characters be truly or falsely drawn in a tragedy; for if there be no manners appearing in the characters, no concernment for the persons can be raised; no pity or horror can be moved, but by vice or virtue; therefore, without them, no person can have any business in the play. If the inclinations be obscure, 'tis a sign the poet is in the dark, and knows not what manner of man he presents to you; and consequently you can have no idea, or very imperfect, of that man; nor can judge what resolutions he ought to take; or what words or actions are proper for him. Most comedies made up of accidents or adventures are liable to fall into this error; and tragedies with many turns are subject to it; for the manners never can be evident where the surprises of fortune take up all the business of the stage; and where the poet is more in pain to tell you what happened to such a man than what he was. 'Tis one of the excellencies of Shakespeare that the manners of his persons are generally apparent, and you see their bent and inclinations. Fletcher comes far short of him in this, as indeed he does almost in everything: there are but glimmerings of manners in most of his comedies, which run upon adventures: and in his tragedies, *Rollo, Otto, A King and No King,* Melantius,[11] and many others of his best, are but pictures shown you in the twilight; you know not whether they resemble vice or virtue, and they are either good, bad, or indifferent, as the present scene requires it. But of all poets, this commendation is to be given to Ben Jonson, that the manners even of the most inconsiderable persons in his plays are everywhere apparent.

By considering the second quality of manners, which is that they be suitable to the age, quality, country, dignity, etc., of the character, we may likewise judge whether a poet has followed nature. In this kind, Sophocles and Euripides have more excelled among the Greeks than Aeschylus; and Terence more than Plautus among the Romans. Thus Sophocles gives to Oedipus the true qualities of a king, in both those plays which bear his name; but in the latter, which is the *Oedipus Colonœus,* he lets fall on purpose his tragic style; his hero speaks not in the arbitrary tone, but remembers, in the softness of his complaints, that he is an unfortunate blind old man, that he is banished from his country, and persecuted by his next relations. The present French poets are generally accused that wheresoever they lay the scene, or in whatsoever age, the manners of their heroes are wholly French. Racine's Bajazet is bred at Constantinople, but his civilities are conveyed to him, by some secret passage, from Versailles into the Seraglio. But our Shakespeare, having as-

cribed to Henry the Fourth the character of a king and of a father, gives him the perfect manners of each relation, when either he transacts with his son or with his subjects. Fletcher, on the other side, gives neither to Arbaces, nor to his King in the *Maid's Tragedy,* the qualities which are suitable to a monarch; though he may be excused a little in the latter, for the King there is not uppermost in the character; 'tis the lover of Evadne, who is King only in a second consideration; and though he be unjust, and has other faults which shall be nameless, yet he is not the hero of the play. 'Tis true, we find him a lawful prince (though I never heard of any King that was in Rhodes), and therefore Mr. Rymer's criticism stands good; that he should not be shown in so vicious a character. Sophocles has been more judicious in his *Antigone;* for though he represents in Creon a bloody prince, yet he makes him not a lawful king, but an usurper, and Antigona herself is the heroine of the tragedy. But when Philaster wounds Arethusa and the boy; and Perigot his mistress, in the *Faithful Shepherdess,* both these are contrary to the character of manhood. Nor is Valentinian managed much better, for though Fletcher has taken his picture truly, and shown him as he was, an effeminate, voluptuous man, yet he has forgotten that he was an Emperor, and has given him none of those royal marks which ought to appear in a lawful successor of the throne. If it be inquired what Fletcher should have done on this occasion: ought he not to have represented Valentinian as he was? Bossu shall answer this question for me, by an instance of the like nature: Mauritius, the Greek Emperor, was a prince far surpassing Valentinian, for he was endued with many kingly virtues; he was religious, merciful, and valiant, but withal he was noted of extreme covetousness, a vice which is contrary to the character of a hero, or a prince: therefore, says the critic, that emperor was no fit person to be represented in a tragedy, unless his good qualities were only to be shown, and his covetousness (which sullied them all) were slurred over by the artifice of the poet.[12] To return once more to Shakespeare: no man ever drew so many characters, or generally distinguished 'em better from one another, excepting only Jonson. I will instance but in one, to show the copiousness of his invention: 'tis that of Caliban, or the Monster in the *Tempest.* He seems there to have created a person which was not in nature, a boldness which at first sight would appear intolerable; for he makes him a species of himself, begotten by an incubus on a witch; but this, as I have elsewhere proved, is not wholly beyond the bounds of credibility, at least the vulgar still believe it. We have the separated notions of a spirit, and of a witch (and spirits,

---

[11]Otto is Rollo's brother; Melantius is a character in *The Maid's Tragedy.*

[12]*Traité du poème épique,* 4.7.

according to Plato, are vested with a subtle body; according to some of his followers, have different sexes); therefore, as from the distinct apprehensions of a horse, and of a man, imagination has formed a centaur; so from those of an incubus and a sorceress, Shakespeare has produced his monster. Whether or no his generation can be defended, I leave to philosophy; but of this I am certain, that the poet has most judiciously furnished him with a person, a language, and a character, which will suit him, both by father's and mother's side: he has all the discontents and malice of a witch, and of a devil, besides a convenient proportion of the deadly sins; gluttony, sloth, and lust are manifest; the dejectedness of a slave is likewise given him, and the ignorance of one bred up in a desert island. His person is monstrous, as he is the product of unnatural lust; and his language is as hobgoblin as his person; in all things he is distinguished from other mortals. The characters of Fletcher are poor and narrow, in comparison of Shakespeare's; I remember not one which is not borrowed from him; unless you will except that strange mixture of a man in the *King and No King;* so that in this part Shakespeare is generally worth our imitation; and to imitate Fletcher is but to copy after him who was a copier.

Under this general head of manners, the passions are naturally included, as belonging to the characters. I speak not of pity and of terror, which are to be moved in the audience by the plot; but of anger, hatred, love, ambition, jealousy, revenge, etc., as they are shown in this or that person of the play. To describe these naturally, and to move them artfully, is one of the greatest commendations which can be given to a poet: to write pathetically, says Longinus, cannot proceed but from a lofty genius. A poet must be born with this quality; yet, unless he help himself by an acquired knowledge of the passions, what they are in their own nature, and by what springs they are to be moved, he will be subject either to raise them where they ought not to be raised, or not to raise them by the just degrees of nature, or to amplify them beyond the natural bounds, or not to observe the crisis and turns of them, in their cooling and decay: all which errors proceed from want of judgment in the poet, and from being unskilled in the principles of moral philosophy. Nothing is more frequent in a fanciful writer than to foil himself by not managing his strength; therefore, as in a wrestler, there is first required some measure of force, a well-knit body, and active limbs, without which all instruction would be vain; yet, these being granted, if he want the skill which is necessary to a wrestler, he shall make but small advantage of his natural robustuousness: so, in a poet, his inborn vehemence and force of spirit will only run him out of breath the sooner, if it be not supported by the help of art. The roar of passion indeed may please an audience, three parts of which are igno-

rant enough to think all is moving which is noise, and it may stretch the lungs of an ambitious actor, who will die upon the spot for a thundering clap; but it will move no other passion than indignation and contempt from judicious men. Longinus, whom I have hitherto followed, continues thus: *If the passions be artfully employed, the discourse becomes vehement and lofty: if otherwise, there is nothing more ridiculous than a great passion out of season:* and to this purpose he animadverts severely upon Aeschylus, who writ nothing in cold blood, but was always in a rapture, and in fury with his audience:[13] the inspiration was still upon him, he was ever tearing it upon the tripos[14]; or (to run off as madly as he does, from one similitude to another) he was always at high flood of passion, even in the dead ebb and lowest water-mark of the scene. He who would raise the passion of a judicious audience, says a learned critic, must be sure to take his hearers along with him; if they be in a calm, 'tis in vain for him to be in a huff: he must move them by degrees, and kindle with 'em; otherwise he will be in danger of setting his own heap of stubble on a fire, and of burning out by himself without warming the company that stand about him. They who would justify the madness of poetry from the authority of Aristotle have mistaken the text, and consequently the interpretation: I imagine it to be false read, where he says of poetry that it is εὐφυοῦς ἤ μανικοῦ, that it had always somewhat in it either of a genius, or of a madman. 'Tis more probable that the original ran thus, that poetry was εὐφυοῦς οὐ μανικοῦ, that it belongs to a witty man, but not to a madman.[15] Thus then the passions, as they are considered simply and in themselves, suffer violence when they are perpetually maintained at the same height; for what melody can be made on that instrument, all whose strings are screwed up at first to their utmost stretch, and to the same sound? But this is not the worst: for the characters likewise bear a part in the general calamity, if you consider the passions embodied in them; for it follows of necessity that no man can be distinguished from another by his discourse, when every man is ranting, swaggering, and exclaiming with the same excess: as if it were the only business of all the characters to contend with each other for the prize at Billingsgate; or that the scene of the tragedy lay in Bet'lem.[16] Suppose the poet should intend this man to be choleric, and that man to be patient; yet when they are confounded in the writing, you cannot distinguish

---

[13] *On the Sublime,* 3.

[14] A reference to the tripod at Delphi on which the priestess of Apollo delivered her raving oracles.

[15] Aristotle, *The Poetics,* 17.

[16] Bedlam, a London hospital for the insane.

them from one another: for the man who was called patient and tame is only so before he speaks; but let his clack be set a-going, and he shall tongue it as impetuously, and as loudly, as the errantest hero in the play. By this means, the characters are only distinct in name; but, in reality, all the men and women in the play are the same person. No man should pretend to write who cannot temper his fancy with his judgment: nothing is more dangerous to a raw horseman than a hot-mouthed jade without a curb.

'Tis necessary therefore for a poet who would concern an audience by describing of a passion, first to prepare it, and not to rush upon it all at once. Ovid has judiciously shown the difference of these two ways, in the speeches of Ajax and Ulysses: Ajax, from the very beginning, breaks out into his exclamations, and is swearing by his Maker, "'By Jupiter,' he cried."[17] Ulysses, on the contrary, prepares his audience with all the submissiveness he can practice, and all the calmness of a reasonable man; he found his judges in a tranquillity of spirit, and therefore set out leisurely and softly with 'em, till he had warmed 'em by degrees; and then he began to mend his pace, and to draw them along with his own impetuousness: yet so managing his breath, that it might not fail him at his need, and reserving his utmost proofs of ability even to the last. The success, you see, was answerable; for the crowd only applauded the speech of Ajax:

and the applause of the crowd followed his closing words.[18]

But the judges awarded the prize for which they contended to Ulysses:

the assembly was very moved; and the power of eloquence was revealed, and the skillful orator carried off the hero's arms.[19]

The next necessary rule is to put nothing into the discourse which may hinder your moving of the passions. Too many accidents, as I have said, encumber the poet, as much as the arms of Saul did David; for the variety of passions which they produce are ever crossing and jostling each other out of the way. He who treats of joy and grief together is in a fair way of causing neither of those effects. There is yet another obstacle to be removed, which is pointed wit, and sentences affected out of season; these are nothing of kin to the violence of passion: no man is at leisure to make sentences

and similes when his soul is in an agony. I the rather name this fault that it may serve to mind me of my former errors; neither will I spare myself, but give an example of this kind from my *Indian Emperor*. Montezuma, pursued by his enemies, and seeking sanctuary, stands parleying without the fort, and describing his danger to Cydaria, in a simile of six lines:

As on the sands the frighted traveller
Sees the high seas come rolling from afar, etc.[20]

My Indian potentate was well skilled in the sea for an inland prince, and well improved since the first act, when he sent his son to discover it. The image had not been amiss from another man, at another time: "but not now, in this place"[21]; he destroyed the concernment which the audience might otherwise have had for him; for they could not think the danger near when he had the leisure to invent a simile.

If Shakespeare be allowed, as I think he must, to have made his characters distinct, it will easily be inferred that he understood the nature of the passions: because it has been proved already that confused passions make undistinguishable characters. Yet I cannot deny that he has his failings; but they are not so much in the passions themselves as in his manner of expression: he often obscures his meaning by his words, and sometimes makes it unintelligible. I will not say of so great a poet that he distinguished not the blown puffy style from true sublimity; but I may venture to maintain that the fury of his fancy often transported him beyond the bounds of judgment, either in coining of new words and phrases or racking words which were in use into the violence of a catachresis.[22] 'Tis not that I would explode[23] the use of metaphors from passions, for Longinus thinks 'em necessary to raise it: but to use 'em at every word, to say nothing without a metaphor, a simile, an image, or description, is I doubt to smell a little too strongly of the buskin. I must be forced to give an example of expressing passion figuratively; but that I may do it with respect to Shakespeare, it shall not be taken from anything of his: 'tis an exclamation against Fortune, quoted in his *Hamlet*, but written by some other poet:

Out, out, thou strumpet Fortune! all you gods,
In general synod, take away her power;
Break all the spokes and felleys from her wheel,
And bowl the round nave down the hill of Heav'n,
As low as to the fiends.

---

[17]*agimus, pro Jupiter, inquit* (*Metamorphoses*, 13.5).

[18]   *vulgique secutum*
ultima mumur erat.
         Ibid., 123.

[19]*mota manus procerum est; et quid facundia posset*
tum patuit, fortisque viri tulit arma disertus.
         Ibid., 282–83.

---

[20]Act 5.

[21]*sed nunc non erat hisce locus* (*Ars poetica*, 1.19).

[22]A misuse of terms.

[23]Banish, reject.

And immediately after, speaking of Hecuba, when Priam was killed before her eyes:

> The mobled queen ran up and down,
> Threatening the flame with bisson rheum; a clout about that head
> Where late the diadem stood; and for a robe,
> About her lank and all o'er-teemed loins,
> A blanket in th' alarm of fear caught up.
> Who this had seen, with tongue in venom steep'd
> 'Gainst Fortune's state would treason have pronounced;
> But if the gods themselves did see her then,
> When she saw Pyrrhus make malicious sport
> In mincing with his sword her husband's limbs,
> The instant burst of clamour that she made
> (Unless things mortal move them not at all)
> Would have made milch the burning eyes of Heaven,
> And passion in the gods.[24]

What a pudder is here kept in raising the expression of trifling thoughts! Would not a man have thought that the poet had been bound prentice to a wheelwright, for his first rant? and had followed a ragman for the clout and blanket, in the second? Fortune is painted on a wheel, and therefore the writer, in a rage, will have poetical justice down upon every member of that engine: after this execution, he bowls the nave down hill, from Heaven to the fiends (an unreasonable long mark, a man would think); 'tis well there are no solid orbs to stop it in the way, or no element of fire to consume it: but when it came to the earth, it must be monstrous heavy, to break ground as low as to the center. His making milch the burning eyes of Heaven was a pretty tolerable flight too: and I think no man ever drew milk out of eyes before him: yet to make the wonder greater, these eyes were burning. Such a sight indeed were enough to have raised passion in the gods; but to excuse the effects of it, he tells you perhaps they did not see it. Wise men would be glad to find a little sense couched under all those pompous words; for bombast is commonly the delight of that audience which loves poetry, but understands it not: and as commonly has been the practice of those writers who, not being able to infuse a natural passion into the mind, have made it their business to ply the ears and to stun their judges by the noise. But Shakespeare does not often thus; for the passions in his scene between Brutus and Cassius are extremely natural, the thoughts are such as arise from the matter, and the expression of 'em not viciously figurative. I cannot leave this subject before I do justice to that divine poet by giving you one of his passionate descriptions:

'tis of Richard the Second when he was deposed, and led in triumph through the streets of London by Henry of Bolingbroke: the painting of it is so lively, and the words so moving, that I have scarce read anything comparable to it in any other language. Suppose you have seen already the fortunate usurper passing through the crowd, and followed by the shouts and acclamations of the people; and now behold King Richard entering upon the scene: consider the wretchedness of his condition, and his carriage in it; and refrain from pity if you can:

> As in a theater, the eyes of men,
> After a well-graced actor leaves the stage,
> Are idly bent on him that enters next,
> Thinking his prattle to be tedious:
> Even so, or with much more contempt, men's eyes
> Did scowl on Richard: no man cried, God save him:
> No joyful tongue gave him his welcome home,
> But dust was thrown upon his sacred head,
> Which with such gentle sorrow he shook off,
> His face still combating with tears and smiles
> (The badges of his grief and patience),
> That had not God (for some strong purpose) steel'd
> The hearts of men, they must perforce have melted,
> And barbarism itself have pitied him.[25]

To speak justly of this whole matter: 'tis neither height of thought that is discommended, nor pathetic vehemence, nor any nobleness of expression in its proper place; but 'tis a false measure of all these, something which is like 'em, and is not them; 'tis the Bristol-stone,[26] which appears like a diamond; 'tis an extravagant thought, instead of a sublime one; 'tis roaring madness, instead of vehemence; and a sound of words, instead of sense. If Shakespeare were stripped of all the bombast in his passions, and dressed in the most vulgar words, we should find the beauties of his thoughts remaining; if his embroideries were burnt down, there would still be silver at the bottom of the melting-pot: but I fear (at least let me fear it for myself) that we who ape his sounding words have nothing of his thought, but are all outside; there is not so much as a dwarf within our giant's clothes. Therefore, let not Shakespeare suffer for our sakes; 'tis our fault, who succeed him in an age which is more refined, if we imitate him so ill that we copy his failings only, and make a virtue of that in our writings which in his was an imperfection.

For what remains, the excellency of that poet was, as I have said, in the more manly passions; Fletcher's in the softer: Shakespeare writ better betwixt man and man; Fletcher, betwixt man and woman: consequently, the one described friendship better; the other love: yet Shakespeare

---

[24]*Hamlet*, 2.2.475–79, 487–500. [Line numbers cited here are those in this anthology; the lines that Dryden quotes differ slightly from this anthology because of his use of another version of Shakespeare's play.—Editor]

[25]*Richard II*, 5.2.23–36.

[26]A rock crystal.

taught Fletcher to write love: and Juliet, and Desdemona, are originals. 'Tis true, the scholar had the softer soul; but the master had the kinder. Friendship is both a virtue and a passion essentially; love is a passion only in its nature, and is not a virtue but by accident: good nature makes friendship, but effeminacy love. Shakespeare had an universal mind, which comprehended all characters and passions; Fletcher a more confined and limited: for though he treated love in perfection, yet honor, ambition, revenge, and generally all the stronger passions, he either touched not, or not masterly. To conclude all, he was a limb of Shakespeare.

I had intended to have proceeded to the last property of manners, which is that they must be constant, and the characters maintained the same from the beginning to the end; and from thence to have proceeded to the thoughts and expressions suitable to a tragedy: but I will first see how this will relish with the age. 'Tis, I confess, but cursorily written; yet the judgment which is given here is generally founded upon experience: but because many men are shocked at the name of rules, as if they were a kind of magisterial prescription upon poets, I will conclude with the words of Rapin, in his reflections on Aristotle's work of poetry: "If the rules be well considered, we shall find them to be made only to reduce nature into method, to trace her step by step, and not to suffer the least mark of her to escape us: 'tis only by these that probability in fiction is maintained, which is the soul of poetry. They are founded upon good sense, and sound reason, rather than on authority; for though Aristotle and Horace are produced, yet no man must argue that what they write is true because they writ it; but 'tis evident, by the ridiculous mistakes and gross absurdities which have been made by those poets who have taken their fancy only for their guide, that if this fancy be not regulated, 'tis a mere caprice, and utterly incapable to produce a reasonable and judicious poem."[27]

---

[27] *Réflexions*, 12.

CRITICAL PERSPECTIVES

KATHARINE EISAMAN MAUS

from "'Playhouse Flesh and Blood': Sexual Ideology and the Restoration Actress" (1979)

Katharine Eisaman Maus has written widely about seventeenth-century literature, including a book on the playwright Ben Jonson. In this essay, Maus explores the relationship between Restoration actresses, their reputation for sexual promiscuity, and the politics of gender in the Restoration theater and society.

Sometime in the fall of 1660—no one is quite sure when or at which theater—the first professional English actress made her debut on the public stage. Her appearance was not entirely without precedents. In the first half of the seventeenth century, Queen Henrietta Maria and her ladies performed extensively in the English court theater. During the interregnum, when the theaters were officially closed, William D'Avenant used at least one woman—a Mrs. Edward Coleman—in his opera *The Siege of Rhodes.* On the Continent, women had been employed on the stage since the sixteenth century, and many royalists became familiar with the French custom when they followed Prince Charles into exile. However, women had never been used on the English stage in any regular or systematic way.

Before the war, adolescent boys had performed the women's parts in the public theater. In November, 1629, when a French company with actresses came to London, Thomas Brand informed Archbishop Laud that "those women . . . giving just offense to all virtuous and well disposed persons in this town . . . were hissed, hooted, and pippin-pelted from the stage."[1] By the Restoration, though, attitudes toward women on the stage seem to have changed radically. The new actresses were accepted almost immediately into the life of the theater, and there was surprisingly little controversy over their suitability for the stage.

What caused this striking reversal of audience attitudes? Was it merely a case of English theater-goers belatedly relinquishing a set of absurd scruples? Discussions of seventeenth-century actresses have assumed that they succeeded on the stage because they could provide a more plausible portrayal of women characters than transvestite actors

could.[2] There are two objections to this kind of explanation. For one thing, there is no evidence which implies that the female impersonators were incompetent. Female parts written by Shakespeare, Webster, Ford, Middleton, and others suggests no mean estimate by the playwrights of the boys' abilities; Elizabethan and Jacobean audiences applauded male Juliets, Rosalinds, and Cleopatras. The usual explanation of the actresses' success further assumes that naturalism is an obvious and desirable goal in theatrical representation—an assumption which is questionable to say the least. E.H. Gombrich has shown that standards of naturalism—what will seem "true to life" in a drawing or painting—vary from generation to generation depending upon the conventions which inform and have informed artistic production. What seems natural or conventional is not universal across time and space, but is historically and culturally conditioned.[3] There is no reason to suppose that naturalism in the theater

[2]e.g., Colley Cibber, *An Apology of the Life of Colley Cibber* (London, 1740), p. 55: "The characters of Women, on former Theatres, were perform'd by Boys, or young Men of the most effeminate Aspect. And what Grace, or Master-Stroke of Action, can we conceive such ungain Hoydens to have been capable of?"

Allardyce Nicoll, *The History of Restoration Drama 1660–1700* (Cambridge: Cambridge U P, 1928), p. 71: "the actresses certainly made possible a more charming presentation of Shakespearean tragedy and comedy, shedding a fresh light on the Desdemonas and Ophelias of the past."

Rosamund Gilder, *Enter the Actresses* (London: George C. Harrup, 1931), pp. 134–35: "In England the curtain of legal prohibition drops in 1642 on a stage peopled by squeaking Cleopatras, and rises eighteen years later on a rout of beautiful, witty, and accomplished actresses."

John Harold Wilson, *All the King's Ladies: Actresses of the Restoration* (Chicago: U Chicago Press, 1958), p. 90: "As creators of character there can be little doubt that the new actresses were superior to their juvenile predecessors . . . the stage life of the female impersonator was usually short, and his interpretation of a character could never be more than superficially correct."

[3]E.H. Gombrich, *Art and Illusion* (New York: Pantheon, 1960), esp. pp. 181–287.

[1]John Payne Collier, *History of Dramatic Poetry to the Time of Shakespeare: And Annals of the Stage to the Restoration* (London: John Murray, 1831), II, pp. 23–24.

is any less problematic than naturalism in the visual arts. Why should male impersonation of women seem more intolerable than other kinds of artificiality—extravagantly exotic sets, or a highly rhetorical acting style? The Restoration audience expected, and enjoyed, stage conventions which grievously ignore the demands of realism as understood by, say, Ibsen or Chekhov.

The orthodox explanation of the actresses' new acceptability is, if not entirely wrong, at least seriously insufficient. What is required is an examination of the issues in terms of the attitudes prevailing in Restoration culture. This examination logically begins with the contemporary accounts of the actresses, and inevitably widens to include analysis of Restoration attitudes toward women and the theater in general.

Unfortunately, there is very little comment upon the actresses in the years when they are first introduced, when the quality of contemporary response might best help illuminate the reasons for their professional success. Since no one seriously questioned women's fitness for the stage, the few attempts to account for the innovation involve no very elaborate process of justification. In 1660, the players and owners of theatrical companies were complaining that the hiatus in the theatrical tradition had created a dearth of well-trained female impersonators. The available actors were all too masculine-looking, they claimed, to excel in women's parts. As Thomas Jordan lamented in his preface to a revival of *Othello*:

> Our women are defective, and so siz'd
> You'ld think they were some of the guard disguis'd
> For to speak truth, men act that are between
> Forty and fifty, wenches of fifteen
> With bone so large and nerve so incompliant
> When you call Desdemona, enter Geant.[4]

According to this line of argument, the peculiar circumstances of the Restoration theater necessitated the employment of women. The closing of the theaters during the interregnum had interrupted the old system of apprenticeship, which had supplied the Elizabethan and Jacobean companies with adequately-trained female impersonators.

This explanation, even if true, would only reveal by what chance women arrived on the stage, and not how and why they were successful once they got there. Furthermore, the plight of the producers was not nearly so severe as Jordan represents it. According to John Downes in *Roscius Angli-*

canus, the King's Company at its inception included four actors "Bred up from Boys, under the Master ACTORS."[5] The Duke's Company included six actors, who "commonly Acted Women's Parts"—notably Edward Kynaston, who "being young made a complete Femal Stage Beauty, performing his part so well . . . that it hath since been disputable among the Judicious, whether any Woman that succeeded him so sensibly touched the audience as he."[6] Pepys and Cibber, as well as Downes, comment upon the excellence of Kynaston's impersonations, as well as upon the more than passable abilities of the lesser actors.[7] Surely if the Restoration audience had greeted the women players with the hisses and orange pips of an earlier generation, the companies would have made do for a while with ungainly performances by untrained adolescent boys. The perceived unsuitability of male actors for female roles is really more a symptom than an explanation of changing attitudes.

As the theaters reopened, actors and producers urged yet another argument for the introduction of actresses, which seems at least in retrospect equally unsatisfactory as a real explanation. Initially some people hoped that the presence of women on the stage would eliminate the obscene and corrupt aspects of English drama, and encourage the adoption of purer standards for theatrical spectacle. The patents issued to William D'Avenant and Thomas Killigrew in 1660, and reissued in 1662, contain the following clause:

> forasmuch as many plays formerly acted, do conteine severall prophane, obscene, and scurrilous passages, and the women's parts therein have been acted by men in the habit of women, at which some have taken offense; for the preventing of these abuses for the future, we doe straitly charge, command, and enjoyn that henceforth no . . . play shall be acted by either of the said companies conteining any passages offensive to piety or good manners . . . And we doe likewise permit and give leave that all the women's parts to be acted in either of the said two companies may be performed by women so long as these recreations, which by reason of the abuses aforesaid were scandalous and offensive, may by such reformation be esteemed not only harmlesse delight but useful instruction.[8]

By this account the actresses were introduced in order to help the dramatic arts exert a beneficial effect upon the community. Whether or not this apparently pious hope was initially a sincere one, it remained unrealized on the Restoration

---

[4]Thomas Jordan, "A Prologue, to introduce the first Woman that came to act on the Stage, in the tragedy called *The Moor of Venice*," in *A Royal Arbour of Loyal Poesie* (London, 1664), p. 22.

[5]John Downes, *Roscius Anglicanus, or An Historical View of the Stage* (London, 1708), p. 2.

[6]Ibid., p. 19.

[7]Samuel Pepys, *The Diary of Samuel Pepys,* ed. R. Latham and W. Matthews (London: G. Bell, 1970), I, 224 (August 18, 1660) and II, 7 (January 7, 1660–61). Cibber, p. 71.

[8]Nicoll, pp. 285–86n.

stage. Restoration drama, especially comedy, tends to be sexually more explicit and morally more subversive than the drama of earlier decades—and the sexual explicitness, at least, largely depends upon the physical presence of genuine women on the stage. "We can only conclude," writes a twentieth century critic, "that [the actresses'] chief effect on dramatic literature was to push it steadily in the direction of sex and sensuality."[9] The threat implied in the language of the patents—that the women's continued employment depended upon their moral efficacy—was of course never carried out. If women were now considered appropriate on the public stage, it was not for their purifying influence, any more than it was due to a shortage of teenage boys.

Since the overt attempts at contemporary justification seem inadequate, it is reasonable to suspect that the new acceptability of actresses is associated with ideological changes more fundamental or far-reaching than a mere modification of theatrical custom might indicate. The first such change which needs to be examined is the transformation in audience attitudes toward players in the latter part of the seventeenth century—a change which makes the success of the Restoration actress even more striking. Before the war, even the most appreciative playgoers seem not have been particularly interested in the offstage lives of Burbage, Kempe, or Alleyn. In the more intimate Restoration theater, though, the personalities of both male and female players intrigued the comparatively small and loyal audience. Actresses as well as actors were praised not for their ability to depict any character with equal skill, but for their ability to inform their dramatic portrayals with the force of their personal talent and idiosyncratic vision. In James Wright's *Historia Histrionica* (London, 1699), Truewit assumes that even in reading an old play one is curious about the personalities of the original actors:

> I wish they had printed in the last age (so I call the times before the rebellion) the actors names over against the parts they acted, as they have done since the restoration: and thus one might have guess'd at the action of the men, by the parts which we now read in the old plays. (p. 3)

Restoration theater did not really challenge the actor to submit himself to the demands of a fictional role; rather it provided, at least for the leading players, manifold opportunities for self-expression. In the case of women like Nell Gwynn, Elizabeth Barry, or Ann Bracegirdle, this kind of attention constituted a virtually unprecedented celebration of female personality—at least of middle- and lower-class female personality.

As Restoration playwrights worked very closely with the theatrical companies, they inevitably wrote with particular performers in mind. They were thus able to play upon the spectator's sense of the relationship between an actor's personality and the roles he was required to enact. Nell Gwynn and Charles Hart, lovers behind the scenes, played witty, amoral "mad couples" together—Florimel and Celadon in Dryden's *Secret Love*, Miridia and Philidor in Howard's *All Mistaken*, Jacintha and Wildblood in Dryden's *Evening's Love*, Olivia and Wildish in Sedley's *Mulberry Garden*. Ann Bracegirdle, who resisted the advances of enamored aristocrats throughout her career, and who was the object of a melodramatic rape attempt, became famous for her portrayal of chaste women in distress. She was applauded when, as Cordelia in the revised *Lear*, she described herself as "Arm'd in my Virgin Innocence"—although the promiscuous Mrs. Barry, "in the same part, more fam'd for her Stage Performance than the other, at the words, *Virgin Innocence*, has created a Horse-laugh . . . and the scene of generous Pity and Compassion at the close turn'd to Ridicule."[10]

Prologues and epilogues, with their ambiguous position between the fictional and the real, provided ideal opportunities to exploit the relation between the player and the part. The most extreme, and probably the funniest, example occurs at the end of Dryden's *Tyrannic Love*. Nell Gwynn, playing a doomed princess despite her generally recognized ineptitude in tragic roles, finally expires. Servants load her corpse onto a litter and are carrying it out when she suddenly sits bolt upright and exclaims, "Hold, are you mad? You damn'd confounded Dog! I am to rise, and speak the Epilogue!" She leaps off the bier and begins the final speech:

> I come, kind Gentlemen, strange news to tell ye
> I am the ghost of poor departed Nelly . . .
> To tell you truth, I walk because I die
> Out of my calling, in a Tragedy.
> O Poet, dam'd dull Poet, who could prove
> So senseless to make Nelly die for love! . . .
> As for my epitaph when I am gone,
> I'll trust no poet, but will write my own:
> "Here Nelly lies, who, though she liv'd a Slattern
> Yet dy'd a princess, acting in Saint Cathar'n."[11]

In *An Essay of Dramatic Poetry, and The Grounds of Criticism in Tragedy*, Dryden's qualified admiration for the French tradition testifies to his interest in and sensitivity to the require-

---

[9]Wilson, p. 107.

[10]William Chetwood, *A General History of the Stage* (London, 1749), p. 28.

[11]John Dryden, *The Dramatic Works*, ed. Montague Summers (London: Nonesuch, 1931), II, p. 395.

ments of theatrical decorum. But the demands of the tragic situation, even for Dryden, are overridden by the demands of Nell's personality.

It is tempting to think of the new acceptance of female assertiveness on the stage as part of a general revaluation of women's status—a reassessment that would eventually allow them to participate more fully in all aspects of public life. Certainly all the evidence suggests that although the actresses were never as numerous or as well-paid as their male colleagues, they participated extensively in the life of the companies to which they belonged. They were granted the same special privileges as the actors—most significantly a relative immunity from prosecution for debt. And with the formation of the Lincoln's Inn Fields Company in 1695, two actresses—Ann Bracegirdle and Mary Saunderson Betterton—became shareholders, with a right to a certain percentage of the company's profits.

The employment of actresses does not, however, coincide with a more general broadening of female participation in public life. In fact, during the second half of the seventeenth century women seem to have been losing rather than acquiring opportunities for gainful employment. Men were encroaching upon such traditionally female occupations as brewing, textile manufacture, dressmaking, and midwifery. Women were less and less likely to run businesses or enter trades independently of their husbands, to help their husbands in a family venture, or to continue such a venture when they were widowed. By the beginning of the eighteenth century, there were few alternatives for undowered, unmarried women—or married women whose husbands could not support them—other than domestic service or prostitution.[12] The success of the actress has to be explained in ways which take into account the drastically different experience of women in other professions.

Actresses, in other words, seem to be anomalous rather than typical; the task is to isolate the factors that make their case so special. It is reasonable to look more closely to the audience's actual response to the women on the stage, in order to establish revealing patterns of assumptions. One such pattern is so obvious as to be unavoidable. Everyone from Dryden on has remarked upon the audience's extraordinarily lively, even obsessive, concern with the actresses' sexuality.

John Downes, in *Roscius Angelicanus,* regales the reader with sly anecdotes:

> And all the Women's Parts admirably Acted: chiefly *Celia* [Moll Davis], a Shepherdess being Mad for Love; especially in Singing several Wild and Mad Songs. *My Lodging is on the Cold Ground,* etc. She perform'd that so Charmingly, that not long after, it Rais'd her from her Bed on the Cold Ground, to a Bed Royal.

> *Note, Mrs. Johnson in this Comedy, Dancing a Jigg so Charming Well, Love's power in a little time after Coerc'd her to Dance more Charming else where.*[13]

Others were less delicate. The anonymous author of "Satyr on Players" (London, c. 1685), declares that actresses are "so lewd in every kind / You'd swear that Rogue and Whore had both combin'd," and goes on to support his claim in explicit detail:

> Sue Percival so long has known the Stage
> She grows in Lewdness faster, than in Age:
> From Eight or Nine she there has swiving been;
> So calls that Nature, which is truly Sin. (page 2)

Despite the difference in tone, Downes and the author of the "Satyr" both assume that the sexual exploits of the actress are an extension of her histrionic function rather than an irrelevant side-issue. Moll Davis's change of beds is described as the direct result of her fine performance; Mrs. Johnson gets invited to dance elsewhere because she has danced so well on the stage; Sue Percival's theatrical and sexual exploits coincide. Modern critics like John Harold Wilson and Allardyce Nicoll conclude that the presence of the actresses debased the theater, by lending it the atmosphere of a brothel. . . .[14]

No doubt the fuss is partly due to the fact that the actresses' sex lives really were fairly unorthodox. As Allardyce Nicoll primly declares, "very few of these women led chaste lives."[15] Elizabeth Barry was the mistress of John, Earl of Rochester; Elizabeth Hall the mistress of Sir Philip Howard; the Mrs. Johnson of Downes's anecdote the mistress of Henry, Earl of Peterborough. Margaret Hughes was the mistress of Prince Rupert, Susannah Hall the mistress of Sir Robert Howard, Ann Reeves the mistress of Dryden, Elizabeth Barry (again) of Otway, and Ann Bracegirdle (perhaps) of Congreve. Hester Davenport was irregularly married to the Earl of Oxford—when she refused to become his mistress he dressed up one of his servants as a parson, and had an invalid marriage ceremony performed. Nell Gwynn and Moll Davis went all the way to the top, and became mistresses of Charles

---

[12]The standard work on the subject is still Alice Clark's *Working Life of Women in the Seventeenth Century* (London: Routledge and Sons, 1919). Her conclusion—that women were progressively excluded from the job market during the seventeenth century—though not her Marxist analysis, has recently been supported by Roger Thompson, *Women In Stuart England and America* (London: Routledge and Kegan Paul, 1974), pp. 74–75.

[13]Downes, pp. 23–24, page 33.

[14]Wilson, *passim.;* Nicoll, p. 72.

[15]Nicoll, p. 72.

II. Others, like Elizabeth Boutell and Rebecca Marshall, played the field.

Nonetheless, there were alternative models, like Mary Saunderson Betterton, who was the leading tragic actress before Mrs. Barry, and who seems to have led a faithful married life throughout her long career. An actress like Nell Gwynn, however, whose stage career lasted only five years, and whose histrionic talents were probably much smaller, seemed a much more exemplary specimen. When Ann Bracegirdle proved unexpectedly chaste, the audience did not divert its attention from her sexuality, but focused upon it all the more sharply.

> RAMBLE: And Mrs. Bracegirdle . . .
> CRITIC: Is a haughty conceited Woman, that has got more Money by dissembling her Lewdness, than others by professing it.
> SULLEN: But does that Romantick Virgin still keep up her great reputation?
> CRITIC: D'ye mean her Reputation for Acting?
> SULLEN: I mean her Reputation for not acting; you understand me.—[16]

By contrast, audience interest in the male players tended not to involve such an avid concern with their sex lives. Actors like Charles Hart, Edward Kynaston, and Cardell Goodman were "kept" by aristocratic ladies—in Goodman's case his connection with Lady Castlemaine obtained him a pardon after he had been convicted of highway robbery, a capital crime. But contemporary comment on their situation is muted; their sexuality is not considered part and parcel with their histrionic vocation. . . .

If hierarchical assumptions dominate conceptions of gender difference, boys and women occupy a similar position—they are inferior versions of mature men, *hommes manqués*. From one point of view, as *As You Like It*'s Rosalind-Ganymede knows, boys and women are cattle of the same color. The convention of the boy-actress has a certain logic; at any rate it does not pose a profound or necessary challenge to the audience's ideological convictions. If sexual difference is understood in terms of opposition, however, transvestite role-playing involves a much greater rupture of decorum—a rupture which may be ludicrous, implausible, or titillating depending upon the context. Boys no longer seem appropriate in women's tragic roles; a Cleopatra who shaves is the occasion for a jest.[17] The Restoration audience was more eager to see women in male disguise, but arguably this eagerness is rooted in the same attitudes which make the boy impersonators seem obsolete. John Harold Wilson has remarked upon the surprisingly "indelicate" methods by which women players in male disguise were unmasked in Restoration comedy.[18] Surely all the loosened hair, all the naked breasts in the fifth act are meant to heighten an incongruity of which the audience was already aware; the unmasking reinforces a histrionic appeal which depends upon the seductive appeal of female difference.

From this perspective one can see why the actresses appeared on the public stage for the first time at the Restoration; why their success could coincide with a more general withdrawal of women from public life; and also why their achievement took the specific forms that it did. It is not merely new attitudes toward women and the theater, but the persistence of old ones, which make possible the novel phenomenon of the Restoration actress, and which condition the highly selective enthusiasm of her audience.

---

[16]Anon. (sometimes ascribed to Charles Gildon), *A Comparison between The Two Stages* (London, 1702), p. 17.

[17]Cibber, p. 71.

[18]Wilson, p. 85.

Modern Europe

Hamm in one of the definitive spaces of modern drama, the empty room of Samuel Beckett's *Endgame,* in the 2000 Rude Mechanicals Theater Company production.

In many ways the world we live in today was forged between 1850 and 1950. Since the mid-nineteenth century, enormous political changes have redrawn the map of the planet: two world wars; the rise of the United States and the rise and fall of the Union of Soviet Socialist Republics as world superpowers; revolutions in Russia and China; worldwide liberation from European colonial rule in Mexico, the Philippines, Latin America, Africa, India, and Southeast Asia. Political change was spurred by a series of industrial and technological revolutions. This century saw the introduction of the telephone, radio, film, and television; of the automobile and the highway; of the airplane and the rocket; of penicillin, anesthetics, vaccinations, and artificial organs; of the assembly line and mass production; of multinational corporations extending their markets and influence around the globe. The acceleration of technological change altered the fabric of daily life, creating new forms of living, working, and relating to one another, and new ways of measuring our lives: suburbs and housing developments, trade unions and public corporations, the time clock and the wristwatch, public education and compulsory retirement. It witnessed huge changes in the landscape of life: the growth of the modern cityscape, of modern slums, skyscrapers, subways, and even city streets; of massive public projects like the Panama and Suez canals, the Empire State Building, the Eiffel Tower, and their grim cousins—the gas chambers of Auschwitz and the nuclear bombing of Hiroshima and Nagasaki.

Political and social changes were rivaled by the intellectual and cultural revolutions that gave—or attempted to give—meaning to modern experience. This was the century of Darwin and the theory of evolution; of Marx and Lenin; of Gandhi's nonviolent resistance; of Einstein, Oppenheimer, and Teller, and a revolution in our understanding of the physical cosmos; of Freud's discovery of the unconscious; of Proust, Joyce, Stein, Eliot, and Woolf; of the Impressionist painters, and of Picasso, and Pollock; of Diaghilev and Nijinsky, of Fred Astaire and Ginger Rogers, of Isadora Duncan and Martha Graham; of Wagner, of Stravinsky and Schoenberg, of ragtime and jazz.

This complex of revolutions extends to the modern theater. Technological innovation, political developments, and two major wars encouraged an increasing internationalism across the arts of Europe, evident in the "international" style of architecture popularized by Le Corbusier, the Bauhaus, and their followers; in Cubist painting and sculpture; and in modernist writing and music. This internationalism, however, hardly fostered a single, monolithic sense of "modernism" in the arts. Instead, it gave rise to a series of fragmentary **AVANT-GARDE** movements—imagism, cubism, vorticism, futurism, symbolism, surrealism, Dada, and so on—each with its own ideals, esthetics, and audience, and usually with its own resistant posture toward society as well. The fragment—the poetic image, Joyce's "epiphanies," Schoenberg's twelve-tone row, montage in film—came to be valued as a means of expression in itself. Since the 1950s, a variety of social, political, and esthetic challenges have been made to modernism—usually under the general rubric of **POSTMODERNISM.** These challenges are discussed later in this essay.

Modernist art also developed a distinction between "high art" and the esthetics of mass culture that parallels the modern division of labor and implies a division between highbrow and lowbrow, the elite and the popular. In many respects, the modernist theater became definitive of "high art" as it was edged from the center of cultural life by other performance media—film, radio, and later, television—which claimed greater immediacy and wider distribution. After the turn of the twentieth century, the modern theater and drama were increasingly pressed to define what is germane, special, essential to live dramatic performance.

Units V, VI, and VII survey the theater more widely than previous units, focusing not on a single city or site of performance, but instead on the broader developments of national and international movements. For although the theaters of Chekhov's Moscow, Shaw's London, and Brecht's Berlin reflected very different social dynamics, they were engaged in a common, distinctly modernist project: bringing the stage into a critical relation to the forms of modern life by taking an experimental attitude toward theatrical production. And many of these projects have a visible legacy in the work of their successors: in Beckett's sterile chambers, in Müller's assault on the dynamics of temporality and identity, in Churchill's parallel between sexual and colonial politics, in the critical **HYBRIDIZATION** of Soyinka's drama.

The Modern Theater

Theatrical innovation always takes place on three fronts: as technology, as esthetics, and as ideology. The history of the modern theater is in one sense a history of new strategies and techniques for stage production: electric lighting, revolving stages, increasingly spectacular and illusionistic stage machinery, and new techniques of stage design, acting, and direction. What makes these changes meaningful is how they are used to represent and explain the world around us.

Reviewing the history of nineteenth-century drama, Brander Matthews, the first professor of dramatic literature in the United States, remarked in 1910 that modern drama owed its innovation more to Edison than to Ibsen, that the new drama was "the inevitable consequence of the incandescent bulb." The technological revolutions that brought engines and electricity to the public transformed theater throughout Europe and America: the replacement of candle lighting and gas lighting with more flexible electric lighting; the installation of the **PROSCENIUM** frame, emphasizing the pictorial coherence of the stage; the gradual disappearance of galleries and boxes in favor of seating the audience in darkened, fan-shaped theaters, emphasizing a perspective view of the proscenium; elevators to raise and lower sets; revolving stages on which several settings could be placed at one time. This technology could be put to a variety of uses, and the nineteenth-century theaters of Europe and America had an extraordinarily spectacular dimension, fostering a taste for **EXTRAVAGANZAS, MELODRAMAS, NAUTICAL SHOWS, PANTOMIMES,** and **TABLEAUX.** However, the apparatus of the modern theater came increasingly to be dominated by the notion of **SCENIC UNITY,** the idea that the stage set, the costumes, the behavior of the actors, and the dramatic action all should correspond to a single historical era and social milieu. Shakespeare's actors had mixed contemporary Elizabethan dress with "antique" costumes in the production of plays with classical settings. Throughout the eighteenth century, actors wore contemporary clothing regardless of the historical era of the play. By the late nineteenth century, however—following the example of Charles Kean and Henry Irving in England, the company of George II, the Duke of Saxe-Meiningen in Germany, and others—productions increasingly strove to establish a unified style on the stage, in which the dialogue, acting style, costumes, setting, and dramatic action all conformed to a single point of view.

The use of a unified theatrical style to assert a thorough **VERISIMILITUDE,** a photographic "slice of life" onstage, became the cornerstone of modern **REALISM** in drama and theater and of the movement called **NATURALISM** in which it began. In a series of essays calling for a "naturalism in the theater," published in the 1870s, the French novelist and playwright Émile Zola argued that the technology of the late nineteenth-century theater could be used to represent a more clinical or scientific attitude toward the world. He urged the stage to adopt a more lifelike and "naturalistic" style by adopting the "objective" methods and perspective of the natural sciences. By filling the stage with objects—real doors, real walls, pictures, furniture, fireplaces—the theater could place men and women in their "environment" rather than in the idealized "setting" of the classical theater, and the characters could then be

A PROSCENIUM STAGE: SHAKESPEARE MEMORIAL THEATRE

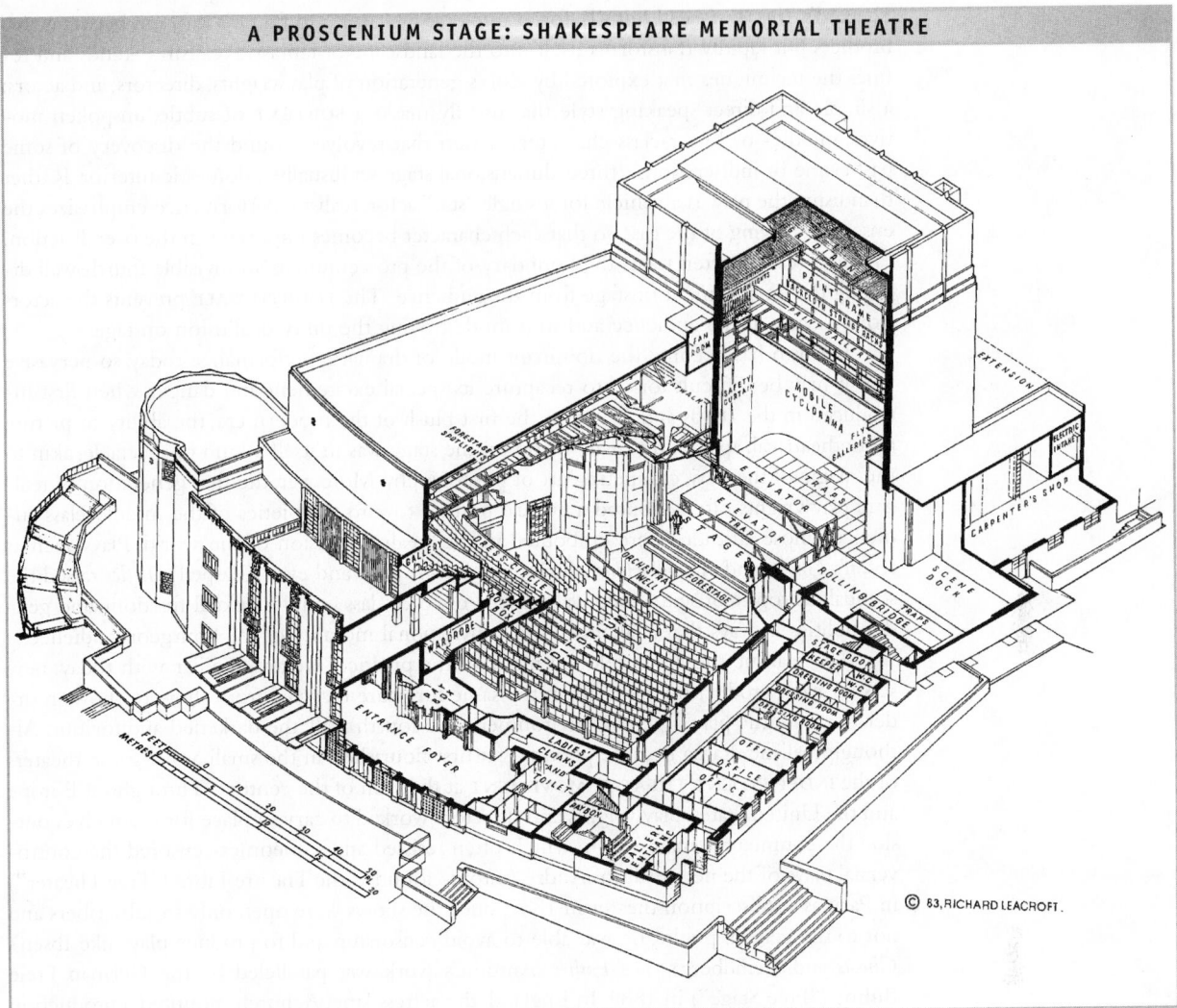

© 63, RICHARD LEACROFT.

The Shakespeare Memorial Theatre, Stratford-upon-Avon, 1932, displays an extensive backstage area used for scenic machinery.

seen as influenced by that material environment. In contrast to the ideal heroes of earlier drama, the characters of modern plays would become part of that stage milieu, influenced by the forces of history, society, economy, and psychology. Naturalism uses the technology of the stage to claim a "scientific" attitude toward social problems, usually emphasizing the determining role that the social environment plays in the characters' actions. It organized the theater's new technology and the idea of scenic unity it made possible, and provided modern theater with a characteristic kind of meaning: the achievement of verisimilitude.

Naturalism and realism are notoriously difficult to distinguish; here we can describe them as two phases in the history of modern theater and drama. In this sense, naturalism provides the thematic inspiration and many of the dramatic techniques we now associate with modern realistic drama. Realism in the theater is also committed to verisimilitude, but usually develops a wider range of style and a more problematic sense of the relationship of character and environment. While naturalistic plays tend to be preoccupied with the duplication of material reality onstage, realistic plays sometimes distort the verisimilitude of the stage picture in order to dramatize an inner, psychological truth. The domestic space of Sam

Shepard's *True West* (see Unit VI), for example, at first seems to frame a reunion between two brothers but rapidly transforms itself into the landscape of fantasy. Realism extends and refines the techniques first explored by Zola's generation of playwrights, directors, and actors: a simple and direct speaking style that usually masks a SUBTEXT of subtle, unspoken motives; middle- or lower-class characters; action that revolves around the discovery of some past crime or indiscretion; a three-dimensional stage set, usually a domestic interior. Rather than using the play as a vehicle for a single "star" actor, realistic performance emphasizes the ensemble playing of the cast, so that each character becomes important in the overall action. Onstage, realism often treats the boundary of the proscenium as an invisible fourth wall dividing the environment onstage from the audience. The FOURTH WALL prevents the actors from playing to the audience and so from destroying the unity of illusion onstage.

Realism has become the dominant mode of dramatic performance today, so pervasive that it may be difficult for us to recapture its special excitement and danger when first introduced in the 1880s and 1890s. In the first blush of the modern era, the ability to picture an untheatrical, apparently "real" world on the stage was in itself a kind of spectacle, akin to the magic of the new, competing art of photography. Moreover, the first generation of realistic playwrights often adopted a critical posture toward the pieties of the middle-class audience whose attitudes were embodied in the "realistic" vision of the world. Plays such as Ibsen's *Ghosts* and *A Doll House,* Strindberg's *Miss Julie,* and even Glaspell's *Trifles* raised the scandalous topics of sexual betrayal, marital discord, class conflict, sexual freedom, and gender politics in ways that challenged the conventional morality of the bourgeois audience.

The realistic theater developed many of the practices we are familiar with today: new sets for each production, rather than the same furniture recycled from show to show, in order to create the play's specific environment; the fourth wall; the darkened auditorium. Although realistic drama became pervasive, it first flourished in the small avant-garde theaters of the INDEPENDENT THEATER MOVEMENT at the turn of the century. Throughout Europe and the United States, playwrights and directors worked to carve a place for themselves outside the commercial mainstream, which often resisted and sometimes censored the controversial plays of the new realism. André Antoine founded the Théâtre Libre ("Free Theater") in Paris as a subscription theater in 1887; since the shows were open only to subscribers and not to the general public, he was able to avoid censorship and to produce plays like Ibsen's *Ghosts* and Strindberg's *The Father.* Antoine's work was paralleled by the German Freie Bühne ("Free Stage") in 1889. In England, the actress Janet Achurch mounted a production of Ibsen's *A Doll House* in 1889; J.T. Grein's Independent Theater opened in 1891 with a production of *Ghosts* and went on to produce plays by Ibsen, Shaw, and other contemporary playwrights. In Russia, Constantin Stanislavski and Vladimir Nemirovich-Danchenko founded the Moscow Art Theater in 1898, launching one of the most influential of modern theaters with their production of Chekhov's *The Seagull.* Independent theaters were often part of nationalist movements as well, especially in Norway, Sweden, Finland, Italy, and Ireland. In Ireland, W. B. Yeats, Lady Augusta Gregory, John Millington Synge, and a solid cast of amateur actors established a nationalist theater company in 1902 and opened The Abbey Theater in 1904. Here, the artistic resistance of the independent theater was allied to political resistance and national self-definition. The influence of these theaters was felt in the United States throughout the first decades of the twentieth century. David Belasco's minute fidelity to detail had firmly established a realistic idiom in the American theater, but it took the LITTLE THEATER MOVEMENT, inaugurated by Eugene O'Neill, Susan Glaspell, and the Provincetown Playhouse in 1915, to establish a repertoire of modern drama in the United States, and they were soon followed by other companies.

Forms of Modern Drama

The rise of the independent theaters also points to the theater's fragmentation and its marginalization in modern society. The theater no longer commands the cultural centrality that it had in classical Athens or in London and Paris in the sixteenth and seventeenth centuries.

SHAKESPEARE MEMORIAL THEATRE, INTERIOR VIEW

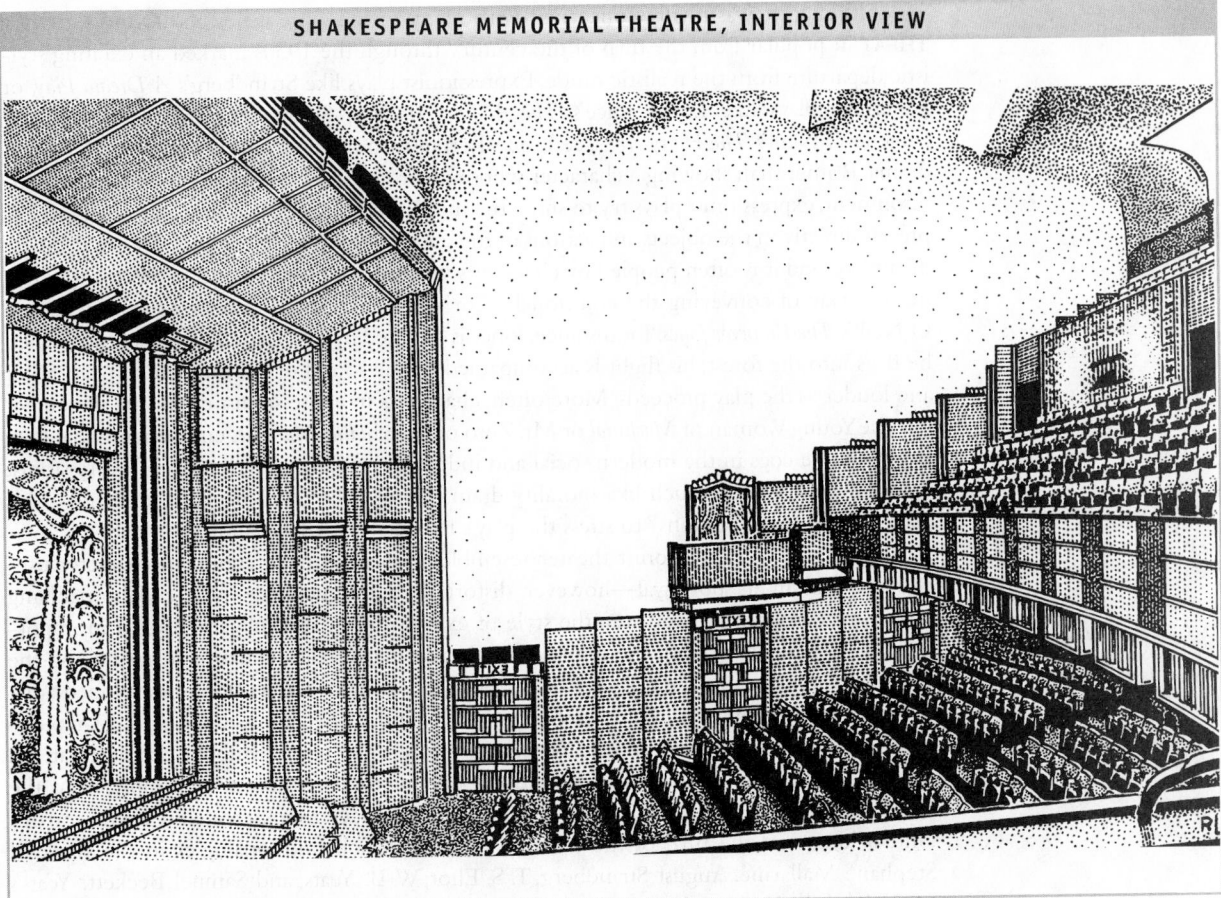

Although the Shakespeare Memorial Theatre has a forestage apron extending toward the audience, it is in many respects typical of the proscenium theaters of the early twentieth century. The audience is seated in a fan-shaped auditorium, in fixed seats, facing the illuminated stage.

Instead, it has become the site for a diverse, sometimes confusing array of artistic experiments. Naturalism and realism were the first dramatic modes to consider themselves not as expressing the dominant political and ideological order, but as criticizing the values and institutions of middle-class society. The major plays of the realistic canon often tend to criticize modern life, particularly its dehumanizing, exploitative routine. The major heroes of the realistic mode—Nora Helmer, Major Barbara, Laura Wingfield—are all characters whose desire for freedom, vitality, and life is threatened by the deadening, deceptive world in which they live. Because realistic drama usually sees that world as an all-embracing "environment," though, its social themes don't finally lead to a call for social change. Modern society may be a prison, but the liberation urged by realistic drama is imagined on the individual level; the characters' search for freedom, value, and meaning leaves the world unchanged. Despite its critical stance toward modern society, realistic drama tacitly accepts the world and its values as an unchanging, and unchangeable, environment in which the characters live out their lives.

For this reason, realistic drama has often seemed an inadequate vehicle for a sustained critique of the forces of modern life, and almost from the moment of its inception in the 1880s and 1890s, realism inspired antagonistic forms of drama and theater. The history of modern drama is a series of reactions against bourgeois society and its values, and against the realistic drama that seemed to represent it and its vision of the world.

Although it was finally concerned with many of the same issues, the **EXPRESSIONIST THEATER** popular from the turn of the century through the 1930s marked an exciting stylistic departure from the realistic mode. Expressionist plays like Strindberg's *A Dream Play,* or American plays like Elmer Rice's *The Adding Machine,* Sophie Treadwell's *Machinal,* or Eugene O'Neill's *The Hairy Ape* (see Unit VI), transformed the terms of realistic theater and drama. Rather than showing a character whose inner vitality is crushed by the bourgeois environment, expressionist plays try to show the mind and heart of the character visually, to express it directly in the objects and actions of the stage. The stage set becomes distorted, nearly dreamlike, and it is often peopled by characters who are exaggerated, mechanized, or fantastic, as a way of conveying the emotional coloring of the central character's experience. In O'Neill's *The Emperor Jones,* for instance, Jones is haunted by his "Little Formless Fears" when he flees into the forest; his flight is accompanied by the sound of a drum, which beats faster and louder as the play proceeds. More often, characters in expressionist drama are unnamed, like the Young Woman of *Machinal* or Mr. Zero of *The Adding Machine,* emphasizing that they have become cogs in the modern social and industrial machine. The action of expressionist drama is episodic and much like morality drama. Ernst Toller even named the scenes of his play *Transfiguration* "stations" to stress the play's likeness to a Christian passion play.

Thematically, expressionist theater resembles realism in its attention to character psychology and in its portrayal—however distorted or exaggerated—of the dehumanizing process of modern life. However, the style of expressionism also subverts realism in important ways, challenging both the logical, causal ordering of realistic dramatic action and the visual verisimilitude of the realistic theater. The **SYMBOLIST THEATER** also developed antirealistic attitudes toward drama and staging and extended the expressionist theater's repudiation of the drama of modern life. Written in prose or in verse, symbolic drama created a dim and mysterious other world, sometimes drawn from mythology or simply from the poet's imagination. The Belgian playwright Maurice Maeterlinck created a vogue for this kind of drama at the turn of the century, a drama which finds analogies in the work of Stéphane Mallarmé, August Strindberg, T. S. Eliot, W. B. Yeats, and Samuel Beckett. Yeats's mythological plays—such as *On Baile's Strand*—are typical of this special and influential mode. Relatively static in action, the plays rely on a densely figurative language to enlarge and energize the "poetic" meaning of events onstage.

Finally, an explicitly Marxist theory of the ideologically coercive dimension of realism— the sense that realism claims that its special perspective of the world is *natural;* that is, unavoidable and *real*—stands at the center of modern **EPIC THEATER.** Though usually associated with Bertolt Brecht, many of the techniques of epic theater were developed by Erwin Piscator in Berlin during the 1920s and early 1930s and by Vsevolod Meyerhold in his brilliant experiments with **CONSTRUCTIVIST THEATER** after the Russian Revolution of 1917. Brecht assimilated these techniques to a political purpose that he called epic theater. Rather than claiming to represent reality directly onstage by concealing the workings of the theater, epic theater alerts the audience to the ideological dimension of theater practice by constantly keeping the stage's "means of production" in view. Brecht developed the **ALIENATION EFFECT** as a way of alerting the audience to the constructed nature of stage events. While the realistic theater claims that the theater and drama, actor and character, stage and dramatic locale are the same, epic theater shows how they are different. In so doing, Brecht argued, the epic theater enables the audience to ask how—with what purpose, to what effect—stage practice is making this dramatic effect come about, and so leads the audience to take a more critical view of the process of the theater. Epic acting, then, comments on itself as "acting." The stage is not unified as a single dramatic locale, but always remains visibly a stage. Brecht also argued that epic drama should be structured differently than realistic plays. Instead of the apparently organic, "causal" action of realistic drama, Brecht's plays are written in a series of episodes. This technique, Brecht argued, allows the actors and the audience to reconsider the character's possibilities for action and change afresh in each scene. By calling the audience's attention to how the play comes into being onstage, epic theater encourages the audience to develop a dialectical sense of how social reality—in the theater and in the world at large—comes into being, how it is made through the interaction of individual and social forces and the interaction of material reality and **IDEOLOGY.** Epic theater has had an enormous influence on drama and theater around the world.

Stage practice has developed its own rich history, too—again often in reaction to realistic verisimilitude. Throughout the twentieth century, for instance, designers and architects have experimented with different ways of orienting the audience to the stage, in **THEATER IN THE ROUND** and in **ENVIRONMENTAL THEATER,** for instance. To see the dramatic action surrounded by spectators or to have the play take place among the audience members alters the audience's relationship to both the drama and its performance and changes how they can read the production. The Constructivist experiments of Vsevolod Meyerhold following the Russian Revolution placed a nonrepresentational "construction" onstage, a structure that the actors used as a "machine for acting" rather than as a realistic set. Similarly, experimental performance altered notions of what dramatic and theatrical representation could be like. Following World War I, writers such as Tristan Tzara called for an art that was formless and irrational, a process rather than a product; such "Dada"—a nonsense term—poems, plays, and monologues were often given **CABARET PERFORMANCE** in Zurich, Berlin, and Paris. **DADA** and **SURREALIST THEATER** developed a kind of hallucinatory intimacy between stage and audience, laying the foundations for Artaud's **THEATER OF CRUELTY.** In all of these experiments, the theater worked to disperse the visual unity characteristic of the realistic stage in ways that led to new configurations of the relationship between the audience and the performers and to new interpretive perspectives on drama and the possibilities of theater.

Realism, expressionism, symbolist theater, and *epic theater*—these useful labels necessarily limit and categorize the rich variety of the stage in ways that are artificial and untrue to the dynamics of change in the modern theater, for new innovations tend to draw their techniques from several of these modes. Modern plays, for instance, often blend representational techniques as a way of challenging the audience's understanding of the drama and its implication in the world. Despite their "realistic" anchoring in a material, lifelike setting, for example, Chekhov's plays sometimes disturb the stability of that illusion with odd, almost "symbolic" effects—the breaking string in *The Cherry Orchard,* for instance. The action of Strindberg's *Miss Julie,* too, for all the play's emphasis on domestic and social environment, seems to lurch and accelerate in ways more characteristic of an "expressionist" linking of the dramatic form to the characters' psychological experience. In Pirandello's *Six Characters in Search of an Author*—a play indebted in many ways to the "symbolist" theater—the Characters want the Actors to produce a play much in the manner of Ibsen's drama, a realistic drama of hidden crime and its discovery. These labels are useful in helping us to describe some of the outlines of a given play, but we should remember that many modern playwrights wrote in a variety of modes, and that each play is itself a kind of experiment.

The modern theater's radical redefinitions of the style and purpose of drama required similar redefinitions of acting and performance. At the turn of the century, a theatrical company would have been organized according to each actor's typical **LINE OF BUSINESS.** Something like the company in Pirandello's *Six Characters,* companies had a leading comic actor, a villain or "heavy," a leading man, a leading lady, a comic old man, a comic woman, and a variety of other parts. Unlike *commedia dell' arte,* actors each played a variety of different characters; nonetheless, each actor would have elaborated some relatively conventional "business" for acting the kind of character he or she usually played. The unity of illusion demanded by the realistic theater, however, required each character to be more finely individualized. Much as the stage designer provided a new set for each production and the

Acting And Performance

Although most of the plays included in *The Wadsworth Anthology of Drama* have been popular in the theater, they are all to some extent plays that have been canonized for their qualities as dramatic "literature": rich language and characterization, complex engagement with social and moral issues, deft and original use of dramatic convention, and so on. However, theater and drama pose special problems to the idea of a single literary canon. As popular entertainments, plays have not always been regarded as having "literary" merit. Plays were published only irregularly in Shakespeare's era partly for this reason, and even today few publishers have much commitment to keeping contemporary plays in print—which makes it particularly difficult for contemporary drama to become part of *any* literary canon. More important, plays are produced under very different conditions than novels and poems. Plays are made to be meaningful in a specific theater; their "literary" impact on readers is often secondary to their original purpose, which is to make a theatrical impact on a given body of spectators.

In late-eighteenth and nineteenth-century Europe—in part as a result of the relaxing of restrictions on theatrical performance, and in part as a reflection of a sense of "literature" as part of a circumscribed sphere of "high culture"—a variety of new dramatic genres became popular, of which the most important is **MELODRAMA.** The term was initially used to indicate plays in which music was used to accentuate the emotional coloring of the action; the term became more generally applied to plays with a conventionalized set of characters, a clear narrative structure, and a distinct moral cosmos. In the nineteenth-century theater, melodrama was an extremely popular genre, fusing the theater's increasing capacity for visual spectacle with a strongly colored and direct dramatic action. The world of melodrama is a world of clear-cut moral absolutes: the hero and heroine are thoroughly virtuous and are threatened by villains who are proportionately unscrupulous. The action is organized in a series of episodes, in each of which the hero/heroine's happiness, virtue, fortune, or life is threatened with destruction; each act of a melodrama usually ends with some striking crisis, often calling for an elaborate stage effect—an explosion, train wreck, or storm. The action of melodrama is often highly involved and coincidental, yet usually works eventually toward a happy—or at least sentimental—ending. If the hero must die, he usually dies in the heroine's arms; more often, the couple are restored to one another and live happily ever after.

Melodrama is usually dated from the popularity of plays like Johann Christoph Friedrich von Schiller's (1759–1805) *The Robbers* (1782), August Friedrich Ferdinand von Kotzebue's (1761–1819) *Menschenhass und Reue* (1789), and René Charles Guilbert de Pixérécourt's (1773–1844) *Coelina* (1800); although Kotzebue and Pixérécourt are now rarely read, their plays were widely adapted throughout Europe. Thirty-six of Kotzebue's plays were translated into English, and several remained popular throughout the nineteenth century. Richard Brinsley Sheridan (1751–1816) adapted Kotzebue's *Der Spanier in Peru* as *Pizarro* in 1799, which became a brilliant success for the actor John Philip Kembel; Thomas Holcroft (1744–1809) adapted Pixérécourt's *Coelina* as *A Tale of Mystery* in 1802. While early nineteenth-century melodrama tended toward Gothic settings—mysterious castles, ghostly visitors, and the like—by later in the century melodrama's typical formal and moral patterns were applied to plays with local and contemporary settings. Pierce Egan's novel *Life in London* was adapted as *Tom and Jerry; or, Life in London* in 1821; Edward George Bulwer-Lytton's (1803–1873) *Money* (1840) was one of several plays that held

costume designer provided clothing appropriate to the character and his or her setting, so the actors were forced to particularize their performances in new ways.

A second stimulus for this innovation was the drama itself. Playwrights like Ibsen and Chekhov typically created characters against the grain of theatrical stereotypes. Nora Helmer, for example, seems like a typical **SOUBRETTE** at the opening of *A Doll House,* the pert and clever young woman of light comedy. However, as the play develops, Ibsen challenges this convention and forces the actress to discover new ways of producing the character. Realistic plays frequently ask actors to work against the apparent "type" of the role, to discover the psychological subtext of will and desire beneath the spoken words that motivates the character's actions. Actors and actresses at the turn of the century frequently had difficulty reading the new realistic plays, precisely because they could not see how to represent the more indirect action and individualized characters through the kinds of stage behavior they had been trained to use.

the stage through the end of the century.

Since melodrama drew a wide audience, and often centered on poor-but-virtuous heroes and heroines, it has sometimes been thought to articulate social resistance. For while early versions like Douglas Jerrold's (1803–1857) hugely popular nautical melodrama *Black Ey'd Susan* (1829) emphasized the undying loyalty and patriotism of British navy sailors (or "tars"), the polarized moral ethos of melodrama could be turned into a vehicle for social critique. In the United States, melodrama became one vehicle for dramatizing ethnic and racial conflict. John Augustus Stone's (1800–1834) *Metamora; or, The Last of the Wampanoags* (1829), dramatized a heroic Indian chief's losing battle to save the land of his ancestors from his rapacious white enemies. In *The Octoroon* (1859), Dion Boucicault (1820–1890) staged the fatal love story between the octoroon Zoe, the virtuous plantation owner who loves her, and the wicked Yankee overseer, McCloskey, who threatens to buy her when it emerges that Zoe was never actually freed from slavery. Although these plays end with "tragic" consequences for their heroes and heroines, melodrama tends to locate its evils in the character of its villains, rather than in the structure of society itself: for this reason, melodrama is usually unable to

MELODRAMA: THE BELLS

Sir Henry Irving's (1838–1905) performance in Leopold Lewis's melodrama *The Bells* was one of his greatest roles. The illustration presents both the emotionally exaggerated quality of melodramatic acting and melodrama's use of special effects. In the play, Mathias (Irving's role) has murdered and concealed the body of a Polish Jew. Although many years have passed since the murder, Mathias is haunted by the sound of his victim's sleigh bells. In this scene, he staggers before a vision of the crime itself.

develop a deeper analysis of the social institutions—racism, for example—that afflict its characters' lives. When Bernard Shaw turned to melodrama as a vehicle for his own drama of social critique, he strategically inverted its patterns of characterization as a way of opening its social order to criticism: one way *Major Barbara*, for example, attempts to jolt the audience into examining its attitudes about society at large is by casting Andrew Undershaft—so similar to the scheming and all-powerful industrialist villain of countless popular melodramas—as the moral "hero" of the play.

A new kind of drama requires a new kind of acting, and companies throughout Europe developed ways of acting more behavioristically onstage. The most systematic approach to acting was undertaken by the actor and director Constantin Stanislavski at the Moscow Art Theater around the turn of the twentieth century. Although Stanislavski thought that his techniques could be applied to any play, he discovered the need for such acting largely in his work on Chekhov's plays. Chekhov's plays were frustrating to actors of the old school, because the characters did not conform to traditional types and the action seemed so indirect and inconsequential, lacking familiar dramatic rhythms and climaxes. Stanislavski developed techniques for approaching each character as an individual, techniques that were later systematized as a "method" of actor-training. Stanislavski trained the actor to associate his or her personal history with the invented actions of the dramatic character so that the actor could tap that emotional spontaneity, a "life in art," as part of the performance. By using the **MAGIC IF**—imagining themselves *as* the character, rather than applying a stock line of business—and using their own **EMOTION MEMORY** to vivify the character's inner life, Stanislavski's actors were taught to bring authentic emotional experience into their performances. Of course, Stanislavski also emphasized the many other abilities that an actor must develop—physical training, vocal control, grace, concentration—but his real contribution to the modern stage is the emphasis on the actor's emotional reality in performance. The realistic theater uses real objects to create a persuasive material environment, and its characters come alive through the actor's real feeling. Stanislavski's work has been extremely influential, particularly in the United States, where it was adapted as the school of **METHOD ACTING** in the 1930s, and it remains—in very different and modified forms—at the center of much actor-training today.

Antirealistic drama also called for the development of new styles of performance. Meyerhold developed **BIOMECHANICS** as a way to make the actor's performance more physical, less directly concerned with the behavioral and psychological verisimilitude typical of Stanislavskian realistic acting. His work has analogies in the use of dance and ritualized performance in symbolist theater and in the nonrepresentational physicality of Antonin Artaud's Theater of Cruelty. Symbolist theater also repudiated the lifelike quality of realistic acting. It required a highly artificial and statuesque stillness from performers, allowing the actors to strike powerful but ethereal poses in order to deliver the densely poetic language of the play without interference. Yeats—whose antipathy to realism was profound—thought of training his actors in barrels, to keep them from moving and gesturing as they would do in everyday life: the art of the symbolist theater should be emphatically artificial, thoroughly apart from the conduct of life beyond the stage.

Brecht, again, voiced the most thorough critique of realistic acting. To Brecht, the problem of realistic acting was that it showed the "character" as a finished product, a commodity, rather than revealing *how* the character had come into being, both through the social forces described in the drama and through the decisions taken by the actor as part of the performance. Brecht argued that the actor should acknowledge that he or she both empathizes with the character and demonstrates the character to the audience, that acting is both feeling and showing at the same time. This dialectical approach invites the audience to see how the actor is making the "character" and allows the public to interpret both the process and the product of theater art, the dramatic "character" and the actor's labor.

Women in Modern Drama and Theater

Most readers of modern drama immediately note the prominence of women characters in the plays—Nora Helmer in *A Doll House,* Anna-Liisa in *Anna-Liisa*, Barbara in *Major Barbara,* Courage in *Mother Courage.* Playwrights frequently associated the political and social limitations of middle-class life with male characters and used female characters to pose subversive questions about that social order. However, in the drama, as in society, this subversive freedom sometimes emerges as illusory or problematic. Ibsen, for instance, enables Nora to recognize how she has been defined by the men in her life, but the world outside her home hardly seems inviting; is there really anywhere for her to go? Many of the women— the Stepdaughter of Pirandello's *Six Characters,* Major Barbara—are also assigned an erotic power opposed to the "reason" of their male antagonists. While this power, too, can be disruptive, it sometimes also reinforces traditional gender stereotypes. Feminine erotic power in the drama carries with it other ascribed values, defining women as more emotional, as more subject to the influence of the body, as closer to "nature." Men retain a pragmatic, "rational" authority that places them at the center of society, and that defines the arena of culture and civilization as an implicitly male domain. The apparent freedom of these stage women, that is, often signals their deeper captivity to the gendered economy of modern society, a captivity shared by actresses in the period as well. Although this is also a period in which actresses—Sarah Bernhardt, Eleonora Duse, Elizabeth Robins, or Ellen Terry, for example—could earn an international reputation, they worked in a theater in which men greatly outnumbered women in the audience and in which nearly all of the managers and producers were men. Women were also important playwrights throughout Europe in the first decades of the twentieth century: Elizabeth Robins's *Votes for Women!* brought the "woman question" to the English stage in 1907; Minna Canth was the leading playwright of the Finnish Theater (her portrait graces the proscenium of the National Theater today); Marieluise Fleisser's *Pioneers in Ingolstadt* (1924) in many ways rivaled Brecht's early vision of epic theater. In a male-dominated industry like the modern theater, it is not surprising that women onstage—both dramatic characters and performers—should reflect fundamentally masculine attitudes about the place of women in society.

To think of the history of theater and drama since Ibsen is to think of an increasingly large and problematic array of dramatic styles, modes of theatrical production, and conceptions of the audience and its world. Many of these innovations were local at first, responding to the social and theatrical conditions of a specific time and place: Brecht's Marxist theater arose in the cabaret culture of Berlin in the late 1920s; Pirandello's **METATHEATER** was part of the lively Italian avant-garde following World War I; Shaw's drama was informed by the progressive politics of the British Fabian Society and by dramatic conventions drawn from the popular plays of the late Victorian stage. The drama of modern Europe develops a posture of resistant inquiry toward the pieties of contemporary social life. It works both to represent that world and to change it, to affect our ideas about character and personality, about the political realities of our world, and even about the metaphysical certainties we have come to believe. But it is the impact of global political and cultural change that marks the theater of the second half of the twentieth century.

THEATER AND CULTURE SINCE 1950

The impact of film and television has forced the theater to work to define what kinds of performance are specific to the stage, how live dramatic performances can offer something unique, something not already available in other performance media. For this reason, perhaps, theater and drama since 1950 have necessarily been "experimental," working to develop new kinds of plays, new practices of stage production, and new kinds of theatrical experience for their audiences. Much as the proscenium theaters of the early twentieth century have given way to other, more flexible kinds of theater spaces, so dramatic writing has become much more varied and experimental. Even stage realism—the mode of Ibsen and Chekhov, Miller and Williams—has undergone an important reworking in the plays of Sam Shepard, Harold Pinter, Heiner Müller, and others.

Here, we can identify three patterns of innovation as a way of organizing our thinking about the diversity of the contemporary stage. One strategy—inspired most directly by Antonin Artaud's **THEATER OF CRUELTY**—attacks the notion that the theater is essentially a *representational* medium, emphasizing instead the *experiential* aspect of theater. Rather than staging images of some fictive world to an audience of passive spectators, this kind of theater works to structure the *present experience* of the audience in new ways, as in the participatory and ritualistic theater experiments of the 1960s and 1970s. The influence of Artaud's assault on representation is evident in the contemporary theater in several ways: in absurdist drama, in the focus on the body in Griselda Gambaro's *Information for Foreigners,* in the dreamlike density of Müller's *Hamletmachine,* or in the imagistic violence of Sarah Kane's *Blasted.*

The second mode of innovation, **THEATER OF THE ABSURD,** originated as a new form of playwriting rather than as theatrical experimentation. The plays of Samuel Beckett, Slawomir Mrozek, Eugène Ionesco, Boris Vian, Edward Albee, Harold Pinter, Václav Havel, and others create a strangely dislocated dramatic world, in which arbitrary or "absurd" events both confront and mystify the characters.

While Artaud inspired an existential or experiential theater, Bertolt Brecht—whose work became widely known and imitated only after World War II—inspired a different kind

THEATER IN THE ROUND

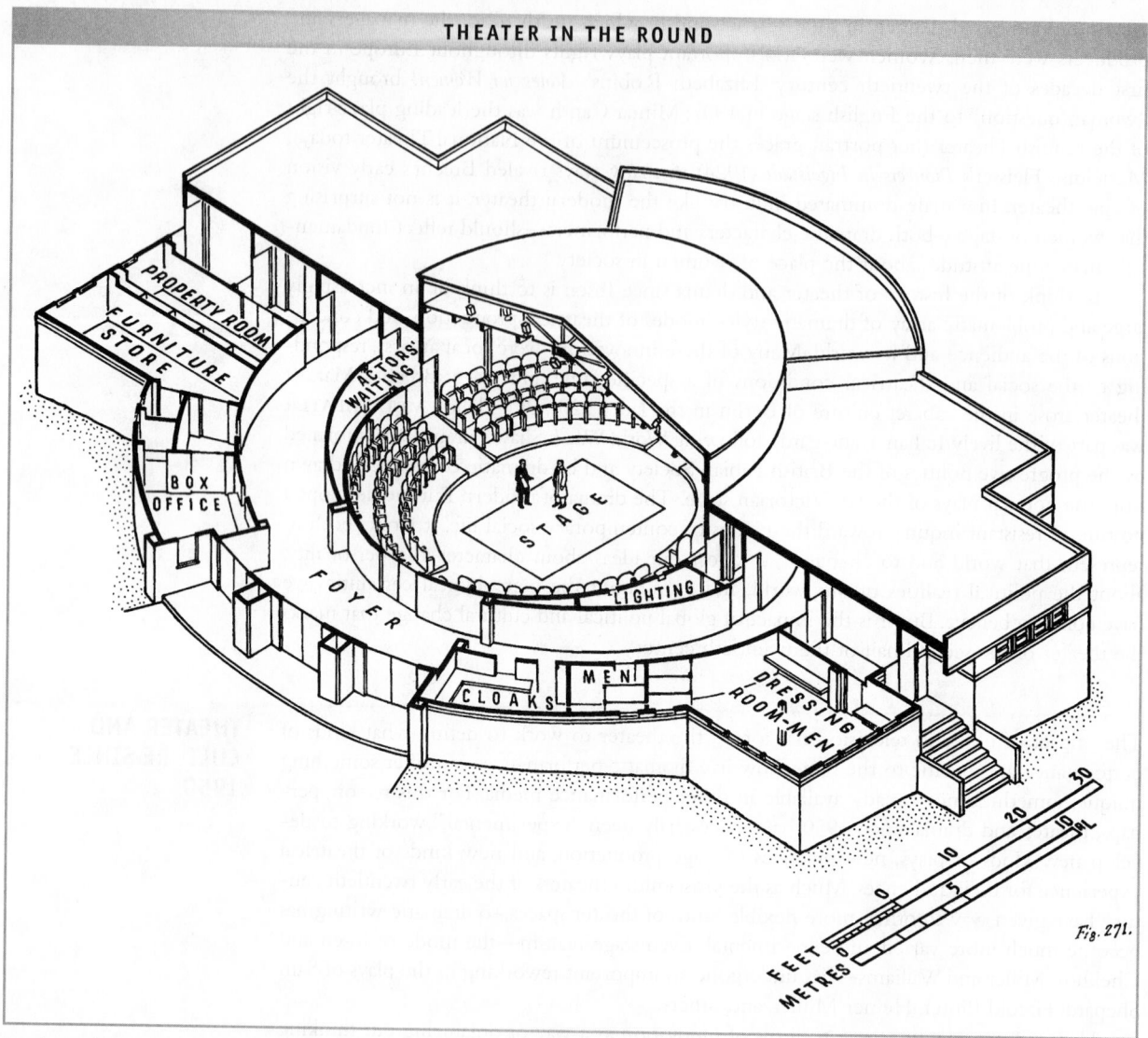

In a theater in the round, the audience surrounds the action, rather than facing the stage as in a proscenium theater. Theater space of this kind lends itself to greater immediacy and contact between the performers and the audience.

of assault on the conventions of realistic theater. Contemporary **POLITICAL THEATER** also criticizes the notion of "representation," but in different terms than Artaud or theater of the absurd, *representation* is a word with two senses: in "representing" a picture of the world, the arts necessarily claim that their images are "representative" in some way. Political theater frequently shows how a social or political order uses its power to "represent" others coercively—for example, by depicting those others through demeaning or limiting stereotypes. For this reason, political theater today is intent on using live performance to change the prejudicial attitudes concealed in conventional ideas of representation.

Of course, no plays fit easily or fully into these three categories, but to think of the drama of the postwar period as raising questions of our existential or our political relation to the theater—and so to the world—provides a useful and powerful way of opening that drama to our understanding. Each of these modes of theater creates a different relationship between the stage and its audience, and we should examine each of them in some detail.

The writings of Antonin Artaud, particularly the essays collected in the volume *The Theater and Its Double* (written in the late 1920s and 1930s, published in France in 1938, translated to English in 1958), have had an extraordinary impact on our sense of theater. Like many innovators of his generation—think of Brecht or Pirandello—Artaud worked to undermine the notion that the theater can only show its audiences realistic vignettes of daily life. Instead, Artaud argued that the theater should alter the balance between presentation—the actual, immediate activities of actors and audiences, their *presence* in the theater—and representation, the fictive "drama" that had seemed to define the purpose and scope of theater. Artaud—who used the term *theater of cruelty* for this project—advocated transforming the theater into an all-consuming spectacle, akin both to rituals like the Catholic Mass and to public festivals, in which the boundaries between acting and observing, actor and spectator, fiction and reality, conscious and unconscious would be broken or transgressed. The idea that the theater would "communicate," but not through rational means, is captured in one of Artaud's most powerful metaphors for this nearly unimaginable theater: the plague. Artaud envisioned a theater that would transmit its experiences corporeally, through the body, like disease, like mystical wisdom, alchemically transforming all of its participants. To avoid staging conventional dramas, Artaud called for a theater of "no more masterpieces," one that would use the dramatic text to transform the relations between stage and spectator by making the production a total experience—visual, auditory, gustatory, olfactory, tactile, physical—for the audience.

Stage director Peter Brook once remarked that "Artaud applied is Artaud betrayed," and it is true that Artaud's sense of theater is deeply metaphorical, a kind of theater experience that is almost unimaginable to us, and certainly not imaginable to us as theater. Artaud rarely offers a practical description of how this theater could come into being. Instead, the value and influence of Artaud's writing has been indirect and inspirational, bearing in a variety of tangential ways on kinds of theater that are not in any literal sense "Artaudian." In that Artaud imagines a theater of *presence*—not of representation—involving the audience in an experience rather than showing them a picture, his theater comes into contact with several very different kinds of innovation. Although the American experimental theater of the 1960s and 1970s is the most direct application—and betrayal—of Artaud, Artaud's conception of theater stands distantly behind a variety of more formally constructed plays: the dislocating imagery of Beckett and Müller; the ritualized, hallucinatory violence of Pinter's plays; the elaborate physical rituals of Gao Xingjian's *The Other Shore*. Of course, as *written* plays, "masterpieces," these plays are specifically opposed to the ideals of Artaud's unrealizable theater, while at the same time they explore part of the terrain opened by Artaud's vision.

Coined by the theater critic Martin Esslin in 1961, the phrase *theater of the absurd* tries to capture the special irrationality and unpredictability of a certain wave of dramatic writing of the late 1950s and 1960s, including the plays of Samuel Beckett and Harold Pinter, for example. Taking as his keynote Beckett's famous play *Waiting for Godot* (1953)—a play in which two Chaplinesque tramps wait for a mysterious man named Godot, who never arrives—Esslin finds the theater of the absurd to have certain stylistic and thematic characteristics. It rejects the sense of causality found in realistic plays, the sense that it is possible to find the causes for events either in the environment or in the psychological motives of the characters themselves. Instead, theater of the absurd tends to be about a world in which inexplicable, arbitrary, or irrational events happen. Although the events usually seem to be part of some kind of order or scheme, it is an order that the characters and their audience cannot quite grasp. As Hamm says in Beckett's play *Endgame*, "Something is taking its course," but neither the characters nor the audience are ever sure what that "something" is. In Eugène Ionesco's play *Rhinoceros* (1960), the inhabitants of a small French village begin to turn inexplicably into rhinoceroses. In each act of Boris Vian's *The Empire Builders* (1959), a family moves to a smaller room in an apartment building, always accompanied by a mysterious, bandaged figure. In Slawomir Mrozek's

Artaud and the Theater of Cruelty

Theater of the Absurd

Striptease (1961), two men are commanded by a huge, silent finger to remove their clothes and don huge conical hats that conceal and blind them. As Esslin suggests, this drama insists that the fictions we use to make sense of our world—ideas of order, causality, rationality—are just that: fictions imposed on an arbitrary and mysterious reality, whose meanings remain fugitive and elusive.

Absurdist drama treats its audience somewhat differently than realistic plays do, rejecting the "dramatic irony" of the traditional theater, in which the audience understands more than the characters onstage. Instead, the theater of the absurd refuses to provide this privilege to its spectators. We are as baffled and frustrated by our attempts to make the events mean something as the characters are; "Mean something!" a character remarks in *Endgame*, "You and I, mean something! (*Brief laugh*)." Our *present* experience as an audience is structured and made significant by absurdist theatrical production. In the theater, we don't just observe the "absurd" drama onstage, we are forced to undergo it, to live it through. For this reason, both the drama onstage and the audience's experience in the theater are sometimes described as *existential*. We have to *decide* the meaning of our being in the theater, without the comfort, solace, or guidance of some transcendent, predetermined world view.

Political Theater   Much as theater of the absurd works to make the spectators' situation in the theater an extension of the characters' situation on the stage, political theater since Brecht has worked to make the audience's performance in the theater a recognizably political one. By fragmenting the stage space, by showing how the illusion is made rather than concealing its means of production, and by involving the audience more overtly in deciding the meaning of the play's events, the theater is shown to be a political instrument. Like television, newspapers, universities, the courts, and so on, the theater is an institution that produces the ideas and images with which we govern our lives. Both the example of Brecht's plays and his challenging theory of performance have been absorbed and redefined by the world theater. In common with theater of the absurd, political theater works to resist and complicate realistic representation, the "slice of life" of Ibsen, Chekhov, and Miller. Instead of staging an arbitrarily unreal and absurd world, political theater examines "representative" images of reality. Who makes those images? Who benefits from them? Who is injured, governed, or oppressed by them? How do they help to maintain the social *status quo*?

For this reason, much political theater connects representation onstage with representation in society, showing how various social groups—women, gay men, lesbians, ethnic and racial groups, the poor—have been staged in society and in the theater. A fundamental assumption of political theater is that these stereotypes are part of the larger system of discrimination that operates in society, and that they reveal the dominant attitudes of those who govern, control, or influence society from positions of power. In plays like Amiri Baraka's *Dutchman,* Caryl Churchill's *Cloud Nine,* and Wole Soyinka's *Death and the King's Horseman,* the racial conflicts informing contemporary society and culture are explored in very different ways: in relation to colonialism, to the mythologies of imperial history, to women's experience. These plays are very different in style, ranging from a kind of realism in *Death and the King's Horseman* to the testifying monologues of Anna Deavere Smith. It is not a single point of view or a single dramatic style that defines political theater, but the use of theatrical representation itself as a way to analyze representation in society at large.

A similar approach to theater informs many of the modern plays gathered in this anthology, for many of them explore the issue of representation: how Asia is represented in the minds of the West in David Henry Hwang's *M. Butterfly,* how the English remapped and so represented the Irish in their own language and political system in Brian Friel's *Translations,* how African tribal traditions are tragically misunderstood by British imperialists in Wole Soyinka's *Death and the King's Horseman,* how the Chicano and Anglo cultures interact in Luis Valdez's *Zoot Suit,* how torture and tourism are connected in Griselda Gambaro's *Infor-*

mation for Foreigners, or the literal consumption of the Third World by the First in Manjula Padmanabhan's *Harvest.* Political theater sometimes seems highly message oriented, overtly didactic to readers and audiences used to the more subtle instruction offered by realistic plays. Yet the messages of contemporary political theater tend to be fused into the process of theater, so that the politics of the play come into being not in the prepared script of the play but in our experience as an audience. All of these plays disrupt the expectations, attitudes, and preconceptions of the empowered audience and invite the audience to develop different ways of reading their society as part of their involvement in the play.

Drama, Theater, and the "Postmodern"

On the contemporary stage, though, these modes of theater do not work in isolation from one another, but interact with one another, as part of the dynamic means the theater uses to engage its audiences in an understanding of the world. Indeed, to describe the contemporary theater in terms of its historical inheritance from the modernist theater of Brecht, Artaud, and the absurdists is in an important sense to overlook what is most significant about the stage today: its break from the traditions of modernism. If we look at the range of contemporary performance activity, much of it has little to do with traditional drama. Think of the performance-art monologues of Spalding Gray (one of his best-known, *Swimming to Cambodia,* was made into a film by Jonathan Demme) or Karen Finley (whose work was at the center of the 1990 censorship controversy at the National Endowment for the Arts); of the music of Laurie Anderson; of video art and film; of music television and advertising; of the disorienting stage spectacles of Robert Wilson; even of "plays" like Peter Handke's *Offending the Audience* and *The Ride Across Lake Constance,* or Heiner Müller's *Hamletmachine,* or Samuel Beckett's later work for the theater, *Not I, Footfalls,* and *Ohio Impromptu.*

Theorists of culture and the arts have related these developments to innovations in the visual arts, in architecture, and in writing, characterizing their common features as **POST-MODERN.** The term itself is a difficult one, suggesting that these works often share some of the features of earlier, "modernist" art; the literary and cultural theorist Fredric Jameson suggests that the distinguishing feature of postmodern art is its attitude toward history. Jameson points out that postmodern works frequently invoke or appropriate the style of earlier historical periods, as in the use of neoclassical ornamentation in recent architecture, or the recollection of earlier film styles in more recent movies (**FILM NOIR** in *Chinatown* or *L.A. Confidential*). Jameson labels this technique **PASTICHE.** What is striking about these postmodern quotations of style, though, is not any systematic reinterpretation of tradition or any statement of value, but their tonelessness, their neutrality, the absence of the kind of moral and historical sense we might expect from the act of confronting history. In postmodern pastiche, the recollection of an earlier style does not provide a new understanding of the past, nor does it illuminate our contemporary historical situation. Instead, pastiche denatures that style by removing it from history, and history from it. Style becomes exactly that: simply another option. Hamm's many quotations from English literature in *Endgame* or the pastiche of Gilbert and Sullivan operetta in Churchill's *Cloud Nine* are perhaps part of this complex problem, for in each case the "past" is presented to the audience in terms of an artistic style that is largely emptied of its force as history.

Moreover, Jameson's discussion of pastiche also emphasizes the importance of the esthetic *surface* in postmodern art. Music video and advertising are sometimes taken as the paradigmatic postmodern forms, forms whose "message" lies almost exclusively in a rapidly changing, brilliantly seductive, series of images. Although this technique relates to the modernist use of **MONTAGE** in film and theater, it is different in several important ways. Modernist montage uses a series of images narratively, to tell a story. Although the camera cuts quickly from image to image, the audience assembles the images in a single complete narrative. Both the narrative and the interpreting spectator achieve a sense of wholeness. In contrast, postmodern images are juxtaposed in striking, sometimes contradictory combinations that resist our ability to impose a single narrative explanation, a single story line. Postmodern performance—on film or video or in the theater—is insistently fragmentary; it asserts the incompletion of the artistic object and the incomplete quality of the spectator's experience as well. Postmodern arts resist imposing a single explanatory interpretation that would both complete the narrative and confirm the audience's sense of wholeness, of self-integration. In this sense, postmodern arts are sometimes described as concerned with the "death of the subject." They question the possibility both of a comprehensible world and of a comprehending individual. By disorienting language, fragmenting narrative, and dispensing with such organizing principles as "plot" and "character," postmodern art claims that we have entered a new age in which the complex disconnections of modern culture have made obsolete many of our beliefs about the world and our ways of representing the world and ourselves.

MODERN EUROPEAN DRAMA IN PERFORMANCE AND HISTORY

The understanding of theater that was inaugurated in the mid-nineteenth century is in many respects continuous with our own today: although various experiments—environmental theater, theater of cruelty, performance art—have contributed to a rich sense of the diversity of theatrical performance forms today, to many people "going to the theater" means going to a specially designated building, sitting in a darkened auditorium, and watching the events that take place on the stage. Of course, this activity is shaped today by social and economic forces still just emerging in the early-modern period: whereas earlier audiences usually had a small number of theaters to turn to for performance, performances are available today in a wide range of spaces—subsidized state and municipal theaters throughout Europe, commercial theaters like those in London's West End and New York's Broadway, college and university playhouses, festival theaters like the annual festival at Grahamstown in South Africa or the Shaw Festival in Stratford, Ontario, and many more. Theater in the twentieth century is characterized by its "optional" character: we choose theater from among a range of other forms of dramatic performance, like film and television; the theaters we attend are positioned in their ambient cultures in a much wider variety of ways; and the performances we see tend to value their "uniqueness" rather than their conventionality in typically modern ways.

Moreover, while the performance practices of earlier European theaters were highly conventionalized—masks and *cothurni* for tragedy in Athens, the phallus for comedy; a standard comic or tragic stage set in the neoclassical theaters of France and Italy—in the modern period, the style of dramatic production has become much more varied, not only as a sign of the director's and designer's artistic signature in the production, but also as part of what the play has to sell to its audiences. Indeed, the invention of the stage director in the late nineteenth century is symptomatic of a trend in modernist esthetics more generally, a trend from the polished deployment of convention to an emphasis on the artwork's originality—an originality that signals the individual creative presence of an author or *auteur*. In earlier theaters, of course, someone usually had the responsibility of organizing and rehearsing the actors: this was sometimes the playwright in classical Athenian theater, or the company's leading actor, like David Garrick, in the later eighteenth century. But in these theaters, performance practice was extremely conventionalized: actors, like Shakespeare's, who have a solid line of business, don't really need much rehearsal—an actor whose typical line of business is comic old men will more or less have an approach ready for characters like Polonius. In the modern theater, however, the director has the responsibility for shaping the diverse talents of the company—set, costume, and lighting designs; acting; music—into a single whole, one that seems to deploy the performance in a unique way. Much as we think of a film as embodying the director's vision, so too in the theater the performance is often understood as an expression of the director's ability to shape the play, the players, and the physical milieu of the stage into a uniquely expressive whole.

For this reason, the modern theater is often called the "director's theater," and in many respects the history of modern stage practice is the history of the innovations of brilliant directors. Although naturalistic or realistic drama—the plays of Ibsen and Chekhov and O'Neill—are duly appreciated for their striking departures from the standard practices of nineteenth-century playwriting, transforming these innovations from the page to the stage required a generation of brilliant directors: Antoine, Stanislavski, Meyerhold, Max Reinhardt. Indeed, throughout the history of the modern theater, actors and directors have sometimes been baffled by the new demands of these scripts; Stanislavski, for example, can be understood to have devised his famous Method in response to the obliquity of Chekhov's plays. Similarly, when one thinks of the landmark theatrical productions of the twentieth-century European theater, they are always associated with the director: Stanislavski's productions of Chekhov at the turn of the century; Meyerhold's brilliant *Hedda Gabler,* with its white set and Hedda's brilliant, snakelike green dress; Piscator's work with Brecht in the 1920s, and Brecht's direction of the Berliner Ensemble in his own and others' plays after World War II; Peter Brook's use of the circus to realize the "magic" of Shakespeare's *A Midsummer Night's Dream* in 1970; Robert Wilson's visualization of Heiner Müller's *Hamletmachine* in the 1980s. As a consequence, one of the most energetic kinds of experiment in the later part of the century has been in the area of a more collaborative theater practice. Like Complicite, many contemporary theater companies are organized as collectives, in which responsibility for the "artistic" decisions is shared, rather than given over to a single person. But even in more conventional circumstances, companies often work to make the playwright's, actors', and designers' work have a more direct impact on the final stage of theater work. Caryl Churchill's play *Cloud Nine,* for example, arose from a series of workshops undertaken by members of the Joint Stock Company, in which the actors experimented by playing different gender, sexual, or racial roles in a variety of situations: Churchill wrote the text of the play out of the workshops, and director Max Stafford-Clark used the results of the workshops as a foundation for the play's theatrical performance. Given the increasing complexity of theatrical production—the use not only of complex technology backstage, but the inclusion of multimedia production as part of the performance itself—we can expect that this struggle to shape the authority of the stage will continue well into the future.

READING THE MATERIAL THEATER

Compared with the documentary record of earlier theaters, the modern theater offers an embarrassment of riches: not only is the print tradition rich in reviews, memoirs, and other accounts of the production and reception of plays in the theater, but also playwrights themselves have often left working drafts of their plays. Henrik Ibsen is particularly notable in this regard: an extremely disciplined and methodical writer, Ibsen not only began most of his plays with a detailed scenario; he retained many of the successive drafts of his plays. These materials provide a unique insight into the process of Ibsen's imagination, and indeed into his practice as a writer as well.

What follows are Ibsen's "Notes for the Modern Tragedy," dated 19 October 1878, and his original scenario for *A Doll House.* Not surprisingly, perhaps, many of the elements of the finished play remain in this outline. At the same time, this document differs from the final drama in a number of respects (including some of the characters' names). Granted that a scenario necessarily tends to streamline the action and emphasize the plot of the play, do you find this scenario surprising in any way? Does it seem to present the same kinds of moral or ethical emphases you find in the play? Are there elements of the finished play that seem larger or more powerful than you might have expected from this scenario alone? Are there elements of the scenario that are less prominent in the final draft? The final lines of the scenario are particularly chilling: "Five: —seven hours till midnight. Twenty-four hours till the next midnight. Twenty-four and seven—thirty-one. Thirty-one hours to live. . . ." How do these lines figure in Ibsen's final imagining of the action of the finale of *A Doll House?*

Notes for the Modern Tragedy

Rome, 19. 10, 78.

There are two kinds of spiritual law, two kinds of conscience, one in man and another, altogether different, in woman. They do not understand each other; but in practical life the woman is judged by man's law, as though she were not a woman but a man.

The wife in the play ends by having no idea of what is right or wrong; natural feeling on the one hand and belief in authority on the other have altogether bewildered her.

A woman cannot be herself in the society of the present day, which is an exclusively masculine society, with laws framed by men and with a judicial system that judges feminine conduct from a masculine point of view.

She has committed forgery, and she is proud of it; for she did it out of love for her husband, to save his life. But this husband with his commonplace principles of honour is on the side of the law and regards the question with masculine eyes.

Spiritual conflicts. Oppressed and bewildered by the belief in authority, she loses faith in her moral right and ability to bring up her children. Bitterness. A mother in modern society, like certain insects who go away and die when she has done her duty in the propagation of the race.[1] Love of life, of home, of husband and children and family. Here and there a womanly shaking-off of her thoughts. Sudden return of anxiety and terror. She must bear it all alone. The catastrophe approaches, inexorably, inevitably. Despair, conflict and destruction.

(Krogstad has acted dishonourably and thereby become well-to-do; now his prosperity does not help him, he cannot recover his honour.)

PERSONS

STENBORG, a Government clerk.

NORA, his wife.

MISS (MRS.) LIND (, a widow).

ATTORNEY KROGSTAD.

KAREN, nurse at the Stenborgs'.

A PARLOUR-MAID at the Stenborgs'.

A PORTER.

THE STENBORGS' THREE LITTLE CHILDREN.

DOCTOR HANK.

SCENARIO

FIRST ACT

A room comfortably, but not showily, furnished. In the back, on the right, a door leads to the hall; on the left another door leads to the room or office of the master of the house, which can be seen when the door is opened. A fire in the stove. Winter day.

She enters from the back, humming gaily; she is in outdoor dress and carries several parcels, has been shopping. As she opens the door, a Porter is seen in the hall, carrying a Christmas-tree. She: Put it down there for the present. (Taking out her purse) How much? Porter: Fifty öre. She: Here is a crown. No, keep the change. The Porter thanks her and goes. She continues humming and smiling with quiet glee as she opens several of the parcels she has brought. Calls off, is he at home? Yes! At first, conversation through the closed door; then he opens it and goes on talking to her while continuing to work most of the time, standing at his desk. There is a ring at the hall-door; he does not want to be disturbed; shuts himself in. The maid opens the door to her mistress's friend, just arrived in town. Happy surprise. Mutual explanation of the position of affairs. He has received the post of manager in the new joint-stock bank and is to enter on his duties at the New Year; all financial worries are at an end. The friend has come to town to look for some small employment in an office or whatever may present itself. Mrs. Stenborg gives her

---

[1]The sentence is elliptical in the original.

good hopes, is certain that all will turn out well. The maid opens the front-door to the debt-collector. Mrs. Stenborg terrified; they exchange a few words; he is shown into the office. Mrs. Stenborg and her friend; the circumstances of the debt-collector are touched upon. Stenborg enters in his overcoat; has sent the collector out the other way. Conversation about the friend's affairs; hesitation on his part. He and the friend go out; his wife follows them into the hall; the Nurse enters with the children. Mother and children play. The collector enters. Mrs. Stenborg sends the children out to the left. Great scene between her and him. He goes. Stenborg enters; has met him on the stairs; displeased; wants to know what he came back for? Her support? No intrigues. His wife cautiously tries to pump him. Strict legal answers. Exit to his room. She (repeating her words when the collector went out) But that's impossible. Why, I did it from love!

SCENARIO

SECOND ACT

The last day of the year. Midday. Nora and the old Nurse. Nora, impelled by uneasiness, is putting on her things to go out. Anxious random questions of one kind and another give a hint that thoughts of death are in her mind. Tries to banish these thoughts, to turn it off, hopes that something or other may intervene. But what? The Nurse goes off to the left.—Stenborg enters from his room. Short dialogue between him and Nora.—The Nurse re-enters, looking for Nora; the youngest child is crying. Annoyance and questioning on Stenborg's part; exit the Nurse; Stenborg is going in to the children.—Doctor Hank enters. Scene between him and Stenborg.—Nora soon re-enters; she has turned back; anxiety has driven her home again. Scene between her, the Doctor and Stenborg. Stenborg goes into his room.—Scene between Nora and the Doctor. The Doctor goes out.—Nora alone.—Mrs. Linde enters. Scene between her and Nora.—Krogstad enters. Short scene between him, Mrs. Linde and Nora. Mrs. Linde goes in to the children.—Scene between Krogstad and Nora.—she entreats and implores him for the sake of her little children; in vain. Krogstad goes out. The letter is seen to fall from outside into the letter-box.—Mrs. Linde re-enters after a short pause. Scene between her and Nora. Half confession. Mrs. Linde goes out.—Nora alone.—Stenborg enters. Scene between him and Nora. He wants to empty the letter-box. Entreaties, jests, half playful persuasion. He promises to let business wait till after New Year's Day; but at 12 o'clock midnight—! Exit. Nora alone. Nora (looking at the clock:) It is five o'clock. Five;—seven hours till midnight. Twenty-four hours till the next midnight. Twenty-four and seven—thirty-one. Thirty-one hours to live.—

THIRD ACT

A muffled sound of dance music is heard from the floor above. A lighted lamp on the table. Mrs. Linde sits in an armchair and absently turns the pages of a book, tries to read, but seems unable to fix her attention; once or twice she looks at her watch. Nora comes down from the dance; uneasiness has driven her; surprise at finding Mrs. Linde, who pretends that she wanted to see Nora in her costume. Helmer, displeased at her going away, comes to fetch her back. The Doctor also enters, but to say good-bye. Meanwhile Mrs. Linde has gone into the side room on the right. Scene between the Doctor, Helmer and Nora. He is going to bed, he says, never to get up again; they are not to come and see him; there is ugliness about a death-bed. He goes out. Helmer goes upstairs again with Nora, after the latter has exchanged a few words of farewell with Mrs. Linde. Mrs. Linde alone. Then Krogstad. Scene and explanation between them. Both go out. Nora and the children. Then she alone. Then Helmer. He takes the letters out of the letter-box. Short scene; good-night; he goes into his room. Nora in despair prepares for the final step; is ready at the door when Helmer enters with the open letter in his hand. Great scene. A ring. Letter to Nora from Krogstad. Final scene. Divorce. Nora leaves the house.—

In this production of Luigi Piran-dello's *Six Characters in Search of an Author,* the statuesque "characters" arrive at the stage door, clothed in black and bathed in an eerie light.

In this scene from Henrik Ibsen's *A Doll House,* Doctor Rank, Helmer, and Nora have just re-turned from the party; Nora wears her tarantella costume, and Helmer has been given a "mask" of middle-class respectability.

The photograph of the Moscow Art Theater's original production of Anton Chekhov's *The Cherry Orchard* shows the naturalistic detail for which Constantin Stanislavski's company was fa-mous; Stanislavski is at the left in the role of Gaev, gesturing to the bookcase.

Henrik Ibsen

At the turn of the century, Henrik Ibsen's name was synonymous with modernity in the European theater; much of the territory of modern drama was first explored in Ibsen's work. Born into a mercantile family in provincial Norway, Ibsen (1828–1906) had planned to study medicine; however, after failing to matriculate at the university, he turned to a career as a writer. From 1850 through 1864, Ibsen worked for the nationalist Norwegian Theater in Bergen and then for the Mollergate Theater in Christiania (now Oslo). As literary manager, stage manager, and assistant to the director, Ibsen learned the craft of practical theater firsthand. He also wrote a series of romantic history plays, some in prose and some in verse. Although his fame now rests on the realistic plays he wrote later in his career, in his own lifetime these history plays—such as *The Vikings at Helgeland* (1858)—were quite popular, especially in Norway.

In 1864, Ibsen left Norway and settled in Rome, where he wrote two pivotal plays, *Brand* (1866) and *Peer Gynt* (1867). The story of an idealistic minister, *Brand* established Ibsen as an important European writer and announced one of his central themes: the cost of moral idealism in the modern world. *Peer Gynt* is often taken as a companion-piece to *Brand*, for Peer's picaresque journey throughout Europe is undertaken simply for the purpose of his own self-satisfaction: while Brand's motto is "Be wholly what you are," Peer Gynt's is "To thine own self be . . . enough." In 1877, after extensive work on the Hegelian history drama *Emperor and Galilean*, Ibsen wrote *Pillars of Society*, a prose drama of modern life, inaugurating the stunning series of plays that made him famous and established the contours of modern realistic drama. In *A Doll House* (1879), *Ghosts* (1881), and *An Enemy of the People* (1882), Ibsen explored the conflict between the social and moral restrictions of bourgeois society and the psychological, often unconscious, demands of individual freedom. Ibsen adapted the suspenseful, rigorously plotted form of the **WELL-MADE PLAY** (or *pièce bien faite*) popularized throughout Europe by French playwrights Eugène Scribe and Victorien Sardou and used it in plays of modern life critical of bourgeois morality and society. The well-made play is notoriously difficult to define, even though its features are familiar: a rigorously "causal" plot, a secret gradually revealed to the audience, a "necessary scene" (the *scène-à-faire*) in which the secret is revealed to the characters, a character (the *raisonneur*) who explains and moralizes the action to the others, and a predominance of coincidental events. In his earlier plays, Ibsen takes these formal conventions and makes them function as forces in the dramatic world. The world of the play comes to seem mechanistic, determined by a secret that will out, full of busybodies explaining and interpreting the action. The mechanics of the well-made play, that is, are identified with the deadening force of social convention, which painfully threatens to extinguish the vitality of the central characters. This conflict between deadening social convention and a mysterious inner vitality pervades Ibsen's mature plays as well, which increasingly moved away from the "well-made" form: *The Wild Duck* (1885), *Rosmersholm* (1887), *The Lady from the Sea* (1888), and *Hedda Gabler* (1890). Ibsen's last plays seem more poetic or symbolic, though they take place in the familiar milieu of the realistic stage: *The Master Builder* (1892), *Little Eyolf* (1894), *John Gabriel Borkman* (1896), and the unfinished *When We Dead Awaken* (1900). Ibsen suffered a paralyzing series of strokes in 1900 that left him unable to write. He died in 1906.

Ibsen's effect on his contemporaries and his influence on the course of modern drama were immediate and profound. His plays were rapidly translated into the major European languages, and stage productions—which often inaugurated the new "independent" theaters—frequently became the subject of sensation and controversy. Indeed, "Ibsenism" came to be a catchword for a variety of social causes, though Ibsen himself generally avoided politics. Although Ibsen's plays brought new issues to the stage, it was his practice as a playwright that proved truly revolutionary. Many playwrights had adopted the realistic theater's use of a material stage environment, its emphasis on the burden of the past, and its sense of a mechanized and constricting society. Ibsen not only used this material with powerful subtlety and resonance, he gave the stage its first distinctively modern characters: complex, contradictory individuals driven by a desire for something—the "joy of life," a sense of themselves—that they can barely recognize or name.

A DOLL HOUSE

A Doll House was inspired by a series of incidents that came to Ibsen's attention in 1878 when a woman named Laura Kieler contacted him. Kieler had signed a secret—and illegal—loan to raise money for a cure for her tubercular husband. She wrote to Ibsen asking him to recommend the novel she had written to his publisher, in hopes that the profits from its sale would allow her to repay the loan. Ibsen refused. Kieler forged a check and was caught. Her husband committed her to an asylum, had her charged as an unfit mother, and demanded a legal separation. When she was released from the asylum, however, the family remained together.

We can see the shaping power of Ibsen's imagination in his transformation of Laura Kieler's tragedy into the ironic masterpiece, *A Doll House*. The play, which by the turn of the century was a rallying point for international feminist demands for the vote and for other legal rights and protections for women, organizes the conflict between Nora and Helmer around a subtle set of contrasts: the childlike and protected Nora and the world-weary Mrs. Linde; the upright and protective Helmer and the shady—yet finally generous—Krogstad; the privations of the past and the financial freedom Nora sees on the horizon. However, as the play proceeds, the stable, bourgeois world that Helmer represents is revealed as a tissue of deception; the institutions of marriage, respectability, and social justice turn out to be fictions that the privileged use to manipulate their world. Nora comes to seem effective, efficient, worldly wise, and finally independent, while Helmer readily compromises his principles to save his reputation. The world of financial freedom Nora glimpses at the play's outset turns out to be a kind of prison and is replaced by another kind of freedom at the end of the play: the frightening freedom to cut herself loose from the bonds of marriage, family, and society.

Helmer had more authority with audiences in the 1880s and 1890s than he does today, and Nora was conventionally criticized as an "unwomanly woman" for taking the loan, deceiving her husband, and leaving her family. Indeed, the first English actress to be offered

Owen Teale and Janet McTeer in Henrik Ibsen's *A Doll House*, in the 1997 production using a new translation by Frank McGuinness.

the part turned it down, because she didn't want audiences to think of her as the kind of woman who would desert her children. Yet the play tends to validate Nora's personal growth and her final decision to leave her family and cannily uses the material environment of the stage setting to convey the suffocating situation in which Nora finds herself.

The play takes place in one room: the drawing room where the upwardly mobile Helmers (deluxe books on the shelf, piano against the wall, framed art prints) receive their guests and conduct their lives. The room itself represents the Helmers' concern for social status and assumes a symbolic importance as well: it stands between the unseen privacy of the kitchen and bedroom—the domestic world of marriage and children—and the threatening public world beyond the front door, the world of Krogstad, of the dark and icy river, of Nora's final escape. The room becomes a kind of prison, a room in which Rank's declaration of love for Nora seems inappropriate, in which Helmer criticizes her dizzying tarantella—a Sicilian dance thought to imitate the death throes of someone bitten by a tarantula—as too abandoned, and in which Nora's final discussion with Helmer makes her submission to him impossible. That is, the room makes concrete the play's concern for the social constraints on a woman's life, becoming a visual image of how Helmer's masculine, bourgeois moral authority imprisons Nora. It is not entirely clear that Nora can survive in the harsh social and economic climate outside the comfortable parlor, but it is clear that escape from the parlor is her final alternative.

A Doll House was a successful—and a scandalous—play throughout Europe in the last decades of the nineteenth century, and it has remained in the repertoire ever since. Nora has always been associated with feminist politics, and several productions in the 1960s and 1970s saw in *A Doll House* an anticipatory allegory of the women's movement. Indeed, whereas Helmer appeared to 1880s audiences as a romantic leading man, the challenge for contemporary productions is to make him appear sympathetic, someone worth Nora's years of sacrifice, and someone she will have to struggle to leave.

A DOLL HOUSE

Henrik Ibsen

TRANSLATED BY ROLF FJELDE

CHARACTERS

TORVALD HELMER, *a lawyer*
NORA, *his wife*
DR. RANK
MRS. LINDE
NILS KROGSTAD, *a bank clerk*
THE HELMERS' THREE SMALL CHILDREN

ANNE-MARIE, *their nurse*
A MAID, *Helene*
A DELIVERY BOY

The action takes place in Helmer's residence.

ACT ONE

A comfortable room, tastefully but not expensively furnished. A door to the right in the back wall leads to the entryway; another to the left leads to HELMER's *study. Between these doors, a piano. Midway in the left-hand wall a door, and further back a window. Near the window a round table with an armchair and a small sofa. In the right-hand wall, toward the rear, a door, and nearer the foreground a porcelain stove with two armchairs and a rocking chair beside it. Between the stove and the side door, a small table. Engravings on the walls. An etagère with china figures and other small art objects; a small bookcase with richly bound books; the floor carpeted; a fire burning in the stove. It is a winter day.*

A bell rings in the entryway; shortly after we hear the door being unlocked. NORA *comes into the room, humming happily to herself; she is wearing street clothes and carries an armload of packages, which she puts down on the table to the right. She has left the hall door open; and through it a* DELIVERY BOY *is seen, holding a Christmas tree and a basket, which he gives to the* MAID *who let them in.*

NORA: Hide the tree well, Helene. The children mustn't get a glimpse of it till this evening, after it's trimmed. (*To the* DELIVERY BOY, *taking out her purse.*) How much?

DELIVERY BOY: Fifty, ma'am.

5 NORA: There's a crown. No, keep the change. (*The* BOY *thanks her and leaves.* NORA *shuts the door. She laughs softly to herself while taking off her street things. Drawing a bag of macaroons from her pocket, she eats a couple, then steals over and listens at her husband's study door.*) Yes, he's home. (*Hums again as she*

10 *moves to the table right.*)

HELMER: (*From the study.*) Is that my little lark twittering out there?

NORA: (*Busy opening some packages.*) Yes, it is.

HELMER: Is that my squirrel rummaging around?

15 NORA: Yes!

HELMER: When did my squirrel get in?

NORA: Just now. (*Putting the macaroon bag in her pocket and wiping her mouth.*) Do come in, Torvald, and see what I've bought.

20 HELMER: Can't be disturbed. (*After a moment he opens the door and peers in, pen in hand.*) Bought, you say? All that there? Has the little spendthrift been out throwing money around again?

NORA: Oh, but Torvald, this year we really should let ourselves

25 go a bit. It's the first Christmas we haven't had to economize.

HELMER: But you know we can't go squandering.

NORA: Oh yes, Torvald, we can squander a little now. Can't we? Just a tiny, wee bit. Now that you've got a big salary and are going to make piles and piles of money.

HELMER: Yes—starting New Year's. But then it's a full three 30 months till the raise comes through.

NORA: Pooh! We can borrow that long.

HELMER: Nora! (*Goes over and playfully takes her by the ear.*) Are your scatterbrains off again? What if today I borrowed a thousand crowns, and you squandered them over Christ- 35 mas week, and then on New Year's Eve a roof tile fell on my head, and I lay there—

NORA: (*Putting her hand on his mouth.*) Oh! Don't say such things!

HELMER: Yes, but what if it happened—then what? 40

NORA: If anything so awful happened, then it just wouldn't matter if I had debts or not.

HELMER: Well, but the people I'd borrowed from?

NORA: Them? Who cares about them! They're strangers.

HELMER: Nora, Nora, how like a woman! No, but seriously, 45 Nora, you know what I think about that. No debts! Never borrow! Something of freedom's lost—and something of beauty, too—from a home that's founded on borrowing and debt. We've made a brave stand up to now, the two of us; and we'll go right on like that the little while we have to. 50

NORA: (*Going toward the stove.*) Yes, whatever you say, Torvald.

HELMER: (*Following her.*) Now, now, the little lark's wings mustn't droop. Come on, don't be a sulky squirrel. (*Taking out his wallet.*) Nora, guess what I have here.

NORA: (*Turning quickly.*) Money! 55

HELMER: There, see. (*Hands her some notes.*) Good grief, I know how costs go up in a house at Christmastime.

NORA: Ten—twenty—thirty—forty. Oh, thank you, Torvald; I can manage no end on this.

HELMER: You really will have to. 60

NORA: Oh yes, I promise I will! But come here so I can show you everything I bought. And so cheap! Look, new clothes for Ivar here—and a sword. Here a horse and a trumpet for Bob. And a doll and a doll's bed here for Emmy; they're nothing much, but she'll tear them to bits in no time any 65 way. And here I have dress material and handkerchiefs for the maids. Old Anne-Marie really deserves something more.

HELMER: And what's in that package there?

NORA: (*With a cry.*) Torvald, no! You can't see that till tonight!

HELMER: I see. But tell me now, you little prodigal, what have 70 you thought of for yourself?

NORA: For myself? Oh, I don't want anything at all.

HELMER: Of course you do. Tell me just what—within reason—you'd most like to have.

75 NORA: I honestly don't know. Oh, listen, Torvald—

HELMER: Well?

NORA: (*Fumbling at his coat buttons, without looking at him.*) If you want to give me something, then maybe you could—you could—

80 HELMER: Come on, out with it.

NORA: (*Hurriedly.*) You could give me money, Torvald. No more than you think you can spare; then one of these days I'll buy something with it.

HELMER: But Nora—

85 NORA: Oh, please, Torvald darling, do that! I beg you, please. Then I could hang the bills in pretty gilt paper on the Christmas tree. Wouldn't that be fun?

HELMER: What are those little birds called that always fly through their fortunes?

90 NORA: Oh yes, spendthrifts; I know all that. But let's do as I say, Torvald; then I'll have time to decide what I really need most. That's very sensible, isn't it?

HELMER: (*Smiling.*) Yes, very—that is, if you actually hung onto the money I give you, and you actually used it to buy your-

95 self something. But it goes for the house and for all sorts of foolish things, and then I only have to lay out some more.

NORA: Oh, but Torvald—

HELMER: Don't deny it, my dear little Nora. (*Putting his arm around her waist.*) Spendthrifts are sweet, but they use up a

100 frightful amount of money. It's incredible what it costs a man to feed such birds.

NORA: Oh, how can you say that! Really, I save everything I can.

HELMER: (*Laughing.*) Yes, that's the truth. Everything you can.

105 But that's nothing at all.

NORA: (*Humming, with a smile of quiet satisfaction.*) Hm, if you only knew what expenses we larks and squirrels have, Torvald.

HELMER: You're an odd little one. Exactly the way your father

110 was. You're never at a loss for scaring up money; but the moment you have it, it runs right out through your fingers; you never know what you've done with it. Well, one takes you as you are. It's deep in your blood. Yes, these things are hereditary, Nora.

115 NORA: Ah, I could wish I'd inherited many of Papa's qualities.

HELMER: And I couldn't wish you anything but just what you are, my sweet little lark. But wait; it seems to me you have a very—what should I call it?—a very suspicious look to-day—

120 NORA: I do?

HELMER: You certainly do. Look me straight in the eye.

NORA: (*Looking at him.*) Well?

HELMER: (*Shaking an admonitory finger.*) Surely my sweet tooth hasn't been running riot in town today, has she?

125 NORA: No. Why do you imagine that?

HELMER: My sweet tooth really didn't make a little detour through the confectioner's?

NORA: No, I assure you, Torvald—

HELMER: Hasn't nibbled some pastry?

130 NORA: No, not at all.

HELMER: Not even munched a macaroon or two?

NORA: No, Torvald, I assure you, really—

HELMER: There, there now. Of course I'm only joking.

NORA: (*Going to the table, right.*) You know I could never think of going against you. 135

HELMER: No, I understand that; and you *have* given me your word. (*Going over to her.*) Well, you keep your little Christmas secrets to yourself, Nora darling. I expect they'll come to light this evening, when the tree is lit.

NORA: Did you remember to ask Dr. Rank? 140

HELMER: No. But there's no need for that; it's assumed he'll be dining with us. All the same, I'll ask him when he stops by here this morning. I've ordered some fine wine. Nora, you can't imagine how I'm looking forward to this evening.

NORA: So am I. And what fun for the children, Torvald! 145

HELMER: Ah, it's so gratifying to know that one's gotten a safe, secure job, and with a comfortable salary. It's a great satisfaction, isn't it?

NORA: Oh, it's wonderful!

HELMER: Remember last Christmas? Three whole weeks be- 150 fore, you shut yourself in every evening till long after midnight, making flowers for the Christmas tree, and all the other decorations to surprise us. Ugh, that was the dullest time I've ever lived through.

NORA: It wasn't at all dull for me. 155

HELMER: (*Smiling.*) But the outcome *was* pretty sorry, Nora.

NORA: Oh, don't tease me with that again. How could I help it that the cat came in and tore everything to shreds.

HELMER: No, poor thing, you certainly couldn't. You wanted so much to please us all, and that's what counts. But it's 160 just as well that the hard times are past.

NORA: Yes, it's really wonderful!

HELMER: Now I don't have to sit here alone, boring myself, and you don't have to tire your precious eyes and your fair little delicate hands— 165

NORA: (*Clapping her hands.*) No, is it really true, Torvald, I don't have to? Oh, how wonderfully lovely to hear! (*Taking his arm.*) Now I'll tell you just how I've thought we should plan things. Right after Christmas—(*The doorbell rings.*) Oh, the bell. (*Straightening the room up a bit.*) Some- 170 body would have to come. What a bore!

HELMER: I'm not at home to visitors, don't forget.

MAID: (*From the hall doorway.*) Ma'am, a lady to see you—

NORA: All right, let her come in.

MAID: (*To* HELMER.) And the doctor's just come too. 175

HELMER: Did he go right to my study?

MAID: Yes, he did.

(HELMER *goes into his room. The* MAID *shows in* MRS. LINDE, *dressed in traveling clothes, and shuts the door after her.*)

MRS. LINDE: (*In a dispirited and somewhat hesitant voice.*) Hello, Nora.

NORA: (*Uncertain.*) Hello— 180

MRS. LINDE: You don't recognize me.

NORA: No, I don't know—but wait, I think—(*Exclaiming.*) What! Kristine! Is it really you?

MRS. LINDE: Yes, it's me.

NORA: Kristine! To think I didn't recognize you. But then, 185 how could I? (*More quietly.*) How you've changed, Kristine!

MRS. LINDE: Yes, no doubt I have. In nine—ten long years.

NORA: Is it so long since we met! Yes, it's all of that. Oh, these last eight years have been a happy time, believe me. And

190 so now you've come in to town, too. Made the long trip in the winter. That took courage.

MRS. LINDE: I just got here by ship this morning.

NORA: To enjoy yourself over Christmas, of course. Oh, how lovely! Yes, enjoy ourselves, we'll do that. But take your
195 coat off. You're not still cold? (*Helping her.*) There now, let's get cozy here by the stove. No, the easy chair there! I'll take the rocker here. (*Seizing her hands.*) Yes, now you have your old look again; it was only in that first moment. You're a bit more pale, Kristine—and maybe a bit thinner.

200 MRS. LINDE: And much, much older, Nora.

NORA: Yes, perhaps a bit older; a tiny, tiny bit; not much at all. (*Stopping short; suddenly serious.*) Oh, but thoughtless me, to sit here, chattering away. Sweet, good Kristine, can you forgive me?

205 MRS. LINDE: What do you mean, Nora?

NORA: (*Softly.*) Poor Kristine, you've become a widow.

MRS. LINDE: Yes, three years ago.

NORA: Oh, I knew it, of course; I read it in the papers. Oh, Kristine, you must believe me; I often thought of writing
210 you then, but I kept postponing it, and something always interfered.

MRS. LINDE: Nora dear, I understand completely.

NORA: No, it was awful of me, Kristine. You poor thing, how much you must have gone through. And he left you noth-
215 ing?

MRS. LINDE: No.

NORA: And no children?

MRS. LINDE: No.

NORA: Nothing at all, then?

220 MRS. LINDE: Not even a sense of loss to feed on.

NORA: (*Looking incredulously at her.*) But Kristine, how could that be?

MRS. LINDE: (*Smiling wearily and smoothing her hair.*) Oh, sometimes it happens, Nora.

225 NORA: So completely alone. How terribly hard that must be for you. I have three lovely children. You can't see them now; they're out with the maid. But now you must tell me everything—

MRS. LINDE: No, no, no, tell me about yourself.

230 NORA: No, you begin. Today I don't want to be selfish. I want to think only of you today. But there *is* something I must tell you. Did you hear of the wonderful luck we had recently?

MRS. LINDE: No, what's that?

235 NORA: My husband's been made manager in the bank, just think!

MRS. LINDE: Your husband? How marvelous!

NORA: Isn't it? Being a lawyer is such an uncertain living, you know, especially if one won't touch any cases that aren't
240 clean and decent. And of course Torvald would never do that, and I'm with him completely there. Oh, we're simply delighted, believe me! He'll join the bank right after New Year's and start getting a huge salary and lots of commissions. From now on we can live quite differently—just
245 as we want. Oh, Kristine, I feel so light and happy! Won't it be lovely to have stacks of money and not a care in the world?

MRS. LINDE: Well, anyway, it would be lovely to have enough for necessities.

250 NORA: No, not just for necessities, but stacks and stacks of money!

MRS. LINDE: (*Smiling.*) Nora, Nora, aren't you sensible yet? Back in school you were such a free spender.

NORA: (*With a quiet laugh.*) Yes, that's what Torvald still says. (*Shaking her finger.*) But "Nora, Nora" isn't as silly as you
255 all think. Really, we've been in no position for me to go squandering. We've had to work, both of us.

MRS. LINDE: You too?

NORA: Yes, at odd jobs—needlework, crocheting, embroidery, and such—(*Casually.*) and other things too. You remem-
260 ber that Torvald left the department when we were married? There was no chance of promotion in his office, and of course he needed to earn more money. But that first year he drove himself terribly. He took on all kinds of extra work that kept him going morning and night. It wore
265 him down, and then he fell deathly ill. The doctors said it was essential for him to travel south.

MRS. LINDE: Yes, didn't you spend a whole year in Italy?

NORA: That's right. It wasn't easy to get away, you know. Ivar had just been born. But of course we had to go. Oh, that
270 was a beautiful trip, and it saved Torvald's life. But it cost a frightful sum, Kristine.

MRS. LINDE: I can well imagine.

NORA: Four thousand, eight hundred crowns it cost. That's really a lot of money.
275

MRS. LINDE: But it's lucky you had it when you needed it.

NORA: Well, as it was, we got it from Papa.

MRS. LINDE: I see. It was just about the time your father died.

NORA: Yes, just about then. And, you know, I couldn't make that trip out to nurse him. I had to stay here, expecting
280 Ivar any moment, and with my poor sick Torvald to care for. Dearest Papa, I never saw him again, Kristine. Oh, that was the worst time I've known in all my marriage.

MRS. LINDE: I know how you loved him. And then you went off to Italy?
285

NORA: Yes. We had the means now, and the doctors urged us. So we left a month after.

MRS. LINDE: And your husband came back completely cured?

NORA: Sound as a drum!

MRS. LINDE: But—the doctor?
290

NORA: Who?

MRS. LINDE: I thought the maid said he was a doctor, the man who came in with me.

NORA: Yes, that was Dr. Rank—but he's not making a sick call. He's our closest friend, and he stops by at least once a day.
295 No, Torvald hasn't had a sick moment since, and the children are fit and strong, and I am, too. (*Jumping up and clapping her hands.*) Oh, dear God, Kristine, what a lovely thing to live and be happy! But how disgusting of me—I'm talking of nothing but my own affairs. (*Sits on a stool close by
300 KRISTINE, arms resting across her knees.*) Oh, don't be angry with me! Tell me, is it really true that you weren't in love with your husband? Why did you marry him, then?

MRS. LINDE: My mother was still alive, but bedridden and helpless—and I had my two younger brothers to look af-
305 ter. In all conscience, I didn't think I could turn him down.

NORA: No, you were right there. But was he rich at the time?

MRS. LINDE: He was very well off, I'd say. But the business was shaky, Nora. When he died, it all fell apart, and nothing was left.
310

NORA: And then—?

MRS. LINDE: Yes, so I had to scrape up a living with a little shop and a little teaching and whatever else I could find. The last

315 three years have been like one endless workday without a rest for me. Now it's over, Nora. My poor mother doesn't need me, for she's passed on. Nor the boys, either; they're working now and can take care of themselves.

NORA: How free you must feel—

MRS. LINDE: No—only unspeakably empty. Nothing to live
320 for now. (*Standing up anxiously.*) That's why I couldn't take it any longer out in that desolate hole. Maybe here it'll be easier to find something to do and keep my mind occupied. If I could only be lucky enough to get a steady job, some office work—

325 NORA: Oh, but Kristine, that's so dreadfully tiring, and you already look so tired. It would be much better for you if you could go off to a bathing resort.

MRS. LINDE: (*Going toward the window.*) I have no father to give me travel money, Nora.

330 NORA: (*Rising.*) Oh, don't be angry with me.

MRS. LINDE: (*Going to her.*) Nora dear, don't you be angry with me. The worst of my kind of situation is all the bitterness that's stored away. No one to work for, and yet you're always having to snap up your opportunities. You
335 have to live; and so you grow selfish. When you told me the happy change in your lot, do you know I was delighted less for your sakes than for mine?

NORA: How so? Oh, I see. You think maybe Torvald could do something for you.

340 MRS. LINDE: Yes, that's what I thought.

NORA: And he will, Kristine! Just leave it to me; I'll bring it up so delicately—find something attractive to humor him with. Oh, I'm so eager to help you.

MRS. LINDE: How very kind of you, Nora, to be so concerned
345 over me—doubly kind, considering you really know so little of life's burdens yourself.

NORA: I—? I know so little—?

MRS. LINDE: (*Smiling.*) Well, my heavens—a little needlework and such—Nora, you're just a child.

350 NORA: (*Tossing her head and pacing the floor.*) You don't have to act so superior.

MRS. LINDE: Oh?

NORA: You're just like the others. You all think I'm incapable of anything serious—

355 MRS. LINDE: Come now—

NORA: That I've never had to face the raw world.

MRS. LINDE: Nora dear, you've just been telling me all your troubles.

NORA: Hm! Trivia! (*Quietly.*) I haven't told you the big thing.
360 MRS. LINDE: Big thing? What do you mean?

NORA: You look down on me so, Kristine, but you shouldn't. You're proud that you worked so long and hard for your mother.

MRS. LINDE: I don't look down on a soul. But it is true: I'm
365 proud—and happy, too—to think it was given to me to make my mother's last days almost free of care.

NORA: And you're also proud thinking of what you've done for your brothers.

MRS. LINDE: I feel I've a right to be.

370 NORA: I agree. But listen to this, Kristine—I've also got something to be proud and happy for.

MRS. LINDE: I don't doubt it. But whatever do you mean?

NORA: Not so loud. What if Torvald heard! He mustn't, not for anything in the world. Nobody must know, Kristine.
375 No one but you.

MRS. LINDE: But what is it, then?

NORA: Come here. (*Drawing her down beside her on the sofa.*) It's true—I've also got something to be proud and happy for. I'm the one who saved Torvald's life.

MRS. LINDE: Saved—? Saved how?   380

NORA: I told you about the trip to Italy. Torvald never would have lived if he hadn't gone south—

MRS. LINDE: Of course; your father gave you the means—

NORA: (*Smiling.*) That's what Torvald and all the rest think, but—   385

MRS. LINDE: But—?

NORA: Papa didn't give us a pin. I was the one who raised the money.

MRS. LINDE: You? That whole amount?

NORA: Four thousand, eight hundred crowns. What do you 390 say to that?

MRS. LINDE: But Nora, how was it possible? Did you win the lottery?

NORA: (*Disdainfully.*) The lottery? Pooh! No art to that.

MRS. LINDE: But where did you get it from then?   395

NORA: (*Humming, with a mysterious smile.*) Hmm, tra-la-la-la.

MRS. LINDE: Because you couldn't have borrowed it.

NORA: No? Why not?

MRS. LINDE: A wife can't borrow without her husband's consent.

NORA: (*Tossing her head.*) Oh, but a wife with a little business 400 sense, a wife who knows how to manage—

MRS. LINDE: Nora, I simply don't understand—

NORA: You don't have to. Whoever said I borrowed the money? I could have gotten it other ways. (*Throwing herself back on the sofa.*) I could have gotten it from some ad- 405 mirer or other. After all, a girl with my ravishing appeal—

MRS. LINDE: You lunatic.

NORA: I'll bet you're eaten up with curiosity, Kristine.

MRS. LINDE: Now listen here, Nora—you haven't done something indiscreet?   410

NORA: (*Sitting up again.*) Is it indiscreet to save your husband's life?

MRS. LINDE: I think it's indiscreet that without his knowledge you—

NORA: But that's the point: he mustn't know! My Lord, can't 415 you understand? He mustn't ever know the close call he had. It was to *me* the doctors came to say his life was in danger—that nothing could save him but a stay in the south. Didn't I try strategy then! I began talking about how lovely it would be for me to travel abroad like other 420 young wives; I begged and I cried; I told him please to remember my condition, to be kind and indulge me; and then I dropped a hint that he could easily take out a loan. But at that, Kristine, he nearly exploded. He said I was frivolous, and it was his duty as man of the house not to 425 indulge me in whims and fancies—as I think he called them. Aha, I thought, now you'll just have to be saved— and that's when I saw my chance.

MRS. LINDE: And your father never told Torvald the money wasn't from him?   430

NORA: No, never. Papa died right about then. I'd considered bringing him into my secret and begging him never to tell. But he was too sick at the time—and then, sadly, it didn't matter.

MRS. LINDE: And you've never confided in your husband since? 435

NORA: For heaven's sake, no! Are you serious? He's so strict on that subject. Besides—Torvald, with all his masculine

pride—how painfully humiliating for him if he ever found out he was in debt to me. That would just ruin our relation-
440   ship. Our beautiful, happy home would never be the same.

MRS. LINDE: Won't you ever tell him?

NORA: (*Thoughtfully, half smiling.*) Yes—maybe sometime, years from now, when I'm no longer so attractive. Don't laugh! I only mean when Torvald loves me less than now,
445   when he stops enjoying my dancing and dressing up and reciting for him. Then it might be wise to have something in reserve—(*Breaking off.*) How ridiculous! That'll never happen—Well, Kristine, what do you think of my big se-cret? I'm capable of something too, hm? You can imagine,
450   of course, how this thing hangs over me. It really hasn't been easy meeting the payments on time. In the business world there's what they call quarterly interest and what they call amortization, and these are always so terribly hard to manage. I've had to skimp a little here and there,
455   wherever I could, you know. I could hardly spare anything from my house allowance, because Torvald has to live well. I couldn't let the children go poorly dressed; whatever I got for them, I felt I had to use up completely—the dar-lings!

460   MRS. LINDE: Poor Nora, so it had to come out of your own budget, then?

NORA: Yes, of course. But I was the one most responsible, too. Every time Torvald gave me money for new clothes and such, I never used more than half; always bought the sim-
465   plest, cheapest outfits. It was a godsend that everything looks so well on me that Torvald never noticed. But it did weigh me down at times, Kristine. It *is* such a joy to wear fine things. You understand.

MRS. LINDE: Oh, of course.

470   NORA: And then I found other ways of making money. Last winter I was lucky enough to get a lot of copying to do. I locked myself in and sat writing every evening till late in the night. Ah, I was tired so often, dead tired. But still it was wonderful fun, sitting and working like that, earning
475   money. It was almost like being a man.

MRS. LINDE: But how much have you paid off this way so far?

NORA: That's hard to say, exactly. These accounts, you know, aren't easy to figure. I only know that I've paid out all I could scrape together. Time and again I haven't known
480   where to turn. (*Smiling.*) Then I'd sit here dreaming of a rich old gentleman who had fallen in love with me—

MRS. LINDE: What! Who is he?

NORA: Oh, really! And that he'd died, and when his will was opened, there in big letters it said, "All my fortune shall be
485   paid over in cash, immediately, to that enchanting Mrs. Nora Helmer."

MRS. LINDE: But Nora dear—who was this gentleman?

NORA: Good grief, can't you understand? The old man never existed; that was only something I'd dream up time and
490   again whenever I was at my wits' end for money. But it makes no difference now; the old fossil can go where he pleases for all I care; I don't need him or his will—because now I'm free. (*Jumping up.*) Oh, how lovely to think of that, Kristine! Carefree! To know you're carefree, utterly
495   carefree; to be able to romp and play with the children, and to keep up a beautiful, charming home—everything just the way Torvald likes it! And think, spring is coming, with big blue skies. Maybe we can travel a little then.

Maybe I'll see the ocean again. Oh yes, it is so marvelous to live and be happy!   500

(*The front doorbell rings.*)

MRS. LINDE: (*Rising.*) There's the bell. It's probably best that I go.

NORA: No, stay. No one's expected. It must be for Torvald.

MAID: (*From the hall doorway.*) Excuse me, ma'am—there's a gentleman here to see Mr. Helmer, but I didn't know—   505
since the doctor's with him—

NORA: Who is the gentleman?

KROGSTAD: (*From the doorway.*) It's me, Mrs. Helmer.

(MRS. LINDE *starts and turns away toward the window.*)

NORA: (*Stepping toward him, tense, her voice a whisper.*) You? What is it? Why do you want to speak to my husband?   510

KROGSTAD: Bank business—after a fashion. I have a small job in the investment bank, and I hear now your husband is going to be our chief—

NORA: In other words, it's—

KROGSTAD: Just dry business, Mrs. Helmer. Nothing but that. 515

NORA: Yes, then please be good enough to step into the study. (*She nods indifferently as she sees him out by the hall door, then returns and begins stirring up the stove.*)

MRS. LINDE: Nora—who was that man?

NORA: That was a Mr. Krogstad—a lawyer.   520

MRS. LINDE: Then it really was him.

NORA: Do you know that person?

MRS. LINDE: I did once—many years ago. For a time he was a law clerk in our town.

NORA: Yes, he's been that.   525

MRS. LINDE: How he's changed.

NORA: I understand he had a very unhappy marriage.

MRS. LINDE: He's a widower now.

NORA: With a number of children. There now, it's burning. (*She closes the stove door and moves the rocker a bit to one side.*) 530

MRS. LINDE: They say he has a hand in all kinds of business.

NORA: Oh? That may be true; I wouldn't know. But let's not think about business. It's so dull.

(DR. RANK *enters from* HELMER'*s study.*)

RANK: (*Still in the doorway.*) No, no, really—I don't want to intrude, I'd just as soon talk a little while with your wife. 535
(*Shuts the door, then notices* MRS. LINDE.) Oh, beg pardon. I'm intruding here too.

NORA: No, not at all. (*Introducing him.*) Dr. Rank, Mrs. Linde.

RANK: Well now, that's a name much heard in this house. I believe I passed the lady on the stairs as I came.   540

MRS. LINDE: Yes, I take the stairs very slowly. They're rather hard on me.

RANK: Uh-hm, some touch of internal weakness?

MRS. LINDE: More overexertion, I'd say.

RANK: Nothing else? Then you're probably here in town to 545
rest up in a round of parties?

MRS. LINDE: I'm here to look for work.

RANK: Is that the best cure for overexertion?

MRS. LINDE: One has to live, Doctor.

RANK: Yes, there's a common prejudice to that effect.   550

NORA: Oh, come on, Dr. Rank—you really do want to live yourself.

RANK: Yes, I really do. Wretched as I am, I'll gladly prolong my torment indefinitely. All my patients feel like that. And it's quite the same, too, with the morally sick. Right at this moment there's one of those moral invalids in there with Helmer—

MRS. LINDE: (*Softly.*) Ah!

NORA: Who do you mean?

RANK: Oh, it's a lawyer, Krogstad, a type you wouldn't know. His character is rotten to the root—but even he began chattering all-importantly about how he had to *live.*

NORA: Oh? What did he want to talk to Torvald about?

RANK: I really don't know. I only heard something about the bank.

NORA: I didn't know that Krog—that this man Krogstad had anything to do with the bank.

RANK: Yes, he's gotten some kind of berth down there. (*To* MRS. LINDE.) I don't know if you also have, in your neck of the woods, a type of person who scuttles about breathlessly, sniffing out hints of moral corruption, and then maneuvers his victim into some sort of key position where he can keep an eye on him. It's the healthy these days that are out in the cold.

MRS. LINDE: All the same, it's the sick who most need to be taken in.

RANK: (*With a shrug.*) Yes, there we have it. That's the concept that's turning society into a sanatorium.

(NORA, *lost in her thoughts, breaks out into quiet laughter and claps her hands.*)

RANK: Why do you laugh at that? Do you have any real idea of what society is?

NORA: What do I care about dreary old society? I was laughing at something quite different—something terribly funny. Tell me, Doctor—is everyone who works in the bank dependent now on Torvald?

RANK: Is that what you find so terribly funny?

NORA: (*Smiling and humming.*) Never mind, never mind! (*Pacing the floor.*) Yes, that's really immensely amusing: that we—that Torvald has so much power now over all those people. (*Taking the bag out of her pocket.*) Dr. Rank, a little macaroon on that?

RANK: See here, macaroons! I thought they were contraband here.

NORA: Yes, but these are some that Kristine gave me.

MRS. LINDE: What? I—?

NORA: Now, now, don't be afraid. You couldn't possibly know that Torvald had forbidden them. You see, he's worried they'll ruin my teeth. But hmp! Just this once! Isn't that so, Dr. Rank? Help yourself! (*Puts a macaroon in his mouth.*) And you too, Kristine. And I'll also have one, only a little one—or two, at the most. (*Walking about again.*) Now I'm really tremendously happy. Now there's just one last thing in the world that I have an enormous desire to do.

RANK: Well! And what's that?

NORA: It's something I have such a consuming desire to say so Torvald could hear.

RANK: And why can't you say it?

NORA: I don't dare. It's quite shocking.

MRS. LINDE: Shocking?

RANK: Well, then it isn't advisable. But in front of us you certainly can. What do you have such a desire to say so Torvald could hear?

NORA: I have such a huge desire to say—to hell and be damned!

RANK: Are you crazy?

MRS. LINDE: My goodness, Nora!

RANK: Go on, say it. Here he is.

NORA: (*Hiding the macaroon bag.*) Shh, shh, shh!

(HELMER *comes in from his study, hat in hand, overcoat over his arm.*)

NORA: (*Going toward him.*) Well, Torvald dear, are you through with him?

HELMER: Yes, he just left.

NORA: Let me introduce you—this is Kristine, who's arrived here in town.

HELMER: Kristine—? I'm sorry, but I don't know—

NORA: Mrs. Linde, Torvald dear. Mrs. Kristine Linde.

HELMER: Of course. A childhood friend of my wife's, no doubt?

MRS. LINDE: Yes, we knew each other in those days.

NORA: And just think, she made the long trip down here in order to talk with you.

HELMER: What's this?

MRS. LINDE: Well, not exactly—

NORA: You see, Kristine is remarkably clever in office work, and so she's terribly eager to come under a capable man's supervision and add more to what she already knows—

HELMER: Very wise, Mrs. Linde.

NORA: And then when she heard that you'd become a bank manager—the story was wired out to the papers—then she came in as fast as she could and—Really, Torvald, for my sake you can do a little something for Kristine, can't you?

HELMER: Yes, it's not at all impossible. Mrs. Linde, I suppose you're a widow?

MRS. LINDE: Yes.

HELMER: Any experience in office work?

MRS. LINDE: Yes, a good deal.

HELMER: Well, it's quite likely that I can make an opening for you—

NORA: (*Clapping her hands.*) You see, you see!

HELMER: You've come at a lucky moment, Mrs. Linde.

MRS. LINDE: Oh, how can I thank you?

HELMER: Not necessary. (*Putting his overcoat on.*) But today you'll have to excuse me—

RANK: Wait, I'll go with you. (*He fetches his coat from the hall and warms it at the stove.*)

NORA: Don't stay out long, dear.

HELMER: An hour; no more.

NORA: Are you going too, Kristine?

MRS. LINDE: (*Putting on her winter garments.*) Yes, I have to see about a room now.

HELMER: Then perhaps we can all walk together.

NORA: (*Helping her.*) What a shame we're so cramped here, but it's quite impossible for us to—

MRS. LINDE: Oh, don't even think of it! Good-bye, Nora dear, and thanks for everything.

NORA: Good-bye for now. Of course you'll be back this evening. And you too, Dr. Rank. What? If you're well enough? Oh, you've got to be! Wrap up tight now.

(*In a ripple of small talk the company moves out into the hall; children's voices are heard outside on the steps.*)

665 NORA: There they are! There they are! (*She runs to open the door. The* CHILDREN *come in with their nurse,* ANNE-MARIE.) Come in, come in! (*Bends down and kisses them.*) Oh, you darlings—! Look at them, Kristine. Aren't they lovely!

RANK: No loitering in the draft here.

670 HELMER: Come, Mrs. Linde—this place is unbearable now for anyone but mothers.

(DR. RANK, HELMER, *and* MRS. LINDE *go down the stairs.* ANNE-MARIE *goes into the living room with the* CHILDREN. NORA *follows, after closing the hall door.*)

NORA: How fresh and strong you look. Oh, such red cheeks you have! Like apples and roses. (*The* CHILDREN *interrupt her throughout the following.*) And it was so much fun? That's 675 wonderful. Really? You pulled both Emmy and Bob on the sled? Imagine, all together! Yes, you're a clever boy, Ivar. Oh, let me hold her a bit, Anne-Marie. My sweet little doll baby! (*Takes the smallest from* ANNE-MARIE *and dances with her.*) Yes, yes, Mama will dance with Bob as well. What? Did you 680 throw snowballs? Oh, if I'd only been there! No, don't bother, Anne-Marie—I'll undress them myself. Oh yes, let me. It's such fun. Go in and rest; you look half frozen. There's hot coffee waiting for you on the stove. (ANNE-MARIE *goes into the room to the left.* NORA *takes the* CHILDREN'S 685 *winter things off, throwing them about, while the children talk to her all at once.*) Is that so? A big dog chased you? But it didn't bite? No, dogs never bite little, lovely doll babies. Don't peek in the packages, Ivar! What is it? Yes, wouldn't you like to know. No, no, it's an ugly something. Well? Shall we play? 690 What shall we play? Hide-and-seek? Yes, let's play hide-and-seek. Bob must hide first. I must? Yes, let me hide first. (*Laughing and shouting, she and the* CHILDREN *play in and out of the living room and the adjoining room to the right. At last* NORA *hides under the table. The* CHILDREN *come storming in, search,* 695 *but cannot find her, then hear her muffled laughter, dash over to the table, lift the cloth up and find her. Wild shouting. She creeps forward as if to scare them. More shouts. Meanwhile, a knock at the hall door; no one has noticed it. Now the door half opens, and* KROGSTAD *appears. He waits a moment; the game goes on.*)

700 KROGSTAD: Beg pardon, Mrs. Helmer—

NORA: (*With a strangled cry, turning and scrambling to her knees.*) Oh! What do you want?

KROGSTAD: Excuse me. The outer door was ajar; it must be someone forgot to shut it—

705 NORA: (*Rising.*) My husband isn't home, Mr. Krogstad.

KROGSTAD: I know that.

NORA: Yes—then what do you want here?

KROGSTAD: A word with you.

NORA: With—? (*To the* CHILDREN, *quietly.*) Go in to Anne-710 Marie. What? No, the strange man won't hurt Mama. When he's gone, we'll play some more. (*She leads the* CHILDREN *into the room to the left and shuts the door after them. Then, tense and nervous:*) You want to speak to me?

KROGSTAD: Yes, I want to.

715 NORA: Today? But it's not yet the first of the month—

KROGSTAD: No, it's Christmas Eve. It's going to be up to you how merry a Christmas you have.

NORA: What is it you want? Today I absolutely can't—

KROGSTAD: We won't talk about that till later. This is something else. You do have a moment to spare, I suppose? 720

NORA: Oh yes, of course—I do, except—

KROGSTAD: Good. I was sitting over at Olsen's Restaurant when I saw your husband go down the street—

NORA: Yes?

KROGSTAD: With a lady. 725

NORA: Yes. So?

KROGSTAD: If you'll pardon my asking: wasn't that lady a Mrs. Linde?

NORA: Yes.

KROGSTAD: Just now come into town? 730

NORA: Yes, today.

KROGSTAD: She's a good friend of yours?

NORA: Yes, she is. But I don't see—

KROGSTAD: I also knew her once.

NORA: I'm aware of that. 735

KROGSTAD: Oh? You know all about it. I thought so. Well, then let me ask you short and sweet: is Mrs. Linde getting a job in the bank?

NORA: What makes you think you can cross-examine me, Mr. Krogstad—you, one of my husband's employees? But 740 since you ask, you might as well know—yes, Mrs. Linde's going to be taken on at the bank. And I'm the one who spoke for her, Mr. Krogstad. Now you know.

KROGSTAD: So I guessed right.

NORA: (*Pacing up and down.*) Oh, one does have a tiny bit of 745 influence, I should hope. Just because I am a woman, don't think it means that—When one has a subordinate position, Mr. Krogstad, one really ought to be careful about pushing somebody who—hm—

KROGSTAD: Who has influence? 750

NORA: That's right.

KROGSTAD: (*In a different tone.*) Mrs. Helmer, would you be good enough to use your influence on my behalf?

NORA: What? What do you mean?

KROGSTAD: Would you please make sure that I keep my sub-755 ordinate position in the bank?

NORA: What does that mean? Who's thinking of taking away your position?

KROGSTAD: Oh, don't play the innocent with me. I'm quite aware that your friend would hardly relish the chance of 760 running into me again; and I'm also aware now whom I can thank for being turned out.

NORA: But I promise you—

KROGSTAD: Yes, yes, yes, to the point: there's still time, and I'm advising you to use your influence to prevent it. 765

NORA: But Mr. Krogstad, I have absolutely no influence.

KROGSTAD: You haven't? I thought you were just saying—

NORA: You shouldn't take me so literally. I! How can you believe that I have any such influence over my husband?

KROGSTAD: Oh, I've known your husband from our student 770 days. I don't think the great bank manager's more steadfast than any other married man.

NORA: You speak insolently about my husband, and I'll show you the door.

KROGSTAD: The lady has spirit. 775

NORA: I'm not afraid of you any longer. After New Year's, I'll soon be done with the whole business.

KROGSTAD: (*Restraining himself.*) Now listen to me, Mrs. Helmer. If necessary, I'll fight for my little job in the bank
780 as if it were life itself.

NORA: Yes, so it seems.

KROGSTAD: It's not just a matter of income; that's the least of it. It's something else—All right, out with it! Look, this is the thing. You know, just like all the others, of course, that
785 once, a good many years ago, I did something rather rash.

NORA: I've heard rumors to that effect.

KROGSTAD: The case never got into court; but all the same, every door was closed in my face from then on. So I took up those various activities you know about. I had to grab
790 hold somewhere; and I dare say I haven't been among the worst. But now I want to drop all that. My boys are growing up. For their sakes, I'll have to win back as much respect as possible here in town. That job in the bank was like the first rung in my ladder. And now your husband
795 wants to kick me right back down in the mud again.

NORA: But for heaven's sake, Mr. Krogstad, it's simply not in my power to help you.

KROGSTAD: That's because you haven't the will to—but I have the means to make you.

800 NORA: You certainly won't tell my husband that I owe you money?

KROGSTAD: Hm—what if I told him that?

NORA: That would be shameful of you. (*Nearly in tears.*) This secret—my joy and my pride—that he should learn it in
805 such a crude and disgusting way—learn it from you. You'd expose me to the most horrible unpleasantness—

KROGSTAD: Only unpleasantness?

NORA: (*Vehemently.*) But go on and try. It'll turn out the worse for you, because then my husband will really see what a
810 crook you are, and then you'll *never* be able to hold your job.

KROGSTAD: I asked if it was just domestic unpleasantness you were afraid of?

NORA: If my husband finds out, then of course he'll pay what I owe at once, and then we'd be through with you for good.

815 KROGSTAD: (*A step closer.*) Listen, Mrs. Helmer—you've either got a very bad memory, or else no head at all for business. I'd better put you a little more in touch with the facts.

NORA: What do you mean?

KROGSTAD: When your husband was sick, you came to me
820 for a loan of four thousand, eight hundred crowns.

NORA: Where else could I go?

KROGSTAD: I promised to get you that sum—

NORA: And you got it.

KROGSTAD: I promised to get you that sum, on certain condi-
825 tions. You were so involved in your husband's illness, and so eager to finance your trip, that I guess you didn't think out all the details. It might just be a good idea to remind you. I promised you the money on the strength of a note I drew up.

NORA: Yes, and that I signed.

830 KROGSTAD: Right. But at the bottom I added some lines for your father to guarantee the loan. He was supposed to sign down there.

NORA: Supposed to? He did sign.

KROGSTAD: I left the date blank. In other words, your father
835 would have dated his signature himself. Do you remember that?

NORA: Yes, I think—

KROGSTAD: Then I gave you the note for you to mail to your father. Isn't that so?

840 NORA: Yes.

KROGSTAD: And naturally you sent it at once—because only some five, six days later you brought me the note, properly signed. And with that, the money was yours.

NORA: Well, then; I've made my payments regularly, haven't I?

845 KROGSTAD: More or less. But—getting back to the point— those were hard times for you then, Mrs. Helmer.

NORA: Yes, they were.

KROGSTAD: Your father was very ill, I believe.

NORA: He was near the end.

850 KROGSTAD: He died soon after?

NORA: Yes.

KROGSTAD: Tell me, Mrs. Helmer, do you happen to recall the date of your father's death? The day of the month, I mean.

NORA: Papa died the twenty-ninth of September.

855 KROGSTAD: That's quite correct; I've already looked into that. And now we come to a curious thing—(*Taking out a paper.*) which I simply cannot comprehend.

NORA: Curious thing? I don't know—

KROGSTAD: This is the curious thing: that your father co-
860 signed the note for your loan three days after his death.

NORA: How—? I don't understand.

KROGSTAD: Your father died the twenty-ninth of September. But look. Here your father dated his signature October second. Isn't that curious, Mrs. Helmer? (NORA *is silent.*)
865 Can you explain it to me? (NORA *remains silent.*) It's also remarkable that the words "October second" and the year aren't written in your father's hand, but rather in one that I think I know. Well, it's easy to understand. Your father forgot perhaps to date his signature, and then someone or
870 other added it, a bit sloppily, before anyone knew of his death. There's nothing wrong in that. It all comes down to the signature. And there's no question about *that,* Mrs. Helmer. It really *was* your father who signed his own name here, wasn't it?

875 NORA: (*After a short silence, throwing her head back and looking squarely at him.*) No, it wasn't. *I* signed Papa's name.

KROGSTAD: Wait, now—are you fully aware that this is a dangerous confession?

NORA: Why? You'll soon get your money.

880 KROGSTAD: Let me ask you a question—why didn't you send the paper to your father?

NORA: That was impossible. Papa was so sick. If I'd asked him for his signature, I also would have had to tell him what the money was for. But I couldn't tell him, sick as he was, that
885 my husband's life was in danger. That was just impossible.

KROGSTAD: Then it would have been better if you'd given up the trip abroad.

NORA: I couldn't possibly. The trip was to save my husband's life. I couldn't give that up.

890 KROGSTAD: But didn't you ever consider that this was a fraud against me?

NORA: I couldn't let myself be bothered by that. You weren't any concern of mine. I couldn't stand you, with all those cold complications you made, even though you knew
895 how badly off my husband was.

KROGSTAD: Mrs. Helmer, obviously you haven't the vaguest idea of what you've involved yourself in. But I can tell you this: it was nothing more and nothing worse that I once did—and it wrecked my whole reputation.

900 NORA: You? Do you expect me to believe that you ever acted bravely to save your wife's life?

KROGSTAD: Laws don't inquire into motives.

NORA: Then they must be very poor laws.

KROGSTAD: Poor or not—if I introduce this paper in court,
905 you'll be judged according to law.

NORA: This I refuse to believe. A daughter hasn't a right to protect her dying father from anxiety and care? A wife hasn't a right to save her husband's life? I don't know much about laws, but I'm sure that somewhere in the
910 books these things are allowed. And you don't know anything about it—you who practice the law? You must be an awful lawyer, Mr. Krogstad.

KROGSTAD: Could be. But business—the kind of business we two are mixed up in—don't you think I know about that?
915 All right. Do what you want now. But I'm telling you *this:* if I get shoved down a second time, you're going to keep me company. (*He bows and goes out through the hall.*)

NORA: (*Pensive for a moment, then tossing her head.*) Oh, really! Trying to frighten me! I'm not so silly as all that. (*Begins*
920 *gathering up the* CHILDREN's *clothes, but soon stops.*) But—? No, but that's impossible! I did it out of love.

THE CHILDREN: (*In the doorway, left.*) Mama, that strange man's gone out the door.

NORA: Yes, yes, I know it. But don't tell anyone about the
925 strange man. Do you hear? Not even Papa!

THE CHILDREN: No, Mama. But now will you play again?

NORA: No, not now.

THE CHILDREN: Oh, but Mama, you promised.

NORA: Yes, but I can't now. Go inside; I have too much to do.
930 Go in, go in, my sweet darlings. (*She herds them gently back in the room and shuts the door after them. Settling on the sofa, she takes up a piece of embroidery and makes some stitches, but soon stops abruptly.*) No! (*Throws the work aside, rises, goes to the hall door and calls out.*) Helene! Let me have the tree in
935 here. (*Goes to the table, left, opens the table drawer, and stops again.*) No, but that's utterly impossible!

MAID: (*With the Christmas tree.*) Where should I put it, ma'am?

NORA: There. The middle of the floor.

MAID: Should I bring anything else?
940 NORA: No, thanks. I have what I need.

(*The* MAID, *who has set the tree down, goes out.*)

NORA: (*Absorbed in trimming the tree.*) Candles here—and flowers here. That terrible creature! Talk, talk, talk! There's nothing to it at all. The tree's going to be lovely. I'll do anything to please you, Torvald. I'll sing for you, dance for you—
945

(HELMER *comes in from the hall, with a sheaf of papers under his arm.*)

NORA: Oh! You're back so soon?

HELMER: Yes. Has anyone been here?

NORA: Here? No.

HELMER: That's odd. I saw Krogstad leaving the front door.
950 NORA: So? Oh yes, that's true. Krogstad was here a moment.

HELMER: Nora, I can see by your face that he's been here, begging you to put in a good word for him.

NORA: Yes.

HELMER: And it was supposed to seem like your own idea? You were to hide it from me that he'd been here. He asked
955 you that, too, didn't he?

NORA: Yes, Torvald, but—

HELMER: Nora, Nora, and you could fall for that? Talk with that sort of person and promise him anything? And then in the bargain, tell me an untruth.
960

NORA: An untruth—?

HELMER: Didn't you say that no one had been here? (*Wagging his finger.*) My little songbird must never do that again. A songbird needs a clean beak to warble with. No false notes. (*Putting his arm about her waist.*) That's the way it
965 should be, isn't it? Yes, I'm sure of it. (*Releasing her.*) And so, enough of that. (*Sitting by the stove.*) Ah, how snug and cozy it is here. (*Leafing among his papers.*)

NORA: (*Busy with the tree, after a short pause.*) Torvald!

HELMER: Yes.
970

NORA: I'm so much looking forward to the Stenborgs' costume party, day after tomorrow.

HELMER: And I can't wait to see what you'll surprise me with.

NORA: Oh, that stupid business!

HELMER: What?
975

NORA: I can't find anything that's right. Everything seems so ridiculous, so inane.

HELMER: So my little Nora's come to *that* recognition?

NORA: (*Going behind his chair, her arms resting on its back.*) Are you very busy, Torvald?
980

HELMER: Oh—

NORA: What papers are those?

HELMER: Bank matters.

NORA: Already?

HELMER: I've gotten full authority from the retiring manage-
985 ment to make all necessary changes in personnel and procedure. I'll need Christmas week for that. I want to have everything in order by New Year's.

NORA: So that was the reason this poor Krogstad—

HELMER: Hm.
990

NORA: (*Still leaning on the chair and slowly stroking the nape of his neck.*) If you weren't so very busy, I would have asked you an enormous favor, Torvald.

HELMER: Let's hear. What is it?

NORA: You know, there isn't anyone who has your good
995 taste—and I want so much to look well at the costume party. Torvald, couldn't you take over and decide what I should be and plan my costume?

HELMER: Ah, is my stubborn little creature calling for a life-guard?
1000

NORA: Yes, Torvald, I can't get anywhere without your help.

HELMER: All right—I'll think it over. We'll hit on something.

NORA: Oh, how sweet of you. (*Goes to the tree again. Pause.*) Aren't the red flowers pretty—? But tell me, was it really such a crime that this Krogstad committed?
1005

HELMER: Forgery. Do you have any idea what that means?

NORA: Couldn't he have done it out of need?

HELMER: Yes, or thoughtlessness, like so many others. I'm not so heartless that I'd condemn a man categorically for just one mistake.
1010

NORA: No, of course not, Torvald!

HELMER: Plenty of men have redeemed themselves by openly confessing their crimes and taking their punishment.

NORA: Punishment—?

1015 HELMER: But now Krogstad didn't go that way. He got himself out by sharp practices, and that's the real cause of his moral breakdown.

NORA: Do you really think that would—?

HELMER: Just imagine how a man with that sort of guilt in
1020 him has to lie and cheat and deceive on all sides, has to wear a mask even with the nearest and dearest he has, even with his own wife and children. And with the children, Nora—that's where it's most horrible.

NORA: Why?

1025 HELMER: Because that kind of atmosphere of lies infects the whole life of a home. Every breath the children take in is filled with the germs of something degenerate.

NORA: (*Coming closer behind him.*) Are you sure of that?

HELMER: Oh, I've seen it often enough as a lawyer. Almost
1030 everyone who goes bad early in life has a mother who's a chronic liar.

NORA: Why just—the mother?

HELMER: It's usually the mother's influence that's dominant, but the father's works in the same way, of course. Every
1035 lawyer is quite familiar with it. And still this Krogstad's been going home year in, year out, poisoning his own children with lies and pretense; that's why I call him morally lost. (*Reaching his hands out toward her.*) So my sweet little Nora must promise me never to plead his cause. Your hand
1040 on it. Come, come, what's this? Give me your hand. There, now. All settled. I can tell you it'd be impossible for me to work alongside of him. I literally feel physically revolted when I'm anywhere near such a person.

NORA: (*Withdraws her hand and goes to the other side of the Christ-*
1045 *mas tree.*) How hot it is here! And I've got so much to do.

HELMER: (*Getting up and gathering his papers.*) Yes, and I have to think about getting some of these read through before dinner. I'll think about your costume, too. And something to hang on the tree in gilt paper, I may even see about that.
1050 (*Putting his hand on her head.*) Oh you, my darling little songbird. (*He goes into his study and closes the door after him.*)

NORA: (*Softly, after a silence.*) Oh, really! it isn't so. It's impossible. It must be impossible.

ANNE-MARIE: (*In the doorway, left.*) The children are begging
1055 so hard to come in to Mama.

NORA: No, no, no, don't let them in to me! You stay with them, Anne-Marie.

ANNE-MARIE: Of course, ma'am. (*Closes the door.*)

NORA: (*Pale with terror.*) Hurt my children—! Poison my
1060 home? (*A moment's pause; then she tosses her head.*) That's not true. Never. Never in all the world.

ACT TWO

Same room. Beside the piano the Christmas tree now stands stripped of ornament, burned-down candle stubs on its ragged branches. NORA's *street clothes lie on the sofa.* NORA, *alone in the room, moves restlessly about; at last she stops at the sofa and picks up her coat.*

NORA: (*Dropping the coat again.*) Someone's coming! (*Goes toward the door, listens.*) No—there's no one. Of course—nobody's coming today, Christmas Day—or tomorrow, either. But maybe—(*Opens the door and looks out.*) No, nothing in the mailbox. Quite empty. (*Coming forward.*) What nonsense! 5 He won't do anything serious. Nothing terrible could happen. It's impossible. Why, I have three small children.

(ANNE-MARIE, *with a large carton, comes in from the room to the left.*)

ANNE-MARIE: Well, at last I found the box with the masquerade clothes.

NORA: Thanks. Put it on the table. 10

ANNE-MARIE: (*Does so.*) But they're all pretty much of a mess.

NORA: Ahh! I'd love to rip them in a million pieces!

ANNE-MARIE: Oh, mercy, they can be fixed right up. Just a little patience.

NORA: Yes, I'll go get Mrs. Linde to help me. 15

ANNE-MARIE: Out again now? In this nasty weather? Miss Nora will catch cold—get sick.

NORA: Oh, worse things could happen—How are the children?

ANNE-MARIE: The poor mites are playing with their Christmas presents, but— 20

NORA: Do they ask for me much?

ANNE-MARIE: They're so used to having Mama around, you know.

NORA: Yes, but Anne-Marie, I *can't* be together with them as much as I was. 25

ANNE-MARIE: Well, small children get used to anything.

NORA: You think so? Do you think they'd forget their mother if she was gone for good?

ANNE-MARIE: Oh, mercy—gone for good!

NORA: Wait, tell me, Anne-Marie—I've wondered so often— 30 how could you ever have the heart to give your child over to strangers?

ANNE-MARIE: But I had to, you know, to become little Nora's nurse.

NORA: Yes, but how could you *do* it? 35

ANNE-MARIE: When I could get such a good place? A girl who's poor and who's gotten in trouble is glad enough for that. Because that slippery fish, he didn't do a thing for me, you know.

NORA: But your daughter's surely forgotten you. 40

ANNE-MARIE: Oh, she certainly has not. She's written to me, both when she was confirmed and when she was married.

NORA: (*Clasping her about the neck.*) You old Anne-Marie, you were a good mother for me when I was little.

ANNE-MARIE: Poor little Nora, with no other mother but me. 45

NORA: And if the babies didn't have one, then I know that you'd—What silly talk! (*Opening the carton.*) Go in to them. Now I'll have to—Tomorrow you can see how lovely I'll look.

ANNE-MARIE: Oh, there won't be anyone at the party as 50 lovely as Miss Nora. (*She goes off into the room, left.*)

NORA: (*Begins unpacking the box, but soon throws it aside.*) Oh, if I dared to go out. If only nobody would come. If only nothing would happen here while I'm out. What craziness—nobody's coming. Just don't think. This muff— 55 needs a brushing. Beautiful gloves, beautiful gloves. Let it go. Let it go! One, two, three, four, five, six—(*With a cry.*)

Oh, there they are! (*Poises to move toward the door, but remains irresolutely standing.* MRS. LINDE *enters from the hall, where she has removed her street clothes.*)

NORA: Oh, it's you, Kristine. There's no one else out there? How good that you've come.

MRS. LINDE: I hear you were up asking for me.

NORA: Yes, I just stopped by. There's something you really can help me with. Let's get settled on the sofa. Look, there's going to be a costume party tomorrow evening at the Stenborgs' right above us, and now Torvald wants me to go as a Neapolitan peasant girl and dance the tarantella that I learned in Capri.

MRS. LINDE: Really, are you giving a whole performance?

NORA: Torvald says yes, I should. See, here's the dress. Torvald had it made for me down there; but now it's all so tattered that I just don't know—

MRS. LINDE: Oh, we'll fix that up in no time. It's nothing more than the trimmings—they're a bit loose here and there. Needle and thread? Good, now we have what we need.

NORA: Oh, how sweet of you!

MRS. LINDE: (*Sewing.*) So you'll be in disguise tomorrow, Nora. You know what? I'll stop by then for a moment and have a look at you all dressed up. But listen, I've absolutely forgotten to thank you for that pleasant evening yesterday.

NORA: (*Getting up and walking about.*) I don't think it was as pleasant as usual yesterday. You should have come to town a bit sooner, Kristine—Yes, Torvald really knows how to give a home elegance and charm.

MRS. LINDE: And you do, too, if you ask me. You're not your father's daughter for nothing. But tell me, is Dr. Rank always so down in the mouth as yesterday?

NORA: No, that was quite an exception. But he goes around critically ill all the time—tuberculosis of the spine, poor man. You know, his father was a disgusting thing who kept mistresses and so on—and that's why the son's been sickly from birth.

MRS. LINDE: (*Lets her sewing fall to her lap.*) But my dearest Nora, how do you know about such things?

NORA: (*Walking more jauntily.*) Hmp! When you've had three children, then you've had a few visits from—from women who know something of medicine, and they tell you this and that.

MRS. LINDE: (*Resumes sewing; a short pause.*) Does Dr. Rank come here every day?

NORA: Every blessed day. He's Torvald's best friend from childhood, and *my* good friend, too. Dr. Rank almost belongs to this house.

MRS. LINDE: But tell me—is he quite sincere? I mean, doesn't he rather enjoy flattering people?

NORA: Just the opposite. Why do you think that?

MRS. LINDE: When you introduced us yesterday, he was proclaiming that he'd often heard my name in this house; but later I noticed that your husband hadn't the slightest idea who I really was. So how could Dr. Rank—?

NORA: But it's all true, Kristine. You see, Torvald loves me beyond words, and, as he puts it, he'd like to keep me all to himself. For a long time he'd almost be jealous if I even mentioned any of my old friends back home. So of course I dropped that. But with Dr. Rank I talk a lot about such things, because he likes hearing about them.

MRS. LINDE: Now listen, Nora; in many ways you're still like a child. I'm a good deal older than you, with a little more experience. I'll tell you something: you ought to put an end to all this with Dr. Rank.

NORA: What should I put an end to?

MRS. LINDE: Both parts of it, I think. Yesterday you said something about a rich admirer who'd provide you with money—

NORA: Yes, one who doesn't exist—worse luck. So?

MRS. LINDE: Is Dr. Rank well off?

NORA: Yes, he is.

MRS. LINDE: With no dependents?

NORA: No, no one. But—

MRS. LINDE: And he's over here every day?

NORA: Yes, I told you that.

MRS. LINDE: How can a man of such refinement be so grasping?

NORA: I don't follow you at all.

MRS. LINDE: Now don't try to hide it, Nora. You think I can't guess who loaned you the forty-eight hundred crowns?

NORA: Are you out of your mind? How could you think such a thing! A friend of ours, who comes here every single day. What an intolerable situation that would have been!

MRS. LINDE: Then it really wasn't him.

NORA: No, absolutely not. It never even crossed my mind for a moment—And he had nothing to lend in those days; his inheritance came later.

MRS. LINDE: Well, I think that was a stroke of luck for you, Nora dear.

NORA: No, it never would have occurred to me to ask Dr. Rank—Still, I'm quite sure that if I had asked him—

MRS. LINDE: Which you won't, of course.

NORA: No, of course not. I can't see that I'd ever need to. But I'm quite positive that if I talked to Dr. Rank—

MRS. LINDE: Behind your husband's back?

NORA: I've got to clear up this other thing; *that's* also behind his back. I've *got* to clear it all up.

MRS. LINDE: Yes, I was saying that yesterday, but—

NORA: (*Pacing up and down.*) A man handles these problems so much better than a woman—

MRS. LINDE: One's husband does, yes.

NORA: Nonsense. (*Stopping.*) When you pay everything you owe, then you get your note back, right?

MRS. LINDE: Yes, naturally.

NORA: And can rip it into a million pieces and burn it up—that filthy scrap of paper!

MRS. LINDE: (*Looking hard at her, laying her sewing aside, and rising slowly.*) Nora, you're hiding something from me.

NORA: You can see it in my face?

MRS. LINDE: Something's happened to you since yesterday morning. Nora, what is it?

NORA: (*Hurrying toward her.*) Kristine! (*Listening.*) Shh! Torvald's home. Look, go in with the children a while. Torvald can't bear all this snipping and stitching. Let Anne-Marie help you.

MRS. LINDE: (*Gathering up some of the things.*) All right, but I'm not leaving here until we've talked this out. (*She disappears into the room, left, as* TORVALD [HELMER] *enters from the hall.*)

NORA: Oh, how I've been waiting for you, Torvald dear.

HELMER: Was that the dressmaker?

NORA: No, that was Kristine. She's helping me fix up my costume. You know, it's going to be quite attractive.

HELMER: Yes, wasn't that a bright idea I had?

NORA: Brilliant! But then wasn't I good as well to give in to you?

HELMER: Good—because you give in to your husband's judgment? All right, you little goose, I know you didn't mean it like that. But I won't disturb you. You'll want to
185 have a fitting, I suppose.

NORA: And you'll be working?

HELMER: Yes. (*Indicating a bundle of papers.*) See, I've been down to the bank. (*Starts toward his study.*)

NORA: Torvald.

190 HELMER: (*Stops.*) Yes.

NORA: If your little squirrel begged you, with all her heart and soul, for something—?

HELMER: What's that?

NORA: Then would you do it?

195 HELMER: First, naturally, I'd have to know what it was.

NORA: Your squirrel would scamper about and do tricks, if you'd only be sweet and give in.

HELMER: Out with it.

NORA: Your lark would be singing high and low in every
200 room—

HELMER: Come on, she does that anyway.

NORA: I'd be a wood nymph and dance for you in the moonlight.

HELMER: Nora—don't tell me it's that same business from this
205 morning?

NORA: (*Coming closer.*) Yes, Torvald, I beg you, please!

HELMER: And you actually have the nerve to drag that up again?

NORA: Yes, yes, you've got to give in to me; you *have* to let
210 Krogstad keep his job in the bank.

HELMER: My dear Nora, I've slated his job for Mrs. Linde.

NORA: That's awfully kind of you. But you could just fire another clerk instead of Krogstad.

HELMER: This is the most incredible stubbornness! Because
215 you go and give an impulsive promise to speak up for him, I'm expected to—

NORA: That's not the reason, Torvald. It's for your own sake. That man does writing for the worst papers; you said it yourself. He could do you any amount of harm. I'm
220 scared to death of him—

HELMER: Ah, I understand. It's the old memories haunting you.

NORA: What do you mean by that?

HELMER: Of course, you're thinking about your father.

NORA: Yes, all right. Just remember how those nasty gossips
225 wrote in the papers about Papa and slandered him so cruelly. I think they'd have had him dismissed if the department hadn't sent you up to investigate, and if you hadn't been so kind and open-minded toward him.

HELMER: My dear Nora, there's a notable difference between
230 your father and me. Your father's official career was hardly above reproach. But mine is; and I hope it'll stay that way as long as I hold my position.

NORA: Oh, who can ever tell what vicious minds can invent? We could be so snug and happy now in our quiet, care-
235 free home—you and I and the children, Torvald! That's why I'm pleading with you so—

HELMER: And just by pleading for him you make it impossible for me to keep him on. It's already known at the bank that I'm firing Krogstad. What if it's rumored around now
240 that the new bank manager was vetoed by his wife—

NORA: Yes, what then—?

HELMER: Oh yes—as long as our little bundle of stubbornness gets her way—! I should go and make myself ridicu-lous in front of the whole office—give people the idea I can be swayed by all kinds of outside pressure. Oh, you can 245 bet I'd feel the effects of that soon enough! Besides—there's something that rules Krogstad right out at the bank as long as I'm the manager.

NORA: What's that?

HELMER: His moral failings I could maybe overlook if I had 250 to—

NORA: Yes, Torvald, why not?

HELMER: And I hear he's quite efficient on the job. But he was a crony of mine back in my teens—one of those rash friendships that crop up again and again to embarrass you 255 later in life. Well, I might as well say it straight out: we're on a firstname basis. And that tactless fool makes no effort at all to hide it in front of others. Quite the contrary—he thinks that entitles him to take a familiar air around me, and so every other second he comes booming out with 260 his "Yes, Torvald!" and "Sure thing, Torvald!" I tell you, it's been excruciating for me. He's out to make my place in the bank unbearable.

NORA: Torvald, you can't be serious about all this.

HELMER: Oh no? Why not? 265

NORA: Because these are such petty considerations.

HELMER: What are you saying? Petty? You think I'm petty!

NORA: No, just the opposite, Torvald dear. That's exactly why—

HELMER: Never mind. You call my motives petty; then I 270 might as well be just that. Petty! All right! We'll put a stop to this for good. (*Goes to the hall door and calls.*) Helene!

NORA: What do you want?

HELMER: (*Searching among his papers.*) A decision. (*The* MAID *comes in.*) Look here; take this letter; go out with it at once. 275 Get hold of a messenger and have him deliver it. Quick now. It's already addressed. Wait, here's some money.

MAID: Yes, sir. (*She leaves with the letter.*)

HELMER: (*Straightening his papers.*) There, now, little Miss Willful. 280

NORA: (*Breathlessly.*) Torvald, what was that letter?

HELMER: Krogstad's notice.

NORA: Call it back, Torvald! There's still time. Oh, Torvald, call it back! Do it for my sake—for your sake, for the children's sake! Do you hear, Torvald; do it! You don't know 285 how this can harm us.

HELMER: Too late.

NORA: Yes, too late.

HELMER: Nora dear, I can forgive you this panic, even though basically you're insulting me. Yes, you are! Or isn't it an 290 insult to think that I should be afraid of a courtroom hack's revenge? But I forgive you anyway, because this shows so beautifully how much you love me. (*Takes her in his arms.*) This is the way it should be, my darling Nora. Whatever comes, you'll see: when it really counts, I have 295 strength and courage enough as a man to take on the whole weight myself.

NORA: (*Terrified.*) What do you mean by that?

HELMER: The whole weight, I said.

NORA: (*Resolutely.*) No, never in all the world. 300

HELMER: Good. So we'll share it, Nora, as man and wife. That's as it should be. (*Fondling her.*) Are you happy now? There, there, there—not these frightened dove's eyes. It's nothing at all but empty fantasies—Now you should run through your tarantella and practice your tambourine. I'll 305

go to the inner office and shut both doors, so I won't hear a thing; you can make all the noise you like. (*Turning in the doorway.*) And when Rank comes, just tell him where he can find me. (*He nods to her and goes with his papers into the*
310 *study, closing the door.*)

NORA: (*Standing as though rooted, dazed with fright, in a whisper.*) He really could do it. He will do it. He'll do it in spite of everything. No, not that, never, never! Anything but that! Escape! A way out—(*The doorbell rings.*) Dr. Rank! Any-
315 thing but that! Anything, whatever it is! (*Her hands pass over her face, smoothing it; she pulls herself together, goes over and opens the hall doo.* DR. RANK *stands outside, hanging his fur coat up. During the following scene, it begins getting dark.*)

NORA: Hello, Dr. Rank. I recognized your ring. But you
320 mustn't go in to Torvald yet; I believe he's working.

RANK: And you?

NORA: For you, I always have an hour to spare—you know that. (*He has entered, and she shuts the door after him.*)

RANK: Many thanks. I'll make use of these hours while I can.
325 NORA: What do you mean by that? While you can?

RANK: Does that disturb you?

NORA: Well, it's such an odd phrase. Is anything going to happen?

RANK: What's going to happen is what I've been expecting so
330 long—but I honestly didn't think it would come so soon.

NORA: (*Gripping his arm.*) What is it you've found out? Dr. Rank, you have to tell me!

RANK: (*Sitting by the stove.*) It's all over with me. There's nothing to be done about it.
335 NORA: (*Breathing easier.*) Is it you—then—?

RANK: Who else? There's no point in lying to one's self. I'm the most miserable of all my patients, Mrs. Helmer. These past few days I've been auditing my internal accounts. Bankrupt! Within a month I'll probably be laid out and
340 rotting in the churchyard.

NORA: Oh, what a horrible thing to say.

RANK: The thing itself is horrible. But the worst of it is all the other horror before it's over. There's only one final examination left; when I'm finished with that, I'll know about
345 when my disintegration will begin. There's something I want to say. Helmer with his sensitivity has such a sharp distaste for anything ugly. I don't want him near my sickroom.

NORA: Oh, but Dr. Rank—

RANK: I won't have him in there. Under no condition. I'll
350 lock my door to him—As soon as I'm completely sure of the worst, I'll send you my calling card marked with a black cross, and you'll know then the wreck has started to come apart.

NORA: No, today you're completely unreasonable. And I
355 wanted you so much to be in a really good humor.

RANK: With death up my sleeve? And then to suffer this way for somebody else's sins. Is there any justice in that? And in every single family, in some way or another, this inevitable retribution of nature goes on—
360 NORA: (*Her hands pressed over her ears.*) Oh, stuff! Cheer up! Please—be gay!

RANK: Yes, I'd just as soon laugh at it all. My poor, innocent spine, serving time for my father's gay army days.

NORA: (*By the table, left.*) He was so infatuated with asparagus
365 tips and *pâté de foie gras,* wasn't that it?

RANK: Yes—and with truffles.

NORA: Truffles, yes. And then with oysters, I suppose?

RANK: Yes, tons of oysters, naturally.

NORA: And then the port and champagne to go with it. It's so sad that all these delectable things have to strike at our bones. 370

RANK: Especially when they strike at the unhappy bones that never shared in the fun.

NORA: Ah, that's the saddest of all.

RANK: (*Looks searchingly at her.*) Hm.

NORA: (*After a moment.*) Why did you smile? 375

RANK: No, it was you who laughed.

NORA: No, it was you who smiled, Dr. Rank!

RANK: (*Getting up.*) You're even a bigger tease than I'd thought.

NORA: I'm full of wild ideas today.

RANK: That's obvious. 380

NORA: (*Putting both hands on his shoulders.*) Dear, dear Dr. Rank, you'll never die for Torvald and me.

RANK: Oh, that loss you'll easily get over. Those who go away are soon forgotten.

NORA: (*Looks fearfully at him.*) You believe that? 385

RANK: One makes new connections, and then—

NORA: Who makes new connections?

RANK: Both you and Torvald will when I'm gone. I'd say you're well under way already. What was that Mrs. Linde doing here last evening? 390

NORA: Oh, come—you can't be jealous of poor Kristine?

RANK: Oh yes, I am. She'll be my successor here in the house. When I'm down under, that woman will probably—

NORA: Shh! Not so loud. She's right in there.

RANK: Today as well. So you see. 395

NORA: Only to sew on my dress. Good gracious, how unreasonable you are. (*Sitting on the sofa.*) Be nice now, Dr. Rank. Tomorrow you'll see how beautifully I'll dance; and you can imagine then that I'm dancing only for you—yes, and of course for Torvald, too—that's understood. (*Takes various items out of the carton.*) Dr. Rank, sit 400 over here and I'll show you something.

RANK: (*Sitting.*) What's that?

NORA: Look here. Look.

RANK: Silk stockings. 405

NORA: Flesh-colored. Aren't they lovely? Now it's so dark here, but tomorrow—No, no, no, just look at the feet. Oh well, you might as well look at the rest.

RANK: Hm—

NORA: Why do you look so critical? Don't you believe they'll 410 fit?

RANK: I've never had any chance to form an opinion on that.

NORA: (*Glancing at him a moment.*) Shame on you. (*Hits him lightly on the ear with the stockings.*) That's for you. (*Puts them away again.*) 415

RANK: And what other splendors am I going to see now?

NORA: Not the least bit more, because you've been naughty. (*She hums a little and rummages among her things.*)

RANK: (*After a short silence.*) When I sit here together with you like this, completely easy and open, then I don't know— 420 I simply can't imagine—whatever would have become of me if I'd never come into this house.

NORA: (*Smiling.*) Yes, I really think you feel completely at ease with us.

RANK: (*More quietly, staring straight ahead.*) And then to have to 425 go away from it all—

NORA: Nonsense, you're not going away.

RANK: (*His voice unchanged.*)—and not even be able to leave some poor show of gratitude behind, scarcely a fleeting regret—no more than a vacant place that anyone can fill.

430

NORA: And if I asked you now for—? No—

RANK: For what?

NORA: For a great proof of your friendship—

RANK: Yes, yes?

435 NORA: No, I mean—for an exceptionally big favor—

RANK: Would you really, for once, make me so happy?

NORA: Oh, you haven't the vaguest idea what it is.

RANK: All right, then tell me.

NORA: No, but I can't, Dr. Rank—it's all out of reason. It's

440 advice and help, too—and a favor—

RANK: So much the better. I can't fathom what you're hinting at. Just speak out. Don't you trust me?

NORA: Of course. More than anyone else. You're my best and truest friend, I'm sure. That's why I want to talk to you.

445 All right, then, Dr. Rank: there's something you can help me prevent. You know how deeply, how inexpressibly dearly Torvald loves me; he'd never hesitate a second to give up his life for me.

RANK: (*Leaning close to her.*) Nora—do you think he's the only

450 one—

NORA: (*With a slight start.*) Who—?

RANK: Who'd gladly give up his life for you.

NORA: (*Heavily.*) I see.

RANK: I swore to myself you should know this before I'm

455 gone. I'll never find a better chance. Yes, Nora, now you know. And also you know now that you can trust me beyond anyone else.

NORA: (*Rising, natural and calm.*) Let me by.

RANK: (*Making room for her, but still sitting.*) Nora—

460 NORA: (*In the hall doorway.*) Helene, bring the lamp in. (*Goes over to the stove.*) Ah, dear Dr. Rank, that was really mean of you.

RANK: (*Getting up.*) That I've loved you just as deeply as somebody else? Was *that* mean?

NORA: No, but that you came out and told me. That was

465 quite unnecessary—

RANK: What do you mean? Have you known—?

(*The* MAID *comes in with the lamp, sets it on the table, and goes out again.*)

RANK: Nora—Mrs. Helmer—I'm asking you: have you known about it?

NORA: Oh, how can I tell what I know or don't know?

470 Really, I don't know what to say—Why did you have to be so clumsy, Dr. Rank! Everything was so good.

RANK: Well, in any case, you now have the knowledge that my body and soul are at your command. So won't you speak out?

475 NORA: (*Looking at him.*) After that?

RANK: Please, just let me know what it is.

NORA: You can't know anything now.

RANK: I have to. You mustn't punish me like this. Give me the chance to do whatever is humanly possible for you.

480 NORA: Now there's nothing you can do for me. Besides, actually, I don't need any help. You'll see—it's only my fantasies. That's what it is. Of course! (*Sits in the rocker, looks at him, and smiles.*) What a nice one you are, Dr. Rank. Aren't you a little bit ashamed, now that the lamp is here?

RANK: No, not exactly. But perhaps I'd better go—for good? 485

NORA: No, you certainly can't do that. You must come here just as you always have. You know Torvald can't do without you.

RANK: Yes, but *you?*

NORA: You know how much I enjoy it when you're here.

RANK: That's precisely what threw me off. You're a mystery 490 to me. So many times I've felt you'd almost rather be with me than with Helmer.

NORA: Yes—you see, there are some people that one loves most and other people that one would almost prefer being with.

RANK: Yes, there's something to that. 495

NORA: When I was back home, of course I loved Papa most. But I always thought it was so much fun when I could sneak down to the maids' quarters, because they never tried to improve me, and it was always so amusing, the way they talked to each other. 500

RANK: Aha, so it's *their* place that I've filled.

NORA: (*Jumping up and going to him.*) Oh, dear, sweet Dr. Rank, that's not what I meant at all. But you can understand that with Torvald it's just the same as with Papa—

(*The* MAID *enters from the hall.*)

MAID: Ma'am—please! (*She whispers to* NORA *and hands her a* 505 *calling card.*)

NORA: (*Glancing at the card.*) Ah! (*Slips it into her pocket.*)

RANK: Anything wrong?

NORA: No, no, not at all. It's only some—it's my new dress—

RANK: Really? But—there's your dress. 510

NORA: Oh, that. But this is another one—I ordered it— Torvald mustn't know—

RANK: Ah, now we have the big secret.

NORA: That's right. Just go in with him—he's back in the inner study. Keep him there as long as— 515

RANK: Don't worry. He won't get away. (*Goes into the study.*)

NORA: (*To the* MAID.) And he's standing waiting in the kitchen?

MAID: Yes, he came up by the back stairs.

NORA: But didn't you tell him somebody was here?

MAID: Yes, but that didn't do any good. 520

NORA: He won't leave?

MAID: No, he won't go till he's talked with you, ma'am.

NORA: Let him come in, then—but quietly. Helene, don't breathe a word about this. It's a surprise for my husband.

MAID: Yes, yes, I understand—(*Goes out.*) 525

NORA: This horror—it's going to happen. No, no, no, it can't happen, it mustn't. (*She goes and bolts* HELMER'*s door. The* MAID *opens the hall door for* KROGSTAD *and shuts it behind him. He is dressed for travel in a fur coat, boots, and a fur cap.*)

NORA: (*Going toward him.*) Talk softly. My husband's home. 530

KROGSTAD: Well, good for him.

NORA: What do you want?

KROGSTAD: Some information.

NORA: Hurry up, then. What is it?

KROGSTAD: You know, of course, that I got my notice. 535

NORA: I couldn't prevent it, Mr. Krogstad. I fought for you to the bitter end, but nothing worked.

KROGSTAD: Does your husband's love for you run so thin? He knows everything I can expose you to, and all the same he dares to— 540

NORA: How can you imagine he knows anything about this?

KROGSTAD: Ah, no—I can't imagine it either, now. It's not at all like my fine Torvald Helmer to have so much guts—

NORA: Mr. Krogstad, I demand respect for my husband!

545 KROGSTAD: Why, of course—all due respect. But since the lady's keeping it so carefully hidden, may I presume to ask if you're also a bit better informed than yesterday about what you've actually done?

NORA: More than you ever could teach me.

550 KROGSTAD: Yes, I *am* such an awful lawyer.

NORA: What is it you want from me?

KROGSTAD: Just a glimpse of how you are, Mrs. Helmer. I've been thinking about you all day long. A cashier, a night—court scribbler, a—well, a type like me also has a little of

555 what they call a heart, you know.

NORA: Then show it. Think of my children.

KROGSTAD: Did you or your husband ever think of mine? But never mind. I simply wanted to tell you that you don't need to take this thing too seriously. For the present, I'm

560 not proceeding with any action.

NORA: Oh no, really! Well—I knew that.

KROGSTAD: Everything can be settled in a friendly spirit. It doesn't have to get around town at all; it can stay just among us three.

565 NORA: My husband must never know anything of this.

KROGSTAD: How can you manage that? Perhaps you can pay me the balance?

NORA: No, not right now.

KROGSTAD: Or you know some way of raising the money in

570 a day or two?

NORA: No way that I'm willing to use.

KROGSTAD: Well, it wouldn't have done you any good, anyway. If you stood in front of me with a fistful of bills, you still couldn't buy your signature back.

575 NORA: Then tell me what you're going to do with it.

KROGSTAD: I'll just hold onto it—keep it on file. There's no outsider who'll even get wind of it. So if you've been thinking of taking some desperate step—

NORA: I have.

580 KROGSTAD: Been thinking of running away from home—

NORA: I have!

KROGSTAD: Or even of something worse—

NORA: How could you guess that?

KROGSTAD: You can drop those thoughts.

585 NORA: How could you guess I was thinking of *that*?

KROGSTAD: Most of us think about *that* at first. I thought about it too, but I discovered I hadn't the courage—

NORA: (*Lifelessly.*) I don't either.

KROGSTAD: (*Relieved.*) That's true, you haven't the courage?

590 You too?

NORA: I don't have it—I don't have it.

KROGSTAD: It would be terribly stupid, anyway. After that first storm at home blows out, why, then—I have here in my pocket a letter for your husband—

595 NORA: Telling everything?

KROGSTAD: As charitably as possible.

NORA: (*Quickly.*) He mustn't ever get that letter. Tear it up. I'll find some way to get money.

KROGSTAD: Beg pardon, Mrs. Helmer, but I think I just told

600 you—

NORA: Oh, I don't mean the money I owe you. Let me know how much you want from my husband, and I'll manage it.

KROGSTAD: I don't want any money from your husband.

NORA: What do you want, then? 605

KROGSTAD: I'll tell you what. I want to recoup, Mrs. Helmer; I want to get on in the world—and there's where your husband can help me. For a year and a half I've kept myself clean of anything disreputable—all that time struggling with the worst conditions; but I was satisfied, 610 working my way up step by step. Now I've been written right off, and I'm just not in the mood to come crawling back. I tell you, I want to move on. I want to get back in the bank—in a better position. Your husband can set up a job for me— 615

NORA: He'll never do that!

KROGSTAD: He'll do it. I know him. He won't dare breathe a word of protest. And once I'm in there together with him, you just wait and see! Inside of a year, I'll be the manager's righthand man. It'll be Nils Krogstad, not Tor- 620 vald Helmer, who runs the bank.

NORA: You'll never see the day!

KROGSTAD: Maybe you think you can—

NORA: I have the courage now—for *that*.

KROGSTAD: Oh, you don't scare me. A smart, spoiled lady like 625 you—

NORA: You'll see; you'll see!

KROGSTAD: Under the ice, maybe? Down in the freezing, coal-black water? There, till you float up in the spring, ugly, unrecognizable, with your hair falling out— 630

NORA: You don't frighten me.

KROGSTAD: Nor do you frighten me. One doesn't do these things, Mrs. Helmer. Besides, what good would it be? I'd still have him safe in my pocket.

NORA: Afterwards? When I'm no longer—? 635

KROGSTAD: Are you forgetting that *I'll* be in control then over your final reputation? (NORA *stands speechless, staring at him.*) Good; now I've warned you. Don't do anything stupid. When Helmer's read my letter, I'll be waiting for his reply. And bear in mind that it's your husband himself who's 640 forced me back to my old ways. I'll never forgive him for that. Good-bye, Mrs. Helmer. (*He goes out through the hall.*)

NORA: (*Goes to the hall door, opens it a crack, and listens.*) He's gone. Didn't leave the letter. Oh no, no, that's impossible too! (*Opening the door more and more.*) What's that? He's 645 standing outside—not going downstairs. He's thinking it over? Maybe he'll—? (*A letter falls in the mailbox; then* KROGSTAD's *footsteps are heard, dying away down a flight of stairs.* NORA *gives a muffled cry and runs over toward the sofa table. A short pause.*) In the mailbox. (*Slips warily over to the* 650 *hall door.*) It's lying there. Torvald, Torvald—now we're lost!

MRS. LINDE: (*Entering with the costume from the room, left.*) There now, I can't see anything else to mend. Perhaps you'd like to try—

NORA: (*In a hoarse whisper.*) Kristine, come here. 655

MRS. LINDE: (*Tossing the dress on the sofa.*) What's wrong? You look upset.

NORA: Come here. See that letter? *There!* Look—through the glass in the mailbox.

MRS. LINDE: Yes, yes, I see it. 660

NORA: That letter's from Krogstad—

MRS. LINDE: Nora—it's Krogstad who loaned you the money!

NORA: Yes, and now Torvald will find out everything.

MRS. LINDE: Believe me, Nora, it's best for both of you.

665 NORA: There's more you don't know. I forged a name.

MRS. LINDE: But for heaven's sake—?

NORA: I only want to tell you that, Kristine, so that you can be my witness.

MRS. LINDE: Witness? Why should I—?

670 NORA: If I should go out of my mind—it could easily happen—

MRS. LINDE: Nora!

NORA: Or anything else occurred—so I couldn't be present here—

MRS. LINDE: Nora, Nora, you aren't yourself at all!

675 NORA: And someone should try to take on the whole weight, all of the guilt, you follow me—

MRS. LINDE: Yes, of course, but why do you think—?

NORA: Then you're the witness that it isn't true, Kristine. I'm very much myself; my mind right now is perfectly clear;

680 and I'm telling you: nobody else has known about this; I alone did everything. Remember that.

MRS. LINDE: I will. But I don't understand all this.

NORA: Oh, how could you ever understand it? It's the miracle now that's going to take place.

685 MRS. LINDE: The miracle?

NORA: Yes, the miracle. But it's so awful, Kristine. It mustn't take place, not for anything in the world.

MRS. LINDE: I'm going right over and talk with Krogstad.

NORA: Don't go near him; he'll do you some terrible harm!

690 MRS. LINDE: There was a time once when he'd gladly have done anything for me.

NORA: He?

MRS. LINDE: Where does he live?

NORA: Oh, how do I know? Yes. (Searches in her pocket.) Here's

695 his card. But the letter, the letter—!

HELMER: (From the study, knocking on the door.) Nora!

NORA: (With a cry of fear.) Oh! What is it? What do you want?

HELMER: Now, now, don't be so frightened. We're not coming in. You locked the door—are you trying on the dress?

700 NORA: Yes, I'm trying it. I'll look just beautiful, Torvald.

MRS. LINDE: (Who has read the card.) He's living right around the corner.

NORA: Yes, but what's the use? We're lost. The letter's in the box.

705 MRS. LINDE: And your husband has the key?

NORA: Yes, always.

MRS. LINDE: Krogstad can ask for his letter back unread; he can find some excuse—

NORA: But it's just this time that Torvald usually—

710 MRS. LINDE: Stall him. Keep him in there. I'll be back as quick as I can. (She hurries out through the hall entrance.)

NORA: (Goes to HELMER's door, opens it, and peers in.) Torvald!

HELMER: (From the inner study.) Well—does one dare set foot in one's own living room at last? Come on, Rank, now

715 we'll get a look—(In the doorway.) But what's this?

NORA: What, Torvald dear?

HELMER: Rank had me expecting some grand masquerade.

RANK: (In the doorway.) That was my impression, but I must have been wrong.

720 NORA: No one can admire me in my splendor—not till tomorrow.

HELMER: But Nora dear, you look so exhausted. Have you practiced too hard?

NORA: No, I haven't practiced at all yet.

HELMER: You know, it's necessary—   725

NORA: Oh, it's absolutely necessary, Torvald. But I can't get anywhere without your help. I've forgotten the whole thing completely.

HELMER: Ah, we'll soon take care of that.

NORA: Yes, take care of me, Torvald, please! Promise me that?   730 Oh, I'm so nervous. That big party—You must give up everything this evening for me. No business—don't even touch your pen. Yes? Dear Torvald, promise?

HELMER: It's a promise. Tonight I'm totally at your service— you little helpless thing. Hm—but first there's one thing I   735 want to—(Goes toward the hall door.)

NORA: What are you looking for?

HELMER: Just to see if there's any mail.

NORA: No, no, don't do that, Torvald!

HELMER: Now what?   740

NORA: Torvald, please. There isn't any.

HELMER: Let me look, though. (Starts out. NORA, at the piano, strikes the first notes of the tarantella. HELMER, at the door, stops.) Aha!

NORA: I can't dance tomorrow if I don't practice with you.   745

HELMER: (Going over to her.) Nora dear, are you really so frightened?

NORA: Yes, so terribly frightened. Let me practice right now; there's still time before dinner. Oh, sit down and play for me, Torvald. Direct me. Teach me, the way you always   750 have.

HELMER: Gladly, if it's what you want. (Sits at the piano.)

NORA: (Snatches the tambourine up from the box, then a long, vari-colored shawl, which she throws around herself, whereupon she springs forward and cries out:) Play for me now! Now I'll   755 dance!

(HELMER plays and NORA dances. RANK stands behind HELMER at the piano and looks on.)

HELMER: (As he plays.) Slower. Slow down.

NORA: Can't change it.

HELMER: Not so violent, Nora!

NORA: Has to be just like this.   760

HELMER: (Stopping.) No, no, that won't do at all.

NORA: (Laughing and swinging her tambourine.) Isn't that what I told you?

RANK: Let me play for her.

HELMER: (Getting up.) Yes, go on. I can teach her more easily   765 then.

(RANK sits at the piano and plays; NORA dances more and more wildly. HELMER has stationed himself by the stove and repeatedly gives her directions; she seems not to hear them; her hair loosens and falls over her shoulders; she does not notice, but goes on dancing. MRS. LINDE enters.)

MRS. LINDE: (Standing dumbfounded at the door.) Ah—!

NORA: (Still dancing.) See what fun, Kristine!

HELMER: But Nora darling, you dance as if your life were at stake.   770

NORA: And it is.

HELMER: Rank, stop! This is pure madness. Stop it, I say!

(RANK *breaks off playing, and* NORA *halts abruptly*).

HELMER: (*Going over to her.*) I never would have believed it. You've forgotten everything I taught you.

775 NORA: (*Throwing away the tambourine.*) You see for yourself.

HELMER: Well, there's certainly room for instruction here.

NORA: Yes, you see how important it is. You've got to teach me to the very last minute. Promise me that, Torvald?

HELMER: You can bet on it.

780 NORA: You mustn't, either today or tomorrow, think about anything else but me; you mustn't open any letters—or the mailbox—

HELMER: Ah, it's still the fear of that man—

NORA: Oh yes, yes, that too.

785 HELMER: Nora, it's written all over you—there's already a letter from him out there.

NORA: I don't know. I guess so. But you mustn't read such things now; there mustn't be anything ugly between us before it's all over.

790 RANK: (*Quietly to* HELMER.) You shouldn't deny her.

HELMER: (*Putting his arm around her.*) The child can have her way. But tomorrow night, after you've danced—

NORA: Then you'll be free.

MAID: (*In the doorway, right.*) Ma'am, dinner is served.

795 NORA: We'll be wanting champagne, Helene.

MAID: Very good, ma'am. (*Goes out.*)

HELMER: So—a regular banquet, hm?

NORA: Yes, a banquet—champagne till daybreak! (*Calling out.*) And some macaroons, Helene. Heaps of them—just

800 this once.

HELMER: (*Taking her hands.*) Now, now, now—no hysterics. Be my own little lark again.

NORA: Oh, I will soon enough. But go on in—and you, Dr. Rank. Kristine, help me put up my hair.

805 RANK: (*Whispering, as they go.*) There's nothing wrong—really wrong, is there?

HELMER: Oh, of course not. It's nothing more than this childish anxiety I was telling you about. (*They go out, right.*)

NORA: Well?

810 MRS. LINDE: Left town.

NORA: I could see by your face.

MRS. LINDE: He'll be home tomorrow evening. I wrote him a note.

NORA: You shouldn't have. Don't try to stop anything now. After all, it's a wonderful joy, this waiting here for the miracle.

815 MRS. LINDE: What is it you're waiting for?

NORA: Oh, you can't understand that. Go in to them; I'll be along in a moment.

(MRS. LINDE *goes into the dining room.* NORA *stands a short while as if composing herself; then she looks at her watch.*)

NORA: Five. Seven hours to midnight. Twenty-four hours to

820 the midnight after, and then the tarantella's done. Seven and twenty-four? Thirty-one hours to live.

HELMER: (*In the doorway, right.*) What's become of the little lark?

NORA: (*Going toward him with open arms.*) Here's your lark!

ACT THREE

Same scene. The table, with chairs around it, has been moved to the center of the room. A lamp on the table is lit. The hall door stands open. Dance music drifts down from the floor above. MRS. LINDE *sits at the table, absently paging through a book, trying to read, but apparently unable to focus her thoughts. Once or twice she pauses, tensely listening for a sound at the outer entrance.*

MRS. LINDE: (*Glancing at her watch.*) Not yet—and there's hardly any time left. If only he's not—(*Listening again.*) Ah, there he is. (*She goes out in the hall and cautiously opens the outer door. Quiet footsteps are heard on the stairs. She whispers:*) Come in. Nobody's here. 5

KROGSTAD: (*In the doorway.*) I found a note from you at home. What's back of all this?

MRS. LINDE: I just *had* to talk to you.

KROGSTAD: Oh? And it just *had* to be here in this house?

MRS. LINDE: At my place it was impossible; my room hasn't a 10 private entrance. Come in; we're all alone. The maid's asleep, and the Helmers are at the dance upstairs.

KROGSTAD: (*Entering the room.*) Well, well, the Helmers are dancing tonight? Really?

MRS. LINDE: Yes, why not? 15

KROGSTAD: How true—why not?

MRS. LINDE: All right, Krogstad, let's talk.

KROGSTAD: Do we two have anything more to talk about?

MRS. LINDE: We have a great deal to talk about.

KROGSTAD: I wouldn't have thought so. 20

MRS. LINDE: No, because you've never understood me, really.

KROGSTAD: Was there anything more to understand—except what's all too common in life? A calculating woman throws over a man the moment a better catch comes by.

MRS. LINDE: You think I'm so thoroughly calculating? You 25 think I broke it off lightly?

KROGSTAD: Didn't you?

MRS. LINDE: Nils—is that what you really thought?

KROGSTAD: If you cared, then why did you write me the way you did? 30

MRS. LINDE: What else could I do? If I had to break off with you, then it was my job as well to root out everything you felt for me.

KROGSTAD: (*Wringing his hands.*) So that was it. And this—all this, simply for money! 35

MRS. LINDE: Don't forget I had a helpless mother and two small brothers. We couldn't wait for you, Nils; you had such a long road ahead of you then.

KROGSTAD: That may be; but you still hadn't the right to abandon me for somebody else's sake. 40

MRS. LINDE: Yes—I don't know. So many, many times I've asked myself if I did have that right.

KROGSTAD: (*More softly.*) When I lost you, it was as if all the solid ground dissolved from under my feet. Look at me; I'm a half-drowned man now, hanging onto a wreck. 45

MRS. LINDE: Help may be near.

KROGSTAD: It was near—but then you came and blocked it off.

MRS. LINDE: Without my knowing it, Nils. Today for the first time I learned that it's you I'm replacing at the bank.

KROGSTAD: All right—I believe you. But now that you know, 50 will you step aside?

MRS. LINDE: No, because that wouldn't benefit you in the slightest.

KROGSTAD: Not "benefit" me, hm! I'd step aside anyway.

MRS. LINDE: I've learned to be realistic. Life and hard, bitter 55 necessity have taught me that.

KROGSTAD: And life's taught me never to trust fine phrases.

MRS. LINDE: Then life's taught you a very sound thing. But you do have to trust in actions, don't you?

60 KROGSTAD: What does that mean?

MRS. LINDE: You said you were hanging on like a half-drowned man to a wreck.

KROGSTAD: I've good reason to say that.

65 MRS. LINDE: I'm also like a half-drowned woman on a wreck. No one to suffer with; no one to care for.

KROGSTAD: You made your choice.

MRS. LINDE: There wasn't any choice then.

KROGSTAD: So—what of it?

MRS. LINDE: Nils, if only we two shipwrecked people could
70 reach across to each other.

KROGSTAD: What are you saying?

MRS. LINDE: Two on one wreck are at least better off than each on his own.

KROGSTAD: Kristine!

75 MRS. LINDE: Why do you think I came into town?

KROGSTAD: Did you really have some thought of me?

MRS. LINDE: I have to work to go on living. All my born days, as long as I can remember, I've worked, and it's been my best and my only joy. But now I'm completely alone
80 in the world; it frightens me to be so empty and lost. To work for yourself—there's no joy in that. Nils, give me something—someone to work for.

KROGSTAD: I don't believe all this. It's just some hysterical feminine urge to go out and make a noble sacrifice.

85 MRS. LINDE: Have you ever found me to be hysterical?

KROGSTAD: Can you honestly mean this? Tell me—do you know everything about my past?

MRS. LINDE: Yes.

KROGSTAD: And you know what they think I'm worth
90 around here.

MRS. LINDE: From what you were saying before, it would seem that with me you could have been another person.

KROGSTAD: I'm positive of that.

MRS. LINDE: Couldn't it happen still?

95 KROGSTAD: Kristine—you're saying this in all seriousness? Yes, you are! I can see it in you. And do you really have the courage, then—?

MRS. LINDE: I need to have someone to care for; and your children need a mother. We both need each other. Nils, I
100 have faith that you're good at heart—I'll risk everything together with you.

KROGSTAD: (Gripping her hands.) Kristine, thank you, thank you—Now I know I can win back a place in their eyes. Yes—but I forgot—

105 MRS. LINDE: (Listening.) Shh! The tarantella. Go now! Go on!

KROGSTAD: Why? What is it?

MRS. LINDE: Hear the dance up there? When that's over, they'll be coming down.

KROGSTAD: Oh, then I'll go. But—it's all pointless. Of course,
110 you don't know the move I made against the Helmers.

MRS. LINDE: Yes, Nils, I know.

KROGSTAD: And all the same, you have the courage to—?

MRS. LINDE: I know how far despair can drive a man like you.

KROGSTAD: Oh, if I only could take it all back.

115 MRS. LINDE: You easily could—your letter's still lying in the mailbox.

KROGSTAD: Are you sure of that?

MRS. LINDE: Positive. But—

KROGSTAD: (Looks at her searchingly.) Is that the meaning of it, then? You'll save your friend at any price. Tell me straight 120 out. Is that it?

MRS. LINDE: Nils—anyone who's sold herself for somebody else once isn't going to do it again.

KROGSTAD: I'll demand my letter back.

MRS. LINDE: No, no. 125

KROGSTAD: Yes, of course. I'll stay here till Helmer comes down; I'll tell him to give me my letter again—that it only involves my dismissal—that he shouldn't read it—

MRS. LINDE: No, Nils, don't call the letter back.

KROGSTAD: But wasn't that exactly why you wrote me to 130 come here?

MRS. LINDE: Yes, in that first panic. But it's been a whole day and night since then, and in that time I've seen such incredible things in this house. Helmer's got to learn everything; this dreadful secret has to be aired; those two have to come to a 135 full understanding; all these lies and evasions can't go on.

KROGSTAD: Well, then, if you want to chance it. But at least there's one thing I can do, and do right away—

MRS. LINDE: (Listening.) Go now, go, quick! The dance is over. We're not safe another second. 140

KROGSTAD: I'll wait for you downstairs.

MRS. LINDE: Yes, please do; take me home.

KROGSTAD: I can't believe it; I've never been so happy. (He leaves by way of the outer door; the door between the room and the hall stays open.) 145

MRS. LINDE: (Straightening up a bit and getting together her street clothes.) How different now! How different! Someone to work for, to live for—a home to build. Well, it is worth the try! Oh, if they'd only come! (Listening.) Ah, there they are. Bundle up. (She picks up her hat and coat. NORA's and 150 HELMER's voices can be heard outside; a key turns in the lock, and HELMER brings NORA into the hall almost by force. She is wearing the Italian costume with a large black shawl about her; he has on evening dress, with a black domino open over it.)

NORA: (Struggling in the doorway.) No, no, no, not inside! I'm 155 going up again. I don't want to leave so soon.

HELMER: But Nora dear—

NORA: Oh, I beg you, please, Torvald. From the bottom of my heart, please—only an hour more!

HELMER: Not a single minute, Nora darling. You know our 160 agreement. Come on, in we go; you'll catch cold out here. (In spite of her resistance, he gently draws her into the room.)

MRS. LINDE: Good evening.

NORA: Kristine!

HELMER: Why, Mrs. Linde—are you here so late? 165

MRS. LINDE: Yes, I'm sorry, but I did want to see Nora in costume.

NORA: Have you been sitting here, waiting for me?

MRS. LINDE: Yes. I didn't come early enough; you were all upstairs; and then I thought I really couldn't leave without 170 seeing you.

HELMER: (Removing NORA's shawl.) Yes, take a good look. She's worth looking at, I can tell you that, Mrs. Linde. Isn't she lovely?

MRS. LINDE: Yes, I should say— 175

HELMER: A dream of loveliness, isn't she? That's what everyone thought at the party, too. But she's horribly stubborn—this sweet little thing. What's to be done with her?

Can you imagine, I almost had to use force to pry her away.

180 NORA: Oh, Torvald, you're going to regret you didn't indulge me, even for just a half hour more.

HELMER: There, you see. She danced her tarantella and got a tumultuous hand—which was well earned, although the performance may have been a bit too naturalistic—I mean
185 it rather overstepped the proprieties of art. But never mind—what's important is, she made a success, an overwhelming success. You think I could let her stay on after that and spoil the effect? Oh no; I took my lovely little Capri girl—my capricious little Capri girl, I should say—
190 took her under my arm; one quick tour of the ballroom, a curtsy to every side, and then—as they say in novels—the beautiful vision disappeared. An exit should always be effective, Mrs. Linde, but that's what I can't get Nora to grasp. Phew, it's hot in here. (*Flings the domino on a chair and opens*
195 *the door to his room.*) Why's it dark in here? Oh yes, of course. Excuse me. (*He goes in and lights a couple of candles.*)

NORA: (*In a sharp, breathless whisper.*) So?

MRS. LINDE: (*Quietly.*) I talked with him.

NORA: And—?

200 MRS. LINDE: Nora—you must tell your husband everything.

NORA: (*Dully.*) I knew it.

MRS. LINDE: You've got nothing to fear from Krogstad, but you have to speak out.

NORA: I won't tell.

205 MRS. LINDE: Then the letter will.

NORA: Thanks, Kristine. I know now what's to be done. Shh!

HELMER: (*Reentering.*) Well, then, Mrs. Linde—have you admired her?

MRS. LINDE: Yes, and now I'll say good night.

210 HELMER: Oh, come, so soon? Is this yours, this knitting?

MRS. LINDE: Yes, thanks. I nearly forgot it.

HELMER: Do you knit, then?

MRS. LINDE: Oh yes.

HELMER: You know what? You should embroider instead.

215 MRS. LINDE: Really? Why?

HELMER: Yes, because it's a lot prettier. See here, one holds the embroidery so, in the left hand, and then one guides the needle with the right—so—in an easy, sweeping curve—right?

MRS. LINDE: Yes, I guess that's—

220 HELMER: But, on the other hand, knitting—it can never be anything but ugly. Look, see here, the arms tucked in, the knitting needles going up and down—there's something Chinese about it. Ah, that was really a glorious champagne they served.

225 MRS. LINDE: Yes, good night, Nora, and don't be stubborn anymore.

HELMER: Well put, Mrs. Linde!

MRS. LINDE: Good night, Mr. Helmer.

HELMER: (*Accompanying her to the door.*) Good night, good
230 night. I hope you get home all right. I'd be very happy to—but you don't have far to go. Good night, good night. (*She leaves. He shuts the door after her and returns.*) There, now, at last we got her out the door. She's a deadly bore, that creature.

235 NORA: Aren't you pretty tired, Torvald?

HELMER: No, not a bit.

NORA: You're not sleepy?

HELMER: Not at all. On the contrary, I'm feeling quite exhilarated. But you? Yes, you really look tired and sleepy.

NORA: Yes, I'm very tired. Soon now I'll sleep. 240

HELMER: See! You see! I was right all along that we shouldn't stay longer.

NORA: Whatever you do is always right.

HELMER: (*Kissing her brow.*) Now my little lark talks sense. Say, did you notice what a time Rank was having tonight? 245

NORA: Oh, was he? I didn't get to speak with him.

HELMER: I scarcely did either, but it's a long time since I've seen him in such high spirits. (*Gazes at her a moment, then comes nearer her.*) Hm—it's marvelous, though, to be back home again—to be completely alone with you. Oh, you 250 bewitchingly lovely young woman!

NORA: Torvald, don't look at me like that!

HELMER: Can't I look at my richest treasure? At all that beauty that's mine, mine alone—completely and utterly.

NORA: (*Moving around to the other side of the table.*) You mustn't 255 talk to me that way tonight.

HELMER: (*Following her.*) The tarantella is still in your blood, I can see—and it makes you even more enticing. Listen. The guests are beginning to go. (*Dropping his voice.*) Nora—it'll soon be quiet through this whole house. 260

NORA: Yes, I hope so.

HELMER: You do, don't you, my love? Do you realize—when I'm out at a party like this with you—do you know why I talk to you so little, and keep such a distance away; just send you a stolen look now and then—you know why I 265 do it? It's because I'm imagining then that you're my secret darling, my secret young bride-to-be, and that no one suspects there's anything between us.

NORA: Yes, yes; oh, yes, I know you're always thinking of me.

HELMER: And then when we leave and I place the shawl over 270 those fine young rounded shoulders—over that wonderful curving neck—then I pretend that you're my young bride, that we're just coming from the wedding, that for the first time I'm bringing you into my house—that for the first time I'm alone with you—completely alone with you, 275 your trembling young beauty! All this evening I've longed for nothing but you. When I saw you turn and sway in the tarantella—my blood was pounding till I couldn't stand it—that's why I brought you down here so early—

NORA: Go away, Torvald! Leave me alone. I don't want all this. 280

HELMER: What do you mean? Nora, you're teasing me. You will, won't you? Aren't I your husband—?

(*A knock at the outside door.*)

NORA: (*Startled.*) What's that?

HELMER: (*Going toward the hall.*) Who is it?

RANK: (*Outside.*) It's me. May I come in a moment? 285

HELMER: (*With quiet irritation.*) Oh, what does he want now? (*Aloud.*) Hold on. (*Goes and opens the door.*) Oh, how nice that you didn't just pass us by!

RANK: I thought I heard your voice, and then I wanted so badly to have a look in. (*Lightly glancing about.*) Ah, me, these old 290 familiar haunts. You have it snug and cozy in here, you two.

HELMER: You seemed to be having it pretty cozy upstairs, too.

RANK: Absolutely. Why shouldn't I? Why not take in everything in life? As much as you can, anyway, and as long as you can. The wine was superb— 295

HELMER: The champagne especially.

RANK: You noticed that too? It's amazing how much I could guzzle down.

NORA: Torvald also drank a lot of champagne this evening.

300 RANK: Oh?

NORA: Yes, and that always makes him so entertaining.

RANK: Well, why shouldn't one have a pleasant evening after a well-spent day?

HELMER: Well spent? I'm afraid I can't claim that.

305 RANK: (*Slapping him on the back.*) But I can, you see!

NORA: Dr. Rank, you must have done some scientific research today.

RANK: Quite so.

HELMER: Come now—little Nora talking about scientific re-
310   search!

RANK: Indeed you may.

NORA: Then they were good?

RANK: The best possible for both doctor and patient—certainty.

315 NORA: (*Quickly and searchingly.*) Certainty?

RANK: Complete certainty. So don't I owe myself a gay evening afterwards?

NORA: Yes, you're right, Dr. Rank.

HELMER: I'm with you—just so long as you don't have to suf-
320   fer for it in the morning.

RANK: Well, one never gets something for nothing in life.

NORA: Dr. Rank—are you very fond of masquerade parties?

RANK: Yes, if there's a good array of odd disguises—

NORA: Tell me, what should we two go as at the next mas-
325   querade?

HELMER: You little featherhead—already thinking of the next!

RANK: We two? I'll tell you what: you must go as Charmed Life—

HELMER: Yes, but find a costume for *that!*

330 RANK: Your wife can appear just as she looks every day.

HELMER: That was nicely put. But don't you know what you're going to be?

RANK: Yes, Helmer, I've made up my mind.

HELMER: Well?

335 RANK: At the next masquerade I'm going to be invisible.

HELMER: That's a funny idea.

RANK: They say there's a hat—black, huge—have you never heard of the hat that makes you invisible? You put it on, and then no one on earth can see you.

340 HELMER: (*Suppressing a smile.*) Ah, of course.

RANK: But I'm quite forgetting what I came for. Helmer, give me a cigar, one of the dark Havanas.

HELMER: With the greatest pleasure. (*Holds out his case.*)

RANK: Thanks. (*Takes one and cuts off the tip.*)

345 NORA: (*Striking a match.*) Let me give you a light.

RANK: Thank you. (*She holds the match for him; he lights the cigar.*) And now good-bye.

HELMER: Good-bye, good-bye, old friend.

NORA: Sleep well, Doctor.

350 RANK: Thanks for that wish.

NORA: Wish me the same.

RANK: You? All right, if you like—Sleep well. And thanks for the light. (*He nods to them both and leaves.*)

HELMER: (*His voice subdued.*) He's been drinking heavily.

355 NORA: (*Absently.*) Could be. (HELMER *takes his keys from his pocket and goes out in the hall.*) Torvald—what are you after?

HELMER: Got to empty the mailbox; it's nearly full. There won't be room for the morning papers.

NORA: Are you working tonight?

360 HELMER: You know I'm not. Why—what's this? Someone's been at the lock.

NORA: At the lock—?

HELMER: Yes, I'm positive. What do you suppose—? I can't imagine one of the maids—? Here's a broken hairpin. Nora, it's yours— 365

NORA: (*Quickly.*) Then it must be the children—

HELMER: You'd better break them of that. Hm, hm—well, opened it after all. (*Takes the contents out and calls into the kitchen.*) Helene! Helene, would you put out the lamp in the hall. (*He returns to the room, shutting the hall door, then* 370 *displays the handful of mail.*) Look how it's piled up. (*Sorting through them.*) Now what's this?

NORA: (*At the window.*) The letter! Oh, Torvald, no!

HELMER: Two calling cards—from Rank.

NORA: From Dr. Rank? 375

HELMER: (*Examining them.*) "Dr. Rank, Consulting Physician." They were on top. He must have dropped them in as he left.

NORA: Is there anything on them?

HELMER: There's a black cross over the name. See? That's a gruesome notion. He could almost be announcing his 380 own death.

NORA: That's just what he's doing.

HELMER: What! You've heard something? Something he's told you?

NORA: Yes. That when those cards came, he'd be taking his 385 leave of us. He'll shut himself in now and die.

HELMER: Ah, my poor friend! Of course I knew he wouldn't be here much longer. But so soon—And then to hide himself away like a wounded animal.

NORA: If it has to happen, then it's best it happens in si- 390 lence—don't you think so, Torvald?

HELMER: (*Pacing up and down.*) He'd grown right into our lives. I simply can't imagine him gone. He with his suffering and loneliness—like a dark cloud setting off our sunlit happiness. Well, maybe it's best this way. For him, at 395 least. (*Standing still.*) And maybe for us too, Nora. Now we're thrown back on each other, completely. (*Embracing her.*) Oh you, my darling wife, how can I hold you close enough? You know what, Nora—time and again I've wished you were in some terrible danger, just so I could 400 stake my life and soul and everything, for your sake.

NORA: (*Tearing herself away, her voice firm and decisive.*) Now you must read your mail, Torvald.

HELMER: No, no, not tonight. I want to stay with you, dearest.

NORA: With a dying friend on your mind? 405

HELMER: You're right. We've both had a shock. There's ugliness between us—these thoughts of death and corruption. We'll have to get free of them first. Until then—we'll stay apart.

NORA: (*Clinging about his neck.*) Torvald—good night! Good night! 410

HELMER: (*Kissing her on the cheek.*) Good night, little songbird. Sleep well, Nora. I'll be reading my mail now. (*He takes the letters into his room and shuts the door after him.*)

NORA: (*With bewildered glances, groping about, seizing* HELMER's *domino, throwing it around her, and speaking in short, hoarse,* 415 *broken whispers.*) Never see him again. Never, never. (*Putting her shawl over her head.*) Never see the children either—them, too. Never, never. Oh, the freezing black water! The depths—down—Oh, I wish it were over—He has it now; he's reading it—now. Oh no, no, not yet. Tor- 420 vald, good-bye, you and the children—(*She starts for the hall; as she does,* HELMER *throws open his door and stands with an open letter in his hand.*)

HELMER: Nora!

425 NORA: (*Screams.*) Oh—!

HELMER: What is this? You know what's in this letter?

NORA: Yes, I know. Let me go! Let me out!

HELMER: (*Holding her back.*) Where are you going?

NORA: (*Struggling to break loose.*) You can't save me, Torvald!

430 HELMER: (*Slumping back.*) True! Then it's true what he writes? How horrible! No, no, it's impossible—it can't be true.

NORA: It is true. I've loved you more than all this world.

HELMER: Ah, none of your slippery tricks.

NORA: (*Taking one step toward him.*) Torvald—!

435 HELMER: What *is* this you've blundered into!

NORA: Just let me loose. You're not going to suffer for my sake. You're not going to take on my guilt.

HELMER: No more playacting. (*Locks the hall door.*) You stay right here and give me a reckoning. You understand what 440 you've done? Answer! You understand?

NORA: (*Looking squarely at him, her face hardening.*) Yes. I'm beginning to understand everything now.

HELMER: (*Striding about.*) Oh, what an awful awakening! In all these eight years—she who was my pride and joy—a hyp445 ocrite, a liar—worse, worse—a criminal! How infinitely disgusting it all is! The shame! (*NORA says nothing and goes on looking straight at him. He stops in front of her.*) I should have suspected something of the kind. I should have known. All your father's flimsy values—Be still! All your father's flimsy 450 values have come out in you. No religion, no morals, no sense of duty—Oh, how I'm punished for letting him off! I did it for your sake, and you repay me like this.

NORA: Yes, like this.

HELMER: Now you've wrecked all my happiness—ruined my 455 whole future. Oh, it's awful to think of. I'm in a cheap little grafter's hands; he can do anything he wants with me, ask for anything, play with me like a puppet—and I can't breathe a word. I'll be swept down miserably into the depths on account of a featherbrained woman.

460 NORA: When I'm gone from this world, you'll be free.

HELMER: Oh, quit posing. Your father had a mess of those speeches too. What good would that ever do me if you were gone from this world, as you say? Not the slightest. He can still make the whole thing known; and if he does, I could be 465 falsely suspected as your accomplice. They might even think that I was behind it—that I put you up to it. And all that I can thank you for—you that I've coddled the whole of our marriage. Can you see now what you've done to me?

NORA: (*Icily calm.*) Yes.

470 HELMER: It's so incredible, I just can't grasp it. But we'll have to patch up whatever we can. Take off the shawl. I said, take it off! I've got to appease him somehow or other. The thing has to be hushed up at any cost. And as for you and me, it's got to seem like everything between us is just 475 as it was—to the outside world, that is. You'll go right on living in this house, of course. But you can't be allowed to bring up the children; I don't dare trust you with them— Oh, to have to say this to someone I've loved so much, and that I still—! Well, that's done with. From now on 480 happiness doesn't matter; all that matters is saving the bits and pieces, the appearance—(*The doorbell rings.* HELMER *starts.*) What's that? And so late. Maybe the worst—? You think he'd—? Hide, Nora! Say you're sick. (*NORA remains standing motionless.* HELMER *goes and opens the door.*)

MAID: (*Half dressed, in the hall.*) A letter for Mrs. Helmer.   485

HELMER: I'll take it. (*Snatches the letter and shuts the door.*) Yes, it's from him. You don't get it; I'm reading it myself.

NORA: Then read it.

HELMER: (*By the lamp.*) I hardly dare. We may be ruined, you and I. But—I've got to know. (*Rips open the letter, skims* 490 *through a few lines, glances at an enclosure, then cries out joyfully.*) Nora! (NORA *looks inquiringly at him.*) Nora! Wait— better check it again—Yes, yes, it's true. I'm saved. Nora, I'm saved!

NORA: And I?   495

HELMER: You too, of course. We're both saved, both of us. Look. He's sent back your note. He says he's sorry and ashamed—that a happy development in his life—oh, who cares what he says! Nora, we're saved! No one can hurt you. Oh, Nora, Nora—but first, this ugliness all has to go.   500 Let me see—(*Takes a look at the note.*) No, I don't want to see it; I want the whole thing to fade like a dream. (*Tears the note and both letters to pieces, throws them into the stove and watches them burn.*) There—now there's nothing left—He wrote that since Christmas Eve you—Oh, they must have   505 been three terrible days for you, Nora.

NORA: I fought a hard fight.

HELMER: And suffered pain and saw no escape but—No, we're not going to dwell on anything unpleasant. We'll just be grateful and keep on repeating: it's over now, it's   510 over! You hear me, Nora? You don't seem to realize—it's over. What's it mean—that frozen look? Oh, poor little Nora, I understand. You can't believe I've forgiven you. But I have, Nora; I swear I have. I know that what you did, you did out of love for me.   515

NORA: That's true.

HELMER: You loved me the way a wife ought to love her husband. It's simply the means that you couldn't judge. But you think I love you any the less for not knowing how to handle your affairs? No, no—just lean on me; I'll guide   520 you and teach you. I wouldn't be a man if this feminine helplessness didn't make you twice as attractive to me. You mustn't mind those sharp words I said—that was all in the first confusion of thinking my world had collapsed. I've forgiven you, Nora; I swear I've forgiven you.   525

NORA: My thanks for your forgiveness. (*She goes out through the door, right.*)

HELMER: No, wait—(*Peers in.*) What are you doing in there?

NORA: (*Inside.*) Getting out of my costume.

HELMER: (*By the open door.*) Yes, do that. Try to calm yourself   530 and collect your thoughts again, my frightened little songbird. You can rest easy now; I've got wide wings to shelter you with. (*Walking about close by the door.*) How snug and nice our home is, Nora. You're safe here; I'll keep you like a hunted dove I've rescued out of a hawk's claws. I'll   535 bring peace to your poor, shuddering heart. Gradually it'll happen, Nora; you'll see. Tomorrow all this will look different to you; then everything will be as it was. I won't have to go on repeating I forgive you; you'll feel it for yourself. How can you imagine I'd ever conceivably want   540 to disown you—or even blame you in any way? Ah, you don't know a man's heart, Nora. For a man there's something indescribably sweet and satisfying in knowing he's forgiven his wife—and forgiven her out of a full and open heart. It's as if she belongs to him in two ways now: in a   545 sense he's given her fresh into the world again, and she's become his wife and his child as well. From now on that's what you'll be to me—you little, bewildered, helpless thing. Don't be afraid of anything, Nora; just open your 550 heart to me, and I'll be conscience and will to you both— (*NORA enters in her regular clothes.*) What's this? Not in bed? You've changed your dress?

NORA: Yes, Torvald, I've changed my dress.

HELMER: But why now, so late?

555 NORA: Tonight I'm not sleeping.

HELMER: But Nora dear—

NORA: (*Looking at her watch.*) It's still not so very late. Sit down, Torvald; we have a lot to talk over. (*She sits at one side of the table.*)

560 HELMER: Nora—what is this? That hard expression—

NORA: Sit down. This'll take some time. I have a lot to say.

HELMER: (*Sitting at the table directly opposite her.*) You worry me, Nora. And I don't understand you.

NORA: No, that's exactly it. You don't understand me. And 565 I've never understood you either—until tonight. No, don't interrupt. You can just listen to what I say. We're closing out accounts, Torvald.

HELMER: How do you mean that?

NORA: (*After a short pause.*) Doesn't anything strike you about 570 our sitting here like this?

HELMER: What's that?

NORA: We've been married now eight years. Doesn't it occur to you that this is the first time we two, you and I, man and wife, have ever talked seriously together?

575 HELMER: What do you mean—seriously?

NORA: In eight whole years—longer even—right from our first acquaintance, we've never exchanged a serious word on any serious thing.

HELMER: You mean I should constantly go and involve you in 580 problems you couldn't possibly help me with?

NORA: I'm not talking of problems. I'm saying that we've never sat down seriously together and tried to get to the bottom of anything.

HELMER: But dearest, what good would that ever do you?

585 NORA: That's the point right there: you've never understood me. I've been wronged greatly, Torvald—first by Papa, and then by you.

HELMER: What! By us—the two people who've loved you more than anyone else?

590 NORA: (*Shaking her head.*) You never loved me. You've thought it fun to be in love with me, that's all.

HELMER: Nora, what a thing to say!

NORA: Yes, it's true now, Torvald. When I lived at home with Papa, he told me all his opinions, so I had the same ones 595 too; or if they were different I hid them, since he wouldn't have cared for that. He used to call me his doll-child, and he played with me the way I played with my dolls. Then I came into your house—

HELMER: How can you speak of our marriage like that?

600 NORA: (*Unperturbed.*) I mean, then I went from Papa's hands into yours. You arranged everything to your own taste, and so I got the same taste as you—or I pretended to; I can't remember. I guess a little of both, first one, then the other. Now when I look back, it seems as if I'd lived here 605 like a beggar—just from hand to mouth. I've lived by doing tricks for you, Torvald. But that's the way you wanted

it. It's a great sin what you and Papa did to me. You're to blame that nothing's become of me.

HELMER: Nora, how unfair and ungrateful you are! Haven't you been happy here? 610

NORA: No, never. I thought so—but I never have.

HELMER: Not—not happy!

NORA: No, only lighthearted. And you've always been so kind to me. But our home's been nothing but a playpen. I've been your doll-wife here, just as at home I was Papa's 615 doll-child. And in turn the children have been my dolls. I thought it was fun when you played with me, just as they thought it fun when I played with them. That's been our marriage, Torvald.

HELMER: There's some truth in what you're saying—under all 620 the raving exaggeration. But it'll all be different after this. Playtime's over; now for the schooling.

NORA: Whose schooling—mine or the children's?

HELMER: Both yours and the children's, dearest.

NORA: Oh, Torvald, you're not the man to teach me to be a 625 good wife to you.

HELMER: And you can say that?

NORA: And I—how am I equipped to bring up children?

HELMER: Nora!

NORA: Didn't you say a moment ago that that was no job to 630 trust me with?

HELMER: In a flare of temper! Why fasten on that?

NORA: Yes, but you were so very right. I'm not up to the job. There's another job I have to do first. I have to try to educate myself. You can't help me with that. I've got to do 635 it alone. And that's why I'm leaving you now.

HELMER: (*Jumping up.*) What's that?

NORA: I have to stand completely alone, if I'm ever going to discover myself and the world out there. So I can't go on living with you. 640

HELMER: Nora, Nora!

NORA: I want to leave right away. Kristine should put me up for the night—

HELMER: You're insane! You've no right! I forbid you!

NORA: From here on, there's no use forbidding me anything. 645 I'll take with me whatever is mine. I don't want a thing from you, either now or later.

HELMER: What kind of madness is this!

NORA: Tomorrow I'm going home—I mean, home where I came from. It'll be easier up there to find something to do. 650

HELMER: Oh, you blind, incompetent child!

NORA: I must learn to be competent, Torvald.

HELMER: Abandon your home, your husband, your children! And you're not even thinking what people will say.

NORA: I can't be concerned about that. I only know how es- 655 sential this is.

HELMER: Oh, it's outrageous. So you'll run out like this on your most sacred vows.

NORA: What do you think are my most sacred vows?

HELMER: And I have to tell you that! Aren't they your duties 660 to your husband and children?

NORA: I have other duties equally sacred.

HELMER: That isn't true. What duties are they?

NORA: Duties to myself.

HELMER: Before all else, you're a wife and a mother. 665

NORA: I don't believe in that anymore. I believe that, before all else, I'm a human being, no less than you—or anyway,

I ought to try to become one. I know the majority thinks
you're right, Torvald, and plenty of books agree with you,
670 too. But I can't go on believing what the majority says, or
what's written in books. I have to think over these things
myself and try to understand them.

HELMER: Why can't you understand your place in your own
home? On a point like that, isn't there one everlasting
675 guide you can turn to? Where's your religion?

NORA: Oh, Torvald, I'm really not sure what religion is.

HELMER: What—?

NORA: I only know what the minister said when I was confirmed. He told me religion was this thing and that.
680 When I get clear and away by myself, I'll go into that
problem too. I'll see if what the minister said was right,
or, in any case, if it's right for me.

HELMER: A young woman your age shouldn't talk like that. If
religion can't move you, I can try to rouse your con-
685 science. You do have some moral feeling? Or, tell me—
has that gone too?

NORA: It's not easy to answer that, Torvald. I simply don't
know. I'm all confused about these things. I just know I
see them so differently from you. I find out, for one thing,
690 that the law's not at all what I'd thought—but I can't get
it through my head that the law is fair. A woman hasn't a
right to protect her dying father or save her husband's life!
I can't believe that.

HELMER: You talk like a child. You don't know anything of
695 the world you live in.

NORA: No, I don't. But now I'll begin to learn for myself. I'll
try to discover who's right, the world or I.

HELMER: Nora, you're sick; you've got a fever. I almost think
you're out of your head.

700 NORA: I've never felt more clearheaded and sure in my life.

HELMER: And—clearheaded and sure—you're leaving your
husband and children?

NORA: Yes.

HELMER: Then there's only one possible reason.

705 NORA: What?

HELMER: You no longer love me.

NORA: No. That's exactly it.

HELMER: Nora! You can't be serious!

NORA: Oh, this is so hard, Torvald—you've been so kind to
710 me always. But I can't help it. I don't love you anymore.

HELMER: (*Struggling for composure.*) Are you also clearheaded
and sure about that?

NORA: Yes, completely. That's why I can't go on staying here.

HELMER: Can you tell me what I did to lose your love?

715 NORA: Yes, I can tell you. It was this evening when the miraculous thing didn't come—then I knew you weren't the
man I'd imagined.

HELMER: Be more explicit; I don't follow you.

NORA: I've waited now so patiently eight long years—for, my
720 Lord, I know miracles don't come every day. Then this
crisis broke over me, and such a certainty filled me: *now*
the miraculous event would occur. While Krogstad's letter was lying out there, I never for an instant dreamed that
you could give in to his terms. I was so utterly sure you'd
725 say to him: go on, tell your tale to the whole wide world.
And when he'd done that—

HELMER: Yes, what then? When I'd delivered my own wife
into shame and disgrace—!

NORA: When he'd done that, I was so utterly sure that you'd
step forward, take the blame on yourself and say: I am the 730
guilty one.

HELMER: Nora—!

NORA: You're thinking I'd never accept such a sacrifice from
you? No, of course not. But what good would my protests
be against you? That was the miracle I was waiting for, in 735
terror and hope. And to stave that off, I would have taken
my life.

HELMER: I'd gladly work for you day and night, Nora—and
take on pain and deprivation. But there's no one who
gives up honor for love. 740

NORA: Millions of women have done just that.

HELMER: Oh, you think and talk like a silly child.

NORA: Perhaps. But you neither think nor talk like the man
I could join myself to. When your big fright was over—
and it wasn't from any threat against me, only for what 745
might damage you—when all the danger was past, for you
it was just as if nothing had happened. I was exactly the
same, your little lark, your doll, that you'd have to handle
with double care now that I'd turned out so brittle and
frail. (*Gets up.*) Torvald—in that instant it dawned on me 750
that for eight years I've been living here with a stranger,
and that I'd even conceived three children—oh, I can't
stand the thought of it! I could tear myself to bits.

HELMER: (*Heavily.*) I see. There's a gulf that's opened between
us—that's clear. Oh, but Nora, can't we bridge it somehow? 755

NORA: The way I am now, I'm no wife for you.

HELMER: I have the strength to make myself over.

NORA: Maybe—if your doll gets taken away.

HELMER: But to part! To part from you! No, Nora, no—I
can't imagine it. 760

NORA: (*Going out, right.*) All the more reason why it has to be.
(*She reenters with her coat and a small overnight bag, which she
puts on a chair by the table.*)

HELMER: Nora, Nora, not now! Wait till tomorrow.

NORA: I can't spend the night in a strange man's room. 765

HELMER: But couldn't we live here like brother and sister—

NORA: You know very well how long that would last. (*Throws
her shawl about her.*) Good-bye, Torvald. I won't look in on
the children. I know they're in better hands than mine.
The way I am now, I'm no use to them. 770

HELMER: But someday, Nora—someday—?

NORA: How can I tell? I haven't the least idea what'll become
of me.

HELMER: But you're my wife, now and wherever you go.

NORA: Listen, Torvald—I've heard that when a wife deserts 775
her husband's house just as I'm doing, then the law frees
him from all responsibility. In any case, I'm freeing you
from being responsible. Don't feel yourself bound, any
more than I will. There has to be absolute freedom for us
both. Here, take your ring back. Give me mine. 780

HELMER: That too?

NORA: That too.

HELMER: There it is.

NORA: Good. Well, now it's all over. I'm putting the keys
here. The maids know all about keeping up the house— 785
better than I do. Tomorrow, after I've left town, Kristine
will stop by to pack up everything that's mine from home.
I'd like those things shipped up to me.

HELMER: Over! All over! Nora, won't you ever think about me?

790 NORA: I'm sure I'll think of you often, and about the chil-
     dren and the house here.
     HELMER: May I write you?
     NORA: No—never. You're not to do that.
     HELMER: Oh, but let me send you—
795 NORA: Nothing. Nothing.
     HELMER: Or help you if you need it.
     NORA: No. I accept nothing from strangers.
     HELMER: Nora—can I never be more than a stranger to you?
     NORA: (*Picking up the overnight bag.*) Ah, Torvald—it would
800   take the greatest miracle of all—
     HELMER: Tell me the greatest miracle!

NORA: You and I both would have to transform ourselves to the
     point that—Oh, Torvald, I've stopped believing in miracles.
HELMER: But I'll believe. Tell me! Transform ourselves to the
     point that—?   805
NORA: That our living together could be a true marriage.
     (*She goes out down the hall.*)
HELMER: (*Sinks down on a chair by the door, face buried in his
     hands.*) Nora! Nora! (*Looking about and rising.*) Empty. She's
     gone. (*A sudden hope leaps in him.*) The greatest miracle—?   810

(*From below, the sound of a door slamming shut.*)

August Strindberg

The Swedish playwright August Strindberg (1849–1912) was a modern Renaissance man: he wrote some fifty plays, several autobiographical novels, and a variety of scientific and occult works as well. A series of tempestuous marriages marked Strindberg's life and are reflected in his corrosively misogynistic attitudes and in his hostility toward Ibsen, who seemed to Strindberg to advocate a new order of feminine domination. Calling *A Doll House* "sick like its father," Strindberg wrote *The Father* (1887) in reply to Ibsen, a play in which a calculating woman drives her husband into madness. Although Strindberg considered the play to be an experiment in the new "naturalism," it is really a kind of psychological thriller: the characters are so consumed by their sexual combat with one another that the worldly environment hardly seems important. Strindberg sent the play to Émile Zola, who found it absorbing and curious, but lacking in the material social reality he demanded of the new drama. Strindberg then wrote *Miss Julie* (1888) and considered the play's use of naturalism in his famous preface to the play. The battle of the sexes is one of Strindberg's preoccupations, examined in a series of plays including *Creditors* (1888) and *The Dance of Death, Parts 1 and 2* (1901).

The battle of the sexes was also the battle that occupied Strindberg's life outside the theater. His three marriages all involved periods of psychological breakdown and creative fertility. His breakdown of the mid-1890s after marrying his second wife is documented in *The Inferno* (1897) and is symptomatic of Strindberg's volatile and unstable frame of mind. Much of Strindberg's manic energy was focused on women—he believed that his wife was attempting to drive him mad by sending rays through the walls. Strindberg also developed a passion for the occult and for alchemy, and in addition to his plays, poems, and novels, he wrote a number of scientific and pseudoscientific treatises. Unlike Ibsen, Strindberg experimented in a variety of dramatic genres throughout his career. Calling himself the "Zola of the occult," Strindberg wrote an influential series of expressionist and symbolic plays; the best known today are *To Damascus* (in three parts, 1898–1901) and *A Dream Play* (1901). He also wrote several important plays on Swedish history, including *Erik XIV* (1899), *Gustav Adolph* (1900), and *Gustav III* (1902). In 1907 he founded a small theater—the Intimate Theater—which brought the independent theater movement to Sweden and produced his intense and often symbolic series of "chamber plays," including *The Ghost Sonata* (1907) and *The Pelican* (1907). When Strindberg died in 1912, he had become not only the most significant literary and theatrical figure in Swedish history, but also a major influence on the course of modern drama.

MISS JULIE

Despite its setting, *Miss Julie* is a good example of Strindberg's subversive attitude toward the conventions of realistic theater. The play concerns the intense, erotic struggle between Jean and Julie, a struggle that takes place at once in the material world they inhabit and in the shadowy realm of fantasy and desire. This oblique angle on realism is suggested in Strindberg's opening stage directions. Instead of a setting oriented frontally toward the audience, creating the impression of a full and objective disclosure, Strindberg sets the stage at an angle, acknowledging that our vision of the characters will be imbalanced, skewed. The setting creates a real environment for the characters, but Strindberg also includes the symbolic Cupid upstage and the signs of Julie's father, the Count. Throughout the play his absent presence weighs on the scene, a disembodied reminder of the social realities governing the scene, personified by the speaking tube and the elegant, polished riding boots and spurs.

The play is set on Midsummer's Night, traditionally a holiday of festive release, but here the occasion for a duel to the death, as Jean fights to possess and destroy Julie. *Miss Julie* is

Jean confronts Julie in the Yale Repertory Theatre production of *Miss Julie,* 2005.

at once a complex psychological drama and an examination of the dynamics of power governing the relations between classes and between men and women. Much as Julie represents the forbidden pleasures of the upper classes to Jean, she also represents the process of his own degradation; the story of his escape from her garden through the outhouse provides an emblem of his experience in relation to the privileged upper classes of the play. Yet if Jean is trapped in servitude, Julie is no less trapped by the conventional society that hems her in, and by the ferocious erotic combat that Strindberg sees as definitive of mature sexuality.

PREFACE

TRANSLATED BY EVERT SPRINCHORN

Like the arts in general, the theater has for a long time seemed to me a *Biblia Pauperum,* a picture Bible for those who cannot read, and the playwright merely a lay preacher who hawks the latest ideals in popular form, so popular that the middle classes—the bulk of the audiences—can grasp them without racking their brains too much. That explains why the theater has always been an elementary school for youngsters and the half-educated, and for women, who still retain a primitive capacity for deceiving themselves and for letting themselves be deceived, that is, for succumbing to illusions and responding hypnotically to the suggestions of the author. Consequently, now that the rudimentary and undeveloped mental processes that operate in the realm of fantasy appear to be evolving to the level of reflection, research, and experimentation, I believe that the theater, like religion, is about to be replaced as a dying institution for whose enjoyment we lack the necessary qualifications. Support for my view is provided by the theater crisis through which all of Europe is now passing, and still more by the fact that in those highly cultured lands which have produced the finest minds of our time—England and Germany—the drama is dead, as for the most part are the other fine arts.

Other countries, however, have thought to create a new drama by filling the old forms with new contents. But since there has not been enough time to popularize the new ideas, the public cannot understand them. And in the second place, controversy has so stirred up the public that they can no longer look on with a pure and dispassionate interest, especially when they see their most cherished ideals assailed or hear an applauding or booing majority openly exercise its tyrannical power, as can happen in the theater. And in the third place, since the new forms for the new ideas have not been created, the new wine has burst the old bottles.

In the play that follows I have not tried to accomplish anything new—that is impossible. I have only tried to modernize the form to satisfy what I believe up-to-date people expect and demand of this art. And with that in mind I have seized upon—or let myself be seized by—a theme that may be said to lie outside current party strife, since the questions of being on the way up or on the way down the social ladder, of being on the top or on the bottom, superior or inferior, man or woman, is, has been, and will be of perennial interest. When I took this theme from real life—I heard about it a few years ago and it made a deep impression on me—I thought it would be a suitable subject for a tragedy, since it still strikes us as tragic to see a happily favored individual go down in defeat, and even more so to see an entire family line die out. But perhaps a time will come when we shall be so highly developed and so enlightened that we can look with indifference upon the brutal, cynical, and heartless spectacle that life offers us, a time when we shall have laid aside those inferior and unreliable mechanical apparatuses called emotions, which will become superfluous and even harmful as our mental organs develop. The fact that my heroine wins sympathy is due entirely to the fact that we are still too weak to overcome the fear that the same fate might overtake us. The extremely sensitive viewer will of course not be satisfied with mere expressions of sympathy, and the man who believes in progress will demand that certain positive actions be taken for getting rid of this evil, a kind of program, in other words. But in the first place absolute evil does not exist. The decline of one family is the making of another, which now gets its chance to rise. This alternate rising and falling provides one of life's greatest pleasures, for happiness is, after all, relative. As for the man who has a program for changing the disagreeable circumstance that the hawk eats the chicken and that lice eat up the hawk, I should like to ask him why it should be changed. Life is not prearranged with such idiotic mathematical precision that only the larger gets to eat the smaller. Just as frequently the bee destroys the lion (in Aesop's fable)—or at least drives him wild.

If my tragedy makes most people feel sad, that is their fault. When we get to be as strong as the first French Revolutionists were, we shall be perfectly content and happy to watch the forests being cleared of the rotting, superannuated trees that have stood too long in the way of others with just as much right to grow and flourish for a while—as content as we are when we see an incurably ill man finally die.

Recently my tragedy *The Father* was censured for being too unpleasant—as if one wanted merry tragedies. "The joy of life" is now the slogan of the day. Theater managers send out orders for nothing but farces, as if the joy of living lay in behaving like a clown and depicting people as if they were afflicted with St. Vitus's dance or congenital idiocy. I find the joy of living in the fierce and ruthless battles of life, and my pleasure comes from learning something, from being taught something. That is why I have chosen for my play an unusual but instructive case, an exception, in other words—but an important exception of the kind that proves the rule—a choice of subject that I know will offend all lovers of the conventional. The next thing that will bother simple minds is that the motivation for the action is not simple and that the point of view is not single. Usually an event in life—and this is a fairly new discovery—is the result of a whole series of more or less deep-rooted causes. The spectator, however, generally chooses the one that puts the least strain on his mind or reflects most credit on his insight. Consider a case of suicide. "Business failure," says the merchant. "Unhappy love," say the women. "Physical illness," says the sick man. "Lost hopes," says the down-and-out. But it may be that the reason lay in all of these or in none of them, and that the suicide hid his real reason behind a completely different one that would reflect greater glory on his memory.

I have motivated the tragic fate of Miss Julie with an abundance of circumstances: her mother's basic instincts, her father's improper bringing-up of the girl, her own inborn nature, and her fiancé's sway over her weak and degenerate mind. Further and more immediately: the festive atmosphere of Midsummer Eve, her father's absence, her period, her preoccupation with animals, the erotic excitement of the dance, the long summer twilight, the highly aphrodisiac influence of flowers, and finally chance itself, which drives two people together in an out-of-the-way room, plus the boldness of the aroused man.

As one can see, I have not been entirely the physiologist, not been obsessively psychological, not traced everything to her mother's heredity, not found the sole cause in her period, not attributed everything to our "immoral times," and not simply preached a moral lesson. Lacking a priest, I have let the cook handle that.

I am proud to say that this complicated way of looking at things is in tune with the times. And if others have anticipated me in this, I am proud that I am not alone in my paradoxes, as all new discoveries are called. And no one can say this time that I am being one-sided.

As far as the drawing of characters is concerned, I have made the people in my play fairly "characterless" for the following reasons. In the course of time the word *character* has acquired many meanings. Originally it probably meant the dominant and fundamental trait in the soul complex and was confused with temperament. Later the middle class used it to mean an automaton. An individual who once for all had found his own true nature or adapted himself to a certain role in life, who in fact had ceased to grow, was called a man of character, while the man who was constantly developing, who, like a skillful sailor on the currents of life, did not sail with close-tied sheets bu who fell off before the wind in order to luff again, was called a man of no character—derogatorily of course, since he was so difficult to keep track of, to pin down and pigeonhole. This middle-class conception of a fixed character was transferred to the stage, where the middle class has always ruled. A character there came to mean someone who was always one and the same, always drunk, always joking, always melancholy, and who needed to be characterized only by some physical defect such as a club foot, a wooden leg, or a red nose, or by the repetition of some such phrase as, "That's capital," or "Barkis is willin'." This uncomplicated way of viewing people is still to be found in the great Molière. Harpagon is nothing but a miser, although Harpagon could have been both a miser and an exceptional financier, a fine father, and a good citizen. Worse still, his "defect" is extremely advantageous to his son-in-law and his daughter who will be his heirs and who therefore should not find fault with him, even if they do have to wait a while to jump into bed together. So I do not believe in simple stage characters. And the summary judgments that writers pass on people—he is stupid, this one is brutal, that one is jealous, this one is stingy, and so on—should not pass unchallenged by the naturalists who know how complicated the soul is and who realize that vice has a reverse side very much like virtue.

Since the persons in my play are modern characters, living in a transitional era more hectic and hysterical than the previous one at least, I have depicted them as more unstable, as torn and divided, a mixture of the old and the new. Nor does it seem improbable to me that modern ideas might also have seeped down through newspapers and kitchen talk to the level of the servants. Consequently the valet may belch forth from his inherited slave soul certain modern ideas. And if there are those who find it wrong to allow people in a modern drama to talk Darwin and who recommend the practice of Shakespeare to our attention, may I remind them that the gravedigger in *Hamlet* talks the then fashionable philosophy of Giordano Bruno (Bacon's philosophy), which is even more improbable, seeing that the means of spreading ideas were fewer then than now. And besides, the fact of the matter is that Darwinism has always existed, ever since Moses' history of creation from the lower animals up to man, but it was not until recently that we discovered it and formulized it.

My souls—or characters—are conglomerations from various stages of culture, past and present, walking scrapbooks, shreds of human lives, tatters torn from old rags that were once Sunday best—hodgepodges just like the human soul. I have even supplied a little source history into the bargain by letting the weaker steal and repeat words of the stronger, letting them get ideas (suggestions as they are called) from one another, from the environment (the songbird's blood), and from objects (the razor). I have also arranged for *Gedankenübertragung*[1] through an inanimate medium to take place (the count's boots, the servant's bell). And I have even made use of "waking suggestions" (a variation of hypnotic suggestion), which have by now been so popularized that they cannot arouse ridicule or skepticism as they would have done in Mesmer's time.

I say Miss Julie is a modern character not because the man-hating half-woman has not always existed but because she has now been brought out into the open, has taken the stage, and is making a noise about herself. Victim of a superstition (one that has seized even stronger minds) that woman, that stunted form of human being, standing with man, the lord of creation, the creator of culture, is meant to be the equal of man or could ever possibly be, she involves herself in an absurd struggle with him in which she falls. Absurd because of a stunted form, subject to the laws of propagation, will always be born stunted and can never catch up with the one who has the lead. As follows: A (the man) and B (the woman) start from the same point C, A with a speed of let us say 100 and B with a speed of 60. When will B overtake A? Answer: never. Neither with the help of equal education or equal voting rights—nor by universal disarmament and temperance societies—any more than two parallel lines can ever meet. The half-woman is a type that forces itself on others, selling itself for power, medals, recognition, diplomas, as formerly it sold itself for money. It represents degeneration. It is not a strong species for it does not maintain itself, but unfortunately it propagates its misery in the following generation. Degenerate men unconsciously select their mates from among these half-women, so that they breed and spread, producing creatures of indeterminate sex to whom life is a torture, but who fortunately are overcome eventually either by a hostile reality, or by the uncontrolled breaking loose of their repressed instincts, or else by their frustration in not being able to compete with the male sex. It is a tragic type, offering us the spectacle of a desperate fight against nature; a tragic legacy of romanticism, which is now being dissipated by naturalism—a movement that seeks only happiness, and for that strong and healthy species are required.

Miss Julie, however, is also a vestige of the old warrior nobility that is now being superseded by a new nobility of nerve and brain. She is victim of the disorder produced within a family by a mother's "crime," of the mistakes of a whole generation gone wrong, of circumstances, of her own defective constitution—all of which put together is equivalent to the fate or universal law off the ancients. The naturalists have banished guilt along with God, but the consequences of an act—punishment, imprisonment, or the fear of it—cannot be banished for the simple reason that they remain whether or not the naturalist dismisses the case from his court. Those sitting on the sidelines can easily afford to be lenient; but what of the injured parties? And even if her father were compelled to forgo taking his revenge, Miss Julie would take vengence on herself, as she does in the play, because of that inherited or acquired sense of honor that has been transmitted to the upper classes from—well, where does it come from? From the age of barbarism, from the first Aryans, from the chivalry of the Middle Ages. And a very fine code it was, but now inimical to the survival of the race. It is the aristocrat's form of hara-kiri, a law of conscience that bids the Japanese to slice his own stomach when someone else dishonors him. The same sort of thing survives, slightly

---

[1] Telepathy

modified, in that exclusive prerogative of the aristocracy, the duel. (Example: the husband challenges his wife's lover to a duel; the lover shoots the husband and runs off with the wife. Result: the husband has saved his *honor* but lost his wife.) Hence the servant Jean lives on; but not Miss Julie, who cannot live without honor. The advantage that the slave has over his master is that he has not committed himself to this defeatist principle. In all of us Aryans there is enough of the nobleman, or the Don Quixote, to make us sympathize with the man who takes his own life after having dishonored himself by shameful deeds. And we are all of us aristocrats enough to be distressed at the sight of a great man lying like a dead hulk ready for the scrap pile, even, I suppose, if he were to raise himself up again and redeem himself by honorable deeds.

The servant Jean is the beginning of a new species in which noticable differentiation has already taken place. He began as a child of a poor worker and is now evolving through self-education into a future gentleman of the upper classes. He is quick to learn, has highly developed senses (smell, taste, sight), and a keen appreciation of beauty. He has already come up in the world, for he is strong enough not to hesitate to make use of other people. He is already a stranger to his old friends, whom he despises as remainders of past stages in his development, and whom he fears and avoids because they know his secrets, guess his intentions, look with envy on his rise and with joyful expectation towards his fall. Hence his character is unformed and divided. He wavers between an admiration of high positions and a hatred of the men who occupy them. He is an aristocrat—he says so himself—familiar with the ins and outs of good society. He is polished on the outside, but coarse underneath. He wears his frock coat with elegance but offers no guarantee that he keeps his body clean.

Although he respects Miss Julie, he is afraid of Christine, because she knows his innermost secrets. Yet sufficiently hard-hearted not to let the events of the night upset his plans for the future. Possessing both the coarseness of the slave and the toughmindedness of the born ruler, he can look at blood without fainting, shake off the bad luck like water, and take calamity by the horns. Consequentlly he will escape from the battle unwounded, probably ending up as proprietor of a hotel. And if he himself does not get to be a Rumanian count, his son will doubtless go to college and possibly end up as a government official.

Now his observations about life as the lower classes see it, from below, are well worth listening to—that is, they are whenever he is telling the truth, which is not too often, because he is more likely to say what is advantageous to him than what is true. When Miss Julie supposes that everyone in the lower classes must feel greatly oppressed by the weight of the classes above, Jean naturally agrees with her since he wants to win her sympathy. But he promptly takes it all back when he finds it expedient to separate himself from the mob.

Apart from the fact that Jean is coming up in the world, he is also superior to Miss Julie in that he is a man. In the sexual sphere, he is the aristocrat. He has the strength of the male, more highly developed senses, and the ability to take the initiative. His inferiority is merely the result of his social environment, which is only temporary and which he will probably slough off along with his livery.

His slave nature expresses itself in his awe of the count (the boots) and his religious superstitions. But he is awed by the count mainly because the count occupies the place he wants most in life; and this awe is still there even after he has won the daughter of the house and seen how empty that beautiful shell was.

I do not believe that any love in the "higher" sense can be born from the union of two such different souls; so I have let Miss Julie's love be refashioned in her imagination as a love that protects and purifies, and I have let Jean imagine that even his love might have a chance to grow under other social circumstances. For I suppose love is very much like the hyacinth that must strike roots deep in the dark earth *before* it can produce a vigorous blossom. Here it shoots up, bursts into bloom, and turns to seed all at once. Such plants can only be short-lived.

Christine—finally to get her—is a female slave, spineless and phlegmatic after years spent at the kitchen stove, bovinely unconscious of her own hypocrisy, and with a full quota of moral and religious notions that serve as scapegoats and cloaks for her sins—which a stronger soul does not require since he is able either to carry the burden of his own sins or to rationalize them out of existence. She attends church regularly where she deftly unloads unto Jesus her household thefts and picks up from him another load of innocence. She is only a secondary character, and I have deliberately done no more than sketch her in—just as I treated the country doctor and parish priest in *The Father* where I only wanted to draw ordinary everyday people such as most country doctors and parsons are. That some have found my minor characters one-dimensional is due to the fact that ordinary people while at work are to a certain extent one-dimensional and do lack an independent existence, showing only one side of themselves in the performance of their duties. And as long as the audience does not feel it needs to see them from different angles, my abstract sketches will pass muster.

Now as far as the dialogue is concerned, I have broken somewhat with tradition in refusing to make my characters into interlocutors who ask stupid questions to elicit witty answers. I have avoided the symmetrical and mathmatical design of the artfully constructed French dialogue and have let minds work as irregularly as they do in real life, where no subject is quite exhausted before another mind engages at random some cog in the conversation and governs it for a while. My dialogue wanders here and there, gathers material in the first scenes which is later picked up, repeated, reworked, developed, and expanded like the theme in a piece of music.

The action of the play poses no problem. Since it really involves only two people, I have limited myself to these two, introducing only one minor character, the cook, and keeping the unhappy spirit of the father brooding over the action as a whole. I have chosen this course because I have noticed that what interests people most nowadays is the psychological action. Our inveterately curious souls are no longer content to see a thing happen; we want to see how it happens. We want to see the strings, look at the machinery, examine the double-bottom drawer, put on the magic ring to find the hidden seam, look in the deck for the marked cards.

In treating the subject this way I have had in mind the case-history novels of the Goncourt brothers, which appeal to me more than anything else in modern literature.

As far as play construction is concerned, I have made a stab at getting rid of act divisions. I was afraid that the spectator's declining susceptibility to illusion might not carry him through the intermission, when he would have time to think about what he has seen and to escape the suggestive influence of the author-hypnotist. I figure my play lasts about ninety minutes. Since one can listen to a lecture, a sermon, or a political debate for that long or even longer, I have convinced myself that a play should not exhaust an audience in that length of time. As early as 1872 in one of my first attempts at drama, *The Outlaw*, I tried out this concentrated form, although with little success. I had finished the work in five acts when I noticed the disjointed and disturbing effect it produced. I burned it, and from the ashes arose a single, complete reworked act of fifty pages that would run for less than an hour. Although this play form is not completely new, it seems to be my special property and has a good chance of gaining favor with the public when tastes change. My hope is to educate a public to sit through a full evening's show in one act. But this whole question must first be probed more deeply. In the meantime, in order to establish resting places for the audience and the acors without destroying the illusion, I have made use of three arts that belong to the drama: the monologue, the pantomime, and the ballet, all of which were part of classic tragedy, the monody having become the monologue and the choral dance, the ballet.

The realists have banished the monologue from the stage as implausible. But if I can motivate it, I make it plausible, and I can then use it to my advantage. Now it is certainly plausible for a speaker to pace the floor and read his speech aloud to himself. It is plausible for an actor to practice his part aloud, for a child to talk to her cat, a mother to babble to her baby, an old lady to chatter to her parrot, and a sleeping man to talk in his sleep. And in order to give the actor a chance to work on his own for once and for a moment not be obliged to follow the author's directions, I have not written out the monologues in detail but simply outlined them. Since it makes very little difference what is said while asleep, or to the parrot or the cat, inasmuch as it does not affect the main action, a gifted player who is in the midst of the situation and mood of the play can probably improvise the monologue better than the author, who cannot estimate ahead of time how much may be said and for how long before the illusion is broken.

Some theaters in Italy have, as we know, returned to the art of improvisation and have thereby trained actors who are truly inventive—without, however, violating the intentions of the author. This seems to be a step in the right direction and possibly the beginning of a new, fertile form of art that will be genuinely *creative*.

In places where the monolgue cannot be properly motivated, I have restorted to pantomime. Here I have given the actor even more freedom to be creative and win the honor on his own. Nevertheless, not to try the audience beyond its limits, I have relied on music—well motivated by the Midsummer Eve dance—to exercise its hypnotic powers during the pantomime scene. I beg the music director to select his tunes with great care, so that associations foreign to the mood of the play will not be produced by reminders of popular operettas or current dance numbers or by folk music of interest only to ethnologists.

The ballet that I have introduced cannot be replaced by a so-called crowd scene. Such scenes are always badly acted, with a pack of babbling fools taking advantage of the occasion to "gag it up," thereby destroying the illusion. Inasmuch as the country people do not improvise their taunts but make use of material already at hand by giving it a double meaning, I have not composed an original lampoon but have made use of a little known round dance that I noted down in the Stockholm district. The words to not fit the situation exactly, which is what I intended, since the slave in his cunning (that is, weakness) never attacks directly. At any rate, let us have no comedians in this serious story and no obscene smirking over an affair that nails the lid on a family coffin.

As far as the scenery is concerned, I have borrowed from impressionistic painting the idea of asymmetrical and open composition, and I believe that I have thereby gained something in the way of greater illusion. Because the audience cannot see the whole room and all the furniture, they will have to surmise what's missing; that is, their imagination will be stimulated to fill in the rest of the picture. I have gained something else by this: I have avoided those tiresome exits through doors. Stage doors are made of canvas and rock at the slightest touch. They cannot even be used to indicate the wrath of an angry father who storms out of the house after a bad dinner, slamming the door behind him "so that the whole house shakes." (In the theater it sways and billows.) Furthermore, I have confined the action to one set, both to give the characters a chance to become part and parcel of their environment and to cut down on scenic extravagance. If there is only one set, one has a right to expect it to be as realistic as possible. Yet nothing is more difficult than to make a room look like a room, however easy it may be for the scene painter to create waterfalls and erupting volcanos. I suppose we shall have to put up with walls made of canvas, but isn't it about time that we stopped painting shelves and pots and pans on the canvas? There are so many other conventions in the theater that we are told to accept in good faith that we should be spared the strain of believing in painted saucepans.

I have placed the backdrop and the table at an angle to force the actors to play face to face or in half profile when they are seated opposite each other at the table. In a production of *Aida* I saw a flat placed at such an angle, which led the eye out in an unfamiliar perspective. Nor did it look as if it had been set that way simply to be different to avoid those monotonous right angles.

Another desirable innovation would be the removal of the footlights. I understand that the purpose of lighting from below is to make the actors look more full in the face. But may I ask why all actors should have full faces? Doesn't this kind of lighting wipe out many of the finer features in the lower part of the face, especially around the jaws? Doesn't it distort the shape of the nose and throw false shadows above the eyes? If not, it certainly does something else: it hurts the actor's eyes. The footlights hit the retina at an angle from which it is usually shielded (except in sailors who must look at the sunlight reflected in the water), and the result is the loss of any effective play of the eyes. All one ever sees on stage are goggle-eyed glances sideways at the boxes or upward at the balcony, with only the whites of the eyes being visible in the latter case. And this probably also accounts for that tiresome fluttering of the eyelashes that the female performers are particularly guilty of. If an actor nowadays wants to express something with his eyes, he can only do it looking right at the audience, known, justifiably or not, as "saying hello to friends."[2]

I should think that the use of sufficiently strong side lights (though the use of reflectors or something like them) would provide the actor with a new asset: an increased range of expression made possible by the play of the eyes, the most expressive part of the face.

I have scarcely any illusions about getting actors to play for the audience and not directly at them, although this should be the goal. Nor do I dream of ever seeing an actor play through all of an important scene with his back to the audience. But is it too much to hope that crucial scenes could be played where the author indicated and not in front of the prompter's box as if they were duets demanding applause? I am not calling for a revolution, only for some small changes. I am well aware that transforming the stage into a real room with the fourth wall missing and with some of the furniture placed with backs to the auditorium would only upset the audience, at least for the present.

If I bring up the subject of make-up, it is not because I dare hope to be heeded by the ladies, who would rather be beautiful than truthful. But the male actor might do well to consider if it is an advantage to paint his face with character lines that remain there like a mask. Let us imagine an actor who pencils in with soot a few lines between his eyes to indicate great anger, and let us suppose that in that permanently enraged state he finds he has to smile on a certain line. Imagine the horrible grimace! And how can the old character wrinkle his brow in anger when his false bald pate is as smooth as a billiard ball?

In a modern psychological drama, in which every tremor of the soul should be reflected more by facial expressions than by gestures and grunts, it would probably be most sensible to experiment with strong side lighting on a small stage, using actors without any make-up or a minimum of it.

And then, if we could get rid of the visible orchestra with its disturbing lights and the faces turned toward the public; if the auditorium floor could be raised so that the spectator's eyes are not level with the actor's knees; if we could get rid of the proscenium boxes and their occupants, arriving giggling and drunk from their dinners; and if we could have it dark in the auditorium during the performance; and if, above everything else, we could have a *small* stage and an *intimate* auditorium—then possibly a new drama might arise and at least one theater become a refuge for cultured audiences. While we are waiting for such a theater, we shall have to write for the dramatic stockpile and prepare the repertory that one day shall come.

Here is my attempt. If I have failed, there is still time to try again!

August Strindberg
(1888)

---

[2] "Counting the house" would be the equivalent in American theater slang.—*Trans.*

MISS JULIE

August Strindberg

TRANSLATED BY EVERT SPRINCHORN

CHARACTERS

MISS JULIE,[3] *twenty-five years old*
JEAN, *valet, thirty years old*
CHRISTINE, *cook, thirty-five years old*
THE CHORUS, *a party of country folk*

The scene is a country estate in Sweden.

The time: A Midsummer Night in the 1880s. The hours after midnight, June 24, St. John the Baptist's Day.

The scene is the kitchen of the estate belonging to the count, MISS JULIE's *father. It is a large kitchen, situated along with the servants' quarters in the basement of the manor house. The side walls and the ceiling of the kitchen are masked by the tormentors and borders of the set. The rear wall runs obliquely upstage from the left. On this wall to the left are two shelves with pots and pans of copper, iron, and pewter. The shelves are decorated with goffered paper. A little to the right can be seen three-fourths of a deep arched entry with two glass doors, and through them can be seen a fountain with a statue of a cupid, lilac bushes in bloom, and the tops of some Lombardy poplars.*

From the left of the stage the corner of a large, Dutch-tile kitchen stove protrudes with part of the hood showing.

Projecting from the right side of the stage is one end of the servants' dining table of white pine, with a few chairs around it.

The stove is decorated with branches of birch leaves; the floor is strewn with juniper twigs.

On the end of the table is a large Japanese spice jar filled with lilacs.

An icebox, a sink, a washbasin.

Over the door a big old-fashioned bell; and to the left of the door the gaping mouth of a speaking tube.

CHRISTINE *is standing at the stove, frying something in a pan. She is wearing a light-colored cotton dress and an apron.*

JEAN *enters, dressed in livery and carrying a pair of high-top boots with spurs. He sets them where they are clearly visible.*

JEAN: What a night! She's wild again! Miss Julie's absolutely wild!

CHRISTINE: You sure took your time getting back!

JEAN: I took the count down to the station, and on my way
5   back, I passed the barn and went in for a dance. And there was Miss Julie leading the dance with the game warden. Then she noticed me. And she ran right into my arms and chose me for the ladies' waltz. And she's been dancing ever since like—like I don't know what. Wild, I tell you, ab-
10   solutely wild!

CHRISTINE: That's nothing new. But she's been worse than ever during the last two weeks, ever since her engagement was broken off.

JEAN: Yes. I never did hear all there was to that. He was a good
15   man, too, even if he wasn't rich. Well, they've got such crazy ideas. (*He sits down at the end of the table.*) Tell me, isn't it strange that a young girl like her—all right, young woman—prefers to stay home here with the servants rather than go with her father to visit her relatives?

CHRISTINE: I suppose she's ashamed to face them after that fi-
20   asco with her young man.

JEAN: No doubt. He wouldn't take any nonsense from her. Do you know what happened, Christine? I saw the whole thing. Of course, I didn't let on.

CHRISTINE: You were there? I don't believe it.
25
JEAN: Well, I was. They were in the stable yard one evening— and she was training him, that's what she called it. Do you know what? She was making him jump over her riding whip—training him like a dog. He jumped over twice, and she whipped him both times. But the third time, he
30   grabbed the whip from her, [scratched her face with it— long scratch on her left cheek;] then broke it in a thousand pieces—and walked off.

CHRISTINE: I don't believe it! What do you know!

JEAN: Yes, that put an end to that affair. —What have you got
35   for me that's really good, Christine?

CHRISTINE: (*Serving him from the frying pan.*) Just a little bit of kidney. Cut it from the veal roast.

JEAN: (*Smelling it.*) Wonderful! One of my special *délices!* (*Feeling the plate.*) Hey, you didn't warm the plate!
40
CHRISTINE: You're more fussy than the count himself when you set your mind to it. (*She rumples his hair affectionately.*)

JEAN: (*Irritated.*) Cut it out! Don't muss up my hair. You know how particular I am!

CHRISTINE: Oh, don't get mad. Can I help it if I like you?
45
(JEAN *eats.* CHRISTINE *gets out a bottle of beer.*)

JEAN: Beer on Midsummer Eve! No thank you! I've got something much better than that. (*He opens a drawer in the table and takes out a bottle of red wine with a gold seal.*) Do you see that? Gold Seal. Now give me a glass.

---

[3]Julie is not a countess; she is the daughter of a count. Her title "fröken" corresponds to the German "Fräulein" and the French "mademoiselle."

31-32 **scratched . . . left cheek** the passage in brackets was deleted in Strindberg's manuscript, probably by Strindberg himself

(She hands him a tumbler.)

50   —No, a wineglass of course. This has to be drunk properly. No water.

CHRISTINE: *(Goes back to the stove and puts on a small saucepan.)* Lord help the woman who gets you for a husband. You're an old fussbudget!

55 JEAN: Talk, talk! You'd consider yourself lucky if you got yourself a man as good as me. It hasn't done you any harm to have people think I'm your fiancé. *(He tastes the wine.)* Very good. Excellent. But warmed just a little too little. *(Warming the glass in his hands.)* We bought this in Dijon. Four francs a

60 liter, unbottled—and the tax on top of that. . . . What on earth are you cooking? It stinks like hell!

CHRISTINE: Some damn mess that Miss Julie wants for her Diana, that damn dog of hers.

JEAN: You should watch your language, Christine. . . . Why do

65 you have to stand in front of the stove on a holiday, cooking for that mutt? Is it sick?

CHRISTINE: Oh, she's sick, all right! She sneaked out to the gatekeeper's pug and—got herself in a fix. And you know Miss Julie, she can't stand anything like that.

70 JEAN: She's too stuck-up in some ways and not proud enough in others. Just like her mother. The countess felt right at home in the kitchen or down in the barn with the cows, but when she went driving, one horse wasn't enough for her, she had to have a pair. Her sleeves were always dirty, but her

75 buttons had the royal crown on them. As for Miss Julie, she doesn't give a hoot in hell how she looks and acts. I mean, she's not really refined, not really. Just now, down at the barn, she grabbed the game warden right from under Anna's eyes and asked him to dance. You wouldn't see anybody in our

80 class behaving like that. But that's what happens when the gentry try to act like the common people—they become common! . . . However, I'll say one thing for her: she *is* beautiful! Statuesque! Ah, those shoulders—those—and so forth, and so forth!

85 CHRISTINE: Oh, don't exaggerate. Clara tells me all about her, and Clara dresses her.

JEAN: Clara, pooh! You women are always jealous of each other. I've been out riding with her. . . . And how she can dance . . . !

90 CHRISTINE: Listen, Jean, you *are* going to dance with me, aren't you, when I'm finished here?

JEAN: Certainly! Of course I am.

CHRISTINE: Promise?

JEAN: Promise! Listen if I say I'm going to do a thing, I do

95 it. . . . Christine, I thank you for a delicious meal. Superb! *(He shoves the cork back into the bottle.)*

(MISS JULIE appears in the entry, talking to someone outside.)

MISS JULIE: I'll be right back. Don't wait for me.

(JEAN slips the bottle into the table drawer quickly and rises respectfully. MISS JULIE comes in and crosses over to CHRISTINE, who is at the stove.)

MISS JULIE: Did you get it ready?

(CHRISTINE signals that JEAN is present.)

JEAN: *(Polite and charming.)* Are you ladies sharing secrets?

MISS JULIE: *(Flipping her handkerchief in his face.)* Don't be 100 nosy!

JEAN: Oh, that smells good! Violets.

MISS JULIE: *(Flirting with him.)* Don't be impudent! And don't tell me you're an expert on perfumes, too. I love the way you dance!—No, mustn't look! Go away! 105

JEAN: *(Cocky but pleasant.)* What are the ladies cooking up? A witches' brew for Midsummer Eve? So they can tell the future? Read what's in the cards for them, and see who they'll marry?

MISS JULIE: *(Curtly.)* You'd have to have good eyes to see that. 110 *(To CHRISTINE.)* Pour it into a small bottle, and seal it tight. . . . Jean, come and dance a schottische with me.

JEAN: *(Hesitating.)* I hope you don't think I'm being rude, but I've already promised this dance to Christine.

MISS JULIE: She can always find someone. Isn't that so, Christine? 115 You don't mind if I borrow Jean for a minute, do you?

CHRISTINE: It ain't up to me. If Miss Julie is gracious enough to invite you, it ain't right for you to say no, Jean. You go on, and thank her for the honor.

JEAN: Frankly, Miss Julie, I don't want to hurt your feelings, 120 but I wonder if it's wise—I mean for you to dance twice in a row with the same partner. Especially since the people around here love to talk.

MISS JULIE: *(Bridling.)* What do you mean? What kind of talk? What are you trying to say? 125

JEAN: *(Retreating.)* I wish you wouldn't misunderstand me, Miss Julie. It just doesn't look right for you to prefer one of your servants to the others who are hoping for the same unusual honor.

MISS JULIE: Prefer! What an idea! I'm really surprised. I, the 130 mistress of the house, am good enough to come to their dance, and when I feel like dancing, I want to dance with someone who knows how to lead. After all I don't want to look ridiculous.

JEAN: As you wish, Miss Julie. I am at your orders. 135

MISS JULIE: *(Gently.)* Don't take it as an order. Tonight we're all just having a good time. There's no question of rank. Now give me your arm. —Don't worry, Christine. I won't run off with your boyfriend.

(JEAN gives her his arm and leads her out.)

PANTOMIME SCENE

This should be played as if the actress were actually alone. She turns her back on the audience when she feels like it; she does not look out into the auditorium; she does not rush through the scene as if afraid the audience will grow impatient.

CHRISTINE alone. *In the distance the sound of the violins playing the schottische.* CHRISTINE, *humming in time with the music, cleans up after* JEAN, *washes the dishes, dries them, and puts them away in a cupboard. Then she takes off her apron, takes a little mirror from one of the table drawers, and leans it against the jar of lilacs on the table. She lights a tallow candle, heats a curling iron, and curls the bangs on her forehead. Then she goes to the doorway and stands listening to the music. She comes back to the table and finds the handkerchief that* MISS JULIE *left behind. She smells it, spreads it out, and then, as if lost in thought, stretches it, smoothes it out, and folds it in four.*

(JEAN enters alone.)

JEAN: Wild! I told you she was wild! You should have seen the way she was dancing. Everyone was peeking at her from behind the doors and laughing at her. What's the matter with her, Christine?

5   CHRISTINE: You might know it's her monthlies, Jean. She always acts peculiar then. . . . Well, are you going to dance with me?

JEAN: You're not mad at me because I broke my promise?

CHRISTINE: Of course not. Not for a little thing like that, you

10   know that. I know my place.

JEAN: (Grabs her around the waist.) You're a sensible girl, Christine. You're going to make somebody a good wife—

(MISS JULIE, coming in, sees them together. She is unpleasantly surprised.)

MISS JULIE: (With forced gaiety.) Well, aren't you the gallant beau—running away from your partner!

15   JEAN: On the contrary, Miss Julie. As you can see, I've hurried back to the partner I deserted.

MISS JULIE: (Changing tack.) You know, you're the best dancer I've met. —Why are you wearing livery on a holiday? Take it off at once.

20   JEAN: I'd have to ask you to leave for a minute. My black coat is hanging right here—(He moves to the right and points.)

MISS JULIE: You're not embarrassed because I'm here, are you? Just to change your coat? Go in your room and come right back again. Or else stay here and I'll turn my back.

25   JEAN: If you'll excuse me, Miss Julie. (He goes off to the right. His arm can be seen as he changes his coat.)

MISS JULIE: (To CHRISTINE.) Tell me something, Christine. Is Jean your fiancé? He acts so familiar with you.

CHRISTINE: Fiancé? I suppose so. At least we say we are.

30   MISS JULIE: What do you mean?

CHRISTINE: Well, Miss Julie, you have had fiancés yourself, and you know—

MISS JULIE: But we were properly engaged—!

CHRISTINE: I know, but did anything come of it?

(JEAN comes back, wearing a black cutaway coat and derby.)

35   MISS JULIE: Très gentil, monsieur Jean! Très gentil!

JEAN: Vous voulez plaisanter, madame.

MISS JULIE: Et vous voulez parler français! Where did you learn to speak French?

JEAN: In Switzerland. I was sommelier in one of the biggest

40   hotels in Lucerne.

MISS JULIE: My! but you look quite the gentleman in that coat! Charmant! (She sits down at the table.)

JEAN: Flatterer!

MISS JULIE: (stiffening.) Who said I was flattering you?

45   JEAN: My natural modesty would not allow me to presume that you were paying sincere compliments to someone like me, and therefore I could only assume that you were exaggerating, which, in this case, means flattering me.

MISS JULIE: You certainly have a way with words. Where did

50   you learn to talk like that? Seeing plays?

JEAN: And other places. You don't think I stayed in the house for six years when I was a valet in Stockholm, do you?

MISS JULIE: I thought you were born in this district. Weren't you?

55   JEAN: My father worked as a farmhand on the district attorney's estate, next door to yours. I used to see you when you were little. Of course you didn't notice me.

MISS JULIE: Did you really?

JEAN: Yes. I remember one time in particular—. But I can't

60   tell you about that!

MISS JULIE: Of course you can. . . . Oh, come on. Just this once—for me.

JEAN: No. No, I really couldn't. Not now. Some other time maybe.

65   MISS JULIE: Some other time? That means never. What's the harm in telling me now?

JEAN: There's no harm. I just don't feel like it. —Look at her.

(He nods at CHRISTINE, who has fallen asleep in a chair by the stove.)

MISS JULIE: Won't she make somebody a pretty wife! I'll bet she snores, too.

70   JEAN: No, she doesn't. But she talks in her sleep.

MISS JULIE: (Archly.) Now how could you know she talks in her sleep?

JEAN: (Coolly.) I've heard her . . .

(Pause. They look at each other.)

MISS JULIE: Why don't you sit down?

75   JEAN: I wouldn't take the liberty in your presence.

MISS JULIE: Not even if I ordered you?

JEAN: Of course I'd obey.

MISS JULIE: Well then: sit down. —Wait a minute. Could you get me something to drink?

80   JEAN: I don't know what there is in the icebox. Only beer, I suppose.

MISS JULIE: Only beer?! I have simple tastes. I prefer beer to wine.

(JEAN takes a bottle of beer from the icebox and opens it. He looks in the cupboard for a glass and a plate, and serves her.)

JEAN: At your service, mademoiselle.

85   MISS JULIE: Thank you. What about you?

JEAN: I'm not much of a beer-drinker, thank you, but if it's your wish—

MISS JULIE: My wish! I should think a gentleman would want to keep his lady company.

90   JEAN: A point well taken! (He opens another bottle and takes a glass.)

MISS JULIE: Now drink a toast to me!

(JEAN hesitates.)

You're not shy, are you? A big, strong man like you?

(Playfully, JEAN kneels and raises his glass in mock gallantry.)

JEAN: To my lady's health!

MISS JULIE: Bravo! Now you have to kiss my shoe, too. Then

95   you will have hit it off perfectly.

(JEAN hesitates, then boldly grasps her foot and touches it lightly with his lips.)

Superb! You should have been an actor.

JEAN: (*Rising.*) This has got to stop, Miss Julie! Someone might come in and see us.

100 MISS JULIE: So what?

JEAN: People would talk, that's what! If you knew how their tongues were wagging out there just a few minutes ago!

MISS JULIE: What did they say? Tell me. Sit down and tell me.

JEAN: I don't want to hurt your feelings. . . . They used ex-
105   pressions that—that hinted at certain—you know what I mean. You're not a child. And when they see a woman drinking, alone with a man—and a servant at that—in the middle of the night—well . . .

MISS JULIE: Well what?! Besides, we're not alone. Christine is
110   here.

JEAN: Sleeping!

MISS JULIE: I'll wake her up. (*She goes over to* CHRISTINE.) Christine! Are you asleep? (CHRISTINE *babbles in her sleep.*) Christine! —My, how sound she sleeps!

115 CHRISTINE: (*Talking in her sleep.*) Count's boots are brushed . . . put on the coffee . . . right away, right away, right . . . mm-mm . . . pooffff . . .

(MISS JULIE *shakes* CHRISTINE.)

MISS JULIE: Wake up, will you!

JEAN: (*Sternly.*) Let her alone! Let her sleep!

120 MISS JULIE: (*Sharply.*) What?

JEAN: She's been standing over the stove all day. She's worn out when night comes. Anyone asleep is entitled to some consideration.

MISS JULIE: (*Changing her tone.*) That's a very kind thought. It
125   does you credit, Jean. You're right, of course. (*She offers* JEAN *her hand.*) Now come on out and pick some lilacs for me.

(*During the following,* CHRISTINE *wakes up and, drunk with sleep, shuffles off to the right to go to bed. A polka can be heard in the distance.*)

JEAN: With you, Miss Julie?

MISS JULIE: Yes, with me.

130 JEAN: That's no good. Absolutely not.

MISS JULIE: I don't know what you're thinking. Aren't you letting your imagination run away with you?

JEAN: No. Other people are.

MISS JULIE: How? Imagining that I'm—*verliebt* with a servant?

135 JEAN: I'm not conceited, but it's been known to happen. And to these people nothing's sacred.

MISS JULIE: "These people!" Why, I do believe you're an aristocrat!

JEAN: Yes, I am.

140 MISS JULIE: I'm climbing down—

JEAN: Don't climb down, Miss Julie! Take my advice. No one will believe that you climbed down deliberately. They'll say you fell.

MISS JULIE: I have a higher opinion of these people than you
145   do. Let's see who's right! Come on! (*She gives him a long, steady look.*)

JEAN: You know, you're very strange.

MISS JULIE: Perhaps. But then so are you. . . . Besides, everything is strange. Life, people, everything. It's all scrum, drifting and
150   drifting on the water until it sinks—drowns. There's a dream I have every now and then. It's coming back to me now. I'm sitting on top of a pillar. I've climbed up it some-

how and I don't know how to get back down. When I look down I get dizzy. I have to get down but I don't have the courage to jump. I can't hold on much longer and I want 155 to fall; but I don't fall. I know I won't have any peace until I get down; no rest until I get down, down on the ground. And if I ever got down on the ground, I'd want to go far-ther down, right down into the earth. . . . Have you ever felt anything like that? 160

JEAN: Never! I used to dream that I'm lying under a tall tree in a dark woods. I want to get up, up to the very top, to look out over the bright landscape with the sun shining on it, to rob the bird's nest up there with the golden eggs in it. And I climb and I climb, but the trunk is so thick, and so smooth, 165 and it's such a long way to that first branch. But I know that if I could just reach that first branch, I'd go right to the top as if on a ladder. I've never reached it yet, but someday I will—even if only in my dreams.

MISS JULIE: Here I am talking about dreams with you. Come 170 out with me. Only into the park a way. (*She offers him her arm, and they start to go.*)

JEAN: Let's sleep on nine midsummer flowers, Miss Julie, and then our dreams will come true!

(MISS JULIE *and* JEAN *suddenly turn around in the doorway.* JEAN *is holding his hand over one eye.*)

MISS JULIE: You've caught something in your eye. Let me see. 175

JEAN: It's nothing. Just a bit of dust. It'll go away.

MISS JULIE: The sleeve of my dress must have grazed your eye. Sit down and I'll help you. (*She takes him by the arm and sits him down. She takes his head and leans it back. With the corner of her handkerchief she tries to get out the bit of dust.*) Now sit 180 still, absolutely still. (*She slaps his hand.*) Do as you're told. Why, I believe you're trembling—a big, strong man like you. (*She feels his biceps.*) With such big arms!

JEAN: (*Warningly.*) Miss Julie!

MISS JULIE: Yes, *Monsieur Jean?* 185

JEAN: *Attention! Je ne suis qu'un homme!*

MISS JULIE: Sit still, I tell you! . . . There now! It's out. Kiss my hand and thank me!

JEAN: (*Rising to his feet.*) Listen to me, Miss Julie—Christine has gone to bed! —Listen to me, I tell you! 190

MISS JULIE: Kiss my hand first!

JEAN: Listen to me!

MISS JULIE: Kiss my hand first!

JEAN: All right. But you'll have no one to blame but yourself.

MISS JULIE: For what? 195

JEAN: For what! Are you twenty-five years old and still a child? Don't you know it's dangerous to play with fire?

MISS JULIE: Not for me, I'm insured!

JEAN: (*Boldly.*) Oh, no, you're not! And even if you are, there's inflammable stuff next door. 200

MISS JULIE: Meaning you?

---

173 **midsummer flowers** a girl would pick in silence on Mid-summer Eve nine different sorts of flowers, make a bouquet of them, and place them under her pillow. The man who appeared in her dreams would be the man she would marry

JEAN: Yes. Not just because it's me, but because I'm young and—

MISS JULIE: And irresistibly handsome? What incredible con-
205 ceit! A Don Juan, maybe! Or a Joseph! Yes, bless my soul, that's it: you're a Joseph!

JEAN: You think so?!

MISS JULIE: I'm almost afraid so!

(JEAN *boldly steps up to her, grabs her around the waist, tries to kiss her. She slaps his face.*)

None of that!

JEAN: More games? Or are you serious?

210 MISS JULIE: I'm serious.

JEAN: Then you must have been serious a moment ago, too! You take your games too seriously; that's dangerous. Well, I'm tired of your games, and if you'll excuse me, I'll return to my work. (*Takes up the boots and starts to brush them.*) The
215 count will be wanting his boots on time, and it's long past midnight.

MISS JULIE: Put those boots down.

JEAN: No! This is my job. It's what I'm here for. I never undertook to be your playmate. That's something I could
220 never be. I consider myself too good for that.

MISS JULIE: You are proud.

JEAN: In some ways. Not in others.

MISS JULIE: Have you ever been in love?

JEAN: We don't use that word around here. But I've hankered
225 after some girls, if that's what you mean. . . . I even got sick once because I couldn't have the one I wanted—really sick, like the princes in the Arabian Nights—who couldn't eat or drink for love.

MISS JULIE: Who was she?

(JEAN *does not reply.*)

230 Who was the girl?

JEAN: You can't get that out of me.

MISS JULIE: Even if I ask you as an equal—ask you—as a friend? . . . Who was she?

JEAN: You.

235 MISS JULIE: (*Sitting down.*) How—amusing . . .

JEAN: Yes, maybe so. Ridiculous. . . . That's why I didn't want to tell you about it before. Want to hear the whole story? . . . Have you any idea what you and your people look like from down below? Of course not. Like hawks or eagles, that's what: you
240 hardly ever see their backs because they're always soaring so high up. I lived with seven brothers and sisters—and a pig— out on the wasteland where there wasn't even a tree growing. But from my window I could see the wall of the count's gar-den with the apple trees sticking up over it. That was the Gar-
245 den of Eden for me, and there were many angry angels with flaming swords standing guard over it. But in spite of them, I and the other boys found a way to the Tree of Life. . . . How contemptible, that's what you're thinking.

MISS JULIE: For stealing apples? All boys do that.

250 JEAN: That's what you say now. All the same, you think me con-temptible. Never mind. One day I went with my mother into this paradise to weed the onion beds. Next to the veg-etable garden stood a Turkish pavilion, shaded by jasmine and hung all over with honeysuckle. I couldn't imagine what it
255 was used for; I only knew I had never seen such a beautiful building. People went in, and came out again. And then one day the door was left open. I sneaked in. The walls were covered with portraits of kings and emperors, and the win-dows had red curtains with tassels on them. —Recognize it? Yes, the count's private privy. . . . I—(*He breaks off a lilac* 260 *and holds it under* MISS JULIE's *nose.*) I had never been inside a castle, never seen anything besides the church. This was more beautiful. And no matter what I tried to think about, my thoughts always came back—to that little pavilion. And little by little there arose in me a desire to experience just 265 for once the whole pleasure of—. *Enfin,* I sneaked in, looked about, and marveled. And just then I heard someone coming! There was only one way out—for the upper-class people. But for me there was one more—a lower one. And I had no other choice but to take it. (MISS JULIE, *who has* 270 *taken the lilac from* JEAN, *lets it fall to the table.*) Then I began to run like mad, plunging through the raspberry bushes, ploughing through the strawberry patches, and came up on the rose terrace. And there I caught sight of a pink dress and a pair of white stockings. You! I crawled under—well, you 275 can imagine what it was like—under thistles that pricked me and wet dirt that stank to high heaven. And all the while I could see you walking among the roses. I said to myself, "If it's true that a thief can enter heaven and be with the an-gels, isn't it strange that a poor man's child here on God's 280 green earth can't enter the count's park and play with the count's daughter."

MISS JULIE: (*Sentimentally.*) Do you think all poor children have felt that way?

JEAN: (*Hesitatingly at first, then with mounting conviction.*) If all 285 poor ch—? Yes—yes, naturally. Of course!

MISS JULIE: It must be terrible to be poor.

JEAN: (*With exaggerated intensity.*) Oh, Miss Julie! You don't know! A dog can lie on the sofa with its mistress; a horse can have its nose stroked by the hand of a countess; but a servant—! 290 (*Changing his tone.*) Of course, now and then you meet some-body with guts enough to work his way up in the world, but how often? —Anyway, you know what I did afterward? I threw myself into the millstream with all my clothes on. Got fished out and spanked. But the following Sunday, when Pa 295 and everybody else in the house went to visit Grandma, I arranged things so I'd be left behind. Then I washed myself all over with soap and warm water, put on my best clothes, and went off to church—just to see you there once more. I saw you, and then I went home determined to die. But I 300 wanted to die beautifully and comfortably, without pain. I re-membered some stories I had heard about how fatal it was to sleep under an elderberry bush. And we had a big one that had just blossomed out. I stripped it of every leaf and blos-som it had and made a bed of them in a bin of oats. Have 305 you ever noticed how smooth oats are? As smooth to the touch as human skin. . . . So I pulled the lid of the bin shut and closed my eyes. Fell asleep. And when they woke me I was really very sick. However, I didn't die, as you can see. — What was I trying to prove? I don't know. There was no hope 310 of winning you. It was just that you were a symbol of the ab-solute hopelessness of my ever getting out of the class I was born in.

MISS JULIE: You know, you have a real gift for telling stories. Did you go to school? 315

JEAN: A little. But I've read a lot of novels and gone to the theater. And I've also listened to educated people talk. That way I learned the most.

MISS JULIE: You mean to tell me you stand around listening
320   to what we're saying!

JEAN: Certainly! And I've heard an awful lot, I can tell you—
sitting on the coachman's seat or rowing the boat. One
time I heard you and a girlfriend talking—

MISS JULIE: Really? . . . And just what did you hear?

325   JEAN: Well, now, I don't know if I can repeat it. I can tell you I
was a little amazed. I couldn't imagine where you had
learned such words. Maybe at bottom there isn't such a big
difference as you might think, between people and people.

MISS JULIE: How vulgar! At least people in my class don't be-
330   have like you when we're engaged.

JEAN: (*Looking her in the eye.*) Are you sure? —Come on now,
it's no use playing the innocent with me.

MISS JULIE: He was a beast. The man I offered my love was a
beast.

335   JEAN: That's what you all say—afterward.

MISS JULIE: All?

JEAN: I'd say so. I've heard the same expression used several
times before in similar circumstances.

MISS JULIE: What kind of circumstances?

340   JEAN: The kind we're talking about. I remember the last time
I—

MISS JULIE: (*Rising.*) That's enough! I don't want to hear any
more.

JEAN: How strange! Neither did she! . . . Well, now if you'll
345   excuse me, I'll go to bed.

MISS JULIE: (*Softly.*) Go to bed on Midsummer Eve?

JEAN: That's right. Dancing with that crowd up there really
doesn't amuse me.

MISS JULIE: Jean, get the key to the boathouse and row me
350   out on the lake. I want to see the sun come up.

JEAN: Do you think that's wise?

MISS JULIE: You sound as if you were worried about your reputation.

JEAN: Why not? I don't particularly care to be made ridicu-
355   lous, or to be kicked out without a recommendation just
when I'm trying to establish myself. Besides, I have a certain obligation to Christine.

MISS JULIE: Oh, I see. It's Christine now.

JEAN: Yes, but I'm thinking of you, too. Take my advice, Miss
360   Julie. Go up to your room.

MISS JULIE: When did you start giving me orders?

JEAN: Just this once. For your own sake! Please! It's very late.
You're so tired, you're drunk; you don't know what you're
doing. Go to bed, Miss Julie. —Besides, if my ears aren't
365   deceiving me, they're coming this way, looking for me. If
they find us here together, you're done for!

THE CHORUS: (*Is heard coming nearer, singing.*)

Said Jill to Jack, "Soil needs a tilling."
Tri-di-ri-di-ralla, tri-di-ri-di-ra.
370   Said Jack to Jill, "Time's a-spilling."
Tri-di-ri-di-ralla-la.
Said Jill to Jack, "Gold's a-hoarding."
Tri-di-ri-di-ralla, tri-di-ri-di-ra.
Said Jack to Jill, "Tell not my lording."

Tri-di-ri-di-ralla-la.   375
Said Jill to Jack, "Hair is for plaiting."
Tri-di-ri-di-ralla, tri-di-ri-di-ra.
"But Jill for Jack is not waiting."
Tri-di-ri-di-ralla-la!

MISS JULIE: I know these people. I love them just as they love   380
me. Let them come. You'll see.

JEAN: Oh, no, Miss Julie, they don't love you! They take the
food you give them, but they spit on it as soon as your
back is turned. Believe me! Just listen to them. Listen to
what they're singing. —No, you'd better not listen.   385

MISS JULIE: (*Listening.*) What are they singing?

JEAN: A nasty song—about you and me!

Allegretto.

Det kom-mo två fru-ar från sko-gen

Tri di-ri-di-ral-la Tri-di-ri-di-ra

Den en-a var våt om fo-o-ten

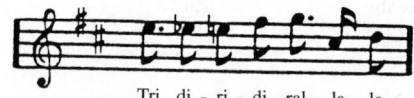

Tri di-ri-di ral-la-la.

De talte om hundra riksdaler
Tri (etc.)
Men ägde knappast en daler
Tri (etc.)
Och kransen jag dig skänker
Tri (etc.)
En annan jag påtänker
Tri (etc.)

MISS JULIE: How disgusting! Oh, what cowardly, sneaking—

JEAN: That's what the mob always is—cowards! You can't fight
them; you can only run away.   390

MISS JULIE: Run away? Where? There's no way out of here.
And we can't go in to Christine.

JEAN: What about my room? What do you say? Rules don't
count in a situation like this. You can trust me. —You said,
let's be friends. Remember? Well, I'm your friend—your   395
true, devoted, respectful friend.

MISS JULIE: But suppose—suppose they looked for you there?

JEAN: I'll bolt the door. If they try to break it down, I'll shoot.
Come, Miss Julie! (*On his knees.*) Please, Miss Julie!

367 **chorus** the Swedish original of this song follows l. 387.
The melody of the peasants' song was not printed in the first Swedish edition, but it did appear in Charles de Casanove's French translation of the play in 1893.

400 MISS JULIE: (*Meaningfully.*) You promise me that you won't—
JEAN: I swear to you!

(MISS JULIE *goes out quickly to the right.* JEAN *follows her impetuously.*)

THE BALLET

The country people enter in festive costumes, with flowers in their hats. The fiddler is in the lead. A keg of small beer and a little keg of liquor, decorated with greenery, are set up on the table. Glasses are brought out. They all drink. Then they form a circle and sing "Said Jill to Jack," dancing the round dance as they sing. At the end of the dance, they all leave singing.

(MISS JULIE *comes in alone; looks at the devastated kitchen; clasps her hands together; then takes out a powder puff and powders her face.* JEAN *enters. He is in high spirits.*)

JEAN: You see! You heard them, didn't you? You've got to admit it's impossible to stay here.
MISS JULIE: No, I don't. But even if I did, what could we do?
JEAN: Go away, travel, get away from here!
5 MISS JULIE: Travel? Yes—but where?
JEAN: Switzerland, the Italian lakes. You've never been there?
MISS JULIE: No. Is it beautiful?
JEAN: Eternal summer, oranges, laurel trees, ah . . . !
MISS JULIE: What do we do when we get there?
10 JEAN: I'll set up a hotel—a first-class hotel with a first-class clientele.
MISS JULIE: Hotel?
JEAN: I tell you that's the life! Always new faces, new languages. Not a minute to think about yourself or worry
15 about your nerves. No looking for something to do. The work keeps you busy. Day and night the bells ring, the trains whistle, the buses come and go. And all the while the money comes rolling in. I tell you it's the life!
MISS JULIE: Yes, that's the life. But what about me?
20 JEAN: The mistress of the whole place, the star of the establishment! With your looks—and your personality—it can't fail. It's perfect! You'll sit in the office like a queen, setting your slaves in motion by pressing an electric button. The guests will file before your throne and timidly lay their treasures
25 on your table. You can't imagine how people tremble when you shove a bill in their face! I'll salt the bills and you'll sugar them with your prettiest smile. Come on, let's get away from here—(*He takes a timetable from his pocket.*)—right away—the next train! We'll be in Malmö at six-thirty,
30 Hamburg eight-forty in the morning; Frankfurt to Basle in one day, and to Como by way of the Gotthard tunnel in—let me see—three days! Three days!
MISS JULIE: You make it sound so wonderful. But, Jean, you have to give me strength. Tell me you love me. Come and
35 put your arms around me.
JEAN: (*Hesitates.*) I want to . . . but I don't dare. Not anymore, not in this house. I do love you—without a shadow of a doubt. How can you doubt that, Miss Julie?
MISS JULIE: (*Shyly, very becomingly.*) You don't have to be for-
40 mal with me, Jean. You can call me Julie. There aren't any barriers between us now. Call me Julie.
JEAN: (*Agonized.*) I can't! There are still barriers between us, Miss Julie, as long as we stay in this house! There's the past, there's the count. I've never met anyone I feel so much respect for.

I've only got to see his gloves lying on a table and I shrivel 45 up. I only have to hear that bell ring and I shy like a frightened horse. I only have to look at his boots standing there so stiff and proud and I feel my spine bending. (*He kicks the boots.*) Superstitions, prejudices that they've drilled into us since we were children! But they can be forgotten just as eas- 50 ily! Just we get to another country where they have a republic! They'll crawl on their hands and knees when they see my uniform. On their hands and knees, I tell you! But not me! Oh, no. I'm not made for crawling. I've got guts, backbone. And once I grab that first branch, you just watch me climb. 55 I may be a valet now, but next year I'll be owning property; in ten years, I'll be living off my investments. Then I'll go to Rumania, get myself some decorations, and maybe—notice I only say maybe—end up as a count!
MISS JULIE: How wonderful, wonderful. 60
JEAN: Listen, in Rumania you can buy titles. You'll be a countess after all. My countess.
MISS JULIE: But I'm not interested in that. I'm leaving all that behind. Tell me you love me, Jean, or else—or else what difference does it make what I am? 65
JEAN: I'll tell you a thousand times—but later! Not now. And not here. Above all, let's keep our feelings out of this or we'll make a mess of everything. We have to look at this thing calmly and coolly, like sensible people. (*He takes out a cigar, clips the end, and lights it.*) Now you sit there and I'll sit here, 70 and we'll talk as if nothing had happened.
MISS JULIE: (*In anguish.*) My God, what are you? Don't you have any feelings?
JEAN: Feelings? Nobody's got more feelings than I have. But I've learned to control them. 75
MISS JULIE: A few minutes ago you were kissing my shoe—and now—!
JEAN: (*Harshly.*) That was a few minutes ago. We've got other things to think about now!
MISS JULIE: Don't speak to me like that, Jean! 80
JEAN: I'm just trying to be sensible. We've been stupid once; let's not be stupid again. Your father might be back at any moment, and we've got to decide our future before then. —Now what do you think about my plans? Do you approve or don't you? 85
MISS JULIE: I don't see anything wrong with them. Except one thing. For a big undertaking like that, you'd need a lot of capital. Have you got it?
JEAN: (*Chewing on his cigar.*) Have I got it? Of course I have. I've got my knowledge of the business, my vast experi- 90 ence, my familiarity with languages. That's capital that counts for something, let me tell you.
MISS JULIE: You can't even buy the railway tickets with it.
JEAN: That's true. That's why I need a backer—someone to put up the money. 95
MISS JULIE: Where can you find him on a moment's notice?
JEAN: You'll find him—if you want to be my partner.
MISS JULIE: I can't. And I don't have a penny to my name.

(*Pause.*)

JEAN: Then you can forget the whole thing.
MISS JULIE: Forget—? 100
JEAN: And things will stay just the way they are.
MISS JULIE: Do you think I'm going to live under the same roof with you as your mistress? Do you think I'm going to have people sneering at me behind my back? How do

105   you think I'll ever be able to look my father in the face after this? No, no! Take me away from here, Jean—the shame, the humiliation. . . . What have I done? Oh, my God, my God! What have I done! (*She bursts into tears.*)

JEAN: Now don't start singing that tune. It won't work. What
110   have you done that's so awful? You're not the first.

MISS JULIE: (*Crying hysterically.*) Now you think me contemptible—I'm falling, falling!

JEAN: Fall down to me, and I'll lift you up again!

MISS JULIE: What awful hold did you have over me? What
115   drove me to you? The weak to the strong? The falling to the rising? Or maybe it was love? Love? This? You don't know what love is!

JEAN: Want to bet? Did you think I was a virgin?

MISS JULIE: You're coarse—vulgar! The things you say, the
120   things you think!

JEAN: That's the way I was brought up. It's the way I am! Now don't get hysterical. And don't play the fine lady with me. We're eating off the same platter now. . . . That's better. Come over here and be a good girl and I'll treat you to something
125   special. (*He opens the table drawer and takes out the wine bottle. He pours the wine into two used glasses.*)

MISS JULIE: Where did you get that wine?

JEAN: From the wine cellar.

MISS JULIE: My father's burgundy!

130 JEAN: Should be good enough for his son-in-law.

MISS JULIE: I was drinking beer and you—!

JEAN: Shows I have better taste than you.

MISS JULIE: Thief!

JEAN: You going to squeal on me?

135 MISS JULIE: Oh, God! Partner in crime with a petty house thief! I must have been drunk; I must have been walking in my sleep. Midsummer Night! Night of innocent games—

JEAN: Yes, very innocent!

MISS JULIE: (*Pacing up and down.*) Is there anyone here on
140   earth as miserable as I am?

JEAN: Why be miserable? Look at the conquest you've made! Think of poor Christine in there. Don't you think she's got any feelings?

MISS JULIE: I thought so a while ago; I don't now. A servant's
145   a servant—

JEAN: And a whore's a whore!

MISS JULIE: (*Falls to her knees and clasps her hands together.*) Oh, God in heaven, put an end to my worthless life! Lift me out of this awful filth I'm sinking in! Save me! Save me!

150 JEAN: I feel sorry for you, I have to admit it. When I was lying in the onion beds, looking up at you on the rose terrace, I—I'm telling you the truth now—I had the same dirty thoughts that all boys have.

MISS JULIE: And you said you wanted to die for me!

155 JEAN: In the oat bin? That was only a story.

MISS JULIE: A lie, you mean.

JEAN: (*Getting sleepy.*) Practically. I think I read it in a paper about a chimney sweep who curled up in a wood-bin with some lilacs because they were going to arrest him for
160   non support of his child.

MISS JULIE: Now I see you as you really are.

JEAN: What did you expect me to do? It's always the fancy talk that gets the women.

MISS JULIE: You dog!

165 JEAN: You bitch!

MISS JULIE: Well, now you've seen the eagle's back—

JEAN: Wasn't exactly its back—!

MISS JULIE: I was going to be the window dressing for your hotel—!

JEAN: And I the hotel—!   170

MISS JULIE: Sitting at the desk, attracting your customers, padding your bills—!

JEAN: I could manage that myself—!

MISS JULIE: How can a human soul be so dirty and filthy?

JEAN: Then why don't you clean it up?   175

MISS JULIE: You lackey! You shoeshine boy! Stand up when I talk to you!

JEAN: You lackey lover! You bootblack's tramp! Shut your mouth and get out of here! Who do you think you are telling me I'm coarse? I've never seen anybody in my class   180 behave as crudely as you did tonight. Have you ever seen any of the girls around here grab at a man like you did? Do you think any of the girls of my class would throw themselves at a man like that! I've never seen the like of it except in animals and prostitutes!   185

MISS JULIE: (*Crushed.*) That's right! Hit me! Walk all over me! It's all I deserve. I'm rotten. But help me! Help me to get out of this—if there is any way out for me!

JEAN: (*Less harsh.*) I'd be doing myself an injustice if I didn't admit that part of the credit for this seduction belongs to   190 me. But do you think a person in my position would have dared to look twice at you if you hadn't asked for it? I'm still amazed—

MISS JULIE: And still proud.

JEAN: Why not? But I've got to confess the victory was a lit-   195 tle too easy to give me any real thrill.

MISS JULIE: Go on, hit me again!

JEAN: (*Standing up.*) No. . . . I'm sorry I said that. I never hit a person who's down, especially a woman. I can't deny that, in one way, it was good to find out that what I saw glittering   200 up above was only fool's gold, to see that the eagle's back was only as gray as its belly, that the smooth cheek was just powder, and that there could be dirt under the manicured nails, that the handkerchief was soiled even though it smelled of perfume. But, in another way, it hurts to find that everything I   205 was striving for wasn't very high above me after all, wasn't even real. It hurts me to see you sink far lower than your own cook. Hurts, like seeing the last flowers cut to pieces by the autumn rains and turned to muck.

MISS JULIE: You talk as if you already stood high above me.   210

JEAN: Well, don't I? Don't forget I could make you a countess but you can never make me a count.

MISS JULIE: I have a father for a count. You can never have that!

JEAN: True. But I might father my own counts—that is, if—   215

MISS JULIE: You're a thief! I'm not!

JEAN: There are worse things than being a thief. A lot worse. And besides, when I take a position in a house, I consider myself a member of the family—in a way, like a child in the house. It's no crime for a child to steal a few ripe cher-   220 ries when they're falling off the trees, is it? (*He begins to feel passionate again.*) Miss Julie, you're a beautiful woman, much too good for the likes of me. You got carried away by your emotions and now you want to cover up your mistake by telling yourself that you love me. You don't   225 love me. Maybe you were attracted by my looks—in which case your kind of love is no better than mine. But I could never be satisfied to be just an animal for you, and I could never make you love me.

230 MISS JULIE: How do you know that for sure?

JEAN: You mean there's a chance? I could love you, there's no doubt about that. You're beautiful, you're refined— (*He goes up to her and takes her hand.*) —educated, lovable when you want to be, and once you set a man's heart on fire, I'll

235 bet it burns forever. (*He puts his arm around her waist.*) You're like hot wine with strong spices. One of your kisses is enough to—

(*He attempts to lead her out, but she rather reluctantly breaks away from him.*)

MISS JULIE: Let me go. You don't get me that way.

JEAN: Then how? Not by petting you and not with pretty

240 words, not by planning for the future, not by saving you from humiliation! Then how, tell me how?

MISS JULIE: How? How? I don't know how! I don't know at all!— I hate you like I hate rats, but I can't get away from you.

JEAN: Then come away with me!

245 MISS JULIE: (*Pulling herself together.*) Away? Yes, we'll go away!— But I'm so tired. Pour me a glass of wine, will you?

(*JEAN pours the wine, MISS JULIE looks at her watch.*)

Let's talk first. We still have a little time. (*She empties the glass of wine and holds it out for more.*)

JEAN: Don't overdo it. You'll get drunk.

250 MISS JULIE: What difference does it make?

JEAN: What difference? It looks cheap. —What did you want to say to me?

MISS JULIE: We're going to run away together, right? But we'll talk first—that is, I'll talk. So far you've done all the talk-

255 ing. You've told me your life, now I'll tell you mine. That way we'll know each other through and through before we become . . . traveling companions.

JEAN: Wait a minute. Are you sure you won't regret this afterward—surrendering your secrets to me?

260 MISS JULIE: I thought you were my friend.

JEAN: I am—sometimes. Just don't count on it.

MISS JULIE: You don't mean that. Anyway, everybody knows my secrets. —My mother's parents were very ordinary people, just commoners. She was brought up, according to the theo-

265 ries of her time, to believe in equality, the independence of women, and all that. And she had a strong aversion to marriage. When my father proposed to her, she swore she would never become his wife but that she might possibly consent to become his mistress. So he told her he didn't want to see the

270 woman he loved enjoy less respect than he did. But she said she didn't care what the world thought—and he, believing that he couldn't live without her, accepted her conditions. That did it. From then on he was cut off from his old circle of friends and left without anything to do in the house,

275 which couldn't have kept him occupied anyway. Then I came into the world—against my mother's wishes, as far as I can make out. My mother decided to bring me up as a nature child. And on top of that I had to learn everything a boy learns, so I could be living proof that women were just as

280 good as men. I had to wear boy's clothes, learn to handle horses—but not to milk the cows! Girls did that! I was made

to groom the horses and harness them, and learn farming and go hunting—I even had to learn how to slaughter the animals. It was disgusting. Awful! And on the estate all the men were set to doing women's chores, and the women to doing 285 men's work—with the result that the whole place fell to pieces, and we became the local laughing-stock. Finally, my father must have come out of his trance. He rebelled, and everything was changed according to his wishes. They got married—very quietly. Then my mother got sick. I don't 290 know what kind of sickness it was, but she often had convulsions, and she would hide herself in the attic or in the garden, and sometimes she would stay out all night. Then there occurred that big fire you've heard about. The house, the stables, the cowsheds, all burned down—and under very pecu- 295 liar circumstances that led one to suspect arson. You see, the accident occurred the day after the insurance expired, and the premiums on the new policy, which my father had sent in, were delayed through the messenger's carelessness, and didn't arrive in time. 300

(*She refills her glass and drinks.*)

JEAN: You've had enough.

MISS JULIE: Who cares! —We were left without a penny to our name. We had to sleep in the carriages. My father didn't know where to turn for money to rebuild the house. Then Mother suggested to him that he might try 305 to borrow money from an old friend of hers, who owned a brick factory not far from here. Father took out a loan, but there wasn't any interest charged, which surprised him. So the place was rebuilt. (*She drinks some more.*) Do you know who set fire to the place? 310

JEAN: Your honorable mother!

MISS JULIE: Do you know who the brick manufacturer was?

JEAN: Your mother's lover?

MISS JULIE: Do you know whose money it was?

JEAN: Let me think a minute. . . . No, I give up. 315

MISS JULIE: It was my mother's!

JEAN: The count's, you mean. Or was there a marriage settlement?

MISS JULIE: There wasn't a settlement. My mother had a little money of her own which she didn't want under my fa- 320 ther's control, so she invested it with her—friend.

JEAN: Who pinched it!

MISS JULIE: Right! He kept it for himself. Well, my father found out what happened. But he couldn't go to court, couldn't pay his wife's lover, couldn't prove that it was his wife's 325 money. That was how my mother got her revenge because he had taken control of the house. He was on the verge of shooting himself. There was even a rumor that he tried and failed. But somehow he took a new lease on life and he forced my mother to pay for her mistakes. Can you imag- 330 ine what those five years were like for me? I loved my father, but I took my mother's side because I didn't know the whole story. She had taught me to hate all men—I'm sure you've heard how she hated men—and I swore to her that I'd never be slave to any man. 335

JEAN: You got engaged to the attorney, didn't you?

MISS JULIE: Only to make him my slave.

JEAN: I guess he didn't go for that, did he?

MISS JULIE: Oh, he wanted to well enough. I didn't give him the chance. I got bored with him. 340

JEAN: Yes, so I noticed—in the stable yard.

MISS JULIE: What did you notice?

JEAN: I saw how he—. [Still see it on your cheek.

MISS JULIE: What!

345 JEAN: The stripe on your cheek.] He broke it off.

MISS JULIE: It's a lie! I broke it off! Did he tell you that? He's beneath contempt!

JEAN: Come on now, as bad as that? So you hate men, hm?

MISS JULIE: Yes, I do. . . . Most of the time. But sometimes, when
350 I can't help myself—oh . . . (*She shudders in disgust.*)

JEAN: Then you hate me, too?

MISS JULIE: You have no idea how much! I'd like to see you killed like an animal—

JEAN: Like when you're caught having sex with an animal: you
355 get two years at hard labor and the animal is killed. Right?

MISS JULIE: Right.

JEAN: But there's no one to catch us—*and no animal!*—So what are we going to do?

MISS JULIE: Go away from here.

360 JEAN: To torture ourselves to death?

MISS JULIE: No. To enjoy ourselves for a day or two, or a week, for as long as can—and then—to die—

JEAN: Die? That's stupid! I've got a better idea: start a hotel!

MISS JULIE: (*Continuing without hearing* JEAN.) —on the shores
365 of Lake Como, where the sun is always shining, where the laurels bloom at Christmas, and the golden oranges glow on the trees.

JEAN: Lake Como is a stinking wet hole, and the only oranges I saw there were on the fruit stands. But it's a good tourist
370 spot with a lot of villas and cottages that are rented out to lovers. Now there's a profitable business. You know why? They rent the villa for the whole season, but they leave after three weeks.

MISS JULIE: (*Naively.*) Why after only three weeks?

375 JEAN: Because that's about as long as they can stand each other. Why else? But they still have to pay the rent. You see? Then you rent it out again to another couple, and so on. There's no shortage of love—even if it doesn't last very long.

MISS JULIE: Then you don't want to die with me?

380 JEAN: I don't want to die at all! I enjoy life too much. And moreover, I consider taking your own life a sin against the Providence that gave us life.

MISS JULIE: You believe in God? You?

JEAN: Yes, certainly I do! I go to church every other Sunday—.
385 Honestly, I've had enough of this talk. I'm going to bed.

MISS JULIE: Really? You think you're going to get off that easy? Don't you know that a man owes something to the woman he's dishonored?

JEAN: (*Takes out his purse and throws a silver coin on the table.*)
390 There you are. I don't want to owe anybody anything.

MISS JULIE: (*Pretending not to notice.*) Do you know what the law says—?

JEAN: Lucky for you the law says nothing about women who seduce men!

395 MISS JULIE: (*As before.*) What else can we do but go away from here, get married, and get divorced?

343–345 **Still . . . cheek** the passage in brackets was deleted in Strindberg's manuscript, probably by Strindberg himself

JEAN: Suppose I refuse to enter into this *mésalliance?*

MISS JULIE: *Mésalliance?*

JEAN: For me! I've got better ancestors than you. I don't have a female arsonist in my family. 400

MISS JULIE: You can't prove that.

JEAN: You can't prove the opposite—because we don't have any family records—except in the police files. But I've read the whole history of your family in that peerage book in the drawing room. Do you know who the 405 founder of your family line was? A miller—who let his wife sleep with the king one night during the Danish war. I don't have any ancestors like that. I don't have any ancestors at all! But I can become an ancestor myself.

MISS JULIE: This is what I get for baring my heart and soul to 410 someone too low to understand, for sacrificing the honor of my family—

JEAN: Dishonor! —I warned you, remember? Drinking makes one talk, and talking's bad.

MISS JULIE: Oh, how sorry I am! . . . If only it had never hap- 415 pened! . . . If only you at least loved me!

JEAN: For the last time—what do you want me to do? Cry? Jump over your whip? Kiss you? Lure you to Lake Como for three weeks and then—? What am I supposed to do? What do you want? I've had more than I can take. This is 420 what I get for involving myself with women. . . . Miss Julie, I can see that you're unhappy; I know that you're suffering; but I simply cannot understand you. My people don't behave like this. We don't hate each other. We make love for the fun of it, when we can get any time off from our work. 425 But we don't have time for it all day and all night like you do. If you ask me, you're sick, Miss Julie. Your mother's mind was affected, you know. There are whole counties affected with pietism. That was your mother's trouble—pietism. It's spreading like the plague. 430

MISS JULIE: You can be understanding, Jean. You're talking to me like a human being now.

JEAN: Well, be human yourself. You spit on me, but you don't let me wipe it off—on you.

MISS JULIE: Help me, Jean. Help me. Tell me what I should 435 do, that's all—which way to go.

JEAN: For Christ's sake, if only I knew myself!

MISS JULIE: I've been crazy—I've been out of my mind—but does that mean there's no way out for me?

JEAN: Stay here as if nothing had happened. Nobody knows 440 anything.

MISS JULIE: Impossible! Everybody who works here knows. Christine knows.

JEAN: They don't know a thing. Anyhow they'd never believe it.

MISS JULIE: (*Slowly, significantly.*) But . . . it might happen 445 again.

JEAN: That's true!

MISS JULIE: And one time there might be . . . consequences.

JEAN: (*Stunned.*) Consequences!! What on earth have I been thinking of? You're right. There's only one thing to do: get 450 away from here! Immediately! I can't go with you—that would give the whole game away. You'll have to go by yourself. Somewhere—I don't care where!

MISS JULIE: By myself? Where? —Oh, no, Jean, I can't. I can't!

JEAN: You've got to! Before the count comes back. You know as 455 well as I do what will happen if you stay here. After one mistake, you figure you might as well go on—the damage is al-

ready done. Then you get more and more careless until—finally you're exposed. I tell you, you've got to get out of the
460 country. Afterward you can write to the count and tell him everything—leaving me out, of course. He'd never figure it was me. He wouldn't even let himself think it was me.

MISS JULIE: I'll go—if you'll come with me!

JEAN: Lady, are you out of your mind? "Miss Julie elopes with
465 her footman." The day after tomorrow it would be in all the papers. The count would never live it down.

MISS JULIE: I can't go away. I can't stay. Help me. I'm so tired, so awfully tired. . . . Tell me what to do. Order me. Start me going. I can't think anymore, can't move anymore . . .

470 JEAN: Now do you realize how weak you all are? What gives you the right to go strutting around with your noses in the air as if you owned the world? All right, I'll give you your orders. Go up and get dressed. Get some traveling money. And come back down here.

475 MISS JULIE: (*Almost in a whisper.*) Come up with me!

JEAN: To your room? . . . You're going crazy again! (*He hesitates a moment.*) No! No! Go! Right now! (*He takes her hand and leads her out.*)

MISS JULIE: (*As she is leaving.*) Don't be so harsh, Jean.

480 JEAN: Orders always sound harsh. You've never had to take them.

(JEAN, *left alone, heaves a sigh of relief and sits down at the table. He takes out a notebook and a pencil and begins to calculate, counting aloud now and then. The pantomime continues until* CHRISTINE *enters, dressed for church, and carrying* JEAN's *white tie and shirtfront in her hand.*)

CHRISTINE: Lord in Heaven, what a mess! What on earth have you been doing?

JEAN: It was Miss Julie. She dragged the whole crowd in here.
485 You must have been sleeping awfully sound if you didn't hear anything.

CHRISTINE: I slept like a log.

JEAN: You already dressed for church?

CHRISTINE: Yes, indeed. Don't you remember you promised
490 to go to communion with me today?

JEAN: Oh, yes. Of course, I remember. I see you've brought my things. All right. Come on, put it on me. (*He sits down, and* CHRISTINE *starts to put the white tie and shirtfront on him. Pause.*)

495 JEAN: (*Yawning.*) What's the lesson for today?

CHRISTINE: The beheading of John the Baptist, what else? It's Midsummer. It's his feast day.

JEAN: My God, that will go on forever. —Hey, you're choking me! . . . Oh, I'm so sleepy, so sleepy.

500 CHRISTINE: What were you doing up all night? You look green in the face.

JEAN: I've been sitting here talking with Miss Julie.

CHRISTINE: That girl! She doesn't know how to behave herself!

(*Pause.*)

JEAN: Tell me something, Christine . . .

505 CHRISTINE: Well, what?

JEAN: Isn't it strange when you think about it? Her, I mean.

CHRISTINE: What's so strange?

JEAN: Everything!

(*Pause.* CHRISTINE *looks at the half-empty glasses on the table.*)

CHRISTINE: Have you been drinking with her?

JEAN: Yes!   510

CHRISTINE: Shame on you! —Look me in the eyes! You haven't . . .?

JEAN: Yes!

CHRISTINE: Is it possible? Is it really possible?

JEAN: (*Thinking about it.*) Yes. It is.   515

CHRISTINE: Oh, how disgusting! I could never have believed anything like this would happen! No. No. This is too much!

JEAN: Don't tell me you're jealous of her?

CHRISTINE: No, not of her. If it had been Clara—or Sophie—I would have scratched your eyes out! But her—? That's dif-   520
ferent. I don't know why. . . . But it's still disgusting!

JEAN: You're not mad at her?

CHRISTINE: No. Mad at you. You were mean and cruel to do a thing like that, very mean. The poor girl! . . . Let me tell you, I'm not going to stay in this house a moment longer, not   525
when I can't have any respect for my employers.

JEAN: Why do you want to respect them?

CHRISTINE: Don't try to be smart. You don't want to work for people who behave like pigs, do you? Well, do you? If you ask me, you'd be lowering yourself by doing that.   530

JEAN: Oh, I don't know. I think it's rather comforting to find out that they're not one damn bit better than we are.

CHRISTINE: Well, I don't. If they're not any better, there's no point in us trying to be like them. —And think of the count. Think of all the sorrows he's been through in his   535
time. My God! I won't stay in this house any longer. . . . Imagine! You, of all people! If it had been the attorney fellow; if it had been somebody respectable—

JEAN: Now just a minute—!

CHRISTINE: Oh, you're all right in your own way. But there's a   540
big difference between one class and another. You can't deny that. —No, this is something I can never get over. She was so proud, and so sarcastic about men, you'd never believe she'd go and throw herself at one. And at somebody like you! And she was going to have Diana shot because the   545
poor thing ran after the gatekeeper's mongrel! —Well, I tell you, I've had enough! I'm not going to stay here any longer. When my term's up, I'm leaving.

JEAN: Then what'll you do?

CHRISTINE: Well, since you brought it up, it's about time that you   550
got yourself a decent place, if we're going to get married.

JEAN: Why should I go looking for another place? I could never get a job like this if I'm married.

CHRISTINE: Well, I know that! But you could get a job as a porter, or maybe try to get a government job as a care-   555
taker somewhere. A square deal and a square meal, that's what you get from the government—and a pension for the wife and children.

JEAN: (*Wryly.*) Fine, fine! But I'm not the kind of guy who thinks about dying for his wife and children this early in   560
the game. Let me tell you, I've got slightly bigger plans than that.

CHRISTINE: Plans! Ha! What about your obligations? You'd better start giving them a little thought!

JEAN: Don't start nagging me about obligations! I know what   565
I have to do without you telling me. (*He hears a sound upstairs.*) Anyhow, we'll have plenty of chance to talk about this later. You just go and get yourself ready, and we'll be off to church.

570   CHRISTINE: Who is that walking around up there?

JEAN: I don't know. Clara, I suppose. Who else?

CHRISTINE: (*Starting to leave.*) It can't be the count, can it? Could he have come back without anybody hearing him?

JEAN: (*Frightened.*) The count? No, it can't be. He would have
575   rung.

CHRISTINE: (*Leaving.*) God help us! I've never heard the like of this.

(*The sun has now risen and strikes the tops of the trees in the park. As the scene progresses, the light shifts gradually until it is shining very obliquely through the windows.* JEAN *goes to the door and signals.* MISS JULIE *enters, dressed for travel, and carrying a small birdcage, covered with a towel. She sets the cage down on a chair.*)

MISS JULIE: I'm ready now.

JEAN: Shh! Christine's awake.

580   MISS JULIE: (*Extremely tense and nervous during the following.*) Did she suspect anything?

JEAN: She doesn't know a thing. —My God, what happened to you?

MISS JULIE: What do you mean? Do I look so strange?

585   JEAN: You're white as a ghost, and you've—excuse me— you've got dirt on your face.

MISS JULIE: Let me wash it off. (*She goes over to the washbasin and washes her face and hands.*) There! Do you have a towel? . . . Oh, look, the sun's coming up!

590   JEAN: That breaks the magic spell!

MISS JULIE: Yes, we were spellbound last night, weren't we? Midsummer madness . . . Jean, listen to me! Come with me. I've got the money!

JEAN: (*Suspiciously.*) Enough?

595   MISS JULIE: Enough for a start. Come with me, Jean. I can't travel alone today. Midsummer Day on a stifling hot train, packed in with crowds of people, all staring at me—stopping at every station when I want to be flying. I can't, Jean, I can't! . . . And everything will remind me of the past. Midsummer Day
600   when I was a child and the church was decorated with leaves—birch leaves and lilacs . . . the table spread for dinner with friends and relatives . . . and after dinner, dancing in the park, with flowers and games. Oh, no matter how far you travel, the memories tag right along in the baggage car . . .
605   and the regrets and the remorse.

JEAN: All right, I'll go with you! But it's got to be now—before it's too late! This very instant!

MISS JULIE: Hurry and get dressed! (*She picks up the birdcage.*)

JEAN: No baggage! It would give us away.

610   MISS JULIE: Nothing. Only what we can take to our seats.

JEAN: (*As he gets his hat.*) What in the devil have you got there? What is that?

MISS JULIE: It's only my canary. I can't leave it behind.

JEAN: A canary! My God, do you expect us to carry a bird-
615   cage around with us? You're crazy. Put that cage down!

MISS JULIE: It's the only thing I'm taking with me from my home—the only living thing who loves me since Diana was unfaithful to me! Don't be cruel, Jean. Let me take it with me.

620   JEAN: I told you to put that cage down! —And don't talk so loud. Christine can hear us.

MISS JULIE: No, I won't leave it with a stranger. I won't. I'd rather have you kill it.

JEAN: Give it here, the little pest. I'll wring its neck.

MISS JULIE: Oh, don't hurt it. Don't—. No, I can't do it!   625

JEAN: Don't worry, I can. Give it here.

(MISS JULIE *takes the bird out of the cage and kisses it.*)

MISS JULIE: Oh, my little Serena, must you die and leave your mistress?

JEAN: You don't have to make a scene of it. It's a question of your whole life and future. You're wasting time!   630

(JEAN *grabs the canary from her, carries it to the chopping block, and picks up a meat cleaver.* MISS JULIE *turns away.*)

You should have learned how to kill chickens instead of shooting revolvers—(*He brings the cleaver down.*)—then a drop of blood wouldn't make you faint.

MISS JULIE: (*Screaming.*) Kill me too! Kill me! You can kill an innocent creature without turning a hair—then kill me.   635 Oh, how I hate you! I loathe you! There's blood between us. I curse the moment I first laid eyes on you! I curse the moment I was conceived in my mother's womb.

JEAN: What good does your cursing do? Let's get out of here!

MISS JULIE: (*Approaches the chopping block, drawn to it against her*   640 *will.*) No, I don't want to go yet. I can't. —I have to see. — Shh! (*She listens but keeps her eyes fastened on the chopping block and cleaver.*) You don't think I can stand the sight of blood, do you? You think I'm so weak, don't you? Oh, how I'd love to see your blood, your brains on that chopping block. I'd   645 love to see the whole of your sex swimming in a sea of blood just like that. I could drink blood out of your skull. Use your chest as a foot bath, dip my toes in your guts! I could eat your heart roasted whole! —You think I'm weak! You think I loved you because my womb hungered for   650 your semen. You think I want to carry your brood under my heart and feed it with my blood? Bear your child and take your name? —Come to think of it, what is your name? I've never even heard your last name. I'll bet you don't have one. I'd be Mrs. Doorman or Madame Garbageman. You   655 dog with *my n*ame on your collar—you lackey with *my* initials on your buttons! Do you think I'm going to share you with my cook and fight over you with my maid?! Ohh!— You think I'm a coward who's going to run away! No, I'm going to stay—come hell or high water. My father will   660 come home—find his desk broken into—his money gone. He'll ring—on that bell—two rings for the valet. And then he'll send for the sheriff—and I'll tell him everything. Everything! Oh, what a relief it'll be to have it all over . . . over and done with . . . if only it will be over. . . . He'll have   665 a stroke and die . . . and there'll be an end to all of us. There'll be peace . . . and quiet . . . forever. . . . The coat of arms will be broken on his coffin; the count's line will be extinct—while the valet's breed will continue in an orphanage, win triumphs in the gutter, and end in jail!   670

(CHRISTINE *enters, dressed for church and with a hymn-book in her hand.* MISS JULIE *rushes over to her and throws herself into her arms as if seeking protection.*)

MISS JULIE: Help me, Christine! Protect me against this man!

CHRISTINE: (*Cold and unmoved.*) This is a fine way to behave on a holy day! (*She sees the chopping block.*) Just look at the

675 mess you've made there! How do you explain that? And what's all this shouting and screaming about?

MISS JULIE: Christine, you're a woman, you're my friend! I warn you, watch out for this—this monster!

JEAN: (*Feeling awkward.*) If you ladies are going to talk, you won't want me around. I think I'll go and shave. (*He slips*
680 *out to the right.*)

MISS JULIE: You've got to understand, Christine! You've got to listen to me!

CHRISTINE: No, I don't. I don't understand this kind of shenani-gans at all. Where do you think you're going dressed like that?
685 And Jean with his hat on? —Well? —Well?

MISS JULIE: Listen to me, Christine! If you'll just listen to me, I'll tell you everything.

CHRISTINE: I don't want to know anything.

MISS JULIE: You've got to listen to me—!

690 CHRISTINE: What about? About your stupid behavior with Jean? I tell you that doesn't bother me at all, because it's none of my business. But if you have any silly idea about talking him into skipping out with you, I'll soon put a stop to that.

695 MISS JULIE: (*Extremely tense.*) Christine, please don't get upset. Listen to me. I can't stay here, and Jean can't stay here. So you see, we have to go away.

CHRISTINE: Hm, hm, hm.

MISS JULIE: (*Suddenly brightening up.*) Wait! I've got an idea!
700 Why couldn't all three of us go away together? —out of the country—to Switzerland—and start a hotel? I've got the money, you see. Jean and I would be responsible for the whole affair—and Christine, you could run the kitchen, I thought. Doesn't that sound wonderful! Say
705 you'll come, Christine, then everything will be settled. Say you will! Please! (*She throws her arms around* CHRISTINE *and pats her.*)

CHRISTINE: (*Remaining aloof and unmoved.*) Hm. Hm.

MISS JULIE: (*Presto tempo.*) You've never been traveling, Chris-
710 tine. You have to get out and see the world. You can't imag-ine how wonderful it is to travel by train—constantly new faces, new countries. We'll go to Hamburg, and stop over to look at the zoo—it's famous, has everything—you'll love that. And we'll go to the theater and the opera. And then
715 when we get to Munich, we'll go to the museums, Chris-tine. They have Rubenses and Raphaels there—those great painters, you know. Of course you've heard about Munich where King Ludwig lived—you know, the king who went mad. And then we can go and see his castles—they're just
720 like the ones you read about in fairy tales. And from there it's just a short trip to Switzerland—with the Alps. Think of the Alps, Christine, covered with snow in the middle of summer. And oranges grow there, and laurel trees that are green the whole year round—

(JEAN *can be seen in the wings at the right, sharpening his straight razor on a strop held between his teeth and his left hand. He listens to* MISS JULIE *with a satisfied expression on his face, now and then nodding approvingly.* MISS JULIE *continues tempo prestissimo.*)

725 —and that's where we'll get a hotel. I'll sit at the desk while Jean stands at the door and receives the guests, goes out shop-ping, writes the letters. What a life that will be! The train whistle blowing, then the bus arriving, then a bell ringing upstairs, then the bell in the restaurant rings—and I'll be making out the bills—and I know just how much to salt 730 them—you can imagine how timid tourists are when you shove a bill in their face!—And you, Christine, you'll run the whole kitchen—there'll be no standing at the stove for you—of course not. If you're going to talk to the people, you'll have to dress. And with your looks—I'm not trying to 735 flatter you, Christine—you'll run off with some man one fine day—a rich Englishman, that's who it'll be, they're so easy to—(*Slowing down.*)—to catch. —Then we'll all be rich. —We'll build a villa on Lake Como. —Maybe it does rain there sometimes, but— (*More and more lifelessly.*) —the sun 740 has to shine sometimes, too—even if it looks cloudy. — And—then . . . or else we can always travel some more—and come back . . . (*Pause.*) —here . . . or somewhere else . . .

CHRISTINE: Do you really believe a word of that yourself, Miss Julie? 745

MY JULIE: (*Completely beaten.*) Do I believe a word of it my-self?

CHRISTINE: Do you?

MISS JULIE: (*Exhausted.*) I don't know. I don't believe anything anymore. (*She sinks down on the bench and lays her head be-* 750 *tween her arms on the table.*) Nothing. Nothing at all.

CHRISTINE: (*Turns to the right and faces* JEAN.) So! You were planning to run away, were you?

JEAN: (*Taken aback, lays his razor down on the table.*) We weren't exactly going to run away! Don't exaggerate. You heard 755 Miss Julie's plans. Even if she's tired now after being up all night, her plans are perfectly practical.

CHRISTINE: Well, just listen to you! Did you really think you could get me to cook for that little—!

JEAN: (*Sharply.*) You keep a respectful tongue in your mouth 760 when you talk to your mistress! Understand?

CHRISTINE: Mistress!

JEAN: Yes, mistress!

CHRISTINE: Well of all the—! I don't have to listen—

JEAN: Yes, you do! You need to listen more and blabber less. 765 Miss Julie is your mistress. Don't you forget that! And if you're going to despise her for what she did, you ought to despise yourself for the same reason.

CHRISTINE: I've always held myself high enough to—

JEAN: High enough to make you look down on others! 770

CHRISTINE: —enough to keep from lowering myself beneath my station. Don't you dare say that the count's cook has ever had anything to do with the stable groom or the swineherd. Don't you dare!

JEAN: Yes, you got yourself a decent man. Lucky you! 775

CHRISTINE: What kind of a decent man is it who sells the oats from the count's stables?

JEAN: Listen to who's talking! You get the gravy on the gro-ceries and take bribes from the butcher!

CHRISTINE: How dare you say a thing like that! 780

JEAN: And you say you can't respect your employers. You of all people! You!

CHRISTINE: Are you going to church or aren't you? You need a good sermon after your great exploits.

JEAN: No, I'm not going to church! Go yourself. Go tell God 785 how bad you are.

CHRISTINE: Yes, I'll do just that. And I'll come back with enough forgiveness for your sins, too. Our Redeemer suf-fered and died on the cross for all our sins, and if we come

790   to Him in faith and with a penitent heart, He will take all
       our sins upon Himself.
       JEAN: Rake-offs included?
       MISS JULIE: Do you really believe that, Christine?
       CHRISTINE: With all my heart, as sure as I'm standing here. It
795   was the faith I was born into, and I've held on to it since
       I was a little girl, Miss Julie. Where sin aboundeth, there
       grace aboundeth also.
       MISS JULIE: If I had your faith, Christine, if only—
       CHRISTINE: But you see, that's something you can't have with
800   out God's special grace. And it is not granted to everyone
       to receive it.
       MISS JULIE: Then who receives it?
       CHRISTINE: That's the secret of the workings of grace, Miss
       Julie, and God is no respecter of persons. With Him the
805   last shall be first—
       MISS JULIE: In that case, he does have respect for the last,
       doesn't he?
       CHRISTINE: (Continuing.) —and it is easier for a camel to go
       through the eye of a needle than for a rich man to enter
810   the kingdom of God. That's how things are, Miss Julie. I'm
       going to leave now—alone. And on my way out I'm go-
       ing to tell the stable boy not to let any horses out, in case
       anyone has any ideas about leaving before the count
       comes home. Goodbye. (She leaves.)
815   JEAN: She's a devil in skirts! —All because of a canary!
       MISS JULIE: (Listlessly.) Never mind the canary. . . . Do you see
       any way out of this, any end to it?
       JEAN: (After thinking for a moment.) No.
       MISS JULIE: What would you do if you were in my place?
820   JEAN: In your place? Let me think. . . . An aristocrat, a woman,
       and—fallen. . . . I don't know. —Or maybe I do.
       MISS JULIE: (Picks up the razor and makes a gesture with it.) Like
       this?
       JEAN: Yes. But I wouldn't do it, you understand. That's the dif-
825   ference between us.
       MISS JULIE: Because you're a man and I'm a woman? What
       difference does that make?
       JEAN: Just the difference that there is—between a man and a
       woman.
830   MISS JULIE: (Holding the razor in her hand.) I want to! But I
       can't do it. My father couldn't do it either, that time when
       he should have.
       JEAN: No, he was right not to. He had to get his revenge first.
       MISS JULIE: And now my mother is getting her revenge again
835   through me.
       JEAN: Didn't you ever love your father, Miss Julie?
       MISS JULIE: Yes, enormously. But I must have hated him too. I
       must have hated him without knowing it. It was he who
       brought me up to despise my own sex, to be half woman
840   and half man. Who's to blame for what has happened? My
       father, my mother, myself? Myself? I don't have a self that's
       my own. I don't have a single thought I didn't get from my
       father, not an emotion I didn't get from my mother. And
       that last idea—about all people being equal—I got that
845   from him, my fiancé. That's why I say he's beneath con-
       tempt. How can it be my own fault? Put the blame on
       Jesus, like Christine does? I'm too proud to do that—and
       too intelligent, thanks to what my father taught me. . . . A
       rich man can't get into heaven? That's a lie. But at least
850   Christine, who's got money in the savings bank, won't get

       in. . . . Who's to blame? What difference does it make who's
       to blame? I'm still the one who has to bear the guilt, suffer
       the consequences—
       JEAN: Yes, but—

       (The bell rings sharply twice. MISS JULIE jumps up. JEAN changes his
       coat.)

       JEAN: The count's back! What if Christine— (He goes to the   855
       speaking tube, taps on it, and listens.)
       MISS JULIE: Has he looked in his desk yet?
       JEAN: This is Jean, sir! (Listens. The audience cannot hear what the
       count says.) Yes, sir! (Listens.) Yes, sir! Yes, as soon as I can.
       (Listens.) Yes, at once, sir! (Listens.) Very good, sir! In half an   860
       hour.
       MISS JULIE: (Trembling with anxiety.) What did he say? For
       God's sake, what did he say?
       JEAN: He ordered his boots and his coffee in half an hour.
       MISS JULIE: Half an hour then! . . . Oh, I'm so tired. I can't   865
       bring myself to do anything. Can't repent, can't run away,
       can't stay, can't live . . . can't die. Help me, Jean. Command
       me, and I'll obey like a dog. Do me this last favor. Save my
       honor, save his name. You know what I ought to do but
       can't force myself to do. Let me use your willpower. You   870
       command me and I'll obey.
       JEAN: I don't know—. I can't either, not now. I don't know
       why. It's as if this coat made me—I can't give you orders
       in this. And now, after the count has spoken to me, I—I
       can't really explain it—but—I've got the backbone of a   875
       damned lackey! If the count came down here now and
       ordered me to cut my throat, I'd do it on the spot.
       MISS JULIE: Then pretend you're him. Pretend I'm you. You
       were such a good actor just a while ago, when you were
       kneeling before me. You were the aristocrat then. Or   880
       else—have you been to the theater and seen a hypnotist?

       (JEAN nods.)

       He says to his subject, "Take this broom!" and he takes it.
       He says, "Now sweep!" and he sweeps.
       JEAN: The person has to be asleep!
       MISS JULIE: (Ecstatic, transported.) I'm already asleep. The   885
       whole room has turned to smoke. You seem like an iron
       stove, a stove that looks like a man in black with a high
       hat. Your eyes are glowing like fading coals in a dying fire.
       Your face is a white smudge, like ashes.

       (The sun is now shining in on the floor and falls on JEAN.)

       It's so good and warm—(She rubs her hands together as if   890
       warming them at a fire.)—and so bright—and so peaceful.
       JEAN: (Takes the razor and puts it in her hand.) There's the
       broom. Go now, when the sun is up—out into the barn—
       and—(He whispers in her ear.)
       MISS JULIE: (Waking up.) Thanks! I'm going to get my rest. But   895
       tell me one thing. Tell me that the first can also receive the
       gift of grace. Tell me that, even if you don't believe it.
       JEAN: The first? I can't tell you that. —Wait a moment, Miss
       Julie. I know what I can tell you. You're no longer one of
       the first. You're one of—the last.   900
       MISS JULIE: That's true! I'm one of the last. I am the very last!
       —oh!—Now I can't go! Tell me just once more, tell me
       to go!

JEAN: Now I can't either. I can't!

905 MISS JULIE: And the first shall be the last . . .

JEAN: Don't think—don't think! You're taking all my strength from me. You're making me a coward. . . . What?! I thought I saw the bell move. No. . . . Let me stuff some paper in it.— Afraid of a bell! But it isn't just a bell. There's somebody be-

910 hind it. A hand that makes it move. And there's something that makes the hand move. —Stop your ears, that's it, stop your ears! But it only rings louder. Rings louder and louder until you answer it. And then it's too late. Then the sheriff comes—and then—(*There are two sharp rings on the bell.* JEAN *gives a start, then straightens himself up.*) It's horrible! But there's 915 no other way for it to end. —Go!

(MISS JULIE *walks resolutely out through the door.*)

Oscar Wilde

Oscar Fingal O'Flahertie Willis Wilde (1854–1900) is best known as the aesthete's aesthete of 1880s and 1890s London, famous for his epigrammatic wit, for his novel *The Picture of Dorian Gray* (1890) and the moody symbolist drama *Salomé* (1892), for the highly polished dramas he produced in the 1890s—*Lady Windermere's Fan* (1892), *A Woman of No Importance* (1893), *An Ideal Husband* (1895)—capped by his transcendent "trivial comedy for serious people," *The Importance of Being Earnest* (1895). However, Wilde is also remembered for the tragedy of his life, the terrible trial in which he was convicted of homosexual practices and sentenced to two years' hard labor, and for the poverty, isolation, and rejection that ensued.

Wilde was born in Dublin, the second son of Sir William Wilde—an author, oculist, and surgeon—and Jane Francesca Elgee, a poet and translator. He was educated at the Portora Royal School, read classics at Trinity College, Dublin, and then matriculated at Magdalen College, Oxford, where he continued to study classics. Leaving Oxford in 1876, Wilde began a career as a poet—his poem "Ravenna" won the Newdigate prize in 1878—and occasional critic on artistic subjects. By 1881, his wit, his pose, his green carnation (already part of the vestimentary code of Victorian gay culture) were so well known that he could be satirized as Bunthorne in Gilbert and Sullivan's operetta *Patience.* In the early 1880s he perfected his lecture performance on tour throughout the United States and Canada, but once he was married to Constance Lloyd in 1884—his two sons, Cyril and Vyvyan, were born in 1885 and 1886—Wilde had need of an income as a regular reviewer and essayist. Through the late 1880s, Wilde gained additional fame as the paradoxical spokesman of aestheticism, writing a brilliant series of articles for the *Pall Mall Gazette,* the *Dramatic Review, Nineteenth Century,* and other magazines, notably "The Decay of Lying" (1889), "The Artist as Critic" (1890), and "The Truth of Masks" (1885).

The posed, paradoxical, masked quality of Wilde's public persona had another dimension, for Wilde's homosexuality forced him to lead an elaborate double life. The passage of the Criminal Law Amendment Act in 1885 made homosexual activity illegal, and Wilde risked—and eventually suffered—both social rejection and legal punishment. As his career and public visibility began to crest in the early 1890s, with the publication of *The Picture of Dorian Gray* and the success of his first plays, Wilde became involved with a young man, Lord Alfred Douglas. In 1895 Douglas's father, the Marquess of Queensberry, left a card at Wilde's club addressed to "Mr. Oscar Wilde, posing as a somdomite [*sic*]." Against the advice of his friends, Wilde sued the Marquess for criminal libel. When Queensberry was acquitted, Wilde was arrested for "acts of gross indecency with other male persons" and subjected to two jury trials, in which a series of young men were put on the stand, testifying to their sexual relations with Wilde. In the first trial, the jury was unable to reach a verdict; in the second, Wilde was found guilty and given the maximum sentence of two years' hard labor. Although he was eventually moved from hard labor in Pentonville to Wandsworth Prison, and then finally to Reading Gaol, prison broke Wilde's health. Constance changed the last names of Cyril and Vyvyan to avoid association with Wilde, and when he was released in 1897 he was bankrupt and alone. Although Wilde's sexual orientation had long been known or suspected by many of his friends, most were unwilling to associate with Wilde after such public scandal. When Wilde returned to society, he was cruelly and systematically shunned. He settled first in France, then joined Alfred Douglas briefly in Italy; in 1898 he published *The Ballad of Reading Gaol* and settled in Paris, where he died two years later.

Despite its energetic "triviality," *The Importance of Being Earnest* is deeply, symbolically involved in the contours of Wilde's life. The opening of *Earnest* in February of 1895 at George Alexander's fashionable St. James's Theatre was something of a society event; fearing the publicity of Wilde's trial, Alexander closed the hugely successful play only weeks later. But *The Importance of Being Earnest* seems to resonate with Wilde's life in other ways as well. In an important sense, *The Importance of Being Earnest* is a play about masking. Much as Wilde's sexual identity had constantly to be negotiated behind the fictive "conventions" of polite society—his sexuality could be tolerated only as long as it was kept discreetly offstage, disacknowleged, unspoken—so in *Earnest* the process of social life in general seems to depend on a tissue of acceptable lies, which occasionally verge on truth: Algernon Moncrieff invents "an invaluable permanent invalid called Bunbury" so that he will have an excuse to escape London; Jack Worthing invents a wastrel younger brother named Ernest as an excuse to escape the country; Cecily invents scenes for her diary and Gwendolen keeps hers handy to "have something sensational to read on the train"; Jack and Algy, both vying to be baptized "Ernest," turn out to be brothers; and Jack, a foundling, turns out to be named Ernest after all.

As Algy remarks in Act One, "The truth is rarely pure and never simple. Modern life would be very tedious if it were either, and modern literature a complete impossibility!" In *Earnest,* Wilde carefully constructs a comedy in which the deceptive surfaces of experience, the manifest fictions and deceptions of "modern life," turn out to provide the only vehicle for truth the play has to offer. Because beneath the constricted, yet infinitely manipulable conventions of polite society surges the powerful force of desire. It is manifest in the elaborate verbal sparring between Jack, Algy, Gwendolen, and Cecily; in the manic, adolescent energy that drives Jack and Algy to the brink of baptism; even in the appetitive fury of the muffin scene. One final way in which these social conventions are marked is through their connection to the conventions of comedy itself—conventions that are forced to the forefront of the audience's attention throughout the play. *Earnest* comes to a climax in a paroxysm of artificiality: making a mockery of the recognition scene between long-lost siblings of romantic comedy, Wilde's Jack Worthing turns out to *be* his fictitious brother Ernest after all. In *The Importance of Being Earnest,* all convention—both social and comic—is shown to be a kind of mask, a fiction that sometimes enables the expression of truth.

Jack and Algernon confront recalcitrant Gwendolyn and Cecily in the McCarter Theatre production of *The Importance of Being Earnest.*

THE IMPORTANCE OF BEING EARNEST

Oscar Wilde

CHARACTERS

JOHN WORTHING, J.P.
ALGERNON MONCRIEFF
REV. CANON CHASUBLE, D.D.
MERRIMAN (*Butler*)
LANE (*Manservant*)

LADY BRACKNELL
HON. GWENDOLEN FAIRFAX
CECILY CARDEW
MISS PRISM (*Governess*)

THE SCENES OF THE PLAY

ACT   I. Algernon Moncrieff's Flat in Half-Moon Street, W.
ACT II. The Garden at the Manor House, Woolton.
ACT III. Drawing-Room of the Manor House, Woolton.

TIME.—*The Present.*   PLACE.—*London.*

ACT ONE

Morning-room in ALGERNON's *flat in Half-Moon Street. The room is luxuriously and artistically furnished. The sound of a piano is heard in the adjoining room.*

(LANE *is arranging afternoon tea on the table, and after the music has ceased,* ALGERNON *enters.*)

ALGERNON: Did you hear what I was playing, Lane?

LANE: I didn't think it polite to listen, sir.

ALGERNON: I'm sorry for that, for your sake. I don't play accurately—anyone can play accurately—but I play with
5   wonderful expression. As far as the piano is concerned,
sentiment is my forte. I keep science for Life.

LANE: Yes, sir.

ALGERNON: And, speaking of the science of Life, have you
got the cucumber sandwiches cut for Lady Bracknell?

10 LANE: Yes, sir. (*Hands them on a salver.*)

ALGERNON: (*Inspects them, takes two, and sits down on the sofa.*)
Oh! . . . by the way, Lane, I see from your book that on
Thursday night, when Lord Shoreman and Mr. Worthing
were dining with me, eight bottles of champagne are en-
15 tered as having been consumed.

LANE: Yes, sir; eight bottles and a pint.

ALGERNON: Why is it that at a bachelor's establishment the
servants invariably drink the champagne? I ask merely for
information.

20 LANE: I attribute it to the superior quality of the wine, sir. I
have often observed that in married households the
champagne is rarely of a first-rate brand.

ALGERNON: Good Heavens! Is marriage so demoralizing as
that?

25 LANE: I believe it *is* a very pleasant state, sir. I have had very
little experience of it myself up to the present. I have only
been married once. That was in consequence of a misunderstanding between myself and a young woman.

ALGERNON: (*Languidly.*) I don't know that I am much inter-
30 ested in your family life, Lane.

LANE: No, sir; it is not a very interesting subject. I never think
of it myself.

ALGERNON: Very natural, I am sure. That will do, Lane, thank
you.

35 LANE: Thank you, sir. (LANE *goes out.*)

ALGERNON: Lane's views on marriage seem somewhat lax.
Really, if the lower orders don't set us a good example,
what on earth is the use of them? They seem, as a class, to
have absolutely no sense of moral responsibility.

(*Enter* LANE.)

LANE: Mr. Ernest Worthing.   40

(*Enter* JACK. LANE *goes out.*)

ALGERNON: How are you, my dear Ernest? What brings you
up to town?

JACK: Oh, pleasure, pleasure! What else should bring one anywhere? Eating as usual, I see, Algy!

ALGERNON: (*Stiffly.*) I believe it is customary in good society 45
to take some slight refreshment at five o'clock. Where
have you been since last Thursday?

JACK: (*Sitting down on the sofa.*) In the country.

ALGERNON: What on earth do you do there?

JACK: (*Pulling off his gloves.*) When one is in town one amuses 50
oneself. When one is in the country one amuses other
people. It is excessively boring.

ALGERNON: And who are the people you amuse?

JACK: (*Airily.*) Oh, neighbours, neighbours.

ALGERNON: Got nice neighbours in your part of Shropshire? 55

JACK: Perfectly horrid! Never speak to one of them.

ALGERNON: How immensely you must amuse them! (*Goes
over and takes sandwich.*) By the way, Shropshire is your
county, is it not?

JACK: Eh? Shropshire? Yes, of course. Hallo! Why all these 60
cups? Why cucumber sandwiches? Why such reckless extravagance in one so young? Who is coming to tea?

ALGERNON: Oh! merely Aunt Augusta and Gwendolen.

JACK: How perfectly delightful!

ALGERNON: Yes, that is all very well; but I am afraid Aunt Au- 65
gusta won't quite approve of your being here.

JACK: May I ask why?

ALGERNON: My dear fellow, the way you flirt with Gwendolen is perfectly disgraceful. It is almost as bad as the way
Gwendolen flirts with you.   70

JACK: I am in love with Gwendolen. I have come up to town
expressly to propose to her.

ALGERNON: I thought you had come up for pleasure? . . . I
call that business.

JACK: How utterly unromantic you are!   75

ALGERNON: I really don't see anything romantic in proposing. It is very romantic to be in love. But there is nothing
romantic about a definite proposal. Why, one may be accepted. One usually is, I believe. Then the excitement is all
over. The very essence of romance is uncertainty. If ever I 80
get married, I'll certainly try to forget the fact.

JACK: I have no doubt about that dear Algy. The Divorce Court was specially invented for people whose memories are so curiously constituted.

85 ALGERNON: Oh! there is no use speculating on that subject. Divorces are made in Heaven—(JACK *puts out his hand to take a sandwich.* ALGERNON *at once interferes.*) Please don't touch the cucumber sandwiches. They are ordered specially for Aunt Augusta. (*Takes one and eats it.*)

90 JACK: Well, you have been eating them all the time.

ALGERNON: That is quite a different matter. She is my aunt. (*Takes plate from below.*) Have some bread and butter. The bread and butter is for Gwendolen. Gwendolen is devoted to bread and butter.

95 JACK: (*Advancing to table and helping himself.*) And very good bread and butter it is, too.

ALGERNON: Well, my dear fellow, you need not eat as if you were going to eat it all. You behave as if you were married to her already. You are not married to her already, and I 100 don't think you ever will be.

JACK: Why on earth do you say that?

ALGERNON: Well, in the first place girls never marry the men they flirt with. Girls don't think it right.

JACK: Oh, that is nonsense!

105 ALGERNON: It isn't. It is a great truth. It accounts for the extraordinary number of bachelors that one sees all over the place. In the second place, I don't give my consent.

JACK: Your consent!

ALGERNON: My dear fellow, Gwendolen is my first cousin. 110 And before I allow you to marry her, you will have to clear up the whole question of Cecily. (*Rings bell.*)

JACK: Cecily! What on earth do you mean? What do you mean, Algy, by Cecily? I don't know anyone of the name of Cecily.

(*Enter* LANE.)

115 ALGERNON: Bring me that cigarette case Mr. Worthing left in the smoking-room the last time he dined here.

LANE: Yes, sir. (LANE *goes out.*)

JACK: Do you mean to say you have had my cigarette case all this time? I wish to goodness you had let me know. I have 120 been writing frantic letters to Scotland Yard about it. I was very nearly offering a large reward.

ALGERNON: Well, I wish you would offer one. I happen to be more than usually hard up.

JACK: There is no good offering a large reward now that the 125 thing is found.

(*Enter* LANE *with the cigarette case on a salver.* ALGERNON *takes it at once.* LANE *goes out.*)

ALGERNON: I think that is rather mean of you, Ernest, I must say. (*Opens case and examines it.*) However, it makes no matter, for, now that I look at the inscription, I find that the thing isn't yours after all.

130 JACK: Of course it's mine. (*Moving to him.*) You have seen me with it a hundred times, and you have no right whatsoever to read what is written inside. It is a very ungentlemanly thing to read a private cigarette case.

ALGERNON: Oh! it is absurd to have a hard-and-fast rule about 135 what one should read and what one shouldn't. More than half of modern culture depends on what one shouldn't read.

JACK: I am quite aware of the fact, and I don't propose to discuss modern culture. It isn't the sort of thing one should talk of in private. I simply want my cigarette case back.

ALGERNON: Yes; but this isn't your cigarette case. This ciga- 140 rette case is a present from someone of the name of Cecily, and you said you didn't know anyone of that name.

JACK: Well, if you want to know, Cecily happens to be my aunt.

ALGERNON: Your aunt!   145

JACK: Yes. Charming old lady she is, too. Lives at Tunbridge Wells. Just give it back to me, Algy.

ALGERNON: (*Retreating to back of sofa.*) But why does she call herself little Cecily if she is your aunt and lives at Tunbridge Wells? (*Reading.*) "From little Cecily with her fondest love."   150

JACK: (*Moving to sofa and kneeling upon it.*) My dear fellow, what on earth is there in that? Some aunts are tall, some aunts are not tall. That is a matter that surely an aunt may be allowed to decide for herself. You seem to think that every aunt should be exactly like your aunt! That is ab- 155 surd! For Heaven's sake give me back my cigarette case. (*Follows* ALGERNON *round the room.*)

ALGERNON: Yes. But why does your aunt call you her uncle? "From little Cecily, with her fondest love to her dear Uncle Jack." There is no objection, I admit, to an aunt being a small 160 aunt, but why an aunt, no matter what her size may be, should call her own nephew her uncle, I can't quite make out. Besides, your name isn't Jack at all; it is Ernest.

JACK: It isn't Ernest; it's Jack.

ALGERNON: You have always told me it was Ernest. I have in- 165 troduced you to everyone as Ernest. You answer to the name of Ernest. You look as if your name was Ernest. You are the most earnest looking person I ever saw in my life. It is perfectly absurd your saying that your name isn't Ernest. It's on your cards. Here is one of them. (*Taking it 170 from case.*) "Mr. Ernest Worthing, B 4, The Albany." I'll keep this as a proof your name is Ernest if ever you attempt to deny it to me, or to Gwendolen, or to anyone else. (*Puts the card in his pocket.*)

JACK: Well, my name is Ernest in town and Jack in the coun- 175 try, and the cigarette case was given to me in the country.

ALGERNON: Yes, but that does not account for the fact that your small Aunt Cecily, who lives at Tunbridge Wells, calls you her dear uncle. Come, old boy, you had much better have the thing out at once.   180

JACK: My dear Algy, you talk exactly as if you were a dentist. It is very vulgar to talk like a dentist when one isn't a dentist. It produces a false impression.

ALGERNON: Well, that is exactly what dentists always do. Now, go on! Tell me the whole thing. I may mention that 185 I have always suspected you of being a confirmed and secret Bunburyist; and I am quite sure of it now.

JACK: Bunburyist? What on earth do you mean by a Bunburyist?

ALGERNON: I'll reveal to you the meaning of that incompara- ble expression as soon as you are kind enough to inform me 190 why you are Ernest in town and Jack in the country.

JACK: Well, produce my cigarette case first.

ALGERNON: Here it is. (*Hands cigarette case.*) Now produce your explanation, and pray make it improbable. (*Sits on sofa.*)   195

JACK: My dear fellow, there is nothing improbable about my explanation at all. In fact it's perfectly ordinary. Old Mr.

Thomas Cardew, who adopted me when I was a little boy, made me in his will guardian to his grand-daughter, Miss
200 Cecily Cardew. Cecily, who addresses me as her uncle from motives of respect that you could not possibly appreciate, lives at my place in the country under the charge of her admirable governess, Miss Prism.

ALGERNON: Where is that place in the country, by the way?

205 JACK: That is nothing to you, dear boy. You are not going to be invited. . . . I may tell you candidly that the place is not in Shropshire.

ALGERNON: I suspected that, my dear fellow! I have Bunburyed all over Shropshire on two separate occasions. Now, go on.
210 Why are you Ernest in town and Jack in the country?

JACK: My dear Algy, I don't know whether you will be able to understand my real motives. You are hardly serious enough. When one is placed in the position of guardian, one has to adopt a very high moral tone on all subjects. It's one's duty
215 to do so. And as a high moral tone can hardly be said to conduce very much to either one's health or one's happiness, in order to get up to town I have always pretended to have a younger brother of the name of Ernest, who lives in the Albany, and gets into the most dreadful scrapes. That, my dear
220 Algy, is the whole truth pure and simple.

ALGERNON: The truth is rarely pure and never simple. Modern life would be very tedious if it were either, and modern literature a complete impossibility!

JACK: That wouldn't be at all a bad thing.

225 ALGERNON: Literary criticism is not your forte, my dear fellow. Don't try it. You should leave that to people who haven't been at a University. They do it so well in the daily papers. What you really are is a Bunburyist. I was quite right in saying you were a Bunburyist. You are one of the
230 most advanced Bunburyists I know.

JACK: What on earth do you mean?

ALGERNON: You have invented a very useful younger brother called Ernest, in order that you may be able to come up to town as often as you like. I have invented an invaluable per-
235 manent invalid called Bunbury, in order that I may be able to go down into the country whenever I choose. Bunbury is perfectly invaluable. If it wasn't for Bunbury's extraordinary bad health, for instance, I wouldn't be able to dine with you at Willis's to-night, for I have been really engaged
240 to Aunt Augusta for more than a week.

JACK: I haven't asked you to dine with me anywhere to-night.

ALGERNON: I know. You are absolutely careless about sending out invitations. It is very foolish of you. Nothing annoys people so much as not receiving invitations.

245 JACK: You had much better dine with your Aunt Augusta.

ALGERNON: I haven't the smallest intention of doing anything of the kind. To begin with, I dined there on Monday, and once a week is quite enough to dine with one's own relatives. In the second place, whenever I do dine there I am al-
250 ways treated as a member of the family, and sent down with either no woman at all, or two. In the third place, I know perfectly well whom she will place me next to, to-night. She will place me next Mary Farquhar, who always flirts with her own husband across the dinner-table. That is not very
255 pleasant. Indeed, it is not even decent . . . and that sort of thing is enormously on the increase. The amount of women in London who flirt with their own husbands is perfectly scandalous. It looks so bad. It is simply washing one's clean linen in public. Besides, now that I know you to be a con-

firmed Bunburyist I naturally want to talk to you about 260 Bunburying. I want to tell you the rules.

JACK: I'm not a Bunburyist at all. If Gwendolen accepts me, I am going to kill my brother, indeed I think I'll kill him in any case. Cecily is a little too much interested in him. It is rather a bore. So I am going to get rid of Ernest. And 265 I strongly advise you to do the same with Mr. . . . with your invalid friend who has the absurd name.

ALGERNON: Nothing will induce me to part with Bunbury, and if you ever get married, which seems to be extremely problematic, you will be very glad to know Bunbury. A 270 man who marries without knowing Bunbury has a very tedious time of it.

JACK: That is nonsense. If I marry a charming girl like Gwendolen, and she is the only girl I ever saw in my life that I would marry, I certainly won't want to know Bunbury. 275

ALGERNON: Then your wife will. You don't seem to realize, that in married life three is company and two is none.

JACK: (*Sententiously.*) That, my dear young friend, is the theory that the corrupt French Drama has been propounding for the last fifty years. 280

ALGERNON: Yes; and that the happy English home has proved in half the time.

JACK: For heaven's sake, don't try to be cynical. It's perfectly easy to be cynical.

ALGERNON: My dear fellow, it isn't easy to be anything now-a- 285 days. There's such a lot of beastly competition about. (*The sound of an electric bell is heard.*) Ah! that must be Aunt Augusta. Only relatives, or creditors, ever ring in that Wagnerian manner. Now, if I get her out of the way for ten minutes, so that you can have an opportunity for proposing to Gwendolen, 290 may I dine with you to-night at Willis's?

JACK: I suppose so if you want to.

ALGERNON: Yes, but you must be serious about it. I hate people who are not serious about meals. It is so shallow of them.

(*Enter* LANE.)

LANE: Lady Bracknell and Miss Fairfax. (ALGERNON *goes* 295 *forward to meet them. Enter* LADY BRACKNELL *and* GWENDOLEN.)

LADY BRACKNELL: Good afternoon, dear Algernon, I hope you are behaving very well.

ALGERNON: I'm feeling very well, Aunt Augusta. 300

LADY BRACKNELL: That's not quite the same thing. In fact the two things rarely go together. (*Sees* JACK *and bows to him with icy coldness.*)

ALGERNON: (*To* GWENDOLEN.) Dear me, you are smart!

GWENDOLEN: I am always smart! Aren't I, Mr. Worthing? 305

JACK: You're quite perfect, Miss Fairfax.

GWENDOLEN: Oh! I hope I am not that. It would leave no room for developments, and I intend to develop in *many directions.* (GWENDOLEN *and* JACK *sit down together in the corner.*) 310

LADY BRACKNELL: I'm sorry if we are a little late, Algernon, but I was obliged to call on dear Lady Harbury. I hadn't been there since her poor husband's death. I never saw a woman so altered; she looks quite twenty years younger. And now I'll have a cup of tea, and one of those nice cu- 315 cumber sandwiches you promised me.

ALGERNON: Certainly, Aunt Augusta. (*Goes over to tea-table.*)

LADY BRACKNELL: Won't you come and sit here, Gwendolen?

GWENDOLEN: Thanks, mamma, I'm quite comfortable where
320   I am.
ALGERNON: (*Picking up empty plate in horror.*) Good heavens!
        Lane! Why are there no cucumber sandwiches? I ordered
        them specially.
LANE: (*Gravely.*) There were no cucumbers in the market this
325   morning, sir. I went down twice.
ALGERNON: No cucumbers!
LANE: No, sir. Not even for ready money.
ALGERNON: That will do, Lane, thank you.
LANE: Thank you sir. (*Goes out.*)
330 ALGERNON: I am greatly distressed, Aunt Augusta, about there
        being no cucumbers, not even for ready money.
LADY BRACKNELL: It really makes no matter, Algernon. I had
        some crumpets with Lady Harbury, who seems to me to
        be living entirely for pleasure now.
335 ALGERNON: I hear her hair has turned quite gold from grief.
LADY BRACKNELL: It certainly has changed its colour. From
        what cause I, of course, cannot say. (ALGERNON *crosses and
        hands tea.*) Thank you. I've quite a treat for you to-night,
        Algernon. I am going to send you down with Mary Far-
340   quhar. She is such a nice woman, and so attentive to her
        husband. It's delightful to watch them.
ALGERNON: I am afraid, Aunt Augusta, I shall have to give up
        the pleasure of dining with you to-night after all.
LADY BRACKNELL: (*Frowning.*) I hope not, Algernon. It would
345   put my table completely out. Your uncle would have to dine
        upstairs. Fortunately he is accustomed to that.
ALGERNON: It is a great bore, and, I need hardly say, a terri-
        ble disappointment to me, but the fact is I have just had a
        telegram to say that my poor friend Bunbury is very ill
350   again. (*Exchanges glances with* JACK.) They seem to think I
        should be with him.
LADY BRACKNELL: It is very strange. This Mr. Bunbury seems
        to suffer from curiously bad health.
ALGERNON: Yes; poor Bunbury is a dreadful invalid.
355 LADY BRACKNELL: Well, I must say, Algernon, that I think it
        is high time that Mr. Bunbury made up his mind whether
        he was going to live or to die. This shilly-shallying with
        the question is absurd. Nor do I in any way approve of the
        modern sympathy with invalids. I consider it morbid. Ill-
360   ness of any kind is hardly a thing to be encouraged in oth-
        ers. Health is the primary duty of life. I am always telling
        that to your poor uncle, but he never seems to take much
        notice . . . as far as any improvement in his ailments goes.
        I should be much obliged if you would ask Mr. Bunbury,
365   from me, to be kind enough not to have a relapse on Sat-
        urday, for I rely on you to arrange my music for me. It is
        my last reception and one wants something that will en-
        courage conversation, particularly at the end of the season
        when everyone has practically said whatever they had to
370   say, which, in most cases, was probably not much.
ALGERNON: I'll speak to Bunbury, Aunt Augusta, if he is still
        conscious, and I think I can promise you he'll be all right
        by Saturday. You see, if one plays good music, people don't
        listen, and if one plays bad music people don't talk. But I'll
375   run over the programme I've drawn out, if you will kindly
        come into the next room for a moment.
LADY BRACKNELL: Thank you, Algernon. It is very thought-
        ful of you. (*Rising, and following* ALGERNON.) I'm sure the
        programme will be delightful, after a few expurgations.
380   French songs I cannot possibly allow. People always seem

to think that they are improper, and either look shocked,
which is vulgar, or laugh, which is worse. But German
sounds a thoroughly respectable language, and indeed, I
believe is so. Gwendolen, you will accompany me.
GWENDOLEN: Certainly, mamma. (LADY BRACKNELL *and*   385
ALGERNON *go into the music-room,* GWENDOLEN *remains
behind.*)
JACK: Charming day it has been, Miss Fairfax.
GWENDOLEN: Pray don't talk to me about the weather, Mr.
Worthing. Whenever people talk to me about the   390
weather, I always feel quite certain that they mean some-
thing else. And that makes me so nervous.
JACK: I do mean something else.
GWENDOLEN: I thought so. In fact, I am never wrong.
JACK: And I would like to be allowed to take advantage of   395
Lady Bracknell's temporary absence . . .
GWENDOLEN: I would certainly advise you to do so. Mamma
has a way of coming back suddenly into a room that I
have often had to speak to her about.
JACK: (*Nervously.*) Miss Fairfax, ever since I met you I have ad-   400
mired you more than any girl . . . I have ever met since . . .
I met you.
GWENDOLEN: Yes, I am quite aware of the fact. And I often wish
that in public, at any rate, you had been more demonstrative.
For me you have always had an irresistible fascination. Even   405
before I met you I was far from indifferent to you. (JACK *looks
at her in amazement.*) We live, as I hope you know, Mr. Worthing, in an age of ideals. The fact is constantly mentioned in
the more expensive monthly magazines, and has reached the
provincial pulpits I am told: and my ideal has always been to   410
love some one of the name of Ernest. There is something in
that name that inspires absolute confidence. The moment
Algernon first mentioned to me that he had a friend called
Ernest, I knew I was destined to love you.
JACK: You really love me, Gwendolen?   415
GWENDOLEN: Passionately!
JACK: Darling! You don't know how happy you've made me.
GWENDOLEN: My own Ernest!
JACK: But you don't really mean to say that you couldn't love
me if my name wasn't Ernest?   420
GWENDOLEN: But your name is Ernest.
JACK: Yes, I know it is. But supposing it was something else?
Do you mean to say you couldn't love me then?
GWENDOLEN: (*Glibly.*) Ah! that is clearly a metaphysical spec-
ulation, and like most metaphysical speculations has very   425
little reference at all to the actual facts of real life, as we
know them.
JACK: Personally, darling, to speak quite candidly, I don't
much care about the name of Ernest . . . I don't think that
name suits me at all.   430
GWENDOLEN: It suits you perfectly. It is a divine name. It has
a music of its own. It produces vibrations.
JACK: Well, really, Gwendolen, I must say that I think there are
lots of other much nicer names. I think, Jack, for instance,
a charming name.   435
GWENDOLEN: Jack? . . . No, there is very little music in the
name Jack, if any at all, indeed. It does not thrill. It produces absolutely no vibration. . . . I have known several
Jacks, and they all, without exception, were more than
usually plain. Besides, Jack is a notorious domesticity for   440
John! And I pity any woman who is married to a man
called John. She would probably never be allowed to

know the entrancing pleasure of a single moment's solitude. The only really safe name is Ernest.

445 JACK: Gwendolen, I must get christened at once—I mean we must get married at once. There is no time to be lost.

GWENDOLEN: Married, Mr. Worthing?

JACK: (*Astounded.*) Well . . . surely. You know that I love you, and you led me to believe, Miss Fairfax, that you were not
450 absolutely indifferent to me.

GWENDOLEN: I adore you. But you haven't proposed to me yet. Nothing has been said at all about marriage. The subject has not even been touched on.

JACK: Well . . . may I propose to you now?

455 GWENDOLEN: I think it would be an admirable opportunity. And to spare you any possible disappointment, Mr. Worthing, I think it only fair to tell you quite frankly beforehand that I am fully determined to accept you.

JACK: Gwendolen!

460 GWENDOLEN: Yes, Mr. Worthing, what have you got to say to me?

JACK: You know what I have got to say to you.

GWENDOLEN: Yes, but you don't say it.

JACK: Gwendolen, will you marry me? (*Goes on his knees.*)

465 GWENDOLEN: Of course I will, darling. How long you have been about it! I am afraid you have had very little experience in how to propose.

JACK: My own one, I have never loved anyone in the world but you.

470 GWENDOLEN: Yes, but men often propose for practice. I know my brother Gerald does. All my girl-friends tell me so. What wonderfully blue eyes you have, Ernest! They are quite, quite blue. I hope you will always look at me just like that, especially when there are other people present.

(*Enter* LADY BRACKNELL.)

475 LADY BRACKNELL: Mr. Worthing! Rise, sir, from this semirecumbent posture. It is most indecorous.

GWENDOLEN: Mamma! (*He tries to rise; she restrains him.*) I must beg you to retire. This is no place for you. Besides, Mr. Worthing has not quite finished yet.

480 LADY BRACKNELL: Finished what, may I ask?

GWENDOLEN: I am engaged to Mr. Worthing, mamma.

(*They rise together.*)

LADY BRACKNELL: Pardon me, you are not engaged to anyone. When you do become engaged to some one, I, or your father, should his health permit him, will inform you
485 of the fact. An engagement should come on a young girl as a surprise, pleasant or unpleasant, as the case may be. It is hardly a matter that she could be allowed to arrange for herself. . . . And now I have a few questions to put to you, Mr. Worthing. While I am making these inquiries, you,
490 Gwendolen, will wait for me below in the carriage.

GWENDOLEN: (*Reproachfully.*) Mamma!

LADY BRACKNELL: In the carriage, Gwendolen! (GWENDOLEN *goes to the door. She and* JACK *blow kisses to each other behind* LADY BRACKNELL'*s back.* LADY BRACKNELL *looks vaguely*
495 *about as if she could not understand what the noise was. Finally turns round.*) Gwendolen, the carriage!

GWENDOLEN: Yes, mamma. (*Goes out, looking back at* JACK.)

LADY BRACKNELL: (*Sitting down.*) You can take a seat, Mr. Worthing. (*Looks in her pocket for note-book and pencil.*)

JACK: Thank you, Lady Bracknell, I prefer standing. 500

LADY BRACKNELL: (*Pencil and note-book in hand.*) I feel bound to tell you that you are not down on my list of eligible young men, although I have the same list as the dear Duchess of Bolton has. We work together, in fact. However, I am quite ready to enter your name, should your answers be what a re 505
ally affectionate mother requires. Do you smoke?

JACK: Well, yes, I must admit I smoke.

LADY BRACKNELL: I am glad to hear it. A man should always have an occupation of some kind. There are far too many idle men in London as it is. How old are you? 510

JACK: Twenty-nine.

LADY BRACKNELL: A very good age to be married at. I have always been of opinion that a man who desires to get married should know either everything or nothing. Which do you know? 515

JACK: (*After some hesitation.*) I know nothing, Lady Bracknell.

LADY BRACKNELL: I am pleased to hear it. I do not approve of anything that tampers with natural ignorance. Ignorance is like a delicate exotic fruit; touch it and the bloom is gone. The whole theory of modern education is radically un 520
sound. Fortunately in England, at any rate, education produces no effect whatsoever. If it did, it would prove a serious danger to the upper classes, and probably lead to acts of violence in Grosvenor Square. What is your income?

JACK: Between seven and eight thousand a year. 525

LADY BRACKNELL: (*Makes a note in her book.*) In land, or in investments?

JACK: In investments, chiefly.

LADY BRACKNELL: That is satisfactory. What between the duties expected of one during one's life-time, and the duties exacted 530
from one after one's death, land has ceased to be either a profit or a pleasure. It gives one position, and prevents one from keeping it up. That's all that can be said about land.

JACK: I have a country house with some land, of course, attached to it, about fifteen hundred acres, I believe; but I 535
don't depend on that for my real income. In fact, as far as I can make out, the poachers are the only people who make anything out of it.

LADY BRACKNELL: A country house! How many bedrooms? Well, that point can be cleared up afterwards. You have a 540
town house, I hope? A girl with a simple, unspoiled nature, like Gwendolen, could hardly be expected to reside in the country.

JACK: Well, I own a house in Belgrave Square, but it is let by the year to Lady Bloxham. Of course, I can get it back 545
whenever I like, at six months' notice.

LADY BRACKNELL: Lady Bloxham? I don't know her.

JACK: Oh, she goes about very little. She is a lady considerably advanced in years.

LADY BRACKNELL: Ah, now-a-days that is no guarantee of re 550
spectability of character. What number in Belgrave Square?

JACK: 149.

LADY BRACKNELL: (*Shaking her head.*) The unfashionable side. I thought there was something. However, that could easily be altered. 555

JACK: Do you mean the fashion, or the side?

LADY BRACKNELL: (*Sternly.*) Both, if necessary, I presume. What are your politics?

JACK: Well, I am afraid I really have none. I am a Liberal Unionist.

LADY BRACKNELL: Oh, they count as Tories. They dine with us. Or comes in the evening, at any rate. Now to minor matters. Are your parents living?

JACK: I have lost both my parents.

LADY BRACKNELL: Both? . . . That seems like carelessness. Who was your father? He was evidently a man of some wealth. Was he born in what the Radical papers call the purple of commerce, or did he rise from the ranks of the aristocracy?

JACK: I am afraid I really don't know. The fact is, Lady Bracknell, I said I had lost my parents. It would be nearer the truth to say that my parents seem to have lost me . . . I don't actually know who I am by birth. I was . . . well, I was found.

LADY BRACKNELL: Found!

JACK: The late Mr. Thomas Cardew, an old gentleman of a very charitable and kindly disposition, found me, and gave me the name of Worthing, because he happened to have a first-class ticket for Worthing in his pocket at the time. Worthing is a place in Sussex. It is a seaside resort.

LADY BRACKNELL: Where did the charitable gentleman who had a first-class ticket for this seaside resort find you?

JACK: (*Gravely.*) In a hand-bag.

LADY BRACKNELL: A hand-bag?

JACK: (*Very seriously.*) Yes, Lady Bracknell. I was in a hand-bag—a somewhat large, black leather hand-bag, with handles to it—an ordinary hand-bag in fact.

LADY BRACKNELL: In what locality did Mr. James, or Thomas, Cardew come across this ordinary hand-bag?

JACK: In the cloak-room at Victoria Station. It was given to him in mistake for his own.

LADY BRACKNELL: The cloak-room at Victoria Station?

JACK: Yes. The Brighton line.

LADY BRACKNELL: The line is immaterial. Mr. Worthing, I confess I feel somewhat bewildered by what you have just told me. To be born, or at any rate bred, in a hand-bag, whether it had handles or not, seems to me to display a contempt for the ordinary decencies of family life that remind one of the worst excesses of the French Revolution. And I presume you know what that unfortunate movement led to? As for the particular locality in which the hand-bag was found, a cloak-room at a railway station might serve to conceal a social indiscretion—has probably, indeed, been used for the purpose before now—but it could hardly be regarded as an assured basis for a recognized position in good society.

JACK: May I ask you then what you would advise me to do? I need hardly say I would do anything in the world to ensure Gwendolen's happiness.

LADY BRACKNELL: I would strongly advise you, Mr. Worthing, to try and acquire some relations as soon as possible, and to make a definite effort to produce at any rate one parent, of either sex, before the season is quite over.

JACK: Well, I don't see how I could possibly manage to do that. I can produce the hand-bag at any moment. It is in my dressing-room at home. I really think that should satisfy you, Lady Bracknell.

LADY BRACKNELL: Me, sir! What has it to do with me? You can hardly imagine that I and Lord Bracknell would dream of allowing our only daughter—a girl brought up with the utmost care—to marry into a cloak-room, and form an alliance with a parcel? Good morning, Mr. Worthing! (LADY BRACKNELL *sweeps out in majestic indignation.*)

JACK: Good morning! (ALGERNON, *from the other room, strikes up the Wedding March.* JACK *looks perfectly furious, and goes to the door.*) For goodness' sake don't play that ghastly tune, Algy! How idiotic you are! (*The music stops, and* ALGERNON *enters cheerily.*)

ALGERNON: Didn't it go off all right, old boy? You don't mean to say Gwendolen refused you? I know it is a way she has. She is always refusing people. I think it is most ill-natured of her.

JACK: Oh, Gwendolen is as right as a trivet. As far as she is concerned, we are engaged. Her mother is perfectly unbearable. Never met such a Gorgon . . . I don't really know what a Gorgon is like, but I am quite sure that Lady Bracknell is one. In any case, she is a monster, without being a myth, which is rather unfair. . . . I beg your pardon, Algy, I suppose I shouldn't talk about your own aunt in that way before you.

ALGERNON: My dear boy, I love hearing my relations abused. It is the only thing that makes me put up with them at all. Relations are simply a tedious pack of people, who haven't got the remotest knowledge of how to live, nor the smallest instinct about when to die.

JACK: Oh, that is nonsense!

ALGERNON: It isn't!

JACK: Well, I won't argue about the matter. You always want to argue about things.

ALGERNON: That is exactly what things were originally made for.

JACK: Upon my word, if I thought that, I'd shoot myself . . . (*A pause.*) You don't think there is any chance of Gwendolen becoming like her mother in about a hundred and fifty years, do you, Algy?

ALGERNON: All women become like their mothers. That is their tragedy. No man does. That's his.

JACK: Is that clever?

ALGERNON: It is perfectly phrased! and quite as true as any observation in civilized life should be.

JACK: I am sick to death of cleverness. Everybody is clever now-a-days. You can't go anywhere without meeting clever people. The thing has become an absolute public nuisance. I wish to goodness we had a few fools left.

ALGERNON: We have.

JACK: I should extremely like to meet them. What do they talk about?

ALGERNON: The fools? Oh! about the clever people, of course.

JACK: What fools!

ALGERNON: By the way, did you tell Gwendolen the truth about your being Ernest in town, and Jack in the country?

JACK: (*In a very patronising manner.*) My dear fellow, the truth isn't quite the sort of thing one tells to a nice, sweet, refined girl. What extraordinary ideas you have about the way to behave to a woman!

ALGERNON: The only way to behave to a woman is to make love to her, if she is pretty, and to someone else if she is plain.

JACK: Oh, that is nonsense.

ALGERNON: What about your brother? What about the profligate Ernest?

JACK: Oh, before the end of the week I shall have got rid of him. I'll say he died in Paris of apoplexy. Lots of people die of apoplexy, quite suddenly, don't they?

ALGERNON: Yes, but it's hereditary, my dear fellow. It's a sort of thing that runs in families. You had much better say a severe chill.

685 JACK: You are sure a severe chill isn't hereditary, or anything of that kind?

ALGERNON: Of course it isn't!

JACK: Very well, then. My poor brother Ernest is carried off suddenly in Paris, by a sever chill. That gets rid of him.

ALGERNON: But I thought you said that . . . Miss Cardew was 690 a little too interested in your poor brother Ernest? Won't she feel his loss a good deal?

JACK: Oh, that is all right. Cecily is not a silly, romantic girl, I am glad to say. She has got a capital appetite, goes for long walks, and pays no attention at all to her lessons.

695 ALGERNON: I would rather like to see Cecily.

JACK: I will take very good care you never do. She is excessively pretty, and she is only just eighteen.

ALGERNON: Have you told Gwendolen yet that you have an excessively pretty ward who is only just eighteen?

700 JACK: Oh! one doesn't blurt these things out to people. Cecily and Gwendolen are perfectly certain to be extremely great friends. I'll bet you anything you like that half an hour after they have met, they will be calling each other sister.

ALGERNON: Women only do that when they have called each 705 other a lot of other thing first. Now, my dear boy, if we want to get a good table at Willis's, we really must go and dress. Do you know it is nearly seven?

JACK: (Irritably.) Oh! it always is nearly seven.

ALGERNON: Well, I'm hungry.

710 JACK: I never knew you when you weren't. . . .

ALGERNON: What shall we do after dinner? Go to a theatre?

JACK: Oh, no! I loathe listening.

ALGERNON: Well, let us go to the Club?

JACK: Oh, no! I hate talking.

715 ALGERNON: Well, we might trot round to the Empire at ten?

JACK: Oh, no! can't bear looking at things. It is so silly.

ALGERNON: Well, what shall we do?

JACK: Nothing!

ALGERNON: It is awfully hard work doing nothing. However, 720 I don't mind hard work where there is no definite object of any kind.

(Enter LANE.)

LANE: Miss Fairfax.

(Enter GWENDOLEN. LANE goes out.)

ALGERNON: Gwendolen, upon my word!

GWENDOLEN: Algy, kindly turn your back. I have something 725 very particular to say to Mr. Worthing.

ALGERNON: Really, Gwendolen, I don't think I can allow this at all.

GWENDOLEN: Algy, you always adopt a strictly immoral attitude towards life. You are not quite old enough to do that. 730 (ALGERNON retires to the fireplace.)

JACK: My own darling!

GWENDOLEN: Ernest, we may never be married. From the expression on mamma's face I fear we never shall. Few parents now-a-days pay any regard to what their children 735 say to them. The old-fashioned respect for the young is fast dying out. Whatever influence I ever had over

mamma, I lost at the age of three. But although she may prevent us from becoming man and wife, and I may marry someone else, and marry often, nothing that she can possibly do can alter my eternal devotion to you. 740

JACK: Dear Gwendolen.

GWENDOLEN: The story of your romantic origin, as related to me by mamma, with unpleasing comments, has naturally stirred the deeper fibers of my nature. Your Christian name has an irresistible fascination. The simplicity of your 745 character make you exquisitely incomprehensible to me. Your town address at the Albany I have. What is your address in the country?

JACK: The Manor House, Woolton, Hertfordshire. (ALGERNON, who has been carefully listening, smiles to himself, and 750 writes the address on his shirt-cuff. Then picks up the Railway Guide.)

GWENDOLEN: There is a good postal service, I suppose? It may be necessary to do something desperate. That, of course, will require serious consideration. I will commu- 755 nicate with you daily.

JACK: My own one!

GWENDOLEN: How long do you remain in town?

JACK: Till Monday.

GWENDOLEN: Good! Algy, you may turn round now. 760

ALGERNON: Thanks, I've turned round already.

GWENDOLEN: You may also ring the bell.

JACK: You will let me see you to your carriage, my own darling?

GWENDOLEN: Certainly. 765

JACK: (To LANE, who now enters.) I will see Miss Fairfax out.

LANE: Yes, sir. (JACK and GWENDOLEN go off. LANE presents several letters on a salver to ALGERNON. It is to be surmised that they are bills, as ALGERNON, after looking at the envelopes, tears them up.) 770

ALGERNON: A glass of sherry, Lane.

LANE: Yes, sir.

ALGERNON: To-morrow, Lane, I'm going Bunburying.

LANE: Yes, sir.

ALGERNON: I shall probably not be back till Monday. You can 775 put up my dress clothes, my smoking jacket, and all the Bunbury suits . . .

LANE: Yes, sir. (Handing sherry.)

ALGERNON: I hope to-morrow will be a fine day, Lane.

LANE: It never is, sir. 780

ALGERNON: Lane, you're a perfect pessimist.

LANE: I do my best to give satisfaction, sir.

(Enter JACK. LANE goes off.)

JACK: There's a sensible, intellectual girl! the only girl I ever cared for in my life. (ALGERNON is laughing immoderately.) What on earth are you so amused at? 785

ALGERNON: Oh, I'm a little anxious about poor Bunbury, that's all.

JACK: If you don't take care, your friend Bunbury will get you into a serious scrape some day.

ALGERNON: I love scrapes. They are the only things that are 790 never serious.

JACK: Oh, that's nonsense, Algy. You never talk anything but nonsense.

ALGERNON: Nobody ever does. (JACK looks indignantly at him,

795   *and leaves the room.* ALGERNON *lights a cigarette, reads his shirt-cuff and smiles.*)

ACT TWO

Garden at the Manor House. A flight of gray stone steps leads up to the house. The garden, an old-fashioned one, full of roses. Time of year, July. Basket chairs, and a table covered with books, are set under a large yew tree.

(MISS PRISM *discovered seated at the table.* CECILY *is at the back watering flowers.*)

MISS PRISM: (*Calling.*) Cecily, Cecily! Surely such a utilitarian occupation as the watering of flowers is rather Moulton's duty than yours? Especially at a moment when intellectual pleasures await you. Your German grammar is on the table.
5   Pray open it at page fifteen. We will repeat yesterday's lesson.
CECILY: (*Coming over very slowly.*) But I don't like German. It isn't at all a becoming language. I know perfectly well that I look quite plain after my German lesson.
MISS PRISM: Child, you know how anxious your guardian is
10   that you should improve yourself in every way. He laid particular stress on your German, as he was leaving for town yesterday. Indeed, he always lays stress on your German when he is leaving for town.
CECILY: Dear Uncle Jack is so very serious! Sometimes he is
15   so serious that I think he cannot be quite well.
MISS PRISM: (*Drawing herself up.*) Your guardian enjoys the best of health, and his gravity of demeanour is especially to be commended in one so comparatively young as he is. I know no one who has a higher sense of duty and responsibility.
20   CECILY: I suppose that is why he often looks a little bored when we three are together.
MISS PRISM: Cecily! I am surprised at you. Mr. Worthing has many troubles in his life. Idle merriment and triviality would be out of place in his conversation. You must re-
25   member his constant anxiety about that unfortunate young man, his brother.
CECILY: I wish Uncle Jack would allow that unfortunate young man, his brother, to come down here sometimes. We might have a good influence over him, Miss Prism. I
30   am sure you certainly would. You know German, and geology, and things of that kind influence a man very much. (CECILY *begins to write in her diary.*)
MISS PRISM: (*Shaking her head.*) I do not think that even I could produce any effect on a character that, according to his own
35   brother's admission, is irretrievably weak and vacillating. Indeed, I am not sure that I would desire to reclaim him. I am not in favour of this modern mania for turning bad people into good people at a moment's notice. As a man sows so let him reap. You must put away your diary, Cecily. I really
40   don't see why you should keep a diary at all.
CECILY: I keep a diary in order to enter the wonderful secrets of my life. If I didn't write them down I should probably forget all about them.
MISS PRISM: Memory, my dear Cecily, is the diary that we all
45   carry about with us.
CECILY: Yes, but it usually chronicles the things that have never happened, and couldn't possibly have happened. I believe that Memory is responsible for nearly all the three-volume novels that Mudie sends us.

MISS PRISM: Do not speak slightingly of the three-volume   50
novel, Cecily. I wrote one myself in earlier days.
CECILY: Did you really, Miss Prism? How wonderfully clever you are! I hope it did not end happily? I don't like novels that end happily. They depress me so much.
MISS PRISM: The good ended happily, and the bad unhappily.   55
That is what Fiction means.
CECILY: I suppose so. But it seems very unfair. And was your novel ever published?
MISS PRISM: Alas! no. The manuscript unfortunately was abandoned. I use the word in the sense of lost or mislaid.   60
To your work, child, these speculations are profitless.
CECILY: (*Smiling.*) But I see dear Dr. Chasuble coming up through the garden.
MISS PRISM: (*Rising and advancing.*) Dr. Chasuble! This is indeed a pleasure.   65

(*Enter* CANON CHASUBLE.)

CHASUBLE: And how are we this morning? Miss Prism, you are, I trust, well?
CECILY: Miss Prism has just been complaining of a slight headache. I think it would do her so much good to have a short stroll with you in the park, Dr. Chasuble.   70
MISS PRISM: Cecily, I have not mentioned anything about a headache.
CECILY: No, dear Miss Prism, I know that, but I felt instinctively that you had a headache. Indeed I was thinking about that, and not about my German lesson, when the   75
Rector came in.
CHASUBLE: I hope, Cecily, you are not inattentive.
CECILY: Oh, I am afraid I am.
CHASUBLE: That is strange. Were I fortunate enough to be Miss Prism's pupil, I would hang upon her lips. (MISS   80
PRISM *glares.*) I spoke metaphorically.—My metaphor was drawn from bees. Ahem! Mr. Worthing, I suppose, has not returned from town yet?
MISS PRISM: We do not expect him till Monday afternoon.
CHASUBLE: Ah yes, he usually likes to spend his Sunday in   85
London. He is not one of those whose sole aim is enjoyment, as, by all accounts, that unfortunate young man, his brother, seems to be. But I must not disturb Egeria and her pupil any longer.
MISS PRISM: Egeria? My name is Lætitia, Doctor.   90
CHASUBLE: (*Bowing.*) A classical allusion merely, drawn from the Pagan authors. I shall see you both no doubt at Evensong.
MISS PRISM: I think, dear Doctor, I will have a stroll with you. I find I have a headache after all, and a walk might do it good.   95
CHASUBLE: With pleasure, Miss Prism, with pleasure. We might go as far as the schools and back.
MISS PRISM: That would be delightful. Cecily, you will read your Political Economy in my absence. The chapter on the Fall of the Rupee you may omit. It is somewhat too   100
sensational. Even these metallic problems have their melodramatic side.

(*Goes down the garden with* DR. CHASUBLE.)

CECILY: (*Picks up books and throws them back on table.*) Horrid Political Economy! Horrid Geography! Horrid, horrid German!   105

(*Enter* MERRIMAN *with a card on a salver.*)

MERRIMAN: Mr. Ernest Worthing has just driven over from the station. He has brought his luggage with him.

CECILY: (*Takes the card and reads it.*) "Mr. Ernest Worthing, B 4 The Albany, W." Uncle Jack's brother! Did you tell him Mr. Worthing was in town?

110

MERRIMAN: Yes, Miss. He seemed very much disappointed. I mentioned that you and Miss Prism were in the garden. He said he was anxious to speak to you privately for a moment.

CECILY: Ask Mr. Ernest Worthing to come here. I suppose you had better talk to the housekeeper about a room for him.

115

MERRIMAN: Yes, Miss.

(MERRIMAN *goes off.*)

CECILY: I have never met any really wicked person before. I feel rather frightened. I am so afraid he will look just like everyone else.

(*Enter* ALGERNON, *very gay and debonair.*)

He does!

120

ALGERNON: (*Raising his hat.*) You are my little cousin Cecily, I'm sure.

CECILY: You are under some strange mistake. I am not little. In fact, I am more than usually tall for my age. (ALGERNON *is rather taken aback.*) But I am your cousin Cecily. You, I see from your card, are Uncle Jack's brother, my cousin Ernest, my wicked cousin Ernest.

125

ALGERNON: Oh! I am not really wicked at all, cousin Cecily. You mustn't think that I am wicked.

130

CECILY: If you are not, then you have certainly been deceiving us all in a very inexcusable manner. I hope you have not been leading a double life, pretending to be wicked and being really good all the time. That would be hypocrisy.

ALGERNON: (*Looks at her in amazement.*) Oh! of course I have been rather reckless.

135

CECILY: I am glad to hear it.

ALGERNON: In fact, now you mention the subject, I have been very bad in my own small way.

CECILY: I don't think you should be so proud of that, though I am sure it must have been very pleasant.

140

ALGERNON: It is much pleasanter being here with you.

CECILY: I can't understand how you are here at all. Uncle Jack won't be back till Monday afternoon.

ALGERNON: That is a great disappointment. I am obliged to go up by the first train on Monday morning. I have a business appointment that I am anxious . . . to miss.

145

CECILY: Couldn't you miss it anywhere but in London?

ALGERNON: No; the appointment is in London.

CECILY: Well, I know, of course, how important it is not to keep a business engagement, if one wants to retain any sense of the beauty of life, but still I think you had better wait till Uncle Jack arrives. I know he wants to speak to you about your emigrating.

150

ALGERNON: About my what?

155

CECILY: Your emigrating. He has gone up to buy your outfit.

ALGERNON: I certainly wouldn't let Jack buy my outfit. He has no taste in neckties at all.

CECILY: I don't think you will require neckties. Uncle Jack is sending you to Australia.

ALGERNON: Australia! I'd sooner die.

160

CECILY: Well, he said at dinner on Wednesday night, that you would have to choose between this world, the next world, and Australia.

ALGERNON: Oh, well! The accounts I have received of Australia and the next world, are not particularly encouraging. This world is good enough for me, cousin Cecily.

165

CECILY: Yes, but are you good enough for it?

ALGERNON: I'm afraid I'm not that. That is why I want you to reform me. You might make that your mission, if you don't mind, cousin Cecily.

170

CECILY: I'm afraid I've not time, this afternoon.

ALGERNON: Well, would you mind my reforming myself this afternoon?

CECILY: That is rather Quixotic of you. But I think you should try.

175

ALGERNON: I will. I feel better already.

CECILY: You are looking a little worse.

ALGERNON: That is because I am hungry.

CECILY: How thoughtless of me. I should have remembered that when one is going to lead an entirely new life, one requires regular and wholesome meals. Won't you come in?

180

ALGERNON: Thank you. Might I have a button-hole first? I never have any appetite unless I have a button-hole first.

CECILY: A Maréchal Niel? (*Picks up scissors.*)

ALGERNON: No, I'd sooner have a pink rose.

185

CECILY: Why? (*Cuts a flower.*)

ALGERNON: Because you are like a pink rose, cousin Cecily.

CECILY: I don't think it can be right for you to talk to me like that. Miss Prism never says such things to me.

ALGERNON: Then Miss Prism is a short-sighted old lady. (CECILY *puts the rose in his button-hole.*) You are the prettiest girl I ever saw.

190

CECILY: Miss Prism says that all good looks are a snare.

ALGERNON: They are a snare that every sensible man would like to be caught in.

195

CECILY: Oh! I don't think I would care to catch a sensible man. I shouldn't know what to talk to him about.

(*They pass into the house.* MISS PRISM *and* DR. CHASUBLE *return.*)

MISS PRISM: You are too much alone, dear Dr. Chasuble. You should get married. A misanthrope I can understand—a womanthrope, never!

200

CHASUBLE: (*With a scholar's shudder.*) Believe me, I do not deserve so neologistic a phrase. The precept as well as the practice of the Primitive Church was distinctly against matrimony.

MISS PRISM: (*Sententiously.*) That is obviously the reason why the Primitive Church has not lasted up to the present day. And you do not seem to realize, dear Doctor, that by persistently remaining single, a man converts himself into a permanent public temptation. Men should be careful; this very celibacy leads weaker vessels astray.

205

210

CHASUBLE: But is a man not equally attractive when married?

MISS PRISM: No married man is ever attractive except to his wife.

CHASUBLE: And often, I've been told, not even to her.

MISS PRISM: That depends on the intellectual sympathies of the woman. Maturity can always be depended on. Ripeness can be trusted. Young women are green. (DR.

215

CHASUBLE *starts*.) I spoke horticulturally. My metaphor was drawn from fruits. But where is Cecily?

220 CHASUBLE: Perhaps she followed us to the schools.

(*Enter* JACK *slowly from the back of the garden. He is dressed in the deepest mourning, with crepe hatband and black gloves.*)

MISS PRISM: Mr. Worthing!

CHASUBLE: Mr. Worthing?

MISS PRISM: This is indeed a surprise. We did not look for you till Monday afternoon.

225 JACK: (*Shakes* MISS PRISM'*s hand in a tragic manner*.) I have returned sooner than I expected. Dr. Chasuble, I hope you are well?

CHASUBLE: Dear Mr. Worthing, I trust this garb of woe does not betoken some terrible calamity?

230 JACK: My brother.

MISS PRISM: More shameful debts and extravagance?

CHASUBLE: Still leading his life of pleasure?

JACK: (*Shaking his head*.) Dead!

CHASUBLE: Your brother Ernest dead?

235 JACK: Quite dead.

MISS PRISM: What a lesson for him! I trust he will profit by it.

CHASUBLE: Mr. Worthing, I offer you my sincere condolence. You have at least the consolation of knowing that you were always the most generous and forgiving of brothers.

240 JACK: Poor Ernest! He had many faults, but it is a sad, sad blow.

CHASUBLE: Very sad indeed. Were you with him at the end?

JACK: No. He died abroad; in Paris, in fact. I had a telegram last night from the manager of the Grand Hotel.

245 CHASUBLE: Was the cause of death mentioned?

JACK: A severe chill, it seems.

MISS PRISM: As a man sows, so shall he reap.

CHASUBLE: (*Raising his hand*.) Charity, dear Miss Prism, charity! None of us are perfect. I myself am peculiarly suscepti-

250 ble to draughts. Will the interment take place here?

JACK: No. He seems to have expressed a desire to be buried in Paris.

CHASUBLE: In Paris! (*Shakes his head*.) I fear that hardly points to any very serious state of mind at the last. You would no

255 doubt wish me to make some slight allusion to this tragic domestic affliction next Sunday. (JACK *presses his hand convulsively*.) My sermon on the meaning of the manna in the wilderness can be adapted to almost any occasion, joyful, or, as in the present case, distressing. (*All sigh*.) I have

260 preached it at harvest celebrations, christenings, confirmations, on days of humiliation and festal days. The last time I delivered it was in the Cathedral, as a charity sermon on behalf of the Society for the Prevention of Discontentment among the Upper Orders. The Bishop, who was

265 present, was much struck by some of the analogies I drew.

JACK: Ah, that reminds me, you mentioned christenings I think, Dr. Chasuble? I suppose you know how to christen all right? (DR. CHASUBLE *looks astounded*.) I mean, of course, you are continually christening, aren't you?

270 MISS PRISM: It is, I regret to say, one of the Rector's most constant duties in this parish. I have often spoken to the poorer classes on the subject. But they don't seem to know what thrift is.

CHASUBLE: But is there any particular infant in whom you are

interested, Mr. Worthing? Your brother was, I believe, un- 275
married, was he not?

JACK: Oh, yes.

MISS PRISM: (*Bitterly*.) People who live entirely for pleasure usually are.

JACK: But it is not for any child, dear Doctor. I am very fond 280
of children. No! the fact is, I would like to be christened myself, this afternoon, if you have nothing better to do.

CHASUBLE: But surely, Mr. Worthing, you have been christened already?

JACK: I don't remember anything about it. 285

CHASUBLE: But have you any grave doubts on the subject?

JACK: I certainly intend to have. Of course, I don't know if the thing would bother you in any way, or if you think I am a little too old now.

CHASUBLE: Not at all. The sprinkling, and, indeed, the im- 290
mersion of adults is a perfectly canonical practice.

JACK: Immersion!

CHASUBLE: You need have no apprehensions. Sprinkling is all that is necessary, or indeed I think advisable. Our weather is so changeable. At what hour would you wish the cere- 295
mony performed?

JACK: Oh, I might trot around about five if that would suit you.

CHASUBLE: Perfectly, perfectly! In fact I have two similar ceremonies to perform at that time. A case of twins that oc- 300
curred recently in one of the outlying cottages on your own estate. Poor Jenkins the carter, a most hard-working man.

JACK: Oh! I don't see much fun in being christened along with other babies. It would be childish. Would half-past 305
five do?

CHASUBLE: Admirably! Admirably! (*Takes out watch*.) And now, dear Mr. Worthing, I will not intrude any longer into a house of sorrow. I would merely beg you not to be too much bowed down by grief. What seem to us bitter trials at the moment are often blessings in disguise.

MISS PRISM: This seems to me a blessing of an extremely obvious kind. 310

(*Enter* CECILY *from the house*.)

CECILY: Uncle Jack! Oh, I am pleased to see you back. But what horrid clothes you have on! Do go and change them.

MISS PRISM: Cecily!

CHASUBLE: My child! my child! (CECILY *goes towards* JACK; *he kisses her brow in a melancholy manner*.) 315

CECILY: What is the matter, Uncle Jack? Do look happy! You look as if you had a toothache and I have such a surprise for you. Who do you think is in the dining-room? Your brother!

JACK: Who?

CECILY: Your brother Ernest. He arrived about half an hour 320
ago.

JACK: What nonsense! I haven't got a brother.

CECILY: Oh, don't say that. However badly he may have behaved to you in the past he is still your brother. You couldn't be so heartless as to disown him. I'll tell him to 325
come out. And you will shake hands with him, won't you, Uncle Jack? (*Runs back into the house*.)

CHASUBLE: These are very joyful tidings.

MISS PRISM: After we had all been resigned to his loss, his sudden return seems to me peculiarly distressing. 330

JACK: My brother is in the dining-room? I don't know what it all means. I think it is perfectly absurd.

(*Enter* ALGERNON *and* CECILY *hand in hand. They come slowly up to* JACK.)

JACK: Good heavens! (*Motions* ALGERNON *away.*)
ALGERNON: Brother John, I have come down from town to
335   tell you that I am very sorry for all the trouble I have given you, and that I intend to lead a better life in the future. (JACK *glares at him and does not take his hand.*)
CECILY: Uncle Jack, you are not going to refuse your own brother's hand?
340   JACK: Nothing will induce me to take his hand. I think his coming down here disgraceful. He knows perfectly well why.
CECILY: Uncle Jack, do be nice. There is some good in everyone. Ernest has just been telling me about his poor invalid friend, Mr. Bunbury, whom he goes to visit so often. And
345   surely there must be much good in one who is kind to an invalid, and leaves the pleasures of London to sit by a bed of pain.
JACK: Oh, he has been talking about Bunbury, has he?
CECILY: Yes, he has told me all about poor Mr. Bunbury, and
350   his terrible state of health.
JACK: Bunbury! Well, I won't have him talk to you about Bunbury or about anything else. It is enough to drive one perfectly frantic.
ALGERNON: Of course I admit that the faults were all on my
355   side. But I must say that I think that Brother John's coldness to me is peculiarly painful. I expected a more enthusiastic welcome, especially considering it is the first time I have come here.
CECILY: Uncle Jack, if you don't shake hands with Ernest I
360   will never forgive you.
JACK: Never forgive me?
CECILY: Never, never, never!
JACK: Well, this is the last time I shall ever do it. (*Shakes hands with* ALGERNON *and glares.*)
365   CHASUBLE: It's pleasant, is it not, to see so perfect a reconciliation? I think we might leave the two brothers together.
MISS PRISM: Cecily, you will come with us.
CECILY: Certainly, Miss Prism. My little task of reconciliation is over.
370   CHASUBLE: You have done a beautiful action to-day, dear child.
MISS PRISM: We must not be premature in our judgments.
CECILY: I feel very happy. (*They all go off.*)
JACK: You young scoundrel, Algy, you must get out of this place as soon as possible. I don't allow any Bunburying here.

(*Enter* MERRIMAN.)

375   MERRIMAN: I have put Mr. Ernest's things in the room next to yours, sir. I suppose that is all right?
JACK: What?
MERRIMAN: Mr. Ernest's luggage, sir. I have unpacked it and put it in the room next to your own.
380   JACK: His luggage?
MERRIMAN: Yes, sir. Three portmanteaus, a dressing-case, two hat-boxes, and a large luncheon-basket.
ALGERNON: I am afraid I can't stay more than a week this time.

JACK: Merriman, order the dog-cart at once. Mr. Ernest has   385
been suddenly called back to town.
MERRIMAN: Yes, sir. (*Goes back into the house.*)
ALGERNON: What a fearful liar you are, Jack. I have not been called back to town at all.
JACK: Yes, you have.   390
ALGERNON: I haven't heard anyone call me.
JACK: Your duty as a gentleman calls you back.
ALGERNON: My duty as a gentleman has never interfered with my pleasures in the smallest degree.
JACK: I can quite understand that.   395
ALGERNON: Well, Cecily is a darling.
JACK: You are not to talk of Miss Cardew like that. I don't like it.
ALGERNON: Well, I don't like your clothes. You look perfectly ridiculous in them. Why on earth don't you go up and change? It is perfectly childish to be in deep mourning for   400
a man who is actually staying for a whole week with you in your house as a guest. I call it grotesque.
JACK: You are certainly not staying with me for a whole week as a guest or anything else. You have got to leave . . . by the four-five train.   405
ALGERNON: I certainly won't leave you so long as you are in mourning. It would be most unfriendly. If I were in mourning you would stay with me, I suppose. I should think it very unkind if you didn't.
JACK: Well, will you go if I change my clothes?   410
ALGERNON: Yes, if you are not too long. I never saw anybody take so long to dress, and with such little result.
JACK: Well, at any rate, that is better than being always over-dressed as you are.
ALGERNON: If I am occasionally a little over-dressed, I make   415
up for it by being always immensely over-educated.
JACK: Your vanity is ridiculous, your conduct an outrage, and your presence in my garden utterly absurd. However, you have got to catch the four-five, and I hope you will have a pleasant journey back to town. This Bunburying, as you call   420
it, has not been a great success for you. (*Goes into the house.*)
ALGERNON: I think it has been a great success. I'm in love with Cecily, and that is everything. (*Enter* CECILY *at the back of the garden. She picks up the can and begins to water the flowers.*) But I must see her before I go, and make arrange-   425
ments for another Bunbury. Ah, there she is.
CECILY: Oh, I merely came back to water the roses. I thought you were with Uncle Jack.
ALGERNON: He's gone to order the dog-cart for me.
CECILY: Oh, is he going to take you for a nice drive?   430
ALGERNON: He's going to send me away.
CECILY: Then have we got to part?
ALGERNON: I am afraid so. It's a very painful parting.
CECILY: It is always painful to part from people whom one has known for a very brief space of time. The absence of old   435
friends one can endure with equanimity. But even a momentary separation from anyone to whom one has just been introduced is almost unbearable.
ALGERNON: Thank you.

(*Enter* MERRIMAN.)

MERRIMAN: The dog-cart is at the door, sir. (ALGERNON *looks*   440
appealingly at CECILY.)
CECILY: It can wait, Merriman . . . for . . . five minutes.

MERRIMAN: Yes, miss.

(*Exit* MERRIMAN.)

ALGERNON: I hope, Cecily, I shall not offend you if I state quite
445 frankly and openly that you seem to me to be in every way
the visible personification of absolute perfection.
CECILY: I think your frankness does you great credit, Ernest.
If you will allow me I will copy your remarks into my diary. (*Goes over to table and begins writing in diary.*)
450 ALGERNON: Do you really keep a diary? I'd give any thing to
look at it. May I?
CECILY: Oh, no. (*Puts her hand over it.*) You see, it is simply a
very young girl's record of her own thoughts and impressions, and consequently meant for publication. When it
455 appears in volume form I hope you will order a copy. But
pray, Ernest, don't stop. I delight in taking down from dictation. I have reached "absolute perfection." You can go
on. I am quite ready for more.
ALGERNON: (*Somewhat taken aback.*) Ahem! Ahem!
460 CECILY: Oh, don't cough, Ernest. When one is dictating one
should speak fluently and not cough. Besides, I don't
know how to spell a cough. (*Writes as* ALGERNON *speaks.*)
ALGERNON: (*Speaking very rapidly.*) Cecily, ever since I first
looked upon your wonderful and incomparable beauty, I
465 have dared to love you wildly, passionately, devotedly,
hopelessly.
CECILY: I don't think that you should tell me that you love
me wildly, passionately, devotedly, hopelessly. Hopelessly
doesn't seem to make much sense, does it?
470 ALGERNON: Cecily!

(*Enter* MERRIMAN.)

MERRIMAN: The dog-cart is waiting, sir.
ALGERNON: Tell it to come round next week, at the same hour.
MERRIMAN: (*Looks at* CECILY, *who makes no sign.*) Yes, sir.

(MERRIMAN *retires.*)

CECILY: Uncle Jack would be very much annoyed if he knew
475 you were staying on till next week, at the same hour.
ALGERNON: Oh, I don't care about Jack. I don't care for anybody in the whole world but you. I love you, Cecily. You
will marry me, won't you?
CECILY: You silly you! Of course. Why, we have been engaged
480 for the last three months.
ALGERNON: For the last three months?
CECILY: Yes, it will be exactly three months on Thursday.
ALGERNON: But how did we become engaged?
CECILY: Well, ever since dear Uncle Jack first confessed to us
485 that he had a younger brother who was very wicked and
bad, you of course have formed the chief topic of conversation between myself and Miss Prism. And of course a
man who is much talked about is always very attractive.
One feels there must be something in him after all. I dare-
490 say it was foolish of me, but I fell in love with you, Ernest.
ALGERNON: Darling! And when was the engagement actually
settled?
CECILY: On the 14th of February last. Worn out by your entire
ignorance of my existence, I determined to end the matter

one way or the other, and after a long struggle with myself 495
I accepted you under this dear old tree here. The next day I
bought this little ring in your name, and this is the little ban-
gle with the true lovers' knot I promised you always to wear.
ALGERNON: Did I give you this? It's very pretty, isn't it?
CECILY: Yes, you've wonderfully good taste, Ernest. It's the 500
excuse I've always given for your leading such a bad life.
And this is the box in which I keep all your dear letters.
(*Kneels at table, opens box, and produces letters tied up with
blue ribbon.*)
ALGERNON: My letters! But my own sweet Cecily, I have 505
never written you any letters.
CECILY: You need hardly remind me of that, Ernest. I remember only too well that I was forced to write your letters for you. I wrote always three times a week, and
sometimes oftener. 510
ALGERNON: Oh, do let me read them, Cecily?
CECILY: Oh, I couldn't possibly. They would make you far too
conceited. (*Replaces box.*) The three you wrote me after I
had broken off the engagement are so beautiful, and so
badly spelled, that even now I can hardly read them with- 515
out crying a little.
ALGERNON: But was our engagement ever broken off?
CECILY: Of course it was. On the 22nd of last March. You can
see the entry if you like. (*Shows diary.*) "Today I broke off 520
my engagement with Ernest. I feel it is better to do so. The
weather still continues charming."
ALGERNON: But why on earth did you break it off? What had
I done? I had done nothing at all. Cecily, I am very much
hurt indeed to hear you broke it off. Particularly when the 525
weather was so charming.
CECILY: It would hardly have been a really serious engage-
ment if it hadn't been broken off at least once. But I for-
gave you before the week was out.
ALGERNON: (*Crossing to her, and kneeling.*) What a perfect an- 530
gel you are, Cecily.
CECILY: You dear romantic boy. (*He kisses her, she puts her fin-
gers through his hair.*) I hope your hair curls naturally, does
it?
ALGERNON: Yes, darling, with a little help from others. 535
CECILY: I am so glad.
ALGERNON: You'll never break off our engagement again,
Cecily?
CECILY: I don't think I could break it off now that I have actually met you. Besides, of course, that is the question of 540
your name.
ALGERNON: Yes, of course. (*Nervously.*)
CECILY: You must not laugh at me, darling, but it had always
been a girlish dream of mine to love some one whose
name was Ernest. (ALGERNON *rises,* CECILY *also.*) There is 545
something in that name that seems to inspire absolute
confidence. I pity any poor married woman whose husband is not called Ernest.
ALGERNON: But, my dear child, do you mean to say you
could not love me if I had some other name? 550
CECILY: But what name?
ALGERNON: Oh, any name you like—Algernon, for instance.
. . .
CECILY: But I don't like the name of Algernon.
ALGERNON: Well, my own dear, sweet, loving little darling, I re- 555
ally can't see why you should object to the name of Alger-

non. It is not at all a bad name. In fact, it is rather an aristocratic name. Half of the chaps who get into the Bankruptcy
Court are called Algernon. But seriously, Cecily . . . (*Moving*
560 *to her.*) . . . if my name was Algy, couldn't you love me?

CECILY: I might respect you, Ernest, I might admire your
character, but I fear that I should not be able to give you
my undivided attention.

ALGERNON: Ahem! Cecily! (*Picking up hat.*) Your Rector here
565 is, I suppose, thoroughly experienced in the practice of all
the rites and ceremonials of the church?

CECILY: Oh, yes. Dr. Chasuble is a most learned man. He has
never written a single book, so you can imagine how
much he knows.

570 ALGERNON: I must see him at once on a most important
christening—I mean on most important business.

CECILY: Oh!

ALGERNON: I sha'n't be away more than half an hour.

CECILY: Considering that we have been engaged since Feb-
575 ruary the 14th, and that I only met you to-day for the first
time, I think it is rather hard that you should leave me for
so long a period as half an hour. Couldn't you make it
twenty minutes?

ALGERNON: I'll be back in no time. (*Kisses her and rushes down*
580 *the garden.*)

CECILY: What an impetuous boy he is. I like his hair so much.
I must enter his proposal in my diary.

(*Enter* MERRIMAN.)

MERRIMAN: A Miss Fairfax has just called to see Mr. Worthing.
On very important business, Miss Fairfax states.

585 CECILY: Isn't Mr. Worthing in his library?

MERRIMAN: Mr. Worthing went over in the direction of the
Rectory some time ago.

CECILY: Pray ask the lady to come out here; Mr. Worthing is
sure to be back soon. And you can bring tea.

590 MERRIMAN: Yes, miss.

(*Goes out.*)

CECILY: Miss Fairfax! I suppose one of the many good elderly
women who are associated with Uncle Jack in some of his
philanthropic work in London. I don't quite like women
who are interested in philanthropic work. I think it is so
595 forward of them.

(*Enter* MERRIMAN.)

MERRIMAN: Miss Fairfax.

(*Enter* GWENDOLEN. *Exit* MERRIMAN.)

CECILY: (*Advancing to meet her.*) Pray let me introduce myself
to you. My name is Cecily Cardew.

GWENDOLEN: Cecily Cardew? (*Moving to her and shaking hands.*)
600 What a very sweet name! Something tells me that we are
going to be great friends. I like you already more than I can
say. My first impressions of people are never wrong.

CECILY: How nice of you to like me so much after we have
known each other such a comparatively short time. Pray
605 sit down.

GWENDOLEN: (*Still standing up.*) I may call you Cecily, may I
not?

CECILY: With pleasure!

GWENDOLEN: And you will always call me Gwendolen, won't
you? 610

CECILY: If you wish.

GWENDOLEN: Then that is all quite settled, is it not?

CECILY: I hope so. (*A pause. They both sit down together.*)

GWENDOLEN: Perhaps this might be a favorable opportunity
for my mentioning who I am. My father is Lord Brack- 615
nell. You have never heard of papa, I suppose?

CECILY: I don't think so.

GWENDOLEN: Outside the family circle, papa, I am glad to say,
is entirely unknown. I think that is quite as it should be.
The home seems to me to be the proper sphere for the 620
man. And certainly once a man begins to neglect his domestic duties he becomes painfully effeminate, does he
not? And I don't like that. It makes men so very attractive.
Cecily, mamma, whose views on education are remarkably
strict, has brought me up to be extremely short-sighted; it 625
is part of her system; so do you mind my looking at you
through my glasses?

CECILY: Oh, not at all, Gwendolen. I am very fond of being
looked at.

GWENDOLEN: (*After examining* CECILY *carefully through a* 630
lorgnette.) You are here on a short visit, I suppose.

CECILY: Oh, no, I live here.

GWENDOLEN: (*Severely.*) Really? Your mother, no doubt, or
some female relative of advanced years, resides here also?

CECILY: Oh, no. I have no mother, nor, in fact, any relations. 635

GWENDOLEN: Indeed?

CECILY: My dear guardian, with the assistance of Miss Prism,
has the arduous task of looking after me.

GWENDOLEN: Your guardian?

CECILY: Yes, I am Mr. Worthing's ward. 640

GWENDOLEN: Oh! It is strange he never mentioned to me
that he had a ward. How secretive of him! He grows more
interesting hourly. I am not sure, however, that the news
inspires me with feelings of unmixed delight. (*Rising and
going to her.*) I am very fond of you, Cecily; I have liked 645
you ever since I met you. But I am bound to state that
now that I know that you are Mr. Worthing's ward, I cannot help expressing a wish you were—well, just a little
older than you seem to be—and not quite so very allur-
ing in appearance. In fact, if I may speak candidly— 650

CECILY: Pray do! I think that whenever one has anything unpleasant to say, one should always be quite candid.

GWENDOLEN: Well, to speak with perfect candour, Cecily, I
wish that you were fully forty-two, and more than usually
plain for your age. Ernest has a strong upright nature. He 655
is the very soul of truth and honour. Disloyalty would be
as impossible to him as deception. But even men of the
noblest possible moral character are extremely susceptible
to the influence of the physical charms of others. Modern,
no less than Ancient History, supplies us with many most 660
painful examples of what I refer to. If it were not so, indeed, History would be quite unreadable.

CECILY: I beg your pardon, Gwendolen, did you say Ernest?

GWENDOLEN: Yes.

CECILY: Oh, but it is not Mr. Ernest Worthing who is my 665
guardian. It is his brother—his elder brother.

GWENDOLEN: (*Sitting down again.*) Ernest never mentioned to me that he had a brother.

CECILY: I am sorry to say they have not been on good terms for a long time.

GWENDOLEN: Ah! that accounts for it. And now that I think of it I have never heard any man mention his brother. The subject seems distasteful to most men. Cecily, you have lifted a load from my mind. I was growing almost anxious. It would have been terrible if any cloud had come across a friendship like ours, would it not? Of course you are quite, quite sure that it is not Mr. Ernest Worthing who is your guardian?

CECILY: Quite sure. (*A pause.*) In fact, I am going to be his.

GWENDOLEN: (*Enquiringly.*) I beg your pardon?

CECILY: (*Rather shy and confidingly.*) Dearest Gwendolen, there is no reason why I should make a secret of it to you. Our little county newspaper is sure to chronicle the fact next week. Mr. Ernest Worthing and I are engaged to be married.

GWENDOLEN: (*Quite politely, rising.*) My darling Cecily, I think there must be some slight error. Mr. Ernest Worthing is engaged to me. The announcement will appear in the *Morning Post* on Saturday at the latest.

CECILY: (*Very politely, rising.*) I am afraid you must be under some misconception. Ernest proposed to me exactly ten minutes ago. (*Shows diary.*)

GWENDOLEN: (*Examines diary through her lorgnette carefully.*) It is certainly very curious, for he asked me to be his wife yesterday afternoon at 5:30. If you would care to verify the incident, pray do so. (*Produces diary of her own.*) I never travel without my diary. One should always have something sensational to read in the train. I am so sorry, dear Cecily, if it is any disappointment to you, but I am afraid *I* have the prior claim.

CECILY: It would distress me more than I can tell you, dear Gwendolen, if it caused you any mental or physical anguish, but I feel bound to point out that since Ernest proposed to you he clearly has changed his mind.

GWENDOLEN: (*Meditatively.*) If the poor fellow has been entrapped into any foolish promise I shall consider it my duty to rescue him at once, and with a firm hand.

CECILY: (*Thoughtfully and sadly.*) Whatever unfortunate entanglement my dear boy may have got into, I will never reproach him with it after we are married.

GWENDOLEN: Do you allude to me, Miss Cardew, as an entanglement? You are presumptuous. On an occasion of this kind it becomes more than a moral duty to speak one's mind. It becomes a pleasure.

CECILY: Do you suggest, Miss Fairfax, that I entrapped Ernest into an engagement? How dare you? This is no time for wearing the shallow mask of manners. When I see a spade I call it a spade.

GWENDOLEN: (*Satirically.*) I am glad to say that I have never seen a spade. It is obvious that our social spheres have been widely different.

(*Enter* MERRIMAN, *followed by the footman. He carries a salver, table-cloth, and plate-stand.* CECILY *is about to retort. The presence of the servants exercises a restraining influence, under which both girls chafe.*)

MERRIMAN: Shall I lay tea here as usual, miss?

CECILY: (*Sternly, in a calm voice.*) Yes, as usual. (MERRIMAN *begins to clear and lay cloth. A long pause.* CECILY *and* GWENDOLEN *glare at each other.*)

GWENDOLEN: Are there many interesting walks in the vicinity, Miss Cardew?

CECILY: Oh, yes, a great many. From the top of one of the hills quite close one can see five counties.

GWENDOLEN: Five counties! I don't think I should like that. I hate crowds.

CECILY: (*Sweetly.*) I suppose that is why you live in town? (GWENDOLEN *bites her lip, and beats her foot nervously with her parasol.*)

GWENDOLEN: (*Looking around.*) Quite a well-kept garden this is, Miss Cardew.

CECILY: So glad you like it, Miss Fairfax.

GWENDOLEN: I had no idea there were any flowers in the country.

CECILY: Oh, flowers are as common here, Miss Fairfax, as people are in London.

GWENDOLEN: Personally I cannot understand how anybody manages to exist in the country, if anybody who is anybody does. The country always bores me to death.

CECILY: Ah! This is what the newspapers call agricultural depression, is it not? I believe the aristocracy are suffering very much from it just at present. It is almost an epidemic amongst them, I have been told. May I offer you some tea, Miss Fairfax?

GWENDOLEN: (*With elaborate politeness.*) Thank you. (*Aside.*) Detestable girl! But I require tea!

CECILY: (*Sweetly.*) Sugar?

GWENDOLEN: (*Superciliously.*) No, thank you. Sugar is not fashionable any more. (CECILY *looks angrily at her, takes up the tongs and puts four lumps of sugar into the cup.*)

CECILY: (*Severely.*) Cake or bread and butter?

GWENDOLEN: (*In a bored manner.*) Bread and butter, please. Cake is rarely seen at the best houses nowadays.

CECILY: (*Cuts a very large slice of cake, and puts it on the tray.*) Hand that to Miss Fairfax. (MERRIMAN *does so, and goes out with footman.* GWENDOLEN *drinks the tea and makes a grimace. Puts down cup at once, reaches out her hand to the bread and butter, looks at it, and finds it is cake. Rises in indignation.*)

GWENDOLEN: You have filled my tea with lumps of sugar, and though I asked most distinctly for bread and butter, you have given me cake. I am known for the gentleness of my disposition, and the extraordinary sweetness of my nature, but I warn you, Miss Cardew, you may go too far.

CECILY: (*Rising.*) To save my poor, innocent, trusting boy from the machinations of any other girl there are no lengths to which I would not go.

GWENDOLEN: From the moment I saw you I distrusted you. I felt that you were false and deceitful. I am never deceived in such matters. My first impressions of people are invariably right.

CECILY: It seems to me, Miss Fairfax, that I am trespassing on your valuable time. No doubt you have many other calls of a similar character to make in the neighbourhood.

(*Enter* JACK.)

GWENDOLEN: (*Catching sight of him.*) Ernest! My own Ernest!

JACK: Gwendolen! Darling! (*Offers to kiss her.*)

GWENDOLEN: (*Drawing back.*) A moment! May I ask if you are engaged to be married to this young lady? (*Points to* CECILY.)

JACK: (*Laughing.*) To dear little Cecily! Of course not! What could have put such an idea into your pretty little head?

785 GWENDOLEN: Thank you. You may. (*Offers her cheek.*)

CECILY: (*Very sweetly.*) I knew there must be some misunderstanding, Miss Fairfax. The gentleman whose arm is at present around your waist is my dear guardian, Mr. John Worthing.

790 GWENDOLEN: I beg your pardon?

CECILY: This is Uncle Jack.

GWENDOLEN: (*Receding.*) Jack! Oh!

(*Enter* ALGERNON.)

CECILY: Here is Ernest.

ALGERNON: (*Goes straight over to* CECILY *without noticing anyone*
795 *else.*) My own love! (*Offers to kiss her.*)

CECILY: (*Drawing back.*) A moment, Ernest! May I ask you—are you engaged to be married to this young lady?

ALGERNON: (*Looking round.*) To what young lady? Good heavens! Gwendolen!

800 CECILY: Yes, to good heavens, Gwendolen, I mean to Gwendolen.

ALGERNON: (*Laughing.*) Of course not! What could have put such an idea into your pretty little head?

CECILY: Thank you. (*Presenting her cheek to be kissed.*) You may.
805 (ALGERNON *kisses her.*)

GWENDOLEN: I felt there was some slight error, Miss Cardew. The gentleman who is now embracing you is my cousin, Mr. Algernon Moncrieff.

CECILY: (*Breaking away from* ALGERNON.) Algernon Moncrieff!
810 Oh! (*The two girls move towards each other and put their arms round each other's waists as if for protection.*)

CECILY: Are you called Algernon?

ALGERNON: I cannot deny it.

CECILY: Oh!

815 GWENDOLEN: Is your name really John?

JACK: (*Standing rather proudly.*) I could deny it if I liked. I could deny anything if I liked. But my name certainly is John. It has been John for years.

CECILY: (*To* GWENDOLEN.) A gross deception has been prac-
820 ticed on both of us.

GWENDOLEN: My poor wounded Cecily!

CECILY: My sweet, wronged Gwendolen!

GWENDOLEN: (*Slowing and seriously.*) You will call me sister, will you not? (*They embrace.* JACK *and* ALGERNON *groan and*
825 *walk up and down.*)

CECILY: (*Rather brightly.*) There is just one question I would like to be allowed to ask my guardian.

GWENDOLEN: An admirable idea! Mr. Worthing, there is just one question I would like to be permitted to put to you.
830 Where is your brother Ernest? We are both engaged to be married to your brother Ernest, so it is a matter of some importance to us to know where your brother Ernest is at present.

JACK: (*Slowly and hesitatingly.*) Gwendolen—Cecily—it is very
835 painful for me to be forced to speak the truth. It is the first time in my life that I have ever been reduced to such a painful position, and I am really quite inexperienced in doing anything of the kind. However I will tell you quite frankly that I have no brother Ernest. I have no brother at
840 all. I never had a brother in my life, and I certainly have not the smallest intention of ever having one in the future.

CECILY: (*Surprised.*) No brother at all?

JACK: (*Cheerily.*) None!

GWENDOLEN: (*Severely.*) Had you never a brother of any kind?

JACK: (*Pleasantly.*) Never. Not even of any kind. 845

GWENDOLEN: I am afraid it is quite clear, Cecily, that neither of us is engaged to be married to anyone.

CECILY: It is not a very pleasant position for a young girl suddenly to find herself in. Is it?

GWENDOLEN: Let us go into the house. They will hardly ven- 850 ture to come after us there.

CECILY: No, men are so cowardly, aren't they? (*They retire into the house with scornful looks.*)

JACK: This ghastly state of things is what you call Bunbury-ing, I suppose? 855

ALGERNON: Yes, and a perfectly wonderful Bunbury it is. The most wonderful Bunbury I have ever had in my life.

JACK: Well, you've no right whatsoever to Bunbury here.

ALGERNON: That is absurd. One has a right to Bunbury any-where one chooses. Every serious Bunburyist knows that. 860

JACK: Serious Bunburyist! Good heavens!

ALGERNON: Well, one must be serious about something, if one wants to have any amusement in life. I happen to be seri-ous about Bunburying. What on earth you are serious about I haven't got the remotest idea. About everything, I 865 should fancy. You have such an absolutely trivial nature.

JACK: Well, the only small satisfaction I have in the whole of this wretched business is that your friend Bunbury is quite exploded. You won't be able to run down to the country quite so often as you used to do, dear Algy. And a very 870 good thing, too.

ALGERNON: Your brother is a little off colour, isn't he, dear Jack? You won't be able to disappear to London quite so frequently as your wicked custom was. And not a bad thing, either. 875

JACK: As for your conduct towards Miss Cardew, I must say that your taking in a sweet, simple, innocent girl like that is quite inexcusable. To say nothing of the fact that she is my ward.

ALGERNON: I can see no possible defence at all for your de- 880 ceiving a brilliant, clever, thoroughly experienced young lady like Miss Fairfax. To say nothing of the fact that she is my cousin.

JACK: I wanted to be engaged to Gwendolen, that is all. I love her. 885

ALGERNON: Well, I simply wanted to be engaged to Cecily. I adore her.

JACK: There is certainly no chance of your marrying Miss Cardew.

ALGERNON: I don't think there is much likelihood, Jack, of 890 you and Miss Fairfax being united.

JACK: Well, that is no business of yours.

ALGERNON: If it was my business, I wouldn't talk about it. (*Begins to eat muffins.*) It is very vulgar to talk about one's business. Only people like stock-brokers do that, and then 895 merely at dinner parties.

JACK: How you can sit there, calmly eating muffins, when we are in this horrible trouble, I can't make out. You seem to me to be perfectly heartless.

ALGERNON: Well, I can't eat muffins in an agitated manner. The 900 butter would probably get on my cuffs. One should always eat muffins quite calmly. It is the only way to eat them.

JACK: I say it's perfectly heartless your eating muffins at all, under the circumstances.

905 ALGERNON: When I am in trouble, eating is the only thing that consoles me. Indeed, when I am in really great trouble, as anyone who knows me intimately will tell you, I refuse everything except food and drink. At the present moment I am eating muffins because I am unhappy. Besides, I am particularly fond of muffins. (*Rising.*)

910 JACK: (*Rising.*) Well, that is no reason why you should eat them all in that greedy way. (*Takes muffin from* ALGERNON.)

ALGERNON: (*Offering tea-cake.*) I wish you would have tea-cake instead. I don't like tea-cake.

915 JACK: Good heavens! I suppose a man may eat his own muffins in his own garden.

ALGERNON: But you have just said it was perfectly heartless to eat muffins.

JACK: I said it was perfectly heartless of you, under the circumstances. That is a very different thing.

920 ALGERNON: That may be. But the muffins are the same. (*He seizes the muffin dish from* JACK.)

JACK: Algy, I wish to goodness you would go.

ALGERNON: You can't possibly ask me to go without having some dinner. It's absurd. I never go without my dinner. No one ever does, except vegetarians and people like that. Besides I have just made arrangements with Dr. Chasuble to be christened at a quarter to six under the name of Ernest.

925

JACK: My dear fellow, the sooner you give up that nonsense the better. I made arrangements this morning with Dr. Chasuble to be christened myself at 5:30, and I naturally will take the name of Ernest. Gwendolen would wish it. We can't both be christened Ernest. It's absurd. Besides, I have a perfect right to be christened if I like. There is no evidence at all that I ever have been christened by anybody. I should think it extremely probable I never was, and so does Dr. Chasuble. It is entirely different in your case. You have been christened already.

930

935

ALGERNON: Yes, but I have not been christened for years.

940 JACK: Yes, but you have been christened. That is the important thing.

ALGERNON: Quite so. So I know my constitution can stand it. If you are not quite sure about your ever having been christened, I must say I think it rather dangerous your venturing on it now. It might make you very unwell. You can hardly have forgotten that someone very closely connected with you was very nearly carried off this week in Paris by a severe chill.

945

JACK: Yes, but you said yourself that a severe chill was not hereditary.

950

ALGERNON: It usedn't to be, I know—but I daresay it is now. Science is always making wonderful improvements in things.

JACK: (*Picking up the muffin-dish.*) Oh, that is nonsense; you are always talking nonsense.

955

ALGERNON: Jack, you are at the muffins again! I wish you wouldn't. There are only two left. (*Takes them.*) I told you I was particularly fond of muffins.

JACK: But I hate tea-cake.

960 ALGERNON: Why on earth then do you allow tea-cake to be served up for your guests? What ideas you have of hospitality!

JACK: Algernon! I have already told you to go. I don't want you here. Why don't you go?

ALGERNON: I haven't quite finished my tea yet, and there is 965 still one muffin left. (JACK *groans, and sinks into a chair.* ALGERNON *still continues eating.*)

ACT THREE

Morning-room at the Manor House. GWENDOLEN *and* CECILY *are at the window, looking out into the garden.*

GWENDOLEN: The fact that they did not follow us at once into the house, as anyone else would have done, seems to me to show that they have some sense of shame left.

CECILY: They have been eating muffins. That looks like repentance. 5

GWENDOLEN: (*After a pause.*) They don't seem to notice us at all. Couldn't you cough?

GWENDOLEN: They're looking at us. What effrontery!

CECILY: They're approaching. That's very forward of them.

GWENDOLEN: Let us preserve a dignified silence. 10

CECILY: Certainly. It's the only thing to do now.

(*Enter* JACK, *followed by* ALGERNON. *They whistle some dreadful popular air from a British opera.*)

GWENDOLEN: This dignified silence seems to produce an unpleasant effect.

CECILY: A most distasteful one.

GWENDOLEN: But we will not be the first to speak. 15

CECILY: Certainly not.

GWENDOLEN: Mr. Worthing, I have something very particular to ask you. Much depends on your reply.

CECILY: Gwendolen, your common sense is invaluable. Mr. Moncrieff, kindly answer me the following question. Why 20 did you pretend to be my guardian's brother?

ALGERNON: In order that I might have an opportunity of meeting you.

CECILY: (*To* GWENDOLEN.) That certainly seems a satisfactory explanation, does it not? 25

GWENDOLEN: Yes, dear, if you can believe him.

CECILY: I don't. But that does not affect the wonderful beauty of his answer.

GWENDOLEN: True. In matters of grave importance, style, not sincerity, is the vital thing. Mr. Worthing, what explanation 30 can you offer to me for pretending to have a brother? Was it in order that you might have an opportunity of coming up to town to see me as often as possible?

JACK: Can you doubt it, Miss Fairfax?

GWENDOLEN: I have the gravest doubts upon the subject. But 35 I intend to crush them. This is not the moment for German skepticism. (*Moving to* CECILY.) Their explanations appear to be quite satisfactory, especially Mr. Worthing's. That seems to me to have the stamp of truth upon it.

CECILY: I am more than content with what Mr. Moncrieff 40 said. His voice alone inspires one with absolute credulity.

GWENDOLEN: Then you think we should forgive them?

CECILY: Yes. I mean no.

GWENDOLEN: True! I had forgotten. There are principles at stake that one cannot surrender. Which of us should tell 45 them? The task is not a pleasant one.

CECILY: Could we not both speak at the same time?

GWENDOLEN: An excellent idea! I nearly always speak at the same time as other people. Will you take the time from me?

50 CECILY: Certainly. (GWENDOLEN *beats time with uplifted finger.*)

GWENDOLEN *and* CECILY: (*Speaking together.*) Your Christian names are still an insuperable barrier. That is all!

JACK *and* ALGERNON: (*Speaking together.*) Our Christian
55 names! Is that all? But we are going to be christened this afternoon.

GWENDOLEN: (*To* JACK.) For my sake you are prepared to do this terrible thing?

JACK: I am.

60 CECILY: (*To* ALGERNON.) To please me you are ready to face this fearful ordeal?

ALGERNON: I am!

GWENDOLEN: How absurd to talk of the equality of the sexes! Where questions of self-sacrifice are concerned, men are
65 infinitely beyond us.

JACK: We are. (*Clasps hands with* ALGERNON.)

CECILY: They have moments of physical courage of which we women know absolutely nothing.

GWENDOLEN: (*To* JACK.) Darling!

70 ALGERNON: (*To* CECILY.) Darling! (*They fall into each other's arms.*)

(*Enter* MERRIMAN. *When he enters he coughs loudly, seeing the situation.*)

MERRIMAN: Ahem! Ahem! Lady Bracknell!

JACK: Good heavens!

(*Enter* LADY BRACKNELL. *The couples separate in alarm. Exit* MERRIMAN.)

LADY BRACKNELL: Gwendolen! What does this mean?

75 GWENDOLEN: Merely that I am engaged to be married to Mr. Worthing, Mamma.

LADY BRACKNELL: Come here. Sit down. Sit down immediately. Hesitation of any kind is a sign of mental decay in the young, of physical weakness in the old. (*Turns to* JACK.) Ap-
80 prised, sir, of my daughter's sudden flight by her trusty maid, whose confidence I purchased by means of a small coin, I followed her at once by a luggage train. Her unhappy father is, I am glad to say, under the impression that she is attending a more than usually lengthy lecture by the
85 University Extension Scheme on the Influence of a Permanent Income on Thought. I do not propose to undeceive him. Indeed I have never undeceived him on any question. I would consider it wrong. But of course, you will clearly understand that all communication between yourself and
90 my daughter must cease immediately from this moment. On this point, as indeed on all points, I am firm.

JACK: I am engaged to be married to Gwendolen, Lady Bracknell!

LADY BRACKNELL: You are nothing of the kind, sir. And now,
95 as regards Algernon! . . . Algernon!

ALGERNON: Yes, Aunt Augusta.

LADY BRACKNELL: May I ask if it is in this house that your invalid friend Mr. Bunbury resides?

ALGERNON: (*Stammering.*) Oh, no! Bunbury doesn't live here.
100 Bunbury is somewhere else at present. In fact, Bunbury is dead.

LADY BRACKNELL: Dead! When did Mr. Bunbury die? His death must have been extremely sudden.

ALGERNON: (*Airily.*) Oh, I killed Bunbury this afternoon. I
105 mean poor Bunbury died this afternoon.

LADY BRACKNELL: What did he die of?

ALGERNON: Bunbury? Oh, he was quite exploded.

LADY BRACKNELL: Exploded! Was he the victim of a revolutionary outrage? I was not aware that Mr. Bunbury was
110 interested in social legislation. If so, he is well punished for his morbidity.

ALGERNON: My dear Aunt Augusta, I mean he was found out! The doctors found out that Bunbury could not live, that is what I mean—so Bunbury died.

115 LADY BRACKNELL: He seems to have had great confidence in the opinion of his physicians. I am glad, however, that he made up his mind at the last to some definite course of action, and acted under proper medical advice. And now that we have finally got rid of this Mr. Bunbury, may I ask,
120 Mr. Worthing, who is that young person whose hand my nephew Algernon is now holding in what seems to me a peculiarly unnecessary manner?

JACK: That lady is Miss Cecily Cardew, my ward. (LADY BRACKNELL *bows coldly to* CECILY.)

125 ALGERNON: I am engaged to be married to Cecily, Aunt Augusta.

LADY BRACKNELL: I beg your pardon?

CECILY: Mr. Moncrieff and I are engaged to be married, lady Bracknell.

130 LADY BRACKNELL: (*With a shiver, crossing to the sofa and sitting down.*) I do not know whether there is anything peculiarly exciting in the air of this particular part of Hertfordshire, but the number of engagements that go on seems to me considerably above the proper average that statistics have
135 laid down for our guidance. I think some preliminary enquiry on my part would not be out of place. Mr. Worthing, is Miss Cardew at all connected with any of the larger railway stations in London? I merely desire information. Until yesterday I had no idea that there were any
140 families or persons whose origin was a Terminus. (JACK *looks perfectly furious, but restrains himself.*)

JACK: (*In a clear, cold voice.*) Miss Cardew is the granddaughter of the late Mr. Thomas Cardew of 149, Belgrave Square, S.W.; Gervase Park, Dorking, Surrey; and the Sporran,
145 Fifeshire, N.B.

LADY BRACKNELL: That sounds not unsatisfactory. Three addresses always inspire confidence, even in tradesmen. But what proof have I of their authenticity?

JACK: I have carefully preserved the Court Guide of the pe-
150 riod. They are open to your inspection, Lady Bracknell.

LADY BRACKNELL: (*Grimly.*) I have known strange errors in that publication.

JACK: Miss Cardew's family solicitors are Messrs. Markby, Markby, and Markby.

155 LADY BRACKNELL: Markby, Markby, and Markby? A firm of the very highest position in their profession. Indeed I am told that one of the Mr. Markbys is occasionally to be seen at dinner parties. So far I am satisfied.

JACK: (*Very irritably.*) How extremely kind of you, Lady Brack-
160 nell! I have also in my possession, you will be pleased to hear, certificates of Miss Cardew's birth, baptism, whooping cough, registration, vaccination, confirmation, and the measles; both the German and the English variety.

LADY BRACKNELL: Ah! A life crowded with incident, I see;
165 though perhaps somewhat too exciting for a young girl. I

am not myself in favour of premature experiences. (*Rises, looks at her watch.*) Gwendolen! the time approaches for our departure. We have not a moment to lose. As a matter of form, Mr. Worthing, I had better ask you if Miss
170 Cardew has any little fortune?

JACK: Oh, about a hundred and thirty thousand pounds in the Funds. That is all. Good-bye, Lady Bracknell. So pleased to have seen you.

LADY BRACKNELL: (*Sitting down again.*) A moment, Mr. Wor-
175 thing. A hundred and thirty thousand pounds! And in the Funds! Miss Cardew seems to me a most attractive young lady, now that I look at her. Few girls of the present day have any really solid qualities, any of the qualities that last, and improve with time. We live, I regret to say, in an age of
180 surfaces. (*To* CECILY.) Come over here, dear. (CECILY *goes across.*) Pretty child! your dress is sadly simple, and your hair seems almost as Nature might have left it. But we can soon alter all that. A thoroughly experienced French maid produces a really marvelous result in a very brief space of time.
185 I remember recommending one to young Lady Lancing, and after three months her own husband did not know her.

JACK: (*Aside.*) And after six months nobody knew her.

LADY BRACKNELL: (*Glares at* JACK *for a few moments. Then bends, with a practised smile, to* CECILY.) Kindly turn round, sweet
190 child. (CECILY *turns completely round.*) No, the side view is what I want. (CECILY *presents her profile.*) Yes, quite as I expected. There are distinct social possibilities in your profile. The two weak points in our age are its want of principle and its want of profile. The chin a little higher, dear. Style
195 largely depends on the way the chin is worn. They are worn very high, just at present. Algernon!

ALGERNON: Yes, Aunt Augusta!

LADY BRACKNELL: There are distinct social possibilities in Miss Cardew's profile.
200 ALGERNON: Cecily is the sweetest, dearest, prettiest girl in the whole world. And I don't care twopence about social possibilities.

LADY BRACKNELL: Never speak disrespectfully of society, Algernon. Only people who can't get into it do that. (*To* CE-
205 CILY.) Dear child, of course you know that Algernon has nothing but his debts to depend upon. But I do not approve of mercenary marriages. When I married Lord Bracknell I had no fortune of any kind. But I never dreamed for a moment of allowing that to stand in my
210 way. Well, I suppose I must give my consent.

ALGERNON: Thank you, Aunt Augusta.

LADY BRACKNELL: Cecily, you may kiss me!

CECILY: (*Kisses her.*) Thank you, Lady Bracknell.

LADY BRACKNELL: You may also address me as Aunt Augusta
215 for the future.

CECILY: Thank you, Aunt Augusta.

LADY BRACKNELL: The marriage, I think, had better take place quite soon.

ALGERNON: Thank you, Aunt Augusta.
220 CECILY: Thank you, Aunt Augusta.

LADY BRACKNELL: To speak frankly, I am not in favour of long engagements. They give people the opportunity of finding out each other's character before marriage, which I think is never advisable.
225 JACK: I beg your pardon for interrupting you, Lady Bracknell, but this engagement is quite out of the question. I am Miss Cardew's guardian, and she cannot marry without

my consent until she comes of age. That consent I absolutely decline to give.

LADY BRACKNELL: Upon what grounds, may I ask? Algernon 230 is an extremely, I may almost say an ostentatiously, eligible young man. He has nothing, but he looks everything. What more can one desire?

JACK: It pains me very much to have to speak frankly to you, Lady Bracknell, about your nephew, but the fact is that I 235 do not approve at all of his moral character. I suspect him of being untruthful. (ALGERNON *and* CECILY *look at him in indignant amazement.*)

LADY BRACKNELL: Untruthful! My nephew Algernon? Impossible! He is an Oxonian. 240

JACK: I fear there can be no possible doubt about the matter. This afternoon, during my temporary absence in London on an important question of romance, he obtained admission to my house by means of the false pretence of being my brother. Under an assumed name he drank, I've just 245 been informed by my butler, an entire pint bottle of my Perrier-Jouet, Brut, '89; a wine I was specially reserving for myself. Continuing his disgraceful deception, he succeeded in the course of the afternoon in alienating the affections of my only ward. He subsequently stayed to tea, and devoured 250 every single muffin. And what makes his conduct all the more heartless is, that he was perfectly well aware from the first that I have no brother, that I never had a brother, and that I don't intend to have a brother, not even of any kind. I distinctly told him so myself yesterday afternoon. 255

LADY BRACKNELL: Ahem! Mr. Worthing, after careful consideration I have decided entirely to overlook my nephew's conduct to you.

JACK: That is very generous of you, Lady Bracknell. My own decision, however, is unalterable. I decline to give my con- 260 sent.

LADY BRACKNELL: (*To* CECILY.) Come here, sweet child. (CE-CILY *goes over.*) How old are you, dear?

CECILY: Well, I am really only eighteen, but I always admit to twenty when I go to evening parties. 265

LADY BRACKNELL: You are perfectly right in making some slight alteration. Indeed, no woman should ever be quite accurate about her age. It looks so calculating . . . (*In meditative manner.*) Eighteen, but admitting to twenty at evening parties. Well, it will not be very long before you are of age 270 and free from the restraints of tutelage. So I don't think your guardian's consent is, after all, a matter of any importance.

JACK: Pray excuse me, Lady Bracknell, for interrupting you again, but it is only fair to tell you that according to the terms of her grandfather's will Miss Cardew does not 275 come legally of age till she is thirty-five.

LADY BRACKNELL: That does not seem to me to be a grave objection. Thirty-five is a very attractive age. London society is full of women of the very highest birth who have, of their own free choice, remained thirty-five for years. Lady Dum- 280 bleton is an instance in point. To my own knowledge she has been thirty-five ever since she arrived at the age of forty, which was many years ago now. I see no reason why our dear Cecily should not be even still more attractive at the age you mention than she is at present. There will be a 285 large accumulation of property.

CECILY: Algy, could you wait for me till I was thirty-five?

ALGERNON: Of course I could, Cecily. You know I could.

CECILY: Yes, I felt it instinctively, but I couldn't wait all that time. I hate waiting even five minutes for anybody. It al- 290 ways makes me rather cross. I am not punctual myself, I know, but I do like punctuality in others, and waiting, even to be married, is quite out of the question.

ALGERNON: Then what is to be done, Cecily?

295 CECILY: I don't know, Mr. Moncrieff.

LADY BRACKNELL: My dear Mr. Worthing, as Miss Cardew states positively that she cannot wait till she is thirty-five—a remark which I am bound to say seems to me to show a somewhat impatient nature—I would beg of you 300 to reconsider your decision.

JACK: But my dear Lady Bracknell, the matter is entirely in your own hands. The moment you consent to my marriage with Gwendolen, I will most gladly allow your nephew to form an alliance with my ward.

305 LADY BRACKNELL: (*Rising and drawing herself up.*) You must be quite aware that what you propose is out of the question.

JACK: Then a passionate celibacy is all that any of us can look forward to.

LADY BRACKNELL: That is not the destiny I propose for 310 Gwendolen. Algernon, of course, can choose for himself. (*Pulls out her watch.*) Come, dear, (GWENDOLEN *rises.*) we have already missed five, if not six, trains. To miss any more might expose us to comment on the platform.

(*Enter* DR. CHASUBLE.)

CHASUBLE: Everything is quite ready for the christenings.

315 LADY BRACKNELL: The christenings, sir! Is not that somewhat premature?

CHASUBLE: (*Looking rather puzzled, and pointing to* JACK *and* ALGERNON.) Both these gentlemen have expressed a desire for immediate baptism.

320 LADY BRACKNELL: At their age? The idea is grotesque and irreligious! Algernon, I forbid you to be baptized. I will not hear of such excesses. Lord Bracknell would be highly displeased if he learned that that was the way in which you wasted your time and money.

325 CHASUBLE: Am I to understand then that there are to be no christenings at all this afternoon?

JACK: I don't think that, as things are now, it would be of much practical value to either of us, Dr. Chasuble.

CHASUBLE: I am grieved to hear such sentiments from you, 330 Mr. Worthing. They savour of the heretical views of the Anabaptists, views that I have completely refuted in four of my unpublished sermons. However, as your present mood seems to be one peculiarly secular, I will return to the church at once. Indeed, I have just been informed by 335 the pewopener that for the last hour and a half Miss Prism has been waiting for me in the vestry.

LADY BRACKNELL: (*Starting.*) Miss Prism! Did I hear you mention a Miss Prism?

CHASUBLE: Yes, Lady Bracknell. I am on my way to join her.

340 LADY BRACKNELL: Pray allow me to detain you for a moment. This matter may prove to be one of vital importance to Lord Bracknell and myself. Is this Miss Prism a female of repellent aspect, remotely connected with education?

CHASUBLE: (*Somewhat indignantly.*) She is the most cultivated 345 of ladies, and the very picture of respectability.

LADY BRACKNELL: It is obviously the same person. May I ask what position she holds in your household?

CHASUBLE: (*Severely.*) I am a celibate, madam.

JACK: (*Interposing.*) Miss Prism, Lady Bracknell, has been for the last three years Miss Cardew's esteemed governess and 350 valued companion.

LADY BRACKNELL: In spite of what I hear of her, I must see her at once. Let her be sent for.

CHASUBLE: (*Looking off.*) She approaches; she is nigh.

(*Enter* MISS PRISM *hurriedly.*)

MISS PRISM: I was told you expected me in the vestry, dear 355 Canon. I have been waiting for you there for an hour and three-quarters. (*Catches sight of* LADY BRACKNELL, *who has fixed her with a stony glare.* MISS PRISM *grows pale and quails. She looks anxiously round as if desirous to escape.*)

LADY BRACKNELL: (*In a severe, judicial voice.*) Prism! (MISS 360 PRISM *bows her head in shame.*) Come here, Prism! (MISS PRISM *approaches in a humble manner.*) Prism! Where is that baby? (*General consternation. The Canon starts back in horror.* ALGERNON *and* JACK *pretend to be anxious to shield* CECILY *and* GWENDOLEN *from hearing the details of a terrible public* 365 *scandal.*) Twenty-eight years ago, Prism, you left Lord Bracknell's house, Number 104, Upper Grosvenor Street, in charge of a perambulator that contained a baby, of the male sex. You never returned. A few weeks later, through the elaborate investigations of the Metropolitan police, the 370 perambulator was discovered at midnight, standing by itself in a remote corner of Bayswater. It contained the manuscript of a three-volume novel of more than usually revolting sentimentality. (MISS PRISM *starts in involuntary indignation.*) But the baby was not there! (*Everyone looks at* 375 MISS PRISM.) Prism, where is that baby? (*A pause.*)

MISS PRISM: Lady Bracknell, I admit with shame that I do not know. I only wish I did. The plain facts of the case are these. On the morning of the day you mention, a day that is forever branded on my memory, I prepared as usual to take the baby 380 out in its perambulator. I had also with me a somewhat old but capacious hand-bag in which I had intended to place the manuscript of a work of fiction that I had written during my few unoccupied hours. In a moment of mental abstraction, for which I never can forgive myself, I deposited the manuscript 385 in the bassinette, and placed the baby in the hand-bag.

JACK: (*Who has been listening attentively.*) But where did you deposit the hand-bag?

MISS PRISM: Do not ask me, Mr. Worthing.

JACK: Miss Prism, this is a matter of no small importance to 390 me. I insist on knowing where you deposited the hand-bag that contained that infant.

MISS PRISM: I left it in the cloak-room of one of the larger railway stations in London.

JACK: What railway station? 395

MISS PRISM: (*Quite crushed.*) Victoria. The Brighton line. (*Sinks into a chair.*)

JACK: I must retire to my room for a moment. Gwendolen, wait here for me.

GWENDOLEN: If you are not too long, I will wait here for you 400 all my life.

(*Exit* JACK *in great excitement.*)

CHASUBLE: What do you think this means, Lady Bracknell?

LADY BRACKNELL: I dare not even suspect, Dr. Chasuble. I need hardly tell you that in families of high position

405 strange coincidences are not supposed to occur. They are hardly considered the thing. (*Noises heard overhead as if someone was throwing trunks about. Everybody looks up.*)

CECILY: Uncle Jack seems strangely agitated.

CHASUBLE: Your guardian has a very emotional nature.

410 LADY BRACKNELL: This noise is extremely unpleasant. It sounds as if he was having an argument. I dislike arguments of any kind. They are always vulgar, and often convincing.

CHASUBLE: (*Looking up.*) It has stopped now. (*The noise is redoubled.*)

415 LADY BRACKNELL: I wish he would arrive at some conclusion.

GWENDOLEN: The suspense is terrible. I hope it will last.

(*Enter* JACK *with a hand-bag of black leather in his hand.*)

JACK: (*Rushing over to* MISS PRISM.) Is this the hand-bag, Miss Prism? Examine it carefully before you speak. The happiness of more than one life depends on your answer.

420 MISS PRISM: (*Calmly.*) It seems to be mine. Yes, here is the injury it received through the upsetting of a Gower Street omnibus in younger and happier days. Here is the stain on the lining caused by the explosion of a temperance beverage, an incident that occurred at Leamington. And here,

425 on the lock, are my initials. I had forgotten that in an extravagant mood I had had them placed there. The bag is undoubtedly mine. I am delighted to have it so unexpectedly restored to me. It has been a great inconvenience being without it all these years.

430 JACK: (*In a pathetic voice.*) Miss Prism, more is restored to you than this hand-bag. I was the baby you placed in it.

MISS PRISM: (*Amazed.*) You?

JACK: (*Embracing her.*) Yes . . . mother!

MISS PRISM: (*Recoiling in indignant astonishment.*) Mr. Wor-

435 thing! I am unmarried!

JACK: Unmarried! I do not deny that is a serious blow. But after all, who has the right to cast a stone against one who has suffered? Cannot repentance wipe out an act of folly? Why should there be one law for men and another for women?

440 Mother, I forgive you. (*Tries to embrace her again.*)

MISS PRISM: (*Still more indignant.*) Mr. Worthing, there is some error. (*Pointing to* LADY BRACKNELL.) There is the lady who can tell you who you really are.

JACK: (*After a pause.*) Lady Bracknell, I hate to seem inquisi-

445 tive, but would you kindly inform me who I am?

LADY BRACKNELL: I am afraid that the news I have to give you will not altogether please you. You are the son of my poor sister, Mrs. Moncrieff, and consequently Algernon's elder brother.

450 JACK: Algy's elder brother! Then I have a brother after all. I knew I had a brother! I always said I had a brother! Cecily,— how could you have ever doubted that I had a brother? (*Seizes hold of* ALGERNON.) Dr. Chasuble, my unfortunate brother. Miss Prism, my unfortunate brother. Gwendolen,

455 my unfortunate brother. Algy, you young scoundrel, you will have to treat me with more respect in the future. You have never behaved to me like a brother in all your life.

ALGERNON: Well, not till to-day, old boy, I admit. I did my best, however, though I was out of practice. (*Shakes hands.*)

460 GWENDOLEN: (*To* JACK.) My own! But what own are you? What is your Christian name, now that you have become someone else?

JACK: Good heavens! . . . I had quite forgotten that point. Your decision on the subject of my name is irrevocable, I suppose?

465 GWENDOLEN: I never change, except in my affections.

CECILY: What a noble nature you have, Gwendolen!

JACK: Then the question had better be cleared up at once. Aunt Augusta, a moment. At the time when Miss Prism left me in the hand-bag, had I been christened already?

470 LADY BRACKNELL: Every luxury that money could buy, including christening, had been lavished on you by your fond and doting parents.

JACK: Then I was christened! That is settled. Now, what name was I given? Let me know the worst.

475 LADY BRACKNELL: Being the eldest son you were naturally christened after your father.

JACK: (*Irritably.*) Yes, but what was my father's Christian name?

LADY BRACKNELL: (*Meditatively.*) I cannot at the present mo-

480 ment recall what the General's Christian name was. But I have no doubt he had one. He was eccentric, I admit. But only in later years. And that was the result of the Indian climate, and marriage, and indigestion, and other things of that kind.

485 JACK: Algy! Can't you recollect what our father's Christian name was?

ALGERNON: My dear boy, we were never even on speaking terms. He died before I was a year old.

JACK: His name would appear in the Army Lists of the pe-

490 riod, I suppose, Aunt Augusta?

LADY BRACKNELL: The General was essentially a man of peace, except in his domestic life. But I have no doubt his name would appear in any military directory.

JACK: The Army Lists of the last forty years are here. These

495 delightful records should have been my constant study. (*Rushes to bookcase and tears the books out.*) M. Generals . . . Mallam, Maxbohm, Magley, what ghastly names they have—Markby, Migsby, Mobbs, Moncrieff! Lieutenant 1840, Captain, Lieutenant-Colonel, Colonel, General

500 1869, Christian names, Ernest John. (*Puts book very quietly down and speaks quite calmly.*) I always told you, Gwendolen, my name was Ernest didn't I? Well, it is Ernest after all, I mean it naturally is Ernest.

LADY BRACKNELL: Yes, I remember the General was called

505 Ernest. I knew I had some particular reason for disliking the name.

GWENDOLEN: Ernest! My own Ernest! I felt from the first that you could have no other name!

JACK: Gwendolen, it is a terrible thing for a man to find out

510 suddenly that all his life he has been speaking nothing but the truth. Can you forgive me?

GWENDOLEN: I can. For I feel sure that you are sure to change.

JACK: My own one!

CHASUBLE: (*To* MISS PRISM.) Lætitia! (*Embraces her.*)   515

MISS PRISM: (*Enthusiastically.*) Frederick! At last!

ALGERNON: Cecily! (*Embraces her.*) At last!

JACK: Gwendolen! (*Embraces her.*) At last!

LADY BRACKNELL: My nephew, you seem to be displaying signs of triviality.   520

JACK: On the contrary, Aunt Augusta, I've now realized for the first time in my life the vital Importance of Being Earnest.

Minna Canth

Born Ulrika Wilhemina (Mina) Johnson, Minna Canth (1844–1897) was one of the most celebrated playwrights of her era, and was closely tied to the dominant movements of late-nineteenth-century theatrical culture: nationalism, theatrical experiment, and the emancipation of women. Born into a working-class family in Tampere, Finland, Canth was fortunate to move to the smaller, yet more educated city of Kuopio in 1853. Among the first generation of formally educated Finnish women, she was sent to study at the Jyväskylä Teachers' Seminary, but left to marry Johann Ferdinand Canth in 1865 and had seven children before his death in 1879. Living in Jyväskylä, she also began to write for the newspaper; Finland's first female journalist, she wrote both news stories and essays on women's education, temperance, and the national awareness movement. She also began to read widely in contemporary European literature, notably studying the Norwegian playwrights Henrik Ibsen and Bjørnstierne Bjørnson, the Danish literary critic Georg Brandes, and the British philosopher John Stuart Mill. When her husband died, Minna Canth moved back to Kuopio and went to work in her father's fabric store, shortly turning it into a successful business. She also held an important literary and intellectual salon in her home that drew influential people—and the region's few literate women—together to discuss the critical topics of the era: religion, social progress, Darwinism, literature, and nationalism. Canth also began to publish her writing more widely, beginning with her first collection of short stories in 1878. In the following year, Canth's first play, *Robbery,* was written, and she brought it to the attention of the nationalistic director of the young Finnish Theater, Kaarlo Bergbom, who staged it in 1882; for the next several years, Bergbom worked closely with Canth, bringing several of her plays to the stage, including *In Roinila's House* (staged 1883). Much as in Norway and Ireland, the turn-of-the-century drama tended to be both nationalistic and socially progressive; yet Canth's most influential plays—*The Workingman's Wife* (1885), *Children of Misfortune* (staged 1888), *The Pastor's Family* (staged 1891), and *Anna-Liisa* (staged 1895)—drew the ire of the more conservative Finnish nationalists, the Fennomen. *Sylvi* (staged 1893)—written in Swedish for the Swedish Theater in Helsinki (Finland was and remains a bilingual nation)—confirmed her renegade status to the Fennomen, though it was staged in Finnish shortly thereafter. Canth continued to agitate for women's rights and freedom, notably publishing a journal with A. B. Mäkelä, *Free Ideas,* that brought the writing of contemporary European "freethinkers" to a Finnish audience. When she died in 1897, Canth had published ten plays, seven novels, and many short stories and journalistic articles. Regarded as one of Finland's two greatest playwrights, when the National Theater was constructed in 1906, the proscenium was graced by two portrait reliefs, one of Aleksis Kivi, and one of Minna Canth.

ANNA-LIISA

Anna-Liisa is representative of the ways women and their confined circumstances in nineteenth-century bourgeois culture became powerful symbols of the need for social change. In plays from Ibsen's *A Doll House* to Harley Granville Barker's *Waste* to Elizabeth Robins's *Votes for Women!,* the "fallen woman"—the woman who takes action in the masculine spheres of finance, philosophy, or sex—reveals the hypocrisy of conventional society. Canth's play makes several unusual departures from the "fallen woman" genre, departures implied by the unusual plot structure of the play. While most plays in the "well-made" tradition save the revelation of the dramatic secret until the play's finale, Canth reveals early in the play the secret of Anna-Liisa's past sexual encounter with the farmworker Mikko and the murder of her baby; moreover, the secret is revealed to the rest of the rural village in Act Two. In this sense, rather than being driven by its sensational plot, *Anna-Liisa* centers on the psychological consequences of the heroine's crime, Anna-Liisa's efforts to keep her secret, her attempted suicide when it is revealed, and the ways she comes to accept her guilt and punishment. At the same time, Canth sets Anna-Liisa's story in the claustrophobic environment of a small Finnish village, where the violation of social propriety is, for much of the play, Anna-Liisa's main "crime." After all, Anna-Liisa was forced to conceal her love for Mikko because he was just a hired hand on the farm; when her sexual past is revealed, her father threatens to kill her with his axe, and even when her real crime—killing the baby—is revealed, her parents, her now-displaced fiancé, Mikko, and his mother (who will now inherit the farm) all conspire to keep it secret. In Canth's play, the heroine at once accepts and makes public her guilt, achieving a kind of moral freedom from her hypocritical social world, even while it sentences her to prison.

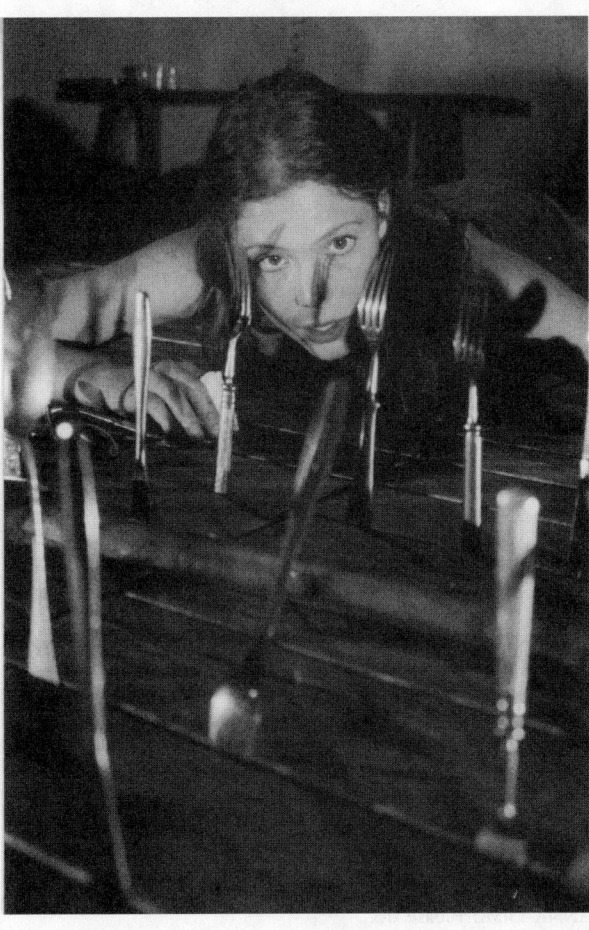

Outi Condit as Anna-Liisa in Tukka-teatteri's experimental production of Minna Canth's *Anna-Liisa,* 2002.

ANNA-LIISA

A Play in Three Acts

Minna Canth

TRANSLATED BY AILI AND AUSTIN FLINT

CHARACTERS

KORTESUO, *farm owner*
RIIKKA, *his wife*
ANNA-LIISA ⎫
PIRKKO ⎭ *their daughters*
JOHANNES KIVIMAA, *Anna-Liisa's fiancé*
MIKKO, *lumberman, Kortesuo's former farmhand*
HUSSO, *mother of Mikko*

PARSON
DOCTOR
SHERIFF
SHOPKEEPER
MRS. RISTOLA, *of the Ristola farm*
MRS. HEIMONEN, *of the Heimonen farm*
MR. KATAJAMÄKI, *farm owner*
VILLAGERS

ACT 1

The main room of the Kortesuo family's farmhouse. A door on the back wall. To its right, hearth and stove. Downstage left, a table with latticed legs; on the right, a high warping reel for the loom. Benches run along the walls and around the tables. Two windows on the left wall, one on the right.

ANNA-LIISA is setting a warp for the loom. She has a fair complexion, and is a slim woman with big sad eyes. She is beautiful but a little pale; her fair hair is in a thick braid down the back. After a moment, Johannes enters.

JOHANNES: Hello there, Anna-Liisa.

ANNA-LIISA: Johannes! How nice.

JOHANNES: Oh, I'm glad I found you alone. Are you still planning to weave something new on the loom?

5 ANNA-LIISA: I am.

JOHANNES: And are you planning to finish it too?

ANNA-LIISA: Oh, yes! You see, this is going to be my wedding dress.

JOHANNES: Really? Your wedding dress! Well, you'll certainly
10   have to get to work on it in a hurry. Do you know why? Do you know what I have in mind?

ANNA-LIISA: Well? Let's hear it.

JOHANNES: Oh, no! Not while you're deep in your work. This is very important. Sit down over there at the table
15   and I'll tell you.

ANNA-LIISA: (*Startled*) Very important? What is it?

JOHANNES: Nothing bad. Don't be afraid. You really do get frightened very easily.

ANNA-LIISA: (*Wipes her forehead, calms down.*) Isn't it silly? My
20   heart skips a beat at the slightest little thing. (*Beat*) You sit on the bench. I'll get myself a stool.

JOHANNES: (*Strokes her hair.*) Is that where you're going to sit again? I wish you'd sit right here, on my knee.

ANNA-LIISA: No, I'll just sit down over here. I feel so good sit-
25   ting by your feet.

JOHANNES: But it would feel much better in my lap. Come on, give it a try.

ANNA-LIISA: No, I won't.

JOHANNES: Why not? Tell me.

30 ANNA-LIISA: Not now. Maybe another time.

JOHANNES: After I've had my say, will you come then?

ANNA-LIISA: Maybe.

JOHANNES: All right, I'll hold you to it.

ANNA-LIISA: Well, then, what's on your mind?

JOHANNES: Only that our wedding banns should be an- 35
nounced in church next Sunday, and in three weeks we'll get married.

ANNA-LIISA: As soon as that?

JOHANNES: Sure, why wait any longer? The sooner the better, I say. What do you think? 40

ANNA-LIISA: I agree. But what will Mother and Father say?

JOHANNES: I'll ask them. Are they home?

ANNA-LIISA: They must be somewhere around the farm.

JOHANNES: Then we'll find out soon enough. But now I
want you here, in my lap. 45

ANNA-LIISA: Don't. Not just yet. We still have a lot to talk about, Johannes.

JOHANNES: We can do it with you sitting on my knee.

ANNA-LIISA: That won't work. You know that from before.

JOHANNES: Well, let's talk directly then—right away. 50

ANNA-LIISA: I don't know where to start.

JOHANNES: Start at the end.

ANNA-LIISA: Oh, please don't joke about this. Let's be serious.

JOHANNES: All right, go ahead. I'll listen, and I promise I
won't laugh. 55

ANNA-LIISA: Before we go to the parsonage, I have to ask you, Johannes: are you sure you'll never regret this?

JOHANNES: Why should I regret it when I love you so much?

ANNA-LIISA: But do you love me with the kind of love the Bible talks about—that endures all, suffers all, forgives all? 60

JOHANNES: And lasts forever. (*Beat*) That very love, my girl. And now it's my turn to speak.

ANNA-LIISA: Please do.

JOHANNES: First of all, I want to tell you that . . .

ANNA-LIISA: That . . .? 65

JOHANNES: You are so . . . so very beautiful, Anna-Liisa.

ANNA-LIISA: Is that all?

JOHANNES: No, I have a lot more to tell you. I want to say that no girl anywhere in the world is equal to you . . . not
in any respect. 70

ANNA-LIISA: Oh, Johannes, that's just what I . . .

JOHANNES: Don't interrupt. Let me finish. (*Beat*) No, not in any respect, just as I said. You see, I'm speaking seriously now. You know what I love about you—even than

75 your beauty and your slim body? It's your quiet nature, your even temper. You're so different from other young people. Much deeper, more grown up. As if you thought and felt more than anyone else. As if you were high above the rest of us . . .

80 ANNA-LIISA: No, no! Stop, Johannes, please stop.

JOHANNES: Yes, above us in spirit. In spirit and morals, I mean.

ANNA-LIISA: Don't talk that way. It upsets me.

JOHANNES: What's true is true.

85 ANNA-LIISA: It's not true. I'm no better than anybody else. In fact, I'm worse. It frightens me that you think so well of me.

JOHANNES: What do you mean? Do you think I would have fallen in love with you if I hadn't thought well of you?

90 ANNA-LIISA: That's just it!

JOHANNES: Or that I would have grown more and more fond of you if I'd felt differently?

ANNA-LIISA: I try to be good, Johannes. I try as hard as I can.

JOHANNES: You don't have to try. You're good anyway. You
95 don't know how to be anything but good. (*Looks her in the eye.*) Now what is it, Anna-Liisa? You're crying!

ANNA-LIISA: No, I'm not!

JOHANNES: But you are. Don't tell me you're not. Those are tears.

100 ANNA-LIISA: They dried up right away. See, no more tears. Are there?

JOHANNES: No, and I won't let them flow ever again, no matter what! (*Snatches her into his lap.*) Well, now! Sit tight, so I can get a good look at you. Oh, my God, how wonder-
105 ful you are! I feel like squeezing you to bits.

ANNA-LIISA: Oh, Johannes, you'll be satisfied with less than that, won't you?

JOHANNES: Now, Anna-Liisa, listen to me. I have to ask you something.

110 ANNA-LIISA: And what would that be?

JOHANNES: Do you like me very, very much?

ANNA-LIISA: You know I do. How many times do you have to ask?

JOHANNES: I won't ask any more, just this once.

115 ANNA-LIISA: And if I answered that I don't like you, then what?

JOHANNES: I wouldn't believe you, since your eyes tell me something different.

ANNA-LIISA: Why do you keep asking, when you know per-
120 fectly well?

JOHANNES: Because I so much like to hear it from you, again and again. (*Beat*) But actually, I was going to put it another way. You know, I've often wondered whether you ever liked anyone else the way you like me. Or am I the first
125 man you've fallen in love with?

ANNA-LIISA: Have you heard something like that?

JOHANNES: I haven't heard anything. I was just thinking.

ANNA-LIISA: So you were just thinking? For no special reason?

JOHANNES: Right, for no reason at all. But still, I'm just curi-
130 ous. You know, I might be a bit of a jealous type. I wouldn't want you to fancy any other man.

ANNA-LIISA: I never would. Not now, not in the future.

JOHANNES: But in the past? Before me? Did you fancy anyone?

ANNA-LIISA: I was only a child then. A senseless child. You
135 know I've just turned twenty.

JOHANNES: That's true. A child—that's what you were then. A quiet child, thoughtful and serious, not one of those flighty girls. I'm the only one you've ever loved! No one else! It makes me feel so good to know that. Can you be-
140 lieve I'm now twice as happy?

ANNA-LIISA: (*Anxious*) Yes, Johannes.

JOHANNES: Why are you squirming so? What's the matter? Don't you believe me?

ANNA-LIISA: Yes, I do—but please, let me go.

145 JOHANNES: Why are you in such a hurry?

ANNA-LIISA: I have to put in the warp. I have to get started on this fabric. At this rate, the wedding dress will never get finished.

JOHANNES: Of course, the wedding dress! Just think, in three
150 weeks we'll be married! Less than a month away! No, no, I won't let you go until you wrap your arms around me and give me a great big hug. You've never hugged me close, Anna-Liisa, but now you really have to . . . or else.

ANNA-LIISA: Oh, Johannes, dearest!

155 JOHANNES: Come on, now, wrap your arms around my neck. You won't get away with anything less. Now the other arm, like that. And now squeeze, hard—or I'll give you such a squeeze that you'll let out a yell. In three weeks I'll be taking you to my own home! Can you believe it?

HUSSO, *an old woman with a dark complexion, pushes the door open and stops at the threshold. Her clothes are shabby; a tattered scarf partly covers her unkempt black hair.*

160 HUSSO: Oh, death and damnation, what love!

ANNA-LIISA: (*Jumps up, frightened.*) Husso!

HUSSO: Yes—Husso, that's me.

JOHANNES: What are you up to?

HUSSO: Just looking and wondering.

165 JOHANNES: Go away! You have no business here.

HUSSO: What makes you so sure?

JOHANNES: Just a guess.

HUSSO: Well, you're wrong. I have something important to say to this young bride.

170 ANNA-LIISA: To me? What is it?

HUSSO: It's confidential.

JOHANNES: You can tell her some other time. It's not convenient for Anna-Liisa right now.

HUSSO: Maybe she could just make it convenient. As I said, I
175 have some important business to talk over with her.

JOHANNES: (*To* ANNA-LIISA) Do you want me to throw her out?

HUSSO: Throw me out? Oh, no, I don't think so. But what does Anna-Liisa say to that?

180 JOHANNES: Just say the word and I'll do it!

ANNA-LIISA: Johannes, don't. I want to hear what's on her mind.

HUSSO: You heard her! That's what I thought she'd say.

ANNA-LIISA: Come on in. Why are you standing in the door-
185 way?

JOHANNES: All right, then. I'll go and have a word with your parents. But get the old hag out of here as soon as you can.

HUSSO: What did you say?

JOHANNES: (*Pushes her aside and goes out.*) Get out of my way!

190 HUSSO: Don't be too proud now. Before you know it, the nasty pig is going to eat up your dinner.

ANNA-LIISA: Husso, what does that mean?

HUSSO: (*Slyly*) I bring you greetings.

ANNA-LIISA: Who from?

195   HUSSO: You have to ask?! Mikko, of course.

ANNA-LIISA: You sure could have left those greetings for another time.

HUSSO: Wait till you hear. There's something else too.

ANNA-LIISA: What is it?

200   HUSSO: Mikko will be coming back home before you know it.

ANNA-LIISA: He's coming here? Why just now?

HUSSO: You go ahead and guess why just now.

ANNA-LIISA: It's only a coincidence. Isn't that right?

205   HUSSO: Oh, no. It's not at all a coincidence. He's coming to collect you before anyone else has a chance to carry you off.

ANNA-LIISA: Coming to collect me? After all this time?

HUSSO: Before, it didn't happen to be convenient. As it is, he's
210   had to leave right in the middle of the logging season.

ANNA-LIISA: Doesn't he know I'm going to be married to someone else?

HUSSO: Of course he knows! I was the one who made sure he got the word. Why do you think he's in such a hurry
215   to get here?

ANNA-LIISA: There's no point. He's too late.

HUSSO: What do you mean, too late? You're not married yet.

ANNA-LIISA: But I'm promised to Johannes. We have a close bond. No one is going to tear us apart.

220   HUSSO: But you had an earlier bond with Mikko. And it was the kind of bond that should last a lifetime. I'll bet you haven't gone that far with this other one. Or have you?

ANNA-LIISA: Be quiet! If you don't have anything else to say, then . . . (*Turns away, annoyed.*)

225   HUSSO: I'm only asking. You don't have to answer if you don't want to. In any case, Mikko's coming to take back what belongs to him. He'll hold you to the promises you made.

ANNA-LIISA: I made them when I was a child, all of fifteen. Why does he even talk about it now?

230   HUSSO: Mikko hasn't forgotten you. Likes you as much as ever.

ANNA-LIISA: It's a waste of time to boast about his affection.

HUSSO: Oh, my God, a waste of time to boast about it? Mikko, who fell head over heels in love with you! You
235   surely can't have forgotten.

ANNA-LIISA: And how did he show this great affection? Ran off and left me all alone just when I needed his support. Didn't show one little bit of sympathy for my youth, my inexperience. Dear Lord, how ruthlessly he behaved!

240   HUSSO: Don't talk rubbish! What else could the poor boy do but run away? You know perfectly well your father would never have given you to his farmhand. If it had come out that you were in a bad way, the boy would have got all the blame for it. Everyone would have shouted that he'd se-
245   duced you. They'd have said that for sure.

ANNA-LIISA: And that's why he ran off to save his own skin. Well, well, he sure was clever.

HUSSO: And you had nothing to worry about at the time. It was for Mikko's sake that I helped you as much as I could.
250   To this day I haven't said a word to anyone. It'll stay a secret among the three of us.

ANNA-LIISA: Let's just forget about it. Let's say it never happened.

HUSSO: The foetus hasn't turned up either. That's how deep I buried it.

ANNA-LIISA: Please, please! That's enough!   255

HUSSO: Let it stay buried for all I care. But you have to go to Mikko. Don't even think of anything else. Your father will give his consent now. Mikko's earned enough money logging in Saarijärvi. Your father's getting old, he's not up to taking care of the farm all by himself. He'll be happy to   260 have a son-in-law to help out. And where do you think you'll find anyone better than Mikko? There's no harder worker anywhere, I tell you.

ANNA-LIISA: Stop! You're only wasting your time. Nothing's going to come of it, anyway.   265

HUSSO: Oh, yes it will, I promise you!

ANNA-LIISA: It won't! Even if Father gives his consent, I won't have him.

HUSSO: You? You say you won't have him? I call that very strange.   270

ANNA-LIISA: How could I accept him when I no longer care for him at all? And I haven't cared for him since the moment he went away.

HUSSO: Now you can't be sure of that. It's been four years since you've seen him; I'll bet you hardly remember what he   275 looks like. You just wait until you see Mikko standing in front of you. Your heart's going to start beating faster all over again. Old love never gets rusty, you know.

ANNA-LIISA: I never loved him at all. It was childish nonsense. Childish, that's all it was.   280

HUSSO: Now, now, let's not quarrel about it. We'll soon see. We'll soon see what's to become of the girl. So you think you've cooled on Mikko! Such a fine, strapping boy! Even if I am his own mother, I dare say this other one's a useless good-for-nothing compared to Mikko! Yes, a   285 useless good-for-nothing, a worn-out old boot! And you'd forsake your own darling, handsome Mikko for the likes of him! Oh, no, my girl, don't mistake bones for meat. Mikko will win out over Johannes any day, that's for sure. And even if there were ten Johanneses, he'd   290 drive them off faster than you can blink. It wouldn't take much.

ANNA-LIISA: I tell you that's not going to happen. Mikko'd better not get his hopes up or start anything like that—I forbid it! If he makes any trouble for Johannes, I'll . . .   295

HUSSO: You'll what?

ANNA-LIISA: I'll never forgive him.

HUSSO: Yes, you will forgive him, and happily too. As soon as Mikko gets his hands on you, you'll melt right away.

ANNA-LIISA: Mikko get his hands on me?! Never! Not ever!   300 Do you hear? Never!

HUSSO: Are you really going to be that stubborn?

ANNA-LIISA: I sure am!

HUSSO: Anna-Liisa, I warn you. Think a bit about your relationships and only then decide what you'll do. Otherwise   305 you might just find yourself up a tree.

ANNA-LIISA: What do you mean by that?

HUSSO: I mean those old matters.

ANNA-LIISA: What are you driving at? What do they have to do with this?   310

HUSSO: Quite a lot. Don't you understand?

ANNA-LIISA: No, I don't understand, not at all.

HUSSO: What if certain secrets should come to light?

ANNA-LIISA: Come to light? How could they, when it was so
315 long ago—four years now!

HUSSO: Might just as well be forty. It has nothing to do with
that.

ANNA-LIISA: But how could it come out? When no one but
the three of us knows about it—the two of you and me.

320 HUSSO: That's just it.

ANNA-LIISA: You would? No, it's impossible.

HUSSO: What's impossible about it? At least we'd keep you
from marrying Johannes. Do you think he'll still want you
when he hears how you carried on with your father's
325 farmhand? Oh, that young Johannes Kivimaa—such a
proud, stuck-up man!

ANNA-LIISA: You could bring yourselves to do that! And
you'd have the heart to ruin all my happiness?

HUSSO: You'll have even more happiness with Mikko. Believe
330 me, he'll treat you like a treasure. And you'll never have to
be afraid of anyone spilling the beans. You'll live the rest of
your days in peace. So you just go to Mikko, and do it right
away. That'll keep you out of all kinds of trouble.

ANNA-LIISA: But I can't do that! I love someone else, not him!
335 Please, Husso, why are you doing this to me? I know you
wouldn't really tell Johannes, any more than you'd tell anyone else. You'd never do such a nasty thing. And you
wouldn't even gain anything by it. Because if Johannes did
walk away from me, I'd never marry anyone else. You're just
340 trying to scare me, right? Oh, you old woman, you thought
you were being so clever. But you can't fool me.

HUSSO: For God's sake! You ought to know I don't fool
around. You'll soon find out what'll happen if you don't
give in.

345 ANNA-LIISA: I don't believe you, I just don't. Mikko would
never let you do it. Wait till he comes, he'll tell you.

HUSSO: Mikko won't stop me, I know that for sure. And besides, I don't have to ask his permission. If he dawdles
along the way here and you're in a rush to get married, I'll
350 take things into my own hands. Believe me, whatever I
have to do, I'll do.

ANNA-LIISA: You'd have the nerve? What if it led to something bad for you too? You'd better think about it.

HUSSO: How could it bring me any trouble? And even if it
355 did, so what? Misery, that's all I've known my whole life
long. I'm not afraid of a few years of jail time, if it should
come to that.

ANNA-LIISA: But if there's nothing to gain from it? For I
swear, I'll never go to Mikko. Never! I'll—I'll do away
360 with myself first!

HUSSO: Do away with yourself! Try and make other people
believe that, not me. You didn't do away with yourself
when you were in worse trouble, and you won't do it this
time, either.

365 ANNA-LIISA: I didn't have the courage then. I was too young.
But now I do.

HUSSO: We'll see about that.

ANNA-LIISA: You're a despicable human being. You have no
heart and no conscience.

370 HUSSO: You talk about heart and conscience? You, who have
murdered your child and now want to pass for a decent
woman? You're deceiving your fiancé, you're deceiving
the whole world. You're a good one to talk about heart
and conscience!—Ha, ha, ha! Makes me laugh! What if my

conscience forces me to tell the truth? What do you say to   375
that?

ANNA-LIISA: Go away! Do what you will. You know my
decision.

HUSSO: And you're going to stick to it!

ANNA-LIISA: I will.   380

PIRKKO, *a twelve-year-old girl, comes running in, barefooted. She is
smart and lively.*

PIRKKO: Anna-Liisa, is it true? Tell me quick, is it true?

ANNA-LIISA: Is what true?

PIRKKO: That they're going to announce the wedding banns
for you next Sunday? Father and Johannes are talking
about it out there.   385

HUSSO: So things are that far along! Well, well, it's only Friday. There's still time before Sunday. Goodbye, Anna-Liisa,
goodbye! (*She leaves.*)

PIRKKO: Tell me, come on, tell me! Is it true?

ANNA-LIISA: Oh—! I don't know. (*She goes to the warping reel,*   390
gives it a few spins.)

PIRKKO: You do know, you can't fool me. I heard Johannes
say the two of you had talked about it. Will lots of
guests be coming to the wedding, Anna-Liisa, will they?
Tell!   395

ANNA-LIISA: Leave me alone. You're always shooting off at the
mouth. (*Leaves the warping reel and goes over to the window.*)

PIRKKO: Why are you in such a bad mood? Did you quarrel
with Husso?

ANNA-LIISA: Pirkko! Run out and see where Husso went off   400
to. And listen, come back and tell me right away if you see
her talking to Johannes.

PIRKKO: Sure! (*She runs out and returns right away.*)

ANNA-LIISA: Well?

PIRKKO: She was going along the forest path towards her own   405
hut.

ANNA-LIISA: And she didn't talk to Johannes?

PIRKKO: No. Johannes was at the other end of the yard.

ANNA-LIISA: Thank God! (*She goes back to the warping reel.*)

PIRKKO: Would it have been so dangerous?   410

ANNA-LIISA: Don't ask so many questions.

PIRKKO: Are you afraid she'll ruin things between you and
Johannes? That she'll tell gossip?

ANNA-LIISA: That's exactly what I'm afraid of.

PIRKKO: You don't have to worry. I'll make sure she never gets   415
anywhere near Johannes.

ANNA-LIISA: Oh, Pirkko, if you do that, I'll always be grateful
to you.

PIRKKO: Trust me. I'll get rid of that old hag if she shows up
here before Sunday. (*Beat*) But listen, Anna-Liisa. When's   420
the wedding going to be? As soon as they've called the
banns three times?

ANNA-LIISA: Yes, right after that.

PIRKKO: Will it be a big wedding? And will there be dancing?
Of course there'll be dancing, what sort of wedding   425
would it be without it! Oh, I've got to learn how to dance
by then! I already know how to do the reel and the schottische and "press-the-bench" and the old maid. But I don't
know any of the new dances, the "Francies," or what do
they call it? I don't know that and I don't know the polka,   430
but you'll teach me, won't you?

ANNA-LIISA: Pirkko, just think, maybe she turned around and came back. (*She goes to the door and looks out.*)

PIRKKO: You mean Husso? No way. She was going so fast she 435 didn't even look back.

ANNA-LIISA: I can't see anyone there. No Johannes, no Father.

PIRKKO: (*Kneeling on the bench, opens the window and looks out.*) They were there only a minute ago, over by the shed. And that's where they are still. No sign of Husso, nowhere at 440 all. Don't worry, I've promised to keep an eye on her.

PIRKKO *keeps swinging her legs and sticking her neck out the window.*

ANNA-LIISA: (*To herself*) Friday, Saturday, Sunday! If those two days would only pass without anything bad happening, then I wouldn't be afraid any more. She wouldn't dare then, not after the banns are announced. Just these two days!

445 PIRKKO: (*Closes the window.*) What are you babbling about?

ANNA-LIISA: Oh, just talking to myself. (*Goes back to the warping reel.*)

PIRKKO: Boy, you're something, talking to yourself. I guess I should get used to doing it, too. When you go away, I 450 won't have anyone to talk to like this. Oh, my, I'm going to miss you, Anna-Liisa. I feel like crying when I think how you'll be going away so soon.

ANNA-LIISA: Poor Pirkko. What fun have I ever been for you?

PIRKKO: You've always been good to me. Who's going to take 455 my side when Mother and Father scold me? And then, when I can't see you, that'll be the worst.

ANNA-LIISA: You'll just have to come over to the Kivimaas' place very often. Come every day. It's not that far.

PIRKKO: I'll come, you can be sure of that. I'll come over to 460 help you with your work. And listen, when you have a baby, I'll take care of it for you.

ANNA-LIISA: A baby? Oh, Pirkko, how do I know whether I'll have a baby or not?

PIRKKO: You'll have one. Why wouldn't you? All the others 465 that get married get one. You'll have a little one just like Mrs. Ristola did a while back. In the beginning, it was so, so tiny. And couldn't hold her head up, she was only nodding, look, like this, like this. That's why you mustn't hold a small child upright, but always lying down like this, on 470 your arm. And you always have to support the neck. Oh, I can take care of a little one, don't you believe me?

ANNA-LIISA: Of course I do.

PIRKKO: You'll have me over to take care of it all the time?

ANNA-LIISA: No, Pirkko, if I do have a child, I'll take care of 475 it myself. I won't trust it to anyone.

PIRKKO: But now and then? You can't be looking after the child all the time. And besides, I'd take care of it as well as you, maybe even better since I like little children so much. From what I've seen, you can't stand them.

480 ANNA-LIISA: How can you say that?

PIRKKO: Because you don't even want to see them. You wouldn't go see little Eeva at the Ristolas' farm, no matter how many times her mother asked you. And when she did come over and put her in your arms you got real 485 scared and almost dropped the baby on the floor. It was lucky Mrs. Ristola caught her in time. That's when they said, "If God lets her have children, how in the world is she going to manage to take care of them?"

ANNA-LIISA: Is that what they said?

PIRKKO: But I thought to myself: don't you worry, I'll take 490 care of Anna-Liisa's children. Oh, it'll be so lovely when they learn to speak and call me Auntie. Auntie Pikko, Auntie Pikko, pick me up. That's what little Elsa from Ristola called me. She couldn't say her *r*'s.

ANNA-LIISA: You're not keeping an eye on the window, 495 Pirkko. You're only looking this way. If Husso had sneaked past you, you'd have missed her.

PIRKKO: She hasn't snuck past me. I'll look after that, all right.

ANNA-LIISA: But I hear some people talking out there.

PIRKKO: (*Peering out the window again*) Of course you can. It's 500 Mother and Father and Johannes coming in.

ANNA-LIISA: Oh, it's them! That gave me a real scare. Pirkko, will you remember to make sure she doesn't come in while they're all here?

PIRKKO: I'll remember, I'll remember. I won't move from this 505 window, or maybe I'll keep watch out in the yard.

ANNA-LIISA: All right, but make sure no one notices. Shh! Here they are.

KORTESUO, RIIKKA, *and* JOHANNES *enter.*

RIIKKA: (*Carries in a pail of water and puts a pot on to boil.*) So, you've been thinking you'll have your banns announced 510 this Sunday, and in three weeks there'll be a wedding! I only wonder how we'll ever get ready for it. And there's Anna-Liisa, just starting on the wedding dress.

KORTESUO: You'll be ready if you keep at it. Nothing to it. And you can get some help if you don't have time to do 515 it yourselves.

RIIKKA: Guess that's what we'll have to do. Sit down, Johannes. I'll get the coffee started. It'll be done before you know it, while I'm boiling the potatoes.

JOHANNES: Don't make coffee just for me. 520

KORTESUO: Go ahead, put the coffee on. The rest of us could use some too.

JOHANNES: So, we'll go to the parsonage tomorrow, right?

KORTESUO: Sure thing, sure thing! And we'll have to pick up something to drink from town. The rest of it we can get 525 right here, from the store.

RIIKKA: So, are we going to make a big celebration of it?

KORTESUO: As big as we can make it!

RIIKKA: You mean for the banns too?

KORTESUO: First the banns and then the wedding. When 530 Anna-Liisa is taken away from us, it will be done with full honors. Just remember, Johannes, this girl has been the apple of my eye ever since she was a little one.

JOHANNES: I can believe that, all right.

KORTESUO: So, even though I'm her father, I can say there's 535 no girl like her.

ANNA-LIISA: Oh, dear Father!

KORTESUO: What's true is true.

JOHANNES: Never you mind, Anna-Liisa. You deserve every word of that praise. There are a lot of malicious tongues 540 around here, and you pick up all sorts of things about other girls, but nobody's ever found fault with you. About Anna-Liisa, nothing but good.

RIIKKA: That's because she gives no reason for talk. The other girls her age are always going to parties or flying off to 545 dances, but this one, never, not even if you tell her to go.

KORTESUO: For a person so young, our Anna-Liisa is very serious and even-tempered, everyone will tell you that. Always responsible and hard-working. But that other one,
550 she's always up to something.

JOHANNES: You mean Pirkko?

KORTESUO: You sure wouldn't take them for sisters, they're
that different.

PIRKKO: Oh, now it's starting again. (*Tries to sneak off.*)

555 RIIKKA: Wait a minute Where are you off to?

PIRKKO: To take the horses to pasture.

RIIKKA: That's the farmhands' job. You take up your knitting.

PIRKKO: But I promised Matti I'd do it.

RIIKKA: You promised! As if Matti had asked you to.

560 PIRKKO: I'll be right back.

KORTESUO: You do as your mother tells you to, or I'll teach
you.

PIRKKO: (*Looking along the bench*) I don't even know where
that knitting is. Who could have taken it?

565 RIIKKA: Who could have taken it! It's wherever you left it.
You'd better find it or you'll be in trouble!

PIRKKO: (*Crawling on the floor*) There it is! Someone's thrown
it on the floor, there, under the bench. And the knitting
needles have been yanked out. The cat, that devil . . . Or
570 could Husso have been so mean?

JOHANNES: Oh, I meant to ask: what business did Husso have
here?

ANNA-LIISA: Nothing special. She just happened to stop
by.

575 KORTESUO: Was that woman here again? That good-for-
nothing gossip! I can't stand the sight of her. I send her
packing every time I set eyes on her. But you just can't get
rid of that woman, not so long as people here keep favor-
ing her.

580 RIIKKA: I don't favor her! Haven't had a word with her for
ages.

KORTESUO: So who is it she wants to see here? Anna-Liisa?

RIIKKA: I don't think it's Anna-Liisa, either. I think she just
comes by without wanting to see anyone special.

585 PIRKKO: Well, only a few minutes ago she was quarreling
with Anna-Liisa. And Anna-Liisa had just asked me to
send her away as soon as I saw her coming.

KORTESUO: That's just what you should do, because we sure
don't need her here. She's one of those end-of-the-world
590 people.

PIRKKO: And Anna-Liisa is afraid—

ANNA-LIISA: Pirkko!

PIRKKO: What does it matter? I can say that much.—Anna-
Liisa's afraid Husso will ruin things between her and
595 Johannes.

JOHANNES: (*Smiling*) Oh? So you're afraid of people like her?
She'd never be able to do that. No, not even—

KORTESUO: Of course not.

MIKKO *enters.*

RIIKKA: Heaven preserve us—it's Mikko!

600 MIKKO: Hello!

KORTESUO: Well, hello!

RIIKKA: So, when was it that you came home? I had no idea.

MIKKO: Just now. Thought I'd drop in at the house of my old
master to say hello.

KORTESUO: You did right to come. Well, hello! Come on in, 605
sit down, the wife will bring us some coffee. It's a long
time since we saw you in these parts.

MIKKO: Four years now. Well, hello, Pirkko! My, my, how
you've grown. Do you still remember me, Mikko the
farmhand?   610

PIRKKO: Of course I remember you. You were the one who
first taught me how to ride a horse.

MIKKO: So you haven't forgotten. Now, what else is new here?

KORTESUO: Not much.

MIKKO: And Johannes has as smooth a face as he ever did. No 615
beard growing in for you yet?

JOHANNES: Sure it would, if I let it grow.

MIKKO: Well, buddy, you should let it grow, so you'd look a
little more like a man.

JOHANNES: What does that have to do with anything?   620

KORTESUO: Johannes is quite a man, even though he doesn't
have a beard.—But Mikko, tell us about your travels. Did
you do well out there?

MIKKO: Very well indeed. Made money hand over fist.

KORTESUO: Really? You must be a rich man by now.   625

MIKKO: Well, got several thousand behind me now.

KORTESUO: Could be you came here with plans to buy a
farm?

MIKKO: How much would you want for the Kivimaa farm?

JOHANNES: That's not for sale.   630

MIKKO: I wouldn't want it, anyway. If I'm going to buy one,
it's got to be a lot bigger than that.

KORTESUO: Bigger than Kivimaa?

MIKKO: Bigger and better all around. There's not even enough
forest land in Kivimaa.   635

JOHANNES: Quite enough for what's needed.

MIKKO: That's too little for me. What in the world can you
do with a farm that's only got forest land to keep the place
going?

RIIKKA: (*Brings in the coffee and sets it on the table.*) Please, have 640
some coffee. Anna-Liisa, you too. Come, help yourself to
some.

MIKKO: Oh, is it Anna-Liisa hiding there behind the warping
reel? I could see the reel turning and guessed somebody
had to be there, on the other side.   645

RIIKKA: Come on, come have some coffee and say hello to
old friends.

MIKKO: (*Goes over to shake hands with* ANNA-LIISA.) No need
to be shy.

JOHANNES: Why would she be shy with you?   650

MIKKO: Right—who else could she be shy with here?

JOHANNES: Her former farmhand.

MIKKO: (*Takes* ANNA-LIISA *by the hand.*) That's right. Her former farmhand who's now become as good as a
landowner.—So, what's new?   655

ANNA-LIISA: Nothing special.

Meets MIKKO's *eyes and withdraws her hand.*

KORTESUO: But Mikko, I don't think you'll find any farm to
your liking in these parts, since you seem to have such big
demands.

MIKKO: (*Returns to the table.*) Who says I've come here to buy 660
a farm?

KORTESUO: Well, that's what I gathered.

MIKKO: No, I have very different plans.

RIIKKA: Perhaps Mikko's thinking of getting married?

665 MIKKO: That's more like it.

KORTESUO: I see! Thinking of getting married. Well, did you already have a girl in mind before you left four years ago?

MIKKO: Sure did.

RIIKKA: Oh, my! And there was no talk at all. So that business

670   had already got started?

MIKKO: It got started all right.

ANNA-LIISA: Johannes, would you like to go for a walk?

RIIKKA: Let Johannes have some coffee first.

KORTESUO: Why would you go for a walk just now? Why

675   don't you both stay here and let Mikko tell us about his plans.

JOHANNES: All right, let's do that.

ANNA-LIISA: It's so stiflingly hot in here.

KORTESUO: Hot? Don't talk nonsense.

680 RIIKKA: But what I wonder is how Mikko's managed to keep that girl in his mind all this time. Four years! Could she have remained as faithful as that, I wonder?

MIKKO: That's just what I came home to find out.

KORTESUO: You don't know? Well then, you're on very shaky

685   ground.

RIIKKA: What if she's taken up with another man? What then?

MIKKO: She'll just have to get rid of him.

KORTESUO: Even if she's already married?

690 MIKKO: Even then.

KORTESUO: But what if she doesn't want to?

MIKKO: Then I'd have to insist.

KORTESUO: You wouldn't?! Is that proper?

MIKKO: I don't ask what's proper. I just want to take back

695   what belongs to me.

ANNA-LIISA: Johannes, let's go! You've finished your coffee by now.

RIIKKA: What is it with you, girl? Johannes can't go until he's had his second cup of coffee. Here's some for you, too.

700   (*Shoves a full cup in front of* ANNA-LIISA.)

KORTESUO: I can see Mikko's been off among the lumbermen. People don't act so rough when they settle matters in our peaceful village.

RIIKKA: And Mikko won't have to be as rough as he sounds,

705   if the girl has kept him in her mind, too.

MIKKO: What do you think? Has she remained faithful to me?

KORTESUO: You're asking us?

MIKKO: Yes, I'm asking you.

RIIKKA: (*Smiling*) If you'd at least let us know the girl's name,

710   then maybe we could answer.

MIKKO: And otherwise you can't?

KORTESUO: How could we? It's impossible.

MIKKO: Can't anyone here give me an answer? Not even Anna-Liisa?

715 JOHANNES: Anna-Liisa? Why Anna-Liisa exactly?

MIKKO: Just in case she'd happen to know.

RIIKKA: What? Do you know who Mikko's been thinking of? And you haven't said a word to me?

MIKKO: So, what kind of answer is Anna-Liisa going to give me?

720 RIIKKA: Well, let's hear.

ANNA-LIISA: Mikko should know. He's just joking.

MIKKO: Now, tell me straight out. Don't beat around the bush. Do you think the girl still loves me?

ANNA-LIISA: I don't think she does.

MIKKO: Is that right? So, you don't think she does? But why 725 wouldn't she love me any more?

ANNA-LIISA: Because you don't deserve it.

JOHANNES: Sounds like Anna-Liisa knows a lot about this.

RIIKKA: She sure seems to.

MIKKO: I don't deserve it? Even though I've been faithful to 730 her for four years and have now come to fetch her? Are you saying I still haven't earned her love?

ANNA-LIISA: You haven't.

JOHANNES: Well, you've heard the truth.

MIKKO: Anna-Liisa, please explain this to me a little more 735 clearly. I'm afraid I don't quite understand it yet.

ANNA-LIISA: I'll explain it to you later, some other time.

RIIKKA: But the rest of us can't make head or tail of what you're talking about.

KORTESUO: Mikko, the best thing for you to do is go straight 740 to your girl and ask her. How could Anna-Liisa really know the answer? That's something to be settled between two people. Anyone else is just a third wheel.

MIKKO: That's what I'll do. As soon as I can talk to her alone, I believe she'll give in to me. 745

RIIKKA: Why wouldn't she give in? To such a fine-looking man as Mikko.

KORTESUO: By the way, have you heard that Anna-Liisa's going to be whisked away from us?

ANNA-LIISA *goes to her warping reel.*

MIKKO: One would have to know that without hearing any- 750 thing—or did you think she was on the way to becoming an old maid?

KORTESUO: Of course not, but I'm trying to tell you she's going to be taken away very soon. Her banns will be announced this Sunday. 755

MIKKO: Well, I can believe it.

KORTESUO: With this Johannes, here, you see.

MIKKO: Johannes? This beardless Johannes? That I can't believe!

JOHANNES: It may not be an article of faith, but it can still come to pass. 760

MIKKO: Not on a day in heaven. You mean to say Anna-Liisa would really fall for this young whippersnapper?

JOHANNES: What do you mean, pal? I have the feeling you're trying to get me all stirred up.

KORTESUO: Now, now, let's not quarrel. I'm sure Mikko's 765 only joking.

MIKKO: By God, I'm not joking.

KORTESUO: You'll see for yourself on Sunday. You'll be right welcome here when we celebrate the banns.

MIKKO: There's plenty of time before Sunday. 770

RIIKKA: No need to wait that long. Anna-Liisa's right here, let her say herself whether it's true or not.

JOHANNES: Right, Anna-Liisa, you say it out loud.

ANNA-LIISA: (*From behind the warping reel*) I wonder if he'll believe me, either. 775

MIKKO: Not much. A young girl's mind is like water in a trough. It spills this way and that. Anna-Liisa's thoughts may well take another direction before she's gone as far as having her banns announced.

ANNA-LIISA: They won't change. You can be sure of that—my 780 thoughts will not change.

JOHANNES: Now, what do you say to that?

MIKKO: Well, I'll just say that if Anna-Liisa's thoughts don't change, yours will.

785 JOHANNES: You're lying!

MIKKO: I swear I'm not! If Anna-Liisa doesn't change her mind before Sunday, then you'll change yours.

RIIKKA: Please, now don't be bickering for no reason at all. We'll soon see . . . Let me pour some more coffee for you.

790 There's still some more in the pot.

PIRKKO: (*Goes to* ANNA-LIISA.) Listen, Anna-Liisa, I'm having a lot of trouble with this knitting.

ANNA-LIISA: Get that man out of here, Pirkko. Please, think of something.

795 PIRKKO: You mean Mikko?

ANNA-LIISA: Yes, him exactly. Right away!

PIRKKO: And will you then knit up my sock for me?

ANNA-LIISA: I will, I will!

PIRKKO: That's a deal!

Slips the knitting into ANNA-LIISA'*s hand, stealthily winds her way to the door and sneaks out.*

800 KORTESUO: Well, now—I say the same as Riikka: why are you bickering for no reason at all? We'll soon see.

JOHANNES: Mikko's up to something with all this.

KORTESUO: Not at all! What could it be! A little joke, that's all—or, at most, some kind of lumberman's trick.

805 RIIKKA: Sure, it couldn't be anything else. He's been gone four years, has just come back here. Mikko's teasing you just for fun.

PIRKKO: (*Tears the door open.*) Mikko, the horse ran off!

MIKKO: (*Jumps up.*) You mean my horse?

810 PIRKKO: Yes, that's right, your horse! Come quick!

MIKKO: Who the hell let him out?

PIRKKO: I was just loosening the reins from the ladder,—I thought I could ride it just a little, but then it took off like anything. (MIKKO *and* KORTESUO *rush out.*)

815 RIIKKA: You're always causing trouble. (*Yanks her by the hair.*) I'll teach you!—Go ahead and holler, you'll get a beating yet. (*Rushes out the door after the men.*)

PIRKKO: (*Cries loudly, but then suddenly calms down.*) But listen, Anna-Liisa, you'd better finish knitting the whole sock for

820 me. (*She runs out.*)

ANNA-LIISA: Johannes—you're not angry at me, are you?

JOHANNES: Oh, Lord no. Why should I be angry with you?

ANNA-LIISA: I just thought—because you're looking so serious.

825 JOHANNES: Mikko was just getting on my nerves, that troublemaker! But never mind. Now, come here. When you're with me, fusses like that soon fade away.

ANNA-LIISA: (*Comes to him.*) I would just like to ask you for one thing, Johannes. If only you would promise me!

830 JOHANNES: I promise—I promise ahead of time, if it isn't impossible.

ANNA-LIISA: It's not impossible. What I'm asking you, what I am fervently asking you, Johannes, is—please stay away from Mikko. Don't start going around with him, don't even

835 let him come near you! If he says something to you, act like you don't even hear it, and try, try your very hardest to see that he doesn't run into you. Will you do that, Johannes? My own sweet darling, will you do that? Tell me!

JOHANNES: But Anna-Liisa, you're acting as if your life had been threatened. So he really did frighten you? 840

ANNA-LIISA: He's a nasty man. You have no idea how nasty.

JOHANNES: I can believe he's nasty, all right. But what can all his nastiness do to us?

ANNA-LIISA: You never know. You never know what ideas he can get into his head. But you do promise to stay away 845 from him, don't you, Johannes?

JOHANNES: Are you afraid Mikko and I will get into an argument, maybe even a fight?

ANNA-LIISA: Yes, I'm afraid. I'm afraid of that too.

JOHANNES: And I guess you think I might be on the losing 850 side.

ANNA-LIISA: That could happen. Mikko is so strong. For all you know he could reach for his knife.

JOHANNES: Mikko's no stronger than I am, even though he called me a whippersnapper. Anyway, big words can't split 855 anyone's lip.

ANNA-LIISA: It's best to keep away from him in any case. Don't you think so, Johannes? You can see that for yourself.

JOHANNES: I'm not so sure.

ANNA-LIISA: But you already half-promised. If it isn't impos- 860 sible, you said. And this is not impossible. You could see that if you'd only want to.

JOHANNES: Sure, sure. But there's just one thing. He might get to think I'm afraid of him.

ANNA-LIISA: Let him think that if he wants to. What does it 865 matter to us? We needn't give it a thought.

JOHANNES: And I'd sure like to punish him a bit for all his big talk a while ago. He'd certainly deserve that.

ANNA-LIISA: If you do that, we'll be doomed! Oh, Johannes, why won't you believe me? 870

JOHANNES: All I'd do is show him he can't toy with me.

ANNA-LIISA: And for that you'd risk everything! Oh, Johannes, this is the first time I've ever asked you for anything, and you refuse me!

JOHANNES: I just think you're being childish. Making moun- 875 tains out of molehills.

ANNA-LIISA: All our happiness depends on it. I know it does.

JOHANNES: Not at all! But since you absolutely insist, then sure, I can stay away from him.

ANNA-LIISA: You promise? 880

JOHANNES: Yes, I promise, I promise. Just to please you. Are you happy now?

ANNA-LIISA: (*Puts her arms around him.*) Oh, yes, I am. Thank you, Johannes. I thank you from the bottom of my heart! 885

JOHANNES: My own sweet darling! Do you love me?

ANNA-LIISA: Oh, I do! You're the one I love most in all the world.

ACT 2

Setting: the same room as in Act 1, except that the warping mill has been removed. RIIKKA *is cooking for the family.* ANNA-LIISA *is looking out the window.* KORTESUO *enters.*

KORTESUO: Hello, we're just back from the parsonage! So now it's done! I've asked for Anna-Liisa's banns to be published.

RIIKKA: Already? What did the old parson have to say about that?

KORTESUO: Nothing much. Just sent his congratulations. He's a nice man, that parson of ours. There aren't many like him.

RIIKKA: Did he mention whether he'd heard of their intentions before?

10 KORTESUO: He seemed to know everything. And he was singing Anna-Liisa's praises. Said the girl's an honor to the whole town. And a good example for others. Said there wasn't anyone else in the confirmation class who knew it as well as Anna-Liisa, neither before or since. Said she'd

15 just rattled it off like that, no matter what part of the catechism he asked about.

RIIKKA: So he was singing her praise Anna-Liisa, do you hear what your father's telling us?

ANNA-LIISA: (*Not turning from the window*) I hear.

20 RIIKKA: And you're no happier than that? What a strange girl!

KORTESUO: She's got so used to people singing her praise. But you should have seen how happy it made Johannes.

RIIKKA: Well, I can imagine. But why didn't he come back here with you? We could have celebrated the registration

25 of the banns with some coffee.

KORTESUO: Said he had to look after something. But he did say he'd come by later in the day. Well, I did invite the parson to the celebration when the banns are published.

RIIKKA: You did? What did he say?

30 KORTESUO: He thanked me right humbly and accepted. And can you guess who else I stopped by to invite?

RIIKKA: Could it be the sheriff?

KORTESUO: The sheriff and the doctor.

RIIKKA: Why so many? I wish you'd invited them only to the

35 wedding.

KORTESUO: We'll invite them to the wedding too, of course. All the people we've invited to the banns, and a lot of others besides.

RIIKKA: My goodness, what ever will we serve them? We

40 haven't made any arrangements for getting provisions yet.

KORTESUO: Haven't made any arrangements! Well, I've already ordered liquor to be delivered from town.

RIIKKA: How in the world did you . . .?

KORTESUO: I asked the shopkeeper to telephone and have

45 them sent from Liknell's with the postman.

RIIKKA: Well, that's good. We can get everything else right here.

KORTESUO: I think he's already delivered them to the store. If you'd get lunch ready, I'll eat and then go for them. I

50 could buy the rest of the things while I'm at it.

RIIKKA: Lunch'll be ready soon. But we have such a lot to do today. Anna-Liisa, do start tidying up the house. Why are you looking out the window all the time?

ANNA-LIISA: No reason.

55 RIIKKA: She's been standing right there all day long. Yesterday too. Doesn't seem to have time for anything else. And she's supposed to be the busy bride.

KORTESUO: I don't think she's looking for anything. She's just standing there deep in thought.

60 RIIKKA: So what are you thinking about? Tell us.

KORTESUO: Do you have to ask? The change in her life, of course.

RIIKKA: Is this the time to think about it, when things are so far along that the banns will be announced tomorrow?

KORTESUO: You won't have any regrets, Anna-Liisa. Johannes 65 will make a good husband.

RIIKKA: That's for sure. They don't make them any better. You should thank your lucky stars, girl.

ANNA-LIISA: He's really too good for me.

KORTESUO: Now I wouldn't say that. But we can be happy 70 anyhow. That's why we'll have a joyous celebration tomorrow.

ANNA-LIISA: Who can tell that ahead of time? I'm so scared of tomorrow, because Father has asked Mikko to come too. Who knows what he'll do? 75

RIIKKA: Are you afraid there'll be some kind of argument or fight?

ANNA-LIISA: Well, that could happen.

RIIKKA: You're right, there's no guarantee it won't. He certainly seemed ready to pick a fight yesterday. 80

KORTESUO: He's turned so rude since he was off at the lumber camp. But never mind, he'll behave tomorrow when we have the parson here, and the sheriff too. And men don't really fight much when they're sober. We just won't serve enough liquor for anyone to get drunk. 85

RIIKKA: Oh, by the way, that Mikko came by again last night. He was asking for you, Anna-Liisa, but you didn't happen to be home. He sat and waited a while, but finally left when you didn't return.

KORTESUO: What did he want with Anna-Liisa? 90

RIIKKA: Said he had something to talk to her about.

ANNA-LIISA: Did he threaten to come back?

RIIKKA: He said he'd come back today.

ANNA-LIISA: Do you think he still means to do that?

RIIKKA: That's what I thought he said. But if he comes, he'll 95 meet up with Johannes and there could be another quarrel.

KORTESUO: What if there is? If they argue, let them. A little quarrel never hurt anybody.—Isn't that soup ready yet?

RIIKKA: Oh yes, it is. Go on into the other room. I'll bring 100 the stewpot in there. (KORTESUO *exits.* RIIKKA *follows him carrying the stewpot. Turns to* ANNA-LIISA *on her way out.*) Why don't you come and have something to eat too, Anna-Liisa.

ANNA-LIISA: So he'll be here today! Could be here any 105 minute now. Oh, my God, what's going to save me from him?

PIRKKO: (*Opens the door and whispers.*) Anna-Liisa! Anna-Liisa!

ANNA-LIISA: (*Frightened*) What is it?

PIRKKO: He's here. 110

ANNA-LIISA: Who?

PIRKKO: Mikko, and he's got Husso along with him. They asked for you and I said they should just go away and come another time, after Sunday. I said you weren't home. But Husso looked me in the eye and said: "You're lying." 115 Threatened to come in and see for herself. Now if you really want to avoid them, you'd better go up quickly and hide on the hearth.

ANNA-LIISA: No, let them come in. I guess I'll have to speak with them sooner or later. They're not going to let me get 120 out of it.

PIRKKO: Should I tell them to come in here, then?

ANNA-LIISA: (*Sinks down on the bench, dejected.*) Go ahead.

PIRKKO: Listen, if you don't want to see them, I'll think of some trick to get them away from here. 125

ANNA-LIISA: No, no. That won't be any help in the long run. They'd just be right back. Let them in right now so they'll be out of the way by the time Johannes gets here.

PIRKKO: I'll keep watch outside and won't let Johannes in un-
130 til they've gone.

ANNA-LIISA: Oh, please do, Pirkko dear.

PIRKKO: Sure! (*Opens the door to go.*) Well, here's Mikko right at the door, keeping watch. Come on in. Anna-Liisa seems to be home.

MIKKO enters.

135 MIKKO: Good evening!

ANNA-LIISA: You've been looking for me?

MIKKO: Yes, I stopped by yesterday afternoon. I waited for you quite a while, but there was not sign of you. Thought you were staying out of my way on purpose.

140 ANNA-LIISA: What do you want with me?

MIKKO: You don't have to ask what I want. Mother's already been by to talk to you about it.

ANNA-LIISA: Then you must know my answer. Let's leave it at that. There's no point going over it again and again. We
145 both know where we stand.

MIKKO: You think it's that easy to get rid of me? Well, well! You sure don't know me very well.

ANNA-LIISA: What more do you want with me? What do I owe you?

150 MIKKO: All I ask is that you honor the bond you made with me, some four, five years ago now.

ANNA-LIISA: You have the nerve to bring that up? Do you have no shame?! Didn't you yourself break that bond when you went off and left me alone in my great misfor-
155 tune?

MIKKO: I didn't go away for good. I promised to come back. And here I am, as you see.

ANNA-LIISA: But now I don't care for you any more. You know I'm about to be married to another man.

160 MIKKO: But you promised to wait for me. You promised to be faithful.

ANNA-LIISA: I promised—because I was a fool.

MIKKO: You said you loved me more than anyone else in the world. And I think you really did, even though you've for-
165 gotten all about it.

ANNA-LIISA: Childishness, sheer childishness! What did I know of love, or anything else at that time? It was easy enough for you to trap and seduce me.

MIKKO: Did it take very much to seduce you? Try to remem-
170 ber it right!

ANNA-LIISA: You were older than I was. You should have understood better where it would lead. But no, you took advantage of my youth and inexperience.

MIKKO: So, you heap all the blame on me? Who was it who
175 would slip out of her bedroom while everyone else was asleep and go to meet me at the end of the cape over there? I didn't have to ask you twice. All it took was a whisper in your ear, and right away you'd promise to come. Can you deny it? If you really think about it, it was
180 your own desire that led you there, more than any temp-
tation I offered.

ANNA-LIISA: It must have been the Devil that tempted me!

MIKKO: It was love, Anna-Liisa, not any evil spirit.

ANNA-LIISA: No, no! Whatever it may have been, it wasn't love. If only I could live through that time again, I'd do it 185 differently. If only I could wipe it away, wash it off like dirt so there wouldn't be a trace of it left. But no, I can't. I can't even if I repent and cry my eyes out. It will always be a stain on my life, for ever and ever.

MIKKO: Now don't talk nonsense! What stain was that? Those 190 were good times, no need to regret them. But after we knew, it was really stupid that we didn't go to your father and tell him straight out how things were and ask his permission for us to get married, since there was nothing else to do. But you were so deathly afraid of your father. 195

ANNA-LIISA: Yes, I certainly was afraid. Of both Mother and Father—Father most of all.

MIKKO: And I wasn't brave enough either. I knew well enough what a storm it would bring on.

ANNA-LIISA: But you shouldn't have gone off and left me all 200 alone. Maybe what happened could have been prevented if I'd had someone to talk to about my sorrows. But I didn't have a soul, no one on the face of the earth.

MIKKO: How could I guess you'd go and do something like that? I thought I'd come back after it was all over and ask 205 your father for your hand. Maybe he'd have given in by then and that would have been the end of it. But you got all scared for no good reason and took the child's life. There was nothing I could do anymore.

ANNA-LIISA: I was out of my mind! My God, I was out of my 210 mind. I was all messed up with worry and fear. And I didn't think I'd really kill the child—God in heaven knows I didn't think that. What I did want to do away with was my own life. Often I stood at the very edge of the Huuhka rocks and was about to throw myself down into the lake. But the wa- 215 ter was so black and deep that I didn't dare. I'd keep putting it off. And then it was too late.

MIKKO: Thank God you didn't! So you were thinking of that? Well, I'll be . . . ! Now that would have been really crazy.

ANNA-LIISA: I didn't realize that my time was getting so close. 220 That's why it came so suddenly. I was so afraid, I didn't know what to do. I tried to get to your mother's, to her cottage on the other side of the woods. But I didn't make it all the way there. There still was a stretch to go when the child came—oh my God, that moment! 225

MIKKO: And the child was alive? Are you sure the child was alive?

ANNA-LIISA: The poor thing was alive, all right. Moved its arms and legs and cried. That's when I—oh my God, oh my God, oh my God. 230

MIKKO: I can imagine the rest. Don't say another thing.

ANNA-LIISA: I pressed my hand to the child's mouth—I have no idea for how long. I was half-fainting and the world turned black before my eyes, but I still kept my hand there. Then—oh my God! 235

MIKKO: Stop it. You're tormenting yourself for no good reason.

ANNA-LIISA: Yes, that's when I felt the little body twitch under my hand and then it was still. I took my hand away—
no more sounds, life had gone out. I don't remember 240 anything more. I became conscious only when I fell down on the floor at your mother's house.

MIKKO: And then you had nothing to worry about. Mother took good care of you, you know.

245 ANNA-LIISA: Your mother went out to dig a grave and cover all the traces. That's what was so horrible—that the poor little one wasn't buried in hallowed ground. Died without being baptized. Buried somewhere in the forest.

250 MIKKO: It's all the same, isn't it? Many a man is lying at the bottom of the sea and can still be blessed. And as for baptism, there are some sects that don't baptize their children at all. The main thing is that you were safe and nothing about this came out. Thanks be to God. No one suspected anything. Then you could be at peace.

255 ANNA-LIISA: At peace? Could I be at peace? My God, what are you saying?

MIKKO: Sure, sure! I mean you weren't caught, no one was after you. And that was all thanks to Mother.

ANNA-LIISA: Oh, it would have been better if I'd been put in
260 prison right away. Because what came later was so terrible that I still can't understand how I could ever bear it. I don't know why I didn't go utterly mad.

MIKKO: Go mad? Why? What was it, then?

ANNA-LIISA: I couldn't get any rest at night, or any peace dur-
265 ing the day. This went on for years. I lived in constant fear and trembling. In the daytime, whenever I heard footsteps or a knock on the door I'd be so frightened that my blood would stand still. I always thought it was the sheriff coming to get me. And when I'd see people talking quietly to-
270 gether I'd be afraid they'd somehow got wind of it and were spreading the word. That's what my peace was like in those days.

MIKKO: Oh, that was all because you were so timid. Why did you have to be so afraid for no reason?

275 ANNA-LIISA: Nights were the worst of all. The child would always be there in front of me and I would keep my hand on its mouth just as I did then. And if I dozed off, the child's cry would ring in my ears and I'd wake up with a start. Sometimes its cry was so loud and clear that I be-
280 lieved the child was right there, next to me. I'd fumble around the empty bed and wouldn't believe it was really empty until I grabbed hold of a light and looked around. Oh, what I would have given to have had the child there beside me, alive again!

285 MIKKO: If I'd been here I sure could have driven those hallucinations away. Do you believe me?

ANNA-LIISA: They haven't haunted me for quite a while now. And I've banished those painful memories. Whatever could have brought them back again? Let's not say any
290 more about it.

MIKKO: You're right, let's not talk. Talking doesn't make things any better. But we'll start fresh, won't we, Anna-Liisa? We'll forget about all those unhappy things and it'll be as if they'd never happened. We'll have good times together.
295 Dear Lord, you'll never have another worry. I'll keep you so very well, so well you can't even imagine. I'll even put you in a glass case, if you wish.

ANNA-LIISA: How can you talk like that? You know as well as I do that my banns with another man will be published
300 tomorrow.

MIKKO: That's no problem. A little money will buy him off.

ANNA-LIISA: But I don't want to get out of it. Leave well enough alone, Mikko. I'll never go along with your ideas.

MIKKO: You needn't worry about Johannes or your father. I'll
305 take care of them, just so long as I know you're on my side.

ANNA-LIISA: My God, don't you understand that I love Johannes and not you? And I never want to break with him, neither by your temptations nor by anyone else's. Do you finally believe me?

310 MIKKO: But I love you, Anna-Liisa, and I want to get you back. I'll do whatever I have to do to get you. By God, I'm not going to give you up to another man. I will not!

ANNA-LIISA: And that's what you call love? Call it anything else, but not love.

315 MIKKO: It certainly is love, the most passionate kind of love in the whole world. Listen to me, Anna-Liisa. I've had you on my mind all the time I've been away in Saarijärvi. I made a firm decision that one day I'd come to collect you. When I heard Johannes had interfered and you were planning to
320 marry him, I flew into such a rage I didn't know what to do. I dropped everything and came straight here. And I won't leave until this matter is cleared up. I'll drive the other one away or the devil take me!

ANNA-LIISA: You have no power to do that. He loves me and
325 won't give me up to you, you can be sure of that.

MIKKO: Loves you! That miserable mush-mouth! What does he know about love?

ANNA-LIISA: What does it have to do with you, whether he does or doesn't? He pleases me, and that's all there is to it.

330 MIKKO: Sure, he pleases you, since you don't know anything better. And since you can't remember the good side of our old times together.

ANNA-LIISA: You promised not to speak about that anymore.

MIKKO: No, Anna-Liisa, it'll be different if you come to me.
335 That's when you'll learn what a real man's love is.

He moves closer to ANNA-LIISA *and tries to touch her.*

ANNA-LIISA: Stay away from me! Go away, go away!

MIKKO: Don't shout! They'll hear you.

ANNA-LIISA: (*Shoving him aside*) You beast! Is that how you thought you'd win me over? Go away! Get out of here
340 right now! I hate you! I loathe the sight of you!

MIKKO: Be quiet! Quiet! I'll break you down yet. This isn't the end of this game. Since you won't give in when I try nicely, let's try another way.

ANNA-LIISA: Just you try! I'm not afraid of you. There's no
345 way you can hurt me.

MIKKO: No way I can hurt you? Think it over a bit. Is there really no way?

ANNA-LIISA: No. You can't do anything to me.

MIKKO: What about the murder of that child?

350 ANNA-LIISA: You want to scare me with that, just like your mother. But it's no use! It doesn't have any effect at all. You won't report it, since you yourself are an accomplice.

MIKKO: I an accomplice? In the child's murder?

ANNA-LIISA: If not directly in that, then—

355 MIKKO: But that's just the point. No one's sentenced to hard labor for giving birth to a child. You must know that much about the law.

ANNA-LIISA *is silent.*

MIKKO: But they do give that sentence for child-murder.

ANNA-LIISA: So, you intend to have me sentenced to hard la-
360 bor? I must say, you really are very noble.

MIKKO: Maybe we don't have to go quite that far. Perhaps it will be enough if your father and Johannes know your secrets. (ANNA-LIISA, *perplexed, falls silent.*) So, what do you think? Won't there be a parting of the ways for the two of

365 you?

ANNA-LIISA: Oh, yes, I guess there'll be a parting of the ways.

MIKKO: That's what I thought. Johannes's love will be snuffed out like the light of a candle. It goes no deeper than that.

ANNA-LIISA: Can I never hope for happiness? When all other

370 people have it, why not me.

MIKKO: You sure won't get it from him.

ANNA-LIISA: Mikko, have pity on me, I've suffered enough.

MIKKO: That's up to you. You can keep me from speaking out if you want to.

375 ANNA-LIISA: Don't make me unhappy again. Not just now, when I have the chance for a better future. What good will it do if you crush my life once again? You spoiled my youth, isn't that enough? I haven't had any happiness, like other people my age—only worry and sorrow all the

380 time. I can't bear anything more, I'm sure I can't.

MIKKO: You won't have any trouble so long as you do what I've told you. Just break with Johannes and come to me.

ANNA-LIISA: I can't do that.

MIKKO: Then you'll have only yourself to blame.

385 ANNA-LIISA: What have I ever done to you that you should persecute me like this? You have no conscience at all. You're a beast, that's what you are, not a human being.

MIKKO: Now listen to me, Anna-Liisa. How can you think of going to a man who doesn't know what sort of secret

390 you're covering up? It could come out at any time, and what would happen then? You and I have the secret in common, and that binds us together forever—much more surely than the words of any pastor.

ANNA-LIISA: The crime binds us together?! No, that's just what

395 separates us, if anything. It would be a curse on us, not a blessing, don't you understand? And how could I possibly love you—you with whom I've sinned and who have made me so miserable? Never! It would be impossible. To tie myself to you—oh my God—that would mean I would bind

400 myself to those horrible memories for the rest of my days. No, no, I cannot! Let anything happen but not that!

MIKKO: Think it over once again before you make up your mind.

ANNA-LIISA: Leave me alone, Mikko. Let me go to Johannes.

405 With him I could forget all this and still have a chance at happiness.

MIKKO: No! I won't give you up to Johannes or anyone else. By fair means or foul, you'll have to be mine!

ANNA-LIISA: Hush! Oh, good heavens, someone's at the door.

410 Hush!

The voices of PIRKKO *and* JOHANNES *are heard outside.*

MIKKO: So, now you know. If you want to avoid unfortunate consequences, don't waste time making a clean break with Johannes. Right away, or else you'll come to grief!

ANNA-LIISA: Quiet, can't you hear . . . ?

415 PIRKKO: (*Still outside*) You're not allowed to go in! Anna-Liisa said not to, no, no, no! You're just—

JOHANNES: (*Also outside*) Pirkko, what is this? Let go of me, I'm going in anyway. You think you can keep me from go-

ing in, you little slip of a girl? Come on, let's go in together. 420

Both enter, PIRKKO *trying to pull him back by the arm.*

PIRKKO: Oh, this rascal won't listen to me. It wasn't my fault, Anna-Liisa, he just slipped past me as I was harnessing father's horse.

JOHANNES: And when she saw me, she screamed so loud I thought someone was holding a knife to her throat! She 425 jumped and stuck onto my arm like a burdock. I'll bet your nails will leave my arm all black and blue.

PIRKKO: I wish they would! It would serve you right, forcing your way in here.

ANNA-LIISA: Pirkko, don't be silly! 430

PIRKKO: Me—silly? Is that right? So I'm silly! All right! Well, from now on I won't take care of your business. That's the end of it, if that's all the thanks I get from you!

ANNA-LIISA: Oh, be quiet!

PIRKKO: (*Suddenly in a different mood*) Do you know where 435 I'm going now? I'll bet you can't guess.

JOHANNES: To the store with your father. To get all the things for the party celebrating the banns.

PIRKKO: I didn't ask you, I asked Anna-Liisa. Why did you have to butt in? Why? 440

JOHANNES: Wasn't it all right for the one who guessed it first to speak out?

PIRKKO: Did you really guess? You must have heard people talking out there. No, got to go. Bye for now.

JOHANNES: Are you going to get to hold the reins too? 445

PIRKKO: Sure!

JOHANNES: Then the wagon'll be sure to turn over.

PIRKKO: You should be ashamed!

ANNA-LIISA: Pirkko, that's no way to talk!

PIRKKO: Then why is he talking nonsense? Says I'll drive so 450 badly the wagon'll turn over. Oh, you big rascal!

MIKKO: (*Laughing*) Serves you right!

JOHANNES: There's no trouble between us. We're good pals, Pirkko and me.

MIKKO: Then you should have stayed out there and played 455 with her. You barged in here at a bad time.

JOHANNES: Is that right, Anna-Liisa?

ANNA-LIISA: Oh, no! For no reason at all Mikko just—

JOHANNES: When Pirkko didn't want to let me in, I thought she was just playing tricks. But I understood why when I 460 saw Mikko here.

MIKKO: So you understood? I guess you're smarter than you look.

JOHANNES: Don't worry, Anna-Liisa, he can shoot off his mouth all he wants. I'm not going to let it get 465 to me.

ANNA-LIISA: You won't? Oh, that's good! No matter what he says, just pretend you don't hear it. Promise!

JOHANNES: (*Sits down with his back to* MIKKO.) Don't worry. I can't see him or hear him. 470

MIKKO: Well, in that case, we can go right on with our conversation, Anna-Liisa. Maybe he'll turn deaf and blind to you too.

ANNA-LIISA: Mikko, stop it! I beg you, please stop!

JOHANNES: Don't you go begging him to do anything. That 475 won't get us anywhere.

MIKKO: Anna-Liisa knows perfectly well where she can get help. Whenever she's ready to take it up. It's all up to her.

480 ANNA-LIISA: They've invited a great many guests here for tomorrow, Johannes.

JOHANNES: That's what your father was just saying out in the yard.

ANNA-LIISA: They're planning a very festive celebration. Father has ordered drinks to be delivered all the way from 485 the city.

JOHANNES: I heard about that too.

ANNA-LIISA: Father has such a good nature. He wishes only joy to everybody.

MIKKO: I wonder if he would wish that to me, too.

490 ANNA-LIISA: Of course, for you too. You know how warmly he welcomed you here yesterday.

MIKKO: But I'm not satisfied with so little. What I demand is even greater joy.

ANNA-LIISA: And right then and there he invited you to the 495 party celebrating the banns tomorrow.

MIKKO: And I guess you wish I wouldn't come. Is that how it is?

ANNA-LIISA: Oh, if you'd only behave, if you wouldn't keep teasing me all the time and wouldn't cause trouble, I'd be 500 glad to see you here among the others.

MIKKO: But not at your side?

JOHANNES: What? You'd try to stand by her side?

MIKKO: Well, well, you seem to be getting your hearing back. That was quick!

505 ANNA-LIISA: If you carry on like that, you'll spoil all the pleasure for yourself and others.

MIKKO: I asked whether you would let me stand by your side tomorrow.

JOHANNES: That's my place, as you very well know.

510 MIKKO: So it is, right now. But others have been there before you.

JOHANNES: What did you say?

ANNA-LIISA: Johannes, you promised not to pay any attention to whatever he says.

515 JOHANNES: I know I promised, but—

MIKKO: But it's a bit difficult, isn't it?

JOHANNES: No, no. Go ahead and talk. I can take it.

ANNA-LIISA: It wasn't nice of you, Mikko, to bring trouble to a house that has always treated you well. If you think 520 about it a minute, you'll have to agree.

MIKKO: You don't treat me as well as you used to, that's the heart of it.

ANNA-LIISA: I leave you in peace. You could do the same for me.

525 MIKKO: Who cares about peace? It's love I demand from you.

JOHANNES: Don't you have any shame? I guessed it. That's what he's been aiming at all along.

ANNA-LIISA: Johannes!

JOHANNES: Well, I'm not going to get mad. Go ahead and 530 talk. Just to spite you, I won't get mad.

MIKKO: Whether you get mad or not is all the same to me. But you'll have to give up Anna-Liisa. And it's best if you do it right now.

JOHANNES: Just because you say so? Well, you can just wait, 535 but don't get too tired waiting.

ANNA-LIISA: (*Sits down next to* JOHANNES *and takes his hand.*) Johannes, he's trying to make us break up.

JOHANNES: Well, he's not going to succeed. Never.

ANNA-LIISA: If you could only stay strong, Johannes. And not 540 abandon me, whatever happens.

JOHANNES: Do you think I'd ever abandon you? Just because of Mikko's scheming? Well, now!

ANNA-LIISA: If only I could trust that you won't ever forsake me! That you won't ever leave me, no matter what!

JOHANNES: In the name of God, how could you ever think 545 of something like that? You know how very deeply I love you. How could I possibly forsake you?

ANNA-LIISA: Johannes, will you be my support, even if something stranger than strange should happen?

JOHANNES: You can trust me. But what stranger than strange 550 thing could possibly happen to us?

ANNA-LIISA: You see, there's no one else in the whole world that I can trust.

JOHANNES: My own sweet darling! You're like a terrified little bird. 555

MIKKO: All right, bill and coo for a minute there. That'll be the last billing and cooing you'll ever do.

JOHANNES: You're still afraid of him?

ANNA-LIISA: Yes, I am.

JOHANNES: You have no reason to be afraid. If you want, I'll 560 send him packing right away.

ANNA-LIISA: No, don't start a quarrel, or we'll be lost.

JOHANNES: I can't understand why you're so afraid. That's no help at all. It only encourages him to act twice as badly.

ANNA-LIISA: Let's try to calm him down by being nice. Be- 565 lieve me, it's the only way.

MIKKO: That's enough, now.

JOHANNES: Enough what?

MIKKO: Enough of these farewells.

JOHANNES: You're mistaken. We're not saying any farewells. 570

MIKKO: Well then, you can skip them, because now you've got to get out of here.

JOHANNES: What did you say?

MIKKO: That you've got to get out of here. Right now!

JOHANNES: Me? Are you telling me to get out? What am I 575 supposed to make of that?

MIKKO: Anna-Liisa and I have to talk privately about some things, just the two of us. You barged in and interrupted us in the middle of it.

JOHANNES: That's nonsense! What private matters do the two 580 of you have? What?

MIKKO: Anna-Liisa, get him out of her now or things will take a different turn.

JOHANNES: Have you gone mad?

MIKKO: Did you hear what I said? 585

ANNA-LIISA: Do as he says, Johannes. Go into the other room for a little while.

JOHANNES: I don't understand you. Wasn't I supposed to be your strength and support here?

ANNA-LIISA: No, I didn't mean that. 590

JOHANNES: What did you mean, then?

ANNA-LIISA: I meant something else. I'll explain later.

JOHANNES: Now, this is going too far.

ANNA-LIISA: Please, dear Johannes. Please go.

JOHANNES: So you're in this with him and are sending me 595 out of the way.

ANNA-LIISA: I'm not sending you away. I'm only asking you to go.

JOHANNES: What's the difference? In any case, you want
600   to stay here with him. Just the two of you, I can't be-
    lieve it!

ANNA-LIISA: If you'd only go off for a little while. So he can
    say what he has to say. Right, Mikko? Just for a little
    while—that'll be all right with you, won't it?

605 MIKKO: Let him stay away a long time while he's at it.

JOHANNES: I'm not going.

MIKKO: So you won't go?

JOHANNES: No.

ANNA-LIISA: Johannes!

610 JOHANNES: Don't ask me to go. I won't. I won't even budge.
    Mikko has nothing to say to you that I couldn't hear.

MIKKO: We can't put it off till later. I want it all cleared up to-
    day, right now.

JOHANNES: What has to be cleared up?

615 MIKKO: Whether the girl's yours or mine.

JOHANNES: What girl are you talking about?

MIKKO: Anna-Liisa, of course. Who else?

JOHANNES: You should know the answer to that without asking.

ANNA-LIISA: No quarreling, now! Oh please stop all this
620   quarreling!

MIKKO: All right, then. You decide which one of us you want
    to belong to.

JOHANNES: She's done that already. Go to church tomorrow
    and hear for yourself.

625 MIKKO: (*To* ANNA-LIISA) You know the consequences. Make
    up your mind!

ANNA-LIISA: Oh, my God!

JOHANNES: Go ahead and tell him, since he insists.

ANNA-LIISA: Stop tormenting me. Leave me alone, both of
630   you.

JOHANNES: It's your own fault. If you'd let me do as I wanted,
    I'd have driven him out of here long before this.

MIKKO: Oh, would you now? You'd have driven me out of
    here? You miserable little puppy! But well, if you'd done
635   that, you'd have been quite a man.

JOHANNES: Stop it, or I'll show you.

ANNA-LIISA: Don't, please! Men, don't! Johannes, you
    promised!

MIKKO: Come on, then, if you dare. I'll knock you over with
640   one punch. And I'll be glad to do it!

ANNA-LIISA: No fighting! No, no! Johannes, Mikko! (*A horse
    stops in front of the house. Voices and footsteps can be heard out-
    side.*) Listen! Oh, thank God! That's Father coming.

KORTESUO, RIIKKA, *and* PIRKKO *enter; carrying bottles of drink,
sugar loaves, and other things.* PIRKKO *is carrying a big sack of flour
on her back. She lets it flop onto the floor.*

PIRKKO: "Aha!" said the old woman as they lowered her into
645   the grave.

KORTESUO: Here comes the supplies for tomorrow.

PIRKKO: Should certainly last us till the wedding. Anna-Liisa,
    do you see how much flour? This will be more than
    enough for you to bake big round rings and a lot of other
650   things.

RIIKKA: We should have done that for the banns, too. Now
    we've gone and spent good money at the baker's.

KORTESUO: Well, do you think we got the flour free? I guess
    these should be enough, or what do you think, men?

These drinks, I mean. But people no longer drink the way   655
    they used to.

RIIKKA: I've heard it's fashionable to have temperance feasts
    now. No liquor at all.

KORTESUO: Oh, I don't give a hoot about the new fashions.
    We have it and we're going to serve it. At least a few   660
    drinks, so the guests will have a good time. If a few peo-
    ple get high, that doesn't hurt anyone.

PIRKKO: Father, may I take the harness off the horse and take
    it to the pasture? And may I ride it just a little bit along
    the road first?   665

KORTESUO: All right, since you want to so badly.

PIRKKO: (*Squeals and jumps for joy.*) Oh, what fun! Now,
    everybody, look out the window when I make it go at full
    gallop. (*Runs out.*)

RIIKKA: Shouldn't have let her. She'll never grow even-   670
    tempered that way.

KORTESUO: Well, what does it mater if she gets to do it just
    this once?

RIIKKA: Whatever will become of that girl? She certainly isn't
    going to become a reasonable adult.   675

KORTESUO: Well, men, why are you looking so serious? You
    haven't been quarreling here, now have you?

ANNA-LIISA: What else! Thank God you came home when
    you did, Father. I don't know what would have happened
    here if you hadn't.   680

RIIKKA: You mean they were picking a fight?

ANNA-LIISA: It just about came to that. I was certainly in a
    tight spot with them here. Well, aren't you embarrassed
    about the whole thing, both of you?

KORTESUO: So, you were about to get into a fight? Oh, my!   685
    And such sensible men!

ANNA-LIISA: Now listen to what Father's saying. Sensible men
    simply don't act like that. And you're really sensible, not
    just a couple of rowdies, aren't you?

RIIKKA: What in the world is this grudge between you two?   690
    Mikko's been away for four years. Even if there was some
    trouble between you, you certainly should have forgotten
    it by now.

MIKKO: It's not an old grudge. It just came out now.

KORTESUO: Old or new, go ahead and make up. You can get   695
    mad, but then be reconciled. Never let the sun set over a
    quarrel. That's what Paul the Apostle says.

JOHANNES: I'm not seeking a quarrel.

KORTESUO: So it comes from Mikko, I guess. Listen here,
    brother silver, you may have a bit of your mother's tem-   700
    per. Forgive me, but I've never been able to stand that
    woman. She seems to be standing around out there in the
    yard again.

MIKKO: What bad has she ever done to you, that you can't
    stand her?   705

KORTESUO: Nothing bad. No, nothing bad.

MIKKO: In fact, she's done you good. Yes, she's done you good,
    but you don't even know it.

KORTESUO: No, I don't know that she's done any good.

MIKKO: Do you want to hear it? I can tell you!   710

ANNA-LIISA: Mikko, did you know there'll be dancing here
    tomorrow? Do you still know how to dance? You used to
    be very good at it. We both were. We'll have to see
    whether we can still do it as well.

MIKKO: You really want to? Do I understand you correctly?   715

ANNA-LIISA: Yes, I want to dance with you tomorrow.

JOHANNES: How can you, Anna-Liisa? After Mikko and I have been fighting, you go and suggest something like that? I just can't believe it!

720 ANNA-LIISA: All that's been settled. Settled and forgotten. Right, Mikko? We're not going to argue any more now, are we? We're all good friends again.

MIKKO: You mean you and me?

JOHANNES: You have nothing to do with each other. No
725 need for anger, but not friendship either.

ANNA-LIISA: No, no, I mean real reconciliation. Harmonious, like any other old friendship. You don't take offence at that, do you, Johannes?

MIKKO: So you're trying to play up to both of us? That won't
730 get you far. One or the other but not both.

JOHANNES: Stay away from him, Anna-Liisa. That would be best.

ANNA-LIISA: I'll just dance with him a few times tomorrow. Nothing more dangerous than that. Then he'll promise to
735 behave himself all evening long.

MIKKO: Oh, I see! So it was just a trap. Oh, how very clever she is! But you can trap others, not me. I'm not the kind of man you can fool. And anyway, it's time to put a stop to all this. Nothing but straight talk will do now.

740 ANNA-LIISA: Not yet, Mikko! Not yet! Let it rest till the day after tomorrow!

MIKKO: We're not going to leave it til the day after tomorrow. It has to come out now.

ANNA-LIISA: Mikko!

745 JOHANNES: What's the matter with you, Anna-Liisa? What are you afraid of?

ANNA-LIISA: Oh, nothing, nothing. Be a support for me, Johannes. Here it comes.

KORTESUO: Hell and damnation! I don't understand any of
750 this. What are you going to put a stop to? And what are you going to talk straight about? If something's been kept hidden from me, I want to know it right now.

ANNA-LIISA: Don't let him speak, Johannes! Don't let him say a word! Oh, do try to shut him up.

755 KORTESUO: Why? Explain yourself!

MIKKO: Well, sir, the fact is that Anna-Liisa was my bride about four years ago, and now I've come to collect her. But that fellow over there has mixed up our relationship.

KORTESUO: Anna-Liisa your bride? You're lying!

760 RIIKKA: God save us! What do I have to hear? Anna-Liisa was only fifteen years old then. Johannes, don't believe a word of it. It's nothing but nonsense. I promise you, there's nothing to it. Other people would have noticed if anything had been going on between them.

765 MIKKO: Well, you didn't notice. We covered it up so well, no one had an inkling.

KORTESUO: Mikko, now just stop it before I get angry. Are you trying to tell me that my daughter had secret relations with a farmhand? Shame on you! You should be ashamed
770 to be spreading such lies. If it were a question of some wanton girl! But Anna-Liisa, whom everybody knows is the most serious and well-behaved girl in the whole village. You have some nerve! And I'll say it once more—you should be ashamed of yourself.

775 MIKKO: Why don't you ask Anna-Liisa whether I've been lying or telling the truth?

RIIKKA: Can't you open your mouth, girl? Why do you let him insult you like that?

KORTESUO: Defend yourself, Anna-Liisa.

JOHANNES: Tell him he's lying, and I'll believe you. 780

ANNA-LIISA: Oh, my God!

JOHANNES: Be brave. Don't be afraid, you're in no danger. You can trust us.

KORTESUO: Well, this is certainly strange. Please, go ahead and answer him! Whose bride are you? Do you belong to Jo- 785 hannes, or to that one over there?

ANNA-LIISA: I'm Johannes's bride. I've never loved anyone else. I was only a child at the time—an ignorant child— only fifteen years old.

RIIKKA: Well, there it is. You can all hear. 790

ANNA-LIISA: Don't forsake me, Johannes.

JOHANNES: Don't worry, since you have nothing on your conscience.

KORTESUO: Mikko, I welcomed you here like an old ac- quaintance, and a former servant. But now that you've 795 plotted like this, I'm going to forbid you to enter my house every again. I will not tolerate such behavior.

MIKKO: Anna-Liisa, will you go on, or is it my turn to talk? You can still have things take another turn if you want to. It's all in your hands. 800

RIIKKA: What in God's name are these threats? You have to understand you won't get her by force.

MIKKO: I won't give up Anna-Liisa. I will not give her to an- other man because she is as good as being my wife, even if we haven't stood before a pastor. 805

JOHANNES: His wife? Anna-Liisa, is that true? Tell me quickly.

RIIKKA: You shameless man!

KORTESUO: Take back those words this minute, or you'll come to a bad end. Take back those words, do you hear me? And then get down on your knees! Get right down 810 and ask forgiveness, first of Anna-Liisa and then of us. Or else, or else!

MIKKO: Do you give in, now, Anna-Liisa? Or shall I tell everything?

ANNA-LIISA: You monster! Just kill me while you're at it! 815

MIKKO: So you won't, Anna-Liisa? Have you got such a hard nature? Well then, there's nothing left but to put my last card on the table. You have only yourself to blame!

He goes to the door.

ANNA-LIISA: What are you going to—?

MIKKO: Mother, come on in! 820

RIIKKA: Husso? She's the last one we need in here! Goes around the village spreading gossip about everything that's going on, and adds a good bit besides.

ANNA-LIISA: Now it's over, Johannes.

JOHANNES: What's over? 825

ANNA-LIISA: Everything, everything!

JOHANNES: You didn't answer me. Was it true, what he just said?

ANNA-LIISA: Oh, if only the earth would swallow me up!

JOHANNES: Answer me, Anna-Liisa, or I'll go mad.

MIKKO: Come on in, come on in! 830

HUSSO: I'm coming. I'm coming as fast as I can. So, do they know everything now?

MIKKO: Not yet. But they will soon. Now you may tell them what you know.

835 HUSSO: So it's come to that, after all? What did I tell you? She doesn't give in easily.

KORTESUO: I don't think Husso has any business here. I'd really want her to go away.

HUSSO: You hear that, Mikko? That's how much they trust
840 us. That's how they've treated me all this time. They don't invite you in, don't ask you to sit down. That's the thanks I get for saving their daughter from shame and hard labor.

RIIKKA: My God, have both of them lost their senses?

845 KORTESUO: You'd better weigh your words carefully, old woman. This isn't going to end here, I promise you.

RIIKKA: Mother and son, they're both in cahoots. No, we don't offer thanks. But let's see what's going to come of it.

KORTESUO: This isn't the end. I'll make them answer for it
850 yet!

HUSSO: Go ahead and take us to court if you dare! I'll stand behind my words. I'll say the same thing there that I say here, that if it hadn't been for me, your daughter would be doing time in prison, and that's the truth. She can thank
855 this poor old woman that she's out free. And what's been my reward from her? Nothing, nothing at all. Once in a dog's age she's cast off some old rags, that's all. Take my word for it, that's how it is.

KORTESUO: You've been scaring her with some dirty trick
860 and have demanded gifts from her? It's a good thing I found out—

HUSSO: A few raggedy pieces of clothing, as I said, nothing else. And for all this time, four long years, I've kept it quiet, haven't breathed so much as a word to a living
865 soul. Anna-Liisa's been able to pass for a proper farmer's daughter and she pretends not to know it, even though the child she killed lies under a fir tree in the forest, not far from here.

RIIKKA: And she dares say things like that to our faces! Men,
870 get her out of here. Grab her by the elbows and throw her out!

MIKKO: Not as long as I'm here.

HUSSO: Go ahead, throw me out! Go ahead! Then I'll go straight to the sheriff and tell him the place. Let them dig
875 up the body so we'll see whether or not I've been lying.

RIIKKA: If they do find a child's body there, it belongs to someone else, not to Anna-Liisa.

HUSSO: The sheriff and the court can clear that up, if Anna-Liisa doesn't confess. But it seems she's not able to contra-
880 dict it here either. She just stands there like a condemned woman. Well, if you'd only believed me and stayed true to Mikko, and not started up any courtship with someone else, you wouldn't have had to end up in a spot like this. Nothing would ever have come out.

885 JOHANNES: You can hear what they're accusing you of, but you don't say a word. There's nothing to it, not even the littlest bit, is there?

MIKKO: Now you know how things stand. Sir, be reasonable and give Anna-Liisa to me. That's the only way out of this.
890 That way, things can even turn out well.

ANNA-LIISA: To him? Never! Anything else, but—

RIIKKA: What did you say, Anna-Liisa? Speak up so that we can all hear you. Don't be afraid, dear child, don't be afraid at all. No one, not even a crazy person, would believe
895 those lies.

KORTESUO: You're innocent, Anna-Liisa. I know you're innocent. I only want to hear it from your own mouth before I see they get the punishment they deserve. You are quite innocent, aren't you?

JOHANNES: In the name of God, answer!   900

RIIKKA: Why do you even ask? You're just tormenting her for no reason at all. The poor thing is almost fainting. You can see that for yourselves.

ANNA-LIISA: Oh, merciful God!

KORTESUO: It's all lies, nothing but lies from beginning to   905
end, isn't it? Just tell us that it is, I'm not asking you for a longer explanation.

RIIKKA: Dear child, good child, can't you hear what your father is asking? "It's a lie"—if only you could get out those words.   910

JOHANNES: (*With a heavy heart*) She can't say it!

KORTESUO: Anna-Liisa, what is this? Can't you hear, or do you just not understand?

ANNA-LIISA: Father—forgive me—Father!

KORTESUO: Don't worry. You won't be judged unfairly. And   915
they will have to answer for this.

ANNA-LIISA: Mother, Father, Johannes, have mercy on me!

KORTESUO: Have mercy? Have mercy for what? If you're innocent, then—(*Sinks down onto a bench, trembling.*) What was I going to say? Riikka, she is innocent, isn't she?   920

RIIKKA: Oh, dear God, don't doubt that!

KORTESUO: Come here, my child, come here. Don't stay down there on the floor, that's not your place. You haven't done anything like they're saying. You've lived right here under our eyes, your parents' eyes. Come here, come.   925
Don't be afraid of them. I'll make them go away. (*Rises.*)
You liars and scoundrels, get out of here! There's the door!
Both of you, out!

ANNA-LIISA: Father, let them stay. They haven't been lying. It's all true.   930

KORTESUO: True? What?

ANNA-LIISA: Everything they've told you here.

RIIKKA: Even that you killed your child?

ANNA-LIISA: Yes, yes! That's also true. Do with me what you will.   935

RIIKKA: Lord have mercy upon us!

JOHANNES: You? You, Anna-Liisa?

KORTESUO: What did she say? I must have got everything mixed up. What was she saying? Did she say she murdered her child?   940

ANNA-LIISA: Father! Hear me out, Father!

KORTESUO: Murdered her child? Murdered! All these years she's been living a lie right in front of me. Deceived me, deceived us all! You filthy snake! (*Fumbles around the bench for an axe.*)   945

ANNA-LIISA: Mother! Mother!

KORTESUO: You snake, I'll kill you!

ANNA-LIISA: Father! For the love of God, men, help!

MIKKO: Calm down, sir! Give me that axe!

KORTESUO: I'll kill you, too. I'll kill both of you!   950

RIIKKA: (*Takes hold of* ANNA-LIISA.) Get away from here, you poor wretch, until he calms down. Away! Away! (*Leads her out.*)

MIKKO: (*Tears the axe from* KORTESUO'*s hands and throws it onto the floor.*) You won't kill Ana-Liisa, and you won't kill me   955
either. That won't help matters at all.

KORTESUO *slumps down on the bench.*

JOHANNES: Won't help matters at all. It's all over.

ACT 3

The same interior, the main room of the farmhouse, RIIKKA *is standing at a window, looking out.*

RIIKKA: There she sits like a statue. Doesn't move, not even a twitch of the hand.

KORTESUO *enters.*

KORTESUO: I've sent for Johannes and Mikko. We've got to get to the bottom of this. Last night everything was left up
5   in the air.
RIIKKA: And Anna-Liisa won't move a muscle. All night long she's been sitting by the side of the lake. Hasn't moved from there one bit.
KORTESUO: Go get her. Bring her in.
10 RIIKKA: Oh, I've gone out several times and tried to persuade her, but it's no use.
KORTESUO: What does she say?
RIIKKA: Not a thing. All she does is stare ahead, with her eyes wide open, and she doesn't take in a single thing one says.
15   She's brooding about something out there.
KORTESUO: What could it be?
RIIKKA: If only she wouldn't throw herself into the lake in the end. That's what I've been watching out for all this time, ever since yesterday. I haven't taken my eyes off her for a minute.
20 KORTESUO: That's all we need! For the miserable girl to go and kill herself on top of everything else.
RIIKKA: Well, you did scare her pretty badly last night. I wonder how you'll feel if the girl goes out of her mind.
KORTESUO: I see! So now it's all my fault. All of it?
25 RIIKKA: No, it's not your fault, not at all. But you could've treated her a little more decently. She's your own child, after all.
KORTESUO: That's just why I have to punish her. What would I care about her crime if she were a stranger?
30 RIIKKA: I have to think the poor girl has suffered quite enough all these years. I don't think there's any need for more punishment from you.
KORTESUO: She's suffered? Sure thing! If she had, would she have covered everything up the way she did? And been
35   able to put on such an act? Hell and damnation, when I just think of it!
RIIKKA: You poor man, you just don't understand these things.
KORTESUO: Are you saying you understand them any better? Tell me!
40 RIIKKA: I think I do.
KORTESUO: So, maybe you knew about this business? Maybe she told you all about it? So you were both in cahoots and kept me in the dark. Fess up—come on, confess this minute or I'll—!
45 RIIKKA: All right, you just go ahead and shoot your mouth off again. As if we didn't have more than enough grief already.

KORTESUO: Did you know about it or didn't you?! Come on, tell me!
RIIKKA: I promise you, I had no idea. I didn't know any more 50 about it than you did. Don't get all worked up for no reason.
KORTESUO: Well, you're her mother. You should have known what your own daughter was up to.
RIIKKA: How could I possibly think of something like that? 55
KORTESUO: You should have been able to see it if you'd had eyes in your head.
RIIKKA: Well, you didn't notice anything either. You could see her as well as I could.
KORTESUO: But it was your duty to look after the girl, not 60 mine. Do you understand?
RIIKKA: I understand! I understand! But please stop all this for now. If you don't stop raging over it, we won't clear things up any better than we did yesterday. And you'll have wasted your time bringing Johannes and Mikko here. 65
KORTESUO: Who's raging now, you or me?
RIIKKA: Let's not quarrel. It won't make things any better.
KORTESUO: What *will* make things better? If you know, tell me.
RIIKKA: Hush! Johannes is coming. 70

JOHANNES *enters.*

JOHANNES: So, what's the news here?
RIIKKA: Bad, just bad. What else? The old man is quarreling and Anna-Liisa—(*She wipes away tears.*) may be lost to us.
JOHANNES: Seems she was sitting by the shore of the lake. Didn't notice me even though I went right past her. 75
RIIKKA: The poor thing can't see or hear anything any more.

She cries and keeps peering out the window.

KORTESUO: Well, Johannes, what are we to do? You'll want to break with Anna-Liisa, of course?
JOHANNES: (*Dejected*) What else can I do? She's not the person I thought she was. 80
KORTESUO: Yes, she pretended to be someone she wasn't. She deceived all of us.
JOHANNES: That's just it—that's why it's such a hard blow— when we thought she was the very best of them all. And then all of a sudden we find out it was the other way around. 85 That she was the worst, and that the loosest girl in the district is like an angel compared to her. It almost made me lose my mind last night. I don't know if I've fully recovered yet. There I was, walking through the forest all night long, lashing at the trees, lashing at the ground. If anyone had seen me, 90 they'd have thought I was out of my mind.
KORTESUO: Well, it's hurt you too, I do understand that. Though come to think of it, you have nothing to worry about. You're rid of her, and soon you'll get another one, a better one in her place. 95
JOHANNES: I don't think I'll ever start courting again. I've had quite enough with this first attempt.
KORTESUO: Oh, I think you will. Just let some time pass. Then it'll all be forgotten.
JOHANNES: I don't think I'll ever forget. 100
KORTESUO: That's what you say now, but I know what I'm talking about. No, I'll say it again—you have nothing to

worry about. It's different for us old people who've lived
our lives as honest and honorable folks and haven't
105   wronged anyone. And now, near the end of our days, we
have to endure such shame. Can you guess how that feels?

JOHANNES: Yes, I can, but you and your wife are innocent.
Everybody who knows you will know that.

KORTESUO: We are innocent, and I dare to say that even be-
110   fore God. Neither of us ever taught her to do anything
like that. But what does that help? The world will judge
as it always judges, and it doesn't take everything into
account.

JOHANNES: But does the world know anything about this?
115   That wouldn't help matters any.

KORTESUO: If we could only keep it hidden! Then the poor
thing wouldn't have to go to prison.

JOHANNES: I'll never say a word. You can trust that.

KORTESUO: Thank you for that promise. I know you'll keep
120   your word.

RIIKKA: But what are we going to do about today?

KORTESUO: That's why we wanted you to join us. I guess we
should call off the banns.

JOHANNES: I don't see how we can manage that, sir. Let them
125   announce the banns. We'll just dissolve them quietly later
on.

RIIKKA: But what about all the guests?

JOHANNES: Let them come. We won't say anything yet. It
would only start their tongues wagging. They'd only be
130   asking questions—and gossiping til kingdom come.

KORTESUO: Yes, why should people have to know yet?
They'll hear about it all in good time.

RIIKKA: Maybe it won't turn out as badly as we thought. With
Johannes helping us out like this, and all.

135   KORTESUO: If only Mikko would get himself here, so we
could talk it over with him too.

JOHANNES: Are you waiting for Mikko? Then I'm getting out
of here.

KORTESUO: Don't go. You have to be here when the guests
140   arrive, or it'll raise all kinds of doubts.

JOHANNES: I can't bear to set eyes on that man. My blood begins to boil as soon as I think of him.

KORTESUO: Now, would you do us this big favor, Johannes?
Would you be under the same roof with him for only one
145   more day?

JOHANNES: And listen to him mock me? Watch his triumph?
No, please don't ask me to do that!

RIIKKA: Wait a minute—! She got up—! Quick, quick! She's
heading for the lake. All is lost! (*Runs out.*)

150   JOHANNES: Anna-Liisa!

KORTESUO: She's trying to drown herself! Oh merciful God,
save us! Oh my legs are buckling under me! (*Tries to rush
out but cannot, sinks to his knees.*)

JOHANNES: Don't worry, I'll go. (*Runs out.*)

155   KORTESUO: Run, run as fast as you can! Oh, God, may they
make it in time! (*Goes to the window and shakes his fist.*) Anna-
Liisa! Just you try it! Oh, no, she's going farther out, in the
boat. Run as fast as you can—take the other boat! Well now,
all right, all right! It'll be all right, thanks be to God.

MIKKO *enters.*

160   KORTESUO: (*Still at the window*) Thank God they got her. She's
out of danger. (*Turns around.*) Mikko, I see you're here.

MIKKO: You sent for me?

KORTESUO: I did. I wanted to ask you whether you'll stick to
what you said yesterday. Do you still want to marry Anna-
Liisa?   165

MIKKO: Of course. I wouldn't change my mind overnight,
since I haven't managed to do it in four years.

KORTESUO: Well, now you can have her.

MIKKO: I can have her at last?

KORTESUO: We no longer have any objection to it. And that   170
goes for Johannes as well as me. As soon as the old banns
have been broken, you can go to the parsonage with her.
Let's try to keep this whole unhappy affair secret if we
possibly can. Even Johannes has given his word not to talk
about it.   175

MIKKO: I see! Well then, all is well. It went just the way I said
it would. If you'd only believed me right away, we'd have
been spared all kinds of unhappiness. But that's water over
the dam. We'll soon forget all about it, won't we?

KORTESUO: I don't think we'll ever forget it. It'll send me to   180
my grave, I'm sure. How could one go on living in constant fear?

MIKKO: What have you got to fear? If Johannes should ever
shoot off his mouth, who would believe such wild stories?
And how could he prove it? It sure wouldn't do him any   185
good to go spill things. We'll say he's just saying it out of
spite, since Anna-Liisa gave him the brush-off.

KORTESUO: But just knowing it weighs on me. How could I
possibly look anyone in the eye from now on?

MIKKO: Nonsense! What's done is done. Why let it bother you   190
anymore? It's no use.

KORTESUO: If I could just manage to get through this day.

MIKKO: Why this day exactly? Oh, yes, the banns are going to
be announced and guests are coming. (*Whistles.*) How are
we going to get out of that one?   195

KORTESUO: We thought we wouldn't say anything about the
breaking-off yet. We'll welcome the guests and act as if
nothing had happened. That way there'll be less fuss.

MIKKO: Hell, that's the best idea! Anna-Liisa and I celebrate
our engagement, but we keep it to ourselves. Not a word   200
to anyone else. Let them believe they're celebrating the
banns and that Johannes will be the groom. By heaven, we
can sure play some tricks on them!

KORTESUO: Play what tricks? That's the last thing I want.
Well, there they come.   205

RIIKKA *and* JOHANNES *drag* ANNA-LIISA *in against her will.*

ANNA-LIISA: Oh, leave me alone! Let me be! I don't want to
come in.

RIIKKA: You must come in. We won't leave you alone out
there anymore.

ANNA-LIISA: Why didn't you let me go? I would have taken   210
the little one in my arms, far out there on the lake, crying, crying just like back then.

KORTESUO: Who was out on the lake? Who was crying?

ANNA-LIISA: My child. My own little child. Out there, and
still crying. Let go of me, let me go out there.   215

RIIKKA: My dearest daughter, believe me, no child was out
there. It was just fatigue that brought the image to your
eyes, and it's no wonder, with you sitting out all night, not
eating, not sleeping. You were just seeing things, that's all.

220 ANNA-LIISA: I could see her so clearly, and then she vanished under the water when you came. Why didn't you let me go? Why did you hold me back?

RIIKKA: Because you would have thrown yourself into the lake, you poor thing.

225 ANNA-LIISA: Yes, into the lake, to my child! Am I not to be granted that joy? (*Weeps softly.*)

KORTESUO: Girl, girl! Would you heap that sorrow on us too?

ANNA-LIISA: I want to die. Let me die. Let me go where my child is.

230 RIIKKA: You wouldn't reach your child that way.

KORTESUO: Now you can forget thoughts like that, Anna-Liisa. Everything's turning out all right, now. You don't have to be afraid ever again, not of prison or anything else. You can go on living in peace.

235 MIKKO: You won't have any time to die, Anna-Liisa. Oh no, you're not going to die at all. Life is just beginning for us now. For you and me. I wonder if you even know it yet, but today we're going to be celebrating our engagement.

ANNA-LIISA: Couldn't I have reached my child? Couldn't I,
240 Mother?

RIIKKA: No! Certainly not.

ANNA-LIISA: But I would have found rest. There I would be, lying in peace at the bottom of the lake. Everything would have been over. All the suffering and all the trouble. I
245 wouldn't know anything anymore.

RIIKKA: And think where you'd end up in the life to come! Lord have mercy on us. Aren't you thinking of that at all, dear child?

ANNA-LIISA: In the life to come? I don't know. But it would
250 be away from here. Away, away! All I've done here is sinned. I've brought shame on myself and on others. I have no place here anymore. Everyone has forsaken me, everyone hates me. I'm no better than a withered branch in a tree or a weed in a field. I give no joy, I'm no use to
255 anyone. Oh, Mother, it's a pity you stopped me from drowning. It would be all over now, and you'd have been rid of me.

KORTESUO: Please, please, don't talk that way. No one hates you. There's no need to speak about the matter ever again,
260 so long as you promise not to go into the lake and not to take your own life in any other way.

MIKKO: We'll have a lot of beautiful days together, Anna-Liisa, the kind not many people are ever given. When I take you as my wife and keep you so very well, I promise that your
265 wish to die will vanish.

ANNA-LIISA: It will not vanish. Mother, please let me go, please let me. I can't go on living. Even if people should forgive me, God will never forgive.

RIIKKA: Oh, yes, He will. Be certain that He will. You're still
270 living in God's grace.

ANNA-LIISA: What does He demand of me, then? I have cried and I have prayed. I have crawled at His feet. But he remains fierce in His anger. What must I do, Mother, for my sin to be washed clean? Please, tell me,
275 Mother!

RIIKKA: Pray that God's holy spirit will light up your soul. I can't advise you, my poor child.

ANNA-LIISA: (*Quietly and slowly, looking upwards*) God's holy spirit?

280 KORTESUO: It does not tell you to kill yourself, that's for sure.

ANNA-LIISA: No, no! It does not. Mother, now the heavenly light has fallen on my soul! Now I know what I must do to have God's grace and forgiveness.

RIIKKA: Thanks be to God! She's calming down.

ANNA-LIISA: Yes, thanks be to God in His glory. And thank 285 you, Mother and Johannes, for preventing me from committing still another sin. Now I want to live. I have found God. I hear His voice in my soul.

KORTESUO: All is well! We no longer have anything to fear. But you'd better go in and get dressed, Anna-Liisa. The 290 church service will be over any minute now, and the guests will be here.

RIIKKA: Put on your very best clothes.

ANNA-LIISA: Yes, Mother! I'll put on my nicest dress! Oh, how blessed life is now. And how quickly it's changed! It 295 came on like a sunrise from the east.

KORTESUO: Yes, yes! But go on now, so you'll be ready.

MIKKO: Just one word before you go, Anna-Liisa. You don't hate me anymore, do you, like you said yesterday?

ANNA-LIISA: No, I don't hate you, Mikko. Not you or any- 300 body else.

MIKKO: Now, did you hear that? What did I say!

KORTESUO: Don't be long, Anna-Lisa. Please go and come back right away in your Sunday best and in a happy mood. 305

ANNA-LIISA: Yes, Father, I will. In my Sunday best and in a happy mood.

RIIKKA: I'll go and get changed, too. (*She and* ANNA-LIISA *leave.*)

MIKKO: So long, so long. Don't be gone too long. She's like a 310 different person. Did you see how her eyes were shining?

JOHANNES: Right. She doesn't seem weighed down by sorrow anymore.

MIKKO: Before the day is over, I'll drive away the last worries. Do you believe me? 315

JOHANNES: Possibly so. I no longer have any idea what to expect.

MIKKO: Johannes, I guess you're still sore at me about yesterday. Don't bother! I don't hold anything against you anymore, now that I'll get back what's rightfully mine. But no 320 power on earth could have made me give up Anna-Liisa.

JOHANNES: You sure let us know that.

MIKKO: Well, yes! You all made me go a bit too far. But that doesn't matter. Let bygones be bygones. Let's all have a good time tonight. 325

HUSSO *enters.*

HUSSO: Is it true what Riikka whispered into my ear as she went by me?

MIKKO: You mean about the change in bridegrooms? It sure is true.

HUSSO: Well, Lord love us! Does that mean you're going to 330 be Kortesuo's son-in-law? Oh, heaven preserve us! Who'd have thought it in the old days, when you had to come here so often to beg for bread. And often get thrown out for your trouble! But now the poor little tenant boy has grown up and will be master of the farm! I say it again: 335 heaven preserve us! That I should get the chance to see this joyous day! Did they give her to you of their own free will?

MIKKO: They sure did, of their own free will.

340 HUSSO: Oh, my! So they really did give her to you freely. Well, I'll have to say my thanks, too. (*Goes over to Kortesuo and shakes his hand.*) Many thanks, sir, God save you! Now you can call me all the names you want and I won't mind at all. Won't say a word. It doesn't matter what happens to me, de-
345 crepit old woman, so long as my son makes out all right.

MIKKO: Now, I won't let anyone get away with treating Mother badly.

KORTESUO: And I won't do it, that's for sure. You'll remember, not a word of this to anyone.

350 HUSSO: Not a word, no. What reason would I have to do that? (*Looks at* MIKKO *with shining eyes.*) But I bet Mikko is happy! Lord, love us! But what does Johannes have to say about it?

JOHANNES: Nothing. I've given her up willingly.

355 HUSSO: Willingly? You mean it? I wonder if you really did it on your own. I don't believe you.

JOHANNES: Whether you believe it or not is all the same to me.

KORTESUO: Now don't start quarreling.

HUSSO: No, no, certainly not. What's it to me, anyway? The
360 main thing is that Mikko got Anna-Liisa. I don't care about anything else.

PIRKKO: (*Enters in church clothes, hymnal in hand.*) Well, greetings from church! So, they dropped it down from the pulpit and it made a giant thud.

365 MIKKO: A giant thud!

PIRKKO: You should have been there to hear it, Johannes. The church was chock full of people, and when they mentioned the names of these two, everyone was so quiet you could have heard a pin drop.

370 MIKKO: You're pulling our legs.

PIRKKO: You keep your mouth shut! Why do you always interrupt when someone's talking?

MIKKO: All right, go on, go on! So you could have heard a pin drop.

375 PIRKKO: It felt so great that my heart started pounding when the parson read out loud, "Young man, farmer Johannes Kivimaa and farmer's daughter, virtuous young maiden—" "Virtuous young maiden." Now, that has a wonderful ring to it!

380 MIKKO: Who's interrupting now?

PIRKKO: You be quiet! I'm not talking to you. I'm talking to the other people. Well yes, "virtuous young Miss Anna-Liisa Kortesuo, whose intended marriage is hereby announced."

385 MIKKO: So they were announcing the banns for Anna-Liisa? All this time I thought it was for Pirkko.

PIRKKO: (*Turns around to face* MIKKO *and with hands behind her back, makes a mocking face at him.*) Nyanyanya!

KORTESUO: Now, Pirkko!

390 PIRKKO: Why does he have to be so mean?

MIKKO: That's quite a girl!

PIRKKO: Where are Mother and Anna-Liisa? Why haven't they decorated the house and hung up the wreaths? Everything's still sitting on the porch and here I spent all
395 last night making them.

KORTESUO: You'll have time to get them up on the walls if you hurry.

PIRKKO: Then get out of here, all of you, and don't come in until I tell you.

HUSSO: I can stay here and help you, can't I?   400

PIRKKO: All right, you can stay. But everyone else, out of here and quickly, too!

KORTESUO: Let's clear out of here while that's going on.

MIKKO: You just wait, Pirkko, I'll show you yet!

JOHANNES, MIKKO, *and* KORTESUO *exit.*

PIRKKO: You'll show me! Show me what? No be quick,   405
Husso. Let's carry in these garlands.

They go to the veranda and bring in green garlands, small trees, and other decorations.

HUSSO: Well, Pirkko, I guess you're really pleased Anna-Liisa's getting married.

PIRKKO: Sure, I am. As happy as a three-thousand mark horse!

HUSSO: Well, well! So I guess you like your new brother-in-   410
law a lot.

PIRKKO: Do I like Johannes? Why wouldn't I? There's no other man as good as him, not in the whole-wide world.

HUSSO: So you wouldn't give Anna-Liisa to anyone else?

PIRKKO: No. Not to anyone besides Johannes.   415

HUSSO: Not even to Mikko?

PIRKKO: To Mikko? Yuck! Least of all to him.

HUSSO: Why least of all?

PIRKKO: Why? Why do you ask? You should understand.

HUSSO: Because Mikko doesn't have a farm?   420

PIRKKO: I don't care one bit about a farm!

HUSSO: What's the mater with him, then?

PIRKKO: Well, if you really want to know, Anna-Liisa can't stand him.

HUSSO: Is that so? Are things really so bad that Anna-Liisa   425
can't stand Mikko after all?

PIRKKO: That's how it is. Why are you laughing, Husso?

HUSSO: Oh, for no reason at all! This is a pretty funny business.

PIRKKO: What is? You've got to tell me, too.   430

HUSSO: What would you say if Anna-Liisa should break up with Johannes and go to Mikko instead?

PIRKKO: Now, don't talk nonsense, old woman.

HUSSO: But Mikko's a much more handsome fellow than Johannes.   435

PIRKKO: Oh, go jump in the lake!

HUSSO: You're saying he isn't?

PIRKKO: Come off it! Go jump in the lake! That's what I say!

HUSSO: I don't think Anna-Liisa is all that anxious to hitch up with Johannes. I hear she's been down in the dumps all   440
morning long, even though it's the day her banns were announced.

PIRKKO: If you don't stop talking like that, I'll send you packing.

HUSSO: Hush! Now you be quiet. The guests are already   445
coming into the yard. (*Settles herself in front of the window, right in the middle, and leans on the window still with both hands.*) Many, many horses. I see them coming from Ristola, Heimonen, Katajamäki—

PIRKKO: And who else? (*Pushes* HUSSO *aside.*) Get out of the   450
way so I can see too. Oh, there are all five of my horses— and the fiddlers, and all the rest of them! (*She runs to the door.*)

MRS. HEIMONEN, MRS. RISTOLA, *and* MR. KATAJAMÄKI, *[all from their farms]*, KORTESUO, MIKKO, JOHANNES, *and* RIIKKA *enter, followed by many other guests, young and old, while the fiddler is playing a tune.*

RIIKKA: Please, come on in, everyone. Please do!

455 MRS. RISTOLA: My, my, and here's Pirkko too. Well, hello. My, how you've grown since I last saw you.

PIRKKO: I'm getting there.

MRS. HEIMONEN: That's right. Pretty soon you'll be a real grown-up. And after they whisk Anna-Liisa away, suitors

460 will start coming around for the other daughter.

MIKKO: Not until then? I've been trying my best for the past few days.

PIRKKO: Oh, cut it out!

RIIKKA: Pirkko's only a child. She's not ready for things like

465 that yet. Oh, please, dear guests, do sit down.

MIKKO: Go ahead. Gents at the end of the table here, ladies on the back bench, and girls, you little fibbertigibbets, you'd better run off to some back corner. That's the right place for you.

470 PIRKKO: Says who? We're not about to go there. We'll sit right here on the bench with the men. Now, what do you say about that?!

RIIKKA: Child, you'd better be quiet, or else! She's got such a big mouth, that live wire of ours!

475 MR. KATAJAMÄKI: Come here and sit beside me, Pirkko. Got a seat for you right here.

PIRKKO: I don't know if I have time to sit around right now. I think the dancing's got to start pretty soon.

MRS. RISTOLA: I don't think they'll start quite yet. We haven't

480 even paid our respects to the bride.

MRS. HEIMONEN: Yes, where's Anna-Liisa? There's been no sign of her.

MRS. KATAJAMÄKI: I was just going to ask the same thing.

RIIKKA: She went in to get dressed just a few minutes ago.

485 PIRKKO: A few minutes ago! And in all that time I've decorated the house, had a bit of a scrap with Husso, done other stuff, and I haven't seen hide nor hair of her.

RIIKKA: She'll be here just as soon as she's ready.

MIKKO: How about it, girls? Why don't we start off with a reel

490 while we're waiting? I see the girls' toes are itching to dance.

PIRKKO: What about your own? Are you saying they're not itching?

MIKKO: Oh, they're itching all right, itching like the very devil.

KORTESUO: Well, go right ahead. Why don't you start danc-

495 ing? I think Riikka's waiting for the gentlemen to come, the pastor, the doctor, and the sheriff. I don't think she'll give us anything to put in our mouths until they get here.

RIIKKA: Oh, they'll probably be here very soon.

MIKKO: Pirkko, will you be my partner?

500 PIRKKO: No, I'm going to dance with Johannes.

MIKKO: Well then, I'll have to pick another one. (*Ogles the girls.*) I wonder which one I should choose. Each one's prettier than the next. Enough to turn a man's head. I'd rather take every one of them.

505 MR. KATAJAMÄKI: I guess Mikko here is doing the duty of the go-between.

MIKKO: After all, I am the go-between. These two wouldn't be where they are without me. You know Johannes. Such a quiet man. He'd never have had the gumption to propose.

KORTESUO: Well, go ahead and start the dance.   510

MIKKO: How about it, ladies and gents? Everybody's got to dance today, no way out of it.

MRS. RISTOLA: Us old folks won't be joining in so early. We'll do it at the end.

MIKKO: You'll dance the quadrille with me, won't you,   515
ma'am? (*Goes and snatches a girl by the crook of his arm.*)

MRS. RISTOLA: Oh, my, he's such a jolly fellow, that Mikko. But the groom, he's a real serious one, and so even-tempered.

MRS. HEIMONEN: A good man indeed. Johannes will make a   520
good son-in-law.

RIIKKA: (*Quietly and sadly*) I know. Johannes is a good man, a good man all around.

MRS. RISTOLA: And he has such a good farm. It will be quite something for Anna-Liisa to be mistress of such a farm.   525

MRS. HEIMONEN: Some people have all the luck and can take pleasure in their children. Others have only worry and sorrow.

RIIKKA *sighs and turns away. The young people dance a short reel.*

MR. KATAJAMÄKI: That's how we used to hop around too. But the old legs have stiffened up on us.   530

KORTESUO: Right. The legs have gone stiff, and the mind too.

MR. KATAJAMÄKI: Later on in the evening we'll join the dancing, won't we?

KORTESUO: I'm no good for that anymore.

MR. KATAJAMÄKI: No way of knowing till you try. Let's prac-   535
tice tonight, so we'll be really good at it at the wedding. Now, when's the wedding set for?

KORTESUO: Oh, the wedding?

MR. KATAJAMÄKI: Right, right. Anna-Liisa's and Johannes's wedding.   540

KORTESUO: Don't rightly know yet. Now, who's coming there? Oh, it's the parson and the sheriff.

MR. KATAJAMÄKI: And the doctor and the shopkeeper. All the town gentlemen. Oh, my, with such a big celebration of the banns, just think what the wedding'll be like!   545

THE PARSON, SHERIFF, DOCTOR, *and* SHOPKEEPER *enter. The dancing stops.*

SHERIFF: Well, well! Such a jolly scene! Don't stop dancing on our account. Go on, go on!

PARSON: Did we frighten you?

MIKKO: We didn't exactly get frightened. The reel just happened to end.   550

PARSON: (*To* KORTESUO) Good day to you, sir. I wish you all the best. (*To* RIIKKA) And to you, ma'am.

SHOPKEEPER: I wonder. Were you at church to hear the banns announced?

KORTESUO: No, we weren't.   555

SHOPKEEPER: Well, I was there. And I can assure you that everything was done just right. The young men sure felt the sting.

MIKKO: Felt the sting? That's what I thought. May I ask you— perhaps it stung the good shopkeeper's heart too?   560

SHOPKEEPER: Well, why wouldn't it? To have the prettiest girl in town taken away like that.

PARSON: Now where's the bridal couple?

SHERIFF: I see the groom over there. Come on out, Kivimaa.
565   Why are you hiding behind the others?
MIKKO: Maybe he's afraid he'll be punished for pulling such
        a trick on us.
DOCTOR: Let's not bear a grudge over something like that. All
        honor to the winner.
570 SHOPKEEPER: No help for it. We'll just wish them luck. But
        Johannes, you'll have to put on quite a wedding for us.
        Make sure you do.
MIKKO: Oh, he's getting off easy. Now if I were the shop-
        keeper, I'd sure beat him to it.
575 PARSON: Now, now! You wouldn't do any such thing.
MIKKO: (*To* PARSON) I wouldn't, sir? Is that what you think?
        Oh, well, all he has to do is pay a little fine—no need for
        anything more.
JOHANNES: Why are we wasting time on such nonsense?
580 MIKKO: Ahaa! He's getting worried!
PARSON: But the bride? Where is the bride?
SHERIFF: That's right. We haven't had the chance to pay our
        respects.
KORTESUO: She'll be here any minute now.
585 RIIKKA: Pirkko, please go tell her to hurry up! Tell her she has
        to come right away! The parson and other guests are wait-
        ing to see her.
PIRKKO: All right, I will. (*Turns and runs off.*)
MIKKO: Now let's welcome her with a real ceremony! We'll
590   divide up on both sides of the room, women on that side,
        men on this. Just like this. When she comes in, we'll all
        shout "long live!" all together.
KORTESUO: Mikko, are you up to your old tricks? Now, let it
        be.
595 RIIKKA: For heaven's sake, don't start setting up anything like
        that. She'll get all frightened, who knows how badly.
SHOPKEEPER: Oh, no! There's no harm in it, even if it fright-
        ens her a little. Remember, we do have the doctor here.
DOCTOR: I'll take care of any fright.
600 SHERIFF: A splendid idea indeed! If the parson would then
        make a little speech, wish her luck from all of us, and so
        on.
PARSON: I'd be glad to.
SHOPKEEPER: Listen. As soon as the parson has finished his
605   speech, we'll all shout "long live!" again, and then we'll sit
        her down in a chair and carry her all around.
MIKKO: Around the room first, then out the door and around
        the yard and then back into the house.—A good deal, said
        the man when he got beat up!
610 RIIKKA: Oh, my, I'm afraid—
PIRKKO: Her door was locked, but I yelled in through the
        keyhole.
RIIKKA: (*Anxiously*) And what did she say? Did she promise
        to come?
615 PIRKKO: She said she was ready.
HUSSO: (*At the window*) There she comes. Oh, my, how slowly
        she's walking!
MIKKO: Now, everybody be quiet! Mother, you watch out,
        and open the door when she comes. But do it quickly, and
620   open it wide!
HUSSO: All right, all right! I'll do as I'm told.

All stand still. HUSSO *suddenly pulls the door wide open.* ANNA-
LIISA *appears. They shout "long live!" to her.*

ANNA-LIISA: Long live God's Holy Spirit in us!
MRS. RISTOLA: What did she say?! God's—?
MRS. HEIMONEN: God's Holy Spirit.
MRS. RISTOLA: What, has she turned devout?   625
MRS. HEIMONEN: Listen. The parson's speaking.
PARSON: That's right. May God's Holy Spirit live in us. And
        may the flesh die, with all its passion and lust. That is the
        highest goal for all of us. And now, on my own behalf, and
        on behalf of all those gathered here, I would like to say a 630
        few words to the bride.
ANNA-LIISA: You are mistaken, if you call me a bride. I am no
        one's bride.
MRS. RISTOLA: No one's bride?
KORTESUO: Now, Anna-Liisa, what's all this about?   635
RIIKKA: Dear Lord, what's got into her head?
MIKKO: Oh, she's just a bit bashful.
PARSON: Why are you denying it? You know your banns were
        announced today. Of course that makes you a bride.
SHERIFF: Now, now, there's no reason to be bashful.   640
SHOPKEEPER: I guess you got embarrassed, with us welcom-
        ing you in this unusual way. But please, don't mind—
DOCTOR: We only wanted to honor you.
MIKKO: Yes, honor you. That's what we, the guests at this cel-
        ebration of the banns—   645
ANNA-LIISA: It's true that my banns were announced today.
        But still, I am not a bride. It has all fallen through.
MRS. HEIMONEN: Now, that's nothing to praise! Oh, my, how
        sad!
MRS. RISTOLA: You said it! My head's all mixed up. Soon I'll   650
        have no idea what's going on.
KORTESUO: What are you thinking of, Anna-Liisa? How can
        you spoil the guests' pleasure like that?
RIIKKA: I don't understand her. (*Looks helplessly at* KORTESUO.)
        What's going to come of this?   655
PARSON: So, you've solemnly decided to break it off?
ANNA-LIISA: It's already been broken off. It had to be so.
HUSSO: There you've got it, Pirkko. What have I been saying
        all this time? Anna-Liisa didn't love Johannes, after all.
        What's so surprising about that? That kind of thing hap-   660
        pens often enough. I've even seen a bride turn back from
        the altar, let alone after announcing the banns. You just tell
        them the truth, Anna-Liisa. No need to be shy.
PARSON: What does the bridegroom have to say about this?
JOHANNES: Anna-Liisa is right. What existed between us has   665
        been broken.
PIRKKO: (*Tugging at* RIIKKA's *skirt*) Mother, Mother, isn't Anna-
        Liisa going to get married, after all? Isn't she, Mother?
RIIKKA: Hush, now you be quiet.
MR. KATAJAMÄKI: So, is this how it all turned out? Oh, well. 670
        But the jolly party sure came to a quick end. Damn them
        all!
MIKKO: Now, sir, don't you worry. We'll go right on with the
        feast. And with any luck, we'll have an engagement party
        instead of a celebration of the banns. What do you say,   675
        Anna-Liisa?
MRS. RISTOLA: Stranger and stranger.
MIKKO: Well, I think she's got someone else in mind.
MR. KATAJAMÄKI: Well, then!
PARSON: I don't know what to say about this. Since both par- 680
        ties wish a separation—
ANNA-LIISA: There's something more I want to say.

MIKKO: Now we're going to hear it!

PARSON: Why don't you leave it at that? I think we've heard
685   quite enough for the time being. Or, what do the parents
think?

KORTESUO: I quite agree with the parson. It's been quite
enough for now. We should let it be for a while.

ANNA-LIISA: I can no longer leave it at that. It weighs on my
690   conscience. It's been withering under that burden of sin
for too long—four long years.

KORTESUO: Now come over here and behave yourself. Didn't
you hear what the parson said?

ANNA-LIISA: Don't try to stop me. Let me follow the voice of
695   the Holy Spirit.

RIIKKA: You can do that some other time.

MIKKO: Right, when you've had the chance to think about it
more and when we've talked about it together.

HUSSO: (Nudges MIKKO.) What's she up to?

700   MIKKO: Don't you get it? She's going to blurt it all out.

HUSSO: Heavens preserve us! Is she crazy?

PARSON: I think she's going to say something quite different
from what I first thought. If her conscience compels her
to speak, then I certainly don't want to forbid her.

705   ANNA-LIISA: And my parents will not want to, either, if they
really think about it. Isn't it true? You don't want to forbid me?

RIIKKA: All I ask is that you let it be for now and come rest
a while. The guests will excuse you. She hasn't slept all
710   night, she's not quite in her senses.

MIKKO: Yes, that's best. Please, ma'am, take her to her room
and let her rest. And if the doctor would please prescribe
something calming for her so she can get some sleep. I'll
be glad to run to the pharmacy.

715   ANNA-LIISA: No, let me speak. I don't need any medicine. You
can see I'm quite calm and fully in my senses.

PARSON: Do you want to speak right here, in everyone's hearing?

ANNA-LIISA: Yes, I do. Freely and honestly, before God and
720   man.

HUSSO: Oh, hell! Don't, Anna-Liisa! You'd better keep your
mouth shut or you'll regret it. Why in the world are you
going to spill everything?

PARSON: Be quiet! Now you stay out of this. Go on, Anna-Liisa,
725   don't be afraid. Freely and honestly, before God and man.

MIKKO: If the parson would let me—Could I speak to her
first?

PARSON: You can do that later, afterwards.

MIKKO: (To ANNA-LIISA) Why don't you step out for a breath
730   of fresh air, just for a moment.

PARSON: (Becoming angry, hits the table with his fist.) Get away!
She mustn't be disturbed, I tell you! Anna-Liisa, you may
start now.

ANNA-LIISA: I have committed a grave sin which I must con-
735   fess now. Until this moment I have grievously hidden it
from everyone in order to spare myself pain and punishment. But covering it up has not made me happy.

PARSON: I'm certain it hasn't. The inner anguish has been all
the greater, hasn't it?

740   ANNA-LIISA: It was so great I could hardly bear it. My conscience hasn't given me a moment's rest.

PARSON: Have courage, my child! What was the sin you committed?

ANNA-LIISA: Four years ago, I gave birth to a child, over there
in the forest, and miserable creature that I am, I killed that   745
child.

MRS. RISTOLA: Oh, my God!

MRS. HEIMONEN: Anna-Liisa? Killed her child?

RIIKKA: I don't know why people listen to the ravings of a
sick person and think they're true.   750

HUSSO: Now, good people, don't you believe a word of it.
She'll take her words back tomorrow, after she's had a
chance to sleep.

ANNA-LIISA: It is as I have said. If you want, I can show you
the place where the child is buried.   755

SHERIFF: Now, in my official capacity I have to ask you a few
questions. Did your parents know anything about this?

ANNA-LIISA: No, they didn't. They are innocent. They believed only the best of me. They didn't have any idea
about my crime.   760

HUSSO: Mikko, let's go. Why should we bother hanging
around here anymore?

MIKKO: Let's wait and see how it turns out.

SHERIFF: Is it the case, then, that this confession comes to you,
the parents, unexpected?   765

KORTESUO: The confession? Yes, this confession was unexpected.

SHERIFF: But you knew of the crime before this, didn't you?

KORTESUO: Not until last night. We've been in a daze ever
since. Haven't known which way to turn.   770

RIIKKA: We couldn't become informers and turn our own
child in, could we now? The law can't demand that.

KORTESUO: Especially since it was such a long time ago.

ANNA-LIISA: I'm the only guilty one. Do not trouble my parents; they didn't know anything about this. I hid it from   775
them, just as I hid it from everyone else.

SHERIFF: You don't have to worry about them if what you say
is true. But I can't leave it at that with you. My sad duty
is to put you under arrest.

ANNA-LIISA: And make me serve the punishment I have   780
earned. Please, Sheriff, do it. That's what I want. What I
have done, I cannot undo, even though I will grieve over
it until the end of my days. But let me suffer, let me suffer the most severe punishment so that I can atone for
my crime, at least in some measure. Come, I will go to   785
prison or do hard labor in the penitentiary—or even be
put to death—whatever justice decrees I will gladly
accept.

RIIKKA: Oh, my child, my child. Dear Lord, take this cup
from me. I cannot bear to drink from it. (Fainting, she falls   790
to the floor, moaning.)

PIRKKO: (Weeping) Mother, Mother!

KORTESUO: (Wipes tears from his eyes.) That I had to live to see
this! That I didn't go to the grave before this!

ANNA-LIISA: Father, Mother, don't grieve for me! Don't   795
grieve! I have nothing to fear. Can't you see how happy I
am now? Never in my life have I felt so happy.

JOHANNES: (Moved) Anna-Liisa!

KORTESUO: Don't you care at all about the stain that you've
brought down upon our grey heads?   800

ANNA-LIISA: Please, forgive me! Oh, if I could somehow
atone for all my transgressions against you.

MRS. RISTOLA: It's such a pity about the parents.

MRS. HEIMONEN: Surely this will destroy them.

805 MRS. RISTOLA: My goodness, you never know what grief your children can bring you.

MR. KATAJAMÄKI: Things have come to grief for you, that's for sure.

MIKKO: (*Quietly, to* HUSSO) There's nothing more we can do now.
810 Better let matters take their course. Let's get out of here!

They exit.

KORTESUO: If only I could die! That's all I wish for.

PARSON: No, dear friends, that's not so! At this moment you have no reason for grief. No, this is a time for rejoicing. God's spirit has done its work in your daughter and has
815 gained a victory. Don't look at this matter with the eyes of the world. Look at it from a higher perspective. Until now, Anna-Liisa has been lost. Now she has found the true path. Let us praise the Lord.

MRS. RISTOLA: I guess that's how it is if you rightly think
820 about it. It's punishment to the flesh, but not to the spirit.

KORTESUO: We're shortsighted, we people. We don't always understand the ways of the Almighty.

RIIKKA: And the flesh always tries to get the upper hand with us.

825 PARSON: Let us endeavor to walk all the more devoutly in the life of the spirit so that we can be victorious, with God's help, as Anna-Liisa has done. (*Takes* ANNA-LIISA *by the hand.*) Go in peace, my child. Go where your conscience leads you. And may the heavenly Father give you strength, so that you may remain strong to the very end. A few mo-
830 ments ago, we offered you congratulations on entering a small, earthly stage of life. But a thousand times more ardently do we now congratulate you on your inner change.

DOCTOR: I agree with the Parson. Goodbye!
835

ANNA-LIISA: (*Puts her arms around her Father and then her Mother.*) Goodbye, Father. Goodbye, Mother. And Pirkko. Goodbye, everyone!

ALL: Goodbye! Farewell!

JOHANNES: Anna-Liisa, wouldn't you like to shake my
840 hand?

ANNA-LIISA: Of course! Goodbye, Johannes, goodbye!

JOHANNES: May God be with you, Anna-Liisa! Just one word more—you are, after all, the person I thought you were from the very beginning.
845

ANNA-LIISA: Thank you for your kindness. Now, Sheriff, I am ready.

SHERIFF: All right, then, it's time to go.

They exit.

PARSON: She is setting out on the road to eternal life. Oh, happy one!
850

Anton Chekhov

The work of Anton Chekhov (1860–1904) is noted for its objectivity, its sympathetic yet almost clinical examination of turn-of-the-century Russian life. Born in the provincial town of Taganrog, Chekhov trained for a career in medicine and began practicing as a physician in the mid-1880s. At that time he also began to write his first short stories. In his fiction, as in his later plays, Chekhov adopted a mildly ironic attitude toward his subjects, one that resisted sensation and melodrama in favor of a more neutral stance; as he wrote in a letter, "It is necessary that on stage everything should be as complex and as simple as in life. People are having dinner, and while they're having it, their future happiness may be decided or their lives may be about to be shattered." Chekhov's life was shattered in just this way, simply, suddenly, and casually. In 1884 he coughed up blood, the sure sign that he had contracted tuberculosis. The disease could not be cured and required repeated periods of convalescence; an early death was a certainty.

Chekhov began writing plays in the 1880s as well, mainly short comic sketches he called "vaudevilles," among them *The Bear* (1888), *The Proposal* (1889), and *The Wedding* (1890). In 1896, the Alexandrinsky Theater in St. Petersburg performed his full-length drama, *The Seagull*. The play's indirect plotting and its avoidance of the conventional climaxes of melodrama confused actors and audiences alike, and it failed. Chekhov was persuaded by Constantin Stanislavski and Vladimir Nemirovich-Danchenko to mount the play in their newly founded Moscow Art Theater (MAT) in 1898. Stanislavski's commitment to a restrained style of performance, emphasizing psychological complexity and balanced playing by the entire ensemble is generally credited with making the MAT production a success; a seagull became the company's signature. Chekhov produced three more major plays with the MAT. He revised *The Wood Demon* (1889) as *Uncle Vanya* in 1899 and then produced *Three Sisters* (1901) and *The Cherry Orchard* (1904). Chekhov married the actress Olga Knipper, who played leading roles in his plays, including Madame Ranevskaya in *The Cherry Orchard* in 1901, and spent the final years of his life convalescing in Yalta.

THE CHERRY ORCHARD

The action of Chekhov's plays is usually indirect, not progressive and consequential, in the manner of Ibsen's work. Instead, a Chekhov play generally opens with the arrival of some well-to-do characters in the provincial scene of the play and closes with their departure: Yelena and Serbryakov in *Uncle Vanya*, the regiment and its romantic Lieutenant Colonel Vershinin in *Three Sisters*, Madame Ranevskaya and her entourage in *The Cherry Orchard*. In between, we see how the lives of the characters are changed and yet somehow remain the same, as though their interaction worked to reveal the fundamentally static condition of their lives.

More than Chekhov's earlier plays, perhaps, *The Cherry Orchard* also seems to prefigure the fall of a class: the leisured, ineffectual, yet attractive Madame Ranevskaya and her brother, who own the estate but are incapable of bringing it into the twentieth century. We are left with the final vision of the ancient servant Firs, himself a relic of the emancipation of the serfs half a century before, locked in the house while the orchard falls to the axes. The future seems to promise a brutal and sudden change, which the main characters of the play are unable to face. The play takes, at best, an ironic attitude toward the fortunes of Lyubov and Gaev. Tragedies in Chekhov's plays occur in the momentary actions of daily life; they are casual and haphazard, almost accidental, and yet alter the course of life irrevocably. Varya and Lopakhin, for example, bumble their way through the long-expected scene of their engagement, but the scene doesn't come off. Lopakhin remains uncommitted and Varya remains a poor relation dependent on the charity of her family, soon to be sent away to work as a governess. For Varya, the misplayed scene has a bitter and tragic finality.

A scene from Anton Chekhov's *The Cherry Orchard*.

Chekhov calls the play a "comedy," and despite its mournful tone we might consider what he might have had in mind. Chekhov seems sympathetic to the tragedies of daily life, but often trains a skeptical eye on characters who assume the self-regarding accents of high tragedy, or whose sense of themselves verges on self-delusion, the solipsistic inability to see the world around them. Throughout *The Cherry Orchard,* some characters seem lost in a world of dreams: think of Gaev and his sister arriving in their childhood nursery, of Trofimov's vague and clumsy plans for the future, of kindly old Firs. Chekhov forces us to regard his characters with a certain distance, largely by weaving a texture of comedy into the fabric of the play. Everyone ridicules Gaev's sentimental apostrophe to the bookcase in act 1, and Chekhov adds a list of vaudeville tricks to his characters' performances: Lopakhin's "Ba-a-a" at the opening of the play, Yepikhodov crushing the hatbox with the suitcase in act 4, Trofimov tumbling down the stairs, Charlotta's music-hall turns, Firs's feeble efforts to keep everyone warm. The famous, inexplicable sound effect of act 2—the breaking string— may work in this way as well. It both underscores the mournful tone of the scene and interrupts the illusionistic surface of the action, forcing the audience out of a fully sympathetic engagement with Chekhov's sentimental characters. The play, in this light, seems "tragic" only if we accept the main characters' view of their predicament and accept their idle, self-absorbed fantasies as the stuff of tragedy.

Chekhov went to some lengths to keep the play's tone unsettled, in part because he knew that Stanislavski tended to regard his work as high tragedy. Chekhov suggested to Stanislavski that he play the part of Lopakhin: "When I was writing Lopakhin," he wrote in a letter to the actor, "I thought of it as a part for you. . . . Lopakhin is a merchant, of course, but he is a very decent person in every sense. He must behave with perfect decorum, like an educated man, with no petty ways or tricks of any sort, and it seemed to me that this part, the central one of the play, would come out brilliantly in your hands. . . . you must remember that Varya, a serious and religious girl, is in love with Lopakhin; she wouldn't be in love with a mere money-grubber." Describing Lopakhin in terms of Varya is typical of

Chekhov's tendency to think of the ensemble as a whole, rather than in terms of individual characters; but we might also think that Chekhov has strategic designs on Stanislavski as well. Fearing that Stanislavski would want to play the part of Gaev, and would play the part too sympathetically, Chekhov tried to persuade him to train his talents on the comic part of Lopakhin. Imagining Stanislavski as Lopakhin, we begin to see the kind of drama Chekhov had imagined: had he taken the part (Stanislavski played Gaev after all), Stanislavski would have played against the grain of broad humor that underlies Lopakhin, humanizing the role, creating neither a fully sympathetic character nor a vulgar comedian, but something in between. Similarly, *The Cherry Orchard* as a whole strikes a balance somewhere between comedy and tragedy, in which comic and tragic possibilities strain against one another as ways of interpreting the play and the experience of our lives.

As it turned out, Stanislavski's direction emphasized the play's sombre tone, the sense of a generation falling before modern progress as the orchard falls to the axes. After the Russian Revolution in 1917, *The Cherry Orchard* came to be regarded as nearly a prophetic allegory of the progress of history, the displacing of the feudal past by the modern, industrial present.

A pronunciation guide for Russian names appears on pp. 666–667.

THE CHERRY ORCHARD

Anton Chekhov

TRANSLATED BY CAROL ROCAMORA

CHARACTERS

RANEVSKAYA, LYUBOV ANDREEVNA, *a landowner*
ANYA, *her daughter, age seventeen*
VARYA, *her adopted daughter, age twenty-four*
GAEV, *Leonid Andreevich, Ranevskaya's brother*
LOPAKHIN, *Yermolai Alekseevich, a merchant*
TROFIMOV, *Pyotr Sergeevich, a student*
SIMEONOV-PISHCHIK, *Boris Borisovich, a landowner*
CHARLOTTA IVANOVNA, *a governess*
YEPIKHODOV, *Semyon Panteleevich, a clerk*
DUNYASHA, *a maid*

FIRS, *a servant, an old man of eighty-seven*
YASHA, *a young servant*
A PASSERBY
A STATIONMASTER
A POST OFFICE CLERK
GUESTS, SERVANTS, CARRIAGE DRIVERS

The action takes place on the estate of Lyubov Andreevna Ranevskaya

ACT ONE

A room, which is still called the nursery. One of the doors leads to ANYA's *room. It is dawn, just before sunrise. It is already May, the cherry trees are all in bloom, but outside it is still cold; there is an early morning frost in the orchard. The windows in the room are closed.*

Enter DUNYASHA *with a candle, and* LOPAKHIN *with a book in his hand.*

LOPAKHIN: The train's arrived, thank God. What time is it?
DUNYASHA: Almost two. (*Puts out the candle.*) It's already getting light out.
LOPAKHIN: So how late is the train, then? A couple of hours,
5   at least. (*Yawns and stretches.*) Well, I've made a fool of myself, then, haven't I! Hm? Came all the way out here, just to meet the train, and fell fast asleep . . . Sat here waiting and dozed right off. Annoying, isn't it . . . You should have woken me up.
10 DUNYASHA: I thought you'd already gone. (*Listens.*) Listen, I think they're here.
LOPAKHIN: (*Listens.*) No . . . They've got to get their baggage first, you know, that sort of thing . . .

(*Pause.*)

Lyubov Andreevna, she's been living abroad for five years,
15   I don't know, I can't even imagine what's become of her now . . . She's a fine person, you know . . . a warm, kind person. I remember, once, when I was a boy, oh, about fifteen years old, say, and my father—he had a shop here in the village then—my father, he hit me in the face with his
20   fist, blood was pouring from my nose . . . We'd come out into the courtyard together, somehow, and he was drunk. And there was Lyubov Andreevna, I remember her so vividly, so young then, so graceful, so slender, she took me by the hand, brought me over to the washstand, right into
25   this very room, into the nursery. "Don't cry, little peasant," she said, "it will heal before your wedding day . . ."

(*Pause.*)

Little peasant . . . Yes, my father was a peasant, it's true enough, and here I am in a three-piece suit and fancy shoes. A silk purse from a sow's ear, or something like that, isn't that how the expression goes . . . Yes . . . The only dif- 30 ference is, now I'm rich, I've got a lot of money, but don't look too closely, once a peasant . . . (*Leafs through the book.*) Look at me, I read through this entire book and didn't understand a word of it. Read it and dozed right off.

(*Pause.*)

DUNYASHA: The dogs didn't sleep at all last night, they can 35 sense their masters are coming home.
LOPAKHIN: What's wrong with you, Dunyasha . . .
DUNYASHA: My hands are trembling. I'm going to faint, I know I am.
LOPAKHIN: You're much too high-strung, Dunyasha. And 40 look at you, all dressed up like a young lady, hair done up, too. You mustn't do that. Remember who you are.

(*Enter* YEPIKHODOV *with a bouquet; he is wearing a jacket and highly polished boots, which squeak loudly; upon entering, he drops the bouquet.*)

YEPIKHODOV: (*Picks up the bouquet.*) Look what the gardener sent. Put them on the dining room table. That's what he said. (*Gives the bouquet to* DUNYASHA.) 45
LOPAKHIN: And bring me some kvass, will you?
DUNYASHA: Yes, sir. (*Leaves.*)
YEPIKHODOV: We have an early morning frost, we have three degrees below zero, and we have the cherry blossoms all in bloom. I don't approve of our climate. (*Sighs.*) Really, I 50 don't. Our climate doesn't work, it just doesn't work. It's not conducive. And would you like to hear more, Yermolai Alekseich, well, then you will, because the day before yesterday, I bought these boots, and, trust me, they squeak so much, that they are beyond hope. Now how can I oil 55 them? Tell me? How?
LOPAKHIN: Enough. You're getting on my nerves.
YEPIKHODOV: Every day some new disaster befalls me. A new day, a new disaster. But do I grumble, do I complain, no, I don't, I accept it, look, I'm smiling, even. 60

(DUNYASHA *enters, gives* LOPAKHIN *some kvass.*)

I'm going now. (*Stumbles against a chair, which falls down.*) There . . . (*As if vindicated.*) You see? I mean, that's the situation, and excuse me for saying so . . . Remarkable, even . . . isn't it! (*Exits.*)

65 DUNYASHA: Yermolai Alekseich, I have something to tell you . . . Yepikhodov has proposed to me.

LOPAKHIN: Ah!

DUNYASHA: But I don't know, really . . . He's a nice enough fellow, you know, quiet and all, it's just that whenever he
70 starts to talk, I can't understand a word he's saying. I mean, it all sounds so sweet and sincere, only it just doesn't make any sense. I like him, I mean, I think I like him. And he? He adores me. But he's such an unfortunate fellow, you know, really, every day it's something else. They even have
75 a name for him, do you know what they call him: "Mister Disaster" . . .

LOPAKHIN: (*Listens.*) I think they're coming . . .

DUNYASHA: They're coming! What's happening to me . . . I'm freezing, look, I'm shivering all over.

80 LOPAKHIN: They're really coming! Let's go meet them. Will she recognize me? We haven't seen each other in five years.

DUNYASHA: (*Agitated.*) I'm going to faint, I know I am . . . Look, I'm fainting!

(*Two carriages are heard pulling up to the house.* LOPAKHIN *and* DUNYASHA *exit quickly. The stage is empty. Then there is noise in the adjacent rooms.* FIRS *hurries across the stage to meet* LYUBOV ANDREEVNA; *he is leaning on a cane, and is dressed in old-fashioned livery and a high hat; he mutters something to himself, but it is impossible to make out a single word. The offstage noise crescendos. A voice calls out; "Let's go this way through here . . ." Enter* LYUBOV ANDREEVNA, ANYA, *and* CHARLOTTA IVANOVNA *with a little dog on a leash; they are all dressed in traveling clothes. Enter* VARYA, *wearing a coat and a shawl,* GAEV, SIMEONOV-PISHCHIK, LOPAKHIN, DUNYASHA *carrying a bundle and an umbrella,* SERVANTS *carrying luggage—they all come through the room.*)

ANYA: This way! Mama, do you remember what room this is?
85 LYUBOV ANDREEVNA: (*Ecstatic, in tears.*) The nursery!

VARYA: How cold it is, my hands are numb. (*To* LYUBOV ANDREEVNA.) Look, Mamochka, your rooms, violet and white, just as you left them.

LYUBOV ANDREEVNA: My nursery, my darling nursery, my
90 beautiful room . . . I slept here, when I was a child . . . (*Weeps.*) And now, I'm a child again . . . (*Kisses her brother,* VARYA, *and her brother again.*) And Varya looks the same as ever, just like a little nun. And Dunyasha I recognize, of course . . . (*Kisses* DUNYASHA.)

95 GAEV: The train was two hours late. How do you like that? How's that for efficiency!

CHARLOTTA: (*To* PISHCHIK.) My dog eats walnuts, too.

PISHCHIK: (*Amazed.*) Imagine that!

(*They all exit, except for* ANYA *and* DUNYASHA.)

DUNYASHA: We've been waiting forever . . . (*Takes* ANYA's *coat*
100 *and hat.*)

ANYA: I didn't sleep one moment the whole journey long, four whole nights . . . and now I'm absolutely frozen!

DUNYASHA: You left during Lent, we had snow then, and frost, and now! My darling! (*Bursts out laughing, kisses her.*) I've waited forever for you, my precious, my joy . . . And I've got 105 something to tell you, I can't wait one minute longer. . . .

ANYA: (*Listlessly.*) Now what . . .

DUNYASHA: Yepikhodov, the clerk, proposed to me just after Easter.

ANYA: Not again . . . (*Adjusts her hair.*) I've lost all my hair- 110 pins . . . (*She is exhausted; she almost sways on her feet.*)

DUNYASHA: No, really, I don't know what to think, any more. He adores me, God, how he adores me!

ANYA: (*Gazes at the door to her room, tenderly.*) My very own room, my windows, it's as if I never left. I'm home! And to- 115 morrow I'll wake up, and I'll run out into the orchard . . . Oh, if only I could rest! I'm so exhausted—I didn't sleep one moment the whole way, I was so worried.

DUNYASHA: Pyotr Sergeich arrived the day before yesterday.

ANYA: (*Overjoyed.*) Petya! 120

DUNYASHA: He's out in the bathhouse, asleep, that's where he's staying. "I'm afraid of being in the way," he said. (*Glances at her pocket watch.*) We ought to wake him up, but Varvara Mikhailovna gave us strict orders not to. "Don't you dare wake him up," she said. 125

(*Enter* VARYA, *a bunch of keys hanging from her belt.*)

VARYA: Dunyasha, go, quickly, bring the coffee . . . Mamochka wants coffee.

DUNYASHA: Right away. (*Exits.*)

VARYA: So, thank God, you're here. You're home at last! (*Embracing her.*) My darling's home! My angel is home! 130

ANYA: I've been through so much.

VARYA: I can imagine.

ANYA: I left during Holy Week, it was so cold then, remember? And Charlotta Ivanovna talked the whole way, talked and played card tricks. How could you have stuck me 135 with Charlotta! . . .

VARYA: You can't travel alone, darling. At seventeen!

ANYA: When we arrived in Paris, it was cold there, too, and snowing. My French is terrible. Mama lived on the fifth floor, and when I finally got there, the flat was filled with 140 all sorts of French people, ladies, an old Catholic priest with a little book, and, oh, it was so uncomfortable there, so stuffy, the room was filled with smoke. And suddenly I felt sorry for Mama, so very sorry, I threw my arms around her neck, I held her so tight, I couldn't let go. And Mama 145 kept clinging to me, and weeping . . .

VARYA: (*In tears.*) Enough, enough . . .

ANYA: She had already sold the dacha near Menton, she had nothing left, nothing at all. And neither did I, not a single kopek, we hardly had enough money to get home. And 150 Mama just doesn't understand it, still! There we are, sitting in the station restaurant, and she orders the most expensive thing on the menu, she gives the waiter a ruble tip for tea. Charlotta, too. And Yasha orders a complete dinner, it's simply terrible. Yasha is Mama's butler, you know. We 155 brought him with us . . .

VARYA: I've seen him, the devil . . .

ANYA: So, tell me! Have we paid the interest yet?

VARYA: With what?

ANYA: Dear God, dear God . . . 160

VARYA: And in August, the estate will be sold . . .

ANYA: Dear God . . .

LOPAKHIN: (*Peeks through the door and makes a 'bleating' sound.*) Ba-a-a . . . (*Exits.*)

165 VARYA: (*In tears.*) I'd like to give him such a . . . (*Makes a threatening gesture with her fist.*)

ANYA: (*Embraces* VARYA, *softly.*) Varya, has he proposed yet? (VARYA *shakes her head "no."*) But he loves you, he does . . . Why don't you talk about it, what are you two waiting

170 for?

VARYA: I know nothing will ever come of it, nothing. He's so busy, he has no time for me, really . . . he pays no attention to me at all. Well, God bless him, but it's too painful for me even to look at him . . . Everyone talks about our wed-

175 ding, everyone congratulates us, but the fact is, there's absolutely nothing to it, it's all a dream . . . (*Changes tone.*) Your brooch looks just like a little bee.

ANYA: (*Sadly.*) Mama bought it. (*She goes to her room, speaking in a gay, child-like voice.*) And in Paris, I went up in a hot air

180 balloon!

VARYA: My darling's home! My angel is home!

(DUNYASHA *has already returned with the coffee pot and prepares the coffee.*)

(*Stands by the doorway.*) All day long, darling, I go about my business, I run the household, I do my chores, but all the time I'm thinking, dreaming. If only we could marry you

185 off to a rich man, then I'd find peace, I'd go to a cloister, and then on a pilgrimage to Kiev, to Moscow, and on and on, from one holy place to the next . . . on and on. A blessing!

ANYA: The birds are singing in the orchard. What time is it?

VARYA: After two, it must be . . . Time for you to sleep, dar-

190 ling. (*Goes into* ANYA'*s room.*) Yes, a blessing!

(YASHA *enters with a rug, and a traveling bag.*)

YASHA: (*Crosses the stage, discreetly.*) May I?

DUNYASHA: I wouldn't have recognized you, Yasha. How you've changed, since you've been abroad.

YASHA: Hm . . . And who are you?

195 DUNYASHA: When you left, I was about 'so' high . . . (*Indicates.*) Dunyasha, Fyodor Kozoedov's daughter. Don't you remember!

YASHA: Hm . . . Ripe as a cucumber! (*Glances around, and then grabs her and embraces her; she screams and drops a saucer.*

200 YASHA *exits quickly.*)

VARYA: (*In the doorway, displeased.*) What's going on here?

DUNYASHA: (*In tears.*) I broke a saucer . . .

VARYA: That means good luck.

ANYA: (*Coming out of her room.*) We'd better warn Mama:

205 Petya's here . . .

VARYA: I gave strict orders not to wake him up.

ANYA: (*Deep in thought.*) Father died six years ago, and one month later my little brother Grisha drowned in the river, a lovely little seven-year-old boy. Mama couldn't endure it,

210 she ran away, she ran away without once looking back . . . (*Shudders.*) How well I understand her, if only she knew!

(*Pause.*)

And Petya Trofimov was Grisha's tutor, he might remind her of it all . . .

(*Enter* FIRS, *in a jacket and white waistcoat.*)

FIRS: (*Goes to the coffee pot, anxiously.*) The mistress will take her coffee here . . . (*Puts on white gloves.*) Is the coffee 215 ready? (*Sternly, to* DUNYASHA.) You! Where is the cream?

DUNYASHA: Oh, my God . . . (*Rushes out.*)

FIRS: (*Fusses with the coffee pot.*) Pathetic fool . . . (*Mutters to himself under his breath.*) They've just returned from Paris . . . Now in the old days, the master used to go to Paris, too . . . 220 by horse and carriage . . . (*Bursts out laughing.*)

VARYA: What is it, Firs?

FIRS: Yes, and what may I do for you? (*Overjoyed.*) My mistress has come home! I've waited for so long! Now I can die . . . (*Weeps with joy.*) 225

(*Enter* LYUBOV ANDREEVNA, GAEV, LOPAKHIN, *and* SIMEONOV-PISHCHIK; SIMEONOV-PISHCHIK *wears a lightweight coat, fitted at the waist, and wide trousers. As he walks,* GAEV *gestures, as if he were playing a game of billiards.*)

LYUBOV ANDREEVNA: How does it go? Wait—don't tell me, let me think . . . "Yellow into the corner pocket! Double into the middle!"

GAEV: "Cut shot into the corner!" Once upon a time, sister dearest, we slept in this very room, you and I, and now I'm 230 fifty-one years old, strange, isn't? . . .

LOPAKHIN: Yes, time flies.

GAEV: Beg pardon?

LOPAKHIN: As I was saying, time flies.

GAEV: It smells of patchouli in here. 235

ANYA: I'm going to bed. Good night, Mama. (*Kisses her mother.*)

LYUBOV ANDREEVNA: My beloved child. (*Kisses her hands.*) Are you glad you're home? I simply can't get hold of myself.

ANYA: Good night, Uncle.

GAEV: (*Kisses her face, hands.*) God bless you. You are the im- 240 age of your mother! (*To his sister.*) Lyuba, you looked exactly like this at her age.

(ANYA *gives her hand to* LOPAKHIN *and* PISHCHIK; *she exits, and closes the door behind her.*)

LYUBOV ANDREEVNA: She's exhausted, really.

PISHCHIK: A tiring journey, no doubt.

VARYA: (*To* LOPAKHIN *and* PISHCHIK.) So, gentlemen? It's almost 245 three o'clock in the morning, let's not overstay our welcome.

LYUBOV ANDREEVNA: (*Laughs.*) You're the same as ever, Varya. (*Draws her close and kisses her.*) First I'll have my coffee, then we'll all go, yes?

(FIRS *places a cushion under her feet.*)

Thank you, dearest. I've gotten so used to coffee. I drink 250 it day and night. Thank you, my darling old man. (*Kisses* FIRS.)

VARYA: I'll go see if they've brought everything in . . . (*Exits.*)

LYUBOV ANDREEVNA: Am I really sitting here? (*Bursts out laughing.*) I feel like jumping up and down, and waving my 255 arms in the air! (*Covers her face with her hands.*) No, really, I must be dreaming! God knows, I love my country, I love it passionately, I couldn't even see out of the train window, I wept the whole way. (*In tears.*) Never mind, we must have our coffee. Thank you, Firs, thank you, my darling 260 old man. I'm so glad you're still alive.

FIRS: The day before yesterday.

GAEV: He's hard of hearing.

LOPAKHIN: I'd better be going; I leave for Kharkov at five this morning. What a nuisance! I only wanted to see you, that's all, to talk to you a little . . . You're as lovely as ever . . .

PISHCHIK: (*Sighs heavily.*) Even lovelier . . . All dressed up, Parisian style . . . I'm head-over-heels, as they say!

LOPAKHIN: People like Leonid Andreich here, they say all sorts of things about me, call me a boor, a kulak, but really, it doesn't matter, I couldn't care less. Let them say whatever they like. I only want you to believe in me, as you always did, to look at me with those beautiful, soulful eyes, as you used to, once. Merciful God! My father was a serf, he belonged to your grandfather and then to your father, but it was you, yes, you, who did so much for me once, so much, and I've forgotten everything now, I love you like my own flesh and blood . . . more, even, than my own flesh and blood.

LYUBOV ANDREEVNA: I can't sit still, I'm in such a state . . . (*Jumps up and walks around the room, agitated.*) I simply can't bear all this joy . . . Go ahead, laugh at me, I'm being foolish, I know it . . . My dear little bookcase . . . (*Kisses the bookcase.*) My own little table.

GAEV: Nanny died while you were gone.

LYUBOV ANDREEVNA: (*Sits and drinks coffee.*) Yes, God rest her soul. They wrote me.

GAEV: Anastasy died, too. And cross-eyed Petrushka—you remember him—he ran away, he lives in town now, at the district superintendent's. (*Takes a box of fruit drops out of his pocket, pops one into his mouth.*)

PISHCHIK: My daughter, Dashenka . . . she sends her regards . . .

LOPAKHIN: I'd like to tell you some good news, if I may, some cheerful news, all right? (*Looks at his watch.*) I've got to go, there's no time to talk . . . so, very briefly, then. As you already know, your cherry orchard is being sold to pay off the debts, the auction date has been set for the twenty-second of August, but don't you worry, my dear, you don't have to lose any sleep over this, rest assured, there is a way out . . . Here's my plan. Your attention, please! Your estate is located only thirteen miles from town, roughly, a railroad runs nearby, so if the cherry orchard and the land along the river are divided up into plots and then leased for summer homes, why then you'll receive at least 25,000 in yearly income.

GAEV: Forgive me, but what nonsense!

LYUBOV ANDREEVNA: I don't quite understand you, Yermolai Alekseich.

LOPAKHIN: You'll receive at least twenty-five rubles a year per three acre plot from the summer tenants, and if you advertise right away, I'll guarantee you, by autumn, there won't be a single plot left, they'll all be bought up. In a word, congratulations, you're saved. The site is marvelous, the river is deep. Only, of course, you'll have to clear it out, get rid of some things . . . for example, let us say, tear down all the old buildings, and this house, too, which isn't much good for anything any more, cut down the old cherry orchard . . .

LYUBOV ANDREEVNA: Cut it down? Forgive me, my darling, but you have no idea what you're talking about. If there is one thing in the entire province that's of interest, that's remarkable, even, why it's our own cherry orchard.

LOPAKHIN: The only thing remarkable about this orchard is that it's so big. There's a cherry crop once every two years, and yes, there are a lot of them, but what good are they, nobody buys them.

GAEV: There is a reference to this cherry orchard in the Encyclopaedia.

LOPAKHIN: (*Looks at his watch.*) Unless we come up with a plan, unless we reach a decision, then on the twenty-second of August the cherry orchard and the entire estate will be auctioned off. Make up your minds, will you, please! There is no other way, I swear to you. None. Absolutely none.

FIRS: Once upon a time, forty—fifty years ago, they used to dry the cherries, soak them, marinate them, preserve them, and often . . .

GAEV: Hush, Firs.

FIRS: And often, they would send cart loads of dried cherries to Moscow and Kharkov. Brought in heaps of money! And those dried cherries, oh, how soft they were, soft, sweet, plump, juicy, fragrant . . . They knew the recipe in those days . . .

LYUBOV ANDREEVNA: Yes, where is that recipe now?

FIRS: Forgotten. No one remembers it any more.

PISHCHIK: (*To* LYUBOV ANDREEVNA.) Tell us! What is it like in Paris? Did you eat frogs' legs?

LYUBOV ANDREEVNA: I ate crocodile.

PISHCHIK: Imagine that . . .

LOPAKHIN: Up until now, we've only had landowners and peasants living in our countryside, but now, the summer people are starting to appear among us. All the towns, even the smallest ones, are surrounded by summer homes now. And, it's possible to predict that, in twenty years or so, the summer population will multiply beyond our wildest dreams. Now they're just sitting out on their balconies, drinking their tea, but just wait, soon it will come to pass, you'll see, they'll start cultivating their little plots of land, and your cherry orchard will bloom again with wealth, prosperity, happiness . . .

GAEV: (*Indignant.*) What nonsense!

(*Enter* VARYA *and* YASHA.)

VARYA: Two telegrams came for you, Mamochka. (*Takes keys and unlocks the antique bookcase; the keys make a clinking sound.*) Here they are.

LYUBOV ANDREEVNA: From Paris. (*Rips them up, without reading them.*) I'm through with Paris.

GAEV: And do you know, Lyuba, how old this bookcase is? Only one week ago, I pull out the bottom drawer, I look, and what do I see—a mark burned into it, a number. This bookcase was built exactly one hundred years ago. How do you like that? Eh? We may now celebrate the jubilee anniversary of this bookcase, ladies and gentlemen. Yes, it's an inanimate object, of course, but nevertheless, it is still a *book* case.

PISHCHIK: (*Amazed.*) One hundred years old. Imagine that! . . .

GAEV: Yes . . . a work of art . . . (*Touching the bookcase.*) O venerable bookcase! I salute thy existence. For over a century, thou hast sought the pure ideals of truth and justice; thy silent exhortation for fruitful labor has not yet faltered these one hundred years, inspiring courage and hope for the brightest future (*In tears.*) in generation after generation of our kin, and fostering in us the noble ideals of charity and good.

(*Pause.*)

LOPAKHIN: Yes . . .

LYUBOV ANDREEVNA: You haven't changed a bit, Lyonya.

GAEV: (*A bit embarrassed.*) "Off the ball . . . right-hand corner! Cut shot into the middle."

385 LOPAKHIN: (*Glances at his watch.*) Time for me to go.

YASHA: (*Gives* LYUBOV ANDREEVNA *medicine.*) Perhaps you'll take your pills now . . .

PISHCHIK: Why bother taking medicine, lovely lady . . .
390 doesn't do any harm, doesn't do any good either . . . Do let me have them . . . dearest lady. (*Takes the pills, pours them into the palm of his hand, blows on them, puts them in his mouth, and washes them down with kvass.*) There!

LYUBOV ANDREEVNA: (*Frightened.*) You've gone mad!

395 PISHCHIK: Took them all.

LOPAKHIN: There's an appetite.

(*Everyone laughs.*)

FIRS: When he was here during Holy Week, he ate half a bucket of cucumbers . . . (*Mutters to himself.*)

LYUBOV ANDREEVNA: What is he saying?

400 VARYA: He's been muttering like that for three years now. We're used to it.

YASHA: Old age.

(*Enter* CHARLOTTA IVANOVNA *wearing a white dress; she is very thin and tightly laced, with a lorgnette on her belt; she crosses the stage.*)

LOPAKHIN: Forgive me, Charlotta Ivanovna, I didn't have the chance to greet you. (*Goes to kiss her hand.*)

405 CHARLOTTA IVANOVNA: (*Takes her hand away.*) If I let you kiss my hand, next you'll want to kiss my elbow, then my shoulder . . .

LOPAKHIN: Not my lucky day.

(*Everyone laughs.*)

So, Charlotta Ivanovna, show us a trick!

410 LYUBOV ANDREEVNA: Yes, Charlotta, show us a trick!

CHARLOTTA: I don't want to. I wish to sleep. (*Exits.*)

LOPAKHIN: We'll see each other again in three weeks. (*Kisses* LYUBOV ANDREEVNA'*s hand.*) Farewell for now. Time to go. (*To* GAEV.) A very good-bye to you. (*Kisses* PISHCHIK.)

415 And to you. (*Shakes hands with* VARYA, *then with* FIRS *and* YASHA.) I don't feel like going. (*To* LYUBOV ANDREEVNA.) If you make up your mind about the summer homes, if you decide to proceed, just let me know, I'll lend you 50,000. Think about it, seriously.

420 VARYA: (*Angrily.*) So go, then!

LOPAKHIN: I'm going, I'm going. . . . (*Exits.*)

GAEV: What a boor. Oh, wait, "pardon" . . . Our Varya's going to marry him. That's our Varya's fiancé.

VARYA: Don't talk so much, Uncle.

425 LYUBOV ANDREEVNA: Why not, Varya, I'd be so pleased. He's a good man.

PISHCHIK: And a most worthy man, as they say, truth be told . . . Now my Dashenka . . . she also says, that . . . well, she says a variety of things. (*Snores, then suddenly awakes*
430 *with a start.*) Nevertheless, dearest lady, oblige me, would

you, please . . . lend me two hundred and forty rubles . . . tomorrow I must pay off the interest on my mortgage.

VARYA: (*Startled.*) We have no money! None!

LYUBOV ANDREEVNA: As a matter of fact, I don't, I have nothing, really.   435

PISHCHIK: Some will turn up, you'll see! (*Bursts out laughing.*) I never lose hope. There, I say to myself, all is lost, all is ruined, and then suddenly, what do you know—they build a railroad right through my land, and . . . they pay me for it! So just wait and see, something will happen, if   440 not today, then tomorrow. My Dashenka is going to win 200,000 . . . she has a lottery ticket.

LYUBOV ANDREEVNA: The coffee's finished, now we can go to bed.

FIRS: (*Brushes* GAEV'*s clothes, scolding him.*) And you've gone   445 and put on the wrong trousers again. What I am going to do with you?

VARYA: (*Softly.*) Anya's sleeping. (*Quietly opens the window.*) The sun is up now, it isn't cold any more. Look, Mamochka: what glorious trees! My God, the air! And the   450 starlings are singing!

GAEV: (*Opens another window.*) The orchard is all in white. You haven't forgotten, Lyuba, have you? Look—that long row of trees stretching on and on, like a silver cord, on and on, do you remember, how it gleams on moonlit nights? You   455 haven't forgotten, have you?

LYUBOV ANDREEVNA: (*Looks out the window onto the orchard.*) O, my childhood, my innocence! Once I slept in this very nursery, I'd look out on the orchard, right from here, and happiness would awaken with me, every morning, every   460 morning, and look, it's all the same, nothing has changed. (*Laughs with joy.*) White, all white! O, my orchard! After the dark, dreary autumn, the cold winter, you're young again, blooming with joy, the heavenly angels have not forsaken you . . . If only this terrible weight could be lifted   465 from my soul, if only I could forget my past!

GAEV: Yes, and the orchard will be sold to pay off our debts, strange, isn't it . . .

LYUBOV ANDREEVNA: Look, there's my mother, walking through the orchard . . . all in white! (*Laughs with joy.*)   470 There she is.

GAEV: Where?

VARYA: God bless you, Mamochka.

LYUBOV ANDREEVNA: There's no one there, I only dreamed it . . . Look, to the right, on the way to the summer-house,   475 a white sapling, bowing low, I thought it was a woman . . .

(TROFIMOV *enters, wearing a shabby, threadbare student's uniform, and spectacles.*)

What an astonishing orchard! Masses of white blossoms, radiant blue sky . . .

TROFIMOV: Lyubov Andreevna!

(*She turns and looks at him.*)

I only came to pay my respects, I'll go, right away. (*Kisses*   480 *her hand passionately.*) They told me I had to wait till morning, but I couldn't bear it any longer . . .

(LYUBOV ANDREEVNA *looks at him with bewilderment.*)

VARYA: (*In tears.*) It's Petya Trofimov . . .

TROFIMOV: Petya Trofimov, former tutor to your Grisha . . .
485   Have I really changed that much?

(LYUBOV ANDREEVNA *embraces him and weeps softly.*)

GAEV: (*Embarrassed.*) Now, now, Lyuba.

VARYA: (*Weeps.*) You see, Petya, didn't I tell you to wait till
tomorrow.

LYUBOV ANDREEVNA: My Grisha . . . my little boy . . .
490   Grisha . . . son . . .

VARYA: But what can we do, Mamochka. It's God's will.

TROFIMOV: (*Gently, in tears.*) There, there . . .

LYUBOV ANDREEVNA: (*Weeps softly.*) My little boy . . . lost . . .
drowned . . . Why? Why, my friend? (*Softer.*) Anya's sleep-
495   ing, and here I am, raising my voice . . . carrying on . . . So,
now, Petya, tell me! Why have you grown so ugly? And so
old, too!

TROFIMOV: There was an old peasant woman on the train
once, she called me "a shabby-looking gentleman."

500   LYUBOV ANDREEVNA: You were just a boy then, a sweet,
young student, and now look at you, you're hair's gotten
thin, you wear glasses . . . Don't tell me you're still a student? (*Goes to the door.*)

TROFIMOV: And I shall be an eternal student, so it seems.

505   LYUBOV ANDREEVNA: (*Kisses her brother, then* VARYA.) Better
go to bed now . . . You've gotten old, too, Leonid.

PISHCHIK: (*Follows her.*) Yes, time for bed . . . Ach, this gout of
mine . . . I'll stay the night with you . . . Lyubov Andreevna, lovely lady, tomorrow morning, if only you
510   would . . . two hundred and forty rubles . . .

GAEV: He never gives up.

PISHCHIK: Two hundred and forty rubles . . . to pay the interest on the mortgage.

LYUBOV ANDREEVNA: But I don't have any money, really, my
515   sweet, I don't.

PISHCHIK: I'll pay you back, charming lady . . . Such a small
amount . . .

LYUBOV ANDREEVNA: Oh, all right, Leonid will give it to
you . . . Give it to him, Leonid.

520   GAEV: I should give it to him? Don't hold your pockets open.

LYUBOV ANDREEVNA: Give it to him, what else can we do . . .
He needs it . . . He'll pay it back.

(*Exeunt* LYUBOV ANDREEVNA, TROFIMOV, PISHCHIK, *and* FIRS,
GAEV, VARYA, *and* YASHA *remain.*)

GAEV: My sister just can't seem to hold on to her money. (*To*
YASHA.) Move away, good fellow, you smell like a chicken
525   coop.

YASHA: (*With a grin.*) And you, Leonid Andreich, you haven't
changed a bit.

GAEV: Beg pardon? (*To* VARYA.) What did he say?

VARYA: (*To* YASHA.) Your mother's come from the village to
530   see you, she's been waiting since yesterday in the servants'
quarters . . .

YASHA: Good for her!

VARYA: Shame on you!

YASHA: Who needs her? She could have waited till tomorrow
535   to come. (*Exits.*)

VARYA: Mamochka's the same as she's always been, she hasn't
changed at all. If she could, she'd give away everything.

GAEV: Yes . . .

(*Pause.*)

If there are many remedies offered for a disease, then that
means the disease is incurable. Now, I've been thinking,   540
wracking my brain, and I've got lots of remedies, oh yes,
lots and lots of remedies, and you know what that means,
don't you, in essence, that means I don't have any. Wouldn't
it be nice, for example, if we received a large inheritance
from somebody or other, wouldn't it be nice to marry our   545
Anya off to a very rich fellow, wouldn't it be nice to go to
Yaroslavl and try and get some money from our aunt, the
countess. Our aunty's very very rich, you know.

VARYA: (*Weeps.*) If only God would help us.

GAEV: Stop weeping. The old lady's very rich, it's true, but   550
the fact is, she doesn't like us. For one thing, my dear sister went off and married a lawyer, and not a gentleman . . .

(ANYA *appears in the doorway.*)

She didn't marry a gentleman, and you can't really say
she's led a particularly conventional life. I mean, she's a
good, kind person, a splendid person, and I love her very   555
very much, of course, but, whatever the extenuating circumstances may have been, let's face it, she hasn't exactly
been the model of virtue. Why, you can sense it in everything about her, her slightest gesture, her movements.

VARYA: (*In a whisper.*) Anya's standing in the doorway.   560

GAEV: Beg pardon?

(*Pause.*)

Amazing, there's something in my right eye . . . I can't see a
thing. And on Thursday, when I was at the circuit court . . .

(ANYA *enters.*)

VARYA: Why aren't you in bed, Anya?

ANYA: I can't fall asleep. I just can't.   565

GAEV: My little one. (*Kisses* ANYA'*s face, hands.*) My child . . .
(*In tears.*) You're not my niece, you're my angel, you're
everything to me. Believe me, believe me . . .

ANYA: I believe you, Uncle, I do. Everyone loves you, everyone reveres you . . . but, darling Uncle, you must try to be   570
quiet, really, just be quiet. What were you saying just now
about my Mama, about your own sister? Why would you
say such a thing?

GAEV: Yes, yes . . . (*Covers his face with her hand.*) As a matter of
fact, it's terrible! My God! My God, save me! And today, I   575
made a speech before a bookcase . . . how foolish of me!
And it was only after I'd finished, that I realized how foolish it was.

VARYA: It's true, Uncle dear, you should try to be quiet. Just
be very quiet, that's all.   580

ANYA: And if you're quiet, you'll feel much better, really.

GAEV: I'll be quiet. (*Kisses* ANYA'*s and* VARYA'*s hands.*) I'll be
quiet. Just one small matter. On Thursday I was at the circuit court, and, well, some people got together and started
talking, you know, about this, that, the other thing, and so   585
on and so on, and one thing led to another, and so it seems
that a loan might be arranged, to pay off the interest to the
bank.

VARYA: God willing!

590 GAEV: And, on Tuesday, I'm going to have another little talk with them again. (*To* VARYA.) Stop weeping. (*To* ANYA.) Your mama will have a word with Lopakhin; he won't refuse her, of course . . . As for you, as soon as you've had your rest, off you'll go to Yaroslavl to see the countess,

595 your great-aunt. So that way, we'll mount a three-pronged attack—and presto! it's in the bag. We'll pay off that interest, I'm sure of it . . . (*Pops a fruit drop into his mouth.*) On my honor, I swear to you, if you like, this estate will not be sold! (*Excited.*) I swear on my happiness! I give you my

600 hand, call me a worthless good-for-nothing, a dishonorable fellow, if I allow it to go up for auction! I swear on my entire being!

ANYA: (*She regains her composure: she is happy.*) How good you are, Uncle, how wise! (*Embraces her uncle.*) Now I'm con-

605 tent! I'm content! I'm happy, now!

(*Enter* FIRS.)

FIRS: (*Reproachfully.*) Leonid Andreich, have you no fear of God in you? When are you going to bed?

GAEV: In a minute, in a minute. Go on, Firs. Yes, it's all right, I'm quite capable of undressing myself. So, children dear,

610 night-night . . . Details tomorrow, but now, it's time for bed. (*Kisses* ANYA *and* VARYA.) I am a man of the eighties . . . These are not laudable times, but nevertheless, I can say that I've suffered greatly for my convictions in this life. It's not without reason that the peasants love me. One must

615 give the peasant his due! Give him his due, for . . .

ANYA: You're off again, Uncle!

VARYA: Uncle, be quiet!

FIRS: (*Angrily.*) Leonid Andreich!

GAEV: I'm coming, I'm coming . . . And so, to bed. "Off two

620 cushions into the middle. Pocket the white . . . clean shot." (*Exits, with* FIRS *shuffling behind him.*)

ANYA: Now, I'm content. I don't want to go to Yaroslavl, not really, I don't like my great-aunt that much, but, all the same, I'm content. Thanks to Uncle. (*Sits.*)

625 VARYA: We must get to bed. I know I'm going to . . . Oh, an awful thing happened here while you were gone. You remember the old servants' quarters, well, only the old ones live there now: you know, Yefimyushka, Polya, Yevstigney, oh, and don't forget Karp . . . Anyway, they started letting

630 some homeless folks stay the night with them—I didn't say anything at first. But then, I hear, they're spreading this rumor, that I'd been giving orders to feed them nothing but dried peas. Because I was being stingy, you see . . . And all this coming from Yevstigney . . . So I say to myself, fine.

635 If that's the way you want it, I say, just you wait and see. So I call for Yevstigney . . . (*Yawns.*) And he comes in . . . And I say to him, how dare you, Yevstigney . . . you're such a fool . . . (*Looks at* ANYA.) Anechka!

(*Pause.*)

She's asleep! (*Takes* ANYA *by the arm.*) Come to bed . . .

640 Come ! . . . (*Leads her.*) My darling's sleeping! Come . . .

(*They go.*)

(*Far beyond the orchard, a shepherd plays on a pipe.* TROFIMOV *enters, crosses the stage, and, seeing* VARYA *and* ANYA, *stops.*)

VARYA: Shh . . . She's asleep . . . fast asleep . . . Come, my precious.

ANYA: (*Softly, half-asleep.*) I'm so tired . . . do you hear the bells . . . Dearest Uncle . . . Mama and Uncle . . .

VARYA: Come, my precious, come . . . (*Exits into* ANYA*'s room.*) 645

TROFIMOV: (*Tenderly.*) My sunlight! My springtime!

ACT TWO

A field. There is a small, dilapidated old chapel, long deserted, and beside it, a well, an old bench, and several large stones, once apparently gravestones. The road to GAEV*'s country estate is visible. To the side, towering poplar trees loom darkly, where the cherry orchard begins. In the distance, there is a row of telegraph poles, and far beyond that, on the horizon, is the indistinct outline of a large town, visible only in very clear, fine weather. Soon, it will be sunset.* CHARLOTTA, YASHA, *and* DUNYASHA *sit on the bench;* YEPIKHODOV *stands nearby and plays the guitar; all are lost in thought.* CHARLOTTA *is wearing an old, peaked military cap; she removes the rifle from her shoulder and adjusts the buckle on the rifle sling.*

CHARLOTTA: (*Deep in thought.*) I have no passport, no real one . . . no one ever told me how old I was, not really . . . but I always have this feeling that I'm still very young. When I was a little girl, Papa and Mama traveled in a circus, they were acrobats, good ones. And I performed the 5 "salto-mortale," the dive of death, and all kinds of tricks. And when Papa and Mama died, a German lady took me in, she raised me, gave me lessons. "Gut." I grew up, I became a governess. But where I am from, and who I am— I don't know . . . Who were my parents, were they ever 10 married . . . I don't know. (*Takes a cucumber out of her pocket and eats it.*) I don't know anything.

(*Pause.*)

So now I feel like talking, but to whom . . . I have no one to talk to.

YEPIKHODOV: (*Plays guitar and sings.*) "What care I for worldly 15 woe, / What care I for friend and foe . . ." How pleasant it is to play upon the mandolin!

DUNYASHA: That's a guitar, not a mandolin. (*Looks in a little mirror and powders her nose.*)

YEPIKHODOV: For the man, who is mad with love, it's a man- 20 dolin. (*Sings.*) "If my true love were requited, / It would set my heart aglow . . ."

(YASHA *joins in, harmonizing.*)

CHARLOTTA: These people sing terribly . . . Phooey! Like jackals.

DUNYASHA: (*To* YASHA.) How blissful, to have been abroad. 25

YASHA: Well, of course. I'm not going to disagree with you on that one. (*Yawns, then lights a cigar.*)

YEPIKHODOV: But we know that already. Everything abroad is very well organized, and has been so for a long long time.

YASHA: Right. 30

YEPIKHODOV: I am a man of the world. I am. I read many many remarkable books. But, speaking for myself, personally, I have no clue, no clue as to what direction I, personally, want my life to take, I mean: Do I want to live, or do I want to shoot myself, in the head . . . So just in case, I 35 always carry a revolver around with me. Here it is . . . (*Shows them a revolver.*)

CHARLOTTA: I'm finished. And now, I'm leaving. (*Puts on the rifle.*) You, Yepikhodov, you are a very intelligent man and also a very dangerous one; women must be mad for you. Brrr! (*Starts to leave.*) These clever people, they're all such fools, no one for me to talk to . . . Alone, all alone, I have no one . . . and who I am, why I am on this earth, no one knows . . . (*Exits, without hurrying.*)

YEPIKHODOV: Now. Speaking for myself, personally, again, putting all else aside, that is, if I may, when it comes to me, I mean, personally, again, I ask myself: Does fate care? No, fate doesn't care, very much as a terrible storm doesn't care about a tiny boat upon the sea. Now. Let us assume I am wrong in this regard, so then, tell me, would you, please, why is it that this morning, yes, this morning, I wake up, just to give you an example, I look up, and there, sitting right on my chest, is this huge and terrifying spider . . . About 'so' big. (*Indicates with both hands.*) And then, to give you yet another example, I go to pick up a glass of kvass, you know, to drink it, I look inside it, and what do I see? Possibly the most offensive species on the face of this earth—like a cockroach.

(*Pause.*)

Have you ever read Buckle?

(*Pause.*)

May I trouble you, Avdotya Fyodorovna, for a word or two.

DUNYASHA: Speak.

YEPIKHODOV: It would be far more desirable to speak to you in private . . . (*Sighs.*)

DUNYASHA: (*Embarrassed.*) Oh, all right . . . only first, bring me my cloak . . . I left it near the cupboard . . . it's a bit chilly out . . .

YEPIKHODOV: Of course . . . Right away . . . Of course. Now I know what to do with my revolver . . . (*Takes the guitar and exits, strumming.*)

YASHA: Mister Disaster! He's hopeless, just between you and me. (*Yawns.*)

DUNYASHA: God forbid he should shoot himself.

(*Pause.*)

I'm so nervous, I worry all the time. I was just a girl when they took me in, you know, I'm not used to the simple life any more, look at my hands, how lily-white they are, like a young lady's. Can't you see, I've become so delicate, so fragile, so . . . so sensitive, every little thing upsets me . . . It's just awful. And if you deceive me, Yasha, I just don't know what will happen to my nerves.

YASHA: (*Kisses her.*) My little cucumber! Of course, a girl should know how to behave, I can't stand a girl who doesn't know how to behave.

DUNYASHA: I've fallen madly in love with you, you are so refined, you can talk about anything.

(*Pause.*)

YASHA: (*Yawns.*) Right! . . . Now, in my opinion, if a girl falls in love, that means she's immoral.

(*Pause.*)

Nice, isn't it, to smoke a cigar in the fresh, open air . . . (*Listens.*) Someone's coming . . . It's the ladies and gentlemen . . .

(DUNYASHA *embraces him impetuously.*)

Go home, pretend you've gone for a swim in the river, take that path there, or else they'll run into you and think I arranged this little rendezvous. I can't have that.

DUNYASHA: (*Coughs quietly.*) I've got a headache from all this cigar smoke . . . (*Exits.*)

(YASHA *remains; he sits by the chapel. Enter* LYUBOV ANDREEVNA, GAEV, *and* LOPAKHIN.)

LOPAKHIN: You must decide, once and for all—time waits for no one. The question's quite simple, you know. Will you or won't you agree to lease your land for conversion into summer homes? Answer in one word: yes or no? One word, that's all!

LYUBOV ANDREEVNA: Who has been smoking those disgusting cigars here . . . (*Sits.*)

GAEV: Since they've built the railroad, it's all become so convenient. (*Sits down.*) We took a little ride into town, we had our lunch . . . "yellow into the middle pocket!" Now, if only I'd gone home first, and played one little game . . .

LYUBOV ANDREEVNA: You'll have plenty of time.

LOPAKHIN: One word, that's all! (*Entreating.*) Give me your answer!

GAEV: (*Yawns.*) Beg pardon?

LYUBOV ANDREEVNA: (*Looks in her purse.*) Yesterday I had so much money, and today I have hardly any at all. My poor, thrifty Varya feeds everyone milk soup, the old folks in the kitchen get nothing but dried peas to eat, and I manage to let money slip right through my fingers. (*Drops her purse, gold coins scatter.*) There, you see, now I've gone and spilled it. . . (*She is annoyed.*)

YASHA: I'll get them, allow me. (*Collects the coins.*)

LYUBOV ANDREEVNA: Please do, Yasha. And why on earth did I go out to lunch . . . That ridiculous restaurant of yours with the music, and the tablecloths that smell of soap . . . And why drink so much, Lyonya? Why eat so much? Why talk so much? Today in the restaurant you went on and on again, on and on . . . About the seventies, about the decadents. And to whom? Talking to the waiters about the decadents!

LOPAKHIN: Yes.

GAEV: (*Waves his hand.*) I'm incorrigible, it's obvious . . . (*Irritably, to* YASHA.) What is it with you, you're always disturbing my line of vision . . .

YASHA: (*Laughs.*) I can't hear the sound of your voice without laughing.

GAEV: (*To his sister.*) It's either him or me . . .

LYUBOV ANDREEVNA: Go away, Yasha, go on . . .

YASHA: (*Gives* LYUBOV ANDREEVNA *her purse.*) Right away. (*Barely contains his laughter.*) At once . . . (*Exits.*)

LOPAKHIN: Your estate is going to be bought by that millionaire, Deriganov. He's coming to the auction himself, they say, in person.

LYUBOV ANDREEVNA: And where did you hear that?

LOPAKHIN: They were talking about it in town.

140 GAEV: Our aunty from Yaroslavl promised to send us something, but when and how much she will send, who knows . . .

LOPAKHIN: How much is she sending? One hundred thousand? Two hundred thousand?

LYUBOV ANDREEVNA: Oh, well, . . . ten–fifteen thousand, at
145 most, and that much we can be thankful for . . .

LOPAKHIN: Forgive me, but such frivolous people as you, my friends, such strange, impractical people, I have never before met in my entire life. I'm speaking to you in the Russian language, I'm telling you that your estate is about
150 to be sold, and you simply don't understand.

LYUBOV ANDREEVNA: But what on earth are we to do? Tell us, what?

LOPAKHIN: Every day I've been telling you. Every day I've been repeating the same thing, over and over again. The
155 cherry orchard and the land must be leased for summer homes, it must be done immediately, as soon as possible— the auction is imminent! Do you understand! As soon as you decide, once and for all, about the summer homes, you'll have as much money as you'll ever want, and then
160 you will be saved.

LYUBOV ANDREEVNA: Summer homes, summer people— forgive me, please, it all sounds so vulgar.

GAEV: I agree with you, absolutely.

LOPAKHIN: Either I'm going to burst out sobbing, or scream-
165 ing, or else I'm going to fall on the ground, right here in front of you. I can't stand it any more! You're driving me mad! (*To* GAEV.) And you, you act like an old woman!

GAEV: Beg pardon?

LOPAKHIN: An old woman! (*Wants to leave.*)
170 LYUBOV ANDREEVNA: (*Frightened.*) No, don't go, please, stay, dearest. I beg of you. Who knows, perhaps we'll think of something!

LOPAKHIN: What's there to think of!

LYUBOV ANDREEVNA: Don't go, I beg of you. It's so much
175 more cheerful when you're here . . .

(*Pause.*)

I keep waiting for something to happen, as if the house were going to tumble down on top of us.

GAEV: (*Deep in thought.*) "Double into the corner pocket . . . Croisé into the middle . . ."
180 LYUBOV ANDREEVNA: How we have sinned . . .

LOPAKHIN: What are you talking about, what sins . . .

GAEV: (*Pops a fruit drop in his mouth.*) They say I've squandered a entire fortune on fruit drops . . . (*Laughs.*)

LYUBOV ANDREEVNA: O my sins, my sins . . . I've always
185 thrown money around, uncontrollably, like a madwoman, and I married a man, who did nothing but keep us in debt. My husband died from too much champagne—he drank himself to death,—then, for my next misfortune, I fell in love with another man, I began living with him . . . and just
190 at that time, there came my first great punishment, and what a blow it dealt me—right here in this river. . . my little boy drowned, and so I fled, abroad, I simply fled, never to return, never to see this river again . . . I closed my eyes and I ran, not knowing where I was going, what I was do-
195 ing, and *he* following after . . . ruthlessly, relentlessly. I bought a dacha near Menton, *he* had fallen ill there, and for three years I knew no rest, neither day nor night; his illness

exhausted me, wasted me, my soul withered away. And then last year, when the dacha was sold to pay off the debts, I fled again, to Paris, and there he robbed me, he left me for 200 another woman, I tried to poison myself . . . How stupid, how shameful . . . And suddenly I felt drawn again to Russia, to my homeland, to my daughter . . . (*Wipes away her tears.*) Dear God, dear God, be merciful, forgive me my sins! Don't punish me any longer! (*Pulls a telegram from her* 205 *pocket.*) Today, I received this from Paris . . . He begs my forgiveness, beseeches me to return . . . (*Rips up the telegram.*) There's music playing, somewhere. (*Listens.*)

GAEV: It's our celebrated Jewish orchestra. Don't you remember, four violins, flute, and contrabass. 210

LYUBOV ANDREEVNA: Does it still exist? We ought to invite them sometime, plan a little soirée.

LOPAKHIN: (*Listens.*) I don't hear anything. (*Hums softly.*)

An enterprising man, the Prussian,
He'll make a Frenchman from a Russian! 215

(*Laughs.*) What a play I saw at the theatre last night, it was very funny, really.

LYUBOV ANDREEVNA: There probably wasn't anything funny about it. Why go to the theatre to see a play! Better to see yourselves more often. How grey your lives are, how end- 220 lessly you talk.

LOPAKHIN: It's the truth. And the truth must be told, our lives are foolish . . .

(*Pause.*)

My papa was a peasant, an ignorant fool, he understood nothing, taught me nothing, he only beat me when he was 225 drunk, and always with a stick. And the fact of the matter is, I'm the same kind of ignorant fool that he was. I never learned anything, I'm ashamed of my own handwriting, it's not even human, it's more like a hoof-mark than a signature.

LYUBOV ANDREEVNA: You ought to get married, my friend. 230

LOPAKHIN: Yes . . . It's the truth.

LYUBOV ANDREEVNA: Why not to our Varya? She's a good girl.

LOPAKHIN: Yes.

LYUBOV ANDREEVNA: She's of simple origin, she works all day long, but the important thing is, she loves you. And 235 you've been fond of her for a long time now.

LOPAKHIN: Well . . . I have nothing against it . . . She's a good girl.

(*Pause.*)

GAEV: They've offered me a job at the bank. 6,000 a year . . . Have you heard? 240

LYUBOV ANDREEVNA: You, in a bank! Stay where you are . . .

(FIRS *enters; he is carrying a coat.*)

FIRS: (*To* GAEV.) Please, sir, better put this on . . . it's chilly out.

GAEV: (*Puts on the coat.*) You get on my nerves, old man.

FIRS: Now, there's no need for that . . . You went out this morning, without telling anyone. (*Looks him over.*) 245

LYUBOV ANDREEVNA: How old you've grown, Firs!

FIRS: Yes, what may I do for you?

LOPAKHIN: She said: How old you've grown!

FIRS: Well, I've lived a long time. They were marrying me off, and your papa wasn't even in this world yet . . . 250

(*Laughs.*) Then, when the emancipation came, I was already head valet . . . I didn't want my freedom, so I stayed with my masters . . .

(*Pause.*)

255 I remember how glad everyone was, but what they were glad about, they didn't even know themselves.

LOPAKHIN: Ah yes, the good old days. At least there was flogging.

FIRS: (*Not hearing.*) I'll say. The servants belonged to the masters, the masters belonged to the servants, but now every-260 thing's all mixed up, you can't tell one from the other.

GAEV: Hush, Firs. Tomorrow I've got to go to town. They've promised to introduce me to some general, he might give us a loan on a promissory note.

LOPAKHIN: Nothing will come of it. And you won't pay off 265 the interest, rest assured.

LYUBOV ANDREEVNA: He's delirious. There are no generals, they don't exist.

(*Enter* TROFIMOV, ANYA, *and* VARYA.)

GAEV: Ah, here they come.

ANYA: Here's Mama.

270 LYUBOV ANDREEVNA: (*Tenderly.*) Come, come . . . My darling children . . . (*Embraces* ANYA *and* VARYA.) If only you knew how much I love you both. Sit here, right next to me.

(*They all get settled.*)

LOPAKHIN: Our eternal student is always in the company of the young ladies.

275 TROFIMOV: Mind your own business.

LOPAKHIN: And when he's fifty, he'll still be a student.

TROFIMOV: Stop your foolish joking.

LOPAKHIN: You're such a peculiar fellow! Why are you so angry with me, anyway?

280 TROFIMOV: Because you won't stop bothering me.

LOPAKHIN: (*Laughs.*) Permit me to ask you, if I may, what do you think of me?

TROFIMOV: Here is what I think of you, Yermolai Alekseich: You are a rich man, soon you'll be a millionaire. So, in the 285 general scheme of things, that is, according to the laws of nature, we need you, we need predatory beasts, who devour everything which stands in their path, so in that sense you are a necessary evil.

(*All laugh.*)

VARYA: Petya, you do better when you talk about astronomy.

290 LYUBOV ANDREEVNA: No, let's continue yesterday's conversation.

TROFIMOV: What about?

GAEV: About pride. Pride in man.

TROFIMOV: That. We talked about that forever, but we did not come to any conclusion. According to your way of 295 thinking, there is something mystical about the proud man, an aura, almost. Perhaps you are correct in your beliefs, but if you analyze the issue clearly, without complicating things, then why does this pride even exist, what reason can there be for pride, if a man is not physically dis-300 tinguished, if the vast majority of mankind is coarse, stu-pid, or profoundly miserable. There is no time for the admiration of self. There is only time for work.

GAEV: We're all going to die, anyway, so what difference does it make?

TROFIMOV: Who knows? And what does it really mean—to 305 die? For all we know, man is endowed with a hundred sensibilities, and when he dies, only the five known to us perish along with him, while the other ninety-five remain alive.

LYUBOV ANDREEVNA: How intelligent you are, Petya! . . . 310

LOPAKHIN: (*Ironically.*) Yes, terribly!

TROFIMOV: Mankind marches onward, ever onward, strength-ening his skills, his capacities. All that has up until now been beyond his reach may one day be attainable, only he must work, indeed, he must do everything in his power to help 315 those who seek the truth. In Russia, however, very few peo-ple actually do work. The vast majority of the intelligentsia, as I know them, do nothing, pursue nothing, and, mean-while, have no predisposition whatsoever to work, they're completely incapable of it. They call themselves 'the intelli- 320 gentsia,' and yet they address their servants with disrespect, they treat the peasants as if they were animals, they're dismal students, they're poorly educated, they never read serious literature, they're absolutely idle, they don't do a thing ex-cept sit around talking about science and art, about which 325 they know nothing at all. And they're all so grim looking, they have tense, taut faces, they only talk about 'important things,' they spend all their time philosophizing, and mean-while, right before their very eyes, the workers live atro-ciously, eat abominably, sleep without bedding, thirty-forty 330 to a room, together with bedbugs, stench, dankness, deprav-ity . . . And so it seems that all this lofty talk is simply meant to conceal the truth from themselves and others. Show me, please, where are the day nurseries, about which they speak so much and so often, where are the public reading rooms? 335 They only write about them in novels, they never become a reality, never. There is only filth, vulgarity, barbarism . . . I dread their serious countenances, their serious conversa-tions, I despise them. Better to be silent!

LOPAKHIN: You know, I get up before five every morning, I 340 work from dawn until night, I deal with money, con-stantly, mine and others, and yes, I see how people really are. You only have to try to get something done to real-ize how few honest, decent people there are in this world. Sometimes, when I can't fall asleep, I lie there thinking: 345 "Dear Lord, you have given us the vast forests, the bound-less plains, the endless horizons, and we who live here on this earth, we should be true giants . . ."

LYUBOV ANDREEVNA: What good are giants . . . They're very nice in fairy tales, you know, but in true life, they're terri- 350 fying.

(YEPIKHODOV *crosses upstage, playing the guitar.*)

(*Pensively.*) There goes Yepikhodov.

ANYA: (*Pensively.*) There goes Yepikhodov.

GAEV: The sun has set, ladies and gentlemen.

TROFIMOV: Yes. 355

GAEV: (*Softly, as if reciting.*) O nature, wondrous nature, you shine on, radiant and eternal, beauteous and indifferent, you whom we call mother, you embody birth and death, you create and you destroy, you . . .

360 VARYA: (*Imploring.*) Uncle, dear!

ANYA: Not again, Uncle!

TROFIMOV: You're better off "pocketing the yellow . . ."

GAEV: I'll be quiet, I'll be quiet.

(*All sit, deep in thought. Silence. Only* FIRS's *muttering can be heard. Suddenly from far, far away, a sound is heard, as if coming from the sky, the sound of a breaking string, dying away in the distance, a mournful sound.*)

LYUBOV ANDREEVNA: What was that?

365 LOPAKHIN: Don't know. Somewhere far away, deep in the mines, a bucket broke loose and fell . . . But somewhere very far away.

GAEV: Or a bird of some kind . . . a heron, perhaps.

TROFIMOV: Or an owl . . .

370 LYUBOV ANDREEVNA: (*Shudders.*) Disturbing, somehow.

(*Pause.*)

FIRS: Right before the time of trouble, it was the same thing: The owl screeched, and the samovar hissed, it never stopped.

GAEV: What time of trouble?

FIRS: Why, before the emancipation of the serfs.

(*Pause.*)

375 LYUBOV ANDREEVNA: Let's go, dear friends, shall we, it's getting dark. (*To* ANYA.) You've got tears in your eyes . . . What is it, my pet? (*Embraces her.*)

ANYA: I'm fine, Mama. It's nothing.

TROFIMOV: Someone's coming.

(*A* PASSERBY *appears in a shabby, white cap and a coat; he is slightly drunk.*)

380 PASSERBY: Permit me to inquire, may I pass through here to get to the train station?

GAEV: You may. Go down that road.

PASSERBY: I'm deeply grateful. (*Coughs.*) What superb weather we're having . . . (*Recites.*) "My brother, my suffering

385 brother . . . Come down to the Volga, whose moan . . ." (*To* VARYA.) Mademoiselle, please, give a poor starving Russian thirty kopeks. . .

(VARYA *cries out in fear.*)

LOPAKHIN: (*Angrily.*) This has gone too far!

LYUBOV ANDREEVNA: (*Stunned.*) Here . . . take this . . .

390 (*Searches in her purse.*) I have no silver . . . Never mind, here's a gold piece . . .

PASSERBY: I'm deeply grateful! (*Exits.*)

(*Laughter.*)

VARYA: (*Frightened.*) I'm leaving . . . I'm leaving . . . Oh, Mamochka, the servants at home have nothing to eat, and

395 you gave him a gold piece.

LYUBOV ANDREEVNA: What are you going to do with me, I'm such a silly fool! I'll give you everything I have. Yermolai Alekseich, please, lend me some more money! . . .

LOPAKHIN: Yes, madam.

LYUBOV ANDREEVNA: Come, ladies and gentlemen, time to 400 go. Oh, yes, Varya, we've just made a match for you. Congratulations.

VARYA: (*In tears.*) Mama, you musn't joke about that.

LOPAKHIN: "Oh-phel-i-a, get thee to a nunnery . . ."

GAEV: It's been so long since I've played a game of billiards, 405 my hands are shaking.

LOPAKHIN: "Oh-phel-i-a, o nymph, remember me in thy prayers!"

LYUBOV ANDREEVNA: Come, ladies and gentlemen. It's almost suppertime.   410

VARYA: How he frightened me. My heart is pounding.

LOPAKHIN: May I remind you, ladies and gentlemen: On the twenty-second of August, the cherry orchard will be sold. Think about it! Think! . . .

(*They all leave, except* TROFIMOV *and* ANYA.)

ANYA: (*Laughing.*) The stranger frightened Varya off, thank 415 goodness, now we're alone.

TROFIMOV: Varya's afraid we'll fall madly in love, she hasn't let us out of her sight for days. She's so narrow-minded, she can't understand we're above love. To overcome all obstacles, real and imagined, which stand in the path of free- 420 dom and happiness,—that is our quest in life. Onward! We set forth, undaunted, toward that star, burning bright in the distance! Onward! Don't fall behind, my friends!

ANYA: (*Clasps her hands.*) How beautifully you talk!

(*Pause.*)

It's glorious here today!   425

TROFIMOV: Yes, the weather is amazing.

ANYA: What have you done to me, Petya, why don't I love the cherry orchard, as I did, once? I loved it so tenderly, I couldn't imagine any other place on earth more lovely than our orchard.   430

TROFIMOV: All Russia is our orchard. The land is vast and beautiful, there are many marvelous places in it.

(*Pause.*)

Just think, Anya: Your grandfather, your great-grandfather, and his forefathers before him, all were serf-owners, they all owned living souls, so isn't it possible, then, that in every 435 blossom, every leaf, every tree trunk in the orchard, a human soul now gazes down upon us, can't you hear their voices . . . To own human souls—can't you see how this has transformed each and every one of us, those who have lived before and those who live today, so that you, your mother, 440 your uncle, all of you, are no longer aware that you are alive at the expense of others, at the expense of those whom you would not even permit beyond your front hall . . . We have fallen behind, by two hundred years or so, at least, we have nothing left, absolutely nothing, no clear understanding of 445 the past, we only philosophize, complain about our boredom, or drink vodka. And it's all so clear, can't you see, that to begin a new life, to live in the present, we must first redeem our past, put an end to it, and redeem it we shall, but only with suffering, only with extraordinary, everlasting toil 450 and suffering. You must understand this, Anya.

ANYA: The house, in which we live, is no longer our house, and I shall leave it, I give you my word.

TROFIMOV: If you have the key, throw it in the well and run, run far, far away. Be free, like the wind.

ANYA: (*Ecstatic.*) How wonderfully you say it!

TROFIMOV: Believe me, Anya, believe me! I'm not even thirty yet, I'm young, I'm still a student, and yet, I've endured so much! Come winter, I'm hungry, sick, anxiety-ridden, poverty-stricken, like a beggar, and wherever fate carries me, there I shall be! And yet, all the while, every waking moment, day and night, my soul is filled with an indescribable premonition, a vision. A vision of happiness, Anya, I can see it now . . .

ANYA: (*Pensively.*) The moon is rising.

(YEPIKHODOV *is heard playing the guitar, the same melancholy song as before. The moon is rising. Somewhere near the poplars,* VARYA *is looking for* ANYA *and calling: "Anya! Where are you?"*)

TROFIMOV: Yes, the moon is rising.

(*Pause.*)

Here comes happiness, here it comes, closer and closer, I can already hear its footsteps. And if we don't see it, if we don't recognize it, then what does it matter? Others will!

(VARYA*'s voice: "Anya! Where are you?"*)

Varya, again! (*Angrily.*) It's disgraceful!

ANYA: I know! Let's go down to the river. It's lovely there.

TROFIMOV: Let's go.

(*They go.*)

(VARYA*'s voice: "Anya! Anya!"*)

ACT THREE

The drawing room, separated from the ballroom by an archway. A chandelier burns brightly. A Jewish orchestra, the same one referred to in Act Two, is heard playing in the entrance hall. It is evening. In the ballroom, the crowd is dancing the 'grand-rond.' The voice of SIMEONOV-PISHCHIK *is heard: "Promenade à une paire!" The couples dance through the drawing room, as follows: first* PISHCHIK *and* CHARLOTTA IVANOVNA; *then* TROFIMOV *and* LYUBOV ANDREEVNA; *then* ANYA *and the* POST OFFICE CLERK; *then* VARYA *and the* STATIONMASTER, *and so on.* VARYA *is weeping quietly and wipes away her tears as she dances.* DUNYASHA *is in the last couple. They dance around the drawing room.* PISHCHIK *calls out: "Grand-rond, balancez!" and "Les cavaliers à genoux et remerciez vos dames!"*

FIRS, *wearing a tailcoat, carries a tray with seltzer water.* PISHCHIK *and* TROFIMOV *enter the drawing room.*

PISHCHIK: I have high blood pressure, I've had two strokes already, it's difficult for me to dance, but, you know what they say: "If you run in a pack, whether you bark or not, you'd better wag your tail." Never you mind, I'm as healthy as a horse. My dear departed father, joker that he was, God rest his soul, always used to say, on the subject of our ancestry, that the Simeonov-Pishchiks are descended from the same horse that Caligula appointed to the Senate . . . (*Sits.*) The only trouble is: We don't have any money! And you know what they say: "A hungry dog believes only in meat . . ." (*Snores and suddenly wakes up.*) And that's my problem . . . all I ever dream about is money . . .

TROFIMOV: As a matter of fact, you do bear some resemblance to a horse.

PISHCHIK: And why not . . . a horse is a good animal . . . you can get a very good price for a horse, you know . . .

(*In the next room, the sound of a billiard game is heard.* VARYA *appears in the archway to the ballroom.*)

TROFIMOV: (*Teasing.*) Madame Lopakhina! Madame Lopakhina! . . .

VARYA: (*Angrily.*) The shabby-looking gentleman!

TROFIMOV: Yes, I'm a shabby-looking gentleman, and proud of it!

VARYA: (*Bitterly.*) We've gone and hired the musicians, now how are we going to pay for them? (*Exits.*)

TROFIMOV: (*To* PISHCHIK.) Think about it: The energy you've wasted your whole life through in search of money to pay off the interest on your debts, if only you'd spent that energy elsewhere, then, no doubt, you could have changed the world.

PISHCHIK: Nietzsche . . . the philosopher . . . the supreme, the exalted . . . a man of the greatest genius, this man once said, in his own writings, that it's all right to forge banknotes.

TROFIMOV: Have you ever read Nietzsche?

PISHCHIK: Well . . . Dashenka told me that one. And anyway, given my situation, even if I could forge banknotes . . . Day after tomorrow, I owe a payment of three hundred and ten rubles . . . I've already scraped up one hundred and thirty so far . . . (*Searches in his pockets, anxiously.*) My money's gone! I've lost my money! (*In tears.*) Where is my money! (*Overjoyed.*) Here it is, in the lining . . . Look, I even broke into a sweat . . .

(*Enter* LYUBOV ANDREEVNA *and* CHARLOTTA IVANOVNA.)

LYUBOV ANDREEVNA: (*Humming the 'lezginka.'*) Why has Leonid been gone so long? What is he doing in town? (*To* DUNYASHA.) Dunyasha, offer the musicians some tea . . .

TROFIMOV: The auction didn't take place, in all probability.

LYUBOV ANDREEVNA: And of all times to invite the musicians and give a ball . . . Oh well, never mind . . . (*Sits and hums softly.*)

CHARLOTTA: (*Gives* PISHCHIK *a deck of cards.*) Here is a deck of cards, think of a card, any card.

PISHCHIK: I've got one.

CHARLOTTA: Now shuffle the deck. Very good. Give it to me, oh my dear Mr. Pishchik, Eins, zwei, drei! Now go look, it's in your side pocket . . .

PISHCHIK: (*Takes a card from his side pocket.*) The eight of spades, you're absolutely right! (*Amazed.*) Imagine that!

CHARLOTTA: (*Holds out the deck of cards in her palm to* TROFIMOV.) Tell me, quickly, which card is the top card?

TROFIMOV: What? Oh, the queen of spades.

CHARLOTTA: Right! (*To* PISHCHIK.) So? Which card is the top card?

PISHCHIK: The ace of hearts.

CHARLOTTA: Right! (*Claps her hands, and the deck of cards disappears.*) My, what lovely weather we're having today!

(*A mysterious female voice answers her as if coming from underneath the floor:* "Oh yes, the weather is splendid, dear lady.")

You are the image of perfection . . .

(*Voice:* "And you I like very much too, dear lady.")

65 STATIONMASTER: (*Applauds.*) Madame Ventriloquist, bravo!

PISHCHIK: (*Amazed.*) Imagine that! Most enchanting Charlotta Ivanovna . . . I'm head-over-heels in love . . .

CHARLOTTA: In love? (*Shrugs her shoulders.*) How could you possibly be in love? "Guter Mensch, aber schlechter Musikant."

70 TROFIMOV: (*Claps* PISHCHIK *on the shoulder.*) Well done, old horse . . .

CHARLOTTA: Your attention please, for one more trick. (*Gets a lap robe from a chair.*) Here is a very lovely lap robe, I wish to sell it . . . (*Shakes it.*) Doesn't anyone wish to buy it?

75 PISHCHIK: (*Amazed.*) Imagine that!

CHARLOTTA: Eins, zwei, drei! (*Quickly lifts the lap robe.*)

(ANYA *appears behind the lap robe; she curtsies, runs to her mother, embraces her, and runs out into the ballroom, amidst general delight.*)

LYUBOV ANDREEVNA: (*Applauds.*) Bravo, bravo! . . .

CHARLOTTA: Once more! Eins, zwei, drei! (*Lifts the lap robe.*)

(VARYA *appears behind the lap robe; she bows.*)

PISHCHIK: (*Amazed.*) Imagine that!

80 CHARLOTTA: The end! (*Throws the lap robe over* PISHCHIK, *curtsies, and runs out into the ballroom.*)

PISHCHIK: (*Hurries after her.*) Sorceress . . . how did you do it? How? (*Exits.*)

LYUBOV ANDREEVNA: And Leonid is still not back. What can
85 he be doing in town this long, I don't understand it! Surely everything is over by now, either the estate has been sold or else the auction never took place, one or the other, so why must we be kept in the dark forever!

VARYA: (*Attempting to console her.*) Uncle has bought it, I'm
90 sure of it.

TROFIMOV: (*Sarcastically.*) Yes.

VARYA: Great-aunt sent him power of attorney to buy the estate in her name and transfer the mortgage to her. She did it for Anya. And Uncle will buy it, with God's help, I'm sure of it.

95 LYUBOV ANDREEVNA: Great-aunt in Yaroslavl sent 50,000 to buy the estate in her name because she doesn't trust us— and that wasn't even enough to pay the interest. (*Covers her face with her hands.*) Today my destiny will be decided, my destiny . . .

100 TROFIMOV: (*Teasing* VARYA.) Madame Lopakhina!

VARYA: (*Angrily.*) The eternal student! Twice you've been expelled from the university.

LYUBOV ANDREEVNA: Why are you so angry, Varya? He's teasing you about Lopakhin, but what does it matter? If you
105 want to—marry Lopakhin, he's a fine man, a fascinating man. And if you don't want to—don't; no one is forcing you to, darling . . .

VARYA: I take this matter very seriously, Mamochka, I must tell you. He is a good man, I like him, I do.

110 LYUBOV ANDREEVNA: Then marry him. What are you waiting for, I don't understand!

VARYA: But Mamochka, I can't propose to him myself. For two years now everyone's been talking to me about him, every-

one, and either he says nothing, or else he jokes about it. I
115 understand. He's busy getting rich, he's preoccupied with his affairs, he has no time for me. Oh, if only I had money, only a little, a hundred rubles even, I'd give up everything, I'd run away as far as I could. I'd enter a convent.

TROFIMOV: Blessings on you!

120 VARYA: (*To* TROFIMOV.) A student's supposed to be intelligent! (*Gently, in tears.*) How ugly you've grown, Petya, and how old, too! (*To* LYUBOV ANDREEVNA, *no longer crying.*) I simply can't live without work, Mamochka. I must be doing something, every minute.

(*Enter* YASHA.)

YASHA: (*Hardly able to contain his laughter.*) Yepikhodov has
125 broken a billiard cue! . . . (*Exits.*)

VARYA: Why is Yepikhodov here? Who allowed him to play billiards? I don't understand these people . . . (*Exits.*)

LYUBOV ANDREEVNA: Don't tease her, Petya, can't you see how miserable she is.   130

TROFIMOV: She's overbearing, that's what she is . . . always poking her nose into other people's business. She hasn't given Anya and me a moment's peace all summer, she's afraid we might fall in love. What business is it of hers, anyway? And how could she even think that of me, I'm far 135
beyond such vulgarity. We are above love!

LYUBOV ANDREEVNA: And I suppose that means I must be beneath love. (*Tremendously agitated.*) Why isn't Leonid back yet? I only want to know: Is the estate sold or isn't it? This terrible business has gone too far, I don't know   140
what to think any more, I'm at my wits' end . . . I might scream any minute . . . I might do something foolish. Save me, Petya. Say something, anything . . .

TROFIMOV: Whether the estate is sold today or not—does it really matter? It's over, it's been so for a long time, there's no 145
turning back again, that path is long overgrown. Face it, dear friend. You mustn't delude yourself any longer, for once in your life you must look the truth straight in the eye.

LYUBOV ANDREEVNA: What truth? Oh, yes, of course, you see what is true and what is not true, while I have lost my vi- 150
sion, I see nothing. You boldly solve all the problems of the world, don't you, but tell me, my darling, isn't that because you're still so young, because you haven't even suffered through one of life's problems yet, not even one? You boldly look to the future, but isn't that because you see 155
nothing so terrible lying ahead, because life is still safely hidden from your young eyes? You have more courage, more character, more honesty than any of us, so then why not have compassion, find it, somewhere in a corner of your heart, have mercy on me. I was born here, my mother 160
and father lived here, my grandfather, too, I love this house, I can't comprehend a life without the cherry orchard, and if it must be sold, then sell me with it . . . (*Embraces* TROFIMOV, *kisses him on the forehead.*) My son drowned here . . . (*Weeps.*) Have pity on me, my good, kind fellow.   165

TROFIMOV: You know I do, with all my heart.

LYUBOV ANDREEVNA: Yes, but there must be another way to say it, another way . . . (*Takes out a handkerchief, a telegram falls on the floor.*) My soul is so heavy today, you can't possibly imagine. There is such a din here, I'm trembling 170
with each and every sound, trembling all over, but I can't

be alone, the silence would be terrifying. Don't judge me, Petya . . . I love you, as if you were my own child. And I'd gladly let you marry Anya, I would, I swear to you, only
175 first you must finish your education, darling, get your degree. You don't do a thing, you just let fate carry you from place to place, and that's such a strange way to live . . . Isn't it? Well? And you simply must do something about that beard, to make it grow, somehow . . . (*Bursts out laughing.*)
180 How funny-looking you are!

TROFIMOV: (*Picks up the telegram.*) I don't wish to be handsome.

LYUBOV ANDREEVNA: It's a telegram from Paris. Every day I receive one. Yesterday, and today, too. That terrible man is
185 ill again, he's in trouble again . . . He begs my forgiveness, he beseeches me to return to him, I really ought to be going to Paris, to be near him. You should see your face now, Petya, so severe, so judgmental, but, really, what am I to do, darling, tell me, what can I do, he's ill, he's alone, un-
190 happy, and who will take care of him, who will keep him from harm, who will nurse him through his illness? Oh, why hide it, why keep silent, I love him, it's the truth. I love him, I love him . . . He is the stone around my neck, and I shall sink with him to the bottom, and how I love this stone, I can't live without it! (*Presses* TROFIMOV'S
195 *hand.*) Don't think ill of me, Petya, and don't speak, please, not a word . . .

TROFIMOV: (*In tears.*) Forgive me for saying it, but for God's sake: This man robbed you, he cleaned you out!

LYUBOV ANDREEVNA: No, no, no, you mustn't talk like that . . .
200 (*Covers her ears.*)

TROFIMOV: He's an absolute scoundrel, and you're the only one who doesn't know it! A petty thief, a good-for-nothing . . .

LYUBOV ANDREEVNA: (*With controlled anger.*) And you're twenty-six or twenty-seven years old, and still a schoolboy!
205 TROFIMOV: So be it!

LYUBOV ANDREEVNA: You're supposed to be a man, at your age you're supposed to understand how lovers behave. Why don't you know this by now . . . why haven't you fallen in love yourself? (*Angrily.*) Yes, yes! You and all your
210 talk about purity . . . why, you're nothing but a prude, that's what you are, an eccentric, a freak . . .

TROFIMOV: (*Horrified.*) What is she saying!

LYUBOV ANDREEVNA: "I am above love." You're not above love, no, as Firs says, you're pathetic! At your age, not to
215 have a lover! . . .

TROFIMOV: (*Horrified.*) This is terrible! What is she saying?! (*Rushes out into the ballroom, holding his head.*) This is terrible . . . I can't bear it, I'm leaving . . . (*Exits, but returns again immediately.*) It's all over between us! (*Exits into the front*
220 *hall.*)

LYUBOV ANDREEVNA: (*Calls after him.*) Petya, wait! Don't be silly, I was only joking! Petya!

(*In the front hall, someone is heard dashing down the stairs, and suddenly falling the rest of the way with a crash.* ANYA *and* VARYA *cry out, but then, almost immediately, laughter is heard.*)

What happened?

(ANYA *runs in.*)

ANYA: (*Laughing.*) Petya fell down the stairs! (*Runs out.*)
225 LYUBOV ANDREEVNA: What a peculiar fellow that Petya is . . .

(*The* STATIONMASTER *stands in the middle of the ballroom, and starts to recite a poem: 'The Fallen Woman' by Alexey Konstantinovich Tolstoy. Everyone stops to listen, but after a few lines, the strains of a waltz are heard coming from the front hall, and the recitation is interrupted. Everyone dances.* TROFIMOV, ANYA, VARYA, *and* LYUBOV ANDREEVNA *pass through from the entrance hall.*)

Petya . . . my pure Petya . . . I beg your forgiveness . . . Come, dance with me . . . (*Dances with him.*)

(ANYA *and* VARYA *dance together.* FIRS *enters, and places his cane near the side door.* YASHA *also enters, and watches the dancing.*)

YASHA: So, what's new, grandpa?

FIRS: I don't feel very well. In the old days, we used to have generals, barons, admirals dancing at our balls; nowadays 230 we have to send for the postal clerk and the stationmaster, and even they come reluctantly. And I'm getting weaker, somehow. In the old days, when anyone of us fell ill, my old master—that would be their grandfather—he would treat us all with sealing wax. I've taken a dose of sealing 235 wax every day for twenty years now, even more, who knows; perhaps that's why I'm still alive.

YASHA: You get on my nerves, grandpa. (*Yawns.*) Maybe it's time for you to kick the bucket.

FIRS: And you're a pathetic fool, that's what you are. (*Mumbles.*) 240

(TROFIMOV *and* LYUBOV ANDREEVNA *dance in the ballroom, and then in the drawing room.*)

LYUBOV ANDREEVNA: "Merci." Let me sit down . . . (*Sits.*) I'm exhausted.

(*Enter* ANYA.)

ANYA: (*Agitated.*) There's a man out in the kitchen, he was just saying that the cherry orchard was sold today.

LYUBOV ANDREEVNA: To whom? 245

ANYA: He didn't say. He left. (*Dances with* TROFIMOV.)

(*Both exit into the ballroom.*)

YASHA: Some old fellow jabbering, that's all. A stranger.

FIRS: And Leonid Andreich is still not here, he's still not back yet. All he has on is a lightweight overcoat, one for in-between seasons, he's bound to catch cold. Oh, these 250 young people nowadays!

LYUBOV ANDREEVNA: I think I'm going to die. Go, Yasha, hurry, find out to whom it was sold.

YASHA: Oh, he left a long time ago, that old fellow. (*Laughs.*)

LYUBOV ANDREEVNA: (*Slightly annoyed.*) And what are you 255 laughing about? What's so funny?

YASHA: That Yepikhodov, he's a clown. The man is pitiful. "Mister Disaster."

LYUBOV ANDREEVNA: Firs, if the estate is sold, where will you go? 260

FIRS: Wherever you tell me, that's where I'll go.

LYUBOV ANDREEVNA: Why do you look like that? Are you ill? You should be in bed, you know . . .

FIRS: Yes . . . (*With a grin.*) I'll go to bed, and who will serve, who will manage everything? Hm? One servant for the 265 whole household.

YASHA: (*To* LYUBOV ANDREEVNA.) Lyubov Andreevna! One small request, allow me, please! If you go to Paris again, take

me with you, I beg of you. I can't stay here any more, it's
270 absolutely impossible. (*Looks around, in a low voice.*) What
can I say, you see for yourself, this is an ignorant country,
the people are immoral, and anyway, life here is boring, the
food they give you in the kitchen is disgusting, and you
have Firs wandering around everywhere, muttering all
275 kinds of nonsense. Take me with you, I beg of you!

(*Enter* PISHCHIK.)

PISHCHIK: May I have the pleasure . . . a little waltz, most
charming lady . . .

(LYUBOV ANDREEVNA *joins him.*)

But, don't forget, one hundred eighty rubles, enchanting
lady . . . That, I'll take . . . (*They dance.*) One hundred and
280 eighty sweet little rubles . . .

(*They cross into the ballroom.*)

YASHA: (*Sings softly.*) "O, do you know how my heart is
yearning . . ."

(*In the ballroom, a figure in a grey top hat and checkered trousers
waves her hands and jumps up and down; there are cries of: "Bravo,
Charlotta Ivanovna!"*)

DUNYASHA: (*Stops to powder her face.*) The mistress told me to
dance—too many gentlemen, too few ladies,—but now my
285 head is spinning from too much waltzing, my heart is
pounding, and, do you know what else, Firs Nikolaevich, the
postmaster just told me something that took my breath away.

(*The music dies down.*)

FIRS: What did he say?
DUNYASHA: "You," he said, "are like a little flower."
290 YASHA: (*Yawns.*) What ignorance . . . (*Exits.*)
DUNYASHA: "A little flower" . . . I'm such a sensitive young
woman, you know, I adore a few tender words.
FIRS: You'll get yourself into a lot of trouble.

(*Enter* YEPIKHODOV.)

YEPIKHODOV: Avdotya Fyodorovna, you keep avoiding me . . .
295 what am I, some sort of insect? (*Sighs.*) Ach, life!
DUNYASHA: Yes, what may I do for you?
YEPIKHODOV: And no doubt, probably, you're right. Of
course. (*Sighs.*) Who can blame you. And yet, look at it
from my point, of view, I mean, if I may say so myself, and
300 I shall, so excuse me, but you have reduced me to a complete state of mind. Now I know my destiny in life, every
day some new disaster befalls me, and have I accepted
this?—yes, I have, I look upon my fate with a smile. You
have given me your word, and though . . .
305 DUNYASHA: Can we have our little talk later, please? Leave
me alone now. I'm in a fantasy. (*Plays with her fan.*)
YEPIKHODOV: A new day, a new disaster, and excuse me, I just
keep smiling, I even laugh, sometimes.

(*Enter* VARYA *from the ballroom.*)

VARYA: You still haven't left yet, Semyon? Who do you think
310 you are, really. (*To* DUNYASHA.) Get out of here, Dunyasha.

(*To* YEPIKHODOV.) First you play billiards and you break a
cue, then you parade around the drawing room like a guest.
YEPIKHIDOV: You should not reprimand me. Excuse me.
VARYA: I'm not reprimanding you, I'm telling you. All you do
is float from one place to the next, you don't do a blessed 315
bit of work. Why we keep you as clerk, God only knows.
YEPIKHODOV: (*Offended.*) Whether I work, or float, or eat, or
play billiards, for that matter, excuse me, but that's a subject of discussion only for our elders.
VARYA: How dare you speak to me like that! (*Enraged.*) How 320
dare you? Do you mean to tell me I don't know what I'm
doing? Get out of here! This minute!
YEPIKHODOV: (*Cowering.*) Excuse me, may I ask that you express yourself in a more delicate fashion?
VARYA: (*Beside herself.*) Get out, this minute! Out! 325

(*He goes to the door, she follows him.*)

"Mister Disaster!" Never set foot in here again, do you
hear! I never want to lay eyes on you!

(YEPIKHODOV *has exited; from behind the door, his voice is heard:
"I am going to file a complaint against you."*)

So, you're think you're coming back, eh? (*Grabs the cane,
which* FIRS *has left by the door.*) Come on . . . come on . . .
come on, I'll show you . . . So, are you coming back? Are 330
you? This is for you, then . . . (*Swings the cane.*)

(*Just at this moment* LOPAKHIN *enters.*)

LOPAKHIN: I humbly thank you.
VARYA: (*Angrily and sarcastically.*) Sorry!
LOPAKHIN: Please, it's nothing. I'm most grateful for the
warm reception. 335
VARYA: Don't mention it. (*She turns to go, then looks around and
asks, meekly.*) I didn't hurt you, did I?
LOPAKHIN: No, of course not, it's nothing. Just a bump, an
enormous one, that's all.

(*Voices in the ballroom: "Lopakhin has returned! Yermolai Alekseich!"*)

PISHCHIK: Well, well, well, and speaking of the devil! . . . 340
(*Kisses* LOPAKHIN.) I smell a touch of brandy, my dear,
good fellow, yes, I do! And we've been celebrating here,
too!

(*Enter* LYUBOV ANDREEVNA.)

LYUBOV ANDREEVNA: Yermolai Alekseich, you're back. Why
did it take you so long? Where is Leonid? 345
LOPAKHIN: Leonid Andreich returned with me, he's coming . . .
LYUBOV ANDREEVNA: (*Upset.*) So? Was there an auction? Tell me!
LOPAKHIN: (*Disconcerted, afraid to reveal his excitement.*) The
auction was over at four o'clock . . . We missed the train,
we had to wait till nine-thirty. (*Sighs heavily.*) Oh! My 350
head is spinning . . .

(*Enter* GAEV. *In his right hand he carries some packages; he wipes
away the tears with his left hand.*)

LYUBOV ANDREEVNA: Lyonya, what is it? Lyonya? (*Impatiently,
in tears.*) Tell me, quickly, for God's sake . . .

355 GAEV: (*Doesn't answer her, simply waves his hands; weeping, to* FIRS.) Here, take it ... anchovies, and some kerch herring ... I haven't had a thing to eat all day ... What I have lived through!

(*The door to the billiard room is open; the clicking of billiard balls is heard, and* YASHA's *voice: "Seven and eighteen!"* GAEV's *expression changes; he is no longer crying.*)

I'm terribly tired. Help me change my clothes, Firs. (*Exits through the ballroom to his room,* FIRS *follows behind.*)
360 PISHCHIK: What happened at the auction? Tell us! Please!
LYUBOV ANDREEVNA: Is the cherry orchard sold?
LOPAKHIN: It is sold.
LYUBOV ANDREEVNA: Who bought it?
LOPAKHIN: I bought it.

(*Pause.* LYUBOV ANDREEVNA *is stunned; she might have fallen, were she not standing near an armchair and table.* VARYA *takes the keys off her belt, throws them on the floor in the middle of the drawing room, and exits.*)

365 I bought it! Wait, ladies and gentlemen, bear with me, please, my head is spinning, I can't speak ... (*Laughs.*) We arrived at the auction, and Deriganov was already there. Leonid Andreich only had 15,000, so right away Deriganov bid 30,000 over and above the debt on the mortgage.
370 I saw how it was going, so I decided to take him on, I bid forty. And he bid forty-five. Then I bid fifty-five. You see—he'd raise it by five, I'd raise it by ten ... And then, it was all over. I bid ninety over and above the debt, and that was it, it went to me. And now, the cherry orchard is mine!
375 Mine! (*Roars with laughter.*) My God, ladies and gentlemen, the cherry orchard is mine! Tell me that I'm drunk, that I'm out of my mind, that I've made it all up ... (*Stamps his feet.*) Don't you laugh at me! If only my father and my grandfather could get up from their graves and witness all these
380 events, how their Yermolai, their ignorant little Yermolai, the one who was beaten, the one who ran barefoot in the bitter winter, how this same little Yermolai bought the estate, the most beautiful estate in the world. I bought the estate, where my grandfather and my father were slaves,
385 where they were forbidden to set foot in the kitchen. No, I'm dreaming, I'm hallucinating, it's only an illusion ... a figment of the imagination, shrouded in a cloak of mystery ... (*Picks up the keys, smiles tenderly.*) She threw down the keys, she's saying she's not the mistress of the house any
390 more ... (*Jingles the keys.*) Ah, well, what does it matter.

(*The orchestra can be heard tuning up.*)

Eh, musicians, play, I want to hear you play! Everyone, come and see, how Yermolai Lopakhin will take an axe out into the cherry orchard, and all the trees will come crashing to the ground! And we'll build summer homes,
395 and our grandchildren and great grandchildren will see a new life ... Let's have music, play!

(*The music plays.* LYUBOV ANDREEVNA *lowers herself into a chair and weeps bitterly.*)

(*Reproachfully.*) Why, why didn't you listen to me? My, poor, dear friend, you'll never get it back now, never. (*In*

tears.) Oh, the sooner all this is behind us, the sooner we can change our chaotic lives, our absurd, unhappy lives. 400
PISHCHIK: (*Takes him by the hand, in a low voice.*) She is weeping. Come into the ballroom, let's leave her alone ... Come ... (*Takes him by the hand and leads him into the ballroom.*)
LOPAKHIN: What's going on here? Let there be music! Loud, the way I want it! Let everything be the way I want it! 405 (*With irony.*) Here comes the new master, the owner of the cherry orchard! (*Accidentally shoves against a table, almost turning over a candelabrum.*) I can pay for it all, for everything! (*Exits with* PISHCHIK.)

(*There is no one left in the ballroom or the drawing room, except* LYUBOV ANDREEVNA, *who is sitting, huddled over weeping bitterly. The music plays softly.* ANYA *and* TROFIMOV *rush in.* ANYA *goes to her mother and kneels before her.* TROFIMOV *stays at the entrance to the ballroom.*)

ANYA: Mama! ... Mama, are you crying? My dear, good, kind 410 Mama, my beautiful Mama, I love you ... I bless you. The cherry orchard is sold, it's gone, it's true, it's true, but don't cry, Mama, you still have your whole life before you to live, and your pure and beautiful soul ... Come with me, come, my darling, away from here, come! ... We'll plant 415 a new orchard, more glorious than this one, you'll see, you'll understand, and joy, a deep, peaceful, gentle joy will settle into your soul, like the warm, evening sun, and you will smile, Mama! Come, darling! Come! ...

ACT FOUR

The same setting as Act One. There are no curtains on the windows, no pictures on the walls; only a few pieces of furniture remain, stacked in a corner, as if for sale. There is a feeling of emptiness. There are suitcases, travel bags, etc. piled high upstage by the door leading to the outside. The door to stage left is open, from which the voices of VARYA *and* ANYA *can be heard.* LOPAKHIN *stands there, waiting.* YASHA *holds a tray of glasses, filled with champagne. In the entrance hall,* YEPIKHODOV *is packing a case. Offstage, voices are heard—the peasants have come to say good-bye.* GAEV's *voice is heard: "Thank you, my friends, I thank you."*

YASHA: The peasants have come to say good-bye. Now here's my opinion on that subject, Yermolai Alekseich: The people are good, but what do *they* know.

(*The noise dies down.* LYUBOV ANDREEVNA *and* GAEV *enter through the entrance hall; she is no longer crying, but she is very pale: she is trembling, and it is difficult for her to speak.*)

GAEV: You gave them everything in your purse, Lyuba. No! You mustn't do that! 5
LYUBOV ANDREEVNA: I couldn't help it! I couldn't help it!

(*Both exit.*)

LOPAKHIN: (*At the door, following after them.*) Please, I humbly beg you! A farewell toast! I didn't think to bring any from town ... and I could only find one bottle at the station. Please! 10

(*Pause.*)

So, my friends! You don't want any? (*Steps away from the door.*) If I'd known, I wouldn't have bought it. Never mind, I won't have any, either.

(YASHA *carefully places the tray on the table.*)

Drink up, Yasha, why don't you.

15 YASHA: To those who are leaving! And to those who are staying behind! (*Drinks.*) This isn't real champagne, that much I can tell you.

LOPAKHIN: Eight rubles a bottle.

(*Pause.*)

Wickedly cold in here, isn't it.

20 YASHA: They didn't stoke up the stoves today, what's the point, everybody's leaving. (*Laughs.*)

LOPAKHIN: What are you laughing about?

YASHA: I'm happy.

LOPAKHIN: It's October, but outside it's sunny and mild, like

25 summertime. Good weather for construction. (*Looks at his watch, at the door.*) Ladies and gentlemen, bear in mind, only forty-six minutes left until the train departs! That means we have to leave for the station in twenty minutes. Hurry, everyone!

(TROFIMOV *enters from the outside, wearing a coat.*)

30 TROFIMOV: I think it's time to go now. They've already brought the horses around. Where are my galoshes, damn it! They've disappeared. (*At the door.*) Anya, my galoshes aren't here! I can't find them!

LOPAKHIN: And I've got to get to Kharkov. I'll go with you as

35 far as the station. I'm going to spend the winter in Kharkov. Yes. Here I am, standing around, talking to you, I'm lost when I'm not working. I can't live without work, I don't know what to do with my hands; isn't it strange, look, they're hanging there, as if they belonged to someone else.

40 TROFIMOV: We'll be leaving momentarily, and you'll return to all your worthy enterprises.

LOPAKHIN: Have a glass with me.

TROFIMOV: I can't.

LOPAKHIN: So, it's off to Moscow, then?

45 TROFIMOV: Yes, that's right, I'll go with them into town, and tomorrow, it's off to Moscow.

LOPAKHIN: Yes . . . Well, the professors haven't started their lectures yet, no doubt they're all waiting for you!

TROFIMOV: That's none of your business.

50 LOPAKHIN: How many years is it, then, since you've been at the university?

TROFIMOV: Think up something new, why don't you? That's a stale and feeble joke, it's not funny any more. (*Searches for his galoshes.*) It's very likely we may never see each other again,

55 you know, so allow me, please, to give you some parting advice: Don't wave your arms around so much! Try to get out of the habit of waving your arms when you talk, if you can. All this planning of yours, you know, building summer houses, creating a new generation of independent landown-

60 ers, and so on and so forth,—why, that's just another form of waving your arms . . . Oh, well, never mind, all things considered, I like you . . . I do. You have delicate, sensitive fingers, the fingers of an artist . . . you have a delicate, sensitive soul . . .

LOPAKHIN: (*Embraces him.*) Good-bye, my friend. Thanks for everything. Just in case, here, take some money for the 65 journey.

TROFIMOV: Why should I? I don't need it.

LOPAKHIN: But you don't have any!

TROFIMOV: Yes, I do, thank you very much. I've just received some money for a translation. Here it is, right here, in my 70 pocket. (*Anxiously.*) Now where are my galoshes!

VARYA: (*From the other room.*) Here, take the filthy things! (*Tosses a pair of rubber galoshes on the stage.*)

TROFIMOV: Why are you so angry, Varya? Hm . . . These are not my galoshes! 75

LOPAKHIN: This spring I planted almost 3,000 acres of poppies, and made a clean profit of 40,000. And when my poppies bloomed, now what a sight that was! So, here's what I'm saying, I've just made 40,000 rubles, and I'm offering you a loan because I can afford to. Why do you look down your 80 nose at me? I'm a peasant . . . what do you expect?

TROFIMOV: Your father was a peasant, mine was a chemist, none of it means a thing.

(LOPAKHIN *takes out his wallet.*)

Stop that, stop . . . Even if you were to give me 200,000, I wouldn't take it. I am a free man. And everything that is 85 so sacred and dear to all of you, rich and poor alike, hasn't the slightest significance to me, it's all dust, adrift in the wind. I can survive without you, I can even surpass you, I am proud and strong. Mankind is on a quest to seek the highest truth, the greatest happiness possible on this earth, 90 and I am in the front ranks!

LOPAKHIN: And will you reach your destination?

TROFIMOV: Yes, I shall.

(*Pause.*)

I shall, or else I'll show others the way.

(*In the distance, the sound is heard of an axe falling on a tree.*)

LOPAKHIN: So, good-bye, my friend. Time to go. Here we are, 95 looking down our noses at one another, and all the while, life goes on, in spite of any of us. When I work, for days on end, without any rest, that's when my thoughts come most clearly, that's when I know why I am on this earth, why I exist. And how many of us are there in Russia, my friend, 100 who still don't know why they exist. Ah well, what does it matter, that's not the point, is it. They say that Leonid Andreich has taken a position at a bank, 6,000 a year . . . He won't be able to keep it, though, he's too lazy . . .

ANYA: (*At the door.*) Mama asks you not to cut down the or- 105 chard till after she's gone.

TROFIMOV: Isn't it possible to show some tact . . . (*Exits through the entrance hall.*)

LOPAKHIN: Yes, yes, right away . . . Really.

ANYA: Have they sent Firs to the hospital yet? 110

YASHA: I told them about it this morning. I'm sure they did.

ANYA: (*To* YEPIKHODOV, *who is walking through the hall.*) Semyon Panteleich, please, go find out, would you, if they've taken Firs to the hospital yet.

YASHA: (*Offended.*) I told Yegor this morning. Why ask the 115 same question over and over!

YEPIKHODOV: The ancient Firs, in my final opinion, is beyond repair; he should return to his forefathers. And I can only envy him. (*Places the suitcase on a hat box, and crushes it.*)
120 Oh, well, of course. I knew it. (*Exits.*)
YASHA: (*Mocking.*) "Mister Disaster" . . .
VARYA: (*From behind the door.*) Have they taken Firs to the hospital?
ANYA: Yes, they have.
125 VARYA: Why didn't they bring the letter to the doctor?
ANYA: We'll just have to send it along . . . (*Exits.*)
VARYA: (*From the adjacent room.*) Where's Yasha? Tell him his mother's here, she wants to say good-bye to him.
YASHA: (*Waves his hand.*) I'm losing my patience.

(*During this,* DUNYASHA *has been busying herself with the luggage; now that* YASHA *is alone, she goes up to him.*)

130 DUNYASHA: Just one last look, Yasha. You're leaving . . . you're abandoning me . . . (*Weeps and throws her arms around his neck.*)
YASHA: What's there to cry about? (*Drinks champagne.*) In six days, I'll be in Paris again. Tomorrow we'll board an ex-
135 press train, and off we'll go, that's the last you'll ever see of us. I just can't believe it. "Vive la France!" . . . This place is not for me, I can't live here . . . and that's all there is to it. I've seen a lot of ignorance—and I've had enough. (*Drinks champagne.*) What's there to cry about? Behave
140 yourself properly, then you won't cry so much.
DUNYASHA: (*Powders her face, looks at herself in the mirror.*) Send me a letter from Paris. You know much I have loved you, Yasha, I have loved you very, very much! I'm a sensitive creature, Yasha!
145 YASHA: They're coming. (*Busies himself with the luggage, hums softly.*)

(*Enter* LYUBOV ANDREEVNA, GAEV, ANYA, *and* CHARLOTTA IVANOVNA.)

GAEV: We really ought to be going. There's hardly any time left. (*Looks at* YASHA.) Who smells of herring in here?
LYUBOV ANDREEVNA: In ten minutes time we'll be getting
150 into the carriages . . . (*Glances around the room.*) Good-bye, beloved home, home of my forefathers. Winter will pass, spring will come, and you'll no longer be here, they will have destroyed you. How much these walls have seen! (*Kisses her daughter passionately.*) My treasure, you're radi-
155 ant, your eyes are sparkling, like two diamonds. Are you happy? Very happy?
ANYA: Very! We're starting a new life, Mama!
GAEV: (*Cheerfully.*) Everything's turned out quite well, as a matter of fact, yes, indeed. Before the cherry orchard was sold,
160 we were all upset, we suffered a great deal, but then, when everything was settled, once and for all, finally and irrevocably, we all calmed down, we were even glad . . . And now I'm a bank official, a financier . . . "yellow into the middle pocket," and you, Lyuba, for all that we've been through,
165 you're looking better than ever, no doubt about it.
LYUBOV ANDREEVNA: Yes, I'm calmer, it's true.

(*She is given her hat and coat.*)

I can sleep better now. Take my things out, Yasha. It's time. (*To* ANYA.) My darling child, we shall see each other again,

soon . . . I am going to Paris, I shall live there on the money your great-aunt from Yaroslavl sent to buy the estate—God 170
bless great-aunt!—but that money won't last very long.
ANYA: You'll come home soon, Mama, soon . . . won't you? And I'll study, take my examinations, and then I'll work, I'll take care of you. And we'll read all sorts of marvelous books together, Mama . . . Won't we? (*Kisses her mother's* 175
hands.) We'll read through the long autumn evenings, we'll read so many books, and a wonderful new world will open before us . . . (*Dreaming.*) Come home, Mama . . .
LYUBOV ANDREEVNA: I'll come, my jewel. (*Embraces her daughter.*)

(*Enter* LOPAKHIN, *and* CHARLOTTA, *who is softly humming a tune.*)

GAEV: Charlotta is happy: she's singing! 180
CHARLOTTA: (*Picks up a bundle, resembling an infant in swaddling clothes.*) "My sweet little baby, 'bye, 'bye . . ."

(*The child's cry:* "Wa, wa! . . ." *can be heard.*)

"Hushabye, baby, my sweet little boy."

(*The child's cry:* "Wa! . . . wa! . . .")

Poor baby! I feel so sorry for you! (*Throws the bundle down.*) Now, please, find me another job. I can't go on like this. 185
LOPAKHIN: We shall, Charlotta Ivanovna, don't worry.
GAEV: We're all being cast out, Varya's going away . . . suddenly no one needs us any more.
CHARLOTTA: There's nowhere for me to live in town. I must go away . . . (*Hums.*) It doesn't matter . . . 190

(*Enter* PISHCHIK.)

LOPAKHIN: One of nature's wonders! . . .
PISHCHIK: (*Out of breath.*) Oy, let me catch my breath . . . I'm all worn out . . . Most honorable friends . . . Give me some water . . .
GAEV: Looking for money, by any chance? I remain your 195
humble servant, but, forgive me, I really must avoid the temptation . . . (*Exits.*)
PISHCHIK: I haven't been here in such a long, long, time . . . loveliest lady . . . (*To* LOPAKHIN.) And you are here, too . . . so good to see you . . . a man of the highest intelligence . . . 200
here, take it . . . it's yours . . . (*Gives* LOPAKHIN *some money.*) Four hundred rubles . . . I still owe you eight hundred and forty . . .
LOPAKHIN: (*Shrugs his shoulders in amazement.*) I must be dreaming . . . Where on earth did you get this? 205
PISHCHIK: Wait . . . So hot . . . Most extraordinary circumstances. Some Englishmen came to visit my estate, and what do you know, they found white clay in the earth . . . whatever that is . . . (*To* LYUBOV ANDREEVNA.) And here's four hundred for you . . . elegant, exquisite lady . . . (*Gives* 210
her some money.) The rest will come later. (*Drinks the water.*) Just now, a young man on the train was telling us about this great philosopher . . . how he's advising everyone to jump off the roof . . . "Jump!" he says, and that will solve everything. (*Amazed.*) Imagine that! Water! . . . 215
LOPAKHIN: What Englishmen are you talking about?
PISHCHIK: I leased them a plot of the land with the white clay for twenty-four years . . . But now, forgive me, please, I've run out of time . . . a long ride ahead . . . I'm going to the

220   Znoykovs . . . to the Kardamonovs . . . I owe everybody . . .
       (*Drinks.*) Good day to you all . . . I'll drop by again on
       Thursday . . .

       LYUBOV ANDREEVNA: We're just moving into town now, and
       tomorrow I'm going abroad . . .

225   PISHCHIK: What? (*Anxiously.*) Why to town? What's this I see
       . . . furniture . . . suitcases . . . Well, never mind . . . (*In tears.*)
       Never mind . . . Very very smart people, these Englishmen
       . . . people of the highest intelligence . . . Never mind . . .
       I wish you happiness . . . God will watch over you . . .

230   Never mind . . . Everything on this earth must come to an
       end . . . (*Kisses* LYUBOV ANDREEVNA*s hand.*) And when you
       hear the news that my own end has come, remember this
       good old horse, won't you, and say: "Once upon a time
       there lived an old so-and-so . . . Simeonov-Pishchik . . .

235   God rest his soul" . . . Magnificent weather we're having
       . . . Yes . . . (*Exits in great confusion, and immediately returns
       and speaks from the doorway.*) Dashenka sends her regards!
       (*Exits.*)

       LYUBOV ANDREEVNA: And now we can go. But I'm leaving
240   with two worries. The first is Firs—he's ill. (*Looks at her
       watch.*) We still have five minutes . . .

       ANYA: Mama, they've already sent Firs to the hospital. Yasha
       sent him this morning.

       LYUBOV ANDREEVNA: My second sorrow is Varya. She's used
245   to getting up early and working, and now, without work,
       she's like a fish out of water. She's grown thin and pale,
       she weeps all the time, poor thing . . .

       (*Pause.*)

       You know very well, Yermolai Alekseich, I have dreamed
       . . . that one day she would marry you, in fact, it was ob-
250   vious to everyone that you would be married. (*She whis-
       pers to* ANYA, *who motions to* CHARLOTTA, *and both exit.*) She
       loves you, you seem to be fond of her, and I don't know
       why, I simply don't know why it is that you go out of your
       way to avoid one other. I don't understand it!

255   LOPAKHIN: I don't understand it myself, to tell the truth. It's all
       so strange, somehow . . . If there's still time, then I'm ready
       to do it now . . . Basta! Let's settle it once and for all; with-
       out you here, I don't think I could possibly propose to her.

       LYUBOV ANDREEVNA: Excellent. It only takes a minute, you
260   know. I'll call her in right away . . .

       LOPAKHIN: Oh yes, and there's champagne, too. (*Looks at
       glasses.*) It's empty, someone drank it all up.

       (YASHA *coughs.*)

       Or, should I say, lapped it all up . . .

       LYUBOV ANDREEVNA: (*Excited.*) Splendid. We're leaving . . .
265   Yasha, "allez"! I'll call her . . . (*At the door.*) Varya, stop what
       you're doing, and come here. Come! (*Exits with* YASHA.)

       LOPAKHIN: (*Looks at his watch.*) Yes . . .

       (*Pause.*)

       (*Muffled laughter and whispering is heard from behind the door; fi-
       nally,* VARYA *enters.*)

       VARYA: (*In a lengthy search for something.*) That's strange, I can't
       find it anywhere . . .

270   LOPAKHIN: What are you looking for?

VARYA: I put it away myself, I can't remember where.

(*Pause.*)

LOPAKHIN: So where will you go now, Varvara Mikhailovna?

VARYA: Me? To the Ragulins' . . . I've agreed to work for them
       . . . you know . . . as a housekeeper.

LOPAKHIN: Aren't they in Yashnevo? That's about forty-five   275
       miles from here.

(*Pause.*)

And so, life has come to an end in this house . . .

VARYA: (*Searching among the things.*) Where can it be . . . Per-
       haps I put it in the trunk . . . Yes, life has come to an end
       in this house . . . and will be no more . . .   280

LOPAKHIN: And I'm off to Kharkov now . . . on the same train.
       I've got a lot of business there. But I'm leaving Yepikhodov
       here to look after things . . . I've hired him, you know.

VARYA: Really!

LOPAKHIN: Last year at this time it was already snowing, if you   285
       remember, and now it's so sunny and calm. Only it's quite
       cold . . . Three degrees of frost, almost.

VARYA: I hadn't noticed.

(*Pause.*)

Anyway, our thermometer's broken . . .

(*Pause.*)

(*A voice is heard calling from outside: "Yermolai Alekseich! . . ."*)

LOPAKHIN: (*As if he'd long been waiting for this call.*) Coming!   290
       (*He hurries out.*)

(VARYA *sits on the floor, puts her head on a bundle of clothing, and
sobs quietly. The door opens, and* LYUBOV ANDREEVNA *enters cautiously.*)

LYUBOV ANDREEVNA: So?

(*Pause.*)

We'd better go.

VARYA: (*No longer weeping, wipes her eyes.*) Yes, Mamochka, it's
       time. If I don't miss the train, I might even get to the Rag-   295
       ulins' today . . .

LYUBOV ANDREEVNA: (*At the door.*) Anya, put your coat on!

(*Enter* ANYA, *then* GAEV, CHARLOTTA IVANOVNA. GAEV *is wearing a warm coat with a hood. The* SERVANTS *and* CARRIAGE
DRIVERS *assemble.* YEPIKHODOV *is busy with the luggage.*)

Now, we can be on our way.

ANYA: (*Overjoyed.*) We're on our way!

GAEV: My friends, my dear, kind friends! Upon leaving this   300
       house forever, how can I be silent, how can I refrain, upon
       this our departure, from expressing those feelings, which
       now fill my very being . . .

ANYA: (*Imploring.*) Uncle!

VARYA: Uncle, must you!   305

GAEV: (*Dejected.*) "Double the yellow into the middle . . ." I'll
       be quiet . . .

(*Enter* TROFIMOV, *then* LOPAKHIN.)

TROFIMOV: All right, ladies and gentlemen, time to depart!

LOPAKHIN: Yepikhodov, my coat!

310 LYUBOV ANDREEVNA: I want to sit for just one minute longer. I never really noticed before, what walls this house has, what ceilings, and now I look at them with such longing, with such tender love . . .

315 GAEV: I remember, when I was six, on Trinity Sunday, I sat at this window and watched my father walking to church . . .

LYUBOV ANDREEVNA: Have they taken everything out?

LOPAKHIN: I think so. (*To* YEPIKHODOV, *who is putting on his coat.*) Yepikhodov, see to it that everything's been taken care of.

YEPIKHODOV: (*Speaking in a hoarse voice.*) Don't you worry, 320 Yermolai Alekseich.

LOPAKHIN: What's the matter with your voice?

YEPIKHODOV: I just drank some water, and I must have swallowed something.

YASHA: (*Contemptuously.*) What ignorance . . .

325 LYUBOV ANDREEVNA: We're leaving—and not a soul will be left here . . .

LOPAKHIN: Until springtime.

VARYA: (*Pulls an umbrella out of a bundle—it appears as if she were about to strike someone;* LOPAKHIN *pretends to be frightened.*)

330 What's wrong with you? . . . I wouldn't think of it . . .

TROFIMOV: Ladies and gentlemen, please, let's get into the carriages now . . . It's time to go! The train will arrive any minute!

VARYA: Petya, here they are, your galoshes, beside the suitcase.

335 (*In tears.*) Look how old and muddy they are . . .

TROFIMOV: (*Putting on the galoshes.*) We're off, ladies and gentlemen!

GAEV: (*Very confused, afraid of bursting into tears.*) Train . . . station . . . "Croisé into the middle pocket, Double the white 340 into the corner . . ."

LYUBOV ANDREEVNA: We're off!

LOPAKHIN: Is everyone here? No one left behind? (*Locks the side door stage left.*) There are some things stored in here, better lock up. We're off!

345 ANYA: Good-bye, house! Good-bye, old life!

TROFIMOV: Hello, new life . . . (*Exits with* ANYA.)

(VARYA *glances around the room and exits without hurrying. Exit* YASHA, *and* CHARLOTTA, *with the little dog.*)

LOPAKHIN: And so, until springtime. Come now, ladies and gentlemen, we'd better be going . . . Once more, a very good-bye!! . . . (*Exits.*)

(LYUBOV ANDREEVNA *and* GAEV *are left alone together. It is as if they have been waiting for this moment; they throw themselves into each others' arms and sob quietly, with restraint, fearing they might be heard.*)

GAEV: (*In despair.*) My sister, my sister . . . 350

LYUBOV ANDREEVNA: O my precious orchard, my sweet, lovely orchard! . . . My life, my youth, my happiness, farewell! . . . Farewell! . . .

(ANYA's *voice calls out, merrily:* "Mama! . . .")

(TROFIMOV's *voice calls out, gaily, excitedly:* "A-oo! . . .")

LYUBOV ANDREEVNA: For the last time, let me look at these walls, these windows . . . how my mother loved to walk 355 about this room . . .

GAEV: My sister, my sister! . . .

(ANYA's *voice:* "Mama! . . .")

(TROFIMOV's *voice:* "A-oo . . .")

LYUBOV ANDREEVNA: We're off! . . .

(*They exit.*)

(*The stage is empty. There is the sound of all the doors being locked, and then of the carriages pulling away. It grows very still. Through the stillness comes the remote sound of the axe falling on a tree, a lonely, melancholy sound. Footsteps are heard.* FIRS *appears at the door, stage right. He is dressed, as always, in a jacket and a white waistcoat, with slippers on his feet. He is ill.*)

FIRS: (*Goes to the door, tries the handle.*) Locked. They've gone . . . (*Sits on the sofa.*) They've forgotten about me . . . Never 360 mind . . . I'll sit here for a just a bit . . . And Leonid Andreich, most likely, didn't put his fur coat on, went off wearing his light one . . . (*Sighs, anxiously.*) Just slipped my notice . . . These young people nowadays! (*Mutters something incomprehensible.*) And life has passed by, somehow, as 365 if I never lived it at all. (*Lies down.*) I'll lie down for just a bit . . . Don't have too much strength left, now, do you, no, not much, not much at all . . . You pathetic old fool, you! . . . (*Lies there, immobile.*)

(*A distant sound is heard, as if coming from the sky, the sound of a breaking string, dying away, a mournful sound. Silence falls, and all that is heard, far off in the orchard, is the sound of the axe falling on a tree.*)

PRONUNCIATION GUIDE TO RUSSIAN NAMES

Cast of Characters

Lyubov (Lyuba) Andreevna Ranevskaya, Lyoo-bof´ (Lyoo´-ba) An-drey´-ev-na Ra-nyef´-ska-ya
("drey" rhymes with the English word "grey")

Anya (Anechka), An´-ya (An´-yech-ka)

Varya (Varvara Mikhailovna), Va´-rya (Var-var´-a Mee-khai´-lov-na)
("khai" rhymes with the word "why")

Leonid (Lyonya) Andreevich (Andreich) Gaev, Le-o-need´ (Lyon´-ya) Andrey´-e-veech (An-drey´-eech) Ga´-yef

Yermolai Alekseevich (Alekseich) Lopakhin, Yer-mo-lai´ A-lek-syey´-e-veech (A-lek-sey´-eech) Lo-pa´-kheen
("lai" in "Yermolai" rhymes with the word "why")
("syey" rhymes with the word "grey")

Pyotr (Petya) Sergeevich (Sergeich) Trofimov, Pyo´-tr (Pye´-tya) Syer-gey´-e-veech (Syer-gey´-eech) Tro-fee´-mof

Boris Borisovich Simeonov-Pishchik, Bo-rees´ Bo-rees´-o-veech See-myon´-of-Peesh´-cheek

Charlotta Ivanovna, Shar-lo´-ta Ee-van´-ov-na
Semyon Panteleevich (Panteleich) Yepikhodov, Se-myon´ Pan-te-lyey´-e-veech (Pan-te-lyey´-eech) Ye-pee-khod´-of ("lyey" rhymes with the word "grey")

Dunyasha (Avdotya Fyodorovna), Doon-ya´-sha (Av-do´-tya Fyo´-do-rov-na)
Firs Nikolaevich, Feers Nee-ko-la´-ye-veech
Yasha, Ya´-sha

Other Russian Names Appearing in the Text

Anastasy, A-na-sta´-see
Dashenka, Da´-shen-ka
Deriganov, Dye-ree-ga´-nof
Grisha, Gree´-sha
Kardamonov, Kar-da-mo´-nof
Karp, Karp
Kharkov, Khar´-kof
Kozoedov (Fyodor), Ko-zo-ye´-dof (Fyo´-dor)
Lopakhina, Lo-pa´-khee-na
Mama (Mamochka), Ma´-ma (Ma´-moch-ka)
Papa, Pa´-pa

Petrushka, Pye-troosh´-ka
Polya, Po´-lya
Ragulin, Ra-goo´-leen
Yaroslavl, Ya-ro-slavl´
Yashnevo, Yash´-nye-vo
Yefimyushka, Ye-fee´-myoosh-ka
Yegor, Ye-gor´
Yevstigney, Yev-steeg-nyey´
("nyey" rhymes with the word "grey")
Znoykov, Znoy´-kof

Bernard Shaw

George Bernard Shaw (1856–1950) was a man of wide-ranging passions and huge abilities (Shaw disliked the name "George" and never used it, preferring "Bernard" or simply "G.B.S."). By his fortieth birthday he had written five novels, three volumes of classic music criticism, and three volumes of incendiary theater reviews; he had become visible in the influential socialist political organization, the **FABIAN SOCIETY;** he had written the first books in English on Wagner's operas and on Ibsen's plays; and he had just started his career as a dramatist, a career that would eventually include more than fifty plays.

Shaw was born in Dublin. Like Jonathan Swift and Richard Brinsley Sheridan before him, Shaw retained the satiric perspective of the Irish outsider in England. His mother was a music teacher and his sister was a promising singer when they left for London while Shaw was in his teens. He followed them to London in 1876. A shy and self-effacing young man, Shaw took a variety of jobs that brought him into contact with the public, and he used the opportunity of lecturing for the Fabian Society to develop the brilliantly articulate persona we recognize today as "G.B.S." Throughout the 1880s, Shaw worked with the Fabians, adopting their plan of gradual social reform in place of a more rigorously Marxist call for social revolution. The Fabians strove to change society through a strategy of permeation, working to get their members elected into prominent offices, where their educational and social reforms might be put into effect. Shaw was deeply influenced by the Fabians' gradualist scheme for social improvement—a scheme that underlies the utopian project of his greatest plays—for Fabian gradualism synchronized with Shaw's other passion, Creative Evolution. Appalled by what he regarded as the mindless mechanism of Darwinian natural selection, Shaw resisted the notion that human evolution followed a random and inevitable process. He urged instead that humanity take command of its future by willing itself to evolve in certain humane directions, and he advocated eugenics, capital punishment, and other ideas in the interest of the development of the species. Shaw attempted an uneasy synthesis of the Fabian socialist project of gradual social evolution with the individualist metaphysics of Creative Evolution: the improvement of society through the improvement of each of its members.

Shaw's friend William Archer once described seeing Shaw in the British Museum reading room simultaneously reading Marx's *Das Kapital* and the score of Wagner's *Ring of the Niebelung* cycle. The blending of political substance with a rich and deeply harmonized verbal music became a constant feature of Shaw's drama. Writing as a theater critic in the 1890s, Shaw became the champion of Ibsen in England. Vowing to lay siege to the conventions of the nineteenth-century theater, he touted Ibsen's plays and lambasted the corny tearjerkers, simplistic melodramas, and overstuffed Shakespearean productions that were the theater's common fare. Not incidentally, he worked to create a taste for his own plays, an operatic drama of the intellectual passions.

Shaw's career as a playwright falls into three main phases. Shaw's earliest plays— *Widowers' Houses* (1892) and *Mrs. Warren's Profession* (1893)—attacked specific social problems, like slum landlords and international prostitution. But Shaw more often linked social ills to the smug pieties of conventional morality. His plays generally work to disillusion his main characters—and his audience—from the ready acceptance of bourgeois ideology as a natural "reality." This process of disillusionment informs Shaw's lighter comedies of the 1890s, plays like *Arms and the Man* (1894), *Candida* (1894), and *Caesar and Cleopatra* (1898). After the turn of the century, however, Shaw entered on his maturity as a playwright, undertaking a series of major comedies that place this process of disillusionment directly in conflict with society's most important institutions: marriage and sexuality in *Man and Superman* (1903); British imperialism in Ireland in *John Bull's Other Island* (1904); salvation, damnation, and raw power in *Major Barbara* (1905); medicine in *The Doctor's Dilemma* (1906); language and class in *Pygmalion* (1912). Several of these plays were first produced at the Court Theater, under the management of Shaw's close friend Harley Granville Barker, who originated the part of Cusins in *Major Barbara* and other Shavian roles. Under Barker and his partner J.E. Vedrenne, the Court Theater in 1904–1907 became the most influential theater in London before World War I. Through its efforts, and Shaw's own energy as playwright, director, and advisor, the Court made Shaw's reputation as a major dramatist. With the coming of World War I, and the violent waste of civilization it brought with it, Shaw's confidence in the eventual perfection of humanity was deeply shaken, and the plays of his final half-century are much bleaker, more uncertain in tone: his magnificent "fantasia in the Russian manner on English themes," *Heartbreak House* (1919), modeled on Chekhov's *The Cherry Orchard; Saint Joan* (1923), perhaps his best-loved play; his five-play quintet on the origin and future of the species, *Back to Methuselah* (1921); and many others. In contrast to the confidence of Shaw's earlier plays, the later dramas generally seem to ask the question that Shaw gave to his Saint Joan: "O God that madest this beautiful earth, when will it be ready to receive Thy saints? How long, O Lord, how long?"

MAJOR BARBARA

Shaw was born before the publication of Darwin's *Origin of Species* in 1859, and he died after the dropping of the atomic bomb on Hiroshima. His major plays, like *Major Barbara,* treat the problems of the twentieth century in the dramatic vocabulary of Edwardian **COMEDY OF MANNERS.** *Major Barbara* is typical of the dialectical process of Shaw's plays. From the

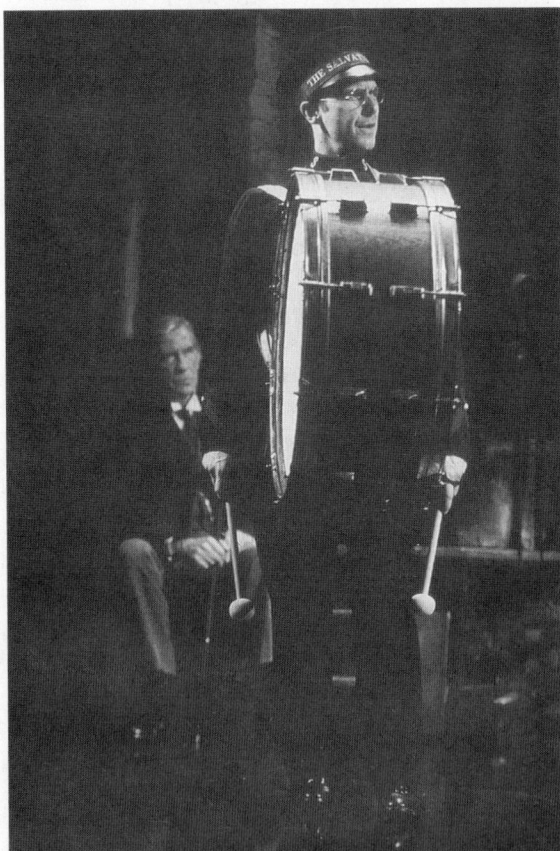

Adolphus Cusins beats the big drum in the finale of Act 2 of Bernard Shaw's *Major Barbara.*

outset—when Stephen learns that his income is derived from his father's munitions empire—Shaw forces the audience and his characters to question the nature of their values, particularly the sense that good and evil, morality and economics, the power to save and the power to destroy can be easily or conveniently distinguished from one another. As a result, the play forces a deeply ironic experience on its characters and on the audience. For Shaw is interested in salvation, not simply the moralizing salvation promised by the Salvation Army, but a Nietzschean transvaluation of values, a salvation beyond the conventional abstractions of good and evil that he regards as necessary to the transformation of English society.

The play is structured dialectically, progressing from thesis, to antithesis, to a problematic synthesis. The "thesis" of act 1 concerns the values of Wilton Crescent: the comfortable morality of the English upper classes. As the scene proceeds, though, Shaw suggests that conventional morality, the innate knowledge of right and wrong, is in fact supported by Undershaft's money and gunpowder. The "antithesis" of act 2 offers the unconventional morality of the Salvation Army; Barbara's shelter in West Ham claims to provide true salvation by requiring a more sincere form of religious conviction. However, as it turns out, both Wilton Crescent and West Ham are equally in the grip of Bodger and Undershaft. The distiller and the munitions-maker determine the material realities on which society erects its illusory social "ideals" and calls them "reality." The Dionysian sacrifice of Barbara at the end of act 2—with its echoes of Christ's crucifixion as well—prepares us for her resurrection in the "synthesis" offered by act 3; in Perivale St Andrews, the spiritual Barbara and the intellectual Cusins are married with the blessing of the explosive Undershaft. We might be troubled, though, by the "synthesis" offered by the utopian factory town, for Undershaft's utopia hardly seems revolutionary. In many ways, Perivale St Andrews largely duplicates turn-of-the-century English class society and industrial capitalism, with the poverty and dirt cleaned up. The play's last act is often said to be unconvincing, and we might wonder whether that is in fact part of Shaw's purpose in *Major Barbara.* Once Shaw instructs us in the process of dialectical criticism, perhaps he invites us to scrutinize even Undershaft's bourgeois utopia, to see Perivale St Andrews as itself in need of further (r)evolution.

Shaw made Andrew Undershaft a magnificently melodramatic, attractive, amoral munitions-maker, whose creative ability is harnessed to the power to destroy. Moreover, Shaw drew a parallel between Undershaft and a crucial dramatic precursor, the Dionysus of Euripides' *The Bacchae.* The character of Cusins was modeled on Shaw's friend, the well-known classical scholar Gilbert Murray, and in the original production, Cusins was even played to resemble Murray. In act 2, Cusins quotes a brief passage adapted from Murray's translation of *The Bacchae,* part of the choral speech delivered just before Pentheus is led out to spy on the Bacchae and be killed. We might take this invocation of Dionysus as a final clue to the play's attitude. Much like Euripides, Shaw prevents his audience from sympathizing entirely with his hero, from readily accepting the terrible power necessary to change the world. Although the play ends with a ceremonial marriage characteristic of **ROMANTIC COMEDY**—symbolizing the union of intellect, spirit, and power—the fact that Dionysus Undershaft presides over this union should give us pause. Can the power he wields really be harnessed for our salvation?

Shaw, not surprisingly, had a systematic but unconventional approach to English spelling and punctuation, and insisted that publisher's observe it when printing his plays; this edition of *Major Barbara* accordingly preserves Shaw's style.

MAJOR BARBARA

Bernard Shaw

CHARACTERS

STEPHEN UNDERSHAFT	CHARLES LOMAX
LADY BRITOMART	RUMMY MITCHENS
BARBARA UNDERSHAFT	SNOBBY PRICE
SARAH UNDERSHAFT	PETER SHIRLEY
ANDREW UNDERSHAFT	BILTON
JENNY HILL	MRS BAINES
BILL WALKER	ADOLPHUS CUSINS
MORRISON	

ACT ONE

It is after dinner in January 1906, in the library in LADY BRITO-MART UNDERSHAFT's *house in Wilton Crescent. A large and comfortable settee is in the middle of the room, upholstered in dark leather. A person sitting on it (it is vacant at present) would have, on his right,* LADY BRITOMART's *writing table, with the lady herself busy at it; a smaller writing table behind him on his left; the door behind him on* LADY BRITOMART's *side; and a window with a window seat directly on his left. Near the window is an armchair.*

LADY BRITOMART *is a woman of fifty or thereabouts, well dressed and yet careless of her dress, well bred and quite reckless of her breeding, well mannered and yet appallingly outspoken and indifferent to the opinion of her interlocutors, amiable and yet peremptory, arbitrary, and high-tempered to the last bearable degree, and withal a very typical managing matron of the upper class, treated as a naughty child until she grew into a scolding mother, and finally settling down with plenty of practical ability and worldly experience, limited in the oddest way with domestic and class limitations, conceiving the universe exactly as if it were a large house in Wilton Crescent, though handling her corner of it very effectively on that assumption, and being quite enlightened and liberal as to the books in the library, the pictures on the walls, the music in the portfolios, and the articles in the papers.*

Her son, STEPHEN, *comes in. He is a gravely correct young man under 25, taking himself very seriously, but still in some awe of his mother, from childish habit and bachelor shyness rather than from any weakness of character.*

STEPHEN: Whats the matter?

LADY BRITOMART: Presently, Stephen.

(STEPHEN *submissively walks to the settee and sits down. He takes up a Liberal weekly called* The Speaker.)

LADY BRITOMART: Dont begin to read, Stephen. I shall require all your attention.

5 STEPHEN: It was only while I was waiting—

LADY BRITOMART: Dont make excuses, Stephen. (*He puts down* The Speaker.) Now! (*She finishes her writing; rises; and comes to the settee.*) I have not kept you waiting very long, I think.

STEPHEN: Not at all, mother.

10 LADY BRITOMART: Bring me my cushion. (*He takes the cushion from the chair at the desk and arranges it for her as she sits down on the settee.*) Sit down. (*He sits down and fingers his tie nervously.*) Dont fiddle with your tie, Stephen: there is nothing the matter with it.

STEPHEN: I beg your pardon. (*He fiddles with his watch chain instead.*) 15

LADY BRITOMART: Now are you attending to me, Stephen?

STEPHEN: Of course, mother.

LADY BRITOMART: No: it's not of course. I want something much more than your everyday matter-of-course attention. 20 I am going to speak to you very seriously, Stephen. I wish you would let that chain alone.

STEPHEN: (*Hastily relinquishing the chain.*) Have I done anything to annoy you, mother? If so, it was quite unintentional.

LADY BRITOMART: (*Astonished.*) Nonsense! (*With some remorse.*) My poor boy, did you think I was angry with you? 25

STEPHEN: What is it, then, mother? You are making me very uneasy.

LADY BRITOMART: (*Squaring herself at him rather aggressively.*) Stephen: may I ask how soon you intend to realize that 30 you are a grown-up man, and that I am only a woman?

STEPHEN: (*Amazed.*) Only a—

LADY BRITOMART: Dont repeat my words, please: it is a most aggravating habit. You must learn to face life seriously, Stephen. I really cannot bear the whole burden of our 35 family affairs any longer. You must advise me: you must assume the responsibility.

STEPHEN: I!

LADY BRITOMART: Yes, you, of course. You were 24 last June. Youve been at Harrow and Cambridge. Youve been to In- 40 dia and Japan. You must know a lot of things, now; unless you have wasted your time most scandalously. Well, advise me.

STEPHEN: (*Much perplexed.*) You know I have never interfered in the household—

LADY BRITOMART: No: I should think not. I dont want you 45 to order the dinner.

STEPHEN: I mean in our family affairs.

LADY BRITOMART: Well, you must interfere now; for they are getting quite beyond me.

STEPHEN: (*Troubled.*) I have thought sometimes that perhaps I 50 ought; but really, mother, I know so little about them; and what I do know is so painful! it is so impossible to mention some things to you—(*He stops, ashamed.*)

LADY BRITOMART: I suppose you mean your father.

STEPHEN: (*Almost inaudibly.*) Yes. 55

LADY BRITOMART: My dear: we cant go on all our lives not mentioning him. Of course you were quite right not to

671

open the subject until I asked you to; but you are old enough now to be taken into my confidence, and to help me to deal with him about the girls.

STEPHEN: But the girls are all right. They are engaged.

LADY BRITOMART: (*Complacently.*) Yes: I have made a very good match for Sarah. Charles Lomax will be a millionaire at 35. But that is ten years ahead; and in the meantime his trustees cannot under the terms of his father's will allow him more than £800 a year.

STEPHEN: But the will says also that if he increases his income by his own exertions, they may double the increase.

LADY BRITOMART: Charles Lomax's exertions are much more likely to decrease his income than to increase it. Sarah will have to find at least another £800 a year for the next ten years; and even then they will be as poor as church mice. And what about Barbara? I thought Barbara was going to make the most brilliant career of all of you. And what does she do? Joins the Salvation Army; discharges her maid; lives on a pound a week and walks in one evening with a professor of Greek whom she has picked up in the street, and who pretends to be a Salvationist, and actually plays the big drum for her in public because he has fallen head over ears in love with her.

STEPHEN: I was certainly rather taken aback when I heard they were engaged. Cusins is a very nice fellow, certainly: nobody would ever guess that he was born in Australia; but—

LADY BRITOMART: Oh, Adolphus Cusins will make a very good husband. After all, nobody can say a word against Greek: it stamps a man at once as an educated gentleman. And my family, thank Heaven, is not a pig-headed Tory one. We are Whigs, and believe in liberty. Let snobbish people say what they please: Barbara shall marry, not the man they like, but the man *I* like.

STEPHEN: Of course I was thinking only of his income. However, he is not likely to be extravagant.

LADY BRITOMART: Dont be too sure of that, Stephen. I know your quiet, simple, refined, poetic people like Adolphus: quite content with the best of everything! They cost more than your extravagant people, who are always as mean as they are second rate. No: Barbara will need at least £2000 a year. You see it means two additional households. Besides, my dear, you must marry soon. I dont approve of the present fashion of philandering bachelors and late marriages; and I am trying to arrange something for you.

STEPHEN: It's very good of you, mother; but perhaps I had better arrange that for myself.

LADY BRITOMART: Nonsense! you are much too young to begin matchmaking: you would be taken in by some pretty little nobody. Of course I dont mean that you are not to be consulted: you know that as well as I do. (STEPHEN *closes his lips and is silent.*) Now dont sulk, Stephen.

STEPHEN: I am not sulking, mother. What has all this got to do with—with—with my father?

LADY BRITOMART: My dear Stephen: where is the money to come from? It is easy enough for you and the other children to live on my income as long as we are in the same house; but I cant keep four families in four separate houses. You know how poor my father is: he has barely seven thousand a year now; and really, if he were not the Earl of Stevenage, he would have to give up society. He can do nothing for us. He says, naturally enough, that it is absurd that he should be asked to provide for the children of a man who is rolling in money. You see, Stephen, your father must be fabulously wealthy, because there is always a war going on somewhere.

STEPHEN: You need not remind me of that, mother. I have hardly ever opened a newspaper in my life without seeing our name in it. The Undershaft torpedo! The Undershaft quick firers! The Undershaft ten inch! the Undershaft disappearing rampart gun! the Undershaft submarine! and now the Undershaft aerial battleship! At Harrow they called me the Woolwich Infant. At Cambridge it was the same. A little brute at King's who was always trying to get up revivals, spoilt my Bible—your first birthday present to me—by writing under my name, "Son and heir to Undershaft and Lazarus, Death and Destruction Dealers: address Christendom and Judea." But that was not so bad as the way I was kowtowed to everywhere because my father was making millions by selling cannons.

LADY BRITOMART: It is not only the cannons, but the war loans that Lazarus arranges under cover of giving credit for the cannons. You know, Stephen, it's perfectly scandalous. Those two men, Andrew Undershaft and Lazarus, positively have Europe under their thumbs. That is why your father is able to behave as he does. He is above the law. Do you think Bismarck or Gladstone or Disraeli could have openly defied every social and moral obligation all their lives as your father has? They simply wouldnt have dared. I asked Gladstone to take it up. I asked The Times to take it up. I asked the Lord Chamberlain to take it up. But it was just like asking them to declare war on the Sultan. They wouldnt. They said they couldnt touch him. I believe they were afraid.

STEPHEN: What could they do? He does not actually break the law.

LADY BRITOMART: Not break the law! He is always breaking the law. He broke the law when he was born: his parents were not married.

STEPHEN: Mother! Is that true?

LADY BRITOMART: Of course it's true: that was why we separated.

STEPHEN: He married without letting you know that!

LADY BRITOMART: (*Rather taken aback by this inference.*) Oh no. To do Andrew justice, that was not the sort of thing he did. Besides, you know the Undershaft motto: Unashamed. Everybody knew.

STEPHEN: But you said that was why you separated.

LADY BRITOMART: Yes, because he was not content with being a foundling himself: he wanted to disinherit you for another foundling. That was what I couldnt stand.

STEPHEN: (*Ashamed.*) Do you mean for—for—for—

LADY BRITOMART: Dont stammer, Stephen. Speak distinctly.

STEPHEN: But this is so frightful to me, mother. To have to speak to you about such things!

LADY BRITOMART: It's not pleasant for me, either, especially if you are still so childish that you must make it worse by a display of embarrassment. It is only in the middle classes, Stephen, that people get into a state of dumb helpless horror when they find that there are wicked people in the world. In our class, we have to decide what is to be done with wicked people; and nothing should disturb our self-possession. Now ask your question properly.

STEPHEN: Mother: have you no consideration for me? For Heaven's sake either treat me as a child, as you always do, and tell me nothing at all or tell me everything and let me take it as best I can.

LADY BRITOMART: Treat you as a child! What do you mean? It is most unkind and ungrateful of you to say such a thing. You know I have never treated any of you as chil-
185 dren. I have always made you my companions and friends, and allowed you perfect freedom to do and say whatever you like, so long as you liked what I could approve of.

STEPHEN: (*Desperately.*) I daresay we have been the very imperfect children of a very perfect mother; but I do beg you to
190 let me alone for once, and tell me about this horrible business of my father wanting to set me aside for another son.

LADY BRITOMART: (*Amazed.*) Another son! I never said anything of the kind. I never dreamt of such a thing. This is what comes of interrupting me.

195 STEPHEN: But you said—

LADY BRITOMART: (*Cutting him short.*) Now be a good boy, Stephen, and listen to me patiently. The Undershafts are descended from a foundling in the parish of St Andrew Undershaft in the city. That was long ago, in the reign of
200 James the First. Well, this foundling was adopted by an armorer and gun-maker. In the course of time the foundling succeeded to the business; and from some notion of gratitude, or some vow or something, he adopted another foundling, and left the business to him. And that
205 foundling did the same. Ever since that, the cannon business has always been left to an adopted foundling named Andrew Undershaft.

STEPHEN: But did they never marry? Were there no legitimate sons?

210 LADY BRITOMART: Oh yes: they married just as your father did; and they were rich enough to buy land for their own children and leave them well provided for. But they always adopted and trained some foundling to succeed them in the business; and of course they always quarrelled with
215 their wives furiously over it. Your father was adopted in that way; and he pretends to consider himself bound to keep up the tradition and adopt somebody to leave the business to. Of course I was not going to stand that. There may have been some reason for it when the Undershafts
220 could only marry women in their own class, whose sons were not fit to govern great estates. But there could be no excuse for passing over my son.

STEPHEN: (*Dubiously.*) I am afraid I should make a poor hand of managing a cannon foundry.

225 LADY BRITOMART: Nonsense! you could easily get a manager and pay him a salary.

STEPHEN: My father evidently had no great opinion of my capacity.

LADY BRITOMART: Stuff, child! you were only a baby: it had
230 nothing to do with your capacity. Andrew did it on principle, just as he did every perverse and wicked thing on principle. When my father remonstrated, Andrew actually told him to his face that history tells us of only two successful institutions: one the Undershaft firm, and the other the Ro-
235 man Empire under the Antonines. That was because the Antonine emperors all adopted their successors. Such rubbish! The Stevenages are as good as the Antonines, I hope; and you are a Stevenage. But that was Andrew all over. There you have the man! Always clever and unanswerable when he
240 was defending nonsense and wickedness: always awkward and sullen when he had to behave sensibly and decently!

STEPHEN: Then it was on my account that your home life was broken up, mother. I am sorry.

LADY BRITOMART: Well, dear, there were other differences. I
245 really cannot bear an immoral man. I am not a Pharisee, I hope; and I should not have minded his merely doing wrong things: we are none of us perfect. But your father didnt exactly do wrong things: he said them and thought them: that was what was so dreadful. He really had a sort
250 of religion of wrongness. Just as one doesnt mind men practising immorality so long as they own that they are in the wrong by preaching morality; so I couldnt forgive Andrew for preaching immorality while he practised morality. You would all have grown up without principles,
255 without any knowledge of right and wrong, if he had been in the house. You know, my dear, your father was a very attractive man in some ways. Children did not dislike him; and he took advantage of it to put the wickedest ideas into their heads, and make them quite unmanage-
260 able. I did not dislike him myself: very far from it; but nothing can bridge over moral disagreement.

STEPHEN: All this simply bewilders me, mother. People may differ about matters of opinion, or even about religion; but how can they differ about right and wrong? Right is
265 right; and wrong is wrong; and if a man cannot distinguish them properly, he is either a fool or a rascal: thats all.

LADY BRITOMART: (*Touched.*) Thats my own boy! (*She pats his cheek.*) Your father never could answer that: he used to laugh and get out of it under cover of some affectionate
270 nonsense. And now that you understand the situation, what do you advise me to do?

STEPHEN: Well, what can you do?

LADY BRITOMART: I must get the money somehow.

STEPHEN: We cannot take money from him. I had rather go
275 and live in some cheap place like Bedford Square or even Hampstead than take a farthing of his money.

LADY BRITOMART: But after all, Stephen, our present income comes from Andrew.

STEPHEN: (*Shocked.*) I never knew that.

280 LADY BRITOMART: Well, you surely didnt suppose your grandfather had anything to give me. The Stevenages could not do everything for you. We gave you social position. Andrew had to contribute something. He had a very good bargain, I think.

285 STEPHEN: (*Bitterly.*) We are utterly dependent on him and his cannons, then?

LADY BRITOMART: Certainly not: the money is settled. But he provided it. So you see it is not a question of taking money from him or not: it is simply a question of how
290 much. I dont want any more for myself.

STEPHEN: Nor do I.

LADY BRITOMART: But Sarah does; and Barbara does. That is, Charles Lomax and Adolphus Cusins will cost them more. So I must put my pride in my pocket and ask for it, I sup-
295 pose. That is your advice, Stephen, is it not?

STEPHEN: No.

LADY BRITOMART: (*Sharply.*) Stephen!

STEPHEN: Of course if you are determined—

LADY BRITOMART: I am not determined: I ask your advice;
300 and I am waiting for it. I will not have all the responsibility thrown on my shoulders.

STEPHEN: (*Obstinately.*) I would die sooner than ask him for another penny.

LADY BRITOMART: (*Resignedly.*) You mean that I must ask him.
305 Very well, Stephen: it shall be as you wish. You will be glad

to know that your grandfather concurs. But he thinks I ought to ask Andrew to come here and see the girls. After all, he must have some natural affection for them.

STEPHEN: Ask him here!!!

310 LADY BRITOMART: Do not repeat my words, Stephen. Where else can I ask him?

STEPHEN: I never expected you to ask him at all.

LADY BRITOMART: Now dont tease, Stephen. Come! you see that it is necessary that he should pay us a visit, dont you?

315 STEPHEN: (*Reluctantly.*) I suppose so, if the girls cannot do without his money.

LADY BRITOMART: Thank you, Stephen: I knew you would give me the right advice when it was properly explained to you. I have asked your father to come this evening. (STEPHEN

320 *bounds from his seat.*) Dont jump, Stephen: it fidgets me.

STEPHEN: (*In utter consternation.*) Do you mean to say that my father is coming here tonight—that he may be here at any moment?

LADY BRITOMART: (*Looking at her watch.*) I said nine. (*He gasps.*

325 *She rises.*) Ring the bell, please. (STEPHEN *goes to the smaller writing table; presses a button on it; and sits at it with his elbows on the table and his head in his hands, outwitted and overwhelmed.*) It is ten minutes to nine yet; and I have to prepare the girls. I asked Charles Lomax and Adolphus to dinner on purpose

330 that they might be here. Andrew had better see them in case he should cherish any delusions as to their being capable of supporting their wives. (*The butler enters:* LADY BRITOMART *goes behind the settee to speak to him.*) Morrison: go up to the drawing room and tell everybody to come down here at

335 once. (MORRISON *withdraws.* LADY BRITOMART *turns to* STEPHEN.) Now remember, Stephen: I shall need all your countenance and authority. (*He rises and tries to recover some vestige of these attributes.*) Give me a chair, dear. (*He pushes a chair forward from the wall to where she stands, near the smaller*

340 *writing table. She sits down; and he goes to the armchair, into which he throws himself.*) I dont know how Barbara will take it. Ever since they made her a major in the Salvation Army she has developed a propensity to have her own way and order people about which quite cows me sometimes. It's not ladylike:

345 I'm sure I dont know where she picked it up. Anyhow, Barbara shant bully me; but still it's just as well that your father should be here before she has time to refuse to meet him or make a fuss. Dont look nervous, Stephen: it will only encourage Barbara to make difficulties. I am nervous enough,

350 goodness knows; but I dont shew it.

(SARAH *and* BARBARA *come in with their respective young men,* CHARLES LOMAX *and* ADOLPHUS CUSINS. SARAH *is slender, bored, and mundane.* BARBARA *is robuster, jollier, much more energetic.* SARAH *is fashionably dressed:* BARBARA *is in Salvation Army uniform.* LOMAX, *a young man about town, is like many other young men about town. He is afflicted with a frivolous sense of humor which plunges him at the most inopportune moments into paroxysms of imperfectly suppressed laughter.* CUSINS *is a spectacled student, slight, thin haired, and sweet voiced, with a more complex form of* LOMAX'S *complaint. His sense of humor is intellectual and subtle, and is complicated by an appalling temper. The lifelong struggle of a benevolent temperament and a high conscience against impulses of inhuman ridicule and fierce impatience has set up a chronic strain which has visibly wrecked his constitution. He is a most implacable, determined, tenacious, intolerant person who by mere force of character presents*

himself as—and indeed actually is—considerate, gentle, explanatory, even mild and apologetic, capable possibly of murder, but not of cruelty or coarseness. By the operation of some instinct which is not merciful enough to blind him with the illusions of love, he is obstinately bent on marrying BARBARA. LOMAX *likes* SARAH *and thinks it will be rather a lark to marry her. Consequently he has not attempted to resist* LADY BRITOMART's *arrangements to that end.*)

(*All four look as if they had been having a good deal of fun in the drawing room. The girls enter first, leaving the swains outside.* SARAH *comes to the settee.* BARBARA *comes in after her and stops at the door.*)

BARBARA: Are Cholly and Dolly to come in?

LADY BRITOMART: (*Forcibly.*) Barbara: I will not have Charles called Cholly: the vulgarity of it positively makes me ill.

BARBARA: It's all right, mother: Cholly is quite correct nowa-

355 days. Are they to come in?

LADY BRITOMART: Yes, if they will behave themselves.

BARBARA: (*Through the door.*) Come in, Dolly; and behave yourself.

(BARBARA *comes to her mother's writing table.* CUSINS *enters smiling, and wanders towards* LADY BRITOMART.)

SARAH: (*Calling.*) Come in, Cholly. (LOMAX *enters, controlling his features very imperfectly, and places himself vaguely between* 360 SARAH *and* BARBARA.)

LADY BRITOMART: (*Peremptorily.*) Sit down, all of you. (*They sit.* CUSINS *crosses to the window and seats himself there.* LOMAX *takes a chair.* BARBARA *sits at the writing table and* SARAH *on the settee.*) I dont in the least know what you are 365 laughing at, Adolphus. I am surprised at you, though I expected nothing better from Charles Lomax.

CUSINS: (*In a remarkably gentle voice.*) Barbara has been trying to teach me the West Ham Salvation March.

LADY BRITOMART: I see nothing to laugh at in that; nor 370 should you if you are really converted.

CUSINS: (*Sweetly.*) You were not present. It was really funny, I believe.

LOMAX: Ripping.

LADY BRITOMART: Be quiet, Charles. Now listen to me, chil- 375 dren. Your father is coming here this evening.

(*General stupefaction.* LOMAX, SARAH, *and* BARBARA *rise:* SARAH *scared, and* BARBARA *amused and expectant.*)

LOMAX: (*Remonstrating.*) Oh I say!

LADY BRITOMART: You are not called on to say anything, Charles.

SARAH: Are you serious, mother? 380

LADY BRITOMART: Of course I am serious. It is on your account, Sarah, and also on Charles's. (*Silence.* SARAH *sits, with a shrug.* CHARLES *looks painfully unworthy.*) I hope you are not going to object, Barbara.

BARBARA: I! why should I? My father has a soul to be saved 385 like anybody else. He's quite welcome as far as I am concerned. (*She sits on the table, and softly whistles 'Onward, Christian Soldiers.'*)

LOMAX: (*Still remonstrant.*) But really, dont you know! Oh I say!

LADY BRITOMART: (*Frigidly.*) What do you wish to convey, 390 Charles?

LOMAX: Well, you must admit that this is a bit thick.

LADY BRITOMART: (*Turning with ominous suavity to* CUSINS.)
395 Adolphus: you are a professor of Greek. Can you translate
Charles Lomax's remarks into reputable English for us?

CUSINS: (*Cautiously.*) If I may say so, Lady Brit, I think
Charles has rather happily expressed what we all feel.
Homer, speaking of Autolycus, uses the same phrase.
400 πυκινὸν δόμον ελθεῖν means a bit thick.

LOMAX: (*Handsomely.*) Not that I mind, you know, if Sarah
dont. (*He sits.*)

LADY BRITOMART: (*Crushingly.*) Thank you. Have I your permission, Adolphus, to invite my own husband to my own
house?

405 CUSINS: (*Gallantly.*) You have my unhesitating support in
everything you do.

LADY BRITOMART: Tush! Sarah: have you nothing to say?

SARAH: Do you mean that he is coming regularly to live here?

LADY BRITOMART: Certainly not. The spare room is ready
410 for him if he likes to stay for a day or two and see a little
more of you; but there are limits.

SARAH: Well, he cant eat us, I suppose. *I* dont mind.

LOMAX: (*Chuckling.*) I wonder how the old man will take it.

LADY BRITOMART: Much as the old woman will, no doubt,
415 Charles.

LOMAX: (*Abashed.*) I didnt mean—at least—

LADY BRITOMART: You didnt think, Charles. You never do;
and the result is, you never mean anything. And now
please attend to me, children. Your father will be quite a
420 stranger to us.

LOMAX: I suppose he hasnt seen Sarah since she was a little kid.

LADY BRITOMART: Not since she was a little kid, Charles, as
you express it with that elegance of diction and refinement
of thought that seem never to desert you. Accordingly—
425 er—(*Impatiently.*) Now I have forgotten what I was going
to say. That comes of your provoking me to be sarcastic,
Charles. Adolphus: will you kindly tell me where I was.

CUSINS: (*Sweetly.*) You were saying that as Mr Undershaft has
not seen his children since they were babies, he will form
430 his opinion of the way you have brought them up from
their behavior tonight, and that therefore you wish us all
to be particularly careful to conduct ourselves well, especially Charles.

LADY BRITOMART: (*With emphatic approval.*) Precisely.

435 LOMAX: Look here, Dolly: Lady Brit didnt say that.

LADY BRITOMART: (*Vehemently.*) I did, Charles. Adolphus's
recollection is perfectly correct. It is most important that
you should be good; and I do beg you for once not to pair
off into opposite corners and giggle and whisper while I
440 am speaking to your father.

BARBARA: All right, mother. We'll do you credit. (*She comes
off the table, and sits in her chair with ladylike elegance.*)

LADY BRITOMART: Remember, Charles, that Sarah will want
to feel proud of you instead of ashamed of you.

445 LOMAX: Oh I say! theres nothing to be exactly proud of, dont
you know.

LADY BRITOMART: Well, try and look as if there was.

(MORRISON, *pale and dismayed, breaks into the room in uncon-
cealed disorder.*)

MORRISON: Might I speak a word to you, my lady?

LADY BRITOMART: Nonsense! Shew him up.

MORRISON: Yes, my lady. (*He goes.*)

450 LOMAX: Does Morrison know who it is?

LADY BRITOMART: Of course. Morrison has always been with us.

LOMAX: It must be a regular corker for him, dont you know.

LADY BRITOMART: Is this a moment to get on my nerves,
Charles, with your outrageous expressions?

455 LOMAX: But this is something out of the ordinary, really—

MORRISON: (*At the door.*) The—er—Mr Undershaft. (*He retreats in confusion.*)

(ANDREW UNDERSHAFT *comes in. All rise.* LADY BRITOMART
meets him in the middle of the room behind the settee.)

(ANDREW *is, on the surface, a stoutish, easygoing elderly man, with
kindly patient manners, and an engaging simplicity of character. But
he has a watchful, deliberate, waiting, listening face, and formidable reserves of power, both bodily and mental, in his capacious chest and long
head. His gentleness is partly that of a strong man who has learnt by
experience that his natural grip hurts ordinary people unless he handles them very carefully, and partly the mellowness of age and success.
He is also a little shy in his present very delicate situation.*)

LADY BRITOMART: Good evening, Andrew.

460 UNDERSHAFT: How d'ye do, my dear.

LADY BRITOMART: You look a good deal older.

UNDERSHAFT: (*Apologetically.*) I am somewhat older. (*Taking her
hand with a touch of courtship.*) Time has stood still with you.

LADY BRITOMART: (*Throwing away his hand.*) Rubbish! This is
465 your family.

UNDERSHAFT: (*Surprised.*) Is it so large? I am sorry to say my
memory is failing very badly in some things. (*He offers his
hand with paternal kindness to* LOMAX.)

LOMAX: (*Jerkily shaking his hand.*) Ahdedoo.

470 UNDERSHAFT: I can see you are my eldest. I am very glad to
meet you again, my boy.

LOMAX: (*Remonstrating.*) No, but look here dont you know—
(*Overcome.*) Oh I say!

LADY BRITOMART: (*Recovering from momentary speechlessness.*)
475 Andrew: do you mean to say that you dont remember
how many children you have?

UNDERSHAFT: Well, I am afraid I—. They have grown so
much—er. Am I making any ridiculous mistake? I may as
well confess: I recollect only one son. But so many things
480 have happened since, of course—er—

LADY BRITOMART: (*Decisively.*) Andrew: you are talking nonsense. Of course you have only one son.

UNDERSHAFT: Perhaps you will be good enough to introduce
me, my dear.

485 LADY BRITOMART: That is Charles Lomax, who is engaged to
Sarah.

UNDERSHAFT: My dear sir, I beg your pardon.

LOMAX: Notatall. Delighted, I assure you.

LADY BRITOMART: This is Stephen.

490 UNDERSHAFT: (*Bowing.*) Happy to make your acquaintance,
Mr Stephen. Then (*Going to* CUSINS.) you must be my son.
(*Taking* CUSINS' *hands in his.*) How are you, my young
friend? (*To* LADY BRITOMART.) He is very like you, my love.

CUSINS: You flatter me, Mr Undershaft. My name is Cusins:
495 engaged to Barbara. (*Very explicitly.*) That is Major Barbara
Undershaft, of the Salvation Army. That is Sarah, your
second daughter. This is Stephen Undershaft, your son.

UNDERSHAFT: My dear Stephen, I beg your pardon.

STEPHEN: Not at all.

500 UNDERSHAFT: Mr Cusins: I am much indebted to you for explaining so precisely. (*Turning to* SARAH.) Barbara, my dear—

SARAH: (*Prompting him.*) Sarah.

UNDERSHAFT: Sarah, of course. (*They shake hands. He goes over* 505 *to* BARBARA.) Barbara—I am right this time, I hope?

BARBARA: Quite right. (*They shake hands.*)

LADY BRITOMART: (*Resuming command.*) Sit down, all of you. Sit down, Andrew. (*She comes forward and sits on the settee.* CUSINS *also brings his chair forward on her left.* BARBARA *and* 510 STEPHEN *resume their seats.* LOMAX *gives his chair to* SARAH *and goes for another.*)

UNDERSHAFT: Thank you, my love.

LOMAX: (*Conversationally, as he brings a chair forward between the writing table and the settee, and offers it to* UNDERSHAFT.) Takes 515 you some time to find out exactly where you are, dont it?

UNDERSHAFT: (*Accepting the chair, but remaining standing.*) That is not what embarrasses me, Mr Lomax. My difficulty is that if I play the part of a father, I shall produce the effect of an intrusive stranger; and if I play the part of a discreet 520 stranger, I may appear a callous father.

LADY BRITOMART: There is no need for you to play any part at all, Andrew. You had much better be sincere and natural.

UNDERSHAFT: (*Submissively.*) Yes, my dear: I daresay that will be best. (*He sits down comfortably.*) Well, here I am. Now 525 what can I do for you?

LADY BRITOMART: You need not do anything, Andrew. You are one of the family. You can sit with us and enjoy yourself.

(*A painfully conscious pause.* BARBARA *makes a face at* LOMAX, *whose too long suppressed mirth immediately explodes in agonized neighings.*)

LADY BRITOMART: (*Outraged.*) Charles Lomax: if you can behave yourself, behave yourself. If not, leave the room.

530 LOMAX: I'm awfully sorry, Lady Brit; but really you know, upon my soul! (*He sits on the settee between* LADY BRITOMART *and* UNDERSHAFT, *quite overcome.*)

BARBARA: Why dont you laugh if you want to, Cholly? It's good for your inside.

535 LADY BRITOMART: Barbara: you have had the education of a lady. Please let your father see that; and dont talk like a street girl.

UNDERSHAFT: Never mind me, my dear. As you know, I am not a gentleman; and I was never educated.

540 LOMAX: (*Encouragingly.*) Nobody'd know it, I assure you. You look all right, you know.

CUSINS: Let me advise you to study Greek, Mr Undershaft. Greek scholars are privileged men. Few of them know Greek; and none of them know anything else; but their 545 position is unchallengeable. Other languages are the qualifications of waiters and commercial travellers: Greek is to a man of position what the hallmark is to silver.

BARBARA: Dolly: dont be insincere. Cholly: fetch your concertina and play something for us.

550 LOMAX: (*Jumps up eagerly, but checks himself to remark doubtfully to* UNDERSHAFT.) Perhaps that sort of thing isnt in your line, eh?

UNDERSHAFT: I am particularly fond of music.

LOMAX: (*Delighted.*) Are you? Then I'll get it. (*He goes upstairs for the instrument.*)

UNDERSHAFT: Do you play, Barbara? 555

BARBARA: Only the tambourine. But Cholly's teaching me the concertina.

UNDERSHAFT: Is Cholly also a member of the Salvation Army?

BARBARA: No: he says it's bad form to be a dissenter. But I dont despair of Cholly. I made him come yesterday to a meeting 560 at the dock gates, and take the collection in his hat.

UNDERSHAFT: (*Looks whimsically at his wife.*)!!

LADY BRITOMART: It is not my doing, Andrew. Barbara is old enough to take her own way. She has no father to advise her.

BARBARA: Oh yes she has. There are no orphans in the Sal- 565 vation Army.

UNDERSHAFT: Your father there has a great many children and plenty of experience, eh?

BARBARA: (*Looking at him with quick interest and nodding.*) Just so. How did you come to understand that? (LOMAX *is* 570 *heard at the door trying the concertina.*)

LADY BRITOMART: Come in, Charles. Play us something at once.

LOMAX: Righto! (*He sits down in his former place, and preludes.*)

UNDERSHAFT: One moment, Mr Lomax. I am rather interested in the Salvation Army. Its motto might be my own: 575 Blood and Fire.

LOMAX: (*Shocked.*) But not your sort of blood and fire, you know.

UNDERSHAFT: My sort of blood cleanses: my sort of fire purifies.

BARBARA: So do ours. Come down tomorrow to my shel- 580 ter—the West Ham shelter—and see what we're doing. We're going to march to a great meeting in the Assembly Hall at Mile End. Come and see the shelter and then march with us: it will do you a lot of good. Can you play anything?

UNDERSHAFT: In my youth I earned pennies, and even 585 shillings occasionally, in the streets and in public house parlors by my natural talent for stepdancing. Later on, I became a member of the Undershaft orchestral society, and performed passably on the tenor trombone.

LOMAX: (*Scandalized—putting down the concertina.*) Oh I say! 590

BARBARA: Many a sinner has played himself into heaven on the trombone, thanks to the Army.

LOMAX: (*To* BARBARA, *still rather shocked.*) Yes; but what about the cannon business, dont you know? (*To* UNDERSHAFT.) Getting into heaven is not exactly in your line, is it? 595

LADY BRITOMART: Charles!!!

LOMAX: Well; but it stands to reason, dont it? The cannon business may be necessary and all that: we cant get on without cannons; but it isnt right, you know. On the other hand, there may be a certain amount of tosh about the 600 Salvation Army—I belong to the Established Church myself—but still you cant deny that it's religion; and you cant go against religion, can you? At least unless youre downright immoral, dont you know.

UNDERSHAFT: You hardly appreciate my position, Mr Lomax— 605

LOMAX: (*Hastily.*) I'm not saying anything against you personally—

UNDERSHAFT: Quite so, quite so. But consider for a moment. Here I am, a profiteer in mutilation and murder. I find myself in a specially amiable humor just now because, this 610 morning, down at the foundry, we blew twenty-seven dummy soldiers into fragments with a gun which formerly destroyed only thirteen.

LOMAX: (*Leniently.*) Well, the more destructive war becomes, the sooner it will be abolished, eh? 615

UNDERSHAFT: Not at all. The more destructive war becomes the more fascinating we find it. No, Mr Lomax: I am obliged to you for making the usual excuse for my trade; but I am not ashamed of it. I am not one of those men who keep their morals and their business in watertight compartments. All the spare money my trade rivals spend on hospitals, cathedrals, and other receptacles for conscience money, I devote to experiments and researches in improved methods of destroying life and property. I have always done so; and I always shall. Therefore your Christmas card moralities of peace on earth and goodwill among men are of no use to me. Your Christianity, which enjoins you to resist not evil, and to turn the other cheek, would make me a bankrupt. My morality—my religion—must have a place for cannons and torpedoes in it.

STEPHEN: (*Coldly—almost sullenly.*) You speak as if there were half a dozen moralities and religions to choose from, instead of one true morality and one true religion.

UNDERSHAFT: For me there is only one true morality; but it might not fit you, as you do not manufacture aerial battleships. There is only one true morality for every man; but every man has not the same true morality.

LOMAX: (*Overtaxed.*) Would you mind saying that again? I didnt quite follow it.

CUSINS: It's quite simple. As Euripides says, one man's meat is another man's poison morally as well as physically.

UNDERSHAFT: Precisely.

LOMAX: Oh, that! Yes, yes, yes. True. True.

STEPHEN: In other words, some men are honest and some are scoundrels.

BARBARA: Bosh! There are no scoundrels.

UNDERSHAFT: Indeed? Are there any good men?

BARBARA: No. Not one. There are neither good men nor scoundrels: there are just children of one Father; and the sooner they stop calling one another names the better. You neednt talk to me: I know them. I've had scores of them through my hands: scoundrels, criminals, infidels, philanthropists, missionaries, county councillors, all sorts. Theyre all just the same sort of sinner; and theres the same salvation ready for them all.

UNDERSHAFT: May I ask have you ever saved a maker of cannons?

BARBARA: No. Will you let me try?

UNDERSHAFT: Well, I will make a bargain with you. If I go to see you tomorrow in your Salvation Shelter, will you come the day after to see me in my cannon works?

BARBARA: Take care. It may end in your giving up the cannons for the sake of the Salvation Army.

UNDERSHAFT: Are you sure it will not end in your giving up the Salvation Army for the sake of the cannons?

BARBARA: I will take my chance of that.

UNDERSHAFT: And I will take my chance of the other. (*They shake hands on it.*) Where is your shelter?

BARBARA: In West Ham. At the sign of the cross. Ask anybody in Canning Town. Where are your works?

UNDERSHAFT: In Perivale St Andrews. At the sign of the sword. Ask anybody in Europe.

LOMAX: Hadnt I better play something?

BARBARA: Yes. Give us 'Onward, Christian Soldiers.'

LOMAX: Well, thats rather a strong order to begin with, dont you know. Suppose I sing 'Thou'rt passing hence, my brother.' It's much the same tune.

BARBARA: It's too melancholy. You get saved, Cholly; and youll pass hence, my brother, without making such a fuss about it.

LADY BRITOMART: Really, Barbara, you go on as if religion were a pleasant subject. Do have some sense of propriety.

UNDERSHAFT: I do not find it an unpleasant subject, my dear. It is the only one that capable people really care for.

LADY BRITOMART: (*Looking at her watch.*) Well, if you are determined to have it, I insist on having it in a proper and respectable way. Charles: ring for prayers.

(*General amazement.* STEPHEN *rises in dismay.*)

LOMAX: (*Rising.*) Oh I say!

UNDERSHAFT: (*Rising.*) I am afraid I must be going.

LADY BRITOMART: You cannot go now, Andrew: it would be most improper. Sit down. What will the servants think?

UNDERSHAFT: My dear: I have conscientious scruples. May I suggest a compromise? If Barbara will conduct a little service in the drawing room, with Mr Lomax as organist, I will attend it willingly. I will even take part, if a trombone can be procured.

LADY BRITOMART: Dont mock, Andrew.

UNDERSHAFT: (*Shocked—to* BARBARA.) You dont think I am mocking, my love, I hope.

BARBARA: No, of course not; and it wouldnt matter if you were: half the Army came to their first meeting for a lark. (*Rising.*) Come along. (*She throws her arm round her father and sweeps him out, calling to the others from the threshold.*) Come, Dolly. Come, Cholly.

(CUSINS *rises.*)

LADY BRITOMART: I will not be disobeyed by everybody. Adolphus: sit down. (*He does not.*) Charles: you may go. You are not fit for prayers: you cannot keep your countenance.

LOMAX: Oh I say! (*He goes out.*)

LADY BRITOMART: (*Continuing.*) But you, Adolphus, can behave yourself if you choose to. I insist on your staying.

CUSINS: My dear Lady Brit: there are things in the family prayer book that I couldnt bear to hear you say.

LADY BRITOMART: What things, pray?

CUSINS: Well, you would have to say before all the servants that we have done things we ought not to have done, and left undone things we ought to have done, and that there is no health in us. I cannot bear to hear you doing yourself such an injustice, and Barbara such an injustice. As for myself, I flatly deny it: I have done my best. I shouldnt dare to marry Barbara—I couldnt look you in the face—if it were true. So I must go to the drawing room.

LADY BRITOMART: (*Offended.*) Well, go. (*He starts for the door.*) And remember this, Adolphus (*He turns to listen.*): I have a very strong suspicion that you went to the Salvation Army to worship Barbara and nothing else. And I quite appreciate the very clever way in which you systematically humbug me. I have found you out. Take care Barbara doesnt. Thats all.

CUSINS: (*With unruffled sweetness.*) Dont tell on me. (*He steals out.*)

LADY BRITOMART: Sarah: if you want to go, go. Anything's better than to sit there as if you wished you were a thousand miles away.

SARAH: (*Languidly.*) Very well, mamma. (*She goes.*)

735   (LADY BRITOMART, *with a sudden flounce, gives way to a little gust of tears.*)

STEPHEN: (*Going to her.*) Mother: whats the matter?

740   LADY BRITOMART: (*Swishing away her tears with her handkerchief.*) Nothing. Foolishness. You can go with him, too, if you like, and leave me with the servants.

STEPHEN: Oh, you mustnt think that, mother. I—I dont like him.

745   LADY BRITOMART: The others do. That is the injustice of a woman's lot. A woman has to bring up her children; and that means to restrain them, to deny them things they want, to set them tasks, to punish them when they do wrong, to do all the unpleasant things. And then the father, who has nothing to do but pet them and spoil them, comes in when
750   all her work is done and steals their affection from her.

STEPHEN: He has not stolen our affection from you. It is only curiosity.

LADY BRITOMART: (*Violently.*) I wont be consoled, Stephen. There is nothing the matter with me. (*She rises and goes to-*
755   *wards the door.*)

STEPHEN: Where are you going, mother?

LADY BRITOMART: To the drawing room, of course. (*She goes out. 'Onward, Christian Soldiers,' on the concertina, with tambourine accompaniment, is heard when the door opens.*) Are you coming, Stephen?

STEPHEN: No. Certainly not. (*She goes. He sits down on the settee, with compressed lips and an expression of strong dislike.*)

ACT TWO

The yard of the West Ham shelter of the Salvation Army is a cold place on a January morning. The building itself, an old warehouse, is newly whitewashed. Its gabled end projects into the yard in the middle, with a door on the ground floor, and another in the loft above it without any balcony or ladder, but with a pulley rigged over it for hoisting sacks. Those who come from this central gable end into the yard have the gateway leading to the street on their left, with a stone horse-trough just beyond it, and, on the right, a penthouse shielding a table from the weather. There are forms at the table; and on them are seated a man and a woman, both much down on their luck, finishing a meal of bread (one thick slice each, with margarine and golden syrup) and diluted milk.

The man, a workman out of employment, is young, agile, a talker, a poser, sharp enough to be capable of anything in reason except honesty or altruistic considerations of any kind. The woman is a commonplace old bundle of poverty and hard-worn humanity. She looks sixty and probably is forty-five. If they were rich people, gloved and muffed and well wrapped up in furs and overcoats, they would be numbed and miserable; for it is a grindingly cold raw January day; and a glance at the background of grimy warehouses and leaden sky visible over the whitewashed walls of the yard would drive any idle rich person straight to the Mediterranean. But these two, being no more troubled with visions of the Mediterranean than of the moon, and being compelled to keep more of their clothes in the pawnshop, and less on their persons, in winter than in summer, are not depressed by the cold: rather are they stung into vivacity, to which their meal has just now given an almost jolly turn. The man takes a pull at his mug, and then gets up and moves about the yard with his hands deep in his pockets, occasionally breaking into a stepdance.

THE WOMAN: Feel better arter your meal, sir?

THE MAN: No. Call that a meal! Good enough for you, praps; but wot is it to me, an intelligent workin man.

THE WOMAN: Workin man! Wot are you?

THE MAN: Painter.   5

THE WOMAN: (*Sceptically.*) Yus, I dessay.

THE MAN: Yus, you dessay! I know. Every loafer that cant do nothink calls isself a painter. Well, I'm a real painter: grainer, finisher, thirty-eight bob a week when I can get it.

THE WOMAN: Then why dont you go and get it?   10

THE MAN: I'll tell you why. Fust: I'm intelligent—fffff! it's rotten cold here (*He dances a step or two.*)—yes: intelligent beyond the station o life into which it has pleased the capitalists to call me; and they dont like a man that sees through em. Second, an intelligent bein needs a doo share   15 of appiness; so I drink somethink cruel when I get the chawnce. Third, I stand by my class and do as little as I can so's to leave arf the job for me fellow workers. Fourth, I'm fly enough to know wots inside the law and wots outside it; and inside it I do as the capitalists do: pinch wot I can   20 lay me ands on. In a proper state of society I am sober, industrious and honest: in Rome, so to speak, I do as the Romans do. Wots the consequence? When trade is bad—and it's rotten bad just now—and the employers az to sack arf their men, they generally start on me.   25

THE WOMAN: Whats your name?

THE MAN: Price. Bronterre O'Brien Price. Usually called Snobby Price, for short.

THE WOMAN: Snobby's a carpenter, aint it? You said you was a painter.   30

PRICE: Not that kind of snob, but the genteel sort. I'm too uppish, owing to my intelligence, and my father being a Chartist and a reading, thinking man: a stationer, too. I'm none of your common hewers of wood and drawers of water; and dont you forget it. (*He returns to his seat at the*   35 *table, and takes up his mug.*) Wots your name?

THE WOMAN: Rummy Mitchens, sir.

PRICE: (*Quaffing the remains of his milk to her.*) Your elth, Miss Mitchens.

RUMMY: (*Correcting him.*) Missis Mitchens.   40

PRICE: Wot! Oh Rummy, Rummy! Respectable married woman, Rummy, gittin rescued by the Salvation Army by pretendin to be a bad un. Same old game!

RUMMY: What am I to do? I cant starve. Them Salvation lasses is dear good girls; but the better you are, the worse they   45 likes to think you were before they rescued you. Why shouldnt we av a bit o credit, poor loves? theyre worn to rags by their work. And where would they get the money to rescue us if we was to let on we're no worse than other people? You know what ladies and gentlemen are.   50

PRICE: Thievin swine! Wish I ad their job, Rummy, all the same. Wot does Rummy stand for? Pet name praps?

RUMMY: Short for Romola.

PRICE: For wot!?

RUMMY: Romola. It was out of a new book. Somebody me   55 mother wanted me to grow up like.

PRICE: We're companions in misfortune, Rummy. Both on us got names that nobody cawnt pronounce. Consequently I'm Snobby and youre Rummy because Bill and Sally wasnt good enough for our parents. Such is life!   60

RUMMY: Who saved you, Mr Price? Was it Major Barbara?

PRICE: No: I come here on my own. I'm going to be Bronterre O'Brien Price, the converted painter. I know wot
they like. I'll tell em how I blasphemed and gambled and
65   wopped my poor old mother—

RUMMY: (Shocked.) Used you to beat your mother?

PRICE: Not likely. She used to beat me. No matter: you come
and listen to the converted painter, and youll hear how she
was a pious woman that taught me me prayers at er knee,
70   an how I used to come home drunk and drag her out o
bed be er snow white airs, an lam into er with the poker.

RUMMY: Thats whats so unfair to us women. Your confessions is just as big lies as ours: you dont tell what you really done no more than us; but you men can tell your lies
75   right out at the meetins and be made much of for it; while
the sort o confessions we az to make az to be wispered to
one lady at a time. It aint right, spite of all their piety.

PRICE: Right! Do you spose the Army'd be allowed if it went
and did right? Not much. It combs our air and makes us
80   good little blokes to be robbed and put upon. But I'll play
the game as good as any of em. I'll see somebody struck
by lightnin, or hear a voice sayin 'Snobby Price: where
will you spend eternity?' I'll av a time of it, I tell you.

RUMMY: You wont be let drink, though.

85   PRICE: I'll take it out in gorspellin, then. I dont want to drink
if I can get fun enough any other way.

(JENNY HILL, a pale, overwrought, pretty Salvation lass of 18, comes
in through the yard gate, leading PETER SHIRLEY, a half hardened,
half worn-out elderly man, weak with hunger.)

JENNY: (Supporting him.) Come! pluck up. I'll get you something to eat. Youll be all right then.

PRICE: (Rising and hurrying officiously to take the old man off
90   JENNY's hands.) Poor old man! Cheer up, brother: youll find
rest and peace and appiness ere. Hurry up with the food,
miss: e's fair done. (JENNY hurries into the shelter.) Ere, buck
up, daddy! she's fetchin y'a thick slice o breadn treacle, an a
mug o skyblue. (He seats him at the corner of the table.)

95   RUMMY: (Gaily.) Keep up your old art! Never say die!

SHIRLEY: I'm not an old man. I'm only 46. I'm as good as ever I
was. The grey patch come in my hair before I was thirty. All
it wants is three pennorth o hair dye: am I to be turned on
the streets to starve for it? Holy God! I've worked ten to
100   twelve hours a day since I was thirteen, and paid my way all
through; and now am I to be thrown into the gutter and my
job given to a young man that can do it no better than me
because Ive black hair that goes white at the first change?

PRICE: (Cheerfully.) No good jawrin about it. Youre only a
105   jumped-up, jerked-off, orspittle-turned-out incurable of
an ole workin man: who cares about you? Eh? Make the
thievin swine give you a meal: theyve stole many a one
from you. Get a bit o your own back. (JENNY returns with
the usual meal.) There you are, brother. Awsk a blessin an
110   tuck that into you.

SHIRLEY: (Looking at it ravenously but not touching it, and crying
like a child.) I never took anything before.

JENNY: (Petting him.) Come, come! the Lord sends it to you:
he wasnt above taking bread from his friends; and why
115   should you be? Besides, when we find you a job you can
pay us for it if you like.

SHIRLEY: (Eagerly.) Yes, yes: thats true. I can pay you back: it's
only a loan. (Shivering.) O Lord! oh Lord! (He turns to the
table and attacks the meal ravenously.)

JENNY: Well, Rummy, are you more comfortable now?   120

RUMMY: God bless you, lovey! youve fed my body and saved
my soul, havnt you? (JENNY, touched, kisses her.) Sit down
and rest a bit: you must be ready to drop.

JENNY: Ive been going hard since morning. But theres more
work than we can do. I mustnt stop.   125

RUMMY: Try a prayer for just two minutes. Youll work all the
better after.

JENNY: (Her eyes lighting up.) Oh isnt it wonderful how a few
minutes prayer revives you! I was quite lightheaded at
twelve o'clock, I was so tired; but Major Barbara just sent   130
me to pray for five minutes; and I was able to go on as if
I had only just begun. (To PRICE.) Did you have a piece of
bread?

PRICE: (With unction.) Yes, miss; but Ive got the piece that I
value more; and thats the peace that passeth hall hanner-   135
stennin.

RUMMY: (Fervently.) Glory Hallelujah!

(BILL WALKER, a rough customer of about 25, appears at the yard
gate and looks malevolently at JENNY.)

JENNY: That makes me so happy. When you say that, I feel
wicked for loitering here. I must get to work again.

(She is hurrying to the shelter, when the new-comer moves quickly
up to the door and intercepts her. His manner is so threatening that
she retreats as he comes at her truculently, driving her down the yard.)

BILL: Aw knaow you. Youre the one that took awy maw girl.   140
Youre the one that set er agen me. Well, I'm gowin to ev
er aht. Not that Aw care a carse for er or you: see? Bat
Aw'll let er knaow; and Aw'll let you knaow. Aw'm gowing to give her a doin thatll teach er to cat awy from me.
Nah in wiv you and tell er to cam aht afore Aw cam in   145
and kick er aht. Tell er Bill Walker wants er. She'll knaow
wot thet means; and if she keeps me witin itll be worse.
You stop to jawr beck at me; and Aw'll stawt on you: d'ye
eah? Theres your wy. In you gow. (He takes her by the arm
and slings her towards the door of the shelter. She falls on her   150
hand and knee. RUMMY helps her up again.)

PRICE: (Rising, and venturing irresolutely towards BILL.) Easy
there, mate. She aint doin you no arm.

BILL: Oo are you callin mite? (Standing over him threateningly.)
Youre gowin to stend ap for er, aw yer? Put ap your ends.   155

RUMMY: (Running indignantly to him to scold him.) Oh, you
great brute—(He instantly swings his left hand back against
her face. She screams and reels back to the trough, where she sits
down, covering her bruised face with her hands and rocking herself and moaning with pain.)   160

JENNY: (Going to her.) Oh, God forgive you! How could you
strike an old woman like that?

BILL: (Seizing her by the hair so violently that she also screams, and
tearing her away from the old woman.) You Gawd forgimme
again an Aw'll Gawd forgive you one on the jawr thetll   165
stop you pryin for a week. (Holding her and turning fiercely
on PRICE.) Ev you ennything to sy agen it?

PRICE: (Intimidated.) No, matey: she aint anything to do with
me.

170 BILL: Good job for you! Aw'd pat two meals into you and fawt you with one finger arter, you stawved cur. (*To* JENNY.) Nah are you gowin to fetch aht Mog Ebbijem; or em Aw to knock your fice off you and fetch her meself?

JENNY: (*Writhing in his grasp.*) Oh please someone go in and
175 tell Major Barbara—(*She screams again as he wrenches her head down; and* PRICE *and* RUMMY *flee into the shelter.*)

BILL: You want to gow in and tell your Mijor of me, do you?

JENNY: Oh please dont drag my hair. Let me go.

BILL: Do you or downt you? (*She stifles a scream.*) Yus or nao?

180 JENNY: God give me strength—

BILL: (*Striking her with his fist in the face.*) Gow an shaow her thet, and tell her if she wants one lawk it to cam and interfere with me. (JENNY, *crying with pain, goes into the shed. He goes to the form and addresses the old man.*) Eah: finish
185 your mess; an git aht o maw wy.

SHIRLEY: (*Springing up and facing him fiercely, with the mug in his hand.*) You take a liberty with me, and I'll smash you over the face with the mug and cut your eye out. Aint you satisfied—young whelps like you—with takin the bread out
190 o the mouths of your elders that have brought you up and slaved for you, but you must come shovin and cheekin and bullyin in here, where the bread o charity is sickenin in our stummicks?

BILL: (*Contemptuously, but backing a little.*) Wot good are you,
195 you aold palsy mag? Wot good are you?

SHIRLEY: As good as you and better. I'll do a day's work agen you or any fat young soaker of your age. Go and take my job at Horrockses, where I worked for ten year. They want young men there: they cant afford to keep men over
200 forty-five. Theyre very sorry—give you a character and happy to help you to get anything suited to your years—sure a steady man wont be long out of a job. Well, let em try you. Theyll find the differ. What do you know? Not as much as how to beeyave yourself—layin your dirty fist
205 across the mouth of a respectable woman!

BILL: Downt provowk me to ly it acrost yours: d'ye eah?

SHIRLEY: (*With blighting contempt.*) Yes: you like an old man to hit, dont you, when youve finished with the women. I aint seen you hit a young one yet.

210 BILL: (*Stung.*) You loy, you aold soupkitchener, you. There was a yang menn eah. Did Aw offer to itt him or did Aw not?

SHIRLEY: Was he starvin or was he not? Was he a man or only a crosseyed thief an a loafer? Would you hit my son-in-law's brother?

215 BILL: Oo's ee?

SHIRLEY: Todger Fairmile o Balls Pond. Him that won £20 off the Japanese wrastler at the music hall by standin out 17 minutes 4 seconds agen him.

BILL: (*Sullenly.*) Aw'm nao music awl wrastler. Ken he box?

220 SHIRLEY: Yes: an you cant.

BILL: Wot! Aw cawnt, cawnt Aw? Wots thet you sy (*Threatening him.*)?

SHIRLEY: (*Not budging an inch.*) Will you box Todger Fairmile if I put him on to you? Say the word.

225 BILL: (*Subsiding with a slouch.*) Aw'll stend ap to enny menn alawv, if he was ten Todger Fairmawls. But Aw dont set ap to be a perfeshnal.

SHIRLEY: (*Looking down on him with unfathomable disdain.*) You box! Slap an old woman with the back o your hand! You
230 hadnt even the sense to hit her where a magistrate couldnt see the mark of it, you silly young lump of conceit and ig-

norance. Hit a girl in the jaw and ony make her cry! If Todger Fairmile'd done it, she wouldnt a got up inside o ten minutes, no more than you would if he got on to you. Yah! I'd set about you myself if I had a week's feedin in 235
me instead o two months' starvation. (*He turns his back on him and sits down moodily at the table.*)

BILL: (*Following him and stooping over him to drive the taunt in.*) You loy! youve the bread and treacle in you that you cam eah to beg. 240

SHIRLEY: (*Bursting into tears.*) Oh God! it's true: I'm only an old pauper on the scrap heap. (*Furiously.*) But youll come to it yourself; and then youll know. Youll come to it sooner than a teetotaller like me, fillin yourself with gin at this hour o the mornin! 245

BILL: Aw'm nao gin drinker, you oald lawr; bat wen Aw want to give my girl a bloomin good awdin Aw lawk to ev a bit o devil in me: see? An eah Aw emm, talkin to a rotten aold blawter like you sted o givin her wot for. (*Working himself into a rage.*) Aw'm gowin in there to fetch her aht. (*He* 250
makes vengefully for the shelter door.)

SHIRLEY: Youre going to the station on a stretcher, more likely; and theyll take the gin and the devil out of you there when they get you inside. You mind what youre about: the major here is the Earl o Stevenage's granddaughter. 255

BILL: (*Checked.*) Garn!

SHIRLEY: Youll see.

BILL: (*His resolution oozing.*) Well, Aw aint dan nathin to er.

SHIRLEY: Spose she said you did! who'd believe you?

BILL: (*Very uneasy, skulking back to the corner of the penthouse.*) 260
Gawd! theres no jastice in this cantry. To think wot them people can do! Aw'm as good as er.

SHIRLEY: Tell her so. It's just what a fool like you would do.

(BARBARA, *brisk and businesslike, comes from the shelter with a note book, and addresses herself to* SHIRLEY. BILL, *cowed, sits down in the corner on a form, and turns his back on them.*)

BARBARA: Good morning.

SHIRLEY: (*Standing up and taking off his hat.*) Good morning, 265
miss.

BARBARA: Sit down: make yourself at home. (*He hesitates; but she puts a friendly hand on his shoulder and makes him obey.*) Now then! since youve made friends with us, we want to know all about you. Names and addresses and trades. 270

SHIRLEY: Peter Shirley. Fitter. Chucked out two months ago because I was too old.

BARBARA: (*Not at all surprised.*) Youd pass still. Why didnt you dye your hair?

SHIRLEY: I did. Me age come out at a coroner's inquest on 275
me daughter.

BARBARA: Steady?

SHIRLEY: Teetotaller. Never out of a job before. Good worker. And sent to the knackers like an old horse!

BARBARA: No matter: if you did your part God will do his. 280

SHIRLEY: (*Suddenly stubborn.*) My religion's no concern of anybody but myself.

BARBARA: (*Guessing.*) I know. Secularist?

SHIRLEY: (*Hotly.*) Did I offer to deny it?

BARBARA: Why should you? My own father's a Secularist, I 285
think. Our Father—yours and mine—fulfils himself in many ways; and I daresay he knew what he was about when he made a Secularist of you. So buck up, Peter! we

can always find a job for a steady man like you. (SHIRLEY,
*disarmed and a little bewildered, touches his hat. She turns from
him to* BILL.) Whats your name?

BILL: (*Insolently.*) Wots thet to you?

BARBARA: (*Calmly making a note.*) Afraid to give his name.
Any trade?

BILL: Oo's afride to give is nime? (*Doggedly, with a sense of heroically defying the House of Lords in the person of Lord Stevenage.*) If you want to bring a chawge agen me, bring it.
(*She waits, unruffled.*) Moy nime's Bill Walker.

BARBARA: (*As if the name were familiar: trying to remember how.*)
Bill Walker? (*Recollecting.*) Oh, I know: you're the man that
Jenny Hill was praying for inside just now. (*She enters his
name in her note book.*)

BILL: Oo's Jenny Ill? And wot call as she to pry for me?

BARBARA: I dont know. Perhaps it was you that cut her lip.

BILL: (*Defiantly.*) Yus, it was me that cat her lip. Aw aint afride
o you.

BARBARA: How could you be, since youre not afraid of God?
Youre a brave man, Mr Walker. It takes some pluck to do
our work here; but none of us dare lift our hand against a
girl like that, for fear of her father in heaven.

BILL: (*Sullenly.*) I want nan o your kentin jawr. I spowse you think
Aw cam eah to beg from you, like this demmiged lot eah. Not
me. Aw downt want your bread and scripe and ketlep. Aw
dont blieve in your Gawd, no more than you do yourself.

BARBARA: (*Sunnily apologetic and ladylike, as on a new footing
with him.*) Oh, I beg your pardon for putting your name
down, Mr Walker. I didnt understand. I'll strike it out.

BILL: (*Taking this as a slight, and deeply wounded by it.*) Eah! you
let maw nime alown. Aint it good enaff to be in your book?

BARBARA: (*Considering.*) Well, you see, theres no use putting
down your name unless I can do something for you, is
there? Whats your trade?

BILL: (*Still smarting.*) Thets nao concern o yours.

BARBARA: Just so. (*Very businesslike.*) I'll put you down as
(*Writing.*) the man who—struck—poor little Jenny Hill—
in the mouth.

BILL: (*Rising threateningly.*) See eah. Awve ed enaff o this.

BARBARA: (*Quite sunny and fearless.*) What did you come to us
for?

BILL: Aw cam for maw gel, see? Aw cam to tike her aht o this
and to brike er jawr for er.

BARBARA: (*Complacently.*) You see I was right about your
trade. (BILL, *on the point of retorting furiously, finds himself, to
his great shame and terror, in danger of crying instead. He sits
down again suddenly.*) Whats her name?

BILL: (*Dogged.*) Er nime's Mog Ebbijem: thets wot her nime is.

BARBARA: Mog Habbijam! Oh, she's gone to Canning Town,
to our barracks there.

BILL: (*Fortified by his resentment of Mog's perfidy.*) Is she? (*Vindictively.*) Then Aw'm gowin to Kennintahn arter her. (*He
crosses to the gate; hesitates; finally comes back at* BARBARA.)
Are you loyin to me to git shat o me?

BARBARA: I dont want to get shut of you. I want to keep you
here and save your soul. Youd better stay: youre going to
have a bad time today, Bill.

BILL: Oo's gowin to give it to me? You, preps?

BARBARA: Someone you dont believe in. But youll be glad
afterwards.

BILL: (*Slinking off.*) Aw'll gow to Kennintahn to be aht o reach
o your tangue. (*Suddenly turning on her with intense malice.*)

And if Aw downt fawnd Mog there, Aw'll cam beck and
do two years for you, selp me Gawd if Aw downt!

BARBARA: (*A shade kindlier, if possible.*) It's no use, Bill. She's
got another bloke.

BILL: Wot!

BARBARA: One of her own converts. He fell in love with her
when he saw her with her soul saved, and her face clean,
and her hair washed.

BILL: (*Surprised.*) Wottud she wash it for, the carroty slat? It's
red.

BARBARA: It's quite lovely now, because she wears a new look
in her eyes with it. It's a pity youre too late. The new
bloke has put your nose out of joint, Bill.

BILL: Aw'll put his nowse aht o joint for him. Not that Aw
care a carse for er, mawnd thet. But Aw'll teach her to
drop me as if Aw was dirt. And Aw'll teach him to meddle with maw judy. Wots iz bleedin nime?

BARBARA: Sergeant Todger Fairmile.

SHIRLEY: (*Rising with grim joy.*) I'll go with him, miss. I want
to see them two meet. I'll take him to the infirmary when
it's over.

BILL: (*To* SHIRLEY, *with undissembled misgiving.*) Is thet im you
was speakin on?

SHIRLEY: Thats him.

BILL: Im that wrastled in the music awl?

SHIRLEY: The competitions at the National Sportin Club was
worth nigh a hundred a year to him. He's gev em up now
for religion; so he's a bit fresh for want of the exercise he
was accustomed to. He'll be glad to see you. Come along.

BILL: Wots is wight?

SHIRLEY: Thirteen four. (BILL's *last hope expires.*)

BARBARA: Go and talk to him, Bill. He'll convert you.

SHIRLEY: He'll convert your head into a mashed potato.

BILL: (*Sullenly.*) Aw aint afride of im. Aw aint afride of ennybody. Bat e can lick me. She's dan me. (*He sits down moodily on the edge of the horse trough.*)

SHIRLEY: You aint going. I thought not. (*He resumes his seat.*)

BARBARA: (*Calling.*) Jenny!

JENNY: (*Appearing at the shelter door with a plaster on the corner
of her mouth.*) Yes, Major.

BARBARA: Send Rummy Mitchens out to clear away here.

JENNY: I think she's afraid.

BARBARA: (*Her resemblance to her mother flashing out for a moment.*) Nonsense! she must do as she's told.

JENNY: (*Calling into the shelter.*) Rummy: the Major says you
must come.

(JENNY *comes to* BARBARA, *purposely keeping on the side next to*
BILL, *lest he should suppose that she shrank from him or bore malice.*)

BARBARA: Poor little Jenny! Are you tired? (*Looking at the
wounded cheek.*) Does it hurt?

JENNY: No: it's all right now. It was nothing.

BARBARA: (*Critically.*) It was as hard as he could hit, I expect.
Poor Bill! You dont feel angry with him, do you?

JENNY: Oh no, no, no: indeed I dont, Major, bless his poor
heart! (BARBARA *kisses her; and she runs away merrily into the
shelter.* BILL *writhes with an agonizing return of his new and
alarming symptoms, but says nothing.* RUMMY MITCHENS *comes
from the shelter.*)

BARBARA: (*Going to meet* RUMMY.) Now Rummy, bustle.
Take in those mugs and plates to be washed; and throw
the crumbs about for the birds.

(RUMMY *takes the three plates and mugs; but* SHIRLEY *takes back his mug from her, as there is still some milk left in it.*)

410 RUMMY: There aint any crumbs. This aint a time to waste good bread on birds.

PRICE: (*Appearing at the shelter door.*) Gentleman come to see the shelter, Major. Says he's your father.

BARBARA: All right. Coming. (SNOBBY [PRICE] *goes back into*
415 *the shelter, followed by* BARBARA.)

RUMMY: (*Stealing across to* BILL *and addressing him in a subdued voice, but with intense conviction.*) I'd av the lor of you, you flat eared pignosed potwalloper, if she'd let me. Youre no gentleman, to hit a lady in the face. (BILL, *with greater things*
420 *moving in him, takes no notice.*)

SHIRLEY: (*Following her.*) Here! in with you and dont get yourself into more trouble by talking.

RUMMY: (*With hauteur.*) I aint ad the pleasure o being hintroduced to you, as I can remember. (*She goes into the shelter*
425 *with the plates.*)

SHIRLEY: Thats the—

BILL: (*Savagely.*) Downt you talk to me, d'ye eah? You lea me alown, or Aw'll do you a mischief. Aw'm not dirt under your feet, ennywy.

430 SHIRLEY: (*Calmly.*) Dont you be afeerd. You aint such prime company that you need expect to be sought after. (*He is about to go into the shelter when* BARBARA *comes out, with* UNDERSHAFT *on her right.*)

BARBARA: Oh, there you are, Mr Shirley! (*Between them.*) This
435 is my father: I told you he was a Secularist, didnt I? Perhaps youll be able to comfort one another.

UNDERSHAFT: (*Startled.*) A Secularist! Not the least in the world: on the contrary, a confirmed mystic.

BARBARA: Sorry, I'm sure. By the way, papa, what is your re-
440 ligion? in case I have to introduce you again.

UNDERSHAFT: My religion? Well, my dear, I am a Millionaire. That is my religion.

BARBARA: Then I'm afraid you and Mr Shirley wont be able to comfort one another after all. Youre not a Millionaire,
445 are you, Peter?

SHIRLEY: No; and proud of it.

UNDERSHAFT: (*Gravely.*) Poverty, my friend, is not a thing to be proud of.

SHIRLEY: (*Angrily.*) Who made your millions for you? Me and
450 my like. Whats kep us poor? Keepin you rich. I wouldnt have your conscience, not for all your income.

UNDERSHAFT: I wouldnt have your income, not for all your conscience, Mr Shirley. (*He goes to the penthouse and sits down on a form.*)

455 BARBARA: (*Stopping* SHIRLEY *adroitly as he is about to retort.*) You wouldnt think he was my father, would you, Peter? Will you go into the shelter and lend the lasses a hand for a while: we're worked off our feet.

SHIRLEY: (*Bitterly.*) Yes: I'm in their debt for a meal, aint I?

460 BARBARA: Oh, not because youre in their debt, but for love of them, Peter, for love of them. (*He cannot understand, and is rather scandalized.*) There! dont stare at me. In with you; and give that conscience of yours a holiday (*Bustling him into the shelter.*)

465 SHIRLEY: (*As he goes in.*) Ah! it's a pity you never was trained to use your reason, miss. Youd have been a very taking lecturer on Secularism.

(BARBARA *turns to her father.*)

UNDERSHAFT: Never mind me, my dear. Go about your work; and let me watch it for a while.

BARBARA: All right. 470

UNDERSHAFT: For instance, whats the matter with that outpatient over there?

BARBARA: (*Looking at* BILL, *whose attitude has never changed, and whose expression of brooding wrath has deepened.*) Oh, we shall cure him in no time. Just watch. (*She goes over to* BILL *and* 475 *waits. He glances up at her and casts his eyes down again, uneasy, but grimmer than ever.*) It would be nice to just stamp on Mog Habbijam's face, wouldnt it, Bill?

BILL: (*Starting up from the trough in consternation.*) It's a loy: Aw never said so. (*She shakes her head.*) Oo taold you wot was 480 in moy mawnd?

BARBARA: Only your new friend.

BILL: Wot new friend?

BARBARA: The devil, Bill. When he gets round people they get miserable, just like you. 485

BILL: (*With a heartbreaking attempt at devil-may-care cheerfulness.*) Aw aint miserable. (*He sits down again, and stretches his legs in an attempt to seem indifferent.*)

BARBARA: Well, if youre happy, why dont you look happy, as we do? 490

BILL: (*His legs curling back in spite of him.*) Aw'm eppy enaff, Aw tell you. Woy cawnt you lea me alown? Wot ev I dan to you? Aw aint smashed your fice, ev Aw?

BARBARA: (*Softly: wooing his soul.*) It's not me thats getting at you, Bill. 495

BILL: Oo else is it?

BARBARA: Somebody that doesnt intend you to smash women's faces, I suppose. Somebody or something that wants to make a man of you.

BILL: (*Blustering.*) Mike a menn o me! Aint Aw a menn? eh? 500 Oo sez Aw'm not a menn?

BARBARA: Theres a man in you somewhere, I suppose. But why did he let you hit poor little Jenny Hill? That wasnt very manly of him, was it?

BILL: (*Tormented.*) Ev dan wiv it, Aw tell you. Chack it. Aw'm 505 sick o your Jenny Ill and er silly little fice.

BARBARA: Then why do you keep thinking about it? Why does it keep coming up against you in your mind? Youre not getting converted, are you?

BILL: (*With conviction.*) Not ME. Not lawkly. 510

BARBARA: Thats right, Bill. Hold out against it. Put out your strength. Dont lets get you cheap. Todger Fairmile said he wrestled for three nights against his salvation harder than he ever wrestled with the Jap at the music hall. He gave in to the Jap when his arm was going to break. But he didnt 515 give in to his salvation until his heart was going to break. Perhaps youll escape that. You havnt any heart, have you?

BILL: Wot d'ye mean? Woy aint Aw got a awt the sime as ennybody else?

BARBARA: A man with a heart wouldnt have bashed poor lit- 520 tle Jenny's face, would he?

BILL: (*Almost crying.*) Ow, will you lea me alown? Ev Aw ever offered to meddle with you, that you cam neggin and provowkin me lawk this? (*He writhes convulsively from his eyes to his toes.*) 525

BARBARA: (*With a steady soothing hand on his arm and a gentle voice that never lets him go.*) It's your soul thats hurting you, Bill, and not me. Weve been through it all ourselves. Come with us, Bill. (*He looks wildly round.*) To brave man-

530 hood on earth and eternal glory in heaven. (*He is on the point of breaking down.*) Come. (*A drum is heard in the shelter; and* BILL, *with a gasp, escapes from the spell as* BARBARA *turns quickly.* ADOLPHUS [CUSINS] *enters from the shelter with a big drum.*) Oh! there you are, Dolly. Let me introduce a
535 new friend of mine, Mr Bill Walker. This is my bloke, Bill: Mr Cusins. (CUSINS *salutes with his drumstick.*)

BILL: Gowin to merry im?

BARBARA: Yes.

BILL: (*Fervently.*) Gawd elp im! Gaw-aw-aw-awd elp im!

540 BARBARA: Why? Do you think he wont be happy with me?

BILL: Awve aony ed to stend it for a mawnin: e'll ev to stend it for a lawftawm.

CUSINS: That is a frightful reflection, Mr Walker. But I cant tear myself away from her.

545 BILL: Well, Aw ken. (*To* BARBARA.) Eah! do you knaow where Aw'm gowin to, and wot Aw'm gowin to do?

BARBARA: Yes: youre going to heaven; and youre coming back here before the week's out to tell me so.

BILL: You loy. Aw'm gowin to Kennintahn, to spit in Todger
550 Fairmawl's eye. Aw beshed Jenny Ill's fice; an nar Aw'll git me aown fice beshed and cam beck and shaow it to er. Ee'll itt me ardern Aw itt her. Thatll mike us square. (*To* ADOLPHUS [CUSINS].) Is thet fair or is it not? Youre a genlmn: you oughter knaow.

555 BARBARA: Two black eyes wont make one white one, Bill.

BILL: Aw didnt awst you. Cawnt you never keep your mahth shat? Oy awst the genlmn.

CUSINS: (*Reflectively.*) Yes: I think youre right, Mr Walker. Yes: I should do it. It's curious: it's exactly what an ancient
560 Greek would have done.

BARBARA: But what good will it do?

CUSINS: Well, it will give Mr Fairmile some exercise; and it will satisfy Mr Walker's soul.

BILL: Rot! there aint nao sach a thing as a saoul. Ah kin you
565 tell wevver Awve a saoul or not? You never seen it.

BARBARA: Ive seen it hurting you when you went against it.

BILL: (*With compressed aggravation.*) If you was maw gel and took the word aht o me mahth lawk thet, Aw'd give you sathink youd feel urtin, Aw would. (*To* CUSINS.) You tike
570 maw tip, mite. Stop er jawr; or youll doy afoah your tawm (*With intense expression.*) Wore aht: thets wot youll be: wore aht. (*He goes away through the gate.*)

CUSINS: (*Looking after him.*) I wonder!

BARBARA: Dolly! (*Indignant, in her mother's manner.*)

575 CUSINS: Yes, my dear, it's very wearing to be in love with you. If it lasts, I quite think I shall die young.

BARBARA: Should you mind?

CUSINS: Not at all. (*He is suddenly softened, and kisses her over the drum, evidently not for the first time, as people cannot kiss
580 over a big drum without practice.* UNDERSHAFT *coughs.*)

BARBARA: It's all right, papa, weve not forgotten you. Dolly: explain the place to papa: I havnt time. (*She goes busily into the shelter.*)

(UNDERSHAFT *and* ADOLPHUS [CUSINS] *now have the yard to themselves.* UNDERSHAFT, *seated on a form, and still keenly attentive, looks hard at* ADOLPHUS [CUSINS]. ADOLPHUS [CUSINS] *looks hard at him.*)

UNDERSHAFT: I fancy you guess something of what is in my
585 mind, Mr Cusins. (CUSINS *flourishes his drumsticks as if in the*

act of beating a lively rataplan, but makes no sound.) Exactly so. But suppose Barbara finds you out!

CUSINS: You know, I do not admit that I am imposing on Barbara. I am quite genuinely interested in the views of the Salvation Army. The fact is, I am a sort of collector of 590 religions; and the curious thing is that I find I can believe them all. By the way, have you any religion?

UNDERSHAFT: Yes.

CUSINS: Anything out of the common?

UNDERSHAFT: Only that there are two things necessary to 595 Salvation.

CUSINS: (*Disappointed, but polite.*) Ah, the Church Catechism. Charles Lomax also belongs to the Established Church.

UNDERSHAFT: The two things are—

CUSINS: Baptism and—   600

UNDERSHAFT: No. Money and gunpowder.

CUSINS: (*Surprised, but interested.*) That is the general opinion of our governing classes. The novelty is in hearing any man confess it.

UNDERSHAFT: Just so.   605

CUSINS: Excuse me: is there any place in your religion for honor, justice, truth, love, mercy and so forth?

UNDERSHAFT: Yes: they are the graces and luxuries of a rich, strong, and safe life.

CUSINS: Suppose one is forced to choose between them and 610 money or gunpowder?

UNDERSHAFT: Choose money and gunpowder; for without enough of both you cannot afford the others.

CUSINS: That is your religion?

UNDERSHAFT: Yes.   615

(*The cadence of this reply makes a full close in the conversation,* CUSINS *twists his face dubiously and contemplates* UNDERSHAFT. UNDERSHAFT *contemplates him.*)

CUSINS: Barbara wont stand that. You will have to choose between your religion and Barbara.

UNDERSHAFT: So will you, my friend. She will find out that that drum of yours is hollow.

CUSINS: Father Undershaft: you are mistaken: I am a sincere 620 Salvationist. You do not understand the Salvation Army. It is the army of joy, of love, of courage: it has banished the fear and remorse and despair of the old hell-ridden evangelical sects: it marches to fight the devil with trumpet and drum, with music and dancing, with banner and palm, as 625 becomes a sally from heaven by its happy garrison. It picks the waster out of the public house and makes a man of him: it finds a worm wriggling in a back kitchen, and lo! a woman! Men and women of rank too, sons and daughters of the Highest. It takes the poor professor of Greek, 630 the most artificial and self-suppressed of human creatures, from his meal of roots, and lets loose the rhapsodist in him; reveals the true worship of Dionysos to him; sends him down the public street drumming dithyrambs (*He plays a thundering flourish on the drum.*)   635

UNDERSHAFT: You will alarm the shelter.

CUSINS: Oh, they are accustomed to these sudden ecstasies. However, if the drum worries you—(*He pockets the drumsticks; unhooks the drum; and stands it on the ground opposite the gateway.*)   640

UNDERSHAFT: Thank you.

CUSINS: You remember what Euripides says about your money and gunpowder?

UNDERSHAFT: No.

645 CUSINS: (*Declaiming.*)

> One and another
> In money and guns may outpass his brother;
> And men in their millions float and flow
> And seethe with a million hopes as leaven;
650 > And they win their will; or they miss their will;
> And their hopes are dead or are pined for still;
> But who'er can know
> As the long days go
> That to live is happy, has found his heaven.

655 My translation: what do you think of it?

UNDERSHAFT: I think, my friend, that if you wish to know, as the long days go, that to live is happy, you must first acquire money enough for a decent life, and power enough to be your own master.

660 CUSINS: You are damnably discouraging. (*He resumes his declamation.*)

> Is it so hard a thing to see
> That the spirit of God—whate'er it be—
> The law that abides and changes not, ages long,
665 > The Eternal and Nature-born: these things be strong?
> What else is Wisdom? What of Man's endeavor,
> Or God's high grace so lovely and so great?
> To stand from fear set free? to breathe and wait?
> To hold a hand uplifted over Fate?
670 > And shall not Barbara be loved for ever?

UNDERSHAFT: Euripides mentions Barbara, does he?

CUSINS: It is a fair translation. The word means Loveliness.

UNDERSHAFT: May I ask—as Barbara's father—how much a year she is to be loved for ever on?

675 CUSINS: As for Barbara's father, that is more your affair than mine. I can feed her by teaching Greek: that is about all.

UNDERSHAFT: Do you consider it a good match for her?

CUSINS: (*With polite obstinacy.*) Mr Undershaft: I am in many ways a weak, timid, ineffectual person; and my health is far 680 from satisfactory. But whenever I feel that I must have anything, I get it, sooner or later. I feel that way about Barbara. I dont like marriage: I feel intensely afraid of it; and I dont know what I shall do with Barbara or what she will do with me. But I feel that I and nobody else must marry 685 her. Please regard that as settled.—Not that I wish to be arbitrary; but why should I waste your time in discussing what is inevitable?

UNDERSHAFT: You mean that you will stick at nothing: not even the conversion of the Salvation Army to the worship 690 of Dionysos.

CUSINS: The business of the Salvation Army is to save, not to wrangle about the name of the pathfinder. Dionysos or another: what does it matter?

UNDERSHAFT: (*Rising and approaching him.*) Professor Cusins: 695 you are a young man after my own heart.

CUSINS: Mr Undershaft: you are, as far as I am able to gather, a most infernal old rascal; but you appeal very strongly to my sense of ironic humor.

(UNDERSHAFT *mutely offers his hand. They shake.*)

UNDERSHAFT: (*Suddenly concentrating himself.*) And now to business. 700

CUSINS: Pardon me. We are discussing religion. Why go back to such an uninteresting and unimportant subject as business?

UNDERSHAFT: Religion is our business at present, because it is through religion alone that we can win Barbara.

CUSINS: Have you, too, fallen in love with Barbara? 705

UNDERSHAFT: Yes, with a father's love.

CUSINS: A father's love for a grown-up daughter is the most dangerous of all infatuations. I apologize for mentioning my own pale, coy, mistrustful fancy in the same breath with it.

UNDERSHAFT: Keep to the point. We have to win her; and 710 we are neither of us Methodists.

CUSINS: That doesnt matter. The power Barbara wields here—the power that wields Barbara herself—is not Calvinism, not Presbyterianism, not Methodism—

UNDERSHAFT: Not Greek Paganism either, eh? 715

CUSINS: I admit that. Barbara is quite original in her religion.

UNDERSHAFT: (*Triumphantly.*) Aha! Barbara Undershaft would be. Her inspiration comes from within herself.

CUSINS: How do you suppose it got there?

UNDERSHAFT: (*In towering excitement.*) It is the Undershaft in- 720 heritance. I shall hand on my torch to my daughter. She shall make my converts and preach my gospel—

CUSINS: What! Money and gunpowder!

UNDERSHAFT: Yes, money and gunpowder. Freedom and power. Command of life and command of death. 725

CUSINS: (*Urbanely: trying to bring him down to earth.*) This is extremely interesting, Mr Undershaft. Of course you know that you are mad.

UNDERSHAFT: (*With redoubled force.*) And you?

CUSINS: Oh, mad as a hatter. You are welcome to my secret 730 since I have discovered yours. But I am astonished. Can a madman make cannons?

UNDERSHAFT: Would anyone else than a madman make them? And now (*With surging energy.*) question for question. Can a sane man translate Euripides? 735

CUSINS: No.

UNDERSHAFT: (*Seizing him by the shoulder.*) Can a sane woman make a man of a waster or a woman of a worm?

CUSINS: (*Reeling before the storm.*) Father Colossus—Mammoth Millionaire— 740

UNDERSHAFT: (*Pressing him.*) Are there two mad people or three in this Salvation shelter today?

CUSINS: You mean Barbara is as mad as we are?

UNDERSHAFT: (*Pushing him lightly off and resuming his equanimity suddenly and completely.*) Pooh, Professor! let us call 745 things by their proper names. I am a millionaire; you are a poet; Barbara is a savior of souls. What have we three to do with the common mob of slaves and idolators? (*He sits down again with a shrug of contempt for the mob.*)

CUSINS: Take care! Barbara is in love with the common peo- 750 ple. So am I. Have you never felt the romance of that love?

UNDERSHAFT: (*Cold and sardonic.*) Have you ever been in love with Poverty, like St Francis? Have you ever been in love with Dirt, like St Simeon? Have you ever been in love with disease and suffering, like our nurses and philanthropists? 755 Such passions are not virtues, but the most unnatural of all the vices. This love of the common people may please an earl's granddaughter and a university professor; but I have been a common man and a poor man; and it has no ro-

760 mance for me. Leave it to the poor to pretend that poverty is a blessing: leave it to the coward to make a religion of his cowardice by preaching humility: we know better than that. We three must stand together above the common peo-
765 ple: how else can we help their children to climb up beside us? Barbara must belong to us, not to the Salvation Army.

CUSINS: Well, I can only say that if you think you will get her away from the Salvation Army by talking to her as you have been talking to me, you dont know Barbara.

UNDERSHAFT: My friend: I never ask for what I can buy.

770 CUSINS: (*In a white fury.*) Do I understand you to imply that you can buy Barbara?

UNDERSHAFT: No; but I can buy the Salvation Army.

CUSINS: Quite impossible.

UNDERSHAFT: You shall see. All religious organizations exist
775 by selling themselves to the rich.

CUSINS: Not the Army. That is the Church of the poor.

UNDERSHAFT: All the more reason for buying it.

CUSINS: I dont think you quite know what the Army does for the poor.

780 UNDERSHAFT: Oh yes I do. It draws their teeth: that is enough for me as a man of business.

CUSINS: Nonsense! It makes them sober—

UNDERSHAFT: I prefer sober workmen. The profits are larger.

CUSINS: —honest—

785 UNDERSHAFT: Honest workmen are the most economical.

CUSINS: —attached to their homes—

UNDERSHAFT: So much the better: they will put up with anything sooner than change their shop.

CUSINS: —happy—

790 UNDERSHAFT: An invaluable safeguard against revolution.

CUSINS: —unselfish—

UNDERSHAFT: Indifferent to their own interests, which suits me exactly.

CUSINS: —with their thoughts on heavenly things—

795 UNDERSHAFT: (*Rising.*) And not on Trade Unionism nor Socialism. Excellent.

CUSINS: (*Revolted.*) You really are an infernal old rascal.

UNDERSHAFT: (*Indicating* PETER SHIRLEY, *who has just come from the shelter and strolled dejectedly down the yard between*
800 *them.*) And this is an honest man!

SHIRLEY: Yes; and what av I got by it? (*He passes on bitterly and sits on the form, in the corner of the penthouse.*)

(SNOBBY PRICE, *beaming sanctimoniously, and* JENNY HILL, *with a tambourine full of coppers, come from the shelter and go to the drum, on which* JENNY *begins to count the money.*)

UNDERSHAFT: (*Replying to* SHIRLEY.) Oh, your employers must have got a good deal by it from first to last. (*He sits*
805 *on the table, with one foot on the side form,* CUSINS, *overwhelmed, sits down on the same form nearer the shelter.* BARBARA *comes from the shelter to the middle of the yard. She is excited and a little overwrought.*)

BARBARA: Weve just had a splendid experience meeting at the
810 other gate in Cripps's lane. Ive hardly ever seen them so much moved as they were by your confession, Mr Price.

PRICE: I could almost be glad of my past wickedness if I could believe that it would elp to keep hathers stright.

BARBARA: So it will, Snobby. How much, Jenny?

JENNY: Four and tenpence, Major.   815

BARBARA: Oh Snobby, if you had given your poor mother just one more kick, we should have got the whole five shillings!

PRICE: If she heard you say that, miss, she'd be sorry I didnt. But I'm glad. Oh what a joy it will be to her when she hears I'm saved!   820

UNDERSHAFT: Shall I contribute the odd twopence, Barbara? The millionaire's mite, eh? (*He takes a couple of pennies from his pocket.*)

BARBARA: How did you make that twopence?

UNDERSHAFT: As usual. By selling cannons, torpedoes, sub-   825
marines, and my new patent Grand Duke hand grenade.

BARBARA: Put it back in your pocket. You cant buy your salvation here for twopence: you must work it out.

UNDERSHAFT: Is twopence not enough? I can afford a little more, if you press me.   830

BARBARA: Two million millions would not be enough. There is bad blood on your hands; and nothing but good blood can cleanse them. Money is no use. Take it away. (*She turns to* CUSINS.) Dolly: you must write another letter for me to the papers. (*He makes a wry face.*) Yes: I know you dont like   835
it; but it must be done. The starvation this winter is beating us: everybody is unemployed. The General says we must close this shelter if we cant get more money. I force the collections at the meetings until I am ashamed: dont I, Snobby?   840

PRICE: It's a fair treat to see you work it, miss. The way you got them up from three-and-six to four-and-ten with that hymn, penny by penny and verse by verse, was a caution. Not a Cheap Jack on Mile End Waste could touch you at it.

BARBARA: Yes; but I wish we could do without it. I am getting   845
at last to think more of the collection than of the people's souls. And what are those hatfuls of pence and halfpence? We want thousands! tens of thousands! hundreds of thousands! I want to convert people, not to be always begging for the Army in a way I'd die sooner than beg for myself.   850

UNDERSHAFT: (*In profound irony.*) Genuine unselfishness is capable of anything, my dear.

BARBARA: (*Unsuspectingly, as she turns away to take the money from the drum and put it in a cash bag she carries.*) Yes, isnt it? (UNDERSHAFT *looks sardonically at* CUSINS.)   855

CUSINS: (*Aside to* UNDERSHAFT.) Mephistopheles! Machiavelli!

BARBARA: (*Tears coming into her eyes as she ties the bag and pockets it.*) How are we to feed them? I cant talk religion to a man with bodily hunger in his eyes. (*Almost breaking down.*) It's frightful.   860

JENNY: (*Running to her.*) Major, dear—

BARBARA: (*Rebounding.*) No: dont comfort me. It will be all right. We shall get the money.

UNDERSHAFT: How?

JENNY: By praying for it, of course. Mrs Baines says she prayed   865
for it last night; and she has never prayed for it in vain: never once. (*She goes to the gate and looks out into the street.*)

BARBARA: (*Who has dried her eyes and regained her composure.*) By the way, dad, Mrs Baines has come to march with us to our big meeting this afternoon; and she is very anxious to meet   870
you, for some reason or other. Perhaps she'll convert you.

UNDERSHAFT: I shall be delighted, my dear.

JENNY: (*At the gate: excitedly.*) Major! Major! heres that man back again.

BARBARA: What man?   875

JENNY: The man that hit me. Oh, I hope he's coming back to join us.

(BILL WALKER, *with frost on his jacket, comes through the gate, his hands deep in his pockets and his chin sunk between his shoulders, like a cleaned-out gambler. He halts between* BARBARA *and the drum.*)

BARBARA: Hullo, Bill! Back already!

BILL: (*Nagging at her.*) Bin talkin ever sence, ev you?

880 BARBARA: Pretty nearly. Well, has Todger paid you out for poor Jenny's jaw?

BILL: Nao e aint.

BARBARA: I thought your jacket looked a bit snowy.

BILL: Sao it is snaowy. You want to knaow where the snaow 885 cam from, downt you?

BARBARA: Yes.

BILL: Well, it cam from orf the grahnd in Pawkinses Corner in Kennintahn. It got rabbed orf be maw shaoulders: see?

BARBARA: Pity you didnt rub some off with your knees, Bill! 890 That would have done you a lot of good.

BILL: (*With sour mirthless humor.*) Aw was sivin anather menn's knees at the tawm. E was kneelin on moy ed, e was.

JENNY: Who was kneeling on your head?

BILL: Todger was. E was pryin for me: pryin comfortable wiv 895 me as a cawpet. Sow was Mog. Sao was the aol bloomin meetin. Mog she sez 'Ow Lawd brike is stabborn sperrit; bat downt urt is dear art.' Thet was wot she said. 'Downt urt is dear art'! An er blowk—thirteen stun four!— kneelin wiv all is wight on me. Fanny, aint it?

900 JENNY: Oh no. We're so sorry, Mr Walker.

BARBARA: (*Enjoying it frankly.*) Nonsense! of course it's funny. Served you right, Bill! You must have done something to him first.

BILL: (*Doggedly.*) Aw did wot Aw said Aw'd do. Aw spit in is eye. 905 E looks ap at the skoy and sez, 'Ow that Aw should be fahnd worthy to be spit upon for the gospel's sike!' e sez; an Mog sez 'Glaory Allelloolier!'; an then e called me Braddher, an dahned me as if Aw was a kid and e was me mather worshin me a Setterda nawt. Aw ednt jast nao shaow wiv im at all. 910 Arf the street pryed; an the tather arf larfed fit to split theirselves. (*To* BARBARA.) There! are you settisfawd nah?

BARBARA: (*Her eyes dancing.*) Wish I'd been there, Bill.

BILL: Yus: youd a got in a hextra bit o talk on me, wouldnt you?

JENNY: I'm so sorry, Mr Walker.

915 BILL: (*Fiercely.*) Downt you gow being sorry for me: youve no call. Listen eah. Aw browk your jawr.

JENNY: No, it didn't hurt me: indeed it didnt, except for a moment. It was only that I was frightened.

BILL: Aw downt want to be forgive be you, or be ennybody. 920 Wot Aw did Aw'll py for. Aw trawd to gat me aown jawr browk to settisfaw you—

JENNY: (*Distressed.*) Oh no—

BILL: (*Impatiently.*) Tell y' Aw did: cawnt you listen to wots bein taold you? All Aw got be it was bein mide a sawt of 925 in the pablic street for me pines. Well, if Aw cawnt settisfaw you one wy, Aw ken anather. Listen eah! Aw ed two quid sived agen the frost; an Awve a pahnd of it left. A mite o mawn last week ed words with the judy e's gowing to merry. E give er wot-for; an e's bin fawnd fifteen 930 bob. E ed a rawt to itt er cause they was gowin to be mer-

rid; but Aw ednt nao rawt to itt you; sao put anather fawv bob on an call it a pahnd's worth. (*He produces a sovereign.*) Eahs the manney. Tike it; and lets ev no more o your forgivin an prying and your Mijor jawrin me. Let wot Aw dan be dan an pide for; and let there be a end of it. 935

JENNY: Oh, I couldnt take it, Mr Walker. But if you would give a shilling or two to poor Rummy Mitchens! you really did hurt her; and she's old.

BILL: (*Contemptuously.*) Not lawkly. Aw'd give her anather as soon as look at er. Let her ev the lawr o me as she threat- 940 ened! She aint forgiven me: not mach. Wot Aw dan to er is not on me mawnd—wot she (*Indicating* BARBARA.) mawt call on me conscience—no more than stickin a pig. It's this Christian gime o yours that Aw wownt ev plyed agen me: this bloomin forgivin an neggin an jawrin that 945 mikes a menn thet sore that iz lawf's a burdn to im. Aw wownt ev it, Aw tell you; sao tike your manney and stop thraowin your silly beshed fice hap agen me.

JENNY: Major: may I take a little of it for the Army?

BARBARA: No: the Army is not to be bought. We want your 950 soul, Bill; and we'll take nothing less.

BILL: (*Bitterly.*) Aw knaow. Me an maw few shillins is not good enaff for you. Youre a earl's grendorter, you are. Nathink less than a andered pahnd for you.

UNDERSHAFT: Come, Barbara! you could do a great deal of 955 good with a hundred pounds. If you will set this gentleman's mind at ease by taking his pound, I will give the other ninety-nine.

(BILL, *dazed by such opulence, instinctively touches his cap.*)

BARBARA: Oh, youre too extravagant, papa. Bill offers twenty pieces of silver. All you need offer is the other ten. That 960 will make the standard price to buy anybody who's for sale. I'm not; and the Army's not. (*To* BILL.) Youll never have another quiet moment, Bill, until you come round to us. You cant stand out against your salvation.

BILL: (*Sullenly.*) Aw cawnt stend aht agen music awl wrastlers 965 and awful tangued women. Awve offered to py. Aw can do no more. Tike it or leave it. There it is. (*He throws the sovereign on the drum, and sits down on the horse-trough. The coin fascinates* SNOBBY PRICE, *who takes an early opportunity of dropping his cap on it.*) 970

(MRS BAINES *comes from the shelter. She is dressed as a Salvation Army Commissioner. She is an earnest looking woman of about 40, with a caressing, urgent voice, and an appealing manner.*)

BARBARA: This is my father, Mrs Baines. (UNDERSHAFT *comes from the table, taking his hat off with marked civility.*) Try what you can do with him. He wont listen to me, because he remembers what a fool I was when I was a baby. (*She leaves them together and chats with* JENNY.) 975

MRS BAINES: Have you been shewn over the shelter, Mr Undershaft? You know the work we're doing, of course.

UNDERSHAFT: (*Very civilly.*) The whole nation knows it, Mrs Baines.

MRS BAINES: No, sir: the whole nation does not know it, or 980 we should not be crippled as we are for want of money to carry our work through the length and breadth of the land. Let me tell you that there would have been rioting this winter in London but for us.

985   UNDERSHAFT: You really think so?

MRS BAINES: I know it. I remember 1886, when you rich gentlemen hardened your hearts against the cry of the poor. They broke the windows of your clubs in Pall Mall.

UNDERSHAFT: (*Gleaming with approval of their method.*) And
990   the Mansion House Fund went up next day from thirty thousand pounds to seventy-nine thousand! I remember quite well.

MRS BAINES: Well, wont you help me to get at the people? They wont break windows then. Come here, Price. Let
995   me shew you to this gentleman (PRICE *comes to be inspected.*) Do you remember the window breaking?

PRICE: My ole father thought it was the revolution, maam.

MRS BAINES: Would you break windows now?

PRICE: Oh no, maam. The windows of eaven av bin opened to
1000   me. I know now that the rich man is a sinner like myself.

RUMMY: (*Appearing above at the loft door.*) Snobby Price!

SNOBBY: Wot is it?

RUMMY: Your mother's askin for you at the other gate in Cripps's Lane. She's heard about your confession (PRICE *turns pale.*)

1005   MRS BAINES: Go, Mr Price; and pray with her.

JENNY: You can go through the shelter, Snobby.

PRICE: (*To* MRS BAINES.) I couldnt face her now, maam, with all the weight of my sins fresh on me. Tell her she'll find her son at ome, waitin for her in prayer. (*He skulks off*
1010   *through the gate, incidentally stealing the sovereign on his way out by picking up his cap from the drum.*)

MRS BAINES: (*With swimming eyes.*) You see how we take the anger and the bitterness against you out of their hearts, Mr Undershaft.

1015   UNDERSHAFT: It is certainly most convenient and gratifying to all large employers of labor, Mrs Baines.

MRS BAINES: Barbara: Jenny: I have good news: most wonderful news. (JENNY *runs to her.*) My prayers have been answered. I told you they would, Jenny, didnt I?

1020   JENNY: Yes, yes.

BARBARA: (*Moving nearer to the drum.*) Have we got money enough to keep the shelter open?

MRS BAINES: I hope we shall have enough to keep all the shelters open. Lord Saxmundham has promised us five
1025   thousand pounds—

BARBARA: Hooray!

JENNY: Glory!

MRS BAINES: —if—

BARBARA: 'If!' If what?

1030   MRS BAINES: —if five other gentlemen will give a thousand each to make it up to ten thousand.

BARBARA: Who is Lord Saxmundham? I never heard of him.

UNDERSHAFT: (*Who has pricked up his ears at the peer's name, and is now watching* BARBARA *curiously.*) A new creation, my
1035   dear. You have heard of Sir Horace Bodger?

BARBARA: Bodger! Do you mean the distiller? Bodger's whisky?

UNDERSHAFT: That is the man. He is one of the greatest of our public benefactors. He restored the cathedral at Hakington. They made him a baronet for that. He gave half a million to
1040   the funds of his party: they made him a baron for that.

SHIRLEY: What will they give him for the five thousand?

UNDERSHAFT: There is nothing left to give him. So the five thousand, I should think, is to save his soul.

MRS BAINES: Heaven grant it may! Oh Mr Undershaft, you
1045   have some very rich friends. Cant you help us towards the

other five thousand? We are going to hold a great meeting this afternoon at the Assembly Hall in the Mile End Road. If I could only announce that one gentleman had come forward to support Lord Saxmundham, others would follow. Dont you know somebody? couldnt you?   1050
wouldnt you? (*Her eyes fill with tears.*) oh, think of those poor people, Mr Undershaft: think of how much it means to them, and how little to a great man like you.

UNDERSHAFT: (*Sardonically gallant.*) Mrs Baines: you are irresistible. I cant disappoint you; and I cant deny myself the   1055
satisfaction of making Bodger pay up. You shall have your five thousand pounds.

MRS BAINES: Thank God!

UNDERSHAFT: You dont thank me?

MRS BAINES: Oh sir, dont try to be cynical: dont be ashamed   1060
of being a good man. The Lord will bless you abundantly; and our prayers will be like a strong fortification round you all the days of your life. (*With a touch of caution.*) You will let me have the cheque to shew at the meeting, wont you? Jenny: go in and fetch a pen and ink. (JENNY *runs to*   1065
the shelter door.)

UNDERSHAFT: Do not disturb Miss Hill: I have a fountain pen. (JENNY *halts. He sits at the table and writes the cheque.* CUSINS *rises to make room for him. They all watch him silently.*)

BILL: (*Cynically, aside to* BARBARA, *his voice and accent horribly*   1070
debased.) Wot prawce selvytion nah?

BARBARA: Stop. (UNDERSHAFT *stops writing: they all turn to her in surprise.*) Mrs Baines: are you really going to take this money?

MRS BAINES: (*Astonished.*) Why not, dear?   1075

BARBARA: Why not! Do you know what my father is? Have you forgotten that Lord Saxmundham is Bodger the whisky man? Do you remember how we implored the County Council to stop him from writing Bodger's Whisky in letters of fire against the sky; so that the poor drink-   1080
ruined creatures on the Embankment could not wake up from their snatches of sleep without being reminded of their deadly thirst by that wicked sky sign? Do you know that the worst thing I have had to fight here is not the devil, but Bodger, Bodger, Bodger, with his whisky, his distilleries,   1085
and his tied houses? Are you going to make our shelter another tied house for him, and ask me to keep it?

BILL: Rotten dranken whisky it is too.

MRS BAINES: Dear Barbara: Lord Saxmundham has a soul to be saved like any of us. If heaven has found the way to   1090
make a good use of his money, are we to set ourselves up against the answer to our prayers?

BARBARA: I know he has a soul to be saved. Let him come down here; and I'll do my best to help him to his salvation. But he wants to send his cheque down to buy us, and   1095
go on being as wicked as ever.

UNDERSHAFT: (*With a reasonableness which* CUSINS *alone perceives to be ironical.*) My dear Barbara: alcohol is a very necessary article. It heals the sick—

BARBARA: It does nothing of the sort.   1100

UNDERSHAFT: Well, it assists the doctor: that is perhaps a less questionable way of putting it. It makes life bearable to millions of people who could not endure their existence if they were quite sober. It enables Parliament to do things at eleven at night that no sane person would do at eleven in   1105
the morning. Is it Bodger's fault that this inestimable gift is

deplorably abused by less than one per cent of the poor? (*He turns again to the table; signs the cheque; and crosses it.*)

MRS BAINES: Barbara: will there be less drinking or more if all those poor souls we are saving come tomorrow and find the doors of our shelters shut in their faces? Lord Saxmundham gives us the money to stop drinking—to take his own business from him.

CUSINS: (*Impishly.*) Pure self-sacrifice on Bodger's part, clearly! Bless dear Bodger! (BARBARA *almost breaks down as* ADOLPHUS, *too, fails her.*)

UNDERSHAFT: (*Tearing out the cheque and pocketing the book as he rises and goes past* CUSINS *to* MRS BAINES.) I also, Mrs Baines, may claim a little disinterestedness. Think of my business! think of the widows and orphans! the men and lads torn to pieces with shrapnel and poisoned with lyddite! (MRS BAINES *shrinks; but he goes on remorselessly.*) the oceans of blood, not one drop of which is shed in a really just cause! the ravaged crops! the peaceful peasants forced, women and men, to till their fields under the fire of opposing armies on pain of starvation! the bad blood of the fierce little cowards at home who egg on others to fight for the gratification of their national vanity! All this makes money for me: I am never richer, never busier than when the papers are full of it. Well, it is your work to preach peace on earth and good will to men. (MRS BAINES's *face lights up again.*) Every convert you make is a vote against war. (*Her lips move in prayer.*) Yet I give you this money to help you to hasten my own commercial ruin. (*He gives her the cheque.*)

CUSINS: (*Mounting the form in an ecstasy of mischief.*) The millennium will be inaugurated by the unselfishness of Undershaft and Bodger. Oh be joyful! (*He takes the drum-sticks from his pocket and flourishes them.*)

MRS BAINES: (*Taking the cheque.*) The longer I live the more proof I see that there is an Infinite Goodness that turns everything to the work of salvation sooner or later. Who would have thought that any good could have come out of war and drink? And yet their profits are brought today to the feet of salvation to do its blessed work. (*She is affected to tears.*)

JENNY: (*Running to* MRS BAINES *and throwing her arms round her.*) Oh dear! how blessed, how glorious it all is!

CUSINS: (*In a convulsion of irony.*) Let us seize this unspeakable moment. Let us march to the great meeting at once. Excuse me just an instant. (*He rushes into the shelter.* JENNY *takes her tambourine from the drum head.*)

MRS BAINES: Mr Undershaft: have you ever seen a thousand people fall on their knees with one impulse and pray? Come with us to the meeting. Barbara shall tell them that the Army is saved, and saved through you.

CUSINS: (*Returning impetuously from the shelter with a flag and a trombone, and coming between* MRS BAINES *and* UNDERSHAFT.) You shall carry the flag down the first street, Mrs Baines. (*He gives her the flag.*) Mr Undershaft is a gifted trombonist: he shall intone an Olympian diapason to the West Ham Salvation March. (*Aside to* UNDERSHAFT, *as he forces the trombone on him.*) Blow, Machiavelli, blow.

UNDERSHAFT: (*Aside to him, as he takes the trombone.*) The trumpet in Zion! (CUSINS *rushes to the drum, which he takes up and puts on.* UNDERSHAFT *continues, aloud.*) I will do my best. I could vamp a bass if I knew the tune.

CUSINS: It is a wedding chorus from one of Donizetti's operas; but we have converted it. We convert everything to good here, including Bodger. You remember the chorus. 'For thee immense rejoicing—immenso giubilo—immenso giubilo.' (*With drum obbligato.*) Rum tum ti tum tum, tum tum ti ta—

BARBARA: Dolly: you are breaking my heart.

CUSINS: What is a broken heart more or less here? Dionysos Undershaft has descended. I am possessed.

MRS BAINES: Come, Barbara: I must have my dear Major to carry the flag with me.

JENNY: Yes, yes, Major darling.

(CUSINS *snatches the tambourine out of* JENNY's *hand and mutely offers it to* BARBARA.)

BARBARA: (*Coming forward a little as she puts the offer behind her with a shudder, whilst* CUSINS *recklessly tosses the tambourine back to* JENNY *and goes to the gate.*) I cant come.

JENNY: Not come!

MRS BAINES: (*With tears in her eyes.*) Barbara: do you think I am wrong to take the money?

BARBARA: (*Impulsively going to her and kissing her.*) No, no: God help you, dear, you must: you are saving the Army. Go; and may you have a great meeting!

JENNY: But arnt you coming?

BARBARA: No. (*She begins taking off the silver S brooch from her collar.*)

MRS BAINES: Barbara: what are you doing?

JENNY: Why are you taking your badge off? You cant be going to leave us, Major.

BARBARA: (*Quietly.*) Father: come here.

UNDERSHAFT: (*Coming to her.*) My dear! (*Seeing that she is going to pin the badge on his collar, he retreats to the penthouse in some alarm.*)

BARBARA: (*Following him.*) Dont be frightened. (*She pins the badge on and steps back towards the table, shewing him to the others.*) There! It's not much for £5000, is it?

MRS BAINES: Barbara: if you wont come and pray with us, promise me you will pray for us.

BARBARA: I cant pray now. Perhaps I shall never pray again.

MRS BAINES: Barbara!

JENNY: Major!

BARBARA: (*Almost delirious.*) I cant bear any more. Quick march!

CUSINS: (*Calling to the procession in the street outside.*) Off we go. Play up, there! Immenso giubilo. (*He gives the time with his drum; and the band strikes up the march, which rapidly becomes more distant as the procession moves briskly away.*)

MRS BAINES: I must go, dear. Youre overworked: you will be all right tomorrow. We'll never lose you. Now Jenny: step out with the old flag. Blood and Fire! (*She marches out through the gate with her flag.*)

JENNY: Glory Hallelujah! (*Flourishing her tambourine and marching.*)

UNDERSHAFT: (*To* CUSINS, *as he marches out past him easing the slide of his trombone.*) 'My ducats and my daughter'!

CUSINS: (*Following him out.*) Money and gunpowder!

BARBARA: Drunkenness and Murder! My God: why hast thou forsaken me?

(*She sinks on the form with her face buried in her hands. The march passes away into silence.* BILL WALKER *steals across to her.*)

BILL: (*Taunting.*) Wot prawce selvytion nah?

SHIRLEY: Dont you hit her when she's down.

1225 BILL: She itt me wen aw wiz dahn. Waw shouldnt Aw git a bit o me aown beck?

BARBARA: (*Raising her head.*) I didnt take your money, Bill. (*She crosses the yard to the gate and turns her back on the two men to hide her face from them.*)

1230 BILL: (*Sneering after her.*) Naow, it warnt enaff for you. (*Turning to the drum, he misses the money.*) Ellow! If you aint took it sammun else ez. Weres it gorn? Bly me if Jenny Ill didnt tike it after all!

RUMMY: (*Screaming at him from the loft.*) You lie, you dirty black-

1235 guard! Snobby Price pinched it off the drum when he took up his cap. I was up here all the time an see im do it.

BILL: Wot! Stowl maw manney! Waw didnt you call thief on him, you silly aold macker you?

RUMMY: To serve you aht for ittin me across the fice. It's cost

1240 y'pahnd, that az. (*Raising a pæan of squalid triumph.*) I done you. I'm even with you. Uve ad it aht o y—(BILL *snatches up* SHIRLEY's *mug and hurls it at her. She slams the loft door and vanishes. The mug smashes against the door and falls in fragments.*)

1245 BILL: (*Beginning to chuckle.*) Tell us, aol menn, wot o'clock this mawnin was it wen im as they call Snobby Prawce was sived?

BARBARA: (*Turning to him more composedly, and with unspoiled sweetness.*) About half past twelve, Bill. And he pinched

1250 your pound at a quarter to two. *I* know. Well, you cant afford to lose it. I'll send it to you.

BILL: (*His voice and accent suddenly improving.*) Not if Aw wiz to stawve for it. Aw aint to be bought.

SHIRLEY: Aint you? Youd sell yourself to the devil for a pint

1255 o beer; only there aint no devil to make the offer.

BILL: (*Unashamed.*) Sao Aw would, mite, and often ev, cheerful. But she cawnt baw me. (*Approaching* BARBARA.) You wanted maw saoul, did you? Well, you aint got it.

BARBARA: I nearly got it, Bill. But weve sold it back to you

1260 for ten thousand pounds.

SHIRLEY: And dear at the money!

BARBARA: No, Peter: it was worth more than money.

BILL: (*Salvationproof.*) It's nao good: you cawnt get rahnd me nah. Aw downt blieve in it; and Awve seen tody that Aw

1265 was rawt. (*Going.*) Sao long, aol soupkitchener! Ta, ta, Major Earl's Grendorter! (*Turning at the gate.*) Wot prawce selvytion nah? Snobby Prawce! Ha! ha!

BARBARA: (*Offering her hand.*) Goodbye, Bill.

BILL: (*Taken aback, half plucks his cap off; then shoves it on again*

1270 *defiantly.*) Git aht. (BARBARA *drops her hand, discouraged. He has a twinge of remorse.*) But thets aw rawt, you knaow. Nathink pasnl. Naow mellice. Sao long, Judy. (*He goes.*)

BARBARA: No malice. So long, Bill.

SHIRLEY: (*Shaking his head.*) You make too much of him, miss,

1275 in your innocence.

BARBARA: (*Going to him.*) Peter: I'm like you now. Cleaned out, and lost my job.

SHIRLEY: Youve youth an hope. Thats two better than me.

BARBARA: I'll get you a job, Peter. Thats hope for you: the youth will have to be enough for me. (*She counts her money.*) 1280 I have just enough left for two teas at Lockharts, a Rowton doss for you, and my tram and bus home. (*He frowns and rises with offended pride. She takes his arm.*) Dont be proud, Peter: it's sharing between friends. And promise me youll talk to me and not let me cry. (*She draws him towards the gate.*) 1285

SHIRLEY: Well, I'm not accustomed to talk to the like of you—

BARBARA: (*Urgently.*) Yes, yes: you must talk to me. Tell me about Tom Paine's books and Bradlaugh's lectures. Come along.

SHIRLEY: Ah, if you would only read Tom Paine in the proper 1290 spirit, miss! (*They go out through the gate together.*)

ACT THREE

Next day after lunch LADY BRITOMART *is writing in the library in Wilton Crescent.* SARAH *is reading in the armchair near the window.* BARBARA, *in ordinary fashionable dress, pale and brooding, is on the settee.* CHARLES LOMAX *enters. He starts on seeing* BARBARA *fashionably attired and in low spirits.*

LOMAX: Youve left off your uniform!

(BARBARA *says nothing; but an expression of pain passes over her face.*)

LADY BRITOMART: (*Warning him in low tones to be careful.*) Charles!

LOMAX: (*Much concerned, coming behind the settee and bending sympathetically over* BARBARA.) I'm awfully sorry, Barbara. 5 You know I helped you all I could with the concertina and so forth. (*Momentously.*) Still, I have never shut my eyes to the fact that there is a certain amount of tosh about the Salvation Army. Now the claims of the Church of England—

LADY BRITOMART: Thats enough, Charles. Speak of some- 10 thing suited to your mental capacity.

LOMAX: But surely the Church of England is suited to all our capacities.

BARBARA: (*Pressing his hand.*) Thank you for your sympathy, Cholly. Now go and spoon with Sarah. 15

LOMAX: (*Dragging a chair from the writing table and seating himself affectionately by* SARAH's *side.*) How is my ownest today?

SARAH: I wish you wouldnt tell Cholly to do things, Barbara. He always comes straight and does them. Cholly: we're going to the works this afternoon. 20

LOMAX: What works?

SARAH: The cannon works.

LOMAX: What? your governor's shop!

SARAH: Yes.

LOMAX: Oh I say! 25

(CUSINS *enters in poor condition. He also starts visibly when he sees* BARBARA *without her uniform.*)

BARBARA: I expected you this morning, Dolly. Didnt you guess that?

CUSINS: (*Sitting down beside her.*) I'm sorry. I have only just breakfasted.

SARAH: But weve just finished lunch. 30

BARBARA: Have you had one of your bad nights?

CUSINS: No: I had rather a good night: in fact, one of the most remarkable nights I have ever passed.

BARBARA: The meeting?

35 CUSINS: No: after the meeting.

LADY BRITOMART: You should have gone to bed after the meeting. What were you doing?

CUSINS: Drinking.

LADY BRITOMART: ⎫   Adolphus!
40 SARAH: ⎬   Dolly!
BARBARA: ⎪   Dolly!
LOMAX: ⎭   Oh I say!

LADY BRITOMART: What were you drinking, may I ask?

CUSINS: A most devilish kind of Spanish burgundy, warranted
45   free from added alcohol: a Temperance burgundy in fact. Its richness in natural alcohol made any addition superfluous.

BARBARA: Are you joking, Dolly?

CUSINS: (*Patiently.*) No. I have been making a night of it with the nominal head of this household: that is all.

50 LADY BRITOMART: Andrew made you drunk!

CUSINS: No: he only provided the wine. I think it was Dionysos who made me drunk. (*To* BARBARA.) I told you I was possessed.

LADY BRITOMART: Youre not sober yet. Go home to bed at
55   once.

CUSINS: I have never before ventured to reproach you, Lady Brit; but how could you marry the Prince of Darkness?

LADY BRITOMART: It was much more excusable to marry him than to get drunk with him. That is a new accom-
60   plishment of Andrew's, by the way. He usent to drink.

CUSINS: He doesnt now. He only sat there and completed the wreck of my moral basis, the rout of my convictions, the purchase of my soul. He cares for you, Barbara. That is what makes him so dangerous to me.

65 BARBARA: That has nothing to do with it, Dolly. There are larger loves and diviner dreams than the fireside ones. You know that, dont you?

CUSINS: Yes: that is our understanding. I know it. I hold to it. Unless he can win me on that holier ground he may amuse me
70   for a while; but he can get no deeper hold, strong as he is.

BARBARA: Keep to that; and the end will be right. Now tell me what happened at the meeting?

CUSINS: It was an amazing meeting. Mrs Baines almost died of emotion. Jenny Hill simply gibbered with hysteria. The
75   Prince of Darkness played his trombone like a madman: its brazen roarings were like the laughter of the damned. 117 conversions took place then and there. They prayed with the most touching sincerity and gratitude for Bodger, and for the anonymous donor of the £5000. Your
80   father would not let his name be given.

LOMAX: That was rather fine of the old man, you know. Most chaps would have wanted the advertisement.

CUSINS: He said all the charitable institutions would be down on him like kites on a battle-field if he gave his name.

85 LADY BRITOMART: Thats Andrew all over. He never does a proper thing without giving an improper reason for it.

CUSINS: He convinced me that I have all my life been doing improper things for proper reasons.

LADY BRITOMART: Adolphus: now that Barbara has left the
90   Salvation Army, you had better leave it too. I will not have you playing that drum in the streets.

CUSINS: Your orders are already obeyed, Lady Brit.

BARBARA: Dolly: were you ever really in earnest about it? Would you have joined if you had never seen me?

CUSINS: (*Disingenuously.*) Well—er—well, possibly, as a collec-   95
tor of religions—

LOMAX: (*Cunningly.*) Not as a drummer, though, you know. You are a very clearheaded brainy chap, Dolly; and it must have been apparent to you that there is a certain amount of tosh about—   100

LADY BRITOMART: Charles: if you must drivel, drivel like a grown-up man and not like a schoolboy.

LOMAX: (*Out of countenance.*) Well, drivel is drivel, dont you know, whatever a man's age.

LADY BRITOMART: In good society in England, Charles, men   105
drivel at all ages by repeating silly formulas with an air of wisdom. Schoolboys make their own formulas out of slang, like you. When they reach your age, and get polit-ical private secretaryships and things of that sort, they drop slang and get their formulas out of the *Spectator* or *The*   110
Times. You had better confine yourself to *The Times.* You will find that there is a certain amount of tosh about *The Times;* but at least its language is reputable.

LOMAX: (*Overwhelmed.*) You are so awfully strong-minded, Lady Brit—   115

LADY BRITOMART: Rubbish! (MORRISON *comes in.*) What is it?

MORRISON: If you please, my lady, Mr Undershaft has just drove up to the door.

LADY BRITOMART: Well, let him in. (MORRISON *hesitates.*) Whats the matter with you?   120

MORRISON: Shall I announce him, my lady; or is he at home here, so to speak, my lady?

LADY BRITOMART: Announce him.

MORRISON: Thank you, my lady. You wont mind my asking, I hope. The occasion is in a manner of speaking new to me.   125

LADY BRITOMART: Quite right. Go and let him in.

MORRISON: Thank you, my lady. (*He withdraws.*)

LADY BRITOMART: Children: go and get ready. (SARAH *and* BARBARA *go upstairs for their out-of-door wraps.*) Charles: go and tell Stephen to come down here in five minutes: you   130
will find him in the drawing room. (CHARLES *goes.*) Adol-phus: tell them to send round the carriage in about fifteen minutes. (ADOLPHUS [CUSINS] *goes.*)

MORRISON: (*At the door.*) Mr Undershaft.

(UNDERSHAFT *comes in.* MORRISON *goes out.*)

UNDERSHAFT: Alone! How fortunate!   135

LADY BRITOMART: (*Rising.*) Dont be sentimental, Andrew. Sit down. (*She sits on the settee: he sits beside her, on her left. She comes to the point before he has time to breathe.*) Sarah must have £800 a year until Charles Lomax comes into his property. Barbara will need more, and need it perma-   140
nently, because Adolphus hasnt any property.

UNDERSHAFT: (*Resignedly.*) Yes, my dear: I will see to it. Any-thing else? for yourself, for instance?

LADY BRITOMART: I want to talk to you about Stephen.

UNDERSHAFT: (*Rather wearily.*) Dont, my dear. Stephen doesnt   145
interest me.

LADY BRITOMART: He does interest me. He is our son.

UNDERSHAFT: Do you really think so? He has induced us to bring him into the world; but he chose his parents very incongruously, I think. I see nothing of myself in him, and   150
less of you.

LADY BRITOMART: Andrew: Stephen is an excellent son, and a most steady, capable, highminded young man. You are simply trying to find an excuse for disinheriting him.

155 UNDERSHAFT: My dear Biddy: the Undershaft tradition disinherits him. It would be dishonest of me to leave the cannon foundry to my son.

LADY BRITOMART: It would be most unnatural and improper of you to leave it to anyone else, Andrew. Do you suppose
160 this wicked and immoral tradition can be kept up for ever? Do you pretend that Stephen could not carry on the foundry just as well as all the other sons of the big business houses?

UNDERSHAFT: Yes: he could learn the office routine without
165 understanding the business, like all the other sons; and the firm would go on by its own momentum until the real Undershaft—probably an Italian or a German—would invent a new method and cut him out.

LADY BRITOMART: There is nothing that any Italian or Ger-
170 man could do that Stephen could not do. And Stephen at least has breeding.

UNDERSHAFT: The son of a foundling! Nonsense!

LADY BRITOMART: My son, Andrew! And even you may have good blood in your veins for all you know.

175 UNDERSHAFT: True. Probably I have. That is another argument in favour of a foundling.

LADY BRITOMART: Andrew: dont be aggravating. And dont be wicked. At present you are both.

UNDERSHAFT: This conversation is part of the Undershaft tra-
180 dition, Biddy. Every Undershaft's wife has treated him to it ever since the house was founded. It is mere waste of breath. If the tradition be ever broken it will be for an abler man than Stephen.

LADY BRITOMART: (*Pouting.*) Then go away.

185 UNDERSHAFT: (*Deprecatory.*) Go away!

LADY BRITOMART: Yes: go away. If you will do nothing for Stephen, you are not wanted here. Go to your foundling, whoever he is; and look after him.

UNDERSHAFT: The fact is, Biddy—

190 LADY BRITOMART: Dont call me Biddy. I dont call you Andy.

UNDERSHAFT: I will not call my wife Britomart: it is not good sense. Seriously, my love, the Undershaft tradition has landed me in a difficulty. I am getting on in years; and my partner Lazarus has at last made a stand and insisted that the succes-
195 sion must be settled one way or the other; and of course he is quite right. You see, I havent found a fit successor yet.

LADY BRITOMART: (*Obstinately.*) There is Stephen.

UNDERSHAFT: Thats just it: all the foundlings I can find are exactly like Stephen.

200 LADY BRITOMART: Andrew!!

UNDERSHAFT: I want a man with no relations and no schooling: that is, a man who would be out of the running altogether if he were not a strong man. And I cant find him. Every blessed foundling nowadays is snapped up in his in-
205 fancy by Barnardo homes, or School Board officers, or Boards of Guardians; and if he shews the least ability he is fastened on by schoolmasters; trained to win scholarships like a racehorse; crammed with secondhand ideas; drilled and disciplined in docility and what they call good taste;
210 and lamed for life so that he is fit for nothing but teaching. If you want to keep the foundry in the family, you had better find an eligible foundling and marry him to Barbara.

LADY BRITOMART: Ah! Barbara! Your pet! You would sacrifice Stephen to Barbara.

UNDERSHAFT: Cheerfully. And you, my dear, would boil Bar- 215 bara to make soup for Stephen.

LADY BRITOMART: Andrew: this is not a question of our likings and dislikings: it is a question of duty. It is your duty to make Stephen your successor.

UNDERSHAFT: Just as much as it is your duty to submit to 220 your husband. Come, Biddy! these tricks of the governing class are of no use with me. I am one of the governing class myself; and it is waste of time giving tracts to a missionary. I have the power in this matter; and I am not to be hum-bugged into using it for your purposes. 225

LADY BRITOMART: Andrew: you can talk my head off; but you cant change wrong into right. And your tie is all on one side. Put it straight.

UNDERSHAFT: (*Disconcerted.*) It wont stay unless it's pinned (*He fumbles at it with childish grimaces.*)— 230

(STEPHEN *comes in.*)

STEPHEN: (*At the door.*) I beg your pardon. (*About to retire.*)

LADY BRITOMART: No: come in, Stephen. (STEPHEN *comes forward to his mother's writing table.*)

UNDERSHAFT: (*Not very cordially.*) Good afternoon.

STEPHEN: (*Coldly.*) Good afternoon. 235

UNDERSHAFT: (*To* LADY BRITOMART.) He knows all about the tradition, I suppose?

LADY BRITOMART: Yes. (*To* STEPHEN.) It is what I told you last night, Stephen.

UNDERSHAFT: (*Sulkily.*) I understand you want to come into 240 the cannon business.

STEPHEN: *I* go into trade! Certainly not.

UNDERSHAFT: (*Opening his eyes, greatly eased in mind and manner.*) Oh! in that case—

LADY BRITOMART: Cannons are not trade, Stephen. They are 245 enterprise.

STEPHEN: I have no intention of becoming a man of business in any sense. I have no capacity for business and no taste for it. I intend to devote myself to politics.

UNDERSHAFT: (*Rising.*) My dear boy: this is an immense re- 250 lief to me. And I trust it may prove an equally good thing for the country. I was afraid you would consider yourself disparaged and slighted. (*He moves towards* STEPHEN *as if to shake hands with him.*)

LADY BRITOMART: (*Rising and interposing.*) Stephen: I cannot 255 allow you to throw away an enormous property like this.

STEPHEN: (*Stiffly.*) Mother: there must be an end of treating me as a child, if you please. (LADY BRITOMART *recoils, deeply wounded by his tone.*) Until last night I did not take your attitude seriously, because I did not think you meant it se- 260 riously. But I find now that you left me in the dark as to matters which you should have explained to me years ago. I am extremely hurt and offended. Any further discussion of my intentions had better take place with my father, as between one man and another. 265

LADY BRITOMART: Stephen! (*She sits down again, her eyes filling with tears.*)

UNDERSHAFT: (*With grave compassion.*) You see, my dear, it is only the big men who can be treated as children.

270   STEPHEN: I am sorry, mother, that you have forced me—

UNDERSHAFT: (*Stopping him.*) Yes, yes, yes, yes: thats all right, Stephen. She wont interfere with you any more: your independence is achieved: you have won your latchkey. Dont rub it in; and above all, dont apologize. (*He resumes*
275   *his seat.*) Now what about your future, as between one man and another—I beg your pardon, Biddy: as between two men and a woman.

LADY BRITOMART: (*Who has pulled herself together strongly.*) I quite understand, Stephen. By all means go your own way if
280   you feel strong enough. (STEPHEN *sits down magisterially in the chair at the writing table with an air of affirming his majority.*)

UNDERSHAFT: It is settled that you do not ask for the succession to the cannon business.

STEPHEN: I hope it is settled that I repudiate the cannon business.

285   UNDERSHAFT: Come, come! dont be so devilishly sulky: it's boyish. Freedom should be generous. Besides, I owe you a fair start in life in exchange for disinheriting you. You cant become prime minister all at once. Havnt you a turn for something? What about literature, art, and so forth?

290   STEPHEN: I have nothing of the artist about me, either in faculty or character, thank Heaven!

UNDERSHAFT: A philosopher, perhaps? Eh?

STEPHEN: I make no such ridiculous pretension.

UNDERSHAFT: Just so. Well, there is the army, the navy, the
295   Church, the Bar. The Bar requires some ability. What about the Bar?

STEPHEN: I have not studied law. And I am afraid I have not the necessary push—I believe that is the name barristers give to their vulgarity—for success in pleading.

300   UNDERSHAFT: Rather a difficult case, Stephen. Hardly anything left but the stage, is there? (STEPHEN *makes an impatient movement.*) Well, come! is there anything you know or care for?

STEPHEN: (*Rising and looking at him steadily.*) I know the difference between right and wrong.

305   UNDERSHAFT: (*Hugely tickled.*) You dont say so! What! no capacity for business, no knowledge of law, no sympathy with art, no pretension to philosophy; only a simple knowledge of the secret that has puzzled all the philosophers, baffled all the lawyers, muddled all the men of busi-
310   ness, and ruined most of the artists: the secret of right and wrong. Why, man, youre a genius, a master of masters, a god! At twentyfour, too!

STEPHEN: (*Keeping his temper with difficulty.*) You are pleased to be facetious. I pretend to nothing more than any honor-
315   able English gentleman claims as his birthright (*He sits down angrily.*)

UNDERSHAFT: Oh, thats everybody's birthright. Look at poor little Jenny Hill, the Salvation lassie! she would think you were laughing at her if you asked her to stand up in the
320   street and teach grammar or geography or mathematics or even drawing room dancing; but it never occurs to her to doubt that she can teach morals and religion. You are all alike, you respectable people. You cant tell me the bursting strain of a ten-inch gun, which is a very simple mat-
325   ter; but you all think you can tell me the bursting strain of a man under temptation. You darent handle high explosives; but youre all ready to handle honesty and truth and justice and the whole duty of man, and kill one another at that game. What a country! What a world!

330   LADY BRITOMART: (*Uneasily.*) What do you think he had better do, Andrew?

UNDERSHAFT: Oh, just what he wants to do. He knows nothing and he thinks he knows everything. That points clearly to a political career. Get him a private secretaryship to someone who can get him an Under Secretaryship; and 335 then leave him alone. He will find his natural and proper place in the end on the Treasury Bench.

STEPHEN: (*Springing up again.*) I am sorry, sir, that you force me to forget the respect due to you as my father. I am an Englishman and I will not hear the Government of my 340 country insulted. (*He thrusts his hands in his pockets, and walks angrily across to the window.*)

UNDERSHAFT: (*With a touch of brutality.*) The government of your country! I am the government of your country: I, and Lazarus. Do you suppose that you and half a dozen ama- 345 teurs like you, sitting in a row in that foolish gabble shop, can govern Undershaft and Lazarus? No, my friend: you will do what pays us. You will make war when it suits us, and keep peace when it doesnt. You will find out that trade requires certain measures when we have decided on those 350 measures. When I want anything to keep my dividends up, you will discover that my want is a national need. When other people want something to keep my dividends down, you will call out the police and military. And in return you shall have the support and applause of my newspapers, and 355 the delight of imagining that you are a great statesman. Government of your country! Be off with you, my boy, and play with your caucuses and leading articles and historic parties and great leaders and burning questions and the rest of your toys. *I* am going back to my counting- 360 house to pay the piper and call the tune.

STEPHEN: (*Actually smiling, and putting his hand on his father's shoulder with indulgent patronage.*) Really, my dear father, it is impossible to be angry with you. You dont know how absurd all this sounds to me. You are very properly proud 365 of having been industrious enough to make money; and it is greatly to your credit that you have made so much of it. But it has kept you in circles where you are valued for your money and deferred to for it, instead of in the doubtless very old-fashioned and behind-the-times public 370 school and university where I formed my habits of mind. It is natural for you to think that money governs England; but you must allow me to think I know better.

UNDERSHAFT: And what does govern England, pray?

STEPHEN: Character, father, character. 375

UNDERSHAFT: Whose character? Yours or mine?

STEPHEN: Neither yours nor mine, father, but the best elements in the English national character.

UNDERSHAFT: Stephen: Ive found your profession for you. Youre a born journalist. I'll start you with a high-toned 380 weekly review. There!

(*Before* STEPHEN *can reply,* SARAH, BARBARA, LOMAX, *and* CUSINS *come in ready for walking.* BARBARA *crosses the room to the window and looks out.* CUSINS *drifts amiably to the armchair.* LOMAX *remains near the door, whilst* SARAH *comes to her mother.*)

(STEPHEN *goes to the smaller writing table and busies himself with his letters.*)

SARAH: Go and get ready, mamma: the carriage is waiting. (LADY BRITOMART *leaves the room.*)

UNDERSHAFT: (*To* SARAH.) Good day, my dear. Good afternoon, Mr Lomax. 385

LOMAX: (*Vaguely.*) Ahdedoo.

UNDERSHAFT: (*To* CUSINS.) Quite well after last night, Euripides, eh?

CUSINS: As well as can be expected.

390 UNDERSHAFT: Thats right. (*To* BARBARA.) So you are coming to see my death and devastation factory, Barbara?

BARBARA: (*At the window.*) You came yesterday to see my salvation factory. I promised you a return visit.

LOMAX: (*Coming forward between* SARAH *and* UNDERSHAFT.)
395   Youll find it awfully interesting. Ive been through the Woolwich Arsenal; and it gives you a ripping feeling of security, you know, to think of the lot of beggars we could kill if it came to fighting. (*To* UNDERSHAFT, *with sudden solemnity.*) Still, it must be rather an awful reflection for
400   you, from the religious point of view as it were. Youre getting on, you know, and all that.

SARAH: You dont mind Cholly's imbecility, papa, do you?

LOMAX: (*Much taken aback.*) Oh I say!

UNDERSHAFT: Mr Lomax looks at the matter in a very proper
405   spirit, my dear.

LOMAX: Just so. Thats all I meant, I assure you.

SARAH: Are you coming, Stephen?

STEPHEN: Well, I am rather busy—er—(*Magnanimously.*) Oh well, yes: I'll come. That is, if there is room for me.

410 UNDERSHAFT: I can take two with me in a little motor I am experimenting with for field use. You wont mind its being rather unfashionable. It's not painted yet; but it's bullet proof.

LOMAX: (*Appalled at the prospect of confronting Wilton Crescent in*
415   *an unpainted motor.*) Oh I say!

SARAH: The carriage for me, thank you. Barbara doesnt mind what she's seen in.

LOMAX: I say, Dolly, old chap: do you really mind the car being a guy? Because of course if you do I'll go in it. Still—

420 CUSINS: I prefer it.

LOMAX: Thanks awfully, old man. Come, my ownest. (*He hurries out to secure his seat in the carriage.* SARAH *follows him.*)

CUSINS: (*Moodily walking across to* LADY BRITOMART's *writing table.*) Why are we two coming to this Works Department
425   of Hell? that is what I ask myself.

BARBARA: I have always thought of it as a sort of pit where lost creatures with blackened faces stirred up smoky fires and were driven and tormented by my father? Is it like that, dad?

UNDERSHAFT: (*Scandalized.*) My dear! It is a spotlessly clean
430   and beautiful hillside town.

CUSINS: With a Methodist chapel? Oh do say theres a Methodist chapel.

UNDERSHAFT: There are two: a Primitive one and a sophisticated one. There is even an Ethical Society; but it is not
435   much patronized, as my men are all strongly religious. In the High Explosives Sheds they object to the presence of Agnostics as unsafe.

CUSINS: And yet they dont object to you!

BARBARA: Do they obey all your orders?

440 UNDERSHAFT: I never give them any orders. When I speak to one of them it is 'Well, Jones, is the baby doing well? and has Mrs Jones made a good recovery?' 'Nicely, thank you, sir.' And thats all.

CUSINS: But Jones has to be kept in order. How do you maintain
445   tain discipline among your men?

UNDERSHAFT: I dont. They do. You see, the one thing Jones wont stand is any rebellion from the man under him, or any

assertion of social equality between the wife of the man with 4 shillings a week less than himself, and Mrs Jones! Of course they all rebel against me, theoretically. Practically, 450 every man of them keeps the man just below him in his place. I never meddle with them. I never bully them. I dont even bully Lazarus. I say that certain things are to be done; but I dont order anybody to do them. I dont say, mind you, that there is no ordering about and snubbing and even bul- 455 lying. The men snub the boys and order them about; the carmen snub the sweepers; the artisans snub the unskilled laborers; the foremen drive and bully both the laborers and artisans; the assistant engineers find fault with the foremen; the chief engineers drop on the assistants; the departmen- 460 tal managers worry the chiefs; and the clerks have tall hats and hymnbooks and keep up the social tone by refusing to associate on equal terms with anybody. The result is a colossal profit, which comes to me.

CUSINS: (*Revolted.*) You really are a—well, what I was saying 465 yesterday.

BARBARA: What was he saying yesterday?

UNDERSHAFT: Never mind, my dear. He thinks I have made you unhappy. Have I?

BARBARA: Do you think I can be happy in this vulgar silly 470 dress? I! who have worn the uniform. Do you understand what you have done to me? Yesterday I had a man's soul in my hand. I set him in the way of life with his face to salvation. But when we took your money he turned back to drunkenness and derision. (*With intense conviction.*) I 475 will never forgive you that. If I had a child, and you destroyed its body with your explosives—if you murdered Dolly with your horrible guns—I could forgive you if my forgiveness would open the gates of heaven to you. But to take a human soul from me, and turn it into the soul of a 480 wolf! that is worse than any murder.

UNDERSHAFT: Does my daughter despair so easily? Can you strike a man to the heart and leave no mark on him?

BARBARA: (*Her face lighting up.*) Oh, you are right: he can never be lost now: where was my faith? 485

CUSINS: Oh, clever clever devil!

BARBARA: You may be a devil; but God speaks through you sometimes. (*She takes her father's hands and kisses them.*) You have given me back my happiness: I feel it deep down now, though my spirit is troubled. 490

UNDERSHAFT: You have learnt something. That always feels at first as if you had lost something.

BARBARA: Well, take me to the factory of death; and let me learn something more. There must be some truth or other behind all this frightful irony. Come, Dolly. (*She goes out.*) 495

CUSINS: My guardian angel! (*To* UNDERSHAFT.) Avaunt! (*He follows* BARBARA.)

STEPHEN: (*Quietly, at the writing table.*) You must not mind Cusins, father. He is a very amiable good fellow; but he is a Greek scholar and naturally a little eccentric. 500

UNDERSHAFT: Ah, quite so. Thank you, Stephen. Thank you. (*He goes out.*)

(STEPHEN *smiles patronizingly; buttons his coat responsibly; and crosses the room to the door.* LADY BRITOMART, *dressed for out-of-doors, opens it before he reaches it. She looks round for others; looks at* STEPHEN; *and turns to go without a word.*)

STEPHEN: (*Embarrassed.*) Mother—

505 LADY BRITOMART: Dont be apologetic, Stephen. And dont forget that you have outgrown your mother. (*She goes out.*)

(*Perivale St Andrews lies between two Middlesex hills, half climbing the northern one. It is an almost smokeless town of white walls, roofs of narrow green slates or red tiles, tall trees, domes, campaniles, and slender chimney shafts, beautifully situated and beautiful in itself. The best view of it is obtained from the crest of a slope about half a mile to the east, where the high explosives are dealt with. The foundry lies hidden in the depths between, the tops of its chimneys sprouting like huge skittles into the middle distance. Across the crest runs an emplacement of concrete, with a firestep, and a parapet which suggests a fortification, because there is a huge cannon of the obsolete Woolwich Infant pattern peering across it at the town. The cannon is mounted on an experimental gun carriage: possibly the original model of the Undershaft disappearing rampart gun alluded to by STEPHEN. The firestep, being a convenient place to sit, is furnished here and there with straw disc cushions; and at one place there is the additional luxury of a fur rug.*)

(*BARBARA is standing on the firestep, looking over the parapet towards the town. On her right is the cannon; on her left the end of a shed raised on piles, with a ladder of three or four steps up to the door, which opens outwards and has a little wooden landing at the threshold, with a fire bucket in the corner of the landing. Several dummy soldiers more or less mutilated, with straw protruding from their gashes, have been shoved out of the way under the landing. A few others are nearly upright against the shed; and one has fallen forward and lies, like a grotesque corpse, on the emplacement. The parapet stops short of the shed, leaving a gap which is the beginning of the path down the hill through the foundry to the town. The rug is on the firestep near this gap. Down on the emplacement behind the cannon is a trolley carrying a huge conical bombshell with a red band painted on it. Further to the right is the door of an office, which, like the sheds, is of the lightest possible construction.*)

(*CUSINS arrives by the path from the town.*)

BARBARA: Well?

CUSINS: Not a ray of hope. Everything perfect! wonderful! real! It only needs a cathedral to be a heavenly city instead of a hellish one.

510 BARBARA: Have you found out whether they have done anything for old Peter Shirley?

CUSINS: They have found him a job as gatekeeper and timekeeper. He's frightfully miserable. He calls the timekeeping brainwork, and says he isnt used to it; and his gate

515 lodge is so splendid that he's ashamed to use the rooms, and skulks in the scullery.

BARBARA: Poor Peter!

(*STEPHEN arrives from the town. He carries a fieldglass.*)

STEPHEN: (*Enthusiastically.*) Have you two seen the place? Why did you leave us?

520 CUSINS: I wanted to see everything I was not intended to see; and Barbara wanted to make the men talk.

STEPHEN: Have you found anything discreditable?

CUSINS: No. They call him Dandy Andy and are proud of his being a cunning old rascal; but it's all horribly, frightfully,

525 immorally, unanswerably perfect.

(SARAH *arrives.*)

SARAH: Heavens! what a place! (*She crosses to the trolley.*) Did you see the nursing home!? (*She sits down on the shell.*)

STEPHEN: Did you see the libraries and schools!?

SARAH: Did you see the ball room and the banqueting chamber in the Town Hall!?   530

STEPHEN: Have you gone into the insurance fund, the pension fund, the building society, the various applications of cooperation!?

(UNDERSHAFT *comes from the office, with a sheaf of telegrams in his hand.*)

UNDERSHAFT: Well, have you seen everything? I'm sorry I was called away. (*Indicating the telegrams.*) Good news from   535 Manchuria.

STEPHEN: Another Japanese victory?

UNDERSHAFT: Oh, I dont know. Which side wins does not concern us here. No: the good news is that the aerial battleship is a tremendous success. At the first trial it has   540 wiped out a fort with three hundred soldiers in it.

CUSINS: (*From the platform.*) Dummy soldiers?

UNDERSHAFT: (*Striding across to STEPHEN and kicking the prostrate dummy brutally out of his way.*) No: the real thing.

(CUSINS *and* BARBARA *exchange glances. Then* CUSINS *sits on the step and buries his face in his hands.* BARBARA *gravely lays her hand on his shoulder. He looks up at her in whimsical desperation.*)

UNDERSHAFT: Well, Stephen, what do you think of the place?   545

STEPHEN: Oh, magnificent. A perfect triumph of modern industry. Frankly, my dear father, I have been a fool: I had no idea of what it all meant: of the wonderful forethought, the power of organization, the administrative capacity, the financial genius, the colossal capital it represents. I have   550 been repeating to myself as I came through your streets 'Peace hath her victories no less renowned than War.' I have only one misgiving about it all.

UNDERSHAFT: Out with it.

STEPHEN: Well, I cannot help thinking that all this provision   555 for every want of your workmen may sap their independence and weaken their sense of responsibility. And greatly as we enjoyed our tea at that splendid restaurant— how they gave us all that luxury and cake and jam and cream for threepence I really cannot imagine!—still you   560 must remember that restaurants break up home life. Look at the continent, for instance! Are you sure so much pampering is really good for the men's characters?

UNDERSHAFT: Well you see, my dear boy, when you are organizing civilization you have to make up your mind   565 whether trouble and anxiety are good things or not. If you decide that they are, then, I take it, you simply dont organize civilization; and there you are, with trouble and anxiety enough to make us all angels! But if you decide the other way, you may as well go through with it. However,   570 Stephen, our characters are safe here. A sufficient dose of anxiety is always provided by the fact that we may be blown to smithereens at any moment.

SARAH: By the way, papa, where do you make the explosives?

575 UNDERSHAFT: In separate little sheds, like that one. When one of them blows up, it costs very little; and only the people quite close to it are killed.

(STEPHEN, *who is quite close to it, looks at it rather scaredly, and moves away quickly to the cannon. At the same moment the door of the shed is thrown abruptly open; and a foreman in overalls and list slippers comes out on the little landing and holds the door for* LOMAX, *who appears in the doorway.*)

LOMAX: (*With studied coolness.*) My good fellow: you neednt get into a state of nerves. Nothing's going to happen to
580 you; and I suppose it wouldnt be the end of the world if anything did. A little bit of British pluck is what you want, old chap. (*He descends and strolls across to* SARAH.)
UNDERSHAFT: (*To the foreman.*) Anything wrong, Bilton?
BILTON: (*With ironic calm.*) Gentleman walked into the high
585 explosives shed and lit a cigaret, sir: thats all.
UNDERSHAFT: Ah, quite so. (*Going over to* LOMAX.) Do you happen to remember what you did with the match?
LOMAX: Oh come! I'm not a fool. I took jolly good care to blow it out before I chucked it away.
590 BILTON: The top of it was red hot inside, sir.
LOMAX: Well, suppose it was! I didnt chuck it into any of your messes.
UNDERSHAFT: Think no more of it, Mr Lomax. By the way, would you mind lending me your matches.
595 LOMAX: (*Offering his box.*) Certainly.
UNDERSHAFT: Thanks. (*He pockets the matches.*)
LOMAX: (*Lecturing to the company generally.*) You know, these high explosives dont go off like gunpowder, except when theyre in a gun. When theyre spread loose, you can put a
600 match to them without the least risk: they just burn quietly like a bit of paper. (*Warming to the scientific interest of the subject.*) Did you know that, Undershaft? Have you ever tried?
UNDERSHAFT: Not on a large scale, Mr Lomax. Bilton will
605 give you a sample of gun cotton when you are leaving if you ask him. You can experiment with it at home. (BILTON *looks puzzled.*)
SARAH: Bilton will do nothing of the sort, papa. I suppose it's your business to blow up the Russians and Japs; but you
610 might really stop short of blowing up poor Cholly. (BILTON *gives it up and retires into the shed.*)
LOMAX: My ownest, there is no danger. (*He sits beside her on the shell.*)

(LADY BRITOMART *arrives from the town with a bouquet.*)

LADY BRITOMART: (*Impetuously.*) Andrew: you shouldnt have
615 let me see this place.
UNDERSHAFT: Why, my dear?
LADY BRITOMART: Never mind why: you shouldnt have: thats all. To think of all that (*Indicating the town.*) being yours! and that you have kept it to yourself all these years!
620 UNDERSHAFT: It does not belong to me. I belong to it. It is the Undershaft inheritance.
LADY BRITOMART: It is not. Your ridiculous cannons and that noisy banging foundry may be the Undershaft inheritance; but all that plate and linen, all that furniture and those
625 houses and orchards and gardens belong to us. They be-

long to me: they are not a man's business. I wont give them up. You must be out of your senses to throw them all away; and if you persist in such folly, I will call in a doctor.
UNDERSHAFT: (*Stooping to smell the bouquet.*) Where did you get the flowers, my dear? 630
LADY BRITOMART: Your men presented them to me in your William Morris Labor Church.
CUSINS: Oh! It needed only that. A Labor Church! (*He mounts the firestep distractedly, and leans with his elbows on the parapet, turning his back to them.*) 635
LADY BRITOMART: Yes, with Morris's words in mosaic letters ten feet high round the dome. NO MAN IS GOOD ENOUGH TO BE ANOTHER MAN'S MASTER. The cynicism of it!
UNDERSHAFT: It shocked the men at first, I am afraid. But now they take no more notice of it than of the ten com- 640 mandments in church.
LADY BRITOMART: Andrew: you are trying to put me off the subject of the inheritance by profane jokes. Well, you shant. I dont ask it any longer for Stephen: he has inherited far too much of your perversity to be fit for it. But Barbara has rights 645 as well as Stephen. Why should not Adolphus succeed to the inheritance? I could manage the town for him; and he can look after the cannons, if they are really necessary.
UNDERSHAFT: I should ask nothing better if Adolphus were a foundling. He is exactly the sort of new blood that is 650 wanted in English business. But he's not a foundling; and theres an end of it. (*He makes for the office door.*)
CUSINS: (*Turning to them.*) Not quite. (*They all turn and stare at him.*) I think—Mind! I am not committing myself in any way as to my future course—but I think the foundling dif- 655 ficulty can be got over. (*He jumps down to the emplacement.*)
UNDERSHAFT: (*Coming back to him.*) What do you mean?
CUSINS: Well, I have something to say which is in the nature of a confession.
SARAH: 660
LADY BRITOMART:
BARBARA: } Confession!
STEPHEN:
LOMAX: Oh I say!
CUSINS: Yes, a confession. Listen, all. Until I met Barbara I 665 thought myself in the main an honorable, truthful man, because I wanted the approval of my conscience more than I wanted anything else. But the moment I saw Barbara, I wanted her far more than the approval of my conscience. 670
LADY BRITOMART: Adolphus!
CUSINS: It is true. You accused me yourself, Lady Brit, of joining the Army to worship Barbara; and so I did. She bought my soul like a flower at a street corner; but she bought it for herself. 675
UNDERSHAFT: What! Not for Dionysos or another?
CUSINS: Dionysos and all the others are in herself. I adored what was divine in her, and was therefore a true worshipper. But I was romantic about her too. I thought she was a woman of the people, and that a marriage with a professor of Greek 680 would be far beyond the wildest social ambitions of her rank.
LADY BRITOMART: Adolphus!!
LOMAX: Oh I say!!!
CUSINS: When I learnt the horrible truth—
LADY BRITOMART: What do you mean by the horrible truth, 685 pray?

CUSINS: That she was enormously rich; that her grandfather was an earl; that her father was the Prince of Darkness—

UNDERSHAFT: Chut!

690 CUSINS: —and that I was only an adventurer trying to catch a rich wife, then I stooped to deceive her about my birth.

BARBARA: (*Rising.*) Dolly!

LADY BRITOMART: Your birth! Now Adolphus, dont dare to make up a wicked story for the sake of these wretched

695 cannons. Remember: I have seen photographs of your parents; and the Agent General for South Western Australia knows them personally and has assured me that they are most respectable married people.

CUSINS: So they are in Australia; but here they are outcasts.

700 Their marriage is legal in Australia, but not in England. My mother is my father's deceased wife's sister; and in this island I am consequently a foundling. (*Sensation.*)

BARBARA: Silly! (*She climbs to the cannon, and leans, listening, in the angle it makes with the parapet.*)

705 CUSINS: Is the subterfuge good enough, Machiavelli?

UNDERSHAFT: (*Thoughtfully.*) Biddy: this may be a way out of the difficulty.

LADY BRITOMART: Stuff! A man cant make cannons any the better for being his own cousin instead of his proper self

710 (*She sits down on the rug with a bounce that expresses her downright contempt for their casuistry.*)

UNDERSHAFT: (*To* CUSINS.) You are an educated man. That is against the tradition.

CUSINS: Once in ten thousand times it happens that the

715 schoolboy is a born master of what they try to teach him. Greek has not destroyed my mind: it has nourished it. Besides, I did not learn it at an English public school.

UNDERSHAFT: Hm! Well, I cannot afford to be too particular: you have cornered the foundling market. Let it pass. You

720 are eligible, Euripides: you are eligible.

BARBARA: Dolly: yesterday morning, when Stephen told us all about the tradition, you became very silent; and you have been strange and excited ever since. Were you thinking of your birth then?

725 CUSINS: When the finger of Destiny suddenly points at a man in the middle of his breakfast, it makes him thoughtful.

UNDERSHAFT: Aha! You have had your eye on the business, my young friend, have you?

CUSINS: Take care! There is an abyss of moral horror between

730 me and your accursed aerial battleships.

UNDERSHAFT: Never mind the abyss for the present. Let us settle the practical details and leave your final decision open. You know that you will have to change your name. Do you object to that?

735 CUSINS: Would any man named Adolphus—any man called Dolly!—object to be called something else?

UNDERSHAFT: Good. Now, as to money! I propose to treat you handsomely from the beginning. You shall start at a thousand a year.

740 CUSINS: (*With sudden heat, his spectacles twinkling with mischief.*) A thousand! You dare offer a miserable thousand to the son-in-law of a millionaire! No, by Heavens, Machiavelli! you shall not cheat me. You cannot do without me; and I can do without you. I must have two thousand five hun-

745 dred a year for two years. At the end of that time, if I am a failure, I go. But if I am a success, and stay on, you must give me the other five thousand.

UNDERSHAFT: What other five thousand?

CUSINS: To make the two years up to five thousand a year. The two thousand five hundred is only half pay in case I 750 should turn out a failure. The third year I must have ten per cent on the profits.

UNDERSHAFT: (*Taken aback.*) Ten per cent! Why, man, do you know what my profits are?

CUSINS: Enormous, I hope: otherwise I shall require twenty- 755 five per cent.

UNDERSHAFT: But, Mr Cusins, this is a serious matter of business. You are not bringing any capital into the concern.

CUSINS: What! no capital! Is my mastery of Greek no capital? Is my access to the subtlest thought, the loftiest poetry yet 760 attained by humanity, no capital? My character! my intellect! my life! my career! what Barbara calls my soul! are these no capital? Say another word; and I double my salary.

UNDERSHAFT: Be reasonable—

CUSINS: (*Peremptorily.*) Mr Undershaft: you have my terms. 765 Take them or leave them.

UNDERSHAFT: (*Recovering himself.*) Very well. I note your terms; and I offer you half.

CUSINS: (*Disgusted.*) Half!

UNDERSHAFT: (*Firmly.*) Half. 770

CUSINS: You call yourself a gentleman; and you offer me half!!

UNDERSHAFT: I do not call myself a gentleman; but I offer you half.

CUSINS: This to your future partner! your successor! your son-in-law! 775

BARBARA: You are selling your own soul, Dolly, not mine. Leave me out of the bargain, please.

UNDERSHAFT: Come! I will go a step further for Barbara's sake. I will give you three fifths; but that is my last word.

CUSINS: Done! 780

LOMAX: Done in the eye! Why, *I* get only eight hundred, you know.

CUSINS: By the way, Mac, I am a classical scholar, not an arithmetical one. Is three fifths more than half or less?

UNDERSHAFT: More, of course. 785

CUSINS: I would have taken two hundred and fifty. How you can succeed in business when you are willing to pay all that money to a University don who is obviously not worth a junior clerk's wages!—well! What will Lazarus say?

UNDERSHAFT: Lazarus is a gentle romantic Jew who cares for 790 nothing but string quartets and stalls at fashionable theatres. He will be blamed for your rapacity in money matters, poor fellow! as he has hitherto been blamed for mine. You are a shark of the first order, Euripides. So much the better for the firm! 795

BARBARA: Is the bargain closed, Dolly? Does your soul belong to him now?

CUSINS: No: the price is settled: that is all. The real tug of war is still to come. What about the moral question?

LADY BRITOMART: There is no moral question in the matter 800 at all, Adolphus. You must simply sell cannons and weapons to people whose cause is right and just, and refuse them to foreigners and criminals.

UNDERSHAFT: (*Determinedly.*) No: none of that. You must keep the true faith of an Armorer, or you dont come in here. 805

CUSINS: What on earth is the true faith of an Armorer?

UNDERSHAFT: To give arms to all men who offer an honest price for them, without respect of persons or principles: to

810 aristocrat and republican, to Nihilist and Tsar, to Capitalist and Socialist, to Protestant and Catholic, to burglar and policeman, to black man, white man and yellow man, to all sorts and conditions, all nationalities, all faiths, all follies, all causes and all crimes. The first Undershaft wrote up in his shop IF GOD GAVE THE HAND, LET NOT MAN WITHHOLD THE

815 SWORD. The second wrote up ALL HAVE THE RIGHT TO FIGHT: NONE HAVE THE RIGHT TO JUDGE. The third wrote up TO MAN THE WEAPON: TO HEAVEN THE VICTORY. The fourth had no literary turn; so he did not write up anything; but he sold cannons to Napoleon under the nose of George the

820 Third. The fifth wrote up PEACE SHALL NOT PREVAIL SAVE WITH A SWORD IN HER HAND. The sixth, my master, was the best of all. He wrote up NOTHING IS EVER DONE IN THIS WORLD UNTIL MEN ARE PREPARED TO KILL ONE ANOTHER IF IT IS NOT DONE. After that, there was nothing left for the

825 seventh to say. So he wrote up, simply, UNASHAMED.

CUSINS: My good Machiavelli, I shall certainly write something up on the wall; only, as I shall write it in Greek, you wont be able to read it. But as to your Armorer's faith, if I take my neck out of the noose of my own morality I am not

830 going to put it into the noose of yours. I shall sell cannons to whom I please and refuse them to whom I please. So there!

UNDERSHAFT: From the moment when you become Andrew Undershaft, you will never do as you please again. Dont come here lusting for power, young man.

835 CUSINS: If power were my aim I should not come here for it. You have no power.

UNDERSHAFT: None of my own, certainly.

CUSINS: I have more power than you, more will. You do not drive this place: it drives you. And what drives the place?

840 UNDERSHAFT: (*Enigmatically.*) A will of which I am a part.

BARBARA: (*Startled.*) Father! Do you know what you are saying; or are you laying a snare for my soul?

CUSINS: Dont listen to his metaphysics, Barbara. The place is driven by the most rascally part of society, the money

845 hunters, the pleasure hunters, the military promotion hunters; and he is their slave.

UNDERSHAFT: Not necessarily. Remember the Armorer's Faith. I will take an order from a good man as cheerfully as from a bad one. If you good people prefer preaching and

850 shirking to buying my weapons and fighting the rascals, dont blame me. I can make cannons: I cannot make courage and conviction. Bah! you tire me, Euripides, with your morality mongering. Ask Barbara: she understands. (*He suddenly reaches up and takes* BARBARA'*s hands, looking powerfully*

855 *into her eyes.*) Tell him, my love, what power really means.

BARBARA: (*Hypnotized.*) Before I joined the Salvation Army, I was in my own power; and the consequence was that I never knew what to do with myself. When I joined it, I had not time enough for all the things I had to do.

860 UNDERSHAFT: (*Approvingly.*) Just so. And why was that, do you suppose?

BARBARA: Yesterday I should have said, because I was in the power of God. (*She resumes her self-possession, withdrawing her hands from his with a power equal to his own.*) But you

865 came and shewed me that I was in the power of Bodger and Undershaft. Today I feel—oh! how can I put it into words? Sarah: do you remember the earthquake at Cannes, when we were little children?—how little the surprise of the first shock mattered compared to the dread

870 and horror of waiting for the second? That is how I feel in this place today. I stood on the rock I thought eternal; and without a word of warning it reeled and crumbled under me. I was safe with an infinite wisdom watching me, an army marching to Salvation with me; and in a

875 moment, at a stroke of your pen in a cheque book, I stood alone; and the heavens were empty. That was the first shock of the earthquake: I am waiting for the second.

UNDERSHAFT: Come, come, my daughter! dont make too much of your little tinpot tragedy. What do we do here when we spend years of work and thought and thousands

880 of pounds of solid cash on a new gun or an aerial battleship that turns out just a hairsbreadth wrong after all? Scrap it. Scrap it without wasting another hour or another pound on it. Well, you have made for yourself something that you call a morality or a religion or what not. It doesnt fit the

885 facts. Well, scrap it. Scrap it and get one that does fit. That is what is wrong with the world at present. It scraps its obsolete steam engines and dynamos; but it wont scrap its old prejudices and its old moralities and its old religions and its old political constitutions. Whats the result? In machinery

890 it does very well; but in morals and religion and politics it is working at a loss that brings it nearer bankruptcy every year. Dont persist in that folly. If your old religion broke down yesterday, get a newer and a better one for tomorrow.

BARBARA: Oh how gladly I would take a better one to my soul!

895 But you offer me a worse one. (*Turning on him with sudden vehemence.*) Justify yourself: shew me some light through the darkness of this dreadful place, with its beautifully clean workshops, and respectable workmen, and model homes.

UNDERSHAFT: Cleanliness and respectability do not need jus-

900 tification, Barbara: they justify themselves. I see no darkness here, no dreadfulness. In your Salvation shelter I saw poverty, misery, cold and hunger. You gave them bread and treacle and dreams of heaven. I give from thirty shillings a week to twelve thousand a year. They find their

905 own dreams; but I look after the drainage.

BARBARA: And their souls?

UNDERSHAFT: I save their souls just as I saved yours.

BARBARA: (*Revolted.*) You saved my soul! What do you mean?

UNDERSHAFT: I fed you and clothed you and housed you. I

910 took care that you should have money enough to live handsomely—more than enough; so that you could be wasteful, careless, generous. That saved your soul from the seven deadly sins.

BARBARA: (*Bewildered.*) The seven deadly sins!

915 UNDERSHAFT: Yes, the deadly seven. (*Counting on his fingers.*) Food, clothing, firing, rent, taxes, respectability and children. Nothing can lift those seven millstones from Man's neck but money; and the spirit cannot soar until the millstones are lifted. I lifted them from your spirit. I enabled

920 Barbara to become Major Barbara; and I saved her from the crime of poverty.

CUSINS: Do you call poverty a crime?

UNDERSHAFT: The worst of crimes. All the other crimes are virtues beside it: all the other dishonors are chivalry itself by

925 comparison. Poverty blights whole cities; spreads horrible pestilences; strikes dead the very souls of all who come within sight, sound, or smell of it. What you call crime is nothing: a murder here and a theft there, a blow now and a curse then: what do they matter? they are only the accidents 930

and illnesses of life: there are not fifty genuine professional criminals in London. But there are millions of poor people, abject people, dirty people, ill fed, ill clothed people. They poison us morally and physically: they kill the happiness of 935 society: they force us to do away with our own liberties and to organize unnatural cruelties for fear they should rise against us and drag us down into their abyss. Only fools fear crime: we all fear poverty. Pah! (*Turning on* BARBARA.) you talk of your halfsaved ruffian in West Ham: you accuse me of 940 dragging his soul back to perdition. Well, bring him to me here; and I will drag his soul back again to salvation for you. Not by words and dreams; but by thirty-eight shillings a week, a sound house in a handsome street, and a permanent job. In three weeks he will have a fancy waistcoat; in three 945 months a tall hat and a chapel sitting; before the end of the year he will shake hands with a duchess at a Primrose League meeting, and join the Conservative Party.

BARBARA: And will he be the better for that?

UNDERSHAFT: You know he will. Dont be a hypocrite, Barbara. 950 He will be better fed, better housed, better clothed, better behaved; and his children will be pounds heavier and bigger. That will be better than an American cloth mattress in a shelter, chopping firewood, eating bread and treacle, and being forced to kneel down from time to time to thank heaven 955 for it: knee drill, I think you call it. It is cheap work converting starving men with a Bible in one hand and a slice of bread in the other. I will undertake to convert West Ham to Mahometanism on the same terms. Try your hand on my men: their souls are hungry because their bodies are full.

960 BARBARA: And leave the east end to starve?

UNDERSHAFT: (*His energetic tone dropping into one of bitter and brooding remembrance.*) I was an east ender. I moralized and starved until one day I swore that I would be a full-fed free man at all costs; that nothing should stop me except 965 a bullet, neither reason nor morals nor the lives of other men. I said 'Thou shalt starve ere I starve'; and with that word I became free and great. I was a dangerous man until I had my will: now I am a useful, beneficent, kindly person. That is the history of most self-made millionaires, 970 I fancy. When it is the history of every Englishman we shall have an England worth living in.

LADY BRITOMART: Stop making speeches, Andrew. This is not the place for them.

UNDERSHAFT: (*Punctured.*) My dear: I have no other means of 975 conveying my ideas.

LADY BRITOMART: Your ideas are nonsense. You got on because you were selfish and unscrupulous.

UNDERSHAFT: Not at all. I had the strongest scruples about poverty and starvation. Your moralists are quite unscrupu- 980 lous about both: they make virtues of them. I had rather be a thief than a pauper. I had rather be a murderer than a slave. I dont want to be either; but if you force the alternative on me, then, by Heaven, I'll choose the braver and more moral one. I hate poverty and slavery worse than any other crimes 985 whatsoever. And let me tell you this. Poverty and slavery have stood up for centuries to your sermons and leading articles: they will not stand up to my machine guns. Dont preach at them: dont reason with them. Kill them.

BARBARA: Killing. Is that your remedy for everything?

990 UNDERSHAFT: It is the final test of conviction, the only lever strong enough to overturn a social system, the only way of saying Must. Let six hundred and seventy fools loose in the streets; and three policemen can scatter them. But huddle them together in a certain house in Westminster; and let them go through certain ceremonies and call themselves 995 certain names until at last they get the courage to kill; and your six hundred and seventy fools become a government. Your pious mob fills up ballot papers and imagines it is governing its masters; but the ballot paper that really governs is the paper that has a bullet wrapped up in it. 1000

CUSINS: That is perhaps why, like most intelligent people, I never vote.

UNDERSHAFT: Vote! Bah! When you vote, you only change the names of the cabinet. When you shoot, you pull down governments, inaugurate new epochs, abolish old orders 1005 and set up new. Is that historically true, Mr Learned Man, or is it not?

CUSINS: It is historically true. I loathe having to admit it. I repudiate your sentiments. I abhor your nature. I defy you in every possible way. Still, it is true. But it ought not to be true. 1010

UNDERSHAFT: Ought! ought! ought! ought! ought! Are you going to spend your life saying ought, like the rest of our moralists? Turn your oughts into shalls, man. Come and make explosives with me. Whatever can blow men up can blow society up. The history of the world is the history of 1015 those who had courage enough to embrace this truth. Have you the courage to embrace it, Barbara?

LADY BRITOMART: Barbara: I positively forbid you to listen to your father's abominable wickedness. And you, Adolphus, ought to know better than to go about saying that wrong 1020 things are true. What does it matter whether they are true if they are wrong?

UNDERSHAFT: What does it matter whether they are wrong if they are true?

LADY BRITOMART: (*Rising.*) Children: come home instantly. 1025 Andrew: I am exceedingly sorry I allowed you to call on us. You are wickeder than ever. Come at once.

BARBARA: (*Shaking her head.*) It's no use running away from wicked people, mamma.

LADY BRITOMART: It is every use. It shews your disapproba- 1030 tion of them.

BARBARA: It does not save them.

LADY BRITOMART: I can see that you are going to disobey me. Sarah: are you coming home or are you not?

SARAH: I daresay it's very wicked of papa to make cannons; 1035 but I dont think I shall cut him on that account.

LOMAX: (*Pouring oil on the troubled waters.*) The fact is, you know, there is a certain amount of tosh about this notion of wickedness. It doesnt work. You must look at facts. Not that I would say a word in favor of anything wrong; 1040 but then, you see, all sorts of chaps are always doing all sorts of things; and we have to fit them in somehow, dont you know. What I mean is that you cant go cutting everybody; and thats about what it comes to. (*Their rapt attention to his eloquence makes him nervous.*) Perhaps I dont make 1045 myself clear.

LADY BRITOMART: You are lucidity itself, Charles. Because Andrew is successful and has plenty of money to give to Sarah, you will flatter him and encourage him in his wickedness.

LOMAX: (*Unruffled.*) Well, where the carcase is, there will the 1050 eagles be gathered, dont you know. (*To* UNDERSHAFT.) Eh? What?

UNDERSHAFT: Precisely. By the way, may I call you Charles?

LOMAX: Delighted. Cholly is the usual ticket.

1055 UNDERSHAFT: (*To* LADY BRITOMART.) Biddy—

LADY BRITOMART: (*Violently.*) Dont dare call me Biddy. Charles Lomax: you are a fool. Adolphus Cusins: you are a Jesuit. Stephen: you are a prig. Barbara: you are a lunatic. Andrew: you are a vulgar tradesman. Now you all know
1060 my opinion; and my conscience is clear, at all events. (*She sits down with a vehemence that the rug fortunately softens.*)

UNDERSHAFT: My dear: you are the incarnation of morality. (*She snorts.*) Your conscience is clear and your duty done when you have called everybody names. Come, Euripides! it is getting
1065 late; and we all want to go home. Make up your mind.

CUSINS: Understand this, you old demon—

LADY BRITOMART: Adolphus!

UNDERSHAFT: Let him alone, Biddy. Proceed, Euripides.

CUSINS: You have me in a horrible dilemma. I want Barbara.

1070 UNDERSHAFT: Like all young men, you greatly exaggerate the difference between one young woman and another.

BARBARA: Quite true, Dolly.

CUSINS: I also want to avoid being a rascal.

UNDERSHAFT: (*With biting contempt.*) You lust for personal
1075 righteousness, for self-approval, for what you call a good conscience, for what Barbara calls salvation, for what I call patronizing people who are not so lucky as yourself.

CUSINS: I do not: all the poet in me recoils from being a good man. But there are things in me that I must reckon with. Pity—

1080 UNDERSHAFT: Pity! The scavenger of misery.

CUSINS: Well, love.

UNDERSHAFT: I know. You love the needy and the outcast: you love the oppressed races, the negro, the Indian ryot, the underdog everywhere. Do you love the Japanese? Do
1085 you love the French? Do you love the English?

CUSINS: No. Every true Englishman detests the English. We are the wickedest nation on earth; and our success is a moral horror.

UNDERSHAFT: That is what comes of your gospel of love, is it?

1090 CUSINS: May I not love even my father-in-law?

UNDERSHAFT: Who wants your love, man? By what right do you take the liberty of offering it to me? I will have your due heed and respect, or I will kill you. But your love! Damn your impertinence!

1095 CUSINS: (*Grinning.*) I may not be able to control my affections, Mac.

UNDERSHAFT: You are fencing, Euripides. You are weakening: your grip is slipping. Come! try your last weapon. Pity and love have broken in your hand: forgiveness is still left.

1100 CUSINS: No: forgiveness is a beggar's refuge. I am with you there: we must pay our debts.

UNDERSHAFT: Well said. Come! you will suit me. Remember the words of Plato.

CUSINS: (*Starting.*) Plato! You dare quote Plato to me!

1105 UNDERSHAFT: Plato says, my friend, that society cannot be saved until either the Professors of Greek take to making gunpowder, or else the makers of gunpowder become Professors of Greek.

CUSINS: Oh, tempter, cunning tempter!

1110 UNDERSHAFT: Come! choose, man, choose.

CUSINS: But perhaps Barbara will not marry me if I make the wrong choice.

BARBARA: Perhaps not.

CUSINS: (*Desperately perplexed.*) You hear!

BARBARA: Father: do you love nobody?   1115

UNDERSHAFT: I love my best friend.

LADY BRITOMART: And who is that, pray?

UNDERSHAFT: My bravest enemy. That is the man who keeps me up to the mark.

CUSINS: You know, the creature is really a sort of poet in his 1120 way. Suppose he is a great man, after all!

UNDERSHAFT: Suppose you stop talking and make up your mind, my young friend.

CUSINS: But you are driving me against my nature. I hate war.

UNDERSHAFT: Hatred is the coward's revenge for being in- 1125 timidated. Dare you make war on war? Here are the means: my friend Mr Lomax is sitting on them.

LOMAX: (*Springing up.*) Oh I say! You dont mean that this thing is loaded, do you? My ownest: come off it.

SARAH: (*Sitting placidly on the shell.*) If I am to be blown up, the 1130 more thoroughly it is done the better. Dont fuss, Cholly.

LOMAX: (*To* UNDERSHAFT, *strongly remonstrant.*) Your own daughter, you know!

UNDERSHAFT: So I see! (*To* CUSINS.) Well, my friend, may we expect you here at six tomorrow morning?   1135

CUSINS: (*Firmly.*) Not on any account. I will see the whole establishment blown up with its own dynamite before I will get up at five. My hours are healthy, rational hours: eleven to five.

UNDERSHAFT: Come when you please: before a week you will 1140 come at six and stay until I turn you out for the sake of your health. (*Calling.*) Bilton! (*He turns to* LADY BRITO- MART, *who rises.*) My dear: let us leave these two young people to themselves for a moment. (BILTON *comes from the shed.*) I am going to take you through the gun cotton shed. 1145

BILTON: (*Barring the way.*) You cant take anything explosive in here, sir.

LADY BRITOMART: What do you mean? Are you alluding to me?

BILTON: (*Unmoved.*) No, maam. Mr Undershaft has the other gentleman's matches in his pocket.   1150

LADY BRITOMART: (*Abruptly.*) Oh! I beg your pardon. (*She goes into the shed.*)

UNDERSHAFT: Quite right, Bilton, quite right: here you are. (*He gives* BILTON *the box of matches.*) Come, Stephen. Come, Charles. Bring Sarah. (*He passes into the shed.*)   1155

(BILTON *opens the box and deliberately drops the matches into the fire-bucket.*)

LOMAX: Oh! I say (BILTON *stolidly hands him the empty box.*) Infernal nonsense! Pure scientific ignorance! (*He goes in.*)

SARAH: Am I all right, Bilton?

BILTON: Youll have to put on list slippers, miss: thats all. Weve got em inside. (*She goes in.*)   1160

STEPHEN: (*Very seriously to* CUSINS.) Dolly, old fellow, think. Think before you decide. Do you feel that you are a suf- ficiently practical man? It is a huge undertaking, an enor- mous responsibility. All this mass of business will be Greek to you.   1165

CUSINS: Oh, I think it will be much less difficult than Greek.

STEPHEN: Well, I just want to say this before I leave you to your- selves. Dont let anything I have said about right and wrong prejudice you against this great chance in life. I have satisfied myself that the business is one of the highest character and a 1170 credit to our country. (*Emotionally.*) I am very proud of my father. I—(*Unable to proceed, he presses* CUSINS' *hand and goes hastily into the shed, followed by* BILTON.)

(BARBARA *and* CUSINS, *left alone together, look at one another silently.*)

CUSINS: Barbara: I am going to accept this offer.

1175 BARBARA: I thought you would.

CUSINS: You understand, dont you, that I had to decide without consulting you. If I had thrown the burden of the choice on you, you would sooner or later have despised me for it.

BARBARA: Yes: I did not want you to sell your soul for me any
1180 more than for this inheritance.

CUSINS: It is not the sale of my soul that troubles me: I have sold it too often to care about that. I have sold it for a professorship. I have sold it for an income. I have sold it to escape being imprisoned for refusing to pay taxes for
1185 hangmen's ropes and unjust wars and things that I abhor. What is all human conduct but the daily and hourly sale of our souls for trifles? What I am now selling it for is neither money nor position nor comfort, but for reality and for power.

1190 BARBARA: You know that you will have no power, and that he has none.

CUSINS: I know. It is not for myself alone. I want to make power for the world.

BARBARA: I want to make power for the world too; but it
1195 must be spiritual power.

CUSINS: I think all power is spiritual: these cannons will not go off by themselves. I have tried to make spiritual power by teaching Greek. But the world can never be really touched by a dead language and a dead civilization. The people
1200 must have power; and the people cannot have Greek. Now the power that is made here can be wielded by all men.

BARBARA: Power to burn women's houses down and kill their sons and tear their husbands to pieces.

CUSINS: You cannot have power for good without having
1205 power for evil too. Even mother's milk nourishes murderers as well as heroes. This power which only tears men's bodies to pieces has never been so horribly abused as the intellectual power, the imaginative power, the poetic, religious power that can enslave men's souls. As a teacher of
1210 Greek I gave the intellectual man weapons against the common man. I now want to give the common man weapons against the intellectual man. I love the common people. I want to arm them against the lawyers, the doctors, the priests, the literary men, the professors, the artists,
1215 and the politicians, who, once in authority, are more disastrous and tyrannical than all the fools, rascals, and impostors. I want a power simple enough for common men to use, yet strong enough to force the intellectual oligarchy to use its genius for the general good.

1220 BARBARA: Is there no higher power than that? (*Pointing to the shell.*)

CUSINS: Yes; but that power can destroy the higher powers just as a tiger can destroy a man: therefore Man must master that power first. I admitted this when the Turks and
1225 Greeks were last at war. My best pupil went out to fight for Hellas. My parting gift to him was not a copy of Plato's

Republic, but a revolver and a hundred Undershaft cartridges. The blood of every Turk he shot—if he shot any—is on my head as well as on Undershaft's. That act committed me to this place for ever. Your father's chal- 1230 lenge has beaten me. Dare I make war on war? I must. I will. And now, is it all over between us?

BARBARA: (*Touched by his evident dread of her answer.*) Silly baby Dolly! How could it be!

CUSINS: (*Overjoyed.*) Then you—you—you—Oh for my 1235 drum! (*He flourishes imaginary drumsticks.*)

BARBARA: (*Angered by his levity.*) Take care, Dolly, take care. Oh, if only I could get away from you and from father and from it all! if I could have the wings of a dove and fly away to heaven! 1240

CUSINS: And leave me!

BARBARA: Yes, you, and all the other naughty mischievous children of men. But I cant. I was happy in the Salvation Army for a moment. I escaped from the world into a paradise of enthusiasm and prayer and soul saving; but the 1245 moment our money ran short, it all came back to Bodger: it was he who saved our people: he, and the Prince of Darkness, my papa. Undershaft and Bodger: their hands stretch everywhere: when we feed a starving fellow creature, it is with their bread, because there is no other bread; 1250 when we tend the sick, it is in the hospitals they endow; if we turn from the churches they build, we must kneel on the stones of the streets they pave. As long as that lasts, there is no getting away from them. Turning our backs on Bodger and Undershaft is turning our backs on life. 1255

CUSINS: I thought you were determined to turn your back on the wicked side of life.

BARBARA: There is no wicked side: life is all one. And I never wanted to shirk my share in whatever evil must be endured, whether it be sin or suffering. I wish I could cure 1260 you of middle-class ideas, Dolly.

CUSINS: (*Gasping.*) Middle cl——! A snub! A social snub to me! from the daughter of a foundling!

BARBARA: That is why I have no class, Dolly: I come straight out of the heart of the whole people. If I were middle- 1265 class I should turn my back on my father's business; and we should both live in an artistic drawing room, with you reading the reviews in one corner, and I in the other at the piano, playing Schumann: both very superior persons, and neither of us a bit of use. Sooner than that, I would 1270 sweep out the guncotton shed, or be one of Bodger's barmaids. Do you know what would have happened if you had refused papa's offer?

CUSINS: I wonder!

BARBARA: I should have given you up and married the man 1275 who accepted it. After all, my dear old mother has more sense than any of you. I felt like her when I saw this place—felt that I must have it—that never, never, never could I let it go; only she thought it was the houses and the kitchen ranges and the linen and china, when it was really all the 1280 human souls to be saved: not weak souls in starved bodies, sobbing with gratitude for a scrap of bread and treacle, but fullfed, quarrelsome, snobbish, uppish creatures, all standing on their little rights and dignities, and thinking that my father ought to be greatly obliged to them for making so 1285 much money for him—and so he ought. That is where salvation is really wanted. My father shall never throw it in my teeth again that my converts were bribed with bread. (*She is transfigured.*) I have got rid of the bribe of bread. I have got rid of the bribe of heaven. Let God's work be done for its own sake: the work he had to create us to do because it cannot be done except by living men and women. When I die, let him be in my debt, not I in his; and let me forgive him as becomes a woman of my rank.

CUSINS: Then the way of life lies through the factory of death?

BARBARA: Yes, through the raising of hell to heaven and of man to God, through the unveiling of an eternal light in the Valley of The Shadow. (*Seizing him with both hands.*) Oh, did you think my courage would never come back? did you believe that I was a deserter? that I, who have stood in the streets, and taken my people to my heart, and talked of the holiest and greatest things with them, could ever turn back and chatter foolishly to fashionable people about nothing in a drawing room? Never, never, never, never: Major Barbara will die with the colors. Oh! and I have my dear little Dolly boy still; and he has found me my place and my work. Glory Hallelujah! (*She kisses him.*)

CUSINS: My dearest: consider my delicate health. I cannot stand as much happiness as you can.

BARBARA: Yes: it is not easy work being in love with me, is it? But it's good for you. (*She runs to the shed, and calls, childlike.*) Mamma! Mamma! (BILTON *comes out of the shed, followed by* UNDERSHAFT.) I want Mamma.

UNDERSHAFT: She is taking off her list slippers, dear. (*He passes on to* CUSINS.) Well? What does she say?

CUSINS: She has gone right up into the skies.

LADY BRITOMART: (*Coming from the shed and stopping on the steps, obstructing* SARAH, *who follows with* LOMAX. BARBARA *clutches like a baby at her mother's skirt.*) Barbara: when will you learn to be independent and to act and think for yourself? I know as well as possible what that cry of 'Mamma, Mamma,' means. Always running to me!

SARAH: (*Touching* LADY BRITOMART's *ribs with her finger tips and imitating a bicycle horn.*) Pip! pip!

LADY BRITOMART: (*Highly indignant.*) How dare you say Pip! pip! to me, Sarah? You are both very naughty children. What do you want, Barbara?

BARBARA: I want a house in the village to live in with Dolly. (*Dragging at the skirt.*) Come and tell me which one to take.

UNDERSHAFT: (*To* CUSINS.) Six o'clock tomorrow morning, Euripides.

Luigi Pirandello

Luigi Pirandello (1867–1936) created a diverse and influential body of plays, but his work is now most often associated with the preoccupations of his *Six Characters in Search of an Author.* Like *Six Characters,* Pirandello's plays use **METATHEATER**—roleplaying, plays-within-plays, and a flexible sense of the limits of stage illusion—to examine a highly theatricalized vision of identity. Can any of us be certain of our identity when others hold radically different perspectives on our actions, on who we are?

Pirandello was born in Sicily. He studied language and literature and received his doctoral degree in 1891 from the University of Rome. He then married the daughter of his father's business partner, but the collapse of the business forced him into a career as a writer. He wrote hundreds of stories in the 1890s and in the first decades of the twentieth century, as well as critical and scholarly articles. Pirandello's dramatic interest in the uncertainty of identity can be traced partly to his troubled marriage. His wife suffered a long mental illness and constantly accused him of adultery, despite his careful and constant attention to her health. In a sense, Pirandello was caught between his own sense of himself and the role he was given in this domestic tragedy.

Pirandello's use of the theater as a metaphor for representing this conflict pervades his mature plays: *Six Characters in Search of an Author* (1921; extensively revised 1925), *Enrico IV* (1922), *Each in His Own Way* (1924), and *Tonight We Improvise* (1930). In these plays, the struggle to discover and maintain identity is subjected to the pressure of performance in the world, performance that renders the "self" a kind of fiction. Yet while all behavior seems to verge on mere "acting," undermining our confidence in the authority or reality of a "self," Pirandello's plays do not seem nostalgic for the fixed and determined characters of realistic drama. For in Pirandello's drama, the "self" can also become a kind of prison, a role that traps the individual in a single and confining performance. This is the tragedy that the nameless hero of *Enrico IV* discovers at the close of that play, much as the hero—a famous author like Pirandello himself—of *When One Is Somebody* (1933) is gradually transformed from a man into a statue by the force of his admirers' adulation.

Pirandello became the director of his own company, the Art Theater of Rome, in 1924, and his major plays entered the world repertoire almost immediately. Pirandello's company toured throughout Europe and the Americas, influencing a generation of playwrights with the power of his theatrical conception of modern life. In addition to his short stories and criticism, Pirandello wrote over forty plays. He was awarded the Nobel Prize in 1934 in recognition of his achievement in the modern theater.

SIX CHARACTERS IN SEARCH OF AN AUTHOR

Six Characters seems at first to elaborate a simple and striking idea. What would happen if a cast of dramatic "characters" confronted the actors who gave them life on the stage? Pirandello had toyed with the idea for some time and had sketched it out as a short story. Onstage, though, the story develops a new and challenging dimension, for the confrontation between the Characters and Actors explores the nature of theatrical representation itself. As the play proceeds, it becomes clear that the Actors and Characters represent opposed versions of reality and of the theater, and their contest calls our understanding of the difference between them into question. The Characters need completion. Their melodramatic incest drama has defined each of them in an imprisoning role, as though the climactic moment of their unfinished play—when the Father nearly (or does he?) procures the Stepdaughter in Madame Pace's brothel—was definitive of the identity of each character. That is, Pirandello questions our fundamental notions of how dramatic characters represent the lives of real people, how they represent the rich complexity of a "life" through a short series of a few typical deeds. As the Father asks at one point, who of us would want his or her life summed up in one moment, one act?

The Father tells the story of the Characters standing in profile just upstage in Luigi Pirandello's *Six Characters in Search of an Author*.

The Actors, on the other hand, seem even less real than the Characters. Although the Characters are "fixed" by the design of their common story, that very consistency gives them a coherence and weight that the flighty Actors seem to lack. The Actors are entirely absorbed in the conventions of their lines of business and the petty jealousies of working together; the Leading Actor must always be "acting" the "Leading Actor," whether he is onstage or not, and so on through the rest of the cast. Oddly enough, then, *Six Characters* does not seem to allow us to choose between the Actors or Characters, to decide which kind of representation—narrative or stage performance—provides a more accurate depiction of "reality." The drama of *Six Characters* arises from the unresolved collision between these two perspectives. In the theater, the process of *Six Characters* insistently disorients its audience from the stable categories of "reality" and "illusion," which is perhaps why audiences rioted when the play was first produced. The Characters are, of course, played by actors, while the Actors are clearly "characters" to the audience. Are we, in the audience, any more "real?" Are we outside the play looking in, or has Pirandello managed to place us onstage, showing the audience also to be playing a role in the endless roleplaying of the theater? For this reason, when reading the play we should resist locating its "meanings" in the Father's philosophical monologues, those moments of *pirandellismo* that seem to sum up the play's confrontation between illusion and reality. The play's meaning arises through the entire process of its action, the baffling, inconclusive, and frustrating confrontation between Characters, Actors, and audience, a confrontation that finally prevents the Characters' drama from ever taking the stage.

Students should note that this version of *Six Characters* represents Pirandello's 1925 revision of the play and that it differs in several ways—especially in the play's brilliant finale— from the earlier 1921 version. Also, this translation was first performed in England, where the role of "Producer" is what Americans generally call the "Director."

SIX CHARACTERS IN SEARCH OF AN AUTHOR

Luigi Pirandello

TRANSLATED BY JOHN LINSTRUM

CHARACTERS

THE FATHER	THE BOY (*non-speaking*)
THE MOTHER	THE LITTLE GIRL (*non-speaking*)
THE STEPDAUGHTER	MADAME PACE
THE SON	

ACTORS

THE PRODUCER	THE STAGE MANAGER
THE LEADING ACTRESS	THE PROMPTER
THE LEADING ACTOR	THE PROPERTY MAN
THE SECOND ACTRESS	THE STAGE HAND
THE YOUNG ACTRESS	THE PRODUCER'S SECRETARY
THE JUVENILE LEAD	THE DOORKEEPER
OTHER ACTORS AND	OTHER THEATRE STAFF
ACTRESSES (*a variable number*)	

The action of the play takes place on the stage of a theatre. There are no act or scene divisions, but there are two interruptions: when the PRODUCER *and the* CHARACTERS *go to the office to write the scenario, giving the* ACTORS *a break in rehearsal, and when a* STAGE HAND *lowers the front curtain by mistake.*

References to 'prompt-box,' 'curtains' and 'letting down trees' will need to be altered if they are not appropriate to the theatre where the performance is taking place.

ACT ONE

When the audience enters, the curtain is already up and the stage is just as it would be during the day. There is no set; it is empty, in almost total darkness. This is so that from the beginning the audience will have the feeling of being present, not at a performance of a properly rehearsed play, but at a performance of a play that happens spontaneously. Two small sets of steps, one on the right and one on the left, lead up to the stage from the auditorium. On the stage, the top is off the PROMPTER's box and is lying next to it. Downstage, there is a small table and a chair with arms for the PRODUCER: it is turned with its back to the audience.

Also downstage there are two small tables, one a little bigger than the other, and several chairs, ready for the rehearsal if needed. There are more chairs scattered on both left and right for the ACTORS: to one side at the back and nearly hidden is a piano.

When the houselights go down, the STAGE HAND comes on through the back door. He is in blue overalls and carries a tool bag. He brings some pieces of wood on, comes to the front, kneels down and starts to nail them together.

The STAGE MANAGER rushes on from the wings.

STAGE MANAGER: Hey! What are you doing?
STAGE HAND: What do you think I'm doing? I'm banging nails in.
STAGE MANAGER: Now? (*He looks at his watch.*) It's half-past ten already. The Producer will be here in a moment to rehearse.
5 STAGE HAND: I've got to do my work some time, you know.
STAGE MANAGER: Right—but not now.
STAGE HAND: When?
STAGE MANAGER: When the rehearsal's finished. Come on,
10 get all this out of the way and let me set for the second act of 'The Rules of the Game.'

(*The* STAGE HAND *picks up his tools and wood and goes off, grumbling and muttering. The* ACTORS *of the company come in through the door, men and women, first one then another, then two together and so on: there will be nine or ten, enough for the parts for the rehearsal of a play by Pirandello, 'The Rules of the Game,' today's rehearsal. They come in, say their 'Good-mornings' to the* STAGE MANAGER *and each other. Some go off to the dressing-rooms; others, among them the* PROMPTER *with the text rolled up under his arm, scatter about the stage waiting for the* PRODUCER *to start the rehearsal. Meanwhile, sitting or standing in groups, they chat together; some smoke, one complains about his part, another one loudly reads something from 'The Stage.' It would be as well if the* ACTORS *and* ACTRESSES *were dressed in colourful clothes, and this first scene should be improvised naturally and vivaciously. After a while somebody might sit down at the piano and play a song; the younger* ACTORS *and* ACTRESSES *start dancing.*)

STAGE MANAGER: (*Clapping his hands to call their attention.*) Come on everybody! Quiet please. The Producer's here.

(*The piano and the dancing both stop. The* ACTORS *turn to look out into the theatre and through the door at the back comes the* PRODUCER; *he walks down the gangway between the seats and, calling 'Good-morning' to the* ACTORS, *climbs up one of the sets of stairs onto the stage. The* SECRETARY *gives him the post, a few magazines, a script. The* ACTORS *move to one side of the stage.*)

PRODUCER: Any letters?
SECRETARY: No. That's all the post there is. (*Giving him the* 15 *script.*)
PRODUCER: Put it in the office. (*Then looking round and turning to the* STAGE MANAGER.) I can't see a thing here. Let's have some lights please.
STAGE MANAGER: Right. (*Calling.*) Workers please! 20

(*In a few seconds the side of the stage where the* ACTORS *are standing is brilliantly lit with white light. The* PROMPTER *has gone into his box and spread out his script.*)

PRODUCER: Good. (*Clapping hands.*) Well then, let's get started. Anybody missing?

STAGE MANAGER: (*Heavily ironic.*) Our leading lady.

PRODUCER: Not again! (*Looking at his watch.*) We're ten minutes late already. Send her a note to come and see me. It might teach her to be on time for rehearsals. (*Almost before he has finished, the* LEADING ACTRESS*'s voice is heard from the auditorium.*)

LEADING ACTRESS: Morning everybody. Sorry I'm late. (*She is very expensively dressed and is carrying a lap-dog. She comes down the aisle and goes up on to the stage.*)

PRODUCER: You're determined to keep us waiting, aren't you?

LEADING ACTRESS: I'm sorry. I just couldn't find a taxi anywhere. But you haven't started yet and I'm not on at the opening anyhow. (*Calling the* STAGE MANAGER, *she gives him the dog.*) Put him in my dressing-room for me will you?

PRODUCER: And she's even brought her lap-dog with her! As if we haven't enough lap-dogs here already. (*Clapping his hands and turning to the* PROMPTER.) Right then, the second act of 'The Rules of the Game.' (*Sits in his arm-chair.*) Quiet please! Who's on?

(*The* ACTORS *clear from the front of the stage and sit to one side, except for three who are ready to start the scene—and the* LEADING ACTRESS. *She has ignored the* PRODUCER *and is sitting at one of the little tables.*)

PRODUCER: Are you in this scene, then?

LEADING ACTRESS: No—I've just told you.

PRODUCER: (*Annoyed.*) Then get off, for God's sake. (*The* LEADING ACTRESS *goes and sits with the others. To the* PROMPTER.) Come on then, let's get going.

PROMPTER: (*Reading his script.*) 'The house of Leone Gala. A peculiar room, both dining-room and study.'

PRODUCER: (*To the* STAGE MANAGER.) We'll use the red set.

STAGE MANAGER: (*Making a note.*) The red set—right.

PROMPTER: (*Still reading.*) 'The table is laid and there is a desk with books and papers. Bookcases full of books and china cabinets full of valuable china. An exit at the back leads to Leone's bedroom. An exit to the left leads to the kitchen. The main entrance is on the right.'

PRODUCER: Right. Listen carefully everybody: there, the main entrance, there, the kitchen. (*To the* LEADING ACTOR *who plays Socrates.*) Your entrances and exits will be from there. (*To the* STAGE MANAGER.) We'll have the French windows there and put the curtains on them.

STAGE MANAGER: (*Making a note.*) Right.

PROMPTER: (*Reading.*) 'Scene One. Leone Gala, Guido Venanzi, and Filippo, who is called Socrates.' (*To* PRODUCER.) Have I to read the directions as well?

PRODUCER: Yes, you have! I've told you a hundred times.

PROMPTER: (*Reading.*) 'When the curtain rises, Leone Gala, in a cook's hat and apron, is beating an egg in a dish with a little wooden spoon. Filippo is beating another and he is dressed as a cook too. Guido Venanzi is sitting listening.'

LEADING ACTOR: Look, do I really have to wear a cook's hat?

PRODUCER: (*Annoyed by the question.*) I expect so! That's what it says in the script. (*Pointing to the script.*)

LEADING ACTOR: If you ask me it's ridiculous.

PRODUCER: (*Leaping to his feet furiously.*) Ridiculous? It's ridiculous, is it? What do you expect me to do if nobody writes good plays any more and we're reduced to putting on plays by Pirandello? And if you can understand them you must be very clever. He writes them on purpose so nobody enjoys them, neither actors nor critics nor audience. (*The* ACTORS *laugh. Then crosses to* LEADING ACTOR *and shouts at him.*) A cook's hat and you beat eggs. But don't run away with the idea that that's all you are doing—beating eggs. You must be joking! You have to be symbolic of the shells of the eggs you are beating. (*The* ACTORS *laugh again and start making ironical comments to each other.*) Be quiet! Listen carefully while I explain. (*Turns back to* LEADING ACTOR.) Yes, the shells, because they are symbolic of the empty form of reason, without its content, blind instinct! You are reason and your wife is instinct: you are playing a game where you have been given parts and in which you are not just yourself but the puppet of yourself. Do you see?

LEADING ACTOR: (*Spreading his hands.*) Me? No.

PRODUCER: (*Going back to his chair.*) Neither do I! Come on, let's get going; you wait till you see the end! You haven't seen anything yet! (*Confidentially.*) By the way, I should turn almost to face the audience if I were you, about three-quarters face. Well, what with the obscure dialogue and the audience not being able to hear you properly in any case, the whole lot'll go to hell. (*Clapping hands again.*) Come on. Let's get going!

PROMPTER: Excuse me, can I put the top back on the prompt-box? There's a bit of a draught.

PRODUCER: Yes, yes, of course. Get on with it.

(*The* STAGE DOORKEEPER, *in a braided cap, has come into the auditorium, and he comes all the way down the aisle to the stage to tell the* PRODUCER *the* SIX CHARACTERS *have come, who, having come in after him, look about them a little puzzled and dismayed. Every effort must be made to create the effect that the* SIX CHARACTERS *are very different from the* ACTORS *of the company. The placings of the two groups, indicated in the directions, once the* CHARACTERS *are on the stage, will help this; so will using different coloured lights. But the most effective idea is to use masks for the* CHARACTERS, *masks specially made of a material that will not go limp with perspiration and light enough not to worry the actors who wear them: they should be made so that the eyes, the nose and the mouth are all free. This is the way to bring out the deep significance of the play. The* CHARACTERS *should not appear as ghosts, but as created realities, timeless creations of the imagination, and so more real and consistent than the changeable realities of the* ACTORS. *The masks are designed to give the impression of figures constructed by art, each one fixed forever in its own fundamental emotion; that is, Remorse for the* FATHER, *Revenge for the* STEPDAUGHTER, *Scorn for the* SON, *Sorrow for the* MOTHER. *Her mask should have wax tears in the corners of the eyes and down the cheeks like the sculptured or painted weeping Madonna in a church. Her dress should be of a plain material, in stiff folds, looking almost as if it were carved and not of an ordinary material you can buy in a shop and have made up by a dressmaker.*)

(*The* FATHER *is about fifty: his reddish hair is thinning at the temples, but he is not bald: he has a full moustache that almost covers his young-looking mouth, which often opens in an uncertain and empty smile. He is pale, with a high forehead: he has blue oval eyes, clear and sharp: he is dressed in light trousers and a dark jacket: his voice is sometimes rich, at other times harsh and loud.)*

(The MOTHER *appears crushed by an intolerable weight of shame and humiliation. She is wearing a thick black veil and is dressed simply in black; when she raises her veil she shows a face like wax, but not suffering, with her eyes turned down humbly.)*

(The STEPDAUGHTER, *who is eighteen years old, is defiant, even insolent. She is very beautiful, dressed in mourning as well, but with striking elegance. She is scornful of the timid, suffering, dejected air of her young brother, a grubby little* BOY *of fourteen, also dressed in black; she is full of a warm tenderness, on the other hand, for the* LITTLE SISTER, *a girl of about four, dressed in white with a black silk sash round her waist.)*

(The SON *is twenty-two, tall, almost frozen in an air of scorn for the* FATHER *and indifference to the* MOTHER: *he is wearing a mauve overcoat and a long green scarf round his neck.)*

DOORMAN: Excuse me, sir.
105 PRODUCER: *(Angrily.)* What the hell is it now?
DOORMAN: There are some people here—they say they want to see you, sir.

(The PRODUCER *and the* ACTORS *are astonished and turn to look out into the auditorium.)*

PRODUCER: But I'm rehearsing! You know perfectly well that no-one's allowed in during rehearsals. *(Turning to face out*
110 *front.)* Who are you? What do you want?
FATHER: *(Coming forward, followed by the others, to the foot of one of the sets of steps.)* We're looking for an author.
PRODUCER: *(Angry and astonished.)* An author? Which author?
FATHER: Any author will do, sir.
115 PRODUCER: But there isn't an author here because we're not rehearsing a new play.
STEPDAUGHTER: *(Excitedly as she rushes up the steps.)* That's better still, better still! We can be your new play.
ACTORS: *(Lively comments and laughter from the* ACTORS.) Oh,
120 listen to that, etc.
FATHER: *(Going up on the stage after the* STEPDAUGHTER.) Maybe, but if there isn't an author here . . . *(To the* PRODUCER.) Unless you'd like to be . . .

(Hand in hand, the MOTHER *and the* LITTLE GIRL, *followed by the little* BOY, *go up on the stage and wait. The* SON *stays sullenly behind.)*

PRODUCER: Is this some kind of joke?
125 FATHER: Now, how can you think that? On the contrary, we are bringing you a story of anguish.
STEPDAUGHTER: We might make your fortune for you!
PRODUCER: Do me a favour, will you? Go away. We haven't time to waste on idiots.
130 FATHER: *(Hurt but answering gently.)* You know very well, as a man of the theatre, that life is full of all sorts of odd things which have no need at all to pretend to be real because they are actually true.
PRODUCER: What the devil are you talking about?
135 FATHER: What I'm saying is that you really must be mad to do things the opposite way round: to create situations that

obviously aren't true and try to make them seem to be really happening. But then I suppose that sort of madness is the only reason for your profession.

(The ACTORS *are indignant.)*

140 PRODUCER: *(Getting up and glaring at him.)* Oh, yes? So ours is a profession of madmen, is it?
FATHER: Well, if you try to make something look true when it obviously isn't, especially if you're not forced to do it, but do it for a game . . . Isn't it your job to give life on the
145 stage to imaginary people?
PRODUCER: *(Quickly answering him and speaking for the* ACTORS *who are growing more indignant.)* I should like you to know, sir, that the actor's profession is one of great distinction. Even if nowadays the new writers only give us dull plays to act and puppets to present instead of men, I'd have you
150 know that it is our boast that we have given life, here on this stage, to immortal works.

(The ACTORS, *satisfied, agree with and applaud the* PRODUCER.)

FATHER: *(Cutting in and following hard on his argument.)* There! You see? Good! You've given life! You've created living beings with more genuine life than people have who
155 breathe and wear clothes! Less real, perhaps, but nearer the truth. We are both saying the same thing.

(The ACTORS *look at each other, astonished.)*

PRODUCER: But just a moment! You said before . . .
FATHER: I'm sorry, but I said that before, about acting for fun,
160 because you shouted at us and said you'd no time to waste on idiots, but you must know better than anyone that Nature uses human imagination to lift her work of creation to even higher levels.
PRODUCER: All right then: but where does all this get us?
165 FATHER: Nowhere. I want to try to show that one can be thrust into life in many ways, in many forms: as a tree or a stone, as water or a butterfly—or as a woman. It might even be as a character in a play.
PRODUCER: *(Ironic, pretending to be annoyed.)* And you, and
170 these other people here, were thrust into life, as you put it, as characters in a play?
FATHER: Exactly! And alive, as you can see.

(The PRODUCER *and the* ACTORS *burst into laughter as if at a joke.)*

FATHER: I'm sorry you laugh like that, because we carry in us, as I said before, a story of terrible anguish as you can
175 guess from this woman dressed in black.

(Saying this, he offers his hand to the MOTHER *and helps her up the last steps and, holding her still by the hand, leads her with a sense of tragic solemnity across the stage which is suddenly lit by a fantastic light.)*

(The LITTLE GIRL *and the* BOY *follow the* MOTHER: *then the* SON *comes up and stands to one side in the background: then the* STEPDAUGHTER *follows and leans against the proscenium arch: the*

ACTORS *are astonished at first, but then, full of admiration for the 'entrance,' they burst into applause—just as if it were a performance specially for them.*)

PRODUCER: (*At first astonished and then indignant.*) My God! Be quiet all of you. (*Turns to the* CHARACTERS.) And you lot get out! Clear off! (*To the* STAGE MANAGER.) Jesus! Get them out of here.

180 STAGE MANAGER: (*Comes forward but stops short as if held back by something strange.*) Go on out! Get out!

FATHER: (*To* PRODUCER.) Oh no, please, you see, we . . .

PRODUCER: (*Shouting.*) We came here to work, you know.

LEADING ACTOR: We really can't be messed about like this.

185 FATHER: (*Resolutely, coming forward.*) I'm astonished! Why don't you believe me? Perhaps you are not used to seeing the characters created by an author spring into life up here on the stage face to face with each other. Perhaps it's because we're not in a script? (*He points to the* PROMPTER'*s box.*)

190 STEPDAUGHTER: (*Coming down to the* PRODUCER, *smiling and persuasive.*) Believe me, sir, we really are six of the most fascinating characters. But we've been neglected.

FATHER: Yes, that's right, we've been neglected. In the sense that the author who created us, living in his mind, wouldn't
195 or couldn't make us live in a written play for the world of art. And that really is a crime sir, because whoever has the luck to be born a character can laugh even at death. Because a character will never die! A man will die, a writer, the instrument of creation: but what he has created will
200 never die! And to be able to live for ever you don't need to have extraordinary gifts or be able to do miracles. Who was Sancho Panza? Who was Prospero? But they will live for ever because—living seeds—they had the luck to find a fruitful soil, an imagination which knew how to grow
205 them and feed them, so that they will live for ever.

PRODUCER: This is all very well! But what do you want here?

FATHER: We want to live, sir.

PRODUCER: (*Ironically.*) For ever!

FATHER: No, no: only for a few moments—in you.

210 AN ACTOR: Listen to that!

LEADING ACTRESS: They want to live in us!

YOUNG ACTOR: (*Pointing to the* STEPDAUGHTER.) I don't mind . . . so long as I get her.

FATHER: Listen, listen: the play is all ready to be put together
215 and if you and your actors would like to, we can work it out now between us.

PRODUCER: (*Annoyed.*) But what exactly do you want to do? We don't make up plays like that here! We present comedies and tragedies here.

220 FATHER: That's right, we know that of course. That's why we've come.

PRODUCER: And where's the script?

FATHER: It's in us, sir. (*The* ACTORS *laugh.*) The play is in us: we are the play and we are impatient to show it to you:
225 the passion inside us is driving us on.

STEPDAUGHTER: (*Scornfully, with the tantalising charm of deliberate impudence.*) My passion, if only you knew! My passion for him! (*She points at the* FATHER *and suggests that she is going to embrace him: but stops and bursts into a screeching laugh.*)

230 FATHER: (*With sudden anger.*) You keep out of this for the moment! And stop laughing like that!

STEPDAUGHTER: Really? Then with your permission, ladies and gentlemen; even though it's only two months since I became an orphan, just watch how I can sing and dance.

(*The* ACTORS, *especially the younger, seem strangely attracted to her while she sings and dances and they edge closer and reach out their hands to catch hold of her. She eludes them, and when the* ACTORS *applaud her and the* PRODUCER *speaks sharply to her she stays still quite removed from them all.*)

AN ACTOR: Very good! etc.   235

PRODUCER: (*Angrily.*) Be quiet! Do you think this is a night-club? (*Turns to* FATHER *and asks with some concern.*) Is she a bit mad?

FATHER: Mad? Oh no—it's worse than that.

STEPDAUGHTER: (*Suddenly running to the* PRODUCER.) Yes. It's   240
worse, much worse! Listen please! Let's put this play on at once, because you'll see that at a particular point I—when this darling little girl here—(*Taking the* LITTLE GIRL *by the hand from next to the* MOTHER *and crossing with her to the* PRODUCER.) Isn't she pretty? (*Takes her in her arms.*) Darling!   245
Darling! (*Puts her down again and adds, moved very deeply but almost without wanting to.*) Well, this lovely little girl here, when God suddenly takes her from this poor Mother: and this little idiot here (*Turning to the* LITTLE BOY *and seizing him roughly by the sleeve.*) does the most stupid thing, like the   250
half-wit he is,—then you will see me run away! Yes, you'll see me rush away! But not yet, not yet! Because, after all the intimate things there have been between him and me (*In the direction of the* FATHER, *with a horrible vulgar wink.*) I can't stay with them any longer, to watch the insult to this   255
mother through that supercilious cretin over there. (*Pointing to the* SON.) Look at him! Look at him! Condescending, standoffish, because he's the legitimate son, him! Full of contempt for me, for the boy and for the little girl: because we are bastards. Do you understand? Bastards. (*Running to*   260
the MOTHER *and embracing her.*) And this poor mother—she—who is the mother of all of us—he doesn't want to recognise her as his own mother—and he looks down on her, he does, as if she were only the mother of the three of us who are bastards—the traitor. (*She says all this quickly,*   265
with great excitement, and after having raised her voice on the word 'bastards' she speaks quietly, half-spitting the word 'traitor.')

MOTHER: (*With deep anguish to the* PRODUCER.) Sir, in the name of these two little ones, I beg you . . . (*Feels herself grow faint and sways.*) Oh, my God.   270

FATHER: (*Rushing to support her with almost all the* ACTORS *bewildered and concerned.*) Get a chair someone . . . quick, get a chair for this poor widow.

(*One of the* ACTORS *offers a chair: the others press urgently around. The* MOTHER, *seated now, tries to stop the* FATHER *lifting her veil.*)

ACTORS: Is it real? Has she really fainted? etc.

FATHER: Look at her, everybody, look at her.   275

MOTHER: No, for God's sake, stop it.

FATHER: Let them look!

MOTHER: (*Lifting her hands and covering her face, desperately.*) Oh, please, I beg you, stop him from doing what he is trying to do; it's hateful.   280

PRODUCER: (*Overwhelmed, astounded.*) It's no use, I don't understand this any more. (*To the* FATHER.) Is this woman your wife?

FATHER: (*At once.*) That's right, she is my wife.

285 PRODUCER: How is she a widow, then, if you're still alive?

(*The* ACTORS *are bewildered too and find relief in a loud laugh.*)

FATHER: (*Wounded, with rising resentment.*) Don't laugh! Please don't laugh like that! That's just the point, that's her own drama. You see, she had another man. Another man who ought to be here.

290 MOTHER: No, no! (*Crying out.*)

STEPDAUGHTER: Luckily for him he died. Two months ago, as I told you: we are in mourning for him, as you can see.

FATHER: Yes, he's dead: but that's not the reason he isn't here. He isn't here because—well just look at her, please, and

295 you'll understand at once—hers is not a passionate drama of the love of two men, because she was incapable of love, she could feel nothing—except, perhaps a little gratitude (but not to me, to him). She's not a woman; she's a mother. And her drama—and, believe me, it's a powerful

300 one—her drama is focused completely on these four children of the two men she had.

MOTHER: I had them? How dare you say that I had them, as if I wanted them myself? It was him, sir! He forced the other man on me. He made me go away with him!

305 STEPDAUGHTER: (*Leaping up, indignantly.*) It isn't true!

MOTHER: (*Bewildered.*) How isn't it true?

STEPDAUGHTER: It isn't true, it just isn't true.

MOTHER: What do you know about it?

STEPDAUGHTER: It isn't true. (*To the* PRODUCER.) Don't be-

310 lieve it! Do you know why she said that? She said it because of him, over there. (*Pointing to the* SON.) She tortures herself, she exhausts herself with worry and all because of the indifference of that son of hers. She wants to make him believe that she abandoned him when he was two

315 years old because the Father made her do it.

MOTHER: (*Passionately.*) He did! He made me! God's my witness. (*To the* PRODUCER.) Ask him if it isn't true. (*Pointing to the* FATHER.) Make him tell our son it's true. (*Turning to the* STEPDAUGHTER.) You don't know anything about it.

320 STEPDAUGHTER: I know that when my father was alive you were always happy and contented. You can't deny it.

MOTHER: No, I can't deny it.

STEPDAUGHTER: He was always full of love and care for you. (*Turning to the* LITTLE BOY *with anger.*) Isn't it true? Admit

325 it. Why don't you say something, you little idiot?

MOTHER: Leave the poor boy alone! Why do you want to make me appear ungrateful? You're my daughter. I don't in the least want to offend your father's memory. I've already told him that it wasn't my fault or even to please

330 myself that I left his house and my son.

FATHER: It's quite true. It was my fault.

LEADING ACTOR: (*To other actors.*) Look at this. What a show!

LEADING ACTRESS: And we're the audience.

YOUNG ACTOR: For a change.

335 PRODUCER: (*Beginning to be very interested.*) Let's listen to them! Quiet! Listen!

(*He goes down the steps into the auditorium and stands there as if to get an idea of what the scene will look like from the audience's viewpoint.*)

SON: (*Without moving, coldly, quietly, ironically.*) Yes, listen to his little scrap of philosophy. He's going to tell you all about the Daemon of Experiment.

FATHER: You're a cynical idiot, and I've told you so a hundred 340 times. (*To the* PRODUCER *who is now in the stalls.*) He sneers at me because of this expression I've found to defend myself.

SON: Words, words.

FATHER: Yes words, words! When we're faced by something we don't understand, by a sense of evil that seems as if it's 345 going to swallow us, don't we all find comfort in a word that tells us nothing but that calms us?

STEPDAUGHTER: And dulls your sense of remorse, too. That more than anything.

FATHER: Remorse? No, that's not true. It'd take more than 350 words to dull the sense of remorse in me.

STEPDAUGHTER: It's taken a little money too, just a little money. The money that he was going to offer as payment, gentlemen.

(*The* ACTORS *are horrified.*)

SON: (*Contemptuously to his stepsister.*) That's a filthy trick. 355

STEPDAUGHTER: A filthy trick? There it was in a pale blue envelope on the little mahogany table in the room behind the shop at Madam Pace's. You know Madame Pace, don't you? One of those Madames who sell 'Robes et Manteaux' so that they can attract poor girls like me from de- 360 cent families into their workroom.

SON: And she's bought the right to tyrannise over the whole lot of us with that money—with what he was going to pay her: and luckily—now listen carefully—he had no reason to pay it to her. 365

STEPDAUGHTER: But it was close!

MOTHER: (*Rising up angrily.*) Shame on you, daughter! Shame!

STEPDAUGHTER: Shame? Not shame, revenge! I'm desperate, desperate to live that scene! The room . . . over here the showcase of coats, there the divan, there the mirror, and 370 the screen, and over there in front of the window, that little mahogany table with the pale blue envelope and the money in it. I can see it all quite clearly. I could pick it up! But you should turn your faces away, gentlemen: because I'm nearly naked! I'm not blushing any longer—I leave 375 that to him. (*Pointing at the* FATHER.) But I tell you he was very pale, very pale then. (*To the* PRODUCER.) Believe me.

PRODUCER: I don't understand any more.

FATHER: I'm not surprised when you're attacked like that! Why don't you put your foot down and let me have my 380 say before you believe all these horrible slanders she's so viciously telling about me.

STEPDAUGHTER: We don't want to hear any of your longwinded fairy-stories.

FATHER: I'm not going to tell any fairy-stories! I want to ex- 385 plain things to him.

STEPDAUGHTER: I'm sure you do. Oh, yes! In your own special way.

(The PRODUCER *comes back up on stage to take control.)*

FATHER: But isn't that the cause of all the trouble? Words! We
390 all have a world of things inside ourselves and each one of
us has his own private world. How can we understand each
other if the words I use have the sense and the value that I
expect them to have, but whoever is listening to me inevitably thinks that those same words have a different sense
395 and value, because of the private world he has inside himself too. We think we understand each other: but we never
do. Look! All my pity, all my compassion for this woman
(Pointing to the MOTHER.) she sees as ferocious cruelty.

MOTHER: But he turned me out of the house!

400 FATHER: There, do you hear? I turned her out! She really believed that I had turned her out.

MOTHER: You know how to talk. I don't . . . But believe me,
sir, *(Turning to the* PRODUCER.) after he married me . . . I
can't think why! I was a poor, simple woman.

405 FATHER: But that was the reason! I married you for your simplicity, that's what I loved in you, believing—*(He stops because she is making gestures of contradiction. Then, seeing the
impossibility of making her understand, he throws his arms wide
in a gesture of desperation and turns back to the* PRODUCER.)
410 No, do you see? She says no! It's terrifying, sir, believe me,
terrifying, her deafness, her mental deafness. *(He taps his
forehead.)* Affection for her children, oh yes. But deaf,
mentally deaf, deaf, sir, to the point of desperation.

STEPDAUGHTER: Yes, but make him tell you what good all his
415 cleverness has brought us.

FATHER: If only we could see in advance all the harm that can
come from the good we think we are doing.

(The LEADING ACTRESS, *who has been growing angry watching the*
LEADING ACTOR *flirting with the* STEPDAUGHTER, *comes forward
and snaps at the* PRODUCER.)

LEADING ACTRESS: Excuse me, are we going to go on with
our rehearsal?

420 PRODUCER: Yes, of course. But I want to listen to this first.

YOUNG ACTOR: It's such a new idea.

YOUNG ACTRESS: It's fascinating.

LEADING ACTRESS: For those who are interested. *(She looks
meaningfully at the* LEADING ACTOR.)

425 PRODUCER: *(To the* FATHER.) Look here, you must explain
yourself more clearly. *(He sits down.)*

FATHER: Listen then. You see, there was a rather poor fellow
working for me as my assistant and secretary, very loyal: he
understood her in everything. *(Pointing to the* MOTHER.)
430 But without a hint of deceit, you must believe that: he was
good and simple, like her: neither of them was capable
even of thinking anything wrong, let alone doing it.

STEPDAUGHTER: So instead he thought of it for them and did
it too!

435 FATHER: It's not true! What I did was for their good—oh yes
and mine too, I admit it! The time had come when I
couldn't say a word to either of them without there immediately flashing between them a sympathetic look: each
one caught the other's eye for advice, about how to take
440 what I had said, how not to make me angry. Well, that was
enough, as I'm sure you'll understand, to put me in a bad
temper all the time, in a state of intolerable exasperation.

PRODUCER: Then why didn't you sack this secretary of yours?

FATHER: Right! In the end I did sack him! But then I had to
watch this poor woman wandering about in the house on 445
her own, forlorn, like a stray animal you take in out of pity.

MOTHER: It's quite true.

FATHER: *(Suddenly, turning to her, as if to stop her.)* And what
about the boy? Is that true as well?

MOTHER: But first he tore my son from me, sir. 450

FATHER: But not out of cruelty! It was so that he could grow
up healthy and strong, in touch with the earth.

STEPDAUGHTER: *(Pointing to the* SON *jeeringly.)* And look at the
result!

FATHER: *(Quickly.)* And is it my fault, too, that he's grown up 455
like this? I took him to a nurse in the country, a peasant,
because his mother didn't seem strong enough to me, although she is from a humble family herself. In fact that
was what made me marry her. Perhaps it was superstitious
of me; but what was I to do? I've always had this dreadful 460
longing for a kind of sound moral healthiness.

(The STEPDAUGHTER *breaks out again into noisy laughter.)*

Make her stop that! It's unbearable.

PRODUCER: Stop it will you? Let me listen, for God's sake.

(When the PRODUCER *has spoken to her, she resumes her previous
position . . . absorbed and distant, a half-smile on her lips. The* PRO-
DUCER *comes down into the auditorium again to see how it looks
from there.)*

FATHER: I couldn't bear the sight of this woman near me.
(Pointing to the MOTHER.) Not so much because of the an- 465
noyance she caused me, you see, or even the feeling of being stifled, being suffocated that I got from her, as for the
sorrow, the painful sorrow that I felt for her.

MOTHER: And he sent me away.

FATHER: With everything you needed, to the other man, to 470
set her free from me.

MOTHER: And to set yourself free!

FATHER: Oh, yes, I admit it. And what terrible things came
out of it. But I did it for the best, and more for her than
for me: I swear it! *(Folds his arms: then turns suddenly to the* 475
MOTHER.) I never lost sight of you did I? Until that fellow, without my knowing it, suddenly took you off to another town one day. He was idiotically suspicious of my
interest in them, a genuine interest, I assure you, without
any ulterior motive at all. I watched the new little family 480
growing up round her with unbelievable tenderness, she'll
confirm that. *(He points to the* STEPDAUGHTER.)

STEPDAUGHTER: Oh yes, I can indeed. I was a pretty little girl,
you know, with plaits down to my shoulders and my little
frilly knickers showing under my dress—so pretty—he 485
used to watch me coming out of school. He came to see
how I was maturing.

FATHER: That's shameful! It's monstrous.

STEPDAUGHTER: No it isn't! Why do you say it is?

FATHER: It's monstrous! Monstrous. *(He turns excitedly to the* 490
PRODUCER *and goes on in explanation.)* After she'd gone
away *(Pointing to the* MOTHER.), my house seemed empty.
She'd been like a weight on my spirit but she'd filled the

house with her presence. Alone in the empty rooms I wan-
495 dered about like a lost soul. This boy here, (*Indicating the*
SON.) growing up away from home—whenever he came
back to the home—I don't know—but he didn't seem to
be mine any more. We needed the mother between us, to
link us together, and so he grew up by himself, apart, with
500 no connection to me either through intellect or love. And
then—it must seem odd, but it's true—first I was curious
about and then strongly attracted to the little family that
had come about because of what I'd done. And the
thought of them began to fill all the emptiness that I felt
505 around me. I needed, I really needed to believe that she was
happy, wrapped up in the simple cares of her life, lucky because she was better off away from the complicated torments of a soul like mine. And to prove it, I used to watch
that child coming out of school.

510 STEPDAUGHTER: Listen to him! He used to follow me along the
street; he used to smile at me and when we came near the
house he'd wave his hand—like this! I watched him, wide-
eyed, puzzled. I didn't know who he was. I told my mother
about him and she knew at once who it must be. (MOTHER
515 *nods agreement.*) At first, she didn't let me go to school again,
at any rate for a few days. But when I did go back, I saw him
standing near the door again—looking ridiculous—with a
brown paper bag in his hand. He came close and petted me:
then he opened the bag and took out a beautiful straw hat
520 with a hoop of rosebuds round it—for me!

PRODUCER: All this is off the point, you know.

SON: (*Contemptuously.*) Yes . . . literature, literature.

FATHER: What do you mean, literature? This is real life: real
passions.

525 PRODUCER: That may be! But you can't put it on the stage
just like that.

FATHER: That's right you can't. Because all this is only leading up to the main action. I'm not suggesting that this part
should be put on the stage. In any case, you can see for
530 yourself, (*Pointing at the* STEPDAUGHTER.) she isn't a pretty
little girl any longer with plaits down to her shoulders.

STEPDAUGHTER: —and with frilly knickers showing under
her frock.

FATHER: The drama begins now: and it's new and complex.

535 STEPDAUGHTER: (*Coming forward, fierce and brooding.*) As soon
as my father died . . .

FATHER: (*Quickly, not giving her time to speak.*) They were so
miserable. They came back here, but I didn't know about
it because of the Mother's stubbornness. (*Pointing to the*
540 MOTHER.) She can't really write you know; but she could
have got her daughter to write, or the boy, or tell me that
they needed help.

MOTHER: But tell me, sir, how could I have known how he felt?

FATHER: And hasn't that always been your fault? You've never
545 known anything about how I felt.

MOTHER: After all the years away from him and after all that
had happened.

FATHER: And was it my fault if that fellow took you so far
away? (*Turning back to the* PRODUCER.) Suddenly,
550 overnight, I tell you, he'd found a job away from here without my knowing anything about it. I couldn't possibly trace
them; and then, naturally I suppose, my interest in them

grew less over the years. The drama broke out, unexpected
and violent, when they came back: when I was driven in
misery by the needs of my flesh, still alive with desire . . . 555
and it is misery, you know, unspeakable misery for the man
who lives alone and who detests sordid, casual affairs; not
old enough to do without women, but not young enough
to be able to go and look for one without shame! Misery?
Is that what I called it. It's horrible, it's revolting, because 560
there isn't a woman who will give her love to him any
more. And when he realises this, he should do without . . .
It's easy to say though. Each of us, face to face with other
men, is clothed with some sort of dignity, but we know
only too well all the unspeakable things that go on in the 565
heart. We surrender, we given in to temptation: but afterwards we rise up out of it very quickly, in a desperate hurry
to rebuild our dignity, whole and firm as if it were a grave-
stone that would cover every sign and memory of our
shame, and hide it from even our own eyes. Everyone's like 570
that, only some of us haven't the courage to talk about it.

STEPDAUGHTER: But they've all got the courage to do it!

FATHER: Yes! But only in secret! That's why it takes more
courage to talk about it! Because if a man does talk about
it—what happens then?—everybody says he's a cynic. 575
And it's simply not true; he's just like everybody else; only
better perhaps, because he's not afraid to use his intelligence to point out the blushing shame of human bestiality, that man, the beast, shuts his eyes to, trying to pretend
it doesn't exist. And what about woman—what is she 580
like? She looks at you invitingly, teasingly. You take her in
your arms. But as soon as she feels your arms round her
she closes her eyes. It's the sign of her mission, the sign by
which she says to a man, 'Blind yourself—I'm blind!'

STEPDAUGHTER: And when she doesn't close her eyes any 585
more? What then? When she doesn't feel the need to hide
from herself any more, to shut her eyes and hide her own
shame. When she can see instead, dispassionately and dry-
eyed this blushing shame of a man who has blinded himself, who is without love. What then? Oh, then what 590
disgust, what utter disgust she feels for all these intellectual complications, for all this philosophy that points to
the bestiality of man and then tries to defend him, to excuse him . . . I can't listen to him, sir. Because when a man
says he needs to 'simplify' life like this—reducing it to 595
bestiality—and throws away every human scrap of innocent desire, genuine feeling, idealism, duty, modesty,
shame, then there's nothing more contemptible and nau-
seating than his remorse—crocodile tears!

PRODUCER: Let's get to the point, let's get to the point. This 600
is all chat.

FATHER: Right then! But a fact is like a sack—it won't stand up
if it's empty. To make it stand up, first you have to put in it all
the reasons and feelings that caused it in the first place. I
couldn't possibly have known that when that fellow died 605
they'd come back here, that they were desperately poor and
that the Mother had gone out to work as a dressmaker, nor
that she'd gone to work for Madame Pace, of all people.

STEPDAUGHTER: She's a very high-class dressmaker—you
must understand that. She apparently has only high-class 610
customers, but she has arranged things carefully so that

these high-class customers in fact serve her—they give her a respectable front . . . without spoiling things for the other ladies at the shop, who are not quite so high-class at all.

615 MOTHER: Believe me, sir, the idea never entered my head that the old hag gave me work because she had an eye on my daughter . . .

STEPDAUGHTER: Poor Mummy! Do you know what that woman would do when I took back the work that my
620 mother had been doing? She would point out how the dress had been ruined by giving it to my mother to sew: she bargained, she grumbled. So, you see, I paid for it, while this poor woman here thought she was sacrificing herself for me and these two children, sewing dresses all night for Madame Pace.

(The ACTORS *make gestures and noises of disgust.)*

625 PRODUCER: *(Quickly.)* And there one day, you met . . .

STEPDAUGHTER: *(Pointing at the* FATHER.) Yes, him. Oh, he was an old customer of hers! What a scene that's going to be, superb!

FATHER: With her, the mother, arriving—

STEPDAUGHTER: *(Quickly, viciously.)*—Almost in time!

630 FATHER: *(Crying out.)*—No, just in time, just in time! Because, luckily, I found out who she was in time. And I took them all back to my house, sir. Can you imagine the situation now, for the two of us living in the same house? She, just as you see her here: and I, not able to look her in the face.

635 STEPDAUGHTER: It's so absurd! Do you think it's possible for me, sir, after what happened at Madame Pace's, to pretend that I'm a modest little miss, well brought up and virtuous just so that I can fit in with his damned pretensions to a 'sound moral healthiness'?

640 FATHER: This is the real drama for me; the belief that we all, you see, think of ourselves as one single person: but it's not true: each of us is several different people, and all these people live inside us. With one person we seem like this and with another we seem very different. But we always
645 have the illusion of being the same person for everybody and of always being the same person in everything we do. But it's not true! It's not true! We find this out for ourselves very clearly when by some terrible chance we're suddenly stopped in the middle of doing something and
650 we're left dangling there, suspended. We realise then, that every part of us was not involved in what we'd been doing and that it would be a dreadful injustice of other people to judge us only by this one action as we dangle there, hanging in chains, fixed for all eternity, as if the whole of
655 one's personality were summed up in that single, interrupted action. Now do you understand this girl's treachery? She accidentally found me somewhere I shouldn't have been, doing something I shouldn't have been doing! She discovered a part of me that shouldn't have existed for
660 her: and now she wants to fix on me a reality that I should never have had to assume for her: it came from a single brief and shameful moment in my life. This is what hurts me most of all. And you'll see that the play will make a tremendous impact from this idea of mine. But then,
665 there's the position of the others. His . . .

(Pointing to the SON.)

SON: *(Shrugging his shoulders scornfully.)* Leave me out of it. I don't come into this.

FATHER: Why don't you come into this?

SON: I don't come into it and I don't want to come into it, because you know perfectly well that I wasn't intended to 670 be mixed up with you lot.

STEPDAUGHTER: We're vulgar, common people, you see! He's a fine gentleman. But you've probably noticed that every now and then I look at him contemptuously, and when I do, he lowers his eyes—he knows the harm he's done me. 675

SON: *(Not looking at her.)* I have?

STEPDAUGHTER: Yes, you. It's your fault, dearie, that I went on the streets! Your fault! *(Movement of horror from the* ACTORS.) Did you or didn't you, with your attitude, deny us—I won't say the intimacy of your home—but that simple hospital- 680 ity that makes guests feel comfortable? We were intruders who had come to invade the country of your 'legitimacy'! *(Turning to the* PRODUCER.) I'd like you to have seen some of the little scenes that went on between him and me, sir. He says that I tyrannised over everyone. But don't you see? 685 It was because of the way he treated us. He called it 'vile' that I should insist on the right we had to move into his house with my mother—and she's his mother too. And I went into the house as its mistress.

SON: *(Slowly coming forward.)* They're really enjoying them- 690 selves, aren't they, sir? It's easy when they all gang up against me. But try to imagine what happened: one fine day, there is a son sitting quietly at home and he sees arrive as bold as brass, a young woman like this, who cheek- ily asks for his father, and heaven knows what business she 695 has with him. Then he sees her come back with the same brazen look in her eye accompanied by that little girl there: and he sees her treat his father—without knowing why—in a most ambiguous and insolent way—asking him for money in a tone that leads one to suppose he re- 700 ally ought to give it, because he is obliged to do so.

FATHER: But I was obliged to do so: I owed it to your mother.

SON: And how was I to know that? When had I ever seen her before? When had I ever heard her mentioned? Then one day I see her come in with her *(Pointing at the* STEP- 705 DAUGHTER.), that boy and that little girl: they say to me, 'Oh, didn't you know? This is your mother, too.' Little by little I began to understand, mostly from her attitude *(Points to* STEPDAUGHTER.) why they'd come to live in the house so suddenly. I can't and I won't say what I feel, and 710 what I think. I wouldn't even like to confess it to myself. So I can't take any active part in this. Believe me, sir, I am a character who has not been fully developed dramatically, and I feel uncomfortable, most uncomfortable, in their company. So please leave me out of it. 715

FATHER: What! But it's precisely because you feel like this . . .

SON: *(Violently exasperated.)* How do you know what I feel? When have you ever bothered yourself about me?

FATHER: All right! I admit it! But isn't that a situation in itself? This withdrawing of yourself, it's cruel to me and to your 720 mother: when she came back to the house, seeing you al- most for the first time, not recognising you, but knowing that you're her own son . . . *(Turning to point out the* MOTHER *to the* PRODUCER.) There, look at her: she's weeping.

725 STEPDAUGHTER: (*Angrily, stamping her foot.*) Like the fool she is!

FATHER: (*Quickly pointing at the* STEPDAUGHTER *to the* PRO-DUCER.) She can't stand that young man, you know. (*Turning and referring to the* SON.) He says that he doesn't come into it, but he's really the pivot of the action! Look here at this lit-

730 tle boy, who clings to his mother all the time, frightened, hu-miliated. And it's because of him over there! Perhaps this little boy's problem is the worst of all: he feels an outsider, more than the others do; he feels so mortified, so humiliated just being in the house,—because it's charity, you see. (*Qui-*

735 *etly.*) He's like his father: timid; he doesn't say anything . . .

PRODUCER: It's not a good idea at all, using him: you don't know what a nuisance children are on the stage.

FATHER: He won't need to be on the stage for long. Nor will the little girl—she's the first to go.

740 PRODUCER: That's good! Yes. I tell you all this interests me—it interests me very much. I'm sure we've the material here for a good play.

STEPDAUGHTER: (*Trying to push herself in.*) With a character like me you have!

745 FATHER: (*Driving her off, wanting to hear what the* PRODUCER *has decided.*) You stay out of it!

PRODUCER: (*Going on, ignoring the interruption.*) It's new, yes.

FATHER: Oh, it's absolutely new!

PRODUCER: You've got a nerve, though, haven't you, coming

750 here and throwing it at me like this?

FATHER: I'm sure you understand. Born as we are for the stage . . .

PRODUCER: Are you amateur actors?

FATHER: No! I say we are born for the stage because . . .

755 PRODUCER: Come on now! You're an old hand at this, at acting!

FATHER: No I'm not. I only act, as everyone does, the part in life that he's chosen for himself, or that others have chosen for him. And you can see that sometimes my own passion gets a bit out of hand, a bit theatrical, as it does with all of us.

760 PRODUCER: Maybe, maybe . . . But you do see, don't you, that without an author . . . I could give you someone's address . . .

FATHER: Oh no! Look here! You do it.

PRODUCER: Me? What are you talking about?

FATHER: Yes, you. Why not?

765 PRODUCER: Because I've never written anything!

FATHER: Well, why not start now, if you don't mind my sug-gesting it? There's nothing to it. Everybody's doing it. And your job is even easier, because we're here, all of us, alive before you.

770 PRODUCER: That's not enough.

FATHER: Why isn't it enough? When you've seen us live our drama . . .

PRODUCER: Perhaps so. But we'll still need someone to write it.

FATHER: Only to write it down, perhaps, while it happens in

775 front of him—live—scene by scene. It'll be enough to sketch it out simply first and then run through it.

PRODUCER: (*Coming back up, tempted by the idea.*) Do you know I'm almost tempted . . . just for fun . . . it might work.

FATHER: Of course it will. You'll see what wonderful scenes

780 will come right out of it! I could tell you what they will be!

PRODUCER: You tempt me . . . you tempt me! We'll give it a chance. Come with me to the office. (*Turning to the* ACTORS.) Take a break: but don't go far away. Be back in a quarter of an hour or twenty minutes. (*To the* FATHER.) Let's see, let's try

785 it out. Something extraordinary might come out of this.

FATHER: Of course it will! Don't you think it'd be better if the others came too? (*Indicating the other* CHARACTERS.)

PRODUCER: Yes, come on, come on. (*Going, then turning to speak to the* ACTORS.) Don't forget: don't be late: back in a quarter of an hour.   790

(*The* PRODUCER *and the* SIX CHARACTERS *cross the stage and go. The* ACTORS *look at each other in astonishment.*)

LEADING ACTOR: Is he serious? What's he going to do?

YOUNG ACTOR: I think he's gone round the bend.

ANOTHER ACTOR: Does he expect to make up a play in five minutes?

YOUNG ACTOR: Yes, like the old actors in the commedia   795 del'arte!

LEADING ACTRESS: Well if he thinks I'm going to appear in that sort of nonsense . . .

YOUNG ACTOR: Nor me!

FOURTH ACTOR: I should like to know who they are.   800

THIRD ACTOR: Who do you think? They're probably escaped lunatics—or crooks.

YOUNG ACTOR: And is he taking them seriously?

YOUNG ACTRESS: It's vanity. The vanity of seeing himself as an author.   805

LEADING ACTOR: I've never heard of such a thing! If the the-atre, ladies and gentlemen, is reduced to this . . .

FIFTH ACTOR: I'm enjoying it!

THIRD ACTOR: Really? We shall have to wait and see what happens next I suppose.   810

(*Talking, they leave the stage. Some go out through the back door, some to the dressing-rooms.*)

(*The Curtain stays up.*)

(*The interval lasts twenty minutes.*)

ACT TWO

The theatre warning-bell sounds to call the audience back. From the dressing-rooms, the door at the back and even from the auditorium, the ACTORS, *the* STAGE MANAGER, *the* STAGE HANDS, *the* PROMPTER, *the* PROPERTY MAN *and the* PRODUCER, *accompa-nied by the* SIX CHARACTERS *all come back on to the stage.*

The house lights go out and the stage lights come on again.

PRODUCER: Come on, everybody! Are we all here? Quiet now! Listen! Let's get started! Stage manager?

STAGE MANAGER: Yes, I'm here.

PRODUCER: Give me that little parlour setting, will you? A couple of plain flats and a door flat will do. Hurry up with it!   5

(*The* STAGE MANAGER *runs off to order someone to do this immedi-ately and at the same time the* PRODUCER *is making arrangements with the* PROPERTY MAN, *the* PROMPTER, *and the* ACTORS: *the two flats and the door flat are painted in pink and gold stripes.*)

PRODUCER: (*To* PROPERTY MAN.) Go see if we have a sofa in stock.

PROPERTY MAN: Yes, there's that green one.

STEPDAUGHTER: No, no, not a green one! It was yellow, yel-low velvet with flowers on it: it was enormous! And so   10 comfortable!

PROPERTY MAN: We haven't got one like that.

PRODUCER: It doesn't matter! Give me whatever there is.

STEPDAUGHTER: What do you mean, it doesn't matter? It was
15   Mme. Pace's famous sofa.

PRODUCER: It's only for a rehearsal! Please, don't interfere. (*To
the* STAGE MANAGER.) Oh, and see if there's a shop window, will you—preferably a long, low one.

STEPDAUGHTER: And a little table, a little mahogany table for
20   the blue envelope.

STAGE MANAGER: (*To the* PRODUCER.) There's that little gold one.

PRODUCER: That'll do—bring it.

FATHER: A mirror!

STEPDAUGHTER: And a screen! A screen, please, or I won't be
25   able to manage, will I?

STAGE MANAGER: All right. We've lots of big screens, don't
you worry.

PRODUCER: (*To* STEPDAUGHTER.) Then don't you want some
coat-hangers and some clothes racks.

30 STEPDAUGHTER: Yes, lots of them, lots of them.

PRODUCER: (*To the* STAGE MANAGER.) See how many there
are and have them brought up.

STAGE MANAGER: Right, I'll see to it.

(*The* STAGE MANAGER *goes off to do it: and while the* PRODUCER
is talking to the PROMPTER, *the* CHARACTERS *and the* ACTORS,
the STAGE MANAGER *is telling the* SCENE SHIFTERS *where to set
up the furniture they have brought.*)

PRODUCER: (*To the* PROMPTER.) Now you, go sit down, will
35   you? Look, this is an outline of the play, act by act. (*He
hands him several sheets of paper.*) But you'll need to be on
your toes.

PROMPTER: Shorthand?

PRODUCER: (*Pleasantly surprised.*) Oh, good! You know short-
40   hand?

PROMPTER: I don't know much about prompting, but I do
know about shorthand.

PRODUCER: Thank God for that anyway! (*He turns to a* STAGE
HAND.) Go fetch me some paper from my office—lots of
45   it—as much as you can find!

(*The* STAGE HAND *goes running off and then comes back shortly
with a bundle of paper that he gives to the* PROMPTER.)

PRODUCER: (*Crossing to the* PROMPTER.) Follow the scenes,
one after another, as they are played and try to get the lines
down . . . at least the most important ones. (*Then turning to
the* ACTORS.) Get out of the way everybody! Here, go over
50   to the prompt side (*Pointing to stage left.*) and pay attention!

LEADING ACTRESS: But, excuse me, we . . .

PRODUCER: (*Anticipating her.*) You won't be expected to improvise, don't worry!

LEADING ACTOR: Then what are we expected to do?

55 PRODUCER: Nothing! Just go over there, listen and watch.
You'll all be given your parts later written out. Right now
we're going to rehearse, as well as we can. And they will
be doing the rehearsal. (*He points to the* CHARACTERS.)

FATHER: (*Rather bewildered, as if he had fallen from the clouds into
60   the middle of the confusion on the stage.*) We are? Excuse me,
but what do you mean, a rehearsal?

PRODUCER: I mean a rehearsal—a rehearsal for the benefit of
the actors. (*Pointing to the* ACTORS.)

FATHER: But if we are the characters . . .

PRODUCER: That's right, you're the 'characters': but characters   65
don't act here, my dear chap. It's actors who act here. The
characters are there in the script—(*Pointing to the*
PROMPTER.) that's when there is a script.

FATHER: That's the point! Since there isn't one and you have
the luck to have the characters alive in front of you . . .   70

PRODUCER: Great! You want to do everything yourselves, do
you? To act your own play, to produce your own play!

FATHER: Well yes, just as we are.

PRODUCER: That would be an experience for us, I can tell you!

LEADING ACTOR: And what about us? What would we be do-   75
ing then?

PRODUCER: Don't tell me you think you know how to act!
Don't make me laugh! (*The* ACTORS *in fact laugh.*) There
you are, you see, you've made them laugh. (*Then remembering.*) But let's get back to the point! We need to cast the   80
play. Well, that's easy: it almost casts itself. (*To the* SECOND
ACTRESS.) You, the mother. (*To the* FATHER.) You'll need to
give her a name.

FATHER: Amalia.

PRODUCER: But that's the real name of your wife isn't it? We   85
can't use her real name.

FATHER: But why not? That is her name . . . But perhaps if
this lady is to play the part . . . (*Indicating the* SECOND AC-
TRESS *vaguely with a wave of his hand.*) I think of her as
Amalia . . . (*Pointing to the* MOTHER.) But do as you like . . .   90
(*A little confused.*) I don't know what to say . . . I'm already
starting to . . . how can I explain it . . . to sound false, my
own words sound like someone else's.

PRODUCER: Now don't worry yourself about it, don't worry
about it at all. We'll work out the right tone of voice. As   95
for the name, if you want it to be Amalia, then Amalia it
shall be: or we can find another. For the moment we'll refer to the characters like this: (*To the* YOUNG ACTOR, *the juvenile lead.*) you are The Son. (*To the* LEADING ACTRESS.)
You, of course, are The Stepdaughter.   100

STEPDAUGHTER: (*Excitedly.*) What did you say? That woman is
me? (*Bursts into laughter.*)

PRODUCER: (*Angrily.*) What are you laughing at?

LEADING ACTRESS: (*Indignantly.*) Nobody has ever dared to
laugh at me before! Either you treat me with respect or   105
I'm walking out! (*Starting to go.*)

STEPDAUGHTER: I'm sorry. I wasn't really laughing at you.

PRODUCER: (*To the* STEPDAUGHTER.) You should feel proud to
be played by . . .

LEADING ACTRESS: (*Quickly, scornfully.*) . . . that woman!   110

STEPDAUGHTER: But I wasn't thinking about her, honestly. I
was thinking about me: I can't see myself in you at all . . .
you're not a bit like me!

FATHER: Yes, that's right: you see, our meaning . . .

PRODUCER: What are you talking about, 'our meaning'? Do   115
you think you have exclusive rights to what you represent?
Do you think it can only exist inside you? Not a bit of it!

FATHER: What? Don't we even have our own meaning?

PRODUCER: Not a bit of it! Whatever you mean is only material here, to which the actors give form and body, voice   120
and gesture, and who, through their art, have given expression to much better material than what you have to
offer: yours is really very trivial and if it stands up on the
stage, the credit, believe me, will all be due to my actors.

125   FATHER: I don't dare to contradict you. But you for your part, must believe me—it doesn't seem trivial to us. We are suffering terribly now, with these bodies, these faces . . .

PRODUCER: (*Interrupting impatiently.*) Yes, well, the make-up will change that, make-up will change that, at least as far

130   as the faces are concerned.

FATHER: Yes, but the voices, the gestures . . .

PRODUCER: That's enough! You can't come on the stage here as yourselves. It is our actors who will represent you here: and let that be the end of it!

135   FATHER: I understand that. But now I think I see why our author who saw us alive as we are here now, didn't want to put us on the stage. I don't want to offend your actors. God forbid that I should! But I think that if I saw myself represented . . . by I don't know whom . . .

140   LEADING ACTOR: (*Rising majestically and coming forward, followed by a laughing group of* YOUNG ACTRESSES.) By me, if you don't object.

FATHER: (*Respectfully, smoothly.*) I shall be honoured, sir. (*He bows.*) But I think, that no matter how hard this gentleman

145   works with all his will and all his art to identify himself with me . . . (*He stops, confused.*)

LEADING ACTOR: Yes, go on.

FATHER: Well, I was saying the performance he will give, even if he is made up to look like me . . . I mean with the dif-

150   ference in our appearance . . . (*All the* ACTORS *laugh.*) it will be difficult for it to be a performance of me as I really am. It will be more like—well, not just because of his figure—it will be more an interpretation of what I am, what he believes me to be, and not how I know myself to

155   be. And it seems to me that this should be taken into account by those who are going to comment on us.

PRODUCER: So you are already worrying about what the critics will say, are you? And I'm still waiting to get this thing started! The critics can say what they like: and we'll

160   worry about putting on the play. If we can! (*Stepping out of the group and looking around.*) Come on, come on! Is the scene set for us yet? (*To the* ACTORS *and* CHARACTERS.) Out of the way! Let's have a look at it. (*Climbing down off the stage.*) Don't let's waste any more time. (*To the* STEP-

165   DAUGHTER.) Does it look all right to you?

STEPDAUGHTER: What? That? I don't recognise it at all.

PRODUCER: Good God! Did you expect us to reconstruct the room at the back of Mme. Pace's shop here on the stage? (*To the* FATHER.) Did you say the room had flowered wallpaper?

170   FATHER: White, yes.

PRODUCER: Well it's not white: it's striped. That sort of thing doesn't matter at all! As for furniture, it looks to me as if we have nearly everything we need. Move that little table a bit further downstage. (*A* STAGE HAND *does it. To the*

175   PROPERTY MAN.) Go and fetch an envelope, pale blue if you can find one, and give it to that gentleman there. (*Pointing to the* FATHER.)

STAGE HAND: An envelope for letters?

PRODUCER: ⎱
FATHER: ⎰   Yes, an envelope for letters!

180   STAGE HAND: Right. (*He goes off.*)

PRODUCER: Now then, come on! The first scene is the young lady's. (*The* LEADING ACTRESS *comes to the centre.*) No, no, not yet. I said the young lady's. (*He points to the* STEP-DAUGHTER.) You stay there and watch.

185   STEPDAUGHTER: (*Adding quickly.*) . . . how I bring it to life.

LEADING ACTRESS: (*Resenting this.*) I shall know how to bring it to life, don't you worry, when I am allowed to.

PRODUCER: (*His head in his hands.*) Ladies, please, no more arguments! Now then. The first scene is between the young

190   lady and Mme. Pace. Oh! (*Worried, turning round and looking out into the auditorium.*) Where is Mme. Pace?

FATHER: She isn't here with us.

PRODUCER: So what do we do now?

FATHER: But she is real. She's real too!

195   PRODUCER: All right. So where is she?

FATHER: May I deal with this? (*Turns to the* ACTRESSES.) Would each of you ladies be kind enough to lend me a hat, a coat, a scarf or something?

ACTRESSES: (*Some are surprised or amused.*) What? My scarf? A

200   coat? What's he want my hat for? What are you wanting to do with them? (*All the* ACTRESSES *are laughing.*)

FATHER: Oh, nothing much, just hang them up here on the racks for a minute or two. Perhaps someone would be kind enough to lend me a coat?

205   ACTORS: Just a coat? Come on, more! The man must be mad.

AN ACTRESS: What for? Only my coat?

FATHER: Yes, to hang up here, just for a moment. I'm very grateful to you. Do you mind?

ACTRESSES: (*Taking off various hats, coats, scarves, laughing and go-*

210   *ing to hang them on the racks.*) Why not? Here you are. I really think it's crazy. Is it to dress the set?

FATHER: Yes, exactly. It's to dress the set.

PRODUCER: Would you mind telling me what you are doing?

FATHER: Yes, of course: perhaps, if we dress the set better, she

215   will be drawn by the articles of her trade and, who knows, she may even come to join us . . . (*He invites them to watch the door at the back of the set.*) Look! Look!

(*The door at the back opens and* MME. PACE *takes a few steps downstage: she is a gross old harridan wearing a ludicrous carroty-coloured wig with a single red rose stuck in at one side, Spanish fashion: garishly made-up: in a vulgar but stylish red silk dress, holding an ostrich-feather fan in one hand and a cigarette between two fingers in the other. At the sight of this Apparition, the* ACTORS *and the* PRODUCER *immediately jump off the stage with cries of fear, leaping down into the auditorium and up the aisles. The* STEPDAUGHTER, *however, runs across to* MME. PACE, *and greets her respectfully, as if she were the mistress.*)

STEPDAUGHTER: (*Running across to her.*) Here she is! Here she is!

FATHER: (*Smiling broadly.*) It's her! What did I tell you? Here

220   she is!

PRODUCER: (*Recovering from his shock, indignantly.*) What sort of trick is this?

LEADING ACTOR: (*Almost at the same time as the others.*) What the hell is happening?

225   JUVENILE LEAD: Where on earth did they get that extra from?

YOUNG ACTRESS: They were keeping her hidden!

LEADING ACTRESS: It's a game, a conjuring trick!

FATHER: Wait a minute! Why do you want to spoil a miracle by being factual. Can't you see this is a miracle of reality, that is born, brought to life, lured here, reproduced, just

230   for the sake of this scene, with more right to be alive here than you have? Perhaps it has more truth than you have yourselves. Which actress can improve on Mme. Pace there? Well? That is the real Mme. Pace. You must admit

235 that the actress who plays her will be less true than she is herself—and there she is in person! Look! My daughter recognised her straight away and went to meet her. Now watch—just watch this scene.

(*Hesitantly, the* PRODUCER *and the* ACTORS *move back to their original places on the stage.*)

(*But the scene between the* STEPDAUGHTER *and* MME. PACE *has already begun while the* ACTORS *were protesting and the* FATHER *explaining: it is being played under their breaths, very quietly, very naturally, in a way that is obviously impossible on stage. So when the* ACTORS' *attention is recalled by the* FATHER *they turn and see that* MME. PACE *has just put her hand under the* STEPDAUGHTER's *chin to make her lift her head up: they also hear her speak in a way that is unintelligible to them. They watch and listen hard for a few moments, then they start to make fun of them.*)

PRODUCER: Well?
240 LEADING ACTOR: What's she saying?
LEADING ACTRESS: Can't hear a thing!
JUVENILE LEAD: Louder! Speak up!
STEPDAUGHTER: (*Leaving* MME. PACE *who has an astonishing smile on her face, and coming down to the* ACTORS.) Louder?
245 What do you mean, 'Louder'? What we're talking about you can't talk about loudly. I could shout about it a moment ago to embarrass him (*Pointing to the* FATHER.) to shame him and to get my own back on him! But it's a different matter for Mme. Pace. It would mean prison for her.
250 PRODUCER: What the hell are you on about? Here in the theatre you have to make yourself heard! Don't you see that? We can't hear you even from here, and we're on the stage with you! Imagine what it would be like with an audience out front! You need to make the scene go! And after all,
255 you would speak normally to each other when you're alone, and you will be, because we shan't be here anyway. I mean we're only here because it's a rehearsal. So just imagine that there you are in the room at the back of the shop, and there's no one to hear you.

(*The* STEPDAUGHTER, *with a knowing smile, wags her finger and her head rather elegantly, as if to say no.*)

260 PRODUCER: Why not?
STEPDAUGHTER: (*Mysteriously, whispering loudly.*) Because there is someone who will hear if she speaks normally. (*Pointing to* MME. PACE.)
PRODUCER: (*Anxiously.*) You're not going to make someone
265 else appear are you?

(*The* ACTORS *get ready to dive off the stage again.*)

FATHER: No, no. She means me. I ought to be over there, waiting behind the door: and Mme. Pace knows I'm there, so excuse me will you: I'll go there now so that I shall be ready for my entrance.

(*He goes towards the back of the stage.*)

270 PRODUCER: (*Stopping him.*) No, no wait a minute! You must remember the stage conventions! Before you can go on to that part . . .

STEPDAUGHTER: (*Interrupts him.*) Oh yes, let's get on with that part. Now! Now! I'm dying to do that scene. If he wants to go through it now, I'm ready!
275
PRODUCER: (*Shouting.*) But before that we must have, clearly stated, the scene between you and her. (*Pointing to* MME. PACE.) Do you see?
STEPDAUGHTER: Oh God! She's only told me what you already know, that my mother's needlework is badly done 280 again, the dress is spoilt and that I shall have to be patient if I want her to go on helping us out of our mess.
MME. PACE: (*Coming forward, with a great air of importance.*) Ah, yes, sir, for that I do not wish to make a profit, to make advantage. 285
PRODUCER: (*Half frightened.*) What? Does she really speak like that?

(*All the* ACTORS *burst out laughing.*)

STEPDAUGHTER: (*Laughing too.*) Yes, she speaks like that, half in Spanish, in the silliest way imaginable!
MME. PACE: Ah it is not good manners that you laugh at me 290 when I make myself to speak, as I can, English, señor.
PRODUCER: No, no, you're right! Speak like that, please speak like that, madam. It'll be marvellous. Couldn't be better! It'll add a little touch of comedy to a rather crude situation. Speak like that! It'll be great! 295
STEPDAUGHTER: Great! Why not? When you hear a proposition made in that sort of accent, it'll almost seem like a joke, won't it? Perhaps you'll want to laugh when you hear that there's an 'old señor' who wants to 'amuse himself with me'—isn't that right, Madame? 300
MME. PACE: Not so old . . . but not quite young, no? But if he is not to your taste . . . he is, how you say, discreet!

(*The* MOTHER *leaps up, to the astonishment and dismay of the* ACTORS *who had not been paying any attention to her, so that when she shouts out they are startled and then smilingly restrain her; however, she has already snatched off* MME. PACE's *wig and flung it on the floor.*)

MOTHER: You witch! Witch! Murderess! Oh, my daughter!
STEPDAUGHTER: (*Running across and taking hold of the* MOTHER.) No! No! Mother! Please! 305
FATHER: (*Running across to her as well.*) Calm yourself, calm yourself! Come and sit down.
MOTHER: Get her away from here!
STEPDAUGHTER: (*To the* PRODUCER *who has also crossed to her.*) My mother can't bear to be in the same place with her. 310
FATHER: (*Also speaking quietly to the* PRODUCER.) They can't possibly be in the same place! That's why she wasn't with us when we first came, do you see! If they meet, everything's given away from the very beginning.
PRODUCER: It's not important, that's not important! This is 315 only a first run-through at the moment! It's all useful stuff, even if it is confused. I'll sort it all out later. (*Turning to the* MOTHER *and taking her to sit down on her chair.*) Come on my dear, take it easy, take it easy: come and sit down again.
STEPDAUGHTER: Go on, Mme. Pace. 320
MME. PACE: (*Offended.*) Oh no, thank-you! I no longer do nothing here with your mother present.
STEPDAUGHTER: Get on with it, bring in this 'old señor' who wants to 'amuse himself with me'! (*Turning majestically to*

325   *the others.*) You see, this next scene has got to be played out—we must do it now. (*To* MME. PACE.) Oh, you can go!

MME. PACE: Ah, I go, I go—I go! Most probably I go!

(*She leaves banging her wig back into place, glaring furiously at the* ACTORS *who applaud her exit, laughing loudly.*)

STEPDAUGHTER: (*To the* FATHER.) Now you come on! No, you don't need to go off again! Come back! Pretend

330   you've just come in! Look, I'm standing here with my eyes on the ground, modestly—well, come on, speak up! Use that special sort of voice, like somebody who has just come in. 'Good afternoon, my dear.'

PRODUCER: (*Off the stage by now.*) Look here, who's the direc-

335   tor here, you or me? (*To the* FATHER *who looks uncertain and bewildered.*) Go on, do as she says: go upstage—no, no don't bother to make an entrance. Then come down stage again.

(*The* FATHER *does as he is told, half mesmerised. He is very pale but already involved in the reality of his recreated life, smiles as he draws near the back of the stage, almost if he genuinely is not aware of the drama that is about to sweep over him. The* ACTORS *are immediately intent on the scene that is beginning now.*)

THE SCENE

FATHER: (*Coming forward with a new note in his voice.*) Good afternoon, my dear.

STEPDAUGHTER: (*Her head down trying to hide her fright.*) Good afternoon.

5   FATHER: (*Studying her a little under the brim of her hat which partly hides her face from him and seeing that she is very young, he exclaims to himself a little complacently and a little guardedly because of the danger of being compromised in a risky adventure.*) Ah . . . but . . . tell me, this won't be the first time, will it?

10   The first time you've been here?

STEPDAUGHTER: No, sir.

FATHER: You've been here before? (*And after the* STEPDAUGH-TER *has nodded an answer.*) More than once? (*He waits for her reply: tries again to look at her under the brim of her hat,*

15   *smiles, then says.*) Well then . . . it shouldn't be too . . . May I take off your hat?

STEPDAUGHTER: (*Quickly, to stop him, unable to conceal her shudder of fear and disgust.*) No, don't! I'll do it!

(*She takes it off unsteadily.*)

(*The* MOTHER *watches the scene intently with the* SON *and the two smaller children who cling close to her all the time: they make a group on one side of the stage opposite the* ACTORS. *She follows the words and actions of the* FATHER *and the* STEPDAUGHTER *in this scene with a variety of expressions on her face—sadness, dismay, anxiety, horror: sometimes she turns her face away and sobs.*)

MOTHER: Oh God! Oh God!

20   FATHER: (*He stops as if turned to stone by the sobbing: then he goes on in the same tone of voice.*) Here, give it to me. I'll hang it up for you. (*He takes the hat in his hand.*) But such a pretty, dear little head like yours should have a much smarter hat than this! Would you like to help me choose one, then,

25   from these hats of Madame's hanging up here? Would you?

YOUNG ACTRESS: (*Interrupting.*) Be careful! Those are our hats!

PRODUCER: (*Quickly and angrily.*) For God's sake, shut up! Don't try to be funny! We're rehearsing! (*Turns back to the* STEPDAUGHTER.) Please go on, will you, from where you were interrupted.   30

STEPDAUGHTER: (*Going on.*) No, thank you, sir.

FATHER: Oh, don't say no to me please! Say you'll have one—to please me. Isn't this a pretty one—look! And then it will please Madame too, you know. She's put them out here on purpose, of course.   35

STEPDAUGHTER: No, look, I could never wear it.

FATHER: Are you thinking of what they would say at home when you went in wearing a new hat? Goodness me! Don't you know what to do? Shall I tell you what to say at home?

STEPDAUGHTER: (*Furiously, nearly exploding.*) That's not why! I 40 couldn't wear it because . . . as you can see: you should have noticed it before. (*Indicating her black dress.*)

FATHER: You're in mourning! Oh, forgive me. You're right, I see that now. Please forgive me. Believe me, I'm really very sorry.   45

STEPDAUGHTER: (*Gathering all her strength and making herself overcome her contempt and revulsion.*) That's enough. Don't go on, that's enough. I ought to be thanking you and not letting you blame yourself and get upset. Don't think any more about what I told you, please. And I should do the 50 same. (*Forcing herself to smile and adding.*) I should try to forget that I'm dressed like this.

PRODUCER: (*Interrupting, turning to the* PROMPTER *in the box and jumping up on the stage again.*) Hold it, hold it! Don't put that last line down, leave it out. (*Turning to the* FATHER 55 *and the* STEPDAUGHTER.) It's going well! It's going well! (*Then to the* FATHER *alone.*) Then we'll put in there the bit that we talked about. (*To the* ACTORS.) That scene with the hats is good, isn't it?

STEPDAUGHTER: But the best bit is coming now! Why can't 60 we get on with it?

PRODUCER: Just be patient, wait a minute. (*Turning and moving across to the* ACTORS.) Of course, it'll all have to be made a lot more light-hearted.

LEADING ACTOR: We shall have to play it a lot quicker, I think. 65

LEADING ACTRESS: Of course: there's nothing particularly difficult in it. (*To the* LEADING ACTOR.) Shall we run through it now?

LEADING ACTOR: Yes right . . . Shall we take it from my entrance? (*He goes to his position behind the door upstage.*) 70

PRODUCER: (*To the* LEADING ACTRESS.) Now then, listen, imagine the scene between you and Mme. Pace is finished. I'll write it up myself properly later on. You ought to be over here I think—(*She goes the opposite way.*) Where are you going now? 75

LEADING ACTRESS: Just a minute, I want to get my hat—(*She crosses to take her hat from the stand.*)

PRODUCER: Right, good, ready now? You are standing here with your head down.

STEPDAUGHTER: (*Very amused.*) But she's not dressed in black! 80

LEADING ACTRESS: Oh, but I shall be, and I'll look a lot better than you do, darling.

PRODUCER: (*To the* STEPDAUGHTER.) Shut up, will you! Go over there and watch! You might learn something! (*Clapping his hands.*) Right! Come on! Quiet please! Take it 85 from his entrance.

(*He climbs off stage so that he can see better. The door opens at the back of the set and the* LEADING ACTOR *enters with the lively, knowing air of an ageing roué. The playing of the following scene by the* ACTORS *must seem from the very beginning to be something quite different from the earlier scene, but without having the faintest air of parody in it.*)

(*Naturally the* STEPDAUGHTER *and the* FATHER, *unable to see themselves in the* LEADING ACTOR *and* LEADING ACTRESS, *hearing their words said by them, express their reactions in different ways, by gestures, or smiles or obvious protests so that we are aware of their suffering, their astonishment, their disbelief.*)

(*The* PROMPTER's *voice is heard clearly between every line in the scene, telling the* ACTORS *what to say next.*)

LEADING ACTOR: Good afternoon, my dear.
FATHER: (*Immediately, unable to restrain himself.*) Oh, no!

(*The* STEPDAUGHTER, *watching the* LEADING ACTOR *enter this way, bursts into laughter.*)

PRODUCER: (*Furious.*) Shut up, for God's sake! And don't you
90   dare laugh like that! We're never going to get anywhere at this rate.
STEPDAUGHTER: (*Coming to the front.*) I'm sorry, I can't help it! The lady stands exactly where you told her to stand and she never moved. But if it were me and I heard someone
95   say good afternoon to me in that way and with a voice like that I should burst out laughing—so I did.
FATHER: (*Coming down a little too.*) Yes, she's right, the whole manner, the voice . . .
PRODUCER: To hell with the manner and the voice! Get out
100   of the way, will you, and let me watch the rehearsal!
LEADING ACTOR: (*Coming down stage.*) If I have to play an old man who has come to a knocking shop—
PRODUCER: Take no notice, ignore them. Go on please! It's going well, it's going well! (*He waits for the* ACTOR *to begin*
105   *again.*) Right, again!
LEADING ACTOR: Good afternoon, my dear.
LEADING ACTRESS: Good afternoon.
LEADING ACTOR: (*Copying the gestures of the* FATHER, *looking under the brim of the hat, but expressing distinctly the two emo-*
110   *tions, first, complacent satisfaction and then anxiety.*) Ah! But tell me . . . this won't be the first time I hope.
FATHER: (*Instinctively correcting him.*) Not 'I hope'—'will it,' 'will it.'
PRODUCER: Say 'will it'—and it's a question.
115 LEADING ACTOR: (*Glaring at the* PROMPTER.) I distinctly heard him say 'I hope.'
PRODUCER: So what? It's all the same, 'I hope' or 'isn't it.' It doesn't make any difference. Carry on, carry on. But perhaps it should still be a little bit lighter; I'll show you—
120   watch me! (*He climbs up on the stage again, and going back to the entrance, he does it himself.*) Good afternoon, my dear.
LEADING ACTRESS: Good afternoon.
PRODUCER: Ah, tell me . . . (*He turns to the* LEADING ACTOR *to make sure that he has seen the way he has demonstrated of look-ing under the brim of the hat.*) You see—surprise . . . anxiety
125   and self-satisfaction. (*Then, starting again, he turns to the* LEADING ACTRESS.) This won't be the first time, will it? The first time you've been here? (*Again turns to the* LEADING

ACTOR, *questioningly.*) Right? (*To the* LEADING ACTRESS.) And then she says, 'No, sir.' (*Again to* LEADING ACTOR.) See 130 what I mean? More subtlety. (*And he climbs off the stage.*)
LEADING ACTRESS: No, sir.
LEADING ACTOR: You've been here before? More than once?
PRODUCER: No, no, no! Wait for it, wait for it. Let her answer first. 'You've been here before?' 135

(*The* LEADING ACTRESS *lifts her head a little, her eyes closed in pain and disgust, and when the* PRODUCER *says 'Now' she nods her head twice.*)

STEPDAUGHTER: (*Involuntarily.*) Oh, my God! (*And she immediately claps her hand over her mouth to stifle her laughter.*)
PRODUCER: What now?
STEPDAUGHTER: (*Quickly.*) Nothing, nothing!
PRODUCER: (*To* LEADING ACTOR.) Come on, then, now it's you. 140
LEADING ACTOR: More than once? Well then, it shouldn't be too . . . May I take off your hat?

(*The* LEADING ACTOR *says this last line in such a way and adds to it such a gesture that the* STEPDAUGHTER, *even with her hand over her mouth trying to stop herself laughing, can't prevent a noisy burst of laughter.*)

LEADING ACTRESS: (*Indignantly turning.*) I'm not staying any longer to be laughed at by that woman!
LEADING ACTOR: Nor am I! That's the end—no more! 145
PRODUCER: (*To* STEPDAUGHTER, *shouting.*) Once and for all, will you shut up! Shut up!
STEPDAUGHTER: Yes, I'm sorry . . . I'm sorry.
PRODUCER: You're an ill-mannered little bitch! That's what you are! And you've gone too far this time! 150
FATHER: (*Trying to interrupt.*) Yes, you're right, she went too far, but please forgive her . . .
PRODUCER: (*Jumping on the stage.*) Why should I forgive her? Her behaviour is intolerable!
FATHER: Yes, it is, but the scene made such a peculiar impact 155 on us . . .
PRODUCER: Peculiar? What do you mean peculiar? Why peculiar?
FATHER: I'm full of admiration for your actors, for this gentleman (*To the* LEADING ACTOR.) and this lady. (*To the* 160 LEADING ACTRESS.) But, you see, well . . . they're not us!
PRODUCER: Right! They're not! They're actors!
FATHER: That's just the point—they're actors. And they are acting our parts very well, both of them. But that's what's different. However much they want to be the same as us, 165 they're not.
PRODUCER: But why aren't they? What is it now?
FATHER: It's something to do with . . . being themselves, I suppose, not being us.
PRODUCER: Well we can't do anything about that! I've told 170 you already. You can't play the parts yourselves.
FATHER: Yes, I know, I know . . .
PRODUCER: Right then. That's enough of that. (*Turning back to the* ACTORS.) We'll rehearse this later on our own, as we usually do. It's always a bad idea to have rehearsals with 175 authors there! They're never satisfied. (*Turns back to the* FATHER *and the* STEPDAUGHTER.) Come on, let's get on with it; and let's see if it's possible to do it without laughing.

STEPDAUGHTER: I won't laugh any more, I won't really. My
180   best bit's coming up now, you wait and see!

PRODUCER: Right: when you say 'Don't think any more about
what I told you, please. And I should do the same.' (*Turning to the* FATHER.) then you come in immediately with the
line 'I understand, ah yes, I understand' and then you ask . . .

185 STEPDAUGHTER: (*Interrupting.*) Ask what? What does he ask?

PRODUCER: Why you're in mourning.

STEPDAUGHTER: No! No! That's not right! Look: when I said
that I should try not to think about the way I was dressed,
do you know what he said? 'Well then, let's take it off,
190   we'll take it off at once, shall we, your little black dress.'

PRODUCER: That's great! That'll be wonderful! That'll bring
the house down!

STEPDAUGHTER: But it's the truth!

PRODUCER: The truth! Do me a favour will you? This is the
195   theatre you know! Truth's all very well up to a point but . . .

STEPDAUGHTER: What do you want to do then?

PRODUCER: You'll see! You'll see! Leave it all to me.

STEPDAUGHTER: No. No I won't. I know what you want to
do! Out of my feeling of revulsion, out of all the vile and
200   sordid reasons why I am what I am, you want to make a
sugary little sentimental romance. You want him to ask me
why I'm in mourning and you want me to reply with the
tears running down my face that it is only two months
since my father died. No. No. I won't have it! He must say
205   to me what he really did say. 'Well then, let's take it off,
we'll take it off at once, shall we, your little black dress.' And
I, with my heart still grieving for my father's death only
two months before, I went behind there, do you see? Behind that screen and with my fingers trembling with shame
210   and loathing I took off the dress, unfastened my bra . . .

PRODUCER: (*His head in his hands.*) For God's sake! What are
you saying!

STEPDAUGHTER: (*Shouting excitedly.*) The truth! I'm telling
you the truth!

215 PRODUCER: All right then. Now listen to me. I'm not denying it's the truth. Right. And believe me I understand
your horror, but you must see that we can't really put a
scene like that on the stage.

STEPDAUGHTER: You can't? Then thanks very much. I'm not
220   stopping here.

PRODUCER: No, listen . . .

STEPDAUGHTER: No, I'm going. I'm not stopping. The pair
of you have worked it all out together, haven't you, what
to put in the scene. Well, thank you very much! I understand
225   stand everything now! He wants to get to the scene where
he can talk about his spiritual torments but I want to show
you my drama! Mine!

PRODUCER: (*Shaking with anger.*) Now we're getting to the real
truth of it, aren't we? Your drama—yours! But it's not only
230   yours, you know. It's drama for the other people as well! For
him (*Pointing to the* FATHER.) and for your mother! You can't
have one character coming on like you're doing, trampling
over the others, taking over the play. Everything needs to be
balanced and in harmony so that we can show what has to
235   be shown! I know perfectly well that we've all got a life inside us and that we all want to parade it in front of other
people. But that's the difficulty, how to present only the bits

that are necessary in relation to the other characters: and in
the small amount we show, to hint at all the rest of the inner
life of the character! I agree, it would be so much simpler, if   240
each character, in a soliloquy or in a lecture could pour out
to the audience what's bubbling away inside him. But that's
not the way we work. (*In an indulgent, placating tone.*) You
must restrain yourself, you see. And believe me, it's in your
own interests: because you could so easily make a bad im-   245
pression, with all this uncontrollable anger, this disgust and
exasperation. That seems a bit odd, if you don't mind my
saying so, when you've admitted that you'd been with other
men at Mme. Pace's and more than once.

STEPDAUGHTER: I suppose that's true. But you know, all the   250
other men were all him as far as I was concerned.

PRODUCER: (*Not understanding.*) Uum—? What? What are
you talking about?

STEPDAUGHTER: If someone falls into evil ways, isn't the responsibility for all the evil which follows to be laid at the   255
door of the person who caused the first mistake? And in
my case, it's him, from before I was even born. Look at
him: see if it isn't true.

PRODUCER: Right then! What about the weight of remorse
he's carrying? Isn't that important? Then, give him the   260
chance to show it to us.

STEPDAUGHTER: But how? How on earth can he show all his
long-suffering remorse, all his moral torments as he calls
them, if you don't let him show his horror when he finds
me in his arms one fine day, after he had asked me to take   265
my dress off, a black dress for my father who had just died:
and he finds that I'm the child he used to go and watch
as she came out of school, me, a woman now, and a
woman he could buy. (*She says these last words in a voice
trembling with emotion.*)   270

(*The* MOTHER, *hearing her say this, is overcome and at first gives
way to stifled sobs: but then she bursts out into uncontrollable crying.
Everyone is deeply moved. There is a long pause.*)

STEPDAUGHTER: (*As soon as the* MOTHER *has quietened herself
she goes on, firmly and thoughtfully.*) At the moment we are
here on our own and the public doesn't know about us.
But tomorrow you will present us and our story in whatever way you choose, I suppose. But wouldn't you like to   275
see the real drama? Wouldn't you like to see it explode
into life, as it really did?

PRODUCER: Of course, nothing I'd like better, then I can use
as much of it as possible.

STEPDAUGHTER: Then persuade my mother to leave.   280

MOTHER: (*Rising and her quiet weeping changing to a loud cry.*)
No! No! Don't let her! Don't let her do it!

PRODUCER: But they're only doing it for me to watch—only
for me, do you see?

MOTHER: I can't bear it, I can't bear it!   285

PRODUCER: But if it's already happened, I can't see what's the
objection.

MOTHER: No! It's happening now, as well: it's happening all
the time. I'm not acting my suffering! Can't you understand that? I'm alive and here now but I can never forget   290
that terrible moment of agony, that repeats itself endlessly
and vividly in my mind. And these two little children here,

you've never heard them speak have you? That's because
they don't speak any more, not now. They just cling to me
295 all the time: they help to keep my grief alive, but they don't
really exist for themselves any more, not for themselves.
And she (*Indicating the* STEPDAUGHTER.) . . . she has gone
away, left me completely, she's lost to me, lost . . . you see her
here for one reason only: to keep perpetually before me, al-
300 ways real, the anguish and the torment I've suffered on her
account.
FATHER: The eternal moment, as I told you, sir. She is here
(*Indicating the* STEPDAUGHTER.) to keep me too in that
moment, trapped for all eternity, chained and suspended
305 in that one fleeting shameful moment of my life. She can't
give up her role and you cannot rescue me from it.
PRODUCER: But I'm not saying that we won't present that
bit. Not at all! It will be the climax of the first act, when
she (*He points to the* MOTHER.) surprises you.
310 FATHER: That's right, because that is the moment when I am
sentenced: all our suffering should reach a climax in her
cry. (*Again indicating the* MOTHER.)
STEPDAUGHTER: I can still hear it ringing in my ears! It
was that cry that sent me mad! You can have me played
315 just as you like: it doesn't matter! Dressed, too, if you
want, so long as I can have at least an arm—only an
arm—bare, because, you see, as I was standing like this
(*She moves across to the* FATHER *and leans her head on his
chest.*) with my head like this and my arms round his
320 neck, I saw a vein, here in my arm, throbbing: and then
it was almost as if that throbbing vein filled me with
a shivering fear, and I shut my eyes tightly like this,
like this and buried my head in his chest. (*Turning to
the* MOTHER.) Scream, Mummy, scream. (*She buries her
325 head in the* FATHER'*s chest, and with her shoulders raised as
if to try not to hear the scream, she speaks with a voice tense
with suffering.*) Scream, as you screamed then!
MOTHER: (*Coming forward to pull them apart.*) No! She's my
daughter! My daughter! (*Tearing her from him.*) You brute,
330 you animal, she's my daughter! Can't you see she's my
daughter?
PRODUCER: (*Retreating as far as the footlights while the* ACTORS
are full of dismay.) Marvellous! Yes, that's great! And then
curtain, curtain!
335 FATHER: (*Running downstage to him, excitedly.*) That's it, that's it!
Because it really was like that!
PRODUCER: (*Full of admiration and enthusiasm.*) Yes, yes, that's
got to be the curtain line! Curtain! Curtain!

(*At the repeated calls of the* PRODUCER, *the* STAGE MANAGER *lowers the curtain, leaving on the apron in front, the* PRODUCER *and
the* FATHER.)

PRODUCER: (*Looking up to heaven with his arms raised.*) The id-
340 iots! I didn't mean now! The bloody idiots—dropping it
in on us like that! (*To the* FATHER, *and lifting up a corner of
the curtain.*) That's marvellous! Really marvellous! A terrific effect! We'll end the act like that! It's the best tag line
I've heard for ages. What a First Act ending! I couldn't
345 have done better if I'd written it myself!

(*They go through the curtain together.*)

ACT THREE

When the curtain goes up we see that the STAGE MANAGER *and*
STAGE HANDS *have struck the first scene and have set another, a
small garden fountain.*

From one side of the stage the ACTORS *come on and from the other
the* CHARACTERS. *The* PRODUCER *is standing in the middle of the
stage with his hand over his mouth, thinking.*

PRODUCER: (*After a short pause, shrugging his shoulders.*) Well,
then: let's get on to the second act! Leave it all to me, and
everything will work out properly.
STEPDAUGHTER: This is where we go to live at his house
(*Pointing to the* FATHER.) in spite of the objections of him 5
over there. (*Pointing to the* SON.)
PRODUCER: (*Getting impatient.*) All right, all right! But leave
it all to me, will you?
STEPDAUGHTER: Provided that you make it clear that he objected!   10
MOTHER: (*From the corner, shaking her head.*) That doesn't matter! The worse it was for us, the more he suffered from remorse.
PRODUCER: (*Impatiently.*) I know, I know! I'll take it all into
account. Don't worry!   15
MOTHER: (*Pleading.*) To set my mind at rest, sir, please do
make sure it's clear that I tried all I could—
STEPDAUGHTER: (*Interrupting her scornfully and going on.*)—to
pacify me, to persuade me that this despicable creature
wasn't worth making trouble about! (*To the* PRODUCER.) 20
Go on, set her mind at rest, because it's true, she tried very
hard. I'm having a whale of a time now! You can see, can't
you, that the meeker she was and the more she tried to
worm her way into his heart, the more lofty and distant
he became! How's that for a dramatic situation!   25
PRODUCER: Do you think that we can actually begin the
Second Act?
STEPDAUGHTER: I won't say another word! But you'll see that
it won't be possible to play everything in the garden, like
you want to do.   30
PRODUCER: Why not?
STEPDAUGHTER: (*Pointing to the* SON.) Because to start with,
he stays shut up in his room in the house all the time! And
then all the scenes for this poor little devil of a boy happen in the house. I've told you once.   35
PRODUCER: Yes, I know that! But on the other hand we can't
put up a notice to tell the audience where the scene is taking place, or change the set three or four times in each Act.
LEADING ACTOR: That's what they used to do in the good old
days.   40
PRODUCER: Yes, when the audience was about as bright as
that little girl over there!
LEADING ACTRESS: And it makes it easier to create an illusion.
FATHER: (*Leaping up.*) An illusion? For pity's sake don't talk
about illusions! Don't use that word, it's especially hurtful 45
to us!
PRODUCER: (*Astonished.*) And why, for God's sake?
FATHER: It's so hurtful, so cruel! You ought to have realised
that!

50 PRODUCER: What else should we call it? That's what we do
    here—create an illusion for the audience . . .
    LEADING ACTOR: With our performance . . .
    PRODUCER: A perfect illusion of reality!
    FATHER: Yes, I know that, I understand. But on the other
55   hand, perhaps you don't understand us yet. I'm sorry! But
    you see, for you and for your actors what goes on here on
    the stage is, quite rightly, well, it's only a game.
    LEADING ACTRESS: (*Interrupting indignantly.*) A game! How
    dare you! We're not children! What happens here is serious!
60 FATHER: I'm not saying that it isn't serious. And I mean, re-
    ally, not just a game but an art, that tries, as you've just said,
    to create the perfect illusion of reality.
    PRODUCER: That's right!
    FATHER: Now try to imagine that we, as you see us here, (*He
65   indicates himself and the other* CHARACTERS.) that we have
    no other reality outside this illusion.
    PRODUCER: (*Astonished and looking at the* ACTORS *with the
    same sense of bewilderment as they feel themselves.*) What the
    hell are you talking about now?
70 FATHER: (*After a short pause as he looks at them, with a faint
    smile.*) Isn't it obvious? What other reality is there for us?
    What for you is an illusion you create, for us is our only
    reality. (*Brief pause. He moves towards the* PRODUCER *and goes
    on.*) But it's not only true for us, it's true for others as well,
75   you know. Just think about it. (*He looks intently into the
    PRODUCER's eyes.*) Do you really know who you are? (*He
    stands pointing at the* PRODUCER.)
    PRODUCER: (*A little disturbed but with a half smile.*) What? Who
    I am? I am me!
80 FATHER: What if I told you that that wasn't true: what if I told
    you that you were me?
    PRODUCER: I would tell you that you were mad!

(*The* ACTORS *laugh.*)

    FATHER: That's right, laugh! Because everything here is a game!
    (*To the* PRODUCER.) And yet you object when I say that it is
85   only for a game that the gentleman there (*Pointing to the
    LEADING ACTOR.*) who is 'himself' has to be 'me,' who, on
    the contrary, am 'myself.' You see, I've caught you in a trap.

(*The* ACTORS *start to laugh.*)

    PRODUCER: Not again! We've heard all about this a little
    while ago.
90 FATHER: No, no. I didn't really want to talk about this. I'd like
    you to forget about your game, (*Looking at the* LEADING
    ACTRESS *as if to anticipate what she will say.*) I'm sorry—
    your artistry! Your art!—that you usually pursue here with
    your actors; and I am going to ask you again in all seri-
95   ousness, who are you?
    PRODUCER: (*Turning with a mixture of amazement and annoyance,
    to the* ACTORS.) Of all the bloody nerve! A fellow who
    claims he is only a character comes and asks me who I am!
    FATHER: (*With dignity but without annoyance.*) A character, my
100   dear sir, can always ask a man who he is, because a char-
    acter really has a life of his own, a life full of his own spe-
    cific qualities, and because of these he is always 'someone.'
    While a man—I'm not speaking about you personally, of
    course, but man in general—well, he can be an absolute
105   'nobody.'

    PRODUCER: All right, all right! Well, since you've asked me,
    I'm the Director, the Producer—I'm in charge! Do you
    understand?
    FATHER: (*Half smiling, but gently and politely.*) I'm only asking to
    try to find out if you really see yourself now in the same way   110
    that you saw yourself, for instance, once upon a time in the
    past, with all the illusions you had then, with everything in-
    side and outside yourself as it seemed then—and not only
    seemed, but really was! Well then, look back on those illu-
    sions, those ideas that you don't have any more, on all those   115
    things that no longer seem the same to you. Don't you feel
    that not only this stage is falling away from under your feet
    but so is the earth itself, and that all these realities of today
    are going to seem tomorrow as if they had been an illusion?
    PRODUCER: So? What does that prove?   120
    FATHER: Oh, nothing much. I only want to make you see that
    if we (*Pointing to himself and the other* CHARACTERS.) have
    no other reality outside our own illusion, perhaps you
    ought to distrust your own sense of reality: because what-
    ever is a reality today, whatever you touch and believe in   125
    and that seems real for you today, is going to be—like the
    reality of yesterday—an illusion tomorrow.
    PRODUCER: (*Deciding to make fun of him.*) Very good! So now
    you're saying that you as well as this play you're going to
    show me here, are more real than I am?   130
    FATHER: (*Very seriously.*) There's no doubt about that at all.
    PRODUCER: Is that so?
    FATHER: I thought you'd realised that from the beginning.
    PRODUCER: More real than I am?
    FATHER: If your reality can change between today and   135
    tomorrow—
    PRODUCER: But everybody knows that it can change, don't
    they? It's always changing! Just like everybody else's!
    FATHER: (*Crying out.*) But ours doesn't change! Do you see?
    That's the difference! Ours doesn't change, it can't change, it   140
    can never be different, never, because it is already determined,
    like this, for ever, that's what's so terrible! We are an eternal re-
    ality. That should make you shudder to come near us.
    PRODUCER: (*Jumping up, suddenly struck by an idea, and standing
    directly in front of the* FATHER.) Then I should like to know   145
    when anyone saw a character step out of his part and make
    a speech like you've done, proposing things, explaining
    things. Tell me when, will you? I've never seen it before.
    FATHER: You've never seen it because an author usually hides
    all the difficulties of creating. When the characters are   150
    alive, really alive and standing in front of their author, he
    has only to follow their words, the actions that they suggest
    to him: and he must want them to be what they want to
    be: and it's his bad luck if he doesn't do what they want!
    When a character is born he immediately assumes such an   155
    independence even of his own author that everyone can
    imagine him in scores of situations that his author hadn't
    even thought of putting him in, and he sometimes acquires
    a meaning that his author never dreamed of giving him.
    PRODUCER: Of course I know all that.   160
    FATHER: Well, then. Why are you surprised by us? Imagine
    what a disaster it is for a character to be born in the imag-
    ination of an author who then refuses to give him life in
    a written script. Tell me if a character, left like this, sus-
    pended, created but without a final life, isn't right to do   165
    what we are doing now, here in front of you. We spent

such a long time, such a very long time, believe me, urging our author, persuading him, first me, then her, (*Pointing to the* STEPDAUGHTER.) then this poor Mother . . .

170 STEPDAUGHTER: (*Coming down the stage as if in a dream.*) It's true, I would go, would go and tempt him, time after time, in his gloomy study just as it was growing dark, when he was sitting quietly in an armchair not even both-
175 ering to switch a light on but leaving the shadows to fill the room: the shadows were swarming with us, we had come to tempt him. (*As if she could see herself there in the study and is annoyed by the presence of the* ACTORS.) Go away will you! Leave us alone! Mother there, with that son of hers—me with the little girl—that poor little kid always
180 on his own—and then me with him (*Pointing to the* FATHER.) and then at last, just me, on my own, all on my own, in the shadows. (*She turns quickly as if she wants to cling on to the vision she has of herself, in the shadows.*) Ah, what scenes, what scenes we suggested to him! What a life I
185 could have had! I tempted him more than the others!
     FATHER: Oh yes, you did! And it was probably all your fault that he did nothing about it! You were so insistent, you made too many demands.
     STEPDAUGHTER: But he wanted me to be like that! (*She comes
190 closer to the* PRODUCER *to speak to him in confidence.*) I think it's more likely that he felt discouraged about the theatre and even despised it because the public only wants to see . . .
     PRODUCER: Let's get on, for God's sake, let's get on. Come to the point will you?
195 STEPDAUGHTER: I'm sorry, but if you ask me, we've got too much happening already, just with our entry into his house. (*Pointing to the* FATHER.) You said that we couldn't put up a notice or change the set every five minutes.
     PRODUCER: Right! Of course we can't! We must combine
200 things, group them together in one continuous flowing action: not the way you've been wanting, first of all seeing your little brother come home from school and wander about the house like a lost soul, hiding behind the doors and brooding on some plan or other that would—what
205 did you say it would do?
     STEPDAUGHTER: Wither him . . . shrivel him up completely.
     PRODUCER: That's good! That's a good expression. And then you 'can see it there in his eyes, getting stronger all the time'—isn't that what you said?
210 STEPDAUGHTER: Yes, that's right. Look at him! (*Pointing to him as he stands next to his* MOTHER.)
     PRODUCER: Yes, great! And then, at the same time, you want to show the little girl playing in the garden, all innocence. One in the house and the other in the garden—we can't
215 do it, don't you see that?
     STEPDAUGHTER: Yes, playing in the sun, so happy! It's the only pleasure I have left, her happiness, her delight in playing in the garden: away from the misery, the squalor of that sordid flat where all four of us slept and where she slept with
220 me—with me! Just think of it! My vile, contaminated body close to hers, with her little arms wrapped tightly round my neck, so lovingly, so innocently. In the garden, whenever she saw me, she would run and take my hand. She never wanted to show me the big flowers, she would
225 run about looking for the 'little weeny' ones, so that she could show them to me; she was so happy, so thrilled! (*As she says this, tortured by the memory, she breaks out into a long*

desperate cry, dropping her head on her arms that rest on a little table. Everybody is very affected by her. The* PRODUCER *comes to her almost paternally and speaks to her in a soothing voice.*) 230

PRODUCER: We'll have the garden scene, we'll have it, don't worry: and you'll see, you'll be very pleased with what we do! We'll play all the scenes in the garden! (*He calls out to a* STAGE HAND *by name.*) Hey . . . . , let down a few bits of tree, will you? A couple of cypresses will do, in front of the 235
fountain. (*Someone drops in the two cypresses and a* STAGE HAND *secures them with a couple of braces and weights.*)
PRODUCER: (*To the* STEPDAUGHTER.) That'll do for now, won't it? It'll just give us an idea. (*Calling out to a* STAGE HAND *by name again.*) Hey, ... give me something for the sky will you? 240
STAGE HAND: What's that?
PRODUCER: Something for the sky! A small cloth to come in behind the fountain. (*A white cloth is dropped from the flies.*) Not white! I asked for a sky! Never mind: leave it! I'll do something with it. (*Calling out.*) Hey lights! Kill everything 245
will you? Give me a bit of moonlight—the blues in the batten and a blue spot on the cloth . . . (*They do.*) That's it! That'll do! (*Now on the scene there is the light he asked for, a mysterious blue light that makes the* ACTORS *speak and move as if in the garden in the evening under a moon. To the* STEPDAUGHTER.) Look 250
here now: the little boy can come out here in the garden and hide among the trees instead of hiding behind the doors in the house. But it's going to be difficult to find a little girl to play the scene with you where she shows you the flowers. (*Turning to the* LITTLE BOY.) Come on, come on, son, come 255
across here. Let's see what it'll look like. (*But the* BOY *doesn't move.*) Come on will you, come on. (*Then he pulls him forward and tries to make him hold his head up, but every time it falls down again on his chest.*) There's something very odd about this lad . . . What's wrong with him? My God, he'll have to 260
say something sometime! (*He comes over to him again, puts his hand on his shoulder and pushes him between the trees.*) Come a bit nearer: let's have a look. Can you hide a bit more? That's it. Now pop your head out and look round. (*He moves away to look at the effect and as the* BOY *does what he has been told to do,* 265
the ACTORS *watch impressed and a little disturbed.*) Ahh, that's good, very good . . . (*He turns to the* STEPDAUGHTER.) How about having the little girl, surprised to see him there, run across. Wouldn't that make him say something?
STEPDAUGHTER: (*Getting up.*) It's no use hoping he'll speak, 270
not as long as that creature's there. (*Pointing to the* SON.) You'll have to get him out of the way first.
SON: (*Moving determinedly to one of the sets of steps leading off the stage.*) With pleasure! I'll go now! Nothing will please me better!
PRODUCER: (*Stopping him immediately.*) Hey, no! Where are 275
you going? Hang on!

(*The* MOTHER *gets up, anxious at the idea that he is really going and instinctively raising her arms as if to hold him back, but without moving from where she is.*)

SON: (*At the footlights, to the* PRODUCER *who is restraining him there.*) There's no reason why I should be here! Let me go will you? Let me go!
PRODUCER: What do you mean there's no reason for you to 280
be here?
STEPDAUGHTER: (*Calmly, ironically.*) Don't bother to stop him. He won't go!

FATHER: You have to play that terrible scene in the garden
285   with your mother.

SON: (*Quickly, angry and determined.*) I'm not going to play
    anything! I've said that all along! (*To the* PRODUCER.) Let
    me go will you?

STEPDAUGHTER: (*Crossing to the* PRODUCER.) It's all right. Let
290   him go. (*She moves the* PRODUCER's *hand from the* SON. *Then
    she turns to the* SON *and says.*) Well, go on then! Off you go!

(*The* SON *stays near the steps but as if pulled by some strange force
he is quite unable to go down them: then to the astonishment and
even the dismay of the* ACTORS, *he moves along the front of the stage
towards the other set of steps down into the auditorium: but having
got there, he again stays near and doesn't actually go down them.
The* STEPDAUGHTER *who has watched him scornfully but very intently, bursts into laughter.*)

STEPDAUGHTER: He can't, you see? He can't! He's got to stay
    here! He must. He's chained to us for ever! No, I'm the
    one who goes, when what must happen does happen, and
295   I run away, because I hate him, because I can't bear the
    sight of him any longer. Do you think it's possible for him
    to run away? He has to stay here with that wonderful fa-
    ther of his and his mother there. She doesn't think she has
    any other son but him. (*She turns to the* MOTHER.) Come
300   on, come on, Mummy, come on! (*Turning back to the* PRO-
    DUCER *to point her out to him.*) Look, she's going to try to
    stop him . . . (*To the* MOTHER, *half compelling her, as if by
    some magic power.*) Come on, come on. (*Then to the* PRO-
    DUCER *again.*) Imagine how she must feel at showing her
305   affection for him in front of your actors! But her longing
    to be near him is so strong that—look! She's going to go
    through that scene with him again! (*The* MOTHER *has now
    actually come close to the* SON *as the* STEPDAUGHTER *says the
    last line: she gestures to show that she agrees to go on.*)

310 SON: (*Quickly.*) But I'm not! I'm not! If I can't get away then
    I suppose I shall have to stay here; but I repeat that I will
    not have any part in it.

FATHER: (*To the* PRODUCER, *excitedly.*) You must make him!

SON: Nobody's going to make me do anything!

315 FATHER: I'll make you!

STEPDAUGHTER: Wait! Just a minute! Before that, the little girl
    has to go to the fountain. (*She turns to take the* LITTLE GIRL,
    drops on her knees in front of her and takes her face between her
    hands.*) My poor little darling, those beautiful eyes, they look
320   so bewildered. You're wondering where you are, aren't
    you? Well, we're on a stage, my darling! What's a stage? Well,
    it's a place where you pretend to be serious. They put on
    plays here. And now we're going to put on a play. Seriously!
    Oh, yes! Even you . . . (*She hugs her tightly and rocks her gently
325   for a moment.*) Oh, my little one, my little darling, what a ter-
    rible play it is for you! What horrible things have been
    planned for you! The garden, the fountain . . . Oh, yes, it's
    only a pretend fountain, that's right. That's part of the game,
    my pretty darling: everything is pretends here. Perhaps
330   you'll like a pretends fountain better than a real one: you can
    play here then. But it's only a game for the others; not for
    you, I'm afraid, it's real for you, my darling, and your game is
    in a real fountain, a big beautiful green fountain with bam-

boos casting shadows, looking at your own reflection, with
lots of baby ducks paddling about, shattering the reflections. You want to stroke one! (*With a scream that electrifies
and terrifies everybody.*) No, Rosetta, no! Your mummy isn't
watching you, she's over there with that selfish bastard! Oh,
God, I feel as if all the devils in hell were tearing me apart
inside . . . And you . . . (*Leaving the* LITTLE GIRL *and turning to
the* LITTLE BOY *in the usual way.*) What are you doing here,
hanging about like a beggar? It'll be your fault too, if that little girl drowns; you're always like this, as if I wasn't paying
the price for getting all of you into this house. (*Shaking his
arm to make him take his hand out of his pocket.*) What have you
got there? What are you hiding? Take it out, take your hand
out! (*She drags his hand out of his pocket and to everyone's horror
he is holding a revolver. She looks at him for a moment, almost with
satisfaction: then she says, grimly.*) Where on earth did you get
that? (*The* BOY, *looking frightened, with his eyes wide and empty,
doesn't answer.*) You idiot, if I'd been you, instead of killing
myself, I'd have killed one of those two: either or both, the
father and the son. (*She pushes him towards the cypress trees
where he then stands watching: then she takes the* LITTLE GIRL
*and helps her to climb in to the fountain, making her lie so that she
is hidden: after that she kneels down and puts her head and arms on
the rim of the fountain.*)

PRODUCER: That's good! It's good! (*Turning to the* STEP-
    DAUGHTER.) And at the same time . . .

SON: (*Scornfully.*) What do you mean, at the same time? There
    was nothing at the same time! There wasn't any scene be-
    tween her and me. (*Pointing to the* MOTHER.) She'll tell
    you the same thing herself, she'll tell you what happened.

(*The* SECOND ACTRESS *and the* JUVENILE LEAD *have left the
group of* ACTORS *and have come to stand nearer the* MOTHER *and
the* SON *as if to study them so as to play their parts.*)

MOTHER: Yes, it's true. I'd gone to his room . . .

SON: Room, do you hear? Not the garden!

PRODUCER: It's not important! We've got to reorganise the
    events anyway. I've told you that already.

SON: (*Glaring at the* JUVENILE LEAD *and the* SECOND ACTRESS.)
    What do you want?

JUVENILE LEAD: Nothing. I'm just watching.

SON: (*Turning to the* SECOND ACTRESS.) You as well! Getting
    ready to play her part are you? (*Pointing to the* MOTHER.)

PRODUCER: That's it. And I think you should be grateful—
    they're paying you a lot of attention.

SON: Oh, yes, thank you! But haven't you realised yet that
    you'll never be able to do this play? There's nothing of us
    inside you and you actors are only looking at us from the
    outside. Do you think we could go on living with a mir-
    ror held up in front of us that didn't only freeze our re-
    flection for ever, but froze us in a reflection that laughed
    back at us with an expression that we didn't even recog-
    nise as our own?

FATHER: That's right! That's right!

PRODUCER: (*To* JUVENILE LEAD *and* SECOND ACTRESS.) Okay.
    Go back to the others.

SON: It's quite useless. I'm not prepared to do anything.

PRODUCER: Oh, shut up, will you, and let me listen to your mother. (*To the* MOTHER.) Well, you'd gone to his room, you said.

390 MOTHER: Yes, to his room. I couldn't bear it any longer. I wanted to empty my heart to him, tell him about all the agony that was crushing me. But as soon as he saw me come in . . .

SON: Nothing happened. I got away! I wasn't going to get involved. I never have been involved. Do you understand?

395 MOTHER: It's true! That's right!

PRODUCER: But we must make up the scene between you, then. It's vital!

MOTHER: I'm ready to do it! If only I had the chance to talk to him for a moment, to pour out all my troubles to him.

400 FATHER: (*Going to the* SON *and speaking violently.*) You'll do it! For your Mother! For your Mother!

SON: (*More than ever determined.*) I'm doing nothing!

FATHER: (*Taking hold of his coat collar and shaking him.*) For God's sake, do as I tell you! Do as I tell you! Do you hear

405 what she's saying? Haven't you any feelings for her?

SON: (*Taking hold of his* FATHER.) No I haven't! I haven't! Let that be the end of it!

(*There is a general uproar. The* MOTHER *frightened out of her wits, tries to get between them and separate them.*)

MOTHER: Please stop it! Please!

FATHER: (*Hanging on.*) Do as I tell you! Do as I tell you!

410 SON: (*Wrestling with him and finally throwing him to the ground near the steps. Everyone is horrified.*) What's come over you? Why are you so frantic? Do you want to parade our disgrace in front of everybody? Well, I'm having nothing to do with it! Nothing! And I'm doing what our author

415 wanted as well—he never wanted to put us on the stage.

PRODUCER: Then why the hell did you come here?

SON: (*Pointing to the* FATHER.) He wanted to, I didn't.

PRODUCER: And aren't you here now?

SON: He was the one who wanted to come and he dragged

420 all of us here with him and agreed with you in there about what to put in the play: and that meant not only what had really happened, as if that wasn't bad enough, but what hadn't happened as well.

PRODUCER: All right, then, you tell me what happened. You tell

425 me! Did you rush out of your room without saying anything?

SON: (*After a moment's hesitation.*) Without saying anything. I didn't want to make a scene.

PRODUCER: (*Needling him.*) What then? What did you do then?

SON: (*He is now the centre of everyone's agonised attention and he

430 crosses the stage.*) Nothing . . . I went across the garden . . . (*He breaks off gloomy and absorbed.*)

PRODUCER: (*Urging him to say more, impressed by his reluctance to speak.*) Well? What then? You crossed the garden?

SON: (*Exasperated, putting his face into the crook of his arm.*) Why

435 do you want me to talk about it? It's horrible! (*The* MOTHER *is trembling with stifled sobs and looking towards the fountain.*)

PRODUCER: (*Quietly, seeing where she is looking and turning to the* SON *with growing apprehension.*) The little girl?

SON: (*Looking straight in front, out to the audience.*) There, in the

440 fountain . . .

FATHER: (*On the floor still, pointing with pity at the* MOTHER.) She was trailing after him!

PRODUCER: (*To the* SON, *anxiously.*) What did you do then?

SON: (*Still looking out front and speaking slowly.*) I dashed across. I was going to jump in and pull her out . . . But something 445 else caught my eye: I saw something behind the tree that made my blood run cold: the little boy, he was standing there with a mad look in his eyes: he was standing looking into the fountain at his little sister, floating there, drowned.

(*The* STEPDAUGHTER *is still bent at the fountain hiding the* LITTLE GIRL, *and she sobs pathetically, her sobs sounding like an echo.*)

(*There is a pause.*)

SON: (*Continued.*) I made a move towards him: but then . . . 450

(*From behind the trees where the little* BOY *is standing there is the sound of a shot.*)

MOTHER: (*With a terrible cry she runs along with the* SON *and all the* ACTORS *in the midst of a great general confusion.*) My son! My son! (*And then from out of the confusion and crying her voice comes out.*) Help! Help me!

PRODUCER: (*Amidst the shouting he tries to clear a space whilst the* 455 *little* BOY *is carried by his feet and shoulders behind the white skycloth.*) Is he wounded? Really wounded? (*Everybody except the* PRODUCER *and the* FATHER *who is still on the floor by the steps, has gone behind the skycloth and stays there talking anxiously. Then independently the* ACTORS *start to come back* 460 *into view.*)

LEADING ACTRESS: (*Coming from the right, very upset.*) He's dead! The poor boy! He's dead! What a terrible thing!

LEADING ACTOR: (*Coming back from the left and smiling.*) What do you mean, dead? It's all make-believe. It's a sham! He's 465 not dead. Don't you believe it!

OTHER ACTORS FROM THE RIGHT: Make-believe? It's real! Real! He's dead!

OTHER ACTORS FROM THE LEFT: No, he isn't. He's pretending! It's all make-believe. 470

FATHER: (*Running off and shouting at them as he goes.*) What do you mean, make-believe? It's real! It's real, ladies and gentlemen! It's reality! (*And with desperation on his face he too goes behind the skycloth.*)

PRODUCER: (*Not caring any more.*) Make-believe?! Reality?! 475 Oh, go to hell the lot of you! Lights! Lights! Lights!

(*At once all the stage and auditorium is flooded with light. The* PRODUCER *heaves a sigh of relief as if he has been relieved of a terrible weight and they all look at each other in distress and with uncertainty.*)

PRODUCER: God! I've never known anything like this! And we've lost a whole day's work! (*He looks at the clock.*) Get off with you, all of you! We can't do anything now! It's too late to start a rehearsal. (*When the* ACTORS *have gone,* 480 *he calls out.*) Hey, lights! Kill everything! (*As soon as he has said this, all the lights go out completely and leave him in the pitch dark.*) For God's sake!! You might have left the workers! I can't see where I'm going!

(*Suddenly, behind the skycloth, as if because of a bad connection, a green light comes up to throw on the cloth a huge sharp shadow of the* CHARACTERS, *but without the little* BOY *and the* LITTLE GIRL. *The* PRODUCER, *seeing this, jumps off the stage, terrified. At the same time the flood of light on them is switched off and the stage is again bathed in the same blue light as before. Slowly the* SON *comes on from the right, followed by the* MOTHER *with her arms raised towards him. Then from the left, the* FATHER *enters.*)

(*They come together in the middle of the stage and stand there as if transfixed. Finally from the left the* STEPDAUGHTER *comes on and moves towards the steps at the front: on the top step she pauses for a moment to look back at the other three and then bursts out in a raucous laugh, dashes down the steps and turns to look at the three figures still on the stage. Then she runs out of the auditorium and we can still hear her manic laughter out into the foyer and beyond.*)

(*After a pause the curtain falls slowly.*)

Bertolt Brecht

Bertolt Brecht (1898–1956) changed the course of the modern European theater—and theater around the world—more than any playwright since Ibsen. However, Brecht's sphere of influence extends beyond his career as a playwright. As a dramatist, he wrote an unsurpassed body of plays; as a theoretician, Brecht's conception of "alienation" in the epic theater opened the way for sweeping innovation in our understanding of the possibilities of the stage; as a director, Brecht's work with his company, the Berliner Ensemble, made it the most influential and important theater in postwar Europe. The challenge of understanding Brecht is to understand the dialectical interplay between theory and practice that informs his assault on stage realism, and on the bourgeois theater itself.

Eugen Berthold Brecht (he later changed his name to Bertolt) was born in Augsburg, Bavaria, in 1898 to a prosperous family. In 1917, he enrolled at Munich University in the natural sciences and worked as a drama critic on the side. He also began work on several plays, including *Baal* (1917). In 1918 he was conscripted into military service for the remainder of World War I and worked in a military hospital. He returned briefly to the university after the war, but soon turned his attention full time to the theater. He moved to Berlin—Germany's theatrical capital at the time—and had the good fortune to work with two influential directors, Max Reinhardt and Erwin Piscator. Piscator advocated the use of new technologies in the theater, as a way of developing a kind of performance more responsive to the mechanized and accelerated routines of modern life. Brecht acknowledged that many of his own staging techniques were derived from his work with Piscator in the 1920s. Throughout the 1920s and early 1930s, Brecht wrote a series of plays that brought him notoriety, largely for their satire of the bourgeois establishment: *Drums in the Night* (1919), *In the Jungle of Cities* (1921), *Man Is Man* (1926), and the musical plays he wrote in collaboration with the composer Kurt Weill, *The Threepenny Opera* (1928) and *The Rise and Fall of the City of Mahagonny* (1930). In the 1920s, Brecht also began to collaborate with Margarete Steffin, one of several women—including Elisabeth Hauptmann, Hella Wuolijoki, and Ruth Berlau—with whom he collaborated as playwright.

Brecht also began his serious reading of Marx in the 1920s, and it was his application of Marxist dialectic to the process of theater that gave rise to his most powerful and original ideas for the stage. From Marx, Brecht adopted a revolutionary posture, not only toward the class struggle, but toward the stage of bourgeois "realism." To Brecht, the realistic theater was not an unbiased window on social reality. Instead, Brecht argued that realistic theater presented a particular political vision, a view of society as inevitably determined by history and evolution, and therefore not susceptible to change. In order to displace "realism," and to demonstrate these hidden politics, Brecht redefined Marx's conception of "alienation" as a theatrical practice. In *Das Kapital*, Marx argues that the division of labor in modern industrial production has altered the relationship between mankind and the world. In modern industry, workers sell their labor in order to produce commodities. These commodities, Marx contends, then seem "alien" in that they appear to have arisen magically. Capitalist production conceals the signs of how they were produced, so that commodities come to have a "natural" life of their own. Yet, even as commodities seem to come alive, the workers become dehumanized, incorporated into the machinery of production. In the world of capital, where everything is for sale, all human relations, lives, and desires become commodified. The prevailing view of the world—in which commodities confront workers as something natural and entirely separate from their makers—is, to Marx, a *false* view, perpetuated within the bourgeois social order to the political advantage of the ruling classes.

Brecht's theater works to provide its audience with ways of regarding bourgeois reality—including realistic theater and drama—as "unnatural," as a political vision, as an ideological view of the world produced in the interest of profit. Brecht's theater, that is, works to "alienate" or "estrange" the audience from the commonplace "realities" of daily life—which we have unreflectively come to regard as "natural" and "inevitable"—in order to train us to question the world made by modern capitalism and the society it sustains. As he wrote in "The Modern Theater Is the Epic Theater," his theater is based on a "radical separation of the elements" of production, rather than on the scenic unity typical of realism. The seamless illusion of the realistic stage is that theater's most seductive commodity: it constantly and subliminally urges the audience to accept its "picture" of reality as a natural, apolitical image of the world as it is. Brecht's theater, in contrast, always shows both the dramatic illusion (the character, the setting, the action) and the process of its making (the work of the actor, the machinery of the theater, the activities of the stage). Brecht works to show the "means of production" in his theater, as a way of suggesting that stage realism, like social reality outside the theater, is *made*, not given.

Brecht called this theater by a variety of names, including **EPIC THEATER,** the term now generally used for Brecht's body of theory and technique. Brecht's plays tend to be episodic, a disconnected, open-ended **MONTAGE** of scenes: The audience must arrive at its own understanding of how the events are linked together, rather than being given an apparently inevitable narrative. Brecht generally left the stage bare in his productions, as a way of preventing the audience from seeing a complete illusion of some fictional dramatic locale. He exposed the lights above the stage, so the audience could see how lights influence the mood of the scene and so influence the audience's judgment. Brecht fragmented the "realistic" unity of the setting in other ways, too. Films could be projected on screens above the stage, forcing the audience to hold the drama in counterpoint to more recent events; placards onstage described the action to take place before the scene began. Finally, Brecht also urged his actors not to empathize entirely with the characters they played, but to strike a balance between a Stanislavskian identification with the character (being "in character," acting the character entirely from his or her point of view) and a more demonstrative attitude, one that enables the actor to represent the character from a variety of perspectives. Through these means, Brecht worked to involve the audience in the process of the play's production. Rather than being seduced by a commodified illusion of reality, the audience of epic theater is invited to consider, and enjoy, how the theater makes its fictions—as a way of teaching the audience to adopt a more critical, "alienated" way of seeing life outside the theater.

Brecht used many of these devices in *The Threepenny Opera* and in the series of plays he wrote in exile. Forced to flee Germany by Nazi purges of left-wing writers in 1933, Brecht spent the greater part of his creative life on the run, living briefly in Sweden, in Finland, and finally in Santa Monica, California, from 1941 to 1947. Although he had drafted *Life of Galileo* in 1938, Brecht continued to work on the play in California, collaborating on an English version with the actor Charles Laughton. He was also questioned by the House Un-American Activities Committee in 1947, as part of its infamous investigation of communism in the entertainment industry. Brecht was not charged and left the United States the following day to return to Europe and Germany. Living in exile, with no theater and little support, Brecht wrote his major plays: *Life of Galileo* (1938), *The Good Person of Szechwan* (1939), *Mother Courage and Her Children* (1939), and *The Caucasian Chalk Circle* (1944). He also wrote his most important theoretical essays, including *A Short Organum for the Theater,* written in Zurich, Switzerland in 1947, but published in 1948 after Brecht returned to Germany.

Brecht returned to East Berlin in 1947 and established his company, the Berliner Ensemble. Brecht's antirealist plays had long been the source of conflict with the **SOCIAL REALISM** advocated by the Communist Party, and even after the war Brecht had to work with a wary eye on the East German authorities. Nonetheless, the Berliner Ensemble—under Brecht's guidance and with the talents of his wife, Helene Weigel—became the leading European production company of the 1950s, sowing the seeds of innovation in every country they visited. Brecht died in August of 1956, just before the Berliner Ensemble's stunning visit to London, but the influence of his conception of theater has become worldwide, visible in plays from Luis Valdez's *Los Vendidos* to Caryl Churchill's *Cloud Nine* to Tony Kushner's *Angels in America* to Maishe Maponya's *Gangsters*.

Mother Courage and Her Children is typical of Brecht's innovative approach to theater and to "political theater" as well. Rather than presenting a thesis, the play works to question the audience's attitudes about a variety of social institutions: warfare, business, motherhood, morality. In a parable-like series of scenes reminiscent both of expressionist theater and of morality drama, *Mother Courage and Her Children* invites the audience to estrange, and so reconsider, its ways of mapping the world.

In his model-book of the play, Brecht wrote that he wanted to show that "war, which is a continuation of business by other means, makes the human virtues fatal to their possessors." The play considers this problem in a variety of challenging ways. Although it is perhaps tempting to see Courage—Why is she called Courage? Was she courageous?—as a tragic heroine, the play relentlessly questions her "heroic" survival, and our own attitudes about the distinctions between war, business, and morality. As Scene I demonstrates, war and business create an all-embracing market in which everything is commodified, that is, for sale. Mother Courage sells a belt buckle and loses a son as part of the same transaction.

Much of the play's power onstage arises through its use of physical space and a few significant properties. The wagon—Courage's home, her means of survival, her mode of production—becomes in a sense the play's central "character." Placing it on a turntable, most productions convey the sense that the wagon is almost always in motion, yet never actually getting anywhere, much as Courage herself enters the play and leaves it singing the same song. Courage's fortunes are emblematized by the wagon as well. Loaded with goods and pulled by her two strong sons in the first scene, it is battered, barren, and empty in the last,

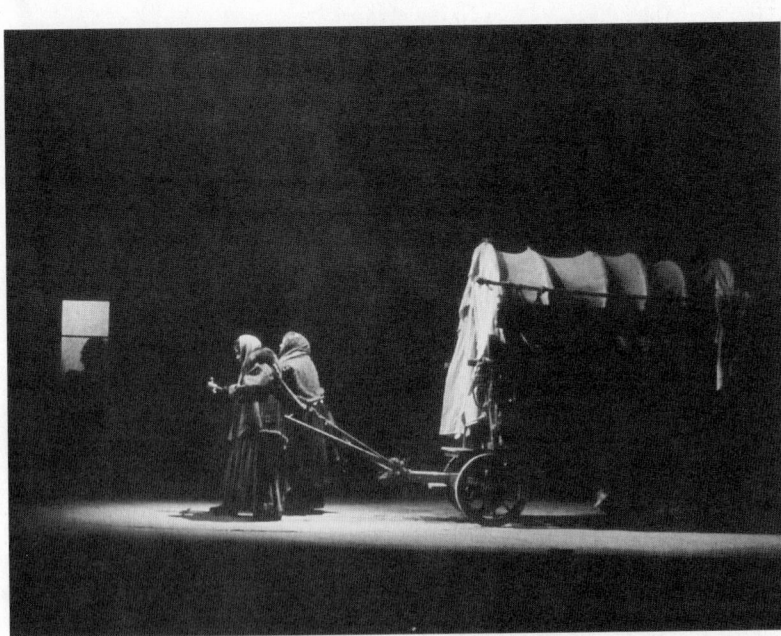

Mother Courage and Kattrin harness themselves to the wagon in Bertolt Brecht's *Mother Courage and Her Children*.

pulled by Mother Courage herself as she struggles to catch up with the army. Brecht was attracted to the idea of using the wagon, the play's economic and material "base," so to speak, to elucidate some of the play's symbolic or moral themes. He used Courage's wash-line to link the wagon to the cannon at the opening of scene 3, tying warfare, the economy, and the domestic sphere together. He raised the harness-poles to form a kind of crucifix after the death of her son Swiss Cheese. Many of the most ironic moments of the Berliner Ensemble production of the play were Weigel's invention: as Mother Courage, she bit the coin in Scene I and slowly measured her pennies out of her purse when she paid the peasants to bury Kattrin at the end of the play. This is the kind of moment that Brecht worked—in theory, as a playwright, in directing productions—to make happen in the theater, a moment when a single gesture forces the audience to consider the scene in a new light, to question the relationship between its ideas of identity and morality and the society that gives them shape and meaning.

MOTHER COURAGE AND HER CHILDREN
A CHRONICLE OF THE THIRTY YEARS' WAR
Bertolt Brecht
TRANSLATED BY JOHN WILLETT

CHARACTERS

MOTHER COURAGE	A CLERK
KATTRIN, *her dumb daughter*	A YOUNG SOLDIER
EILIF, *the elder son*	AN OLDER SOLDIER
SWISS CHEESE, *the younger son*	A PEASANT
THE RECRUITER	THE PEASANT'S WIFE
THE SERGEANT	THE YOUNG MAN
THE COOK	THE OLD WOMAN
THE GENERAL	ANOTHER PEASANT
THE CHAPLAIN	HIS WIFE
THE ARMOURER	THE YOUNG PEASANT
YVETTE POTTIER	THE ENSIGN
THE MAN WITH THE PATCH	SOLDIERS
ANOTHER SERGEANT	A VOICE
THE ANCIENT COLONEL	

SCENE ONE

Spring 1624. The Swedish Commander-in-Chief Count Oxenstierna is raising troops in Dalecarlia for the Polish campaign. The canteen woman Anna Fierling, known under the name of Mother Courage, loses one son.

Country road near a town.

A SERGEANT *and a* RECRUITER *stand shivering.*

RECRUITER: How can you muster a unit in a place like this? I've been thinking about suicide, sergeant. Here am I, got to find our commander four companies before the twelfth of the month, and people round here are so nasty I can't
5 sleep nights. S'pose I get hold of some bloke and shut my eye to his pigeon chest and varicose veins, I get him proper drunk, he signs on the line, I'm just settling up, he goes for a piss, I follow him to the door because I smell a rat; bob's your uncle, he's off like a flea with the itch. No notion of
10 word of honour, loyalty, faith, sense of duty. This place has shattered my confidence in the human race, sergeant.
SERGEANT: It's too long since they had a war here; stands to reason. Where's their sense of morality to come from? Peace—that's just a mess; takes a war to restore order.
15 Peacetime, the human race runs wild. People and cattle get buggered about, who cares? Everyone eats just as he feels inclined, a hunk of cheese on top of his nice white bread, and a slice of fat on top of the cheese. How many young blokes and good horses in that town there, nobody knows;
20 they never thought of counting. I been in places ain't seen a war for nigh seventy years: folks hadn't got names to them, couldn't tell one another apart. Takes a war to get proper nominal rolls and inventories—shoes in bundles and corn in bags, and man and beast properly numbered
25 and carted off, cause it stands to reason: no order, no war.
RECRUITER: Too true.

SERGEANT: Same with all good things, it's a job to get a war going. But once it's blossomed out there's no holding it; folk start fighting shy of peace like punters what can't stop for fear of having to tot up what they lost. Before that it's 30 war they're fighting shy of. It's something new to them.
RECRUITER: Hey, here's a cart coming. Two tarts with two young fellows. Stop her, sergeant. If this one's a flop I'm not standing around in your spring winds any longer, I can tell you. 35

(Sound of a jew's-harp. Drawn by two young fellows, a covered cart rolls in. On it sit MOTHER COURAGE *and her dumb daughter* KATTRIN.)

MOTHER COURAGE: Morning, sergeant.
SERGEANT: *(Blocking the way.)* Morning, all. And who are you?
MOTHER COURAGE: Business folk. *(Sings.)*

> You captains, tell the drums to slacken
> And give your infanteers a break: 40
> It's Mother Courage with her waggon
> Full of the finest boots they make.
> With crawling lice and looted cattle
> With lumbering guns and straggling kit—
> How can you flog them into battle 45
> Unless you get them boots that fit?
> The new year's come. The watchmen shout.
> The thaw sets in. The dead remain.
> Whatever life has not died out
> It staggers to its feet again. 50
>
> Captains, how can you make them face it—
> Marching to death without a brew?
> Courage has rum with which to lace it
> And boil their souls and bodies through.
> Their musket primed, their stomach hollow— 55
> Captains, your men don't look so well.
> So feed them up and let them follow

While you command them into hell.
The new year's come. The watchmen shout.
60   The thaw sets in. The dead remain.
Wherever life has not died out
It staggers to its feet again.

SERGEANT: Halt! Who are you with, you trash?

THE ELDER SON: Second Finnish Regiment.

65   SERGEANT: Where's your papers?

MOTHER COURAGE: Papers?

THE YOUNGER SON: What, mean to say you don't know Mother Courage?

SERGEANT: Never heard of her. What's she called Courage for?

70   MOTHER COURAGE: Courage is the name they gave me because I was scared of going broke, sergeant, so I drove me cart right through the bombardment of Riga with fifty loaves of bread aboard. They were going mouldy, it was high time, hadn't any choice really.

75   SERGEANT: Don't be funny with me. Your papers.

MOTHER COURAGE: (*Pulling a bundle of papers from a tin box and climbing down off the cart.*) That's all my papers, sergeant. You'll find a whole big missal from Altötting in Bavaria for wrapping gherkins in, and a road map of Moravia, the Lord
80   knows when I'll ever get there, might as well chuck it away, and here's a stamped certificate that my horse hasn't got foot-and-mouth, only he's dead worse luck, cost fifteen florins he did—not me luckily. That enough paper for you?

SERGEANT: You pulling my leg? I'll knock that sauce out of
85   you. S'pose you know you got to have a licence.

MOTHER COURAGE: Talk proper to me, do you mind, and don't you dare say I'm pulling your leg in front of my unsullied children, 'tain't decent, I got no time for you. My honest face, that's me licence with the Second Regiment,
90   and if it's too difficult for you to read there's nowt I can do about it. Nobody's putting a stamp on that.

RECRUITER: Sergeant, methinks I smell insubordination in this individual. What's needed in our camp is obedience.

MOTHER COURAGE: Sausage, if you ask me.

95   SERGEANT: Name.

MOTHER COURAGE: Anna Fierling.

SERGEANT: You all called Fierling then?

MOTHER COURAGE: What d'you mean? It's me's called Fierling, not them.

100   SERGEANT: Aren't all this lot your children?

MOTHER COURAGE: You bet they are, but why should they all have to be called the same, eh? (*Pointing to her elder son.*) For instance, that one's called Eilif Nojocki—Why? his father always claimed he was called Kojocki or Mojocki or some-
105   thing. The boy remembers him clearly, except that the one he remembers was someone else, a Frenchie with a little beard. Aside from that he's got his father's wits; that man knew how to snitch a peasant's pants off his bum without him noticing. This way each of us has his own name, see.

110   SERGEANT: What, each one different?

MOTHER COURAGE: Don't tell me you ain't never come across that.

SERGEANT: So I s'pose he's a Chinaman? (*Pointing to the younger son.*)

115   MOTHER COURAGE: Wrong. Swiss.

SERGEANT: After the Frenchman?

MOTHER COURAGE: What Frenchman? I never heard tell of no Frenchman. You keep muddling things up, we'll be hanging around here till dark. A Swiss, but called Fejos,
120   and the name has nowt to do with his father. He was called something quite different and was a fortifications engineer, only drunk all the time.

(SWISS CHEESE *beams and nods; dumb* KATTRIN *too is amused.*)

SERGEANT: How in hell can he be called Fejos?

MOTHER COURAGE: I don't like to be rude, sergeant, but you ain't got much imagination, have you? Course he's called
125   Fejos, because when he arrived I was with a Hungarian, very decent fellow, had terrible kidney trouble though he never touched a drop. The boy takes after him.

SERGEANT: But he wasn't his father . . .

MOTHER COURAGE: Took after him just the same. I call him
130   Swiss Cheese. (*Pointing to her daughter.*) And that's Kattrin Haupt, she's half German.

SERGEANT: Nice family, I must say.

MOTHER COURAGE: Aye, me cart and me have seen the world.

SERGEANT: I'm writing all this down. (*He writes.*) And you're
135   from Bamberg in Bavaria; how d'you come to be here?

MOTHER COURAGE: Can't wait till war chooses to visit Bamberg, can I?

RECRUITER: (*To* EILIF.) You two should be called Jacob Ox and Esau Ox, pulling the cart like that. I s'pose you never
140   get out of harness?

EILIF: Ma, can I clobber him one? I wouldn't half like to.

MOTHER COURAGE: And I says you can't; just you stop where you are. And now two fine officers like you, I bet you could use a good pistol, or a belt buckle, yours is on its last
145   legs, sergeant.

SERGEANT: I could use something else. Those boys are healthy as young birch trees, I observe: chests like barrels, solid leg muscles. So why are they dodging their military service, may I ask?
150

MOTHER COURAGE: (*Quickly.*) Nowt doing, sergeant. Yours is no trade for my kids.

RECRUITER: But why not? There's good money in it, glory too. Flogging boots is women's work. (*To* EILIF.) Come here, let's see if you've muscles in you or if you're a chicken.
155

MOTHER COURAGE: He's a chicken. Give him a fierce look, he'll fall over.

RECRUITER: Killing a young bull that happens to be in his way. (*Wants to lead him off.*)

MOTHER COURAGE: Let him alone, will you? He's nowt for
160   you folk.

RECRUITER: He was crudely offensive and talked about clobbering me. The two of us are going to step into that field and settle it man to man.

EILIF: Don't you worry, mum, I'll fix him.
165

MOTHER COURAGE: Stop there! You varmint! I know you, nowt but fights. There's a knife down his boot. A slasher, that's what he is.

RECRUITER: I'll draw it out of him like a milk-tooth. Come along, sonny.
170

MOTHER COURAGE: Sergeant, I'll tell the colonel. He'll have you both in irons. The lieutenant's going out with my daughter.

SERGEANT: No rough stuff, chum. (*To* MOTHER COURAGE.)
175   What you got against military service? Wasn't his own father a soldier? Died a soldier's death, too? Said it yourself.

MOTHER COURAGE: He's nowt but a child. You want to take
him off to slaughterhouse, I know you lot. They'll give
you five florins for him.

180 RECRUITER: First he's going to get a smart cap and boots, eh?

EILIF: Not from you.

MOTHER COURAGE: Let's both go fishing, said angler to
worm. (*To* SWISS CHEESE.) Run off, call out they're trying
to kidnap your brother. (*She pulls a knife.*) Go on, you kid-
185   nap him, just try. I'll slit you open, trash. I'll teach you to
make war with him. We're doing an honest trade in ham
and linen, and we're peaceable folk.

SERGEANT: Peaceable I don't think; look at your knife. You
should be ashamed of yourself; put that knife away, you
190   old harridan. A minute back you were admitting you live
off the war, how else should you live, what from? But
how's anyone to have war without soldiers?

MOTHER COURAGE: No need for it to be my kids.

SERGEANT: Oh, you'd like war to eat the pips but spit out the
195   apple? It's to fatten up your kids, but you won't invest in
it. Got to look after itself, eh? And you called Courage,
fancy that. Scared of the war that keeps you going? Your
sons aren't scared of it, I can see that.

EILIF: Take more than a war to scare me.

200 SERGEANT: And why? Look at me: has army life done all that
badly by me? Joined up at seventeen.

MOTHER COURAGE: Still got to reach seventy.

SERGEANT: I don't mind waiting.

MOTHER COURAGE: Under the sod, eh?

205 SERGEANT: You trying to insult me, saying I'll die?

MOTHER COURAGE: S'pose it's true? S'pose I can see the mark's
on you? S'pose you look like a corpse on leave to me? Eh?

SWISS CHEESE: She's got second sight, Mother has.

RECRUITER: Go ahead, tell the sergeant's fortune, might
210   amuse him.

MOTHER COURAGE: Gimme helmet. (*He gives it to her.*)

SERGEANT: It don't mean a bloody sausage. Anything for a
laugh though.

MOTHER COURAGE: (*Taking out a sheet of parchment and tearing it
215   up.*) Eilif, Swiss Cheese and Kattrin, may all of us be torn apart
like this if we lets ourselves get too mixed up in the war. (*To
the* SERGEANT.) Just for you I'm doing it for free. Black's for
death. I'm putting a big black cross on this slip of paper.

SWISS CHEESE: Leaving the other one blank, see?

220 MOTHER COURAGE: Then I fold them across and shake them.
All of us is jumbled together like this from our mother's
womb, and now draw a slip and you'll know. (*The
SERGEANT hesitates.*)

RECRUITER: (*To* EILIF.) I don't take just anybody, they all know
225   I'm choosey, but you got the kind of fire I like to see.

SERGEANT: (*Fishing in the helmet.*) Too silly. Load of eyewash.

SWISS CHEESE: Drawn a black cross, he has. Write him off.

RECRUITER: They're having you on; not everybody's name's
on a bullet.

230 SERGEANT: (*Hoarsely.*) You've put me in the shit.

MOTHER COURAGE: Did that yourself the day you became a
soldier. Come along, let's move on now. 'Tain't every day
we have a war, I got to get stirring.

SERGEANT: God damn it, you can't kid me. We're taking that
bastard of yours for a soldier.   235

EILIF: Swiss Cheese'd like to be a soldier too.

MOTHER COURAGE: First I've heard of that. You'll have to
draw too, all three of you. (*She goes to the rear to mark crosses
on further slips.*)

RECRUITER: (*To* EILIF.) One of the things they say against us is   240
that it's all holy-holy in the Swedish camp; but that's a malicious rumour to do us down. There's no hymn-singing but
Sundays, just a single verse, and then only for those got voices.

MOTHER COURAGE: (*Coming back with the slips, which she drops
into the* SERGEANT's *helmet.*) Trying to get away from their   245
ma, the devils, off to war like calves to salt-lick. But I'm
making you draw lots, and that'll show you the world is no
vale of joys with 'Come along, son, we need a few more
generals'. Sergeant, I'm so scared they won't get through
the war. Such dreadful characters, all three of them. (*She   250
hands the helmet to* EILIF.) Hey, come on, fish out your slip.
(*He fishes one out, unfolds it. She snatches it from him.*) There
you are, it's a cross. Oh, wretched mother that I am, o pain-
racked giver of birth! Shall he die? Aye, in the springtime
of life he is doomed. If he becomes a soldier he shall bite   255
the dust, it's plain to see. He is too foolhardy, like his dad
was. And if he ain't sensible he'll go the way of all flesh, his
slip proves it. (*Shouts at him.*) You going to be sensible?

EILIF: Why not?

MOTHER COURAGE: Sensible thing is stay with your mother,   260
never mind if they poke fun at you and call you chicken,
just you laugh.

RECRUITER: If you're pissing in your pants I'll make do with
your brother.

MOTHER COURAGE: I told you laugh. Go on, laugh. Now you   265
draw, Swiss Cheese. I'm not so scared on your account,
you're honest. (*He fishes in the helmet.*) Oh, why look at
your slip in that strange way? It's got to be a blank. There
can't be any cross on it. Surely I'm not going to lose *you*.
(*She takes the slip.*) A cross? What, you too? Is that because   270
you're so simple, perhaps? O Swiss Cheese, you too will
be sunk if you don't stay utterly honest all the while, like
I taught you from childhood when you brought the
change back from the baker's. Else you can't save yourself.
Look, sergeant, that's a black cross, ain't it?   275

SERGEANT: A cross, that's right. Can't think how I come to
get one. I always stay in the rear. (*To the* RECRUITER.)
There's no catch. Her own family get it too.

SWISS CHEESE: I get it too. But I listen to what I'm told.

MOTHER COURAGE: (*To* KATTRIN.) And now you're the only   280
one I know's all right, you're a cross yourself; got a kind
heart you have. (*Holds the helmet up to her on the cart, but
takes the slip out herself.*) No, that's too much. That can't be
right; must have made a mistake shuffling. Don't be too
kindhearted, Kattrin, you'll have to give it up, there's a   285
cross above your path too. Lie doggo, girl, it can't be that
hard once you're born dumb. Right, all of you know now.
Look out for yourselves, you'll need to. And now up we
get and on we go. (*She climbs on to the cart.*)

RECRUITER: (*To the* SERGEANT.) Do something.   290

SERGEANT: I don't feel very well.

RECRUITER: Must of caught a chill taking your helmet off in
that wind. Involve her in a deal. (*Aloud.*) Might as well

295 have a look at that belt-buckle, sergeant. After all, our friends here have to live by their business. Hey, you people, the sergeant wants to buy that belt-buckle.

MOTHER COURAGE: Half a florin. Two florins is what a belt like that's worth. (*Climbs down again.*)

300 SERGEANT: 'Tain't new. Let me get out of this damned wind and have a proper look at it. (*Goes behind the cart with the buckle.*)

MOTHER COURAGE: Ain't what I call windy.

SERGEANT: I s'pose it might be worth half a florin, it's silver.

MOTHER COURAGE: (*Joining him behind the cart.*) It's six solid ounces.

305 RECRUITER: (*To* EILIF.) And then we men'll have one together. Got your bounty money here, come along. (EILIF *stands undecided.*)

MOTHER COURAGE: Half a florin it is.

SERGEANT: It beats me. I'm always at the rear. Sergeant's the
310 safest job there is. You can send the others up front, cover themselves with glory. Me dinner hour's properly spoiled. Shan't be able to hold nowt down, I know.

MOTHER COURAGE: Mustn't let it prey on you so's you can't eat. Just stay at the rear. Here, take a swig of brandy, man.
315 (*Gives him a drink.*)

RECRUITER: (*Has taken* EILIF *by the arm and is leading him away up stage.*) Ten florins bounty money, then you're a gallant fellow fighting for the king and women'll be after you like flies. And you can clobber me for free for insulting you.

(*Exeunt both.*)

(*Dumb* KATTRIN *leans down from the cart and makes hoarse noises.*)

320 MOTHER COURAGE: All right, Kattrin, all right. Sergeant's just paying. (*Bites the half-florin.*) I got no faith in any kind of money. Burnt child, that's me, sergeant. This coin's good, though. And now let's get moving. Where's Eilif?

SWISS CHEESE: Went off with the recruiter.

325 MOTHER COURAGE: (*Stands quite still, then.*) You simpleton. (*To* KATTRIN.) 'Tain't your fault, you can't speak, I know.

SERGEANT: Could do with a swig yourself, ma. That's life. Plenty worse things than being a soldier. Want to live off war, but keep yourself and family out of it, eh?

330 MOTHER COURAGE: You'll have to help your brother pull now, Kattrin.

(*Brother and sister hitch themselves to the cart and start pulling.* MOTHER COURAGE *walks alongside. The cart rolls on.*)

SERGEANT: (*Looking after them.*)
Like the war to nourish you?
Have to feed it something too.

SCENE TWO

In the years 1625 and 1626 Mother Courage crosses Poland in the train of the Swedish armies. Before the fortress of Wallhof she meets her son again. Successful sale of a capon and heyday of her dashing son.

The GENERAL's *tent.*

Beside it, his kitchen. Thunder of cannon. The COOK *is arguing with* MOTHER COURAGE, *who wants to sell him a capon.*

THE COOK: Sixty hellers for a miserable bird like that?

MOTHER COURAGE: Miserable bird? This fat brute? Mean to say some greedy old general—and watch your step if you got nowt for his dinner—can't afford sixty hellers for him?

THE COOK: I can get a dozen like that for ten hellers just 5 down the road.

MOTHER COURAGE: What, a capon like this you can get just down the road? In time of siege, which means hunger that tears your guts. A rat you might get: 'might' I say because they're all being gobbled up, five men spending best part 10 of day chasing one hungry rat. Fifty hellers for a giant capon in time of siege!

THE COOK: But it ain't us having the siege, it's t'other side. We're conducting the siege, can't you get that in your head?

MOTHER COURAGE: But we got nowt to eat too, even worse 15 than them in the town. Took it with them, didn't they? They're having a high old time, everyone says. And look at us! I been to the peasants, there's nowt there.

THE COOK: There's plenty. They're sitting on it.

MOTHER COURAGE: (*Triumphantly.*) They ain't. They're bust, 20 that's what they are. Just about starving. I saw some, were grubbing up roots from sheer hunger, licking their fingers after they boiled some old leather strap. That's way it is. And me got a capon here and supposed to take forty hellers for it. 25

THE COOK: Thirty, not forty. I said thirty.

MOTHER COURAGE: Here, this ain't just any old capon. It was such a gifted beast, I been told, it could only eat to music, had a military march of its own. It could count, it was that intelligent. And you say forty hellers is too much? General 30 will make mincemeat of you if there's nowt on his table.

THE COOK: See what I'm doing? (*He takes a piece of beef and puts his knife to it.*) Here I got a bit of beef, I'm going to roast it. Make up your mind quick.

MOTHER COURAGE: Go on, roast it. It's last year's. 35

THE COOK: Last night's. That animal was still alive and kicking, I saw him myself.

MOTHER COURAGE: Alive and stinking, you mean.

THE COOK: I'll cook him five hours if need be. I'll just see if he's still tough. (*He cuts into it.*) 40

MOTHER COURAGE: Put plenty of pepper on it so his lordship the general don't smell the pong.

(*The* GENERAL, *a* CHAPLAIN *and* EILIF *enter the tent.*)

THE GENERAL: (*Slapping* EILIF *on the shoulder.*) Now then, Eilif my son, into your general's tent with you and sit thou at my right hand. For you accomplished a deed of heroism, 45 like a pious cavalier; and doing what you did for God, and in a war of religion at that, is something I commend in you most highly, you shall have a gold bracelet as soon as we've taken this town. Here we are, come to save their souls for them, and what do those insolent dung- 50 encrusted yokels go and do? Drive their beef away from us. They stuff it into those priests of theirs all right, back and front, but you taught 'em manners, ha! So here's a pot of red wine for you, the two of us'll knock it back at one gulp. (*They do so.*) Piss all for the chaplain, the old bigot. 55 And now, what would you like for dinner, my darling?

EILIF: A bit of meat, why not?

THE GENERAL: Cook! Meat!

THE COOK: And then he goes and brings guests when there's
60   nowt there.

(MOTHER COURAGE *silences him so she can listen.*)

EILIF: Hungry job cutting down peasants.
MOTHER COURAGE: Jesus Christ, it's my Eilif.
THE COOK: Your what?
MOTHER COURAGE: My eldest boy. It's two years since I lost
65   sight of him, they pinched him from me on the road, must
     think well of him if the general's asking him to dinner, and
     what kind of a dinner can you offer? Nowt. You heard
     what the visitor wishes to eat: meat. Take my tip, you set-
     tle for the capon, it'll be a florin.
70 THE GENERAL: (*Has sat down with* EILIF, *and bellows.*) Food,
     Lamb, you foul cook, or I'll have your hide.
     THE COOK: Give it over, dammit, this is blackmail.
     MOTHER COURAGE: Didn't someone say it was a miserable bird?
     THE COOK: Miserable; give it over, and a criminal price, fifty
75   hellers.
     MOTHER COURAGE: A florin, I said. For my eldest boy, the
     general's guest, no expense is too great for me.
     THE COOK: (*Gives her the money.*) You might at least pluck it
     while I see to the fire.
80 MOTHER COURAGE: (*Sits down to pluck the fowl.*) He won't
     half be surprised to see me. He's my dashing clever son.
     Then I got a stupid one too, he's honest though. The girl's
     nowt. One good thing, she don't talk.
     THE GENERAL: Drink up, my son, this is my best Falernian;
85   only got a barrel or two left, but that's nothing to pay for
     a sign that's there's still true faith to be found in my army.
     As for that shepherd of souls he can just look on, because
     all he does is preach, without the least idea how it's to be
     carried out. And now, my son Eilif, tell us more about the
90   neat way you smashed those yokels and captured the
     twenty oxen. Let's hope they get here soon.
     EILIF: A day or two at most.
     MOTHER COURAGE: Thoughtful of our Eilif not to bring the
     oxen in till tomorrow, else you lot wouldn't have looked
95   twice at my capon.
     EILIF: Well, it was like this, see. I'd heard peasants had been
     driving the oxen they'd hidden, out of the forest into one
     particular wood, on the sly and mostly by night. That's
     where people from the town were s'posed to come and
100 pick them up. So I holds off and lets them drive their oxen
     together, reckoning they'd be better than me at finding
     'em. I had my blokes slavering after the meat, cut their
     emergency rations even further for a couple of days till
     their mouths was watering at the least sound of any word
105 beginning with 'me-', like 'measles' say.
     THE GENERAL: Very clever of you.
     EILIF: Possibly. The rest was a piece of cake. Except that the
     peasants had cudgels and outnumbered us three to one
     and made a murderous attack on us. Four of 'em shoved
110 me into a thicket, knocked my sword from my hand and
     bawled out 'Surrender!' What's the answer, I wondered;
     they're going to make mincemeat of me.
     THE GENERAL: What did you do?
     EILIF: I laughed.
115 THE GENERAL: You did what?
     EILIF: Laughed. So we got talking. I put it on a business foot-
     ing from the start, told them 'Twenty florins a head's too

much. I'll give you fifteen'. As if I was meaning to pay.
That threw them, and they began scratching their heads.
In a flash I'd picked up my sword and was hacking 'em to   120
pieces. Necessity's the mother of invention, eh, sir?
THE GENERAL: What is your view, pastor of souls?
THE CHAPLAIN: That phrase is not strictly speaking in the
     Bible, but when Our Lord turned the five loaves into five
     hundred there was no war on and he could tell people to   125
     love their neighbours as they'd had enough to eat. Today
     it's another story.
THE GENERAL: (*Laughs.*) Quite another story. You can have a
     swig after all for that, you old Pharisee. (*To* EILIF.) Hacked
     'em to pieces, did you, so my gallant lads can get a proper   130
     bite to eat? What do the Scriptures say? 'Whatsoever thou
     doest for the least of my brethren, thou doest for me'. And
     what did you do for them? Got them a good square meal
     of beef, because they're not accustomed to mouldy bread,
     the old way was to fix a cold meal of rolls and wine in   135
     your helmet before you went out to fight for God.
EILIF: Aye, in a flash I'd picked up my sword and was hacking
     them to pieces.
THE GENERAL: You've the makings of a young Caesar. You
     ought to see the King.   140
EILIF: I have from a distance. He kind of glows. I'd like to
     model myself on him.
THE GENERAL: You've got something in common already. I
     appreciate soldiers like you, Eilif, men of courage. Some-
     body like that I treat as I would my own son. (*He leads him*   145
     over to the map.) Have a look at the situation, Eilif; it's a
     long haul still.
MOTHER COURAGE: (*Who has been listening and now angrily*
     plucks the fowl.) That must be a rotten general.
THE COOK: He's ravenous all right, but why rotten?   150
MOTHER COURAGE: Because he's got to have men of courage,
     that's why. If he knew how to plan a proper campaign what
     would he be needing men of courage for? Ordinary ones
     would do. It's always the same; whenever there's a load of
     special virtues around it means something stinks.   155
THE COOK: I thought it meant things is all right.
MOTHER COURAGE: No, that they stink. Look, s'pose some
     general or king is bone stupid and leads his men up shit
     creek, then those men've got to be fearless, there's another
     virtue for you. S'pose he's stingy and hires too few soldiers,   160
     then they got to be a crowd of Hercules's. And s'pose he's
     slapdash and don't give a bugger, then they got to be clever
     as monkeys else their number's up. Same way they got to
     show exceptional loyalty each time he gives them impossi-
     ble jobs. Nowt but virtues no proper country and no decent   165
     king or general would ever need. In decent countries folk
     don't have to have virtues, the whole lot can be perfectly or-
     dinary, average intelligence, and for all I know cowards.
THE GENERAL: I'll wager your father was a soldier.
EILIF: A great soldier, I been told. My mother warned me   170
     about it. There's a song I know.
THE GENERAL: Sing it to us. (*Roars.*) When's that dinner coming?
EILIF: It's called The Song of the Girl and the Soldier. (*He*
     sings it, dancing a war dance with his sabre.)

The guns blaze away, and the bay'nit'll slay   175
And the water can't hardly be colder.
What's the answer to ice? Keep off's my advice!

That's what the girl told the soldier.
Next thing the soldier, wiv' a round up the spout
180 Hears the band playing and gives a great shout:
Why, it's marching what makes you a soldier!
So it's down to the south and then northwards once more:
See him catching that bay'nit in his naked paw!
That's what his comrades done told her.

185 Oh, do not despise the advice of the wise
Learn wisdom from those that are older
And don't try for things that are out of your reach—
That's what the girl told the soldier.
Next thing the soldier, his bay'nit in place
190 Wades into the river and laughs in her face
Though the water comes up to his shoulder.
When the shingle roof glints in the light o' the moon
We'll be wiv' you again, not a moment too soon!
That's what his comrades done told her.

195 MOTHER COURAGE: (*Takes up the song in the kitchen, beating on a pot with her spoon.*)

You'll go out like a light! And the sun'll take flight
For your courage just makes us feel colder.
Oh, that vanishing light! May God see that it's right!—
200 That's what the girl told the soldier.

EILIF: What's that?
MOTHER COURAGE: (*Continues singing.*)

Next thing the soldier, his bay'nit in place
Was caught by the current and went down without trace
205 And the water couldn't hardly be colder.
Then the shingle roof froze in the light o' the moon
As both soldier and ice drifted down to their doom—
And d'you know what his comrades done told her?

He went out like a light. And the sunshine took flight
210 For his courage just made 'em feel colder.
Oh, do not despise the advice of the wise!
That's what the girl told the soldier.

THE GENERAL: The things they get up to in my kitchen these days.
215 EILIF: (*Has gone into the kitchen. He flings his arms round his mother.*) Fancy seeing you again, ma! Where's the others?
MOTHER COURAGE: (*In his arms.*) Snug as a bug in a rug. They made Swiss Cheese paymaster of the Second Finnish; any road he'll stay out of fighting that way, I
220 couldn't keep him out altogether.
EILIF: How's the old feet?
MOTHER COURAGE: Bit tricky getting me shoes on of a morning.
THE GENERAL: (*Has joined them.*) So you're his mother, I hope you've got plenty more sons for me like this one.
225 EILIF: Ain't it my lucky day? You sitting out there in the kitchen, ma, hearing your son commended . . .
MOTHER COURAGE: You bet I heard. (*Slaps his face.*)
EILIF: (*Holding his cheek.*) What's that for? Taking the oxen?
MOTHER COURAGE: No. Not surrendering when those four
230 went for you and wanted to make mincemeat of you. Didn't I say you should look after yourself? You Finnish devil!

(*The GENERAL and the CHAPLAIN stand in the doorway laughing.*)

SCENE THREE

Three years later Mother Courage is taken prisoner along with elements of a Finnish regiment. She manages to save her daughter, likewise her covered cart, but her honest son is killed.

Military camp.

Afternoon. A flagpole with the regimental flag. From her cart, festooned now with all kinds of goods, MOTHER COURAGE has stretched a washing line to a large cannon, across which she and KATTRIN are folding the washing. She is bargaining at the same time with an ARMOURER over a sack of shot. SWISS CHEESE, now wearing a paymaster's uniform, is looking on.

A comely person, YVETTE POTTIER, is sewing a gaily coloured hat, a glass of brandy before her. She is in her stockinged feet, having laid aside her red high-heeled boots.

THE ARMOURER: I'll let you have that shot for a couple of florins. It's cheap at the price, I got to have the money because the colonel's been boozing with his officers since two days back, and the drink's run out.
MOTHER COURAGE: That's troops' munitions. They catch me 5 with that, I'm for court-martial. You crooks flog the shot, and troops got nowt to fire at enemy.
THE ARMOURER: Have a heart, can't you; you scratch my back and I'll scratch yours.
MOTHER COURAGE: I'm not taking army property. Not at 10 that price.
THE ARMOURER: You can sell it on the q.t. tonight to the Fourth Regiment's armourer for five florins, eight even, if you let him have a receipt for twelve. He's right out of ammunition. 15
MOTHER COURAGE: Why not you do it?
THE ARMOURER: I don't trust him, he's a pal of mine.
MOTHER COURAGE: (*Takes the sack.*) Gimme. (*To KATTRIN.*) Take it away and pay him a florin and a half. (*The ARMOURER protests.*) I said a florin and a half. (KATTRIN *drags* 20 *the sack upstage, the* ARMOURER *following her* MOTHER COURAGE *addresses* SWISS CHEESE.) Here's your woollies, now look after them, it's October and autumn may set in any time. I ain't saying it's got to, cause I've learned nowt's got to come when you think it will, not even seasons of 25 the year. But your regimental accounts got to add up right, come what may. Do they add up right?
SWISS CHEESE: Yes, mother.
MOTHER COURAGE: Don't you forget they made you paymaster cause you was honest, not dashing like your 30 brother, and above all so stupid I bet you ain't even thought of clearing off with it, no not you. That's a big consolation to me. And don't lose those woollies.
SWISS CHEESE: No, mother, I'll put them under my mattress. (*Begins to go.*) 35
THE ARMOURER: I'll go along with you, paymaster.
MOTHER COURAGE: And don't you start learning him none of your tricks.

(*The* ARMOURER *leaves with* SWISS CHEESE *without any farewell gesture.*)

YVETTE: (*Waving to him.*) No reason not to say goodbye, ar-
40   mourer.

MOTHER COURAGE: (*To* YVETTE.) I don't like to see them together. He's wrong company for our Swiss Cheese. Oh
well, war's off to a good start. Easily take four, five years
before all countries are in. A bit of foresight, don't do
45   nothing silly, and business'll flourish. Don't you know you
ain't s'posed to drink before midday with your complaint?

YVETTE: Complaint, who says so, it's a libel.

MOTHER COURAGE: They all say so.

YVETTE: Because they're all telling lies, Mother Courage, and
50   me at my wits' end cause they're all avoiding me like
something the cat brought in thanks to those lies, what
the hell am I remodelling my hat for? (*She throws it away.*)
That's why I drink before midday. Never used to, gives
you crows' feet, but now what the hell? All the Second
55   Finnish know me. Ought to have stayed at home when
my first fellow did me wrong. No good our sort being
proud. Eat shit, that's what you got to do, or down you go.

MOTHER COURAGE: Now don't you start up again about that
Pieter of yours and how it all happened, in front of my in-
60   nocent daughter too.

YVETTE: She's the one should hear it, put her off love.

MOTHER COURAGE: Nobody can put 'em off that.

YVETTE: Then I'll go on, get it off my chest. It all starts with
yours truly growing up in lovely Flanders, else I'd never of
65   seen him and wouldn't be stuck here now in Poland, cause
he was an army cook, fair-haired, a Dutchman but thin for
once. Kattrin, watch out for the thin ones, only in those
days I didn't know that, or that he'd got a girl already, or
that they all called him Puffing Piet cause he never took his
70   pipe out of his mouth when he was on the job, it meant
that little to him. (*She sings the Song of Fraternisation.*)

When I was only sixteen
The foe came into our land.
He laid aside his sabre
75   And with a smile he took my hand.
After the May parade
The May light starts to fade.
The regiment dressed by the right
The drums were beaten, that's the drill.
80   The foe took us behind the hill
And fraternised all night.

There were so many foes then
But mine worked in the mess.
I loathed him in the daytime.
85   At night I loved him none the less.
After the May parade
The May light starts to fade.
The regiment dressed by the right
The drums were beaten, that's the drill.
90   The foe took us behind the hill
And fraternised all night.

The love which came upon me
Was wished on me by fate.
My friends could never grasp why
95   I found it hard to share their hate.
The fields were wet with dew
When sorrow first I knew.

The regiment dressed by the right
The drums were beaten, that's the drill.
And then the foe, my lover still   100
Went marching out of sight.

I followed him, fool that I was, but I never found him, and
that was five years back. (*She walks unsteadily behind the cart.*)

MOTHER COURAGE: You left your hat here.

YVETTE: Anyone wants it can have it.   105

MOTHER COURAGE: Let that be a lesson, Kattrin. Don't you
start anything with them soldiers. Love makes the world
go round, I'm warning you. Even with fellows not in the
army it's no bed of roses. He says he'd like to kiss the
ground your feet walk on—reminds me, did you wash   110
them yesterday?—and after that you're his skivvy. Be
thankful you're dumb, then you can't contradict yourself
and won't be wanting to bite your tongue off for speaking the truth; it's a godsend, being dumb is. And here
comes the general's cook, now what's he after?   115

(*Enter the* COOK *and the* CHAPLAIN.)

THE CHAPLAIN: I have a message for you from your son Eilif,
and the cook has come along because you made such a
profound impression on him.

THE COOK: I just came along to get a bit of air.

MOTHER COURAGE: That you can always do here if you be-   120
have yourself, and if you don't I can deal with you. What
does he want? I got no spare cash.

THE CHAPLAIN: Actually I had a message for his brother the
paymaster.

MOTHER COURAGE: He ain't here now nor anywhere else   125
neither. He ain't his brother's paymaster. He's not to lead
him into temptation nor be clever at his expense. (*Giving
him money from the purse slung round her.*) Give him this, it's
a sin, he's banking on mother's love and ought to be
ashamed of himself.   130

THE COOK: Not for long, he'll have to be moving off with
the regiment, might be to his death. Give him a bit extra,
you'll be sorry later. You women are tough, then later on
you're sorry. A little glass of brandy wouldn't have been a
problem, but it wasn't offered and, who knows, a bloke   135
may lie beneath the green sod and none of you people
will ever be able to dig him up again.

THE CHAPLAIN: Don't give way to your feelings, cook. To fall
in battle is a blessing, not an inconvenience, and why? It is
a war of faith. None of your common wars but a special   140
one, fought for the faith and therefore pleasing to God.

THE COOK: Very true. It's a war all right in one sense, what
with requisitioning, murder and looting and the odd bit of
rape thrown in, but different from all the other wars because it's a war of faith; stands to reason. But it's thirsty   145
work at that, you must admit.

THE CHAPLAIN: (*To* MOTHER COURAGE, *indicating the* COOK.)
I tried to stop him, but he says he's taken a shine to you,
you figure in his dreams.

THE COOK: (*Lighting a stumpy pipe.*) Just want a glass of   150
brandy from a fair hand, what harm in that? Only I'm
groggy already cause the chaplain here's been telling such
jokes all the way along you bet I'm still blushing.

MOTHER COURAGE: Him a clergyman too. I'd best give the pair of you a drink or you'll start making me immoral suggestions cause you've nowt else to do.

THE CHAPLAIN: Behold a temptation, said the court preacher, and fell. (*Turning back to look at* KATTRIN *as he leaves.*) And who is this entrancing young person?

MOTHER COURAGE: That ain't an entrancing but a decent young person. (*The* CHAPLAIN *and the* COOK *go behind the cart with* MOTHER COURAGE. KATTRIN *looks after them, then walks away from her washing towards the hat. She picks it up and sits down, pulling the red boots towards her.* MOTHER COURAGE *can be heard in the background talking politics with the* CHAPLAIN *and the* COOK.)

MOTHER COURAGE: Those Poles here in Poland had no business sticking their noses in. Right, our king moved in on them, horse and foot, but did they keep the peace? no, went and stuck their noses into their own affairs, they did, and fell on king just as he was quietly clearing off. They committed a breach of peace, that's what, so blood's on their own head.

THE CHAPLAIN: All our king minded about was freedom. The emperor had made slaves of them all, Poles and Germans alike, and the king had to liberate them.

THE COOK: Just what I say, your brandy's first rate, I weren't mistaken in your face, but talk of the king, it cost the king dear trying to give freedom to Germany, what with giving Sweden the salt tax, what cost the poor folk a bit, so I've heard, on top of which he had to have the Germans locked up and drawn and quartered cause they wanted to carry on slaving for the emperor. Course the king took a serious view when anybody didn't want to be free. He set out by just trying to protect Poland against bad people, particularly the emperor, then it started to become a habit till he ended up protecting the whole of Germany. They didn't half kick. So the poor old king's had nowt but trouble for all his kindness and expenses, and that's something he had to make up for by taxes of course, which caused bad blood, not that he'd let a little matter like that depress him. One thing he had on his side, God's word, that was a help. Because otherwise folk would of been saying he done it all for himself and to make a bit on the side. So he's always had a good conscience, which was the main point.

MOTHER COURAGE: Anyone can see you're no Swede or you wouldn't be talking that way about the Hero King.

THE CHAPLAIN: After all he provides the bread you eat.

THE COOK: I don't eat it, I bake it.

MOTHER COURAGE: They'll never beat him, and why, his men got faith in him. (*Seriously.*) To go by what the big shots say, they're waging war for almighty God and in the name of everything that's good and lovely. But look closer, they ain't so silly, they're waging it for what they can get. Else little folk like me wouldn't be in it at all.

THE COOK: That's the way it is.

THE CHAPLAIN: As a Dutchman you'd do better to glance at the flag above your head before venting your opinions here in Poland.

MOTHER COURAGE: All good Lutherans here. Prosit!

(KATTRIN *has put on* YVETTE's *hat and begun strutting around in imitation of her way of walking.*)

(*Suddenly there is a noise of cannon fire and shooting. Drums.* MOTHER COURAGE, *the* COOK *and the* CHAPLAIN *rush out from behind the cart, the two last-named still carrying their glasses. The* ARMOURER *and another* SOLDIER *run up to the cannon and try to push it away.*)

MOTHER COURAGE: What's happening? Wait till I've taken my washing down, you louts! (*She tries to rescue her washing.*)

THE ARMOURER: The Catholics! Broken through. Don't know if we'll get out of here. (*To the* SOLDIER.) Get that gun shifted! (*Runs on.*)

THE COOK: God, I must find the general. Courage, I'll drop by in a day or two for another talk.

MOTHER COURAGE: Wait, you forgot your pipe.

THE COOK: (*In the distance.*) Keep it for me. I'll be needing it.

MOTHER COURAGE: Would happen just as we're making a bit of money.

THE CHAPLAIN: Ah well, I'll be going too. Indeed, if the enemy is so close as that it might be dangerous. Blessèd are the peacemakers is the motto in wartime. If only I had a cloak to cover me.

MOTHER COURAGE: I ain't lending no cloaks, not on your life. I been had too often.

THE CHAPLAIN: But my faith makes it particularly dangerous for me.

MOTHER COURAGE: (*Gets him a cloak.*) Goes against my conscience, this does. Now you run along.

THE CHAPLAIN: Thank you, dear lady, that's very generous of you, but I think it might be wiser for me to remain seated here; it could arouse suspicion and bring the enemy down on me if I were seen to run.

MOTHER COURAGE: (*To the* SOLDIER.) Leave it, you fool, who's going to pay you for that? I'll look after it for you, you're risking your neck.

THE SOLDIER: (*Running away.*) You can tell 'em I tried.

MOTHER COURAGE: Cross my heart. (*Sees her daughter with the hat.*) What you doing with that strumpet's hat? Take that lid off, you gone crazy? And the enemy arriving any minute! (*Pulls the hat off* KATTRIN's *head.*) Want 'em to pick you up and make a prostitute of you? And she's gone and put those boots on, whore of Babylon! Off with those boots! (*Tries to tug them off her.*) Jesus Christ, chaplain, gimme a hand, get those boots off her, I'll be right back. (*Runs to the cart.*)

YVETTE: (*Arrives, powdering her face.*) Fancy that, the Catholics are coming. Where's my hat? Who's been kicking it around? I can't go about looking like this if the Catholics are coming. What'll they think of me? No mirror either. (*To the* CHAPLAIN.) How do I look? Too much powder?

THE CHAPLAIN: Exactly right.

YVETTE: And where are them red boots? (*Fails to find them as* KATTRIN *hides her feet under her skirt.*) I left them here all right. Now I'll have to get to me tent barefoot. It's an outrage.

(*Exit.*)

(SWISS CHEESE *runs in carrying in a small box.*)

MOTHER COURAGE: (*Arrives with her hands full of ashes. To* KATTRIN.) Here some ashes. (*To* SWISS CHEESE.) What's that you're carrying?

SWISS CHEESE: Regimental cash box.

MOTHER COURAGE: Chuck it away. No more paymastering for you.

265 SWISS CHEESE: I'm responsible. (*He goes to the rear.*)

MOTHER COURAGE: (*To the* CHAPLAIN.) Take your clerical togs off, padre, or they'll spot you under that cloak. (*She rubs* KATTRIN'*s face with ash.*) Keep still, will you? There you are, a bit of muck and you'll be safe. What a disaster.
270 Sentries were drunk. Hide your light under a bushel, it says. Take a soldier, specially a Catholic one, add a clean face, and there's your instant whore. For weeks they get nowt to eat, then soon as they manage to get it by looting they're falling on anything in skirts. That ought to do.
275 Let's have a look. Not bad. Looks like you been grubbing in muckheap. Stop trembling. Nothing'll happen to you like that. (*To* SWISS CHEESE.) Where d'you leave cash box?

SWISS CHEESE: Thought I'd put it in cart.

MOTHER COURAGE: (*Horrified.*) What, my cart? Sheer crimi-
280 nal idiocy. Only take me eyes off you one instant. Hang us all three, they will.

SWISS CHEESE: I'll put it somewhere else then, or clear out with it.

MOTHER COURAGE: You sit on it, it's too late now.

285 THE CHAPLAIN: (*Who is changing his clothes downstage.*) For heaven's sake, the flag!

MOTHER COURAGE: (*Hauls down the regimental flag.*) Bozhe moi! I'd given up noticing it were there. Twenty-five years I've had it.

(*The thunder of cannon intensifies.*)

(*A morning three days later. The cannon has gone.* MOTHER COURAGE, KATTRIN, *the* CHAPLAIN *and* SWISS CHEESE *are sitting gloomily over a meal.*)

290 SWISS CHEESE: That's three days I been sitting around with nowt to do, and sergeant's always been kind to me but any moment now he'll start asking where's Swiss Cheese with the pay box?

MOTHER COURAGE: You thank your stars they ain't after you.

295 THE CHAPLAIN: What can I say? I can't even hold a service here, it might make trouble for me. Whosoever hath a full heart, his tongue runneth over, it says, but heaven help me if mine starts running over.

MOTHER COURAGE: That's how it goes. Here they sit, one
300 with his faith and the other with his cash box. Dunno which is more dangerous.

THE CHAPLAIN: We are all of us in God's hands.

MOTHER COURAGE: Oh, I don't think it's as bad as that yet, though I must say I can't sleep nights. If it weren't for you,
305 Swiss Cheese, things'd be easier. I think I got meself cleared. I told 'em I didn't hold with Antichrist, the Swedish one with horns on, and I'd observed left horn was a bit unserviceable. Half way through their interrogation I asked where I could get church candles not too dear. I knows the
310 lingo cause Swiss Cheese's dad were Catholic, often used to make jokes about it, he did. They didn't believe me all that much, but they ain't got no regimental canteen lady. So they're winking an eye. Could turn out for the best, you know. We're prisoners, but same like fleas on dog.

THE CHAPLAIN: That's good milk. But we'll need to cut down 315 our Swedish appetites a bit. After all, we've been defeated.

MOTHER COURAGE: Who's been defeated? Look, victory and defeat ain't bound to be same for the big shots up top as for them below, not by no means. Can be times the bottom lot find a defeat really pays them. Honour's lost, nowt else. I re- 320 member once up in Livonia our general took such a beating from enemy I got a horse off our baggage train in the confusion, pulled me cart seven months, he did, before we won and they checked up. As a rule you can say victory and defeat both come expensive to us ordinary folk. Best thing for us is when 325 politics get bogged down solid. (*To* SWISS CHEESE.) Eat up.

SWISS CHEESE: Got no appetite for it. What's sergeant to do when pay day comes round?

MOTHER COURAGE: They don't have pay days on a retreat.

SWISS CHEESE: It's their right, though. They needn't retreat if 330 they don't get paid. Needn't stir a foot.

MOTHER COURAGE: Swiss Cheese, you're that conscientious it makes me quite nervous. I brought you up to be honest, you not being clever, but you got to know where to stop. Chaplain and me, we're off now to buy Catholic flag 335 and some meat. Dunno anyone so good at sniffing meat, like sleepwalking it is, straight to target. I'd say he can pick out a good piece by the way his mouth starts watering. Well, thank goodness they're letting me go on trading. You don't ask tradespeople their faith but their prices. 340 And Lutheran trousers keep cold out too.

THE CHAPLAIN: What did the mendicant say when he heard the Lutherans were going to turn everything in town and country topsy-turvy? 'They'll always need beggars'. (MOTHER COURAGE *disappears into the cart.*) So she's still 345 worried about the cash box. So far they've taken us all for granted as part of the cart, but how long for?

SWISS CHEESE: I can get rid of it.

THE CHAPLAIN: That's almost more dangerous. Suppose you're seen. They have spies. Yesterday a fellow popped 350 up out of the ditch in front of me just as I was relieving myself first thing. I was so scared I only just suppressed an ejaculatory prayer. That would have given me away all right. I think what they'd like best is to go sniffing people's excrement to see if they're Protestants. The spy was 355 a little runt with a patch over one eye.

MOTHER COURAGE: (*Clambering out of the cart with a basket.*) What have I found, you shameless creature? (*She holds up the red boots in triumph.*) Yvette's red high-heeled boots! Coolly went and pinched them, she did. Cause you put it in her 360 head she was an enchanting young person. (*She lays them in the basket.*) I'm giving them back. Stealing Yvette's boots! She's wrecking herself for money. That's understandable. But you'd do it for nothing, for pleasure. What did I tell you: you're to wait till it's peace. No soldiers for you. You're 365 not to start exhibiting yourself till it's peacetime.

THE CHAPLAIN: I don't find she exhibits herself.

MOTHER COURAGE: Too much for my liking. Let her be like a stone in Dalecarlia, where there's nowt else, so folk say 'Can't see that cripple', that's how I'd lief have her. Then 370 nowt'll happen to her. (*To* SWISS CHEESE.) You leave that box where it is, d'you hear? And keep an eye on your sister, she needs it. The pair of you'll have me in grave yet. Sooner be minding a bagful of fleas.

(She leaves with the CHAPLAIN. KATTRIN *clears away the dishes.)*

375 SWISS CHEESE: Won't be able to sit out in the sun in shirt-sleeves much longer. (KATTRIN *points at a tree.*) Aye, leaves turning yellow. (KATTRIN *asks by gestures if he wants a drink.*) Don't want no drink. I'm thinking. (*Pause.*) Said she can't sleep. Best if I got rid of that box, found a good
380 place for it. All right, let's have a glass. (KATTRIN *goes behind the cart.*) I'll stuff it down the rat-hole by the river for the time being. Probably pick it up tonight before first light and take it to Regiment. How far can they have retreated in three days? Bet sergeant's surprised. I'm agree-
385 ably disappointed in you, Swiss Cheese, he'll say. I make you responsible for the cash, and you go and bring it back.

(As KATTRIN *emerges from behind the cart with a full glass in her hand, two men confront her. One is a* SERGEANT, *the other doffs his hat to her. He has a patch over one eye.)*

THE MAN WITH THE PATCH: God be with you, mistress. Have you seen anyone round here from Second Finnish Regimental Headquarters?

(KATTRIN, badly frightened, runs downstage, spilling the brandy. The two men look at one another, then withdraw on seeing SWISS CHEESE *sitting there.)*

390 SWISS CHEESE: (*Interrupted in his thoughts.*) You spilt half of it. What are those faces for? Jabbed yourself in eye? I don't get it. And I'll have to be off, I've thought it over, it's the only way. (*He gets up. She does everything possible to make him realise the danger. He only shrugs her off.*) Wish I knew what
395 you're trying to say. Sure you mean well, poor creature, just can't get words out. What's it matter your spilling my brandy, I'll drink plenty more glasses yet, what's one more or less? (*He gets the box from the cart and takes it under his tunic.*) Be back in a moment. Don't hold me up now, or I'll
400 be angry. I know you mean well. Too bad you can't speak.

(As she tries to hold him back he kisses her and tears himself away. Exit. She is desperate, running hither and thither uttering little noises. The CHAPLAIN *and* MOTHER COURAGE *return.* KATTRIN *rushes to her mother.)*

MOTHER COURAGE: What's all this? Pull yourself together, love. They done something to you? Where's Swiss Cheese? Tell it me step by step, Kattrin. Mother understands you. What, so that bastard did take the box? I'll
405 wrap it round his ears, the little hypocrite. Take your time and don't gabble, use your hands, I don't like it when you howl like a dog, what'll his reverence say? Makes him uncomfortable. What, a one-eyed man came along?

THE CHAPLAIN: That one-eyed man is a spy. Have they ar-
410 rested Swiss Cheese? (KATTRIN *shakes her head, shrugs her shoulders.*) We're done for.

MOTHER COURAGE: (*Fishes in her basket and brings out a Catholic flag, which the* CHAPLAIN *fixes to the mast.*) Better hoist new flag.

415 THE CHAPLAIN: (*Bitterly.*) All good Catholics here.

(Voices are heard from the rear. The two men bring in SWISS CHEESE.)*

SWISS CHEESE: Let me go, I got nowt. Don't twist my shoulder, I'm innocent.

SERGEANT: Here's where he came from. You know each other.

MOTHER COURAGE: Us? How?

SWISS CHEESE: I don't know her. Got no idea who she is, had 420 nowt to do with them. I bought me dinner here, ten hellers it cost. You might have seen me sitting here, it was too salty.

SERGEANT: Who are you people, eh?

MOTHER COURAGE: We're law-abiding folk. That's right, he 425 bought a dinner. Said it was too salty.

SERGEANT: Trying to pretend you don't know each other, that it?

MOTHER COURAGE: Why should I know him? Can't know everyone. I don't go asking 'em what they're called and are 430 they a heretic; if he pays he ain't a heretic. You a heretic?

SWISS CHEESE: Go on.

THE CHAPLAIN: He sat there very properly, never opening his mouth except when eating. Then he had to.

SERGEANT: And who are you? 435

MOTHER COURAGE: He's just my potboy. Now I expect you gentlemen are thirsty, I'll get you a glass of brandy, you must be hot and tired with running.

SERGEANT: No brandy on duty. (*To* SWISS CHEESE.) You were carrying something. Must have hidden it by the river. Was 440 a bulge in your tunic when you left here.

MOTHER COURAGE: You sure it was him?

SWISS CHEESE: You must be thinking of someone else. I saw someone bounding off with a bulge in his tunic. I'm the wrong man. 445

MOTHER COURAGE: I'd say it was a misunderstanding too, such things happen. I'm a good judge of people, I'm Courage, you heard of me, everyone knows me, and I tell you that's an honest face he has.

SERGEANT: We're on the track of the Second Finnish Regi- 450 ment's cash box. We got the description of the fellow responsible for it. Been trailing him two days. It's you.

SWISS CHEESE: It's not me.

SERGEANT: And you better cough it up, or you're a goner, you know. Where is it? 455

MOTHER COURAGE: (*Urgently.*) Of course he'd give it over rather than be a goner. Right out he'd say: I got it, here it is, you're too strong. He ain't all that stupid. Speak up, stupid idiot, here's the sergeant giving you a chance.

SWISS CHEESE: S'pose I ain't got it. 460

SERGEANT: Then come along. We'll get it out of you. (*They lead him off.*)

MOTHER COURAGE: (*Calls after them.*) He'd tell you. He's not that stupid. And don't you twist his shoulder! (*Runs after them.*) 465

(Evening of the same day. The CHAPLAIN *and dumb* KATTRIN *are cleaning glasses and polishing knives.)*

THE CHAPLAIN: Cases like that, where somebody gets caught, are not unknown in religious history. It reminds me of the Passion of Our Lord and Saviour. There's an old song about that. (*He sings the Song of the Hours.*)

---

469 **Song of the Hours** translated by Ralph Manheim

470 In the first hour Jesus mild
     Who had prayed since even
     Was betrayed and led before
     Pontius the heathen.

475 Pilate found him innocent
     Free from fault and error
     Therefore, having washed his hands
     Sent him to King Herod.

     In the third hour he was scourged
     Stripped and clad in scarlet
480 And a plaited crown of thorns
     Set upon his forehead.

     On the Son of Man they spat
     Mocked him and made merry.
     Then the cross of death was brought
485 Given him to carry.

     At the sixth hour with two thieves
     To the cross they nailed him
     And the people and the thieves
     Mocked him and reviled him.

490 This is Jesus King of Jews
     Cried they in derision
     Till the sun withdrew its light
     From that awful vision.

     At the ninth hour Jesus wailed
495 Why hast thou me forsaken?
     Soldiers brought him vinegar
     Which he left untaken.

     Then he yielded up the ghost
     And the earth was shaken.
500 Rended was the temple's veil
     And the saints were wakened.

     Soldiers broke the two thieves' legs
     As the night descended.
     Thrust a spear in Jesus' side
505 When his life had ended.

     Still they mocked, as from his wound
     Flowed the blood and water
     And blasphemed the Son of Man
     With their cruel laughter.

510 MOTHER COURAGE: (*Entering excitedly.*) It's touch and go. They
     say sergeant's open to reason though. Only we mustn't let on
     it's Swiss Cheese else they'll say we helped him. It's a matter
     of money, that's all. But where's money to come from? Hasn't
     Yvette been round? I ran into her, she's got her hooks on
515 some colonel, maybe he'd buy her a canteen business.
     THE CHAPLAIN: Do you really wish to sell?
     MOTHER COURAGE: Where's money for sergeant to come from?
     THE CHAPLAIN: What'll you live on, then?
     MOTHER COURAGE: That's just it.

     (YVETTE POTTIER *arrives with an extremely ancient* COLONEL.)

520 YVETTE: (*Embracing* MOTHER COURAGE.) My dear Courage,
     fancy seeing you so soon. (*Whispers.*) He's not unwilling.
     (*Aloud.*) This is my good friend who advises me in busi-

ness matters. I happened to hear you wanted to sell your
cart on account of circumstances. I'll think it over.
MOTHER COURAGE: Pledge it, not sell, just not too much   525
hurry, 'tain't every day you find a cart like this in wartime.
YVETTE: (*Disappointed.*) Oh, pledge. I thought it was for sale.
I'm not so sure I'm interested. (*To the* COLONEL.) How do
you feel about it?
THE COLONEL: Just as you feel, pet.   530
MOTHER COURAGE: I'm only pledging it.
YVETTE: I thought you'd got to have the money.
MOTHER COURAGE: (*Firmly.*) I got to have it, but sooner run
myself ragged looking for a bidder than sell outright. And
why? The cart's our livelihood. It's a chance for you,   535
Yvette; who knows when you'll get another like it and
have a special friend to advise you, am I right?
YVETTE: Yes, my friend thinks I should clinch it, but I'm not
sure. If it's only a pledge . . . so you agree we ought to buy
outright?   540
THE COLONEL: I agree, pet.
MOTHER COURAGE: Best look and see if you can find anything for sale then; maybe you will if you don't rush it,
take your friend along with you, say a week or fortnight,
might find something suits you.   545
YVETTE: Then let's go looking. I adore going around looking
for things, I adore going around with you, Poldi, it's such
fun, isn't it? No matter if it takes a fortnight. How soon
would you pay the money back if you got it?
MOTHER COURAGE: I'd pay back in two weeks, maybe one.   550
YVETTE: I can't make up my mind, Poldi chéri, you advise
me. (*Takes the* COLONEL *aside.*) She's got to sell, I know, no
problem there. And there's that ensign, you know, the fair-
haired one, he'd be glad to lend me the money. He's crazy
about me, says there's someone I remind him of. What do   555
you advise?
THE COLONEL: You steer clear of him. He's no good. He's
only making use of you. I said I'd buy you something,
didn't I, pussykins?
YVETTE: I oughtn't to let you. Of course if you think the ensign 560
might try to take advantage . . . Poldi, I'll accept it from you.
THE COLONEL: That's how I feel too.
YVETTE: Is that your advice?
THE COLONEL: That is my advice.
YVETTE: (*To* COURAGE *once more.*) My friend's advice would   565
be to accept. Make me out a receipt saying the cart's mine
once two weeks are up, with all its contents, we'll check
it now, I'll bring the two hundred florins later. (*To the*
COLONEL.) You go back to the camp, I'll follow, I got to
check it all and see there's nothing missing from my cart. 570
(*She kisses him. He leaves. She climbs up on the cart.*) Not all
that many boots, are there?
MOTHER COURAGE: Yvette, it's no time for checking your
cart, s'posing it is yours. You promised you'd talk to
sergeant about Swiss Cheese, there ain't a minute to lose, 575
they say in an hour he'll be courtmartialled.
YVETTE: Just let me count the shirts.
MOTHER COURAGE: (*Pulling her down by the skirt.*) You bloody
vampire. Swiss Cheese's life's at stake. And not a word about
who's making the offer, for God's sake, pretend it's your   580
friend, else we're all done for cause we looked after him.
YVETTE: I fixed to meet that one-eyed fellow in the copse, he
should be there by now.

THE CHAPLAIN: It doesn't have to be the whole two hundred either, I'd go up to a hundred and fifty, that may be enough.

585

MOTHER COURAGE: Since when has it been your money? You kindly keep out of this. You'll get your hotpot all right, don't worry. Hurry up and don't haggle, it's life or death. (*Pushes* YVETTE *off*.)

590 THE CHAPLAIN: Far be it from me to interfere, but what are we going to live on? You're saddled with a daughter who can't earn her keep.

MOTHER COURAGE: I'm counting on regimental cash box, Mr. Clever. They'll allow it as his expenses.

595 THE CHAPLAIN: But will she get the message right?

MOTHER COURAGE: It's her interest I should spend her two hundred so she gets the cart. She's set on that, God knows how long that colonel of hers'll last. Kattrin, polish the knives, there's the pumice. And you, stop hanging round

600 like Jesus on Mount of Olives, get moving, wash them glasses, we'll have fifty or more of cavalry in tonight and I don't want to hear a lot of 'I'm not accustomed to having to run about, oh my poor feet, we never ran in church'. Thank the Lord they're corruptible. After all, they ain't

605 wolves, just humans out for money. Corruption in humans is same as compassion in God. Corruption's our only hope. Long as we have it there'll be lenient sentences and even an innocent man'll have a chance of being let off.

YVETTE: (*Comes in panting.*) They'll do it for two hundred.

610 But it's got to be quick. Soon be out of their hands. Best thing is I go right away to my colonel with the one-eyed man. He's admitted he had the box, they put the thumb-screws on him. But he chucked it in the river soon as he saw they were on his track. The box is a write-off. I'll go

615 and get the money from my colonel, shall I?

MOTHER COURAGE: Box is a write-off? How'm I to pay back two hundred then?

YVETTE: Oh, you thought you'd get it from the box, did you? And I was to be Joe Soap I suppose? Better not count on

620 that. You'll have to pay up if you want Swiss Cheese back, or would you sooner I dropped the whole thing so's you can keep your cart?

MOTHER COURAGE: That's something I didn't allow for. Don't worry, you'll get your cart, I've said goodbye to it, had it

625 seventeen years, I have. I just need a moment to think, it's bit sudden, what'm I to do, two hundred's too much for me, pity you didn't beat 'em down. Must keep a bit back, else any Tom, Dick and Harry'll be able to shove me in ditch. Go and tell them I'll pay hundred and twenty florins,

630 else it's all off, either way I'm losing me cart.

YVETTE: They won't do it. That one-eyed man's impatient already, keeps looking over his shoulder, he's so worked up. Hadn't I best pay them the whole two hundred?

MOTHER COURAGE: (*In despair.*) I can't pay that. Thirty years

635 I been working. She's twenty-five already, and no husband. I got her to think of too. Don't push me, I know what I'm doing. Say a hundred and twenty, or it's off.

YVETTE: It's up to you. (*Rushes off.*)

(*Without looking at either the* CHAPLAIN *or her daughter,* MOTHER COURAGE *sits down to help* KATTRIN *polish knives.*)

MOTHER COURAGE: Don't smash them glasses, they ain't ours

640 now. Watch what you're doing, you'll cut yourself. Swiss Cheese'll be back, I'll pay two hundred if it comes to the pinch. You'll get your brother, love. For eighty florins we could fill a pack with goods and start again. Plenty of folk has to make do.

THE CHAPLAIN: The Lord will provide, it says.   645

MOTHER COURAGE: See they're properly dry. (*She cleans knives in silence.* KATTRIN *suddenly runs behind the cart, sobbing.*)

YVETTE: (*Comes running in.*) They won't do it. I told you so. The one-eyed man wanted to leave right away, said there was no point. He says he's just waiting for the drum-roll;   650 that means sentence has been pronounced. I offered a hundred and fifty. He didn't even blink. I had to convince him to stay there so's I could have another word with you.

MOTHER COURAGE: Tell him I'll pay the two hundred. Hurry! (YVETTE *runs off. They sit in silence. The* CHAPLAIN *has stopped*   655 *polishing the glasses.*) I reckon I bargained too long.

(*In the distance drumming is heard. The* CHAPLAIN *gets up and goes to the rear.* MOTHER COURAGE *remains seated. It grows dark. The drumming stops. It grows light once more.* MOTHER COURAGE *is sitting exactly as before.*)

YVETTE: (*Arrives, very pale.*) Well, you got what you asked for, with your haggling and trying to keep your cart. Eleven bullets they gave him, that's all. You don't deserve I should bother any more about you. But I did hear they don't be-   660 lieve the box really is in the river. They've an idea it's here and anyhow that you're connected with him. They're going to bring him here, see if you gives yourself away when you sees him. Thought I'd better warn you so's you don't recognise him, else you'll all be for it. They're right on my   665 heels, best tell you quick. Shall I keep Kattrin away? (MOTHER COURAGE *shakes her head.*) Does she know? She mayn't have heard the drumming or know what it meant.

MOTHER COURAGE: She knows. Get her.

(YVETTE *fetches* KATTRIN, *who goes to her mother and stands beside her.* MOTHER COURAGE *takes her hand. Two lansequenets come carrying a stretcher with something lying on it covered by a sheet. The* SERGEANT *marches beside them. They set down the stretcher.*)

SERGEANT: Here's somebody we dunno the name of. It's got to   670 be listed, though, so everything's shipshape. He had a meal here. Have a look, see if you know him. (*He removes the sheet.*) Know him? (MOTHER COURAGE *shakes her head.*) What, never see him before he had that meal here? (MOTHER COURAGE *shakes her head.*) Pick him up. Chuck him in the   675 pit. He's got nobody knows him. (*They carry him away.*)

SCENE FOUR

Mother Courage sings the Song of the Grand Capitulation.

Outside an officer's tent.

MOTHER COURAGE *is waiting. A* CLERK *looks out of the tent.*

THE CLERK: I know you. You had a paymaster from the Lutherans with you, what was in hiding. I'd not complain if I were you.

MOTHER COURAGE: But I got a complaint to make. I'm innocent, would look as how I'd a bad conscience if I let this   5 pass. Slashed everything in me cart to pieces with their sabres, they did, then wanted I should pay five taler fine for nowt, I tell you, nowt.

THE CLERK: Take my tip, better shut up. We're short of can-
10 teens, so we let you go on trading, specially if you got a bad conscience and pay a fine now and then.

MOTHER COURAGE: I got a complaint.

THE CLERK: Have it your own way. Then you must wait till the captain's free. (*Withdraws inside the tent.*)

15 YOUNG SOLDIER: (*Enters aggressively.*) Bouque la Madonne! Where's that bleeding pig of a captain what's took my reward money to swig with his tarts? I'll do him.

OLDER SOLDIER: (*Running after him.*) Shut up. They'll put you in irons.

20 YOUNG SOLDIER: Out of there, you thief! I'll slice you into pork chops, I will. Pocketing my prize money after I'd swum the river, only one in the whole squadron, and now I can't even buy meself a beer. I'm not standing for that. Come on out there so I can cut you up!

25 OLDER SOLDIER: Blessed Mother of God, he's asking for trouble.

MOTHER COURAGE: Is it some reward he weren't paid?

YOUNG SOLDIER: Lemme go, I'll slash you too while I'm at it.

OLDER SOLDIER: He rescued the colonel's horse and got no
30 reward for it. He's young yet, still wet behind the ears.

MOTHER COURAGE: Let him go, he ain't a dog you got to chain up. Wanting your reward is good sound sense. Why be a hero otherwise?

YOUNG SOLDIER: So's he can sit in there and booze. You're
35 shit-scared, the lot of you. I done something special and I want my reward.

MOTHER COURAGE: Don't you shout at me, young fellow. Got me own worries, I have; any road you should spare your voice, be needing it when captain comes, else there he'll be
40 and you too hoarse to make a sound, which'll make it hard for him to clap you in irons till you turn blue. People what shouts like that can't keep it up ever; half an hour, and they have to be rocked to sleep, they're so tired.

YOUNG SOLDIER: I ain't tired and to hell with sleep. I'm hun-
45 gry. They make our bread from acorns and hemp-seed, and they even skimp on that. He's whoring away my reward and I'm hungry. I'll do him.

MOTHER COURAGE: Oh I see, you're hungry. Last year that general of yours ordered you all off roads and across fields
50 so corn should be trampled flat; I could've got ten florins for a pair of boots s'pose I'd had boots and s'pose anyone'd been able to pay ten florins. Thought he'd be well away from that area this year, he did, but here he is, still there, and hunger is great. I see what you're angry about.

55 YOUNG SOLDIER: I won't have it, don't talk to me, it ain't fair and I'm not standing for that.

MOTHER COURAGE: And you're right; but how long? How long you not standing for unfairness? One hour, two hours? Didn't ask yourself that, did you, but it's the whole
60 point, and why, once you're in irons it's too bad if you suddenly finds you can put up with unfairness after all.

YOUNG SOLDIER: What am I listening to you for, I'd like to know? Bouque la Madonne, where's that captain?

MOTHER COURAGE: You been listening to me because you
65 knows it's like what I say, your anger has gone up in smoke already, it was just a short one and you needed a long one, but where you going to get it from?

YOUNG SOLDIER: Are you trying to tell me asking for my reward is wrong?

MOTHER COURAGE: Not a bit. I'm just telling you your anger 70 ain't long enough, it's good for nowt, pity. If you'd a long one I'd be trying to prod you on. Cut him up, the swine, would be my advice to you in that case; but how about if you don't cut him up cause you feels your tail going between your legs? Then I'd look silly and captain'd take it 75 out on me.

OLDER SOLDIER: You're perfectly right, he's just a bit crazy.

YOUNG SOLDIER: Very well, let's see if I don't cut him up. (*Draws his sword.*) When he arrives I'm going to cut him up.

THE CLERK: (*Looks out.*) The captain'll be here in one minute. 80 Sit down.

(*The* YOUNG SOLDIER *sits down.*)

MOTHER COURAGE: He's sitting now. See, what did I say? You're sitting now. Ah, how well they know us, no one need tell 'em how to go about it. Sit down! and, bingo, we're sitting. And sitting and sedition don't mix. Don't try 85 to stand up, you won't stand the way you was standing before. I shouldn't worry about what I think; I'm no better, not one moment. Bought up all our fighting spirit, they have. Eh? S'pose I kick back, might be bad for business. Let me tell you a thing or two about the Grand Capitu- 90 lation. (*She sings the Song of the Grand Capitulation.*)

Back when I was young, I was brought to realise
What a very special person I must be
(Not just any old cottager's daughter, what with my looks
    and my talents and my urge towards Higher Things)
And insisted that my soup should have no hairs in it.   95
No one makes a sucker out of me!
(All or nothing, only the best is good enough, each man
    for himself, nobody's telling *me* what to do.)
Then I heard a tit
Chirp: Wait a bit!
    And you'll be marching with the band   100
    In step, responding to command
    And striking up your little dance:
    Now we advance.
    And now: parade, form square!
    Then men swear God's there—   105
    Not the faintest chance!

In no time at all anyone who looked could see
That I'd learned to take my medicine with good grace.
(Two kids on my hands and look at the price of bread,
    and things they expect of you!)
When they finally came to feel that they were through   110
    with me
They'd got me grovelling on my face.
(Takes all sorts to make a world, you scratch my back
    and I'll scratch yours, no good banging your head
    against a brick wall.)
Then I heard that tit
Chirp: Wait a bit!
    And you'll be marching with the band   115
    In step, responding to command
    And striking up your little dance:
    Now they advance.
    And now: parade, form square!

120   Then men swear God's there—
      Not the faintest chance!

      I've known people tried to storm the summits:
      There's no star too bright or seems too far away.
      (Dogged does it, where there's a will there's a way, by
      hook or by crook.)
125   As each peak disclosed fresh peaks to come, it's
      Strange how much a plain straw hat could weigh.
      (You have to cut your coat according to your cloth.)
      Then I hear the tit
      Chirp: Wait a bit!
130   And they'll be marching with the band
            In step, responding to command
            And striking up their little dance:
            Now they advance
            And now: parade, form square!
135   Then men swear God's there—
      Not the faintest chance!

      MOTHER COURAGE: (*To the* YOUNG SOLDIER.) That's why I
      reckon you should stay there with your sword drawn if
      you're truly set on it and your anger's big enough, because
140   you got grounds, I agree, but if your anger's a short one
      best leave right away.
      YOUNG SOLDIER: Oh stuff it. (*He staggers off with the* OLDER
      SOLDIER *following.*)
      THE CLERK: (*Sticks his head out.*) Captain's here now. You can
145   make your complaint.
      MOTHER COURAGE: I changed me mind. I ain't complaining.
      (*Exit.*)

SCENE FIVE

Two years have gone by. The war is spreading to new
areas. Ceaselessly on the move, Courage's little cart
crosses Poland, Moravia, Bavaria, Italy, then Bavaria
again. 1631. Tilly's victory at Magdeburg costs Mother
Courage four officers' shirts.

MOTHER COURAGE'*s cart has stopped in a badly shot-up village.
Thin military music in the distance. Two* SOLDIERS *at the bar being served by* KATTRIN *and* MOTHER COURAGE. *One of them has
a lady's fur coat over his shoulders.*

MOTHER COURAGE: Can't pay, that it? No money, no
schnapps. They give us victory parades, but catch them
giving men their pay.
FIRST SOLDIER: I want my schnapps. I missed the looting.
5   That double-crossing general only allowed an hour's looting in the town. He ain't an inhuman monster, he said.
Town must of paid him.
THE CHAPLAIN: (*Stumbles in.*) There are people still lying in
that yard. The peasant's family. Somebody give me a hand.
10   I need linen.

(*The* SECOND SOLDIER *goes off with him.* KATTRIN *becomes very
excited and tries to make her mother produce linen.*)

MOTHER COURAGE: I got none. All my bandages was sold to
regiment. I ain't tearing up my officer's shirts for that lot.
THE CHAPLAIN: (*Calling back.*) I need linen, I tell you.
MOTHER COURAGE: (*Blocking* KATTRIN'*s way into the cart by
sitting on the step.*) I'm giving nowt. They'll never pay, and   15
why, nowt to pay with.
THE CHAPLAIN: (*Bending over a woman he has carried in.*) Why
d'you stay around during the gunfire?
PEASANT WOMAN: (*Feebly.*) Farm.
MOTHER COURAGE: Catch them abandoning anything. But   20
now I'm s'posed to foot the bill. I won't do it.
FIRST SOLDIER: Those are Protestants. What they have to be
Protestants for?
MOTHER COURAGE: They ain't bothering about faith. They
lost their farm.   25
SECOND SOLDIER: They're no Protestants. They're Catholics
like us.
FIRST SOLDIER: No way of sorting 'em out in a bombardment.
A PEASANT: (*Brought in by the* CHAPLAIN.) My arm's gone.
THE CHAPLAIN: Where's that linen?   30
MOTHER COURAGE: I can't give nowt. What with expenses,
taxes, loan interest and bribes. (*Making guttural noises,* KAT-
TRIN *raises a plank and threatens her mother with it.*) You
gone plain crazy? Put that plank away or I'll paste you
one, you cow. I'm giving nowt, don't want to, got to think   35
of meself. (*The* CHAPLAIN *lifts her off the steps and sets her on
the ground, then starts pulling out shirts and tearing them into
strips.*) My officers' shirts! Half a florin apiece! I'm ruined.
(*From the house comes the cry of a child in pain.*)
THE PEASANT: The baby's in there still. (KATTRIN *dashes in.*)   40
THE CHAPLAIN: (*To the woman.*) Don't move. They'll get it out.
MOTHER COURAGE: Stop her, roof may fall in.
THE CHAPLAIN: I'm not going back in there.
MOTHER COURAGE: (*Torn both ways.*) Don't waste my pre-
cious linen.   45

(KATTRIN *brings a baby out of the ruins.*)

MOTHER COURAGE: How nice, found another baby to cart
around? Give it to its ma this instant, unless you'd have me
fighting for hours to get it off you, like last time, d'you
hear? (*To the* SECOND SOLDIER.) Don't stand there gaw-
ping, you go back and tell them cut out that music, we can   50
see it's a victory with our own eyes. All your victories
mean to me is losses.
THE CHAPLAIN: (*Tying a bandage.*) Blood's coming through.

(KATTRIN *is rocking the baby and making lullaby noises.*)

MOTHER COURAGE: Look at her, happy as a queen in all this
misery; give it back at once, its mother's coming round. (*She*   55
catches the FIRST SOLDIER, *who has been attacking the drinks and
is trying to make off with one of the bottles.*) Psia krew! Thought
you'd score another victory, you animal? Now pay.
FIRST SOLDIER: I got nowt.
MOTHER COURAGE: (*Pulling the fur coat off his back.*) Then   60
leave that coat, it's stolen any road.
THE CHAPLAIN: There's still someone under there.

SCENE SIX

Outside the Bavarian town of Ingolstadt Courage participates in the funeral of the late Imperial commander Tilly. Discussions are held about war heroes and the war's duration. The Chaplain complains that his talents are lying fallow, and dumb Kattrin gets the red boots. The year is 1632.

Inside a canteen tent.

It has a bar towards the rear. Rain. Sound of drums and Funeral music. The CHAPLAIN *and the regimental* CLERK *are playing a board game.* MOTHER COURAGE *and her daughter are stocktaking.*

THE CHAPLAIN: Now the funeral procession will be moving off.
MOTHER COURAGE: Too bad about commander in chief—twenty-two pairs those socks—he fell by accident, they say. Mist over fields, that was the trouble. General had just
5   been haranguing a regiment saying they must fight to last man and last round, he was riding back when mist made him lose direction so he was up front and a bullet got him in midst of battle—only four hurricane lamps left. (*A whistle from the rear. She goes to the bar.*) You scrimshankers,
10   dodging your commander in chief's funeral, scandal I call it. (*Pours drinks.*)
THE CLERK: They should never of paid troops out before the funeral. Instead of going now they're all getting pissed.
THE CHAPLAIN: (*To the* CLERK.) Aren't you supposed to go to
15   the funeral?
THE CLERK: Dodged it cause of the rain.
MOTHER COURAGE: It's different with you, your uniform might get wet. I heard they wanted to toll bells for funeral as usual, except it turned out all churches had been blown
20   to smithereens by his orders, so poor old commander in chief won't be hearing no bells as they let the coffin down. They're going to let off three salvoes instead to cheer things up—seventeen belts.
SHOUTS: (*From the bar.*) Hey, Missis, a brandy!
25   MOTHER COURAGE: Let's see your money. No, I ain't having you in my tent with your disgusting boots. You can drink outside, rain or no rain. (*To the* CLERK.) I'm only letting in sergeants and up. Commander in chief had been having his worries, they say. S'posed to have been trouble with
30   Second Regiment cause he stopped their pay, said it was a war of faith and they should do it for free. (*Funeral march. All look to the rear.*)
THE CHAPLAIN: Now they'll be filing past the noble corpse.
MOTHER COURAGE: Can't help feeling sorry for those gener-
35   als and emperors, there they are maybe thinking they're doing something extra special what folk'll talk about in years to come, and earning a public monument, like conquering the world for instance, that's a fine ambition for a general, how's he to know any better? I mean, he plagues
40   hisself to death, then it all breaks down on account of ordinary folk what just wants their beer and bit of a chat, nowt higher. Finest plans get bolloxed up by the pettiness of them as should be carrying them out, because emperors can't do nowt themselves, they just counts on soldiers
45   and people to back 'em up whatever happens, am I right?
THE CHAPLAIN: (*Laughs.*) Courage, you're right, aside from the soldiers. They do their best. Give me that lot outside

there, for instance, drinking their brandy in the rain, and I'd guarantee to make you one war after another for a hundred years if need be, and I'm no trained general.   50
MOTHER COURAGE: You don't think war might end, then?
THE CHAPLAIN: What, because the commander in chief's gone? Don't be childish. They're two a penny, no shortage of heroes.
MOTHER COURAGE: Ee, I'm not asking for fun of it, but because I'm thinking whether to stock up, prices are low   55
now, but if war's going to end it's money down the drain.
THE CHAPLAIN: I realise it's a serious question. There've always been people going round saying 'the war can't go on for ever'. I tell you there's nothing to stop it going on for ever. Of course there can be a bit of a breathing space. The war   60
may need to get its second wind, it may even have an accident so to speak. There's no guarantee against that; nothing's perfect on this earth of ours. A perfect war, the sort you might say couldn't be improved on, that's something we shall probably never see. It can suddenly come to a   65
standstill for some quite unforeseen reason, you can't allow for everything. A slight case of negligence, and it's bogged down up to the axles. And then it's a matter of hauling the war out of the mud again. But emperor and kings and popes will come to its rescue. So on the whole it has noth-   70
ing serious to worry about, and will live to a ripe old age.
A SOLDIER: (*Sings at the bar.*)

> A schnapps, landlord, you're late!
> A soldier cannot wait
> To do his emperor's orders.   75

Make it a double, this is a holiday.
MOTHER COURAGE: S'pose I went by what you say . . .
THE CHAPLAIN: Think it out for yourself. What's to compete with the war?
THE SOLDIER: (*At the rear.*)   80

> Your breast, my girl, you're late!
> A soldier cannot wait
> To ride across the borders.

THE CLERK: (*Unexpectedly.*) And what about peace? I'm from Bohemia and I'd like to go home some day.   85
THE CHAPLAIN: Would you indeed? Ah, peace. Where is the hole once the cheese has been eaten?
THE SOLDIER: (*At the rear.*)

> Lead trumps, my friend, you're late!
> A soldier cannot wait.   90
> His emperor needs him badly.
>
> Your blessing, priest, you're late!
> A soldier cannot wait.
> Must lay his life down gladly.

THE CLERK: In the long run life's impossible if there's no peace.   95
THE CHAPLAIN: I'd say there's peace in war too; it has its peaceful moments. Because war satisfies all requirements, peaceable ones included, they're catered for, and it would simply fizzle out if they weren't. In war you can do a crap like in the depths of peacetime, then between one battle 100
and the next you can have a beer, then even when you're moving up you can lay your head on your arms and have a bit of shuteye in the ditch, it's entirely possible. During a charge you can't play cards maybe, but nor can you in the

105 depths of peacetime when you're ploughing, and after a victory there are various openings. You may get a leg blown off, then you start by making a lot of fuss as though it were serious, but afterwards you calm down or get given a schnapps, and you end up hopping around and the war's

110 no worse off than before. And what's to stop you being fruitful and multiplying in the middle of all the butchery, behind a barn or something, in the long run you can't be held back from it, and then the war will have your progeny and can use them to carry on with. No, the war will always

115 find an outlet, mark my words. Why should it ever stop?

(KATTRIN *has ceased working and is staring at the* CHAPLAIN.)

MOTHER COURAGE: I'll buy fresh stock then. If you say so. (KATTRIN *suddenly flings a basket full of bottles to the ground and runs off.*) Kattrin! (*Laughs.*) Damn me if she weren't waiting for peace. I promised her she'd get a husband soon

120 as peace came. (*Hurries after her.*)

THE CLERK: (*Standing up.*) I won. You been talking too much. Pay up.

MOTHER COURAGE: (*Returning with* KATTRIN.) Don't be silly, war'll go on a bit longer, and we'll make a bit more

125 money, and peacetime'll be all the nicer for it. Now you go into town, that's ten minutes' walk at most, fetch things from Golden Lion, the expensive ones, we can fetch rest in cart later, it's all arranged, regimental clerk here will go with you. Nearly everybody's attending commander in

130 chief's funeral, nowt can happen to you. Careful now, don't let them steal nowt, think of your dowry.

(KATTRIN *puts a cloth over her head and leaves with the* CLERK.)

THE CHAPLAIN: Is that all right to let her go with the clerk?

MOTHER COURAGE: She's not that pretty they'd want to ruin her.

THE CHAPLAIN: I admire the way you run your business and

135 always win through. I see why they called you Courage.

MOTHER COURAGE: Poor folk got to have courage. Why, they're lost. Simply getting up in morning takes some doing in their situation. Or ploughing a field, and in a war at that. Mere fact they bring kids into world shows they got

140 courage, cause there's no hope for them. They have to hang one another and slaughter one another, so just looking each other in face must call for courage. Being able to put up with emperor and pope shows supernatural courage, cause those two cost 'em their lives. (*She sits down, takes a little pipe from*

145 *her purse and smokes.*) You might chop us a bit of kindling.

THE CHAPLAIN: (*Reluctantly removing his coat and preparing to chop up sticks.*) I happen to be a pastor of souls, not a woodcutter.

MOTHER COURAGE: I got no soul, you see. Need firewood, though.

150 THE CHAPLAIN: Where's that stumpy pipe from?

MOTHER COURAGE: Just a pipe.

THE CHAPLAIN: What d'you mean, 'just', it's a quite particular pipe, that.

MOTHER COURAGE: Aha?

155 THE CHAPLAIN: That stumpy pipe belongs to the Oxenstierna Regiment's cook.

MOTHER COURAGE: If you know that already why ask, Mr Clever?

THE CHAPLAIN: Because I didn't know if you were aware

160 what you're smoking. You might just have been rummag-

ing around in your things, come across some old pipe or other, and used it out of sheer absence of mind.

MOTHER COURAGE: And why not?

THE CHAPLAIN: Because you didn't. You're smoking that de-

165 liberately.

MOTHER COURAGE: And why shouldn't I?

THE CHAPLAIN: Courage, I'm warning you. It's my duty. Probably you'll never clap eyes on the gentleman again, and that's no loss but your good fortune. He didn't make

170 at all a reliable impression on me. Quite the opposite.

MOTHER COURAGE: Really? Nice fellow that.

THE CHAPLAIN: So he's what you would call a nice fellow? I wouldn't. Far be it from me to bear him the least ill-will, but nice is not what I would call him. More like one of

175 those Don Juans, a slippery one. Have a look at that pipe if you don't believe me. You must admit it tells you a good deal about his character.

MOTHER COURAGE: Nowt that I can see. Worn out, I'd call it.

THE CHAPLAIN: Practically bitten through, you mean. A man

180 of wrath. That is the pipe of an unscrupulous man of wrath; you must see that if you have any discrimination left.

MOTHER COURAGE: Don't chop my chopping block in two.

THE CHAPLAIN: I told you I'm not a woodcutter by trade. I studied to be a pastor of souls. My talent and abilities are

185 being abused in this place, by manual labour. My God-given endowments are denied expression. It's a sin. You have never heard me preach. One sermon of mine can put a regiment in such a frame of mind it'll treat the enemy like a flock of sheep. Life to them is a smelly old foot-

190 cloth which they fling away in a vision of final victory. God has given me the gift of speech. I can preach so you'll lose all sense of sight and hearing.

MOTHER COURAGE: I don't wish to lose my sense of sight and hearing. Where'd that leave me?

195 THE CHAPLAIN: Courage, I have often thought that your dry way of talking conceals more than just a warm heart. You too are human and need warmth.

MOTHER COURAGE: Best way for us to get this tent warm is have plenty of firewood.

200 THE CHAPLAIN: Don't change the subject. Seriously, Courage, I sometimes ask myself what it would be like if our relationship were to become somewhat closer. I mean, given that the whirlwind of war has so strangely whirled us together.

MOTHER COURAGE: I'd say it was close enough. I cook meals

205 for you and you run around and chop firewood for instance.

THE CHAPLAIN: (*Coming closer.*) You know what I mean by closer; it's not a relationship founded on meals and wood-chopping and other such base necessities. Let your head speak, harden thyself not.

210 MOTHER COURAGE: Don't you come at me with that axe. That'd be too close a relationship.

THE CHAPLAIN: You shouldn't make a joke of it. I'm a serious person and I've thought about what I'm saying.

MOTHER COURAGE: Be sensible, padre. I like you. I don't want

215 to row you. All I'm after is get myself and children through all this with my cart. I don't see it as mine, and I ain't in the mood for private affairs. Right now I'm taking a gamble, buying stores just when commander in chief's fallen and all the talk's of peace. Where d'you reckon you'd turn if I'm

220 ruined? Don't know, do you? You chop us some kindling wood, then we can keep warm at night, that's quite some-

thing these times. What's this? (*She gets up. Enter* KATTRIN, *out of breath, with a wound above her eye. She is carrying a variety of stuff: parcels, leather goods, a drum and so on.*)

225 MOTHER COURAGE: What happened, someone assault you? On way back? She was assaulted on her way back. Bet it was that trooper was getting drunk here. I shouldn't have let you go, love. Drop that stuff. Not too bad, just a flesh wound you got. I'll bandage it and in a week it'll be all right. Worse than
230 wild beasts, they are. (*She ties up the wound.*)

THE CHAPLAIN: It's not them I blame. They never went raping back home. The fault lies with those that start wars, it brings humanity's lowest instincts to the surface.

MOTHER COURAGE: Calm down. Didn't clerk come back
235 with you? That's because you're respectable, they don't bother. Wound ain't a deep one, won't leave no mark. There you are, all bandaged up. You'll get something, love, keep calm. Something I put aside for you, wait till you see. (*She delves into a sack and brings out* YVETTE's *red high-heeled*
240 *boots.*) Made you open your eyes, eh? Something you always wanted. They're yours. Put 'em on quick, before I change me mind. Won't leave no mark, and what if it does? Ones I'm really sorry for's the ones they fancy. Drag them around till they're worn out, they do. Those they
245 don't care for they leaves alive. I seen girls before now had pretty faces, then in no time looking fit to frighten a hyaena. Can't even go behind a bush without risking trouble, horrible life they lead. Same like with trees, straight well-shaped ones get chopped down to make beams for
250 houses and crooked ones live happily ever after. So it's a stroke of luck for you really. Them boots'll be all right, I greased them before putting them away.

(KATTRIN *leaves the boots where they are and crawls into the cart.*)

THE CHAPLAIN: Let's hope she's not disfigured.

MOTHER COURAGE: She'll have a scar. No use her waiting for
255 peacetime now.

THE CHAPLAIN: She didn't let them steal the things.

MOTHER COURAGE: Maybe I shouldn't have dinned that into her so. Wish I knew what went on in that head of hers. Just once she stayed out all night, once in all those years.
260 Afterwards she went around like before, except she worked harder. Couldn't get her to tell what had happened. Worried me quite a while, that did. (*She collects the articles brought by* KATTRIN, *and sorts them angrily.*) That's war for you. Nice way to get a living!

(*Sound of cannon fire.*)

265 THE CHAPLAIN: Now they'll be burying the commander in chief. This is a historic moment.

MOTHER COURAGE: What I call a historic moment is them bashing my daughter over the eye. She's half wrecked already, won't get no husband now, and her so crazy about
270 kids; any road she's only dumb from war, soldier stuffed something in her mouth when she was little. As for Swiss Cheese I'll never see him again, and where Eilif is God alone knows. War be damned.

SCENE SEVEN

Mother Courage at the peak of her business career.

High road.

The CHAPLAIN, MOTHER COURAGE *and* KATTRIN *are pulling the cart, which is hung with new wares.* MOTHER COURAGE *is wearing a necklace of silver coins.*

MOTHER COURAGE: I won't have you folk spoiling my war for me. I'm told it kills off the weak, but they're write-off in peacetime too. And war gives its people a better deal. (*She sings.*)

And if you feel your forces fading   5
You won't be there to share the fruits.
But what is war but private trading
That deals in blood instead of boots?

And what's the use of settling down? Them as does are first to go. (*Sings.*)   10

Some people think to live by looting
The goods some others haven't got.
You think it's just a line they're shooting
Until you hear they have been shot.

And some I saw dig six feet under   15
In haste to lie down and pass out.
Now they're at rest perhaps they wonder
Just what was all their haste about.

(*They pull it further.*)

SCENE EIGHT

The same year sees the death of the Swedish king Gustavus Adolphus at the battle of Lützen. Peace threatens to ruin Mother Courage's business. Courage's dashing son performs one heroic deed too many and comes to a sticky end.

Camp.

A summer morning. In front of the cart stand an OLD WOMAN *and her son. The son* [YOUNG MAN] *carries a large sack of bedding.*

MOTHER COURAGE'S VOICE: (*From inside the cart.*) Does it need to be this ungodly hour?

THE YOUNG MAN: We walked twenty miles in the night and got to be back today.

MOTHER COURAGE'S VOICE: What am I to do with bedding?   5
Folk've got no houses.

THE YOUNG MAN: Best have a look first.

THE OLD WOMAN: This place is no good either. Come on.

THE YOUNG MAN: What, and have them sell the roof over our head for taxes? She might pay three florins if you throw   10
in the bracelet. (*Bells start ringing.*) Listen, mother.

VOICES: (*From the rear.*) Peace! Swedish king's been killed.

MOTHER COURAGE: (*Sticks her head out of the cart. She has not yet done her hair.*) What's that bell-ringing about in mid-week?

THE CHAPLAIN: (*Crawling out from under the cart.*) What are   15
they shouting? Peace?

MOTHER COURAGE: Don't tell me peace has broken out just after I laid in new stock.

THE CHAPLAIN: (*Calling to the rear.*) That true? Peace?

20 VOICES: Three weeks ago, they say, only no one told us.

THE CHAPLAIN: (*To* COURAGE.) What else would they be ringing the bells for?

VOICES: A whole lot of Lutherans have driven into town, they brought the news.

25 THE YOUNG MAN: Mother, it's peace. What's the matter?

(*The* OLD WOMAN *has collapsed.*)

MOTHER COURAGE: (*Speaking into the cart.*) Holy cow! Kattrin, peace! Put your black dress on, we're going to church. Least we can do for Swiss Cheese. Is it true, though?

THE YOUNG MAN: The people here say so. They've made
30   peace. Can you get up? (*The* OLD WOMAN *stands up dumbfounded.*) I'll get the saddlery going again, I promise. It'll all work out. Father will get his bedding back. Can you walk? (*To the* CHAPLAIN.) She came over queer. It's the news. She never thought there'd be peace again. Father al-
35   ways said so. We're going straight home. (*They go off.*)

MOTHER COURAGE'S VOICE: Give her a schnapps.

THE CHAPLAIN: They've already gone.

MOTHER COURAGE'S VOICE: What's up in camp?

THE CHAPLAIN: They're assembling. I'll go on over. Shouldn't
40   I put on my clerical garb?

MOTHER COURAGE'S VOICE: Best check up before parading yourself as heretic. I'm glad about peace, never mind if I'm ruined. Any road I'll have got two of me children through the war. Be seeing Eilif again now.

45 THE CHAPLAIN: And who's that walking down the lines? Bless me, the army commander's cook.

THE COOK: (*Somewhat bedraggled and carrying a bundle.*) What do I behold? The padre!

THE CHAPLAIN: Courage, we've got company.

(MOTHER COURAGE *clambers out.*)

50 THE COOK: I promised I'd drop over for a little talk soon as I had the time. I've not forgotten your brandy, Mrs Fierling.

MOTHER COURAGE: Good grief, the general's cook! After all these years! Where's my eldest boy Eilif?

THE COOK: Hasn't he got here? He left before me, he was on
55   his way to see you too.

THE CHAPLAIN: I shall don my clerical garb, just a moment.

(*Goes off behind the cart.*)

MOTHER COURAGE: Then he may be here any minute. (*Calls into the cart.*) Kattrin, Eilif's on his way. Get cook a glass of brandy, Kattrin! (KATTRIN *does not appear.*) Drag your hair
60   down over it, that's all right. Mr Lamb's no stranger. (*Fetches the brandy herself.*) She don't like to come out, peace means nowt to her. Took too long coming, it did. They gave her a crack over one eye, you barely notice it now but she thinks folks are staring at her.

65 THE COOK: Ah yes. War. (*He and* MOTHER COURAGE *sit down.*)

MOTHER COURAGE: Cooky, you caught me at bad moment. I'm ruined.

THE COOK: What? That's hard.

MOTHER COURAGE: Peace'll wring my neck. I went and took Chaplain's advice, laid in fresh stocks only t'other day. And
70   now they're going to demobilise and I'll be left sitting on me wares.

THE COOK: What d'you want to go and listen to padre for? If I hadn't been in such a hurry that time, the Catholics arriving so quickly and all, I'd warned you against that man. All piss
75   and wind, he is. So he's the authority around here, eh?

MOTHER COURAGE: He's been doing washing-up for me and helping pull.

THE COOK: Him pull! I bet he told you some of those jokes of his too, I know him, got a very unhealthy view of
80   women, he has, all my good influence on him went for nowt. He ain't steady.

MOTHER COURAGE: You steady then?

THE COOK: Whatever else I ain't, I'm steady. Mud in your eye!

MOTHER COURAGE: Steady, that's nowt. I only had one steady
85   fellow, thank God. Hardest I ever had to work in me life; he flogged the kids' blankets soon as autumn came, and he called me mouth-organ an unchristian instrument. Ask me, you ain't saying much for yourself admitting you're steady.

THE COOK: Still tough as nails, I see; but that's what I like
90   about you.

MOTHER COURAGE: Now don't tell me you been dreaming of me nails.

THE COOK: Well, well, here we are, along with armistice bells and your brandy like what nobody else ever serves, it's fa-
95   mous, that is.

MOTHER COURAGE: I don't give two pins for your armistice bells just now. Can't see 'em handing out all the back pay what's owing, so where does that leave me with my famous brandy? Had your pay yet?
100

THE COOK: (*Hesitantly.*) Not exactly. That's why we all shoved off. If that's how it is, I thought, I'll go and visit friends. So here I am sitting with you.

MOTHER COURAGE: Other words you got nowt.

THE COOK: High time they stopped that bloody clanging.
105   Wouldn't mind getting into some sort of trade. I'm fed up being cook to that lot. I'm s'posed to rustle them up meals out of tree roots and old bootsoles, then they fling the hot soup in my face. Cook these days is a dog's life. Sooner do war service, only of course it's peacetime now. (*He sees the*
110   CHAPLAIN *reappearing in his old garments.*) More about that later.

THE CHAPLAIN: It's still all right, only had a few moths in it.

THE COOK: Can't see why you bother. You won't get your old job back, who are you to inspire now to earn his pay hon-
115   ourably and lay down his life? What's more I got a bone to pick with you, cause you advised this lady to buy a lot of unnecessary goods saying war would go on for ever.

THE CHAPLAIN: (*Heatedly.*) I'd like to know what concern that is of yours.
120

THE COOK: Because it's unscrupulous, that sort of thing is. How dare you meddle in other folks' business arrangements with your unwanted advice?

THE CHAPLAIN: Who's meddling? (*To* COURAGE.) I never knew this gentleman was such an intimate you had to ac-
125   count to him for everything.

MOTHER COURAGE: Keep your hair on, cook's only giving his personal opinion and you can't deny your war was a flop.

THE CHAPLAIN: You should not blaspheme against peace, Courage. You are a hyaena of the battlefield.

MOTHER COURAGE: I'm what?

THE COOK: If you're going to insult this lady you'll have to settle with me.

THE CHAPLAIN: It's not you I'm talking to. Your intentions are only too transparent. (*To* COURAGE.) But when I see you picking up peace betwixt your finger and your thumb like some dirty old snot-rag, then my humanity feels outraged; for then I see that you don't want peace but war, because you profit from it; in which case you shouldn't forget the ancient saying that whosoever sups with the devil needs a long spoon.

MOTHER COURAGE: I got no use for war, and war ain't got much use for me. But I'm not being called no hyaena, you and me's through.

THE CHAPLAIN: Then why grumble about peace when everybody's breathing sighs of relief? Because of some old junk in your cart?

MOTHER COURAGE: My goods ain't old junk but what I lives by, and you too up to now.

THE CHAPLAIN: Off war, in other words. Aha.

THE COOK: (*To the* CHAPLAIN.) You're old enough to know it's always a mistake offering advice. (*To* COURAGE.) Way things are, your best bet's to get rid of certain goods quick as you can before prices hit rock-bottom. Dress yourself and get moving, not a moment to lose.

MOTHER COURAGE: That ain't bad advice. I'll do that, I guess.

THE CHAPLAIN: Because cooky says it.

MOTHER COURAGE: Why couldn't you say it? He's right, I'd best go off to market. (*Goes inside the cart.*)

THE COOK: That's one to me, padre. You got no presence of mind. What you should of said was: what, me offer advice, all I done was discuss politics. Better not take me on. Cock-fighting don't suit that get-up.

THE CHAPLAIN: If you don't stop your gob I'll murder you, get-up or no get-up.

THE COOK: (*Pulling off his boots and unwrapping his foot-cloths.*) Pity the war made such a godless shit of you, else you'd easily get another parsonage now it's peacetime. Cooks won't be needed, there's nowt to cook, but faith goes on just the same, nowt changed in that direction.

THE CHAPLAIN: Mr Lamb, I'm asking you not to elbow me out. Since I came down in the world I've become a better person. I couldn't preach to anyone now.

(*Enter* YVETTE POTTIER *in black, dressed up to the nines, carrying a cane. She is much older and fatter, and heavily powdered. She is followed by a manservant.*)

YVETTE: Hullo there, everybody. Is this Mother Courage's establishment?

THE CHAPLAIN: It is. And with whom have we the honour ...?

YVETTE: With the Countess Starhemberg, my good man. Where's Courage?

THE CHAPLAIN: (*Calls into the cart.*) The Countess Starhemberg wishes to speak to you.

MOTHER COURAGE'S VOICE: Just coming.

YVETTE: It's Yvette.

MOTHER COURAGE'S VOICE: Oh, Yvette!

YVETTE: Come to see how you are. (*Sees the* COOK *turn round aghast.*) Pieter!

THE COOK: Yvette!

YVETTE: Well I never! How d'you come to be here?

THE COOK: Got a lift.

THE CHAPLAIN: You know each other then? Intimately?

YVETTE: I should think so. (*She looks the* COOK *over.*) Fat.

THE COOK: Not all that skinny yourself.

YVETTE: All the same I'm glad to see you, you shit. Gives me a chance to say what I think of you.

THE CHAPLAIN: You say it, in full; but don't start till Courage is out here.

MOTHER COURAGE: (*Coming out with all kinds of goods.*) Yvette! (*They embrace.*) But what are you in mourning for?

YVETTE: Suits me, don't it? My husband the colonel died a few years back.

MOTHER COURAGE: That old fellow what nearly bought the cart?

YVETTE: His elder brother.

MOTHER COURAGE: Then you're sitting pretty. Nice to find somebody what's made it in this war.

YVETTE: Up and down and up again, that's the way it went.

MOTHER COURAGE: I'm not hearing a word against colonels, they make a mint of money.

THE CHAPLAIN: I would put my boots back on if I were you. (*To* YVETTE.) You promised you would say what you think of the gentleman.

THE COOK: Don't kick up a stink here, Yvette.

MOTHER COURAGE: Yvette, this is a friend of mine.

YVETTE: That's old Puffing Piet.

THE COOK: Let's drop the nicknames. I'm called Lamb.

MOTHER COURAGE: (*Laughs.*) Puffing Piet! Him as made all the women crazy! Here, I been looking after your pipe for you.

THE CHAPLAIN: Smoking it, too.

YVETTE: What luck I can warn you against him. Worst of the lot, he was, rampaging along the whole Flanders coastline. Got more girls in trouble than he has fingers.

THE COOK: That's all a long while ago. 'Tain't true anyhow.

YVETTE: Stand up when a lady brings you into the conversation! How I loved this man! All the time he had a little dark girl with bandy legs, got her in trouble too of course.

THE COOK: Got you into high society more like, far as I can see.

YVETTE: Shut your trap, you pathetic remnant! Better watch out for him, though; fellows like that are still dangerous even when on their last legs.

MOTHER COURAGE: (*To* YVETTE.) Come along, got to get rid of my stuff afore prices start dropping. You might be able to put a word in for me at regiment, with your connections. (*Calls into the cart.*) Kattrin, church is off, I'm going to market instead. When Eilif turns up, one of you give him a drink. (*Exit with* YVETTE.)

YVETTE: (*As she leaves.*) Fancy a creature like that ever making me leave the straight and narrow path. Thank my lucky stars I managed to reach the top all the same. But I've cooked your goose, Puffing Piet, and that's something that'll be credited to me one day in the world to come.

THE CHAPLAIN: I would like to take as a text for our little talk 'The mills of God grind slowly'. Weren't you complaining about my jokes?

THE COOK: Dead out of luck, I am. It's like this, you see: I thought I might get a hot meal. Here am I starving, and

245 now they'll be talking about me and she'll get quite a wrong picture. I think I'll clear out before she's back.

THE CHAPLAIN: I think so too.

THE COOK: Padre, I'm fed up already with this bloody peace. Human race has to go through fire and sword cause it's sinful from the cradle up. I wish I could be roasting a fat 250 capon once again for the general, wherever he's got to, in mustard sauce with a carrot or two.

THE CHAPLAIN: Red cabbage. Red cabbage for a capon.

THE COOK: You're right, but carrots was what he had to have.

THE CHAPLAIN: No sense of what's fitting.

255 THE COOK: Not that it stopped you guzzling your share.

THE CHAPLAIN: With misgivings.

THE COOK: Anyway you must admit those were the days.

THE CHAPLAIN: I might admit it if pressed.

THE COOK: Now you've called her a hyaena your days here 260 are finished. What you staring at?

THE CHAPLAIN: Eilif! (EILIF *arrives, followed by* SOLDIERS *with pikes. His hands are fettered. His face is chalky-white.*) What's wrong?

EILIF: Where's mother?

265 THE CHAPLAIN: Gone into town.

EILIF: I heard she was around. They've allowed me to come and see her.

THE COOK: (*To the* SOLDIERS.) What you doing with him?

A SOLDIER: Something not nice.

270 THE CHAPLAIN: What's he been up to?

THE SOLDIER: Broke into a peasant's place. The wife's dead.

THE CHAPLAIN: How could you do a thing like that?

EILIF: It's what I did last time, ain't it?

THE COOK: Aye, but it's peace now.

275 EILIF: Shut up. All right if I sit down till she comes?

THE SOLDIER: We've no time.

THE CHAPLAIN: In wartime they recommended him for that, sat him at the general's right hand. Dashing, it was, in those days. Any chance of a word with the provost-marshal?

280 THE SOLDIER: Wouldn't do no good. Taking some peasant's cattle, what's dashing about that?

THE COOK: Dumb, I call it.

EILIF: If I'd been dumb you'd starved, clever bugger.

THE COOK: But as you were clever you're going to be shot.

285 THE CHAPLAIN: We'd better fetch Kattrin out anyhow.

EILIF: Sooner have a glass of schnapps, could do with that.

THE SOLDIER: No time, come along.

THE CHAPLAIN: And what shall we tell your mother?

EILIF: Tell her it wasn't any different, tell her it was the same 290 thing. Or tell her nowt. (*The* SOLDIERS *propel him away.*)

THE CHAPLAIN: I'll accompany you on your grievous journey.

EILIF: Don't need any bloody parsons.

THE CHAPLAIN: Wait and see. (*Follows him.*)

THE COOK: (*Calls after them.*) I'll have to tell her, she'll want 295 to see him.

THE CHAPLAIN: I wouldn't tell her anything. At most that he was here and will come again, maybe tomorrow. By then I'll be back and can break it to her. (*Hurries off.*)

(*The* COOK *looks after him, shaking his head, then walks restlessly around. Finally he comes up to the cart.*)

THE COOK: Hoy! Don't you want to come out? I can under- 300 stand you hiding away from peace. Like to do the same myself. Remember me, I'm general's cook? I was wondering if you'd a bit of something to eat while I wait for your mum. I don't half feel like a bit of pork, or bread even, just to fill the time. (*Peers inside.*) Head under blanket. (*Sound of gunfire off.*) 305

MOTHER COURAGE: (*Runs in, out of breath and with all her goods still.*) Cooky, peacetime's over. War's been on again three days now. Heard news before selling me stuff, thank God. They're having a shooting match with Lutherans in town. We must get cart away at once. Kattrin, pack up! What 310 you in the dumps for? What's wrong?

THE COOK: Nowt.

MOTHER COURAGE: Something is. I see it way you look.

THE COOK: Cause war's starting up again, I s'pose. Looks as if it'll be tomorrow night before I get next hot food inside me. 315

MOTHER COURAGE: You're lying, cooky.

THE COOK: Eilif was here. Had to leave almost at once, though.

MOTHER COURAGE: Was he now? Then we'll be seeing him on march. I'm joining our side this time. How's he look?

THE COOK: Same as usual. 320

MOTHER COURAGE: Oh, he'll never change. Take more than war to steal him from me. Clever, he is. You going to help me get packed? (*Begins to pack up.*) What's his news? Still in general's good books? Say anything about his deeds of valour? 325

THE COOK: (*Glumly.*) Repeated one of them, I'm told.

MOTHER COURAGE: Tell it me later, we got to move off. (KATTRIN *appears.*) Kattrin, peacetime's finished now. We're moving on. (*To the* COOK.) How about you?

THE COOK: Have to join up again. 330

MOTHER COURAGE: Why don't you . . . Where's padre?

THE COOK: Went into town with Eilif.

MOTHER COURAGE: Then you come along with us a way. Need somebody to help me.

THE COOK: That business with Yvette, you know . . . 335

MOTHER COURAGE: Done you no harm in my eyes. Opposite. Where there's smoke there's fire, they say. You coming along?

THE COOK: I won't say no.

MOTHER COURAGE: The Twelfth moved off already. Take the 340 shaft. Here's a bit of bread. We must get round behind to Lutherans. Might even be seeing Eilif tonight. He's my favourite one. Short peace, wasn't it? Now we're off again. (*She sings as the* COOK *and* KATTRIN *harness themselves up.*)

From Ulm to Metz, from Metz to Munich 345
Courage will see the war gets fed.
The war will show a well-filled tunic
Given its daily shot of lead.
But lead alone can hardly nourish
It must have soldiers to subsist. 350
It's you it needs to make it flourish.
The war's still hungry. So enlist!

SCENE NINE

It is the seventeenth year of the great war of faith. Germany has lost more than half her inhabitants. Those who survive the bloodbath are killed off by terrible epidemics. Once fertile areas are ravaged by famine, wolves roam the burnt-out towns. In autumn 1634 we find Courage in the Fichtelgebirge, off the main axis of the Swedish armies. The winter this year is early and harsh. Business is bad, so that there is nothing to do but beg. The cook gets a letter from Utrecht and is sent packing.

Outside a semi-dilapidated parsonage.

Grey morning in early winter. Gusts of wind. MOTHER COURAGE *and the* COOK *in shabby sheepskins, drawing the cart.*

THE COOK: It's all dark, nobody up yet.

MOTHER COURAGE: Except it's parson's house. Have to crawl out of bed to ring bells. Then he'll have hot soup.

THE COOK: What from when whole village is burnt, we
5   seen it.

MOTHER COURAGE: It's lived in, though, dog was barking.

THE COOK: S'pose parson's got, he'll give nowt.

MOTHER COURAGE: Maybe if we sing. . . .

THE COOK: I've had enough. (*Abruptly.*) Got a letter from
10   Utrecht saying mother died of cholera and inn's mine. Here's letter if you don't believe me. No business of yours the way aunty goes on about my mode of existence, but have a look.

MOTHER COURAGE: (*Reads the letter.*) Lamb, I'm tired too of
15   always being on the go. I feel like butcher's dog, dragging meat round customers and getting nowt off it. I got nowt left to sell, and folk got nowt left to buy nowt with. Saxony a fellow in rags tried landing me a stack of old books for two eggs, Württemberg they wanted to swap their
20   plough for a titchy bag of salt. What's to plough for? Nowt growing no more, just brambles. In Pomerania villages are s'posed to have started in eating the younger kids, and nuns have been caught sticking folk up.

THE COOK: World's dying out.

25 MOTHER COURAGE: Sometimes I sees meself driving through hell with me cart selling brimstone, or across heaven with packed lunches for hungry souls. Give me my kids what's left, let's find some place they ain't shooting, and I'd like a few more years undisturbed.

30 THE COOK: You and me could get that inn going, Courage, think it over. Made up me mind in the night, I did: back to Utrecht with or without you, and starting today.

MOTHER COURAGE: Have to talk to Kattrin. That's a bit quick for me; I'm against making decisions all freezing cold and
35   nowt inside you. Kattrin! (KATTRIN *climbs out of the cart.*) Kattrin, got something to tell you. Cook and I want to go to Utrecht. He's been left an inn there. That'd be a settled place for you, let you meet a few people. Lots of 'em respect somebody mature, looks ain't everything. I'd like it
40   too. I get on with cook. Say one thing for him, got a head for business. We'd have our meals for sure, not bad, eh? And your own bed too; like that, wouldn't you? Road's no life really. God knows how you might finish up. Lousy already, you are. Have to make up our minds, see, we could move
45   with the Swedes, up north, they're somewhere up that way. (*She points to the left.*) Reckon that's fixed, Kattrin.

THE COOK: Anna, I got something private to say to you.

MOTHER COURAGE: Get back in cart, Kattrin.

(KATTRIN *climbs back.*)

THE COOK: I had to interrupt, cause you don't understand, far as I can see. I didn't think there was need to say it, 50 sticks out a mile. But if it don't, then let me tell you straight, no question of taking her along, not on your life. You get me, eh?

(KATTRIN *sticks her head out of the cart behind them and listens.*)

MOTHER COURAGE: You mean I'm to leave Kattrin back here?

THE COOK: Use your imagination. Inn's got no room. It ain't 55 one of the sort got three bar parlours. Put our backs in it we two'll get a living, but not three, no chance of that. She can keep cart.

MOTHER COURAGE: Thought she might find husband in Utrecht. 60

THE COOK: Go on, make me laugh. Find a husband, how? Dumb and that scar on top of it. And at her age?

MOTHER COURAGE: Don't talk so loud.

THE COOK: Loud or soft, no getting over facts. And that's another reason why I can't have her in the inn. Customers 65 don't want to be looking at that all the time. Can't blame them.

MOTHER COURAGE: Shut your big mouth. I said not so loud.

THE COOK: Light's on in parson's house. We can try singing.

MOTHER COURAGE: Cooky, how's she to pull the cart on her 70 own? War scares her. She'll never stand it. The dreams she must have . . . I hear her nights groaning. Mostly after a battle. What's she seeing in those dreams, I'd like to know. She's got a soft heart. Lately I found she'd got another hedgehog tucked away what we'd run over. 75

THE COOK: Inn's too small. (*Calls out.*) Ladies and gentlemen, domestic staff and other residents! We are now going to give you a song concerning Solomon, Julius Caesar and other famous personages what had bad luck. So's you can see we're respectable folk, which makes it difficult to carry 80 on, particularly in winter. (*They sing.*)

> You saw sagacious Solomon
> You know what came of him.
> To him complexities seemed plain.
> He cursed the hour that gave birth to him   85
> And saw that everything was vain.
> How great and wise was Solomon!
> The world however didn't wait
> But soon observed what followed on.
> It's wisdom that had brought him to this state—   90
> How fortunate the man with none!

Yes, the virtues are dangerous stuff in this world, as this fine song proves, better not to have them and have a pleasant life and breakfast instead, hot soup for instance. Look at me: I haven't any but I'd like some. I'm a serving soldier 95 but what good did my courage do me in all them battles, nowt, here I am starving and better have been shit-scared and stayed at home. For why?

> You saw courageous Caesar next
> You know what he became.   100
> They deified him in his life
> Then had him murdered just the same.
> And as they raised the fatal knife
> How loud he cried: You too, my son!

105　　　The world however didn't wait
　　　　But soon observed what followed on.
　　　　It's courage that had brought him to that state.
　　　　How fortunate the man with none!

110　(*Sotto voce.*) Don't even look out. (*Aloud.*) Ladies and gentlemen, domestic staff and other inmates! All right, you
may say, gallantry never cooked a man's dinner, what
about trying honesty? You can eat all you want then, or
anyhow not stay sober. How about it?

　　　　You heard of honest Socrates
115　　　The man who never lied:
　　　　They weren't so grateful as you'd think
　　　　Instead the rulers fixed to have him tried
　　　　And handed him the poisoned drink.
　　　　How honest was the people's noble son!
120　　　The world however didn't wait
　　　　But soon observed what followed on.
　　　　It's honesty that brought him to that state.
　　　　How fortunate the man with none!

Ah yes, they say, be unselfish and share what you've got,
125　but how about if you got nowt? It's all very well to say the
dogooders have a hard time, but you still got to have
something. Aye, unselfishness is a rare virtue, cause it just
don't pay.

　　　　Saint Martin couldn't bear to see
130　　　His fellows in distress.
　　　　He met a poor man in the snow
　　　　And shared his cloak with him, we know.
　　　　Both of them therefore froze to death.
　　　　His place in Heaven was surely won!
135　　　The world however didn't wait
　　　　But soon observed what followed on.
　　　　Unselfishness had brought him to that state.
　　　　How fortunate the man with none!

That's how it is with us. We're respectable folk, stick to-
140　gether, don't steal, don't murder, don't burn places down.
And all the time you might say we're sinking lower and
lower, and it's true what the song says, and soup is few and
far between, and if we weren't like this but thieves and
murderers I dare say we'd be eating our fill. For virtues
145　aren't their own reward, only wickednesses are, that's how
the world goes and it didn't ought to.

　　　　Here you can see respectable folk
　　　　Keeping to God's own laws.
　　　　So far he hasn't taken heed.
150　　　You who sit safe and warm indoors
　　　　Help to relieve our bitter need!
　　　　How virtuously we had begun!
　　　　The world however didn't wait
　　　　But soon observed what followed on.
155　　　It's fear of God that brought us to that state.
　　　　How fortunate the man with none!

VOICE: (*From above.*) Hey, you there! Come on up! There's
hot soup if you want.
160　MOTHER COURAGE: Lamb, me stomach won't stand nowt.
'Tain't that it ain't sensible, what you say, but is that your
last word? We got on all right.

THE COOK: Last word. Think it over.
MOTHER COURAGE: I've nowt to think. I'm not leaving her here.
THE COOK: That's proper senseless, nothing I can do about it
though. I'm not a brute, just the inn's a small one. So now　165
we better get on up, or there'll be nowt here either and
wasted time singing in the cold.
MOTHER COURAGE: I'll get Kattrin.
THE COOK: Better bring a bit back for her. Scare them if they
sees three of us coming. (*Exeunt both.*)　170

(KATTRIN *climbs out of the cart with a bundle. She looks around to
see if the other two have gone. Then she takes an old pair of trousers
of the* COOK's *and a skirt of her mother's, and lays them side by side
on one of the wheels, so that they are easily seen. She has finished
and is picking up her bundle to go, when* MOTHER COURAGE *comes
back from the house.*)

MOTHER COURAGE: (*With a plate of soup.*) Kattrin! Will you
stop there? Kattrin! Where you off to with that bundle? Has
devil himself taken you over? (*She examines the bundle.*) She's
packed her things. You been listening? I told him nowt doing, Utrecht, his rotten inn, what'd we be up to there? You　175
and me, inn's no place for us. Still plenty to be got out of
war. (*She sees the trousers and the skirt.*) You're plain stupid.
S'pose I'd seen that, and you gone away? (*She holds* KATTRIN
back as she tries to break away.*) Don't you start thinking it's on
your account I given him the push. It was cart, that's it.　180
Catch me leaving my cart I'm used to, it ain't you, it's for
cart. We'll go off in t'other direction, and we'll throw cook's
stuff out so he finds it, silly man. (*She climbs in and throws out
a few other articles in the direction of the trousers.*) There, he's out
of our business now, and I ain't having nobody else in, ever.　185
You and me'll carry on now. This winter will pass, same as
all the others. Get hitched up, it looks like snow.

(*They both harness themselves to the cart, then wheel it round and
drag it off. When the* COOK *arrives he looks blankly at his kit.*)

SCENE TEN

During the whole of 1635 Mother Courage and her
daughter Kattrin travel over the highroads of central
Germany, in the wake of the increasingly bedraggled
armies.

High road.

MOTHER COURAGE *and* KATTRIN *are pulling the cart. They pass
a* PEASANT's *house inside which there is a voice singing.*

THE VOICE:　The roses in our arbour
　　　　Delight us with their show:
　　　　They have such lovely flowers
　　　　Repaying all our labour
　　　　After the summer showers.　　　　　　　　　　　5
　　　　Happy are those with gardens now:
　　　　They have such lovely flowers.

　　　　When winter winds are freezing
　　　　As through the woods they blow
　　　　Our home is warm and pleasing.　　　　　　　　10
　　　　We fixed the thatch above it

With straw and moss we wove it.
Happy are those with shelter now
When winter winds are freezing.

(MOTHER COURAGE *and* KATTRIN *pause to listen, then continue pulling.*)

SCENE ELEVEN

January 1636. The emperor's troops are threatening the Protestant town of Halle. The stone begins to speak. Mother Courage loses her daughter and trudges on alone. The war is a long way from being over.

The cart is standing, much the worse for wear, alongside a PEASANT's *house with a huge thatched roof, backing on a wall of rock. It is night.*

An ENSIGN *and* THREE SOLDIERS *in heavy armour step out of the wood.*

THE ENSIGN: I want no noise now. Anyone shouts, shove your pike into him.
FIRST SOLDIER: Have to knock them up, though, if we're to find a guide.
5 THE ENSIGN: Knocking sounds natural. Could be a cow bumping the stable wall.

(*The* SOLDIERS *knock on the door of the house. The* PEASANT's *wife opens it. They stop her mouth.* TWO SOLDIERS *go in.*)

MAN'S VOICE: (*Within.*) What is it?

(*The* SOLDIERS *bring out the* PEASANT *and his son* [THE YOUNG PEASANT].)

THE ENSIGN: (*Pointing at the cart, where* KATTRIN's *head has appeared.*) There's another one. (*A* SOLDIER *drags her out.*)
10 Anyone else live here beside you lot?
THE PEASANTS: This is our son. And she's dumb. Her mother's gone into town to buy stuff. For their business, cause so many people's getting out and selling things cheap. They're just passing through. Canteen folk.
15 THE ENSIGN: I'm warning you, keep quiet, or if there's the least noise you get a pike across your nut. Now I want someone to come with us and show us the path to the town. (*Points to the* YOUNG PEASANT.) Here, you.
THE YOUNG PEASANT: I don't know no path.
20 SECOND SOLDIER: (*Grinning.*) He don't know no path.
THE YOUNG PEASANT: I ain't helping Catholics.
THE ENSIGN: (*To the* SECOND SOLDIER.) Stick your pike in his ribs.
THE YOUNG PEASANT: (*Forced to his knees, with the pike threatening him.*) I won't do it, not to save my life.
25 FIRST SOLDIER: I know what'll change his mind. (*Goes towards the stable.*) Two cows and an ox. Listen, you: if you're not reasonable I'll chop up your cattle.
THE YOUNG PEASANT: No, not that!
30 THE PEASANT'S WIFE: (*Weeps.*) Please spare our cattle, captain, it'd be starving us to death.
THE ENSIGN: They're dead if he goes on being obstinate.
FIRST SOLDIER: I'm taking the ox first.

THE YOUNG PEASANT: (*To his father.*) Have I got to? (*The* WIFE *nods.*) Right.   35
THE PEASANT'S WIFE: And thank you kindly, captain, for sparing us, for ever and ever, Amen.

(*The* PEASANT *stops his* WIFE *from further expressions of gratitude.*)

FIRST SOLDIER: I knew the ox was what they minded about most, was I right?

(*Guided by the* YOUNG PEASANT, *the* ENSIGN *and his* SOLDIERS *continue on their way.*)

THE PEASANT: What are they up to, I'd like to know. Nowt good.   40
THE PEASANT'S WIFE: Perhaps they're just scouting. What you doing?
THE PEASANT: (*Putting a ladder against the roof and climbing up it.*) Seeing if they're on their own. (*From the top.*) Something moving in the wood. Can see something down by   45 the quarry. And there are men in armour in the clearing. And a gun. That's at least a regiment. God's mercy on the town and everyone in it!
THE PEASANT'S WIFE: Any lights in the town?
THE PEASANT: No. They'll all be asleep. (*Climbs down.*) If   50 those people get in they'll butcher the lot.
THE PEASANT'S WIFE: Sentries're bound to spot them first.
THE PEASANT: Sentry in the tower up the hill must have been killed, or he'd have blown his bugle.
THE PEASANT'S WIFE: If only there were more of us.   55
THE PEASANT: Just you and me and that cripple.
THE PEASANT'S WIFE: Nowt we can do, you'd say. . . .
THE PEASANT: Nowt.
THE PEASANT'S WIFE: Can't possibly run down there in the blackness.   60
THE PEASANT: Whole hillside's crawling with 'em. We could give a signal.
THE PEASANT'S WIFE: What, and have them butcher us too?
THE PEASANT: You're right, nowt we can do.
THE PEASANT'S WIFE: (*To* KATTRIN.) Pray, poor creature, pray!   65 Nowt we can do to stop bloodshed. You can't talk, maybe, but at least you can pray. He'll hear you if no one else can. I'll help you. (*All kneel,* KATTRIN *behind the two* PEASANTS.) Our Father, which art in Heaven, hear Thou our prayer, let not the town be destroyed with all what's in it sound   70 asleep and suspecting nowt. Arouse Thou them that they may get up and go to the walls and see how the enemy approacheth with picks and guns in the blackness across fields below the slope. (*Turning to* KATTRIN.) Guard Thou our mother and ensure that the watchman sleepeth not   75 but wakes up, or it will be too late. Succour our brother-in-law also, he is inside there with his four children, spare Thou them, they are innocent and know nowt. (*To* KATTRIN, *who gives a groan.*) One of them's not two yet, the eldest's seven. (KATTRIN *stands up distractedly.*) Our Father,   80 hear us, for only Thou canst help; we look to be doomed, for why, we are weak and have no pike and nowt and can risk nowt and are in Thy hand along with our cattle and all the farm, and same with the town, it too is in Thy hand and the enemy is before the walls in great strength.   85

(*Unobserved,* KATTRIN *has slipped away to the cart and taken from it something which she hides beneath her apron; then she climbs up the ladder on to the stable roof.*)

THE PEASANT'S WIFE: Forget not the children, what are in danger, the littlest ones especially, the old folk what can't move, and every living creature.

90 THE PEASANT: And forgive us our trespasses as we forgive them that trespass against us. Amen.

(*Sitting on the roof,* KATTRIN *begins to beat the drum which she has pulled out from under her apron.*)

THE PEASANT'S WIFE: Jesus Christ, what's she doing?
THE PEASANT: She's out of her mind.
THE PEASANT'S WIFE: Quick, get her down.

(*The* PEASANT *hurries to the ladder, but* KATTRIN *pulls it up on to the roof.*)

THE PEASANT'S WIFE: She'll do us in.
95 THE PEASANT: Stop drumming at once, you cripple!
THE PEASANT'S WIFE: Bringing the Catholics down on us!
THE PEASANT: (*Looking for stones to throw.*) I'll stone you.
THE PEASANT'S WIFE: Where's your feelings? Where's your heart? We're done for if they come down on us. Slit our
100 throats, they will.

(KATTRIN *stares into the distance towards the town and carries on drumming.*)

THE PEASANT'S WIFE: (*To her husband.*) I told you we shouldn't have allowed those vagabonds on to farm. What do they care if our last cows are taken?
105 THE ENSIGN: (*Runs in with his* SOLDIERS *and the* YOUNG PEAS-ANT.) I'll cut you to ribbons, all of you!
THE PEASANT'S WIFE: Please, sir, it's not our fault, we couldn't help it. It was her sneaked up there. A foreigner.
THE ENSIGN: Where's the ladder?
THE PEASANT: There.
110 THE ENSIGN: (*Calls up.*) I order you, throw that drum down.

(KATTRIN *goes on drumming.*)

THE ENSIGN: You're all in this together. It'll be the end of you.
THE PEASANT: They been cutting pine trees in that wood. How about if we got one of the trunks and poked her off....
FIRST SOLDIER: (*To the* ENSIGN.) Permission to make a sug-
115 gestion, sir! (*He whispers something in the* ENSIGN'S *ear.*) Listen, we got a suggestion could help you. Get down off there and come into town with us right away. Show us which your mother is and we'll see she ain't harmed.

(KATTRIN *goes on drumming.*)

THE ENSIGN: (*Pushes him roughly aside.*) She doesn't trust you;
120 with a mug like yours it's not surprising. (*Calls up.*) Suppose I gave you my word? I can give my word of honour as an officer.

(KATTRIN *drums harder.*)

THE ENSIGN: Is nothing sacred to her?
THE YOUNG PEASANT: There's more than her mother involved, sir.
125 FIRST SOLDIER: This can't go on much longer. They're bound to hear in the town.
THE ENSIGN: We'll have somehow to make a noise that's louder than her drumming. What can we make a noise with?

FIRST SOLDIER: Thought we weren't s'posed to make no noise.
THE ENSIGN: A harmless one, you fool. A peaceful one.   130
THE PEASANT: I could chop wood with my axe.
THE ENSIGN: Good: you chop. (*The* PEASANT *fetches his axe and attacks a tree-trunk.*) Chop harder! Harder! You're chopping for your life.

(KATTRIN *has been listening, drumming less loudly the while. She now looks wildly round, and goes on drumming.*)

THE ENSIGN: Not loud enough. (*To the* FIRST SOLDIER.) You   135 chop too.
THE PEASANT: Only got the one axe. (*Stops chopping.*)
THE ENSIGN: We'll have to set the farm on fire. Smoke her out, that's it.
THE PEASANT: It wouldn't help, captain. If the townspeople   140 see a fire here they'll know what's up.

(KATTRIN *has again been listening as she drums. At this point she laughs.*)

THE ENSIGN: Look at her laughing at us. I'm not having that. I'll shoot her down, and damn the consequences. Fetch the harquebus.

(THREE SOLDIERS *hurry off.* KATTRIN *goes on drumming.*)

THE PEASANT'S WIFE: I got it, captain. That's their cart. If we   145 smash it up she'll stop. Cart's all they got.
THE ENSIGN: (*To the* YOUNG PEASANT.) Smash it up. (*Calls up.*) We're going to smash up your cart if you don't stop drumming. (*The* YOUNG PEASANT *gives the cart a few feeble blows.*)
THE PEASANT'S WIFE: Stop it, you animal!   150

(*Desperately looking towards the cart,* KATTRIN *emits pitiful noises. But she goes on drumming.*)

THE ENSIGN: Where are those clodhoppers with the harquebus?
FIRST SOLDIER: Can't have heard nowt in town yet, else we'd be hearing their guns.
THE ENSIGN: (*Calls up.*) They can't hear you at all. And now we're going to shoot you down. For the last time: throw   155 down that drum!
THE YOUNG PEASANT: (*Suddenly flings away his plank.*) Go on drumming! Or they'll all be killed! Go on, go on....

(*The* FIRST SOLDIER *knocks him down and beats him with his pike.* KATTRIN *starts to cry, but she goes on drumming.*)

THE PEASANT'S WIFE: Don't strike his back! For God's sake, you're beating him to death!   160

(*The* SOLDIERS *hurry in with the arquebus.*)

SECOND SOLDIER: Colonel's frothing at the mouth, sir. We're all for court-martial.
THE ENSIGN: Set it up! Set it up! (*Calls up while the gun is being erected.*) For the very last time: stop drumming! (KATTRIN, *in tears, drums as loud as she can.*) Fire! (*The* SOLDIERS *fire.* KAT-   165 TRIN *is hit, gives a few more drumbeats and then slowly crumples.*)
THE ENSIGN: That's the end of that.

(*But* KATTRIN's *last drumbeats are taken up by the town's cannon. In the distance can be heard a confused noise of tocsins and gunfire.*)

FIRST SOLDIER: She's made it.

SCENE TWELVE

Before first light. Sound of the fifes and drums of troops marching off into the distance.

In front of the cart MOTHER COURAGE *is squatting by her daughter. The peasant family are standing near her.*

THE PEASANTS: (*With hostility.*) You must go, missis. There's only one more regiment behind that one. You can't go on your own.

MOTHER COURAGE: I think she's going to sleep. (*She sings.*)

5   Lullaby baby
           What's that in the hay?
           Neighbours' kids grizzle
           But my kids are gay.
           Neighbours' are in tatters
10   And you're dressed in lawn
           Cut down from the raiment an
           Angel has worn.
           Neighbours' kids go hungry
           And you shall eat cake
15   Suppose it's too crumbly
           You've only to speak.
           Lullaby baby
           What's that in the hay?
           The one lies in Poland
20   The other—who can say?

Better if you'd not told her nowt about your brother-in-law's kids.

THE PEASANT: If you'd not gone into town to get your cut it might never of happened.

25 MOTHER COURAGE: Now she's asleep.

THE PEASANT'S WIFE: She ain't asleep. Can't you see she's passed over?

THE PEASANT: And it's high time you got away yourself. There are wolves around and, what's worse, marauders.

MOTHER COURAGE: Aye.   30

(*She goes and gets a tarpaulin to cover the dead girl with.*)

THE PEASANT'S WIFE: Ain't you got nobody else? What you could go to?

MOTHER COURAGE: Aye, one left. Eilif.

THE PEASANT: (*As* MOTHER COURAGE *covers the dead girl.*) Best look for him, then. We'll mind her, see she gets 35 proper burial. Don't you worry about that.

MOTHER COURAGE: Here's money for expenses.

(*She counts out coins into the* PEASANT's *hands. The* PEASANT *and his* SON *shake hands with her and carry* KATTRIN *away.*)

THE PEASANT'S WIFE: (*As she leaves.*) I'd hurry.

MOTHER COURAGE: (*Harnessing herself to the cart.*) Hope I can pull cart all right by meself. Be all right, nowt much in- 40 side it. Got to get back in business again.

(*Another regiment with its fifes and drums marches past in the background.*)

MOTHER COURAGE: (*Tugging the cart.*) Take me along!

(*Singing is heard from offstage.*)

           With all its luck and all its danger
           The war is dragging on a bit
           Another hundred years or longer   45
           The common man won't benefit.
           Filthy his food, no soap to shave him
           The regiment steals half his pay.
           But still a miracle may save him:
           Tomorrow is another day!   50
               The new year's come. The watchmen shout.
               The thaw sets in. The dead remain.
               Wherever life has not died out
               It staggers to its feet again.

Jean Genet

Jean Genet (1910–1986) is perhaps as famous for his life as for his important work as a novelist and playwright. Born the illegitimate son of a Parisian prostitute, he was abandoned at birth and raised by the state. At the age of 15 he was convicted of theft and sent to a reformatory in Mettray. He served briefly in the French Foreign Legion, then deserted and wandered Europe throughout the 1930s, making a living as a beggar, smuggler, thief, and homosexual prostitute, until his arrest and imprisonment in 1941. In prison, Genet wrote his first poem, "The Man Condemned to Death," and his first novel, *Our Lady of the Flowers;* he was again sentenced in 1947, but the playwright Jean Cocteau and the philosopher Jean-Paul Sartre launched an appeal to secure his pardon. Genet's career became more closely entwined with Sartre in 1952, when Sartre's biography, *Saint-Genet: Actor and Martyr,* was published as volume 1 of Genet's *Complete Works.* Sartre takes Genet as an example of existential man, forced to enact the role of "criminal" that existence has arbitrarily assigned to him. Genet wrote several other novels, including *Miracle of the Rose* (1946), *Funeral Rites* (1947), and *Querrelle of Brest* (1947), and in 1947 wrote his first play, *The Maids,* followed by *Deathwatch* (1949), *The Balcony* (1956), *The Blacks* (1958), and *The Screens* (1966). Genet's dramatization of Algerian resistance to French rule in *The Screens* caused riots in Paris when it was first produced there, and throughout his flamboyant career as a writer, Genet worked to support a number of oppositional political organizations, including the Black Panthers in the United States and the Palestine Liberation Organization. Genet's memoir of his travel to the Middle East and life among the Palestinians, *A Prisoner of Love,* was published posthumously in 1989.

THE BALCONY

The Balcony is one of the most celebrated plays in the modern canon, admired for its richly baroque dialogue, for its forthright staging of the nature of desire, and for its determined subversion of any "safe" notion of theatrical representation. From the outset, Genet intertwines Madame Irma's brothel, The Balcony—"Le balcon," a salacious pun in French—and the situation of the theater audience. In the opening stage direction, for instance, Genet describes the room in which one of Madame Irma's clients enacts his erotic fantasies:

> The set seems to represent a sacristy, formed by three blood-red, cloth folding screens. The one at the rear has a built-in door. Above, a huge Spanish crucifix, drawn in *trompe l'oeil.* On the right wall, a mirror, with a carved gilt frame, reflects an unmade bed which, if the room were arranged logically, would be in the first rows of the orchestra.

The mirror of the opening stage direction suggests that the studio extends out into the auditorium, at once displacing the audience and *including* the space we inhabit within Madame Irma's erotic theater.

Throughout the play, Genet correlates the practice of theater with the strategies of fantasy. For Madame Irma's clients come to the brothel not—or at least not explicitly—for sex, but to purchase illusions, performances. The petit-bourgeois clients come to see themselves reflected in the images of the Bishop, the Judge, the General, a process of erotic fulfillment that is at the same time a kind of self-erasure: to perform the role completely, as the General recognizes in Scene 3, is to be transformed into an "image," to achieve a kind of death: "close to death . . . where I shall be nothing, though reflected *ad infinitum* in these mirrors, nothing but my image." The clients' performances suggest that the boundary between self and role, reality and enactment is insistently blurred by the force of desire, a desire in Genet's play—like all desire, perhaps—which carries the force of absence.

Moreover, as the play progresses, it becomes increasingly difficult to circumscribe the limits of theater, performance, and erotics, for Madame Irma's brothel and the illusions it

The General, the Bishop, the Judge, the Chief of Police, and Madame Irma in the American Repertory Theatre production of *The Balcony*.

sells come to seem nearly coextensive with the world. Irma, for example, at first seems to be the manager of reality and fantasy, directing the work of The Balcony. And yet her relationship with Carmen and with the Chief of Police in Scene 5 seems artificial, "performed," as though she, too, plays the part of the savvy yet kindhearted madam, acting out her own fantasy scenario. Similarly, the revolution that seems to be taking place "outside" The Balcony has as its final effect the death and deification of the Chief of Police: is the revolution also a performance invented to satisfy the Chief's desire to assume a place in the "nomenclature" of the social order, and the order of fantasy? As the play proceeds, it seems as though there is no "outside" The Balcony, no "reality" that isn't produced as part of Madame Irma's theater: even the Queen and her staff (the Bishop, the Judge, the General) come to be performed by The Balcony's inhabitants.

The "revolution" that Genet proposes in *The Balcony* is only partly a political one; it is more urgently a critique of ontology, of the notions of "presence" that enable us confidently—and wrongly, the play argues—to distinguish between true and false, real and enacted, the actual and the artificial, the spectator and the actor. And, of course, in the play's stunning finale, Madame Irma turns to us, the theater audience, and addresses us as she has addressed her other clients throughout the play: "You must now go home, where everything—you can be quite sure—will be falser than here."

THE BALCONY

Jean Genet

TRANSLATED BY BERNARD FRECHTMAN

CHARACTERS

THE BISHOP
THE JUDGE
THE EXECUTIONER (*Arthur*)
THE GENERAL
THE CHIEF OF POLICE
THE BEGGAR
ROGER
THE COURT ENVOY
THE FIRST PHOTOGRAPHER

THE SECOND PHOTOGRAPHER
THE THIRD PHOTOGRAPHER
IRMA (*the queen*)
THE WOMAN (*Rosine*)
THE THIEF
THE GIRL
CARMEN
CHANTAL

SCENE I

On the ceiling, a chandelier, which will remain the same in each scene. The set seems to represent a sacristy, formed by three blood-red, cloth folding-screens. The one at the rear has a built-in door. Above, a huge Spanish crucifix, drawn in trompe l'oeil. On the right wall, a mirror, with a carved gilt frame, reflects an unmade bed which, if the room were arranged logically, would be in the first rows of the orchestra. A table with a large jug. A yellow armchair. On the chair, a pair of black trousers, a shirt and a jacket. THE BISHOP, *in mitre and gilded cope, is sitting in the chair. He is obviously larger than life. The role is played by an actor wearing tragedian's cothurni about twenty inches high. His shoulders, on which the cope lies, are inordinately broadened so that when the curtain rises he looks huge and stiff, like a scarecrow. He wears garish make-up. At the side, a woman, rather young, highly made up and wearing a lace dressing-gown, is drying her hands with a towel. Standing by is another woman,* IRMA. *She is about forty, dark, severe-looking, and is wearing a black tailored suit and a hat with a tight string (like a chin-strap).*

THE BISHOP: (*sitting in the chair, middle of the stage. In a low but fervent voice*) In truth, the mark of a prelate is not mildness or unction, but the most rigorous intelligence. Our heart is our undoing. We think we are master of our kindness; 5 we are the slaves of a serene laxity. It is something quite other than intelligence that is involved. . . . (*He hesitates.*) It may be cruelty. And beyond that cruelty—and through it—a skillful, vigorous course towards Absence. Towards Death. God? (*Smiling*) I can read your mind! (*To his mitre*) 10 Mitre, bishop's bonnet, when my eyes close for the last time, it is you that I shall see behind my eyelids, you, my beautiful gilded hat . . . you, my handsome ornaments, copes, laces. . . .
IRMA: (*bluntly*) An agreement's an agreement. When a deal's 15 been made. . . .

(*Throughout the scene she hardly moves. She is standing very near the door.*)

THE BISHOP: (*very gently, waving her aside with a gesture*) And when the die is cast. . . .
IRMA: No. Twenty. Twenty and no nonsense. Or I'll lose my temper. And that's not like me. . . . Now, if you have any 20 difficulties. . . .

THE BISHOP: (*curtly, and tossing away the mitre*) Thank you.
IRMA: And don't break anything. We need that. (*To the woman*) Put it away.

(*She lays the mitre on the table, near the jug.*)

THE BISHOP: (*after a deep sigh*) I've been told that this house is going to be besieged. The rebels have already crossed the 25 river.
IRMA: There's blood everywhere. . . . You can slip round behind the Archbishop's Palace. Then, down Fishmarket Street. . . .

(*Suddenly a scream of pain, uttered by a woman offstage.*)

IRMA: (*annoyed*) But I told them to be quiet. Good thing I re- 30 membered to cover the windows with padded curtains.

(*Suddenly amiable, insidious*)

Well, and what was it this evening? A blessing? A prayer? A mass? A perpetual adoration?
THE BISHOP: (*gravely*) Let's not talk about that now. It's over. I'm concerned only about getting home. . . . You say the 35 city's splashed with blood. . . .
THE WOMAN: There was a blessing, Madame. Then, my confession. . . .
IRMA: And that after?
THE BISHOP: That'll do! 40
THE WOMAN: That was all. At the end, my absolution.
IRMA: Won't anyone be able to witness it? Just once?
THE BISHOP: (*frightened*) No, no. Those things must remain secret, and they shall. It's indecent enough to talk about them while I'm being undressed. Nobody. And all the 45 doors must be closed. Firmly closed, shut, buttoned, laced, hooked, sewn. . . .
IRMA: I merely asked. . . .
THE BISHOP: Sewn, Madame.
IRMA: (*annoyed*) You'll allow me at least, won't you, to feel a 50 little uneasy . . . professionally? I said twenty.
THE BISHOP: (*his voice suddenly grows clear and sharp, as if he were awakening. He displays a little annoyance*) We didn't tire ourselves. Barely six sins, and far from my favourite ones. 55

756

THE WOMAN: Six, but deadly ones! And it was a job finding *those.*

THE BISHOP: (*uneasy*) What? You mean they were false?

THE WOMAN: They were real, all right! I mean it was a job
60   committing them. If only you realized what it takes, what
      a person has to go through, in order to reach the point of
      disobedience.

THE BISHOP: I can imagine, my child. The order of the world
      is so lax that you can do as you please there—or almost.
65   But if your sins were false, you may say so now.

IRMA: Oh no! I can hear you complaining already the next
      time you come. No. they were real. (*To* THE WOMAN) Un-
      tie his laces. Take off his shoes. And when you dress him,
      be careful he doesn't catch cold. (*To* THE BISHOP) Would
70   you like a toddy, a hot drink?

THE BISHOP: Thank you. I haven't time. I must be going.

(*Dreamily*)

      Yes, six, but deadly ones!

IRMA: Come here, we'll undress you!

THE BISHOP: (*pleading, almost on his knees*) No, no, not yet.
75 IRMA: It's time. Come on! Quick! Make it snappy!

(*While they talk, the women undress him. Or rather they merely
remove pins and untie cords that seem to secure the cope, stole and
surplice.*)

THE BISHOP: (*to* THE WOMAN) About the sins, you really did
      commit them?

THE WOMAN: I did.

THE BISHOP: You really made the gestures? All the gestures?
80 THE WOMAN: I did.

THE BISHOP: When you moved towards me with your face
      forward, was it really aglow with the light of the flames?

THE WOMAN: It was.

THE BISHOP: And when my ringed hand came down on your
85   forehead, forgiving it. . . .

THE WOMAN: It was.

THE BISHOP: And when my gaze pierced your lovely eyes?

THE WOMAN: It was.

IRMA: Was there at least a glimmer of repentance in her
90   lovely eyes, my Lord?

THE BISHOP: (*standing up*) A fleeting glimmer. But was I seek-
      ing repentance in them? I saw there the greedy longing
      for transgression. In flooding it, evil all at once baptized it.
      Her big eyes opened on the abyss . . . a deathly pallor lit
95   up—yes, Madame—lit up her face. But our holiness lies
      only in our being able to forgive you your sins. Even if
      they're only make-believe.

THE WOMAN: (*suddenly coy*) And what if my sins were real?

THE BISHOP: (*in a different, less theatrical tone*) You're mad! I
100   hope you really didn't do all that!

IRMA: (*to* THE BISHOP) Don't listen to her. As for her sins, don't
      worry. Here there's no. . .

THE BISHOP: (*interrupting her*) I'm quite aware of that. Here
      there's no possibility of doing evil. You live in evil. In the ab-
105   sence of remorse. How could you do evil? The Devil makes
      believe. That's how one recognizes him. He's the great Ac-
      tor. And that's why the Church has anathematized actors.

THE WOMAN: Reality frightens you, doesn't it?

THE BISHOP: If your sins were real, they would be crimes, and
      I'd be a fine mess.   110

THE WOMAN: Would you go to the police?

(IRMA *continues to undress him. However, he still has the cope on
his shoulders.*)

IRMA: Stop plaguing her with all those questions.

(*The same terrible scream is heard again.*)

      They're at it again! I'll go and shut them up.

THE BISHOP: That wasn't a make-believe scream.

IRMA: (*anxiously*) I don't know. . . . Who knows and what does 115
      it matter?

THE BISHOP: (*going slowly to the mirror. He stands in front of it*)
      Now answer, mirror, answer me. Do I come here to dis-
      cover evil and innocence? (*To* IRMA, *very gently*) Leave the
      room! I want to be by myself.   120

IRMA: It's late. And the later it gets, the more dangerous it'll
      be . . .

THE BISHOP: (*pleading*) Just one more minute.

IRMA: You've been here two hours and twenty minutes. In
      other words, twenty minutes too long. . . .   125

THE BISHOP: (*suddenly incensed*) I want to be by myself. Eaves-
      drop, if you want to—I know you do, anyway—and don't
      come back till I've finished.

(*The two women leave with a sigh, looking as if they were out of patience.* THE BISHOP *remains alone.*)

THE BISHOP: (*after making a visible effort to calm himself, in front
      of the mirror and holding his surplice*) Now answer, mirror,   130
      answer me. Do I come here to discover evil and inno-
      cence? And in your gilt-edged glass, what was I? Never—
      I affirm it before God Who sees me—I never desired the
      Episcopal throne. To become bishop, to work my way
      up—by means of virtues or vices—would have been to   135
      turn away from the ultimate dignity of bishop. I shall ex-
      plain: (THE BISHOP *speaks in a tone of great precision, as if pur-
      suing a line of logical reasoning*) in order to become a bishop,
      I should have had to make a zealous effort not to be one,
      but to do what would have resulted in my being one.   140
      Having become a bishop, in order to be one I should have
      had—in order to be one for myself, of course!—I should
      have had to be constantly aware of being one so as to per-
      form my function. (*He seizes the flap of his surplice and kisses
      it.*) Oh laces, laces, fashioned by a thousand little hands to 145
      veil ever so many panting bosoms, buxom bosoms, and
      faces, and hair, you illustrate me with branches and flow-
      ers! Let us continue. But—there's the crux!

(*He laughs.*)

      So I speak Latin!—a function is a function. It's not a mode
      of being. But a bishop—that's a mode of being. It's a trust. 150
      A burden. Mitres, lace, gold-cloth and glass trinkets, gen-
      uflexions. . . . To hell with the function!

(*Crackling of machine-gun fire.*)

IRMA: (*putting her head through the door*) Have you finished?

THE BISHOP: For Christ's sake, leave me alone. Get the hell
      out! I'm probing myself.   155

(IRMA *shuts the door.*)

THE BISHOP: (*to the mirror*) The majesty, the dignity, that light up my person, do not emanate from the attributions of my function.—No more, good heavens! than from my personal merits.—The majesty, the dignity that light me up
160 come from a more mysterious brilliance: the fact that the bishop precedes me. Do I make myself clear, mirror, gilded image, ornate as a box of Mexican cigars? And I wish to be bishop in solitude, for appearance alone. . . . And in order to destroy all function, I want to cause a scandal and feel
165 you up, you slut, you bitch, you trollop, you tramp. . . .
IRMA: (*entering*) That'll do now. You've got to leave.
THE BISHOP: You're crazy! I haven't finished.

(*Both women have entered.*)

IRMA: I'm not trying to pick an argument, and you know it, but you've no time to waste. . . .
170 THE BISHOP: (*ironically*) What you mean is that you need the room for someone else and you've got to arrange the mirrors and jugs.
IRMA: (*very irritated*) That's no business of yours. I've given you every attention while you've been here. And I repeat
175 that it's dangerous for anyone to loiter in the streets.

(*Sound of gun-fire in the distance.*)

THE BISHOP: (*bitterly*) That's not true. You don't give a damn about my safety. When the job's finished, you don't give a damn about anyone!
IRMA: (*to the girl*) Stop listening to him and undress him.
180 IRMA: (*to* THE BISHOP, *who has stepped down from his cothurni and has now assumed the normal size of an actor, of the most ordinary of actors*) Lend a hand. You're stiff.
THE BISHOP: (*with a foolish look*) Stiff? I'm stiff? A solemn stiffness! Final immobility. . . .
185 IRMA: (*to the girl*) Hand him his jacket. . . .
THE BISHOP: (*looking at his clothes, which are heaped on the floor*) Ornaments, laces, through you I re-enter myself. I reconquer a domain. I beleaguer a very ancient place from which I was driven. I install myself in a clearing where
190 suicide at last becomes possible. The judgment depends on me, and here I stand, face to face with my death.
IRMA: That's all very fine, but you've got to go. You left your car at the front door, near the power-station.
THE BISHOP: (*to* IRMA) Because our Chief of Police, that
195 wretched incompetent, is letting us be slaughtered by the rabble! (*Turning to the mirror and declaiming*) Ornaments! Mitres! Laces! You, above all, oh gilded cope, you protect me from the world. Where are my legs, where are my arms? Under your scalloped, lustrous flaps, what have my hands
200 been doing? Fit only for fluttering gestures, they've become mere stumps of wings—not of angels, but of partridges!— rigid cope, you make it possible for the most tender and luminous sweetness to ripen in warmth and darkness. My charity, a charity that will flood the world—it was under
205 this carapace that I distilled it. . . . Would my hand emerge at times, knife-like, to bless? Or cut, mow down? My hand, the head of a turtle, would push aside the flaps. A turtle or a cautious snake? And go back into the rock. Underneath, my hand would dream. . . . Ornaments, gilded copes. . . .

(*The stage moves from left to right, as if it were plunging into the wings. The following set then appears.*)

SCENE II

Same chandelier. Three brown folding-screens. Bare walls. At right, same mirror, in which is reflected the same unmade bed as in the first scene. A woman, young and beautiful, seems to be chained, with her wrists bound. Her muslin dress is torn. Her breasts are visible. Standing in front of her is the executioner. He is a giant, stripped to the waist. Very muscular. His whip has been slipped through the loop of his belt, in back, so that he seems to have a tail. A JUDGE, *who, when he stands up, will seem larger than life (he, too, is mounted on cothurni, which are invisible beneath his robe, and his face is made up) is crawling, on his stomach, towards the woman, who shrinks as he approaches.*

THE THIEF: (*holding out her foot*) Not yet! Lick it! Lick it first. . . .

(THE JUDGE *makes an effort to continue crawling. Then he stands up and, slowly and painfully, though apparently happy, goes and sits down on a stool.* THE THIEF (*the woman described above*) *drops her domineering attitude and becomes humble.*)

THE JUDGE: (*severely*) For you're a thief! You were caught. . . . Who? The police. . . . Have you forgotten that your movements are hedged about by a strong and subtle network, my 5 strong-arm cops? They're watchful, swivel-eyed insects that lie in wait for you. All of you! And they bring you captive, all of you, to the Bench. . . . What have you to say for yourself? You were caught. . . . Under your skirt. . . . (*To* THE EXECUTIONER.) Put your hand under her skirt. You'll find 10 the pocket, the notorious Kangaroo Pocket. . . . (*To* THE THIEF) that you fill with any old junk you pick up. Because you're an idiot to boot. . . . (*To* THE EXECUTIONER.) What was there in that notorious Kangaroo Pocket? In that enormous paunch? 15
THE EXECUTIONER: Bottles of scent, my Lord, a flashlight, a bottle of Fly-tox, some oranges, several pairs of socks, bearskins, a Turkish towel, a scarf. (*To* THE JUDGE.) Do you hear me? I said: a scarf.
THE JUDGE: (*with a start*) A scarf? Ah ha, so that's it? Why the 20 scarf? Eh? What were you going to do with it? Whom were you planning to strangle? Answer. Who? . . . Are you a thief or a strangler? (*Very gently, imploringly*) Tell me, my child, I beg of you, tell me you're a thief.
THE THIEF: Yes, my Lord. 25
THE EXECUTIONER: No!
THE THIEF: (*looking at him in surprise*) No?
THE EXECUTIONER: That's for later.
THE THIEF: Eh?
THE EXECUTIONER: I mean the confession is supposed to 30 come later. Plead not guilty.
THE THIEF: What, and get beaten again!
THE JUDGE: (*mealy-mouthed*) Exactly, my child: and get beaten. You must first deny, then admit and repent. I want to see hot tears gush from your lovely eyes. Oh! 35 I want you to be drenched in them. The power of tears! . . . Where's my statute-book? (*He fishes under his robe and pulls out a book.*)
THE THIEF: I've already cried. . . .

40 THE JUDGE: (*he seems to be reading*) Under the blows. I want tears of repentance. When I see you wet as a meadow I'll be utterly satisfied!

THE THIEF: It's not easy. I tried to cry before. . . .

THE JUDGE: (*no longer reading. In a half-theatrical, almost familiar*
45 *tone*) You're quite young. Are you new here? (*Anxiously*) At least you're not a minor?

THE THIEF: Oh no, sir.

THE JUDGE: Call me my Lord. How long have you been here?

THE EXECUTIONER: Since the day before yesterday, my Lord.

50 THE JUDGE: (*reassuming the theatrical tone and resuming the reading*) Let her speak. I like that puling voice of hers, that voice without resonance. . . . Look here: you've got to be a model thief if I'm to be a model judge. If you're a fake thief, I become a fake judge. Is that clear?

55 THE THIEF: Oh yes, my Lord.

THE JUDGE: (*he continues reading*) Good. Thus far everything has gone off well. My executioner has hit hard . . . for he too has his function. We are bound together, you, he and I. For example, if he didn't hit, how could I stop him from
60 hitting? Therefore, he must strike so that I can intervene and demonstrate my authority. And you must deny your guilt so that he can beat you.

(*A noise is heard, as of something having fallen in the next room. In a natural tone*)

What's that? Are all the doors firmly shut? Can anyone see us, or hear us?

65 THE EXECUTIONER: No, no, you needn't worry. I bolted the door.

(*He goes to examine a huge bolt on the rear door.*)

And the corridor's out of bounds.

THE JUDGE: (*in a natural tone*) Are you sure?

THE EXECUTIONER: You can take my word for it.

(*He puts his hand into his pocket.*)

70 Can I have a smoke?

THE JUDGE: (*in a natural tone*) The smell of tobacco inspires me. Smoke away.

(*Same noise as before.*)

Oh, what *is* that? What *is* it? Can't they leave me in peace?

(*He gets up.*)

What's going on?

75 THE EXECUTIONER: (*curtly*) Nothing at all. Someone must have dropped something. You're getting nervous.

THE JUDGE: (*in a natural tone*) That may be, but my nervousness makes me aware of things. It keeps me on the alert.

(*He gets up and moves towards the wall.*)

May I have a look?

80 THE EXECUTIONER: Just a quick one, because it's getting late.

(*THE EXECUTIONER shrugs his shoulders and exchanges a wink with the thief.*)

THE JUDGE: (*after looking*) It's lit up. Brightly lit, but empty.

THE EXECUTIONER: (*shrugging his shoulders*) Empty!

THE JUDGE: (*in an even more familiar tone*) You seem anxious. Has anything new happened?

THE EXECUTIONER: This afternoon, just before you arrived, 85 the rebels took three key-positions. They set fire to several places. Not a single fireman came out. Everything went up in flames. The Palace. . . .

THE JUDGE: What about the Chief of Police? Twiddling his thumbs as usual? 90

THE THIEF: There's been no news of him for four hours. If he can get away, he's sure to come here. He's expected at any moment.

THE JUDGE: (*to THE THIEF, and sitting down*) In any case, he'd better not plan to come by way of Queen's Bridge. It was 95 blown up last night.

THE THIEF: We know that. We heard the explosion from here.

THE JUDGE: (*resuming his theatrical tone. He reads the statute-book*) All right. Let's get on with it. Thus, taking advantage of the sleep of the just, taking advantage of a moment's 100 inattention, you rob them, you ransack, you pilfer and purloin. . . .

THE THIEF: No, my Lord, never. . . .

THE EXECUTIONER: Shall I tan her hide?

THE THIEF: (*crying out*) Arthur! 105

THE EXECUTIONER: What's eating you? Don't address me. Answer his Lordship. And call me Mr. Executioner.

THE THIEF: Yes, Mr. Executioner.

THE JUDGE: (*reading*) I continue: did you steal?

THE THIEF: I did, I did, my Lord. 110

THE JUDGE: (*reading*) Good. Now answer quickly, and to the point: what else did you steal?

THE THIEF: Bread, because I was hungry.

THE JUDGE: (*he draws himself up and lays down the book*) Sublime! Sublime function! I'll have all that to judge. Oh, 115 child, you reconcile me with the world. A judge! I'm going to be judge of your acts! On me depends the weighing, the balance. The world is an apple. I cut it in two: the good, the bad. And you agree, thank you, you agree to be the bad! (*Facing the audience*) Right before your eyes: noth- 120 ing in my hands, nothing up my sleeve, remove the rot and cast it off. But it's a painful occupation. If every judgment were delivered seriously, each one would cost me my life. That's why I'm dead. I inhabit that region of exact freedom. I, King of Hell, weigh those who are dead, like me. 125 She's a dead person, like myself.

THE THIEF: You frighten me, sir.

THE JUDGE: (*very bombastically*) Be still. In the depths of Hell I sort out the humans who venture there. Some to the flames, the others to the boredom of the fields of aspho- 130 del. You, thief, spy, she-dog, Minos is speaking to you, Minos weighs you. (*To THE EXECUTIONER*) Cerberus?

THE EXECUTIONER: (*imitating the dog*) Bow-wow, bow-wow!

THE JUDGE: You're handsome! And the sight of a fresh victim makes you even handsomer. (*He curls up THE EXECU- 135 TIONER's lips.*) Show your fangs. Dreadful. White. (*Suddenly he seems anxious. To THE THIEF*) But at least you're not lying about those thefts—you did commit them, didn't you?

THE EXECUTIONER: Don't worry. She committed them, all right. She wouldn't have dared not to. I'd have made her. 140

THE JUDGE: I'm almost happy. Continue. What did you steal? (*Suddenly, machine-gun fire.*)

THE JUDGE: There's simply no end to it. Not a moment's rest.

THE THIEF: I told you: the rebellion has spread all over the north of the city....

THE EXECUTIONER: Shut up!

THE JUDGE: (*irritated*) Are you going to answer, yes or no? What else have you stolen? Where? When? How? How much? Why? For whom?

THE THIEF: I very often entered houses when the maids were off. I used the tradesmen's entrance.... I stole from drawers, I broke into children's piggy-banks. (*She is visibly trying to find words.*) Once I dressed up as a lady. I put on a dark-brown suit, a black straw hat with cherries, a veil and a pair of black shoes—with Cuban heels—then I went in....

THE JUDGE: (*in a rush*) Where? Where? Where? Where—where—where? Where did you go in?

THE THIEF: I can't remember. Forgive me.

THE EXECUTIONER: Shall I let her have it?

THE JUDGE: Not yet. (*To the girl*) Where did you go in? Tell me where?

THE THIEF: (*in a panic*) But I swear to you, I don't remember.

THE EXECUTIONER: Shall I let her have it? Shall I, my Lord?

THE JUDGE: (*to THE EXECUTIONER, and going up to him*) Ah! ah! your pleasure depends on me. You like to thrash, eh? I'm pleased with you, Executioner! Masterly mountain of meat, hunk of beef that's set in motion at a word from me! (*He pretends to look at himself in THE EXECUTIONER.*) Mirror that glorifies me! Image that I can touch, I love you. Never would I have the strength or skill to leave streaks of fire on her back. Besides, what could I do with such strength and skill? (*He touches him.*) Are you there? You're all there, my huge arm, too heavy for me, too big, too fat for my shoulder, walking at my side all by itself! Arm, hundredweight of meat, without you I'd be nothing.... (*To THE THIEF*) And without you too, my child. You're my two perfect complements....Ah, what a fine trio we make! (*To THE THIEF*) But you, you have a privilege that he hasn't, nor I either, that of priority. My being a judge is an emanation of your being a thief. You need only refuse—but you'd better not!—need only refuse to be who you are—what you are, therefore who you are—for me to cease to be ... to vanish, evaporated. Burst. Volatilized. Denied. Hence: good born of.... What then? What then? But you won't refuse, will you? You won't refuse to be a thief? That would be wicked. It would be criminal. You'd deprive me of being! (*Imploringly*) Say it, my child, my love, you won't refuse?

THE THIEF: (*coyly*) I might.

THE JUDGE: What's that? What's that you say? You'd refuse? Tell me where. And tell me again what you've stolen.

THE THIEF: (*curtly, and getting up*) I won't.

THE JUDGE: Tell me where. Don't be cruel....

THE THIEF: Your tone is getting too familiar. I won't have it!

THE JUDGE: Miss.... Madame. I beg of you. (*He falls to his knees.*) Look, I beseech you. Don't leave me in this position, waiting to be a judge. If there were no judge, what would become of us, but what if there were no thieves?

THE THIEF: (*ironically*) And what if there weren't?

THE JUDGE: It would be awful. But you won't do that to me, will you? Please understand me: I don't mind your hiding, for as long as you can and as long as my nerves can bear it, behind the refusal to confess—it's all right to be mean and make me yearn, even prance, make me dance, drool, sweat, whinny with impatience, crawl ... do you want me to crawl?

THE EXECUTIONER: (*to THE JUDGE*) Crawl.

THE JUDGE: I'm proud!

THE EXECUTIONER: (*threateningly*) Crawl!

(THE JUDGE, *who was on his knees, lies flat on his stomach and crawls slowly towards* THE THIEF. *As he crawls forward,* THE THIEF *moves back.*)

THE EXECUTIONER: Good. Continue.

THE JUDGE: (*to THE THIEF*) You're quite right, you rascal, to make me crawl after my judgeship, but if you were to refuse for good, you hussy, it would be criminal....

THE THIEF: (*haughtily*) Call me Madame, and ask politely.

THE JUDGE: Will I get what I want?

THE THIEF: (*coyly*) It cost a lot—stealing does.

THE JUDGE: I'll pay! I'll pay whatever I have to, Madame. But if I no longer had to divide the Good from the Evil, of what use would I be? I ask you?

THE THIEF: I ask myself.

THE JUDGE: (*is infinitely sad*) A while ago I was going to be Minos. My Cerberus was barking. (*To THE EXECUTIONER*) Do you remember? (THE EXECUTIONER *interrupts* THE JUDGE *by cracking his whip.*) You were so cruel, so mean! So good! And me, I was pitiless. I was going to fill Hell with the souls of the damned, to fill prisons. Prisons! Prisons! Prisons, dungeons. Blessed places where evil is impossible since they are the crossroads of all the malediction in the world. One cannot commit evil in evil. Now, what I desire above all is not to condemn, but to judge ... (*He tries to get up.*)

THE EXECUTIONER: Crawl! And hurry up, I've got to go and get dressed.

THE JUDGE: (*to the girl*) Madame! Madame, please, I beg of you. I'm willing to lick your shoes, but tell me you're a thief....

THE THIEF: (*in a cry*) Not yet! Lick! Lick! Lick first!

(*The stage moves from left to right, as at the end of the preceding scene, and plunges into the right wing. In the distance, machine-gun fire.*)

SCENE III

Three dark-green folding-screens, arranged as in the preceding scenes. The same chandelier. The same mirror reflecting the unmade bed. On an armchair, a horse of the kind used by folk-dancers, with a little kilted skirt. In the room, a timid-looking gentleman: the GENERAL. *He removes his jacket, then his bowler hat and his gloves.* IRMA *is near him.*

THE GENERAL: (*He points to the hat, jacket and gloves*) Have that cleared out.

IRMA: It'll be folded and wrapped.

THE GENERAL: Have it removed from sight.

IRMA: It'll be put away. Even burned.

THE GENERAL: Yes, yes, of course, I'd like it to burn! Like cities at twilight.

IRMA: Did you notice anything on the way?

THE GENERAL: I ran very serious risks. The populace has blown up dams. Whole areas are flooded. The arsenal in particular. So that all the powder supplies are wet. And the weapons rusty. I had to make some rather wide detours—though I didn't trip over a single drowned body.

15   IRMA: I wouldn't take the liberty of asking you your opinions. Everyone is free, and I'm not concerned with politics.

THE GENERAL: Then let's talk of something else. The important thing is how I'm going to get out of this place. It'll be late by the time I leave. . . .

IRMA: About it's being late. . . .

20   THE GENERAL: That does it.

(He reaches into his pocket, takes out some banknotes, counts them and gives some to IRMA. *She keeps them in her hand.)*

THE GENERAL: I'm not keen about being shot down in the dark when I leave. For, of course, there won't be anyone to escort me?

IRMA: I'm afraid not. Unfortunately Arthur's not free. *(A long*
25   *pause.)*

THE GENERAL: *(suddenly impatient)* But . . . isn't she coming?

IRMA: I can't imagine what she's doing. I gave instructions that everything was to be ready by the time you arrived. The horse is already here. . . . I'll ring.

30   THE GENERAL: Don't, I'll attend to that. *(He rings.)* I like to ring! Ringing's authoritative. Ah, to ring out commands.

IRMA: In a little while, General. Oh, I'm so sorry, here am I giving you your rank. . . . In a little while you'll. . . .

THE GENERAL: Sh! Don't say it.

35   IRMA: You have such force, such youth! such dash!

THE GENERAL: And spurs. Will I have spurs? I said they were to be fixed to my boots. Oxblood boots, right?

IRMA: Yes, General. And patent-leather.

THE GENERAL: Oxblood. Patent-leather, very well, but with
40   mud?

IRMA: With mud and perhaps a little blood. I've had the decorations prepared.

THE GENERAL: Authentic ones?

IRMA: Authentic ones. *(Suddenly a woman's long scream.)*

45   THE GENERAL: What's that?

(He starts going to the right wall and is already bending down to look, as if there were a small crack, but IRMA *steps in front of him.)*

IRMA: Nothing. There's always some carelessness, on both sides.

THE GENERAL: But that cry? A woman's cry. A call for help perhaps? My heart skips a beat. . . . I spring forward. . . .

50   IRMA: *(icily)* I want no trouble here. Calm down. For the time being, you're in mufti.

THE GENERAL: That's right.

(A woman's scream again.)

THE GENERAL: All the same, it's disturbing. Besides, it'll be awkward.

55   IRMA: What on earth can she be doing?

(She goes to ring, but by the rear door enters a very beautiful young woman, red-headed, hair undone, dishevelled. Her bosom is almost bare. She is wearing a black corset, black stockings and very high-heeled shoes. She is holding a general's uniform, complete with sword, cocked hat and boots.)

THE GENERAL: *(severely)* So you finally got here? Half an hour late. That's more than's needed to lose a battle.

IRMA: She'll redeem herself, General, I know her.

THE GENERAL: *(looking at the boots)* What about the blood? I
60   don't see any blood.

IRMA: It dried. Don't forget that it's the blood of your past battles. Well, then, I'll leave you. Do you have everything you need?

THE GENERAL: *(looking to the right and left)* You're forget-
65   ting. . . .

IRMA: Good God! yes, I was forgetting.

(She lays on the chair the towels she has been carrying on her arm. Then she leaves by the rear. THE GENERAL *goes to the door, then locks it. But no sooner is the door closed than someone knocks.* THE GIRL *goes to open it. Behind, and standing slightly back,* THE EXECUTIONER, *sweating, wiping himself with a towel.)*

THE EXECUTIONER: Is Mme Irma here?

THE GIRL: *(curtly)* In the Rose-garden. *(Correcting herself)* I'm sorry, in the Funeral Chapel.

(She closes the door.)

THE GENERAL: *(irritated)* I'll be left in peace, I hope. And
70   you're late. Where the hell were you? Didn't they give you your feed-bag? You're smiling, are you? Smiling at your rider? You recognize his hand, gentle but firm? *(He strokes her.)* My proud steed! My handsome mare, we've had
75   many a spirited gallop together!

THE GIRL: And that's not all! I want to trip through the world with my nervous legs and well-shod hooves. Take off your trousers and shoes so I can dress you.

THE GENERAL: *(he has taken the cane)* All right, but first, down
80   on your knees! Come on, come on, bend your knees, bend them. . . .

*(*THE GIRL *rears, utters a whinny of pleasure and kneels like a circus horse before* THE GENERAL.)*

THE GENERAL: Bravo! Bravo, Dove! You haven't forgotten a thing. And now, you're going to help me and answer my questions. It's fitting and proper for a nice filly to help her master unbutton himself and take off his gloves, and to be
85   at his beck and call. Now start by untying my laces.

(During the entire scene that follows, THE GIRL *helps* THE GENERAL *remove his clothes and then dress up as a general. When he is completely dressed, he will be seen to have taken on gigantic proportions, by means of trick effects: invisible footgear, broadened shoulders, excessive make-up.)*

THE GIRL: Left foot still swollen?

THE GENERAL: Yes. It's my leading-foot. The one that prances. Like your hoof when you toss your head.

THE GIRL: What am I doing? Unbutton yourself.
90

THE GENERAL: Are you a horse or an illiterate? If you're a horse, you toss your head. Help me. Pull. Don't pull so hard. See here, you're not a plough-horse.

THE GIRL: I do what I have to do.

THE GENERAL: Are you rebelling? Already? Wait till I'm ready.
95   When I put the bit into your mouth. . . .

THE GIRL: Oh no, not that.

THE GENERAL: A general reprimanded by his horse! You'll have the bit, the bridle, the harness, the saddlegirth, and I, in boots and helmet, will whip and plunge!

THE GIRL: The bit is awful. It makes the gums and the corners of the lips bleed. I'll drool blood.

THE GENERAL: Foam pink and spit fire! But what a gallop! Along the rye-fields, through the alfalfa, over the meadows and dusty roads, over hill and dale, awake or asleep, from dawn to twilight and from twilight. . . .

THE GIRL: Tuck in your shirt. Pull up your braces. It's quite a job dressing a victorious general who's to be buried. Do you want the sabre?

THE GENERAL: Let it lie on the table, like Lafayette's. Conspicuously, but hide the clothes. Where? How should *I* know? Surely there's a hiding-place somewhere.

(THE GIRL *bundles up his clothes and hides them behind the armchair.*)

THE GENERAL: The tunic? Good. Got all the medals? Count 'em.

THE GIRL: (*after counting them, very quickly*) They're all here, sir.

THE GENERAL: What about the war? Where's the war?

THE GIRL: (*very softly*) It's approaching, sir. It's evening in an apple-orchard. The sky is calm and pink. The earth is bathed in a sudden peace—the moan of doves—the peace that precedes battles. The air is very still. An apple has fallen to the grass. A yellow apple. Things are holding their breath. War is declared. The evening is very mild. . . .

THE GENERAL: But suddenly?

THE GIRL: We're at the edge of the meadow. I keep myself from flinging out, from whinnying. Your thighs are warm and you're pressing my flanks. Death. . . .

THE GENERAL: But suddenly?

THE GIRL: Death has pricked up her ears. She puts a finger to her lips, asking for silence. Things are lit up with an ultimate goodness. You yourself no longer heed my presence. . . .

THE GENERAL: But suddenly?

THE GIRL: Button up by yourself, sir. The water lay motionless in the pools. The wind itself was awaiting an order to unfurl the flags. . . .

THE GENERAL: But suddenly?

THE GIRL: Suddenly? Eh? Suddenly? (*She seems to be trying to find the right words.*) Ah yes, suddenly all was fire and sword! Widows! Miles of crêpe had to be woven to put on the standards. The mothers and wives remained dry-eyed behind their veils. The bells came clattering down the bombed towers. As I rounded a corner I was frightened by a blue cloth. I reared, but, steadied by your gentle and masterful hand, I ceased to quiver. I started forward again. How I loved you, my hero!

THE GENERAL: But . . . the dead? Weren't there any dead?

THE GIRL: The soldiers died kissing the standard. You were all victory and kindness. One evening, remember. . . .

THE GENERAL: I was so mild that I began to snow. To snow on my men, to shroud them in the softest of winding-sheets. To snow. Moskova!

THE GIRL: Splinters of shell had gashed the lemons. Now death was in action. She moved nimbly from one to the other, deepening a wound, dimming an eye, tearing off an arm, opening an artery, discolouring a face, cutting short a cry, a song. Death was ready to drop. Finally, exhausted, herself dead with fatigue, she grew drowsy and rested lightly on your shoulder, where she fell asleep.

THE GENERAL: (*drunk with joy*) Stop, stop, it's not time for that yet, but I feel it'll be magnificent. The cross-belt? Good. (*He looks at himself in the mirror.*) Austerlitz! General! Man of war and in full regalia, behold me in my pure appearance. Nothing, no contingent trails behind me. I appear, purely and simply. If I went through wars without dying, went through sufferings without dying, if I was promoted, without dying, it was for this minute close to death.

(*Suddenly he stops; he seems troubled by an idea.*)

Tell me, Dove?

THE GIRL: What is it, sir?

THE GENERAL: What's the Chief of Police been doing?

(THE GIRL *shakes her head.*)

Nothing? Still nothing? In short, everything slips through his fingers. And what about us, are we wasting our time?

THE GIRL: (*imperiously*) Not at all. And, in any case, it's no business of ours. Continue. You were saying: for this minute close to death . . . and then?

THE GENERAL: (*hesitating*) . . . close to death . . . where I shall be nothing, though reflected *ad infinitum* in these mirrors, nothing but my image. . . . Quite right, comb your mane. Curry yourself. I require a well-groomed filly. So, in a little while, to the blare of trumpets, we shall descend—I on your back—to death and glory, for I am about to die. It is indeed a descent to the grave. . . .

THE GIRL: But, sir, you've been dead since yesterday.

THE GENERAL: I know . . . but a formal and picturesque descent, by unexpected stairways. . . .

THE GIRL: You are a dead general, but an eloquent one.

THE GENERAL: Because I'm dead, prating horse. What is now speaking, and so beautifully, is Example. I am now only the image of my former self. Your turn, now. Lower your head and hide your eyes, for I want to be a general in solitude. Not even for myself, but for my image, and my image for its image, and so on. In short, we'll be among equals. Dove, are you ready?

(THE GIRL *nods.*)

Come now. Put on your bay dress, horse, my fine Arab steed.

(THE GENERAL *slips the mock-horse over her head. Then he cracks his whip.*)

We're off!

(*He bows to his image in the mirror.*)

Farewell, general!

(*Then he stretches out in the arm-chair with his feet on another chair and bows to the audience, holding himself rigid as a corpse.* THE GIRL *places herself in front of the chair and, on the spot, makes the movements of a horse in motion.)*

THE GIRL: The procession has begun. . . . We're passing through the City. . . . We're going along the river. I'm sad. . . . The sky is overcast. The nation weeps for that splendid
200   hero who died in battle. . . .
THE GENERAL: *(starting)* Dove!
THE GIRL: *(turning around, in tears)* Sir?
THE GENERAL: Add that I died with my boots on!

(He then resumes his pose.)

THE GIRL: My hero died with his boots on! The procession
205   continues. Your aides-de-camp precede me. . . . Then come I, Dove, your war-horse. . . . The military band plays a funeral march. . . .

(Marching in place, THE GIRL sings Chopin's Funeral March, which is continued by an invisible orchestra [with brasses]. Far off, machine-gun fire.)

SCENE IV

A room, the three visible panels of which are three mirrors in which is reflected a little old man, dressed as a tramp though neatly combed. He is standing motionless in the middle of the room. Near him, looking very indifferent, a very beautiful red-haired girl. Leather corselet, leather boots. Naked and beautiful thighs. Fur jacket. She is waiting. So is the man. He is impatient, nervous. THE GIRL is motionless.

THE MAN *removes his torn gloves tremblingly. He takes from his pocket a handkerchief and mops his face. He takes off his glasses, folds them and puts them into a case, which he then slips into his pocket.*

He wipes his hands with his handkerchief.

All the gestures of the little old man are reflected in the three mirrors.

(Three actors are needed to play the roles of the reflections.)

At length, there are three raps at the rear door.

The red-haired girl goes to the door. She says: "Yes."

The door opens a little and through the opening appear IRMA's *hand and arm holding a whip and a very dirty and shaggy wig.*

THE GIRL *takes them. The door closes.*

THE MAN's *face lights up.*

The red-haired girl has an exaggeratedly lofty and cruel air.

She puts the wig on his head roughly.

THE MAN *takes a bouquet of artificial flowers from his pocket. He holds it as if he were going to offer it to the girl, who whips him and lashes it from his hand.*

THE MAN's *face is lit up with tenderness.*

Very near-by, machine-gun fire.

THE MAN *touches his wig.*

THE MAN: What about the lice?
THE GIRL: *(very coarsely)* They're there.

SCENE V

IRMA's *room. Very elegant. It is the same room that was reflected in the mirrors in the first three scenes. The same chandelier. Large lace hangings suspended from the flies. Three arm-chairs. At left, large window near which is an apparatus by means of which* IRMA *can see what is going on in the studios. Door at right. Door at left.* IRMA *is sitting at her dressing-table, going over her accounts. Near her, a girl:* CARMEN. *Machine-gun fire.*

CARMEN: *(counting)* The bishop, twenty . . . the judge, twenty. . . . *(She raises her head.)* No, Madame, nothing yet. No Chief of Police.
IRMA: *(irritated)* He's going to turn up, *if* he turns up . . . fit to be tied! And yet!   5
CARMEN: Yes, I know: it takes all kinds to make a world. But no Chief of Police. *(She counts again.)* The general, twenty . . . the sailor, twenty . . . the brat, thirty. . . .
IRMA: I've told you, Carmen, I don't like that. And I demand respect for the visitors. Vi-si-tors! I don't allow myself—   10 my own self *(she stresses the word "own")*—even to refer to them as clients. And yet! . . . *(She flashily snaps the sheaf of fresh banknotes that she has in her hand.)*
CARMEN: *(severely; she has turned around and is glaring at* IRMA) For you, yes: cash and refinement.   15
IRMA: *(trying to be conciliatory)* Those eyes! Don't be unjust. You've been irritable for some time now. I realize we're on edge because of what's going on, but things will quiet down. The sun will come out again. George. . . .
CARMEN: Ah, him!   20
IRMA: Don't sneer at the Chief of Police. If not for him we'd be in a fine mess. Yes, we, because you're tied up with me. And with him. *(A long pause.)* What disturbs me most is your sadness. *(Wisely.)* You've changed, Carmen. And even before the rebellion started. . . .   25
CARMEN: There's nothing much left for me to do at your place, Mme. Irma.
IRMA: *(disconcerted)* But . . . I've put you in charge of my book-keeping. You sit down at my desk and all at once my entire life opens out before you. I haven't a secret left, and   30 you're not happy?
CARMEN: Of course, I'm grateful to you for your confidence, but . . . it's not the same thing.
IRMA: Do you miss "that," Carmen? (CARMEN *is silent.)* come, Come, Carmen, when you mounted the snow-covered   35 rock with the yellow paper rose-bush—by the way, I'm going to have to store that in the cellar—and when the miraculously-healed leper swooned at the sight of you, you didn't take yourself seriously, did you, Carmen? *(Brief silence.)*
CARMEN: When our sessions are over, Madame, you never al-   40 low anyone to talk about them. So you have no idea of how we really feel. You observe it all from a distance. But if ever you once put on the dress and the blue veil, or if you were the unbuttoned penitent, or the general's mare, or the country girl tumbled in the hay. . . .   45
IRMA: *(shocked)* Me!
CARMEN: Or the maid in a pink apron, or the archduchess deflowered by the policeman, or . . . but I'm not going to run through the whole list . . . you'd know what that does to a girl's soul, and that she's got to use a little irony in self-   50 deference. But no, you don't even want us to talk about it among ourselves. You're afraid of a smile, of a joke.

IRMA: (*very severely*) True, I don't allow any joking. A giggle, or even a smile, spoils everything. A smile means doubt.
55   The clients want sober ceremonies. With sighs. My house is a severe place. You're allowed to play cards.

CARMEN: Then don't be surprised that we're sad. (*A pause.*) But I'm thinking of my daughter.

IRMA: (*She stands—for a bell has buzzed—and goes to a curious*
60   *piece of furniture at the left, a kind of switchboard with a view-finder and earphone. While talking, she looks into the view-finder, after pushing down a switch*) Every time I ask you a slightly intimate question, you shut up like a clam, and you throw your daughter up to me. Are you still set on go-
65   ing to see her? Don't be a fool. Between this place and the nursery in the country there's fire and water, rebellion and bullets. I even wonder whether . . . (*The bell buzzes again. MME IRMA pulls up the switch and pushes down another*) . . . whether they didn't get George on the way. Though a
70   Chief of Police knows how to take care of himself. (*She looks at a watch that she takes from her bosom.*) He's late. (*She looks anxious.*) Or else he hasn't dared to go out.

CARMEN: In order to get to your studios, those gentlemen of yours go through gunfire without fear, whereas I, in order
75   to see my daughter. . . .

IRMA: Without fear? In a state of jitters that excites them. Their nostrils can sniff the orgy behind the wall of flame and steel. . . . Let's get back to the accounts, shall we?

CARMEN: In all, counting the sailor and the simple jobs, it
80   comes to three hundred and twenty.

IRMA: The more killing there is in the working-class districts, the more the men roll into my studios.

CARMEN: The men?

IRMA: (*after a pause*) Some men. Drawn by my mirrors and
85   chandeliers, always the same ones. As for the others, hero-ism takes the place of women.

CARMEN: (*bitterly*) Women?

IRMA: What shall I call you, my big, long, sterile girls? Their seed never ripens in you, and yet . . . if you weren't there?
90 CARMEN: You have your revels, Mme Irma.

IRMA: Be still. It's this chilling game that makes me sad and melancholy. Fortunately I have my jewels. Which, as it happens, are in great danger. (*Dreamily*) I have my jew-els . . . and you, the orgies of your heart. . . .
95 CARMEN: . . . they don't help matters, Madame. My daughter loves me.

IRMA: You're the fairy godmother who comes to see her with toys and perfumes. She pictures you in Heaven. (*Bursting out laughing*) Ah, that's the limit—to think there's someone
100   for whom my brothel—which is Hell—is Heaven! It's Heaven for your brat! (*She laughs.*) Are you going to make a whore of her later on?

CARMEN: Mme Irma!

IRMA: That's right! I ought to leave you to your secret
105   brothel, your precious pink cat-house, your soulful whore-house. . . . You think I'm cruel? This rebellion is getting me down, too. You may not realize it, but I have moments of fear and panic. . . . It looks to me as if the aim of the rebellion weren't to capture the Royal Palace, but
110   to sack my studios. I'm afraid, Carmen. Yet I've tried everything, even prayer. (*She smiles painfully.*) Like your miraculously-healed leper. Have I wounded you?

CARMEN: (*with decision*) Twice a week, on Tuesdays and Fri-days, I had to be the Immaculate Conception of Lourdes

and appear to a bank-clerk of the National Provincial. For 115 you it meant money in the bank and justified your brothel, whereas for me it was. . . .

IRMA: (*astonished*) You agreed to it. You didn't seem to mind it.

CARMEN: I was happy. 120

IRMA: Well? Where's the harm?

CARMEN: I saw the effect I had on my bank-clerk. I saw his state of terror, how he'd break out in a sweat, I heard the rattle in his throat. . . .

IRMA: That'll do. He doesn't come any more. I wonder why? 125 Maybe the danger. Or maybe his wife found out. (*A pause.*) Maybe he's dead. Attend to my accounts.

CARMEN: Your book-keeping will never replace my appear-ing to the bank-clerk. It had become as real as at Lourdes. Everything inside me now yearns for my daughter. She's 130 in a real garden. . . .

IRMA: You'll have a hard time getting to her, and before long the garden will be in your heart.

CARMEN: Be still!

IRMA: (*inexorably*) The city is full of corpses. All the roads are 135 cut off. The peasants are also going over to the rebels. I wonder why? Contagion? The rebellion is an epidemic. It has the same fatal and sacred character. In any case, we're going to find ourselves more and more isolated. The rebels have it in for the Clergy, for the Army, for the Magistracy, 140 for me, Irma, a bawd and madame of a whore-house. As for you, you'll be killed, disembowelled, and your daugh-ter will be adopted by some virtuous rebel. And that's what's in store for all of us. (*She shudders.*)

(*Suddenly a buzz.* IRMA *runs to the apparatus and looks and lis-tens as before.*)

IRMA: Studio 24, Chamber of the Sands. What's going on? 145

(*She watches very attentively. A long pause.*)

CARMEN: (*She has sat down at* IRMA's *table and gone back to the accounts. Without raising her head*) The Foreign Le-gion?

IRMA: (*with her eye still glued to the apparatus*) Yes. It's the heroic Legionnaire falling to the sand. And that idiot Rachel has 150 thrown a dart at his ear. He might have been disfigured. What an idea, having himself shot as if by an Arab, and dying—if you want to call it that!—at attention, on a sand-pile! (*A silence. She watches attentively.*) Ah, Rachel's doctoring him. She's preparing a dressing for him, and he has a happy 155 look. (*Very much interested.*) My, my, he seems to like it. I have a feeling he wants to alter his scenario and that starting to-day he's going to die in the military hospital, tucked in by his nurse. . . . Another uniform to buy. Always expenses. (*Sud-denly anxious.*) Say, I don't like that. Not one bit. I'm getting 160 more and more worried about Rachel. She'd better not double-cross me the way Chantal did. (*Turning around, to* CARMEN.) By the way, no news of Chantal?

CARMEN: None.

IRMA: (*picks up the apparatus again*) And the machine's 165 not working right! What's he saying to her? He's ex-plaining . . . she's listening . . . she understands. I'm afraid he understands too. (*Buzzing again. She pushes down another switch and looks.*) False alarm. It's the plumber leaving.

170 CARMEN: Which one?

IRMA: The real one.

CARMEN: Which is the real one?

IRMA: The one who repairs the taps.

CARMEN: Is the other one fake?

175 IRMA: (*shrugs her shoulders and pushes down the first switch*) Ah, I told you so: the three or four drops of blood from his ear have inspired him. Now he's having her pamper him. Tomorrow morning he'll be in fine fettle for going to his Embassy.

180 CARMEN: He's married, isn't he?

IRMA: As a rule, I don't like to talk about the private life of my visitors. The Grand Balcony has a world-wide reputation. It's the most artful, yet the most decent house of illusions. . . .

185 CARMEN: Decent?

IRMA: Discreet. But I might as well be frank with you, you inquisitive girl. Most of them are married.

(*A pause.*)

CARMEN: When they're with their wives, whom they love, do they keep a tiny, small-scale version of their revels in a
190 brothel. . . .

IRMA: (*reprimanding her*) Carmen!

CARMEN: Excuse me, Madame . . . in a house of illusions. I was saying: do they keep their revels in a house of illusions tucked away in the back of their heads in miniature form,
195 far off? But present?

IRMA: It's possible, child. No doubt they do. Like a Chinese lantern left over from a carnival, and waiting for the next one, or, if you prefer, like an imperceptible light in the imperceptible window of an imperceptible castle that they
200 can enlarge instantly whenever they feel like going there to relax. (*Machine-gun fire.*) You hear that? They're approaching. They're out to get me.

CARMEN: (*continuing her train of thought*) All the same, it must be nice in a real house.

205 IRMA: (*more and more frightened*) They'll succeed in surrounding the house before George arrives. . . . One thing we mustn't forget—if ever we get out of this mess—is that the walls aren't sufficiently padded and the windows aren't well sealed. . . . One can hear all that's going on in the
210 street. Which means that from the street one can hear what's going on in the house.

CARMEN: (*still pensive*) In a real house, it must be nice. . . .

IRMA: Who knows! But Carmen, if my girls start bothering their heads about such things, it'll be the ruin of the
215 brothel. I really think you miss your apparition. Look, I can do something for you. I did promise it to Regina, but I offer it to you. if you want to, of course. Someone rang me up yesterday and asked for a Saint Theresa. . . . (*A pause.*) Ah, obviously, it's a come-down from the Immac-
220 ulate Conception to Saint Theresa, but it's not bad either. . . . (*A pause.*) Well, what do you say? It's for a banker. Very clean, you know. Not demanding. I offer it to you. If the rebels are crushed, naturally.

CARMEN: I liked my dress and veil and rose-bush.

225 IRMA: There's a rose-bush in the "Saint Theresa" too. Think it over.

(*A pause.*)

CARMEN: And what'll the authentic detail be?

IRMA: The ring. He's got it all worked out. The wedding ring. You know that every nun wears a wedding ring, as a bride of God. (CARMEN *makes a gesture of astonishment.*) That's so. 230 That's how he'll know he's dealing with a real nun.

CARMEN: What about the fake detail?

IRMA: It's almost always the same: black lace under the homespun skirt. Well, how about it? You have the kind of gentleness he likes. He'll be pleased. 235

CARMEN: It's really very kind of you, to think of him.

IRMA: I'm thinking of you.

CARMEN: You're so kind, Madame—I wasn't being ironic. The thing to be said for your house is that it brings consolation. You set up and prepare their secret theatres. . . . You've got 240 your feet on the ground. The proof is that you rake in the money. Whereas they . . . their awakening must be brutal. No sooner is it finished than it starts all over again.

IRMA: Luckily for me.

CARMEN: . . . starts all over again, and always the same adven- 245 ture. They'd like it never to end.

IRMA: You miss the entire point. When it's over, their minds are clear. I can tell from their eyes. Suddenly they understand mathematics. They love their children and their country. Like you. 250

CARMEN: (*puffing herself up*) I'm the daughter of a high-ranking officer. . . .

IRMA: I know. There always has to be one in a brothel. But bear in mind that General, Bishop and Judge are, in real life. . . .

CARMEN: Which are you talking about? 255

IRMA: Real ones.

CARMEN: Which are real? The ones here?

IRMA: The others. In real life they're props of a display that they have to drag in the mud of the real and commonplace. Here, Comedy and Appearance remain pure, and 260 the Revels intact.

CARMEN: The revels that I indulge in. . . .

IRMA: (*interrupting her*) I know what they are: to forget theirs.

CARMEN: Do you blame me for that?

IRMA: And theirs are to forget yours. They, too, love their 265 children. Afterwards.

(*Buzzing again, as before,* IRMA, *who has been sitting all the while near the apparatus, turns about, looks into the viewfinder and puts the receiver to her ear.* CARMEN *goes back to her accounts.*)

CARMEN: (*without raising her head*) The Chief of Police?

IRMA: (*describing the scene*) No. The waiter who just arrived. He's going to start complaining again . . . there he goes, he's flaring up because Elyane is handing him a white apron. 270

CARMEN: I warned you. He wants a pink one.

IRMA: Go to the Five-and-Ten tomorrow, if it's open. And buy a duster for the railwayman. A green one.

CARMEN: If only Elyane doesn't forget to drop the tip on the floor. He demands a true revolt. And dirty glasses. 275

IRMA: They all want everything to be as true as possible. . . . Minus something indefinable, so that it won't be true. (*Changing her tone.*) Carmen, it was I who decided to call my establishment a house of illusions, but I'm only the manager. Each individual, when he rings the bell and en- 280 ters, brings his own scenario, perfectly thought out. My job is merely to rent the hall and furnish the props, actors and actresses. My dear, I've succeeded in lifting it from the

ground—do you see what I mean? I unloosed it long ago
285 and it's flying. I cut the moorings. It's flying. Or, if you
like, it's sailing in the sky, and I with it. Well, my darling . . . may I say something tender—every madame always, traditionally, has a slight partiality for one of her
young ladies. . . .
290 CARMEN: I had noticed it, Madame, and I too, at times. . . .

(*She looks at* IRMA *languidly.*)

IRMA: (*standing up and looking at her*) I have a strange feeling,
Carmen. (*A long pause.*) But let's continue. Darling, the
house really does take off, leaves the earth, sails in the sky
295 when, in the secrecy of my heart, I call myself, but with
great precision, a keeper of a bawdy-house. Darling, when
secretly, in silence, I repeat to myself silently, "You're a bawd,
boss of a whore-house," darling, everything (*suddenly lyrical*),
everything flies off—chandeliers, mirrors, carpets, pianos,
caryatids and my studios, my famous studios: the studio
300 known as the Hay Studio, hung with rustic scenes, the Studio of the Hangings, spattered with blood and tears, the
Throne-room Studio, draped in velvet with a fleur-de-lis
pattern, the Studio of Mirrors, the Studio of State, the Studio of Perfumed Foundations, the Urinal Studio, the Am-
305 phitrite Studio, the Moonlight Studio, everything flies off:
studios—Oh! I was forgetting the studio of the beggars, of
the tramps, where filth and poverty are magnified. To continue: studio, girls, . . . (*she thinks again.*) Oh! I was forgetting: the most beautiful of all, ultimate adornment, crown of
310 the edifice—if the construction of it is ever completed. I
speak of the Funeral Studio, adorned with marble urns, my
Studio of Solemn Death, the Tomb! The Mausoleum Studio. . . . To continue: studios, girls, crystals, laces, balconies,
everything takes it on the lam, rises up and carries me off!

(*A long pause. The two women are standing motionless, facing each
other.*)

315 CARMEN: How well you speak.
IRMA: (*modestly*) I went through elementary school.
CARMEN: So I assumed. My father, the artillery colonel. . . .
IRMA: (*correcting her sharply*) You mean cavalry, my dear.
CARMEN: Excuse me. That's right. The cavalry colonel wanted
320 me to have an education. Alas. . . . As for you, you've been
successful. You've been able to surround your loveliness
with a sumptuous theatre, a gala, the splendours of which
envelop you and hide you from the world. Your whoredom
required such pomp. But what about me, am I to have only
325 myself and be only myself? No, Madame. Thanks to vice
and men's heartache, I too have had my moment of glory!
With the receiver at your ear, you could see me through the
view-finder, standing erect, sovereign and kind, maternal
yet feminine, with my heel on the cardboard snake and the
330 pink paper-roses. You could also see the bank-clerk from
the National City kneeling before me and swooning when
I appeared to him. Unfortunately he had his back to you
and so you weren't aware of the ecstasy on his face and the
wild pounding of my heart. My blue veil, my blue robe, my
335 blue apron, my blue eyes. . . .
IRMA: They're hazel.
CARMEN: They were blue that day. For him I was Heaven in
person descending on his brow. I was a Madonna to

whom a Spaniard might have prayed and sworn an oath.
He hymned me, fusing me with his beloved colour, and 340
when he carried me to bed, it was into the blue that he
penetrated. But I won't ever appear to him again.
IRMA: I've offered you Saint Theresa.
CARMEN: I'm not prepared, Mme Irma. One has to know
what the client's going to require. Has everything been 345
worked out?
IRMA: Every whore should be able—I hope you'll excuse me,
but since we've gone so far, let's talk man to man—should
be able to handle any situation.
CARMEN: I'm one of your whores, Mme Irma, and one of your 350
best. I boast of it. In the course of an evening, I can . . .
IRMA: I'm aware of your feats. But when you start glorifying
yourself as soon as you hear the word whore, which you
keep repeating to yourself and which you flaunt as if it were
a title, it's not quite the same as when I use the word to des- 355
ignate a function. But you're right, darling, to extol your
profession and to glory in it. Make it shine. Let it illuminate
you, if that's the only thing you have. (*Tenderly*) I'll do all I
can to help you. . . . You're not only the purest jewel of all
my girls, you're the one on whom I bestow all my tender- 360
ness. But stay with me. . . . Would you dare leave me when
everything is cracking up everywhere? Death—the real
thing—is at my door, it's beneath my windows. . . .

(*Machine-gun fire.*)

You hear?
CARMEN: The Army is fighting bravely. 365
IRMA: And the Rebels even more bravely. And we're in the
shadow of the cathedral, a few feet from the Archbishop's
Palace. There's no price on my head. No, that would be
too much to expect, but it's known that I serve supper to
prominent people. So they're out to get me. And there are 370
no men in the house.
CARMEN: There's Arthur.
IRMA: Are you trying to be funny? He's no man, he's my
stage-prop. Besides, as soon as his session is over, I'll send
him to look for George. 375
CARMEN: Assuming the worst. . . .
IRMA: If the rebels win? I'm a goner. They're workers. Without imagination. Prudish and maybe chaste.
CARMEN: It won't take them long to get used to debauchery.
Just wait till they get a little bored. . . . 380
IRMA: You're wrong. Or else they won't let themselves get
bored. But I'm the one who's most exposed. For you it's
different. In every revolution there's the glorified whore
who sings an anthem and is virginified. That'll be you. The
others'll piously bring water for the dying to drink. After- 385
wards . . . they'll marry you off. Would you like to get married?
CARMEN: Orange blossoms, tulle . . .
IRMA: Wonderful! To you, getting married means masquerading. Darling, you certainly are one of us. No, I can't 390
imagine you married either. Besides, what they're really
dreaming of doing is murdering us. We'll have a lovely
death, Carmen. It will be terrible and sumptuous. They
may break into my studios, shatter the crystals, tear the
brocades and slit our throats. . . . 395
CARMEN: They'll take pity. . . .
IRMA: They won't. They'll thrill at the thought that their fury
is sacrilegious. All bedraggled, with caps on their heads, or

400 in helmets and boots, they'll destroy us by fire and sword. It'll be very beautiful. We oughtn't to wish for any other kind of end, and you, you're thinking of leaving. . . .

CARMEN: But Mme Irma. . . .

IRMA: Yes, yes. When the house is about to go up in flames, 405 when the rose is about to be stabbed, all you think of, Carmen, is fleeing.

CARMEN: If I wanted to be elsewhere, you know very well why.

IRMA: Your daughter is dead. . . .

CARMEN: Madame!

IRMA: Whether dead or alive, your daughter is dead. Think of 410 the charming grave, adorned with daisies and artificial wreaths, at the far end of the garden . . . and that garden in your heart, where you'll be able to look after it. . . .

CARMEN: I'd have loved to see her again. . . .

IRMA: You'll keep her image in the image of the garden and 415 the garden in your heart under the flaming robe of Saint Theresa. And you hesitate? I offer you the very finest of deaths, and you hesitate? Are you a coward?

CARMEN: You know very well I'm devoted to you.

IRMA: I'll teach you figures! The wonderful figures that we'll 420 spend the nights together calligraphing.

CARMEN: (softly) The war is raging. As you said, it's the horde.

IRMA: (triumphantly) The horde, but we have our cohorts, our armies, our hosts, legions, battalions, vessels, heralds, clarions, trumpets, our colours, streamers, standards, ban-425 ners . . . to lead us to catastrophe! Death? It's certain death, but with what speed and with what dash! . . . (Melancholically) Unless George is still all-powerful. . . . and above all if he can get through the horde and come and save us. (A deep sigh.) Now come and dress me. But first I want to see 430 how Rachel's getting on.

(Same business as before. IRMA glues her eye to the view-finder. A pause. She peers.)

With this gadget I can see them and even hear their sighs.

(A pause. She looks into the apparatus.)

Christ is leaving with his paraphernalia. I've never been able to understand why he has himself tied to the cross with ropes he brings in a valise. Maybe they're ropes that 435 have been blessed. Where does he put them when he gets home? Who the hell cares! Let's take a look at Rachel. (She pushes down another switch.) Ah, they've finished. They're talking. They're putting away the little arrows, the bow, the gauze bandages, the white officer's cap. . . . No, I 440 don't at all like the way they're looking at each other: it's too candid and straightforward. (She turns to CARMEN.) There you have the dangers of regularity. It would be a catastrophe if my clients and girls smiled at each other affectionately. It would be an even greater catastrophe than 445 if it were a question of love. (She presses the switch mechanically and lays down the receiver. Pensively:) Arthur's session must be over. He'll be along in a minute. . . . Dress me.

CARMEN: What are you wearing?

IRMA: The cream-coloured négligé.

(CARMEN opens the door of a closet and takes out the négligé, while IRMA unhooks her suit.)

450 Tell me, Carmen, what about Chantal? . . .

CARMEN: Madame?

IRMA: Yes. About Chantal, tell me, what do you know about her?

CARMEN: I've questioned all the girls: Rosine, Elyane, Flo-455 rence, Marlyse. They've each prepared a little report. I'll let you have them. But I didn't get much out of them. It's possible to spy beforehand. During the fighting, it's harder. For one thing, the camps are more sharply defined. You can choose. When there's peace, it's too vague. You don't quite know whom you're betraying. Nor even whether 460 you're betraying. There's no news about Chantal. They don't even know whether she's still alive.

IRMA: But, tell me, you wouldn't have any scruples about it?

CARMEN: None at all. Entering a brothel means rejecting the world. Here I am and here I stay. Your mirrors and orders and 465 the passions are my reality. What jewels are you wearing?

IRMA: The diamonds. My jewels. They're the only things I have that are real. I feel everything else is sham. I have my jewels as others have little girls in gardens. Who's double-crossing? You're hesitating. 470

CARMEN: The girls all mistrust me. I collect their little report. I pass it on to you. You pass it on to the police. The police check on it. . . . Me, I know nothing.

IRMA: You're cautious. Give me a handkerchief.

CARMEN: (bringing a lace handkerchief) Viewed from here, 475 where, in any case, men show their naked selves, life seems to me so remote, so profound, that it has all the unreality of a film or of the birth of Christ in the manger. When I'm in a room with a man and he forgets himself so far as to say to me: "The arsenal will be taken tomorrow night," 480 I feel as if I were reading an obscene scrawl. His act becomes as mad, as . . . voluminous as those described in a certain way on certain walls. . . . No, I'm not cautious.

(A knocking. IRMA gives a start. She rushes to the apparatus and, by means of a mechanism operated by a button, conceals it in the wall. In the course of the scene with ARTHUR, CARMEN undresses and then dresses IRMA, so that the latter is ready just when THE CHIEF OF POLICE arrives.)

IRMA: Come in!

(The door opens. Enter THE EXECUTIONER, whom hereafter we shall call ARTHUR. Classical pimp's outfit: light grey suit, white felt hat, etc. He finishes knotting his tie.)

IRMA: (examining him minutely) Is the session over? He went 485 through it fast.

ARTHUR: Yes, the little geezer's buttoning up. He's pooped. Two sessions in half an hour. With all that shooting in the street, I wonder whether he'll get back to his hotel. (He imitates the JUDGE in Scene Two.) Minos judges you. . . . Minos 490 weighs you . . . Cerberus? Bow-wow! Bow-wow! (He shows his fangs and laughs.) Hasn't the Chief of Police arrived?

IRMA: You went easy, I hope? Last time, the poor girl was laid up for two days.

(CARMEN has brought the cream-coloured négligé. IRMA is now in her chemise.)

ARTHUR: Don't pull that kind-hearted-whore stuff on me. 495 Both last time and tonight she got what was coming to her: in dough and in wallops. Right on the line. The banker wants to see stripes on her back. So I stripe it.

IRMA: At least you don't get any pleasure out of it?

500 ARTHUR: Not with her. You're my only love. And a job's a job. I'm conscientious about my work.

IRMA: (*sternly*) I'm not jealous of the girl, but I wouldn't want you to disable the personnel. It's getting harder and harder to replace.

505 ARTHUR: I tried a couple of times to draw marks on her back with purple paint, but it didn't work. The old guy inspects her when he arrives and insists I deliver her in good shape.

IRMA: Paint? Who gave you permission? (*To* CARMEN) My Turkish slippers, darling.

510 ARTHUR: (*shrugging his shoulders*) What's one illusion more or less! I thought I was doing the right thing. But don't worry. Now I whip, I flagellate, she screams, and he crawls.

IRMA: See to it she doesn't scream so loud. The house is being watched.

515 ARTHUR: The radio has just announced that all the north part of town was taken last night. And the Judge wants screaming. The Bishop's less dangerous. He's satisfied with pardoning sins.

CARMEN: Though he gets pleasure out of pardoning, he ex-
520 pects you to commit them. No, the best of the lot is the one you tie up, spank, whip and soothe, and then he snores.

ARTHUR: Who cuddles him? (*To* CARMEN) You? Do you give him your breast?

CARMEN: (*curtly*) I do my job right. And in any case, Mr.
525 Arthur, you're wearing an outfit that doesn't allow you to joke. The pimp has a grin, never a smile.

IRMA: She's right.

ARTHUR: How much did you take in today?

IRMA: (*on the defensive*) Carmen and I haven't finished the ac-
530 counts.

ARTHUR: But I have. According to my calculations, it runs to a good two hundred.

IRMA: That's possible. In any case, don't worry. I don't cheat.

ARTHUR: I believe you, my love, but I can't help it: the fig-
535 ures arrange themselves in my head. Two hundred! War, rebellion, shooting, frost, hail, rain, showers of shit, nothing stops them! On the contrary. People are killing each other in the streets, the joint's being watched, but all the same, they come charging in. As for me, I've got you right
540 at home, sweetie-pie, otherwise. . . .

IRMA: (*bluntly*) You'd be cowering in a cellar, paralysed with fear.

ARTHUR: (*ambiguously*) I'd do as the others do, my love. I'd wait to be saved by the Chief of Police. You're not forget-
545 ting my little percentage?

IRMA: I give you what you need.

ARTHUR: My love! I've ordered the silk shirts. And do you know what kind of silk? And what colour? In the purple silk of your blouse!

550 IRMA: (*tenderly*) All right, cut it. Not in front of Carmen.

ARTHUR: Then it's O.K.?

IRMA: (*weakening*) Yes.

ARTHUR: How much?

IRMA: (*regaining her self-possession*) We'll see. I have to go over
555 the accounts with Carmen. (*Winningly*) It'll be as much as I can. For the moment, you've absolutely got to go to meet George. . . .

ARTHUR: (*with insolent irony*) I beg your pardon, my beloved?

IRMA: (*curtly*) To go to meet Mr. George. To Police Headquarters, if necessary, and to let him know that I'm rely-   560
ing only on him.

ARTHUR: (*slightly uneasy*) You're kidding, I hope? . . .

IRMA: (*with sudden sternness*) The tone of my last remark should answer your question. I'm no longer playing. Or, if you like, not the same role. And there's no longer any need   565
for you to play the mean, soft-hearted pimp. Do as I tell you, but first take the atomizer. (*To* CARMEN, *who brings the object*) Give it to him. (*To* ARTHUR) And on your knees!

ARTHUR: (*he puts one knee on the floor and sprays* IRMA) In the street? All by myself? . . . Me? . . .   570

IRMA: (*standing in front of him*) I've got to know what's happening to George. I can't remain unprotected.

ARTHUR: I'm here . . .

IRMA: (*shrugging*) I've got to defend my jewels, my studios, my girls. The Chief of Police should have been here a half-   575
hour ago. . . .

ARTHUR: (*woefully*) Me in the street! . . . But it's hailing . . . they're shooting. . . . (*He points to his suit.*) And I got dressed up to stay here, to go walking through the corridors and look at myself in your mirrors. And also for you   580
to see me dressed up as a pimp. . . . All I've got to protect me is the silk. . . .

IRMA: (*to* CARMEN) Let me have my bracelets, Carmen. (*To* ARTHUR) And you, spray.

ARTHUR: I'm not meant for outdoors. I've been living within   585
your walls too long. Even my skin couldn't tolerate the fresh air . . . maybe if I had a veil. . . . What if I were recognized? . . .

IRMA: (*irritated, and pivoting in front of the atomizer*) Hug the walls. (*A pause.*) Take this revolver.   590

ARTHUR: (*frightened*) On me?

IRMA: In your pocket.

ARTHUR: My pocket! Imagine me having to shoot? . . .

IRMA: (*gently*) So now you're crammed full of what you are? Gorged?   595

ARTHUR: Gorged, that's right. . . . (*A pause.*) Rested, gorged . . . but if I go out into the street. . . .

IRMA: (*commandingly, but gently*) You're right. No revolver. But take off your hat and go where I tell you, and come back and let me know what's going on. You have a session this   600
evening. Did you know? (*He tosses his hat away.*)

ARTHUR: (*on his way to the door*) This evening? Another one? What is it?

IRMA: I thought I told you: a corpse.

ARTHUR: (*with disgust*) What am I supposed to do with it?   605

IRMA: Nothing. You're to remain motionless, and you'll be buried. You'll be able to rest.

ARTHUR: Ah, because I'm the one who . . . ? Ah, O.K. All right. Who's the client? Someone new?

IRMA: (*mysteriously*) A very important person, and stop asking   610
questions. Get going.

ARTHUR: (*starting to leave, then hesitating, timidly*) Don't I get a kiss?

IRMA: When we come back. If we come back.

(*Exit* ARTHUR, *still on his knees.*)
(*But the door at the right has already opened and, without knocking,* THE CHIEF OF POLICE *enters. Heavy fur-lined coat, hat, cigar.* CARMEN *starts running to call* ARTHUR *back, but* THE CHIEF OF POLICE *steps in front of her.*)

615 THE CHIEF OF POLICE: No, no, stay, Carmen. I like having you around. As for the gigolo, let him find me.

(He keeps his hat and coat on, does not remove his cigar from his mouth, but bows to IRMA *and kisses her hand.)*

IRMA: *(breathlessly)* Put your hand here. *(On her breast.)* I'm all tense. I'm still wrought up. I knew you were on your way, which meant you were in danger. I waited for you all 620 a-tremble . . . while perfuming myself. . . .

THE CHIEF OF POLICE: *(while taking off his hat, coat, gloves, and jacket)* All right, that'll do. Let's cut the comedy. The situation's getting more and more serious—it's not desperate, but it will be before long—hap-pi-ly! The Royal Palace is 625 surrounded. The Queen's in hiding. The city—it's a miracle that I got through—the city's being ravaged by fire and sword. Out there the rebellion is tragic and joyous, whereas in this house everything's dying a slow death. So, today's my day. By tonight I'll be in the grave or on a 630 pedestal. So whether I love you or desire you is unimportant. How are things going at the moment?

IRMA: Marvellously. I had some great performances.

THE CHIEF OF POLICE: *(impatiently)* What kind?

IRMA: Carmen has a talent for description. Ask her.

635 THE CHIEF OF POLICE: *(to* CARMEN*)* Tell me, Carmen, still . . .?

CARMEN: Yes, sir, still. Still the pillars of the Empire: the Judge. . . .

THE CHIEF OF POLICE: *(ironically)* Our allegories, our talking weapons. And is there also . . .?

640 CARMEN: As every week, a new theme.

*(THE CHIEF OF POLICE *makes a gesture of curiosity.)*

This time it's the baby who gets slapped, spanked, tucked in, then cries and is cuddled.

THE CHIEF OF POLICE: *(impatiently)* Fine. But. . . .

CARMEN: He's charming, Sir. And so sad!

645 THE CHIEF OF POLICE: *(irritably)* Is that all?

CARMEN: And so pretty when you unswaddle him. . . .

THE CHIEF OF POLICE: *(with rising fury)* Are you pulling my leg, Carmen? I'm asking you whether I'm in it?

CARMEN: Whether you're in it?

650 IRMA: *(ironically, though we do not know with whom she is ironic)* You're not in it.

THE CHIEF OF POLICE: Not yet? *(To* CARMEN.*)* Well, yes or no, is there a simulation. . . .

CARMEN: *(bewildered)* Simulation?

655 THE CHIEF OF POLICE: You idiot! Yes! An impersonation of the Chief of Police?

(Very heavy silence.)

IRMA: The time's not ripe. My dear, your function isn't noble enough to offer dreamers an image that would console them. Perhaps because it lacks illustrious ancestors? No, 660 my dear fellow. . . . You have to resign yourself to the fact that your image does not yet conform to the liturgies of the brothel.

THE CHIEF OF POLICE: Who's represented in them?

IRMA: You know who. You have your index-cards. *(She enu-* 665 *merates on her fingers.)* There are two kings of France with coronation ceremonies and different rituals, an admiral at the stern of his sinking destroyer, a dey of Algiers surren-

dering, a fireman putting out a fire, a goat attached to a stake, a housewife returning from market, a pickpocket, a robbed man who's bound and beaten up, a Saint Sebast- 670 ian, a farmer in his barn . . . but no chief of police . . . nor colonial administrator, though there *is* a missionary dying on the cross, and Christ in person.

THE CHIEF OF POLICE: *(after a pause)* You're forgetting the mechanic. 675

IRMA: He doesn't come any more. What with tightening screws, he'd have ended by constructing a machine. And it might have worked. Back to the factory!

THE CHIEF OF POLICE: So not a single one of your clients has had the idea . . . the remotest idea, the barest suggest- 680 ion. . . .

IRMA: No. I know you do what you can. You try hatred and love. But glory gives you the cold shoulder.

THE CHIEF OF POLICE: *(forcefully)* My image is growing bigger and bigger. It's becoming colossal. Everything around 685 me repeats and reflects it. And you've never seen it represented in this place?

IRMA: In any case, even if it were celebrated here, I wouldn't see anything. The ceremonies are secret.

THE CHIEF OF POLICE: You liar. You've got secret peep-holes 690 in every wall. Every partition, every mirror, is rigged. In one place, you can hear the sighs, in another the echo of the moans. You don't need me to tell you that brothel tricks are mainly mirror tricks. . . . *(Very sadly)* Nobody yet! But I'll make my image detach itself from me. I'll 695 make it penetrate into your studios, force its way in, reflect and multiply itself. Irma, my function weighs me down. Here, it will appear to me in the blazing light of pleasure and death. *(Musingly)* Of death.

IRMA: You must keep killing, my dear George. 700

THE CHIEF OF POLICE: I do what I can, I assure you. People fear me more and more.

IRMA: Not enough. You must plunge into darkness, into shit and blood. *(With sudden anguish)* And must kill whatever remains of our love. 705

THE CHIEF OF POLICE: *(curtly)* Everything's dead.

IRMA: That's a fine victory. So you've got to kill what's around you.

THE CHIEF OF POLICE: *(very irritated)* I repeat: I do what I can to prove to the nation that I'm a leader, a lawgiver, a 710 builder. . . .

IRMA: *(uneasily)* You're raving. Or else you really do expect to build an empire. In which case you're raving.

THE CHIEF OF POLICE: *(with conviction)* When the rebellion's been put down, and put down by me, when I've the na- 715 tion behind me and been appealed to by the Queen, nothing can stop me. Then, and only then, will you see who I now am! *(Musingly)* Yes, my dear, I want to build an empire . . . so that the empire will, in exchange, build *me.* . . .

IRMA: . . . a tomb. 720

THE CHIEF OF POLICE: *(somewhat taken aback)* But, after all, why not? Doesn't every conqueror have one? So? *(Exalted)* Alexandria! I'll have my tomb, Irma. And when the cornerstone is laid, you'll be my guest of honour.

IRMA: Thank you. *(To* CARMEN.*)* Carmen, the tea. 725

THE CHIEF OF POLICE: *(to* CARMEN, *who is about to leave)* Just a minute, Carmen. What do you think of the idea?

CARMEN: That you want to merge your life with one long funeral, sir.

730   THE CHIEF OF POLICE: (aggressively) Is life anything else? You seem to know everything—so tell me: in this sumptuous theatre where every moment a drama is performed—in the sense that the outside world says a mass is celebrated—what have you observed?

735   CARMEN: (after a hesitation) As for anything serious, anything worth reporting, only one thing: that without the thighs it contained, a pair of pants on a chair is beautiful, sir. Emptied of our little old men, our ornaments are deathly sad. They're the ones that are placed on the catafalques of

740   high dignitaries. They cover only corpses that never stop dying. And yet. . . .

IRMA: (To CARMEN) That's not what the Chief of Police is asking.

THE CHIEF OF POLICE: I'm used to Carmen's speeches. (To

745   CARMEN) You were saying: and yet . . . ?

CARMEN: And yet, I'm sure that the sudden joy in their eyes when they see the cheap finery is really the gleam of innocence. . . .

THE CHIEF OF POLICE: People claim that our house sends

750   them to Death. (Suddenly a ringing. IRMA starts. A pause.)

IRMA: Someone's opened the door. Who can it be at this hour? (To CARMEN) Carmen, go down and shut the door.

(CARMEN exits. A rather long silence between IRMA and THE CHIEF OF POLICE, who remain alone.)

THE CHIEF OF POLICE: My tomb!

IRMA: It was I who rang. I wanted to be alone with you for

755   a moment. (A pause, during which they look into each other's eyes seriously.) Tell me, George. . . . (She hesitates.) Do you still insist on keeping up the game? No, no, don't be impatient. Aren't you tired of it?

THE CHIEF OF POLICE: But. . . . In a little while I'll be going

760   home.

IRMA: If you can. If the rebellion leaves you free to go.

THE CHIEF OF POLICE: The rebellion is a game. From here you can't see anything of the outside, but every rebel is playing a game. And he loves his game.

765   IRMA: But supposing they let themselves be carried beyond the game? I mean if they get so involved in it that they destroy and replace everything. Yes, yes, I know, there's always the false detail that reminds them that at a certain moment, at a certain point in the drama, they have to stop,

770   and even withdraw. . . . but what if they're so carried away by passion that they no longer recognize anything and leap, without realizing it, into. . . .

THE CHIEF OF POLICE: You mean into reality? What of it? Let them try. I do as they do, I penetrate right into the reality

775   that the game offers us, and since I have the upper hand, it's I who score.

IRMA: They'll be stronger than you.

THE CHIEF OF POLICE: Why do you say "they'll be"? I've left the members of my bodyguard in one of your studios. So

780   I'm always in contact with my various departments. All right, enough of that. Are you or aren't you the mistress of a house of illusions? Good. If I come to your place, it's to find satisfaction in your mirrors and their trickery. (Tenderly) Don't worry. Everything will be just as it's always been.

785   IRMA: I don't know why, but today I feel uneasy. Carmen seems strange to me. The rebels—how shall I put it?—have a kind of gravity. . . .

THE CHIEF OF POLICE: Their role requires it.

IRMA: No, no . . . of determination. They walk by the windows threateningly, but they don't sing. The threat is in their eyes.   790

THE CHIEF OF POLICE: What of it? Supposing it is, do you take me for a coward? Do you think I should give up and go home?

IRMA: (pensively) No. Besides, I think it's too late.

THE CHIEF OF POLICE: Do you have any news?   795

IRMA: From Chantal, before she lit out. The power-house will be occupied around 3 a.m.

THE CHIEF OF POLICE: Are you sure? Who told her?

IRMA: The partisans of the Fourth Sector.

THE CHIEF OF POLICE: That's plausible. How did she find out?   800

IRMA: It's through her that there were leaks, and through her alone. So don't belittle my house. . . .

THE CHIEF OF POLICE: Your cat-house, my love.

IRMA: Cat-house, whore-house, bawdy-house. Brothel. Fuckery. Call it anything you like. So Chantal's the only one   805
who's on the other side. . . . She lit out. But before she did, she confided in Carmen, and Carmen's no fool.

THE CHIEF OF POLICE: Who tipped her off?

IRMA: Roger. The plumber. How do you imagine him? Young and handsome? No. He's forty. Thick-set. Serious, with   810
ironic eyes. Chantal spoke to him. I put him out: too late. He belongs to the Andromeda network.

THE CHIEF OF POLICE: Andromeda? Splendid. The rebellion's riding high, it's moving out of this world. If it gives its sectors the names of constellations, it'll evaporate in no time   815
and be metamorphosed into song. Let's hope the songs are beautiful.

IRMA: And what if their songs give the rebels courage? What if they're willing to die for them?

THE CHIEF OF POLICE: The beauty of their songs will make   820
them soft. Unfortunately, they haven't yet reached the point of either beauty or softness. In any case, Chantal's tender passions were providential.

IRMA: Don't bring God into. . . .

THE CHIEF OF POLICE: I'm a freemason. Therefore. . . .   825

IRMA: You? You never told me.

THE CHIEF OF POLICE: (solemnly) Sublime Prince of the Royal Secret.

IRMA: (ironically) You, a brother in a little apron! With a hood and taper and a little mallet! That's odd. (A pause.) You too?   830

THE CHIEF OF POLICE: Why? You too?

IRMA: (with mock solemnity) I'm a guardian of far more solemn rites. (Suddenly sad) Since that's all I am now.

THE CHIEF OF POLICE: As usual, you're going to bring up our grand passion.   835

IRMA: (gently) No, not our passion, but the time when we loved each other.

THE CHIEF OF POLICE: Well, would you like to give a historical account of it and deliver a eulogy? You think my visits would have less zest if you didn't flavour them with the   840
memory of a pretended innocence?

IRMA: It's a question of tenderness. Neither the wildest concoctions of my clients nor my own fancies nor my constant endeavour to enrich my studios with new themes nor the passing of time nor the gilding and crystals nor   845
bitter cold can dispel the moments when you cuddled in my arms or keep me from remembering them.

THE CHIEF OF POLICE: Do you really miss them?

IRMA: (*tenderly*) I'd give my kingdom to relive a single one of
850   them! And you know which one. I need just one word of
truth—as when one looks at one's wrinkles at night, or
rinses one's mouth. . . .

THE CHIEF OF POLICE: It's too late. (*A pause.*) Besides, we
couldn't cuddle each other eternally. You don't know what
855   I was already secretly moving towards when I was in your
arms.

IRMA: I know that I loved you.

THE CHIEF OF POLICE: It's too late. Could you give up Arthur?

IRMA: It was you who forced him on me. You insisted on there
860   being a man here—against my better judgment—in a domain that should have remained virgin. . . . You fool, don't
laugh. Virgin, that is, sterile. But you wanted a pillar, a shaft,
a phallus present—an upright bulk. Well, it's here. You saddled me with that hunk of congested meat, that milksop
865   with wrestler's arms. He may look like a strongman at a fair,
but you don't realize how fragile he is. You stupidly forced
him on me because you felt yourself ageing.

THE CHIEF OF POLICE: Be still.

IRMA: (*shrugging her shoulders*) And you relaxed here through
870   Arthur. I need him now. I have no illusions. I'm his man
and he relies on me, but I need that rugged shop-window
dummy hanging on to my skirts. He's my body, as it were,
but set beside me.

THE CHIEF OF POLICE: (*ironically*) What if I were jealous?

875 IRMA: Of that big doll made up as an executioner in order to
satisfy a phony judge? You're kidding, but the spectacle of
me under the spectacle of that magnificent body never
used to bother you. . . . Let me repeat. . . .

THE CHIEF OF POLICE: (*he slaps* IRMA, *who falls on the sofa*) And
880   don't blubber or I'll break your jaw, and I'll send your
joint up in smoke. I'll set fire to your hair and bush and
I'll turn you loose. I'll light up the town with blazing
whores. (*very gently*) Do you think I'm capable of it?

IRMA: (*in a panting whisper*) Yes, darling.

885 THE CHIEF OF POLICE: All right, add up the accounts for me.
If you like, you can deduct Apollo's crêpe de Chine. And
hurry up. I've got to get back to my post. For the time being, I have to act. Afterwards. . . . Afterwards, things'll run
themselves. My name will act in my place. Well, what
890   about Arthur?

IRMA: (*submissively*) He'll be dead this evening.

THE CHIEF OF POLICE: Dead? You mean . . . really . . . really
dead?

IRMA: (*with resignation*) Come, come, George, the way one
895   dies here.

THE CHIEF OF POLICE: Indeed? Meaning. . . .

IRMA: The Minister. . . . (*She is interrupted by the voice of*
CARMEN.)

CARMEN: (*in the wings*) Lock Studio 17! Elyane, hurry up!
900   And lower the studio . . . no, no, wait . . . (*We hear the sound
of a rusty cog-wheel, the kind made by certain old lifts. Enter
CARMEN.*) Madame, the Queen's Envoy is in the drawing-
room. . . .

(*The door opens, left, and* ARTHUR *appears, trembling and with his
clothes torn.*)

ARTHUR: (*noticing* THE CHIEF OF POLICE) You here! You man-
905   aged to get through?

IRMA: (*rushing to his arms*) Darling! What's the matter? Are you
hurt? Speak!

ARTHUR: (*panting*) I tried to get to Police Headquarters. Impossible. The whole city's lit up with fires. The rebels are in
control practically everywhere. I don't think you can get   910
back, sir. I was able to reach the Royal Palace, and I saw the
Grand Chamberlain. He said he'd try to come. I might add
that he shook my hand. And then I left. The women are the
most excited. They're urging the men to loot and kill. But
what was most awful was a girl who was singing. . . .   915

(*A shot is heard. A window-pane is shivered. Also a mirror near the
bed.* ARTHUR *falls down, hit in the forehead by a bullet coming from
outside.* CARMEN *bends over him, then rises to her feet again. Then*
IRMA *bends over him and strokes his forehead.*)

THE CHIEF OF POLICE: In short, I'm stuck in the whore-
house. That means I'll have to act from the whore-house.

IRMA: (*to herself, bent over* ARTHUR) Can it be that everything's
slipping away? Slipping between my fingers? . . . (*bitterly*) I
still have my jewels . . . my rocks . . . and perhaps not for   920
long. . . .

CARMEN: (*softly*) If the house is to be blown up. . . . Is Saint
Theresa's costume in the closet, Mme Irma?

IRMA: (*anxiously*) At the left. But first have Arthur removed.
I'm going to receive the Envoy.   925

SCENE VI

*A public square, with patches of shadow. In the background, at some
distance, we perceive the façade of the Grand Balcony, the blinds of
which are drawn.* CHANTAL *and* ROGER *are locked in embrace. Three
men seem to be watching over them. Black suits. Black sweaters. They
are holding machine-guns which are pointed at the Grand Balcony.*

CHANTAL: Keep me, if you will, my love, but keep me in your
heart. And wait for me.

ROGER: I love you with your body, with your hair, your bosom, your belly, your guts, your fluids, your smells. Chantal, I love you in my bed. They. . . .   5

CHANTAL: (*smiling*) They don't care a rap about me. But without them, *I'd* be nothing.

ROGER: You're mine. I . . .

CHANTAL: (*annoyed*) I know. You dragged me from the grave.
And no sooner do I shake off my wrappings than, ungrate-   10
ful wretch that I am, I gad about like a trollop. I plunge into
the adventure, and I escape you. (*Suddenly with tender irony.*)
But Roger, my love, you know I love you, you and only you.

ROGER: You've just said the word: you're escaping me. I can't
follow you in your heroic and stupid course.   15

CHANTAL: Ah ha! You're jealous of whom, or what? People
say that I soar above the insurrection, that I'm its soul and
voice, and you—you're rooted to the ground. That's why
you're sad. . . .

ROGER: Chantal, please, don't be vulgar. If you can help. . . .   20

(*One of the men draws near.*)

THE MAN: (*to* ROGER) Well, is it yes or is it no?

ROGER: What if she stays there?

THE MAN: I'm asking you to let us have her for two hours.

ROGER: Chantal belongs. . . .

25   CHANTAL: (*standing up*) To nobody!

ROGER: . . . To my section.

THE MAN: To the insurrection!

ROGER: If you want a woman to lead your men forward, then create one.

30   THE MAN: We looked for one, but there aren't any. We tried to build one up: nice voice, nice bosom, with the right kind of free and easy manner. But her eyes lacked fire, and you know that without fire. . . . We asked the North Section and the Port Section to let us have theirs; they weren't free.

35   CHANTAL: A woman like me? Another one? All I have is a hoarse voice and a face like an owl's. I give them or lend them for hatred's sake. I'm nothing, only my face, my voice, and inside me a sweet, poisonous kindness. D'you mean to tell me I have two popular rivals, two other poor

40   devils? Let them come, I'll show them! I have no rival.

ROGER: (*exploding*) I snatched her—snatched her from a grave. She's already escaping me and mounting to the sky. If I lend her to you. . . .

THE MAN: We're not asking you for that. If we take her, we're

45   hiring her.

CHANTAL: (*amused*) How much?

ROGER: Even if we let you have her to sing and spur on your district, if she gets bumped off we'll lose everything. No one can replace her.

50   THE MAN: She agreed to it.

ROGER: She doesn't belong to herself any more. She's ours. She's our sign. All that your women are good for is tearing up and carrying stones or reloading guns. I know that's useful, but. . . .

55   THE MAN: How many women do you want in exchange?

ROGER: (*thoughtfully*) Is a singer on the barricades as precious as all that?

THE MAN: How many? Ten women for Chantal?

(*A pause.*)

Twenty?

60   ROGER: Twenty women? You'd pay me twenty measly women, twenty oxen, twenty head of cattle? So Chantal's something special? And do you know where she comes from?

CHANTAL: (*to Roger, violently*) Every morning I go back—because at night I'm ablaze—I go back to a hovel and

65   sleep—chastely, my love!—and drink myself into a stupor on red wine. And I, with my grating voice, my sham anger, my cameo eyes, my painted illumination, my Andalusian hair, I comfort and enchant the rabble. They'll win and my victory will be a strange one.

70   ROGER: (*thoughtfully*) Twenty women for Chantal?

THE MAN: (*sharply*) A hundred.

ROGER: (*still pensively*) And it's probably because of her that we'll win. She already embodies the Revolution. . . .

THE MAN: A hundred. You agree?

75   ROGER: Where are you taking her? And what'll she have to do?

CHANTAL: We'll see. Don't worry, I was born under a lucky star. As for the rest of it, I realize my power. The people love me, they listen to me, they follow me.

ROGER: What will she do?

80   THE MAN: Hardly anything. As you know, we're attacking the Palace at dawn. Chantal will go in first. She'll sing from a balcony. That's all.

ROGER: A hundred women. A thousand and maybe more. So she's no longer a woman. The creature they make of her out of rage and despair has her price. In order to fight against   85 an image Chantal has frozen into an image. The fight is no longer taking place in reality, but in the lists. Field azure. It's the combat of allegories. None of us know any longer why we revolted. So she was bound to come around to that.

THE MAN: Well, is it yes? Answer, Chantal. It's for you to an-   90 swer.

CHANTAL: (*to THE MAN*) I'd like us to be alone for a moment. I've got something else to say.

(THE MAN *moves off and goes back into the shadow.*)

ROGER: (*violently*) I didn't steal you for you to become a unicorn or a two-headed eagle.   95

CHANTAL: You don't like unicorns.

ROGER: I've never been able to make love to them. (*He caresses her.*) Nor to you either.

CHANTAL: You mean I don't know how to love. I disappoint you. Yet I love you. And you hired me out for a hundred   100 female diggers.

ROGER: Forgive me. I need them. And yet I love you. I love you and I don't know how to tell you. I can't sing. And singing is the last resort.

CHANTAL: I'll have to leave before day-break. If the North   105 Section has come through, the Queen will be dead in an hour. It'll be the end of the Chief of Police. If not, we'll never get out of this bedlam.

ROGER: One minute more, my love, my life. It's still night.

CHANTAL: It's the hour when night breaks away from the day,   110 my dove, let me go.

ROGER: The minutes without you will be unbearable.

CHANTAL: We won't be separated, I swear to you. I'll speak to them in an icy tone and at the same time I'll murmur words of love for you. You'll hear them from here, and I'll   115 hear yours.

ROGER: They may keep you, Chantal. They're strong—strong as death.

CHANTAL: Don't be afraid, my love. I know their power. Your sweetness and tenderness are stronger. I'll speak to them   120 with severity. I'll tell them what the people demand. They'll listen to me because they'll be afraid. Let me go.

ROGER: (*screaming*) Chantal, I love you!

CHANTAL: Ah, my love, it's because I love you that I must hurry.   125

ROGER: You love me?

CHANTAL: I love you because you're tender and sweet, you the hardest and sternest of men. And your sweetness and tenderness are such that they make you as light as a shred of tulle, subtle as a flake of mist, airy as a caprice. Your   130 thick muscles, your arms, your thighs, your hands, are more unreal than the melting of day into night. You envelop me and I contain you.

ROGER: Chantal, I love you because you're hard and stern, you the tenderest and sweetest of women. And your   135 sweetness and tenderness are such that they make you as stern as a lesson, hard as hunger, inflexible as a block of ice. Your breasts, your skin, your hair are more real than the certainty of noon. You envelop me and I contain you.

140 CHANTAL: When I stand before them, when I speak to them, I'll be hearing your sighs and moans and the beating of your heart. Let me go.

(He holds her back.)

ROGER: You still have time. There's still some shadow along the walls. You'll go round the back of the Archbishop's
145 Palace. You know the way.

ONE OF THE REBELS: *(in a low voice)* It's time, Chantal. Day is breaking.

CHANTAL: Do you hear? They're calling me.

ROGER: *(suddenly irritated)* But why you? You'll never be able
150 to speak to them.

CHANTAL: I, better than anyone. I'm gifted.

ROGER: They're clever, cunning. . . .

CHANTAL: I'll invent gestures, postures, phrases. Before they even say a word, I'll understand, and you'll be proud of my
155 victory.

ROGER: Let the others go. *(He cries out to the rebels.)* You go! Or me, if you're afraid. I'll tell them they must give in, because we're the law.

CHANTAL: Don't listen to him. He's drunk. *(To ROGER)* All
160 *they* can do is fight, and all *you* can do is love me. That's the role you've learned to play. As for me, it's something else. At least the brothel has been of some use to me: it's taught me the art of pretence, of acting, I've had to play so many roles that I know almost all of them. And I've had
165 so many partners. . . .

ROGER: Chantal!

CHANTAL: And such artful ones, such cunning and eloquent ones, that my skill and trickery and eloquence are incomparable. I can be familiar with the Queen, the Hero, the
170 General, the heroic Troops . . . and can fool them all.

ROGER: You know all the roles, don't you? Just now, you were reciting lines to me, weren't you?

CHANTAL: One learns fast. You yourself. . . .

(The three rebels have drawn close.)

ONE OF THE REBELS: *(pulling CHANTAL)* Cut the speeches. Get
175 going.

ROGER: Chantal, stay!

(CHANTAL goes off, led by the rebels.)

CHANTAL: I envelop you and I contain you, my love. . . .

(She disappears in the direction of The Balcony, pushed by the three men.)

ROGER: *(alone)* . . . and I've had so many partners, and such artful ones, such cunning ones . . . that she did, after all,
180 have to try to give them an answer. The one they wanted. In a little while she'll have cunning and artful partners. She'll be the answer they're waiting for.

(As he speaks, the setting moves toward the left, the stage grows dark, and he himself, still speaking, moves off and into the wings. When the light goes on again, the setting of the next scene is in place.)

SCENE VII

The Funeral Studio in MME IRMA's *listing of the Studios. The studio is in ruins. The lace and velvet are torn. The artificial wreaths are tattered. An impression of desolation.* IRMA's *dress is in rags. So is the suit of* THE CHIEF OF POLICE. ARTHUR's *corpse is lying on a kind of fake tomb of fake black marble. Nearby, a new character,* THE COURT ENVOY. *embassy uniform. He is the only one unscathed.* CARMEN *is dressed as at the beginning. A tremendous explosion. Everything shatters.*

THE ENVOY: *(in a tone both airy and grave)* For more centuries than I can tell, the centuries have worn themselves thin refining me . . . subtilizing me . . . *(He smiles.)* From something or other about the explosion, from its power, in which was mingled a clinking of jewels and broken mir- 5 rors, I rather think it was the Royal Palace. *(The characters all look at each other, horror-stricken.)* Let us not display any emotion. So long as we are not like that. . . . *(He points to the corpse of Arthur.)*

IRMA: He didn't think he'd be acting his role of corpse this 10 evening in earnest.

THE ENVOY: *(smiling)* Our dear Minister of the Interior would have been delighted had not he himself met the same fate. It is unfortunately I who have had to replace him in his mission here, and I have no taste for pleasures of this kind. 15 *(He touches Arthur's corpse with his foot.)* Yes, this body would have sent our dear Minister into raptures.

IRMA: Not at all, your Excellency. It's make-believe that these gentlemen want. The Minister desired a fake corpse. But this one is real. Look at it: it's truer than life. His entire be- 20 ing is speeding towards immobility.

THE ENVOY: he was therefore meant for grandeur.

THE CHIEF OF POLICE: Him? He was a spineless dummy.

THE ENVOY: He was, like us, haunted by a quest of immobil- ity. By what we call the hieratic. And, in passing, allow me 25 to pay tribute to the imagination responsible for there be- ing a funeral parlour in this house.

IRMA: *(proudly)* And you see only part of it.

THE ENVOY: Whose idea was it?

IRMA: The Wisdom of Nations, your Excellency. 30

THE ENVOY: it does things well. But we were talking about the Queen, to protect whom is my mission.

THE CHIEF OF POLICE: You're going about it in a curious way. The Palace, according to what you say. . . .

THE ENVOY: *(smiling)* For the time being, Her Majesty is in 35 safety. But time is pressing. The prelate is said to have been beheaded. The Archbishop's Palace has been ransacked. The Law Court and Military Headquarters have been routed. . . .

THE CHIEF OF POLICE: But what about the Queen? 40

THE ENVOY: *(in a very light tone)* She's embroidering. For a moment she thought of nursing the wounded. But it was pointed out to her that, as the throne was threatened, she had to carry to an extreme the Royal prerogatives.

IRMA: Which are? 45

THE ENVOY: Absence. Her Majesty has retired to a chamber, in solitude. The disobedience of her people saddens her. She is embroidering a handkerchief. The design of it is as follows: the four corners will be adorned with poppy heads. In the middle of the handkerchief, embroidered in 50 pale blue silk, will be a swan, resting on the water of a lake. That's the only point about which Her Majesty is troubled: will it be the water of a lake, a pond or a pool? Or simply of a tank or a cup? It is a grave problem. We have

55 chosen it because it is insoluble, and the Queen can engross herself in an infinite meditation.

IRMA: Is the Queen amused?

THE ENVOY: Her Majesty is occupying herself in becoming entirely what she must be: the Queen. (*He looks at the*

60 *corpse.*) She, too, is moving rapidly towards immobility.

IRMA: And she's embroidering.

THE ENVOY: No, Madame, I say the Queen is embroidering a handkerchief, for though it is my duty to describe her, it is also my duty to conceal her.

65 IRMA: Do you mean she's not embroidering?

THE ENVOY: I mean that the Queen is embroidering and that she is not embroidering. She picks her nose, examines the pickings and lies down again. Then, she dries the dishes.

IRMA: The Queen?

70 THE ENVOY: She is not nursing the wounded. She is embroidering an invisible handkerchief. . . .

THE CHIEF OF POLICE: By God! What have you done with Her Majesty? I want a straight answer. I'm not amused. . . .

THE ENVOY: She is in a chest. She is sleeping. Wrapped in the

75 folds of royalty, she is snoring. . . .

THE CHIEF OF POLICE: (*threateningly*) Is the Queen dead?

THE ENVOY: (*unperturbed*) She is snoring and she is not snoring. Her head, which is tiny, supports, without wavering, a crown of metal and stones.

80 THE CHIEF OF POLICE: (*more and more threateningly*) Enough of that. You said the Palace was in danger. . . . What's to be done? I still have almost the entire police force behind me. Those who are still with me are ready to die for me. . . . They know who I am and what I'll do for them. . . . I, too,

85 have my role to play. But if the Queen is dead, everything is jeopardized. *She's* my support, it's in her name that I'm working to make a name for myself. How far has the rebellion gone? I want a clear answer.

THE ENVOY: You can judge from the state of this house. And

90 from your own. . . . All seems lost.

IRMA: You belong to the Court, your Excellency. Before coming here, I was with the troops. That's where I won my first spurs. I can assure you that I've known worse situations. The populace—from which I broke away with a kick of

95 my heels—the populace is howling beneath my windows, which have been multiplied by the bombs: my house stands its ground. My rooms aren't intact, but they've held up. My whores, except for one lunatic, are on the job. If the centre of the palace is a woman like me. . . .

100 THE ENVOY: (*imperturbably*) The Queen is standing on one foot in the middle of an empty room, and she. . .

THE CHIEF OF POLICE: That'll do! I've had enough of your riddles. For me, the Queen has to be someone. And the situation has to be concrete. Describe it to me exactly. I've

105 no time to waste.

THE ENVOY: Whom do you want to save?

THE CHIEF OF POLICE: The Queen!

CARMEN: The flag!

IRMA: My hide!

110 THE ENVOY: (*to* THE CHIEF OF POLICE) If you're eager to save the Queen—and, beyond her, our flag, and all its gold

fringe, and its eagle, cords and pole, would you describe them to me?

THE CHIEF OF POLICE: Until now I've served the things you mention, and served them with distinction, and without 115 bothering to know any more about them than what I saw. And I'll continue. What's happening about the rebellion?

THE ENVOY: (*resignedly*) The garden gates will, for a moment longer, hold back the crowd. The guards are devoted, like us, with an obscure devotion. They'll die for their sovereign. 120 They'll give their blood. Unhappily there won't be enough of it to drown the rebellion. Sand bags have been piled up in front of the doors. In order to confuse even reason, Her Majesty removes herself from one secret chamber to another, from the servants' hall to the Throne Room, from the 125 latrines to the chicken-coop, the chapel, the guardroom. . . . She makes herself unfindable and thus attains a threatened invisibility. So much for the inside of the palace.

THE CHIEF OF POLICE: What about the Generalissimo?

THE ENVOY: Gone mad. He wanders among the crowd, 130 where nobody will harm him, protected by his madness.

THE CHIEF OF POLICE: What about the Attorney-General?

THE ENVOY: Died of fright.

THE CHIEF OF POLICE: And the Bishop?

THE ENVOY: His case is more difficult. The Church is secre- 135 tive. Nothing is known about him. Nothing definite. His decapitated head was said to have been seen on the handlebars of a bicycle. Of course, the rumour was false. We're therefore relying entirely on you. But your orders aren't getting through. 140

THE CHIEF OF POLICE: Down below, in the corridors and studios, I have enough loyal men to protect us all. They can remain in contact with my offices. . . .

THE ENVOY: (*interrupting him*) Are your men in uniform?

THE CHIEF OF POLICE: Of course. They're my bodyguard. Do 145 you imagine me with a bodyguard in sport jackets? They're in uniform. Black ones. With my emblem. They're brave. They, too, want to win.

THE ENVOY: To save what?

(*A pause.*)

Won't you answer? Would it perturb you to see things as 150 they are? To gaze at the world tranquilly and accept responsibility for your gaze, whatever it might see?

THE CHIEF OF POLICE: But, after all, in coming to see me, you did have something definite in mind, didn't you? You had a plan? Let's hear it. 155

(*Suddenly a terrific blast. Both men, but not* IRMA, *fall flat on the floor, then stand up again and dust each other off.*)

THE ENVOY: That may have been the Royal Palace. Long live the royal Palace!

IRMA: But then, just before . . . the explosion?

THE ENVOY: A royal palace is forever blowing up. In fact, that's exactly what it is: a continuous explosion. 160

(*Enter* CARMEN. *She throws a black sheet over the corpse of* ARTHUR *and tidies things up a bit.*)

THE CHIEF OF POLICE: (*aghast*) But the Queen. . . . Then the Queen's under the rubble?

THE ENVOY: (*smiling mysteriously*) You need not worry. Her Majesty is in a safe place. And that phoenix, when dead,
165 can rise up from the ashes of a royal palace. I can understand your impatience to prove your valour, your devotion . . . but the Queen will wait for you as long as necessary. (*To* IRMA) I must pay tribute, Madame, to your coolness. And to your courage. They are worthy of the highest re-
170 spect. . . . (*Musingly*) of the highest. . . .

IRMA: You're forgetting to whom you're speaking. I may run a brothel, but I wasn't born of the marriage of the moon and a crocodile. I've lived among the people. . . . All the same, it was quite a blast. And the people. . . .

175 THE ENVOY: (*severely*) That's behind you. When life departs, the hands cling to a sheet. What significance has that rag when you're about to penetrate into the providential fixity?

IRMA: Sir? Do you mean I'm at my last gasp?

THE ENVOY: (*examining her, part by part*) Splendid head! Study
180 thighs! Solid shoulders!

IRMA: (*laughing*) So I've been told, and it didn't make me lose my head. In short, I'll make a presentable corpse if the rebels act fast and if they leave me intact. But if the Queen is dead. . . .

185 THE ENVOY: (*bowing*) Long live the Queen, Madame.

IRMA: (*first taken aback, then irritated*) I don't like to be kidded! Pack up your nonsense, and clear out.

THE ENVOY: (*spiritedly*) I've described the situation. The populace, in its joy and fury, is at the brink of ecstasy. It's for
190 us to press it forward.

IRMA: Instead of standing here and talking drivel, go poke around for the Queen in the rubble of the Palace and pull her out. Even if slightly roasted. . . .

THE ENVOY: (*severely*) No. A queen who's been cooked and
195 mashed up isn't presentable. And even when alive she was less beautiful than you.

IRMA: Her lineage was more ancient . . . she was older. . . . And, after all, maybe she was just as frightened as I.

THE CHIEF OF POLICE: It is in order to approach her, to be
200 worthy of her, that one makes such a mighty effort. But what if one is Herself?

(CARMEN *stops in order to listen.*)

IRMA: I don't know how to talk. I'm always hemming and hawing.

THE ENVOY: All must unfold in a silence that etiquette allows
205 no one to break.

THE CHIEF OF POLICE: I'm going to have the rubble of the Palace cleared away. If, as you said, the Queen was in a chest, it may be possible to save her.

THE ENVOY: (*shrugging his shoulders*) It was made of rosewood!
210 And it was so old, so worn. . . . (*To* IRMA, *running his hand over the back of her neck*) Yes, it requires solid vertebrae . . . they've got to carry several pounds . . .

THE CHIEF OF POLICE: . . . and resist the axe, don't they? Irma, don't listen to him! (*To* THE ENVOY.) And what about me?
215 I'm the strong-man of this country, but it's because I've based my power on the crown. I bamboozle the great majority, but it's because I had the smart idea of serving the Queen . . . even if at times I've seemed to do some shabby things . . . seemed to, d'you hear? . . . It's not Irma. . . .

220 IRMA: (*to* THE ENVOY) I'm really very weak, your Excellency, and very frail. Though a while ago I was boasting. . . .

THE ENVOY: (*with authority*) Around this delicate and precious kernel we'll forge a shell of gold and iron. But you must make up your mind quickly.

THE CHIEF OF POLICE: (*furiously*) Above me! So Irma would 225 be above *me*! All the trouble I've gone to in order to be master would be wasted effort. Whereas, nice and snug in her studio, all she'd have to do is nod her head. . . . If I'm in power, I'm willing to impose Irma. . . .

THE ENVOY: Impossible. It's from her that you must derive 230 your authority. She must appear by divine right. Don't forget that you're not yet represented in her studios.

IRMA: Allow me just a little more respite. . . .

THE ENVOY: A few seconds, for time is pressing.

THE CHIEF OF POLICE: If only there were some way of know- 235 ing what the late sovereign would have thought of it. We can't decide just like that. To appropriate a heritage. . . .

THE ENVOY: (*scornfully*) You're knuckling under already. Do you tremble if there's no authority above you to decide? But it's for Mme Irma to declare. . . . 240

IRMA: (*in a highfalutin tone*) In the records of our family, which goes a long way back, there was some question of. . . .

THE ENVOY: (*severely*) Nonsense, Mme Irma. In our vaults, genealogists are working day and night. History is submis- 245 sive to them. I said we hadn't a minute to waste in conquering our people, but beware! Although the populace may worship you, its high-flown pride is capable of sacrificing you. It sees you as red, either crimson or blood-red. If it kills its idols and thrusts them into the sewers, it 250 will sweep you up with them. . . .

(*The same explosion is heard again.* THE ENVOY *smiles.*)

THE CHIEF OF POLICE: It's an enormous risk. . . .

CARMEN: That's for Mme Irma to decide. (*To* IRMA.) The ornaments are ready.

IRMA: (*to* THE ENVOY) Are you quite sure of what you're saying? 255 Do you really know what's going on? What about your spies?

THE ENVOY: They inform us as accurately as the peep-holes that peer into your studios. (*Smiling.*) And I may add that we consult them with the same pleasurable thrill. But we must act fast. We're engaged in a race against the clock. It's 260 we or they. Mme. Irma, think speedily.

IRMA: (*holding her head in her hands*) I'm hurrying, sir. I'm approaching my destiny as fast as I can. (*To* CARMEN) Go see what they're doing.

CARMEN: I've locked them up. 265

IRMA: Get them ready.

THE ENVOY: (*to* CARMEN) What about you, what's to be done with you?

CARMEN: I'm here for eternity.

(*Exit* CARMEN.)

THE ENVOY: One other matter, a more delicate one. I men- 270 tioned an image that for some days now has been mounting in the sky of the revolution.

IRMA: The revolution has its sky too?

THE ENVOY: Don't envy it. Chantal's image is circulating in the streets. An image that resembles her and does not resemble 275 her. She towers above the battles. At first, people were fighting against illustrious and illusory tyrants, then for freedom. Tomorrow they'll be ready to die for Chantal alone.

280 IRMA: The ungrateful wretch! She who was in such demand as Lucrezia Borgia.

THE CHIEF OF POLICE: She won't last. She's like me: she has neither father nor mother. And if she becomes an image, we'll make use of it. (*A pause.*) . . . A mask. . . .

THE ENVOY: Everything beautiful on earth you owe to masks.

(*Suddenly a bell rings. irma is about to dart forward, but stops.*)

285 IRMA: (*to* THE CHIEF OF POLICE) It's Carmen. What's she saying? What are they doing?

(THE CHIEF OF POLICE *lifts one of the earphones.*)

THE CHIEF OF POLICE: (*transmitting the message*) While waiting to go home, they're standing around looking at themselves in the mirrors.

290 IRMA: Tell her to smash the mirrors or veil them.

(*A silence. Then a burst of machine-gun fire.*)

My mind's made up. I presume I've been summoned from all eternity and that God will bless me. I'm going to prepare myself by prayer.

THE ENVOY: (*gravely*) Do you have the outfits?

295 IRMA: My closets are as famous as my studios. (*Suddenly worried.*) But everything must be in an awful state! The bombs, the plaster, the dust. Tell Carmen to brush the costumes! (*To* THE CHIEF OF POLICE) George . . . this is our last minute together! From now on, we'll no longer be us. . . .

(THE ENVOY *discreetly moves off and goes to the window.*)

300 THE CHIEF OF POLICE: (*tenderly*) But I love you.

THE ENVOY: (*turning around, and in a tone of detachment*) Think of that mountain north of the city. All the labourers were at work when the rebellion broke out. . . . (*A pause.*) I refer to a project for a tomb. . . .

305 THE CHIEF OF POLICE: (*greedily*) What's the plan of it?

THE ENVOY: Later. A mountain of red marble hollowed out with rooms and niches, and in the middle a tiny diamond sentry-box.

THE CHIEF OF POLICE: Will I be able to stand there—or sit—

310 and keep vigil over my entire death?

THE ENVOY: He who gets it will be there—dead—for eternity. The world will centre about it. About it will rotate the planets and the suns. From a secret point of the same room will run a road that will lead, after many and many

315 a complication, to another room where mirrors will reflect to infinity . . . I say infinity. . . .

THE CHIEF OF POLICE: O.K.!

THE ENVOY: . . . the image of a dead man.

IRMA: (*hugging* THE CHIEF OF POLICE *to her*) So I'll be real? My

320 robe will be real? My lace, my jewels will be real? The rest of the world. . . .

(*Machine-gun fire.*)

THE ENVOY: (*after a last glance through the shutters*) Yes, but make haste. Go to your apartments. Embroider an inter-

minable handkerchief. . . . (*To* THE CHIEF OF POLICE) You, give your last orders to your last men. (*He goes to a mirror,* 325 *takes from his pocket a whole collection of decorations and fastens them to his tunic.*) (*In a vulgar tone*) And make it snappy. I don't have time to listen to your crap.

SCENE VIII

The scene is the balcony itself, which projects beyond the façade of the brothel. The shutters, which face the audience, are closed. Suddenly, all the shutters open by themselves. The edge of the balcony is at the very edge of the footlights. Through the windows can be seen THE BISHOP, THE GENERAL, *and* THE JUDGE, *who are getting ready. Finally, the French windows are flung wide open. The three men come out on the balcony. First* THE BISHOP, *then* THE GENERAL, *then* THE JUDGE. *They are followed by the Hero. Then comes* THE QUEEN: MME IRMA, *wearing a diadem on her brow and an ermine cloak. All the characters step forward and take their positions with great timidity. They are silent. They simply show themselves. All are of huge proportions, gigantic—except the Hero, that is,* THE CHIEF OF POLICE—*and are wearing their ceremonial garments, which are torn and dusty. Then, near them, but not on the balcony, appears the beggar. In a gentle voice, he cries out:*

THE BEGGAR: Long live the Queen! (*He goes off timidly, as he came.*)

(*Finally, a strong wind stirs the curtains:* CHANTAL *appears.* THE QUEEN *bows to her. A shot.* CHANTAL *falls.* THE GENERAL *and* THE QUEEN *carry her away dead.*)

SCENE IX

IRMA's *room, which looks as if it had been hit by a hurricane. Rear, a large two-panelled mirror which forms the wall. Right, a door; left, another. Three cameras on tripods. Next to each is a photographer, three very wide-awake young men with ironic expressions. Each is wearing a black leather jacket and close-fitting blue jeans. Enter, in turn, very timidly, right,* THE BISHOP *and, left,* THE JUDGE *and* THE GENERAL. *On seeing each other, they bow deeply. Then,* THE GENERAL *salutes and* THE BISHOP *blesses* THE GENERAL.

THE JUDGE: (*with a sign of relief*) What we've been through!

THE GENERAL: And it's not over! We have to invent an entire life . . . That's hard. . . .

THE BISHOP: Hard or not, we've got to go through with it. We can no longer back out. Before entering the carriage. . . . 5

THE GENERAL: The slowness of the carriage!

THE BISHOP: . . . entering the carriage, it was still possible to chuck the whole business. But now. . . .

THE JUDGE: Do you think we were recognized? I was in the middle, hidden by your profiles. Opposite me, Irma. . . . 10 (*The name astonishes him.*) Irma? The Queen. . . . The Queen hid my face. . . . do you think we were?

THE BISHOP: No danger of that. You know whom I saw . . . at the right (*unable to keep from laughing*) with his fat, good-natured mug and pink cheeks, though the town was in 15 smithereens? (*The other two smile.*) With his dimples and decayed teeth? And who threw himself on my hand . . . I thought to bite me, and I was about to pull away my fingers . . . to kiss my ring? Who? My fruit-and-vegetable man.

(THE JUDGE *laughs.*)

20 THE GENERAL: (*grimly*) The slowness of the carriage. The carriage wheels on the people's feet and hands! The dust!

THE JUDGE: (*uneasily*) I was opposite the Queen. Through the back window, a woman. . . .

THE BISHOP: (*continuing his account*) I saw her too, at the left-
25 hand door, she was running along and throwing kisses at us!

THE GENERAL: (*more and more grimly*) The slowness of the carriage! We moved forward so slowly amidst the sweaty mob! Their roars were like threats, but they were only cheering. Someone could have hamstrung the horses,
30 fired a shot, could have unhitched the traces and harnessed *us*, attached us to the shaft or the horses, could have drawn and quartered us or turned us into draught-horses. But no. Just flowers tossed from a window, and a people hailing its queen, who stood upright beneath her golden
35 crown. (*A pause.*) And the horses going at a walking pace . . . and the Envoy standing on the footboard!

(*A silence.*)

THE BISHOP: (*ironically*) No one could have recognized us. We were in the gold and glitter. They were blinded. It hit them in the eye. . . .
40 THE JUDGE: it wouldn't have taken much. . . .

THE BISHOP: (*same*) Exhausted by the fighting, choked by the dust, the people stood waiting for the procession. The procession was all they saw. In any case, we can no longer back out. We've been chosen.
45 THE GENERAL: By whom?

THE BISHOP: (*with sudden grandiloquence*) By glory in person.

THE GENERAL: This masquerade?

THE BISHOP: It lies with us for this masquerade to change meaning. First, we must use words that magnify. We must
50 act fast, and with precision. No errors allowed. (*With authority*) As for me, instead of being merely the symbolic head of the country's church, I've decided to become its actual head. Instead of blessing and blessing and blessing until I've had my fill, I'm going to sign decrees and ap-
55 point priests. The clergy is being organized. A basilica is under construction. It's all in there. (*He points to a folder under his arm.*) Full of plans and projects. (*To* THE JUDGE) What about you?

THE JUDGE: (*looking at his wristwatch*) I have an appointment
60 with a number of magistrates. We're drafting bills, we're revising the legal code. (*To* THE GENERAL) What about you?

THE GENERAL: Oh, me, your ideas drift through my poor head like smoke through a log shanty. The art of war's not something you can master just like that. The general-staffs. . . .
65 THE BISHOP: (*interrupting*) Like everything else, the fate of arms can be read in your stars. Read your stars, damn it!

THE GENERAL: That's easy to say. But when the Hero comes back, planted firmly on his rump, as if on a horse. . . . For, of course, nothing's happened yet?
70 THE BISHOP: Nothing. But let's not crow too soon. Though his image hasn't yet been consecrated by the brothel, it still may. If so, we're done for. Unless you make a positive effort to seize power.

(*Suddenly, he breaks off. One of the photographers has cleared his throat, as if to spit. Another has snapped his fingers like a Spanish dancer.*)

THE BISHOP: (*severely*) Indeed, you're here. Please do your job quickly, and in silence, if possible. You're to take each of 75 our profiles, one smiling, the other rather stern.

FIRST PHOTOGRAPHER: We'll do our job, don't worry. (*To* THE BISHOP) Get set for prayer, because the world ought to be bombarded with the picture of a pious man.

THE BISHOP: (*without moving*) In fervent meditation. 80

FIRST PHOTOGRAPHER: Right, fervent. Get set.

THE BISHOP: (*ill at ease*) But . . . how?

FIRST PHOTOGRAPHER: Don't you know how to compose yourself for prayer? Okay, facing both God and the camera. Hands together. Head up. Eyes down. That's the clas- 85 sical pose. A return to order, a return to classicism.

THE BISHOP: (*kneeling*) Like this?

FIRST PHOTOGRAPHER: (*looking at him with curiosity*) That's it. . . . (*He looks at the camera.*) No you're not in the frame. . . . (*Shuffling on his knees,* THE BISHOP *places himself in front* 90 *of the camera.*) Okay.

SECOND PHOTOGRAPHER: (*to* THE JUDGE) Would you mind pulling a longer face? You don't quite look like a judge. A little longer.

THE JUDGE: Horselike? Sullen? 95

SECOND PHOTOGRAPHER: Horselike and sullen, my Lord. And both hands in front, on your brief. What I want is a shot of *the* Judge. A good photographer is one who gives a definitive image. Perfect.

FIRST PHOTOGRAPHER: (*to* THE BISHOP) Turn your head . . . just 100 a little. . . . (*He turns* THE BISHOP's *head.*)

THE BISHOP: (*angrily*) You're unscrewing the neck of a prelate!

FIRST PHOTOGRAPHER: I want a three-quarter view of you praying, my Lord.

SECOND PHOTOGRAPHER: (*to* THE JUDGE) My Lord, if you 105 possibly can, a little more severity. . . . with a pendulous lip. (*Crying out*) That's it! Perfect! Stay that way! (*He rushes behind his camera, but there is a flash before he gets there.* THE FIRST PHOTOGRAPHER *has just taken his shot.* THE SECOND PHOTOGRAPHER *puts his head under the black hood of his* 110 *camera.*)

THE GENERAL: (*to* THE THIRD PHOTOGRAPHER) The finest pose is Poniatovsky's.

THIRD PHOTOGRAPHER: (*striking a pose*) With the sword?

THE GENERAL: No, no. That's Lafayette. No, with the arm ex- 115 tended and the marshal's baton. . . .

THIRD PHOTOGRAPHER: Ah, you mean Wellington?

THE GENERAL: Unfortunately, I don't have a baton. . . .

(*Meanwhile,* THE FIRST PHOTOGRAPHER *has gone back to* THE 120 BISHOP, *who has not moved, and looks him over silently.*)

THIRD PHOTOGRAPHER: (*to* THE GENERAL) We've got just what we need. Here, now strike the pose. (*Rolls up a sheet of paper in the form of a marshal's baton. He hands it to* THE GENERAL, *who strikes a pose, and then dashes to his camera. A* 125 *flash:* THE SECOND PHOTOGRAPHER *has just taken his shot.*)

THE BISHOP: (*to* THE FIRST PHOTOGRAPHER) I hope the negative comes out well. Now we'll have to flood the world with a picture of me receiving the Eucharist. Unfortunately, we don't have a Host on hand. . . . 130

FIRST PHOTOGRAPHER: leave it to us, Monsignor. Newspapermen are a resourceful bunch. (*Calls out*) My Lord!

(THE JUDGE *approaches.*)

I'm going to try a stunt. Lend me a hand a minute. (*Without further ado, he takes him by the hand and sets him in place.*)
135 But I want only your hand to show . . . there . . . roll up your sleeve a little . . . above Monsignor's tongue. More. Okay. (*Still fumbling in his pocket. To the bishop.*) Stick out your tongue. More. Okay. (*Still fumbling in his pocket. A flash:* THE GENERAL *has just been photographed; he resumes his natural pose.*) Damn it! I don't have a thing! (*He looks*
140 *about. To* THE GENERAL) That's perfect. May I? (*Without waiting for an answer, he takes* THE GENERAL's *monocle from his eye and goes back to the group formed by* THE BISHOP *and* THE JUDGE. *He makes the* judge *hold the monocle above* THE
145 BISHOP's *tongue as if it were a Host, and he rushes to his camera. A flash.*)

(THE QUEEN, *who has entered with* THE ENVOY, *has been watching these proceedings for some moments.*)

THE ENVOY: It's a true image, born of a false spectacle.
FIRST PHOTOGRAPHER: (*cynically*) That's common practice,
150 your Majesty. When some rebels were captured, we paid a militiaman to bump off a chap I'd just sent to buy me a packet of cigarettes. The photo shows a rebel shot down while trying to escape.
THE QUEEN: Monstrous!
THE ENVOY: But have things ever happened otherwise? His-
155 tory was lived so that a glorious page might be written, and then read. It's reading that counts. (*To the photographers*) Gentlemen, the Queen informs me that she congratulates you. She asks that you return to your posts.

(*The* THREE PHOTOGRAPHERS *puts their heads under the black hoods of their cameras.*)
(*A silence.*)

THE QUEEN: (*in a low voice, as if to herself*) Isn't he here?
160 THE ENVOY: (*to the Three Figures*) The Queen would like to know what you're doing, what you plan to do.
THE BISHOP: We've been recovering as many dead bodies as possible. We were planning to embalm them and lodge them in our heaven. Your grandeur requires your having
165 slaughtered the rebels wholesale. We shall keep for ourselves only a few of our fallen martyrs, to whom we shall pay honour that will honour us.
THE QUEEN: (*to* THE ENVOY) That will serve my glory, will it not?
THE ENVOY: (*smiling*) The massacres, too, are revels wherein
170 the people indulge to their heart's content in the pleasure of hating us. I am speaking, to be sure, of "our" people. They can at last set up a statute to us in their hearts so as to shower it with blows. At least, I hope so.
THE QUEEN: Does that mean that leniency and kindness are
175 of no avail?
THE ENVOY: (*smiling*) A St. Vincent de Paul Studio?
THE QUEEN: (*testily to* THE JUDGE) You, my Lord, what's being done? I'd ordered fewer death penalties and more sentences to forced labour. I hope the underground galleries
180 are finished? (*To* THE ENVOY) It's the word galley-slaves that made me think of the galleries of the Mausoleum. Are they finished?
THE JUDGE: Completely. And open to the public on Sundays. Some of the arches are completely adorned with the
185 skeletons of prisoners who died during the digging.

THE QUEEN: (*in the direction of* THE BISHOP) Very good. What about the Church? I suppose that anyone who hasn't done at least a week's work on this extraordinary chapel is in a state of mortal sin?
(THE BISHOP *bows. To the General*) As for you, I'm aware of 190 your severity. Your soldiers are watching over the workers, and they thoroughly deserve the fine name of builders. (*Smiling gently, with feigned fatigue.*) For, as you know, gentlemen, I plan to present this tomb to the Hero. You know how downcast he feels, don't you, and how he suffers at 195 not yet having been impersonated?
THE GENERAL: (*plucking up courage*) He'll have a hard time attaining glory. The places have been filled for ages. Every niche has its statue. (*Fatuously*) We, at least. . . .
THE JUDGE: That's how it always is when one wants to start 200 from the bottom. And particularly by rejecting or neglecting the traditional. The established order of things, as it were.
THE QUEEN: (*suddenly vibrant*) Yet it was he who saved everything. He wants glory. He insists on breaking open the gates of legend, but he has allowed you to carry on with 205 your ceremonies.
THE BISHOP: (*arrogantly*) To be frank, Madame, we're no longer concerned with that. As for me, my skirt hampers me, and my hands get caught in the lace. We're going to have to act. 210
THE QUEEN: (*indignantly*) Act? You? You mean to say you're going to strip us of our power?
THE JUDGE: We have to fulfill our functions, don't we?
THE QUEEN: Functions! You're planning to overthrow him, to lower, him to take his place! 215
THE BISHOP: Somewhere in time—in time or in space!— perhaps there exist high dignitaries invested with absolute dignity and attired with veritable ornaments. . . .
THE QUEEN: (*very angrily*) Veritable! And what about those? You mean that those you're wrapped and swathed in—my 220 whole paraphernalia!—which come from my closets, aren't veritable?
THE BISHOP: (*pointing to* THE JUDGE's *ermine, the silk of his robe, etc.*) Rabbit, sateen, machine-made lace . . . you think we're going to be satisfied with make-believe to the end 225 of our days?
THE QUEEN: (*outraged*) But this morning . . . (*She breaks off. Enter* THE CHIEF OF POLICE, *quietly, humbly.*) George, beware of them.
THE CHIEF OF POLICE: (*trying to smile*) I think that . . . victory 230 . . . we've won the day. May I sit down?

(*He sits down. Then he looks about, as if questioning everyone.*)

THE ENVOY: (*ironically*) No, nobody's come yet. Nobody has yet felt the need to abolish himself in your fascinating image.
THE CHIEF OF POLICE: That means the projects you submit- 235 ted to me aren't every effective. (*To* THE QUEEN) Nothing? Nobody?
THE QUEEN: (*very gently*) Nobody. And yet, the blinds have been drawn again. The men ought to be coming in. Besides, the apparatus has been set up; so we'll be informed 240 by a full peal of bells.
THE ENVOY: (*to* THE CHIEF OF POLICE) You didn't care for the project I submitted to you this morning. Yet that's the image that haunts you and that ought to haunt others.

245 THE CHIEF OF POLICE: Ineffectual.

THE ENVOY: (*showing a photographic negative*) The executioner's red coat and his axe. I suggested amaranth red and the steel axe.

THE QUEEN: (*testily*) Studio 14, known as the Studio of Exe-
250 cutions. Already been done.

THE JUDGE: (*making himself agreeable, to* THE CHIEF OF POLICE) Yet you're feared.

THE CHIEF OF POLICE: I'm afraid that they fear and envy a man, but . . . (*groping for words*) . . . but not a wrinkle, for example,
255 or a curl . . . or a cigar . . . or a whip. The latest image that was proposed to me. . . . I hardly dare mention it to you.

THE JUDGE: Was it . . . very audacious?

THE CHIEF OF POLICE: Very. Too audacious. I'd never dare tell you what it was. (*Suddenly, he seems to make up his mind.*)
260 Gentlemen, I have sufficient confidence in your judgment and devotion. After all, I want to carry on the fight by bold-ness of ideas as well. It was this: I've been advised to appear in the form of a gigantic phallus, a prick of great stature. . . .

(*The Three Figures and* THE QUEEN *are dumbfounded.*)

THE QUEEN: George! You?
265 THE CHIEF OF POLICE: What do you expect? If I'm to sym-bolize the nation, your joint. . . .

THE ENVOY: (*to* THE QUEEN) Allow him, Madame. It's the tone of the age.

THE JUDGE: A phallus? Of great stature? You mean—enor-
270 mous?

THE CHIEF OF POLICE: Of my stature.

THE JUDGE: But that'll be very difficult to bring off.

THE ENVOY: Not so very. What with new techniques and our rubber industry, remarkable things can be worked out. No
275 I'm not worried about that, but rather . . . (*turning to* THE BISHOP) . . . what the Church will think of it?

THE BISHOP: (*after reflection, shrugging his shoulders*) No definite pronouncement can be made this evening. To be sure, the idea is a bold one. (*To* THE CHIEF OF POLICE) But if your
280 case is desperate, we shall have to examine the matter. For . . . it would be a formidable figure-head, and if you were to transmit yourself in that guise to posterity. . . .

THE CHIEF OF POLICE: (*gently*) Would you like to see the model?
285 THE JUDGE: (*to* THE CHIEF OF POLICE) It's wrong of you to be impatient. *We* waited two thousand years to perfect our roles. Keep hoping. . . .

THE GENERAL: (*interrupting him*) Glory is achieved in combat. You haven't enough illustrious Waterloos to your credit.
290 Keep fighting, or sit down and wait out the regulation two thousand years.

(*Everyone laughs.*)

THE QUEEN: (*violently*) You don't care a damn about his suf-fering. And it was I who singled you out! I who fished you out of the rooms of my brothel and hired you for his
295 glory. And you agreed to serve him.

(*A pause.*)

THE BISHOP: (*firmly*) It is at this point that a question, and a very serious one, arises: are you going to use what we rep-resent, or are we (*he points to the other two Figures*) going to use you to serve what we represent?

300 THE QUEEN: (*flaring up*) Your conditions, you? Puppets who without their rabbit, as you put it, would be nothing, you, a man who was made to dance naked—in other words, skinned!—on the public squares of Seville and Toledo! and who danced! To the click of castanets! Your condi-
305 tions, my Lord?

THE BISHOP: That day I *had* to dance. As for the rabbit, it's what it *must* be—the sacred image of ermine—it has the same power.

THE CHIEF OF POLICE: For the time being, but. . . .

310 THE BISHOP: (*getting excited*) Exactly. So long as we were in a room in a brothel, we belonged to our own fantasies. But once having exposed them, having named them, having proclaimed them, we're now tied up with human beings, tied to you, and forced to go on with this adventure ac-
315 cording to the laws of visibility.

THE CHIEF OF POLICE: You have no power. I alone. . . .

THE BISHOP: Then we shall go back to our rooms and there continue the quest of an absolute dignity. We ought never to have left them. For we were content there, and it was you
320 who came and dragged us away. For ours was a happy state. And absolutely safe. In peace, in comfort, behind shutters, behind padded curtains, protected by a police force that pro-tects brothels, we were able to be a general, judge and bishop to the point of perfection and to the point of rapture! You
325 tore us brutally from that delicious, untroubled state.

THE GENERAL: (*interrupting* THE BISHOP) My breeches! What joy when I pulled on my breeches! I now sleep in my general's breeches. I eat in my breeches, I waltz—*when* I waltz—in my breeches, I live in my general's breeches. I'm
330 a general the way one is a priest.

THE JUDGE: I'm just a dignity represented by a skirt.

THE GENERAL: (*to* THE BISHOP) At no moment can I prepare myself—I used to start a month in advance!—prepare my-self for pulling on my general's boots and breeches. I'm
335 rigged in them for all eternity. By Jove, I no longer dream.

THE BISHOP: (*to* THE CHIEF OF POLICE) You see, he no longer dreams. Our ornamental purity, our luxurious and barren—and sublime—appearance has been eaten away. It's gone for-ever. Well and good. But the taste of that bitter delight of
340 responsibility of which I've spoken has remained with us, and we find it to our liking. Our rooms are no longer secret. You hurt us by dragging us into the light. But as for danc-ing? You spoke of dancing? You referred to that notorious af-ternoon when, stripped—or skinned, whichever word
345 amuses you—stripped of our priestly ornaments, we had to dance naked on the cathedral square. I danced, I admit it, with people laughing at me, but at least I danced. Whereas now, if ever I have an itch for that kind of thing, I'll have to go on the sly to the Balcony, where there probably is a room
350 prepared for prelates who like to be ballerinas a few hours a week. No, no. . . . We're going to live in the light, but with all that that implies. We—magistrate, soldier, prelate—we're going to act in such a way as to impoverish our ornaments unceasingly! We're going to render them useful! But in or-
355 der that they be of use, and of use to us—since it's your or-der that we've chosen to defend—you must be the first to recognize them and pay homage to them.

THE CHIEF OF POLICE: (*calmly*) I shall be not the hundred-thousandth-reflection-within-a-reflection in a mirror, but

360 the One and Only, into whom a hundred thousand want to merge. If not for me, you'd have all been done for. The expression "beaten hollow" would have had meaning. (*He is going to regain his authority increasingly.*)

THE QUEEN: (*To* THE BISHOP, *insinuatingly*) You happen to be
365 wearing that robe this evening simply because you were unable to clear out of the studios in time. You just couldn't tear yourself away from one of your hundred thousand reflections, but the clients are beginning to come back. . . . There's no rush yet, but Carmen has recorded several en-
370 tries. . . . (*To* THE CHIEF OF POLICE) Don't let them intimidate you. Before the revolt, there were lots of them. . . . (*To* THE BISHOP) If you hadn't had the abominable idea of having Chantal assassinated. . . .

THE BISHOP: (*frightened*) A stray bullet!

375 THE QUEEN: Stray or not, Chantal was assassinated on *my* balcony! When she came back here to see me, to visit her boss. . . .

THE BISHOP: I had the presence of mind to make her one of our saints.

380 THE CHIEF OF POLICE: A traditional attitude. A churchman's reflex. But there's no need to congratulate yourself. The image of her on our flag has hardly any power. Or rather. . . . I've had reports from all quarters that owing to the possibility that she was playing a double game,
385 Chantal has been condemned by those she was supposed to save. . . .

THE QUEEN: (*anxiously*) But then the whole business is starting all over again?

(*From this point on* THE QUEEN *and* THE CHIEF OF POLICE *will seem very agitated.* THE QUEEN *will go to a window and draw the curtains after trying to look out into the street.*)

THE ENVOY: All of it.

390 THE GENERAL: Are we going to have to . . . to get into the carriage again? The slowness of the carriage!

THE BISHOP: If I had Chantal shot, and then canonized, if I had her image blazoned on our flag. . . .

THE QUEEN: It's *my* image that ought to be there. . . .

395 THE ENVOY: You're already on the postage stamps, on the banknotes, on the seals in the police-stations.

THE GENERAL: The slowness of the carriage . . .

THE QUEEN: Will I therefore never be who I am?

THE ENVOY: Never again.

400 THE QUEEN: Every event of my life—my blood that trickles if I scratch myself. . . .

THE ENVOY: Everything will be written for you with a capital letter.

THE QUEEN: But that's Death?

405 THE ENVOY: It is indeed.

THE CHIEF OF POLICE: (*with sudden authority*) It means death for all of you. And that's why I'm sure of you. At least, as long as I've not been impersonated, because after that I'll just sit back and take it easy. (*Inspired*) Besides, I'll know by a sud-
410 den weakness of my muscles that my image is escaping from me to go and haunt men's minds. When that happens my visible end will be near. For the time being, and if we have to act . . . (*To* THE BISHOP) who will assume real responsibilities? You? (*He shrugs.*) Be logical: if you are what you are,
415 judge, general, bishop, it's because you wanted to become

that and wanted it known that you had become it. You therefore did what was necessary to achieve your purpose and to be a focus of attention. Is that right?

THE JUDGE: Pretty much.

THE CHIEF OF POLICE: Very well. That means you've never
420 performed an act for its own sake, but always so that, when linked with other acts, it would make a bishop, a judge, a general. . . .

THE BISHOP: That's both true and false. For each act contained within itself its leaven of novelty.
425

THE JUDGE: We acquired greater dignity thereby.

THE CHIEF OF POLICE: No doubt, my Lord, but this dignity, which has become as inhuman as a crystal, makes you unfit for governing men. No, no, gentlemen, above you, more sublime than you, is the Queen. It's from her, for the time
430 being, that you derive your power and your rights. Above her—that to which she refers—is our standard, on which I've blazoned the image of Chantal Victorious, our saint.

THE BISHOP: (*aggressively*) Above Her Majesty, whom we venerate, and above her flag, is God, Who speaks through my
435 voice.

THE CHIEF OF POLICE: (*irritably*) And above God? (*A silence.*) Well, gentlemen, above God are you, without whom God would be nothing. And above you am I, without whom. . . .

THE JUDGE: What about the people? The photographers?
440

THE CHIEF OF POLICE: On their knees before the people who are on their knees before God. Therefore. . . .

(*They all burst out laughing.*)

That's why I want you to serve me. But a while ago you were holding forth quite volubly. I should therefore like to pay homage to your eloquence, your facility of elocution,
445 the limpidity of your timbre, the potency of your organ. As for me, I'm a mere man of action who gets tangled up in words and ideas when they're not immediately applied. That's why I was wondering whether to send you back to your kennel. I won't do it. In any case, not right away,
450 since you're already there.

THE GENERAL: Sir!

THE CHIEF OF POLICE: (*He pushes* THE GENERAL, *who topples over and remains sitting on the floor, flabbergasted*) Lie down! Lie down, General!
455

THE JUDGE: My skirt can be tucked up. . . .

THE CHIEF OF POLICE: (*He pushes* THE JUDGE, *who topples over*) Lie down! Since you want to be recognized as a judge, do you want to hold on to your dignity according to my idea of it? And according to the general meaning attached to
460 your dignities? Very well. Must I therefore grant you increasing recognition along these lines? Yes or no?

(*No one answers.*)

Well, gentlemen, yes or no? (THE BISHOP *steps aside, prudently.*)

THE QUEEN: (*very blandly*) Excuse him, if he gets carried away.
465 I'm quite aware of what you used to come here for: (*to* THE BISHOP) you, my Lord, to seek by quick, decisive ways a manifest saintliness. No, no, I'm not being ironic. The gold of my chasubles had little to do with it, I'm sure. It wasn't mere gross ambition that brought you behind my
470

closed shutters. Love of God was hidden there. I realize that. You, my Lord, you were indeed guided by a concern for justice, since it was the image of a magistrate that you wished to see reflected a thousand times in my mirrors.
475 And you, General, it was bravery and military glory and the heroic deed that haunted you. So let yourselves go, relax, without too many scruples. . . .

(*One after the other, the three men heave a deep sigh.*)

THE CHIEF OF POLICE: (*continuing*) That's relief to you, isn't it? You never really wanted to get out of yourselves and com-
480 municate, if only by acts of meanness, with the world. I understand you. (*Amiably*) My role, unfortunately, is in motion. In short, as you probably know, it's not in the nomenclature of the brothels. . . .
THE QUEEN: In the pink handbook.
485 THE CHIEF OF POLICE: Yes, in the pink handbook. (*To the Three Figures*) Come now, gentlemen, don't you feel sorry for a poor fellow like me? (*He looks at them one after the other.*) Come, come, gentlemen, you're not hardhearted, are you? It's for you that these Studios and Illustrious
490 Rites were perfected, by means of exquisite experimentation. They required long labour, infinite patience, and you want to go back to the light of day? (*Almost humble, and suddenly looking very very tired*) Wait just a little while. For the time being, I'm still loaded with future acts, loaded
495 with actions . . . but as soon as I feel I'm being multiplied ad infinitum, then . . . then, ceasing to be hard, I'll go and rot in people's minds. And you, get into your skirts again if you want to, and get back on the job. (*To* THE BISHOP) You're silent. (*A long silence.*) That's right. . . . Let's be silent,
500 and let's wait. . . . (*A long and heavy silence.*) Perhaps it's now . . . (*In a low, humble voice*) that my apotheosis is being prepared. . . . (*Everybody is visibly expectant. Then,* CARMEN *enters, as if furtively, by the left door.* THE ENVOY *is the first to see her. He silently indicates her presence to* THE QUEEN. THE
505 QUEEN *motions to* CARMEN *to withdraw, but* CARMEN *nevertheless takes a step forward.*)
THE QUEEN: (*in an almost low voice*) I gave orders that we were not to be disturbed. What do you want?

(CARMEN *goes to her.*)

CARMEN: I tried to ring, but the apparatus is out of order. I
510 beg your pardon. I'd like to speak with you.
THE QUEEN: Well, what is it? Speak up!
CARMEN: (*hesitantly*) It's . . . I don't know. . . .
THE QUEEN: (*resignedly*) Well, when at Court do as the Court does. Let's speak in an undertone. (*She conspicuously lends*
515 *ear to* CARMEN, *who leans forward and murmurs a few words.* THE QUEEN *seems very upset.*)
THE QUEEN: Are you sure?
CARMEN: Quite, Madame.

(THE QUEEN *bolts from the room, followed by* CARMEN. THE CHIEF OF POLICE *starts to follow them, but* THE ENVOY *intervenes.*)

THE ENVOY: One does not follow Her Majesty.
520 THE CHIEF OF POLICE: What's going on? Where's she going?
THE ENVOY: (*ironically*) To embroider. The Queen is embroi-

dering, and she is not embroidering. . . . You know the refrain? The Queen attains her reality when she withdraws, absents herself, or dies.
THE CHIEF OF POLICE: What's happening outside? (*To* THE 525
JUDGE) Do you have any news?
THE JUDGE: What you call outside is as mysterious to us as we are to it.
THE BISHOP: I shall try to depict the grief of this people which thought it had liberated itself by rebelling. Alas—or 530
rather, thank Heaven!—there will never be a movement powerful enough to destroy our imagery.
THE CHIEF OF POLICE: (*almost tremblingly*) So you think I have a chance?
THE BISHOP: You're in the best possible position. There's con- 535
sternation everywhere, in all families, in all institutions. People have trembled so violently that your image is beginning to make them doubt themselves.
THE CHIEF OF POLICE: Am I their only hope?
THE BISHOP: Their only hope lies in utter collapse. 540
THE CHIEF OF POLICE: In short, I'm like a pool in which they behold themselves?
THE GENERAL: (*delighted, with a burst of laughter*) And if they lean over too far, they fall in and drown. Before long, you'll be full of drowned bodies! (*No one seems to share his* 545
merriment.) Oh well . . . they're not yet at the brink! (*Embarrassed*) Let's wait.

(*A silence.*)

THE CHIEF OF POLICE: So you really think the people had a wild hope? And that in losing all hope they lose everything? And that in losing everything they'll come and lose 550
themselves in me? . . .
THE BISHOP: That may very well happen. But, believe me, not if we can help it.
THE CHIEF OF POLICE: When I am offered that final consecration. . . . 555
THE ENVOY: (*ironically*) For you, but for you alone, for a second the Earth will stop rotating. . . .

(*Suddenly the door at the left opens and* THE QUEEN *appears, beaming.*)

THE QUEEN: George! (*She falls into the arms of* THE CHIEF OF POLICE.)
THE CHIEF OF POLICE: (*incredulous*) It's not true. (THE QUEEN 560
nods yes.) But where? . . . When?
THE QUEEN: (*deeply moved*) There! . . . Now! The Studio. . . .
THE CHIEF OF POLICE: You're pulling my leg. I didn't hear anything.

(*Suddenly a tremendous ringing, a kind of peal of bells.*)

So it's true? It's for me? (*He pushes* THE QUEEN *away.* 565
Solemnly, as the ringing stops) Gentlemen, I belong to the Nomenclature! (*To* THE QUEEN) But are you really sure?

(*The ringing starts again, then stops.*)

THE QUEEN: It was I who received him and ushered him into the Mausoleum Studio. The one that's being built in your

570   honour. I left Carmen behind to attend to the preparations
and I ran to let you know. I'm trembling like a leaf. . . .

(*The ringing starts again, then stops.*)

THE BISHOP: (*gloomily*) We're up the creek.
THE CHIEF OF POLICE: The apparatus is working. You can
see. . . .

(*He goes to the left, followed by* THE QUEEN.)

575   THE ENVOY: That is not the practice. It's filthy. . . .
THE CHIEF OF POLICE: (*shrugging his shoulders*) Where's the
mechanism? (*To the Queen*) Let's watch together.

(*She stands at the left, facing a small port-hole. After a brief hesitation,* THE JUDGE, GENERAL *and* BISHOP *place themselves at the
right, at another port-hole symmetrical with the first. Then, the two
panels of the double mirror forming the back of the stage silently draw
apart, revealing the interior of the Special Studio.* THE ENVOY, *with
resignation, joins* THE CHIEF OF POLICE.)
DESCRIPTION OF THE MAUSOLEUM STUDIO: *The stones of the
wall, which is circular, are visible. At the rear, a stairway that descends. In the centre of this well there seems to be another, in which
the steps of a stairway are visible. On the walls, four laurel wreaths,
adorned with crépe. When the panels separate,* ROGER *is at the middle of the stairway, which he is descending.* CARMEN *seems to be
guiding him.* ROGER *is dressed like* THE CHIEF OF POLICE, *though,
mounted on the same cothurni as the Three Figures, he looks taller.
His shoulders have also been broadened. He descends the stairs to the
rhythm of a drum.*

CARMEN: (*approaching, and handing him a cigar*) It's on the
house.
580   ROGER: (*putting the cigar into his mouth*) Thanks.
CARMEN: (*taking the cigar from him*) That end's for the light.
This one's for the mouth. (*She turns the cigar around.*) Is this
your first cigar?
ROGER: Yes. . . . (*A pause.*) I'm not asking for your advice.
585   You're here to serve me, I've paid. . . .
CARMEN: I beg your pardon, sir.
ROGER: The slave?
CARMEN: He's being untied.
ROGER: He knows what it's about?
590   CARMEN: Completely. You're the first. You're inaugurating this
Studio, but, you know, the scenarios are all reducible to a
major theme. . . .
ROGER: Which is . . . ?
CARMEN: Death.
595   ROGER: (*touching the walls*) And so this is my tomb?
CARMEN: (*correcting him*) Mausoleum.
ROGER: How many slaves are working on it?
CARMEN: The entire people, sir. Half of the population dur-
ing the day and the other half at night. As you have re-
600   quested, the whole mountain will be burrowed and
tunneled. The interior will have the complexity of a ter-
mite nest or of the Basilica of Lourdes—we don't know
yet. No one will be able to see anything from the outside.
All they'll know is that the mountain is sacred, but, inside,
605   the tombs are already being enshrined in tombs, the cenotaphs in cenotaphs, the coffins in coffins, the urns. . . .

ROGER: What about here, where I am now?
CARMEN: (*with a gesture of disdain*) An antechamber. An antechamber called the Valley of the Fallen. (*She mounts the
underground stairway.*) In a little while, you'll go farther   610
down.
ROGER: I'm not to hope to see the light of day again?
CARMEN: But . . . do you still want to?

(*A silence.*)

ROGER: It's really true that no one's ever been here before me?
CARMEN: In this . . . tomb, or in this . . . Studio?   615

(*A silence.*)

ROGER: Is everything really on right? My outfit? My toupet?

(THE CHIEF OF POLICE *turns to* THE QUEEN.)

THE CHIEF OF POLICE: He knew I wear a toupet?
THE BISHOP: (*snickering, to* THE JUDGE, *and* THE GENERAL) He's
the only one who doesn't know that everyone knows it.
CARMEN: (*to* ROGER) Everything was carefully planned long   620
ago. It's all been worked out. The rest is up to you.
ROGER: (*anxiously*) You realize I'm feeling my way too. I've
got to imagine what the Hero's like, and he's never shown
himself much.
CARMEN: That's why we've taken you to the Mausoleum   625
Studio. It's not possible to make many errors here, nor indulge your imagination.

(*A pause.*)

ROGER. Will I be alone?
CARMEN: Everything is padded. The doors are lined. So are
the walls.   630
ROGER: (*hesitantly*) What about . . . the mausoleum?
CARMEN: (*forcefully*) Built into the rock. The proof is that
there's water oozing from the walls. Deathly silent. As for
light, the darkness is so thick that your eyes have developed astounding qualities. The cold? Yes, the coldness of   635
death. It's been a gigantic job drilling through the mountain. Men are still groaning in order to hollow out a gigantic niche for you. Everything proves that you're loved
and that you're a conqueror.
ROGER: Groaning? Could . . . could I hear the groaning?   640

(CARMEN *turns toward a hole dug out at the foot of the wall, from
which emerges the head of* THE BEGGAR, *the character seen in Scene
4. He is now* THE SLAVE.)

CARMEN: Come here!

(THE SLAVE *crawls in.*)

ROGER: (*looking the slave over*) Is that it?
CARMEN: A fine specimen, isn't he? Skinny. With lice and sores.
He dreams of dying for you. I'll leave you alone now.
ROGER: With him? No, no. (*A pause.*) Stay. Everything always   645
takes place in the presence of a woman. It's in order for a
woman's face to be a witness that, usually. . . .

(*Suddenly, the sound of a hammer striking an anvil. Then a cock crows.*)

Is life so near?

CARMEN: (*in a normal voice, not acting*) As I've told you, everything's padded, but some sounds always manage to filter
through. Does it bother you? Life's starting up again little
by little . . . as before. . . .

ROGER: (*he seems anxious*) Yes, as before. . . .

CARMEN: (*gently*) You were. . . .

ROGER: Yes. Everything's washed up. . . . And what's saddest
of all is people's saying: "The rebellion was wonderful!"

CARMEN: You mustn't think about it any more. And you must
stop listening to the sounds from outside. Besides, it's raining. The whole mountain has been swept by a tornado.
(*Stage voice*) You are at home here. (*Pointing to* THE SLAVE)
Make him talk.

ROGER: (*playing his role*) For you can talk? And what else can
you do?

THE SLAVE: (*lying on his belly*) First, bow; then, shrink into myself a little more (*He takes* ROGER's *foot and places it on his
own back.*) like this! . . . and even. . . .

ROGER: (*impatiently*) Yes . . . and even?

THE SLAVE: Sink into the earth, if it's possible.

ROGER: (*drawing on his cigar*) Sink in, really? But there's no
mud?

THE QUEEN: (*To the others*) He's right. We should have provided mud. In a well-run house. . . . But it's opening day,
and he's the first client to use the Studio. . . .

THE SLAVE: (*To* ROGER) I feel it all over my body, sir. It's all over
me, except in my mouth, which is open so that I can sing
your praises and utter the groans that made me famous.

ROGER: Famous? You're famous, you?

THE SLAVE: Famous for my chants, sir, which are hymns to
your glory.

ROGER: So your glory accompanies mine? (*To* CARMEN) Does
he mean that my reputation will be kept going by his
words? And . . . if he says nothing, I'll cease to exist . . . ?

CARMEN: (*curtly*) I'd like very much to satisfy you, but you ask
questions that aren't in the scenario.

ROGER: (*To* THE SLAVE) But what about you, who sings to you?

THE SLAVE: Nobody. I'm dying.

ROGER: But without me, without my sweat, without my tears
and blood, what would you be?

THE SLAVE: Nothing.

ROGER: (*To* THE SLAVE) You sing? But what else do you do?

THE SLAVE: We do all we possibly can to be more and more
unworthy of you.

ROGER: What, for example?

THE SLAVE: We try hard just to stand and rot. And, believe me,
it's not always easy. Life tries to prevail. . . . But we stand
our ground. We keep shrinking more and more every. . . .

ROGER: Day?

THE SLAVE: Week.

THE CHIEF OF POLICE: (*To the others*) That's not much. With a
little effort. . . .

THE ENVOY: (*To* THE CHIEF OF POLICE) Be still. Let them play
out their roles.

ROGER: That's not much. With a little effort. . . .

THE SLAVE: (*with exaltation*) With joy, Your Excellency! You're
so splendid! So splendid that I wonder whether you're
aglow or whether you're all the darkness of all the nights?

ROGER: What does it matter, since I'm no longer to have any
reality except in the reality of your phrases.

THE SLAVE: (*crawling in the direction of the upper stairway*) You
have not mouth nor ears nor eyes, but all of you is a thundering mouth and at the same time a dazzling and watchful eye. . . .

ROGER: *You* see it, but do the others know it? Does the night
know it? Does death? Do the stones? What do the stones
say?

THE SLAVE: (*still dragging on his belly and beginning to crawl up
the stairs*) The stones say. . . .

ROGER: Well, I'm listening.

THE SLAVE: (*he stops crawling, and faces the audience*) The cement
that holds us together to form your tomb. . . .

THE CHIEF OF POLICE: (*facing the audience and joyfully beating
his breast*) The stones venerate me!

THE SLAVE: (*continuing*) . . . the cement is moulded of tears,
spit and blood. The workers' eyes and hands that rested
upon us have matted us with grief. We are yours, and only
yours.

(THE SLAVE *starts crawling up the stairs again.*)

ROGER: (*with rising exaltation*) Everything proclaims me!
Everything breathes me and everything worships me! My
history was lived so that a glorious page might be written
and then read. It's reading that counts. (*He suddenly notices
that* THE SLAVE *has disappeared. To* CARMEN) But . . . where's
he going? . . . Where is he? . . .

CARMEN: He's gone off to sing. He's going up into the light
of day. He'll tell . . . that he carried your footsteps . . . and
that. . . .

ROGER: (*anxiously*) Yes, and that? What else will he tell?

CARMEN: The truth; that you're dead, or rather than you
don't stop dying and that your image, like your name, re-
verberates to infinity.

ROGER: He knows that my image is everywhere?

CARMEN: Yes, everywhere, inscribed and engraved and imposed by fear.

ROGER: In the palms of stevedores? In the games of children?
On the teeth of soldiers? In war?

CARMEN: Everywhere.

THE CHIEF OF POLICE: (*to the others*) So I've made it?

THE QUEEN: (*fondly*) Are you happy?

THE CHIEF OF POLICE: You've done a good job. That puts the
finishing touch to your house.

ROGER: (*To* CARMEN) Is it in prisons? In the wrinkles of old
people?

CARMEN: It is.

ROGER: In the curves of roads?

CARMEN: You mustn't ask the impossible.

(*Same sounds as earlier: the cock and the anvil.*)

It's time to go, sir. The session's over. Turn left, and when
you reach the corridor. . . .

(*The sound of the anvil again, a little louder.*)

You hear? You've got to go home. . . . What are you doing?

ROGER: Life is nearby . . . and far away. Here all the women
are beautiful. Their purpose is purely ornamental. . . . One
can lose oneself in them. . . .

CARMEN: (*curtly*) That's right. In ordinary language, we're called whores. But you've got to leave. . . .

ROGER: And go where? Into life? To carry on, as they say, with my activities. . . .

765 CARMEN: (*a little anxiously*) I don't know what you're doing, and I haven't the right to inquire. But you've got to leave. Your time's up.

(*The sound of the anvil and other sounds indicate an activity: cracking of a whip, humming of a motor, etc.*)

ROGER: They give you the rush in this place! Why do you want me to go back where I came from?

770 CARMEN: You've nothing further to do. . . .

ROGER: There? No. Nothing further. Nor here either. And outside, in what you call life, everything has crashed. No truth was possible. . . . Did you know Chantal?

CARMEN: (*suddenly frightened*) Get going! Clear out of here!

775 THE QUEEN: I won't allow him to create a rumpus in my studios! Who was it who sent me that individual? Whenever there are disturbances, the riff-raff always crop up. I hope that Carmen. . . .

CARMEN: (*To* ROGER) Get out! You've no right to ask questions either. You know that brothels are very strictly regulated and that we're protected by the police.

780 ROGER: No! Since I'm playing the Chief of Police and since you allow me to be here. . . .

CARMEN: (*pulling him away*) You're crazy! You wouldn't be the first who thought he'd risen to power. . . . Come along!

785 ROGER: (*disengaging himself*) If the brothel exists and if I've a right to go there, then I've a right to lead the character I've chosen to the very limit of his destiny . . . no, of mine . . . of merging his destiny with mine. . . .

790 CARMEN: Stop shouting, sir. All the studios are occupied. Come along. . . .

(CARMEN *tries to make him leave. She opens a door, then another, then a third, unable to find the right one.* ROGER *takes out a knife and, with his back to the audience, makes the gesture of castrating himself.*)

THE QUEEN: On my rugs! On the new carpet! He's a lunatic!

CARMEN: (*crying out*) Doing that here! (*She yells*) Madame!

795 Mme Irma! (CARMEN *finally manages to drag* ROGER *out.*)

(THE QUEEN *rushes from the room. All the characters—the* CHIEF OF POLICE, THE ENVOY, THE JUDGE, THE GENERAL, THE BISHOP— *turn and leave the port-holes.* THE CHIEF OF POLICE *moves forward to the middle of the stage.*)

THE CHIEF OF POLICE: Well played. He thought he had me. (*He places his hand on his fly, very visibly feels his balls and, reassured, heaves a sigh.*) Mine are here. So which of us is washed up? He or I? Though my image he castrated in

800 every brothel in the world, I remain intact. Intact, gentlemen. (*A pause.*) That plumber didn't know how to handle his role, that was all. (*He calls out, joyfully*) Irma! Irma! . . . Where is she? It's not her job to dress wounds.

THE QUEEN: (*entering*) George! The vestibule . . . the rugs are

805 covered with blood . . . the vestibule's full of clients. . . . We're wiping up as best we can. . . . Carmen doesn't know where to put them. . . .

THE ENVOY: (*bowing to* THE CHIEF OF POLICE) Nice work.

THE CHIEF OF POLICE: An image of me will be perpetuated in secret. Mutilated? (*He shrugs his shoulders.*) Yet a low 810 Mass will be said to my glory. Notify the kitchens! Have them send me enough grub for two thousand years.

THE QUEEN: What about me? George, *I'm* alive!

THE CHIEF OF POLICE: (*without hearing her*) So. . . . I'm. . . . Where? Here, or . . . a thousand times there? (*He points* 815 *to the tomb.*) Now I can be kind . . . and pious . . . and just. . . . Did you see? Did you see me? There, just before, larger than large, stronger than strong, deader than dead? So I've nothing more to do with you.

THE QUEEN: George! But I still love you! 820

THE CHIEF OF POLICE: (*moving towards the tomb*) I've won the right to go and sit and wait for two thousand years. (*To the photographers*) You! Watch me live, and die. For posterity: shoot! (*Three almost simultaneous flashes.*) I've won! (*He walks backwards into the tomb, very slowly, while* THE 825 THREE PHOTOGRAPHERS *casually leave by the left wing, with their cameras slung over their backs. They wave before disappearing.*)

THE QUEEN: But it was I who did everything, who organized everything. . . . Stay. . . . What will. . . . 830

(*Suddenly a burst of machine-gun fire.*)

You hear!

THE CHIEF OF POLICE: (*with a burst of laughter*) Think of me!

(THE JUDGE *and* THE GENERAL *rush forward to stop him, but the doors start closing as the* THE CHIEF OF POLICE *descends the first steps. A second burst of machine-gun fire.*)

THE JUDGE: (*clinging to the door*) Don't leave us alone!

THE GENERAL: (*gloomily*) That carriage again!

THE ENVOY: (*to* THE JUDGE) Be careful, you'll get your fingers 835 caught.

(*The door has definitely closed. The characters remain bewildered for a moment. A third burst of machine-gun fire.*)

THE QUEEN: Gentlemen, you are free.

THE BISHOP: But . . . in the middle of the night?

THE QUEEN: (*interrupting him*) You'll leave by the narrow door that leads into the alley. There's a car waiting for you. 840

(*She nods courteously. The Three Figures exeunt right. A fourth burst of machine-gun fire.*)

Who is it? . . . Our side? . . . Or rebels? . . . Or? . . .

THE ENVOY: Someone dreaming. Madame. . . .

(THE QUEEN *goes to various parts of the room and presses buttons. Each time, a light goes out.*)

THE QUEEN: (*continuing to extinguish lights*). . . . Irma. . . . Call me Mme Irma and go home. Good night, sir.

THE ENVOY: Good night, Mme Irma. 845

(THE ENVOY *exits.*)

IRMA: (*alone, and continuing to extinguish lights*) It took so much light . . . two pounds' worth of electricity a day! Thirty-eight studios! Every one of them gilded, and all of them rigged with machinery so as to be able to fit into and combine with each other. . . . And all these performances so that I can remain alone, mistress and assistant mistress of this house and of myself. (*She pushes in a button, then pushes it out again.*) Oh no, that's the tomb. He needs lights, for two thousand years! . . . and food for two thousand years. . . . (*She shrugs her shoulders.*) Oh well, everything's in working order, and dishes have been prepared. Glory means descending into the grave with tons of victuals! . . . (*She calls out, facing the wings*) Carmen? Carmen? . . . Bolt the doors, my dear, and put the furniture-covers on. . . . (*She continues extinguishing.*) In a little while, I'll have to start all over again . . . put all the lights on again . . . dress up. . . . (*A cock crows.*) Dress up . . . ah, the disguises! Distribute roles again . . . assume my own. . . . (*She stops in the middle of the stage, facing the audience.*) . . . Prepare yours . . . judges, generals, bishops, chamberlains, rebels who allow the revolt to congeal, I'm going to prepare my costumes and studios for tomorrow. . . . You must now go home, where everything—you can be quite sure—will be falser than here. . . . You must go now. You'll leave by the right, through the alley. . . . (*She extinguishes the last light.*) It's morning already.

(*A burst of machine-gun fire.*)

Samuel Beckett

Samuel Beckett (1906–1989) is the most influential European dramatist of the postwar period. Born near Dublin, Ireland, Beckett was educated at Trinity College, Dublin, where he studied modern languages. Taking his B.A. in 1928, Beckett received an appointment as *lecteur* at l'École Normale Supérieure in Paris. While in Paris, Beckett met the Irish novelist James Joyce. Beckett assisted Joyce (who was nearly blind) in a variety of ways and became a close friend. Joyce also exerted a profound influence on Beckett's writing. In 1929, Beckett contributed an essay entitled "Dante . . . Bruno . Vico . . Joyce" to a volume on Joyce's *Finnegans Wake*. Throughout the 1930s, Beckett was associated with Joyce and with a variety of avant-garde movements in Paris. He wrote a series of poems—including the prize-winning "Whoroscope"—as well as a study of Proust (1931), the volume of short stories *More Pricks than Kicks* (1934), and the novel *Murphy* (1938). Although Beckett returned briefly to Ireland on a few occasions, he had settled permanently in Paris. During World War II, Beckett served in the French Resistance. He was discovered by the Nazis and forced to flee Paris in 1942. He worked in the unoccupied zone of southern France for the remainder of the war, where he wrote the novel *Watt* (1953). After the war, Beckett received the Croix de Guerre and the Médaille de la Résistance for his services. He began to write exclusively in French, starting work on a major trilogy of novels—*Molloy* (1951), *Malone Dies* (1951), and *The Unnameable* (1953).

Beckett had experimented with drama during the 1930s and 1940s, but his first staged play, *Waiting for Godot* (first written in French, as *En attendant Godot*), produced at the tiny Théâtre de Babylone in January of 1953, impelled him in a new direction. Although Beckett continued to write fiction—including *From an Abandoned Work* (1956), *How It Is* (1964), *Imagination Dead Imagine* (1965), and *Company* (1979)—his major writing of the 1960s, 1970s, and 1980s was for the theater. His second play, *Endgame*, also written in French, was produced in 1957 and was followed by a series of challenging works for the stage: *Krapp's Last Tape* (1958), *Happy Days* (1962), *Play* (1963), *Not I* (1972), *Footfalls* (1975), *Rockaby* (1981), and *Catastrophe* (1982). For his extraordinarily diverse and influential body of work, Beckett won the Nobel Prize for Literature in 1970. Beckett also wrote several plays for radio and television, as well as a film starring Buster Keaton, *Film* (1965). Beginning in the mid-1960s, Beckett directed productions of his plays, and several productions he directed in France and in Germany now have the status of classics—something like Elia Kazan's productions of Tennessee Williams's plays, or Stanislavski's productions of Chekhov.

Beckett's impact on the contemporary theater can hardly be overestimated and can be seen in the work of Sam Shepard, Harold Pinter, and many others. *Waiting for Godot* signaled new possibilities for stage action—or inaction—and developed the implications of Chekhov's static stage in a more symbolic direction. Each of Beckett's plays explores the nature and limitations of its medium in new and challenging ways. *Endgame* refigures the claustral box of realistic drama, for its characters are trapped in a room of endless—or possibly ending—routine. In *Play*, Beckett puts three urns onstage, from which three heads emerge to deliver, more or less simultaneously, a jarring, repetitive monologue of seduction and betrayal. Once the play has finished, Beckett directs his performers—and his audience—to "Repeat play," and so calls the relationship between actors and spectators, theater and reality into question: If we cannot leave the theater when the play is over, is it possible that there is no way out of the purgatory on the stage and in the auditorium? This sense that the self is always in flight is the theme of several of Beckett's later plays. In *Not I*, for instance, all that the audience sees is a Mouth eight feet above the stage, reciting an endless narrative in which she avoids claiming the speech as her own. In *Ohio Impromptu* (1981), an identical reader and listener relate a painful narrative of loss, in which it is unclear whether they are two individuals or parts of a single person. The power of Beckett's spare, minimalist theater, the beauty of his sculptural use of actors and stage space, and the harsh exigency of the action of his plays have transformed the stage of our time.

Endgame is Beckett's second full-length play to reach the stage; although its simplicity and repetitiveness are in some ways reminiscent of *Waiting for Godot,* the tone of *Endgame* is bleaker, harsher. As Beckett wrote to Alan Schneider, the play's first American director, *Endgame*'s power is "the power of the text to claw."

The "endgame" of a chess match is the final portion of the game, at which either a checkmate or a stalemate has become inevitable. In *Endgame,* Beckett literalizes the uncertainty of the endgame—will the tortuous nothingness of the characters' lives continue indefinitely, move after move, or will it somehow end? Although some critics have taken the "shelter" and the empty landscape outside as an indication that the play takes place in a bomb shelter after a nuclear bombing, *Endgame* seems to present a microcosm of postmodern life, in which the futile search for fugitive "meanings" raises the despairing feeling that our lives are meaningless, "absurd" after all. Hamm is a kind of ham actor and recalls Shakespeare's Richard III ("My kingdom for a nightman") and Prospero ("Our revels now are ended"), as well as perhaps King Lear and Hamlet in his performance. Hamm is perhaps the first **POSTMODERN** dramatic hero, less a full "character" than a *pastiche* of dramatic roles and possibilities, which exist now only in bits and pieces, recollected fragments (on **PASTICHE,** see Fredric Jameson's essay). Hamm's blindness also recalls both Oedipus—who also struggled with his father—and Ham the son of Noah, who was blinded when he saw his father naked. Hamm continually reminds us that his performance—it's full of asides, a "last soliloquy," and many self-regarding comments on Hamm's success or failure—is an attempt to impose meaning on the process of the play's action. This recollection of the dramatic and literary tradition also points to the problematic place—or absence—of history in *Endgame.* If there is a kind of past ("Once!") in *Endgame,* it is recalled most clearly by Hamm's parents: Nagg and Nell, legless in their garbage cans, describe an earlier, more sentimental or

Nagg and Nell in their ashbins in Samuel Beckett's *Endgame,* in the 2000 Rude Mechanicals Theater Company production.

romantic era, when couples rode tandems in the Ardennes and rowed on Lake Como. Overall, though, time seems to be an endless present moment in *Endgame,* a moment disconnected from the past that once gave it meaning, and from the future which gave it closure. It may be that the play is postnuclear (although Beckett's draft manuscripts suggest that the inspiration was really a war hospital), but this setting is less important than the sense of time that this tiny world contains. For *Endgame* is finally about time and its passing, the painfully slow passage of moment to moment, and its finality once it is past.

Endgame was originally written in French as *Fin de partie* and was rewritten into English by Beckett himself; there are several small differences in dialogue and action between the two versions.

ENDGAME

Samuel Beckett

CHARACTERS

NAGG   HAMM
NELL   CLOV

Bare interior.

Grey light.

Left and right back, high up, two small windows, curtains drawn.

Front right, a door. Hanging near door, its face to wall, a picture.

Front left, touching each other, covered with an old sheet, two ashbins.

Center, in an armchair on castors, covered with an old sheet, HAMM.

Motionless by the door, his eyes fixed on HAMM, CLOV. *Very red face.*

Brief tableau.

CLOV *goes and stands under window left. Stiff, staggering walk. He looks up at window left. He turns and looks at window right. He goes and stands under window right. He looks up at window right. He turns and looks at window left. He goes out, comes back immediately with a small step-ladder, carries it over and sets it down under window left, gets up on it, draws back curtain. He gets down, takes six steps (for example) towards window right, goes back for ladder, carries it over and sets it down under window right, gets up on it, draws back curtain. He gets down, takes three steps towards window left, goes back for ladder, carries it over and sets it down under window left, gets up on it, looks out of window. Brief laugh. He gets down, takes one step towards window right, goes back for ladder, carries it over and sets it down under window right, gets up on it, looks out of window. Brief laugh. He gets down, goes with ladder towards ashbins, halts, turns, carries back ladder and sets it down under window right, goes to ashbins, removes sheet covering them, folds it over his arm. He raises one lid, stoops and looks into bin. Brief laugh. He closes lid. Same with other bin. He goes to* HAMM, *removes sheet covering him, folds it over his arm. In a dressing-gown, a stiff toque on his head, a large blood-stained handkerchief over his face, a whistle hanging from his neck, a rug over his knees, thick socks on his feet,* HAMM *seems to be asleep.* CLOV *looks him over. Brief laugh. He goes to door, halts, turns towards auditorium.*

CLOV: *(Fixed gaze, tonelessly.)* Finished, it's finished, nearly finished, it must be nearly finished.

(Pause.)

Grain upon grain, one by one, and one day, suddenly, there's a heap, a little heap, the impossible heap.

(Pause.)

5   I can't be punished any more.

(Pause.)

I'll go now to my kitchen, ten feet by ten feet by ten feet, and wait for him to whistle me.

(Pause.)

Nice dimensions, nice proportions, I'll lean on the table, and look at the wall, and wait for him to whistle me.

(He remains a moment motionless, then goes out. He comes back immediately, goes to window right, takes up the ladder and carries it out. Pause. HAMM *stirs. He yawns under the handkerchief. He removes the handkerchief from his face. Very red face. Black glasses.)*

HAMM: Me—   10
(He yawns.)
—to play.
(He holds the handkerchief spread out before him.)
Old stancher!
(He takes off his glasses, wipes his eyes, his face, the glasses, puts them on again, folds the handkerchief and puts it back neatly in the breast-pocket of his dressing-gown. He clears his throat, joins the tips of his fingers.)
Can there be misery—
(He yawns.)
—loftier than mine? No doubt. Formerly. But now?
(Pause.)
My father?   15
(Pause.)
My mother?
(Pause.)
My . . . dog?
(Pause.)
Oh I am willing to believe they suffer as much as such creatures can suffer. But does that mean their sufferings equal mine? No doubt.   20
(Pause.)
No, all is a—
(He yawns.)
—bsolute,
(Proudly.)
the bigger a man is the fuller he is.
(Pause. Gloomily.)
And the emptier.
(He sniffs.)
Clov!   25
(Pause.)
No, alone.
(Pause.)
What dreams! Those forests!
(Pause.)
Enough, it's time it ended, in the shelter too.
(Pause.)
And yet I hesitate, I hesitate to . . . to end. Yes, there it is, it's time it ended and yet I hesitate to—   30
(He yawns.)
—to end.
(Yawns.)
God, I'm tired, I'd better off in bed.
(He whistles. Enter CLOV *immediately. He halts beside the chair.)*

You pollute the air!
(*Pause.*)
     Get me ready, I'm going to bed.
35 CLOV: I've just got you up.
HAMM: And what of it?
CLOV: I can't be getting you up and putting you to bed every
     five minutes, I have things to do.

(*Pause.*)

HAMM: Did you ever see my eyes?
40 CLOV: No.
HAMM: Did you never have the curiosity, while I was sleep-
     ing, to take off my glasses and look at my eyes?
CLOV: Pulling back the lids?
(*Pause.*)
     No.
45 HAMM: One of these days I'll show them to you.
(*Pause.*)
     It seems they've gone all white.
(*Pause.*)
     What time is it?
CLOV: The same as usual.
HAMM: (*Gesture towards window right.*) Have you looked?
50 CLOV: Yes.
HAMM: Well?
CLOV: Zero.
HAMM: It'd need to rain.
CLOV: It won't rain.

(*Pause.*)

55 HAMM: Apart from that, how do you feel?
CLOV: I don't complain.
HAMM: You feel normal?
CLOV: (*Irritably.*) I tell you I don't complain.
HAMM: I feel a little queer.
(*Pause.*)
60   Clov!
CLOV: Yes.
HAMM: Have you not had enough?
CLOV: Yes!
(*Pause.*)
     Of what?
65 HAMM: Of this . . . this . . . thing.
CLOV: I always had.
(*Pause.*)
     Not you?
HAMM: (*Gloomily.*) Then there's no reason for it to change.
CLOV: It may end.
(*Pause.*)
70   All life long the same questions, the same answers.
HAMM: Get me ready.
(CLOV *does not move.*)
     Go and get the sheet.
(CLOV *does not move.*)
     Clov!
CLOV: Yes.
75 HAMM: I'll give you nothing more to eat.
CLOV: Then we'll die.
HAMM: I'll give you just enough to keep you from dying.
     You'll be hungry all the time.

CLOV: Then we won't die.
(*Pause.*)
     I'll go and get the sheet.   80

(*He goes towards the door.*)

HAMM: No!
(CLOV *halts.*)
     I'll give you one biscuit per day.
(*Pause.*)
     One and a half.
(*Pause.*)
     Why do you stay with me?
CLOV: Why do you keep me?   85
HAMM: There's no one else.
CLOV: There's nowhere else.

(*Pause.*)

HAMM: You're leaving me all the same.
CLOV: I'm trying.
HAMM: You don't love me.   90
CLOV: No.
HAMM: You loved me once.
CLOV: Once!
HAMM: I've made you suffer too much.
(*Pause.*)
     Haven't I?   95
CLOV: It's not that.
HAMM: (*Shocked.*) I haven't made you suffer too much?
CLOV: Yes!
HAMM: (*Relieved.*) Ah you gave me a fright!
(*Pause. Coldly.*)
     Forgive me.   100
(*Pause. Louder.*)
     I said, Forgive me.
CLOV: I heard you.
(*Pause.*)
     Have you bled?
HAMM: Less.
(*Pause.*)
     Is it not time for my pain-killer?   105
CLOV: No.

(*Pause.*)

HAMM: How are your eyes?
CLOV: Bad.
HAMM: How are your legs?
CLOV: Bad.   110
HAMM: But you can move.
CLOV: Yes.
HAMM: (*Violently.*) Then move!
(CLOV *goes to back wall, leans against it with his forehead and
hands.*)
     Where are you?
CLOV: Here.   115
HAMM: Come back!
(CLOV *returns to his place beside the chair.*)
     Where are you?
CLOV: Here.
HAMM: Why don't you kill me?

120 CLOV: I don't know the combination of the cupboard.

(*Pause.*)

HAMM: Go and get two bicycle-wheels.
CLOV: There are no more bicycle-wheels.
HAMM: What have you done with your bicycle?
CLOV: I never had a bicycle.
125 HAMM: The thing is impossible.
CLOV: When there were still bicycles I wept to have one. I crawled at your feet. You told me to go to hell. Now there are none.
HAMM: And your rounds? When you inspected my paupers.
130 Always on foot?
CLOV: Sometimes on horse.
(*The lid of one of the bins lifts and the hands of* NAGG *appear, gripping the rim. Then his head emerges. Nightcap. Very white face.* NAGG *yawns, then listens.*)
I'll leave you, I have things to do.
HAMM: In your kitchen?
CLOV: Yes.
135 HAMM: Outside of here it's death.
(*Pause.*)
All right, be off.
(*Exit* CLOV. *Pause.*)
We're getting on.
NAGG: Me pap!
HAMM: Accursed progenitor!
140 NAGG: Me pap!
HAMM: The old folks at home! No decency left! Guzzle, guzzle, that's all they think of.
(*He whistles. Enter* CLOV. *He halts beside the chair.*)
Well! I thought you were leaving me.
CLOV: Oh not just yet, not just yet.
145 NAGG: Me pap!
HAMM: Give him his pap.
CLOV: There's no more pap.
HAMM: (*To* NAGG.) Do you hear that? There's no more pap. You'll never get any more pap.
150 NAGG: I want me pap!
HAMM: Give him a biscuit.
(*Exit* CLOV.)
Accursed fornicator! How are your stumps?
NAGG: Never mind me stumps.

(*Enter* CLOV *with biscuit.*)

CLOV: I'm back again, with the biscuit.

(*He gives biscuit to* NAGG *who fingers it, sniffs it.*)

155 NAGG: (*Plaintively.*) What is it?
CLOV: Spratt's medium.
NAGG: (*As before.*) It's hard! I can't!
HAMM: Bottle him!

(CLOV *pushes* NAGG *back into the bin, closes the lid.*)

CLOV: (*Returning to his place beside the chair.*) If age but knew!
160 HAMM: Sit on him!
CLOV: I can't sit.
HAMM: True. And I can't stand.
CLOV: So it is.

HAMM: Every man his speciality.
(*Pause.*)
No phone calls?   165
(*Pause.*)
Don't we laugh?
CLOV: (*After reflection.*) I don't feel like it.
HAMM: (*After reflection.*) Nor I.
(*Pause.*)
Clov!
CLOV: Yes.   170
HAMM: Nature has forgotten us.
CLOV: There's no more nature.
HAMM: No more nature! You exaggerate.
CLOV: In the vicinity.
HAMM: But we breathe, we change! We lose our hair, our 175
teeth! Our bloom! Our ideals!
CLOV: Then she hasn't forgotten us.
HAMM: But you say there is none.
CLOV: (*Sadly.*) No one that ever lived ever thought so crooked as we.   180
HAMM: We do what we can.
CLOV: We shouldn't.

(*Pause.*)

HAMM: You're a bit of all right, aren't you?
CLOV: A smithereen.

(*Pause.*)

HAMM: This is slow work.   185
(*Pause.*)
Is it not time for my pain-killer?
CLOV: No.
(*Pause.*)
I'll leave you, I have things to do.
HAMM: In your kitchen?
CLOV: Yes.   190
HAMM: What, I'd like to know.
CLOV: I look at the wall.
HAMM: The wall! And what do you see on your wall? Mene, mene? Naked bodies?
CLOV: I see my light dying.   195
HAMM: Your light dying! Listen to that! Well, it can die just as well here, *your* light. Take a look at me and then come back and tell me what you think of *your* light.

(*Pause.*)

CLOV: You shouldn't speak to me like that.

(*Pause.*)

HAMM: (*Coldly.*) Forgive me.   200
(*Pause. Louder.*)
I said, Forgive me.
CLOV: I heard you.

(*The lid of* NAGG'*s bin lifts. His hands appear, gripping the rim. Then his head emerges. In his mouth the biscuit. He listens.*)

HAMM: Did your seeds come up?
CLOV: No.

205 HAMM: Did you scratch round them to see if they had sprouted?
CLOV: They haven't sprouted.
HAMM: Perhaps it's still too early.
CLOV: If they were going to sprout they would have sprouted. (*Violently.*)
     They'll never sprout!

(*Pause.* NAGG *takes biscuit in his hand.*)

210 HAMM: This is not much fun.
(*Pause.*)
     But that's always the way at the end of the day, isn't it, Clov?
CLOV: Always.
HAMM: It's the end of the day like any other day, isn't it, Clov?
215 CLOV: Looks like it.

(*Pause.*)

HAMM: (*Anguished.*) What's happening, what's happening?
CLOV: Something is taking its course.

(*Pause.*)

HAMM: All right, be off.
(*He leans back in his chair, remains motionless.* CLOV *does not move, heaves a great groaning sigh.* HAMM *sits up.*)
     I thought I told you to be off.
220 CLOV: I'm trying.
(*He goes to door, halts.*)
     Ever since I was whelped.

(*Exit* CLOV.)

HAMM: We're getting on.

(*He leans back in his chair, remains motionless.* NAGG *knocks on the lid of the other bin. Pause. He knocks harder. The lid lifts and the hands of* NELL *appear, gripping the rim. Then her head emerges. Lace cap. Very white face.*)

NELL: What is it, my pet?
(*Pause.*)
     Time for love?
225 NAGG: Were you asleep?
NELL: Oh no!
NAGG: Kiss me.
NELL: We can't.
NAGG: Try.

(*Their heads strain towards each other, fail to meet, fall apart again.*)

230 NELL: Why this farce, day after day?

(*Pause.*)

NAGG: I've lost me tooth.
NELL: When?
NAGG: I had it yesterday.
NELL: (*Elegiac.*) Ah yesterday!

(*They turn painfully towards each other.*)

235 NAGG: Can you see me?
NELL: Hardly. And you?

NAGG: What?
NELL: Can you see me?
NAGG: Hardly.
NELL: So much the better, so much the better.   240
NAGG: Don't say that.
(*Pause.*)
     Our sight has failed.
NELL: Yes.

(*Pause. They turn away from each other.*)

NAGG: Can you hear me?
NELL: Yes. And you?   245
NAGG: Yes.
(*Pause.*)
     Our hearing hasn't failed.
NELL: Our what?
NAGG: Our hearing.
NELL: No.   250
(*Pause.*)
     Have you anything else to say to me?
NAGG: Do you remember—
NELL: No.
NAGG: When we crashed on our tandem and lost our shanks.

(*They laugh heartily.*)

NELL: It was in the Ardennes.   255

(*They laugh less heartily.*)

NAGG: On the road to Sedan.
(*They laugh still less heartily.*)
     Are you cold?
NELL: Yes, perished. And you?
NAGG: (*Pause.*) I'm freezing.
(*Pause.*)
     Do you want to go in?   260
NELL: Yes.
NAGG: Then go in.
(NELL *does not move.*)
     Why don't you go in?
NELL: I don't know.

(*Pause.*)

NAGG: Has he changed your sawdust?   265
NELL: It isn't sawdust.
(*Pause. Wearily.*)
     Can you not be a little accurate, Nagg?
NAGG: Your sand then. It's not important.
NELL: It is important.

(*Pause.*)

NAGG: It was sawdust once.   270
NELL: Once!
NAGG: And now it's sand.
(*Pause.*)
     From the shore.
(*Pause. Impatiently.*)
     Now it's sand he fetches from the shore.
NELL: Now it's sand.   275

NAGG: Has he changed yours?

NELL: No.

NAGG: Nor mine.

(*Pause.*)

I won't have it!

(*Pause. Holding up the biscuit.*)

280 Do you want a bit?

NELL: No.

(*Pause.*)

Of what?

NAGG: Biscuit. I've kept you half.

(*He looks at the biscuit. Proudly.*)

Three quarters. For you. Here.

(*He proffers the biscuit.*)

285 No?

(*Pause.*)

Do you not feel well?

HAMM: (*Wearily.*) Quiet, quiet, you're keeping me awake.

(*Pause.*)

Talk softer.

(*Pause.*)

If I could sleep I might make love. I'd go into the woods.

290 My eyes would see . . . the sky, the earth. I'd run, run, they wouldn't catch me.

(*Pause.*)

Nature!

(*Pause.*)

There's something dripping in my head.

(*Pause.*)

A heart, a heart in my head.

(*Pause.*)

295 NAGG: (*Soft.*) Do you hear him? A heart in his head!

(*He chuckles cautiously.*)

NELL: One mustn't laugh at those things, Nagg. Why must you always laugh at them?

NAGG: Not so loud!

NELL: (*Without lowering her voice.*) Nothing is funnier than un-

300 happiness, I grant you that. But—

NAGG: (*Shocked.*) Oh!

NELL: Yes, yes, it's the most comical thing in the world. And we laugh, we laugh, with a will, in the beginning. But it's always the same thing. Yes, it's like the funny story we

305 have heard too often, we still find it funny, but we don't laugh any more.

(*Pause.*)

Have you anything else to say to me?

NAGG: No.

NELL: Are you quite sure?

(*Pause.*)

310 Then I'll leave you.

NAGG: Do you not want your biscuit?

(*Pause.*)

I'll keep it for you.

(*Pause.*)

I thought you were going to leave me.

NELL: I am going to leave you.

315 NAGG: Could you give me a scratch before you go?

NELL: No.

(*Pause.*)

Where?

NAGG: In the back.

NELL: No.

(*Pause.*)

Rub yourself against the rim. 320

NAGG: It's lower down. In the hollow.

NELL: What hollow?

NAGG: The hollow!

(*Pause.*)

Could you not?

(*Pause.*)

Yesterday you scratched me there. 325

NELL: (*Elegiac.*) Ah yesterday!

NAGG: Could you not?

(*Pause.*)

Would you like me to scratch you?

(*Pause.*)

Are you crying again?

NELL: I was trying. 330

(*Pause.*)

HAMM: Perhaps it's a little vein.

(*Pause.*)

NAGG: What was that he said?

NELL: Perhaps it's a little vein.

NAGG: What does that mean?

(*Pause.*)

That means nothing. 335

(*Pause.*)

Will I tell you the story of the tailor?

NELL: No.

(*Pause.*)

What for?

NAGG: To cheer you up.

NELL: It's not funny. 340

NAGG: It always made you laugh.

(*Pause.*)

The first time I thought you'd die.

NELL: It was on Lake Como.

(*Pause.*)

One April afternoon.

(*Pause.*)

Can you believe it? 345

NAGG: What?

NELL: That we once went out rowing on Lake Como.

(*Pause.*)

One April afternoon.

NAGG: We had got engaged the day before.

NELL: Engaged! 350

NAGG: You were in such fits that we capsized. By rights we should have been drowned.

NELL: It was because I felt happy.

NAGG: (*Indignant.*) It was not, it was not, it was my story and nothing else. Happy! Don't you laugh at it still? Every 355 time I tell it. Happy!

NELL: It was deep, deep. And you could see down to the bottom. So white. So clean.

NAGG: Let me tell it again.

(*Raconteur's voice.*)

360   An Englishman, needing a pair of striped trousers in a hurry for the New Year festivities, goes to his tailor who takes his measurements.

(*Tailor's voice.*)

    "That's the lot, come back in four days, I'll have it ready." Good. Four days later.

(*Tailor's voice.*)

365   "So sorry, come back in a week, I've made a mess of the seat." Good, that's all right, a neat seat can be very ticklish. A week later.

(*Tailor's voice.*)

    "Frightfully sorry, come back in ten days, I've made a hash of the crotch." Good, can't be helped, a snug crotch is al-

370   ways a teaser. Ten days later.

(*Tailor's voice.*)

    "Dreadfully sorry, come back in a fortnight, I've made a balls of the fly." Good, at a pinch, a smart fly is a stiff proposition.

(*Pause. Normal voice.*)

    I never told it worse.

(*Pause. Gloomy.*)

    I tell this story worse and worse.

(*Pause. Raconteur's voice.*)

375   Well, to make it short, the bluebells are blowing and he ballockses the buttonholes.

(*Customer's voice.*)

    "God damn you to hell, Sir, no, it's indecent, there are limits! In six days, do you hear me, six days, God made the world. Yes Sir, no less Sir, the WORLD! And you are not

380   bloody well capable of making me a pair of trousers in three months!"

(*Tailor's voice, scandalized.*)

    "But my dear Sir, my dear Sir, look—

(*Disdainful gesture, disgustedly.*)

    —at the world—

(*Pause.*)

    and look—

(*Loving gesture, proudly.*)

385   —at my TROUSERS!"

(*Pause. He looks at* NELL *who has remained impassive, her eyes unseeing, breaks into a high forced laugh, cuts it short, pokes his head towards* NELL, *launches his laugh again.*)

HAMM: Silence!

(NAGG *starts, cuts short his laugh.*)

NELL: You could see down to the bottom.

HAMM: (*Exasperated.*) Have you not finished? Will you never finish?

(*With sudden fury.*)

390   Will this never finish?

(NAGG *disappears into his bin, closes the lid behind him.* NELL *does not move. Frenziedly.*)

    My kingdom for a nightman!

(*He whistles. Enter* CLOV.)

    Clear away this muck! Chuck it in the sea!

(CLOV *goes to bins, halts.*)

NELL: So white.

HAMM: What? What's she blathering about?

(CLOV *stoops, takes* NELL's *hand, feels her pulse.*)

NELL: (*To* CLOV.) Desert!   395

(CLOV *lets go her hand, pushes her back in the bin, closes the lid.*)

CLOV: (*Returning to his place beside the chair.*) She has no pulse.

HAMM: What was she drivelling about?

CLOV: She told me to go away, into the desert.

HAMM: Damn busybody! Is that all?

CLOV: No.   400

HAMM: What else?

CLOV: I didn't understand.

HAMM: Have you bottled her?

CLOV: Yes.

HAMM: Are they both bottled?   405

CLOV: Yes.

HAMM: Screw down the lids.

(CLOV *goes towards door.*)

    Time enough.

(CLOV *halts.*)

    My anger subsides, I'd like to pee.

CLOV: (*With alacrity.*) I'll go and get the catheter.   410

(*He goes towards door.*)

HAMM: Time enough.

(CLOV *halts.*)

    Give me my pain-killer.

CLOV: It's too soon.

(*Pause.*)

    It's too soon on top of your tonic, it wouldn't act.

HAMM: In the morning they brace you up and in the evening   415 they calm you down. Unless it's the other way round.

(*Pause.*)

    That old doctor, he's dead naturally?

CLOV: He wasn't old.

HAMM: But he's dead?

CLOV: Naturally.   420

(*Pause.*)

    You ask *me* that?

(*Pause.*)

HAMM: Take me for a little turn.

(CLOV *goes behind the chair and pushes it forward.*)

    Not too fast!

(CLOV *pushes chair.*)

    Right round the world!

(CLOV *pushes chair.*)

    Hug the walls, then back to the center again.   425

(CLOV *pushes chair.*)

    I was right in the center, wasn't I?

CLOV: (*Pushing.*) Yes.

HAMM: We'd need a proper wheel-chair. With big wheels. Bicycle wheels!

(*Pause.*)

    Are you hugging?   430

CLOV: (*Pushing.*) Yes.

HAMM: (*Groping for wall.*) It's a lie! Why do you lie to me?

CLOV: (*Bearing closer to wall.*) There! There!

HAMM: Stop!

(CLOV *stops chair close to back wall.* HAMM *lays his hand against wall.*)

435   Old wall!

(*Pause.*)

      Beyond is the . . . other hell.

(*Pause. Violently.*)

      Closer! Closer! Up against!

CLOV: Take away your hand.

(HAMM *withdraws his hand.* CLOV *rams chair against wall.*)

      There!

(HAMM *leans towards wall, applies his ear to it.*)

440   HAMM: Do you hear?

(*He strikes the wall with his knuckles.*)

      Do you hear? Hollow bricks!

(*He strikes again.*)

      All that's hollow!

(*Pause. He straightens up. Violently.*)

      That's enough. Back!

CLOV: We haven't done the round.

445   HAMM: Back to my place!

(CLOV *pushes chair back to center.*)

      Is that my place?

CLOV: Yes, that's your place.

HAMM: Am I right in the center?

CLOV: I'll measure it.

450   HAMM: More or less! More or less!

CLOV: (*Moving chair slightly.*) There!

HAMM: I'm more or less in the center?

CLOV: I'd say so.

HAMM: You'd say so! Put me right in the center!

455   CLOV: I'll go and get the tape.

HAMM: Roughly! Roughly!

(CLOV *moves chair slightly.*)

      Bang in the center!

CLOV: There!

(*Pause.*)

HAMM: I feel a little too far to the left.

(CLOV *moves chair slightly.*)

460   Now I feel a little too far to the right.

(CLOV *moves chair slightly.*)

      I feel a little too far forward.

(CLOV *moves chair slightly.*)

      Now I feel a little too far back.

(CLOV *moves chair slightly.*)

      Don't stay there,

(*i.e., Behind the chair.*)

      you give me the shivers.

(CLOV *returns to his place beside the chair.*)

465   CLOV: If I could kill him I'd die happy.

(*Pause.*)

HAMM: What's the weather like?

CLOV: As usual.

HAMM: Look at the earth.

CLOV: I've looked.

HAMM: With the glass?   470

CLOV: No need of the glass.

HAMM: Look at it with the glass.

CLOV: I'll go and get the glass.

(*Exit* CLOV.)

HAMM: No need of the glass!

(*Enter* CLOV *with telescope.*)

CLOV: I'm back again, with the glass.   475

(*He goes to window right, looks up at it.*)

      I need the steps.

HAMM: Why? Have you shrunk?

(*Exit* CLOV *with telescope.*)

      I don't like that, I don't like that.

(*Enter* CLOV *with ladder, but without telescope.*)

CLOV: I'm back again, with the steps.

(*He sets down ladder under window right, gets up on it, realizes he has not the telescope, gets down.*)

      I need the glass.   480

(*He goes towards door.*)

HAMM: (*Violently.*) But you have the glass!

CLOV: (*Halting, violently.*) No, I haven't the glass!

(*Exit* CLOV.)

HAMM: This is deadly.

(*Enter* CLOV *with telescope. He goes towards ladder.*)

CLOV: Things are livening up.

(*He gets up on ladder, raises the telescope, lets it fall.*)

      I did it on purpose.   485

(*He gets down, picks up the telescope, turns it on auditorium.*)

      I see . . . a multitude . . . in transports . . . of joy.

(*Pause.*)

      That's what I call a magnifier.

(*He lowers the telescope, turns towards* HAMM.)

      Well? Don't we laugh?

HAMM: (*After reflection.*) I don't.

CLOV: (*After reflection.*) Nor I.   490

(*He gets up on ladder, turns the telescope on the without.*)

      Let's see.

(*He looks, moving the telescope.*)

      Zero . . .

(*He looks.*)

      . . . zero . . .

(*He looks.*)

      . . . and zero.

HAMM: Nothing stirs. All is—   495

CLOV: Zer—

HAMM: (*Violently.*) Wait till you're spoken to!

(*Normal voice.*)

      All is . . . all is . . . all is what?

(*Violently.*)

      All is what?

CLOV: What all is? In a word? Is that what you want to know?   500

      Just a moment.

(*He turns the telescope on the without, looks, lowers the telescope, turns towards* HAMM.)

    Corpsed.

(*Pause.*)

    Well? Content?

HAMM: Look at the sea.

505 CLOV: It's the same.

HAMM: Look at the ocean!

(CLOV *gets down, takes a few steps towards window left, goes back for ladder, carries it over and sets it down under window left, gets up on it, turns the telescope on the without, looks at length. He starts, lowers the telescope, examines it, turns it again on the without.*)

CLOV: Never seen anything like that!

HAMM: (*Anxious.*) What? A sail? A fin? Smoke?

CLOV: (*Looking.*) The light is sunk.

510 HAMM: (*Relieved.*) Pah! We all knew that.

CLOV: (*Looking.*) There was a bit left.

HAMM: The base.

CLOV: (*Looking.*) Yes.

HAMM: And now?

515 CLOV: (*Looking.*) All gone.

HAMM: No gulls?

CLOV: (*Looking.*) Gulls!

HAMM: And the horizon? Nothing on the horizon?

CLOV: (*Lowering the telescope, turning towards* HAMM, *exasperated.*) What in God's name could there be on the horizon?

(*Pause.*)

520 HAMM: The waves, how are the waves?

CLOV: The waves?

(*He turns the telescope on the waves.*)

    Lead.

HAMM: And the sun?

CLOV: (*Looking.*) Zero.

525 HAMM: But it should be sinking. Look again.

CLOV: (*Looking.*) Damn the sun.

HAMM: Is it night already then?

CLOV: (*Looking.*) No.

HAMM: Then what is it?

530 CLOV: (*Looking.*) Gray.

(*Lowering the telescope, turning towards* HAMM, *louder.*)

    Gray!

(*Pause. Still louder.*)

    GRRAY!

(*Pause. He gets down, approaches* HAMM *from behind, whispers in his ear.*)

HAMM: (*Starting.*) Gray! Did I hear you say gray?

CLOV: Light black. From pole to pole.

535 HAMM: You exaggerate.

(*Pause.*)

    Don't stay there, you give me the shivers.

(CLOV *returns to his place beside the chair.*)

CLOV: Why this farce, day after day?

HAMM: Routine. One never knows.

(*Pause.*)

    Last night I saw inside my breast. There was a big sore.

CLOV: Pah! You saw your heart.   540

HAMM: No, it was living.

(*Pause. Anguished.*)

    Clov!

CLOV: Yes.

HAMM: What's happening?

CLOV: Something is taking its course.   545

(*Pause.*)

HAMM: Clov!

CLOV: (*Impatiently.*) What is it?

HAMM: We're not beginning to . . . to . . . mean something?

CLOV: Mean something! You and I, mean something!

(*Brief laugh.*)

    Ah that's a good one!   550

HAMM: I wonder.

(*Pause.*)

    Imagine if a rational being came back to earth, wouldn't he be liable to get ideas into his head if he observed us long enough.

(*Voice of rational being.*)

    Ah, good, now I see what it is, yes, now I understand what 555 they're at!

(CLOV *starts, drops the telescope and begins to scratch his belly with both hands. Normal voice.*)

    And without going so far as that, we ourselves . . .

(*With emotion.*)

    . . . we ourselves . . . at certain moments . . .

(*Vehemently.*)

    To think perhaps it won't all have been for nothing!

CLOV: (*Anguished, scratching himself.*) I have a flea!   560

HAMM: A flea! Are there still fleas?

CLOV: On me there's one.

(*Scratching.*)

    Unless it's a crablouse.

HAMM: (*Very perturbed.*) But humanity might start from there all over again! Catch him, for the love of God!   565

CLOV: I'll go and get the powder.

(*Exit* CLOV.)

HAMM: A flea! This is awful! What a day!

(*Enter* CLOV *with a sprinkling-tin.*)

CLOV: I'm back again, with the insecticide.

HAMM: Let him have it!

(CLOV *loosens the top of his trousers, pulls it forward and shakes powder into the aperture. He stoops, looks, waits, starts, frenziedly shakes more powder, stoops, looks, waits.*)

CLOV: The bastard!   570

HAMM: Did you get him?

CLOV: Looks like it.

(*He drops the tin and adjusts his trousers.*)

    Unless he's laying doggo.

HAMM: Laying! Lying you mean. Unless he's *lying* doggo.

CLOV: Ah? One says lying? One doesn't say laying?   575

HAMM: Use your head, can't you. If he was laying we'd be bitched.

CLOV: Ah.

(*Pause.*)
     What about that pee?
580 HAMM: I'm having it.
     CLOV: Ah that's the spirit, that's the spirit!

(*Pause.*)

     HAMM: (*With ardour.*) Let's go from here, the two of us!
          South! You can make a raft and the currents will carry us
          away, far away, to other . . . mammals!
585 CLOV: God forbid!
     HAMM: Alone, I'll embark alone! Get working on that raft
          immediately. Tomorrow I'll be gone for ever.
     CLOV: (*Hastening towards door.*) I'll start straight away.
     HAMM: Wait!
     (CLOV *halts.*)
590   Will there be sharks, do you think?
     CLOV: Sharks? I don't know. If there are there will be.

(*He goes towards door.*)

     HAMM: Wait!
     (CLOV *halts.*)
          Is it not yet time for my pain-killer?
     CLOV: (*Violently.*) No!

(*He goes towards door.*)

595 HAMM: Wait!
     (CLOV *halts.*)
          How are your eyes?
     CLOV: Bad.
     HAMM: But you can see.
     CLOV: All I want.
600 HAMM: How are your legs?
     CLOV: Bad.
     HAMM: But you can walk.
     CLOV: I come . . . and go.
     HAMM: In my house.
     (*Pause. With prophetic relish.*)
605   One day you'll be blind, like me. You'll be sitting there, a
          speck in the void, in the dark, for ever, like me.
     (*Pause.*)
          One day you'll say to yourself, I'm tired, I'll sit down, and
          you'll go and sit down. Then you'll say, I'm hungry, I'll get
          up and get something to eat. But you won't get up. You'll
610   say, I shouldn't have sat down, but since I have I'll sit on a
          little longer, then I'll get up and get something to eat. But
          you won't get up and you won't get anything to eat.
     (*Pause.*)
          You'll look at the wall a while, then you'll say, I'll close my
          eyes, perhaps have a little sleep, after that I'll feel better,
615   and you'll close them. And when you open them again
          there'll be no wall any more.
     (*Pause.*)
          Infinite emptiness will be all around you, all the resur-
          rected dead of all the ages wouldn't fill it, and there you'll
          be like a little bit of grit in the middle of the steppe.
     (*Pause.*)
620   Yes, one day you'll know what it is, you'll be like me, ex-
          cept that you won't have anyone with you, because you

won't have had pity on anyone and because there won't
be anyone left to have pity on.

(*Pause.*)

CLOV: It's not certain.
(*Pause.*)
     And there's one thing you forget.   625
HAMM: Ah?
CLOV: I can't sit down.
HAMM: (*Impatiently.*) Well you'll lie down then, what the hell!
     Or you'll come to a standstill, simply stop and stand still,
     the way you are now. One day you'll say, I'm tired, I'll   630
     stop. What does the attitude matter?

(*Pause.*)

CLOV: So you all want me to leave you.
HAMM: Naturally.
CLOV: Then I'll leave you.
HAMM: You can't leave us.   635
CLOV: Then I won't leave you.

(*Pause.*)

HAMM: Why don't you finish us?
(*Pause.*)
     I'll tell you the combination of the cupboard if you
     promise to finish me.
CLOV: I couldn't finish you.   640
HAMM: Then you won't finish me.

(*Pause.*)

CLOV: I'll leave you, I have things to do.
HAMM: Do you remember when you came here?
CLOV: No. Too small, you told me.
HAMM: Do you remember your father.   645
CLOV: (*Wearily.*) Same answer.
(*Pause.*)
     You've asked me these questions millions of times.
HAMM: I love the old questions.
(*With fervour.*)
     Ah the old questions, the old answers, there's nothing like
     them!   650
(*Pause.*)
     It was I was a father to you.
CLOV: Yes.
(*He looks at* HAMM *fixedly.*)
     You were that to me.
HAMM: My house a home for you.
CLOV: Yes.   655
(*He looks about him.*)
     This was that for me.
HAMM: (*Proudly.*) But for me,
(*Gesture towards himself.*)
     no father. But for Hamm,
(*Gesture towards surroundings.*)
     no home.

(*Pause.*)

CLOV: I'll leave you.   660

HAMM: Did you ever think of one thing?

CLOV: Never.

HAMM: That here we're down in a hole.

(*Pause.*)

But beyond the hills? Eh? Perhaps it's still green. Eh?

(*Pause.*)

665   Flora! Pomona!

(*Ecstatically.*)

Ceres!

(*Pause.*)

Perhaps you won't need to go very far.

CLOV: I can't go very far.

(*Pause.*)

I'll leave you.

670 HAMM: Is my dog ready?

CLOV: He lacks a leg.

HAMM: Is he silky?

CLOV: He's a kind of Pomeranian.

HAMM: Go and get him.

675 CLOV: He lacks a leg.

HAMM: Go and get him!

(*Exit* CLOV.)

We're getting on.

(*Enter* CLOV *holding by one of its three legs a black toy dog.*)

CLOV: Your dogs are here.

(*He hands the dog to* HAMM *who feels it, fondles it.*)

HAMM: He's white, isn't he?

680 CLOV: Nearly.

HAMM: What do you mean, nearly? Is he white or isn't he?

CLOV: He isn't.

(*Pause.*)

HAMM: You've forgotten the sex.

CLOV: (*Vexed.*) But he isn't finished. The sex goes on at the end.

(*Pause.*)

685 HAMM: You haven't put on his ribbon.

CLOV: (*Angrily.*) But he isn't finished, I tell you! First you finish your dog and then you put on his ribbon!

(*Pause.*)

HAMM: Can he stand?

CLOV: I don't know.

690 HAMM: Try.

(*He hands the dog to* CLOV *who places it on the ground.*)

Well?

CLOV: Wait!

(*He squats down and tries to get the dog to stand on its three legs, fails, lets it go. The dog falls on its side.*)

HAMM: (*Impatiently.*) Well?

CLOV: He's standing.

695 HAMM: (*Groping for the dog.*) Where? Where is he?

(CLOV *holds up the dog in a standing position.*)

CLOV: There.

(*He takes* HAMM's *hand and guides it towards the dog's head.*)

HAMM: (*His hand on the dog's head.*) Is he gazing at me?

CLOV: Yes.

HAMM: (*Proudly.*) As if he were asking me to take him for a walk?   700

CLOV: If you like.

HAMM: (*As before.*) Or as if he were begging me for a bone.

(*He withdraws his hand.*)

Leave him like that, standing there imploring me.

(CLOV *straightens up. The dog falls on its side.*)

CLOV: I'll leave you.

HAMM: Have you had your visions?   705

CLOV: Less.

HAMM: Is Mother Pegg's light on?

CLOV: Light! How could anyone's light be on?

HAMM: Extinguished!

CLOV: Naturally it's extinguished. If it's not on it's extin-   710
guished.

HAMM: No, I mean Mother Pegg.

CLOV: But naturally she's extinguished!

(*Pause.*)

What's the matter with you today?

HAMM: I'm taking my course.   715

(*Pause.*)

Is she buried?

CLOV: Buried! Who would have buried her?

HAMM: You.

CLOV: Me! Haven't I enough to do without burying people?

HAMM: But you'll bury me.   720

CLOV: No I won't bury you.

(*Pause.*)

HAMM: She was bonny once, like a flower of the field.

(*With reminiscent leer.*)

And a great one for the men!

CLOV: We too were bonny—once. It's a rare thing not to have been bonny—once.   725

(*Pause.*)

HAMM: Go and get the gaff.

(CLOV *goes to door, halts.*)

CLOV: Do this, do that, and I do it. I never refuse. Why?

HAMM: You're not able to.

CLOV: Soon I won't do it any more.

HAMM: You won't be able to any more.   730

(*Exit* CLOV.)

Ah the creatures, the creatures, everything has to be explained to them.

(*Enter* CLOV *with gaff.*)

CLOV: Here's your gaff. Stick it up.

(*He gives the gaff to* HAMM *who, wielding it like a puntpole, tries to move his chair.*)

HAMM: Did I move?
735   CLOV: No.

(HAMM *throws down the gaff.*)

HAMM: Go and get the oilcan.
CLOV: What for?
HAMM: To oil the castors.
CLOV: I oiled them yesterday.
740   HAMM: Yesterday! What does that mean? Yesterday!
      CLOV: (*Violently.*) That means that bloody awful day, long ago, before this bloody awful day. I use the words you taught me. If they don't mean anything any more, teach me others. Or let me be silent.

(*Pause.*)

745   HAMM: I once knew a madman who thought the end of the world had come. He was a painter—and engraver. I had a great fondness for him. I used to go and see him, in the asylum. I'd take him by the hand and drag him to the window. Look! There! All that rising corn! And there! Look!
750   The sails of the herring fleet! All that loveliness!
      (*Pause.*)
      He'd snatch away his hand and go back into his corner. Appalled. All he had seen was ashes.
      (*Pause.*)
      He alone had been spared.
      (*Pause.*)
      Forgotten.
      (*Pause.*)
755   It appears the case is . . . was not so . . . so unusual.
      CLOV: A madman? When was that?
      HAMM: Oh way back, way back, you weren't in the land of the living.
      CLOV: God be with the days!

(*Pause.* HAMM *raises his toque.*)

760   HAMM: I had a great fondness for him.
      (*Pause. He puts on his toque again.*)
      He was a painter—and engraver.
      CLOV: There are so many terrible things.
      HAMM: No, no, there are not so many now.
      (*Pause.*)
      Clov!
765   CLOV: Yes.
      HAMM: Do you not think this has gone on long enough?
      CLOV: Yes!
      (*Pause.*)
      What?
      HAMM: This . . . this . . . thing.
770   CLOV: I've always thought so.
      (*Pause.*)
      You not?
      HAMM: (*Gloomily.*) Then it's a day like any other day.
      CLOV: As long as it lasts.
      (*Pause.*)

All life long the same inanities.
HAMM: I can't leave you.   775
CLOV: I know. And you can't follow me.

(*Pause.*)

HAMM: If you leave me how shall I know?
CLOV: (*Briskly.*) Well you simply whistle me and if I don't come running it means I've left you.

(*Pause.*)

HAMM: You won't come and kiss me goodbye?   780
CLOV: Oh I shouldn't think so.

(*Pause.*)

HAMM: But you might be merely dead in your kitchen.
CLOV: The result would be the same.
HAMM: Yes, but how would I know, if you were merely dead in your kitchen?   785
CLOV: Well . . . sooner or later I'd start to stink.
HAMM: You stink already. The whole place stinks of corpses.
CLOV: The whole universe.
HAMM: (*Angrily.*) To hell with the universe.
(*Pause.*)
      Think of something.   790
CLOV: What?
HAMM: An idea, have an idea.
(*Angrily.*)
      A bright idea!
CLOV: Ah good.
(*He starts pacing to and fro, his eyes fixed on the ground, his hands behind his back. He halts.*)
      The pains in my legs! It's unbelievable! Soon I won't be   795
      able to think any more.
HAMM: You won't be able to leave me.
(CLOV *resumes his pacing.*)
      What are you doing?
CLOV: Having an idea.
(*He paces.*)
      Ah!   800

(*He halts.*)

HAMM: What a brain!
(*Pause.*)
      Well?
CLOV: Wait!
(*He meditates. Not very convinced.*)
      Yes . . .
(*Pause. More convinced.*)
      Yes!   805
(*He raises his head.*)
      I have it! I set the alarm.

(*Pause.*)

HAMM: This is perhaps not one of my bright days, but frankly—
CLOV: You whistle me. I don't come. The alarm rings. I'm gone. It doesn't ring. I'm dead.   810

(*Pause.*)

HAMM: Is it working?
(*Pause. Impatiently.*)
    The alarm, is it working?
CLOV: Why wouldn't it be working?
HAMM: Because it's worked too much.
815 CLOV: But it's hardly worked at all.
HAMM: (*Angrily.*) Then because it's worked too little!
CLOV: I'll go and see.
(*Exit* CLOV. *Brief ring of alarm off. Enter* CLOV *with alarm-clock. He holds it against* HAMM's *ear and releases alarm. They listen to it ringing to the end. Pause.*)
    Fit to wake the dead! Did you hear it?
HAMM: Vaguely.
820 CLOV: The end is terrific!
HAMM: I prefer the middle.
(*Pause.*)
    Is it not time for my pain-killer?
CLOV: No!
(*He goes to door, turns.*)
    I'll leave you.
825 HAMM: It's time for my story. Do you want to listen to my
    story.
CLOV: No.
HAMM: Ask my father if he wants to listen to my story.

(CLOV *goes to bins, raises the lid of* NAGG's, *stoops, looks into it. Pause. He straightens up.*)

CLOV: He's asleep.
830 HAMM: Wake him.

(CLOV *stoops, wakes* NAGG *with the alarm. Unintelligible words.* CLOV *straightens up.*)

CLOV: He doesn't want to listen to your story.
HAMM: I'll give him a bon-bon.

(CLOV *stoops. As before.*)

CLOV: He wants a sugar-plum.
HAMM: He'll get a sugar-plum.

(CLOV *stoops. As before.*)

835 CLOV: It's a deal.
(*He goes towards door.* NAGG's *hands appear, gripping the rim. Then the head emerges.* CLOV *reaches door, turns.*)
    Do you believe in the life to come?
HAMM: Mine was always that.
(*Exit* CLOV.)
    Got him that time!
NAGG: I'm listening.
840 HAMM: Scoundrel! Why did you engender me?
NAGG: I didn't know.
HAMM: What? What didn't you know?
NAGG: That it'd be you.
(*Pause.*)
    You'll give me a sugar-plum?
845 HAMM: After the audition.

NAGG: You swear?
HAMM: Yes.
NAGG: On what?
HAMM: My honor.

(*Pause. They laugh heartily.*)

NAGG: Two.   850
HAMM: One.
NAGG: One for me and one for—
HAMM: One! Silence!
(*Pause.*)
    Where was I?
(*Pause. Gloomily.*)
    It's finished, we're finished.   855
(*Pause.*)
    Nearly finished.
(*Pause.*)
    There'll be no more speech.
(*Pause.*)
    Something dripping in my head, ever since the fontanelles.
(*Stifled hilarity of* NAGG.)
    Splash, splash, always on the same spot.
(*Pause.*)
    Perhaps it's a little vein.   860
(*Pause.*)
    A little artery.
(*Pause. More animated.*)
    Enough of that, it's story time, where was I?
(*Pause. Narrative tone.*)
    The man came crawling towards me, on his belly. Pale,
    wonderfully pale and thin, he seemed on the point of—
(*Pause. Normal tone.*)
    No, I've done that bit.   865
(*Pause. Narrative tone.*)
    I calmly filled my pipe—the meerschaum, lit it with . . .
    let us say a vesta, drew a few puffs. Aah!
(*Pause.*)
    Well, what is it *you* want?
(*Pause.*)
    It was an extra-ordinarily bitter day, I remember, zero by
    the thermometer. But considering it was Christmas Eve   870
    there was nothing . . . extra-ordinary about that. Season-
    able weather, for once in a way.
(*Pause.*)
    Well, what ill wind blows you my way? He raised his face
    to me, black with mingled dirt and tears.
(*Pause. Normal tone.*)
    That should do it.   875
(*Narrative tone.*)
    No no, don't look at me, don't look at me. He dropped his
    eyes and mumbled something, apologies I presume.
(*Pause.*)
    I'm a busy man, you know, the final touches, before the
    festivities, you know what it is.
(*Pause. Forcibly.*)
    Come on now, what is the object of this invasion?   880
(*Pause.*)
    It was a glorious bright day, I remember, fifty by the he-
    liometer, but already the sun was sinking down into the . . .
    down among the dead.

(*Normal tone.*)
Nicely put, that.
(*Narrative tone.*)
885 Come on now, come on, present your petition and let me
resume my labors.
(*Pause. Normal tone.*)
There's English for you. Ah well . . .
(*Narrative tone.*)
It was then he took the plunge. It's my little one, he said.
Tsstss, a little one, that's bad. My little boy, he said, as if the
890 sex mattered. Where did he come from? He named the
hole. A good half-day, on horse. What are you insinuating? That the place is still inhabited? No no, not a soul, except himself and the child—assuming he existed. Good. I
enquired about the situation at Kov, beyond the gulf. Not
895 a sinner. Good. And you expect me to believe you have
left your little one back there, all alone, and alive into the
bargain? Come now!
(*Pause.*)
It was a howling wild day, I remember, a hundred by the
anenometer. The wind was tearing up the dead pines and
900 sweeping them . . . away.
(*Pause. Normal tone.*)
A bit feeble, that.
(*Narrative tone.*)
Come on, man, speak up, what is it you want from me, I
have to put up my holly.
(*Pause.*)
Well to make it short it finally transpired that what he wanted
905 from me was . . . bread for his brat? Bread? But I have no bread,
it doesn't agree with me. Good. Then perhaps a little corn?
(*Pause. Normal tone.*)
That should do it.
(*Narrative tone.*)
Corn, yes, I have corn, it's true, in my granaries. But use
your head. I give you some corn, a pound, a pound and a
910 half, you bring it back to your child and you make him—
if he's still alive—a nice pot of porridge,
(NAGG *reacts.*)
a nice pot and a half of porridge, full of nourishment.
Good. The colors come back into his little cheeks—per-
haps. And then?
(*Pause.*)
915 I lost patience.
(*Violently.*)
Use your head, can't you, use your head, you're on earth,
there's no cure for that!
(*Pause.*)
It was an exceedingly dry day, I remember, zero by the hy-
grometer. Ideal weather, for my lumbago.
(*Pause. Violently.*)
920 But what in God's name do you imagine? That the earth
will awake in spring? That the rivers and seas will run with
fish again? That there's manna in heaven still for imbeciles
like you?
(*Pause.*)
Gradually I cooled down, sufficiently at least to ask him how
925 long he had taken on the way. Three whole days. Good. In
what condition he had left the child. Deep in sleep.
(*Forcibly.*)
But deep in what sleep, deep in what sleep already?

(*Pause.*)
Well to make it short I finally offered to take him into my
service. He had touched a chord. And then I imagined al-
ready that I wasn't much longer for this world. 930
(*He laughs. Pause.*)
Well?
(*Pause.*)
Well? Here if you were careful you might die a nice nat-
ural death, in peace and comfort.
(*Pause.*)
Well?
(*Pause.*)
In the end he asked me would I consent to take in the 935
child as well—if he were still alive.
(*Pause.*)
It was the moment I was waiting for.
(*Pause.*)
Would I consent to take in the child . . .
(*Pause.*)
I can see him still, down on his knees, his hands flat on the
ground, glaring at me with his mad eyes, in defiance of my 940
wishes.
(*Pause. Normal tone.*)
I'll soon have finished with this story.
(*Pause.*)
Unless I bring in other characters.
(*Pause.*)
But where would I find them?
(*Pause.*)
Where would I look for them? 945
(*Pause. He whistles. Enter* CLOV.)
Let us pray to God.
NAGG: Me sugar-plum!
CLOV: There's a rat in the kitchen!
HAMM: A rat! Are there still rats?
CLOV: In the kitchen there's one. 950
HAMM: And you haven't exterminated him?
CLOV: Half. You disturbed us.
HAMM: He can't get away?
CLOV: No.
HAMM: You'll finish him later. Let us pray to God. 955
CLOV: Again!
NAGG: Me sugar-plum!
HAMM: God first!
(*Pause.*)
Are you right?
CLOV: (*Resigned.*) Off we go. 960
HAMM: (*To* NAGG.) And you?
NAGG: (*Clasping his hands, closing his eyes, in a gabble.*) Our Fa-
ther which art—
HAMM: Silence! In silence! Where are your manners?
(*Pause.*)
Off we go. 965
(*Attitudes of prayer. Silence. Abandoning his attitude, discouraged.*)
Well?
CLOV: (*Abandoning his attitude.*) What a hope! And you?
HAMM: Sweet damn all!
(*To* NAGG.)
And you?
NAGG: Wait! 970
(*Pause. Abandoning his attitude.*)

Nothing doing!

HAMM: The bastard! He doesn't exist!

CLOV: Not yet.

NAGG: Me sugar-plum!

975   HAMM: There are no more sugar-plums!

(*Pause.*)

NAGG: It's natural. After all I'm your father. It's true if it hadn't been me it would have been someone else. But that's no excuse.

(*Pause.*)

980   Turkish Delight, for example, which no longer exists, we all know that, there is nothing in the world I love more. And one day I'll ask you for some, in return for a kindness, and you'll promise it to me. One must live with the times.

(*Pause.*)

Whom did you call when you were a tiny boy, and were frightened, in the dark? Your mother? No. Me. We let you

985   cry. Then we moved you out of earshot, so that we might sleep in peace.

(*Pause.*)

I was asleep, as happy as a king, and you woke me up to have me listen to you. It wasn't indispensable, you didn't really need to have me listen to you.

(*Pause.*)

990   I hope the day will come when you'll really need to have me listen to you, and need to hear my voice, any voice.

(*Pause.*)

Yes, I hope I'll live till then, to hear you calling me like when you were a tiny boy, and were frightened, in the dark, and I was your only hope.

(*Pause.* NAGG *knocks on lid of* NELL's *bin. Pause.*)

995   Nell!

(*Pause. He knocks louder. Pause. Louder.*)

Nell!

(*Pause.* NAGG *sinks back into his bin, closes the lid behind him. Pause.*)

HAMM: Our revels now are ended.

(*He gropes for the dog.*)

The dog's gone.

CLOV: He's not a real dog, he can't go.

1000   HAMM: (*Groping.*) He's not there.

CLOV: He's lain down.

HAMM: Give him up to me.

(CLOV *picks up the dog and gives it to* HAMM. HAMM *holds it in his arms. Pause.* HAMM *throws away the dog.*)

Dirty brute!

(CLOV *begins to pick up the objects lying on the ground.*)

What are you doing?

1005   CLOV: Putting things in order.

(*He straightens up. Fervently.*)

I'm going to clear everything away!

(*He starts picking up again.*)

HAMM: Order!

CLOV: (*Straightening up.*) I love order. It's my dream. A world where all would be silent and still and each thing in its last

1010   place, under the last dust.

(*He starts picking up again.*)

HAMM: (*Exasperated.*) What in God's name do you think you are doing?

CLOV: (*Straightening up.*) I'm doing my best to create a little order.

HAMM: Drop it!   1015

(CLOV *drops the objects he has picked up.*)

CLOV: After all, there or elsewhere.

(*He goes towards door.*)

HAMM: (*Irritably.*) What's wrong with your feet?

CLOV: My feet?

HAMM: Tramp! Tramp!

CLOV: I must have put on my boots.   1020

HAMM: Your slippers were hurting you?

(*Pause.*)

CLOV: I'll leave you.

HAMM: No!

CLOV: What is there to keep me here?

HAMM: The dialogue.   1025

(*Pause.*)

I've got on with my story.

(*Pause.*)

I've got on with it well.

(*Pause. Irritably.*)

Ask me where I've got to.

CLOV: Oh, by the way, your story?

HAMM: (*Surprised.*) What story?   1030

CLOV: The one you've been telling yourself all your days.

HAMM: Ah you mean my chronicle?

CLOV: That's the one.

(*Pause.*)

HAMM: (*Angrily.*) Keep going, can't you, keep going!

CLOV: You've got on with it, I hope.   1035

HAMM: (*Modestly.*) Oh not very far, not very far.

(*He sighs.*)

There are days like that, one isn't inspired.

(*Pause.*)

Nothing you can do about it, just wait for it to come.

(*Pause.*)

No forcing, no forcing, it's fatal.

(*Pause.*)

I've got on with it a little all the same.   1040

(*Pause.*)

Technique, you know.

(*Pause. Irritably.*)

I say I've got on with it a little all the same.

CLOV: (*Admiringly.*) Well I never! In spite of everything you were able to get on with it!

HAMM: (*Modestly.*) Oh not very far, you know, not very far,   1045
but nevertheless, better than nothing.

CLOV: Better than nothing! Is it possible?

HAMM: I'll tell you how it goes. He comes crawling on his belly—

1050 CLOV: Who?

HAMM: What?

CLOV: Who do you mean, he?

HAMM: Who do I mean! Yet another.

CLOV: Ah him! I wasn't sure.

1055 HAMM: Crawling on his belly, whining for bread for his brat. He's offered a job as gardener. Before—

(CLOV *bursts out laughing.*)

What is there so funny about that?

CLOV: A job as gardener!

HAMM: Is that what tickles you?

1060 CLOV: It must be that.

HAMM: It wouldn't be the bread?

CLOV: Or the brat.

(*Pause.*)

HAMM: The whole thing is comical, I grant you that. What about having a good guffaw the two of us together?

1065 CLOV: (*After reflection.*) I couldn't guffaw again today.

HAMM: (*After reflection.*) Nor I.

(*Pause.*)

I continue then. Before accepting with gratitude he asks if he may have his little boy with him.

CLOV: What age?

1070 HAMM: Oh tiny.

CLOV: He would have climbed the trees.

HAMM: All the little odd jobs.

CLOV: And then he would have grown up.

HAMM: Very likely.

(*Pause.*)

1075 CLOV: Keep going, can't you, keep going!

HAMM: That's all. I stopped there.

(*Pause.*)

CLOV: Do you see how it goes on.

HAMM: More or less.

CLOV: Will it not soon be the end?

1080 HAMM: I'm afraid it will.

CLOV: Pah! You'll make up another.

HAMM: I don't know.

(*Pause.*)

I feel rather drained.

(*Pause.*)

The prolonged creative effort.

(*Pause.*)

1085 If I could drag myself down to the sea! I'd make a pillow of sand for my head and the tide would come.

CLOV: There's no more tide.

(*Pause.*)

HAMM: Go and see is she dead.

(CLOV *goes to bins, raises the lid of* NELL*'s, stoops, looks into it. Pause.*)

CLOV: Looks like it.

(*He closes the lid, straightens up.* HAMM *raises his toque. Pause. He puts it on again.*)

HAMM: (*With his hand to his toque.*) And Nagg?   1090

(CLOV *raises lid of* NAGG*'s bin, stoops, looks into it. Pause.*)

CLOV: Doesn't look like it.

(*He closes the lid, straightens up.*)

HAMM: (*Letting go his toque.*) What's he doing?

(CLOV *raises lid of* NAGG*'s bin, stoops, looks into it. Pause.*)

CLOV: He's crying.

(*He closes lid, straightens up.*)

HAMM: Then he's living.

(*Pause.*)

Did you ever have an instant of happiness?   1095

CLOV: Not to my knowledge.

(*Pause.*)

HAMM: Bring me under the window.

(CLOV *goes towards chair.*)

I want to feel the light on my face.

(CLOV *pushes chair.*)

Do you remember, in the beginning, when you took me for a turn? You used to hold the chair too high. At every   1100 step you nearly tipped me out.

(*With senile quaver.*)

Ah great fun, we had, the two of us, great fun.

(*Gloomily.*)

And then we got into the way of it.

(CLOV *stops the chair under window right.*)

There already?

(*Pause. He tilts back his head.*)

Is it light?   1105

CLOV: It isn't dark.

HAMM: (*Angrily.*) I'm asking you is it light.

CLOV: Yes.

(*Pause.*)

HAMM: The curtain isn't closed?

CLOV: No.   1110

HAMM: What window is it?

CLOV: The earth.

HAMM: I knew it!

(*Angrily.*)

But there's no light there! The other!

(CLOV *pushes chair towards window left.*)

The earth!   1115

(CLOV *stops the chair under window left.* HAMM *tilts back his head.*)

That's what I call light!

(*Pause.*)

Feels like a ray of sunshine.

(*Pause.*)

No?
CLOV: No.
1120 HAMM: It isn't a ray of sunshine I feel on my face?
CLOV: No.

(*Pause.*)

HAMM: Am I very white?
(*Pause. Angrily.*)
    I'm asking you am I very white!
CLOV: Not more so than usual.

(*Pause.*)

1125 HAMM: Open the window.
CLOV: What for?
HAMM: I want to hear the sea.
CLOV: You wouldn't hear it.
HAMM: Even if you opened the window?
1130 CLOV: No.
HAMM: Then it's not worth while opening it?
CLOV: No.
HAMM: (*Violently.*) Then open it!
(CLOV *gets up on the ladder, opens the window. Pause.*)
    Have you opened it?
1135 CLOV: Yes.

(*Pause.*)

HAMM: You swear you've opened it?
CLOV: Yes.

(*Pause.*)

HAMM: Well . . . !
(*Pause.*)
    It must be very calm.
(*Pause. Violently.*)
1140   I'm asking you is it very calm!
CLOV: Yes.
HAMM: It's because there are no more navigators.
(*Pause.*)
    You haven't much conversation all of a sudden. Do you
    not feel well?
1145 CLOV: I'm cold.
HAMM: What month are we?
(*Pause.*)
    Close the window, we're going back.
(CLOV *closes the window, gets down, pushes the chair back to its
place, remains standing behind it, head bowed.*)
    Don't stay there, you give me the shivers!
(CLOV *returns to his place beside the chair.*)
    Father!
(*Pause. Louder.*)
1150   Father!
(*Pause.*)
    Go and see did he hear me.

(CLOV *goes to* NAGG's *bin, raises the lid, stoops. Unintelligible words.*
CLOV *straightens up.*)

CLOV: Yes.
HAMM: Both times?

(CLOV *stoops. As before.*)

CLOV: Once only.
HAMM: The first time or the second?   1155

(CLOV *stoops. As before.*)

CLOV: He doesn't know.
HAMM: It must have been the second.
CLOV: We'll never know.

(*He closes lid.*)

HAMM: Is he still crying?
CLOV: No.   1160
HAMM: The dead go fast.
(*Pause.*)
    What's he doing?
CLOV: Sucking his biscuit.
HAMM: Life goes on.
(CLOV *returns to his place beside the chair.*)
    Give me a rug, I'm freezing.   1165
CLOV: There are no more rugs.

(*Pause.*)

HAMM: Kiss me.
(*Pause.*)
    Will you not kiss me?
CLOV: No.
HAMM: On the forehead.   1170
CLOV: I won't kiss you anywhere.

(*Pause.*)

HAMM: (*Holding out his hand.*) Give me your hand at least.
(*Pause.*)
    Will you not give me your hand?
CLOV: I won't touch you.

(*Pause.*)

HAMM: Give me the dog.   1175
(CLOV *looks round for the dog.*)
    No!
CLOV: Do you not want your dog?
HAMM: No.
CLOV: Then I'll leave you.
HAMM: (*Head bowed, absently.*) That's right.   1180

(CLOV *goes to door, turns.*)

CLOV: If I don't kill that rat he'll die.
HAMM: (*As before.*) That's right.
(*Exit* CLOV. *Pause.*)
    Me to play.
(*He takes out his handkerchief, unfolds it, holds it spread out before
him.*)
    We're getting on.
(*Pause.*)
    You weep, and weep, for nothing, so as not to laugh, and   1185
little by little . . . you begin to grieve.
(*He folds the handkerchief, puts it back in his pocket, raises his
head.*)
    All those I might have helped.

(*Pause.*)
    Helped!
(*Pause.*)
    Saved.
(*Pause.*)
1190   Saved!
(*Pause.*)
    The place was crawling with them!
(*Pause. Violently.*)
    Use your head, can't you, use your head, you're on earth, there's no cure for that!
(*Pause.*)
    Get out of here and love one another! Lick your neigh-
1195 bor as yourself!
(*Pause. Calmer.*)
    When it wasn't bread they wanted it was crumpets.
(*Pause. Violently.*)
    Out of my sight and back to your petting parties!
(*Pause.*)
    All that, all that!
(*Pause.*)
    Not even a real dog!
(*Calmer.*)
1200   The end is in the beginning and yet you go on.
(*Pause.*)
    Perhaps I could go on with my story, end it and begin an-other.
(*Pause.*)
    Perhaps I could throw myself out on the floor.
(*He pushes himself painfully off his seat, falls back again.*)
    Dig my nails into the cracks and drag myself forward with
1205 my fingers.
(*Pause.*)
    It will be the end and there I'll be, wondering what can have brought it on and wondering what can have . . .
(*He hesitates.*)
    . . . why it was so long coming.
(*Pause.*)
    There I'll be, in the old shelter, alone against the silence
1210 and . . .
(*He hesitates.*)
    . . . the stillness. If I can hold my peace, and sit quiet, it will be all over with sound, and motion, all over and done with.
(*Pause.*)
    I'll have called my father and I'll have called my . . .
(*He hesitates.*)
    . . . my son. And even twice, or three times, in case they
1215 shouldn't have heard me, the first time, or the second.
(*Pause.*)
    I'll say to myself, He'll come back.
(*Pause.*)
    And then?
(*Pause.*)
    And then?
(*Pause.*)
    He couldn't, he has gone too far.
(*Pause.*)
1220   And then?
(*Pause. Very agitated.*)
    All kinds of fantasies! That I'm being watched! A rat! Steps! Breath held and then . . .

(*He breathes out.*)
    Then babble, babble, words, like the solitary child who turns himself into children, two, three, so as to be together, and whisper together, in the dark.   1225
(*Pause.*)
    Moment upon moment, pattering down, like the millet grains of . . .
(*He hesitates.*)
    . . . that old Greek, and all life long you wait for that to mount up to a life.
(*Pause. He opens his mouth to continue, renounces.*)
    Ah let's get it over!   1230
(*He whistles. Enter* CLOV *with alarm-clock. He halts beside the chair.*)
    What? Neither gone nor dead?
CLOV: In spirit only.
HAMM: Which?
CLOV: Both.
HAMM: Gone from me you'd be dead.   1235
CLOV: And vice versa.
HAMM: Outside of here it's death!
(*Pause.*)
    And the rat?
CLOV: He's got away.
HAMM: He can't go far.   1240
(*Pause. Anxious.*)
    Eh?
CLOV: He doesn't need to go far.

(*Pause.*)

HAMM: Is it not time for my pain-killer?
CLOV: Yes.
HAMM: Ah! At last! Give it to me! Quick!   1245

(*Pause.*)

CLOV: There's no more pain-killer.

(*Pause.*)

HAMM: (*Appalled.*) Good . . . !
(*Pause.*)
    No more pain-killer!
CLOV: No more pain-killer. You'll never get any more pain-killer.   1250

(*Pause.*)

HAMM: But the little round box. It was full!
CLOV: Yes. But now it's empty.

(*Pause.* CLOV *starts to move about the room. He is looking for a place to put down the alarm-clock.*)

HAMM: (*Soft.*) What'll I do?
(*Pause. In a scream.*)
    What'll I do?
(CLOV *sees the picture, takes it down, stands it on the floor with its face to the wall, hangs up the alarm-clock in its place.*)
    What are you doing?   1255
CLOV: Winding up.
HAMM: Look at the earth.

CLOV: Again!

HAMM: Since it's calling to you.

1260 CLOV: Is your throat sore?

(*Pause.*)

Would you like a lozenge?

(*Pause.*)

No.

(*Pause.*)

Pity.

(CLOV *goes, humming, towards window right, halts before it, looks up at it.*)

HAMM: Don't sing.

1265 CLOV: (*Turning towards* HAMM.) One hasn't the right to sing any more?

HAMM: No.

CLOV: Then how can it end?

HAMM: You want it to end?

1270 CLOV: I want to sing.

HAMM: I can't prevent you.

(*Pause.* CLOV *turns towards window right.*)

CLOV: What did I do with that steps?

(*He looks around for ladder.*)

You didn't see that steps?

(*He sees it.*)

Ah, about time.

(*He goes towards window left.*)

1275 Sometimes I wonder if I'm in my right mind. Then it passes over and I'm as lucid as before.

(*He gets up on ladder, looks out of window.*)

Christ, she's under water!

(*He looks.*)

How can that be?

(*He pokes forward his head, his hand above his eyes.*)

It hasn't rained.

(*He wipes the pane, looks. Pause.*)

1280 Ah what a fool I am! I'm on the wrong side!

(*He gets down, takes a few steps towards window right.*)

Under water!

(*He goes back for ladder.*)

What a fool I am!

(*He carries ladder towards window right.*)

Sometimes I wonder if I'm in my right senses. Then it passes off and I'm as intelligent as ever.

(*He sets down ladder under window right, gets up on it, looks out of window. He turns towards* HAMM.)

1285 Any particular sector you fancy? Or merely the whole thing?

HAMM: Whole thing.

CLOV: The general effect? Just a moment.

(*He looks out of window. Pause.*)

HAMM: Clov.

1290 CLOV: (*Absorbed.*) Mmm.

HAMM: Do you know what it is?

CLOV: (*As before.*) Mmm.

HAMM: I was never there.

(*Pause.*)

Clov!

CLOV: (*Turning towards* HAMM, *exasperated.*) What is it? 1295

HAMM: I was never there.

CLOV: Lucky for you.

(*He looks out of window.*)

HAMM: Absent, always. It all happened without me. I don't know what's happened.

(*Pause.*)

Do you know what's happened? 1300

(*Pause.*)

Clov!

CLOV: (*Turning towards* HAMM, *exasperated.*) Do you want me to look at this muckheap, yes or no?

HAMM: Answer me first.

CLOV: What? 1305

HAMM: Do you know what's happened?

CLOV: When? Where?

HAMM: (*Violently.*) When! What's happened? Use your head, can't you! What has happened?

CLOV: What for Christ's sake does it matter? 1310

(*He looks out of window.*)

HAMM: I don't know.

(*Pause.* CLOV *turns towards* HAMM.)

CLOV: (*Harshly.*) When old Mother Pegg asked you for oil for her lamp and you told her to get out to hell, you knew what was happening then, no?

(*Pause.*)

You know what she died of, Mother Pegg? Of darkness. 1315

HAMM: (*Feebly.*) I hadn't any.

CLOV: (*As before.*) Yes, you had.

(*Pause.*)

HAMM: Have you the glass?

CLOV: No, it's clear enough as it is.

HAMM: Go and get it. 1320

(*Pause.* CLOV *casts up his eyes, brandishes his fists. He loses balance, clutches on to the ladder. He starts to get down, halts.*)

CLOV: There's one thing I'll never understand.

(*He gets down.*)

Why I always obey you. Can you explain that to me?

HAMM: No. . . . Perhaps it's compassion.

(*Pause.*)

A kind of great compassion.

(*Pause.*)

Oh you won't find it easy, you won't find it easy. 1325

(*Pause.* CLOV *begins to move about the room in search of the telescope.*)

CLOV: I'm tired of our goings on, very tired.

(*He searches.*)

You're not sitting on it?

(*He moves the chair, looks at the place where it stood, resumes his search.*)

HAMM: (*Anguished.*) Don't leave me there!
(*Angrily* CLOV *restores the chair to its place.*)
   Am I right in the center?
1330 CLOV: You'd need a microscope to find this—
(*He sees the telescope.*)
   Ah, about time.

(*He picks up the telescope, gets up on the ladder, turns the telescope on the without.*)

HAMM: Give me the dog.
CLOV: (*Looking.*) Quiet!
HAMM: (*Angrily.*) Give me the dog!

(CLOV *drops the telescope, clasps his hands to his head. Pause. He gets down precipitately, looks for the dog, sees it, picks it up, hastens towards* HAMM *and strikes him violently on the head with the dog.*)

1335 CLOV: There's your dog for you!

(*The dog falls to the ground. Pause.*)

HAMM: He hit me!
CLOV: You drive me mad, I'm mad!
HAMM: If you must hit me, hit me with the axe.
(*Pause.*)
   Or with the gaff, hit me with the gaff. Not with the dog.
1340   With the gaff. Or with the axe.

(CLOV *picks up the dog and gives it to* HAMM *who takes it in his arms.*)

CLOV: (*Imploringly.*) Let's stop playing!
HAMM: Never!
(*Pause.*)
   Put me in my coffin.
CLOV: There are no more coffins.
1345 HAMM: Then let it end!
(CLOV *goes towards ladder.*)
   With a bang!
(CLOV *gets up on ladder, gets down again, looks for telescope, sees it, picks it up, gets up ladder, raises telescope.*)
   Of darkness! And me? Did anyone ever have pity on me?
CLOV: (*Lowering the telescope, turning towards* HAMM.) What?
(*Pause.*)
   Is it me you're referring to?
1350 HAMM: (*Angrily.*) An aside, ape! Did you never hear an aside before?
(*Pause.*)
   I'm warming up for my last soliloquy.
CLOV: I warn you. I'm going to look at this filth since it's an order. But it's the last time.
(*He turns the telescope on the without.*)
1355   Let's see.
(*He moves the telescope.*)
   Nothing . . . nothing . . . good . . . good . . . nothing . . . goo—
(*He starts, lowers the telescope, examines it, turns it again on the without. Pause.*)
   Bad luck to it!
HAMM: More complications!
(CLOV *gets down.*)
   Not an underplot, I trust.

(CLOV *moves ladder nearer window, gets up on it, turns telescope on the without.*)

CLOV: (*Dismayed.*) Looks like a small boy!   1360
HAMM: (*Sarcastic.*) A small . . . boy!
CLOV: I'll go and see.
(*He gets down, drops the telescope, goes towards door, turns.*)
   I'll take the gaff.

(*He looks for the gaff, sees it, picks it up, hastens towards door.*)

HAMM: No!

(CLOV *halts.*)

CLOV: No? A potential procreator?   1365
HAMM: If he exists he'll die there or he'll come here. And if he doesn't . . .

(*Pause.*)

CLOV: You don't believe me? You think I'm inventing?

(*Pause.*)

HAMM: It's the end, Clov, we've come to the end. I don't need you any more.   1370

(*Pause.*)

CLOV: Lucky for you.

(*He goes towards door.*)

HAMM: Leave me the gaff.

(CLOV *gives him the gaff, goes towards door, halts, looks at alarm-clock, takes it down, looks round for a better place to put it, goes to bins, puts it on lid of* NAGG'S *bin. Pause.*)

CLOV: I'll leave you.

(*He goes towards door.*)

HAMM: Before you go . . .
(CLOV *halts near door.*)
   . . . say something.   1375
CLOV: There is nothing to say.
HAMM: A few words . . . to ponder . . . in my heart.
CLOV: Your heart!
HAMM: Yes.
(*Pause. Forcibly.*)
   Yes!   1380
(*Pause.*)
   With the rest, in the end, the shadows, the murmurs, all the trouble, to end up with.
(*Pause.*)
   Clov. . . . He never spoke to me. Then, in the end, before he went, without my having asked him, he spoke to me. He said . . .   1385
CLOV: (*Despairingly.*) Ah . . . !
HAMM: Something . . . from your heart.
CLOV: My heart!
HAMM: A few words . . . from your heart.

(Pause.)

1390 CLOV: (Fixed gaze, tonelessly, towards auditorium.) They said to
me, That's love, yes, yes, not a doubt, now you see how—
HAMM: Articulate!
CLOV: (As before.) How easy it is. They said to me, That's
friendship, yes, yes, no question, you've found it. They said
1395 to me, Here's the place, stop, raise your head and look at all
that beauty. That order! They said to me, Come now, you're
not a brute beast, think upon these things and you'll see
how all becomes clear. And simple! They said to me, What
skilled attention they get, all these dying of their wounds.
1400 HAMM: Enough!
CLOV: (As before.) I say to myself—sometimes, Clov, you must
learn to suffer better than that if you want them to weary
of punishing you—one day. I say to myself—sometimes,
Clov, you must be there better than that if you want them
1405 to let you go—one day. But I feel too old, and too far, to
form new habits. Good, it'll never end, I'll never go.
(Pause.)
Then one day, suddenly, it ends, it changes, I don't understand, it dies, or it's me, I don't understand, that either. I
ask the words that remain—sleeping, waking, morning,
1410 evening. They have nothing to say.
(Pause.)
I open the door of the cell and go. I am so bowed I only
see my feet, if I open my eyes, and between my legs a little trail of black dust. I say to myself that the earth is extinguished, though I never saw it lit.
(Pause.)
1415 It's easy going.
(Pause.)
When I fall I'll weep for happiness.

(Pause. He goes towards door.)

HAMM: Clov!
(CLOV halts, without turning.)
Nothing.
(CLOV moves on.)
Clov!

(CLOV halts, without turning.)

1420 CLOV: This is what we call making an exit.
HAMM: I'm obliged to you, Clov. For your services.
CLOV: (Turning, sharply.) Ah pardon, it's I am obliged to you.
HAMM: It's we are obliged to each other.
(Pause. CLOV goes towards door.)
One thing more.
(CLOV halts.)
1425 A last favor.
(Exit CLOV.)
Cover me with the sheet.
(Long pause.)
No? Good.
(Pause.)
Me to play.
(Pause. Wearily.)
Old endgame lost of old, play and lose and have done
1430 with losing.
(Pause. More animated.)

Let me see.
(Pause.)
Ah yes!
(He tries to move the chair, using the gaff as before. Enter CLOV,
dressed for the road. Panama hat, tweed coat, raincoat over his arm,
umbrella, bag. He halts by the door and stands there, impassive and
motionless, his eyes fixed on HAMM, till the end. HAMM gives up.)
Good.
(Pause.)
Discard.
(He throws away the gaff, makes to throw away the dog, thinks bet-
ter of it.)
Take it easy.   1435
(Pause.)
And now?
(Pause.)
Raise hat.
(He raises his toque.)
Peace to our . . . arses.
(Pause.)
And put on again.
(He puts on his toque.)
Deuce.   1440
(Pause. He takes off his glasses.)
Wipe.
(He takes out his handkerchief and, without unfolding it, wipes his
glasses.)
And put on again.
(He puts on his glasses, puts back the handkerchief in his pocket.)
We're coming. A few more squirms like that and I'll call.
(Pause.)
A little poetry.
(Pause.)
You prayed—   1445
(Pause. He corrects himself.)
You CRIED for night; it comes—
(Pause. He corrects himself.)
It FALLS: now cry in darkness.
(He repeats, chanting.)
You cried for night; it falls: now cry in darkness.
(Pause.)
Nicely put, that.
(Pause.)
And now?   1450
(Pause.)
Moments for nothing, now as always, time was never and
time is over, reckoning closed and story ended.
(Pause. Narrative tone.)
If he could have his child with him. . . .
(Pause.)
It was the moment I was waiting for.
(Pause.)
You don't want to abandon him? You want him to bloom   1455
while you are withering? Be there to solace your last mil-
lion last moments?
(Pause.)
He doesn't realize, all he knows is hunger, and cold, and
death to crown it all. But you! You ought to know what
the earth is like, nowadays. Oh I put him before his re-   1460
sponsibilities!
(Pause. Normal tone.)

Well, there we are, there I am, that's enough.
(*He raises the whistle to his lips, hesitates, drops it. Pause.*)
    Yes, truly!
(*He whistles. Pause. Louder. Pause.*)
    Good.
(*Pause.*)
1465   Father!
(*Pause. Louder.*)
    Father!
(*Pause.*)
    Good.
(*Pause.*)
    We're coming.
(*Pause.*)
    And to end up with?
(*Pause.*)
1470   Discard.
(*He throws away the dog. He tears the whistle from his neck.*)
    With my compliments.
(*He throws whistle towards auditorium. Pause. He sniffs. Soft.*)

    Clov!
(*Long pause.*)
    No? Good.
(*He takes out the handkerchief.*)
    Since that's the way we're playing it . . .
(*He unfolds handkerchief.*)
    . . . let's play it that way . . .
1475
(*He unfolds.*)
    . . . and speak no more about it . . .
(*He finishes unfolding.*)
    . . . speak no more.
(*He holds handkerchief spread out before him.*)
    Old stancher!
(*Pause.*)
    You . . . remain.
(*Pause. He covers his face with handkerchief, lowers his arms to armrests, remains motionless.*)

(*Brief tableau.*)

Harold Pinter

Harold Pinter (b. 1930) has had an extensive career as an actor, playwright, and screenwriter, but is best-known for his strikingly disorienting stage plays. Pinter was born and raised in Hackney, a working-class neighborhood just beyond London's East End. He studied briefly at the Royal Academy of Dramatic Art and pursued a career as a stage and radio actor in the early 1950s before becoming a playwright. His early plays—notably *The Room* (1957), *The Birthday Party* (1958), and *The Dumb Waiter* (1960)—are inflected by the theater of the absurd in the indirect, often menacing, and finally inexplicable quality of their action. However, Pinter's drama is set in a much more recognizable locale than are many of Beckett's or Ionesco's plays; his plays often work by frustrating our "realistic" expectations of characters and their stage world. This is particularly true of Pinter's two major successes of the 1960s, *The Caretaker* (1960) and *The Homecoming* (1965). In both of these plays, a visitor disturbs the delicate balance of relations that bind a family together. What is characteristically "Pinteresque" about the action is the way that Pinter's spare and oblique dialogue makes the characters' motives and intentions nearly unreadable, often despite the violence with which they are expressed. If the poverty of language in most realistic drama tends to imply the emptiness of the characters, in Pinter's drama it seems most often to imply their explosive potential to erupt.

Pinter went through a period of profound writer's block in the late 1960s, writing only the short plays *Landscape* (1969) and *Silence* (1969). In the 1970s, though, he wrote a series of major dramas: *Old Times* (1971), *No Man's Land* (1975), and *Betrayal* (1978). These plays take memory and the past as their subject, examining how, in the words of Anna in *Old Times,* "There are things I remember which may never have happened but as I recall them so they take place." More recently, Pinter has written *A Kind of Alaska* (1982), a play based on Oliver Sachs's *Awakenings,* and several plays, sometimes on more political subjects: *One for the Road* (1984), *Mountain Language* (1988), *Party Time* (1990), *Moonlight* (1993), *Ashes to Ashes* (1996), and *Celebration* (2000). Pinter also has written a number of screenplays, both for his own plays, such as *Betrayal,* and for other projects, including *The French Lieutenant's Woman* and *Turtle Diary.* Pinter is also an accomplished poet and it was reported in 2005 that he had decided to stop writing plays and turn his attention to poetry. Pinter won the Nobel Prize in Literature in 2005.

THE HOMECOMING

The Homecoming is typical of Pinter's earlier drama in that it provides us with a recognizable situation—Teddy, an American college professor, returns home to London with his wife Ruth to visit his family—that immediately twists in new and surprising directions. For much like the room onstage, with its missing upstage wall, something is missing in this family that determines the structure of their relationships. The most obvious missing element of family life here is the absent mother, Jessie, whose absence informs the relationships between the men of the play: Max, who does the cleaning and cooking, to everyone's ridicule; Sam, who is accused of homosexual prostitution; Lenny, the pimp; Joey, the macho boxer. When Ruth appears in this scenario, she seems suddenly to take the role vacated by Jessie, becoming the controlling figure in the house of crippled men. Ruth assumes the two roles attributed to Jessie—mother and whore. The question, as Max asks at the end, is will she prove "adaptable" to the men's fantasies or will she—as Ruth's independence suggests—adapt the men to her own designs?

The Homecoming clearly plays with the formalities and conventions of realistic drama. The secret that often motivates the action of an Ibsen play (Nora's forgery in *A Doll House,* for example) seems to be disclosed in the play by Sam—"MacGregor had Jessie in the back

Sam "dies" in Harold Pinter's *The Homecoming,* staged by the American Repertory Theatre.

of my cab as I drove them along"—but finally this "secret" loses its power to explain. It is either already known or finally irrelevant to the characters. Indeed, the past in *The Homecoming* seems to be largely improvised or invented. The characters frequently seem to make up stories of the "past" that function more as maneuverings in the present than as reliable accounts of something that actually happened. Lenny's story of beating up a prostitute underneath an arch in act 1, for instance, seems not really to have happened. It is instead an effort to intimidate the seductive Ruth, also a woman standing underneath an arch in the living room. The past in *The Homecoming* is one that the characters invent and reinvent as the action progresses. The past becomes a fantasy that the characters work to re-create in the present action of the play.

THE HOMECOMING

Harold Pinter

CHARACTERS

MAX, *a man of seventy*
LENNY, *a man in his early thirties*
SAM, *a man of sixty-three*
JOEY, *a man in his middle twenties*
TEDDY, *a man in his middle thirties*
RUTH, *a woman in her early thirties*

Summer: An old house in North London.

A large room, extending the width of the stage.

The back wall, which contained the door, has been removed. A square arch shape remains. Beyond it, the hall. In the hall a staircase, ascending upstage left, well in view. The front door upstage right. A coatstand, hooks, etc.

In the room a window, right. Odd tables, chairs. Two large armchairs. A large sofa, left. Against right wall a large sideboard, the upper half of which contains a mirror. Upstage left, a radiogram.

ACT ONE

Evening.

LENNY *is sitting on the sofa with a newspaper, a pencil in his hand. He wears a dark suit. He makes occasional marks on the back page.*

MAX *comes in, from the direction of the kitchen. He goes to sideboard, opens top drawer, rummages in it, closes it.*

He wears an old cardigan and a cap, and carries a stick.

He walks downstage, stands, looks about the room.

MAX: What have you done with the scissors?

(*Pause.*)

I said I'm looking for the scissors. What have you done with them?

(*Pause.*)

Did you hear me? I want to cut something out of the paper.
5 LENNY: I'm reading the paper.
MAX: Not that paper. I haven't even read that paper. I'm talking about last Sunday's paper. I was just having a look at it in the kitchen.

(*Pause.*)

Do you hear what I'm saying? I'm talking to you! Where's
10 the scissors?
LENNY: (*Looking up, quietly.*) Why don't you shut up, you daft prat?

(MAX *lifts his stick and points it at him.*)

MAX: Don't you talk to me like that. I'm warning you.

(*He sits in large armchair.*)

There's an advertisement in the paper about flannel vests.
15 Cut price. Navy surplus. I could do with a few of them.

(*Pause.*)

I think I'll have a fag. Give me a fag.

(*Pause.*)

I just asked you to give me a cigarette.

(*Pause.*)

Look what I'm lumbered with.

(*He takes a crumpled cigarette from his pocket.*)

I'm getting old, my word of honour.

(*He lights it.*)

You think I wasn't a tearaway? I could have taken care of you, 20
twice over. I'm still strong. You ask your Uncle Sam what I
was. But at the same time I always had a kind heart. Always.

(*Pause.*)

I used to knock about with a man called MacGregor. I
called him Mac. You remember Mac? Eh?

(*Pause.*)

Huhh! We were two of the worst hated men in the West 25
End of London. I tell you, I still got the scars. We'd walk
into a place, the whole room'd stand up, they'd make way
to let us pass. You never heard such silence. Mind you, he
was a big man, he was over six foot tall. His family were
all MacGregors, they came all the way from Aberdeen, but 30
he was the only one they called Mac.

(*Pause.*)

He was very fond of your mother, Mac was. Very fond.
He always had a good word for her.

(*Pause.*)

Mind you, she wasn't such a bad woman. Even though it
made me sick just to look at her rotten stinking face, she 35
wasn't such a bad bitch. I gave her the best bleeding years
of my life, anyway.
LENNY: Plug it, will you, you stupid sod, I'm trying to read
the paper.

40   MAX: Listen! I'll chop your spine off, you talk to me like that! You understand? Talking to your lousy filthy father like that!

LENNY: You know what, you're getting demented.

(*Pause.*)

What do you think of Second Wind for the three-thirty?

45   MAX: Where?

LENNY: Sandown Park.

MAX: Don't stand a chance.

LENNY: Sure he does.

MAX: Not a chance.

50   LENNY: He's the winner.

(LENNY *ticks the paper.*)

MAX: He talks to me about horses.

(*Pause.*)

I used to live on the course. One of the loves of my life. Epsom? I knew it like the back of my hand. I was one of the best-known faces down at the paddock. What a mar-
55   vellous open-air life.

(*Pause.*)

He talks to me about horses. You only read their names in the papers. But I've stroked their manes, I've held them, I've calmed them down before a big race. I was the one they used to call for. Max, they'd say, there's a horse here, he's
60   highly strung, you're the only man on the course who can calm him. It was true. I had a . . . I had an instinctive un-derstanding of animals. I should have been a trainer. Many times I was offered the job—you know, a proper post, by the Duke of . . . I forget his name . . . one of the Dukes. But
65   I had family obligations, my family needed me at home.

(*Pause.*)

The times I've watched those animals thundering past the post. What an experience. Mind you, I didn't lose, I made a few bob out of it, and you know why? Because I always had the smell of a good horse. I could smell him. And not
70   only the colts but the fillies. Because the fillies are more highly strung than the colts, they're more unreliable, did you know that? No, what do you know? Nothing. But I was always able to tell a good filly by one particular trick. I'd look her in the eye. You see? I'd stand in front of her
75   and look her straight in the eye, it was a kind of hypno-tism, and by the look deep down in her eye I could tell whether she was a stayer or not. It was a gift. I had a gift.

(*Pause.*)

And he talks to me about horses.

LENNY: Dad, do you mind if I change the subject?

(*Pause.*)

80   I want to ask you something. That dinner we had before, what was the name of it? What do you call it?

(*Pause.*)

Why don't you buy a dog? You're a dog cook. Honest. You think you're cooking for a lot of dogs.

MAX: If you don't like it get out.

LENNY: I am going out. I'm going out to buy myself a proper   85   dinner.

MAX: Well, get out! What are you waiting for?

(LENNY *looks at him.*)

LENNY: What did you say?

MAX: I said shove off out of it, that's what I said.

LENNY: You'll go before me, Dad, if you talk to me in that   90   tone of voice.

MAX: Will I, you bitch?

(MAX *grips his stick.*)

LENNY: Oh, Daddy, you're not going to use your stick on me, are you? Eh? Don't use your stick on me, Daddy. No, please. It wasn't my fault, it was one of the others. I haven't   95   done anything wrong, Dad, honest. Don't clout me with that stick, Dad.

(*Silence.*)

(MAX *sits hunched.* LENNY *reads the paper.*)

(SAM *comes in the front door. He wears a chauffeur's uniform. He hangs his hat on a hook in the hall and comes into the room. He goes to a chair, sits in it and sighs.*)

Hullo, Uncle Sam.

SAM: Hullo.

LENNY: How are you, Uncle?   100

SAM: Not bad. A bit tired.

LENNY: Tired? I bet you're tired. Where you been?

SAM: I've been to London Airport.

LENNY: All the way up to London Airport? What, right up the M4?   105

SAM: Yes, all the way up there.

LENNY: Tch, tch, tch. Well, I think you're entitled to be tired, Uncle.

SAM: Well, it's the drivers.

LENNY: I know. That's what I'm talking about. I'm talking   110   about the drivers.

SAM: Knocks you out.

(*Pause.*)

MAX: I'm here, too, you know.

(SAM *looks at him.*)

I said I'm here, too. I'm sitting here.

SAM: I know you're here.   115

(*Pause.*)

SAM: I took a Yankee out there today . . . to the Airport.

LENNY: Oh, a Yankee, was it?

SAM: Yes, I been with him all day. Picked him up at the Savoy at half past twelve, took him to the Caprice for his lunch. After lunch I picked him up again, took him down to a   120   house in Eaton Square—he had to pay a visit to a friend

there—and then round about tea-time I took him right
the way out to the Airport.

LENNY: Had to catch a plane there, did he?

125 SAM: Yes. Look what he gave me. He gave me a box of cigars.

(SAM *takes a box of cigars from his pocket.*)

MAX: Come here. Let's have a look at them.

(SAM *shows* MAX *the cigars.* MAX *takes one from the box, pinches it and sniffs it.*)

It's a fair cigar.

SAM: Want to try one?

(MAX *and* SAM *light cigars.*)

You know what he said to me? He told me I was the best
130 chauffeur he'd ever had. The best one.

MAX: From what point of view?

SAM: Eh?

MAX: From what point of view?

LENNY: From the point of view of his driving, Dad, and his
135 general sense of courtesy, I should say.

MAX: Thought you were a good driver, did he, Sam? Well, he
gave you a first-class cigar.

SAM: Yes, he thought I was the best he'd ever had. They all say
that, you know. They won't have anyone else, they only ask
140 for me. They say I'm the best chauffeur in the firm.

LENNY: I bet the other drivers tend to get jealous, don't they,
Uncle?

SAM: They do get jealous. They get very jealous.

MAX: Why?

(*Pause.*)

145 SAM: I just told you.

MAX: No, I just can't get it clear, Sam. Why do the other drivers get jealous?

SAM: Because (a) I'm the best driver, and because . . . (b) I
don't take liberties.

(*Pause.*)

150 I don't press myself on people, you see. These big businessmen, men of affairs, they don't want the driver jawing
all the time, they like to sit in the back, have a bit of peace
and quiet. After all, they're sitting in a Humber Super
Snipe, they can afford to relax. At the same time, though,
155 this is what really makes me special . . . I do know how to
pass the time of day when required.

(*Pause.*)

For instance, I told this man today I was in the second
world war. Not the first. I told him I was too young for
the first. But I told him I fought in the second.

(*Pause.*)

160 So did he, it turned out.

(LENNY *stands, goes to the mirror and straightens his tie.*)

LENNY: He was probably a colonel, or something, in the
American Air Force.

SAM: Yes.

LENNY: Probably a navigator, or something like that, in a Flying Fortress. Now he's most likely a high executive in a 165
worldwide group of aeronautical engineers.

SAM: Yes.

LENNY: Yes, I know the kind of man you're talking about.

(LENNY *goes out, turning to his right.*)

SAM: After all, I'm experienced. I was driving a dust cart at
the age of nineteen. Then I was in long-distance haulage. 170
I had ten years as a taxi-driver and I've had five as a private chauffeur.

MAX: It's funny you never got married, isn't it? A man with
all your gifts.

(*Pause.*)

Isn't it? A man like you? 175

SAM: There's still time.

MAX: Is there?

(*Pause.*)

SAM: You'd be surprised.

MAX: What you been doing, banging away at your lady customers, have you? 180

SAM: Not me.

MAX: In the back of the Snipe? Been having a few crafty reefs
in a layby, have you?

SAM: Not me.

MAX: On the back seat? What about the armrest, was it up or 185
down?

SAM: I've never done that kind of thing in my car.

MAX: Above all that kind of thing, are you, Sam?

SAM: Too true.

MAX: Above having a good bang on the back seat, are you? 190

SAM: Yes, I leave that to others.

MAX: You leave it to others? What others? You paralysed prat!

SAM: I don't mess up my car! Or my . . . my boss's car! Like
other people.

MAX: Other people? What other people? 195

(*Pause.*)

What other people?

(*Pause.*)

SAM: Other people.

(*Pause.*)

MAX: When you find the right girl, Sam, let your family
know, don't forget, we'll give you a number one send-off,
I promise you. You can bring her to live here, she can 200
keep us all happy. We'd take it in turns to give her a walk
around the park.

SAM: I wouldn't bring her here.

MAX: Sam, it's your decision. You're welcome to bring your
bride here, to the place where you live, or on the other hand 205
you can take a suite at the Dorchester. It's entirely up to you.

SAM: I haven't got a bride.

(SAM *stands, goes to the sideboard, takes an apple from the bowl, bites into it.*)

Getting a bit peckish.

(*He looks out of the window.*)

210   Never get a bride like you had, anyway. Nothing like your bride . . . going about these days. Like Jessie.

(*Pause.*)

After all, I escorted her once or twice, didn't I? Drove her round once or twice in my cab. She was a charming woman.

(*Pause.*)

215   All the same, she was your wife. But still . . . they were some of the most delightful evenings I've ever had. Used to just drive her about. It was my pleasure.
MAX: (*Softly, closing his eyes.*) Christ.
SAM: I used to pull up at a stall and buy her a cup of coffee. She was a very nice companion to be with.

(*Silence.*)

(JOEY *comes in the front door. He walks into the room, takes his jacket off, throws it on a chair and stands.*)

(*Silence.*)

JOEY: Feel a bit hungry.
220   SAM: Me, too.
MAX: Who do you think I am, your mother? Eh? Honest. They walk in here every time of the day and night like bloody animals. Go and find yourself a mother.

(LENNY *walks into the room, stands.*)

JOEY: I've been training down at the gym.
225   SAM: Yes, the boy's been working all day and training all night.
MAX: What do you want, you bitch? You spend all the day sitting on your arse at London Airport, buy yourself a jam-roll. You expect me to sit here waiting to rush into the kitchen the moment you step in the door? You've been
230   living sixty-three years, why don't you learn to cook?
SAM: I can cook.
MAX: Well, go and cook!

(*Pause.*)

LENNY: What the boys want, Dad, is your own special brand of cooking, Dad. That's what the boys look forward to. The
235   special understanding of food, you know, that you've got.
MAX: Stop calling me Dad. Just stop all that calling me Dad, do you understand?
LENNY: But I'm your son. You used to tuck me up in bed every night. He tucked you up, too, didn't he, Joey?

(*Pause.*)

240   He used to like tucking up his sons.

(LENNY *turns and goes towards the front door.*)

MAX: Lenny.
LENNY: (*Turning.*) What?
MAX: I'll give you a proper tuck up one of these nights, son. You mark my word.

(*They look at each other.*)

(LENNY *opens the front door and goes out.*)

(*Silence.*)

JOEY: I've been training with Bobby Dodd.   245

(*Pause.*)

And I had a good go at the bag as well.

(*Pause.*)

I wasn't in bad trim.
MAX: Boxing's a gentleman's game.

(*Pause.*)

I'll tell you what you've got to do. What you've got to do is you've got to learn how to defend yourself, and you've   250
got to learn how to attack. That's your only trouble as a boxer. You don't know how to defend yourself, and you don't know how to attack.

(*Pause.*)

Once you've mastered those arts you can go straight to   255
the top.

(*Pause.*)

JOEY: I've got a pretty good idea . . . of how to do that.

(JOEY *looks round for his jacket, picks it up, goes out of the room and up the stairs.*)

(*Pause.*)

MAX: Sam . . . why don't you go, too, eh? Why don't you just go upstairs? Leave me quiet. Leave me alone.
SAM: I want to make something clear about Jessie, Max. I want to. I do. When I took her out in the cab, round the   260
town, I was taking care of her, for you. I was looking after her for you, when you were busy, wasn't I? I was showing her the West End.

(*Pause.*)

You wouldn't have trusted any of your other brothers. You wouldn't have trusted Mac, would you? But you   265
trusted me. I want to remind you.

(*Pause.*)

Old Mac died a few years ago, didn't he? Isn't he dead?

(*Pause.*)

He was a lousy stinking rotten loudmouth. A bastard uncouth sodding runt. Mind you, he was a good friend of yours.   270

(Pause.)

MAX: Eh, Sam . . .

SAM: What?

MAX: Why do I keep you here? You're just an old grub.

SAM: Am I?

275 MAX: You're a maggot.

SAM: Oh yes?

MAX: As soon as you stop paying your way here, I mean when you're too old to pay your way, you know what I'm going to do? I'm going to give you the boot.

280 SAM: You are, eh?

MAX: Sure. I mean, bring in the money and I'll put up with you. But when the firm gets rid of you—you can flake off.

SAM: This is my house as well, you know. This was our mother's house.

285 MAX: One lot after the other. One mess after the other.

SAM: Our father's house.

MAX: Look what I'm lumbered with. One cast-iron bunch of crap after another. One flow of stinking pus after another.

(Pause.)

290   Our father? I remember him. Don't worry. You kid yourself. He used to come over to me and look down at me. My old man did. He'd bend right over me, then he'd pick me up. I was only that big. Then he'd dandle me. Give me the bottle. Wipe me clean. Give me a smile. Pat me on the bum. Pass me around, pass me from hand to hand. Toss me

295   up in the air. Catch me coming down. I remember my father.

(Blackout.)

(Lights up. Night. TEDDY *and* RUTH *stand at the threshold of the room.)*

(They are both well dressed in light summer suits and light raincoats. Two suitcases are by their side.)

(They look at the room. TEDDY *tosses the key in his hand, smiles.)*

TEDDY: Well, the key worked.

(Pause.)

They haven't changed the lock.

(Pause.)

RUTH: No one's here.

300 TEDDY: *(Looking up.)* They're asleep.

(Pause.)

RUTH: Can I sit down?

TEDDY: Of course.

RUTH: I'm tired.

(Pause.)

TEDDY: Then sit down.

(She does not move.)

That's my father's chair.   305

RUTH: That one?

TEDDY: *(Smiling.)* Yes, that's it. Shall I go up and see if my room's still there?

RUTH: It can't have moved.

TEDDY: No, I mean if my bed's still there.   310

RUTH: Someone might be in it.

TEDDY: No. They've got their own beds.

(Pause.)

RUTH: Shouldn't you wake someone up? Tell them you're here?

TEDDY: Not at this time of night. It's too late.

(Pause.)

Shall I go up?   315

(He goes into the hall, looks up the stairs, comes back.)

Why don't you sit down?

(Pause.)

I'll just go up . . . have a look.

(He goes up the stairs, stealthily.)

*(*RUTH *stands, then slowly walks across the room.)*

*(*TEDDY *returns.)*

It's still there. My room. Empty. The bed's there. What are you doing?

(She looks at him.)

Blankets, no sheets. I'll find some sheets. I could hear   320 snores. Really. They're all still here, I think. They're all snoring up there. Are you cold?

RUTH: No.

TEDDY: I'll make something to drink, if you like. Something hot.   325

RUTH: No, I don't want anything.

*(*TEDDY *walks about.)*

TEDDY: What do you think of the room? Big, isn't it? It's a big house. I mean, it's a fine room, don't you think? Actually there was a wall, across there . . . with a door. We knocked it down . . . years ago . . . to make an open living area. The   330 structure wasn't affected, you see. My mother was dead.

*(*RUTH *sits.)*

Tired?

RUTH: Just a little.

TEDDY: We can go to bed if you like. No point in waking anyone up now. Just go to bed. See them all in the morn-   335 ing . . . see my father in the morning . . .

(Pause.)

RUTH: Do you want to stay?

TEDDY: Stay?

(*Pause.*)

We've come to stay. We're bound to stay . . . for a few days.

340 RUTH: I think . . . the children . . . might be missing us.
TEDDY: Don't be silly.
RUTH: They might.
TEDDY: Look, we'll be back in a few days, won't we?

(*He walks about the room.*)

Nothing's changed. Still the same.

(*Pause.*)

345 Still, he'll get a surprise in the morning, won't he? The old man. I think you'll like him very much. Honestly. He's a . . . well, he's old, of course. Getting on.

(*Pause.*)

I was born here, do you realize that?
RUTH: I know.

(*Pause.*)

350 TEDDY: Why don't you go to bed? I'll find some sheets. I feel . . . wide awake, isn't it odd? I think I'll stay up for a bit. Are you tired?
RUTH: No.
TEDDY: Go to bed. I'll show you the room.
355 RUTH: No, I don't want to.
TEDDY: You'll be perfectly all right up there without me. Really you will. I mean, I won't be long. Look, it's just up there. It's the first door on the landing. The bathroom's right next door. You . . . need some rest, you know.

(*Pause.*)

360 I just want to . . . walk about for a few minutes. Do you mind?
RUTH: Of course I don't.
TEDDY: Well . . . Shall I show you the room?
RUTH: No, I'm happy at the moment.
365 TEDDY: You don't have to go to bed. I'm not saying you have to. I mean, you can stay up with me. Perhaps I'll make a cup of tea or something. The only thing is we don't want to make too much noise, we don't want to wake anyone up.
RUTH: I'm not making any noise.
370 TEDDY: I know you're not.

(*He goes to her.*)

(*Gently.*) Look, it's all right, really. I'm here. I mean . . . I'm with you. There's no need to be nervous. Are you nervous?
RUTH: No.
TEDDY: There's no need to be.

(*Pause.*)

375 They're very warm people, really. Very warm. They're my family. They're not ogres.

(*Pause.*)

Well, perhaps we should go to bed. After all, we have to be up early, see Dad. Wouldn't be quite right if he found us in bed, I think. (*He chuckles.*) Have to be up before six, come down, say hullo.   380

(*Pause.*)

RUTH: I think I'll have a breath of air.
TEDDY: Air?

(*Pause.*)

What do you mean?
RUTH: (*Standing.*) Just a stroll.
TEDDY: At this time of night? But we've . . . only just got here.   385 We've got to go to bed.
RUTH: I just feel like some air.
TEDDY: But I'm going to bed.
RUTH: That's all right.
TEDDY: But what am I going to do?   390

(*Pause.*)

The last thing I want is a breath of air. Why do you want a breath of air?
RUTH: I just do.
TEDDY: But it's late.
RUTH: I won't go far. I'll come back.   395

(*Pause.*)

TEDDY: I'll wait up for you.
RUTH: Why?
TEDDY: I'm not going to bed without you.
RUTH: Can I have the key?

(*He gives it to her.*)

Why don't you go to bed?   400

(*He puts his arms on her shoulders and kisses her.*)

(*They look at each other, briefly. She smiles.*)

I won't be long.

(*She goes out of the front door.*)

(TEDDY *goes to the window, peers out after her, half turns from the window, stands, suddenly chews his knuckles.*)

(LENNY *walks into the room from upstage left. He stands. He wears pyjamas and dressing-gown. He watches* TEDDY.)

(TEDDY *turns and sees him.*)

(*Silence.*)

TEDDY: Hullo, Lenny.
LENNY: Hullo, Teddy.

(*Pause.*)

TEDDY: I didn't hear you come down the stairs.
LENNY: I didn't.   405

(*Pause.*)

I sleep down here now. Next door. I've got a kind of study, workroom cum bedroom next door now, you see.
TEDDY: Oh. Did I . . . wake you up?
LENNY: No. I just had an early night tonight. You know how
410   it is. Can't sleep. Keep waking up.

(*Pause.*)

TEDDY: How are you?
LENNY: Well, just sleeping a bit restlessly, that's all. Tonight, anyway.
TEDDY: Bad dreams?
415   LENNY: No, I wouldn't say I was dreaming. It's not exactly a dream. It's just that something keeps waking me up. Some kind of tick.
TEDDY: A tick?
LENNY: Yes.
420   TEDDY: Well, what is it?
LENNY: I don't know.

(*Pause.*)

TEDDY: Have you got a clock in your room?
LENNY: Yes.
TEDDY: Well, maybe it's the clock.
425   LENNY: Yes, could be, I suppose.

(*Pause.*)

Well, if it's the clock I'd better do something about it. Stifle it in some way, or something.

(*Pause.*)

TEDDY: I've . . . just come back for a few days.
LENNY: Oh yes? Have you?

(*Pause.*)

430   TEDDY: How's the old man?
LENNY: He's in the pink.

(*Pause.*)

TEDDY: I've been keeping well.
LENNY: Oh, have you?

(*Pause.*)

Staying the night then, are you?
435   TEDDY: Yes.
LENNY: Well, you can sleep in your old room.
TEDDY: Yes, I've been up.
LENNY: Yes, you can sleep there.

(LENNY *yawns.*)

Oh well.
440   TEDDY: I'm going to bed.
LENNY: Are you?
TEDDY: Yes, I'll get some sleep.
LENNY: Yes, I'm going to bed, too.

(TEDDY *picks up the cases.*)

I'll give you a hand.
TEDDY: No, they're not heavy.   445

(TEDDY *goes into the hall with the cases.* LENNY *turns out the light in the room.*)

(*The light in the hall remains on.*)

(LENNY *follows into the hall.*)

LENNY: Nothing you want?
TEDDY: Mmmm?
LENNY: Nothing you might want, for the night? Glass of water, anything like that?
TEDDY: Any sheets anywhere?   450
LENNY: In the sideboard in your room.
TEDDY: Oh, good.
LENNY: Friends of mine occasionally stay there, you know, in your room, when they're passing through this part of the world.   455

(LENNY *turns out the hall light and turns on the first landing light.*)

(TEDDY *begins to walk up the stairs.*)

TEDDY: Well, I'll see you at breakfast, then.
LENNY: Yes, that's it. Ta-ta.

(TEDDY *goes upstairs.*)

(LENNY *goes off left.*)

(*Silence.*)

(*The landing light goes out. Slight night light in the hall and room.*)

(LENNY *comes back into the room, goes to the window and looks out.*)

(*He leaves the window and turns on a lamp. He is holding a small clock.*)

(*He sits, places the clock in front of him, lights a cigarette and sits.* RUTH *comes in the front door.*)

(*She stands still.* LENNY *turns his head, smiles. She walks slowly into the room.*)

LENNY: Good evening.
RUTH: Morning, I think.
LENNY: You're right there.   460

(*Pause.*)

My name's Lenny. What's yours?
RUTH: Ruth.

(*She sits, puts her coat collar around her.*)

LENNY: Cold?
RUTH: No.
LENNY: It's been a wonderful summer, hasn't it? Remarkable.   465

(*Pause.*)

Would you like something? Refreshment of some kind? An aperitif, anything like that?

RUTH: No, thanks.

470 LENNY: I'm glad you said that. We haven't got a drink in the house. Mind you, I'd soon get some in, if we had a party or something like that. Some kind of celebration . . . you know.

(Pause.)

You must be connected with my brother in some way. The one who's been abroad.

475 RUTH: I'm his wife.

LENNY: Eh listen, I wonder if you can advise me. I've been having a bit of a rough time with this clock. The tick's been keeping me up. The trouble is I'm not all that convinced it was the clock. I mean there are lots of things which tick in
480 the night, don't you find that? All sorts of objects, which, in the day, you wouldn't call anything else but commonplace. They give you no trouble. But in the night any given one of a number of them is liable to start letting out a bit of a tick. Whereas you look at these objects in the day and they're just
485 commonplace. They're as quiet as mice during the daytime. So . . . all things being equal . . . this question of me saying it was the clock that woke me up, well, that could very easily prove something of a false hypothesis.

(He goes to the sideboard, pours from a jug into a glass, takes the glass to RUTH.)

Here you are. I bet you could do with this.

490 RUTH: What is it?

LENNY: Water.

(She takes it, sips, places the glass on a small table by her chair.)

(LENNY watches her.)

Isn't it funny? I've got my pyjamas on and you're fully dressed?

(He goes to the sideboard and pours another glass of water.)

Mind if I have one? Yes, it's funny seeing my old brother
495 again after all these years. It's just the sort of tonic my Dad needs, you know. He'll be chuffed to his bollocks in the morning, when he sees his eldest son. I was surprised myself when I saw Teddy, you know. Old Ted. I thought he was in America.

500 RUTH: We're on a visit to Europe.

LENNY: What, both of you?

RUTH: Yes.

LENNY: What, you sort of live with him over there, do you?

RUTH: We're married.

505 LENNY: On a visit to Europe, eh? Seen much of it?

RUTH: We've just come from Italy.

LENNY: Oh, you went to Italy first, did you? And then he brought you over here to meet the family, did he? Well, the old man'll be pleased to see you, I can tell you.

510 RUTH: Good.

LENNY: What did you say?

RUTH: Good.

(Pause.)

LENNY: Where'd you go to in Italy?

RUTH: Venice.

LENNY: Not dear old Venice? Eh? That's funny. You know, 515 I've always had a feeling that if I'd been a soldier in the last war—say in the Italian campaign—I'd probably have found myself in Venice. I've always had that feeling. The trouble was I was too young to serve, you see. I was only a child, I was too small, otherwise I've got a pretty shrewd 520 idea I'd probably have gone through Venice. Yes, I'd almost certainly have gone through it with my battalion. Do you mind if I hold your hand?

RUTH: Why?

LENNY: Just a touch.   525

(He stands and goes to her.)

Just a tickle.

RUTH: Why?

(He looks down at her.)

LENNY: I'll tell you why.

(Slight pause.)

One night, not too long ago, one night down by the docks, I was standing alone under an arch, watching all the men 530 jibbing the boom, out in the harbour, and playing about with the yardarm, when a certain lady came up to me and made me a certain proposal. This lady had been searching for me for days. She'd lost track of my whereabouts. However, the fact was she eventually caught up with me, and 535 when she caught up with me she made me this certain proposal. Well, this proposal wasn't entirely out of order and normally I would have subscribed to it. I mean I would have subscribed to it in the normal course of events. The only trouble was she was falling apart with the pox. So I 540 turned it down. Well, this lady was very insistent and started taking liberties with me down under this arch, liberties which by any criterion I couldn't be expected to tolerate, the facts being what they were, so I clumped her one. It was on my mind at the time to do away with her, you 545 know, to kill her, and the fact is, that as killings go, it would have been a simple matter, nothing to it. Her chauffeur, who had located me for her, he'd popped around the corner to have a drink, which just left this lady and myself, you see, alone, standing underneath this arch, watching all the 550 steamers steaming up, no one about, all quiet on the Western Front, and there she was up against the wall—well, just sliding down the wall, following the blow I'd given her. Well, to sum up, everything was in my favour, for a killing. Don't worry about the chauffeur. The chauffeur would 555 never have spoken. He was an old friend of the family. But . . . in the end I thought . . . Aaah, why go to all the bother . . . you know, getting rid of the corpse and all that, getting yourself into a state of tension. So I just gave her another belt in the nose and a couple of turns of the boot and sort 560 of left it at that.

RUTH: How did you know she was diseased?

LENNY: How did I know?

(*Pause.*)

I decided she was.

(*Silence.*)

565   You and my brother are newly-weds, are you?
RUTH: We've been married six years.
LENNY: He's always been my favourite brother, old Teddy. Do
you know that? And my goodness we are proud of him here,
I can tell you. Doctor of Philosophy and all that . . . leaves
570   quite an impression. Of course, he's a very sensitive man, isn't
he? Ted. Very. I've often wished I was as sensitive as he is.
RUTH: Have you?
LENNY: Oh yes. Oh yes, very much so. I mean, I'm not say-
ing I'm not sensitive. I am. I could just be a bit more so,
575   that's all.
RUTH: Could you?
LENNY: Yes, just a bit more so, that's all.

(*Pause.*)

I mean, I am very sensitive to atmosphere, but I tend to get
desensitized, if you know what I mean, when people make
580   unreasonable demands on me. For instance, last Christmas
I decided to do a bit of snow-clearing for the Borough
Council, because we had a heavy snow over here that year
in Europe. I didn't have to do this snow-clearing—I mean
I wasn't financially embarrassed in any way—it just ap-
585   pealed to me, it appealed to something inside me. What I
anticipated with a good deal of pleasure was the brisk cold
bite in the air in the early morning. And I was right. I had
to get my snowboots on and I had to stand on a corner, at
about five-thirty in the morning, to wait for the lorry to
590   pick me up, to take me to the allotted area. Bloody freezing. Well, the lorry came, I jumped on the tailboard, headlights on, dipped, and off we went. Got there, shovels up,
fags on, and off we went, deep into the December snow,
hours be-fore cockcrow. Well, that morning, while I was
595   having my mid-morning cup of tea in a neighboring cafe,
the shovel standing by my chair, an old lady approached me
and asked me if I would give her a hand with her iron mangle. Her brother-in-law, she said, had left it for her, but he'd
left it in the wrong room, he'd left it in the front room.
600   Well, naturally, she wanted it in the back room. It was a present he'd given her, you see, a mangle, to iron out the washing. But he'd left it in the wrong room, he'd left it in the
front room, well that was a silly place to leave it, it couldn't
stay there. So I took time off to give her a hand. She only
605   lived up the road. Well, the only trouble was when I got
there I couldn't move this mangle. It must have weighed
about half a ton. How this brother-in-law got it up there
in the first place I can't even begin to envisage. So there I
was, doing a bit of shoulders on with the mangle, risking a
610   rupture, and this old lady just standing there, waving me
on, not even lifting a little finger to give me a helping hand.
So after a few minutes I said to her, now look here, why
don't you stuff this iron mangle up your arse? Anyway, I
said, they're out of date, you want to get a spin drier. I had
615   a good mind to give her a workover there and then, but as
I was feeling jubilant with the snow-clearing I just gave her

a short-arm jab to the belly and jumped on a bus outside.
Excuse me, shall I take this ashtray out of your way?
RUTH: It's not in my way.
LENNY: It seems to be in the way of your glass. The glass was   620
about to fall. Or the ashtray. I'm rather worried about the
carpet. It's not me, it's my father. He's obsessed with order
and clarity. He doesn't like mess. So, as I don't believe
you're smoking at the moment, I'm sure you won't object
if I move the ashtray.   625

(*He does so.*)

And now perhaps I'll relieve you of your glass.
RUTH: I haven't quite finished.
LENNY: You've consumed quite enough, in my opinion.
RUTH: No, I haven't.
LENNY: Quite sufficient, in my own opinion.   630
RUTH: Not in mine, Leonard.

(*Pause.*)

LENNY: Don't call me that, please.
RUTH: Why not?
LENNY: That's the name my mother gave me.

(*Pause.*)

Just give me the glass.   635
RUTH: No.

(*Pause.*)

LENNY: I'll take it, then.
RUTH: If you take the glass . . . I'll take you.

(*Pause.*)

LENNY: How about me taking the glass without you taking
me?   640
RUTH: Why don't I just take you?

(*Pause.*)

LENNY: You're joking.

(*Pause.*)

You're in love, anyway, with another man. You've had a
secret liaison with another man. His family didn't even
know. Then you come here without a word of warning   645
and start to make trouble.

(*She picks up the glass and lifts it towards him.*)

RUTH: Have a sip. Go on. Have a sip from my glass.

(*He is still.*)

Sit on my lap. Take a long cool sip.

(*She pats her lap.*)

(*Pause. She stands, moves to him with the glass.*)

Put your head back and open your mouth.

650   LENNY: Take that glass away from me.
      RUTH: Lie on the floor. Go on. I'll pour it down your throat.
      LENNY: What are you doing, making me some kind of proposal?

(She laughs shortly, drains the glass.)

      RUTH: Oh, I was thirsty.

(She smiles at him, puts the glass down, goes into the hall and up the stairs.)

(He follows into the hall and shouts up the stairs.)

655   LENNY: What was that supposed to be? Some kind of proposal?

(Silence.)

(He comes back into the room, goes to his own glass, drains it.)

(A door slams upstairs. The landing light goes on.)

(MAX comes down the stairs, in pyjamas and cap. He comes into the room.)

      MAX: What's going on here? You drunk?

(He stares at LENNY.)

      What are you shouting about? You gone mad?

(LENNY pours another glass of water.)

      Prancing about in the middle of the night shouting your head off. What are you, a raving lunatic?
660   LENNY: I was thinking aloud.
      MAX: Is Joey down here? You been shouting at Joey?
      LENNY: Didn't you hear what I said, Dad? I said I was thinking aloud.
      MAX: You were thinking so loud you got me out of bed.
665   LENNY: Look, why don't you just . . . pop off, eh?
      MAX: Pop off? He wakes me up in the middle of the night, I think we got burglars here, I think he's got a knife stuck in him, I come down here, he tells me to pop off.

(LENNY sits down.)

      He was talking to someone. Who could he have been
670   talking to? They're all asleep. He was having a conversation with someone. He won't tell me who it was. He pretends he was thinking aloud. What are you doing, hiding someone here?
      LENNY: I was sleepwalking. Get out of it, leave me alone, will
675   you?
      MAX: I want an explanation, you understand? I asked you who you got hiding here.

(Pause.)

      LENNY: I'll tell you what, Dad, since you're in the mood for a bit of a . . . chat, I'll ask you a question. It's a question
680   I've been meaning to ask you for some time. That night . . . you know . . . the night you got me . . . that night with Mum, what was it like? Eh? When I was just a glint in your eye. What was it like? What was the background to it? I mean, I want to know the real facts about my background. I mean, for instance, is it a fact that you had me 685 in mind all the time, or is it a fact that I was the last thing you had in mind?

(Pause.)

      I'm only asking this in a spirit of inquiry, you understand that, don't you? I'm curious. And there's lots of people of my age share that curiosity, you know that, Dad? They of- 690 ten ruminate, sometimes singly, sometimes in groups, about the true facts of that particular night—the night they were made in the image of those two people at it. It's a question long overdue, from my point of view, but as we happen to be passing the time of day here tonight I 695 thought I'd pop it to you.

(Pause.)

      MAX: You'll drown in your own blood.
      LENNY: If you prefer to answer the question in writing I've got no objection.

(MAX stands.)

      I should have asked my dear mother. Why didn't I ask my 700 dear mother? Now it's too late. She's passed over to the other side.

(MAX spits at him.)

(LENNY looks down at the carpet.)

      Now look what you've done. I'll have to Hoover that in the morning, you know.

(MAX turns and walks up the stairs.)

(LENNY sits still.)

(Blackout.)

(Lights up.)

(Morning.)

(JOEY in front of the mirror. He is doing some slow limbering-up exercises. He stops, combs his hair, carefully. He then shadowboxes, heavily, watching himself in the mirror.)

(MAX comes in from upstage left.)

(Both MAX and JOEY are dressed. MAX watches JOEY in silence. JOEY stops shadowboxing, picks up a newspaper and sits.)

(Silence.)

      MAX: I hate this room. 705

(Pause.)

      It's the kitchen I like. It's nice in there. It's cosy.

(Pause.)

But I can't stay in there. You know why? Because he's always washing up in there, scraping the plates, driving me out of the kitchen, that's why.

710 JOEY: Why don't you bring your tea in here?

MAX: I don't want to bring my tea in here. I hate it here. I want to drink my tea in there.

(*He goes into the hall and looks towards the kitchen.*)

What's he doing in there?

(*He returns.*)

What's the time?

715 JOEY: Half past six.

MAX: Half past six.

(*Pause.*)

I'm going to see a game of football this afternoon. You want to come?

(*Pause.*)

I'm talking to you.

720 JOEY: I'm training this afternoon. I'm doing six rounds with Blackie.

MAX: That's not till five o'clock. You've got time to see a game of football before five o'clock. It's the first game of the season.

725 JOEY: No, I'm not going.

MAX: Why not?

(*Pause.*)

(MAX *goes into the hall.*)

Sam! Come here!

(MAX *comes back into the room.*)

(SAM *enters with a cloth.*)

SAM: What?

MAX: What are you doing in there?

730 SAM: Washing up.

MAX: What else?

SAM: Getting rid of your leavings.

MAX: Putting them in the bin, eh?

SAM: Right in.

735 MAX: What point you trying to prove?

SAM: No point.

MAX: Oh yes, you are. You resent making my breakfast, that's what it is, isn't it? That's why you bang round the kitchen like that, scraping the frying-pan, scraping all the leavings
740 into the bin, scraping all the plates, scraping all the tea out of the teapot . . . that's why you do that, every single stinking morning. I know. Listen, Sam. I want to say something to you. From my heart.

(*He moves closer.*)

I want you to get rid of these feelings of resentment
745 you've got towards me. I wish I could understand them.

Honestly, have I ever given you cause? Never. When Dad died he said to me, Max, look after your brothers. That's exactly what he said to me.

SAM: How could he say that when he was dead?

MAX: What?   750

SAM: How could he speak if he was dead?

(*Pause.*)

MAX: Before he died, Sam. Just before. They were his last words. His last sacred words, Sammy. A split second after he said those words . . . he was a dead man. You think I'm joking? You think when my father spoke—on his death-bed—   755
I wouldn't obey his words to the last letter? You hear that, Joey? He'll stop at nothing. He's even prepared to spit on the memory of our Dad. What kind of a son were you, you wet wick? You spent half your time doing crossword puzzles! We took you into the butcher's shop, you couldn't even   760
sweep the dust off the floor. We took MacGregor into the shop, he could run the place by the end of a week. Well, I'll tell you one thing. I respected my father not only as a man but as a number one butcher! And to prove it I followed him into the shop. I learned to carve a carcass at his knee. I com-   765
memorated his name in blood. I gave birth to three grown men! All on my own bat. What have you done?

(*Pause.*)

What have you done? You tit!

SAM: Do you want to finish the washing up? Look, here's the cloth.   770

MAX: So try to get rid of these feelings of resentment, Sam. After all, we are brothers.

SAM: Do you want the cloth? Here you are. Take it.

(TEDDY *and* RUTH *come down the stairs. They walk across the hall and stop just inside the room.*)

(*The others turn and look at them.* JOEY *stands.*)

(TEDDY *and* RUTH *are wearing dressing-gowns.*)

(*Silence.*)

(TEDDY *smiles.*)

TEDDY: Hullo . . . Dad . . . We overslept.

(*Pause.*)

What's for breakfast?   775

(*Silence.*)

(TEDDY *chuckles.*)

Huh. We overslept.

(MAX *turns to* SAM.)

MAX: Did you know he was here?

SAM: No.

(MAX *turns to* JOEY.)

MAX: Did you know he was here?

(*Pause.*)

780   I asked you if you knew he was here.
JOEY: No.
MAX: Then who knew?

(*Pause.*)

Who knew?

(*Pause.*)

I didn't know.
785   TEDDY: I was going to come down, Dad, I was going to . . .
be here, when you came down.

(*Pause.*)

How are you?

(*Pause.*)

Uh . . . look, I'd . . . like you to meet . . .
MAX: How long you been in this house?
790   TEDDY: All night.
MAX: All night? I'm a laughing-stock. How did you get in?
TEDDY: I had my key.

(MAX *whistles and laughs.*)

MAX: Who's this?
TEDDY: I was just going to introduce you.
795   MAX: Who asked you to bring tarts in here?
TEDDY: Tarts?
MAX: Who asked you to bring dirty tarts into this house?
TEDDY: Listen, don't be silly—
MAX: You been here all night?
800   TEDDY: Yes, we arrived from Venice—
MAX: We've had a smelly scrubber in my house all night.
We've had a stinking pox-ridden slut in my house all night.
TEDDY: Stop it! What are you talking about?
MAX: I haven't seen the bitch for six years, he comes home
805   without a word, he brings a filthy scrubber off the street,
he shacks up in my house!
TEDDY: She's my wife! We're married!

(*Pause.*)

MAX: I've never had a whore under this roof before. Ever since
your mother died. My word of honour. (*To* JOEY.) Have you
810   ever had a whore here? Has Lenny ever had a whore here?
They come back from America, they bring the slopbucket
with them. They bring the bedpan with them. (*To* TEDDY.)
Take that disease away from me. Get her away from me.
TEDDY: She's my wife.
815   MAX: (*To* JOEY.) Chuck them out.

(*Pause.*)

A Doctor of Philosophy. Sam, you want to meet a Doctor
of Philosophy? (*To* JOEY.) I said chuck them out.

(*Pause.*)

What's the matter? You deaf?
JOEY: You're an old man. (*To* TEDDY.) He's an old man.

(LENNY *walks into the room, in a dressing-gown.*)

(*He stops.*)

(*They all look round.* MAX *turns back, hits* JOEY *in the stomach
with all his might.*)

(JOEY *contorts, staggers across the stage.* MAX, *with the exertion of
the blow, begins to collapse. His knees buckle. He clutches his stick.*)

(SAM *moves forward to help him.*)

(MAX *hits him across the head with his stick.*)

(SAM *sits, head in hands.*)

(JOEY, *hands pressed to his stomach, sinks down at the feet of*
RUTH.)

(*She looks down at him.* LENNY *and* TEDDY *are still.*)

(JOEY *slowly stands. He is close to* RUTH. *He turns from* RUTH,
looks round at MAX.)

(SAM *clutches his head.* MAX *breathes heavily, very slowly gets to his
feet.* JOEY *moves to him.*)

(*They look at each other.*)

(*Silence.*)

(MAX *moves past* JOEY, *walks towards* RUTH. *He gestures with his
stick.*)

MAX: Miss.   820

(RUTH *walks toward him.*)

RUTH: Yes?

(*He looks at her.*)

MAX: You a mother?
RUTH: Yes.
MAX: How many you got?
RUTH: Three.   825

(*He turns to* TEDDY.)

MAX: All yours, Ted?

(*Pause.*)

Teddy, why don't we have a nice cuddle and kiss, eh? Like
the old days? What about a nice cuddle and kiss, eh?
TEDDY: Come on, then.

(*Pause.*)

MAX: You want to kiss your old father? Want a cuddle with 830
your old father?
TEDDY: Come on, then.

(TEDDY *moves a step towards him.*)

Come on.

(*Pause.*)

MAX: You still love your old Dad, eh?

(*They face each other.*)

835 TEDDY: Come on, Dad. I'm ready for the cuddle.

(MAX *begins to chuckle, gurgling.*)

(*He turns to the family and addresses them.*)

MAX: He still loves his father!

(*Curtain.*)

ACT TWO

Afternoon.

MAX, TEDDY, LENNY and SAM *are about the stage, lighting cigars.*

JOEY *comes in from upstage left with a coffee tray, followed by* RUTH. *He puts the tray down.* RUTH *hands coffee to all the men. She sits with her cup.* MAX *smiles at her.*

RUTH: That was a very good lunch.
MAX: I'm glad you liked it. (*To the others.*) Did you hear that? (*To* RUTH.) Well, I put my heart and soul into it, I can tell you. (*He sips.*) And this is a lovely cup of coffee.
5 RUTH: I'm glad.

(*Pause.*)

MAX: I've got the feeling you're a first-rate cook.
RUTH: I'm not bad.
MAX: No, I've got the feeling you're a number one cook. Am I right, Teddy?
10 TEDDY: Yes, she's a very good cook.

(*Pause.*)

MAX: Well, it's a long time since the whole family was to-gether, eh? If only your mother was alive. Eh, what do you say, Sam? What would Jessie say if she was alive? Sitting here with her three sons. Three fine grown-up lads. And
15 a lovely daughter-in-law. The only shame is her grand-children aren't here. She'd have petted them and cooed over them, wouldn't she, Sam? She'd have fussed over them and played with them, told them stories, tickled them—I tell you she'd have been hysterical. (*To* RUTH.)
20 Mind you, she taught those boys everything they know. She taught them all the morality they know. I'm telling you. Every single bit of the moral code they live by—was taught to them by their mother. And she had a heart to go with it. What a heart. Eh, Sam? Listen, what's the use
25 of beating round the bush? That woman was the back-bone to this family. I mean, I was busy working twenty-four hours a day in the shop, I was going all over the country to find meat, I was making my way in the world, but I left a woman at home with a will of iron, a heart of
30 gold and a mind. Right, Sam?

(*Pause.*)

What a mind.

(*Pause.*)

Mind you, I was a generous man to her. I never left her short of a few bob. I remember one year I entered into negotiations with a top-class group of butchers with con-tinental connections. I was going into association with 35 them. I remember the night I came home, I kept quiet. First of all I gave Lenny a bath, then Teddy a bath, then Joey a bath. What fun we used to have in the bath, eh, boys? Then I came downstairs and I made Jessie put her feet up on a pouffe—what happened to that pouffe, I 40 haven't seen it for years—she put her feet up on the pouffe and I said to her, Jessie, I think our ship is going to come home, I'm going to treat you to a couple of items, I'm going to buy you a dress in pale corded blue silk, heavily encrusted in pearls, and for casual wear, a pair of 45 pantaloons in lilac flowered taffeta. Then I gave her a drop of cherry brandy. I remember the boys came down, in their pyjamas, all their hair shining, their faces pink, it was before they started shaving, and they knelt down at our feet, Jessie's and mine. I tell you, it was like Christmas. 50

(*Pause.*)

RUTH: What happened to the group of butchers?
MAX: The group? They turned out to be a bunch of crimi-nals like everyone else.

(*Pause.*)

This is a lousy cigar.

(*He stubs it out.*)

(*He turns to* SAM.)

What time you going to work?   55
SAM: Soon.
MAX: You've got a job on this afternoon, haven't you?
SAM: Yes, I know.
MAX: What do you mean, you know? You'll be late. You'll lose your job? What are you trying to do, humiliate me? 60
SAM: Don't worry about me.
MAX: It makes the bile come up in my mouth. The bile—you understand. (*To* RUTH.) I worked as a butcher all my life, using the chopper and the slab, the slab, you know what I mean, the chopper and the slab! To keep my fam- 65 ily in luxury. Two families! My mother was bedridden, my brothers were all invalids. I had to earn the money for the leading psychiatrists. I had to read books! I had to study the disease, so that I could cope with an emergency at every stage. A crippled family, three bastard sons, a slut- 70 bitch of a wife—don't talk to me about the pain of child-birth—I suffered the pain, I've still got the pangs—when I give a little cough my back collapses—and here I've got a lazy idle bugger of a brother won't even get to work on time. The best chauffeur in the world. All his life he's sat 75 in the front seat giving lovely hand signals. You call that work? This man doesn't know his gearbox from his arse!

SAM: You go and ask my customers! I'm the only one they ever ask for.

80 MAX: What do the other drivers do, sleep all day?

SAM: I can only drive one car. They can't all have me at the same time.

MAX: Anyone could have you at the same time. You'd bend over for half a dollar on Blackfriars Bridge.

85 SAM: Me!

MAX: For two bob and a toffee apple.

SAM: He's insulting me. He's insulting his brother. I'm driving a man to Hampton Court at four forty-five.

MAX: Do you want to know who could drive? MacGregor!

90 MacGregor was a driver.

SAM: Don't you believe it.

(MAX *points his stick at* SAM.)

MAX: He didn't even fight in the war. This man didn't even fight in the bloody war!

SAM: I did!

95 MAX: Who did you kill?

(*Silence.*)

(SAM *gets up, goes to* RUTH, *shakes her hand and goes out of the front door.*)

(MAX *turns to* TEDDY.)

Well, how you been keeping, son?

TEDDY: I've been keeping very well, Dad.

MAX: It's nice to have you with us, son.

TEDDY: It's nice to be back, Dad.

(*Pause.*)

100 MAX: You should have told me you were married, Teddy. I'd have sent you a present. Where was the wedding, in America?

TEDDY: No. Here. The day before we left.

MAX: Did you have a big function?

TEDDY: No, there was no one there.

105 MAX: You're mad. I'd have given you a white wedding. We'd have had the cream of the cream here. I'd have been only too glad to bear the expense, my word of honour.

(*Pause.*)

TEDDY: You were busy at the time. I didn't want to bother you.

MAX: But you're my own flesh and blood. You're my first

110 born. I'd have dropped everything. Sam would have driven you to the reception in the Snipe, Lenny would have been your best man, and then we'd have all seen you off on the boat. I mean, you don't think I disapprove of marriage, do you? Don't be daft. (*To* RUTH.) I've been begging my two

115 youngsters for years to find a nice feminine girl with proper credentials—it makes life worth living. (*To* TEDDY.) Anyway, what's the difference, you did it, you made a wonderful choice, you've got a wonderful family, a marvellous career . . . so why don't we let bygones be bygones?

(*Pause.*)

120 You know what I'm saying? I want you both to know that you have my blessing.

TEDDY: Thank you.

MAX: Don't mention it. How many other houses in the district have got a Doctor of Philosophy sitting down drinking a cup of coffee? 125

(*Pause.*)

RUTH: I'm sure Teddy's very happy . . . to know that you're pleased with me.

(*Pause.*)

I think he wondered whether you would be pleased with me.

MAX: But you're a charming woman. 130

(*Pause.*)

RUTH: I was . . .

MAX: What?

(*Pause.*)

What she say?

(*They all look at her.*)

RUTH: I was . . . different . . . when I met Teddy . . . first.

TEDDY: No you weren't. You were the same. 135

RUTH: I wasn't.

MAX: Who cares? Listen, live in the present, what are you worrying about? I mean, don't forget the earth's about five thousand million years old, at least. Who can afford to live in the past? 140

(*Pause.*)

TEDDY: She's a great help to me over there. She's a wonderful wife and mother. She's a very popular woman. She's got lots of friends. It's a great life, at the University . . . you know . . . it's a very good life. We've got a lovely house . . . we've got all . . . we've got everything we want. It's a very 145 stimulating environment.

(*Pause.*)

My department . . . is highly successful.

(*Pause.*)

We've got three boys, you know.

MAX: All boys? Isn't that funny, eh? You've got three, I've got three. You've got three nephews, Joey. Joey! You're an un- 150 cle, do you hear? You could teach them how to box.

(*Pause.*)

JOEY: (*To* RUTH.) I'm a boxer. In the evenings, after work. I'm in demolition in the daytime.

RUTH: Oh?

JOEY: Yes. I hope to be full time, when I get more bouts. 155

MAX: (*To* LENNY.) He speaks so easily to his sister-in-law, do you notice? That's because she's an intelligent and sympathetic woman.

(*He leans to her.*)

160   Eh, tell me, do you think the children are missing their mother?

(*She looks at him.*)

TEDDY: Of course they are. They love her. We'll be seeing them soon.

(*Pause.*)

LENNY: (*To* TEDDY.) Your cigar's gone out.
TEDDY: Oh, yes.
165   LENNY: Want a light?
TEDDY: No. No.

(*Pause.*)

So has yours.
LENNY: Oh, yes.

(*Pause.*)

Eh, Teddy, you haven't told us much about your Doctor-
170   ship of Philosophy. What do you teach?
TEDDY: Philosophy.
LENNY: Well, I want to ask you something. Do you detect a certain logical incoherence in the central affirmations of Christian theism?
175   TEDDY: That question doesn't fall within my province.
LENNY: Well, look at it this way . . . you don't mind my asking you some questions, do you?
TEDDY: If they're within my province.
LENNY: Well, look at it this way. How can the unknown merit
180   reverence? In other words, how can you revere that of which you're ignorant? At the same time, it would be ridiculous to propose that what we *know* merits reverence. What we know merits any one of a number of things, but it stands to reason reverence isn't one of them. In other words,
185   apart from the known and the unknown, what else is there?

(*Pause.*)

TEDDY: I'm afraid I'm the wrong person to ask.
LENNY: But you're a philosopher. Come on, be frank. What do you make of all this business of being and not-being?
TEDDY: What do you make of it?
190   LENNY: Well, for instance, take a table. Philosophically speak-ing. What is it?
TEDDY: A table.
LENNY: Ah. You mean it's nothing else but a table. Well, some people would envy your certainty, wouldn't they, Joey?
195   For instance, I've got a couple of friends of mine, we of-ten sit round the Ritz Bar having a few liqueurs, and they're always saying things like that, you know, things like: Take a table, take it. All right, I say, *take* it, *take* a table, but once you've taken it, what you going to do with it?
200   Once you've got hold of it, where you going to take it?
MAX: You'd probably sell it.
LENNY: You wouldn't get much for it.
JOEY: Chop it up for firewood.

(*LENNY looks at him and laughs.*)

RUTH: Don't be too sure though. You've forgotten some-thing. Look at me. I . . . move my leg. That's all it is. But   205
I wear . . . underwear . . . which moves with me . . . it . . . captures your attention. Perhaps you misinterpret. The ac-tion is simple. It's a leg . . . moving. My lips move. Why don't you restrict . . . your observations to that? Perhaps the fact that they move is more significant . . . than the   210
words which come through them. You must bear that . . . possibility . . . in mind.

(*Silence.*)

(TEDDY *stands.*)

I was born quite near here.

(*Pause.*)

Then . . . six years ago, I went to America.

(*Pause.*)

It's all rock. And sand. It stretches . . . so far . . . everywhere   215
you look. And there's lots of insects there.

(*Pause.*)

And there's lots of insects there.

(*Silence.*)

(*She is still.*)

(MAX *stands.*)

MAX: Well, it's time to go to the gym. Time for your work-out, Joey.
LENNY: (*Standing.*) I'll come with you.   220

(JOEY *sits looking at* RUTH.)

MAX: Joe.

(JOEY *stands. The three go out.*)

(TEDDY *sits by* RUTH, *holds her hand. She smiles at him.*)

(*Pause.*)

TEDDY: I think we'll go back. Mmnn?

(*Pause.*)

Shall we go home?
RUTH: Why?
TEDDY: Well, we were only here for a few days, weren't we?   225
We might as well . . . cut it short, I think.
RUTH: Why? Don't you like it here?
TEDDY: Of course I do. But I'd like to go back and see the boys now.

(*Pause.*)

RUTH: Don't you like your family?   230
TEDDY: Which family?
RUTH: Your family here.

TEDDY: Of course I like them. What are you talking about?

(*Pause.*)

RUTH: You don't like them as much as you thought you did?

235 TEDDY: Of course I do. Of course I . . . like them. I don't know what you're talking about.

(*Pause.*)

Listen. You know what time of the day it is there now, do you?

RUTH: What?

240 TEDDY: It's morning. It's about eleven o'clock.

RUTH: Is it?

TEDDY: Yes, they're about six hours behind us . . . I mean . . . behind the time here. The boys'll be at the pool . . . now . . . swimming. Think of it. Morning over there. Sun. We'll

245 go anyway, mmnn? It's so clean there.

RUTH: Clean.

TEDDY: Yes.

RUTH: Is it dirty here?

TEDDY: No, of course not. But it's cleaner there.

(*Pause.*)

250 Look, I just brought you back to meet the family, didn't I? You've met them, we can go. The fall semester will be starting soon.

RUTH: You find it dirty here?

TEDDY: I didn't say I found it dirty here.

(*Pause.*)

255 I didn't say that.

(*Pause.*)

Look. I'll go and pack. You rest for a while. Will you? They won't be back for at least an hour. You can sleep. Rest. Please.

(*She looks at him.*)

You can help me with my lectures when we get back. I'd

260 love that. I'd be so grateful for it, really. We can bathe till October. You know that. Here, there's nowhere to bathe, except the swimming bath down the road. You know what it's like? It's like a urinal. A filthy urinal!

(*Pause.*)

You liked Venice, didn't you? It was lovely, wasn't it? You

265 had a good week. I mean . . . I took you there. I can speak Italian.

RUTH: But if I'd been a nurse in the Italian campaign I would have been there before.

(*Pause.*)

TEDDY: You just rest. I'll go and pack.

(TEDDY *goes out and up the stairs.*)

(*She closes her eyes.*)

(LENNY *appears from upstage left. He walks into the room and sits near her.*)

(*She opens her eyes.*)

(*Silence.*)

LENNY: Well, the evenings are drawing in.   270

RUTH: Yes, it's getting dark.

(*Pause.*)

LENNY: Winter'll soon be upon us. Time to renew one's wardrobe.

(*Pause.*)

RUTH: That's a good thing to do.

LENNY: What?   275

(*Pause.*)

RUTH: I always . . .

(*Pause.*)

Do you like clothes?

LENNY: Oh, yes. Very fond of clothes.

(*Pause.*)

RUTH: I'm fond . . .

(*Pause.*)

What do you think of my shoes?   280

LENNY: They're very nice.

RUTH: No, I can't get the ones I want over there.

LENNY: Can't get them over there, eh?

RUTH: No . . . you don't get them there.

(*Pause.*)

I was a model before I went away.   285

LENNY: Hats?

(*Pause.*)

I bought a girl a hat once. We saw it in a glass case, in a shop. I tell you what it had. It had a bunch of daffodils on it, tied with a black satin bow, and then it was covered with a cloche of black veiling. A cloche. I'm telling you.   290
She was made for it.

RUTH: No . . . I was a model for the body. A photographic model for the body.

LENNY: Indoor work?

RUTH: That was before I had . . . all my children.   295

(*Pause.*)

No, not always indoors.

(*Pause.*)

Once or twice we went to a place in the country, by train. Oh, six or seven times. We used to pass a . . . a large white water tower. This place . . . this house . . . was very big . . . the trees . . . there was a lake, you see . . . we used to change and walk down towards the lake . . . we went down a path . . . on stones . . . there were . . . on this path. Oh, just . . . wait . . . yes . . . when we changed in the house we had a drink. There was a cold buffet.

(*Pause.*)

305 Sometimes we stayed in the house but . . . most often . . . we walked down to the lake . . . and did our modelling there.

(*Pause.*)

Just before we went to America I went down there. I walked from the station to the gate and then I walked up 310 the drive. There were lights on . . . I stood in the drive . . . the house was very light.

(TEDDY *comes down the stairs with the cases. He puts them down, looks at* LENNY.)

TEDDY: What have you been saying to her?

(*He goes to* RUTH.)

Here's your coat.

(LENNY *goes to the radiogram and puts on a record of slow jazz.*)

Ruth. Come on. Put it on.

315 LENNY: (*To* RUTH.) What about one dance before you go?
TEDDY: We're going.
LENNY: Just one.
TEDDY: No. We're going.
LENNY: Just one dance, with her brother-in-law, before she
320 goes.

(LENNY *bends to her.*)

Madam?

(RUTH *stands. They dance, slowly.*)

(TEDDY *stands, with* RUTH's *coat.*)

(MAX *and* JOEY *come in the front door and into the room. They stand.*)

(LENNY *kisses* RUTH. *They stand, kissing.*)

JOEY: Christ, she's wide open. Dad, look at that.

(*Pause.*)

She's a tart.

(*Pause.*)

Old Lenny's got a tart in here.

(JOEY *goes to them. He takes* RUTH's *arm. He smiles at* LENNY. *He sits with* RUTH *on the sofa, embraces and kisses her.*)

(*He looks up at* LENNY.)

Just up my street. 325

(*He leans her back until she lies beneath him. He kisses her. He looks up at* TEDDY *and* MAX.)

It's better than a rubdown, this.

(LENNY *sits on the arm of the sofa. He caresses* RUTH's *hair as* JOEY *embraces her.*)

(MAX *comes forward, looks at the cases.*)

MAX: You going, Teddy? Already?

(*Pause.*)

Well, when you coming over again, eh? Look, next time you come over, don't forget to let us know beforehand whether you're married or not. I'll always be glad to meet 330 the wife. Honest. I'm telling you.

(JOEY *lies heavily on* RUTH.)

(*They are almost still.*)

(LENNY *caresses her hair.*)

Listen, you think I don't know why you didn't tell me you were married? I know why. You were ashamed. You thought I'd be annoyed because you married a woman beneath you. You should have known me better. I'm 335 broadminded. I'm a broadminded man.

(*He peers to see* RUTH's *face under* JOEY, *turns back to* TEDDY.)

Mind you, she's a lovely girl. A beautiful woman. And a mother too. A mother of three. You've made a happy woman out of her. It's something to be proud of. I mean, we're talking about a woman of quality. We're talking 340 about a woman of feeling.

(JOEY *and* RUTH *roll off the sofa on to the floor.*)

(JOEY *clasps her.* LENNY *moves to stand above them. He looks down on them. He touches* RUTH *gently with his foot.*)

(RUTH *suddenly pushes* JOEY *away.*)

(*She stands up.* JOEY *gets to his feet, stares at her.*)

RUTH: I'd like something to eat. (*To* LENNY.) I'd like a drink. Did you get any drink?
LENNY: We've got drink.
RUTH: I'd like one, please.
LENNY: What drink? 345
RUTH: Whisky.
LENNY: I've got it.

(*Pause.*)

RUTH: Well, get it.

(LENNY *goes to the sideboard, takes out bottle and glasses.*)

(JOEY *moves towards her.*)

Put the record off. 350

(*He looks at her, turns, puts the record off.*)

I want something to eat.

(*Pause.*)

JOEY: I can't cook. (*Pointing to* MAX.) He's the cook.

(LENNY *brings her a glass of whisky.*)

LENNY: Soda on the side?
RUTH: What's this glass? I can't drink out of this. Haven't you
355   got a tumbler?
LENNY: Yes.
RUTH: Well, put it in a tumbler.

(*He takes the glass back, pours whisky into a tumbler, brings it to her.*)

LENNY: On the rocks? Or as it comes?
RUTH: Rocks? What do you know about rocks?
360 LENNY: We've got rocks. But they're frozen stiff in the fridge.

(RUTH *drinks.*)

(LENNY *looks round at the others.*)

      Drinks all round?

(*He goes to the sideboard and pours drinks.*)

(JOEY *moves closer to* RUTH.)

JOEY: What food do you want?

(RUTH *walks round the room.*)

RUTH: (*To* TEDDY.) Have your family read your critical works?
MAX: That's one thing I've never done. I've never read one of
365   his critical works.
TEDDY: You wouldn't understand them.

(LENNY *hands drinks all round.*)

JOEY: What sort of food do you want? I'm not the cook, anyway.
LENNY: Soda, Ted? Or as it comes?
370 TEDDY: You wouldn't understand my works. You wouldn't have
      the faintest idea of what they were about. You wouldn't ap-
      preciate the points of reference. You're way behind. All of
      you. There's no point in my sending you my works. You'd
      be lost. It's nothing to do with the question of intelligence.
375   It's a way of being able to look at the world. It's a question of
      how far you can operate on things and not in things. I mean
      it's a question of your capacity to ally the two, to relate the
      two, to balance the two. To see, to be able to see! I'm the one
      who can see. That's why I can write my critical works.
380   Might do you good . . . have a look at them . . . see how cer-
      tain people can view . . . things . . . how certain people can
      maintain . . . intellectual equilibrium. Intellectual equilib-
      rium. You're just objects. You just . . . move about. I can ob-
      serve it. I can see what you do. It's the same as I do. But you're
385   lost in it. You won't get me being . . . I won't be lost in it.

      (*Blackout.*)

(*Lights up.*)

(*Evening.*)

(TEDDY *sitting, in his coat, the cases by him.* SAM.)

(*Pause.*)

SAM: Do you remember MacGregor, Teddy?
TEDDY: Mac?
SAM: Yes.
TEDDY: Of course I do.
SAM: What did you think of him? Did you take to him?   390
TEDDY: Yes. I liked him. Why?

(*Pause.*)

SAM: You know, you were always my favourite, of the lads. Al-
      ways.

(*Pause.*)

      When you wrote to me from America I was very
      touched, you know. I mean you'd written to your father a   395
      few times but you'd never written to me. But then, when
      I got that letter from you . . . well, I was very touched. I
      never told him. I never told him I'd heard from you.

(*Pause.*)

      (*Whispering.*) Teddy, shall I tell you something? You were
      always your mother's favourite. She told me. It's true. You   400
      were always the . . . you were always the main object of
      her love.

(*Pause.*)

      Why don't you stay for a couple more weeks, eh? We
      could have a few laughs.

(LENNY *comes in the front door and into the room.*)

LENNY: Still here, Ted? You'll be late for your first seminar.   405

(*He goes to the sideboard, opens it, peers in it, to the right and the left, stands.*)

      Where's my cheese-roll?

(*Pause.*)

      Someone's taken my cheese-roll. I left it there. (*To* SAM.)
      You been thieving?
TEDDY: I took your cheese-roll, Lenny.

(*Silence.*)

(SAM *looks at them, picks up his hat and goes out of the front door.*)

(*Silence.*)

LENNY: You took my cheese-roll?   410
TEDDY: Yes.
LENNY: I made that roll myself. I cut it and put the butter on.
      I sliced a piece of cheese and put it in between. I put it on

415 a plate and I put it in the sideboard. I did all that before I went out. Now I come back and you've eaten it.

TEDDY: Well, what are you going to do about it?

LENNY: I'm waiting for you to apologize.

TEDDY: But I took it deliberately, Lenny.

LENNY: You mean you didn't stumble on it by mistake?

420 TEDDY: No, I saw you put it there. I was hungry, so I ate it.

(*Pause.*)

LENNY: Barefaced audacity.

(*Pause.*)

What led you to be so . . . vindictive against your own brother? I'm bowled over.

(*Pause.*)

425 Well, Ted, I would say this is something approaching the naked truth, isn't it? It's a real cards on the table stunt. I mean, we're in the land of no holds barred now. Well, how else can you interpret it? To pinch your younger brother's specially made cheese-roll when he's out doing a spot of work, that's not equivocal, it's unequivocal.

(*Pause.*)

430 Mind you, I will say you do seem to have grown a bit sulky during the last six years. A bit sulky. A bit inner. A bit less forthcoming. It's funny, because I'd have thought that in the United States of America, I mean with the sun and all that, the open spaces, on the old campus, in your position, lectur-
435 ing, in the centre of all the intellectual life out there, on the old campus, all the social whirl, all the stimulation of it all, all your kids and all that, to have fun with, down by the pool, the Greyhound buses and all that, tons of iced water, all the comfort of those Bermuda shorts and all that, on the old
440 campus, no time of the day or night you can't get a cup of coffee or a Dutch gin, I'd have thought you'd have grown more forthcoming, not less. Because I want you to know that you set a standard for us, Teddy. Your family looks up to you, boy, and you know what it does? It does its best to fol-
445 low the example you set. Because you're a great source of pride to us. That's why we were so glad to see you come back, to welcome you back to your birthplace. That's why.

(*Pause.*)

No, listen, Ted, there's no question that we live a less rich life here than you do over there. We live a closer life. We're
450 busy, of course. Joey's busy with his boxing, I'm busy with my occupation, Dad still plays a good game of poker, and he does the cooking as well, well up to his old standard, and Uncle Sam's the best chauffeur in the firm. But nevertheless we do make up a unit, Teddy, and you're an integral part
455 of it. When we all sit round the backyard having a quiet gander at the night sky, there's always an empty chair stand-ing in the circle, which is in fact yours. And so when you at length return to us, we do expect a bit of grace, a bit of je ne sais quoi, a bit of generosity of mind, a bit of liberal-
460 ity of spirit, to reassure us. We do expect that. But do we get it? Have we got it? Is that what you've given us?

(*Pause.*)

TEDDY: Yes.

(JOEY *comes down the stairs and into the room, with a newspaper.*)

LENNY: (*To* JOEY.) How'd you get on?

JOEY: Er . . . not bad.

LENNY: What do you mean? 465

(*Pause.*)

What do you mean?

JOEY: Not bad.

LENNY: I want to know what you mean—by not bad.

JOEY: What's it got to do with you?

LENNY: Joey, you tell your brother everything. 470

(*Pause.*)

JOEY: I didn't get all the way.

LENNY: You didn't get all the way?

(*Pause.*)

(*With emphasis.*) You didn't get all the way?
But you've had her up there for two hours.

JOEY: Well? 475

LENNY: You didn't get all the way and you've had her up there for two hours!

JOEY: What about it?

(LENNY *moves closer to him.*)

LENNY: What are you telling me?

JOEY: What do you mean? 480

LENNY: Are you telling me she's a tease?

(*Pause.*)

She's a tease!

(*Pause.*)

What do you think of that, Ted? Your wife turns out to be a tease. He's had her up there for two hours and he didn't go the whole hog. 485

JOEY: I didn't say she was a tease.

LENNY: Are you joking? It sounds like a tease to me, don't it to you, Ted?

TEDDY: Perhaps he hasn't got the right touch.

LENNY: Joey? Not the right touch? Don't be ridiculous. He's 490 had more dolly than you've had cream cakes. He's irre-sistible. He's one of the few and far between. Tell him about the last bird you had, Joey.

(*Pause.*)

JOEY: What bird?

LENNY: The last bird! When we stopped the car . . . 495

JOEY: Oh, that . . . yes . . . well, we were in Lenny's car one night last week . . .

LENNY: The Alfa.

JOEY: And er . . . bowling down the road . . .

500 LENNY: Up near the Scrubs.
JOEY: Yes, up over by the Scrubs . . .
LENNY: We were doing a little survey of North Paddington.
JOEY: And er . . . it was pretty late, wasn't it?
LENNY: Yes, it was late. Well?

(*Pause.*)

505 JOEY: And then we . . . well, by the kerb, we saw this parked
       car . . . with a couple of girls in it.
LENNY: And their escorts.
JOEY: Yes, there were two geezers in it. Anyway . . .

(*Pause.*)

       What we do then?
510 LENNY: We stopped the car and got out!
JOEY: Yes . . . we got out . . . and we told the . . . two escorts
       . . . to go away . . . which they did . . . and then we . . . got
       the girls out of the car . . .
LENNY: We didn't take them over the Scrubs.
515 JOEY: Oh, no. Not over the Scrubs. Well, the police would
       have noticed us there . . . you see. We took them over a
       bombed site.
LENNY: Rubble. In the rubble.
JOEY: Yes, plenty of rubble.

(*Pause.*)

520   Well . . . you know . . . then we had them.
LENNY: You've missed out the best bit. He's missed out the
       best bit!
JOEY: What bit?
LENNY: (*To* TEDDY.) His bird says to him, I don't mind, she
525   says, but I've got to have some protection. I've got to have
       some contraceptive protection. I haven't got any contra-
       ceptive protection, old Joey says to her. In that case I won't
       do it, she says. Yes you will says Joey, never mind about the
       contraceptive protection.

(LENNY *laughs.*)

530   Even my bird laughed when she heard that. Yes, even she
       gave out a bit of a laugh. So you can't say old Joey isn't a
       bit of a knockout when he gets going, can you? And here
       he is upstairs with your wife for two hours and he hasn't
       even been the whole hog. Well, your wife sounds like a
535   bit of a tease to me, Ted. What do you make of it, Joey?
       You satisfied? Don't tell me you're satisfied without going
       the whole hog?

(*Pause.*)

JOEY: I've been the whole hog plenty of times. Sometimes . . .
       you can be happy . . . and not go the whole hog. Now and
540   again . . . you can be happy . . . without going any hog.

(LENNY *stares at him.*)

(MAX *and* SAM *come in the front door and into the room.*)

MAX: Where's the whore? Still in bed? She'll make us all an-
       imals.

LENNY: The girl's a tease.
MAX: What?
LENNY: She's had Joey on a string.   545
MAX: What do you mean?
TEDDY: He had her up there for two hours and he didn't go
       the whole hog.

(*Pause.*)

MAX: My Joey? She did that to my boy?

(*Pause.*)

       To my youngest son? Tch, tch, tch, tch. How you feeling, 550
       son? Are you all right?
JOEY: Sure I'm all right.
MAX: (*To* TEDDY.) Does she do that to you, too?
TEDDY: No.
LENNY: He gets the gravy.   555
MAX: You think so?
JOEY: No he don't.

(*Pause.*)

SAM: He's her lawful husband. She's his lawful wife.
JOEY: No he don't! He don't get no gravy! I'm telling you.
       I'm telling all of you. I'll kill the next man who says he 560
       gets the gravy.
MAX: Joey . . . what are you getting so excited about? (*To*
       LENNY.) It's because he's frustrated. You see what happens?
JOEY: Who is?
MAX: Joey. No one's saying you're wrong. In fact, everyone's 565
       saying you're right.

(*Pause.*)

(MAX *turns to the others.*)

       You know something? Perhaps it's not a bad idea to have
       a woman in the house. Perhaps it's a good thing. Who
       knows? Maybe we should keep her.

(*Pause.*)

       Maybe we'll ask her if she wants to stay.   570

(*Pause.*)

TEDDY: I'm afraid not, Dad. She's not well, and we've got to
       get home to the children.
MAX: Not well? I told you, I'm used to looking after people
       who are not so well. Don't worry about that. Perhaps we'll
       keep her here.   575

(*Pause.*)

SAM: Don't be silly.
MAX: What's silly?
SAM: You're talking rubbish.
MAX: Me?
SAM: She's got three children.   580
MAX: She can have more! Here. If she's so keen.
TEDDY: She doesn't want any more.
MAX: What do you know about what she wants, eh, Ted?

TEDDY: (*Smiling.*) The best thing for her is to come home
585   with me, Dad. Really. We're married, you know.

(MAX *walks about the room, clicks his fingers.*)

MAX: We'd have to pay her, of course. You realize that? We
    can't leave her walking about without any pocket money.
    She'll have to have a little allowance.
JOEY: Of course we'll pay her. She's got to have some money
590   in her pocket.
MAX: That's what I'm saying. You can't expect a woman to
    walk about without a few bob to spend on a pair of stock-
    ings.

(*Pause.*)

LENNY: Where's the money going to come from?
595   MAX: Well, how much is she worth? What we talking about,
    three figures?
LENNY: I asked you where the money's going to come from.
    It'll be an extra mouth to feed. It'll be an extra body to
    clothe. You realize that?
600   JOEY: I'll buy her clothes.
LENNY: What with?
JOEY: I'll put in a certain amount out of my wages.
MAX: That's it. We'll pass the hat round. We'll make a dona-
    tion. We're all grown-up people, we've got a sense of re-
605   sponsibility. We'll all put a little in the hat. It's democratic.
LENNY: It'll come to a few quid, Dad.

(*Pause.*)

I mean, she's not a woman who likes walking around in
    second-hand goods. She's up to the latest fashion. You
    wouldn't want her walking about in clothes which don't
610   show her off at her best, would you?
MAX: Lenny, do you mind if I make a little comment? It's not
    meant to be critical. But I think you're concentrating too
    much on the economic considerations. There are other
    considerations. There are the human considerations. You
615   understand what I mean? There are the human consider-
    ations. Don't forget them.
LENNY: I won't.
MAX: Well don't.

(*Pause.*)

Listen, we're bound to treat her in something approxi-
620   mating, at least, to the manner in which she's accustomed.
    After all, she's not someone off the street, she's my
    daughter-in-law!
JOEY: That's right.
MAX: There you are, you see. Joey'll donate, Sam'll donate. . . .

(SAM *looks at him.*)

625   I'll put in a few bob out of my pension, Lenny'll cough
    up. We're laughing. What about you, Ted? How much
    you going to put in the kitty?
TEDDY: I'm not putting anything in the kitty.
MAX: What? You won't even help to support your own wife?
630   I thought he was a son of mine. You lousy stinkpig. Your
    mother would drop dead if she heard you take that attitude.

LENNY: Eh, Dad.

(LENNY *walks forward.*)

I've got a better idea.
MAX: What?
LENNY: There's no need for us to go to all this expense. I   635
    know these women. Once they get started they ruin your
    budget. I've got a better idea. Why don't I take her up
    with me to Greek Street?

(*Pause.*)

MAX: You mean put her on the game?

(*Pause.*)

We'll put her on the game. That's a stroke of genius, that's   640
    a marvellous idea. You mean she can earn the money
    herself—on her back?
LENNY: Yes.
MAX: Wonderful. The only thing is, it'll have to be short
    hours. We don't want her out of the house all night.   645
LENNY: I can limit the hours.
MAX: How many?
LENNY: Four hours a night.
MAX: (*Dubiously.*) Is that enough?
LENNY: She'll bring in a good sum for four hours a night.   650
MAX: Well, you should know. After all, it's true, the last thing
    we want to do is wear the girl out. She's going to have her
    obligations this end as well. Where you going to put her
    in Greek Street?
LENNY: It doesn't have to be right in Greek Street, Dad. I've   655
    got a number of flats all around that area.
MAX: You have? Well, what about me? Why don't you give
    me one?
LENNY: You're sexless.
JOEY: Eh, wait a minute, what's all this?   660
MAX: I know what Lenny's saying. Lenny's saying she can pay
    her own way. What do you think, Teddy? That'll solve all
    our problems.
JOEY: Eh, wait a minute. I don't want to share her.
MAX: What did you say?   665
JOEY: I don't want to share her with a lot of yobs!
MAX: Yobs! You arrogant git! What arrogance. (*To* LENNY.)
    Will you be supplying her with yobs?
LENNY: I've got a very distinguished clientèle, Joey. They're
    more distinguished than you'll ever be.   670
MAX: So you can count yourself lucky we're including you in.
JOEY: I didn't think I was going to have to share her!
MAX: Well, you *are* going to have to share her! Otherwise she
    goes straight back to America. You understand?

(*Pause.*)

It's tricky enough as it is, without you shoving your oar   675
    in. But there's something worrying me. Perhaps she's not
    so up to the mark. Eh? Teddy, you're the best judge. Do
    you think she'd be up to the mark?

(*Pause.*)

I mean what about all this teasing? Is she going to make a
    habit of it? That'll get us nowhere.   680

(*Pause.*)

TEDDY: It was just love play . . . I suppose . . . that's all I suppose it was.

MAX: Love play? Two bleeding hours? That's a bloody long time for love play!

685 LENNY: I don't think we've got anything to worry about on that score, Dad.

MAX: How do you know?

LENNY: I'm giving you a professional opinion.

(LENNY *goes to* TEDDY.)

LENNY: Listen, Teddy, you could help us, actually. If I were to
690 send you some cards, over to America . . . you know, very nice ones, with a name on, and a telephone number, very discreet, well, you could distribute them . . . to various parties, who might be making a trip over here. Of course, you'd get a little percentage out of it.

695 MAX: I mean, you needn't tell them she's your wife.

LENNY: No, we'd call her something else. Dolores, or something.

MAX: Or Spanish Jacky.

LENNY: No, you've got to be reserved about it, Dad. We could
700 call her something nice . . . like Cynthia . . . or Gillian.

(*Pause.*)

JOEY: Gillian.

(*Pause.*)

LENNY: No, what I mean, Teddy, you must know lots of professors, heads of departments, men like that. They pop over here for a week at the Savoy, they need somewhere
705 they can go to have a nice quiet poke. And of course you'd be in a position to give them inside information.

MAX: Sure. You can give them proper data. You know, the kind of thing she's willing to do. How far she'd be prepared to go with their little whims and fancies. Eh, Lenny? To what ex-
710 tent she's various. I mean if you don't know who does?

(*Pause.*)

I bet you before two months we'd have a waiting list.

LENNY: You could be our representative in the States.

MAX: Of course. We're talking in international terms! By the time we've finished Pan-American'll give us a discount.

(*Pause.*)

715 TEDDY: She'd get old . . . very quickly.

MAX: No . . . not in this day and age! With the health service? Old! How could she get old? She'll have the time of her life.

(RUTH *comes down the stairs, dressed.*)

(*She comes into the room.*)

(*She smiles at the gathering, and sits.*)

(*Silence.*)

TEDDY: Ruth . . . the family have invited you to stay, for a little while longer. As a . . . as a kind of guest. If you like the

idea I don't mind. We can manage very easily at home . . .   720
until you come back.

RUTH: How very nice of them.

(*Pause.*)

MAX: It's an offer from our heart.

RUTH: It's very sweet of you.

MAX: Listen . . . it would be our pleasure.   725

(*Pause.*)

RUTH: I think I'd be too much trouble.

MAX: Trouble? What are you talking about? What trouble? Listen, I'll tell you something. Since poor Jessie died, eh, Sam? we haven't had a woman in the house. Not one. In-   730
side this house. And I'll tell you why. Because their mother's image was so dear any other woman would have . . . tarnished it. But you . . . Ruth . . . you're not only lovely and beautiful, but you're kin. You're kin. You belong here.

(*Pause.*)

RUTH: I'm very touched.

MAX: Of course you're touched. I'm touched.   735

(*Pause.*)

TEDDY: But Ruth, I should tell you . . . that you'll have to pull your weight a little, if you stay. Financially. My father isn't very well off.

RUTH: (*To* MAX.) Oh, I'm sorry.

MAX: No, you'd just have to bring in a little, that's all. A few   740
pennies. Nothing much. It's just that we're waiting for Joey to hit the top as a boxer. When Joey hits the top . . . well . . .

(*Pause.*)

TEDDY: Or you can come home with me.

LENNY: We'd get you a flat.   745

(*Pause.*)

RUTH: A flat?

LENNY: Yes.

RUTH: Where.

LENNY: In town.

(*Pause.*)

But you'd live here, with us.   750

MAX: Of course you would. This would be your home. In the bosom of the family.

LENNY: You'd just pop up to the flat a couple of hours a night, that's all.

MAX: Just a couple of hours, that's all. That's all.   755

LENNY: And you make enough money to keep you going here.

(*Pause.*)

RUTH: How many rooms would this flat have?

LENNY: Not many.

RUTH: I would want at least three rooms and a bathroom.

760 LENNY: You wouldn't need three rooms and a bathroom.
MAX: She'd need a bathroom.
LENNY: But not three rooms.

(*Pause.*)

RUTH: Oh, I would. Really.
LENNY: Two would do.
765 RUTH: No. Two wouldn't be enough.

(*Pause.*)

I'd want a dressing-room, a rest-room, and a bedroom.

(*Pause.*)

LENNY: All right, we'll get you a flat with three rooms and a
bathroom.
RUTH: With what kind of conveniences?
770 LENNY: All conveniences.
RUTH: A personal maid?
LENNY: Of course.

(*Pause.*)

We'd finance you, to begin with, and then, when you
were established, you could pay us back, in instalments.
775 RUTH: Oh, no, I wouldn't agree to that.
LENNY: Oh, why not?
RUTH: You would have to regard your original outlay simply
as a capital investment.

(*Pause.*)

LENNY: I see. All right.
780 RUTH: You'd supply my wardrobe, of course?
LENNY: We'd supply everything. Everything you need.
RUTH: I'd need an awful lot. Otherwise I wouldn't be content.
LENNY: You'd have everything.
RUTH: I would naturally want to draw up an inventory of
785 everything I would need, which would require your sig-
natures in the presence of witnesses.
LENNY: Naturally.
RUTH: All aspects of the agreement and conditions of em-
ployment would have to be clarified to our mutual satis-
790 faction before we finalized the contract.
LENNY: Of course.

(*Pause.*)

RUTH: Well, it might prove a workable arrangement.
LENNY: I think so.
MAX: And you'd have the whole of your daytime free, of
795 course. You could do a bit of cooking here if you wanted to.
LENNY: Make the beds.
MAX: Scrub the place out a bit.
TEDDY: Keep everyone company.

(SAM *comes forward.*)

SAM: (*In one breath.*) MacGregor had Jessie in the back of my
800 cab as I drove them along.

(*He croaks and collapses.*)

(*He lies still.*)

(*They look at him.*)

MAX: What's he done? Dropped dead?
LENNY: Yes.
MAX: A corpse? A corpse on my floor? Get him out of here!
Clear him out of here!

(JOEY *bends over* SAM.)

JOEY: He's not dead.   805
LENNY: He probably was dead, for about thirty seconds.
MAX: He's not even dead!

(LENNY *looks down at* SAM.)

LENNY: Yes, there's still some breath there.
MAX: (*Pointing at* SAM.) You know what that man had?
LENNY: Has.   810
MAX: Has! A diseased imagination.

(*Pause.*)

RUTH: Yes, it sounds a very attractive idea.
MAX: Do you want to shake on it now, or do you want to
leave it till later?
RUTH: Oh, we'll leave it till later.   815

(TEDDY *stands.*)

(*He looks down at* SAM.)

TEDDY: I was going to ask him to drive me to London Airport.

(*He goes to the cases, picks one up.*)

Well, I'll leave your case, Ruth. I'll just go up the road to
the Underground.
MAX: Listen, if you go the other way, first left, first right, you
remember, you might find a cab passing there.   820
TEDDY: Yes, I might do that.
MAX: Or you can take the tube to Piccadilly Circus, won't
take you ten minutes, and pick up a cab from there out to
the Airport.
TEDDY: Yes, I'll probably do that.   825
MAX: Mind you, they'll charge you double fare. They'll
charge you for the return trip. It's over the six-mile limit.
TEDDY: Yes. Well, bye-bye, Dad. Look after yourself.

(*They shake hands.*)

MAX: Thanks, son. Listen. I want to tell you something. It's
been wonderful to see you.   830

(*Pause.*)

TEDDY: It's been wonderful to see you.
MAX: Do your boys know about me? Eh? Would they like to
see a photo, do you think, of their grandfather?
TEDDY: I know they would.

(MAX *brings out his wallet.*)

MAX: I've got one on me. I've got one here. Just a minute. 835
Here you are. Will they like that one?

TEDDY: (*Taking it.*) They'll be thrilled.

(*He turns to* LENNY.)

    Good-bye, Lenny.

(*They shake hands.*)

LENNY: Ta-ta, Ted. Good to see you. Have a good trip.

840 TEDDY: Bye-bye, Joey.

(JOEY *does not move.*)

JOEY: Ta-ta.

(TEDDY *goes to the front door.*)

RUTH: Eddie.

(TEDDY *turns.*)

(*Pause.*)

    Don't become a stranger.

(TEDDY *goes, shuts the front door.*)

(*Silence.*)

(*The three men stand.*)

(RUTH *sits relaxed in her chair.* SAM *lies still.*)

(JOEY *walks slowly across the room. He kneels at her chair.*)

(*She touches his head, lightly.*)

(*He puts his head in her lap.*)

(MAX *begins to move above them, backwards and forwards.*)

(LENNY *stands still.* MAX *turns to* LENNY.)

MAX: I'm too old, I suppose. She thinks I'm an old man.

(*Pause.*)

845   I'm not such an old man.

(*Pause.*)

    (*To* RUTH.) You think I'm too old for you?

(*Pause.*)

Listen. You think you're just going to get that big slag all the time? You think you're just going to have him . . . you're going to just have him all the time? You're going to have to work! You'll have to take them on, you understand?   850

(*Pause.*)

Does she realize that?

(*Pause.*)

Lenny, do you think she understands . . .

(*He begins to stammer.*)

What . . . what . . . what . . . we're getting at? What . . . we've got in mind? Do you think she's got it clear?

(*Pause.*)

I don't think she's got it clear.   855

(*Pause.*)

You understand what I mean? Listen, I've got a funny idea she'll do the dirty on us, you want to bet? She'll use us, she'll make use of us, I can tell you! I can smell it! You want to bet?

(*Pause.*)

She won't . . . be adaptable!   860

(*He falls to his knees, whimpers, begins to moan and sob. He stops sobbing, crawls past* SAM's *body round her chair, to the other side of her.*)

I'm not an old man.

(*He looks up at her.*)

Do you hear me?

(*He raises his face to her.*)

Kiss me.

(*She continues to touch* JOEY's *head, lightly.*)

(LENNY *stands, watching.*)

(*Curtain.*)

Heiner Müller

Since the 1970s, Heiner Müller (1929–1996) has been widely considered the most provocative playwright in Germany, East or West. Müller was born in 1929 and spent his youth watching the Weimar Republic give way to the rise of Nazism in Germany. He was drafted into the German army in 1945 and taken prisoner by the U.S. forces, but escaped into the Soviet-controlled zone near Neubrandenberg. Müller and his family settled after the war in East Germany, where his father briefly worked as a political functionary but then defected to the West in 1952. Müller, however, remained in East Germany, where he finished school and—under the influence of Brecht's Berliner Ensemble—began to pursue a career as a playwright. He wrote two short plays at this time, *The Battle* (1949) and *Tractor* (1949), before becoming closely involved with the journal *New German Literature* and the League of German Writers. Never an apologist for the Communist party, Müller was nonetheless a deeply committed socialist playwright. In the 1950s he wrote a series of "Productionsstücke," plays set in farms or factories dealing with the daily problems of workers' lives and the difficulties of achieving a truly socialist state.

His first full-length play to be staged was a dramatization of John Reed's *Ten Days That Shook the World* (1957), which was followed by *The Wage Cutter* and *The Correction* (1958). In 1964, Müller adapted Erik Neutsch's novel *The Construction Project* for the stage, a play about the sacrifices required of workers in rebuilding East Germany. The Communist party attacked the play as subversive, and Müller's plays were officially banned from 1965 to 1969; Müller suffered the suicide of his wife, Ingeborg Schwenker, in 1965 as well. At this time, Müller concentrated on a series of brilliant translations and adaptations, of Sophocles' *Oedipus the King* (1967), an adaptation of *Philoctetes* written in 1966 but not permitted to be staged in East Germany until 1979, and a translation of Aeschylus' *Prometheus* (1969). In 1969, Müller was officially "rehabilitated," and was invited to serve as dramaturg for the Berliner Ensemble. Working with the Berliner Ensemble—and Erich Honecker's lifting of some of the restrictions on writers—spurred Müller's most productive period in the theater: *Cement* (1973), *Germania Death in Berlin* (1977), *Mauser* (written while visiting at the University of Texas–Austin in 1978), *The Farmers* (1978), *Hamletmachine* (1978), *Quartett* (1981), *Ruined Shoreline—Medea-Material—Landscape with Argonauts* (1983). Many of these plays deal with the challenges both of patriotism and of finding a true form of revolution; given the fact that Müller's dramatic style in this period became more dense, elliptical, and poetic, it is perhaps not surprising that he continued to have difficulties with the party, and many of his plays—including *Hamletmachine*—continued to be banned in East Germany until the fall of the Berlin Wall in 1989. Müller's drama now receives as much attention in Germany as in the rest of the West, and the idiom of his work—its imagistic and fragmentary quality, as well as its glancing engagement with "history"—has come to define the possibilities of postmodern theater. Müller died in 1996.

HAMLETMACHINE

Hamletmachine is one of the most celebrated performance "texts" of the 1970s and 1980s. Originally drafted under the working title "Shakespeare's Factory," *Hamletmachine* has been produced in both Europe and the United States, notably in a 1986 production at New York University designed by Robert Wilson. Both as a dramatic text and in performance, *Hamletmachine* is a brilliant instance of one way postmodern "pastiche" operates in the theater. As a text, the play invokes, "quotes," and distorts a variety of texts from the history of literature and culture. It opens with the actor declaring "I was Hamlet," and is structured around five confrontations between Hamlet and Ophelia. Shakespeare, Marx, and other writers are invoked throughout. Müller closes the play by laminating Ophelia to Electra to the radical

Heiner Müller's *Hamletmachine*, directed by Robert Wilson at the Thalia Theater in Hamburg, Germany (1989).

terrorist Ulrike Meinhoff and to the would-be assassin of President Gerald Ford, Squeaky Fromm. In performance, this dense and elliptical script intersects with the other "languages" of the stage: Ophelia appears with a clock in her heart; the actor playing Hamlet declares "I'm not Hamlet" and proceeds to tear up photographs of the author; the visual field of the stage is distributed among live action, film, and video; three naked women speak the words of Marx, Lenin, and Mao, then have their heads split by Hamlet; scenes include an "*Ice Age*" and "*The deep sea.* OPHELIA *in a wheelchair. Fish, debris, dead bodies and limbs drift by.*"

Hamletmachine is divided into five sections; in each, Hamlet and Ophelia—or, more accurately, voices identified with Hamlet's famous indecision and Ophelia's innocent victimization—confront the necessity of acting, and the impossibility of acting among the contemporary "ruins of Europe." Müller's densely imagistic imagination resists summary, but it is clear that *Hamletmachine* is at once about the incoherence of modern life and about the specific political failures of socialism in Eastern Europe, where "SOMETHING IS ROTTEN IN THIS AGE OF HOPE." Hamlet, for instance, is haunted by "the ghost who made me," a ghost whose armor he assumes at the end of the play to destroy the icons of Marxist history, Marx, Lenin, Mao; in section 4, "PEST IN BUDA/BATTLE FOR GREENLAND," Hamlet seems to confront and criticize the failed Hungarian revolt of 1956. He seems specifically alienated from a world in which the possibility of revolution has become merely theatrical: "I don't take part any more. My words have nothing to tell me any more. My thoughts suck the blood out of the images. My drama doesn't happen anymore. Behind me a set is put up. By people who aren't interested in my drama, for people to whom it means nothing." This vision of a "world without mothers," where we "could butcher each other in peace and quiet" is complemented by Ophelia's function in the play, for Ophelia becomes a figure for the metaphysical evacuation of a world without ideals, where to "walk into the street clothed in my blood" is the only form of resistance left. In her final speech,

Ophelia is identified with Aeschylus' Electra, returning with vengeance on the hopeless world destroyed around her; she quotes both Ulrike Meinhoff ("long live hate and contempt, rebellion and death") and Squeaky Fromm, who had tried to assassinate U.S. President Gerald Ford ("When she walks through your bedrooms carrying butcher knives you'll know the truth").

It might also be noted that *Hamletmachine* is a densely autobiographical play, in which the "Hamlet" figure articulates many of Müller's own reservations about the future of socialism in Europe and the possibility about ongoing revolution. As Müller noted in an interview in 1982, "*Hamletmachine* = H.M. = Heiner Müller"; he also notes, perhaps with a touch of irony, "I carefully disseminated this interpretation."

HAMLETMACHINE

Heiner Müller

TRANSLATED BY CARL WEBER

I FAMILY SCRAPBOOK

I was Hamlet. I stood at the shore and talked with the surf
BLABLA, the ruins of Europe in back of me. The bells
tolled the state-funeral, murderer and widow a couple, the
councillors goose-stepping behind the highranking car-
5 cass' coffin, bawling with badly paid grief WHO IS THE
CORPSE IN THE HEARSE / ABOUT WHOM
THERE'S SUCH A HUE AND CRY / 'TIS THE
CORPSE OF A GREAT / GIVER OF ALMS the lane
formed by the populace, creation of his statecraft HE WAS
10 A MAN HE TOOK THEM ALL FOR ALL. I stopped
the funeral procession, I pried open the coffin with my
sword, the blade broke, yet with the blunt reminder I succeeded, and I dispensed my dead procreator FLESH
LIKES TO KEEP THE COMPANY OF FLESH among
15 the bums around me. The mourning turned into rejoic-
ing, the rejoicing into lip-smacking, on top of the empty
coffin the murderer humped the widow LET ME HELP
YOU UP, UNCLE, OPEN YOUR LEGS, MAMA. I laid
down on the ground and listened to the world doing its
20 turns in step with the putrefaction.
I'M GOOD HAMLET GI'ME A CAUSE FOR GRIEF★
AH THE WHOLE GLOBE FOR A REAL SORROW★
RICHARD THE THIRD I THE PRINCE-KILLING
KING★
25 OH MY PEOPLE WHAT HAVE I DONE UNTO THEE★
I'M LUGGING MY OVERWEIGHT BRAIN LIKE A
HUNCHBACK
CLOWN NUMBER TWO IN THE SPRING OF
COMMUNISM
30 SOMETHING IS ROTTEN IN THIS AGE OF HOPE★
LET'S DELVE IN EARTH AND BLOW HER AT THE
MOON★
Here comes the ghost who made me, the ax still in his
skull. Keep your hat on, I know you've got one hole too
35 many. I would my mother had one less when you were
still of flesh: I would have been spared myself. Women
should be sewed up—a world without mothers. We could
butcher each other in peace and quiet, and with some
confidence, if life gets too long for us or our throats too
40 tight for our screams. What do you want of me? Is one
state-funeral not enough for you? You old sponger. Is
there no blood on your shoes? What's your corpse to me?
Be glad the handle is sticking out, maybe you'll go to
heaven. What are you waiting for? All the cocks have been
45 butchered. Tomorrow morning has been cancelled.
SHALL I
AS IS THE CUSTOM STICK A PIECE OF IRON INTO
THE NEAREST FLESH OR THE SECOND BEST
TO LATCH UNTO IT SINCE THE WORLD IS
50 SPINNING

★The lines with an asterisk are in English in the German text.

LORD BREAK MY NECK WHILE I'M FALLING
FROM AN
ALEHOUSE BENCH

Enters Horatio. Confidant of my thoughts so full of blood
since the morning is curtained by the empty sky. 55
YOU'LL BE TOO LATE MY FRIEND FOR YOUR
PAY-CHECK / NO PART FOR YOU IN THIS MY
TRAGEDY. Horatio, do you know me? Are you my
friend, Horatio? If you know me how can you be my
friend? Do you want to play Polonius who wants to sleep 60
with his daughter, the delightful Ophelia, here she enters
right on cue, look how she shakes her ass, a tragic character. Horatio Polonius. I knew you're an actor. I am too, I'm
playing Hamlet. Denmark is a prison, a wall is growing
between the two of us. Look what's growing from that 65
wall. Exit Polonius. My mother the bride. Her breasts a
rosebed, her womb the snakepit. Have you forgotten your
lines, Mama. I'll prompt you. WASH THE MURDER
OFF YOUR FACE MY PRINCE / AND OFFER THE
NEW DENMARK YOUR GLAD EYE. I'll change you 70
back into a virgin mother, so your king will have a blood-
wedding. A MOTHER'S WOMB IS NOT A ONE-
WAY STREET. Now, I tie your hands on your back with
your bridal veil since I'm sick of your embrace. Now, I
tear the wedding dress. Now, I smear the shreds of the 75
wedding dress with the dust my father turned into, and
with the soiled shreds your face your belly your breasts.
Now, I take you, my mother, in his, my father's invisible
tracks. I stifle your scream with my lips. Do you recognize
the fruit of your womb? Now go to your wedding, whore, 80
in the broad Danish sunlight which shines on the living
and the dead. I want to cram the corpse down the latrine
so the palace will choke in royal shit. Then let me eat your
heart, Ophelia, which weeps my tears.

II THE EUROPE OF WOMEN

Enormous room.★ OPHELIA. *Her heart is a clock.*

OPHELIA (CHORUS/HAMLET): I am Ophelia. The one the 85
river didn't keep. The woman dangling from the rope.
The woman with her arteries cut open. The woman with
the overdose. SNOW ON HER LIPS. The woman with
her head in the gas stove. Yesterday I stopped killing myself. I'm alone with my breasts my thighs my womb. I 90
smash the tools of my captivity, the chair the table the bed.
I destroy the battlefield that was my home. I fling open the
doors so the wind gets in and the scream of the world. I
smash the window. With my bleeding hands I tear the
photos of the men I loved and who used me on the bed 95
on the table on the chair on the ground. I set fire to my
prison. I throw my clothes into the fire. I wrench the
clock that was my heart out of my breast. I walk into the
street clothed in my blood.

III SCHERZO

The university of the dead. Whispering and muttering. From their gravestones (lecterns), the dead philosophers throw their books at HAMLET. *Gallery (ballet) of the dead women. The woman dangling from the rope. The woman with her arteries cut open, etc. . . .* HAMLET *views them with the attitude of a visitor in a museum (theatre). The dead women tear his clothes off his body. Out of an upended coffin, labeled* HAMLET 1 *step* CLAUDIUS *and* OPHELIA, *the latter dressed and made up like a whore. Striptease by* OPHELIA.

100 OPHELIA: Do you want to eat my heart, Hamlet? (*Laughs.*)
HAMLET: (*Face in his hands.*) I want to be a woman.

(HAMLET *dresses in* OPHELIA's *clothes,* OPHELIA *puts the make-up of a whore on his face,* CLAUDIUS—*now* HAMLET's *father—laughs without uttering a sound,* OPHELIA *blows* HAMLET *a kiss and steps with* CLAUDIUS/HAMLET'S FATHER *back into the coffin.* HAMLET *poses as a whore. An* ANGEL, *his face at the back of his head:* HORATIO. *He dances with* HAMLET.)

VOICES: (*From the coffin.*) What thou killed thou shalt love.

(*The dance grows faster and wilder. Laughter from the coffin. On a swing, the madonna with breast cancer.* HORATIO *opens an umbrella, embraces* HAMLET. *They freeze under the umbrella, embracing. The breast cancer radiates like a sun.*)

IV PEST IN BUDA / BATTLE FOR GREENLAND

Space 2, as destroyed by OPHELIA. *An empty armor, an ax stuck in the helmet.*

HAMLET: The stove is smoking in quarrelsome October
A BAD COLD HE HAD OF IT JUST THE WORST
    TIME★
105 JUST THE WORST TIME OF THE YEAR FOR A
    REVOLUTION★
Cement in bloom walks through the slums
Doctor Zhivago weeps
For his wolves
SOMETIMES IN WINTER THEY CAME INTO
    THE VILLAGE
110 AND TORE APART A PEASANT

(*He takes off make-up and costume.*)

THE ACTOR PLAYING HAMLET: I'm not Hamlet. I don't take part any more. My words have nothing to tell me anymore. My thoughts suck the blood out of the images. My drama doesn't happen anymore. Behind me the set is put up. By
115 people who aren't interested in my drama, for people to whom it means nothing. I'm not interested in it anymore either. I won't play along anymore. (*Unnoticed by the* ACTOR PLAYING HAMLET, STAGEHANDS *place a refrigerator and three TV-sets on the stage. Humming of the refrigerator. Three TV-*
120 *channels without sound.*) The set is a monument. It presents a man who made history, enlarged a hundred times. The petrification of a hope. His name is interchangeable, the hope has not been fulfilled. The monument is toppled into the dust, razed by those who succeeded him in power three

years after the state funeral of the hated and most honored 125
leader. The stone is inhabited. In the spacy nostrils and auditory canals, in the creases of skin and uniform of the demolished monument, the poorer inhabitants of the capital are dwelling. After an appropriate period, the uprising follows the toppling of the monument. My drama, if it still 130
would happen, would happen in the time of the uprising. The uprising starts with a stroll. Against the traffic rules, during the working hours. The street belongs to the pedestrians. Here and there, a car is turned over. Nightmare of a knife thrower: Slowly driving down a one-way street 135
towards an irrevocable parking space surrounded by armed pedestrians. Policemen, if in the way, are swept to the curb. When the procession approaches the government district it is stopped by a police line. People form groups, speakers arise from them. On the balcony of a government build- 140
ing, a man in badly fitting mufti appears and begins to speak too. When the first stone hits him, he retreats behind the double doors of bullet-proof glass. The call for more freedom turns into the cry for the overthrow of the government. People begin to disarm the policemen, to storm 145
two, three buildings, a prison a police precinct an office of the secret police, they string up a dozen henchmen of the rulers by their heels, the government brings in troops, tanks. My place, if my drama would still happen, would be on both sides of the front, between the frontlines, over and 150
above them. I stand in the stench of the crowd and hurl stones at policemen soldiers tanks bullet-proof glass. I look through the double doors of bullet-proof glass at the crowd pressing forward and smell the sweat of my fear. Choking with nausea, I shake my fist at myself who stands behind 155
the bullet-proof glass. Shaking with fear and contempt, I see myself in the crowd pressing forward, foaming at the mouth, shaking my fist at myself. I string up my uniformed flesh by my own heels. I am the soldier in the gun turret, my head is empty under the helmet, the stifled scream un- 160
der the tracks. I am the typewriter. I tie the noose when the ringleaders are strung up, I pull the stool from under their feet, I break my own neck. I am my own prisoner. I feed my own data into the computers. My parts are the spittle and the spittoon the knife and the wound the fang and the 165
throat the neck and the rope. I am the data bank. Bleeding in the crowd. Breathing again behind the double doors. Oozing wordslime in my soundproof blurb over and above the battle. My drama didn't happen. The script has been lost. The actors put their faces on the rack in the dressing 170
room. In his box, the prompter is rotting. The stuffed corpses in the house don't stir a hand. I go home and kill the time, at one with my undivided self.

Television The daily nausea Nausea
Of prefabricated babble Of decreed cheerfulness 175
How do you spell GEMÜTLICHKEIT
Give us this day our daily murder
Since thine is nothingness Nausea
Of the lies which are believed
By the liars and nobody else 180
Nausea
Of the lies which are believed Nausea
Of the mugs of the manipulators marked
By their struggle for positions votes bank accounts

185 Nausea A chariot armed with scythes sparkling with
    punchlines
I walk through street stores Faces
Scarred by the consumers battle Poverty
Without dignity Poverty without the dignity
Of the knife the knuckleduster the clenched fist
190 The humiliated bodies of women
Hope of generations
Stifled in blood cowardice stupidity
Laughter from dead bellies
Hail Coca Cola
195 A kingdom
For a murderer
I WAS MACBETH
THE KING HAD OFFERED HIS THIRD MISTRESS
TO ME
200 I KNEW EVERY MOLE ON HER HIPS
RASKOLNIKOV CLOSE TO THE
HEART UNDER THE ONLY COAT THE AX FOR
THE
ONLY
205 SKULL OF THE PAWNBROKER
In the solitude of airports
I breathe again I am
A privileged person My nausea
Is a privilege
210 Protected by torture
Barbed wire Prisons

(*Photograph of the author.*)

I don't want to eat drink breathe love a woman a man a
child an animal anymore. I don't want to die anymore. I
don't want to kill anymore.

(*Tearing of the author's photograph.*)

215 I force open my sealed flesh. I want to dwell in my veins,
in the marrow of my bones, in the maze of my skull. I retreat into my entrails. I take my seat in my shit, in my blood.
Somewhere bodies are torn apart so I can dwell in my shit.

---

*English-language productions could use the entire quote from
Karl Marx: Introduction to *Critique of Hegel's Philosophy of Law.*

Somewhere bodies are opened so I can be alone with my
blood. My thoughts are lesions in my brain. My brain is a 220
scar. I want to be a machine. Arms for grabbing Legs to
walk on, no pain no thoughts.

(*TV screens go black. Blood oozes from the refrigerator. Three naked
women:* MARX, LENIN, MAO. *They speak simultaneously, each one
in his own language, the text:*)

THE MAIN POINT IS TO OVERTHROW ALL
EXISTING CONDITIONS . . .*

(*The* ACTOR OF HAMLET *puts on make-up and costume.*)

HAMLET THE DANE PRINCE AND MAGGOT'S 225
FODDER STUMBLING FROM HOLE TO HOLE
TOWARDS THE FINAL HOLE LISTLESS IN HIS
BACK THE GHOST THAT ONCE MADE HIM
GREEN LIKE OPHELIA'S FLESH IN CHILDBED
AND SHORTLY ERE THE THIRD COCK'S 230
CROW A CLOWN WILL TEAR THE FOOL'S CAP
OFF THE PHILOSOPHER A BLOATED BLOOD-
HOUND'LL CRAWL INTO THE ARMOR

(*He steps into the armor, splits with the ax the heads of* MARX,
LENIN, MAO. *Snow. Ice Age.*)

V FIERCELY ENDURING MILLENIUMS IN THE FEARFUL ARMOR

The deep sea. OPHELIA *in a wheelchair. Fish, debris, dead bodies and
limbs drift by.*

OPHELIA: (*While two* MEN *in white smocks wrap gauze around her
and the wheelchair, from bottom to top.*) This is Electra speak- 235
ing. In the heart of darkness. Under the sun of torture. To
the capitals of the world. In the name of the victims. I
eject all the sperm I have received. I turn the milk of my
breasts into lethal poison. I take back the world I gave
birth to. I choke between my thighs the world I gave birth 240
to. I bury it in my womb. Down with the happiness of
submission. Long live hate and contempt, rebellion and
death. When she walks through your bedrooms carrying
butcher knives you'll know the truth.

(*The men exit.* OPHELIA *remains on stage, motionless in her white
wrappings.*)

Caryl Churchill

Caryl Churchill (b. 1938) was born in England and began her education in Canada during World War II; she returned to study at Oxford University, taking her B.A. in 1960. At Oxford, Churchill began her career as a playwright, producing several plays: *Downstairs* (1958), *Having a Wonderful Time* (1960), and *Early Death* (1962). During the 1960s, she wrote a series of brilliant radio plays. She also studied radical politics and returned to the theater in the 1970s with a series of striking political dramas: *Owners* (1972), *Objections to Sex and Violence* (1975), and *A Light Shining in Buckinghamshire* (1976). In the mid-1970s, Churchill began to work more closely with experimental theater companies, collaborating with actors and directors in the writing of her plays. Working with the feminist theater company Monstrous Regiment (the name alludes to the Calvinist preacher John Knox's 1558 diatribe against Queen Mary of England, "The First Blast of the Trumpet against the Monstrous Regiment of Women"), she wrote *Vinegar Tom* (1976), a play about witchcraft and sexual politics in seventeenth-century England. With the Joint Stock company, she investigated the politics of sexuality more extensively in *Cloud Nine* (1979), a pastiche of melodrama, Gilbert and Sullivan operetta, and modern realistic theater that uses CROSS-DRESSING and ROLE-DOUBLING to explore the relationship between colonial and sexual oppression in the nineteenth century and today. The history of gender oppression and the options for contemporary women are the subject of *Top Girls* (1982), and Churchill has continued to write challenging plays on the relationship between class, race, and gender in British social life, including *Fen* (1983), *Serious Money* (1987), and *Three More Sleepless Nights* (1995). *Mad Forest* (1990) concerns the revolution in Rumania and *Skryker* (1994) was developed from Lancashire folktales; *Blue Heart* (1997) was written after Churchill collaborated on several music-theater pieces, including *Lives of the Great Poisoners* (1993) and *Hotel* (1997). Her most recent plays have been short, nearly allegorical dramas: *Far Away* (2001) concerns the problems of political resistance and represents yet another new departure for Churchill, political allegory in the mode of magical realism; *A Number* (2003) takes on the subject of human cloning through the relationship between a father and several identical "sons."

CLOUD NINE

Onstage, the most exciting and interesting device in *Cloud Nine* is its use of CROSS-DRESSING and ROLE-DOUBLING. In the first act, for instance, Betty must be played by a man, Joshua by a white man, and Edward by a woman. By "alienating" actors from the characters they play, Churchill clearly intends to raise the questions of gender, sexual orientation, and race as ideological issues, for in each of these cases the difference between the performer and the role marks what Clive wants to see as real. Betty is played by a man because Clive—and his patriarchal society—cannot envision women's identity; women are constructed on the model of male attitudes. Joshua is played by a white man because imperial and racist culture reduces African identity to the construction of white, European attitudes. Edward is played by a woman to express the impossibility of Edward's conforming to Clive's heterosexual standards. In all three cases, the "identity" of the character is compromised or even erased, to be filled in and embodied by the attitudes that Clive and his society want them to hold. This performative dimension of the play's politics is echoed by the play's doubling of parts—each of the actors in act 1 takes a part in act 2, inviting the audience to draw comparisons between the two characters. Although other doubling patterns are possible, Churchill has suggested doubling Harry Bagley, the explorer, with Martin, the superficially liberated man; Clive, the father, with Cathy, the child; Betty with Edward; and so on. Doubling and cross-dressing are familiar conventions in the theater, but in *Cloud Nine* they have a specific dramatic purpose in developing the themes of the play. By denaturalizing the categories of gender, race, and sexuality, *Cloud*

Danny Scheie as Betty, waving to Harry Bagley in Caryl Churchill's *Cloud Nine*, produced by the Trinity Repertory Theatre.

Nine undertakes a typically postmodern inquiry into the construction of social reality, asking what meanings are created by these categories, and how they work to structure the relationship between self and society.

Author's Note

Cloud Nine was written for Joint Stock Theatre Group in 1978–1979. The company's usual work method is to set up a workshop in which the writer, director and actors research a particular subject. The writer then goes away to write the play, before returning to the company for a rehearsal and rewrite period. In the case of *Cloud Nine* the workshop lasted for three weeks, the writing period for twelve, and the rehearsal for six.

The workshop for *Cloud Nine* was about sexual politics. This meant that the starting point for our research was to talk about ourselves and share our very different attitudes and experiences. We also explored stereotypes and role reversals in games and improvisations, read books and talked to other people. Though the play's situations and characters were not developed in the workshop, it draws deeply on this material, and I wouldn't have written the same play without it.

When I came to write the play, I returned to an idea that had been touched on briefly in the workshop—the parallel between colonial and sexual oppression, which Genet calls "the colonial or feminine mentality of interiorised repression." So the first act of *Cloud Nine* takes place in Victorian Africa, where Clive, the white man, imposes his ideals on his family and the natives. Betty, Clive's wife, is played by a man because she wants to be what men want her to be, and, in the same way, Joshua, the black servant, is played by a white man because he wants to be what whites want him to be. Betty does not value herself as a woman, nor does Joshua value himself as a black. Edward, Clive's son, is played by a woman for a different reason—partly to do with the stage convention of having boys played by women (Peter Pan, radio plays, etc.) and partly with highlighting the way Clive tries to impose traditional male behaviour on him. Clive struggles throughout the act to maintain the world he wants to see—a faithful wife, a manly son. Harry's homosexuality is reviled, Ellen's is invisible. Rehearsing the play for the first time, we were initially taken by how funny the first act was and then by the painfulness of the relationships—which then became more funny than when they had seemed purely farcical.

The second act is set in London in 1979—this is where I wanted the play to end up, in the changing sexuality of our own time. Betty is middle-aged, Edward and Victoria have grown up. A hundred years have passed, but for the characters only twenty-five years. There were two reasons for this. I felt the first act would be stronger set in Victorian times, at the height of colonialism, rather than in Africa during the 1950s. And when the company talked about their childhoods and the attitudes to sex and marriage that they had been given when they were young, everyone felt that they had received very conventional, almost Victorian expectations and that they had made great changes and discoveries in their lifetimes.

The first act, like the society it shows, is male dominated and firmly structured. In the second act, more energy comes from the women and the gays. The uncertainties and changes of society, and a more feminine and less authoritarian feeling, are reflected in the looser structure of the act. Betty, Edward and Victoria all change from the rigid positions they had been left in by the first act, partly because of their encounters with Gerry and Lin.

In fact, all the characters in this act change a little for the better. If men are finding it hard to keep control in the first act, they are finding it hard to let go in the second: Martin dominates Victoria, despite his declarations of sympathy for feminism, and the bitter end of colonialism is apparent in Lin's soldier brother, who dies in Northern Ireland. Betty is now played by a woman, as she gradually becomes real to herself. Cathy is played by a man, partly as a simple reversal of Edward being played by a woman, partly because the size and presence of a man on stage seemed appropriate to the emotional force of young children, and partly, as with Edward, to show more clearly the issues involved in learning what is considered correct behaviour for a girl.

It is essential for Joshua to be played by a white, Betty (I) by a man, Edward (I) by a woman, and Cathy by a man. The soldier should be played by the actor who plays Cathy. The doubling of Mrs Saunders and Ellen is not intended to make a point so much as for sheer fun—and of course to keep the company to seven in each act. The doubling can be done in any way that seems right for any particular production. The first production went Clive-Cathy, Betty-Edward, Edward-Betty, Maud-Victoria, Mrs Saunders/Ellen-Lin, Joshua-Gerry, Harry-Martin. When we did the play again, at the Royal Court in 1980, we decided to try a different doubling: Clive-Edward, Betty-Gerry, Edward-Victoria, Maud-Lin, Mrs Saunders/Ellen-Betty, Joshua-Cathy, Harry-Martin. I've a slight preference for the first way because I like seeing Clive become Cathy, and enjoy the Edward-Betty connections. Some doublings aren't practicable, but any way of doing the doubling seems to set up some interesting resonances between the two acts.

C.C. 1983

THE TEXT

The first edition of *Cloud Nine* (Pluto/Joint Stock 1979) went to press before the end of rehearsal. Further changes were made within the first week or two of production, and these were incorporated in the Pluto/Joint Stock/Royal Court edition (1980). This edition also went to press during rehearsal, so although it may include some small changes made for that production, others don't turn up till the Pluto Plays edition (1983), which also includes a few changes from the American production, a few lines cut here or reinstated there. Other changes for the American production can be found in French's American acting edition—

the main ones are the position of Betty's monologue and some lines of the 'ghosts'. For the Fireside Bookclub and Methuen Inc. (1984) in America I did another brushing up, not very different from Pluto '83, and I have kept almost the same text for this edition. The scenes I tinker with most are the flogging scene and Edward's and Gerry's last scene—I no longer know what's the final version except by looking at the text.

There's a problem with the Maud and Ellen reappearances in Act Two. If Ellen is doubled with Betty, obviously only Maud can appear. Equally Maud-Betty would mean only Ellen could, though that seems a dull doubling. This text gives both Maud and Ellen. In the production at the Court in 1981 only Maud appeared and she has some extra lines so she can talk about sex as well as work; they can be found in Pluto (1983).

C.C. 1984

CLOUD NINE
Caryl Churchill

CHARACTERS

ACT ONE

CLIVE, *a colonial administrator*
BETTY, *his wife, played by a man*
JOSHUA, *his black servant, played by a white*
EDWARD, *his son, played by a woman*
VICTORIA, *his daughter, a dummy*
MAUD, *his mother-in-law*
ELLEN, *Edward's governess*
HARRY BAGLEY, *an explorer*
MRS SAUNDERS, *a widow*

ACT TWO

BETTY
EDWARD, *her son*

VICTORIA, *her daughter*
MARTIN, *Victoria's husband*
LIN
CATHY, *Lin's daughter, age 5, played by a man*
GERRY, *Edward's lover*

Except for CATHY, characters in Act Two are played by actors of their own sex.

Act One takes place in a British colony in Africa in Victorian times.

Act Two takes place in London in 1979. But for the characters it is twenty-five years later.

ACT ONE

SCENE I

Low bright sun. Verandah. Flagpole with union jack. The Family—
CLIVE, BETTY, EDWARD, VICTORIA, MAUD, ELLEN, JOSHUA.

ALL: (*Sing.*)

> Come gather, sons of England, come gather in your pride.
> Now meet the world united, now face it side by side;
> Ye who the earth's wide corners, from veldt to prairie, roam.
> From bush and jungle muster all who call old England "home."
> 5 Then gather round for England,
> Rally to the flag,
> From North and South and East and West
> Come one and all for England!

CLIVE: This is my family. Though far from home
10 We serve the Queen wherever we may roam
I am a father to the natives here,
And father to my family so dear.

(*He presents* BETTY. *She is played by a man.*)

> My wife is all I dreamt a wife should be,
> And everything she is she owes to me.

15 BETTY: I live for Clive. The whole aim of my life
Is to be what he looks for in a wife.
I am a man's creation as you see,
And what men want is what I want to be.

(CLIVE *presents* JOSHUA. *He is played by a white.*)

CLIVE: My boy's a jewel. Really has the knack.
20 You'd hardly notice that the fellow's black.
JOSHUA: My skin is black but oh my soul is white.
I hate my tribe. My master is my light.
I only live for him. As you can see,
What white men want is what I want to be.

(CLIVE *presents* EDWARD. *He is played by a woman.*)

CLIVE: My son is young. I'm doing all I can
To teach him to grow up to be a man.   25
EDWARD: What father wants I'd dearly like to be.
I find it rather hard as you can see.

(CLIVE *presents* VICTORIA, *who is a dummy,* MAUD, *and* ELLEN.)

CLIVE: No need for any speeches by the rest.
My daughter, mother-in-law, and governess.   30
ALL: (*Sing.*)

> O'er countless numbers she, our Queen,
> Victoria reigns supreme;
> O'er Africa's sunny plains, and o'er
> Canadian frozen stream;
> The forge of war shall weld the chains of brotherhood   35
> secure;
> So to all time in ev'ry clime our Empire shall endure.
> Then gather round for England,
> Rally to the flag,
> From North and South and East and West
> Come one and all for England!   40

(*All go except* BETTY. CLIVE *comes.*)

BETTY: Clive?
CLIVE: Betty. Joshua!

(JOSHUA *comes with a drink for* CLIVE.)

BETTY: I thought you would never come. The day's so long
without you.
CLIVE: Long ride in the bush.   45
BETTY: Is anything wrong? I heard drums.
CLIVE: Nothing serious. Beauty is a damned good mare. I
must get some new boots sent from home. These ones
have never been right. I have a blister.
BETTY: My poor dear foot.   50
CLIVE: It's nothing.
BETTY: Oh but it's sore.

CLIVE: We are not in this country to enjoy ourselves. Must have ridden fifty miles. Spoke to three different headmen
55   who would all gladly chop off each other's heads and wear them round their waists.

BETTY: Clive!

CLIVE: Don't be squeamish, Betty, let me have my joke. And what has my little dove done today?

60 BETTY: I've read a little.

CLIVE: Good. Is it good?

BETTY: It's poetry.

CLIVE: You're so delicate and sensitive.

BETTY: And I played the piano. Shall I send for the children?

65 CLIVE: Yes, in a minute. I've a piece of news for you.

BETTY: Good news?

CLIVE: You'll certainly think it's good. A visitor.

BETTY: From home?

CLIVE: No. Well of course originally from home.

70 BETTY: Man or woman?

CLIVE: Man.

BETTY: I can't imagine.

CLIVE: Something of an explorer. Bit of a poet. Odd chap but brave as a lion. And a great admirer of yours.

75 BETTY: What do you mean? Whoever can it be?

CLIVE: With an H and a B. And does conjuring tricks for little Edward.

BETTY: That sounds like Mr Bagley.

CLIVE: Harry Bagley.

80 BETTY: He certainly doesn't admire me, Clive, what a thing to say. How could I possibly guess from that. He's hardly explored anything at all, he's just been up a river, he's done nothing at all compared to what you do. You should have said a heavy drinker and a bit of a bore.

85 CLIVE: But you like him well enough. You don't mind him coming?

BETTY: Anyone at all to break the monotony.

CLIVE: But you have your mother. You have Ellen.

BETTY: Ellen is a governess. My mother is my mother.

90 CLIVE: I hoped when she came to visit she would be company for you.

BETTY: I don't think mother is on a visit. I think she lives with us.

CLIVE: I think she does.

95 BETTY: Clive you are so good.

CLIVE: But are you bored my love?

BETTY: It's just that I miss you when you're away. We're not in this country to enjoy ourselves. If I lack society that is my form of service.

100 CLIVE: That's a brave girl. So today has been all right? No fainting? No hysteria?

BETTY: I have been very tranquil.

CLIVE: Ah what a haven of peace to come home to. The coolth, the calm, the beauty.

105 BETTY: There is one thing, Clive, if you don't mind.

CLIVE: What can I do for you, my dear?

BETTY: It's about Joshua.

CLIVE: I wouldn't leave you alone here with a quiet mind if it weren't for Joshua.

110 BETTY: Joshua doesn't like me.

CLIVE: Joshua has been my boy for eight years. He has saved my life. I have saved his life. He is devoted to me and to mine. I have said this before.

BETTY: He is rude to me. He doesn't do what I say. Speak to him.

CLIVE: Tell me what happened.   115

BETTY: He said something improper.

CLIVE: Well, what?

BETTY: I don't like to repeat it.

CLIVE: I must insist.

BETTY: I had left my book inside on the piano. I was in the   120
hammock. I asked him to fetch it.

CLIVE: And did he not fetch it?

BETTY: Yes, he did eventually.

CLIVE: And what did he say?

BETTY: Clive—   125

CLIVE: Betty.

BETTY: He said Fetch it yourself. You've got legs under that dress.

CLIVE: Joshua!

(JOSHUA *comes.*)

Joshua, madam says you spoke impolitely to her this afternoon. 130

JOSHUA: Sir?

CLIVE: When she asked you to pass her book from the piano.

JOSHUA: She has the book, sir.

BETTY: I have the book now, but when I told you—

CLIVE: Betty, please, let me handle this. You didn't pass it at   135
once?

JOSHUA: No sir, I made a joke first.

CLIVE: What was that?

JOSHUA: I said my legs were tired, sir. That was funny because the book was very near, it would not make my legs tired   140
to get it.

BETTY: That's not true.

JOSHUA: Did madam hear me wrong?

CLIVE: She heard something else.

JOSHUA: What was that, madam?   145

BETTY: Never mind.

CLIVE: Now Joshua, it won't do you know. Madam doesn't like that kind of joke. You must do what madam says, just do what she says and don't answer back. You know your place, Joshua. I don't have to say any more.   150

JOSHUA: No sir.

BETTY: I expect an apology.

JOSHUA: I apologise, madam.

CLIVE: There now. It won't happen again, my dear. I'm very shocked Joshua, very shocked.   155

(CLIVE *winks at* JOSHUA, *unseen by* BETTY. JOSHUA *goes.*)

CLIVE: I think another drink, and send for the children, and isn't that Harry riding down the hill? Wave, wave. Just in time before dark. Cuts it fine, the blighter. Always a hothead, Harry.

BETTY: Can he see us?   160

CLIVE: Stand further forward. He'll see your white dress. There, he waved back.

BETTY: Do you think so? I wonder what he saw. Sometimes sunset is so terrifying I can't bear to look.

CLIVE: It makes me proud. Elsewhere in the empire the sun   165
is rising.

BETTY: Harry looks so small on the hillside.

(ELLEN *comes.*)

ELLEN: Shall I bring the children?

BETTY: Shall Ellen bring the children?

170   CLIVE: Delightful.

BETTY: Yes, Ellen, make sure they're warm. The night air is deceptive. Victoria was looking pale yesterday.

CLIVE: My love.

(MAUD comes from inside the house.)

MAUD: Are you warm enough Betty?

175   BETTY: Perfectly.

MAUD: The night air is deceptive.

BETTY: I'm quite warm. I'm too warm.

MAUD: You're not getting a fever, I hope? She's not strong, you know, Clive. I don't know how long you'll keep her

180   in this climate.

CLIVE: I look after Her Majesty's domains. I think you can trust me to look after my wife.

(ELLEN comes carrying VICTORIA, age 2. EDWARD, age 9, lags behind.)

BETTY: Victoria, my pet, say good evening to papa.

(CLIVE takes VICTORIA on his knee.)

CLIVE: There's my sweet little Vicky. What have we done today?

185   BETTY: She wore Ellen's hat.

CLIVE: Did she wear Ellen's big hat like a lady? What a pretty.

BETTY: And Joshua gave her a piggy back. Tell papa. Horsy with Joshy?

ELLEN: She's tired.

190   CLIVE: Nice Joshy played horsy. What a big strong Joshy. Did you have a gallop? Did you make him stop and go? Not very chatty tonight are we?

BETTY: Edward, say good evening to papa.

CLIVE: Edward my boy. Have you done your lessons well?

195   EDWARD: Yes papa.

CLIVE: Did you go riding?

EDWARD: Yes papa.

CLIVE: What's that you're holding?

BETTY: It's Victoria's doll. What are you doing with it, Edward?

200   EDWARD: Minding her.

BETTY: Well I should give it to Ellen quickly. You don't want papa to see you with a doll.

CLIVE: No, we had you with Victoria's doll once before, Edward.

ELLEN: He's minding it for Vicky. He's not playing with it.

205   BETTY: He's not playing with it, Clive. He's minding it for Vicky.

CLIVE: Ellen minds Victoria, let Ellen mind the doll.

ELLEN: Come, give it to me.

(ELLEN takes the doll.)

EDWARD: Don't pull her about. Vicky's very fond of her. She

210   likes me to have her.

BETTY: He's a very good brother.

CLIVE: Yes, it's manly of you Edward, to take care of your little sister. We'll say no more about it. Tomorrow I'll take you riding with me and Harry Bagley. Would you like that?

215   EDWARD: Is he here?

CLIVE: He's just arrived. There Betty, take Victoria now. I must go and welcome Harry.

(CLIVE tosses VICTORIA to BETTY, who gives her to ELLEN.)

EDWARD: Can I come, papa?

BETTY: Is he warm enough?

EDWARD: Am I warm enough?   220

CLIVE: Never mind the women, Ned. Come and meet Harry.

(They go. The women are left. There is a silence.)

MAUD: I daresay Mr Bagley will be out all day and we'll see nothing of him.

BETTY: He plays the piano. Surely he will sometimes stay at home with us.   225

MAUD: We can't expect it. The men have their duties and we have ours.

BETTY: He won't have seen a piano for a year. He lives a very rough life.

ELLEN: Will it be exciting for you, Betty?   230

MAUD: Whatever do you mean, Ellen?

ELLEN: We don't have very much society.

BETTY: Clive is my society.

MAUD: It's time Victoria went to bed.

ELLEN: She'd like to stay up and see Mr Bagley.   235

MAUD: Mr Bagley can see her tomorrow.

(ELLEN goes.)

MAUD: You let that girl forget her place, Betty.

BETTY: Mother, she is governess to my son. I know what her place is. I think my friendship does her good. She is not very happy.   240

MAUD: Young women are never happy.

BETTY: Mother, what a thing to say.

MAUD: Then when they're older they look back and see that comparatively speaking they were ecstatic.

BETTY: I'm perfectly happy.   245

MAUD: You are looking very pretty tonight. You were such a success as a young girl. You have made a most fortunate marriage. I'm sure you will be an excellent hostess to Mr Bagley.

BETTY: I feel quite nervous at the thought of entertaining.   250

MAUD: I can always advise you if I'm asked.

BETTY: What a long time they're taking. I always seem to be waiting for the men.

MAUD: Betty you have to learn to be patient. I am patient. My mama was very patient.   255

(CLIVE approaches, supporting CAROLINE SAUNDERS.)

CLIVE: It is a pleasure. It is an honour. It is positively your duty to seek my help. I would be hurt, I would be insulted by any show of independence. Your husband would have been one of my dearest friends if he had lived. Betty, look who has come, Mrs Saunders. She has ridden here all   260
alone, amazing spirit. What will you have? Tea or something stronger? Let her lie down, she is overcome. Betty, you will know what to do.

(MRS SAUNDERS lies down.)

MAUD: I knew it. I heard drums. We'll be killed in our beds.

CLIVE: Now, please, calm yourself.   265

MAUD: I am perfectly calm. I am just outspoken. If it comes to being killed I shall take it as calmly as anyone.

CLIVE: There is no cause for alarm. Mrs Saunders has been alone since her husband died last year, amazing spirit. Not
270 surprisingly, the strain has told. She has come to us as her nearest neighbours.

MAUD: What happened to make her come?

CLIVE: This is not an easy country for a woman.

MAUD: Clive, I heard drums. We are not children.

275 CLIVE: Of course you heard drums. The tribes are constantly at war, if the term is not too grand to grace their squabbles. Not unnaturally Mrs Saunders would like the company of white women. The piano. Poetry.

BETTY: We are not her nearest neighbours.

280 CLIVE: We are among her nearest neighbours and I was a dear friend of her late husband. She knows that she will find a welcome here. She will not be disappointed. She will be cared for.

MAUD: Of course we will care for her.

285 BETTY: Victoria is in bed. I must go and say goodnight. Mother, please, you look after Mrs Saunders.

CLIVE: Harry will be here at once.

(BETTY *goes*.)

MAUD: How rash to go out after dark without a shawl.

CLIVE: Amazing spirit. Drink this.

290 MRS SAUNDERS: Where am I?

MAUD: You are quite safe.

MRS SAUNDERS: Clive? Clive? Thank God. This is very kind. How do you do? I am sorry to be a nuisance. Charmed. Have you a gun? I have a gun.

295 CLIVE: There is no need for guns I hope. We are all friends here.

MRS SAUNDERS: I think I will lie down again.

(HARRY BAGLEY *and* EDWARD *have approached*.)

MAUD: Ah, here is Mr Bagley.

EDWARD: I gave his horse some water.

CLIVE: You don't know Mrs Saunders, do you Harry? She has at
300 present collapsed, but she is recovering thanks to the good offices of my wife's mother who I think you've met before. Betty will be along in a minute. Edward will go home to school shortly. He is quite a young man since you saw him.

HARRY: I hardly knew him.

305 MAUD: What news have you for us, Mr Bagley?

CLIVE: Do you know Mrs Saunders, Harry? Amazing spirit.

EDWARD: Did you hardly know me?

HARRY: Of course I knew you. I mean you have grown.

EDWARD: What do you expect?

310 HARRY: That's quite right, people don't get smaller.

MAUD: Edward. You should be in bed.

EDWARD: No, I'm not tired, I'm not tired am I Uncle Harry?

HARRY: I don't think he's tired.

CLIVE: He is overtired. It is past his bedtime. Say goodnight.

315 EDWARD: Goodnight, sir.

CLIVE: And to your grandmother.

EDWARD: Goodnight, grandmother.

(EDWARD *goes*.)

MAUD: Shall I help Mrs Saunders indoors? I'm afraid she may get a chill.

CLIVE: Shall I give her an arm? 320

MAUD: How kind of you, Clive. I think I am strong enough.

(MAUD *helps* MRS SAUNDERS *into the house*.)

CLIVE: Not a word to alarm the women.

HARRY: Absolutely.

CLIVE: I did some good today I think. Kept up some alliances. There's a lot of affection there. 325

HARRY: They're affectionate people. They can be very cruel of course.

CLIVE: Well they are savages.

HARRY: Very beautiful people many of them.

CLIVE: Joshua! (*To* HARRY.) I think we should sleep with guns. 330

HARRY: I haven't slept in a house for six months. It seems extremely safe.

(JOSHUA *comes*.)

CLIVE: Joshua, you will have gathered there's a spot of bother. Rumours of this and that. You should be armed I think.

JOSHUA: There are many bad men, sir. I pray about it. Jesus 335 will protect us.

CLIVE: He will indeed and I'll also get you a weapon. Betty, come and keep Harry company. Look in the barn, Joshua, every night.

(CLIVE *and* JOSHUA *go*. BETTY *comes*.)

HARRY: I wondered where you were. 340

BETTY: I was singing lullabies.

HARRY: When I think of you I always think of you with Edward in your lap.

BETTY: Do you think of me sometimes then?

HARRY: You have been thought of where no white woman 345 has ever been thought of before.

BETTY: It's one way of having adventures. I suppose I will never go in person.

HARRY: That's up to you.

BETTY: Of course it's not. I have duties. 350

HARRY: Are you happy, Betty?

BETTY: Where have you been?

HARRY: Built a raft and went up the river. Stayed with some people. The king is always very good to me. They have a lot of skulls around the place but not white men's I think. 355 I made up a poem one night. If I should die in this forsaken spot, There is a loving heart without a blot, Where I will live—and so on.

BETTY: When I'm near you it's like going out into the jungle. It's like going up the river on a raft. It's like going out 360 in the dark.

HARRY: And you are safety and light and peace and home.

BETTY: But I want to be dangerous.

HARRY: Clive is my friend.

BETTY: I am your friend. 365

HARRY: I don't like dangerous women.

BETTY: Is Mrs Saunders dangerous?

HARRY: Not to me. She's a bit of an old boot.

(JOSHUA *comes, unobserved*.)

BETTY: Am I dangerous?

370 HARRY: You are rather.

BETTY: Please like me.

HARRY: I worship you.

BETTY: Please want me.

HARRY: I don't want to want you. Of course I want you.

375 BETTY: What are we going to do?

HARRY: I should have stayed on the river. The hell with it.

(He goes to take her in his arms, she runs away into the house. HARRY *stays where he is. He becomes aware of* JOSHUA.*)*

HARRY: Who's there?

JOSHUA: Only me sir.

HARRY: Got a gun now have you?

380 JOSHUA: Yes sir.

HARRY: Where's Clive?

JOSHUA: Going round the boundaries sir.

HARRY: Have you checked there's nobody in the barns?

JOSHUA: Yes sir.

385 HARRY: Shall we go in a barn and fuck? It's not an order.

JOSHUA: That's all right, yes.

(They go off.)

SCENE II

An open space some distance from the house. MRS SAUNDERS *alone, breathless. She is carrying a riding crop.* CLIVE *arrives.*

CLIVE: Why? Why?

MRS SAUNDERS: Don't fuss, Clive, it makes you sweat.

CLIVE: Why ride off now? Sweat, you would sweat if you were in love with somebody as disgustingly capricious as

5   you are. You will be shot with poisoned arrows. You will miss the picnic. Somebody will notice I came after you.

MRS SAUNDERS: I didn't want you to come after me. I wanted to be alone.

CLIVE: You will be raped by cannibals.

10 MRS SAUNDERS: I just wanted to get out of your house.

CLIVE: My God, what women put us through. Cruel, cruel. I think you are the sort of woman who would enjoy whipping somebody. I've never met one before.

MRS SAUNDERS: Can I tell you something, Clive?

15 CLIVE: Let me tell you something first. Since you came to the house I have had an erection twenty-four hours a day except for ten minutes after the time we had intercourse.

MRS SAUNDERS: I don't think that's physically possible.

CLIVE: You are causing me appalling physical suffering. Is this

20   the way to treat a benefactor?

MRS SAUNDERS: Clive, when I came to your house the other night I came because I was afraid. The cook was going to let his whole tribe in through the window.

CLIVE: I know that, my poor sweet. Amazing—

25 MRS SAUNDERS: I came to you although you are not my nearest neighbour—

CLIVE: Rather than to the old major of seventy-two.

MRS SAUNDERS: Because the last time he came to visit me I had to defend myself with a shotgun and I thought you

30   would take no for an answer.

CLIVE: But you've already answered yes.

MRS SAUNDERS: I answered yes once. Sometimes I want to say no.

CLIVE: Women, my God. Look the picnic will start, I have to go to the picnic. Please Caroline— 35

MRS SAUNDERS: I think I will have to go back to my own house.

CLIVE: Caroline, if you were shot with poisoned arrows do you know what I'd do? I'd fuck your dead body and poison myself. Caroline, you smell amazing. You terrify me. You are dark like this continent. Mysterious. Treacherous. 40 When you rode to me through the night. When you fainted in my arms. When I came to you in your bed, when I lifted the mosquito netting, when I said let me in, let me in. Oh don't shut me out, Caroline, let me in.

(He has been caressing her feet and legs. He disappears completely under her skirt.)

MRS SAUNDERS: Please stop. I can't concentrate. I want to go 45 home. I wish I didn't enjoy the sensation because I don't like you, Clive. I do like living in your house where there's plenty of guns. But I don't like you at all. But I do like the sensation. Well I'll have it then. I'll have it, I'll have it—

(Voices are heard singing The First Noël.)

Don't stop. Don't stop. 50

(CLIVE comes out from under her skirt.)

CLIVE: The Christmas picnic. I came.

MRS SAUNDERS: I didn't.

CLIVE: I'm all sticky.

MRS SAUNDERS: What about me? Wait.

CLIVE: All right, are you? Come on. We mustn't be found. 55

MRS SAUNDERS: Don't go now.

CLIVE: Caroline, you are so voracious. Do let go. Tidy yourself up. There's a hair in my mouth.

(CLIVE and MRS SAUNDERS go off. BETTY *and* MAUD *come, with* JOSHUA *carrying hamper.)*

MAUD: I never would have thought a guinea fowl could taste so like a turkey. 60

BETTY: I had to explain to the cook three times.

MAUD: You did very well dear.

(JOSHUA sits apart with gun. EDWARD *and* HARRY *with* VICTORIA *on his shoulder, singing The First Noël.* MAUD *and* BETTY *are unpacking the hamper.* CLIVE *arrives separately.)*

MAUD: This tablecloth was one of my mama's.

BETTY: Uncle Harry playing horsy.

EDWARD: Crackers crackers. 65

BETTY: Not yet, Edward.

CLIVE: And now the moment we have all been waiting for.

(CLIVE opens champagne. General acclaim.)

CLIVE: Oh dear, stained my trousers, never mind.

EDWARD: Can I have some?

MAUD: Oh no Edward, not for you. 70

CLIVE: Give him half a glass.

MAUD: If your father says so.

CLIVE: All rise please. To Her Majesty Queen Victoria, God bless her, and her husband and all her dear children.

75 ALL: The Queen.
EDWARD: Crackers crackers.

(*General cracker pulling, hats.* CLIVE *and* HARRY *discuss champagne.*)

HARRY: Excellent, Clive, wherever did you get it?
CLIVE: I know a chap in French Equatorial Africa.
EDWARD: I won, I won mama.

(ELLEN *arrives.*)

80 BETTY: Give a hat to Joshua, he'd like it.

(EDWARD *takes hat to* JOSHUA. BETTY *takes a ball from the hamper and plays catch with* ELLEN. *Murmurs of surprise and congratulations from the men whenever they catch the ball.*)

EDWARD: Mama, don't play. You know you can't catch a ball.
BETTY: He's perfectly right. I can't throw either.

(BETTY *sits down.* ELLEN *has the ball.*)

EDWARD: Ellen, don't you play either. You're no good. You
    spoil it.

(EDWARD *takes* VICTORIA *from* HARRY *and gives her to* ELLEN. *He takes the ball and throws it to* HARRY. HARRY, CLIVE *and* EDWARD *play ball.*)

85 BETTY: Ellen come and sit with me. We'll be spectators and
    clap.

(EDWARD *misses the ball.*)

CLIVE: Butterfingers.
EDWARD: I'm not.
HARRY: Throw straight now.
90 EDWARD: I did, I did.
CLIVE: Keep your eye on the ball.
EDWARD: You can't throw.
CLIVE: Don't be a baby.
EDWARD: I'm not, throw a hard one, throw a hard one—
95 CLIVE: Butterfingers. What will Uncle Harry think of you?
EDWARD: It's your fault. You can't throw. I hate you.

(*He throws the ball wildly in the direction of* JOSHUA.)

CLIVE: Now you've lost the ball. He's lost the ball.
EDWARD: It's Joshua's fault. Joshua's butterfingers.
CLIVE: I don't think I want to play any more. Joshua, find the
100   ball will you?
EDWARD: Yes, please play. I'll find the ball. Please play.
CLIVE: You're so silly and you can't catch. You'll be no good
    at cricket.
MAUD: Why don't we play hide and seek?
105 EDWARD: Because it's a baby game.
BETTY: You've hurt Edward's feelings.
CLIVE: A boy has no business having feelings.
HARRY: Hide and seek. I'll be it. Everybody must hide. This
    is the base, you have to get home to base.
110 EDWARD: Hide and seek, hide and seek.
HARRY: Can we persuade the ladies to join us?
MAUD: I'm playing. I love games.

BETTY: I always get found straight away.
ELLEN: Come on, Betty, do. Vicky wants to play.
EDWARD: You won't find me ever.   115

(*They all go except* CLIVE, HARRY, JOSHUA.)

HARRY: It is safe, I suppose?
CLIVE: They won't go far. This is very much my territory and
    it's broad daylight. Joshua will keep an open eye.
HARRY: Well I must give them a hundred. You don't know
    what this means to me, Clive. A chap can only go on so   120
    long alone. I can climb mountains and go down rivers, but
    what's it for? For Christmas and England and games and
    women singing. This is the empire, Clive. It's not me
    putting a flag in new lands. It's you. The empire is one big
    family. I'm one of its black sheep, Clive. And I know you 125
    think my life is rather dashing. But I want you to know I
    admire you. This is the empire, Clive, and I serve it. With
    all my heart.
CLIVE: I think that's about a hundred.
HARRY: Ready or not, here I come!   130

(*He goes.*)

CLIVE: Harry Bagley is a fine man, Joshua. You should be
    proud to know him. He will be in history books.
JOSHUA: Sir, while we are alone.
CLIVE: Joshua of course, what is it? You always have my ear.
    Any time.   135
JOSHUA: Sir, I have some information. The stable boys are not
    to be trusted. They whisper. They go out at night. They
    visit their people. Their people are not my people. I do
    not visit my people.
CLIVE: Thank you, Joshua. They certainly look after Beauty.   140
    I'll be sorry to have to replace them.
JOSHUA: They carry knives.
CLIVE: Thank you, Joshua.
JOSHUA: And, sir.
CLIVE: I appreciate this, Joshua, very much.   145
JOSHUA: Your wife.
CLIVE: Ah, yes?
JOSHUA: She also thinks Harry Bagley is a fine man.
CLIVE: Thank you, Joshua.
JOSHUA: Are you going to hide?   150
CLIVE: Yes, yes I am. Thank you. Keep your eyes open Joshua.
JOSHUA: I do, sir.

(CLIVE *goes.* JOSHUA *goes.* HARRY *and* BETTY *race back to base.*)

BETTY: I can't run, I can't run at all.
HARRY: There, I've caught you.
BETTY: Harry, what are we going to do?   155
HARRY: It's impossible, Betty.
BETTY: Shall we run away together?

(MAUD *comes.*)

MAUD: I give up. Don't catch me. I have been stung.
HARRY: Nothing serious I hope.
MAUD: I have ointment in my bag. I always carry ointment. I   160
    shall just sit down and rest. I am too old for all this fun.
    Hadn't you better be seeking, Harry?

(HARRY *goes.* MAUD *and* BETTY *are alone for some time. They don't speak.* HARRY *and* EDWARD *race back.*)

EDWARD: I won, I won, you didn't catch me.
HARRY: Yes I did.
165 EDWARD: Mama, who was first?
BETTY: I wasn't watching. I think it was Harry.
EDWARD: It wasn't Harry. You're no good at judging. I won, didn't I grandma?
MAUD: I expect so, since it's Christmas.
170 EDWARD: I won, Uncle Harry. I'm better than you.
BETTY: Why don't you help Uncle Harry look for the others?
EDWARD: Shall I?
HARRY: Yes, of course.
BETTY: Run along then. He's just coming.

(EDWARD *goes.*)

175   Harry, I shall scream.
HARRY: Ready or not, here I come.

(HARRY *runs off.*)

BETTY: Why don't you go back to the house, mother, and rest your insect-bite?
MAUD: Betty, my duty is here. I don't like what I see. Clive
180   wouldn't like it, Betty. I am your mother.
BETTY: Clive gives you a home because you are my mother.

(HARRY *comes back.*)

HARRY: I can't find anyone else. I'm getting quite hot.
BETTY: Sit down a minute.
HARRY: I can't do that. I'm he. How's your sting?
185 MAUD: It seems to be swelling up.
BETTY: Why don't you go home and rest? Joshua will go with you. Joshua!
HARRY: I could take you back.
MAUD: That would be charming.
190 BETTY: You can't go. You're he.

(JOSHUA *comes.*)

Joshua, my mother wants to go back to the house. Will you go with her please.
JOSHUA: Sir told me I have to keep an eye.
BETTY: I am telling you to go back to the house. Then you
195   can come back here and keep an eye.
MAUD: Thank you Betty. I know we have our little differences, but I always want what is best for you.

(JOSHUA *and* MAUD *go.*)

HARRY: Don't give way. Keep calm.
BETTY: I shall kill myself.
200 HARRY: Betty, you are a star in my sky. Without you I would have no sense of direction. I need you, and I need you where you are, I need you to be Clive's wife. I need to go up rivers and know you are sitting here thinking of me.
BETTY: I want more than that. Is that wicked of me?
205 HARRY: Not wicked, Betty. Silly.

(EDWARD *calls in the distance.*)

EDWARD: Uncle Harry, where are you?
BETTY: Can't we ever be alone?
HARRY: You are a mother. And a daughter. And a wife.
BETTY: I think I shall go and hide again.

(BETTY *goes.* HARRY *goes.* CLIVE *chases* MRS SAUNDERS *across the stage.* EDWARD *and* HARRY *call in the distance.*)

EDWARD: Uncle Harry!   210
HARRY: Edward!

(EDWARD *comes.*)

EDWARD: Uncle Harry!

(HARRY *comes.*)

   There you are. I haven't found anyone have you?
HARRY: I wonder where they all are.
EDWARD: Perhaps they're lost forever. Perhaps they're dead. 215
   There's trouble going on isn't there, and nobody says because of not frightening the women and children.
HARRY: Yes, that's right.
EDWARD: Do you think we'll be killed in our beds?
HARRY: Not very likely.   220
EDWARD: I can't sleep at night. Can you?
HARRY: I'm not used to sleeping in a house.
EDWARD: If I'm awake at night can I come and see you? I won't wake you up. I'll only come in if you're awake.
HARRY: You should try to sleep.   225
EDWARD: I don't mind being awake because I make up adventures. Once we were on a raft going down to the rapids. We've lost the paddles because we used them to fight off the crocodiles. A crocodile comes at me and I stab it again and again and the blood is everywhere and it tips up the raft and 230
   it has you by the leg and it's biting your leg right off and I take my knife and stab it in the throat and rip open its stomach and it lets go of you but it bites my hand but it's dead. And I drag you onto the river bank and I'm almost fainting with pain and we lie there in each other's arms.   235
HARRY: Have I lost my leg?
EDWARD: I forgot about the leg by then.
HARRY: Hadn't we better look for the others?
EDWARD: Wait. I've got something for you. It was in mama's box but she never wears it.   240

(EDWARD *gives* HARRY *a necklace.*)

   You don't have to wear it either but you might like to look at.
HARRY: It's beautiful. But you'll have to put it back.
EDWARD: I wanted to give it to you.
HARRY: You did. It can go back in the box. You still gave it 245
   to me. Come on now, we have to find the others.
EDWARD: Harry, I love you.
HARRY: Yes I know. I love you too.
EDWARD: You know what we did when you were here before. I want to do it again. I think about it all the time. I try to do it 250
   to myself but it's not as good. Don't you want to any more?
HARRY: I do, but it's a sin and a crime and it's also wrong.
EDWARD: But we'll do it anyway won't we?
HARRY: Yes of course.

255 EDWARD: I wish the others would all be killed. Take it out
        now and let me see it.
    HARRY: No.
    EDWARD: Is it big now?
    HARRY: Yes.
260 EDWARD: Let me touch it.
    HARRY: No.
    EDWARD: Just hold me.
    HARRY: When you can't sleep.
    EDWARD: We'd better find the others then. Come on.
265 HARRY: Ready or not, here we come.

(They go out with whoops and shouts. BETTY *and* ELLEN *come.)*

    BETTY: Ellen, I don't want to play any more.
    ELLEN: Nor do I, Betty.
    BETTY: Come and sit here with me. Oh Ellen, what will be-
        come of me?
270 ELLEN: Betty, are you crying? Are you laughing?
    BETTY: Tell me what you think of Harry Bagley.
    ELLEN: He's a very fine man.
    BETTY: No, Ellen, what you really think.
    ELLEN: I think you think he's very handsome.
275 BETTY: And don't you think he is? Oh Ellen, you're so good
        and I'm so wicked.
    ELLEN: I'm not so good as you think.

*(*EDWARD *comes.)*

    EDWARD: I've found you.
    ELLEN: We're not hiding Edward.
280 EDWARD: But I found you.
    ELLEN: We're not playing, Edward, now run along.
    EDWARD: Come on, Ellen, do play. Come on, mama.
    ELLEN: Edward, don't pull your mama like that.
    BETTY: Edward, you must do what your governess says. Go
285   and play with Uncle Harry.
    EDWARD: Uncle Harry!

*(*EDWARD *goes.)*

    BETTY: Ellen, can you keep a secret?
    ELLEN: Oh yes, yes please.
    BETTY: I love Harry Bagley. I want to go away with him.
290   There, I've said it, it's true.
    ELLEN: How do you know you love him?
    BETTY: I kissed him.
    ELLEN: Betty.
    BETTY: He held my hand like this. Oh I want him to do it
295   again. I want him to stroke my hair.
    ELLEN: Your lovely hair. Like this, Betty?
    BETTY: I want him to put his arm around my waist.
    ELLEN: Like this, Betty?
    BETTY: Yes, oh I want him to kiss me again.
300 ELLEN: Like this Betty?

*(*ELLEN *kisses* BETTY.)*

    BETTY: Ellen, whatever are you doing? It's not a joke.
    ELLEN: I'm sorry, Betty. You're so pretty. Harry Bagley doesn't
        deserve you. You wouldn't really go away with him?
    BETTY: Oh Ellen, you don't know what I suffer. You don't
305   know what love is. Everyone will hate me, but it's worth
        it for Harry's love.

ELLEN: I don't hate you, Betty, I love you.
BETTY: Harry says we shouldn't go away. But he says he wor-
    ships me.
ELLEN: I worship you Betty.   310
BETTY: Oh Ellen, you are my only friend.

(They embrace. The others have all gathered together. MAUD *has re-
joined the party, and* JOSHUA.)*

CLIVE: Come along everyone, you mustn't miss Harry's con-
    juring trick.

*(*BETTY *and* ELLEN *go to join the others.)*

MAUD: I didn't want to spoil the fun by not being here.
HARRY: What is it that flies all over the world and is up my   315
    sleeve?

*(*HARRY *produces a union jack from up his sleeve. General acclaim.)*

CLIVE: I think we should have some singing now. Ladies, I
    rely on you to lead the way.
ELLEN: We have a surprise for you. I have taught Joshua a
    Christmas carol. He has been singing it at the piano but   320
    I'm sure he can sing it unaccompanied, can't you, Joshua?
JOSHUA: In the deep midwinter
               Frosty wind made moan,
               Earth stood hard as iron,
               Water like a stone.   325
               Snow had fallen snow on snow
               Snow on snow,
               In the deep midwinter
               Long long ago.

               What can I give him   330
               Poor as I am?
               If I were a shepherd
               I would bring a lamb.
               If I were a wise man
               I would do my part   335
               What can I give him,
               Give my heart.

SCENE III

Inside the house. BETTY, MRS SAUNDERS, MAUD *with* VICTORIA.
*The blinds are down so the light isn't bright though it is day out-
side.* CLIVE *looks in.*

CLIVE: Everything all right? Nothing to be frightened of.

*(*CLIVE *goes. Silence.)*

MAUD: Clap hands, daddy comes, with his pockets full of
    plums. All for Vicky.

(Silence.)

MRS SAUNDERS: Who actually does the flogging?
MAUD: I don't think we want to imagine.   5
MRS SAUNDERS: I imagine Joshua.
BETTY: Yes I think it would be Joshua. Or would Clive do it
    himself?
MRS SAUNDERS: Well we can ask them afterwards.

10 MAUD: I don't like the way you speak of it, Mrs Saunders.
MRS SAUNDERS: How should I speak of it?
MAUD: The men will do it in the proper way, whatever it is.
We have our own part to play.
MRS SAUNDERS: Harry Bagley says they should just be sent
15 away. I don't think he likes to see them beaten.
BETTY: Harry is so tender hearted. Perhaps he is right.
MAUD: Harry Bagley is not altogether—He has lived in this
country a long time without any responsibilities. It is part
of his charm but it hasn't improved his judgment. If the
20 boys were just sent away they would go back to the vil-
lage and make more trouble.
MRS SAUNDERS: And what will they say about us in the village if they've been flogged?
BETTY: Perhaps Clive should keep them here.
25 MRS SAUNDERS: That is never wise.
BETTY: Whatever shall we do?
MAUD: I don't think it is up to us to wonder. The men don't
tell us what is going on among the tribes, so how can we
possibly make a judgment?
30 MRS SAUNDERS: I know a little of what is going on.
BETTY: Tell me what you know. Clive tells me nothing.
MAUD: You would not want to be told about it, Betty. It is
enough for you that Clive knows what is happening. Clive
will know what to do. Your father always knew what to do.
35 BETTY: Are you saying you would do something different,
Caroline?
MRS SAUNDERS: I would do what I did at my own home. I
left. I can't see any way out except to leave. I will leave
here. I will keep leaving everywhere I suppose.
40 MAUD: Luckily this household has a head. I am squeamish
myself. But luckily Clive is not.
BETTY: You are leaving here then, Caroline?
MRS SAUNDERS: Not immediately. I'm sorry.

(*Silence.*)

MRS SAUNDERS: I wonder if it's over.

(EDWARD *comes in.*)

45 BETTY: Shouldn't you be with the men, Edward?
EDWARD: I didn't want to see any more. They got what they
deserved. Uncle Harry said I could come in.
MRS SAUNDERS: I never allowed the servants to be beaten in
my own house. I'm going to find out what's happening.

(MRS SAUNDERS *goes out.*)

50 BETTY: Will she go and look?
MAUD: Let Mrs Saunders be a warning to you, Betty. She is
alone in the world. You are not, thank God. Since your
father died, I know what it is to be unprotected. Vicky is
such a pretty little girl. Clap hands, daddy comes, with his
55 pockets full of plums. All for Vicky.

(EDWARD, *meanwhile, has found the doll and is playing clap hands
with her.*)

BETTY: Edward, what have you got there?
EDWARD: I'm minding her.

BETTY: Edward, I've told you before, dolls are for girls.
MAUD: Where is Ellen? She should be looking after Edward.
(*She goes to the door.*) Ellen! Betty, why do you let that girl 60
mope about in her own room? That's not what she's come
to Africa for.
BETTY: You must never let the boys at school know you like
dolls. Never, never. No one will talk to you, you won't be
on the cricket team, you won't grow up to be a man like 65
your papa.
EDWARD: I don't want to be like papa. I hate papa.
MAUD: Edward! Edward!
BETTY: You're a horrid wicked boy and papa will beat you.
Of course you don't hate him, you love him. Now give 70
Victoria her doll at once.
EDWARD: She's not Victoria's doll, she's my doll. She doesn't
love Victoria and Victoria doesn't love her. Victoria never
even plays with her.
MAUD: Victoria will learn to play with her. 75
EDWARD: She's mine and she loves me and she won't be
happy if you take her away, she'll cry, she'll cry, she'll cry.

(BETTY *takes the doll away, slaps him, bursts into tears.* ELLEN *comes in.*)

BETTY: Ellen, look what you've done. Edward's got the doll
again. Now, Ellen, will you please do your job.
ELLEN: Edward, you are a wicked boy. I am going to lock you 80
in the nursery until supper time. Now go upstairs this
minute.

(*She slaps* EDWARD, *who bursts into tears and goes out.*)

I do try to do what you want. I'm so sorry.

(ELLEN *bursts into tears and goes out.*)

MAUD: There now, Vicky's got her baby back. Where did
Vicky's naughty baby go? Shall we smack her? Just a little 85
smack. (MAUD *smacks the doll hard.*) There, now she's a
good baby. Clap hands, daddy comes, with his pockets full
of plums. All for Vicky's baby. When I was a child we honoured our parents. My mama was an angel.

(JOSHUA *comes in. He stands without speaking.*)

BETTY: Joshua? 90
JOSHUA: Madam?
BETTY: Did you want something?
JOSHUA: Sent to see the ladies are all right, madam.

(MRS SAUNDERS *comes in.*)

MRS SAUNDERS: We're very well thank you, Joshua, and how
are you? 95
JOSHUA: Very well thank you, Mrs Saunders.
MRS SAUNDERS: And the stable boys?
JOSHUA: They have had justice, madam.
MRS SAUNDERS: So I saw. And does your arm ache?
MAUD: This is not a proper conversation, Mrs Saunders. 100
MRS SAUNDERS: You don't mind beating your own people?
JOSHUA: Not my people, madam.
MRS SAUNDERS: A different tribe?
JOSHUA: Bad people.

(HARRY *and* CLIVE *come in.*)

105 CLIVE: Well this is all very gloomy and solemn. Can we have the shutters open? The heat of the day has gone, we could have some light, I think. And cool drinks on the verandah, Joshua. Have some lemonade yourself. It is most refreshing.

(*Sunlight floods in as the shutters are opened.* EDWARD *comes.*)

EDWARD: Papa, papa, Ellen tried to lock me in the nursery.
110 Mama is going to tell you of me. I'd rather tell you myself. I was playing with Vicky's doll again and I know it's very bad of me. And I said I didn't want to be like you and I said I hated you. And it's not true and I'm sorry, I'm sorry and please beat me and forgive me.

115 CLIVE: Well there's a brave boy to own up. You should always respect and love me, Edward, not for myself, I may not deserve it, but as I respected and loved my own father, because he was my father. Through our father we love our Queen and our God, Edward. Do you understand? It is
120 something men understand.

EDWARD: Yes papa.

CLIVE: Then I forgive you and shake you by the hand. You spend too much time with the women. You may spend more time with me and Uncle Harry, little man.

125 EDWARD: I don't like women. I don't like dolls. I love you, papa, and I love you, Uncle Harry.

CLIVE: There's a fine fellow. Let us go out onto the verandah.

(*They all start to go.* EDWARD *takes* HARRY's *hand and goes with him.* CLIVE *draws* BETTY *back. They embrace.*)

BETTY: Poor Clive.

CLIVE: It was my duty to have them flogged. For you and Ed-
130 ward and Victoria, to keep you safe.

BETTY: It is terrible to feel betrayed.

CLIVE: You can tame a wild animal only so far. They revert to their true nature and savage your hand. Sometimes I feel the natives are the enemy. I know that is wrong. I know I
135 have a responsibility towards them, to care for them and bring them all to be like Joshua. But there is something dangerous. Implacable. This whole continent is my enemy. I am pitching my whole mind and will and reason and spirit against it to tame it, and I sometimes feel it will
140 break over me and swallow me up.

BETTY: Clive, Clive, I am here. I have faith in you.

CLIVE: Yes, I can show you my moments of weakness, Betty, because you are my wife and because I trust you. I trust you, Betty, and it would break my heart if you did not de-
145 serve that trust. Harry Bagley is my friend. It would break my heart if he did not deserve my trust.

BETTY: I'm sorry, I'm sorry. Forgive me. It is not Harry's fault, it is all mine. Harry is noble. He has rejected me. It is my wickedness, I get bored, I get restless, I imagine things.
150 There is something so wicked in me, Clive.

CLIVE: I have never thought of you having the weakness of your sex, only the good qualities.

BETTY: I am bad, bad, bad—

CLIVE: You are thoughtless, Betty, that's all. Women can be
155 treacherous and evil. They are darker and more dangerous than men. The family protects us from that, you protect me

from that. You are not that sort of woman. You are not unfaithful to me, Betty. I can't believe you are. It would hurt me so much to cast you off. That would be my duty.

BETTY: No, no, no.   160

CLIVE: Joshua has seen you kissing.

BETTY: Forgive me.

CLIVE: But I don't want to know about it. I don't want to know. I wonder of course, I wonder constantly. If Harry Bagley was not my friend I would shoot him. If I shot you 165
every British man and woman would applaud me. But no. It was a moment of passion such as women are too weak to resist. But you must resist it, Betty, or it will destroy us. We must fight against it. We must resist this dark female lust, Betty, or it will swallow us up.   170

BETTY: I do, I do resist. Help me. Forgive me.

CLIVE: Yes I do forgive you. But I can't feel the same about you as I did. You are still my wife and we still have duties to the household.

(*They go out arm in arm. As soon as they have gone* EDWARD *sneaks back to get the doll, which has been dropped on the floor. He picks it up and comforts it.* JOSHUA *comes through with a tray of drinks.*)

JOSHUA: Baby. Sissy. Girly.   175

(JOSHUA *goes.* BETTY *calls from off.*)

BETTY: Edward?

(BETTY *comes in.*)

BETTY: There you are, my darling. Come, papa wants us all to be together. Uncle Harry is going to tell how he caught a crocodile. Mama's sorry she smacked you.

(*They embrace.* JOSHUA *comes in again, passing through.*)

BETTY: Joshua, fetch me some blue thread from my sewing 180
box. It is on the piano.

JOSHUA: You've got legs under that skirt.

BETTY: Joshua.

JOSHUA: And more than legs.

BETTY: Edward, are you going to stand there and let a servant 185
insult your mother?

EDWARD: Joshua, get my mother's thread.

JOSHUA: Oh little Eddy, playing at master. It's only a joke.

EDWARD: Don't speak to my mother like that again.

JOSHUA: Ladies have no sense of humour. You like a joke 190
with Joshua.

EDWARD: You fetch her sewing at once, do you hear me? You move when I speak to you, boy.

JOSHUA: Yes sir, master Edward sir.

(JOSHUA *goes.*)

BETTY: Edward, you were wonderful.   195

(*She goes to embrace him but he moves away.*)

EDWARD: Don't touch me.

Song
A BOY'S BEST FRIEND

ALL: While plodding on our way, the toilsome road of life,
How few the friends that daily there we meet.
Not many will stand in trouble and in strife,
200   With counsel and affection ever sweet.
But there is one whose smile will ever on us beam,
Whose love is dearer far than any other;
And wherever we may turn
This lesson we will learn
205   A boy's best friend is his mother.

Then cherish her with care
And smooth her silv'ry hair,
When gone you will never get another.
And wherever we may turn
210   This lesson we shall learn,
A boy's best friend is his mother.

SCENE IV

The verandah as in Scene One. Early morning. Nobody there. JOSHUA comes out of the house slowly and stands for some time doing nothing. EDWARD comes out.

EDWARD: Tell me another bad story, Joshua. Nobody else is even awake yet.

JOSHUA: First there was nothing and then there was the great goddess. She was very large and she had golden eyes and
5   she made the stars and the sun and the earth. But soon she was miserable and lonely and she cried like a great waterfall and her tears made all the rivers in the world. So the great spirit sent a terrible monster, a tree with hundreds of eyes and a long green tongue, and it came chasing after
10   her and she jumped into a lake and the tree jumped in after her, and she jumped right up into the sky. And the tree couldn't follow, he was stuck in the mud. So he picked up a big handful of mud and he threw it at her, up among the stars, and it hit her on the head. And she fell down onto
15   the earth into his arms and the ball of mud is the moon in the sky. And then they had children which is all of us.

EDWARD: It's not true, though.

JOSHUA: Of course it's not true. It's a bad story. Adam and Eve is true. God made man white like him and gave him the bad
20   woman who liked the snake and gave us all this trouble.

(CLIVE *and* HARRY *come out.*)

CLIVE: Run along now, Edward. No, you may stay. You mustn't repeat anything you hear to your mother or your grandmother or Ellen.

EDWARD: Or Mrs Saunders?

25 CLIVE: Mrs Saunders is an unusual woman and does not require protection in the same way. Harry, there was trouble last night where we expected it. But it's all over now. Everything is under control but nobody should leave the house today I think.

30 HARRY: Casualties?

CLIVE: No, none of the soldiers hurt thank God. We did a certain amount of damage, set a village on fire and so forth.

HARRY: Was that necessary?

CLIVE: Obviously, it was necessary, Harry, or it wouldn't have happen. The army will come and visit, no doubt. You'll 35 like that, eh, Joshua, to see the British army? And a treat for you, Edward, to see the soldiers. Would you like to be a soldier?

EDWARD: I'd rather be an explorer.

CLIVE: Ah, Harry, like you, you see. I didn't know an explorer 40 at his age. Breakfast, I think, Joshua.

(CLIVE *and* JOSHUA *go in.* HARRY *is following.*)

EDWARD: Uncle.

(HARRY *stops.*)

EDWARD: Harry, why won't you talk to me?

HARRY: Of course I'll talk to you.

EDWARD: If you won't be nice to me I'll tell father. 45

HARRY: Edward, no, not a word, never, not to your mother, nobody, please. Edward, do you understand? Please.

EDWARD: I won't tell. I promise I'll never tell. I've cut my finger and sworn.

HARRY: There's no need to get so excited Edward. We can't 50 be together all the time. I will have to leave soon anyway, and go back to the river.

EDWARD: You can't, you can't go. Take me with you.

ELLEN: Edward!

HARRY: I have my duty to the Empire. 55

(HARRY *goes in.* ELLEN *comes out.*)

ELLEN: Edward, breakfast time. Edward.

EDWARD: I'm not hungry.

ELLEN: Betty, please come and speak to Edward.

(BETTY *comes.*)

BETTY: Why what's the matter?

ELLEN: He won't come in for breakfast. 60

BETTY: Edward, I shall call your father.

EDWARD: You can't make me eat.

(*He goes in.* BETTY *is about to follow.*)

ELLEN: Betty.

(BETTY *stops.*)

ELLEN: Betty, when Edward goes to school will I have to leave?

BETTY: Never mind, Ellen dear, you'll get another place. I'll 65 give you an excellent reference.

ELLEN: I don't want another place, Betty. I want to stay with you forever.

BETTY: If you go back to England you might get married, Ellen. You're quite pretty, you shouldn't despair of getting 70 a husband.

ELLEN: I don't want a husband. I want you.

BETTY: Children of your own, Ellen, think.

ELLEN: I don't want children, I don't like children. I just want to be alone with you, Betty, and sing for you and kiss you 75 because I love you, Betty.

BETTY: I love you too, Ellen. But women have their duty as soldiers have. You must be a mother if you can.

ELLEN: Betty, Betty, I love you so much. I want to stay with
80   you forever, my love for you is eternal, stronger than
      death. I'd rather die than leave you, Betty.
BETTY: No you wouldn't, Ellen, don't be silly. Come, don't
      cry. You don't feel what you think you do. It's the loneli-
      ness here and the climate is very confusing. Come and
85   have breakfast, Ellen dear, and I'll forget all about it.

(ELLEN *goes*, CLIVE *comes*.)

BETTY: Clive, please forgive me.
CLIVE: Will you leave me alone?

(BETTY *goes back into the house*. HARRY *comes*.)

CLIVE: Women, Harry. I envy you going into the jungle, a
      man's life.
90   HARRY: I envy you.
CLIVE: Harry, I know you do. I have spoken to Betty.
HARRY: I assure you, Clive—
CLIVE: Please say nothing about it.
HARRY: My friendship for you—
95   CLIVE: Absolutely. I know the friendship between us, Harry,
      is not something that could be spoiled by the weaker sex.
      Friendship between men is a fine thing. It is the noblest
      form of relationship.
HARRY: I agree with you.
100   CLIVE: There is the necessity of reproduction. The family is
      all important. And there is the pleasure. But what we put
      ourselves through to get that pleasure, Harry. When I
      heard about our fine fellows last night fighting those sav-
      ages to protect us I thought yes, that is what I aspire to. I
105   tell you Harry, in confidence, I suddenly got out of Mrs
      Saunders' bed and came out here on the verandah and
      looked at the stars.
HARRY: I couldn't sleep last night either.
CLIVE: There is something dark about women, that threatens
110   what is best in us. Between men that light burns brightly.
HARRY: I didn't know you felt like that.
CLIVE: Women are irrational, demanding, inconsistent,
      treacherous, lustful, and they smell different from us.
HARRY: Clive—
115   CLIVE: Think of the comradeship of men, Harry, sharing ad-
      ventures, sharing danger, risking their lives together.

(HARRY *takes hold of* CLIVE.)

CLIVE: What are you doing?
HARRY: Well, you said—
CLIVE: I said what?
120   HARRY: Between men.

(CLIVE *is speechless*.)

      I'm sorry, I misunderstood, I would never have dreamt, I
      thought—
CLIVE: My God, Harry, how disgusting.
HARRY: You will not betray my confidence.
125   CLIVE: I feel contaminated.
HARRY: I struggle against it. You cannot imagine the shame.
      I have tried everything to save myself.
CLIVE: The most revolting perversion. Rome fell, Harry, and
      this sin can destroy an empire.

HARRY: It is not a sin, it is a disease.   130
CLIVE: A disease more dangerous than diphtheria. Effeminacy
      is contagious. How I have been deceived. Your face does
      not look degenerate. Oh Harry, how did you sink to this?
HARRY: Clive, help me, what am I to do?
CLIVE: You have been away from England too long.   135
HARRY: Where can I go except into the jungle to hide?
CLIVE: You don't do it with the natives, Harry? My God, what
      a betrayal of the Queen.
HARRY: Clive, I am like a man born crippled. Please help me.
CLIVE: You must repent.   140
HARRY: I have thought of killing myself.
CLIVE: That is a sin too.
HARRY: There is no way out. Clive, I beg of you, do not be-
      tray my confidence.
CLIVE: I cannot keep a secret like this. Rivers will be named after 145
      you, it's unthinkable. You must save yourself from depravity.
      You must get married. You are not unattractive to women.
      What a relief that you and Betty were not after all—good
      God, how disgusting. Now Mrs Saunders. She's a woman of
      spirit, she could go with you on your expeditions.   150
HARRY: I suppose getting married wouldn't be any worse
      than killing myself.
CLIVE: Mrs Saunders! Mrs Saunders! Ask her now, Harry.
      Think of England.

(MRS SAUNDERS *comes*. CLIVE *withdraws*. HARRY *goes up to* MRS
SAUNDERS.)

HARRY: Mrs Saunders, will you marry me?   155
MRS SAUNDERS: Why?
HARRY: We are both alone.
MRS SAUNDERS: I choose to be alone, Mr Bagley. If I can look
      after myself, I'm sure you can. Clive, I have something im-
      portant to tell you. I've just found Joshua putting earth on   160
      his head. He tells me his parents were killed last night by
      the British soldiers. I think you owe him an apology on
      behalf of the Queen.
CLIVE: Joshua! Joshua!
MRS SAUNDERS: Mr Bagley, I could never be a wife again.   165
      There is only one thing about marriage that I like.

(JOSHUA *comes*.)

CLIVE: Joshua, I am horrified to hear what has happened.
      Good God!
MRS SAUNDERS: His father was shot. His mother died in the
      blaze.   170

(MRS SAUNDERS *goes*.)

CLIVE: Joshua, do you want a day off? Do you want to go to
      your people?
JOSHUA: Not my people, sir.
CLIVE: But you want to go to your parents' funeral?
JOSHUA: No sir.   175
CLIVE: Yes, Joshua, yes, your father and mother. I'm sure they
      were loyal to the crown. I'm sure it was all a terrible mistake.
JOSHUA: My mother and father were bad people.
CLIVE: Joshua, no.
JOSHUA: You are my father and mother.   180

CLIVE: Well really. I don't know what to say. That's very decent of you. Are you sure there's nothing I can do? You can have the day off you know.

(BETTY *comes out followed by* EDWARD.)

BETTY: What's the matter? What's happening?
185   CLIVE: Something terrible has happened. No, I mean some relatives of Joshua's met with an accident.
JOSHUA: May I go sir?
CLIVE: Yes, yes of course. Good God, what a terrible thing. Bring us a drink will you Joshua?

(JOSHUA *goes.*)

190   EDWARD: What? What?
BETTY: Edward, go and do your lessons.
EDWARD: What is it, Uncle Harry?
HARRY: Go and do your lessons.
ELLEN: Edward, come in here at once.
195   EDWARD: What's happened, Uncle Harry?

(HARRY *has moved aside,* EDWARD *follows him.* ELLEN *comes out.*)

HARRY: Go away. Go inside. Ellen!
ELLEN: Go inside, Edward. I shall tell your mother.
BETTY: Go inside, Edward at once. I shall tell your father.
CLIVE: Go inside, Edward. And Betty you go inside too.

(BETTY, EDWARD *and* ELLEN *go.* MAUD *comes out.*)

200   CLIVE: Go inside. And Ellen, you come outside.

(ELLEN *comes out.*)

  Mr Bagley has something to say to you.
HARRY: Ellen. I don't suppose you would marry me?
ELLEN: What if I said yes?
CLIVE: Run along now, you two want to be alone.

(HARRY *and* ELLEN *go out.* JOSHUA *brings* CLIVE *a drink.*)

205   JOSHUA: The governess and your wife, sir.
CLIVE: What's that, Joshua?
JOSHUA: She talks of love to your wife, sir. I have seen them. Bad women.
CLIVE: Joshua, you go too far. Get out of my sight.

SCENE V

The verandah. A table with a white cloth. A wedding cake and a large knife. Bottles and glasses. JOSHUA *is putting things on the table.* EDWARD *has the doll.* JOSHUA *sees him with it. He holds out his hand.* EDWARD *gives him the doll.* JOSHUA *takes the knife and cuts the doll open and shakes the sawdust out of it.* JOSHUA *throws the doll under the table.*

MAUD: Come along Edward, this is such fun.

(*Everyone enters, triumphal arch for* HARRY *and* ELLEN.)

MAUD: Your mama's wedding was a splendid occasion, Edward. I cried and cried.

(ELLEN *and* BETTY *go aside.*)

ELLEN: Betty, what happens with a man? I don't know what to do.   5
BETTY: You just keep still.
ELLEN: And what does he do?
BETTY: Harry will know what to do.
ELLEN: And is it enjoyable?
BETTY: Ellen, you're not getting married to enjoy yourself.   10
ELLEN: Don't forget me, Betty.

(ELLEN *goes.*)

BETTY: I think my necklace has been stolen Clive. I did so want to wear it at the wedding.
EDWARD: It was Joshua. Joshua took it.
CLIVE: Joshua?   15
EDWARD: He did, he did, I saw him with it.
HARRY: Edward, that's not true.
EDWARD: It is, it is.
HARRY: Edward, I'm afraid you took it yourself.
EDWARD: I did not.   20
HARRY: I have seen him with it.
CLIVE: Edward, is that true? Where is it? Did you take your mother's necklace? And to try and blame Joshua, good God.

(EDWARD *runs off.*)

BETTY: Edward, come back. Have you got my necklace?
HARRY: I should leave him alone. He'll bring it back.   25
BETTY: I wanted to wear it. I wanted to look my best at your wedding.
HARRY: You always look your best to me.
BETTY: I shall get drunk.

(MRS SAUNDERS *comes.*)

MRS SAUNDERS: The sale of my property is completed. I shall   30
leave tomorrow.
CLIVE: That's just as well. Whose protection will you seek this time?
MRS SAUNDERS: I shall go to England and buy a farm there. I shall introduce threshing machines.   35
CLIVE: Amazing spirit.

(*He kisses her.* BETTY *launches herself on* MRS SAUNDERS. *They fall to the ground.*)

CLIVE: Betty—Caroline—I don't deserve this—Harry, Harry.

(HARRY *and* CLIVE *separate them.* HARRY *holding* MRS SAUNDERS, CLIVE, BETTY.)

CLIVE: Mrs Saunders, how can you abuse my hospitality? How dare you touch my wife? You must leave here at once.
BETTY: Go away, go away. You are a wicked woman.   40
MAUD: Mrs Saunders, I am shocked. This is your hostess.
CLIVE: Pack your bags and leave the house this instant.
MRS SAUNDERS: I was leaving anyway. There's no place for me here. I have made arrangements to leave tomorrow, and tomorrow is when I will leave. I wish you joy, Mr Bagley.   45

(MRS SAUNDERS *goes.*)

CLIVE: No place for her anywhere I should think. Shocking behaviour.

BETTY: Oh Clive, forgive me, and love me like you used to.
CLIVE: Were you jealous my dove? My own dear wife!
50 MAUD: Ah, Mr Bagley, one flesh, you see.

(EDWARD *comes back with the necklace.*)

CLIVE: Good God, Edward, it's true.
EDWARD: I was minding it for mama because of the troubles.
CLIVE: Well done, Edward, that was very manly of you. See
    Betty? Edward was protecting his mama's jewels from the
55 rebels. What a hysterical fuss over nothing. Well done, lit-
    tle man. It is quite safe now. The bad men are dead.
    Edward, you may do up the necklace for mama.

(EDWARD *does up* BETTY's *necklace, supervised by* CLIVE, JOSHUA
is drinking steadily. ELLEN *comes back.*)

MAUD: Ah, here's the bride. Come along, Ellen, you don't cry
    at your own wedding, only at other people's.
60 CLIVE: Now, speeches, speeches. Who is going to make a
    speech? Harry, make a speech.
HARRY: I'm no speaker. You're the one for that.
ALL: Speech, speech.
HARRY: My dear friends—what can I say—the empire—the
65 family—the married state to which I have always
    aspired—your shining example of domestic bliss—my
    great good fortune in winning Ellen's love—happiest day
    of my life.

(*Applause.*)

CLIVE: Cut the cake, cut the cake.

(HARRY *and* ELLEN *take the knife to cut the cake.* HARRY *steps on
the doll under the table.*)

70 HARRY: What's this?
ELLEN: Oh look.
BETTY: Edward.
EDWARD: It was Joshua. It was Joshua. I saw him.
CLIVE: Don't tell lies again.

(*He hits* EDWARD *across the side of the head.*)

75   Unaccustomed as I am to public speaking—

(*Cheers.*)

        Harry, my friend. So brave and strong and supple.
        Ellen, from neath her veil so shyly peeking.
        I wish you joy. A toast—the happy couple.
        Dangers are past. Our enemies are killed.
80   —Put your arm round her, Harry, have a kiss—
        All murmuring of discontent is stilled.
        Long may you live in peace and joy and bliss.

(*While he is speaking* JOSHUA *raises his gun to shoot* CLIVE. *Only*
EDWARD *sees. He does nothing to warn the others. He puts his
hands over his ears.*)

(*Black.*)

ACT TWO

SCENE I

*Winter afternoon. Inside the hut of a one o'clock club, a children's
playcentre in a park,* VICTORIA *and* LIN, *mothers.* CATHY, LIN's
daughter, age 5, played by a man, clinging to LIN. VICTORIA *reading a book.*

CATHY: Yum yum bubblegum.
    Stick it up your mother's bum.
    When it's brown
    Pull it down
    Yum yum bubblegum.   5
LIN: Like your shoes, Victoria.
CATHY: Jack be nimble, Jack be quick,
    Jack jump over the candlestick.
    Silly Jack, he should jump higher,
    Goodness gracious, great balls of fire.   10
LIN: Cathy, do stop. Do a painting.
CATHY: You do a painting.
LIN: You do a painting.
CATHY: What shall I paint?
LIN: Paint a house.   15
CATHY: No.
LIN: Princess.
CATHY: No.
LIN: Pirates.
CATHY: Already done that.   20
LIN: Spacemen.
CATHY: I never paint spacemen. You know I never.
LIN: Paint a car crash and blood everywhere.
CATHY: No, don't tell me. I know what to paint.
LIN: Go on then. You need an apron, where's an apron. Here. 25
CATHY: Don't want an apron.
LIN: Lift up your arms. There's a good girl.
CATHY: I don't want to paint.
LIN: Don't paint. Don't paint.
CATHY: What shall I do? You paint. What shall I do mum?   30
VICTORIA: There's nobody on the big bike, Cathy, quick.

(CATHY *goes out.* VICTORIA *is watching the children playing outside.*)

VICTORIA: Tommy, it's Jimmy's gun. Let him have it. What
    the hell.

(*She goes on reading. She reads while she talks.*)

LIN: I don't know how you can concentrate.
VICTORIA: You have to or you never do anything.   35
LIN: Yeh, well. It's really warm in here, that's one thing. It's
    better than standing out there. I got chilblains last winter.
VICTORIA: It is warm.
LIN: I suppose Tommy doesn't let you read much. I expect he
    talks to you while you're reading.   40
VICTORIA: Yes, he does.
LIN: I didn't get very far with that book you lent me.
VICTORIA: That's all right.
LIN: I was glad to have it, though. I sit with it on my lap while
    I'm watching telly. Well, Cathy's off. She's frightened I'm 45
    going to leave her. It's the babyminder didn't work out
    when she was two, she still remembers. You can't get

them used to other people if you're by yourself. It's no good blaming me. She clings round my knees every
50 morning up the nursery and they don't say anything but they make you feel you're making her do it. But I'm desperate for her to go to school. I did cry when I left her the first day. You wouldn't, you're too fucking sensible. You'll call the teacher by her first name. I really fancy you.
55 VICTORIA: What?
    LIN: Put your book down will you for five minutes. You didn't hear a word I said.
    VICTORIA: I don't get much time to myself.
    LIN: Do you ever go to the movies?
60 VICTORIA: Tommy's very funny who he's left with. My mother babysits sometimes.
    LIN: Your husband could babysit.
    VICTORIA: But then we couldn't go to the movies.
    LIN: You could go to the movies with me.
65 VICTORIA: Oh I see.
    LIN: Couldn't you?
    VICTORIA: Well yes, I could.
    LIN: Friday night?
    VICTORIA: What film are we talking about?
70 LIN: Does it matter what film?
    VICTORIA: Of course it does.
    LIN: You choose then. Friday night.

(CATHY comes in with gun, shoots them saying Kiou kiou kiou, and runs off again.)

Not in a foreign language, ok. You don't go in the movies to read.

(LIN watches the children playing outside.)

75 Don't hit him, Cathy, kill him. Point the gun, kiou, kiou, kiou. That's the way.
    VICTORIA: They've just banned war toys in Sweden.
    LIN: The kids'll just hit each other more.
    VICTORIA: Well, psychologists do differ in their opinions as to
80 whether or not aggression is innate.
    LIN: Yeh?
    VICTORIA: I'm afraid I do let Tommy play with guns and just hope he'll get it out of his system and not end up in the army.
    LIN: I've got a brother in the army.
85 VICTORIA: Oh I'm sorry. Whereabouts is he stationed?
    LIN: Belfast.
    VICTORIA: Oh dear.
    LIN: I've got a friend who's Irish and we went on a Troops Out march. Now my dad won't speak to me.
90 VICTORIA: I don't get on too well with my father either.
    LIN: And your husband? How do you get on with him?
    VICTORIA: Oh, fine. Up and down. You know. Very well. He helps with the washing up and everything.
    LIN: I left mine two years ago. He let me keep Cathy and I'm
95 grateful for that.
    VICTORIA: You shouldn't be grateful.
    LIN: I'm a lesbian.
    VICTORIA: You still shouldn't be grateful.
    LIN: I'm grateful he didn't hit me harder than he did.
100 VICTORIA: I suppose I'm very lucky with Martin.
    LIN: Don't get at me about how I bring up Cathy, ok?
    VICTORIA: I didn't.

LIN: Yes you did. War toys. I'll give her a rifle for Christmas and blast Tommy's pretty head off for a start.

(VICTORIA goes back to her book.)

LIN: I hate men.   105
VICTORIA: You have to look at it in a historical perspective in terms of learnt behaviour since the industrial revolution.
LIN: I just hate the bastards.
VICTORIA: Well it's a point of view.

(By now CATHY has come back in and started painting in many colours, without an apron. EDWARD comes in.)

EDWARD: Victoria, mother's in the park. She's walking round 110
    all the paths very fast.
VICTORIA: By herself?
EDWARD: I told her you were here.
VICTORIA: Thanks.
EDWARD: Come on.   115
VICTORIA: Ten minutes talking to my mother and I have to spend two hours in a hot bath.

(VICTORIA goes out.)

LIN: Shit, Cathy, what about an apron. I don't mind you having paint on your frock but if it doesn't wash off just don't tell me you can't wear your frock with paint on, ok?   120
CATHY: Ok.
LIN: You're gay, aren't you?
EDWARD: I beg your pardon?
LIN: I really fancy your sister. I thought you'd understand. You do but you can go on pretending you don't, I don't   125
    mind. That's lovely Cathy, I like the green bit.
EDWARD: Don't go around saying that. I might lose my job.
LIN: The last gardener was ever so straight. He used to flash at all the little girls.
EDWARD: I wish you hadn't said that about me. It's not true. 130
LIN: It's not true and I never said it and I never thought it and I never will think it again.
EDWARD: Someone might have heard you.
LIN: Shut up about it then.

(BETTY and VICTORIA come up.)

BETTY: It's quite a nasty bump.   135
VICTORIA: He's not even crying.
BETTY: I think that's very worrying. You and Edward always cried. Perhaps he's got concussion.
VICTORIA: Of course he hasn't mummy.
BETTY: That other little boy was very rough. Should you   140
    speak to somebody about him?
VICTORIA: Tommy was hitting him with a spade.
BETTY: Well he's a real little boy. And so brave not to cry. You must watch him for signs of drowsiness. And nausea. If he's sick in the night, phone an ambulance. Well, you're 145
    looking very well darling, a bit tired, a bit peaky. I think the fresh air agrees with Edward. He likes the open air life because of growing up in Africa. He misses the sunshine, don't you, darling? We'll soon have Edward back on his feet. What fun it is here.   150
VICTORIA: This is Lin. And Cathy.

BETTY: Oh Cathy what a lovely painting. What is it? Well I think it's a house on fire. I think all that red is a fire. Is that right? Or do I see legs, is it a horse? Can I have the lovely
155   painting or is it for mummy? Children have such imagination, it makes them so exhausting. (*To* LIN.) I'm sure you're wonderful, just like Victoria. I had help with my children. One does need help. That was in Africa of course so there wasn't the servant problem. This is my son
160   Edward. This is—
EDWARD: Lin.
BETTY: Lin, this is Lin. Edward is doing something such fun, he's working in the park as a gardener. He does look exactly like a gardener.
165   EDWARD: I am a gardener.
BETTY: He's certainly making a stab at it. Well it will be a story to tell. I expect he will write a novel about it, or perhaps a television series. Well what a pretty child Cathy is. Victoria was a pretty child just like a little doll—you can't be cer-
170   tain how they'll grow up. I think Victoria's very pretty but she doesn't make the most of herself, do you darling, it's not the fashion I'm told but there are still women who dress out of *Vogue,* well we hope that's not what Martin looks for, though in many ways I wish it was, I don't know what
175   it is Martin looks for and nor does he I'm afraid poor Martin. Well I am rattling on. I like your skirt dear but your shoes won't do at all. Well do they have lady gardeners, Edward, because I'm going to leave your father and I think I might need to get a job, not a gardener really of course. I
180   haven't got green fingers I'm afraid, everything I touch shrivels straight up. Vicky gave me a poinsettia last Christmas and the leaves all fell off on Boxing Day. Well good heavens, look what's happened to that lovely painting.

(CATHY *has slowly and carefully been going over the whole sheet with black paint. She has almost finished.*)

LIN: What you do that for silly? It was nice.
185   CATHY: I like your earrings.
VICTORIA: Did you say you're leaving Daddy?
BETTY: Do you darling? Shall I put them on you? My ears aren't pierced, I never wanted that, they just clip on the lobe.
LIN: She'll get paint on you, mind.
190   BETTY: There's a pretty girl. It doesn't hurt does it. Well you'll grow up to know you have to suffer a little bit for beauty.
CATHY: Look mum I'm pretty, I'm pretty, I'm pretty.
LIN: Stop showing off Cathy.
VICTORIA: It's time we went home. Tommy, time to go
195   home. Last go then, all right.
EDWARD: Mum did I hear you right just now?
CATHY: I want my ears pierced.
BETTY: Ooh, not till you're big.
CATHY: I know a girl got her ears pierced and she's three.
200   She's got real gold.
BETTY: I don't expect she's English, darling. Can I give her a sweety? I know they're not very good for the teeth, Vicky gets terribly cross with me. What does mummy say?
LIN: Just one, thank you very much.
205   CATHY: I like your beads.
BETTY: Yes they are pretty. Here you are.

(*It is the necklace from Act One.*)

CATHY: Look at me, look at me. Vicky, Vicky, Vicky look at me.
LIN: You look lovely, come on now.
CATHY: And your hat, and your hat.
LIN: No, that's enough.   210
BETTY: Of course she can have my hat.
CATHY: Yes, yes, hat, hat. Look look look.
LIN: That's enough, please, stop it now. Hat off, bye bye hat.
CATHY: Give me my hat.
LIN: Bye bye beads.   215
BETTY: It's just fun.
LIN: It's very nice of you.
CATHY: I want my beads.
LIN: Where's the other earring?
CATHY: I want my beads.   220

(CATHY *has the other earring in her hand. Meanwhile* VICTORIA *and* EDWARD *look for it.*)

EDWARD: Is it on the floor?
VICTORIA: Don't step on it.
EDWARD: Where?
CATHY: I want my beads. I want my beads.
LIN: You'll have a smack.   225

(LIN *gets the earring from* CATHY.)

CATHY: I want my beads.
BETTY: Oh dear oh dear. Have you got the earring? Thank you darling.
CATHY: I want my beads, you're horrid, I hate you, mum, you smell.   230
BETTY: This is the point you see where one had help. Well it's been lovely seeing you dears and I'll be off again on my little walk.
VICTORIA: You're leaving him? Really?
BETTY: Yes you hear alright, Vicky, yes. I'm finding a little flat,   235
that will be fun.

(BETTY *goes.*)

Bye bye Tommy, granny's going now. Tommy don't hit that little girl, say goodbye to granny.
VICTORIA: Fucking hell.
EDWARD: Puking Jesus.   240
LIN: That was news was it, leaving your father?
EDWARD: They're going to want so much attention.
VICTORIA: Does everybody hate their mothers?
EDWARD: Mind you, I wouldn't live with him.
LIN: Stop snivelling, pigface. Where's your coat? Be quiet   245
now and we'll have doughnuts for tea and if you keep on we'll have dogshit on toast.

(CATHY *laughs so much she lies on the floor.*)

VICTORIA: Tommy, you've had two last goes. Last last last go.
LIN: Not that funny, come on, coat on.
EDWARD: Can I have your painting?   250
CATHY: What for?
EDWARD: For a friend of mine.
CATHY: What's his name?
EDWARD: Gerry.
CATHY: How old is he?   255
EDWARD: Thirty-two.

CATHY: You can if you like. I don't care. Kiou kiou kiou kiou.

(CATHY *goes out.* EDWARD *takes the painting and goes out.*)

LIN: Will you have sex with me?
VICTORIA: I don't know what Martin would say. Does it
260   count as adultery with a woman?
LIN: You'd enjoy it.

SCENE II

Spring. Swing, bench, pond nearby. EDWARD *is gardening.* GERRY *sitting on a bench.*

EDWARD: I sometimes pretend we don't know each other. And you've come to the park to eat your sandwiches and look at me.
GERRY: That would be more interesting, yes. Come and sit
5   down.
EDWARD: If the superintendent comes I'll be in trouble. It's not my dinner time yet. Where were you last night? I think you owe me an explanation. We always do tell each other everything.
10   GERRY: Is that a rule?
EDWARD: It's what we agreed.
GERRY: It's a habit we've got into. Look, I was drunk. I woke up at 4 o'clock on somebody's floor. I was sick. I hadn't any money for a cab. I went back to sleep.
15   EDWARD: You could have phoned.
GERRY: There wasn't a phone.
EDWARD: Sorry.
GERRY: There was a phone and I didn't phone you. Leave it alone, Eddy, I'm warning you.
20   EDWARD: What are you going to do to me, then?
GERRY: I'm going to the pub.
EDWARD: I'll join you in ten minutes.
GERRY: I didn't ask you to come. (EDWARD *goes.*) Two years I've been with Edward. You have to get away sometimes or you
25   lose sight of yourself. The train from Victoria to Clapham still has those compartments without a corridor. As soon as I got on the platform I saw who I wanted. Slim hips, tense shoulders, trying not to look at anyone. I put my hand on my packet just long enough so that he couldn't miss it.
30   The train came in. You don't want to get in too fast or some straight dumbo might get in with you. I sat by the window. I couldn't see where the fuck he'd got to. Then just as the whistle went he got in. Great. It's a six-minute journey so you can't start anything you can't finish. I stared
35   at him and he unzipped his flies. Then he stopped. So I stood up and took my cock out. He took me in his mouth and shut his eyes tight. He was sort of mumbling it about as if he wasn't sure what to do, so I said, 'A bit tighter son' and he said 'Sorry' and then got on with it. He was jerking
40   off with his left hand, and I could see he'd got a fairsized one. I wished he'd keep still so I could see his watch. I was getting really turned on. What if we pulled into Clapham Junction now. Of course by the time we sat down again the train was just slowing up. I felt wonderful. Then he started
45   talking. It's better if nothing is said. Once you find he's a librarian in Walthamstow with a special interest in science fiction and lives with his aunt, then forget it. He said I hope you don't think I do this all the time. I said I hope you will

from now on. He said he would if I was on the train, but
50   why don't we go out for a meal? I opened the door before the train stopped. I told him I live with somebody, I don't want to know. He was jogging sideways to keep up. He said 'What's your phone number, you're my ideal physical type, what sign of the zodiac are you? Where do you live? Where
55   are you going now?' It's not fair, I saw him at Victoria a couple of months later and I went straight down to the end of the platform and I picked up somebody really great who never said a word, just smiled.

(CATHY *is on the swing.*)

CATHY: Batman and Robin
Had a batmobile.   60
Robin done a fart
And paralysed the wheel.
The wheel couldn't take it,
The engine fell apart,
All because of Robin   65
And his supersonic fart.

(CATHY *goes.* MARTIN, VICTORIA *and* BETTY *walking slowly.*)

MARTIN: Tom!
BETTY: He'll fall in.
VICTORIA: No he won't.
MARTIN: Don't go too near the edge Tom. Throw the bread   70
from there. The ducks can get it.
BETTY: I'll never be able to manage. If I can't even walk down the street by myself. Everything looks so fierce.
VICTORIA: Just watch Tommy feeding the ducks.
BETTY: He's going to fall in. Make Martin make him move back.   75
VICTORIA: He's not going to fall in.
BETTY: It's since I left your father.
VICTORIA: Mummy, it really was the right decision.
BETTY: Everything comes at me from all directions. Martin despises me.   80
VICTORIA: Of course he doesn't, mummy.
BETTY: Of course he does.
MARTIN: Throw the bread. That's the way. The duck can get it. Quack quack quack quack quack.
BETTY: I don't want to take pills. Lin says you can't trust doctors.   85
VICTORIA: You're not taking pills. You're doing very well.
BETTY: But I'm so frightened.
VICTORIA: What are you frightened of?
BETTY: Victoria, you always ask that as if there was suddenly going to be an answer.   90
VICTORIA: Are you all right sitting there?
BETTY: Yes, yes. Go and be with Martin.

(VICTORIA *joins* MARTIN, BETTY *stays sitting on the bench.*)

MARTIN: You take the job, you go to Manchester. You turn it down, you stay in London. People are making decisions like this every day of the week. It needn't be for more than   95
a year. You get long vacations. Our relationship might well stand the strain of that, and if it doesn't we're better out of it. I don't want to put any pressure on you. I'd just like to know so we can sell the house. I think we're moving into an entirely different way of life if you go to Man-   100
chester because it won't end there. We could keep the

house as security for Tommy but he might as well get used
to the fact that life nowadays is insecure. You should ask
your mother what she thinks and then do the opposite. I
105 could just take that room in Barbara's house, and then we
could babysit for each other. You think that means I want
to fuck Barbara. I don't. Well, I do, but I won't. And even
if I did, what's a fuck between friends? What are we meant
to do it with, strangers? Whatever you want to do, I'll be
110 delighted. If you could just let me know what it is I'm to
be delighted about. Don't cry again, Vicky, I'm not the
sort of man who makes women cry.

(LIN *has come in and sat down with* BETTY, CATHY *joins them. She
is wearing a pink dress and carrying a rifle.*)

LIN: I've bought her three new frocks. She won't wear jeans to
school any more because Tracy and Mandy called her a boy.
115 CATHY: Tracy's got a perm.
LIN: You should have shot them.
CATHY: They're coming to tea and we've got to have trifle.
Not trifle you make, trifle out of a packet. And you've got
to wear a skirt. And tights.
120 LIN: Tracy's mum wears jeans.
CATHY: She does not. She wears velvet.
BETTY: Well I think you look very pretty. And if that gun has
caps in it please take it a long way away.
CATHY: It's got red caps. They're louder.
125 MARTIN: Do you think you're well enough to do this job? You
don't have to do it. No one's going to think any the less of
you if you stay here with me. There's no point being so liberated you make yourself cry all the time. You stay and
we'll get everything sorted out. What it is about sex, when
130 we talk while it's happening I get to feel it's like a driving
lesson. Left, right, a little faster, carry on, slow down—

(CATHY *shoots* VICTORIA.)

CATHY: You're dead Vicky.
VICTORIA: Aaaargh.
CATHY: Fall over.
135 VICTORIA: I'm not falling over, the ground's wet.
CATHY: You're dead.
VICTORIA: Yes, I'm dead.
CATHY: The Dead Hand Gang fall over. They said I had to fall
over in the mud or I can't play. That duck's a mandarin.
140 MARTIN: Which one? Look, Tommy.
CATHY: That's a diver. It's got a yellow eye and it dives. That's
a goose. Tommy doesn't know it's a goose, he thinks it's a
duck. The babies get eaten by weasels. Kiou kiou.

(CATHY *goes.*)

MARTIN: So I lost my erection last night not because I'm not
145 prepared to talk, it's just that taking in technical information is a different part of the brain and also I don't like to
feel that you do it better to yourself. I have read the Hite
report. I do know that women have to learn to get their
pleasure despite our clumsy attempts at expressing undying
150 devotion and ecstasy, and that what we spent our adolescence thinking was an animal urge we had to suppress is in
fact a fine art we have to acquire. I'm not like whatever
percentage of American men have become impotent as a

direct result of women's liberation, which I am totally in
favour of, more I sometimes think than you are yourself. 155
Nor am I one of your villains who sticks it in, bangs away,
and falls asleep. My one aim is to give you pleasure. My one
aim is to give you rolling orgasms like I do other women.
So why the hell don't you have them? My analysis for what
it's worth is that despite all my efforts you still feel domi- 160
nated by me. I in fact think it's very sad that you don't feel
able to take that job. It makes me feel very guilty. I don't
want you to do it just because I encourage you to do it. But
don't you think you'd feel better if you did take the job?
You're the one who's talked about freedom. You're the one 165
who's experimenting with bisexuality, and I don't stop you,
I think women have something to give each other. You
seem to need the mutual support. You find me too overwhelming. So follow it through, go away, leave me and
Tommy alone for a bit, we can manage perfectly well with- 170
out you. I'm not putting any pressure on you but I don't
think you're being a whole person. God knows I do everything I can to make you stand on your own two feet. Just
be yourself. You don't seem to realise how insulting it is to
me that you can't get yourself together. 175

(MARTIN *and* VICTORIA *go.*)

BETTY: You must be very lonely yourself with no husband.
You don't miss him?
LIN: Not really, no.
BETTY: Maybe you like being on your own.
LIN: I'm seeing quite a lot of Vicky. I don't live alone. I live 180
with Cathy.
BETTY: I would have been frightened when I was your age. I
thought, the poor children, their mother all alone.
LIN: I've a lot of friends.
BETTY: I find when I'm making tea I put out two cups. It's 185
strange not having a man in the house. You don't know
who to do things for.
LIN: Yourself.
BETTY: Oh, that's very selfish.
LIN: Have you any women friends? 190
BETTY: I've never been so short of men's company that I've
had to bother with women.
LIN: Don't you like women?
BETTY: They don't have such interesting conversations as
men. There has never been a woman composer of genius. 195
They don't have a sense of humour. They spoil things for
themselves with their emotions. I can't say I do like
women very much, no.
LIN: But you're a woman.
BETTY: There's nothing says you have to like yourself. 200
LIN: Do you like me?
BETTY: There's no need to take it personally, Lin.

(MARTIN *and* VICTORIA *come back.*)

MARTIN: Did you know if you put cocaine on your prick you
can keep it up all night? The only thing is of course it goes
numb so you don't feel anything. But you would, that's 205
the main thing. I just want to make you happy.
BETTY: Vicky, I'd like to go home.
VICTORIA: Yes, mummy, of course.
BETTY: I'm sorry, dear.

210 VICTORIA: I think Tommy would like to stay out a bit longer.
LIN: Hello, Martin. We do keep out of each other's way.
MARTIN: I think that's the best thing to do.
BETTY: Perhaps you'd walk home with me, Martin. I do feel safer with a man. The park is so large the grass seems to tilt.
215 MARTIN: Yes, I'd like to go home and do some work. I'm writing a novel about women from the women's point of view.

(MARTIN and BETTY go. LIN and VICTORIA are alone. They embrace.)

VICTORIA: Why the hell can't he just be a wife and come with me? Why does Martin make me tie myself in knots? No wonder we can't just have a simple fuck. No, not Mar-
220 tin, why do I make myself tie myself in knots. It's got to stop, Lin. I'm not like that with you. Would you love me if I went to Manchester?
LIN: Yes.
VICTORIA: Would you love me if I went on a climbing expe-
225 dition in the Andes mountains?
LIN: Yes.
VICTORIA: Would you love me if my teeth fell out?
LIN: Yes.
VICTORIA: Would you love me if I loved ten other people?
230 LIN: And me?
VICTORIA: Yes.
LIN: Yes.
VICTORIA: And I feel apologetic for not being quite so subordinate as I was. I am more intelligent than him. I am brilliant.
235 LIN: Leave him Vic. Come and live with me.
VICTORIA: Don't be silly.
LIN: Silly, Christ, don't then. I'm not asking because I need to live with someone. I'd enjoy it, that's all, we'd both enjoy it. Fuck you. Cathy, for fuck's sake stop throwing stones at
240 the ducks. The man's going to get you.
VICTORIA: What man? Do you need a man to frighten your child with?
LIN: My mother said it.
VICTORIA: You're so inconsistent, Lin.
245 LIN: I've changed who I sleep with, I can't change everything.
VICTORIA: Like when I had to stop you getting a job in a boutique and collaborating with sexist consumerism.
LIN: I should have got that job, Cathy would have liked it. Why shouldn't I have some decent clothes? I'm sick of dressing
250 like a boy, why can't I look sexy, wouldn't you love me?
VICTORIA: Lin, you've no analysis.
LIN: No but I'm good at kissing aren't I? I give Cathy guns, my mum didn't give me guns. I dress her in jeans, she wants to wear dresses. I don't know. I can't work it out, I
255 don't want to. You read too many books, you get at me all the time, you're worse to me than Martin is to you, you piss me off, my brother's been killed. I'm sorry to win the argument that way but there it is.
VICTORIA: What do you mean win the argument?
260 LIN: I mean be nice to me.
VICTORIA: In Belfast?
LIN: I heard this morning. Don't don't start. I've hardly seen him for two years. I rung my father. You'd think I'd shot myself. He doesn't want me to go to the funeral.

(CATHY approaches.)

VICTORIA: What will you do?
LIN: Go of course.
CATHY: What is it? Who's killed? What?
LIN: It's Bill. Your uncle. In the army. Bill that gave you the blue teddy.
270 CATHY: Can I have his gun?
LIN: It's time we went home. Time you went to bed.
CATHY: No it's not.
LIN: We go home and you have tea and you have a bath and you go to bed.
275 CATHY: Fuck off.
LIN: Cathy, shut up.
VICTORIA: It's only half past five, why don't we—
LIN: I'll tell you why she has to go to bed—
VICTORIA: She can come home with me.
280 LIN: Because I want her out of the fucking way.
VICTORIA: She can come home with me.
CATHY: I'm not going to bed.
LIN: I want her home with me not home with you, I want her in bed, I want today over.
285 CATHY: I'm not going to bed.

(LIN hits CATHY, CATHY cries.)

LIN: And shut up or I'll give you something to cry for.
CATHY: I'm not going to bed.
VICTORIA: Cathy—
LIN: You keep out of it.
290 VICTORIA: Lin for God's sake.

(They are all shouting. CATHY runs off. LIN and VICTORIA are silent. Then they laugh and embrace.)

LIN: Where's Tommy?
VICTORIA: What? Didn't he go with Martin?
LIN: Did he?
VICTORIA: God oh God.
295 LIN: Cathy! Cathy!
VICTORIA: I haven't thought about him. How could I not think about him? Tommy!
LIN: Cathy! Come on, quick, I want some help.
VICTORIA: Tommy! Tommy!

(CATHY comes back.)

300 LIN: Where's Tommy? Have you seen him? Did he go with Martin? Do you know where he is?
CATHY: I showed him the goose. We went in the bushes.
LIN: Then what?
CATHY: I came back on the swing.
305 VICTORIA: And Tommy? Where was Tommy?
CATHY: He fed the ducks.
LIN: No that was before.
CATHY: He did a pee in the bushes. I helped him with his trousers.
310 VICTORIA: And after that?
CATHY: He fed the ducks.
VICTORIA: No no.
CATHY: He liked the ducks. I expect he fell in.
LIN: Did you see him fall in?
315 VICTORIA: Tommy! Tommy!
LIN: What's the last time you saw him?

CATHY: He did a pee.

VICTORIA: Mummy said he would fall in. Oh God, Tommy!

LIN: We'll go round the pond. We'll go opposite ways round
320   the pond.

ALL: (*Shout.*) Tommy!

(VICTORIA *and* LIN *go off opposite sides.* CATHY *climbs the bench.*)

CATHY: Georgie Best, superstar
      Walks like a woman and wears a bra.
        There he is! I see him! Mum! Vicky! There he is! He's
325   in the bushes.

(LIN *comes back.*)

LIN: Come on Cathy love, let's go home.

CATHY: Vicky's got him.

LIN: Come on.

CATHY: Is she cross?

330 LIN: No. Come on.

CATHY: I found him.

LIN: Yes. Come on.

(CATHY *gets off the bench.* CATHY *and* LIN *hug.*)

CATHY: I'm watching telly.

LIN: Ok.

335 CATHY: After the news.

LIN: Ok.

CATHY: I'm not going to bed.

LIN: Yes you are.

CATHY: I'm not going to bed now.

340 LIN: Not now but early.

CATHY: How early?

LIN: Not late.

CATHY: How not late?

LIN: Early.

345 CATHY: How early?

LIN: Not late.

(*They go off together.* GERRY *comes on. He waits.* EDWARD *comes.*)

EDWARD: I've got some fish for dinner. I thought I'd make a
      cheese sauce.

GERRY: I won't be in.

350 EDWARD: Where are you going?

GERRY: For a start I'm going to a sauna. Then I'll see.

EDWARD: All right. What time will you be back? We'll eat
      then.

GERRY: You're getting like a wife.

355 EDWARD: I don't mind that.

GERRY: Why don't I do the cooking sometime?

EDWARD: You can if you like. You're just not so good at it
      that's all. Do it tonight.

GERRY: I won't be in tonight.

360 EDWARD: Do it tomorrow. If we can't eat it we can always
      go to a restaurant.

GERRY: Stop it.

EDWARD: Stop what?

GERRY: Just be yourself.

365 EDWARD: I don't know what you mean. Everyone's always
      tried to stop me being feminine and now you are too.

GERRY: You're putting it on.

EDWARD: I like doing the cooking. I like being fucked. You
      do like me like this really.

GERRY: I'm bored, Eddy.   370

EDWARD: Go to the sauna.

GERRY: And you'll stay home and wait up for me.

EDWARD: No, I'll go to bed and read a book.

GERRY: Or knit. You could knit me a pair of socks.

EDWARD: I might knit. I like knitting.   375

GERRY: I don't mind if you knit. I don't want to be married.

EDWARD: I do.

GERRY: Well I'm divorcing you.

EDWARD: I wouldn't want to keep a man who wants his
      freedom.   380

GERRY: Eddy, do stop playing the injured wife, it's not funny.

EDWARD: I'm not playing. It's true.

GERRY: I'm not the husband so you can't be the wife.

EDWARD: I'll always be here, Gerry, if you want to come
      back. I know you men like to go off by yourselves. I don't   385
      think I could love deeply more than once. But I don't
      think I can face life on my own so don't leave it too long
      or it may be too late.

GERRY: What are you trying to turn me into?

EDWARD: A monster, darling, which is what you are.   390

GERRY: I'll collect my stuff from the flat in the morning.

(GERRY *goes.* EDWARD *sits on the bench. It gets darker.* VICTORIA
comes.)

VICTORIA: Tommy dropped a toy car somewhere, you haven't
      seen it? It's red. He says it's his best one. Oh the hell with
      it. Martin's reading him a story. There, isn't it quiet?

(*They sit on the bench, holding hands.*)

EDWARD: I like women.   395

VICTORIA: That should please mother.

EDWARD: No listen Vicky. I'd rather be a woman. I wish I had
      breasts like that, I think they're beautiful. Can I touch
      them?

VICTORIA: What, pretending they're yours?   400

EDWARD: No, I know it's you.

VICTORIA: I think I should warn you I'm enjoying this.

EDWARD: I'm sick of men.

VICTORIA: I'm sick of men.

EDWARD: I think I'm a lesbian.   405

SCENE III

The park. Summer night. VICTORIA, LIN *and* EDWARD *drunk.*

LIN: Where are you?

VICTORIA: Come on.

EDWARD: Do we sit in a circle?

VICTORIA: Sit in a triangle.

EDWARD: You're good at mathematics. She's good at mathe-   5
      matics.

VICTORIA: Give me your hand. We all hold hands.

EDWARD: Do you know what to do?

LIN: She's making it up.

VICTORIA: We start off by being quiet.   10

EDWARD: What?

LIN: Hush.

EDWARD: Will something appear?

VICTORIA: It was your idea.

15 EDWARD: It wasn't my idea. It was your book.

LIN: You said call up the goddess.

EDWARD: I don't remember saying that.

LIN: We could have called her on the telephone.

EDWARD: Don't be so silly, this is meant to be frightening.

20 LIN: Kiss me.

VICTORIA: Are we going to do it?

LIN: We're doing it.

VICTORIA: A ceremony.

LIN: It's very sexy, you said it is. You said the women were priests in the temples and fucked all the time. I'm just
25 helping.

VICTORIA: As long as it's sacred.

LIN: It's very sacred.

VICTORIA: Innin, Innana, Nana, Nut, Anat, Anahita, Istar, Isis.

30 LIN: I can't remember all that.

VICTORIA: Lin! Innin, Innana, Nana, Nut, Anat, Anahita, Istar, Isis.

(LIN *and* EDWARD *join in and continue the chant under* VICTORIA's *speech.*)

Goddess of many names, oldest of the old, who walked in chaos and created life, hear us calling you back through
35 time, before Jehovah, before Christ, before men drove you out and burnt your temples, hear us, Lady, give us back what we were, give us the history we haven't had, make us the women we can't be.

ALL: Innin, Innana, Nana, Nut, Anat, Anahita, Istar, Isis.

(*Chant continues under other speeches.*)

40 LIN: Come back, goddess.

VICTORIA: Goddess of the sun and the moon her brother, little goddess of Crete with snakes in your hands.

LIN: Goddess of breasts.

VICTORIA: Goddess of cunts.

45 LIN: Goddess of fat bellies and babies. And blood blood blood.

(*Chant continues.*)

I see her.

EDWARD: What?

(*They stop chanting.*)

LIN: I see her. Very tall. Snakes in her hands. Light light light—look out! Did I give you a fright?
50 EDWARD: I was terrified.

VICTORIA: Don't spoil it Lin.

LIN: It's all out of a book.

VICTORIA: Innin Innana—I can't do it now. I was really enjoying myself.

55 LIN: She won't appear with a man here.

VICTORIA: They had men, they had sons and lovers.

EDWARD: They had eunuchs.

LIN: Don't give us ideas.

VICTORIA: There's Attis and Tammuz, they're torn to pieces.

60 EDWARD: Tear me to pieces, Lin.

VICTORIA: The priestess chose a lover for a year and he was king because she chose him and then he was killed at the end of the year.

EDWARD: Hurray.

VICTORIA: And the women had the children and nobody 65 knew it was done by fucking so they didn't know about fathers and nobody cared who the father was and the property was passed down through the maternal line—

LIN: Don't turn it into a lecture, Vicky, it's meant to be an orgy.

VICTORIA: It never hurts to understand the theoretical back- 70 ground. You can't separate fucking and economics.

LIN: Give us a kiss.

EDWARD: Shut up, listen.

LIN: What?

EDWARD: There's somebody there. 75

LIN: Where?

EDWARD: There.

VICTORIA: The priestesses used to make love to total strangers.

LIN: Go on then, I dare you.

EDWARD: Go on, Vicky. 80

VICTORIA: He won't know it's a sacred rite in honour of the goddess.

EDWARD: We'll know.

LIN: We can tell him.

EDWARD: It's not what he thinks, it's what we think. 85

LIN: Don't tell him till after, he'll run a mile.

VICTORIA: Hello. We're having an orgy. Do you want me to suck your cock?

(*The stranger approaches. It is* MARTIN.)

MARTIN: There you are. I've been looking everywhere. What the hell are you doing? Do you know what the time is? 90 You're all pissed out of your minds.

(*They leap on* MARTIN, *pull him down and start to make love to him.*)

MARTIN: Well that's all right. If all we're talking about is having a lot of sex there's no problem. I was all for the sixties when liberation just meant fucking.

(*Another stranger approaches.*)

LIN: Hey you, come here. Come and have sex with us. 95

VICTORIA: Who is it?

(*The stranger is a soldier.*)

LIN: It's my brother.

EDWARD: Lin, don't.

LIN: It's my brother.

VICTORIA: It's her sense of humour, you get used to it. 100

LIN: Shut up Vicky, it's my brother. Isn't it? Bill?

SOLDIER: Yes it's me.

LIN: And you are dead.

SOLDIER: Fucking dead all right yeh.

LIN: Have you come back to tell us something? 105

SOLDIER: No I've come for a fuck. That was the worst thing in the fucking army. Never fucking let out. Can't fucking talk to Irish girls. Fucking bored out of my fucking head. That or shit scared. For five minutes I'd be glad I wasn't bored, then I was fucking scared. Then we'd come in and I'd be 110 glad I wasn't scared and then I was fucking bored. Spent the day reading fucking porn and the fucking night wanking. Man's fucking life in the fucking army? No fun when the fucking kids hate you. I got so I fucking wanted to kill someone and I got fucking killed myself and I want a fuck.

LIN: I miss you. Bill. Bill.

(LIN *collapses.* SOLDIER *goes.* VICTORIA *comforts* LIN.)

EDWARD: Let's go home.

LIN: Victoria, come home with us. Victoria's coming to live with me and Edward.

MARTIN: Tell me about it in the morning.

LIN: It's true.

VICTORIA: It is true.

MARTIN: Tell me when you're sober.

(EDWARD, LIN, VICTORIA *go off together.* MARTIN *goes off alone.* GERRY *comes on.*)

GERRY: I come here sometimes at night and pick somebody up. Sometimes I come here at night and don't pick anybody up. I do also enjoy walking about at night. There's never any trouble finding someone. I can have sex any time. You might not find the type you most fancy every day of the week, but there's plenty of people about who just enjoy having a good time. I quite like living alone. If I live with someone I get annoyed with them. Edward always put on Capital radio when he got up. The silence gets wasted. I wake up at four o'clock sometimes. Birds. Silence. If I bring somebody home I never let them stay the night. Edward! Edward!

(EDWARD *from Act One comes on.*)

EDWARD: Gerry I love you.

GERRY: Yes, I know. I love you, too.

EDWARD: You know what we did? I want to do it again. I think about it all the time. Don't you want to any more?

GERRY: Yes, of course.

Song
CLOUD NINE

ALL: It'll be fine when you reach Cloud Nine.

Mist was rising and the night was dark.
Me and my baby took a walk in the park.
He said Be mine and you're on Cloud Nine.

Better watch out when you're on Cloud Nine.

Smoked some dope on the playground swings
Higher and higher on true love's wings
He said Be mine and you're on Cloud Nine.

Twenty-five years on the same Cloud Nine.

Who did she meet on her first blind date?
The guys were no surprise but the lady was great
They were women in love, they were on Cloud Nine.

Two the same, they were on Cloud Nine.

The bride was sixty-five, the groom was seventeen,
They fucked in the back of the black limousine.
It was divine in their silver Cloud Nine.

Simply divine in their silver Cloud Nine.

The wife's lover's children and my lover's wife,
Cooking in my kitchen, confusing my life.
And it's upside down when you reach Cloud Nine.

Upside down when you reach Cloud Nine.

SCENE IV

The park. Afternoon in late summer. MARTIN, CATHY, EDWARD.

CATHY: Under the bramble bushes,
Under the sea boom boom boom,
True love for you my darling,
True love for me my darling,
When we are married,
We'll raise a family.
Boy for you, girl for me,
Boom tiddley oom boom
SEXY.

EDWARD: You'll have Tommy and Cathy tonight then ok? Tommy's still on antibiotics, do make him finish the bottle, he takes it in Ribena. It's no good in orange, he spits it out. Remind me to give you Cathy's swimming things.

CATHY: I did six strokes, didn't I Martin? Did I do a width? How many strokes is a length? How many miles is a swimming pool? I'm going to take my bronze and silver and gold and diamond.

MARTIN: Is Tommy still wetting the bed?

EDWARD: Don't get angry with him about it.

MARTIN: I just need to go to the launderette so I've got a spare sheet. Of course I don't get fucking angry, Eddy, for God's sake. I don't like to say he is my son but he is my son. I'm surprised I'm not wetting the bed myself.

CATHY: I don't wet the bed ever. Do you wet the bed Martin?

MARTIN: No.

CATHY: You said you did.

(BETTY *comes.*)

BETTY: I do miss the sun living in England but today couldn't be more beautiful. You appreciate the weekend when you're working. Betty's been at work this week, Cathy. It's terrible tiring, Martin, I don't know how you've done it all these years. And the money, I feel like a child with the money, Clive always paid everything but I do understand it perfectly well. Look Cathy let me show you my money.

CATHY: I'll count it. Let me count it. What's that?

BETTY: Five pounds, Five and five is—

CATHY: One two three—

BETTY: Five and five is ten, and five—

CATHY: If I get it right can I have one?

EDWARD: No you can't.

(CATHY *goes on counting the money.*)

BETTY: I never like to say anything, Martin, or you'll think I'm being a mother-in-law.

EDWARD: Which you are.

BETTY: Thank you, Edward, I'm not talking to you. Martin, I think you're being wonderful. Vicky will come back. Just let her stay with Lin till she sorts herself out. It's very nice for a girl to have a friend; I had friends at school, that was very nice. But I'm sure Lin and Edward don't want her with them all the time. I'm not at all shocked that Lin and Edward aren't married and she already has a child, we all 50 know first marriages don't always work out. But really Vicky must be in the way. And poor little Tommy. I hear he doesn't sleep properly and he's had a cough.

MARTIN: No, he's fine, Betty, thank you.

CATHY: My bed's horrible. I want to sleep in the big bed with 55 Lin and Vicky and Eddy and I do get in if I've got a bad dream, and my bed's got a bump right in my back. I want to sleep in a tent.

BETTY: Well Tommy has got a nasty cough, Martin, whatever you say.

60 EDWARD: He's over that. He's got some medicine.

MARTIN: He takes it in Ribena.

BETTY: Well I'm glad to hear it. Look what a lot of money, Cathy, and I sit behind a desk of my own and I answer the telephone and keep the doctor's appointment book and it 65 really is great fun.

CATHY: Can we go camping, Martin, in a tent? We could take the Dead Hand Gang.

BETTY: Not those big boys, Cathy? They're far too big and rough for you. They climb back into the park after dark. 70 I'm sure mummy doesn't let you play with them, does she Edward? Well I don't know.

(*Ice cream bells.*)

CATHY: Ice cream. Martin you promised. I'll have a double ninety-nine. No I'll have a shandy lolly. Betty, you have a shandy lolly and I'll have a lick. No, you have a double 75 ninety-nine and I'll have the chocolate.

(MARTIN, CATHY *and* BETTY *go, leaving* EDWARD. GERRY *comes.*)

GERRY: Hello, Eddy. Thought I might find you here.

EDWARD: Gerry.

GERRY: Not working today then?

EDWARD: I don't work here any more.

80 GERRY: Your mum got you into a dark suit?

EDWARD: No of course not. I'm on the dole. I am working, though, I do housework.

GERRY: Whose wife are you now then?

EDWARD: Nobody's. I don't think like that any more. I'm liv- 85 ing with some women.

GERRY: What women?

EDWARD: It's my sister, Vic, and her lover. They go out to work and I look after the kids.

GERRY: I thought for a moment you said you were living 90 with women.

EDWARD: We do sleep together, yes.

GERRY: I was passing the park anyway so I thought I'd look in. I was in the sauna the other night and I saw someone who looked like you but it wasn't. I had sex with him anyway. 95 EDWARD: I do go to the sauna sometimes.

(CATHY *comes, gives* EDWARD *an ice cream, goes.*)

GERRY: I don't think I'd like living with children. They make a lot of noise don't they?

EDWARD: I tell them to shut up and they shut up. I wouldn't want to leave them at the moment.

GERRY: Look why don't we go for a meal sometime? 100

EDWARD: Yes I'd like that. Where are you living now?

GERRY: Same place.

EDWARD: I'll come round for you tomorrow night about 7:30.

GERRY: Great.

(EDWARD *goes.* HARRY *comes.* HARRY *and* GERRY *pick each other up. They go off.* BETTY *comes back.*)

BETTY: No, the ice cream was my treat, Martin. Off you go. 105 I'm going to have a quiet sit in the sun.

(MAUD *comes.*)

MAUD: Let Mrs Saunders be a warning to you, Betty. I know what it is to be unprotected.

BETTY: But mother, I have a job. I earn money.

MAUD: I know we have our little differences but I always 110 want what is best for you.

(ELLEN *comes.*)

ELLEN: Betty, what happens with a man?

BETTY: You just keep still.

ELLEN: And is it enjoyable? Don't forget me, Betty.

(MAUD *and* ELLEN *go.*)

BETTY: I used to think Clive was the one who liked sex. But 115 then I found I missed it. I used to touch myself when I was very little, I thought I'd invented something wonderful. I used to do it to go to sleep with or to cheer myself up, and one day it was raining and I was under the kitchen table, and my mother saw me with my hand under my dress rub- 120 bing away, and she dragged me out so quickly I hit my head and it bled and I was sick, and nothing was said, and I never did it again till this year. I thought if Clive wasn't looking at me there wasn't a person there. And one night in bed in my flat I was so frightened I started touching myself. I 125 thought my hand might go through space. I touched my face, it was there, my arm, my breast, and my hand went down where I thought it shouldn't, and I thought well there is somebody there. It felt very sweet, it was a feeling from very long ago, it was very soft, just barely touching, 130 and I felt myself gathering together more and more and I felt angry with Clive and angry with my mother and I went on and on defying them, and there was this vast feel- ing growing in me and all round me and they couldn't stop me and no one could stop me and I was there and coming 135 and coming. Afterwards I thought I'd betrayed Clive. My mother would kill me. But I felt triumphant because I was a separate person from them. And I cried because I didn't want to be. But I don't cry about it any more. Sometimes I do it three times in one night and it really is great fun. 140

(VICTORIA *and* LIN *come in.*)

VICTORIA: So I said to the professor, I don't think this is an oc- casion for invoking the concept of structural causality—oh hello mummy.

BETTY: I'm going to ask you a question, both of you. I have
145   a little money from your grandmother. And the three of
you are living in that tiny flat with two children. I wonder if we could get a house and all live in it together? It
would give you more room.

VICTORIA: But I'm going to Manchester anyway.

150 LIN: We'd have a garden, Vicky.

BETTY: You do seem to have such fun all of you.

VICTORIA: I don't want to.

BETTY: I didn't think you would.

LIN: Come on, Vicky, she knows we sleep together, and Eddy.

155 BETTY: I think I've known for quite a while but I'm not sure.
I don't usually think about it, so I don't know if I know
about it or not.

VICTORIA: I don't want to live with my mother.

LIN: Don't think of her as your mother, think of her as Betty.

160 VICTORIA: But she thinks of herself as my mother.

BETTY: I am your mother.

VICTORIA: But mummy we don't even like each other.

BETTY: We might begin to.

(CATHY comes on howling with a nosebleed.)

LIN: Oh Cathy what happened?

165 BETTY: She's been assaulted.

VICTORIA: It's a nosebleed.

CATHY: Took my ice cream.

LIN: Who did?

CATHY: Took my money.

(MARTIN comes.)

170 MARTIN: Is everything all right?

LIN: I thought you were looking after her.

CATHY: They hit me. I can't play. They said I'm a girl.

BETTY: Those dreadful boys, the gang, the Dead Hand.

MARTIN: What do you mean you thought I was looking after her?

175 LIN: Last I saw her she was with you getting an ice cream. It's
your afternoon.

MARTIN: Then she went off to play. She goes off to play. You
don't keep an eye on her every minute.

LIN: She doesn't get beaten up when I'm looking after her.

180 CATHY: Took my money.

MARTIN: Why the hell should I look after your child anyway?
I just want Tommy. Why should he live with you and
Vicky all week?

LIN: I don't mind if you don't want to look after her but don't

185   say you will and then this happens.

VICTORIA: When I get to Manchester everything's going to be
different anyway, Lin's staying here, and you're staying here,
we're all going to have to sit down and talk it through.

MARTIN: I'd really enjoy that.

190 CATHY: Hit me on the face.

LIN: You were the one looking after her and look at her now,
that's all.

MARTIN: I've had enough of you telling me.

LIN: Yes you know it all.

195 MARTIN: Now stop it. I work very hard at not being like this,
I could do with some credit.

LIN: Ok you're quite nice, try and enjoy it. Don't make me
sorry for you, Martin, it's hard for me too. We've better
things to do than quarrel. I've got to go and sort those little bastards out for a start. Where are they, Cathy?   200

CATHY: Don't kill them, mum, hit them. Give them a nosebleed, mum.

(LIN goes.)

VICTORIA: Tommy's asleep in the pushchair. We'd better
wake him up or he won't sleep tonight.

MARTIN: Sometimes I keep him up watching television till he   205
falls asleep on the sofa so I can hold him. Come on, Cathy,
we'll get another ice cream.

CATHY: Chocolate sauce and nuts.

VICTORIA: Betty, would you like an ice cream?

BETTY: No thank you, the cold hurts my teeth, but what a   210
nice thought, Vicky, thank you.

(VICTORIA goes. BETTY alone. GERRY comes.)

BETTY: I think you used to be Edward's flatmate.

GERRY: You're his mother. He's talked about you.

BETTY: Well never mind. Children are always wrong about
their parents. It's a great problem knowing where to live   215
and who to share with. I live by myself just now.

GERRY: Good. So do I. You can do what you like.

BETTY: I don't really know what I like.

GERRY: You'll soon find out.

BETTY: What do you like?   220

GERRY: Waking up at four in the morning.

BETTY: I like listening to music in bed and sometimes for supper I just have a big piece of bread and dip it in very hot
lime pickle. So you don't get lonely by yourself? Perhaps
you have a lot of visitors. I've been thinking I should have   225
some visitors, I could give a little dinner party. Would you
come? There wouldn't just be bread and lime pickle.

GERRY: Thank you very much.

BETTY: Or don't wait to be asked to dinner. Just drop in informally. I'll give you the address shall I? I don't usually   230
give strange men my address but then you're not a strange
man, you're a friend of Edward's. I suppose I seem a different generation to you but you are older than Edward. I
was married for so many years it's quite hard to know how
to get acquainted. But if there isn't a right way to do   235
things you have to invent one. I always thought my
mother was far too old to be attractive but when you get
to an age yourself it feels quite different.

GERRY: I think you could be quite attractive.

BETTY: If what?   240

GERRY: If you stop worrying.

BETTY: I think when I do more about things I worry about
them less. So perhaps you could help me do more.

GERRY: I might be going to live with Edward again.

BETTY: That's nice, but I'm rather surprised if he wants to   245
share a flat. He's rather involved with a young woman he
lives with, or two young women, I don't understand Edward but never mind.

GERRY: I'm very involved with him.

250 BETTY: I think Edward did try to tell me once but I didn't listen. So what I'm being told now is that Edward is 'gay' is
that right? And you are too. And I've been making rather
a fool of myself. But Edward does also sleep with women.
GERRY: He does, yes, I don't.
255 BETTY: Well people always say it's the mother's fault but I don't
intend to start blaming myself. He seems perfectly happy.
GERRY: I could still come and see you.
BETTY: So you could, yes. I'd like that. I've never tried to pick
up a man before.
260 GERRY: Not everyone's gay.

BETTY: No, that's lucky isn't it.

(GERRY goes. CLIVE comes.)

CLIVE: You are not that sort of woman, Betty. I can't believe
you are. I can't feel the same about you as I did. And
Africa is to be communist I suppose. I used to be proud
to be British. There was a high ideal. I came out onto the   265
verandah and looked at the stars.

(CLIVE goes. BETTY from Act One comes. BETTY and BETTY
embrace.)

SARAH KANE

A brilliant young playwright, Sarah Kane (1971–1999) changed the landscape of British theater in the 1990s with her series of brilliant, violent parables. The daughter of British journalists, Kane was raised in an environment of religious evangelism; she studied playwriting and acting at the University of Bristol, and then enrolled in the playwriting course founded by the playwright David Edgar at the University of Birmingham. Her first play, *Blasted* (1995), was denounced by the press with a ferocity reminiscent of the reception of earlier landmarks in the British stage—Edward Bond's *Saved* in 1965, John Osborne's *Look Back in Anger* in 1956, or even the first production of Ibsen's *Ghosts* in 1891, when Clement Scott famously called the play "An open drain; a loathsome sore unbandaged; a dirty act done publicly." At the same time, though, Kane's mastery both of an intensity of dramatic action and visual imagery immediately drew defenders as well, among them Edward Bond and Caryl Churchill. In the course of the late 1990s, Kane continued to explore the intersection between language and image in an increasingly experimental series of plays—*Phaedra's Love* (1996), *Skin* (a television play, 1997), *Cleansed* (1998), and *Crave* (1998). Kane suffered from severe depression, and she wrote her final play, *4.48 Psychosis*—a play in free verse without given speakers—about the moment at which she would awaken each morning, clinging to a moment of mental clarity and conviction. Written in the autumn of 1998, the play presaged Kane's suicide on February 20, 1999. *4.48 Psychosis* was produced by the Royal Court Theatre in 2000 as part of a retrospective season that brought earlier work, including *Blasted,* back to the London stage.

BLASTED

By any measure, *Blasted* is an elegant, horrific play. Taking place in the claustrophobic environment of "*a very expensive hotel room in Leeds,*" Kane's nearly surreal violence is perhaps implied in the phrase she uses to qualify that setting: "*the kind that is so expensive it could be anywhere in the world.*" For while the action of the play seems initially confined to the domestic naturalism characteristic of much British drama—the naturalism typical of socially critical drama from Shaw and Barker and Galsworthy to Osborne to Kane's contemporaries Mark Ravenhill and Patrick Marber—it immediately swerves into another register, as the brutal relationship between Ian and Cate explodes into a new level of violence with the arrival of the Soldier, the apparent bombing of the hotel, and the transformation of the English landscape to a setting that could indeed be "anywhere in the world." Kane's drama proves challenging precisely because the characters' relationships—Ian's brutal rape of Cate, the Soldier's equally brutal rape of Ian—are set against a shifting social and political backdrop. Ian's irritated muttering in Scene Two—"Speak the Queen's English fucking nigger"—alerts us to a resonant class and racial oppression, a political violence that Kane locates at the core of English culture. With the arrival of the Soldier and the bombing of the hotel, the landscape seems to shift to a different kind of battlefield, reminiscent of the ethnic and political strife of Bosnia in the late 1990s. With a kind of surreal dream logic, Ian's petty prejudice is translated into the Soldier's militarized violence, evoked both in his hardened accounts of mutilation—"Insides of people's heads came out of their eyes. Saw a child most of his face blown off, young girl I fucked hand up inside her trying to claw my liquid out, starving man eating his dead wife's leg"—and in the actions he performs, raping Ian, sucking out his eyes, and then committing suicide. In Kane's world, the cycle of inhuman violence is unalterable; yet while individuals brutalize each other, Kane seems to hold out the hope for tiny acts of community, as when Cate returns to Ian at the end of the play. In its evocative imagery and language, and in the way it enfolds a political critique into a series of brilliant, brutal images, Kane's *Blasted* was the signal work of British theater in the 1990s.

The soldier stands over Ian in the Rude Gorilla Theatre production of Sarah Kane's *Blasted*.

BLASTED

Sarah Kane

FOR VINCENT O'CONNELL, WITH THANKS.

CHARACTERS

IAN
CATE
SOLDIER

SCENE ONE

A very expensive hotel room in Leeds—the kind that is so expensive it could be anywhere in the world.

There is a large double bed.
A mini-bar and champagne on ice.
A telephone.
A large bouquet of flowers.
Two doors—one is the entrance from the corridor, the other leads off to the bathroom.

Two people enter—IAN and CATE.

IAN is 45, Welsh born but lived in Leeds much of his life and picked up the accent.

CATE is 21, a lower-middle-class Southerner with a south London accent and a stutter when under stress.

They enter.

CATE stops at the door, amazed at the classiness of the room. IAN comes in, throws a small pile of newspapers on the bed, goes straight to the mini-bar and pours himself a large gin. He looks briefly out of the window at the street, then turns back to the room.

IAN: I've shat in better places than this.

(He gulps down the gin.)

    I stink.
    You want a bath?
CATE: *(Shakes her head.)*

IAN goes into the bathroom and we hear him run the water. He comes back in with only a towel around his waist and a revolver in his hand. He checks it is loaded and puts it under his pillow.

5 IAN: Tip that wog when he brings up the sandwiches.

He leaves fifty pence and goes into the bathroom.
CATE comes further into the room.
She puts her bag down and bounces on the bed.
She goes around the room, looking in every drawer, touching everything.
She smells the flowers and smiles.

CATE: Lovely.

IAN comes back in, hair wet, towel around his waist, drying himself off.
He stops and looks at CATE who is sucking her thumb.
He goes back in the bathroom where he dresses.
We hear him coughing terribly in the bathroom.
He spits in the sink and re-enters.

CATE: You all right?
IAN: It's nothing.

He pours himself another gin, this time with ice and tonic, and sips it at a more normal pace.
He collects his gun and puts it in his under-arm holster.
He smiles at CATE.

IAN: I'm glad you've come. Didn't think you would.

(He offers her champagne.)

CATE: *(Shakes her head.)*   10
    I was worried.
IAN: This? *(He indicates his chest.)* Don't matter.
CATE: I didn't mean that. You sounded unhappy.
IAN: *(Pops the champagne. He pours them both a glass.)*
CATE: What we celebrating?   15
IAN: *(Doesn't answer. He goes to the window and looks out.)*
    Hate this city. Stinks. Wogs and Pakis taking over.
CATE: You shouldn't call them that.
IAN: Why not?
CATE: It's not very nice.   20
IAN: You a nigger-lover?
CATE: Ian, don't.
IAN: You like our coloured brethren?
CATE: Don't mind them.
IAN: Grow up.   25
CATE: There's Indians at the day centre where my brother goes. They're really polite.
IAN: So they should be.
CATE: He's friends with some of them.
IAN: Retard, isn't he?   30
CATE: No, he's got learning difficulties.
IAN: Aye. Spaz.
CATE: No he's not.
IAN: Glad my son's not a Joey.
CATE: Don't c- call him that.   35

IAN: Your mother I feel sorry for. Two of you like it.
CATE: Like wh- what?
IAN: (*Looks at her, deciding whether or not to continue. He decides against it.*)
40   You know I love you.
CATE: (*Smiles a big smile, friendly and non-sexual.*)
IAN: Don't want you ever to leave.
CATE: I'm here for the night.
IAN: (*Drinks.*)
45   Sweating again. Stink. You ever thought of getting married?
CATE: Who'd marry me?
IAN: I would.
CATE: I couldn't.
IAN: You don't love me. I don't blame you, I wouldn't.
50   CATE: I couldn't leave Mum.
IAN: Have to one day.
CATE: Why?
IAN: (*Opens his mouth to answer but can't think of one.*)

There is a knock at the door.
IAN *starts, and* CATE *goes to answer it.*

IAN: Don't.
55   CATE: Why not?
IAN: I said.

He takes his gun from the holster and goes to the door.
He listens.
Nothing.

CATE: (*Giggles.*)
IAN: Shh.

He listens.
Still nothing.

IAN: Probably the wog with the sarnies. Open it.

CATE *opens the door.*
There's no one there, just a tray of sandwiches on the floor.
She brings them in and examines them.

60   CATE: Ham. Don't believe it.
IAN: (*Takes a sandwich and eats it.*)

Champagne?

CATE: (*Shakes her head.*)
IAN: Got something against ham?
65   CATE: Dead meat. Blood. Can't eat an animal.
IAN: No one would know.
CATE: No, I can't, I actually can't, I'd puke all over the place.
IAN: It's only a pig.
CATE: I'm hungry.
70   IAN: Have one of these.
CATE: I CAN'T.
IAN: I'll take you out for an Indian.
Jesus, what's this? Cheese.

CATE *beams.*
She separates the cheese sandwiches from the ham ones, and eats.
IAN *watches her.*

IAN: Don't like your clothes.
CATE: (*Looks down at her clothes.*)   75
IAN: You look like a lesbos.
CATE: What's that?
IAN: Don't look very sexy, that's all.
CATE: Oh.

(*She continues to eat.*)

Don't like your clothes either.   80
IAN: (*Looks down at his clothes.
Then gets up, takes them all off and stands in front of her, naked.*)
Put your mouth on me.
CATE: (*Stares. Then bursts out laughing.*)
IAN: No?   85
Fine.
Because I stink?
CATE: (*Laughs even more.*)

IAN *attempts to dress, but fumbles with embarrassment.*
He gathers his clothes and goes into the bathroom where he dresses.
CATE *eats, and giggles over the sandwiches.*
IAN *returns, fully dressed.*
He picks up his gun, unloads and reloads it.

IAN: You got a job yet?
CATE: No.   90
IAN: Still screwing the taxpayer.
CATE: Mum gives me money.
IAN: When are you going to stand on your own feet?
CATE: I've applied for a job at an advertising agency.
IAN: (*Laughs genuinely.*)   95
No chance.
CATE: Why not?
IAN: (*Stops laughing and looks at her.*)
Cate. You're stupid. You're never going to get a job.
CATE: I am. I am not.   100
IAN: See.
CATE: St- Stop it. You're doing it deliberately.
IAN: Doing what?
CATE: C- Confusing me.
IAN: No, I'm talking, you're just too thick to understand.   105
CATE: I am not, I am not.

CATE *begins to tremble.* IAN *is laughing.*
CATE *faints.*
IAN *stops laughing and stares at her motionless body.*

IAN: Cate?

(*He turns her over and lifts up her eyelids.
He doesn't know what to do.
He gets a glass of gin and dabs some on her face.*)

CATE: (*Sits bolt upright, eyes open but still unconscious.*)
IAN: Fucking Jesus.
CATE: (*Bursts out laughing, unnaturally, hysterically, uncontrollably.*)   110
IAN: Stop fucking about.
CATE: (*Collapses again and lies still.*)

IAN *stands by helplessly.*
After a few moments, CATE *comes round as if waking up in the morning.*

IAN: What the Christ was that?
CATE: Have to tell her.
115 IAN: Cate?
CATE: She's in danger.

(*She closes her eyes and slowly comes back to normal.*
She looks at IAN *and smiles.*)

IAN: What now?
CATE: Did I faint?
IAN: That was real?
120 CATE: Happens all the time.
IAN: What, fits?
CATE: Since Dad came back.
IAN: Does it hurt?
CATE: I'll grow out of it the doctor says.
125 IAN: How do you feel?
CATE: (*Smiles.*)
IAN: Thought you were dead.
CATE: [I] Suppose that's what it's like.
IAN: Don't do it again, fucking scared me.
130 CATE: Don't know much about it, I just go. Feels like I'm
    away for minutes or months sometimes, then I come back
    just where I was.
IAN: It's terrible.
CATE: I didn't go far.
135 IAN: What if you didn't come round?
CATE: Wouldn't know. I'd stay there.
IAN: Can't stand it.

(*He goes to the mini-bar and pours himself another large gin and
lights a cigarette.*)

CATE: What?
IAN: Death. Not being.
140 CATE: You fall asleep and then you wake up.
IAN: How do you know?
CATE: Why don't you give up smoking?
IAN: (*Laughs.*)
CATE: You should. They'll make you ill.
145 IAN: Too late for that.
CATE: Whenever I think of you it's with a cigarette and a gin.
IAN: Good.
CATE: They make your clothes smell.
IAN: Don't forget my breath.
150 CATE: Imagine what your lungs must look like.
IAN: Don't need to imagine. I've seen.
CATE: When?
IAN: Last year. When I came round, surgeon brought in this
    lump of rotting pork, stank. My lung.
155 CATE: He took it out?
IAN: Other one's the same now.
CATE: But you'll die.
IAN: Aye.
CATE: Please stop smoking.
160 IAN: Won't make any difference.
CATE: Can't they do something?
IAN: No. It's not like your brother, look after him he'll be all
    right.
CATE: They die young.
165 IAN: I'm fucked.

CATE: Can't you get a transplant?
IAN: Don't be stupid. They give them to people with a life. Kids.
CATE: People die in accidents all the time, they must have
    some spare.
IAN: Why? What for? Keep me alive to die of cirrhosis in 170
    three months' time?
CATE: You're making it worse, speeding it up.
IAN: Enjoy myself while I'm here.

(*He inhales deeply on his cigarette and swallows the last of the gin neat.*)

    [I'll] Call that coon, get some more sent up.
CATE: (*Shakes.*)   175
IAN: Wonder if the conker understands English.

He notices CATE's *distress and cuddles her.*
He kisses her.
She pulls away and wipes her mouth.

CATE: Don't put your tongue in, I don't like it.
IAN: Sorry.

The telephone rings loudly. IAN *starts, then answers it.*

IAN: Hello?
CATE: Who is it?   180
IAN: (*Covers the mouthpiece.*) Shh.
    (*Into the mouthpiece.*) Got it here.

(*He takes a notebook from the pile of newspapers and dictates
down the phone.*)

A serial killer slaughtered British tourist Samantha Scrace,
S – C – R – A – C – E, in a sick murder ritual comma,
police revealed yesterday point new par. The bubbly nine- 185
teen year old from Leeds was among seven victims found
buried in identical triangular tombs in an isolated New
Zealand forest point new par. Each had been stabbed
more than twenty times and placed face down comma,
hands bound behind their backs point new par. Caps up, 190
ashes at the site showed the maniac had stayed to cook a
meal, caps down point new par. Samantha comma, a
beautiful redhead with dreams of becoming a model
comma, was on the trip of a lifetime after finishing her A
levels last year point. Samantha's heartbroken mum said 195
yesterday colon quoting, we pray the police will come up
with something dash, anything comma, soon point still
quoting. The sooner this lunatic is brought to justice the
better point end quote new par. The Foreign Office
warned tourists Down Under to take extra care point. A 200
spokesman said colon quoting, common sense is the best
rule point end quote, copy ends.

(*He listens. Then he laughs.*)

    Exactly.

(*He listens.*)

    That one again, I went to see her. Scouse tart, spread her
    legs. No. Forget it. Tears and lies, not worth the space. 205

(*He presses a button on the phone to connect him to room service.*)

    Tosser.

CATE: How do they know you're here?

IAN: Told them.

CATE: Why?

210 IAN: In case they needed me.

CATE: Silly. We came here to be away from them.

IAN: Thought you'd like this. Nice hotel.

(Into the mouthpiece.)

Bring a bottle of gin up, son.

(He puts the phone down.)

CATE: We always used to go to yours.

215 IAN: That was years ago. You've grown up.

CATE: *(Smiles.)*

IAN: I'm not well any more.

CATE: *(Stops smiling.)*

IAN *kisses her.*
She responds.
He puts his hand under her top and moves it towards her breast.
With the other hand he undoes his trousers and starts masturbating.
He begins to undo her top.
She pushes him away.

CATE: Ian, d- don't.

220 IAN: What?

CATE: I don't w- want to do this.

IAN: Yes you do.

CATE: I don't.

IAN: Why not? You're nervous, that's all.

(He starts to kiss her again.)

225 CATE: I t- t- t- t- t- t- t- told you. I really like you but I c-
c- c- c- can't do this.

IAN: *(Kissing her.)* Shhh.

(He starts to undo her trousers.)
CATE *panics.*
She starts to tremble and make inarticulate crying sounds.
IAN *stops, frightened of bringing another 'fit' on.*

IAN: All right, Cate, it's all right. We don't have to do anything.

He strokes her face until she has calmed down.
She sucks her thumb.
Then.

IAN: That wasn't very fair.

230 CATE: What?

IAN: Leaving me hanging, making a prick of myself.

CATE: I f- f- felt—

IAN: Don't pity me, Cate. You don't have to fuck me 'cause
I'm dying, but don't push your cunt in my face then take

235 it away 'cause I stick my tongue out.

CATE: I- I- Ian.

IAN: What's the m- m- matter?

CATE: I k- k- kissed you, that's all. I l- l- like you.

IAN: Don't give me a hard-on if you're not going to finish me

240 off. It hurts.

CATE: I'm sorry.

IAN: Can't switch it on and off like that. If I don't come my
cock aches.

CATE: I didn't mean it.

IAN: Shit. *(He appears to be in considerable pain.)*   245

CATE: I'm sorry. I am. I won't do it again.

IAN, *apparently still in pain, takes her hand and grasps it around his*
penis, keeping his own hand over the top.
Like this, he masturbates until the comes with some genuine pain.
He releases CATE's *hand and she withdraws it.*

CATE: Is it better?

IAN: *(Nods.)*

CATE: I'm sorry.

IAN: Don't worry. Can we make love tonight?   250

CATE: No.

IAN: Why not?

CATE: I'm not your girlfriend any more.

IAN: Will you be my girlfriend again?

CATE: I can't.   255

IAN: Why not?

CATE: I told Shaun I'd be his.

IAN: Have you slept with him?

CATE: No.

IAN: Slept with me before. You're more mine than his.   260

CATE: I'm not.

IAN: What was that about then, wanking me off?

CATE: I d- d- d- d-

IAN: Sorry. Pressure, pressure. I love you, that's all.

CATE: You were horrible to me.   265

IAN: I wasn't.

CATE: Stopped phoning me, never said why.

IAN: It was difficult, Cate.

CATE: Because I haven't got a job?

IAN: No, pet, not that.   270

CATE: Because of my brother?

IAN: No, no, Cate. Leave it now.

CATE: That's not fair.

IAN: I said leave it.

(He reaches for his gun.)
There is a knock at the door.
IAN *starts, then goes to answer it.*

IAN: I'm not going to hurt you, just leave it. And keep quiet.   275
It'll only be Sooty after something.

CATE: Andrew.

IAN: What do you want to know a conker's name for?

CATE: I thought he was nice.

IAN: After a bit of black meat, eh? Won't do it with me but   280
you'll go with a whodat.

CATE: You're horrible.

IAN: Cate, love, I'm trying to look after you. Stop you getting
hurt.

CATE: You hurt me.   285

IAN: No, I love you.

CATE: Stopped loving me.

IAN: I've told you to leave that. Now.

He kisses her passionately, then goes to the door.

When his back is turned, CATE *wipes her mouth.*
IAN *opens the door. There is a bottle of gin outside on a tray.*
IAN *brings it in and stands, unable to decide between gin and champagne.*

CATE: Have champagne, better for you.
290 IAN: Don't want it better for me.

(He pours himself a gin.)

CATE: You'll die quicker.
IAN: Thanks. Don't it scare you?
CATE: What?
IAN: Death.
295 CATE: Whose?
IAN: Yours.
CATE: Only for Mum. She'd be unhappy if I died. And my
      brother.
IAN: You're young.
300   When I was your age—
         Now.
CATE: Will you have to go to hospital?
IAN: Nothing they can do.
CATE: Does Stella know?
305 IAN: What would I want to tell her for?
CATE: You were married.
IAN: So?
CATE: She'd want to know.
IAN: So she can throw a party at the coven.
310 CATE: She wouldn't do that. What about Matthew?
IAN: What about Matthew?
CATE: Have you told him?
IAN: I'll send him an invite for the funeral.
CATE: He'll be upset.
315 IAN: He hates me.
CATE: He doesn't.
IAN: He fucking does.
CATE: Are you upset?
IAN: Yes. His mother's a lesbos. Am I not preferable to that?
320 CATE: Perhaps she's a nice person.
IAN: She don't carry a gun.
CATE: I expect that's it.
IAN: I loved Stella till she became a witch and fucked off with
      a dyke, and I love you, though you've got the potential.
325 CATE: For what?
IAN: Sucking gash.
CATE: *(Utters an inarticulate sound.)*
IAN: You ever had a fuck with a woman?
CATE: No.
330 IAN: You want to?
CATE: Don't think so. Have you? With a man.
IAN: You think I'm a cocksucker? You've seen me. *(He vaguely
      indicates his groin.)* How can you think that?
CATE: I don't. I asked. You asked me.
335 IAN: You dress like a lesbos. I don't dress like a cocksucker.
CATE: What do they dress like?
IAN: Hitler was wrong about the Jews who have they hurt the
      queers he should have gone for scum them and the wogs
      and fucking football fans send a bomber over Elland Road
340   finish them off.

(He pours champagne and toasts the idea.)

CATE: I like football.
IAN: Why?
CATE: It's good.
IAN: And when was the last time you went to a football
      match?   345
CATE: Saturday. United beat Liverpool 2–0.
IAN: Didn't you get stabbed?
CATE: Why should I?
IAN: That's what football's about. It's not fancy footwork and
      scoring goals. It's tribalism.   350
CATE: I like it.
IAN: You would. About your level.
CATE: I go to Elland Road sometimes. Would you bomb me?
IAN: What do you want to ask a question like that for?
CATE: Would you though?   355
IAN: Don't be thick.
CATE: But would you?
IAN: Haven't got a bomber.
CATE: Shoot me, then. Could you do that?
IAN: Cate.   360
CATE: Do you think it's hard to shoot someone?
IAN: Easy as shitting blood.
CATE: Could you shoot me?
IAN: Could you shoot me stop asking that could you shoot
      me you could shoot me.   365
CATE: I don't think so.
IAN: If I hurt you.
CATE: Don't think you would.
IAN: But if.
CATE: No, you're soft.   370
IAN: With people I love.

(He stares at her, considering making a pass.)

CATE: *(Smiles at him, friendly.)*
IAN: What's this job, then?
CATE: Personal Assistant.
IAN: Who to?   375
CATE: Don't know.
IAN: Who did you write the letter to?
CATE: Sir or madam.
IAN: You have to know who you're writing to.
CATE: It didn't say.   380
IAN: How much?
CATE: What?
IAN: Money. How much do you get paid.
CATE: Mum said it was a lot. I don't mind about that as long
      as I can go out sometimes.   385
IAN: Don't despise money. You got it easy.
CATE: I haven't got any money.
IAN: No and you haven't got kids to bring up neither.
CATE: Not yet.
IAN: Don't even think about it. Who would have children.   390
      You have kids, they grow up, they hate you and you die.
CATE: I don't hate Mum.
IAN: You still need her.
CATE: You think I'm stupid. I'm not stupid.
IAN: I worry.   395
CATE: Can look after myself.
IAN: Like me.
CATE: No.

IAN: You hate me, don't you.
400 CATE: You shouldn't have that gun.
IAN: May need it.
CATE: What for?
IAN: (*Drinks.*)
CATE: Can't imagine it.
405 IAN: What?
CATE: You. Shooting someone. You wouldn't kill anything.
IAN: (*Drinks.*)
CATE: Have you ever shot anyone?
IAN: Your mind.
410 CATE: Have you though?
IAN: Leave it now, Cate.

She takes the warning.
IAN *kisses her and lights a cigarette.*

IAN: When I'm with you I can't think about anything else.
    You take me to another place.
CATE: It's like that when I have a fit.
415 IAN: Just you.
CATE: The world don't exist, not like this.
    Looks the same but—
    Time slows down.
    A dream I get stuck in, can't do nothing about it.
420   One time—
IAN: Make love to me.
CATE: Blocks out everything else.
        Once—
IAN: [I'll] Make love to you.
425 CATE: It's like that when I touch myself.

IAN *is embarrassed.*

CATE: Just before I'm wondering what it'll be like, and just af-
    ter I'm thinking about the next one, but just as it happens
    it's lovely, I don't think of nothing else.
IAN: Like the first cigarette of the day.
430 CATE: That's bad for you though.
IAN: Stop talking now, you don't know anything about it.
CATE: Don't need to.
IAN: Don't know nothing. That's why I love you, want to
    make love to you.
435 CATE: But you can't.
IAN: Why not?
CATE: I don't want to.
IAN: Why did you come here?
CATE: You sounded unhappy.
440 IAN: Make me happy.
CATE: I can't.
IAN: Please.
CATE: No.
IAN: Why not?
445 CATE: Can't.
IAN: Can.
CATE: How?
IAN: You know.
CATE: Don't.
450 IAN: Please.
CATE: No.
IAN: I love you.

CATE: I don't love you.
IAN: (*Turns away. He sees the bouquet of flowers and picks it up.*)
    These are for you.   455

Blackout.
The sound of spring rain.

SCENE TWO

The same.
Very early the following morning.
Bright and sunny—it's going to be a very hot day.
The bouquet of flowers is now ripped apart and scattered around the room.

CATE *is still asleep.*
IAN *is awake, glancing through the newspapers.*
IAN *goes to the mini-bar. It is empty.*
He finds the bottle of gin under the bed and pours half of what is left into a glass.
He stands looking out of the window at the street.
He takes the first sip and is overcome with pain.
He waits for it to pass, but it doesn't. It gets worse.
IAN *clutches his side—it becomes extreme.*
He begins to cough and experiences intense pain in his chest, each cough tearing at his lung.
CATE *wakes and watches* IAN.
IAN *drops to his knees, puts the glass down carefully, and gives in to the pain.*
It looks very much as if he is dying.
His heart, lung, liver and kidneys are all under attack and he is making involuntary crying sounds.
Just at the moment when it seems he cannot survive this, it begins to ease.
Very slowly, the pain decreases until it has all gone.
IAN *is a crumpled heap on the floor.*
He looks up and sees CATE *watching him.*

CATE: Cunt.
IAN: (*Gets up slowly, picks up the glass and drinks.*
    He lights his first cigarette of the day.)
    I'm having a shower.
CATE: It's only six o'clock.   5
IAN: Want one?
CATE: Not with you.
IAN: Suit yourself. Cigarette?
CATE: (*Makes a noise of disgust.*)

They are silent.
IAN *stands, smoking and drinking neat gin.*
When he's sufficiently numbed, he comes and goes between the bedroom and bathroom, undressing and collecting discarded towels.
He stops, towel around his waist, gun in hand, and looks at CATE.
She is staring at him with hate.

IAN: Don't worry, I'll be dead soon.   10

(*He tosses the gun onto the bed.*)

    Have a pop.

CATE *doesn't move.*

IAN *waits, then chuckles and goes into the bathroom.*
We hear the shower running.
CATE *stares at the gun.*
She gets up very slowly and dresses.
She packs her bag.
She picks up IAN's *leather jacket and smells it.*
She rips the arms off at the seams.
She picks up his gun and examines it.
We hear IAN *coughing up in the bathroom.*
CATE *puts the gun down and he comes in.*
He dresses.
He looks at the gun.

IAN: No?

(*He chuckles, unloads and reloads the gun and tucks it in his holster.*)

   We're one, yes?
CATE: (*Sneers.*)
15 IAN: We're one.
   Coming down for breakfast? It's paid for.
CATE: Choke on it.
IAN: Sarky little tart this morning, aren't we?

He picks up his jacket and puts one arm through a hole.
He stares at the damage, then looks at CATE.
A beat, then she goes for him, slapping him around the head hard and fast.
He wrestles her onto the bed, her still kicking, punching and biting.
She takes the gun from his holster and points it at his groin.
He backs off rapidly.

IAN: Easy, easy, that's a loaded gun.
20 CATE: I d- d- d- d- d- d- d- d-
IAN: Catie, come on.
CATE: d- d- d- d- d- d- d- d-
IAN: You don't want an accident. Think about your mum.
   And your brother. What would they think?
25 CATE: I d- d- d- d- d- d- d- d- d- d-

CATE *trembles and starts gasping for air.*
She faints.
IAN *goes to her, takes the gun and puts it back in the holster.*
Then lies her on the bed on her back.
He puts the gun to her head, lies between her legs, and simulates sex.
As he comes, CATE *sits bolt upright with a shout.*
IAN *moves away, unsure what to do, pointing the gun at her from behind.*
She laughs hysterically, as before, but doesn't stop.
She laughs and laughs and laughs until she isn't laughing any more, she's crying her heart out.
She collapses again and lies still.

IAN: Cate? Catie?

IAN *puts the gun away.*
He kisses her and she comes round.
She stares at him.

IAN: You back?
CATE: Liar.

IAN *doesn't know if this means yes or no, so he just waits.*
CATE *closes her eyes for a few seconds, then opens them.*

IAN: Cate?
CATE: Want to go home now.   30
IAN: It's not even seven. There won't be a train.
CATE: I'll wait at the station.
IAN: It's raining.
CATE: It's not.
IAN: Want you to stay here. Till after breakfast at least.   35
CATE: No.
IAN: Cate. After breakfast.
CATE: No.
IAN: (*Locks the door and pockets the key.*)
   I love you.   40
CATE: I don't want to stay.
IAN: Please.
CATE: Don't want to.
IAN: You make me feel safe.
CATE: Nothing to be scared of.   45
IAN: I'll order breakfast.
CATE: Not hungry.
IAN: (*Lights a cigarette.*)
CATE: How can you smoke on an empty stomach?
IAN: It's not empty. There's gin in it.   50
CATE: Why can't I go home?
IAN: (*Thinks.*)
   It's too dangerous.

Outside, a car backfires-there is an enormous bang.
IAN *throws himself flat on the floor.*

CATE: (*Laughs.*)
   It's only a car.   55
IAN: You. You're fucking thick.
CATE: I'm not. You're scared of things when there's nothing
   to be scared of. What's thick about not being scared of
   cars?
IAN: I'm not scared of cars. I'm scared of dying.   60
CATE: A car won't kill you. Not from out there.
   Not unless you ran out in front of it.
   (*She kisses him.*)
   What's scaring you?
IAN: Thought it was a gun.   65
CATE: (*Kisses his neck.*)
   Who'd have a gun?
IAN: Me.
CATE: (*Undoes his shirt.*)
   You're in here.   70
IAN: Someone like me.
CATE: (*Kisses his chest.*)
   Why would they shoot at you?
IAN: Revenge.
CATE: (*Runs her hands down his back.*)   75
IAN: For things I've done.
CATE: (*Massages his neck.*)
   Tell me.
IAN: Tapped my phone.
CATE: (*Kisses the back of his neck.*)   80
IAN: Talk to people and I know I'm being listened to. I'm
   sorry I stopped calling you but—

CATE: (*Strokes his stomach and kisses between his shoulder blades.*)

IAN: Got angry when you said you loved me, talking soft on
85   the phone, people listening to that.

CATE: (*Kisses his back.*)
       Tell me.

IAN: In before you know it.

CATE: (*Licks his back.*)

90 IAN: Signed the Official Secrets Act, shouldn't be telling you
       this.

CATE: (*Claws and scratches his back.*)

IAN: Don't want to get you into trouble.

CATE: (*Bites his back.*)

95 IAN: Think they're trying to kill me. Served my purpose.

CATE: (*Pushes him onto his back.*)

IAN: Done the jobs they asked. Because I love this land.

CATE: (*Sucks his nipples.*)

IAN: Stood at stations, listened to conversations and given the
100   nod.

CATE: (*Undoes his trousers.*)

IAN: Driving jobs. Picking people up, disposing of bodies, the
       lot.

CATE: (*Begins to perform oral sex on* IAN.)

105 IAN: Said you were dangerous.
       So I stopped.
       Didn't want you in any danger.
       But
       Had to call you again
110   Missed
       This
       Now
       I do
       The real job
115   I
       Am
       A
       Killer

On the word 'killer' he comes.
As soon as CATE *hears the word she bites his penis as hard as she*
can.
IAN's *cry of pleasure turns into a scream of pain.*
He tries to pull away but CATE *holds on with her teeth.*
He hits her and she lets go.
IAN *lies in pain, unable to speak.*
CATE *spits frantically, trying to get every trace of him out of her*
mouth.
She goes to the bathroom and we hear her cleaning her teeth.
IAN *examines himself. He is still in one piece.*
CATE *returns.*

CATE: You should resign.
120 IAN: Don't work like that.
CATE: Will they come here?
IAN: I don't know.
CATE: (*begins to panic.*)
IAN: Don't start that again.
125 CATE: I c- c- c- c- c-
IAN: Cate, I'll shoot you myself you don't stop.
       I told you because I love you, not to scare you.
CATE: You don't.
IAN: Don't argue I do. And you love me.

CATE: No more.   130
IAN: Loved me last night.
CATE: I didn't want to do it.
IAN: Thought you liked that.
CATE: No.
IAN: Made enough noise.   135
CATE: It was hurting.
IAN: Went down on Stella all the time, didn't hurt her.
CATE: You bit me. It's still bleeding.
IAN: Is that what this is all about?
CATE: You're cruel.   140
IAN: Don't be stupid.
CATE: Stop calling me that.
IAN: You sleep with someone holding hands and kissing you
       wank me off then say we can't fuck get into bed but don't
       want me to touch you what's wrong with you Joey?   145
CATE: I'm not. You're cruel. I wouldn't shoot someone.
IAN: Pointed it at me.
CATE: Wouldn't shoot.
IAN: It's my job. I love this country. I won't see it destroyed
       by slag.   150
CATE: It's wrong to kill.
IAN: Planting bombs and killing little kiddies, that's wrong.
       That's what they do. Kids like your brother.
CATE: It's wrong.
IAN: Yes, it is.   155
CATE: No. You. Doing that.
IAN: When are you going to grow up?
CATE: I don't believe in killing.
IAN: You'll learn.
CATE: No I won't.   160
IAN: Can't always be taking it backing down letting them
       think they've got a right turn the other cheek SHIT some
       things are worth more than that have to be protected from
       shite.
CATE: I used to love you.   165
IAN: What's changed?
CATE: You.
IAN: No. Now you see me. That's all.
CATE: You're a nightmare.

She shakes.
IAN *watches a while, then hugs her.*
She is still shaking so he hugs tightly to stop her.

CATE: That hurts.   170
IAN: Sorry.

He hugs her less tightly.
He has a coughing fit.
He spits into his handkerchief and waits for the pain to subside.
Then he lights a cigarette.

IAN: How you feeling?
CATE: I ache.
IAN: (*Nods.*)
CATE: Everywhere.   175
       I stink of you.
IAN: You want a bath?

CATE *begins to cough and retch.*
She puts her fingers down her throat and produces a hair.

She holds it up and looks at IAN *in disgust. She spits.*
IAN *goes into the bathroom and turns on one of the bath taps.*
CATE *stares out of the window.*
IAN *returns.*

CATE: Looks like there's a war on.
IAN: (*Doesn't look.*)
180   Turning into Wogland.
         You coming to Leeds again?
CATE: Twenty-sixth.
IAN: Will you come and see me?
CATE: I'm going to the football.

She goes to the bathroom.
IAN *picks up the phone.*

185 IAN: Two English breakfasts, son.

He finishes the remainder of the gin.
CATE *returns.*

CATE: I can't piss. It's just blood.
IAN: Drink lots of water.
CATE: Or shit. It hurts.
IAN: It'll heal.

There is a knock at the door. They both jump.

190 CATE: DON'T ANSWER IT DON'T ANSWER IT
         DON'T ANSWER IT

She dives on the bed and puts her head under the pillow.

IAN: Cate, shut up.

He pulls the pillow off and puts the gun to her head.

CATE: Do it. Go on, shoot me. Can't be no worse than what
         you've done already. Shoot me if you want, then turn it on
195   yourself and do the world a favour.
IAN: (*Stares at her.*)
CATE: I'm not scared of you, Ian. Go on.
IAN: (*Gets off her.*)
CATE: (*Laughs.*)
200 IAN: Answer the door and suck the cunt's cock.

CATE *tries to open the door. It is locked.*
IAN *throws the key at her.*
She opens the door.
The breakfasts are outside on a tray. She brings them in.
IAN *locks the door.*
CATE *stares at the food.*

CATE: Sausages. Bacon.
IAN: Sorry. Forgot. Swap your meat for my tomatoes and
         mushrooms. And toast.
CATE: (*Begins to retch.*)
205   The smell.

IAN *takes a sausage off the plate and stuffs it in his mouth and keeps
a rasher of bacon in his hand.*
He puts the tray of food under the bed with a towel over it.

IAN: Will you stay another day?

CATE: I'm having a bath and going home.

She picks up her bag and goes into the bathroom, closing the door.
We hear the other bath tap being turned on.
There are two loud knocks at the outer door.
IAN *draws his gun, goes to the door and listens.*
The door is tried from outside. It is locked.
There are two more loud knocks.

IAN: Who's there?

Silence.
Then two more loud knocks.

IAN: Who's there?

Silence.
Then two more knocks.
IAN *looks at the door.*
Then he knocks twice.
Silence.
Then two more knocks from outside.
IAN *thinks.*
Then he knocks three times.
Silence.
Three knocks from outside.
IAN *knocks once.*
One knock from outside.
IAN *knocks twice.*
Two knocks.
IAN *puts his gun back in the holster and unlocks the door.*

IAN: (*Under his breath.*) Speak the Queen's English fucking 210
         nigger.

He opens the door.
Outside is a SOLDIER *with a sniper's rifle.*
IAN *tries to push the door shut and draw his revolver.*
The SOLDIER *pushes the door open and takes* IAN's *gun easily.*
The two stand, both surprised, staring at each other.
Eventually.

SOLDIER: What's that?

IAN *looks down and realizes he is still holding a rasher of bacon.*

IAN: Pig.

The SOLDIER *holds out his hand.*
IAN *gives him the bacon and he eats it quickly, rind and all.*
The SOLDIER *wipes his mouth.*

SOLDIER: Got any more?
IAN: No.   215
SOLDIER: Got any more?
IAN: I–
         No.
SOLDIER: Got any more?
IAN: (*Points to the tray under the bed.*)   220

The SOLDIER *bends down carefully, never taking his eyes or rifle off*
IAN, *and takes the tray from under the bed.*
He straightens up and glances down at the food.

SOLDIER: Two.
IAN: I was hungry.
SOLDIER: I bet.

The SOLDIER *sits on the edge of the bed and very quickly devours both breakfasts.*
He sighs with relief and burps.
He nods towards the bathroom.

SOLDIER: She in there?
225 IAN: Who?
SOLDIER: I can smell the sex.

(He begins to search the room.)

You a journalist?
IAN: I—
SOLDIER: Passport.
230 IAN: What for?
SOLDIER: *(Looks at him.)*
IAN: In the jacket.

The SOLDIER *is searching a chest of drawers.*
He finds a pair of CATE's *knickers and holds them up.*

SOLDIER: Hers?
IAN: *(Doesn't answer.)*
235 SOLDIER: Or yours.

(He closes his eyes and rubs them gently over his face, smelling with pleasure.)

What's she like?
IAN: *(Doesn't answer.)*
SOLDIER: Is she soft?
Is she—?
240 IAN: *(Doesn't answer.)*

The SOLDIER *puts* CATE's *knickers in his pocket and goes to the bathroom.*
He knocks on the door. No answer.
He tries the door. It is locked.
He forces it and goes in.
IAN *waits, in a panic.*
We hear the bath taps being turned off.
IAN *looks out of the window.*

IAN: Jesus Lord.

The SOLDIER *returns.*

SOLDIER: Gone. Taking a risk. Lot of bastard soldiers out there.

IAN *looks in the bathroom.* CATE *isn't there.*
The SOLDIER *looks in* IAN's *jacket pockets and takes his keys, wallet and passport.*

SOLDIER: *(Looks at* IAN's *press card.)*
245   Ian Jones.
         Journalist.
IAN: Oi.
SOLDIER: Oi.

They stare at each other.

IAN: If you've come to shoot me—
SOLDIER: *(reaches out to touch* IAN's *face but stops short of physi-* 250
    cal contact.)
IAN: You taking the piss?
SOLDIER: Me?

(He smiles.)

    Our town now.

(He stands on the bed and urinates over the pillows.)
IAN *is disgusted.*
There is a blinding light, then a huge explosion.
Blackout.
The sound of summer rain.

SCENE THREE
The hotel has been blasted by a mortar bomb.
There is a large hole in one of the walls, and everything is covered in dust which is still falling.
The SOLDIER *is unconscious, rifle still in hand.*
He has dropped IAN's *gun which lies between them.*
IAN *lies very still, eyes open.*

IAN: Mum?

Silence.
The SOLDIER *wakes and turns his eyes and rifle on* IAN *with the minimum possible movement.*
He instinctively runs his free hand over his limbs and body to check that he is still in one piece. He is.

SOLDIER: The drink.

IAN *looks around. There is a bottle of gin lying next to him with the lid off.*
He holds it up to the light.

IAN: Empty.
SOLDIER: *(Takes the bottle and drinks the last mouthful.)*
IAN: *(Chuckles.)*   5
    Worse than me.

The SOLDIER *holds the bottle up and shakes it over his mouth, catching any remaining drops.*
IAN *finds his cigarettes in his shirt pocket and lights up.*

SOLDIER: Give us a cig.
IAN: Why?
SOLDIER: 'Cause I've got a gun and you haven't.

IAN *considers the logic.*
Then takes a single cigarette out of the packet and tosses it at the SOLDIER.
The SOLDIER *picks up the cigarette and puts it in his mouth.*
He looks at IAN, *waiting for a light.*
IAN *holds out his cigarette.*
The SOLDIER *leans forward, touching the tip of his cigarette against the lit one, eyes always on* IAN.
He smokes.

SOLDIER: Never met an Englishman with a gun before, most 10
    of them don't know what a gun is. You a soldier?
IAN: Of sorts.

SOLDIER: Which side, if you can remember.

IAN: Don't know what the sides are here.

15   Don't know where . . .

(*He trails off confused, and looks at the* SOLDIER.)

    Think I might be drunk.

SOLDIER: No, It's real.

(*He picks up the revolver and examines it.*)

    Come to fight for us?

IAN: No, I—

20 SOLDIER: No, course not. English.

IAN: I'm Welsh.

SOLDIER: Sound English, fucking accent.

IAN: I live there.

SOLDIER: Foreigner?

25 IAN: English and Welsh is the same. British. I'm not an import.

SOLDIER: What's fucking Welsh, never heard of it.

IAN: Come over from God knows where have their kids and call them English they're not English born in England don't make you English.

30 SOLDIER: Welsh as in Wales?

IAN: It's attitude.

(*He turns away.*)

    Look at the state of my fucking jacket. The bitch.

SOLDIER: Your girlfriend did that, angry was she?

IAN: She's not my girlfriend.

35 SOLDIER: What, then?

IAN: Mind your fucking own.

SOLDIER: Haven't been here long have you.

IAN: So?

SOLDIER: Learn some manners, Ian.

40 IAN: Don't call me that.

SOLDIER: What shall I call you?

IAN: Nothing.

Silence.
The SOLDIER *looks at* IAN *for a very long time, saying nothing.*
IAN *is uncomfortable.*
Eventually.

IAN: What?

SOLDIER: Nothing.

Silence.
IAN *is uneasy again.*

45 IAN: My name's Ian.

SOLDIER: I
        Am
        Dying to make love
        Ian

50 IAN: (*Looks at him.*)

SOLDIER: You got a girlfriend?

IAN: (*Doesn't answer.*)

SOLDIER: I have.
    Col.

55   Fucking beautiful.

IAN: Cate-

SOLDIER: Close my eyes and think about her.
    She's—
    She's—
    She's—   60
    She's—
    She's—
    She's—
    She's—
    When was the last time you—?   65

IAN: (*Looks at him.*)

SOLDIER: When? I know it was recent, smell it, remember.

IAN: Last night. I think.

SOLDIER: Good?

IAN: Don't know. I was pissed. Probably not.   70

SOLDIER: Three of us—

IAN: Don't tell me.

SOLDIER: Went to a house just outside town. All gone. Apart from a small boy hiding in the corner. One of the others took him outside. Lay him on the ground and 75 shot him through the legs. Heard crying in the basement. Went down. Three men and four women. Called the others. They held the men while I fucked the women. Youngest was twelve. Didn't cry, just lay there. Turned her over and—Then she cried. Made her lick 80 me clean. Closed my eyes and thought of—Shot her father in the mouth. Brothers shouted. Hung them from the ceiling by their testicles.

IAN: Charming.

SOLDIER: Never done that?   85

IAN: No.

SOLDIER: Sure?

IAN: I wouldn't forget.

SOLDIER: You would.

IAN: Couldn't sleep with myself.   90

SOLDIER: What about your wife?

IAN: I'm divorced.

SOLDIER: Didn't you ever—

IAN: No.

SOLDIER: What about that girl locked herself in the bathroom. 95

IAN: (*Doesn't answer.*)

SOLDIER: Ah.

IAN: You did four in one go, I've only ever done one.

SOLDIER: You killed her?

IAN: (*Makes a move for his gun.*)   100

SOLDIER: Don't I'll have to shoot you. Then I'd be lonely.

IAN: Course I haven't.

SOLDIER: Why not, don't seem to like her very much.

IAN: I do.
    She's . . . a woman.   105

SOLDIER: So?

IAN: I've never—
    It's not—

SOLDIER: What?

IAN: (*Doesn't answer.*)   110

SOLDIER: Thought you were a soldier.

IAN: Not like that.

SOLDIER: Not like that, they're all like that.

IAN: My job-

SOLDIER: Even me. Have to be.   115
    My girl—

Not going back to her. When I go back.
She's dead, see. Fucking bastard soldier, he—

He stops.
Silence.

IAN: I'm sorry.
120 SOLDIER: Why?
IAN: It's terrible.
SOLDIER: What is?
IAN: Losing someone, a woman, like that.
SOLDIER: You know, do you?
125 IAN: I—
SOLDIER: Like what?
IAN: Like—
    you said—
    A soldier—
130 SOLDIER: You're a soldier.
IAN: I haven't—
SOLDIER: What if you were ordered to?
IAN: Can't imagine it.
SOLDIER: Imagine it.
135 IAN: (*Imagines it.*)
SOLDIER: In the line of duty. For your country. Wales.
IAN: (*Imagines harder.*)
SOLDIER: Foreign slag.
IAN: (*Imagines harder. Looks sick.*)
140 SOLDIER: Would you?
IAN: (*Nods.*)
SOLDIER: How.
IAN: Quickly. Back of the head. Bam.
SOLDIER: That's all.
145 IAN: It's enough.
SOLDIER: You think?
IAN: Yes.
SOLDIER: You never killed anyone.
IAN: Fucking have.
150 SOLDIER: No.
IAN: Don't you fucking—
SOLDIER: Couldn't talk like this. You'd know.
IAN: Know what?
SOLDIER: Exactly. You don't know.
155 IAN: Know fucking what?
SOLDIER: Stay in the dark.
IAN: What? Fucking what? What don't I know?
SOLDIER: You think—

(*He stops and smiles.*)

    I broke a woman's neck. Stabbed up between her legs,
160   on the fifth stab snapped her spine.
IAN: (*Looks sick.*)
SOLDIER: You couldn't do that.
IAN: No.
SOLDIER: You never killed.
165 IAN: Not like that.
SOLDIER: Not
    Like
    That
IAN: I'm not a torturer.
170 SOLDIER: You're close to them, gun to head. Tie them up, tell
    them what you're going to do to them, make them wait

for it, then . . . what?
IAN: Shoot them.
SOLDIER: You haven't got a clue.
IAN: What then?   175
SOLDIER: You never fucked a man before you killed him?
IAN: No.
SOLDIER: Or after?
IAN: Course not.
SOLDIER: Why not?   180
IAN: What for, I'm not queer.
SOLDIER: Col, they buggered her. Cut her throat. Hacked her
    ears and nose off, nailed them to the front door.
IAN: Enough.
SOLDIER: Ever seen anything like that?   185
IAN: Stop.
SOLDIER: Not in photos?
IAN: Never.
SOLDIER: Some journalist, that's your job.
IAN: What?   190
SOLDIER: Proving it happened. I'm here, got no choice. But
    you. You should be telling people.
IAN: No one's interested.
SOLDIER: You can do something, for me—
IAN: No.   195
SOLDIER: Course you can.
IAN: I can't do anything.
SOLDIER: Try.
IAN: I write . . . stories. That's all. Stories. This isn't a story
    anyone wants to hear.   200
SOLDIER: Why not?
IAN: (*Takes one of the newspapers from the bed and reads.*)
    'Kinky car dealer Richard Morris drove two teenage
    prostitutes into the country, tied them naked to fences
    and whipped them with a belt before having sex.   205
    Morris, from Sheffield, was jailed for three years for un-
    lawful sexual intercourse with one of the girls, aged
    thirteen.'

(*He tosses the paper away.*)

    Stories.
SOLDIER: Doing to them what they done to us, what good is   210
    that? At home I'm clean. Like it never happened.
    Tell them you saw me.
    Tell them . . . you saw me.
IAN: It's not my job.
SOLDIER: Whose is it?   215
IAN: I'm a home journalist, for Yorkshire. I don't cover for-
    eign affairs.
SOLDIER: Foreign affairs, what you doing here?
IAN: I do other stuff. Shootings and rapes and kids getting
    fiddled by queer priests and schoolteachers. Not soldiers 220
    screwing each other for a patch of land. It has to be . . .
    personal. Your girlfriend, she's a story. Soft and clean. Not
    you. Filthy, like the wogs. No joy in a story about blacks
    who gives a shit? Why bring you to light?
SOLDIER: You don't know fuck all about me.   225
    I went to school.
    I made love with Col.
    Bastards killed her, now I'm here.
    Now I'm here.

(*He pushes the rifle in* IAN's *face.*)

230   Turn over, Ian.
IAN: Why?
SOLDIER: Going to fuck you.
IAN: No.
SOLDIER: Kill you then.
235 IAN: Fine.
SOLDIER: See. Rather be shot than fucked and shot.
IAN: Yes.
SOLDIER: And now you agree with anything I say.

He kisses IAN *very tenderly on the lips.*
They stare at each other.

SOLDIER: You smell like her. Same cigarettes.

The SOLDIER *turns* IAN *over with one hand.*
He holds the revolver to IAN's *head with the other.*
He pulls down IAN's *trousers, undoes his own and rapes him—eyes*
closed and smelling IAN's *hair.*
The SOLDIER *is crying his heart out.*
IAN's *face registers pain but he is silent.*
When the SOLDIER *has finished he pulls up his trousers and pushes*
the revolver up IAN's *anus.*

240 SOLDIER: Bastard pulled the trigger on Col.
        What's it like?
IAN: (*Tries to answer. He can't.*)
SOLDIER: (*Withdraws the gun and sits next to* IAN.)
        You never fucked by a man before?
245 IAN: (*Doesn't answer.*)
SOLDIER: Didn't think so. It's nothing. Saw thousands of
        people packing into trucks like pigs trying to leave
        town. Women threw their babies on board hoping
        someone would look after them. Crushing each other to
250   death. Insides of people's heads came out of their eyes.
        Saw a child most of his face blown off, young girl I
        fucked hand up inside her trying to claw my liquid out,
        starving man eating his dead wife's leg. Gun was born
        here and won't die. Can't get tragic about your arse.
255   Don't think your Welsh arse is different to any other arse
        I fucked. Sure you haven't got any more food, I'm
        fucking starving.
IAN: Are you going to kill me?
SOLDIER: Always covering your own arse.

The SOLDIER *grips* IAN's *head in his hands.*
He puts his mouth over one of IAN's *eyes, sucks it out, bites it off*
and eats it.
He does the same to the other eye.

260 SOLDIER: He ate her eyes.
        Poor bastard.
        Poor love.
        Poor fucking bastard.

Blackout.
The sound of autumn rain.

SCENE FOUR
The same.
The SOLDIER *lies close to* IAN, *the revolver in his hand.*
He has blown his own brain out.

CATE *enters through the bathroom door, soaking wet and carrying a baby.*
She steps over the SOLDIER *with a glance.*
Then she sees IAN.

CATE: You're a nightmare.
IAN: Cate?
CATE: It won't stop.
IAN: Catie? You here?
CATE: Everyone in town is crying.   5
IAN: Touch me.
CATE: Soldiers have taken over.
IAN: They've won?
CATE: Most people gave up.
IAN: You seen Matthew?   10
CATE: No.
IAN: Will you tell him for me?
CATE: He isn't here.
IAN: Tell him—
    Tell him—   15
CATE: No.
IAN: Don't know what to tell him.
    I'm cold.
    Tell him—
    You here?   20
CATE: A woman gave me her baby.
IAN: You come for me, Catie? Punish me or rescue me makes
    no difference I love you Cate tell him for me do it for me
    touch me Cate.
CATE: Don't know what to do with it.   25
IAN: I'm cold.
CATE: Keeps crying.
IAN: Tell him—
CATE: I CAN'T.
IAN: Will you stay with me, Cate?   30
CATE: No.
IAN: Why not?
CATE: I have to go back soon.
IAN: Shaun know what we did?
CATE: No.   35
IAN: Better tell him.
CATE: No.
IAN: He'll know. Even if you don't.
CATE: How?
IAN: Smell it. Soiled goods. Don't want it, not when you can   40
    have someone clean.
CATE: What's happened to your eyes?
IAN: I need you to stay, Cate. Won't be for long.
CATE: Do you know about babies?
IAN: No.   45
CATE: What about Matthew?
IAN: He's twenty-four.
CATE: When he was born.
IAN: They shit and cry. Hopeless.
CATE: Bleeding.   50
IAN: Will you touch me?
CATE: No.
IAN: So I know you're here.
CATE: You can hear me.
IAN: Won't hurt you, I promise.   55
CATE: (*Goes to him slowly and touches the top of his head.*)
IAN: Help me.
CATE: (*Strokes his hair.*)

IAN: Be dead soon anyway, Cate.
60   And it hurts.
    Help me to—
    Help me—
    Finish
    It
65 CATE: (*Withdraws her hand.*)
    IAN: Catie?
    CATE: Got to get something for Baby to eat.
    IAN: Won't find anything.
    CATE: May as well look.
70 IAN: Fucking bastards ate it all.
    CATE: It'll die.
    IAN: Needs its mother's milk.
    CATE: Ian.
    IAN: Stay.
75   Nowhere to go, where are you going to go?
        Bloody dangerous on your own, look at me.
        Safer here with me.

    CATE *considers.*
    Then sits down with the baby some distance from IAN.
    He relaxes when he hears her sit.
    CATE *rocks the baby.*

    IAN: Not as bad as all that, am I?
    CATE: (*Looks at him.*)
80 IAN: Will you help me, Catie?
    CATE: How.
    IAN: Find my gun?

    CATE *thinks.*
    Then gets up and searches around, baby in arms.
    She sees the revolver in the SOLDIER's *hand and stares at it for some time.*

    IAN: Found it?
    CATE: No.

    She takes the revolver from the SOLDIER *and fiddles with it.*
    It springs open and she stares in at the bullets.
    She removes them and closes the gun.

85 IAN: That it?
    CATE: Yes.
    IAN: Can I have it?
    CATE: I don't think so.
    IAN: Catie.
90 CATE: What?
    IAN: Come on.
    CATE: Don't tell me what to do.
    IAN: I'm not, love. Can you keep that baby quiet.
    CATE: It's not doing anything. It's hungry.
95 IAN: We're all bloody hungry, don't shoot myself I'll starve to
        death.
    CATE: It's wrong to kill yourself.
    IAN: No it's not.
    CATE: God wouldn't like it.
100 IAN: There isn't one.
    CATE: How do you know?
    IAN: No God. No Father Christmas. No fairies. No Narnia.
        No fucking nothing.
    CATE: Got to be something.
105 IAN: Why?

CATE: Doesn't make sense otherwise.
IAN: Don't be fucking stupid, doesn't make sense anyway. No
    reason for there to be a God just because it would be bet-
    ter if there was.
CATE: Thought you didn't want to die.   110
IAN: I can't see.
CATE: My brother's got blind friends. You can't give up.
IAN: Why not?
CATE: It's weak.
IAN: I know you want to punish me, trying to make me live.   115
CATE: I don't.
IAN: Course you fucking do, I would. There's people I'd love
    to suffer but they don't, they die and that's it.
CATE: What if you're wrong?
IAN: I'm not.   120
CATE: But if.
IAN: I've seen dead people. They're dead. They're not some-
    where else, they're dead.
CATE: What about people who've seen ghosts?
IAN: What about them? Imagining it. Or making it up or   125
    wishing the person was still alive.
CATE: People who've died and come back say they've seen
    tunnels and lights—
IAN: Can't die and come back. That's not dying, it's fainting.
    When you die, it's the end.   130
CATE: I believe in God.
IAN: Everything's got a scientific explanation.
CATE: No.
IAN: Give me my gun.
CATE: What are you going to do?   135
IAN: I won't hurt you.
CATE: I know.
IAN: End it.
    Got to, Cate, I'm ill.
    Just speeding it up a bit.   140
CATE: (*Thinks hard.*)
IAN: Please.
CATE: (*Gives him the gun.*)
IAN: (*Takes the gun and puts it in his mouth.*
    He takes it out again.)   145
    Don't stand behind me.

He puts the gun back in his mouth.
He pulls the trigger. The gun clicks, empty.
He shoots again. And again and again and again.
He takes the gun out of his mouth.

IAN: Fuck.
CATE: Fate, see. You're not meant to do it. God—
IAN: The cunt.

(*He throws the gun away in despair.*)

CATE: (*Rocks the baby and looks down at it.*)   150
    Oh no.
IAN: What.
CATE: It's dead.
IAN: Lucky bastard.
CATE: (*Bursts out laughing, unnaturally, hysterically, uncontrollably.* 155
    She laughs and laughs and laughs and laughs and laughs.)
Blackout.
The sound of heavy winter rain.

SCENE FIVE

The same.
CATE is burying the baby under the floor.
She looks around and finds two pieces of wood.
She rips the lining out of IAN's jacket and binds the wood together in a cross which she sticks into the floor.
She collects a few of the scattered flowers and places them under the cross.

CATE: I don't know her name.
IAN: Don't matter. No one's going to visit.
CATE: I was supposed to look after her.
IAN: Can bury me next to her soon. Dance on my grave.
5 CATE: Don't feel no pain or know nothing you shouldn't know—
IAN: Cate?
CATE: Shh.
IAN: What you dong?
10 CATE: Praying. Just in case.
IAN: Will you pray for me?
CATE: No.
IAN: When I'm dead, not now.
CATE: No point when you're dead.
15 IAN: You're praying for her.
CATE: She's baby.
IAN: So?
CATE: Innocent.
IAN: Can't you forgive me?
20 CATE: Don't see bad things or go bad places—
IAN: She's dead, Cate.
CATE: Or meet anyone who'll do bad things.
IAN: She won't, Cate, she's dead.
CATE: Amen.

(*She starts to leave.*)

25 IAN: Where you going?
CATE: I'm hungry.
IAN: Cate, it's dangerous. There's no food.
CATE: Can get some off a soldier.
IAN: How?
30 CATE: (*Doesn't answer.*)
IAN: Don't do that.
CATE: Why not?
IAN: That's not you.
CATE: I'm hungry.
35 IAN: I know so am I.
    But.
    I'd rather—
    It's not—
    Please, Cate.
40   I'm blind.
CATE: I'm hungry.

(*She goes.*)

IAN: Cate? Catie?
    If you get some food—
    Fuck.

Darkness.
Light.
IAN masturbating.

IAN: cunt cunt cunt cunt cunt cunt cunt cunt cunt cunt 45
    cunt

Darkness.
Light.
IAN strangling himself with his bare hands.
Darkness.
Light.
IAN shitting.
And then trying to clean it up with newspaper.
Darkness.
Light.
IAN laughing hysterically.
Darkness
Light.
IAN having a nightmare.
Darkness.
Light.
IAN crying, huge bloody tears.
He is hugging the SOLDIER's body for comfort.
Darkness.
Light.
IAN lying very still, weak with hunger.
Darkness.
Light.
IAN tears the cross out of the ground, rips up the floor and lifts the baby's body out.
He eats the baby.
He puts the remains back in the baby's blanket and puts the bundle back in the hole.
A beat, then he climbs in after it and lies down, head poking out of the floor.
He dies with relief.
It starts to rain on him, coming through the roof.
Eventually.

IAN: Shit.

CATE enters carrying some bread, a large sausage and a bottle of gin.
There is blood seeping from between her legs.

CATE: You're sitting under a hole.
IAN: I know.
CATE: Get wet.   50
IAN: Aye.
CATE: Stupid bastard.

She pulls a sheet off the bed and wraps it around her.
She sits next to IAN's head.
She eats her fill of the sausage and bread, then washes it down with gin.
IAN listens.
She feeds IAN with the remaining food.
She pours gin in IAN's mouth.
She finishes feeding IAN and sits apart from him huddled for warmth.
She drinks the gin.
She sucks her thumb.
Silence.
It rains.

IAN: Thank you.

Blackout.

David Hare

Sir David Hare (b. 1947) is one of Britain's most visible and accomplished playwrights and has long been engaged in political theater. After studying at Jesus College, Cambridge University, Hare co-founded the Portable Theatre Company, where he worked with playwrights Howard Brenton and Snoo Wilson, and with Max Stafford-Clark, the co-founder of one of the most influential theater companies of the 1970s and 1980s, Joint Stock Theatre Group. In the course of his long career as a playwright, Hare has mastered a range of dramatic and theatrical styles, ranging from the epic theater of *Fanshen* (1975) to the political realism of *A Map of the World* (1983) and *Saigon: Year of the Cat* (1983), to the lyrical irony of *Plenty* (1978), to the savage cartoon-like parody of *Pravda* (written with Howard Brenton, 1985), to the monologue *Via Dolorosa* (1998), about his encounter with Israeli-Palestinian politics on a visit to Israel. Nonetheless, Hare is best known for his complex interrogations of contemporary British life: the postwar malaise of *Plenty,* the critique of Thatcherism in *The Secret Rapture* (1988), the series of plays on British public institutions—*Racing Demon* (1990), on the Church of England; *Murmuring Judges* (1991), on the legal system; *Absence of War* (1993), on the Labour party—and more recently, *The Permanent Way* (2003), on the decline of British Rail, and *Stuff Happens* (2004), on the negotiations between the United States and the United Kingdom on their joint plans to declare war on Iraq. At the same time, Hare has been celebrated for the deft character studies that stand at the center of his work, particularly in plays such as *Skylight* (1995) and *Amy's View* (1997). Hare is the author of over thirty plays, screenplays (*Weatherby* [1985], *Paris by Night* [1988], *Damage* [1992]), and adaptations (notably of Chekhov's *Platonov* and *Ivanov,* and of Brecht's *Mother Courage and Her Children*). He was knighted in 1998.

STUFF HAPPENS

Stuff Happens opened at Britain's Royal National Theatre on September 1, 2004, about 18 months after United States, United Kingdom, and coalition forces invaded Iraq. As Hare notes at the outset of the play, much of the action is composed of information given in public or reported widely in the press. At the same time, Hare's play is hardly a documentary. Instead, like many of Hare's plays, *Stuff Happens* focuses on a central character; in this case it is Colin Powell, the U.S. Secretary of State, and the extent to which his efforts to promote diplomacy were outmaneuvered and finally overcome by an early and apparently arbitrary decision to invade Iraq. After briefly introducing the play's central characters—Colin Powell, Condoleeza Rice, Donald Rumsfeld, Paul Wolfowitz, George W. Bush, Tony Blair, Jack Straw, David Manning, Dominique de Villepin, Hans Blix—the play traces the course of the plan of invasion: the decision to turn arms, attention, and resources away from pursuing Osama bin Laden; the desire to ensure that bin Laden would be captured by American rather than coalition forces; the early pressure from Cheney, Rice, Rumsfeld, and Wolfowitz to invade Iraq; the flimsiness of the evidence that Iraq was manufacturing weapons of mass destruction; the systematic efforts to undermine the United Nations, compromise the authority of the Security Council, and coerce the inspection efforts led by Hans Blix; the callousness with which the political cost of Blair's contribution to the alliance was dismissed; and, finally, the extent to which Powell's military experience and commitment to negotiation were simply sold out. Although the trajectory of this history is well known, to some people Hare's view may seem merely to articulate a "European" perspective, one in which Europe's great sympathy for the United States in the wake of the attack on the World Trade Center was itself sacrificed in favor of the Bush administration's go-it-alone pursuit of an arguably unjustified and unnecessary war: "On September 11, America changed. Yes, it got much stupider," as a British tourist in New York remarks. Hare's condemnation of the sys-

George W. Bush in his flight suit, prematurely announcing the successful completion of the war in Iraq, in the Royal National Theatre production of *Stuff Happens*, 2004.

tematic deception with which the war was imagined and prosecuted, and of the hubris with which the rest of world opinion was simply ignored, certainly represents an attitude widely held outside and inside the United States. Yet Hare's drama is far from political satires like David Edgar's Shakespearean parody of Richard Nixon, *Dick Deterred*. Instead, *Stuff Happens* trains a skeptical eye on the human process of political decision-making, particularly on the conflict between alternative world views, the conflict between an imaginative, informed, morally committed desire to avoid war and the attraction of military conflict for short-term political advantage. Characteristically enough, the play's moral ballast is evoked in a brief discussion between Colin Powell and Bush:

POWELL: Maybe because my whole life has been in the army I'm less impressed than some people
    by the use of force. I see it for what it is.
BUSH: What is it?
POWELL: Failure

STUFF HAPPENS

David Hare

IN MEMORIAM
MARY, HELEN, RORY

AUTHOR'S NOTE

Stuff Happens is a history play, which happens to center on very recent history. The events within it have been authenticated from multiple sources, both private and public. What happened happened. Nothing in the narrative is knowingly untrue. Scenes of direct address quote people verbatim. When the doors close on the world's leaders and on their entourages, then I have used my imagination. This is surely a play, not a documentary, and driven, I hope, by its themes as much as by its characters and story.

I must thank all those people—some at the heart of these events, others to the side—who generously gave so much of their time and their knowledge to help my understanding. I owe much to Dr Christopher Turner, visiting scholar at Columbia University, who assisted me throughout. No bland formulation of thanks can do justice to the depth and detail of his research.

CHARACTERS

GEORGE W. BUSH
LAURA BUSH
DICK CHENEY
COLIN POWELL
CONDOLEEZZA RICE
DONALD RUMSFELD
GEORGE TENET
PAUL WOLFOWITZ
PAUL O'NEILL
MICHAEL GERSON
MARK DAYTON
DAN BARTLETT
JOHN NEGROPONTE
JOHN MCCAIN
JESSICA STERN
DAVID KAY
ARI FLEISCHER
INTERVIEWER

TONY BLAIR
JACK STRAW
DAVID MANNING
JONATHAN POWELL
ALASTAIR CAMPBELL
RICHARD DEARLOVE
PHILIP BASSETT

TREVOR MCDONALD
ALAN SIMPSON
JEREMY GREENSTOCK
GEOFF HOON
ROBIN COOK

JACQUES CHIRAC
DOMINIQUE DE VILLEPIN
MAURICE GOURDAULT-MONTAGNE
JEAN-DAVID LEVITTE
GÉRARD ERRERA

SADDAM HUSSEIN
GENERAL HASSAN MUHAMMAD AMIN

HANS BLIX
KOFI ANNAN
IGOR IVANOV
SERGEI LAVROV
MOHAMMED EIBARADE
RICARDO LAGOS
YO-YO MA

VIEWPOINTS

Other parts played by members of the company

STUFF HAPPENS

All of us have heard this term "preventive war" since the earliest days of Hitler. In this day and time . . . I don't believe there is such a thing; and frankly I wouldn't even listen to anyone seriously that came in and talked about such a thing.

Dwight Eisenhower

It is useless to attempt to reason a man out of a thing he was never reasoned into.

Jonathan Swift

ACT ONE

ONE

As the audience arrive, the cast are already assembling onstage. Then the lights change and one of the ACTORs speaks.

AN ACTOR: The Inevitable is what will seem to happen to you purely by chance.
The Real is what will strike you as really absurd.
Unless you are certain you are dreaming, it is certainly a dream of your own.
Unless you exclaim—'There must be some mistake'—you must be mistaken.

5

TWO

Another ACTOR *steps forward.*

AN ACTOR: Stuff. Happens. The response of Donald Rums-feld, the American Secretary of Defense, when asked to comment on the widespread looting and pillage that fol-lowed the American conquest of Baghdad—Friday, April
5   11th 2003:

JOURNALIST: What's your response, sir? Mr Secretary, how do you respond to the news of looting and pillage in Bagh-dad?

RUMSFELD: I've seen the pictures. I've seen those pictures. I
10   could take pictures in any city in America. Think what's happened in our cities when we've had riots, and prob-lems, and looting. Stuff happens! But in terms of what's going on in that country, it is a fundamental misunder-standing to see those images over and over and over again
15   of some boy walking out with a vase and say, 'Oh, my goodness, you didn't have a plan.' That's nonsense. They know what they're doing, and they're doing a terrific job. And it's untidy, and freedom's untidy, and free people are free to make mistakes and commit crimes and do bad
20   things. They're also free to live their lives and do wonder-ful things, and that's what's going to happen here.

THREE

A line of civilians and soldiers head for a helicopter on a rooftop to evacuate Saigon.

AN ACTOR: So where to begin? To take the story back—April 25th 1975, the unforgettable event: the fall of Saigon. At last there are limits to American power.

COLIN POWELL *steps forward.*

POWELL: In Vietnam I learned a certain attitude, a certain dis-
5   trust . . .

AN ACTOR: Major Colin Powell is pulled out of Vietnam six years earlier. By his own description, a serving soldier, schooled in obedience . . .

POWELL: The army is the most democratic institution in
10   America.

AN ACTOR: November 1968: Powell is in a helicopter which falls to the ground, in his words, 'like an elevator with a snapped cable'.

POWELL: After Vietnam, many in my generation vowed that
15   when our turn came to call the shots, we would not qui-etly acquiesce in half-hearted warfare for half-baked rea-sons. Politicians start wars; soldiers fight and die in them.

AN ACTOR: He is awarded the Legion of Merit and evolves what becomes known as the Powell doctrine:

20   POWELL: War should be the politics of last resort.

DONALD RUMSFELD, *peppy, in trifocals, steps forward.*

AN ACTOR: Also in the seventies, Donald Rumsfeld, one-time champion wrestler, University of Chicago, is an assistant to Richard Nixon.

RUMSFELD: I'd always worried about politicians who spent
25   most of their time getting ready to *be* something as opposed

to doing something. And I questioned whether that was a great way to live a life, getting ready as opposed to doing.

AN ACTOR: One friend says of Rumsfeld:

RUMSFELD'S FIRST FRIEND: When you play squash with him, you are lucky not to have your head taken off with his   30 racquet. The court is a finite place. If you are between him and the wall, Rumsfeld always fires away.

AN ACTOR: A second friend says:

RUMSFELD'S SECOND FRIEND: In locker-room terms, Don is a towel-snapper.   35

DICK CHENEY, *rock-hard, bland, steps forward.*

AN ACTOR: In the same White House, jostling for position, is the young Dick Cheney, who has achieved a total of five student deferments in order to avoid being drafted to Vietnam.

CHENEY: I had other priorities in the sixties than military ser-   40 vice.

AN ACTOR: Cheney proves himself willing to take on re-sponsibilities others shirk.

CHENEY: Memo from Dick Cheney, October 12th 1974. We will be unable in the short term to fix the drainage prob-   45 lem in the sink in the first-floor bathroom. The White House plumbing is very old and we have had the General Services Administration working for some time to figure out how to improve this problem.

AN ACTOR: When Cheney moves into elected politics, he is   50 already uncompromising.

CHENEY: I never met a weapons system I didn't vote for.

CONDOLEEZZA RICE, *splendid, always alone, steps forward.*

AN ACTOR: At the same time, at Stanford University, a min-ister's daughter from Birmingham, Alabama, Condoleezza Rice, is choosing between a professional music career or a   55 life in academia studying the Soviet bloc.

RICE: Like most Americans I listened with some skepticism to the Cold War claim that America was a 'beacon of democracy'. My ancestors were property—a fraction of a man. Women were not included in those immortal con-   60 stitutional phrases concerning the right of the people 'in the course of human events' to choose who would rule.

AN ACTOR: When asked by Yo-Yo Ma:

YO-YO MA: Who is your favourite composer?

RICE: Brahms.   65

YO-YO MA: Why? Why Brahms?

RICE: He's passionate without being sentimental.

YO-YO MA: Do you think it's also this irresolution in Brahms, the tension that is never resolved?

AN ACTOR: In her office Rice keeps two mirrors, so she can   70 see her back as well as her front.

PAUL WOLFOWITZ, *suited, intent, steps forward.*

At another university, a Yale professor, Paul Wolfowitz, spends the nineteen seventies chewing over the implica-tions of the involvement in Vietnam which he describes as:

WOLFOWITZ: An over-expenditure of American power.   75

AN ACTOR: An ex-maths whiz, Wolfowitz is in love with the idea of national greatness.

892   UNIT V • MODERN EUROPE

WOLFOWITZ: I focus on geo-strategic issues. I consider my-
self conceptual. I am willing to re-examine entire precepts
80   of US foreign policy.
AN ACTOR: One colleague remarks:
COLLEAGUE: The word 'hawk' doesn't do Wolfowitz justice.
What about velociraptor?

TONY BLAIR, *direct, vigorous, steps forward.*

AN ACTOR: At the same time, in England, a fledgling lawyer,
85   just down from Oxford, is recovering from the sudden,
premature death of his mother and beginning a relationship with another lawyer in the same chambers.
BLAIR: It was late before I had any politics at all.
AN ACTOR: A friend remarks:
90   BLAIR'S FRIEND: You'd be at a party and you'd turn round
and find that Tony had gone. He'd slipped away a couple
of hours before. You'd find he was getting up at five
o'clock to finish an essay.
AN ACTOR: Fired up by an original mix of theology and so-
95   cial duty, Blair will become Britain's youngest Labour MP.
BLAIR: I particularly resent the assumption that if you find
Neanderthal elements in the Labour Party, you have
found the real party.
AN ACTOR: He refuses to list his early positions in *Who's Who.*
100   BLAIR: I do not regard being a Shadow Cabinet front-bench
spokesman as a real job. I did not join the Labour Party to
join a party of protest. I joined it as a party of government
and I will make sure that it is a party of government.

KOFI ANNAN, *gentle, imposing, steps forward.*

AN ACTOR: In the nineteen seventies, Kofi Annan, the son of
105   a Fanti tribal chief, whose name means—
ANNAN: Born on a Friday.
AN ACTOR: —is working as Managing Director of the Ghanaian Tourist Development Company, operating duty-free
shops at the Kotoka International Airport, Accra.
110   ANNAN: I wanted to make a contribution to Ghana but I
found myself constantly fighting the military, so I went
back to the UN.
AN ACTOR: His keen sense of the possible, Annan says, comes
from watching the Ghanaian struggle for independence.
115   ANNAN: I feel profoundly African, my roots are deeply
African.
AN ACTOR: Most people are drawn to him by the timbre of
voice, like an amplified whisper:
ANNAN: Imagine a pool of fresh, clear water. Beyond the
120   pool, there are some steps, and you are going down the
steps . . .

HANS BLIX, *with an air of mild amusement, steps forward.*

AN ACTOR: And finally, in Sweden, a graduate of Uppsala
university, Hans Blix, is finding his way in Liberal Party
politics.
125   BLIX: I was an amateur actor when I was a student. Theatre
teaches you the value of collaboration, of getting on with
other people. As well, of course, as being damned enjoyable.
AN ACTOR: Blix is already developing an attitude to life
which Colin Powell will one day find praiseworthy.

POWELL: He's as reliable as a Volvo.   130
BLIX: Being aware that one of Powell's favourite hobbies is
working on Volvo engines, I took this as praise.

The eight central characters step forward.

AN ACTOR: These are the actors, these are the men and
women who will play parts in a defining drama of the
new century. And at their head is a snappish young man,   135
seeking his fortune in the oil-rich Permian Basin of West
Texas, who will, one day, like forty-six per cent of his fellow Americans, say he has been born again.

BUSH *steps among them.*

BUSH: My faith frees me. Frees me to put the problem of the
moment in proper perspective. Frees me to make deci-   140
sions which others might not like. Frees me to enjoy life
and not worry about what comes next.
You know I had a drinking problem. Right now I should
be in a bar in Texas, not in the Oval Office. There is only
one reason I am in the Oval Office and not a bar. I found   145
God. I am here because of the power of prayer.
AN ACTOR: The elder son of a Kennebunkport dynasty,
George W. Bush is considered the joke of the family, beside his more favoured brother Jeb. He only enters politics
at the age of forty-seven.   150
BUSH: I could not be governor if I did not believe in a divine
plan which supersedes all human plans.
AN ACTOR: When he runs for President, he observes:
BUSH: I feel like God wants me to run for President. I can't
explain it, but I sense my country is going to need me.   155
Something is going to happen and at that time my country is going to need me. I know it won't be easy, on me or
on my family, but God wants me to do it.
AN ACTOR: His Deputy Under-Secretary for Defense will
observe: 160
LT GENERAL: Why is this man in the White House? The ma-
jority of Americans did not vote for him. Why is he there?
And I tell you this morning that he's in the White House
because God put him there for a time such as this.
AN ACTOR: Bush will lose the popular vote by a margin of   165
539,898. Upon his taking up office, he will observe:
BUSH: I'm the commander—see, I don't need to explain. I
don't need to explain why I say things. That's the interesting thing about being the President. Maybe somebody
needs to explain to me why they say something. But I   170
don't feel like I owe anybody an explanation.

FOUR

BUSH, *fastidiously punctual, is already in place, sitting alone at the
head of a torpedo-shaped table.*

AN ACTOR: The new administration hits the ground running.
Ten days after his inauguration, on January 30th 2001,
President Bush presides at a meeting of the National Se-
curity Council for the first time.

BUSH *is joined by a group including* POWELL, CHENEY, RUMSFELD,
TENET, RICE, O'NEILL *and a rank of generals. Behind, everyone has
deputies.*

5   BUSH: I believe we all have a piece of paper. This first meeting, we take the Middle East. Condi?
RICE: If I can express what the President is feeling, we wish
to start by sharply differentiating ourselves from the previous administration. President Clinton's attempts to bro-
10   ker a deal between the Israelis and the Palestinians not
only took up a huge amount of time, they also left this
country looking weak. The President's view is that the
time has come to tilt back towards Israel. You'll say, sir, if I
misrepresent you?

BUSH *says nothing.*

15   CHENEY: Please continue.
RICE: The President feels that the fortunes of the region need
to be decided by the players themselves. This present administration isn't going to take on problems it knows it
can't solve.
20   BUSH: Anybody here met Sharon?

COLIN POWELL *lifts a hand.*

POWELL: I've met him. I know him.
BUSH: I want to take the guy at face value. With Sharon we
have this policy: we don't go by past reputation.
RICE: The President feels very strongly that we're a new ad-
25   ministration. The relationship should be judged not by
how it's been in the past but how it proceeds.
BUSH: Sharon flew me in a helicopter over the Palestinian
camps. Looked real bad down there.

There is a short silence.

I think this is one we want to get out of.

There is another short silence.

30   RICE: Any comments?
POWELL: If I may, sir.

They all look at POWELL.

I don't need to give a lecture about the intensity of feelings in the Middle East. This is a problem with deep historical roots. We're not prisoners of history, but on the
35   other hand we can't pretend history never happened.
RUMSFELD: What's your point?
POWELL: On the ground there's a conflict. Left to himself,
Sharon's instincts are always to rack up that conflict—and
always by military means. If we disengage, the risk is, we
40   unleash Sharon. The consequences of that will be dire for
the Palestinians.
BUSH: Well, maybe that's what's needed. Maybe that's the best
way to get things back in balance.

There's a silence.

You know, sometimes, in my experience, a real show of
45   strength by just one side can clarify things. It can make
things really clear.

POWELL *looks at him a moment.*

Now let's move on. Iraq.

O'NEILL: Iraq?
AN ACTOR: Paul O'Neill. Secretary of the Treasury.
O'NEILL: Iraq?   50

But TENET *is already unfurling a large aerial photograph onto the
table.*

RICE: Yeah, that's right, we're going to have a briefing. The
CIA Director's going to brief us, get us up to speed on the
latest intelligence.
AN ACTOR: George Tenet. Director, CIA.
TENET: I'm going to ask you all to take a look at this photo-   55
graph.
RICE: The real danger to the region . . .
TENET: If we can all study this photograph . . .
RICE: Correctly analysed, when you correctly analyse the re-
gion, the real threat is destabilization.   60
TENET: Here's the photograph.
RICE: And where's that going to come from? It's going to
come from Saddam Hussein.
TENET: I hope everyone can see the photograph.
RICE: I think we ought to keep our eye on that.   65
TENET: There's the railroad, there are the tracks . . . look over
here and you'll see the trucks coming in . . .
RUMSFELD: There's the trucks . . .
TENET: There's the water-cooler. This was taken by surveil-
lance planes, so the quality is kind of grainy . . .   70

CHENEY *signals to military deputies sitting behind.*

CHENEY: Everyone come see this. You don't want to miss this.
RUMSFELD: It's grainy, but you can see . . .
TENET: This looks to us . . .
RUMSFELD: You can see clearly . . .
TENET: I think the CIA believes . . .   75
RUMSFELD: Even I can see, and I'm nearly seventy . . .
TENET: This might well be a plant which produces either
chemical or biological materials for weapons manufac-
ture.

Everyone is crowded round the photograph.

BUSH: Yeah, Yeah.   80
RICE: Everyone see?
O'NEILL: I can see. But—I'm asking, I'm just asking: I've seen
an awful lot of factories round the world that look an aw-
ful lot like this. What's the evidence, what's the evidence
of what this factory's producing?   85
TENET: Well, it's rhythm.
O'NEILL: Rhythm?
TENET: Rhythm of shipment. Round the clock. In and out of
the plant. Trucks coming and going all night. The rhythm
is consistent. Look, let's be clear: I'm not saying it is, I'm   90
not saying they are . . .
RUMSFELD: You're not saying it's not.
TENET: I'm not.
RUMSFELD: He's not saying anything.
TENET: Not quite.   95
RUMSFELD: He's from the CIA.

They all laugh.

TENET: There is no confirming intelligence, no, that they are definitely producing chemical or biological weapons. I am not claiming that. I'm saying, 'Look at the photo—look at 100 it—and what you will see is a factory clearly consistent.' And if they were producing such weapons—*if*—if they were, if such weapons were being produced, then this—seen here—would be the kind of factory, this looks just like the factory from which such weapons would come.

There is a silence.

105 BUSH: We need to know more about this. We need to know more about the weapons.

FIVE

An angry British Journalist appears.

JOURNALIST: The absurdity of it. The absurdity and the irrelevance. The idea of discussing even . . . a historical event, an invasion already more than a year old. A country groaning under a dictator, its people oppressed, liberated
5 at last from a twenty-five year tyranny—and freed. Free on the streets, and free one day to vote.

How obscene it is, how decadent, to give your attention not to the now, not to the liberation, not to the people freed, but to the relentless archaic discussion of the
10 *manner* of the liberation. Was it lawful? Was it not? How was it done? What were the details of its doing? Whose views were overridden? Whose views condoned?

Do I like the people who did it? Are they my kind of people? Hey—are they stupider than me?
15 How spoiled, how indulged we are to discuss the manner—oh yes, we discuss the manner, late into the night, candles guttering, our faces sweating, reddening with wine and hatred—but the act itself—the thing done—the splendid thing done—freedom given to peo-
20 ple who were not free—this thing is ignored, preferring as we do to fight among ourselves—our own disputes, our own resentment of each other elevated way above the needs of the victims. 'I trust Blair/I don't.' 'I like Bush/I don't.' 'Bush is stupid/Bush is clever.' This obses-
25 sion with ourselves! How Western we are. From what height of luxury and excess we look down to condemn the exact style in which even a little was given to those who had nothing.

Saddam Hussein attacked every one of his neighbours
30 except Jordan. Imagine, if you will, if you are able, a dictator in Europe, murdering his own people, attacking his neighbours, killing half a million people for no other offence but proximity. Do you really then imagine, hand on heart, that the finer feelings of the international commu-
35 nity, the exact procedures of the United Nations would need to be tested, would the finer points of sovereignty detain us, before we rose, as a single force, to overthrow the offender? Would we ask, faced with the bodies, faced with the gas, faced with the ditches and the murders,
40 would we really stop to say, 'Can we do this?' What is the word, then, for those of us in the West who apply one standard to ourselves, and another to others? What is the word for those who claim to love democracy and yet who will not fight to extend democracy to Arabs as well?

A people hitherto suffering now suffer less. This is the 45 story. No other story obtains.

SIX

BUSH *sits on a low chair reading to children in a kindergarten.*

AN ACTOR: September 11th 2001. At 8.46 a.m. American Airlines Flight 11 from Boston, hijacked by suicide bombers, crashes into the North Tower of the World Trade Center in New York. Seventeen minutes later, United Airlines Flight 175, also from Boston, crashes into the South. 5

An aide leans in to BUSH'*s ear.*

AN ACTOR: In Sarasota, Florida, the President makes a brief statement.
BUSH: The full resources of the federal government will be employed to investigate and find those folks who committed this act. Terrorism against our nation will not stand. 10
AN ACTOR: At 9.39 a.m., a third plane, American Airlines Flight 77, smashes into the Pentagon. A fourth, United Airlines Flight 93, aimed at the White House, is diverted by the bravery of its passengers and also crashes. President Bush is flow to Barksdale Air Force Base in Louisiana, 15 where he records a statement to be broadcast only when he is once again airborne.
BUSH: Make no mistake. The United States will hunt down and punish those responsible for these cowardly acts. Freedom itself was attacked this morning by a faceless coward. 20 And freedom will be defended.
AN ACTOR: The President is moved to an underground bunker at Strategic Command, Offutt Air Base, Nebraska. At his own insistence, he is flown back to the White House, whence he broadcasts live to the nation at 8.30 p.m. 25
BUSH: We will make no distinction between the terrorists who committed these acts and those who harbour them. None of us will forget this day. Yet we go forward to defend freedom and all that is good and just in our world.

Exhausted staff gather to hear the President.

AN ACTOR: He then addresses his team in the Presidential 30 Emergency Operations Center:
BUSH: I want you all to understand that we are at war, and we will stay at war until this is done. Nothing else matters. Everything is available for the pursuit of this war. Any barriers in your way, they're gone. Any money you need, you 35 have it. This is our only agenda.

The staff dissolve.

AN ACTOR: On Iraqi television a spokesman for Saddam Hussein declares:
IRAQI SPOKESMAN: The massive explosions in the centres of power are a painful slap in the face of US politicians to 40 stop their illegitimate hegemony and attempts to impose custodianship on peoples. The American cowboy is reaping the fruits of his crimes against humanity.
AN ACTOR: In England Tony Blair declares:
BLAIR: This is not a battle between the United States of 45 America and terrorism, but between the free and democratic world and terrorism.

AN ACTOR: The French newspaper *Le Monde* has a headline:
LE MONDE: We are all Americans now.
50 AN ACTOR: By nightfall, 2,948 people of ninety-one different nationalities are dead. Four days later, on September
15th, the President assembles his War Cabinet for a weekend at Camp David.

SEVEN

The War Cabinet—including BUSH, RICE, WOLFOWITZ, POWELL,
O'NEILL, TENET, CHENEY *and* RUMSFELD, *now in casual clothes—
assembles in a wood-panelled room at Camp David.*

BUSH: We'll begin this meeting as we always do.

Everyone closes their eyes.

Oh God, who gives everything and knows everything, direct our thoughts, give our thoughts direction, make us
wise, give us wisdom, that we may surely do good. In thy
5   name.
ALL: Amen.

Everyone resettles.

BUSH: I'm going to be asking everyone to make reports, I'm
going to be asking everyone to talk informally, so we can
look at options, different ways of going . . .
10 O'NEILL: I'm proud to be able to say: the New York Stock Exchange is indeed going to be open on Monday.
BUSH: I've said that's important.
O'NEILL: We're sending out a signal, and the signal is: business
as usual.
15 AN ACTOR: As the day went on, the War Cabinet began to
hear of a global network of terror in over fifty countries,
of which Osama bin Laden and Al Qaeda were only one
part . . .

TENET *gets up and hands out identical intelligence dossiers to
everyone.*

TENET: Within this dossier you'll find up-to-date informa-
20   tion of terror organizations. The plan inside focuses on expanded powers for the CIA. We're asking for a kind of
global charge—the right to attack any aspect of a terrorist network without specific case-by-case clearance from
the President.
25 BUSH: This is a war. This is a war on terror.
TENET: The most important objective for us is to concentrate
our efforts providing money and resources for the Northern Alliance within Afghanistan, to make sure that if we
go in, we can energise support, we can make sure there are
30   people ready to take over the running of the country
when the Taliban falls.
BUSH: I tell you how I see Afghanistan. I see it as a 'demonstration model'.
RICE: Speaking with the President, what the President's been
35   saying to me is that Afghanistan can be used as a kind of
example . . .
BUSH: That's what it is.
RICE: That's right.
BUSH: An example.

RICE: That's right.   40
BUSH: A model, it's a kind of model . . .
RICE: Afghanistan is a kind of demonstration model, so that
other countries can look and say, 'Oh I see. That's what
happens . . .'
BUSH: 'I see . . .'   45
RICE: 'That's what happens.'
O'NEILL: What other countries d'you have in mind?
BUSH: Iran.
O'NEILL: OK.
BUSH: For example.   50

There's a silence.

RICE: We want to send a message to countries which are considering actions hostile to the United States.
BUSH: Wolfie . . .
WOLFOWITZ: Well, I want to talk about another country, it's
another country in the Middle East, let's talk about that   55
category of countries which is considering actions hostile
to the United States. And if you take a good look at that
category then I think there's one egregious member. It's
been in violation of United Nations resolutions for over
ten years.   60
RUMSFELD: I sent a memo, if you remember, Mr President, in
January, before this happened, I sent a memo with a list of
countries who I considered were eager to exploit any
lapses in US capability. China, North Korea, Russia, Iran.
My conclusion was we should take any actions necessary 65
to dissuade nations from challenging American interests.
Top of that list was Iraq.

BUSH *nods.*

WOLFOWITZ: We're talking a corrupt dictatorship, run by a
man who oppresses his own people and thumbs his nose
at American power. We're talking about going in and es-   70
tablishing democracy. This is a country which is now very
brittle. It will break very easily. It's sitting there, waiting to
fall. This is something we can do with very little effort. For
a minimum expenditure of effort, we can get maximum
result. Take out Saddam and we blow fresh air into the   75
Middle East.
RUMSFELD: I mean, Jumping Jiminy, look at it strategically . . .
WOLFOWITZ: That's it . . .
RUMSFELD: Look at it: Afghanistan's a big country, but what   80
are we going to bomb? Tommy Franks says there are only
three dozen targets. Three dozen! Have you looked at
Afghanistan? Terracotta pots and straw roofs! It isn't easy.
You can do it . . .
WOLFOWITZ: Oh sure, you can do it . . .   85
RUMSFELD: We'll do it. Anything we're asked to do, we'll do.
But it's hard. The only thing you can say for it, at least it
isn't the Balkans. We're not like Clinton . . .
CHENEY: We're not . . .
BUSH: Hell, we're not . . .   90
RUMSFELD: It's not the Balkans . . .
CHENEY: If there's one thing we can agree on . . .
RUMSFELD: Wasting time in a place full of ethnic hatreds.
Pounding sand. But that doesn't mean it's easy. It isn't easy.

95 WOLFOWITZ: Attacking Afghanistan will be uncertain. I'm not saying we won't succeed . . .

RUMSFELD: We'll succeed.

WOLFOWITZ: Yeah. But what I'm concerned about is, OK, there we are in maybe six months' time with a hundred
100 thousand American soldiers—

RUMSFELD: Don't say 'bogged down' . . .

WOLFOWITZ: All right, let's say 'snarled up'—a hundred thousand American soldiers snarled up! OK? In mountain fighting. What message does that send? What example? Whereas,
105 look . . . Iraq's a country we know. We've been there. And more important—talking about sending messages—I'd say there's a good percentage chance Saddam Hussein was directly involved in the attacks on the World Trade Center.

BUSH: Reckon that, Paul. What percentage?

110 WOLFOWITZ: Ten to fifty. That's where I'd put it. A ten to fifty per cent chance.

Everyone is thoughtful.

RICE: Mr President, Afghanistan is a country—this is a place with a history. It was nemesis for the British in the nine-teenth century. It was nemesis for the Russians in the
115 twentieth. All I'm concerned is it isn't our turn in the twenty-first.

Nobody says anything.

WOLFOWITZ: That's what's good about Iraq. It's do-able.

The Cabinet breaks up and goes for soup and sandwiches.

AN ACTOR: They stopped for lunch.

BUSH: There's chicken noodle soup. Home-made.

120 WOLFOWITZ: Wonderful . . .

O'NEILL: Smells good.

RUMSFELD: I could eat a baby through the bars of a cot.

BUSH: We bake our own bread here. They bake the bread.

O'NEILL: Kind of thing your mother served you.

125 BUSH: Not my mother. Not my mother at all. She never cooked. That woman had frostbite on her fingers. Everything out of the freezer.

Everyone laughs.

It's good to be eating this kind of food. It's comfort food. It's good to be eating it now.

130 AN ACTOR: Then in the afternoon they went back to it.

The meeting resumes.

RUMSFELD: I'd like to move on to a subject I think important. It's not a subject. It's an approach. There's a mistake they made during the first Gulf War. They were too specific. Remember? They talked all the time about Saddam Hus-
135 sein. That had an effect. It elevated the guy. Now he's still there and everyone says, 'Hey—they screwed up.' We want to avoid that mistake.

BUSH: Huh.

RUMSFELD: Look, sir, understand—not to pre-empt any deci-
140 sion . . .

BUSH *raises a hand in permission.*

But I think we're all beginning to feel a consensus. OK, we accept what we have to do first. We have to go after Al Qaeda and get its leader. We want to take out Osama bin Laden, we want to take out Mohammad Omar, we want to isolate them in their camps and destroy them. But I'm 145 not sure that's the rhetoric we should be using. Because I'm just point out—if we set targets, if we make targets, specific targets, if we make objectives and then we don't hit them—(*Rumsfeld waits a moment.*) If we turn this guy into some kind of monster—this great monster Osama 150 bin Laden—I mean, I'm saying I don't think the President should even mention him.

BUSH: Huh.

RUMSFELD: I liked what you said earlier, sir. A war on terror. That's good. That's vague. 155

CHENEY: It's good.

RUMSFELD: That way we can do anything.

There's a short silence.

AN ACTOR: By nightfall they were tired. Nobody summed up. But, towards the end: 160

POWELL: We've heard a lot of plans . . .

BUSH: Colin.

POWELL: We've heard a lot of different ideas. And that's OK. But one thing I'd say: we have to be take care. Step by step. If we go into Afghanistan, we're going to need Pakistan. 165 And that's going to be a risk for Musharraf.

BUSH: Is he ready to take that risk?

POWELL: I believe he is, sir. The guy is genuine. He wants a secular, Westernised country. That's what Musharraf wants and he's willing to risk a lot to get it. But there 170 are also dangers for us. Afghanistan is already a mess. Pakistan sides with us and the danger is that country's destabilised as well. Suddenly the whole region's on fire. The point I'm making: this exercise is going to need patience. How we do things is going to be just as impor- 175 tant as what we do. My job will be to assemble an international coalition. A coalition of countries who want to show their support for us and for the values we share in common. Here, today, we can talk among our-selves, we can say, 'Oh let's go do Iraq, or hey, it's time 180 to fix Iran . . .' But. Since Tuesday we have the support of the whole world. People don't want to go for one thing, and then find they've signed up for another. No-body likes bait and switch. Who we go against is going to decide who goes with us. 185

BUSH: Sure. (*Bush nods.*) You know, Colin, finally this is a war on terror. And at some point we may be the only ones left. That's fine with me.

There's a silence. Then they break up.

AN ACTOR: The meeting broke up.

BUSH: Here they come . . . 190

RUMSFELD: Good evening, ladies.

*In come the wives—*LAURA BUSH, JOYCE RUMSFELD, NANCY O'NEILL, *etc.*

AN ACTOR: Their wives joined them and they all had supper.

TENET: What have we got tonight?

LAURA: Fried chicken, corn-bread, mashed potatoes and
195   gravy.

RUMSFELD: Hey, OK. I'll have the fried chicken, the corn-
bread, the mashed potatoes and the gravy.

Everyone laughs.

AN ACTOR: An artist had made a jigsaw of the White House
with the Bushes standing in front of it. So, after dinner, the
200   President sat with his wife and they worked quietly, putting
the little bits of their family and their house together.

BUSH *sits with* LAURA *assembling the jigsaw.*

BUSH: That looks like you, Laura. That looks like a bit of you,
sweetheart.

LAURA: I'll work on the columns, you work on the people.

205 AN ACTOR: Nobody knew what to do, but nobody wanted
to leave.

Everyone is now sitting around, relaxed.

RICE: Anyone want to go bowling?

BUSH: I'm not bowling tonight, no way. Oh no.

LAURA: Anyone know any hymns?

210 RICE: Yeah. Yeah. I know some hymns.

The room falls silent. RICE *begins to sing.*

Amazing grace! How sweet the sound
That saved a wretch like me!
I once was lost, but now am found;
Was blind, but now I see.

Everyone joins in.

215   Through many dangers, toils and snares
I have already come;
'Tis grace hath brought me safe thus far,
And grace will lead me home.

EIGHT

Congress. Legislators greet the arrival of BUSH, *accompanied by*
TONY BLAIR.

AN ACTOR: On September 17th the President signs an executive order authorizing attacks on Afghanistan. Three days
later he addresses Congress:

BUSH: Every nation, in every region, now has a decision to
5   make. Either you are with us or you are with the terrorists.

AN ACTOR: In the balcony above him is the British Prime
Minister. At one point Bush looks up:

BUSH: Thank you for coming, friend.

BLAIR *receives a standing ovation in Congress, then moves to a*
lectern in Brighton.

AN ACTOR: Soon after, back in England, Blair addresses the
10   Labour Party conference:

BLAIR: The state of Africa is a scar on the conscience of the
world. But if the world as a community focused on it,
we could heal it. And if we don't, it will become deeper
and angrier. This is the moment to tackle problems
from the slums of Gaza to the mountain ranges of 15
Afghanistan. This is a moment to seize. The kaleido-
scope has been shaken. The pieces are in flux. Soon they
will settle again. Before they do, let us reorder this world
around us.

AN ACTOR: On October 7th the US and Britain begin air 20
and missile strikes against thirty-one Al Qaeda and Taliban
targets.

RUMSFELD *appears for a press conference, flanked by generals.*

RUMSFELD: The campaign's going well, couldn't be going
better. After two days we are now able to carry out strikes
more or less round the clock and we've been hitting 25
eighty-five per cent of our targets. Some of the targets we
hit need to be re-hit.

Laughter.

JOURNALIST: What are you saying, Mr Secretary? Are you
saying you're running out of targets?

RUMSFELD: We're not running out of targets. Afghanistan is. 30

More laughter.

You know, if you try to quantify what we're doing today
in terms of previous conventional wars, you're making a
huge mistake. That is 'old think' and that will not help you
analyse what we're doing. It's a different kind of conflict.

The press conference becomes a swanky Washington dinner.

AN ACTOR: One month later, Rumsfeld is thunderously re- 35
ceived when he addresses a black-tie dinner of defence
contractors:

RUMSFELD: The coalition will not determine the mission.
The mission will determine the coalition. We will not stop
for Ramadan. We will not stop for winter. And after the 40
Taliban and Al Qaeda we'll get after the rest.

JACK STRAW *steps forward.*

AN ACTOR: In Europe, the British Foreign Secretary, Jack
Straw, is regularly put forward to control the impact of
statements from Rumsfeld and the Pentagon:

STRAW: There are always statements coming out of Washing- 45
ton. Washington is a very large place. But this military
coalition is about action in respect of military and terrorist targets in Afghanistan.

AN ACTOR: On November 13th, after five years under an extreme religious regime, the Northern Alliance enter and 50
liberate the capital, Kabul.

BUSH *is in the Oval Office,* CHENEY *and* RICE *with him, listening*
to the call on speakerphone. BLAIR, DAVID MANNING, JONATHAN
POWELL, *and* ALASTAIR CAMPBELL *are in* BLAIR'*s den in Down-*
ing Street.

BUSH: Tony. Hi. Good to hear you.

BLAIR: Hello.

BUSH: You've heard the good news? You've been hearing the
55 good news?

BLAIR: Yes. It's all very good, I agree. It's mostly good. But there's one issue I need to raise.

There's a silence. BUSH *looks straight ahead.*

BUSH: Raise your issue.

BLAIR: It's this. As you know, British special forces have been
60 working on the Pakistani border, around Tora Bora . . .

BUSH: I know that.

BLAIR: Seeking out bin Laden. I'm sure you've also been told that just a few days ago, we found him. We tracked him.

BUSH: I got those reports.

65 BLAIR: The point is this: when we found him, our special forces received a request from the US special forces. We were ordered to pull out.

There's another silence. RICE *looks to* CHENEY.

Now I don't know where that particular order came from . . .

70 BUSH: It's an operational decision . . .

BLAIR: Of course . . .

BUSH: It's not taken at this level.

BLAIR: No. I accept that. But I also have great respect for my military . . .

75 BUSH: I respect my military.

BLAIR: That's the reason I'm calling. As of now, I've got some angry generals. A decision was made—George, I'm not saying you made it, I'm sure it wasn't you—whoever—

BLAIR *is offering* BUSH *the chance to speak, but he says nothing.*

In fact, I don't know if you even know who took it—who
80 took that decision—

BLAIR *waits again.* BUSH *looks to* CHENEY, *who shakes his head very slightly.*

BUSH: Go on.

BLAIR: We're both—you and I both—look, it's clear—capturing bin Laden has tremendous significance . . .

BUSH: That could be.

85 BLAIR: Tremendous impact. And in the world as it is, the British army capturing him would not ring the same bells as if you had caught him. I accept that.

There is another silence. Both groups on either side of the Atlantic are still.

I don't want to labour this.

BUSH: You're not labouring it, Tony. You're making a point.
90 We don't ever not hear you.

BLAIR *looks to* MANNING, *who rolls his eyes.*

BLAIR: As of December 11th,, bin Laden has gone off the map. Intelligence has lost him. In the time between when

we were ordered to withdraw and you going in, bin Laden escaped.

BUSH: Yes. 95

There is silence. BUSH *nods slightly.*

Thank you for raising that, Tony. What other matters are you thinking to raise?

The two camps dissolve.

AN ACTOR: Not long after, the President remarks:

BUSH: Our objective is more than bin Laden. I just don't spend that much time on him, to be honest. Focusing on 100 one person indicates to me that people don't understand the scope of this mission. Terror is bigger than one man.

AN ACTOR: By the end of 2001, the US will have spent $6.46 billion on the bombing of Afghanistan.

BUSH *takes* RUMSFELD's *arm and leads him from a corridor into a small office.*

BUSH: Donald, I need to see you alone. 105

AN ACTOR: On November 21st 2001, George Bush leads Donald Rumsfeld into an empty office next to the Situation Room.

BUSH: Donald, I know you're doing a worldwide review. I've been thinking: it could provide a very good cover. 110

RUMSFELD: What sort of cover?

BUSH: What kind of war plan do you have for Iraq? How do you feel about the war plan for Iraq? Let's get started on this. Get Tommy Franks looking at it.

AN ACTOR: It is seventy-two days after September 11th. 115

BUSH: And Donald—don't tell anyone else.

NINE

A New Labour Politician appears. She is direct, to the point.

POLITICIAN: We know the world. We know how the world is. Something is decided. Something has to be done. If each of us waited for the perfect circumstances, nothing would ever be achieved.

At a certain moment, Dick Cheney, Donald Rumsfeld, 5
Paul Wolfowitz—three different men, but all wishing the world better, wishing the world changed—prompt the President. 'Do it now. If it is not done now, it will never be done.'

They saw an opening, and in they went. 10

I understand the feelings of those who wish things might have been done differently. In a different way. At a different time. we may all wish that. But who said 'Politics is the art of the possible'? You do what you can. Because in politics, in life, one thing is certain: there will always be 15 reasons not to act.

I can't put my hand on my heart and say things are going to work out in Iraq. How do I know? How can anyone say that? We walk backwards into the future. A dictator was removed. Reasons were offered for that re- 20 moval which have proved, with hindsight, not to be justified. Weapons believed to exist turned out not to exist. A flawless military victory was compromised by sloppy Pen-

25 tagon planning for peace. Practices evolved on the ground which everyone admits were unworthy of a great cause. But the action itself remains pure.

Do you know, do you have any idea how rare it is, for even one moment in the disorderly unfolding of events, to achieve purpose?

30 And now? Now we can only wait.

TEN

A team of sweating speech-writers circle, reading out explosive rhetorical sections of the forthcoming speech. MICHAEL GERSON *is in charge.*

AN ACTOR: January 29th 2002: George Bush uses his State of the Union address to rack up the rhetoric. The President's chief speech-writer, Michael Gerson, calls this:
GERSON: A plastic, teachable moment.
5 AN ACTOR: Gerson instructs his team:
GERSON: Make the best case for war in Iraq. But leave exit ramps.

BUSH *enters a cheering Congress and shakes eager hands.*

AN ACTOR: Dick Cheney sits directly behind as the President reads the result:
10 BUSH: Iraq continues to flaunt its hostility towards America and to support terror. States like these, and their terrorist allies, constitute an axis of evil, arming to threaten the peace of the world. By seeking weapons of mass destruction, these regimes pose a grave and growing danger.
15 All nations should know: America will do what is necessary to ensure our nation's security. I will not wait on events, while dangers gather. I will not stand by as peril draws closer and closer.
History has called America and our allies to action.
20 Steadfast in our purpose, we now press on. We have known freedom's price. We have shown freedom's power. And in this great conflict, my fellow Americans, we will see freedom's victory.
AN ACTOR: Paul Wolfowitz recalls:
25 WOLFOWITZ: It was when I heard that speech I thought: the President really gets it.
AN ACTOR: The President himself says of the phrase 'axis of evil':
BUSH: It just kind of resonates.
30 AN ACTOR: At once, alarm bells start to go off in European capitals. The French Foreign Minister calls the speech:
FRENCH FOREIGN MINISTER: Simplistic.
AN ACTOR: The German Foreign Minister warns:
GERMAN FOREIGN MINISTER: Alliance partners are not satel-
35 lites.
AN ACTOR: A British Foreign Office official observes:
FOREIGN OFFICE OFFICIAL: We all smiled at the jejune language. It sounded straight out of *Lord of the Rings.*
AN ACTOR: The Iraqi Vice-President comments:
40 IRAQI VICE-PRESIDENT: This statement of President Bush is stupid.
AN ACTOR: The British Foreign Minister, Jack Straw, adds:
STRAW: The President's speech can be best understood by the fact there are mid-term Congressional elections coming
45 up in November.

AN ACTOR: Condoleezza Rice is enraged:
RICE: This is not about American politics, and I assume that when the British government speaks about foreign policy, it's not about British politics.
AN ACTOR: Blair instructs his personal foreign policy adviser 50 David Manning to make a conciliatory call.

MANNING *and* RICE *are on mobile phones.*

MANNING: The Prime Minister has asked me to apologise for his Foreign Secretary. I mean, for what his Foreign Secretary said.
RICE: The President understands. This is a war, David. We 55 know better than anyone: nobody gets it right all the time.

They laugh. At once a helicopter arrives to deposit BLAIR, CHERIE BLAIR, CHERIE BLAIR'S *mother, baby* LEO, DAVID MANNING, JONATHAN POWELL *and* ALASTAIR CAMPBELL *at Crawford, Texas. The Englishmen are all in dark suits with black ties.* BUSH, RICE *and their team are all in jeans and T-shirts.*

BUSH: Tony. Hi.
BLAIR: George. You know David Manning?
BUSH: Sure do.   60
BLAIR: Condoleezza. Alastair Campbell?
CAMPBELL: Of course.
RICE: Hello, Alastair.
JONATHAN POWELL: Jonathan Powell. Tony's Chief of Staff.

They turn to face a barrage of cameras.

BUSH: Interesting style for Texas.   65
BLAIR: The Queen Mother.
BUSH: Ah yes. I forgot. The Queen Mother. They say a beautiful woman.
BLAIR: Well. Yes. In her way.

They smile. BUSH *gestures* BLAIR *into the informal surroundings of his ranch.*

AN ACTOR: In Crawford, Texas, a town which is little more 70 than a crossroads in a scorpion-infested wilderness, the President meets Tony Blair to take him to the Prairie Chapel Ranch, his family retreat—sixteen hundred acres of oak groves, cattle, creeks and freshly stocked ponds . . .

BUSH *and* BLAIR, *alone, walk together in the grounds.*

BUSH: Nobody's looking. You can undo your tie. And it's an 75 open agenda.

BLAIR *smiles and loosens his tie.*

BLAIR: In that case: urgently, I'd like to thank you, George, for some of the forthright things you've been saying about Israeli incursions into the Palestinian territory.
BUSH: Go on.   80
BLAIR: I think it's important. The more even-handed America can be between Israel and the Palestinians—the fairer you can be seen to be . . .
BUSH: I've condemned the incursions.
BLAIR: You have.   85

BUSH: I've told them to stop. I've told them to withdraw.

BLAIR: You have. (BLAIR *waits*.) They haven't actually stopped. They haven't withdrawn.

BUSH: No. They haven't.

BLAIR *waits again.* BUSH *shrugs.*

90 Israel's an independent nation. Sharon's a tough guy.

BLAIR: Anyway, I think you can discern what I'm saying. You and I both have some sort of vision, I think . . .

BUSH: That's right . . .

BLAIR: About how things might be reshaped in the Middle

95 East . . .

BUSH: That's the very thing I want to talk to you about. That very thing.

BLAIR: Well. The only way we're going to make progress is by bringing serious pressure. On the Israelis and the Pales-

100 tinians equally. That's vital.

BUSH *looks at him a moment.*

BUSH: My concern is this, Tony. At this moment, just at this very moment, I'm finding the subject of Iraq seems to be moving up the agenda.

BLAIR: That's clear.

105 BUSH: It's moving up all the time.

BLAIR: We've begun to sense that.

BUSH: I'm sitting here and since 9/11 I've been getting very strong feelings that this is something we can't leave alone.

BLAIR: I understand those feelings.

110 BUSH: Saddam has to be dealt with. My view is, we're moving into the second phase. We did Afghanistan. Now we move on. The second phase.

BLAIR: And I agree. There is no question of leaving him alone. He's been left alone for far too long.

115 BUSH: This is a guy who gassed his own people.

BLAIR: Quite.

There is a short silence.

Quite. You and I want the same things.

BUSH: I'm sure we do.

BLAIR: The only discussion is going to be about method. Be-

120 cause . . . well, back at home, you probably know, you've probably heard . . . you've been taking soundings of your own . . .

BUSH: Matter of fact, yes.

BLAIR: It's true, I'm going through one of those periods—you

125 haven't had one yet—when political problems come together.

BUSH: Give me an example.

BLAIR: Well, for example, I know it sounds silly, but foxhunt-ing. Also, there's something called Railtrack . . .

130 BUSH: Is that a railroad company?

BLAIR: Look, you really don't want to know. My point is this: I'm in rough water, there's an accumulation—foreign and domestic. A first term is easy, George. A hundred and forty-six MPs have already signed what we call an early-

135 day motion. It's a kind of warning. And a hundred and thirty of them are in my own party. They're expressing their opposition to British support for a US-led war on Iraq. The phrase they're using is 'deep unease'.

BUSH *thinks a moment.*

BUSH: Deep unease? Huh.

BLAIR: Now you and I know we're way ahead of ourselves. 140

BUSH: Way ahead.

BLAIR: Any war, any conceivable war, is a long way off. It isn't going to happen tomorrow . . .

BUSH: Not tomorrow, no.

BLAIR: It's an option. 145

BUSH: That's what it is. It's an option.

BLAIR: But I have to give you my judgement.

BUSH: Please. I welcome your judgement.

BLAIR: In the event of your considering armed action against Iraq, the British Parliament—and I'd say still 150 more the British people—won't go along without UN support.

There is a silence.

From the British point of view this has to be approached in a certain way. On Afghanistan you had a coalition. There were tensions, definite tensions, but we agreed on 155 the aim. So it is here.

BUSH: Say more.

BLAIR: I have an Attorney-General who is advising me that any invasion of Iraq without UN support is going to be in breach of international law. 160

BUSH: Is that what he says?

BLAIR: That's it. That's what he says. In fact, he says more than that.

BUSH: Do I know this guy?

BLAIR: You don't. 165

BUSH: Tell me what he says.

BLAIR: What he says is this: even with UN support, any inva-sion may still be illegal unless we can demonstrate that the threat to British national security from Iraq is what he calls 'real and imminent'. 170

BUSH *is impassive.*

Real and imminent, George. If Britain is involved, we will need evidence that Iraq can and will launch a nuclear, bi-ological or chemical attack on a Western country. We can't go to war because of what we fear. Only because of what we know. 175

BUSH: I see. (*Bush thinks a moment.*) I see. That's putting the bar quite high.

BLAIR: Yes. It's high.

They both think.

Now plainly, if you so choose you can set out on your own. You can do it all on your own. That's your choice. 180 But, frankly, I wouldn't advise it.

BUSH: I understand.

BLAIR: And selfishly I don't want it, because I think the whole undertaking is far too important. If we do reach the point where we one day have to contemplate military ac- 185 tion, then I would want that action to be unarguably le-gitimate. I want it to have authority.

BUSH: Sure.

BLAIR: And in Britain—in other parts of the world—that
190   means the UN.

There is a silence.

Now I don't know what you feel about that. To be honest
. . . if I'm honest, we're getting contradictory impressions
from different parts of your administration.
BUSH: I can believe that.
195 BLAIR: That's right. It's not unknown . . .
BUSH: It isn't unknown . . .
BLAIR: We both know: a little confusion can sometimes be
creative in government.
BUSH: It can be useful, yeah.
200 BLAIR: Some of your people genuinely respect the UN.
Whereas, with others, let's say, there's a contempt, an al-
most obsessive hatred . . .
BUSH: It's me that'll take the decision. I'll take the decision.
I'm the President.
205 BLAIR: Yeah. To me, it's an opportunity. The UN is an
American-built institution. America built it.

BUSH *doesn't reply.*

Internationally—well, in Europe, in Russia, I can help.
I think I can chip in with a good deal of personal
persuasion—with Chirac, with Putin. My relationships are
210   excellent. One of the advantages of being a bit longer in
office . . .
BUSH: Sure.
BLAIR: Knowing the people. Knowing the personalities. I
have a history, remember? Sierra Leone . . .
215 BUSH: Sure.
BLAIR: Kosovo . . .
BUSH: Sure.
BLAIR: Kosovo was a tough sell. People didn't believe in it.
Believe me, I'm not scared of being unpopular . . .
220 BUSH: I know that.
BLAIR: Going out on a limb. Military intervention for humane purposes, it's something I've believed in for a long
time. I find it abhorrent, the idea the West stands by and
just watches as less fortunate people suffer.

Again, BUSH *doesn't answer.*

225   There's a speech of mine, in fact, I made in Chicago . . .
BUSH: I know that speech . . .
BLAIR: Way before 9/11 even . . .
BUSH: I've read the digest.
BLAIR: It's something I've argued. A moral duty. And I be-
230   lieve in it. The West has the right—no, more than a
right, a responsibility—to intervene against regimes
which are committing offences against their own citizens. It's simple humanity. At some point we're all going
to have to articulate a new code. In my view, there's
235   such a thing as progressive war. But when it comes to
Iraq, it's difficult. Because people are asking: why Iraq?
Why now? To the British, a unilateral attack is going to
seem like an act of unprovoked aggression against a sovereign power. But a multilateral force, sanctioned by the
240   UN, well, that's a different thing. That's a force for

something more important than nation. That's a force
for justice.

BUSH *nods slightly, non-committal.*

BUSH: I'm going to think about this.
BLAIR: Good.
BUSH: I'm going to talk to my people. (*Bush smiles.*) you're al-   245
ways eloquent, Tony.

BLAIR *is tense now.*

BLAIR: I have one other request.
BUSH: Of course.
BLAIR: There's one other thing I have to ask.
BUSH: Ask.   250
BLAIR: We're at the beginning of a process. I've told you: I'm
going to try and persuade you to go through the UN.
BUSH: I accept that.
BLAIR: That means new resolutions. That means honest diplo-
macy. So. Nothing could be more disastrous to me—to my   255
position—than any suggestion—any possible suggestion—
from any single member of your administration—that a decision to resort to military means has already been taken. I
can't describe the harm that would do.
BUSH: Tell me.   260
BLAIR: I have to go back, I have to face my Cabinet. I have
to look my colleagues in the eye and tell them the truth.
I can very easily lose Cabinet members over this. If my
enemies can say, 'This is a war which was cooked up a
long time ago by a group in Washington who are just go-   265
ing through the motions . . .' If they can say, 'America decided this, they decided it, it's fixed, and nothing you do,
Tony, will have any effect . . .' (*Blair pauses.*) If people can
say that, then my position becomes untenable.
BUSH: You need to be in good faith.   270
BLAIR: It's important to me.

BUSH *nods slightly.*

BUSH: I've been clear with you. We're just discussing the options.
BLAIR: Good.
BUSH: I can say that: we're looking at the options.
BLAIR: Good.   275
BUSH: No war plan's on the table. It's not on the table.
BLAIR: I think that's important. I don't just mean it's impor-
tant, it's true. I know it's true. It's also important you say it.

There is a silence.

BUSH: It's what I'm saying.
BLAIR: Good.   280

BUSH *and* BLAIR *walk out to face a press conference.*

BUSH: Good morning. Laura and I are very honoured to have
our friends, Tony and Cherie Blair and their family, visit
us here in Crawford. We appreciate the rain that the Prime
Minister brought with him. And so do the other farmers
and ranchers in the area. Mr Prime Minister, thanks for   285
bringing it.

BLAIR: My pleasure, George.

Laughter.

JOURNALIST: Mr President, you have yet to build an international coalition for military action against Iraq. Has the violence in the Middle East thwarted your efforts? And Prime Minister Blair, has Bush convinced you on the need for a military action against Iraq?

BUSH: Adam, the Prime Minister and I, of course, talked about Iraq. We both recognise the danger of a man who's willing to kill his own people harbouring and developing weapons of mass destruction. This guy, Saddam Hussein, is a leader who gasses his own people.

SECOND JOURNALIST: Prime Minister, we've heard the President say what his policy is directly about Saddam Hussein, which is to remove him. Can I ask you whether that is now the policy of the British government?

BLAIR: Well, John, you know it has always been our policy that Iraq would be a better place without Saddam Hussein. But how we now proceed in this situation, that is a matter that is open.

BUSH: Maybe I should be a little less direct and be a little more nuanced, and say we support regime change.

SECOND JOURNALIST: That's a change though, isn't it, a change in policy?

BUSH: No, it's really not. Regime change was the policy of my predecessor, as well.

SECOND JOURNALIST: And your father?

BUSH: You know, I can't remember that far back.

Laughter.

I think regime change sounds a lot more civil, doesn't it? The world would be better off without him. Let me put it that way, though. And so will the future.

They shake hands, wave and part.

AN ACTOR: On his return to England, Blair is restless, unsure of what's been agreed.

BLAIR *is back in his den with* MANNING, JONATHAN POWELL *and* CAMPBELL.

BLAIR: He's tricky, isn't he?

MANNING: Oh yes. He's tricky.

BLAIR: You don't know exactly what's been agreed. You don't know where you are.

MANNING: Cheney'll get to him. You wait.

CAMPBELL: You wait.

MANNING: Cheney. Rummy. Wolfie. It always happens. You agree something and then they get to him.

BLAIR: Yes.

MANNING *smiles.*

MANNING: Shame we don't live there, really.

MANNING *stares ahead, thoughtful.* BLAIR *sips his mug of tea, seemingly casual.*

AN ACTOR: Worried, uncertain, Blair issues a fatal order:

BLAIR: I've been thinking. I've had this idea. I need—I don't know—tell me if you think this is crazy, David—I think it might help if we had some sort of dossier. A kind of *dossier*.

MANNING: What kind of dossier?

BLAIR: I'd have thought, I don't know, surely the intelligence services can put something together?

MANNING: You mean, from sources?

BLAIR: Just the facts. Spelt out—very simply, very clearly, about the dangers of Iraq developing and using their weapons of mass destruction.

MANNING: You mean we publish intelligence? The services don't like that. They don't like doing that.

BLAIR: Yes. But this is important. This is unusual. *We* know the dangers. The public doesn't. The facts have never been marshaled, they've never been put together . . .

MANNING: No.

BLAIR: In one document. I'm just thinking: I'm going to need to be armed—

MANNING: I see that.

BLAIR: —with something you can actually look at . . .

CAMPBELL: It's a good idea.

BLAIR: A4, photos, facts. Something you can actually read, you can actually look at. Hold. 'Oh, I see, there it is. That's how it is.'

There is a silence.

That's what we need. If we had that.

MANNING *says nothing.*

Could you? Would you?

The graduating class of 2002 at the United States Military Academy at West Point passes by in a splendour of military uniforms and martial music.

AN ACTOR: In June 2002, President Bush takes the passing-out parade at West Point.

BUSH *inspects the parade.*

In his address, he repudiates the core idea of the United Nations Charter which forbids the use of force not undertaken in self-defence. He introduces a concept new in international law: the doctrine of the pre-emptive strike.

BUSH *addresses the seated graduates.*

BUSH: For much of the last century, America's defence relied on Cold War doctrines of deterrence and containment. But new threats require new thinking. Deterrence—the promise of massive retaliation against nations—means nothing against shadowy terrorist networks with no nation or citizens to defend. Containment is not possible when unbalanced dictators with weapons of mass destruction can deliver those weapons on missiles or secretly provide them to terrorist allies.

375   We cannot defend America by hoping for the best. If we wait for threats to fully materialize we will have waited too long.

We are in a conflict between good and evil, and America will call evil by its name. By confronting evil and lawless regimes, we do not create a problem, we reveal a problem. And we will lead the world in opposing it.

380   AN ACTOR: By August, Colin Powell has become nervous of the direction his government is taking. On a plane back from a tour of the Far East, he makes four pages of notes, then next day asks to see the President.

A muggy night at the White House. BUSH *is casually dressed.* POWELL *and* RICE *are more formal.*

BUSH: Happy to see you, Colin. Always happy to take time.
385   POWELL: This is good of you, sir.
BUSH: You're always welcome.
AN ACTOR: They have dinner together in the President's quarters, then afterwards:

They all settle in armchairs, relaxed.

BUSH: You've been where?
390   POWELL: Indonesia.
BUSH: That's right.
POWELL: The Philippines. I'm looking for a post with less foreign travel.

They all smile.

RICE: Colin was saying earlier he's not sure he'd have taken
395   the job if he'd known what it was.
BUSH: Why's that? Why d'you say that?
POWELL: Oh, simple. Aren't I always the guy who brings the bad news?

BUSH *looks at him a moment.*

Funny, I was laughing about it with Jack Straw.
400   BUSH: That's the—
POWELL: Yeah. Nice man.
BUSH: Yeah.
POWELL: My opposite number.
BUSH: Why were you laughing?
405   POWELL: Jack was asking, 'Don't you get tired? Because it's always our job to go to the leader and say, "The French don't like it," or "The Russians won't wear it" . . .' The boss never wants to see you. Why should he see you when you're always the person telling him what he doesn't want
410   to hear?
BUSH: Yeah.
POWELL: The opinion of foreigners.
BUSH: Yeah
POWELL: That's what you do.
415   RICE: Sure.
POWELL: You tell him what foreigners are thinking. You explain the French position. After a while, you've explained the French position so often it begins to feel like you *are* French. And you can see everyone in the room thinking:
420   'OK. Then why didn't you tell the French to fuck off?'

They all laugh.

'Well, why didn't you?' And it's worse in this country—it's worse for me than it is for Jack, because here everyone's also thinking: 'Hey—this is the most powerful country in the world, we're the world's only superpower, and we're wasting time while this guy tells us what some hippy
425   Euro-peacenik foreign minister wants—why do we have to listen to him?' (*Powell looks amused.*) You can't win. In this job. You always seem weak.
BUSH: Not you, Colin. You don't seem weak.

The two men look at each other, level.

Tell me what's bothering you.
430   POWELL: Forgive me, sir, you'll understand, but I think I know a little about the military . . .
BUSH: Why, sure.
POWELL: One thing I know: armies make plans. That's what they do. Constantly. When you're back in the barracks,
435   you plan. Mostly for situations which will never arise. I met an Israeli general once who told me he had a plan for the Israeli army to capture the North Pole. He thought it would work, too. It was a good plan. But that's all it was. A plan.
440
BUSH: What are you saying?
POWELL: I'm saying nowadays we seem to be full of plans.

There's a silence.

BUSH: I'm a war President. We're at war.
POWELL: Maybe because my whole life has been in the army I'm less impressed than some people by the use of force. I
445   see it for what it is.
BUSH: What is it?
POWELL: Failure.

BUSH *smiles.*

BUSH: I'm going to take some persuading.
POWELL: That's why I wanted to see you. Privately.
450

The two men look at each other. BUSH *gestures at* RICE.

BUSH: Just Condi.
POWELL: All right, then I'll tell you: I'm getting frustrated by all these military plans. I can't help noticing the most enthusiastic advocates of these plans seem to be men who—strangely—weren't around last time. These men weren't
455   on duty when their country asked them to fight.
BUSH: That gives you credentials. Of course it does.
POWELL: Armchair generals. Intellectuals. Sometimes I think all the trouble in the world is caused by intellectuals who have an 'idea'. They have some idea of action with no pos-
460   sible regard for its consequences. (*Powell sits forward, specific.*) We need to get a balance here.
BUSH: What sort of balance?
POWELL: Between the military and the diplomatic. Because at this moment far too little attention is being paid to the
465   latter.
BUSH: Go on.

POWELL: If we go into Iraq without a coalition and without the UN, then we're going to find ourselves in trouble. The
470 whole region is a tinderbox. And the current level of thinking from some people in this administration seems to be, 'OK, so let's throw in a match and see what happens . . .' It's at that level. Truly. It's nihilistic.

POWELL is angry. BUSH shifts.

BUSH: We need to make an example.
475 POWELL: I know. I know that argument.
BUSH: We need to do that.
POWELL: Sure.
BUSH: We need to show these people that we mean business.
POWELL: The Roman Empire. I'm familiar with the analogy.
480 The Romans would always go out of their way to make an announcement: 'You are now dealing with the Roman Empire.' Yeah. So if you pricked a senator in Rome, if you just pricked him through his toga with a pin, then Roman soldiers would seek out the village you came from—
485 wherever it was—anywhere in the empire—however far-flung—and they would kill all your family and burn down your house, they'd slaughter everyone in sight and rape all your daughters, just to make the point, just to put a message across: don't prick senators. But, sir, we're not Ro-
490 mans. And last time I looked at the constitution, we were still a republic, not an empire.

BUSH looks chastened, as if POWELL has finally reached him.

These are issues. These are large issues. And I'm the one who's going to have to pick up the pieces. (*Powell shakes his head.*) You sent me out to the Middle East to see
495 Sharon and Arafat, I was meant to be setting out a road-map . . .
BUSH: OK . . .
POWELL: The President's much-touted new initiative for peace . . . this big road-map . . .
500 BUSH: This was unfortunate . . .
POWELL: And while I'm in the region, while I'm actually in the area, back home the Secretary of Defense—
BUSH: All right . . .
POWELL: —is briefing against me, he's speaking openly, saying
505 Arafat's a busted flush and I shouldn't even be meeting him.
BUSH: All right, I've spoken to Donald . . .
POWELL: He says Colin Powell is soft on Arafat. Well, as a matter of fact Colin Powell isn't soft on Arafat—I don't have
510 any attitude to Arafat except he's the elected leader of 3.3 million Palestinians, and my President has personally asked me to negotiate with him.
RICE: It was a bad episode.
POWELL: You could say!
515 RICE: None of us come well out of it.
POWELL: We looked like some tenth-rate African dictatorship.
BUSH: I spoke strongly to Donald. It's not going to happen again.
520 POWELL: It should never have happened at all! Rumsfeld cut my legs off.

There is an angry silence. BUSH shifts again, uncomfortable.

OK, so I've had this experience, and now I'm looking at the current planning—planning for Iraq—and all I can see is a group of people getting a hard-on about the idea of war, and no one giving a damn for the reality. Ten times 525 more excitement about going in than there is about how the hell we get out! (*Powell is firm now, clear.*) We invade Iraq, the whole region can be destabilised. Friends of ours like Saudi Arabia, Egypt, Jordan—all going to be put in danger. The oxygen's going to be sucked out of everything 530 the United States is trying to do—not just the war on terror—every other diplomatic, defence and intelligence arrangement we have. And the economic implications are staggering—not least on the price of oil. In fact, there's a thousand questions nobody wants to consider, let alone 535 answer. How will we be received? By the Iraqis themselves? Wolfowitz has some nancy-boy banker in tow. He hasn't been back to his home country for forty-four years. This guy's a certified fraud—he's on the run from embezzlement charges in Jordan—and he's the one who, from 540 his profound ignorance of his homeland, is telling us that Iraqis are going to run out into the streets and greet us as liberators. Oh yes? And we're going on *his* word, are we? And once we go, how long will we stay? Rumsfeld wants the State Department to toy with some dicked-up plan 545 for post-war reconstruction. Has anyone put a figure on it? And most of all, has anyone stopped for a moment— have they stopped for one moment to consider the implications? If you go into Iraq, you're going to be the proud owner of twenty-five million people. Their lives. All their 550 hopes and aspirations. All their problems. Has anyone begun to think about that?

POWELL *shakes his head in disbelief.*

RICE: I don't understand. What do you want? You want us to do nothing?
POWELL: No. I want my country to be less arrogant. 555
RICE: OK.
POWELL: I want us to go about this in a different way.

BUSH *and* RICE *wait for* POWELL *to calm.*

Three thousand of our citizens died. They died in an unforgivable attack. But that doesn't license us to behave like idiots. If we reach the point where everyone is secretly 560 hoping that America gets a bloody nose, then we're going to find it very hard indeed to call on friends when we need them.

The other two are silenced by the depth of POWELL's *feelings. Then* BUSH *speaks.*

BUSH: I've said before: this isn't a popularity contest, Colin. It isn't about being popular. 565
POWELL: No, it isn't. You're right.
BUSH: No.
POWELL: It's about being effective. And the present policy of being as high-handed as possible with as many countries

570 as possible is profoundly counter-productive. It won't
work.

BUSH *is silent.*

There's an element of hypocrisy, George. We were trading
with the guy! Not long ago. People keep asking, how do
575 we know he's got weapons of mass destruction? How do
we know? Because we've still got the receipts. (*Powell
shakes his head.*) It'd be nice to pretend we even have a
choice. It would be great to say we can invade Iraq uni-
laterally. Except we can't. We need access to bases, facili-
580 ties. Overflight rights. For that you need allies. Not allies
you buy, not allies you bribe: allies you can actually trust,
because they believe in what you're doing and they're
signed up to it. We need a coalition. And if that takes time,
amen. And the only place to do it is at the UN. With the
help of a new UN resolution.

BUSH *gets up. The other two follow.*

585 BUSH: I'm not going to decide on this. I'm not going to decide on this tonight.
POWELL: I'm going to remind you, sir. Sixty-four per cent of
the American public favour this. So long as it's with the
support of the international community. Without that
590 support, the figure drops to thirty-three.
BUSH: I've seen the figures. They showed me the polls.
POWELL: OK, I'm arguing it as principle. But whatever—
even as politics—go to the UN and you take the American people with you. You might even avoid war. You say
595 I'm always looking for a downside, but I can't see the
downside of that. (POWELL *turns to* RICE.) You going my
way?
RICE: I am.
POWELL: I'll run you home.

POWELL *turns back to* BUSH.

600 BUSH: Sounded like you'd been waiting a long time.
POWELL: I'm sorry?
BUSH: To say what you said.
POWELL: Probably thirty years.

They both smile.

Goodnight, sir.
605 BUSH: Goodnight.

BUSH *goes.* POWELL *and* RICE *walk together down deserted White
House corridors.*

RICE: That was good stuff.
POWELL: Thank you.
RICE: We need a few more evenings like that.

POWELL *looks at her sideways. He can't tell if she supports him.*

POWELL: It's past his bedtime, isn't it?
610 RICE: Yes. Yes. He likes to be in bed by ten.

They walk on. Silence. Then:

Listen, if you don't mind, I'm going to take a rain check.
I'm going to work a little longer.
POWELL: Sure. You do that. (POWELL *nods.*) Goodnight, then.
RICE: Goodnight.

*The stage darkens. The White House glows in the night, creamy, sur-
real. An August evening in a Southern town.*

TWELVE

The image holds, floating, dream-like. AN ACTOR *speaks quietly.*

AN ACTOR: So it was. In August, the decision was taken. The
United States would go back to the United Nations to
demand a new resolution setting out guidelines for fresh
weapons inspections and promising harsh penalties if
Baghdad failed to co-operate.   5

*Quietly, the NSC begins to reassemble—*BUSH, POWELL, RICE,
TENET, *etc.* RUMSFELD *comes in with* CHENEY.

RUMSFELD: You're looking cheerful, Dick.
CHENEY: Am I?
RUMSFELD: For a man who just lost.
CHENEY: Did I lose?

Everyone has taken their place at the table. They close their eyes.

BUSH: Oh God, guide us and guide the USA, that the right-   10
eous may triumph and we may do good, in thy name, oh
Lord.
ALL: Amen.

BUSH *smiles.*

BUSH: Good morning, gentlemen. I've had a special request.
The Vice-President has asked if he can speak first. Kind of 15
a special occasion. We don't often hear from Dick, do we?
RUMSFELD: Not at length.
BUSH: Pretty special when he speaks, never mind first.

Everyone laughs.

Fire away, Dick.
CHENEY: Well . . . the President's made a decision. I'm going 20
to stand by that decision, even though I've argued against
it.
BUSH: You certainly have.
CHENEY: I don't think anyone in this room begins to understand what we've let ourselves in for. But. The decision's 25
been taken and I'm going to offer a notion of how it
should be presented. I mean, to the world.
BUSH: Go on.
CHENEY: The way we do this is: crisis at the UN.
BUSH: Say that again.   30
CHENEY: Crisis at the UN. (CHENEY *smiles.*) We turn it round,
see? That's my notion. Nothing to do with American intentions. No longer a question of American foreign policy—its wisdom, its legality. No. Saddam Hussein has

35 violated seventeen UN agreements. The UN has 173 pages of concerns about weapons of mass destruction. Therefore. The only question is: 'Does the UN still have a role?' That's the question. Is the UN an East River chattering factory? Is it an expensive irrelevance? Is this or is

40 this not an organisation which still has the authority to enforce its own resolutions? Does it have the chops? (CHENEY *looks round.*) Yes, we'll go through the UN. We go to the UN. We walk right in that glass door. Yes, we're supporting the UN. 'What, us? Sure, we support the UN.' But

45 all the time we're asking the question: 'Can the UN deliver?'

There is a silence.

BUSH: I think it's good. This way it's not about us. It's about them. That's good. We put the monkey on Annan's back.

Nobody moves for a moment. A wind begins to blow. Two anoraked figures with walking sticks appear, blinking genially in the wind. They are HANS *and* EVA BLIX.

BLIX: I had been walking in Patagonia with my wife in Jan-
50 uary 2000. We were on our way to the Antarctic. At a sweet town called El Calafate—it means 'The Blueberry'—I was waiting for a plane to Ushuaia—it's the southern-most town in the world—when I was given a message from a Mr Kofi Annan, please to call him. The
55 telephonist had never heard of him.

KOFI ANNAN *at the United Nations is having to raise his voice on the telephone.*

ANNAN: Hello. Hello, I'm trying to speak to Mr Hans Blix. He's walking in Patagonia.
BLIX: I managed to call him back. Kofi asked me if I'd be interested in resuming my old job of leading the Iraqi
60 weapons inspections. (BLIX *hesitates for only a moment.*) I said yes. I'd be interested.

End of Act One.

ACT TWO

THIRTEEN

A PALESTINIAN ACADEMIC *waits for the audience to return. She speaks when they are ready.*

PALESTINIAN ACADEMIC: For the Palestinian, there is no other context. We see everything in the context of Palestine.
Why Iraq? The question has been asked a thousand times. And a thousand answers have been given. Why was
5 the only war in history ever to be based purely on intelligence—and doubtful intelligence at that—launched against a man who was ten years past his peak of belligerence?
Why Iraq? Why now? Here comes the familiar list of
10 explanations. Because an Arab democracy would serve as a model. Because it was unfinished business—'He tried to kill my dad.' Because Osama bin Laden had served notice on the dictatorship in Saudi Arabia, and now America

needed a new military base. Because Cheney worked for Halliburton. 'It was all about oil!'
15 For us, no. For Palestinians, it's about one thing: defending the interests of America's three-billion-dollar-a-year colony in the Middle East.
This is a President whose knowledge of Palestine is confined to one helicopter flight in the company of 20 Sharon, from which he looked down on the suffering of the refugees. UN resolutions which are offered as the gold standard to legitimise war on Iraq are ignored when they conflict with the territorial advancement of Israel. Justice and freedom are the ostensible cause of the West—but 25 never extended to a people expelled from their land and forbidden any right to return. Terror is condemned, but state-sanctioned murder is green-lit.
The Jewish poet Claim Nahman Bialik dreamt of a state where there would be Zionist murderers, Zionist 30 prostitutes, Zionist crooks. Israel, he said, would only be normal when it was as corrupt and human as any other state in the world. Well, it's human now.
The victims of the conflict have become the problem. We are the Jews of the Jews. 35

FOURTEEN

Fleets of black cars. Angry hooting and honking. NYPD out in force. Urban chaos.

AN ACTOR: September 12th 2002. Gridlock on the streets of New York. A motorcade glides towards the glass matchbox on Sutton Place. In his hand, George Bush has the bitterly contested text of what some say will be the most important speech of his life. 5
BUSH: You know, you've got to remember, every speech is now 'the speech of my life'. I've had about six of those from my trusted advisers. So I'm immune to the 'speech of your life' stuff.
AN ACTOR: In the dog days of August, members of his ad- 10 ministration have been on a linguistic offensive which seems to Colin Powell seriously at odds with what has been agreed—
POWELL: We had an agreement! I thought we had an agreement! 15

DICK CHENEY *moves into a TV studio.*

AN ACTOR: To Powell's dismay the airwaves are full of colleagues aiming to discredit the principle of a return to inspections:
CHENEY: A return of inspectors would provide no assurance whatsoever of Saddam's compliance with UN resolutions. 20 On the contrary, there is a great danger that it would provide false comfort that Saddam was somehow 'back in the box'.
AN ACTOR: Cheney pre-empts the findings of any future inspections:
CHENEY: Simply stated, there is no doubt that Saddam Hus- 25 sein now has weapons of mass destruction.

RUMSFELD *appears before a Senate hearing.*

AN ACTOR: At a Senate hearing, Donald Rumsfeld joins in. When asked by Senator Mark Dayton:

DAYTON: What is compelling us now to make a precipitous
30   decision and take precipitous action?
RUMSFELD: What's different? What's different is three thou-
      sand people got killed.

The Senate hearing disappears.

AN ACTOR: Paul Wolfowitz throws in his own definition of
      weapons of mass destruction:
35 WOLFOWITZ: It's like the judge said about pornography: I
      can't define it but I will know it when I see it.
AN ACTOR: Cheney goes on to make a direct connection be-
      tween the attack on the Twin Towers and Saddam Hus-
      sein.
40 CHENEY: Success in Iraq means we will have struck a blow
      right at the heart of the base, if you will, the geographic
      base of the terrorists who had us under assault now for
      many years, but most especially on 9/11.
AN ACTOR: He asserts:
45 CHENEY: Many of us are convinced that Saddam will acquire
      nuclear weapons fairly soon. Just how soon we cannot
      gauge.
AN ACTOR: Even Condoleezza Rice seems to side with Cheney.
RICE: There will always be some uncertainty about how
50   quickly he can acquire nuclear weapons. But we don't
      want the smoking gun to be a mushroom cloud.

BLAIR *paces, sheaves of paper in hand.*

AN ACTOR: On the other side of the Atlantic, Tony Blair has
      finally received a draft of his proposed dossier which
      seems to him seriously disappointing in its lack of con-
55   clusive evidence.
BLAIR: Really! I mean, really! I mean, come on!

MANNING, CAMPBELL, JONATHAN POWELL *and* BASSETT *all pace,
the same sheaves in hand.*

AN ACTOR: Special adviser Philip Bassett writes to Alastair
      Campbell:
BASSETT: Needs much more weight, writing, detail. We need
60   *better* intelligence material, *more* material, and better
      flagged-up, more *convincing* material.
AN ACTOR: On September 11th an anonymous e-mail goes
      round the intelligence community:

A Spook reads the e-mail on a note of rising urgency.

SPOOK: Number Ten, through the Chairman of the Joint In-
65   telligence Committee, want the document to be as strong
      as possible within the bounds of available intelligence. This
      is therefore a last call for any items of intelligence agencies
      think can and should be included! Responses needed by
      12.00 tomorrow!

The door of 10 Downing Street is opened at night to admit SIR
RICHARD DEARLOVE.

70 BLAIR: Sir Richard. Welcome. Come in. Do.
AN ACTOR: That night, Sir Richard Dearlove, Head of MI6,
      visits the Prime Minister.

MANNING, CAMPBELL, JONATHAN POWELL *and* BLAIR *are with*
Dearlove in the den.

BLAIR: Well?
DEARLOVE: I do . . . I do have one new source you might be
      interested in.   75
BLAIR: That's why we asked you.
DEARLOVE: It isn't corroborated. (DEARLOVE *shifts.*) This is
      highly unusual. As you know, I don't usually like to de-
      pend on a single supplier. There are procedures . . .
BLAIR: Plainly.   80
DEARLOVE: The protocol of intelligence . . .
BLAIR: Essential.
DEARLOVE: We don't like to offer information from just one
      line of reporting.

BLAIR *waits again.*

      We have a source who is saying that the Iraqi military are   85
      able to deploy chemical or biological weapons within
      twenty to forty-five minutes of an order to do so.

There is a moment's silence.

BLAIR: This is a source of your own?
DEARLOVE: Not exactly.
BLAIR: We'll need to know more.   90
DEARLOVE: It's come to us through an Iraqi organisation.
MANNING: An exiles' organization?
DEARLOVE: The original source is in the Iraqi army.

There is another brief silence.

BLAIR: Richard, it's not in anyone's interests that this infor-
      mation should be wrong.   95
DEARLOVE: Clearly.
BLAIR: If the weapons inspectors go back in, and—God for-
      bid—any of these weapons are found not to exist, then my
      life as Prime Minister will become very difficult indeed.

DEARLOVE *waits.*

      Can you—what I'm asking—can you promise this informa-   100
      tion is sound?
DEARLOVE: No. No, I can't promise. It's a judgement.
BLAIR: And what is your own judgement?

DEARLOVE *hesitates to phrase with care.*

DEARLOVE: My judgement is that this is a significant piece of
      raw intelligence.   105

BLAIR *nods, pleased.*

BLAIR: We'll talk more. You'll give David here the details.
DEARLOVE: I will. Goodnight, Prime Minister.
BLAIR: Goodnight.

Everyone says 'Goodnight'. DEARLOVE *goes.* BLAIR *paces a few mo-*
ments, thinking.

      There it is.

Nobody speaks.

110   David? Well?
MANNING: You asked for something. He brought it. That's
service, I suppose.

BLAIR *considers the implications of this remark.*

BLAIR: It's an instinct, isn't it? It's a feeling.

Everyone waits for the decision.

What did he say? 'Twenty to forty-five'?
115 MANNING: Yes.
BLAIR: Use forty-five.

Downing Street dissolves.

AN ACTOR: As the dossier is prepared, the forty-five-minute
claim gains a life of its own, gathering momentum with
each new draft. It is mentioned four times in the pub-
120   lished dossier and emphasised by Blair in his own introduction.
BLAIR: This document discloses that Saddam's military planning allows for some of the WMD to be ready within
forty-five minutes of an order to use them.
125 AN ACTOR: It becomes a headline all over the world. That
night in the London *Evening Standard:*
EVENING STANDARD: Forty-five minutes to attack!
AN ACTOR: In private, George Tenet, Head of the CIA, refers
to the claim as:
130 TENET: The 'they-can-attack-in-forty-five-minutes' shit.

The General Assembly arrives, POWELL *taking his place among
them.*

AN ACTOR: Meanwhile in New York, George Bush walks
through the glass doors, first to listen to Kofi Annan—
ANNAN: The existence of an effective international security
system depends on the Council's authority—and there-
135   fore on the Council having the political will to act.
AN ACTOR: —and then, finally, to address the General Assembly, in the presence of his Secretary of State—

POWELL *puts on his headphones.*

—who uses headphones even though they speak a common language.

BUSH *steps up to the podium.*

140   Bush makes an early claim:
BUSH: Should Iraq acquire fissile material, it would be able to
build a nuclear weapon within a year.
AN ACTOR: Then goes on to insist:
BUSH: The history, the logic and the facts lead to one con-
145   clusion: Saddam Hussein's regime is a grave and gathering
danger.
Delegates to the General Assembly, we have been more
than patient. We've tried sanctions. We've tried the carrot
of oil for food, and the stick of coalition military strikes.

But Saddam Hussein has defied all these efforts and con- 150
tinues to develop weapons of mass destruction. The first
time we may be completely certain he has a nuclear
weapon is when, God forbids, he uses one.
AN ACTOR: As the speech goes on—
BUSH: My nation will work with the UN Security Council . . . 155
AN ACTOR: —Powell becomes restless, waiting for the President's promise to work through a new UN resolution.
Powell checks delivery against Draft 24 of the speech,
agreed the previous night.

POWELL *whispers to* JOHN NEGROPONTE, *US Ambassador to the
UN.*

POWELL: What's going on?   160
AN ACTOR: In his panic, Powell believes that Dick Cheney
has deliberately removed the vital pledge.
POWELL: He didn't say it!
AN ACTOR: But Bush himself realises that the most important
words have not appeared on the teleprompter. Two lines 165
late he inserts the undertaking from memory.
BUSH: We will work with UN Security Council for the nec-
essary resolutions.
AN ACTOR: The unscripted use of the plural—
BUSH: 'Necessary resolutions.'   170
AN ACTOR: —will unleash a process of diplomacy which will
last six months.

FIFTEEN

At the Hotel Pierre, POWELL *is sitting at an elegant dining table
with* JOHN NEGROPONTE, JACK STRAW, JEREMY GREENSTOCK,
IGOR IVANOV *and* SERGEY LAVROV. *They sit in silence for a mo-
ment, white-jacketed waiters attendant. And then in comes* DO-
MINIQUE DE VILLEPIN, *accompanied by* JEAN-DAVID LEVITTE.
Everyone stands, and shakes hands.

DE VILLEPIN: Good morning, gentlemen . . .
AN ACTOR: Enter the French.
POWELL: Everyone here knows Dominique de Villepin . . .
STRAW: Of course . . .
DE VILLEPIN: Jean-David Levite, our Ambassador at the   5
UN . . .
AN ACTOR: The Hotel Pierre, New York, September 13th
2002 . . .
POWELL: John Negroponte, our Ambassador . . .
DE VILLEPIN: John . . .   10
POWELL: Igor, Sergei . . .
IVANOV: Dominique . . .
LAVROV: Jean-David . . . .
DE VILLEPIN: Jack . . .
STRAW: Dominique . . .   15
POWELL: I thought it would be useful to have some kind of
meeting in advance—
DE VILLEPIN: I think it's an excellent idea . . .
POWELL: —while we're all in New York, so we can just gently
find our way to each others' positions   20
STRAW: Everyone knows Jeremy Greenstock?
DE VILLEPIN: It's always a pleasure to be with Jeremy.
GREENSTOCK: Dominique. Jean-David.
DE VILLEPIN: What a charming hotel. This is a charming place
to meet.   25

POWELL *opens his arms to say 'Let's sit.'*

Are we going to eat first?
POWELL: I thought not. I thought talk first, then enjoy lunch.
DE VILLEPIN: Why not?

They all sit. Waiters retire.

POWELL: To be clear: the President obviously sees yesterday's
30 address as an act of faith in the United Nations.
DE VILLEPIN: Good.
POWELL: But it's also a test. A test of resolve. I'm reluctant to
say that at this table we hold the future of the UN in our
hands. Should the Security Council fail to get compliance
35 from Saddam Hussein, it's going to be very bad news for
the prestige and standing of the organisation.
DE VILLEPIN: Yes.
POWELL: We see this process as clearly asking the question:
how effective can the UN be?

DE VILLEPIN *smiles.*

40 DE VILLEPIN: Shall I speak?
IVANOV: You go ahead.
DE VILLEPIN: Yes, I can see this is what you've been saying in
public . . .
POWELL: I'm saying it at the Hotel Pierre . . .
45 DE VILLEPIN: Of course you are.
POWELL: In private.
DE VILLEPIN: Yes. But I notice you use the word 'compliance'
. . .
POWELL: Yes.
50 DE VILLEPIN: 'The purpose of any resolution being to enforce
compliance . . .'
POWELL: Yes.
DE VILLEPIN: 'To work towards the disarmament of Iraq . . .'
POWELL: Well?
55 DE VILLEPIN: Forgive me, but there's a confusion here, isn't
there? I listened attentively to your President's speech yesterday and I found this same confusion.
POWELL: What confusion is that?
DE VILLEPIN: It's as if, yes, you've decided to go through a
60 process, but you haven't quite decided what the purpose
of this process is.

POWELL *looks at him a moment.*

POWELL: I thought we had. I thought we'd decided.
DE VILLEPIN: Have you? Look, believe me, I think I speak for
all of us when I say we're delighted you're here.
65 IVANOV: We couldn't be happier.
DE VILLEPIN: All of us have had to endure the taunts of
Americans who've taken to saying that the only people
who believe in international organisations are the people who are weak enough to need them. The only coun-
70 tries who insist on international law are the countries
who won't spend the money to get their way by physical force.
POWELL: I admit: I've heard that said.
DE VILLEPIN: To be honest, in Europe we get a little tired of
75 that kind of remark.

POWELL: I understand.
DE VILLEPIN: Belief in the United Nations isn't a sign of
weakness, it's a sign of strength.
POWELL: So it is for us.
DE VILLEPIN: Good. (DE VILLEPIN *smiles.*) You see in the last two 80
years, since Mr Bush came to power, there have been—
what would you call them? Little signs—indicators—
POWELL: Yes, I know.
DE VILLEPIN: What are they? *Straws in the wind?* Little ges-
tures—like the repudiation of the Kyoto protocol on the 85
environment, withdrawal from the Anti-Ballistic Missile
Treaty, rejection of the comprehensive Test Ban Treaty, repudiation of the protocol to the Biological Weapons Convention, refusal to recognise or take part in the
International Criminal Court—presumably so that your 90
Mr Kissinger can continue climbing onto aeroplanes
without fear of arrest . . .
POWELL: Very funny . . .
DE VILLEPIN: Call us over-sensitive, but some of us find it hard
to believe you're now getting wholeheartedly behind the 95
idea of international law.

POWELL *looks at him mistrustfully.*

Speaking for myself—I think the world outside America
has felt a little like a rejected lover these past two years.
Now it's one o'clock in the morning and you're coming
to our door with a bunch of flowers and whisky on your 100
breath. You can see why some of us are feeling just a little
bit cautious.
POWELL: We wouldn't have come if we didn't believe in it.
DE VILLEPIN: No. (DE VILLEPIN *looks at* POWELL *a moment, almost challenging him.*) However. We can't ignore the facts. 105
Even as we sit in this room, as we start to enjoy our lunch,
your Defense Secretary is already embarking on a substantial military build-up. Am I wrong?

POWELL *doesn't answer.*

By our reckoning, by the time we get to the pastry you'll
be on your way to putting some sixty thousand military 110
personnel into the region.
POWELL: Certainly.
DE VILLEPIN: So?
POWELL: Dominique, even Kofi welcomes our presence. He
has no problem with it. Why should he? He sees it as a 115
way of exerting pressure to enforce the will of the UN.
DE VILLEPIN: Pressure. Of course.
POWELL: It's coercive diplomacy.
DE VILLEPIN: If that's what it is—coercive—then of course it's
welcome. 120
POWELL: Force isn't force unless you threaten to use it.

There's a chilly silence. DE VILLEPIN *shifts.*

DE VILLEPIN: Yes. I was talking about this last night to
Igor . . .
POWELL: You were?
DE VILLEPIN: Yes. Just briefly. 125
IVANOV: We met briefly.
DE VILLEPIN: In advance of this meeting.

POWELL: Ah, you mean, you met in advance of the meeting in advance of the meetings?

They all smile.

130 DE VILLEPIN: Yes, exactly.
POWELL: Go on.
DE VILLEPIN: We were saying: you're on what I think you call a twin-track, aren't you? The military and the diplomatic.
POWELL: Yes. Yes, we are.
135 DE VILLEPIN: Clearly it's going to need an extraordinary balance of skill to keep those two tracks running. Rather than crashing into each other.
POWELL: That's what I'm here for.
DE VILLEPIN: And believe me—I wanted to say this—we're
140 most of all pleased it's you. That means a great deal to us.
POWELL: Thank you. (POWELL *is watchful, mistrusting* DE VILLEPIN's *flattery.*)
DE VILLEPIN: The most popular man in America.
POWELL: I'm sorry?
145 DE VILLEPIN: According to the polls.

POWELL *is icy.*

More popular even than the President.
POWELL: They're just polls.
DE VILLEPIN: All the same. All the same. It's not a bad thing to be, is it? More popular than your own President? Virtually
150 the only uncontested hero in America. It puts you in a remarkably strong position.

There is a silence. DE VILLEPIN *drums his fingers on the table.*

STRAW: Dominique, I'm an averagely intelligent person and I'm not sure where you're heading.
DE VILLEPIN: No? It must be my English.
155 STRAW: Must be.
DE VILLEPIN: I'll make myself clear. (DE VILLEPIN *turns to* POWELL, *now focused.*) There's all the difference in the world between coming to the UN with the aim of getting Saddam to disarm through peaceful means, and coming to the UN in or-
160 der simply to get a stamp of approval for an invasion.
POWELL: That's not what we're asking for.
DE VILLEPIN: Isn't it?
POWELL: No. No, I don't think it is. I mean, we haven't yet specified the wording of the resolution . . .
165 DE VILLEPIN: Exactly . . .
POWELL: That lies ahead.
DE VILLEPIN: Exactly.
POWELL: The framing of the resolution, that's the very subject of this lunch . . .

DE VILLEPIN *smiles again.*

170 DE VILLEPIN: All it is: I'm looking at this contradiction and trying to make some sense of it. On the one hand, the US says it's giving the Security Council the chance to handle the process. On the other hand, certain members of the administration—not you, Colin—are implying that only
175 one outcome is going to be acceptable. My point is this: you can't come to the UN, then announce that the UN

has failed if it gives you any result but the one you want. You can't do that. Put it another way: you can't play football and be the referee as well. That isn't—I'm using the English expression—'playing fair'. 180
POWELL: That's not what we're doing. We're not doing that. This is a negotiation. Genuine. With equal partners. There are fifteen countries on the Security Council. We want fifteen votes. Freely given. We're in good faith.
DE VILLEPIN: I would hope. 185
POWELL: Do you think I'd be here if we weren't?

DE VILLEPIN *opens his hands, as if to say he doesn't know the answer.*

DE VILLEPIN: I'm going to make a suggestion in the hope of defusing any possible tension.
POWELL: Go ahead.
DE VILLEPIN: Though I'm becoming embarrassed at being the 190
only person who speaks.
STRAW: Believe me, we're enjoying listening.
POWELL: What's your suggestion?

DE VILLEPIN *smiles.*

DE VILLEPIN: I suggest two resolutions.
POWELL: Two? 195
DE VILLEPIN: Yes. One to effect disarmament. And the second . . . the second to trigger war if, after a reasonable time, disarmament is not proved to have taken place. It seems the easiest way of disentangling your two different aims.
POWELL: I see. (POWELL *looks at him a moment.*) I see. You want 200
me to get a resolution, then come back and get another?
DE VILLEPIN: That's it exactly.
POWELL: Do you . . . do you have any idea how hard it was to get here in the first place?
DE VILLEPIN: I have some idea, yes. 205
POWELL: And now you want me to come back?

But DE VILLEPIN *is not fazed.*

DE VILLEPIN: France won't consider a first resolution which contains any kind of hidden trigger, and mechanism which might trigger war. The French are genuinely delighted to help the United States if your purpose is, in- 210
deed, disarmament. Nothing would make us happier. If you have a second purpose—to license an attack—to seek international cover for an American invasion—then no. We deal with a new situation only when and as disarmament is shown not to occur. 215

POWELL *is looking at him in dismay.*

Please. What I'm suggesting is not unreasonable. It can hardly come as a surprise. If you remember, your own President referred to 'resolutions' in the plural.
NEGROPONTE: That was a glitch!
DE VILLEPIN: He used the plural. 220
NEGROPONTE: It was a technical glitch!
DE VILLEPIN: Whatever.
NEGROPONTE: You know perfectly well: when the President said he was going to 'bring forward resolutions' what he meant was 'resolution'. Single. 225
LEVITTE: It's a pity that's not what he said.

NEGROPONTE: He was improvising. He had to improvise. The machine went down and he did very well to say anything at all!

LEVITTE *is taking out a transcript.*

230 LEVITTE: If there's a problem, I have a transcript here. I can check.

POWELL: There's no need to check! (POWELL *has spoken with unexpected sharpness. Now he turns to* DE VILLEPIN, *measured, cool.*) Good. Very well. We've laid out preliminary posi-
235 tions, and now we're all going to eat our lunch. Afterwards I'm going to think things over.

DE VILLEPIN: Thank you.

POWELL: Because there's some kind of contract here, I think.

DE VILLEPIN: Contract?

240 POWELL: Yes. Between us. (POWELL *stops, deliberate.*) Think. Consider. The questions you might have asked me: 'Do I personally want to see the inspectors back in?' 'Yes.' 'Do I genuinely want the inspections to succeed?' 'Yes.' 'Do I want war?' 'Emphatically, no.' Now if these are the out-
245 comes we all desire, it's up to you to make my life liveable. You have to give me something I can take back to the President.

DE VILLEPIN: I accept that.

POWELL: Push me too hard and you'll end up with an out-
250 come the opposite of what you want. Remember that. This is a two-way street. Your good faith is to be tested as much as mine. (POWELL *smiles, still chilly.*) If anyone's stupid enough to think this is payback time for what-ever grudge they happen to be nursing against the
255 US—be it Kyoto or the Criminal Court or—I don't know—how they hate McDonald's—then what they'll be doing in effect is condemning Iraqi women and chil-dren to the sort of bombardment which is going to make them wish they'd never been born. And possibly
260 civil chaos after. That's what I'm trying to avoid. (POW-ELL *waits for this to sink in.*) As to two resolutions, well, it's a technical question, because although we're going to fight about words, it won't ultimately be about words. It'll be a fight about attitude: wanting to help or
265 not.

The table is silenced.

Yes, America's a great power. The only great power. You may see this as the moment when America has to submit to the international will. And you may be relishing that prospect.
270 DE VILLEPIN: I didn't say that.

POWELL: But I don't see it that way. (*Powell smiles.*) I know you're a lover of history . . .

DE VILLEPIN: I am . . .

POWELL: I think it's Hobbes, isn't it? who says 'Covenants
275 without swords are but words . . .'

DE VILLEPIN: I think it's Hobbes.

POWELL: So. For the moment, America has the swords and is therefore—whether we like it or not—the enforcer of covenants. In France, I don't know, you may wish for the
280 day when that's no longer so. But, with the best will in the world, I don't see that day arriving in the next few

months. (POWELL *reaches across and touches* DE VILLEPIN's *wrist.*) We have to work together.

DE VILLEPIN: We'll work together.

POWELL: Good. I'm going to hold you to that. (POWELL *gets up* 285 *to get the waiters back. He goes to the door, then turns.*) Oh, and by the way—about working together. If we do go for two resolutions—*if*—one for proof of disarmament, the other for war—I warn you now, don't vote for the first unless you're going to be ready one day to vote for the second. 290 We'd take that very badly. (POWELL *looks a moment.*) Lunch.

POWELL *opens the door and the waiters in white coats pour in, bear-ing food and drink.*

SIXTEEN

Groups of Senators and Congressmen arrive to be briefed by BUSH.

AN ACTOR: Soon after his address to the UN the President goes to Congress to seek the authorization he needs. First, he embarks on a lobbying campaign, inviting a hundred and ninety-five Congressmen and all hundred Senators to the White House for personal briefings: 5

BUSH: You can't distinguish between Al Qaeda and Saddam when you talk about the war on terror.

AN ACTOR: After two days of debate in the House, the Pres-ident has a vote of 266 to 133 to allow him carte blanche to deploy the US armed forces 'as he deems to be neces- 10 sary and appropriate'.

The Senate assembles.

In the Senate, John McCain captures the mood:

MCCAIN: There is no greater responsibility we face than vot-ing to place this country on a course that could send young Americans to war in her defence. All of us must 15 weigh our consciences carefully. The very fact that we are holding this free debate serves as a reminder that we are a great nation, united in freedom's defence, and called once again to make the world safe for freedom's blessings to flourish. The quality of our greatness will determine the 20 character of our response.

Parliament assembles.

AN ACTOR: In Britain, Parliament is recalled to debate the growing crisis. Fifty-three Labour MPs rebel. One says:

SIMPSON: Bush will hit Iraq in much the same way that a drunk will hit a bottle—to satisfy his thirst for power and 25 oil. I must tell the Prime Minister that the role of a friend in such circumstances is not to pass the drunk the bottle!

BLIX *and* MOHAMMED ELBARADEI *arrive, smiling at a piece of pa-per they both hold.*

AN ACTOR: America draws up the first draft of a startlingly tough resolution which insists on the right to send US troops into Iraq to guard inspectors as they go about their 30 work.

BLIX: It was so remote from reality. It was written by some-one who doesn't understand how inspections function.

POWELL *lifts a phone to* BLIX.

POWELL: Hans. It's Colin Powell. The President and I were
35   thinking it would it would be nice if you dropped by to
      see him.
BLIX: I'd be delighted.
POWELL: We'll send a van to your hotel at 8 a.m. That way
      we can get you right in and avoid security.

BLIX *and* ELBARADEI *walk with* POWELL *down White House corridors.* CHENEY *gets up and shakes their hands. They all sit down.*

40   AN ACTOR: Hans Blix and his colleague Mohammed
      ElBaradei are invited to the White House. First, they are
      taken to the Vice-President's office for what turns out to
      be a brief meeting.
CHENEY: You know, we're sure there are weapons there. I
45   don't think you're going to have any trouble finding
      them. And if you do have any trouble, understand, we're
      ready to discredit you.

Everyone gets up.

AN ACTOR: Moments later, they are ushered into the Oval
      Office.

BUSH *gets up from behind the desk to shake hands.* POWELL *hovers.*

50   BUSH: It's a great honour to meet you both. I'm honoured to
      meet you, sir.
BLIX: No, the honour is mine.
ELBARADEI: Good morning, Mr President.

BUSH *gestures them to sit down.*

BUSH: I'm hearing you're thinking you can start in two
55   months.
BLIX: Two months, yes. We've known for some time we
      might go back in. So it's a practical question. Reassembling the team.

BUSH *sits back behind his desk.*

BUSH: A lot of things get said, there's a lot of noise in the air,
60   hyperventilation, this is—you know—stuff that goes on. I
      tune it out. I don't listen. They say I'm a mad Texan bent
      on war. That's not so. That's what I wanted to say to you.
      I want to go through the UN and I want him disarmed.
BLIX: I'm happy to hear that.
65   BUSH: We have confidence in you.
BLIX: Thank you, Mr President. That means a great deal to us.

BUSH *nods and looks at him a moment.*

BUSH: You can be assured, Mr Blix, you've got the force of
      the United States behind you.
BLIX: Yes.
70   BUSH: The only mistake you could make is to imagine that
      when you come to report, it's you that's making the decision. About whether to take further action.
BLIX: Of course not. I agree with you. That's not my role.

BUSH: No. It isn't you that makes that decision. It's me.

They all get up.

AN ACTOR: Blix and ElBaradei are now ushered into a third   75
      and final meeting, this time with Condoleezza Rice.

They all sit down.

RICE: What I want to put to you, is: it's understood, you work
      for the UN, they're your masters, we accept that. But we
      feel there can also be input from individual members of
      the Security Council.   80
BLIX: Which members do you have in mind?
RICE: Naturally, the United States.

BLIX *nods, as if thinking seriously.*

BLIX: What sort of input? I mean, intelligence, yes, the more
      the better. Materiel. We're grateful. But beyond that?
RICE: This is a very big job, it's an important job . . .   85
BLIX: Believe me, I don't need persuading . . .
RICE: And we have a lot of ideas on how you can be helped.
BLIX: Helped?
RICE: Yes. We're proposing some sort of philosophical agreement. On paper. A signed agreement. About what you're   90
      going to do. And the way you're going to do it.

BLIX *nods again, considering.*

BLIX: I don't think I can do that, Dr Rice. I work for the UN.

BLIX *stares at her.* WOLFOWITZ *comes in.*

AN ACTOR: Later, in the meeting, Paul Wolfowitz arrives.
RICE: You don't know Paul Wolfowitz?
BLIX: I haven't had the pleasure. How do you do?   95

ELBAREDEI, BLIX *and* WOLFOWITZ *stand round shaking hands.*

AN ACTOR: Nine months earlier Wolfowitz has ordered a secret CIA investigation to discredit Hans Blix.

WOLFOWITZ *has sat down and is looking hard at* BLIX.

WOLFOWITZ: You do know they have the weapons, don't
      you? I mean, you are starting from that position, I hope?
BLIX: I go in with a great deal of knowledge.   100
WOLFOWITZ: It's not your knowledge, it's your position I'm
      interested in.
BLIX: My position?
WOLFOWITZ: Yes. What's your position? What is it?
BLIX: Well, I have experience, I hope I have judgement, but   105
      professionally, I see it as a matter of principle: I have no
      position.

WOLFOWITZ *just stares at him.*

WOLFOWITZ: You remember, the problems we had last
      time . . .
BLIX: I do.   110

WOLFOWITZ: Last time we couldn't get scientists to travel abroad.

BLIX: It's true. It's always a problem.

WOLFOWITZ: Everyone's terrified. If you leave the country to
115   talk to you guys, then Saddam will kill you when you get back. He'll kill your family. It's a dictatorship.

BLIX: I agree.

WOLFOWITZ: So I've been thinking about it. I've got a solution.

120 BLIX: We'd like to hear it.

WOLFOWITZ: It'll work like a subpoena. A sort of international subpoena. We have the right to slap an injunction on a scientist, we take him out, we talk to him abroad and this time we get what we need.

BLIX says nothing.

125   What do you think?

BLIX: Forgive me, but somehow I've never seen the UN as being in the kidnapping business.

They all shake hands, making polite goodbyes.

RICE: It's been a great privilege to meet you.

BLIX: It's certainly been a very useful meeting.

130 AN ACTOR: Colin Powell spends the next four weeks in negotiation after the first US draft is rejected by all fourteen other members of the Security Council. After seven weeks, arguments about wording have reached a bitter stand-off. The French insist that there may be serious con-
135   sequences should Iraq be in material breach of the resolution, as evidenced by:

LEVITTE: A false declaration 'and' a general failure to cooperate.

AN ACTOR: The Americans prefer the word:

NEGROPONTE: 'Or'.

140 AN ACTOR: The dispute over this single word lasts five days.

RICE is in her office at night. POWELL *appears.*

POWELL: Condi . . . You busy?

RICE: I'm busy. Busy enough. Come in.

They both smile.

How you getting on? You close?

POWELL: Still that word.

145 RICE: The President's very firm about this. Lose the little things, you start losing the big ones.

POWELL *nods slightly.*

POWELL: Condi, the French aren't stupid. They know we'll go to war if we have to.

RICE: So?

150 POWELL: I'm trying to avoid war.

RICE: We're all trying to avoid war.

POWELL: Yeah. (POWELL *looks at her, not believing her.*) Look, they're offering a formula. It's words. Words set out in a certain order. It satisfies their honour and it satisfies us.
155   They're going to say we need a second resolution, we're going to say we don't. You can read it either way.

RICE: That good, eh?

They both smile.

POWELL: All we want is a headline: 'US Achieves Iraq Resolution'. I can get fourteen votes . . .

RICE: Fourteen?   160

POWELL: Maybe fifteen. Even Syria. Who knows? But I have to give in to the French. On this one thing. It's a way of saying, 'Look, we're not going to give you nothing.'

RICE *stares, undecided.*

We were going to do this in two weeks, remember? Do we want it to take longer? Do we want it to fail? I don't 165
think so.

RICE: Do you like this guy?

POWELL: He's a self-defined intellectual who writes biographies of Napoleon. He destroyed my daughter's wedding to discuss 'and' or 'or'.   170

RICE: You like him.

POWELL *looks her in the eye.*

POWELL: Condi, I'm telling you: he gave me his word.

RICE: OK.

POWELL: That means something.

They stare at one another a moment.

Do you think . . . do you think you could speak to the 175
President?

RICE: Why don't you speak to him?

They both know the answer, so neither speaks.

POWELL: No point in being a trusted adviser unless she gives some trusted advice.

RICE *smiles in assent.*

Thank you.   180

POWELL *goes.* RICE *sits alone.*

AN ACTOR: On November 8th Powell concedes the word 'or' and the Security Council unanimously adopts Resolution 1441. Immediately afterwards the Americans and the French brief the press, giving contradictory readings of the same document.   185

Diplomats at the UN brief separate pools of journalists.

NEGROPONTE: Resolution 1441 contains no hidden triggers and does not constrain any member state from taking any action to defend itself against the threat posed by Iraq.

LEVITTE: By insisting on two stages, the resolution makes it 190
clear that it is only the Security Council which can handle this matter.

AN ACTOR: Dominique de Villepin adds:

DE VILLEPIN: I have signed nothing which locks us in to war.
195 AN ACTOR: This is widely seen as the moment of Powell's greatest triumph.

SEVENTEEN

GENERAL HASSAN MUHAMMAD AMIN *sets out a table with twelve thousand pages of documents for the world's press to photograph.*

AN ACTOR: Within the required week, Iraq re-admits inspectors and commits to producing a full description of their chemical facilities within thirty days. On December 7th, General Hassan Muhammad Amin has a photo call.

A media scrum, flash photos and a proud General.

5   Piled on a table are forty-three spiral-bound volumes of documents, containing 12,159 pages, six folders and twelve CD-ROMs.
AMIN: We are a country devoid of weapons of mass destruction.
10 AN ACTOR: Saddam Hussein makes a statement on Iraqi television:

SADDAM *speaks in Arabic, a translator renders it in English.*

SADDAM: We apologise to God about any act which has angered him in the past, and that was held against us, and we apologise to the Kuwaitis on the same basis.
15 AN ACTOR: Amin then drives to the UN compound and hands the papers over. They are thence flown on to the UN in New York.

Another media scrum as two young men arrive with huge bags.

The US insists that the submission will be a cookbook for lethal chemical weapons and rules that not all members of
20 the Council can be trusted to read the whole document.
BLIX: To be honest, I was happy for the document to go first to Washington. They have the logistical capacity to make fifteen copies of twelve thousand pages. We don't.
AN ACTOR: During the week in Washington the names of the
25 two companies which, before the 1991 Gulf War, secretly supplied Iraq with seventeen types of biological agents are removed. One company is American. The other French.

In BLAIR's *den,* JONATHAN POWELL *and* MANNING *sit reading a résumé.* BLAIR *pacing moodily, the same résumé in hand.* CAMPBELL *sitting at a desk, quietly working.*

BLAIR: I don't know. I just don't know. I knew it'd be bad, but not this bad!
30 MANNING: It's bad.
BLAIR: He's blown it. He's really blown it, hasn't he? I thought Saddam would give us *something.* I did genuinely believe he'd give us *something.*
MANNING: Twelve thousand pages—the whole thing a point-
35 less re-hash.
BLAIR: The Americans are going to go crazy. They're going to say he's not in compliance . . .
MANNING: Cheney, Rummy, Wolfie . . .

BLAIR: Exactly. He's playing into their hands. They're all going to say, 'Oh great, now we can go to war!' I mean, re- 40
ally! This was Saddam's chance. Why didn't he take it?
CAMPBELL: Because he's got the IQ of parsley.

But BLAIR *ignores this, pacing.*

BLAIR: And now where are we? Blix is running round Mesopotamia like Hercule Poirot. The whole world is watching and everyone seems to think it's some kind of 45
game. Everyone thinks: 'If Blix doesn't find the weapons, then Saddam wins.' The man is a murderous dictator, and we've turned the whole thing into Cluedo. Tell me I'm wrong.
MANNING: You're not wrong. 50

BLAIR *shakes his head.*

BLAIR: It's all Blix's fault. He's letting himself be used. Why can't people understand? It isn't Blix's job to find the weapons—it's Saddam's job to prove they've been destroyed.
MANNING: Of course. 55
BLAIR: It's perfectly simple. Why don't people get it? I've explained it. God knows I've explained it.
CAMPBELL: You have. Often.
BLAIR: It's not up to us to prove they exist! It's up to them to prove they don't! 60

MANNING *looks at his fingernails, the diplomat.*

MANNING: There was always a danger. We knew that. We went in knowing that inspections could be misconstrued.
BLAIR: David, I promised the British people: no war without the UN. (BLAIR *moves away, insistent.*) There's one rule. With the Americans there's one rule. You get in early. The 65
earlier you join, the more influence you have. You prove your loyalty. And that way they listen.
MANNING: It's true.
BLAIR: You remember what happened to Kinnock?
MANNING: I do. 70
BLAIR: My God! The humiliation! Ronald Reagan gave him twenty minutes! We're a Labour government. The one thing we've learnt: if for a moment, if even for a moment we come adrift from Washington, our credibility is gone. It's gone! 75

CAMPBELL *looks up as* BLAIR *paces.*

I've got my military saying to me, 'Are we in or are we out?' They're saying, 'We need time to prepare.' And I've got the British public saying, 'You promised you'd wait.' I've got the British public saying, 'Well you haven't found the weapons, so you can't be going to war.' How many 80
times can I lift the phone? How many times can I say, 'George, hold on, just hold on . . .' (BLAIR *bursts out again at the injustice.*) Saddam was meant to give me something! He was meant to help!
MANNING: Yes. Yes. It's tricky. 85
BLAIR: I can't believe where we are. Every bad thing that could have happened has happened.

The advisers are looking one to another, lost for advice. POWELL *is quiet, conciliatory.*

JONATHAN POWELL: You think the world's reasonable, Prime Minister. It's not reasonable.

90 BLAIR: I'm not asking Saddam to be clever. I'm just asking him to have some elementary cunning. Some vestigial instinct for survival. At least have that! Every politician has that! (BLAIR *looks away, lost.*) What am I meant to do?

95 MANNING: You have to do what you're doing. You have to leave it with Blix.

BLAIR *shakes his head.*

BLAIR: It's wrong. It's so wrong.

Downing Street disappears.

AN ACTOR: In the second week of the New Year, Rice flags up an issue which has been disturbing her.

The Oval Office, BUSH *alone at his desk.* RICE *comes in.*

100 RICE: There's something I need to mention to you, sir.
BUSH: Whatever.
RICE: An imbalance.
BUSH: Tell me.
RICE: It's my job to balance out separate needs, separate re-
105 quirements. The different departments. To listen. As of this moment, the Secretary of Defense knows your plans, sir. Donald's been party to them. You could say, some time back. (RICE *waits a moment.*) The Secretary of State doesn't know your plans.
110 BUSH: I understand.
RICE: He's not been party to them. (*Rice shifts.*) Colin works every day . . .
BUSH: Yes.
RICE: At the UN.
115 BUSH: Yes.
RICE: Among foreign ministers. Hitting the phones. Taking the diplomatic route.
BUSH: Yes.
RICE: I'm not sure this situation can go on as it is.

BUSH *stares, at his most enigmatic.* RICE *goes.*

120 AN ACTOR: On January 13th, Powell is summoned to the Oval Office.

BUSH *gets up as* POWELL *arrives.*

BUSH: Welcome, Colin.
POWELL: Mr President.
BUSH: Come in. Make yourself comfortable.
125 POWELL: Alone?
BUSH: Yes.
POWELL: No Condi?
BUSH: No. No Condi.

POWELL *has said it lightly, but* BUSH's *tone alerts him. Tense, he sits.*

POWELL: Sir?
BUSH: Colin, I think we've reached a fork in the road. We're   130
at that fork. I don't think there's a way round this. These inspections are a distraction. They weaken us. They weaken our purpose.

POWELL *looks at him a moment.*

POWELL: In what way?
BUSH: We've got ourselves into a situation where we're in-   135
sisting he's guilty until he proves he's innocent. That's not good. That's not good for us. He's making a monkey of us.
POWELL: What you're saying: you've made up your mind.
BUSH: I'm saying that.
POWELL: You've thought this through?   140

BUSH *nods.*

BUSH: I've taken a decision. If you have a problem with that decision, best thing is you should speak. You should say something now. I've invited you in. I'm giving you the chance to say something now.

They look at each other. There is a long silence.

It would be a big thing. It would be a big thing if you dis-   145
agreed. Well?
POWELL: I don't disagree.

BUSH *nods, satisfied.* POWELL *gets up.*

Thank you, sir. Thank you for telling me. (POWELL *goes out.*)
AN ACTOR: Later, Bush recalls:
BUSH: It was a very cordial conversation. I would describe it   150
as cordial. I think the log will show that it was relatively short.
AN ACTOR: White House records show that the encounter lasted twelve minutes.

BUSH, *alone, looks at us a moment.*

BUSH: I didn't need his permission.   155

EIGHTEEN

A BRIT IN NEW YORK *appears.*

BRIT IN NEW YORK: 'America changed.' That's what we're told. 'On September 11th everything changed.' 'If you're not American, you can't understand.'
     The infantile psycho-babble of popular culture is grafted opportunistically onto America's politics. The lan-   5
guage of childish entitlement becomes the lethal rhetoric of global wealth and privilege.
     Asked how you are as president, on the first day of a war which will kill around thirty thousand people: 'I feel good.'   10
     I was in Saks Fifth Avenue the morning they bombed Baghdad. 'Isn't it wonderful?' says the saleswoman. 'At last we're hitting back.' 'Yes,' I reply. 'At the wrong people. Somebody steals your handbag, so you kill their second cousin, on the grounds they live close. Explain to me,' I   15

say, 'Saudi Arabia is financing Al Qaeda. Iran, Lebanon and
Syria are known to shelter terrorists. North Korea is developing a nuclear weapons programme. All these you
leave alone. No, you go to war with the one place in the
20 region admitted to have no connection with terrorism.'
'You're not American,' says the saleswoman. 'You don't
understand.'

Oh, a question, then. If 'You're not American. You don't
understand' is the new dispensation, then why not 'You're
25 not Chechen'? Are the Chechens also now licensed? Are
Basques? Theatres, restaurants, public squares? Do Israeli
milk-bars filled with women and children become fair
game on the grounds that 'You don't understand. We're
Palestinian, we're Chechen, we're Irish, we're Basque'? If
30 the principle of international conduct is now to be that
you may go against anyone you like on the grounds that
you've been hurt by somebody else, does that apply to
everyone? Or just to America?

On September 11th, America changed. Yes. It got much
35 stupider.

NINETEEN

RICE *welcomes* MAURICE GOURDAULT-MONTAGNE *and* JEAN-
DAVID LEVITTE *to her office.*

AN ACTOR: On the very same day that Powell is informed of
his President's intentions, Condoleezza Rice entertains
Chirac's personal envoy, Maurice Gourdault-Montagne,
nicknamed MGM, accompanied by Ambassador Levitte.
5 MGM: President Chirac sends his compliments.
RICE: Please send him mine. D'you mind if we eat in the office?

They move to a small lunch table.

AN ACTOR: At lunch, the French run through their reservations. At the end of the meal:
10 MGM: Forgive me, but my sense is that even if a decision to invade hasn't actually been taken, it is at least imminent.
Please, I don't expect you to comment. (GOURDAULT-MON-
TAGNE *puts up a hand.*) France came here to express our
anxieties. We've expressed them. But thanks to the skill of
15 Mr Powell, France has so far managed to avoid having to
take up a position of public opposition to American plans.
RICE: We've noted that. We're grateful.
MGM: My President feels that it's in neither country's interest
that France and America quarrel.
20 RICE: We don't want that either.
MGM: Nobody wants it. These are two great countries. Two
of the greatest countries in the world.
RICE: Are you making a deal?
LEVITTE: We're making an offer.
25 RICE: I see. Carry on.
MGM: You have one reading of Resolution 1441. We have another. We've made our point. Put it like this: we have no
desire, we have no need to go on making it.

RICE *frowns.*

RICE: All right. Let's be clear. You're saying . . .

MGM: We're saying we would happy to help the temperature 30
to fall.
RICE: We'd certainly appreciate that.
MGM: We're happy to be silent.
RICE: That would be welcome.
MGM: We agree. Why force an issue which doesn't need to be 35
forced?

They wait a moment while RICE *takes this in.*

LEVITTE: Naturally, the only problem . . .
MGM: Yes . . .
LEVITTE: The only problem would be if anyone were stupid
enough to try and bring forward a second resolution. 40
MGM: Yes.
LEVITTE: We would take that badly.
MGM: Yes.
LEVITTE: The first was difficult enough.

The Frenchmen smile.

RICE: I don't understand. It was you who insisted on a sec- 45
ond resolution in the first place. It was France.
MGM: That's right.
RICE: Now you seem to be saying you're happy to let it go.
LEVITTE: That's right. Why not? The French are realists. We
see how the future is likely to develop. A second resolu- 50
tion and France would be put in an impossible position.
France would be forced to use its veto, which it has no
wish to do.
RICE: No.
MGM: What our President is saying is: if you wish to declare 55
the diplomatic process over, France will have no problem
with that.
RICE: Thank you.

There is a silence.

Thank you.

The Frenchmen leave. RICE *goes to* POWELL'*s office.*

AN ACTOR: At once Rice goes to see Powell. 60
POWELL: No. It's not going to work. We can't do it. Blair!
RICE: It's always Blair.
POWELL: Blair promised a second resolution. He doesn't have
a choice. Nor does Howard in Australia. Nor does Aznar.
They're fighting their own public. 65

RICE *is about to speak.* POWELL *cuts her off.*

Blair's swimming upstream, Condi. We can't let him
drown.

They look at each other a moment.

AN ACTOR: The news of the rejection of their offer is conveyed to the French. One week later:

DE VILLEPIN *on the phone to* POWELL.

70 DE VILLEPIN: Colin, we were wondering if you were going to
      come to New York. We're calling a special meeting—
   POWELL: I know . . .
   DE VILLEPIN: —of foreign ministers in the Security Council.
      To discuss global terrorism. I think it's going to look odd
75   if you're not there.
   POWELL: Dominique, the meeting's on January 20th.
   DE VILLEPIN: Yes, I'm sorry about that.
   POWELL: It's not . . . I have a number of speaking engage-
      ments. It's also . . .
80 DE VILLEPIN: Yes?

POWELL is reluctant to speak.

POWELL: It's Martin Luther King day.

Silence. Neither man moves.

AN ACTOR: On January 20th Powell travels specially to New
      York. The session passes unremarkably but afterwards, in
      front of the world's press and without prior warning,
85   France publicly hardens its position.

Press mob. DE VILLEPIN holds up his hands.

DE VILLEPIN: Gentlemen, gentlemen . . .
AN ACTOR: The incident is known in diplomatic circles as
      'the ambush'.

DE VILLEPIN raises his voice.

DE VILLEPIN: We believe today that nothing justifies military
90   intervention. Military action is a dead end. Nothing justi-
      fies an American adventure. Nothing! Nothing!
JOURNALIST: Will France use its veto in the case of any new
      resolution?
DE VILLEPIN: France is a permanent member of the Security
95   Council. It will shoulder all of its responsibilities faithful
      to all the principles it has.
AN ACTOR: In response, the American people go into a frenzy
      of French-bashing. French tourism, French wine, French
      fries.

POWELL is raging round his office.

100 POWELL: What is this? What the hell is this? I've got a bunch
      of right-wing nutcases in the White House, I've got the
      treacherous French in the Security Council. I'm standing
      in the fucking road! And the shit is all flowing one way!
      (*POWELL turns incensed.*) We had an agreement! I thought
105   we had an agreement!

DONALD RUMSFELD is surrounded by the press mob.

AN ACTOR: Happy to see the row escalate, Donald Rumsfeld
      fans the flames when asked about European dissent:
RUMSFELD: You're thinking of Europe as Germany and
      France. I don't. That's old Europe. If you look to the east,
110   Germany has been a problem, France has been a problem.
      But you look at the vast numbers of other countries in
      Europe. They're not with France and Germany on this,
      they're with the United States.
AN ACTOR: As a deliberate provocation, a few days later he
      proclaims: 115
RUMSFELD: There are four countries that will never support
      us. Never. Cuba, Libya and Germany.
AN ACTOR: Asked to name the fourth:
RUMSFELD: I forgot the fourth.

The press mob go.

AN ACTOR: Noticing a sudden hardening in Colin Powell's   120
      attitudes, a reporter asks:
REPORTER: You've now become a hawk in Iraqi issues and
      speak just like Rumsfeld, so why did you change?
AN ACTOR: Powell replies:
POWELL: It's very unwise to stereotype people with one-   125
      word labels.

TWENTY

*The Oval Office. BUSH is already there, as RICE, POWELL, RUMS-
FELD and CHENEY assemble quickly and sit down.*

RICE: Gentlemen, good morning. The President's called this
      meeting—informal meeting—because we have a problem
      to discuss. Prime Minister Blair's going to be here in
      twenty-four hours. And he's going to be making a request.

CHENEY smirks.

CHENEY: Yeah, I think we know what that request is going to   5
      be.
RICE: And we have to take it seriously because—clearly—he's
      our principal ally. He's committed. He's committed to the
      cause.

BUSH turns to POWELL.

BUSH: Colin?   10
POWELL: Well, I think as everyone's guessed . . .
RUMSFELD: Yeah, we've guessed . . .
POWELL: Blair is going to be asking us to help him secure a
      second resolution. Which he needs for domestic political
      reasons.   15
BUSH: How you feeling about that, Colin?
POWELL: I'll tell you frankly, sir, I don't relish the prospect.
      But on the other hand . . . I want to see diplomacy ex-
      hausted. I don't want to see it terminated.

BUSH turns to CHENEY.

BUSH: Dick?   20
CHENEY: I don't know. I don't understand what we're doing.
      We've got a resolution, haven't we?
POWELL: Yeah. 1441.
CHENEY: If you remember, I didn't want to go get that one . . .
RICE: We remember . . .   25
CHENEY: But at last we got it, and now—I'm trying to make
      sense of this—don't we look stupid if we go back for an-
      other?

POWELL: Well . . .

30 CHENEY: In fact, go back for a second, the only thing we're doing is admitting that the first one didn't give us authorisation in the first place.

POWELL: That's not so. We're not admitting that. I'm making that plain.

CHENEY *ignores him, gathering force.*

35 CHENEY: In fact, can I ask something here? Exactly what craziness are we getting ourselves into? I see no logic. If the first one was good enough—which we always said it was—what the fuck is the point of a second?

POWELL: It's not us that needs it.

40 CHENEY: Exactly. So OK, so we go back, do we? We put ourselves back in the diplomatic mudpit, is that right? And we say, 'The first is fine, the first is just beautiful, but now we've decided we'd like a second, just like the cream and nuts on top of the sundae—so the dish *looks* better.' I

45 mean, are we serious?

RUMSFELD: We're not serious.

CHENEY: We're going to war! The whole country's furious with the French. They're furious with the Germans. We've got the resolution. We've got the troops. Let's go!

CHENEY *has sounded final and now his emotion is infectious.*

50 RUMSFELD: Can I say something? With respect, sir. Isn't this moment now for a little reality? Before we commit? Before we commit young Americans to give their lives? Isn't this the moment just to do the obvious thing and maybe stop listening to Europe? Because we can see—we're get-

55 ting used to this—Europeans are always more worried about how exactly America *reacts* to the threat of Saddam than they are about Saddam himself. Man's coming at you with a knife. All they're worrying about is which hand we use to take it away.

60 POWELL: But *is* he coming at us? We believe he is. But we've got to persuade everyone else. By facts. It's not such a terrible instinct, Donald. People want things to be legitimate.

RUMSFELD: I'll tell you what's legitimate. What we do is legitimate. Read the American Constitution. It was written

65 by Thomas Jefferson and he said—and I'll remind you of his words—that what makes governments legitimate is the consent of the people.

CHENEY: That's right.

RUMSFELD: The authority to act comes from the will of the

70 people.

CHENEY: The American people.

RUMSFELD: That's right. (RUMSFELD *speaks from deep, suppressed emotion.*) Power in this country doesn't come from its institutions, and it sure as hell doesn't come from abroad.

75 There's a lot of talk going on about 'The UN wants this' and 'The UN's allowing that'. Well no, actually. And once we start thinking like that, we're dead.

POWELL: I'm not thinking like that.

RUMSFELD: The United Nations has no power, or is it meant

80 to.

POWELL: Of course not.

RUMSFELD: It's a facility. That's all it is. It's a setting, it's a context. The United Nations never achieved anything, not in

or of itself. Something isn't right because the UN says it is. (RUMSFELD *is quiet, persuasive.*) I know why we're going 85 to war. And so do you, Colin. Because the man is a lunatic and we can't afford the risk that one day he might team up with terrorists.

BUSH: That's what it is.

RUMSFELD: Yeah.   90

BUSH: It's about risk.

RUMSFELD: That's what it's about. In this new world, in this new post-9/11 world. (RUMSFELD *shakes his head.*) And that is something which all grown-up people understand.

CHENEY: Everyone understands.   95

RUMSFELD: Yeah. Which is why the dishonesty gets to me.

CHENEY: Sure.

RUMSFELD: It gets to me.

CHENEY: It gets to me as well.

RUMSFELD: Because what can you say about these people in 100 Europe except that they live their lives under the American umbrella? Every time it rains they come running for shelter. And yet they still think that they're entitled to say, 'Hey you're not holding that umbrella right.' Or more often, 'I want a share of that umbrella.' Or even, 'You're not 105 allowed an umbrella because not everybody's got one.' And that's the dishonesty, that's the rank dishonesty.

CHENEY: It's such dishonesty.

RUMSFELD: They talk about the American empire! How can we be an empire? Who ever heard of an empire that 110 spends day after day discussing exit strategies? (RUMSFELD *shakes his head.*) We don't need lectures from Europe on how to hold our knives and forks. (RUMSFELD *turns back to* POWELL.) They pretend all the time that they're upset because we're not consulting. 'They're not consulting,' they 115 say! Are you fooled by that? I'm not. Because what they really hate, what's really bugging them, is not the *way* we do things. It's that we're the only people in the world that can do them. It's not our manner, it's our power. And all they want, all anyone wants, is to put a brake on that 120 power. And that is the purpose of this exercise. That is the purpose of getting us snared up in yet another fucking resolution.

POWELL *is not buying it.*

POWELL: This is different.

RUMSFELD: Why? Why's it different?   125

POWELL: Because you can't put Blair in with the French.

RUMSFELD: Can't I?

POWELL: You can't put him in with the Germans.

RUMSFELD: You going to give me a reason?

This is all joshing, but now POWELL *raises his voice.*

POWELL: Blair's been with us! He's been with us all along! 130

CHENEY: So?

CHENEY *is grinning. Now* BUSH *joins in.*

BUSH: Dick doesn't like him.

CHENEY: I don't trust him. New Labour. What the hell does that mean? We don't call ourselves the New Republicans.

135

RUMSFELD: We're not a friggin' girl band.

POWELL: All right, come on, this is ridiculous. This isn't worthy of you, Dick.

CHENEY: Not worthy? You want me to be serious?

140 POWELL: I do.

CHENEY: You want me to tell you what I really think?

POWELL: Yes.

CHENEY: All right. I'll tell you. (CHENEY *pauses a moment before taking aim.*) Tony Blair? I've read his stuff. I've heard him

145 talk. This is a man on a mission. This is a man with a history.

POWELL: Sure.

CHENEY: He knows what he wants: he wants to build some new world order out of the ruins of the World Trade Center. He wants the right to go into any country anywhere

150 and bring relief from suffering and pain wherever he finds it. And I don't. What I want is to follow this country's legitimate security concerns. And, for me, those come above everything.

RUMSFELD: Me, too.

155 CHENEY: Now: if those interests happen to coincide with an Englishman's fantasy of how he's one day going to introduce some universal penalty system—three strikes and the UN says you can overthrow any regime you like—then that's fine. If not, not, and we won't miss him.

160 POWELL: That isn't fair. (POWELL *shakes his head.*) Blair's loyal. He's been loyal from the start.

CHENEY: OK, I admit, if we want him, Blair's good at the high moral tone. If you want to go into battle with a preacher sitting on top of the tank, that's fine by me. But bear in

165 mind, preacher's one more to carry. Needs rations, needs a latrine, just like everyone else.

POWELL: I like Blair.

CHENEY: Maybe you do. But we don't need him. And as of this moment he's bringing us nothing but trouble.

170 (CHENEY *smiles, definitive.*) It's a good rule. When the cat shit gets bigger than the cat, get rid of the cat.

RUMSFELD: Nice.

CHENEY: This guy is putting himself halfway between American power and international diplomacy. And sorry—but

175 that's a place where people get mashed.

POWELL: That's where I am, Dick. In that same place.

CHENEY: No. No, Colin. It's different for you.

POWELL: Why? Why's it different for me?

POWELL *waits. A real nastiness has come into the room.*

CHENEY: Because you can come running home whenever

180 you need.

There's a deadly silence. Nobody says anything. RICE *shifts, tactful.*

RICE: OK. OK, we're going to wrap this up soon. Sir? Do you want to conclude?

BUSH *is thoughtful, seemingly immune to the atmosphere between his colleagues.*

BUSH: Blair wants to keep on the right side of us.

RICE: That's right.

185 BUSH: If he's not pro-American, he's nothing. Look at it his way round. He's staked the house. He's not going to quit.

On the other hand, his government can fall. That's a real thing. It may really fall. So. (BUSH *looks round.*) I'm sorry, gentlemen. We have to do what we can.

POWELL *gets up and stands a moment by himself.*

TWENTY-ONE

The Security Council arrives. The Foreign Ministers and their Ambassadors.

AN ACTOR: On February 5th Powell is prevailed upon to make a presentation to the UN, using a sound-and-light show to demonstrate his case for the 'imminent threat'.

POWELL *sits down, then holds up a small vial of anthrax.*

POWELL: My colleagues, every statement I make today is backed up by sources, solid sources.   5

AN ACTOR: The Head of White House Communications team, Dan Bartlett, remarks:

BARTLETT: We called it 'the Powell buy-in'.

POWELL: These are not assertions. What we are giving you are facts and conclusions based on solid intelligence.   10

AN ACTOR: Although Powell has spent the previous four days angrily throwing out much of the two-hundred-minute speech Cheney, the CIA and the Pentagon have given him to read, he does raise the spectre of mobile laboratories to make biological agents: 15

POWELL: The source is an eyewitness, an Iraqi chemical engineer who supervised one of these facilities.

AN ACTOR: It turns out the supposed eyewitness is actually in Germany. The CIA has never spoken to him. Hans Blix comments: 20

BLIX: I knew they'd cut a lot of stuff they claimed to have, and that left me thinking: if this is the best they've got, what on earth was the rest like?

AN ACTOR: When his turn comes, Blix offers the Council a rather different assessment.   25

BLIX: Since we have arrived in Iraq we have conducted more than four hundred inspections, covering more than three hundred sites. The inspectors have not found any weapons of mass destruction.

AN ACTOR: Later, Blix comments: 30

BLIX: I was often asked later why there was such a change in tone with my previous speech, and I used to explain that if you are asked to talk about the weather, your reports must be different when the weather changes.

BLIX *sits down. There is a flurry of excitement.*

AN ACTOR: In the charged atmosphere Dominique de 35 Villepin seizes his opportunity:

DE VILLEPIN: War is always the sanction of failure. France has never ceased to stand upright in the face of history and before mankind. In this temple of the United Nations, we are the guardians of an ideal, the guardians of a con- 40 science.

AN ACTOR: De Villepin turns to Colin Powell:

DE VILLEPIN: This message comes to you today from an old country, France, from a continent like mine, Europe, that has known wars, occupation and barbarity. Let us give the 45

United Nations inspectors the time they need for their mission to succeed.

AN ACTOR: As de Villepin finishes, there is an unknown noise, starting in the galleries and rippling down, a stream becoming a flood.

The sound of applause. People rise to their feet. POWELL *pushes away his papers.*

Buoyed up by Blix's report, next day, people all over the world take to the streets.

The Council disappears.

Saturday 15th February sees the largest anti-war demonstration of all time. A hundred million protestors in six hundred cities demand the right of the inspectors to complete their work.

BLIX *steps out for milk.*

In New York, Hans Blix goes out to get milk and finds Second and Third Avenues jammed with two hundred thousand people.

BLIX: I was worried I might be recognized and risk being hoisted to some demonstrator's truck as a mascot. In fact the Swedish Ambassador gave me a poster he picked up after the demonstration.

BLIX *shows us the poster. It says: BLIX NOT BOMBS.*

It hangs on my wall now.

TWENTY-TWO

BLAIR's *office assembles*—CAMPBELL, MANNING, JONATHAN POWELL, *etc.*

AN ACTOR: On February 24th, Britain, Spain and the US table the long-awaited second resolution which will unambiguously authorize the use of force. They then begin the attempt to gather the votes they need from what come to be called 'the swinging six'.

GREENSTOCK: For weeks I was on the phones and went to endless dinners.

AN ACTOR: Jeremy Greenstock—a former Classics master at Eton—is British Ambassador to the UN:

GREENSTOCK: Cocktail parties are the best, you can get round twenty-five of the smaller countries in an hour. Your mind whirls the whole time, you have to remember all the names, the alliances, it's like a gigantic switchboard in your head. The faster you can make the connections the better, but it all needs to look effortless.

AN ACTOR: Blair embarks on a four-week marathon of whirlwind diplomacy. Baroness Amos is sent to Africa for the votes of Cameroon, Angola and Guinea. Blair calls the President of Chile, offering to make the seven-thousand-mile round-trip himself:

BLAIR *is on the phone to* RICARDO LAGOS.

BLAIR: I can come in person if you like.

LAGOS: I don't think that'll be necessary. (LAGOS *puts down the phone.*)

AN ACTOR: A senior Whitehall figure remarks:

SENIOR WHITEHALL FIGURE: We underestimated the dislike of the US around the world. Many small countries didn't like being pushed around. We failed to pick up the warning signs of what was a kind of peasants' revolt.

AN ACTOR: One African official:

AFRICAN OFFICIAL: What can the Americans do to us? Are they going to bomb us? Invade us?

GREENSTOCK: I got used to hearing the Prime Minister's voice every day:

BLAIR: How many votes will we get? Guinea? Cameroon? Angola? Mexico? Chile? Pakistan?

GREENSTOCK: I could only say, 'Four, Prime Minister: the United States, Britain, Spain and Bulgaria.' He'd say:

BLAIR: Crumbs.

BLAIR *goes into a TV studio.*

AN ACTOR: Noting that America has promised $20.7 million and Britain £6.2 million in aid to Guinea, Trevor Macdonald asks Tony Blair:

TREVOR MACDONALD: What is the going rate for a vote in the Security Council these days?

AN ACTOR: Blair has embarked on what he calls his 'masochism strategy' directly confronting critics of the war:

A BEREAVED MOTHER *is in the audience.*

MOTHER: I lost my only child in the World Trade Center. I can't describe to you how I will feel for the rest of my life. They killed three thousand innocent victims. How many innocent victims are you and Mr Bush going to kill? Mr Blair, don't do it. Don't do it!

BLAIR *leaves the studio.*

AN ACTOR: During the credits Blair is slow-handclapped by the audience. On his return to Downing Street, he asks his advisers:

BLAIR: Who the fuck fixed that up? Thanks very much, guys.

There is bitter laughter in the den. GEOFF HOON *is on the phone to* RUMSFELD.

HOON: Donald. Donald, it's Geoff Hoon. I'm sorry to be making this call. It's not a call anyone wants to make. But I have a duty to tell you that there is a danger we may lose the next vote in Parliament. And if we do, I'm going to be unable to commit British troops in Iraq.

AN ACTOR: Rumsfeld next day gives one of his regular briefings to the press where he is asked:

JOURNALIST: Would the US go to war without Britain?

RUMSFELD: To the extent they're able to participate, that would be welcome. To the extent they're not, there are workarounds and they would not be involved, at least in that phase of it.

AN ACTOR: Blair flies into a rage, calling Bush directly.

BUSH *with* CHENEY, RICE *and* RUMSFELD *on one end,* BLAIR *with* MANNING, JONATHAN POWELL *and* CAMPBELL *on the other.*

BLAIR: I can't believe this! Here I am, staking my entire political existence, we're on the verge of committing British
70   troops, I've worked—I've worked now for over eighteen
months to help you on this, George, I've risked everything, I've been at your side from beginning to end, and
your Secretary of Defense, George, your Secretary of Defense goes on television and says—
75   BUSH: I know. I heard. I heard what he said.
BLAIR: He says: 'Oh don't worry, we don't need the British
anyway.'
BUSH: Yeah, I saw that. I did see that. (BUSH *looks deadpan at*
CHENEY *and* RUMSFELD.)
80   BLAIR: I have to say, if you set out deliberately to destroy the
coalition, I can't think of anything more disastrous and
damaging.
BUSH: Yeah. No. Yeah, I take your point.
BLAIR: Well?
85   BUSH: I've spoken to Donald. He says he was trying to be
helpful. But he admits . . . it came out wrong.

CHIRAC *goes into a TV studio.*

AN ACTOR: But that same night it is a speech of Jacques
Chirac which finally gives Blair a political lifeline.
CHIRAC: My position is that whatever the circumstances
90   France will vote 'No', because she considers tonight that
there are no grounds for waging war.
AN ACTOR: Chirac uses the word . . .
CHIRAC: 'Tonight' . . .
AN ACTOR: . . . to mean he is open to argument, should the
95   situation change. But Downing Street senses an escape
route at last.

*The Downing Street group—*BLAIR, CAMPBELL, MANNING—
arguing flat out.

BLAIR: Do you think we can do this?
MANNING: Of course we can do it.
BLAIR: Are you sure?
100 MANNING: Look, we're defending the Alamo. This is life and
death. You heard what he said.
CAMPBELL: I've got his words here.
BLAIR: I know the words.
CAMPBELL: 'Whatever the circumstances.' France will vote no
105 'whatever the circumstances'.
BLAIR: But he did say 'tonight'. That's the position *tonight.*
CAMPBELL: Of course he said 'tonight'! Of course he said
'tonight'! But he also said 'whatever the circumstances'.

The room has reached shouting pitch. CAMPBELL *is standing in dis-*
belief.

What are you saying? Are you saying we have to play fair
110 with the French? With the *French?* And when exactly did
the fucking French play fair with us?

Downing Street dissolves.

AN ACTOR: Blair announces that attempts to pass the resolution may now have to be abandoned, not, he says, because
the votes are not there, but because Chirac has rendered

further diplomacy pointless. The French Ambassador in   115
London warns David Manning:
ERRERA: You can't really be going to use this? This is like the
Soviet Union! You're deliberately distorting the President's
words.
MANNING: Gérard, it's too good not to use.   120
AN ACTOR: The French Ambassador tells the BBC:
ERRERA: We feel sorry for Tony Blair. But if it helps him to
blame us for the failure of his resolution, we will not hold
it against him.

STRAW *and* POWELL *on phones in their separate offices.*

STRAW: Colin.   125
POWELL: Jack.
STRAW: I've been asked to explain to you, the Prime Minister is facing the most difficult occasion of his life.
POWELL: We're following it closely.
STRAW: He's facing a full-scale rebellion in Parliament. Tony's 130
asked me to make clear—he cannot survive, he has no
chance of survival, he cannot even go into that debate, unless your President offers a cast-iron commitment to work
for peace in the Middle East.

There is a charged silence.

Colin, I can't be clearer.   135

There is a silence. BUSH *and* POWELL *walk out together.*

AN ACTOR: Next day Bush steps into the Rose Garden—
BUSH: We have reached a hopeful moment for progress . . .
AN ACTOR: —and promises that he will at last publish the
long-delayed road-map for Israel and Palestine.

House of Commons. ROBIN COOK *stands.*

The following day the US and the UK formally renege on   140
their promise to seek a second resolution. The leader of
the House of Commons, Robin Cook, stands up to resign.
COOK: I cannot support a war without international agreement or domestic support. On Iraq, I believe that the pre- 145
vailing mood of the British people is sound. They do not
doubt that Saddam is a brutal dictator, but they are not
persuaded that he is a clear and present danger to Britain.
They want inspections to be given a chance, and they suspect they are being pushed too quickly into conflict by a   150
US administration with an agenda of its own.
    Only a year ago we and the United States were part of a
coalition against terrorism that was wider and more diverse
than I could ever have imagined possible. History will be
astonished at the diplomatic miscalculations that led so   155
quickly to the disintegration of that powerful coalition.

COOK *is cheered as he sits.*

AN ACTOR: Next day, Blair has a chance to respond when the
government wins the vote for war:
BLAIR: If this House now demands that at this moment, faced
with this threat from this regime, that British troops are   160

pulled back, that we turn away at the point of reckoning—what then? What will Saddam feel? What will the
other states who tyrannise their people, the terrorists who
threaten our existence, what will they take from that?
165   Who will celebrate and who will weep?

The House of Commons disappears.

AN ACTOR: On March 20th, air-raid sirens announce the beginning of war just before dawn in Baghdad.

The sound of sirens, wailing in the distance.

TWENTY-THREE

The sirens fade.

AN ACTOR: The invasion begins. On March 27th, one week
in, Paul Wolfowitz reassures Congress that Iraq will not
cost a penny once it has been conquered:
WOLFOWITZ: We're dealing with a country that can really fi-
5   nance its own reconstruction and relatively soon.
AN ACTOR: The military campaign is over in just forty-two
days. At the end of April, President Bush does an underwater survival training course in the White House swimming pool to prepare for his tailhook landing from an
10   S-3B Viking jet onto the aircraft carrier USS *Abraham Lincoln,* just thirty miles off the coast of San Diego.

An aircraft carrier. A huge banner saying MISSION ACCOMPLISHED.

Thanks to an artful arrangement of jump-suit groin-
straps, George W. Bush, 43rd President of the United
States, shows his balls to the world.

BUSH *gets out of his plane and struts across the deck to inspect the
troops. Military bands. Parade. Then* BUSH *speaks.*

15   BUSH: We have removed an ally of Al Qaeda, and cut off a
source of terrorist funding. And this much is certain. No
terrorist network will gain weapons of mass destruction
from inside the Iraqi regime, because that regime is no
more. In these nineteen months that changed the world,
20   our actions have been focused and deliberate and propor-
tionate to the offence.
        All of you, all in this generation of our military, have
taken up the highest calling of history. And wherever you
go, you carry a message of hope, a message that is ancient
25   and ever new. In the words of the prophet Isaiah, 'To the
captives, come out; and to those in darkness, be free.'
AN ACTOR: Donald Rumsfeld adds:
RUMSFELD: There is, I am certain, among the Iraqi people a
respect for the care and the precision that went into the
30   bombing campaign.
AN ACTOR: Paul Wolfowitz comments:
WOLFOWITZ: Like the people of France in the nineteen forties, they view us as their hoped-for liberator.

The aircraft carrier disappears.

AN ACTOR: One of the Americans' first actions is to disband
35   the Iraqi army and police force, flooding several hundred

thousand young men onto the unemployment market,
unpaid and discontented. Meanwhile, Condoleezza Rice
reveals her strategy for dealing with those countries who
led opposition to US invasion:
RICE: Punish France, ignore Germany and forgive Russia.   40
AN ACTOR: In May 2003, Paul Wolfowitz admits weapons of
mass destruction had originally been chosen only for
what he terms 'bureaucratic reasons':
WOLFOWITZ: The Bush administration focused on alleged
weapons of mass destruction as the primary justification   45
for toppling Saddam Hussein by force because it was politically convenient, because it was the one reason everyone could agree on.
AN ACTOR: Blair asserts:
BLAIR: You are just going to have to have a little bit of pa-   50
tience. I have absolutely no doubt at all when we present
the full evidence, that evidence will be found and I have
absolutely no doubt it exists because Saddam's history of
weapons of mass destruction is not some invention of the
British security services.   55
AN ACTOR: On July 23rd 2003, with the security situation
worsening daily, Paul Wolfowitz explains why Americans
were not greeted, as he had promised, with flowers and offers of sweets.
WOLFOWITZ: Some important assumptions turned out to un-   60
derestimate the problem.
AN ACTOR: As resistance to the occupation hardens, the
counter-terrorist expert Jessica Stern observes:
STERN: America has taken a country that was not a terrorist
threat and turned it into one. Even if there weren't any Al   65
Qaeda in Iraq before the Americans went in, there most
certainly are now.
AN ACTOR: On September 7th 2003, the President reveals
that the reconstruction of Iraq which Wolfowitz has said
will be—   70
WOLFOWITZ: Self-financing.
AN ACTOR: —will, in fact, cost at least:
BUSH: Eighty-seven billion dollars.
AN ACTOR: By September 14th, Dick Cheney is also willing
to make an admission: 75
INTERVIEWER: Vice-President, this time last year you claimed
Saddam Hussein was developing nuclear capability.
CHENEY: Yeah, I did misspeak. We never had any evidence
that Hussein had acquired a nuclear weapon.
AN ACTOR: On October 2nd, the head of Iraqi survey group,   80
David Kay, is asked whether, after six months, he has
found any weapons of mass destruction.
KAY: I've barely found lunch.
AN ACTOR: Even Colin Powell is ready to confess about the
mobile biological labs which were at the centre of his UN   85
speech:
POWELL: Unfortunately our multiple sourcing has turned out
not to be accurate.
AN ACTOR: As to US assertions that Iraq possessed bombs,
rockets, and shells for poison agents, unmanned aerial   90
vehicles for delivering biological and chemical
weapons, nuclear weapon materials, sarin, tabun, mustard agent, precursor chemicals, VX nerve agent, anthrax, aflotoxins, ricin and surface-to-surface Al Hussein
missiles, not one has so far been found. One vial of   95
Strain B Botulinum toxin is found in the domestic re-

frigerator of an Iraqi scientist. It is ten years old. Hans Blix comments:

100 BLIX: They wanted to come to the conclusion that there were weapons. Like the former days of the witch-hunt, they are convinced that they exist. And if you see a black cat, well, that's evidence of the witch.

AN ACTOR: When asked about going to war on falsified intelligence, the President's spokesman replies:

105 FLEISCHER: The President has moved on. And I think, frankly, much of the country has moved on as well.

AN ACTOR: When asked where Osama bin Laden is, the President replies:

BUSH: I don't know where he is. I have no idea and I really

110 don't care.

AN ACTOR: When asked on February 2nd 2004 by a reporter:

REPORTER: Do you think the country is owed an explanation about the Iraqi intelligence failure before the election so the voters have this information before they elect a new

115 President?

AN ACTOR: The President replies:

BUSH: First of all I want to know all the facts.

AN ACTOR: The previous September, Colin Powell attends a lunch of *New York Times* editors.

POWELL *is at a lunch with Editors.*

120 He is asked:

EDITOR: Do you think Americans would have supported this war if weapons of mass destruction had not been the issue?

POWELL: Your question is too hypothetical to answer.

125 AN ACTOR: An editor then asks:

EDITOR: Would you personally have supported it?

AN ACTOR: Powell smiles and reaches out his hand.

POWELL *smiles and reaches out his hand.*

POWELL: It was good to meet you.

All the ACTORs *stand like a line of inspection on either side. In silence,* POWELL *turns and, without turning back, leaves the play.*

AN ACTOR: On June 4th 2003, George Bush, who, by then,

130 has used the word 'evil' in 319 separate speeches since becoming President, reveals to the Palestinian Prime Minister:

BUSH: God told me to strike at Al Qaeda and I struck them, and then He instructed me to strike at Saddam, which I

135 did.

BUSH *and* SHARON *appear before microphones.*

AN ACTOR: On April 14th 2004, President Bush invites Ariel Sharon to the White House. He formally abandons the so-called road-map and gives Israel permission to implement a plan of its own, with no representation or right of negotiation offered to Palestinians.   140

BUSH: Good job, Prime Minister. Good job.

AN ACTOR: Tony Blair refuses to dissent from the new policy.

BUSH *and* SHARON *shake hands and leave.*

BLAIR: After the war, I did consider apologizing. But I wasn't sure what I'd be apologizing for. And besides, the moment has gone.   145

BLAIR *looks at us a moment, then goes. Only* AN ACTOR *remains.*

AN ACTOR: Eighteen months after the invasion of Iraq, seventy per cent of the American electorate still believe that Saddam Hussein was directly involved in the planning of the 9/11 attacks.

An ACTOR *leaves. An* IRAQI EXILE *comes on, alone.*

IRAQI EXILE: I left my country twenty-seven years ago. I   150 longed for the fall of the dictator. In exile, I worked for it. Then Donald Rumsfeld said, 'Stuff happens.' It seemed to me the most racist remark I had ever heard.

A vacuum was created. Was it created deliberately? I cannot comprehend. They came to save us, but they had   155 no plans.

And now the American dead are counted, their numbers recorded, their coffins draped in flags. How many Iraqis have died? How many civilians? No figure is given. Our dead are uncounted.   160

We opposed Saddam Hussein, many of us, because he harmed people, and anybody who harms innocent Iraqis I feel equally passionately and strongly about, and I will oppose them. And I will.

I mean, if there is a word, Iraq has been crucified. By   165 Saddam's sins, by ten years of sanctions, and then this. Basically it's a story of a nation that failed in only one thing. But it's a big sin. It failed to take charge of itself. And that meant the worst person in the country took charge. Until this nation takes charge of itself, it will continue to   170 suffer.

I mean, Iraqis say to me, 'Look, tell America.' I tell them: 'You are putting your faith in the wrong person. Don't expect America or anybody will do it for you.

'If you don't do it yourself, this is what you get.'   175

CRITICAL CONTEXTS

FRIEDRICH NIETZSCHE (1844–1900)

from *The Birth of Tragedy* (1872)

TRANSLATED BY WALTER KAUFMANN

*Throughout his career, the German philosopher and poet Friedrich Nietzsche criticized the limitations of modern conceptual and moral categories. This revolutionary subversion of the premises of philosophy forms the core of his most famous works—*The Gay Science *(1882),* Also Spoke Zarathustra *(1883–92), and* Beyond Good and Evil *(1886). In* The Birth of Tragedy *(1872), Nietzsche argues that Greek tragedy arose from the collision between Athenian rationalism—symbolized by Apollo, Socrates, and Euripides—and an earlier, irrational mysticism, symbolized by Dionysus. Although Nietzsche's reading of Greek history has been generally discredited, the essay offers a powerful and influential reading of the tension between the rational and irrational informing Greek drama. Nietzsche was admired by several modern playwrights represented in this volume, including Bernard Shaw, August Strindberg, and Eugene O'Neill.*

Despite its symbolic contours, Nietzsche's representation of tragedy shares in the dialectical imagination that also drives other major theorists of tragic drama, including Aristotle. In what ways are the Appolinian and the Dionysian complicit in one another? What are the aspects of tragic experience that Nietzsche means to capture in these two images? Why do you think the full title of the essay is The Birth of Tragedy from the Spirit of Music?

SECTION 1

We shall have gained much for the science of aesthetics, once we perceive not merely by logical inference, but with the immediate certainty of vision, that the continuous development of art is bound up with the *Apollinian* and *Dionysian* duality—just as procreation depends on the duality of the sexes, involving perpetual strife with only periodically intervening reconciliations. The terms Dionysian and Apollinian we borrow from the Greeks, who disclose to the discerning mind the profound mysteries of their view of art, not, to be sure, in concepts, but in the intensely clear figures of their gods. Through Apollo and Dionysus, the two art deities of the Greeks, we come to recognize that in the Greek world there existed a tremendous opposition, in origin and aims, between the Apollinian art of sculpture, and the nonimagistic, Dionysian art of music. These two different tendencies run parallel to each other, for the most part openly at variance; and they continually incite each other to new and more powerful births, which perpetuate an antagonism, only superficially reconciled by the common term "art"; till eventually, by a metaphysical miracle of the Hellenic "will," they appear coupled with each other and through this coupling ultimately generate an equally Dionysian and Apollinian form of art—Attic tragedy.

In order to grasp these two tendencies, let us first conceive of them as the separate art worlds of *dreams* and *intoxication*. These physiological phenomena present a contrast analogous to that existing between the Apollinian and the Dionysian. It was in dreams, says Lucretius, that the glorious divine figures first appeared to the souls of men; in dreams the great shaper beheld the splendid bodies of superhuman beings; and the Hellenic poet, if questioned about the mysteries of poetic inspiration, would likewise have suggested dreams and he might have given an explanation like that of Hans Sachs in the *Meistersinger*:

> The poet's task is this, my friend,
> to read his dreams and comprehend.
> The truest human fancy seems
> to be revealed to us in dreams:
> all poems and versification
> are but true dreams' interpretation.

The beautiful illusion of the dream worlds, in the creation of which every man is truly an artist, is the prerequisite of all plastic art, and, as we shall see, of an important part of poetry also. In our dreams we delight in the immediate understanding of figures; all forms speak to us; there is nothing unimportant or superfluous. But even when this dream reality is most intense, we still have, glimmering through it, the sensation that it is *mere appearance:* at least this is my experience, and for its frequency—indeed, normality—I could adduce many proofs, including the sayings of the poets.

Philosophical men even have a presentiment that the reality in which we live and have our being is also mere appearance, and that another, quite different reality lies beneath it. Schopenhauer actually indicates as the criterion of philosophical ability the occasional ability to view men and things as mere phantoms or dream images. Thus the aesthetically sensitive man stands in the same relation to the reality of dreams as the philosopher does to the reality of existence; he is a close and willing observer, for these images afford him an interpretation of life, and by reflecting on these processes he trains himself for life.

It is not only the agreeable and friendly images that he experiences as something universally intelligible: the serious, the troubled, the sad, the gloomy, the sudden restraints, the tricks of accident, anxious expectations, in short, the whole divine comedy of life, including the inferno, also pass before him, not like mere shadows on a wall—for he lives and suffers with these scenes—and yet not without that fleeting sensation of illusion. And perhaps many will, like myself, recall how amid the dangers and terrors of dreams they have occasionally said to themselves in self-encouragement, and not without success: "It is a dream! I will dream on!" I have likewise heard of people who were able to continue one and the same dream for three and even more successive nights—facts which indicate clearly how our innermost being, our common ground, experiences dreams with profound delight and a joyous necessity.

This joyous necessity of the dream experience has been embodied by the Greeks in their Apollo: Apollo, the god of all plastic energies, is at the same time the soothsaying god. He, who (as the etymology of the name indicates) is the "shining one," the deity of light, is also ruler over the beautiful illusion of the inner world of fantasy. The higher truth, the perfection of these states in contrast to the incompletely intelligible everyday world, this deep consciousness of nature, healing and helping in sleep and dreams, is at the same time the symbolical analogue of the soothsaying faculty and of the arts generally, which make life possible and worth living. But we must also include in our image of Apollo that delicate boundary which the dream image must not overstep lest it have a pathological effect (in which case mere appearance would deceive us as if it were crude reality). We must keep in mind that measured restraint, that freedom from the wilder emotions, that calm of the sculptor god. His eye must be "sunlike," as befits his origin; even when it is angry and distempered it is still hallowed by beautiful illusion. And so, in one sense, we might apply to Apollo the words of Schopenhauer when he speaks of the man wrapped in the veil of *māyā* [illusion]: "Just as in a stormy sea that, unbounded in all directions, raises and drops mountainous waves, howling, a sailor sits in a boat and trusts in his frail bark: so in the midst of a world of torments the individual human being sits quietly, supported by and trusting in the *principium individuationis*." In fact, we might say of Apollo that in him the unshaken faith in this *principium* and the calm repose of the man wrapped up in it receive their most sublime expression; and we might call Apollo himself the glorious divine image of

the *principium individuationis*, through whose gestures and eyes all the joy and wisdom of "illusion," together with its beauty, speak to us.

In the same work Schopenhauer has depicted for us the tremendous terror which seizes man when he is suddenly dumbfounded by the cognitive form of phenomena because the principle of sufficient reason, in some one of its manifestations, seems to suffer an exception. If we add to this terror the blissful ecstasy that wells from the innermost depths of man, indeed of nature, at this collapse of the *principium individuationis*, we steal a glimpse into the nature of the *Dionysian*, which is brought home to us most intimately by the analogy of intoxication.

Either under the influence of the narcotic draught, of which the songs of all primitive men and peoples speak, or with the potent coming of spring that penetrates all nature with joy, these Dionysian emotions awake, and as they grow in intensity everything subjective vanishes into complete self-forgetfulness. In the German Middle Ages, too, singing and dancing crowds, ever increasing in number, whirled themselves from place to place under this same Dionysian impulse. In these dancers of St. John and St. Vitus, we rediscover the Bacchic choruses of the Greeks, with their prehistory in Asia Minor, as far back as Babylon and the orgiastic Sacaea. There are some who, from obtuseness or lack of experience, turn away from such phenomena as from "folk-diseases," with contempt or pity born of the consciousness of their own "healthy-mindedness." But of course such poor wretches have no idea how corpselike and ghostly their so-called "healthy-mindedness" looks when the glowing life of the Dionysian revelers roars past them.

Under the charm of the Dionysian not only is the union between man and man reaffirmed, but nature which has become alienated, hostile, or subjugated, celebrates once more her reconciliation with her lost son, man. Freely, earth proffers her gifts, and peacefully the beasts of prey of the rocks and desert approach. The chariot of Dionysus is covered with flowers and garlands; panthers and tigers walk under its yoke. Transform Beethoven's "Hymn to Joy" into a painting; let your imagination conceive the multitudes bowing to the dust, awestruck—then you will approach the Dionysian. Now the slave is a free man; now all the rigid, hostile barriers that necessity, caprice, or "impudent convention" have fixed between man and man are broken. Now, the gospel of universal harmony, each one feels himself not only united, reconciled, and fused with his neighbor, but as one with him, as if the veil of *māyā* had been torn aside and were now merely fluttering in tatters before the mysterious primordial unity.

In song and in dance man expresses himself as a member of a higher community; he has forgotten how to walk and speak and is on the way toward flying into the air, dancing. His very gestures express enchantment. Just as the animals now talk, and the earth yields milk and honey, supernatural sounds emanate from him, too: he feels himself a god, he himself now walks about enchanted, in ecstasy, like the gods he saw walking in his dreams. He is no longer an artist, he has become a work of art: in these paroxysms of intoxication the artistic power of all nature reveals itself to the highest gratification of the primordial unity. The noblest clay, the most costly marble, man, is here kneaded and cut, and to the sound of the chisel stokes of the Dionysian world-artist rings out the cry of the Eleusinian mysteries: "Do you prostrate yourselves, millions? Do you sense your Maker, world?" . . .

SECTION 10

The tradition is undisputed that Greek tragedy in its earliest form had for its sole theme the sufferings of Dionysus and that for a long time the only stage hero was Dionysus himself. But it may be claimed with equal confidence that until Euripides, Dionysus never ceased to be the tragic hero; that all the celebrated figures of the Greek stage—Prometheus, Oedipus, etc.—are mere masks of this original hero, Dionysus. That behind all these masks there is a deity, that is one essential reason for the typical "ideality" of these famous figures which has caused so much astonishment. Somebody, I do not know who, has claimed that all individuals, taken as individuals, are comic and hence untragic—from which it would follow that the Greeks simply *could* not suffer individuals on the tragic stage. In fact, this is what they seem to have felt; and the Platonic distinction and evaluation of the "idea" and the "idol," the mere image, is very deeply rooted in the Hellenic character.

Using Plato's terms we should have to speak of the tragic figures of the Hellenic stage somewhat as follows: the one truly real Dionysus appears in a variety of forms, in the mask of a fighting hero, and entangled, as it were, in the net of the individual will. The god who appears talks and acts so as to resemble an erring, striving, suffering individual. That he *appears* at all with such epic precision and clarity is the work of the dream-interpreter, Apollo, who through this symbolic appearance interprets to the chorus its Dionysian state. In truth, however, the hero is the suffering Dionysus of the Mysteries, the god experiencing in himself the agonies of individuation, of whom wonderful myths tell that as a boy he was torn to pieces by the Titans and now is worshiped in this state as Zagreus. Thus it is intimated that this dismemberment, the properly Dionysian *suffering*, is like a transformation into air, water, earth, and fire, that we are therefore to regard the state of individuation as the origin and primal cause of all suffering, as something objectionable in itself. From the

smile of this Dionysus sprang the Olympian gods, from his tears sprang man. In this existence as a dismembered god, Dionysus possesses the dual nature of a cruel, barbarized demon and a mild, gentle ruler. But the hope of the epopts [initiates] looked toward a rebirth of Dionysus, which we must now dimly conceive as the end of individuation. It was for this coming third Dionysus that the epopts' roaring hymns of joy resounded. And it is this hope alone that casts a gleam of joy upon the features of a world torn asunder and shattered into individuals; this is symbolized in the myth of Demeter, sunk in eternal sorrow, who *rejoices* again for the first time when told that she may *once more* give birth to Dionysus. This view of things already provides us with all the elements of a profound and pessimistic view of the world, together with the *mystery doctrine of tragedy:* the fundamental knowledge of the oneness of everything existent, the conception of individuation as the primal cause of evil, and of art as the joyous hope that the spell of individuation may be broken in augury of a restored oneness.

We have already suggested that the Homeric epos is the poem of Olympian culture, in which this culture has sung its own song of victory over the terrors of the war of the Titans. Under the predominating influence of tragic poetry, these Homeric myths are now born anew; and this metempsychosis reveals that in the meantime the Olympian culture also has been conquered by a still more profound view of the world. The defiant Titan Prometheus has announced to his Olympian tormentor that some day the greatest danger will menace his rule, unless Zeus should enter into an alliance with him in time. In Aeschylus we recognize how the terrified Zeus, fearful of his end, allies himself with the Titan. Thus the former age of the Titans is once more recovered from Tartarus and brought to the light.

The philosophy of wild and naked nature beholds with the frank, undissembling gaze of truth the myths of the Homeric world as they dance past: they turn pale, they tremble under the piercing glance of this goddess—till the powerful fist of the Dionysian artist forces them into the service of the new deity. Dionysian truth takes over the entire domain of myth as the symbolism of *its* knowledge which it makes known partly in the public cult of tragedy and partly in the secret celebrations of dramatic mysteries, but always in the old mythical garb.

What power was it that freed Prometheus from his vultures and transformed the myth into a vehicle of Dionysian wisdom? It is the Heraclean power of music: having reached its highest manifestation in tragedy, it can invest myths with a new and most profound significance. This we have already characterized as the most powerful function of music. For it is the fate of every myth to creep by degrees into the narrow limits of some alleged historical reality, and to be treated by some later generation as a unique fact with historical claims: and the Greeks were already fairly on the way toward re-stamping the whole of their mythical juvenile dream saga-ciously and arbitrarily into a historico-pragmatical *juvenile history*. For this is the way in which religions are wont to die out: under the stern, intelligent eyes of an orthodox dogma-tism, the mythical premises of a religion are systematized as a sum total of historical events; one begins apprehensively to defend the credibility of the myths, while at the same time one opposes any continuation of their natural vitality and growth; the feeling for myth perishes, and its place is taken by the claim of religion to historical foundations. This dying myth was now seized by the new-born genius of Dionysian music; and in these hands it flourished once more with colors such as it had never yet displayed, with a fragrance that awak-ened a longing anticipation of a metaphysical world. After this final effulgence it collapses, its leaves wither, and soon the mocking Lucians of antiquity catch at the discolored and faded flowers carried away by the four winds. Through tragedy the myth attains its most profound content, its most expres-sive form; it rises once more like a wounded hero, and its whole excess of strength, together with the philosophic calm of the dying, burns in its eyes with a last powerful gleam.

What did you want, sacrilegious Euripides, when you sought to compel this dying myth to serve you once more? It died under your violent hands—and then you needed a copied, masked myth that, like the ape of Heracles, merely knew how to deck itself out in the ancient pomp. And just as the myth died on you, the genius of music died on you, too. Though with greedy hands you plundered all the gardens of music, you still managed only copied, masked music. And be-cause you had abandoned Dionysus, Apollo abandoned you: rouse all the passions from their resting places and conjure them into your circle, sharpen and whet a sophistical dialec-tic for the speeches of your heroes—your heroes, too, have only copied, masked passions and speak only copied, masked speeches. . . .

ÉMILE ZOLA (1840–1902)

from *Naturalism in the Theatre* (1878)

TRANSLATED BY ALBERT BERMEL

An influential novelist, playwright, and literary theorist, Zola became the spokesman for naturalism in the theater in a series of articles he wrote in the 1870s, collected as Naturalism in the Theatre *in 1878. In these essays, Zola urged the theater to adopt an attitude of scientific objectivity, an attitude reflected in the development of a new dramatic style. The naturalistic theater asserted such objectivity through its choice of subject matter (middle-class life), its treatment of characters (driven by "physiological" motives, not by "metaphysical" passions), its use of a prosaic, antiliterary language, and by the importance attached to the material environment. Zola's energy in summoning a new form of theatrical representation is evident here: what will be the signs of that new theatre onstage? What is the value that Zola ascribes to life-like representation, and how will it become visible onstage? How will this new theater be distinguished from the classical and romantic past?*

It seems impossible that the movement of inquiry and analy-sis, which is precisely the movement of the nineteenth cen-tury, can have revolutionized all the sciences and arts and left dramatic art to one side, as if isolated. The natural sci-ences date from the end of the last century; chemistry and physics are less than a hundred years old; history and criti-cism have been renovated, virtually re-created since the Rev-olution; an entire world has arisen; it has sent us back to the study of documents, to experience, made us realize that to start afresh we must first take things back to the beginning, become familiar with man and nature, verify what is. Thence-forward, the great naturalistic school, which has spread se-cretly, irrevocably, often making its way in darkness but always advancing, can finally come out triumphantly into the light of day. To trace the history of this movement, with the misunderstandings that might have impeded it and the mul-tiple causes that have thrust it forward or slowed it down, would be to trace the history of the century itself. An irre-sistible current carries our society towards the study of real-ity. In the novel Balzac has been the bold and mighty innovator who has replaced the observation of the scholar with the imagination of the poet. But in the theatre the evo-lution seems slower. No eminent writer has yet formulated the new idea with any clarity.

I certainly do not say that some excellent works have not been produced, with characters in them who are ingeniously examined and bold truths taken right on to the stage. Let me, for instance, cite certain plays by M. Dumas *fils*, whose talent I scarcely admire, and M. Émile Augier, the most hu-mane and powerful of all. Still, they are midgets beside

Balzac; they lack the genius to lay down the formula. It must be said that one can never tell quite when a movement is getting under way; generally its source is remote and lost in the earlier movement from which it emerged. In a manner of speaking, the naturalistic current has always existed. It brings with it nothing absolutely novel. But it has finally flowed into a period favourable to it; it is succeeding and expanding because the human mind has attained the necessary maturity. I do not, therefore, deny the past; I affirm the present. The strength of naturalism is precisely that it has deep roots in our national literature which contains plenty of wisdom. It comes from the very entrails of humanity; it is that much the stronger because it has taken longer to grow and is found in a greater number of our masterpieces.

Certain things have come to pass and I point them out. Can we believe that *L'Ami Fritz* would have been applauded at the Comédie-Française twenty years ago? Definitely not! This play, in which people eat all the time and the lover talks in such homely language, would have disgusted both the classicists and the romantics. To explain its success we must concede that as the years have gone by a secret fermentation has been at work. Lifelike paintings, which used to repel the public, today attract them. The majority has been won over and the stage is open to every experiment. This is the only conclusion to draw.

So that is where we stand. To explain my point better—am not afraid of repeating myself—I will sum up what I have said. Looking closely at the history of our dramatic literature, one can detect several clearly separated periods. First, there was the infancy of the art, farces and the mystery plays of the Middle Ages, the reciting of simple dialogues which developed as part of a naïve convention, with primitive staging and sets. Gradually, the plays became more complex but in a crude fashion. When Corneille appeared he was acclaimed most of all for his status as an innovator, for refining the dramatic formula of the time, and for hallowing it by means of his genius. It would be very interesting to study the pertinent documents and discover how our classical formula came to be created. It corresponded to the social spirit of the period. Nothing is solid that is not built on necessity. Tragedy reigned for two centuries because it satisfied the exact requirements of those centuries. Geniuses of differing temperaments had buttressed it with their masterpieces. And it continued to impose itself long afterwards, even when second-rate talents were producing inferior work. It acquired a momentum. It persisted also as the literary expression of that society, and nothing would have overthrown it if the society, had not itself disappeared. After the Revolution, after that profound disturbance that was meant to transform everything and give birth to a new world, tragedy struggled

to stay alive for a few more years. Then the formula cracked and romanticism broke through. A new formula asserted itself. We must look back at the first half of the century to understand the meaning of this cry for liberty. The young society was in the tremor of its infancy. The excited, bewildered, violently unleashed people were still racked by a dangerous fever; and in the first flush of their new liberty they yearned for prodigious adventures and superhuman love affairs. They gaped at the stars; some committed suicide, a very curious reaction to the social enfranchisement which had just been declared at the cost of so much blood. Turning specifically to dramatic literature, I maintain that romanticism in the theatre was an uncomplicated revolt, the invasion by a victorious group who took over the stage violently with drums beating and flags flying. In these early moments the combatants dreamed of making their imprint with a new form; to one rhetoric they opposed another: the Middle Ages to Antiquity, the exalting of passion to the exalting of duty. And that was all, for only the scenic conventions were altered. The characters remained marionettes in new clothing. Only the exterior aspect and the language were modified. But for the period that was enough. Romanticism had taken possession of the theatre in the name of literary freedom and it carried out its revolutionary task with incomparable bravura. But who does not see today that its role could extend no farther than that? Does romanticism have anything whatever to say about our present society? Does it meet one of our requirements? Obviously not. It is as outmoded as a jargon we no longer follow. It confidently expected to replace classical literature which had lasted for two centuries because it was based on social conditions. But romanticism was based on nothing but the fantasy of a few poets or, if you will, on the passing malady of minds overwhelmed by historical events; it was bound to disappear with the malady. It provided the occasion for a magnificent flowering of lyricism; that will be its eternal glory. Today, however, with the evolution accomplished, it is plain that romanticism was no more than the necessary link between classicism and naturalism. The struggle is over; now we must found a secure state. Naturalism flows out of classical art, just as our present society has arisen from the wreckage of the old society. Naturalism alone corresponds to our social needs; it alone has deep roots in the spirit of our times; and it alone can provide a living, durable formula for our art, because this formula will express the nature of our contemporary intelligence. There may be fashions and passing fantasies that exist outside naturalism but they will not survive for long. I say again, naturalism is the expression of our century and it will not die until a new upheaval transforms our democratic world.

Only one thing is needed now: men of genius who can fix the naturalistic formula. Balzac has done it for the novel and the novel is established. When will our Corneilles, Molières and Racines appear to establish our new theatre? We must hope and wait.

• • •

The period when romantic drama ruled now seems distant. In Paris five or six of its playhouses prospered. The demolition of the old theatres along the Boulevard du Temple was a catastrophe of the first order. The theatres became separated from one another, the public changed, different fashions arose. But the discredit into which the drama has fallen proceeds mostly from the exhaustion of the genre—ridiculous, boring plays have gradually taken over from the potent works of 1830.

To this enfeeblement we must add the absolute lack of new actors who understand and can interpret these kinds of plays, for every dramatic formula that vanishes carries away its interpreters with it. Today the drama, hunted from stage to stage, has only two houses that really belong to it, the Ambigu and the Théâtre-Historique. Even at the Saint-Martin the drama is lucky to win a brief showing for itself, between one great spectacle and the next.

An occasional success may renew its courage. But its decline is inevitable; romantic drama is sliding into oblivion, and if it seems sometimes to check its descent, it does so only to roll even lower afterwards. Naturally, there are loud complaints. The tail-end romanticists are desperately unhappy. They swear that except in the drama—meaning their kind of drama—there is no salvation for dramatic literature. I believe, on the contrary, that we must find a new formula that will transform the drama, just as the writers in the first half of the century transformed tragedy. That is the essence of the matter. Today the battle is between romantic drama and naturalistic drama. By romantic drama I mean every play that mocks truthfulness in its incidents and characterization, that struts about in its puppet-box, stuffed to the belly with noises that flounder, for some idealistic reason or other, in pastiches of Shakespeare and Hugo. Every period has its formula; ours is certainly not that of 1830. We are an age of method, of experimental science; our primary need is for precise analysis. We hardly understand the liberty we have won if we use it only to imprison ourselves in a new tradition. The way is open: we can now return to man and nature.

Finally, there have been great efforts to revive the historical drama. Nothing could be better. A critic cannot roundly condemn the choice of historical subjects, even if his own preferences are entirely for subjects that are modern. It is

simply that I am full of distrust. The manager one gives this sort of play to frightens me in advance. It is a question of how history is treated, what unusual characters are presented bearing the names of kings, great captains or great artists, and what awful sauce they are served up in to make the history palatable. As soon as the authors of these concoctions move into the past they think everything is permitted: improbabilities, cardboard dolls, monumental idiocies, the hysterical scribblings that falsely represent local colour. And what strange dialogue—François I talking like a haberdasher straight out of the Rue Saint-Denis, Richelieu using the words of a criminal from the Boulevard du Crime, Charlotte Corday with the weeping sentimentalities of a factory girl.

What astounds me is that our playwrights do not seem to suspect for a moment that the historical genre is unavoidably the least rewarding, the one that calls most strongly for research, integrity, a consummate gift of intuition, a talent for reconstruction. I am all for historical drama when it is in the hands of poets of genius or men of exceptional knowledge who are capable of making the public see an epoch come alive with its special quality, its manners, its civilization. In that case we have a work of prophecy or of profoundly interesting criticism.

But unfortunately I know what it is these partisans of historical drama want to revive: the swaggering and swordplay, the big spectacle with big words, the play of lies that shows off in front of the crowd, the gross exhibition that saddens honest minds. Hence my distrust. I think that all this antiquated business is better left in our museum of dramatic history under a pious layer of dust.

There are, undeniably, great obstacles to original experiments: we run up against the hypocrisies of criticism and the long education in idiocies that has been foisted on the public. This public, which titters at every childishness in melodramas, nevertheless lets itself be carried away by outbursts of fine sentiment. But the public is changing. Shakespeare's public and Molière's are no longer ours. We must reckon with shifts in outlook, with the need for reality which is everywhere getting more insistent. The last few romantics vainly repeat that the public wants this and the public wants that; the day is coming when the public will want the truth.

• • •

The old formulas, classical and romantic, were based on the rearrangement and systematic amputation of the truth. They determined on principle that the truth is not good enough; they tried to draw out of it an essence, a 'poetry', on the pretext that nature must be expurgated and magnified. Up to the present the different literary schools disputed only over the question of the best way to disguise the truth so that it might not look too brazen to the public. The classicists adopted the toga; the romantics fought a revolution to impose the coat of mail and the doublet. Essentially the change of dress made little difference; the counterfeiting of nature went on. But today the naturalistic thinkers are telling us that the truth does not need clothing; it can walk naked. That, I repeat, is the quarrel.

Writers with any sense understand perfectly that tragedy and romantic drama are dead. The majority, though, are badly troubled when they turn their minds to the as-yet-unclear formula of tomorrow. Does the truth seriously ask them to give up the grandeur, the poetry, the traditional epic effects that their ambition tells them to put into their plays? Does naturalism demand that they shrink their horizons and risk not one flight into fantasy?

I will try to reply. But first we must determine the methods used by the idealists to lift their works into poetry. They begin by placing their chosen subject in a distant time. That provides them with costumes and makes the framework of the story vague enough to give them full scope for lying. Next, they generalize instead of particularizing; their characters are no longer living people but sentiments, arguments, passions that have been induced by reasoning. This false framework calls for heroes of marble or cardboard. A man of flesh and bone with his own originality would jar in such a legendary setting. Moreover, when we see the characters in romantic drama or tragedy walking about they are stiffened into an attitude, one representing duty, another patriotism, a third superstition, a fourth maternal love; thus, all the abstract ideas file by. Never the thorough analysis of an organism, never a character whose muscles and brain function as in nature.

These, then, are the mannerisms that writers with epic inclinations do not want to give up. For them poetry resides in the past and in abstraction, in the idealizing of facts and characters. As soon as one confronts them with daily life, with the people who fill our streets, they blink, they stammer, they are afraid; they no longer see clearly; they find everything ugly and not good enough for art. According to them, a subject must enter the lies of legend, men must harden and turn to stone like statues before the artist can accept them and make them fit the disguises he has prepared.

Now, it is at this point that the naturalistic movement comes along and says squarely that poetry is everywhere, in everything, even more in the present and the real than in the past and the abstract. Each event at each moment has its poetic, superb aspect. We brush up against heroes who are great and powerful in different respects from the puppets of the epic-makers. Not one playwright in this century has

brought to life figures as lofty as Baron Hulot, Old Grandet, César Birotteau, and all the other characters of Balzac, who are so individual and so alive. Beside these real, giant creations Greek and Roman heroes quake; the heroes of the Middle Ages fall flat on their faces like lead soldiers.

With the superior works being produced in these times by the naturalistic school—works of high endeavour, pulsing with life—it is ridiculous and false to park our poetry in some antiquated temple and bury it in cobwebs. Poetry flows at its full force through everything that exists; the truer to life, the greater it becomes. And I mean to give the word poetry its widest definition, not to pin it down exclusively to the cadence of two rhymes, nor to burn it in a narrow coterie of dreamers, but to restore its real human significance which concerns the expansion and encouragement of every kind of truth.

Take our present environment, then, and try to make men live in it: you will write great works. It will undoubtedly call for some effort; it means sifting out of the confusion of life the simple formula of naturalism. Therein lies the difficulty: to do great things with the subjects and characters that our eyes, accustomed to the spectacle of the daily round, have come to see as small. I am aware that it is more convenient to present a marionette to the public and name it Charlemagne and puff it up with such tirades that the public believes it is watching a colossus; it is more convenient than taking a bourgeois of our time, a grotesque, unsightly man, and drawing sublime poetry out of him, making him, for example, Père Goriot, the father who gives his guts for his daughters, a figure so gigantic with truth and love that no other literature can offer his equal.

Nothing is as easy as persuading the managers with known formulas; and heroes in the classical or romantic taste cost so little labour that they are manufactured by the dozen, and have become standardized articles that clutter up our literature. But it takes hard work to create a real hero, intelligently analysed, alive and performing. That is probably why naturalism terrifies those authors who are used to fishing up great men from the troubled waters of history. They would have to burrow too deeply into humanity, learn about life, go straight for the greatness of reality and make it function with all their power. And let nobody gainsay this true poetry of humanity; it has been sifted out in the novel and can be in the theatre; only the method of adaptation remains to be found.

I am troubled by a comparison; it has been haunting me and I will now free myself of it. For two long months a play called *Les Danicheff* has been running at the Odéon. It takes place in Russia. It has been very successful here, but is apparently so dishonest, so packed with gross improbabilities, that the author, a Russian, has not even dared to show it in his country. What can you think of this work which is applauded in Paris and would be booed in St Petersburg? Well, imagine for a moment that the Romans could come back to life and see a performance of *Rome vaincue*. Can you hear their roars of laughter? Do you think the play would complete one performance? It would strike them as a parody; it would sink under the weight of mockery. And is there one historical play that could be performed before the society it claims to portray? A strange theatre, this, which is plausible only among foreigners, is based on the disappearance of the generations it deals with, and is made up of so much misinformation that it is good only for the ignorant!

The future is with naturalism. The formula will be found; it will be proved that there is more poetry in the little apartment of a bourgeois than in all the empty, worm-eaten palaces of history; in the end we will see that everything meets in the real: lovely fantasies that are free of capriciousness and whimsy, and idylls, and comedies, and dramas. Once the soil has been turned over, the task that seems alarming and unfeasible today will become easy.

I am not qualified to pronounce on the form that tomorrow's drama will take; that must be left to the voice of some genius to come. But I will allow myself to indicate the path I consider our theatre will follow.

First, the romantic drama must be abandoned. It would be disastrous for us to take over its outrageous acting, its rhetoric, its inherent thesis of action at the expense of character analysis. The finest models of the genre are, as has been said, mere operas with big effects. I believe, then, that we must go back to tragedy—not, heaven forbid, to borrow more of its rhetoric, its system of confidants, its declaiming, its endless speeches, but to return to its simplicity of action and its unique psychological and physiological study of the characters. Thus understood, the tragic framework is excellent; one deed unwinds in all its reality, and moves the characters to passions and feelings, the exact analysis of which constitutes the sole interest of the play—and in a contemporary environment, with the people who surround us.

My constant concern, my anxious vigil, has made me wonder which of us will have the strength to raise himself to the pitch of genius. If the naturalistic drama must come into being, only a genius can give birth to it. Corneille and Racine made tragedy. Victor Hugo made romantic drama. Where is the as-yet-unknown author who must make the naturalistic drama? In recent years experiments have not been wanting. But either because the public was not ready or because none of the beginners had the necessary staying-power, not one of these attempts has had decisive results.

In battles of this kind, small victories mean nothing; we need triumphs that overwhelm the adversary and win the public to the cause. Audiences would give way before the onslaught of a really strong man. This man would come with the expected word, the solution to the problem, the formula for a real life on stage, combining it with the illusions necessary in the theatre. He would have what the newcomers have as yet lacked: the cleverness or the might to impose himself and to remain so close to truth that his cleverness could not lead him into lies.

And what an immense place this innovator would occupy in our dramatic literature! He would be at the peak. He would build his monument in the middle of the desert of mediocrity that we are crossing, among the jerry-built houses strewn about our most illustrious stages. He would put everything in question and remake everything, scour the boards, create a world whose elements he would lift from life, from outside our traditions. Surely there is no more ambitious dream that a writer of our time could fulfil. The domain of the novel is crowded; the domain of the theatre is free. At this time in France an imperishable glory awaits the man of genius who takes up the work of Molière and finds in the reality of living comedy the full, true drama of modern society.

• • •

PHYSIOLOGICAL MAN

. . . In effect, the great naturalistic evolution, which comes down directly from the fifteenth century to ours has everything to do with the gradual substitution of physiological man for metaphysical man. In tragedy metaphysical man, man according to dogma and logic, reigned absolutely. The body did not count; the soul was regarded as the only interesting piece of human machinery; drama took place in the air, in pure mind. Consequently, what use was the tangible world? Why worry about the place where the action was located? Why be surprised at a baroque costume or false declaiming? Why notice that Queen Dido was a boy whose budding beard forced him to wear a mask? None of that mattered; these trifles were not worth stooping to; the play was heard out as if it were a school essay or a law case; it was on a higher plane than man, in the world of ideas, so far away from real man that any intrusion of reality would have spoiled the show.

Such is the point of departure—in Mystery plays, the religious point; the philosophical point in tragedy. And from that beginning natural man, stifling under the rhetoric and dogma, struggled secretly, tried to break free, made lengthy, futile efforts, and in the end asserted himself, limb by limb. The whole history of our theatre is in this conquest by the physiological man, who emerged more clearly in each period from behind the dummy of religious and philosophical idealism. Corneille, Molière, Racine, Voltaire, Beaumarchais and, in our day, Victor Hugo, Émile Augier, Alexandre Dumas *fils*, even Sardou, have had only one task, even when they were not completely aware of it: to increase the reality of our corpus of drama, to progress towards truth, to sift out more and more of the natural man and impose him on the public. And inevitably, the evolution will not end with them. It continues; it will continue forever. Mankind is very young. . . .

COSTUME, STAGE DESIGN, SPEECH

Modern clothes make a poor spectacle. If we depart from bourgeois tragedy, shut in between its four walls, and wish to use the breadth of larger stages for crowd scenes we are embarrassed and constrained by the monotony and the uniformly funereal look of the extras. In this case, I think, we should take advantage of the variety of garb offered by the different classes and occupations. To elaborate: I can imagine an author setting one act in the main marketplace of les Halles in Paris. The setting would be superb, with its bustling life and bold possibilities. In this immense setting we could have a very picturesque ensemble by displaying the porters wearing their large hats, the saleswomen with their white aprons and vividly-coloured scarves, the customers dressed in silk or wool or cotton prints, from the ladies accompanied by their maids to the female beggars on the prowl for anything they can pick up off the street. For inspiration it would be enough to go to les Halles and look about. Nothing is gaudier or more interesting. All of Paris would enjoy seeing this set if it were realized with the necessary accuracy and amplitude.

And how many other settings for popular drama there are for the taking! Inside a factory, the interior of a mine, the gingerbread market, a railway station, flower stalls, a racetrack, and so on. All the activities of modern life can take place in them. It will be said that such sets have already been tried. Unquestionably we have seen factories and railway stations in fantasy plays; but these were fantasy stations and factories. I mean, these sets were thrown together to create an illusion that was at best incomplete. What we need is detailed reproduction: costumes supplied by tradespeople, not sumptuous but adequate for the purposes of truth and for the interest of the scenes. Since everybody mourns the death of the drama our playwrights certainly ought to make a try at this type of popular, contemporary drama. At one stroke they could satisfy the public hunger for spectacle and the need for exact studies which grows more pressing every day. Let us hope, though, that the playwrights will show us real people and not those whining members of the working class who play such strange roles in boulevard melodrama.

As M. Adolphe Jullien has said—and I will never be tired of repeating it—everything is interdependent in the theatre. Lifelike costumes look wrong if the sets, the diction, the plays themselves are not lifelike. They must all march in step along the naturalistic road. When costume becomes more accurate, so do sets; actors free themselves from bombastic declaiming; plays study reality more closely and their characters are more true to life. I could make the same observations about sets I have just made about costume. With them too, we may seem to have reached the highest possible degree of truth, but we still have long strides to take. Most of all we would need to intensify the illusion in reconstructing the environments, less for their picturesque quality than for dramatic utility. The environment must determine the character. When a set is planned so as to give the lively impression of a description by Balzac; when, as the curtain rises, one catches the first glimpse of the characters, their personalities and behaviour, if only to see the actual locale in which they move, the importance of exact reproduction in the decor will be appreciated. Obviously, that is the way we are going. Environment, the study of which has transformed science and literature, will have to take a large role in the theatre. And here I may mention again the question of metaphysical man, the abstraction who had to be satisfied with his three walls in tragedy—whereas the physiological man in our modern works is asking more and more compellingly to be determined by his setting, by the environment that produced him. We see then that the road to progress is still long, for sets as well as costume. We are coming upon the truth but we can hardly stammer it out.

Another very serious matter is diction. True, we have got away from the chanting, the plainsong, of the seventeenth century. But we now have a "theatre voice," a false recitation that is very obtrusive and very annoying. Everything that is wrong with it comes from the fixed traditional code set up by the majority of critics. They found the theatre in a certain state and, instead of looking to the future, and judging the progress we are making and the progress we shall make by the progress we have already made, they stubbornly defend the relics of the old conventions, swearing that these relics must be preserved. Ask them why, make them see how far we have travelled; they will give you no logical reason. They will reply with assertions based on a set of conditions that are disappearing.

In diction the errors come from what the critics call "theatre language." Their theory is that on stage you must not speak as you do in everyday life. To support this viewpoint they pick examples from traditional practices, from what was happening yesterday—and is happening still—without taking account of the naturalistic movement, the phases of which have been established for us by M. Jullien's book.[1] Let us realize that there is no such thing as "theatre language." There

---

[1] Adolphe Jullien 1845–1932, writer on music and the theatre. The book Zola cites is *Histoire du costume au théâtre*, 1880.

has been a rhetoric which grew more and more feeble and is now dying out. Those are the facts. If you compare the declaiming of actors under Louis XIV with that of Lekain, and if you compare Lekain's with that of our own artists today, you will clearly distinguish the phases from tragic chanting down to our search for the natural, precise tone, the cry of truth. It follows that "theatre language," that language of booming sonority, is vanishing. We are moving towards simplicity, the exact word spoken without emphasis, quite naturally. How many examples I could give if I had unlimited space! Consider the powerful effect that Geoffroy has on the public; all his talent comes from his natural personality. He holds the public because he speaks on stage as he does at home. When a sentence sounds outlandish he cannot pronounce it; the author has to find another one. That is the fundamental criticism of so-called "theatre language." Again, follow the diction of a talented actor and at the same time watch the public; the cheers go up, the house is in raptures when a truthful accent gives the words the exact value they must have. All the great successes of the stage are triumphs over convention.

Alas, yes, there is a "theatre language." It is the clichés, the resounding platitudes, the hollow words that roll about like empty barrels, all that intolerable rhetoric of our vaudevilles and dramas, which is beginning to make us smile. It would be very interesting to study the style of such talented authors as MM. Augier, Dumas and Sardou. I could find much to criticize, especially in the last two with their conventional language, a language of their own that they put into the mouths of all their characters, men, women, children, old folk, both sexes and all ages. This irritates me, for each character has his own language, and to create living people you must give them to the public not merely in accurate dress and in the environments that have made them what they are, but with their individual ways of thinking and expressing themselves. I repeat that that is the obvious aim of our theatre. There is no theatre language regulated by such a code as "cadenced sentences" or sonority. There is simply a kind of dialogue that is growing more precise and is following—or rather, leading—sets and costumes towards naturalistic progress. When plays are more truthful, the actors' diction will gain enormously in simplicity and naturalness.

To conclude, I will repeat that the battle of the conventions is far from being finished, and that it will no doubt last forever. Today we are beginning to see clearly where we are going, but our steps are still impeded by the melting slush of rhetoric and metaphysics.

CONSTANTIN STANISLAVSKI (1863–1938)

"Direction and Acting" (1929)

One of the founders of the Moscow Art Theater, Stanislavski developed a systematic approach to acting that involved working both on the actor's psychological and on his or her physical portrayal of character. In this article, originally written for the Encyclopedia Britannica, Stanislavski outlines some of the central features of his "system": public solitude, concentration, internal technique.

Theatrical art has always been collective, arising only where poetical-dramatic talent was actively combined with the actor's. The basis of a play is always a dramatic conception; a general artistic sense is imparted to the theatrical action by the unifying, creative genius of the actor. Thus the actor's dramatic activity begins at the foundation of the play. In the first place, each actor, either independently or through the theatre manager, must probe for the fundamental motive in the finished play—the creative idea that is characteristic of the author and that reveals itself as the germ from which his work grows organically. The motive of the play always keeps the character developing before the spectator; each personality in the work takes a part conforming to his own character; the work, then developing in the appointed direction, flows on to the final point conceived by the author. The first stage in the work of the actor and theatre manager is to probe for the germ of the play, investigating the fundamental line of action that traverses all of its episodes and is therefore called by the writer its transparent effect or action. In contrast to some theatrical directors, who consider every play only as material for theatrical repetition, the writer believes that in the production of every important drama the director and actor must go straight for the most exact and profound conception of the mind and ideal of the dramatist, and must not change that ideal for their own. The interpretation of the play and the character of its artistic incarnation inevitably appear in a certain measure subjective, and bear the mark of the individual peculiarities of the manager and actors; but only by profound attention to the artistic individuality of the author and to his ideal and mentality, which have been disclosed as the creative germ of the play, can the theatre realize all its artistic depth and transmit, as in a poetical production, completeness and harmony of composition. Every part of the future spectacle is then unified in it by its own artistic work; each part, in the measure of its own genius, will flow on to the artistic realization aimed at by the dramatist.

The actor's task, then, begins with the search for the play's artistic seed. All artistic action—organic action, as in every constructive operation of nature—starts from this seed at the moment when it is conveyed to the mind. On reaching the actor's mind, the seed must wander around, germinate, put out roots, drinking in the juices of the soil in which it is planted, grow and eventually bring forth a lively flowering plant. Artistic process must in all cases flow very rapidly, but usually, in order that it may preserve the character of the true organic action and may lead to the creation of life, of a clear truly artistic theatrical image, and not of a trade substitute, it demands much more time than is allotted to it in the best European theatres. That is why in the writer's theatre every dramatization passes through eight to ten revisions, as is also done in Germany by the famous theatre manager and theorist, K. Hagemann. Sometimes even more than ten revisions are needed, occasionally extending over several months. But even under these conditions, the creative genius of the actor does not appear so freely as does, for instance, the creative genius of the dramatist. Bound by the strict obligations of his *collectif,* the actor must not postpone his work to the moment when his physical and psychic condition appears propitious for creative genius. Meanwhile, his exacting and capricious artistic nature is prompted by aspirations of his artistic intuition, and in the absence of creative genius is not reached by any effort of his will. He is not aided in that respect by outward technique—his skill in making use of his body, his vocal equipment and his powers of speech.

THE ARTISTIC CONDITION

But is it really impossible? Are there no means, no processes that sensibly would help us, and spontaneously lead to that artistic condition which is born of genius without any effort on its part? If that capacity is unattainable all at once, by some process or other, it may, perhaps, be acquired in parts, and through progressive stages may perfect those elements out of which the artistic condition is composed, and which are subject to our will. Of course the general run of acting does not come into being from this genius, but cannot such acting, in some measure, be brought by it near to what is evidence of genius? These are the problems which presented themselves to the writer about 20 years ago, when reflecting on the external obstacles that hamper actors' artistic genius, and partly compel substitution of the crude outward marks of the actor's profession for its results. They drove

him to the rediscovery of processes of external technique, i.e., methods proceeding form consciousness to subconsciousness, in which domain flow nine-tenths of all real artistic processes. Observations both upon himself and other actors with whom he happened to rehearse, but chiefly upon growing theatrical skill in Russia and abroad, allowed him to do some generalizing, which thereupon he verified in practice.

The first is that, in an artistic condition, full freedom of body plays a principal rôle; i.e., the freedom from that muscular strain which, without our knowing it, fetters us not only on the stage but also in ordinary life, hindering us from being obedient conductors of our psychic action. This muscular strain, reaching its maximum at those times when the actor is called upon to perform something especially difficult in his theatrical work, swallows up the bulk of this external energy, diverting him from activity of the higher centres. This teaches us the possibility of availing ourselves of the muscular energy of our limbs only as necessity demands, and in exact conformity with our creative efforts.

PUBLIC SOLITUDE

The second observation is that the flow of the actor's artistic force is considerably retarded by the visual auditorium and the public, whose presence may hamper his outward freedom of movement, and powerfully hinder his concentration on his own artistic taste. It is almost unnecessary to remark that the artistic achievement of great actors is always bound by the concentration of attention to the action of their own performance, and that when in that condition, i.e., just when the actor's attention is taken away from the spectator, he gains a particular power over the audience, grips it, and compels it to take an active share in his artistic existence. This does not mean, of course, that the actor must altogether cease to feel the public; but the public is concerned only in so far as it neither exerts pressure on him nor diverts him unnecessarily from the artistic demands of the moment, which last might happen to him even while knowing how to regulate his attention. The actor suitably disciplined must automatically restrict the sphere of his attention, concentrating on what comes within this sphere, and only half consciously seizing on what comes within its aura. If need be, he must restrict that sphere to such an extent that it reaches a condition that may be called *public solitude.* But as a rule this sphere of attention is elastic, it expands or contracts for the actor, with regard to the course of his theatrical actions. Within the boundary of this sphere, as one of the actual aspects of the play, there is also the actor's immediate central *object of attention,* the object on which, somehow or other, his will is concentrated at the moment with which, in the course of the play, he is in inward communication. This theatrical sympathy with the object can only be complete when the actor has trained himself by long practice to surrender himself in his own impressions, and also in his reactions to those impressions, with maximum intensity: only so does theatrical action attain the necessary force, only so is created between the actual aspects of the play, i.e., between the actors, that link, that living bond, which is essential for the carrying through of the play to its goal, with the general maintenance of the rhythm and time of each performance.

CONCENTRATION

But whatever may be the sphere of the actor's attention, whether it confines him at some moments to public solitude, or whether it grips the faces of all those before the stage, dramatic artistic genius, as in the preparation of the part so in its repeated performance, requires a full concentration of all the mental and physical talents of the actor, and the participation of the whole of his physical and psychic capacity. It takes hold of his sight and hearing, all his external senses; it draws out not only the periphery but also the essential depth of his existence, and it evokes to activity his memory, imagination, emotions, intelligence and will. The whole mental and physical being of the actor must be directed to that which is derived from his facial expression. At the moment of inspiration, of the involuntary use of all the actor's qualities, at that moment he actually exists. On the other hand, in the absence of this employment of his qualities, the actor is gradually led astray along the road leading to time-honored theatrical traditions; he begins to "produce" wherever he sees them, or, glancing at his own image, imitates the inward manifestations of his emotions, or tries to draw from himself the emotions of the perfected part, to "inspire" them within himself. But when forcing such an image by his own psychic equipment, with its unchanging organic laws, he by no means attains that desired result of artistic genius; he must present only the rough counterfeit of emotion, because emotions do not come to order. By no effort of conscious will can one awake them in oneself at a moment, nor can they ever be of use for creative genius striving to bring this about by searching the depths of its mind. A fundamental axiom, therefore, for the actor who wishes to be a real artist on the stage, may be stated thus: he must not play to produce emotions, and he must not involuntarily evoke them in himself.

ACTIVITY OF IMAGINATION

Considerations on the nature of artistically gifted people, however, inevitably open up the road to the possession of the

emotion of the part. This road traverses activity of imagination, which in most of its stages is subject to the action of consciousness. One must not suddenly begin to operate on emotion; one must put oneself in motion in the direction of artistic imagination, but imagination—as is also shown by observations of scientific psychology—disturbs our aberrant memory, and, luring from the hidden recesses beyond the boundaries of its sense of harmony whatever elements there may be of proved emotions, organizes them afresh in sympathy with those that have arisen in our imagery. So surrounded within our figures of imagination, without effort on our part, the answer to our aberrant memory is found and the sounds of sympathetic emotion are called out from us. This is why the creative imagination presents itself afresh, the indispensable gift of the actor. Without a well developed, mobile imagination, creative faculty is by no means possible, not by instinct nor intuition nor the aid of external technique. In the acquiring of it, that which has lain dormant in the mind of the artist is, when immersed in his sphere of unconscious imagery and emotion, completely harmonized within him.

This practical method for the artistic education of the actor, directed by means of his imagination to the storing up of affective memory, is sufficiently enlarged upon; his individual emotional experience, by its limits, actually leads to the restriction of the sphere of his creative genius, and does not allow him to play parts dissimilar to those of his psychic harmony. This opinion is fundamental for the clearing away of misunderstandings of those elements of reality from which are produced fictitious creations of imagination; these are also derived from organic experience, but a wealth and variety of these creations are only obtained by combinations drawn from a trial of elements. The musical scale has only its basic notes, the solar spectrum its radical colors, but the combination of sounds in music and of colors in painting are infinite. One can in the same way speak of radical emotions preserved in imaginative memory, just as the reception in imagination of outward harmony remains in the intellectual memory; the sum of these radical emotions in the inner experience of each person is limited, but the shades and combinations are as infinite as the combinations that create activity of imagination out of the elements of inward experience.

Certainly, but the actor's outward experience—i.e., his sphere of vital sensations and reflections—must always be elastic, for only in that condition can the actor enlarge the sphere of his creative faculty. On the other hand, he must judiciously develop his imagination, harnessing it again and again to new propositions. But, in order that that imaginary union which is the actor's very foundation, produced by the creative genius of the dramatist, should take hold of him emotionally and lead him on to theatrical action, it is necessary that the actor should "swing toward" that union, as toward something as real as the union of reality surrounding him.

THE EMOTION OF TRUTH

This does not mean that the actor must surrender himself on the stage to some such hallucination as that when playing he should lose the sense of reality around him, to take scenery for real trees, etc. On the contrary, some part of his senses must remain free from the grip of the play to control everything that he attempts and achieves as the performer of his part. He does not forget that surrounding him on the stage are decorations, scenery, etc., but they have no meaning for him. He says to himself, as it were: "I know that all around me on the stage is a rough counterfeit of reality. It is false. But if all should be real, see how I might be carried away to some such scene; then I would act." And at that instant, when there arises in his mind that artistic "suppose," encircling his real life, he loses interest in it, and is transported to another plane, created for him, of imaginary life. Restored to real life again, the actor must perforce modify the truth, as in the actual construction of his invention, so also in the survivals connected to it. His invention can be shown to be illogical, wide of the truth—and then he ceases to believe it. Emotion rises in him with invention; i.e., his outward regard for imagined circumstances may be shown as "determined" without relation to the individual nature of a given emotion. Finally, in the expression of the outward life of his part, the actor, as a living complex emotion, never making use of sufficient perfection of all his bodily equipment, may give an untrue intonation, may not keep the artistic mean in gesticulation and may through the temptation of cheap effect drift into mannerism or awkwardness.

Only by a strongly developed sense of truth may he achieve a single inward beauty in which, unlike the conventional theatrical gestures and poses, the true condition of the character is expressed in every one of his attitudes and outward gestures.

INTERNAL TECHNIQUE

The combination of all the above-named procedure and habits also composes the actor's external technique. Parallel with its development must go also the development of internal technique—the perfecting of that bodily equipment which serves for the incarnation of the theatrical image created by the actor, and the exact, clear expression of his external consciousness. With this aim in view the actor must work out within himself not only the ordinary flexibility and mobility of action, but also the particular consciousness that directs all his groups of muscles, and the ability to feel the energy trans-

fused within him, which, arising from his highest creative centres, forms in a definite manner his mimicry and gestures, and, radiating from him, brings into the circle of its influence his partners on the stage and in the auditorium. The same growth of consciousness and fineness of internal feelings must be worked out by the actor in relation to his vocal equipment. Ordinary speech—as in life, so on the stage—is prosaic and monotonous; in it words sound disjointed, without any harmonious stringing together in a vocal melody as continuous as that of a violin, which by the hand of a master violinist can become fuller, deeper, finer and more transparent, and can without difficulty run from the higher to the lower notes and vice versa, and can alternate from pianissimo to forte. To counteract the wearisome monotony of reading, actors often elaborate, especially when declaiming poetry, with those artificial vocal *fioriture,* cadences and sudden raising and lowering of the voice, which are so characteristic of the conventional, pompous declamation, and which are not influenced by the corresponding emotion of the part, and therefore impress the more sensitive auditors with a feeling of unreality.

But there exists another natural musical sonorousness of speech, which we may see in great actors at the moment of their own true artistic elation, and which is closely knit to the internal sonorousness of their rôle. The actor must develop within himself this natural musical speech by practising his voice with due regard to his sense of reality, almost as much as a singer. At the same time he must perfect his elocution. It is possible to have a strong, flexible, impressive voice, and still distort speech, on the one hand by incorrect pronunciation, on the other by neglect of those almost imperceptible pauses and emphasis through which are attained the exact transmission of the sense of the sentence, and also its particular emotional coloring. In the perfect production of the dramatist, every word, every letter, every punctuation mark has its part in transmitting his inward reality; the actor in his interpretation of the play, according to his intelligence, introduces into each sentence his individual nuances, which must be transmitted not only by the motions of his body, but also by artistically developed speech. He must bear this in mind, that every sound which goes to make a word appears as a separate note, which has its part in the harmonious sound of the word, and which is the expression of one or other particle of the soul drawn out through the word. The perfecting, therefore, of the phonetics of speech cannot be limited to mechanical exercise of the vocal equipment, but must also be directed in such a way that the actor learns to feel each separate sound in a word as an instrument of artistic expression. But in regard to the musical tone of the voice, freedom, elasticity, rhythm of movement and generally all external technique of dramatic art, to say nothing of internal technique, the present day actor is still on a low rung of the ladder of artistic culture, still far behind in this re-spect, from many causes, the masters of music, poetry and painting, with an almost infinite road of development to travel.

It is evident that under these conditions, the staging of a play, which will satisfy highly artistic demands, cannot be achieved at the speed that economic factors unfortunately make necessary in most theatres. This creative process, which every actor must go through, from his conception of the part to its artistic incarnation, is essentially very compli-cated, and is hampered by lack of perfection of outward and inward technique. It is also much hindered by the necessity of fitting in the actors one with another—the adjustment of their artistic individualities into an artistic whole.

PRODUCTION

Responsibility for bringing about this accord, and the artistic integrity and expression of the performance rests with the theatre manager. During the period when the manager exer-cised a despotic rule in the theatre, a period starting with the Meiningen players and still in force even in many of the fore-most theatres, the manager worked out in advance all the plans for staging a play, and, while certainly having regard to the existing cast, indicated to the actors the general outlines of the scenic effects, and the *mise-en-scène*. The writer also ad-hered to this system, but now he has come to the conclusion that the creative work of the manager must be done in collab-oration with the actor's work, neither ignoring nor confirming it. To encourage the actor's creative genius, to control and ad-just it, ensuring that this creative genius grows out of the unique artistic germ of the drama, as much as the external building up of the performance—that in the opinion of the writer is the problem of the theatre director to-day.

The joint work of the director and actor begins with the analysis of the drama and the discovery of its artistic germ, and with the investigation of its *transparent effect*. The next step is the discovery of the transparent effect of individual parts—of that fundamental will direction of each individual ac-tor, which, organically derived from his character, determines his place in the general action of the play. If the actor cannot at once secure this transparent effect, then it must be traced bit by bit with the manager's aid—by dividing the part into sections corresponding to the separate stages of the life of the particular actor—from the separate problems developing be-fore him in his struggle for the attainment of his goal. Each such section of a part of each problem, can, if necessary, be subjected to further psychological analysis, and sub-divided into problems even more detailed, corresponding to those separate mind actions of the performer out of which stage life is summed up. The actor must catch the *mind axes* of the emo-tions and temperaments, but not the emotions and tempera-ments that give color to these sections of the part. In other words, when studying each portion of his part, he must ask himself what he wants, what he requires as a performer of the play and which definite partial problem he is putting before himself at a given moment. The answer to this question should not be in the form of a noun, but rather of a verb: "I wish to ob-tain possession of the heart of this lady"—"I wish to enter her house"—"I wish to push aside the servants who are protecting her," etc. Formulated in this manner, the mind problem, of which the object and setting, thanks to the working of his cre-ative imagination, are forming a brighter and clearer picture for the actor, begins to grip him and to excite him, extracting from the recesses of his working memory the combinations of emotions necessary to the part, of emotions that have an ac-tive character and mould themselves into dramatic action. In this way the different sections of the actor's part grow more lively and richer by degrees, owing to the involuntary play of the complicated organic survivals. By joining together and grafting these sections, the *score of the part* is formed; the scores of the separate parts, after the continual joint work of the actors during rehearsals and by the necessary adjustment of them one with another, are summed up in a single *score of the performance*.

THE SCORE CONDENSED

Nevertheless, the work of the actors and manager is still un-finished. The actor is studying and living in the part and the play deeper and deeper still, finding their deeper artistic mo-tives; so he lives in the score of his part still more profoundly. But the score of the part itself and of the play are actually subject by degrees during the work to further alterations. As in a perfect poetical production there are no superfluous words but only those necessary to the poet's artistic scheme, so in a score of the part there must not be a single superflu-ous emotion but only emotions necessary for the *transparent effect*. The score of each part must be condensed, as also the form of its transmitting, and bright, simple and compelling forms of its incarnation must be found. Only then, when in each actor every part not only organically ripens and comes to life but also all emotions are stripped of the superfluous, when they all crystallize and sum up into a live contact, when they harmonize amongst themselves in the general tune, rhythm and time of the performance, then the play may be presented to the public.

During repeated presentations the theatrical score of the play and each part remains in general unaltered. But that does not mean that from the moment the performance is shown to the public the actor's creative process is to be considered ended, and that there remains for him only the mechanical repetition of his achievement at the first presentation. On the contrary, every performance imposes on him creative condi-tions; all his psychical forces must take part in it, because only in these conditions can they creatively adapt the score of the part to those capricious changes which may develop in them from hour to hour, as in all living nervous creatures influencing one another by their emotions, and only then can they transmit to the spectator that invisible something, inexpressible in words, which forms the spiritual content of the play. And that is the whole origin of the substance of dramatic art.

As regards the outward arrangements of the play—scenery, theatrical properties, etc.—all are of value in so far as they correspond to the expression of dramatic action, i.e., to the actors' talents; in no case may they claim to have an independent artistic importance in the theatre, although up to now they have been so considered by many great scene painters. The art of scene painting, as well as the music included in the play, is on the stage only an auxiliary art, and the manager's duty is to get from each what is necessary for the illumination of the play performed before an audience, while subordinating each to the problems of the actors.

BERTOLT BRECHT (1898–1956)
"Theatre for Pleasure or Theatre for Instruction" (1935–1936)
TRANSLATED BY JOHN WILLETT

In this essay, Brecht attacks the bourgeois notion that the theater can be divided into two kinds of art, as though drama were either instructive or entertaining. As he does in his plays, Brecht dialecticizes these categories, showing that they define one another and therefore exist within one another. Realistic plays, after all, not only entertain their audiences, but also offer an image of the world, a kind of instruction. On the other hand, intellectual or critical activity is not only pleasurable in itself, but it also can lead to a lively kind of theater as well, as Brecht's plays illustrate. This essay was unpublished in Brecht's lifetime: John Willett dates it from 1935 or 1936. He notes that Brecht uses the word Entfremdung *here for "alienation," the same word used by Marx and Hegel. Brecht later coined his own word* Verfremdungseffekt *for "alienation effect."*

A few years back, anybody talking about the modern theatre meant the theatre in Moscow, New York and Berlin. He might have thrown in a mention of one of Jouvet's productions in Paris or Cochran's in London, or *The Dybbuk* as given by the Habima (which is to all intents and purposes part of the Russian theatre, since Vakhtangov was its director). But broadly speaking there were only three capitals so far as modern theatre was concerned.

Russian, American and German theatres differed widely from one another, but were alike in being modern, that is to say in introducing technical and artistic innovations. In a sense they even achieved a certain stylistic resemblance, probably because technology is international (not just that part which is directly applied to the stage but also that which influences it, the film for instance), and because large progressive cities in large industrial countries are involved. Among the older capitalist countries it is the Berlin theatre that seemed of late to be in the lead. For a period all that is common to the modern theatre received its strongest and (so far) maturest expression there.

The Berlin theatre's last phase was the so-called epic theatre, and it showed the modern theatre's trend of development in its purest form. Whatever was labelled '*Zeitstück*' or '*Piscatorbühne*' or '*Lehrstück*' belongs to the epic theatre.

THE EPIC THEATRE
Many people imagine that the term 'epic theatre' is self-contradictory, as the epic and dramatic ways of narrating a story are held, following Aristotle, to be basically distinct. The difference between the two forms was never thought simply to lie in the fact that the one is performed by living beings while the other operates via the written word; epic works such as those of Homer and the medieval singers were at the same time theatrical performances, while dramas like Goethe's *Faust* and Byron's *Manfred* are agreed to have been more effective as books. Thus even by Aristotle's definition the difference between the dramatic and epic forms was attributed to their different methods of construction, whose laws were dealt with by two different branches of aesthetics. The method of construction depended on the different way of presenting the work to the public, sometimes via the stage, sometimes through a book; and independently of that there was the 'dramatic element' in epic works and the 'epic element' in dramatic. The bourgeois novel in the last century developed much that was 'dramatic,' by which was meant the strong centralization of the story, a momentum that drew the separate parts into a common relationship. A particular passion of utterance, a certain emphasis on the clash of forces are hallmarks of the 'dramatic'. The epic writer Döblin provided an excellent criterion when he said that with an epic work, as opposed to a dramatic, one can as it were take a pair of scissors and cut it into individual pieces, which remain fully capable of life.

This is no place to explain how the opposition of epic and dramatic lost its rigidity after having long been held to be irreconcilable. Let us just point out that the technical advances alone were enough to permit the stage to incorporate an element of narrative in its dramatic productions. The possibility of projections, the greater adaptability of the stage due to mechanization, the film, all completed the theatre's equipment, and did so at a point where the most important transactions between people could no longer be shown simply by personifying the motive forces or subjecting the characters to invisible metaphysical powers.

To make these transactions intelligible the environment in which the people lived had to be brought to bear in a big and 'significant' way.

This environment had of course been shown in the existing drama, but only as seen from the central figure's point of view, and not as an independent element. It was defined by the hero's reactions to it. It was seen as a storm can be seen when one sees the ships on a sheet of water unfolding their sails, and the sails filling out. In the epic theatre it was to appear standing on its own.

The stage began to tell a story. The narrator was no longer missing, along with the fourth wall. Not only did the background adopt an attitude to the events on the stage—by big screens recalling other simultaneous events elsewhere, by projecting documents which confirmed or contradicted what the characters said, by concrete and intelligible figures to accompany abstract conversations, by figures and sentences to support mimed transactions whose sense was unclear—but the actors too refrained from going over wholly into their role, remaining detached from the character they were playing and clearly inviting criticism of him.

The spectator was no longer in any way allowed to submit to an experience uncritically (and without practical consequences) by means of simple empathy with the characters in a play. The production took the subject-matter and the incidents shown and put them through a process of alienation: the alienation that is necessary to all understanding. When something seems 'the most obvious thing in the world' it means that any attempt to understand the world has been given up.

What is 'natural' must have the force of what is startling. This is the only way to expose the laws of cause and effect. People's activity must simultaneously be so and be capable of being different.

It was all a great change.

The dramatic theatre's spectator says: Yes, I have felt like that too—Just like me—It's only natural—It'll never change—The sufferings of this man appal me, because they are inescapable—That's great art; it all seems the most obvious thing in the world—I weep when they weep, I laugh when they laugh.

The epic theatre's spectator says: I'd never have thought it—That's not the way—That's extraordinary, hardly believable—It's got to stop—The sufferings of this man appal me, because they are unnecessary—That's great art: nothing obvious in it—I laugh when they weep, I weep when they laugh.

THE INSTRUCTIVE THEATRE

The stage began to be instructive.

Oil, inflation, war, social struggles, the family, religion, wheat, the meat market, all became subjects for theatrical representation. Choruses enlightened the spectator about facts unknown to him. Films showed a montage of events from all over the world. Projections added statistical material. And as the 'background' came to the front of the stage so people's activity was subjected to criticism. Right and wrong courses of action were shown. People were shown who knew what they were doing, and others who did not. The theatre became an affair for philosophers, but only for such philosophers as wished not just to explain the world but also to change it. So we had philosophy, and we had instruction. And where was the amusement in all that? Were they sending us back to school, teaching us to read and write? Were we supposed to pass exams, work for diplomas?

Generally there is felt to be a very sharp distinction between learning and amusing oneself. The first may be useful, but only the second is pleasant. So we have to defend the epic theatre against the suspicion that it is a highly disagreeable, humourless, indeed strenuous affair.

Well: all that can be said is that the contrast between learning and amusing oneself is not laid down by divine rule; it is not one that has always been and must continue to be.

Undoubtedly there is much that is tedious about the kind of learning familiar to us from school, from our professional training, etc. But it must be remembered under what conditions and to what end that takes place.

It is really a commercial transaction. Knowledge is just a commodity. It is acquired in order to be resold. All those who have grown out of going to school have to do their learning virtually in secret, for anyone who admits that he still has something to learn devalues himself as a man whose knowledge is inadequate. Moreover the usefulness of learning is very much limited by factors outside the learner's control. There is unemployment, for instance, against which no knowledge can protect one. There is the division of labour, which makes generalized knowledge unnecessary and impossible. Learning is often among the concerns of those whom no amount of concern will get any forwarder. There is not much knowledge that leads to power, but plenty of knowledge to which only power can lead.

Learning has a very different function for different social strata. There are strata who cannot imagine any improvement in conditions: they find the conditions good enough for them. Whatever happens to oil they will benefit from it. And: they feel the years beginning to tell. There can't be all that many years more. What is the point of learning a lot now? They have said their final word: a grunt. But there are also strata 'waiting their turn' who are discontented with conditions, have a vast interest in the practical side of learning, want at all costs to find out where they stand, and know that they are lost without learning; these are the best and keenest learners. Similar differences apply to countries and peoples. Thus the pleasure of learning depends on all sorts of things; but none the less there is such a thing as pleasurable learning, cheerful and militant learning.

If there were not such amusement to be had from learning the theatre's whole structure would unfit it for teaching.

Theatre remains theatre even when it is instructive theatre, and in so far as it is good theatre it will amuse.

THEATRE AND KNOWLEDGE

But what has knowledge got to do with art? We know that knowledge can be amusing, but not everything that is amusing belongs in the theatre.

I have often been told, when pointing out the invaluable services that modern knowledge and science, if properly applied, can perform for art and specially for the theatre, that art and knowledge are two estimable but wholly distinct fields of human activity. This is a fearful truism, of course, and it is as well to agree quickly that, like most truisms, it is perfectly true. Art and science work in quite different ways: agreed. But, bad as it may sound, I have to admit that I cannot get along as an artist without the use of one or two sciences. This may well arouse serious doubts as to my artistic capacities. People are used to seeing poets as unique and slightly unnatural beings who reveal with a truly godlike assurance things that other people can only recognize after much sweat and toil. It is naturally distasteful to have to admit that one does not belong to this select band. All the same, it must be admitted. It must at the same time be made clear that the scientific occupations just confessed to are not pardonable side interests, pursued on days off after a good week's work. We all know how Goethe was interested in natural history, Schiller in history: as a kind of hobby, it is charitable to assume. I have no wish promptly to accuse these two of having needed these sciences for their poetic activity; I am not trying to shelter behind them; but I must say that I do need the sciences. I have to admit, however, that I look askance at all sorts of people who I know do not operate on the level of scientific understanding: that is to say, who sing as the birds sing, or as people imagine the birds to sing. I don't mean by that that I would reject a charming poem about the taste of fried fish or the delights of a boating party just because the writer had not studied gastronomy or navigation. But in my view the great and complicated things that go on in the world cannot be adequately recognized by people who do not use every possible aid to understanding.

Let us suppose that great passions or great events have to be shown which influence the fate of nations. The lust for power is nowadays held to be such a passion. Given that a poet 'feels' this lust and wants to have someone strive for power, how is he to show the exceedingly complicated machinery within which the struggle for power nowadays takes place? If his hero is a politician, how do politics work? If he is a business man, how does business work? And yet there are writers who find business and politics nothing like so passionately interesting as the individual's lust for power. How are they to acquire the necessary knowledge? They are scarcely likely to learn enough by going round and keeping their eyes open, though even then it is more than they would get by just rolling their eyes in an exalted frenzy. The foundation of a paper like the *Völkischer Beobachter* or a business like Standard Oil is a pretty complicated affair, and such things cannot be conveyed just like that. One important field for the playwright is psychology. It is taken for granted that a poet, if not an ordinary man, must be able without further instruction to discover the motives that lead a man to commit murder; he must be able to give a picture of a murderer's mental state 'from within himself.' It is taken for granted that one only has to look inside oneself in such a case; and then there's always one's imagination. . . . There are various reasons why I can no longer surrender to this agreeable hope of getting a result quite so simply. I can no longer find in myself all those motives which the press or scientific reports show to have been observed in people. Like the average judge when pronouncing sentence, I cannot without further ado conjure up an adequate picture of a murderer's mental state. Modern psychology, from psychoanalysis to behaviourism, acquaints me with facts that lead me to judge the case quite differently, especially if I bear in mind the findings of sociology and do not overlook economics and history. You will say: but that's getting complicated. I have to answer that it *is* complicated. Even if you let yourself be convinced, and agree with me that a large slice of literature is exceedingly primitive, you may still ask with profound concern: won't an evening in such a theatre be a most alarming affair? The answer to that is: no.

Whatever knowledge is embodied in a piece of poetic writing has to be wholly transmuted into poetry. Its utilization fulfils the very pleasure that the poetic element provokes. If it does not at the same time fulfil that which is fulfilled by the scientific element, none the less in an age of great discoveries and inventions one must have a certain inclination to penetrate deeper into things—a desire to make the world controllable—if one is to be sure of enjoying its poetry.

IS THE EPIC THEATRE SOME KIND OF 'MORAL INSTITUTION'?

According to Friedrich Schiller the theatre is supposed to be a moral institution. In making this demand it hardly occurred to Schiller that by moralizing from the stage he might drive the audience out of the theatre. Audiences had no objection to moralizing in his day. It was only later that Friedrich Nietzsche attacked him for blowing a moral trumpet. To Nietzsche any concern with morality was a depressing affair; to Schiller it seemed thoroughly enjoyable. He knew of nothing that could give greater amusement and satisfaction than the propagation of ideas. The bourgeoisie was setting about forming the ideas of the nation.

Putting one's house in order, patting oneself on the back, submitting one's account, is something highly agreeable. But describing the collapse of one's house, having pains in the back, paying one's account, is indeed a depressing affair, and that was how Friedrich Nietzsche saw things a century later. He was poorly disposed towards morality, and thus towards the previous Friedrich too.

The epic theatre was likewise often objected to as moralizing too much. Yet in the epic theatre moral arguments only took second place. Its aim was less to moralize than to observe. That is to say it observed, and then the thick end of the wedge followed: the story's moral. Of course we cannot pretend that we started our observations out of a pure passion for observing and without any more practical motive, only to be completely staggered by their results. Undoubtedly there were some painful discrepancies in our environment, circumstances that were barely tolerable, and this not merely on account of moral considerations. It is not only moral considerations that make hunger, cold and oppression hard to bear. Similarly, the object of our inquiries was not just to arouse moral objections to such circumstances (even though they could easily be felt—though not by all the audience alike; such objections were seldom for instance felt by those who profited by the circumstances in question) but to discover means for their

elimination. We were not in fact speaking in the name of morality but in that of the victims. These truly are two distinct matters, for the victims are often told that they ought to be contented with their lot, for moral reasons. Moralists of this sort see man as existing for morality, not morality for man. At least it should be possible to gather from the above to what degree and in what sense the epic theatre is a moral institution.

CAN EPIC THEATRE BE PLAYED ANYWHERE?

Stylistically speaking, there is nothing all that new about the epic theatre. Its expository character and its emphasis on virtuosity bring it close to the old Asiatic theatre. Didactic tendencies are to be found in the medieval mystery plays and the classical Spanish theatre, and also in the theatre of the Jesuits.

These theatrical forms corresponded to particular trends of their time, and vanished with them. Similarly the modern epic theatre is linked with certain trends. It cannot by any means be practised universally. Most of the great nations today are not disposed to use the theatre for ventilating their problems. London, Paris, Tokyo and Rome maintain their theatres for quite different purposes. Up to now favourable circumstances for an epic and didactic theatre have only been found in a few places and for a short period of time. In Berlin Fascism put a very definite stop to the development of such a theatre.

It demands not only a certain technological level but a powerful movement in society which is interested to see vital questions freely aired with a view to their solution, and can defend this interest against every contrary trend.

The epic theatre is the broadest and most far-reaching attempt at large-scale modern theatre, and it has all those immense difficulties to overcome that always confront the vital forces in the sphere of politics, philosophy, science and art.

ANTONIN ARTAUD (1896–1948)

from *The Theater and Its Double* (1938)

TRANSLATED BY MARY CAROLINE RICHARDS

An early member of the surrealist movement in Paris, Antonin Artaud was well-known between the wars as an actor, playwright, and essayist of the avant-garde theater, and he is one of the formative influences on the modern European theater. Artaud is most often associated with the "theater of cruelty," his label for a theater that would assault the representational dynamics of traditional theater and break the boundaries between actor and audience, stage and spectacle. Artaud was declared insane and committed to a mental hospital in 1939. He remained institutionalized for most of the remainder of his life.

THE THEATER AND CULTURE

Never before, when it is life itself that is in question, has there been so much talk of civilization and culture. And there is a curious parallel between this generalized collapse of life at the root of our present demoralization and our concern for a culture which has never been coincident with life, which in fact has been devised to tyrannize over life.

Before speaking further about culture, I must remark that the world is hungry and not concerned with culture, and that the attempt to orient toward culture thoughts turned only toward hunger is a purely artificial expedient.

What is most important, it seems to me, is not so much to defend a culture whose existence has never kept a man from going hungry, as to extract, from what is called culture, ideas whose compelling force is identical with that of hunger.

We need to live first of all; to believe in what makes us live and that something *makes* us live—to believe that whatever is produced from the mysterious depths of ourselves need not forever haunt us as an exclusively digestive concern.

I mean that if it is important for us to eat first of all, it is even more important for us not to waste in the sole concern for eating our simple power of being hungry.

If confusion is the sign of the times, I see at the root of this confusion a rupture between things and words, between things and the ideas and signs that are their representation.

Not, of course, for lack of philosophical systems; their number and contradictions characterize our old French and European culture: but where can it be shown that life, our life, has ever been affected by these systems? I will not say that philosophical systems must be applied directly and immediately: but of the following alternatives, one must be true:

Either these systems are within us and permeate our being to the point of supporting life itself (and if this is the case, what use are books?), or they do *not* permeate us and therefore do not have the capacity to support life (and in this case what does their disappearance matter?).

We must insist upon the idea of culture-in-action, of culture growing within us like a new organ, a sort of second breath; and on civilization as an applied culture controlling even our subtlest actions, a *presence of mind;* the distinction between culture and civilization is an artificial one, providing two words to signify an identical function.

A civilized man judges and is judged according to his behavior, but even the term "civilized" leads to confusion: a cultivated "civilized" man is regarded as a person instructed in systems, a person who thinks in forms, signs, representations—a monster whose faculty of deriving thoughts from acts, instead of identifying acts with thoughts, is developed to an absurdity.

If our life lacks brimstone, i.e., a constant magic, it is because we choose to observe our acts and lose ourselves in considerations of their imagined form instead of being impelled by their force.

And this faculty is an exclusively human one. I would even say that it is this infection of the human which contaminates ideas that should have remained divine; for far from believing that man invented the supernatural and the divine, I think it is man's age-old intervention which has ultimately corrupted the divine within him.

All our ideas about life must be revised in a period when nothing any longer adheres to life; it is this painful cleavage which is responsible for the revenge of *things;* the poetry which is no longer within us and which we no longer succeed in finding in things suddenly appears on their wrong side: consider the unprecedented number of crimes whose perverse gratuitousness is explained only by our powerlessness to take complete possession of life.

If the theater has been created as an outlet for our repressions, the agonized poetry expressed in its bizarre corruptions of the facts of life demonstrates that life's intensity is still intact and asks only to be better directed.

But no matter how loudly we clamor for magic in our lives, we are really afraid of pursuing an existence entirely under its influence and sign.

Hence our confirmed lack of culture is astonished by certain grandiose anomalies; for example, on an island without any contact with modern civilization, the mere passage of a ship carrying only healthy passengers may provoke the sudden outbreak of diseases unknown on that island but a specialty of nations like our own: shingles, influenza, grippe, rheumatism, sinusitis, polyneuritis, etc.

Similarly, if we think Negroes smell bad, we are ignorant of the fact that anywhere but in Europe it is we whites who "smell bad." And I would even say that we give off an odor as white as the gathering of pus in an infected wound.

As iron can be heated until it turns white, so it can be said that everything excessive is white; for Asiatics white has become the mark of extreme decomposition.

This said, we can begin to form an idea of culture, an idea which is first of all a protest.

A protest against the senseless constraint imposed upon the idea of culture by reducing it to a sort of inconceivable Pantheon, producing an idolatry no different from the image-worship of those religions which relegate their gods to Pantheons.

A protest against the idea of culture as distinct from life—as if there were culture on one side and life on the other, as if true culture were not a refined means of understanding and *exercising* life.

The library at Alexandria can be burnt down. There are forces above and beyond papyrus: we may temporarily be deprived of our ability to discover these forces, but their energy will not be suppressed. It is good that our excessive facilities are no longer available, that forms fall into oblivion: a culture without space or time, restrained only by the capacity of our own nerves, will reappear with all the more energy. It is right that from time to time cataclysms occur which compel us to return to nature, i.e., to rediscover life. The old totemism of animals, stones, objects capable of discharging thunderbolts, costumes impregnated with bestial essences—everything, in short, that might determine, disclose, and direct the secret forces of the universe—is for us a dead thing, from which we derive nothing but static and aesthetic profit, the profit of an audience, not of an actor.

Yet totemism is an actor, for it moves, and has been created in behalf of actors; all true culture relies upon the barbaric and primitive means of totemism whose savage, i.e., entirely spontaneous, life I wish to worship.

What has lost us culture is our Occidental idea of art and the profits we seek to derive from it. Art and culture cannot be considered together, contrary to the treatment universally accorded them!

True culture operates by exaltation and force, while the European ideal of art attempts to cast the mind into an attitude distinct from force but addicted to exaltation. It is a lazy, unserviceable notion which engenders an imminent death. If the Serpent Quetzalcoatl's multiple twists and turns are harmonious, it is because they express the equilibrium and fluctuations of a sleeping force; the intensity of the forms is there only to seduce and direct a force which, in music, would produce an insupportable range of sound.

The gods that sleep in museums: the god of fire with his incense burner that resembles an Inquisition tripod; Tlaloc, one of the manifold Gods of the Waters, on his wall of green granite; the Mother Goddess of Waters, the Mother Goddess of Flowers; the immutable expression, echoing from beneath many layers of water, of the Goddess robed in green jade; the enraptured, blissful expression, features crackling with incense, where atoms of sunlight circle—the countenance of the Mother Goddess of Flowers; this world of obligatory servitude in which a stone comes alive when it has been properly carved, the world of organically civilized men whose vital organs too awaken from their slumber, this human world enters into us, participating in the dance of the gods without turning round or looking back, on pain of becoming, like ourselves, crumbled pillars of salt.

In Mexico, since we are talking about Mexico, there is no art: things are made for use. And the world is in perpetual exaltation.

To our disinterested and inert idea of art an authentic culture opposes a violently egoistic and magical, i.e., *interested* idea. For the Mexicans seek contact with the *Manas*, forces latent in every form, unreleased by contemplation of the forms for themselves, but springing to life by magic identification with these forms. And the old Totems are there to hasten the communication.

How hard it is, when everything encourages us to sleep, though we may look about us with conscious, clinging eyes, to wake and yet look about us as in a dream, with eyes that no longer know their function and whose gaze is turned inward.

This is how our strange idea of disinterested action originated, though it is action nonetheless, and all the more violent for skirting the temptation of repose.

Every real effigy has a shadow which is its double; and art must falter and fail from the moment the sculptor believes he has liberated the kind of shadow whose very existence will destroy his repose.

Like all magic cultures expressed by appropriate hieroglyphs, the true theater has its shadows too, and, of all languages and all arts, the theater is the only one left whose shadows have shattered their limitations. From the beginning, one might say its shadows did not tolerate limitations.

Our petrified idea of the theater is connected with our petrified idea of a culture without shadows, where, no matter which way it turns, our mind *(esprit)* encounters only emptiness, though space is full.

But the true theater, because it moves and makes use of living instruments, continues to stir up shadows where life has never ceased to grope its way. The actor does not make the same gestures twice, but he makes gestures, he moves; and although he brutalizes forms, nevertheless behind them and through their destruction he rejoins that which outlives forms and produces their continuation.

The theater, which is in *no thing*, but makes use of everything—gestures, sounds, words, screams, light, darkness—rediscovers itself at precisely the point where the mind requires a language to express its manifestations.

And the fixation of the theater in one language—written words, music, lights, noises—betokens its imminent ruin, the choice of any one language betraying a taste for the special effects of that language; and the dessication of the language accompanies its limitation.

For the theater as for culture, it remains a question of naming and directing shadows: and the theater, not confined to a fixed language and form, not only destroys false shadows but prepares the way for a new generation of shadows, around which assembles the true spectacle of life.

To break through language in order to touch life is to create or recreate the theater; the essential thing is not to believe that this act must remain sacred, i.e., set apart—the essential thing is to believe that not just anyone can create it, and that there must be a preparation.

This leads to the rejection of the usual limitations of man and man's powers, and infinitely extends the frontiers of what is called reality.

We must believe in a sense of life renewed by the theater, a sense of life in which man fearlessly makes himself master of what does not yet exist, and brings it into being. And everything that has not been born can still be brought to life if we are not satisfied to remain mere recording organisms.

Furthermore, when we speak the word "life," it must be understood we are not referring to life as we know it from its surface of fact, but to that fragile, fluctuating center which forms never reach. And if there is still one hellish, truly accursed thing in our time, it is our artistic dallying with forms, instead of being like victims burnt at the stake, signaling through the flames.

• • •

NO MORE MASTERPIECES

One of the reasons for the asphyxiating atmosphere in which we live without possible escape or remedy—and in which we all share, even the most revolutionary among us—is our respect for what has been written, formulated, or painted, what has been given form, as if all expression were not at last exhausted, were not at a point where things must break apart if they are to start anew and begin fresh.

We must have done with this idea of masterpieces reserved for a self-styled elite and not understood by the general public; the mind has no such restricted districts as those so often used for clandestine sexual encounters.

Masterpieces of the past are good for the past: they are not good for us. We have the right to say what has been said and even what has not been said in a way that belongs to us, a way that is immediate and direct, corresponding to present modes of feeling, and understandable to everyone.

It is idiotic to reproach the masses for having no sense of the sublime, when the sublime is confused with one or another of its formal manifestations, which are moreover always defunct manifestations. And if for example a contemporary public does not understand *Oedipus Rex*, I shall make bold to say that it is the fault of *Oedipus Rex* and not of the public.

In *Oedipus Rex* there is the theme of incest and the idea that nature mocks at morality and that there are certain unspecified powers at large which we would do well to beware of, call them *destiny* or anything you choose.

There is in addition the presence of a plague epidemic which is a physical incarnation of these powers. But the whole in a manner and language that have lost all touch with the rude and epileptic rhythm of our time. Sophocles speaks grandly perhaps, but in a style that is no longer timely. His language is too refined for this age. It is as if he were speaking beside the point.

However, a public that shudders at train wrecks, that is familiar with earthquakes, plagues, revolutions, wars; that is sensitive to the disordered anguish of love, can be affected by all these grand notions and asks only to become aware of them, but on condition that it is addressed in its own language, and that its knowledge of these things does not come to it through adulterated trappings and speech that belong to extinct eras which will never live again.

Today as yesterday, the public is greedy for mystery: it asks only to become aware of the laws according to which destiny manifests itself, and to divine perhaps the secret of its apparitions.

Let us leave textual criticism to graduate students, formal criticism to esthetes, and recognize that what has been said is not still to be said; that an expression does not have the same value twice, does not live two lives; that all words, once spoken, are dead and function only at the moment when they are uttered, that a form, once it has served, cannot be used again and asks only to be replaced by another, and that the theater is the only place in the world where a gesture, once made, can never be made the same way twice.

If the public does not frequent our literary masterpieces, it is because those masterpieces are literary, that is to say, fixed; and fixed in forms that no longer respond to the needs of the time.

Far from blaming the public, we ought to blame the formal screen we interpose between ourselves and the public, and this new form of idolatry, the idolatry of fixed masterpieces which is one of the aspects of bourgeois conformism.

This conformism makes us confuse sublimity, ideas, and things with the forms they have taken in time and in our minds—in our snobbish, precious, aesthetic mentalities which the public does not understand.

How pointless in such matters to accuse the public of bad taste because it relishes insanities, so long as the public is not shown a valid spectacle; and I defy anyone to show me *here* a spectacle valid—valid in the supreme sense of the theater—since the last great romantic melodramas, i.e., since a hundred years ago.

The public, which takes the false for the true, has the sense of the true and always responds to it when it is manifested. However it is not upon the stage that the true is to be sought nowadays, but in the street; and if the crowd in the street is offered an occasion to show its human dignity, it will always do so.

If people are out of the habit of going to the theater, if we have all finally come to think of theater as an inferior art, a means of popular distraction, and to use it as an outlet for our worst instincts, it is because we have learned too well what the theater has been, namely, falsehood and illusion. It is because we have been accustomed for four hundred years, that is since the Renaissance, to a purely descriptive and narrative theater—storytelling psychology; it is because every possible ingenuity has been exerted in bringing to life on the stage plausible but detached beings, with the spectacle on one side, the public on the other—and because the public is no longer shown anything but the mirror of itself.

Shakespeare himself is responsible for this aberration and decline, this disinterested idea of the theater which wishes a theatrical performance to leave the public intact, without setting off one image that will shake the organism to its foundations and leave an ineffaceable scar.

If, in Shakespeare, a man is sometimes preoccupied with what transcends him, it is always in order to determine the ultimate consequences of this preoccupation within him, i.e., psychology.

Psychology, which works relentlessly to reduce the un-known to the known, to the quotidian and the ordinary, is the cause of the theater's abasement and its fearful loss of energy, which seems to me to have reached its lowest point. And I think both the theater and we ourselves have had enough of psychology.

I believe furthermore that we can all agree on this matter sufficiently so that there is no need to descend to the re-pugnant level of the modern and French theater to condemn the theater of psychology.

Stories about money, worry over money, social careerism, the pangs of love unspoiled by altruism, sexuality sugar-coated with an eroticism that has lost its mystery have nothing to do with the theater, even if they do belong to psychology. These torments, seductions, and lusts before which we are nothing but Peeping Toms gratifying our cravings, tend to go bad, and their rot turns to revolution: we must take this into account.

But this is not our most serious concern.

If Shakespeare and his imitators have gradually insinuated the idea of art for art's sake, with art on one side and life on the other, we can rest on this feeble and lazy idea only as long as the life outside endures. But there are too many signs that everything that used to sustain our lives no longer does so, that we are all mad, desperate, and sick. And I call for us to react.

This idea of a detached art, of poetry as a charm which exists only to distract our leisure, is a decadent idea and an unmistakable symptom of our power to castrate.

Our literary admiration for Rimbaud, Jarry, Lautréamont, and a few others, which has driven two men to suicide, but turned into café gossip for the rest, belongs to this idea of literary poetry, of detached art, of neutral spiritual activity which creates nothing and produces nothing; and I can bear witness that at the very moment when that kind of personal poetry which involves only the man who creates it and only at the moment he creates it broke out in its most abusive fashion, the theater was scorned more than ever before by poets who have never had the sense of direct and concerted action, nor of efficacity, nor of danger.

We must get rid of our superstitious valuation of texts and *written* poetry. Written poetry is worth reading once, and then should be destroyed. Let the dead poets make way for others. Then we might even come to see that it is our veneration for what has already been created, however beautiful and valid it may be, that petrifies us, deadens our responses, and prevents us from making contact with that underlying power, call it thought-energy, the life force, the determinism of change, lunar menses, or anything you like. Beneath the poetry of the texts, there is the actual poetry, without form and without text. And just as the efficacity of masks in the magic practices of certain tribes is exhausted—and these masks are no longer good for anything except museums—so the poetic efficacity of a text is exhausted; yet the poetry and the efficacity of the theater are exhausted least quickly of all, since they permit the *action* of what is gesticulated and pronounced, and which is never made the same way twice.

It is a question of knowing what we want. If we are prepared for war, plague, famine, and slaughter we do not even need to say so, we have only to continue as we are; continue behaving like snobs, rushing en masse to hear such and such a singer, to see such and such an admirable performance which never transcends the realm of art (and even the Russian ballet at the height of its splendor never transcended the realm of art), to marvel at such and such an exhibition of painting in which exciting shapes explode here and there but at random and without any genuine consciousness of the forces they could rouse.

This empiricism, randomness, individualism, and anarchy must cease.

Enough of personal poems, benefitting those who create them much more than those who read them.

Once and for all, enough of this closed, egoistic, and personal art.

Our spiritual anarchy and intellectual disorder is a function of the anarchy of everything else—or rather, everything else is a function of this anarchy.

I am not one of those who believe that civilization has to change in order for the theater to change; but I do believe that the theater, utilized in the highest and most difficult sense possible, has the power to influence the aspect and formation of things: and the encounter upon the stage of two passionate manifestations, two living centers, two nervous magnetisms is something as entire, true, even decisive, as, in life, the encounter of one epidermis with another in a time-less debauchery.

That is why I propose a theater of cruelty.—With this mania we all have for depreciating everything, as soon as I have said "cruelty," everybody will at once take it to mean "blood." But *theater of cruelty* means a theater difficult and cruel for myself first of all. And, on the level of performance, it is not the cruelty we can exercise upon each other by hacking at each other's bodies, carving up our personal anatomies, or, like Assyrian emperors, sending parcels of human ears, noses, or neatly detached nostrils through the mail, but the much more terrible and necessary cruelty which things can exercise against us. We are not free. And the sky can still fall on our heads. And the theater has been created to teach us that first of all.

Either we will be capable of returning by present-day means to this superior idea of poetry and poetry-through-theater which underlies the Myths told by the great ancient tragedians, capable once more of entertaining a religious idea of the theater (without meditation, useless contemplation, and vague dreams), capable of attaining awareness and a possession of certain dominant forces, of certain notions that control all others, and (since ideas, when they are effective, carry their energy with them) capable of recovering within ourselves those energies which ultimately create order and increase the value of life, or else we might as well abandon ourselves now, without protest, and recognize that we are no longer good for anything but disorder, famine, blood, war, and epidemics.

Either we restore all the arts to a central attitude and necessity, finding an analogy between a gesture made in painting or the theater, and a gesture made by lava in a volcanic explosion, or we must stop painting, babbling, writing, or doing whatever it is we do.

I propose to bring back into the theater this elementary magical idea, taken up by modern psychoanalysis, which consists in effecting a patient's cure by making him assume the apparent and exterior attitudes of the desired condition.

I propose to renounce our empiricism of imagery, in which the unconscious furnishes images at random, and which the poet arranges at random too, calling them poetic and hence hermetic images, as if the kind of trance that poetry provides did not have its reverberations throughout the whole sensibility, in every nerve, and as if poetry were some vague force whose movements were invariable.

I propose to return through the theater to an idea of the physical knowledge of images and the means of inducing trances, as in Chinese medicine which knows, over the entire extent of the human anatomy, at what points to puncture in order to regulate the subtlest functions.

Those who have forgotten the communicative power and magical mimesis of a gesture, the theater can reinstruct, because a gesture carries its energy with it, and there are still human beings in the theater to manifest the force of the gesture made.

To create art is to deprive a gesture of its reverberation in the organism, whereas this reverberation, if the gesture is made in the conditions and with the force required, incites the organism and, through it, the entire individuality, to take attitudes in harmony with the gesture.

The theater is the only place in the world, the last general means we still possess of directly affecting the organism and, in periods of neurosis and petty sensuality like the one in which we are immersed, of attacking this sensuality by physical means it cannot withstand.

If music affects snakes, it is not on account of the spiritual notions it offers them, but because snakes are long and coil their length upon the earth, because their bodies touch the earth at almost every point; and because the musical vibrations which are communicated to the earth affect them like a very subtle, very long massage; and I propose to treat the spectators like the snakecharmer's subjects and conduct them *by means of their organisms* to an apprehension of the subtlest notions.

At first by crude means, which will gradually be refined. These immediate crude means will hold their attention at the start.

That is why in the "theater of cruelty" the spectator is in the center and the spectacle surrounds him.

In this spectacle the sonorisation is constant: sounds, noises, cries are chosen first for their vibratory quality, then for what they represent.

Among these gradually refined means light is interposed in its turn. Light which is not created merely to add color or to brighten, and which brings its power, influence, suggestions with it. And the light of a green cavern does not sensually dispose the organism like the light of a windy day.

After sound and light there is action, and the dynamism of action: here the theater, far from copying life, puts itself whenever possible in communication with pure forces. And whether you accept or deny them, there is nevertheless a way of speaking which gives the name of "forces" to whatever brings to birth images of energy in the unconscious, and gratuitous crime on the surface.

A violent and concentrated action is a kind of lyricism: it summons up supernatural images, a bloodstream of images, a bleeding spurt of images in the poet's head and in the spectator's as well.

Whatever the conflicts that haunt the mind of a given period, I defy any spectator to whom such violent scenes will have transferred their blood, who will have felt in himself the transit of a superior action, who will have seen the extraordinary and essential movements of his thought illuminated in extraordinary deeds—the violence and blood having been placed at the service of the violence of the thought—I defy that spectator to give himself up, once outside the theater, to ideas of war, riot, and blatant murder.

So expressed, this idea seems dangerous and sophomoric. It will be claimed that example breeds example, that if the attitude of cure induces cure, the attitude of murder will induce murder. Everything depends upon the manner and the purity with which the thing is done. There is a risk. But let it not be forgotten that though a theatrical gesture is violent, it is disinterested; and that the theater teaches precisely the uselessness of the action which, once done, is not to be done, and the superior use of the state unused by the action and which, *restored,* produces a purification.

I propose then a theater in which violent physical images crush and hypnotize the sensibility of the spectator seized by the theater as by a whirlwind of higher forces.

A theater which, abandoning psychology, recounts the extraordinary, stages natural conflicts, natural and subtle forces, and presents itself first of all as an exceptional power of redirection. A theater that induces trance, as the dances of Dervishes induce trance, and that addresses itself to the organism by precise instruments, by the same means as those of certain tribal music cures which we admire on records but are incapable of originating among ourselves.

There is a risk involved, but in the present circumstances I believe it is a risk worth running. I do not believe we have managed to revitalize the world we live in, and I do not believe it is worth the trouble of clinging to; but I do propose something to get us out of our marasmus, instead of continuing to complain about it, and about the boredom, inertia, and stupidity of everything.

AUGUSTO BOAL

from *Theatre of the Oppressed* (1974)

TRANSLATED BY CHARLES A. McBRIDE AND MARIA-ODILIA LEAL McBRIDE

One of contemporary world theater's most influential figures, Augusto Boal (b. 1931) pioneered the use of theatrical performance as a means of direct social change. Closely associated with the liberationist educational philosophy of his Brazilian countryman Paolo Friere, Boal's work explores the ways theater games and street theater can be used as pedagogy—instructing even illiterate audiences to become agents of social change, what Boal calls "spect-actors"—and so as direct social practice. In 1971, Boal was apprehended and tortured by Brazilian authorities, and then exiled; he returned to Brazil in 1986, founding the Center for the Theater of the Oppressed in Rio de Janeiro, and continuing to develop the practice of Forum Theater. Boal has published several books on liberationist theater, including Games for Actors and Non-Actors *(1992),* The Rainbow of Desire *(1995), and* Legislative Theater *(1998).*

In this selection from Theater of the Oppressed, *"Poetics of the Oppressed," Boal describes some of the techniques he used with peasants and workers in the cities of Lima and Chiclayo, Peru, in 1973, particularly focusing on the development of the "spect-actor."*

EXPERIMENTS WITH THE PEOPLE'S THEATER IN PERU

These experiments were carried out in August of 1973, in the cities of Lima and Chiclayo, with the invaluable collaboration of Alicia Saco, within the program of the Integral Literacy Operation (*Operación Alfabetización Integral* [ALFIN]), directed by Alfonso Lizarzaburu and with the participation, in the various sectors, of Estela Liñares, Luis Garrido Lecca, Ramón Vilcha, and Jesús Ruiz Durand. The method used by ALFIN in the literacy program was, of course, derived from Paulo Freire.

In 1973, the revolutionary government of Peru began a national literacy campaign called *Operación Alfabetización Integral* with the objective of eradicating illiteracy within the span of four years. It is estimated that in Peru's population of 14 million people, between three and four million are illiterate or semi-illiterate.

In any country the task of teaching an adult to read and write poses a difficult and delicate problem. In Peru the problem is magnified because of the vast number of languages and dialects spoken by its people. Recent studies point to the existence of at least 41 dialects of the two principal languages, besides Spanish, which are the Quechua and the Aymara. Research carried out in the province of Loreto in the north of the country, verified the existence of 45 different languages in that region. Forty-five *languages,* not mere dialects! And this is what is perhaps the least populated province in the country.

This great variety of languages has perhaps contributed to an understanding on the part of the organizers of ALFIN, that the illiterate are not people who are unable to express themselves: they are simply people unable to express themselves in a particular language, which in this case is Spanish. All idioms are "languages," but there is an infinite number of languages that are not idiomatic. There are many languages besides those that are written or spoken. By learning a new language, a person acquires a new way of knowing reality and of passing that knowledge on to others. Each language is absolutely irreplaceable. All languages complement each other in achieving the widest, most complete knowledge of what is real.

Assuming this to be true, the ALFIN project formulated two principal aims:

1) to teach literacy in both the first language and in Spanish without forcing the abandonment of the former in favor of the latter;

2) to teach literacy in all possible languages, especially the artistic ones, such as theater, photography, puppetry, films, journalism, etc.

The training of the educators, chosen from the same regions where literacy was to be taught, was developed in four stages according to the special characteristics of each social group:

1) *barrios* (neighborhoods) or new villages, corresponding to our slums *(cantegril, favela, . . .);*

2) rural areas;

3) mining areas;

4) areas where Spanish is not the first language, which embrace 40 percent of the population. Of this 40 percent, half is made up of bilingual citizens who learned Spanish after acquiring fluency in their own indigenous language. The other half speaks no Spanish.

It is too early to evaluate the results of the ALFIN plan since it is still in its early stages. What I propose to do here is to relate my personal experience as a participant in the theatrical sector and to outline the various experiments we made in considering the theater as language, capable of being utilized by any person, with or without artistic talent. We tried to show in practice how the theater can be placed at the service of the oppressed, so that they can express themselves and so that, by using this new language, they can also discover new concepts.

In order to understand this *poetics of the oppressed* one must keep in mind its main objective: to change the people— "spectators," passive beings in the theatrical phenomenon— into subjects, into actors, transformers of the dramatic action. I hope that the differences remain clear. Aristotle proposes a poetics in which the spectator delegates power to the dramatic character so that the latter may act and think for him. Brecht proposes a poetics in which the spectator delegates power to the character who thus acts in his place but the spectator reserves the right to think for himself, often in opposition to the character. In the first case, a "catharsis" occurs; in the second, an awakening of critical conscious-

ness. But the *poetics of the oppressed* focuses on the action itself: the spectator delegates no power to the character (or actor) either to act or to think in his place; on the contrary, he himself assumes the protagonic role, changes the dramatic action, tries out solutions, discusses plans for change—in short, trains himself for real action. In this case, perhaps the theater is not revolutionary in itself, but it is surely a rehearsal for the revolution. The liberated spectator, as a whole person, launches into action. No matter that the action is fictional; what matters is that it is action!

I believe that all the truly revolutionary theatrical groups should transfer to the people the means of production in the theater so that the people themselves may utilize them. The theater is a weapon, and it is the people who should wield it.

But how is this transference to be achieved? As an example I cite what was done by Estela Liñares, who was in charge of the photography section of the ALFIN Plan.

What would be the old way to utilize photography in a literacy project? Without doubt, it would be to photograph things, streets, people, landscapes, stores, etc., then show the pictures and discuss them. But who would take these pictures? The instructors, group leaders, or coordinators. On the other hand, if we are going to give the people the means of production, it is necessary to hand over to them, in this case, the camera. This is what was done in ALFIN. The educators would give a camera to members of the study group, would teach them how to use it, and propose to them the following:

We are going to ask you some questions. For this purpose we will speak in Spanish. And you must answer us. But you can not speak in Spanish: you must speak in "photography." We ask you things in Spanish, which is a language. You answer us in photography, which is also a language.

The questions asked were very simple, and the answers— that is, the photos—were discussed later by the group. For example, when people were asked, where do you live?, they responded with the following types of photo-answers:

1) A picture showing the interior of a shack. In Lima it rarely rains and for this reason the shacks are made of straw mats, instead of with more permanent walls and roofs. In general they have only one room that serves as kitchen, living room, and bedroom; the families live in great promiscuity and very often young children watch their parents engage in sexual intercourse, which commonly leads to sexual acts between brothers and sisters as young as ten or eleven years old, simply as an imitation of their parents. A photo showing the interior of a shack fully answers the question, where do you live? Every element of each photo has a special meaning, which must be discussed by the group: the objects focused on, the angle from which the picture is taken, the presence or absence of people in it, etc.

2) To answer the same question, a man took a picture of the bank of a river. The discussion clarified its meaning. The river Rímac,

which passes through Lima, overflows at certain times of the year. This makes life on its banks extremely dangerous, since shacks are often swept away, with a consequent loss of human lives. It is also very common for children to fall into the river while playing and the rising waters make rescue difficult. When a man answers the question with that picture, he is fundamentally expressing anguish: how can he work with peace of mind knowing that his child may be drowning in the river?

3) Another man photographed a part of the river where pelicans come to eat garbage in times of great hunger; the people, equally hungry, capture, kill and eat the pelicans. Showing this photo, the man communicated his awareness of living in a place where ironically the people welcomed hunger, because it attracted the pelicans which then served to satisfy their hunger.

4) A woman who had recently emigrated from a small village in the interior answered with a picture of the main street in her *barrio*: the old natives of Lima lived on one side of the street, while those from the interior lived on the other. On one side were those who saw their jobs threatened by the newcomers; on the other, the poor who had left everything behind in search of work. The street was a dividing line between brothers equally exploited, who found themselves facing each other as if they were enemies. The picture helped to reveal their common condition: poverty on both sides—while pictures of the wealthier neighborhoods showed who were their true enemies. The picture of the divided street showed the need to redirect their violent resentment. . . . Studying the picture of her street helped the woman to understand her own reality.

5) One day a man, in answer to the same question, took a picture of a child's face. Of course everyone thought that the man had made a mistake and repeated the question to him:

"You didn't understand; what we want is that you show us where you live. Take a picture and show us where you live. Any picture; the street, the house, the town, the river . . ."

"Here is my answer. Here is where I live."

"But it's a child. . . ."

"Look at his face: there is blood on it. This child, as all the others who live here, have their lives threatened by the rats that infest the whole bank of the river Rímac. They are protected by dogs that attack the rats and scare them away. But there was a mange epidemic and the city dog-catcher came around here catching lots of dogs and taking them away. This child had a dog who protected him. During the day his parents used to go to work and he was left with his dog. But now he doesn't have it any more. A few days ago, when you asked me where I lived, the rats had come while the child was sleeping and had eaten part of his nose. This is why there's so much blood on his face. Look at the picture; it is my answer. I live in a place where things like this still happen."

I could write a novel about the children of the *barrios* along the river Rímac; but only photography, and no other language, could express the pain of that child's eyes, of those tears mixed with blood. And, as if the irony and outrage were not enough, the photograph was in Kodachrome, "Made in U.S.A."

The use of photography may help also to discover valid symbols for a whole community or social group. It happens many times that well intentioned theatrical groups are unable to communicate with a mass audience because they use symbols that are meaningless for that audience. A royal crown may symbolize power, but a symbol only functions as such if its meaning is shared. For some a royal crown may produce a strong impact and yet be meaningless for others.

What is exploitation? The traditional figure of Uncle Sam is, for many social groups throughout the world, the ultimate symbol of exploitation. It expresses to perfection the rapacity of "Yankee" imperialism.

In Lima the people were also asked, what is exploitation? Many photographs showed the grocer; others the landlord; still others, some government office. On the other hand, a child answered with the picture of a nail on a wall. For him that was the perfect symbol of exploitation. Few adults understood it, but all the other children were in complete agreement that the picture expressed their feelings in relation to exploitation. The discussion explained why. The simplest work boys engage in at the age of five or six is shining shoes. Obviously, in the *barrios* where they live there are no shoes to shine and, for this reason, they must go to downtown Lima in order to find work. Their shine-boxes and other tools of the trade are of course an absolute necessity, and yet these boys cannot be carrying their equipment back and forth every day between work and home. So they must rent a nail on the wall of some place of business, whose owner charges them two or three *soles* per night and per nail. Looking at a nail, those children are reminded of oppression and their hatred of it; the sight of a crown, Uncle Sam, or Nixon, however, probably means nothing to them.

It is easy enough to give a camera to someone who has never taken a picture before, tell him how to focus it and which button to press. With this alone the means of photographic production are in the hands of that person. But what is to be done in the case of the theater?

The means for producing a photograph are embodied in the camera, which is relatively easy to handle, but the means of producing theater are made up of man himself, obviously more difficult to manage.

We can begin by stating that the first word of the theatrical vocabulary is the human body, the main source of sound and movement. Therefore, to control the means of theatrical production, man must, first of all, control his own body, know his own body, in order to be capable of making it more expressive. Then he will be able to practice theatrical forms in which by stages he frees himself from his condition of spectator and takes on that of actor, in which he ceases to be an object and becomes a subject, is changed from witness into protagonist.

The plan for transforming the spectator into actor can be systematized in the following general outline of four stages:

First stage: *Knowing the body:* a series of exercises by which one gets to know one's body, its limitations and possibilities, its social distortions and possibilities of rehabilitation.

Second stage: *Making the body expressive:* a series of games by which one begins to express one's self through the body, abandoning other, more common and habitual forms of expression.

Third stage: *The theater as language:* one begins to practice theater as a language that is living and *present,* not as a finished product displaying images form the past:

First degree: *Simultaneous dramaturgy:* the spectators "write" simultaneously with the acting of the actors;

Second degree: *Image theater:* the spectators intervene directly, "speaking" through images made with the actors' bodies;

Third degree: *forum theater:* the spectators intervene directly in the dramatic action and act.

Fourth stage: *The theater as discourse:* simple forms in which the spectator-actor creates "spectacles" according to his need to discuss certain themes or rehearse certain actions.

Examples:

1) *Newspaper theater*

2) *Invisible theater*

3) *Photo-romance theater*

4) *Breaking of repression*

5) *Myth theater*

6) *Trial theater*

7) *Masks and Rituals*

First Stage: Knowing the Body.

The initial contact with a group of peasants, workers, or villagers—if they are confronted with the proposal to put on a theatrical performance—can be extremely difficult. They have quite likely never heard of theater and if they have heard of it, their conception of it will probably have been distorted by television, with its emphasis on sentimentality, or by some traveling circus group. It is also very common for those people to associate theater with leisure or frivolity. Thus caution is required even when the contact takes place through an educator who belongs to the same class as the illiterates or semi-illiterates, even if he lives among them in a shack and shares their comfortless life. The very fact that the educator comes with the mission of eradicating illiteracy (which presupposes a coercive, forceful action) is in itself an alienating factor between the agent and the local people. For this reason the theatrical experience should begin not with something alien to the people (theatrical techniques that are taught or imposed) but with the *bodies* of those who agree to participate in the experiment.

There is a great number of exercises designed with the objective of making each person aware of his own body, of his bodily possibilities, and of deformations suffered because of the type of work he performs. That is, it is necessary for each one to feel the "muscular alienation" imposed on his body by work.

A simple example will serve to clarify this point: compare the muscular structure of a typist with that of the night watchman of a factory. The first performs his or her work seated in a chair: from the waist down the body becomes, during working hours, a kind of pedestal, while arms and fingers are active. The watchman, on the other hand, must walk continually during his eight-hour shift and consequently will develop muscular structures that facilitate walking. The bodies of both become alienated in accordance with their respective types of work.

The same is true of any person whatever the work or social status. The combination of roles that a person must perform imposes on him a "mask" of behavior. This is why those who perform the same roles end up resembling each other: artists, soldiers, clergymen, teachers, workers, peasants, landlords, decadent noblemen, etc.

Compare the angelical placidity of a cardinal walking in heavenly bliss through the Vatican Gardens with, on the other hand, an aggressive general giving orders to his inferiors. The former walks softly, listening to celestial music, sensitive to colors of the purest impressionistic delicacy: if by chance a small bird crosses the cardinal's path, one easily imagines him talking to the bird and addressing it with some amiable word of Christian inspiration. By contrast, it does not befit the general to talk with little birds, whether he cares to or not. No soldier would respect a general who talks to the birds. A general must talk as someone who gives orders, even if it is to tell his wife that he loves her. Likewise, a military man is expected to use spurs, whether he be a brigadier or an admiral. Thus all military officers resemble each other, just as do all cardinals; but vast differences separate generals from cardinals.

The exercises of this first stage are designed to "undo" the muscular structure of the participants. That is, to take them apart, to study and analyze them. Not to weaken or destroy them, but to raise them to the level of consciousness. So that each worker, each peasant understands, sees, and feels to what point his body is governed by his work.

If one is able, in this way, to disjoint one's own muscular structures, one will surely be able to assemble structures characteristic of other professions and social classes; that is, one will be able to physically "interpret" characters different from oneself.

All the exercises of this series are in fact designed to disjoint. Acrobatic and athletic exercises that serve to create muscular structures characteristic of athletes or acrobats are irrelevant here. I offer the following as examples of disjunctive exercises:

1) *Slow motion race*. The participants are invited to run a race with the aim of losing: the last one is the winner. Moving in slow motion, the body will find its center of gravity dislocated at each successive moment and so must find again a new muscular structure which will maintain its balance. The participants must never interrupt the motion or stand still; also they must take the longest step they can and their feet must rise above knee level. In this exercise, a 10-meter run can be more tiring than a conventional 500-meter run, for the effort needed to keep one's balance in each new position is intense.

2) *Cross-legged race*. The participants form pairs, embrace each other and intertwine their legs (the left of one with the right of the other, and vice versa). In the race, each pair acts as if it were a single person and each person acts as if his mate were his leg. The "leg" doesn't move alone: it must be put in motion by its mate!

3) *Monster race*. "Monsters" of four legs are formed: each person embraces the thorax of his mate but in reverse position; so that the legs of one fit around the neck of the other, forming a headless monster with four legs. The monsters then run a race.

4) *Wheel race*. The pairs form wheels, each one grabbing the ankles of the other, and run a race of human wheels.

5) *Hypnosis*. The pairs face each other and one puts his hand a few centimeters from the nose of his partner, who must keep this distance: the first one starts to move his hand in all directions, up and down, from left to right, slowly or faster, while the other moves his body in order to maintain the same distance between his nose and his partner's hand. During these movements he is forced to assume bodily positions that he never takes in his daily life, thus reforming permanently his muscular structures.

Later, groups of three are formed: one leads and the other two follow, one at each hand of the leader. The latter can do anything—cross his arms, separate his hands, etc., while the other two must try to maintain the distance. Afterward, groups of five are formed, one as leader and the other four keeping the distance in relation to the two hands and feet of the leader, while the latter can do what he pleases, even dance, etc.

6) *Boxing match*. The participants are invited to box, but they cannot touch each other under any circumstances; each one must fight as if he were really fighting but without touching his partner, who nevertheless must react as if he had received each blow.

7) *Out West*. A variation of the preceding exercises. The participants improvise a scene typical of bad western movies, with the pianist, the swaggering young cowboy, the dancers, the drunks, the villains who come in kicking the saloon doors, etc. The whole scene is performed in silence; the participants are not allowed to touch each other, but must react to every gesture or action. For example, an *imaginary* chair is thrown against a row of bottles (also imaginary), the pieces of which fly in all directions, and the participants react to the chair, the falling bottles, etc. At the end of the scene all must engage in a free-for-all fight.

All these exercises are included in my book *200 Exercises and Games for the Actor and for the Non-Actor Who Wants to Say Something Through Theater*. There are many more exercises that can be used in the same manner. In proposing exercises it's always advisable to ask the participants to describe or invent others: in this stage, the type that would serve to analyze the muscular structures of each participant. At every stage, however, the maintenance of a creative atmosphere is extremely important.

Second Stage: Making the Body Expressive.

In the second stage the intention is to develop the expressive ability of the body. In our culture we are used to expressing everything through words, leaving the enormous expressive capabilities of the body in an underdeveloped state. A series of "games" can help the participants to begin to use their bodily resources for self-expression. I am talking about parlor games and not necessarily those of a theatrical laboratory. The participants are invited to "play," not to "interpret," characters but they will "play" better to the extent that they "interpret" better.

For example: In one game pieces of paper containing names of animals, male and female, are distributed, one to each participant. For ten minutes, each person tries to give a physical, bodily impression of the animal named on his piece of paper. Talking or making noises that would suggest the animal is forbidden. The communication must be effected entirely through the body. After the first ten minutes, each participant must find his mate among the others who are imitating the animals, since there will always be a male and a female for each one. When two participants are convinced that they constitute a pair, they leave the stage, and the game is over when all participants find their mates through a purely physical communication, without the utilization of words or recognizable sounds.

What is important in games of this type is not to guess right but rather that all the participants try to express themselves through their bodies, something they are not used to doing. Without realizing it they will in fact be giving a "dramatical performance."

I remember one of these games played in a slum area, when a man drew the name *hummingbird*. Not knowing how to express it physically, he remembered nevertheless that this bird flies very rapidly from one flower to another, stops and sucks on a flower while producing a peculiar sound. So with his hands the man imitated the frenetic wings of the hummingbird and, "flying" from participant to participant, halted before each one of them making that sound. After ten minutes, when it was time for him to look for his mate, this man looked all around him and found no one who seemed to be enough of a hummingbird to attract him. Finally he saw a tall, fat man who was making a pendular movement with his hands and, setting aside his doubts, decided that there was his beloved mate; he went straight to "her," making turns around "her" and throwing little kisses to the air while singing joyfully. The fat man, upset, tried to escape, but the other fellow went after him, more and more in love with his hummingbird mate and singing with ever more amorous glee. Finally, though convinced that the other man was not his mate, the fat one—while the others roared with laughter—decided to follow his persistent suitor off stage simply to end the ordeal. Then (for only then were they allowed to talk) the first man, full of joy, cried out:

"I am the male hummingbird, and you are the female? Isn't that right?"

The fat one, very discouraged, looked at him and said: "No, dummy, I'm the bull. . . ."

How the fat man could give an impression of a delicate hummingbird while trying to portray a bull, we will never know. But, no matter: what does matter is that for 15 or 20 minutes all those people tried to "speak" with their bodies.

This type of game can be varied *ad infinitum;* the slips of paper can bear, for example, the names of occupations or professions. If the participants depict an animal, it will perhaps have little to do with their ideology. But if a peasant is called upon to act as a landlord; a worker, the owner of a factory; or if a woman must portray a policeman, all their ideology counts and finds physical expression through the game. The names of the participants themselves may be written on slips of paper, requiring them to convey impressions of each other and thus revealing, physically, their opinions and mutual criticisms.

In this stage, as in the first, regardless of how many games one proposes to the participants, the latter should always be encouraged to invent other games and not to be passive recipients of an entertainment that comes from the outside.

Third Stage: The Theater as Language.

This stage is divided into three parts, each one representing a different degree of direct participation of the spectator in the performance. The spectator is encouraged to intervene in the action, abandoning his condition of object and assuming fully the role of subject. The two preceding stages are preparatory, centering around the work of the participants with their own bodies. Now this stage focuses on the theme to be discussed and furthers the transition from passivity to action.

CRITICAL PERSPECTIVES

MARTIN ESSLIN

from *The Theatre of the Absurd* (1961)

In his seminal study of the postwar theater of Eugène Ionesco, Samuel Beckett, Harold Pinter, and other playwrights, Martin Esslin (1918–2002) coined the phrase "theater of the absurd" to describe the disorienting quality of their plays. The book has been widely influential and provided the first generation of postwar theatergoers with a way of understanding the new drama. Esslin wrote several books on modern drama and theater, including Brecht: A Choice of Evils *(1959),* Pinter: A Study of His Plays *(1976), and* An Anatomy of Drama *(1976). He also worked for the British Broadcasting Corporation and taught drama at Stanford University and elsewhere.*

On 19 November 1957, a group of worried actors were preparing to face their audience. The actors were members of the company of the San Francisco Actors' Workshop. The audience consisted of fourteen hundred convicts at the San Quentin penitentiary. No live play had been performed at San Quentin since Sarah Bernhardt appeared there in 1913. Now, forty-four years later, the play that had been chosen, largely because no woman appeared in it, was Samuel Beckett's *Waiting for Godot*.

No wonder the actors and Herbert Blau, the director, were apprehensive. How were they to face one of the toughest audiences in the world with a highly obscure, intellectual play that had produced near riots among a good many highly sophisticated audiences in Western Europe? Herbert Blau decided to prepare the San Quentin audience for what was to come. He stepped on to the stage and addressed the packed, darkened North Dining Hall—a sea of flickering matches that the convicts tossed over their shoulders after lighting their cigarettes. Blau compared the play to a piece of jazz music "to which one must listen for whatever one may find in it." In the same way, he hoped, there would be some meaning, some personal significance for each member of the audience in *Waiting for Godot*.

The curtain parted. The play began. And what had bewildered the sophisticated audiences of Paris, London, and New York was immediately grasped by an audience of convicts. As the writer of "Memos of a first-nighter" put it in the columns of the prison paper, the *San Quentin News*:

> The trio of muscle-men, biceps overflowing, . . . parked all 642 lbs on the aisle and waited for the girls and funny stuff. When this didn't appear they audibly fumed and audibly decided to wait until the house lights dimmed before escaping. They made one error. They listened and looked two minutes too long and stayed. Left at the end. All shook . . .[1]

Or as the writer of the lead story of the same paper reported, under the headline, "San Francisco Group Leaves S.Q. Audience Waiting for Godot":

> From the moment Robin Wagner's thoughtful and limbo-like set was dressed with light, until the last futile and expectant handclasp was hesitantly activated between the two searching vagrants, the San Francisco company had its audience of captives in its collective hand. . . . Those that had felt a less controversial vehicle should be attempted as a first play here had their fears allayed a short five minutes after the Samuel Beckett piece began to unfold.[2]

A reporter from the San Francisco *Chronicle* who was present noted that the convicts did not find it difficult to understand the play. One prisoner told him, "Godot is society." Said another: "He's the outside."[3] A teacher at the prison was quoted as saying, "They know what is meant by waiting . . . and they knew if Godot finally came, he would only be a disappointment."[4] The leading article of the prison paper showed how clearly the writer had understood the meaning of the play:

> It was an expression, symbolic in order to avoid all personal error, by an author who expected each member of his audience to draw his own conclusions, make his own errors. It asked nothing in point, it forced no dramatized moral on the viewer, it held out no specific hope. . . . We're still waiting for Godot, and shall continue to wait. When the scenery gets too drab and the action too slow, we'll call each other names and swear to part forever—but then, there's no place to go![5]

It is said that Godot himself, as well as turns of phrase and characters from the play, have since become a permanent part of the private language, the institutional mythology of San Quentin.

---

[1] *San Quentin News*, San Quentin, Calif., 28 November 1957.

[2] Ibid.

[3] *Theatre Arts*, New York, July 1958.

[4] Ibid.

[5] *San Quentin News*, 28 November 1957.

Why did a play of the supposedly esoteric avant-garde make so immediate and so deep an impact on an audience of convicts? Because it confronted them with a situation in some ways analogous to their own? Perhaps. Or perhaps because they were unsophisticated enough to come to the theatre without any preconceived notions and ready-made expectations, so that they avoided the mistake that trapped so many established critics who condemned the play for its lack of plot, development, characterization, suspense, or plain common sense. Certainly the prisoners of San Quentin could not be suspected of the sin of intellectual snobbery, for which a sizeable proportion of the audiences of *Waiting for Godot* have often been reproached; of pretending to like a play they did not even begin to understand, just to appear in the know.

The reception of *Waiting for Godot* at San Quentin, and the wide acclaim given to plays by Ionesco, Adamov, Pinter, and others, testify that these plays, which are so often superciliously dismissed as nonsense or mystification, have something to say and can be understood. Most of the incomprehension with which plays of this type are still being received by critics and theatrical reviewers, most of the bewilderment they have caused and to which they still give rise, come from the fact that they are part of a new, and still developing stage convention that has not yet been generally understood and has hardly ever been defined. Inevitably, plays written in this new convention will, when judged by the standards and criteria of another, be regarded as impertinent and outrageous impostures. If a good play must have a cleverly constructed story, these have no story or plot to speak of; if a good play is judged by subtlety of characterization and motivation, these are often without recognizable characters and present the audience with almost mechanical puppets; if a good play has to have a fully explained theme, which is neatly exposed and finally solved, these often have neither a beginning nor an end; if a good play is to hold the mirror up to nature and portray the manners and mannerisms of the age in finely observed sketches, these seem often to be reflections of dreams and nightmares; if a good play relies on witty repartee and pointed dialogue, these often consists of incoherent babblings.

But the plays we are concerned with here pursue ends quite different from those of the conventional play and therefore use quite different methods. They can be judged only by the standards of the Theatre of the Absurd. . . .

It must be stressed, however, that the dramatists whose work is here discussed do not form part of any self-proclaimed or self-conscious school or movement. On the contrary, each of the writers in question is an individual who regards himself as a lone outsider, cut off and isolated in his private world. Each has his own personal approach to both subject-matter and form; his own roots, sources, and background. If they also, very clearly and in spite of themselves, have a good deal in common, it is because their work most sensitively mirrors and reflects the preoccupations and anxieties, the emotions and thinking of many of their contemporaries in the Western world.

This is not to say that their works are representative of mass attitudes. It is an oversimplification to assume that any age presents a homogeneous pattern. Ours being, more than most others, an age of transition, it displays a bewilderingly stratified picture: medieval beliefs still held and overlaid by eighteenth-century rationalism and mid-nineteenth-century Marxism, rocked by sudden volcanic eruptions of prehistoric fanaticisms and primitive tribal cults. Each of these components of the cultural pattern of the age finds its own artistic expression. The Theatre of the Absurd, however, can be seen as the reflection of what seems to be the attitude most genuinely representative of our own time.

The hallmark of this attitude is its sense that the certitudes and unshakable basic assumptions of former ages have been swept away, that they have been tested and found wanting, that they have been discredited as cheap and somewhat childish illusions. The decline of religious faith was masked until the end of the Second World War by the substitute religions of faith in progress, nationalism, and various totalitarian fallacies. All this was shattered by the war. By 1942, Albert Camus was calmly putting the question why, since life had lost all meaning, man should not seek escape in suicide. In one of the great, seminal heart-searchings of our time, *The Myth of Sisyphus,* Camus tried to diagnose the human situation in a world of shattered beliefs:

> A world that can be explained by reasoning, however faulty, is a familiar world. But in a universe that is suddenly deprived of illusions and of light, man feels a stranger. His is an irremediable exile, because he is deprived of memories of a lost homeland as much as he lacks the hope of a promised land to come. This divorce between man and his life, the actor and his setting, truly constitutes the feeling of Absurdity.[6]

"Absurd" originally means "out of harmony," in a musical context. Hence its dictionary definition: "out of harmony with reason or propriety; incongruous, unreasonable, illogical." In common usage, "absurd" may simply mean "ridiculous," but this is not the sense in which Camus uses the word, and in which it is used when we speak of the Theatre of the Absurd. In an essay on Kafka, Ionesco defined his understanding of the term as follows: "Absurd is that which is devoid of purpose. . . . Cut off from his religious, metaphysical,

---

[6]Albert Camus, *Le Mythe de Sisyphe* (Paris: Gallimard, 1942), p. 18.

and transcendental roots, man is lost; all his actions become senseless, absurd, useless."[7]

This sense of metaphysical anguish at the absurdity of the human condition is, broadly speaking, the theme of the plays of Beckett, Adamov, Ionesco, Genet, and the other writers. . . . But it is not merely the subject-matter that defines what is here called the Theatre of the Absurd. A similar sense of the senselessness of life, of the inevitable devaluation of ideals, purity, and purpose, is also the theme of much of the work of dramatists like Giraudoux, Anouilh, Salacrou, Sartre, and Camus himself. Yet these writers differ from the dramatists of the Absurd in an important respect: they present their sense of the irrationality of the human condition in the form of highly lucid and logically constructed reasoning, while the Theatre of the Absurd strives to express its sense of the senselessness of the human condition and the inadequacy of the rational approach by the open abandonment of rational devices and discursive thought. While Sartre or Camus express the new content in the old convention, the Theatre of the Absurd goes a step further in trying to achieve a unity between its basic assumptions and the form in which these are expressed. In some senses, the *theatre* of Sartre and Camus is less adequate as an expression of the *philosophy* of Sartre and Camus—in artistic, as distinct from philosophic, terms—than the Theatre of the Absurd.

If Camus argued that in our disillusioned age the world has ceased to make sense, he did so in the elegantly rationalistic and discursive style of an eighteenth-century moralist, in well-constructed and polished plays. If Sartre argues that existence comes before essence and that human personality can be reduced to pure potentiality and the freedom to choose itself anew at any moment, he presents his ideas in plays based on brilliantly drawn characters who remain wholly consistent and thus reflect the old convention that each human being has a core of immutable, unchanging essence—in fact, an immortal soul. And the beautiful phrasing and argumentative brilliance of both Sartre and Camus in their relentless probing still, by implication, proclaim a tacit conviction that logical discourse can offer valid solutions, that the analysis of language will lead to the uncovering of basic concepts—Platonic ideas.

This is an inner contradiction that the dramatists of the Absurd are trying, by instinct and intuition rather than by conscious effort, to overcome and resolve. The Theatre of the

Absurd has renounced arguing *about* the absurdity of the human condition; it merely *presents* it in being—that is, in terms of concrete stage images. This is the difference between the approach of the philosopher and that of the poet; the difference, to take an example from another sphere, between the *idea* of God in the works of Thomas Aquinas or Spinoza and the *intuition* of God in those of St John of the Cross or Meister Eckhart—the difference between theory and experience.

It is this striving for an integration between the subject-matter and the form in which it is expressed that separates the Theatre of the Absurd from the Existentialist theatre.

It must also be distinguished from another important, and parallel, trend in the contemporary French theatre, which is equally preoccupied with the absurdity and uncertainty of the human condition: the "poetic avant-garde" theatre of dramatists like Michel de Ghelderode, Jacques Audiberti, Georges Neveux, and, in the younger generation, Georges Schehadé, Henri Pichette, and Jean Vauthier, to name only some of its most important exponents. This is an even more difficult dividing line to draw, for the two approaches overlap a good deal. The "poetic avant-garde" relies on fantasy and dream reality as much as the Theatre of the Absurd does; it also disregards such traditional axioms as that of the basic unity and consistency of each character or the need for a plot. Yet basically the "poetic avant-garde" represents a different mood; it is more lyrical, and far less violent and grotesque. Even more important is its different attitude toward language: the "poetic avant-garde" relies to a far greater extent on consciously "poetic" speech; it aspires to plays that are in effect poems, images composed of a rich web of verbal associations.

The Theatre of the Absurd, on the other hand, tends toward a radical devaluation of language, toward a poetry that is to emerge from the concrete and objectified images of the stage itself. The element of language still plays an important part in this conception, but what *happens* on the stage transcends, and often contradicts, the *words* spoken by the characters. In Ionesco's *The Chairs*, for example, the poetic content of a powerfully poetic play does not lie in the banal words that are uttered but in the fact that they are spoken to an ever-growing number of empty chairs.

The Theatre of the Absurd is thus part of the "anti-literary" movement of our time, which has found its expression in abstract painting, with its rejection of "literary" elements in pictures; or in the "new novel" in France, with its reliance on the description of objects and its rejection of empathy and anthropomorphism. It is no coincidence that, like all these movements and so many of the efforts to create new forms of expression in all the arts, the Theatre of the Absurd should be centred in Paris. . . .

[7]Eugène Ionesco, "Dans les armes de la ville," *Cahiers de la Compagnie Madeleine Renaud-Jean-Louis Barrault*, Paris, no. 20, October 1957.

FREDRIC JAMESON

from "Postmodernism and Consumer Society" (1983)

Fredric Jameson (b. 1934) is probably the most prominent Marxist cultural critic writing in the United States today and is the author of several important books, including Marxism and Form *(1971),* The Prison-House of Language *(1972),* The Political Unconscious *(1988), and* Postmodernism, or, The Cultural Logic of Late Capitalism *(1991). This section is from one of Jameson's many essays on postmodern art, culture, and society. Jameson uses the term* pastiche *to characterize the problematic ways contemporary arts invoke the imagery and style of earlier historical eras, paradoxically erasing "history" in the process. How does Jameson identify pastiche as both a feature of a work's style and as an index of its broader political, social, and cultural meaning? How does the movement from parody to pastiche epitomize the movement from modernism to postmodernism?*

PASTICHE ECLIPSES PARODY

One of the most significant features or practices in postmodernism today is pastiche. I must first explain this term, which people generally tend to confuse with or assimilate to that related verbal phenomenon called parody. Both pastiche and parody involve the imitation or, better still, the mimicry of other styles and particularly of the mannerisms and stylistic twitches of other styles. It is obvious that modern literature in general offers a very rich field for parody, since the great modern writers have all been defined by the invention or production of rather unique styles: think of the Faulknerian long sentence or of D.H. Lawrence's characteristic nature imagery; think of Wallace Stevens's peculiar way of using abstractions; think also of the mannerisms of the philosophers, of Heidegger for example, or Sartre; think of the musical styles of Mahler or Prokofiev. All of these styles, however different from each other, are comparable in this: each is quite unmistakable; once one is learned, it is not likely to be confused with something else.

Now parody capitalizes on the uniqueness of these styles and seizes on their idiosyncrasies and eccentricities to produce an imitation which mocks the original. I won't say that the satiric impulse is conscious in all forms of parody. In any case, a good or great parodist has to have some secret sympathy for the original, just as a great mimic has to have the capacity to put himself/herself in the place of the person imitated. Still, the general effect of parody is—whether in sympathy or with malice—to cast ridicule on the private nature of these stylistic mannerisms and their excessiveness and eccentricity with respect to the way people normally speak or write. So there remains somewhere behind all parody the feeling that there is a linguistic norm in contrast to which the styles of the great modernists can be mocked.

But what would happen if one no longer believed in the existence of normal language, of ordinary speech, of the linguistic norm (the kind of clarity and communicative power celebrated by Orwell in his famous essay, say)? One could think of it in this way; perhaps the immense fragmentation and privatization of modern literature—its explosion into a host of distinct private styles and mannerisms—foreshadows deeper and more general tendencies in social life as a whole. Supposing that modern art and modernism—far from being a kind of specialized aesthetic curiosity—actually anticipated social developments along these lines; supposing that in the decades since the emergence of the great modern styles society has itself begun to fragment in this way, each group coming to speak a curious private language of its own, each profession developing its private code or idiolect, and finally each individual coming to be a kind of linguistic island, separated from everyone else? But then in that case, the very possibility of any linguistic norm in terms of which one could ridicule private languages and idiosyncratic styles would vanish, and we would have nothing but stylistic diversity and heterogeneity.

That is the moment at which pastiche appears and parody has become impossible. Pastiche is, like parody, the imitation of a peculiar or unique style, the wearing of a stylistic mask, speech in a dead language: but it is a neutral practice of such mimicry, without parody's ulterior motive, without the satirical impulse, without laughter, without that still latent feeling that there exists something *normal* compared to which what is being imitated is rather comic. Pastiche is blank parody, parody that has lost its sense of humor: pastiche is to parody what that curious thing, the modern practice of a kind of blank irony, is to what Wayne Booth calls the stable and comic ironies of, say, the eighteenth century.

THE DEATH OF THE SUBJECT

But now we need to introduce a new piece into this puzzle, which may help to explain why classical modernism is a thing of the past and why postmodernism should have taken its place. This new component is what is generally called the 'death of the subject' or, to say it in more conventional language, the end of individualism as such. The great modernisms were, as we have said, predicated on the invention of a personal, private style, as unmistakable as your finger-print, as incomparable as your own body. But this means that the modernist aesthetic is in some way organically linked to the conception of a unique self and private identity, a unique personality and individuality, which can be expected to gen-erate its own unique vision of the world and to forge its own unique, unmistakable style.

Yet today, from any number of distinct perspectives, the social theorists, the psychoanalysts, even the linguists, not to speak of those of us who work in the area of culture and cultural and formal change, are all exploring the notion that that kind of individualism and personal identity is a thing of the past; that the old individual or individualist subject is 'dead'; and that one might even describe the concept of the unique individual and the theoretical basis of individualism as ideological. There are in fact two positions on all this, one of which is more radical than the other. The first one is con-tent to say: yes, once upon a time, in the classic age of com-petitive capitalism, in the heyday of the nuclear family and the emergence of the bourgeoisie as the hegemonic social class, there was such a thing as individualism, as individual subjects. But today, in the age of corporate capitalism, of the so-called organization man, of bureaucracies in business as well as in the state, of demographic explosion—today, that older bourgeois individual subject no longer exists.

Then there is a second position, the more radical of the two, what one might call the poststructuralist position. It adds: not only is the bourgeois individual subject a thing of the past, it is also a myth: it *never* really existed in the first place; there have never been autonomous subjects of that type. Rather, this construct is merely a philosophical and cul-tural mystification which sought to persuade people that they 'had' individual subjects and possessed this unique per-sonal identity.

For our purposes, it is not particularly important to de-cide which of these positions is correct (or rather, which is more interesting and productive). What we have to retain from all this is rather an aesthetic dilemma: because if the experience and the ideology of the unique self, an experi-ence and ideology which informed the stylistic practice of classical modernism, is over and done with, then it is no longer clear what the artists and writers of the present pe-riod are supposed to be doing. What is clear is merely that the older models—Picasso, Proust, T. S. Eliot—do not work any more (or are positively harmful), since nobody has that kind of unique private world and style to express any longer. And this is perhaps not merely a 'psychological' matter: we also have to take into account the immense weight of sev-enty or eighty years of classical modernism itself. There is another sense in which the writers and artists of the present

day will no longer be able to invent new styles and worlds—they've already been invented; only a limited number of combinations are possible; the unique ones have been thought of already. So the weight of the whole modernist aesthetic tradition—now dead—also 'weighs like a night-mare on the brains of the living,' as Marx said in another context.

Hence, once again, pastiche: in a world in which stylistic innovation is no longer possible, all that is left is to imitate dead styles, to speak through the masks and with the voices of the styles in the imaginary museum. But this means that contemporary or postmodernist art is going to be about art itself in a new kind of way: even more, it means that one of its essential messages will involve the necessary failure of art and the aesthetic, the failure of the new, the imprisonment in the past.

THE NOSTALGIA MODE

As this may seem very abstract, I want to give a few exam-ples, one of which is so omnipresent that we rarely link it with the kinds of developments in high art discussed here. This particular practice of pastiche is not high-cultural but very much within mass culture, and it is generally known as the 'nostalgia film' (what the French neatly call *la mode rétro*—retrospective styling). We must conceive of this category in the broadest way: narrowly, no doubt, it consists merely of films about the past and about specific generational mo-ments of that past. Thus, one of the inaugural films in this new 'genre' (if that's what it is) was Lucas's *American Graffiti*, which in 1973 set out to recapture all the atmosphere and stylistic peculiarities of the 1950s United States, the United States of the Eisenhower era. Polanski's great film *Chinatown* does something similar for the 1930s, as does Bertolucci's *The Conformist* for the Italian and European context of the same period, the fascist era in Italy; and so forth. We could go on listing these films for some time: why call them pas-tiche? Are they not rather work in the more traditional genre known as the historical film—work which can more simply be theorized by extrapolating that other well-known form which is the historical novel?

I have my reasons for thinking that we need new cate-gories for such films. But let me first add some anomalies: supposing I suggested that *Star Wars* is also a nostalgia film. What could that mean? I presume we can agree that this is not a historical film about our own intergalactic past. Let me put it somewhat differently: one of the most important cul-tural experiences of the generations that grew up from the 1930s to the 1950s was the Saturday afternoon serial of the Buck Rogers type—alien villains, true American heroes, hero-ines in distress, the death ray or the doomsday box, and the cliffhanger at the end whose miraculous resolution was to be witnessed next Saturday afternoon. *Star Wars* reinvents this experience in the form of a pastiche: that is, there is no longer any point to a parody of such serials since they are long extinct. *Star Wars,* far from being a pointless satire of such now dead forms, satisfies a deep (might I even say repressed?) longing to experience them again: it is a complex object in which on some first level children and adolescents can take the adventures straight, while the adult public is able to gratify a deeper and more properly nostalgic desire to return to that older period and to live its strange old aesthetic artifacts through once again. This film is thus *metonymically* a historical or nostalgia film: unlike *American Graffiti,* it does not reinvent a picture of the past in its lived totality; rather, by reinventing the feel and shape of characteristic art objects of an older period (the serials), it seeks to reawaken a sense of the past associated with those objects. *Raiders of the Lost Ark,* meanwhile, occupies an intermediary position here: on some level it is about the 1930s and 1940s, but in reality it too conveys that period metonymically through its own characteristic adventure stories (which are no longer ours).

Now let me discuss another interesting anomaly which may take us further towards understanding nostalgia film in particular and pastiche generally. This one involves a recent film called *Body Heat,* which, as has abundantly been pointed out by the critics, is a kind of distant remake of *The Postman Always Rings Twice* or *Double Indemnity.* (The allusive and elusive plagiarism of older plots is, of course, also a feature of pastiche.) Now *Body Heat* is technically not a nostalgia film, since it takes place in a contemporary setting, in a little Florida village near Miami. On the other hand, this technical contemporaneity is most ambiguous indeed: the credits—always our first cue—are lettered and scripted in a 1930s Art-Deco style which cannot but trigger nostalgic reactions (first to *Chinatown,* no doubt, and then beyond it to some more historical referent). Then the very style of the hero himself is ambiguous: William Hurt is a new star but has nothing of the distinctive style of the preceding generation of male superstars like Steve McQueen or even Jack Nicholson, or rather, his persona here is a kind of mix of their characteristics with an older role of the type generally associated with Clark Gable. So here too there is a faintly archaic feel to all this. The spectator begins to wonder why this story, which could

have been situated anywhere, is set in a small Florida town, in spite of its contemporary reference. One begins to realize after a while that the small town setting has a crucial strategic function: it allows the film to do without most of the signals and references which we might associate with the contemporary world, with consumer society—the appliances and artifacts, the high rises, the object world of late capitalism. Technically, then, its objects (its cars, for instance) are 1980s products, but everything in the film conspires to blur that immediate contemporary reference and to make it possible to receive this too as nostalgia work—as a narrative set in some indefinable nostalgic past, an eternal 1930s, say, beyond history. It seems to me exceedingly symptomatic to find the very style of nostalgia films invading and colonizing even those movies today which have contemporary settings: as though, for some reason, we were unable today to focus our own present, as though we have become incapable of achieving aesthetic representations of our own current experience. But if that is so, then it is a terrible indictment of consumer capitalism itself—or, at the very least, an alarming and pathological symptom of a society that has become incapable of dealing with time and history.

So now we come back to the question of why nostalgia film or pastiche is to be considered different from the older historical novel or film. (I should also include in this discussion the major literary example of all this, to my mind: the novels of E.L. Doctorow—*Ragtime,* with its turn-of-the-century atmosphere, and *Loon Lake,* for the most part about our 1930s. But these are, in my opinion, historical novels in appearance only. Doctorow is a serious artist and one of the few genuinely left or radical novelists at work today. It is no disservice to him, however, to suggest that his narratives do not represent our historical past so much as they represent our ideas or cultural stereotypes about that past.) Cultural production has been driven back inside the mind, within the monadic subject: it can no longer look directly out of its eyes at the real world for the referent but must, as in Plato's cave, trace its mental images of the world on its confining walls. If there is any realism left here, it is a 'realism' which springs from the shock of grasping that confinement and of realizing that, for whatever peculiar reasons, we seem condemned to seek the historical past through our own pop images and stereotypes about that past, which itself remains forever out of reach.

UNA CHAUDHURI

from *Staging Place: The Geography of Modern Drama* (1995)

THE POLITICS OF HOME AND THE POETICS OF EXILE

Una Chaudhuri has written widely on modern drama and performance, and is the author of a well-known book on Genet, as well as of Staging Place. *In this selection from the opening chapter of* Staging Place, *Chaudhuri explores the many places of modern drama, elaborating the relationship between the ongoing thematics of home and exile.*

> I think that it is at least empirically arguable that our daily life, our psychic experience, our cultural languages, are today dominated by categories of space rather than categories of time, as in the period of high modernism.
>
> —Fredric Jameson, *Postmodernism, or The Cultural Logic of Late Capitalism*

The prevalence of space-based studies in the social sciences and in cultural studies is a response to an increasingly complex cultural experience of space and place, one that has decisively displaced the older paradigms of spatial intelligibility not only in the realm of art but also, thanks to the mass media, in that of public culture, and hence in contemporary consciousness. Therefore, the conceptual horizon for considering the theater's use of space and the drama's discourse on place is an ever-changing one, reflecting changes in the cultural, technological, and even the theoretical processing of space.

For example: during the time this book was being written, an inescapable element of the American popular culture scene was an ad campaign for Pepsi-Cola. The original TV commercials featured Ray Charles accompanied by three gorgeous female backup singers (the Raylettes) in short, shiny, skintight dresses. The main lyric asserted that Pepsi-Cola was "the right one, Baby," to which Ray, supported by the Raylettes, added an enthusiastic (and cinematographically punched-in) "Uh-huh." The commercial became (or was made, through the efforts of the ad agency) so popular that T-shirts and other consumer goods appeared bearing the legend "Uh-huh!" A news item in the *Wall Street Journal* reported that executives at the rival company, Coca-Cola, were going around trying to avoid using the expression "uh-huh" in their conversations! As time went on, the original commercial was expanded and extended and varied in a number of highly effective ways. One of these showed other famous people, including Jerry Lewis, Charo, and Tiny Tim, "auditioning" for Ray's role, doing hilariously bad renditions of the by now famous lyric.

One quite extraordinary installment, for which much anticipation was whipped up by the ad company, and which first aired during the half-time period of the Super Bowl, extended the range of jingle singers far beyond the American pop-cultural scene. This lengthy commercial showed huge gatherings of people in foreign lands—China, India, Japan—singing the jingle in their own various stereotypical ways, with a variety of accents and music styles. One of the scenes showed a group of Buddhist monks sitting cross-legged on the ground in formal rows in a monastery, intoning "uh-huh, uh-huh" in deep and solemn tones, as if it were a mantra or prayer.

The technical brilliance of this commercial, as well as its appropriation of the seductive and stereotypical images often used by the airline and tourist industries of the world, was partly responsible for the pleasure it gave. But there was another, less benign, element in its success as well. Under its cheery good humor and its apparently generous sharing of the pleasures of Pepsi with the peoples of the world, the ad was a blatant inscription of American economic imperialism, and it revealed quite precisely what the semiological—that is, the ideological, aesthetic, and psychological—terms of this imperialism are. In this semiotic, which is also the semiotic of Walt Disney World's World Showcase, parts of the world are isolated and double coded as different and yet the same, their difference being a matter of spectacle, while their sameness is a matter of desire. The spectacular Other, whose otherness is contained within—and figured purely as—superficial *style* (of clothes, architecture, music, etc.) is the necessary foundation for a figuration of universal consumerist desire.

How successful this figuration has been in material terms is now depressingly well known. The triumph of American consumerism goes beyond its undeniable monuments—the McDonald's in Moscow, the Disneyland near Paris, the Pizza Hut in Calcutta, and so on—to the realm of representation itself. The full import of the Pepsi commercial as universalizing discourse did not become clear to me until I saw, on a trip to India, the Indian version of the commercial. Gone were Ray and the Raylettes; in their place a number of Indian actors in different situations sang the same jingle, while the aforementioned Buddhist monks (on loan from the American version of the ad?) intoned their solemn "uh-huhs."

The West's construction of otherness takes a dizzying turn when, supported by the power of multinational capital, it dictates the self-construction of non-Western identities. This spiral of misrepresentation and self-misrepresentation—

which has its origins in the orientalist discourse of the earliest colonialisms—is now well established. The logic it obeys is similar to the traditional logic of gender difference, according to which the best woman is a man, because (as Song Liling says in *M. Butterfly*) "only a man knows how a woman is supposed to act." Unlike gender, however, national and ethnic identities are often derived from or directed toward a *geography;* there is a *location* of identity based on race, nation, ethnicity, language—in short, all the elements that together or in part designate the notion of a culture—that is often absent from the discourse of gender. To put it bluntly, the construction of cultural otherness is also a *mapping of the world,* a fact that contributes powerfully to the literalization of accounts of ethnic difference.

A book on place and the representation of place such as this one cannot avoid acknowledging the discourse of the Pepsi commercial as one of its horizons; no contemporary inquiry into the nature of place can ignore the placement and displacement wrought by the global mass media operating in support of a global consumer economy. The images of otherness set to the music of Ray Charles are simply the quintessential summarizing of the current state of the category of place, a category this century has seen beset by extraordinary challenges and changes. As Brecht's astonishing prologue to *The Caucasian Chalk Circle* makes clear, the *meaning* (not merely the ownership) of place has given this century its politics; we should not be surprised to find, as this book argues, that it has also given it its theater, and that a complex engagement with the significance, determinations, and potentialities of place courses through the body of modern drama.

Besides the mass media's capture of otherness—within a web of implied sameness disguised as difference—the second major source of the gradual reinscription of place in the late twentieth century is the revolution in electronic communications. In the modern world of computerized data management and instantaneous information dispersal, a person's basic mode of location is altered. Instead of experiencing life from a fixed point in space and time, the subject of the electronic society is, as Mark Poster writes, "multiplied by databases, dispersed by computer messaging and conferencing, decontextualized and reidentified by TV ads, dissolved and materialized continuously in the electronic transmission of symbols." So thoroughgoing and ubiquitous is this dispersal of subjective experience over multiple electronic channels that human beings can be said to be returning to a nomadic form of existence, wandering over vast global distances daily as they change channels, fax letters, leave messages on answering machines, and have the facts of their socioeconomic lives gathered, stored, and analyzed by myriad marketing concerns.

As Mark Poster puts it, the new version of "who am I?" is firmly anchored in a new form of "*where* am I?"

> If I can speak directly to a friend in Paris while sitting in California, if I can witness political and cultural events as they occur across the globe without leaving my home, if a database at a remote location contains my profile and informs government agencies which make the decisions that affect my life without any knowledge on my part of these events, if I can shop in my home using my TV or computer, then where am I and who am I? In these circumstances, I cannot consider myself centered in my rational, autonomous subjectivity or bordered by a defined ego, but I am disrupted, subverted, and dispersed across social space.

The erasure of spatial particularity, one of the hallmarks of post-modernism, is represented in drama (and elsewhere) through the figure of America. As we shall see in a later chapter, the America of the modern theater's imagination is a principle of dispersal, of dissolution. This America, which we shall meet in various guises throughout this book, is a complex and ultimately redemptive figure, for it is the hinge, the turning point in a more than century-long neglect of the very principle that it seems to erase: space. The rise in the nineteenth century of what Edward Soja calls a "destabilizing historicism" had, by the twentieth, deprivileged space to the point of denying it any explanatory or theoretical force whatsoever. Michel Foucault summarized the situation, asking, "Did it start with Bergson or before? Space was treated as the dead, the fixed, the undialectical, the immobile. Time, on the contrary, was richness, fecundity, life."

The category of space reenters the field of critical and social theory, as Soja has argued, through the works of Foucault, through structuralism, and through the writings of Henri Lefebvre. The formulation of a "postmodern critical geography" to counter and complement the rigid historicism of twentieth-century thought is a vast and vital project, of which one of the crucial goals is the recovery of *place.* It is in this area that the figure of America functions as a hinge, for it both *reproduces* and *displaces* the dominant theoretical bias against space. Through its alliance with the principles of progress and of homogeneity, the figure of America first signified a kind of ultimate placelessness, a guarantee of the absolute *un*meaning of place as a component of human experience. But the very success of this figuration—what one might call the hyperbole of American utopianism—proved to be its undoing. In the late twentieth century the figure of America has begun to be required, increasingly, to make good its utopian claims, and the principle of placelessness is confronted by the multivoiced demand for new *placements.* The movement known generally as multiculturalism is in fact a call for America to be reimagined: not, this time, as a utopia, but as what Foucault would call a "heterotopia," a place capable of containing within it many different, even incompatible, places.

As Soja explains it, Foucault's move was to navigate beyond several already ongoing efforts to respatialize social theory:

> Foucault outlined his notion of "heterotopias" as the characteristic spaces of the modern world, superseding the hierarchic "ensemble of places" of the Middle Ages and the enveloping "space of emplacement" opened up by Galileo into an early-modern, infinitely folding, "space of extension" and measurement. Moving away from both the "internal space" of Bachelard's brilliant poetics . . . and the intentional regional descriptions of the phenomenologists, Foucault focused our attention on another spatiality of social life, an "external space," the actually lived (and socially produced) space of sites and the relations between them.

This other spatiality is actually (to apply a neologism) a new *platiality,* a recognition of the signifying power and political potential of *specific places.*

In the theater (to return to the place that concerns me here) the encounter between this new platiality and the figure of America occurs most memorably in the drama of immigration and multiculturalism, which is the subject of the latter part of this book. But before this recent drama can replace the old accounts of space, place, and identity, the drama that supported those accounts must be thoroughly understood, which is to say, in terms of theatrical practice: deconstructed. The figure (or idea, or image, or myth) of America, then, is frequently used in contemporary drama as the vehicle for a critique, an engagement with and finally a revisioning of place. The figure of America is able to serve in this way—that is, in the deconstruction of place as traditionally conceived—because the discourse this figure disrupts most decisively is one that has structured—and continues to structure—traditional dramatic paradigms of place and identity most profoundly: the discourse of home.

The privileged setting of modern drama is the family home. The domestic interior contains the history of a process, begun in the nineteenth century and still unconcluded as the twentieth century nears its end, of a locational stage practice, a way of filling the signifying space of theater with an *environment.* This kind of environmentalism, which enters the drama through realism and naturalism (and which is intimately related to the figure of home), relies on and propagates a very special account of space and place. According to (and then thanks to) this environmentalism, placement becomes available to rational understanding and explanation. That is to say, place enters the positivist project as a factor of knowledge and a code of representation.

The first sign of this new coding of place is the ready divisibility of the world into what Philip Fisher calls "a spectrum of environments," a set of discrete economic zones each with "its local features, types, common languages, heroes and catastrophes." The theater responds to this new view of space by developing a stage practice based on the principle of spatial intelligibility, on the idea that *where* an action unfolds goes a long way toward explaining it. The name of this stage practice is, of course, naturalism, but (as Raymond Williams argued in what remains the most sophisticated discussion of theatrical naturalism) it is not only as *stage* practice but also as a dramatic discourse that naturalism engages and revisions the category of space: "In high naturalism," writes Williams, "the lives of the characters have soaked into their environment. . . . Moreover, the environment has soaked into their lives."

Recognizing that this environmentalism determines dramatic discourse at a deep structural level, Williams singles out a plot device that will become central to the evolving discourse of modern drama: escape, or, more generally, creative displacement. For Williams, naturalism marks only the exhaustion or contradiction of this device. "The pre-naturalist conventions of providential escape or of resolution through recognition," he writes, "fall away in the face of this sombre assessment of the weight of the world: not a world which is background, nor an illustrative setting; but one which has entwined itself in the deepest layers of the personality." But the figure of escape is not so quickly depleted. From the late nineteenth century on, the image or idea of escape, of creative displacement, develops into a full-blown poetics of exile, from which the drama of the later twentieth century is still seeking to free itself.

THE POLITICS OF HOME

That there is a politics to simply being at home is no longer an unfamiliar idea: in terms of recent cultural practice, we saw one aspect of that politics in the transformation of the word *housewife* into the word *homemaker,* a substitution that played out a whole reconceptualization of the power relations between women and domesticity. The historical backgrounds of this shift and its far-reaching theoretical implications are being charted by feminist scholars today. In the area that concerns me directly here, that of theatrical representation, a similar political thematic of home has prevailed. Indeed, as far as the stage is concerned, the ideology we recognize as modern humanism was inaugurated by a decision not to remain in a home as artificial and stifling as a doll's house.

However, as both these examples show, there has long been a certain reductive literalness in this conceptualization of home, one that, for all its desire to liberate or liberalize, will inevitably produce only a limited and ultimately reactionary account of identity. One of the cleverest (and earliest) schemas of this mode of self-production, as well as its disastrous consequences, is to be found in Poe's story "The Fall of the House of Usher," which suggests that the figure of home has long involved a denial of difference. The story shows the damage that unchecked literalism can do, as it forces an unwanted equivalence on several distinct entities: two individuals, a family, a family history, and a house. Poe's account of destruction by sheer reductiveness—all the Ushers collapse together into one undifferentiated heap—is also a deconstruction of the grotesque late-Romantic politics of singular identity, identity that feels itself too securely "housed" in a place where it can no longer be at home.

The theatrical version of the literalized home is to be found in realism, which from its inception has staged both the deterministic power as well as the crisis of this concept. One sign of the crisis is the violent ambiguity, in realism, of spatial signs. Ibsen's famous interactive architectural symbols—his climbable towers, slammable doors, and burnable buildings—help to construct domestic space as a problematic: both the *condition for* and the *obstacle to* psychological coherence. Again and again in Ibsen, the crisis of the concept of home appears as the collision therein of two incommensurable desires: the desire for a stable container for identity and the desire to deterritorialize the self.

The figure of home lends itself to one of the basic impulses of realism—the attempt to locate a space of personal experimentation: experimentation with the definition of persons, and with selfhood. This project dovetails nicely with the sense we have, from the nuclear family setups of the twentieth century, that home is a space of obligatory self-fashioning. As James Ellenwood expressed it in 1939, when the bourgeois discourse of home was at its most unreflective and unproblematized:

> Because, and this is basic, we learn by doing, . . . the home is the one ideal place for working things out realistically. It is the laboratory where most experiments are tried. Other agencies lecture and teach us about good living, but here we are up against life itself. . . . In a home one HAS to work out problems and relationships that, elsewhere, are only theorized over. Here you have to make good.

But Ellenwood also isolates a few other characteristics of the figure of home that play into the increasingly paradoxical discourse of realism. Home is both a site of *difference* ("It would take no less than a genius to interest all the members of a family in many common programs," says Ellenwood) and a site of *compulsion* ("It is the place where you have to go when there is no other place you can or want to go. . . . Only rarely does one run away or resign. The normal home is a long sentence"). As we shall see in chapter 2, this contradictory conditionality of the figure of home—its status as both shel-

ter and prison, security and as entrapment—is crucial to its dramatic meaning.

The theatrical conventions of the realist drama made their own contribution to the practice of deriving identity from environment. Under realism's rich re-creation of actual environments lay an attempted closure of fictionality, a will to close the gap between the world of the stage and the world of the spectator (the same will that led, later, to the hyperinclusive theatrology of environmental theater; see chap. 1). Several of the practices of the early naturalists sought to erase the difference between the public nature of theater and the private world of experience. André Antoine, founder of the Théâtre-Libre, recalls that "For our second production, we decided to emphasize that this is no public playhouse, but a special private society, by sending out announcements folded in the form of wedding invitations" (quoted by Waxman). Antoine also had Strindberg's preface to *Miss Julie* translated and distributed to his audiences. As Samuel Waxman notes, "It was another step forward toward the twentieth century 'little' theatre that has become almost universal."

Needless to say, the public was not always ready to be drawn into the imagined intimacy dreamed of by the theater practitioners. Nemirovich-Danchenko, writing on the need to regulate late arrivals, exposes this conflict with spectators, reading so trivial a fact as lateness as a deliberate attempt on the spectator's part "to violate my will." He asserts that he "can't allow it," calling one such spectator a "bourgeois of the first water," and when the problem persists after the Russian Revolution, that kind of spectator is an "imbecile" who thinks "that the revolution gave him the right to do as he liked." He concludes by insisting that "our attitude to the public" is not the attitude of a "master," but that the spectator should be happy and grateful for the privilege of entering. The audience should behave like "charming guests," or "we [will] force it to submit to rules essential for the artistic unity of the spectacle."

The realist stage installed a logic of representation to which the spectator was, essentially, an obstacle, a hindrance, an inconvenience. As I will show in my discussion of *Miss Julie* in chapter 1, the paradox of this drama—the paradox of shared (i.e., public) private experience—involved the spectator in an impossible displacement, where s/he was asked to play the role of ultimate hermeneutic authority while being reminded simultaneously of the authorizing but invisible presence of the omnipotent puppet master/playwright, creator of all meaning.

Certainly the most significant intervention that realism made into the developing discourse on space was through its commitment to what we could now call a platiality of the stage, an emphasis on the particularity and materiality of each dramatic environment. How great a revolution this was is memorably expressed by Nemirovich-Danchenko in the following detailed account of what had been the scenic norm before realism:

> every play must have its own setting. . . . At present in every theatre of the Soviet Union this is commonly accepted as the ABC of the business, but then it seemed like a revolution. The old theatre had its "garden," its "wood"—as the officials themselves contended, "of the most approved verdure"; it had a reception room with soft-lined chairs and a tall lamp in the corner with a yellow shade eminently suited for a comfortable love passage; a large reception room with pillars, painted of course; a middle-class room with red mahogany furniture. In the storeroom of decorations there were "Gothic" and "Renaissance" properties for "classical" plays, as all costume-plays were called by the director, even though they were written by contemporary authors. They had, correspondingly, chairs with high backs, a black carved table, and a curule chair, which the director stubbornly persisted in calling the "culture" chair. All these properties were used now in one play, now in its successor.

The fully iconic, single-set, middle-class living room of realism produced so closed and so *complete* a stage world that it supported the new and powerful fantasy of the stage not as a place to pretend in or to perform on but a place to *be,* a fully existential arena. We tend to associate this fantasy primarily with acting theory, and specifically with Stanislavsky, but its effects can also be seen in the new structural emphasis, in realist drama, on arrivals and departures. So literally global is the signification of the stage-home of realism, that simply to enter or leave it becomes a decisive—perhaps *the* decisive—dramatic act.

This is precisely what Chekhov ironizes in his drama. In Chekhov's plays as in Ibsen's, arrivals and departures are used as macrostructural devices, but Chekhov's arrivals and departures, unlike Ibsen's, are marked by a certain comic-pathetic arbitrariness. In historical terms, they look forward to the random wanderings of absurdist characters, led famously by Beckett's vagabonds Didi and Gogo. They initiate a figure of motiveless meandering that gains, much later, a political meaning when it is associated with such overpowering external determinants of movement as governments and technologies: thus, in David Rabe's *Streamers,* the soldiers waiting in boot camp to be shipped off to Vietnam express the meaninglessness of arrivals and departures:

> BILLY: How long you think we got?
> ROGER: What do you mean?
> BILLY: Till they pack us up, man, ship us out.
> ROGER: To the war, you mean? To Disneyland? Man, I dunno; that up to them IBMs. Them machines is figurin' that. Maybe tomorrow, maybe next week, maybe never.

The surprising intrusion of Disneyland into this account of a malevolent and absurd exilic condition is not the merely decorative flourish it might appear to be: as we shall see later, the figure of the artificial environment, of which Disneyland is the most powerful and complex exemplar, haunts the imagination of modern drama from *The Wild Duck* onward, marking the sense of an increasingly catastrophic dispossession of nature, which is the end point and inevitable outcome of that crisis of place we are tracking through the discourse of home.

But already in Chekhov, the act of displacement, shorn of its decisiveness, ceases to be a strategy for the formulation of a stable identity and becomes instead a symptom of its loss. In the legendary dispute between Chekhov and Stanislavsky what was being contested, in part, was the whole politics of deriving individual identities from environments, of grounding in a stage-home characters who were essentially homeless. By contrast, the more stylized, less realistic stagings of Chekhov's plays by contemporary directors like Andre Serban and Peter Brook recover the problematic of identity that naturalism tends to bracket out. To the degree that the stage-home is deliteralized, it reveals itself as a complex and contradictory thematic, precisely an *idea* of home—not a place but a discursive field laid out in such a way as to guarantee its inhabitants a certain psychological homelessness.

In Chekhov's drama, the discourse of home is deconstructed to produce the image of a *static* exilic consciousness, experienced by the characters as a feeling of being homesick while at home. Here the sentimental image of home—as an actual place correlated with a strong and desirable emotional experience (the sense of "belonging")—unravels as the logic linking belonging with exile is revealed to be not a logic of opposition but rather one of supplementarity: the emotional structure that is most familiar, most habitual and homelike, to these characters is the feeling of being displaced from somewhere else. They are not exiled *from* where they belong but exiled *to* where they belong.

However, the literalistic and domestic space of naturalism contained Chekhov's deconstruction and stopped it short of any ideological reformulation of the politics of identity. Exilic consciousness, read either as upper-class malaise or as universal tragic alienation, was ultimately something the spectator could be *at home* with. Once situated in terms of an already well coded "milieu and moment," the contradiction embodied by these characters is easily absorbed into a modernist account of psychological fragmentation and alienation, the same account, indeed, that has made exile itself a privileged poetic figure.

The realist discourse of home relies on a long-standing conceptual structure in which two figures are balanced—and constructed—as opposites: the figures of belonging and exile. The home as house (and, behind it, the home as homeland) is the site of a claim to affiliation whose incontestability has been established by a thick web of economic, juridical, and scientific discourses—which also construct the meaning of exile. It is a usefully ambivalent meaning: on the one hand, exile is branded by the negatives of loss and separation; on the other, it is distinguished by distance, detachment, perspective. For the individual (and exile is a decidedly individualistic figure) the poetics of exile offers a mechanism whereby suffering is exchanged for a certain moral authority, personal rupture for aesthetic rapture, as heard, for example, in Nabokov's reflection that "the break in my destiny affords me in retrospect a syncopal kick that I would not have missed for worlds."

The conjunction of naturalism and certain proxemic compulsions—exile, homelessness—inhabits one of the originary moments of the myth of dramatic modernism, the story of the first production of André Antoine's Théâtre-Libre. As is well known, one of the plays to be presented on the first evening, March 30, 1887, was *Jacques Damour,* adapted by M. Leon Hennique from a novel by Emile Zola. For his part, Antoine regarded this association with the name of the controversial father of naturalism not only as the aesthetic and ideological cornerstone of his theater-to-be, but also as a badge of artistic relevance, if not revolutionary correctness: "I realized instantly," he claims, "that Zola's name on our program would guarantee us the attention of [the influential critic] Sarcey." The amateur group with whom Antoine performed, however, felt differently: "Zola's name was already causing some misgivings in our society. Certain of the members were disturbed by the notoriety I was gaining. Finally, the club's name and meeting place were both refused me for such a presentation."

In a sense, then, the Théâtre-Libre is created out of an experience of loss, disenfranchisement, *homelessness.* Certainly that is how it seemed to Antoine himself, who frames his narrative with the image of dispossession. The story of the Théâtre-Libre, as its founder tells it, begins with this first exile and ends with another, more literal one:

> Here ends the odyssey of the Thèâtre-Libre. Having set out seven years ago from my garret in the Rue de Dunkerque with forty sous in my pocket, to rehearse our first production in the little wine shop in the Rue des Abesses, I at last find myself in Rome, with almost the same sum in my pocket, surrounded by fifteen companions as dejected as myself, with a hundred thousand francs of debts awaiting me in Paris, and with no idea of what we will do tomorrow.

Antoine's memoir reproduces a characteristic association of modern dramatic thought: spatial specificity is combined with figures of exile and displacement, street and city names mark the *loss* of place. Of course, spatial specificity,

indeed literalism, is one of the things the Théâtre-Libre is famous for, and Antoine is justly celebrated for his attention to the details of the spaces his stage re-created. At this level too, an originary moment from the Théâtre-Libre legend links the stage with the discourse of home. Three days before the opening of the first production, Antoine writes: "I had a lot of trouble this morning finding the furniture and properties, since I scarcely had the means to rent them. I spoke to my mother about it, and she allowed me to take the furniture from her dining room—chairs and table—for the room behind the shop in *Jacques Damour.*" Thus the first production of Antoine's theater involves him in a literal re-creation of home; later on the situation is reversed, and the stage becomes the site of a "creative" homelessness: "I no longer have a cent or a home; for the time being, I will sleep on a small cot which is folded up during the day and passes for a property."

Homelessness is only the most graphic version of the many displacements that constitute the insistent and pervasive challenges to home, transforming this apparently simple figure into a powerful irreality, something on the order of a fantasy, fable, myth, or impossible dream. Other displacements, all of which will be discussed in the following pages and all of which are complex figures, even whole discourses, are exile, immigration, and refugeehood. Of these exile is certainly the most fully theorized and poeticized concept, having become nothing short of a symbol for modern culture itself. According to George Steiner, the literature of the twentieth century is best understood as an "extraterritorial" art, expressing the universal experience of exile and refugeehood: "It seems proper that those who create art in a civilization of quasi-barbarism, which has made so many homeless, should themselves be poets unhoused and wanderers across language. Eccentric, aloof, nostalgic, deliberately untimely" (quoted by Said). The names of Conrad, Joyce, Kafka, and Nabokov are sufficient to evoke the principle of a potent exilic consciousness as the shaping force of modern literature. The history of drama supplies its own names: Ibsen, Strindberg, Chekhov, Beckett, Brecht—all experienced and were marked by exile or other displacements; all made dislocation one of the central themes of their drama.

But, as Edward Said points out in his essay "Reflections on Exile," the unparalleled scale of contemporary displacements removes the figure of exile from its earlier status as literary and cultural motif, signifying heightened consciousness and privileged perspective:

> But the difference between earlier exiles and those of our own times is, it bears stressing, scale: our age with its modern warfare, imperialism and quasi-theological ambitions of totalitarian rulers—is indeed the age of the refugee, the displaced person,

mass immigration. . . . On the twentieth-century scale, exile is neither aesthetically nor humanistically comprehensible: at most the literature about exile objectifies an anguish and a predicament most people rarely experience at first hand. . . . Is it not true that the views of exile in literature and, moreover, in religion obscure what is truly horrendous: that exile is irremediably secular and unbearably historical; that it is produced by human beings for other human beings; and that, like death but without death's ultimate mercy, it has torn millions of people from the nourishment of tradition, family and geography?

This terrible truth of actual exile makes its way into Western drama quite late, but when it does, it illuminates the terms of a century-long struggle with the problem of place. This struggle, to which I have given the label geopathology, unfolds as an incessant dialogue between belonging and exile, home and homelessness. At midcentury, a new discourse enters the dialogue and changes the established terms of the drama's engagement with place, displacing as well the dramatic structures that had served the geopathic model. The new discourse centers upon the figure of America, explicating it, first, as a *betrayal* of place, and then finding in it a muted celebration of placelessness. Out of this celebration there emerges, finally, a kind of solution—or at least the beginnings of a new formulation that might redirect, if not entirely overcome, that painful politics of place I am calling geopathology. In the emerging drama of multiculturalism, it seems to me, are the outlines of a new *heterotopic* account of the relationship between persons and places. This account begins by creatively confronting the problem of place, regarding it as a challenge and an invitation rather than as a tragic impasse.

A work that exemplifies this evolving new attitude toward place is Laurie Anderson's epic piece, *United States*. As Henry Sayre points out, Anderson uses performance to realize the postmodern experience of what Gilles Deleuze, describing the logic of Nietzsche's texts, has called "nomadism":

> The only conceivable key [to these texts], perhaps, would be in the concept of "embarkation." . . . We embark, then, in a kind of raft of "the Medusa"; bombs fall all around the raft as it drifts towards icy subterranean streams—or towards torrid rivers, the Orinoco, the Amazon; the passengers row together. They are not supposed to like one another, they fight with one another, they eat one another. To row together is to share, to share something beyond law, contract or institution. It is a period of drifting, of "deterritorialization."

According to Sayre, Anderson "manages to 'deterritorialize' the United States, to give her audience a sense that they are in some measure *outside*—or wanderers within—the very place they live."

Employing two tropes that have been involved in the figuration of place from the beginning of the modern period—

the tropes of dislocation and of the technologies of representation—Anderson in effect completes what has been a halting but nevertheless progressive reinscription of the figure of home, as well as of the general category of place. That process, begun in midcentury (when it was figured as the failure of homecoming), concludes when, in Sayre's words, "we recognize in [Anderson's] wanderings our own homelessness." Her lavish use of technology—technologies for manipulating sound, image, and even voice—is the extreme realization of a century-long rebellion against the naturalistic theater's dream of total visibility (the inner logic of that dream and the theatrical functioning it dictates are discussed in chap. 1). One playful passage in *United States* encapsulates the whole complex relation between *seeing* and *place*:

> Over the river
> And through the woods
> Whose woods these are
> Long time no see
> Long time no see[9]

The multiple experiences of place invoked here—as home and origin (Grandmother's house), as property (whose woods these are), as travel (miles to go before I sleep)—the copresence of high and low culture (Robert Frost and Little Red Riding Hood), as well as, finally, the muted reference to the dispossession of nature (the river and woods no longer seen): all these are part of the gradually evolving postgeopathological drama of the past two decades. Among the many aspects of geopathic drama that are revisioned in the contemporary theater is one that Anderson (like most other avant-garde practitioners of theater) deeply engages, the problematic of visibility. As Sayre articulates it: "Are we meeting someone we have not seen for a long time, or have we been, for a long time, blind?"

The chapters that follow describe a development that is also, at every "stage," a forecast and a memory. The conventionality of dramatic discourse—dictated by both its public nature as well as its material contextualization in an ongoing theater culture—makes the drama powerfully intertextual. This book traces that intertextuality by tracking not only the figures of home, homelessness, exile, and immigration, but also an apparently unconnected collection of recurring figures that insistently accompany the dramatic discourse of place: addiction, photography, performance, and burial.

Chapter 1, "Plays and Place," presents a theoretical model for the relationship of theatrical space and dramatic place by considering the habitual—and, I argue, false—opposition between naturalism and the experimental stage practice known as environmental theater. An exploration of the theoretics of naturalism as refracted through *Miss Julie* and Strindberg's preface to the play leads to a recognition that naturalism rested on a fantasy of total visibility, of the impossible translation of private experience into public expression. This problematic of a public privacy survives long after naturalism, persisting into environmental theater, where its presence is occluded by new spatial arrangements designed to create "shared experiences" (shared, that is, between the audience and the actors). These spatial arrangements, I argue, are deceptive, and the ideology sustaining them is the subject of Jim Cartwright's play *Road*. As I read it, *Road* stages the politics of place that link environmentalism to its supposed opposite, naturalism, and these politics are intimately connected to the dramatic discourse of home.

Chapter 2, "Geopathology," lays out the terms and consequences of a foundational semiology of place based on the idea of ill placement. Several of the themes and motifs that enter the drama through this semiology persist long into the future; among these, the figures of photography and of performance surface with interesting variations even after the discourse of home has been thoroughly revised through what I have called the "multicultural imagination," the topic of my final chapter. In the last play that I examine in that chapter, Ping Chong's *Nuit Blanche,* the figures of photography and performance are fused into the play's basic expressive strategy, its combination of slides and live action. In this play also, one of the most vibrant undercurrents running through the whole history of this thematic, namely, an ecological current, is brought to the surface. The relation between ecology and geopathology, discovered as early as Ibsen's *Wild Duck,* emerges as crucial to the deterritorialized theatrology of postmodernism.

Before the drama of multiculturalism can reconfigure place, the terms of geopathology have to be confronted. Chapter 3, "America and the Limits of Homecoming," traces the effects of the figure of America on the unraveling discourse of home. Focusing on two transatlantic pairs of plays—first Pinter's *The Homecoming* and Shepard's *Buried Child* and then Caryl Churchill's *Ice Cream* and George C. Wolfe's *The Colored Museum*—this chapter presents an encapsulated history of the dramatic discourse of home, its past and future condensed into the figure of failed homecoming and the dramaturgy of the hidden (and now worthless) secret.

From this analysis, an unexpected image, the image of the buried child, emerges as a privileged—even obsessional—device of the modern dramatic imagination. The figure of the buried child occurs again and again in modern drama, tempting one to turn to psychoanalysis for an explanation. I have preferred simply to track the fate of this strange figure in the evolving postgeopathic platial discourse of modern drama and to link it, finally, to a peculiar figure in the discourse of what Harold Bloom calls "the American religion." According to Bloom, America's obsession with the unborn child marks this culture's unacknowledged commitment to an essentially Gnostic belief system, whereby the essential self is as old as God himself and, like God, no part of the creation. George Bush's apparently contradictory concern for fetuses and unconcern for unwanted infants make a kind of sense from this point of view, valuing the uncreated—or precreated—divine being over the unwanted child who "is sadly fallen away from freedom": "One sees why the fetus and the flag are one; the baby is not alone, and will drain the pious taxpayer, but the fetus can wave over the land of the free, whose Fundamentalists will remain solitary and godlike, poised always *before* the Creation."

Bloom's reading of the American obsession with the unborn child helps to explain the painful contradiction this figure registers when brought into line with another powerful American mythology, America's view of itself as a *place* of exceptional potentiality, a land of unimagined progress and plenty. Bloom's reading would suggest that, for George Bush and his unwitting Gnostic constituency, this land—like the unwanted starving infant over whom the innocent fetus takes precedence—is part of the fallen creation and as such of little intrinsic concern to those whose minds and hearts are turned to the Hereafter. For them, as for Joseph Smith, the Mormon prophet, America is merely the ancient burial ground of a truth awaiting revelation. (The Book of Mormon was said to have lain buried for centuries in upstate New York until the Angel Moroni led Joseph Smith to it.) But another imagination of America, one that celebrates the land itself, its majestic landscapes and its vast spaces, contests this religious vision, substituting another, perhaps secular, faith, whose greatest manifestation has been American ecological thinking. The desecration of America, figured time and time again through the imagery of waste and garbage—the all-American figure of *junk*—provokes a reconsideration of the figure of the buried child. In this ongoing reformulation, the buried child is precious not for its links to a divinity that preexists creation but for its figuration of *recovery:* the hope, however hopeless, that what has been lost or destroyed by industrialization, technology, modernism can somehow be reclaimed, "dug up," revived, and acknowledged for the precious gift it always was.

Once again, it is Laurie Anderson's *United States* that seems to summarize the contradictory logic of the figure of the buried child and its relation to America, to the present, and (if our luck as a species holds out) to the future. In a section entitled "Song for Two Jims," Anderson tells of visiting a family in Kentucky, two parents and four children:

> One day Mrs Taylor told me that she used to have another kid, but that he had apparently fallen down one of the holes. Her description was very abstract. Nobody tried to rescue him. He just fell down the hole. She said: "Well one
> day I saw him out there
> and I was watching
> and then I didn't see him out there no more."

The abstraction of the mother's description of this extraordinary event is the key to its meaning. It is not only, as Sayre says, that "the 'meaning' of the narrative lies in the very meaninglessness of the Taylors' lives," but also that their defective access to meaning (and hence to affect, to feeling) takes the form of—precisely—a sudden invisibility. The buried child of modern drama is the unseen and unseeable force of circumstance; and circumstance, as we shall see, has long been understood as place, or rather as ill placement. In Anderson's text, however, a very precise characterization is given to the traditionally abstract discourse of geopathology, and we should not be surprised to find that that characterization consists of the two major unacknowledged or unconscious themes of geopathic drama: technology and ecology. The hole into which the "kid" falls is one of many deep holes drilled in the shale surrounding the Taylor household—by Standard Oil. The buried child is the covictim—with the land, with the earth itself—of unbridled technological progress.

The midcentury drama of failed homecoming is also the drama in which the figure of the buried child, and the related dramaturgy of discovery, begins to unravel and betray its hitherto invisible functioning. The process is completed in Laurie Anderson's piece, where the buried child finally speaks and, speaking, exposes the logic of its invisibility, naming that which is destroying, erasing, "burying" it:

> So hold me, Mom, in your long arms,
> in your automatic arms,
> your electronic arms . . .
> your petrochemical arms,
> your military arms,
> in your electronic arms.

After the failure of homecoming, the drama embarks on a quest for new places, and language is among the privileged sites of this exploration. Chapter 4, "The Places of Language," looks at the idea of language as place in three plays that also extend the dramatic discourse on America. Eric Overmyer's On the Verge links language, place, and the future, a connection that is then reengaged in a more material and historical mode by Caryl Churchill's Mad Forest and in a more apocalyptic and ecological mode by Maria Irene Fornes's The Danube. The newly awakened desire for a new platiality to replace the geopathic idealization of ill placement moves beyond language in the plays of immigration and multiculturalism that are the subjects of chapters 5 and 6, respectively. In the plays discussed in these chapters, the discourse of place begins to shift—more or less decisively—toward a recognition of the power of actual and specific places, although the old figuration of America as the principle of placelessness is never far away, never finally overcome.

The figures of home and exile have developed, in the course of this century, far beyond the scope of the literary figures with which they were first associated. The massive and agonizing dislocations of the modern age have left the poetics of exile far behind. The question I finally ask, in the epilogue of this book but also from the beginning, is this: How is the experience of dislocation making its voice heard in the theatrical language of the West? Two recent plays serve to outline an answer: Tony Kushner's monumental (and hugely successful) Angels in America and Suzan-Lori Parks's fragile (and largely unheralded) The America Play allow for a tentative formulation of where the journey beyond geopathology has led us. That both plays focus their reflections on the figure of America suggests that the modern drama's discourse of place has now transmuted itself into something quite site-specific. Both plays' meditations on the approaching millennium, their shared irony toward the morbid seductions of closure, their playful refusal of the logic of last words—all this makes them the ideal vehicle for what a book like this one must seek: a non-ending, an "other" place from which the otherness of place can continue to be explored and enjoyed.

Jeffrey Wright as Lincoln and Don Cheadle as Booth in the 2002 Joseph Papp Public Theater production of Suzan-Lori Parks's play *Topdog/Underdog*.

Social and technological change transformed the world in the late nineteenth and early twentieth centuries. Between 1860 and today, the United States emerged from a crippling civil war, two world wars, and the anxieties of the Cold War to become a dominant global power. However, despite the nation's emergence as a major player on the world stage, the arts in the United States were shaped by divided and contradictory impulses. The desire to imitate European models competed with a desire to bring distinctively American arts into being. Even as the Civil War threatened to destroy the nation itself, writers such as Walt Whitman, Ralph Waldo Emerson, Henry David Thoreau, and others gave voice to a national literature that both incorporated and redefined European traditions. With the global expansion of U.S. influence, especially after World War I, the question of an "American culture" became a pressing one; after World War II, certain forms of culture became one of the United States' most significant exports, exports at once assimilated, resisted, and redefined in the contemporary era of globalized culture.

In the theater, the modern era has brought with it the search for a quintessentially "American" drama in which theme, setting, and characterization explore American experience, often by invoking and then discarding styles and attitudes derived from the European stage. In a sense, American drama in the twentieth century translated the idea of American political freedom into more abstract, metaphorical, even Romantic terms, as a conflict between individual freedom and the pressures of confining social realities, such as economic hardship, social class, gender, and race. The search for an American idiom in the theater absorbs the stylistic experiments of European modernism and reshapes them, bending the formal innovation of the European theater to American issues and concerns.

"THE" AMERICAN THEATER?

The democratic experience and populist rhetoric of American public life has generally resisted the idea of a national culture emanating from a single center like New York City or Washington, D.C. For this reason, perhaps, the dream of a national theater has repeatedly failed. In the nineteenth century, westward expansion brought theater from New York, Philadelphia, and Boston to the Midwestern cities of Chicago, St. Louis, and Kansas City, and then to Los Angeles and San Francisco, and to scores of smaller towns between the Mississippi River and the Pacific Ocean. The theater was a widely dispersed local affair. Towns often boasted theaters that could be used for opera, drama, or vaudeville and that supported local companies while also catering to touring shows with stars drawn from New York and Europe. Although a lively local theater thrived throughout the country, offering melodrama, classical plays, comedies, and other entertainments, the appetite for touring shows created a demand for organizations capable of handling scheduling problems for local theaters and regional booking agencies.

In 1896 a group of theatrical entrepreneurs headed by Charles Frohman formed a nationwide organization of booking agents called the SYNDICATE. In a sense, they created the first model of how a national theater might work in the United States. The Syndicate offered theater managers a full season of touring shows—provided that the manager contracted to deal only with the Syndicate. By gaining exclusive control over theaters on key travel routes, the Syndicate thwarted competition from other touring producers and often even denied local companies the use of local theaters. At its height, the Syndicate had exclusive rights to more than 700 theaters. It could blackball non-Syndicate performers from working by threatening producers who hired them, and it could withdraw Syndicate support from any manager who booked non-Syndicate shows or performers.

The effects of the Syndicate were profound and shaped the American theater for the next half-century. The Syndicate's grip on the theater effectively extinguished major professional theater outside New York as a source of new plays and productions; it also influenced playwriting, since the Syndicate developed plays only as commercial properties that could be successfully marketed to a general audience coast-to-coast. Although the Syndicate's power was resisted by a few famous actors and powerful producers, its approach was imitated by other groups. The parochial interests of the New York stage—where the shows of such organizations originated—became in practice the interests of the American theater, and New York became the center of theatrical production and theatrical investment. The revival of significant, professional "regional" theaters as centers of new productions—Margo Jones's Theater 47 in Dallas, the Alley Theater of Houston, the Arena Stage in Washington, D.C., the Actors Workshop of San Francisco, the Guthrie Theater in Minneapolis—had to wait until the 1940s and 1950s. The Syndicate's fortunes also point out the fallacy inherent in the notion of *an* American theater. Throughout its history, the American theater has embraced a range of dynamic and contradictory attitudes toward the stage and its place in society: New York versus the "provinces," mainstream versus elite, conventional versus experimental, commercial versus artistic. Theatrical innovation has been spurred primarily by theaters outside the commercial mainstream, especially by small, amateur "little theaters," by university and college theaters, by community theaters, and by ethnic theaters.

EUROPEAN INFLUENCE AND AMERICAN INNOVATION

The growth of American drama and theater was decisively shaped by the commercial climate of the stage and also by the United States' isolation from the energetic traditions of European theater. While there had long been a homegrown playwriting tradition, many of the most successful plays in nineteenth-century America were—in an era before copyright protection was extended to dramatic authors—productions, adaptations, or piracies of European novels and plays, as well as of American classics like Harriet Beecher Stowe's *Uncle Tom's Cabin*. Moreover, given the lucrative opportunities of touring, British and European actor/managers frequently brought shows to the United States, and some—notably the prolific playwright and actor Dion Boucicault, whose plays *The Poor of New York* (1857) and *The Octoroon* (1859) were written and successfully staged in the United States—developed plays on American themes. Although turn-of-the-century Broadway developed a homegrown version of theatrical realism—epitomized by writer/producer David Belasco's *The Governor's Lady* (1912), which reproduced the interior of a familiar theater district restaurant onstage—European experimentation made its impact on America in more indirect ways, usually only after those experiments had crystallized into a body of theatrical practices and conventions. Many major companies toured the United States. The Abbey Theater came with John Millington Synge's *The Playboy of the Western World* in 1911–1912, and the German producer Max Reinhardt brought his spectacular productions to the United States in 1912, 1914, 1924, and 1927–1928. The British director Harley Granville Barker, who sponsored Shaw's plays and had gained fame as an innovative director of Shakespeare, directed in New York in 1915; the Ballets Russes toured in 1916; and the Moscow Art Theater, whose disciples Richard Boleslavsky and Maria Ouspenskaya founded the American Laboratory Theater in 1923, performed in 1923–1924.

Many of these companies, the Abbey and the Moscow Art Theater in particular, had begun as small, independent, amateur theaters, and their work was most directly implemented in the United States by similar groups. Some innovation came from the new college and university programs in drama: George Pierce Baker's famous playwriting course at Harvard University in the first decades of the century (taken by Eugene O'Neill, among many others) and Montgomery T. Gregory's program for black writers and performers at Howard University in the 1920s were only the beginning of a concerted effort to bring theater and drama into the university curriculum and to develop a greater awareness of progressive theater. However, it largely fell to the **LITTLE THEATER MOVEMENT** to assimilate this new work and redirect it toward particularly American concerns. Innovation in the American theater came largely from these small companies, committed to mounting new and uncommercial work. The Chicago Little Theater, the Toy Theater of Boston, the Neighborhood Playhouse and the Washington Square Playhouse of New York, and Detroit's Arts and Crafts Theater were all in operation by 1917, and the Little Negro Theater Movement was producing plays in Harlem and Washington, D.C., as well.

The Provincetown Playhouse provides a model of the "little theaters" and their fortunes in the early twentieth century. Founded in 1915 in Provincetown, Massachusetts—an artists' retreat at the tip of Cape Cod—the company was initially a group of young amateurs intent on theater, including the playwright Susan Glaspell; her husband, George Cram Cook; and, later, Eugene O'Neill. In the first year, the players produced plays in their summer homes. In 1916 they converted an old wharf building into a small theater and produced, among other plays, O'Neill's *Bound East for Cardiff.* In the autumn, the players returned to New York and opened a small theater in Greenwich Village. The company could hardly afford complex and expensive sets and turned its efforts instead toward a simple and realistic kind of performance. Eugene O'Neill's early plays were produced by the Provincetown company, and after he became a successful Broadway playwright, he continued to open many of his plays there. Like all of the "little theaters," the Provincetown had difficulty managing the transition from a small amateur company to the larger demands of a self-sustaining professional company. It went through a series of transformations before closing in 1929, having introduced O'Neill to the stage and having staged plays by John Reed, Edna St. Vincent Millay, Susan Glaspell, Djuna Barnes, Edmund Wilson, Paul Green, Wallace Stevens, Theodore Dreiser, August Strindberg, and many others.

In the United States, the freedom to make theater has always been qualified by the need to make it pay. The trials of sustaining artistic ambition in the commercial environment of the theater is the central narrative of the most innovative theatrical companies of the modern era. The ideal of an American theater remained tantalizing yet elusive and was often pursued in several ways, usually by developing a distinctive repertoire of plays, or by trying to define a typically American performance idiom. "Little theaters" like the Provincetown emphasized the production of American drama. Other theaters tried to produce American drama, the new European drama, and the classics for a larger audience than the "little theaters" could reach. The Theater Guild, for example, was organized in 1919 in New York as a subscription company specifically for the purpose of producing noncommercial plays. In the course of the next decade, the Guild staged plays by Shaw, Pirandello, Ibsen, and Strindberg, as well as plays by Americans like O'Neill and Elmer Rice. The Guild succeeded in incorporating American plays like O'Neill's *Strange Interlude* (1928) and Rice's *The Adding Machine* (1923) into the repertoire of serious modern drama and in bringing it to a significant public. However, following the stock market crash of 1929 and the economic depression that ensued, the Guild invested in a less adventuresome repertoire in the hopes of drawing a larger audience and so lost its original mission.

Although it sponsored an innovative selection of plays, the Theater Guild did not develop an original style of production. In 1931, several Guild members began a spin-off company—called simply the Group—for the purpose of investigating different kinds of drama and different approaches to performance. Eventually including Harold Clurman, Cheryl Crawford, Lee Strasberg, Elia Kazan, Sanford Meisner, and many others, the Group at first worked on plays examining the social ferment of the 1930s and the hardship of the Great Depression. Much as Chekhov became the centerpiece of Stanislavski's Moscow Art Theater, so the plays of Clifford Odets became the Group's standards: *Awake and Sing!, Waiting for Lefty,* and *Golden Boy.* However, the Group's most extensive contribution to the American theater was its systematic importation of Stanislavskian acting techniques. In the Group, and later in the Actors Studio, actors were trained in Stanislavski's approach to **EMOTION MEMORY** and **GIVEN CIRCUMSTANCES,** laying the groundwork for what became a distinctly "American" style of acting, acting that was emotionally spontaneous, grounded in subtext, psychologically realistic and nuanced. Nonetheless, the Group, the Studio, and the training they devised produced a generation of actors ready to meet the challenges of the burgeoning American drama of the 1940s and 1950s: Marlon Brando, Ben Gazzara, Karl Malden, Geraldine Page, Kim Stanley, Maureen Stapleton, and many others.

The impact of this acting can be seen in the great stage productions of the post-war period. The 1940s and early 1950s saw the development of a distinctively American approach to stage realism, balancing nuanced characterization with a concern for the social environment. Arthur Miller's *Death of a Salesman* and *The Crucible,* Tennessee Williams's *A Streetcar Named Desire* and *The Glass Menagerie,* and Eugene O'Neill's *The Iceman Cometh* and *Long Day's Journey into Night* demanded the subtle realism that became the hallmark of American acting and of American drama in the world repertoire. These plays—and their descendants, like the plays of Beth Henley, David Mamet, Maria Irene Fornes, August Wilson, or Sam Shepard—succeeded by criticizing American ideals and institutions while at the same time exploring the psyche of the American character. Indeed, in these plays the American character often seems to be thwarted precisely by the process of American society. The fragile beauty of Tennessee Williams's Southern belles is usually crushed by the sordid realities of modern urban life; in Shepard's *True West,* the American West becomes a mythic battleground, where a yuppie and a drifter shoot it out for control of the image.

POSTWAR EXPERIMENTS

After World War II, the most significant innovations in American theater have come from small "experimental" theater companies. In part through the influence of Antonin Artaud's conception of a **THEATER OF CRUELTY** (see Unit V), and the several tours of Jerzy Grotowski's Lab Theater of Poland, experimental theater in the 1960s and 1970s tended to reject the esthetic of stage realism in favor of producing an immediate, quintessentially *theatrical* experience for its audiences. As a result, many productions in the 1960s and 1970s—the Living Theater's *Paradise Now,* the Performance Group's *Dionysus in 69,* the Open Theater's *The Serpent,* the work of the Bread and Puppet Theater, of the San Francisco Mime Troup, of Mabou Mines, and many others—incorporated the audience as participants in the action. Many of these experiments also led to new forms of playwriting, in which classical notions of representation also were broken down. Moreover, these experiments not only led to the incorporation of a more immediate, physical esthetic into American drama (visible, too, in performance art), but also to the exploration of Brechtian epic theater: experiments with narrative (Fornes's *Fefu and Her Friends*), with an episodic epic form (Kushner's *Angels in America*), or with a more politicized performance of "character" (Anna Deavere Smith's monologues).

Indeed, American drama continued to strike a compromise with the innovations of the European theater after World War II. Eric Bentley—a brilliant scholar, director, playwright, and translator—worked indefatigably to bring Bertolt Brecht to the attention of the American theater. Brecht became particularly important in the United States as the Vietnam War and widespread civil and social discontent spurred the theater in more agitational, political directions. Feminist theater, ethnic theater, and gay and lesbian theater have all at times availed themselves of Brecht's theater theory and practice. The work of Luis Valdez and El Teatro Campesino in California in the 1960s and 1970s is a direct extension of Brecht's sense of theater. Bringing a flatbed truck to farmworkers' strikes, Teatro Campesino produced its short, political dramas to an active, involved audience and became part of the process of social change. "Absurdist" playwrights like Samuel Beckett, Harold Pinter, and Eugène Ionesco were also both produced and imitated in the United States, influencing the work of American playwrights like Edward Albee, Maria Irene Fornes, Jack Gelber, Adrienne Kennedy, David Mamet, and Sam Shepard. Indeed, in plays like Amiri Baraka's *Dutch-*

man or Sam Shepard's *True West,* we can see the inflections of **THEATER OF THE ABSURD** in plays that are recognizably "American" in style and subject matter.

In 1935, an act of Congress established the Federal Theater Project, as a way to employ workers left unemployed by the Depression (see Aside box). The Federal Theater Project also sponsored a Negro Unit, directed by John Houseman and Orson Welles, which operated in ten cities around the United States; two of its productions, an all-black *Macbeth* and *The Swing Mikado,* were among the Federal Theater's most successful productions. The fact of a separate Negro Unit points to a different crisis in the idea of an American theater. How could a theater largely in the hands of the white, Anglo, male, middle class adequately represent the diversity of the nation's experience, particularly the experience of the oppressed? As the poet and playwright Langston Hughes observed in "Notes on Commercial Theater," published in 1940, the stage had in many ways appropriated African-American culture, systematically absorbing it into its own dominant values:

> *Yep, you done taken my blues and gone.*
> *You also took my spirituals and gone.*
> *You put me in Macbeth and Carmen Jones*
> *And all kinds of Swing Mikados*
> *And in everything but what's about me—*
> *But someday somebody'll*
> *Stand up and talk about me,*
> *And write about me—*
> *Black and beautiful—*

Far from representing authentic black experience in America, such theater more often confirmed the discriminatory fantasies already prominent on the stage and in society. Such stereotypes as the boozy Irishman, the dull Swede, the sunny and/or murderous Italian, and the greedy Jew—appearing even in "realistic" plays like Rice's *Street Scene* (1929), and dating back through the stereotyped slaves and Indians of Boucicault's *Octoroon*—work to reinforce the "normative" perspective of dominant culture, reflecting the attitudes, behavior, and social practices that oppress such groups in the world outside the theater. It is not surprising, then, that throughout the history of the United States, ethnic theaters have played a prominent part in maintaining the cultural identity of America's minority populations: the Yiddish theater of New York, Polish theaters in Chicago, Scandinavian theaters throughout the Midwest, a thriving circuit of Spanish-language theaters shared by Mexico and Southwestern states from Texas to California, Cuban-influenced theater in Florida, and Puerto Rican theater in New York. Some of these theaters produced versions of classic European plays in their own accents, but most developed their own dramatic forms, as ways of maintaining themselves in the face of a brutally exclusive "American" culture.

The experience of slavery places African Americans in a different position vis-à-vis the culture of the United States, and the black theater has had a profound impact on the course of the American stage. Although an African Theater Company was founded in New York in 1821—sponsoring, among others, the brilliant Shakespearean actor Ira Aldridge (1807–1867) who left the United States for a distinguished career in Europe—in the main, African Americans had little direct access to the theater before the twentieth century. Black characters had long figured as stage villains and comic buffoons in American drama. Played by white actors in blackface makeup, these abusive types literally enacted white attitudes toward racial difference. "Jim Crow" was first popularized by the white song-and-dance man T. D. Rice in the 1830s, and more "sympathetic" characters, like Tom in the hugely popular stage adaptations of Harriet Beecher Stowe's *Uncle Tom's Cabin* (1832), were devised by white authors and played by white actors. The minstrel troupes that became popular after the Civil

THE FEDERAL THEATER PROJECT

If the Group Theater and the Actors Studio created an identifiably "American" approach to acting, the Federal Theater Project succeeded—briefly—in creating a truly national theater. An act of Congress established the Federal Theater Project in 1935 under the Works Projects Administration, with Hallie Flanagan Davis (1890–1969) as director. Like other WPA projects, the Federal Theater was designed both to employ workers idled by the Depression and to provide service to the community. It was an enormous undertaking; in New York City alone, half the theaters were closed by 1933 and half its population of actors unemployed. Given the mission of providing employment by hiring large casts and supporting personnel, and a commitment to dramatizing contemporary social issues, the Federal Theater developed its most notable genre, the Living Newspaper. Living Newspapers incorporated dialogue taken from newspapers and other public media into a series of vignettes, readings, films, and other techniques to a problem in current national and world affairs: the farm crisis in *Triple A Plowed Under* (1936), housing in *One-Third of a Nation* (1938), rural electrification in *Power* (1937). At its height, the Federal Theater had branches in forty states; these branches staged productions devised by the project's directors, using their own local resources, and often developed their own material. In 1936, for instance, a stage adaptation of Sinclair Lewis's *It Can't Happen Here* opened simultaneously in twenty-one theaters around the country, including black-cast and Yiddish productions. The Federal Theater ran for four full seasons be-

fore being terminated by Congress in 1939: it financed 1,200 productions of 830 major works, at times employing more than ten thousand people, most of whom had been unemployed. Admission to its shows was inexpensive, and in an average week 500,000 people saw its productions; over its four years of production, its audiences numbered more than 30 million people. In New York alone, more than 12 million people saw its productions. However, in an era of labor unrest and the pervasive fear of outside agitation, the Newspapers were seen by the Project's enemies in government—many of whom opposed the WPA altogether—as too left-wing for government support.

Despite its demise, the United State's' only truly national theater had significant influence on the course of American theater and drama. Not only did the Federal Theater have huge audiences, but it brought new audiences into the theater: 65 percent of its audiences were seeing a stage play for the first time. The Living

Newspapers developed a home-grown adaptation of the techniques of European experimental theater (including Brechtian epic theater) in the United States. In this sense, the Federal Theater inspired the work of several distinguished theater companies that survived its demise, notably John Houseman's (1915–1985) Mercury Theater, which produced Mark Blitzstein's *The Cradle Will Rock,* and a distinguished series of productions of modern and classic plays—by Shaw, Büchner, Shakespeare, and others. In addition, the Negro Units of the Federal Theater operated in Seattle, Hartford, Philadelphia, Newark, Los Angeles, Boston, Birmingham, Raleigh, San Francisco, and Chicago, employing more than 800 people and staging seventy-five productions in the project's four years of operation. Most importantly, the Federal Theater enabled a generation of actors, designers, directors, and playwrights to survive the Depression, and it brought the theater powerfully into the national scene.

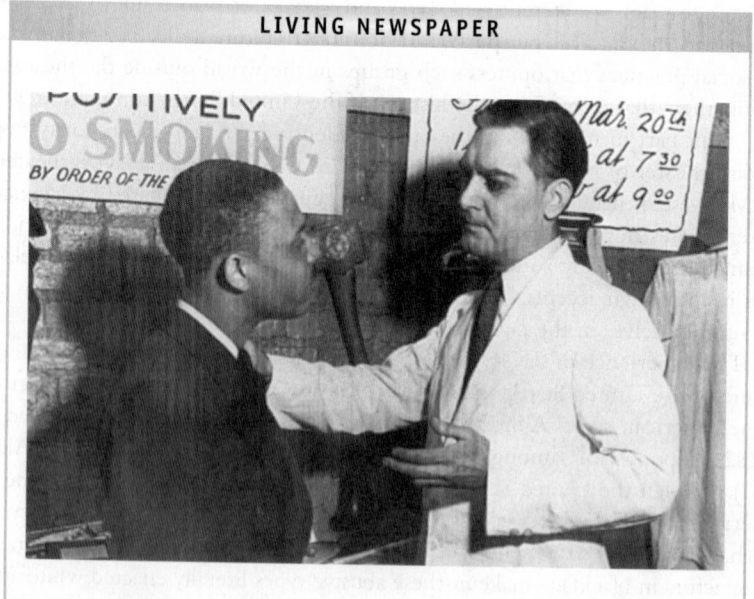

LIVING NEWSPAPER

The Federal Theater Project dramatizes news events in the New York production of 1935.

War for depicting romanticized vignettes of plantation life were also first performed by white actors. Later, black performers—in minstrel troupes, or in the newly popular "Negro musicals"—often had little choice other than to enact these stereotypes themselves, for such roles were the only openings available on the stage (even black theaters were usually financed and operated by white entrepreneurs). Despite small inroads like the Lafayette Theater (founded in Harlem in 1915), representing black experience to America at large was almost exclusively the prerogative of white actors, producers, playwrights, and performers. In this regard, the theater—like the institutions of literature, the press, the legal system, and state and federal government—denied African Americans their own voice.

Spurred in part by successful plays by white dramatists that self-consciously attempted to "humanize" black characters for white audiences—O'Neill's *The Emperor Jones* (1920) and *All God's Chillun Got Wings* (1924), Marc Connelly's *The Green Pastures* (1930), Paul Green's *In Abraham's Bosom* (1926), and Dubose and Dorothy Heyward's *Porgy* (1920; transformed into the Gershwin musical *Porgy and Bess* in 1935)—black actors and writers became galvanized to "stand up and talk" about themselves. Throughout the 1920s the LITTLE NEGRO THEATER MOVEMENT sponsored plays of black life largely for black audiences. The Lafayette Theater, for example, opened Willis Richardson's *The Chipwoman's Fortune* in 1923; it later became the first play by a black playwright to reach Broadway. In the 1920s and 1930s, black drama increasingly addressed the politics of racism in the United States, while also depicting the effect of racism in daily life. Several organizations worked to sponsor African-American drama and theater. W.E.B. DuBois, a founder of the National Association for the Advancement of Colored People (NAACP), used his *Crisis* magazine—in collaboration with the National Urban League's *Opportunity*—to give a series of prizes to promising African American playwrights; winners included Eulalie Spence's *Foreign Mail* (1926), Zora Neale Hurston's *Colorstruck* and *Spears* (1925), and Georgia Douglas Johnson's *Blue Blood* (1926). The NAACP also sponsored the production of plays, including Angelina Weld Grimké's influential drama of a young woman's reaction to the lynching of her father and brother, *Rachel* (1916). *Rachel* was one of the first of a series of plays about lynching. How this important genre of black theater—and a crucial element of black experience in the United States—was both overlooked and distorted by white theater is the subject of Alice Childress's brilliant play *Trouble in Mind,* which opened off-Broadway in 1955. Finally, black colleges, universities, and even high schools also became centers for a new dramatic repertoire. In 1921, Montgomery T. Gregory formed a department of Dramatic Arts at Howard University in Washington, D.C., and with Alain Locke developed an influential program in acting, playwriting, and theatrical production, offering the first institutionalized training for black writers and performers in the United States.

In a 1926 playbill for Harlem's Krigwa Players, W.E.B. DuBois described the goals of a black theater:

> The plays of a real Negro theater must be: *One: About us.* That is, they must have plots which reveal Negro life as it is. *Two: By us.* That is, they must be written by Negro authors who understand from birth and continual association just what it means to be a Negro today. *Three: For us.* That is, the theater must cater primarily to Negro audiences and be supported and sustained by their entertainment and approval. *Fourth: Near us.* The theater must be in a Negro neighborhood near the mass of ordinary Negro people.

Throughout the 1930s and 1940s, African American playwrights and actors came into increasing national prominence, both by developing DuBois's agenda and by working to bring an authentic black drama to a wider audience. Langston Hughes wrote a number of plays in the 1930s, including the well-known *Mulatto* (1935); the Federal Theater Project produced W.E.B. DuBois's *Haiti* at the Lafayette Theater; and playwrights trained at Howard were produced in New York and elsewhere. The founding of the companies like the American Negro Theater in 1939, the Negro Playwrights Company in 1940, and the Negro Ensemble Company in 1957 began to meet DuBois's charge, developing the actors, the production experience, and the financing that would sustain the explosive growth of black American drama after World War II. When Lorraine Hansberry's *A Raisin in the Sun* opened in 1959, it was the first play written by a black woman to reach Broadway, the first directed by a black director (Lloyd Richards), and the first financed predominantly by African Americans. The success of *Raisin* foretold the success of black theater in the coming decades, as black playwrights—Amiri Baraka, Adrienne Kennedy, Charles Gordone, Ed Bullins, Charles Fuller, Ntozake Shange, August Wilson, Anna Deavere Smith, Suzan-Lori Parks, and many others—came to shape the American theater.

POPULAR THEATER AND MASS CULTURE

The tension between commercial viability and dramatic achievement is perhaps best symbolized by Broadway itself, the American theater's "magnificent invalid," where even the greatest American plays can hardly compare in terms of commercial and popular success with Broadway's most uniquely American genre: the musical. Musical theater has a long history in the United States, and in many respects its fortunes parallel those of the dramatic theater. Musical theater also witnessed the tyranny of national producing syndicates, the impact of European innovation, and the powerful contributions of black and ethnic cultures. However, the integration of song and dance, orchestral music, and (usually) a romantic plot characteristic of the Broadway musical really dates to the period of World War II, probably to Richard Rodgers and Oscar Hammerstein's *Oklahoma!* (1943), which ran for 2,248 performances (*Death of a Salesman,* in contrast, ran for 742). *Oklahoma!* provided the model not only for other Rodgers and Hammerstein hits—*Carousel* (1945), *South Pacific* (1949), *The King and I* (1951)—but for other musicals as well: Alan Jay Lerner and Frederick Loewe's updating of Shaw's *Pygmalion* in *My Fair Lady* (1956), Frank Loesser's *Guys and Dolls* (1950), and Leonard Bernstein, Stephen Sondheim, and Arthur Laurents's *West Side Story* (1957). Although the form of the Broadway musical underwent significant changes in the 1970s and 1980s, its popularity points to one of the ways that the theater has sought to recapture an audience from film and television: by emphasizing the unique excitement of a dazzling live spectacle. This is as true of Broadway hits like *High Society* (1997), which used the Cole Porter music from the 1956 film of the same name, as it is of several musicals adapted from animated films—notably *The Lion King* (1997). The musical theater also points to the fundamental conditions of the Broadway theatrical economy as well. Musicals remain popular with producers because the huge financial investment required to mount a musical can repay much larger returns for investors than any "straight" play.

Throughout the history of the stage in the West, important theaters have succeeded both in creating innovative drama and in creating a public. However, the American theater—if there is *an* American theater—is a different entity altogether from the citizens' theater of classical Athens, the courtly theater of Racine and Molière, or even the educated circle of subscribers to Shaw's Court Theater. In a sense, this difference can be traced to the fact that the American theater first came into force only in the twentieth century, at just the moment when other dramatic media—film and television—began to compete with it. The American theater has had to define itself in the environment of modern mass culture. Not only are film and television more accessible to most people, but the technology and distribution of such mass media have fundamentally altered our understanding both of drama and performance, and of what an audience *is*. "The American theater" has always been a critical fiction, homogenizing the diversity of stage activity in the United States, writing some forms of drama—chiefly American realistic plays—into history, and writing others out of it. Today, it may be equally artificial to separate live theater from other forms of dramatic production, forms that have massively changed the terrain where dramatic performance takes place.

With the global expansion of the United States in the first two thirds of the twentieth century, the development of new modes of commerce and trade in the 1960s and 1970s (notably the multinational corporation), and especially with the breakup of the Soviet Union and its satellite states symbolized by the fall of the Berlin Wall in 1989, "American" culture has become a widely exported commodity. Much as American culture has absorbed both immigrant and conquered cultures as part of the development of the United States, so now the image of "America" is projected around the world, on T-shirts, in cartoons, in the imagery of Mickey Mouse and Michael Jordan, in television programs, in films.

Drama and theater are also part of that projected image, and American drama has rapidly become part of a global canon of modern theater: plays such as *Death of a Salesman* and *Fences* have been performed in the People's Republic of China; *Angels in America* was produced in London before it opened in New York, and has since been produced around the world. One of the most challenging aspects of American theater, however, is what might be called its *diversity,* the way different playwrights have worked to challenge a monolithic notion of "American" culture, and the values—white, masculinist, heterosexual, middle-class, English-speaking—it asserts as definitive. This diversity emerges in several ways, not only through a writer's or a company's decision to make their own alternative perspective *count*—as Luis Valdez and El Teatro Campesino do in *Zoot Suit*—but to use theatrical production to mark, make visible, "alienate" in Brecht's sense the ways the normative values of "American" culture are produced, and the kinds of work those values do.

For this reason, while there remains a large "mainstream" of stage style, much of the most adventurous work in the American theater has experimented with new, alternative ways of representing drama on the stage, and new ways of engaging its audience. The "rep and rev" of Suzan-Lori Parks's plays, the ways they "repeat and revise" a single gesture in order to highlight the *constructedness* of the body and the ways it represents itself culturally is one of these techniques; Anna Deavere Smith's effort to imitate the gestural conventions of her interview subjects does a similar kind of work, implying that those gestures are part of a common cultural repertoire, an individual act of expression that uses social means. This "alienating" of the ways "identity" is produced onstage extends to a wide range of contemporary performance. In 1983, for example, the Wooster Group's *L.S.D.—Just the High Points* set portions of Arthur Miller's *The Crucible* as a trial, literalizing the parallel with the McCarthy hearings that the play was widely thought to allegorize; in *Routes 1 & 9,* the company integrated scenes from Thornton Wilder's *Our Town* into a blackface minstrel show, in effect staging the racist attitudes that "our town"—white America in this case—has both produced and disowned.

This use of the stage to expose dominant or oppressive attitudes that are concealed within the monuments of American culture is also characteristic of performance works like Coco Fusco and Guillermo Gómez-Peña's *Two Undiscovered Amerindians Visit . . . ,* (which has been filmed as *The Couple in the Cage*). In the early 1990s, Gómez-Peña (a performance artist born in Mexico) and Fusco (a Cuban-American) devised a performance in which they portrayed "native" or "indigenous" inhabitants of the (fictitious) Carribean island of Guatinaui. Wearing deeply layered costumes—basketball sneakers, feathered headdresses, sunglasses, bottle-cap-studded vests—Fusco and Gómez-Peña were displayed in a cage, as anthropological "discoveries." During the course of the performance, which was produced in several art museums around the United States, as well as in the Field Museum of Natural History in Chicago, and on a plaza in Madrid, Gómez-Peña and Fusco exhibited behavior: they watched TV, they ate, for a fee they had their photo taken with spectators, or danced, and so on. The purpose of the production, however, was less to portray an exoticized native "other," than it was to *stage* the attitudes of their audiences to the spectacle of these imprisoned, displayed people. Although we might think this an extreme or at least a special case, it might be said that what Gómez-Peña and Fusco did here—stage the audience—is a task that stretches back to Valdez's work in the 1960s, and has become one of the principal innovations of contemporary American performance.

Since the mid-1960s, a variety of non-dramatic performance modes have developed in Western theater that are commonly known by the generic label of "performance art." Although it is difficult to generalize about this wide range of performances, most performance-art works share certain features: many (though certainly not all) are solo works, in which a performer (or performers) relates directly to an audience; the performer(s) may be working from a plan or script, but the performance is not a traditional "drama," enacting a fictitious narrative of the deeds of a fictitious "character" through "acting." Instead, in performance art, the performer uses a variety of means—monologue, physical performance, music, dance—to produce a spectacle that is "really happening" between himself or herself and the spectators.

Many performance-art works of the 1970s and 1980s used the performers' bodies to explore the limits of "theater." Chris Burden, for example, staged several events in which he wounded himself before an audience: in one 1970 work, he shot himself in the arm with a pistol; in another, he was crucified on top of a Volkswagen. In one of Carolee Schneeman's works, she unwinds a long scroll from her vagina, reading it to the audience. Annie Sprinkle, once a pornographic film star, openly objectifies her body on-stage for a visible audience of men (and women), as she had once done in the more covert and coercive scene of pornography; in one performance, she invites the audience onstage while she conducts her own cervical examination. Many performance art works take place outside theatrical venues, so that the performance becomes part of the everyday "performance" of street life. Linda Montano spent one year connected by a short rope to Teching Tsieh; the artists' lack of privacy was constantly on display in the streets of New York. In one of her early performances, Laurie Anderson stood on a large block of ice on a New York City street, playing her violin until the ice melted.

Several performance artists have become well-known for their monologue-performances, which range widely in technique and strategy. Anna Deavere Smith's works—such as *Fires in the Mirror: Crown Heights, Brooklyn and Other Identities* and *Twilight—Los Angeles, 1992*—differ from many performance art monologues in that Smith impersonates and represents a range of speakers; yet both in the brilliance of her individual performance and in her effort to perform the speakers faithfully (rather than "act" them in a theatrical sense), Smith's work touches on the "authentic" aspect of performance art. This emphasis on the "authentic," the "real," enables several performance artists to explore the relationship between identity politics and performance. In *Memory Tricks,* Marga Gomez, daughter of a Cuban theater impresario and a Puerto Rican "exotic dancer," recalls her family and childhood to interrogate the formation of Latina identity in the United States. David Drake's *The Night Larry Kramer Kissed Me* dramatizes the performer's understanding and exploration of his gay sexuality from the time of his sixth birthday, on the night of the 1969 Stonewall Riots in New York's Greenwich Village—in which gay men and lesbians protested abusive treatment by the police—through the AIDS crisis of the 1980s and 1990s.

Many artists use performance to foreground and criticize the everyday racist, sexist, and/or homophobic "performance" commonly accepted as "normal behavior" in U.S. society, and to bring into view other ways of performing identity. Adrian Piper, a light-skinned African American woman, sometimes hands out business cards to people who "ignore" her race:

I am black. I am sure that you did not realize this when you made / laughed at / agreed with that racist remark. In the past, I have attempted to alert white people to my racial identity in advance. Unfortunately, this invariably causes them to react to me as pushy, manipulative, or socially inappropriate. Therefore, my policy is to assume that white people do not make these remarks, even when they believe there are no black people present, and to distribute this card when they do. I regret any discomfort my presence is causing you, just as I am sure you regret the discomfort your racism is causing me.

Lesbian playwright Holly Hughes had written several plays—notably *The Well of Horniness, The Lady Dick,* and *Dress Suits for Hire,* which was performed by Peggy Shaw and Lois Weaver at the WOW Cafe—before developing her well-known performance piece *World Without End* in 1989. In *My Queer Body,* Tim Miller narrates the history of his sexual experience and the formation of his identity as a gay man; he undresses during the performance and performs part of *My Queer Body* in the nude, sometimes moving about the audience. Karen Finley's performances often express her outrage at the implicit and explicit violence against women in American culture; in monologues like *Constant State of Desire* and *We Keep Our Victims Ready,* she uses her body to enact and physicalize the "obscenity" of such violence. In a section of *We Keep Our Victims Ready* entitled "St. Valentine's Massacre," Finley examines the way patriarchal culture encodes a subtle hatred of women, one that women can self-destructively internalize. In performance, while Finley monologues, "My life is worth nothing but shit," she smears her naked body with chocolate pudding and studs it with spermlike bean sprouts, a stunning and physical image of the sexualization of violence.

As the performance continues, though, she layers herself with tinsel and red candies, transforming her abjection into a strange beauty. Such performances purposefully transgress the boundaries of decorous social behavior, in part to dramatize the kind of oppression that lurks in "everyday" performance. By all accounts, audiences who have seen Finley's or Miller's performances have found them powerful and moving; but to some critics (who often proudly claim that they have not seen the performance), such performance verges on "obscenity." In 1990, conservative politicians led by then Senator Jesse Helms (R–North Carolina) pressured the National Endowment for the Arts to withdraw funding from four performance artists who had been recommended by the peer-review process for support. Not only were Tim Miller, Karen Finley, Holly Hughes, and John Fleck denied funding, but the Endowment's head, John Frohnmayer, subsequently resigned, and a "general standards of decency" restriction of dubious constitutionality was required of subsequent recipients of NEA support.

Perhaps the best-known autobiographical performer, however, is Spalding Gray. Gray began his career with The Performance Group, an avant-garde company working with **ENVIRONMENTAL THEATER** in the late 1960s and 1970s. With Elizabeth LeCompte and other members of the group, Gray collaborated on a series of performances, collectively called *The Rhode Island Trilogy—Sakonnet Point* (1975), *Rumstick Road* (1977), and *Nyatt School* (1978), followed by an epilogue, *Point Judith* (1979). The Performance Group was committed to authentic "performance" (in which the actors behave as themselves, rather than "acting" in a theatrical sense), and Gray found a sequence of *Rumstick Road*—in which he narrated events of his life to the audience—to be a particularly fertile ground for continued exploration. In the course of the next several years, Gray developed a se-

PERFORMANCE ART

Anna Deavere Smith portrays Angela King at the world premier of Smith's *Twilight—Los Angeles, 1992*.

ries of autobiographical performances. In some of these works, Gray structures a certain degree of randomness in the performance: in *India and After (America)* (1979), for example, he randomly chooses words from a dictionary to key part of his monologue; in *A Personal History of the American Theatre* (1980), he shuffles a collection of index cards with play titles on them and uses the series to direct his performance. Gray's more recent work has been made into films, and so has become known to a wider audience. The film versions of *Swimming to Cambodia* (1984) and *Monster in a Box* (1990) preserve much of the ambience of Gray's performance. In the opening sequence of *Swimming to Cambodia,* for example, we see Gray walking through

the streets of the Village, entering the Performance Garage, seating himself onstage at a long table, and opening the notebook that seems to provide the score for his performance. Gray addresses the camera and, as in his stage performances, seems to occupy a startling and fascinating middle ground between acting and being: he is clearly shaping the story, representing and constructing the narrative of his life as a kind of fiction, while at the same time claiming that quasi-fictive narrative as his own, as himself. Like other postmodern art forms, performance art evocatively explores the edge between representation and "reality," refusing to demarcate a fixed difference between them.

READING THE
MATERIAL THEATER

As writing, drama is part of the wide horizon of literature, and throughout its history, the stage has been the site of adaptation; the Greek playwrights adapted their dramas from familiar myths, the medieval craft guilds developed original dramas from Biblical narratives, and Shakespeare famously adapted existing narratives—from classical and contemporary literature, as well as from English history—and plays. With the rise of print, however, a different kind of "adaptation" began to take place, as playwrights and theater managers could turn a quick profit by bringing a famous novel to the stage, typically in a pirated version. In the nineteenth century, for instance, Charles Dickens's novels were frequently pirated for the stage; in versions that not only outraged Dickens, but that paid him no fees or royalties. Susan Glaspell's *Trifles,* however, represents an alternative phenomenon: the translation to the page of a work that had first found success on the stage. In 1917, Glaspell adapted her short story "A Jury of Her Peers" from her play *Trifles.* While the story has been, perhaps, even more widely celebrated than the play, it also raises some important questions about the place of dramatic writing in the age of print. Although both works tell the same "story," they do so through very different means: how do the resources of the stage and the resources of the page contribute to the creation of a *different* work of art?

SUSAN GLASPELL
"A Jury of Her Peers" (1917)

After the success of Trifles, *Glaspell wrote a short, narrative version of the play, which has been justly celebrated for the ways it deploys a woman's narrative "point of view." Moreover, the short story also dramatizes the different resources that the theater and narrative fiction have available in order to tell the "same" story.*

When Martha Hale opened the storm-door and got the north wind, she ran back for her big woolen scarf. As she hurriedly wound that round her head her eye made a scandalized sweep of her kitchen. It was no ordinary thing that called her away—it was probably farther from ordinary than anything that had ever happened in Dickson County. But her kitchen was in no shape for leaving: bread ready for mixing, half the flour sifted and half unsifted.

She hated to see things half done; but she had been at that when they stopped to get Mr. Hale, and the sheriff came in to say his wife wished Mrs. Hale would come too—adding, with a grin, that he guessed she was getting scarey and wanted another woman along. So she had dropped everything right were it was.

"Martha!" now came her husband's impatient voice. "Don't keep folks waiting out here in the cold."

She joined the three men and the one woman waiting for her in the sheriff's car.

After she had the robes tucked in she took another look at the woman beside her. She had met Mrs. Peters the year before, at the county fair, and the thing she remembered about her was that she didn't seem like a sheriff's wife. She was small and thin and didn't have a strong voice. Mrs. Gorman, sheriff's wife before Gorman went out and Peters came in, had a voice that seemed to be backing up the law with every word. But if Mrs. Peters didn't look like a sheriff's wife, Peters made it up in looking like a sheriff—a heavy man with a big voice, who was particularly genial with the law-abiding, as if to make it plain that he knew the difference between criminals and non-criminals. And right there it came into Mrs. Hale's mind that this man who was so lively with all of them was going to the Wrights' now as a sheriff.

"The country's not very pleasant this time of year," Mrs. Peters at last ventured.

Mrs. Hale scarcely finished her reply, for they had gone up a little hill and could see the Wright place, and seeing it did not make her feel like talking. It looked very lonely this cold March morning. It had always been a lonesome-looking place. It was down in a hollow, and the poplar trees around it were lonely-looking trees. The men were looking at it and talking about what had happened. The county attorney was bending to one side, scrutinizing the place as they drew up to it.

"I'm glad you came with me," Mrs. Peters said nervously, as the two women were about to follow the men in through the kitchen door.

Even after she had her foot on the doorstep, Martha Hale had a moment of feeling she could not cross this threshold. And the reason it seemed she couldn't cross it now was because she hadn't crossed it before. Time and time again it had been in her mind, "I ought to go over and see Minnie Foster"—she still thought of her as Minnie Foster, though for twenty years she had been Mrs. Wright. And then there was always something to do and Minnie Foster would go from her mind. But *now* she could come.

The men went over to the stove. The women stood close together by the door. Young Henderson, the county attorney, turned around and said, "Come up to the fire, ladies."

Mrs. Peters took a step forward, then stopped. "I'm not—cold," she said.

And so the two women stood by

the door, at first not even so much as looking around the kitchen.

The men talked about what a good thing it was the sheriff had sent his deputy out that morning to make a fire for them, and then Sheriff Peters stepped back from the stove, unbuttoned his outer coat, and leaned his hands on the kitchen table in a way that seemed to mark the beginning of official business. "Now, Mr. Hale," he said in a sort of semi-official voice, "before we move things about, you tell Mr. Henderson just what it was you saw when you came here yesterday morning."

The county attorney was looking around the kitchen.

"By the way," he asked, "has anything been moved?" He turned to the sheriff. "Are things just as you left them yesterday?"

Peters looked from cupboard to sink; to a small worn rocker a little to one side of the kitchen table.

"It's just the same."

"Well, Mr. Hale," said the county attorney, "tell just what happened when you came here yesterday morning."

Mrs. Hale, still leaning against the door, had that sinking feeling of the mother whose child is about to speak a piece. Lewis often wandered along and got things mixed up in a story. She hoped he would tell this straight and plain, and not say unnecessary things that would make it harder for Minnie Foster. He didn't begin at once, and she noticed that he looked queer, as if thinking of what he had seen here yesterday.

"Yes, Mr. Hale?" the county attorney reminded.

"Harry and I had started to town with a load of wood," Mrs. Hale's husband began.

Harry was Mrs. Hale's oldest boy. He wasn't with them now, for the wood never got to town yesterday and he was taking it this morning, so he hadn't been home when the sheriff stopped to say he wanted Mr. Hale to come over to the Wright place and tell the county attorney his story there, where he could point it all out. With all Mrs. Hale's other emotions came the fear Harry wasn't dressed warm enough—they hadn't any of them realized how that north wind did bite.

"We come along this road," Hale was going on, "and as we got in sight of the house I says to Harry, 'I'm goin' to see if I can't get John Wright to take a telephone.' You see," he explained to Henderson, "unless I can get somebody to go in with me they won't come out this branch road except for a price *I* can't pay. I'd spoke to Wright about it before; but he put me off, saying folks talked too much anyway, and all he asked was peace and quiet—guess you know about how much he talked himself. But I thought maybe if I went to the house and talked about it before his wife, and said all the women—folks liked the telephones, and that in this lonesome stretch of road it would be a good thing—well, I said to Harry that that was what I was going to say—though I said at the same time that I didn't know as what his wife wanted made much difference to John—"

Now, there he was!—saying things he didn't need to say. Mrs. Hale tried to catch her husband's eye, but fortunately the county attorney interrupted with:

"Let's talk about that a little later, Mr. Hale. I do want to talk about that, but I'm anxious now to know just what happened when you got here."

When he began this time, it was deliberately, as if he knew it were important.

"I didn't see or hear anything. I knocked at the door. And still it was all quiet inside. I knew they must be up—it was past eight o'clock. So I knocked again, louder, and I thought I heard somebody say, 'Come in.' I wasn't sure—I'm not sure yet. But I opened the door—this door," jerking a hand toward the door by which the two women stood, "and there, in that rocker"—pointing to it—"sat Mrs. Wright."

Everyone in the kitchen looked at the rocker. It came into Mrs. Hale's mind that this chair didn't look in the least like Minnie Foster—the Minnie Foster of twenty years before. It was a dingy red, with wooden rungs up the back, and the middle rung gone; the chair sagged to one side.

"How did she—look?" the county attorney was inquiring.

"Well," said Hale, "she looked—queer?"

"How do you mean—queer?"

He took out note-book and pencil. Mrs. Hale did not like the sight of that pencil. She kept her eye on her husband, as if to keep him from saying unnecessary things that would go into the book and make trouble.

Hale spoke guardedly: "Well, as if she didn't know what she was going to do next. And kind of—done up."

"How did the seem to feel about your coming?"

"Why, I don't think she minded—one way or other. She didn't pay much attention. I said, 'Ho' do, Mrs. Wright. It's cold, ain't it?' And she said, 'Is it?'—and went on pleatin' of her apron.

"Well, I was surprised. She didn't ask me to come up to the stove, but just set there, not even lookin' at me. And so I said, 'I want to see John.'

"And then she—laughed. I guess you would call it a laugh.

"I thought of Harry and the team outside, so I said, a little sharp, 'Can I see John?' 'No,' says she—kind of dull like. 'Ain't he home?' says I. Then she looked at me. 'Yes,' says she, 'he's home.' 'Then why can't I see him?' I asked her, out of patience with her now. ''Cause he's dead,' says she, just as quiet and dull—and fell to pleatin' her apron. 'Dead?' says I, like you do when you can't take in what you've heard.

"She just nodded her head, not getting a bit excited, but rockin' back and forth.

"'Why—where is he?'" says I, not knowing *what* to say.

"She just pointed upstairs—like this"—pointing to the room above.

"I got up, with the idea of going up there myself. By this time I—didn't know what to do. I walked from there to here, then I says "'Why, what did he die of?'"

"'He died of a rope round his neck,' says she; and just went on pleatin' at her apron."

Hale stopped speaking, staring at the rocker. Nobody spoke; it was as if all were seeing the woman who had sat there the morning before.

"And what did you do then?" the attorney asked.

"I went out and called Harry, I though I might—need help. I got Harry in, and we went upstairs." His voice fell almost to a whisper. "There he was—lying over the—"

"I think I'd rather have you go into that upstairs," the county attorney interrupted, "where you can point it all out. Just go on now with the rest of the story."

"Well, my first thought was to get that rope off. It looked—"

He stopped; he did not say how it looked.

"But Harry, he went up to him and he said, 'No, he's dead all right, and we'd better not touch anythin'.' So we went downstairs.

"She was still sitting that same way. 'Has anybody been notified?' I asked. 'No,' says she, unconcerned.

"'Who did this, Mrs. Wright?' said Harry. He said it business-like, and she stopped pleatin' at her apron. 'I don't know,' she says. 'You don't *know?*' says Harry. 'Weren't you sleepin' in the bed with him?' 'Yes,' says she, 'but I was on the inside.' 'Somebody slipped a rope round his neck and strangled him, and you didn't wake up?' says Harry. 'I didn't wake up,' she said after him.

"We may have looked as if we didn't see how that could be, for after a minute she said, 'I sleep sound.'

"Harry was going to ask her more questions, but I said maybe that weren't our business; maybe we ought to let her tell her story first to the coroner or the sheriff. So Harry went fast as he could over to High Road—the Rivers' place, where there's a telephone."

"And what did she do when she knew you had gone for the coroner?"

"She moved from that chair to this one over here, and just sat there with her hands held together and looking down. I got a feeling that I ought to make some conversation, so I said I had come in to see if John wanted to put in a telephone; and at that she started to laugh, and then she stopped and looked at me—scared."

At sound of a moving pencil the man who was telling the story looked up.

"I dunno—maybe it wasn't scared; I wouldn't like to say it was. Soon Harry got back, and then Dr. Lloyd came, and you, Mr. Peters, and so I guess that's all I know that you don't."

He said this with relief, moved as if relaxing. The county attorney walked to the stair door.

"I guess we'll go upstairs first—then out to the barn and around there."

He paused and looked around the kitchen.

"You're convinced there was nothing important here?" he asked the sheriff. "Nothing that would—point to any motive?"

The sheriff too looked all around. "Nothing here but kitchen things," he said, with a little laugh for the insignificance of kitchen things.

The county attorney was looking at the cupboard. He opened the upper part and looked in. After a moment he drew his hand away sticky.

"Here's a nice mess," he said resentfully.

The two women had drawn nearer, and now the sheriff's wife spoke.

"Oh—her fruit," she said, looking to Mrs. Hale for understanding. "She worried about that when it turned so cold last night. She said the fire would go out and her jars might burst."

Mrs. Peters' husband broke into a laugh.

"Well, can you beat the women! Held for murder, and worrying about her preserves!"

The young attorney set his lips.

"I guess before we're through with her she may have something more serious than preserves to worry about."

"Oh, well," said Mrs. Hale's husband, with good-natured superiority, "women are used to worrying over trifles."

The two women moved a little closer together. Neither of them spoke. The county attorney seemed to remember his manners—and think of his future.

"And yet," said he, with the gallantry of a young politician, "for all their worries, what would we do without the ladies?"

The women did not speak. He went to the sink to wash his hands, turned to wipe them on the roller towel, pulled it for a cleaner place.

"Dirty towels! Not much of a housekeeper, would you say, ladies?" He kicked his foot against some dirty pans under the sink.

"There's a great deal of work to be done on a farm," said Mrs. Hale stiffly.

"To be sure. And yet"—with a little bow to her—"I know there are some Dickson County farm-houses that do not have such roller towels."

"Those towels get dirty awful quick. Men's hands aren't always as clean as they might be."

"Ah, loyal to your sex, I see," he laughed. He gave her a keen look. "But you and Mrs. Wright were neighbours. I suppose you were friends too."

Martha Hale shook her head.

"I've seen little enough of her of late years. I've not been in this house—it's more than a year."

"And why was that? You didn't like her?"

"I liked her well enough," she replied with spirit. "Farmers' wives have their hands full, Mr. Henderson. And then—" She looked around the kitchen.

"Yes?" he encouraged.

"It never seemed a very cheerful place," said she, more to herself than to him.

"No," he agreed; "I don't think anyone would call it cheerful. I shouldn't say she had the home-making instinct."

"Well, I don't know as Wright had either," she muttered.

"You mean they didn't get on very well?"

"No; I don't mean anything," she answered, with decision. "But I don't think a place would be any the cheer-fuler for John Wright's bein' in it."

"I'd like to talk to you about that a little later, Mrs. Hale." He moved towards the stair door, followed by the two men.

"I suppose anything Mrs. Peters does'll be all right?" the sheriff in-quired. "She was to take in some clothes for her, you know—and a few little things. We left in such a hurry yesterday."

The county attorney looked at the two women they were leaving alone among the kitchen things.

"Yes—Mrs. Peters," he said, his glance resting on the woman who was not Mrs. Peters, the big farmer woman who stood behind the sher-iff's wife. "Of course Mrs. Peters is one of us," he added in a manner of entrusting responsibility. "And keep your eye out, Mrs. Peters, for anything that might be of use. No telling; you women might come upon a clue to the motive—and that's the thing we need."

Mr. Hale rubbed his face in the fashion of a slow man getting ready for a pleasantry. "But would the women know a clue if they did come upon it?" he said. Having delivered himself of this, he followed the others through the stair door.

The women stood motionless, lis-tening to the footsteps, first upon the stairs, then in the room above them.

Then, as if releasing herself from something too strange, Mrs. Hale be-gan to arrange the dirty pans under the sink, which the county attorney's disdainful push of the foot had upset.

"I'd hate to have men coming into my kitchen, snoopin' round and criti-cizing."

"Of course it's no more than their duty," said the sheriff's wife, in her timid manner.

"Duty's all right, but I guess that deputy sheriff that come out to make the fire might have got a little of this on." She gave the roller towel a pull. "Wish I'd thought of that sooner! Seems mean to talk about her for not having things slicked up, when she had to come away in such a hurry."

She looked around the kitchen. Certainly it was not "slicked up." Her eye was held by a bucket of sugar on a low shelf. The cover was off the wooden bucket, and beside it was a paper bag—half full.

Mrs. Hale moved towards it.

"She was putting this in there," she said to herself—slowly.

She thought of the flour in her kitchen at home—half sifted, half not sifted. She had been interrupted, and had left things half done. What had in-terrupted Minnie Foster? Why had that work been left half done? She made a move as if to finish it—unfinished things always bothered her, and then she saw that Mrs. Peters was watching her, and she didn't want Mrs. Peters to get that feeling she had of work be-gun and then—for some reason—not finished.

"It's a shame about her fruit," she said, going to the cupboard. "I wonder if it's all gone.

"Here's one that's all right," she said at last. She held it towards the light. "This is cherries, too." She

looked again. "I declare I believe that's the only one.

"She'll feel awful bad, after all her hard work in the hot weather. I re-member the afternoon I put up my cherries last summer."

She put the bottle on the table, and was about to sit down in the rocker. But something kept her from sitting in that chair. She stood looking at it, seeing the woman who had sat there "pleatin' at her apron."

The thin voice of the sheriff's wife broke in upon her: "I must be getting those things from the front room closet." She opened the door into the other room, started in, stepped back. "You coming with me, Mrs. Hale?" she asked nervously. "You—you could help me get them."

They were soon back. "My!" said Mrs. Peters, dropping the things on the table and hurrying to the stove.

Mrs. Hale stood examining the clothes the woman who was being detained in town had said she wanted.

"Wright was close!" she ex-claimed, holding up a shabby black skirt that bore the marks of much making over. "I think maybe that's why she kept so much to herself. I s'pose she felt she couldn't do her part; and then, you don't enjoy things when you feel shabby. She used to wear pretty clothes and be lively— when she was Minnie Foster, one of the town girls, singing in the choir. But that—oh, that was twenty years ago."

With a carefulness in which there was something tender, she folded the shabby clothes and piled them at one corner of the table. She looked up at Mrs. Peters, and there was something in the other woman's look that irri-tated her.

"She don't care," she said to her-self. "Much difference it makes to her whether Minnie Foster had pretty clothes when she was a girl."

Then she looked again, and she wasn't so sure; in fact, she hadn't at any time been sure about Mrs. Peters.

She had that shrinking manner, and yet her eyes looked as if they could see a long way into things.

"This all you was to take in?" asked Mrs. Hale.

"No," said the sheriff's wife; "she said she wanted an apron. Funny thing to want," she ventured in her nervous way, "for there's not much to get you dirty in jail, goodness knows. But I suppose just to make her feel more natural. She said they were in the bottom drawer of this cupboard. Yes—here they are. And then her little shawl that always hung on the stair door."

She took the small grey shawl from behind the door leading upstairs.

Suddenly Mrs. Hale took a quick step towards the other woman.

"Mrs. Peters!"

"Yes, Mrs. Hale?"

"Do you think she—did it?"

Mrs. Peters looked frightened. "Oh, I don't know," she said, in a voice that seemed to shrink from the subject.

"Well, I don't think she did," affirmed Mrs. Hale. "Asking for an apron, and her little shawl. Worryin' about her fruit."

"Mr. Peters says—" Footsteps were heard in the room above; she stopped, looked up, then went on in a lowered voice: "Mr. Peters says—it looks bad for her. Mr. Henderson is awful sarcastic in a speech, and he's going to make fun of her saying she didn't wake up."

For a moment Mrs. Hale had no answer. Then, "Well, I guess John Wright didn't wake up—when they was slippin' that rope under his neck," she muttered.

"No, it's *strange*," breathed Mrs. Peters. "They think it was such a—funny way to kill a man."

"That's just what Mr. Hale said," said Mrs. Hale, in a resolutely natural voice. "There was a gun in the house. He says that's what he can't understand."

"Mr. Henderson said, coming out, that what was needed for the case was a motive. Something to show anger—or sudden feeling."

"Well, I don't see any signs of anger around here," said Mrs. Hale. "I don't—"

She stopped. Her eye was caught by a dishtowel in the middle of the kitchen table. Slowly she moved towards the table. One half of it was wiped clean, the other half untidy. Her eyes made a slow, almost unwilling turn to the bucket of sugar and the half-empty bag beside it. Things begun—and not finished.

She stepped back. "Wonder how they're finding things upstairs? I hope she had it in better shape up there. Seems kind of *sneaking*, locking her up in town and coming out here to get her own house to turn against her!"

"But, Mrs. Hale," said the sheriff's wife, "the law is the law."

"I s'pose it is," answered Mrs. Hale shortly.

She turned to the stove, saying something about that fire not being much to brag of.

"The law is the law—and a bad stove is a bad stove. How'd you like to cook on this?" with the poker pointing to the broken lining. She opened the oven door. The thought of Minnie Foster trying to bake in that oven—and the thought of her never going over to see Minnie Foster—

She was startled by hearing Mrs. Peters say, "A person gets discouraged—and loses heart."

The sheriff's wife had looked from the stove to the sink—the pail of water which has been carried in from outside. The two women stood there silent, above them the footsteps of the men who were looking for evidence against the woman who had worked in that kitchen. That look of seeing into things, of seeing through a thing to something else, was in the eyes of the sheriff's wife now. When Mrs. Hale next spoke to her, it was gently.

"Better loosen up your things, Mrs. Peters. We'll not feel them when we go out."

Mrs. Peters went to the back of the room to hang up the fur tippet she was wearing. "Why, she was piecing a quilt," she exclaimed, and held up a large sewing basket piled high with quilt pieces.

Mrs. Hale spread some of the blocks on the table.

"It's log-cabin pattern," she said, putting several of them together. "Pretty, isn't it?"

They were so engaged with the quilt that they did not hear the footsteps on the stairs. As the stair door opened Mrs. Hale was saying, "Do you suppose she was going to quilt it, or just knot it?"

The sheriff threw up his hands.

"They wonder whether she was going to quilt it, or just knot it!"

There was a laugh for the ways of women, a warming of hands over the stove, and then the county attorney said briskly, "Well, let's go right out to the barn and get that cleared up."

"I don't see as there's anything so strange," Mrs. Hale said resentfully, after the outside door had closed on the three men—"our taking up our time with little things while we're waiting for them to get the evidence. I don't see as it's anything to laugh about."

"Of course they've got awful important things on their minds," said the sheriff's wife apologetically.

They returned to an inspection of the blocks for the quilt. Mrs. Hale was looking at the fine, even sewing, preoccupied with thoughts of the woman who had done that sewing, when she heard the sheriff's wife say, in a startled tone, "Why, look at this one."

"The sewing," said Mrs. Peters, in a troubled way. "All the rest of them have been so nice and even—but—

this one. Why, it looks as if she didn't know what she was about!"

Their eyes met—something flashed to life, passed between them; then, as if with an effort, they seemed to pull away from each other. A moment Mrs. Hale sat there, her fingers upon those stitches so unlike the rest of the sewing. Then she had pulled a knot and drawn the threads.

"Oh, what are you doing. Mrs. Hale?" asked the sheriff's wife.

"Just pulling out a stitch or two that's not sewed very good," said Mrs. Hale mildly.

"I don't think we ought to touch things," Mrs. Peters said.

"I'll just finish up this end," answered Mrs. Hale.

She threaded a needle and started to replace bad sewing with good. Then in that thin, timid voice, she heard: "Mrs. Hale!"

"Yes, Mrs. Peters?"

"What do you suppose she was so—nervous about?"

"Oh, *I* don't know," said Mrs. Hale, as if dismissing a thing not important enough to spend much time on. "I don't know as she was—nervous. I sew awful queer sometimes when I'm just tired."

"Well, I must get these clothes wrapped. They may be through sooner than we think. I wonder where I could find a piece of paper—and string."

"In that cupboard, maybe," suggested Mrs. Hale.

One piece of the crazy sewing remained unripped. Mrs. Peters' back turned. Martha Hale scrutinized that piece, compared it with the dainty, accurate stitches of the other blocks. The difference was startling. Holding this block it was hard to remain quiet, as if the distracted thoughts of the woman who had perhaps turned to it to try and quiet herself were communicating themselves to her.

"Here's a bird-cage," Mrs. Peters said. "Did she have a bird, Mrs. Hale?"

"Why, I don't know whether she did or not." She turned to look at the cage Mrs. Peters was holding up. "I've

not been here in so long." She sighed. "There was a man round last year selling canaries cheap—but I don't know as she took one. Maybe she did. She used to sing real pretty herself."

"Seems kind of funny to think of a bird here. But she must have had one—or why would she have a cage? I wonder what happened to it."

"I suppose maybe the cat got it," suggested Mrs. Hale, resuming her sewing.

"No; she didn't have a cat. She's got that feeling some people have about cats—being afraid of them. When they brought her to our house yesterday, my cat got in the room, and she was real upset and asked me to take it out."

"My sister Bessie was like that," laughed Mrs. Hale.

The sheriff's wife did not reply. The silence made Mrs. Hale turn. Mrs. Peters was examining the bird-cage.

"Look at this door," she said slowly. "It's broke. One hinge has been pulled apart."

Mrs. Hale came nearer.

"Looks as if someone must have been—rough with it."

Again their eyes met—startled, questioning, apprehensive. For a moment neither spoke nor stirred. Then Mrs. Hale, turning away, said brusquely. "If they're going to find any evidence, I wish they'd be about it. I don't like this place."

"But I'm awful glad you came with me, Mrs. Hale." Mrs. Peters put the bird-cage on the table and sat down. "It would be lonesome for me—sitting here alone."

"Yes, it would, wouldn't it?" agreed Mrs. Hale. She had picked up the sewing, but now it dropped to her lap, and she murmured: "But I tell you what I *do* wish, Mrs. Peters. I wish I had come over sometimes when she was here. I wish—I had."

"But of course you were awful busy, Mrs. Hale. Your house—and your children."

"I could've come. I stayed away because it weren't cheerful—and that's why I ought to have come. I"—she

looked around—"I've never liked this place. Maybe because it's down in a hollow and you don't see the road. I don't know what it is, but it's a lonesome place, and always was. I wish I had come over to see Minnie Foster sometimes. I can see now—"

"Well, you mustn't reproach yourself. Somehow we just don't see how it is with other folks till—something comes up."

"Not having children makes less work," mused Mrs. Hale, "but it makes a quiet house. And Wright out to work all day—and no company when he did come in. Did you know John Wright, Mrs. Peters?"

"Not to know him. I've seen him in town. They say he was a good man."

"Yes—good," conceded John Wright's neighbour grimly. "He didn't drink, and kept his word as well as most, I guess, and paid his debts. But he was a hard man, Mrs. Peters. Just to pass the time of day with him—" She shivered. "Like a raw wind that gets to the bone." Her eye fell upon the cage on the table before her, and she added, "I should think she would've wanted a bird!"

Suddenly she leaned forward, looking intently at the cage. "But what do you s'pose went wrong with it?"

"I don't know," returned Mrs. Peters; "unless it got sick and died."

But after she said this she reached over and swung the broken door. Both women watched it.

"You didn't know—her?" Mrs. Hale asked.

"Not till they brought her yesterday," said the sheriff's wife.

"She—come to think of it, she was kind of like a bird herself. Real sweet and pretty, but kind of timid and—flutterly. How—she—did—change."

Finally, as if struck with a happy thought and relieved to get back to every-day things: "Tell you what, Mrs. Peters, why don't you take the quilt in with you? It might take up her mind."

"Why, I think that's a real nice idea, Mrs. Hale. There couldn't possibly be any objection to that, could there?

Now, just what will I take? I wonder if her patches are in here?" They turned to the sewing basket.

"Here's some red," said Mrs. Hale, bringing out a roll of cloth. Underneath this was a box. "Here, maybe her scissors are in here—and her things." She held it up. "What a pretty box! I'll warrant that was something she had a long time ago—when she was a girl."

She held it in her hand a moment; then, with a little sigh, opened it.

Instantly her hand went to her nose. "Why!"

Mrs. Peters drew nearer—then turned away.

"There's something wrapped up in this piece of silk," faltered Mrs. Hale.

"This isn't her scissors," said Mrs. Peters, in a shrinking voice.

Mrs. Hale raised the piece of silk. "Oh, Mrs. Peters!" she cried. "It's—"

Mrs. Peters bent closer.

"It's the bird," she whispered.

"But, Mrs. Peters!" cried Mrs. Hale. "*Look* at it! Its *neck*—look at its neck! It's all—other side *to*."

The sheriff's wife again bent closer.

"Somebody wrung its neck," said she, in a voice that was slow and deep.

The eyes of the two women met—this time clung together in a look of dawning comprehension, of growing horror. Mrs. Peters looked from the dead bird to the broken door of the cage. Again their eyes met. And just then there was a sound at the outside door.

Mrs. Hale slipped the box under the quilt pieces in the basket. The county attorney and sheriff came in.

"Well, ladies," said the attorney, as one turning from serious things to little pleasantries, "have you decided whether she was going to quilt it or knot it?"

"We think," said the sheriff's wife hastily, "that she was going to knot it."

"Well, that's very interesting, I'm sure." He caught sight of the cage. "Has the bird flown?"

"We think the cat got it," said Mrs. Hale in a prosaic voice.

He was walking up and down, as if thinking something out.

"Is there a cat?" he asked absently.

Mrs. Hale shot a look up at the sheriff's wife.

"Well, not *now*," said Mrs. Peters. "They're superstitious, you know; they leave."

The county attorney did not heed her. "No sign at all of anyone having come in from the outside," he said to Peters, continuing an interrupted conversation. "Their own rope. Now let's go upstairs again and go over it, piece by piece. It would have to have been someone who knew just the—"

The stair door closed behind them and their voices were lost.

The two women sat motionless, not looking at each other, but as if peering into something and at the same time holding back. When they spoke now it was as if they were afraid of what they were saying, but could not help saying it.

"She liked the bird," said Martha Hale. "She was going to bury it in that pretty box."

"When I was a girl," said Mrs. Peters, under her breath, "my kitten—there was a boy took a hatchet, and before my eyes—before I could get there—" She covered her face an instant. "If they hadn't held me back I would have"—she caught herself, and finished weakly—"hurt him."

Then they sat without speaking or moving.

"I wonder how it would seem," Mrs. Hale began, as if feeling her way over strange ground—"never to have had any children around." Her eyes made a sweep of the kitchen. "No, Wright wouldn't like the bird—a thing that sang. She used to sing. He killed that too."

Mrs. Peters moved. "Of course we don't know who killed the bird."

"I knew John Wright," was the answer.

"It was an awful thing was done in this house that night, Mrs. Hale," said the sheriff's wife. "Killing a man while he slept—slipping a thing round his neck that choked the life out of him."

Mrs. Hale's hand went to the bird-cage. "His neck. Choked the life out of him."

"We don't *know* who killed him," whispered Mrs. Peters wildly. "We don't *know*."

Mrs. Hale had not moved. "If there had been years and years of nothing, then a bird to sing to you, it would be awful—still, after the bird was still."

"I know what stillness is," whispered Mrs. Peters. "When we homesteaded in Dakota, and my first baby died—after he was two years old—and me with no other then—"

Mrs. Hale stirred. "How soon do you suppose they'll be through looking for the evidence?"

"I know what stillness is," repeated Mrs. Peters. Then she too pulled back. "The law has got to punish crime, Mrs. Hale."

"I wish you'd seen Minnie Foster when she wore a white dress with blue ribbons, and stood up there in the choir and sang."

The picture of that girl, the thought that she had lived neighbour to her for twenty years, and had let her die for lack of life, was suddenly more than the woman cold bear.

"Oh, I *wish* I'd come over here once in a while!" she cried. "That was a crime! That was a crime! Who's going to punish *that?*"

"We mustn't—take on," said Mrs. Peters, with a frightened look towards the stairs.

"I might 'a' *known* she needed help! I tell you, it's *queer,* Mrs. Peters. We live close together, and we live far apart. We all go through the same things—it's all just a different kind of the same thing! If it weren't—why do you and I *know*—what we know this minute?"

Seeing the jar of fruit on the table, she reached for it. "If I was you I wouldn't *tell* her her fruit was gone! Tell her it *ain't.* Tell her it's all right—all of it. Here—take this in to prove it to her! She—she may never know whether it was broke or not."

Mrs. Peters took the bottle of fruit as if glad to take it—as if touching a familiar thing, having something to do, could keep her from something else. She looked about for something to wrap the fruit in, took a petticoat from the pile of clothes she had brought from the front room, nervously started winding that round the bottle.

"My!" she began, in a high voice, "it's a good thing the men couldn't hear us! Getting all stirred up over a little thing like a—dead canary. As if that could have anything to do with—with—My, wouldn't they *laugh?*"

There were footsteps on the stairs.

"Maybe they would," muttered Mrs. Hale—"maybe they wouldn't."

"No, Peters," said the county attorney, "it's all perfectly clear, except the reason for doing it. But you know juries when it comes to women. If there was some definite thing—something to *show.* Something to make a story about. A thing that would connect up with this clumsy way of doing it."

Mrs. Hale looked at Mrs. Peters. Mrs. Peters was looking at her. Quickly they looked away from one another. The outer door opened and Mr. Hale came in.

"I've nailed back that board we ripped off," he said.

"Much obliged, Mr. Hale," said the sheriff. "We'll be getting along now."

"I'm going to stay here awhile by myself," the county attorney suddenly announced. "You can send Frank out for me, can't you?" he asked the sheriff. "I want to go over everything. I'm not satisfied we can't do better."

Again, for one brief moment, the women's eyes met.

The sheriff came up to the table.

"Did you want to see what Mrs. Peters was going to take in?"

The county attorney picked up the apron. He laughed.

"Oh, I guess they're not very dangerous things the ladies have picked out."

Mrs. Hale's hand was on the sewing basket in which the box was concealed. She felt that she ought to take her hand off the basket. She did not seem able to. She picked up one of the quilt blocks she had piled on to cover the box. She had a fear that if he took up the basket she would snatch it from him.

But he did not take it. With another laugh he turned away, saying, "No, Mrs. Peters doesn't need supervising. For that matter, a sheriff's wife is married to the law. Ever think of it that way, Mrs. Peters?"

Mrs. Peters had turned her face away. "Not—just that way," she said.

"Married to the law!" chuckled Mrs. Peters' husband. He moved towards the door into the front room, and said to the county attorney, "I just want you to come here a minute, George. We ought to take a look at these windows."

"Oh—windows!" scoffed the county attorney.

"We'll be leaving in a second, Mr. Hale," Mr. Peters told the farmer, as he followed the county attorney into the other room.

"Can't be leavin' too soon to suit me," muttered Hale, and went out.

Again, for one final moment, the two women were alone in that kitchen.

Martha Hale sprang up, her hands tight together, looking at that other woman, with whom it rested. At first she could not see her eyes, for the sheriff's wife had not turned back since she turned away at that suggestion of being married to the law. Slowly, unwillingly, Mrs. Peters turned her head until her eyes met the eyes of the other woman. There was a moment when they held each other in a steady, burning look in which there was no evasion nor flinching. Then Martha Hale's eyes pointed the way to the basket in which was hidden the thing that would convict the third woman—that woman who was not there, and yet who had been there with them through that hour.

For a moment Mrs. Peters did not move. And then she did it. Threw back the quilt pieces, got the box, tried to put it in her hand-bag. It was too big. Desperately she opened it, started to take the bird out. But there she broke—she could not touch the bird. She stood there helpless, foolish.

There was a sound at the door. Martha Hale snatched the box from the sheriff's wife and got it in the pocket of her big coat just as the sheriff and the county attorney came back into the kitchen.

"Well, Henry," said the county attorney, facetiously, "at least we found out that she was not going to quilt it. She was going to—what is it you call it, ladies?"

Mrs. Hale's hand was against the pocket of her coat.

"We call it—knot it," was her answer.

THE END

The conflict in Sam Shepard's *True West* escalates when Austin (Gary Sinise) confronts Lee (John Malkovitch) after a night of stealing toasters.

The Angel appears above Prior Walter in Tony Kushner's *Angels in America, Part I: Millennium Approaches.*

This scene from August Wilson's *Fences* shows how Wilson's attention to the play's social environment has been translated into a detailed mise-en-scène; here, James Earl Jones plays the role of Troy Maxon.

Dion Boucicault

Dion Boucicault (1822–1890) was one of the most prominent and successful playwrights of the nineteenth-century English-speaking world. Born Dionysus Lardner Boursiquot in Dublin, Boucicault was first educated there, and later in England, after his family moved to London in 1828 or 1829. The family was accompanied by Dr. Dionysus Lardner, who remained with and supported Boucicault's mother Anne and her children after Boucicault's father Samuel returned to Dublin; he was probably her lover as well. Although Boucicault was apprenticed as an engineer to Lardner, he fled to the theater where he pursued a long and successful career as playwright, actor, and manager. Boucicault, like most of his contemporaries, was an inventive adapter, and many of his 230 plays are based on the novels and French plays he was paid to bring to the English stage. But he was also a shrewd and original playwright. His first real success as a writer, *London Assurance,* was one of the most popular plays of the century, and was innovative in several respects: staged by Madame Vestris in 1841, it used a **BOX SET,** with practical doors and real furniture onstage, creating a new level of naturalism in the theater. He adapted the durable *Corsican Brothers* for the stage in 1852, providing a great success for the actor/manager Charles Kean, and later for Henry Irving. In 1852 he also met the actress Agnes Robertson—who became his lover and had several children with Boucicault—and left England with her for his first American tour.

Although Boucicault was not an American, many of his most important plays were written and produced in the United States, and take American social issues as their subject. Living in the United States in the 1850s, Boucicault wrote *The Poor of New York* (1857); the play was hugely popular, and Boucicault later adapted it to play in whatever city he was visiting (later versions included *The Poor of Liverpool, The Poor of London,* and so on). He also wrote (and acted in, alongside Agnes) *The Octoroon* in 1859, as well as one of the first of his important Irish melodramas, *The Colleen Bawn,* in 1860. Returning to England, Boucicault capitalized on the vogue of sensation melodrama with *Arrah-na-Pogue* in 1864 and writing, starring in, and touring the United States in *The Shaughraun* in 1874.

Boucicault was involved in all aspects of theater as playwright, actor, and manager (in the era before the rise of the stage director, the actor/manager was typically in charge of assembling the company and of directing the play). Moreover, he was centrally involved in changing the financing of play-production, insisting that the playwright should be granted a percentage of a play's profit onstage, rather than being paid a straight fee or receiving the "benefit" of receipts of a single night's performance; and while he had often been involved in pirating work for the stage, he also pressed for copyright protection for playwrights, whose writing was not protected by copyright legislation. An efficient master of popular theater, Boucicault nonetheless adapted those forms—especially **MELODRAMA**—to original purposes. Although Boucicault's drama slipped into obscurity in the later nineteenth century, several of his plays—especially his American and Irish melodramas—are seen to deploy the conventions of popular theater toward a critique of social injustice.

THE OCTOROON

Adapted from Mayne Reid's novel, *The Quadroon,* and performed on the eve of the American Civil War, *The Octoroon* addresses the "American problem"—slavery—in the sentimental accents of nineteenth-century melodrama. Following the lead of Harriet Beecher Stowe's massively popular novel, *Uncle Tom's Cabin*—a novel that was widely adapted to the stage, and helped to turn popular feeling against slavery—Boucicault develops the standard devices of melodrama: a strong and sensational plot; a central conflict between a malevolent villain and his virtuous and vulnerable victims; and a highly-colored emotional palette. Boucicault's mastery of the form can be seen most easily in the structure of the play: each scene ends with a striking **TABLEAU,** a highly charged scene that focuses on a change in the plot and that usually involves some elaborate stage effects—McClosky discovering the error in Zoe's manumission papers and vowing to own the Octoroon himself; McClosky murdering Paul and seizing the fateful letter that would save Terrebone Plantation (and Zoe) from sale to creditors; McClosky fleeing in his canoe, pursued by the relentless Indian Wahnotee.

Much of Boucicault's skill as a dramatist lies in his ingenious adaptation of the character stereotypes of melodrama, which are given a clearly "American" spin in *The Octoroon*. The heroine of the play—Zoe, played by Agnes Robertson—is an octoroon, one eighth African American, and so is by law susceptible to enslavement and prohibited from marrying a white man (in this case, the play's virtuous hero, George Peyton). Although raised in the Peyton family as a white woman, she is Judge Peyton's "natural"—i.e., illegitimate—daughter by one of his "quadroon" slaves, and so is treated much less formally than the other women; several of the characters—McClosky in particular—order her about much as they would order a household servant, despite her evident refinement. George Peyton arrives at the outset of the play to assume his inheritance: the Terrebone Plantation, which has suffered from years of mismanagement, and is now facing sale to its creditors. Educated in Paris, George has developed both the effete manners and the cultivated sensibilities of a European: while George is the only character onstage to notice—and object to—the way Zoe is treated by others, he has to learn "American" directness in the course of the play. If Zoe and George adapt the conventional heroine and hero of melodrama to the American grain, Boucicault adapts a quintessentially American character-type—the Yankee—to the conventions of melodrama. There are two Yankee types in the play: the current overseer Scudder, a kindly inventor whose good intentions are partly responsible for the collapse of the plantation, and McClosky, the murderous villain of the piece (who, as the previous overseer, took advantage of Judge Peyton and gradually acquired part of the plantation himself). Boucicault's use of "American" stereotypes extends, of course, to characters prominent on the nineteenth-century stage: slaves and Indians. Here, it is a measure of Boucicault's larger aims that the slaves (played in blackface by white actors) are consistently represented as virtuous, loving, and beloved members of the Peyton extended family (this doesn't prevent Boucicault from portraying them as simple, fun-loving, and often lazy), and the Indian Wahnotee—played by Boucicault himself—as the implacable agent of justice (if, again playing to a familiar stereotype, addicted to rum).

Written by an Irishman whose Irish plays reveal a canny critique of British oppression, *The Octoroon* frames the central issue of American history—slavery—in the forms of popular theater. Not surprisingly, then, the ethical and sentimental axes of the play often seem conflicted. Like many melodramas, *The Octoroon* is a "rent-day" play: the tragedy is framed as the virtuous family's loss of their property, the Terrebone Plantation and its slaves. Yet while Boucicault amply visualizes the tragedies associated with slavery onstage—splitting up slave families in the auction scene in act 3, the legal barriers to Zoe's marriage to George, McClosky's purchase of Zoe to be his mistress—the play is not finally able to mount a political critique of the tragedy of slavery itself. Zoe's reluctance to be sold to McClosky is figured in the play in both sentimental terms (she is in love with another man) and in class terms (she is much more refined than the low-class McClosky); she barely mentions the institution of slavery itself, and Boucicault goes out of his way to show her loving sense of gratitude to the deceased Judge Peyton for taking her into his home (the fact that her mother, a "quadroon" slave owned by the Peytons, was probably raped by the Judge, is bypassed in the play). Indeed, the theme of "justice" that runs through the play—How should Zoe be treated by white society? Who owns the plantation? Should McClosky be given the rough justice of a lynching when the murder is discovered? Should George be allowed to marry Zoe?—never quite touches on the fundamental injustice of slavery itself.

Given the political and social context of 1859—the play opened during John Brown's raid on Harper's Ferry, one of the ignition points of the Civil War—it is perhaps not surprising that Zoe kills herself at the end of the play. Although we understand that the Plantation may be saved by the discovery of McClosky's deception (he found and concealed the letter from Liverpool that would have bailed the plantation out of debt, murdering little Paul to get it), no playwright, and no theater, could risk staging miscegenation positively onstage, as the marriage—or even the plausible romance—of George and Zoe would have required. Miscegenation figures in the play, of course, in the mixed-race "problem" posed by Zoe herself, a problem the play is finally unwilling to confront by proposing a "legitimate" marriage between the play's sentimental hero and heroine.

When he brought the play to England, however, Boucicault rewrote the ending of the play. Instead of showing Zoe stealing to the plantation's slave quarters and taking poison, the new version ends the play with the capture of McClosky, revealed in his crime—spectacularly enough—by the photographic plate showing his murderous triumph over the body of Paul. In this version, as the steamship explodes in fire in the background and Wahnotee struggles with and finally kills McClosky, George carries the prostrate body of Zoe—dead? or simply fainted?—ambiguously onstage.

THE OCTOROON
Dion Boucicault

CHARACTERS

GEORGE PEYTON

SALEM SCUDDER

MR SUNNYSIDE

JACOB M'CLOSKY

WAHNOTEE

LAFOUCHE

CAPTAIN RATTS

COLONEL POINTDEXTER

JULES THIBODEAUX

JUDGE CAILLOU

JACKSON

OLD PETE

PAUL, *a boy slave*

SOLON

MRS PEYTON

ZOE

DORA SUNNYSIDE

GRACE

MINNIE

DIDO

ACT ONE

The scene opens on a view of the Plantation Terrebonne, in Louisiana. A branch of the Mississippi is seen winding through the estate. A low-built but extensive planter's dwelling, surrounded with a veranda, and raised a few feet from the ground, occupies the left side. On the right stand a table and chairs. GRACE *is discovered sitting at breakfast-table with the Negro children.*

SOLON: (*Enters, from the house.*) Yah! you bomn'ble fry—git out—a gen'leman can't pass for you.

GRACE: (*Seizing a fly whisk.*) Hee!—ha git out! (*She drives the children away. In escaping, they tumble against* SOLON, *who falls*
5 *with the tray; the children steal the bananas and rolls that fall about.*)

PETE: (*Who is lame, enters; he carries a mop and pail.*) Hey! laws a massey! why, clar out! drop dat banana! I'll murder this yer crowd. (*He chases children about; they leap over railing at*
10 *back.*)

(*Exit* SOLON.)

Dem little niggers is a judgment upon dis generation.

GEORGE: (*Enters, from the house.*) What's the matter, Pete?

PETE: It's dem black trash, Mas'r George; dis ere property wants claring; dem's getting too numerous round: when I
15 gets time I'll kill some on 'em, sure!

GEORGE: They don't seem to be scared by the threat.

PETE: Stop, you varmin! stop till I get enough of you in one place!

GEORGE: Were they all born on this estate?

20 PETE: Guess they nebber was born—dem tings! what, dem?— get away! Born here—dem darkies? What, on Terrebonne! Don't b'lieve it, Mas'r George; dem black tings never was born at all; dey swarmed one mornin' on a sassafras tree in the swamp; I cotched 'em; dey ain't no 'count. Don't be-
25 lieve dey'll turn out niggers when dey're growed; dey'll come out sunthin' else.

GRACE: Yes, Mas'r George, dey was born here; and old Pete is fonder on 'em dan he is of his fiddle on a Sunday.

PETE: What? dem tings—dem? get away. (*Makes blow at the*
30 *children.*) Born here! dem darkies! What, on Terrebonne? Don't b'lieve it, Mas'r George—no. One morning dey swarmed on a sassafras tree in de swamp, and I cotched 'em all in a sieve—dat's how dey come on top of dis yearth—git out, you—ya, ya! (*Laughs.*)

(*Exit* GRACE.)

MRS PEYTON: (*Enters from the house.*) So, Pete, you are spoil- 35 ing those children as usual!

PETE: Dat's right, missus! gib it to ole Pete! he's allers in for it! Git away dere! Ya! if dey ain't all lighted, like coons, on dat snake fence, just out of shot. Look dar! Ya, ya! Dem de-
bils. Ya! 40

MRS PEYTON: Pete, do you hear?

PETE: Git down dar! I'm arter you! (*Hobbles off.*)

MRS PEYTON: You are out early this morning, George.

GEORGE: I was up before daylight. We got the horses saddled, and galloped down the shell road over the Piney Patch; 45 then coasting the Bayou Lake, we crossed the long swamps, by Paul's Path, and so came home again.

MRS PEYTON: (*Laughing.*) You seem already familiar with the names of every spot on the estate.

(*Enter* PETE, *who arranges breakfast.*)

GEORGE: Just one month ago I quitted Paris. I left that siren 50 city as I would have left a beloved woman.

MISS PEYTON: No wonder! I dare say you left at least a dozen beloved women there, at the same time.

GEORGE: I feel that I departed amid universal and sincere re-gret. I left my loves and my creditors equally inconsolable. 55

MRS PEYTON: George, you are incorrigible. Ah! you remind me so much of your uncle, the judge.

GEORGE: Bless his dear old handwriting, it's all I ever saw of him. For ten years his letters came every quarter-day, with a remittance and a word of advice in his formal cavalier style; 60 and then a joke in the postscript, that upset the dignity of the foregoing. Aunt, when he died, two years ago, I read over those letters of his, and if I didn't cry like a baby—

MRS PEYTON: No, George; say you wept like a man. And so you really kept those foolish letters? 65

GEORGE: Yes; I kept the letters, and squandered the money.

MRS PEYTON: (*Embracing him.*) Ah! why were you not my son—you are so like my dear husband.

SCUDDER: (*Enters.*) Ain't he! Yes—when I saw him and Miss Zoe galloping through the green sugar crop, and doing 70 ten dollars' worth of damage at every stride, says I, how like his old uncle he do make the dirt fly.

GEORGE: O, aunt! what a bright, gay creature she is!

SCUDDER: What, Zoe! Guess that you didn't leave anything
75　female in Europe that can lift an eyelash beside that gal. When she goes along, she just leaves a streak of love behind her. It's a good drink to see her come into the cotton fields—the niggers get fresh on the sight of her. If she ain't worth her weight in sunshine you may take one of
80　my fingers off, and choose which you like.

MRS PEYTON: She need not keep us waiting breakfast, though. Pete, tell Miss Zoe that we are waiting.

PETE: Yes, missus. Why, Minnie, why don't you run when you hear, you lazy crittur?

(MINNIE runs off.)

85　Dat's de laziest nigger on dis yere property. (Sitting down.) Don't do nuffin.

MRS PEYTON: My dear George, you are left in your uncle's will heir to this estate.

GEORGE: Subject to your life interest and an annuity to Zoe,
90　is it not so?

MRS PEYTON: I fear that the property is so involved that the strictest economy will scarcely recover it. My dear husband never kept any accounts, and we scarcely know in what condition the estate really is.

95　SCUDDER: Yes, we do, ma'am; it's in a darned bad condition. Ten years ago the judge took as overseer a bit of Connecticut hardware called M'Closky. The judge didn't understand accounts—the overseer did. For a year or two all went fine. The judge drew money like Bourbon whisky from a bar-
100　rel, and never turned off the tap. But out it flew, free for everybody or anybody to beg, borrow, or steal. So it went, till one day the judge found the tap wouldn't run. He looked in to see what stopped it, and pulled out a big mortgage. 'Sign that,' says the overseer; 'it's only a formality.' 'All
105　right,' says the judge, and away went a thousand acres; so at the end of eight years, Jacob M'Closky, Esquire, finds himself proprietor of the richest half of Terrebonne—

GEORGE: But the other half is free.

SCUDDER: No, it ain't; because, just then, what does the judge
110　do, but hire another overseer—a Yankee—a Yankee named Salem Scudder.

MRS PEYTON: O, no, it was—

SCUDDER: Hold on, now! I'm going to straighten this account clear out. What was this here Scudder? Well, he
115　lived in New York by sittin' with his heels up in front of French's Hotel, and inventin'—

GEORGE: Inventing what?

SCUDDER: Improvements—anything, from a stay-lace to a fire-engine. Well, he cut that for the photographing line.
120　He and his apparatus arrived here, took the judge's likeness and his fancy, who made him overseer right off. Well, sir, what does this Scudder do but introduces his inventions and improvements on this estate. His new cotton gins broke down, the steam sugarmills burst up, until he
125　finished off with his folly what Mr M'Closky with his knavery began.

MRS PEYTON: O, Salem! how can you say so? Haven't you worked like a horse?

SCUDDER: No, ma'am, I worked like an ass—an honest one,
130　and that's all. Now, Mr George, between the two overseers, you and that good lady have come to the ground; that is the state of things, just as near as I can fix it.

(ZOE sings without.)

GEORGE: 'Tis Zoe.

SCUDDER: O, I have not spoiled that anyhow. I can't introduce any darned improvement there. Ain't that a cure for 135 old age; it kinder lifts the heart up, don't it?

MRS PEYTON: Poor child! what will become of her when I am gone? If you haven't spoiled her, I fear I have. She has had the education of a lady.

GEORGE: I have remarked that she is treated by the neighbours 140 with a kind of familiar condescension that annoyed me.

SCUDDER: Don't you know that she is the natural daughter of the judge, your uncle, and that old lady thar just adored anything her husband cared for; and this girl, that another woman would 'a' hated, she loves as if she'd been her own 145 child.

GEORGE: Aunt, I am prouder and happier to be your nephew and heir to the ruins of Terrebonne, than I would have been to have had half Louisiana without you.

ZOE: (Enters from the house.) Am I late? Ah! Mr Scudder, good 150 morning.

SCUDDER: Thank'ye. I'm from fair to middlin', like a bamboo cane, much the same all the year round.

ZOE: No; like a sugar cane; so dry outside, one would never think there was so much sweetness within. 155

SCUDDER: Look here: I can't stand that gal! if I stop here, I shall hug her right off. (He sees PETE, who has set his pail down up stage, and gone to sleep on it.) If that old nigger ain't asleep, I'm blamed. Hillo! (He kicks pail from under PETE, and lets him down. Exit.) 160

PETE: Hi! Debbel's in de pail! Whar's breakfass?

(Enter SOLON and DIDO with coffeepot and dishes.)

DIDO: Bless'ee, Missey Zoe, here it be. Dere's a dish of penpans—jess taste, Mas'r George—and here's fried bananas; smell 'em do, sa glosh.

PETE: Hole yer tongue, Dido. Whar's de coffee? (He pours it 165 out.) If it don't stain de cup, your wicked ole life's in danger, sure! dat right! black as nigger; clar as ice. You may drink dat, Mas'r George. (Looks off.) Yah! here's Mas'r Sunnyside, and Missey Dora, jist drove up. Some of you niggers run and hole de hosses; and take dis, Dido. (He gives her cof- 170 feepot to hold, and hobbles off, followed by SOLON and DIDO.)

(Enter SUNNYSIDE and DORA.)

SUNNYSIDE: Good day, ma'am. (He shakes hands with George.) I see we are just in time for breakfast. (He sits.)

DORA: O, none for me; I never eat. (She sits.)

GEORGE: (Aside.) They do not notice Zoe. (Aloud.) You don't 175 see Zoe, Mr Sunnyside.

SUNNYSIDE: Ah! Zoe, girl; are you there?

DORA: Take my shawl, Zoe. (ZOE helps her.) What a good creature she is.

SUNNYSIDE: I dare say, now, that in Europe you have never 180 met any lady more beautiful in person, or more polished in manners, than that girl.

GEORGE: You are right, sir; though I shrank from expressing that opinion in her presence, so bluntly.

185 SUNNYSIDE: Why so?

GEORGE: It may be considered offensive.

SUNNYSIDE: (*Astonished.*) What? I say, Zoe, do you hear that?

DORA: Mr Peyton is joking.

MRS PEYTON: My nephew is not acquainted with our cus-
190   toms in Louisiana, but he will soon understand.

GEORGE: Never, Aunt! I shall never understand how to wound the feelings of any lady; and, if that is the custom here, I shall never acquire it.

DORA: Zoe, my dear, what does he mean?

195 ZOE: I don't know.

GEORGE: Excuse me, I'll light a cigar. (*He goes up.*)

DORA: (*Aside to* ZOE.) Isn't he sweet! O, dear, Zoe, is he in love with anybody?

ZOE: How can I tell?

200 DORA: Ask him, I want to know; don't say I told you to in-
quire, but find out. Minnie, fan me, it is so nice—and his clothes are French, ain't they?

ZOE: I think so; shall I ask him that too?

DORA: No, dear. I wish he would make love to me. When he
205   speaks to one he does it so easy, so gentle; it isn't bar-room style; love lined with drinks, sighs tinged with tobacco— and they say all the women in Paris were in love with him, which I feel *I* shall be. Stop fanning me; what nice boots he wears.

210 SUNNYSIDE: (*To* MRS PEYTON.) Yes, ma'am, I hold a mortgage over Terrebonne; mine's a ninth, and pretty near covers all the property, except the slaves. I believe Mr M'Closky has a bill of sale on them. O, here he is.

(*Enter* M'CLOSKY.)

SUNNYSIDE: Good morning. Mr M'Closky.

215 M'CLOSKY: Good morning, Mr Sunnyside; Miss Dora, your servant.

DORA: (*Seated.*) Fan me, Minnie.— (*Aside.*) I don't like that man.

M'CLOSKY: (*Aside.*) Insolent as usual.—(*Aloud.*) You begged
220   me to call this morning. I hope I'm not intruding.

MRS PEYTON: My nephew, Mr Peyton.

M'CLOSKY: O, how d'ye do, sir? (*He offers his hand,* GEORGE *bows coldly. Aside.*) A puppy—if he brings any of his European airs here we'll fix him.—(*Aloud.*) Zoe, tell Pete to
225   give my mare a feed, will ye?

GEORGE: (*Angrily.*) Sir!

M'CLOSKY: Hillo! did I tread on ye?

MRS PEYTON: What is the matter with George?

ZOE: (*Takes fan from* MINNIE.) Go, Minnie, tell Pete; run! (*Exit*
230   MINNIE.)

MRS PEYTON: Grace, attend to Mr M'Closky.

M'CLOSKY: A julep, gal, that's my breakfast, and a bit of cheese.

GEORGE: (*Aside to* MRS PEYTON.) How can you ask that vul-
235   gar ruffian to your table!

MRS PEYTON: Hospitality in Europe is a courtesy: here, it is an obligation. We tender food to a stranger, not because he is a gentleman, but because he is hungry.

GEORGE: Aunt, I will take my rifle down to the Atchafalaya.
240   Paul has promised me a bear and a deer or two. I see my

little Nimrod yonder, with his Indian companion. Excuse me, ladies. Ho! Paul! (*He enters house.*)

PAUL: (*Outside.*) I'ss, Mas'r George.

(*Enter* PAUL *with the Indian.*)

SUNNYSIDE: It's a shame to allow that young cub to run over the swamps and woods, hunting and fishing his life away 245 instead of hoeing cane.

MRS PEYTON: The child was a favourite of the judge, who encouraged his gambols. I couldn't bear to see him put to work.

GEORGE: (*Returning with rifle.*) Come, Paul, are you ready? 250

PAUL: I'ss Mas'r George. O, golly! ain't that a pooty gun.

M'CLOSKY: See here, you imp; if I catch you, and your redskin yonder, gunning in my swamps, I'll give you rats, mind. Them vagabonds, when the game's about, shoot my pigs.

(GEORGE *goes into house.*)

PAUL: You gib me rattan, Mas'r Clostry, but I guess you take a 255 berry long stick to Wahnotee. Ugh, he make bacon of you.

M'CLOSKY: Make bacon of me, you young whelp! Do you mean that I'm a pig? Hold on a bit. (*He seizes whip and holds* PAUL.)

ZOE: O, sir! don't, pray, don't. 260

M'CLOSKY: (*Slowly lowering his whip.*) Darn you, redskin, I'll pay you off some day, both of ye. (*He returns to table and drinks.*)

SUNNYSIDE: That Indian is a nuisance. Why don't he return to his nation out West? 265

M'CLOSKY: He's too fond of thieving and whiskey.

ZOE: No; Wahnotee is a gentle, honest creature, and remains here because he loves that boy with the tenderness of a woman. When Paul was taken down with the swamp fever the Indian sat outside the hut, and neither ate, slept, 270 nor spoke for five days, till the child could recognise and call him to his bedside. He who can love so well is hon-est—don't speak ill of poor Wahnotee.

MRS PEYTON: Wahnotee, will you go back to your people?

WAHNOTEE: Sleugh. 275

PAUL: He don't understand; he speaks a mash-up of Indian and Mexican. Wahnotee Patira na sepau assa wigiran?

WAHNOTEE: Weal Omenee.

PAUL: Says he'll go if I'll go with him. He calls me Omenee, the Pigeon, and Miss Zoe is Ninemoosha, the Sweetheart. 280

WAHNOTEE: (*Pointing to* ZOE.) Ninemoosha.

ZOE: No, Wahnotee, we can't spare Paul.

PAUL: If Omenee remain, Wahnotee will die in Terrebonne.

(*During the dialogue,* WAHNOTEE *has taken* GEORGE's *gun.*)

GEORGE: (*Enters.*) Now I'm ready. (GEORGE *tries to regain his gun;* WAHNOTEE *refuses to give it up;* PAUL *quietly takes it from* 285 *him and remonstrates with him.*)

DORA: Zoe, he's going; I want him to stay and make love to me, that's what I came for today.

MRS PEYTON: George, I can't spare Paul for an hour or two; he must run over to the landing; the steamer from New 290 Orleans passed up the river last night, and if there's a mail they have thrown it ashore.

SUNNYSIDE: I saw the mailbags lying in the shed this morning.

MRS PEYTON: I expect an important letter from Liverpool; away with you, Paul; bring the mailbags here.

295 PAUL: I'm 'most afraid to take Wahnotee to the shed, there's rum there.

WAHNOTEE: Rum!

PAUL: Come, then, but if I catch you drinkin', O, laws a mussey, you'll get snakes! I'll gib it you! now mind. (*Exits*

300 *with Indian.*)

GEORGE: Come, Miss Dora, let me offer you my arm.

DORA: Mr George, I am afraid, if all we hear is true, you have led a dreadful life in Europe.

GEORGE: That's a challenge to begin a description of my fem-

305 inine adventures.

DORA: You have been in love, then?

GEORGE: Two hundred and forty-nine times! Let me relate you the worst cases.

DORA: No! no!

310 GEORGE: I'll put the naughty parts in French.

DORA: I won't hear a word! O, you horrible man! go on. (GEORGE *and* DORA *go into the house.*)

M'CLOSKY: Now, ma'am, I'd like a little business, if agreeable. I bring you news; your banker, old Lafouche, of New Or-

315 leans, is dead; the executors are winding up his affairs, and have foreclosed on all overdue mortgages, so Terrebonne is for sale. Here's the *Picayune* (*Producing paper.*) with the advertisement.

ZOE: Terrebonne for sale!

320 MRS PEYTON: Terrebonne for sale, and you, sir, will doubtless become its purchaser.

M'CLOSKY: Well, ma'am, I s'pose there's no law agin my bidding for it. The more bidders, the better for you. You'll take care, I guess, it don't go too cheap.

325 MRS PEYTON: O, sir, I don't value the place for its price, but for the many happy days I've spent here; that landscape, flat and uninteresting though it may be, is full of charm for me, those poor people, born around me, growing up about my heart, have bounded my view of life; and now

330 to lose that homely scene, lose their black, ungainly faces! O, sir, perhaps you should be as old as I am, to feel as I do, when my past life is torn away from me.

M'CLOSKY: I'd be darned glad if somebody would tear my past life away from *me*. Sorry I can't help you, but the fact

335 is, you're in such an all-fired mess that you couldn't be pulled out without a derrick.

MRS PEYTON: Yes, there is a hope left yet, and I cling to it. The house of Mason Brothers, of Liverpool, failed some twenty years ago in my husband's debt.

340 M'CLOSKY: They owed him over fifty thousand dollars.

MRS PEYTON: I cannot find the entry in my husband's accounts; but you, Mr M'Closky, can doubtless detect it. Zoe, bring here the judge's old desk; it is in the library.

(*Exit* ZOE *to the house.*)

M'CLOSKY: You don't expect to recover any of this old debt,

345 do you?

MRS PEYTON: Yes; the firm has recovered itself, and I received a notice two months ago that some settlement might be anticipated.

SUNNYSIDE: Why, with principal and interest this debt has

350 been more than doubled in twenty years.

MRS PEYTON: But it may be years yet before it will be paid off, if ever.

SUNNYSIDE: If there's a chance of it, there's not a planter round here who wouldn't lend you the whole cash, to keep your name and blood amongst us. Come, cheer up, 355 old friend.

MRS PEYTON: Ah! Sunnyside, how good you are; so like my poor Peyton. (*Exit* MRS PEYTON *and* SUNNYSIDE *to the house.*)

M'CLOSKY: Curse their old families—they cut me—a bilious, 360 conceited, thin lot of dried-up aristocracy. I hate 'em. Just because my grandfather wasn't some broken-down Virginia transplant, or a stingy old Creole, I ain't fit to sit down to the same meat with them. It makes my blood so hot I feel my heart hiss. I'll sweep these Peytons from this section 365 of the country. Their presence keeps alive the reproach against me that I ruined them. Yet, if this money should come! Bah! There's no chance of it. Then, if they go, they'll take Zoe—she'll follow them. Darn that girl; she makes me quiver when I think of her; she's took me for all I'm worth. 370

(*Enter* ZOE *from house, with the desk.*)

M'CLOSKY: O, here, do you know what the annuity the old judge left you is worth today? Not a picayune.

ZOE: It is surely worth the love that dictated it: here are the papers and accounts. (*Putting the desk on the table.*)

M'CLOSKY: Stop, Zoe; come here! How would you like to 375 rule the house of the richest planter on Atchafalaya—eh? or say the word, and I'll buy this old barrack, and you shall be mistress of Terrebonne.

ZOE: O, sir, do not speak so to me!

M'CLOSKY: Why not! look here, these Peytons are bust; cut 380 'em; I am rich, jine me; I'll set you up grand, and we'll give these first families here our dust, until you'll see their white skins shrivel up with hate and rage; what d'ey say?

ZOE: Let me pass! O, pray, let me go!

M'CLOSKY: What, you won't, won't ye? If young George Pey- 385 ton was to make you the same offer, you'd jump at it pretty darned quick, I guess. Come, Zoe, don't be a fool; I'd marry you if I could, but you know I can't; so just say what you want. Here, then, I'll put back these Peytons in Terrebonne, and they shall know you done it; yes, they'll 390 have you to thank for saving them from ruin.

ZOE: Do you think they would live here on such terms?

M'CLOSKY: Why not? We'll hire out our slaves, and live on their wages.

ZOE: But I'm not a slave. 395

M'CLOSKY: No; if you were I'd buy you, if you cost all I'm worth.

ZOE: Let me pass!

M'CLOSKY: Stop.

SCUDDER: (*Enters.*) Let her pass. 400

M'CLOSKY: Eh?

SCUDDER: Let her pass! (*He takes out his knife. Exit* ZOE *to house.*)

M'CLOSKY: Is that you, Mr Overseer? (*He examines paper.*)

SCUDDER: Yes, I'm here, somewhere, interferin'. 405

M'CLOSKY: (*Sitting.*) A pretty mess you've got this estate in—

SCUDDER: Yes—me and Co.— we done it; but, as you were senior partner in the concern, I reckon you got the big lick.

M'CLOSKY: What d'ye mean?

410 SCUDDER: Let me proceed by illustration. (*Sits.*) Look thar! (*Points with his knife off.*) D'ye see that tree?—it's called a live oak, and is a native here; beside it grows a creeper; year after year that creeper twines its long arms round and round the tree—sucking the earth dry all about its roots—

415 living on its life—overrunning its branches, until at last the live oak withers and dies out. Do you know what the niggers round here call that sight? they call it the Yankee hugging the Creole.

M'CLOSKY: Mr. Scudder, I've listened to a great many of your

420 insinuations, and now I'd like to come to an understanding what they mean. If you want a quarrel!—

SCUDDER: No, I'm the skurriest crittur at a fight you ever see; my legs have been too well brought up to stand and see my body abused; I take good care of myself, I can tell you.

425 M'CLOSKY: Because I heard that you had traduced my character.

SCUDDER: Traduced! Whoever said so lied. I always said you were the darndest thief that ever escaped a white jail to misrepresent the North to the South.

430 M'CLOSKY: (*Raises hand to back of his neck.*) What!

SCUDDER: Take your hand down—take it down.(M'CLOSKY *lowers his hand.*) Whenever I gets into company like yours, I always start with the advantage on my side.

M'CLOSKY: What d'ye mean?

435 SCUDDER: I mean that before you could draw that bowie knife, you wear down your back, I'd cut you into shingles. Keep quiet, and let's talk sense. You wanted to come to an understanding, and I'm coming thar as quick as I can. Now, Jacob M'Closky, you despise me because you think

440 I'm a fool; I despise you because I know you to be a knave. Between us we've ruined these Peytons; you fired the judge, and I finished off the widow. Now, I feel bad about my share in the business. I'd give half the balance of my life to wipe out my part of the work. Many a night

445 I've laid awake and thought how to pull them through, till I've cried like a child over the sum I couldn't do; and you know how darned hard 'tis to make a Yankee cry.

M'CLOSKY: Well, what's that to me?

SCUDDER: Hold on, Jacob, I'm coming to that—I tell ye, I'm

450 such a fool—I can't bear the feeling, it keeps at me like a skin complaint, and if this family is sold up—

M'CLOSKY: What then?

SCUDDER: (*Rising.*) I'd cut my throat—or yours—yours I'd prefer.

455 M'CLOSKY: Would you now? why don't you do it?

SCUDDER: 'Cos I's skeered to try! I never killed a man in my life—and civilisation is so strong in me I guess I couldn't do it—I'd like to, though!

M'CLOSKY: And all for the sake of that old woman and that

460 young puppy—eh? No other cause to hate—to envy me—to be jealous of me—eh?

SCUDDER: Jealous? what for?

M'CLOSKY: Ask the colour in your face: d'ye think I can't read you, like a book? With your New England hypocrisy, you

465 would persuade yourself that it was this family alone you cared for; it ain't—you know it ain't—'t is the 'Octoroon'; and you love her as I do; and you hate me because I'm your rival—that's where the tears come from, Salem Scudder, if you ever shed any—that's where the shoe pinches.

470 SCUDDER: Wal, I do like the gal; she's a—

M'CLOSKY: She's in love with young Peyton; it make me curse whar it made you cry, as it does now; I see the tears on your cheeks now.

SCUDDER: Look at 'em Jacob, for they are honest water from

475 the well of truth. I ain't ashamed of it—I do love the gal; but I ain't jealous of you, because I believe the only sincere feeling about you is your love for Zoe, and it does your heart good to have her image thar; but I believe you put it thar to spile. By fair means I don't think you can get

480 her, and don't you try foul with her, 'cause if you do, Jacob, civilisation be darned, I'm on you like a painter, and when I'm drawed out I'm pizin.

(*Exit* SCUDDER *to house.*)

M'CLOSKY: Fair or foul, I'll have her—take that home with you! (*He opens desk.*) What's here—judgment? yes, plenty of 'em; bill of costs; account with Citizens' Bank—what's

485 this? "Judgment, $40,000, 'Thibodeaux against Peyton,'"—surely, that is the judgment under which this estate is now advertised for sale—(*He takes up paper and examines it.*) yes, 'Thibodeaux against Peyton, 1838.' Hold

490 on! whew! this is worth taking to—in this desk the judge used to keep one paper I want—this should be it. (*Reads.*) 'The free papers of my daughter Zoe, registered February 4th, 1841.' Why, Judge, wasn't you lawyer enough to know that while a judgment stood against you it was a lien on

495 your slaves? Zoe is your child by a quadroon slave, and you didn't free her; blood! if this is so, she's mine! this old Liverpool debt—that may cross me—if it only arrive too late—if it don't come by this mail—Hold on! this letter the old lady expects—that's it; let me only head off that

500 letter, and Terrebonne will be sold before they can recover it. That boy and the Indian have gone down to the landing for the post-bags; they'll idle on the way as usual? my mare will take me across the swamp, and before they can reach the shed, I'll have purified them bags—ne'er a let-

505 ter shall show this mail. Ha, ha!—(*Calls.*) Pete, you old turkey-buzzard, saddle my mare. Then, if I sink every dollar I'm worth in her purchase, I'll own that Octoroon.

ACT TWO

The wharf with goods, boxes, and bales scattered about—a camera on a stand; DORA *being photographed by* SCUDDER, *who is arranging photographic apparatus,* GEORGE *and* PAUL *looking on at back.*

SCUDDER: Just turn your face a leetle this way—fix your—let's see—look here.

DORA: So?

SCUDDER: That's right. (*Putting his head under the darkening apron.*) It's such a long time since I did this sort of thing, and this old machine has got so dirty and stiff, I'm afraid

5 it won't operate. That's about right. Now don't stir.

PAUL: Ugh! she looks as though she war gwine to have a tooth drawed!

SCUDDER: I've got four plates ready, in case we miss the first shot. One of them is prepared with a self-developing liq-

10 uid that I've invented. I hope it will turn out better than most of my notions. Now fix yourself. Are you ready?

DORA: Ready!

SCUDDER: Fire!—one, two, three. (SCUDDER *takes out watch*.)

15 PAUL: Now it's cooking; laws mussey? I feel it all inside, as if I was at a lottery.

SCUDDER: So! (*Throws down apron.*) That's enough. (*Withdrawing slide, turns and sees* PAUL.) What! what are you doing there, you young varmint! Ain't you took them bags
20 to the house yet?

PAUL: Now, it ain't no use trying to get mad, Mas'r Scudder. I'm gwine! I only come back to find Wahnotee; whar is dat ign'ant Injiun?

SCUDDER: You'll find him scenting round the rum store,
25 hitched up by the nose. (*Goes into the room.*)

PAUL: (*Calling at the door.*) Say, Mas'r Scudder, take me in dat telescope?

SCUDDER: (*Inside the room.*) Get out, you cub! clar out!

PAUL: You got four of dem dishes ready. Gosh, wouldn't I like
30 to hab myself took! What's de charge, Mas'r Scudder? (*He runs off.*)

SCUDDER: (*Enters from the room.*) Job had none of them critters on his plantation, else he'd never ha' stood through so many chapters. Well, that has come out clear, ain't it?
35 (*Showing the plate.*)

DORA: O, beautiful! Look, Mr Peyton.

GEORGE: (*Looking.*) Yes, very fine!

SCUDDER: The apparatus can't mistake. When I traveled round with this machine, the homely folks used to sing
40 out, 'Hillo, mister, this ain't like me!' 'Ma'am,' says I, 'the apparatus can't mistake.' 'But, mister, that ain't my nose.' 'Ma'am, your nose drawed it. The machine can't err—you may mistake your phiz but the apparatus don't.' 'But, sir, it ain't agreeable.' 'No, ma'am, the truth seldom is.'

45 PETE: (*Enters, puffing.*) Mas'r Scudder! Mas'r Scudder!

SCUDDER: Hillo! what are you blowing about like a steamboat with one wheel for?

PETE: *You* blow, Mas'r Scudder, when I tole you: dere's a man from Noo Aleens just arriv'd at de house, and he's
50 stuck up two papers on de gates: 'For sale—dis yer property,' and a heap of oder tings—an he seen missus, and arter he shown some papers she burst out crying— I yelled; den de corious of little niggers dey set up, den de hull plantation children—de live stock reared up and
55 created a purpiration of lamentation as did de ole heart good to har.

DORA: What's the matter?

SCUDDER: He's come.

PETE: Dass it—I saw 'm!

60 SCUDDER: The sheriff from New Orleans has taken possession—Terrebonne is in the hands of the law.

ZOE: (*Enters.*) O, Mr Scudder! Dora! Mr Peyton! come home—there are strangers in the house.

DORA: Stay, Mr Peyton: Zoe, a word! (*She leads her forward—*
65 *aside.*) Zoe, the more I see of George Peyton the better I like him; but he is too modest—that is a very impertinent virtue in a man.

ZOE: I'm no judge, dear.

DORA: Of course not, you little fool; no one ever made love
70 to you, and you can't understand; I mean, that George knows I am an heiress; my fortune would release this estate from debt.

ZOE: O, I see!

DORA: If he would only propose to marry me I would accept him, but he don't know that, and he will go on fooling, in 75 his slow European way, until it is too late.

ZOE: What's to be done?

DORA: You tell him.

ZOE: What? that he isn't to go on fooling in his slow—

DORA: No, you goose! twit him on his silence and abstrac- 80 tion—I'm sure it's plain enough, for he has not spoken two words to me all the day; then joke round the subject, and at last speak out.

SCUDDER: Pete, as you came here, did you pass Paul and the Indian with the letter-bags? 85

PETE: No, sar; but dem vagabonds neber take the 'specable straight road, dey goes by de swamp. (*Exits up the path.*)

SCUDDER: Come, sir!

DORA: (*To* ZOE.) Now's your time.—(*Aloud.*) Mr Scudder, take us with you—Mr Peyton is so slow, there's no getting 90 him on.

(*Exit* DORA *and* SCUDDER.)

ZOE: They are gone!—(*Glancing at* GEORGE.) Poor fellow, he has lost all.

GEORGE: Poor child! how sad she looks now she has no resource. 95

ZOE: How shall I ask him to stay?

GEORGE: Zoe, will you remain here? I wish to speak to you.

ZOE: (*Aside.*) Well, that saves trouble.

GEORGE: By our ruin you lose all.

ZOE: O, I'm nothing; think of yourself. 100

GEORGE: I can think of nothing but the image that remains face to face with me; so beautiful, so simple, so confiding, that I dare not express the feelings that have grown up so rapidly in my heart.

ZOE: (*Aside.*) He means Dora. 105

GEORGE: If I dared to speak!

ZOE: That's just what you must do, and do it at once, or it will be too late.

GEORGE: Has my love been divined?

ZOE: It has been more than suspected. 110

GEORGE: Zoe, listen to me, then. I shall see this estate pass from me without a sigh, for it possesses no charm for me; the wealth I covet is the love of those around me—eyes that are rich in fond looks, lips that breathe endearing words; the only estate I value is the heart of one true 115 woman, and the slaves I'd have are her thoughts.

ZOE: George, George, your words take away my breath!

GEORGE: The world, Zoe, the free struggle of minds and hands is before me; the education bestowed on me by my dear uncle is a noble heritage which no sheriff can seize; 120 with that I can build up a fortune, spread a roof over the heads I love, and place before them the food I have earned; I will work—

ZOE: Work! I thought none but coloured people worked.

GEORGE: Work, Zoe, is the salt that gives savour to life. 125

ZOE: Dora said you were slow; if she could hear you now—

GEORGE: Zoe, you are young; your mirror must have told you that you are beautiful. Is your heart free?

ZOE: Free? of course it is!

GEORGE: We have known each other but a few days, but to 130 me those days have been worth all the rest of my life. Zoe, you have suspected the feeling that now commands an utterance—you have seen that I love you.

ZOE: Me! you love *me*?

135 GEORGE: As my wife—the sharer of my hopes, my ambitions, and my sorrows; under the shelter of your love I could watch the storms of fortune pass unheeded by.

ZOE: *My* love! *My* love? George, you know not what you say! *I* the sharer of your sorrows—your wife! Do you know 140 what I am?

GEORGE: Your birth—I know it. Has not my dear aunt forgotten it—she who had the most right to remember it? You are illegitimate, but love knows no prejudice.

ZOE: (*Aside.*) Alas! he does not know, he does not know! and 145 will despise me, spurn me, loathe me, when he learns who, what, he has so loved—(*Aloud.*) George, O, forgive me! Yes, I love you—I did not know it until your words showed me what has been in my heart; each of them awoke a new sense, and now I know how unhappy—how 150 very unhappy I am.

GEORGE: Zoe, what have I said to wound you?

ZOE: Nothing; but you must learn what I thought you already knew. George you cannot marry me; the laws forbid it!

155 GEORGE: Forbid it?

ZOE: There is a gulf between us, as wide as your love, as deep as my despair; but, O, tell me, say you will pity me! that you will not throw me from you like a poisoned thing!

GEORGE: Zoe, explain yourself—your language fills me with 160 shapeless fears.

ZOE: And what shall I say?—I—my mother was—no, no—not her! Why should I refer the blame to her? George, do you see that hand you hold? look at these fingers; do you see the nails are of a bluish tinge?

165 GEORGE: Yes, near the quick there is a faint blue mark.

ZOE: Look in my eyes; is not the same colour in the white?

GEORGE: It is their beauty.

ZOE: Could you see the roots of my hair you would see the same dark, fatal mark. Do you know what that is?

170 GEORGE: No.

ZOE: That is the ineffaceable curse of Cain. Of the blood that feeds my heart, one drop in eight is black—bright red as the rest may be, that one drop poisons all the flood; those seven bright drops give me love like yours—hope like 175 yours—ambition like yours—life hung with passions like dewdrops on the morning flowers; but the one black drop gives me despair, for I'm an unclean thing—forbidden by the laws—I'm an Octoroon!

GEORGE: Zoe, I love you none the less; this knowledge brings 180 no revolt to my heart, and I can overcome the obstacle.

ZOE: But *I* cannot.

GEORGE: We can leave this country, and go far away where none can know.

ZOE: And you mother, she who from infancy treated me with 185 such fondness, she who, as you said, has most reason to spurn me, can she forget what I am? Will she gladly see you wedded to the child of her husband's slave? No! she would revolt from it, as all but you would; and if I consented to hear the cries of my heart, if I did not crush out 190 my infant love, what would she say to the poor girl on whom she had bestowed so much? No, no!

GEORGE: Zoe, must we immolate our lives on her prejudice?

ZOE: Yes, for I'd rather be black than ungrateful! Ah, George, our race has at least one virtue—it knows how to suffer!

GEORGE: Each word you utter makes my love sink deeper 195 into my heart.

ZOE: And I remained here to induce you to offer that heart to Dora!

GEORGE: If you bid me do so I will obey you—

ZOE: No, no! if you cannot be mine, O, let me not blush 200 when I think of you.

GEORGE: Dearest Zoe! (*Exit* GEORGE *and* ZOE. *As they exit,* M'CLOSKY *rises from behind a rock and looks after them.*)

M'CLOSKY: She loves him! I felt it—and how she can love! (*Advances.*) That one black drop of blood burns in her 205 veins and lights up her heart like a foggy sun. O, how I lapped up her words, like a thirsty bloodhound! I'll have her, if it costs me my life! Yonder the boy still lurks with those mail-bags; the devil still keeps him here to tempt me, darn his yellow skin! I arrived just too late, he had 210 grabbed the prize as I came up. Hillo! he's coming this way, fighting with his Injiun. (*Conceals himself.*)

PAUL: (*Enters, wrestling with* WAHNOTEE.) It ain't no use now: you got to gib it up!

WAHNOTEE: Ugh! 215

PAUL: It won't do! You got dat bottle of rum hid under your blanket—gib it up now, you—Yar! (*Wrenching it from him.*) You nasty, lying Injiun! It's no use you putting on airs; I ain't gwine to sit up wid you all night and you drunk. Hillo! war's de crowd gone? And dar's de 'paratus—O, 220 gosh, if I could take a likeness ob dis child! Uh—uh, let's have a peep. (*Looking through camera.*) O, golly! yar, you Wahnotee! you stan' dar, I see you. Ta demine usti. (*He looks at* WAHNOTEE *through the camera;* WAHNOTEE *springs back with an expression of alarm.*) 225

WAHNOTEE: No tue Wahnotee.

PAUL: Ha, ha! he tinks it's a gun. You ign'ant Injiun, it can't hurt you! Stop, here's dem dishes—plates—dat's what he call 'em, all fix: I see Mas'r Scudder do it often—tink I can take likeness—stay dere, Wahnotee. 230

WAHNOTEE: No, carabine tue.

PAUL: I must operate and take my own likeness too—how debbel I do dat? Can't be ober dar an' here too—I ain't twins. Ugh! ach! 'Top; you look, you Wahnotee; you see dis rag, eh? Well when I say go, den lift dis rag like dis, see! 235 den run to dat pine tree up dar (*Points.*) and back ag'in, and den pull down de rag so, d'ye see?

WAHNOTEE: Hugh!

PAUL: Den you hab glass ob rum.

WAHNOTEE: Rum! 240

PAUL: Dat wakes him up. Coute, Wahnotee in omenee dit go Wahnotee, poina la fa, comb a pine tree, la revieut sala, la fa.

WAHNOTEE: Firewater!

PAUL: Yes, den a glass ob firewater; now den. (*Throwing mail-* 245 *bags down and sitting on them.*) Pret, now den go.

(WAHNOTEE *raises the apron and runs off.* PAUL *sits for his picture—*M'CLOSKY *appears.*)

M'CLOSKY: Where are they? Ah, yonder goes the Indian!

PAUL: De time he gone just 'bout enough to cook dat dish plate.

250 M'CLOSKY: Yonder is the boy—now is my time! What's he doing; is he asleep? (*Advancing.*) He is sitting on my prize! darn his carcass! I'll clear him off there—he'll never know what stunned him. (*He takes Indian's tomahawk and steals to* PAUL.)

255 PAUL: Dam dat Injiun! is dat him creeping dar? I daren't move fear to spile myself. (M'CLOSKY *strikes him on the head—he falls dead.*)

M'CLOSKY: Horraw; the bags are mine—now for it!—(*Opening the mail-bags.*) What's here? Sunnyside, Pointdexter,
260 Jackson, Peyton; here it is—the Liverpool postmark, sure enough!—(*Opening letter—reads.*) 'Madam, we are instructed by the firm of Mason and Co., to inform you that a dividend of forty per cent is payable on the first prox-
265 imo, this amount in consideration of position, they send herewith, and you will find enclosed by draft to your order, on the Bank of Louisiana, which please acknowledge—the balance will be paid in full, with interest, in three, six, and nine months—your drafts on Mason Broth-
270 ers at those dates will be accepted by La Palisse and Compagnie, N. O., so that you may command immediate use of the whole amount at once, if required. Yours, etc., James Brown.' What a find! this infernal letter would have saved all. (*During the reading of the letter, he remains nearly motionless under the focus of the camera.*) But now I guess it will
275 arrive too late—these darned U.S. mails are to blame. The Injiun! he must not see me. (*Exits rapidly.*)

(WAHNOTEE *runs on, and pulls down the apron. He sees* PAUL, *lying on the ground, and speaks to him, thinking that he is shamming sleep. He gesticulates and jabbers to him and moves him with his feet, then kneels down to rouse him. To his horror he finds him dead. Expressing great grief he raises his eyes and they fall upon the camera. Rising with a savage growl, he seizes the tomahawk and smashes the camera to pieces. Going to* PAUL *he expresses in pantomime grief, sorrow, and fondness, and takes him in his arms to carry him away.*)

ACT THREE

A room in MRS PEYTON's *house showing the entrance on which an auction bill is pasted.* SOLON *and* GRACE *are there.*

PETE: (*Outside.*) Dis way—dis way.

(*Enter* PETE, POINTDEXTER, JACKSON, LAFOUCHE, *and* CAILLOU.)

PETE: Dis way, gen'l'men; now, Solon—Grace—dey's hot and tirsty—sangaree, brandy, rum.
JACKSON: Well, what d'ye say, Lafouche—d'ye smile?

(*Enter* THIBODEAUX *and* SUNNYSIDE.)

5 THIBODEAUX: I hope we don't intrude on the family.
PETE: You see dat hole in dar, sar? I was raised on dis yar plantation—nebber see no door in it—always open, sar, for stranger to walk in.
SUNNYSIDE: And for substance to walk out.
10 RATTS: (*Enters.*) Fine southern style that, eh!
LAFOUCHE: (*Reading the bill.*) 'A fine, well-built old family mansion, replete with every comfort.'
RATTS: There's one name on the list of slaves scratched, I see.

LAFOUCHE: Yes; No. 49, Paul, a quadroon boy, aged thirteen.
SUNNYSIDE: He's missing. 15
POINTDEXTER: Run away, I suppose.
PETE: (*Indignantly.*) No, sar; nigger nebber cut stick on Terrebonne; dat boy's dead, sure.
RATTS: What, Picayune Paul, as we called him, that used to come abroad my boat?—poor little darkey, I hope not; 20 many a picayune he picked up for his dance and nigger songs, and he supplied our table with fish and game from the Bayous.
PETE: Nebber supply no more, sar—nebber dance again. Mas'r Ratts, you hard him sing about de place where de 25 good niggers go, de last time.
RATTS: Well!
PETE: Well, he gone dar hisself; why I tink so—'cause we missed Paul for some days, but nebber tout nothin' till one night dat Injiun Wahnotee suddenly stood right dar 30 'mongst us—was in his war paint, and mighty cold and grave—he sit down by de fire. 'Whar's Paul?' I say—he smoke and smoke, but nebber look out ob de fire; well knowing dem critters, I wait a long time—den he say, 'Wahnotee great chief'; den I say nothing—smoke anoder 35 time—last, rising to go, he turn round at door, and say berry low—O, like a woman's voice he say, 'Omenee Pangeuk'—dat is, Paul is dead—nebber see him since.
RATTS: That redskin killed him.
SUNNYSIDE: So we believe; and so mad are the folks around, 40 if they catch the redskin they'll lynch him sure.
RATTS: Lynch him! Darn his copper carcass, I've got a set of Irish deck-hands abroad that just loved that child; and after I tell them this, let them get a sight of the redskin, I believe they would eat him, tomahawk and all. Poor little 45 Paul!
THIBODEAUX: What was he worth?
RATTS: Well, near on five hundred dollars.
PETE: (*Scandalised.*) What, sar! You p'tend to be sorry for Paul, and prize him like dat! Five hundred dollars! (*To* THI- 50 BODEAUX.) T'ousand dollars, Massa Thibodeau.
SCUDDER: (*Enters.*) Gentlemen, the sale takes place at three. Good morning, Colonel. It's near that now, and there's still the sugarhouses to be inspected. Good day, Mr Thibodeaux—shall we drive down that way? Mr Lafouche, why, 55 how do you do, sir? you're looking well.
LAFOUCHE: Sorry I can't return the compliment.
RATTS: Salem's looking a kinder hollowed out.
SCUDDER: What, Mr Ratts, are you going to invest in swamps? 60
RATTS: No; I want a nigger.
SCUDDER: Hush.
PETE: Eh! wass dat?
SCUDDER: Mr Sunnyside, I can't do this job of showin' round the folks; my stomach goes agin it. I want Pete here a 65 minute.
SUNNYSIDE: I'll accompany them certainly.
SCUDDER: (*Eagerly.*) Will ye? Thank ye; thank ye.
SUNNYSIDE: We must excuse Scudder, friends. I'll see you round the estate. 70

(*Enter* GEORGE *and* MRS PEYTON.)

LAFOUCHE: Good morning, Mrs Peyton.

(All salute.)

SUNNYSIDE: This way, gentlemen.

RATTS: (*Aside to* SUNNYSIDE.). I say, I'd like to say summit soft to the old woman; perhaps it wouldn't go well, would it?

75 THIBODEAUX: No; leave it alone.

RATTS: Darn it, when I see a woman in trouble, I feel like selling the skin off my back.

(*Exit* THIBODEAUX, SUNNYSIDE, RATTS, POINTDEXTER, GRACE, JACKSON, LAFOUCHE, CAILLOU, SOLON.)

SCUDDER: (*Aside to* PETE.) Go outside there; listen to what you hear, then go down to the quarters and tell the boys,

80 for I can't do it. O, get out.

PETE: He said 'I want a nigger.' Laws, a mussey! What am goin' to cum ob us! (*Exits slowly, as if trying to conceal himself.*)

GEORGE: My dear aunt, why do you not move from this

85 painful scene? Go with Dora to Sunnyside.

MRS PEYTON: No, George; your uncle said to me with his dying breath, 'Nellie, never leave Terrebonne,' and I never *will* leave it, till the law compels me.

SCUDDER: Mr George, I'm going to say somethin' that has

90 been chokin' me for some time. I know you'll excuse it. Thar's Miss Dora—that girl's in love with you; yes, sir, her eyes are startin' out of her head with it: now her fortune would redeem a good part of this estate.

MRS PEYTON: Why, George, I never suspected this!

95 GEORGE: I did, Aunt, I confess but—

MRS PEYTON: And you hesitated from motives of delicacy?

SCUDDER: No, ma'am; here's the plan of it. Mr George is in love with Zoe.

GEORGE: Scudder!

100 MRS PEYTON: George!

SCUDDER: Hold on, now! things have got so jammed in on top of us, we ain't got time to put kid gloves on to handle them. He loves Zoe, and has found out that she loves him. (*Sighing.*) Well, that's all right; but as he can't marry

105 her, and as Miss Dora would jump at him—

MRS PEYTON: Why didn't you mention this before?

SCUDDER: Why, because *I* love Zoe, too, and I couldn't take that young feller from her; and she's jist living on the sight of him, as I saw her do; and they so happy in spite of this

110 yer misery around them, and they reproachin' themselves with not feeling as they ought. I've seen it, I tell you; and darn it, ma'am, can't you see that's what's been a hollowing me out so—I beg your pardon.

MRS PEYTON: O, George—my son, let me call you—I do not

115 speak for my own sake, nor for the loss of the estate, but for the poor people here: they will be sold, divided, and taken away—they have been born here. Heaven has denied me children; so all the strings of my heart have grown around and amongst them, like the fibres and roots of an

120 old tree in its native earth. O, let all go, but save them! With them around us, if we have not wealth, we shall at least have the home that they alone can make—

GEORGE: My dear mother—Mr Scudder—you teach me what I ought to do; if Miss Sunnyside will accept me as I

125 am, Terrebonne shall be saved: I will sell myself, but the slaves shall be protected.

MRS PEYTON: *Sell* yourself, George! Is not Dora worth any man's—

SCUDDER: Don't say that, ma'am; don't say that to a man that loves another gal. He's going to do an heroic act; don't 130 spile it.

MRS PEYTON: But Zoe is only an Octoroon.

SCUDDER: She's won this race agin the white, anyhow; it's too late now to start her pedigree. (*As* DORA *enters.*) Come, Mrs Peyton, take my arm. Hush! here's the other one: she's 135 a little too thoroughbred— too much of the greyhound; but the heart's there, I believe.

(*Exeunt* SCUDDER *and* MRS PEYTON.)

DORA: Poor Mrs Peyton.

GEORGE: Miss Sunnyside, permit me a word: a feeling of delicacy has suspended upon my lips an avowal, which— 140

DORA: (*Aside.*) O, dear, has he suddenly come to his senses?

(*Enter* ZOE, *stopping at back.*)

GEORGE: In a word, I have seen and admired you!

DORA: (*Aside.*) He has a strange way of showing it. European, I suppose.

GEORGE: If you would pardon the abruptness of the question, 145 I would ask you. Do you think the sincere devotion of my life to make yours happy would succeed?

DORA: (*Aside.*) Well, he has the oddest way of making love.

GEORGE: You are silent?

DORA: Mr Peyton, I presume you have hesitated to make this 150 avowal because you feared, in the present condition of affairs here, your object might be misconstrued, and that your attention was rather to my fortune than myself. (*A pause.*) Why don't he speak?—I mean, you feared I might not give you credit for sincere and pure feelings. Well, you 155 wrong me. I don't think you capable of anything else but—

GEORGE: No, I hesitated because an attachment I had formed before I had the pleasure of seeing you had not altogether died out. 160

DORA: (*Smiling.*) Some of those sirens of Paris, I presume. (*Pausing.*) I shall endeavour not to be jealous of the past; perhaps I have no right to be. (*Pausing.*) But now that vagrant love is—eh, faded—is it not? Why don't you speak, sir? 165

GEORGE: Because, Miss Sunnyside, I have not learned to lie.

DORA: Good gracious—who wants you to?

GEORGE: I do, but I can't do it. No, the love I speak of is not such as you suppose—it is a passion that has grown up here since I arrived; but it is a hopeless, mad, wild feeling, 170 that must perish.

DORA: Here! since you arrived! Impossible: you have seen no one; whom can you mean?

ZOE: (*Advancing.*) Me.

GEORGE: Zoe! 175

DORA: You!

ZOE: Forgive him, Dora; for he knew no better until I told him. Dora, you are right. He is incapable of any but sincere and pure feelings—so are you. He loves me—what of that? You know you can't be jealous of a poor creature like 180 me. If he caught the fever, were stung by a snake, or possessed of any other poisonous or unclean thing, you could

pity, tend, love him through it, and for your gentle care he
would love you in return. Well, is he not thus afflicted
185 now? I am his love—he loves an Octoroon.

GEORGE: O, Zoe, you break my heart!

DORA: At college they said I was a fool—I must be. At New
Orleans, they said, 'She's pretty, very pretty, but no brains.'
I'm afraid they must be right; I can't understand a word of
190 all this.

ZOE: Dear Dora, try to understand it with your heart. You
love George; you love him dearly; I know it; and you deserve to be loved by him. He will love you—he must. His
love for me will pass away—it shall. You heard him say it
195 was hopeless. O, forgive him and me!

DORA: (*Weeping.*) O, why did he speak to me at all then?
You've made me cry, then, and I hate you both! (*Exits
through room.*)

(*Enter* MRS PEYTON *and* SCUDDER, M'CLOSKY *and* POINTDEX-
TER.)

M'CLOSKY: I'm sorry to intrude, but the business I came
200 upon will excuse me.

MRS PEYTON: Here is my nephew, sir.

ZOE: Perhaps I had better go.

M'CLOSKY: Wal, as it consarns you, perhaps you better had.

SCUDDER: Consarns Zoe?

205 M'CLOSKY: I don't know; she may as well hear the hull of it.
Go on, Colonel—Colonel Pointdexter, ma'am—the
mortgagee, auctioneer, and general agent.

POINTDEXTER: Pardon me, madam, but do you know these
papers? (*He hands the papers to* MRS PEYTON.)

210 MRS PEYTON: (*Taking them.*) Yes, sir; they were the free papers
of the girl Zoe; but they were in my husband's secretary.
How came they in your possession?

M'CLOSKY: I—I found them.

GEORGE: And you purloined them?

215 M'CLOSKY: Hold on, you'll see. Go on, Colonel.

POINTDEXTER: The list of your slaves is incomplete—it wants
one.

SCUDDER: The boy Paul—we know it.

POINTDEXTER: No, sir, you have omitted the Octoroon girl,
220 Zoe.

MRS PEYTON: } Zoe!
ZOE: } Me!

POINTDEXTER: At the time the judge executed those free papers to his infant slave, a judgment stood recorded against
225 him; while that was on record he had no right to make
away with his property. That judgment still exists: under
it and others this estate is sold today. Those free papers
ain't worth the sand that's on 'em.

MRS PEYTON: Zoe a slave! It is impossible!

230 POINTDEXTER: It is certain, madam: the judge was negligent,
and doubtless forgot this small formality.

SCUDDER: But the creditors will not claim the gal?

M'CLOSKY: Excuse me; one of the principal mortgagees has
made the demand.

(*Exeunt* M'CLOSKY *and* POINTDEXTER.)

235 SCUDDER: Hold on yere, George Peyton; you sit down there.
You're trembling so, you'll fall down directly. This blow
has staggered me some.

MRS PEYTON: O, Zoe, my child! don't think too hard of your
poor father.

ZOE: I shall do so if you weep. See, I'm calm.   240

SCUDDER: Calm as a tombstone, and with about as much life.
I see it in your face.

GEORGE: It cannot be! It shall not be!

SCUDDER: Hold your tongue—it must. Be calm—darn the
things; the proceeds of this sale won't cover the debts of   245
the estate. Consarn those Liverpool English fellers, why
couldn't they send something by the last mail? Even a letter, promising something—such is the feeling round
amongst the planters. Darn me, if I couldn't raise thirty
thousand on the envelope alone, and ten thousand more   250
on the postmark.

GEORGE: Zoe, they shall not take you from us while I live.

SCUDDER: Don't be a fool; they'd kill you, and then take her,
just as soon as—stop: old Sunnyside, he'll buy her; that'll
save her.   255

ZOE: No, it won't; we have confessed to Dora that we love
each other. How can she then ask her father to free me?

SCUDDER: What in thunder made you do that?

ZOE: Because it was the truth, and I had rather be a slave with
a free soul, than remain free with a slavish, deceitful heart.   260
My father gives me freedom—at least he thought so. May
Heaven bless him for the thought, bless him for the happiness he spread around my life. You say the proceeds of
the sale will not cover his debts. Let me be sold then, that
I may free his name. I give him back the liberty he be-   265
stowed upon me; for I can never repay him the love he
bore his poor Octoroon child, on whose breast his last
sigh was drawn, into whose eyes he looked with the last
gaze of affection.

MRS PEYTON: O, my husband! I thank Heaven you have not   270
lived to see this day.

ZOE: George, leave me! I would be alone a little while.

GEORGE: Zoe! (*Turns away, overpowered.*)

ZOE: Do not weep, George. Dear George, you now see what
a miserable thing I am.   275

GEORGE: Zoe!

SCUDDER: I wish they could sell *me!* I brought half this ruin on
this family, with my all-fired improvements. I deserve to be
a nigger this day—I feel like one, inside. (*Exit* SCUDDER.)

ZOE: Go now, George—leave me—take her with you.   280

(*Exit* MRS PEYTON *and* GEORGE.)

A slave! a slave! Is this a dream—for my brain reels with
the blow? He said so. What! then I shall be sold—sold!
and my master—O! (*She falls on her knees, with her face in
her hands.*) No—no master but one. George—George—
hush—they come! save me! No, (*Looks off.*) 't is Pete and   285
the servants—they come this way. (*Enters the inner room.*)

(*Enter* PETE, GRACE, MINNIE, SOLON, DIDO, *and all the* NE-
GROES.)

PETE: Cum yer now—stand round, 'cause I've got to talk to
you darkies—keep dem chil'n quiet—don't make no
noise, de missus up dar har us.

SOLON: Go on, Pete.   290

PETE: Gen'l'men, my coloured frens and ladies, dar's mighty
bad news gone round. Dis yer prop'ty to be sold—old

Terrebonne—whar we all been raised, is gwine—dey's gwine to tak it away—can't stop here nohow.

295 ALL: O-o!—O-o!

PETE: Hold quiet, you trash o' niggers! Tink anybody wants you to cry? Who's you to set up screeching?—Be quiet! But dis ain't all. Now, my culled brethren, gird up your lines, and listen—hold on yer bref—it's a comin'. We

300 t'ought dat de niggers would belong to de ole missus, and if she lost Terrebonne, we must live dere allers, and we would hire out, and bring our wages to ole Missus Peyton.

ALL: Ya! ya! Well—

PETE: Hush! I tell ye, 't ain't so—we can't do it—we've got to

305 be sold—

ALL: Sold!

PETE: Will you hush? she will har you. Yes! I listen dar jess now—dar was ole lady cryin'—Mas'r George—ah! you seen dem big tears in his eyes. O, Mas'r Scudder, he didn't

310 cry zackly; both ob his eyes and cheek look like de bad Bayou in low season—so dry dat I cry for him. (*Raising his voice.*) Den say de missus, ''T ain't for de land I keer, but for dem poor niggers—dey'll be sold—dat wot stagger me.' 'No,' say Mas'r George, 'I'd rather sell myself fuss; but

315 dey shan't suffer, nohow—I see 'em dam fuss.'

ALL: O, bless 'um! Bless Mas'r George.

PETE: Hole yer tongues. Yes, for you, for me, for dem little ones, dem folks cried. Now, den, if Grace dere wid her chil'n were all sold, she'll begin screechin' like a cat. She

320 didn't mind how kind old judge was to her; and Solon, too, he'll holler, and break de ole lady's heart.

GRACE: No, Pete; no, I won't. I'll bear it.

PETE: I don't tink you will any more, but dis here will; 'cause de family spile Dido, dey has. She nebber was worth much

325 a' dat nigger.

DIDO: How dar you say dat, you black nigger, you? I fetch as much as any odder cook in Louisiana.

PETE: What's de use of your takin' it kind, and comfortin' de missus' heart, if Minnie dere, and Louise, and Marie, and

330 Julie is to spile it?

MINNIE: We won't, Pete; we won't.

PETE: (*To the men.*) Dar, do ye hear dat, ye mis'able darkies; dem gals is worth a boat load of kinder men dem is. Cum, for de pride of de family, let every darky look his best for

335 the judge's sake—dat ole man so good to us, and dat ole woman—so dem strangers from New Orleans shall say, dem's happy darkies, dem's a fine set of niggers; every one say when he's sold, 'Lor' bless dis yer family I'm gwine out of, and send me as good a home.'

340 ALL: We'll do it, Pete; we'll do it.

PETE: Hush! hark! I tell ye dar's somebody in dar. Who is it?

GRACE: It's Missy Zoe. See! see!

PETE: Come along; she har what we say, and she's cryin' for us. None o' ye ign'rant niggers could cry for yerselves like

345 dat. Come here quiet: now quiet.

(*Exeunt* PETE *and all the* NEGROES, *slowly.*)

ZOE: (*Who is supposed to have overheard the last scene, enters.*) O! must I learn from these poor wretches how much I owe, and how I ought to pay the debt? Have I slept upon the benefits I received, and never saw, never felt, never knew

350 that I was forgetful and ungrateful? O, my father! my dear, dear father! forgive your poor child. You made her life too happy, and now these tears will flow. Let me hide them till I teach my heart. O, my—my heart! (*Exits, with a low, wailing, suffocating cry.*)

(*Enter* M'CLOSKY, LAFOUCHE, JACKSON, SUNNYSIDE, *and* POINTDEXTER.)

POINTDEXTER: (*Looking at his watch.*) Come, the hour is past. 355 I think we may begin business. Where is Mr Scudder?

JACKSON: I want to get to Ophelensis tonight.

DORA: (*Enters.*) Father, come here.

SUNNYSIDE: Why, Dora, what's the matter? Your eyes are red.

DORA: Are they? Thank you. I don't care, they were blue this 360 morning, but it don't signify now.

SUNNYSIDE: My darling! Who has been teasing you?

DORA: Never mind. I want you to buy Terrebonne.

SUNNYSIDE: Buy Terrebonne! What for?

DORA: No matter—buy it! 365

SUNNYSIDE: It will cost me all I'm worth. This is folly, Dora.

DORA: Is my plantation at Comptableau worth this?

SUNNYSIDE: Nearly—perhaps.

DORA: Sell it, then, and buy this.

SUNNYSIDE: Are you mad, my love? 370

DORA: Do you want *me* to stop here and *bid* for it?

SUNNYSIDE: Good gracious, no!

DORA: Then I'll do it if you don't.

SUNNYSIDE: I will! I will! But for Heaven's sake go—here comes the crowd. (*Exit* DORA.) What on earth does that 375 child mean or want?

(*Enter* SCUDDER, GEORGE, RATTS, CAILLOU, PETE, GRACE, MINNIE, *and all the* NEGROES. *A large table is in the centre of the background.* POINTDEXTER *mounts the table with his hammer, his clerk sitting at his feet. The Negro mounts the table from behind. The rest sit down.*)

POINTDEXTER: Now, gentlemen, we shall proceed to business. It ain't necessary for me to dilate, describe or enumerate; Terrebonne is known to you as one of the richest bits of sile in Louisiana, and its condition reflects credit on them 380 as had to keep it. I'll trouble you for that piece of baccy, Judge—thank you—so, gentlemen, as life is short, we'll start right off. The first lot on here is the estate in block, with its sugar-houses, stock, machines, implements, good dwelling-houses and furniture. If there is no bid for the es- 385 tate and stuff, we'll sell it in smaller lots. Come, Mr Thibodeaux, a man has a chance once in his life—here's yours.

THIBODEAUX: Go on. What's the reserve bid?

POINTDEXTER: The first mortgagee bids forty thousand dollars.

THIBODEAUX: Forty-five thousand. 390

SUNNYSIDE: Fifty thousand.

POINTDEXTER: When you have done joking, gentlemen, you'll say one hundred and twenty thousand. It carried that easy on mortgage.

LAFOUCHE: Then why don't you buy it yourself, Colonel? 395

POINTDEXTER: I'm waiting on your fifty thousand bid.

CAILLOU: Eighty thousand.

POINTDEXTER: Don't be afraid: it ain't going for that, Judge.

SUNNYSIDE: Ninety thousand.

POINTDEXTER: We're getting on. 400

THIBODEAUX: One hundred—

POINTDEXTER: One hundred thousand bid for this mag—
CAILLOU: One hundred and ten thousand—
POINTDEXTER: Good again—one hundred and—
405 SUNNYSIDE: Twenty.
POINTDEXTER: And twenty thousand bid. Squire Sunnyside is
     going to sell this at fifty thousand advance tomorrow.
     (*Looking round.*) Where's that man from Mobile that
     wanted to give one hundred and eighty thousand?
410 THIBODEAUX: I guess he ain't left home yet, Colonel.
POINTDEXTER: I shall knock it down to the Squire—going—
     gone—for one hundred and twenty thousand dollars.
     (*Raising hammer.*) Judge, you can raise the hull on mort-
     gage—going for half its value. (*Knocking on the table.*)
415 Squire Sunnyside, you've got a pretty bit o' land, Squire.
     Hillo, darkey, hand me a smash dar.
SUNNYSIDE: I got more than I can work now.
POINTDEXTER: Then buy the hands along with the property.
     Now, gentlemen, I'm proud to submit to you the finest lot
420 of field hands and house servants that was ever offered for
     competition: they speak for themselves, and do credit to
     their owners. (*Reading.*) 'No. 1, Solon, a guest boy, and a
     good waiter.'
PETE: That's my son—buy him, Mas'r Ratts; he's sure to sarve
425 you well.
POINTDEXTER: Hold your tongue!
RATTS: Let the old darkey alone—eight hundred for that boy.
CAILLOU: Nine.
RATTS: A thousand.
430 SOLON: Thank you, Mas'r Ratts: I die for you sar; hold up for
     me, sar.
RATTS: Look here, the boy knows and likes me, Judge; let him
     come my way?
CAILLOU: Go on—I'm dumb.
435 POINTDEXTER: One thousand bid. He's yours, Captain Ratts,
     Magnolia steamer.

(SOLON *goes and stands behind* RATTS.)

     'No. 2, the yellow girl, Grace, with two children—Saul,
     aged four, and Victoria, five.' (*They get on table.*)
SCUDDER: That's Solon's wife and children, Judge.
440 GRACE: (*To* RATTS.) Buy me, Mas'r Ratts, do buy me, sar?
RATTS: What in thunder should I do with you and those dev-
     ils on board my boat?
GRACE: Wash, sar—cook, sar—anyting.
RATTS: Eight hundred agin, then—I'll go it.
445 JACKSON: Nine.
RATTS: I'm broke, Solon—I can't stop the Judge.
THIBODEAUX: What's the matter, Ratts? I'll lend you all you
     want. Go it, if you're a mind to.
RATTS: Eleven.
450 JACKSON: Twelve.
SUNNYSIDE: O, O!
SCUDDER: (*To* JACKSON.) Judge, my friend. The Judge is a lit-
     tle deaf. Hello! (*Speaking in his ear trumpet.*) This gal and
     them children belong to that boy Solon there. You're bid-
455 ding to separate them, Judge.
JACKSON: The devil I am! (*Rising.*) I'll take back my bid,
     Colonel.
POINTDEXTER: All right, Judge; I thought there was a mistake.
     I must keep you, Captain, to the eleven hundred.

460 RATTS: Go it.
POINTDEXTER: Eleven hundred—going—going—sold! 'No.
     3, Pete, a house servant.'
PETE: Dat's me—yer, I'm comin'—stand around dar. (*Tumbles
     upon the table.*)
465 POINTDEXTER: Aged seventy-two.
PETE: What's dat? A mistake, sar—forty-six.
POINTDEXTER: Lame.
PETE: But don't mount to nuffin—kin work cannel. Come,
     Judge, pick up. Now's your time, sar.
470 JACKSON: One hundred dollars.
PETE: What, sar? me! for me!—look ye here! (*He dances.*)
GEORGE: Five hundred.
PETE: Mas'r George—ah, no, sar—don't buy me—keep your
     money for some udder dat is to be sold. I ain't no 'count, sar.
475 POINTDEXTER: Five hundred bid—it's a good price. He's
     yours, Mr George Peyton. (PETE *goes down.*) 'No. 4, the
     Octoroon girl, Zoe.'

(*Enter* ZOE, *very pale, and stands on table.* M'CLOSKY *who hitherto
has taken no interest in the sale, now turns his chair.*)

SUNNYSIDE: (*Rising.*) Gentlemen, we are all acquainted with
     the circumstances of this girl's position, and I feel sure that
     no one here will oppose the family who desires to redeem
480 the child of our esteemed and noble friend, the late Judge
     Peyton.
ALL: Hear! bravo! hear!
POINTDEXTER: While the proceeds of this sale promises to re-
     alise less than the debts upon it, it is my duty to prevent
485 any collusion for the depreciation of the property.
RATTS: Darn ye! You're a man as well as an auctioneer, ain't ye?
POINTDEXTER: What is offered for the slave?
SUNNYSIDE: One thousand dollars.
M'CLOSKY: Two thousand.
490 SUNNYSIDE: Three thousand.
M'CLOSKY: Five thousand.
GEORGE: Demon!
SUNNYSIDE: I bid seven thousand, which is the last dollar this
     family possesses.
495 M'CLOSKY: Eight.
THIBODEAUX: Nine.
ALL: Bravo!
M'CLOSKY: Ten. It's no use, Squire.
SCUDDER: Jacob M'Closky, you shan't have that girl. Now,
500 take care what you do. Twelve thousand.
M'CLOSKY: Shan't I! Fifteen thousand. Beat that any of ye.
POINTDEXTER: Fifteen thousand bid for the Octoroon.
DORA: (*Enters.*) Twenty thousand.
ALL: Bravo!
505 M'CLOSKY: Twenty-five thousand.
ALL: (*Groan.*) O! O!
GEORGE: Yelping hound—take that. (*He rushes on* M'CLOSKY.
     M'CLOSKY *draws his knife.*)
SCUDDER: (*Darting between them.*) Hold on, George Peyton—
510 stand back. This is your own house; we are under your
     uncle's roof; recollect yourself. And, strangers, ain't we for-
     getting there's a lady present? (*The knives disappear.*) If we
     can't behave like Christians, let's try and act like gentle-
     men. Go on, Colonel.
515 LAFOUCHE: He didn't ought to bid against a lady.

M'CLOSKY: O, that's it, is it? Then I'd like to hire a lady to go to auction and buy my hands.

POINTDEXTER: Gentlemen, I believe none of us have two
520 feelings about the conduct of that man; but he has the law on his side—we may regret, but we must respect it. Mr M'Closky has bid twenty-five thousand dollars for the Octoroon. Is there any other bid? For the first time, twenty-five thousand—last time! (*Brings hammer down.*) To
525 Jacob M'Closky, the Octoroon girl, Zoe, twenty-five thousand dollars.

ACT FOUR

The wharf. The steamer, Magnolia, *alongside a bluff rock.* RATTS *discovered, superintending the loading of ship. Enter* LAFOUCHE *and* JACKSON.

JACKSON: How long before we start, captain?

RATTS: Just as soon as we put this cotton on board.

(*Enter* PETE, *with a lantern, and* SCUDDER, *with notebook.*)

SCUDDER: One hundred and forty-nine bales. Can you take any more?

5 RATTS: Not a bale. I've got engaged eight hundred bales at the next landing, and one hundred hogsheads of sugar at Patten's Slide—that'll take my guards under—hurry up thar.

VOICE: (*Outside.*) Wood's aboard.

10 RATTS: All aboard then.

(*Enter* M'CLOSKY.)

SCUDDER: Sign that receipt, Captain, and save me going up to the clerk.

M'CLOSKY: See here—there's a small freight of turpentine in the fore hold there, and one of the barrels leaks; a spark
15 from your engines might set the ship on fire, and you'll go with it.

RATTS: You be darned! Go and try it, if you've a mind to.

LAFOUCHE: Captain, you've loaded up here until the boat is sunk so deep in the mud she won't float.

20 RATTS: (*Calling off.*) Wood up thar, you Pollo—hang on to the safety valve—guess she'll crawl off on her paddles. (*Shouts heard.*)

JACKSON: What's the matter?

SOLON: (*Enters.*) We got him!

25 SCUDDER: Who?

SOLON: The Injiun!

SCUDDER: Wahnotee? Where is he? D'ye call running away from a fellow catching him?

RATTS: Here he comes.

30 ALL: Where? Where?

(*Enter* WAHNOTEE. *They are all about to rush on him.*)

SCUDDER: Hold on! stan' round thar! no violence—the crittur don't know what we mean.

JACKSON: Let him answer for the boy then.

M'CLOSKY: Down with him—lynch him.

35 ALL: Lynch him!

(*Exit* LAFOUCHE.)

SCUDDER: Stan' back, I say! I'll nip the first that lays a finger on him. Pete, speak to the redskin.

PETE: Whar's Paul, Wahnotee? What's come ob de child?

WAHNOTEE: Paul wunce—Paul pangeuk.

PETE: Pangeuk—dead!   40

WAHNOTEE: Mort!

M'CLOSKY: And you killed him? (*They approach him.*)

SCUDDER: Hold on!

PETE: Um, Paul reste?

WAHNOTEE: Hugh vieu. (*Goes.*) Paul reste ci!   45

SCUDDER: Here, stay! (*Examines the ground.*) The earth has been stirred here lately.

WAHNOTEE: Weenee Paul. (*He points down, and shows by pantomime how he buried* PAUL.)

SCUDDER: The Injiun means that he buried him there! Stop!   50
here's a bit of leather. (*Drawing out the mail-bags.*) The mail-bags that were lost! (*Sees the tomahawk in* WAHNOTEE's *belt—draws it out and examines it.*) Look! here are marks of blood—look thar, redskin, what's that?

WAHNOTEE: Paul! (*Makes a sign that* PAUL *was killed by a blow* 55
on the head.)

M'CLOSKY: He confesses it; the Indian got drunk, quarreled with him, and killed him.

LAFOUCHE: (*Re-enters with smashed apparatus.*) Here are evidences of the crime; this rum-bottle half emptied—this   60
photographic apparatus smashed—and there are marks of blood and footsteps around the shed.

M'CLOSKY: What more d'ye want—ain't that proof enough? Lynch him!

ALL: Lynch him! Lynch him!   65

SCUDDER: Stan' back, boys! He's an Injiun—fair play.

JACKSON: Try him, then—try him on the spot of his crime.

ALL: Try him! Try him!

LAFOUCHE: Don't let him escape!

RATTS: I'll see to that. (*Drawing revolver.*) If he stirs, I'll put a   70
bullet through his skull, mighty quick.

M'CLOSKY: Come, form a court then, choose a jury—we'll fix this varmin.

(*Enter* THIBODEAUX *and* CAILLOU.)

THIBODEAUX: What's the matter?

LAFOUCHE: We've caught this murdering Injiun, and are go-   75
ing to try him.

(WAHNOTEE *sits, rolled in blanket.*)

PETE: Poor little Paul—poor little nigger!

SCUDDER: This business goes agin me, Ratts—'t ain't right.

LAFOUCHE: We're ready; the jury's impanelled—go ahead—
who'll be accuser?   80

RATTS: M'Closky.

M'CLOSKY: Me?

RATTS: Yes; you was the first to hail Judge Lynch.

M'CLOSKY: Well, what's the use of argument whar guilt sticks out so plain; the boy and Injiun were alone when last   85
seen.

SCUDDER: Who says that?

M'CLOSKY: Everybody—that is, I heard so.

SCUDDER: Say what you know—not what you heard.

M'CLOSKY: I know then that the boy was killed with that   90
tomahawk—the redskin owns it—the signs of violence

are all round the shed—this apparatus smashed—ain't it plain that in a drunken fit he slew the boy, and when sober concealed the body yonder?

95 ALL: That's it—that's it.

RATTS: Who defends the Injiun?

SCUDDER: I will; for it is agin my natur' to b'lieve him guilty; and if he be, this ain't the place, nor you the authority to try him. How are we sure the boy is dead at all? There are

100 no witnesses but a rum bottle and an old machine. Is it on such evidence you'd hang a human being?

RATTS: His own confession.

SCUDDER: I appeal against your usurped authority. This lynch law is a wild and lawless proceeding. Here's a pic-

105 tur' for a civilised community to afford; yonder, a poor, ignorant savage, and round him a circle of hearts, white with revenge and hate, thirsting for his blood: you call yourselves judges—you ain't—you're a jury of executioners. It is such scenes as these that bring disgrace upon our West-

110 ern life.

M'CLOSKY: Evidence! Evidence! Give us evidence. We've had talk enough; now for proof.

ALL: Yes, yes! Proof, proof!

SCUDDER: Where am I to get it? The proof is here, in my

115 heart.

PETE: (*Who has been looking about the camera.*) 'Top, sar! 'Top a bit! O, laws-a-mussey, see dis! here's a pictur' I found stickin' in that yar telescope machine, sar! look, sar!

SCUDDER: A photographic plate.

(PETE *holds his lantern up.*)

120 What's this, eh! two forms! The child—'t is he! dead—and above him—Ah! ah! Jacob M'Closky, 't was you murdered that boy!

M'CLOSKY: Me?

SCUDDER: You! You slew him with that tomahawk; and as you

125 stood over his body with the letter in your hand, you thought that no witness saw the deed, that no eye was on you—but there was, Jacob M'Closky, there was. The eye of the Eternal was on you—the blessed sun in heaven, that, looking down, struck upon this plate the image of

130 the deed. Here you are, in the very attitude of your crime!

M'CLOSKY: 'T is false!

SCUDDER: 'T is true! the apparatus can't lie. Look there, jurymen. (*Showing plate to jury.*) Look there. O, you wanted evidence—you called for proof—Heaven has answered

135 and convicted you.

M'CLOSKY: What court of law would receive such evidence? (*Going.*)

RATTS: Stop! *This* would! You called it yourself; you wanted to make us murder that Injiun; and since we've got our

140 hands in for justice, we'll try it on *you.* What say ye? shall we have one law for the redskin and another for the white?

ALL: Try him! Try him!

RATTS: Who'll be accuser?

145 SCUDDER: I will! Fellow citizens, you are convened and assembled here under a higher power than the law. What's the law? When the ship's abroad on the ocean, when the army is before the enemy, where in thunder's the law? It is in the hearts of brave men, who can tell right from

wrong, and from whom justice can't be bought. So it is 150 here, in the wilds of the West, where our hatred of crime is measured by the speed of our executions—where necessity is law! I say, then, air you honest men? air you true? Put your hands on your naked breasts, and let every man as don't feel a real American heart there, bustin' up with 155 freedom, truth, and right, let that man step out—that's the oath I put to ye—and then say, Darn ye, go it!

ALL: Go on! Go on!

SCUDDER: No! I won't go on; that man's down. I won't strike him, even with words. Jacob, your accuser is that picter of 160 the crime—let that speak—defend yourself.

M'CLOSKY: (*Drawing knife.*) I will, quicker than lightning.

RATTS: Seize him, then!

(*They rush on* M'CLOSKY, *and disarm him.*)

He can fight though he's a painter: claws all over.

SCUDDER: Stop! Search him, we may find more evidence.   165

M'CLOSKY: Would you rob me first, and murder me afterwards?

RATTS: (*Searching him.*) That's his programme—here's a pocketbook.

SCUDDER: (*Opening it.*) What's here? Letters! Hello! To 'Mrs 170 Peyton, Terrebonne, Louisiana, United States.' Liverpool postmark. Ho! I've got hold of the tail of a rat—come out. (*Reads.*) What's this? A draft for eighty-five thousand dollars, and credit on Palisse and Co., of New Orleans, for the balance. Hi! the rat's out. You killed the boy to steal this 175 letter from the mail-bags—you stole this letter, that the money should not arrive in time to save the Octoroon; had it done so, the lien on the estate would have ceased, and Zoe be free.

ALL: Lynch him! Lynch him! Down with him!   180

SCUDDER: Silence in the court: stand back, let the gentlemen of the jury retire, consult, and return their verdict.

RATTS: I'm responsible for the crittur—go on.

PETE: (*To* WAHNOTEE.) See, Injiun; look dar, (*Showing him the plate.*) see dat innocent; look, dar's de murderer of poor 185 Paul.

WAHNOTEE: Ugh! (*Examining the plate.*)

PETE: Ya! as he? Closky tue Paul—kill de child with your tomahawk dar: 't wasn't you, no—ole Pete allus say so. Poor Injiun lub our little Paul.   190

(WAHNOTEE *rises and looks at* M'CLOSKY—*he is in his war paint and fully armed.*)

SCUDDER: What say ye, gentlemen? Is the prisoner guilty, or is he not guilty?

ALL: Guilty!

SCUDDER: And what is to be his punishment?   195

ALL: Death! (*All advance.*)

WAHNOTEE: (*Crosses to* M'CLOSKY). Ugh!

SCUDDER: No, Injiun; we deal out justice here, not revenge. 'T ain't you he has injured, 't is the white man, whose laws he has offended.   200

RATTS: Away with him—put him down the aft hatch, till we rig his funeral.

M'CLOSKY: Fifty against one! O! if I had you one by one alone in the swamp, I'd rip ye all. (*He is borne off in boat, struggling.*)   205

SCUDDER: Now, then, to business.

PETE: (*Re-enters from boat.*) O, law, sir, dat debil Closky, he tore hisself from de gen'lam, knock me down, take my light, and trows it on de turpentine barrels, and de shed's all afire!

(*Fire seen.*)

210 JACKSON: (*Re-entering.*) We are catching fire forward: quick, cut free from the shore.

RATTS: All hands aboard there—cut the starn ropes—give her headway!

ALL: Ay, ay!

(*Cry of 'Fire' heard—engine bells heard—steam whistle noise.*)

215 RATTS: Cut all away, for'ard—overboard with every bale afire.

(*The steamer moves off with the fire still blazing.*)

M'CLOSKY: (*Re-enters, swimming.*) Ha! have I fixed ye? Burn! burn! that's right. You thought you had cornered me, did ye? As I swam down, I thought I heard something in the water, as if pursuing me—one of them darned alligators, I
220 suppose—they swarm hereabout—may they crunch every limb of ye. (*Exits.*)

(WAHNOTEE *is seen swimming. He finds trail and follows* M'CLOSKY. *The steamer floats on at back, burning.*)

ACT FIVE

SCENE I

Negroes' quarters.

ZOE: (*Enters.*) It wants an hour yet to daylight—here is Pete's hut—(*Knocks.*) He sleeps—no: I see a light.

DIDO: (*Enters from hut.*) Who dat?

ZOE: Hush, Aunty 'T is I—Zoe.

5 DIDO: Miss Zoe? Why you out in de swamp dis time ob night; you catch de fever sure—you is all wet.

ZOE: Where's Pete?

DIDO: He gone down to de landing last night wid Mas'r Scudder; not come back since—kint make it out.

10 ZOE: Aunty, there is sickness up at the house; I have been up all night beside one who suffers, and I remembered that when I had the fever you gave me a drink, a bitter drink, that made me sleep—do you remember it?

DIDO: Didn't I? Dem doctors ain't no 'count; dey don't know
15 nuffin.

ZOE: No; but you, Aunty, you are wise—you know every plant, don't you, and what it is good for?

DIDO: Dat you drink is fust rate for red fever. Is de folks' head bad?

20 ZOE: Very bad, Aunty; and the heart aches worse, so they can get no rest.

DIDO: Hold on a bit, I get you de bottle. (*Exits.*)

ZOE: In a few hours that man, my master, will come for me: he has paid my price, and he only consented to let me re-
25 main here this one night, because Mrs Peyton promised to give me up to him today.

DIDO: (*Re-enters with phial.*) Here 't is—now you give one timble-full—dat's nuff.

ZOE: All there is there would kill one, wouldn't it?

DIDO: Guess it kill a dozen—nebber try. 30

ZOE: It's not a painful death, Aunty, is it? You told me it pro-duced a long, long sleep.

DIDO: Why you tremble so? Why you speak so wild? What you's gwine to do, missey?

ZOE: Give me the drink. 35

DIDO: No. Who dat sick at de house?

ZOE: Give it to me.

DIDO: No. You want to hurt yourself. O, Miss Zoe, why you ask old Dido for dis pizen?

ZOE: Listen to me. I love one who is here, and he loves me— 40
George. I sat outside his door all night—I heard his sighs—his agony—torn from him by my coming fate; and he said, 'I'd rather see her dead than his!'

DIDO: Dead!

ZOE: He said so—then I rose up, and stole from the house, 45
and ran down to the bayou: but its cold, black, silent stream terrified me—drowning must be so horrible a death. I could not do it. Then, as I knelt there, weeping for courage, a snake rattled beside me. I shrunk from it and fled. Death was there beside me, and I dared not take it. 50
O! I'm afraid to die; yet I am more afraid to live.

DORA: Die!

ZOE: So I came here to you; to you, my own dear nurse; to you, who so often hushed me to sleep when I was a child; who dried my eyes and put your little Zoe to rest. Ah! 55
give me the rest that no master but One can disturb—the sleep from which I shall awake free! You can protect me from that man—do let me die without pain.

DIDO: No, no—life is good for young t'ing like you.

ZOE: O! good, good nurse: you will you, will. 60

DIDO: No— g' way.

ZOE: Then I shall never leave Terrebonne—the drink, nurse; the drink; that I may never leave my home—my dear, dear home. You will not give me to that man? Your own Zoe, that loves you, Aunty, so much, so much. (*She gets the* 65
phial.) Ah! I have it.

DIDO: No, missey. O! no—don't.

ZOE: Hush! (*Runs off.*)

DIDO: Here, Solon, Minnie, Grace.

(*They enter.*)

ALL: Was de matter? 70

DIDO: Miss Zoe got de pizen. (*Exits.*)

ALL: O! O! (*Exeunt.*)

SCENE II

In a canebrake bayou, on a bank, with a canoe nearby, M'CLOSKY *is seen asleep.*

M'CLOSKY: Burn, burn! blaze away! How the flames crack. I'm not guilty; would ye murder me? Cut, cut the rope— I choke—choke—Ah! (*Wakes.*) Hello! where am I? Why, I was dreaming—curse it! I can never sleep now without dreaming. Hush! I thought I heard the sound of a paddle 5
in the water. All night, as I fled through the canebrake, I heard footsteps behind me. I lost them in the cedar swamp—again they haunted my path down the bayou,

moving as I moved, resting when I rested—hush! there
again!—no; it was only the wind over the canes. The sun
is rising. I must launch my dug-out, and put for the bay,
and in a few hours I shall be safe from pursuit on board of
one of the coasting schooners that run from Galveston to
Matagorda. In a little time this darned business will blow
over, and I can show again. Hark! there's that noise again!
If it was the ghost of that murdered boy haunting me!
Well—I didn't mean to kill him, did I? Well, then, what
has my all-cowardly heart got to skeer me so far? (*He gets
in canoe and rows off.* WAHNOTEE *appears in another canoe. He
gets out and finds trail and paddles off after* M'CLOSKY.)

SCENE III

A cedar swamp. Enter SCUDDER *and* PETE.

SCUDDER: Come on, Pete, we shan't reach the house before
midday.

PETE: Nebber mind, sa, we bring good news—it won't spile
for de keeping.

SCUDDER: Ten miles we've had to walk, because some blamed
varmin onhitched our dug-out. I left it last night all safe.

PETE: P'r'aps it floated away itself.

SCUDDER: No; the hitching line was cut with a knife.

PETE: Say, Mas'r Scudder, s'pose we go in round by de quarters and raise de darkies, den dey cum long wid us, and we
'proach dat ole house like Gin'ral Jackson when he took
London out dar.

SCUDDER: Hello, Pete, I never heard of that affair.

PETE: I tell you, sa—hush!

SCUDDER: What?

PETE: Was dat?—a cry out dar in the swamp—dar again!

SCUDDER: So it is. Something forcing its way through the
undergrowth—it comes this way—it's either a bear or a
runaway nigger. (*He draws a pistol.* M'CLOSKY *rushes on, and
falls at* SCUDDER's *feet.*)

SCUDDER: Stand off—what are ye?

PETE: Mas'r Clusky.

M'CLOSKY: Save me—save me! I can go no farther. I heard
voices.

SCUDDER: Who's after you?

M'CLOSKY: I don't know, but I feel it's death! In some form,
human, or wild best, or ghost, it has tracked me through
the night. I fled; it followed. Hark! there it comes—it
comes—don't you hear a footstep on the dry leaves!

SCUDDER: Your crime has driven you mad.

M'CLOSKY: D'ye hear it—nearer—nearer—ah!

(WAHNOTEE *rushes on, and attacks* M'CLOSKY.)

SCUDDER: The Injiun! By thunder.

PETE: You'se a dead man, Mas'r Clusky—you got to b'lieve
dat.

M'CLOSKY: No—no. If I must die, give me up to the law; but
save me from the tomahawk. You are a white man; you'll
not leave one of your own blood to be butchered by the
redskin?

SCUDDER: Hold on now, Jacob; we've got to figure on that—
let us look straight at the thing. Here we are on the sel-
vage of civilisation. It ain't our side, I believe, rightly; but

Nature has said that where the white man sets his foot, the
red man and the black man shall up sticks and stand
around. But what do we pay for that possession? In cash?
No—in kind—that is, in protection, forbearance, gentleness, in all them goods that show the critters the difference between the Christian and the savage. Now, what
have you done to show them the distinction? For, darn
me, if I can find out.

M'CLOSKY: For what I have done, let me be tried.

SCUDDER: You have been tried—honestly tried and convicted. Providence has chosen your executioner. I shan't
interfere.

PETE: O, no; Mas'r Scudder, don't leave Mas'r Closky like
dat—don't, sa—'t ain't what good Christian should do.

SCUDDER: D'ye hear that, Jacob? This old nigger, the grandfather of the boy you murdered, speaks for you—don't that
go through you? D'ye feel it? Go on, Pete, you've waked
up the Christian here, and the old hoss responds. (*He throws
bowie knife to* M'CLOSKY.) Take that, and defend yourself.

(*Exeunt* SCUDDER *and* PETE. WAHNOTEE *faces him. They fight,*
M'CLOSKY *runs off,* WAHNOTEE *follows him.—Screams outside.*)

SCENE IV

Parlour at Terrebonne.

ZOE: (*Enters.*) My home, my home! I must see you no more.
Those little flowers can live, but I cannot. Tomorrow they'll
bloom the same—all will be here as now, and I shall be cold.
O! my life, my happy life; why has it been so bright?

(*Enter* MRS PEYTON *and* DORA.)

DORA: Zoe, where have you been?

MRS PEYTON: We felt quite uneasy about you.

ZOE: I've been to the Negro quarters. I suppose I shall go before long, and I wished to visit all the places, once again,
to see the poor people.

MRS PEYTON: Zoe, dear, I'm glad to see you more calm this
morning.

DORA: But how pale she looks, and she trembles so.

ZOE: Do I? (*Enter* GEORGE.) Ah! he is here.

DORA: George, here she is.

ZOE: I have come to say good bye, sir; two hard words—so
hard, they might break many a heart; mightn't they?

GEORGE: O, Zoe! can you smile at this moment?

ZOE: You see how easily I have become reconciled to my
fate—so it will be with you. You will not forget poor
Zoe! but her image will pass away like a little cloud that
obscured your happiness a while—you will love each
other? you are both too good not to join your hearts.
Brightness will return amongst you. Dora, I once made
you weep; those were the only tears I caused anybody.
Will you forgive me?

DORA: Forgive you—(*Kisses her.*)

GEORGE: Zoe, you are pale. Zoe!—she faints!

ZOE: No; a weakness, that's all—a little water. (DORA *gets some
water.*) I have a restorative here—will you pour it in the
glass? (DORA *attempts to take it.*) No; not you—George.
(GEORGE *pours the contents of the phial into glass.*) Now, give
it to me. George, dear George, do you love me?

GEORGE: Do you doubt it, Zoe?

ZOE: No! (*She drinks.*)

35 DORA: Zoe, if all I possess would buy your freedom, I would gladly give it.

ZOE: I am free! I had but one Master on earth, and he has given me my freedom!

DORA: Alas! but the deed that freed you was not lawful.

40 ZOE: Not lawful—no—but I am going to where there is no law—where there is only justice.

GEORGE: Zoe, you are suffering—your lips are white—your cheeks are flushed.

ZOE: I must be going—it is late. Farewell, Dora. (*Retires.*)

45 PETE: (*Outside.*) Whar's Missus—whar's Mas'r George?

GEORGE: They come.

SCUDDER: (*Enters.*) Stand around and let me pass—room thar! I feel so big with joy, creation ain't wide enough to hold me. Mrs Peyton, George Peyton, Terrebonne is

50 yours. It was that rascal M'Closky—but he got rats, I swow—he killed the boy, Paul, to rob this letter from the mail-bags—the letter from Liverpool you know—he sot fire to the shed—that was how the steamboat got burned up.

55 MRS PEYTON: What d' ye mean?

SCUDDER: Read—read that. (*He gives letter to them.*)

GEORGE: Explain yourself.

SUNNYSIDE: (*Enters.*) Is it true?

SCUDDER: Every word of it, Squire. Here, you tell it, since

60 you know it. If I was to try, I'd bust.

MRS PEYTON: Read, George. Terrebonne is yours.

(*Enter PETE, DIDO, SOLON, MINNIE, and GRACE.*)

PETE: War is she—war is Miss Zoe?

SCUDDER: What's the matter?

PETE: Don't ax me. Whar's de gal? I say.

65 SCUDDER: Here she is—Zoe!—water—she faints.

PETE: No—no. 'T ain't no faint—she's a dying, sa: she got pi-zon from old Dido here, this mornin'.

GEORGE: Zoe!

SCUDDER: Zoe! is this true?—no, it ain't—darn it, say it ain't.

70 Look here, you're free, you know; nary a master to hurt you now: you will stop here as long as you're a mind to, only don't look so.

DORA: Her eyes have changed colour.

PETE: Dat's what her soul's gwine to do. It's going up dar,

75 whar dere's no line atween folks.

GEORGE: She revives.

ZOE: (*On the sofa.*) George—where—where—

GEORGE: O, Zoe! what have you done?

ZOE: Last night I overheard you weeping in your room, and

80 you said, 'I'd rather see her dead than so!'

GEORGE: Have I then prompted you to this?

ZOE: No; but I loved you so, I could not bear my fate; and then I stood between your heart and hers. When I am dead she will not be jealous of your love for me,

85 no laws will stand between us. Lift me; so—(GEORGE *raises her head.*)—let me look at you, that your face may be the last I see of this world. O! George, you may, without a blush, confess your love for the Octoroon. (*She dies.* GEORGE *lowers her head gently and kneels beside*

90 *her.*)

The English Happy Ending

ACT FOUR

SCENE: *The wharf.—The Steamer 'Magnolia' alongside,* L.—*A bluff rock,* R.U.E. RATTS *discovered, superintending the loading of ship. Enter* LAFOUCHE *and* JACKSON, L.

JACKSON: How long before we start, captain?

RATTS: Just as soon as we put this cotton on board.

(*Enter* PETE, *with lantern, and* SCUDDER, *with notebook.* R.)

SCUDDER: One hundred and forty-nine bales. Can you take any more?

RATTS: Not a bale. I've got engaged eight hundred bales at the next landing, and one hundred hogsheads of sugar at Pat-ten's Slide—that'll take my guards under—hurry up thar! 5

VOICE: (*Outside.*) Wood's aboard.

RATTS: All aboard then.

(*Enter* M'CLOSKY, R.)

SCUDDER: Sign that receipt, captain, and save me going up to the clerk.

M'CLOSKY: See here—there's a small freight of turpentine in 10 the fore-hold there, and one of the barrels leaks; a spark from your engines might set the ship on fire, and you'd go with it.

RATTS: You be darned! Go and try if you've a mind to.

LAFOUCHE: Captain, you've loaded up here until the boat is 15 sunk so deep in the mud she won't float.

RATTS: (*Calls off.*) Wood up thar, you Pollo—hang on to the safety valve—guess she'll crawl off on her paddles. (*Shouts heard,* R.)

JACKSON: What's the matter? 20

(*Enter* SOLON, R.)

SOLON: We got him!

SCUDDER: Who?

SOLON: The Inginn!

SCUDDER: Wahnotee? where is he? d'ye call running away from a fellow catching him? 25

RATTS: Here he comes.

OMNES: Where? where?

(*Enter* WAHNOTEE, R., *they are all about to rush on him.*)

SCUDDER: Hold on! stan' round thar! no violence—the crit-ter don't know what we mean.

JACKSON: Let him answer for the boy then. 30

M'CLOSKY: Down with him—lynch him.

OMNES: Lynch him!

(*Exit* LAFOUCHE, R.)

SCUDDER: Stan' back, I say! I'll nip the first that lays a finger on him. Pete, speak to the redskin.

PETE: Whar's Paul, Wahnotee? What's come ob de child? 35

WAHNOTEE: Paul wunce—Paul pangeuk.

PETE: Pangeuk—dead.

WAHNOTEE: Mort!

M'CLOSKY: And you killed him? (*They approach again.*)

40 SCUDDER: Hold on!

PETE: Um, Paul reste?

WAHNOTEE: Hugh vieu—(*Goes L.*)—Paul reste ci!

SCUDDER: Here, stay! (*Examines the ground.*) The earth has been stirred here lately.

45 WAHNOTEE: Weenee Paul. (*Points down and shows by pantomime how he buried* PAUL.)

SCUDDER: The Inginn means that he buried him there! Stop, here's a bit of leather. (*Draws out mail-bags.*) The mail-bags that were lost! (*Sees tomahawk in* WAHNOTEE's *belt—draws*

50 *it out and examines it.*) Look! here are marks of blood— look thar, red-skin, what's that?

WAHNOTEE: Paul! (*Makes sign that* PAUL *was killed by a blow on the head.*)

M'CLOSKY: He confesses it; the Indian got drunk, quarreled

55 with him, and killed him.

(*Re-enter* LAFOUCHE, R., *with smashed apparatus.*)

LAFOUCHE: Here are evidences of the crime; this rum bottle half emptied—this photographic apparatus smashed—and there are marks of blood and footsteps around the shed.

M'CLOSKY: What more d'ye want—ain't that proof enough?

60 Lynch him!

OMNES: Lynch him! Lynch him!

SCUDDER: Stan' back, boys! he's an Inginn—fair play.

JACKSON: Try him then— try him on the spot of his crime.

OMNES: Try him! try him!

65 LAFOUCHE: Don't let him escape!

RATTS: I'll see to that. (*Draws revolver.*) If he stirs, I'll put a bullet through his skull, mighty quick.

M'CLOSKY: Come—form a court, then, choose a jury—we'll fix this varmin.

(*Enter* THIBODEAUX *and* CAILLOU, L.)

70 THIBODEAUX: What's the matter?

LAFOUCHE: We've caught this murdering Inginn, and are going to try him.

(WAHNOTEE *sits* L., *rollen in blanket.*)

PETE: Poor little Paul—poor little nigger!

SCUDDER: This business goes agin me, Ratts—'taint right.

75 LAFOUCHE: We're ready, the jury is empannelled—go ahead— who'll be accuser?

RATTS: M'Closky.

M'CLOSKY: Me!

RATTS: Yes; you was the first to hail Judge Lynch.

80 M'CLOSKY: (R.) Well, what's the use of argument, whar guilt sticks out so plain; the boy and Inginn were alone when last seen.

SCUDDER: (L. C.) Who says that?

M'CLOSKY: Everybody—that is, I heard so.

85 SCUDDER: Say what you know—not what you heard.

M'CLOSKY: I know then, that the boy was killed with that tomahawk—the redskin owns it—the signs of violence are all round the shed—this apparatus smashed—ain't it plain that in a drunken fit he slew the boy, and when sober

90 concealed the body yonder?

OMNES: That's it—that's it.

RATTS: Who defends the Indian?

SCUDDER: I will; for it's agin my natur' to b'lieve him guilty; and if he be, this ain't the place, nor you the authority, to try him. How are we sure the boy is dead at all? There are 95 no witnesses but a rum-bottle and an old machine. Is it on such evidence you'd hang a human being?

RATTS: His own confession.

SCUDDER: I appeal against your usurped authority; this lynch law is a wild and lawless proceeding. Here's a picture for a 100 civilised community to afford; yonder, a poor ignorant savage, and round him a circle of hearts, white with revenge and hate, thirsting for his blood; you call yourselves judges—you ain't—you're a jury of executioners. It is such scenes as these that bring disgrace upon our Western life. 105

M'CLOSKY: Evidence! Evidence! give us evidence, we've had talk enough; now for proof.

OMNES: Yes, yes! Proof, proof!

SCUDDER: Where am I to get it? the proof is here, in my heart! 110

PETE: (*Who has been looking about the camera.*) Top sar! top a bit! Oh, laws-a-mussey, see dis, here's a pictur' I found sticking in that yar telescope machine, sar! look, sar!

SCUDDER: A photographic plate. (PETE *holds lantern up.*) What's this, eh? two forms! the child—'tis he! dead—and 115 above him—Ah, ah! Jacob M'Closky—'twas you murdered the boy!

M'CLOSKY: Me?

SCUDDER: You! You slew him with that tomahawk, and as you stood over his body with the letter in your hand, you 120 thought that no witness saw the deed, that no eye was on you; but there was, Jacob M'Closky, there was—the eye of the Eternal was on you—the blessed sun in heaven, that, looking down, struck upon this plate the image of the deed. Here you are, in the very attitude of your crime! 125

M'CLOSKY: 'Tis false!

SCUDDER: 'Tis true! the apparatus can't lie. Look there, jurymen—(*shows plate to jury*)—look there. Oh, you wanted evidence—you called for proof—heaven has answered and convicted you. 130

M'CLOSKY: What court of law would receive such evidence? (*Going.*)

RATTS: Stop, *this* would—you called it yourself; you wanted to make us murder that Inginn, and since we've got our hands in for justice, we'll try it on you. What say ye? Shall we 135 have one law for the redskin and another for the white?

OMNES: Try him! try him!

RATTS: Who'll be accuser?

SCUDDER: I will! Fellow citizens, you have convened and assembled here under a higher power than the law. What's 140 the law? When the ship's abroad on the ocean—when the army is before the enemy—where in thunder's the law? It is in the hearts of brave men who can tell right from wrong, and from whom justice can't be bought. So it is here, in the Wilds of the West, where out hatred of crime 145 is measured by the speed of our executions—where necessity is law!—I say, then, air you honest men? air you true? put your hands on your naked breasts, and let every man as don't feel a real American heart there, bustin' up with freedom, truth and right, let that man step out— 150 that's the oath I put to ye—and then say, darn ye, go it!

OMNES: Go on—Go on.

SCUDDER: No! I won't go on, that man's down, I won't strike him even with words. Jacob, your accuser is that picter of
155 the crime—let that speak—defend yourself.

M'CLOSKY: (*Draws knife.*) I will, quicker than lightning.

RATTS: Seize him, then! (*They rush on* M'CLOSKY *and disarm him.*) He can fight though—he's a painter, claws all over.

SCUDDER: Stop! Search him, we may find more evidence.

160 M'CLOSKY: Would you rob me first, and murder me afterwards?

RATTS: (*Searching him.*) That's his programme—here's a pocketbook.

SCUDDER: (*Opens it.*) What's here? Letters! Hello! to 'Mrs Pey-
165 ton, Terrebonne, Louisiana, United States' Liverpool post mark. Ho! I've got hold of the tail of a rat—come out. (*Reads.*) What's this?—a draft for 85,000 dollars and credit on Palisse and Co., of New Orleans, for the balance. Hi! the rat's out—you killed the boy to steal this letter from the
170 mail-bags—you stole this letter that the money should not arrive in time to save the Octoroon; had it done so, the lien on the estate would have ceased, and Zoe be free.

OMNES: Lynch him!—lynch him!—down with him!

SCUDDER: Silence in the court—stand back, let the gentle-
175 men of the jury retire, consult, and return their verdict.

RATTS: I'm responsible for the crittur—go on.

PETE: (*To* WAHNOTEE.) See, Inginn, look dar. (*Shows him plate.*) See dat innocent, look, dare's the murderer of poor Paul.

WAHNOTEE: Ugh! (*Examines plate.*)

180 PETE: Ya! as he? Closky tue Paul—kill de child with your tomahawk dar, 'twasn't you, no—ole Pete allus say so. Poor Inginn lub our little Paul.

(WAHNOTEE *rises and looks at* M'CLOSKY—*he is in his war paint and fully armed.*)

SCUDDER: What say ye, gentlemen? Is the prisoner guilty, or is he not guilty?

185 OMNES: Guilty!

SCUDDER: And what is to be his punishment?

OMNES: Death!

WAHNOTEE: (*Crosses to* M'CLOSKY.) Ugh!

SCUDDER: The Inginn, by thunder!

190 PETE: (*To* M'CLOSKY.) You's a dead man, mas'r; you've got to b'lieve dat.

M'CLOSKY: No! If I must die, give me up to the laws, but save me from the tomahawk of the savage; you are a white man, you'll not leave one of your own blood to be
195 butchered by the scalping knife of the redskin.

SCUDDER: Hold on now, Jacob, we've got to figure that out; let us look straight at the thing. Here we are on the confines of civilisation; it ain't our sile, I believe, rightly; Natur' has said that where the white man sets his foot the
200 red man and the black man shall up sticks and stan' round. Now, what do we pay for that possession? In cash? No— in kind—that is, in protection and forbearance, in gentleness, and in all them goods that show the critturs the difference between the Christian and the Savage. Now what
205 have you done to show 'em the distinction? for darn me if I can find out.

M'CLOSKY: For what I've done let me be tried.

SCUDDER: Oh, you have been fairly and honestly tried, and convicted: Providence has chosen your executioner—I
210 shan't interfere.

PETE: Oh! sar! hi, Mas'r Scudder, don't leave Mas'r 'Closky like date—don't, sar—tain't what a good Christian would do.

SCUDDER: D'ye hear that, Jacob?—this old nigger, the grandfather of the boy you murdered, speaks for you—don't that go through ye—d'ye feel it? Go on, Pete, you've 215 woke up the Christian here, and the old hoss responds.

WAHNOTEE: (*Placing his hand on* M'CLOSKY*'s head.*) Wahnotee!

SCUDDER: No, Inginn, we deal justice here, not revenge; tain't you he has injured, 'tis the white man, whose laws he has offended. 220

RATTS: Away with him! put him down the hatch till we rig his funeral.

M'CLOSKY: Fifty against one! Oh! if you were alone—if I had ye one by one in the swamp, I'd rip ye all.

PETE: (*Lighting him off,* R.) Dis way, Mas'r 'Closky, take care, sar. 225

(*Exit with* M'CLOSKY *and* JACKSON *to steamer.*)

LAFOUCHE: Off with him quick—here comes the ladies.

(*Enter* MRS CLAIBORNE, R 1 E.)

MRS CLAIBORNE: Shall we soon start, Captain?

RATTS: Yes, ma'am; we've only got a—Take my hand, ma'am, to steady you—a little account to square, and we're off.

MRS CLAIBORNE: A fog is rising. 230

RATTS: Swamp mist; soon clear off. (*Hands her to steamer.*)

MRS CLAIBORNE: Good night.

RATTS: Good night, ma'am—good night.

SCUDDER: Now to business.

(PETE *appears on deck.*)

PETE: Oh! law, sar. Dat debbel, 'Closky—he tore hisself from 235 de gentleman—knock me down—take away my light, and throwed it on de turpentine barrels—de ship's on fire!

(*All hurry off to ship—alarm bell rings—loud shouts; a hatch in the deck is opened—a glare of red—and* M'CLOSKY *emerges from the aperture; he is without his coat, and carries a bowie knife; he rushes down—*WAHNOTEE *alone is watching him from* R. U. E.).

M'CLOSKY: Ha, ha ha! I've given them something to remember how they treated Jacob M'Closky. Made my way from one end of the vessel to the other, and now the road to es- 240 cape is clear before me—and thus to secure it! (*He goes to* R. C., *and is met by* WAHNOTEE, *who silently confronts him.*)

WAHNOTEE: Paul.

M'CLOSKY: Devils!—you here!—stand clear!

WAHNOTEE: Paul. 245

M'CLOSKY: You won't—die, fool!

(*Thrusts at him—*WAHNOTEE, *with his tomahawk, strikes the knife out of his hand;* M'CLOSKY *starts back;* WAHNOTEE *throws off his blanket, and strikes at* M'CLOSKY *several times, who avoids him; at last he catches his arm, and struggles for the tomahawk, which falls; a violent struggle and fight takes place, ending with the triumph of* WAHNOTEE, *who drags* M'CLOSKY *along the ground, takes up the knife and stabs him repeatedly;* GEORGE *enters, bearing* ZOE *in his arms—all the* CHARACTERS *rush on—noise increasing—The steam vessel blows up—grand Tableau, and*

(*Curtain.*)

Susan Glaspell

Susan Glaspell (1882–1948) was born in Iowa, studied at Drake University in Des Moines and at the University of Chicago, and then briefly pursued a career as a journalist. With her husband, George Cram Cook, she founded the Provincetown Playhouse and wrote many of the plays it produced: *Suppressed Desires* (1914, written with Cook), a spoof of the vogue for psychoanalysis among New York's intellectual elite; *Trifles* (1916); *Close the Book* (1917); *A Woman's Honor* (1918); and *Tickless Time* (1918, again written with Cook). After the reorganization of the Provincetown in 1921, Glaspell wrote a series of full-length, often experimental, plays: *Inheritors* (1920), *The Verge* (1921), and *Alison's House* (1930). *Alison's House,* based loosely on the life of Emily Dickinson and her family, won Glaspell the Pulitzer Prize in 1930. Glaspell then retired from playwriting and largely from the theater as well, returning briefly to serve as the director of the Mid-West Play Bureau for the Federal Theater Project.

TRIFLES

Trifles is an important play in the development of American realism. It poses a distinct contrast to Eugene O'Neill's early plays, with which it shared the Provincetown stage. O'Neill's realistic plays attempt to filter an abstract, metaphysical longing into the drab world of his down-and-out drifters and sailors. Glaspell's drama more directly examines the values and behavior of the society she brings to the stage. In *Trifles*—and in the short story "A Jury of Her Peers," which she adapted from the play the following year—Glaspell considers the relationship between truth, power, and gender. The play is a murder mystery. A local man, John Wright, has been found dead, and his wife, Minnie, is suspected of killing him. Called to investigate, County Attorney George Henderson, Sheriff Henry Peters, and neighbor Lewis Hale readily assume a masculine prerogative to discover the truth of John Wright's murder, telling their wives to remain in the kitchen out of the way. How-

The Provincetown Players' 1917 production of Susan Glaspell's *Trifles*.

ever, the truth of the crime is in fact concealed *in* the kitchen, and only the women are able to discover it. Glaspell shows the audience that the "trifles" of the women's world are the signs of a reality wholly unreadable to the men, precisely because it is a world they regard as feminine, and therefore unimportant and uninteresting. *Trifles,* that is, works to subvert our notions of reality and truth by suggesting how such ideas are constructed within a specific social order—the masculine order of modern society.

TRIFLES

A PLAY IN ONE ACT

Susan Glaspell

CHARACTERS

COUNTY ATTORNEY, *George Henderson*
SHERIFF, *Henry Peters*
LEWIS HALE, *a neighboring farmer*
MRS. PETERS

MRS. HALE

THE SETTING: *The kitchen in the now abandoned farmhouse of John Wright*

SCENE: *The kitchen in the now abandoned farmhouse of John Wright, a gloomy kitchen, and left without having been put in order—unwashed pans under the sink, a loaf of bread outside the breadbox, a dish towel on the table—other signs of incompleted work. At the rear the outer door opens and the SHERIFF comes in followed by the COUNTY ATTORNEY and HALE. The SHERIFF and HALE are men in middle life, the COUNTY ATTORNEY is a young man; all are much bundled up and go at once to the stove. They are followed by the two women—the SHERIFF's wife first; she is a slight wiry woman, a thin nervous face. MRS. HALE is larger and would ordinarily be called more comfortable looking, but she is disturbed now and looks fearfully about as she enters. The women have come in slowly, and stand close together near the door.*

COUNTY ATTORNEY: (*Rubbing his hands.*) This feels good. Come up to the fire, ladies.

MRS. PETERS: (*After taking a step forward.*) I'm not—cold.

5   SHERIFF: (*Unbuttoning his overcoat and stepping away from the stove as if to mark the beginning of official business.*) Now, Mr. Hale, before we move things about, you explain to Mr. Henderson just what you saw when you came here yesterday morning.

COUNTY ATTORNEY: By the way, has anything been moved?
10   Are things just as you left them yesterday?

SHERIFF: (*Looking about.*) It's just the same. When it dropped below zero last night I thought I'd better send Frank out this morning to make a fire for us—no use getting pneumonia with a big case on, but I told him not to touch any-
15   thing except the stove—and you know Frank.

COUNTY ATTORNEY: Somebody should have been left here yesterday.

SHERIFF: Oh—yesterday. When I had to send Frank to Morris Center for that man who went crazy—I want you to
20   know I had my hands full yesterday, I knew you could get back from Omaha by today and as long as I went over everything here myself—

COUNTY ATTORNEY: Well, Mr. Hale, tell just what happened when you came here yesterday morning.

25   HALE: Harry and I had started to town with a load of potatoes. We came along the road from my place and as I got here I said, "I'm going to see if I can't get John Wright to go in with me on a party telephone." I spoke to Wright about it once before and he put me off, saying folks talked too
30   much anyway, and all he asked was peace and quiet—I guess you know about how much he talked himself; but I thought maybe if I went to the house and talked about it before his wife, though I said to Harry that I didn't know as what his wife wanted made much difference to John—

COUNTY ATTORNEY: Let's talk about that later, Mr. Hale. I do   35
want to talk about that, but tell now just what happened
when you got to the house.

HALE: I didn't hear or see anything; I knocked at the door, and still it was all quiet inside. I knew they must be up, it was past eight o'clock. So I knocked again, and I thought   40
I heard somebody say, "Come in." I wasn't sure, I'm not sure yet, but I opened the door—this door (*Indicating the door by which the two women are still standing.*) and there in that rocker—(*Pointing to it.*) sat Mrs. Wright.

(*They all look at the rocker.*)

COUNTY ATTORNEY: What—was she doing?   45

HALE: She was rockin' back and forth. She had her apron in her hand and was kind of—pleating it.

COUNTY ATTORNEY: And how did she—look?

HALE: Well, she looked queer.

COUNTY ATTORNEY: How do you mean—queer?   50

HALE: Well, as if she didn't know what she was going to do next. And kind of done up.

COUNTY ATTORNEY: How did she seem to feel about your coming?

HALE: Why, I don't think she minded—one way or other. She didn't pay much attention. I said, "How do, Mrs. Wright,   55
it's cold, ain't it?" And she said, "Is it?"—and went on kind of pleating at her apron. Well, I was surprised; she didn't ask me to come up to the stove, or to set down, but just sat there, not even looking at me, so I said, "I want to see John." And then she—laughed. I guess you would call it a   60
laugh. I thought of Harry and the team outside, so I said a little sharp: "Can't I see John?" "No," she says, kind o' dull like. "Ain't he home?" says I. "Yes," says she, "he's home." "Then why can't I see him?" I asked her, out of patience. "'Cause he's dead," says she. "*Dead?*" says I. She just   65
nodded her head, not getting a bit excited, but rockin' back and forth. "Why—where is he?" says I, not knowing what to say. She just pointed upstairs—like that (*Himself pointing to the room above.*) I got up, with the idea of going up there. I walked from there to here—then I says, "Why,   70
what did he die of?" "He died of a rope round his neck," says she, and just went on pleatin' at her apron. Well, I went out and called Harry. I thought I might—need help. We went upstairs and there he was lyin'—

COUNTY ATTORNEY: I think I'd rather have you go into that   75
upstairs, where you can point it all out. Just go on now
with the rest of the story.

HALE: Well, my first thought was to get that rope off. It looked
... (*Stops, his face twitches.*) ... but Harry, he went up to him,

80 and he said, "No, he's dead all right, and we'd better not touch anything." So we went back down stairs. She was still sitting that same way. "Has anybody been notified?" I asked. "No," says she, unconcerned. "Who did this, Mrs. Wright?" said Harry. He said it businesslike—and she

85 stopped pleatin' of her apron. "I don't know," she says. "You don't *know?*" says Harry. "No," says she. "Weren't you sleepin' in the bed with him?" says Harry. "Yes," says she, "but I was on the inside." "Somebody slipped a rope round his neck and strangled him and you didn't wake up?" says

90 Harry. "I didn't wake up," she said after him. We must 'a looked as if we didn't see how that could be, for after a minute she said, "I sleep sound." Harry was going to ask her more questions but I said maybe we ought to let her tell her story first to the coroner, or the sheriff, so Harry went fast as

95 he could to Rivers' place, where there's a telephone.

COUNTY ATTORNEY: And what did Mrs. Wright do when she knew that you had gone for the coroner?

HALE: She moved from that chair to this one over here (*Pointing to a small chair in the corner.*) and just sat there with her

100 hands held together and looking down. I got a feeling that I ought to make some conversation, so I said I had come in to see if John wanted to put in a telephone, and at that she started to laugh, and then she stopped and looked at me—scared. (*The* COUNTY ATTORNEY, *who has had his

105 notebook out, makes a note.*) I dunno, maybe it wasn't scared. I wouldn't like to say it was. Soon Harry got back, and then Dr. Lloyd came, and you, Mr. Peters, and so I guess that's all I know that you don't.

COUNTY ATTORNEY: (*Looking around.*) I guess we'll go up-

110 stairs first—and then out to the barn and around there. (*To the* SHERIFF.) You're convinced that there was nothing important here—nothing that would point to any motive.

SHERIFF: Nothing here but kitchen things.

(*The* COUNTY ATTORNEY *after again looking around the kitchen, opens the door of a cupboard closet. He gets up on a chair and looks on a shelf. Pulls his hand away, sticky.*)

COUNTY ATTORNEY: Here's a nice mess.

(*The women draw nearer.*)

115 MRS. PETERS: (*To the other woman.*) Oh, her fruit; it did freeze. (*To the* COUNTY ATTORNEY.) She worried about that when it turned so cold. She said the fire'd go out and her jars would break.

SHERIFF: Well, can you beat the women! Held for murder and

120 worryin' about her preserves.

COUNTY ATTORNEY: I guess before we're through she may have something more serious than preserves to worry about.

HALE: Well, women are used to worrying over trifles.

(*The two women move a little closer together.*)

COUNTY ATTORNEY: (*With the gallantry of a young politician.*)

125 And yet, for all their worries, what would we do without the ladies? (*The women do not unbend. He goes to the sink, takes a dipperful of water from the pail and pouring it into a basin, washes his hands. Starts to wipe them on the roller towel, turns it for a cleaner place.*) Dirty towels! (*Kicks his foot against

the pans under the sink.*) Not much of a housekeeper, would 130 you say, ladies?

MRS. HALE: (*Stiffly.*) There's a great deal of work to be done on a farm.

COUNTY ATTORNEY: To be sure. And yet (*With a little bow to her.*) I know there are some Dickson county farmhouses 135 which do not have such roller towels.

(*He gives it a pull to expose its full length again.*)

MRS. HALE: Those towels get dirty awful quick. Men's hands aren't always as clean as they might be.

COUNTY ATTORNEY: Ah, loyal to your sex, I see. But you and Mrs. Wright were neighbors. I suppose you were friends, 140 too.

MRS. HALE: (*Shaking her head.*) I've not seen much of her of late years. I've not been in this house—it's more than a year.

COUNTY ATTORNEY: And why was that? You didn't like her?

MRS. HALE: I liked her all well enough. Farmers' wives have 145 their hands full, Mr. Henderson. And then—

COUNTY ATTORNEY: Yes—?

MRS. HALE: (*Looking about.*) It never seemed a very cheerful place.

COUNTY ATTORNEY: No—it's not cheerful. I shouldn't say she had the homemaking instinct. 150

MRS. HALE: Well, I don't know as Wright had, either.

COUNTY ATTORNEY: You mean that they didn't get on very well?

MRS. HALE: No, I don't mean anything. But I don't think a place'd be any cheerfuller for John Wright's being in it.

COUNTY ATTORNEY: I'd like to talk more of that a little later. 155 I want to get the lay of things upstairs now.

(*He goes to the left, where three steps lead to a stair door.*)

SHERIFF: I suppose anything Mrs. Peters does'll be all right. She was to take in some clothes for her, you know, and a few little things. We left in such a hurry yesterday.

COUNTY ATTORNEY: Yes, but I would like to see what you 160 take, Mrs. Peters, and keep an eye out for anything that might be of use to us.

MRS. PETERS: Yes, Mr. Henderson.

(*The women listen to the men's steps on the stairs, then look about the kitchen.*)

MRS. HALE: I'd hate to have men coming into my kitchen, snooping around and criticising. 165

(*She arranges the pans under sink which the* COUNTY ATTORNEY *had shoved out of place.*)

MRS. PETERS: Of course it's no more than their duty.

MRS. HALE: Duty's all right, but I guess that deputy sheriff that came out to make the fire might have got a little of this on. (*Gives the roller towel a pull.*) Wish I'd thought of that sooner. Seems mean to talk about her for not having things slicked 170 up when she had to come away in such a hurry.

MRS. PETERS: (*Who has gone to a small table in the left rear corner of the room, and lifted one end of a towel that covers a pan.*) She had bread set.

(*Stands still.*)

175 MRS. HALE: (*Eyes fixed on a loaf of bread beside the breadbox, which is on a low shelf at the other side of the room. Moves slowly toward it.*) She was going to put this in there. (*Picks up loaf, then abruptly drops it. In a manner of returning to familiar things.*) It's a shame about her fruit. I wonder if it's all gone. (*Gets*
180 *up on the chair and looks.*) I think there's some here that's all right, Mrs. Peters. Yes—here; (*Holding it toward the window.*) this is cherries, too. (*Looking again.*) I declare I believe that's the only one. (*Gets down, bottle in her hand. Goes to the sink and wipes it off on the outside.*) She'll feel awful bad after all
185 her hard work in the hot weather. I remember the afternoon I put up my cherries last summer.

(*She puts the bottle on the big kitchen table, center of the room. With a sigh, is about to sit down in the rocking-chair. Before she is seated realizes what chair it is; with a slow look at it, steps back. The chair which she has touched rocks back and forth.*)

MRS. PETERS: Well, I must get those things from the front room closet. (*She goes to the door at the right, but after looking into the other room, steps back.*) You coming with me,
190 Mrs. Hale? You could help me carry them.

(*They go in the other room; reappear, MRS. PETERS carrying a dress and skirt, MRS. HALE following with a pair of shoes.*)

MRS. PETERS: My, it's cold in there.

(*She puts the clothes on the big table, and hurries to the stove.*)

MRS. HALE: (*Examining the skirt.*) Wright was close. I think maybe that's why she kept so much to herself. She didn't even belong to the Ladies Aid. I suppose she felt she
195 couldn't do her part, and then you don't enjoy things when you feel shabby. She used to wear pretty clothes and be lively, when she was Minnie Foster, one of the town girls singing in the choir. But that—oh, that was thirty years ago. This all you was to take in?
200 MRS. PETERS: She said she wanted an apron. Funny thing to want, for there isn't much to get you dirty in jail, goodness knows. But I suppose just to make her feel more natural. She said they was in the top drawer in this cupboard. Yes, here. And then her little shawl that always hung be-
205 hind the door. (*Opens stair door and looks.*) Yes, here it is.

(*Quickly shuts door leading upstairs.*)

MRS. HALE: (*Abruptly moving toward her.*) Mrs. Peters?
MRS. PETERS: Yes, Mrs. Hale?
MRS. HALE: Do you think she did it?
MRS. PETERS: (*In a frightened voice.*) Oh, I don't know.
210 MRS. HALE: Well, I don't think she did. Asking for an apron and her little shawl. Worrying about her fruit.
MRS. PETERS: (*Starts to speak, glances up, where footsteps are heard in the room above. In a low voice.*) Mr. Peters says it looks bad for her. Mr. Henderson is awful sarcastic in a speech and
215 he'll make fun of her sayin' she didn't wake up.
MRS. HALE: Well, I guess John Wright didn't wake when they was slipping that rope under his neck.
MRS. PETERS: No, it's strange. It must have been done awful crafty and still. They say it was such a—funny way to kill
220 a man, rigging it all up like that.

MRS. HALE: That's just what Mr. Hale said. There was a gun in the house. He says that's what he can't understand.
MRS. PETERS: Mr. Henderson said coming out that what was needed for the case was a motive; something to show anger, or—sudden feeling. 225
MRS. HALE: (*Who is standing by the table.*) Well, I don't see any signs of anger around here. (*She puts her hand on the dish towel which lies on the table, stands looking down at table, one half of which is clean, the other half messy.*) It's wiped to here. (*Makes a move as if to finish work, then turns and looks at loaf 230 of bread outside the breadbox. Drops towel. In that voice of coming back to familiar things.*) Wonder how they are finding things upstairs. I hope she had it a little more red-up up there. You know, it seems kind of *sneaking*. Locking her up in town and then coming out here and trying to get her 235 own house to turn against her!
MRS. PETERS: But Mrs. Hale, the law is the law.
MRS. HALE: I s'pose 'tis. (*Unbuttoning her coat.*) Better loosen up your things, Mrs. Peters. You won't feel them when you go out. 240

(MRS. PETERS *takes off her fur tippet, goes to hang it on hook at back of room, stands looking at the under part of the small corner table.*)

MRS. PETERS: She was piecing a quilt.

(*She brings the large sewing basket and they look at the bright pieces.*)

MRS. HALE: It's log cabin pattern. Pretty, isn't it? I wonder if she was goin' to quilt it or just knot it?

(*Footsteps have been heard coming down the stairs. The* SHERIFF *enters followed by* HALE *and the* COUNTY ATTORNEY.)

SHERIFF: They wonder if she was going to quilt it or just knot it!

(*The men laugh; the women look abashed.*)

COUNTY ATTORNEY: (*Rubbing his hands over the stove.*) Frank's 245 fire didn't do much up there, did it? Well, let's go out to the barn and get that cleared up.

(*The men go outside.*)

MRS. HALE: (*Resentfully.*) I don't know as there's anything so strange, our takin' up our time with little things while we're waiting for them to get the evidence. (*She sits down 250 at the big table smoothing out a block with decision.*) I don't see as it's anything to laugh about.
MRS. PETERS: (*Apologetically.*) Of course they've got awful important things on their minds.

(*Pulls up a chair and joins* MRS. HALE *at the table.*)

MRS. HALE: (*Examining another block.*) Mrs. Peters, look at this 255 one. Here, this is the one she was working on, and look at that sewing! All the rest of it has been so nice and even. And look at this! It's all over the place! Why, it looks as if she didn't know what she was about!

(*After she has said this they look at each other, then start to glance back at the door. After an instant* MRS. HALE *has pulled at a knot and ripped the sewing.*)

260   MRS. PETERS: Oh, what are you doing, Mrs. Hale?

MRS. HALE: (*Mildly.*) Just pulling out a stitch or two that's not sewed very good. (*Threading a needle.*) Bad sewing always made me fidgety.

MRS. PETERS: (*Nervously.*) I don't think we ought to touch things.

265   MRS. HALE: I'll just finish up this end. (*Suddenly stopping and leaning forward.*) Mrs. Peters?

MRS. PETERS: Yes, Mrs. Hale?

MRS. HALE: What do you suppose she was so nervous about?

MRS. PETERS: Oh—I don't know. I don't know as she was

270   nervous. I sometimes sew awful queer when I'm just tired. (MRS. HALE *starts to say something, looks at* MRS. PETERS, *then goes on sewing.*) Well, I must get these things wrapped up. They may be through sooner than we think. (*Putting apron and other things together.*) I wonder where I can find a piece

275   of paper, and string.

MRS. HALE: In that cupboard, maybe.

MRS. PETERS: (*Looking in cupboard.*) Why, here's a birdcage. (*Holds it up.*) Did she have a bird, Mrs. Hale?

MRS. HALE: Why, I don't know whether she did or not—I've

280   not been here for so long. There was a man around last year selling canaries cheap, but I don't know as she took one; maybe she did. She used to sing real pretty herself.

MRS. PETERS: (*Glancing around.*) Seems funny to think of a bird here. But she must have had one, or why would she

285   have a cage? I wonder what happened to it.

MRS. HALE: I s'pose maybe the cat got it.

MRS. PETERS: No, she didn't have a cat. She's got that feeling some people have about cats—being afraid of them. My cat got in her room and she was real upset and asked me to take it out.

290   MRS. HALE: My sister Bessie was like that. Queer, ain't it?

MRS. PETERS: (*Examining the cage.*) Why, look at this door. It's broke. One hinge is pulled apart.

MRS. HALE: (*Looking too.*) Looks as if someone must have been rough with it.

295   MRS. PETERS: Why, yes.

(*She brings the cage forward and puts it on the table.*)

MRS. HALE: I wish if they're going to find any evidence they'd be about it. I don't like this place.

MRS. PETERS: But I'm awful glad you came with me, Mrs. Hale. It would be lonesome for me sitting here alone.

300   MRS. HALE: It would, wouldn't it? (*Dropping her sewing.*) But I tell you what I do wish, Mrs. Peters. I wish I had come over sometimes when *she* was here. I—(*Looking around the room.*)— wish I had.

MRS. PETERS: But of course you were awful busy, Mrs.

305   Hale— your house and your children.

MRS. HALE: I could've come. I stayed away because it weren't cheerful—and that's why I ought to have come. I—I've never liked this place. Maybe because it's down in a hollow and you don't see the road. I dunno what it is, but it's

310   a lonesome place and always was. I wish I had come over to see Minnie Foster sometimes. I can see now—

(*Shakes her head.*)

MRS. PETERS: Well you mustn't reproach yourself, Mrs. Hale. Somehow we just don't see how it is with other folks until—something comes up.

MRS. HALE: Not having children makes less work—but it   315
makes a quiet house, and Wright out to work all day, and no company when he did come in. Did you know John Wright, Mrs. Peters?

MRS. PETERS: Not to know him; I've seen him in town. They say he was a good man.   320

MRS. HALE: Yes—good; he didn't drink, and kept his word as well as most, I guess, and paid his debts. But he was a hard man, Mrs. Peters. Just to pass the time of day with him— (*Shivers.*) Like a raw wind that gets to the bone. (*Pauses, her eye falling on the cage.*) I should think she would 'a wanted   325
a bird. But what do you suppose went with it?

MRS. PETERS: I don't know, unless it got sick and died.

(*She reaches over and swings the broken door, swings it again. Both women watch it.*)

MRS. HALE: You weren't raised round here, were you? (MRS. PETERS *shakes her head.*) You didn't know—her?

MRS. PETERS: Not till they brought her yesterday.   330

MRS. HALE: She—come to think of it, she was kind of like a bird herself—real sweet and pretty, but kind of timid and— fluttery. How—she—did—change. (*Silence; then as if struck by a happy thought and relieved to get back to every day things.*) Tell you what, Mrs. Peters, why don't you take the   335
quilt in with you? It might take up her mind.

MRS. PETERS: Why, I think that's a real nice idea, Mrs. Hale. There couldn't possibly be any objection to it, could there? Now, just what would I take? I wonder if her patches are in here—and her things.   340

(*They look in the sewing basket.*)

MRS. HALE: Here's some red. I expect this has got sewing things in it. (*Brings out a fancy box.*) What a pretty box. Looks like something somebody would give you. Maybe her scissors are in here. (*Opens box. Suddenly puts her hand to her nose.*) Why—(MRS. PETERS *bends nearer, then turns her face*   345
away.) There's something wrapped up in this piece of silk.

MRS. PETERS: Why, this isn't her scissors.

MRS. HALE: (*Lifting the silk.*) Oh, Mrs. Peters—its—

(MRS. PETERS *bends closer.*)

MRS. PETERS: It's the bird.

MRS. HALE: (*Jumping up.*) But, Mrs. Peters—look at it! Its   350
neck! Look at its neck! It's all—other side *to*.

MRS. PETERS: Somebody—wrung—its—neck.

(*Their eyes meet. A look of growing comprehension, of horror. Steps are heard outside.* MRS. HALE *slips box under quilt pieces, and sinks into her chair. Enter* SHERIFF *and* COUNTY ATTORNEY. MRS. PETERS *rises.*)

COUNTY ATTORNEY: (*As one turning from serious things to little pleasantries.*) Well, ladies, have you decided whether she was going to quilt it or knot it?   355

MRS. PETERS: We think she was going to—knot it.

COUNTY ATTORNEY: Well, that's interesting, I'm sure. (*Seeing the birdcage.*) Has the bird flown?

MRS. HALE: (*Putting more quilt pieces over the box.*) We think the—cat got it.   360

COUNTY ATTORNEY: (*Preoccupied.*) Is there a cat?

(MRS. HALE *glances in a quick covert way at* MRS. PETERS.)

MRS. PETERS: Well, not now. They're superstitious, you know. They leave.

COUNTY ATTORNEY: (*To* SHERIFF PETERS, *continuing an inter-*
365 *rupted conversation.*) No sign at all of anyone having come from the outside. Their own rope. Now let's go up again and go over it piece by piece. (*They start upstairs.*) It would have to have been someone who knew just the—

(MRS. PETERS *sits down. The two women sit there not looking at one another, but as if peering into something and at the same time holding back. When they talk now it is in the manner of feeling their way over strange ground, as if afraid of what they are saying, but as if they cannot help saying it.*)

MRS. HALE: She liked the bird. She was going to bury it in
370 that pretty box.

MRS. PETERS: (*In a whisper.*) When I was a girl—my kitten—there was a boy took a hatchet, and before my eyes—and before I could get there—(*Covers her face an instant.*) If they hadn't held me back I would have—(*Catches herself,*
375 *looks upstairs where steps are heard, falters weakly.*)—hurt him.

MRS. HALE: (*With a slow look around her.*) I wonder how it would seem never to have had any children around. (*Pause.*) No, Wright wouldn't like the bird—a thing that sang. She used to sing. He killed that, too.

380 MRS. PETERS: (*Moving uneasily.*) We don't know who killed the bird.

MRS. HALE: I knew John Wright.

MRS. PETERS: It was an awful thing was done in this house that night, Mrs. Hale. Killing a man while he slept, slipping a
385 rope around his neck that choked the life out of him.

MRS. HALE: His neck. Choked the life out of him.

(*Her hand goes out and rests on the birdcage.*)

MRS. PETERS: (*With rising voice.*) We don't know who killed him. We don't know.

MRS. HALE: (*Her own feeling not interrupted.*) If there'd been
390 years and years of nothing, then a bird to sing to you, it would be awful—still, after the bird was still.

MRS. PETERS: (*Something within her speaking.*) I know what stillness is. When we homesteaded in Dakota, and my first baby died—after he was two years old, and me with no
395 other then—

MRS. HALE: (*Moving.*) How soon do you suppose they'll be through, looking for the evidence?

MRS. PETERS: I know what stillness is. (*Pulling herself back.*) The law has got to punish crime, Mrs. Hale.

400 MRS. HALE: (*Not as if answering that.*) I wish you'd seen Minnie Foster when she wore a white dress with blue ribbons and stood up there in the choir and sang. (*A look around the room.*) Oh, I *wish* I'd come over here once in a while! That was a crime! That was a crime! Who's going to punish that?

405 MRS. PETERS: (*Looking upstairs.*) We mustn't—take on.

MRS. HALE: I might have known she needed help! I know how things can be—for women. I tell you, it's queer, Mrs. Peters. We live close together and we live far apart. We all go

through the same things—it's all just a different kind of the same thing. (*Brushes her eyes; noticing the bottle of fruit, reaches* 410
out for it.) If I was you I wouldn't tell her her fruit was gone. Tell her it *ain't.* Tell her it's all right. Take this in to prove it to her. She—she may never know whether it was broke or not.

MRS. PETERS: (*Takes the bottle, looks about for something to wrap it in, takes petticoat from the clothes brought from the other room,* 415
very nervously begins winding this around the bottle. In a false voice.) My, it's a good thing the men couldn't hear us. Wouldn't they just laugh! Getting all stirred up over a little thing like a—dead canary. As if that could have anything to do with—with—wouldn't they *laugh!* 420

(*The men are heard coming down stairs.*)

MRS. HALE: (*Under her breath.*) Maybe they would—maybe they wouldn't.

COUNTY ATTORNEY: No, Peters, it's all perfectly clear except a reason for doing it. But you know juries when it comes to women. If there was some definite thing. Something to 425
show—something to make a story about—a thing that would connect up with this strange way of doing it—

(*The women's eyes meet for an instant. Enter* HALE *from outer door.*)

HALE: Well, I've got the team around. Pretty cold out there.

COUNTY ATTORNEY: I'm going to stay here a while by myself. (*To the* SHERIFF.) You can send Frank out for me, can't you? I want 430
to go over everything. I'm not satisfied that we can't do better.

SHERIFF: Do you want to see what Mrs. Peters is going to take in?

(*The* COUNTY ATTORNEY *goes to the table, picks up the apron, laughs.*)

COUNTY ATTORNEY: Oh, I guess they're not very dangerous things the ladies have picked out. (*Moves a few things about, disturbing the quilt pieces which cover the box. Steps back.*) No, 435
Mrs. Peters doesn't need supervising. For that matter, a sheriff's wife is married to the law. Ever think of it that way, Mrs. Peters?

MRS. PETERS: Not—just that way.

SHERIFF: (*Chuckling.*) Married to the law. (*Moves toward the* 440
other room.) I just want you to come in here a minute, George. We ought to take a look at these windows.

COUNTY ATTORNEY: (*Scoffingly.*) Oh, windows!

SHERIFF: We'll be right out, Mr. Hale.

(HALE *goes outside. The* SHERIFF *follows the* COUNTY ATTORNEY *into the other room. Then* MRS. HALE *rises, hands tight together, looking intensely at* MRS. PETERS, *whose eyes make a slow turn, finally meeting* MRS. HALE's. *A moment* MRS. HALE *holds her, then her own eyes point the way to where the box is concealed. Suddenly* MRS. PETERS *throws back quilt pieces and tries to put the box in the bag she is wearing. It is too big. She opens box, starts to take bird out, cannot touch it, goes to pieces, stands there helpless. Sound of a knob turning in the other room.* MRS. HALE *snatches the box and puts it in the pocket of her big coat. Enter* COUNTY ATTORNEY *and* SHERIFF.)

COUNTY ATTORNEY: (*Facetiously.*) Well, Henry, at least we 445
found out that she was not going to quilt it. She was going to—what is it you call it, ladies?

MRS. HALE: (*Her hand against her pocket.*) We call it—knot it, Mr. Henderson.

Eugene O'Neill

Born the son of the famous turn-of-the-century actor James O'Neill, Eugene O'Neill (1888–1953) became America's greatest dramatist. Much of O'Neill's younger life is described in his late play, *Long Day's Journey into Night:* how he spent his first several years touring with his family following his father's career on the stage; his stints in boarding school and at Princeton; some time spent working on ships sailing to South America and Africa, and bumming around in Buenos Aires and New York; a serious bout with tuberculosis. In the play, O'Neill leaves the future of his young poet-hero uncertain, but in fact illness provided O'Neill with the time to begin writing seriously. When he recovered, O'Neill attended George Pierce Baker's playwriting classes at Harvard. He worked briefly in Greenwich Village and then joined the Provincetown Playhouse company on Cape Cod in 1916, where his first plays were produced.

O'Neill had a long and tumultuous career in the theater. An admirer of Strindberg's drama, and widely read in Nietzsche, Freud, and Jung, O'Neill experimented in a variety of different theatrical styles, always searching for new ways to reveal the complex working of a character's psychology. He wrote a series of short realistic plays that were produced at the Provincetown and other "little theaters," the best of which concern life at sea: *Bound East for Cardiff* (1916), *Fog* (1917), *In the Zone* (1917), *The Long Voyage Home* (1917), and *The Moon of the Caribbees* (1918). His first Broadway production, *Beyond the Horizon* (1920) won him the first of four Pulitzer Prizes; he later won for *Anna Christie* (1921), *Strange Interlude* (1928), and *Long Day's Journey into Night* (awarded posthumously in 1956). Throughout the 1920s, the period of his greatest success in the theater, O'Neill both wrote realistic plays like *Desire Under the Elms* (1924) and experimented in a variety of other modes. He tried expressionistic techniques in *The Hairy Ape* (1922) and *The Emperor Jones* (1920); masks in *The Great God Brown* (1926); and revealing "asides" in *Strange Interlude,* in which characters speak their unspoken "thoughts" directly to the audience. He also took a chance with comedy in *Ah, Wilderness!* (1932), something of a study for *Long Day's Journey.*

O'Neill's decade of success was followed by a series of impressive failures. Some of these plays are nonetheless fascinating. Although it played well in 1928, the asides and length (more than eight hours) of *Strange Interlude* have militated against many revivals; the parallels between Aeschylus' *Oresteia* and O'Neill's *Mourning Becomes Electra* (1931) still attract comment and discussion. Much of O'Neill's work from the late 1920s and 1930s is inflated and bombastic, and plays like *Lazarus Laughed* (1928), *Marco Millions* (1929), *Dynamo* (1929), and *Days Without End* (1934) seemed to mark his flagging powers as a writer. When O'Neill won the Nobel Prize in 1936, his career was widely regarded as finished. His plays had become empty and grandiose, and he suffered from Parkinson's disease, which made it increasingly difficult for him to write. Throughout the 1930s and 1940s, though, O'Neill planned a massive cycle of plays concerning the fortunes of an American family, called *A Tale of Possessors Self-Dispossessed;* of these he completed only *A Touch of the Poet* (written 1935–1942) and a draft of *More Stately Mansions* (1935–1940). However, in the 1940s, O'Neill also wrote his greatest plays, realistic dramas based for the most part on his family's history and on his own life. These hard-won plays may have been out of keeping with the national mood in the aftermath of World War II: when *The Iceman Cometh* opened in 1946, it ran for only 136 performances, and *A Moon for the Misbegotten* (1947) closed in Ohio before reaching New York. Yet when *Iceman* was revived in 1956, directed by Jose Quintero, it was a huge success and prompted a widespread reevaluation of O'Neill's drama.

Since O'Neill was raised on his father's melodramatic portrayal of *The Count of Monte Cristo,* it is not surprising that he was at times also infected with the spirit of melodrama. O'Neill's plays often recall melodrama's emphasis on the passions of the characters, its striking moments of stage action, its penchant for the romantic and the sentimental. O'Neill's experimentation and sure sense of the stage enabled him to achieve an unparalleled body of work and to define the course of drama in the United States in the first half of the twentieth century.

THE HAIRY APE

Although O'Neill is today most often remembered for the realistic plays he wrote late in his career, *The Hairy Ape* testifies to his ongoing experiments with the form and purpose of theatrical representation. O'Neill was an admirer of Strindberg's drama, and throughout his career experimented with various **EXPRESSIONIST THEATER** techniques, ways of expressing a character's state of mind directly in the setting: the offstage drumming that's heard in *Moon of the Caribbees,* the Little Formless Fears in *The Emperor Jones,* the convention that lets characters speak their "real" thoughts directly to the audience as asides in *Strange Interlude.* In *The Hairy Ape,* O'Neill develops another aspect of expressionist theater, its use of a morality-play structure and a distorted stage set to allegorize the predicament of "modern man." But while later plays—Elmer Rice's *The Adding Machine* or Sophie Treadwell's *Machinal*—take the plight of the faceless, routinized office worker as their model, O'Neill locates the problem of identity in modern culture in an industrial worker, the coal-stoker Yank. *The Hairy Ape* begins by showing Yank in his element, the ship's forecastle, and O'Neill emphasizes the play's evocation of Yank's perspective in his stage directions. Much as the play will show the vital Yank to be hemmed in on every side by imprisoning social conventions, so here in the ship, *"The lines of bunks, the uprights supporting them, cross each other like the steel framework of a cage. The ceiling crushes down upon the men's heads."* From the outset, Yank is the creature of industrial society, a man transformed into a kind of machine, breathing the smoke of the stokehole, reveling in its heat: "Hell, sure, dat's my fav'rite climate. I eat it up! I git fat on it!

Kate Valk as Mildred and Willem Dafoe as Yank in Eugene O'Neill's *The Hairy Ape,* by the Wooster Group.

It's me makes it hot! It's me makes it roar! It's me makes it move!" In the scenes that follow, however, Yank goes on a kind of pilgrimage: when Mildred is brought to the stokehole in scene 3, Yank is insulted, and vows to "show her who's a ape!"; in the subsequent scenes he leaves the ship, encounters the riches of Fifth Avenue, is thrown in jail and firehosed, is attacked and beaten by labor organizers who take him for a spy, and winds up at the gorilla cage in the zoo. The language of industrial protest—indeed, of a Marxist industrial proletariat—suffuses the play, and O'Neill takes Yank's predicament to represent both a social and a kind of existential crisis; like Charlie Chaplin in his film *Modern Times*—but with a harder, less sentimental edge—O'Neill sees modern industrial culture as a new form of social production: a social order that requires the destruction of its Yanks even as it depends on their creation.

Although some readers may find O'Neill's language here quaint or off-putting—both in its stagey imitation of a 1920s dialect and in its accurate use of racist epithets—the play has had a continuing vitality on the stage; it was produced by the avant-garde Wooster Group in the 1990s and starred Willem Dafoe as Yank.

THE HAIRY APE

A COMEDY OF ANCIENT AND MODERN LIFE IN EIGHT SCENES

Eugene O'Neill

CHARACTERS

ROBERT SMITH, "YANK"
PADDY
LONG
MILDRED DOUGLAS
HER AUNT
SECOND ENGINEER
FOURTH ENGINEER
A GUARD
A SECRETARY OF AN ORGANIZATION
STOKERS, LADIES, GENTLEMEN, ETC.

Scene I   The firemen's forecastle of an ocean liner an hour after sailing from New York.

Scene II   Section of promenade deck, two days out—morning.

Scene III   The stokehole. A few minutes later.

Scene IV   Same as Scene I. Half an hour later.

Scene V   Fifth Avenue, New York. Three weeks later.

Scene VI   An island near the city. The next night.

Scene VII   In the city. About a month later.

Scene VIII   In the city. Twilight of the next day.

SCENE ONE

SCENE: *The firemen's forecastle of a transatlantic liner an hour after sailing from New York for the voyage across. Tiers of narrow, steel bunks, three deep, on all sides. An entrance in rear. Benches on the floor before the bunks. The room is crowded with men, shouting, cursing, laughing, singing—a confused, inchoate uproar swelling into a sort of unity, a meaning—the bewildered, furious, baffled defiance of a beast in a cage. Nearly all the men are drunk. Many bottles are passed from hand to hand. All are dressed in dungaree pants, heavy ugly shoes. Some wear singlets, but the majority are stripped to the waist.*

The treatment of this scene, or of any other scene in the play, should by no means be naturalistic. The effect sought after is a cramped space in the bowels of a ship, imprisoned by white steel. The lines of bunks, the uprights supporting them, cross each other like the steel framework of a cage. The ceiling crushes down upon the men's heads. They cannot stand upright. This accentuates the natural stooping posture which shoveling coal and the resultant overdevelopment of back and shoulder muscles have given them. The men themselves should resemble those pictures in which the appearance of Neanderthal Man is guessed at. All are hairy-chested, with long arms of tremendous power, and low, receding brows above their small, fierce, resentful eyes. All the civilized white races are represented, but except for the slight differentiation in color of hair, skin, eyes, all these men are alike.

The curtain rises on a tumult of sound. YANK is seated in the foreground. He seems broader, fiercer, more truculent, more powerful, more sure of himself than the rest. They respect his superior strength—the grudging respect of fear. Then, too, he represents to them a self-expression, the very last word in what they are, their most highly developed individual.

VOICES: Gif me trink dere, you!
'Ave a wet!
Salute!
Gesundheit!
5   Skoal!
Drunk as a lord, God stiffen you!
Here's how!
Luck!

Pass back that bottle, damn you!
Pourin' it down his neck!
Ho, Froggy! Where the devil have you been?   10
La Touraine.
I hit him smash in yaw, py Gott!
Jenkins the First he's a rotten swine—
And the coppers nabbed him—and I run—   15
I like peer better. It don't pig head gif you.
A slut, I'm sayin'. She robbed me aslape—
To hell with 'em all!
You're a bloody liar!
Say dot again! (*Commotion. Two men about to fight are*   20
pulled apart.)
No scrappin' now!
Tonight—
See who's the best man!
Bloody Dutchman!
Tonight on the for'ard square.   25
I'll bet on Dutchy.
He packa da wallop, I tell you!
Shut up, Wop!
No fightin', maties. We're all chums, ain't we?

(*A voice starts bawling a song.*)

    Beer, beer, glorious beer!   30
    Fill yourselves right up to here.

YANK: (*For the first time seeming to take notice of the uproar about him, turns around threateningly—in a tone of contemptuous authority.*) Choke off dat noise! Where d'yuh get dat beer stuff? Beer, hell! Beer's for goils—and Dutchmen. Me for   35 somep'n wit a kick to it! Gimme a drink, one of youse guys. (*Several bottles are eagerly offered. He takes a tremendous gulp at one of them; then, keeping the bottle in his hand, glares belligerently at the owner, who hastens to acquiesce in this robbery by saying.*) All righto, Yank. Keep it and have another.   40 (*YANK contemptuously turns his back on the crowd again. For a second there is an embarrassed silence. Then—.*)
VOICES: We must be passing the Hook.
She's beginning to roll to it.

45   Six days in hell—and then Southampton.
      Py Yesus, I vish somepody take my first vatch for me!
      Gittin' seasick, Square-head?
      Drink up and forget it!
      What's in your bottle?
50   Gin.
      Dot's a nigger trink.
      Absinthe? It's doped. You'll go off your chump, Froggy!
      Cochon!
      Whisky, that's the ticket!
55   Where's Paddy?
      Going asleep.
      Sing us that whisky song, Paddy.

(*They all turn to an old, wizened Irishman who is dozing, very drunk, on the benches forward. His face is extremely monkey-like with all the sad, patient pathos of that animal in his small eyes.*)

      Singa da song, Caruso Pat!
      He's gettin' old. The drink is too much for him.
60   He's too drunk.
PADDY: (*Blinking about him, starts to his feet resentfully, swaying, holding on to the edge of a bunk.*) I'm never too drunk to sing. 'Tis only when I'm dead to the world I'd be wishful to sing at all. (*With a sort of sad contempt.*) "Whisky
65   Johnny," ye want? A chanty, ye want? Now that's a queer wish from the ugly like of you. God help you. But no mather, (*He starts to sing in a thin, nasal, doleful tone.*)

      Oh, whisky is the life of man!
          Whisky! O Johnny! (*They all join in on this.*)
70   Oh, whisky is the life of man!
          Whisky for my Johnny! (*Again chorus.*)
      Oh, whisky drove my old man mad!
          Whisky! O Johnny!
      Oh, whisky drove my old man mad!
75   Whisky for my Johnny!

YANK: (*Again turning around scornfully.*) Aw hell! Nix on dat old sailing ship stuff! All dat bull's dead, see? And you're dead, too, yuh damned old Harp, on'y yuh don't know it. Take it easy, see. Give us a rest. Nix on de loud noise.
80   (*With a cynical grin.*) Can't youse see I'm tryin' to t'ink?
ALL: (*Repeating the word after him as one with the same cynical amused mockery.*) Think! (*The chorused word has a brazen metallic quality as if their throats were phonograph horns. It is followed by a general uproar of hard, barking laughter.*)
85 VOICES: Don't be cracking your head wit ut, Yank.
      You gat headache, py yingo!
      One thing about it—it rhymes with drink!
      Ha, ha, ha!
      Drink, don't think!
90   Drink, don't think!
      Drink, don't think! (*A whole chorus of voices has taken up this refrain, stamping on the floor, pounding on the benches with fists.*)
YANK: (*Taking a gulp from his bottle—good-naturedly.*) Aw right. Can de noise. I got yuh de foist time. (*The uproar subsides. A very drunken sentimental tenor begins to sing.*)

95   Far away in Canada,
              Far across the sea,
          There's a lass who fondly waits
              Making a home for me—

YANK: (*Fiercely contemptuous.*) Shut up, yuh lousy boob! Where d'yuh get dat tripe? Home? Home, hell! I'll make a home 100 for yuh! I'll knock yuh dead. Home! T'hell wit home! Where d'yuh get dat tripe? Dis is home, see? What d'yuh want wit home? (*Proudly.*) I runned away from mine when I was a kid. On'y too glad to beat it, dat was me. Home was lickings for me, dat's all. But yuh can bet your shoit no one 105 ain't never licked me since! Wanter try it, any of youse? Huh! I guess not. (*In a more placated but still contemptuous tone.*) Goils waitin' for yuh, huh? Aw, hell! Dat's all tripe. Dey don't wait for no one. Dey'd double-cross yuh for a nickel. Dey're all tarts, get me? Treat 'em rough, dat's me. 110 To hell wit 'em. Tarts, dat's what, de whole bunch of 'em.
LONG: (*Very drunk, jumps on a bench excitedly, gesticulating with a bottle in his hand.*) Listen 'ere, Comrades. Yank 'ere is right. 'E says this 'ere stinkin' ship is our 'ome. And 'e says as 'ome is 'ell. And 'e's right! This is 'ell. We lives in 'ell, 115 Comrades—and right enough we'll die in it. (*Raging.*) And who's ter blame, I arsks yer? We ain't. We wasn't born this rotten way. All men is born free and ekal. That's in the bleedin' Bible, maties. But what d'they care for the Bible—them lazy, bloated swine what travels first cabin? 120 Them's the ones. They dragged us down 'til we're on'y wage slaves in the bowels of a bloody ship, sweatin', burnin' up, eatin' coal dust! Hit's them's ter blame—the damned Capitalist clarss! (*There had been a gradual murmur of contemptuous resentment rising among the men until now he 125 is interrupted by a storm of catcalls, hisses, boos, hard laughter.*)
VOICES: Turn it off!
      Shut up!
      Sit down!
      Closa da face!   130
      Tamn fool! (*Etc.*)
YANK: (*Standing up and glaring at LONG.*) Sit down before I knock yuh down! (LONG *makes haste to efface himself.* YANK *goes on contemptuously.*) De Bible, huh? De Cap'tlist class, huh? Aw nix on dat Salvation Army–Socialist bull. Git a 135 soapbox! Hire a hall! Come and be saved, huh? Jerk us to Jesus, huh? Aw g'wan! I've listened to lots of guys like you, see. Yuh're all wrong. Wanter know what I t'ink? Yuh ain't no good for no one. Yuh're de bunk. Yuh ain't got no noive, get me? Yuh're yellow, dat's what. Yellow, dat's you. 140 Say! What's dem slobs in de foist cabin got to do wit us? We're better men dan dey are, ain't we? Sure! One of us guys could clean up de whole mob wit one mit. Put one of 'em down here for one watch in de stokehole, what'd happen? Dey'd carry him off on a stretcher. Dem boids 145 don't amount to nothin'. Dey're just baggage. Who makes dis old tub run? Ain't it us guys? Well den, we belong, don't we? We belong and dey don't. Dat's all. (*A loud chorus of approval.* YANK *goes on.*) As for dis bein' hell—aw, nuts! Yuh lost your noive, dat's what. Dis is a man's job, get 150 me? It belongs. It runs dis tub. No stiffs need apply. But yuh're a stiff, see? Yuh're yellow, dat's you.
VOICES: (*With a great hard pride in them.*)
      Righto!
      A man's job!   155
      Talk is cheap, Long.
      He never could hold up his end.
      Divil take him!
      Yank's right. We make it go.
      Py Gott, Yank say right ting!   160

We don't need no one cryin' over us.
Makin' speeches.
Throw him out!
Yellow!
165 Chuck him overboard!
I'll break his jaw for him!

(*They crowd around* LONG *threateningly.*)

YANK: (*Half good-natured again—contemptuously.*) Aw, take it easy. Leave him alone. He ain't woith a punch. Drink up. Here's how, whoever owns dis. (*He takes a long swallow from*
170 *his bottle. All drink with him. In a flash all is hilarious amiability again, back-slapping, loud talk, etc.*)

PADDY: (*Who has been sitting in a blinking, melancholy daze— suddenly cries out in a voice full of old sorrow.*) We belong to this, you're saying? We make the ship to go, you're saying?
175 Yerra then, that Almighty God have pity on us! (*His voice runs into the wail of a keen, he rocks back and forth on his bench. The men stare at him, startled and impressed in spite of themselves.*)—Oh, to be back in the fine days of my youth, ochone! Oh, there was fine beautiful ships them days—
180 clippers wid tall masts touching the sky—fine strong men in them—men that was sons of the sea as if 'twas the mother that bore them. Oh, the clean skins of them, and the clear eyes, the straight backs and full chests of them! Brave men they was, and bold men surely! We'd be sailing out,
185 bound down round the Horn maybe. We'd be making sail in the dawn, with a fair breeze, singing a chanty song wid no care to it. And astern the land would be sinking low and dying out, but we'd give it no heed but a laugh, and never a look behind. For the day that was, was enough, for
190 we was free men—and I'm thinking 'tis only slaves do be giving heed to the day that's gone or the day to come— until they're old like me. (*With a sort of religious exaltation.*) Oh, to be scudding south again wid the power of the Trade Wind driving her on steady through the nights and
195 the days! Full sail on her! Nights and days! Nights when the foam of the wake would be flaming wid fire, when the sky'd be blazing and winking wid stars. Or the full of the moon maybe. Then you'd see her driving through the gray night, her sails stretching aloft all silver and white, not
200 a sound on the deck, the lot of us dreaming dreams, till you'd believe 'twas no real ship at all you was on but a ghost ship like the *Flying Dutchman* they say does be roaming the seas forevermore widout touching a port. And there was the days, too. A warm sun on the clean decks.
205 Sun warming the blood of you, and wind over the miles of shiny green ocean like strong drink to your lungs. Work—aye, hard work—but who'd mind that at all? Sure, you worked under the sky and 'twas work wid skill and daring to it. And wid the day done, in the dog watch,
210 smoking me pipe at ease, the lookout would be raising land maybe, and we'd see the mountains of South Americy wid the red fire of the setting sun painting their white tops and the clouds floating by them! (*His tone of exaltation ceases. He goes on mournfully.*) Yerra, what's the use of
215 talking? 'Tis a dead man's whisper. (*To* YANK *resentfully.*) 'Twas them days men belonged to ships, not now. 'Twas them days a ship was part of the sea, and a man was part of a ship, and the sea joined all together and made it one. (*Scornfully.*) Is it one wid this you'd be, Yank—black smoke

220 from the funnels smudging the sea, smudging the decks— the bloody engines pounding and throbbing and shaking-wid—divil a sight of sun or a breath of clean air—choking our lungs wid coal dust—breaking our backs and hearts in the hell of the stokehole—feeding the bloody furnace—
225 feeding our lives along wid the coal, I'm thinking—caged in by steel from a sight of the sky like bloody apes in the Zoo! (*With a harsh laugh.*) Ho-ho, divil mend you! Is it to belong to that you're wishing? Is it a flesh and blood wheel of the engines you'd be?

230 YANK: (*Who has been listening with a contemptuous sneer, barks out the answer.*) Sure ting! Dat's me. What about it?

PADDY: (*As if to himself—with great sorrow.*) Me time is past due. That a great wave wid sun in the heart of it may sweep me over the side sometime I'd be dreaming of the
235 days that's gone!

YANK: Aw, yuh crazy Mick! (*He springs to his feet and advances on* PADDY *threateningly—then stops, fighting some queer struggle within himself—lets his hands fall to his sides—contemptuously.*) Aw, take it easy. Yuh're aw right, at dat. Yuh're bugs, dat's
240 all—nutty as a cuckoo. All dat tripe yuh been pullin'—Aw, dat's all right. On'y it's dead, get me? Yuh don't belong no more, see. Yuh don't get de stuff. Yuh're too old. (*Disgustedly.*) But aw say, come up for air onct in a while, can't yuh? See what's happened since yuh croaked. (*He suddenly bursts*
245 *forth vehemently, growing more and more excited.*) Say! Sure! Sure I meant it! What de hell—Say, lemme talk! Hey! Hey, you old Harp! Hey, youse guys! Say, listen to me—wait a moment—I gotta talk, see. I belong and he don't. He's dead but I'm livin'. Listen to me! Sure I'm part of de engines!
250 Why de hell not? Dey move, don't dey? Dey're speed, ain't dey? Dey smash trou, don't dey? Twenty-five knots a hour! Dat's goin' some! Dat's new stuff! Dat belongs! But him, he's too old. He gets dizzy. Say, listen. All dat crazy tripe about nights and days; all dat crazy tripe about stars and moons; all
255 dat crazy tripe about suns and winds, fresh air and de rest of it—Aw hell, dat's all a dope dream! Hittin' de pipe of de past, dat's what he's doin'. He's old and don't belong no more. But me, I'm young! I'm in de pink! I move wit it! It, get me! I mean de ting dat's de guts of all dis. It ploughs trou
260 all de tripe he's been sayin'. It blows dat up! It knocks dat dead! It slams dat offen de face of de oith! It, get me! De engines and de coal and de smoke and all de rest of it! He can't breathe and swallow coal dust, but I kin, see? Dat's fresh air for me! Dat's food for me! I'm new, get me? Hell in de
265 stokehole? Sure! It takes a man to work in hell. Hell, sure, dat's my fav'rite climate. I eat it up! I git fat on it! It's me makes it hot! It's me makes it roar! It's me makes it move! Sure, on'y for me everyting stops. It all goes dead, get me? De noise and smoke and all de engines movin' de woild, dey
270 stop. Dere ain't nothin' no more! Dat's what I'm sayin'. Everything else dat makes de woild move, somep'n makes it move. It can't move witout somep'n else, see? Den yuh get down to me. I'm at de bottom, get me! Dere ain't nothin' foither. I'm de end! I'm de start! I start somep'n and de
275 woild moves! It—dat's me!—de new dat's moiderin' de old! I'm de ting in coal dat makes it boin; I'm steam and oil for de engines; I'm de ting in noise dat makes yuh hear it; I'm smoke and express trains and steamers and factory whistles; I'm de ting in gold dat makes money! And I'm what makes
280 iron into steel! Steel, dat stands for de whole ting! And I'm steel—steel—steel! I'm de muscles in steel, de punch

behind it. (*As he says this he pounds with his fist against the steel bunks. All the men, roused to a pitch of frenzied self-glorification by his speech, do likewise. There is a deafening metallic roar,*
285 *through which* YANK's *voice can be heard bellowing.*) Slaves, hell! We run de whole woiks. All de rich guys dat tink dey're somep'n, dey ain't nothin'! Dey don't belong. But us guys, we're in de move, we're at de bottom, de whole ting is us! (PADDY *from the start of* YANK's *speech has been taking one gulp*
290 *after another from his bottle, at first frightenedly, as if he were afraid to listen, then desperately, as if to drown his senses, but finally has achieved complete indifferent, even amused, drunkenness.* YANK *sees his lips moving. He quells the uproar with a shout.*) Hey, youse guys, take it easy! Wait a moment! De nutty Harp is
295 sayin' somep'n.

PADDY: (*Is heard now—throws his head back with a mocking burst of laughter.*) Ho-ho-ho-ho-ho—

YANK: (*Drawing back his fist, with a snarl.*) Aw! Look out who yuh're givin' the bark!

300 PADDY: (*Begins to sing "The Miller of Dee" with enormous good nature.*)

> I care for nobody, no, not I,
> And nobody cares for me.

YANK: (*Good-natured himself in a flash, interrupts* PADDY *with a*
305 *slap on the bare back like a report.*) Dat's de stuff! Now yuh're gettin' wise to somep'n. Care for nobody, dat's de dope! To hell wit 'em all! And nix on nobody else carin'. I kin care for myself, get me! (*Eight bells sound; muffled, vibrating through the steel walls as if some enormous brazen gong were*
310 *imbedded in the heart of the ship. All the men jump up mechanically, file through the door silently close upon each other's heels in what is very like a prisoners' lockstep.* YANK *slaps* PADDY *on the back.*) Our watch, yuh old Harp! (*Mockingly.*) Come on down in hell. Eat up de coal dust. Drink in de heat. It's
315 it, see! Act like yuh like it, yuh better—or croak yuhself.

PADDY: (*With jovial defiance.*) To the divil wid it! I'll not report this watch. Let thim log me and be damned. I'm no slave the like of you. I'll be sittin' here at me ease, and drinking, and thinking, and dreaming dreams.

320 YANK: (*Contemptuously.*) Tinkin' and dreamin', what'll that get yuh? What's tinkin' got to do wit it? We move, don't we? Speed, ain't it? Fog, dat's all you stand for. But we drive trou dat, don't we? We split dat up and smash trou— twenty-five knots a hour! (*Turns his back on* PADDY *scorn-*
325 *fully.*) Aw, yuh make me sick! Yuh don't belong! (*He strides out the door in rear.* PADDY *hums to himself, blinking drowsily.*)

(*The curtain falls.*)

SCENE TWO

SCENE: *Two days out. A section of the promenade deck.* MILDRED DOUGLAS *and her* AUNT *are discovered reclining in deck chairs. The former is a girl of twenty, slender, delicate, with a pale, pretty face marred by a self-conscious expression of disdainful superiority. She looks fretful, nervous and discontented, bored by her own anemia.* HER AUNT *is a pompous and proud—and fat—old lady. She is a type even to the point of a double chin and lorgnettes. She is dressed pretentiously, as if afraid her face alone would never indicate her position in life.* MILDRED *is dressed all in white.*

The impression to be conveyed by this scene is one of the beautiful, vivid life of the sea all about—sunshine on the deck in a great flood, the fresh sea wind blowing across it. In the midst of this, these two incongruous, artificial figures, inert and disharmonious, the elder like a gray lump of dough touched up with rouge, the younger looking as if the vitality of her stock had been sapped before she was conceived, so that she is the expression not of its life energy but merely of the artificialities that energy had won for itself in the spending.

MILDRED: (*Looking up with affected dreaminess.*) How the black smoke swirls back against the sky! Is it not beautiful?

AUNT: (*Without looking up.*) I dislike smoke of any kind.

MILDRED: My great-grandmother smoked a pipe—a clay pipe.

AUNT: (*Ruffling.*) Vulgar!   5

MILDRED: She was too distant a relative to be vulgar. Time mellows pipes.

AUNT: (*Pretending boredom but irritated.*) Did the sociology you took up at college teach you that—to play the ghoul on every possible occasion, excavating old bones? Why not 10 let your great-grandmother rest in her grave?

MILDRED: (*Dreamily.*) With her pipe beside her—puffing in Paradise.

AUNT: (*With spite.*) Yes, you are a natural born ghoul. You are even getting to look like one, my dear. 15

MILDRED: (*In a passionless tone.*) I detest you, Aunt. (*Looking at her critically.*) Do you know what you remind me of? Of a cold pork pudding against a background of linoleum tablecloth in the kitchen of a—but the possibilities are wearisome. (*She closes her eyes.*) 20

AUNT: (*With a bitter laugh.*) Merci for your candor. But since I am and must be your chaperon—in appearance—at least—let us patch up some sort of armed truce. For my part you are quite free to indulge any pose of eccentricity that beguiles you—as long as you observe the amenities 25

MILDRED: (*Drawling.*) The inanities?

AUNT: (*Going on as if she hadn't heard.*) After exhausting the morbid thrills of social service work on New York's East Side—how they must have hated you, by the way, the poor that you made so much poorer in their own eyes!— 30 you are now bent on making your slumming international. Well, I hope Whitechapel will provide the needed nerve tonic. Do not ask me to chaperon you there, however. I told your father I would not. I loathe deformity. We will hire an army of detectives and you may investi- 35 gate everything—they allow you to see.

MILDRED: (*Protesting with a trace of genuine, earnestness.*) Please do not mock at my attempts to discover how the other half lives. Give me credit for some sort of groping sincerity in that at least. I would like to help them. I would like to be 40 of some use in the world. Is it my fault I don't know how? I would like to be sincere, to touch life somewhere. (*With weary bitterness.*) But I'm afraid I have neither the vitality nor integrity. All that was burnt out in our stock before I was born. Grandfather's blast furnaces, flaming to the sky, 45 melting steel, making millions—then father keeping those home fires burning, making more millions—and little me at the tail-end of it all. I'm a waste product in the Bessemer process—like the millions. Or rather, I inherit the acquired trait of the by-product, wealth, but none of the energy, 50 none of the strength of the steel that made it. I am sired by gold and damned by it, as they say at the race track—damned in more ways than one. (*She laughs mirthlessly.*)

AUNT: (*Unimpressed—superciliously.*) You seem to be going in for sincerity today. It isn't becoming to you, really—except as an obvious pose. Be as artificial as you are, I advise. There's a sort of sincerity in that, you know. And, after all, you must confess you like that better.

MILDRED: (*Again affected and bored.*) Yes, I suppose I do. Pardon me for my outburst. When a leopard complains of its spots, it must sound rather grotesque. (*In a mocking tone.*) Purr, little leopard. Purr, scratch, tear, kill, gorge yourself and be happy—only stay in the jungle, where your spots are camouflage. In a cage they make you conspicuous.

AUNT: I don't know what you are talking about.

MILDRED: It would be rude to talk about anything to you. Let's just talk. (*She looks at her wrist watch.*) Well, thank goodness, it's about time for them to come for me. That ought to give me a new thrill, Aunt.

AUNT: (*Affectedly troubled.*) You don't mean to say you're going? The dirt—the heat must be frightful—

MILDRED: Grandfather started as a puddler. I should have inherited an immunity to heat that would make a salamander shiver. It will be fun to put it to the test.

AUNT: But don't you have to have the captain's—or someone's—permission to visit the stokehole?

MILDRED: (*With a triumphant smile.*) I have it—both his and the chief engineer's. Oh, they didn't want to at first, in spite of my social service credentials. They didn't seem a bit anxious that I should investigate how the other half lives and works on a ship. So I had to tell them that my father, the president of Nazareth Steel, chairman of the board of directors of this line, had told me it would be all right.

AUNT: He didn't.

MILDRED: How naïve age makes one! But I said he did, Aunt. I even said he had given me a letter to them—which I had lost. And they were afraid to take the chance that I might be lying. (*Excitedly.*) So it's ho! for the stokehole. The second engineer is to escort me. (*Looking at her watch again.*) It's time. And here he comes, I think. (*The* SECOND ENGINEER *enters. He is a husky, fine-looking man of thirty-five or so. He stops before the two and tips his cap, visibly embarrassed and ill-at-ease.*)

SECOND ENGINEER: Miss Douglas?

MILDRED: Yes. (*Throwing off her rugs and getting to her feet.*) Are we all ready to start?

SECOND ENGINEER: In just a second, ma'am. I'm waiting for the Fourth. He's coming along.

MILDRED: (*With a scornful smile.*) You don't care to shoulder this responsibility alone, is that it?

SECOND ENGINEER: (*Forcing a smile.*) Two are better than one. (*Disturbed by her eyes, glances out to sea—blurts out.*) A fine day we're having.

MILDRED: Is it?

SECOND ENGINEER: A nice warm breeze—

MILDRED: It feels cold to me.

SECOND ENGINEER: But it's hot enough in the sun—

MILDRED: Not hot enough for me. I don't like Nature. I was never athletic.

SECOND ENGINEER: (*Forcing a smile.*) Well, you'll find it hot enough where you're going.

MILDRED: Do you mean hell?

SECOND ENGINEER: (*Flabbergasted, decides to laugh.*) Ho-ho! No, I mean the stokehole.

MILDRED: My grandfather was a puddler. He played with boiling steel.

SECOND ENGINEER: (*All at sea—uneasily.*) Is that so? Hum, you'll excuse me, ma'am, but are you intending to wear that dress?

MILDRED: Why not?

SECOND ENGINEER: You'll likely rub against oil and dirt. It can't be helped.

MILDRED: It doesn't matter. I have lots of white dresses.

SECOND ENGINEER: I have an old coat you might throw over—

MILDRED: I have fifty dresses like this. I will throw this one into the sea when I come back. That ought to wash it clean, don't you think?

SECOND ENGINEER: (*Doggedly.*) There's ladders to climb down that are none too clean—and dark alleyways—

MILDRED: I will wear this very dress and none other.

SECOND ENGINEER: No offense meant. It's none of my business. I was only warning you—

MILDRED: Warning? That sounds thrilling.

SECOND ENGINEER: (*Looking down the deck—with a sigh of relief.*) There's the Fourth now. He's waiting for us. If you'll come—

MILDRED: Go on. I'll follow you. (*He goes.* MILDRED *turns a mocking smile on her* AUNT.) An oaf—but a handsome, virile oaf.

AUNT: (*Scornfully.*) Poser!

MILDRED: Take care. He said there were dark alleyways—

AUNT: (*In the same tone.*) Poser!

MILDRED: (*Biting her lips angrily.*) You are right. But would that my millions were not so anemically chaste!

AUNT: Yes, for a fresh pose I have no doubt you would drag the name of Douglas in the gutter!

MILDRED: From which it sprang. Good-by, Aunt. Don't pray too hard that I may fall into the fiery furnace.

AUNT: Poser!

MILDRED: (*Viciously.*) Old hag! (*She slaps her* AUNT *insultingly across the face and walks off, laughing gaily.*)

AUNT: (*Screams after her.*) I said poser!

(*The curtain falls.*)

SCENE THREE

SCENE: *The stokehole. In the rear, the dimly-out-lined bulks of the furnaces and boilers. High overhead one hanging electric bulb sheds just enough light through the murky air laden with coal dust to pile up masses of shadows everywhere. A line of men, stripped to the waist, is before the furnace doors. They bend over, looking neither to right nor left, handling their shovels as if they were part of their bodies, with a strange, awkward, swinging rhythm. They use the shovels to throw open the furnace doors. Then from these fiery round holes in the black a flood of terrific light and heat pours full upon the men who are outlined in silhouette in the crouching, inhuman attitudes of chained gorillas. The men shovel with a rhythmic motion, swinging as on a pivot from the coal which lies in heaps on the floor behind to hurl it into the flaming mouths before them. There is a tumult of noise—the brazen clang of the furnace doors as they are flung open or slammed shut, the grating, teeth-gritting grind of steel against steel, of crunching coal. This clash of sounds stuns one's ears with its rending dissonance. But there is order in it, rhythm, a mechanical regulated recurrence, a tempo. And rising above all, making the air hum with the quiver of liberated energy, the roar of leaping flames in the furnaces, the monotonous throbbing beat of the engines.*

As the curtain rises, the furnace doors are shut. The men are taking a breathing spell. One or two are arranging the coal behind them, pulling it into more accessible heaps. The others can be dimly made out leaning on their shovels in relaxed attitudes of exhaustion.

PADDY: (*From somewhere in the line—plaintively.*) Yerra, will this divil's own watch nivir end? Me back is broke. I'm destroyed entirely.

YANK: (*From the center of the line—with exuberant scorn.*) Aw,
5   yuh make me sick! Lie down and croak, why don't yuh? Always beefin', dat's you! Say, dis is a cinch! Dis was made for me! It's my meat, get me! (*A whistle is blown—a thin, shrill note from somewhere overhead in the darkness.* YANK *curses without resentment.*) Dere's de damn engineer crackin' de
10   whip. He tinks we're loafin'.

PADDY: (*Vindictively.*) God stiffen him!

YANK: (*In an exultant tone of command.*) Come on, youse guys! Git into de game! She's gettin' hungry! Pile some grub in her. Trow it into her belly! Come on now, all of youse!
15   Open her up! (*At this last all the men, who have followed his movements of getting into position, throw open their furnace doors with a deafening clang. The fiery light floods over their shoulders as they bend round for the coal. Rivulets of sooty sweat have traced maps on their backs. The enlarged muscles form bunches of
20   high light and shadow.*)

YANK: (*Chanting a count as he shovels without seeming effort.*) One—two—tree—(*His voice rising exultantly in the joy of battle.*) Dat's de stuff! Let her have it! All togedder now! Sling it into her! Let her ride! Shoot de piece now! Call
25   de toin on her! Drive her into it! Feel her move. Watch her smoke! Speed, dat's her middle name! Give her coal, youse guys! Coal, dat's her booze! Drink it up, baby! Let's see yuh sprint! Dig in and gain a lap! Dere she go-o-es. (*This last in the chanting formula of the galley gods at the six-
30   day bike race. He slams his furnace door shut. The others do likewise with as much unison as their wearied bodies will permit. The effect is of one fiery eye after another being blotted out with a series of accompanying bangs.*)

PADDY: (*Groaning.*) Me back is broke. I'm bate out—bate—
35   (*There is a pause. Then the inexorable whistle sounds again from the dim regions above, the electric light. There is a growl of cursing rage from all sides.*)

YANK: (*Shaking his fist upward—contemptuously.*) Take it easy dere, you! Who d'yuh tinks runnin' dis game, me or you?
40   When I git ready, we move. Not before! When I git ready, get me!

VOICES: (*Approvingly.*)
   That's the stuff!
   Yank tal him, py golly!
45   Yank ain't afeerd.
   Goot poy, Yank!
   Give him hell!
   Tell'im 'e's a bloody swine!
   Bloody slave-driver!

50 YANK: (*Contemptuously.*) He ain't got no noive. He's yellow, get me? All de engineers is yellow. Dey got streaks a mile wide. Aw, to hell with him! Let's move, youse guys. We

had a rest. Come on, she needs it! Give her pep! It ain't for him. Him and his whistle, dey don't belong. But we belong, see! We gotter feed de baby! Come on! (*He turns   55 and flings his furnace door open. They all follow his lead. At this instant the* SECOND *and* FOURTH ENGINEERS *enter from the darkness on the left with* MILDRED *between them. She starts, turns paler, her pose is crumbling, she shivers with fright in spite of the blazing heat, but forces herself to leave the* ENGINEERS *and   60 take a few steps near the men. She is right behind* YANK. *All this happens quickly while the men have their backs turned.*)

YANK: Come on, youse guys! (*He is turning to get coal when the whistle sounds again in a peremptory, irritating note. This drives* YANK *into a sudden fury. While the other men have turned full   65 around and stopped dumbfounded by the spectacle of* MILDRED *standing there in her white dress,* YANK *does not turn far enough to see her. Besides, his head is thrown back, he blinks upward through the murk trying to find the owner of the whistle, he brandishes his shovel murderously over his head in one hand, pound-   70 ing on his chest, gorilla-like, with the other, shouting.*) Toin off dat whistle! Come down outa dere, yuh yellow, brass-buttoned, Belfast bum, yuh! Come down and I'll knock yer brains out! Yuh lousy, stinkin, yellow mut of a Catholic-moiderin' bastard! Come down and I'll moider yuh!   75 Pullin' dat whistle on me, huh? I'll show yuh! I'll crash yer skull in! I'll drive yer teet' down yer troat! I'll slam yer nose trou de back of yer head! I'll cut yer guts out for a nickel, yuh lousy boob, yuh dirty, crummy, muck-eatin' son of a— (*Suddenly he becomes conscious of all the other men staring at   80 something directly behind his back. He whirls defensively with a snarling, murderous growl, crouching to spring, his lips drawn back over his teeth, his small eyes gleaming ferociously. He sees* MIL-DRED, *like a white apparition in the full light from the open furnace doors. He glares into her eyes, turned to stone. As for her,   85 during his speech she has listened, paralyzed with horror, terror, her whole personality crushed, beaten in, collapsed, by the terrific impact of this unknown, abysmal brutality, naked and shameless. As she looks at his gorilla face, as his eyes bore into hers, she utters a low, choking cry and shrinks away from him, putting both hands   90 up before her eyes to shut out the sight of his face, to protect her own. This startles* YANK *to a reaction. His mouth falls open, his eyes grow bewildered.*)

MILDRED: (*About to faint—to the* ENGINEERS, *who now have her one by each arm—whimperingly.*) Take me away! Oh, the   95 filthy beast! (*She faints. They carry her quickly back, disappearing in the darkness at the left, rear. An iron door clangs shut. Rage and bewildered fury rush back on* YANK. *He feels himself insulted in some unknown fashion in the very heart of his pride. He roars.*) God damn yuh! (*And hurls his shovel after them at   100 the door which has just closed. It hits the steel bulkhead with a clang and falls clattering on the steel floor. From overhead the whistle sounds again in a long, angry, insistent command.*)

(*The curtain falls.*)

SCENE FOUR

SCENE: *The firemen's forecastle.* YANK's *watch has just come off duty and had dinner. Their faces and bodies shine from a soap and water scrubbing but around their eyes, where a hasty dousing does not touch, the coal dust sticks like black make-up, giving them a queer, sinister expression.* YANK *has not washed either face or body. He stands out in contrast to them, a blackened, brooding figure. He is seated forward on a bench in the exact attitude of Rodin's "The Thinker." The others, most of them smoking pipes, are staring at* YANK *half-apprehensively, as if fearing an outburst; half-amusedly, as if they saw a joke somewhere that tickled them.*

VOICES: He ain't ate nothin'.
  Py golly, a fallar gat to gat grub in him.
  Divil a lie.
  Yank feeda da fire, no feeda da face.
5   Ha-ha.
  He ain't even washed hisself.
  He's forgot.
  Hey, Yank, you forgot to wash.
YANK: (*Sullenly.*) Forgot nothin'! To hell wit washin'.
10 VOICES: It'll stick to you.
  It'll get under your skin.
  Give yer the bleedin' itch, that's wot.
  It makes spots on you—like a leopard.
  Like a piebald nigger, you mean.
15   Better wash up, Yank.
  You sleep better.
  Wash up, Yank.
  Wash up! Wash up!
YANK: (*Resentfully.*) Aw say, youse guys. Lemme alone. Can't
20   youse see I'm tryin' to tink?
ALL: (*Repeating the word after him as one with cynical mockery.*) Think! (*The word has a brazen, metallic quality as if their throats were phonograph horns. It is followed by a chorus of hard, barking, laughter.*)
25 YANK: (*Springing to his feet and glaring at them belligerently.*) Yes, tink! Tink, dat's what I said! What about it? (*They are silent, puzzled by his sudden resentment at what used to be one of his jokes.* YANK *sits down again in the same attitude of "The Thinker."*)
30 VOICES: Leave him alone.
  He's got a grouch on.
  Why wouldn't he?
PADDY: (*With a wink at the others.*) Sure I know what's the matther. 'Tis aisy to see. He's fallen in love, I'm telling you.
35 ALL: (*Repeating the word after him as one with cynical mockery.*) Love! (*The word has a brazen, metallic quality as if their throats were phonograph horns. It is followed by a chorus of hard, barking laughter.*)
YANK: (*With a contemptuous snort.*) Love, hell! Hate, dat's what.
40   I've fallen in hate, get me?
PADDY: (*Philosophically.*) 'Twould take a wise man to tell one from the other. (*With a bitter, ironical scorn, increasing as he goes on.*) But I'm telling you it's love that's in it. Sure what else but love for us poor bastes in the stokehole would be
45   bringing a fine lady, dressed like a white quane, down a mile of ladders and steps to be havin' a look at us? (*A growl of anger goes up from all sides.*)
LONG: (*Jumping on a bench—hectically.*) Hinsultin' us! Hinsultin' us, the bloody cow! And them bloody engineers! What
50   right 'as they got to be exhibitin' us 's if we was bleedin' monkeys in a menagerie? Did we sign for hinsults to our dignity as 'onest workers? Is that in the ship's articles? You kin bloody well bet it ain't! But I knows why they done it. I arsked a deck steward 'o she was and 'e told me. 'Er
55   old man's a bleedin' millionaire, a bloody Capitalist! 'E's got enuf bloody gold to sink this bleedin' ship! 'E makes arf the bloody steel in the world! 'E owns this bloody boat! And you and me, Comrades, we're 'is slaves! And the skipper and mates and engineers, they're 'is slaves! And she's 'is bloody daughter and we're all 'er slaves, too! And 60 she gives 'er orders as 'ow she wants to see the bloody animals below decks and down they take 'er! (*There is a roar of rage from all sides.*)
YANK: (*Blinking at him bewilderedly.*) Say! Wait a moment! Is all dat straight goods? 65
LONG: Straight as string! The bleedin' steward as waits on 'em, 'e told me about 'er. And what're we goin' ter do, I arsks yer? 'Ave we got ter swaller 'er hinsults like dogs? It ain't in the ship's articles. I tell yer we got a case. We kin go to law— 70
YANK: (*With abysmal contempt.*) Hell! Law!
ALL: (*Repeating the word after him as one with cynical mockery.*) Law! (*The word has a brazen metallic quality as if their throats were phonograph horns. It is followed by a chorus of hard, barking laughter.*) 75
LONG: (*Feeling the ground slipping from under his feet—desperately.*) As voters and citizens we kin force the bloody governments—
YANK: (*With abysmal contempt.*) Hell! Governments!
ALL: (*Repeating the word after him as one with cynical mockery.*) Governments! (*The word has a brazen metallic quality as if* 80 *their throats were phonograph horns. It is followed by a chorus of hard, barking laughter.*)
LONG: (*Hysterically.*) We're free and equal in the sight of God—
YANK: (*With abysmal contempt.*) Hell! God!
ALL: (*Repeating the word after him as one with cynical mockery.*) 85 God! (*The word has a brazen metallic quality as if their throats were phonograph horns. It is followed by a chorus of hard, barking, laughter.*)
YANK: (*Witheringly.*) Aw, join de Salvation Army!
ALL: Sit down! Shut up! Damn fool! Sea-lawyer! (LONG *slinks* 90 *back out of sight.*)
PADDY: (*Continuing the trend of his thoughts as if he had never been interrupted—bitterly.*) And there she was standing behind us, and the Second pointing at us like a man you'd hear in a circus would be saying: In this cage is a queerer 95 kind of baboon than ever you'd find in darkest Africy. We roast them in their own sweat—and be damned if you won't hear some of thim saying they like it! (*He glances scornfully at* YANK.)
YANK: (*With a bewildered uncertain growl.*) Aw! 100
PADDY: And there was Yank roarin' curses and turning round wid his shovel to brain her—and she looked at him, and him at her—
YANK: (*Slowly.*) She was all white. I thought she was a ghost. Sure. 105
PADDY: (*With heavy, biting sarcasm.*) 'Twas love at first sight, divil a doubt of it! If you'd seen the endearin' look on her pale mug when she shriveled away with her hands over her eyes to shut out the sight of him! Sure, 'twas as if she'd seen a great hairy ape escaped from the Zoo! 110
YANK: (*Stung—with a growl of rage.*) Aw!
PADDY: And the loving way Yank heaved his shovel at the skull of her, only she was out the door! (*A grin breaking over his face.*) 'Twas touching, I'm telling you! It put the touch of home, swate home in the stokehole. (*There is a roar of* 115 *laughter from all.*)

YANK: (*Glaring at* PADDY *menacingly.*) Aw, choke dat off, see!

PADDY: (*Not heeding him—to the others.*) And her grabbin' at the Second's arm for protection. (*With a grotesque imitation of a woman's voice.*) Kiss me, Engineer, dear, for it's dark down here and me old man's in Wall Street making money! Hug me tight, darlin', for I'm afeerd in the dark and me mother's on deck makin' eyes at the skipper! (*Another roar of laughter.*)

YANK: (*Threateningly.*) Say! What yuh tryin' to do, kid me, yuh old Harp?

PADDY: Divil a bit! Ain't I wishin' myself you'd brained her?

YANK: (*Fiercely.*) I'll brain her! I'll brain her yet, wait 'n' see! (*Coming over to* PADDY *slowly.*) Say, is dat what she called me—a hairy ape?

PADDY: She looked it at you if she didn't say the word itself.

YANK: (*Grinning horribly.*) Hairy ape, huh? Sure! Dat's de way she looked at me, aw right. Hairy ape! So dat's me, huh? (*Bursting into rage—as if she were still in front of him.*) Yuh skinny tart! Yuh white-faced bum, yuh! I'll show yuh who's a ape! (*Turning to the others, bewilderment seizing him again.*) Say, youse guys. I was bawlin' him out for pullin' de whistle on us. You heard me. And den I seen youse lookin' at somep'n and I tought he'd sneaked down to come up in back of me, and I hopped round to knock him dead wit de shovel. And dere she was wit de light on her! Christ, yuh coulda pushed me over with a finger! I was scared, get me? Sure! I tought she was a ghost, see? She was all in white like dey wrap around stiffs. You seen her. Kin yuh blame me? She didn't belong, dat's what. And den when I come to and seen it was a real skoit and seen de way she was lookin' at me—like Paddy said—Christ, I was sore, get me? I don't stand for dat stuff from nobody. And I flung de shovel—on'y she'd beat it. (*Furiously.*) I wished it'd banged her! I wished it'd knocked her block off!

LONG: And be 'anged for murder or 'lectrocuted? She ain't bleedin' well worth it.

YANK: I don't give a damn what! I'd be square wit her, wouldn't I? Tink I wanter let her put somep'n over on me? Tink I'm goin' to let her git away wit dat stuff? Yuh don't know me! No one ain't never put nothin' over on me and got away wit it, see!—not dat kind of stuff—no guy and no skoit neither! I'll fix her! Maybe she'll come down again—

VOICE: No chance, Yank. You scared her out of a year's growth.

YANK: I scared her? Why de hell should I scare her? Who de hell is she? Ain't she de same as me? Hairy ape, huh? (*With his old confident bravado.*) I'll show her I'm better'n her, if she on'y knew it. I belong and she don't, see! I move and she's dead! Twenty-five knots a hour, dat's me! Dat carries her but I make dat. She's on'y baggage. Sure! (*Again bewilderedly.*) But, Christ, she was funny lookin'! Did yuh pipe her hands? White and skinny. Yuh could see de bones through 'em. And her mush, dat was dead white, too. And her eyes, dey was like dey'd seen a ghost. Me, dat was! Sure! Hairy ape! Ghost, huh? Look at dat arm! (*He extends his right arm, swelling out the great muscles.*) I coulda took her wit dat, wit' just my little finger even, and broke her in two. (*Again bewilderedly.*) Say, who is dat skoit, huh? What is she? What's she come from? Who made her? Who give her de noive to look at me like dat? Dis ting's got my goat right. I don't get her. She's new to me. What does a skoit like her mean, huh? She don't belong, get me! I can't see her. (*With growing anger.*) But one ting I'm wise to, aw right, aw right! Youse all kin bet your shoits I'll git even wit her. I'll show her if she tinks she—She grinds de organ and I'm on de string, huh? I'll fix her! Let her come down again and I'll fling her in de furnace! She'll move den! She won't shiver at nothin' den! Speed, dat'll be her! She'll belong den! (*He grins horribly.*)

PADDY: She'll never come. She's had her bellyfull, I'm telling you. She'll be in bed now, I'm thinking, wid ten doctors and nurses feedin' her salts to clean the fear out of her.

YANK: (*Enraged.*) Yuh tink I made her sick, too, do yuh? Just lookin' at me, huh? Hairy ape, huh? (*In a frenzy of rage.*) I'll fix her! I'll tell her where to git off! She'll git down on her knees and take it back or I'll bust de face offen her! (*Shaking one fist upward and beating on his chest with the other.*) I'll find yuh! I'm comin', d'yuh hear? I'll fix yuh, God damn yuh! (*He makes a rush for the door.*)

VOICES: Stop him!
He'll get shot!
He'll murder her!
Trip him up!
Hold him!
He's gone crazy!
Gott, he's strong!
Hold him down!
Look out for a kick!
Pin his arms!

(*They have all piled on him and, after a fierce struggle, by sheer weight of numbers have borne him to the floor just inside the door.*)

PADDY: (*Who has remained detached.*) Kape him down till he's cooled off. (*Scornfully.*) Yerra, Yank, you're a great fool. Is it payin' attention at all you are to the like of that skinny sow widout one drop of rale blood in her?

YANK: (*Frenziedly, from the bottom of the heap.*) She's done me doit! She done me doit, didn't she? I'll git square wit her! I'll get her some way! Git offen me, youse guys! Lemme up! I'll show her who's a ape!

(*The curtain falls.*)

SCENE FIVE

SCENE: *Three weeks later. A corner of Fifth Avenue in the Fifties on a fine Sunday morning. A general atmosphere of clean, well-tidied, wide street; a flood of mellow, tempered sunshine; gentle, genteel breezes. In the rear, the show windows of two shops, a jewelry establishment on the corner, a furrier's next to it. Here the adornments of extreme wealth are tantalizingly displayed. The jeweler's window is gaudy with glittering diamonds, emeralds, rubies, pearls, etc., fashioned in ornate tiaras, crowns, necklaces, collars, etc. From each piece hangs an enormous tag from which a dollar sign and numerals in intermittent electric lights wink out the incredible prices. The same in the furrier's. Rich furs of all varieties hang there bathed in a downpour of artificial light. The general effect is of a background of magnificence cheapened and made grotesque by commercialism, a background in tawdry disharmony with the clear light and sunshine on the street itself.*

Up the side street YANK *and* LONG *come swaggering.* LONG *is dressed in shore clothes, wears a black Windsor tie, cloth cap.* YANK *is in his dirty dungarees. A fireman's cap with black peak is cocked defiantly on the side of his head. He has not shaved for days and around his fierce, resentful eyes—as around those of* LONG *to a lesser degree—the black smudge of coal dust still sticks like make-up. They hesitate and stand together at the corner, swaggering, looking about them with a forced, defiant contempt.*

LONG: (*Indicating it all with an oratorical gesture.*) Well, 'ere we are. Fif' Avenoo. This 'ere's their bleedin' private lane, as yer might say. (*Bitterly.*) We're trespassers 'ere. Proletarians keep orf the grass!

5   YANK: (*Dully.*) I don't see no grass, yuh boob. (*Staring at the sidewalk.*) Clean, ain't it? Yuh could eat a fried egg offen it. The white wings got some job sweepin' dis up. (*Looking up and down the avenue—surlily.*) Where's all de white-collar stiffs yuh said was here—and de skoits—*her* kind?

10 LONG: In church, blarst 'em! Arskin' Jesus to give 'em more money.

YANK: Choich, huh? I useter go to choich onct—sure—when I was a kid. Me old man and woman, dey made me. Dey never went demselves, dough. Always got too big a head on

15 Sunday mornin', dat was dem. (*With a grin.*) Dey was scrappers for fair, bot' of dem. On Satiday nights when dey bot' got a skinful dey could put up a bout oughter been staged at de Garden. When dey got trough dere wasn't a chair or table with a leg under it. Or else dey bot' jumped on me for

20 somep'n. Dat was where I loined to take punishment. (*With a grin and a swagger.*) I'm a chip offen de old block, get me?

LONG: Did yer old man follow de sea?

YANK: Naw. Worked along shore. I runned away when me old lady croaked with de tremens. I helped at truckin' and

25 in de market. Den I shipped in de stokehole. Sure. Dat belongs. De rest was nothin'. (*Looking around him.*) I ain't never seen dis before. De Brooklyn waterfront, dat was where I was dragged up. (*Taking a deep breath.*) Dis ain't so bad at dat, huh?

30 LONG: Not bad? Well, we pays for it wiv our bloody sweat, if yer wants to know!

YANK: (*With sudden angry disgust.*) Aw, hell! I don't see no one, see—like her. All dis gives me a pain. It don't belong. Say, ain't dere a back room around dis dump? Let's go shoot a

35 ball. All dis is too clean and quiet and dolled-up, get me? It gives me a pain.

LONG: Wait and yer'll bloody well see—

YANK: I don't wait for no one. I keep on de move. Say, what yuh drag me up here for, anyway? Tryin' to kid me, yuh

40 simp, yuh?

LONG: Yer wants to get back at 'er, don't yer? That's what yer been sayin' every bloomin' hour since she hinsulted yer.

YANK: (*Vehemently.*) Sure ting I do! Didn't I try to get even wit her in Southampton? Didn't I sneak on de dock and wait

45 for her by de gangplank? I was goin' to spit in her pale mug, see! Sure, right in her pop-eyes! Dat woulda made me even, see? But no chanct. Dere was a whole army of plain-clothes bulls around. Dey spotted me and gimme de bum's rush. I never seen her. But I'll git square wit her yet, you

50 watch! (*Furiously.*) De lousy tart! She tink she kin get away with moider—but not wit me! I'll fix her! I'll tink of a way!

LONG: (*As disgusted as he dares to be.*) Ain't that why I brought yer up 'ere—to show yer? Yer been lookin' at this 'ere 'ole affair wrong. Yer been actin' an' talkin' 's if it was all a

55 bleedin' personal matter between yer and that bloody cow.

I wants to convince yer she was on'y a representative of 'er clarss. I wants to awaken yer bloody clarss consciousness. Then yer'll see it's 'er clarss yer've got to fight, not 'er alone. There's a 'ole mob of 'em like 'er, Gawd blind 'em!

60 YANK: (*Spitting on his hands—belligerently.*) De more de merrier when I gits started. Bring on de gang!

LONG: Yer'll see 'em in arf a mo', when that church lets out. (*He turns and sees the window display in the two stores for the first time.*) Blimey! Look at that, will yer? (*They both walk back and

65 stand looking in the jeweler's.* LONG *flies into a fury.*) Just look at this 'ere bloomin' mess! Just look at it! Look at the bleedin' prices on 'em—more'n our 'ole bloody stokehole makes in ten voyages sweatin' in 'ell! And they—'er and 'er bloody clarss—buys 'em for toys to dangle on 'em! One of these

70 'ere, would buy scoff for a starvin' family for a year!

YANK: Aw, cut de sob stuff! T' hell wit de starvin' family! Yuh'll be passin' de hat to me next. (*With naïve admiration.*) Say, dem tings is pretty, huh? Bet yuh dey'd hock for a piece of change aw right. (*Then turning away, bored.*) But

75 aw hell, what good are dey? Let 'er have 'em. Dey don't belong no more'n she does. (*With a gesture of sweeping the jewelers into oblivion.*) All dat don't count, get me?

LONG: (*Who has moved to the furrier's—indignantly.*) And I s'pose this 'ere don't count neither—skins of poor, 'arm-

80 less animals slaughtered so as 'er and 'ers can keep their bleedin' noses warm!

YANK: (*Who has been staring at something inside—with queer excitement.*) Take a slant at dat! Give it de once-over! Monkey fur—two t'ousand bucks! (*Bewilderedly.*) Is dat straight

85 goods—monkey fur? What de hell—?

LONG: (*Bitterly.*) It's straight enuf. (*With grim humor.*) They wouldn't bloody well pay that for 'airy ape's skin—no, nor for the 'ole livin' ape with all 'is 'ead, and body, and soul thrown in!

90 YANK: (*Clenching his fists, his face growing pale with rage as if the skin in the window were a personal insult.*) Trowin' it up in my face! Christ! I'll fix her!

LONG: (*Excitedly.*) Church is out. 'Ere they come, the bleedin' swine. (*After a glance at* YANK's *lowering face—uneasily.*) Easy

95 goes, Comrade. Keep yer bloomin' temper. Remember force defeats itself. It ain't our weapon. We must impress our demands through peaceful means—the votes of the on-marching proletarians of the bloody world!

YANK: (*With abysmal contempt.*) Votes, hell! Votes is a joke, see.

100 Votes for women! Let dem do it!

LONG: (*Still more uneasily.*) Calm, now. Treat 'em wiv the proper contempt. Observe the bleedin' parasites but 'old yer 'orses.

YANK: (*Angrily.*) Git away from me! Yuh're yellow, dat's what. Force, dat's me! De punch, dat's me every time, see! (*The

105 crowd from church enter from the right, sauntering slowly and affectedly, their heads held stiffly up, looking neither to right nor left, talking in toneless, simpering voices. The women are rouged, calcimined, dyed, overdressed to the nth degree. The men are in Prince Alberts, high hats, spats, canes, etc. A procession of gaudy mari-

110 onettes, yet with something of the relentless horror of Frankenstein monsters in their detached, mechanical unawareness.*)

VOICES: Dear Doctor Caiaphas! He is so sincere!

What was the sermon? I dozed off.

About the radicals, my dear—and the false doctrines that are being preached.

115 We must organize a hundred per cent American bazaar.

And let everyone contribute one one-hundredth per cent
of their income tax.
What an original idea!
We can devote the proceeds to rehabilitating the veil of
the temple.
But that has been done so many times.

120 YANK: (*Glaring from one to the other of them—with an insulting
snort of scorn.*) Huh! Huh! (*Without seeming to see him, they
make wide detours to avoid the spot where he stands in the middle of the sidewalk.*)

LONG: (*Frightenedly.*) Keep yer bloomin' mouth shut, I tells yer.

125 YANK: (*Viciously.*) G'wan! Tell it to Sweeney! (*He swaggers
away and deliberately lurches into a top-hatted gentleman, then
glares at him pugnaciously.*) Say, who d'yuh tink yuh're
bumpin'? Tink yuh own de oith?

GENTLEMAN: (*Coldly and affectedly.*) I beg your pardon. (*He has
130   not looked at* YANK *and passes on without a glance, leaving him
bewildered.*)

LONG: (*Rushing up and grabbing* YANK's *arm.*) 'Ere! Come
away! This wasn't what I meant. Yer'll 'ave the bloody
coppers down on us.

135 YANK: (*Savagely—giving him a push that sends him sprawling.*)
G'wan!

LONG: (*Picks himself up—hysterically.*) I'll pop orf then. This
ain't what I meant. And whatever 'appens yer can't blame
me. (*He slinks off left.*)

140 YANK: T' hell wit youse! (*He approaches a lady—with a vicious
grin and a smirking wink.*) Hello, Kiddo. How's every little
ting? Got anyting on for tonight? I know an old boiler
down to de docks we kin crawl into. (*The lady stalks by without a look, without a change of pace.* YANK *turns to others—*
145   *insultingly.*) Holy smokes, what a mug! Go hide yuhself
before de horses shy at yuh. Gee, pipe de heine on dat one!
Say, youse, yuh look like de stoin of a ferryboat. Paint and
powder! All dolled up to kill! Yuh look like stiffs laid out for
de boneyard! Aw, g'wan, de lot of youse! Yuh give me de
150   eyeache. Yuh don't belong, get me! Look at me, why don't
youse dare? I belong, dat's me! (*Pointing to skyscraper across
the street which is in process of construction—with bravado.*) See
dat building goin' up dere? See de steel work? Steel, dat's
me! Youse guys live on it and tink yuh're somep'n. But I'm
155   in it, see! I'm de-hoistin' engine dat makes it go up! I'm it—
de inside and bottom of it! Sure! I'm steel and steam and
smoke and de rest of it! It moves—speed—twenty-five stories up—and me at de top and bottom—movin'! Youse
simps don't move. Yuh're on'y dolls I winds up to see 'm
160   spin. Yuh're de garbage, get me—de leavins—der ashes we
dump over de side! Now, what's 'a' yuh gotta say? (*But as
they seem neither to see nor hear him, he flies into a fury.*) Bums!
Pigs! Tarts! Bitches! (*He turns in rage on the men, bumping viciously into them but not jarring them the least bit. Rather it is he
165   who recoils after each collision. He keeps growling.*) Git off de
oith! G'wan, yuh bum! Look where yuh're goin', can't
yuh? Git outa here! Fight, why don't yuh? Put up yer mits!
Don't be a dog! Fight or I'll knock yuh dead! (*But, without
seeming to see him, they all answer with mechanical affected po-
170   liteness.*) I beg your pardon. (*Then at a cry from one of the
women they all scurry to the furrier's window.*)

THE WOMAN: (*Ecstatically, with a gasp of delight.*) Monkey fur!
(*The whole crowd of men and women chorus after her in the
same tone of affected delight.*) Monkey fur!

175 YANK: (*With a jerk of his head back on his shoulders, as if he had received a punch full in the face—raging.*) I see yuh, all in white!
I see yuh, yuh white-faced tart, yuh! Hairy ape, huh? I'll
hairy ape yuh! (*He bends down and grips at the street curbing as
if to pluck it out and hurl it. Foiled in this, snarling with passion,
180   he leaps to the lamppost on the corner and tries to pull it up for a
club. Just at that moment a bus is heard rumbling up. A fat, high-
hatted, spatted gentleman runs out from the side street. He calls
out plaintively.*) Bus! Bus! Stop there! (*And runs full tilt into
the bending straining* YANK, *who is bowled off his balance.*)

185 YANK: (*Seeing a fight—with a roar of joy as he springs to his feet.*)
At last! Bus, huh! I'll bust yuh! (*He lets drive a terrific swing,
his fist landing full on the fat gentleman's face. But the gentleman stands unmoved as if nothing had happened.*)

GENTLEMAN: I beg your pardon. (*Then irritably.*) You have
190   made me lose my bus. (*He claps his hands and begins to
scream.*) Officer! Officer! (*Many police whistles shrill out on
the instant and a whole platoon of policemen rush in on* YANK
*from all sides. He tries to fight but is clubbed to the pavement and
fallen upon. The crowd at the window have not moved or noticed
195   this disturbance. The clanging gong of the patrol wagon approaches with a clamoring din.*)

(*The curtain falls.*)

SCENE SIX

SCENE: *Night of the following day. A row of cells in the prison on
Blackwell's Island. The cells extend back diagonally from right front
to left rear. They do not stop, but disappear in the dark background
as if they ran on, numberless, into infinity. One electric bulb from the
low ceiling of the narrow corridor sheds its light through the heavy
steel bars of the cell at the extreme front and reveals part of the interior.* YANK *can be seen within, crouched on the edge of his cot in
the attitude of Rodin's "The Thinker." His face is spotted with black
and blue bruises. A blood-stained bandage is wrapped around his
head.*

YANK: (*Suddenly starting as if awakening from a dream, reaches out
and shakes the bars—aloud to himself, wonderingly.*) Steel. Dis
is de Zoo, huh? (*A burst of hard barking laughter comes from
the unseen occupants of the cells, runs back down the tier, and
abruptly ceases.*)   5

VOICES: (*Mockingly.*) The Zoo? That's a new name for this
coop—a damn good name!
Steel, eh? You said a mouthful. This is the old iron
house.
Who is that boob talkin'?
He's the bloke they brung in out of his head. The bulls
had beat him up fierce.

YANK: (*Dully.*) I musta been dreamin'. I tought I was in a cage   10
at de Zoo—but de apes don't talk, do dey?

VOICES: (*With mocking laughter.*) You're in a cage aw right.
A coop!
A pen!
A sty!
A kennel! (*Hard laughter—a pause.*)   15
Say, guy! Who are you? No, never mind lying. What are
you?

Yes, tell us your sad story. What's your game?
What did they jug yuh for?

YANK: (*Dully.*) I was a fireman—stokin' on de liners. (*Then with
20   sudden rage, rattling his cell bars.*) I'm a hairy ape, get me? And
I'll bust youse all in de jaw if yuh don't lay off kiddin' me.

VOICES: Huh! You're a hard-boiled duck, ain't you!
When you spit, it bounces! (*Laughter.*)
Aw, can it. He's a regular guy. Ain't you?
25   What did he say he was—a ape?

YANK: (*Defiantly.*) Sure ting! Ain't dat what youse all are—
apes? (*A silence. Then a furious rattling of bars from down the
corridor.*)

A VOICE: (*Thick with rage.*) I'll show yuh who's a ape, yuh bum!

30 VOICES: Ssshh! Nix!
Can de noise!
Piano!
You'll have the guard down on us!

YANK: (*Scornfully.*) De guard? Yuh mean de keeper don't yuh?
35   (*Angry exclamations from all the cells.*)

VOICE: (*Placatingly.*) Aw, don't pay no attention to him. He's off
his nut from the beatin'-up he got. Say, you guy! We're waitin'
to hear what they landed you for—or ain't yuh tellin'?

YANK: Sure, I'll tell youse. Sure! Why de hell not? On'y—
40   youse won't get me. Nobody gets me but me, see? I
started to tell de Judge and all he says was: "Toity days to
tink it over." Tink it over! Christ, dat's all I been doin' for
weeks! (*After a pause.*) I was tryin' to git even with someone, see?—someone dat done me doit.

45 VOICES: (*Cynically.*) De old stuff, I bet. Your goil, huh?
Give yuh the double-cross, huh?
That's them every time!
Did yuh beat up de odder guy?

YANK: (*Disgustedly.*) Aw, yuh're all wrong! Sure dere was a skoit
50   in it—but not what youse mean, not dat old tripe. Dis was
a new kind of skoit. She was dolled up all in white—in de
stokehole. I tought she was a ghost. Sure. (*A pause.*)

VOICES: (*Whispering.*) Gee, he's still nutty.
Let him rave. It's fun listenin'.

55 YANK: (*Unheeding—groping in his thoughts.*) Her hands—dey
was skinny and white like dey wasn't real but painted on
somep'n. Dere was a million miles from me to her—
twenty-five knots an hour. She was like some dead ting de
cat brung in. Sure, dat's what. She didn't belong. She be-
60   longed in de window of a toy store, or on de top of a
garbage can, see! Sure! (*He breaks out angrily.*) But would
yuh believe it, she had de noive to do me doit. She lamped
me like she was seein' somep'n broke loose from de
menagerie. Christ, yuh'd oughter seen her eyes! (*He rattles
65   the bars of his cell furiously.*) But I'll get back at her yet, you
watch! And if I can't find her I'll take it out on de gang
she runs wit. I'm wise to where dey hangs out now. I'll
show her who belongs! I'll show her who's in de move
and who ain't. You watch my smoke!

70 VOICES: (*Serious and joking.*) Dat's de talkin'!
Take her for all she's got!
What was this dame, anyway? Who was she, eh?

YANK: I dunno. First cabin stiff. Her old man's a millionaire,
dey says—name of Douglas.

75 VOICES: Douglas? That's the president of the Steel Trust, I bet.
Sure. I seen his mug in de papers.
He's filthy with dough.

VOICE: Hey, feller, take a tip from me. If you want to get back
at that dame, you better join the Wobblies. You'll get some
action, then.   80

YANK: Wobblies? What de hell's dat?

VOICE: Ain't you ever heard of the I. W. W.?

YANK: Naw. What is it?

VOICE: A gang of blokes—a tough gang. I been readin' about
'em today in the paper. The guard give me the *Sunday Times.*   85
There's a long spiel about 'em. It's from a speech made in the
Senate by a guy named Senator Queen. (*He is in the cell next
to* YANK's. *There is a rustling of paper.*) Wait'll I see if I got light
enough and I'll read you. Listen. (*He reads.*) "There is a menace existing in this country today which threatens the vitals 90
of our fair Republic—as foul a menace against the very life-
blood of the American Eagle as was the foul conspiracy of
Cataline against the eagles of ancient Rome!"

VOICE: (*Disgustedly.*) Aw, hell! Tell him to salt de tail of dat
eagle!   95

VOICE: (*Reading.*) "I refer to that devil's brew of rascals, jail-
birds, murderers and cutthroats who libel all honest working men by calling themselves the Industrial Workers of
the World; but in the light of their nefarious plots, I call
them the Industrious Wreckers of the World!"   100

YANK: (*With vengeful satisfaction.*) Wreckers, dat's de right
dope! Dat belongs! Me for dem!

VOICE: Ssshh! (*Reading.*) "This fiendish organization is a foul
ulcer on the fair body of our Democracy—"

VOICE: Democracy, hell! Give him de boid, fellers—the rasp-   105
berry! (*They do.*)

VOICE: Ssshh! (*Reading.*) "Like Cato I say to this Senate, the I.
W. W. must be destroyed! For they represent an ever-
present dagger pointed at the heart of the greatest nation
the world has ever known, where all men are born free and 110
equal, with equal opportunities to all, where the Founding
Fathers have guaranteed to each one happiness, where
Truth, Honor, Liberty, Justice, and the Brotherhood of
Man are a religion absorbed with one's mother's milk,
taught at our father's knee, sealed, signed, and stamped   115
upon in the glorious Constitution of these United States!"
(*A perfect storm of hisses, catcalls, boos, and hard laughter.*)

VOICES: (*Scornfully.*) Hurrah for de Fort' of July!
Pass de hat!
Liberty!   120
Justice!
Honor!
Opportunity!
Brotherhood!

ALL: (*With abysmal scorn.*) Aw, hell!   125

VOICE: Give that Queen Senator guy the bark! All togedder
now— one—two—tree—(*A terrific chorus of barking and yapping.*)

GUARD: (*From a distance.*) Quiet, there, youse—or I'll get the
hose. (*The noise subsides.*)   130

YANK: (*With growling rage.*) I'd like to catch dat senator guy
alone for a second. I'd loin him some trute!

VOICE: Ssshh! Here's where he gits down to cases on the Wobblies. (*Reads.*) "They plot with fire in one hand and dynamite in the other. They stop not before murder to gain   135
their ends, nor at the outraging of defenseless womanhood.
They would tear down society, put the lowest scum in the
seats of the mighty, turn Almighty God's revealed plan for

140   the world topsy-turvy, and make of our sweet and lovely
       civilization a shambles, a desolation where man, God's mas-
       terpiece, would soon degenerate back to the ape!"

VOICE: (*To* YANK.) Hey, you guy. There's ape stuff again.

YANK: (*With a growl of fury.*) I got him. So dey blow up tings,
145   do dey? Dey turn tings round, do dey? Hey, lend me dat
       paper, will yuh?

VOICE: Sure. Give it to him. On'y keep it to yourself, see. We
       don't wanter listen to no more of that slop.

VOICE: Here you are. Hide it under your mattress.

YANK: (*Reaching out.*) Tanks. I can't read much but I kin man-
150   age. (*He sits, the paper in the hand at his side, in the attitude of
       Rodin's "The Thinker." A pause. Several snores from down the
       corridor. Suddenly* YANK *jumps to his feet with a furious groan as
       if some appalling thought had crashed on him—bewilderedly.*)
       Sure—her old man—president of de Steel Trust—makes
155   half de steel in de world—steel—where I tought I be-
       longed—drivin' trou—movin'—in dat—to make* her*—
       and cage me in for her to spit on! Christ! (*He shakes the bars
       of his cell door till the whole tier trembles. Irritated, protesting ex-
       clamations from those awakened or trying to get to sleep.*) He
160   made dis—dis cage! Steel! *It* don't belong, dat's what!
       Cages, cells, locks, bolts, bars—dat's what it means!—
       holdin' me down wit him at de top! But I'll manage trou!
       Fire, dat melts it! I'll be fire—under de heap—fire dat
       never goes out—hot as hell—breakin' out in de night—
165   (*While he has been saying this last he has shaken his cell door to
       a clanging accompaniment. As he comes to the "breakin' out" he
       seizes one bar with both hands and, putting his two feet up against
       the others so that his position is parallel to the floor like a mon-
       key's, he gives a great wrench backwards. The bar bends like a
170   licorice stick under his tremendous strength. Just at this moment
       the* PRISON GUARD *rushes in dragging a hose behind him.*)

GUARD: (*Angrily.*) I'll loin youse bums to wake me up! (*Sees
       YANK.) Hello, it's you, huh? Got the D.Ts., hey? Well, I'll cure
       'em. I'll drown your snakes for yuh! (*Noticing the bar.*) Hell,
175   look at dat bar bended! On'y a bug is strong enough for dat!

YANK: (*Glaring at him.*) Or a hairy ape, yuh big yellow bum!
       Look out! Here I come! (*He grabs another bar.*)

GUARD: (*Scared now—yelling off left.*) Toin de hose on, Ben!—
       full pressure! And call de others—and a straitjacket! (*The
180   curtain is falling. As it hides* YANK *from view, there is a splatter-
       ing smash as the stream of water hits the steel of* YANK's *cell.*)

(*The curtain falls.*)

SCENE SEVEN

SCENE: *Nearly a month later. An I. W. W. local near the waterfront,
showing the interior of a front room on the ground floor, and the
street outside. Moonlight on the narrow street, buildings massed in
black shadow. The interior of the room, which is general assembly
room, office; and reading room, resembles some dingy settlement boys'
club. A desk and high stool are in one corner. A table with papers,
stacks of pamphlets, chairs about it, is at center. The whole is decidedly cheap, banal, commonplace and unmysterious as a room could
well be. The Secretary is perched on the stool making entries in a
large ledger. And eye shade casts his face into shadows. Eight or ten
men, longshoremen, iron workers, and the like are grouped about the*

table. *Two are playing checkers. One is writing a letter. Most of them
are smoking pipes. A big signboard is on the wall at the rear, "Industrial Workers of the World—Local No. 57."*

YANK: (*Comes down the street outside. He is dressed as in Scene
       Five. He moves cautiously, mysteriously. He comes to a point op-
       posite the door; tiptoes softly up to it, listens, is impressed by the
       silence within, knocks carefully, as if he were guessing at the pass-
       word to some secret rite. Listens. No answer. Knocks again a bit   5
       louder. No answer. Knocks impatiently, much louder.*)

SECRETARY: (*Turning around on his stool.*) What the hell is
       that—someone knocking? (*Shouts.*) Come in, why don't
       you? (*All the men in the room look up.* YANK *opens the door
       slowly, gingerly, as if afraid of an ambush. He looks around for   10
       secret doors, mystery, is taken aback by the commonplaceness of
       the room and the men in it, thinks he may have gotten in the
       wrong place, then sees the signboard on the wall and is reassured.*)

YANK: (*Blurts out.*) Hello.

MEN: (*Reservedly.*) Hello.   15

YANK: (*More easily.*) I tought I'd bumped into de wrong dump.

SECRETARY: (*Scrutinizing him carefully.*) Maybe you have. Are
       you a member?

YANK: Naw, not yet. Dat's what I come for—to join.

SECRETARY: That's easy. What's your job—long-shore?   20

YANK: Naw. Fireman—stoker on de liners.

SECRETARY: (*With satisfaction.*) Welcome to our city. Glad to
       know you people are waking up at last. We haven't got
       many members in your line.

YANK: Naw. Dey're all dead to de woild.   25

SECRETARY: Well, you can help to wake 'em. What's your
       name? I'll make out your card.

YANK: (*Confused.*) Name? Lemme tink.

SECRETARY: (*Sharply.*) Don't you know your own name?

YANK: Sure; but I been just Yank for so long—Bob, dat's it— 30
       Bob Smith.

SECRETARY: (*Writing.*) Robert Smith. (*Fills out the rest of the
       card.*) Here you are. Cost you half a dollar.

YANK: Is dat all—four bits? Dat's easy. (*Gives the* SECRETARY
       the money.)   35

SECRETARY: (*Throwing it in drawer.*) Thanks. Well, make your-
       self at home. No introductions needed. There's literature
       on the table. Take some of those pamphlets with you to
       distribute aboard ship. They may bring results. Sow the
       seed, only go about it right. Don't get caught and fired.   40
       We got plenty out of work. What we need is men who
       can hold their jobs—and work for us at the same time.

YANK: Sure. (*But he still stands, embarrassed and uneasy.*)

SECRETARY: (*Looking at him—curiously.*) What did you knock
       for? Think we had a coon in uniform to open doors?   45

YANK: Naw. I tought it was locked—and dat yuh'd wanter
       give me the once-over trou a peephole or somep'n to see
       if I was right.

SECRETARY: (*Alert and suspicious but with an easy laugh.*) Think
       we were running a crap game?   50
That door is never locked. What put that in your nut?

YANK: (*With a knowing grin, convinced that this is all camouflage,
       a part of the secrecy.*) Dis burg is full of bulls, ain't it?

SECRETARY: (*Sharply.*) What have the cops got to do with us?
       We're breaking no laws.   55

YANK: (*With a knowing wink.*) Sure. Youse wouldn't for woilds. Sure. I'm wise to dat.

SECRETARY: You seem to be wise to a lot of stuff none of us knows about.

60   YANK: (*With another wink.*) Aw, dat's aw right, see. (*Then made a bit resentful by the suspicious glances from all sides.*) Aw, can it! Youse needn't put me trou de toid degree. Can't youse see I belong? Sure! I'm reg'lar. I'll stick, get me? I'll shoot de woiks for youse. Dat's why I wanted to join in.

65   SECRETARY: (*Breezily, feeling him out.*) That's the right spirit. Only are you sure you understand what you've joined? It's all plain and aboveboard; still, some guys get a wrong slant on us. (*Sharply.*) What's your notion of the purpose of the I.W.W.?

70   YANK: Aw, I know all about it.

SECRETARY: (*Sarcastically.*) Well, give us some of your valuable information.

YANK: (*Cunningly.*) I know enough not to speak outa my toin. (*Then resentfully again.*) Aw, say! I'm reg'lar. I'm wise to de
75   game. I know yuh got to watch your step wit a stranger. For all youse know, I might be a plain-clothes dick, or somep'n, dat's what yuh're tinkin', huh? Aw, forget it! I belong, see? Ask any guy down to de docks if I don't.

SECRETARY: Who said you didn't?

80   YANK: After I'm 'nitiated, I'll show yuh.

SECRETARY: (*Astounded.*) Initiated? There's no initiation.

YANK: (*Disappointed.*) Ain't there no password—no grip nor nothin'?

SECRETARY: What'd you think this is—the Elks—or the
85   Black Hand?

YANK: De Elks, hell! De Black Hand, dey're a lot of yellow backstickin' Ginees. Naw. Dis is a man's gang, ain't it?

SECRETARY: You said it! That's why we stand on our two feet in the open. We got no secrets.

90   YANK: (*Surprised but admiringly.*) Yuh mean to say yuh always run wide open—like dis?

SECRETARY: Exactly.

YANK: Den yuh sure got your noive wit youse!

SECRETARY: (*Sharply.*) Just what was it made you want to join
95   us? Come out with that straight.

YANK: Yuh call me? Well, I got noive, too! Here's my hand. Yuh wanter blow tings up, don't yuh? Well, dat's me! I belong!

SECRETARY: (*With pretended carelessness.*) You mean change the
100   unequal conditions of society by legitimate direct action—or with dynamite?

YANK: Dynamite! Blow it offen de oith—steel—all de cages—all de factories, steamers, buildings, jails—de Steel Trust and all dat makes it go.

105   SECRETARY: So—that's your idea, eh? And did you have any special job in that line you wanted to propose to us? (*He makes a sign to the men, who get up cautiously one by one and group behind* YANK.)

YANK: (*Boldly.*) Sure, I'll come out wit it. I'll show youse I'm
110   one of de gang. Dere's dat millionaire guy, Douglas—

SECRETARY: President of the Steel Trust, you mean? Do you want to assassinate him?

YANK: Naw, dat don't get yuh nothin'. I mean blow up de factory, de woiks, where he makes de steel. Dat's what I'm

after—to blow up de steel, knock all de steel in de woild   115
up to de moon. Dat'll fix tings! (*Exactly, with a touch of bravado.*) I'll do it by me lonesome! I'll show yuh! Tell me where his woiks is, how to git there, all de dope. Gimme de stuff, de old butter—and watch me do de rest! Watch de smoke and see it move! I don't give a damn if dey nab   120
me—long as it's done! I'll soive life for it—and give 'em de laugh! (*Half to himself.*) And I'll write her a letter and tell her de hairy ape done it. Dat'll square tings.

SECRETARY: (*Stepping away from* YANK.) Very interesting. (*He gives a signal. The men, huskies all, throw themselves on* YANK   125
and before he knows it they have his legs and arms pinioned. But he is too flabbergasted to make a struggle, anyway. They feel him over for weapons.)

MAN: No gat, no knife. Shall we give him what's what and put the boots to him?   130

SECRETARY: No. He isn't worth the trouble we'd get into. He's too stupid. (*He comes closer and laughs mockingly in* YANK's *face.*) Ho-ho! By God, this is the biggest joke they've put up on us yet. Hey, you Joke! Who sent you— Burns or Pinkerton? No, by God, you're such a bonehead   135
I'll bet you're in the Secret Service! Well, you dirty spy, you rotten agent provocator, you can go back and tell whatever skunk is paying you blood-money for betraying your brothers that he's wasting his coin. You couldn't catch a cold. And tell him that all he'll ever get on us, or   140
ever has got, is just his own sneaking plots that he's framed up to put us in jail. We are what our manifesto says we are, neither more nor less—and we'll give him a copy of that any time he calls. And as for you—(*He glares scornfully at* YANK, *who is sunk in an oblivious stupor.*) Oh, hell, what's   145
the use of talking? You're a brainless ape.

YANK: (*Aroused by the word to fierce but futile struggles.*) What's dat, yuh Sheeny bum, yuh!

SECRETARY: Throw him out, boys. (*In spite of his struggles, this is done with gusto and éclat. Propelled by several parting kicks,*   150
YANK *lands sprawling in the middle of the narrow cobbled street. With a growl he starts to get up and storm the closed door, but stops bewildered by the confusion in his brain, pathetically impotent. He sits there, brooding, in as near to the attitude of Rodin's "Thinker" as he can get in his position.*)   155

YANK: (*Bitterly.*) So dem boids don't tink I belong, neider. Aw, to hell wit 'em! Dey're in de wrong pew—de same old bull—soapboxes and Salvation Army—no guts! Cut out an hour offen de job a day and make me happy! Gimme a dollar more a day and make me happy! Tree   160
square a day, and cauliflowers in de front yard—ekal rights—a woman and kids—a lousy vote—and I'm all fixed for Jesus, huh? Aw, hell! What does dat get yuh? Dis ting's in your inside, but it ain't your belly. Feedin' your face—sinkers and coffee—dat don't touch it. It's way   165
down—at de bottom. Yuh can't grab it, and yuh can't stop it. It moves, and everything moves. It stops and de whole woild stops. Dat's me now—I don't tick, see?—I'm a busted Ingersoll, dat's what. Steel was me, and I owned de woild. Now I ain't steel, and de woild owns me. Aw, hell!   170
I can't see—it's all dark, get me? It's all wrong! (*He turns a bitter mocking face up like an ape gibbering at the moon.*) Say, youse up dere, Man in de Moon, yuh look so wise, gimme

175 de answer, huh? Slip me de inside dope, de information right from de stable—where do I get off at, huh?

A POLICEMAN: (*Who has come up the street in time to hear this last with grim humor.*) You'll get off at the station, you boob, if you don't get up out of that and keep movin'.

YANK: (*Looking up at him—with a hard, bitter laugh.*) Sure!
180 Lock me up! Put me in a cage! Dat's de on'y answer yuh know. G'wan, lock me up!

POLICEMAN: What you been doin'?

YANK: Enuf to gimme life for! I was born, see? Sure, dat's de charge. Write it in de blotter. I was born, get me!

185 POLICEMAN: (*Jocosely.*) God pity your old woman! (*Then matter-of-fact.*) But I've no time for kidding. You're soused. I'd run you in but it's too long a walk to the station. Come on now, get up, or I'll fan your ears with this club. Beat it now! (*He hauls* YANK *to his feet.*)

190 YANK: (*In a vague mocking tone.*) Say, where do I go from here?

POLICEMAN: (*Giving him a push—with a grin, indifferently.*) Go to hell.

(*The curtain falls.*)

SCENE EIGHT

SCENE: *Twilight of the next day. The monkey house at the Zoo. One spot of clear gray light falls on the front of one cage so that the interior can be seen. The other cages are vague, shrouded in shadow from which chatterings pitched in a conversational tone can be heard. On the one cage a sign from which the word "gorilla" stands out. The gigantic animal himself is seen squatting on his haunches on a bench in much the same attitude as Rodin's "Thinker."* YANK *enters from the left. Immediately a chorus of angry chattering and screeching breaks out. The gorilla turns his eyes but makes no sound or move.*

YANK: (*With a hard, bitter laugh.*) Welcome to your city, huh? Hail, hail, de gang's all here! (*At the sound of his voice the chattering dies away into an attentive silence.* YANK *walks up to the gorilla's cage and, leaning over the railing, stares in at its occupant,*
5 *who stares back at him, silent and motionless. There is a pause of dead stillness. Then* YANK *begins to talk in a friendly confidential tone, half-mockingly, but with a deep undercurrent of sympathy.*) Say, yuh're some hard-lookin' guy, ain't yuh? I seen lots of tough nuts dat de gang called gorillas, but yuh're de foist
10 real one I ever seen. Some chest yuh got, and shoulders, and dem arms and mits! I bet yuh got a punch in eider fist dat'd knock 'em all silly. (*This with genuine admiration. The gorilla, as if he understood, stands upright, swelling out his chest and pounding on it with his fist.* YANK *grins sympathetically.*)
15 Sure, I get yuh. Yuh challenge de whole woild, huh? Yuh got what I was sayin' even if yuh muffed de woids. (*Then bitterness creeping in.*) And why wouldn't yuh get me? Ain't we both members of de same club—de Hairy Apes? (*They stare at each other—a pause—then* YANK *goes on slowly and bit-*
20 *terly.*) So yuh're what she seen when she looked at me, de white-faced tart! I was you to her, get me? On'y outa de cage—broke out—free to moider her, see? Sure! Dat's what she tought. She wasn't wise dat I was in a cage, too—worser'n yours—sure—a damn sight—'cause you got
25 some chanct to bust loose—but me—(*He grows confused.*) Aw, hell! It's all wrong, ain't it? (*A pause.*) I s'pose yuh wan-

ter know what I'm doin' here, huh? I been warmin' a bench down to de Battery—ever since last night. Sure. I seen de sun come up. Dat was pretty, too—all red and pink
30 and green. I was looking' at de skyscrapers—steel—and all de ships comin' in, sailin' out, all over de oith—and dey was steel, too. De sun was warm, dey wasn't no clouds, and dere was a breeze blowin'. Sure, it was great stuff. I got it aw right—what Paddy said about dat bein' de right dope—
35 on'y I couldn't get *in* it, see? I couldn't belong in dat. It was over my head. And I kept tinkin'—and den I beat it up here to see what youse was like. And I waited till dey was all gone to git yuh alone. Say, how d'yuh feel sittin' in dat pen all de time, havin' to stand for 'em comin' and starin'
40 at yuh—de white-faced, skinny tarts and de boobs what marry 'em—makin' fun of yuh, laughin' at yuh, gittin' scared of yuh—damn 'em! (*He pounds on the rail with his fist. The gorilla rattles the bars of his cage and snarls. All the other monkeys set up an angry chattering in the darkness.* YANK *goes*
45 *on excitedly.*) Sure! Dat's de way it hits me, too. On'y yuh're lucky, see? Yuh don't belong with 'em and you know it. But me, I belong wit 'em—but I don't, see? Dey don't belong wit me, dat's what. Get me? Tinkin' is hard—(*He passes one hand across his forehead with a painful gesture. The gorilla growls*
50 *impatiently.* YANK *goes on gropingly.*) It's dis way, what I'm dri-vin' at. Youse can sit and dope dream in de past, green woods, de jungle and de rest of it. Den yuh belong and dey don't. Den yuh kin laugh at 'em, see? Yuh're de champ of de woild. But me—I ain't got no past to tink in, nor
55 nothin' dat's comin', on'y what's now—and dat don't be-long. Sure, you're de best off! Yuh can't tink, can yuh? Yuh can't talk neider. But I kin make a bluff at talkin' and tin-kin'—a'most git away wit it—a'most!—and dat's where de joker comes in. (*He laughs.*) I ain't on oith and I ain't in
60 heaven, get me? I'm in de middle tryin' to separate 'em, takin' all de woist punches from bot' of 'em. Maybe dat's what dey call hell, huh? But you, yuh're at de bottom. You belong! Sure! Yuh're de on'y one in de woild dat does, yuh lucky stiff! (*The gorilla growls proudly.*) And dat's why dey
65 gotter put yuh in a cage, see? (*The gorilla roars angrily.*) Sure! Yuh get me. It beats it when you try to tink it or talk it—it's way down—deep—behind—you 'n' me we feel it. Sure! Bot' members of dis club! (*He laughs—then in a sav-age tone.*) What de hell! T'hell wit it! A little action, dat's our
70 meat! Dat belongs! Knock 'em down and keep bustin' 'em till dey croaks yuh wit a gat—wit steel! Sure! Are yuh game? Dey've looked at youse, ain't dey—in a cage? Wan-ter get even? Wanter wind up like a sport 'stead of croakin' slow in dere? (*The gorilla roars an emphatic affirmative.* YANK
75 *goes on with a sort of furious exaltation.*) Sure! Yuh're reg'lar! Yuh'll stick to de finish! Me 'n' you, huh?—bot' members of this club! We'll put up one last star bout dat'll knock 'em offen deir seats! Dey'll have to make de cages stronger af-ter we're trou! (*The gorilla is straining at his bars, growling, hop-ping from one foot to the other.* YANK *takes a jimmy from under*
80 *his coat and forces the lock on the cage door. He throws this open.*) Pardon from de governor! Step out and shake hands! I'll take yuh for a walk down Fif' Avenoo. We'll knock 'em of-fen de oith and croak wit de band playin'. Come on, Brother. (*The gorilla scrambles gingerly out of his cage. Goes to*
85 YANK *and stands looking at him.* YANK *keeps his mocking tone—holds out his hand.*) Shake—de secret grip of our order.

(*Something, the tone of mockery, perhaps, suddenly enrages the animal. With a spring he wraps his huge arms around* YANK *in a murderous hug. There is a crackling snap of crushed ribs—a gasping cry, still mocking, from* YANK.) Hey, I didn't say kiss me! (*The gorilla lets the crushed body slip to the floor; stands over it uncertainly, considering; then picks it up, throws it in the cage, shuts the door, and shuffles off menacingly into the darkness at left. A great uproar of frightened chattering and whimpering comes from the other cages. Then* YANK *moves, groaning, opening his eyes, and there is silence. He mutters painfully.*) Say—dey oughter match him—wit Zybszko. He got me, aw right. I'm trou. Even him didn't tink I belonged. (*Then, with sudden passionate despair.*) Christ, where do I get off at? Where do I fit in? (*Checking himself as suddenly.*) Aw, what de hell! No squawkin', see! No quittin', get me! Croak wit your boots on! (*He grabs hold of the bars of the cage and hauls himself painfully to his feet—looks around him bewilderedly—forces a mocking laugh.*) In de cage, huh? (*In the strident tones of a circus barker.*) Ladies and gents, step forward and take a slant at de one and only—(*His voice weakened.*)—one and original—Hairy Ape from de wilds of—(*He slips in a heap on the floor and dies. The monkeys set up a chattering, whimpering wail. And, perhaps, the Hairy Ape at last belongs.*)

(*The curtain falls.*)

Tennessee Williams

Like Amanda Wingfield in *The Glass Menagerie,* Tennessee Williams (1911–1983) regarded himself as a product of the Old South and its genteel, rural, and—finally—obsolete traditions. Born Thomas Lanier Williams to a traveling shoe salesman and his wife, Williams was raised in Mississippi before moving to the tenements of St. Louis. As a child, Williams contracted diphtheria, which briefly paralyzed his legs and left him frail and homebound for some time. During his convalescence, Williams read and wrote avidly and published his first story at the age of sixteen. After high school, he briefly attended the University of Missouri, but withdrew when his poor health prevented him from passing the ROTC course. He then worked for three years in a shoe factory, then tried Washington University in St. Louis, but again dropped out. He finally took his degree in playwriting from the University of Iowa in 1938, when he changed his name to "Tennessee." In the 1930s, Williams's embattled relation to the world was deepened by the "loss" of his beloved sister Rose. Rose became chronically depressed, and Williams's mother, unable to cope with her erratic and wild behavior, consented to having a lobotomy performed. Rose was left docile but inert and became the prototype of several of Williams's most memorable dramatic characters, women whose inner beauty is too delicate to be disclosed to the world. At this time Williams also recognized his own homosexuality, a recognition that deepened his sense of the threatening conformity imposed by mainstream American society.

Coming of age in the Great Depression was formative for Williams's drama, particularly the range of themes associated with his mature work: a sexual tension surging beneath the surface of the characters' lives, the collapse of a sustaining family and social order, the attraction of misfits destroyed by a world that will not accept them. Williams wrote several now-lost plays in the late 1930s, and *Battle of Angels* (1940; later revised as *Orpheus Descending* in 1957) was produced by the Theater Guild in Boston, where it failed. Williams scored a major success with his next play, *The Glass Menagerie* (1944). He continued his success with a series of important dramas: *Summer and Smoke* (1947), *A Streetcar Named Desire* (1947), *The Rose Tattoo* (1951), *Camino Real* (1953), *Cat on a Hot Tin Roof* (1955), *Sweet Bird of Youth* (1959), and *Night of the Iguana* (1961). In his later years, Williams's drama became increasingly gothic and sensational, and his personal life suffered as well; Williams became an alcoholic and was institutionalized on several occasions. He continued to write plays to the end of his life, developing his characteristic strengths: a feel for the nuances of character, and a flair for dramatizing the victims of an unfeeling world.

THE GLASS MENAGERIE

First performed in 1944, *The Glass Menagerie* looks back to the 1930s. Its characters are reminiscent of Williams and his family, and their grinding poverty recalls the depression-era plays of Elmer Rice and Clifford Odets. In many ways, *The Glass Menagerie* is a play in the realistic tradition. Laura's menagerie recalls how Ibsen, Chekhov, and Strindberg used stage objects (Nora's Christmas tree in *A Doll House,* the cherry orchard in Chekhov's play) to evoke and symbolize the characters' motives and sensibilities. However, Williams also uses the device of the "memory play" to disrupt the linearity of realistic drama. Tom constructs the scene and the characters for the audience, and slide projections of phrases and images often illustrate the action as it takes place. These devices lend *The Glass Menagerie* the flavor of symbolist theater. Moreover, Tom's anticipation of the Spanish Civil War and World War II sets the play in a larger social and political context that looms foreboddingly over the fragile and self-absorbed characters. Amanda and Laura seem doomed never to escape the drab apartment, and even Tom, wandering the world, finally cannot escape it either. Deeply personal (Williams's given name was Tom), *The Glass Menagerie* also provides a kind of study

Tom, Laura, Jim, and Amanda in Tennessee Williams's *The Glass Menagerie* at the Williamstown Theatre Festival.

for Williams's later plays, for it includes a typical panoply of Williams's characters: the blunt, sexually aggressive, emotionally stunted Jim; Amanda, the faded Southern belle; Laura, more crippled emotionally than physically; and Tom, who falls in love with long distance yet never succeeds in escaping his past or in finding his future.

Production Notes

Being a "memory play," *The Glass Menagerie* can be presented with unusual freedom of convention. Because of its considerably delicate or tenuous material, atmospheric touches and subtleties of direction play a particularly important part. Expressionism and all other unconventional techniques in drama have only one valid aim, and that is a closer approach to truth. When a play employs unconventional techniques, it is not, or certainly shouldn't be, trying to escape its responsibility of dealing with reality, or interpreting experience, but is actually or should be attempting to find a closer approach, a more penetrating and vivid expression of things as they are. The straight realistic play with its genuine Frigidaire and authentic ice-cubes, its characters who speak exactly as its audience speaks, corresponds to the academic landscape and has the same virtue of a photographic likeness. Everyone should know nowadays the unimportance of the photographic in art: that truth, life, or reality is an organic thing which the poetic imagination can represent or suggest, in essence, only through transformation, through changing into other forms than those which were merely present in appearance.

These remarks are not meant as a preface only to this particular play. They have to do with a conception of a new, plastic theatre which must take the place of the exhausted theatre of realistic conventions if the theatre is to resume vitality as a part of our culture.

THE SCREEN DEVICE

There is *only one important difference between the original and the acting version of the play* and that is the *omission* in the latter of the device that I tentatively included in my *original* script. This device was the use of a screen on which were projected magic-lantern slides bearing images or titles. I do not regret the omission of this device from the original Broadway production. The extraordinary power of Miss Taylor's performance made it suitable to have the utmost simplicity in the physical production. But I think it may be interesting to some readers to see how this device was conceived. So I am putting it into the published manuscript. These images and legends, projected from behind, were cast on a section of wall between the front-room and dining-room areas, which should be indistinguishable from the rest when not in use.

The purpose of this will probably be apparent. It is to give accent to certain values in each scene. Each scene contains a particular point (or several) which is structurally the most important. In an episodic play, such as this, the basic structure or narrative line may be obscured from the audience; the effect may seem fragmentary rather than architectural. This may not be the fault of the play so much as a lack of attention in the audience. The legend or image upon the screen will strengthen the effect of what is merely allusion in the writing and allow the primary point to be made more simply and lightly than if the entire responsibility were on the spoken lines. Aside from this structural value, I think the screen will have a definite emotional appeal, less definable but just as important. An imaginative producer or director may invent many other uses for this device than those indicated in the present script. In fact the possibilities of the device seem much larger to me than the instance of this play can possibly utilize.

THE MUSIC

Another extra-literary accent in this play is provided by the use of music. A single recurring tune, "The Glass Menagerie," is used to give emotional emphasis to suitable passages. This tune is like circus music, not when you are on the grounds or in the immediate vicinity of the parade, but when you are at some distance and very likely thinking of something else. It seems under those circumstances to continue almost interminably and it weaves in and out of your preoccupied consciousness; then it is the lightest, most delicate music in the world and perhaps the saddest. It expresses the surface vivacity of life with the underlying strain of immutable and inexpressible sorrow. When you look at a piece of delicately spun glass you think of two things: how beautiful it is and how easily it can be broken. Both of those ideas should be woven into the recurring tune, which dips in and out of the play as if it were carried on a wind that changes. It serves as a thread of connection and allusion between the narrator with his separate point in time and space and the subject of his story. Between each episode it returns as reference to the emotion, nostalgia, which is the first condition of the play. It is primarily Laura's music and therefore comes out most clearly when the play focuses upon her and the lovely fragility of glass which is her image.

THE LIGHTING

The lighting in the play is not realistic. In keeping with the atmosphere of memory, the stage is dim. Shafts of light are focused on selected areas or actors, sometimes in contradistinction to what is the apparent center. For instance, in the quarrel scene between Tom and Amanda, in which Laura has no active part, the clearest pool of light is on her figure. This is also true of the supper scene, when her silent figure on the sofa should remain the visual center. The light upon Laura should be distinct from the others, having a peculiar pristine clarity such as light used in early religious portraits of female saints or madonnas. A certain correspondence to light in religious paintings, such as El Greco's, where the figures are radiant in atmosphere that is relatively dusky, could be effectively used throughout the play. (It will also permit a more effective use of the screen.) A free, imaginative use of light can be of enormous value in giving a mobile, plastic quality to plays of a more or less static nature.

Tennessee Williams

THE GLASS MENAGERIE

Tennessee Williams

CHARACTERS

AMANDA WINGFIELD (*the mother*), *a little woman of great but confused vitality clinging frantically to another time and place. Her characterization must be carefully created, not copied from type. She is not paranoiac, but her life is paranoia. There is much to admire in Amanda, and as much to love and pity as there is to laugh at. Certainly she has endurance and a kind of heroism, and though her foolishness makes her unwittingly cruel at times, there is tenderness in her slight person.*

LAURA WINGFIELD (*her daughter*), *Amanda, having failed to establish contact with reality, continues to live vitally in her illusions, but Laura's situation is even graver. A childhood illness has left her crippled, one leg slightly shorter than the other, and held in a brace. This defect need not be more than suggested on the stage. Stemming from this, Laura's separation increases till she is like a piece of her own glass collection, too exquisitely fragile to move from the shelf.*

TOM WINGFIELD (*her son*), *and the narrator of the play. A poet with a job in a warehouse. His nature is not remorseless, but to escape from a trap he has to act without pity.*

JIM O'CONNOR (*the gentleman caller*), *a nice, ordinary, young man.*

SCENE: *An Alley in St. Louis*

Part I   Preparation for a Gentleman Caller.

Part II The Gentlemen calls.

TIME: *Now and the Past*

SCENE ONE

The Wingfield apartment is in the rear of the building, one of those vast hive-like conglomerations of the cellular living-units that flower as warty growths in overcrowded urban centers of lower middle-class population and are symptomatic of the impulse of this largest and fundamentally enslaved section of American society to avoid fluidity and differentiation and to exist and function as one interfused mass of automatism.

The apartment faces an alley and is entered by a fire escape, a structure whose name is a touch of accidental poetic truth, for all of these huge buildings are always burning with the slow and implacable fires of human desperation. The fire escape is part of what we see—that is, the landing of it and steps descending from it.

The scene is memory and is therefore nonrealistic. Memory takes a lot of poetic license. It omits some details; others are exaggerated, according to the emotional value of the articles it touches, for memory is seated predominantly in the heart. The interior is therefore rather dim and poetic.

At the rise of the curtain, the audience is faced with the dark, grim rear wall of the Wingfield tenement. This building is flanked on both sides by dark, narrow alleys which run into murky canyons of tangled clotheslines, garbage cans, and the sinister latticework of neighboring fire escapes. It is up and down these side alleys that exterior entrances and exits are made during the play. At the end of TOM's opening commentary, the dark tenement wall slowly becomes transparent and reveals the interior of the ground-floor Wingfield apartment.

Nearest the audience is the living room, which also serves as a sleeping room for LAURA, *the sofa unfolding to make her bed. Just beyond, separated from the living room by a wide arch or second proscenium with transparent faded portieres (or second curtain), is the dining room. In an old-fashioned whatnot in the living room are seen scores of transparent glass animals. A blown-up photograph of the father hangs on the wall of the living room, to the left of the archway. It is the face of a very handsome young man in a doughboy's First World War cap. He is gallantly smiling, ineluctably smiling, as if to say "I will be smiling forever."*

Also hanging on the wall, near the photograph, are a typewriter keyboard chart and a Gregg shorthand diagram. An upright typewriter on a small table stands beneath the charts.

The audience hears and sees the opening scene in the dining room through both the transparent fourth wall of the building and the transparent gauze portieres of the dining-room arch. It is during this revealing scene that the fourth wall slowly ascends, out of sight. This transparent exterior wall is not brought down again until the very end of the play, during TOM's *final speech.*

The narrator is an undisguised convention of the play. He takes whatever license with dramatic convention is convenient to his purposes.

TOM *enters, dressed as a merchant sailor, and strolls across to the fire escape. There he stops and lights a cigarette. He addresses the audience.*

TOM: Yes, I have tricks in my pocket, I have things up my sleeve. But I am the opposite of a stage magician. He gives you illusion that has the appearance of truth. I give you truth in the pleasant disguise of illusion.

   To begin with, I turn back time. I reverse it to that 5 quaint period, the thirties, when the huge middle class of America was matriculating in a school for the blind. Their eyes had failed them, or they had failed their eyes, and so they were having their fingers pressed forcibly down on the fiery Braille alphabet of a dissolving economy. 10

   In Spain there was revolution. Here there was only shouting and confusion. In Spain there was Guernica. Here there were disturbances of labor, sometimes pretty violent, in otherwise peaceful cities such as Chicago, Cleveland, Saint Louis . . . This is the social background of the play. 15

(*Music begins to play.*)

   The play is memory. Being a memory play, it is dimly lighted, it is sentimental, it is not realistic. In memory everything seems to happen to music. That explains the fiddle in the wings.

   I am the narrator of the play, and also a character in it. 20 The other characters are my mother, Amanda, my sister, Laura, and a gentleman caller who appears in the final

scenes. He is the most realistic character in the play, being an
emissary from a world of reality that we were somehow set
apart from. But since I have a poet's weakness for symbols, I
am using this character also as a symbol; he is the long-
delayed but always expected something that we live for.

There is a fifth character in the play who doesn't appear except in this larger-than-life-size photograph over
the mantel. This is our father who left us a long time ago.
He was a telephone man who fell in love with long distances; he gave up his job with the telephone company
and skipped the light fantastic out of town . . .

The last we heard of him was a picture postcard from
Mazatlan, on the Pacific coast of Mexico, containing a
message of two words: "Hello—Goodbye!" and no address.

I think the rest of the play will explain itself. . . .

(AMANDA's voice becomes audible through the portieres.)

(Legend on screen: "Ou sont les neiges.")

(TOM divides the portieres and enters the dining room. AMANDA and
LAURA are seated at a drop-leaf table. Eating is indicated by gestures
without food or utensils. AMANDA faces the audience. TOM and
LAURA are seated in profile. The interior has lit up softly and
through the scrim we see AMANDA and LAURA seated at the table.)

AMANDA: (Calling.) Tom?
TOM: Yes, Mother.
AMANDA: We can't say grace until you come to the table!
TOM: Coming, Mother. (He bows slightly and withdraws, reappearing a few moments later in his place at the table.)
AMANDA: (To her son.) Honey, don't push with your fingers. If
you have to push with something, the thing to push with
is a crust of bread. And chew—chew! Animals have se-
cretions in their stomachs which enable them to digest
food without mastication, but human beings are supposed
to chew their food before they swallow it down. Eat food
leisurely, son, and really enjoy it. A well-cooked meal has
lots of delicate flavors that have to be held in the mouth
for appreciation. So chew your food and give your salivary
glands a chance to function!

(TOM deliberately lays his imaginary fork down and pushes his chair
back from the table.)

TOM: I haven't enjoyed one bite of this dinner because of your
constant directions on how to eat it. It's you that make me
rush through meals with your hawklike attention to every
bite I take. Sickening—spoils my appetite—all this discussion of—animals' secretion—salivary glands—mastication!
AMANDA: (Lightly.) Temperament like a Metropolitan star!

(TOM rises and walks toward the living room.)

You're not excused from the table.
TOM: I'm getting a cigarette.
AMANDA: You smoke too much.

(LAURA rises.)

LAURA: I'll bring in the blanc mange.

(TOM remains standing with his cigarette by the portieres.)

AMANDA: (Rising.) No, sister, no, sister—you be the lady this
time and I'll be the darky.
LAURA: I'm already up.
AMANDA: Resume your seat, little sister—I want you to stay
fresh and pretty—for gentlemen callers!
LAURA: (Sitting down.) I'm not expecting any gentlemen callers.
AMANDA: (Crossing out to the kitchenette, airily.) Sometimes
they come when they are least expected! Why, I remember one Sunday afternoon in Blue Mountain—

(She enters the kitchenette.)

TOM: I know what's coming!
LAURA: Yes. But let her tell it.
TOM: Again?
LAURA: She loves to tell it.

(AMANDA returns with a bowl of dessert.)

AMANDA: One Sunday afternoon in Blue Mountain—your
mother received—seventeen!—gentlemen callers! Why,
sometimes there weren't chairs enough to accommodate
them all. We had to send the nigger over to bring in folding chairs from the parish house.
TOM: (Remaining at the portieres.) How did you entertain those
gentlemen callers?
AMANDA: I understood the art of conversation!
TOM: I bet you could talk.
AMANDA: Girls in those days knew how to talk, I can tell you.
TOM: Yes?

(Image on screen: AMANDA as a girl on a porch, greeting callers.)

AMANDA: They knew how to entertain their gentlemen
callers. It wasn't enough for a girl to be possessed of a
pretty face and a graceful figure—although I wasn't
slighted in either respect. She also needed to have a nimble wit and a tongue to meet all occasions.
TOM: What did you talk about?
AMANDA: Things of importance going on in the world!
Never anything coarse or common or vulgar.

(She addresses TOM as though he were seated in the vacant chair at
the table though he remains by the portieres. He plays this scene as
though reading from a script.)

My callers were gentlemen—all! Among my callers were
some of the most prominent young planters of the Mississippi Delta—planters and sons of planters!

(TOM motions for music and a spot of light on AMANDA. Her eyes
lift, her face glows, her voice becomes rich and elegiac.)

(Screen legend: "Ou sont les neiges d'antan?")

There was young Champ Laughlin who later became
vice-president of the Delta Planters Bank. Hadley Steven-
son who was drowned in Moon Lake and left his widow
one hundred and fifty thousand in Government bonds.
There were the Cutrere brothers, Wesley and Bates. Bates
was one of my bright particular beaux! He got in a quarrel with that wild Wainwright boy. They shot it out on the
floor of Moon Lake Casino. Bates was shot through the

stomach. Died in the ambulance on his way to Memphis. His widow was also well provided-for, came into eight or ten thousand acres, that's all. She married him on the rebound—never loved her—carried my picture on him
110 the night he died! And there was that boy that every girl in the Delta had set her cap for! That beautiful, brilliant young Fitzhugh boy from Greene County!

TOM: What did he leave his widow?

AMANDA: He never married! Gracious, you talk as though all
115 of my old admirers had turned up their toes to the daisies!

TOM: Isn't this the first you've mentioned that still survives?

AMANDA: That Fitzhugh boy went North and made a fortune—came to be known as the Wolf of Wall Street! He had the Midas touch, whatever he touched turned to
120 gold! And I could have been Mrs. Duncan J. Fitzhugh, mind you! But—I picked your *father!*

LAURA: (*Rising.*) Mother, let me clear the table.

AMANDA: No, dear, you go in front and study your typewriter chart. Or practice your shorthand a little. Stay fresh and
125 pretty!—It's almost time for our gentlemen callers to start arriving. (*She flounces girlishly toward the kitchenette.*) How many do you suppose we're going to entertain this afternoon?

(TOM *throws down the paper and jumps up with a groan.*)

LAURA: (*Alone in the dining room.*) I don't believe we're going to receive any, Mother.

130 AMANDA: (*Reappearing, airily.*) What? No one—not one? You must be joking!

(LAURA *nervously echoes her laugh. She slips in a fugitive manner through the half-open portieres and draws them gently behind her. A shaft of very clear light is thrown on her face against the faded tapestry of the curtains. Faintly the music of "The Glass Menagerie" is heard as she continues, lightly.*)

Not one gentleman caller? It can't be true! There must be a flood, there must have been a tornado!

LAURA: It isn't a flood, it's not a tornado, Mother. I'm just not
135 popular like you were in Blue Mountain. . . .

(TOM *utters another groan.* LAURA *glances at him with a faint, apologetic smile. Her voice catches a little.*)

Mother's afraid I'm going to be an old maid.

(*The scene dims out with the "Glass Menagerie" music.*)

SCENE TWO

On the dark stage the screen is lighted with the image of blue roses. Gradually LAURA's *figure becomes apparent and the screen goes out. The music subsides.*

LAURA *is seated in the delicate ivory chair at the small claw-foot table. She wears a dress of soft violet material for a kimono—her hair is tied back from her forehead with a ribbon. She is washing and polishing her collection of glass.* AMANDA *appears on the fire escape steps. At the sound of her ascent,* LAURA *catches her breath, thrusts the bowl of ornaments away, and seats herself stiffly before the diagram of the typewriter keyboard as though it held her spellbound. Something has happened to* AMANDA. *It is written in her face as she climbs to the landing: a look that is grim and hopeless and a little*

absurd. *She has on one of those cheap or imitation velvety-looking cloth coats with imitation fur collar. Her hat is five or six years old, one of those dreadful cloche hats that were worn in the late Twenties, and she is clutching an enormous black patent-leather pocketbook with nickel clasps and initials. This is her full-dress outfit, the one she usually wears to the D.A.R. Before entering she looks through the door. She purses her lips, opens her eyes very wide, rolls them upward and shakes her head. Then she slowly lets herself in the door. Seeing her mother's expression* LAURA *touches her lips with a nervous gesture.*

LAURA: Hello, Mother, I was—(*She makes a nervous gesture toward the chart on the wall.* AMANDA *leans against the shut door and stares at* LAURA *with a martyred look.*)

AMANDA: Deception? Deception? (*She slowly removes her hat and gloves, continuing the sweet suffering stare. She lets the hat* 5 *and gloves fall on the floor—a bit of acting.*)

LAURA: (*Shakily.*) How was the D.A.R. meeting?

(AMANDA *slowly opens her purse and removes a dainty white handkerchief which she shakes out delicately and delicately touches to her lips and nostrils.*)

Didn't you go to the D.A.R. meeting, Mother?

AMANDA: (*Faintly, almost inaudibly.*) —No.—No. (*Then more forcibly.*) I did not have the strength—to go to the D.A.R. 10 In fact, I did not have the courage! I wanted to find a hole in the ground and hide myself in it forever! (*She crosses slowly to the wall and removes the diagram of the typewriter keyboard. She holds it in front of her for a second, staring at it sweetly and sorrowfully—then bites her lips and tears it into two pieces.*) 15

LAURA: (*Faintly.*) Why did you do that, Mother?

(AMANDA *repeats the same procedure with the chart of the Gregg Alphabet.*)

Why are you—

AMANDA: Why? Why? How old are you, Laura?

LAURA: Mother, you know my age.

AMANDA: I thought that you were an adult; it seems that I was 20 mistaken. (*She crosses slowly to the sofa and sinks down and stares at* LAURA.)

LAURA: Please don't stare at me, Mother.

(AMANDA *closes her eyes and lowers her head. There is a ten-second pause.*)

AMANDA: What are we going to do, what is going to become of us, what is the future? 25

(*There is another pause.*)

LAURA: Has something happened, Mother?

(AMANDA *draws a long breath, takes out the handkerchief again, goes through the dabbing process.*)

Mother, has—something happened?

AMANDA: I'll be all right in a minute, I'm just bewildered—(*She hesitates.*)—by life. . . .

LAURA: Mother, I wish that you would tell me what's happened! 30

AMANDA: As you know, I was supposed to be inducted into my office at the D.A.R. this afternoon.

(*Screen image:* A swarm of typewriters.)

But I stopped off at Rubicam's Business College to speak to your teachers about your having a cold and ask them what progress they thought you were making down there.

LAURA: Oh . . . .

AMANDA: I went to the typing instructor and introduced myself as your mother. She didn't know who you were. "Wingfield," she said, "We don't have any such student enrolled at the school!"

I assured her she did, that you had been going to classes since early in January.

"I wonder," she said, "If you could be talking about that terribly shy little girl who dropped out of school after only a few days' attendance?"

"No," I said, "Laura, my daughter, has been going to school every day for the past six weeks!"

"Excuse me," she said. She took the attendance book out and there was your name, unmistakably printed, and all the dates you were absent until they decided that you had dropped out of school.

I still said, "No, there must have been some mistake! There must have been some mix-up in the records!"

And she said, "No—I remember her perfectly now. Her hands shook so that she couldn't hit the right keys! The first time we gave a speed test, she broke down completely—was sick at the stomach and almost had to be carried into the wash room! After that morning she never showed up any more. We phoned the house but never got any answer"—While I was working at Famous-Barr, I suppose, demonstrating those—

(*She indicates a brassiere with her hands.*)

Oh! I felt so weak I could barely keep on my feet! I had to sit down while they got me a glass of water! Fifty dollars' tuition, all of our plans—my hopes and ambitions for you—just gone up the spout, just gone up the spout like that.

(LAURA *draws a long breath and gets awkwardly to her feet. She crosses to the Victrola and winds it up.*)

What are you doing?

LAURA: Oh! (*She releases the handle and returns to her seat.*)

AMANDA: Laura, where have you been going when you've gone out pretending that you were going to business college?

LAURA: I've just been going out walking.

AMANDA: That's not true.

LAURA: It is. I just went walking.

AMANDA: Walking? Walking? In winter? Deliberately courting pneumonia in that light coat? Where did you walk to, Laura?

LAURA: All sorts of places—mostly in the park.

AMANDA: Even after you'd started catching that cold?

LAURA: It was the lesser of two evils, Mother.

(*Screen image:* Winter scene in a park.)

I couldn't go back there. I—threw up—on the floor!

AMANDA: From half past seven till after five every day you mean to tell me you walked around in the park, because you wanted to make me think that you were still going to Rubicam's Business College?

LAURA: It wasn't as bad as it sounds. I went inside places to get warmed up.

AMANDA: Inside where?

LAURA: I went in the art museum and the bird houses at the Zoo. I visited the penquins every day! Sometimes I did without lunch and went to the movies. Lately I've been spending most of my afternoons in the Jewel Box, that big glass house where they raise the tropical flowers.

AMANDA: You did all this to deceive me, just for deception? (LAURA *looks down.*) Why?

LAURA: Mother, when you're disappointed, you get that awful suffering look on your face, like the picture of Jesus' mother in the museum!

AMANDA: Hush!

LAURA: I couldn't face it.

(*There is a pause. A whisper of strings is heard. Legend on screen:* "The Crust of Humility.")

AMANDA: (*Hopelessly fingering the huge pocketbook.*) So what are we going to do the rest of our lives? Stay home and watch the parades go by? Amuse ourselves with the glass menagerie, darling? Eternally play those worn-out phonograph records your father left as a painful reminder of him? We won't have a business career—we've given that up because it gave us nervous indigestion! (*She laughs wearily.*) What is there left but dependency all our lives? I know so well what becomes of unmarried women who aren't prepared to occupy a position. I've seen such pitiful cases in the South—barely tolerated spinsters living upon the grudging patronage of sister's husband or brother's wife!—stuck away in some little mousetrap of a room—encouraged by one in-law to visit another—little birdlike women without any nest—eating the crust of humility all their life!

Is that the future that we've mapped out for ourselves? I swear it's the only alternative I can think of! (*She pauses.*) It isn't a very pleasant alternative, is it? (*She pauses again.*) Of course—some girls *do* marry.

(LAURA *twists her hands nervously.*)

Haven't you ever liked some boy?

LAURA: Yes. I liked one once. (*She rises.*) I came across his picture a while ago.

AMANDA: (*With some interest.*) He gave you his picture?

LAURA: No, it's in the yearbook.

AMANDA: (*Disappointed.*) Oh—a high school boy.

(*Screen image:* JIM as the high school hero bearing a silver cup.)

LAURA: Yes. His name was Jim. (*She lifts the heavy annual from the claw-foot table.*) Here he is in *The Pirates of Penzance.*

AMANDA: (*Absently.*) The what?

LAURA: The operetta the senior class put on. He had a wonderful voice and we sat across the aisle from each other Mondays, Wednesdays and Fridays in the Aud. Here he is with the silver cup for debating! See his grin?

AMANDA: (*Absently.*) He must have had a jolly disposition.

LAURA: He used to call me—Blue Roses.

(*Screen image:* Blue roses.)

AMANDA: Why did he call you such a name as that?

LAURA: When I had that attack of pleurosis—he asked me what was the matter when I came back. I said pleurosis—
135 he thought that I said Blue Roses! So that's what he always called me after that. Whenever he saw me, he'd holler, "Hello, Blue Roses!" I didn't care for the girl that he went out with. Emily Meisenbach. Emily was the best-dressed girl at Soldan. She never struck me, though, as being sin-
140 cere . . . It says in the Personal Section—they're engaged. That's—six years ago! They must be married by now.

AMANDA: Girls that aren't cut out for business careers usually wind up married to some nice man. (*She gets up with a spark of revival.*) Sister, that's what you'll do!

(*LAURA utters a startled, doubtful laugh. She reaches quickly for a piece of glass.*)

145 LAURA: But, Mother—

AMANDA: Yes? (*She goes over to the photograph.*)

LAURA: (*In a tone of frightened apology.*) I'm—crippled!

AMANDA: Nonsense! Laura, I've told you never, never to use that word. Why, you're not crippled, you just have a little
150 defect—hardly noticeable, even! When people have some slight disadvantage like that, they cultivate other things to make up for it—develop charm—and vivacity—and— *charm!* That's all you have to do! (*She turns again to the photograph.*) One thing your father had *plenty of*—was charm!

(*The scene fades out with music.*)

SCENE THREE

Legend on screen: "After the fiasco—"

TOM *speaks from the fire escape landing.*

TOM: After the fiasco at Rubicam's Business College, the idea of getting a gentleman caller for Laura began to play a more and more important part in Mother's calculations. It became an obsession. Like some archetype of the univer-
5 sal unconscious, the image of the gentleman caller haunted our small apartment. . . .

(*Screen image:* A young man at the door of a house with flowers.)

An evening at home rarely passed without some allu-sion to this image, this specter, this hope . . . Even when he wasn't mentioned, his presence hung in Mother's preoccu-
10 pied look and in my sister's frightened, apologetic man-ner—hung like a sentence passed upon the Wingfields!
Mother was a woman of action as well as words. She began to take logical steps in the planned direction. Late that winter and in the early spring—realizing that extra
15 money would be needed to properly feather the nest and plume the bird—she conducted a vigorous campaign on the telephone, roping in subscribers to one of those mag-azines for matrons called *The Homemaker's Companion,* the type of journal that features the serialized sublimations of
20 ladies of letters who think in terms of delicate cuplike breasts, slim, tapering waists, rich, creamy thighs, eyes like wood smoke in autumn, fingers that soothe and caress like strains of music, bodies as powerful as Etruscan sculpture.

(*Screen image:* The cover of a glamor magazine.)

(AMANDA *enters with the telephone on a long extension cord. She is spotlighted in the dim stage.*)

AMANDA: Ida Scott? This is Amanda Wingfield! We missed you at the D.A.R. last Monday! I said to myself: She's 25 probably suffering with that sinus condition! How is that sinus condition?
Horrors! Heaven have mercy!—You're a Christian martyr, yes, that's what you are, a Christian martyr!
Well, I just now happened to notice that your subscrip- 30 tion to the *Companion's* about to expire! Yes, it expires with the next issue, honey!—just when that wonderful new serial by Bessie Mae Hopper is getting off to such an exciting start. Oh, honey, it's something that you can't miss! You remember how *Gone with the Wind* took everybody by storm! You sim- 35 ply couldn't go out if you hadn't read it. All everybody *talked* was Scarlett O'Hara. Well, this is a book that critics already compare to *Gone with the Wind.* It's the *Gone with the Wind* of the post–World War generation!—What?—Burning?— Oh, honey, don't let them burn, go take a look in the oven 40 and I'll hold the wire! Heavens—I think she's hung up!

(*The scene dims out.*)

(*Legend on screen:* "You think I'm in love with Continental Shoemakers?")

(*Before the lights come up again, the violent voices of* TOM *and* AMANDA *are heard. They are quarreling behind the portieres. In front of them stands* LAURA *with clenched hands and panicky ex-pression. A clear pool of light is on her figure throughout this scene.*)

TOM: What in Christ's name am I—

AMANDA: (*Shrilly.*) Don't you use that—

TOM: —supposed to do!

AMANDA: —expression! Not in my—   45

TOM: Ohhh!

AMANDA: —presence! Have you gone out of your senses?

TOM: I have, that's true, *driven* out!

AMANDA: What is the matter with you, you—big—big— IDIOT!   50

TOM: Look!—I've got *no thing,* no single thing—

AMANDA: Lower your voice!

TOM: —in my life here that I can call my OWN! Everything is—

AMANDA: Stop that shouting!

TOM: Yesterday you confiscated my books! You had the nerve 55 to—

AMANDA: I took that horrible novel back to the library—yes! That hideous book by that insane Mr. Lawrence.

(TOM *laughs wildly.*)

I cannot control the output of diseased minds or people who cater to them—   60

(TOM *laughs still more wildly.*)

BUT I WON'T ALLOW SUCH FILTH BROUGHT INTO MY HOUSE! No, no, no, no, no!

TOM: House, house! Who pays rent on it, who makes a slave of himself to—

65 AMANDA: (*Fairly screeching.*) Don't you DARE to—
    TOM: No, no, *I* mustn't say things! *I've* got to just—
    AMANDA: Let me tell you—
    TOM: I don't want to hear any more!

(*He tears the portieres open. The dining-room area is lit with a turgid smoky red glow. Now we see* AMANDA; *her hair is in metal curlers and she is wearing a very old bathrobe, much too large for her slight figure, a relic of the faithless Mr. Wingfield. The upright typewriter now stands on the drop-leaf table, along with a wild disarray of manuscripts. The quarrel was probably precipitated by* AMANDA's *interruption of* TOM's *creative labor. A chair lies overthrown on the floor. Their gesticulating shadows are cast on the ceiling by the fiery glow.*)

    AMANDA: You *will* hear more, you—
70 TOM: No, I won't hear more, I'm going out!
    AMANDA: You come right back in—
    TOM: Out, out, out! Because I'm—
    AMANDA: Come back here, Tom Wingfield! I'm not through talking to you!
75 TOM: Oh, go—
    LAURA: (*Desperately.*)—Tom!
    AMANDA: You're going to listen, and no more insolence from you! I'm at the end of my patience!

(*He comes back toward her.*)

    TOM: What do you think I'm at? Aren't I supposed to have
80 any patience to reach the end of, Mother? I know, I know. It seems unimportant to you, what I'm *doing*—what I *want* to do—having a little *difference* between them! You don't think that—
    AMANDA: I think you've been doing things that you're
85 ashamed of. That's why you act like this. I don't believe that you go every night to the movies. Nobody goes to the movies night after night. Nobody in their right minds goes to the movies as often as you pretend to. People don't go to the movies at nearly midnight, and movies don't let
90 out at two A.M. Come in stumbling. Muttering to yourself like a maniac! You get three hours' sleep and then go to work. Oh, I can picture the way you're doing down there. Moping, doping, because you're in no condition.
    TOM: (*Wildly.*) No, I'm in no condition!
95 AMANDA: What right have you got to jeopardize your job? Jeopardize the security of us all? How do you think we'd manage if you were—
    TOM: Listen! You think I'm crazy about the *warehouse?* (*He bends fiercely toward her slight figure.*) You think I'm in love
100 with the Continental Shoemakers? You think I want to spend fifty-five years down there in that—*celotex interior!* with—*fluorescent—tubes!* Look! I'd rather somebody picked up a crowbar and battered out my brains—than go back mornings! I *go!* Every time you come in yelling that
105 Goddamn *"Rise and Shine!" "Rise and Shine!"* I say to myself, "How *lucky dead* people are!" But I get up. I *go!* For sixty-five dollars a month I give up all that I dream of doing and being *ever!* And you say self—*self's* all I ever think of. Why, listen, if self is what I thought of, Mother, I'd be
110 where he is—GONE! (*He points to his father's picture.*) As far as the system of transportation reaches! (*He starts past her. She grabs his arm.*) Don't grab at me, Mother!
    AMANDA: Where are you going?

    TOM: I'm going to the *movies!*
    AMANDA: I don't believe that lie!   115

(TOM *crouches toward her, overtowering her tiny figure. She backs away, gasping.*)

    TOM: I'm going to opium dens! Yes, opium dens, dens of vice and criminals' hangouts, Mother. I've joined the Hogan Gang, I'm a hired assassin, I carry a tommy gun in a violin case! I run a string of cat houses in the Valley! They call me   120
    Killer, Killer Wingfield, I'm leading a double-life, a simple, honest warehouse worker by day, by night a dynamic *czar* of the *underworld*, Mother. I go to gambling casinos, I spin away fortunes on the roulette table! I wear a patch over one eye and a false mustache, sometimes I put on green whiskers.   125
    On those occasions they call me—*El Diablo!* Oh, I could tell you many things to make you sleepless! My enemies plan to dynamite this place. They're going to blow us all sky-high some night! I'll be glad, very happy, and so will you! You'll go up, up on a broomstick, over Blue Mountain   130
    with seventeen gentlemen callers! You ugly—babbling old—witch . . . (*He goes through a series of violent, clumsy movements, seizing his overcoat, lunging to the door, pulling it fiercely open. The women watch him, aghast. His arm catches in the sleeve of the coat as he struggles to pull it on. For a moment he is pinioned by the bulky garment. With an outraged groan he tears the coat off   135
    again, splitting the shoulder of it, and hurls it across the room. It strikes against the shelf of* LAURA's *glass collection, and there is a tinkle of shattering glass.* LAURA *cries out as if wounded.*)

(*Music.*)

(*Screen legend:* "The Glass Menagerie.")

    LAURA: (*Shrilly.*) My glass!—menagerie . . . (*She covers her face and turns away.*)   140

(*But* AMANDA *is still stunned and stupefied by the "ugly witch" so that she barely notices this occurrence. Now she recovers her speech.*)

    AMANDA: (*In an awful voice.*) I won't speak to you—until you apologize!

(*She crosses through the portieres and draws them together behind her.* TOM *is left with* LAURA. LAURA *clings weakly to the mantel with her face averted.* TOM *stares at her stupidly for a moment. Then he crosses to the shelf. He drops awkwardly on his knees to collect the fallen glass, glancing at* LAURA *as if he would speak but couldn't.*)

(*"The Glass Menagerie" music steals in as the scene dims out.*)

SCENE FOUR

The interior of the apartment is dark. There is a faint light in the alley. A deep-voiced bell in a church is tolling the hour of five.

TOM *appears at the top of the alley. After each solemn boom of the bell in the tower, he shakes a little noisemaker or rattle as if to express the tiny spasm of man in contrast to the sustained power and dignity of the Almighty. This and the unsteadiness of his advance make it evident that he has been drinking. As he climbs the few steps to the fire escape landing light steals up inside.* LAURA *appears in the front room in a nightdress. She notices that* TOM's *bed is empty.* TOM *fishes in*

*his pockets for his door key, removing a motley assortment of articles
in the search, including a shower of movie ticket stubs and an empty
bottle. At last he finds the key, but just as he is about to insert it, it
slips from his fingers. He strikes a match and crouches below the door.*

TOM: (*Bitterly.*) One crack—and it falls through!

(LAURA *opens the door.*)

LAURA: Tom! Tom, what are you doing?
TOM: Looking for a door key.
LAURA: Where have you been all this time?
5   TOM: I have been to the movies.
LAURA: All this time at the movies?
TOM: There was a very long program. There was a Garbo
      picture and a Mickey Mouse and a travelogue and a news-
      reel and a preview of coming attractions. And there was
10   an organ solo and a collection for the Milk Fund—
      simultaneously—which ended up in a terrible fight be-
      tween a fat lady and an usher!
LAURA: (*Innocently.*) Did you have to stay through everything?
TOM: Of course! And, oh, I forgot! There was a big stage
15   show! The headliner on this stage show was Malvolio the
      Magician. He performed wonderful tricks, many of them,
      such as pouring water back and forth between pitchers.
      First it turned to wine and then it turned to beer and then
      it turned to whisky. I know it was whisky it finally turned
20   into because he needed somebody to come up out of the
      audience to help him, and I came up—both shows! It was
      Kentucky Straight Bourbon. A very generous fellow, he
      gave souvenirs. (*He pulls from his back pocket a shimmering
      rainbow-colored scarf.*) He gave me this. This is his magic
25   scarf. You can have it, Laura. You wave it over a canary
      cage and you get a bowl of goldfish. You wave it over the
      goldfish bowl and they fly away canaries . . . But the won-
      derfullest trick of all was the coffin trick. We nailed him
      into a coffin and he got out of the coffin without remov-
30   ing one nail. (*He has come inside.*) There is a trick that
      would come in handy for me—get me out of this two-
      by-four situation! (*He flops onto the bed and starts removing
      his shoes.*)
LAURA: Tom—shhh!
35   TOM: What're you shushing me for?
LAURA: You'll wake up Mother.
TOM: Goody, goody! Pay 'er back for all those "Rise an'
      Shines." (*He lies down, groaning.*) You know it don't take
      much intelligence to get yourself into a nailed-up coffin,
40   Laura. But who in hell ever got himself out of one with-
      out removing one nail?

(*As if in answer, the father's grinning photograph lights up. The scene
dims out.*)

(*Immediately following, the church bell is heard striking six. At the
sixth stroke the alarm clock goes off in* AMANDA's *room, and after a
few moments we hear her calling: "Rise and Shine! Rise and Shine!*
LAURA, *go tell your brother to rise and shine!"*)

TOM: (*Sitting up slowly.*) I'll rise—but I won't shine.

(*The light increases.*)

AMANDA: Laura, tell your brother his coffee is ready.

(LAURA *slips into the front room.*)

LAURA: Tom!—It's nearly seven. Don't make Mother nervous.

(*He stares at her stupidly.*)

      (*Beseechingly.*) Tom, speak to Mother this morning. Make   45
      up with her, apologize, speak to her!
TOM: She won't to me. It's her that started not speaking.
LAURA: If you just say you're sorry she'll start speaking.
TOM: Her not speaking—is that such a tragedy?
LAURA: Please—please!   50
AMANDA: (*Calling from the kitchenette.*) Laura, are you going to
      do what I asked you to do, or do I have to get dressed and
      go out myself?
LAURA: Going, going—soon as I get on my coat!

(*She pulls on a shapeless felt hat with a nervous, jerky movement,
pleadingly glancing at* TOM. *She rushes awkwardly for her coat. The
coat is one of* AMANDA's, *inaccurately made-over, the sleeves too short
for* LAURA.)

      Butter and what else?   55
AMANDA: (*Entering from the kitchenette.*) Just butter. Tell them
      to charge it.
LAURA: Mother, they make such faces when I do that.
AMANDA: Sticks and stones can break our bones, but the ex-
      pression on Mr. Garfinkel's face won't harm us! Tell your 60
      brother his coffee is getting cold.
LAURA: (*At the door.*) Do what I asked you, will you, will you,
      Tom?

(*He looks sullenly away.*)

AMANDA: Laura, go now or just don't go at all!
LAURA: (*Rushing out.*) Going—going!   65

(*A second later she cries out.* TOM *springs up and crosses to the door.*
TOM *opens the door.*)

TOM: Laura?
LAURA: I'm all right. I slipped, but I'm all right.
AMANDA: (*Peering anxiously after her.*) If anyone breaks a leg on
      those fire-escape steps, the landlord ought to be sued for
      every cent he possesses! (*She shuts the door. Now she remem-*   70
      bers she isn't speaking to TOM *and returns to the other room.*)

(*As* TOM *comes listlessly for his coffee, she turns her back to him and
stands rigidly facing the window on the gloomy gray vault of the
areaway. Its light on her face with its aged but childish features is cruelly sharp, satirical as a Daumier print.*)

(*The music of "Ave Maria" is heard softly.*)

(TOM *glances sheepishly but sullenly at her averted figure and
slumps at the table. The coffee is scalding hot; he sips it and gasps
and spits it back in the cup. At his gasp,* AMANDA *catches her breath
and half turns. Then she catches herself and turns back to the window.* TOM *blows on his coffee, glancing sidewise at his mother. She
clears her throat.* TOM *clears his. He starts to rise, sinks back down
again, scratches his head, clears his throat again.* AMANDA *coughs.*
TOM *raises his cup in both hands to blow on it, his eyes staring over
the rim of it at his mother for several moments. Then he slowly sets
the cup down and awkwardly and hesitantly rises from the chair.*)

TOM: (*Hoarsely.*) Mother. I—I apologize, Mother.

(AMANDA *draws a quick, shuddering breath. Her face works grotesquely. She breaks into childlike tears.*)

I'm sorry for what I said, for everything that I said, I didn't mean it.

75 AMANDA: (*Sobbingly.*) My devotion has made me a witch and so I make myself hateful to my children!

TOM: *No, you* don't.

AMANDA: I worry so much, don't sleep, it makes me nervous!

TOM: (*Gently.*) I understand that.

80 AMANDA: I've had to put up a solitary battle all these years. But you're my right-hand bower! Don't fall down, don't fail!

TOM: (*Gently.*) I try, Mother.

AMANDA: (*With great enthusiasm.*) Try and you will *succeed!* (*The notion makes her breathless.*) Why, you—you're just *full*

85 of natural endowments! Both of my children—they're *unusual* children! Don't you think I know it? I'm so—*proud!* Happy and—feel I've—so much to be thankful for but—promise me one thing, son!

TOM: What, Mother?

90 AMANDA: Promise, son, you'll—never be a drunkard!

TOM: (*Turns to her grinning.*) I will never be a drunkard, Mother.

AMANDA: That's what frightened me so, that you'd be drinking! Eat a bowl of Purina!

TOM: Just coffee, Mother.

95 AMANDA: Shredded wheat biscuit?

TOM: No. No, Mother, just coffee.

AMANDA: You can't put in a day's work on an empty stomach. You've got ten minutes—don't gulp! Drinking too-hot liquids makes cancer of the stomach . . . Put cream in.

100 TOM: No, thank you.

AMANDA: To cool it.

TOM: No! No, thank you, I want it black.

AMANDA: I know, but it's not good for you. We have to do all that we can to build ourselves up. In these trying times

105 we live in, all that we have to cling to is—each other . . . That's why it's so important to—Tom, I—sent out your sister so I could discuss something with you. If you hadn't spoken I would have spoken to you. (*She sits down.*)

TOM: (*Gently.*) What is it, Mother, that you want to discuss?

110 AMANDA: *Laura!*

(TOM *puts his cup down slowly.*)

(*Legend on screen:* "Laura." *Music:* "The Glass Menagerie.")

TOM: —Oh.—Laura . . .

AMANDA: (*Touching his sleeve.*) You know how Laura is. So quiet but—still water runs deep! She notices things and I think she—broods about them.

(TOM *looks up.*)

115 A few days ago I came in and she was crying.

TOM: What about?

AMANDA: You.

TOM: Me?

AMANDA: She has an idea that you're not happy here.

120 TOM: What gave her that idea?

AMANDA: What gives her any idea? However, you do act strangely. I—I'm not criticizing, understand *that!* I know

your ambitions do not lie in the warehouse, that like everybody in the whole wide world—you've had to—make sacrifices, but—Tom—Tom—life's not easy, it calls 125 for—Spartan endurance! There's so many things in my heart that I cannot describe to you! I've never told you but I—*loved* your father. . . .

TOM: (*Gently.*) I know that, Mother.

AMANDA: And you—when I see you taking after his ways! 130 Staying out late—and—well, you *had* been drinking the night you were in that—terrifying condition! Laura says that you hate the apartment and that you go out nights to get away from it! Is that true, Tom?

TOM: No. You say there's so much in your heart that you 135 can't describe to me. That's true of me, too. There's so much in my heart that I can't describe to *you!* So let's respect each other's—

AMANDA: But, why—*why*, Tom—are you always so *restless?* Where do you *go* to, nights? 140

TOM: I—go to the movies.

AMANDA: Why do you go to the movies so much, Tom?

TOM: I go to the movies because—I like adventure. Adventure is something I don't have much of at work, so I go to the movies. 145

AMANDA: But, Tom, you go to the movies *entirely* too *much!*

TOM: I like a lot of adventure.

(AMANDA *looks baffled, then hurt. As the familiar inquisition resumes,* TOM *becomes hard and impatient again.* AMANDA *slips back into her querulous attitude toward him.*)

(*Image on screen:* A sailing vessel with Jolly Roger.)

AMANDA: Most young men find adventure in their careers.

TOM: Then most young men are not employed in a warehouse.

AMANDA: The world is full of young men employed in warehouses and offices and factories. 150

TOM: Do all of them find adventure in their careers?

AMANDA: They do or they do without it! Not everybody has a craze for adventure.

TOM: Man is by instinct a lover, a hunter, a fighter, and none 155 of those instincts are given much play at the warehouse!

AMANDA: Man is by instinct! Don't quote instinct to me! Instinct is something that people have got away from! It belongs to animals! Christian adults don't want it!

TOM: What do Christian adults want, then, Mother? 160

AMANDA: Superior things! Things of the mind and the spirit! Only animals have to satisfy instincts! Surely your aims are somewhat higher than theirs! Than monkeys—pigs—

TOM: I reckon they're not.

AMANDA: You're joking. However, that isn't what I wanted to 165 discuss.

TOM: (*Rising.*) I haven't much time.

AMANDA: (*Pushing his shoulders.*) Sit down.

TOM: You want me to punch in red at the warehouse, Mother?

AMANDA: You have five minutes. I want to talk about Laura. 170

(*Screen legend:* "Plans and Provisions.")

TOM: All right! What about Laura?

AMANDA: We have to be making some plans and provisions for her. She's older than you, two years, and nothing has

happened. She just drifts along doing nothing. It frightens
175 me terribly how she just drifts along.

TOM: I guess she's the type that people call home girls.

AMANDA: There's no such type, and if there is, it's a pity! That
is unless the home is hers, with a husband!

TOM: What?

180 AMANDA: Oh, I can see the handwriting on the wall as plain as I
see the nose in front of my face! It's terrifying! More and
more you remind me of your father! He was out all hours
without explanation!—Then *left! Goodbye!* And me with
the bag to hold. I saw that letter you got from the Merchant
185 Marine. I know what you're dreaming of. I'm not standing
here blindfolded. (*She pauses.*) Very well, then. Then do it!
But not till there's somebody to take your place.

TOM: What do you mean?

AMANDA: I mean that as soon as Laura has got somebody to
190 take care of her, married, a home of her own, independent—why, then you'll be free to go wherever you please,
on land, on sea, whichever way the wind blows you! But
until that time you've got to look out for your sister. I
don't say me because I'm old and don't matter! I say for
195 your sister because she's young and dependent.

I put her in business college—a dismal failure! Frightened her so it made her sick at the stomach. I took her over
to the Young People's League at the church. Another fiasco.
She spoke to nobody, nobody spoke to her. Now all she
200 does is fool with those pieces of glass and play those worn-
out records. What kind of a life is that for a girl to lead?

TOM: What can I do about it?

AMANDA: Overcome selfishness! Self, self, self is all that you
ever think of!

(TOM *springs up and crosses to get his coat. It is ugly and bulky. He
pulls on a cap with earmuffs.*)

205 Where is your muffler? Put your wool muffler on!

(*He snatches it angrily from the closet, tosses it around his neck and
pulls both ends tight.*)

Tom! I haven't said what I had in mind to ask you.

TOM: I'm too late to—

AMANDA: (*Catching his arm—very importunately; then shyly.*)
Down at the warehouse, aren't there some—nice young
210 men?

TOM: No!

AMANDA: There *must* be—*some.* . . .

TOM: Mother—(*He gestures.*)

AMANDA: Find out one that's clean-living—doesn't drink and
215 ask him out for sister!

TOM: What?

AMANDA: For *sister!* To *meet!* Get *acquainted!*

TOM: (*Stamping to the door.*) Oh, my *go-osh!*

AMANDA: Will you?

(*He opens the door. She says, imploringly:*)

220 Will you?

(*He starts down the fire escape.*)

Will you? *Will* you, dear?

TOM: (*Calling back.*) Yes!

(AMANDA *closes the door hesitantly and with a troubled but faintly
hopeful expression.*)

(*Screen image:* The cover of a glamor magazine.)

(*The spotlight picks up* AMANDA *at the phone.*)

AMANDA: Ella Cartwright? This is Amanda Wingfield!
How are you, honey?
How is that kidney condition? 225

(*There is a five-second pause.*)

Horrors!

(*There is another pause.*)

You're a Christian martyr, yes, honey, that's what you are, a
Christian martyr! Well, I just now happened to notice in my
little red book that your subscription to the *Companion* has
just run out! I knew that you wouldn't want to miss out on 230
the wonderful serial starting in this new issue. It's by Bessie
Mae Hopper, the first thing she's written since *Honeymoon
for Three.* Wasn't that a strange and interesting story? Well,
this one is even lovelier, I believe. It has a sophisticated, society background. It's all about the horsey set on Long Island! 235

(*The light fades out.*)

SCENE FIVE

Legend on the screen: "Annunciation."

Music is heard as the light slowly comes on.

*It is early dusk of a spring evening. Supper has just been finished in
the Wingfield apartment.* AMANDA *and* LAURA, *in light-colored
dresses, are removing dishes from the table in the dining room, which
is shadowy, their movements formalized almost as a dance or ritual,
their moving forms as pale and silent as moths.* TOM, *in white shirt
and trousers, rises from the table and crosses toward the fire escape.*

AMANDA: (*As he passes her.*) Son, will you do me a favor?

TOM: What?

AMANDA: Comb your hair! You look so pretty when your
hair is combed!

(TOM *slouches on the sofa with the evening paper. Its enormous
headline reads:* "Franco Triumphs.")

There is only one respect in which I would like you to 5
emulate your father.

TOM: What respect is that?

AMANDA: The care he always took of his appearance. He
never allowed himself to look untidy.

(*He throws down the paper and crosses to the fire escape.*)

Where are you going? 10

TOM: I'm going out to smoke.

AMANDA: You smoke too much. A pack a day at fifteen cents a
pack. How much would that amount to in a month? Thirty
times fifteen is how much, Tom? Figure it out and you will
be astounded at what you could save. Enough to give you a 15

night-school course in accounting at Washington U! Just think what a wonderful thing that would be for you, son!

(TOM *is unmoved by the thought.*)

TOM: I'd rather smoke. (*He steps out on the landing, letting the screen door slam.*)

20 AMANDA: (*Sharply.*) I know! That's the tragedy of it. . . . (*Alone, she turns to look at her husband's picture.*)

(*Dance music:* "The World Is Waiting for the Sunrise!")

TOM: (*To the audience.*) Across the alley from us was the Paradise Dance-hall. On evenings in spring the windows and doors were open and the music came outdoors. Sometimes the 25 lights were turned out except for a large glass sphere that hung from the ceiling. It would turn slowly about and filter the dusk with delicate rainbow colors. Then the orchestra played a waltz or a tango, something that had a slow and sensuous rhythm. Couples would come outside, to the rela- 30 tive privacy of the alley. You could see them kissing behind ash pits and telephone poles. This was the compensation for lives that passed like mine, without any change or adven- ture. Adventure and change were imminent in this year. They were waiting around the corner for all these kids. Sus- 35 pended in the mist over Berchtesgaden, caught in the folds of Chamberlain's umbrella. In Spain there was Guernica! But here there was only hot swing music and liquor, dance- halls, bars, and movies, and sex that hung in the gloom like a chandelier and flooded the world with brief, deceptive 40 rainbows. . . . All the world was waiting for bombardments!

(AMANDA *turns from the picture and comes outside.*)

AMANDA: (*Sighing.*) A fire escape landing's a poor excuse for a porch. (*She spreads a newspaper on a step and sits down, gracefully and demurely as if she were settling into a swing on a Mississippi veranda.*) What are you looking at?
45 TOM: The moon.
AMANDA: Is there a moon this evening?
TOM: It's rising over Garfinkel's Delicatessen.
AMANDA: So it is! A little silver slipper of a moon. Have you made a wish on it yet?
50 TOM: Um-hum.
AMANDA: What did you wish for?
TOM: That's a secret.
AMANDA: A secret, huh? Well, I won't tell mine either. I will be just as mysterious as you.
55 TOM: I bet I can guess what yours is.
AMANDA: Is my head so transparent?
TOM: You're not a sphinx.
AMANDA: No, I don't have secrets. I'll tell you what I wished for on the moon. Success and happiness for my precious 60 children! I wish for that whenever there's a moon, and when there isn't a moon, I wish for it, too.
TOM: I thought perhaps you wished for a gentleman caller.
AMANDA: Why do you say that?
TOM: Don't you remember asking me to fetch one?
65 AMANDA: I remember suggesting that it would be nice for your sister if you brought home some nice young man from the warehouse. I think that I've made that suggestion more than once.

TOM: Yes, you have made it repeatedly.
AMANDA: Well?   70
TOM: We are going to have one.
AMANDA: *What?*
TOM: A gentleman caller!

(*The annunciation is celebrated with music.*)

(AMANDA *rises.*)

(*Image on screen:* A caller with a bouquet.)

AMANDA: You mean you have asked some nice young man to come over?   75
TOM: Yep. I've asked him to dinner.
AMANDA: You really did?
TOM: I did!
AMANDA: You did, and did he—*accept?*
TOM: He did!   80
AMANDA: Well, well—well, well! That's—lovely!
TOM: I thought that you would be pleased.
AMANDA: It's definite then?
TOM: Very definite.
AMANDA: Soon?   85
TOM: Very soon.
AMANDA: For heaven's sake, stop putting on and tell me some things, will you?
TOM: What things do you want me to tell you?
AMANDA: *Naturally* I would like to know when he's coming! 90
TOM: He's coming tomorrow.
AMANDA: *Tomorrow?*
TOM: Yep. Tomorrow.
AMANDA: But, Tom!
TOM: Yes, Mother?   95
AMANDA: Tomorrow gives me no time!
TOM: Time for what?
AMANDA: Preparations! Why didn't you phone me at once, as soon as you asked him, the minute that he accepted? Then don't you see, I could have been getting ready! 100
TOM: You don't have to make any fuss.
AMANDA: Oh, Tom, Tom, Tom, of course I have to make a fuss! I want things nice, not sloppy! Not thrown together. I'll certainly have to do some fast thinking, won't I?
TOM: I don't see why you have to think at all.   105
AMANDA: You just don't know. We can't have a gentleman caller in a pigsty! All my wedding silver has to be polished, the monogrammed table linen ought to be laundered! The windows have to be washed and fresh curtains put up. And how about clothes? We have to *wear* something, don't we? 110
TOM: Mother, this boy is no one to make a fuss over!
AMANDA: Do you realize he's the first young man we've in- troduced to your sister? It's terrible, dreadful, disgraceful that poor little sister has never received a single gentleman caller! Tom, come inside! (*She opens the screen door.*) 115
TOM: What for?
AMANDA: I want to ask you some things.
TOM: If you're going to make such a fuss, I'll call it off, I'll tell him not to come!
AMANDA: You certainly won't do anything of the kind. Noth- 120 ing offends people worse than broken engagements. It simply means I'll have to work like a Turk! We won't be brilliant, but we will pass inspection. Come on inside.

(TOM *follows her inside, groaning.*)

Sit down.

125 TOM: Any particular place you would like me to sit?

AMANDA: Thank heavens I've got that new sofa! I'm also making payments on a floor lamp I'll have sent out! And put the chintz covers on, they'll brighten things up! Of course I'd hoped to have these walls re-papered. . . . What

130 is the young man's name?

TOM: His name is O'Connor.

AMANDA: That, of course, means fish—tomorrow is Friday! I'll have that salmon loaf—with Durkee's dressing! What does he do? He works at the warehouse?

135 TOM: Of course! How else would I—

AMANDA: Tom, he—doesn't drink?

TOM: Why do you ask me that?

AMANDA: Your father *did!*

TOM: Don't get started on that!

140 AMANDA: He *does* drink, then?

TOM: Not that I know of!

AMANDA: Make sure, be certain! The last thing I want for my daughter's a boy who drinks!

TOM: Aren't you being a little bit premature? Mr. O'Connor

145 has not yet appeared on the scene!

AMANDA: But will tomorrow. To meet your sister, and what do I know about his character? Nothing! Old maids are better off than wives of drunkards!

TOM: Oh, my God!

150 AMANDA: Be still!

TOM: (*Leaning forward to whisper.*) Lots of fellows meet girls whom they don't marry!

AMANDA: Oh, talk sensibly, Tom—and don't be sarcastic! (*She has gotten a hairbrush.*)

155 TOM: What are you doing?

AMANDA: I'm brushing that cowlick down! (*She attacks his hair with the brush.*) What is this young man's position at the warehouse?

TOM: (*Submitting grimly to the brush and the interrogation.*) This

160 young man's position is that of a shipping clerk, Mother.

AMANDA: Sounds to me like a fairly responsible job, the sort of a job *you* would be in if you just had more *get-up.* What is his salary? Have you any idea?

TOM: I would judge it to be approximately eighty-five dol-

165 lars a month.

AMANDA: Well—not princely, but—

TOM: Twenty more than I make.

AMANDA: Yes, how well I know! But for a family man, eighty-five dollars a month is not much more than you can just

170 get by on. . . .

TOM: Yes, but Mr. O'Connor is not a family man.

AMANDA: He might be, mightn't he? Some time in the future?

TOM: I see. Plans and provisions.

AMANDA: You are the only young man that I know of who

175 ignores the fact that the future becomes the present, the present the past, and the past turns into everlasting regret if you don't plan for it!

TOM: I will think that over and see what I can make of it.

AMANDA: Don't be supercilious with your mother! Tell me

180 some more about this—what do you call him?

TOM: James D. O'Connor. The D. is for Delaney.

AMANDA: Irish on *both* sides! *Gracious!* And doesn't drink?

TOM: Shall I call him up and ask him right this minute?

AMANDA: The only way to find out about those things is to 185 make discreet inquiries at the proper moment. When I was a girl in Blue Mountain and it was suspected that a young man drank, the girl whose attentions he had been receiving, if any girl *was,* would sometimes speak to the minister of his church, or rather her father would if her father was 190 living, and sort of feel him out on the young man's character. That is the way such things are discreetly handled to keep a young woman from making a tragic mistake!

TOM: Then how did you happen to make a tragic mistake?

AMANDA: That innocent look of your father's had everyone fooled! He *smiled*—the world was *enchanted!* No girl can do 195 worse than put herself at the mercy of a handsome appearance! I hope that Mr. O'Connor is not too good-looking.

TOM: No, he's not too good-looking. He's covered with freckles and hasn't too much of a nose.

AMANDA: He's not right-down homely, though? 200

TOM: Not right-down homely. Just medium homely, I'd say.

AMANDA: Character's what to look for in a man.

TOM: That's what I've always said, Mother.

AMANDA: You've never said anything of the kind and I suspect you would never give it a thought. 205

TOM: Don't be so suspicious of me.

AMANDA: At least I hope he's the type that's up and coming.

TOM: I think he really goes in for self-improvement.

AMANDA: What reason have you to think so?

TOM: He goes to night school. 210

AMANDA: (*Beaming.*) Splendid! What does he do, I mean study?

TOM: Radio engineering and public speaking!

AMANDA: Then he has visions of being advanced in the world! Any young man who studies public speaking is aiming to have an executive job some day! And radio en- 215 gineering? A thing for the future! Both of these facts are very illuminating. Those are the sort of things that a mother should know concerning any young man who comes to call on her daughter. Seriously or—not.

TOM: One little warning. He doesn't know about Laura. I 220 didn't let on that we had dark ulterior motives. I just said, why don't you come and have dinner with us? He said okay and that was the whole conversation.

AMANDA: I bet it was! You're eloquent as an oyster. However, he'll know about Laura when he gets here. When he sees 225 how lovely and sweet and pretty she is, he'll thank his lucky stars he was asked to dinner.

TOM: Mother, you mustn't expect too much of Laura.

AMANDA: What do you mean?

TOM: Laura seems all those things to you and me because 230 she's ours and we love her. We don't even notice she's crippled any more.

AMANDA: Don't say crippled! You know that I never allow that word to be used!

TOM: But face facts, Mother. She is and—that's not all— 235

AMANDA: What do you mean "not all"?

TOM: Laura is very different from other girls.

AMANDA: I think the difference is all to her advantage.

TOM: Not quite all—in the eyes of others—strangers—she's terribly shy and lives in a world of her own and those things 240 make her seem a little peculiar to people outside the house.

AMANDA: Don't say peculiar.

TOM: Face the facts. She is.

(The dance-hall music changes to a tango that has a minor and somewhat ominous tone.)

AMANDA: In what way is she peculiar—may I ask?

245 TOM: *(Gently.)* She lives in a world of her own—a world of little glass ornaments, Mother. . . .

(He gets up. AMANDA *remains holding the brush, looking at him, troubled.)*

She plays old phonograph records and—that's about all— *(He glances at himself in the mirror and crosses to the door.)*

AMANDA: *(Sharply.)* Where are you going?

250 TOM: I'm going to the movies. *(He goes out the screen door.)*

AMANDA: Not to the movies, every night to the movies! *(She follows quickly to the screen door.)* I don't believe you always go to the movies!

(He is gone. AMANDA *looks worriedly after him for a moment. Then vitality and optimism return and she turns from the door, crossing to the portieres.)*

Laura! Laura!

*(*LAURA *answers from the kitchenette.)*

255 LAURA: Yes, Mother.

AMANDA: Let those dishes go and come in front!

*(*LAURA *appears with a dish towel.* AMANDA *speaks to her gaily.)*

Laura, come here and make a wish on the moon!

(Screen image: The Moon.)

LAURA: *(Entering.)* Moon—moon?

AMANDA: A little silver slipper of a moon. Look over your left
260   shoulder, Laura, and make a wish!

*(*LAURA *looks faintly puzzled as if called out of sleep.* AMANDA *seizes her shoulders and turns her at an angle by the door.)*

Now! Now, darling, *wish!*

LAURA: What shall I wish for, Mother?

AMANDA: *(Her voice trembling and her eyes suddenly filling with tears.)* Happiness! Good fortune!

(The sound of the violin rises and the stage dims out.)

SCENE SIX

The light comes up on the fire escape landing. TOM *is leaning against the grill, smoking.*

Screen image: The high school hero.

TOM: And so the following evening I brought Jim home to dinner. I had known Jim slightly in high school. In high school Jim was a hero. He had tremendous Irish good nature and vitality with the scrubbed and polished look of
5   white chinaware. He seemed to move in a continual spotlight. He was a star in basketball, captain of the debating club, president of the senior class and the glee club and he sang the male lead in the annual light operas. He was always running or bounding, never just walking. He seemed always at the point of defeating the law of gravity. He was 10
shooting with such velocity through his adolescence that you would logically expect him to arrive at nothing short of the White House by the time he was thirty. But Jim apparently ran into more interference after his graduation from Soldan. His speed had definitely slowed. Six years af- 15
ter he left high school he was holding a job that wasn't much better than mine.

(Screen image: The Clerk.)

He was the only one at the warehouse with whom I was on friendly terms. I was valuable to him as someone who could remember his former glory, who had seen him win 20
basketball games and the silver cup in debating. He knew of my secret practice of retiring to a cabinet of the washroom to work on poems when business was slack in the warehouse. He called me Shakespeare. And while the other boys in the warehouse regarded me with suspicious hostil- 25
ity, Jim took a humorous attitude toward me. Gradually his attitude affected the others, their hostility wore off and they also began to smile at me as people smile at an oddly fashioned dog who trots across their path at some distance.
    I knew that Jim and Laura had known each other at Sol- 30
dan, and I had heard Laura speak admiringly of his voice. I didn't know if Jim remembered her or not. In high school Laura had been as unobtrusive as Jim had been astonishing. If he did remember Laura, it was not as my sister, for when I asked him to dinner, he grinned and said, "You know, 35
Shakespeare, I never thought of you as having folks!"
    He was about to discover that I did. . . .

(Legend on screen: "The accent of a coming foot.")

(The light dims out on TOM *and comes up in the Wingfield living room—a delicate lemony light. It is about five on a Friday evening of late spring which comes "scattering poems in the sky.")*

*(*AMANDA *has worked like a Turk in preparation for the gentleman caller. The results are astonishing. The new floor lamp with its rose silk shade is in place, a colored paper lantern conceals the broken light fixture in the ceiling, new billowing white curtains are at the windows, chintz covers are on the chairs and sofa, a pair of new sofa pillows make their initial appearance. Open boxes and tissue paper are scattered on the floor.)*

*(*LAURA *stands in the middle of the room with lifted arms while* AMANDA *crouches before her, adjusting the hem of a new dress, devout and ritualistic. The dress is colored and designed by memory. The arrangement of* LAURA's *hair is changed; it is softer and more becoming. A fragile, unearthly prettiness has come out in* LAURA: *she is like a piece of translucent glass touched by light, given a momentary radiance, not actual, not lasting.)*

AMANDA: *(Impatiently.)* Why are you trembling?

LAURA: Mother, you've made me so nervous!

AMANDA: How have I made you nervous?

LAURA: By all this fuss! You make it seem so important! 40

AMANDA: I don't understand you, Laura. You couldn't be satisfied with just sitting home, and yet whenever I try to arrange something for you, you seem to resist it. *(She gets*

45   up.) Now take a look at yourself. No, wait! Wait just a mo-
     ment—I have an idea!
LAURA: What is it now?

(AMANDA *produces two powder puffs which she wraps in handkerchiefs and stuffs in* LAURA'S *bosom.*)

LAURA: Mother, what are you doing?
AMANDA: They call them "Gay Deceivers"!
50 LAURA: I won't wear them!
AMANDA: You will!
LAURA: Why should I?
AMANDA: Because, to be painfully honest, your chest is flat.
LAURA: You make it seem like we were setting a trap.
55 AMANDA: All pretty girls are a trap, a pretty trap, and men ex-
     pect them to be.

(*Legend on screen:* "A pretty trap.")

     Now look at yourself, young lady. This is the prettiest you
     will ever be! (*She stands back to admire* LAURA.) I've got to
     fix myself now! You're going to be surprised by your
60   mother's appearance!

(AMANDA *crosses through the portieres, humming gaily.* LAURA
*moves slowly to the long mirror and stares solemnly at herself. A
wind blows the white curtains inward in a slow, graceful motion and
with a faint, sorrowful sighing.*)

AMANDA: (*From somewhere behind the portieres.*) It isn't dark
     enough yet.

(LAURA *turns slowly before the mirror with a troubled look.*)

(*Legend on screen:* "This is my sister: Celebrate her with
strings!" *Music plays.*)

AMANDA: (*Laughing, still not visible.*) I'm going to show you
     something. I'm going to make a spectacular appearance!
65 LAURA: What is it, Mother?
AMANDA: Possess your soul in patience—you will see! Some-
     thing I've resurrected from that old trunk! Styles haven't
     changed so terribly much after all.... (*She parts the portieres.*)
     Now just look at your mother! (*She wears a girlish frock of
70   yellowed voile with a blue silk sash. She carries a bunch of jon-
     quils—the legend of her youth is nearly revived. Now she speaks
     feverishly.*) This is the dress in which I led the cotillion. Won
     the cakewalk twice at Sunset Hill, wore one Spring to the
     Governor's Ball in Jackson! See how I sashayed around the
75   ballroom, Laura? (*She raises her skirt and does a mincing step
     around the room.*) I wore it on Sundays for my gentlemen
     callers! I had it on the day I met your father.... I had
     malaria fever all that Spring. The change of climate from
     East Tennessee to the Delta—weakened resistance. I had a
80   little temperature all the time—not enough to be seri-
     ous—just enough to make me restless and giddy! Invita-
     tions poured in—parties all over the Delta! "Stay in bed,"
     said Mother, "you have a fever!"—but I just wouldn't. I
     took quinine but kept on going, going! Evenings, dances!
85   Afternoons, long, long rides! Picnics—lovely! So lovely,
     that country in May—all lacy with dogwood, literally
     flooded with jonquils! That was the spring I had the craze
     for jonquils. Jonquils became an absolute obsession.

Mother said, "Honey, there's no more room for jonquils."
And still I kept on bringing in more jonquils. Whenever,   90
wherever I saw them, I'd say "Stop! Stop! I see jonquils!" I
made the young men help me gather the jonquils! It was a
joke, Amanda and her jonquils. Finally there were no more
vases to hold them, every available space was filled with
jonquils. No vases to hold them? All right, I'll hold them   95
myself! And then I—(*She stops in front of the picture. Music
plays.*) met your father! Malaria fever and jonquils and
then—this—boy.... (*She switches on the rose-colored lamp.*) I
hope they get here before it starts to rain. (*She crosses the
room and places the jonquils in a bowl on the table.*) I gave your   100
brother a little extra change so he and Mr. O'Connor could
take the service car home.
LAURA: (*With an altered look.*) What did you say his name was?
AMANDA: O'Connor.
LAURA: What is his first name?   105
AMANDA: I don't remember. Oh, yes, I do. It was—Jim!

(LAURA *sways slightly and catches hold of a chair.*)

(*Legend on screen:* "Not Jim!")

LAURA: (*Faintly.*) Not—Jim!
AMANDA: Yes, that was it, it was Jim! I've never known a Jim
     that wasn't nice!

(*The music becomes ominous.*)

LAURA: Are you sure his name is Jim O'Connor?   110
AMANDA: Yes. Why?
LAURA: Is he the one that Tom used to know in high school?
AMANDA: He didn't say so. I think he just got to know him
     at the warehouse.
LAURA: There was a Jim O'Connor we both knew in high   115
     school—(*Then, with effort.*) If that is the one that Tom is
     bringing to dinner—you'll have to excuse me, I won't
     come to the table.
AMANDA: What sort of nonsense is this?
LAURA: You asked me once if I'd ever liked a boy. Don't you   120
     remember I showed you this boy's picture?
AMANDA: You mean the boy you showed me in the yearbook?
LAURA: Yes, that boy.
AMANDA: Laura, Laura, were you in love with that boy?
LAURA: I don't know, Mother. All I know is I couldn't sit at   125
     the table if it was him!
AMANDA: It won't be him! It isn't the least bit likely. But
     whether it is or not, you will come to the table. You will
     not be excused.
LAURA: I'll have to be, Mother.   130
AMANDA: I don't intend to humor your silliness, Laura. I've had
     too much from you and your brother, both! So just sit down
     and compose yourself till they come. Tom has forgotten his
     key so you'll have to let them in, when they arrive.
LAURA: (*Panicky.*) Oh, Mother—*you* answer the door!   135
AMANDA: (*Lightly.*) I'll be in the kitchen—busy!
LAURA: Oh, Mother, please answer the door, don't make me
     do it!
AMANDA: (*Crossing into the kitchenette.*) I've got to fix the dress-
     ing for the salmon. Fuss, fuss—silliness!—over a gentle-   140
     man caller!

(*The door swings shut.* LAURA *is left alone.*)

(*Legend on screen:* "Terror!")

(*She utters a low moan and turns off the lamp—sits stiffly on the edge of the sofa, knotting her fingers together.*)

(*Legend on screen:* "The Opening of a Door!")

(TOM *and* JIM *appear on the fire escape steps and climb to the landing. Hearing their approach,* laura *rises with a panicky gesture. She retreats to the portieres. The doorbell rings.* LAURA *catches her breath and touches her throat. Low drums sound.*)

AMANDA: (*Calling.*) Laura, sweetheart! The door!

(LAURA *stares at it without moving.*)

JIM: I think we just beat the rain.
TOM: Uh-huh. (*He rings again, nervously.* JIM *whistles and fishes*
145   *for a cigarette.*)
AMANDA: (*Very, very gaily.*) Laura, that is your brother and Mr. O'Connor! Will you let them in, darling?

(LAURA *crosses toward the kitchenette door.*)

LAURA: (*Breathlessly.*) Mother—you go to the door!

(AMANDA *steps out of the kitchenette and stares furiously at* LAURA. *She points imperiously at the door.*)

LAURA: Please, please!
150   AMANDA: (*In a fierce whisper.*) What is the matter with you, you silly thing?
LAURA: (*Desperately.*) Please, you answer it, *please!*
AMANDA: I told you I wasn't going to humor you, Laura. Why have you chosen this moment to lose your mind?
155   LAURA: Please, please, please, you go!
AMANDA: You'll have to go to the door because I can't!
LAURA: (*Despairingly.*) I can't either!
AMANDA: *Why?*
LAURA: I'm *sick!*
160   AMANDA: I'm sick, too—of your nonsense! Why can't you and your brother be normal people? Fantastic whims and behavior!

(TOM *gives a long ring.*)

Preposterous goings on! Can you give me one reason—(*She calls out lyrically.*) Coming! Just one second!—why you
165   should be afraid to open a door? Now you answer it, Laura!
LAURA: Oh, oh, oh . . . (*She returns through the portieres, darts to the Victrola, winds it frantically and turns it on.*)
AMANDA: Laura Wingfield, you march right to that door!
LAURA: Yes—yes, Mother!

(*A faraway, scratchy rendition of "Dardanella" softens the air and gives her strength to move through it. She slips to the door and draws it cautiously open.* TOM *enters with the caller,* JIM O'CONNOR.)

170   TOM: Laura, this is Jim. Jim, this is my sister, Laura.
JIM: (*Stepping inside.*) I didn't know that Shakespeare had a sister!

LAURA: (*Retreating, stiff and trembling, from the door.*) How—how do you do?
JIM: (*Heartily, extending his hand.*) Okay!

(LAURA *touches it hesitantly with hers.*)

JIM: Your hand's *cold,* Laura!   175
LAURA: Yes, well—I've been playing the Victrola. . . .
JIM: Must have been playing classical music on it! You ought to play a little hot swing music to warm you up!
LAURA: Excuse me—I haven't finished playing the Victrola . . . (*She turns awkwardly and hurries into the front room. She*   180
pauses a second by the Victrola. Then she catches her breath and darts through the portieres like a frightened deer.)
JIM: (*Grinning.*) What was the matter?
TOM: Oh—with Laura? Laura is—terribly shy.
JIM: Shy, huh? It's unusual to meet a shy girl nowadays. I don't   185
believe you ever mentioned you had a sister.
TOM: Well, now you know. I have one. Here is the *Post Dispatch.* You want a piece of it?
JIM: Uh-huh.
TOM: What piece? The comics?   190
JIM: Sports! (*He glances at it.*) Ole Dizzy Dean is on his bad behavior.
TOM: (*Uninterested.*) Yeah? (*He lights a cigarette and goes over to the fire-escape door.*)
JIM: Where are *you* going?   195
TOM: I'm going out on the terrace.
JIM: (*Going after him.*) You know, Shakespeare—I'm going to sell you a bill of goods!
TOM: What goods?
JIM: A course I'm taking.   200
TOM: Huh?
JIM: In public speaking! You and me, we're not the warehouse type.
TOM: Thanks—that's good news. But what has public speaking got to do with it?   205
JIM: It fits you for—executive positions!
TOM: Awww.
JIM: I tell you it's done a helluva lot for me.

(*Image on screen:* Executive at his desk.)

TOM: In what respect?
JIM: In every! Ask yourself what is the difference between   210
you an' me and men in the office down front? Brains?—No!—Ability?—No! Then what? Just one little thing—
TOM: What is that one little thing?
JIM: Primarily it amounts to—social poise! Being able to square up to people and hold your own on any social level!   215
AMANDA: (*From the kitchenette.*) Tom?
TOM: Yes, Mother?
AMANDA: Is that you and Mr. O'Connor?
TOM: Yes, Mother.
AMANDA: Well, you just make yourselves comfortable in there.   220
TOM: Yes, Mother.
AMANDA: Ask Mr. O'Connor if he would like to wash his hands.
JIM: Aw, no—no—thank you—I took care of that at the warehouse. Tom—   225
TOM: Yes?
JIM: Mr. Mendoza was speaking to me about you.

TOM: Favorably?

JIM: What do you think?

230 TOM: Well—

JIM: You're going to be out of a job if you don't wake up.

TOM: I am waking up—

JIM: You show no signs.

TOM: The signs are interior.

(*Image on screen:* The sailing vessel with the Jolly Roger again.)

235 TOM: I'm planning to change. (*He leans over the fire-escape rail, speaking with quiet exhilaration. The incandescent marquees and signs of the first-run movie houses light his face from across the alley. He looks like a voyager.*) I'm right at the point of committing myself to a future that doesn't include the ware-
240   house and Mr. Mendoza or even a night-school course in public speaking.

JIM: What are you gassing about?

TOM: I'm tired of the movies.

JIM: Movies!

245 TOM: Yes, movies! Look at them—(*A wave toward the marvels of Grand Avenue.*) All of those glamorous people—having adventures—hogging it all, gobbling the whole thing up! You know what happens? People go to the *movies* instead of *moving!* Hollywood characters are supposed to have all
250   the adventures for everybody in America, while everybody in America sits in a dark room and watches them have them! Yes, until there's a war. That's when adventure becomes available to the masses! *Everyone's* dish, not only Gable's! Then the people in the dark room come out of
255   the dark room to have some adventures themselves—goody, goody! It's our turn now, to go to the South Sea Island—to make a safari—to be exotic, far-off! But I'm not patient. I don't want to wait till then. I'm tired of the *movies* and I am *about* to *move!*

260 JIM: (*Incredulously.*) Move?

TOM: Yes.

JIM: When?

TOM: Soon!

JIM: Where? Where?

(*The music seems to answer the question, while* TOM *thinks it over. He searches in his pockets.*)

265 TOM: I'm starting to boil inside. I know I seem dreamy, but inside—well, I'm boiling! Whenever I pick up a shoe, I shudder a little thinking how short life is and what I am doing! Whatever that means, I know it doesn't mean shoes—except as something to wear on a traveler's feet!
270   (*He finds what he has been searching for in his pockets and holds out a paper to Jim.*) Look—

JIM: What?

TOM: I'm a member.

JIM: (*Reading.*) The Union of Merchant Seamen.

275 TOM: I paid my dues this month, instead of the light bill.

JIM: You will regret it when they turn the lights off.

TOM: I won't be here.

JIM: How about your mother?

TOM: I'm like my father. The bastard son of a bastard! Did
280   you notice how he's grinning in his picture in there? And he's been absent going on sixteen years!

JIM: You're just talking, you drip. How does your mother feel about it?

TOM: Shhh! Here comes Mother! Mother is not acquainted with my plans!   285

AMANDA: (*Coming through the portieres.*) Where are you all?

TOM: On the terrace, Mother.

(*They start inside. She advances to them.* TOM *is distinctly shocked at her appearance. Even* JIM *blinks a little. He is making his first contact with girlish Southern vivacity and in spite of the night-school course in public speaking is somewhat thrown off the beam by the unexpected outlay of social charm. Certain responses are attempted by* JIM *but are swept aside by* AMANDA's *gay laughter and chatter.* TOM *is embarrassed but after the first shock* JIM *reacts very warmly. He grins and chuckles, is altogether won over.*)

(*Image on screen:* AMANDA *as a girl.*)

AMANDA: (*Coyly smiling, shaking her girlish ringlets.*) Well, well, well, so this is Mr. O'Connor. Introductions entirely unnecessary. I've heard so much about you from my boy. I fi- 290
nally said to him, Tom—good gracious!—why don't you bring this paragon to supper? I'd like to meet this nice young man at the warehouse!—instead of just hearing him sing your praises so much! I don't know why my son is so stand-offish—that's not Southern behavior! 295

Let's sit down and—I think we could stand a little more air in here! Tom, leave the door open. I felt a nice fresh breeze a moment ago. Where has it gone to? Mmm, so warm already! And not quite summer, even. We're going to burn up when summer really gets started. However, 300
we're having—we're having a very light supper. I think light things are better fo' this time of year. The same as light clothes are. Light clothes an' light food are what warm weather calls fo'. You know our blood gets so thick during th' winter—it takes a while fo' us to *adjust* 305
ou'selves!—when the season changes . . . It's come so quick this year. I wasn't prepared. All of a sudden—heavens! Already summer! I ran to the trunk an' pulled out this light dress—terribly old! Historical almost! But feels so good—so good an' co-ol, y' know. . . . 310

TOM: Mother—

AMANDA: Yes, honey?

TOM: How about—supper?

AMANDA: Honey, you go ask Sister if supper is ready! You know that Sister is in full charge of supper! Tell her you hungry 315
boys are waiting for it. (*To* JIM.) Have you met Laura?

JIM: She—

AMANDA: Let you in? Oh, good, you've met already! It's rare for a girl as sweet an' pretty as Laura to be domestic! But Laura is, thank heavens, not only pretty but also very domestic. I'm 320
not at all. I never was a bit. I never could make a thing but angel-food cake. Well, in the South we had so many servants. Gone, gone, gone. All vestige of gracious living! Gone completely! I wasn't prepared for what the future brought me. All of my gentlemen callers were sons of 325
planters and so of course I assumed that I would be married to one and raise my family on a large piece of land with plenty of servants. But man proposes—and woman accepts the proposal! To vary that old, old saying a little bit—I married no planter! I married a man who worked for the 330

telephone company! That gallantly smiling gentleman over there! (*She points to the picture.*) A telephone man who—fell in love with long-distance! Now he travels and I don't even know where! But what am I going on for about my—tribu-
335 lations? Tell me yours—I hope you don't have any! Tom?

TOM: (*Returning.*) Yes, Mother?

AMANDA: Is supper nearly ready?

TOM: It looks to me like supper is on the table.

AMANDA: Let me look—(*She rises prettily and looks through the*
340 *portieres.*) Oh, lovely! But where is Sister?

TOM: Laura is not feeling well and she says that she thinks she'd better not come to the table.

AMANDA: What? Nonsense! Laura? Oh, Laura!

LAURA: (*From the kitchenette, faintly.*) Yes, Mother.

345 AMANDA: You really must come to the table. We won't be seated until you come to the table! Come in, Mr. O'Connor. You sit over there, and I'll . . . . Laura? Laura Wingfield! You're keeping us waiting, honey! We can't say grace until you come to the table!

(*The kitchenette door is pushed weakly open and* LAURA *comes in. She is obviously quite faint, her lips trembling, her eyes wide and staring. She moves unsteadily toward the table.*)

(*Screen legend:* "Terror!")

(*Outside a summer storm is coming on abruptly. The white curtains billow inward at the windows and there is a sorrowful murmur from the deep blue dusk.*)

(LAURA *suddenly stumbles; she catches at a chair with a faint moan.*)

350 TOM: Laura!

AMANDA: Laura!

(*There is a clap of thunder.*)

(*Screen legend:* "Ah!")

(*Despairingly.*) Why, Laura, you *are* ill, darling! Tom, help your sister into the living room, dear! Sit in the living room, Laura—rest on the sofa. Well! (*To* JIM *as* TOM *helps*
355 *his sister to the sofa in the living room.*) Standing over the hot stove made her ill! I told her that it was just too warm this evening, but—

(TOM *comes back to the table.*)

Is Laura all right now?

TOM: Yes.

360 AMANDA: What *is* that? Rain? A nice cool rain has come up! (*She gives* JIM *a frightened look.*) I think we may—have grace—now . . . (TOM *looks at her stupidly.*) Tom, honey— you say grace!

TOM: Oh . . . "For these and all thy mercies—"

(*They bow their heads,* AMANDA *stealing a nervous glance at* JIM. *In the living room* LAURA, *stretched on the sofa, clenches her hand to her lips, to hold back a shuddering sob.*)

365 God's Holy Name be praised—

(*The scene dims out.*)

SCENE SEVEN

It is half an hour later. Dinner is just being finished in the dining room, LAURA *is still huddled upon the sofa, her feet drawn under her, her head resting on a pale blue pillow, her eyes wide and mysteriously watchful. The new floor lamp with its shade of rose-colored silk gives a soft, becoming light to her face, bringing out the fragile, unearthly prettiness which usually escapes attention. From outside there is a steady murmur of rain, but it is slackening and soon stops; the air outside becomes pale and luminous as the moon breaks through the clouds. A moment after the curtain rises, the lights in both rooms flicker and go out.*

JIM: Hey, there, Mr. Light Bulb!

(AMANDA *laughs nervously.*)

(*Legend on screen:* "Suspension of a public service.")

AMANDA: Where was Moses when the lights went out? Ha-ha. Do you know the answer to that one, Mr. O'Connor?

JIM: No, Ma'am, what's the answer?

AMANDA: In the dark!   5

(JIM *laughs appreciatively.*)

Everybody sit still. I'll light the candles. Isn't it lucky we have them on the table? Where's a match? Which of you gentlemen can provide a match?

JIM: Here.

AMANDA: Thank you, Sir.   10

JIM: Not at all, Ma'am!

AMANDA: (*As she lights the candles.*) I guess the fuse has burnt out. Mr. O'Connor, can you tell a burnt-out fuse? I know I can't and Tom is a total loss when it comes to mechanics.

(*They rise from the table and go into the kitchenette, from where their voices are heard.*)

Oh, be careful you don't bump into something. We don't   15
want our gentleman caller to break his neck. Now wouldn't that be a fine howdy-do?

JIM: Ha-ha! Where is the fuse-box?

AMANDA: Right here next to the stove. Can you see anything?

JIM: Just a minute.   20

AMANDA: Isn't electricity a mysterious thing? Wasn't it Benjamin Franklin who tied a key to a kite? We live in such a mysterious universe, don't we? Some people say that science clears up all the mysteries for us. In my opinion it only creates more! Have you found it yet?   25

JIM: No, Ma'am. All these fuses look okay to me.

AMANDA: Tom!

TOM: Yes, Mother?

AMANDA: That light bill I gave you several days ago. The one I told you we got the notices about?   30

(*Legend on screen:* "Ha!")

TOM: Oh—yeah.

AMANDA: You didn't neglect to pay it by any chance?

TOM: Why, I—

AMANDA: Didn't! I might have known it!

JIM: Shakespeare probably wrote a poem on that light bill,   35
Mrs. Wingfield.

AMANDA: I might have known better than to trust him with it! There's such a high price for negligence in this world!

JIM: Maybe the poem will win a ten-dollar prize.

40 AMANDA: We'll just have to spend the remainder of the evening in the nineteenth century, before Mr. Edison made the Mazda lamp!

JIM: Candlelight is my favorite kind of light.

AMANDA: That shows you're romantic! But that's no excuse
45 for Tom. Well, we got through dinner. Very considerate of them to let us get through dinner before they plunged us into everlasting darkness, wasn't it, Mr. O'Connor?

JIM: Ha-ha!

AMANDA: Tom, as a penalty for your carelessness you can help
50 me with the dishes.

JIM: Let me give you a hand.

AMANDA: Indeed you will not!

JIM: I ought to be good for something.

AMANDA: Good for something? (*Her tone is rhapsodic.*) You?
55 Why, Mr. O'Connor, nobody, *nobody's* given me this much entertainment in years—as you have!

JIM: Aw, now, Mrs. Wingfield!

AMANDA: I'm not exaggerating, not one bit! But Sister is all by her lonesome. You go keep her company in the par-
60 lor! I'll give you this lovely old candelabrum that used to be on the altar at the Church of the Heavenly Rest. It was melted a little out of shape when the church burnt down. Lightning struck it one spring. Gypsy Jones was holding a revival at the time and he intimated that the church was
65 destroyed because the Episcopalians gave card parties.

JIM: Ha-ha.

AMANDA: And how about you coaxing Sister to drink a little wine? I think it would be good for her! Can you carry both at once?

70 JIM: Sure. I'm Superman!

AMANDA: Now, Thomas, get into this apron!

(JIM *comes into the dining room, carrying the candelabrum, its candles lighted, in one hand and a glass of wine in the other. The door of the kitchenette swings closed on* AMANDA's *gay laughter; the flickering light approaches the portieres.* LAURA *sits up nervously as* JIM *enters. She can hardly speak from the almost intolerable strain of being alone with a stranger.*)

(*Screen legend:* "I don't suppose you remember me at all!")

(*At first, before* JIM's *warmth overcomes her paralyzing shyness,* LAURA's *voice is thin and breathless, as though she had just run up a steep flight of stairs.* JIM's *attitude is gently humorous. While the incident is apparently unimportant, it is to* LAURA *the climax of her secret life.*)

JIM: Hello there, Laura.

LAURA: (*Faintly.*) Hello.

(*She clears her throat.*)

JIM: How are you feeling now? Better?

75 LAURA: Yes. Yes, thank you.

JIM: This is for you. A little dandelion wine. (*He extends the glass toward her with extravagant gallantry.*)

LAURA: Thank you.

JIM: Drink it—but don't get drunk!

(*He laughs heartily.* LAURA *takes the glass uncertainly; she laughs shyly.*)

Where shall I set the candles?   80

LAURA: Oh—oh, anywhere. . . .

JIM: How about here on the floor? Any objections?

LAURA: No.

JIM: I'll spread a newspaper under to catch the drippings. I like to sit on the floor. Mind if I do?   85

LAURA: Oh, no.

JIM: Give me a pillow?

LAURA: What?

JIM: A pillow!

LAURA: Oh . . . (*She hands him one quickly.*)   90

JIM: How about you? Don't you like to sit on the floor?

LAURA: Oh—yes.

JIM: Why don't you, then?

LAURA: I—will.

JIM: Take a pillow!   95

(LAURA *does. She sits on the floor on the other side of the candelabrum.* JIM *crosses his legs and smiles engagingly at her.*) I can't hardly see you sitting way over there.

LAURA: I can—see you.

JIM: I know, but that's not fair, I'm in the limelight.   100

(LAURA *moves her pillow closer.*)

Good! Now I can see you! Comfortable?

LAURA: Yes.

JIM: So am I. Comfortable as a cow! Will you have some gum?

LAURA: No, thank you.

JIM: I think that I will indulge, with your permission. (*He   105
musingly unwraps a stick of gum and holds it up.*) Think of the fortune made by the guy that invented the first piece of chewing gum. Amazing, huh? The Wrigley Building is one of the sights of Chicago—I saw it when I went up to the Century of Progress. Did you take in the Century of   110
Progress?

LAURA: No, I didn't.

JIM: Well, it was quite a wonderful exposition. What impressed me most was the Hall of Science. Gives you an idea of what the future will be in America, even more wonderful   115
than the present time is! (*There is a pause.* JIM *smiles at her.*) Your brother tells me you're shy. Is that right, Laura?

LAURA: I—don't know.

JIM: I judge you to be an old-fashioned type of girl. Well, I think that's a pretty good type to be. Hope you don't   120
think I'm being too personal—do you?

LAURA: (*Hastily, out of embarrassment.*) I believe I *will* take a piece of gum, if you—don't mind. (*Clearing her throat.*) Mr. O'Connor, have you—kept up with your singing?

JIM: Singing? Me?   125

LAURA: Yes. I remember what a beautiful voice you had.

JIM: When did you hear me sing?

(LAURA *does not answer, and in the long pause which follows a man's voice is heard singing offstage.*)

VOICE: O blow, ye winds, heigh-ho,
                        A-roving I will go!
                           I'm off to my love   130
                              With a boxing glove—
                        Ten thousand miles away!

JIM: You say you've heard me sing?

LAURA: Oh, yes! Yes, very often . . . I—don't suppose—you
135 remember me—at all?

JIM: (*Smiling doubtfully.*) You know I have an idea I've seen
you before. I had that idea soon as you opened the door.
It seemed almost like I was about to remember your
name. But the name that I started to call you—wasn't a
140 name! And so I stopped myself before I said it.

LAURA: Wasn't it—Blue Roses?

JIM: (*Springing up, grinning.*) Blue Roses! My gosh, yes—Blue
Roses! That's what I had on my tongue when you opened
the door! Isn't it funny what tricks your memory plays? I
145 didn't connect you with high school somehow or other.
But that's where it was; it was high school. I didn't even
know you were Shakespeare's sister! Gosh, I'm sorry.

LAURA: I didn't expect you to. You—barely knew me!

JIM: But we did have a speaking acquaintance, huh?

150 LAURA: Yes, we—spoke to each other.

JIM: When did you recognize me?

LAURA: Oh, right away!

JIM: Soon as I came in the door?

LAURA: When I heard your name I thought it was probably you.
155 I knew that Tom used to know you a little in high school. So
when you came in the door—well, then I was—sure.

JIM: Why didn't you *say* something, then?

LAURA: (*Breathlessly.*) I didn't know what to say, I was—too
surprised!

160 JIM: For goodness' sakes! You know, this sure is funny!

LAURA: Yes! Yes, isn't it, though. . . .

JIM: Didn't we have a class in something together?

LAURA: Yes, we did.

JIM: What class was that?

165 LAURA: It was—singing—chorus!

JIM: Aw!

LAURA: I sat across the aisle from you in the Aud.

JIM: Aw.

LAURA: Mondays, Wednesdays, and Fridays.

170 JIM: Now I remember—you always came in late.

LAURA: Yes, it was so hard for me, getting upstairs. I had that
brace on my leg—it clumped so loud!

JIM: I never heard any clumping.

LAURA: (*Wincing at the recollection.*) To me it sounded like—
175 thunder!

JIM: Well, well, well, I never even noticed.

LAURA: And everybody was seated before I came in. I had to
walk in front of all those people. My seat was in the back
row. I had to go clumping all the way up the aisle with
180 everyone watching!

JIM: You shouldn't have been self-conscious.

LAURA: I know, but I was. It was always such a relief when
the singing started.

JIM: Aw, yes, I've placed you now! I used to call you Blue
185 Roses. How was it that I got started calling you that?

LAURA: I was out of school a little while with pleurosis.
When I came back you asked me what was the matter. I
said I had pleurosis—you thought I said *Blue Roses.* That's
what you always called me after that!

190 JIM: I hope you didn't mind.

LAURA: Oh, no—I liked it. You see, I wasn't acquainted with
many—people. . . .

JIM: As I remember you sort of stuck by yourself.

LAURA: I—I—never have had much luck at—making friends.

JIM: I don't see why you wouldn't. 195

LAURA: Well, I—started out badly.

JIM: You mean being—

LAURA: Yes, it sort of—stood between me—

JIM: You shouldn't have let it!

LAURA: I know, but it did, and— 200

JIM: You were shy with people!

LAURA: I tried not to be but never could—

JIM: Overcome it?

LAURA: No, I—I never could!

JIM: I guess being shy is something you have to work out of 205
kind of gradually.

LAURA: (*Sorrowfully.*) Yes—I guess it—

JIM: Takes time!

LAURA: Yes—

JIM: People are not so dreadful when you know them. That's 210
what you have to remember! And everybody has problems, not just you, but practically everybody has got some
problems. You think of yourself as having the only problems, as being the only one who is disappointed. But just
look around you and you will see lots of people as disap- 215
pointed as you are. For instance, I hoped when I was going to high school that I would be further along at this
time, six years later, than I am now. You remember that
wonderful write-up I had in *The Torch?*

LAURA: Yes! (*She rises and crosses to the table.*) 220

JIM: It said I was bound to succeed in anything I went into!

(LAURA *returns with the high school yearbook.*)

Holy Jeez! *The Torch!*

(*He accepts it reverently. They smile across the book with mutual
wonder.* LAURA *crouches beside him and they begin to turn the pages.*
LAURA's *shyness is dissolving in his warmth.*)

LAURA: Here you are in *The Pirates of Penzance!*

JIM: (*Wistfully.*) I sang the baritone lead in that operetta.

LAURA: (*Raptly.*) So—beautifully! 225

JIM: (*Protesting.*) Aw—

LAURA: Yes, yes—beautifully—beautifully!

JIM: You heard me?

LAURA: All three times!

JIM: No! 230

LAURA: Yes!

JIM: All three performances?

LAURA: (*Looking down.*) Yes.

JIM: Why?

LAURA: I—wanted to ask you to—autograph my program. (*She* 235
takes the program from the back of the yearbook and shows it to him.)

JIM: Why didn't you ask me to?

LAURA: You were always surrounded by your own friends so
much that I never had a chance to.

JIM: You should have just— 240

LAURA: Well, I—thought you might think I was—

JIM: Thought I might think you was—what?

LAURA: Oh—

JIM: (*With reflective relish.*) I was beleaguered by females in
those days. 245

LAURA: You were terribly popular!

JIM: Yeah—

LAURA: You had such a—friendly way—

JIM: I was spoiled in high school.

250 LAURA: Everybody—liked you!

JIM: Including you?

LAURA: I—yes, I—did, too—(*She gently closes the book in her lap.*)

JIM: Well, well, well! Give me that program, Laura.

(*She hands it to him. He signs it with a flourish.*)

There you are—better late than never!

255 LAURA: Oh, I—what a—surprise!

JIM: My signature isn't worth very much right now. But some day—maybe—it will increase in value! Being disappointed is one thing and being discouraged is something else. I am disappointed but I am not discouraged. I'm

260 twenty-three years old. How old are you?

LAURA: I'll be twenty-four in June.

JIM: That's not old age!

LAURA: No, but—

JIM: You finished high school?

265 LAURA: (*With difficulty.*) I didn't go back.

JIM: You mean you dropped out?

LAURA: I made bad grades in my final examinations. (*She rises and replaces the book and the program on the table. Her voice is strained.*) How is—Emily Meisenbach getting along?

270 JIM: Oh, that kraut-head!

LAURA: Why do you call her that?

JIM: That's what she was.

LAURA: You're not still—going with her?

JIM: I never see her.

275 LAURA: It said in the "Personal" section that you were—engaged!

JIM: I know, but I wasn't impressed by that—propaganda!

LAURA: It wasn't—the truth?

JIM: Only in Emily's optimistic opinion!

280 LAURA: Oh—

(*Legend: "What have you done since high school?"*)

(JIM *lights a cigarette and leans indolently back on his elbows smiling at* LAURA *with a warmth and charm which lights her inwardly with altar candles. She remains by the table, picks up a piece from the glass menagerie collection, and turns it in her hands to cover her tumult.*)

JIM: (*After several reflective puffs on his cigarette.*) What have you done since high school?

(*She seems not to hear him.*)

Huh?

(LAURA *looks up.*)

I said what have you done since high school, Laura?

285 LAURA: Nothing much.

JIM: You must have been doing something these six long years.

LAURA: Yes.

JIM: Well, then, such as what?

LAURA: I took a business course at business college—

JIM: How did that work out?   290

LAURA: Well, not very—well—I had to drop out, it gave me—indigestion—

(JIM *laughs gently.*)

JIM: What are you doing now?

LAURA: I don't do anything—much. Oh, please don't think I sit around doing nothing! My glass collection takes up a   295 good deal of time. Glass is something you have to take good care of.

JIM: What did you say—about glass?

LAURA: Collection I said—I have one—(*She clears her throat and turns away again, acutely shy.*)   300

JIM: (*Abruptly.*) You know what I judge to be the trouble with you? Inferiority complex! Know what that is? That's what they call it when someone low-rates himself! I understand it because I had it, too. Although my case was not so aggravated as yours seems to be. I had it until I took up pub-   305 lic speaking, developed my voice, and learned that I had an aptitude for science. Before that time I never thought of myself as being outstanding in any way whatsoever! Now I've never made a regular study of it, but I have a friend who says I can analyze people better than doctors that   310 make a profession of it. I don't claim that to be necessarily true, but I can sure guess a person's psychology, Laura! (*He takes out his gum.*) Excuse me, Laura. I always take it out when the flavor is gone. I'll use this scrap of paper to wrap it in. I know how it is to get it stuck on a shoe. (*He wraps*   315 *the gum in paper and puts it in his pocket.*) Yep—that's what I judge to be your principal trouble. A lack of confidence in yourself as a person. You don't have the proper amount of faith in yourself. I'm basing that fact on a number of your remarks and also on certain observations I've made. For in-   320 stance that clumping you thought was so awful in high school. You say that you even dreaded to walk into class. You see what you did? You dropped out of school, you gave up an education because of a clump, which as far as I know was practically non-existent! A little physical defect is what   325 you have. Hardly noticeable even! Magnified thousands of times by imagination! You know what my strong advice to you is? Think of yourself as *superior* in some way!

LAURA: In what way would I think?

JIM: Why, man alive, Laura! Just look about you a little. What   330 do you see? A world full of common people! All of 'em born and all of 'em going to die! Which of them has one-tenth of your good points! Or mine! Or anyone else's, as far as that goes—gosh! Everybody excels in some one thing. Some in many! (*He unconsciously glances at himself in*   335 *the mirror.*) All you've got to do is discover in *what!* Take me, for instance. (*He adjusts his tie at the mirror.*) My interest happens to lie in electro-dynamics. I'm taking a course in radio engineering at night school, Laura, on top of a fairly responsible job at the warehouse. I'm taking that   340 course and studying public speaking.

LAURA: Ohhhh.

JIM: Because I believe in the future of television! (*Turning his back to her.*) I wish to be ready to go up right along with it. Therefore I'm planning to get in on the ground floor.   345 In fact I've already made the right connections and all that remains is for the industry itself to get under way! Full steam—(*His eyes are starry.*) *Knowledge*—Zzzzzp! *Money*—Zzzzzp!—*Power!* That's the cycle democracy is built on!

(*His attitude is convincingly dynamic.* LAURA *stares at him, even her shyness eclipsed in her absolute wonder. He suddenly grins.*)

350   I guess you think I think a lot of myself!
LAURA: No—o-o-o, I—
JIM: Now how about you? Isn't there something you take more interest in than anything else?
LAURA: Well, I do—as I said—have my—glass collection—

(*A peal of girlish laughter rings from the kitchenette.*)

355   JIM: I'm not right sure I know what you're talking about. What kind of glass is it?
LAURA: Little articles of it, they're ornaments mostly! Most of them are little animals made out of glass, the tiniest little animals in the world. Mother calls them a glass menagerie!
360   Here's an example of one, if you'd like to see it! This one is one of the oldest. It's nearly thirteen.

(*Music:* "The Glass Menagerie.")

(*He stretches out his hand.*)

Oh, be careful—if you breathe, it breaks!
JIM: I'd better not take it. I'm pretty clumsy with things.
LAURA: Go on, I trust you with him! (*She places the piece in his*
365   *palm.*) There now—you're holding him gently! Hold him over the light, he loves the light! You see how the light shines through him?
JIM: It sure does shine!
LAURA: I shouldn't be partial, but he is my favorite one.
370   JIM: What kind of a thing is this one supposed to be?
LAURA: Haven't you noticed the single horn on his forehead?
JIM: A unicorn, huh?
LAURA: Mmmm-hmmm!
JIM: Unicorns—aren't they extinct in the modern world?
375   LAURA: I know!
JIM: Poor little fellow, he must feel sort of lonesome.
LAURA: (*Smiling.*) Well, if he does, he doesn't complain about it. He stays on a shelf with some horses that don't have horns and all of them seem to get along nicely together.
380   JIM: How do you know?
LAURA: (*Lightly.*) I haven't heard any arguments among them!
JIM: (*Grinning.*) No arguments, huh? Well, that's a pretty good sign! Where shall I set him?
LAURA: Put him on the table. They all like a change of
385   scenery once in a while!
JIM: Well, well, well, well—(*He places the glass piece on the table, then raises his arms and stretches.*) Look how big my shadow is when I stretch!
LAURA: Oh, oh, yes—it stretches across the ceiling!
390   JIM: (*Crossing to the door.*) I think it's stopped raining. (*He opens the fire-escape door and the background music changes to a dance tune.*) Where does the music come from?
LAURA: From the Paradise Dance-hall across the alley.
JIM: How about cutting the rug a little, Miss Wingfield?
395   LAURA: Oh, I—

JIM: Or is your program filled up? Let me have a look at it. (*He grasps an imaginary card.*) Why, every dance is taken! I'll just have to scratch some out.

(*Waltz music:* "La Golondrina.")

Ahhh, a waltz! (*He executes some sweeping turns by himself, then holds his arms toward* LAURA.)
400   LAURA: (*Breathlessly.*) I—can't dance!
JIM: There you go, that inferiority stuff!
LAURA: I've never danced in my life!
JIM: Come on, try!
405   LAURA: Oh, but I'd step on you!
JIM: I'm not made out of glass.
LAURA: How—how—how do we start?
JIM: Just leave it to me. You hold your arms out a little.
LAURA: Like this?
410   JIM: (*Taking her in his arms.*) A little bit higher. Right. Now don't tighten up, that's the main thing about it—relax.
LAURA: (*Laughing breathlessly.*) It's hard not to.
JIM: Okay.
LAURA: I'm afraid you can't budge me.
415   JIM: What do you bet I can't? (*He swings her into motion.*)
LAURA: Goodness, yes, you can!
JIM: Let yourself go, now, Laura, just let yourself go.
LAURA: I'm—
JIM: Come on!
420   LAURA: —trying!
JIM: Not so stiff—easy does it!
LAURA: I know but I'm—
JIM: Loosen th' backbone! There now, that's a lot better.
LAURA: Am I?
425   JIM: Lots, lots better! (*He moves her about the room in a clumsy waltz.*)
LAURA: Oh, my!
JIM: Ha-ha!
LAURA: Oh, my goodness!
430   JIM: Ha-ha-ha!

(*They suddenly bump into the table, and the glass piece on it falls to the floor.* JIM *stops the dance.*)

What did we hit on?
LAURA: Table.
JIM: Did something fall off it? I think—
LAURA: Yes.
435   JIM: I hope that it wasn't the little glass horse with the horn!
LAURA: Yes. (*She stoops to pick it up.*)
JIM: Aw, aw, aw. Is it broken?
LAURA: Now it is just like all the other horses.
JIM: It's lost its—
440   LAURA: Horn! It doesn't matter. Maybe it's a blessing in disguise.
JIM: You'll never forgive me. I bet that that was your favorite piece of glass.
LAURA: I don't have favorites much. It's no tragedy, Freckles.
445   Glass breaks so easily. No matter how careful you are. The traffic jars the shelves and things fall off them.
JIM: Still I'm awfully sorry that I was the cause.
LAURA: (*Smiling.*) I'll just imagine he had an operation. The horn was removed to make him feel less—freakish!

(They both laugh.)

450   Now he will feel more at home with the other horses, the
        ones that don't have horns. . . .
        JIM: Ha-ha, that's very funny! *(Suddenly he is serious.)* I'm glad
        to see that you have a sense of humor. You know—
        you're—well—very different! Surprisingly different from
455   anyone else I know! *(His voice becomes soft and hesitant with
        a genuine feeling.)* Do you mind me telling you that?

(LAURA is abashed beyond speech.)

        I mean it in a nice way—

(LAURA nods shyly, looking away.)

        You make me feel sort of—I don't know how to put it!
        I'm usually pretty good at expressing things, but—this is
460   something that I don't know how to say!

*(LAURA touches her throat and clears it—turns the broken unicorn
in her hands. His voice becomes softer.)*

        Has anyone ever told you that you were pretty?

*(There is a pause, and the music rises slightly. LAURA looks up
slowly, with wonder, and shakes her head.)*

        Well, you are! In a very different way from anyone else.
        And all the nicer because of the difference, too.

*(His voice becomes low and husky. LAURA turns away, nearly faint
with the novelty of her emotions.)*

        I wish that you were my sister. I'd teach you to have some
465   confidence in yourself. The different people are not like
        other people, but being different is nothing to be ashamed
        of. Because other people are not such wonderful people.
        They're one hundred times one thousand. You're one
        times one! They walk all over the earth. You just stay here.
470   They're common as—weeds, but—you—well, you're—
        Blue Roses!

(Image on screen: Blue Roses.)

(The music changes.)

        LAURA: But blue is wrong for—roses. . . .
        JIM: It's right for you! You're—pretty!
        LAURA: In what respect am I pretty?
475   JIM: In all respects—believe me! Your eyes—your hair—are
        pretty! Your hands are pretty! *(He catches hold of her hand.)*
        You think I'm making this up because I'm invited to din-
        ner and have to be nice. Oh, I could do that! I could put
        on an act for you, Laura, and say lots of things without be-
480   ing very sincere. But this time I am. I'm talking to you sin-
        cerely. I happened to notice you had this inferiority
        complex that keeps you from feeling comfortable with
        people. Somebody needs to build your confidence up and
        make you proud instead of shy and turning away and—
485   blushing. Somebody—ought to—*kiss you, Laura!*

*(His hand slips slowly up her arm to her shoulder as the music swells
tumultuously. He suddenly turns her about and kisses her on the lips.
When he releases her, LAURA sinks on the sofa with a bright, dazed
look. JIM backs away and fishes in his pocket for a cigarette.)*

(Legend on screen: "A souvenir.")

        Stumblejohn!

*(He lights the cigarette, avoiding her look. There is a peal of girlish
laughter from AMANDA in the kitchenette. LAURA slowly raises and
opens her hand. It still contains the little broken glass animal. She
looks at it with a tender, bewildered expression.)*

        Stumblejohn! I shouldn't have done that—that was way
        off the beam. You don't smoke, do you?

*(She looks up, smiling, not hearing the question. He sits beside her
rather gingerly. She looks at him speechlessly—waiting. He coughs
decorously and moves a little farther aside as he considers the situation
and senses her feelings, dimly, with perturbation. He speaks gently.)*

        Would you—care for a—mint?

(She doesn't seem to hear him but her look grows brighter even.)

        Peppermint? Life Saver? My pocket's a regular drug-   490
        store—wherever I go . . . *(He pops a mint in his mouth. Then
        he gulps and decides to make a clean breast of it. He speaks
        slowly and gingerly.)* Laura, you know, if I had a sister like
        you, I'd do the same thing as Tom. I'd bring out fellows
        and—introduce her to them. The right type of boys—of   495
        a type to—appreciate her. Only—well—he made a mis-
        take about me. Maybe I've got no call to be saying this.
        That may not have been the idea in having me over. But
        what if it was? There's nothing wrong about that. The
        only trouble is that in my case—I'm not in a situation   500
        to—do the right thing. I can't take down your number
        and say I'll phone. I can't call up next week and—ask for
        a date. I thought I had better explain the situation in case
        you—misunderstood it and—I hurt your feelings. . . .

*(There is a pause. Slowly, very slowly, LAURA's look changes, her eyes
returning slowly from his to the glass figure in her palm. AMANDA
utters another gay laugh in the kitchenette.)*

        LAURA: *(Faintly.)* You—won't—call again?   505
        JIM: No, Laura, I can't. *(He rises from the sofa.)* As I was just ex-
        plaining, I've—got strings on me. Laura, I've—been going
        steady! I go out all the time with a girl named Betty. She's
        a home-girl like you, and Catholic, and Irish, and in a
        great many ways we—get along fine. I met her last sum-   510
        mer on a moonlight boat trip up the river to Alton, on the
        Majestic. Well—right away from the start it was—love!

(Legend: "Love!")

*(LAURA sways slightly forward and grips the arm of the sofa. He fails
to notice, now enrapt in his own comfortable being.)*

        Being in love has made a new man of me!

*(Leaning stiffly forward, clutching the arm of the sofa, LAURA strug-
gles visibly with her storm. But JIM is oblivious; she is a long way off.)*

        The power of love is really pretty tremendous! Love is
        something that—changes the whole world, Laura!   515

*(The storm abates a little and LAURA leans back. He notices her
again.)*

It happened that Betty's aunt took sick, she got a wire and had to go to Centralia. So Tom—when he asked me to dinner—I naturally just accepted the invitation, not knowing that you—that he—that I—(*He stops awkwardly.*) 520 Huh—I'm a stumblejohn!

(*He flops back on the sofa. The holy candles on the altar of* LAURA'S *face have been snuffed out. There is a look of almost infinite desolation.* JIM *glances at her uneasily.*)

I wish that you would—say something.

(*She bites her lip which was trembling and then bravely smiles. She opens her hand again on the broken glass figure. Then she gently takes his hand and raises it level with her own. She carefully places the unicorn in the palm of his hand, then pushes his fingers closed upon it.*)

What are you—doing that for? You want me to have him? Laura?

(*She nods.*)

What for?
525 LAURA: A—souvenir. . . .

(*She rises unsteadily and crouches beside the Victrola to wind it up.*)

(*Legend on screen:* "Things have a way of turning out so badly!" *Or image: Gentleman caller waving goodbye—gaily.*)

(*At this moment* AMANDA *rushes brightly back into the living room. She bears a pitcher of fruit punch in an old-fashioned cut-glass pitcher, and a plate of macaroons. The plate has a gold border and poppies painted on it.*)

AMANDA: Well, well, well! Isn't the air delightful after the shower? I've made you children a little liquid refreshment. (*She turns gaily to* JIM.) Jim, do you know that song about lemonade?

530   "Lemonade, lemonade
        Made in the shade and stirred with a spade—
        Good enough for any old maid!"

JIM: (*Uneasily.*) Ha-ha! No—I never heard it.
AMANDA: Why, Laura! You look so serious!
535 JIM: We were having a serious conversation.
AMANDA: Good! Now you're better acquainted!
JIM: (*Uncertainly.*) Ha-ha! Yes.
AMANDA: You modern young people are much more seri-ousminded than my generation. I was so gay as a girl!
540 JIM: You haven't changed, Mrs. Wingfield.
AMANDA: Tonight I'm rejuvenated! The gaiety of the occasion, Mr. O'Connor! (*She tosses her head with a peal of laughter, spilling some lemonade.*) Oooo! I'm baptizing myself!
JIM: Here—let me—
545 AMANDA: (*Setting the pitcher down.*) There now. I discovered we had some maraschino cherries. I dumped them in, juice and all!
JIM: You shouldn't have gone to that trouble, Mrs. Wingfield.
AMANDA: Trouble, trouble? Why, it was loads of fun! Didn't
550   you hear me cutting up in the kitchen? I bet your ears were burning! I told Tom how outdone with him I was

for keeping you to himself so long a time! He should have brought you over much, much sooner! Well, now that you've found your way, I want you to be a very frequent caller! Not just occasional but all the time. Oh, we're go- 555 ing to have a lot of gay times together! I see them coming! Mmm, just breathe that air! So fresh, and the moon's so pretty! I'll skip back out—I know where my place is when young folks are having a—serious conversation!
JIM: Oh, don't go out, Mrs. Wingfield. The fact of the mat- 560 ter is I've got to be going.
AMANDA: Going, now? You're joking! Why, it's only the shank of the evening, Mr. O'Connor!
JIM: Well, you know how it is.
AMANDA: You mean you're a young workingman and have to 565 keep workingmen's hours. We'll let you off early tonight. But only on the condition that next time you stay later. What's the best night for you? Isn't Saturday night the best night for you workingmen?
JIM: I have a couple of time-clocks to punch, Mrs. Wingfield. 570 One at morning, another one at night!
AMANDA: My, but you are ambitious! You work at night, too?
JIM: No, Ma'am, not work but—Betty!

(*He crosses deliberately to pick up his hat. The band at the Paradise Dance-hall goes into a tender waltz.*)

AMANDA: Betty? Betty? Who's—Betty!

(*There is an ominous cracking sound in the sky.*)

JIM: Oh, just a girl. The girl I go steady with!   575

(*He smiles charmingly. The sky falls.*)

(*Legend:* "The Sky Falls.")

AMANDA: (*A long-drawn exhalation.*) Ohhhh . . . Is it a serious romance, Mr. O'Connor?
JIM: We're going to be married the second Sunday in June.
AMANDA: Ohhhh—how nice! Tom didn't mention that you were engaged to be married.   580
JIM: The cat's not out of the bag at the warehouse yet. You know how they are. They call you Romeo and stuff like that. (*He stops at the oval mirror to put on his hat. He carefully shapes the brim and the crown to give a discreetly dashing effect.*) It's been a wonderful evening, Mrs. Wingfield. I guess this 585 is what they mean by Southern hospitality.
AMANDA: It really wasn't anything at all.
JIM: I hope it don't seem like I'm rushing off. But I promised Betty I'd pick her up at the Wabash depot, an' by the time I get my jalopy down there her train'll be in. Some 590 women are pretty upset if you keep 'em waiting.
AMANDA: Yes, I know—the tyranny of women! (*She extends her hand.*) Goodbye, Mr. O'Connor. I wish you luck—and happiness—and success! All three of them, and so does Laura! Don't you, Laura?   595
LAURA: Yes!
JIM: (*Taking* LAURA'S *hand.*) Goodbye, Laura. I'm certainly going to treasure that souvenir. And don't you forget the good advice I gave you. (*He raises his voice to a cheery shout.*) So long, Shakespeare! Thanks again, ladies. Good night! 600

(*He grins and ducks jauntily out. Still bravely grimacing,* AMANDA *closes the door on the gentleman caller. Then she turns back to the room with a puzzled expression. She and* LAURA *don't dare to face each other.* LAURA *crouches beside the Victrola to wind it.*)

AMANDA: (*Faintly.*) Things have a way of turning out so badly. I don't believe that I would play the Victrola. Well, well—well! Our gentleman caller was engaged to be married! (*She raises her voice.*) Tom!

605 TOM: (*From the kitchenette.*) Yes, Mother?

AMANDA: Come in here a minute. I want to tell you something awfully funny.

TOM: (*Entering with a macaroon and a glass of the lemonade.*) Has the gentleman caller gotten away already?

610 AMANDA: The gentleman caller has made an early departure. What a wonderful joke you played on us!

TOM: How do you mean?

AMANDA: You didn't mention that he was engaged to be married.

615 TOM: Jim? Engaged?

AMANDA: That's what he just informed us.

TOM: I'll be jiggered! I didn't know about that.

AMANDA: That seems very peculiar.

TOM: What's peculiar about it?

620 AMANDA: Didn't you call him your best friend down at the warehouse?

TOM: He is, but how did I know?

AMANDA: It seems extremely peculiar that you wouldn't know your best friend was going to be married!

625 TOM: The warehouse is where I work, not where I know things about people!

AMANDA: You don't know things anywhere! You live in a dream; you manufacture illusions!

(*He crosses to the door.*)

Where are you going?

630 TOM: I'm going to the movies.

AMANDA: That's right, now that you've had us make such fools of ourselves. The effort, the preparations, all the expense! The new floor lamp, the rug, the clothes for Laura! All for what? To entertain some other girl's fiancé! Go to the movies, go! Don't think about us, a mother deserted, an unmarried sister who's crippled and has no job! Don't let anything interfere with your selfish pleasure! Just go, go, go—to the movies!

635

TOM: All right, I will! The more you shout about my selfishness to me the quicker I'll go, and I won't go to the movies!

640

AMANDA: Go, then! Go to the moon—you selfish dreamer!

(TOM *smashes his glass on the floor. He plunges out on the fire escape, slamming the door.* LAURA *screams in fright. The dance-hall music becomes louder.* TOM *stands on the fire escape, gripping the rail. The moon breaks through the storm clouds, illuminating his face.*)

(*Legend on screen: "And so goodbye . . ."*)

(TOM's *closing speech is timed with what is happening inside the house. We see, as though through soundproof glass, that* AMANDA *appears to be making a comforting speech to* LAURA, *who is huddled upon the sofa. Now that we cannot hear the mother's speech, her silliness is gone and she has dignity and tragic beauty.* LAURA's *hair hides her face until, at the end of the speech, she lifts her head to smile at her mother.* AMANDA's *gestures are slow and graceful, almost dancelike, as she comforts her daughter. At the end of her speech she glances a moment at the father's picture—then withdraws through the portieres. At the close of* TOM's *speech,* LAURA *blows out the candles, ending the play.*)

TOM: I didn't go to the moon, I went much further—for time is the longest distance between two places. Not long after that I was fired for writing a poem on the lid of a shoe-box. I left Saint Louis. I descended the steps of this fire escape 645 for a last time and followed, from then on, in my father's footsteps, attempting to find in motion what was lost in space. I traveled around a great deal. The cities swept about me like dead leaves, leaves that were brightly colored but torn away from the branches. I would have stopped, but I 650 was pursued by something. It always came upon me unawares, taking me altogether by surprise. Perhaps it was a familiar bit of music. Perhaps it was only a piece of transparent glass. Perhaps I am walking along a street at night, in some strange city, before I have found companions. I pass 655 the lighted window of a shop where perfume is sold. The window is filled with pieces of colored glass, tiny transparent bottles in delicate colors, like bits of a shattered rainbow. Then all at once my sister touches my shoulder. I turn around and look into her eyes. Oh, Laura, Laura, I tried to 660 leave you behind me, but I am more faithful than I intended to be! I reach for a cigarette, I cross the street, I run into the movies or a bar, I buy a drink, I speak to the nearest stranger—anything that can blow your candles out!

(LAURA *bends over the candles.*)

For nowadays the world is lit by lightning! Blow out your 665 candles, Laura—and so goodbye. . . .

(*She blows the candles out.*)

Arthur Miller

Arthur Miller (1915–2005) was born in Harlem and raised in Brooklyn. The son of Jewish immigrants, Miller often takes the milieu of urban New York as the substance of his drama. Like Tennessee Williams, Miller was formed by the Depression. He worked a variety of jobs to help his family make ends meet, and eventually gained provisional admission to the University of Michigan, where he studied playwriting and graduated in 1938. He worked briefly for the Federal Theater Project. Although his first play—*The Man Who Had All the Luck* (1944)—failed, Miller went on to write a series of gritty and powerful plays: *All My Sons* (1947), *Death of a Salesman* (1949), an adaptation of Ibsen's *An Enemy of the People* (1950), and *The Crucible* (1953). In 1955, Miller wrote *A View from the Bridge,* a story of honor and betrayal among New York's Italian immigrants. He also married Marilyn Monroe in that year, and his next play, *After the Fall* (1964), is a lightly disguised account of their stormy marriage and its break-up. In 1964 he also produced *Incident at Vichy,* a play concerning the Nazi persecution of the Jews during World War II, and he returned to the subject in his 1981 screenplay, *Playing for Time.* Until his death Miller continued to write and have his plays produced worldwide—including *The Price* (1968), *The Creation of the World and Other Business* (1972—revised as *Up from Paradise* 1974), *The Archbishop's Calling* (1977), *The American Clock* (1980), *Danger: Memory* (1987), *The Ride Down Mount Morgan* (1991), *The Last Yankee* (1993); and *Resurrection Blues* (2002). He also published a memoir (*Timebends*), a series of collected essays, and an account of the production of *Salesman* in the People's Republic of China during the 1980s. He wrote and lectured frequently about his career and about American theater.

DEATH OF A SALESMAN

Something like *Oedipus the King* for the classical theater, or *Hamlet* for the English Renaissance stage, *Death of a Salesman* has become an icon of the American theater: Miller's central characters—Willy Loman, the worn-out, dreaming salesman; his two sons, Biff, the All-American star, who can never quite fit into American society, and Happy, the unhappy younger brother—have entered into the popular lexicon of cultural stereotypes, landmarks for later playwrights. (Think of Troy Maxson in August Wilson's *Fences,* or Lee and Austin in Sam Shepard's *True West,* or even Lincoln and Booth in Suzan-Lori Parks's *Topdog/Underdog.*) And, again like *Hamlet,* the play provides a dominant central role that has tested generations of actors from Lee J. Cobb, who created Willy Loman onstage, to Dustin Hoffman and Brian Dennehy.

As in classical tragedy (see Miller's essay, "Tragedy and the Common Man," later in this unit), the action of *Death of a Salesman* is impelled by a single, climactic event: Willy is approaching the end of his career, his glad-handing sales contacts are all dead or retired, and he's no longer pulling in business for the company—he's about to be fired. While this is perhaps less sensational than the crimes that prompt Oedipus or Hamlet to tragic action, Miller uses the fluidity of his stage and his remarkable ear for the prosaic poetry of everyday speech to give this event an extraordinary resonance. Blending scenes from Willy's past (the affecting scenes of Willy as a young father; the Woman in Boston and Biff's discovery of Willy's hypocrisy) with the Loman family's present straits, *Death of a Salesman* claims Willy as a representative figure, embodying the contradictions of the American dream. As Linda puts it, "Willy Loman never made a lot of money. His name was never in the paper. He's not the finest character that ever lived. But he's a human being, and a terrible thing is happening to him. So attention must be paid." Miller deftly focuses a conflict between the material circumstances of Willy's life, his hard work, his exploitation by the company that finally sends him "to his grave like an old dog," and Willy's nonetheless eager belief in the system, in the salesman's ethic that has sustained and destroyed him. *Death of a Salesman* stages a double perspective on deadly mythology of America: Willy at once believes, and teaches his two sons to believe, that to be "well liked" is more important, more critical than ability or achievement; at the same time, he turns aside from the life represented by his uncle Ben, remaining with his good job and steady income instead of pursuing the intangible fortunes of Alaska like his pioneering father. Although the play stages many of the turning points in Willy's life, the opportunities missed to take a new direction, the central "cause" of the play's action took place years earlier, when Willy met an aging salesman and decided to pursue his career rather than light out for the frontier. What most impressed Willy about *that* salesman was his funeral: he died the "death of a salesman, in his green velvet slippers in the smoker of the New York, New Haven and Hartford, going into Boston—when he died, hundreds of salesmen and buyers were at his funeral." Part of Miller's genius in *Death of a Salesman* lies in the reach he gives to this figure and in the central conflict between the city and the frontier still embodied by the career of the salesman, represented in the play as a kind of Kit Carson or Daniel Boone, a rootless wanderer domesticated and destroyed by his willing acceptance of the demands of business and the society it sustains. As Charlie puts it in the "Requiem" ending the play: "Willy was a salesman. And for a salesman, there is no rock bottom to the life. He don't put a bolt to a nut, he don't tell you the law or give you medicine. He's a man way out there in the blue, riding on a smile and a shoeshine. . . . A salesman is got to dream, boy. It comes with the territory."

Jo Mielziner's celebrated set for the premiere production of Arthur Miller's *Death of a Salesman*, showing the cutaway house and the downstage playing area.

DEATH OF A SALESMAN

Arthur Miller

CHARACTERS

WILLY LOMAN	JENNY
LINDA	STANLEY
BIFF	MISS FORSYTHE
HAPPY	LETTA
BERNARD	
THE WOMAN	
CHARLEY	
UNCLE BEN	
HOWARD WAGNER	

The action takes place in Willy Loman's house and yard and in various places he visits in the New York and Boston of today.

Throughout the play, in the stage directions, left and right mean stage left and stage right.

ACT ONE

A melody is heard, played upon a flute. It is small and fine, telling of grass and trees and the horizon. The curtain rises.

Before us is the Salesman's house. We are aware of towering, angular shapes behind it, surrounding it on all sides. Only the blue light of the sky falls upon the house and forestage; the surrounding area shows an angry glow of orange. As more light appears, we see a solid vault of apartment houses around the small, fragile-seeming home. An air of the dream clings to the place, a dream rising out of reality. The kitchen at center seems actual enough, for there is a kitchen table with three chairs, and a refrigerator. But no other fixtures are seen. At the back of the kitchen there is a draped entrance, which leads to the living-room. To the right of the kitchen, on a level raised two feet, is a bedroom furnished only with a brass bedstead and a straight chair. On a shelf over the bed a silver athletic trophy stands. A window opens onto the apartment house at the side.

Behind the kitchen, on a level raised six and a half feet, is the boys' bedroom, at present barely visible. Two beds are dimly seen, and at the back of the room a dormer window. (This bedroom is above the unseen living-room.) At the left a stairway curves up to it from the kitchen.

The entire setting is wholly, or, in some places, partially transparent. The roof-line of the house is one-dimensional; under and over it we see the apartment buildings. Before the house lies an apron, curving beyond the forestage into the orchestra. This forward area serves as the back yard as well as the locale of all Willy's imaginings and of his city scenes. Whenever the action is in the present the actors observe the imaginary wall-lines, entering the house only through its door at the left. But in the scenes of the past these boundaries are broken, and characters enter or leave a room by stepping "through" a wall onto the forestage.

From the right, Willy Loman, the Salesman, enters, carrying two large sample cases. The flute plays on. He hears but is not aware of it. He is past sixty years of age, dressed quietly. Even as he crosses the stage to the doorway of the house, his exhaustion is apparent. He unlocks the door, comes into the kitchen, and thankfully lets his burden down, feeling the soreness of his palms. A word-sigh escapes his lips—it might be "Oh, boy, oh, boy." He closes the door, then carries his cases out into the living-room, through the draped kitchen doorway.

Linda, his wife, has stirred in her bed at the right. She gets out and puts on a robe, listening. Most often jovial, she has developed an iron repression of her exceptions to Willy's behavior—she more than loves him, she admires him, as though his mercurial nature, his temper, his massive dreams and little cruelties, served her only as sharp reminders of the turbulent longings within him, longings which she shares but lacks the temperament to utter and follow to their end.

LINDA: (*Hearing* WILLY *outside the bedroom, calls with some trepidation.*) Willy!

WILLY: It's all right. I came back.

LINDA: Why? What happened? (*Slight pause.*) Did something happen, Willy? 5

WILLY: No, nothing happened.

LINDA: You didn't smash the car, did you?

WILLY: (*With casual irritation.*) I said nothing happened. Didn't you hear me?

LINDA: Don't you feel well? 10

WILLY: I'm tired to the death. (*The flute has faded away. He sits on the bed beside her, a little numb.*) I couldn't make it. I just couldn't make it, Linda.

LINDA: (*Very carefully, delicately.*) Where were you all day? You look terrible. 15

WILLY: I got as far as a little above Yonkers. I stopped for a cup of coffee. Maybe it was the coffee.

LINDA: What?

WILLY: (*After a pause.*) I suddenly couldn't drive any more. The car kept going off onto the shoulder, y'know? 20

LINDA: (*Helpfully.*) Oh. Maybe it was the steering again. I don't think Angelo knows the Studebaker.

WILLY: No, it's me, it's me. Suddenly I realize I'm goin' sixty miles an hour and I don't remember the last five minutes. I'm—I can't seem to—keep my mind to it. 25

LINDA: Maybe it's your glasses. You never went for your new glasses.

WILLY: No, I see everything. I came back ten miles an hour. It took me nearly four hours from Yonkers.

LINDA: (*Resigned.*) Well, you'll just have to take a rest, Willy, 30 you can't continue this way.

WILLY: I just got back from Florida.

LINDA: But you didn't rest your mind. Your mind is overactive, and the mind is what counts, dear.

35 WILLY: I'll start out in the morning. Maybe I'll feel better in the morning. (*She is taking off his shoes.*) These goddam arch supports are killing me.

LINDA: Take an aspirin. Should I get you an aspirin? It'll soothe you.

40 WILLY: (*With wonder.*) I was driving along, you understand? And I was fine. I was even observing the scenery. You can imagine, me looking at scenery, on the road every week of my life. But it's so beautiful up there, Linda, the trees are so thick, and the sun is warm. I opened the windshield

45 and just let the warm air bathe over me. And then all of a sudden I'm goin' off the road! I'm tellin' ya, I absolutely forgot I was driving. If I'd've gone the other way over the white line I might've killed somebody. So I went on again—and five minutes later I'm dreamin' again, and I

50 nearly— (*He presses two fingers against his eyes.*) I have such thoughts, I have such strange thoughts.

LINDA: Willy, dear. Talk to them again. There's no reason why you can't work in New York.

WILLY: They don't need me in New York. I'm the New En-
55 gland man. I'm vital in New England.

LINDA: But you're sixty years old. They can't expect you to keep traveling every week.

WILLY: I'll have to send a wire to Portland. I'm supposed to see Brown and Morrison tomorrow morning at ten
60 o'clock to show the line. Goddammit, I could sell them! (*He starts putting on his jacket.*)

LINDA: (*Taking the jacket from him.*) Why don't you go down to the place tomorrow and tell Howard you've simply got to work in New York? You're too accommodating,
65 dear.

WILLY: If old man Wagner was alive I'd a been in charge of New York now! That man was a prince, he was a master-ful man. But that boy of his, that Howard, he don't appre-ciate. When I went north the first time, the Wagner
70 Company didn't know where New England was!

LINDA: Why don't you tell those things to Howard, dear?

WILLY: (*Encouraged.*) I will, I definitely will. Is there any cheese?

LINDA: I'll make you a sandwich.

75 WILLY: No, go to sleep. I'll take some milk. I'll be up right away. The boys in?

LINDA: They're sleeping. Happy took Biff on a date tonight.

WILLY: (*Interested.*) That so?

LINDA: It was so nice to see them shaving together, one be-
80 hind the other, in the bathroom. And going out to-gether. You notice? The whole house smells of shaving lotion.

WILLY: Figure it out. Work a lifetime to pay off a house. You finally own it, and there's nobody to live in it.

85 LINDA: Well, dear, life is a casting off. It's always that way.

WILLY: No, no, some people—some people accomplish some-thing. Did Biff say anything after I went this morning?

LINDA: You shouldn't have criticized him, Willy, especially af-ter he just got off the train. You mustn't lose your temper
90 with him.

WILLY: When the hell did I lose my temper? I simply asked him if he was making any money. Is that a criticism?

LINDA: But, dear, how could he make any money?

WILLY: (*Worried and angered.*) There's such an undercurrent in
95 him. He became a moody man. Did he apologize when I left this morning?

LINDA: He was crestfallen, Willy. You know how he admires you. I think if he finds himself, then you'll both be hap-pier and not fight any more.

100 WILLY: How can he find himself on a farm? Is that a life? A farmhand? In the beginning, when he was young, I thought, well, a young man, it's good for him to tramp around, take a lot of different jobs. But it's more than ten years now and he has yet to make thirty-five dollars a
105 week!

LINDA: He's finding himself, Willy.

WILLY: Not finding yourself at the age of thirty-four is a dis-grace!

LINDA: Shh!

110 WILLY: The trouble is he's lazy, goddammit!

LINDA: Willy, please!

WILLY: Biff is a lazy bum!

LINDA: They're sleeping. Get something to eat. Go on down.

WILLY: Why did he come home? I would like to know what
115 brought him home.

LINDA: I don't know. I think he's still lost, Willy. I think he's very lost.

WILLY: Biff Loman is lost. In the greatest country in the world a young man with such—personal attractiveness,
120 gets lost. And such a hard worker. There's one thing about Biff—he's not lazy.

LINDA: Never.

WILLY: (*With pity and resolve.*) I'll see him in the morning; I'll have a nice talk with him. I'll get him a job selling. He could be big in no time. My God! Remember how they
125 used to follow him around in high school? When he smiled at one of them their faces lit up. When he walked down the street. . . (*He loses himself in reminiscences.*)

LINDA: (*Trying to bring him out of it.*) Willy, dear, I got a new kind of American-type cheese today. It's whipped.
130

WILLY: Why do you get American when I like Swiss?

LINDA: I just thought you'd like a change—

WILLY: I don't want a change! I want Swiss cheese. Why am I always being contradicted?

LINDA: (*With a covering laugh.*) I thought it would be a surprise.
135

WILLY: Why don't you open a window in here, for God's sake?

LINDA: (*With infinite patience.*) They're all open, dear.

WILLY: The way they boxed us in here. Bricks and windows, windows and bricks.

LINDA: We should've bought the land next door.
140

WILLY: The street is lined with cars. There's not a breath of fresh air in the neighborhood. The grass don't grow any more, you can't raise a carrot in the back yard. They should've had a law against apartment houses. Remember those two beautiful elm trees out there? When I and Biff
145 hung the swing between them?

LINDA: Yeah, like being a million miles from the city.

WILLY: They should've arrested the builder for cutting those down. They massacred the neighborhood. (*Lost.*) More and more I think of those days, Linda. This time of year
150 it was lilac and wisteria. And then the peonies would come out, and the daffodils. What fragrance in this room!

LINDA: Well, after all, people had to move somewhere.

WILLY: No, there's more people, now.

155 LINDA: I don't think there's more people I think—

WILLY: There's more people! That's what's ruining this country! Population is getting out of control. The competition is maddening! Smell the stink from that apartment house! And another one on the other side . . . How can they whip

160 cheese?

(*On* WILLY's *last line,* BIFF *and* HAPPY *raise themselves up in their beds, listening.*)

LINDA: Go down, try it. And be quiet.

WILLY: (*Turning to* LINDA, *guiltily.*) You're not worried about me, are you, sweetheart?

BIFF: What's the matter?

165 HAPPY: Listen!

LINDA: You've got too much on the ball to worry about.

WILLY: You're my foundation and my support, Linda.

LINDA: Just try to relax, dear. You make mountains out of molehills.

170 WILLY: I won't fight with him any more. If he wants to go back to Texas, let him go.

LINDA: He'll find his way.

WILLY: Sure. Certain men just don't get started till later in life. Like Thomas Edison, I think. Or B. F. Goodrich. One

175 of them was deaf. (*He starts for the bedroom doorway.*) I'll put my money on Biff.

LINDA: And Willy—if it's warm Sunday we'll drive in the country. And we'll open the windshield, and take lunch.

180 WILLY: No, the windshields don't open on the new cars.

LINDA: But you opened it today.

WILLY: Me? I didn't. (*He stops.*) Now isn't that peculiar! Isn't that a remarkable—(*He breaks off in amazement and fright as the flute is heard distantly.*)

LINDA: What, darling?

185 WILLY: That is the most remarkable thing.

LINDA: What, dear?

WILLY: I was thinking of the Chevvy. (*Slight pause.*) Nineteen twenty-eight . . . when I had that red Chevvy—(*Breaks off.*) That funny? I coulda sworn I was driving that Chevvy

190 today.

LINDA: Well, that's nothing. Something must've reminded you.

WILLY: Remarkable. Ts. Remember those days? The way Biff used to simonize that car? The dealer refused to believe

195 there was eighty thousand miles on it. (*He shakes his head.*) Heh! (*To* LINDA.) Close your eyes, I'll be right up. (*He walks out of the bedroom.*)

HAPPY *to* BIFF: Jesus, maybe he smashed up the car again!

LINDA: (*Calling after* WILLY.) Be careful on the stairs, dear! The

200 cheese is on the middle shelf! (*She turns, goes over to the bed, takes his jacket, and goes out of the bedroom.*)

(*Light has risen on the boys' room. Unseen,* WILLY *is heard talking to himself, "Eighty thousand miles," and a little laugh.* BIFF *gets out of bed, comes downstage a bit, and stands attentively.* BIFF *is two years older than his brother* HAPPY, *well built, but in these days bears a worn air and seems less self-assured. He has succeeded less, and his dreams are stronger and less acceptable than* HAPPY's. HAPPY *is tall, powerfully made. Sexuality is like a visible color on him, or a scent that many women have discovered. He, like his brother, is lost, but in*

a different way, for he has never allowed himself to turn his face toward defeat and is thus more confused and hard-skinned, although seemingly more content.

HAPPY: (*Getting out of bed.*) He's going to get his license taken away if he keeps that up. I'm getting nervous about him, y'know, Biff?

BIFF: His eyes are going.   205

HAPPY: No, I've driven with him. He sees all right. He just doesn't keep his mind on it. I drove into the city with him last week. He stops at a green light and then it turns red and he goes. (*He laughs.*)

BIFF: Maybe he's color-blind.   210

HAPPY: Pop? Why he's got the finest eye for color in the business. You know that.

BIFF: (*Sitting down on his bed.*) I'm going to sleep.

HAPPY: You're not still sour on Dad, are you, Biff?

BIFF: He's all right, I guess.   215

WILLY: (*Underneath them, in the living-room.*) Yes, sir, eighty thousand miles—eighty-two thousand!

BIFF: You smoking?

HAPPY: (*Holding out a pack of cigarettes.*) Want one?

BIFF: (*Taking a cigarette.*) I can never sleep when I smell it.   220

WILLY: What a simonizing job, heh!

HAPPY: (*With deep sentiment.*) Funny, Biff, y'know? Us sleeping in here again? The old beds. (*He pats his bed affectionately.*) All the talk that went across those two beds, huh? Our whole lives.   225

BIFF: Yeah. Lotta dreams and plans.

HAPPY: (*With a deep and masculine laugh.*) About five hundred women would like to know what was said in this room.

(*They share a soft laugh.*)

BIFF: Remember that big Betsy something—what the hell was her name—over on Bushwick Avenue?   230

HAPPY: (*Combing his hair.*) With the collie dog!

BIFF: That's the one. I got you in there, remember?

HAPPY: Yeah, that was my first time—I think. Boy, there was a pig! (*They laugh, almost crudely.*) You taught me everything I know about women. Don't forget that.   235

BIFF: I bet you forgot how bashful you used to be. Especially with girls.

HAPPY: Oh, I still am, Biff.

BIFF: Oh, go on.

HAPPY: I just control it, that's all. I think I got less bashful and   240
you got more so. What happened, Biff? Where's the old humor, the old confidence? (*He shakes* BIFF's *knee.* BIFF *gets up and moves restlessly about the room.*) What's the matter?

BIFF: Why does Dad mock me all the time?

HAPPY: He's not mocking you, he—   245

BIFF: Everything I say there's a twist of mockery on his face. I can't get near him.

HAPPY: He just wants you to make good, that's all. I wanted to talk to you about Dad for a long time, Biff. Something's—happening to him. He—talks to himself.   250

BIFF: I noticed that this morning. But he always mumbled.

HAPPY: But not so noticeable. It got so embarrassing I sent him to Florida. And you know something? Most of the time he's talking to you.

BIFF: What's he say about me?   255

HAPPY: I can't make it out.

BIFF: What's he say about me?

HAPPY: I think the fact that you're not settled, that you're still kind of up in the air . . .

260 BIFF: There's one or two other things depressing him, Happy.

HAPPY: What do you mean?

BIFF: Never mind. Just don't lay it all to me.

HAPPY: But I think if you just got started—I mean—is there any future for you out there?

265 BIFF: I tell ya, Hap, I don't know what the future is. I don't know—what I'm supposed to want.

HAPPY: What do you mean?

BIFF: Well, I spent six or seven years after high school trying to work myself up. Shipping clerk, salesman, business of 270 one kind or another. And it's a measly manner of existence. To get on that subway on the hot mornings in summer. To devote your whole life to keeping stock, or making phone calls, or selling or buying. To suffer fifty weeks of the year for the sake of a two-week vacation, 275 when all you really desire is to be outdoors, with your shirt off. And always to have to get ahead of the next fella. And still—that's how you build a future.

HAPPY: Well, you really enjoy it on a farm? Are you content out there?

280 BIFF: (*With rising agitation.*) Hap, I've had twenty or thirty different kinds of jobs since I left home before the war, and it always turns out the same. I just realized it lately. In Nebraska when I herded cattle, and the Dakotas, and Arizona, and now in Texas. It's why I came home now, I 285 guess, because I realized it. This farm I work on, it's spring there now, see? And they've got about fifteen new colts. There's nothing more inspiring or—beautiful than the sight of a mare and a new colt. And it's cool there now, see? Texas is cool now, and it's spring. And whenever 290 spring comes to where I am, I suddenly get the feeling, my God, I'm not gettin' anywhere! What the hell am I doing, playing around with horses, twenty-eight dollars a week! I'm thirty-four years old, I oughta be makin' my future. That's when I come running home. And now, I get 295 here, and I don't know what to do with myself. (*After a pause.*) I've always made a point of not wasting my life, and everytime I come back here I know that all I've done is to waste my life.

HAPPY: You're a poet, you know that, Biff? You're a—you're 300 an idealist!

BIFF: No, I'm mixed up very bad. Maybe I oughta get married. Maybe I oughta get stuck into something. Maybe that's my trouble. I'm like a boy. I'm not married, I'm not in business, I just—I'm like a boy. Are you content, Hap? 305 You're a success, aren't you? Are you content?

HAPPY: Hell, no!

BIFF: Why? You're making money, aren't you?

HAPPY: (*Moving about with energy, expressiveness.*) All I can do now is wait for the merchandise manager to die. And sup310 pose I get to be merchandise manager? He's a good friend of mine, and he just built a terrific estate on Long Island. And he lived there about two months and sold it, and now he's building another one. He can't enjoy it once it's finished. And I know that's just what I would do. I don't 315 know what the hell I'm workin' for. Sometimes I sit in my apartment—all alone. And I think of the rent I'm paying. And it's crazy. But then, it's what I always wanted. My own

apartment, a car, and plenty of women. And still, goddammit, I'm lonely.

BIFF: (*With enthusiasm.*) Listen, why don't you come out West 320 with me?

HAPPY: You and I, heh?

BIFF: Sure, maybe we could buy a ranch. Raise cattle, use our muscles. Men built like we are should be working out in the open.   325

HAPPY: (*Avidly.*) The Loman Brothers, heh?

BIFF: (*With vast affection.*) Sure, we'd be known all over the counties!

HAPPY: (*Enthralled.*) That's what I dream about, Biff. Sometimes I want to just rip my clothes off in the middle of the 330 store and outbox that goddam merchandise manager. I mean I can outbox, outrun, and outlift anybody in that store, and I have to take orders from those common, petty sons-of-bitches till I can't stand it any more.

BIFF: I'm tellin' you, kid, if you were with me I'd be happy 335 out there.

HAPPY: (*Enthused.*) See, Biff, everybody around me is so false that I'm constantly lowering my ideals . . .

BIFF: Baby, together we'd stand up for one another, we'd have someone to trust.   340

HAPPY: If I were around you—

BIFF: Hap, the trouble is we weren't brought up to grub for money. I don't know how to do it.

HAPPY: Neither can I!

BIFF: Then let's go!   345

HAPPY: The only thing is—what can you make out there?

BIFF: But look at your friend. Builds an estate and then hasn't the peace of mind to live in it.

HAPPY: Yeah, but when he walks into the store the waves part in front of him. That's fifty-two thousand dollars a year 350 coming through the revolving door, and I got more in my pinky finger than he's got in his head.

BIFF: Yeah, but you just said—

HAPPY: I gotta show some of those pompous, self-important executives over there that Hap Loman can make the 355 grade. I want to walk into the store the way he walks in. Then I'll go with you, Biff. We'll be together yet, I swear. But take those two we had tonight. Now weren't they gorgeous creatures?

BIFF: Yeah, yeah, most gorgeous I've had in years.   360

HAPPY: I get that any time I want, Biff. Whenever I feel disgusted. The only trouble is, it gets like bowling or something. I just keep knockin' them over and it doesn't mean anything. You still run around a lot?

BIFF: Naa. I'd like to find a girl—steady, somebody with sub- 365 stance.

HAPPY: That's what I long for.

BIFF: Go on! You'd never come home.

HAPPY: I would! Somebody with character, with resistance! Like Mom, y'know? You're gonna call me a bastard when I 370 tell you this. That girl Charlotte I was with tonight is engaged to be married in five weeks. (*He tries on his new hat.*)

BIFF: No kiddin'!

HAPPY: Sure, the guy's in line for the vice-presidency of the store. I don't know what gets into me, maybe I just have 375 an overdeveloped sense of competition or something, but I went and ruined her, and furthermore I can't get rid of her. And he's the third executive I've done that

to. Isn't that a crummy characteristic? And to top it all,
380   I go to their weddings! (*Indignantly, but laughing.*) Like
I'm not supposed to take bribes. Manufacturers offer me
a hundred-dollar bill now and then to throw an order
their way. You know how honest I am, but it's like this
girl, see. I hate myself for it. Because I don't want the
385   girl, and, still, I take it and—I love it!

BIFF: Let's go to sleep.

HAPPY: I guess we didn't settle anything, heh?

BIFF: I just got one idea that I think I'm going to try.

HAPPY: What's that?

390   BIFF: Remember Bill Oliver?

HAPPY: Sure, Oliver is very big now. You want to work for
him again?

BIFF: No, but when I quit he said something to me. He put
his arm on my shoulder, and he said, "Biff, if you ever
395   need anything, come to me."

HAPPY: I remember that. That sounds good.

BIFF: I think I'll go to see him. If I could get ten thousand or
even seven or eight thousand dollars I could buy a beautiful ranch.

400   HAPPY: I bet he'd back you. 'Cause he thought highly of you,
Biff. I mean, they all do. You're well liked, Biff. That's why
I say to come back here, and we both have the apartment.
And I'm tellin' you, Biff, any babe you want . . .

BIFF: No, with a ranch I could do the work I like and still be
405   something. I just wonder though. I wonder if Oliver still
thinks I stole that carton of basketballs.

HAPPY: Oh, he probably forgot that long ago. It's almost ten
years. You're too sensitive. Anyway, he didn't really fire
you.

410   BIFF: Well, I think he was going to. I think that's why I quit.
I was never sure whether he knew or not. I know he
thought the world of me, though. I was the only one he'd
let lock up the place.

WILLY: (*Below.*) You gonna wash the engine, Biff?

415   HAPPY: Shh!

(BIFF *looks at* HAPPY, *who is gazing down, listening.* WILLY *is
mumbling in the parlor.*)

HAPPY: You hear that?

(*They listen.* WILLY *laughs warmly.*)

BIFF: (*Growing angry.*) Doesn't he know Mom can hear that?

WILLY: Don't get your sweater dirty, Biff!

(*A look of pain crosses* BIFF'*s face.*)

HAPPY: Isn't that terrible? Don't leave again, will you? You'll
420   find a job here. You gotta stick around. I don't know what
to do about him, it's getting embarrassing.

WILLY: What a simonizing job!

BIFF: Mom's hearing that!

WILLY: No kiddin', Biff, you got a date? Wonderful!

425   HAPPY: Go on to sleep. But talk to him in the morning, will
you?

BIFF: (*Reluctantly getting into bed.*) With her in the house.
Brother!

HAPPY: (*Getting into bed.*) I wish you'd have a good talk with
430   him.

(*The light on their room begins to fade.*)

BIFF: (*To himself in bed.*) That selfish, stupid . . .

HAPPY: Sh . . . Sleep, Biff.

(*Their light is out. Well before they have finished speaking,* WILLY'*s
form is dimly seen below in the darkened kitchen. He opens the refrigerator, searches in there, and takes out a bottle of milk. The apartment
houses are fading out, and the entire house and surroundings become
covered with leaves. Music insinuates itself as the leaves appear.*)

WILLY: Just wanna be careful with those girls, Biff, that's all.
Don't make any promises. No promises of any kind. Because a girl, y'know, they always believe what you tell 'em,   435
and you're very young, Biff, you're too young to be talking seriously to girls.

(*Light rises on the kitchen.* WILLY, *talking, shuts the refrigerator
door and comes downstage to the kitchen table. He pours milk into
a glass. He is totally immersed in himself, smiling faintly.*)

WILLY: Too young entirely, Biff. You want to watch your
schooling first. Then when you're all set, there'll be plenty
of girls for a boy like you. (*He smiles broadly at a kitchen   440
chair.*) That so? The girls pay for you? (*He laughs.*) Boy, you
must really be makin' a hit.

(WILLY *is gradually addressing—physically—a point offstage, speaking through the wall of the kitchen, and his voice has been rising in
volume to that of a normal conversation.*)

WILLY: I been wondering why you polish the car so careful.
Ha! Don't leave the hubcaps, boys. Get the chamois to the
hubcaps. Happy, use newspaper on the windows, it's the   445
easiest thing. Show him how to do it, Biff! You see,
Happy? Pad it up, use it like a pad. That's it, that's it, good
work. You're doin' all right, Hap. (*He pauses, then nods in
approbation for a few seconds, then looks upward.*) Biff, first
thing we gotta do when we get time is clip that big   450
branch over the house. Afraid it's gonna fall in a storm and
hit the roof. Tell you what. We get a rope and sling her
around, and then we climb up there with a couple of saws
and take her down. Soon as you finish the car, boys, I
wanna see ya. I got a surprise for you, boys.   455

BIFF: (*Offstage.*) Whatta ya got, Dad?

WILLY: No, you finish first. Never leave a job till you're finished—remember that. (*Looking toward the "big trees".*)
Biff, up in Albany I saw a beautiful hammock. I think I'll
buy it next trip, and we'll hang it right between those two   460
elms. Wouldn't that be something? Just swingin' there under those branches. Boy, that would be . . .

(*Young* BIFF *and* YOUNG HAPPY *appear from the direction* WILLY
was addressing. HAPPY *carries rags and a pail of water.* BIFF, *wearing a sweater with a block "S," carries a football.*)

BIFF: (*Pointing in the direction of the car offstage.*) How's that,
Pop, professional?

WILLY: Terrific. Terrific job, boys. Good work, Biff.   465

HAPPY: Where's the surprise, Pop?

WILLY: In the back seat of the car.

HAPPY: Boy! (*He runs off.*)

BIFF: What is it, Dad? Tell me, what'd you buy?

470 WILLY: (*Laughing, cuffs him.*) Never mind, something I want you to have.

BIFF: (*Turns and starts off.*) What is it, Hap?

HAPPY: (*Offstage.*) It's a punching bag!

BIFF: Oh, Pop!

475 WILLY: It's got Gene Tunney's signature on it!

(HAPPY *runs onstage with a punching bag.*)

BIFF: Gee, how'd you know we wanted a punching bag?

WILLY: Well, it's the finest thing for the timing.

HAPPY: (*Lies down on his back and pedals with his feet.*) I'm losing weight, you notice, Pop?

480 WILLY: (*To* HAPPY.) Jumping rope is good too.

BIFF: Did you see the new football I got?

WILLY: (*Examining the ball.*) Where'd you get a new ball?

BIFF: The coach told me to practice my passing.

WILLY: That so? And he gave you the ball, heh?

485 BIFF: Well, I borrowed it from the locker room. (*He laughs confidentially.*)

WILLY: (*Laughing with him at the theft.*) I want you to return that.

HAPPY: I told you he wouldn't like it!

490 BIFF: (*Angrily.*) Well, I'm bringing it back!

WILLY: (*Stopping the incipient argument, to* HAPPY.) Sure, he's gotta practice with a regulation ball, doesn't he? (*To* BIFF.) Coach'll probably congratulate you on your initiative!

BIFF: Oh, he keeps congratulating my initiative all the time,

495 Pop.

WILLY: That's because he likes you. If somebody else took that ball there'd be an uproar. So what's the report, boys, what's the report?

BIFF: Where'd you go this time, Dad? Gee we were lonesome

500 for you.

WILLY: (*Pleased, puts an arm around each boy and they come down to the apron.*) Lonesome, heh?

BIFF: Missed you every minute.

WILLY: Don't say? Tell you a secret, boys. Don't breathe it to

505 a soul. Someday I'll have my own business, and I'll never have to leave home any more.

HAPPY: Like Uncle Charley, heh?

WILLY: Bigger than Uncle Charley! Because Charley is not— liked. He's liked, but he's not—well liked.

510 BIFF: Where'd you go this time, Dad?

WILLY: Well, I got on the road, and I went north to Providence. Met the Mayor.

BIFF: The Mayor of Providence!

WILLY: He was sitting in the hotel lobby.

515 BIFF: What'd he say?

WILLY: He said, "Morning!" And I said, "You got a fine city here, Mayor." And then he had coffee with me. And then I went to Waterbury. Waterbury is a fine city. Big clock city, the famous Waterbury clock. Sold a nice bill there.

520 And then Boston—Boston is the cradle of the Revolution. A fine city. And a couple of other towns in Mass., and on to Portland and Bangor and straight home!

BIFF: Gee, I'd love to go with you sometime, Dad.

WILLY: Soon as summer comes.

525 HAPPY: Promise?

WILLY: You and Hap and I, and I'll show you all the towns. America is full of beautiful towns and fine, upstanding

people. And they know me, boys, they know me up and down New England. The finest people. And when I bring you fellas up, there'll be open sesame for all of us, 530 'cause one thing, boys: I have friends. I can park my car in any street in New England, and the cops protect it like their own. This summer, heh?

BIFF *and* HAPPY: (*Together.*) Yeah! You bet!

WILLY: We'll take our bathing suits.   535

HAPPY: We'll carry your bags, Pop!

WILLY: Oh, won't that be something! Me comin' into the Boston stores with you boys carryin' my bags. What a sensation!

(BIFF *is prancing around, practicing passing the ball.*)

WILLY: You nervous, Biff, about the game?   540

BIFF: Not if you're gonna be there.

WILLY: What do they say about you in school, now that they made you captain?

HAPPY: There's a crowd of girls behind him everytime the classes change.   545

BIFF: (*Taking* WILLY's *hand.*) This Saturday, Pop, this Saturday—just for you, I'm going to break through for a touchdown.

HAPPY: You're supposed to pass.

BIFF: I'm takin' one play for Pop. You watch me, Pop, and   550 when I take off my helmet, that means I'm breakin' out. Then you watch me crash through that line!

WILLY: (*Kisses* BIFF.) Oh, wait'll I tell this in Boston!

(BERNARD *enters in knickers. He is younger than* BIFF, *earnest and loyal, a worried boy.*)

BERNARD: Biff, where are you? You're supposed to study with me today.   555

WILLY: Hey, looka Bernard. What're you lookin' so anemic about, Bernard?

BERNARD: He's gotta study, Uncle Willy. He's got Regents next week.

HAPPY: (*Tauntingly, spinning* BERNARD *around.*) Let's box,   560 Bernard!

BERNARD: Biff! (*He gets away from* HAPPY.) Listen, Biff, I heard Mr. Birnbaum say that if you don't start studyin' math he's gonna flunk you, and you won't graduate. I heard him!

WILLY: You better study with him, Biff. Go ahead now.   565

BERNARD: I heard him!

BIFF: Oh, Pop, you didn't see my sneakers! (*He holds up a foot for* WILLY *to look at.*)

WILLY: Hey, that's a beautiful job of printing!

BERNARD: (*Wiping his glasses.*) Just because he printed Uni- 570 versity of Virginia on his sneakers doesn't mean they've got to graduate him, Uncle Willy!

WILLY: (*Angrily.*) What're you talking about? With scholarships to three universities they're gonna flunk him?

BERNARD: But I heard Mr. Birnbaum say—   575

WILLY: Don't be a pest, Bernard! (*To his boys.*) What an anemic!

BERNARD: Okay, I'm waiting for you in my house, Biff.

(BERNARD *goes off. The* LOMANS *laugh.*)

WILLY: Bernard is not well liked, is he?

BIFF: He's liked, but he's not well liked.

580 HAPPY: That's right, Pop.

WILLY: That's just what I mean. Bernard can get the best marks in school, y'understand, but when he gets out in the business world, y'understand, you are going to be five times ahead of him. That's why I thank Almighty God you're 585 both built like Adonises. Because the man who makes an appearance in the business world, the man who creates personal interest, is the man who gets ahead. Be liked and you will never want. You take me, for instance. I never have to wait in line to see a buyer. "Willy Loman is here!" That's all 590 they have to know, and I go right through.

BIFF: Did you knock them dead, Pop?

WILLY: Knocked 'em cold in Providence, slaughtered 'em in Boston.

HAPPY: (*On his back, pedaling again.*) I'm losing weight, you 595 notice, Pop?

(LINDA *enters, as of old, a ribbon in her hair, carrying a basket of washing.*)

LINDA: (*With youthful energy.*) Hello, dear!

WILLY: Sweetheart!

LINDA: How'd the Chevvy run?

WILLY: Chevrolet, Linda, is the greatest car ever built. (*To the* 600 *boys.*) Since when do you let your mother carry wash up the stairs?

BIFF: Grab hold there, boy!

HAPPY: Where to, Mom?

LINDA: Hang them up on the line. And you better go down 605 to your friends, Biff. The cellar is full of boys. They don't know what to do with themselves.

BIFF: Ah, when Pop comes home they can wait!

WILLY: (*Laughs appreciatively.*) You better go down and tell them what to do, Biff.

610 BIFF: I think I'll have them sweep out the furnace room.

WILLY: Good work, Biff.

BIFF: (*Goes through wall-line of kitchen to doorway at back and calls down.*) Fellas! Everybody sweep out the furnace room! I'll be right down!

615 VOICES: All right! Okay, Biff.

BIFF: George and Sam and Frank, come out back! We're hangin' up the wash! Come on, Hap, on the double! (*He and* HAPPY *carry out the basket.*)

LINDA: The way they obey him!

620 WILLY: Well, that's training, the training. I'm tellin' you, I was sellin' thousands and thousands, but I had to come home.

LINDA: Oh, the whole block'll be at that game. Did you sell anything?

WILLY: I did five hundred gross in Providence and seven hun-625 dred gross in Boston.

LINDA: No! Wait a minute, I've got a pencil. (*She pulls pencil and paper out of her apron pocket.*) That makes your commission . . . Two hundred—my God! Two hundred, and twelve dollars!

630 WILLY: Well, I didn't figure it yet, but . . .

LINDA: How much did you do?

WILLY: Well, I—I did—about a hundred and eighty gross in Providence. Well, no—it came to—roughly two hundred gross on the whole trip.

635 LINDA: (*Without hesitation.*) Two hundred gross. That's . . . (*She figures.*)

WILLY: The trouble was that three of the stores were half closed for inventory in Boston. Otherwise I woulda broke records.

LINDA: Well, it makes seventy dollars and some pennies. 640 That's very good.

WILLY: What do we owe?

LINDA: Well, on the first there's sixteen dollars on the refrigerator—

WILLY: Why sixteen? 645

LINDA: Well, the fan belt broke, so it was a dollar eighty.

WILLY: But it's brand new.

LINDA: Well, the man said that's the way it is. Till they work themselves in, y'know.

(*They move through the wall-line into the kitchen.*)

WILLY: I hope we didn't get stuck on that machine. 650

LINDA: They got the biggest ads of any of them!

WILLY: I know, it's a fine machine. What else?

LINDA: Well, there's nine-sixty for the washing machine. And for the vacuum cleaner there's three and a half due on the fifteenth. Then the roof, you got twenty-one dollars re-655 maining.

WILLY: It don't leak, does it?

LINDA: No, they did a wonderful job. Then you owe Frank for the carburetor.

WILLY: I'm not going to pay that man! That goddam Chevro-660 let, they ought to prohibit the manufacture of that car!

LINDA: Well, you owe him three and a half. And odds and ends, comes to around a hundred and twenty dollars by the fifteenth.

WILLY: A hundred and twenty dollars! My God, if business 665 don't pick up I don't know what I'm gonna do!

LINDA: Well, next week you'll do better.

WILLY: Oh, I'll knock 'em dead next week. I'll go to Hartford. I'm very well liked in Hartford. You know, the trouble is, Linda, people don't seem to take to me. 670

(*They move onto the forestage.*)

LINDA: Oh, don't be foolish.

WILLY: I know it when I walk in. They seem to laugh at me.

LINDA: Why? Why would they laugh at you? Don't talk that way, Willy.

(WILLY *moves to the edge of the stage.* LINDA *goes into the kitchen and starts to darn stockings.*)

WILLY: I don't know the reason for it, but they just pass me 675 by. I'm not noticed.

LINDA: But you're doing wonderful, dear. You're making seventy to a hundred dollars a week.

WILLY: But I gotta be at it ten, twelve hours a day. Other men—I don't know—they do it easier. I don't know 680 why—I can't stop myself—I talk too much. A man oughta come in with a few words. One thing about Charley. He's a man of few words, and they respect him.

LINDA: You don't talk too much, you're just lively.

WILLY: (*Smiling.*) Well, I figure, what the hell, life is short, a 685 couple of jokes (*To himself.*) I joke too much! (*The smile goes.*)

LINDA: Why? You're—

WILLY: I'm fat. I'm very—foolish to look at, Linda. I didn't tell
690   you, but Christmas time I happened to be calling on F. H.
         Stewarts, and a salesman I know, as I was going in to see the
         buyer I heard him say something about—walrus. And I—
         I cracked him right across the face. I won't take that. I sim-
         ply will not take that. But they do laugh at me. I know that.
695 LINDA: Darling . . .
WILLY: I gotta overcome it. I know I gotta overcome it. I'm
         not dressing to advantage, maybe.
LINDA: Willy, darling, you're the handsomest man in the
         world—
700 WILLY: Oh, no, Linda.
LINDA: To me you are. (*Slight pause.*) The handsomest.

(*From the darkness is heard the laughter of a woman.* WILLY *doesn't
turn to it, but it continues through* LINDA's *lines.*)

LINDA: And the boys, Willy. Few men are idolized by their
         children the way you are.

(*Music is heard as behind a scrim, to the left of the house,* THE
WOMAN, *dimly seen, is dressing.*)

WILLY: (*With great feeling.*) You're the best there is, Linda,
705   you're a pal, you know that? On the road—on the road I
         want to grab you sometimes and just kiss the life outa you.

(*The laughter is loud now, and he moves into a brightening area at
the left, where* THE WOMAN *has come from behind the scrim and is
standing, putting on her hat, looking into a "mirror" and laughing.*)

WILLY: 'Cause I get so lonely—especially when business is
         bad and there's nobody to talk to. I get the feeling that I'll
         never sell anything again, that I won't making a living for
710   you, or a business, a business for the boys. (*He talks through*
         THE WOMAN's *subsiding laughter;* THE WOMAN *primps at the
         "mirror."*) There's so much I want to make for—
THE WOMAN: Me? You didn't make me, Willy. I picked you.
WILLY: (*Pleased.*) You picked me?
715 THE WOMAN: (*Who is quite proper-looking,* WILLY's *age.*) I did.
         I've been sitting at that desk watching all the salesmen go
         by, day in, day out. But you've got such a sense of humor,
         and we do have such a good time together, don't we?
WILLY: Sure, sure. (*He takes her in his arms.*) Why do you have
720   to go now?
THE WOMAN: It's two o'clock . . .
WILLY: No, come on in! (*He pulls her.*)
THE WOMAN: . . . my sisters'll be scandalized. When'll you be
         back?
725 WILLY: Oh, two weeks about. Will you come up again?
THE WOMAN: Sure thing. You do make me laugh. It's good
         for me. (*She squeezes his arm, kisses him.*) And I think you're
         a wonderful man.
WILLY: You picked me, heh?
730 THE WOMAN: Sure. Because you're so sweet. And such a kidder.
WILLY: Well, I'll see you next time I'm in Boston.
THE WOMAN: I'll put you right through to the buyers.
WILLY: (*Slapping her bottom.*) Right. Well, bottoms up!
THE WOMAN: (*Slaps him gently and laughs.*) You just kill me,
735   Willy. (*He suddenly grabs her and kisses her roughly.*) You kill
         me. And thanks for the stockings. I love a lot of stockings.
         Well, good night.

WILLY: Good night. And keep your pores open!
THE WOMAN: Oh, Willy!

(THE WOMAN *bursts out laughing, and* LINDA's *laughter blends in.*
THE WOMAN *disappears into the dark. Now the area at the kitchen
table brightens.* LINDA *is sitting where she was at the kitchen table,
but now is mending a pair of her silk stockings.*)

LINDA: You are, Willy. The handsomest man. You've got no   740
         reason to feel that—
WILLY: (*Coming out of* THE WOMAN's *dimming area and going
         over to* LINDA.) I'll make it all up to you, Linda, I'll—
LINDA: There's nothing to make up, dear. You're doing fine,
         better than—   745
WILLY: (*Noticing her mending.*) What's that?
LINDA: Just mending my stockings. They're so expensive—
WILLY: (*Angrily, taking them from her.*) I won't have you mend-
         ing stockings in this house! Now throw them out!

(LINDA *puts the stockings in her pocket.*)

BERNARD: (*Entering on the run.*) Where is he? If he doesn't   750
         study!
WILLY: (*Moving to the forestage, with great agitation.*) You'll give
         him the answers!
BERNARD: I do, but I can't on a Regents! That's a state exam!
         They're liable to arrest me!   755
WILLY: Where is he? I'll whip him, I'll whip him!
LINDA: And he'd better give back that football, Willy, it's not
         nice.
WILLY: Biff! Where is he? Why is he taking everything?
LINDA: He's too rough with the girls, Willy. All the mothers   760
         are afraid of him!
WILLY: I'll whip him!
BERNARD: He's driving the car without a license!

(THE WOMAN's *laugh is heard.*)

WILLY: Shut up!
LINDA: All the mothers—   765
WILLY: Shut up!
BERNARD: (*Backing quietly away and out.*) Mr. Birnbaum says
         he's stuck up.
WILLY: Get outa here!
BERNARD: If he doesn't buckle down he'll flunk math! (*He   770
         goes off.*)
LINDA: He's right, Willy, you've gotta—
WILLY: (*Exploding at her.*) There's nothing the matter with
         him! You want him to be a worm like Bernard? He's got
         spirit, personality . . .   775

(*As he speaks,* LINDA, *almost in tears, exits into the living-room.*
WILLY *is alone in the kitchen, wilting and staring. The leaves are gone.
It is night again, and the apartment houses look down from behind.*)

WILLY: Loaded with it. Loaded! What is he stealing? He's giv-
         ing it back, isn't he? Why is he stealing? What did I tell him?
         I never in my life told him anything but decent things.

(HAPPY *in pajamas has come down the stairs;* WILLY *suddenly becomes aware of* HAPPY's *presence.*)

HAPPY: Let's go now, come on.

780 WILLY: (*Sitting down at the kitchen table.*) Huh! Why did she have to wax the floors herself? Everytime she waxes the floors she keels over. She knows that!

HAPPY: Shh! Take it easy. What brought you back tonight?

WILLY: I got an awful scare. Nearly hit a kid in Yonkers. God!
785   Why didn't I go to Alaska with my brother Ben that time! Ben! That man was a genius, that man was success incarnate! What a mistake! He begged me to go.

HAPPY: Well, there's no use in—

WILLY: You guys! There was a man started with the clothes on
790   his back and ended up with diamond mines!

HAPPY: Boy, someday I'd like to know how he did it.

WILLY: What's the mystery? The man knew what he wanted and went out and got it! Walked into a jungle, and comes out, the age of twenty-one, and he's rich! The world is an
795   oyster, but you don't crack it open on a mattress!

HAPPY: Pop, I told you I'm gonna retire you for life.

WILLY: You'll retire me for life on seventy goddam dollars a week? And your women and your car and your apartment, and you'll retire me for life! Christ's sake, I couldn't
800   get past Yonkers today! Where are you guys, where are you? The woods are burning! I can't drive a car!

(CHARLEY *has appeared in the doorway. He is a large man, slow of speech, laconic, immovable. In all he says, despite what he says, there is pity, and, now, trepidation. He has a robe over pajamas, slippers on his feet. He enters the kitchen.*)

CHARLEY: Everything all right?

HAPPY: Yeah, Charley, everything's . . .

WILLY: What's the matter?

805 CHARLEY: I heard some noise. I thought something happened. Can't we do something about the walls? You sneeze in here, and in my house hats blow off.

HAPPY: Let's go to bed, Dad. Come on.

(CHARLEY *signals to* HAPPY *to go.*)

WILLY: You go ahead, I'm not tired at the moment.

810 HAPPY: (*To* WILLY.) Take it easy, huh? (*He exits.*)

WILLY: What're you doin' up?.

CHARLEY: (*Sitting down at the kitchen table opposite* WILLY.) Couldn't sleep good. I had a heartburn.

WILLY: Well, you don't know how to eat.

815 CHARLEY: I eat with my mouth.

WILLY: No, you're ignorant. You gotta know about vitamins and things like that.

CHARLEY: Come on, let's shoot. Tire you out a little.

WILLY: (*Hesitantly.*) All right. You got cards?

820 CHARLEY: (*Taking a deck from his pocket.*) Yeah, I got them. Someplace. What is it with those vitamins?

WILLY: (*Dealing.*) They build up your bones. Chemistry.

CHARLEY: Yeah, but there's no bones in a heartburn.

WILLY: What are you talkin' about? Do you know the first
825   thing about it?

CHARLEY: Don't get insulted.

WILLY: Don't talk about something you don't know anything about.

(*They are playing. Pause.*)

CHARLEY: What're you doin' home?

WILLY: A little trouble with the car.   830

CHARLEY: Oh. (*Pause.*) I'd like to take a trip to California.

WILLY: Don't say.

CHARLEY: You want a job?

WILLY: I got a job, I told you that. (*After a slight pause.*) What the hell are you offering me a job for?   835

CHARLEY: Don't get insulted.

WILLY: Don't insult me.

CHARLEY: I don't see no sense in it. You don't have to go on this way.

WILLY: I got a good job. (*Slight pause.*) What do you keep   840 comin' in here for?

CHARLEY: You want me to go?

WILLY: (*After a pause, withering.*) I can't understand it. He's going back to Texas again. What the hell is that?

CHARLEY: Let him go.   845

WILLY: I got nothin' to give him, Charley, I'm clean, I'm clean.

CHARLEY: He won't starve. None a them starve. Forget about him.

WILLY: Then what have I got to remember?   850

CHARLEY: You take it too hard. To hell with it. When a deposit bottle is broken you don't get your nickel back.

WILLY: That's easy enough for you to say.

CHARLEY: That ain't easy for me to say.

WILLY: Did you see the ceiling I put up in the living-room?   855

CHARLEY: Yeah, that's a piece of work. To put up a ceiling is a mystery to me. How do you do it?

WILLY: What's the difference?

CHARLEY: Well, talk about it.

WILLY: You gonna put up a ceiling?   860

CHARLEY: How could I put up a ceiling?

WILLY: Then what the hell are you bothering me for?

CHARLEY: You're insulted again.

WILLY: A man who can't handle tools is not a man. You're disgusting.   865

CHARLEY: Don't call me disgusting, Willy.

(UNCLE BEN, *carrying a valise and an umbrella, enters the forestage from around the right corner of the house. He is a stolid man, in his sixties, with a mustache and an authoritative air. He is utterly certain of his destiny, and there is an aura of far places about him. He enters exactly as* WILLY *speaks.*)

WILLY: I'm getting awfully tired, Ben.

(BEN's *music is heard.* BEN *looks around at everything.*)

CHARLEY: Good, keep playing; you'll sleep better. Did you call me Ben?

(BEN *looks at his watch.*)

WILLY: That's funny. For a second there you reminded me of   870 my brother Ben.

BEN: I only have a few minutes. (*He strolls, inspecting the place.* WILLY *and* CHARLEY *continue playing.*)

CHARLEY: You never heard from him again, heh? Since that time?   875

WILLY: Didn't Linda tell you? Couple of weeks ago we got a letter from his wife in Africa. He died.

CHARLEY: That so.

BEN: (*Chuckling.*) So this is Brooklyn, eh?

880 CHARLEY: Maybe you're in for some of his money.

WILLY: Naa, he had seven sons. There's just one opportunity I had with that man . . .

BEN: I must make a train, William. There are several properties I'm looking at in Alaska.

885 WILLY: Sure, sure! If I'd gone with him to Alaska that time, everything would've been totally different.

CHARLEY: Go on, you'd froze to death up there.

WILLY: What're you talking about?

BEN: Opportunity is tremendous in Alaska, William. Surprised you're not up there.

890 WILLY: Sure, tremendous.

CHARLEY: Heh?

WILLY: There was the only man I ever met who knew the answers.

895 CHARLEY: Who?

BEN: How are you all?

WILLY: (*Taking a pot, smiling.*) Fine, fine.

CHARLEY: Pretty sharp tonight.

BEN: Is Mother living with you?

900 WILLY: No, she died a long time ago.

CHARLEY: Who?

BEN: That's too bad. Fine specimen of a lady, Mother.

WILLY: (*To* CHARLEY.) Heh?

BEN: I'd hoped to see the old girl.

905 CHARLEY: Who died?

BEN: Heard anything from Father, have you?

WILLY: (*Unnerved.*) What do you mean, who died?

CHARLEY: (*Taking a pot.*) What're you talkin' about?

BEN: (*Looking at his watch.*) William, it's half-past eight!

910 WILLY: (*As though to dispel his confusion he angrily stops* CHARLEY'S *hand.*) That's my build!

CHARLEY: I put the ace—

WILLY: If you don't know how to play the game I'm not gonna throw my money away on you!

915 CHARLEY: (*Rising.*) It was my ace, for God's sake!

WILLY: I'm through, I'm through!

BEN: When did Mother die?

WILLY: Long ago. Since the beginning you never knew how to play cards.

920 CHARLEY: (*Picks up the cards and goes to the door.*) All right! Next time I'll bring a deck with five aces.

WILLY: I don't play that kind of game!

CHARLEY: (*Turning to him.*) You ought to be ashamed of yourself!

925 WILLY: Yeah?

CHARLEY: Yeah! (*He goes out.*)

WILLY: (*Slamming the door after him.*) Ignoramus!

BEN: (*As* WILLY *comes toward him through the wall-line of the kitchen.*) So you're William.

930 WILLY: (*Shaking* BEN'S *hand.*) Ben! I've been waiting for you so long! What's the answer? How did you do it?

BEN: Oh, there's a story in that.

(LINDA *enters the forestage, as of old, carrying the wash basket.*)

LINDA: Is this Ben?

BEN: (*Gallantly.*) How do you do, my dear.

935 LINDA: Where've you been all these years? Willy's always wondered why you—

WILLY: (*Pulling* BEN *away from her impatiently.*) Where is Dad? Didn't you follow him? How did you get started?

BEN: Well, I don't know how much you remember.

WILLY: Well, I was just a baby, of course, only three or four 940 years old—

BEN: Three years and eleven months.

WILLY: What a memory, Ben!

BEN: I have many enterprises, William, and I have never kept 945 books.

WILLY: I remember I was sitting under the wagon in—was it Nebraska?

BEN: It was South Dakota, and I gave you a bunch of wildflowers.

WILLY: I remember you walking away down some open road. 950

BEN: (*Laughing.*) I was going to find Father in Alaska.

WILLY: Where is he?

BEN: At that age I had a very faulty view of geography, William. I discovered after a few days that I was heading due south, so instead of Alaska, I ended up in Africa. 955

LINDA: Africa!

WILLY: The Gold Coast!

BEN: Principally diamond mines.

LINDA: Diamond mines!

BEN: Yes, my dear. But I've only a few minutes— 960

WILLY: No! Boys! Boys! (YOUNG BIFF *and* HAPPY *appear.*) Listen to this. This is your Uncle Ben, a great man! Tell, my boys, Ben!

BEN: Why, boys, when I was seventeen I walked into the jungle, and when I was twenty-one I walked out. (*He laughs.*) 965 And by God I was rich.

WILLY: (*To the boys.*) You see what I been talking about? The greatest things can happen!

BEN: (*Glancing at his watch.*) I have an appointment in Ketchikan Tuesday week. 970

WILLY: No, Ben! Please tell about Dad. I want my boys to hear. I want them to know the kind of stock they spring from. All I remember is a man with a big beard, and I was in Mamma's lap, sitting around a fire, and some kind of high music. 975

BEN: His flute. He played the flute.

WILLY: Sure, the flute, that's right?

(*New music is heard, a high, rollicking tune.*)

BEN: Father was a very great and a very wild-hearted man. We would start in Boston, and he'd toss the whole family into the wagon, and then he'd drive the team right across 980 the country; through Ohio, and Indiana, Michigan, Illinois, and all the Western states. And we'd stop in the towns and sell the flutes that he'd made on the way. Great inventor, Father. With one gadget he made more in a week than a man like you could make in a lifetime. 985

WILLY: That's just the way I'm bringing them up, Ben— rugged, well liked, all-around.

BEN: Yeah? (*To* BIFF.) Hit that, boy—hard as you can. (*He pounds his stomach.*)

BIFF: Oh, no, sir! 990

BEN: (*Taking boxing stance.*) Come on, get to me! (*He laughs.*)

WILLY: Go to it, Biff! Go ahead, show him!

BIFF: Okay! (*He cocks his fists and starts in.*)

LINDA: (*To* WILLY.) Why must he fight, dear?

995 BEN: (*Sparring with* BIFF.) Good boy! Good boy!
WILLY: How's that, Ben, heh?
HAPPY: Give him the left, Biff!
LINDA: Why are you fighting?
BEN: Good boy! (*Suddenly comes in, trips* BIFF, *and stands over*
1000 *him, the point of his umbrella poised over* BIFF's *eye.*)
LINDA: Look out, Biff!
BIFF: Gee!
BEN: (*Patting* BIFF's *knee.*) Never fight fair with a stranger, boy.
You'll never get out of the jungle that way. (*Taking* LINDA's
1005 *hand and bowing.*) It was an honor and a pleasure to meet
you, Linda.
LINDA: (*Withdrawing her hand coldly, frightened.*) Have a nice—
trip.
BEN: (*To* WILLY.) And good luck with your—what do you do?
1010 WILLY: Selling.
BEN: Yes. Well . . . (*He raises his hand in farewell to all.*)
WILLY: No, Ben, I don't want you to think . . . (*He takes* BEN's
arm to show him.) It's Brooklyn, I know, but we hunt too.
BEN: Really, now.
1015 WILLY: Oh, sure, there's snakes and rabbits and—that's why I
moved out here. Why, Biff can fell any one of these trees
in no time! Boys! Go right over to where they're building
the apartment house and get some sand. We're gonna rebuild the entire front stoop right now! Watch this Ben!
1020 BIFF: Yes, sir! On the double, Hap!
HAPPY: (*As he and* BIFF *run off.*) I lost weight, Pop, you notice?

(CHARLEY *enters in knickers, even before the boys are gone.*)

CHARLEY: Listen, if they steal any more from that building
the watchman'll put the cops on them!
LINDA: (*To* WILLY.) Don't let Biff . . .

(BEN *laughs lustily.*)

1025 WILLY: You shoulda seen the lumber they brought home last
week. At least a dozen six-by-tens worth all kinds a
money.
CHARLEY: Listen, if that watchman—
WILLY: I gave them hell, understand. But I got a couple of
1030 fearless characters there.
CHARLEY: Willy, the jails are full of fearless characters.
BEN: (*Clapping* WILLY *on the back, with a laugh at* CHARLEY.)
And the stock exchange, friend!
WILLY: (*Joining in* BEN's *laughter.*) Where are the rest of your
1035 pants?
CHARLEY: My wife bought them.
WILLY: Now all you need is a golf club and you can go up-
stairs and go to sleep. (*To* BEN.) Great athlete! Between
him and his son Bernard they can't hammer a nail!
1040 BERNARD: (*Rushing in.*) The watchman's chasing Biff!
WILLY: (*Angrily.*) Shut up! He's not stealing anything!
LINDA: (*Alarmed, hurrying off left.*) Where is he? Biff, dear! (*She
exits.*)
WILLY: (*Moving toward the left, away from* BEN.) There's noth-
1045 ing wrong. What's the matter with you?
BEN: Nervy boy. Good!
WILLY: (*Laughing.*) Oh, nerves of iron, that Biff!
CHARLEY: Don't know what it is. My New England man
comes back and he's bleedin', they murdered him up there.
1050 WILLY: It's contacts, Charley, I got important contacts!

CHARLEY: (*Sarcastically.*) Glad to hear it, Willy. Come in later,
we'll shoot a little casino. I'll take some of your Portland
money. (*He laughs at* WILLY *and exits.*)
WILLY: (*Turning to* BEN.) Business is bad, it's murderous. But
not for me, of course. 1055
BEN: I'll stop by on my way back to Africa.
WILLY: (*Longingly.*) Can't you stay a few days? You're just what
I need, Ben, because I—I have a fine position here, but
I—well, Dad left when I was such a baby and I never had
a chance to talk to him and I still feel—kind of temporary 1060
about myself.
BEN: I'll be late for my train.

(*They are at opposite ends of the stage.*)

WILLY: Ben, my boys—can't we talk? They'd go into the jaws
of hell for me, see, but I—
BEN: William, you're being first-rate with your boys. Out- 1065
standing, manly chaps!
WILLY: (*Hanging on to his words.*) Oh, Ben, that's good to hear!
Because sometimes I'm afraid that I'm not teaching them
the right kind of—Ben, how should I teach them?
BEN: (*Giving great weight to each word, and with a certain vicious* 1070
audacity.) William, when I walked into the jungle, I was
seventeen. When I walked out I was twenty-one. And, by
God, I was rich! (*He goes off into the darkness around the right
corner of the house.*)
WILLY: . . . was rich! That's just the spirit I want to imbue 1075
them with! To walk into a jungle! I was right! I was right!
I was right!

(BEN *is gone, but* WILLY *is still speaking to him as* LINDA, *in nightgown and robe, enters the kitchen, glances around for* WILLY, *then
goes to the door of the house, looks out and sees him. Comes down
to his left. He looks at her.*)

LINDA: Willy, dear? Willy?
WILLY: I was right!
LINDA: Did you have some cheese? (*He can't answer.*) It's very 1080
late, darling. Come to bed, heh?
WILLY: (*Looking straight up.*) Gotta break your neck to see a
star in this yard.
LINDA: You coming in?
WILLY: Whatever happened to that diamond watch fob? Re- 1085
member? When Ben came from Africa that time? Didn't
he give me a watch fob with a diamond in it?
LINDA: You pawned it, dear. Twelve, thirteen years ago. For
Biff's radio correspondence course.
WILLY: Gee, that was a beautiful thing. I'll take a walk. 1090
LINDA: But you're in your slippers.
WILLY: (*Starting to go around the house at the left.*) I was right! I
was! (*Half to* LINDA, *as he goes, shaking his head.*) What a
man! There was a man worth talking to. I was right!
LINDA: (*Calling after* WILLY.) But in your slippers, Willy! 1095

(WILLY *is almost gone when* BIFF, *in his pajamas, comes down the
stairs an enters the kitchen.*)

BIFF: What is he doing out there?
LINDA: Sh!
BIFF: God Almighty, Mom, how long has he been doing this?
LINDA: Don't, he'll hear you.

1100 BIFF: What the hell is the matter with him?

LINDA: It'll pass by morning.

BIFF: Shouldn't we do anything?

LINDA: Oh, my dear, you should do a lot of things, but there's nothing to do, so go to sleep.

(HAPPY *comes down the stair and sits on the steps.*)

1105 HAPPY: I never heard him so loud, Mom.

LINDA: Well, come around more often; you'll hear him. (*She sits down at the table and mends the lining of* WILLY'*s jacket.*)

BIFF: Why didn't you ever write me about this, Mom?

LINDA: How would I write to you? For over three months 1110 you had no address.

BIFF: I was on the move. But you know I thought of you all the time. You know that, don't you, pal?

LINDA: I know, dear, I know. But he likes to have a letter. Just to know that there's still a possibility for better things.

1115 BIFF: He's not like this all the time, is he?

LINDA: It's when you come home he's always the worst.

BIFF: When I come home?

LINDA: When you write you're coming, he's all smiles, and talks about the future, and—he's just wonderful. And then 1120 the closer you seem to come, the more shaky he gets, and then, by the time you get here, he's arguing, and he seems angry at you. I think it's just that maybe he can't bring himself to—to open up to you. Why are you so hateful to each other? Why is that?

1125 BIFF: (*Evasively.*) I'm not hateful, Mom.

LINDA: But you no sooner come in the door than you're fighting!

BIFF: I don't know why. I mean to change. I'm tryin', Mom, you understand?

1130 LINDA: Are you home to stay now?

BIFF: I don't know. I want to look around, see what's doin'.

LINDA: Biff, you can't look around all your life, can you?

BIFF: I just can't take hold, Mom. I can't take hold of some kind of a life.

1135 LINDA: Biff, a man is not a bird, to come and go with the springtime.

BIFF: Your hair . . . (*He touches her hair.*) Your hair got so gray.

LINDA: Oh, it's been gray since you were in high school. I just stopped dyeing it, that's all.

1140 BIFF: Dye it again, will ya? I don't want my pal looking old. (*He smiles.*)

LINDA: You're such a boy! You think you can go away for a year and . . . You've got to get it into your head now that one day you'll knock on this door and there'll be strange 1145 people here—

BIFF: What are you talking about? You're not even sixty, Mom.

LINDA: But what about your father?

BIFF: (*Lamely.*) Well, I meant him too.

1150 HAPPY: He admires Pop.

LINDA: Biff, dear, if you don't have any feeling for him, then you can't have any feeling for me.

BIFF: Sure I can, Mom.

LINDA: No. You can't just come to see me, because I love 1155 him. (*With a threat, but only a threat, of tears.*) He's the dearest man in the world to me, and I won't have anyone making him feel unwanted and low and blue. You've got to make up your mind now, darling, there's no leeway any more. Either he's your father and you pay him that respect, or else you're not to come here. I know he's not easy 1160 to get along with—nobody knows that better than me—but . . .

WILLY: (*From the left, with a laugh.*) Hey, hey, Biffo!

BIFF: (*Starting to go out after* WILLY.) What the hell is the matter with him? (HAPPY *stops him.*) 1165

LINDA: Don't—don't go near him!

BIFF: Stop making excuses for him! He always, always wiped the floor with you. Never had an ounce of respect for you.

HAPPY: He's always had respect for— 1170

BIFF: What the hell do you know about it?

HAPPY: (*Surlily.*) Just don't call him crazy!

BIFF: He's got no character—Charley wouldn't do this. Not in his own house—spewing out that vomit from his mind.

HAPPY: Charley never had to cope with what he's got to. 1175

BIFF: People are worse off than Willy Loman. Believe me, I've seen them!

LINDA: Then make Charley your father, Biff. You can't do that, can you? I don't say he's a great man. Willy Loman never made a lot of money. His name was never in the pa- 1180 per. He's not the finest character that ever lived. But he's a human being, and a terrible thing is happening to him. So attention must be paid. He's not to be allowed to fall into his grave like an old dog. Attention, attention must finally be paid to such a person. You called him crazy— 1185

BIFF: I didn't mean—

LINDA: No, a lot of people think he's lost his—balance. But you don't have to be very smart to know what his trouble is. The man is exhausted.

HAPPY: Sure! 1190

LINDA: A small man can be just as exhausted as a great man. He works for a company thirty-six years this March, opens up unheard-of territories to their trademark, and now in his old age they take his salary away.

HAPPY: (*Indignantly.*) I didn't know that, Mom. 1195

LINDA: You never asked, my dear! Now that you get your spending money someplace else you don't trouble your mind with him.

HAPPY: But I gave you money last—

LINDA: Christmas time, fifty dollars! To fix the hot water it 1200 cost ninety-seven fifty! For five weeks he's been on straight commission, like a beginner, an unknown!

BIFF: Those ungrateful bastards!

LINDA: Are they any worse than his sons? When he brought them business, when he was young, they were glad to see 1205 him. But now his old friends, the old buyers that loved him so and always found some order to hand him in a pinch—they're all dead, retired. He used to be able to make six, seven calls a day in Boston. Now he takes his valises out of the car and puts them back and takes them out again and 1210 he's exhausted. Instead of walking he talks now. He drives seven hundred miles, and when he gets there no one knows him any more, no one welcomes him. And what goes through a man's mind, driving seven hundred miles home without having earned a cent? Why shouldn't he talk to 1215 himself? Why? When he has to go to Charley and borrow fifty dollars a week and pretend to me that it's his pay? How long can that go on? How long? You see what I'm sitting

1220 here and waiting for? And you tell me he has no character? The man who never worked a day but for your benefit? When does he get the medal for that? Is this his reward—to turn around at the age of sixty-three and find his sons, who he loved better than his life, one a philandering bum—

HAPPY: Mom!

1225 LINDA: That's all you are, my baby! (*To* BIFF.) And you! What happened to the love you had for him? You were such pals! How you used to talk to him on the phone every night! How lonely he was till he could come home to you!

BIFF: All right, Mom. I'll live here in my room, and I'll get a

1230 job. I'll keep away from him, that's all.

LINDA: No, Biff. You can't stay here and fight all the time.

BIFF: He threw me out of this house, remember that.

LINDA: Why did he do that? I never knew why.

BIFF: Because I know he's a fake and he doesn't like anybody

1235 around who knows!

LINDA: Why a fake? In what way? What do you mean?

BIFF: Just don't lay it all at my feet. It's between me and him— that's all I have to say. I'll chip in from now on. He'll settle for half my pay check. He'll be all right. I'm going to

1240 bed. (*He starts for the stairs.*)

LINDA: He won't be all right.

BIFF: (*Turning on the stairs, furiously.*) I hate this city and I'll stay here. Now what do you want?

LINDA: He's dying, Biff.

(HAPPY *turns quickly to her, shocked.*)

1245 BIFF: (*After a pause.*) Why is he dying?

LINDA: He's been trying to kill himself.

BIFF: (*With great horror.*) How?

LINDA: I live from day to day.

BIFF: What're you talking about?

1250 LINDA: Remember I wrote you that he smashed up the car again? In February?

BIFF: Well?

LINDA: The insurance inspector came. He said that they have evidence. That all these accidents in the last year—

1255 weren't—weren't—accidents.

HAPPY: How can they tell that? That's a lie.

LINDA: It seems there's a woman . . . (*She takes a breath as*

⎰ BIFF: (*Sharply but contained.*) What woman?

⎱ LINDA: (*Simultaneously.*) . . . and this woman . . .

1260 LINDA: What?

BIFF: Nothing. Go ahead.

LINDA: What did you say?

BIFF: Nothing. I just said what woman?

HAPPY: What about her?

1265 LINDA: Well, it seems she was walking down the road and saw his car. She says that he wasn't driving fast at all, and that he didn't skid. She says he came to that little bridge, and then deliberately smashed into the railing, and it was only the shallowness of the water that saved him.

1270 BIFF: Oh, no, he probably just fell asleep again.

LINDA: I don't think he fell asleep.

BIFF: Why not?

LINDA: Last month . . . (*With great difficulty.*) Oh, boys, it's so hard to say a thing like this! He's just a big stupid man to

1275 you, but I tell you there's more good in him than in many other people. (*She chokes, wipes her eyes.*) I was looking for

a fuse. The lights blew out, and I went down the cellar. And behind the fuse box—it happened to fall out—was a length of rubber pipe—just short.

1280 HAPPY: No kidding?

LINDA: There's a little attachment on the end of it. I knew right away. And sure enough, on the bottom of the water heater there's a new little nipple on the gas pipe.

HAPPY: (*Angrily.*) That—jerk.

1285 BIFF: Did you have it taken off?

LINDA: I'm—I'm ashamed to. How can I mention it to him? Every day I go down and take away that little rubber pipe. But, when he comes home, I put it back where it was. How can I insult him that way? I don't know what to do.

1290 I live from day to day, boys. I tell you, I know every thought in his mind. It sounds so old-fashioned and silly, but I tell you he put his whole life into you and you've turned your backs on him. (*She is bent over in the chair, weeping, her face in her hands.*) Biff, I swear to God! Biff, his

1295 life is in your hands!

HAPPY: (*To* BIFF.) How do you like that damned fool!

BIFF: (*Kissing her.*) All right, pal, all right. It's all settled now. I've been remiss. I know that, Mom. But now I'll stay, and I swear to you, I'll apply myself. (*Kneeling in front of her, in a fever of self-reproach.*) It's just—you see, Mom, I don't fit in

1300 business. Not that I won't try. I'll try, and I'll make good.

HAPPY: Sure you will. The trouble with you in business was you never tried to please people.

BIFF: I know, I—

HAPPY: Like when you worked for Harrison's. Bob Harrison

1305 said you were tops, and then you go and do some damn fool thing like whistling whole songs in the elevator like a comedian.

BIFF: (*Against* HAPPY.) So what? I like to whistle sometimes.

HAPPY: You don't raise a guy to a responsible job who whis-

1310 tles in the elevator!

LINDA: Well, don't argue about it now.

HAPPY: Like when you'd go off and swim in the middle of the day instead of taking the line around.

BIFF: (*His resentment rising.*) Well, don't you run off? You take

1315 off sometimes, don't you? On a nice summer day?

HAPPY: Yeah, but I cover myself!

LINDA: Boys!

HAPPY: If I'm going to take a fade the boss can call any number where I'm supposed to be and they'll swear to him

1320 that I just left. I'll tell you something that I hate to say, Biff, but in the business world some of them think you're crazy.

BIFF: (*Angered.*) Screw the business world!

HAPPY: All right, screw it! Great, but cover yourself!

LINDA: Hap, Hap!

1325 BIFF: I don't care what they think! They've laughed at Dad for years, and you know why? Because we don't belong in this nuthouse of a city! We should be mixing cement on some open plain, or—or carpenters. A carpenter is allowed to whistle!

1330

(WILLY *walks in from the entrance of the house, at left.*)

WILLY: Even your grandfather was better than a carpenter. (*Pause. They watch him.*) You never grew up. Bernard does not whistle in the elevator, I assure you.

BIFF: (*As though to laugh* WILLY *out of it.*) Yeah, but you do, Pop.

1335 WILLY: I never in my life whistled in an elevator! And who in the business world thinks I'm crazy?

BIFF: I didn't mean it like that, Pop. Now don't make a whole thing out of it, will ya?

WILLY: Go back to the West! Be a carpenter, a cowboy, enjoy
1340 yourself!

LINDA: Willy, he was just saying—

WILLY: I heard what he said!

HAPPY: (*Trying to quiet* WILLY.) Hey, Pop, come on now . . .

WILLY: (*Continuing over* HAPPY'*s line.*) They laugh at me, heh?
1345 Go to Filene's, go to the Hub, go to Slattery's, Boston. Call out the name Willy Loman and see what happens! Big shot!

BIFF: All right, Pop.

WILLY: Big!
1350 BIFF: All right!

WILLY: Why do you always insult me?

BIFF: I didn't say a word. (*To* LINDA.) Did I say a word?

LINDA: He didn't say anything, Willy.

WILLY: (*Going to the doorway of the living-room.*) All right, good
1355 night, good night.

LINDA: Willy, dear, he just decided . . .

WILLY: (*To* BIFF.) If you get tired hanging around tomorrow, paint the ceiling I put up in the living-room.

BIFF: I'm leaving early tomorrow.
1360 HAPPY: He's going to see Bill Oliver, Pop.

WILLY: (*Interestedly.*) Oliver? For what?

BIFF: (*With reserve, but trying, trying.*) He always said he'd stake me. I'd like to go into business, so maybe I can take him up on it.
1365 LINDA: Isn't that wonderful?

WILLY: Don't interrupt. What's wonderful about it? There's fifty men in the City of New York who'd stake him. (*To* BIFF.) Sporting goods?

BIFF: I guess so. I know something about it and—
1370 WILLY: He knows something about it! You know sporting goods better than Spalding, for God's sake! How much he giving you?

BIFF: I don't know, I didn't even see him yet, but—

WILLY: Then what're you talkin' about?
1375 BIFF: (*Getting angry.*) Well, all I said was I'm gonna see him, that's all!

WILLY: (*Turning away.*) Ah, you're counting your chickens again.

BIFF: (*Starting left for the stairs.*) Oh, Jesus, I'm going to sleep!
1380 WILLY: (*Calling after him.*) Don't curse in this house!

BIFF: (*Turning.*) Since when did you get so clean?

HAPPY: (*Trying to stop them.*) Wait a . . .

WILLY: Don't use that language to me! I won't have it!

HAPPY: (*Grabbing* BIFF, *shouts.*) Wait a minute! I got an idea. I
1385 got a feasible idea. Come here, Biff, let's talk this over now, let's talk some sense here. When I was down in Florida last time, I thought of a great idea to sell sporting goods. It just came back to me. You and I, Biff—we have a line, the Loman Line. We train a couple of weeks, and put on
1390 a couple of exhibitions, see?

WILLY: That's an idea!

HAPPY: Wait! We form two basketball teams, see? Two water-polo teams. We play each other. It's a million dollars' worth of publicity. Two brothers, see? The Loman Broth-
1395 ers. Displays in the Royal Palms—all the hotels. And ban-

ners over the ring and the basketball court: "Loman Brothers." Baby, we could sell sporting goods!

WILLY: That is a one-million-dollar idea!

LINDA: Marvelous!

BIFF: I'm in great shape as far as that's concerned.   1400

HAPPY: And the beauty of it is, Biff, it wouldn't be like a business. We'd be out playin' ball again.

BIFF: (*Enthused.*) Yeah, that's . . .

WILLY: Million-dollar . . .

HAPPY: And you wouldn't get fed up with it, Biff. It'd be the   1405
family again. There'd be the old honor, and comradeship, and if you wanted to go off for a swim or somethin'—well, you'd do it! Without some smart cooky gettin' up ahead of you!

WILLY: Lick the world! You guys together could absolutely   1410
lick the civilized world.

BIFF: I'll see Oliver tomorrow. Hap, if we could work that out . . .

LINDA: Maybe things are beginning to—

WILLY: (*Wildly enthused, to* LINDA.) Stop interrupting! (*To* BIFF.)   1415
But don't wear sport jacket and slacks when you see Oliver.

BIFF: No, I'll—

WILLY: A business suit, and talk as little as possible, and don't crack any jokes.

BIFF: He did like me. Always liked me.   1420

LINDA: He loved you!

WILLY: (*To* LINDA.) Will you stop! (*To* BIFF.) Walk in very serious. You are not applying for a boy's job. Money is to pass. Be quiet, fine, and serious. Everybody likes a kidder, but nobody lends him money.   1425

HAPPY: I'll try to get some myself, Biff. I'm sure I can.

WILLY: I see great things for you kids, I think your troubles are over. But remember, start big and you'll end big. Ask for fifteen. How much you gonna ask for?

BIFF: Gee, I don't know—   1430

WILLY: And don't say "Gee." "Gee" is a boy's word. A man walking in for fifteen thousand dollars does not say "Gee!"

BIFF: Ten, I think, would be top though.

WILLY: Don't be so modest. You always started too low. Walk in with a big laugh. Don't look worried. Start off with a   1435
couple of your good stories to lighten things up. It's not what you say, it's how you say it—because personality always wins the day.

LINDA: Oliver always thought the highest of him—

WILLY: Will you let me talk?   1440

BIFF: Don't yell at her, Pop, will ya?

WILLY: (*Angrily.*) I was talking, wasn't I?

BIFF: I don't like you yelling at her all the time, and I'm tellin' you, that's all.

WILLY: What're you, takin' over this house?   1445

LINDA: Willy—

WILLY: (*Turning on her.*) Don't take his side all the time, goddammit!

BIFF: (*Furiously.*) Stop yelling at her!

WILLY: (*Suddenly pulling on his cheek, beaten down, guilt ridden.*)   1450
Give my best to Bill Oliver—he may remember me. (*He exits through the living-room doorway.*)

LINDA: (*Her voice subdued.*) What'd you have to start that for? (BIFF *turns away.*) You see how sweet he was as soon as you talked hopefully? (*She goes over to* BIFF.) Come up and say   1455
good night to him. Don't let him go to bed that way.

HAPPY: Come on, Biff, let's buck him up.

LINDA: Please, dear. Just say good night. It takes so little to make him happy. Come. (*She goes through the living-room* 1460 *doorway, calling upstairs from within the living-room.*) Your pajamas are hanging in the bathroom, Willy!

HAPPY: (*Looking toward where* LINDA *went out.*) What a woman! They broke the mold when they made her. You know that, Biff?

1465 BIFF: He's off salary. My God, working on commission!

HAPPY: Well, let's face it: he's no hot-shot selling man. Except that sometimes, you have to admit, he's a sweet personality.

BIFF: (*Deciding.*) Lend me ten bucks, will ya? I want to buy some new ties.

1470 HAPPY: I'll take you to a place I know. Beautiful stuff. Wear one of my striped shirts tomorrow.

BIFF: She got gray. Mom got awful old. Gee, I'm gonna go in to Oliver tomorrow and knock him for a—

HAPPY: Come on up. Tell that to Dad. Let's give him a whirl. 1475 Come on.

BIFF: (*Steamed up.*) You know, with ten thousand bucks, boy!

HAPPY: (*As they go into the living-room.*) That's the talk, Biff, that's the first time I've heard the old confidence out of you! (*From within the living-room, fading off.*) You gonna live 1480 with me, kid, and any babe you want just say the word . . . (*The last lines are hardly heard. They are mounting the stairs to their parents' bedroom.*)

LINDA: (*Entering her bedroom and addressing* WILLY, *who is in the bathroom. She is straightening the bed for him.*) Can you do 1485 anything about the shower? It drips.

WILLY: (*From the bathroom.*) All of a sudden everything falls to pieces! Goddam plumbing, oughta be sued, those people. I hardly finished putting it in and the thing . . . (*His words rumble off.*)

1490 LINDA: I'm just wondering if Oliver will remember him. You think he might?

WILLY: (*Coming out of the bathroom in his pajamas.*) Remember him? What's the matter with you, you crazy? If he'd've stayed with Oliver he'd be on top by now! Wait'll Oliver 1495 gets a look at him. You don't know the average caliber any more. The average young man today—(*He is getting into bed.*)—is got a caliber of zero. Greatest thing in the world for him was to bum around.

(BIFF *and* HAPPY *enter the bedroom. Slight pause.*)

WILLY: (*Stops short, looking at* BIFF.) Glad to hear it, boy. 1500 HAPPY: He wanted to say good night to you, sport.

WILLY: (*To* BIFF.) Yeah. Knock him dead, boy. What'd you want to tell me?

BIFF: Just take it easy, Pop. Good night. (*He turns to go.*)

WILLY: (*Unable to resist.*) And if anything falls off the desk while 1505 you're talking to him—like a package or something— don't you pick it up. They have office boys for that.

LINDA: I'll make a big breakfast—

WILLY: Will you let me finish? (*To* BIFF.) Tell him you were in the business in the West. Not farm work.

1510 BIFF: All right, Dad.

LINDA: I think everything—

WILLY: (*Going right through her speech.*) And don't undersell yourself. No less than fifteen thousand dollars.

BIFF: (*Unable to bear him.*) Okay. Good night, Mom. (*He starts moving.*) 1515

WILLY: Because you got a greatness in you, Biff, remember that. You got all kinds a greatness . . . (*He lies back, exhausted.* BIFF *walks out.*)

LINDA: (*Calling after* BIFF.) Sleep well, darling!

HAPPY: I'm gonna get married, Mom. I wanted to tell you. 1520

LINDA: Go to sleep, dear.

HAPPY: (*Going.*) I just wanted to tell you.

WILLY: Keep up the good work. (HAPPY *exits.*) God . . . remember that Ebbets Field game? The championship of the city? 1525

LINDA: Just rest. Should I sing to you?

WILLY: Yeah. Sing to me. (LINDA *hums a soft lullaby.*) When that team came out—he was the tallest, remember?

LINDA: Oh, yes. And in gold.

(BIFF *enters the darkened kitchen, takes a cigarette, and leaves the house. He comes downstage into a golden pool of light. He smokes, staring at the night.*)

WILLY: Like a young god. Hercules—something like that. 1530 And the sun, the sun all around him. Remember how he waved to me? Right up from the field, with the representatives of three colleges standing by? And the buyers I brought, and the cheers when he came out—Loman, Loman, Loman! God Almighty, he'll be great yet. A star like 1535 that, magnificent, can never really fade away!

(*The light on* WILLY *is fading. The gas heater begins to glow through the kitchen wall, near the stairs, a blue flame beneath red coils.*)

LINDA: (*Timidly.*) Willy dear, what has he got against you?

WILLY: I'm so tired. Don't talk any more.

(BIFF *slowly returns to the kitchen. He stops, stares toward the heater.*)

LINDA: Will you ask Howard to let you work in New York?

WILLY: First thing in the morning. Everything'll be all right. 1540

(BIFF *reaches behind the heater and draws out a length of rubber tubing. He is horrified and turns his head toward* WILLY's *room, still dimly lit, from which the strains of* LINDA's *desperate but monotonous humming rise.*)

WILLY: (*Staring through the window into the moonlight.*) Gee, look at the moon moving between the buildings!

(BIFF *wraps the tubing around his hand and quickly goes up the stairs.*)

(*Curtain.*)

ACT TWO

Music is heard, gay and bright. The curtain rises as the music fades away. WILLY, *in shirt sleeves, is sitting at the kitchen table, sipping coffee, his hat in his lap.* LINDA *is filling his cup when she can.*

WILLY: Wonderful coffee. Meal in itself.

LINDA: Can I make you some eggs?

WILLY: No. Take a breath.

LINDA: You look so rested, dear.

5 WILLY: I slept like a dead one. First time in months. Image, sleeping till ten on a Tuesday morning. Boys left nice and early, heh?

LINDA: They were out of here by eight o'clock.

WILLY: Good work!

10 LINDA: It was so thrilling to see them leaving together. I can't get over the shaving lotion in this house!

WILLY: (*Smiling.*) Mmm—

LINDA: Biff was very changed this morning. His whole attitude seemed to be hopeful. He couldn't wait to get down-

15 town to see Oliver.

WILLY: He's heading for a change. There's no question, there simply are certain men that take longer to get—solidified. How did he dress?

LINDA: His blue suit. He's so handsome in that suit. He could

20 be a—anything in that suit!

(WILLY *gets up from the table.* LINDA *holds his jacket for him.*)

WILLY: There's no question, no question at all. Gee, on the way home tonight I'd like to buy some seeds.

LINDA: (*Laughing.*) That'd be wonderful. But not enough sun gets back there. Nothing'll grow any more.

25 WILLY: You wait, kid, before it's all over we're gonna get a little place out in the country, and I'll raise some vegetables, a couple of chickens . . .

LINDA: You'll do it yet, dear.

(WILLY *walks out of his jacket.* LINDA *follows him.*)

WILLY: And they'll get married, and come for a weekend. I'd

30 build a little guest house. 'Cause I got so many fine tools, all I'd need would be a little lumber and some peace of mind.

LINDA: (*Joyfully.*) I sewed the lining . . .

WILLY: I could build two guest houses, so they'd both come.

35 Did he decide how much he's going to ask Oliver for?

LINDA: (*Getting him into the jacket.*) He didn't mention it, but I imagine ten or fifteen thousand. You going to talk to Howard today?

WILLY: Yeah. I'll put it to him straight and simple. He'll just

40 have to take me off the road.

LINDA: And Willy, don't forget to ask for a little advance, because we've got the insurance premium. It's the grace period now.

WILLY: That's a hundred . . . ?

45 LINDA: A hundred and eight, sixty-eight. Because we're a little short again.

WILLY: Why are we short?

LINDA: Well, you had the motor job on the car . . .

WILLY: That goddam Studebaker!

50 LINDA: And you got one more payment on the refrigerator . . .

WILLY: But it just broke again!

LINDA: Well, it's old, dear.

WILLY: I told you we should've bought a well-advertised machine. Charley bought a General Electric and it's twenty

55 years old and it's still good, that son-of-a-bitch.

LINDA: But, Willy—

WILLY: Whoever heard of a Hastings refrigerator? Once in my life I would like to own something outright before it's

broken! I'm always in a race with the junkyard! I just fin-

ished paying for the car and it's on its last legs. The re- 60
frigerator consumes belts like a goddam maniac. They
time those things. They time them so when you finally
paid for them, they're used up.

LINDA: (*Buttoning up his jacket as he unbuttons it.*) All told,
about two hundred dollars would carry us, dear. But that 65
includes the last payment on the mortgage. After this payment, Willy, the house belongs to us.

WILLY: It's twenty-five years!

LINDA: Biff was nine years old when we bought it.

WILLY: Well, that's a great thing. To weather a twenty-five 70
year mortgage is—

LINDA: It's an accomplishment.

WILLY: All the cement, the lumber, the reconstruction I put
in this house! There ain't a crack to be found in it any
more. 75

LINDA: Well, it served its purpose.

WILLY: What purpose? Some stranger'll come along, move in,
and that's that. If only Biff would take this house, and raise
a family . . . (*He starts to go.*) Good-by, I'm late.

LINDA: (*Suddenly remembering.*) Oh, I forgot! You're supposed 80
to meet them for dinner.

WILLY: Me?

LINDA: At Frank's Chop House on Forty-eighth near Sixth
Avenue.

WILLY: Is that so! How about you? 85

LINDA: No, just the three of you. They're gonna blow you to
a big meal!

WILLY: Don't say! Who thought of that?

LINDA: Biff came to me this morning, Willy, and he said, "Tell
Dad, we want to blow him to a big meal." Be there six 90
o'clock. You and your two boys are going to have dinner.

WILLY: Gee whiz! That's really somethin'. I'm gonna knock
Howard for a loop, kid. I'll get an advance, and I'll come
home with a New York job. Goddammit, now I'm gonna
do it! 95

LINDA: Oh, that's the spirit, Willy!

WILLY: I will never get behind a wheel the rest of my life!

LINDA: It's changing, Willy, I can feel it changing!

WILLY: Beyond a question. G'by, I'm late. (*He starts to go
again.*) 100

LINDA: (*Calling after him as she runs to the kitchen table for a
handkerchief.*) You got your glasses?

WILLY: (*Feels for them, then comes back in.*) Yeah, yeah, got my
glasses.

LINDA: (*Giving him the handkerchief.*) And a handkerchief. 105

WILLY: Yeah, handkerchief.

LINDA: And your saccharine?

WILLY: Yeah, my saccharine.

LINDA: Be careful on the subway stairs.

(*She kisses him, and a silk stocking is seen hanging from her hand.*
WILLY *notices it.*)

WILLY: Will you stop mending stockings? At least while I'm 110
in the house. It gets me nervous. I can't tell you. Please.

(LINDA *hides the stocking in her hand as she follows* WILLY *across
the forestage in front of the house.*)

LINDA: Remember, Frank's Chop House.

WILLY: (*Passing the apron.*) Maybe beets would grow out there.

115 LINDA: (*Laughing.*) But you tried so many times.

WILLY: Yeah. Well, don't work hard today. (*He disappears around the right corner of the house.*)

LINDA: Be careful!

(*As* WILLY *vanishes,* LINDA *waves to him. Suddenly the phone rings. She runs across the stage and into the kitchen and lifts it.*)

120 LINDA: Hello? Oh, Biff! I'm so glad you called, I just . . . Yes, sure, I just told him. Yes, he'll be there for dinner at six o'clock, I didn't forget. Listen, I was just dying to tell you. You know that little rubber pipe I told you about? That he connected to the gas heater? I finally decided to go

125 down the cellar this morning and take it away and destroy it. But it's gone! Imagine? He took it away himself, it isn't there! (*She listens.*) When? Oh, then you took it. Oh—nothing, it's just that I'd hoped he'd taken it away himself. Oh, I'm not worried, darling, because this morn-

130 ing he left in such high spirits, it was like the old days! I'm not afraid any more. Did Mr. Oliver see you? . . . Well, you wait there then. And make a nice impression on him, darling. Just don't perspire too much before you see him. And have a nice time with Dad. He may have big news

135 too! . . . That's right, a New York job. And be sweet to him tonight, dear. Be loving to him. Because he's only a little boat looking for a harbor. (*She is trembling with sorrow and joy.*) Oh, that's wonderful, Biff, you'll save his life. Thanks, darling. Just put your arm around him when he comes

140 into the restaurant. Give him a smile. That's the boy . . . Good-by, dear, . . . You got your comb? . . . That's fine. Good-by, Biff dear.

(*In the middle of her speech,* HOWARD WAGNER, *thirty-six, wheels on a small typewriter table on which is a wire-recording machine and proceeds to plug it in. This is on the left forestage. Light slowly fades on* LINDA *as it rises on* HOWARD. HOWARD *is intent on threading the machine and only glances over his shoulder as* WILLY *appears.*)

WILLY: Pst! Pst!

HOWARD: Hello, Willy, come in.

145 WILLY: Like to have a little talk with you, Howard.

HOWARD: Sorry to keep you waiting. I'll be with you in a minute.

WILLY: What's that, Howard?

HOWARD: Didn't you ever see one of these? Wire recorder.

150 WILLY: Oh. Can we talk a minute?

HOWARD: Records things. Just got delivery yesterday. Been driving me crazy, the most terrific machine I ever saw in my life. I was up all night with it.

WILLY: What do you do with it.

155 HOWARD: I bought it for dictation, but you can do anything with it. Listen to this. I had it home last night. Listen to what I picked up. The first one is my daughter. Get this. (*He flicks the switch and "Roll out the Barrel" is heard being whistled.*) Listen to that kid whistle.

160 WILLY: That is lifelike, isn't it?

HOWARD: Seven years old. Get that tone.

WILLY: Ts, ts. Like to ask a little favor if you . . .

(*The whistling breaks off, and the voice of* HOWARD's *daughter is heard.*)

HIS DAUGHTER: "Now you, Daddy."

HOWARD: She's crazy for me! (*Again the same song is whistled.*) That's me! Ha! (*He winks.*) 165

WILLY: You're very good!

(*The whistling breaks off again. The machine runs silent a moment.*)

HOWARD: Sh! Get this now, this is my son.

HIS SON: "The capital of Alabama is Montgomery; the capital of Arizona is Phoenix; the capital of Arkansas is Little Rock; the capital of California is Sacramento . . . (*And on,* 170 *and on.*)

HOWARD: (*Holding up five fingers.*) Five years old, Willy!

WILLY: He'll make an announcer some day!

HIS SON: (*Continuing.*) "The capital . . ."

HOWARD: Get that—alphabetical order! (*The machine breaks* 175 *off suddenly.*) Wait a minute. The maid kicked the plug out.

WILLY: It certainly is a—

HOWARD: Sh, for God's sake!

HIS SON: "It's nine o'clock, Bulova watch time. So I have to go to sleep." 180

WILLY: That really is—

HOWARD: Wait a minute! The next is my wife.

(*They wait.*)

HOWARD'S VOICE: "Go on, say something." (*Pause.*) "Well, you gonna talk?"

HIS WIFE: "I can't think of anything." 185

HOWARD'S VOICE: "Well, talk—it's turning."

HIS WIFE: (*Shyly, beaten.*) "Hello." (*Silence.*) "Oh, Howard, I can't talk into this . . ."

HOWARD: (*Snapping the machine off.*) That was my wife.

WILLY: That is a wonderful machine. Can we— 190

HOWARD: I tell you, Willy, I'm gonna take my camera, and my bandsaw, and all my hobbies, and out they go. This is the most fascinating relaxation I ever found.

WILLY: I think I'll get one myself.

HOWARD: Sure, they're only a hundred and a half. You can't 195 do without it. Supposing you wanna hear Jack Benny, see? But you can't be at home at that hour. So you tell the maid to turn the radio on when Jack Benny comes on, and this automatically goes on with the radio . . .

WILLY: And when you come home you . . . 200

HOWARD: You can come home twelve o'clock, one o'clock, any time you like, and you get yourself a Coke and sit yourself down, throw the switch, and there's Jack Benny's program in the middle of the night!

WILLY: I'm definitely going to get one. Because lots of time 205 I'm on the road, and I think to myself, what I must be missing on the radio!

HOWARD: Don't you have a radio in the car?

WILLY: Well, yeah, but who ever thinks of turning it on?

HOWARD: Say, aren't you supposed to be in Boston? 210

WILLY: That's what I want to talk to you about, Howard. You got a minute? (*He draws a chair in from the wing.*)

HOWARD: What happened? What're you doing here?

WILLY: Well . . .

HOWARD: You didn't crack up again, did you? 215

WILLY: Oh, no. No . . .

HOWARD: Geez, you had me worried there for a minute. What's the trouble?

WILLY: Well, tell you the truth, Howard. I've come to the de-
220   cision that I'd rather not travel any more.

HOWARD: Not travel! Well, what'll you do?

WILLY: Remember, Christmas time, when you had the party here? You said you'd try to think of some spot for me here in town.

225 HOWARD: With us?

WILLY: Well, sure.

HOWARD: Oh, yeah, yeah. I remember. Well, I couldn't think of anything for you, Willy.

WILLY: I tell ya, Howard. The kids are all grown up, y'know.
230   I don't need much any more. If I could take home—well, sixty-five dollars a week, I could swing it.

HOWARD: Yeah, but Willy, see I—

WILLY: I tell ya why, Howard. Speaking frankly and between the two of us, y'know—I'm just a little tired.

235 HOWARD: Oh, I could understand that, Willy. But you're a road man, Willy, and we do a road business. We've only got a half-dozen salesmen on the floor here.

WILLY: God knows, Howard, I never asked a favor of any man. But I was with the firm when your father used to
240   carry you in here in his arms.

HOWARD: I know that, Willy, but—

WILLY: Your father came to me the day you were born and asked me what I thought of the name of Howard, may he rest in peace.

245 HOWARD: I appreciate that, Willy, but there just is no spot here for you. If I had a spot I'd slam you right in, but I just don't have a single solitary spot.

(*He looks for his lighter.* WILLY *has picked it up and gives it to him. Pause.*)

WILLY: (*With increasing anger.*) Howard, all I need to set my
250   table is fifty dollars a week.

HOWARD: But where am I going to put you, kid?

WILLY: Look, it isn't a question of whether I can sell merchandise, is it?

HOWARD: No, but it's a business, kid, and everybody's gotta
255   pull his own weight.

WILLY: (*Desperately.*) Just let me tell you a story, Howard—

HOWARD: 'Cause you gotta admit, business is business.

WILLY: (*Angrily.*) Business is definitely business, but just listen for a minute. You don't understand this. When I was a
260   boy—eighteen, nineteen—I was already on the road. And there was a question in my mind as to whether selling had a future for me. Because in those days I had a yearning to go to Alaska. See, there were three gold strikes in one month in Alaska, and I felt like going out. Just for the ride
265   you might say.

HOWARD: (*Barely interested.*) Don't say.

WILLY: Oh, yeah, my father lived many years in Alaska. He was an adventurous man. We've got quite a little streak of self-reliance in our family. I thought I'd go out with my older
270   brother and try to locate him, and maybe settle in the North with the old man. And I was almost decided to go, when I met a salesman in the Parker House. His name was Dave Singleman. And he was eighty-four years old, and

he'd drummed merchandise in thirty-one states. And old Dave, he'd go up to his room, y'understand, put on his 275 green velvet slippers—I'll never forget—and pick up his phone and call the buyers, and without ever leaving his room, at the age of eighty-four, he made his living. And when I saw that, I realized that selling was the greatest career a man could want. 'Cause what could be more satisfy- 280 ing than to be able to go, at the age of eighty-four, into twenty or thirty different cities, and pick up a phone, and be remembered and loved and helped by so many different people? Do you know? when he died—and by the way he died the death of a salesman, in his green velvet slippers in 285 the smoker of the New York, New Haven and Hartford, going into Boston—when he died, hundreds of salesmen and buyers were at his funeral. Things were sad on a lotta trains for months after that. (*He stands up.* HOWARD *has not looked at him.*) In those days there was personality in it, 290 Howard. There was respect, and comradeship, and gratitude in it. Today, it's all cut and dried, and there's no chance for bringing friendship to bear—or personality. You see what I mean? They don't know me any more.

HOWARD: (*Moving away, to the right.*) That's just the thing, 295 Willy.

WILLY: If I had forty dollars a week—that's all I'd need. Forty dollars, Howard.

HOWARD: Kid, I can't take blood from a stone, I—

WILLY: (*Desperation is on him now.*) Howard, the year Al Smith 300 was nominated, your father came to me and—

HOWARD: (*Starting to go off.*) I've got to see some people, kid.

WILLY: (*Stopping him.*) I'm talking about your father! There were promises made across this desk! You mustn't tell me you've got people to see—I put thirty-four years into this 305 firm, Howard, and now I can't pay my insurance! You can't eat the orange and throw the peel away—a man is not a piece of fruit! (*After a pause.*) Now pay attention. Your father—in 1928 I had a big year. I averaged a hundred and seventy dollars a week in commissions. 310

HOWARD: (*Impatiently.*) Now, Willy, you never averaged—

WILLY: (*Banging his hand on the desk.*) I averaged a hundred and seventy dollars a week in the year of 1928! And your father came to me—or rather, I was in the office here—it was right over this desk—and he put his hand on my 315 shoulder—

HOWARD: (*Getting up.*) You'll have to excuse me, Willy, I gotta see some people. Pull yourself together. (*Going out.*) I'll be back in a little while.

(*On* HOWARD'*s exit, the light on his chair grows very bright and strange.*)

WILLY: Pull myself together! What the hell did I say to him? 320 My God, I was yelling at him! How could I! (WILLY *breaks off, staring at the light, which occupies the chair, animating it. He approaches this chair, standing across the desk from it.*) Frank, Frank, don't you remember what you told me that time? How you put your hand on my shoulder, and Frank . . . 325 (*He leans on the desk and as he speaks the dead man's name he accidentally switches on the recorder, and instantly.*)

HOWARD'S SON: ". . . of New York is Albany. The capital of Ohio is Cincinnati, the capital of Rhode Island is . . ." (*The recitation continues.*) 330

WILLY: (*Leaping away with fright, shouting.*) Ha! Howard! Howard! Howard!

HOWARD: (*Rushing in.*) What happened?

340 WILLY: (*Pointing at the machine, which continues nasally, childishly, with the capital cities.*) Shut it off! Shut it off!

HOWARD: (*Pulling the plug out.*) Look, Willy . . .

WILLY: (*Pressing his hands to his eyes.*) I gotta get myself some coffee. I'll get some coffee . . .

(WILLY *starts to walk out.* HOWARD *stops him.*)

HOWARD: (*Rolling up the cord.*) Willy, look . . .

345 WILLY: I'll go to Boston.

HOWARD: Willy, you can't go to Boston for us.

WILLY: Why can't I go?

HOWARD: I don't want you to represent us. I've been meaning to tell you for a long time now.

350 WILLY: Howard, are you firing me?

HOWARD: I think you need a good long rest, Willy.

WILLY: Howard—

HOWARD: And when you feel better, come back, and we'll see if we can work something out.

355 WILLY: But I gotta earn money, Howard. I'm in no position to—

HOWARD: Where are your sons? Why don't your sons give you a hand?

WILLY: They're working on a very big deal.

360 HOWARD: This is no time for false pride, Willy. You go to your sons and you tell them that you're tired. You've got two great boys, haven't you?

WILLY: Oh, no question, no question, but in the meantime . . .

HOWARD: Then that's that, heh?

365 WILLY: All right, I'll go to Boston tomorrow.

HOWARD: No, no.

WILLY: I can't throw myself on my sons. I'm not a cripple!

HOWARD: Look, kid, I'm busy this morning.

WILLY: (*Grasping* HOWARD's *arm.*) Howard, you've got to let 370 me go to Boston!

HOWARD: (*Hard, keeping himself under control.*) I've got a line of people to see this morning. Sit down, take five minutes, and pull yourself together, and then go home, will ya? I need the office, Willy. (*He starts to go, turns, remembering the* 375 *recorder, starts to push off the table holding the recorder.*) Oh, yeah. Whenever you can this week, stop by and drop off the samples. You'll feel better, Willy, and then come back and we'll talk. Pull yourself together, kid, there's people outside.

(HOWARD *exits, pushing the table off left.* WILLY *stares into space, exhausted. Now the music is heard—* BEN's *music—first distantly, then closer, closer. As* WILLY *speaks,* BEN *enters from the right. He carries valise and umbrella.*)

380 WILLY: Oh, Ben, how did you do it? What is the answer? Did you wind up the Alaska deal already?

BEN: Doesn't take much time if you know what you're doing. Just a short business trip. Boarding ship in an hour. Wanted to say good-by.

385 WILLY: Ben, I've got to talk to you.

BEN: (*Glancing at his watch.*) Haven't the time, William.

WILLY: (*Crossing the apron to Ben.*) Ben, nothing's working out. I don't know what to do.

BEN: Now, look here, William. I've bought timberland in Alaska and I need a man to look after things for me.   390

WILLY: God, timberland! Me and my boys in those grand outdoors!

BEN: You've a new continent at your doorstep, William. Get out of these cities, they're full of talk and time payments and courts of law. Screw on your fists and you can fight   395 for a fortune up there.

WILLY: Yes, yes! Linda, Linda!

(LINDA *enters as of old, with the wash.*)

LINDA: Oh, you're back?

BEN: I haven't much time.

WILLY: No, wait! Linda, he's got a proposition for me in   400 Alaska.

LINDA: But you've got— (*To* BEN.) He's got a beautiful job here.

WILLY: But in Alaska, kid, I could—

LINDA: You're doing well enough, Willy!   405

BEN: (*To* LINDA.) Enough for what, my dear?

LINDA: (*Frightened of* BEN *and angry at him.*) Don't say those things to him! Enough to be happy right here, right now. (*To* WILLY, *while* BEN *laughs.*) Why must everybody conquer the world? You're well liked, and the boys love you,   410 and someday—(*To* BEN.)—why, old man Wagner told him just the other day that if he keeps it up he'll be a member of the firm, didn't he, Willy?

WILLY: Sure, sure. I am building something with this firm, Ben, and if a man is building something he must be on the   415 right track, mustn't he?

BEN: What are you building? Lay your hand on it. Where is it?

WILLY: (*Hesitantly.*) That's true, Linda, there's nothing.

LINDA: Why? (*To* BEN.) There's a man eighty-four years old—

WILLY: That's right, Ben, that's right. When I look at that man   420 I say, what is there to worry about?

BEN: Bah!

WILLY: It's true, Ben. All he has to do is go into any city, pick up the phone, and he's making his living and you know why?   425

BEN: (*Picking up his valise.*) I've got to go.

WILLY: (*Holding* BEN *back.*) Look at this boy!

(BIFF, *in his high school sweater, enters carrying suitcase.* HAPPY *carries* BIFF's *shoulder guards, gold helmet, and football pants.*)

WILLY: Without a penny to his name, three great universities are begging for him, and from there the sky's the limit, because it's not what you do, Ben. It's who you know and   430 the smile on your face! It's contacts, Ben, contacts! The whole wealth of Alaska passes over the lunch table at the Commodore Hotel, and that's the wonder, the wonder of this country, that a man can end with diamonds here on the basis of being liked! (*He turns to* BIFF.) And that's why   435 when you get out on that field today it's important. Because thousands of people will be rooting for you and loving you. (*To* BEN, *who has again begun to leave.*) And Ben! when he walks into a business office his name will sound out like a bell and all the doors will open to him! I've seen   440 it, Ben, I've seen it a thousand times! You can't feel it with your hand like timber, but it's there!

BEN: Good-by, William.

WILLY: Ben, am I right? Don't you think I'm right? I value
445 your advice.

BEN: There's a new continent at your doorstep, William. You
could walk out rich. Rich! (*He is gone.*)

WILLY: We'll do it here, Ben! You hear me? We're gonna do it
here!

(*Young* BERNARD *rushes in. The gay music of the Boys is heard.*)

450 BERNARD: Oh, gee, I was afraid you left already!

WILLY: Why? What time is it?

BERNARD: It's half-past one!

WILLY: Well, come on, everybody! Ebbets Field next stop!
Where's the pennants? (*He rushes through the wall-line of the*
455 *kitchen and out into the living-room.*)

LINDA: (*To* BIFF.) Did you pack fresh underwear?

BIFF: (*Who has been limbering up.*) I want to go!

BERNARD: Biff, I'm carrying your helmet, ain't I?

HAPPY: No, I'm carrying the helmet.

460 BERNARD: Oh, Biff, you promised me.

HAPPY: I'm carrying the helmet.

BERNARD: How am I going to get in the locker room?

LINDA: Let him carry the shoulder guards. (*She puts her coat
and hat on in the kitchen.*)

465 BERNARD: Can I, Biff? 'Cause I told everybody I'm going to
be in the locker room.

HAPPY: In Ebbets Field it's the clubhouse.

BERNARD: I meant the clubhouse. Biff!

HAPPY: Biff!

470 BIFF: (*Grandly, after a slight pause.*) Let him carry the shoulder
guards.

HAPPY: (*As he gives* BERNARD *the shoulder guards.*) Stay close to
us now.

(WILLY *rushes in with the pennants.*)

WILLY: (*Handing them out.*) Everybody wave when Biff comes
475 out on the field. (HAPPY *and* BERNARD *run off.*) You set
now, boy?

(*The music has died away.*)

BIFF: Ready to go, Pop. Every muscle is ready.

WILLY: (*At the edge of the apron.*) You realize what this means?

BIFF: That's right, Pop.

480 WILLY: (*Feeling* BIFF's *muscles.*) You're comin' home this afternoon captain of the All-Scholastic Championship Team of
the City of New York.

BIFF: I got it, Pop. And remember, pal, when I take off my
helmet, that touchdown is for you.

485 WILLY: Let's go! (*He is starting out, with his arm around* BIFF,
when CHARLEY *enters, as of old, in knickers.*) I got no room
for you, Charley.

CHARLEY: Room? For what?

WILLY: In the car.

490 CHARLEY: You goin' for a ride? I wanted to shoot some
casino.

WILLY: (*Furiously.*) Casino! (*Incredulously.*) Don't you realize
what today is?

LINDA: Oh, he knows, Willy. He's just kidding you.

495 WILLY: That's nothing to kid about!

CHARLEY: No. Linda, what's goin' on?

LINDA: He's playing in Ebbets Field.

CHARLEY: Baseball in this weather?

WILLY: Don't talk to him. Come on, come on! (*He is pushing
them out.*)   500

CHARLEY: Wait a minute, didn't you hear the news?

WILLY: What?

CHARLEY: Don't you listen to the radio? Ebbets Field just
blew up.

WILLY: You go to hell! (CHARLEY *laughs. Pushing them out.*) 505
Come on, come on! We're late.

CHARLEY: (*As they go.*) Knock a homer, Biff, knock a homer!

WILLY: (*The last to leave, turning to* CHARLEY.) I don't think
that was funny, Charley. This is the greatest day of his life.

CHARLEY: Willy, when are you going to grow up?   510

WILLY: Yeah, heh? When this game is over, Charley, you'll be
laughing out of the other side of your face. They'll be calling him another Red Grange. Twenty-five thousand a year.

CHARLEY: (*Kidding.*) Is that so?

WILLY: Yeah, that's so.   515

CHARLEY: Well, then, I'm sorry, Willy. But tell me something.

WILLY: What?

CHARLEY: Who is Red Grange?

WILLY: Put up your hands. Goddam you, put up your hands!

(CHARLEY, *chuckling, shakes his head and walks away, around the
left corner of the stage.* WILLY *follows him. The music rises to a
mocking frenzy.*)

WILLY: Who the hell do you think you are, better than every- 520
body else? You don't know everything, you big, ignorant,
stupid . . . Put up your hands!

(*Light rises, on the right side of the forestage, on a small table in the
reception room of* CHARLEY's *office. Traffic sounds are heard.*
BERNARD, *now mature, sits whistling to himself. A pair of tennis
rackets and an overnight bag are on the floor beside him.*)

WILLY: (*Offstage.*) What are you walking away for? Don't walk
away! If you're going to say something say it to my face! I
know you laugh at me behind my back. You'll laugh out 525
of the other side of your goddam face after this game.
Touchdown! Touchdown! Eighty thousand people!
Touchdown! Right between the goal posts.

(BERNARD *is a quiet, earnest, but self-assured young man.* WILLY's
voice is coming from right upstage now. BERNARD *lowers his feet off
the table and listens.* JENNY, *his father's secretary, enters.*)

JENNY: (*Distressed.*) Say, Bernard, will you go out in the hall?

BERNARD: What is that noise? Who is it?   530

JENNY: Mr. Loman. He just got off the elevator.

BERNARD: (*Getting up.*) Who's he arguing with?

JENNY: Nobody. There's nobody with him. I can't deal with
him any more, and your father gets all upset everytime he
comes. I've got a lot of typing to do, and your father's 535
waiting to sign it. Will you see him?

WILLY: (*Entering.*) Touchdown! Touch— (*He sees* JENNY.)
Jenny, Jenny, good to see you. How're ya? Workin'? Or still
honest?

JENNY: Fine. How've you been feeling?   540

WILLY: Not much any more, Jenny. Ha, ha! (*He is surprised to
see the rackets.*)

BERNARD: Hello, Uncle Willy.

WILLY: (*Almost shocked.*) Bernard! Well, look who's here! (*He comes quickly, guiltily, to* BERNARD *and warmly shakes his hand.*)

BERNARD: How are you? Good to see you.

WILLY: What are you doing here?

BERNARD: Oh, just stopped by to see Pop. Get off my feet till my train leaves. I'm going to Washington in a few minutes.

WILLY: Is he in?

BERNARD: Yes, he's in his office with the accountant. Sit down.

WILLY: (*Sitting down.*) What're you going to do in Washington?

BERNARD: Oh, just a case I've got there, Willy.

WILLY: That so? (*Indicating the rackets.*) You going to play tennis there?

BERNARD: I'm staying with a friend who's got a court.

WILLY: Don't say. His own tennis court. Must be fine people, I bet.

BERNARD: They are, very nice. Dad tells me Biff's in town.

WILLY: (*With a big smile.*) Yeah, Biff's in. Working on a very big deal, Bernard.

BERNARD: What's Biff doing?

WILLY: Well, he's been doing very big things in the West. But he decided to establish himself here. Very big. We're having dinner. Did I hear your wife had a boy?

BERNARD: That's right. Our second.

WILLY: Two boys! What do you know!

BERNARD: What kind of a deal has Biff got?

WILLY: Well, Bill Oliver—very big sporting-goods man—he wants Biff very badly. Called him in from the West. Long distance, carte blanche, special deliveries. Your friends have their own private tennis court?

BERNARD: You still with the old firm, Willy?

WILLY: (*After a pause.*) I'm—I'm overjoyed to see how you made the grade, Bernard, overjoyed. It's an encouraging thing to see a young man really—really— Looks very good for Biff—very— (*He breaks off, then.*) Bernard— (*He is so full of emotion, he breaks off again.*)

BERNARD: What is it, Willy?

WILLY: (*Small and alone.*) What—what's the secret?

BERNARD: What secret?

WILLY: How—how did you? Why didn't he ever catch on?

BERNARD: I wouldn't know that, Willy.

WILLY: (*Confidentially, desperately.*) You were his friend, his boyhood friend. There's something I don't understand about it. His life ended after that Ebbets Field game. From the age of seventeen nothing good ever happened to him.

BERNARD: He never trained himself for anything.

WILLY: But he did, he did. After high school he took so many correspondence courses. Radio mechanics; television; God knows what, and never made the slightest mark.

BERNARD: (*Taking off his glasses.*) Willy, do you want to talk candidly?

WILLY: (*Rising, faces* BERNARD.) I regard you as a very brilliant man, Bernard. I value your advice.

BERNARD: Oh, the hell with the advice, Willy. I couldn't advise you. There's just one thing I've always wanted to ask you. When he was supposed to graduate, and the math teacher flunked him—

WILLY: Oh, that son-of-a-bitch ruined his life.

BERNARD: Yeah, but, Willy, all he had to do was go to summer school and make up that subject.

WILLY: That's right, that's right.

BERNARD: Did you tell him not to go to summer school?

WILLY: Me? I begged him to go. I ordered him to go!

BERNARD: Then why wouldn't he go?

WILLY: Why? Why! Bernard, that question has been trailing me like a ghost for the last fifteen years. He flunked the subject, and laid down and died like a hammer hit him!

BERNARD: Take it easy, kid.

WILLY: Let me talk to you—I got nobody to talk to. Bernard, Bernard, was it my fault? Y'see? It keeps going around in my mind, maybe I did something to him. I got nothing to give him.

BERNARD: Don't take it so hard.

WILLY: Why did he lay down? What is the story there? You were his friend!

BERNARD: Willy, I remember, it was June, and our grades came out. And he'd flunked math.

WILLY: That son-of-a-bitch!

BERNARD: No, it wasn't right then. Biff just got very angry, I remember, and he was ready to enroll in summer school.

WILLY: (*Surprised.*) He was?

BERNARD: He wasn't beaten by it at all. But then, Willy, he disappeared from the block for almost a month. And I got the idea that he'd gone up to New England to see you. Did he have a talk with you then?

(WILLY *stares in silence.*)

BERNARD: Willy?

WILLY: (*With a strong edge of resentment in his voice.*) Yeah, he came to Boston. What about it?

BERNARD: Well, just that when he came back—I'll never forget this, it always mystifies me. Because I'd thought so well of Biff, even though he'd always taken advantage of me. I loved him, Willy, y'know? And he came back after that month and took his sneakers—remember those sneakers with "University of Virginia" printed on them? He was so proud of those, wore them every day. And he took them down in the cellar, and burned them up in the furnace. We had a fist fight. It lasted at least half an hour. Just the two of us, punching each other down thee cellar, and crying right through it. I've often thought of how strange it was that I knew he'd given up his life. What happened in Boston, Willy?

(WILLY *looks at him as at an intruder.*)

BERNARD: I just bring it up because you asked me.

WILLY: (*Angrily.*) Nothing. What do you mean, "What happened?" What's that got to do with anything?

BERNARD: Well, don't get sore.

WILLY: What are you trying to do, blame it on me? If a boy lays down is that my fault?

BERNARD: Now, Willy, don't get—

WILLY: Well, don't—don't talk to me that way! What does that mean, "What happened?"

(CHARLEY *enters. He is in his vest, and he carries a bottle of bourbon.*)

CHARLEY: Hey, you're going to miss that train. (*He waves the bottle.*)

660 BERNARD: Yeah, I'm going. (*He takes the bottle.*) Thanks, Pop. (*He picks up his rackets and bag.*) Good-by, Willy, and don't worry about it. You know, "If at first you don't succeed . . ."

WILLY: Yes, I believe in that.

BERNARD: But sometimes, Willy, it's better for a man just to
665 walk away.

WILLY: Walk away?

BERNARD: That's right.

WILLY: But if you can't walk away?

BERNARD: (*After a slight pause.*) I guess that's when it's tough.
670 (*Extending his hand.*) Good-by, Willy.

WILLY: (*Shaking* BERNARD'*s hand.*) Good-by, boy.

CHARLEY: (*An arm on* BERNARD'*s shoulder.*) How do you like this kid? Gonna argue a case in front of the Supreme Court.

675 BERNARD: (*Protesting.*) Pop!

WILLY: (*Genuinely shocked, pained, and happy.*) No! The Supreme Court!

BERNARD: I gotta run. 'By, Dad!

CHARLEY: Knock 'em dead, Bernard!

(BERNARD *goes off.*)

680 WILLY: (*As* CHARLEY *takes out his wallet.*) The Supreme Court! And he didn't even mention it!

CHARLEY: (*Counting out money on the desk.*) He don't have to—he's gonna do it.

WILLY: And you never told him what to do, did you? You
685 never took any interest in him.

CHARLEY: My salvation is that I never took any interest in anything. There's some money—fifty dollars. I got an accountant inside.

WILLY: Charley, look . . . (*With difficulty.*) I got my insurance
690 to pay. If you can manage it—I need a hundred and ten dollars.

(CHARLEY *doesn't reply for a moment; merely stops moving.*)

WILLY: I'd draw it from my bank but Linda would know, and I . . .

CHARLEY: Sit down, Willy.

695 WILLY: (*Moving toward the chair.*) I'm keeping an account of everything, remember. I'll pay every penny back. (*He sits.*)

CHARLEY: Now listen to me, Willy.

WILLY: I want you to know I appreciate . . .

CHARLEY: (*Sitting down on the table.*) Willy, what're you doin'?
700 What the hell is goin' on in your head?

WILLY: Why? I'm simply . . .

CHARLEY: I offered you a job. You can make fifty dollars a week. And I won't send you on the road.

WILLY: I've got a job.

705 CHARLEY: Without pay? What kind of a job is a job without pay? (*He rises.*) Now, look, kid, enough is enough. I'm no genius but I know when I'm being insulted.

WILLY: Insulted!

CHARLEY: Why don't you want to work for me?

710 WILLY: What's the matter with you? I've got a job.

CHARLEY: Then what're you walkin' in here every week for?

WILLY: (*Getting up.*) Well, if you don't want me to walk in here—

CHARLEY: I am offering you a job.

WILLY: I don't want your goddam job! 715

CHARLEY: When the hell are you going to grow up?

WILLY: (*Furiously.*) You big ignoramus, if you say that to me again I'll rap you one! I don't care how big you are! (*He's ready to fight.*)

(*Pause.*)

CHARLEY: (*Kindly, going to him.*) How much do you need, 720 Willy?

WILLY: Charley, I'm strapped, I'm strapped. I don't know what to do. I was just fired.

CHARLEY: Howard fired you?

WILLY: That snotnose. Imagine that? I named him. I named 725 him Howard.

CHARLEY: Willy, when're you gonna realize that them things don't mean anything? You named him Howard, but you can't sell that. The only thing you got in this world is what you can sell. And the funny thing is that you're a 730 salesman, and you don't know that.

WILLY: I've always tried to think otherwise, I guess. I always felt that if a man was impressive, and well liked, that nothing—

CHARLEY: Why must everybody like you? Who liked J. P. Morgan? Was he impressive? In a Turkish bath he'd look 735 like a butcher. But with his pockets on he was very well liked. Now listen, Willy, I know you don't like me, and nobody can say I'm in love with you, but I'll give you a job because—just for the hell of it, put it that way. Now what do you say? 740

WILLY: I—I just can't work for you, Charley.

CHARLEY: What're you, jealous of me?

WILLY: I can't work for you, that's all, don't ask me why.

CHARLEY: (*Angered, takes out more bills.*) You been jealous of me all your life, you damned fool! Here, pay your insur- 745 ance. (*He puts the money in* WILLY'*s hand.*)

WILLY: I'm keeping strict accounts.

CHARLEY: I've got some work to do. Take care of yourself. And pay your insurance.

WILLY: (*Moving to the right.*) Funny, y'know? After all the 750 highways, and the trains, and the appointments, and the years, you end up worth more dead than alive.

CHARLEY: Willy, nobody's worth nothin' dead. (*After a slight pause.*) Did you hear what I said?

(WILLY *stands still, dreaming.*)

CHARLEY: Willy! 755

WILLY: Apologize to Bernard for me when you see him. I didn't mean to argue with him. He's a fine boy. They're all fine boys, and they'll end up big—all of them. Someday they'll all play tennis together. Wish me luck, Charley. He saw Bill Oliver today. 760

CHARLEY: Good luck.

WILLY: (*On the verge of tears.*) Charley, you're the only friend I got. Isn't that a remarkable thing? (*He goes out.*)

CHARLEY: Jesus!

(CHARLEY *stares after him a moment and follows. All light blacks out. Suddenly raucous music is heard, and a red glow rises behind the screen at right.* STANLEY, *a young waiter, appears, carrying a table, followed by* HAPPY, *who is carrying two chairs.*)

765 STANLEY: (*Putting the table down.*) That's all right, Mr. Loman, I can handle it myself. (*He turns and takes the chairs from* HAPPY *and places them at the table.*)

HAPPY: (*Glancing around.*) Oh, this is better.

STANLEY: Sure, in the front there you're in the middle of all
770 kinds a noise. Whenever you got a party, Mr. Loman, you just tell me and I'll put you back here. Y'know, there's a lotta people they don't like it private, because when they go out they like to see a lotta action around them because they're sick and tired to stay in the house by theirself. But
775 I know you, you ain't from Hackensack. You know what I mean?

HAPPY: (*Sitting down.*) So how's it coming, Stanley?

STANLEY: Ah, it's a dog's life. I only wish during the war they'd a took me in the Army. I coulda been dead by now.

780 HAPPY: My brother's back, Stanley.

STANLEY: Oh, he come back, heh? From the Far West.

HAPPY: Yeah, big cattle man, my brother, so treat him right. And my father's coming too.

STANLEY: Oh, your father too!

785 HAPPY: You got a couple of nice lobsters?

STANLEY: Hundred per cent, big.

HAPPY: I want them with the claws.

STANLEY: Don't worry, I don't give you no mice. (HAPPY *laughs.*) How about some wine? It'll put a head on the
790 meal.

HAPPY: No. You remember, Stanley, that recipe I brought you from overseas? With the champagne in it?

STANLEY: Oh, yeah, sure. I still got it tacked up yet in the kitchen. But that'll have to cost a buck apiece anyways.

795 HAPPY: That's all right.

STANLEY: What'd you, hit a number or somethin'?

HAPPY: No, it's a little celebration. My brother is—I think he pulled off a big deal today. I think we're going into business together.

800 STANLEY: Great! That's the best for you. Because a family business, you know what I mean?—that's the best.

HAPPY: That's what I think.

STANLEY: 'Cause what's the difference? Somebody steals? It's in the family. Know what I mean? (*Sotto voce.*) Like this
805 bartender here. The boss is goin' crazy what kinda leak he's got in the cash register. You put it in but it don't come out.

HAPPY: (*Raising his head.*) Sh!

STANLEY: What?

810 HAPPY: You notice I wasn't lookin' right or left, was I?

STANLEY: No.

HAPPY: And my eyes are closed.

STANLEY: So what's the—?

HAPPY: Strudel's comin'.

815 STANLEY: (*Catching on, looks around.*) Ah, no, there's no—

(*He breaks off as a furred, lavishly dressed girl enters and sits at the next table. Both follow her with their eyes.*)

STANLEY: Geez, how'd ya know?

HAPPY: I got radar or something. (*Staring directly at her profile.*) Oooooooo . . . Stanley.

STANLEY: I think that's for you, Mr. Loman.

820 HAPPY: Look at that mouth. Oh, God. And the binoculars.

STANLEY: Geez, you got a life, Mr. Loman.

HAPPY: Wait on her.

STANLEY: (*Going to the girl's table.*) Would you like a menu, ma'am?

GIRL: I'm expecting someone, but I'd like a— 825

HAPPY: Why don't you bring her—excuse me, miss, do you mind? I sell champagne, and I'd like you to try my brand. Bring her a champagne, Stanley.

GIRL: That's awfully nice of you.

HAPPY: Don't mention it. It's all company money. (*He laughs.*) 830

GIRL: That's a charming product to be selling, isn't it?

HAPPY: Oh, gets to be like everything else. Selling is selling, y'know.

GIRL: I suppose.

HAPPY: You don't happen to sell, do you? 835

GIRL: No, I don't sell.

HAPPY: Would you object to a compliment from a stranger? You ought to be on a magazine cover.

GIRL: (*Looking at him a little archly.*) I have been.

(STANLEY *comes in with a glass of champagne.*)

HAPPY: What'd I say before, Stanley? You see? She's a cover 840 girl.

STANLEY: Oh, I could see, I could see.

HAPPY: (*To the* GIRL.) What magazine?

GIRL: Oh, a lot of them. (*She takes the drink.*) Thank you.

HAPPY: You know what they say in France, don't you? 845 "Champagne is the drink of the complexion"—Hya Biff!

(BIFF *has entered and sits with* HAPPY.)

BIFF: Hello, kid. Sorry I'm late.

HAPPY: I just got here. Uh, Miss—?

GIRL: Forsythe.

HAPPY: Miss Forsythe, this is my brother. 850

BIFF: Is Dad here?

HAPPY: His name is Biff. You might've heard of him. Great football player.

GIRL: Really? What team?

HAPPY: Are you familiar with football? 855

GIRL: No, I'm afraid I'm not.

HAPPY: Biff is quarterback with the New York Giants.

GIRL: Well, that is nice, isn't it? (*She drinks.*)

HAPPY: Good health.

GIRL: I'm happy to meet you. 860

HAPPY: That's my name. Hap. It's really Harold, but at West Point they called me Happy.

GIRL: (*Now really impressed.*) Oh, I see. How do you do? (*She turns her profile.*)

BIFF: Isn't Dad coming? 865

HAPPY: You want her?

BIFF: Oh, I could never make that.

HAPPY: I remember the time that idea would never come into your head. Where's the old confidence, Biff?

BIFF: I just saw Oliver— 870

HAPPY: Wait a minute, I've got to see that old confidence again. Do you want her? She's on call.

BIFF: Oh, no. (*He turns to look at the* GIRL.)

HAPPY: I'm telling you. Watch this. (*Turning to the* GIRL.) Honey? (*She turns to him.*) Are you busy? 875

GIRL: Well, I am . . . but I could make a phone call.

HAPPY: Do that, will you, honey? And see if you can get a friend. We'll be here for a while. Biff is one of the greatest football players in the country.

880 GIRL: (*Standing up.*) Well, I'm certainly happy to meet you.

HAPPY: Come back soon.

GIRL: I'll try.

HAPPY: Don't try, honey, try hard.

(*The* GIRL *exits.* STANLEY *follows, shaking his head in bewildered admiration.*)

HAPPY: Isn't that a shame now? A beautiful girl like that?
885 That's why I can't get married. There's not a good woman in a thousand. New York is loaded with them, kid!

BIFF: Hap, look—

HAPPY: I told you she was on call!

BIFF: (*Strangely unnerved.*) Cut it out, will ya? I want to say
890 something to you.

HAPPY: Did you see Oliver?

BIFF: I saw him all right. Now look, I want to tell Dad a couple of things and I want you to help me.

HAPPY: What? Is he going to back you?

895 BIFF: Are you crazy? You're out of your goddam head, you know that?

HAPPY: Why? What happened?

BIFF: (*Breathlessly.*) I did a terrible thing today, Hap. It's been the strangest day I ever went through. I'm all numb, I swear.

900 HAPPY: You mean he wouldn't see you?

BIFF: Well, I waited six hours for him, see? All day. Kept sending my name in. Even tried to date his secretary so she'd get me to him, but no soap.

HAPPY: Because you're not showin' the old confidence, Biff.
905 He remembered you, didn't he?

BIFF: (*Stopping* HAPPY *with a gesture.*) Finally, about five o'clock, he comes out. Didn't remember who I was or anything. I felt like such an idiot, Hap.

HAPPY: Did you tell him my Florida idea?

910 BIFF: He walked away. I saw him for one minute. I got so mad I could've torn the walls down! How the hell did I ever get the idea I was a salesman there? I even believed myself that I'd been a salesman for him! And then he gave me one look and—I realized what a ridiculous lie my whole life
915 has been! We've been talking in a dream for fifteen years. I was a shipping clerk.

HAPPY: What'd you do?

BIFF: (*With great tension and wonder.*) Well, he left, see. And the secretary went out. I was all alone in the waiting-room. I
920 don't know what came over me, Hap. The next thing I know I'm in his office—paneled walls, everything. I can't explain it. I—Hap, I took his fountain pen.

HAPPY: Geez, did he catch you?

BIFF: I ran out. I ran down all eleven flights. I ran and ran and
925 ran.

HAPPY: That was an awful dumb—what'd you do that for?

BIFF: (*Agonized.*) I don't know, I just—wanted to take something, I don't know. You gotta help me, Hap, I'm gonna tell Pop.

930 HAPPY: You crazy? What for?

BIFF: Hap, he's got to understand that I'm not the man somebody lends that kind of money to. He thinks I've been spiting him all these years and it's eating him up.

HAPPY: That's just it. You tell him something nice.

BIFF: I can't.   935

HAPPY: Say you got a lunch date with Oliver tomorrow.

BIFF: So what do I do tomorrow?

HAPPY: You leave the house tomorrow and come back at night and say Oliver is thinking it over. And he thinks it over for a couple of weeks, and gradually it fades away 940 and nobody's the worse.

BIFF: But it'll go on forever!

HAPPY: Dad is never so happy as when he's looking forward to something!

(WILLY *enters.*)

HAPPY: Hello, scout!   945

WILLY: Gee, I haven't been here in years!

(STANLEY *has followed* WILLY *in and sets a chair for him.* STANLEY *starts off but* HAPPY *stops him.*)

HAPPY: Stanley!

(STANLEY *stands by, waiting for an order.*)

BIFF: (*Going to* WILLY *with guilt, as to an invalid.*) Sit down, Pop. You want a drink?

WILLY: Sure, I don't mind.   950

BIFF: Let's get a load on.

WILLY: You look worried.

BIFF: N-no. (*To* STANLEY.) Scotch all around. Make it doubles.

STANLEY: Doubles, right. (*He goes.*)

WILLY: You had a couple already, didn't you?   955

BIFF: Just a couple, yeah.

WILLY: Well, what happened, boy? (*Nodding affirmatively, with a smile.*) Everything go all right?

BIFF: (*Takes a breath, then reaches out and grasps* WILLY's *hand.*) Pal . . . (*He is smiling bravely, and* WILLY *is smiling too*). I had 960 an experience today.

HAPPY: Terrific, Pop.

WILLY: That so? What happened?

BIFF: (*High, slightly alcoholic, above the earth.*) I'm going to tell you everything from first to last. It's been a strange day. 965 (*Silence. He looks around, composes himself as best he can, but his breath keeps breaking the rhythm of his voice.*) I had to wait quite a while for him, and—

WILLY: Oliver?

BIFF: Yeah, Oliver. All day, as a matter of cold fact. And a lot 970 of—instances—facts, Pop, facts about my life came back to me. Who was it, Pop? Who ever said I was a salesman with Oliver?

WILLY: Well, you were.

BIFF: No, Dad, I was a shipping clerk.   975

WILLY: But you were practically—

BIFF: (*With determination.*) Dad, I don't know who said it first, but I was never a salesman for Bill Oliver.

WILLY: What're you talking about?

BIFF: Let's hold onto the facts tonight, Pop. We're not going 980 to get anywhere bullin' around. I was a shipping clerk.

WILLY: (*Angrily.*) All right, now listen to me—

BIFF: Why don't you let me finish?

WILLY: I'm not interested in stories about the past or any crap of that kind because the woods are burning, boys, you 985 understand? There's a big blaze going on all around. I was fired today.

BIFF: (*Shocked.*) How could you be?

990 WILLY: I was fired, and I'm looking for a little good news to tell your mother, because the woman has waited and the woman has suffered. The gist of it is that I haven't got a story left in my head, Biff. So don't give me a lecture about facts and aspects. I am not interested. Now what've you got to say to me?

(STANLEY *enters with three drinks. They wait until he leaves.*)

995 WILLY: Did you see Oliver?

BIFF: Jesus, Dad!

WILLY: You mean you didn't go up there?

HAPPY: Sure he went up there.

BIFF: I did. I—saw him. How could they fire you?

1000 WILLY: (*On the edge of his chair.*) What kind of a welcome did he give you?

BIFF: He won't even let you work on commission?

WILLY: I'm out! (*Driving.*) So tell me, he gave you a warm welcome?

1005 HAPPY: Sure, Pop, sure!

BIFF: (*Driven.*) Well, it was kind of—

WILLY: I was wondering if he'd remember you. (*To* HAPPY.) Imagine, man doesn't see him for ten, twelve years and gives him that kind of a welcome!

1010 HAPPY: Damn right!

BIFF: (*Trying to return to the offensive.*) Pop, look—

WILLY: You know why he remembered you, don't you? Because you impressed him in those days.

BIFF: Let's talk quietly and get this down to the facts, huh?

1015 WILLY: (*As though* BIFF *had been interrupting.*) Well, what happened? It's great news, Biff. Did he take you into his office or'd you talk in the waiting-room?

BIFF: Well, he came in, see, and—

WILLY: (*With a big smile.*) What'd he say? Betcha he threw his

1020 arm around you.

BIFF: Well, he kinda—

WILLY: He's a fine man. (*To* HAPPY.) Very hard man to see, y'know.

HAPPY: (*Agreeing.*) Oh, I know.

1025 WILLY: (*To* BIFF.) Is that where you had the drinks?

BIFF: Yeah, he gave me a couple of—no, no!

HAPPY: (*Cutting in.*) He told him my Florida idea.

WILLY: Don't interrupt. (*To* BIFF.) How'd he react to the Florida idea?

1030 BIFF: Dad, will you give me a minute to explain?

WILLY: I've been waiting for you to explain since I sat down here! What happened? He took you into his office and what?

BIFF: Well—I talked. And—and he listened, see.

1035 WILLY: Famous for the way he listens, y'know. What was his answer?

BIFF: His answer was— (*He breaks off, suddenly angry.*) Dad, you're not letting me tell you what I want to tell you!

WILLY: (*Accusing, angered.*) You didn't see him, did you?

1040 BIFF: I did see him!

WILLY: What'd you insult him or something? You insulted him didn't you?

BIFF: Listen, will you let me out of it, will you just let me out of it!

HAPPY: What the hell!

1045 WILLY: Tell me what happened!

BIFF: (*To* HAPPY.) I can't talk to him!

(*A single trumpet note jars the ear. The light of green leaves stains the house, which holds the air of night and a dream* YOUNG BERNARD *enters and knocks on the door of the house.*)

YOUNG BERNARD: (*Frantically.*) Mrs. Loman, Mrs. Loman!

HAPPY: Tell him what happened!

1050 BIFF: (*To* HAPPY.) Shut up and leave me alone!

WILLY: No, no! You had to go and flunk math!

BIFF: What math? What're you talking about?

YOUNG BERNARD: Mrs. Loman, Mrs. Loman!

(LINDA *appears in the house, as of old.*)

WILLY: (*Wildly.*) Math, math, math!

1055 BIFF: Take it easy, Pop!

YOUNG BERNARD: Mrs. Loman!

WILLY: (*Furiously.*) If you hadn't flunked you'd've been set by now!

1060 BIFF: Now, look, I'm gonna tell you what happened, and you're going to listen to me.

YOUNG BERNARD: Mrs. Loman!

BIFF: I waited six hours—

HAPPY: What the hell are you saying?

1065 BIFF: I kept sending in my name but he wouldn't see me. So finally he . . . (*He continues unheard as light fades low on the restaurant.*)

YOUNG BERNARD: Biff flunked math!

LINDA: No!

1070 YOUNG BERNARD: Birnbaum flunked him! They won't graduate him!

LINDA: But they have to. He's gotta go to the university. Where is he? Biff! Biff!

YOUNG BERNARD: No, he left. He went to Grand Central.

LINDA: Grand— You mean he went to Boston!

1075 YOUNG BERNARD: Is Uncle Willy in Boston?

LINDA: Oh, maybe Willy can talk to the teacher. Oh, the poor, poor boy!

(*Light on house area snaps out.*)

BIFF: (*At the table, now audible, holding up a gold fountain pen.*) . . . so I'm washed up with Oliver, you understand? Are you listening to me?

1080 WILLY: (*At a loss.*) Yeah, sure. If you hadn't flunked—

BIFF: Flunked what? What're you talking about?

WILLY: Don't blame everything on me! I didn't flunk math—you did! What pen?

1085 HAPPY: That was awful dumb, Biff, a pen like that is worth—

WILLY: (*Seeing the pen for the first time.*) You took Oliver's pen?

BIFF: (*Weakening.*) Dad, I just explained it to you.

WILLY: You stole Bill Oliver's fountain pen!

BIFF: I didn't exactly steal it! That's just what I've been explaining to you!

1090 HAPPY: He had it in his hand and just then Oliver walked in, so he got nervous and stuck it in his pocket!

WILLY: My God, Biff!

BIFF: I never intended to do it, Dad!

1095 OPERATOR'S VOICE: Standish Arms, good evening!

WILLY: (*Shouting.*) I'm not in my room!

BIFF: (*Frightened.*) Dad, what's the matter? (*He and* HAPPY *stand up.*)

OPERATOR: Ringing Mr. Loman for you!

1100 WILLY: I'm not there, stop it!

BIFF: (*Horrified, gets down on one knee before* WILLY.) Dad, I'll make good, I'll make good. (WILLY *tries to get to his feet.* BIFF *holds him down.*) Sit down now.

WILLY: No, you're no good, you're no good for anything.

1105 BIFF: I am, Dad, I'll find something else, you understand? Now don't worry about anything. (*He holds up* WILLY's *face.*) Talk to me, Dad.

OPERATOR: Mr. Loman does not answer. Shall I page him?

1110 WILLY: (*Attempting to stand, as though to rush and silence the* OPERATOR.) No, no, no!

HAPPY: He'll strike something, Pop.

WILLY: No, no . . .

BIFF: (*Desperately, standing over* WILLY.) Pop, listen! Listen to me! I'm telling you something good. Oliver talked to his

1115 partner about the Florida idea. You listening? He—he talked to his partner, and he came to me . . . I'm going to be all right, you hear? Dad, listen to me, he said it was just a question of the amount!

WILLY: Then you . . . got it?

1120 HAPPY: He's gonna be terrific, Pop!

WILLY: (*Trying to stand.*) Then you got it, haven't you? You got it! You got it!

BIFF: (*Agonized, holds* WILLY *down.*) No, no. Look, Pop. I'm supposed to have lunch with them tomorrow. I'm just

1125 telling you this so you'll know that I can still make an impression, Pop. And I'll make good somewhere, but I can't go tomorrow, see?

WILLY: Why not? You simply—

BIFF: But the pen, Pop!

1130 WILLY: You give it to him and tell him it was an oversight!

HAPPY: Sure, have lunch tomorrow!

BIFF: I can't say that—

WILLY: You were doing a crosswood puzzle and accidentally used his pen!

1135 BIFF: Listen, kid, I took those balls years ago, now I walk in with his fountain pen? That clinches it, don't you see? I can't face him like that! I'll try elsewhere.

PAGE'S VOICE: Paging Mr. Loman!

WILLY: Don't you want to be anything?

1140 BIFF: Pop, how can I go back?

WILLY: You don't want to be anything, is that what's behind it?

BIFF: (*Now angry at* WILLY *for not crediting his sympathy.*) Don't take it that way! You think it was easy walking into that office after what I'd done to him? A team of horses

1145 couldn't have dragged me back to Bill Oliver!

WILLY: Then why'd you go?

BIFF: Why did I go? Why did I go! Look at you! Look at what's become of you!

(*Off left,* THE WOMAN *laughs.*)

WILLY: Biff, you're going to go to that lunch tomorrow, or—

BIFF: I can't go. I've got no appointment!   1150

HAPPY: Biff, for . . .!

WILLY: Are you spiting me?

BIFF: Don't take it that way! Goddammit!

WILLY: (*Strikes* BIFF *and falters away from the table.*) You rotten little louse! Are you spiting me?   1155

THE WOMAN: Someone's at the door, Willy!

BIFF: I'm no good, can't you see what I am?

HAPPY: (*Separating them.*) Hey, you're in a restaurant! Now cut it out, both of you! (*The girls enter.*) Hello, girls, sit down.

(THE WOMAN *laughs, off left.*)

MISS FORSYTHE: I guess we might as well. This is Letta.   1160

THE WOMAN: Willy, are you going to wake up?

BIFF: (*Ignoring* WILLY.) How're ya, miss, sit down. What do you drink?

MISS FORSYTHE: Letta might not be able to stay long.

LETTA: I gotta get up very early tomorrow. I got jury duty.   1165
I'm so excited! Were you fellows ever on a jury?

BIFF: No, but I been in front of them! (*The girls laugh.*) This is my father.

LETTA: Isn't he cute? Sit down with us, Pop.

HAPPY: Sit him down, Biff!   1170

BIFF: (*Going to him.*) Come on, slugger, drink us under the table. To hell with it! Come on, sit down, pal.

(*On* BIFF's *last insistence,* WILLY *is about to sit.*)

THE WOMAN: (*Now urgently.*) Willy, are you going to answer the door!

(*The* WOMAN's *call pulls* WILLY *back. He starts right, befuddled.*)

BIFF: Hey, where are you going?   1175

WILLY: Open the door.

BIFF: The door?

WILLY: The washroom . . . the door . . . where's the door?

BIFF: (*Leading* WILLY *to the left.*) Just go straight down.

(WILLY *moves left.*)

THE WOMAN: Willy, Willy, are you going to get up, get up, get 1180
up, get up?

(WILLY *exits left.*)

LETTA: I think it's sweet you bring your daddy along.

MISS FORSYTHE: Oh, he isn't really your father!

BIFF: (*At left, turning to her resentfully.*) Miss Forsythe, you've just seen a prince walk by. A fine, troubled prince. A hard- 1185
working, unappreciated prince. A pal, you understand? A good companion. Always for his boys.

LETTA: That's so sweet.

HAPPY: Well, girls, what's the program? We're wasting time. Come on, Biff. Gather round. Where would you like to go? 1190

BIFF: Why don't you do something for him?

HAPPY: Me!

BIFF: Don't you give a damn for him, Hap?

HAPPY: What're you talking about? I'm the one who—

BIFF: I sense it, you don't give a good goddam about him. (*He 1195
takes the rolled-up hose from his pocket and puts it on the table*

in front of HAPPY.) Look what I found in the cellar, for Christ's sake. How can you bear to let it go on?

HAPPY: Me? Who goes away? Who runs off and—

1200 BIFF: Yeah, but he doesn't mean anything to you. You could help him—I can't! Don't you understand what I'm talking about? He's going to kill himself, don't you know that?

HAPPY: Don't I know it! Me!

1205 BIFF: Hap, help him! Jesus . . . help him . . . Help me, help me, I can't bear to look at his face! (*Ready to weep, he hurries out, up right.*)

HAPPY: (*Starting after him.*) Where are you going?

MISS FORSYTHE: What's he so mad about?

1210 HAPPY: Come on, girls, we'll catch up with him.

MISS FORSYTHE: (*As* HAPPY *pushes her out.*) Say, I don't like that temper of his!

HAPPY: He's just a little overstrung, he'll be all right!

WILLY: (*Off left, as* THE WOMAN *laughs.*) Don't answer! Don't

1215 answer!

LETTA: Don't you want to tell your father—

HAPPY: No, that's not my father. He's just a guy. Come on, we'll catch Biff, and, honey, we're going to paint this town! Stanley, where's the check! Hey, Stanley!

(*They exit.* STANLEY *looks toward left.*)

1220 STANLEY: (*Calling to* HAPPY *indignantly.*) Mr. Loman! Mr. Loman!

(STANLEY *picks up a chair and follows them off. Knocking is heard off left.* THE WOMAN *enters, laughing.* WILLY *follows her. She is in a black slip; he is buttoning his shirt. Raw, sensuous music accompanies their speech.*)

WILLY: Will you stop laughing? Will you stop?

THE WOMAN: Aren't you going to answer the door? He'll wake the whole hotel.

1225 WILLY: I'm not expecting anybody.

THE WOMAN: Whyn't you have another drink, honey, and stop being so damn self-centered?

WILLY: I'm so lonely.

THE WOMAN: You know you ruined me, Willy? From now

1230 on, whenever you come to the office, I'll see that you go right through to the buyers. No waiting at my desk any more, Willy. You ruined me.

WILLY: That's nice of you to say that.

THE WOMAN: Gee, you are self-centered! Why so sad? You are

1235 the saddest, self-centeredest soul I ever did see-saw. (*She laughs. He kisses her.*) Come on inside, drummer boy. It's silly to be dressing in the middle of the night. (*As knocking is heard.*) Aren't you going to answer the door?

WILLY: They're knocking on the wrong door.

1240 THE WOMAN: But I felt the knocking. And he heard us talking in here. Maybe the hotel's on fire!

WILLY: (*His terror rising.*) It's a mistake.

THE WOMAN: Then tell him to go away!

WILLY: There's nobody there.

1245 THE WOMAN: It's getting on my nerves, Willy. There's somebody standing out there and it's getting on my nerves!

WILLY: (*Pushing her away from him.*) All right, stay in the bathroom here, and don't come out. I think there's a law in Massachusetts about it, so don't come out. It may be that

new room clerk. He looked very mean. So don't come 1250 out. It's a mistake, there's no fire.

(*The knocking is heard again. He takes a few steps away from her, and she vanishes into the wing. The light follows him, and now he is facing* YOUNG BIFF, *who carries a suitcase.* BIFF *steps toward him. The music is gone.*)

BIFF: Why didn't you answer?

WILLY: Biff! What are you doing in Boston?

BIFF: Why didn't you answer? I've been knocking for five minutes, I called you on the phone— 1255

WILLY: I just heard you. I was in the bathroom and had the door shut. Did anything happen home?

BIFF: Dad—I let you down.

WILLY: What do you mean?

BIFF: Dad . . . 1260

WILLY: Biffo, what's this about? (*Putting his arm around* BIFF.) Come on, let's go downstairs and get you a malted.

BIFF: Dad, I flunked math.

WILLY: Not for the term?

BIFF: The term. I haven't got enough credits to graduate. 1265

WILLY: You mean to say Bernard wouldn't give you the answers?

BIFF: He did, he tried, but I only got a sixty-one.

WILLY: And they wouldn't give you four points?

BIFF: Birnbaum refused absolutely. I begged him, Pop, but he 1270 won't give me those points. You gotta talk to him before they close the school. Because if he saw the kind of man you are, and you just talked to him in your way, I'm sure he'd come through for me. The class came right before practice, see, and I didn't go enough. Would you talk to 1275 him? He'd like you, Pop. You know the way you could talk.

WILLY: You're on. We'll drive right back.

BIFF: Oh, Dad, good work! I'm sure he'll change it for you!

WILLY: Go downstairs and tell the clerk I'm checkin' out. Go 1280 right down.

BIFF: Yes, sir! See, the reason he hates me, Pop—one day he was late for class so I got up at the blackboard and imitated him. I crossed my eyes and talked with a lithp.

WILLY: (*Laughing.*) You did? The kids like it? 1285

BIFF: They nearly died laughing!

WILLY: Yeah? What'd you do?

BIFF: The thquare root of thixthy twee is . . . (WILLY *bursts out laughing;* BIFF *joins him.*) And in the middle of it he walked in!

(WILLY *laughs and* THE WOMAN *joins in offstage.*)

WILLY: (*Without hesitation.*) Hurry downstairs and— 1290

BIFF: Somebody in there?

WILLY: No, that was next door.

(THE WOMAN *laughs offstage.*)

BIFF: Somebody got in your bathroom!

WILLY: No, it's the next room, there's a party—

THE WOMAN: (*Enters, laughing. She lisps this.*) Can I come in? 1295 There's something in the bathtub, Willy, and it's moving!

(WILLY *looks at* BIFF, *who is staring open-mouthed and horrified at* THE WOMAN.)

WILLY: Ah—you better go back to your room. They must be finished painting by now. They're painting her room so I let her take a shower here. Go back, go back . . . (*He*
1300   *pushes her.*)

THE WOMAN: (*Resisting.*) But I've got to get dressed, Willy, I can't—

WILLY: Get out of here! Go back, go back . . . (*Suddenly striving for the ordinary.*) This is Miss Francis, Biff, she's a buyer.
1305   They're painting her room. Go back, Miss Francis, go back . . .

THE WOMAN: But my clothes, I can't go out naked in the hall!

WILLY: (*Pushing her offstage.*) Get outa here! Go back, go back!

(BIFF *slowly sits down on his suitcase as the argument continues offstage.*)

THE WOMAN: Where's my stockings? You promised me stock-
1310   ings, Willy!

WILLY: I have no stockings here!

THE WOMAN: You had two boxes of size nine sheers for me, and I want them!

WILLY: Here, for God's sake, will you get outa here!

1315   THE WOMAN: (*Enters holding a box of stockings.*) I just hope there's nobody in the hall. That's all I hope. (*To* BIFF.) Are you football or baseball?

BIFF: Football.

THE WOMAN: (*Angry, humiliated.*) That's me too. G'night. (*She*
1320   *snatches her clothes from* WILLY, *and walks out.*)

WILLY: (*After a pause.*) Well, better get going. I want to get to the school first thing in the morning. Get my suits out of the closet. I'll get my valise. (BIFF *doesn't move.*) What's the matter? (BIFF *remains motionless, tears falling.*) She's a buyer.
1325   Buys for J.H. Simmons. She lives down the hall—they're painting. You don't imagine—(*He breaks off. After a pause.*) Now listen, pal, she's just a buyer. She sees merchandise in her room and they have to keep it looking just so . . . (*Pause. Assuming command.*) All right, get my suits. (BIFF
1330   *doesn't move.*) Now stop crying and do as I say. I gave you an order. Biff, I gave you an order! Is that what you do when I give you an order? How dare you cry! (*Putting his arm around* BIFF.) Now look, Biff, when you grow up you'll understand about these things. You mustn't—you
1335   mustn't overemphasize a thing like this. I'll see Birnbaum first thing in the morning.

BIFF: Never mind.

WILLY: (*Getting down beside* BIFF.) Never mind! He's going to give you those points. I'll see to it.

1340   BIFF: He wouldn't listen to you.

WILLY: He certainly will listen to me. You need those points for the U. of Virginia.

BIFF: I'm not going there.

WILLY: Heh? If I can't get him to change that mark you'll
1345   make it up in summer school. You've got all summer to—

BIFF: (*His weeping breaking from him.*) Dad . . .

WILLY: (*Infected by it.*) Oh, my boy . . .

BIFF: Dad . . .

WILLY: She's nothing to me, Biff. I was lonely, I was terribly
1350   lonely.

BIFF: You—you gave her Mama's stockings! (*His tears break through and he rises to go.*)

WILLY: (*Grabbing for* BIFF.) I gave you an order!

BIFF: Don't touch me, you—liar!

WILLY: Apologize for that!   1355

BIFF: You fake! You phony little fake! You fake! (*Overcome, he turns quickly and weeping fully goes out with his suitcase.* WILLY *is left on the floor on his knees.*)

WILLY: I gave you an order! Biff, come back here or I'll beat you! Come back here! I'll whip you!   1360

(STANLEY *comes quickly in from the right and stands in front of* WILLY.)

WILLY: (*Shouts at* STANLEY.) I gave you an order . . .

STANLEY: Hey, let's pick it up, pick it up, Mr. Loman. (*He helps* WILLY *to his feet.*) Your boys left with the chippies. They said they'll see you home.

(*A second waiter watches some distance away.*)

WILLY: But we were supposed to have dinner together.   1365

(*Music is heard,* WILLY*'s theme.*)

STANLEY: Can you make it?

WILLY: I'll—sure, I can make it. (*Suddenly concerned about his clothes.*) Do I—I look all right?

STANLEY: Sure, you look all right. (*He flicks a speck off* WILLY*'s lapel.*)   1370

WILLY: Here—here's a dollar.

STANLEY: Oh, your son paid me. It's all right.

WILLY: (*Putting it in* STANLEY*'s hand.*) No, take it. You're a good boy.

STANLEY: Oh, no, you don't have to . . .   1375

WILLY: Here—here's some more, I don't need it any more. (*After a slight pause.*) Tell me—is there a seed store in the neighborhood?

STANLEY: Seeds? You mean like to plant?

(*As* WILLY *turns,* STANLEY *slips the money back into his jacket pocket.*)

WILLY: Yes. Carrots, peas . . .   1380

STANLEY: Well, there's hardware stores on Sixth Avenue, but it may be too late now.

WILLY: (*Anxiously.*) Oh, I'd better hurry. I've got to get some seeds. (*He starts off to the right.*) I've got to get some seeds, right away. Nothing's planted. I don't have a thing in the 1385 ground.

(WILLY *hurries out as the light goes down.* STANLEY *moves over to the right after him, watches him off. The other waiter has been staring at* WILLY.)

STANLEY: (*To the waiter.*) Well, whatta you looking at?

(*The waiter picks up the chairs and moves off right.* STANLEY *takes the table and follows him. The light fades on this area. There is a long pause, the sound of the flute coming over. The light gradually rises on the kitchen, which is empty.* HAPPY *appears at the door of the house, followed by* BIFF. HAPPY *is carrying a large bunch of long-stemmed roses. He enters the kitchen, looks around for* LINDA. *Not seeing her, he turns to* BIFF, *who is just outside the house door, and makes a gesture with his hands, indicating "Not here, I guess." He looks into the living-room and freezes. Inside,* LINDA, *unseen, is seated,* WILLY'*s coat on her lap. She rises ominously and quietly and moves toward* HAPPY, *who backs up into the kitchen, afraid.*)

HAPPY: Hey, what're you doing up? (LINDA *says nothing but moves toward him implacably.*) Where's Pop? (*He keeps back-*
1390 *ing to the right, and now* LINDA *is in full view in the doorway to the living-room.*) Is he sleeping?
LINDA: Where were you?
HAPPY: (*Trying to laugh it off.*) We met two girls, Mom, very fine types. Here, we brought you some flowers. (*Offering*
1395 *them to her.*) Put them in your room, Ma.

(*She knocks them to the floor at* BIFF'*s feet. He has now come inside and closed the door behind him. She stares at* BIFF, *silent.*)

HAPPY: Now what'd you do that for? Mom, I want you to have some flowers—
LINDA: (*Cutting* HAPPY *off, violently to* BIFF.) Don't you care whether he lives or dies?
1400 HAPPY: (*Going to the stairs.*) Come upstairs, Biff.
BIFF: (*With a flare of disgust, to* HAPPY.) Go away from me! (*To* LINDA.) What do you mean, lives or dies? Nobody's dying around here, pal.
LINDA: Get out of my sight! Get out of here!
1405 BIFF: I wanna see the boss.
LINDA: You're not going near him!
BIFF: Where is he? (*He moves into the living-room and* LINDA *follows.*)
LINDA: (*Shouting after* BIFF.) You invite him for dinner. He
1410 looks forward to it all day—(BIFF *appears in his parents' bedroom, looks around, and exits.*)—and then you desert him there. There's no stranger you'd do that to!
HAPPY: Why? He had a swell time with us. Listen, when I—(LINDA *comes back into the kitchen.*)—desert him I hope I
1415 don't outlive the day!
LINDA: Get out of here!
HAPPY: Now look, Mom . . .
LINDA: Did you have to go to women tonight? You and your lousy rotten whores!

(BIFF *re-enters the kitchen.*)

1420 HAPPY: Mom, all we did was follow Biff around trying to cheer him up! (*To* BIFF.) Boy, what a night you gave me!
LINDA: Get out of here, both of you, and don't come back! I don't want you tormenting him any more. Go on now, get your things together! (*To* BIFF.) You can sleep in his apart-
1425 ment. (*She starts to pick up the flowers and stops herself.*) Pick up this stuff, I'm not your maid any more. Pick it up, you bum, you!

(HAPPY *turns his back to her in refusal.* BIFF *slowly moves over and gets down on his knees, picking up the flowers.*)

LINDA: You're a pair of animals! Not one, not another living soul would have had the cruelty to walk out on that man
1430 in a restaurant!
BIFF: (*Not looking at her.*) Is that what he said?
LINDA: He didn't have to say anything. He was so humiliated he nearly limped when he came in.
HAPPY: But, Mom, he had a great time with us—
1435 BIFF: (*Cutting him off violently.*) Shut up!

(*Without another word,* HAPPY *goes upstairs.*)

LINDA: You! You didn't even go in to see if he was all right!
BIFF: (*Still on the floor in front of* LINDA, *the flowers in his hand; with self-loathing.*) No. Didn't. Didn't do a damned thing. How do you like that, heh? Left him babbling in a toilet.
LINDA: You louse. You . . .
1440
BIFF: Now you hit it on the nose! (*He gets up, throws the flowers in the wastebasket.*) The scum of the earth, and you're looking at him!
LINDA: Get out of here!
BIFF: I gotta talk to the boss, Mom. Where is he?
1445
LINDA: You're not going near him. Get out of this house!
BIFF: (*With absolute assurance, determination.*) No. We're gonna have an abrupt conversation, him and me.
LINDA: You're not talking to him!

(*Hammering is heard from outside the house, off right.* BIFF *turns toward the noise.*)

LINDA: (*Suddenly pleading.*) Will you please leave him alone?   1450
BIFF: What's he doing out there?
LINDA: He's planting the garden!
BIFF: (*Quietly.*) Now? Oh, my God!

(BIFF *moves outside,* LINDA *following. The light dies down on them and comes up on the center of the apron as* WILLY *walks into it. He is carrying a flashlight, a hoe, and a handful of seed packets. He raps the top of the hoe sharply to fix it firmly, and then moves to the left, measuring off the distance with his foot. He holds the flashlight to look at the seed packets, reading off the instructions. He is in the blue of night.*)

WILLY: Carrots . . . quarter-inch apart. Rows . . . one-foot rows. (*He measures it off.*) One foot. (*He puts down a package and measures off.*) Beets. (*He puts down another package and measures again.*) Lettuce. (*He reads the package, puts it down.*) One foot—(*He breaks off as* BEN *appears at the right and moves slowly down to him.*) What a proposition, ts, ts. Terrific, terrific. 'Cause she's suffered, Ben, the woman has suffered. You understand me? A man can't go out the way he came in, Ben, a man has got to add up to something. You can't, you can't—(BEN *moves toward him as though to interrupt.*) You gotta consider, now. Don't answer so quick. Remember, it's a guaranteed twenty-thousand-dollar proposition. Now look, Ben, I want you to go through the ins and outs of this thing with me. I've got nobody to talk to, Ben, and the woman has suffered, you hear me?
1455

1460

1465

BEN: (*Standing still, considering.*) What's the proposition?
WILLY: It's twenty thousand dollars on the barrelhead. Guaranteed, gilt-edged, you understand?
1470
BEN: You don't want to make a fool of yourself. They might not honor the policy.
WILLY: How can they dare refuse? Didn't I work like a coolie to meet every premium on the nose? And now they don't pay off? Impossible!
1475
BEN: It's called a cowardly thing, William.
WILLY: Why? Does it take more guts to stand here the rest of my life ringing up a zero?
BEN: (*Yielding.*) That's a point, William. (*He moves, thinking, turns.*) And twenty thousand—that *is* something one can feel with the hand, it is there.
1480

WILLY: (*Now assured, with rising power.*) Oh, Ben, that's the whole beauty of it! I see it like a diamond, shining in the dark, hard and rough, that I can pick up and touch in my hand. Not like—like an appointment! This would not be another damned-fool appointment, Ben, and it changes all the aspects. Because he thinks I'm nothing, see, and so he spites me. But the funeral— (*Straightening up.*) Ben, that funeral will be massive! They'll come from Maine, Massachusetts, Vermont, New Hampshire! All the old-timers with the strange license plates—that boy will be thunderstruck, Ben, because he never realized—I am known! Rhode Island, New York, New Jersey—I am known, Ben, and he'll see it with his eyes once and for all. He'll see what I am, Ben! He's in for a shock, that boy!

BEN: (*Coming down to the edge of the garden.*) He'll call you a coward.

WILLY: (*Suddenly fearful.*) No, that would be terrible.

BEN: Yes. And a damned fool.

WILLY: No, no, he mustn't, I won't have that! (*He is broken and desperate.*)

BEN: He'll hate you, William.

(*The gay music of the Boys is heard.*)

WILLY: Oh, Ben, how do we get back to all the great times? Used to be so full of light, and comradeship, the sleigh-riding in winter, and the ruddiness on his cheeks. And always some kind of good news coming up, always something nice coming up ahead. And never even let me carry the valises in the house, and simonizing, simonizing that little red car! Why, why can't I give him something and not have him hate me?

BEN: Let me think about it. (*He glances at his watch.*) I still have a little time. Remarkable proposition, but you've got to be sure you're not making a fool of yourself.

(BEN *drifts off upstage and goes out of sight.* BIFF *comes down from the left.*)

WILLY: (*Suddenly conscious of* BIFF, *turns and looks up at him, then begins picking up the packages of seeds in confusion.*) Where the hell is that seed? (*Indignantly.*) You can't see nothing out here! They boxed in the whole goddam neighborhood!

BIFF: There are people all around here. Don't you realize that?

WILLY: I'm busy. Don't bother me.

BIFF: (*Taking the hoe from* WILLY.) I'm saying good-by to you, Pop. (WILLY *looks at him, silent, unable to move.*) I'm not coming back any more.

WILLY: You're not going to see Oliver tomorrow?

BIFF: I've got no appointment, Dad.

WILLY: He put his arm around you, and you've got no appointment?

BIFF: Pop, get this now, will you? Everytime I've left it's been a fight that sent me out of here. Today I realized something about myself and I tried to explain it to you and I—I think I'm just not smart enough to make any sense out of it for you. To hell with whose fault it is or anything like that. (*He takes* WILLY's *arm.*) Let's just wrap it up, heh? Come on in, we'll tell Mom. (*He gently tries to pull* WILLY *to left.*)

WILLY: (*Frozen, immobile, with guilt in his voice.*) No, I don't want to see her.

BIFF: Come on! (*He pulls again, and* WILLY *tries to pull away.*)

WILLY: (*Highly nervous.*) No, no, I don't want to see her.

BIFF: (*Tries to look into* WILLY's *face, as if to find the answer there.*) Why don't you want to see her?

WILLY: (*More harshly now.*) Don't bother me, will you?

BIFF: What do you mean, you don't want to see her? You don't want them calling you yellow, do you? This isn't your fault; it's me, I'm a bum. Now come inside! (WILLY *strains to get away.*) Did you hear what I said to you?

(WILLY *pulls away and quickly goes by himself into the house.* BIFF *follows.*)

LINDA: (*To* WILLY). Did you plant, dear?

BIFF: (*At the door, to* LINDA.) All right, we had it out. I'm going and I'm not writing any more.

LINDA: (*Going to* WILLY *in the kitchen.*) I think that's the best way, dear. 'Cause there's no use drawing it out, you'll just never get along.

(WILLY *doesn't respond.*)

BIFF: People ask where I am and what I'm doing, you don't know, and you don't care. That way it'll be off your mind and you can start brightening up again. All right? That clears it, doesn't it? (WILLY *is silent, and* BIFF *goes to him.*) You gonna wish me luck, scout? (*He extends his hand.*) What do you say?

LINDA: Shake his hand, Willy.

WILLY: (*Turning to her, seething with hurt.*) There's no necessity to mention the pen at all, y'know.

BIFF: (*Gently.*) I've got no appointment, Dad.

WILLY: (*Erupting fiercely.*) He put his arm around . . . ?

BIFF: Dad, you're never going to see what I am, so what's the use of arguing? If I strike oil I'll send you a check. Meantime forget I'm alive.

WILLY: (*To* LINDA.) Spite, see?

BIFF: Shake hands, Dad.

WILLY: Not my hand.

BIFF: I was hoping not to go this way.

WILLY: Well, this is the way you're going. Good-by.

(BIFF *looks at him a moment, then turns sharply and goes to the stairs.*)

WILLY: (*Stops him with.*) May you rot in hell if you leave this house!

BIFF: (*Turning.*) Exactly what is it that you want from me?

WILLY: I want you to know, on the train, in the mountains, in the valleys, wherever you go, that you cut down your life for spite!

BIFF: No, no.

WILLY: Spite, spite, is the word of your undoing! And when you're down and out, remember what did it. When you're rotting somewhere beside the railroad tracks, remember, and don't you dare blame it on me!

BIFF: I'm not blaming it on you!

WILLY: I won't take the rap for this, you hear?

(HAPPY *comes down the stairs and stands on the bottom step, watching.*)

BIFF: That's just what I'm telling you!

1585 WILLY: (*Sinking into a chair at the table, with full accusation.*) You're trying to put a knife in me—don't think I don't know what you're doing!

BIFF: All right, phony! Then let's lay it on the line. (*He whips the rubber tube out of his pocket and puts it on the table.*)

1590 HAPPY: You crazy—

LINDA: Biff! (*She moves to grab the hose, but* BIFF *holds it down with his hand.*)

BIFF: Leave it there! Don't move it!

WILLY: (*Not looking at it.*) What is that?

1595 BIFF: You know goddam well what that is.

WILLY: (*Caged, wanting to escape.*) I never saw that.

BIFF: You saw it. The mice didn't bring it into the cellar! What is this supposed to do, make a hero out of you? This supposed to make me sorry for you?

1600 WILLY: Never heard of it.

BIFF: There'll be no pity for you, you hear it? No pity!

WILLY: (*To* LINDA.) You hear the spite!

BIFF: No, you're going to hear the truth—what you are and what I am!

1605 LINDA: Stop it!

WILLY: Spite!

HAPPY: (*Coming down toward* BIFF.) You cut it now!

BIFF: (*To* HAPPY.) The man don't know who we are! The man is gonna know! (*To* WILLY.) We never told the truth for ten

1610 minutes in this house!

HAPPY: We always told the truth!

BIFF: (*Turning on him.*) You big blow, are you the assistant buyer? You're one of the two assistants to the assistant, aren't you?

1615 HAPPY: Well, I'm practically—

BIFF: You're practically full of it! We all are! And I'm through with it. (*To* WILLY.) Now hear this, Willy, this is me.

WILLY: I know you!

BIFF: You know why I had no address for three months? I

1620 stole a suit in Kansas City and I was in jail. (*To* LINDA, *who is sobbing.*) Stop crying. I'm through with it.

(LINDA *turns away from them, her hands covering her face.*)

WILLY: I suppose that's my fault!

BIFF: I stole myself out of every good job since high school!

WILLY: And whose fault is that?

1625 BIFF: And I never got anywhere because you blew me so full of hot air I could never stand taking orders from anybody! That's whose fault it is!

WILLY: I hear that!

LINDA: Don't, Biff!

1630 BIFF: It's goddam time you heard that! I had to be boss big shot in two weeks, and I'm through with it!

WILLY: Then hang yourself! For spite, hang yourself!

BIFF: No! Nobody's hanging himself, Willy! I ran down eleven flights with a pen in my hand today. And suddenly I

1635 stopped, you hear me? And in the middle of that office building, do you hear this? I stopped in the middle of that building and I saw—the sky. I saw the things that I love in this world. The work and the food and time to sit and smoke. And I looked at the pen and said to myself, what

1640 the hell am I grabbing this for? Why am I trying to become what I don't want to be? What am I doing in an office, making a contemptuous, begging fool of myself, when all

I want is out there, waiting for me the minute I say I know who I am! Why can't I say that, Willy? (*He tries to make* WILLY *face him, but* WILLY *pulls away and moves to the left.*) 1645

WILLY: (*With hatred, threateningly.*) The door of your life is wide open!

BIFF: Pop! I'm a dime a dozen, and so are you!

WILLY: (*Turning on him now in an uncontrolled outburst.*) I am not a dime a dozen! I am Willy Loman, and you are Biff 1650 Loman!

(BIFF *starts for* WILLY, *but is blocked by* HAPPY. *In his fury,* BIFF *seems on the verge of attacking his father.*)

BIFF: I am not a leader of men, Willy, and neither are you. You were never anything but a hard-working drummer who landed in the ash can like all the rest of them! I'm one dollar an hour, Willy! I tried seven states and couldn't 1655 raise it. A buck an hour! Do you gather my meaning? I'm not bringing home any prizes any more, and you're going to stop waiting for me to bring them home!

WILLY: (*Directly to* BIFF.) You vengeful, spiteful mut!

(BIFF *breaks from* HAPPY. WILLY, *in fright, starts up the stairs.* BIFF *grabs him.*)

BIFF: (*At the peak of his fury.*) Pop, I'm nothing! I'm nothing, 1660 Pop. Can't you understand that? There's no spite in it any more. I'm just what I am, that's all.

(BIFF'S *fury has spent itself, and he breaks down, sobbing, holding on to* WILLY, *who dumbly fumbles for* BIFF'S *face.*)

WILLY: (*Astonished.*) What're you doing? What're you doing? (*To* LINDA.) Why is he crying?

BIFF: (*Crying, broken.*) Will you let me go, for Christ's sake? 1665 Will you take that phony dream and burn it before something happens? (*Struggling to contain himself, he pulls away and moves to the stairs.*) I'll go in the morning. Put him— put him to bed. (*Exhausted,* BIFF *moves up the stairs to his room.*) 1670

WILLY: (*After a long pause, astonished, elevated.*) Isn't that—isn't that remarkable? Biff—he likes me!

LINDA: He loves you, Willy!

HAPPY: (*Deeply moved.*) Always did, Pop.

WILLY: Oh, Biff! (*Staring wildly.*) He cried! Cried to me. (*He 1675 is choking with his love, and now cries out his promise.*) That boy—that boy is going to be magnificent!

(BEN *appears in the light just outside the kitchen.*)

BEN: Yes, outstanding, with twenty thousand behind him.

LINDA: (*Sensing the racing of his mind, fearfully, carefully.*) Now come to bed, Willy. It's all settled now. 1680

WILLY: (*Finding it difficult not to rush out of the house.*) Yes, we'll sleep. Come on. Go to sleep, Hap.

BEN: And it does take a great kind of a man to crack the jungle.

(*In accents of dread,* BEN'S *idyllic music starts up.*)

HAPPY: (*His arm around* LINDA.) I'm getting married, Pop, don't forget it. I'm changing everything. I'm gonna run 1685 that department before the year is up. You'll see, Mom. (*He kisses her.*)

BEN: The jungle is dark but full of diamonds, Willy.

(WILLY *turns, moves, listening to* BEN.)

LINDA: Be good. You're both good boys, just act that way,
1690 that's all.
HAPPY: 'Night, Pop. (*He goes upstairs.*)
LINDA: (*To* WILLY). Come, dear.
BEN: (*With greater force.*) One must go in to fetch a diamond
      out.
1695 WILLY: (*To* LINDA, *as he moves slowly along the edge of the kitchen,
      toward the door.*) I just want to get settled down, Linda. Let
      me sit alone for a little.
LINDA: (*Almost uttering her fear.*) I want you upstairs.
WILLY: (*Taking her in his arms.*) In a few minutes, Linda. I
1600 couldn't sleep right now. Go on, you look awful tired. (*He
      kisses her.*)
BEN: Not like an appointment at all. A diamond is rough and
      hard to the touch.
WILLY: Go on now. I'll be right up.
1705 LINDA: I think this is the only way, Willy.
WILLY: Sure, it's the best thing.
BEN: Best thing!
WILLY: The only way. Everything is gonna be—go on, kid, get
      to bed. You look so tired.
1710 LINDA: Come right up.
WILLY: Two minutes.

(LINDA *goes into the living-room, then reappears in her bedroom.*
WILLY *moves just outside the kitchen door.*)

WILLY: Loves me. (*Wonderingly.*) Always loved me. Isn't that a
      remarkable thing? Ben, he'll worship me, for it!
BEN: (*With promise.*) It's dark there, but full of diamonds.
1715 WILLY: Can you imagine that magnificence with twenty
      thousand dollars in his pocket?
LINDA: (*Calling from her room.*) Willy! Come up!
WILLY: (*Calling into the kitchen.*) Yes! Yes. Coming! It's very
      smart, you realize that, don't you, sweetheart? Even Ben
1720 sees it. I gotta go, baby. 'By! 'By! (*Going over to* BEN, *almost
      dancing.*) Imagine? When the mail comes he'll be ahead of
      Bernard again!
BEN: A perfect proposition all around.
WILLY: Did you see how he cried to me? Oh, if I could kiss
1725 him, Ben!
BEN: Time, William, time!
WILLY: Oh, Ben, I always knew one way or another we were
      gonna make it, Biff and I!
BEN: (*Looking at his watch.*) The boat. We'll be late. (*He moves
1730 slowly off into the darkness.*)
WILLY: (*Elegiacally, turning to the house.*) Now when you kick
      off, boy, I want a seventy-yard boot, and get right down
      the field under the ball, and when you hit, hit low and hit
      hard, because it's important, boy. (*He swings around and faces
1735 the audience.*) There's all kinds of important people in the
      stands, and the first thing you know . . . (*Suddenly realizing
      he is alone.*) Ben! Ben, where do I . . . ? (*He makes a sudden
      movement of search.*) Ben, how do I . . . ?
LINDA: (*Calling.*) Willy, you coming up?
1740 WILLY: (*Uttering a gasp of fear, whirling about as if to quiet her.*)
      Sh! (*He turns around as if to find his way; sounds, faces, voices,
      seem to be swarming in upon him and he flicks at them, crying.*)

Sh! Sh! (*Suddenly music, faint and high, stops him. It rises in
intensity, almost to an unbearable scream. He goes up and down
on his toes, and rushes off around the house.*) Shhh!   1745
LINDA: Willy?

(*There is no answer.* LINDA *waits.* BIFF *gets up off his bed He is still
in his clothes.* HAPPY *sits up.* BIFF *stands listening.*)

LINDA: (*With real fear.*) Willy, answer me! Willy!

(*There is the sound of a car starting and moving away at full speed.*)

LINDA: No!
BIFF: (*Rushing down the stairs.*) Pop!

(*As the car speeds off, the music crashes down in a frenzy of sound,
which becomes the soft pulsation of a single cello string.* BIFF *slowly returns to his bedroom. He and* HAPPY *gravely don their jackets.* LINDA
*slowly walks out of her room. The music has developed into a dead
march. The leaves of day are appearing over everything.* CHARLEY
and BERNARD, *somberly dressed, appear and knock on the kitchen
door.* BIFF *and* HAPPY *slowly descend the stairs to the kitchen as*
CHARLEY *and* BERNARD *enter. All stop a moment when* LINDA, *in
clothes of mourning, bearing a little bunch of roses, comes through the
draped doorway into the kitchen. She goes to* CHARLEY *and takes his
arm. Now all move toward the audience, through the wall-line of the
kitchen. At the limit of the apron,* LINDA *lays down the flowers,
kneels, and sits back on her heels. All stare down at the grave.*)

REQUIEM

CHARLEY: It's getting dark, Linda.

(LINDA *doesn't react. She stares at the grave.*)

BIFF: How about it, Mom? Better get some rest, heh? They'll
      be closing the gate soon.

(LINDA *makes no move. Pause.*)

HAPPY: (*Deeply angered.*) He had no right to do that. There
      was no necessity for it. We would've helped him.   5
CHARLEY: (*Grunting.*) Hmmm.
BIFF: Come along, Mom.
LINDA: Why didn't anybody come?
CHARLEY: It was a very nice funeral.
LINDA: But where are all the people he knew? Maybe they   10
      blame him.
CHARLEY: Naa. It's a rough world, Linda. They wouldn't
      blame him.
LINDA: I can't understand it. At this time especially. First time
      in thirty-five years we were just about free and clear. He   15
      only needed a little salary. He was even finished with the
      dentist.
CHARLEY: No man only needs a little salary.
LINDA: I can't understand it.
BIFF: There were a lot of nice days. When he'd come home   20
      from a trip; or on Sundays, making the stoop; finishing the
      cellar; putting on the new porch; when he built the extra
      bathroom; and put up the garage. You know something,
      Charley, there's more of him in that front stoop than in all
      the sales he ever made.   25

CHARLEY: Yeah. He was a happy man with a batch of cement.

LINDA: He was so wonderful with his hands.

BIFF: He had the wrong dreams. All, all, wrong.

HAPPY: (*Almost ready to fight* BIFF.) Don't say that!

30 BIFF: He never knew who he was.

CHARLEY: (*Stopping* HAPPY's *movement and reply. To* BIFF.) Nobody dast blame this man. You don't understand: Willy was a salesman. And for a salesman, there is no rock bottom to the life. He don't put a bolt to a nut, he don't tell

35 you the law or give you medicine. He's a man way out there in the blue, riding on a smile and a shoeshine. And when they start not smiling back—that's an earthquake. And then you get yourself a couple of spots on your hat, and you're finished. Nobody dast blame this man. A sales-

40 man is got to dream, boy. It comes with the territory.

BIFF: Charley, the man didn't know who he was.

HAPPY: (*Infuriated.*) Don't say that!

BIFF: Why don't you come with me, Happy?

HAPPY: I'm not licked that easily. I'm staying right in this city,

45 and I'm gonna beat this racket! (*He looks at* BIFF, *his chin set.*) The Loman Brothers!

BIFF: I know who I am, kid.

HAPPY: All right, boy. I'm gonna show you and everybody else that Willy Loman did not die in vain. He had a good

50 dream. It's the only dream you can have—to come out number-one man. He fought it out here, and this is where I'm gonna win it for him.

BIFF: (*With a hopeless glance at* HAPPY, *bends toward his mother.*) Let's go, Mom.

LINDA: I'll be with you in a minute. Go on, Charley. (*He hes-* 55 *itates.*) I want to, just for a minute. I never had a chance to say good-by.

(CHARLEY *moves away, followed by* HAPPY. BIFF *remains a slight distance up and left of* LINDA. *She sits there, summoning herself. The flute begins, not far away, playing behind her speech.*)

LINDA: Forgive me, dear. I can't cry. I don't know what it is, but I can't cry. I don't understand it. Why did you ever do that? Help me, Willy, I can't cry. It seems to me that you're 60 just on another trip. I keep expecting you. Willy, dear, I can't cry. Why did you do it? I search and search and I search, and I can't understand it, Willy. I made the last payment on the house today. Today, dear. And there'll be nobody home. (*A sob rises in her throat.*) We're free and clear. 65 (*Sobbing more fully, released.*) We're free. (BIFF *comes slowly toward her.*) We're free . . . We're free . . .

BIFF *lifts her to her feet and moves out up right with her in his arms.* LINDA *sobs quietly.* BERNARD *and* CHARLEY *come together and follow them, followed by* HAPPY. *Only the music of the flute is left on the darkening stage as over the house the hard towers of the apartment buildings rise into sharp focus, and*

The Curtain Falls

Amiri Baraka / LeRoi Jones

Born Everett LeRoi Jones in Newark, New Jersey, in 1934, Amiri Baraka has become the most important revolutionary voice in contemporary black theater in the United States. He attended Rutgers University and Howard University, taking his B.A. from Howard in 1954. Baraka later said that his education at Howard was too involved with "learning to be white." He served in the United States Air Force before returning to New York in 1958. Living in Greenwich Village, he studied at Columbia University, married his first wife—an interracial marriage, lightly disguised in his play *The Slave*—and worked to develop his talents as a writer. Jones worked everywhere to develop a black esthetic, in his own poetry (in the mode of the Beat poets Gregory Corso and Allen Ginsberg), in essays, and in magazines that he founded and edited. In 1960, Jones was part of a delegation of black Americans invited to Cuba to celebrate Fidel Castro's revolution. That visit had a profound impact on Jones, sharpening his sense of the need both for a distinctive black esthetic and culture, and for a social revolution to eradicate the injustices of white-dominated American society. His plays of the 1960s are, in fact, often directly concerned with this issue and with how white liberalism—ostensibly the ally of black power—finally becomes an obstacle to the more fundamental revolution needed to bring black identity, culture, and power into being. In 1964, three of his plays opened in New York: *The Eighth Ditch, The Baptism,* and *Dutchman,* which won the Obie award for the best American play of the season. He then wrote a series of plays examining black activism and revolution in American life: *The Slave* (1964) and *The Toilet* (1964), *Experimental Death Unit #1* (1965), and *J-e-l-l-o* (1965). The assassination of Malcolm X in 1965 and the Watts riots in Los Angeles also drove Jones toward a more militant position, as articulated in plays like *A Black Mass* (1966), *Slave Ship* (1966), *The Great Goodness of Life* (*A Coon Show*) (1967), *Home on the Range* (1968), and *The Death of Malcolm X* (1969), and later in *The*

Clay strangles Lula in the subway at the climax of Amiri Baraka/LeRoi Jones's *Dutchman,* produced by the Hartford Stage in 2000.

Motion of History (1977) and *Money* (1988). In 1964 Jones established the Black Arts Repertory Theater and School in Harlem and began a program of cultural nationalism there, which he has pursued subsequently in several other organizations and described in several collections of essays. He has been deeply involved in developing a theater that would serve the need for cultural and political revolution in the black community.

As part of his commitment to forging a sustaining system of values for the African American community, Jones became a Kawaidi Muslim minister in 1968, adopting the title Imamu (spiritual leader) and the name Amiri Baraka at that time. Throughout the 1970s and 1980s, Baraka articulated and solidified the claims of cultural nationalism, frequently in a fiercely revolutionary, Marxist rhetoric. Baraka continues to be involved in a variety of political and social activities in the black community.

DUTCHMAN

Dutchman is one of Baraka's most powerful plays, both in its indictment of racist culture and in its straightforward confrontation between Lula and Clay. The title alludes to the legendary *Flying Dutchman*, the ship of the dead said to haunt the high seas. The subway car of the play is at once a ghost ship—where the young black man Clay is murdered—and a ghostly incarnation of racist fantasies. At the beginning of the play, Lula seems attracted to the middle-class Clay, but as the play develops it becomes clear that, to seduce Clay, Lula must transform him into something else, a fantasy figure of the white imagination. When Clay refuses to play along, delivering instead an impassioned statement of his own black identity, Lula murders him, with the implied consent of the white riders of the subway. *Dutchman* is a powerful parable of the problems of black identity in white culture.

DUTCHMAN

Amiri Baraka/LeRoi Jones

CHARACTERS

CLAY, *twenty-year-old Negro*
LULA, *thirty-year-old white woman*
RIDERS OF COACH, *white and black*
YOUNG NEGRO
CONDUCTOR

In the flying underbelly of the city. Steaming hot, and summer on top, outside. Underground. The subway heaped in modern myth.

Opening scene is a man sitting in a subway seat, holding a magazine but looking vacantly just above its wilting pages. Occasionally he looks blankly toward the window on his right. Dim lights and darkness whistling by against the glass. (Or paste the lights, as admitted props, right on the subway windows. Have them move, even dim and flicker. But give the sense of speed. Also stations, whether the train is stopped or the glitter and activity of these stations merely flashes by the windows.)

The man is sitting alone. That is, only his seat is visible, though the rest of the car is outfitted as a complete subway car. But only his seat is shown. There might be, for a time, as the play begins, a loud scream of the actual train. And it can recur throughout the play, or continue on a lower key once the dialogue starts.

The train slows after a time, pulling to a brief stop at one of the stations. The man looks idly up, until he sees a woman's face staring at him through the window; when it realizes that the man has noticed the face, it begins very premeditatedly to smile. The man smiles too, for a moment, without a trace of self-consciousness. Almost an instinctive though undesirable response. Then a kind of awkwardness or embarrassment sets in, and the man makes to look away, is further embarrassed, so he brings back his eyes to where the face was, but by now the train is moving again, and the face would seem to be left behind by the way the man turns his head to look back through the other windows at the slowly fading platform. He smiles then; more comfortably confident, hoping perhaps that his memory of this brief encounter will be pleasant. And then he is idle again.

SCENE ONE

Train roars. Lights flash outside the windows.

LULA *enters from the rear of the car in bright, skimpy summer clothes and sandals. She carries a net bag full of paper books, fruit, and other anonymous articles. She is wearing sunglasses, which she pushes up on her forehead from time to time.* LULA *is a tall, slender, beautiful woman with long red hair hanging straight down her back, wearing only loud lipstick in somebody's good taste. She is eating an apple, very daintily. Coming down the car toward* CLAY.

She stops beside CLAY's *seat and hangs languidly from the strap, still managing to eat the apple. It is apparent that she is going to sit in the seat next to* CLAY, *and that she is only waiting for him to notice her before she sits.*

CLAY *sits as before, looking just beyond his magazine, now and again pulling the magazine slowly back and forth in front of his face in a hopeless effort to fan himself. Then he sees the woman hanging there beside him and he looks up into her face, smiling quizzically.*

LULA: Hello.
CLAY: Uh, hi're you?
LULA: I'm going to sit down. . . . O.K.?
CLAY: Sure.
5 LULA:

(Swings down onto the seat, pushing her legs straight out as if she is very weary.)

Ooooof! Too much weight.
CLAY: Ha, doesn't look like much to me.

(Leaning back against the window, a little surprised and maybe stiff.)

LULA: It's so anyway.

(And she moves her toes in the sandals, then pulls her right leg up on the left knee, better to inspect the bottoms of the sandals and the back of her heel. She appears for a second not to notice that CLAY *is sitting next to her or that she has spoken to him just a second before.* CLAY *looks at the magazine, then out the black window. As he does this, she turns very quickly toward him.)*

Weren't you staring at me through the window?
CLAY: 10

(Wheeling around and very much stiffened.)

What?
LULA: Weren't you staring at me through the window? At the last stop?
CLAY: Staring at you? What do you mean?
LULA: Don't you know what staring means?   15
CLAY: I saw you through the window . . . if that's what it means. I don't know if I was staring. Seems to me you were staring through the window at me.
LULA: I was. But only after I'd turned around and saw you staring through that window down in the vicinity of my 20 ass and legs.
CLAY: Really?
LULA: Really. I guess you were just taking those idle potshots. Nothing else to do. Run your mind over people's flesh.
CLAY: Oh boy. Wow, now I admit I was looking in your di- 25 rection. But the rest of that weight is yours.
LULA: I suppose.
CLAY: Staring through train windows is weird business. Much weirder than staring very sedately at abstract asses.
LULA: That's why I came looking through the window . . . so 30 you'd have more than that to go on. I even smiled at you.
CLAY: That's right.
LULA: I even got into this train, going some other way than mine. Walked down the aisle . . . searching you out.

35   CLAY: Really? That's pretty funny.
     LULA: That's pretty funny. . . . God, you're dull.
     CLAY: Well, I'm sorry, lady, but I really wasn't prepared for
        party talk.
     LULA: No, you're not. What are you prepared for?

(*Wrapping the apple core in a Kleenex and dropping it on the floor.*)

40   CLAY:

(*Takes her conversation as pure sex talk. He turns to confront her
squarely with this idea.*)

     I'm prepared for anything. How about you?
     LULA:

(*Laughing loudly and cutting it off abruptly.*)

     What do you think you're doing?
     CLAY: What?
45   LULA: You think I want to pick you up, get you to take me
        somewhere and screw me, huh?
     CLAY: Is that the way I look?
     LULA: You look like you been trying to grow a beard. That's
        exactly what you look like. You look like you live in New
50   Jersey with your parents and are trying to grow a beard.
        That's what. You look like you've been reading Chinese
        poetry and drinking lukewarm sugarless tea.

(*Laughs, uncrossing and recrossing her legs.*)

     You look like death eating a soda cracker.
     CLAY:

(*Cocking his head from one side to the other, embarrassed and trying to make some comeback, but also intrigued by what the woman
is saying . . . even the sharp city coarseness of her voice, which is still
a kind of gentle sidewalk throb.*)

55   Really? I look like all that?
     LULA: Not all of it.

(*She feigns a seriousness to cover an actual somber tone.*)

     I lie a lot.

(*Smiling.*)

     It helps me control the world.
     CLAY:

(*Relieved and laughing louder than the humor.*)

60   Yeah, I bet.
     LULA: But it's true, most of it, right? Jersey? Your bumpy neck?
     CLAY: How'd you know all that? Huh? Really. I mean about
        Jersey . . . and even the beard. I met you before? You know
        Warren Enright?
65   LULA: You tried to make it with your sister when you were ten.

(CLAY *leans back hard against the back of the seat, his eyes opening
now, still trying to look amused.*)

     But I succeeded a few weeks ago.

(*She starts to laugh again.*)

     CLAY: What're you talking about? Warren tell you that? You're
        a friend of Georgia's?
     LULA: I told you I lie. I don't know your sister. I don't know
        Warren Enright.   70
     CLAY: You mean you're just picking these things out of the air?
     LULA: Is Warren Enright a tall skinny black black boy with a
        phony English accent?
     CLAY: I figured you knew him.
     LULA: But I don't. I just figured you would know somebody   75
        like that.

(*Laughs.*)

     CLAY: Yeah, yeah.
     LULA: You're probably on your way to his house now.
     CLAY: That's right.
     LULA: 80

(*Putting her hand on* CLAY's *closer knee, drawing it from the knee
up to the thigh's hinge, then removing it, watching his face very
closely, and continuing to laugh, perhaps more gently than before.*)

     Dull, dull, dull. I bet you think I'm exciting.
     CLAY: You're O.K.
     LULA: Am I exciting you now?
     CLAY: Right. That's not what's supposed to happen?
     LULA: How do I know?   85

(*She returns her hand, without moving it, then takes it away and
plunges it in her bag to draw out an apple.*)

     You want this?
     CLAY: Sure.
     LULA:

(*She gets one out of the bag for herself.*)

     Eating apples together is always the first step. Or walking up
     uninhabited Seventh Avenue in the twenties on weekends.   90

(*Bites and giggles, glancing at* CLAY *and speaking in loose singsong.*)

     Can get you involved . . . boy! Get us involved. Um-huh.

(*Mock seriousness.*)

     Would you like to get involved with me, Mister Man?
     CLAY:

(*Trying to be as flippant as* LULA, *whacking happily at the apple.*)

     Sure. Why not? A beautiful woman like you. Huh, I'd be
     a fool not to.   95
     LULA: And I bet you're sure you know what you're talking
        about.

(*Taking him a little roughly by the wrist, so he cannot eat the apple,
then shaking the wrist.*)

     I bet you're sure of almost everything anybody ever asked
     you about . . . right?

(Shakes his wrist harder.)

100   Right?

CLAY: Yeah, right. . . . Wow, you're pretty strong, you know? Whatta you, a lady wrestler or something?

LULA: What's wrong with lady wrestlers? And don't answer because you never knew any. Huh.

(Cynically.)

105   That's for sure. They don't have any lady wrestlers in that part of Jersey. That's for sure.

CLAY: Hey, you still haven't tole me how you know so much about me.

LULA: I told you I didn't know anything about *you* . . . you're

110   a well-known type.

CLAY: Really?

LULA: Or at least I know the type very well. And your skinny English friend too.

CLAY: Anonymously?

115 LULA:

(Settles back in seat, single-mindedly finishing her apple and humming snatches of rhythm and blues song.)

What?

CLAY: Without knowing us specifically?

LULA: Oh boy.

(Looking quickly at CLAY.)

What a face. You know, you could be a handsome man.

120 CLAY: I can't argue with you.

LULA:

(Vague, off-center response.)

What?

CLAY:

(Raising his voice, thinking the train noise has drowned part of his sentence.)

I can't argue with you.

125 LULA: My hair is turning gray. A gray hair for each year and type I've come through.

CLAY: Why do you want to sound so old?

LULA: But it's always gentle when it starts.

(Attention drifting.)

Hugged against tenements, day or night.

130 CLAY: What?

LULA:

(Refocusing.)

Hey, why don't you take me to that party you're going to?

LULA: You must be a friend of Warren's to know about the party.

135 LULA: Wouldn't you like to take me to the party?

(Imitates clinging vine.)

Oh, come on, ask me to your party.

CLAY: Of course I'll ask you to come with me to the party. And I'll bet you're a friend of Warren's.

LULA: Why not be a friend of Warren's? Why not?

(Taking his arm.)

Have you asked me yet?   140

CLAY: How can I ask you when I don't know your name?

LULA: Are you talking to my name?

CLAY: What is it, a secret?

LULA: I'm Lena the Hyena.

CLAY: The famous woman poet?   145

LULA: Poetess! The same!

CLAY: Well, you know so much about me . . . what's my name?

LULA: Morris the Hyena.

CLAY: The famous woman poet?

LULA: The same.   150

(Laughing and going into her bag.)

You want another apple?

CLAY: Can't make it, lady. I only have to keep one doctor away a day.

LULA: I bet your name is . . . something like . . . uh, Gerald or Walter. Huh?   155

CLAY: God, no.

LULA: Lloyd, Norman? One of those hopeless colored names creeping out of New Jersey. Leonard? Gag. . . .

CLAY: Like Warren?

LULA: Definitely. Just exactly like Warren. Or Everett.   160

CLAY: Gag. . . .

LULA: Well, for sure, it's not Willie.

CLAY: It's Clay.

LULA: Clay? Really? Clay what?

CLAY: Take your pick. Jackson, Johnson, or Williams.   165

LULA: Oh, really? Good for you. But it's got to be Williams. You're too pretentious to be a Jackson or Johnson.

CLAY: Thass right.

LULA: But Clay's O.K.

CLAY: So's Lena.   170

LULA: It's Lula.

CLAY: Oh?

LULA: Lula the Hyena.

CLAY: Very good.

LULA: 175

(Starts laughing again.)

Now you say to me, "Lula, Lula, why don't you go to this party with me tonight?" It's your turn, and let those be your lines.

CLAY: Lula, why don't you go to this party with me tonight, Huh?

LULA: Say my name twice before you ask, and no huh's.   180

CLAY: Lula, Lula, why don't you go to this party with me tonight?

LULA: I'd like to go, Clay, but how can you ask me to go when you barely know me?

CLAY: That is strange, isn't it?   185

LULA: What kind of reaction is that? You're supposed to say, "Aw, come on, we'll get to know each other better at the party."

CLAY: That's pretty corny.

LULA: What are you into anyway?

(*Looking at him half sullenly but still amused.*)

190   What thing are you playing at, Mister? Mister Clay Williams?

(*Grabs his thigh, up near the crotch.*)

What are you thinking about?

CLAY: Watch it now, you're gonna excite me for real.

LULA:

(*Taking her hand away and throwing her apple core through the window.*)

195   I bet.

(*She slumps in the seat and is heavily silent.*)

CLAY: I thought you knew everything about me? What happened?

(LULA *looks at him, then looks slowly away, then over where the other aisle would be. Noise of the train. She reaches in her bag and pulls out one of the paper books. She puts it on her leg and thumbs the pages listlessly.* CLAY *cocks his head to see the title of the book. Noise of the train.* LULA *flips pages and her eyes drift. Both remain silent.*)

Are you going to the party with me, Lula?

LULA:

(*Bored and not even looking.*)

I don't even know you.

200   CLAY: You said you know my type.

LULA:

(*Strangely irritated.*)

Don't get smart with me, Buster. I know you like the palm of my hand.

CLAY: The one you eat the apples with?

205   LULA: Yeh. And the one I open doors late Saturday evening with. That's my door. Up at the top of the stairs. Five flights. Above a lot of Italians and lying Americans. And scrape carrots with. Also . . .

(*Looks at him.*)

the same hand I unbutton my dress with, or let my skirt

210   fall down. Same hand. Lover.

CLAY: Are you angry about anything? Did I say something wrong?

LULA: Everything you say is wrong.

(*Mock smile.*)

That's what makes you so attractive. Ha. In that funny-book jacket with all the buttons.

(*More animate, taking hold of his jacket.*)

215   What've you got the jacket and tie on in all this heat for? And why're you wearing a jacket and tie like that? Did your people ever burn witches or start revolutions over the price of tea? Boy, those narrow-shoulder clothes come from a tradition you ought to feel oppressed by. A three-button suit. What right do you have to be wearing a   220 three-button suit and striped tie? Your grandfather was a slave, he didn't go to Harvard.

CLAY: My grandfather was a night watchman.

LULA: And you went to a colored college where everybody thought they were Averell Harriman.   225

CLAY: All except me.

LULA: And who did you think you were? Who do you think you are now?

CLAY:

(*Laughs as if to make light of the whole trend of the conversation.*)

Well, in college I thought I was Baudelaire. But I've   230 slowed down since.

LULA: I bet you never once thought you were a black nigger.

(*Mock serious, then she howls with laughter.* CLAY *is stunned but after initial reaction, he quickly tries to appreciate the humor.* LULA *almost shrieks.*)

A black Baudelaire.

CLAY: That's right.

LULA: Boy, are you corny. I take back what I said before.   235 Everything you say is not wrong. It's perfect. You should be on television.

CLAY: You act like you're on television already.

LULA: That's because I'm an actress.

CLAY: I thought so.   240

LULA: Well, you're wrong. I'm no actress. I told you I always lie. I'm nothing, honey, and don't you ever forget it.

(*Lighter.*)

Although my mother was a Communist. The only person in my family ever to amount to anything.

CLAY: My mother was a Republican.   245

LULA: And your father voted for the man rather than the party.

CLAY: Right!

LULA: Yea for him. Yea, yea for him.

CLAY: Yea!

LULA: And yea for America where he is free to vote for the   250 mediocrity of his choice! Yea!

CLAY: Yea!

LULA: And yea for both your parents who even though they differ about so crucial a matter as the body politic still forged a union of love and sacrifice that was destined to flower at the   255 birth of the noble Clay . . . what's your middle name?

CLAY: Clay.

LULA: A union of love and sacrifice that was destined to flower at the birth of the noble Clay Clay Williams. Yea! And most of all yea yea for you. Clay Clay. The Black Baudelaire! Yes!   260

(*And with knifelike cynicism.*)

My Christ. My Christ.

CLAY: Thank you, ma'am.

LULA: May the people accept you as a ghost of the future. And love you, that you might not kill them when you can.

CLAY: What?   265

LULA: You're a murderer, Clay, and you know it.

(*Her voice darkening with significance.*)

You know goddamn well what I mean.

CLAY: I do?

LULA: So we'll pretend the air is light and full of perfume.

270 CLAY:

(*Sniffing at her blouse.*)

It is.

LULA: And we'll pretend the people cannot see you. That is, the citizens. And that you are free of your own history. And I am free of my history. We'll pretend that we are 275 both anonymous beauties smashing along through the city's entrails.

(*She yells as loud as she can.*)

GROOVE!

(*Black.*)

SCENE TWO

Scene is the same as before, though now there are other seats visible in the car. And throughout the scene other people get on the subway. There are maybe one or two seated in the car as the scene opens, though neither CLAY *nor* LULA *notices them.* CLAY's *tie is open.* LULA *is hugging his arm.*

CLAY: The party!

LULA: I know it'll be something good. You can come in with me, looking casual and significant. I'll be strange, haughty, and silent, and walk with long slow strides.

5 CLAY: Right.

LULA: When you get drunk, pat me once, very lovingly on the flanks, and I'll look at you cryptically, licking my lips.

CLAY: It sounds like something we can do.

LULA: You'll go around talking to young men about your 10 mind, and to old men about your plans. If you meet a very close friend who is also with someone like me, we can stand together, sipping our drinks and exchanging codes of lust. The atmosphere will be slithering in love and half-love and very open moral decision.

15 CLAY: Great. Great.

LULA: And everyone will pretend they don't know your name, and then . . .

(*She pauses heavily.*)

later, when they have to, they'll claim a friendship that denies your sterling character.

20 CLAY:

(*Kissing her neck and fingers.*)

And then what?

LULA: Then? Well, then we'll go down the street, late night, eating apples and winding very deliberately toward my house.

25 CLAY: Deliberately?

LULA: I mean, we'll look in all the shop windows, and make fun of the queers. Maybe we'll meet a Jewish Buddhist and flatten his conceits over some pretentious coffee.

CLAY: In honor of whose God?

LULA: Mine. 30

CLAY: Who is . . . ?

LULA: Me . . . and you.

CLAY: A corporate Godhead.

LULA: Exactly. Exactly.

(*Notices one of the other people entering.*)

CLAY: Go on with the chronicle. Then what happens to us? 35

LULA:

(*A mild depression, but she still makes her description triumphant and increasingly direct.*)

To my house, of course.

CLAY: Of course.

LULA: And up the narrow steps of the tenement.

CLAY: You live in a tenement? 40

LULA: Wouldn't live anywhere else. Reminds me specifically of my novel form of insanity.

CLAY: Up the tenement stairs.

LULA: And with my apple-eating hand I push open the door and lead you, my tender big-eyed prey, into my . . . God, 45 what can I call it . . . into my hovel.

CLAY: Then what happens?

LULA: After the dancing and games, after the long drinks and long walks, the real fun begins.

CLAY: Ah, the real fun. 50

(*Embarrassed, in spite of himself.*)

Which is . . . ?

LULA:

(*Laughs at him.*)

Real fun in the dark house. Hah! Real fun in the dark house, high up above the street and the ignorant cowboys. I lead you in, holding your wet hand gently in my hand . . . 55

CLAY: Which is not wet?

LULA: Which is dry as ashes.

CLAY: And cold?

LULA: Don't think you'll get out of your responsibility that way. It's not cold at all. You Fascist! Into my dark living 60 room. Where we'll sit and talk endlessly, endlessly.

CLAY: About what?

LULA: About what? About your manhood, what do you think? What do you think we've been talking about all this time?

CLAY: Well, I didn't know it was that. That's for sure. Every 65 other thing in the world but that.

(*Notices another person entering, looks quickly, almost involuntarily, up and down the car, seeing the other people in the car.*)

Hey, I didn't even notice when those people got on.

LULA: Yeah, I know.

CLAY: Man, this subway is slow.

LULA: Yeah, I know. 70

CLAY: Well, go on. We were talking about my manhood.

LULA: We still are. All the time.

CLAY: We were in your living room.

LULA: My dark living room. Talking endlessly.

75 CLAY: About my manhood.

LULA: I'll make you a map of it. Just as soon as we get to my house.

CLAY: Well, that's great.

LULA: One of the things we do while we talk. And screw.

CLAY:

(*Trying to make his smile broader and less shaky.*)

80   We finally got there.

LULA: And you'll call my rooms black as a grave. You'll say, "This place is like Juliet's tomb."

CLAY:

(*Laughs.*)

I might.

85 LULA: I know. You've probably said it before.

CLAY: And is that all? The whole grand tour?

LULA: Not all. You'll say to me very close to my face, many, many times, you'll say, even whisper, that you love me.

CLAY: Maybe I will.

90 LULA: And you'll be lying.

CLAY: I wouldn't lie about something like that.

LULA: Hah. It's the only kind of thing you will lie about. Especially if you think it'll keep me alive.

CLAY: Keep you alive? I don't understand.

95 LULA:

(*Bursting out laughing, but too shrilly.*)

Don't understand? Well, don't look at me. It's the path I take, that's all. Where both feet take me when I set them down. One in front of the other.

CLAY: Morbid. Morbid. You sure you're not an actress? All
100   that self-aggrandizement.

LULA: Well, I told you I wasn't an actress . . . but I also told you I lie all the time. Draw your own conclusions.

CLAY: And is that all of our lives together you've described? There's no more?

105 LULA: I've told you all I know. Or almost all.

CLAY: There's no funny parts?

LULA: I thought it was all funny.

CLAY: But you mean peculiar, not ha-ha.

LULA: You don't know what I mean.

110 CLAY: Well, tell me the almost part then. You said almost all. What else? I want the whole story.

LULA:

(*Searching aimlessly through her bag. She begins to talk breathlessly, with a light and silly tone.*)

All stories are whole stories. All of 'em. Our whole story
. . . nothing but change. How could things go on like that
115 forever? Huh?

(*Slaps him on the shoulder, begins finding things in her bag, taking them out and throwing them over her shoulder into the aisle.*)

Except I do go on as I do. Apples and long walks with deathless intelligent lovers. But you mix it up. Look out

the window, all the time. Turning pages. Change change change. Till, shit, I don't know you. Wouldn't, for that matter. You're too serious. I bet you're even too serious to be 120 psychoanalyzed. Like all those Jewish poets from Yonkers, who leave their mothers looking for other mothers, or others' mothers, on whose baggy tits they lay their fumbling heads. Their poems are always funny, and all about sex. 125

CLAY: They sound great. Like movies.

LULA: But you change.

(*Blankly.*)

And things work on you till you hate them.

(*More people come into the train. They come closer to the couple, some of them not sitting, but swinging drearily on the straps, staring at the two with uncertain interest.*)

CLAY: Wow. All these people, so suddenly. They must all come from the same place. 130

LULA: Right. That they do.

CLAY: Oh? You know about them too?

LULA: Oh yeah. About them more than I know about you. Do they frighten you?

CLAY: Frighten me? Why should they frighten me? 135

LULA: 'Cause you're an escaped nigger.

CLAY: Yeah?

LULA: 'Cause you crawled through the wire and made tracks to my side.

CLAY: Wire? 140

LULA: Don't they have wire around plantations?

CLAY: You must be Jewish. All you can think about is wire. Plantations didn't have any wire. Plantations were big open whitewashed places like heaven, and everybody on 'em was grooved to be there. Just strummin' and hummin' 145 all day.

LULA: Yes, yes.

CLAY: And that's how the blues was born.

LULA: Yes, yes. And that's how the blues was born.

(*Begins to make up a song that becomes quickly hysterical. As she sings she rises from her seat, still throwing things out of her bag into the aisle, beginning a rhythmical shudder and twistlike wiggle, which she continues up and down the aisle, bumping into many of the standing people and tripping over the feet of those sitting. Each time she runs into a person she lets out a very vicious piece of profanity, wiggling and stepping all the time.*)

And that's how the blues was born. Yes. Yes. Son of a 150 bitch, get out of the way. Yes. Quack. Yes. Yes. And that's how the blues was born. Ten little niggers sitting on a limb, but none of them ever looked like him.

(*Points to* CLAY, *returns toward the seat, with her hands extended for him to rise and dance with her.*)

And that's how blues was born. Yes. Come on. Clay. Let's do the nasty. Rub bellies. Rub bellies. 155

CLAY:

(*Waves his hands to refuse. He is embarrassed, but determined to get a kick out of the proceedings.*)

Hey, what was in those apples? Mirror, mirror on the wall, who's the fairest one of all? Snow White, baby, and don't you forget it.

160   LULA:

(*Grabbing for his hands, which he draws away.*)

Come on, Clay. Let's rub bellies on the train. The nasty. The nasty. Do the gritty grind, like your ol' rag-head mammy. Grind till you lose your mind. Shake it, shake it, shake it, shake it! OOOOweeee! Come on, Clay. Let's do

165   the choo-choo train shuffle, the navel scratcher.

CLAY: Hey, you coming on like the lady who smoked up her grass skirt.

LULA:

(*Becoming annoyed that he will not dance, and becoming more animated as if to embarrass him still further.*)

Come on, Clay . . . let's do the thing. Uhh! Uhh! Clay!

170   Clay! You middle-class black bastard. Forget your social-working mother for a few seconds and let's knock stomachs. Clay, you liver-lipped white man. You would-be Christian. You ain't no nigger, you're just a dirty white man. Get up, Clay. Dance with me, Clay.

175   CLAY: Lula! Sit down, now. Be cool.

LULA:

(*Mocking him, in wild dance.*)

Be cool. Be cool. That's all you know . . . shaking the wild-root cream-oil on your knotty head, jackets buttoning up to your chin, so full of white man's words. Christ!

180   God! Get up and scream at these people. Like scream meaningless shit in these hopeless faces.

(*She screams at people in train, still dancing.*)

Red trains cough Jewish underwear for keeps! Expanding smells of silence. Gravy snot whistling like sea birds. Clay. Clay, you got to break out. Don't sit there dying the way

185   they want you to die. Get up.

CLAY: Oh, sit the fuck down.

(*He moves to restrain her.*)

Sit down, goddamn it.

LULA:

(*Twisting out of his reach.*)

Screw yourself, Uncle Tom. Thomas Woolly-Head.

(*Begins to dance a kind of jig, mocking* CLAY *with loud forced humor.*)

190   There is Uncle Tom . . . I mean, Uncle Thomas Woolly-Head. With old white matted mane. He hobbles on his wooden cane. Old Tom. Old Tom. Let the white man hump his ol' mama, and he jes' shuffle off in the woods and hide his gentle gray head. Ol' Thomas Woolly-Head.

(*Some of the other riders are laughing now. A drunk gets up and joins* LULA *in her dance, singing, as best he can, her "song."* CLAY *gets up out of his seat and visibly scans the faces of the other riders.*)

CLAY: Lula! Lula!   195

(*She is dancing and turning, still shouting as loud as she can. The drunk too is shouting, and waving his hands wildly.*)

Lula . . . you dumb bitch. Why don't you stop it?

(*He rushes half stumbling from his seat, and grabs one of her flailing arms.*)

LULA: Let me go! You black son of a bitch.

(*She struggles against him.*)

Let me go! Help!

(CLAY *is dragging her towards her seat, and the drunk seeks to interfere. He grabs* CLAY *around the shoulders and begins wrestling with him.* CLAY *clubs the drunk to the floor without releasing* LULA, *who is still screaming.* CLAY *finally gets her to the seat and throws her into it.*)

CLAY: Now you shut the hell up.

(*Grabbing her shoulders.*)

Just shut up. You don't know what you're talking about.   200 You don't know anything. So just keep your stupid mouth closed.

LULA: You're afraid of white people. And your father was. Uncle Tom Big Lip!

CLAY: 205

(*Slaps her as hard as he can, across the mouth.* LULA's *head bangs against the back of the seat. When she raises it again,* CLAY *slaps her again.*)

Now shut up and let me talk.

(*He turns toward the other riders, some of whom are sitting on the edge of their seats. The drunk is on one knee, rubbing his head, and singing softly the same song. He shuts up too when he sees* CLAY *watching him. The others go back to newspapers or stare out the windows.*)

Shit, you don't have any sense, Lula, nor feelings either. I could murder you now. Such a tiny ugly throat. I could squeeze it flat, and watch you turn blue, on a humble. For dull kicks. And all these weak-faced ofays squatting   210 around here, staring over their papers at me. Murder them too. Even if they expected it. That man there . . .

(*Points to well-dressed man.*)

I could rip that *Times* right out of his hand, as skinny and middle-classed as I am, I could rip that paper out of his hand and just as easily rip out his throat. It takes no great   215 effort. For what? To kill you soft idiots? You don't understand anything but luxury.

LULA: You fool!

CLAY:

(*Pushing her against the seat.*)

I'm not telling you again, Tallulah Bankhead! Luxury. In your   220 face and your fingers. You telling me what I ought to do.

(Sudden scream frightening the whole coach.)

Well, don't! Don't you tell me anything! If I'm a middle-class fake white man . . . let me be. And let me be in the way I want.

(Through his teeth.)

225   I'll rip your lousy breasts off! Let me be who I feel like being. Uncle Tom. Thomas. Whoever. It's none of your business. You don't know anything except what's there for you to see. An act. Lies. Device. Not the pure heart, the pumping black heart. You don't ever know that. And I sit here,
230   in this buttoned-up suit, to keep myself from cutting all your throats. I mean wantonly. You great liberated whore! You fuck some black man, and right away you're an expert on black people. What a lotta shit that is. The only thing you know is that you come if he bangs you hard enough.
235   And that's all. The belly rub? You wanted to do the belly rub? Shit, you don't even know how. You don't know how. That ol' dipty-dip shit you do, rolling your ass like an elephant. That's not my kind of belly rub. Belly rub is not Queens. Belly rub is dark places, with big hats and over-
240   coats held up with one arm. Belly rub hates you. Old bald-headed four-eyed ofays popping their fingers . . . and don't know yet what they're doing. They say, "I love Bessie Smith." And don't even understand that Bessie Smith is saying, "Kiss my ass, kiss my black unruly ass." Before love,
245   suffering, desire, anything you can explain, she's saying, and very plainly, "Kiss my black ass." And if you don't know that, it's you that's doing the kissing.
      Charlie Parker? Charlie Parker. All the hip white boys scream for Bird. And Bird saying, "Up your ass, feeble-
250   minded ofay! Up your ass." And they sit there talking about the tortured genius of Charlie Parker. Bird would've played not a note of music if he just walked up to East Sixty-seventh Street and killed the first ten white people he saw. Not a note! And I'm the great would-be poet. Yes.
255   That's right! Poet. Some kind of bastard literature . . . all it needs is a simple knife thrust. Just let me bleed you, you loud whore, and one poem vanished. A whole people of neurotics, struggling to keep from being sane. And the only thing that would cure the neurosis would be your
260   murder. Simple as that. I mean if I murdered you, then other white people would begin to understand me. You understand? No. I guess not. If Bessie Smith had killed some white people she wouldn't have needed that music. She could have talked very straight and plain about the
265   world. No metaphors. No grunts. No wiggles in the dark of her soul. Just straight two and two are four. Money. Power. Luxury. Like that. All of them. Crazy niggers turning their backs on sanity. When all it needs is that simple act. Murder. Just murder! Would make us all sane.

(Suddenly weary.)

270   Ahhh. Shit. But who needs it? I'd rather be a fool. Insane. Safe with my words, and no deaths, and clean, hard thoughts, urging me to new conquests. My people's madness. Hah! That's a laugh. My people. They don't need me to claim them. They got legs and arms of their own. Per-
275   sonal insanities. Mirrors. They don't need all those words.

They don't need any defense. But listen, though, one more thing. And you tell this to your father, who's probably the kind of man who needs to know at once. So he can plan ahead. Tell him not to preach so much rationalism and cold logic to these niggers. Let them alone. Let them sing curses 280 at you in code and see your filth as simple lack of style. Don't make the mistake, through some irresponsible surge of Christian charity, of talking too much about the advantages of Western rationalism, or the great intellectual legacy of the white man, or maybe they'll begin to listen. And then, 285 maybe one day, you'll find they actually do understand exactly what you are talking about, all these fantasy people. All these blues people. And on that day, as sure as shit, when you really believe you can "accept" them into your fold, as half-white trusties late of the subject peoples. With no more 290 blues, except the very old ones, and not a watermelon in sight, the great missionary heart will have triumphed, and all of those ex-coons will be stand-up Western men, with eyes for clean hard useful lives, sober, pious and sane, and they'll murder you. They'll murder you, and have very ra- 295 tional explanations. Very much like your own. They'll cut your throats, and drag you out to the edge of your cities so the flesh can fall away from your bones, in sanitary isolation.

LULA:

(Her voice takes on a different, more businesslike quality.)

I've heard enough.   300

CLAY:

(Reaching for his books.)

I bet you have. I guess I better collect my stuff and get off this train. Looks like we won't be acting out that little pageant you outlined before.

LULA: No. We won't. You're right about that, at least.   305

(She turns to look quickly around the rest of the car.)

All right!

(The others respond.)

CLAY:

(Bending across the girl to retrieve his belongings.)

Sorry, baby, I don't think we could make it.

(As he is bending over her, the girl brings up a small knife and plunges it into CLAY's chest. Twice. He slumps across her knees, his mouth working stupidly.)

LULA: Sorry is right.

(Turning to the others in the car who have already gotten up from their seats.)

Sorry is the rightest thing you've said. Get this man off 310 me! Hurry, now!

(The others come and drag CLAY's body down the aisle.)

Open the door and throw his body out.

(They throw him off.)

And all of you get off at the next stop.

(LULA busies herself straightening her things. Getting everything in order. She takes out a notebook and makes a quick scribbling note. Drops it in her bag. The train apparently stops and all the others get off, leaving her alone in the coach. Very soon a YOUNG NEGRO *of about twenty comes into the coach, with a couple of books under his arm. He sits a few seats in back of* LULA. *When he is seated she turns and gives him a long slow look. He looks up from his book and drops the book on his lap. Then an old Negro* CONDUCTOR *comes into the car, doing a sort of restrained soft shoe, and half mumbling the words of some song. He looks at the young man, briefly, with a quick greeting.)*

CONDUCTOR: Hey, brother!
YOUNG NEGRO: Hey.

315

(The CONDUCTOR *continues down the aisle with his little dance and the mumbled song.* LULA *turns to stare at him and follows his movements down the aisle. The* CONDUCTOR *tips his hat when he reaches her seat, and continues out the car.)*

Luis Valdez

Luis Valdez (b. 1940), was born and raised the son of farmworkers in Delano, California. He majored in drama at San Jose State College, taking his B.A. in 1964, and then joined the San Francisco Mime Troup, an important experimental theater company. In 1965, when farm workers at the Delano grape plantations went on strike, Valdez formed El Teatro Campesino ("The Farmworkers' Theater"). Valdez and Teatro Campesino devised two dramatic forms: *ACTOS,* short, satirical plays dramatizing the oppression of the fieldworkers, and *MITOS,* poetic, lyrical plays on Chicano life. *Actos* were improvised by members of El Teatro Campesino playing "stock" characters (the farmworker, the boss, etc.); because they were improvised for each production and each community, *actos* varied considerably from performance to performance. The final versions published by Valdez were written down much later. El Teatro Campesino became one of several important Chicano theater companies that performed throughout the Southwest and in urban areas of the Midwest and Northeast, drawing on both American and European dramatic traditions, as well as traditions of Mexican and Spanish-language theater in the United States that date to the seventeenth century. In the late 1960s and 1970s, Teatro Campesino toured the United States and Europe and gained an international reputation. Valdez's other *actos* with Teatro Campesino include *Las Dos Caras del Patroncito* (1965), *No Saco Nada de la Escuela* (1969), and *Vietnam Campesino* (1970). Valdez produced the stage play *Zoot Suit* in 1978, which was released as a film in 1981. In 1980, Valdez transformed El Teatro Campesino into a production company, a marked shift from its collaborative and activist origins. This version of El Teatro Campesino hired "professional" actors, abandoning the collective esthetic characteristic of the company's earlier work. Valdez developed several new projects in connection with the company's new theater in San Juan Bautista (built in 1981), notably *Bandido!* (1981), *Corridos* (1992), and *I Don't Have to Show You No Stinking Badges* (1990). His film *La Bamba* was released in 1987, and Valdez filmed *Pastorelas* for PBS television in 1990. Valdez has held academic appointments at the University of California, Berkeley, and at the University of California, Santa Cruz. He is teaching at the new campus of the California State University at Monterey.

ZOOT SUIT

Zoot Suit remains the most successful play of the Chicano theater, and presents a vivid re-reading of one of the formative moments in Chicano history: the "Zoot Suit Riots" in Los Angeles during World War II. Valdez stages the play's perspective on history in its opening moments, a kind of Brechtian *GESTUS:* the elegant figure of the Pachuco—the cool urban Latino draped in the refined, dressy zoot suit—enters the stage by slicing through a giant newspaper-curtain, the *Los Angeles Herald,* whose headlines proclaim "ZOOT-SUITER HORDES INVADE LOS ANGELES. U.S. NAVY AND MARINES ARE CALLED IN." The Pachuco instigates the play's central action, not merely to re-stage history, but to interrogate the means of history, the ways in which public history—represented here by the newspaper, later by police reports and trial transcripts—both distorts and finally erases the facts of Chicano history. The events of *Zoot Suit* are taken directly from the Sleepy Lagoon murder trial of 1942 (an excellent video from the "American Experience" series on PBS, *The Zoot Suit Riots,* is available). Los Angeles in the early 1940s was a city at war; 50,000 sailors were in port, and the city was nervous about invasion from Japan and subversion from within. At the same time, it was also a deeply racialized city, in which Mexican-American citizens (the term *Chicano* was not embraced by Mexican Americans until the 1960s) routinely suffered discrimination of all kinds: signs reading "No Mexicans Allowed" were prominent in the city, whose Mexican-American population numbered well over a quarter million. Mexican Americans were routinely stigmatized as a "criminal element" by the city's

Anglo majority, and allegations that subversion might come from the "Mexicans" of the city—most of whom were not "Mexicans" but American citizens—were made casually and repeatedly in the press. At the same time, the zoot suit craze had become popular among younger Mexican Americans, and zoot suits—high-waisted baggy pants gathered into narrow pegged cuffs, an oversize long jacket, dangling watchchain, and wide-brimmed hat—could be seen all over Los Angeles, especially in the jazz and swing clubs downtown.

The Zoot Suit Riots took place against this backdrop of racial conflict. Valdez's play takes the Sleepy Lagoon trial as the centerpiece of the riots. In August of 1942, a young Mexican-American couple—Hank Leyvas and his girlfriend—were beaten by a Mexican-American gang; later that evening Leyvas went to the Sleepy Lagoon swimming hole with some friends from his 38th Street neighborhood to take revenge for the beating. When they arrived, they found a man—José Díaz—who had been beaten and stabbed but was still alive. Leaving their girlfriends to tend to Díaz, the boys went inside for their fight, and then picked up the girls and left Sleepy Lagoon. Díaz died, and when his murder was discovered, the Los Angeles Police Department set up a dragnet, bringing in 600 Mexican-American boys for questioning; they then arrested Hank Leyvas and twenty other boys for Díaz's murder. Held at the 77th Precinct, the boys were routinely and savagely beaten by the police, and when they were brought to trial, Judge Charles Frickie would not allow them to receive haircuts or clean clothes. Although they were unanimous in denying complicity in Díaz's death, on January 12, 1943, seventeen of the boys were found guilty and sent to San Quentin prison outside San Francisco, far from their families or their legal representation; Hank Leyvas, alleged to be the ringleader of the group, was given a life sentence and eventually sent to Folsom prison. Several of the girls were—without legal proceedings of any kind—taken from their families and made wards of the state; they were sent to the prison-like Ventura School for Girls, and remained in state custody until turning 21. Almost immediately a Sleepy Lagoon Defense Committee was formed, spearheaded by Alice Greenfield McGrath, and the Committee succeeded not only in gaining the support of prominent Angelinos, but in raising money nationwide to take the case to appeal. The case was appealed in November 1943 but did not receive a decision for nearly a year. In October 1944, the appeals court ruled that the original trial had been mistried, and that the defendants should be released. Since the City of Los Angeles did not retry the case, the men were released but never cleared of the murder, having spent two years in California prisons. More recently, however, the men's story has been substantiated, even though they have not been formally cleared of the crime. As the *Zoot Suit Riots* program reports, one of the girls, Lorena Encinas, had knowledge of the crime: her brother, Louie Encinas, had been at the party before the 38th Street contingent arrived, and was involved in the fight and stabbing of Díaz.

Meanwhile, the Sleepy Lagoon case was only one in a series of racial hostilities that took place in Los Angeles, and fighting—particularly between servicemen stationed in L.A. and Mexican Americans—was increasingly common. On June 3, 1943, a group of sailors got into a fight with some Mexican-American men, and one of the sailors had his jaw broken and was knocked out. He was brought back to the armory where many of the sailors were stationed, and one of their commanding officers directed the sailors—who hardly needed additional incentive—to take reprisals. On the evening of June 4, a group of sailors headed to downtown Los Angeles with clubs and other weapons to beat Mexican-American men, attacking them randomly on the street as well as going into businesses and movie theaters in search of victims. Rioting escalated over the next few nights, as servicemen (many coming to L.A. explicitly for this purpose) then went into Mexican-American neighborhoods to beat civilians, particularly targeting zoot suiters, stripping them of their suits and burning them. Five thousand civilians were publicly recruited to join with the servicemen in these unprovoked attacks; although the Mexican Americans fought back, they were both outnumbered and undermined by their lack of political or legal support. The Los Angeles Police Department kept a low profile during the rioting; rather than coming to the aid of the Mexican-American neighborhoods, they simply waited until the servicemen and civilians had completed their raids on the *barrios,* and then arrested Mexican Americans for rioting. On June 8, the military declared the city off limits to servicemen, and the riots quickly stopped; the following day the Los Angeles City Council banned the wearing of zoot suits in public—the fine for doing so was thirty days in jail.

Staging these events, Valdez develops a complex critique of the work of ideology in creating "history": this critique is perhaps most evident in the play's use of setting, the ways in which piles of newspaper—the principal organ representing the "meaning" of the riots to contemporary Anglo Angelinos—are used to form the major elements of the set, epitomizing the framing hysteria of the Press. But if the Press and its minions—including the legal system—fashions public history, then Pachuco provides an image of resistant history, at once embodying a moment of cultural pride and a moment of cultural pathos (when he is stripped of the zoot suit by the sailors), as well as a transparent moment of cultural myth-making, when he rises from his beating and his arms *"as an Aztec conch blows."* Valdez here signals a deeper connection between the Pachuco and the myth of Aztlán, the indigenous homeland in the upper Southwest from which the Aztecs were said to have emigrated to Mexico, now often taken as the mythic homeland of Chicanos.

Perhaps the most salient moment of Valdez's historical revision takes place in the play's closing moments, in which the Pachuco refuses to enclose the history of the Zoot Suit Riots within a single narrative. Instead, the play suggests that the history of the Zoot Suit Riots, and by implication the history of Chicanos and Chicanas in America, is still being written. Hank Leyvas died in a bar in 1971, but *Zoot Suit* suggests that Henry Reyna's story might have alternative outcomes: did Henry Reyna return to prison, "where he died of the trauma of his life in 1972" or did he go to Korea in 1950, where "he was killed at Inchon in 1952, being posthumously awarded the Congressional Medal of Honor" or did he marry "Della in 1948 and they have five kids, three of them now going to the University, speaking calo and calling themselves Chicanos"? Outlining the many trajectories of Chicano history in the postwar period, and the many ways in which Chicano history is woven into the fabric of contemporary American history, the Pachuco summons the Zoot Suit Riots as an originating event, one that—like most narratives of origin—has a mythological status in the ways "we"—not only Chicanos and Chicanas, but all Americans—understand our identity today. For all of us, "Henry Reyna . . . El Pachuco . . . The man . . . the myth . . . still lives."

ZOOT SUIT
Luis Valdez

CHARACTERS

EL PACHUCO
HENRY REYNA

HIS FAMILY:
ENRIQUE REYNA
DOLORES REYNA
LUPE REYNA
RUDY REYNA

HIS FRIENDS:
GEORGE SHEARER
ALICE BLOOMFIELD

HIS GANG:
DELLA BARRIOS
SMILEY TORRES
JOEY CASTRO
TOMMY ROBERTS
ELENA TORRES
BERTHA VILLARREAL

THE DOWNEY GANG:
RAFAS
RAGMAN
HOBO
CHOLO
ZOOTER
GÜERA
HOBA
BLONDIE
LITTLE BLUE

DETECTIVES:
LIEUTENANT EDWARDS
SERGEANT SMITH

THE PRESS:
PRESS
CUB REPORTER
NEWSBOY

THE COURT:
JUDGE F.W. CHARLES
BAILIFF

THE PRISON:
GUARD

THE MILITARY:
BOSUN'S MATE
SAILORS
MARINE
SWABBIE
MANCHUKA
SHORE PATROLMAN

OTHERS:
GIRLS
PIMP
CHOLO

SETTING

The giant facsimile of a newspaper front page serves as a drop curtain.

The huge masthead reads: LOS ANGELES HERALD EXPRESS Thursday, June 3, 1943.

A headline cries out: ZOOT-SUITER HORDES INVADE LOS ANGELES. US NAVY AND MARINES ARE CALLED IN.

Behind this are black drapes creating a place of haunting shadows larger than life. The somber shapes and outlines of pachuco images hang subtly, black on black, against a back-ground of heavy fabric evoking memories and feelings like an old suit hanging forgotten in the depths of a closet somewhere, sometime . . . Below this is a sweeping, curving place of levels and rounded corners with the hard, ingrained brilliance of countless spit shines, like the memory of a dance hall.

ACT ONE
PROLOGUE

A switchblade plunges through the newspaper. It slowly cuts a rip to the bottom of the drop. To the sounds of "Perdido" by Duke Ellington, EL PACHUCO emerges from the slit. HE adjusts his clothing, meticulously fussing with his collar, suspenders, cuffs. HE tends to his hair, combing back every strand into a long luxurious ducktail, with infinite loving pains. Then HE reaches into the slit and pulls out his coat and hat. HE dons them. His fantastic costume is complete. It is a zoot suit. HE is transformed into the very image of the pachuco myth, from his pork-pie hat to the tip of his four-foot watch chain. Now HE turns to the audience. His three-soled shoes with metal taps click-clack as HE proudly, slovenly, defiantly makes his way downstage. HE stops and assumes a pachuco stance.

PACHUCO: ¿Que le watcha a mis trapos, ese?
    ¿Sabe qué, carnal?
    Estas garras me las planté porque
    Vamos a dejarnos caer un play, ¿sabe?

(HE crosses to center stage, models his clothes.)

    Watcha mi tacuche, ese. Aliviánese con mis calcos, tando, 5
    lisa, tramos, y carlango, ese.

(Pause.)

    Nel, sabe qué, usted está muy verdolaga. Como se me hace
    que es puro square.

(EL PACHUCO breaks character and addresses the audience in perfect English.)

    Ladies and gentlemen
    the play you are about to see 10
    is a construct of fact and fantasy.
    The Pachuco Style was an act in Life
    and his language a new creation.
    His will to be was an awesome force
    eluding all documentation . . . 15

A mythical, quizzical, frightening being
precursor of revolution
Or a piteous, hideous heroic joke
deserving of absolution?
20 I speak as an actor on the stage.
The Pachuco was existential
for he was an Actor in the streets
both profane and reverential.
It was the secret fantasy of every bato
25 in or out of the Chicanada
to put on a Zoot Suit and play the Myth
más *chucote* que la chingada.

(*Puts hat back on and turns.*)

¡Pos órale!

(*Music. The newspaper drop flies.* EL PACHUCO *begins his chuco stroll upstage, swinging his watch chain.*)

1. ZOOT SUIT

The scene is a barrio dance in the forties. PACHUCOS *and* PACHU-CAS *in zoot suits and pompadours.*
They are members of the 38TH STREET GANG, *led by* HENRY REYNA, *21, dark, Indian-looking, older than his years, and* DELLA BARRIOS, *20, his girlfriend in miniskirt and fingertip coat. A* SAILOR *called* SWABBIE *dances with his girlfriend* MANCHUKA *among the* COUPLES. *Movement. Animation.* EL PACHUCO *sings.*

PACHUCO:
PUT ON A ZOOT SUIT, MAKES YOU FEEL REAL
  ROOT
LOOK LIKE A DIAMOND, SPARKLING, SHINING
READY FOR DANCING
5 READY FOR THE BOOGIE TONIGHT!

(*The* COUPLES, *dancing, join the* PACHUCO *in exclaiming the last term of each line in the next verse.*)

THE HEPCATS UP IN HARLEM WEAR THAT
  DRAPE SHAPE
COMO LOS PACHUCONES DOWN IN L.A.
WHERE HUISAS IN THEIR POMPADOURS
10   LOOK REAL KEEN
ON THE DANCE FLOOR OF THE BALLROOMS
DONDE BAILAN SWING.
YOU BETTER GET HEP TONIGHT
AND PUT ON THAT ZOOT SUIT!

(*The* DOWNEY GANG, *a rival group of pachucos enters upstage left. Their quick dance step becomes a challenge to* 38TH STREET.)

15 DOWNEY GANG: Downey . . . ¡Rifa!
HENRY: (*Gesturing back.*) ¡Toma! (*The music is hot.* EL PACHUCO *slides across the floor and momentarily breaks the tension.* HENRY *warns* RAFAS, *the leader of the* DOWNEY GANG, *when* HE *sees him push his brother* RUDY.) ¡ Rafas!
20 PACHUCO: (*Sings.*)
TRUCHA, ESE LOCO, VAMOS AL BORLO
WEAR THAT CARLANGO, TRAMOS Y TANDO

DANCE WITH YOUR HUISA
DANCE TO THE BOOGIE TONIGHT!
'CAUSE THE ZOOT SUIT IS THE STYLE IN   25
  CALIFORNIA
TAMBIÉN EN COLORADO Y ARIZONA
THEY'RE WEARING THAT TACUCHE EN EL PASO
Y EN TODOS LOS SALONES DE CHICAGO
YOU BETTER GET HEP TONIGHT   30
AND PUT ON THAT ZOOT SUIT!

2. THE MASS ARRESTS

We hear a siren, then another, and another. It sounds like gang-busters. The dance is interrupted. COUPLES *pause on the dance floor.*

PACHUCO: Trucha, la jura. ¡Pélenle! (PACHUCOS *start to run out, but* DETECTIVES *leap onstage with drawn guns. A* CUB RE-PORTER *takes flash pictures.*)
SGT. SMITH: Hold it right there, kids!
LT. EDWARDS: Everybody get your hands up!   5
RUDY: Watcha! This way! (RUDY *escapes with some others.*)
LT. EDWARDS: Stop or I'll shoot! (EDWARDS *fires his revolver into the air. A number of pachucos and their girlfriends freeze. The cops round them up.* SWABBIE, *an American sailor, and* MANCHUKA, *a Japanese-American dancer, are among them.*)   10
SGT. SMITH: ¡Ándale! (*Sees* SWABBIE.) You! Get out of here.
SWABBIE: What about my girl?
SGT. SMITH: Take her with you. (SWABBIE *and* MANCHUKA *exit.*)
HENRY: What about my girl?
LT. EDWARDS: No dice, Henry. Not this time. Back in line.   15
SGT. SMITH: Close it up!
LT. EDWARDS: Spread! (*The* PACHUCOS *turn upstage in a line with their hands up. The sirens fade and give way to the sound of a teletype. The* PACHUCOS *turn and form a lineup, and the* PRESS *starts shooting pictures as* HE *speaks.*)   20
PRESS: The City of the Angels, Monday, August 2, 1942. The Los Angeles Examiner, Headline:
THE LINEUP: (*In chorus.*) Death Awakens Sleepy Lagoon (*Breath.*) LA Shaken by Lurid "Kid" Murder.
PRESS: The City of the Angels, Monday, August 2, 1942. The   25
  Los Angeles Times Headline:
THE LINEUP: One Killed, Ten Hurt in Boy Wars: (*Breath.*) Mexican Boy Gangs Operating Within City.
PRESS: The City of the Angels, August 2, 1942. Los Angeles Herald Express Headline: 30
THE LINEUP: Police Arrest Mexican Youths. Black Widow Girls in Boy Gangs.
PRESS: The City of the Angels . . .
PACHUCO: (*Sharply.*) El Pueblo de Nuestra Señora la Reina de los Ángeles de Porciúncula, pendejo.   35
PRESS: (*Eyeing the* PACHUCO *cautiously.*) The Los Angeles Daily News Headline:
BOYS IN THE LINEUP: Police Nab 300 in Roundup.
GIRLS IN THE LINEUP: Mexican Girls Picked Up in Arrests.
LT. EDWARDS: Press Release, Los Angeles Police Depart-   40
  ment: A huge showup of nearly 300 boys and girls rounded up by the police and sheriff's deputies will be held tonight at eight o'clock in Central Jail at First and Hill Street. Victims of assault, robbery, purse snatching, and similar crimes are asked to be present for the iden-   45
  tification of suspects.

PRESS: Lieutenant . . . ? (EDWARDS *poses as the* PRESS *snaps a picture.*)

LT. EDWARDS: Thank you.

50 PRESS: Thank you. (SMITH *gives a signal, and the lineup moves back, forming a straight line in the rear, leaving* HENRY *up front by himself.*)

LT. EDWARDS: Move! Turn! Out! (*As the rear line moves off to the left following* EDWARDS, SMITH *takes* HENRY *by the arm and*

55 *pulls him downstage, shoving him to the floor.*)

3. PACHUCO YO

SGT. SMITH: Okay, kid, you wait here till I get back. Think you can do that? Sure you can. You pachucos are regular tough guys. (SMITH *exits.* HENRY *sits up on the floor.* EL PACHUCO *comes forward.*)

5 HENRY: Bastards. (HE *gets up and paces nervously. Pause.*) ¿Ese? ¿Ese?

PACHUCO: (*Behind him.*) ¿Qué pues, nuez?

HENRY: (*Turning.*) Where the hell you been, ese?

PACHUCO: Checking out the barrio. Qué desmadre, ¿no?

10 HENRY: What's going on, ese? This thing is big.

PACHUCO: The city's cracking down on pachucos, carnal. Don't you read the newspapers? They're screaming for blood.

HENRY: All I know is they got nothing on me. I didn't do

15 anything.

PACHUCO: You're Henry Reyna, ese—Hank Reyna! The snarling juvenile delinquent. The zootsuiter. The bitter young pachuco gang leader of 38th Street. That's what they got on you.

20 HENRY: I don't like this, ese. (*Suddenly intense.*) I DON'T LIKE BEING LOCKED UP!

PACHUCO: Calmantes montes, chicas patas. Haven't I taught you to survive? Play it cool.

HENRY: They're going to do it again, ese! They're going to

25 charge me with some phony rap and keep me until they make something stick.

PACHUCO: So what's new?

HENRY: (*Pause.*) I'm supposed to report for the Navy tomorrow. (THE PACHUCO *looks at him with silent disdain.*) You

30 don't want me to go, do you?

PACHUCO: Stupid move, carnal.

HENRY: (*Hurt and angered by* PACHUCO's *disapproval.*) I've got to do something.

PACHUCO: Then hang tough. Nobody's forcing you to do

35 shit.

HENRY: I'm forcing me, ese—ME, you understand?

PACHUCO: Muy patriotic, eh?

HENRY: Yeah.

PACHUCO: Off to fight for your country.

40 HENRY: Why not?

PACHUCO: Because this ain't your country. Look what's happening all around you. The Japs have sewed up the Pacific. Rommel is kicking ass in Egypt but the Mayor of L.A. has declared all-out war on Chicanos. On you! ¿Te curas?

45 HENRY: Órale.

PACHUCO: Qué mamada, ¿no? Is that what you want to go out and die for? Wise up. These bastard paddy cops have it in for you. You're a marked man. They think you're the enemy.

50 HENRY: (*Refusing to accept it.*) Screw them bastard cops!

PACHUCO: And as soon as the Navy finds out you're in jail again, ya estuvo, carnal. Unfit for military duty because of your record. Think about it.

HENRY: (*Pause.*) You got a frajo?

PACHUCO: Simón. (HE *pulls out a cigarette, hands it to* HENRY, 55 *lights it for him.* HENRY *is pensive.*)

HENRY: (*Smokes, laughs ironically.*) I was all set to come back a hero, see? Me la rayo. For the first time in my life I really thought Hank Reyna was going someplace.

PACHUCO: Forget the war overseas, carnal. Your war is on the 60 homefront.

HENRY: (*With new resolve.*) What do you mean?

PACHUCO: The barrio needs you, carnal. Fight back! Stand up to them with some style. Show the world a Chicano has balls. Hang tough. You can take it. Remember, Pachuco 65 Yo!

HENRY: (*Assuming the style.*) Con safos, carnal.

4. THE INTERROGATION

The PRESS *enters, followed by* EDWARDS *and* SMITH.

PRESS: (*To the audience.*) Final Edition; The Los Angeles Daily News. The police have arrested twenty-two members of the 38th Street Gang, pending further investigation of various charges.

LT. EDWARDS: Well, son, I was hoping I wouldn't see you in 5 here again.

HENRY: Then why did you arrest me?

LT. EDWARDS: Come on, Hank, you know why you're here.

HENRY: Yeah. I'm a Mexican.

LT. EDWARDS: Don't give me that. How long have I known 10 you? Since '39?

HENRY: Yeah, when you got me for stealing a car, remember?

LT. EDWARDS: All right. That was a mistake. I didn't know it was your father's car. I tried to make it up to you. Didn't I help you set up the youth club? 15

SGT. SMITH: They turned it into a gang, Lieutenant. Everything they touch turns to shit.

LT. EDWARDS: I remember a kid just a couple of years back. Head boy at the Catholic Youth Center. His idea of fun was going to the movies. What happened to that nice kid, 20 Henry?

PRESS: He's "Gone With The Wind," trying to look like Clark Gable.

SGT. SMITH: Now he thinks he's Humphrey Bogart.

PACHUCO: So who are you, puto? Pat O'Brien? 25

LT. EDWARDS: This is the wrong time to be anti-social, son. This country's at war, and we're under strict orders to crack down on all malcontents.

SGT. SMITH: Starting with all pachucos and draft dodgers.

HENRY: I ain't no draft dodger. 30

LT. EDWARDS: I know you're not. I heard you got accepted by the Navy. Congratulations. When do you report?

HENRY: Tomorrow?

SGT. SMITH: Tough break!

LT. EDWARDS: It's still not too late, you know. I could still re- 35 lease you in time to get sworn in.

HENRY: If I do what?

LT. EDWARDS: Tell me, Henry, what do you know about a big gang fight last Saturday night, out at Sleepy Lagoon?

40 PACHUCO: Don't tell 'em shit.

HENRY: Which Sleepy Lagoon?

LT. EDWARDS: You mean there's more than one? Come on, Hank, I know you were out there. I've got a statement from your friends that says you were beaten up. Is that

45 true? Were you and your girl attacked?

HENRY: I don't know anything about it. Nobody's ever beat me up.

SGT. SMITH: That's a lie and you know it. Thanks to your squealer friends, we've got enough dope on you to indict

50 for murder right now.

HENRY: Murder?

SGT. SMITH: Yeah, murder. Another greaser named José Williams.

HENRY: I never heard of the bato.

55 SGT. SMITH: Yeah, sure.

LT. EDWARDS: I've been looking at your record, Hank. Petty theft, assault, burglary, and now murder. Is that what you want? The gas chamber? Play square with me. Give me a statement as to what happened at the Lagoon, and I'll go

60 to bat for you with the Navy. I promise you.

PACHUCO: If that ain't a line of gabacho bullshit, I don't know what is.

LT. EDWARDS: Well?

PACHUCO: Spit in his pinche face.

65 SGT. SMITH: Forget it, Lieutenant. You can't treat these animals like people.

LT. EDWARDS: Shut up! I'm thinking of your family, Hank. Your old man would be proud to see you in the Navy. One last chance, son. What do you say?

70 HENRY: I ain't your son, cop.

LT. EDWARDS: All right, Reyna, have it your way. (EDWARDS and PRESS exit.)

PACHUCO: You don't deserve it, ese, but your going to get it anyway.

75 SGT. SMITH: All right, muchacho, it's just me and you now. I hear tell you pachucos wear these monkey suits as a kind of armor. Is that right? How's it work? This is what you zooters need—a little old-fashioned discipline.

HENRY: Screw you, flatfoot.

80 SGT. SMITH: You greasy son of a bitch. What flatpened at the Sleepy Lagoon? Talk! Talk! Talk! (SMITH beats HENRY with a rubber sap. HENRY passes out and falls to the floor, with his hands still handcuffed behind his back. DOLORES his mother appears in a spot upstage, as he falls.)

85 DOLORES: Henry! (Lights change. Four PACHUCO COUPLES enter, dancing a 40's pasodoble (two-step) around HENRY on the floor, as they swing in a clothesline of newspaper sheets. Music.)

PACHUCO:

Get up and escape, Henry . . .

90 leave reality behind
with your buenas garras
muy chamberlain
escape through the barrio streets of your mind
through a neighborhood of memories

95 all chuckhole lined
and the love
and the pain
as fine as wine . . .

(HENRY sits up, seeing his mother DOLORES folding newspaper sheets like clothes on a clothesline.)

DOLORES: Henry?

PACHUCO: It's a lifetime ago, last Saturday night . . . before 100
Sleepy Lagoon and the big bad fight.

DOLORES: Henry!

PACHUCO: Tu mamá, carnal. (HE recedes into the background.)

DOLORES: (At the clothesline.) Henry, ¿hijo? Ven a cenar.

HENRY: (Gets up off the floor.) Sorry, jefita, I'm not hungry. Be- 105
sides, I got to pick up Della. We're late for the dance.

DOLORES: Dance? In his heat? Don't you muchachos ever think of anything else? God knows I suffer la pena negra seeing you go out every night.

HENRY: This isn't just any night, jefa. It's my last chance to use 110
my tacuche.

DOLORES: Tacuche? Pero tu padre . . .

HENRY: (Revealing a stubborn streak.) I know what mi 'apá said, 'amá. I'm going to wear it anyway.

DOLORES: (Sighs, resigns herself.) Mira, hijo. I know you work 115
hard for your clothes. And I know how much they mean to you. Pero por diosito santo, I just don't know what you see en esa cochinada se "soot zoot."

HENRY: (Smiling.) Drapes, 'amá, we call them drapes.

DOLORES: (Scolding playfully.) Ay sí, drapes, muy funny, ¿ver- 120
dad? And what do the police call them, eh? They've put you in jail so many times. ¿Sabes qué? I'm going to send them all your clothes!

HENRY: A qué mi 'amá. Don't worry. By this time next week, I'll be wearing my Navy blues. Okay? 125

DOLORES: Bendito sea Dios. I still can't believe you're going off to war. I almost wish you were going back to jail.

HENRY: ¡Órale? (LUPE REYNA, 16, enters dressed in a short skirt and baggy coat. She is followed by DELLA BARRIOS, 17, dressed more modestly. LUPE hides behind a newspaper sheet on the line.) 130

LUPE: Hank! Let's go, carnal. Della's here.

HENRY: Della . . . Orale, esa. What are you doing here? I told you I was going to pick you up at your house.

DELLA: You know how my father gets.

HENRY: What happened? 135

DELLA: I'll tell you later.

DOLORES: Della, hija, buenas noches. How pretty you look.

DELLA: Buenas noches. (DOLORES hugs DELLA, then spots LUPE hiding behind the clothesline.)

DOLORES: (To LUPE.) ¿Oye y tú? What's wrong with you? 140
What are you doing back there?

LUPE: Nothing, 'amá.

DOLORES: Well, come out then.

LUPE: We're late 'amá.

DOLORES: Come out, te digo. (LUPE comes out exposing 145
her extremely short skirt. DOLORES gasps.) ¡Válgame Dios! Guadalupe, are you crazy? Why bother to wear any-thing?

LUPE: Ay, 'amá, it's the style. Short skirt and fingertip coat. Huh, Hank? 150

HENRY: Uh, yeah, 'amá.

DOLORES: ¿Oh sí? And how come Della doesn't get to wear the same style?

HENRY: No . . . that's different. No, chale.

ENRIQUE: (Off.) ¡vieja! 155

DOLORES: Ándale. Go change before your father sees you.

ENRIQUE: I'm home. (Coming into the scene.) Buenas noches, everybody. (All respond. ENRIQUE sees LUPE.) ¡Ay, jijo! Where's the skirt?!

LUPE: It's here. 160

ENRIQUE: Where's the rest of it?

DOLORES: She's going to the dance.

ENRIQUE: ¿Y a mí qué me importa? Go and change those clothes. Ándale.

165 LUPE: Please, 'apá?

ENRIQUE: No, señorita.

LUPE: Chihuahua, I don't want to look like a square.

ENRIQUE: ¡Te digo que no! I will not have my daughter looking like a . . .

170 DOLORES: Like a puta . . . I mean, a pachuca.

LUPE: (*Pleading for help.*) Hank . . .

HENRY: Do what they say, sis.

LUPE: But you let Henry wear his drapes.

ENRIQUE: That's different. He's a man. Es hombre.

175 DOLORES: Sí, that's different. You men are all alike. From such a stick, such a splinter. De tal palo, tal astillota.

ENRIQUE: Natural, muy natural, and look how he came out. ¡Bien macho! Like his father. ¿Verdad, m'ijo?

HENRY: If you say so, jefito.

180 ENRIQUE: (*To* DELLA.) Buenas noches.

DELLA: Buenas noches.

HENRY: 'Apá, this is Della Barrios.

ENRIQUE: Mira, mira . . . So this is your new girlfriend, eh? Muy bonita. Quite a change from the last one.

185 DOLORES: Ay, señor.

ENRIQUE: It's true. What was her name?

DELLA: Bertha?

ENRIQUE: That's the one. The one with the tattoo.

DOLORES: Este hombre. We have company.

190 ENRIQUE: That reminds me. I invited the compadres to the house mañana.

DOLORES: ¿Que qué?

ENRIQUE: I'm buying a big keg of cerveza to go along with the menudo.

195 DOLORES: Oye, ¿cuál menudo?

ENRIQUE: (*Cutting him off.*) ¡Qué caray, mujer! It isn't every day a man's son goes off to fight for his country. I should know. Della, m'ija, when I was in the Mexican Revolution, I was not even as old as my son is.

200 DOLORES: N'ombre, don't start with your revolution. We'll be here all night.

HENRY: Yeah, jefe, we've got to go.

LUPE: (*Comes forward. She has rolled down her skirt.*) 'Apá, is this better?

205 ENRIQUE: Bueno. And you leave it that way.

HENRY: Órale, pues. It's getting late. Where's Rudy?

LUPE: He's still getting ready. Rudy! (RUDY REYNA, *19, comes downstage in an old suit made into a tachuche.*)

RUDY: Let's go everybody. I'm ready.

210 ENRIQUE: Oye, oye, ¿y tú? What are you doing with my coat?

RUDY: It's my tachuche, 'apá.

ENRIQUE: ¡Me lleva la chingada!

DOLORES: Enrique . . . ¡por el amor de Dios!

ENRIQUE: (*To* HENRY.) You see what you're doing? First that one and now this one. (*To* RUDY.) Hijo, don't go out like that. Por favor. You look like an idiot, pendejo.

215

RUDY: Órale, Hank. Don't I look all right?

HENRY: Nel, ese, you look fine. Watcha. Once I leave for the service, you can have my tachuche. Then you can really be in style. ¿Cómo la ves?

220

RUDY: Chale. Thanks, carnal, but if I don't join the service myself, I'm gonna get my own tachuche.

HENRY: You sure? I'm not going to need it where I'm going. ¿Tú sabes?

RUDY: Are you serious?   225

HENRY: Simón.

RUDY: I'll think about it.

HENRY: Pos, no hay pedo, ese.

ENRIQUE: ¿Cómo que pedo? Nel, ¿Simón? Since when did we stop speaking Spanish in this house? Have you no respect?   230

DOLORES: Muchachos, muchachos, go to your dance. (HENRY *starts upstage.*)

HENRY: Buenas noches . . . (ENRIQUE *holds out his hand.* HENRY *stops, looks, and then returns to kiss his father's hand. Then* HE *moves to kiss his* MOTHER *and* RUDY *in turn kisses* ENRIQUE'*s hand.* ENRIQUE *says "Buenas Noches" to each of his sons.*)   235

HENRY: Órale, we'd better get going . . . (*General "goodbyes" from everybody.*)

ENRIQUE: (*As* RUDY *goes past him.*) Henry! Don't let your brother drink beer.   240

RUDY: Ay, 'apá. I can take care of myself.

DOLORES: I'll believe that when I see it. (SHE *kisses him on the nose.*)

LUPE: Ahí te watcho, 'amá.   245

ENRIQUE: ¿Que qué?

LUPE: I mean, I'll see you later. (HENRY, DELLA, LUPE *and* RUDY *turn upstage. Music starts.*)

ENRIQUE: Mujer, why didn't you let me talk?

DOLORES: (*Sighing.*) Talk, señor, talk all you want. I'm listening. (ENRIQUE *and* DOLORES *exit up right.* RUDY *and* LUPE *exit up left. Lights change. We hear hot dance music.* HENRY *and* DELLA *dance at center stage.* EL PACHUCO *sings.*)   250

PACHUCO:

CADA SÁBADO EN LA NOCHE   255
YO ME VOY A BORLOTEAR
CON MI LINDA PACHUCONA
LAS CADERAS A MENEAR
ELLA LE HACE MUY DE AQUELLAS
CUANDO EMPIEZA A GUARACHAR   260
AL COMPÁS DE LOS TIMBALES
YO ME SIENTO PETATEAR

(*From upstage right, three pachucos now enter in a line, moving to the beat. They are* JOEY CASTRO, *17;* SMILEY TORRES, *23; and* TOMMY ROBERTS, *19, Anglo. They all come downstage left in a diagonal.*)

LOS CHUCOS SUAVES BAILAN RUMBA
BAILAN LA RUMBA Y LE ZUMBAN
BAILAN GUARACHA SABROSÓN
EL BOTECITO Y EL DANZÓN!

(*Chorus repeats, the music fades.* HENRY *laughs and happily embraces* DELLA.)

5. THE PRESS

Lights change. EL PACHUCO *escorts* DELLA *off right.* THE PRESS *appears at upstage center.*

PRESS: Los Angeles Times: August 8, 1942.

A NEWSBOY *enters, lugging in two more bundles of newspapers, hawking them as he goes.* PEOPLE *of various walks of life enter at intervals and buy newspapers. They arrange themselves in the background reading.*

NEWSBOY: EXTRA! EXTRAAA! READ ALL ABOUT IT. SPECIAL SESSION OF L.A. COUNTY GRAND JURY CONVENES. D.A. CHARGES CONSPIRACY IN SLEEPY LAGOON MURDER. EXTRAAA! (*A* 5 CUB REPORTER *emerges and goes to the* PRESS, *as* LIEUTENANT EDWARDS *enters.*)

CUB REPORTER: Hey, here comes Edwards! (EDWARDS *is besieged by the* PRESS, *joined by* ALICE BLOOMFIELD, *26, a woman reporter.*)

10 PRESS: How about it, Lieutenant? What's the real scoop on the Sleepy Lagoon? Sex, violence . . .

CUB REPORTER: Marijuana?

NEWSBOY: Read all about it! Mexican Crime Wave Engulfs L.A.

15 LT. EDWARDS: Slums breed crime, fellas. That's your story.

ALICE: Lieutenant. What exactly is the Sleepy Lagoon?

CUB REPORTER: A great tune by Harry James, doll. Wanna dance? (ALICE *ignores the* CUB.)

LT. EDWARDS: It's a reservoir. An old abandoned gravel pit, re- 20 ally. It's on a ranch between here and Long Beach. Serves as a swimming hole for the younger Mexican kids.

ALICE: Because they're not allowed to swim in the public plunges?

PRESS: What paper are you with, lady? The Daily Worker?

25 LT. EDWARDS: It also doubles as a sort of lovers' lane at night—which is why the gangs fight over it. Now they've finally murdered somebody.

NEWSBOY: EXTRA! EXTRA! ZOOT-SUITED GOONS OF SLEEPY LAGOON!

30 LT. EDWARDS: But we're not going to mollycoddle these youngsters any more. And you can quote me on that.

PRESS: One final question, Lieutenant. What about the 38th Street Gang—weren't you the first to arrest Henry Reyna?

LT. EDWARDS: I was. And I noticed right away the kid had 35 great leadership potential. However . . .

PRESS: Yes?

LT. EDWARDS: You can't change the spots on a leopard.

PRESS: Thank you, sir. (PEOPLE *with newspapers crush them and throw them down as they exit.* EDWARDS *turns and exits.* ALICE 40 *turns towards* HENRY *for a moment.*)

NEWSBOY: EXTRA, EXTRA. READ ALL ABOUT THE MEXICAN BABY GANGSTERS. EXTRA, EXTRA.

THE PRESS *and* CUB REPORTER *rush out happily to file their stories. The* NEWSBOY *leaves, hawking his papers.* ALICE *exits, with determination. Far upstage,* ENRIQUE *enters with a rolling garbage can.* HE *is a street sweeper. During the next scene* HE *silently sweeps up the newspapers, pausing at the last to read one of the news stories.*

6. THE PEOPLE'S LAWYER

JOEY: ¡Chale, ese, chale! Qué pinche agüite.

SMILEY: Mexican Baby Gangsters?!

TOMMY: Zoot-suited goons! I knew it was coming. Every time the D.A. farts, they throw us in the can.

5 SMILEY: Pos, qué chingados, Hank. I can't believe this. Are they really going to pin us with a murder rap? I've got a wife and kid, man!

JOEY: Well, there's one good thing anyway. I bet you know that we've made the headlines. Everybody knows we got 10 the toughest gang in town.

TOMMY: Listen to this, pip squeak. The biggest heist he ever pulled was a Tootsie Roll.

JOEY: (*Grabbing his privates.*) Here's your Tootsie Roll, ese.

TOMMY: What, that? Get my microscope, Smiley.

JOEY: Why don't you come here and take a little bite, joto. 15

TOMMY: Joto? Who you calling a joto, maricón?

JOEY: You, white boy. Did I ever tell you, you got the finest little duck ass in the world.

TOMMY: No, you didn't tell me that, culero. (JOEY *and* TOMMY *start sparring.*) 20

SMILEY: (*Furious.*) Why don't you batos knock it off?

HENRY: (*Cool.*) Cálmenla.

SMILEY: ¡Pinches chavalos! (*The batos stop.*)

JOEY: We're just cabuliando, ese.

TOMMY: Simón, ese. Horsing around. (*He gives* JOEY *a final punch.*) 25

SMILEY: (*With deep self-pity.*) I'm getting too old for this pedo, Hank. All this farting around con esos chavalillos.

HENRY: Relax, carnal. No te agüites.

SMILEY: You and me have been through a lot, Hank. Parties, chingazos, jail. When you said let's join the pachucada, I 30 joined the pachucada. You and me started the 38th, bato. I followed you even after my kid was born, but what now, carnal? This pinche pedo is serious.

TOMMY: He's right, Hank. They indicted the whole gang.

JOEY: Yeah, you know the only one who ain't here is Rudy. 35 (HENRY *turns sharply.*) He was at the Sleepy Lagoon too, ese. Throwing chingazos.

HENRY: Yeah, but the cops don't know that, do they? Unless one of us turned stoolie.

JOEY: Hey, ese, don't look at me. They beat the shit out of me, 40 but that's all they got. Shit.

TOMMY: That's all you got to give. (*Laughs.*)

HENRY: Okay! Let's keep it that way. I don't want my carnalillo pulled into this. And if anybody asks about him, you batos don't know nothing. You get me? 45

SMILEY: Simón.

TOMMY: Crazy.

JOEY: (*Throwing his palms out.*) Say, Jackson, I'm cool. You know that.

HENRY: There's not a single paddy we can trust. 50

TOMMY: Hey, ese, what about me?

HENRY: You know what I mean.

TOMMY: No, I don't know what you mean. I'm here with the rest of yous.

JOEY: Yeah, but you'll be the first one out, cabrón. 55

TOMMY: Gimme a break, maníaco. ¡Yo soy pachuco!

HENRY: Relax, ese. Nobody's getting personal with you. Don't I let you take out my carnala? Well, don't I?

TOMMY: Simón.

HENRY: That's because you respect my family. The rest of 60 them paddies are after our ass.

PACHUCO: Talk about paddies, ese, you got company. (GEORGE SHEARER *enters upstage right and comes down.* HE *is a middle-aged lawyer, strong and athletic, but with the slightly frazzled look of a people's lawyer.*) 65

GEORGE: Hi, boys.

HENRY: Trucha!

GEORGE: My name is George Shearer. I've been retained by your parents to handle your case. Can we sit and talk for a little bit? (*Pause. The* BOYS *eye* GEORGE *suspiciously.* HE 70 *slides a newspaper bundle a few feet upstage.*)

PACHUCO: Better check him out, ese. He looks like a cop.

HENRY: (*To the* GUYS, *sotto voce.*) Pónganse al alba. Este me huele a chota.

75 GEORGE: What was that? Did you say I could sit down? Thank you. (HE *pulls a bundle upstage.* HE *sits.*) Okay, let me get your names straight first. Who's José Castro?

JOEY: Right here, ese. What do you want to know?

GEORGE: We'll get to that. Ismael Torres?

80 SMILEY: (*Deadpan.*) That's me. But they call me Smiley.

GEORGE: (*A wide grin.*) Smiley? I see. You must be Thomas Roberts.

TOMMY: I ain't Zoot Suit Yokum.

GEORGE: Which means you must be Henry Reyna.

85 HENRY: What if I am. Who are you?

GEORGE: I already told you, my name's George Shearer. Your parents asked me to come.

HENRY: Oh yeah? Where did they get the money for a lawyer?

90 GEORGE: I'm a People's Lawyer, Henry.

SMILEY: People's Lawyer?

JOEY: Simón, we're people.

TOMMY: At least they didn't send no animal's lawyer.

HENRY: So what does that mean? You doing this for free or
95   what?

GEORGE: (*Surprise turning to amusement.*) I try not to work for free, if I can help it, but I do sometimes. In this case, I expect to be paid for my services.

HENRY: So who's paying you? For what? And how much?

100 GEORGE: Hey, hey, hold on there. I'm supposed to ask the questions. You're the one going on trial, not me.

PACHUCO: Don't let him throw you, ese.

GEORGE: I sat in on part of the Grand Jury. It was quite a farce, wasn't it? Murder one indictment and all.

105 SMILEY: You think we stand a chance?

GEORGE: There's always a chance, Smiley. That's what trials are for.

PACHUCO: He didn't answer your question, ese.

HENRY: You still didn't answer my question, mister. Who's
110   paying you? And how much?

GEORGE: (*Getting slightly peeved.*) Well, Henry, it's really none of your damned business. (*The* BOYS *react.*) But for whatever it's worth, I'll tell you a little story. The first murder case I ever tried, and won incidentally, was for a Filipino. I
115   was paid exactly three dollars and fifty cents plus a pack of Lucky Strike cigarettes, and a note for a thousand dollars—never redeemed. Does that answer your question?

HENRY: How do we know you're really a lawyer?

GEORGE: How do I know you're Henry Reyna? What do you
120   really mean, son? Do you think I'm a cop?

HENRY: Maybe.

GEORGE: What are you trying to hide from the cops? Murder? (*The* BOYS *react.*) All right! Aside from your parents, I've been called into this case by a citizens committee
125   that's forming in your behalf, Henry. In spite of evidence to the contrary, there are some people out there who don't want to see you get the shaft.

HENRY: ¿Sabes qué, mister? Don't do us any favors.

GEORGE: (*Starting to leave.*) All right, you want another
130   lawyer? I'll talk to the Public Defender's office.

JOEY: (*Grabbing his briefcase.*) Hey, wait a minute, ese. Where are you going?

TOMMY: De cincho se le va a volar la tapa.

JOEY: Nel, este bolillo no sabe nada.

GEORGE: (*Exploding.*) All right, kids, cut the crap!   135

SMILEY: (*Grabs his briefcase and crosses to* HENRY.) Let's give him a break, Hank. (SMILEY *hands the briefcase to* GEORGE.)

GEORGE: Thank you. (HE *starts to exit. Stops.*) You know, you're making a big mistake. I wonder if you know who your friends are? You boys are about to get a mass trial. You 140 know what that is? Well, it's a new one on me too. The Grand Jury has indicted you all on the same identical crime. Not just you four. The whole so-called 38th Street Gang. And you know who the main target is? You, Henry, because they're saying you're the ringleader. (*Looks around* 145 *at the* GUYS.) And I suppose you are. But you're leading your buddies here down a dead-end street. The D.A.'s coming after you, son, and he's going to put you and your whole gang right into the gas chamber. (GEORGE *turns to leave.* SMILEY *panics.* JOEY *and* TOMMY *react with him.*)   150

SMILEY/JOEY/TOMMY: (*All together.*) Gas chamber! But we didn't do nothing! We're innocent!

HENRY: ¡Cálmenla! (*The batos stop in their tracks.*) Okay. Say we believe you're a lawyer, what does that prove? The press has already tried and convicted us. Think you can change 155 that?

GEORGE: Probably not. But then, public opinion comes and goes, Henry. What matters is our system of justice. I believe it works, however slowly the wheels may grind. It could be a long uphill fight, fellas, but we can make it. I 160 know we can. I've promised your parents the best defense I'm capable of. The question is, Henry, will you trust me?

HENRY: Why should I? You're a gringo.

GEORGE: (*Calmly, deliberately.*) ¿Cómo sabes?

TOMMY: (*Shocked.*) Hey, you speak Spanish?   165

GEORGE: Más o menos.

JOEY: You mean you understood us a while ago?

GEORGE: More or less.

JOEY: (*Embarrassed.*) ¡Híjole, qué gacho, ese!

GEORGE: Don't worry. I'm not much on your pachuco slang. 170 The problem seems to be that I look like an Anglo to you. What if I were to tell you that I had Spanish blood in my veins? That my roots go back to Spain, just like yours? What if I'm an Arab? What if I'm a Jew? What difference does it make? The question is, will you let me help you? 175 (*Pause.* HENRY *glances at the* PACHUCO.)

PACHUCO: ¡Chale!

HENRY: (*Pause.*) Okay!

SMILEY: Me too!

JOEY: Same here!   180

TOMMY: ¡Órale!

GEORGE: (*Eagerly.*) Okay! Let's go to work. I want to know exactly what happened right from the beginning. (GEORGE *sits down and opens his briefcase.*)

HENRY: Well, I think the pedo really started at the dance last 185 Saturday night . . . (*El* PACHUCO *snaps his fingers and we hear dance music. Lights change.* GEORGE *exits.*)

7. THE SATURDAY NIGHT DANCE

SWABBIE *and* MANCHUKA *come running onstage as the barrio dance begins to take shape.* HENRY *and the batos move upstage to join other* PACHUCOS *and* PACHUCAS *coming in.* HENRY *joins* DELLA

BARRIOS; JOEY *teams up with* BERTHA VILLARREAL, TOMMY *picks up* LUPE REYNA; *and* SMILEY *escorts his wife* ELENA TORRES. *They represent the* 38TH STREET *neighborhood. Also entering the dance comes the* DOWNEY GANG, *looking mean.* RUDY *stands upstage, in the background, drinking a bottle of beer.* EL PACHUCO *sings.*

PACHUCO:
> CUANDO SALGO YO A BAILAR
> YO ME PONGO MUY CATRÍN
> LAS HUISITAS TODAS GRITAN, DADDY
> VAMOS A BAILAR EL SWING!

(*The* COUPLES *dance. A lively swing number. The music comes to a natural break and shifts into a slow number.* BERTHA *approaches* HENRY *and* DELLA *downstage on the dance floor.*)

5 BERTHA: Ese, ¡surote! How about a dance for old time's sake? No te hagas gacho.

HENRY: (*Slow dancing with* DELLA.) Sorry, Bertha.

BERTHA: Is this your new huisa? This little fly chick?

DELLA: Listen, Bertha . . .

10 HENRY: (*Stops her.*) Chale. She's just jealous. Beat it, Bertha.

BERTHA: Beat it yourself. Mira. You got no hold on me, cabrón. Not any more. I'm as free as a bird.

SMILEY: (*Coming up.*) Ese, Hank, that's the Downey Gang in the corner. You think they're looking for trouble?

15 HENRY: There's only a couple of them.

BERTHA: That's all we need.

SMILEY: Want me to alert the batos?

HENRY: Nel, be cool.

BERTHA: Be cool? Huy, yu, yui. Forget it, Smiley. Since he
20 joined the Navy, this bato forgot the difference between being cool and being cool-O. (*She laughs and turns but* HENRY *grabs her angrily by the arm.* BERTHA *pulls free and walks away cool and tough. The music changes and the beat picks up.* EL PACHUCO *sings as the* COUPLES *dance.*)

PACHUCO:
25 > CUANDO VOY AL VACILÓN
> Y ME METO YO A UN SALON
> LAS CHAVALAS GRITAN, PAPI VENTE
> VAMOS A BAILAR DANSÓN!

(*The dance turns Latin. The music comes to another natural break and holds.* LUPE *approaches* HENRY *on the dance floor.*)

LUPE: Hank. Rudy's at it again. He's been drinking since we
30 got here.

HENRY: (*Glancing over at* RUDY.) He's okay, sis, let the carnal enjoy himself.

RUDY: (*Staggering over.*) ¡Ese, carnal!

HENRY: What you say, brother?

35 RUDY: I'm flying high, Jackson. Feeling good.

LUPE: Rudy, if you go home drunk again, mi 'apá's going to use you for a punching bag. (RUDY *kisses her on the cheek and moves on.*)

DELLA: How are you feeling?

40 HENRY: Okay.

DELLA: Still thinking about Bertha?

HENRY: Chale, ¿qué traes? Listen, you want to go out to the Sleepy Lagoon? I've got something to tell you.

DELLA: What?

HENRY: Later, later.   45

LUPE: You better tell Rudy to stop drinking.

HENRY: Relax, sis. If he gets too drunk, I'll carry him home. (*Music picks up again.* EL PACHUCO *sings a third verse.*)

PACHUCO:
> TOCAN MAMBO SABROSÓN   50
> SE ALBOROTA EL CORAZÓN
> Y CON UNA CHAVALONA VAMOS
> VAMOS A BAILAR EL MAMBO

(*The* COUPLES *do the mambo. In the background,* RUDY *gets into an argument with* RAFAS, *the leader of the* DOWNEY GANG. *A fight breaks out as the music comes to a natural break.* RAFAS *pushes* RUDY, *half drunk, onto the floor.*)

RAFAS: ¡Y a ti qué te importa, puto!

RUDY: (HE *falls.*) ¡Cabrón!   55

HENRY: (*Reacting immediately.*) Hey! (*The whole dance crowd tenses up immediately, splitting into separate camps. Batos from* 38TH *clearly outnumber the* GUYS *from* DOWNEY.)

RAFAS: He started it, ese. El comenzó a chingar conmigo.

RUDY: You chicken shit, ese! Tú me haces la puñeta, ¡pirujo!   60

RAFAS: Come over here and say that, puto!

HENRY: (*Pulling* RUDY *behind him.*) ¡Agüítala, carnal! (*Faces* RAFAS.) You're a little out of your territory, ¿Que no Rafas?

RAFAS: It's a barrio dance, ese. We're from the barrio.

HENRY: You're from Downey.   65

RAFAS: Vale madre. ¡Downey Rifa!

DOWNEY GANG: ¡SIMÓN!

RAFAS: What are you going to do about it?

HENRY: I'm going to kick your ass. (*The* TWO SIDES *start to attack each other.*) ¡Cálmenla! (ALL *stop.*)   70

RAFAS: (*Pulls out a switchblade.*) You and how many batos?

HENRY: Just me and you, cabrón. That's my carnalillo you started pushing around, see? And nobody chinga con mi familia without answering to me, ese! Hank Reyna! (HE *pulls out another switchblade.*)   75

BERTHA: ALL-RIGHT!

HENRY: Let's see if you can push me around like you did my little brother, ese. Come on . . . COME ON! (*They knife fight.* HENRY *moves in fast. Recoiling,* RAFAS *falls to the floor.* HENRY's *blade is at his throat.* EL PACHUCO *snaps his fingers.* 80 *Everyone freezes.*)

PACHUCO: Qué mamada, Hank. That's exactly what the play needs right now. Two more Mexicans killing each other. Watcha . . . Everybody's looking at you.

HENRY: (*Looks out at the audience.*) Don't give me that bullshit.   85 Either I kill him or he kills me.

PACHUCO: That's exactly what they paid to see. Think about it. (EL PACHUCO *snaps again. Everybody unfreezes.*)

HENRY: (*Kicks* RAFAS.) Get out of here. ¡Píntate!

BERTHA: What?   90

GÜERA: (RAFAS' *girlfriend runs forward.*) Rafas. ¡Vámonos! (SHE *is stopped by other* DOWNEY *batos.*)

RAFAS: Está suave. I'll see you later.

HENRY: Whenever you want, cabrón. (*The* DOWNEY GANG *retreats, as the* 38TH *razzes them all the way out. Insults are ex-* 95 *changed.* BERTHA *shouts "¡Chinga tu madre!" and they are gone. The* 38TH *whoops in victory.*)

SMILEY: Órale, you did it, ese! ¡Se escamaron todos!

TOMMY: We sure chased those jotos out of here.

100 BERTHA: I could have beat the shit out of those two rucas.

JOEY: That pinche Rafas is yellow without his gang, ese.

LUPE: So why didn't you jump out there?

JOEY: Chale, Rudy ain't my baby brother.

RUDY: (*Drunk.*) Who you calling a baby, pendejo? I'll show
105   you who's a baby!

JOEY: Be cool, ese.

TOMMY: Man, you're lucky your brother was here.

BERTHA: Why? He didn't do nothing. The old Hank would
   have slit Rafas' belly like a fat pig.

110 HENRY: Shut your mouth, Bertha!

RUDY: ¿Por qué, carnal? You backed down, ese. I could have
   taken that sucker on by myself.

HENRY: That's enough, Rudy. You're drunk.

DELLA: Hank, what if Rafas comes back with all his gang?

115 HENRY: (*Reclaiming his leadership.*) We'll kill the sons of bitches.

JOEY: ¡Órale! ¡La 38th rifa! (*Music. Everybody gets back with furious energy.* EL PACHUCO *sings.*)

PACHUCO:
120   DE LOS BAILES QUE MENTÉ
   Y EL BOLERO Y EL BEGUÍN
   DE TODOS LOS BAILES JUNTOS
   ME GUSTA BAILAR EL SWING! HEY!

(*The dance ends with a group exclamation: HEY!*)

8. EL DÍA DE LA RAZA

The PRESS *enters upstage level, pushing a small hand truck piled
high with newspaper bundles. The batos and rucas on the dance floor
freeze in their final positions.* EL PACHUCO *is the only one who relaxes and moves.*

PRESS: October 12, 1942: Columbus Day. Four Hundred and
   Fiftieth Anniversary of the Discovery of America. Headlines!

In their places, the COUPLES *now stand straight and recite a headline
before exiting. As they do so, the* PRESS *moves the bundles of newspapers on the floor to outline the four corners of a jail cell.*

SMILEY/ELENA: President Roosevelt Salutes Good Neighbors
5   In Latin America. (SMILEY *and* ELENA *exit.*)

TOMMY/LUPE: British Begin Drive to Oust Rommel From
   North Africa. (TOMMY *and* LUPE *exit.*)

RUDY/CHOLO: Japs In Death Grip On Pacific Isles. (RUDY *and*
   CHOLO *exit.* PRESS *tosses another bundle.*)

10 ZOOTER/LITTLE BLUE: Web Of Zoot Crime Spreads.
   (ZOOTER *and* LITTLE BLUE *exit.*)

MANCHUKA/SWABBIE: U.S. Marines Land Bridgehead On
   Guadalcanal. (MANCHUKA *and* SWABBIE *exit.*)

JOEY/BERTHA: First Mexican Braceros Arrive In U.S.A. (JOEY
15   *and* BERTHA *exit.*)

DELLA: Sleepy Lagoon Murder Trial Opens Tomorrow. (DELLA
   and the PRESS *exit. As they exit,* GEORGE *and* ALICE *enter upstage left.* HENRY *is center, in a "cell" outlined by four newspaper bundles left by the* PRESS.)

20 GEORGE: Henry? How you doing, son? Listen, I've brought
   somebody with me that wants very much to meet you. I
   thought you wouldn't mind. (ALICE *crosses to* HENRY.)

ALICE: Hello! My name is Alice Bloomfield and I'm a reporter from the Daily People's World.

GEORGE: And . . . And, I might add, a red hot member of the   25
   ad hoc committee that's fighting for you guys.

ALICE: Oh, George! I'd hardly call it fighting, for Pete's sake.
   This struggle has just barely begun. But we're sure going
   to win it, aren't we, Henry?

HENRY: I doubt it.   30

GEORGE: Oh come on, Henry. How about it, son? You all set
   for tomorrow? Anything you need, anything I can get for
   you?

HENRY: Yeah. What about the clean clothes you promised
   me? I can't go to court looking like this.   35

GEORGE: You mean they didn't give them to you?

HENRY: What?

GEORGE: Your mother dropped them off two days ago. Clean
   pants, shirt, socks, underwear, the works. I cleared it with
   the Sheriff last week.   40

HENRY: They haven't given me nothing.

GEORGE: I'm beginning to smell something around here.

HENRY: Look, George, I don't like being like this. I ain't dirty.
   Go do something, man!

GEORGE: Calm down. Take it easy, son. I'll check on it right   45
   now. Oh! Uh, Alice?

ALICE: I'll be okay, George.

GEORGE: I'll be right back. (HE *exits.*)

ALICE: (*Pulling out a pad and pencil.*) Now that I have you all
   to myself, mind if I ask you a couple of questions?   50

HENRY: I got nothing to say.

ALICE: How do you know? I haven't asked you anything yet.
   Relax. I'm from the progressive press. Okay? (HENRY *stares
   at her, not knowing quite how to react.* ALICE *sits on a bundle
   and crosses her goodlooking legs.* HENRY *concentrates on that.*) 55
   Now. The regular press is saying the Pachuco Crime Wave
   is fascist inspired—any thoughts about that?

HENRY: (*Bluntly.*) No.

ALICE: What about the American Japanese? Is it true they are
   directing the subversive activities of the pachucos from in- 60
   side the relocation camps? (HENRY *turns to the* PACHUCO
   with a questioning look.)

PACHUCO: This one's all yours, ese.

HENRY: Look, lady, I don't know what the hell you're talking
   about.   65

ALICE: I'm talking about you, Henry Reyna. And what the
   regular press has been saying. Are you aware you're in here
   just because some bigshot up in San Simeon wants to sell
   more papers? It's true.

HENRY: So?   70

ALICE: So, he's the man who started this Mexican Crime
   Wave stuff. Then the police got into the act. Get the picture? Somebody is using you as a patsy.

HENRY: (*His machismo insulted.*) Who you calling a patsy?

ALICE: I'm sorry, but it's true.   75

HENRY: (*Backing her up.*) What makes you so goddamned
   smart?

ALICE: (*Starting to get scared and trying not to show it.*) I'm a reporter. It's my business to know.

PACHUCO: Puro pedo. She's just a dumb broad only good for   80
   you know what.

HENRY: Look, Miss Bloomfield, just leave me alone, all right?
   (HENRY *moves away.* ALICE *takes a deep breath.*)

ALICE: Look, let's back up and start all over, okay? Hello. My name is Alice Bloomfield, and I'm not a reporter. I'm just somebody that wants very much to be your friend. (*Pause. With sincere feeling.*) Can you believe that?

HENRY: Why should I?

ALICE: Because I'm with you.

HENRY: Oh, yeah! Then how come you ain't in jail with me?

ALICE: (*Holding her head up.*) We are all in jail, Henry. Some of us just don't know it.

PACHUCO: Mmm, pues. No comment. (*Pause.* HENRY *stares at her, trying to figure her out.* ALICE *tries a softer approach.*)

ALICE: Believe it or not, I was born in Los Angeles just like you. But for some strange reason I grew up here, not knowing very much about Mexicans at all. I'm just trying to learn.

HENRY: (*Intrigued, but cynical.*) What?

ALICE: Little details. Like that tattooed cross on your hand. Is that the sign of the pachuco? (HENRY *covers his right hand with and automatic reflex, then* HE *realizes what he has done.*)

HENRY: (*Smiles to himself, embarrassed.*) Órale.

ALICE: Did I embarrass you? I'm sorry. Your mother happened to mention it.

HENRY: (*Surprised.*) My mother? You talked to my jefita?

ALICE: (*With enthusiasm.*) Yes! And your father and Lupe and Rudy. The whole family gave me a helluva interview. But your mother was sensational. I especially liked her story about the midnight raid. How the police rushed into your house with drawn guns, looking for you on some trumped up charge, and how your father told them you were already in jail . . . God, I would have paid to have seen the cops' faces.

HENRY: (*Hiding his sentiment.*) Don't believe anything my jefa tells you. (*Then quickly.*) There's a lot she doesn't know. I'm no angel.

ALICE: I'll just bet you're not. But you have been taken in for suspicion a dozen times, kept in jail for a few days, then released for lack of evidence. And it's all stayed on your juvenile record.

HENRY: Yeah, well I ain't no punk, see.

ALICE: I know. You're an excellent mechanic. And you fix all the guys' cars. Well, at least you're not one of the lumpen proletariat.

HENRY: The lumpen what?

ALICE: Skip it. Let's just say you're a classic social victim.

HENRY: Bullshit.

ALICE: (*Pause. A serious question.*) Are you saying you're guilty?

HENRY: Of what?

ALICE: The Sleepy Lagoon Murder.

HENRY: What if I am?

ALICE: Are you?

HENRY: (*Pause, a serious answer.*) Chale. I've pulled a lot of shit in my time, but I didn't do that. (GEORGE *re-enters flushed and angry, trying to conceal his frustration.*)

GEORGE: Henry, I'm sorry, but dammit, something's coming off here, and the clothes have been withheld. I'll have to bring it up in court.

HENRY: In court?

GEORGE: They've left me no choice.

ALICE: What's going on?

HENRY: It's a set up, George. Another lousy set up!

GEORGE: It's just the beginning, son. Nobody said this was going to be a fair fight. Well, if they're going to fight dirty, so am I. Legally, but dirty. Trust me.

ALICE: (*Passionately.*) Henry, no matter what happens in the trial, I want you to know I believe you're innocent. Remember that when you look out, and it looks like some sort of lynch mob. Some of us . . . a lot of us . . . are right there with you.

GEORGE: Okay, Alice, let's scram. I've got a million things to do. Henry, see you tomorrow under the big top, son. Good luck, son.

ALICE: Thumbs up, Henry, we're going to beat this rap! (ALICE *and* GEORGE *exit.* EL PACHUCO *watches them go, then turns to* HENRY.)

PACHUCO: "Thumbs up, Henry, we're going to beat this rap." You really think you're going to beat this one, ese?

HENRY: I don't want to think about it.

PACHUCO: You've got to think about it, Hank. Everybody's playing you for a sucker. Wake up, carnal!

HENRY: Look, bato, what the hell do you expect me to do?

PACHUCO: Hang tough. (*Grabs his scrotum.*) Stop going soft.

HENRY: Who's going soft?

PACHUCO: (*Incisively.*) You're hoping for something that isn't going to happen, ese. These paddies are leading you by the nose. Do you really believe you stand a chance?

HENRY: (*Stubborn all the more.*) Yeah. I think I got a chance.

PACHUCO: Just because that white broad says so?

HENRY: Nel, ese, just because Hank Reyna says so.

PACHUCO: The classic social victim, eh?

HENRY: (*Furious but keeping his cool.*) Mira, ese. Hank Reyna's no loser. I'm coming out of this on top. ¿Me entiendes, Mendez? (HE *walks away with a pachuco gait.*)

PACHUCO: (*Forcefully.*) Don't try to out-pachuco ME, ese! We'll see who comes out on top. (HE *picks up a bundle of newspapers and throws it upstage center. It lands with a thud.*) Let's go to court!

9. OPENING OF THE TRIAL

Music. The JUDGE's *bench, made up of more newspaper bundles piled squarely on a four-wheeled hand truck is pushed in by the batos. The* PRESS *rides it in, holding the State and Federal Flags. A* BAILIFF *puts in place a hand cart: the* JUDGE's *throne. From the sides, spectators enter, including* HENRY's *family and friends:* ALICE, DELLA, BERTHA, ELENA.

PRESS: The largest mass trial in the history of Los Angeles County opens this morning in the Superior Court at ten A.M. The infamous Sleepy Lagoon Murder case involves sixty-six charges against twenty-two defendants with seven lawyers pleading for the defense, two for the prosecution. The District Attorney estimates that over a hundred witnesses will be called and has sworn—I quote—"to put an end to Mexican baby gangsterism." End quote.

BAILIFF: (*Bangs a gavel on the bench.*) The Superior Court of the State of California. In and For the County of Los Angeles. Department forty-three. The honorable F. W. Charles, presiding. All rise! (JUDGE CHARLES *enters. All rise.* EL PACHUCO *squats. The* JUDGE *is played by the same actor that portrays* EDWARDS.)

JUDGE: Please be seated. (*All sit.* PACHUCO *stands.*) Call this case, Bailiff.

BAILIFF: (*Reading from a sheet.*) The people of the State of California Versus Henry Reyna, Ismael Torres, Thomas

120   Roberts, Jose Castro and eighteen other . . . (*Slight hesita-tion.*) . . . pa-coo-cos.

JUDGE: Is Counsel for the Defense present?

GEORGE: (*Rises.*) Yes, Your Honor.

JUDGE: Please proceed. (*Signals the* PRESS.)

125 PRESS: Your Honor . . .

GEORGE: (*Moving in immediately.*) If the Court please, it was reported to me on Friday that the District Attorney has absolutely forbidden the Sheriff's Office to permit these boys to have clean clothes or haircuts. Now, it's been three

130   months since the boys were arrested . . .

PRESS: (*Jumping in.*) Your Honor, there is testimony we expect to develop that he 38th Street Gang are characterized by their style of haircuts . . .

GEORGE: Three months, Your Honor.

135 PRESS: . . . the thick heavy heads of hair, the ducktail comb, the pachuco pants . . .

GEORGE: Your Honor, I can only infer that the Prosecu-tion . . . is trying to make these boys look disreputable, like mobsters.

140 PRESS: Their appearance is distinctive, Your Honor. Essential to the case.

GEORGE: You are trying to exploit the fact that these boys look foreign in appearance! Yet clothes like these are be-ing worn by kids all over America.

145 PRESS: Your Honor . . .

JUDGE: (*Bangs the gavel.*) I don't believe we will have any dif-ficulty if their clothing becomes dirty.

GEORGE: What about the haircuts, Your Honor?

JUDGE: (*Ruling.*) The zoot haircuts will be retained through-

150   out the trial for purposes of identification of defendants by witnesses.

PACHUCO: You hear that one, ese? Listen to it again. (*Snaps.* JUDGE *repeats automatically.*)

JUDGE: The zoot haircuts will be retained throughout the

155   trial for purposes of identification of defendants by wit-nesses.

PACHUCO: He wants to be sure we know who you are.

JUDGE: It has been brought to my attention the Jury is hav-ing trouble telling one boy from another, so I am going to

160   rule the defendants stand each time their names are men-tioned.

GEORGE: I object. If the Prosecution makes an accusation, it will mean self-incrimination.

JUDGE: (*Pause.*) Not necessarily. (*To* PRESS.) Please proceed.

165 GEORGE: (*Still trying to set the stage.*) Then if the Court please, might I request that my clients be allowed to sit with me during the trial so that I might consult with them?

JUDGE: Request denied.

GEORGE: May I inquire of Your Honor, if the defendant

170   Thomas Robert might rise from his seat and walk over to counsel table so as to consult with me during the trial?

JUDGE: I certainly will not permit it.

GEORGE: You will not?

JUDGE: No. This is a small courtroom, Mr. Shearer. We can't

175   have twenty-two defendants all over the place.

GEORGE: Then I object. On the grounds that that is a denial of the rights guaranteed all defendants by both the Fed-eral and State constitutions.

JUDGE: Well, that is your opinion. (*Gavel.*) Call your first witness.

180 PRESS: The prosecution calls Lieutenant Sam Edwards of the Los Angeles Police Department.

PACHUCO: (*Snaps. Does double take on* JUDGE.) You know what. We've already heard from that bato. Let's get on with the defense. (*Snaps.* PRESS *sits.* GEORGE *stands.*)

GEORGE: The defense calls Adela Barrios.   185

BAILIFF: (*Calling out.*) Adeela Barreeos to the stand. (DELLA BARRIOS *comes forth out of the spectators.* BERTHA *leans for-ward.*)

BERTHA: (*Among the spectators.*) Don't tell 'em nothing. (*The* BAILIFF *swears in* DELLA *silently.*)   190

PACHUCO: Look at your gang. They do look like mobsters. Se watchan bien gachos. (HENRY *looks at the batos, who are sprawled out in their places.*)

HENRY: (*Under his breath.*) Come on, Batos, sit up.

SMILEY: We're tired, Hank.   195

JOEY: My butt is sore.

TOMMY: Yeah, look at the soft chairs the jury's got.

HENRY: What did you expect? They're trying to make us look bad. Come on! Straighten up.

SMILEY: Simón, batos, Hank is right.   200

JOEY: ¡Más alba nalga!

TOMMY: Put some class on your ass.

HENRY: Sit up! (*They all sit up.*)

GEORGE: State your name please.

DELLA: Adela Barrios. (*She sits.*)   205

GEORGE: Miss Barrios, were you with Henry Reyna on the night of August 1, 1942?

DELLA: Yes.

JUDGE: (*To* HENRY.) Please stand. (HENRY *stands.*)

GEORGE: Please tell the court what transpired that night.   210

DELLA: (*Pause. Takes a breath.*) Well, after the dance that Satur-day night, Henry and I drove out to the Sleepy Lagoon about eleven-thirty.

10. SLEEPY LAGOON

Music: THE HARRY JAMES THEME. EL PACHUCO *creates the scene. The light changes. We see a shimmering pattern of light on the floor growing to the music. It becomes the image of the Lagoon. As the music soars to a trumpet solo,* HENRY *reaches out to* DELLA, *and she glides to her feet.*

DELLA: There was a full moon that night, and as we drove up to the Lagoon we noticed right away the place was empty . . . (*A pair of headlights silently pulls in from the black back-ground upstage center.*) Henry parked the car on the bank of the reservoir and we relaxed. (*Headlights go off.*) It was such   5 a warm, beautiful night, and the sky was so full of stars, we couldn't just sit in the car. So we got out, and Henry took my hand . . . (HENRY *stands and takes* DELLA's *hand.*) We went for a walk around the Lagoon. Neither of us said anything at first, so the only sounds we could hear were   10 the crickets and the frogs . . . (*Sounds of crickets and frogs, then music faintly in the background.*) When we got to the other side of the reservoir, we began to hear music, so I asked Henry, what's that?

HENRY: Sounds like they're having a party.   15

DELLA: Where?

HENRY: Over at the Williams' Ranch. See the house lights.

DELLA: Who lives there?

HENRY: A couple of families. Mexicanos. I think they work on the ranch. You know, their name used to be Gonzales, 20 but they changed it to Williams.

DELLA: Why?

HENRY: I don't know. Maybe they think it gives 'em more class. (*We hear Mexican music.*) Ay, jijo. They're probably
25   celebrating a wedding or something.

DELLA: As soon as he said wedding, he stopped talking and we both knew why. He had something on his mind, something he was trying to tell me without sounding like a square.

30 HENRY: Della . . . what are you going to do if I don't come back from the war?

DELLA: That wasn't the question I was expecting, so I answered something dumb, like I don't know, what's going to keep you from coming back?

35 HENRY: Maybe wanting too much out of life, see? Ever since I was a kid, I've had this feeling like there's a big party going on someplace, and I'm invited, but I don't know how to get there. And I want to get there so bad, I'll even risk my life to make it. Sounds crazy, huh? (DELLA *and* HENRY
40   *kiss. They embrace and then* HENRY *speaks haltingly.*) If I get back from the war . . . will you marry me?

DELLA: Yes! (SHE *embraces him and almost causes them to topple over.*)

HENRY: ¡Órale! You'll knock us into the Lagoon. Listen, what
45   about your old man? He ain't going to like you marrying me.

DELLA: I know. But I don't care. I'll go to hell with you if you want me to.

HENRY: ¿Sabes qué? I'm going to give you the biggest
50   Pachuco wedding L.A. has ever seen. (*Another pair of headlights comes in from the left.* DELLA *goes back to her narration.*)

DELLA: Just then another car pulled up to the Lagoon. It was Rafas and some drunk guys in a gang from Downey. They got out and started to bust the windows on Henry's car.
55   Henry yelled at them, and they started cussing at us. I told Henry not to say anything, but he cussed them back!

HENRY: You stay here, Della.

DELLA: Henry, no! Don't go down there! Please don't go down there!

60 HENRY: Can't you hear what they're doing to my car?

DELLA: There's too many of them. They'll kill you!

HENRY: ¡Chale! (HENRY *turns and runs upstage, where he stops in a freeze.*)

DELLA: Henry! Henry ran down the back of the Lagoon and
65   attacked the gang by himself. Rafas had about ten guys with him and they jumped on Henry like a pack of dogs. He fought them off as long as he could, then they threw him on the ground hard and kicked him until he passed out . . . (*Headlights pull off.*) After they left, I ran down to
70   Henry and held him in my arms until he came to. And I could tell he was hurt, but the first thing he said was . . .

PACHUCO: Let's go into town and get the guys. (*Music: Glen Miller's "In the Mood."* HENRY *turns to the batos and they stand.* SMILEY, JOEY *and* TOMMY *are joined by* RUDY, BERTHA,
75   LUPE *and* ELENA, *who enter from the side. They turn downstage in a body and freeze.*)

DELLA: It took us about an hour to go into town and come back. We got to the Lagoon with about eight cars, but the Downey gang wasn't there.

80 JOEY: Órale, ¿pos qué pasó? Nobody here.

SMILEY: Then let's go to Downey.

THE BOYS: (*Ad lib.*) Let's go!

HENRY: ¡Chale! ¡Chale! (*Pause. They all stop.*) Ya estuvo. Everybody go home. (*A collective groan from* THE BOYS.) Go home!

DELLA: That's when we heard music coming from the Williams'   85
Ranch again. We didn't know Rafas and his gang had been there too, causing trouble. So when Joey said . . .

JOEY: Hey, there's a party! Bertha, let's crash it.

DELLA: We all went there yelling and laughing. (*The group of batos turns upstage in a mimetic freeze.*) At the Williams'   90
Ranch they saw us coming and thought we were the Downey Gang coming back again . . . They attacked us. (*The group now mimes a series of tableaus showing the fight.*) An old man ran out of the house with a kitchen knife and Henry had to hit him. Then a girl grabbed me by the hair   95
and in a second everybody was fighting! People were grabbing sticks from the fence, bottles, anything! It all happened so fast, we didn't know what hit us, but Henry said let's go!

HENRY: ¡Vámonos! Let's get out of here.   100

DELLA: And we started to back off . . . Before we got to the cars, I saw something out of the corner of my eye . . . It was a guy. He was hitting a man on the ground with a big stick. (EL PACHUCO *mimes this action.*) Henry called to him, but he wouldn't stop. He wouldn't stop . . . He wouldn't stop . . .   105
He wouldn't stop . . . (DELLA *in tears, holds* HENRY *in her arms. The batos and rucas start moving back to their places, quietly.*) Driving back in the car, everybody was quiet, like nothing had happened. We didn't know José Williams had died at the party that night and that the guys would be arrested the   110
next day for murder. (HENRY *separates from her and goes back to stand in his place.* DELLA *resumes the witness stand.*)

11. THE CONCLUSION OF THE TRIAL

Lights change back to courtroom, as JUDGE CHARLES *bangs his gavel. Everyone is seated back in place.*

GEORGE: Your witness.

PRESS: (*Springing to the attack.*) You say Henry Reyna hit the man with his fist. (*Indicates* HENRY *standing.*) Is this the Henry Reyna?

DELLA: Yes. I mean, no. He's Henry, but he didn't . . .   5

PRESS: Please be seated. (HENRY *sits.*) Now, after Henry Reyna hit the old man with his closed fist, is that when he pulled the knife?

DELLA: The old man had the knife.

PRESS: So Henry pulled one out, too?   10

GEORGE: (*Rises.*) Your Honor, I object to counsel leading the witness.

PRESS: I am not leading the witness.

GEORGE: You are.

PRESS: I certainly am not.   15

GEORGE: Yes, you are.

JUDGE: I would suggest, Mr. Shearer, that you look up during the noon hour just what a leading question is.

GEORGE: If the Court please, I am going to assign that remark of Your Honor as misconduct.   20

JUDGE: (*To* PRESS.) Proceed. (GEORGE *crosses back to his chair.*)

PRESS: Where was Smiley Torres during all this? Is it not true that Smiley Torres grabbed a woman by the hair and kicked her to the ground? Will Smiley Torres please stand? (SMILEY *stands.*) Is this the man?   25

DELLA: Yes, it's Smiley, but he . . .

PRESS: Please be seated. (SMILEY *sits.* PRESS *picks up a two-by-four.*) Wasn't José Castro carrying a club of some kind?

GEORGE: (*On his feet again.*) Your Honor, I object! No such
30   club was ever found. The Prosecution is implying that this two-by-four is associated with my client in some way.

PRESS: I'm not implying anything, Your Honor, I'm merely using this stick as an illustration.

JUDGE: Objection overruled.

35 PRESS: Will José Castro please stand? (JOEY *stands.*) Is this man who was carrying a club? (DELLA *refuses to answer.*) Answer the question please.

DELLA: I refuse.

PRESS: You are under oath. You can't refuse.

40 JUDGE: Answer the question, young lady.

DELLA: I refuse.

PRESS: Is this the man you saw hitting another man with a two-by-four? Your Honor . . .

JUDGE: I order you to answer the question.

45 GEORGE: Your Honor, I object. The witness is obviously afraid her testimony will be manipulated by the Prosecution.

PRESS: May I remind the court that we have a signed confession from one José Castro taken while in jail . . .

GEORGE: I object. Those were not confessions! Those are
50   statements. They are false and untrue, Your Honor, obtained through beatings and coercion of the defendants by the police!

JUDGE: I believe the technical term is admissions, Mr. Prosecutor. Objection sustained. (*Applause from spectators.*) At the
55   next outburst, I will clear this courtroom. Go on, Mr. Prosecutor.

PRESS: Sit down please. (JOEY *sits.* GEORGE *goes back to his seat.*) Is Henry Reyna the leader of the 38th Street Gang? (HENRY *stands.*)

60 DELLA: Not in the sense that you mean.

PRESS: Did Henry Reyna, pachuco ringleader of the 38th Street Gang, willfully murder José Williams?

DELLA: No. They attacked us first.

PRESS: I didn't ask for your comment.

65 DELLA: But they did, they thought we were the Downey gang.

PRESS: Just answer my questions.

DELLA: We were just defending ourselves so we could get out of there.

70 PRESS: Your Honor, will you instruct the witness to be cooperative.

JUDGE: I must caution you, young lady, answer the questions or I'll hold you in contempt.

PRESS: Was this the Henry Reyna who was carrying a three-
75   foot lead pipe?

GEORGE: I object!

JUDGE: Overruled.

DELLA: No.

PRESS: Was it a two-foot lead pipe?

80 GEORGE: Objection!

JUDGE: Overruled.

DELLA: No!

PRESS: Did he kick a woman to the ground?

DELLA: No, he was hurt from the beating.

85 PRESS: Sit down. (HENRY *sits.*) Did Tommy Roberts rip stakes from a fence and hit a man on the ground?

GEORGE: Objection!

JUDGE: Overruled.

DELLA: I never saw him do anything.

PRESS: Did Joey Castro have a gun?   90

GEORGE: Objection!

JUDGE: Overruled. (JOEY *stands.*)

PRESS: Sit down. (JOEY *sits.*) Did Henry Reyna have a black-jack in his hand? (HENRY *stands.*)

DELLA: No.   95

PRESS: A switchblade knife?

DELLA: No.

PRESS: A two-by-four?

DELLA: No.

PRESS: Did he run over to José Williams, hit him on the head 100
and kill him?

DELLA: He could barely walk, how could he run to any place?

PRESS: (*Moving in for the kill.*) Did Smiley Torres? (*The batos stand and sit as their names are mentioned.*) Did Joey Castro? Did Tommy Roberts? Did Henry Reyna? Did Smiley 105
Torres? Did Henry Reyna? Did Henry Reyna? Did Henry Reyna kill José Williams?!

DELLA: No, no, no!

GEORGE: (*On HIS feet again.*) Your Honor, I object! The Prosecution is pulling out objects from all over the place, none 110
of which were found at Sleepy Lagoon, and none of which have been proven to be associated with my clients in any way.

JUDGE: Overruled.

GEORGE: If Your Honor please, I wish to make an assignment 115
of misconduct!

JUDGE: We have only had one this morning. We might as well have another now.

GEORGE: You have it, Your Honor.

JUDGE: One more remark like that and I'll hold you in con- 120
tempt. Quite frankly, Mr. Shearer, I am getting rather tired of your repeated useless objections.

GEORGE: I have not made useless objections.

JUDGE: I am sorry. Somebody is using ventriloquism. We have a Charlie McCarthy using Mr. Shearer's voice.   125

GEORGE: I am going to assign that remark of Your Honor as misconduct.

JUDGE: Fine. I would feel rather bad if you did not make an assignment of misconduct at least three times every session. (*Gavel.*) Witness is excused. (DELLA *stands.*) However, I am 130
going to remand her to the custody of the Ventura State School for Girls for a period of one year . . .

HENRY: What?

JUDGE: . . . to be held there as a juvenile ward of the State. Bailiff?   135

GEORGE: If the court please . . . If the court please . . . (BAILIFF *crosses to* DELLA *and takes her off left.*)

JUDGE: Court is in recess until tomorrow morning. (JUDGE *retires.* PRESS *exits.* HENRY *meets* GEORGE *halfway across center stage. The rest of the batos stand and stretch in the background.*) 140

GEORGE: Now, Henry, I want you to listen to me, please. You've got to remember he's the judge, Hank. And this is his courtroom.

HENRY: But he's making jokes, George, and we're getting screwed!   145

GEORGE: I know. I can't blame you for being bitter, but believe me, we'll get him.

HENRY: I thought you said we had a chance.

GEORGE: (*Passionately.*) We do! This case is going to be won
150   on appeal.

HENRY: Appeal! You mean you already know we're going to
    lose?

PACHUCO: So what's new?

GEORGE: Don't you see, Henry, Judge Charles is hanging
155   himself as we go. I've cited over a hundred separate cases
    of misconduct by the bench, and it's all gone into the
    record. Prejudicial error, denial of due process, inadmissi-
    ble evidence, hearsay . . .

HENRY: ¿Sabes qué, George? Don't tell me any more. (HENRY
160   *turns.* ALICE *and* ENRIQUE *approach him.*)

ALICE: Henry . . . ?

HENRY: (*Turns furiously.*) I don't want to hear it, Alice! (HENRY
    sees ENRIQUE, *but neither father nor son can think of anything
    to say.* HENRY *goes back upstage.*)

165 ALICE: George, is there anything we can do?

GEORGE: No. He's bitter, and he has a right to be. (JUDGE
    CHARLES *pounds his gavel. All go back to their places and sit.*)

JUDGE: We'll now hear the Prosecution's concluding statement.

PRESS: Your Honor, ladies and gentlemen of the jury. What
170   you have before you is a dilemma of our times. The City
    of Los Angeles is caught in the midst of the biggest, most
    terrifying crime wave in its history. A crime wave that
    threatens to engulf the very foundations of our civic
    well-being. We are not only dealing with the violent
175   death of one José Williams in a drunken barrio brawl. We
    are dealing with a threat and danger to our children, our
    families, our homes. Set these pachucos free, and you
    shall unleash the forces of anarchy and destruction in our
    society. Set these pachucos free and you will turn them
180   into heroes. Others just like them must be watching us
    at this very moment. What nefarious schemes can they
    be hatching in their twisted minds? Rape, drugs, assault,
    more violence? Who shall be their next innocent victim
    in some dark alley way, on some lonely street? You? You?
185   Your loved ones? No! Henry Reyna and his Latin juve-
    nile cohorts are not heroes. They are criminals, and they
    must be stopped. The specific details of this murder are
    irrelevant before the overwhelming danger of the
    pachuco in our midst. I ask you to find these zoot-suited
190   gangsters guilty of murder and to put them in the gas
    chamber where they belong. (*The* PRESS *sits down.*
    GEORGE *rises and takes center stage.*)

GEORGE: Ladies and gentlemen of the jury, you have heard me
    object to the conduct of this trial. I have tried my best to
195   defend what is most precious in our American society—a
    society now at war against the forces of racial intolerance
    and totalitarian injustice. The prosecution has not provided
    one witness that actually saw, with his own eyes, who actu-
    ally murdered José Williams. These boys are not the
200   Downey gang, yet the evidence suggests that they were at-
    tacked because the people at the ranch thought they were.
    Henry Reyna and Della Barrios were victims of the same
    bunch. Yes, they might have been spoiling for a revenge—
    who wouldn't under the circumstances—but not with the
205   intent to conspire to commit murder. So how did José
    Williams die? Was it an accident? Was it manslaughter? Was
    it murder? Perhaps we may never know. All the prosecution
    has been able to prove is that these boys wear long hair and
    zoot suits. And all the rest has been circumstantial evidence,

hearsay and war hysteria. The prosecution has tried to lead 210
you to believe that they are some kind of inhuman gangsters. Yet they are Americans. Find them guilty of anything
more serious than a juvenile bout of fisticuffs, and you will
condemn all American youth. Find them guilty of murder,
and you will murder the spirit of racial justice in America. 215
(GEORGE *sits down.*)

JUDGE: The jury will retire to consider its verdict. (*The* PRESS
stands and starts to exit with the BAILIFF. EL PACHUCO *snaps. All
freeze.*)

PACHUCO: Chale. Let's have it. (*Snaps again. The* PRESS *turns* 220
and comes back again.)

JUDGE: Has the jury reached a verdict?

PRESS: We have, Your Honor.

JUDGE: How say you?

PRESS: We find the defendants guilty of murder in the first 225
and second degrees.

JUDGE: The defendants will rise. (*The batos come to their feet.*)
Henry Reyna, José Castro, Thomas Roberts, Ismael Torres,
and so forth. You have been tried by a jury of your peers
and found guilty of murder in the first and second degrees. 230
The Law prescribes the capital punishment for this offense.
However, in view of your youth and in consideration of
your families, it is hereby the judgement of this court that
you be sentenced to life imprisonment . . .

RUDY: No! 235

JUDGE: . . . and sent to the State Penitentiary at San Quentin.
Court adjourned. (*Gavel.* JUDGE *exits.* DOLORES, ENRIQUE
and family go to HENRY. BERTHA *crosses to* JOEY; LUPE *goes to*
TOMMY. ELENA *crosses to* SMILEY. GEORGE *and* ALICE *talk.*)

DOLORES: ¡Hijo mío! ¡Hijo de mi alma! (BAILIFF *comes down* 240
with a pair of handcuffs.)

BAILIFF: Okay, boys. (*He puts the cuffs on* HENRY. RUDY *comes up.*)

RUDY: ¿Carnal? (HENRY *looks at the* BAILIFF, *who gives him a nod
of permission to spend a moment with* RUDY. HENRY *embraces
him with the cuffs on.* GEORGE *and* ALICE *approach.*) 245

GEORGE: Henry? I can't pretend to know how you feel, son.
I just want you to know that our fight has just begun.

ALICE: We may have lost this decision, but we're going to appeal immediately. We're going to stand behind you until
your name is absolutely clear. I swear it! 250

PACHUCO: What the hell are they going to do, ese? They just
sent you to prison for life. Once a Mexican goes in, he
never comes out.

BAILIFF: Boys? (*The* BOYS *exit with the* BAILIFF. *As they go*
ENRIQUE *calls after them.*) 255

ENRIQUE: (*Holding back tears.*) Hijo. Be a man, hijo. (*Then to
his family.*) Vámonos . . . ¡Vámonos! (*The family leaves and*
EL PACHUCO *slowly walks to center stage.*)

PACHUCO: We're going to take a short break right now, so you
can all go out and take a leak, smoke a frajo. Ahí los watcho. 260
(*He exits up center and the newspaper backdrop comes down.*)

ACT TWO
PROLOGUE

Lights up and EL PACHUCO *emerges from the shadows. The newspaper drop is still down. Music.*

PACHUCO:
Watchamos pachucos

los batos
the dudes
street-corner warriors who fought and moved
5 like unknown soldiers in wars of their own
El Pueblo de Los was the battle zone
from Sleepy Lagoon to the Zoot Suit wars
when Marines and Sailors made their scores
stomping like Nazis on East L.A. . . .
10 pero ?saben qué?
That's later in the play. Let's pick it up in prison.
We'll begin this scene
inside the walls of San Quintín.

1. SAN QUENTIN

A bell rings as the drop rises. HENRY, JOEY, SMILEY *and* TOMMY *enter accompanied by a* GUARD.

GUARD: All right, people, lock up. (BOYS *move downstage in four directions. They step into "cells" simply marked by shadows of bars on the floor in their separate places. Newspaper handcarts rest on the floor as cots. Sound of cell doors closing. The* GUARD
5   *paces back and forth upstage level.*)
HENRY:
San Quentin, California
March 3, 1943
Dear Family:
10   Coming in from the yard in the evening, we are quickly locked up in our cells. Then the clank and locking of the doors leaves one with a rather empty feeling. You are standing up to the iron door, waiting for the guard to come along and take the count, listening as his footsteps
15   fade away in the distance. By this time there is a tense stillness that seems to crawl over the cellblock. You realize you are alone, so all alone.
PACHUCO: This all sounds rather tragic, doesn't it?
HENRY: But here comes the guard again, and he calls out your
20   number in a loud voice . . .
GUARD: (*Calls numbers;* BOYS *call name.*) 24-545
HENRY: Reyna!
GUARD: 24-546
JOEY: Castro!
25 GUARD: 24-547
TOMMY: Roberts!
GUARD: 24-548
SMILEY: Torres! (GUARD *passes through dropping letters and exits up left.*)
30 HENRY: You jump to your feet, stooping to pick up the letter . . .
JOEY: (*Excited.*) Or perhaps several letters . . .
TOMMY: You are really excited as you take the letters from the envelope.
35 SMILEY: The censor has already broken the seal when he reads it.
HENRY: You make a mental observation to see if you recognize the handwriting on the envelope.
SMILEY: (*Anxious.*) It's always nice to hear from home . . .
JOEY: Or a close comrade . . .
40 TOMMY: Friends that you know on the outside . . .
HENRY: Or perhaps it's from a stranger. (*Pause. Spotlight at upstage center.* ALICE *walks in with casual clothes on. Her hair is in pigtails, and she wears a pair of drapes.* SHE *is cheerful.*)

2. THE LETTERS
Dear Boys,
Announcing the publication (mimeograph) of the Appeal News, your very own newsletter, to be sent to you twice a month for the purpose of keeping you reliably informed of everything—the progress of the Sleeping Lagoon De- 5 fense Committee (We have a name now) and, of course, the matter of your appeal.
                                   Signed,
                                   Your editor
                                   Alice Bloomfield.   10

(*Music. "Perdido" by Duke Ellington.* ALICE *steps down and sits on the lip of the upstage level. The* BOYS *start swinging the bat, dribbling the basketball, shadow-boxing and exercising.* ALICE *mimes typing movements and we hear the sounds of a typewriter. Music fades.* ALICE *rises.*)

ALICE: The Appeal News Volume 1, Number I, April 7, 1943.
Boys,
You can, you must, and you will help us on the outside by what you do on the inside. Don't forget, what you do affects others. You have no control over that. When the time 15 comes, let us be proud to show the record.
                                   Signed,
                                   Your editor.

(*Music up again. The* BOYS *go through their activities.* ALICE *moves downstage center and the music fades.*)

SMILEY: (*Stepping toward her.*)
April 10, 1943   20
Dear Miss Bloomfield,
I have discovered from my wife that you are conducting door-to-door fund-raising campaigns in Los Angeles. She doesn't want to tell you, but she feels bad about doing such a thing. It's not our custom to go around the neigh- 25 borhoods asking for money.
ALICE: (*Turning toward* SMILEY.)
Dear Smiley,
Of course, I understand your feelings . . .
SMILEY: (*Adamant.*) I don't want my wife going around beg- 30 ging.
ALICE: It isn't begging—it's fund-raising.
SMILEY: I don't care what you call it. If that's what it's going to take, count me out.
ALICE: All right. I won't bother your wife if she really doesn't 35 want me to. Okay? (SMILEY *looks at her and turns back to his upstage position. Music. The batos move again.* TOMMY *crosses to* ALICE. *Another fade.*)
TOMMY:
April 18, 1943
Dear Alice,   40
Trying to find the words and expression to thank you for your efforts in behalf of myself and the rest of the batos makes me realize what a meager vocabulary I possess . . .
ALICE:
Dear Tommy,   45
Your vocabulary is just fine. Better than most.
TOMMY: Most what?

ALICE: People.

TOMMY: (*Glances at* HENRY.) Uh, listen, Alice. I don't want to
50   be treated any different than the rest of the batos, see? And
don't expect me to talk to you like some square Anglo,
some *pinche gabacho.* You just better find out what it
means to be Chicano, and it better be pretty damn quick.

ALICE: Look, Tommy, I didn't . . .

55   TOMMY: I know what you're trying to do for us and that's
reet, see? Shit. Most paddies would probably like to see us
locked up for good. I been in jail a couple of times before,
but never nothing this deep. Strange, ain't it, the trial in
Los? I don't really know what happened or why. I don't
60   give a shit what the papers said. We didn't do half the
things I read about. I also know that I'm in here just because I hung around with Mexicans . . . or pachucos. Well,
just remember this, Alicia . . . I grew up right alongside
most of these batos, and I'm pachuco too. *Simón, esa,* you
65   better believe it! (*Music up. Movement.* TOMMY *returns to his
position.* HENRY *stands.* ALICE *turns toward him, but* HE *walks
over to* THE PACHUCO, *giving her his back.*)

JOEY: (*Stepping forward anxiously.*)
May 1, 1943
70   Dear Alice . . . Darling!
I can't help but spend my time thinking about you.
How about sending us your *retra*—that is, your photo-
graph? Even though Tommy would like one of Rita
Hayworth—he's always chasing Mexican skirts (Ha!
75   Ha!)—I'd prefer to see your sweet face any day.

ALICE: (*Directly to him.*)
Dear Joey,
Thank you so much. I really appreciated receiving your
letter.

80   JOEY: That's all reet, Grandma! You mind if I call you
Grandma?

ALICE: Oh, no.

JOEY: *Eres una ruca de aquellas.*

ALICE: I'm a what?

85   JOEY: *Ruca.* A fine chick.

ALICE: (*Pronounces the word.*) *Ruca?*

JOEY: *De aquellas.* (*Makes a cool gesture, palms out at hip level.*)

ALICE: (*Imitating him.*) *De aquellas.*

JOEY: All reet! You got it. (*Pause.*) P.S. Did you forget the pho-
90   tograph?

ALICE: (SHE *hands it to him.*)
Dearest Joey,
Of course not. Here it is, attached to a copy of the Appeal
News. I'm afraid it's not exactly a pin-up.

95   JOEY: (*Kissing the photo.*) Alice, honey, you're a doll! (JOEY *shows the
photo to* TOMMY *then* SMILEY, *who is curious enough to come into
the circle.* ALICE *looks at* HENRY, *but* HE *continues to ignore her.*)

ALICE: (*Back at center.*) The Appeal News, Volume I, Number
3, May 5, 1943.
100 Dear Boys,
Feeling that el Cinco de Mayo is a very appropriate day—
the CIO radio program, "Our Daily Bread," is devoting
the entire time this evening to a discussion of discrimination against Mexicans in general and against you guys in
105 particular.

Music up. The repartee between ALICE *and the batos is now friendly
and warm. Even* SMILEY *is smiling with* ALICE. *They check out her
"drapes."*

3. THE INCORRIGIBLE PACHUCO

HENRY *stands at downstage left, looks at the group, then decides to
speak.*

HENRY:
May 17, 1943
Dear Miss Bloomfield,
I understand you're coming up to Q this weekend, and I
would like to talk to you—in private. Can you arrange it?

(*The batos turn away, taking a hint.*)

ALICE: (*Eagerly.*) Yes, yes, I can. What can I do for you, Henry? 5
(HENRY *and* ALICE *step forward toward each other.* EL PACHUCO
moves in.)

HENRY: For me? ¡Ni madre!

ALICE: (*Puzzled.*) I don't understand.

HENRY: I wanted you to be the first to know, Alice. I'm drop- 10
ping out of the appeal.

ALICE: (*Unbelieving.*) You're what?

HENRY: I'm bailing out, esa. Dropping out of the case, see?

ALICE: Henry, you can't!

HENRY: Why can't I?   15

ALICE: Because you'll destroy our whole case! If we don't
present a united front, how can we ask the public to support us?

HENRY: That's your problem. I never asked for their support.
Just count me out.   20

ALICE: (*Getting nervous, anxious.*) Henry, please, think about
what you're saying. If you drop out, the rest of the boys
will probably go with you. How can you even think of
dropping out of the appeal? What about George and all
the people that have contributed their time and money in 25
the past few months? You just can't quit on them!

HENRY: Oh no? Just watch me.

ALICE: If you felt this way, why didn't you tell me before?

HENRY: Why didn't you ask me? You think you can just move
in and defend anybody you feel like? When did I ever ask 30
you to start a defense committee for me? Or a newspaper?
Or a fundraising drive and all that other shit? I don't need
defending, esa. I can take care of myself.

ALICE: But what about the trial, the sentence. They gave your
life imprisonment?   35

HENRY: It's my life!

ALICE: Henry, honestly—are you kidding me?

HENRY: You think so?

ALICE: But you've seen me coming and going. Writing to
you, speaking for you, traveling up and down the state. 40
You must have known I was doing it for you. Nothing
has come before my involvement, my attachment, my
passion for this case. My boys have been everything
to me.

HENRY: My boys? My boys! What the hell are we—your per- 45
sonal property? Well, let me set you straight, lady, I ain't
your boy.

ALICE: You know I never meant it that way.

HENRY: You think I haven't see through your bullshit? Always
so concerned. Come on, boys. Speak out, boys. Stand up 50
for your people. Well, you leave my people out of this!
Can't you understand that.

ALICE: No, I can't understand that.

HENRY: You're just using Mexicans to play politics.

55 ALICE: Henry, that's the worst thing anyone has ever said to me.

HENRY: Who are you going to help next—the Colored People?

ALICE: No, as a matter of fact, I've already helped the Colored
60   People. What are you going to do next—go to the gas chamber?

HENRY: What the hell do you care?

ALICE: I don't!

HENRY: Then get the hell out of here!

65 ALICE: (*Furious.*) You think you're the only one who doesn't want to be bothered? You ought to try working in the Sleepy Lagoon defense office for a few months. All the haggling, the petty arguments, the lack of cooperation. I've wanted to quit a thousand times. What the hell am I
70   doing here? They're coming at me from all sides. You're too sentimental and emotional about this, Alice. You're too cold hearted, Alice. You're collecting money and turning it over to the lawyers, while the families are going hungry. They're saying you can't be trusted because you're a Com-
75   munist, because you're a Jew. Okay! If that's the way they feel about me, then to hell with them! I hate them too. I hate their language, I hate their enchiladas, and I hate their goddamned mariachi music! (*Pause. They look at each other.* HENRY *smiles, then* ALICE—*feeling foolish—and they both*
80   *break out laughing.*)

HENRY: All right! Now you sound like you mean it.

ALICE: I do.

HENRY: Okay! Now we're talking straight.

ALICE: I guess I have been sounding like some square paddy
85   chick. But, you haven't exactly been Mister Cool yourself . . . ese.

HENRY: So, let's say we're even Steven.

ALICE: Fair enough. What now?

HENRY: Why don't we bury the hatchet, you know what I
90   mean?

ALICE: Can I tell George you'll go on with the appeal?

HENRY: Yeah. I know there's a lot of people out there who are willing and trying to help us. People who feel that our conviction was an injustice. People like George . . . and
95   you. Well, the next time you see them, tell them Hank Reyna sends his thanks.

ALICE: Why don't you tell them?

HENRY: You getting wise with me again?

ALICE: If you write an article—and I know you can—we'll
100   publish it in the People's World. What do you say?

PACHUCO: Article! Pos who told you, you could write, ese?

HENRY: (*Laughs.*) Chale.

ALICE: I'm serious. Why don't you give it a try?

HENRY: I'll think about it. (*Pause.*) Listen, you think you and
105   I could write each other . . . outside the newsletter?

ALICE: Sure.

HENRY: Then it's a deal. (*They shake hands.*)

ALICE: I'm glad we're going to be communicating. I think we're going to be very good friends. (ALICE *lifts her hands*
110   *to* HENRY'S *shoulder in a gesture of comradeship.* HENRY *follows her hand, putting his on top of hers.*)

HENRY: You think so?

ALICE: I know so.

GUARD: Time, miss.

115 ALICE: I gotta go. Think about the article, okay? (SHE *turns to the* BOYS.) I gotta go, boys.

JOEY: Goodbye, Grandma! Say hello to Bertha.

SMILEY: And to my wife!

TOMMY: Give my love to Lupe!

GUARD: Time!   120

ALICE: I've got to go. Goodbye, goodbye. (ALICE *exits, escorted by the* GUARD *upstage left. As* SHE *goes,* JOEY *calls after her.*)

JOEY: See you, Grandma.

TOMMY: (*Turning to* JOEY *and* SMILEY.) She loves me.

PACHUCO: Have you forgotten what happened at the trial?   125
You think the Appeals Court is any different? Some paddy judge sitting in the same fat-ass judgment of your fate.

HENRY: Come on, ese, give me a break!

PACHUCO: One break, coming up! (HE *snaps his fingers. The*
    GUARD *blows his whistle.*)   130

GUARD: Rec time! (*The batos move upstage to the upper level. Music. The* BOYS *mime a game of handball against the backdrop. During the game,* GEORGE *enters at stage right and comes downstage carrying his briefcase. The* GUARD *blows a whistle and stops the game.*)   135

GUARD: Reyna, Castro, Roberts, Torres!—You got a visitor.

4. MAJOR GEORGE

The BOYS *turn and see* GEORGE. *They come down enthusiastically.*

JOEY: ¡Óra-leh! ¡Ese, Cheer!

SMILEY: George!

GEORGE: Hi, guys! (*The* BOYS *shake his hand, pat him on the back.* HENRY *comes to him last.*) How are you all doing? You boys staying in shape.?   5

JOEY: Ese, you're looking at the hero of the San Quentin athletic program. Right, batos? (HE *shadowboxes a little.*)

TOMMY: Ten rounds with a busted ankle.

JOEY: ¡Simón! And I won the bout, too. I'm the terror of the flyweights, ese. The killer fly!   10

TOMMY: They got us doing everything. Cheer. Baseball, basketball.

SMILEY: Watch repairing.

GEORGE: (*Impressed.*) Watch repairing?

SMILEY: I'm also learning to improve my English and arith-   15
metic.

GEORGE: Warden Duffy has quite a program. I hear he's a good man?

JOEY: Simón, he's a good man. We've learned our lesson . . .
Well, anyway, I've learned my lesson, boy. No more   20
pachuquismo for me. Too many people depending on us to help out. The raza here in Los. The whole southwest. Mexico, South America! Like you and Grandma say, this is the people's world. If you get us out of here, I figure the only thing I could do is become a union organizer. Or go   25
into major league baseball.

GEORGE: Baseball?

JOEY: Simón, ese. You're looking at the first Mexican Babe Ruth. Or maybe, "Babe Root." Root! You get it?

TOMMY: How about "Baby Zoot"?   30

JOEY: Solid, Jackson.

GEORGE: Babe Zooter!

JOEY: Solid tudee, that's all reet, ese.

GEORGE: What about you, Henry? What have you been doing?   35

HENRY: Time, George, I've been doing time.

TOMMY: Ain't it the truth?

SMILEY: Yeah, George! When you going to spring us out of here, ese?

40 HENRY: How's the appeal coming?

GEORGE: (*Getting serious.*) Not bad. There's been a development I have to talk to you about. But other than that . . .

HENRY: Other than what?

SMILEY: (*Pause.*) Bad news?

45 GEORGE: (*Hedging.*) It all depends on how you look at it, Smiley. It really doesn't change anything. Work on the brief is going on practically day and night. The thing is, even with several lawyers on the case now, it'll still be several months before we file. I want to be honest about that.

50 HENRY: (*Suspiciously.*) Is that the bad news?

GEORGE: Not exactly. Sit down, boys. (*Pause. HE laughs to himself.*) I really don't mean to make such a big deal out of this thing. Fact is I'm still not quite used to the idea myself. (*Pause.*) You see . . . I've been drafted.

55 JOEY: Drafted?

TOMMY: Into the Army?

SMILEY: You?

GEORGE: That's right. I'm off to war.

JOEY: But . . . you're old, Cheer.

60 HENRY: (*A bitter edge.*) Why you, George? Why did they pick on you?

GEORGE: Well, Henry, I wouldn't say they "picked" on me. There's lots of men my age overseas. After all, it is war time and . . .

65 HENRY: And you're handling our appeal.

GEORGE: (*Pause.*) We have other lawyers.

HENRY: But you're the one who knows the case!

GEORGE: (*Pause.*) I knew you were going to take this hard. Believe me, Henry, my being drafted has nothing to do

70 with your case. It's just a coincidence.

HENRY: Like our being in here for life is a coincidence?

GEORGE: No, that's another . . .

HENRY: Like our being hounded every goddam day of our life is a coincidence?

75 GEORGE: Henry . . . (*HENRY turns away furiously. There is a pause.*) It's useless anger, son, believe me. Actually, I'm quite flattered by your concern, but I'm hardly indispensable.

HENRY: (*Deeply disturbed.*) What the hell are you talking

80 about, George?

GEORGE: I'm talking about all the people trying to get you out. Hundreds, perhaps thousands. Alice and I aren't the only ones. We've got a heck of a fine team of lawyers working on the brief. With or without me, the appeal will

85 be won. I promise you that.

HENRY: It's no use, George.

GEORGE: I realize all that sounds pretty unconvincing under the circumstances, but it's true.

HENRY: Those bastard cops are never going to let us out of

90 here. We're here for life and that's it.

GEORGE: You really believe that?

HENRY: What do you expect me to believe?

GEORGE: I wish I could answer that, son, but that's really for you to say.

95 GUARD: Time, Counselor.

GEORGE: Coming. (*Turns to the other BOYS.*) Listen, boys, I don't know where in the world I'll be the day your appeal is won—and it will be won—whether it's in the Pacific

somewhere or in Europe or in a hole in the ground . . . Take care of yourselves. 100

TOMMY: See you around, George.

SMILEY: So long, George.

JOEY: 'Bye, Cheer.

GEORGE: Yeah. See you around. (*Pause.*) Goodbye, Henry. Good luck and God bless you. 105

HENRY: God bless you, too, George. Take care of yourself.

TOMMY: Say, George, when you come back from the war, we're going to take you outa town and blast some weed.

JOEY: We'll get you a pair of buns you can hold in your hands!

GEORGE: I may just take you up on that. (*The GUARD escorts* 110 *GEORGE out, then turns back to the BOYS.*)

GUARD: All right, new work assignments. Everybody report to the jute mill. Let's go. (SMILEY, JOEY *and* TOMMY *start to exit.* HENRY *hangs back.*) What's the matter with you, Reyna? You got lead in your pants? I said let's go. 115

HENRY: We're supposed to work in the mess hall.

GUARD: You got a new assignment.

HENRY: Since when?

GUARD: Since right now. Get going!

HENRY: (*Hanging back.*) The warden know about this? 120

GUARD: What the hell do you care? You think you're something special? Come on, greaseball. Move!

HENRY: Make me, you bastard!

GUARD: Oh, yeah. (*The GUARD pushes* HENRY. HENRY *pushes back. The batos react, as the GUARD traps* HENRY *with his club* 125 *around the chest. The BOYS move to* HENRY's *defense.*) Back!

HENRY: (*To the batos.*) Back off! BACK OFF! Don't be stupid.

GUARD: Okay, Reyna, you got solitary! Bastard, huh? Into the hole! (HE *pushes* HENRY *onto center stage. Lights down. A single spot.*) Line, greaseballs. Move out! (*As they march.*) 130 Quickly, quickly. You're too slow. Move, move, move. (*The* BOYS *exit with the* GUARD.)

5. SOLITARY

A lone saxophone sets the mood.

PACHUCO: Too bad, ese. He set you up again.

HENRY: (*Long pause.* HE *looks around.*) Solitary, ese . . . they gave me solitary. (HE *sits down on the floor, a forlorn figure.*)

PACHUCO: Better get used to it, carnal. That's what this stretch is going to be about, see? You're in here for life, bato. 5

HENRY: I can't accept it, ese.

PACHUCO:
You've go to, Hank . . .
only this reality is real now,
only this place is real,
sitting in the lonely cell of your will . . . 10

HENRY: I can't see my hands.

PACHUCO:
Then tell your eyes to forget the light, ese
Only the hard floor is there, carnal 15
Only the cold hard edge of this reality
and there is no time . . .
Each second is a raw drop of blood from your brain
that you must swallow
drop by drop 20
and don't even start counting
or you'll lose your mind . . .

HENRY: I've got to know why I'm here, ese! I've got to have a reason for being here.

25 PACHUCO: You're here, Hank, because you chose to be— because you protected your brother and your family. And nobody knows the worth of that effort better than you, ese.

HENRY: I miss them, ese . . . my jefitos, my carnalillo, my sis . . . I miss Della.

30 PACHUCO: (*A spot illuminates* HENRY's *family standing upstage;* EL PACHUCO *snaps it off.*)
Forget them!
Forget them all.
Forget your family and the barrio
35   beyond the wall.

HENRY: There's still a chance I'll get out.

PACHUCO: Fat chance.

HENRY: I'm talking about the appeal!

PACHUCO: And I'm talking about what's real! ¿Qué traes,
40   Hank? Haven't you learned yet?

HENRY: Learned what?

PACHUCO:
Not to expect justice when it isn't there.
No court in the land's going to set you free.
45   Learn to protect your loves by binding them
in hate, ese! Stop hanging on to false hopes.
The moment those hopes come crashing down,
you'll find yourself on the ground foaming at
the mouth. ¡Como loco!

50 HENRY: (*Turning on him furiously.*) ¿Sabes qué? Don't tell me any more. I don't need you to tell me what to do. Fuck off! FUCK OFF! (HENRY *turns away from* EL PACHUCO. *Long pause. An anxious, intense moment.* EL PACHUCO *shifts gears and breaks the tension with a satirical twist.* HE *throws his*
55   *arms out and laughs.*)

PACHUCO:
¡Órale pues!
Don't take the pinche play so seriously, Jesús!
Es puro vacilón!
60   Watcha.

(HE *snaps his fingers. Lights change. We hear the sounds of the city.*)

This is Los, carnal.
You want to see some justice for pachucos?
Check out what's happening back home today.
The Navy has landed, ese—
65   on leave with full pay
and war's breaking out in the streets of L.A.!

6. ZOOT SUIT RIOTS

We hear music: the bugle call from "Bugle Call Rag." Suddenly the stage is awash in colored lights. The city of Los Angeles appears in the background in a panoramic vista of lights tapering into the night horizon. SAILORS *and* GIRLS *jitterbug on the dance floor. It is the Avalon Ballroom. The music is hot, the dancing hotter.* EL PACHUCO *and* HENRY *stand to the side.*

The scene is in dance and mostly pantomime. Occasionally words are heard over the music which is quite loud. On the floor are two SAILORS (SWABBIE *is one.*) *and a* MARINE *dancing with the* GIRLS. *A* SHORE PATROLMAN *speaks to the* CIGARETTE GIRL. *A* PIMP *comes on and watches the action.* LITTLE BLUE *and* ZOOTER *are also*

on the floor. RUDY *enters wearing* HENRY's *zoot suit with* BERTHA *and* LUPE. LUPE *takes their picture, then all three move up center to the rear of the ballroom.* CHOLO *comes in down center, sees them and moves up stage. All four make an entrance onto the dance floor.*

The MARINE *takes his girl aside after paying her.* SHE *passes the money to the* PIMP. *The* SAILORS *try to pick up on* LUPE *and* BERTHA, *and* CHOLO *pushes one back. The* SAILORS *complain to the* SHORE PATROL, *who throws* CHOLO *out the door down center. There is an argument that* RUDY *joins. The* SAILORS *go back to* BERTHA *and* LUPE *who resist.* CHOLO *and* RUDY *go to their defense and a fight develops.* ZOOTER *and* LITTLE BLUE *split.* CHOLO *takes the* GIRLS *out and* RUDY *pulls a knife. He is facing the three* SAILORS *and the* MARINE, *when* THE PACHUCO *freezes the action.*

PACHUCO: (*Forcefully.*) Órale, that's enough! (EL PACHUCO *takes* RUDY's *knife and with a tap sends him off-stage.* RUDY *exits with the* GIRLS. EL PACHUCO *is now facing the angry* SERVICEMEN. *He snaps his fingers. The* PRESS *enters quickly to the beeping sound of a radio broadcast.*)   5

PRESS: Good evening, Mr. and Mrs. North and South America and all the ships at sea. Let's go to press. FLASH. Los Angeles, California, June 3, 1943. Serious rioting broke out here today as flying squadrons of Marines and soldiers joined the Navy in a new assault on zooter-infested dis-   10 tricts. A fleet of twenty taxicabs carrying some two hundred servicemen pulled out of the Naval Armory in Chavez Ravine tonight and assembled a task force that invaded the eastside barrio. (*Unfreeze. The following speeches happen simultaneously.*)   15

MATE: You got any balls in them funny pants, boy?

SAILOR: He thinks he's tough . . .

SWABBIE: How about it, lardhead? You a tough guy or just a draft dodger?

PRESS: The Zoot Suiters, those gamin' dandies . . .   20

PACHUCO: (*Cutting them off.*) Why don't you tell them what I really am, ese, or how you've been forbidden to use the very word . . .

PRESS: We are complying in the interest of the war.

PACHUCO: How have you complied?   25

PRESS: We're using other terms.

PACHUCO: Like "pachuco" and "zoot suiter"?

PRESS: What's wrong with that? The Zoot Suit Crime Wave is even beginning to push the war news off the front page.

PACHUCO: 30
The Press distorted the very meaning of the word "zoot suit."
All it is for you guys is another way to say Mexican.
But the ideal of the original chuco
was to look like a diamond   35
to look sharp
hip
bonaroo
finding a style of urban survival
in the rural skirts and outskirts   40
of the brown metropolis of Los, cabrón.

PRESS: It's an affront to good taste.

PACHUCO: Like the Mexicans, Filipinos and blacks who wear them.

PRESS: Yes!   45

PACHUCO: Even the white kids and the Wops and the Jews are putting on the drape shape.

PRESS: You are trying to outdo the white man in exaggerated white man's clothes!

PACHUCO:
50   Because everybody knows
      that Mexicans, Filipinos and Blacks
      belong to the huarache
      the straw hat and the dirty overall.

PRESS: You savages weren't even wearing clothes when the
55   white man pulled you out of the jungle.

MARINE: My parents are going without collars and cuffs so you can wear that shit.

PRESS: That's going too far, too goddamned far and it's got to be stopped!

60 PACHUCO: Why?

PRESS: Don't you know there's a war on? Don't you fucking well know you can't get away with that shit? What are we fighting for if not to annihilate the enemies of the American way of life?

65 MATE: Let's tear it off his back!

SAILORS/MARINE: Let's strip him! Get him! (Etc.)

PRESS: KILL THE PACHUCO BASTARD!! (*Music: "American Patrol" by Glenn Miller. The* PRESS *gets a searchlight from upstage center while the* FOUR SERVICEMEN *stalk* EL PACHUCO.)

70 SAILOR: Heh, zooter. Come on, zooter!

SWABBIE: You think you're more important than the war, zooter?

MATE: Let's see if you got any balls in them funny pants, boy.

SWABBIE: Watch out for the knife.

75 SAILOR: That's a real chango monkey suit he's got on.

MATE: I bet he's half monkey—just like the Filipinos and Niggers that wear them.

SWABBIE: You trying to outdo the white man in them glad rags, Mex? (*They fight now to the finish.* EL PACHUCO *is over-*
80   *powered and stripped as* HENRY *watches helplessly from his position. The* PRESS *and* SERVICEMEN *exit with pieces of* EL PACHUCO's *zoot suit.* EL PACHUCO *stands. The only item of clothing on his body is a small loincloth.* HE *turns and looks at* HENRY, *with mystic intensity.* HE *opens his arms as an Aztec*
85   *conch blows, and* HE *slowly exits backward with powerful calm into the shadows. Silence.* HENRY *comes downstage.* HE *absorbs the impact of what* HE *has seen and falls to his knees at center stage, spent and exhausted. Lights down.*)

7. ALICE

The GUARD *and* ALICE *enter from opposite sides of the stage. The* GUARD *carries a handful of letters and is reading one of them.*

GUARD: July 2, 1943.

ALICE:
      Dear Henry,
      I hope this letter finds you in good health and good spirits—but I have to assume you've heard about the riots in Los Angeles. It was a nightmare, and it lasted for a week.
5   The city is still in a state of shock.

GUARD: (*Folds letter back into envelope, then opens another.*) August 5, 1943.

ALICE:
      Dear Henry,
10   The riots here in L.A. have touched off race riots all over the country—Chicago, Detroit, even little Beau-

mont, Texas, for Christ's sake. But the one in Harlem was the worst. Millions of dollars worth of property damage. 500 people were hospitalized, and five Negroes were killed.   15

GUARD: Things are rough all over.

ALICE: Please write to me and tell me how you feel.

GUARD: (*The* GUARD *folds up the second letter, stuffs it back into its envelope and opens a third.*) August 20, 1943.

ALICE: 20
      Dear Henry,
      Although I am disappointed not to have heard from you, I thought I would send you some good news for a change. Did you know we had a gala fund-raiser at the Mocambo?

GUARD: The Mocambo . . . Hotcha!   25

ALICE:
      . . . and Rita Hayworth lent your sister Lupe a ball gown for the occasion. She got dressed at Cecil B. DeMille's house, and she looked terrific. Her escort was Anthony Quinn, and Orson Welles said . . .

GUARD: Orson Welles! Well! Sounds like Louella Parsons. (HE 30 *folds up the letter.*) September 1, 1943.

ALICE: Henry, why aren't you answering my letters?

GUARD: He's busy. (HE *continues to stuff the envelope.*)

ALICE: Henry, if there's something I've said or done . . . ? (*The* GUARD *shuffles the envelopes.*) Henry . . . (*Lights change.* 35 GUARD *crosses to center stage, where* HENRY *is still doubled up on the floor.*)

GUARD: Welcome back to the living, Reyna. It's been a long hot summer. Here's your mail. (*The* GUARD *tosses the letters to the floor directly in front of* HENRY's *head.* HENRY *looks up* 40 *slowly and grabs one of the letters.* HE *opens it, trying to focus. The* GUARD *exits.*)

ALICE: Henry, I just found out you did ninety days in solitary. I'm furious at the rest of the guys for keeping it from me. I talked to Warden Duffy, and he said you struck a guard. 45 Did something happen I should know about? I wouldn't ask if it wasn't so important, but a clean record . . . (HENRY *rips up the letter he has been reading and scatters the others. Alarmed.*) Henry? (HENRY *pauses, his instant fury spent and under control.* HE *sounds almost weary, but the anger is still* 50 *there.*)

HENRY: You still don't understand, Alice.

ALICE: (*Softly, compassionate.*) But I do! I'm not accusing you of anything. I don't care what happened or why they sent you there. I'm sure you had your reasons. But you know 55 the public is watching you.

HENRY: (*Frustrated, a deep question.*) Why do you do this, Alice?

ALICE: What?

HENRY: The appeal, the case, all the shit you do. You think the public gives a goddamn?   60

ALICE: (*With conviction.*) Yes! We are going to get you out of here, Henry Reyna. We are going to win!

HENRY: (*Probing.*) What if we lose?

ALICE: (*Surprised but moving on.*) We're not going to lose.

HENRY: (*Forcefully, insistent, meaning more than* HE *is saying.*) 65 What if we do? What if we get another crooked judge, and he nixes the appeal?

ALICE: Then we'll appeal again. We'll take it to the Supreme Court. (*A forced laugh.*) Hell, we'll take it all the way to President Roosevelt!   70

HENRY: (*Backing her up—emotionally.*) What if we still lose?

ALICE: (*Bracing herself against his aggression.*) We can't.

HENRY: Why can't we?

75 ALICE: (*Giving a political response in spite of herself.*) Because we've got too much support. You should see the kinds of people responding to us. Unions, Mexicans, Negroes, Oakies. It's fantastic.

HENRY: (*Driving harder.*) Why can't we lose, Alice?

ALICE: I'm telling you.

80 HENRY: No, you're not.

ALICE: (*Starting to feel vulnerable.*) I don't know what to tell you.

HENRY: Yes, you do!

ALICE: (*Frightened.*) Henry . . . ?

85 HENRY: Tell me why we can't lose, Alice!

ALICE: (*Forced to fight back, with characteristic passion.*) Stop it, Henry! Please stop it! I won't have you treat me this way. I never have been able to accept one person pushing another around . . . pushing me around! Can't you see that's

90 why I'm here? Because I can't stand it happening to you. Because I'm a Jew, goddammit! I have been there . . . I have been there! If you lose, I lose. (*Pause. The emotional tension is immense. ALICE fights to hold back tears. SHE turns away.*)

95 HENRY: I'm sorry . . .

ALICE: (*Pause.*) It's stupid for us to fight like this. I look forward to coming here for weeks. Just to talk to you, to be with you, to see your eyes.

HENRY: (*Pause.*) I thought a lot about you when I was in the

100 hole. Sometimes . . . sometimes I'd even see you walk in, in the dark, and talk to me. Just like you are right now. Same look, same smile, same perfume . . . (*HE pauses.*) Only the other one never gave me so much lip. She just listened. She did say one thing. She said . . .

105 ALICE: (*Trying to make light of it. Then more gently.*) I can't say that to you, Henry. Not the way you want it.

HENRY: Why not?

ALICE: (*SHE means it.*) Because I can't allow myself to be used to fill in for all the love you've always felt and always re-

110 ceived from all your women.

HENRY: (*With no self-pity.*) Give it a chance, Alice.

ALICE: (*Beside herself.*) Give it a chance? You crazy idiot. If I thought making love to you would solve all your problems, I'd do it in a second. Don't you know that? But it

115 won't. It'll only complicate things. I'm trying to help you, goddammit. And to do that, I have to be your friend, not your white woman.

HENRY: (*Getting angry.*) What makes you think I want to go to bed with you. Because you're white? I've had more

120 white pieces of ass than you can count, ¿sabes? Who do you think you are? God's gift to us brown animals.

ALICE: (*ALICE slaps him and stops, horrified. A whirlpool of emotions.*) Oh, Hank. All the love and hate it's taken to get us together in this lousy prison room. Do you realize only

125 Hitler and the Second World War could have accomplished that? I don't know whether to laugh or cry. (*ALICE folds into her emotional spin, her body shaking. Suddenly she turns, whipping herself out of it with a cry, both laughing and weeping. They come to each other and embrace. Then they kiss—*

130 *passionately. The GUARD enters. HE frowns.*)

GUARD: Time, Miss.

ALICE: (*Turning.*) Already? Oh, my God, Henry, there's so many messages I was going to give you. Your mother and father send their love, of course. And Lupe and . . . Della. And . . . oh, yes. They want you to know Rudy's in the 135 Marines.

HENRY: The Marines?

ALICE: I'll write you all about it. Will you write me?

HENRY: (*A glance at the GUARD.*) Yes.

GUARD: (*His tone getting harsher.*) Let's go, lady. 140

HENRY: Goodbye, Licha.

ALICE: I'll see you on the outside . . . Hank. (*ALICE gives HENRY a thumb up gesture, and the GUARD escorts her out. HENRY turns downstage, full of thoughts. HE addresses EL PACHUCO, who is nowhere to be seen.*) 145

HENRY: You were wrong, ese . . . There's something to hope for. I know now we're going to win the appeal. Do you hear me, ese? Ese! (*Pause.*) Are you even there any more? (*The GUARD re-enters at a clip.*)

GUARD: Okay, Reyna, come on. 150

HENRY: Where to?

GUARD: We're letting you go . . . (*HENRY looks at him incredulously. The GUARD smiles.*) . . . to Folsom Prison with all the rest of the hardcore cons. You really didn't expect to walk out of here a free man, did you? Listen, kid, your appeal 155 stands about as much chance as the Japs and Krauts of winning the war. Personally, I don't see what that broad sees in you. I wouldn't give you the sweat off my balls. Come on! (*HENRY and the GUARD turn upstage to leave. Lights change. EL PACHUCO appears halfway up the backdrop,* 160 *fully dressed again and clearly visible. HENRY stops with a jolt as HE sees him. EL PACHUCO lifts his arms. Lights go down as we hear the high sound of a bomb falling to earth.*)

8. THE WINNING OF THE WAR

The aerial bomb explodes with a reverberating sound and a white flash that illuminates the form of pachuco images in the black backdrop. Other bombs fall and all hell breaks loose. Red flashes, artillery, gunfire, ack-ack. HENRY and the GUARD exit. The FOUR SERVICEMEN enter as an honor guard. Music: Glen Miller's "Saint Louis Blues March." As the SERVICEMEN march on we see RUDY down left in his marine uniform, belt undone. ENRIQUE, DOLORES and LUPE join him. DOLORES has his hat, LUPE her camera. ENRIQUE fastens two buttons on the uniform as RUDY does up his belt. DOLORES inspects his collar and gives him his hat. RUDY puts on his hat and all pose for LUPE. She snaps the picture and RUDY kisses them all and is off. HE picks up the giant switchblade from behind a newspaper bundle and joins the SERVICEMEN as they march down in drill formation. The family marches off, looking back sadly. The drill ends and RUDY and the SHORE PATROL move to one side. As RUDY's interrogation goes on, PEOPLE in the barrio come on with newspapers to mime daily tasks. The PRESS enters.

PRESS: The Los Angeles Examiner, July 1, 1943. Headline: WORLD WAR II REACHES TURNING POINT. If the late summer of 1942 was the low point, a year later the war for the Allies is pounding its way to certain victory.

SHORE PATROL: July 10! 5

RUDY: U.S., British and Canadian troops invade Sicily, Sir!

SHORE PATROL: August 6!

RUDY: U.S. troops occupy Solomon Island, Sir!

SHORE PATROL: September 5!

10 RUDY: MacArthur's forces land on New Guinea, Sir!

SHORE PATROL: October 1!

RUDY: U.S. Fifth Army enters Naples, Sir!

PRESS: On and on it goes. From Corsica to Kiev, from Tarawa to Anzio. The relentless advance of the Allied armies can-

15 not be checked. (*One by one,* HENRY's *family and friends enter, carrying newspapers. They tear the papers into small pieces.*) The Los Angeles Times, June 6, 1944. Headline: Allied forces under General Eisenhower land in Normandy.

SHORE PATROL: August 19!

20 RUDY: American First Army reaches Germany, Sir!

SHORE PATROL: October 17!

RUDY: MacArthur returns to the Philippines, Sir!

PRESS: On the homefront, Americans go on with their daily lives with growing confidence and relief, as the war

25 pushes on toward inevitable triumph. (*Pause.*) The Los Angeles Daily News, Wednesday, November 8, 1944. Headline: District Court of Appeals decides in Sleepy Lagoon murder case . . . boys in pachuco murder given . . .

PEOPLE: FREEDOM!!! (*Music bursts forth as the joyous crowd tosses*

30 *the shredded newspaper into the air like confetti. The* BOYS *enter upstage center, and the crowd rushes to them, weeping and cheering. There are kisses and hugs and tears of joy.* HENRY *is swept forward by the triumphal procession.*)

9. RETURN TO THE BARRIO

The music builds and people start dancing. Others just embrace. The tune is "Soldado Razo" played to a lively corrido beat. It ends with joyous applause, laughter and tears.

RUDY: ¡Ese carnal!

HENRY: Rudy!!

DOLORES: ¡Bendito sea Dios! Who would believe this day would ever come? Look at you—you're all home!

5 LUPE: I still can't believe it. We won! We won the appeal! (*Cheers.*)

ENRIQUE: I haven't felt like this since Villa took Zacatecas. (*Laughter, cheers.*) ¡Pero mira! Look who's here. Mis hijos. (*Puts his arm around* HENRY *and* RUDY.) It isn't every day a

10 man has two grown sons come home from so far away— one from the war, the other from . . . bueno, who cares? The Sleepy Lagoon is history, hombre. For a change, los Mexicanos have won! (*Cheers.*)

GEORGE: Well, Henry. I don't want to say I told you so, but

15 we sure taught Judge Charles a lesson in misconduct, didn't we? (*More cheers.*) Do you realize this is the greatest victory the Mexican-American community has ever had in the history of this whole blasted country?

DOLORES: Yes, but if it wasn't for the unselfish thoughtfulness

20 of people like you and this beautiful lady—and all the people who helped out, Mexicanos, Negros, all Americanos—our boys would not be home today.

GEORGE: I only hope you boys realize how important you are now.

25 JOEY: Pos, I realize it, ese. (*Laughter.*)

RUDY: I came all the way from Hawaii just to get here, carnal. I only got a few days, but I'm going to get you drunk.

HENRY: Pos, we'll see who gets who drunk, ese. (*Laughter and hoots.* HENRY *spots* EL PACHUCO *entering from stage right.*)

DOLORES: Jorge, Licha, todos. Let's go into the house, eh? I've 30 made a big pot of menudo, and it's for everybody.

ENRIQUE: There's ice-cold beer too. Vénganse, vamos todos.

GEORGE: (*To* ALICE.) Alice . . . Menudo, that's Mexican chicken soup? (*Everybody exits, leaving* HENRY *behind with* EL PACHUCO.) 35

HENRY: It's good to see you again, ese. I thought I'd lost you.

PACHUCO: H'm pues, it'd take more than the U.S. Navy to wipe me out.

HENRY: Where you been?

PACHUCO: Pos, here in the barrio. Welcome back.   40

HENRY: It's good to be home.

PACHUCO: No hard feelings?

HENRY: Chale—we won, didn't we?

PACHUCO: Simón.

HENRY: Me and the batos have been in a lot of fights to-   45 gether, ese. But we won this one, because we learned to fight in a new way.

PACHUCO: And that's the perfect way to end of this play— happy ending y todo. (PACHUCO *makes a sweeping gesture. Lights come down.* HE *looks up at the lights, realizing some-* 50 *thing is wrong.* HE *flicks his wrist, and the lights go back up again.*)

But life ain't that way, Hank.

The barrio's still out there, waiting and wanting.

The cops are still tracking us down like dogs.   55

The gangs are still killing each other,

Families are barely surviving,

And there in your own backyard . . . life goes on.

(*Soft music.* DELLA *enters.*)

DELLA: Hank? (HENRY *goes to her and they embrace.*)

HENRY: Where were you? Why didn't you come to the Hall   60 of Justice to see us get out?

DELLA: I guess I was a little afraid things had changed. So much has happened to both of us.

PACHUCO: Simón. She's living in your house.

DELLA: After I got back from Ventura, my parents gave me a   65 choice. Forget about you or get out.

HENRY: Why didn't you write to me?

DELLA: You had your own problems. Your jefitos took care of me. Hey, you know what, Hank, I think they expect us to get married.   70

PACHUCO: How about it, ese? You still going to give her that big pachuco wedding you promised?

HENRY: I have to think about it.

ALICE: (*Off-stage.*) Henry?

PACHUCO: (*Snaps fingers.*) Wish you had the time. But here   75 comes Licha.

ALICE: (*Entering.*) Henry, I've just come to say good night. (DELLA *freezes and* HENRY *turns to* ALICE.)

HENRY: Good night? Why are you leaving so soon?

ALICE: Soon? I've been here all afternoon. There'll be other   80 times, Henry. You're home now, with your family, that's what matters.

HENRY: Don't patronize me, Alice.

ALICE: (*Surprised.*) Patronize you?

HENRY: Yeah. I learned a few words in the joint.   85

ALICE: Yo también, Hank. Te quiero. (PACHUCO *snaps.* ALICE *freezes, and* RUDY *enters.*)

RUDY: Ese, carnal, congratulations, the jefita just told me about you and Della. That's great, ese. But if you want me to be best man, you better do it in the next three days.

HENRY: Wait a minute, Rudy, don't push me.

RUDY: Qué pues, getting cold feet already? (HENRY *is beginning to be surrounded by separate conversations.*)

DELLA: If you don't want me here, I can move out.

RUDY: Watcha. I'll let you and Della have our room tonight, bato. I'll sleep on the couch.

ALICE: You aren't expecting me to sleep here, are you?

HENRY: I'm not asking you to.

PACHUCO/ALICE/RUDY/DELLA: Why not?

RUDY: The jefitos will never know, ese.

ALICE: Be honest, Henry.

DELLA: What do you want me to do?

HENRY: Give me a chance to think about it. Give me a second!

PACHUCO: One second! (PACHUCO *snaps.* ENRIQUE *enters.*)

ENRIQUE: Bueno, bueno, pues, what are you doing out here, hijo? Aren't you coming in for menudo?

HENRY: I'm just thinking, jefito.

ENRIQUE: ¿De qué, hombre? Didn't you do enough of that in prison? Andale, this is your house. Come in and live again.

HENRY: 'Apá, did you tell Della I was going to marry her?

ENRIQUE: Yes, but only after you did.

RUDY: ¿Qué traes, carnal? Don't you care about Della anymore?

ALICE: If it was just me and you, Henry, it might be different. But you have to think of your family.

HENRY: I don't need you to tell me my responsibilities.

ALICE: I'm sorry.

RUDY: Sorry, carnal.

DELLA: I don't need anybody to feel sorry for me. I did what I did because I wanted to. All I want to know is what's going to happen now. If you still want me, órale, suave. If you don't, that's okay, too. But I'm not going to hang around like a pendeja all my life.

RUDY: Your huisa's looking finer than ever, carnal.

ALICE: You're acting as if nothing has happened.

ENRIQUE: You have your whole life ahead of you.

ALICE: You belong here, Henry. I'm the one that's out of place.

RUDY: If you don't pick up on her, I'm going to have to step in.

HENRY: That's bullshit. What about what we shared in prison? I've never been that close to anybody.

ALICE: That was in prison.

HENRY: What the hell do you think the barrio is?

RUDY: It's not bullshit!

HENRY: Shut up, carnalillo!

RUDY: Carnalillo? How can you still call me that? I'm not your pinche little brother no more.

GEORGE: (*Entering.*) You guys have got to stop fighting, Henry, or the barrio will never change. Don't you realize you men represent the hope of your people?

ALICE: Della was in prison too. You know you had thousands of people clamoring for your release, but you were Della's only hope.

HENRY: Look, esa, I know you did a year in Ventura. I know you stood up for me when it counted. I wish I could make it up to you.

DELLA: Don't give me your bullshit, Henry. Give it to Alice.

ALICE: I think it's time for Alice Bloomfield to go home.

HENRY: Don't be jealous, esa.

DELLA: Jealous? Mira, cabrón, I know I'm not the only one you ever took to the Sleepy Lagoon.

RUDY: The Sleepy Lagoon ain't shit. I saw real lagoons in those islands, ese—killing Japs! I saw some pachucos go out there that are never coming back.

DELLA: But I was always there when you came back, wasn't I?

DOLORES: (*Entering.*) Henry? Come back inside, hijo. Everybody's waiting for you.

RUDY: Why didn't you tell them I was there, carnal? I was at the Sleepy Lagoon. Throwing chingazos with everybody!

HENRY: Don't you understand, Rudy? I was trying to keep you from getting a record. Those bastard cops are never going to leave us alone.

GEORGE: You've got to forget what happened, Henry.

HENRY: What can I give you, Della? I'm an ex-con.

DELLA: So am I!

SMILEY: (*Entering.*) Let's face it, Hank. There's no future for us in this town. I'm taking my wife and kid and moving to Arizona.

DOLORES: (*Simultaneously.*) I know what you are feeling, hijo, it's home again. I know inside you are afraid that nothing has changed. That the police will never leave you in peace. Pero no le hace. Everything is going to be fine now. Marry Della and fill this house with children. Just do one thing for me—forget the zoot suit clothes.

ENRIQUE: If there's one thing that will keep a man off the streets is his own familia.

GEORGE: Don't let this thing eat your heart out for the rest of your . . .

ALICE: Sometimes the best thing you can do for someone you love is walk away.

DELLA: What do you want, Hank?

RUDY: It cost me more than it did you.

SMILEY: We started the 38th and I'll never forget you, carnal. But I got to think about my family.

HENRY: Wait a minute! I don't know if I'll be back in prison tomorrow or not! I have nothing to give you, Della. Not even a piece of myself.

DELLA: I have my life to live, too, Hank. I love you. I would even die for you. Pero me chingan la madre if I'm going to throw away my life for nothing.

HENRY: But I love you . . . (*Both* GIRLS *turn.* HENRY *looks at* ALICE, *then to the whole group upstage of him. Still turning,* HE *looks at* DELLA *and goes to embrace her. The freeze ends and other people enter.*)

LUPE: ¡Órale, Hank! Watcha Joey. The crazy bato went all the way to his house and put on his drapes.

JOEY: ¡Esos, batooooooosss! ¡Esas, huisaaaaaass!

TOMMY: Look at this cat! He looks all reet.

LUPE: Yeah, like a parakeet!

HENRY: ¿Y tú, ese? How come you put on your tacuche? Where's the party?

JOEY: Pos, ain't the party here?

RUDY: Yeah, ese, but this ain't the Avalon Ballroom. The zoot suit died under fire here in Los. Don't you know that, cabrón?

210   ENRIQUE: Rudolfo!

LUPE: And he was supposed to get Henry drunk.

RUDY: Shut up, esa!

ENRIQUE: ¡Ya pues! Didn't you have any menudo? Vieja, fix him a great big bowl of menudo and put plenty of chile

215   in it. We're going to sweat it out of him.

RUDY: I don't need no pinche menudo.

HENRY: Watch your language, carnal.

RUDY: And I don't need you! I'm a man. I can take care of myself!

220   JOEY: Muy marine el bato . . .

ENRIQUE: Rudy, hijo. Are you going to walk into the kitchen or do I have to drag you.

RUDY: Whatever you say, jefito.

GEORGE: Well, Alice. This looks like the place where we came

225   in. I think it's about time we left.

ALICE: Say the word, George, just say the word.

DOLORES: No, no. You can't leave so soon.

JOEY: Chale, chale, chale. You can't take our Grandma. ¿Qué se trae, carnal? Póngase más abusado, ese. No se haga tan

230   square.

GEORGE: Okay, square I got. What was the rest of it?

JOEY: Pos, le estoy hablando en chicas patas, ese. Es puro chicano.

RUDY: ¿Qué chicano? Ni que madre, cabrón. Why don't you

235   grow up.

JOEY: Grow up, ese?

RUDY: Try walking downtown looking like that. See if the sailors don't skin your ass alive.

JOEY: So what? It's no skin off your ass. Come on, Bertha.

240   RUDY: She's staying with me.

JOEY: She's mine.

RUDY: Prove it, punk. (RUDY attacks JOEY and they fight. The BATOS and RUCAS take out JOEY. HENRY pacifies RUDY, who bursts out crying. ENRIQUE, DELLA, DOLORES, ALICE,

245   LUPE and GEORGE are the only ones left. RUDY in a flush of emotion.) Cabrones, se amontonaron. They ganged up on me, carnal. You left me and they ganged up on me. You shouldn't have done it, carnal. Why didn't you take me with you. For the jefitos? The jefitos lost me

250   anyway.

HENRY: Come on in the house, Rudy . . .

RUDY: No! I joined the Marines. I didn't have to join, but I went. ¿Sabes por qué? Because they got me, carnal. Me chingaron, ese. (Sobs.) I went to the pinche show with

255   Bertha, all chingón in your tachuche, ese. I was wearing your zoot suit, and they got me. Twenty sailors, Marines. We were up in the balcony. They came down from behind. They grabbed me by the neck and dragged me down the stairs, kicking and punching and pulling my

260   greña. They dragged me out into the streets . . . and all the people watched while they stripped me. (Sobs.) They stripped me, carnal. Bertha saw them strip me. Hijos de la chingada, they stripped me. (HENRY goes to RUDY and em-

braces him with fierce love and desperation. Pause. TOMMY comes running in.)

TOMMY: ¡Órale! There's cops outside. They're trying to arrest   265
Joey. (GEORGE crosses to TOMMY.)

GEORGE: (Bursting out.) Joey?

TOMMY: They got him up against your car. They're trying to say he stole it!

GEORGE: Oh, God. I'll take care of this.   270

ALICE: I'll go with you. (GEORGE, TOMMY and ALICE exit.)

HENRY: Those fucking bastards! (HE starts to exit.)

DELLA: Henry, no!

HENRY: What the hell do you mean no? Don't you see what's going on outside?   275

DELLA: They'll get you again! That's what they want.

HENRY: Get out of my way! (HE pushes her out of the way, toward DOLORES.)

ENRIQUE: (Stands up before Henry.) ¡Hijo!

HENRY: Get out of my way, jefe!   280

ENRIQUE: You will stay here!

HENRY: Get out of my way! (ENRIQUE powerfully pushes him back and throws HENRY to the floor and holds.)

ENRIQUE: ¡TE DIGO QUE NO! (Silent moment, HENRY stands up and offers to strike ENRIQUE. But something stops him. The   285
realization that if HE strikes back or even if HE walks out the door, the family bond is irreparably broken. HENRY tenses for a moment, then relaxes and embraces his father. DELLA goes to them and joins the embrace. Then DOLORES, then LUPE, then RUDY. All embrace in a tight little group. PRESS enters right and comes down.)   290

PRESS: Henry Reyna went back to prison in 1947 for robbery and assault with a deadly weapon. While incarcerated, he killed another inmate and he wasn't released until 1955, when he got into hard drugs. He died of the trauma of his life in 1972.   295

PACHUCO: That's the way you see it, ese. But there's other way to end this story.

RUDY: Henry Reyna went to Korea in 1950. He was shipped across in a destroyer and defended the 38th Parallel until he was killed at Inchon in 1952, being posthumously   300
awarded the Congressional Medal of Honor.

ALICE: Henry Reyna married Della in 1948 and they have five kids, three of them now going to the University, speaking calo and calling themselves Chicanos.

GEORGE: Henry Reyna, the born leader . . .   305

JUDGE: Henry Reyna, the social victim . . .

BERTHA: Henry Reyna, the street corner warrior . . .

SMILEY: Henry Reyna, el carnal de aquellas . . .

JOEY: Henry Reyna, the zoot suiter . . .

TOMMY: Henry Reyna, my friend . . .   310

LUPE: Henry Reyna, my brother . . .

ENRIQUE: Henry Reyna . . .

DOLORES: Our son . . .

DELLA: Henry Reyna, my love . . .

PACHUCO: Henry Reyna . . . El Pachuco . . . The man . . . the   315
myth . . . still lives. (Lights down and fade out.)

Sam Shepard

Sam Shepard (b. 1943) is probably the best-known American playwright of his generation. Born Samuel Shepard Rogers to a military family stationed in Illinois, Shepard spent his youth moving from base to base, until his father retired and settled the family in southern California. Shepard was an indifferent student and left college for New York City in 1963. He took a job busing tables at the Village Gate jazz club and began to write plays for off-Broadway, including *Cowboys* (1964), *Red Cross* (1966), *La Turista* (1966), *The Unseen Hand* (1970), *Cowboy Mouth* (1971), and *Tooth of Crime* (1972). In these plays, Shepard invented what became his characteristic idiom: a search for the "West" of myth, an image both fascinating and elusive, somehow undiscoverable amid the consumer trash of suburban society. He also developed a sense of split and fragmented characters, relying on his typically jazzy use of language. This is particularly true of *Tooth of Crime,* in which a kind of shoot-out between the old rock 'n' roll star, Hoss, and the Keith Richards–like Crow is conducted in an invented language of rock music, drugs, cars, gangsters, and old movies. Shepard won six Obie awards between 1964 and 1970, but his work took a great step forward in the major plays of the late 1970s and 1980s: *Curse of the Starving Class* (1978), *Buried Child* (Pulitzer Prize, 1979), *True West* (1980), *Fool for Love* (1982), *A Lie of the Mind* (1985), *States of Shock* (1991), *Simpatico* (1994), and *Eyes for Consuela* (1998). Shepard also has written the screenplay for the Wim Wenders film, *Paris, Texas,* and has starred in several films himself, notably as Chuck Yeager in *The Right Stuff* (1983) and as the Ghost of Old Hamlet in Michael Almereyda's *Hamlet* (2000).

Gary Sinise as Austin and John Malkovitch as Lee in the 1980 Steppenwolf Theater production of Sam Shepard's *True West*.

TRUE WEST

True West is the leanest, most elemental of Shepard's plays and brings the question of identity—individual and cultural—into sharp focus. The play concerns two brothers: Austin, a yuppie screenwriter, and his derelict brother, Lee, a petty thief who spends much of his time in the desert. In the course of the play, however, Austin and Lee subtly change roles and identities: Lee swings a deal to write the screenplay for a Western movie, while Austin seems to abandon the desire to be a writer, working to prove himself to Lee by stealing toasters from the suburban neighbors. *True West* is a kind of Western, though the brothers don't fight it out for any actual piece of territory, since there is no Dodge City, no True West to fight over. What the brothers finally duel for is a mythic terrain, the terrain of their father, of the desert, of Westerns: the "West" of the imagination.

TRUE WEST
Sam Shepard

CHARACTERS

AUSTIN, *early thirties, light blue sports shirt, light tan cardigan sweater, clean blue jeans, white tennis shoes*

LEE, *his older brother, early forties, filthy white t-shirt, tattered brown overcoat covered with dust, dark blue baggy suit pants from the Salvation Army, pink suede belt, pointed black forties dress shoes scuffed up, holes in the soles, no socks, no hat, long pronounced sideburns, "Gene Vincent" hairdo, two days' growth of beard, bad teeth*

SAUL KIMMER, *late forties, Hollywood producer, pink and white flower print sports shirt, white sports coat with matching polyester slacks, black and white loafers*

MOM, *early sixties, mother of the brothers, small woman, conservative white skirt and matching jacket, red shoulder bag, two pieces of matching red luggage*

SCENE: *All nine scenes take place on the same set; a kitchen and adjoining alcove of an older home in a Southern California suburb, about 40 miles east of Los Angeles. The kitchen takes up most of the playing area to stage left. The kitchen consists of a sink, upstage center, surrounded by counter space, a wall telephone, cupboards, and a small window just above it bordered by neat yellow curtains. Stage left of sink is a stove. Stage right, a refrigerator. The alcove adjoins the kitchen to stage right. There is no wall division or door to the alcove. It is open and easily accessible from the kitchen and defined only by the objects in it: a small round glass breakfast table mounted on white iron legs, two matching white iron chairs set across from each other. The two exterior walls of the alcove which prescribe a corner in the upstage right are composed of many small windows, beginning from a solid wall about three feet high and extending to the ceiling. The windows look out to bushes and citrus trees. The alcove is filled with all sorts of house plants in various pots, mostly Boston ferns hanging in planters at different levels. The floor of the alcove is composed of green synthetic grass.*

All entrances and exits are made stage left from the kitchen. There is no door. The actors simply go off and come onto the playing area.

NOTE ON SET AND COSTUME: *The set should be constructed realistically with no attempt to distort its dimensions, shapes, objects, or colors. No objects should be introduced which might draw special attention to themselves other than the props demanded by the script. If a stylistic "concept" is grafted onto the set design it will only serve to confuse the evolution of the characters' situation, which is the most important focus of the play.*

Likewise, the costumes should be exactly representative of who the characters are and not added onto for the sake of making a point to the audience.

NOTE ON SOUND: *The Coyote of Southern California has a distinct yapping, dog-like bark, similar to a Hyena. This yapping grows more intense and maniacal as the pack grows in numbers, which is usually the case when they lure and kill pets from suburban yards. The sense of growing frenzy in the pack should be felt in the background, particularly in Scenes 7 and 8. In any case, these Coyotes never make the long, mournful, solitary howl of the Hollywood stereotype.*

The sound of Crickets can speak for itself.

These sounds should also be treated realistically even though they sometimes grow in volume and numbers.

ACT ONE

SCENE I

Night. Sound of crickets in dark. Candlelight appears in alcove, illuminating AUSTIN, *seated at glass table hunched over a writing notebook, pen in hand, cigarette burning in ashtray, cup of coffee, typewriter on table, stacks of paper, candle burning on table.*

Soft moonlight fills kitchen illuminating LEE, *beer in hand, six-pack on counter behind him. He's leaning against the sink, mildly drunk; takes a slug of beer.*

LEE: So, Mom took off for Alaska, huh?

AUSTIN: Yeah.

LEE: Sorta' left you in charge.

AUSTIN: Well, she knew I was coming down here so she offered me the place.

LEE: You keepin' the plants watered?

AUSTIN: Yeah.

LEE: Keepin' the sink clean? She don't like even a single tea leaf in the sink ya' know.

AUSTIN: (*Trying to concentrate on writing.*) Yeah, I know.

(*Pause.*)

LEE: She gonna' be up there a long time?

AUSTIN: I don't know.

LEE: Kinda' nice for you, huh? Whole place to yourself.

AUSTIN: Yeah, it's great.

LEE: Ya' got crickets anyway. Tons a' crickets out there. (*Looks around kitchen.*) Ya' got groceries? Coffee?

AUSTIN: (*Looking up from writing.*) What?

LEE: You got coffee?

AUSTIN: Yeah.

LEE: At's good. (*Short pause.*) Real coffee? From the bean?

AUSTIN: Yeah. You want some?

LEE: Naw. I brought some uh—(*Motions to beer.*)

AUSTIN: Help yourself to whatever's—(*Motions to refrigerator.*)

LEE: I will. Don't worry about me. I'm not the one to worry about. I mean I can uh—(*Pause.*) You always work by candlelight?

AUSTIN: No—uh—Not always.

LEE: Just sometimes?

AUSTIN: (*Puts pen down, rubs his eyes.*) Yeah. Sometimes it's soothing.

LEE: Isn't that what the old guys did?

AUSTIN: What old guys?

LEE: The Forefathers. You know.

AUSTIN: Forefathers?

35 LEE: Isn't that what they did? Candlelight burning into the night? Cabins in the wilderness.

AUSTIN: (Rubs hand through his hair.) I suppose.

LEE: I'm not botherin' you am I? I mean I don't wanna break into yer uh—concentration or nothin'.

40 AUSTIN: No, it's all right.

LEE: That's good. I mean I realize that yer line a' work demands a lota' concentration.

AUSTIN: It's okay.

LEE: You probably think that I'm not fully able to compre-

45 hend somethin' like that, huh?

AUSTIN: Like what?

LEE: That stuff yer doin'. That art. You know. Whatever you call it.

AUSTIN: It's just a little research.

50 LEE: You may not know it but I did a little art myself once.

AUSTIN: You did?

LEE: Yeah! I did some a' that. I fooled around with it. No future in it.

AUSTIN: What'd you do?

55 LEE: Never mind what I did! Just never mind about that. (Pause.) It was ahead of its time.

(Pause.)

AUSTIN: So, you went out to see the old man, huh?

LEE: Yeah, I seen him.

AUSTIN: How's he doing?

60 LEE: Same. He's doin' just about the same.

AUSTIN: I was down there too, you know.

LEE: What d'ya' want, an award? You want some kinda' medal? You were down there. He told me all about you.

AUSTIN: What'd he say?

65 LEE: He told me. Don't worry.

(Pause.)

AUSTIN: Well—

LEE: You don't have to say nothin'.

AUSTIN: I wasn't.

LEE: Yeah, you were gonna' make somethin' up. Somethin'

70 brilliant.

(Pause.)

AUSTIN: You going to be down here very long, Lee?

LEE: Might be. Depends on a few things.

AUSTIN: You got some friends down here?

LEE: (Laughs.) I know a few people. Yeah.

75 AUSTIN: Well, you can stay here as long as I'm here.

LEE: I don't need your permission do I?

AUSTIN: No.

LEE: I mean she's my mother too, right?

AUSTIN: Right.

80 LEE: She might've just as easily asked me to take care of her place as you.

AUSTIN: That's right.

LEE: I mean I know how to water plants.

(Long pause.)

AUSTIN: So you don't know how long you'll be staying then?

LEE: Depends mostly on houses, ya' know. 85

AUSTIN: Houses?

LEE: Yeah. Houses. Electric devices. Stuff like that. I gotta' make a little tour first.

(Short pause.)

AUSTIN: Lee, why don't you just try another neighborhood, all right? 90

LEE: (Laughs.) What'sa' matter with this neighborhood? This is a great neighborhood. Lush. Good class a' people. Not many dogs.

AUSTIN: Well, our uh—Our mother just happens to live here. That's all. 95

LEE: Nobody's gonna' know. All they know is somethin's missing. That's all. She'll never even hear about it. Nobody's gonna' know.

AUSTIN: You're going to get picked up if you start walking around here at night. 100

LEE: Me? I'm gonna' git picked up? What about you? You stick out like a sore thumb. Look at you. You think yer regular lookin'?

AUSTIN: I've got too much to deal with here to be worrying about— 105

LEE: Yer not gonna' have to worry about me! I've been doin' all right without you. I haven't been anywhere near you for five years! Now isn't that true?

AUSTIN: Yeah.

LEE: So you don't have to worry about me. I'm a free agent. 110

AUSTIN: All right.

LEE: Now all I wanna' do is borrow yer car.

AUSTIN: No!

LEE: Just fer a day. One day.

AUSTIN: No! 115

LEE: I won't take it outside a twenty mile radius. I promise ya'. You can check the speedometer.

AUSTIN: You're not borrowing my car! That's all there is to it.

(Pause.)

LEE: Then I'll just take the damn thing.

AUSTIN: Lee, look—I don't want any trouble, all right? 120

LEE: That's a dumb line. That is a dumb fuckin' line. You git paid fer dreamin' up a line like that?

AUSTIN: Look, I can give you some money if you need money.

(LEE suddenly lunges at AUSTIN, grabs him violently by the shirt and shakes him with tremendous power.)

LEE: Don't you say that to me! Don't you ever say that to me! (Just as suddenly he turns him loose, pushes him away and backs 125 off.) You may be able to git away with that with the Old Man. Git him tanked up for a week! Buy him off with yer Hollywood blood money, but not me! I can git my own money my own way. Big money!

AUSTIN: I was just making an offer. 130

LEE: Yeah, well keep it to yourself!

(Long pause.)

Those are the most monotonous fuckin' crickets I ever heard in my life.

AUSTIN: I kinda' like the sound.

135 LEE: Yeah. Supposed to be able to tell the temperature by the number a' pulses. You believe that?

AUSTIN: The temperature?

LEE: Yeah. The air. How hot it is.

AUSTIN: How do you do that?

140 LEE: I don't know. Some woman told me that. She was a Botanist. So I believed her.

AUSTIN: Where'd you meet her?

LEE: What?

AUSTIN: The woman Botanist?

145 LEE: I met her on the desert. I been spendin' a lota' time on the desert.

AUSTIN: What were you doing out there?

LEE: (*Pause, stares in space.*) I forgit. Had me a Pit Bull there for a while but I lost him.

150 AUSTIN: Pit Bull?

LEE: Fightin' dog. Damn I made some good money off that little dog. Real good money.

(*Pause.*)

AUSTIN: You could come up north with me, you know.

LEE: What's up there?

155 AUSTIN: My family.

LEE: Oh, that's right, you got the wife and kiddies now don't ya'. The house, the car, the whole slam. That's right.

AUSTIN: You could spend a couple days. See how you like it. I've got an extra room.

160 LEE: Too cold up there.

(*Pause.*)

AUSTIN: You want to sleep for a while?

LEE: (*Pause, stares at* AUSTIN.) I don't sleep.

(*Lights to black.*)

SCENE II

Morning. AUSTIN *is watering plants with a vaporizer,* LEE *sits at glass table in alcove drinking beer.*

LEE: I never realized the old lady was so security-minded.

AUSTIN: How do you mean?

LEE: Made a little tour this morning. She's got locks on every-thing. Locks and double-locks and chain locks and—

5   What's she got that's so valuable?

AUSTIN: Antiques I guess. I don't know.

LEE: Antiques? Brought everything with her from the old place, huh. Just the same crap we always had around. Plates and spoons.

10 AUSTIN: I guess they have personal value to her.

LEE: Personal value. Yeah. Just a lota' junk. Most of it's phony anyway. Idaho decals. Now who in the hell wants to eat offa' plate with the State of Idaho starin' ya' in the face. Every time ya' take a bite ya' get to see a little bit more.

15 AUSTIN: Well it must mean something to her or she wouldn't save it.

LEE: Yeah, well personally I don't wann' be invaded by Idaho when I'm eatin'. When I'm eatin' I'm home. Ya' know

what I'm sayin? I'm not driftin', I'm home. I don't need my thoughts swept off to Idaho. I don't need that! 20

(*Pause.*)

AUSTIN: Did you go out last night?

LEE: Why?

AUSTIN: I thought I heard you go out.

LEE: Yeah, I went out. What about it?

AUSTIN: Just wondered. 25

LEE: Damn coyotes kept me awake.

AUSTIN: Oh yeah, I heard them. They must've killed some-body's dog or something.

LEE: Yappin' their fool heads off. They don't yap like that on the desert. They howl. These are city coyotes here. 30

AUSTIN: Well, you don't sleep anyway do you?

(*Pause,* LEE *stares at him.*)

LEE: You're pretty smart aren't ya?

AUSTIN: How do you mean?

LEE: I mean you never had any more on the ball than I did. But here you are gettin' invited into prominent people's 35 houses. Sittin' around talkin' like you know somethin'.

AUSTIN: They're not so prominent.

LEE: They're a helluva' lot more prominent than the houses I get invited into.

AUSTIN: Well you invite yourself. 40

LEE: That's right. I do. In fact I probably got a wider range a' choices than you do, come to think of it.

AUSTIN: I wouldn't doubt it.

LEE: In fact I been inside some pretty classy places in my time. And I never even went to an Ivy League school either. 45

AUSTIN: You want some breakfast or something?

LEE: Breakfast?

AUSTIN: Yeah. Don't you eat breakfast?

LEE: Look, don't worry about me pal. I can take care a' myself. You just go ahead as though I wasn't even here, all right? 50

(AUSTIN *goes into kitchen, makes coffee.*)

AUSTIN: Where'd you walk to last night?

(*Pause.*)

LEE: I went up in the foothills there. Up in the San Gabriels. Heat was drivin' me crazy.

AUSTIN: Well, wasn't it hot out on the desert?

LEE: Different kinda' heat. Out there it's clean. Cools off at 55 night. There's a nice little breeze.

AUSTIN: Where were you, the Mojave?

LEE: Yeah. The Mojave. That's right.

AUSTIN: I haven't been out there in years.

LEE: Out past Needles there. 60

AUSTIN: Oh yeah.

LEE: Up here it's different. This country's real different.

AUSTIN: Well, it's been built up.

LEE: Built up? Wiped out is more like it. I don't even hardly recognize it. 65

AUSTIN: Yeah. Foothills are the same though, aren't they?

LEE: Pretty much. It's funny goin' up in there. The smells and everything. Used to catch snakes up there, remember?

AUSTIN: You caught snakes.

70 LEE: Yeah. And you'd pretend you were Geronimo or some damn thing. You used to go right out to lunch.

AUSTIN: I enjoyed my imagination.

LEE: That what you call it? Looks like yer still enjoyin' it.

AUSTIN: So you just wandered around up there, huh?

75 LEE: Yeah. With a purpose.

AUSTIN: See any houses?

(*Pause.*)

LEE: Couple. Couple a' real nice ones. One of 'em didn't even have a dog. Walked right up and stuck my head in the window. Not a peep. Just a sweet kinda' suburban silence.

80 AUSTIN: What kind of a place was it?

LEE: Like a paradise. Kinda' place that sorta' kills ya' inside. Warm yellow lights. Mexican tile all around. Copper pots hangin' over the stove. Ya' know like they got in the magazines. Blonde people movin' in and outa' the rooms,

85 talkin' to each other. (*Pause.*) Kinda' place you wish you sorta' grew up in, ya' know.

AUSTIN: That's the kind of place you wish you'd grown up in?

LEE: Yeah, why not?

AUSTIN: I thought you hated that kind of stuff.

90 LEE: Yeah, well you never knew too much about me did ya'?

(*Pause.*)

AUSTIN: Why'd you go out to the desert in the first place?

LEE: I was on my way to see the old man.

AUSTIN: You mean you just passed through there?

LEE: Yeah. That's right. Three months of passin' through.

95 AUSTIN: Three months?

LEE: Somethin' like that. Maybe more. Why?

AUSTIN: You lived on the Mojave for three months?

LEE: Yeah. What'sa' matter with that?

AUSTIN: By yourself?

100 LEE: Mostly. Had a couple a' visitors. Had that dog for a while.

AUSTIN: Didn't you miss people?

LEE: (*Laughs.*) People?

AUSTIN: Yeah. I mean I go crazy if I have to spend three nights in a motel by myself.

105 LEE: Yer not in a motel now.

AUSTIN: No, I know. But sometimes I have to stay in motels.

LEE: Well, they got people in motels don't they?

AUSTIN: Strangers.

LEE: Yer friendly aren't ya'? Aren't you the friendly type?

(*Pause.*)

110 AUSTIN: I'm going to have somebody coming by here later, Lee.

LEE: Ah! Lady friend?

AUSTIN: No, a producer.

LEE: Aha! What's he produce?

AUSTIN: Film. Movies. You know.

115 LEE: Oh, movies. Motion Pictures! A Big Wig huh?

AUSTIN: Yeah.

LEE: What's he comin' by here for?

AUSTIN: We have to talk about a project.

LEE: Whadya' mean, "a project"? What's a "project"?

120 AUSTIN: A script.

LEE: Oh. That's what yer doin' with all these papers?

AUSTIN: Yeah.

LEE: Well, what's the project about?

AUSTIN: We're uh—it's a period piece.

LEE: What's "a period piece"?   125

AUSTIN: Look, it doesn't matter. The main thing is we need to discuss this alone. I mean—

LEE: Oh, I get it. You want me outa' the picture.

AUSTIN: Not exactly. I just need to be alone with him for a couple of hours. So we can talk.   130

LEE: Yer afraid I'll embarrass ya' huh?

AUSTIN: I'm not afraid you'll embarrass me!

LEE: Well, I tell ya' what—Why don't you just gimme the keys to yer car and I'll be back here around six o'clock or so. That give ya' enough time?   135

AUSTIN: I'm not loaning you my car, Lee.

LEE: You want me to just git lost huh? Take a hike? Is that it? Pound the pavement for a few hours while you bullshit yer way into a million bucks.

AUSTIN: Look, it's going to be hard enough for me to face   140
this character on my own without—

LEE: You don't know this guy?

AUSTIN: No I don't know—He's a producer. I mean I've been meeting with him for months but you never get to know a producer.   145

LEE: Yer tryin' to hustle him? Is that it?

AUSTIN: I'm not trying to hustle him! I'm trying to work out a deal! It's not easy.

LEE: What kinda' deal?

AUSTIN: Convince him it's a worthwhile story.   150

LEE: He's not convinced? How come he's comin' over here if he's not convinced? I'll convince him for ya'.

AUSTIN: You don't understand the way things work down here.

LEE: How do things work down here?

(*Pause.*)

AUSTIN: Look, if I loan you my car will you have it back here 155
by six?

LEE: On the button. With a full tank a' gas.

AUSTIN: (*Digging in his pocket for keys.*) Forget about the gas.

LEE: Hey, these days gas is gold, old buddy.

(AUSTIN *hands the keys to* LEE.)

You remember that car I used to loan you?   160

AUSTIN: Yeah.

LEE: Forty Ford. Flathead.

AUSTIN: Yeah.

LEE: Sucker hauled ass didn't it?

AUSTIN: Lee, it's not that I don't want to loan you my car—   165

LEE: You are loanin' me yer car.

(LEE *gives* AUSTIN *a pat on the shoulder, pause.*)

AUSTIN: I know. I just wish—

LEE: What? You wish what?

AUSTIN: I don't know. I wish I wasn't—I wish I didn't have to be doing business down here. I'd like to just spend some   170
time with you.

LEE: I thought it was "Art" you were doin'.

(LEE *moves across kitchen toward exit, tosses keys in his hand.*)

AUSTIN: Try to get it back here by six, okay?

175 LEE: No sweat. Hey, ya' know, if that uh—story of yours doesn't go over with the guy—tell him I got a couple a' "projects" he might be interested in. Real commercial. Full a' suspense. True-to-life stuff.

(LEE *exits,* AUSTIN *stares after* LEE *then turns, goes to papers at table, leafs through pages, lights fade to black.*)

SCENE III

Afternoon. Alcove, SAUL KIMMER *and* AUSTIN *seated across from each other at table.*

SAUL: Well, to tell you the truth Austin, I have never felt so confident about a project in quite a long time.

AUSTIN: Well, that's good to hear, Saul.

SAUL: I am absolutely convinced we can get this thing off the
5 ground. I mean we'll have to make a sale to television and that means getting a major star. Somebody bankable. But I think we can do it. I really do.

AUSTIN: Don't you think we need a first draft before we approach a star?

10 SAUL: No, no, not at all. I don't think it's necessary. Maybe a brief synopsis. I don't want you to touch the typewriter until we have some seed money.

AUSTIN: That's fine with me.

SAUL: I mean it's a great story. Just the story alone. You've re-
15 ally managed to capture something this time.

AUSTIN: I'm glad you like it, Saul.

(LEE *enters abruptly into kitchen carrying a stolen television set, short pause.*)

LEE: Aw shit, I'm sorry about that. I am really sorry Austin.

AUSTIN: (*Standing.*) That's all right.

LEE: (*Moving toward them.*) I mean I thought it was way past
20 six already. You said to have it back here by six.

AUSTIN: We were just finishing up. (*To* SAUL.) This is my, uh—brother, Lee.

SAUL: (*Standing.*) Oh, I'm very happy to meet you.

(LEE *sets T.V. on sink counter, shakes hands with* SAUL.)

LEE: I can't tell ya' how happy I am to meet you sir.

25 SAUL: Saul Kimmer.

LEE: Mr. Kipper.

SAUL: Kimmer.

AUSTIN: Lee's been living out on the desert and he just uh—

SAUL: Oh, that's terrific! (*To* LEE.) Palm Springs?

30 LEE: Yeah. Yeah, right. Right around in that area. Near uh—Bob Hope Drive there.

SAUL: Oh I love it out there. I just love it. The air is wonderful.

LEE: Yeah. Sure is. Healthy.

35 SAUL: And the golf. I don't know if you play golf, but the golf is just about the best.

LEE: I play a lota' golf.

SAUL: Is that right?

LEE: Yeah. In fact I was hoping I'd run into somebody out here
40 who played a little golf. I've been lookin' for a partner.

SAUL: Well, I uh—

AUSTIN: Lee's just down for a visit while our mother's in Alaska.

SAUL: Oh, your mother's in Alaska?

AUSTIN: Yes. She went up there on a little vacation. This is
45 her place.

SAUL: I see. Well isn't that something. Alaska.

LEE: What kinda' handicap do ya' have, Mr. Kimmer?

SAUL: Oh I'm just a Sunday duffer really. You know.

LEE: That's good 'cause I haven't swung a club in months.

50 SAUL: Well we ought to get together sometime and have a little game. Austin, do you play?

(SAUL *mimes a Johnny Carson golf swing for* AUSTIN.)

AUSTIN: No. I don't uh—I've watched it on T.V.

LEE: (*To* SAUL.) How 'bout tomorrow morning? Bright and early. We could get out there and put in eighteen holes be-
55 fore breakfast.

SAUL: Well, I've got uh—I have several appointments—

LEE: No, I mean real early. Crack a' dawn. While the dew's still thick on the fairway.

SAUL: Sounds really great.

60 LEE: Austin could be our caddie.

SAUL: Now that's an idea. (*Laughs.*)

AUSTIN: I don't know the first thing about golf.

LEE: There's nothin' to it. Isn't that right, Saul? He'd pick it up in fifteen minutes.

65 SAUL: Sure. Doesn't take long. 'Course you have to play for years to find your true form. (*Chuckles.*)

LEE: (*To* AUSTIN.) We'll give ya' a quick run-down on the club faces. The irons, the woods. Show ya' a couple pointers on the basic swing. Might even let ya' hit the ball a couple
70 times. Whadya' think, Saul?

SAUL: Why not. I think it'd be great. I haven't had any exercise in weeks.

LEE: At's the spirit! We'll have a little orange juice right afterwards.

(*Pause.*)

75 SAUL: Orange juice?

LEE: Yeah! Vitamin C! Nothin' like a shot a' orange juice after a round a' golf. Hot shower. Snappin' towels at each others' privates. Real sense a' fraternity.

SAUL: (*Smiles at* AUSTIN.) Well, you make it sound very invit-
80 ing, I must say. It really does sound great.

LEE: Then it's a date.

SAUL: Well, I'll call the country club and see if I can arrange something.

LEE: Great! Boy, I sure am sorry that I busted in on ya' all in
85 the middle of yer meeting.

SAUL: Oh that's quite all right. We were just about finished anyway.

LEE: I can wait out in the other room if you want.

SAUL: No really—

LEE: Just got Austin's color T.V. back from the shop. I can
90 watch a little amateur boxing now.

(LEE *and* AUSTIN *exchange looks.*)

SAUL: Oh—Yes.

LEE: You don't fool around in Television, do you Saul?

95   SAUL: Uh—I have in the past. Produced some T.V. Specials. Network stuff. But it's mainly features now.

LEE: That's where the big money is, huh?

SAUL: Yes. That's right.

AUSTIN: Why don't I call you tomorrow, Saul and we'll get
100   together. We can have lunch or something.

SAUL: That'd be terrific.

LEE: Right after the golf.

(Pause.)

SAUL: What?

LEE: You can have lunch right after the golf.

105   SAUL: Oh, right.

LEE: Austin was tellin' me that yer interested in stories.

SAUL: Well, we develop certain projects that we feel have commercial potential.

LEE: What kinda' stuff do ya' go in for?

110   SAUL: Oh, the usual. You know. Good love interest. Lots of action. *(Chuckles at AUSTIN.)*

LEE: Westerns?

SAUL: Sometimes.

AUSTIN: I'll give you a ring, Saul.

(AUSTIN tries to move SAUL across the kitchen but LEE blocks their way.)

115   LEE: I got a Western that'd knock yer lights out.

SAUL: Oh really?

LEE: Yeah. Contemporary Western. Based on a true story. 'Course I'm not a writer like my brother here. I'm not a man of the pen.

120   SAUL: Well—

LEE: I mean I can tell ya' a story off the tongue but I can't put it down on paper. That don't make any difference though does it?

SAUL: No, not really.

125   LEE: I mean plenty a' guys have stories don't they? True-life stories. Musta' been a lota' movies made from real life.

SAUL: Yes. I suppose so.

LEE: I haven't seen a good Western since "Lonely Are the Brave." You remember that movie?

130   SAUL: No, I'm afraid I—

LEE: Kirk Douglas. Helluva' movie. You remember that movie, Austin?

AUSTIN: Yes.

LEE: *(To SAUL.)* The man dies for the love of a horse.

135   SAUL: Is that right?

LEE: Yeah. Ya' hear the horse screamin' at the end of it. Rain's comin' down. Horse is screamin'. Then there's a shot. BLAM! Just a single shot like that. Then nothin' but the sound of rain. And Kirk Douglas is ridin' in the ambu-
140   lance. Ridin' away from the scene of the accident. And when he hears that shot he knows that his horse has died. He knows. And you see his eyes. And his eyes die. Right inside his face. And then his eyes close. And you know that he's died too. You know that Kirk Douglas has died
145   from the death of his horse.

SAUL: *(Eyes AUSTIN nervously.)* Well, it sounds like a great movie. I'm sorry I missed it.

LEE: Yeah, you shouldn't a' missed that one.

SAUL: I'll have to try to catch it some time. Arrange a screen-ing or something. Well, Austin, I'll have to hit the freeway before rush hour. 150

AUSTIN: *(Ushers him toward exit.)* It's good seeing you, Saul.

(AUSTIN and SAUL shake hands.)

LEE: So ya' think there's room for a real Western these days? A true-to-life Western?

SAUL: Well, I don't see why not. Why don't you uh—tell the story to Austin and have him write a little outline. 155

LEE: You'd take a look at it then?

SAUL: Yes. Sure. I'll give it a read-through. Always eager for new material. *(Smiles at AUSTIN.)*

LEE: That's great! You'd really read it then huh?

SAUL: It would just be my opinion of course. 160

LEE: That's all I want. Just an opinion. I happen to think it has a lota' possibilities.

SAUL: Well, it was great meeting you and I'll—

(SAUL and LEE shake.)

LEE: I'll call you tomorrow about the golf.

SAUL: Oh. Yes, right. 165

LEE: Austin's got your number, right?

SAUL: Yes.

LEE: So long Saul. *(Gives SAUL a pat on the back.)*

(SAUL exits, AUSTIN turns to LEE, looks at T.V. then back to lee.)

AUSTIN: Give me the keys.

(AUSTIN extends his hand toward LEE, LEE doesn't move, just stares at AUSTIN, smiles, lights to black.)

SCENE IV

Night. Coyotes in distance, fade, sound of typewriter in dark, crick-ets, candlelight in alcove, dim light in kitchen, lights reveal AUSTIN at glass table typing, LEE sits across from him, foot on table, drinking beer and whiskey, the T.V. is still on sink counter, AUSTIN types for a while, then stops.

LEE: All right, now read it back to me.

AUSTIN: I'm not reading it back to you, Lee. You can read it when we're finished. I can't spend all night on this.

LEE: You got better things to do?

AUSTIN: Let's just go ahead. Now what happens when he 5
leaves Texas?

LEE: Is he ready to leave Texas yet? I didn't know we were that far along. He's not ready to leave Texas.

AUSTIN: He's right at the border.

LEE: *(Sitting up.)* No, see this is one a' the crucial parts. Right 10
here. *(Taps paper with beer can.)* We can't rush through this. He's not right at the border. He's a good fifty miles from the border. A lot can happen in fifty miles.

AUSTIN: It's only an outline. We're not writing an entire script now. 15

LEE: Well ya' can't leave things out even if it is an outline. It's one a' the most important parts. Ya' can't go leavin' it out.

AUSTIN: Okay, okay. Let's just—get it done.

LEE: All right. Now. He's in the truck and he's got his horse trailer and his horse. 20

AUSTIN: We've already established that.

LEE: And he sees this other guy comin' up behind him in another truck. And that truck is pullin' a gooseneck.

AUSTIN: What's a gooseneck?

25 LEE: Cattle trailer. You know the kind with a gooseneck, goes right down in the bed a' the pick-up.

AUSTIN: Oh. All right. (*Types.*)

LEE: It's important.

AUSTIN: Okay. I got it.

30 LEE: All these details are important.

(AUSTIN *types as they talk.*)

AUSTIN: I've got it.

LEE: And this other guy's got his horse all saddled up in the back a' the gooseneck.

AUSTIN: Right.

35 LEE: So both these guys have got their horses right along with 'em, see.

AUSTIN: I understand.

LEE: Then this first guy suddenly realizes two things.

AUSTIN: The guy in front?

40 LEE: Right. The guy in front realizes two things almost at the same time. Simultaneous.

AUSTIN: What were the two things?

LEE: Number one, he realizes that the guy behind him is the husband of the woman he's been—

(LEE *makes gesture of screwing by pumping his arm.*)

45 AUSTIN: (*Sees* LEE's *gesture.*) Oh. Yeah.

LEE: And number two, he realizes he's in the middle of Tornado Country.

AUSTIN: What's "Tornado Country"?

LEE: Panhandle.

50 AUSTIN: Panhandle?

LEE: Sweetwater. Around in that area. Nothin'. Nowhere. And number three—

AUSTIN: I thought there was only two.

LEE: There's three. There's a third unforeseen realization.

55 AUSTIN: And what's that?

LEE: That he's runnin' outa' gas.

AUSTIN: (*Stops typing.*) Come on, Lee.

(AUSTIN *gets up, moves to kitchen, gets a glass of water.*)

LEE: Whadya' mean, "come on"? That's what it is. Write it down! He's runnin' outa' gas.

60 AUSTIN: It's too—

LEE: What? It's too what? It's too real! That's what ya' mean isn't it? It's too much like real life!

AUSTIN: It's not like real life! It's not enough like real life. Things don't happen like that.

65 LEE: What! Men don't fuck other men's women?

AUSTIN: Yes. But they don't end up chasing each other across the Panhandle. Through "Tornado Country."

LEE: They do in this movie!

AUSTIN: And they don't have horses conveniently along with them when they run out of gas! And they don't run out of gas either!

70 LEE: These guys run outa' gas! This is my story and one a' these guys runs outa' gas!

AUSTIN: It's just a dumb excuse to get them into a chase scene. It's contrived.   75

LEE: It is a chase scene! It's already a chase scene. They been chasin' each other fer days.

AUSTIN: So now they're supposed to abandon their trucks, climb on their horses and chase each other into the mountains?

LEE: (*Standing suddenly.*) There aren't any mountains in the   80
Panhandle! It's flat!

(LEE *turns violently toward windows in alcove and throws beer can at them.*)

LEE: Goddamn these crickets! (*Yells at crickets.*) Shut up out there! (*Pause, turns back toward table.*) This place is like a fuckin' rest home here. How're you supposed to think!

AUSTIN: You wanna' take a break?   85

LEE: No, I don't wanna' take a break! I wanna' get this done! This is my last chance to get this done.

AUSTIN: (*Moves back into alcove.*) All right. Take it easy.

LEE: I'm gonna' be leavin' this area. I don't have time to mess around here.   90

AUSTIN: Where are you going?

LEE: Never mind where I'm goin'! That's got nothin' to do with you. I just gotta' get this done. I'm not like you. Hangin' around bein' a parasite offa' other fools. I gotta' do this thing and get out.   95

(*Pause.*)

AUSTIN: A parasite? Me?

LEE: Yeah, you!

AUSTIN: After you break into people's houses and take their televisions?

LEE: They don't need their televisions! I'm doin' them a service.   100

AUSTIN: Give me back my keys, Lee.

LEE: Not until you write this thing! You're gonna' write this outline thing for me or that car's gonna' wind up in Arizona with a different paint job.   105

AUSTIN: You think you can force me to write this? I was doing you a favor.

LEE: Git off yer high horse will ya'! Favor! Big favor. Handin' down favors from the mountain top.

AUSTIN: Let's just write it, okay? Let's sit down and not get   110
upset and see if we can just get through this.

(AUSTIN *sits at typewriter.*)

(*Long pause.*)

LEE: Yer not gonna' even show it to him, are ya'?

AUSTIN: What?

LEE: This outline. You got no intention of showin' it to him. Yer just doin' this 'cause yer afraid a' me.   115

AUSTIN: You can show it to him yourself.

LEE: I will, boy! I'm gonna' read it to him on the golf course.

AUSTIN: And I'm not afraid of you either.

LEE: Then how come yer doin' it?

AUSTIN: (*Pause.*) So I can get my keys back.   120

(*Pause as* LEE *takes keys out of his pocket slowly and throws them on table, long pause,* AUSTIN *stares at keys.*)

LEE: There. Now you got yer keys back.

(AUSTIN *looks up at* LEE *but doesn't take keys.*)

LEE: Go ahead. There's yer keys.

(AUSTIN *slowly takes keys off table and puts them back in his own pocket.*)

Now what're you gonna' do? Kick me out?
AUSTIN: I'm not going to kick you out, Lee.
125 LEE: You couldn't kick me out, boy.
AUSTIN: I know.
LEE: So you can't even consider that one. (*Pause.*) You could call the police. That'd be the obvious thing.
AUSTIN: You're my brother.
130 LEE: That don't mean a thing. You go down to the L.A. Police Department there and ask them what kinda' people kill each other the most. What do you think they'd say?
AUSTIN: Who said anything about killing?
LEE: Family people. Brothers. Brothers-in-law. Cousins. Real
135 American-type people. They kill each other in the heat mostly. In the Smog-Alerts. In the Brush Fire Season. Right about this time a' year.
AUSTIN: This isn't the same.
LEE: Oh no? What makes it different?
140 AUSTIN: We're not insane. We're not driven to acts of violence like that. Not over a dumb movie script. Now sit down.

(*Long pause,* LEE *considers which way to go with it.*)

LEE: Maybe not. (*He sits back down at table across from* AUSTIN.) Maybe you're right. Maybe we're too intelligent, huh? (*Pause.*) We got our heads on our shoulders. One of us has
145 even got a Ivy League diploma. Now that means somethin' don't it? Doesn't that mean somethin'?
AUSTIN: Look, I'll write this thing for you, Lee. I don't mind writing it. I just don't want to get all worked up about it. It's not worth it. Now, come on. Let's just get through it, okay?
150 LEE: Nah. I think there's easier money. Lotsa' places I could pick up thousands. Maybe millions. I don't need this shit. I could go up to Sacramento Valley and steal me a diesel. Ten thousand a week dismantling one a' those suckers. Ten thousand a week!

(LEE *opens another beer, puts his foot back up on table.*)

155 AUSTIN: No, really, look, I'll write it out for you. I think it's a great idea.
LEE: Nah, you got yer own work to do. I don't wanna' interfere with yer life.
AUSTIN: I mean it'd be really fantastic if you could sell this.
160 Turn it into a movie. I mean it.

(*Pause.*)

LEE: Ya' think so huh?
AUSTIN: Absolutely. You could really turn your life around, you know. Change things.
LEE: I could get me a house maybe.
165 AUSTIN: Sure you could get a house. You could get a whole ranch if you wanted to.
LEE: (*Laughs.*) A ranch? I could get a ranch?

AUSTIN: 'Course you could. You know what a screenplay sells for these days?
LEE: No. What's it sell for? 170
AUSTIN: A lot. A whole lot of money.
LEE: Thousands?
AUSTIN: Yeah. Thousands.
LEE: Millions?
AUSTIN: Well— 175
LEE: We could get the old man outa' hock then.
AUSTIN: Maybe.
LEE: Maybe? Whadya' mean, maybe?
AUSTIN: I mean it might take more than money.
LEE: You were just tellin' me it'd change my whole life 180 around. Why wouldn't it change his?
AUSTIN: He's different.
LEE: Oh, he's of a different ilk huh?
AUSTIN: He's not gonna' change. Let's leave the old man out of it. 185
LEE: That's right. He's not gonna' change but I will. I'll just turn myself right inside out. I could be just like you then, huh? Sittin' around dreamin' stuff up. Gettin' paid to dream. Ridin' back and forth on the freeway just dreamin' my fool head off. 190
AUSTIN: It's not all that easy.
LEE: It's not, huh?
AUSTIN: No. There's a lot of work involved.
LEE: What's the toughest part? Deciding whether to jog or play tennis? 195

(*Long pause.*)

AUSTIN: Well, look. You can stay here—do whatever you want to. Borrow the car. Come in and out. Doesn't matter to me. It's not my house. I'll help you write this thing or—not. Just let me know what you want. You tell me.
LEE: Oh. So now suddenly you're at my service. Is that it? 200
AUSTIN: What do you want to do Lee?

(*Long pause,* LEE *stares at him then turns and dreams at windows.*)

LEE: I tell ya' what I'd do if I still had that dog. Ya' wanna' know what I'd do?
AUSTIN: What?
LEE: Head out to Ventura. Cook up a little match. God that 205 little dog could bear down. Lota' money in dog fightin'. Big money.

(*Pause.*)

AUSTIN: Why don't we try to see this through, Lee. Just for the hell of it. Maybe you've really got something here. What do you think? 210

(*Pause,* LEE *considers.*)

LEE: Maybe so. No harm in tryin' I guess. You think it's such a hot idea. Besides, I always wondered what'd be like to be you.
AUSTIN: You did?
LEE: Yeah, sure. I used to picture you walkin' around some campus with yer arms fulla' books. Blondes chasin' after ya'. 215
AUSTIN: Blondes? That's funny.
LEE: What's funny about it?

AUSTIN: Because I always used to picture you somewhere.

LEE: Where'd you picture me?

220 AUSTIN: Oh, I don't know. Different places. Adventures. You were always on some adventure.

LEE: Yeah.

AUSTIN: And I used to say to myself, "Lee's got the right idea. He's out there in the world and here I am. What am I do-

225 ing?"

LEE: Well you were settin' yourself up for somethin'.

AUSTIN: I guess.

LEE: We better get started on this thing then.

AUSTIN: Okay.

(AUSTIN *sits up at typewriter, puts new paper in.*)

230 LEE: Oh. Can I get the keys back before I forget?

(AUSTIN *hesitates.*)

You said I could borrow the car if I wanted, right? Isn't that what you said?

AUSTIN: Yeah. Right.

(AUSTIN *takes keys out of his pocket, sets them on table,* LEE *takes keys slowly, plays with them in his hand.*)

LEE: I could get a ranch, huh?

235 AUSTIN: Yeah. We have to write it first though.

LEE: Okay. Let's write it.

(*Lights start dimming slowly to end as* AUSTIN *types,* LEE *speaks.*)

So they take off after each other straight into an endless black prairie. The sun is just comin' down and they can feel the night on their backs. What they don't know is that each one

240 of 'em is afraid, see. Each one separately thinks that he's the only one that's afraid. And they keep ridin' like that straight into the night. Not knowing. And the one who's chasin' doesn't know where the other one is taking him. And the one who's being chased doesn't know where he's going.

(*Lights to black, typing stops in the dark, crickets fade.*)

ACT TWO

SCENE V

Morning. LEE *at the table in alcove with a set of golf clubs in a fancy leather bag,* AUSTIN *at sink washing a few dishes.*

AUSTIN: He really liked it, huh?

LEE: He wouldn't a' gave me these clubs if he didn't like it.

AUSTIN: He gave you the clubs?

LEE: Yeah. I told ya' he gave me the clubs. The bag too.

5 AUSTIN: I thought he just loaned them to you.

LEE: He said it was part a' the advance. A little gift like. Gesture of his good faith.

AUSTIN: He's giving you an advance?

LEE: Now what's so amazing about that? I told ya' it was a

10 good story. You even said it was a good story.

AUSTIN: Well that is really incredible Lee. You know how many guys spend their whole lives down here trying to break into this business? Just trying to get in the door?

LEE: (*Pulling clubs out of bag, testing them.*) I got no idea. How many?   15

(*Pause.*)

AUSTIN: How much of an advance is he giving you?

LEE: Plenty. We were talkin' big money out there. Ninth hole is where I sealed the deal.

AUSTIN: He made a firm commitment?

LEE: Absolutely.   20

AUSTIN: Well, I know Saul and he doesn't fool around when he says he likes something.

LEE: I thought you said you didn't know him.

AUSTIN: Well, I'm familiar with his tastes.

LEE: I let him get two up on me goin' into the back nine. He 25 was sure he had me cold. You shoulda' seen his face when I pulled out the old pitching wedge and plopped it pin-high, two feet from the cup. He 'bout shit his pants. "Where'd a guy like you ever learn how to play golf like that?" he says.   30

(LEE *laughs,* AUSTIN *stares at him.*)

AUSTIN: 'Course there's no contract yet. Nothing's final until it's on paper.

LEE: It's final, all right. There's no way he's gonna' back out of it now. We gambled for it.

AUSTIN: Saul, gambled?   35

LEE: Yeah, sure. I mean he liked the outline already so he wasn't risking that much. I just guaranteed it with my short game.

(*Pause.*)

AUSTIN: Well, we should celebrate or something. I think Mom left a bottle of champagne in the refrigerator. We should have a little toast.   40

(AUSTIN *gets glasses from cupboard, goes to refrigerator, pulls out bottle of champagne.*)

LEE: You shouldn't oughta' take her champagne, Austin. She's gonna' miss that.

AUSTIN: Oh, she's not going to mind. She'd be glad we put it to good use. I'll get her another bottle. Besides, it's perfect for the occasion.   45

(*Pause.*)

LEE: Yer gonna' get a nice fee fer writin' the script a' course. Straight fee.

(AUSTIN *stops, stares at* LEE, *puts glasses and bottle on table, pause.*)

AUSTIN: I'm writing the script?

LEE: That's what he said. Said we couldn't hire a better screen-writer in the whole town.   50

AUSTIN: But I'm already working on a script. I've got my own project. I don't have time to write two scripts.

LEE: No, he said he was gonna' drop that other one.

(*Pause.*)

AUSTIN: What? You mean mine? He's going to drop mine and do yours instead?   55

LEE: (*Smiles.*) Now look, Austin, it's jest beginner's luck ya' know. I mean I sank a fifty foot putt for this deal. No hard feelings.

(AUSTIN *goes to phone on wall, grabs it, starts dialing.*)

60   He's not gonna' be in, Austin. Told me he wouldn't be in 'till late this afternoon.

AUSTIN: (*Stays on phone, dialing, listen.*) I can't believe this. I just can't believe it. Are you sure he said that? Why would he drop mine?

LEE: That's what he told me.

65   AUSTIN: He can't do that without telling me first. Without talking to me at least. He wouldn't just make a decision like that without talking to me!

LEE: Well I was kinda' surprised myself. But he was real enthusiastic about my story.

(AUSTIN *hangs up phone violently, paces.*)

70   AUSTIN: What'd he say! Tell me everything he said!

LEE: I been tellin' ya'! He said he liked the story a whole lot. It was the first authentic Western to come along in a decade.

AUSTIN: He liked that story! Your story?

LEE: Yeah! What's so surprisin' about that?

75   AUSTIN: It's stupid! It's the dumbest story I ever heard in my life.

LEE: Hey, hold on! That's my story yer talkin' about!

AUSTIN: It's a bullshit story! It's idiotic. Two lamebrains chasing each other across Texas! Are you kidding? Who do you

80   think's going to go see a film like that?

LEE: It's not a film! It's a movie. There's a big difference. That's somethin' Saul told me.

AUSTIN: Oh he did, huh?

LEE: Yeah, he said, "In this business we make movies, Ameri-

85   can movies. Leave the films to the French."

AUSTIN: So you got real intimate with old Saul huh? He started pouring forth his vast knowledge of Cinema.

LEE: I think he liked me a lot, to tell ya' the truth. I think he felt I was somebody he could confide in.

90   AUSTIN: What'd you do, beat him up or something?

LEE: (*Stands fast.*) Hey, I've about had it with the insults buddy! You think yer the only one in the brain department here? Yer the only one that can sit around and cook things up? There's other people got ideas too, ya' know!

95   AUSTIN: You must've done something. Threatened him or something. Now what'd you do Lee?

LEE: I convinced him!

(LEE *makes sudden menacing lunge toward* AUSTIN, *wielding golf club above his head, stops himself, frozen moment, long pause,* LEE *lowers club.*)

AUSTIN: Oh, Jesus. You didn't hurt him did you?

(*Long silence,* LEE *sits back down at table.*)

Lee! Did you hurt him?

100   LEE: I didn't do nothin' to him! He liked my story. Pure and simple. He said it was the best story he's come across in a long, long time.

AUSTIN: That's what he told me about my story! That's the same thing he said to me.

LEE: Well, he musta' been lyin'. He musta' been lyin' to one   105
of us anyway.

AUSTIN: You can't come into this town and start pushing people around. They're gonna' put you away!

LEE: I never pushed anybody around! I beat him fair and square. (*Pause.*) They can't touch me anyway. They can't   110
put a finger on me. I'm gone. I can come in through the window and go out through the door. They never knew what hit 'em. You, yer stuck. Yer the one that's stuck. Not me. So don't be warnin' me what to do in this town.

(*Pause,* AUSTIN *crosses to table, sits at typewriter, rests.*)

AUSTIN: Lee, come on, level with me will you? It doesn't   115
make any sense that suddenly he'd throw my idea out the window. I've been talking to him for months. I've got too much at stake. Everything's riding on this project.

LEE: What's yer idea?

AUSTIN: It's just a simple love story.   120

LEE: What kinda' love story?

AUSTIN: (*Stands, cross into kitchen.*) I'm not telling you!

LEE: Ha! 'Fraid I'll steal it huh? Competition's gettin' kinda' close to home isn't it?

AUSTIN: Where did Saul say he was going?   125

LEE: He was gonna' take my story to a couple studios.

AUSTIN: That's *my* outline you know! I wrote that outline! You've got no right to be peddling it around.

LEE: You weren't ready to take credit for it last night.

AUSTIN: Give me my keys!   130

LEE: What?

AUSTIN: The keys! I want my keys back!

LEE: Where you goin'?

AUSTIN: Just give me my keys! I gotta' take a drive. I gotta' get out of here for a while.   135

LEE: Where you gonna' go, Austin?

AUSTIN: (*Pause.*) I might just drive out to the desert for a while. I gotta' think.

LEE: You can think here just as good. This is the perfect setup for thinkin'. We got some writin' to do here, boy. Now   140
let's just have us a little toast. Relax. We're partners now.

(LEE *pops the cork of the champagne bottle, pours two drinks as the lights fade to black.*)

SCENE VI

Afternoon. LEE *and* SAUL *in kitchen,* AUSTIN *in alcove.*

LEE: Now you tell him. You tell him, Mr. Kipper.

SAUL: Kimmer.

LEE: Kimmer. You tell him what you told me. He don't believe me.

AUSTIN: I don't want to hear it.   5

SAUL: It's really not a big issue, Austin. I was simply amazed by your brother's story and—

AUSTIN: Amazed? You lost a bet! You gambled with my material!

SAUL: That's really beside the point, Austin. I'm ready to go all the way with your brother's story. I think it has a great   10
deal of merit.

AUSTIN: I don't want to hear about it, okay? Go tell it to the executives! Tell it to somebody who's going to turn it into a package deal or something. A T.V. series. Don't tell it to me.

15 SAUL: But I want to continue with your project too, Austin. It's not as though we can't do both. We're big enough for that aren't we?

AUSTIN: "We"? *I* can't do both! I don't know about "we."

LEE: (*To* SAUL.) See, what'd I tell ya'. He's totally unsympathetic.

20 SAUL: Austin, there's no point in our going to another screenwriter for this. It just doesn't make sense. You're brothers. You know each other. There's a familiarity with the material that just wouldn't be possible otherwise.

AUSTIN: There's no familiarity with the material! None! I

25 don't know what "Tornado Country" is. I don't know what a "gooseneck" is. And I don't want to know! (*Pointing to* LEE.) He's a hustler! He's a bigger hustler than you are! If you can't see that, then—

LEE: (*To* AUSTIN.) Hey, now hold on. I didn't have to bring

30 this bone back to you, boy. I persuaded Saul here that you were the right man for the job. You don't have to go throwin' up favors in my face.

AUSTIN: Favors! I'm the one who wrote the fuckin' outline! You can't even spell.

35 SAUL: (*To* AUSTIN.) Your brother told me about the situation with your father.

(*Pause.*)

AUSTIN: What? (*Looks at* LEE.)

SAUL: That's right. Now we have a clear-cut deal here, Austin. We have big studio money standing behind this thing. Just

40 on the basis of your outline.

AUSTIN: (*To* SAUL.) What'd he tell you about my father?

SAUL: Well—that he's destitute. He needs money.

LEE: That's right. He does.

(AUSTIN *shakes his head, stares at them both.*)

AUSTIN: (*To* LEE.) And this little assignment is supposed to go

45 toward the old man? A charity project? Is that what this is? Did you cook this up on the ninth green too?

SAUL: It's a big slice, Austin.

AUSTIN: (*To* LEE.) I gave him money! I already gave him money. You know that. He drank it all up!

50 LEE: This is a different deal here.

SAUL: We can set up a trust for your father. A large sum of money. It can be doled out to him in parcels so he can't misuse it.

AUSTIN: Yeah, and who's doing the doling?

SAUL: Your brother volunteered.

(AUSTIN *laughs.*)

55 LEE: That's right. I'll make sure he uses it for groceries.

AUSTIN: (*To* SAUL.) I'm not doing this script! I'm not writing this crap for you or anybody else. You can't blackmail me into it. You can't threaten me into it. There's no way I'm doing it. So just give it up. Both of you.

(*Long pause.*)

60 SAUL: Well, that's it then. I mean this is an easy three hundred grand. Just for a first draft. It's incredible, Austin. We've got three different studios all trying to cut each other's throats to get this material. In one morning. That's how hot it is.

AUSTIN: Yeah, well you can afford to give me a percentage on 65 the outline then. And you better get the genius here an agent before he gets burned.

LEE: Saul's gonna' be my agent. Isn't that right, Saul?

SAUL: That's right. (*To* AUSTIN.) Your brother has really got something, Austin. I've been around too long not to rec- 70 ognize it. Raw talent.

AUSTIN: He's got a lota' balls is what he's got. He's taking you right down the river.

SAUL: Three hundred thousand, Austin. Just for a first draft. Now you've never been offered that kind of money before. 75

AUSTIN: I'm not writing it.

(*Pause.*)

SAUL: I see. Well—

LEE: We'll just go to another writer then. Right, Saul? Just hire us somebody with some enthusiasm. Somebody who can recognize the value of a good story. 80

SAUL: I'm sorry about this, Austin.

AUSTIN: Yeah.

SAUL: I mean I was hoping we could continue both things but now I don't see how it's possible.

AUSTIN: So you're dropping my idea altogether. Is that it? Just 85 trade horses in midstream? After all these months of meetings.

SAUL: I wish there was another way.

AUSTIN: I've got everything riding on this, Saul. You know that. It's my only shot. If this falls through— 90

SAUL: I have to go with what my instincts tell me—

AUSTIN: Your instincts!

SAUL: My gut reaction.

AUSTIN: You lost! That's your gut reaction. You lost a gamble. Now you're trying to tell me you like his story? How 95 could you possibly fall for that story? It's as phony as Hopalong Cassidy. What do you see in it? I'm curious.

SAUL: It has the ring of truth, Austin.

AUSTIN: (*Laughs.*) Truth?

LEE: It is true. 100

SAUL: Something about the real West.

AUSTIN: Why? Because it's got horses? Because it's got grown men acting like little boys?

SAUL: Something about the land. Your brother is speaking from experience. 105

AUSTIN: So am I!

SAUL: But nobody's interested in love these days, Austin. Let's face it.

LEE: That's right.

AUSTIN: (*To* SAUL.) He's been camped out on the desert for 110 three months. Talking to cactus. What's he know about what people wanna' see on the screen! I drive on the freeway every day. I swallow the smog. I watch the news in color. I shop in the Safeway. I'm the one who's in touch! Not him!

SAUL: I have to go now, Austin. 115

(SAUL *starts to leave.*)

AUSTIN: There's no such thing as the West anymore! It's a dead issue! It's dried up, Saul, and so are you.

(SAUL *stops and turns to* AUSTIN.)

SAUL: Maybe you're right. But I have to take the gamble, don't I?

120 AUSTIN: You're a fool to do this, Saul.

SAUL: I've always gone on my hunches. Always. And I've never been wrong. (*To* LEE.) I'll talk to you tomorrow, Lee.

LEE: All right, Mr. Kimmer.

125 SAUL: Maybe we could have some lunch.

LEE: Fine with me. (*Smiles at* AUSTIN.)

SAUL: I'll give you a ring.

(SAUL *exits, lights to black as brothers look at each other from a distance.*)

SCENE VII

Night. Coyotes, crickets, sound of typewriter in dark, candlelight up on LEE *at typewriter struggling to type with one finger system,* AUSTIN *sits sprawled out on kitchen floor with whiskey bottle, drunk.*

AUSTIN: (*Singing, from floor.*)

> "Red sails in the sunset
> Way out on the blue
> Please carry my loved one
> 5 Home safely to me
>
> Red sails in the sunset—"

LEE: (*Slams fist on table.*) Hey! Knock it off will ya'! I'm tryin' to concentrate here.

AUSTIN: (*Laughs.*) You're tryin' to concentrate?

10 LEE: Yeah. That's right.

AUSTIN: Now you're tryin' to concentrate.

LEE: Between you, the coyotes and the crickets a thought don't have much of a chance.

AUSTIN: "Between me, the coyotes and the crickets." What a 15 great title.

LEE: I don't need a title! I need a thought.

AUSTIN: (*Laughs.*) A thought! Here's a thought for ya'—

LEE: I'm not askin' fer yer thoughts! I got my own. I can do this thing on my own.

20 AUSTIN: You're going to write an entire script on your own?

LEE: That's right.

(*Pause.*)

AUSTIN: Here's a thought. Saul Kimmer—

LEE: Shut up will ya'!

AUSTIN: He thinks we're the same person.

25 LEE: Don't get cute.

AUSTIN: He does! He's lost his mind. Poor old Saul. (*Giggles.*) Thinks we're one and the same.

LEE: Why don't you ease up on that champagne.

AUSTIN: (*Holding up bottle.*) This isn't champagne anymore.
30   We went through the champagne a long time ago. This is serious stuff. The days of champagne are long gone.

LEE: Well, go outside and drink it.

AUSTIN: I'm enjoying your company, Lee. For the first time since your arrival I am finally enjoying your company.
35   And now you want me to go outside and drink alone?

LEE: That's right.

(LEE *reads through paper in typewriter, makes an erasure.*)

AUSTIN: You think you'll make more progress if you're alone? You might drive yourself crazy.

LEE: I could have this thing done in a night if I had a little si- 40 lence.

AUSTIN: Well you'd still have the crickets to contend with. The coyotes. The sounds of the Police Helicopters prowl- ing above the neighborhood. Slashing their searchlights down through the streets. Hunting for the likes of you.

LEE: I'm a screenwriter now! I'm legitimate. 45

AUSTIN: (*Laughing.*) A screenwriter!

LEE: That's right. I'm on salary. That's more'n I can say for you. I got an advance coming.

AUSTIN: This is true. This is very true. An advance. (*Pause.*) Well, maybe I oughta' go out and try my hand at your 50 trade. Since you're doing so good at mine.

LEE: Ha!

(LEE *attempts to type some more but gets the ribbon tangled up, starts trying to re-thread it as they continue talking.*)

AUSTIN: Well why not? You don't think I've got what it takes to sneak into people's houses and steal their T.V.s?

LEE: You couldn't steal a toaster without losin' yer lunch. 55

(AUSTIN *stands with a struggle, supports himself by the sink.*)

AUSTIN: You don't think I could sneak into somebody's house and steal a toaster?

LEE: Go take a shower or somethin' will ya!

(LEE *gets more tangled up with the typewriter ribbon, pulling it out of the machine as though it was fishing line.*)

AUSTIN: You really don't think I could steal a crumby toaster? How much you wanna' bet I can't steal a toaster! How 60 much? Go ahead! You're a gambler aren't you? Tell me how much yer willing to put on the line. Some part of your big advance? Oh, you haven't got that yet have you. I forgot.

LEE: All right. I'll bet you your car that you can't steal a toaster without gettin' busted. 65

AUSTIN: You already got my car!

LEE: Okay, your house then.

AUSTIN: What're you gonna' give me! I'm not talkin' about my house and my car, I'm talkin' about what are you gonna' give me. You don't have nothin' to give me. 70

LEE: I'll give you—shared screen credit. How 'bout that? I'll have it put in the contract that this was written by the both of us.

AUSTIN: I don't want my name on that piece of shit! I want something of value. You got anything of value? You got any tidbits from the desert? Any Rattlesnake bones? I'm 75 not a greedy man. Any little personal treasure will suffice.

LEE: I'm gonna' just kick yer ass out in a minute.

AUSTIN: Oh, so now you're gonna' kick me out! Now I'm the intruder. I'm the one who's invading your precious privacy.

LEE: I'm trying to do some screenwriting here!! 80

(LEE *stands, picks up typewriter, slams it down hard on table, pause, silence except for crickets.*)

AUSTIN: Well, you got everything you need. You got plenty a' coffee? Groceries. You got a car. A contract. (*Pause.*)

Might need a new typewriter ribbon but other than that you're pretty well fixed. I'll just leave ya' alone for a while.

(AUSTIN *tries to steady himself to leave,* LEE *makes a move toward him.*)

85 LEE: Where you goin'?
AUSTIN: Don't worry about me. I'm not the one to worry about.

(AUSTIN *weaves toward exit, stops.*)

LEE: What're you gonna' do? Just go wander out into the night?
AUSTIN: I'm gonna' make a little tour.
LEE: Why don't ya' just go to bed for Christ's sake. Yer makin'
90   me sick.
AUSTIN: I can take care a' myself. Don't worry about me.

(AUSTIN *weaves badly in another attempt to exit, he crashes to the floor,* LEE *goes to him but remains standing.*)

LEE: You want me to call your wife for ya' or something?
AUSTIN: (*From floor.*) My wife?
LEE: Yeah. I mean maybe she can help ya' out. Talk to ya' or
95   somethin'.
AUSTIN: (*Struggles to stand again.*) She's five hundred miles away. North. North of here. Up in the North country where things are calm. I don't need any help. I'm gonna' go outside and I'm gonna' steal a toaster. I'm gonna' steal some other
100   stuff too. I might even commit bigger crimes. Bigger than you ever dreamed of. Crimes beyond the imagination!

(AUSTIN *manages to get himself vertical, tries to head for exit again.*)

LEE: Just hang on a minute, Austin.
AUSTIN: Why? What for? You don't need my help, right? You got a handle on the project. Besides, I'm lookin' forward
105   to the smell of the night. The bushes. Orange blossoms. Dust in the driveways. Rain bird sprinklers. Lights in people's houses. You're right about the lights, Lee. Everybody else is livin' the life. Indoors. Safe. This is a Paradise down here. You know that? We're livin' in a Paradise. We've for-
110   gotten about that.
LEE: You sound just like the old man now.
AUSTIN: Yeah, well we all sound alike when we're sloshed. We just sorta' echo each other.
LEE: Maybe if we could work on this together we could bring
115   him back out here. Get him settled down some place.

(AUSTIN *turns violently toward* LEE, *takes a swing at him, misses and crashes to the floor again,* LEE *stays standing.*)

AUSTIN: I don't want him out here! I've had it with him! I went all the way out there! I went out of my way. I gave him money and all he did was play Al Jolson records and spit at me! I gave him money!

(*Pause.*)

120 LEE: Just help me a little with the characters, all right? You know how to do it, Austin.
AUSTIN: (*On floor, laughs.*) The characters!
LEE: Yeah. You know. The way they talk and stuff. I can hear it in my head but I can't get it down on paper.

AUSTIN: What characters?   125
LEE: The guys. The guys in the story.
AUSTIN: Those aren't characters.
LEE: Whatever you call 'em then. I need to write somethin' out.
AUSTIN: Those are illusions of characters.
LEE: I don't give a damn what ya' call 'em! You know what   130
I'm talkin' about!
AUSTIN: Those are fantasies of a long lost boyhood.
LEE: I gotta' write somethin' out on paper!!

(*Pause.*)

AUSTIN: What for? Saul's gonna' get you a fancy screenwriter isn't he?   135
LEE: I wanna' do it myself!
AUSTIN: Then do it! Yer on your own now, old buddy. You bulldogged yer way into contention. Now you gotta' carry it through.
LEE: I will but I need some advice. Just a couple a' things.   140
Come on, Austin. Just help me get 'em talkin' right. It won't take much.
AUSTIN: Oh, now you're having a little doubt huh? What happened? The pressure's on, boy. This is it. You gotta' come up with it now. You don't come up with a winner   145
on your first time out they just cut your head off. They don't give you a second chance ya' know.
LEE: I got a good story! I know it's a good story. I just need a little help is all.
AUSTIN: Not from me. Not from yer little old brother. I'm re-   150
tired.
LEE: You could save this thing for me, Austin. I'd give ya' half the money. I would. I only need half anyway. With this kinda' money I could be a long time down the road. I'd never bother ya' again. I promise. You'd never even see me again.   155
AUSTIN: (*Still on floor.*) You'd disappear?
LEE: I would for sure.
AUSTIN: Where would you disappear to?
LEE: That don't matter. I got plenty a' places.
AUSTIN: Nobody can disappear. The old man tried that.   160
Look where it got him. He lost his teeth.
LEE: He never had any money.
AUSTIN: I don't mean that. I mean his teeth! His real teeth. First he lost his real teeth, then he lost his false teeth. You never knew that did ya'? He never confided in you.   165
LEE: Nah, I never knew that.
AUSTIN: You wanna' drink?

(AUSTIN *offers bottle to* LEE, LEE *takes it, sits down on kitchen floor with* AUSTIN, *they share the bottle.*)

Yeah, he lost his real teeth one at a time. Woke up every morning with another tooth lying on the mattress. Finally, he decides he's gotta' get 'em all pulled out but he doesn't   170
have any money. Middle of Arizona with no money and no insurance and every morning another tooth is lying on the mattress. (*Takes a drink.*) So what does he do?
LEE: I dunno'. I never knew about that.
AUSTIN: He begs the government. G.I. Bill or some damn   175
thing. Some pension plan he remembers in the back of his head. And they send him out the money.
LEE: They did?

(They keep trading the bottle between them, taking drinks.)

AUSTIN: Yeah. They send him the money but it's not enough
180   money. Costs a lot to have all yer teeth yanked. They
charge by the individual tooth, ya' know. I mean one
tooth isn't equal to another tooth. Some are more expensive. Like the big ones in the back—

LEE: So what happened?

185 AUSTIN: So he locates a Mexican dentist in Juarez who'll do
the whole thing for a song. And he takes off hitchhiking
to the border.

LEE: Hitchhiking?

AUSTIN: Yeah. So how long you think it takes him to get to
190   the border? A man his age.

LEE: I dunno.

AUSTIN: Eight days it takes him. Eight days in the rain and the
sun and every day he's droppin' teeth on the blacktop nobody'll pick him up 'cause his mouth's full a' blood.

(Pause, they drink.)

195   So finally he stumbles into the dentist. Dentist takes all his
money and all his teeth. And there he is, in Mexico, with
his gums sewed up and his pockets empty.

(Long silence, AUSTIN drinks.)

LEE: That's it?

AUSTIN: Then I go out to see him, see. I go out there and I
200   take him out for a nice Chinese dinner. But he doesn't eat.
All he wants to do is drink Martinis outa' plastic cups.
And he takes his teeth out and lays 'em on the table 'cause
he can't stand the feel of 'em. And we ask the waitress for
one a' those doggie bags to take the Chop Suey home in.
205   So he drops his teeth in the doggie bag along with the
Chop Suey. And then we go out to hit all the bars up and
down the highway. Says he wants to introduce me to all
his buddies. And in one a' those bars, in one a' those bars
up and down the highway, he left that doggie bag with his
210   teeth laying in the Chop Suey.

LEE: You never found it?

AUSTIN: We went back but we never did find it. *(Pause.)* Now
that's a true story. True to life.

(They drink as lights fade to black.)

SCENE VIII

*Very early morning, between night and day. No crickets, coyotes yap-
ping feverishly in distance before light comes up, a small fire blazes up
in the dark from alcove area, sound of LEE smashing typewriter with
a golf club, lights coming up, LEE seen smashing typewriter methodically then dropping pages of his script into a burning bowl set on the
floor of alcove, flames leap up, AUSTIN has a whole bunch of stolen
toasters lined up on the sink counter along with LEE's stolen T.V., the
toasters are of a wide variety of models, mostly chrome, AUSTIN goes
up and down the line of toasters, breathing on them and polishing
them with a dish towel, both men are drunk, empty whiskey bottles
and beer cans litter floor of kitchen, they share a half empty bottle on
one of the chairs in the alcove, LEE keeps periodically taking deliberate
ax-chops at the typewriter using a nine-iron as AUSTIN speaks, all of
their mother's house plants are dead and drooping.*

AUSTIN: *(Polishing toasters.)* There's gonna' be a general lack of
toast in the neighborhood this morning. Many, many unhappy, bewildered breakfast faces. I guess it's best not to
even think of the victims. Not to even entertain it. Is that
the right psychology?   5

LEE: *(Pauses.)* What?

AUSTIN: Is that the correct criminal psychology? Not to
think of the victims?

LEE: What victims?

*(LEE takes another swipe at typewriter with nine-iron, adds pages to
the fire.)*

AUSTIN: The victims of crime. Of breaking and entering. I 10
mean is it a prerequisite for a criminal not to have a conscience?

LEE: Ask a criminal.

(Pause, LEE stares at AUSTIN.)

What're you gonna' do with all those toasters? That's the
dumbest thing I ever saw in my life.   15

AUSTIN: I've got hundreds of dollars worth of household appliances here. You may not realize that.

LEE: Yeah, and how many hundreds of dollars did you walk
right past?

AUSTIN: It was toasters you challenged me to. Only toasters. 20
I ignored every other temptation.

LEE: I never challenged you! That's no challenge. Anybody
can steal a toaster.

(LEE smashes typewriter again.)

AUSTIN: You don't have to take it out on my typewriter ya'
know. It's not the machine's fault that you can't write. It's 25
a sin to do that to a good machine.

LEE: A sin?

AUSTIN: When you consider all the writers who never even
had a machine. Who would have given an eyeball for a
good typewriter. Any typewriter.   30

(LEE smashes typewriter again.)

AUSTIN: *(Polishing toasters.)* All the ones who wrote on match-
book covers. Paper bags. Toilet paper. Who had their
writing destroyed by their jailers. Who persisted beyond
all odds. Those writers would find it hard to understand
your actions.   35

*(LEE comes down on typewriter with one final crushing blow of the
nine-iron then collapses in one of the chairs, takes a drink from bottle, pause.)*

AUSTIN: *(After pause.)* Not to mention demolishing a perfectly good golf club. What about all the struggling
golfers? What about Lee Trevino? What do you think he
would've said when he was batting balls around with
broomsticks at the age of nine. Impoverished.   40

(Pause.)

LEE: What time is it anyway?

AUSTIN: No idea. Time stands still when you're havin' fun.

LEE: Is it too late to call a woman? You know any women?

AUSTIN: I'm a married man.

45   LEE: I mean a local woman.

(AUSTIN *looks out at light through window above sink.*)

AUSTIN: It's either too late or too early. You're the nature en-
thusiast. Can't you tell the time by the light in the sky?
Orient yourself around the North Star or something?

LEE: I can't tell anything.

50   AUSTIN: Maybe you need a little breakfast. Some toast! How
'bout some toast?

(AUSTIN *goes to cupboard, pulls out loaf of bread and starts dropping
slices into every toaster,* LEE *stays sitting, drinks, watches* AUSTIN.)

LEE: I don't need toast. I need a woman.

AUSTIN: A woman isn't the answer. Never was.

LEE: I'm not talkin' about permanent. I'm talkin' about tem-
55   porary.

AUSTIN: (*Putting toast in toasters.*) We'll just test the merits of
these little demons. See which brands have a tendency to
burn. See which one can produce a perfectly golden piece
of fluffy toast.

60   LEE: How much gas you got in yer car?

AUSTIN: I haven't driven my car for days now. So I haven't
had an opportunity to look at the gas gauge.

LEE: Take a guess. You think there's enough to get me to Bakersfield?

65   AUSTIN: Bakersfield? What's in Bakersfield?

LEE: Just never mind what's in Bakersfield! You think there's
enough goddamn gas in the car!

AUSTIN: Sure.

LEE: Sure. You could care less, right. Let me run outa' gas on
70   the Grapevine. You could give a shit.

AUSTIN: I'd say there was enough gas to get you just about
any-where, Lee. With your determination and guts.

LEE: What the hell time is it anyway?

(LEE *pulls out his wallet, starts going through dozens of small pieces
of paper with phone numbers written on them, drops some on the
floor, drops others in the fire.*)

AUSTIN: Very early. This is the time of morning when the
75   coyotes kill people's cocker spaniels. Did you hear them?
That's what they were doing out there. Luring innocent
pets away from their homes.

LEE: (*Searching through his papers.*) What's the area code for
Bakersfield? You know?

80   AUSTIN: You could always call the operator.

LEE: I can't stand that voice they give ya'.

AUSTIN: What voice?

LEE: That voice that warns you that if you'd only tried harder
to find the number in the phone book you wouldn't have
85   to be calling the operator to begin with.

(LEE *gets up, holding a slip of paper from his wallet, stumbles toward
phone on wall, yanks receiver, starts dialing.*)

AUSTIN: Well I don't understand why you'd want to talk to
anybody else anyway. I mean you can talk to me. I'm your
brother.

LEE: (*Dialing.*) I wanna' talk to a woman. I haven't heard a
woman's voice in a long time.   90

AUSTIN: Not since the Botanist?

LEE: What?

AUSTIN: Nothing. (*Starts singing as he tends toast.*)

"Red sails in the sunset
Way out on the blue   95
Please carry my loved one
Home safely to me"

LEE: Hey, knock it off will ya'! This is long distance here.

AUSTIN: Bakersfield?

LEE: Yeah, Bakersfield. It's Kern County.   100

AUSTIN: Well, what County are *we* in?

LEE: You better get yourself a 7-Up, boy.

AUSTIN: One County's as good as another.

(AUSTIN *hums "Red Sails" softly as* LEE *talks on phone.*)

LEE: (*To phone.*) Yeah, operator look—first off I wanna' know
the area code for Bakersfield. Right. Bakersfield! Okay.   105
Good. Now I wanna' know if you can help me track somebody down. (*Pause.*) No, no I mean a phone number. Just a
phone number. Okay. (*Holds a piece of paper up and reads it.*)
Okay, the name is Melly Ferguson. Melly. (*Pause.*) I dunno'.
Melly. Maybe. Yeah. Maybe Melanie. Yeah. Melanie Fer-   110
guson. Okay. (*Pause.*) What? I can't hear ya' so good. Sounds
like yer under the ocean. (*Pause.*) You got ten Melanie Fergusons? How could that be? Ten Melanie Fergusons in
Bakersfield? Well gimme all of 'em then. (*Pause.*) What d'ya
mean? Gimme all ten Melanie Fergusons! That's right. Just   115
a second. (*To* AUSTIN.) Gimme a pen.

AUSTIN: I don't have a pen.

LEE: Gimme a pencil then!

AUSTIN: I don't have a pencil.

LEE: (*To phone.*) Just a second, operator. (*To* AUSTIN.) Yer a   120
writer and ya' don't have a pen or a pencil!

AUSTIN: I'm not a writer. You're a writer.

LEE: I'm on the phone here! Get me a pen or a pencil.

AUSTIN: I gotta' watch the toast.

LEE: (*To phone.*) Hang on a second, operator.   125

(LEE *lets the phone drop then starts pulling all the drawers in the
kitchen out on the floor and dumping the contents, searching for a
pencil,* AUSTIN *watches him casually.*)

LEE: (*Crashing through drawers, throwing contents around kitchen.*)
This is the last time I try to live with people, boy! I can't believe it. Here I am! Here I am again in a desperate situation!
This would never happen out on the desert. I would never
be in this kinda' situation out on the desert. Isn't there a pen   130
or a pencil in this house! Who lives in this house anyway!

AUSTIN: Our mother.

LEE: How come she don't have a pen or a pencil! She's a social person isn't she? Doesn't she have to make shopping
lists? She's gotta' have a pencil. (*Finds a pencil.*) Aaha! (*He   135
rushes back to phone, picks up receiver.*) All right operator.
Operator? Hey! Operator! Goddamnit!

(LEE *rips the phone off the wall and throws it down, goes back to
chair and falls into it, drinks, long pause.*)

AUSTIN: She hung up?

LEE: Yeah, she hung up. I knew she was gonna' hang up. I
140   could hear it in her voice.

(LEE *starts going through his slips of paper again.*)

AUSTIN: Well, you're probably better off staying here with me
    anyway. I'll take care of you.
LEE: I don't need takin' care of! Not by you anyway.
AUSTIN: Toast is almost ready.

(AUSTIN *starts buttering all the toast as it pops up.*)

145 LEE: I don't want any toast!

(*Long pause.*)

AUSTIN: You gotta' eat something. Can't just drink. How long
    have we been drinking, anyway?
LEE: (*Looking through slips of paper.*) Maybe it was Fresno.
    What's the area code for Fresno? How could I have lost
150   that number! She was beautiful.

(*Pause.*)

AUSTIN: Why don't you just forget about that, Lee. Forget
    about the woman.
LEE: She had green eyes. You know what green eyes do to me?
AUSTIN: I know but you're not gonna' get it on with her now
155   anyway. It's dawn already. She's in Bakersfield for Christ's
    sake.

(*Long pause, LEE considers the situation.*)

LEE: Yeah. (*Looks at windows.*) It's dawn?
AUSTIN: Let's just have some toast and—
LEE: What is this bullshit with the toast anyway! You make it
160   sound like salvation or something. I don't want any god-
    damn toast! How many times I gotta' tell ya'! (LEE *gets up,
    crosses upstage to windows in alcove, looks out,* AUSTIN *butters
    toast.*)
AUSTIN: Well it is like salvation sort of. I mean the smell. I
165   love the smell of toast. And the sun's coming up. It makes
    me feel like anything's possible. Ya' know?
LEE: (*Back to* AUSTIN, *facing windows upstage.*) So go to church
    why don't ya'.
AUSTIN: Like a beginning. I love beginnings.
170 LEE: Oh yeah. I've always been kinda' partial to endings myself.
AUSTIN: What if I come with you, Lee?
LEE: (*Pause as* LEE *turns toward* AUSTIN.) What?
AUSTIN: What if I come with you out to the desert?
LEE: Are you kiddin'?
175 AUSTIN: No. I'd just like to see what it's like.
LEE: You wouldn't last a day out there pal.
AUSTIN: That's what you said about the toasters. You said I
    couldn't steal a toaster either.
LEE: A toaster's got nothin' to do with the desert.
180 AUSTIN: I could make it, Lee. I'm not that helpless. I can cook.
LEE: Cook?
AUSTIN: I can.
LEE: So what! You can cook. Toast.
AUSTIN: I can make fires. I know how to get fresh water from
185   condensation.

(AUSTIN *stacks buttered toast up in a tall stack on plate.*)

(LEE *slams table.*)

LEE: It's not somethin' you learn out of a Boy Scout hand-
    book!
AUSTIN: Well how do you learn it then! How're you supposed
    to learn it!

(*Pause.*)

LEE: Ya' just learn it, that's all. Ya' learn it 'cause ya' have to
    learn it. You don't *have* to learn it.   190
AUSTIN: You could teach me.
LEE: (*Stands.*) What're you, crazy or somethin'? You went to
    college. Here, you are down here, rollin' in bucks. Floatin'
    up and down in elevators. And you wanna' learn how to
    live on the desert!   195
AUSTIN: I do, Lee. I really do. There's nothin' down here for
    me. There never was. When we were kids here it was dif-
    ferent. There was a life here then. But now—I keep
    comin' down here thinkin' it's the fifties or somethin'. I
    keep finding myself getting off the freeway at familiar   200
    landmarks that turn out to be unfamiliar. On the way to
    appointments. Wandering down streets I thought I recog-
    nized that turn out to be replicas of streets I remember.
    Streets I misremember. Streets I can't tell if I lived on or
    saw in a postcard. Fields that don't even exist anymore. 205
LEE: There's no point cryin' about that now.
AUSTIN: There's nothin' real down here, Lee! Least of all me!
LEE: Well I can't save you from that!
AUSTIN: You can let me come with you.
LEE: No dice, pal.   210
AUSTIN: You could let me come with you, Lee!
LEE: Hey, do you actually think I chose to live out in the mid-
    dle a' nowhere? Do ya'? Ya' think it's some kinda' philo-
    sophical decision I took or somethin'? I'm livin' out there
    'cause I can't make it here! And yer bitchin' to me about   215
    all yer success!
AUSTIN: I'd cash it all in in a second. That's the truth.
LEE: (*Pause, shakes his head.*) I can't believe this.
AUSTIN: Let me go with you.
LEE: Stop sayin' that will ya'! Yer worse than a dog.   220

(AUSTIN *offers out the plate of neatly stacked toast to* LEE.)

AUSTIN: You want some toast?

(LEE *suddenly explodes and knocks the plate out of* AUSTIN's *hand,
toast goes flying, long frozen moment where it appears* LEE *might go
all the way this time when* AUSTIN *breaks it by slowly lowering himself to his knees and begins gathering the scattered toast from the floor
and stacking it back on the plate,* LEE *begins to circle* AUSTIN *in a
slow, predatory way, crushing pieces of toast in his wake, no words for
a while,* AUSTIN *keeps gathering toast, even the crushed pieces.*)

LEE: Tell ya' what I'll do, little brother. I might just consider
    makin' you a deal. Little trade. (AUSTIN *continues gathering
    toast as* LEE *circles him through this.*) You write me up this
    screenplay thing just like I tell ya'. I mean you can use all yer 225
    usual tricks and stuff. Yer fancy language. Yer artistic hocus
    pocus. But ya' gotta' write everything like I say. Every move.
    Every time they run outa' gas, they run outa' gas. Every time
    they wanna' jump on a horse, they do just that. If they

230 wanna' stay in Texas, by God they'll stay in Texas! (*Keeps circling.*) And you finish the whole thing up for me. Top to bottom. And you put my name on it. And I own all the rights. And every dime goes in my pocket. You do that and I'll sure enough take ya' with me to the desert. (LEE *stops,* 235 *pause, looks down at* AUSTIN.) How's that sound?

(*Pause as* AUSTIN *stands slowly holding plate of demolished toast, their faces are very close, pause.*)

AUSTIN: It's a deal.

(LEE *stares straight into* AUSTIN's *eyes, then he slowly takes a piece of toast off the plate, raises it to his mouth and takes a huge crushing bite never taking his eyes off* AUSTIN's *as* lee *crunches into the toast the lights black out.*)

SCENE IX

Mid-day. No sound, blazing heat, the stage is ravaged; bottles, toasters, smashed typewriter, ripped out telephone, etc. All the debris from previous scene is now starkly visible in intense yellow light, the effect should be like a desert junkyard at high noon, the coolness of the preceding scenes is totally obliterated. AUSTIN *is seated at table in alcove, shirt open, pouring with sweat, hunched over a writing notebook, scribbling notes desperately with a ballpoint pen.* LEE *with no shirt, beer in hand, sweat pouring down his chest, is walking a slow circle around the table, picking his way through the objects, sometimes kicking them aside.*

LEE: (*As he walks.*) All right, read it back to me. Read it back to me!
AUSTIN: (*Scribbling at top speed.*) Just a second.
LEE: Come on, come on! Just read what ya' got.
5 AUSTIN: I can't keep up! It's not the same as if I had a typewriter.
LEE: Just read what we got so far. Forget about the rest.
AUSTIN: All right. Let's see—okay—(*Wipes sweat from his face, reads as* LEE *circles.*) Luke says uh—
LEE: Luke?
10 AUSTIN: Yeah.
LEE: His name's Luke? All right, all right—we can change the names later. What's he say? Come on, come on.
AUSTIN: He says uh—(*Reading.*) "I told ya' you were a fool to follow me in here. I know this prairie like the back a' my
15 hand."
LEE: No, no, no! That's not what I said. I never said that.
AUSTIN: That's what I wrote.
LEE: It's not what I said. I never said "like the back a' my hand." That's stupid. That's one a' those—whadya' call it?
20 Whadya' call that?
AUSTIN: What?
LEE: Whadya' call it when somethin's been said a thousand times before. Whadya' call that?
AUSTIN: Um—a cliché?
25 LEE: Yeah. That's right. Cliché. That's what that is. A cliché. "The back a' my hand." That's stupid.
AUSTIN: That's what you said.
LEE: I never said that! And even if I did, that's where yer supposed to come in. That's where yer supposed to change it
30 to somethin' better.
AUSTIN: Well how am I supposed to do that and write down what you say at the same time?

LEE: Ya' just do, that's all! You hear a stupid line you change it. That's yer job.
AUSTIN: All right. (*Makes more notes.*) 35
LEE: What're you changin' it to?
AUSTIN: I'm not changing it. I'm just trying to catch up.
LEE: Well change it! We gotta' change that, we can't leave that in there like that. ". . . the back a' my hand." That's dumb.
AUSTIN: (*Stops writing, sits back.*) All right. 40
LEE: (*Pacing.*) So what'll we change it to?
AUSTIN: Um—How 'bout—"I'm on intimate terms with this prairie."
LEE: (*To himself considering line as he walks.*) "I'm on intimate terms with this prairie." Intimate terms, intimate terms. 45
Intimate—that means like uh—sexual right?
AUSTIN: Well—yeah—or—
LEE: He's on sexual terms with the prairie? How dya' figure that?
AUSTIN: Well it doesn't necessarily have to mean sexual.
LEE: What's it mean then? 50
AUSTIN: It means uh—close—personal—
LEE: All right. How's it sound? Put it into the uh—the line there. Read it back. Let's see how it sounds. (*To himself.*) "Intimate terms."
AUSTIN: (*Scribbles in notebook.*) Okay. It'd go something like 55
this: (*Reads.*) "I told ya' you were a fool to follow me in here. I'm on intimate terms with this prairie."
LEE: That's good. I like that. That's real good.
AUSTIN: You do?
LEE: Yeah. Don't you? 60
AUSTIN: Sure.
LEE: Sounds original now. "Intimate terms." That's good. Okay. Now we're cookin! That has a real ring to it.

(AUSTIN *makes more notes,* LEE *walks around, pours beer on his arms and rubs it over his chest feeling good about the new progress, as he does this* MOM *enters unobtrusively down left with her luggage, she stops and stares at the scene still holding luggage as the two men continue, unaware of her presence,* AUSTIN *absorbed in his writing,* LEE *cooling himself off with beer.*)

LEE: (*Continues.*) "He's on intimate terms with this prairie." Sounds real mysterious and kinda' threatening at the same 65
time.
AUSTIN: (*Writing rapidly.*) Good.
LEE: Now—(LEE *turns and suddenly sees* MOM, *he stares at her for a while, she stares back,* AUSTIN *keeps writing feverishly, not noticing,* LEE *walks slowly over to* MOM *and takes a closer look, long pause.*) 70
LEE: Mom?

(AUSTIN *looks up suddenly from his writing, sees* MOM, *stands quickly, long pause,* MOM *surveys the damage.*)

AUSTIN: Mom. What're you doing back?
MOM: I'm back.
LEE: Here, lemme take those for ya.

(LEE *sets beer on counter then takes both her bags but doesn't know where to set them down in the sea of junk so he just keeps holding them.*)

AUSTIN: I wasn't expecting you back so soon. I thought uh— 75
How was Alaska?
MOM: Fine.

LEE: See any igloos?

MOM: No. Just glaciers.

80 AUSTIN: Cold huh?

MOM: What?

AUSTIN: It must've been cold up there?

MOM: Not really.

LEE: Musta' been colder than this here. I mean we're havin' a
85   real scorcher here.

MOM: Oh? (*She looks at damage.*)

LEE: Yeah. Must be in the hundreds.

AUSTIN: You wanna' take your coat off, Mom?

MOM: No. (*Pause, she surveys space.*) What happened in here?

90 AUSTIN: Oh um—Me and Lee were just sort of celebrating
   and uh—

MOM: Celebrating?

AUSTIN: Yeah. Uh—Lee sold a screenplay. A story, I mean.

MOM: Lee did?

95 AUSTIN: Yeah.

MOM: Not you?

AUSTIN: No. Him.

MOM: (*To* LEE.) You sold a screenplay?

LEE: Yeah. That's right. We're just sorta' finishing it up right
100   now. That's what we're doing here.

AUSTIN: Me and Lee are going out to the desert to live.

MOM: You and Lee?

AUSTIN: Yeah. I'm taking off with Lee.

MOM: (*She looks back and forth at each of them, pause.*) You
105   gonna go live with your father?

AUSTIN: No. We're going to a different desert Mom.

MOM: I see. Well, you'll probably wind up on the same desert
   sooner or later. What're all these toasters doing here?

AUSTIN: Well—we had kind of a contest.

110 MOM: Contest?

LEE: Yeah.

AUSTIN: Lee won.

MOM: Did you win a lot of money, Lee?

LEE: Well not yet. It's comin' in any day now.

115 MOM: (*To* LEE.) What happened to your shirt?

LEE: Oh. I was sweatin' like a pig and I took it off.

(AUSTIN *grabs* LEE's *shirt off the table and tosses it to him,* LEE *sets
down suitcases and puts his shirt on.*)

MOM: Well it's one hell of a mess in here isn't it?

AUSTIN: Yeah, I'll clean it up for you, Mom. I just didn't know
   you were coming back so soon.

120 MOM: I didn't either.

AUSTIN: What happened?

MOM: Nothing. I just started missing all my plants.

(*She notices dead plants.*)

AUSTIN: Oh.

MOM: Oh, they're all dead aren't they. (*She crosses toward them,*
125   *examines them closely.*) You didn't get a chance to water I
   guess.

AUSTIN: I was doing it and then Lee came and—

LEE: Yeah I just distracted him a whole lot here, Mom. It's not
   his fault.

(*Pause, as* MOM *stares at plants.*)

MOM: Oh well, one less thing to take care of I guess. (*Turns* 130
toward brothers.) Oh, that reminds me—You boys will
probably never guess who's in town. Try and guess.

(*Long pause, brothers stare at her.*)

AUSTIN: Whadya' mean, Mom?

MOM: Take a guess. Somebody very important has come to
   town. I read it, coming down on the Greyhound. 135

LEE: Somebody very important?

MOM: See if you can guess. You'll never guess.

AUSTIN: Mom—we're trying to uh—(*Points to writing pad.*)

MOM: Picasso. (*Pause.*) Picasso's in town. Isn't that incredible?
   Right now. 140

(*Pause.*)

AUSTIN: Picasso's dead, Mom.

MOM: No, he's not dead. He's visiting the museum. I read it
   on the bus. We have to go down there and see him.

AUSTIN: Mom—

MOM: This is the chance of a lifetime. Can you imagine? We 145
   could all go down and meet him. All three of us.

LEE: Uh—I don't think I'm really up fer meetin' anybody
   right now. I'm uh—What's his name?

MOM: Picasso! Picasso! You've never heard of Picasso? Austin,
   you've heard of Picasso. 150

AUSTIN: Mom, we're not going to have time.

MOM: It won't take long. We'll just hop in the car and go
   down there. An opportunity like this doesn't come along
   every day.

AUSTIN: We're gonna' be leavin' here, Mom! 155

(*Pause.*)

MOM: Oh.

LEE: Yeah.

(*Pause.*)

MOM: You're both leaving?

LEE: (*Looks at* AUSTIN.) Well we were thinkin' about that before but now I— 160

AUSTIN: No, we are! We're both leaving. We've got it all
   planned.

MOM: (*To* AUSTIN.) Well you can't leave. You have a family.

AUSTIN: I'm leaving. I'm getting out of here.

LEE: (*To* MOM.) I don't really think Austin's cut out for the 165
   desert do you?

MOM: No. He's not.

AUSTIN: I'm going with you, Lee!

MOM: He's too thin.

LEE: Yeah, he'd just burn up out there. 170

AUSTIN: (*To* LEE.) We just gotta' finish this screenplay and
   then we're gonna' take off. That's the plan. That's what you
   said. Come on, let's get back to work, Lee.

LEE: I can't work under these conditions here. It's too hot.

AUSTIN: Then we'll do it on the desert. 175

LEE: Don't be tellin' me what we're gonna do!

MOM: Don't shout in the house.

LEE: We're just gonna' have to postpone the whole deal.

AUSTIN: I can't postpone it! It's gone past postponing! I'm
180 doing everything you said. I'm writing down exactly what
  you tell me.
LEE: Yeah, but you were right all along see. It is a dumb story.
  "Two lamebrains chasin' each other across Texas." That's
  what you said, right?
185 AUSTIN: I never said that.

(LEE *sneers in* AUSTIN'S *face then turns to* MOM.)

LEE: I'm gonna' just borrow some a' your antiques, Mom. You
  don't mind do ya'? Just a few plates and things. Silverware.

(LEE *starts going through all the cupboards in kitchen pulling out
plates and stacking them on counter as* MOM *and* AUSTIN *watch.*)

MOM: You don't have any utensils on the desert?
LEE: Nah, I'm fresh out.
190 AUSTIN: (*To* LEE.) What're you doing?
MOM: Well some of those are very old. Bone China.
LEE: I'm tired of eatin' outa' my bare hands, ya' know. It's not
  civilized.
AUSTIN: (*To* LEE.) What're you doing? We made a deal!
195 MOM: Couldn't you borrow the plastic ones instead? I have
  plenty of plastic ones.
LEE: (*As he stacks plates.*) It's not the same. Plastic's not the
  same at all. What I need is somethin' authentic. Somethin'
  to keep me in touch. It's easy to get outa' touch out there.
200 Don't worry I'll get 'em back to ya'.

(AUSTIN *rushes up to* LEE, *grabs him by shoulders.*)

AUSTIN: You can't just drop the whole thing, Lee!

(LEE *turns, pushes* AUSTIN *in the chest knocking him backwards into
the alcove,* MOM *watches numbly, lee returns to collecting the plates,
silverware, etc.*)

MOM: You boys shouldn't fight in the house. Go outside and fight.
LEE: I'm not fightin'. I'm leavin'.
MOM: There's been enough damage done already.
205 LEE: (*His back to* AUSTIN *and* MOM, *stacking dishes on counter.*)
  I'm clearin' outa' here once and for all. All this town does
  is drive a man insane. Look what it's done to Austin there.
  I'm not lettin' that happen to me. Sell myself down the
  river. No sir. I'd rather be a hundred miles from nowhere
210 than let that happen to me.

(*During this* AUSTIN *has picked up the ripped-out phone from the
floor and wrapped the cord tightly around both his hands, he lunges
at* LEE *whose back is still to him, wraps the cord around* LEE'S *neck,
plants a foot in lee's back and pulls back on the cord, tightening it,*
LEE *chokes desperately, can't speak and can't reach* AUSTIN *with his
arms,* AUSTIN *keeps applying pressure on* LEE'S *back with his foot,
bending him into the sink,* MOM *watches.*)

AUSTIN: (*Tightening cord.*) You're not goin' anywhere! You're
  not takin' anything with you. You're not takin' my car!
  You're not takin' the dishes! You're not takin' anything!
  You're stayin' right here!
215 MOM: You'll have to stop fighting in the house. There's plenty
  of room outside to fight. You've got the whole outdoors
  to fight in.

(LEE *tries to tear himself away, he crashes across the stage like an enraged bull dragging* AUSTIN *with him, he snorts and bellows but*
AUSTIN *hangs on and manages to keep clear of* LEE'S *attempts to
grab him, they crash into the table, to the floor,* LEE *is face down
thrashing wildly and choking,* AUSTIN *pulls cord tighter, stands with
one foot planted on* LEE'S *back and the cord stretched taut.*)

AUSTIN: (*Holding cord.*) Gimme back my keys, Lee! Take the
  keys out! Take 'em out!

(LEE *desperately tries to dig in his pockets, searching for the car keys,*
MOM *moves closer.*)

MOM: (*Calmly to* AUSTIN.) You're not killing him are you? 220
AUSTIN: I don't know. I don't know if I'm killing him. I'm
  stopping him. That's all. I'm just stopping him.

(LEE *thrashes but* AUSTIN *is relentless.*)

MOM: You oughta' let him breathe a little bit.
AUSTIN: Throw the keys out, Lee!

(LEE *finally gets keys out and throws them on floor but out of*
AUSTIN'S *reach,* AUSTIN *keeps pressure on cord, pulling* LEE'S *neck
back,* LEE *gets one hand to the cord but can't relieve the pressure.*)

  Reach me those keys would ya', Mom.   225
MOM: (*Not moving.*) Why are you doing this to him?
AUSTIN: Reach me the keys!
MOM: Not until you stop choking him.
AUSTIN: I can't stop choking him! He'll kill me if I stop
  choking him!   230
MOM: He won't kill you. He's your brother.
AUSTIN: Just get me the keys would ya'!

(*Pause.* MOM *picks keys up off floor, hands them to* AUSTIN.)

AUSTIN: (*To* MOM.) Thanks.
MOM: Will you let him go now?
AUSTIN: I don't know. He's not gonna' let me get outa' here. 235
MOM: Well you can't kill him.
AUSTIN: I can kill him! I can easily kill him. Right now. Right
  here. All I gotta' do is just tighten up. See? (*He tightens cord,*
  LEE *thrashes wildly.* AUSTIN *releases pressure a little, maintain-
  ing control.*) Ya' see that?   240
MOM: That's a savage thing to do.
AUSTIN: Yeah well don't tell me I can't kill him because I can.
  I can just twist. I can just keep twisting. (AUSTIN *twists the
  cord tighter,* LEE *weakens, his breathing changes to a short rasp.*)
MOM: Austin!   245

(AUSTIN *relieves pressure,* LEE *breathes easier but* AUSTIN *keeps him
under control.*)

AUSTIN: (*Eyes on* LEE, *holding cord.*) I'm goin' to the desert.
  There's nothing stopping me. I'm going by myself to the
  desert.

(MOM *moving toward her luggage.*)

MOM: Well, I'm going to go check into a motel. I can't stand
  this anymore.   250
AUSTIN: Don't go yet!

(MOM *pauses.*)

MOM: I can't stay here. This is worse than being homeless.

AUSTIN: I'll get everything fixed up for you, Mom. I promise. Just stay for a while.

255 MOM: (*Picking up luggage.*) You're going to the desert.

AUSTIN: Just wait!

(LEE *thrashes,* AUSTIN *subdues him,* MOM *watches holding luggage, pause.*)

MOM: It was the worst feeling being up there. In Alaska. Staring out a window. I never felt so desperate before. That's why when I saw that article on Picasso I thought—

260 AUSTIN: Stay here, Mom. This is where you live.

(*She looks around the stage.*)

MOM: I don't recognize it at all.

(*She exits with luggage,* AUSTIN *makes a move toward her but* LEE *starts to struggle and* AUSTIN *subdues him again with cord, pause.*)

AUSTIN: (*Holding cord.*) Lee? I'll make ya' a deal. You let me get outa' here. Just let me get to my car. All right, Lee?

Gimme a little headstart and I'll turn you loose. Just gimme a little headstart. All right? 265

(LEE *makes no response,* AUSTIN *slowly releases tension cord, still nothing from* LEE.)

AUSTIN: Lee?

(LEE *is motionless,* AUSTIN *very slowly begins to stand, still keeping a tenuous hold on the cord and his eyes riveted to* LEE *for any sign of movement,* AUSTIN *slowly drops the cord and stands, he stares down at* LEE *who appears to be dead.*)

AUSTIN: (*Whispers.*) Lee?

(*Pause,* AUSTIN *considers, looks toward exit, back to* LEE, *then makes a small movement as if to leave. Instantly* LEE *is on his feet and moves toward exit, blocking* AUSTIN's *escape. They square off to each other, keeping a distance between them. Pause, a single coyote heard in distance, lights fade softly into moonlight, the figures of the brothers now appear to be caught in a vast desert-like landscape, they are very still but watchful for the next move, lights go slowly to black as the after-image of the brothers pulses in the dark, coyote fades.*)

August Wilson

August Wilson (1945–2005) was born and raised on "The Hill," the black ghetto of Pittsburgh. He dropped out of school in the ninth grade, but supported himself with odd jobs while he continued his self-education, reading and studying; he also began to write poems and stories on the changing problems of race relations in America. He founded a theater in Pittsburgh in the mid-1960s, and then founded Black Horizons Theater Company there in 1968. His first play, *Jitney,* was staged in 1978. Wilson then applied to study playwriting at the Eugene O'Neill Theater Center's National Playwrights' Conference, where he submitted the text of *Ma Rainey's Black Bottom,* which was read by the eminent African American stage director Lloyd Richards, who had brought Lorraine Hansberry's *A Raisin in the Sun* to Broadway in 1959. Richards read the play and produced it at the Yale Repertory Theater in 1984 before bringing it to Broadway. *Ma Rainey's Black Bottom* is the first of several plays examining African American history in the twentieth century, many of them using jazz as a musical idiom; it was followed by *Fences* (1985)—which won the Pulitzer Prize—*Joe Turner's Come and Gone* (1986), *The Piano Lesson* (1987), *Two Trains Running* (1991), *Seven Guitars* (1995), and *King Hedley II* (1999).

FENCES

Set in 1957, the action of *Fences* sits on the brink of the civil rights movement and outlines the challenges facing African Americans whose legal freedoms had yet to become a social reality. The play is—as its final funeral scene implies—deeply reminiscent of Arthur Miller's *Death of a Salesman,* and suggests that realism is in many way still the dominant mode of American theater. Like Miller's play, it is about a hardworking man whose responsibilities to his family fall athwart his dreams of happiness, a conflict that finally costs him both. However, while Miller's Willy Loman is victimized by his belief in the "American Dream," Wilson's Troy Maxson lives his life on the underside of that dream. Thrown out of his home at fourteen by his father, Troy moved north to Pittsburgh; unable to find work, he made a living through petty crime until he was caught and sentenced to fifteen years' imprisonment. On his release, he found his wife and child and began a career in baseball, playing in the Negro Leagues. Integration came to baseball, and by 1957 Jackie Robinson, Hank Aaron, and a young Roberto Clemente are all playing in the major leagues—but it is too late for Troy. He is now working as a trash collector, fighting the company to let African Americans drive the garbage trucks as well as pick up the trash.

Like Willy Loman, Troy too is a family man. The family is Troy's refuge from the racism and defeat of his daily life, and his proudest accomplishment as well: he has forced himself to shoulder the responsibility of providing for his children and of loving his wife, a responsibility that lends his life purpose and direction. As he says to Rose in act 1, "Woman . . . I do the best I can do. . . . We go upstairs in that room at night . . . and I fall down on you and try to blast a hole into forever. I get up Monday morning . . . find my lunch on the table. I go out. Make my way. Find my strength to carry me through to the next Friday." However, as Rose notes, the world is changing around Troy, and these changes threaten the life that he has made. His son Cory is being recruited on a football scholarship. Troy, his own exploitation by the white-dominated sports industry still in mind, forces Cory to quit the team, and so to pass up the scholarship—and the chance to go to college. Nor does Troy shoulder the rest of his family life easily. He cares for his mentally handicapped brother Gabriel, but eventually has him committed to a mental hospital in order to get half of his government pension. Despite his love for and gratitude to Rose, he has an affair with another woman, who dies delivering their daughter. Although family life has been Troy's salvation, it also has hemmed him in—in the dead-end jobs, the constant poverty, the fence he

James Earl Jones reprises his role as Troy in this 1986 Goodman Theatre production of August Wilson's *Fences*.

builds at the end of the play. He risks it all for the chance of some happiness with Alberta and loses; Rose takes in Troy's daughter: "From right now . . . this child got a mother. But you a womanless man." He fights Cory, and much as his own father had thrown him out of the house, he forces his own son to leave as well.

The joyous, mournful conclusion of *Fences*—when Gabriel dances Troy's soul into heaven—perhaps provides the best commentary on the life of Troy Maxson. Suffering the indignities and humiliation of racism throughout his life, Troy built a stable home for himself, a life. As a defense against the world, perhaps, that life was bound to crumble, particularly as pressure of social change forced Troy to deal with a future he had never imagined. In Wilson's final image, however, Troy's life is celebrated, a thing of rough and rugged beauty, demanding our attention and respect.

FENCES

August Wilson

CHARACTERS

TROY MAXSON
IM BONO, *Troy's friend*
ROSE, *Troy's wife*
LYONS, *Troy's oldest son by previous marriage*
GABRIEL, *Troy's brother*
CORY, *Troy and Rose's son*
RAYNELL, *Troy's daughter*

> When the sins of our fathers visit us
> We do not have to play host.
> We can banish them with forgiveness
> As God, in His Largeness and Laws.
> —AUGUST WILSON

SETTING: *The setting is the yard which fronts the only entrance to the Maxson household, an ancient two-story brick house set back off a small alley in a big-city neighborhood. The entrance to the house is gained by two or three steps leading to a wooden porch badly in need of paint.*

A relatively recent addition to the house and running its full width, the porch lacks congruence. It is a sturdy porch with a flat roof. One or two chairs of dubious value sit at one end where the kitchen window opens onto the porch. An old-fashioned icebox stands silent guard at the opposite end.

The yard is a small dirt yard, partially fenced, except for the last scene, with a wooden sawhorse, a pile of lumber, and other fence-building equipment set off to the side. Opposite is a tree from which hangs a ball made of rags. A baseball bat leans against the tree. Two oil drums serve as garbage receptacles and sit near the house at right to complete the setting.

THE PLAY: *Near the turn of the century, the destitute of Europe sprang on the city with tenacious claws and an honest and solid dream. The city devoured them. They swelled its belly until it burst into a thousand furnaces and sewing machines, a thousand butcher shops and bakers' ovens, a thousand churches and hospitals and funeral parlors and moneylenders. The city grew. It nourished itself and offered each man a partnership limited only by his talent, his guile, and his willingness and capacity for hard work. For the immigrants of Europe, a dream dared and won true.*

The descendants of African slaves were offered no such welcome or participation. They came from places called the Carolinas and the Virginias, Georgia, Alabama, Mississippi, and Tennessee. They came strong, eager, searching. The city rejected them and they fled and settled along the riverbanks and under bridges in shallow, ramshackle houses made of sticks and tar-paper. They collected rags and wood. They sold the use of their muscles and their bodies. They cleaned houses and washed clothes, they shined shoes, and in quiet desperation and vengeful pride, they stole, and lived in pursuit of their own dream. That they could breathe free, finally, and stand to meet life with the force of dignity and whatever eloquence the heart could call upon.

By 1957, the hard-won victories of the European immigrants had solidified the industrial might of America. War had been confronted and won with new energies that used loyalty and patriotism as its fuel. Life was rich, full, and flourishing. The Milwaukee Braves won the World Series, and the hot winds of change that would make the sixties a turbulent, racing, dangerous, and provocative decade had not yet begun to blow full.

ACT ONE

SCENE I

It is 1957. TROY *and* BONO *enter the yard, engaged in conversation.* TROY *is fifty-three years old, a large man with thick, heavy hands; it is this largeness that he strives to fill out and make an accommodation with. Together with his blackness, his largeness informs his sensibilities and the choices he has made in his life.*

Of the two men, BONO *is obviously the follower. His commitment to their friendship of thirty-odd years is rooted in his admiration of* TROY's *honesty, capacity for hard work, and his strength, which* BONO *seeks to emulate.*

It is Friday night, payday, and the one night of the week the two men engage in a ritual of talk and drink. TROY *is usually the most talkative and at times he can be crude and almost vulgar, though he is capable of rising to profound heights of expression. The men carry lunch buckets and wear or carry burlap aprons and are dressed in clothes suitable to their jobs as garbage collectors.*

BONO: Troy, you ought to stop that lying!
TROY: I ain't lying! The nigger had a watermelon this big.

(He indicates with his hands.)

Talking about . . . "What watermelon, Mr. Rand?" I liked to fell out! "What watermelon, Mr. Rand?" . . . And it sitting there big as life. 5
BONO: What did Mr. Rand say?
TROY: Ain't said nothing. Figure if the nigger too dumb to know he carrying a watermelon, he wasn't gonna get much sense out of him. Trying to hide that great big old watermelon under his coat. Afraid to let the white man see him carry it home. 10
BONO: I'm like you . . . I ain't got no time for them kind of people.
TROY: Now what he look like getting mad cause he see the man from the union talking to Mr. Rand?
BONO: He come to me talking about . . . "Maxson gonna get 15 us fired." I told him to get away from me with that. He walked away from me calling you a troublemaker. What Mr. Rand say?
TROY: Ain't said nothing. He told me to go down the Commissioner's office next Friday. They called me down there 20 to see them.
BONO: Well, as long as you got your complaint filed, they can't fire you. That's what one of them white fellows tell me.

TROY: I ain't worried about them firing me. They gonna fire me cause I asked a question? That's all I did. I went to Mr. Rand and asked him, "Why? Why you got the white mens driving and the colored lifting?" Told him, "what's the matter, don't I count? You think only white fellows got sense enough to drive a truck. That ain't no paper job! Hell, anybody can drive a truck. How come you got all whites driving and the colored lifting?" He told me "take it to the union." Well, hell, that's what I done! Now they wanna come up with this pack of lies.

BONO: I told Brownie if the man come and ask him any questions . . . just tell the truth! It ain't nothing but something they done trumped up on you cause you filed a complaint on them.

TROY: Brownie don't understand nothing. All I want them to do is change the job description. Give everybody a chance to drive the truck. Brownie can't see that. He ain't got that much sense.

BONO: How you figure he be making out with that gal be up at Taylors' all the time . . . that Alberta gal?

TROY: Same as you and me. Getting just as much as we is. Which is to say nothing.

BONO: It is, huh? I figure you doing a little better than me . . . and I ain't saying what I'm doing.

TROY: Aw, nigger, look here . . . I know you. If you had got anywhere near that gal, twenty minutes later you be looking to tell somebody. And the first one you gonna tell . . . that you gonna want to brag to . . . is gonna be me.

BONO: I ain't saying that. I see where you be eyeing her.

TROY: I eye all the women. I don't miss nothing. Don't never let nobody tell you Troy Maxson don't eye the women.

BONO: You been doing more than eyeing her. You done bought her a drink or two.

TROY: Hell yeah, I bought her a drink! What that mean? I bought you one, too. What that mean cause I buy her a drink? I'm just being polite.

BONO: It's alright to buy her one drink. That's what you call being polite. But when you wanna be buying two or three . . . that's what you call eyeing her.

TROY: Look here, as long as you known me . . . you ever known me to chase after women?

BONO: Hell yeah! Long as I done known you. You forgetting I knew you when.

TROY: Naw, I'm talking about since I been married to Rose?

BONO: Oh, not since you been married to Rose. Now, that's the truth, there. I can say that.

TROY: Alright then! Case closed.

BONO: I see you be walking up around Alberta's house. You supposed to be at Taylors' and you be walking up around there.

TROY: What you watching where I'm walking for? I ain't watching after you.

BONO: I seen you walking around there more than once.

TROY: Hell, you liable to see me walking anywhere! That don't mean nothing cause you see me walking around there.

BONO: Where she come from anyway? She just kinda showed up one day.

TROY: Tallahassee. You can look at her and tell she one of them Florida gals. They got some big healthy women down there. Grow them right up out the ground. Got a little bit of Indian in her. Most of them niggers down in Florida got some Indian in them.

BONO: I don't know about that Indian part. But she damn sure big and healthy. Woman wear some big stockings. Got them great big old legs and hips as wide as the Mississippi River.

TROY: Legs don't mean nothing. You don't do nothing but push them out of the way. But them hips cushion the ride!

BONO: Troy, you ain't got no sense.

TROY: It's the truth! Like you riding on Goodyears!

(ROSE *enters from the house. She is ten years younger than* TROY, *her devotion to him stems from her recognition of the possibilities of her life without him: a succession of abusive men and their babies, a life of partying and running the streets, the Church, or aloneness with its attendant pain and frustration. She recognizes* TROY's *spirit as a fine and illuminating one and she either ignores or forgives his faults, only some of which she recognizes. Though she doesn't drink, her presence is an integral part of the Friday night rituals. She alternates between the porch and the kitchen, where supper preparations are under way.*)

ROSE: What you all out here getting into?

TROY: What you worried about what we getting into for? This is men talk, woman.

ROSE: What I care what you all talking about? Bono, you gonna stay for supper?

BONO: No, I thank you, Rose. But Lucille say she cooking up a pot of pigfeet.

TROY: Pigfeet! Hell, I'm going home with you! Might even stay the night if you got some pigfeet. You got something in there to top them pigfeet, Rose?

ROSE: I'm cooking up some chicken. I got some chicken and collard greens.

TROY: Well, go on back in the house and let me and Bono finish what we was talking about. This is men talk. I got some talk for you later. You know what kind of talk I mean. You go on and powder it up.

ROSE: Troy Maxson, don't you start that now!

TROY: (*Puts his arm around her.*) Aw, woman . . . come here. Look here, Bono . . . when I met this woman . . . I got out that place, say, "Hitch up my pony, saddle up my mare . . . there's a woman out there for me somewhere. I looked here. Looked there. Saw Rose and latched on to her." I latched on to her and told her—I'm gonna tell you the truth—I told her, "Baby, I don't wanna marry, I just wanna be your man." Rose told me . . . tell him what you told me, Rose.

ROSE: I told him if he wasn't the marrying kind, then move out the way so the marrying kind could find me.

TROY: That's what she told me. "Nigger, you in my way. You blocking the view! Move out the way so I can find me a husband." I thought it over two or three days. Come back—

ROSE: Ain't no two or three days nothing. You was back the same night.

TROY: Come back, told her . . . "Okay, baby . . . but I'm gonna buy me a banty rooster and put him out there in the backyard . . . and when he sees a stranger come, he'll flap his wings and crow . . ." Look here, Bono, I could watch the front door by myself . . . it was that back door I was worried about.

ROSE: Troy, you ought not talk like that. Troy ain't doing nothing but telling a lie.

TROY: Only thing is . . . when we first got married . . . forget the rooster . . . we ain't had no yard!

135 BONO: I hear you tell it. Me and Lucille was staying down there on Logan Street. Had two rooms with the outhouse in the back. I ain't mind the outhouse none. But when that goddamn wind blow through there in the winter . . . that's what I'm talking about! To this day I wonder why in

140 the hell I ever stayed down there for six long years. But see, I didn't know I could do no better. I thought only white folks had inside toilets and things.

ROSE: There's a lot of people don't know they can do no better than they doing now. That's just something you got to

145 learn. A lot of folks still shop at Bella's.

TROY: Ain't nothing wrong with shopping at Bella's. She got fresh food.

ROSE: I ain't said nothing about if she got fresh food. I'm talking about what she charge. She charge ten cents more

150 than the A&P.

TROY: The A&P ain't never done nothing for me. I spends my money where I'm treated right. I go down to Bella, say, "I need a loaf of bread, I'll pay you Friday." She give it to me. What sense that make when I got money to go and spend

155 it somewhere else and ignore the person who done right by me? That ain't in the Bible.

ROSE: We ain't talking about what's in the Bible. What sense it make to shop there when she overcharge?

TROY: You shop where you want to. I'll do my shopping

160 where the people been good to me.

ROSE: Well, I don't think it's right for her to overcharge. That's all I was saying.

BONO: Look here . . . I got to get on. Lucille going be raising all kind of hell.

165 TROY: Where you going, nigger? We ain't finished this pint. Come here, finish this pint.

BONO: Well, hell, I am . . . if you ever turn the bottle loose.

TROY: (*Hands him the bottle.*) The only thing I say about the A&P is I'm glad Cory got that job down there. Help him

170 take care of his school clothes and things. Gabe done moved out and things getting tight around here. He got that job . . . He can start to look out for himself.

ROSE: Cory done went and got recruited by a college football team.

175 TROY: I told that boy about that football stuff. The white man ain't gonna let him get nowhere with that football. I told him when he first come to me with it. Now you come telling me he done went and got more tied up in it. He ought to go and get recruited in how to fix cars or

180 something where he can make a living.

ROSE: He ain't talking about making no living playing football. It's just something the boys in school do. They gonna send a recruiter by to talk to you. He'll tell you he ain't talking about making no living playing football. It's a

185 honor to be recruited.

TROY: It ain't gonna get him nowhere. Bono'll tell you that.

BONO: If he be like you in the sports . . . he's gonna be alright. Ain't but two men ever played baseball as good as you. That's Babe Ruth and Josh Gibson. Them's the only

190 two men ever hit more home runs than you.

TROY: What it ever get me? Ain't got a pot to piss in or a window to throw it out of.

ROSE: Times have changed since you was playing baseball, Troy. That was before the war. Times have changed a lot since then. 195

TROY: How in hell they done changed?

ROSE: They got lots of colored boys playing ball now. Baseball and football.

BONO: You right about that, Rose. Times have changed, Troy. You just come along too early. 200

TROY: There ought not never have been no time called too early! Now you take that fellow . . . what's that fellow they had playing right field for the Yankees back then? You know who I'm talking about, Bono. Used to play right field for the Yankees. 205

ROSE: Selkirk?

TROY: Selkirk! That's it! Man batting .269, understand? .269. What kind of sense that make? I was hitting .432 with thirty-seven home runs! Man batting .269 and playing right field for the Yankees! I saw Josh Gibson's daughter 210 yesterday. She walking around with raggedy shoes on her feet. Now I bet you Selkirk's daughter ain't walking around with raggedy shoes on her feet! I bet you that!

ROSE: They got a lot of colored baseball players now. Jackie Robinson was the first. Folks had to wait for Jackie 215 Robinson.

TROY: I done seen a hundred niggers play baseball better than Jackie Robinson. Hell, I know some teams Jackie Robinson couldn't even make! What you talking about Jackie Robinson. Jackie Robinson wasn't nobody. I'm talking 220 about if you could play ball then they ought to have let you play. Don't care what color you were. Come telling me I come along too early. If you could play . . . then they ought to have let you play.

(TROY *takes a long drink from the bottle.*)

ROSE: You gonna drink yourself to death. You don't need to 225 be drinking like that.

TROY: Death ain't nothing. I done seen him. Done wrassled with him. You can't tell me nothing about death. Death ain't nothing but a fastball on the outside corner. And you know what I'll do to that! Lookee here, Bono . . . am I ly- 230 ing? You get one of them fastballs, about waist high, over the outside corner of the plate where you can get the meat of the bat on it . . . and good god! You can kiss it goodbye. Now, am I lying?

BONO: Naw, you telling the truth there. I seen you do it. 235

TROY: If I'm lying . . . that 450 feet worth of lying!

(*Pause.*)

That's all death is to me. A fastball on the outside corner.

ROSE: I don't know why you want to get on talking about death.

TROY: Ain't nothing wrong with talking about death. That's 240 part of life. Everybody gonna die. You gonna die, I'm gonna die. Bono's gonna die. Hell, we all gonna die.

ROSE: But you ain't got to talk about it. I don't like to talk about it.

TROY: You the one brought it up. Me and Bono was talking 245 about baseball . . . you tell me I'm gonna drink myself to

death. Ain't that right, Bono? You know I don't drink this but one night out of the week. That's Friday night. I'm gonna drink just enough to where I can handle it. Then
250 I cuts it loose. I leave it alone. So don't you worry about me drinking myself to death. 'Cause I ain't worried about Death. I done seen him. I done wrestled with him.

Look here, Bono . . . I looked up one day and Death was marching straight at me. Like Soldiers on Parade! The
255 Army of Death was marching straight at me. The middle of July, 1941. It got real cold just like it be winter. It seem like Death himself reached out and touched me on the shoulder. He touch me just like I touch you. I got cold as ice and Death standing there grinning at me.
260 ROSE: Troy, why don't you hush that talk.
TROY: I say . . . What you want, Mr. Death? You be wanting me? You done brought your army to be getting me? I looked him dead in the eye. I wasn't fearing nothing. I was ready to tangle. Just like I'm ready to tangle now. The
265 Bible say be ever vigilant. That's why I don't get but so drunk. I got to keep watch.
ROSE: Troy was right down there in Mercy Hospital. You remember he had pneumonia? Laying there with a fever talking plumb out of his head.
270 TROY: Death standing there staring at me . . . carrying that sickle in his hand. Finally he say, "You want bound over for another year?" See, just like that . . . "You want bound over for another year?" I told him, "Bound over hell! Let's settle this now!"
275 It seem like he kinda fell back when I said that, and all the cold went out of me. I reached down and grabbed that sickle and threw it just as far as I could throw it . . . and me and him commenced to wrestling.

We wrestled for three days and three nights. I can't say
280 where I found the strength from. Every time it seemed like he was gonna get the best of me, I'd reach way down deep inside myself and find the strength to do him one better.
ROSE: Every time Troy tell that story he find different ways to
285 tell it. Different things to make up about it.
TROY: I ain't making up nothing. I'm telling you the facts of what happened. I wrestled with Death for three days and three nights and I'm standing here to tell you about it.

(Pause.)

Alright. At the end of the third night we done weakened
290 each other to where we can't hardly move. Death stood up, throwed on his robe . . . had him a white robe with a hood on it. He throwed on that robe and went off to look for his sickle. Say, "I'll be back." Just like that. "I'll be back." I told him, say, "Yeah, but . . . you gonna have to find
295 me!" I wasn't no fool. I wasn't going looking for him. Death ain't nothing to play with. And I know he's gonna get me. I know I got to join his army . . . his camp followers. But as long as I keep my strength and see him coming . . . as long as I keep up my vigilance . . . he's gonna
300 have to fight to get me. I ain't going easy.
BONO: Well, look here, since you got to keep up your vigilance . . . let me have the bottle.
TROY: Aw hell, I shouldn't have told you that part. I should have left out that part.

ROSE: Troy be talking that stuff and half the time don't even 305 know what he be talking about.
TROY: Bono know me better than that.
BONO: That's right. I know you. I know you got some Uncle Remus in your blood. You got more stories than the devil got sinners. 310
TROY: Aw hell, I done seen him too! Done talked with the devil.
ROSE: Troy, don't nobody wanna be hearing all that stuff.

(LYONS enters the yard from the street. Thirty-four years old, TROY's son by a previous marriage, he sports a neatly trimmed goatee, sport coat, white shirt, tieless and buttoned at the collar. Though he fancies himself a musician, he is more caught up in the rituals and "idea" of being a musician than in the actual practice of the music. He has come to borrow money from TROY, and while he knows he will be successful, he is uncertain as to what extent his lifestyle will be held up to scrutiny and ridicule.)

LYONS: Hey, Pop.
TROY: What you come "Hey, Popping" me for? 315
LYONS: How you doing, Rose?

(He kisses her.)

Mr. Bono. How you doing?
BONO: Hey, Lyons . . . how you been?
TROY: He must have been doing alright. I ain't seen him around here last week. 320
ROSE: Troy, leave your boy alone. He come by to see you and you wanna start all that nonsense.
TROY: I ain't bothering Lyons.

(Offers him the bottle.)

Here . . . get you a drink. We got an understanding. I know why he come by to see me and he know I know. 325
LYONS: Come on, Pop . . . I just stopped by to say hi . . . see how you was doing.
TROY: You ain't stopped by yesterday.
ROSE: You gonna stay for supper, Lyons? I got some chicken cooking in the oven. 330
LYONS: No, Rose . . . thanks. I was just in then neighborhood and thought I'd stop by for a minute.
TROY: You was in the neighborhood alright, nigger. You telling the truth there. You was in the neighborhood cause it's my payday. 335
LYONS: Well, hell, since you mentioned it . . . let me have ten dollars.
TROY: I'll be damned! I'll die and go to hell and play blackjack with the devil before I give you ten dollars.
BONO: That's what I wanna know about . . . that devil you 340 done seen.
LYONS: What . . . Pop done seen the devil? You too much, Pops.
TROY: Yeah, I done seen him. Talked to him too!
ROSE: You ain't seen no devil. I done told you that man ain't had nothing to do with the devil. Anything you can't un- 345 derstand, you want to call it the devil.
TROY: Look here, Bono . . . I went down to see Hertzberger about some furniture. Got three rooms for two-ninety-eight. That what it say on the radio. "Three rooms . . . two-ninety-eight." Even made up a little song about it. Go 350

down there . . . man tell me I can't get no credit. I'm working every day and can't get no credit. What to do? I got an
empty house with some raggedy furniture in it. Cory ain't
got no bed. He's sleeping on a pile of rags on the floor.
355 Working every day and can't get no credit. Come back
here—Rose'll tell you—madder than hell. Sit down . . . try
to figure what I'm gonna do. Come a knock on the door.
Ain't been living here but three days. Who know I'm here?
Open the door . . . devil standing there bigger than life.
360 White fellow . . . got on good clothes and everything.
Standing there with a clipboard in his hand. I ain't had to
say nothing. First words come out of his mouth was . . . "I
understand you need some furniture and can't get no
credit." I liked to fell over. He say "I'll give you all the credit
365 you want, but you got to pay the interest on it." I told him,
"Give me three rooms worth and charge whatever you
want." Next day a truck pulled up here and two men un-
loaded them three rooms. Man what drove the truck give
me a book. Say send ten dollars, first of every month to the
370 address in the book and everything will be alright. Say if I
miss a payment the devil was coming back and it'll be hell
to pay. That was fifteen years ago. To this day . . . the first
of the month I send my ten dollars, Rose'll tell you.

ROSE: Troy lying.

375 TROY: I ain't never seen that man since. Now you tell me
who else that could have been but the devil? I ain't sold
my soul or nothing like that, you understand. Naw, I
wouldn't have truck with the devil about nothing like
that. I got my furniture and pays my ten dollars the first
380 of the month just like clockwork.

BONO: How long you say you been paying this ten dollars a
month?

TROY: Fifteen years!

BONO: Hell, ain't you finished paying for it yet? How much
385 the man done charged you.

TROY: Aw hell, I done paid for it. I done paid for it ten times
over! The fact is I'm scared to stop paying it.

ROSE: Troy lying. We got that furniture from Mr. Glickman.
He ain't paying no ten dollars a month to nobody.

390 TROY: Aw hell, woman. Bono know I ain't that big a fool.

LYONS: I was just getting ready to say . . . I know where there's
a bridge for sale.

TROY: Look here, I'll tell you this . . . it don't matter to me if
he was the devil. It don't matter if the devil give credit.
395 Somebody has got to give it.

ROSE: It ought to matter. You going around talking about
having truck with the devil . . . God's the one you gonna
have to answer to. He's the one gonna be at the Judgment.

LYONS: Yeah, well, look here, Pop . . . let me have that ten dol-
400 lars. I'll give it back to you. Bonnie got a job working at
the hospital.

TROY: What I tell you, Bono? The only time I see this nigger is
when he wants something. That's the only time I see him.

LYONS: Come on, Pop, Mr. Bono don't want to hear all that.
405 Let me have the ten dollars. I told you Bonnie working.

TROY: What that mean to me? "Bonnie working." I don't care
if she working. Go ask her for the ten dollars if she working. Talking about "Bonnie working." Why ain't you
working?

410 LYONS: Aw, Pop, you know I can't find no decent job. Where
am I gonna get a job at? You know I can't get no job.

TROY: I told you I know some people down there. I can get
you on the rubbish if you want to work. I told you that
the last time you came by here asking me for something.

LYONS: Naw, Pop . . . thanks. That ain't for me. I don't wanna   415
be carrying nobody's rubbish. I don't wanna be punching
nobody's time clock.

TROY: What's the matter, you too good to carry people's rubbish? Where you think that ten dollars you talking about
come from? I'm just supposed to haul people's rubbish and   420
give my money to you cause you too lazy to work. You too
lazy to work and wanna know why you ain't got what I got.

ROSE: What hospital Bonnie working at? Mercy?

LYONS: She's down at Passavant working in the laundry.

TROY: I ain't got nothing as it is. I give you that ten dollars   425
and I got to eat beans the rest of the week. Naw . . . you
ain't getting no ten dollars here.

LYONS: You ain't got to be eating no beans. I don't know why
you wanna say that.

TROY: I ain't got no extra money. Gabe done moved over to   430
Miss Pearl's paying her the rent and things done got tight
around here. I can't afford to be giving you every payday.

LYONS: I ain't asked you to give me nothing. I asked you to
loan me ten dollars. I know you got ten dollars.

TROY: Yeah, I got it. You know why I got it? Cause I don't   435
throw my money away out there in the streets. You living
the fast life . . . wanna be a musician . . . running around
in them clubs and things . . . then, you learn to take care
of yourself. You ain't gonna find me going and asking nobody for nothing. I done spent too many years without.   440

LYONS: You and me is two different people, Pop.

TROY: I done learned my mistake and learned to do what's
right by it. You still trying to get something for nothing.
Life don't owe you nothing. You owe it to yourself. Ask
Bono. He'll tell you I'm right.   445

LYONS: You got your way of dealing with the world . . . I got
mine. The only thing that matters to me is the music.

TROY: Yeah, I can see that! It don't matter how you gonna eat
. . . where your next dollar is coming from. You telling the
truth there.   450

LYONS: I know I got to eat. But I got to live too. I need something that gonna help me to get out of the bed in the
morn-ing. Make me feel like I belong in the world. I don't
bother nobody. I just stay with my music cause that's the
only way I can find to live in the world. Otherwise there   455
ain't no telling what I might do. Now I just come by to ask you for
ten dollars. I don't wanna hear all that about how I live.

TROY: Boy, your mama did a hell of a job raising you.

LYONS: You can't change me, Pop. I'm thirty-four years old. If 460
you wanted to change me, you should have been there
when I was growing up. I come by to see you . . . ask for
ten dollars and you want to talk about how I was raised.
You don't know nothing about how I was raised.

ROSE: Let the boy have ten dollars, Troy.   465

TROY: (To LYONS.) What the hell you looking at me for? I ain't
got no ten dollars. You know what I do with my money.

(To ROSE.)

Give him ten dollars if you want him to have it.

ROSE: I will. Just as soon as you turn it loose.

470   TROY: (*Handing* ROSE *the money.*) There it is. Seventy-six dollars and forty-two cents. You see this, Bono? Now, I ain't gonna get but six of that back.

ROSE: You ought to stop telling that lie. Here, Lyons.

(*She hands him the money.*)

LYONS: Thanks, Rose. Look . . . I got to run . . . I'll see you later.

475   TROY: Wait a minute. You gonna say, "thanks, Rose" and ain't gonna look to see where she got that ten dollars from? See how they do me, Bono?

LYONS: I know she got it from you, Pop. Thanks. I'll give it back to you.

480   TROY: There he go telling another lie. Time I see that ten dollars . . . he'll be owing me thirty more.

LYONS: See you, Mr. Bono.

BONO: Take care, Lyons!

LYONS: Thanks, Pop. I'll see you again.

(LYONS *exits the yard.*)

485   TROY: I don't know why he don't go and get him a decent job and take care of that woman he got.

BONO: He'll be alright, Troy. The boy is still young.

TROY: The *boy* is thirty-four years old.

ROSE: Let's not get off into all that.

490   BONO: Look here . . . I got to be going. I got to be getting on. Lucille gonna be waiting.

TROY: (*Puts his arm around* ROSE.) See this woman, Bono? I love this woman. I love this woman so much it hurts. I love her so much . . . I done run out of ways of loving

495   her. So I got to go back to basics. Don't you come by my house Monday morning talking about time to go to work . . . 'cause I'm still gonna be stroking!

ROSE: Troy! Stop it now!

BONO: I ain't paying him no mind, Rose. That ain't nothing but gin-talk. Go on, Troy. I'll see you Monday.

500   TROY: Don't you come by my house, nigger! I done told you what I'm gonna be doing.

(*The lights go down to black.*)

SCENE II

The lights come up on ROSE *hanging up clothes. She hums and sings softly to herself. It is the following morning.*

ROSE: (*Sings.*)

Jesus, be a fence all around me every day.
Jesus, I want you to protect me as I travel on my way.
Jesus, be a fence all around me every day.

(TROY *enters from the house.*)

5   ROSE: (*Continues.*)

Jesus, I want you to protect me
As I travel on my way.

(*To* TROY.)

'Morning. You ready for breakfast? I can fix it soon as I finish hanging up these clothes?

TROY: I got the coffee on. That'll be alright. I'll just drink some of that this morning.   10

ROSE: That 651 hit yesterday. That's the second time this month. Miss Pearl hit for a dollar . . . seem like those that need the least always get lucky. Poor folks can't get nothing.

TROY: Them numbers don't know nobody. I don't know why   15
you fool with them. You and Lyons both.

ROSE: It's something to do.

TROY: You ain't doing nothing but throwing your money away.

ROSE: Troy, you know I don't play foolishly. I just play a nickel
here and a nickel there.   20

TROY: That's two nickels you done thrown away.

ROSE: Now I hit sometimes . . . that makes up for it. It always comes in handy when I do hit. I don't hear you complaining then.

TROY: I ain't complaining now. I just say it's foolish. Trying   25
to guess out of six hundred ways which way the number gonna come. If I had all the money niggers, these Negroes, throw away on numbers for one week—just one week—I'd be a rich man.

ROSE: Well, you wishing and calling it foolish ain't gonna stop   30
folks from playing numbers. That's one thing for sure. Besides . . . some good things come from playing numbers. Look where Pope done bought him that restaurant off of numbers.

TROY: I can't stand niggers like that. Man ain't had two dimes   35
to rub together. He walking around with his shoes all run over bumming money for cigarettes. Alright. Got lucky there and hit the numbers . . .

ROSE: Troy, I know all about it.

TROY: Had good sense, I'll say that for him. He ain't throwed   40
his money away. I seen niggers hit the numbers and go through two thousand dollars in four days. Man bought him that restaurant down there . . . fixed it up real nice . . . and then didn't want nobody to come in it! A Negro go in there and can't get no kind of service. I seen a white fellow   45
come in there and order a bowl of stew. Pope picked all the meat out the pot for him. Man ain't had nothing but a bowl of meat! Negro come behind him and ain't got nothing but the potatoes and carrots. Talking about what numbers do for people, you picked a wrong example. Ain't done nothing but make a worser fool out of him than he was before.   50

ROSE: Troy, you ought to stop worrying about what happened at work yesterday.

TROY: I ain't worried. Just told me to be down there at the Commissioner's office on Friday. Everybody think they   55
gonna fire me. I ain't worried about them firing me. You ain't got to worry about that.

(*Pause.*)

Where's Cory? Cory in the house? (*Calls.*) Cory?

ROSE: He gone out.

TROY: Out, huh? He gone out 'cause he know I want him to   60
help me with this fence. I know how he is. That boy scared of work.

(GABRIEL *enters. He comes halfway down the alley and, hearing* TROY'*s voice, stops.*)

TROY: (*Continues.*) He ain't done a lick of work in his life.

ROSE: He had to go to football practice. Coach wanted them
65   to get in a little extra practice before the season start.
TROY: I got his practice . . . running out of here before he get
       his chores done.
ROSE: Troy, what is wrong with you this morning? Don't
       nothing set right with you. Go on back in there and go to
70   bed . . . get up on the other side.
TROY: Why something got to be wrong with me? I ain't said
       nothing wrong with me.
ROSE: You got something to say about everything. First it's the
       numbers . . . then it's the way the man runs his restaurant
75   . . . then you done got on Cory. What's it gonna be next?
       Take a look up there and see if the weather suits you . . .
       or is it gonna be how you gonna put up the fence with
       the clothes hanging in the yard.
TROY: You hit the nail on the head then.
80 ROSE: I know you like I know the back of my hand. Go on
       in there and get you some coffee . . . see if that straighten
       you up. 'Cause you ain't right this morning.

(TROY *starts into the house and sees* GABRIEL. GABRIEL *starts
singing.* TROY's *brother, he is seven years younger than* TROY. *Injured in World War II, he has a metal plate in his head. He carries
an old trumpet tied around his waist and believes with every fiber of
his being that he is the Archangel Gabriel. He carries a chipped basket with an assortment of discarded fruits and vegetables he has
picked up in the strip district and which he attempts to sell.*)

GABRIEL: (*Singing.*)

85   Yes, ma'am, I got plums
             You ask me how I sell them
             Oh ten cents apiece
             Three for a quarter
             Come and buy now
             'Cause I'm here today
90   And tomorrow I'll be gone

(GABRIEL *enters.*)

     Hey, Rose!
ROSE: How you doing, Gabe?
GABRIEL: There's Troy . . . Hey, Troy!
TROY: Hey, Gabe.

(*Exit into kitchen.*)

95 ROSE: (*To* GABRIEL.) What you got there?
GABRIEL: You know what I got, Rose. I got fruits and vegetables.
ROSE: (*Looking in basket.*) Where's all these plums you talking
       about?
GABRIEL: I ain't got no plums today, Rose. I was just singing
100   that. Have some tomorrow. Put me in a big order for
       plums. Have enough plums tomorrow for St. Peter and
       everybody.

(TROY *re-enters from kitchen, crosses to steps.*)

(*To* ROSE.)

     Troy's mad at me.
TROY: I ain't mad at you. What I got to be mad at you about?
105   You ain't done nothing to me.

GABRIEL: I just moved over to Miss Pearl's to keep out from
       in your way. I ain't mean no harm by it.
TROY: Who said anything about that? I ain't said anything
       about that.
GABRIEL: You ain't mad at me, is you?   110
TROY: Naw . . . I ain't mad at you, Gabe. If I was mad at you
       I'd tell you about it.
GABRIEL: Got me two rooms. In the basement. Got my own
       door too. Wanna see my key?

(*He holds up a key.*)

     That's my own key! Ain't nobody else got a key like that. 115
     That's my key! My two rooms!
TROY: Well, that's good, Gabe. You got your own key . . . that's
       good.
ROSE: You hungry, Gabe? I was just fixing to cook Troy his
       breakfast.   120
GABRIEL: I'll take some biscuits. You got some biscuits? Did
       you know when I was in heaven . . . every morning me
       and St. Peter would sit down by the gate and eat some big
       fat biscuits? Oh, yeah! We had us a good time. We'd sit
       there and eat us them biscuits and then St. Peter would go 125
       off to sleep and tell me to wake him up when it's time to
       open the gates for the judgment.
ROSE: Well, come on . . . I'll make up a batch of biscuits.

(ROSE *exits into the house.*)

GABRIEL: Troy . . . St. Peter got your name in the book. I seen
       it. It say . . . Troy Maxson. I say . . . I know him! He got   130
       the same name like what I got. That's my brother!
TROY: How many times you gonna tell me that, Gabe?
GABRIEL: Ain't got my name in the book. Don't have to have
       my name. I done died and went to heaven. He got your
       name though. One morning St. Peter was looking at his   135
       book . . . marking it for the judgment . . . and he let me
       see your name. Got it in there under M. Got Rose's name
       . . . I ain't seen it like I seen yours . . . but I know it's in
       there. He got a great big book. Got everybody's name
       what was ever been born. That's what he told me. But I   140
       seen your name. Seen it with my own eyes.
TROY: Go on in the house there. Rose going to fix you
       something to eat.
GABRIEL: Oh, I ain't hungry. I done had breakfast with Aunt
       Jemimah. She come by and cooked me up a whole mess of 145
       flapjacks. Remember how we used to eat them flapjacks.
TROY: Go on in the house and get you something to eat now.
GABRIEL: I got to go sell my plums. I done sold some toma-
       toes. Got me two quarters. Wanna see?

(*He shows* TROY *his quarters.*)

     I'm gonna save them and buy me a new horn so St. Peter   150
     can hear me when it's time to open the gates.

(GABRIEL *stops suddenly. Listens.*)

     Hear that? That's the hellhounds. I got to chase them out
     of here. Go on get out of here! Get out!

(GABRIEL *exits singing.*)

155   Better get ready for the judgment
       Better get ready for the judgment
       My Lord is coming down

(ROSE *enters from the house*.)

TROY: He gone off somewhere.
GABRIEL: (*Offstage*.)

160   Better get ready for the judgment
       Better get ready for the judgment morning
       Better get ready for the judgment
       My God is coming down

ROSE: He ain't eating right. Miss Pearl say she can't get him
    to eat nothing.
165 TROY: What you want me to do about it, Rose? I done did
    everything I can for the man. I can't make him get well.
    Man got half his head blown away . . . what you expect?
ROSE: Seem like something ought to be done to help him.
TROY: Man don't bother nobody. He just mixed up from that
170   metal plate he got in his head. Ain't no sense for him to
    go back into the hospital.
ROSE: Least he be eating right. They can help him take care
    of himself.
TROY: Don't nobody wanna be locked up, Rose. What you
175   wanna lock him up for? Man go over there and fight the
    war . . . messin' around with them Japs, get half his head
    blown off . . . and they give him a lousy three thousand
    dollars. And I had to swoop down on that.
ROSE: Is you fixing to go into that again?
180 TROY: That's the only way I got a roof over my head . . . cause
    of that metal plate.
ROSE: Ain't no sense you blaming yourself for nothing. Gabe
    wasn't in no condition to manage that money. You done
    what was right by him. Can't nobody say you ain't done
185   what was right by him. Look how long you took care of
    him . . . till he wanted to have his own place and moved
    over there with Miss Pearl.
TROY: That ain't what I'm saying, woman! I'm just stating the
    facts. If my brother didn't have that metal plate in his head
190   . . . I wouldn't have a pot to piss in or a window to throw
    it out of. And I'm fifty-three years old. Now see if you
    can understand that!

(TROY *gets up from the porch and starts to exit the yard*.)

ROSE: Where you going off to? You been running out of here
    every Saturday for weeks. I thought you was gonna work
195   on this fence?
TROY: I'm gonna walk down to Taylors'. Listen to the ball
    game. I'll be back in a bit. I'll work on it when I get back.

(*He exits the yard. The lights go to black*.)

SCENE III

The lights come up on the yard. It is four hours later. ROSE *is taking down the clothes from the line.* CORY *enters carrying his football
equipment.*

ROSE: Your daddy like to had a fit with you running out of
    here this morning without doing your chores.

CORY: I told you I had to go to practice.
ROSE: He say you were supposed to help him with this fence.
CORY: He been saying that the last four or five Saturdays, and 5
    then he don't never do nothing, but go down to Taylors'.
    Did you tell him about the recruiter?
ROSE: Yeah, I told him.
CORY: What he say?
ROSE: He ain't said nothing too much. You get in there and 10
    get started on your chores before he gets back. Go on and
    scrub down them steps before he gets back here hollering
    and carrying on.
CORY: I'm hungry. What you got to eat, Mama?
ROSE: Go on and get started on your chores. I got some meat 15
    loaf in there. Go on and make you a sandwich . . . and
    don't leave no mess in there.

(CORY *exits into the house.* ROSE *continues to take down the
clothes.* TROY *enters the yard and sneaks up and grabs her from behind.*)

    Troy! Go on, now. You liked to scared me to death. What
    was the score of the game? Lucille had me on the phone
    and I couldn't keep up with it.   20
TROY: What I care about the game? Come here, woman.

(*He tries to kiss her*.)

ROSE: I thought you went down Taylors' to listen to the game.
    Go on, Troy! You supposed to be putting up this fence.
TROY: (*Attempting to kiss her again*.) I'll put it up when I fin-
    ish with what is at hand.   25
ROSE: Go on, Troy. I ain't studying you.
TROY: (*Chasing after her*.) I'm studying you . . . fixing to do my
    homework!
ROSE: Troy, you better leave me alone.
TROY: Where's Cory? That boy brought his butt home yet?   30
ROSE: He's in the house doing his chores.
TROY: (*Calling*.) Cory! Get your butt out here, boy!

(ROSE *exits into the house with the laundry.* TROY *goes over to the
pile of wood, picks up a board, and starts sawing.* CORY *enters from
the house*.)

TROY: You just now coming in here from leaving this morning?
CORY: Yeah, I had to go to football practice.
TROY: Yeah, what?   35
CORY: Yessir.
TROY: I ain't but two seconds off you noway. The garbage sit-
    ting in there overflowing . . . you ain't done none of your
    chores . . . and you come in here talking about "Yeah."
CORY: I was just getting ready to do my chores now, Pop . . .   40
TROY: Your first chore is to help me with this fence on Sat-
    urday. Everything else come after that. Now get that saw
    and cut them boards.

(CORY *takes the saw and begins cutting the boards.* TROY *continues
working. There is a long pause*.)

CORY: Hey, Pop . . . why don't you buy a TV?
TROY: What I want with a TV? What I want one of them for?   45
CORY: Everybody got one. Earl, Ba Bra . . . Jesse!

TROY: I ain't asked you who had one. I say what I want with one?

CORY: So you can watch it. They got lots of things on TV.
50 Baseball games and everything. We could watch the World Series.

TROY: Yeah . . . and how much this TV cost?

CORY: I don't know. They got them on sale for around two hundred dollars.

55 TROY: Two hundred dollars, huh?

CORY: That ain't that much, Pop.

TROY: Naw, it's just two hundred dollars. See that roof you got over your head at night? Let me tell you something about that roof. It's been over ten years since that roof was
60 last tarred. See now . . . the snow come this winter and sit up there on that roof like it is . . . and it's gonna seep in-side. It's just gonna be a little bit . . . ain't gonna hardly no-tice it. Then the next thing you know, it's gonna be leaking all over the house. Then the wood rot from all
65 that water and you gonna need a whole new roof. Now, how much you think it cost to get that roof tarred?

CORY: I don't know.

TROY: Two hundred and sixty-four dollars . . . cash money. While you thinking about a TV, I got to be thinking about
70 the roof . . . and whatever else go wrong around here. Now if you had two hundred dollars, what would you do . . . fix the roof or buy a TV?

CORY: I'd buy a TV. Then when the roof started to leak . . . when it needed fixing . . . I'd fix it.

75 TROY: Where you gonna get the money from? You done spent it for a TV. You gonna sit up and watch the water run all over your brand new TV.

CORY: Aw, Pop. You got money. I know you do.

TROY: Where I got it at, Huh?

80 CORY: You got it in the bank.

TROY: You wanna see my bankbook? You wanna see that seventy-three dollars and twenty-two cents I got sitting up in there.

CORY: You ain't got to pay for it all at one time. You can put
85 a down payment on it and carry it on home with you.

TROY: Not me. I ain't gonna owe nobody nothing if I can help it. Miss a payment and they come and snatch it right out your house. Then what you got? Now, soon as I get two hundred dollars clear, then I'll buy a TV. Right now,
90 as soon as I get two hundred and sixty-four dollars, I'm gonna have this roof tarred.

CORY: Aw . . . Pop!

TROY: You go on and get you two hundred dollars and buy one if ya want it. I got better things to do with my money.

95 CORY: I can't get no two hundred dollars. I ain't never seen two hundred dollars.

TROY: I'll tell you what . . . you get you a hundred dollars and I'll put the other hundred with it.

CORY: Alright, I'm gonna show you.

100 TROY: You gonna show me how you can cut them boards right now.

(CORY *begins to cut the boards. There is a long pause.*)

CORY: The Pirates won today. That makes five in a row.

TROY: I ain't thinking about the Pirates. Got an all-white team. Got that boy . . . that Puerto Rican boy . . .

Clemente. Don't even half-play him. That boy could be 105
something if they give him a chance. Play him one day and sit him on the bench the next.

CORY: He gets a lot of chances to play.

TROY: I'm talking about playing regular. Playing every day so you can get your timing. That's what I'm talking about. 110

CORY: They got some white guys on the team that don't play every day. You can't play everybody at the same time.

TROY: If they got a white fellow sitting on the bench . . . you can bet your last dollar he can't play! The colored guy got to be twice as good before he get on the team. That's why 115
I don't want you to get all tied up in them sports. Man on the team and what it get him? They got colored on the team and don't use them. Same as not having them. All them teams the same.

CORY: The Braves got Hank Aaron and Wes Covington. Hank 120
Aaron hit two home runs today. That makes forty-three.

TROY: Hank Aaron ain't nobody. That's what you supposed to do. That's how you supposed to play the game. Ain't nothing to it. It's just a matter of timing . . . getting the right follow-through. Hell, I can hit forty-three home 125
runs right now!

CORY: Not off no major-league pitching, you couldn't.

TROY: We had better pitching in the Negro leagues. I hit seven home runs off of Satchel Paige. You can't get no better than that! 130

CORY: Sandy Koufax. He's leading the league in strikeouts.

TROY: I ain't thinking of no Sandy Koufax.

CORY: You got Warren Spahn and Lew Burdette. I bet you couldn't hit no home runs off of Warren Spahn.

TROY: I'm through with it now. You go on and cut them 135
boards.

(*Pause.*)

Your mama tell me you done got recruited by a college football team? Is that right?

CORY: Yeah. Coach Zellman say the recruiter gonna be coming by to talk to you. Get you to sign the permission papers. 140

TROY: I thought you supposed to be working down there at the A&P. Ain't you suppose to be working down there af-ter school?

CORY: Mr. Stawicki say he gonna hold my job for me until after the football season. Say starting next week I can work 145
weekends.

TROY: I thought we had an understanding about this football stuff? You suppose to keep up with your chores and hold that job down at the A&P. Ain't been around here all day on a Saturday. Ain't none of your chores done . . . and now 150
you telling me you done quit your job.

CORY: I'm gonna be working weekends.

TROY: You damn right you are! And ain't no need for nobody coming around here to talk to me about signing nothing.

CORY: Hey, Pop . . . you can't do that. He's coming all the way 155
from North Carolina.

TROY: I don't care where he coming from. The white man ain't gonna let you get nowhere with that football noway. You go on and get your book-learning so you can work yourself up in that A&P or learn how to fix cars or build 160
houses or something, get you a trade. That way you have something can't nobody take away from you. You go on

and learn how to put your hands to some good use. Besides hauling people's garbage.

165 CORY: I get good grades, Pop. That's why the recruiter wants to talk with you. You got to keep up your grades to get recruited. This way I'll be going to college. I'll get a chance . . .

TROY: First you gonna get your butt down there to the A&P
170 and get your job back.

CORY: Mr. Stawicki done already hired somebody else 'cause I told him I was playing football.

TROY: You a bigger fool than I thought . . . to let somebody take away your job so you can play some football. Where
175 you gonna get your money to take out your girlfriend and whatnot? What kind of foolishness is that to let somebody take away your job?

CORY: I'm still gonna be working weekends.

TROY: Naw . . . naw. You getting your butt out of here and
180 finding you another job.

CORY: Come on, Pop! I got to practice. I can't work after school and play football too. The team needs me. That's what Coach Zellman say . . .

TROY: I don't care what nobody else say. I'm the boss . . . you
185 understand? I'm the boss around here. I do the only saying what counts.

CORY: Come on, Pop!

TROY: I asked you . . . did you understand?

CORY: Yeah . . .
190 TROY: What?!

CORY: Yessir.

TROY: You go on down there to that A&P and see if you can get your job back. If you can't do both . . . then you quit the football team. You've got to take the crookeds with
195 the straights.

CORY: Yessir.

(*Pause.*)

Can I ask you a question?

TROY: What the hell you wanna ask me? Mr. Stawicki the one you got the questions for.
200 CORY: How come you ain't never liked me?

TROY: Liked you? Who the hell say I got to like you? What law is there say I got to like you? Wanna stand up in my face and ask a damn fool-ass question like that. Talking about liking somebody. Come here boy, when I talk to you.

(CORY *comes over to where* TROY *is working. He stands slouched over and* TROY *shoves him on his shoulder.*)

205 Straighten up, goddammit! I asked you a question . . . what law is there say I got to like you?

CORY: None.

TROY: Well, alright then! Don't you eat every day?

(*Pause.*)

Answer me when I talk to you! Don't you eat every day?
210 CORY: Yeah.

TROY: Nigger, as long as you in my house, you put that sir on the end of it when you talk to me!

CORY: Yes . . . sir.

TROY: You eat every day.

215 CORY: Yessir!

TROY: Got a roof over your head.

CORY: Yessir!

TROY: Got clothes on your back.

CORY: Yessir.

220 TROY: Why you think that is?

CORY: Cause of you.

TROY: Aw, hell I know it's 'cause of me . . . but why do you think that is?

CORY: (*Hesitant.*) Cause you like me.

225 TROY: Like you? I go out of here every morning . . . bust my butt . . . putting up with them crackers every day . . . cause I like you? You about the biggest fool I ever saw.

(*Pause.*)

It's my job. It's my responsibility! You understand that? A man got to take care of his family. You live in my house
230 . . . sleep you behind on my bedclothes . . . fill you belly up with my food . . . cause you my son. You my flesh and blood. Not 'cause I like you! Cause it's my duty to take care of you. I owe a responsibility to you! Let's get this straight right here . . . before it go along any further . . . I
235 ain't got to like you. Mr. Rand don't give me my money come payday cause he likes me. He gives me cause he owe me. I done give you everything I had to give you. I gave you your life! Me and your mama worked that out between us. And liking your black ass wasn't part of the bar-
240 gain. Don't you try and go through life worrying about if somebody like you or not. You best be making sure they doing right by you. You understand what I'm saying, boy?

CORY: Yessir.

TROY: Then get the hell out of my face, and get on down to
245 that A&P.

(ROSE *has been standing behind the screen door for much of the scene. She enters as* CORY *exits.*)

ROSE: Why don't you let the boy go ahead and play football, Troy? Ain't no harm in that. He's just trying to be like you with the sports.

250 TROY: I don't want him to be like me! I want him to move as far away from my life as he can get. You the only decent thing that ever happened to me. I wish him that. But I don't wish him a thing else from my life. I decided seventeen years ago that boy wasn't getting involved in no sports. Not after what they did to me in the sports.

255 ROSE: Troy, why don't you admit you was too old to play in the major leagues? For once . . . why don't you admit that?

TROY: What do you mean too old? Don't come telling me I was too old. I just wasn't the right color. Hell, I'm fifty-three years old and can do better than Selkirk's .269 right now!

260 ROSE: How's was you gonna play ball when you were over forty? Sometimes I can't get no sense out of you.

TROY: I got good sense, woman. I got sense enough not to let my boy get hurt over playing no sports. You been mothering that boy too much. Worried about if people like him.

265 ROSE: Everything that boy do . . . he do for you. He wants you to say "Good job, son." That's all.

TROY: Rose, I ain't got time for that. He's alive. He's healthy. He's got to make his own way. I made mine. Ain't nobody gonna hold his hand when he get out there in that world.

270 ROSE: Times have changed from when you was young, Troy. People change. The world's changing around you and you can't even see it.

TROY: (*Slow, methodical.*) Woman . . . I do the best I can do. I come in here every Friday. I carry a sack of potatoes and
275 a bucket of lard. You all line up at the door with your hands out. I give you the lint from my pockets. I give you my sweat and my blood. I ain't got no tears. I done spent them. We go upstairs in that room at night . . . and I fall down on you and try to blast a hole into forever. I get up
280 Monday morning . . . find my lunch on the table. I go out. Make my way. Find my strength to carry me through to the next Friday.

(*Pause.*)

That's all I got, Rose. That's all I got to give. I can't give nothing else.

(TROY *exits into the house. The lights go down to black.*)

SCENE IV

It is Friday. Two weeks later. CORY *starts out of the house with his football equipment. The phone rings.*

CORY: (*Calling.*) I got it!

(*He answers the phone and stands in the screen door talking.*)

Hello? Hey, Jesse. Naw . . . I was just getting ready to leave now.

ROSE: (*Calling.*) Cory!
5 CORY: I told you, man, them spikes is all tore up. You can use them if you want, but they ain't no good. Earl got some spikes.

ROSE: (*Calling.*) Cory!

CORY: (*Calling to* ROSE.) Mam? I'm talking to Jesse.

(*Into phone.*)

10 When she say that. (*Pause.*) Aw, you lying, man. I'm gonna tell her you said that.

ROSE: (*Calling.*) Cory, don't you go nowhere!

CORY: I got to go to the game, Ma!

(*Into the phone.*)

Yeah, hey, look, I'll talk to you later. Yeah, I'll meet you
15 over Earl's house. Later. Bye, Ma.

(CORY *exits the house and starts out the yard.*)

ROSE: Cory, where you going off to? You got that stuff all pulled out and thrown all over your room.

CORY: (*In the yard.*) I was looking for my spikes. Jesse wanted to borrow my spikes.
20 ROSE: Get up there and get that cleaned up before your daddy get back in here.

CORY: I got to go to the game! I'll clean it up *when I get back.*

(CORY *exits.*)

ROSE: That's all he need to do is see that room all messed up.

(ROSE *exits into the house.* TROY *and* BONO *enter the yard.* TROY *is dressed in clothes other than his work clothes.*)

BONO: He told him the same thing he told you. Take it to the union.   25

TROY: Brownie ain't got that much sense. Man wasn't thinking about nothing. He wait until I confront them on it . . . then he wanna come crying seniority.

(*Calls.*)

Hey, Rose!

BONO: I wish I could have seen Mr. Rand's face when he told   30 you.

TROY: He couldn't get it out of his mouth! Liked to bit his tongue! When they called me down there to the Commissioner's office . . . he thought they was gonna fire me. Like everybody else.   35

BONO: I didn't think they was gonna fire-you. I thought they was gonna put you on the warning paper.

TROY: Hey, Rose!

(*To* BONO.)

Yeah, Mr. Rand like to bit his tongue.

(TROY *breaks the seal on the bottle, takes a drink, and hands it to* BONO.)

BONO: I see you run right down to Taylors' and told that Al-   40 berta gal.

TROY: (*Calling.*) Hey Rose! (*To* BONO.) I told everybody. Hey, Rose! I went down there to cash my check.

ROSE: (*Entering from the house.*) Hush all that hollering, man! I know you out here. What they say down there at the   45 Commissioner's office?

TROY: You supposed to come when I call you, woman. Bono'll tell you that.

(*To* BONO.)

Don't Lucille come when you call her?

ROSE: Man, hush your mouth. I ain't no dog . . . talk about   50 "come when you call me."

TROY: (*Puts his arm around* ROSE.) You hear this, Bono? I had me an old dog used to get uppity like that. You say, "C'mere, Blue!" . . . and he just lay there and look at you. End up getting a stick and chasing him away trying to   55 make him come.

ROSE: I ain't studying you and your dog. I remember you used to sing that old song.

TROY: (*He sings.*) Hear it ring! Hear it ring! I had a dog his name was Blue.   60

ROSE: Don't nobody wanna hear you sing that old song.

TROY: (*Sings.*) You know Blue was mighty true.

ROSE: Used to have Cory running around here singing that song.

BONO: Hell, I remember that song myself.

TROY: (*Sings.*)   65

You know Blue was a good old dog.
Blue treed a possum in a hollow log.

That was my daddy's song. My daddy made up that song.

ROSE: I don't care who made it up. Don't nobody wanna hear you sing it.

TROY: (*Makes a song like calling a dog.*) Come here, woman.

ROSE: You come in here carrying on, I reckon they ain't fired you. What they say down there at the Commissioner's office?

TROY: Look here, Rose . . . Mr. Rand called me into his office today when I got back from talking to them people down there . . . it come from up top . . . he called me in and told me they was making me a driver.

ROSE: Troy, you kidding!

TROY: No I ain't. Ask Bono.

ROSE: Well, that's great, Troy. Now you don't have to hassle them people no more.

(LYONS *enters from the street.*)

TROY: Aw hell, I wasn't looking to see you today. I thought you was in jail. Got it all over the front page of the *Courier* about them raiding Sefus' place . . . where you be hanging out with all them thugs?

LYONS: Hey, Pop . . . that ain't got nothing to do with me. I don't go down there gambling. I go down there to sit in with the band. I ain't got nothing to do with the gambling part. They got some good music down there.

TROY: They got some rogues . . . is what they got.

LYONS: How you been, Mr. Bono? Hi, Rose.

BONO: I see where you playing down at the Crawford Grill tonight.

ROSE: How come you ain't brought Bonnie like I told you. You should have brought Bonnie with you, she ain't been over in a month of Sundays.

LYONS: I was just in the neighborhood . . . thought I'd stop by.

TROY: Here he come . . .

BONO: Your daddy got a promotion on the rubbish. He's gonna be the first colored driver. Ain't got to do nothing but sit up there and read the paper like them white fellows.

LYONS: Hey, Pop . . . if you knew how to read you'd be alright.

BONO: Naw . . . naw . . . you mean if the nigger knew how to *drive* he'd be all right. Been fighting with them people about driving and ain't even got a license. Mr. Rand know you ain't got no driver's license?

TROY: Driving ain't nothing. All you do is point the truck where you want it to go. Driving ain't nothing.

BONO: Do Mr. Rand know you ain't got no driver's license? That's what I'm talking about. I ain't asked if driving was easy. I asked if Mr. Rand know you ain't got no driver's license.

TROY: He ain't got to know. The man ain't got to know my business. Time he find out, I have two or three driver's licenses.

LYONS: (*Going into his pocket.*) Say, look here, Pop . . .

TROY: I knew it was coming. Didn't I tell you, Bono? I know what kind of "Look here, Pop" that was. The nigger fixing to ask me for some money. It's Friday night. It's my payday. All them rogues down there on the avenue . . . the ones that ain't in jail . . . and Lyons is hopping in his shoes to get down there with them.

LYONS: See, Pop . . . if you give somebody else a chance to talk sometime, you'd see that I was fixing to pay you back your ten dollars like I told you. Here . . . I told you I'd pay you when Bonnie got paid.

TROY: Naw . . . you go ahead and keep that ten dollars. Put it in the bank. The next time you feel like you wanna come by here and ask me for something . . . you go on down there and get that.

LYONS: Here's your ten dollars, Pop. I told you I don't want you to give me nothing. I just wanted to borrow ten dollars.

TROY: Naw . . . you go on and keep that for the next time you want to ask me.

LYONS: Come on, Pop . . . here go your ten dollars.

ROSE: Why don't you go on and let the boy pay you back, Troy?

LYONS: Here you go, Rose. If you don't take it I'm gonna have to hear about it for the next six months.

(*He hands her the money.*)

ROSE: You can hand yours over here too, Troy.

TROY: You see this, Bono. You see how they do me.

BONO: Yeah, Lucille do me the same way.

(GABRIEL *is heard singing offstage. He enters.*)

GABRIEL: Better get ready for the Judgment! Better get ready for . . . Hey! . . . Hey! . . . There's Troy's boy!

LYONS: How you doing, Uncle Gabe?

GABRIEL: Lyons . . . The King of the Jungle! Rose . . . hey, Rose. Got a flower for you.

(*He takes a rose from his pocket.*)

Picked it myself. That's the same rose like you is!

ROSE: That's right nice of you, Gabe.

LYONS: What you been doing, Uncle Gabe?

GABRIEL: Oh, I been chasing hellhounds and waiting on the time to tell St. Peter to open the gates.

LYONS: You been chasing hellhounds, huh? Well . . . you doing the right thing, Uncle Gabe. Somebody got to chase them.

GABRIEL: Oh, yeah . . . I know it. The devil's strong. The devil ain't no pushover. Hellhounds snipping at everybody's heels. But I got my trumpet waiting on the judgment time.

LYONS: Waiting on the Battle of Armageddon, huh?

GABRIEL: Ain't gonna be too much of a battle when God get to waving that Judgment sword. But the people's gonna have a hell of a time trying to get into heaven if them gates ain't open.

LYONS: (*Putting his arm around* GABRIEL.) You hear this, Pop. Uncle Gabe, you alright!

GABRIEL: (*Laughing with* LYONS.) Lyons! King of the Jungle.

ROSE: You gonna stay for supper, Gabe. Want me to fix you a plate?

GABRIEL: I'll take a sandwich, Rose. Don't want no plate. Just wanna eat with my hands. I'll take a sandwich.

ROSE: How about you, Lyons? You staying? Got some short ribs cooking.

LYONS: Naw, I won't eat nothing till after we finished playing.

(*Pause.*)

You ought to come down and listen to me play, Pop.

TROY: I don't like that Chinese music. All that noise.

ROSE: Go on in the house and wash up, Gabe . . . I'll fix you a sandwich.

175 GABRIEL: (*To* LYONS, *as he exits.*) Troy's mad at me.

LYONS: What you mad at Uncle Gabe for, Pop.

ROSE: He thinks Troy's mad at him cause he moved over to Miss Pearl's.

TROY: I ain't mad at the man. He can live where he want to
180 live at.

LYONS: What he move over there for? Miss Pearl don't like nobody.

ROSE: She don't mind him none. She treats him real nice. She just don't allow all that singing.

185 TROY: She don't mind that rent he be paying . . . that's what she don't mind.

ROSE: Troy, I ain't going through that with you no more. He's over there cause he want to have his own place. He can come and go as he please.

190 TROY: Hell, he could come and go as he please here. I wasn't stopping him. I ain't put no rules on him.

ROSE: It ain't the same thing, Troy. And you know it.

(GABRIEL *comes to the door.*)

Now, that's the last I wanna hear about that. I don't wanna hear nothing else about Gabe and Miss Pearl. And next
195 week . . .

GABRIEL: I'm ready for my sandwich, Rose.

ROSE: And next week . . . when that recruiter come from that school . . . I want you to sign that paper and go on and let Cory play football. Then that'll be the last I have to hear
200 about that.

TROY: (*To* ROSE *as she exits into the house.*) I ain't thinking about Cory nothing.

LYONS: What . . . Cory got recruited? What school he going to?

TROY: That boy walking around here smelling his piss . . .
205 thinking he's grown. Thinking he's gonna do what he want, irrespective of what I say. Look here, Bono . . . I left the Commissioner's office and went down to the A&P . . . that boy ain't working down there. He lying to me. Telling me he got his job back . . . telling me he working
210 weekends . . . telling me he working after school . . . Mr. Stawicki tell me he ain't working down there at all!

LYONS: Cory just growing up. He's just busting at the seams trying to fill out your shoes.

TROY: I don't care what he's doing. When he get to the point
215 where he wanna disobey me . . . then it's time for him to move on. Bono'll tell you that. I bet he ain't never disobeyed his daddy without paying the consequences.

BONO: I ain't never had a chance. My daddy came on through . . . but I ain't never knew him to see him . . . or what he
220 had on his mind or where he went. Just moving on through. Searching out the New Land. That's what the old folks used to call it. See a fellow moving around from place to place . . . woman to woman . . . called it searching out the New Land. I can't say if he ever found it. I come along,
225 didn't want no kids. Didn't know if I was gonna be in one place long enough to fix on them right as their daddy. I figured I was going searching too. As it turned out I been hooked up with Lucille near about as long as your daddy been with Rose. Going on sixteen years.

230 TROY: Sometimes I wish I hadn't known my daddy. He ain't cared nothing about no kids. A kid to him wasn't noth-

ing. All he wanted was for you to learn how to walk so he could start you to working. When it come time for eating . . . he ate first. If there was anything left over, that's
235 what you got. Man would sit down and eat two chickens and give you the wing.

LYONS: You ought to stop that, Pop. Everybody feed their kids. No matter how hard times is . . . everybody care about their kids. Make sure they have something to eat.

240 TROY: The only thing my daddy cared about was getting them bales of cotton into Mr. Lubin. That's the only thing that mattered to him. Sometimes I used to wonder why he was living. Wonder why the devil hadn't come and got him. "Get them bales of cotton in to Mr. Lubin" and find
245 out he owe him money . . .

LYONS: He should have just went on and left when he saw he couldn't get nowhere. That's what I would have done.

TROY: How he gonna leave with eleven kids? And where he gonna go? He ain't knew how to do nothing but farm.
250 No, he was trapped and I think he knew it. But I'll say this for him . . . he felt a responsibility toward us. Maybe he ain't treated us the way I felt he should have . . . but without that responsibility he could have walked off and left us . . . made his own way.

255 BONO: A lot of them did. Back in those days what you talking about . . . they walk out their front door and just take on down one road or another and keep on walking.

LYONS: There you go! That's what I'm talking about.

BONO: Just keep on walking till you come to something else. Ain't you never heard of nobody having the walking blues?
260 Well, that's what you call it when you just take off like that.

TROY: My daddy ain't had them walking blues! What you talking about? He stayed right there with his family. But he was just as evil as he could be. My mama couldn't stand him. Couldn't stand that evilness. She run off when I was
265 about eight. She sneaked off one night after he had gone to sleep. Told me she was coming back for me. I ain't never seen her no more. All his women run off and left him. He wasn't good for nobody.

When my turn come to head out, I was fourteen and got
270 to sniffing around Joe Canewell's daughter. Had us an old mule we called Greyboy. My daddy sent me out to do some plowing and I tied up Greyboy and went to fooling around with Joe Canewell's daughter. We done found us a nice little spot, got real cozy with each other. She about thirteen
275 and we done figured we was grown anyway . . . so we down there enjoying ourselves . . . ain't thinking about nothing. We didn't know Greyboy had got loose and wandered back to the house and my daddy was looking for me. We down there by the creek enjoying ourselves when my daddy
280 come up on us. Surprised us. He had them leather straps off the mule and commenced to whupping me like there was no tomorrow. I jumped up, mad and embarrassed. I was scared of my daddy. When he commenced to whupping on me . . . quite naturally I run to get out of the way.
285

(*Pause.*)

Now I thought he was mad cause I ain't done my work. But I see where he was chasing me off so he could have the gal for himself. When I see what the matter of it was,

I lost all fear of my daddy. Right there is where I become a man . . . at fourteen years of age.

(*Pause.*)

Now it was my turn to run him off. I picked up them same reins that he had used on me. I picked up them reins and commenced to whupping on him. The gal jumped up and run off . . . and when my daddy turned to face me, I could see why the devil had never come to get him . . . cause he was the devil himself. I don't know what happened. When I woke up, I was laying right there by the creek, and Blue . . . this old dog we had . . . was licking my face. I thought I was blind. I couldn't see nothing. Both my eyes were swollen shut. I layed there and cried. I didn't know what I was gonna do. The only thing I knew was the time had come for me to leave my daddy's house. And right there the world suddenly got big. And it was a long time before I could cut it down to where I could handle it.

Part of that cutting down was when I got to the place where I could feel him kicking in my blood and knew that the only thing that separated us was the matter of a few years.

(GABRIEL *enters from the house with a sandwich.*)

LYONS: What you got there, Uncle Gabe?

GABRIEL: Got me a ham sandwich. Rose gave me a ham sandwich.

TROY: I don't know what happened to him. I done lost touch with everybody except Gabriel. But I hope he's dead. I hope he found some peace.

LYONS: That's a heavy story, Pop. I didn't know you left home when you was fourteen.

TROY: And didn't know nothing. The only part of the world I knew was the forty-two acres of Mr. Lubin's land. That's all I knew about life.

LYONS: Fourteen's kinda young to be out on your own. (*Phone rings.*) I don't even think I was ready to be out on my own at fourteen. I don't know what I would have done.

TROY: I got up from the creek and walked on down to Mobile. I was through with farming. Figured I could do better in the city. So I walked the two hundred miles to Mobile.

LYONS: Wait a minute . . . you ain't walked no two hundred miles, Pop. Ain't nobody gonna walk no two hundred miles. You talking about some walking there.

BONO: That's the only way you got anywhere back in them days.

LYONS: Shhh. Damn if I wouldn't have hitched a ride with somebody!

TROY: Who you gonna hitch it with? They ain't had no cars and things like they got now. We talking about 1918.

ROSE: (*Entering.*) What you all out here getting into?

TROY: (*To* ROSE.) I'm telling Lyons how good he got it. He don't know nothing about this I'm talking.

ROSE: Lyons, that was Bonnie on the phone. She say you supposed to pick her up.

LYONS: Yeah, okay, Rose.

TROY: I walked on down to Mobile and hitched up with some of them fellows that was heading this way. Got up here and found out . . . not only couldn't you get a job . . . you couldn't find no place to live. I thought I was in freedom. Shhh. Colored folks living down there on the river-banks in whatever kind of shelter they could find for themselves. Right down there under the Brady Street Bridge. Living in shacks made of sticks and tarpaper. Messed around there and went from bad to worse. Started stealing. First it was food. Then I figured, hell, if I steal money I can buy me some food. Buy me some shoes too! One thing led to another. Met your mama. I was young and anxious to be a man. Met your mama and had you. What I do that for? Now I got to worry about feeding you and her. Got to steal three times as much. Went out one day looking for somebody to rob . . . that's what I was, a robber. I'll tell you the truth. I'm ashamed of it today. But it's the truth. Went to rob this fellow . . . pulled out my knife . . . and he pulled out a gun. Shot me in the chest. It felt just like somebody had taken a hot branding iron and laid it on me. When he shot me I jumped at him with my knife. They told me I killed him and they put me in the penitentiary and locked me up for fifteen years. That's where I met Bono. That's where I learned how to play baseball. Got out that place and your mama had taken you and went on to make life without me. Fifteen years was a long time for her to wait. But that fifteen years cured me of that robbing stuff. Rose'll tell you. She asked me when I met her if I had gotten all that foolishness out of my system. And I told her, "Baby, it's you and baseball all what count with me." You hear me, Bono? I meant it too. She say, "Which one comes first?" I told her, "Baby, ain't no doubt it's baseball . . . but you stick and get old with me and we'll both outlive this baseball." Am I right, Rose? And it's true.

ROSE: Man, hush your mouth. You ain't said no such thing. Talking about, "Baby, you know you'll always be number one with me." That's what you was talking.

TROY: You hear that, Bono. That's why I love her.

BONO: Rose'll keep you straight. You get off the track, she'll straighten you up.

ROSE: Lyons, you better get on up and get Bonnie. She waiting on you.

LYONS: (*Gets up to go.*) Hey, Pop, why don't you come on down to the Grill and hear me play?

TROY: I ain't going down there. I'm too old to be sitting around in them clubs.

BONO: You got to be good to play down at the Grill.

LYONS: Come on, Pop . . .

TROY: I got to get up in the morning.

LYONS: You ain't got to stay long.

TROY: Naw, I'm gonna get my supper and go on to bed.

LYONS: Well, I got to go. I'll see you again.

TROY: Don't you come around my house on my payday.

ROSE: Pick up the phone and let somebody know you coming. And bring Bonnie with you. You know I'm always glad to see her.

LYONS: Yeah, I'll do that, Rose. You take care now. See you, Pop. See you, Mr. Bono. See you, Uncle Gabe.

GABRIEL: Lyons! King of the Jungle!

(LYONS *exits.*)

TROY: Is supper ready, woman? Me and you got some business to take care of. I'm gonna tear it up too.

ROSE: Troy, I done told you now!

TROY: (*Puts his arm around* BONO.) Aw hell, woman . . . this is Bono. Bono like family. I done known this nigger since . . . how long I done know you?

405 BONO: It's been a long time.

TROY: I done known this nigger since Skippy was a pup. Me and him done been through some times.

BONO: You sure right about that.

TROY: Hell, I done know him longer than I known you. And 410 we still standing shoulder to shoulder. Hey, look here, Bono . . . a man can't ask for no more than that.

(*Drinks to him.*)

I love you, nigger.

BONO: Hell, I love you too . . . but I got to get home see my woman. You got yours in hand. I got to go get mine.

(BONO *starts to exit as* CORY *enters the yard, dressed in his football uniform. He gives* TROY *a hard, uncompromising look.*)

415 CORY: What you do that for, Pop?

(*He throws his helmet down in the direction of* TROY.)

ROSE: What's the matter? Cory . . . what's the matter?

CORY: Papa done went up to the school and told Coach Zellman I can't play football no more. Wouldn't even let me play the game. Told him to tell the recruiter not to come.

420 ROSE: Troy . . .

TROY: What you Troying me for? Yeah, I did it. And the boy know why I did it.

CORY: Why you wanna do that to me? That was the one chance I had.

425 ROSE: Ain't nothing wrong with Cory playing football, Troy.

TROY: The boy lied to me. I told the nigger if he wanna play football . . . to keep his chores and hold down that job at the A&P. That was the conditions. Stopped down there to see Mr. Stawicki . . .

430 CORY: I can't work after school during the football season, Pop! I tried to tell you that Mr. Stawicki's holding my job for me. You don't never want to listen to nobody. And then you wanna go and do this to me!

TROY: I ain't done nothing to you. You done it to yourself.

435 CORY: Just cause you didn't have a chance! You just scared I'm gonna be better than you, that's all.

TROY: Come here.

ROSE: Troy . . .

(CORY *reluctantly crosses over to* TROY.)

TROY: Alright! See. You done made a mistake.

440 CORY: I didn't even do nothing!

TROY: I'm gonna tell you what your mistake was. See . . . you swung at the ball and didn't hit it. That's strike one. See, you in the batter's box now. You swung and you missed. That's strike one. Don't you strike out!

(*Lights fade to black.*)

ACT TWO

SCENE I

The following morning. CORY *is at the tree hitting the ball with the bat. He tries to mimic* TROY, *but his swing is awkward, less sure.* ROSE *enters from the house.*

ROSE: Cory, I want you to help me with this cupboard.

CORY: I ain't quitting the team. I don't care what Poppa say.

ROSE: I'll talk to him when he gets back. He had to go see about your Uncle Gabe. The police done arrested him. Say he was disturbing the peace. He'll be back directly. Come 5 on in here and help me clean out the top of this cupboard.

(CORY *exits into the house.* ROSE *sees* TROY *and* BONO *coming down the alley.*)

Troy . . . what they say down there?

TROY: Ain't said nothing. I give them fifty dollars and they let him go. I'll talk to you about it. Where's Cory?

ROSE: He's in there helping me clean out these cupboards. 10

TROY: Tell him to get his butt out here.

(TROY *and* BONO *go over to the pile of wood.* BONO *picks up the saw and begins sawing.*)

TROY: (*To* BONO.) All they want is the money. That makes six or seven times I done went down there and got him. See me coming they stick out their hands.

BONO: Yeah. I know what you mean. That's all they care 15 about . . . that money. They don't care about what's right.

(*Pause.*)

Nigger, why you got to go and get some hard wood? You ain't doing nothing but building a little old fence. Get you some soft pine wood. That's all you need.

TROY: I know what I'm doing. This is outside wood. You 20 put pine wood inside the house. Pine wood is inside wood. This here is outside wood. Now you tell me where the fence is gonna be?

BONO: You don't need this wood. You can put it up with pine wood and it's stand as long as you gonna be here 25 looking at it.

TROY: How you know how long I'm gonna be here, nigger? Hell, I might just live forever. Live longer than old man Horsely.

BONO: That's what Magee used to say. 30

TROY: Magee's a damn fool. Now you tell me who you ever heard of gonna pull their own teeth with a pair of rusty pliers.

BONO: The old folks . . . my granddaddy used to pull his teeth with pliers. They ain't had no dentists for the colored 35 folks back then.

TROY: Get clean pliers! You understand? Clean pliers! Sterilize them! Besides we ain't living back then. All Magee had to do was walk over to Doc Goldblums.

BONO: I see where you and that Tallahassee gal . . . that Al- 40 berta . . . I see where you all done got tight.

TROY: What you mean "got tight"?

BONO: I see where you be laughing and joking with her all the time.

45   TROY: I laughs and jokes with all of them, Bono. You know me.
BONO: That ain't the kind of laughing and joking I'm talking about.

(CORY enters from the house.)

CORY: How you doing, Mr. Bono?
TROY: Cory? Get that saw from Bono and cut some wood.
50   He talking about the wood's too hard to cut. Stand back there, Jim, and let that young boy show you how it's done.
BONO: He's sure welcome to it.

(CORY takes the saw and begins to cut the wood.)

Whew-e-e! Look at that. Big old strong boy. Look like Joe Louis. Hell, must be getting old the way I'm watching that
55   boy whip through that wood.
CORY: I don't see why Mama want a fence around the yard noways.
TROY: Damn if I know either. What the hell she keeping out with it? She ain't got nothing nobody want.
60   BONO: Some people build fences to keep people out . . . and other people build fences to keep people in. Rose wants to hold on to you all. She loves you.
TROY: Hell, nigger, I don't need nobody to tell me my wife loves me, Cory . . . go on in the house and see if you can
65   find that other saw.
CORY: Where's it at?
TROY: I said find it! Look for it till you find it!

(CORY exits into the house.)

What's that supposed to mean? Wanna keep us in?
BONO: Troy . . . I done known you seem like damn near my
70   whole life. You and Rose both. I done know both of you all for a long time. I remember when you met Rose. When you was hitting them baseball out the park. A lot of them old gals was after you then. You had the pick of the litter. When you picked Rose, I was happy for you.
75   That was the first time I knew you had any sense. I said . . . My man Troy knows what he's doing . . . I'm gonna follow this nigger . . . he might take me somewhere. I been following you too. I done learned a whole heap of things about life watching you. I done learned how to tell where
80   the shit lies. How to tell it from the alfalfa. You done learned me a lot of things. You showed me how to not make the same mistakes . . . to take life as it comes along and keep putting one foot in front of the other.

(Pause.)

Rose a good woman, Troy.
85   TROY: Hell, nigger, I know she a good woman. I been married to her for eighteen years. What you got on your mind, Bono?
BONO: I just say she a good woman. Just like I say anything. I ain't got to have nothing on my mind.
TROY: You just gonna say she a good woman and leave it
90   hanging out there like that? Why you telling me she a good woman?
BONO: She loves you, Troy. Rose loves you.
TROY: You saying I don't measure up. That's what you trying to say. I don't measure up cause I'm seeing this other gal.
95   I know what you trying to say.

BONO: I know what Rose means to you, Troy. I'm just trying to say I don't want to see you mess up.
TROY: Yeah, I appreciate that, Bono. If you was messing around on Lucille I'd be telling you the same thing.
BONO: Well, that's all I got to say. I just say that because I love   100
you both.
TROY: Hell, you know me . . . I wasn't out there looking for nothing. You can't find a better woman than Rose. I know that. But seems like this woman just stuck onto me where I can't shake her loose. I done wrestled with it,   105
tried to throw her off me . . . but she just stuck on tighter. Now she's stuck on for good.
BONO: You's in control . . . that's what you tell me all the time. You responsible for what you do.
TROY: I ain't ducking the responsibility of it. As long as it sets   110
right in my heart . . . then I'm okay. Cause that's all I listen to. It'll tell me right from wrong every time. And I ain't talking about doing Rose no bad turn. I love Rose. She done carried me a long ways and I love and respect her for that.   115
BONO: I know you do. That's why I don't want to see you hurt her. But what you gonna do when she find out? What you got then? If you try and juggle both of them . . . sooner or later you gonna drop one of them. That's common sense.
TROY: Yeah, I hear what you saying, Bono. I been trying to   120
figure a way to work it out.
BONO: Work it out right, Troy. I don't want to be getting all up between you and Rose's business . . . but work it so it come out right.
TROY: Aw hell, I get all up between you and Lucille's business.   125
When you gonna get that woman that refrigerator she been wanting? Don't tell me you ain't got no money now. I know who your banker is. Mellon don't need that money bad as Lucille want that refrigerator. I'll tell you that.
BONO: Tell you what I'll do . . . when you finish building this   130
fence for Rose . . . I'll buy Lucille that refrigerator.
TROY: You done stuck your foot in your mouth now!

(TROY grabs up a board and begins to saw. BONO starts to walk out the yard.)

Hey, nigger . . . where you going?
BONO: I'm going home. I know you don't expect me to help you now. I'm protecting my money. I wanna see you put   135
that fence up by yourself. That's what I want to see. You'll be here another six month without me.
TROY: Nigger, you ain't right.
BONO: When it comes to my money . . . I'm right as fireworks on the Fourth of July.   140
TROY: Alright, we gonna see now. You better get out your bankbook.

(BONO exits, and TROY continues to work. ROSE enters from the house.)

ROSE: What they say down there? What's happening with Gabe?
TROY: I went down there and got him out. Cost me fifty dol-   145
lars. Say he was disturbing the peace. Judge set up a hearing for him in three weeks. Say to show cause why he shouldn't be re-committed.

ROSE: What was he doing that cause them to arrest him?

150 TROY: Some kids was teasing him and he run them off home. Say he was howling and carrying on. Some folks seen him and called the police. That's all it was.

ROSE: Well, what's you say? What'd you tell the judge?

155 TROY: Told him I'd look after him. It didn't make no sense to recommit the man. He stuck out his big greasy palm and told me to give him fifty dollars and take him on home.

ROSE: Where's he at now? Where'd he go off to?

TROY: He's gone on about his business. He don't need nobody to hold his hand.

160 ROSE: Well, I don't know. Seem like that would be the best place for him if they did put him into the hospital. I know what you're gonna say. But that's what I think would be best.

TROY: The man done had his life ruined fighting for what?

165 And they wanna take and lock him up. Let him be free. He don't bother nobody.

ROSE: Well, everybody got their own way of looking at it I guess. Come on and get your lunch. I got a bowl of lima beans and some cornbread in the oven. Come on get

170 something to eat. Ain't no sense you fretting over Gabe.

(ROSE *turns to go into the house.*)

TROY: Rose . . . got something to tell you.

ROSE: Well, come on . . . wait till I get this food on the table.

TROY: Rose!

(*She stops and turns around.*)

I don't know how to say this.

(*Pause.*)

175 I can't explain it none. It just sort of grows on you till it gets out of hand. It starts out like a little bush . . . and the next thing you know it's a whole forest.

ROSE: Troy . . . what is you talking about?

TROY: I'm talking, woman, let me talk. I'm trying to find a

180 way to tell you . . . I'm gonna be a daddy. I'm gonna be somebody's daddy.

ROSE: Troy . . . you're not telling me this? You're gonna be . . . what?

TROY: Rose . . . now . . . see . . .

185 ROSE: You telling me you gonna be somebody's daddy? You telling your *wife* this?

(GABRIEL *enters from the street. He carries a rose in his hand.*)

GABRIEL: Hey, Troy! Hey, Rose!

ROSE: I have to wait eighteen years to hear something like this.

GABRIEL: Hey, Rose . . . I got a flower for you.

(*He hands it to her.*)

190 That's a rose. Same rose like you is.

ROSE: Thanks, Gabe.

GABRIEL: Troy, you ain't mad at me is you? Them bad mens come and put me away. You ain't mad at me is you?

TROY: Naw, Gabe, I ain't mad at you.

195 ROSE: Eighteen years and you wanna come with this.

GABRIEL: (*Takes a quarter out of his pocket.*) See what I got? Got a brand new quarter.

TROY: Rose . . . it's just . . .

ROSE: Ain't nothing you can say, Troy. Ain't no way of explaining that.

200

GABRIEL: Fellow that give me this quarter had a whole mess of them. I'm gonna keep this quarter till it stop shining.

ROSE: Gabe, go on in the house there. I got some watermelon in the frigidaire. Go on and get you a piece.

GABRIEL: Say, Rose . . . you know I was chasing hellhounds 205 and them bad mens come and get me and take me away. Troy helped me. He come down there and told them they better let me go before he beat them up. Yeah, he did!

ROSE: You go on and get you a piece of watermelon, Gabe. Them bad mens is gone now.

210

GABRIEL: Okay, Rose . . . gonna get me some watermelon. The kind with the stripes on it.

(GABRIEL *exits into the house.*)

ROSE: Why, Troy? Why? After all these years to come dragging this in to me now. It don't make no sense at your age. I could have expected this ten or fifteen years ago, but not 215 now.

TROY: Age ain't got nothing to do with it, Rose.

ROSE: I done tried to be everything a wife should be. Everything a wife could be. Been married eighteen years and I got to live to see the day you tell me you been seeing an- 220 other woman and done fathered a child by her. And you know I ain't never wanted no half nothing in my family. My whole family is half. Everybody got different fathers and mothers . . . my two sisters and my brother. Can't hardly tell who's who. Can't never sit down and talk about 225 Papa and Mama. It's your papa and your mama and my papa and my mama . . .

TROY: Rose . . . stop it now.

ROSE: I ain't never wanted that for none of my children. And now you wanna drag your behind in here and tell me 230 something like this.

TROY: You ought to know. It's time for you to know.

ROSE: Well, I don't want to know, goddamn it!

TROY: I can't just make it go away. It's done now. I can't wish the circumstance of the thing away. 235

ROSE: And you don't want to either. Maybe you want to wish me and my boy away. Maybe that's what you want? Well, you can't wish us away. I've got eighteen years of my life invested in you. You ought to have stayed upstairs in my bed where you belong. 240

TROY: Rose . . . now listen to me . . . we can get a handle on this thing. We can talk this out . . . come to an understanding.

ROSE: All of a sudden it's "we." Where was "we" at when you was down there rolling around with some godforsaken woman? "We" should have come to an understanding be- 245 fore you started making a damn fool of yourself. You're a day late and a dollar short when it comes to an understanding with me.

TROY: It's just . . . She gives me a different idea . . . a different understanding about myself. I can step out of this house 250 and get away from the pressures and problems . . . be a different man. I ain't got to wonder how I'm gonna pay the bills or get the roof fixed. I can just be a part of myself that I ain't never been.

ROSE: What I want to know . . . is do you plan to continue 255 seeing her. That's all you can say to me.

TROY: I can sit up in her house and laugh. Do you understand what I'm saying. I can laugh out loud . . . and it feels good. It reaches all the way down to the bottom of my shoes.

(*Pause.*)

260   Rose, I can't give that up.

ROSE: Maybe you ought to go on and stay down there with her . . . if she a better woman than me.

TROY: It ain't about nobody being a better woman or nothing. Rose, you ain't the blame. A man couldn't ask for no

265   woman to be a better wife than you've been. I'm responsible for it. I done locked myself into a pattern trying to take care of you all that I forgot about myself.

ROSE: What the hell was I there for? That was my job, not somebody else's.

270 TROY: Rose, I done tried all my life to live decent . . . to live a clean . . . hard . . . useful life. I tried to be a good husband to you. In every way I knew how. Maybe I come into the world backwards, I don't know. But . . . you born with two strikes on you before you come to the plate. You got to guard it

275   closely . . . always looking for the curve-ball on the inside corner. You can't afford to let none get past you. You can't afford a call strike. If you going down . . . you going down swinging. Everything lined up against you. What you gonna do. I fooled them, Rose. I bunted. When I found you and

280   Cory and a halfway decent job . . . I was safe. Couldn't nothing touch me. I wasn't gonna strike out no more. I wasn't going back to the penitentiary. I wasn't gonna lay in the streets with a bottle of wine. I was safe. I had me a family. A job. I wasn't gonna get that last strike. I was on first looking

285   for one of them boys to knock me in. To get me home.

ROSE: You should have stayed in my bed, Troy.

TROY: Then when I saw that gal . . . she firmed up my backbone. And I got to thinking that if I tried . . . I just might be able to steal second. Do you understand after eighteen

290   years I wanted to steal second.

ROSE: You should have held me tight. You should have grabbed me and held on.

TROY: I stood on first base for eighteen years and I thought . . . well, goddamn it . . . go on for it!

295 ROSE: We're not talking about baseball! We're talking about you going off to lay in bed with another woman . . . and then bring it home to me. That's what we're talking about. We ain't talking about no baseball.

TROY: Rose, you're not listening to me. I'm trying the best I

300   can to explain it to you. It's not easy for me to admit that I been standing in the same place for eighteen years.

ROSE: I been standing with you! I been right here with you, Troy. I got a life too. I gave eighteen years of my life to stand in the same spot with you. Don't you think I ever wanted

305   other things? Don't you think I had dreams and hopes? What about my life? What about me? Don't you think it ever crossed my mind to want to know other men? That I wanted to lay up somewhere and forget about my responsibilities? That I wanted someone to make me laugh so I

310   could feel good? You not the only one who's got wants and needs. But I held on to you, Troy. I took all my feelings, my wants and needs, my dreams . . . and I buried them inside you. I planted a seed and watched and prayed over it. I planted myself inside you and waited to bloom. And it

315 didn't take me no eighteen years to find out the soil was hard and rocky and it wasn't never gonna bloom.

But I held on to you, Troy. I held you tighter. You was my husband. I owed you everything I had. Every part of me I could find to give you. And upstairs in that room . . .

320 with the darkness falling in on me . . . I gave everything I had to try and erase the doubt that you wasn't the finest man in the world. And wherever you was going . . . I wanted to be there with you. Cause you was my husband. Cause that's the only way I was gonna survive as your

325 wife. You always talking about what you give . . . and what you don't have to give. But you take too. You take . . . and don't even know nobody's giving!

(ROSE *turns to exit into the house;* TROY *grabs her arm.*)

TROY: You say I take and don't give!

ROSE: Troy! You're hurting me!

TROY: You say I take and don't give.   330

ROSE: Troy . . . you're hurting my arm! Let go!

TROY: I done give you everything I got. Don't you tell that lie on me.

ROSE: Troy!

TROY: Don't you tell that lie on me!   335

(CORY *enters from the house.*)

CORY: Mama!

ROSE: Troy. You're hurting me.

TROY: Don't you tell me about no taking and giving.

(CORY *comes up behind* TROY *and grabs him.* TROY, *surprised, is thrown off balance just as* CORY *throws a glancing blow that catches him on the chest and knocks him down.* TROY *is stunned, as is* CORY.)

ROSE: Troy. Troy. No!

(TROY *gets to his feet and starts at* CORY.)

Troy . . . no. Please! Troy!   340

(ROSE *pulls on* TROY *to hold him back.* TROY *stops himself.*)

TROY: (*To* CORY.) Alright. That's strike two. You stay away from around me, boy. Don't you strike out. You living with a full count. Don't you strike out.

(TROY *exits out the yard as the lights go down.*)

SCENE II

It is six months later, early afternoon. TROY *enters from the house and starts to exit the yard.* ROSE *enters from the house.*

ROSE: Troy, I want to talk to you.

TROY: All of a sudden, after all this time, you want to talk to me, huh? You ain't wanted to talk to me for months. You ain't wanted to talk to me last night. You ain't wanted no part of me then. What you wanna talk to me about now? 5

ROSE: Tomorrow's Friday.

TROY: I know what day tomorrow is. You think I don't know tomorrow's Friday? My whole life I ain't done nothing but look to see Friday coming and you got to tell me it's Friday.

10 ROSE: I want to know if you're coming home.

TROY: I always come home, Rose. You know that. There ain't never been a night I ain't come home.

ROSE: That ain't what I mean . . . and you know it. I want to know if you're coming straight home after work.

15 TROY: I figure I'd cash my check . . . hang out at Taylors' with the boys . . . maybe play a game of checkers . . .

ROSE: Troy, I can't live like this. I won't live like this. You livin' on borrowed time with me. It's been going on six months now you ain't been coming home.

20 TROY: I be here every night. Every night of the year. That's 365 days.

ROSE: I want you to come home tomorrow after work.

TROY: Rose . . . I don't mess up my pay. You know that now. I take my pay and I give it to you. I don't have no money but what you give me back. I just want to have a little time to myself . . . a little time to enjoy life.

ROSE: What about me? When's my time to enjoy life?

TROY: I don't know what to tell you, Rose. I'm doing the best I can.

30 ROSE: You ain't been home from work but time enough to change your clothes and run out . . . and you wanna call that the best you can do?

TROY: I'm going over to the hospital to see Alberta. She went into the hospital this afternoon. Look like she might have the baby early. I won't be gone long.

35 ROSE: Well, you ought to know. They went over to Miss Pearl's and got Gabe today. She said you told them to go ahead and lock him up.

TROY: I ain't said no such thing. Whoever told you that is telling a lie. Pearl ain't doing nothing but telling a big fat lie.

40 ROSE: She ain't had to tell me. I read it on the papers.

TROY: I ain't told them nothing of the kind.

ROSE: I saw it right there on the papers.

TROY: What it say, huh?

45 ROSE: It said you told them to take him.

TROY: Then they screwed that up, just the way they screw up everything. I ain't worried about what they got on the paper.

ROSE: Say the government send part of his check to the hospital and the other part to you.

50 TROY: I ain't got nothing to do with that if that's the way it works. I ain't made up the rules about how it work.

ROSE: You did Gabe just like you did Cory. You wouldn't sign the paper for Cory . . . but you signed for Gabe. You signed that paper.

55

(*The telephone is heard ringing inside the house.*)

TROY: I told you I ain't signed nothing, woman! The only thing I signed was the release form. Hell, I can't read, I don't know what they had on that paper! I ain't signed nothing about sending Gabe away.

60 ROSE: I said send him to the hospital . . . you said let him be free . . . now you done went down there and signed him to the hospital for half his money. You went back on yourself, Troy. You gonna have to answer for that.

TROY: See now . . . you been over there talking to Miss Pearl. She done got mad cause she ain't getting Gabe's rent money. That's all it is. She's liable to say anything.

65

ROSE: Troy, I seen where you signed the paper.

TROY: You ain't seen nothing I signed. What she doing got papers on my brother anyway? Miss Pearl telling a big fat lie. And I'm gonna tell her about it too! You ain't seen 70 nothing I signed. Say . . . you ain't seen nothing I signed.

(ROSE *exits into the house to answer the telephone. Presently she returns.*)

ROSE: Troy . . . that was the hospital. Alberta had the baby.

TROY: What she have? What is it?

ROSE: It's a girl.

TROY: I better get on down to the hospital to see her.   75

ROSE: Troy . . .

TROY: Rose . . . I got to go see her now. That's only right . . . what's the matter . . . the baby's alright, ain't it?

ROSE: Alberta died having the baby.

TROY: Died . . . you say she's dead? Alberta's dead?   80

ROSE: They said they done all they could. They couldn't do nothing for her.

TROY: The baby? How's the baby?

ROSE: They say it's healthy. I wonder who's gonna bury her.

TROY: She had family, Rose. She wasn't living in the world 85 by herself.

ROSE: I know she wasn't living in the world by herself.

TROY: Next thing you gonna want to know if she had any insurance.

ROSE: Troy, you ain't got to talk like that.   90

TROY: That's the first thing that jumped out your mouth. "Who's gonna bury her?" Like I'm fixing to take on that task for myself.

ROSE: I am your wife. Don't push me away.

TROY: I ain't pushing nobody away. Just give me some space. 95 That's all. Just give me some room to breathe.

(ROSE *exits into the house.* TROY *walks about the yard.*)

TROY: (*With a quiet rage that threatens to consume him.*) Alright . . . Mr. Death. See now . . . I'm gonna tell you what I'm gonna do. I'm gonna take and build me a fence around this yard. See? I'm gonna build me a fence around what belongs 100 to me. And then I want you to stay on the other side. See? You stay over there until you're ready for me. Then you come on. Bring your army. Bring your sickle. Bring your wrestling clothes. I ain't gonna fall down on my vigilance this time. You ain't gonna sneak up on me no more. When 105 you ready for me . . . when the top of your list say Troy Maxson . . . that's when you come around here. You come up and knock on the front door. Ain't nobody else got nothing to do with this. This is between you and me. Man to man. You stay on the other side of that fence until you 110 ready for me. Then you come up and knock on the front door. Anytime you want. I'll be ready for you.

(*The lights go down to black.*)

SCENE III

The lights come up on the porch. It is late evening three days later. ROSE *sits listening to the ball game waiting for* TROY. *The final out of the game is made and* ROSE *switches off the radio.* TROY *enters the yard carrying an infant wrapped in blankets. He stands back from the house and calls.*

ROSE *enters and stands on the porch. There is a long, awkward silence, the weight of which grows heavier with each passing second.*

TROY: Rose . . . I'm standing here with my daughter in my arms. She ain't but a wee bittie little old thing. She don't know nothing about grownups' business. She innocent . . . and she ain't got no mama.

5 ROSE: What you telling me for, Troy?

(She turns and exits into the house.)

TROY: Well . . . I guess we'll just sit out here on the porch.

(He sits down on the porch. There is an awkward indelicateness about the way he handles the baby. His largeness engulfs and seems to swallow it. He speaks loud enough for ROSE to hear.)

A man's got to do what's right for him. I ain't sorry for nothing I done. It felt right in my heart.

(To the baby.)

What you smiling at? Your daddy's a big man. Got these 10 great big old hands. But sometimes he's scared. And right now your daddy's scared cause we sitting out here and ain't got no home. Oh, I been homeless before. I ain't had no little baby with me. But I been homeless. You just be out on the road by your lonesome and you see one of 15 them trains coming and you just kinda go like this . . .

(He sings as a lullaby.)

> Please, Mr. Engineer let a man ride the line
> Please, Mr. Engineer let a man ride the line
> I ain't got no ticket please let me ride the blinds

(ROSE enters from the house. TROY hearing her steps behind him, stands and faces her.)

She's my daughter, Rose. My own flesh and blood. I can't 20 deny her no more than I can deny them boys.

(Pause.)

You and them boys is my family. You and them and this child is all I got in the world. So I guess what I'm saying is . . . I'd appreciate it if you'd help take care of her.

ROSE: Okay, Troy . . . you're right. I'll take care of your baby 25 for you . . . cause . . . like you say . . . she's innocent . . . and you can't visit the sins of the father upon the child. A motherless child has got a hard time.

(She takes the baby from him.)

From right now . . . this child got a mother. But you a womanless man.

(ROSE turns and exits into the house with the baby. Lights go down to black.)

SCENE IV

It is two months later. LYONS enters from the street. He knocks on the door and calls.

LYONS: Hey, Rose! *(Pause.)* Rose!

ROSE: *(From inside the house.)* Stop that yelling. You gonna wake up Raynell. I just got her to sleep.

LYONS: I just stopped by to pay Papa this twenty dollars I owe 5 him. Where's Papa at?

ROSE: He should be here in a minute. I'm getting ready to go down to the church. Sit down and wait on him.

LYONS: I got to go pick up Bonnie over her mother's house.

ROSE: Well, sit it down there on the table. He'll get it.

LYONS: *(Enters the house and sets the money on the table.)* Tell 10 Papa I said thanks. I'll see you again.

ROSE: Alright, Lyons. We'll see you.

(LYONS starts to exit as CORY enters.)

CORY: Hey, Lyons.

LYONS: What's happening, Cory. Say man, I'm sorry I missed your graduation. You know I had a gig and couldn't get 15 away. Otherwise, I would have been there, man. So what you doing?

CORY: I'm trying to find a job.

LYONS: Yeah I know how that go, man. It's rough out here. Jobs are scarce. 20

CORY: Yeah, I know.

LYONS: Look here, I got to run. Talk to Papa . . . he know some people. He'll be able to help get you a job. Talk to him . . . see what he say.

CORY: Yeah . . . alright, Lyons. 25

LYONS: You take care. I'll talk to you soon. We'll find some time to talk.

(LYONS exits the yard. CORY wanders over to the tree, picks up the bat and assumes a batting stance. He studies an imaginary pitcher and swings. Dissatisfied with the result, he tries again. TROY enters. They eye each other for a beat. CORY puts the bat down and exits the yard. TROY starts into the house as ROSE exits with RAYNELL. She is carrying a cake.)

TROY: I'm coming in and everybody's going out.

ROSE: I'm taking this cake down to the church for the bake-sale. Lyons was by to see you. He stopped by to pay you 30 your twenty dollars. It's laying in there on the table.

TROY: *(Going into his pocket.)* Well . . . here go this money.

ROSE: Put it in there on the table, Troy. I'll get it.

TROY: What time you coming back?

ROSE: Ain't no use in you studying me. It don't matter what 35 time I come back.

TROY: I just asked you a question, woman. What's the matter . . . can't I ask you a question?

ROSE: Troy, I don't want to go into it. Your dinner's in there on the stove. All you got to do is heat it up. And don't you 40 be eating the rest of them cakes in there. I'm coming back for them. We having a bakesale at the church tomorrow.

(ROSE exits the yard. TROY sits down on the steps, takes a pint bottle from his pocket, opens it and drinks. He begins to sing.)

TROY: Hear it ring! Hear it ring!
> Had an old dog his name was Blue
> You know Blue was mighty true 45
> You know Blue as a good old dog
> Blue trees a possum in a hollow log
> You know from that he was a good old dog.

(BONO *enters the yard.*)

BONO: Hey, Troy.

50 TROY: Hey, what's happening, Bono?

BONO: I just thought I'd stop by to see you.

TROY: What you stop by and see me for? You ain't stopped by in a month of Sundays. Hell, I must owe you money or something.

55 BONO: Since you got your promotion I can't keep up with you. Used to see you everyday. Now I don't even know what route you working.

TROY: They keep switching me around. Got me out in Greentree now . . . hauling white folks' garbage.

60 BONO: Greentree, huh? You lucky, at least you ain't got to be lifting them barrels. Damn if they ain't getting heavier. I'm gonna put in my two years and call it quits.

TROY: I'm thinking about retiring myself.

BONO: You got it easy. You can *drive* for another five years.

65 TROY: It ain't the same, Bono. It ain't like working the back of the truck. Ain't got nobody to talk to . . . feel like you working by yourself. Naw, I'm thinking about retiring. How's Lucille?

BONO: She alright. Her arthritis get to acting up on her
70 sometime. Saw Rose on my way in. She going down to the church, huh?

TROY: Yeah, she took up going down there. All them preachers looking for somebody to fatten their pockets.

(*Pause.*)

Got some gin here.

75 BONO: Naw, thanks. I just stopped by to say hello.

TROY: Hell, nigger . . . you can take a drink. I ain't never known you to say no to a drink. You ain't got to work tomorrow.

BONO: I just stopped by. I'm fixing to go over to Skinner's.
80 We got us a domino game going over his house every Friday.

TROY: Nigger, you can't play no dominoes. I used to whup you four games out of five.

BONO: Well, that learned me. I'm getting better.

85 TROY: Yeah? Well, that's alright.

BONO: Look here . . . I got to be getting on. Stop by sometime, huh?

TROY: Yeah, I'll do that, Bono. Lucille told Rose you bought her a new refrigerator.

90 BONO: Yeah, Rose told Lucille you had finally built your fence . . . so I figured we'd call it even.

TROY: I knew you would.

BONO: Yeah . . . okay. I'll be talking to you.

TROY: Yeah, take care, Bono. Good to see you. I'm gonna stop
95 over.

BONO: Yeah. Okay, Troy.

(BONO *exits.* TROY *drinks from the bottle.*)

TROY: Old Blue died and I dig his grave
Let him down with a golden chain
Every night when I hear old Blue bark
I know Blue treed a possum in Noah's Ark.
100 Hear it ring! Hear it ring!

(CORY *enters the yard. They eye each other for a beat.* TROY *is sitting in the middle of the steps.* CORY *walks over.*)

CORY: I got to get by.

TROY: Say what? What's you say?

CORY: You in my way. I got to get by.

TROY: You got to get by where? This is my house. Bought and 105 paid for. In full. Took me fifteen years. And if you wanna go in my house and I'm sitting on the steps . . . you say excuse me. Like your mama taught you.

CORY: Come on, Pop . . . I got to get by.

(CORY *starts to maneuver his way past* TROY. TROY *grabs his leg and shoves him back.*)

TROY: You just gonna walk over top of me?   110

CORY: I live here too!

TROY: (*Advancing toward him.*) You just gonna walk over top of me in my own house?

CORY: I ain't scared of you.

TROY: I ain't asked if you was scared of me. I asked you if you 115 was fixing to walk over top of me in my own house? That's the question. You ain't gonna say excuse me? You just gonna walk over top of me?

CORY: If you wanna put it like that.

TROY: How else am I gonna put it?   120

CORY: I was walking by you to go into the house cause you sitting on the steps drunk, singing to yourself. You can put it like that.

TROY: Without saying excuse me???

(CORY *doesn't respond.*)

I asked you a question. Without saying excuse me???   125

CORY: I ain't got to say excuse me to you. You don't count around here no more.

TROY: Oh, I see . . . I don't count around here no more. You ain't got to say excuse me to your daddy. All of a sudden you done got so grown that your daddy don't count 130 around here no more . . . Around here in his own house and yard that he done paid for with the sweat of his brow. You done got so grown to where you gonna take over. You gonna take over my house. Is that right? You gonna wear my pants. You gonna go in there and stretch out on 135 my bed. You ain't got to say excuse me cause I don't count around here no more. Is that right?

CORY: That's right. You always talking this dumb stuff. Now, why don't you just get out my way.

TROY: I guess you got someplace to sleep and something to 140 put in your belly. You got that, huh? You got that? That's what you need. You got that, huh?

CORY: You don't know what I got. You ain't got to worry about what I got.

TROY: You right! You one hundred percent right! I done 145 spent the last seventeen years worrying about what you got. Now it's your turn, see? I'll tell you what to do. You grown . . . we done established that. You a man. Now, let's see you act like one. Turn your behind around and walk out this yard. And when you get out there in the alley . . . 150 you can forget about this house. See? Cause this is my house. You go on and be a man and get your own house. You can forget about this. Cause this is mine. You go on and get yours cause I'm through with doing for you.

CORY: You talking about what you did for me . . . what'd you 155 ever give me?

TROY: Them feet and bones! That pumping heart, nigger! I give you more than anybody else is ever gonna give you.

CORY: You ain't never gave me nothing! You ain't never done nothing but hold me back. Afraid I was gonna be better than you. All you ever did was try and make me scared of you. I used to tremble every time you called my name. Every time I heard your footsteps in the house. Wondering all the time . . . what's Papa gonna say if I do this? . . . What's he gonna say if I do that? . . . What's Papa gonna say if I turn on the radio? And Mama, too . . . she tries . . . but she's scared of you.

TROY: You leave your mama out of this. She ain't got nothing to do with this.

CORY: I don't know how she stand you . . . after what you did to her.

TROY: I told you to leave your mama out of this!

(He advances toward CORY.)

CORY: What you gonna do . . . give me a whupping? You can't whup me no more. You're too old. You just an old man.

TROY: *(Shoves him on his shoulder.)* Nigger! That's what you are. You just another nigger on the street to me!

CORY: You crazy! You know that?

TROY: Go on now! You got the devil in you. Get on away from me!

CORY: You just a crazy old man . . . talking about I got the devil in me.

TROY: Yeah, I'm crazy! If you don't get on the other side of that yard . . . I'm gonna show you how crazy I am! Go on . . . get the hell out of my yard.

CORY: It ain't your yard. You took Uncle Gabe's money he got from the army to buy this house and then you put him out.

TROY: *(TROY advances on CORY.)* Get your black ass out of my yard!

(TROY's advance backs CORY up against the tree. CORY grabs up the bat.)

CORY: I ain't going nowhere! Come on . . . put me out! I ain't scared of you.

TROY: That's my bat!

CORY: Come on!

TROY: Put my bat down!

CORY: Come on, put me out.

(CORY swings at TROY, who backs across the yard.)

What's the matter? You so bad . . . put me out!

(TROY advances toward CORY.)

CORY: *(Backing up.)* Come on! Come on!

TROY: You're gonna have to use it! You wanna draw that bat back on me . . . you're gonna have to use it.

CORY: Come on! . . . Come on!

(CORY swings the bat at TROY a second time. He misses. TROY continues to advance toward him.)

TROY: You're gonna have to kill me! You wanna draw that bat back on me. You're gonna have to kill me.

(CORY, backed up against the tree, can go no farther. TROY taunts him. He sticks out his head and offers him a target.)

Come on! Come on!

(CORY is unable to swing the bat. TROY grabs it.)

TROY: Then I'll show you.

(CORY and TROY struggle over the bat. The struggle is fierce and fully engaged. TROY ultimately is the stronger, and takes the bat from CORY and stands over him ready to swing. He stops himself.)

Go on and get away from around my house.

(CORY, stung by his defeat, picks himself up, walks slowly out of the yard and up the alley.)

CORY: Tell Mama I'll be back for my things.

TROY: They'll be on the other side of that fence.

(CORY exits.)

TROY: I can't taste nothing. Helluljah! I can't taste nothing no more. *(TROY assumes a batting posture and begins to taunt Death, the fastball in the outside corner.)* Come on! It's between you and me now! Come on! Anytime you want! Come on! I be ready for you . . . but I ain't gonna be easy.

(The lights go down on the scene.)

SCENE V

The time is 1965. The lights come up in the yard. It is the morning of TROY's funeral. A funeral plaque with a light hangs beside the door. There is a small garden plot off to the side. There is noise and activity in the house as ROSE, LYONS and BONO have gathered. The door opens and RAYNELL, seven years old, enters dressed in a flannel nightgown. She crosses to the garden and pokes around with a stick. ROSE calls from the house.

ROSE: Raynell!

RAYNELL: Mam?

ROSE: What you doing out there?

RAYNELL: Nothing.

(ROSE comes to the door.)

ROSE: Girl, get in here and get dressed. What you doing?

RAYNELL: Seeing if my garden growed.

ROSE: I told you it ain't gonna grow overnight. You got to wait.

RAYNELL: It don't look like it never gonna grow. Dag!

ROSE: I told you a watched pot never boils. Get in here and get dressed.

RAYNELL: This ain't even no pot, Mama.

ROSE: You just have to give it a chance. It'll grow. Now you come on and do what I told you. We got to be getting ready. This ain't no morning to be playing around. You hear me?

RAYNELL: Yes, mam.

(ROSE exits into the house. RAYNELL continues to poke at her garden with a stick. CORY enters. He is dressed in a Marine corporal's uniform, and carries a duffel bag. His posture is that of a military man, and his speech has a clipped sternness.)

CORY: (*To* RAYNELL.) Hi.

(*Pause.*)

I bet your name is Raynell.

RAYNELL: Uh huh.

CORY: Is your mama home?

(RAYNELL *runs up on the porch and calls through the screen door.*)

20 RAYNELL: Mama . . . there's some man out here. Mama?

(ROSE *comes to the door.*)

ROSE: Cory? Lord have mercy! Look here, you all!

(ROSE *and* CORY *embrace in a tearful reunion as* BONO *and* LYONS *enter from the house dressed in funeral clothes.*)

BONO: Aw, looka here . . .

ROSE: Done got all grown up!

CORY: Don't cry, Mama. What you crying about?

25 ROSE: I'm just so glad you made it.

CORY: Hey Lyons. How you doing, Mr. Bono.

(LYONS *goes to embrace* CORY.)

LYONS: Look at you, man. Look at you. Don't he look good, Rose. Got them Corporal stripes.

ROSE: What took you so long.

30 CORY: You know how the Marines are, Mama. They got to get all their paperwork straight before they let you do anything.

ROSE: Well, I'm sure glad you made it. They let Lyons come. Your Uncle Gabe's still in the hospital. They don't know

35 if they gonna let him out or not. I just talked to them a little while ago.

LYONS: A Corporal in the United States Marines.

BONO: Your daddy knew you had it in you. He used to tell me all the time.

40 LYONS: Don't he look good, Mr. Bono?

BONO: Yeah, he remind me of Troy when I first met him.

(*Pause.*)

Say, Rose, Lucille's down at the church with the choir. I'm gonna go down and get the pallbearers lined up. I'll be back to get you all.

45 ROSE: Thanks, Jim.

CORY: See you, Mr. Bono.

LYONS: (*With his arm around* RAYNELL.) Cory . . . look at Raynell. Ain't she precious? She gonna break a whole lot of hearts.

50 ROSE: Raynell, come and say hello to your brother. This is your brother, Cory. You remember Cory.

RAYNELL: No, Mam.

CORY: She don't remember me, Mama.

ROSE: Well, we talk about you. She heard us talk about you.

55 (*To* RAYNELL.) This is your brother, Cory. Come on and say hello.

RAYNELL: Hi.

CORY: Hi. So you're Raynell. Mama told me a lot about you.

ROSE: You all come on into the house and let me fix you

60 some breakfast. Keep up your strength.

CORY: I ain't hungry, Mama.

LYONS: You can fix me something, Rose. I'll be in there in a minute.

ROSE: Cory, you sure you don't want nothing. I know they ain't feeding you right.   65

CORY: No, Mama . . . thanks. I don't feel like eating. I'll get something later.

ROSE: Raynell . . . get on upstairs and get that dress on like I told you.

(ROSE *and* RAYNELL *exit into the house.*)

LYONS: So . . . I hear you thinking about getting married.   70

CORY: Yeah, I done found the right one, Lyons. It's about time.

LYONS: Me and Bonnie been split up about four years now. About the time Papa retired. I guess she just got tired of all them changes I was putting her through.

(*Pause.*)

I always knew you was gonna make something out your-   75
self. Your head was always in the right direction. So . . . you gonna stay in . . . make it a career . . . put in your twenty years?

CORY: I don't know. I got six already, I think that's enough.

LYONS: Stick with Uncle Sam and retire early. Ain't nothing   80
out here. I guess Rose told you what happened with me. They got me down the workhouse. I thought I was being slick cashing other people's checks.

CORY: How much time you doing?

LYONS: They give me three years. I got that beat now. I ain't   85
got but nine more months. It ain't so bad. You learn to deal with it like anything else. You got to take the crookeds with the straights. That's what Papa used to say. He used to say that when he struck out. I seen him strike out three times in a row . . . and the next time up he hit   90
the ball over the grandstand. Right out there in Home-stead Field. He wasn't satisfied hitting in the seats . . . he want to hit it over everything! After the game he had two hundred people standing around waiting to shake his hand. You got to take the crookeds with the straights.   95
Yeah, papa was something else.

CORY: You still playing?

LYONS: Cory . . . you know I'm gonna do that. There's some fellows down there we got us a band . . . we gonna try and stay together when we get out . . . but yeah, I'm still play-   100
ing. It still helps me to get out of bed in the morning. As long as it do that I'm gonna be right there playing and trying to make some sense out of it.

ROSE: (*Calling.*) Lyons, I got these eggs in the pan.

LYONS: Let me go on and get these eggs, man. Get ready to   105
go bury Papa.

(*Pause.*)

How you doing? You doing alright?

(CORY *nods.* LYONS *touches him on the shoulder and they share a moment of silent grief.* LYONS *exits into the house.* CORY *wanders about the yard.* RAYNELL *enters.*)

RAYNELL: Hi.

CORY: Hi.

RAYNELL: Did you used to sleep in my room?

CORY: Yeah . . . that used to be my room.

RAYNELL: That's what Papa call it. "Cory's room." It got your football in the closet.

(ROSE *comes to the door.*)

ROSE: Raynell, get in there and get them good shoes on.

RAYNELL: Mama, can't I wear these. Them other ones hurt my feet.

ROSE: Well, they just gonna have to hurt your feet for a while. You ain't said they hurt your feet when you went down to the store and got them.

RAYNELL: They didn't hurt then. My feet done got bigger.

ROSE: Don't you give me no backtalk now. You get in there and get them shoes on.

(RAYNELL *exits into the house.*)

Ain't too much changed. He still got that piece of rag tied to that tree. He was out here swinging that bat. I was just ready to go back in the house. He swung that bat and then he just fell over. Seem like he swung it and stood there with this grin on his face . . . and then he just fell over. They carried him on down to the hospital, but I knew there wasn't no need . . . why don't you come on in the house?

CORY: Mama . . . I got something to tell you. I don't know how to tell you this . . . but I've got to tell you . . . I'm not going to Papa's funeral.

ROSE: Boy, hush your mouth. That's your daddy you talking about. I don't want hear that kind of talk this morning. I done raised you to come to this? You standing there all healthy and grown talking about you ain't going to your daddy's funeral.

CORY: Mama . . . listen . . .

ROSE: I don't want to hear it, Cory. You just get that thought out of your head.

CORY: I can't drag Papa with me everywhere I go. I've got to say no to him. One time in my life I've got to say no.

ROSE: Don't nobody have to listen to nothing like that. I know you and your daddy ain't seen eye to eye, but I ain't got to listen to that kind of talk this morning. Whatever was between you and your daddy . . . the time has come to put it aside. Just take it and set it over there on the shelf and forget about it. Disrespecting your daddy ain't gonna make you a man, Cory. You got to find a way to come to that on your own. Not going to your daddy's funeral ain't gonna make you a man.

CORY: The whole time I was growing up . . . living in his house . . . Papa was like a shadow that followed you everywhere. It weighed on you and sunk into your flesh. It would wrap around you and lay there until you couldn't tell which one was you anymore. That shadow digging in your flesh. Trying to crawl in. Trying to live through you. Everywhere I looked, Troy Maxson was staring back at me . . . hiding under the bed . . . in the closet. I'm just saying I've got to find a way to get rid of that shadow, Mama.

ROSE: You just like him. You got him in you good.

CORY: Don't tell me that, Mama.

ROSE: You Troy Maxson all over again.

CORY: I don't want to be Troy Maxson. I want to be me.

ROSE: You can't be nobody but who you are, Cory. That shadow wasn't nothing but you growing into yourself. You either got to grow into it or cut it down to fit you. But that's all you got to make life with. That's all you got to measure yourself against that world out there. Your daddy wanted you to be everything he wasn't . . . and at the same time he tried to make you into everything he was. I don't know if he was right or wrong . . . but I do know he meant to do more good than he meant to do harm. He wasn't always right. Sometimes when he touched he bruised. And sometimes when he took me in his arms he cut.

When I first met your daddy I thought . . . Here is a man I can lay down with and make a baby. That's the first thing I thought when I seen him. I was thirty years old and had done seen my share of men. But when he walked up to me and said, "I can dance a waltz that'll make you dizzy," I thought, Rose Lee, here is a man that you can open yourself up to and be filled to bursting. Here is a man that can fill all them empty spaces you been tipping around the edges of. One of them empty spaces was being somebody's mother.

I married your daddy and settled down to cooking his supper and keeping clean sheets on the bed. When your daddy walked through the house he was so big he filled it up. That was my first mistake. Not to make him leave some room for me. For my part in the matter. But at that time I wanted that. I wanted a house that I could sing in. And that's what your daddy gave me. I didn't know to keep up his strength I had to give up little pieces of mine. I did that. I took on his life as mine and mixed up the pieces so that you couldn't hardly tell which was which anymore. It was my choice. It was my life and I didn't have to live it like that. But that's what life offered me in the way of being a woman and I took it. I grabbed hold of it with both hands.

By the time Raynell came into the house, me and your daddy had done lost touch with one another. I didn't want to make my blessing off of nobody's misfortune . . . but I took on to Raynell like she was all them babies I had wanted and never had.

(*The phone rings.*)

Like I'd been blessed to relive a part of my life. And if the Lord see fit to keep up my strength . . . I'm gonna do her just like your daddy did you . . . I'm gonna give her the best of what's in me.

RAYNELL: (*Entering, still with her old shoes.*) Mama . . . Reverend Tollivier on the phone.

(ROSE *exits into the house.*)

RAYNELL: Hi.

CORY: Hi.

RAYNELL: You in the Army or the Marines?

CORY: Marines.

RAYNELL: Papa said it was the Army. Did you know Blue?

CORY: Blue? Who's Blue?

RAYNELL: Papa's dog what he sing about all the time.

CORY: (*Singing.*)

220   Hear it ring! Hear it ring!
                  I had a dog his name was Blue
                  You know Blue was mighty true
                  You know Blue was a good old dog
                  Blue treed a possum in a hollow log
225   You know from that he was a good old dog.
                  Hear it ring! Hear it ring!

(RAYNELL *joins in singing.*)

CORY and RAYNELL: Blue treed a possum out on a limb
                  Blue looked at me and I looked at him
                  Grabbed that possum and put him in a sack
230   Blue stayed there till I came back
                  Old Blue's feets was big and round
                  Never allowed a possum to touch the ground.
                  Old Blue died and I dug his grave
                  I dug his grave with a silver spade
235   Let him down with a golden chain
                  And every night I call his name
                  Go on Blue, you good dog you
                  Go on Blue, you good dog you
RAYNELL: Blue laid down and died like a man
240   Blue laid down and died . . .
BOTH: Blue laid down and died like a man
                  Now he's treeing possums in the Promised Land
                  I'm gonna tell you this to let you know
                  Blue's gone where the good dogs go
245   When I hear old Blue bark
                  When I hear old Blue bark
                  Blue treed a possum in Noah's Ark
                  Blue treed a possum in Noah's Ark.

(ROSE *comes to the screen door.*)

ROSE: Cory, we gonna be ready to go in a minute.
250 CORY: (*To* RAYNELL.) You go on in the house and change them shoes like Mama told you so we can go to Papa's funeral.

RAYNELL: Okay, I'll be back.

(RAYNELL *exits into the house.* CORY *gets up and crosses over to the tree.* ROSE *stands in the screen door watching him.* GABRIEL *enters from the alley.*)

GABRIEL: (*Calling.*) Hey, Rose!
ROSE: Gabe?   255
GABRIEL: I'm here, Rose. Hey Rose, I'm here!

(ROSE *enters from the house.*)

ROSE: Lord . . . Look here, Lyons!
LYONS: See, I told you, Rose . . . I told you they'd let him come.
CORY: How you doing, Uncle Gabe?   260
LYONS: How you doing, Uncle Gabe?
GABRIEL: Hey, Rose. It's time. It's time to tell St. Peter to open the gates. Troy, you ready? You ready, Troy. I'm gonna tell St. Peter to open the gates. You get ready now.

(GABRIEL, *with great fanfare, braces himself to blow. The trumpet is without a mouthpiece. He puts the end of it into his mouth and blows with great force, like a man who has been waiting some*   265 *twenty-odd years for this single moment. No sound comes out of the trumpet. He braces himself and blows again with the same result. A third time he blows. There is a weight of impossible description that falls away and leaves him bare and exposed to a frightful realization. It is a trauma that a sane and normal mind would be unable to withstand. He begins to dance. A slow, strange dance, eerie and lifegiving. A dance of atavistic signature and ritual.* LYONS *attempts to embrace him.* GABRIEL *pushes* LYONS *away. He begins to howl in what is an attempt at song, or perhaps a song turning back into itself in an attempt at speech. He finishes his dance and the gates of heaven stand open as wide as God's closet.*)

     That's the way that go!

(*Blackout.*)

David Henry Hwang

David Henry Hwang was born in Los Angeles in 1957. He graduated with a B.A. in English from Stanford University in 1979 and studied at the Yale School of Drama in 1980–81. In the 1980s, Hwang wrote a series of powerful plays concerning the cultural and political experience of Asian Americans in the United States. His first play, *F.O.B.* ("fresh off the boat"), dramatizes the tensions that arise between Chinese immigrants to the United States and their assimilated friends and relatives. The play won an Obie award in 1980. Hwang addressed similar issues in *The Dance of the Railroad* (1981) and in *Rich Relations* (1986), and he collaborated with composer Philip Glass on *1000 Airplanes on the Roof* (1988). Hwang's Tony Award–winning *M. Butterfly* (1988) is a brilliant critique of Western attitudes toward Asia, epitomized by one of Western culture's most powerful and seductive images of the Orient: Giacomo Puccini's opera, *Madame Butterfly*. His recent plays include *Trying to Find Chinatown* (1996) and *Bondage* (1996); he has also written the book for a revival of Rodgers and Hammerstein's musical, *Flower Drum Song* (2001).

M. BUTTERFLY

In *M. Butterfly,* Hwang traces the relationship between the "Orient" of the Western imagination and the political realities that such images help to foster. The play's central character, the diplomat Gallimard, conducts his relationship with China in terms of Puccini's *Madame Butterfly*. In Puccini's 1904 opera, based on the 1900 play by David Belasco, the

John Lithgow as Gallimard and B.D. Wong as Song Liling in the 1988 Broadway production of David Henry Hwang's *M. Butterfly.*

naval officer Pinkerton marries the Japanese geisha girl Butterfly. He leaves for the United States, promising to return, and Butterfly waits for him, meanwhile bearing his child. When Pinkerton returns with his wife from America to collect his child, Butterfly realizes that he will never return to her. She commits suicide.

As Hwang has remarked, Butterfly has become a cultural stereotype of East-West relations—"speaking of an Asian woman, we would sometimes say, 'She's pulling a Butterfly,' which meant playing the submissive Oriental number." This sexist and racist stereotype, Hwang argues, pervades not only Western men's fantasies about Asian women—as the mail-order business in Asian wives suggests, Western men see Asian women as obedient, submissive, and sexually self-sacrificing—but also conditions the political relationship between Asia and the West as well.

M. Butterfly fuses this erotic and political desire for domination in the character of Gallimard, a French diplomat who falls in love with Song Liling, an opera singer whom he first sees singing the death aria from *Madame Butterfly*. However, the play develops a fascinating twist, for Song is in fact a man, who plays female roles in the Beijing Opera, and who—as a woman—develops a love affair with Gallimard in order to spy for the Chinese government. *M. Butterfly* compacts a complex reading of the politics of race, gender, and sexuality in a brilliantly theatrical drama.

M. BUTTERFLY

David Henry Hwang

CHARACTERS

KUROGO
RENE GALLIMARD
SONG LILING
MARC
MAN 2
CONSUL SHARPLESS
RENEE
WOMAN AT PARTY
PINUP GIRL
COMRADE CHIN

SUZUKI
SHU–FANG
HELGA
M. TOULON
MAN 1
JUDGE

The action of the play takes place in a Paris prison in the present, and in recall, during the decade 1960 to 1970 in Beijing, and from 1966 to the present in Paris.

ACT ONE

SCENE I

M. GALLIMARD's *prison cell. Paris. Present.*

Lights fade up to reveal RENE GALLIMARD, *65, in a prison cell. He wears a comfortable bathrobe, and looks old and tired. The sparsely furnished cell contains a wooden crate upon which sits a hot plate with a kettle, and a portable tape recorder.* GALLIMARD *sits on the crate staring at the recorder, a sad smile on his face.*

Upstage SONG, *who appears as a beautiful woman in traditional Chinese garb, dances a traditional piece from the Peking Opera, surrounded by the percussive clatter of Chinese music.*

Then, slowly, lights and sound cross-fade; the Chinese opera music dissolves into a Western opera, the "Love Duet" from Puccini's Madame Butterfly. SONG *continues dancing, now to the Western accompaniment. Though her movements are the same, the difference in music now gives them a balletic quality.*

GALLIMARD *rises, and turns upstage towards the figure of* SONG, *who dances without acknowledging him.*

GALLIMARD: Butterfly, Butterfly . . .

(He forces himself to turn away, as the image of SONG *fades out, and talks to us.)*

GALLIMARD: The limits of my cell are as such: four-and-a-half meters by five. There's one window against the far wall; a door, very strong, to protect me from autograph hounds.
5   I'm responsible for the tape recorder, the hot plate, and this charming coffee table.
    When I want to eat, I'm marched off to the dining room—hot, steaming slop appears on my plate. When I want to sleep, the light bulb turns itself off—the work of
10   fairies. It's an enchanted space I occupy. The French—we know how to run a prison.
    But, to be honest, I'm not treated like an ordinary prisoner. Why? Because I'm a celebrity. You see, I make people laugh.
15   I never dreamed this day would arrive. I've never been considered witty or clever. In fact, as a young boy, in an informal poll among my grammar school classmates, I was

voted "least likely to be invited to a party." It's a title I managed to hold onto for many years. Despite some stiff competition.
20   But now, how the tables turn! Look at me: the life of every social function in Paris. Paris? Why be modest? My fame has spread to Amsterdam, London, New York. Listen to them! In the world's smartest parlors. I'm the one who lifts their spirits!
25

(With a flourish, GALLIMARD *directs our attention to another part of the stage.)*

SCENE II

A party. Present.

Lights go up on a chic-looking parlor, where a well-dressed trio, two men and one woman, make conversation. GALLIMARD *also remains lit; he observes them from his cell.*

WOMAN: And what of Gallimard?
MAN 1: Gallimard?
MAN 2: Gallimard!
GALLIMARD: *(To us.)* You see? They're all determined to say my name, as if it were some new dance.   5
WOMAN: He still claims not to believe the truth.
MAN 1: What? Still? Even since the trial?
WOMAN: Yes. Isn't it mad?
MAN 2: *(Laughing.)* He says . . . it was dark . . . and she was very modest!   10

(The trio break into laughter.)

MAN 1: So—what? He never touched her with his hands?
MAN 2: Perhaps he did, and simply misidentified the equipment. A compelling case for sex education in the schools.
WOMAN: To protect the National Security—the Church can't argue with that.   15
MAN 1: That's impossible! How could he not know?
MAN 2: Simple ignorance.
MAN 1: For twenty years?
MAN 2: Time flies when you're being stupid.
WOMAN: Well, I thought the French were ladies' men.   20
MAN 2: It seems Monsieur Gallimard was overly anxious to live up to his national reputation.

WOMAN: Well, he's not very good-looking.
MAN 1: No, he's not.
25 MAN 2: Certainly not.
WOMAN: Actually, I feel sorry for him.
MAN 2: A toast! To Monsieur Gallimard!
WOMAN: Yes! To Gallimard!
MAN 1: To Gallimard!
30 MAN 2: Vive la différence!

(*They toast, laughing. Lights down on them.*)

SCENE III

M. GALLIMARD's *cell.*

GALLIMARD: (*Smiling.*) You see? They toast me. I've become patron saint of the socially inept. Can they really be so foolish?
Men like that—they should be scratching at my door, begging to learn my secrets! For I, Rene Gallimard, you see, I
5   have known, and been loved by . . . the Perfect Woman.
      Alone in this cell, I sit night after night, watching our story
play through my head, always searching for a new ending, one
which redeems my honor, where she returns at last to my
arms. And I imagine you—my ideal audience—who come
10   to understand and even, perhaps just a little, to envy me.

(*He turns on his tape recorder. Over the house speakers, we hear the
opening phrases of* Madame Butterfly.)

GALLIMARD: In order for you to understand what I did and why,
I must introduce you to my favorite opera: *Madame Butterfly.*
By Giacomo Puccini. First produced at La Scala, Milan, in
1904, it is now beloved throughout the Western world.

(*As* GALLIMARD *describes the opera, the tape segues in and out to
sections he may be describing.*)

15 GALLIMARD: And why not? Its heroine, Cio-Cio-San, also
known as Butterfly, is a feminine ideal, beautiful and
brave. And its hero, the man for whom she gives up everything, is—(*He pulls out a naval officer's cap from under his
crate, pops it on his head, and struts about.*)—not very good-
20   looking, not too bright, and pretty much a wimp: Benjamin Franklin Pinkerton of the U.S. Navy. As the curtain
rises, he's just closed on two great bargains: one on a
house, the other on a woman—call it a package deal.
      Pinkerton purchased the rights to Butterfly for one
25   hundred yen—in modern currency, equivalent to about
. . . sixty-six cents. So, he's feeling pretty pleased with himself as Sharpless, the American consul, arrives to witness
the marriage.

(MARC, *wearing an official cap to designate* SHARPLESS, *enters and
plays the character.*)

SHARPLESS/MARC: Pinkerton!
30 PINKERTON/GALLIMARD: Sharpless! How's it hangin'? It's a
great day, just great. Between my house, my wife, and the
rickshaw ride in from town, I've saved nineteen cents just
this morning.
SHARPLESS: Wonderful. I can see the inscription on your
35   tombstone already: "I saved a dollar, here I lie." (*He looks
around.*) Nice house.

PINKERTON: It's artistic. Artistic, don't you think? Like the way
the shoji screens slide open to reveal the wet bar and disco
mirror ball? Classy, huh? Great for impressing the chicks.
SHARPLESS: "Chicks"? Pinkerton, you're going to be a mar- 40
ried man!
PINKERTON: Well, sort of.
SHARPLESS: What do you mean?
PINKERTON: This country—Sharpless, it is okay. You got all
these geisha girls running around—   45
SHARPLESS: I know! I live here!
PINKERTON: Then, you know the marriage laws, right? I split
for one month, it's annulled!
SHARPLESS: Leave it to you to read the fine print. Who's the
lucky girl?   50
PINKERTON: Cio-Cio-San. Her friends call her Butterfly.
Sharpless, she eats out of my hand!
SHARPLESS: She's probably very hungry.
PINKERTON: Not like American girls. It's true what they say
about Oriental girls. They want to be treated bad!   55
SHARPLESS: Oh, please!
PINKERTON: It's true!
SHARPLESS: Are you serious about this girl?
PINKERTON: I'm marrying her, aren't I?
SHARPLESS: Yes—with generous trade-in terms.   60
PINKERTON: When I leave, she'll know what it's like to have
loved a real man. And I'll even buy her a few nylons.
SHARPLESS: You aren't planning to take her with you?
PINKERTON: Huh? Where?
SHARPLESS: Home!   65
PINKERTON: You mean, America? Are you crazy? Can you see
her trying to buy rice in St. Louis?
SHARPLESS: So, you're not serious.

(*Pause.*)

PINKERTON/GALLIMARD: (*As* PINKERTON.) Consul, I am a
sailor in port. (*As* GALLIMARD.) They then proceed to sing 70
the famous duet, "The Whole World Over."

(*The duet plays on the speakers.* GALLIMARD, *as* PINKERTON, *lip-
syncs his lines from the opera.*)

GALLIMARD: To give a rough translation: "The whole world
over, the Yankee travels, casting his anchor wherever he
wants. Life's not worth living unless he can win the hearts
of the fairest maidens, then hotfoot it off the premises   75
ASAP." (*He turns towards* MARC.) In the preceding scene, I
played Pinkerton, the womanizing cad, and my friend
Marc from school . . . (MARC *bows grandly for our benefit.*)
played Sharpless, the sensitive soul of reason. In life, however, our positions were usually—no, always—reversed.   80

SCENE IV

Ecole Nationale. Aix-en-Provence. 1947.

GALLIMARD: No, Marc, I think I'd rather stay home.
MARC: Are you crazy?! We are going to Dad's condo in Mar-
seille! You know what happened last time?
GALLIMARD: Of course I do.
MARC: Of course you don't! You never know. . . . They   5
stripped, Rene!

GALLIMARD: Who stripped?

MARC: The girls!

GALLIMARD: Girls? Who said anything about girls?

10 MARC: Rene, we're a buncha university guys goin' up to the woods. What are we gonna do—talk philosophy?

GALLIMARD: What girls? Where do you get them?

MARC: Who cares? The point is, they come. On trucks. Packed in like sardines. The back flips open, babes hop

15 out, we're ready to roll.

GALLIMARD: You mean, they just—?

MARC: Before you know it, every last one of them—they're stripped and splashing around my pool. There's no moon out, they can't see what's going on, their boobs are flap-

20 ping, right? You close your eyes, reach out—it's grab bag, get it? Doesn't matter whose ass is between whose legs, whose teeth are sinking into who. You're just in there, go- ing at it, eyes closed, on and on for as long as you can stand. (*Pause.*) Some fun, huh?

25 GALLIMARD: What happens in the morning?

MARC: In the morning, you're ready to talk some philosophy. (*Beat.*) So how 'bout it?

GALLIMARD: Marc, I can't . . . I'm afraid they'll say no—the girls. So I never ask.

30 MARC: You don't have to ask! That's the beauty—don't you see? They don't have to say yes. It's perfect for a guy like you, really.

GALLIMARD: You go ahead . . . I may come later.

MARC: Hey, Rene—it doesn't matter that you're clumsy and

35 got zits—they're not looking!

GALLIMARD: Thank you very much.

MARC: Wimp.

(MARC *walks over to the other side of the stage, and starts waving and smiling at women in the audience.*)

GALLIMARD: (*To us.*) We now return to my version of *Madame Butterfly* and the events leading to my recent conviction

40 for treason.

(GALLIMARD *notices* MARC *making lewd gestures.*)

Marc, what are you doing?

MARC: Huh? (*Sotto voce.*) Rene, there're a lotta great babes out there. They're probably lookin' at me and thinking, "What a dangerous guy."

45 GALLIMARD: Yes—how could they help but be impressed by your cool sophistication?

(GALLIMARD *pops the* SHARPLESS *cap on* MARC's *head, and points him offstage.* MARC *exits, leering.*)

SCENE V

M. GALLIMARD's *cell.*

GALLIMARD: Next, Butterfly makes her entrance. We learn her age—fifteen . . . but very mature for her years.

(*Lights come up on the area where we saw* SONG *dancing at the top of the play. She appears there again, now dressed as* MADAME BUTTERFLY, *moving to the "Love Duet."* GALLIMARD *turns up- stage slightly to watch, transfixed.*)

GALLIMARD: But as she glides past him, beautiful, laughing softly behind her fan, don't we who are men sigh with hope? We, who are not handsome, nor brave, nor power- 5 ful, yet somehow believe, like Pinkerton, that we deserve a Butterfly. She arrives with all her possessions in the folds of her sleeves, lays them all out, for her man to do with as he pleases. Even her life itself—she bows her head as she whispers that she's not even worth the hundred yen he 10 paid for her. He's already given too much, when we know he's really had to give nothing at all.

(*Music and lights on* SONG *out.* GALLIMARD *sits at his crate.*)

GALLIMARD: In real life, women who put their total worth at less than sixty-six cents are quite hard to find. The closest we come is in the pages of these magazines. (*He reaches into* 15 *his crate, pulls out a stack of girlie magazines, and begins flipping through them.*) Quite a necessity in prison. For three or four dollars, you get seven or eight women.

I first discovered these magazines at my uncle's house. One day, as a boy of twelve. The first time I saw them in 20 his closet . . . all lined up—my body shook. Not with lust—no, with power. Here were women—a shelfful— who would do exactly as I wanted.

(*The "Love Duet" creeps in over the speakers. Special comes up, re- vealing, not* SONG *this time, but a* PINUP GIRL *in a sexy negligee, her back to us.* GALLIMARD *turns upstage and looks at her.*)

GIRL: I know you're watching me.

GALLIMARD: My throat . . . it's dry. 25

GIRL: I leave my blinds open every night before I go to bed.

GALLIMARD: I can't move.

GIRL: I leave my blinds open and the lights on.

GALLIMARD: I'm shaking. My skin is hot, but my penis is soft. Why? 30

GIRL: I stand in front of the window.

GALLIMARD: What is she going to do?

GIRL: I toss my hair, and I let my lips part . . . barely.

GALLIMARD: I shouldn't be seeing this. It's so dirty. I'm so bad. 35

GIRL: Then, slowly, I lift off my nightdress.

GALLIMARD: Oh, god. I can't believe it. I can't—

GIRL: I toss it to the ground.

GALLIMARD: Now, she's going to walk away. She's going to—

GIRL: I stand there, in the light, displaying myself. 40

GALLIMARD: No. She's—why is she naked?

GIRL: To you.

GALLIMARD: In front of a window? This is wrong. No—

GIRL: Without shame.

GALLIMARD: No, she must . . . like it. 45

GIRL: I like it.

GALLIMARD: She . . . she wants me to see.

GIRL: I want you to see.

GALLIMARD: I can't believe it! She's getting excited!

GIRL: I can't see you. You can do whatever you want. 50

GALLIMARD: I can't do a thing. Why?

GIRL: What would you like me to do . . . next?

(*Lights go down on her. Music off. Silence, as* GALLIMARD *puts away his magazines. Then he resumes talking to us.*)

GALLIMARD: Act Two begins with Butterfly staring at the ocean. Pinkerton's been called back to the U.S., and he's given his wife a detailed schedule of his plans. In the column marked "return date," he's written "when the robins nest." This failed to ignite her suspicions. Now, three years have passed without a peep from him. Which brings a response from her faithful servant, Suzuki.

(COMRADE CHIN enters, playing SUZUKI.)

SUZUKI: Girl, he's a loser. What'd he ever give you? Nineteen cents and those ugly Day-Glo stockings? Look, it's finished! Kaput! Done! And you should be glad! I mean, the guy was a woofer! He tried before, you know—before he met you, he went down to geisha central and plunked down his spare change in front of the usual candidates—everyone else gagged! These are hungry prostitutes, and they were not interested, get the picture? Now, stop slathering when an American ship sails in, and let's make some bucks—I mean, yen! We are broke!

   Now, what about Yamadori? Hey, hey—don't look away—the man is a prince—figuratively, and, what's even better, literally. He's rich, he's handsome, he says he'll die if you don't marry him—and he's even willing to overlook the little fact that you've been deflowered all over the place by a foreign devil. What do you mean, "But he's Japanese?" You're Japanese! You think you've been touched by the whitey god? He was a sailor with dirty hands!

(SUZUKI stalks offstage.)

GALLIMARD: She's also visited by Consul Sharpless, sent by Pinkerton on a minor errand.

(MARC enters, as SHARPLESS.)

SHARPLESS: I hate this job.
GALLIMARD: This Pinkerton—he doesn't show up personally to tell his wife he's abandoning her. No, he sends a government diplomat . . . at taxpayer's expense.
SHARPLESS: Butterfly? Butterfly? I have some bad—I'm going to be ill. Butterfly, I came to tell you—
GALLIMARD: Butterfly says she knows he'll return and if he doesn't she'll kill herself rather than go back to her own people. (*Beat.*) This causes a lull in the conversation.
SHARPLESS: Let's put it this way . . .
GALLIMARD: Butterfly runs into the next room, and returns holding—

(*Sound cue: a baby crying.* SHARPLESS, "seeing" this, backs away.)

SHARPLESS: Well, good. Happy to see things going so well. I suppose I'll be going now. Ta ta. Ciao. (*He turns away. Sound cue out.*) I hate this job. (*He exits.*)
GALLIMARD: At that moment, Butterfly spots in the harbor an American ship—the *Abramo Lincoln!*

(*Music cue: "The Flower Duet."* SONG, *still dressed as* BUTTERFLY, *changes into a wedding kimono, moving to the music.*)

GALLIMARD: This is the moment that redeems her years of waiting. With Suzuki's help, they cover the room with flowers—

(CHIN, *as* SUZUKI, *trudges onstage and drops a lone flower without much enthusiasm.*)

GALLIMARD: —and she changes into her wedding dress to prepare for Pinkerton's arrival.

(SUZUKI *helps* BUTTERFLY *change.* HELGA *enters, and helps* GALLIMARD *change into a tuxedo.*)

GALLIMARD: I married a woman older than myself—Helga.
HELGA: My father was ambassador to Australia. I grew up among criminals and kangaroos.
GALLIMARD: Hearing that brought me to the altar—

(HELGA *exits.*)

GALLIMARD: —where I took a vow renouncing love. No fantasy woman would ever want me, so, yes, I would settle for a quick leap up the career ladder. Passion, I banish, and in its place—practicality!

   But my vows had long since lost their charm by the time we arrived in China. The sad truth is that all men want a beautiful woman, and the uglier the man, the greater the want.

(SUZUKI *makes final adjustments of* BUTTERFLY's *costume, as does* GALLIMARD *of his tuxedo.*)

GALLIMARD: I married late, at age thirty-one. I was faithful to my marriage for eight years. Until the day when, as a junior-level diplomat in puritanical Peking, in a parlor at the German ambassador's house, during the "Reign of a Hundred Flowers," I first saw her . . . singing the death scene from *Madame Butterfly.*

(SUZUKI *runs offstage.*)

SCENE VI

German ambassador's house. Beijing. 1960.

*The upstage special area now becomes a stage. Several chairs face upstage, representing seating for some twenty guests in the parlor. A few "diplomats"—*RENEE, MARC, TOULON—*in formal dress enter and take seats.*

GALLIMARD *also sits down, but turns towards us and continues to talk. Orchestral accompaniment on the tape is now replaced by a simple piano.* SONG *picks up the death scene from the point where* BUTTERFLY *uncovers the hara-kiri knife.*

GALLIMARD: The ending is pitiful. Pinkerton, in an art of great courage, stays home and sends his American wife to pick up Butterfly's child. The truth, long deferred, has come up to her door.

(SONG, *playing* BUTTERFLY, *sings the lines from the opera in her own voice—which, though not classical, should be decent.*)

SONG: "Con onor muore/ chi non puo serbar/ vita con onore."
GALLIMARD: (*Simultaneously.*) "Death with honor / Is better than life / Life with dishonor."

(*The stage is illuminated; we are now completely within an elegant diplomat's residence.* SONG *proceeds to play out an abbreviated death scene. Everyone in the room applauds.* SONG, *shyly, takes her bows. Others in the room rush to congratulate her.* GALLIMARD *remains with us.*)

GALLIMARD: They say in opera the voice is everything. That's probably why I'd never before enjoyed opera. Here ... here
10 was a Butterfly with little or no voice—but she had the grace, the delicacy ... I believed this girl. I believed her suffering. I wanted to take her in my arms—so delicate, even I could protect her, take her home, pamper her until she smiled.

(*Over the course of the preceding speech,* SONG *has broken from the upstage crowd and moved directly upstage of* GALLIMARD.)

SONG: Excuse me. Monsieur ... ?

(GALLIMARD *turns upstage, shocked.*)

15 GALLIMARD: Oh! Gallimard. Mademoiselle ... ? A beautiful ...
SONG: Song Liling.
GALLIMARD: A beautiful performance.
SONG: Oh, please.
GALLIMARD: I usually—
20 SONG: You make me blush. I'm no opera singer at all.
GALLIMARD: I usually don't like *Butterfly.*
SONG: I can't blame you in the least.
GALLIMARD: I mean, the story—
SONG: Ridiculous.
25 GALLIMARD: I like the story, but ... what?
SONG: Oh, you like it?
GALLIMARD: I ... what I mean is, I've always seen it played by huge women in so much bad makeup.
SONG: Bad makeup is not unique to the West.
30 GALLIMARD: But, who can believe them?
SONG: And you believe me?
GALLIMARD: Absolutely. You were utterly convincing. It's the first time—
SONG: Convincing? As a Japanese woman? The Japanese used
35 hundreds of our people for medical experiments during the war, you know. But I gather such an irony is lost on you.
GALLIMARD: No! I was about to say, it's the first time I've seen the beauty of the story.
SONG: Really?
40 GALLIMARD: Of her death. It's a ... a pure sacrifice. He's unworthy, but what can she do? She loves him ... so much. It's a very beautiful story.
SONG: Well, yes, to a Westerner.
GALLIMARD: Excuse me?
45 SONG: It's one of your favorite fantasies, isn't it? The submissive Oriental woman and the cruel white man.
GALLIMARD: Well, I didn't quite mean ...
SONG: Consider it this way: what would you say if a blonde homecoming queen fell in love with a short Japanese
50 businessman? He treats her cruelly, then goes home for three years, during which time she prays to his picture and turns down marriage from a young Kennedy. Then, when she learns he has remarried, she kills herself. Now, I believe you would consider this girl to be a deranged idiot,
55 correct? But because it's an Oriental who kills herself for a Westerner—ah!—you find it beautiful.

(*Silence.*)

GALLIMARD: Yes ... well ... I see your point ...
SONG: I will never do Butterfly again, Monsieur Gallimard. If you wish to see some real theatre, come to the Peking Opera sometime. Expand your mind.   60

(SONG *walks offstage.*)

GALLIMARD: (*To us.*) So much for protecting her in my big Western arms.

SCENE VII

M. GALLIMARD's *apartment. Beijing. 1960.*

GALLIMARD *changes from his tux into a casual suit.* HELGA *enters.*

GALLIMARD: The Chinese are an incredibly arrogant people.
HELGA: They warned us about that in Paris, remember?
GALLIMARD: Even Parisians consider them arrogant. That's a switch.
HELGA: What is it that Madame Su says? "We are a very old   5
civilization." I never know if she's talking about her country or herself.
GALLIMARD: I walk around here, all I hear every day, everywhere is how *old* this culture is. The fact that "old" may be synonymous with "senile" doesn't occur to them.   10
HELGA: You're not going to change them. "East is east, west is west, and ..." whatever that guy said.
GALLIMARD: It's just that—silly. I met ... at Ambassador Koening's tonight—you should've been there.
HELGA: Koening? Oh god, no. Did he enchant you all again   15
with the history of Bavaria?
GALLIMARD: No. I met, I suppose, the Chinese equivalent of a diva. She's a singer in the Chinese opera.
HELGA: They have an opera, too? Do they sing in Chinese? Or maybe—in Italian?   20
GALLIMARD: Tonight, she did sing in Italian.
HELGA: How'd she manage that?
GALLIMARD: She must've been educated in the West before the Revolution. Her French is very good also. Anyway, she sang the death scene from *Madame Butterfly.*   25
HELGA: *Madame Butterfly!* Then I should have come. (*She begins humming, floating around the room as if dragging long kimono sleeves.*) Did she have a nice costume? I think it's a classic piece of music.
GALLIMARD: That's what *I* thought, too. Don't let her hear   30
you say that.
HELGA: What's wrong?
GALLIMARD: Evidently the Chinese hate it.
HELGA: She hated it, but she performed it anyway? Is she perverse?   35
GALLIMARD: They hate it because the white man gets the girl. Sour grapes if you ask me.
HELGA: Politics again? Why can't they just hear it as a piece of beautiful music? So, what's in their opera?
GALLIMARD: I don't know. But, whatever it is, I'm sure it   40
must be *old.*

(HELGA *exits.*)

SCENE VIII

Chinese opera house and the streets of Beijing. 1960.

The sound of gongs clanging fills the stage.

GALLIMARD: My wife's innocent question kept ringing in my ears. I asked around, but no one knew anything about the Chinese opera. It took four weeks, but my curiosity overcame my cowardice. This Chinese diva—this unwilling
5   Butterfly—what did she do to make her so proud?

The room was hot, and full of smoke. Wrinkled faces, old women, teeth missing—a man with a growth on his neck, like a human toad. All smiling, pipes falling from their mouths, cracking nuts between their teeth, a live
10 chicken pecking at my foot—all looking, screaming, gawking . . . at her.

(The upstage area is suddenly hit with a harsh white light. It has become the stage for the Chinese opera performance. Two dancers enter, along with SONG. GALLIMARD *stands apart, watching.* SONG *glides gracefully amidst the two dancers. Drums suddenly slam to a halt.* SONG *strikes a pose, looking straight at* GALLIMARD. *Dancers exit. Light change. Pause, then* SONG *walks right off the stage and straight up to* GALLIMARD.*)*

SONG: Yes. You. White man. I'm looking straight at you.
GALLIMARD: Me?
SONG: You see any other white men? It was too easy to spot
15   you. How often does a man in my audience come in a tie?

*(*SONG *starts to remove her costume. Underneath, she wears simple baggy clothes. They are now backstage. The show is over.)*

SONG: So, you are an adventurous imperialist?
GALLIMARD: I . . . thought it would further my education.
SONG: It took you four weeks. Why?
GALLIMARD: I've been busy.
20 SONG: Well, education has always been undervalued in the West, hasn't it?
GALLIMARD: *(Laughing.)* I don't think it's true.
SONG: No, you wouldn't. You're a Westerner. How can you objectively judge your own values?
25 GALLIMARD: I think it's possible to achieve some distance.
SONG: Do you? *(Pause.)* It stinks in here. Let's go.
GALLIMARD: These are the smells of your loyal fans.
SONG: I love them for being my fans, I hate the smell they leave behind. I too can distance myself from my people.
30   *(She looks around, then whispers in his ear.)* "Art for the masses" is a shitty excuse to keep artists poor. *(She pops a cigarette in her mouth.)* Be a gentleman, will you? And light my cigarette.

*(*GALLIMARD *fumbles for a match.)*

GALLIMARD: I don't . . . smoke.
35 SONG: *(Lighting her own.)* Your loss. Had you lit my cigarette, I might have blown a puff of smoke right between your eyes. Come.

(They start to walk about the stage. It is a summer night on the Beijing streets. Sounds of the city play on the house speakers.)

SONG: How I wish there were even a tiny cafe to sit in. With cappuccinos, and men in tuxedos and bad expatriate jazz.
GALLIMARD: If my history serves me correctly, you weren't even 40 allowed into the clubs in Shanghai before the Revolution.
SONG: Your history serves you poorly, Monsieur Gallimard. True, there were signs reading "No dogs and Chinamen." But a woman, especially a delicate Oriental woman—we always go where we please. Could you imagine it other- 45 wise? Clubs in China filled with pasty, big-thighed white women, while thousands of slender lotus blossoms wait just outside the door? Never. The clubs would be empty. *(Beat.)* We have always held a certain fascination for you Caucasian men, have we not? 50
GALLIMARD: But . . . that fascination is imperialist, or so you tell me.
SONG: Do you believe everything I tell you? Yes. It is always imperialist. But sometimes . . . sometimes, it is also mutual. Oh—this is my flat. 55
GALLIMARD: I didn't even—
SONG: Thank you. Come another time and we will further expand your mind.

*(*SONG *exits.* GALLIMARD *continues roaming the streets as he speaks to us.)*

GALLIMARD: What was that? What did she mean, "Some-times . . . it is mutual?" Women do not flirt with me. And 60 I normally can't talk to them. But tonight, I held up my end of the conversation.

SCENE IX

GALLIMARD'*s bedroom. Beijing. 1960.*

HELGA *enters.*

HELGA: You didn't tell me you'd be home late.
GALLIMARD: I didn't intend to. Something came up.
HELGA: Oh! Like what?
GALLIMARD: I went to the . . . to the Dutch ambassador's home.
HELGA: Again? 5
GALLIMARD: There was a reception for a visiting scholar. He's writing a six-volume treatise on the Chinese revolution. We all gathered that meant he'd have to live here long enough to actually write six volumes, and we all expressed our deepest sympathies. 10
HELGA: Well, I had a good night too. I went with the ladies to a martial arts demonstration. Some of those men— when they break those thick boards—*(She mimes fanning herself.)* whoo-whoo!

*(*HELGA *exits. Lights dim.)*

GALLIMARD: I lied to my wife. Why? I've never had any rea- 15 son to lie before. But what reason did I have tonight? I didn't do anything wrong. That night, I had a dream. Other people, I've been told, have dreams where angels appear. Or dragons, or Sophia Loren in a towel. In my dream, Marc from school appeared. 20

*(*MARC *enters, in a nightshirt and cap.)*

MARC: Rene! You met a girl!

(GALLIMARD *and* MARC *stumble down the Beijing streets. Night sounds over the speakers.*)

GALLIMARD: It's not that amazing, thank you.

MARC: No! It's so monumental, I heard about it halfway around the world in my sleep!

25 GALLIMARD: I've met girls before, you know.

MARC: Name one. I've come across time and space to congratulate you. (*He hands* GALLIMARD *a bottle of wine.*)

GALLIMARD: Marc, this is expensive.

MARC: On those rare occasions when you become a formless

30   spirit, why not steal the best?

(MARC *pops open the bottle, begins to share it with* GALLIMARD.)

GALLIMARD: You embarrass me. She . . . there's no reason to think she likes me.

MARC: "Sometimes, it is mutual"?

GALLIMARD: Oh.

35 MARC: "Mutual"? "Mutual"? What does that mean?

GALLIMARD: You heard!

MARC: It means the money is in the bank, you only have to write the check!

GALLIMARD: I am a married man!

40 MARC: And an excellent one too. I cheated after . . . six months. Then again and again, until now—three hundred girls in twelve years.

GALLIMARD: I don't think we should hold that up as a model.

MARC: Of course not! My life—it is disgusting! Phooey!

45   Phooey! But, you—you are the model husband.

GALLIMARD: Anyway, it's impossible. I'm a foreigner.

MARC: Ah, yes. She cannot love you, it is taboo, but something deep inside her heart . . . she cannot help herself . . . she must surrender to you. It is her destiny.

50 GALLIMARD: How do you imagine all this?

MARC: The same way you do. It's an old story. It's in our blood. They fear us, Rene. Their women fear us. And their men—their men hate us. And, you know something? They are all correct.

(*They spot a light in a window.*)

55 MARC: There! There, Rene!

GALLIMARD: It's her window.

MARC: Late at night—it burns. The light—it burns for you.

GALLIMARD: I won't look. It's not respectful.

MARC: We don't have to be respectful. We're foreign devils.

(*Enter* SONG, *in a sheer robe. The "One Fine Day" aria creeps in over the speakers. With her back to us,* SONG *mimes attending to her toilette. Her robe comes loose, revealing her white shoulders.*)

60 MARC: All your life you've waited for a beautiful girl who would lay down for you. All your life you've smiled like a saint when it's happened to every other man you know. And you see them in magazines and you see them in movies. And you wonder, what's wrong with me? Will

65   anyone beautiful ever want me? As the years pass, your hair thins and you struggle to hold onto even your hopes. Stop struggling, Rene. The wait is over. (*He exits.*)

GALLIMARD: Marc? Marc?

(*At that moment,* SONG, *her back still towards us, drops her robe. A second of her naked back, then a sound cue: a phone ringing, very loud. Blackout, followed in the next beat by a special up on the bedroom area, where a phone now sits.* GALLIMARD *stumbles across the stage and picks up the phone. Sound cue out. Over the course of his conversation, area lights fill in the vicinity of his bed. It is the following morning.*)

GALLIMARD: Yes? Hello?

SONG: (*Offstage.*) Is it very early?   70

GALLIMARD: Why, yes.

SONG: (*Offstage.*) How early?

GALLIMARD: It's . . . it's 5:30. Why are you—?

SONG: (*Offstage.*) But it's light outside. Already.

GALLIMARD: It is. The sun must be in confusion today.   75

(*Over the course of* SONG's *next speech, her upstage special comes up again. She sits in a chair, legs crossed, in a robe, telephone to her ear.*)

SONG: I waited until I saw the sun. That was as much discipline as I could manage for one night. Do you forgive me?

GALLIMARD: Of course . . . for what?

SONG: Then I'll ask you quickly. Are you really interested in the opera?   80

GALLIMARD: Why, yes. Yes I am.

SONG: Then come again next Thursday. I am playing *The Drunken Beauty*. May I count on you?

GALLIMARD: Yes. You may.

SONG: Perfect. Well, I must be getting to bed. I'm exhausted. 85 It's been a very long night for me.

(SONG *hangs up; special on her goes off.* GALLIMARD *begins to dress for work.*)

SCENE X

SONG LILING's *apartment. Beijing. 1960.*

GALLIMARD: I returned to the opera that next week, and the week after that . . . she keeps our meetings so short— perhaps fifteen, twenty minutes at most. So I am left each week with a thirst which is intensified. In this way, fifteen weeks have gone by. I am starting to doubt the words of my 5 friend Marc. But no, not really. In my heart, I know she has . . . an interest in me. I suspect this is her way. She is outwardly bold and outspoken, yet her heart is shy and afraid. It is the Oriental in her at war with her Western education.

SONG: (*Offstage.*) I will be out in an instant. Ask the servant 10 for anything you want.

GALLIMARD: Tonight, I have finally been invited to enter her apartment. Though the idea is almost beyond belief, I believe she is afraid of me.

(GALLIMARD *looks around the room. He picks up a picture in a frame, studies it. Without his noticing,* SONG *enters, dressed elegantly in a black gown from the twenties. She stands in the doorway looking like Anna May Wong.*)

SONG: That is my father.   15

GALLIMARD: (*Surprised.*) Mademoiselle Song . . .

(*She glides up to him, snatches away the picture.*)

SONG: It is very good that he did not live to see the Revolution. They would, no doubt, have made him kneel on broken glass. Not that he didn't deserve such a punishment.
20 But he is my father. I would've hated to see it happen.
GALLIMARD: I'm very honored that you've allowed me to
visit your home.

(SONG *curtsys.*)

SONG: Thank you. Oh! Haven't you been poured any tea?
GALLIMARD: I'm really not—
25 SONG: (*To her offstage servant.*) Shu-Fang! Cha! Kwai-lah! (*To*
GALLIMARD.) I'm sorry. You want everything to be perfect—
GALLIMARD: Please.
SONG: —and before the evening even begins—
GALLIMARD: I'm really not thirsty.
30 SONG: —it's ruined.
GALLIMARD: (*Sharply.*) Mademoiselle Song!

(SONG *sits down.*)

SONG: I'm sorry.
GALLIMARD: What are you apologizing for now?

(*Pause;* SONG *starts to giggle.*)

SONG: I don't know!

(GALLIMARD *laughs.*)

35 GALLIMARD: Exactly my point.
SONG: Oh, I am silly. Lightheaded. I promise not to apologize
for anything else tonight, do you hear me?
GALLIMARD: That's a good girl!

(SHU-FANG, *a servant girl, comes out with a tea tray and starts to
pour.*)

SONG: (*To* SHU-FANG.) No! I'll pour myself for the gentleman!

(SHU-FANG, *staring at* GALLIMARD, *exits.*)

40 SONG: No, I . . . I don't even know why I invited you up.
GALLIMARD: Well, I'm glad you did.

(SONG *looks around the room.*)

SONG: There is an element of danger to your presence.
GALLIMARD: Oh?
SONG: You must know.
45 GALLIMARD: It doesn't concern me. We both know why I'm
here.
SONG: It doesn't concern me either. No . . . well perhaps . . .
GALLIMARD: What?
SONG: Perhaps I am slightly afraid of scandal.
50 GALLIMARD: What are we doing?
SONG: I'm entertaining you. In my parlor.
GALLIMARD: In France, that would hardly—
SONG: France. France is a country living in the modern era.
Perhaps even ahead of it. China is a nation whose soul is
55 firmly rooted two thousand years in the past. What I do,

even pouring the tea for you now . . . it has . . . implications. The walls and windows say so. Even my own heart,
strapped inside this Western dress . . . even it says things—
things I don't care to hear.

(SONG *hands* GALLIMARD *a cup of tea.* GALLIMARD *puts his hand
over both the teacup and* SONG'S *hand.*)

GALLIMARD: This is a beautiful dress.   60
SONG: Don't.
GALLIMARD: What?
SONG: I don't even know if it looks right on me.
GALLIMARD: Believe me—
SONG: You are from France. You see so many beautiful women. 65
GALLIMARD: France? Since when are the European women—?
SONG: Oh! What am I trying to do, anyway?!

(SONG *runs to the door, composes herself, then turns towards* GALLI-
MARD.)

SONG: Monsieur Gallimard, perhaps you should go.
GALLIMARD: But . . . why?
SONG: There's something wrong about this.   70
GALLIMARD: I don't see what.
SONG: I feel . . . I am not myself.
GALLIMARD: No. You're nervous.
SONG: Please. Hard as I try to be modern, to speak like a man,
to hold a Western woman's strong face up to my own . . . in 75
the end, I fail. A small, frightened heart beats too quickly
and gives me away. Monsieur Gallimard, I'm a Chinese girl.
I've never . . . never invited a man up to my flat before. The
forwardness of my actions makes my skin burn.
GALLIMARD: What are you afraid of? Certainly not me, I hope. 80
SONG: I'm a modest girl.
GALLIMARD: I know. And very beautiful. (*He touches her hair.*)
SONG: Please—go now. The next time you see me, I shall
again be myself.
GALLIMARD: I like you the way you are right now.   85
SONG: You are a cad.
GALLIMARD: What do you expect? I'm a foreign devil.

(GALLIMARD *walks downstage.* SONG *exits.*)

GALLIMARD: (*To us.*) Did you hear the way she talked about
Western women? Much differently than the first night.
She does—she feels inferior to them—and to me.   90

SCENE XI

The French embassy. Beijing. 1960.

GALLIMARD *moves towards a desk.*

GALLIMARD: I determined to try an experiment. In *Madame
Butterfly*, Cio-Cio-San fears that the Western man who
catches a butterfly will pierce its heart with a needle, then
leave it to perish. I began to wonder: had I, too, caught a
butterfly who would writhe on a needle?   5

(MARC *enters, dressed as a bureaucrat, holding a stack of papers. As*
GALLIMARD *speaks,* MARC *hands papers to him. He peruses, then
signs, stamps or rejects them.*)

GALLIMARD: Over the next five weeks, I worked like a dynamo. I stopped going to the opera, I didn't phone or write her. I knew this little flower was waiting for me to call, and, as I wickedly refused to do so, I felt for the first
10 time that rush of power—the absolute power of a man.

(MARC *continues acting as the bureaucrat, but he now speaks as himself.*)

MARC: Rene! It's me!
GALLIMARD: Marc—I hear your voice everywhere now. Even in the midst of work.
MARC: That's because I'm watching you—all the time.
15 GALLIMARD: You were always the most popular guy in school.
MARC: Well, there's no guarantee of failure in life like happiness in high school. Somehow I knew I'd end up in the suburbs working for Renault and you'd be in the Orient picking
20 exotic women off the trees. And they say there's no justice.
GALLIMARD: That's why you were my friend?
MARC: I gave you a little of my life, so that now you can give me some of yours. (*Pause.*) Remember Isabelle?
GALLIMARD: Of course I remember! She was my first experience.
25 MARC: We all wanted to ball her. But she only wanted me.
GALLIMARD: I had her.
MARC: Right. You balled her.
GALLIMARD: You were the only one who ever believed me.
MARC: Well, there's a good reason for that. (*Beat.*) C'mon.
30 You must've guessed.
GALLIMARD: You told me to wait in the bushes by the cafeteria that night. The next thing I knew, she was on me. Dress up in the air.
MARC: She never wore underwear.
35 GALLIMARD: My arms were pinned to the dirt.
MARC: She loved the superior position. A girl ahead of her time.
GALLIMARD: I looked up, and there was this woman . . . bouncing up and down on my loins.
MARC: Screaming, right?
40 GALLIMARD: Screaming, and breaking off the branches all around me, and pounding my butt up and down into the dirt.
MARC: Huffing and puffing like a locomotive.
GALLIMARD: And in the middle of all this, the leaves were getting into my mouth, my legs were losing circulation, I
45 thought, "God. So this is *it?*"
MARC: You thought that?
GALLIMARD: Well, I was worried about my legs falling off.
MARC: You didn't have a good time?
GALLIMARD: No, that's not what I—I had a great time!
50 MARC: You're sure?
GALLIMARD: Yeah. Really.
MARC: 'Cuz I wanted you to have a good time.
GALLIMARD: I did.

(*Pause.*)

MARC: Shit. (*Pause.*) When all is said and done, she was kind
55 of a lousy lay, wasn't she? I mean, there was a lot of energy there, but you never knew what she was doing with it. Like when she yelled "I'm coming!"—hell, it was so loud, you wanted to go "Look, it's not that big a deal."
GALLIMARD: I got scared. I thought she meant someone was
60 actually coming. (*Pause.*) But, Marc?

MARC: What?
GALLIMARD: Thanks.
MARC: Oh, don't mention it.
GALLIMARD: It was my first experience.
MARC: Yeah. You got her.   65
GALLIMARD: I got her.
MARC: Wait! Look at that letter again!

(GALLIMARD *picks up one of the papers he's been stamping, and rereads it.*)

GALLIMARD: (*To us.*) After six weeks, they began to arrive. The letters.

(*Upstage special on* SONG, *as* MADAME BUTTERFLY. *The scene is underscored by the "Love Duet."*)

SONG: Did we fight? I do not know. Is the opera no longer 70 of interest to you? Please come—my audiences miss the white devil in their midst.

(GALLIMARD *looks up from the letter, towards us.*)

GALLIMARD: (*To us.*) A concession, but much too dignified. (*Beat; he discards the letter.*) I skipped the opera again that week to complete a position paper on trade.   75

(*The bureaucrat hands him another letter.*)

SONG: Six weeks have passed since last we met. In this your practice—to leave friends in the lurch? Sometimes I hate you, sometimes I hate myself, but always I miss you.
GALLIMARD: (*To us.*) Better, but I don't like the way she calls me "friend." When a woman calls a man her "friend," 80 she's calling him a eunuch or a homosexual. (*Beat; he discards the letter.*) I was absent from the opera for the seventh week, feeling a sudden urge to clean out my files.

(*Bureaucrat hands him another letter.*)

SONG: Your rudeness is beyond belief. I don't deserve this cruelty. Don't bother to call. I'll have you turned away at the door.   85
GALLIMARD: (*To us.*) I didn't. (*He discards the letter; bureaucrat hands him another.*) And then finally, the letter that concluded my experiment.
SONG: I am out of words. I can hide behind dignity no longer. What do you want? I have already given you my shame.   90

(GALLIMARD *gives the letter back to* MARC, *slowly. Special on* SONG *fades out.*)

GALLIMARD: (*To us.*) Reading it, I became suddenly ashamed. Yes, my experiment had been a success. She was turning on my needle. But the victory seemed hollow.
MARC: Hollow? Are you crazy?
GALLIMARD: Nothing, Marc. Please go away.   95
MARC: (*Exiting, with papers.*) Haven't I taught you anything?
GALLIMARD: "I have already given you my shame." I had to attend a reception that evening. On the way, I felt sick. If there is a God, surely he would punish me now. I had finally gained power over a beautiful woman, only to abuse 100 it cruelly. There must be justice in the world. I had the strange feeling that the ax would fall this very evening.

SCENE XII

AMBASSADOR TOULON's *residence. Beijing. 1960.*

Sound cue: party noises. Light change. We are now in a spacious residence. TOULON, *the French ambassador, enters and taps* GALLIMARD *on the shoulder.*

TOULON: Gallimard? Can I have a word? Over here.
GALLIMARD: (*To us.*) Manuel Toulon. French ambassador to China. He likes to think of us all as his children. Rather like God.
5 TOULON: Look, Gallimard, there's not much to say. I've liked you. From the day you walked in. You were no leader, but you were tidy and efficient.
GALLIMARD: Thank you, sir.
TOULON: Don't jump the gun. Okay, our needs in China are
10 changing. It's embarrassing that we lost Indochina. Someone just wasn't on the ball there. I don't mean you personally, of course.
GALLIMARD: Thank you, sir.
TOULON: We're going to be doing a lot more information-
15 gathering in the future. The nature of our work here is changing. Some people are just going to have to go. It's nothing personal.
GALLIMARD: Oh.
TOULON: Want to know a secret? Vice-Consul LeBon is be-
20 ing transferred.
GALLIMARD: (*To us.*) My immediate superior!
TOULON: And most of his department.
GALLIMARD: (*To us.*) Just as I feared! God has seen my evil heart—
25 TOULON: But not you.
GALLIMARD: (*To us.*)—and he's taking her away just as . . . (*To* TOULON.) Excuse me, sir?
TOULON: Scare you? I think I did. Cheer up, Gallimard. I want you to replace LeBon as vice-consul.
30 GALLIMARD: You—? Yes, well, thank you, sir.
TOULON: Anytime.
GALLIMARD: I . . . accept with great humility.
TOULON: Humility won't be part of the job. You're going to coordinate the revamped intelligence division. Want to
35 know a secret? A year ago, you would've been out. But the past few months, I don't know how it happened, you've become this new aggressive confident . . . thing. And they also tell me you get along with the Chinese. So I think you're a lucky man, Gallimard. Congratulations.

(*They shake hands.* TOULON *exits. Party noises out.* GALLIMARD *stumbles across a darkened stage.*)

40 GALLIMARD: Vice-consul? Impossible! As I stumbled out of the party, I saw it written across the sky: There is no God. Or, no—say that there is a God. But that God . . . understands. Of course! God who creates Eve to serve Adam, who blesses Solomon with his harem but ties Jezebel to a
45 burning bed—that God is a man. And he understands! At age thirty-nine, I was suddenly initiated into the way of the world.

SCENE XIII

SONG LILING's *apartment. Beijing. 1960.*

SONG *enters, in a sheer dressing gown.*

SONG: Are you crazy?
GALLIMARD: Mademoiselle Song—
SONG: To come here—at this hour? After . . . after eight weeks?
GALLIMARD: It's the most amazing—
SONG: You bang on my door? Scare my servants, scandalize 5 the neighbors?
GALLIMARD: I've been promoted. To vice-consul.

(*Pause.*)

SONG: And what is that supposed to mean to me?
GALLIMARD: Are you my Butterfly?
SONG: What are you saying? 10
GALLIMARD: I've come tonight for an answer: are you my Butterfly?
SONG: Don't you know already?
GALLIMARD: I want you to say it.
SONG: I don't want to say it. 15
GALLIMARD: So, that is your answer?
SONG: You know how I feel about—
GALLIMARD: I do remember one thing.
SONG: What?
GALLIMARD: In the letter I received today. 20
SONG: Don't.
GALLIMARD: "I have already given you my shame."
SONG: It's enough that I even wrote it.
GALLIMARD: Well, then—
SONG: I shouldn't have it splashed across my face. 25
GALLIMARD: —if that's all true—
SONG: Stop!
GALLIMARD: Then what is one more short answer?
SONG: I don't want to!
GALLIMARD: Are you my Butterfly? (*Silence; he crosses the room* 30 *and begins to touch her hair.*) I want from you honesty. There should be nothing false between us. No false pride.

(*Pause.*)

SONG: Yes, I am. I am your Butterfly.
GALLIMARD: Then let me be honest with you. It is because of you that I was promoted tonight. You have changed my 35 life forever. My little Butterfly, there should be no more secrets: I love you.

(*He starts to kiss her roughly. She resists slightly.*)

SONG: No . . . no . . . gently . . . please, I've never . . .
GALLIMARD: No?
SONG: I've tried to appear experienced, but . . . the truth 40 is . . . no.
GALLIMARD: Are you cold?
SONG: Yes. Cold.
GALLIMARD: Then we will go very, very slowly.

(*He starts to caress her; her gown begins to open.*)

SONG: No . . . let me . . . keep my clothes . . . 45

GALLIMARD: But . . .

SONG: Please . . . it all frightens me. I'm a modest Chinese girl.

GALLIMARD: My poor little treasure.

SONG: I am your treasure. Though inexperienced, I am not . . .
50   ignorant. They teach us things, our mothers, about pleasing a man.

GALLIMARD: Yes?

SONG: I'll do my best to make you happy. Turn off the lights.

(GALLIMARD *gets up and heads for a lamp.* SONG, *propped up on
one elbow, tosses her hair back and smiles.*)

SONG: Monsieur Gallimard?
55   GALLIMARD: Yes, Butterfly?

SONG: "Vieni, vieni!"

GALLIMARD: "Come, darling."

SONG: "Ah! Dolce notte!"

GALLIMARD: "Beautiful night."
60   SONG: "Tutto estatico d'amor ride il ciel!"

GALLIMARD: "All ecstatic with love, the heavens are filled
with laughter."

(*He turns off the lamp. Blackout.*)

ACT TWO

SCENE I

M. GALLIMARD's *cell. Paris. Present.*

Lights up on GALLIMARD. *He sits in his cell, reading from a leaflet.*

GALLIMARD: This, from a contemporary critic's commentary
on *Madame Butterfly:* "Pinkerton suffers from . . . being an
obnoxious bounder whom every man in the audience
itches to kick." Bully for us men in the audience! Then, in
5   the same note: "Butterfly is the most irresistibly appealing
of Puccini's 'Little Women.' Watching the succession of her
humiliations is like watching a child under torture." (*He
tosses the pamphlet over his shoulder.*) I suggest that, while we
men may all want to kick Pinkerton, very few of us would
10   pass up the opportunity to be Pinkerton.

(GALLIMARD *moves out of his cell.*)

SCENE II

GALLIMARD *and* BUTTERFLY's *flat. Beijing. 1960.*

We are in a simple but well-decorated parlor. GALLIMARD *moves to
sit on a sofa, while* SONG, *dressed in a chong sam, enters and curls
up at his feet.*

GALLIMARD: (*To us.*) We secured a flat on the outskirts of
Peking. Butterfly, as I was calling her now, decorated our
"home" with Western furniture and Chinese antiques.
And there, on a few stolen afternoons or evenings each
5   week, Butterfly commenced her education.

SONG: The Chinese men—they keep us down.

GALLIMARD: Even in the "New Society"?

SONG: In the "New Society," we are all kept ignorant equally.
That's one of the exciting things about loving a Western
10   man. I know you are not threatened by a woman's education.

GALLIMARD: I'm no saint, Butterfly.

SONG: But you come from a progressive society.

GALLIMARD: We're not always reminding each other how
"old" we are, if that's what you mean.

SONG: Exactly. We Chinese—once, I suppose, it is true, we   15
ruled the world. But so what? How much more exciting
to be part of the society ruling the world today. Tell me—
what's happening in Vietnam?

GALLIMARD: Oh, Butterfly—you want me to bring my work
home?   20

SONG: I want to know what you know. To be impressed by my
man. It's not the particulars so much as the fact that you're
making decisions which change the shape of the world.

GALLIMARD: Not the world. At best, a small corner.

(TOULON *enters, and sits at a desk upstage.*)

SCENE III

French embassy. Beijing. 1961.

GALLIMARD *moves downstage, to* TOULON's *desk.* SONG *remains
upstage, watching.*

TOULON: And a more troublesome corner is hard to imagine.

GALLIMARD: So, the Americans plan to begin bombing?

TOULON: This is very secret, Gallimard: yes. The Americans
don't have an embassy here. They're asking us to be their
eyes and ears. Say Jack Kennedy signed an order to bomb   5
North Vietnam, Laos. How would the Chinese react?

GALLIMARD: I think the Chinese will squawk—

TOULON: Uh-huh.

GALLIMARD: —but, in their hearts, they don't even like Ho
Chi Minh.   10

(*Pause.*)

TOULON: What a bunch of jerks. Vietnam was *our* colony.
Not only didn't the Americans help us fight to keep them,
but now, seven years later, they've come back to grab the
territory for themselves. It's very irritating.

GALLIMARD: With all due respect, sir, why should the Amer-   15
icans have won our war for us back in '54 if we didn't
have the will to win it ourselves?

TOULON: You're kidding, aren't you?

(*Pause.*)

GALLIMARD: The Orientals simply want to be associated with
whoever shows the most strength and power. You live with   20
the Chinese, sir. Do you think they like Communism?

TOULON: I live in China. Not with the Chinese.

GALLIMARD: Well, I—

TOULON: *You* live with the Chinese.

GALLIMARD: Excuse me?   25

TOULON: I can't keep a secret.

GALLIMARD: What are you saying?

TOULON: Only that I'm not immune to gossip. So, you're
keeping a native mistress. Don't answer. It's none of my
business. (*Pause.*) I'm sure she must be gorgeous.   30

GALLIMARD: Well . . .

TOULON: I'm impressed. You have the stamina to go out into the streets and hunt one down. Some of us have to be content with the wives of the expatriate community.

35 GALLIMARD: I do feel . . . fortunate.

TOULON: So, Gallimard, you've got the inside knowledge— what *do* the Chinese think?

GALLIMARD: Deep down, they miss the old days. You know, cappuccinos, men in tuxedos—

40 TOULON: So what do we tell the Americans about Vietnam?

GALLIMARD: Tell them there's a natural affinity between the West and the Orient.

TOULON: And that you speak from experience?

GALLIMARD: The Orientals are people too. They want the
45 good things we can give them. If the Americans demonstrate the will to win, the Vietnamese will welcome them into a mutually beneficial union.

TOULON: I don't see how the Vietnamese can stand up to American firepower.

50 GALLIMARD: Orientals will always submit to a greater force.

TOULON: I'll note your opinions in my report. The Americans always love to hear how "welcome" they'll be. (*He starts to exit.*)

GALLIMARD: Sir?

55 TOULON: Mmmm?

GALLIMARD: This . . . rumor you've heard.

TOULON: Uh-huh?

GALLIMARD: How . . . widespread do you think it is?

TOULON: It's only widespread within this embassy. Where
60 nobody talks because everybody is guilty. We were worried about you, Gallimard. We thought you were the only one here without a secret. Now you go and find a lotus blossom . . . and top us all. (*He exits.*)

GALLIMARD: (*To us.*) Toulon knows! And he approves! I was
65 learning the benefits of being a man. We form our own clubs, sit behind thick doors, smoke—and celebrate the fact that we're still boys. (*He starts to move downstage, towards* SONG.) So, over the—

(*Suddenly* COMRADE CHIN *enters.* GALLIMARD *backs away.*)

GALLIMARD: (*To* SONG.) No! Why does she have to come in?
70 SONG: Rene, be sensible. How can they understand the story without her? Now, don't embarrass yourself.

(GALLIMARD *moves down center.*)

GALLIMARD: (*To us.*) Now, you will see why my story is so amusing to so many people. Why they snicker at parties in disbelief. Please—try to understand it from my point of
75 view. We are all prisoners of our time and place. (*He exits.*)

SCENE IV

GALLIMARD *and* BUTTERFLY'S *flat. Beijing. 1961.*

SONG: (*To us.*) 1961. The flat Monsieur Gallimard rented for us. An evening after he has gone.

CHIN: Okay, see if you find out when the Americans plan to start bombing Vietnam. If you can find out what cities,
5 even better.

SONG: I'll do my best, but I don't want to arouse his suspicions.

CHIN: Yeah, sure, of course. So, what else?

SONG: The Americans will increase troops in Vietnam to 170,000 soldiers with 120,000 militia and 11,000 American advisors.   10

CHIN: (*Writing.*) Wait, wait. 120,000 militia and—

SONG: —11,000 American—

CHIN: —American advisors. (*Beat.*) How do you remember so much?

SONG: I'm an actor.   15

CHIN: Yeah. (*Beat.*) Is that how come you dress like that?

SONG: Like what, Miss Chin?

CHIN: Like that dress! You're wearing a dress. And every time I come here, you're wearing a dress. Is that because you're an actor? Or what?   20

SONG: It's a . . . disguise, Miss Chin.

CHIN: Actors, I think they're all weirdos. My mother tells me actors are like gamblers or prostitutes or —

SONG: It helps me in my assignment.

(*Pause.*)

CHIN: You're not gathering information in any way that vio-   25
lates Communist Party principles, are you?

SONG: Why would I do that?

CHIN: Just checking. Remember: when working for the Great Proletarian State, you represent our Chairman Mao in every position you take.   30

SONG: I'll try to imagine the Chairman taking my positions.

CHIN: We all think of him this way. Good-bye, comrade. (*She starts to exit.*) Comrade?

SONG: Yes?

CHIN: Don't forget: there is no homosexuality in China!   35

SONG: Yes, I've heard.

CHIN: Just checking. (*She exits.*)

SONG: (*To us.*) What passes for a woman in modern China.

(GALLIMARD *sticks his head out from the wings.*)

GALLIMARD: Is she gone?

SONG: Yes, Rene. Please continue in your own fashion.   40

SCENE V

Beijing. 1961–63.

GALLIMARD *moves to the couch where* SONG *still sits. He lies down in her lap, and she strokes his forehead.*

GALLIMARD: (*To us.*) And so, over the years 1961, '62, '63, we settled into our routine, Butterfly and I. She would always have prepared a light snack and then, ever so delicately, and only if I agreed, she would start to pleasure me. With her hands, her mouth . . . too many ways to explain, and   5
too sad, given my present situation. But mostly we would talk. About my life. Perhaps there is nothing more rare than to find a woman who passionately listens.

(SONG *remains upstage, listening, as* HELGA *enters and plays a scene downstage with* GALLIMARD.)

HELGA: Rene, I visited Dr. Bolleart this morning.

GALLIMARD: Why? Are you ill?   10

HELGA: No, no. You see, I wanted to ask him . . . that question we've been discussing.

GALLIMARD: And I told you, it's only a matter of time. Why did you bring a doctor into this? We just have to keep try-
15   ing—like a crapshoot, actually.

HELGA: I went, I'm sorry. But listen: he says there's nothing wrong with me.

GALLIMARD: You see? Now, will you stop—?

HELGA: Rene, he says he'd like you to go in and take some tests.

20   GALLIMARD: Why? So he can find there's nothing wrong with both of us?

HELGA: Rene, I don't ask for much. One trip! One visit! And then, whatever you want to do about it—you decide.

GALLIMARD: You're assuming he'll find something defective!

25   HELGA: No! Of course not! Whatever he finds—if he finds nothing, we decide what to do about nothing! But go!

GALLIMARD: If he finds nothing, we keep trying. Just like we do now.

HELGA: But at least we'll know! (*Pause.*) I'm sorry. (*She starts*
30   *to exit.*)

GALLIMARD: Do you really want me to see Dr. Bolleart?

HELGA: Only if you want a child, Rene. We have to face the fact that time is running out. Only if you want a child. (*She exits.*)

35   GALLIMARD: (*To* SONG.) I'm a modern man, Butterfly. And yet, I don't want to go. It's the same old voodoo. I feel like God himself is laughing at me if I can't produce a child.

SONG: You men of the West—you're obsessed by your odd desire for equality. Your wife can't give you a child, and
40   *you're* going to the doctor?

GALLIMARD: Well, you see, she's already gone.

SONG: And because this incompetent can't find the defect, you now have to subject yourself to him? It's unnatural.

GALLIMARD: Well, what is the "natural" solution?

45   SONG: In Imperial China, when a man found that one wife was inadequate, he turned to another—to give him his son.

GALLIMARD: What do you—? I can't . . . marry you, yet.

SONG: Please. I'm not asking you to be my husband. But I am already your wife.

50   GALLIMARD: Do you want to . . . have my child?

SONG: I thought you'd never ask.

GALLIMARD: But, your career . . . your—

SONG: Phooey on my career! That's your Western mind, twist-ing itself into strange shapes again. Of course I love my ca-
55   reer. But what would I love most of all? To feel something inside me—day and night—something I know is yours. (*Pause.*) Promise me . . . you won't go to this doctor. Who is this Western quack to set himself as judge over the man I love? I know who is a man, and who is not. (*She exits.*)

60   GALLIMARD: (*To us.*) Dr. Bolleart? Of course I didn't go. What man would?

SCENE VI

Beijing. 1963.

Party noises over the house speakers. RENEE *enters, wearing a re-vealing gown.*

GALLIMARD: 1963. A party at the Austrian embassy. None of us could remember the Austrian ambassador's name, which seemed somehow appropriate. (*To* RENEE.) So, I tell the Americans, Diem must go. The U.S. wants to be respected by the Vietnamese, and yet they're propping up this nobody   5
seminarian as her president. A man whose claim to fame is his sister-in-law imposing fanatic "moral order" cam-paigns? Oriental women—when they're good, they're very good, but when they're bad, they're Christians.

RENEE: Yeah.   10

GALLIMARD: And what do you do?

RENEE: I'm a student. My father exports a lot of useless stuff to the Third World.

GALLIMARD: How useless?

RENEE: You know. Squirt guns, confectioner's sugar, hula   15
hoops . . .

GALLIMARD: I'm sure they appreciate the sugar.

RENEE: I'm here for two years to study Chinese.

GALLIMARD: Two years?

RENEE: That's what everybody says.   20

GALLIMARD: When did you arrive?

RENEE: Three weeks ago.

GALLIMARD: And?

RENEE: I like it. It's primitive, but . . . well, this is the place to learn Chinese, so here I am.   25

GALLIMARD: Why Chinese?

RENEE: I think it'll be important someday.

GALLIMARD: You do?

RENEE: Don't ask me when, but . . . that's what I think.

GALLIMARD: Well, I agree with you. One hundred percent.   30
That's very farsighted.

RENEE: Yeah. Well of course, my father thinks I'm a complete weirdo.

GALLIMARD: He'll thank you someday.

RENEE: Like when the Chinese start buying hula hoops?   35

GALLIMARD: There're a billion bellies out there.

RENEE: And if they end up taking over the world—well, then I'll be lucky to know Chinese too, right?

(*Pause.*)

GALLIMARD: At this point, I don't see how the Chinese can possibly take—   40

RENEE: You know what I *don't* like about China?

GALLIMARD: Excuse me? No—what?

RENEE: Nothing to do at night.

GALLIMARD: You come to parties at embassies like everyone else.   45

RENEE: Yeah, but they get out at ten. And then what?

GALLIMARD: I'm afraid the Chinese idea of a dance hall is a dirt floor and a man with a flute.

RENEE: Are you married?

GALLIMARD: Yes. Why?   50

RENEE: You wanna . . . fool around?

(*Pause.*)

GALLIMARD: Sure.

RENEE: I'll wait for you outside. What's your name?

GALLIMARD: Gallimard. Rene.

RENEE: Weird. I'm Renee too. (*She exits.*)   55

GALLIMARD: (*To us.*) And so, I embarked on my first extra-extramarital affair. Renee was picture perfect. With a body like those girls in the magazines. If I put a tissue pa-per over my eyes, I wouldn't have been able to tell the dif-ference. And it was exciting to be with someone who   60 wasn't afraid to be seen completely naked. But is it possible for a woman to be *too* uninhibited, *too* willing, so as to seem almost too . . . masculine?

(*Chuck Berry blares from the house speakers, then comes down in volume as* RENEE *enters, toweling her hair.*)

RENEE: You have a nice weenie.
65 GALLIMARD: What?
RENEE: Penis. You have a nice penis.
GALLIMARD: Oh. Well, thank you. That's very . . .
RENEE: What—can't take a compliment?
GALLIMARD: No, it's very . . . reassuring.
70 RENEE: But most girls don't come out and say it, huh?
GALLIMARD: And also . . . what did you call it?
RENEE: Oh. Most girls don't call it a "weenie," huh?
GALLIMARD: It sounds very—
RENEE: Small, I know.
75 GALLIMARD: I was going to say, "young."
RENEE: Yeah. Young, small, same thing. Most guys are pretty, uh, sensitive about that. Like, you know, I had a boyfriend back home in Denmark. I got mad at him once and called him a little weeniehead. He got so mad! He said at least I
80   should call him a great big weeniehead.
GALLIMARD: I suppose I just say "penis."
RENEE: Yeah. That's pretty clinical. There's "cock," but that sounds like a chicken. And "prick" is painful, and "dick" is like you're talking about someone who's not in the room.
85 GALLIMARD: Yes. It's a . . . bigger problem than I imagined.
RENEE: I—I think maybe it's because I really don't know what to do with them—that's why I call them "weenies."
GALLIMARD: Well, you did quite well with . . . mine.
RENEE: Thanks, but I mean, really *do* with them. Like, okay,
90   have you ever looked at one? I mean, really?
GALLIMARD: No, I suppose when it's part of you, you sort of take it for granted.
RENEE: I guess. But, like, it just hangs there. This little . . . flap of flesh. And there's so much fuss that we make about it.
95   Like, I think the reason we fight wars is because we wear clothes. Because no one knows—between the men, I mean—who has the bigger . . . weenie. So, if I'm a guy with a small one, I'm going to build a really big building or take over a really big piece of land or write a really long book
100   so the other men don't know, right? But, see, it never really works, that's the problem. I mean, you conquer the country, or whatever, but you're still wearing clothes, so there's no way to prove absolutely whose is bigger or smaller. And that's what we call a civilized society. The whole world run
105   by a bunch of men with pricks the size of pins. (*She exits.*)
GALLIMARD: (*To us.*) This was simply not acceptable.

(*A high-pitched chime rings through the air.* SONG, *dressed as Butterfly, appears in the upstage special. She is obviously distressed. Her body swoons as she attempts to clip the stems of flowers she's arranging in a vase.*)

GALLIMARD: But I kept up our affair, wildly, for several months. Why? I believe because of Butterfly. She knew the secret I was trying to hide. But, unlike a Western
110   woman, she didn't confront me, threaten, even pout. I remembered the words of Puccini's *Butterfly*:

SONG: "Noi siamo gente avvezza / alle piccole cose / umili e silenziose."
GALLIMARD: "I come from a people / Who are accustomed to little / Humble and silent." I saw Pinkerton and Butterfly, and 115 what she would say if he were unfaithful . . . nothing. She would cry, alone, into those wildly soft sleeves, once full of possessions, now empty to collect her tears. It was her tears and her silence that excited me, every time I visited Renee.
TOULON: (*Offstage.*) Gallimard!   120

(TOULON *enters.* GALLIMARD *turns towards him. During the next section,* SONG, *up center, begins to dance with the flowers. It is a drunken dance, where she breaks small pieces off the stems.*)

TOULON: They're killing him.
GALLIMARD: Who? I'm sorry? What?
TOULON: Bother you to come over at this late hour?
GALLIMARD: No . . . of course not.
TOULON: Not after you hear my secret. Champagne?   125
GALLIMARD: Um . . . thank you.
TOULON: You're surprised. There's something that you've wanted, Gallimard. No, not a promotion. Next time. Something in the world. You're not aware of this, but there's an informal gossip circle among intelligence agents. 130 And some of ours heard from some of the Americans—
GALLIMARD: Yes?
TOULON: That the U.S. will allow the Vietnamese generals to stage a coup . . . and assassinate President Diem.

(*The chime rings again.* TOULON *freezes.* GALLIMARD *turns upstage and looks at* SONG, *who slowly and deliberately clips a flower off its stem.* GALLIMARD *turns back towards* TOULON.)

GALLIMARD: I think . . . that's a very wise move!   135

(TOULON *unfreezes.*)

TOULON: It's what you've been advocating. A toast?
GALLIMARD: Sure. I consider this a vindication.
TOULON: Not exactly. "To the test. Let's hope you pass."

(*They drink. The chime rings again.* TOULON *freezes.* GALLIMARD *turns upstage, and* SONG *clips another flower.*)

GALLIMARD: (*To* TOULON.) The test?
TOULON: (*Unfreezing.*) It's a test of everything you've been 140 saying. I personally think the generals probably will stop the Communists. And you'll be a hero. But if anything goes wrong, then your opinions won't be worth a pig's ear. I'm sure that won't happen. But sometimes it's easier when they don't listen to you.   145
GALLIMARD: They're your opinions too, aren't they?
TOULON: Personally, yes.
GALLIMARD: So we agree.
TOULON: But my opinions aren't on that report. Yours are. Cheers.   150

(TOULON *turns away from* GALLIMARD *and raises his glass. At that instant* SONG *picks up the vase and hurls it to the ground. It shatters.* SONG *sinks down amidst the shards of the vase, in a calm, childlike trance. She sings softly, as if reciting a child's nursery rhyme.*)

SONG: (*Repeat as necessary.*) "The whole world over, the white man travels, setting anchor, wherever he likes. Life's not worth living, unless he finds, the finest maidens, of every land . . ."

(GALLIMARD *turns downstage towards us.* SONG *continues singing.*)

155 GALLIMARD: I shook as I left his house. That coward! That worm! To put the burden for his decisions on my shoulders! I started for Renee's. But no, that was all I needed. A schoolgirl who would question the role of the penis in modern society. What I wanted was revenge. A vessel to
160 contain my humiliation. Though I hadn't seen her in several weeks, I headed for Butterfly's.

(GALLIMARD *enters* SONG's *apartment.*)

SONG: Oh! Rene . . . I was dreaming!
GALLIMARD: You've been drinking?
SONG: If I can't sleep, then yes, I drink. But then, it gives me
165 these dreams which—Rene, it's been almost three weeks since you visited me last.
GALLIMARD: I know. There's been a lot going on in the world.
SONG: Fortunately I am drunk. So I can speak freely. It's not the world, it's you and me. And an old problem. Even the
170 softest skin becomes like leather to a man who's touched it too often. I confess I don't know how to stop it. I don't know how to become another woman.
GALLIMARD: I have a request.
SONG: Is this a solution? Or are you ready to give up the flat?
175 GALLIMARD: It may be a solution. But I'm sure you won't like it.
SONG: Oh well, that's very important. "Like it?" Do you think I "like" lying here alone, waiting, always waiting for your return? Please—don't worry about what I may not "like."
GALLIMARD: I want to see you . . . naked.

(*Silence.*)

180 SONG: I thought you understood my modesty. So you want me to—what—strip? Like a big cowboy girl? Shiny pasties on my breasts? Shall I fling my kimono over my head and yell "ya-hoo" in the process? I thought you respected my shame!
185 GALLIMARD: I believe you gave me your shame many years ago.
SONG: Yes—and it is just like a white devil to use it against me. I can't believe it. I thought myself so repulsed by the passive Oriental and the cruel white man. Now I see—we are always most revolted by the things hidden within us.
190 GALLIMARD: I just mean—
SONG: Yes?
GALLIMARD: —that it will remove the only barrier left between us.
SONG: No, Rene. Don't couch your request in sweet words.
195 Be yourself—a cad—and know that my love is enough, that I submit—submit to the worst you can give me. (*Pause.*) Well, come. Strip me. Whatever happens, know that you have willed it. Our love, in your hands. I'm helpless before my man.

(GALLIMARD *starts to cross the room.*)

200 GALLIMARD: Did I not undress her because I knew, somewhere deep down, what I would find? Perhaps. Happiness is so rare that our mind can turn somersaults to protect it.

At the time, I only knew that I was seeing Pinkerton stalking towards his Butterfly, ready to reward her love with his lecherous hands. The image sickened me, pulled 205 me to my knees, so I was crawling towards her like a worm. By the time I reached her, Pinkerton . . . had vanished from my heart. To be replaced by something new, something unnatural, that flew in the face of all I'd learned in the world—something very close to love. 210

(*He grabs her around the waist; she strokes his hair.*)

GALLIMARD: Butterfly, forgive me.
SONG: Rene . . .
GALLIMARD: For everything. From the start.
SONG: I'm . . .
GALLIMARD: I want to— 215
SONG: I'm pregnant. (*Beat.*) I'm pregnant. (*Beat.*) I'm pregnant.

(*Beat.*)

GALLIMARD: I want to marry you!

SCENE VII

GALLIMARD *and* BUTTERFLY's *flat. Beijing. 1963.*

Downstage, SONG *paces as* COMRADE CHIN *reads from her notepad. Upstage,* GALLIMARD *is still kneeling. He remains on his knees throughout the scene, watching it.*

SONG: I need a baby.
CHIN: (*From pad.*) He's been spotted going to a dorm.
SONG: I need a baby.
CHIN: At the Foreign Language Institute.
SONG: I need a baby. 5
CHIN: The room of a Danish girl . . . What do you mean, you need a baby?!
SONG: Tell Comrade Kang—last night, the entire mission, it could've ended.
CHIN: What do you mean? 10
SONG: Tell Kang—he told me to strip.
CHIN: *Strip?!*
SONG: Write!
CHIN: I tell you, I don't understand nothing about this case anymore. Nothing. 15
SONG: He told me to strip, and I took a chance. Oh, we Chinese, we know how to gamble.
CHIN: (*Writing.*) " . . . told him to strip."
SONG: My palms were wet, I had to make a split-second decision.
CHIN: Hey! Can you slow down?! 20

(*Pause.*)

SONG: You write faster, I'm the artist here. Suddenly, it hit me—"All he wants is for her to submit. Once a woman submits, a man is always ready to become 'generous.'"
CHIN: You're just gonna end up with rough notes.
SONG: And it worked! He gave in! Now, if I can just present 25 him with a baby. A Chinese baby with blond hair—he'll be mine for life!
CHIN: Kang will never agree! The trading of babies has to be a counterrevolutionary act.

30 SONG: Sometimes, a counterrevolutionary act is necessary to counter a counterrevolutionary act.

(*Pause.*)

CHIN: Wait.
SONG: I need one . . . in seven months. Make sure it's a boy.
CHIN: This doesn't sound like something the Chairman would
35   do. Maybe you'd better talk to Comrade Kang yourself.
SONG: Good. I will.

(CHIN *gets up to leave.*)

SONG: Miss Chin? Why, in the Peking Opera, are women's roles played by men?
CHIN: I don't know. Maybe, a reactionary remnant of male—
40 SONG: No. (*Beat.*) Because only a man knows how a woman is supposed to act.

(CHIN *exits.* SONG *turns upstage, towards* GALLIMARD.)

GALLIMARD: (*Calling after* CHIN.) Good riddance! (*To* SONG.) I could forget all that betrayal in an instant, you know. If you'd just come back and become Butterfly again.
45 SONG: Fat chance. You're here in prison, rotting in a cell. And I'm on a plane, winging my way back to China. Your President pardoned me of our treason, you know.
GALLIMARD: Yes, I read about that.
SONG: Must make you feel . . . lower than shit.
50 GALLIMARD: But don't you, even a little bit, wish you were here with me?
SONG: I'm an artist, Rene. You were my greatest . . . acting challenge. (*She laughs.*) It doesn't matter how rotten I answer, does it? You still adore me. That's why I love you,
55   Rene. (*She points to us.*) So—you were telling your audience about the night I announced I was pregnant.

(GALLIMARD *puts his arms around* SONG's *waist. He and* SONG *are in the positions they were in at the end of Scene 6.*)

SCENE VIII

Same.

GALLIMARD: I'll divorce my wife. We'll live together here, and then later in France.
SONG: I feel so . . . ashamed.
GALLIMARD: Why?
5 SONG: I had begun to lose faith. And now, you shame me with your generosity.
GALLIMARD: Generosity? No, I'm proposing for very selfish reasons.
SONG: Your apologies only make me feel more ashamed. My
10   outburst a moment ago!
GALLIMARD: Your outburst? What about my request?!
SONG: You've been very patient dealing with my . . . eccentricities. A Western man, used to women freer with their bodies—
15 GALLIMARD: It was sick! Don't make excuses for me.
SONG: I have to. You don't seem willing to make them for yourself.

(*Pause.*)

GALLIMARD: You're crazy.
SONG: I'm happy. Which often looks like crazy.
GALLIMARD: Then make me crazy. Marry me.   20

(*Pause.*)

SONG: No.
GALLIMARD: What?
SONG: Do I sound silly, a slave, if I say I'm not worthy?
GALLIMARD: Yes. In fact you do. No one has loved me like you.
SONG: Thank you. And no one ever will. I'll see to that.   25
GALLIMARD: So what is the problem?
SONG: Rene, we Chinese are realists. We understand rice, gold, and guns. You are a diplomat. Your career is skyrocketing. Now, what would happen if you divorced your wife to marry a Communist Chinese actress?   30
GALLIMARD: That's not being realistic. That's defeating yourself before you begin.
SONG: We must conserve our strength for the battles we can win.
GALLIMARD: That sounds like a fortune cookie!
SONG: Where do you think fortune cookies come from?   35
GALLIMARD: I don't care.
SONG: You do. So do I. And we should. That is why I say I'm not worthy. I'm worthy to love and even to be loved by you. But I am not worthy to end the career of one of the West's most promising diplomats.   40
GALLIMARD: It's not that great a career! I made it sound like more than it is!
SONG: Modesty will get you nowhere. Flatter yourself, and you flatter me. I'm flattered to decline your offer. (*She exits.*)
GALLIMARD: (*To us.*) Butterfly and I argued all night. And, in   45 the end, I left, knowing I would never be her husband. She went away for several months—to the countryside, like a small animal. Until the night I received her call.

(*A baby's cry from offstage.* SONG *enters, carrying a child.*)

SONG: He looks like you.
GALLIMARD: Oh! (*Beat; he approaches the baby.*) Well, babies are   50 never very attractive at birth.
SONG: Stop!
GALLIMARD: I'm sure he'll grow more beautiful with age. More like his mother.
SONG: "Chi vide mai / a bimbo del Giappon . . ."   55
GALLIMARD: "What baby, I wonder, was ever born in Japan"—or China, for that matter—
SONG: ". . . occhi azzurrini?"
GALLIMARD: "With azure eyes"—they're actually sort of brown, wouldn't you say?   60
SONG: "E il labbro."
GALLIMARD: "And such lips!" (*He kisses* SONG.) And such lips.
SONG: "E i ricciolini d'oro schietto?"
GALLIMARD: "And such a head of golden"—if slightly patchy—"curls?"   65
SONG: I'm going to call him "Peepee."
GALLIMARD: Darling, could you repeat that because I'm sure a rickshaw just flew by overhead.
SONG: You heard me.
GALLIMARD: "Song Peepee"? May I suggest Michael, or   70 Stephan, or Adolph?
SONG: You may, but I won't listen.
GALLIMARD: You can't be serious. Can you imagine the time this child will have in school?

SONG: In the West, yes.

GALLIMARD: It's worse than naming him Ping Pong or Long Dong or—

SONG: But he's never going to live in the West, is he?

(*Pause.*)

GALLIMARD: That wasn't my choice.

SONG: It is mine. And this is my promise to you: I will raise him, he will be our child, but he will never burden you outside of China.

GALLIMARD: Why do you make these promises? I want to be burdened! I want a scandal to cover the papers!

SONG: (*To us.*) Prophetic.

GALLIMARD: I'm serious.

SONG: So am I. His name is as I registered it. And he will never live in the West.

(SONG *exits with the child.*)

GALLIMARD: (*To us.*) It is possible that her stubbornness only made me want her more. That drawing back at the moment of my capitulation was the most brilliant strategy she could have chosen. It is possible. But it is also possible that by this point she could have said, could have done ... anything, and I would have adored her still.

SCENE IX

Beijing. 1966.

A driving rhythm of Chinese percussion fills the stage.

GALLIMARD: And then, China began to change. Mao became very old, and his cult became very strong. And, like many old men, he entered his second childhood. So he handed over the reins of state to those with minds like his own. And children ruled the Middle Kingdom with complete caprice. The doctrine of the Cultural Revolution implied continuous anarchy. Contact between Chinese and foreigners became impossible. Our flat was confiscated. Her fame and my money now counted against us.

(*Two dancers in Mao suits and red-starred caps enter, and begin crudely mimicking revolutionary violence, in an agitprop fashion.*)

GALLIMARD: And somehow the American war went wrong too. Four hundred thousand dollars were being spent for every Viet Cong killed; so General Westmoreland's remark that the Oriental does not value life the way Americans do was oddly accurate. Why weren't the Vietnamese people giving in? Why were they content instead to die and die and die again?

(TOULON *enters.*)

TOULON: Congratulations, Gallimard.

GALLIMARD: Excuse me, sir?

TOULON: Not a promotion. That was last time. You're going home.

GALLIMARD: What?

TOULON: Don't say I didn't warn you.

GALLIMARD: I'm being transferred ... because I was wrong about the American war?

TOULON: Of course not. We don't care about the Americans. We care about your mind. The quality of your analysis. In general, everything you've predicted here in the Orient ... just hasn't happened.

GALLIMARD: I think that's premature.

TOULON: Don't force me to be blunt. Okay, you said China was ready to open to Western trade. The only thing they're trading out there are Western heads. And, yes, you said the Americans would succeed in Indochina. You were kidding, right?

GALLIMARD: I think the end is in sight.

TOULON: Don't be pathetic. And don't take this personally. You were wrong. It's not your fault.

GALLIMARD: But I'm going home.

TOULON: Right. Could I have the number of your mistress? (*Beat.*) Joke! Joke! Eat a croissant for me.

(TOULON *exits.* SONG, *wearing a Mao suit, is dragged in from the wings as part of the upstage dance. They "beat" her, then lampoon the acrobatics of the Chinese opera, as she is made to kneel onstage.*)

GALLIMARD: (*Simultaneously.*) I don't care to recall how Butterfly and I said our hurried farewell. Perhaps it was better to end our affair before it killed her.

(GALLIMARD *exits.* COMRADE CHIN *walks across the stage with a banner reading: "The Actor Renounces His Decadent Profession!" She reaches the kneeling* SONG. *Percussion stops with a thud. Dancers strike poses.*)

CHIN: Actor-oppressor, for years you have lived above the common people and looked down on their labor. While the farmer ate millet—

SONG: I ate pastries from France and sweetmeats from silver trays.

CHIN: And how did you come to live in such an exalted position?

SONG: I was a plaything for the imperialists!

CHIN: What did you do?

SONG: I shamed China by allowing myself to be corrupted by a foreigner ...

CHIN: What does this mean? The People demand a full confession!

SONG: I engaged in the lowest perversions with China's enemies!

CHIN: What perversions? Be more clear!

SONG: I let him put it up my ass!

(*Dancers look over, disgusted.*)

CHIN: Aaaa-ya! How can you use such sickening language?!

SONG: My language ... is only as foul as the crimes I committed ...

CHIN: Yeah. That's better. So—what do you want to do now?

SONG: I want to serve the people.

(*Percussion starts up, with Chinese strings.*)

CHIN: What?

SONG: I want to serve the people!

(*Dancers regain their revolutionary smiles, and begin a dance of victory.*)

CHIN: What?!

SONG: I want to serve the people!

(*Dancers unveil a banner: "The Actor Is Rehabilitated!"* SONG *remains kneeling before* CHIN, *as the dancers bounce around them, then exit. Music out.*)

SCENE X

A commune. Hunan Province. 1970.

CHIN: How you planning to do that?

SONG: I've already worked four years in the fields of Hunan, Comrade Chin.

CHIN: So? Farmers work all their lives. Let me see your hands.

(SONG *holds them out for her inspection.*)

5 CHIN: Goddamn! Still so smooth! How long does it take to turn you actors into good anythings? Hunh. You've just spent too many years in luxury to be any good to the Revolution.

SONG: I served the Revolution.

10 CHIN: Serve the Resolution? Bullshit! You wore dresses! Don't tell me—I was there. I saw you! You and your white vice-consul! Stuck up there in your flat, living off the People's Treasury! Yeah, I knew what was going on! You two . . . homos! Homos! Homos! (*Pause; she composes herself.*) Ah! Well . . . you will serve the people, all right. But

15 not with the Revolution's money. This time, you use your own money.

SONG: I have no money.

CHIN: Shut up! And you won't stink up China anymore with

20 your pervert stuff. You'll pollute the place where pollution begins—the West.

SONG: What do you mean?

CHIN: Shut up! You're going to France. Without a cent in your pocket. You find your consul's house, you make him

25 pay your expenses—

SONG: No.

CHIN: And you give us weekly reports! Useful information!

SONG: That's crazy. It's been four years.

CHIN: Either that, or back to rehabilitation center!

30 SONG: Comrade Chin, he's not going to support me! Not in France! He's a white man! I was just his plaything—

CHIN: Oh yuck! Again with the sickening language. Where's my stick?

SONG: You don't understand the mind of a man.

(*Pause.*)

35 CHIN: Oh no? No I don't? Then how come I'm married, huh? How come I got a man? Five, six years ago, you always tell me those kinds of things, I felt very bad. But not now! Be-cause what does the Chairman say? He tells us *I'm* now the smart one, you're now the nincompoop!

40 *You're* the blackhead, the harebrain, the nitwit! You think you're so smart? You understand "The Mind of a Man"? Good! Then *you* go to France and be a pervert for Chairman Mao!

(CHIN *and* SONG *exit in opposite directions.*)

SCENE XI

Paris. 1968–70.

GALLIMARD *enters.*

GALLIMARD: And what was waiting for me back in Paris? Well, better Chinese food than I'd eaten in China. Friends and relatives. A little accounting, regular schedule, keeping track of traffic violations in the suburbs. . . . And the

5 indignity of students shouting the slogans of Chairman Mao at me—in French.

HELGA: Rene? Rene? (*She enters, soaking wet.*) I've had a . . . a problem. (*She sneezes.*)

GALLIMARD: You're wet.

10 HELGA: Yes, I . . . coming back from the grocer's. A group of students, waving red flags, they—

(GALLIMARD *fetches a towel.*)

HELGA: —they ran by, I was caught up along with them. Before I knew what was happening—

(GALLIMARD *gives her the towel.*)

HELGA: Thank you. The police started firing water cannons at

15 us. I tried to shout, to tell them I was the wife of a diplomat, but—you know how it is . . . (*Pause.*) Needless to say, I lost the groceries. Rene, what's happening to France?

GALLIMARD: What's—? Well, nothing, really.

HELGA: Nothing? The storefronts are in flames, there's glass in

20 the streets, buildings are toppling—and I'm wet!

GALLIMARD: Nothing! . . . that I care to think about.

HELGA: And is that why you stay in this room?

GALLIMARD: Yes, in fact.

HELGA: With the incense burning? You know something? I

25 hate incense. It smells so sickly sweet.

GALLIMARD: Well, I hate the French. Who just smell—period!

HELGA: And the Chinese were better?

GALLIMARD: Please—don't start.

HELGA: When we left, this exact same thing, the riots—

30 GALLIMARD: No, no . . .

HELGA: Students screaming slogans, smashing down doors—

GALLIMARD: Helga—

HELGA: It was all going on in China, too. Don't you remember?!

GALLIMARD: Helga! Please! (*Pause.*) You have never under-

35 stood China, have you? You walk in here with these ridiculous ideas, that the West is falling apart, that China was spitting in our faces. You come in, dripping of the streets, and you leave water all over my floor. (*He grabs* HELGA's *towel, begins mopping up the floor.*)

40 HELGA: But it's the truth!

GALLIMARD: Helga, I want a divorce.

(*Pause;* GALLIMARD *continues, mopping the floor.*)

HELGA: I take it back. China is . . . beautiful. Incense, I like incense.

GALLIMARD: I've had a mistress.

45 HELGA: So?

GALLIMARD: For eight years.

HELGA: I knew you would. I knew you would the day I married you. And now what? You want to marry her?

GALLIMARD: I can't. She's in China.

HELGA: I see. You want to leave. For someone who's not here, is that right?

GALLIMARD: That's right.

HELGA: You can't live with her, but still you don't want to live with me.

GALLIMARD: That's right.

(*Pause.*)

HELGA: Shit. How terrible that I can figure that out. (*Pause.*) I never thought I'd say it. But, in China, I was happy. I knew, in my own way, I knew that you were not everything you pretended to be. But the pretense—going on your arm to the embassy ball, visiting your office and the guards saying, "Good morning, good morning, Madame Gallimard"—the pretense . . . was very good indeed. (*Pause.*) I hope everyone is mean to you for the rest of your life. (*She exits.*)

GALLIMARD: (*To us.*) Prophetic.

(MARC *enters with two drinks.*)

GALLIMARD: (*To* MARC.) In China, I was different from all other men.

MARC: Sure. You were white. Here's your drink.

GALLIMARD: I felt . . . touched.

MARC: In the head? Rene, I don't want to hear about the Oriental love goddess. Okay? One night—can we just drink and throw up without a lot of conversation?

GALLIMARD: You still don't believe me, do you?

MARC: Sure I do. She was the most beautiful, et cetera, et cetera, blasé blasé.

(*Pause.*)

GALLIMARD: My life in the West has been such a disappointment.

MARC: Life in the West is like that. You'll get used to it. Look, you're driving me away. I'm leaving. Happy, now? (*He exits, then returns.*) Look, I have a date tomorrow night. You wanna come? I can fix you up with—

GALLIMARD: Of course. I would love to come.

(*Pause.*)

MARC: Uh—on second thought, no. You'd better get ahold of yourself first.

(*He exits;* GALLIMARD *nurses his drink.*)

GALLIMARD: (*To us.*) This is the ultimate cruelty, isn't it? That I can talk and talk and to anyone listening, it's only air—too rich a diet to be swallowed by a mundane world. Why can't anyone understand? That in China, I once loved, and was loved by, very simply, the Perfect Woman.

(SONG *enters, dressed as Butterfly in wedding dress.*)

GALLIMARD: (*To* SONG.) Not again. My imagination is hell. Am I asleep this time? Or did I drink too much?

SONG: Rene?

GALLIMARD: God, it's too painful! That you speak?

SONG: What are you talking about? Rene—touch me.

GALLIMARD: Why?

SONG: I'm real. Take my hand.

GALLIMARD: Why? So you can disappear again and leave me clutching at the air? For the entertainment of my neighbors who—?

(SONG *touches* GALLIMARD.)

SONG: Rene?

(GALLIMARD *takes* SONG's *hand. Silence.*)

GALLIMARD: Butterfly? I never doubted you'd return.

SONG: You hadn't . . . forgotten—?

GALLIMARD: Yes, actually, I've forgotten everything. My mind, you see—there wasn't enough room in this hard head—not for the world *and* for you. No, there was only room for one. (*Beat.*) Come, look. See? Your bed has been waiting, with the Klimt poster you like, and—see? The xiang lu [incense burner] you gave me?

SONG: I . . . I don't know what to say.

GALLIMARD: There's nothing to say. Not at the end of a long trip. Can I make you some tea?

SONG: But where's your wife?

GALLIMARD: She's by my side. She's by my side at last.

(GALLIMARD *reaches to embrace* SONG. SONG *sidesteps, dodging him.*)

GALLIMARD: Why?

SONG: (*To us.*) So I did return to Rene in Paris. Where I found—

GALLIMARD: Why do you run away? Can't we show them how we embraced that evening?

SONG: Please. I'm talking.

GALLIMARD: You have to do what I say! I'm conjuring you up in *my* mind!

SONG: Rene, I've never done what you've said. Why should it be any different in your mind? Now split—the story moves on, and I must change.

GALLIMARD: I welcomed you into my home! I didn't have to, you know! I could've left you penniless on the streets of Paris! But I took you in!

SONG: Thank you.

GALLIMARD: So . . . please . . . don't change.

SONG: You know I have to. You know I will. And anyway, what difference does it make? No matter what your eyes tell you, you can't ignore the truth. You already know too much.

(GALLIMARD *exits.* SONG *turns to us.*)

SONG: The change I'm going to make requires about five minutes. So I thought you might want to take this opportunity to stretch your legs, enjoy a drink, or listen to the musicians. I'll be here, when you return, right where you left me.

(SONG *goes to a mirror in front of which is a wash basin of water. She starts to remove her makeup as stagelights go to half and houselights come up.*)

ACT THREE

SCENE I

A courthouse in Paris. 1986.

As he promised, SONG *has completed the bulk of his transformation onstage by the time the houselights go down and the stagelights come up full. He removes his wig and kimono, leaving them on the floor. Underneath, he wears a well-cut suit.*

SONG: So I'd done my job better than I had a right to expect. Well, give him some credit, too. He's right—I was in a fix when I arrived in Paris. I walked from the airport into town, then I located, by blind groping, the Chinatown dis-
5 trict. Let me make one thing clear: whatever else may be said about the Chinese, they are stingy! I slept in doorways three days until I could find a tailor who would make me this kimono on credit. As it turns out, maybe I didn't even need it. Maybe he would've been happy to see me in a sim-
10 ple shift and mascara. But . . . better safe than sorry.
   That was 1970, when I arrived in Paris. For the next fif-teen years, yes, I lived in a very comfy life. Some relief, be-lieve me, after four years on a fucking commune in Nowheresville, China. Rene supported the boy and me, and
15 I did some demonstrations around the country as part of my "cultural exchange" cover. And then there was the spying.

(SONG *moves upstage, to a chair.* TOULON *enters as a* JUDGE, *wear-ing the appropriate wig and robes. He sits near* SONG. *It's 1986, and* SONG *is testifying in a courtroom.*)

SONG: Not much at first. Rene had lost all his high-level con-tacts. Comrade Chin wasn't very interested in parking-ticket statistics. But finally, at my urging, Rene got a job as
20 a courier, handling sensitive documents. He'd photograph them for me, and I'd pass them on to the Chinese embassy.
JUDGE: Did he understand the extent of his activity?
SONG: He didn't ask. He knew that I needed those docu-ments, and that was enough.
25 JUDGE: But he must've known he was passing classified in-formation.
SONG: I can't say.
JUDGE: He never asked what you were going to do with them?
SONG: Nope.

(*Pause.*)

30 JUDGE: There is one thing that the court—indeed, that all of France—would like to know.
SONG: Fire away.
JUDGE: Did Monsieur Gallimard know you were a man?
SONG: Well, he never saw me completely naked. Ever.
35 JUDGE: But surely, he must've . . . how can I put this?
SONG: Put it however you like. I'm not shy. He must've felt around?
JUDGE: Mmmmm.
SONG: Not really. I did all the work. He just laid back. Of
40 course we did enjoy more . . . complete union, and I sup-pose he *might* have wondered why I was always on my stomach, but. . . . But what you're thinking is, "Of course a wrist must've brushed . . . a hand hit . . . over twenty

years!" Yeah. Well, Your Honor, it was my job to make him think I was a woman. And chew on this: it wasn't all 45 that hard. See, my mother was a prostitute along the Bundt before the Revolution. And, uh, I think it's fair to say she learned a few things about Western men. So I bor-rowed her knowledge. In service to my country.
JUDGE: Would you care to enlighten the court with this se- 50 cret knowledge? I'm sure we're all very curious.
SONG: I'm sure you are. (*Pause.*) Okay, Rule One is: Men al-ways believe what they want to hear. So a girl can tell the most obnoxious lies and the guys will believe them every time—"This is my first time"—"That's the biggest I've 55 ever seen"—or *both,* which, if you really think about it, is not possible in a single lifetime. You've maybe heard those phrases a few times in your own life, yes, Your Honor?
JUDGE: It's not my life, Monsieur Song, which is on trial today.
SONG: Okay, okay, just trying to lighten up the proceedings. 60 Tough room.
JUDGE: Go on.
SONG: Rule Two: As soon as a Western man comes into con-tact with the East—he's already confused. The West has sort of an international rape mentality towards the East. 65 Do you know rape mentality?
JUDGE: Give us your definition, please.
SONG: Basically, "Her mouth says no, but her eyes say yes." The West thinks of itself as masculine—big guns, big in-dustry, big money—so the East is feminine—weak, deli- 70 cate, poor . . . but good at art, and full of inscrutable wisdom—the feminine mystique.
   Her mouth says no, but her eyes say yes. The West be-lieves the East, deep down, *wants* to be dominated—be-cause a woman can't think for herself. 75
JUDGE: What does this have to do with my question?
SONG: You expect Oriental countries to submit to your guns, and you expect Oriental women to be submissive to your men. That's why you say they make the best wives.
JUDGE: But why would that make it possible for you to fool 80 Monsieur Gallimard? Please—get to the point.
SONG: One, because when he finally met his fantasy woman, he wanted more than anything to believe that she was, in fact, a woman. And second, I am an Oriental. And being an Oriental, I could never be completely a man. 85

(*Pause.*)

JUDGE: Your armchair political theory is tenuous, Monsieur Song.
SONG: You think so? That's why you'll lose in all your deal-ings with the East.
JUDGE: Just answer my question: did he know you were a man? 90

(*Pause.*)

SONG: You know, your Honor, I never asked.

SCENE II

Same.

Music from the "Death Scene" from Butterfly *blares over the house speakers. It is the loudest thing we've heard in this play.*

GALLIMARD *enters, crawling towards* SONG's *wig and kimono.*

GALLIMARD: Butterfly? Butterfly?

(SONG *remains a man, in the witness box, delivering a testimony we do not hear.*)

GALLIMARD: (*To us.*) In my moment of greatest shame, here, in this courtroom—with that . . . person up there, telling the world. . . . What strikes me especially is how shallow
5   he is, how glib and obsequious . . . completely . . . without substance! The type that prowls around discos with a gold medallion stinking of garlic. So little like my Butterfly.
      Yet even in this moment my mind remains agile, flip-flopping like a man on a trampoline. Even now, my pic-
10   ture dissolves, and I see that . . . witness . . . talking to me.

(SONG *suddenly stands straight up in his witness box, and looks at* GALLIMARD.)

SONG: Yes. You. White man.

(SONG *steps out of the witness box, and moves downstage towards* GALLIMARD. *Light change.*)

GALLIMARD: (*To* SONG.) Who? Me?
SONG: Do you see any other white men?
GALLIMARD: Yes. There're white men all around. This is a
15   French courtroom.
SONG: So you are an adventurous imperialist. Tell me, why did it take you so long? To come back to this place?
GALLIMARD: What place?
SONG: This theatre in China. Where we met many years ago.
20   GALLIMARD: (*To us.*) And once again, against my will, I am transported.

(*Chinese opera music comes up on the speakers.* SONG *begins to do opera moves, as he did the night they met.*)

SONG: Do you remember? The night you gave your heart?
GALLIMARD: It was a long time ago.
SONG: Not long enough. A night that turned your world up-
25   side down.
GALLIMARD: Perhaps.
SONG: Oh, be honest with me. What's another bit of flattery when you've already given me twenty years' worth? It's a wonder my head hasn't swollen to the size of China.
30   GALLIMARD: Who's to say it hasn't?
SONG: Who's to say? And what's the shame? In pride? You think I could've pulled this off if I wasn't already full of pride when we met? No, not just pride. Arrogance. It takes arrogance, really—to believe you can will, with your eyes and your lips,
35   the destiny of another. (*He dances.*) C'mon. Admit it. You still want me. Even in slacks and a button-down collar.
GALLIMARD: I don't see what the point of—
SONG: You don't? Well maybe, Rene, just maybe—I want you.
GALLIMARD: You do?
40   SONG: Then again, maybe I'm just playing with you. How can you tell? (*Reprising his feminine character, he sidles up to* GALLIMARD.) "How I wish there were even a small cafe to sit in. With men in tuxedos, and cappuccinos, and bad expatriate jazz." Now you want to kiss me, don't you?

GALLIMARD: (*Pulling away.*) What makes you—?   45
SONG: —so sure? See? I take the words from your mouth. Then I wait for you to come and retrieve them. (*He reclines on the floor.*)
GALLIMARD: Why? Why do you treat me so cruelly?
SONG: Perhaps I *was* treating you cruelly. But now—I'm be-   50   ing nice. Come here, my little one.
GALLIMARD: I'm not your little one!
SONG: My mistake. It's I who am *your* little one, right?
GALLIMARD: Yes, I—
SONG: So come get your little one. If you like. I may even let   55   you strip me.
GALLIMARD: I mean, you were! Before . . . but not like this!
SONG: I was? Then perhaps I still am. If you look hard enough. (*He starts to remove his clothes.*)
GALLIMARD: What—what are you doing?   60
SONG: Helping you to see through my act.
GALLIMARD: Stop that! I don't want to! I don't—
SONG: Oh, but you asked me to strip, remember?
GALLIMARD: What? That was years ago! And I took it back!
SONG: No. You postponed it. Postponed the inevitable. To-   65   day, the inevitable has come calling.

(*From the speakers, cacophony:* Butterfly *mixed in with Chinese gongs.*)

GALLIMARD: No! Stop! I don't want to see!
SONG: Then look away.
GALLIMARD: You're only in my mind! All this is in my mind! I order you! To stop!   70
SONG: To what? To strip? That's just what I'm—
GALLIMARD: No! Stop! I want you—!
SONG: You want me?
GALLIMARD: To stop!
SONG: You know something, Rene? Your mouth says no, but   75   your eyes say yes. Turn them away. I dare you.
GALLIMARD: I don't have to! Every night, you say you're going to strip, but then I beg you and you stop!
SONG: I guess tonight is different.
GALLIMARD: Why? Why should that be?   80
SONG: Maybe I've become frustrated. Maybe I'm saying "Look at me, you fool!" Or maybe I'm just feeling . . . sexy. (*He is down to his briefs.*)
GALLIMARD: Please. This is unnecessary. I know what you are.
SONG: Do you? What am I?   85
GALLIMARD: A—a man.
SONG: You don't really believe that.
GALLIMARD: Yes I do! I knew all the time somewhere that my happiness was temporary, my love a deception. But my mind kept the knowledge at bay. To make the wait bearable.   90
SONG: Monsieur Gallimard—the wait is over.

(SONG *drops his briefs. He is naked. Sound cue out. Slowly, we and* SONG *come to the realization that what we had thought to be* GALLIMARD's *sobbing is actually his laughter.*)

GALLIMARD: Oh god! What an idiot! Of course!
SONG: Rene—what?
GALLIMARD: Look at you! You're a man! (*He bursts into laughter again.*)
SONG: I fail to see what's so funny!   95

GALLIMARD: "You fail to see—!" I mean, you never did have much of a sense of humor, did you? I just think it's ridiculously funny that I've wasted so much time on just a man!

100   SONG: Wait. I'm not "just a man."

GALLIMARD: No? Isn't that what you've been trying to convince me of?

SONG: Yes, but what I mean—

GALLIMARD: And now, I finally believe you, and you tell me

105   it's not true? I think you must have some kind of identity problem.

SONG: Will you listen to me?

GALLIMARD: Why?! I've been listening to you for twenty years. Don't I deserve a vacation?

110   SONG: I'm not just any man!

GALLIMARD: Then, what exactly are you?

SONG: Rene, how can you ask—? Okay, what about this?

(He picks up Butterfly's robes, starts to dance around. No music.)

GALLIMARD: Yes, that's very nice. I have to admit.

(SONG holds out his arm to GALLIMARD.)

SONG: It's the same skin you've worshiped for years. Touch it.

115   GALLIMARD: Yes, it does feel the same.

SONG: Now—close your eyes.

(SONG covers GALLIMARD's eyes with one hand. With the other, SONG draws GALLIMARD's hand up to his face. GALLIMARD, like a blind man, lets his hands run over SONG's face.)

GALLIMARD: This skin, I remember. The curve of her face, the softness of her cheek, her hair against the back of my hand . . .

120   SONG: I'm your Butterfly. Under the robes, beneath everything, it was always me. Now, open your eyes and admit it— you adore me. *(He removes his hand from GALLIMARD's eyes.)*

GALLIMARD: You, who knew every inch of my desires—how could you, of all people, have made such a mistake?

125   SONG: What?

GALLIMARD: You showed me your true self. When all I loved was the lie. A perfect lie, which you let fall to the ground—and now, it's old and soiled.

SONG: So—you never really loved me? Only when I was

130   playing a part?

GALLIMARD: I'm a man who loved a woman created by a man. Everything else—simply falls short.

(Pause.)

SONG: What am I supposed to do now?

GALLIMARD: You were a fine spy, Monsieur Song, with an

135   even finer accomplice. But now I believe you should go. Get out of my life!

SONG: Go where? Rene, you can't live without me. Not after twenty years.

GALLIMARD: I certainly can't live with you—not after twenty

140   years of betrayal.

SONG: Don't be so stubborn! Where will you go?

GALLIMARD: I have a date . . . with my Butterfly.

SONG: So, throw away your pride. And come . . .

GALLIMARD: Get away from me! Tonight, I've finally learned to tell fantasy from reality. And, knowing the difference, I   145 choose fantasy.

SONG: *I'm* your fantasy!

GALLIMARD: You? You're as real as hamburger. Now get out! I have a date with my Butterfly and I don't want your body polluting the room! *(He tosses SONG's suit at him.)*   150 Look at these—you dress like a pimp.

SONG: Hey! These are Armani slacks and—! *(He puts on his briefs and slacks.)* Let's just say . . . I'm disappointed in you, Rene. In the crush of your adoration, I thought you'd become something more. More like . . . a woman.   155

But no. Men. You're like the rest of them. It's all in the way we dress, and make up our faces, and bat our eyelashes. You really have so little imagination!

GALLIMARD: You, Monsieur Song? Accuse me of too little imagination? You, if anyone, should know—I am pure   160 imagination. And in imagination I will remain. Now get out!

(GALLIMARD bodily removes SONG from the stage, taking his kimono.)

SONG: Rene! I'll never put on those robes again! You'll be sorry!

GALLIMARD: *(To SONG.)* I'm already sorry! *(Looking at the ki-*   165 *mono in his hands.)* Exactly as sorry . . . as a Butterfly.

SCENE III

M. GALLIMARD's prison cell. Paris. Present.

GALLIMARD: I've played out the events of my life night after night, always searching for a new ending to my story, one where I leave this cell and return forever to my Butterfly's arms.

Tonight I realize my search is over. That I've looked all   5 along in the wrong place. And now, to you, I will prove that my love was not in vain—by returning to the world of fantasy where I first met her.

(He picks up the kimono; dancers enter.)

GALLIMARD: There is a vision of the Orient that I have. Of slender women in chong sams and kimonos who die for   10 the love of unworthy foreign devils. Who are born and raised to be the perfect women. Who take whatever punishment we give them, and bounce back, strengthened by love, unconditionally. It is a vision that has become my life.

(Dancers bring the wash basin to him and help him make up his face.)

GALLIMARD: In public, I have continued to deny that Song Lil-   15 ing is a man. This brings me headlines, and is a source of great embarrassment to my French colleagues, who can now be sent into a coughing fit by the mere mention of Chinese food. But alone, in my cell, I have long since faced the truth.

And the truth demands a sacrifice. For mistakes made   20 over the course of a lifetime. My mistakes were simple and absolute—the man I loved was a cad, a bounder. He deserved nothing but a kick in the behind, and instead I gave him . . . all my love.

25   Yes—love. Why not admit it all? That was my undoing, wasn't it? Love warped my judgment, blinded my eyes, rearranged the very lines on my face . . . until I could look in the mirror and see nothing but . . . a woman.

(*Dancers help him put on the Butterfly wig.*)

GALLIMARD: I have a vision. Of the Orient. That, deep
30   within its almond eyes, there are still women. Women willing to sacrifice themselves for the love of a man. Even a man whose love is completely without worth.

(*Dancers assist* GALLIMARD *in donning the kimono. They hand him a knife.*)

GALLIMARD: Death with honor is better than life . . . life with dishonor. (*He sets himself center stage, in a seppuku position.*)
35   The love of a Butterfly can withstand many things—unfaithfulness, loss, even abandonment. But how can it face the one sin that implies all others? The devastating knowledge that, underneath it all, the object of her love was nothing more, nothing less than . . . a man. (*He sets the tip of the knife against his body.*) It is 19__. And I have found
40   her at last. In a prison on the outskirts of Paris. My name is Rene Gallimard—also known as Madame Butterfly.

(GALLIMARD *turns upstage and plunges his knife into his body, as music from the "Love Duet" blares over the speakers. He collapses into the arms of the dancers, who lay him reverently on the floor. The image holds for several beats. Then a tight special up on* SONG, *who stands as a man, staring at the dead* GALLIMARD. *He smokes a cigarette; the smoke filters up through the lights. Two words leave his lips.*)

SONG: Butterfly? Butterfly?

(*Smoke rises as lights fade slowly to black.*)

Tony Kushner

Born in 1956, Tony Kushner first came to international prominence with *Angels in America* (1991), a two-part play that was an enormous success both in London and in Los Angeles before moving to New York in 1993. Kushner's "gay fantasia on national themes" is, in a sense, a displaced autobiography: the displaced narrative of his own growing up as a gay man in the American era of Roy Cohn, the decline of the Communist menace, the onset of the AIDS epidemic, and the rise of the conservative political agenda that dominated American politics in the 1980s. Kushner was born in New York, but his family soon moved to New Orleans, where his parents were musicians in the New Orleans Philharmonic. When he was two, the family moved to Lake Charles, Louisiana; his mother, once a prominent New York bassoonist, devoted herself to educating the children in literature, music, and the arts; she also acted in the Lake Charles theater company. Kushner knew that he was gay but concealed it from his parents; when he went to college at Columbia University, he spent some time in psychoanalysis trying to alter his sexual orientation. However, by his mid-twenties, Kushner was able to accept his sexuality and came out. After taking his B.A. at Columbia, he studied theater at New York University. His first play, *A Bright Room Called Day* (1985), was written while he worked as a switchboard operator; it concerns the collapse of the political left and the rise of fascism during the German Weimar Republic; Kushner also adapted a translation of Corneille's play, *The Illusion*. *Angels in America* is his second play. *Slavs* opened in New York in 1994, and an early play, *Hydriotaphia,* opened in 1998. His most recent play, *Homebody/Kabul,* opened in 2001.

The first part of *Angels in America* (the second part is entitled *Perestroika*), *Millennium Approaches* is a complete play in its own right. Kushner began writing the play in 1988 when Oskar Eustis, who had directed his first play for the Eureka Theater Company in San Francisco, asked Kushner for another play. Subtitled "A Gay Fantasia on National Themes," *Millennium*

ANGELS IN AMERICA, PART I: MILLENNIUM APPROACHES

The Angel (Ellen McLaughlin) appears to Prior Walter (Stephen Spinella) at the climax of Tony Kushner's *Angels in America, Part One: Millennium Approaches* in the 1993 Broadway production.

Approaches is at once a deeply personal look at the lives of two couples—Joe and Harper, a young Mormon couple transplanted to New York; Louis and Prior, a gay couple facing (and not facing) the onset of AIDS—and a political "fantasia" in the manner of Shaw's *Heartbreak House* or *The Apple Cart*. Kushner sets the characters' struggles against the background of conservative politics and the increasing power of the conservative right in 1980s America; as Martin remarks in act 2: ". . . we'll get our way on just about everything: abortion, defense, Central America, protecting the family, a live investment climate. . . . It's really the end of Liberalism. The end of New Deal Socialism. The end of ipso facto secular humanism."

While Kushner's play takes aim at the policies of the Republican administration, the play's politics extend deeply into the politics of personal action. The emphasis on individualism, on self-sufficiency, on destroying the liberal consensus, and on eliminating social programs characteristic of the Reagan administration has consequences in the private sphere as well, where freedom looks alternately like selfishness and chaos. Roy Cohn—famous for his anticommunist activities and for prosecuting (and winning) the death sentence for Julius and Ethel Rosenberg for selling secret information to the Soviet Union—in many ways exemplifies this linkage in the play. Unable to give up his view of political power ("the game . . . of being alive"), Cohn refuses to be treated for AIDS because it would mean a public admission that he is gay, something generally known but not acknowledged. Louis, unable to bring himself to care for Prior during his horrifying illness, finds both emptiness and freedom in deserting his lover. Harper, whose valium-induced fantasies summon the cosmic travel agent Mr. Lies (who whisks her off to Antarctica) is in the throes of a nervous breakdown, a literalized response to the decaying world in which she lives, where "everywhere, things are collapsing, lies surfacing, systems of defense giving way."

The hallucinatory style of *Millennium Approaches* enables Kushner to bring this blending of public and private, the grand sweep of history and the narrower compass of individual suffering, into a close juxtaposition. *Millennium Approaches* ends when Prior's ancestors—a medieval monk and a seventeenth-century dandy—appear to announce the coming of a mysterious angel, whose voice is heard intermittently throughout the play. The Angel's arrival is heralded in a number of ways: Prior regards his first lesion of Kaposi's sarcoma as the mark of the angel of death; a feather drops from above and the voice is heard at the end of Harper's/Prior's intertwined dream-hallucination in act 1; Joe alludes to Jacob wrestling with his angel, an image of Joe's fight to recognize and admit his own homosexuality. The Angel is a figure of release and redemption from the isolation in which the characters find themselves.

However, the Angel also has a public, historical significance as well. Kushner has suggested that the Angel alludes to a comment made by the German cultural critic Walter Benjamin. In "Theses on the Philosophy of History," Benjamin makes the following remark on the process of history:

> A Klee painting named "Angelus Novus" shows an angel looking as though he is about to move away from something he is fixedly contemplating. His eyes are staring, his mouth is open, his wings are spread. This is how one pictures the angel of history. His face is turned toward the past. Where we perceive a chain of events, he sees one single catastrophe which keeps piling wreckage upon wreckage and hurls it in front of his feet. The angel would like to stay, awaken the dead, and make whole what has been smashed. But a storm is blowing from Paradise; it has got caught in his wings with such violence that the angel can no longer close them. This storm irresistibly propels him into the future to which his back is turned, while the pile of debris before him grows skyward. This storm is what we call progress.

The Angel is, to Kushner as to Benjamin, a figure for the dialectical force of history, the way that history moves into the future both in antithesis to the past, and yet bearing the past along with it. In *Angels in America*, Tony Kushner provides a sense of how it is we live today, in the midst of this "storm . . . we call progress."

ANGELS IN AMERICA, PART I: MILLENNIUM APPROACHES

Tony Kushner

CHARACTERS

ROY M. COHN, *a successful New York lawyer and unofficial power broker*

JOSEPH (JOE) PORTER PITT, *chief clerk for Justice Theodore Wilson of the Federal Court of Appeals, Second Circuit*

HARPER AMATY PITT, *Joe's wife, an agoraphobic with a mild Valium addiction*

LOUIS IRONSON, *a word processor working for the Second Circuit Court of Appeals*

PRIOR WALTER, *Louis's boyfriend. Occasionally works as a club designer or caterer, otherwise lives very modestly but with great style off a small trust fund*

HANNAH PORTER PITT, *Joe's mother, currently residing in Salt Lake City, living off her deceased husband's army pension*

BELIZE, *a former drag queen and former lover of Prior's: A registered nurse. Belize's name was originally Norman Arriaga; Belize is a drag name that stuck*

THE ANGEL, *four divine emanations, Fluor, Phosphor, Lumen and Candle; manifest in One: the Continental Principality of America. She has magnificent steel-gray wings*

RABBI ISIDOR CHEMELWITZ, *an orthodox Jewish rabbi, played by the actor playing Hannah*

MR. LIES, *Harper's imaginary friend, a travel agent, who in style of dress and speech suggests a jazz musician; he always wears a large lapel badge emblazoned "IOTA" (The International Order of Travel Agents). He is played by the actor playing Belize*

THE MAN IN THE PARK, *played by the actor playing Prior*

THE VOICE, *the voice of The Angel*

HENRY, *Roy's doctor, played by the actor playing Hannah*

EMILY, *a nurse, played by the actor playing The Angel*

MARTIN HELLER, *a Reagan Administration Justice Department flackman, played by the actor playing Harper*

SISTER ELLA CHAPTER, *a Salt Lake City real-estate saleswoman, played by the actor playing The Angel*

PRIOR 1, *the ghost of a dead Prior Walter from the 13th century, played by the actor playing Joe. He is a blunt, gloomy medieval farmer with a gutteral Yorkshire accent*

PRIOR 2, *the ghost of a dead Prior Walter from the 17th century, played by the actor playing Roy. He is a Londoner, sophisticated, with a High British accent*

THE ESKIMO, *played by the actor playing Joe*

THE WOMAN IN THE SOUTH BRONX, *played by the actor playing The Angel*

ETHEL ROSENBERG, *played by the actor playing Hannah*

PLAYWRIGHT'S NOTES

A DISCLAIMER: *Roy M. Cohn, the character, is based on the late Roy M. Cohn (1927–1986), who was all too real; for the most part the acts attributed to the character Roy, such as his illegal conferences with Judge Kaufmann during the trial of Ethel Rosenberg, are to be found in the historical record. But this Roy is a work of dramatic fiction; his words are my invention, and liberties have been taken.*

A NOTE ABOUT THE STAGING: *The play benefits from a pared-down style of presentation, with minimal scenery and scene shifts done rapidly (no blackouts!), employing the cast as well as stagehands—which makes for an actor-driven event, as this must be. The moments of magic—the appearance and disappearance of Mr. Lies and the ghosts, the Book hallucination, and the ending—are to be fully realized, as bits of wonderful theatrical illusion—which means it's OK if the wires show, and maybe it's good that they do, but the magic should at the same time be thoroughly amazing.*

> . . . In a murderous time
> the heart breaks and breaks
> and lives by breaking.
>
> —STANLEY KUNITZ
> "THE TESTING-TREE"

ACT ONE

Bad News October–November 1985

SCENE I

The last days of October. RABBI ISODOR CHEMELWITZ *alone onstage with a small coffin. It is a rough pine box with two wooden pegs, one at the foot and one at the head, holding the lid in place. A prayer shawl embroidered with a Star of David is draped over the lid, and by the head a yarzheit candle is burning.*

RABBI ISIDOR CHEMELWITZ: (*He speaks sonorously, with a heavy Eastern European accent, unapologetically consulting a sheet of notes for the family names.*) Hello and good morning. I am Rabbi Isidor Chemelwitz of the Bronx Home for Aged He- brews. We are here this morning to pay respects at the pass- ing of Sarah Ironson, devoted wife of Benjamin Ironson, also deceased, loving and caring mother of her sons Morris, Abraham, and Samuel, and her daughters Esther and Rachel; beloved grandmother of Max, Mark, Louis, Lisa, Maria . . . uh . . . Lesley, Angela, Doris, Luke and Eric. (*Looks more closely at paper.*) Eric? This is a Jewish name? (*Shrugs.*) Eric. A large and loving family. We assemble that we may mourn collectively this good and righteous woman.

(*He looks at the coffin.*)

This woman. I did not know this woman. I cannot accurately describe her attributes, nor do justice to her dimensions. She was. . . . Well, in the Bronx Home of Aged Hebrews are many like this, the old, and to many I speak but not to be frank with this one. She preferred silence. So I do not know her and yet I know her. She was . . .

(He touches the coffin.)

20 . . . not a person but a whole kind of person, the ones who crossed the ocean, who brought with us to America the villages of Russia and Lithuania—and how we struggled, and how we fought, for the family, for the Jewish home, so that you would not grow up *here*, in this strange
25 place, in the melting pot where nothing melted. Descendants of this immigrant woman, you do not grow up in America, you and your children and their children with the goyische names. You do not live in America. No such place exists. Your clay is the clay of some Litvak shtetl,
30 your air the air of the steppes—because she carried the old world on her back across the ocean, in a boat, and she put it down on Grand Concourse Avenue, or in Flatbush, and she worked that earth into your bones, and you pass it to your children, this ancient, ancient culture and
35 home.

(Little pause.)

You can never make that crossing that she made, for such Great Voyages in this world do not any more exist. But every day of your lives the miles that voyage between that place and this one you cross. Every day. You understand
40 me? In you that journey is.

So . . .

She was the last of the Mohicans, this one was. Pretty soon . . . all the old will be dead.

SCENE II

Same day. ROY *and* JOE *in* ROY's *office.* ROY *at an impressive desk, bare except for a very elaborate phone system, rows and rows of flashing buttons which bleep and beep and whistle incessantly, making chaotic music underneath* ROY's *conversations.* JOE *is sitting, waiting.* ROY *conducts business with great energy, impatience and sensual abandon: gesticulating, shouting, cajoling, crooning, playing the phone, receiver and hold button with virtuosity and love.*

ROY: *(Hitting a button.)* Hold. *(To* JOE.*)* I wish I was an octopus, a fucking octopus. Eight loving arms and all those suckers. Know what I mean?

JOE: No, I . . .

5 ROY: *(Gesturing to a deli platter of little sandwiches on his desk.)* You want lunch?

JOE: No, that's OK really I just . . .

ROY: *(Hitting a button.)* Ailene? Roy Cohn. Now what kind of a greeting is. . . . I thought we were friends, Ai. . . . Look
10 Mrs. Soffer you don't have to get. . . . You're upset. You're yelling. You'll aggravate your condition, you shouldn't yell, you'll pop little blood vessels in your face if you yell. . . . No that was a joke, Mrs. Soffer, I was joking. . . . I already apologized sixteen times for that, Mrs. Soffer, you
15 . . . *(While she's fulminating,* ROY *covers the mouthpiece with his hand and talks to* JOE.*)* This'll take a minute, eat already, what is this tasty sandwich here it's—*(He takes a bite of a sandwich.)* Mmmmm, liver or some. . . . Here.

(He pitches the sandwich to JOE, *who catches it and returns it to the platter.)*

ROY: *(Back to Mrs. Soffer.)* Uh huh, uh huh. . . . No, I already
20 told you, it wasn't a vacation, it was business. Mrs. Soffer, I have clients in Haiti, Mrs. Soffer, I. . . . Listen, Ailene, YOU THINK I'M THE ONLY GODDAM LAWYER IN HISTORY EVER MISSED A COURT DATE? Don't make such a big fucking. . . . Hold. *(He hits the hold button.)* You HAG!
25 JOE: If this is a bad time . . .

ROY: *Bad* time? This is a *good* time! *(Button.)* Baby doll, get me. . . . Oh fuck, wait . . . *(Button, button.)* Hello? Yah. Sorry to keep you holding, Judge Hollins, I. . . . Oh *Mrs.* Hollins, sorry dear deep voice you got. Enjoying your visit? *(Hand
30 over mouthpiece, to* JOE.*)* She sounds like a truckdriver and he sounds like Kate Smith, very confusing. Nixon appointed him, all the geeks are Nixon appointees . . . *(To Mrs. Hollins.)* Yeah yeah right good so how many tickets dear? Seven. For what, *Cats, 42nd Street,* what? No you wouldn't like *La
35 Cage,* trust me, I know. Oh for godsake. . . . Hold. *(Button, button.)* Baby doll, seven for *Cats* or something, anything hard to get, I don't give a fuck what and neither will they. *(Button; to* JOE.*)* You see *La Cage?*

JOE: No, I . . .
40 ROY: Fabulous. Best thing on Broadway. Maybe ever. *(Button.)* Who? Aw, Jesus H. Christ, Harry, *no,* Harry, Judge John Francis Grimes, Manhattan Family Court. Do I have to do every goddam thing myself? *Touch* the bastard, Harry, and don't call me on this line again, I told you not to . . .
45 JOE: *(Starting to get up.)* Roy, uh, should I wait outside or . . .

ROY: *(To* JOE.*)* Oh sit. *(To* HARRY.*)* You hold. I pay you to hold fuck you Harry you jerk. *(Button.)* Half-wit dickbrain. *(Instantly philosophical.)* I see the universe, Joe, as a kind of sandstorm in outer space with winds of mega-
50 hurricane velocity, but instead of grains of sand it's shards and splinters of glass. You ever feel that way? Ever have one of those days?

JOE: I'm not sure I . . .

ROY: So how's life in Appeals? How's the Judge?
55 JOE: He sends his best.

ROY: He's a good man. Loyal. Not the brightest man on the bench, but he has manners. And a nice head of silver hair.

JOE: He gives me a lot of responsibility.

ROY: Yeah, like writing his decisions and signing his name.
60 JOE: Well . . .

ROY: He's a nice guy. And you cover admirably.

JOE: Well, thanks, Roy, I . . .

ROY: *(Button.)* Who is *this?* Well who the fuck are *you?* Hold—*(Button.)* Harry? Eighty-seven grand, something
65 like that. Fuck him. Eat me. New Jersey, chain of porno film stores in, uh, Weehawken. That's—Harry, that's the beauty of the law. *(Button.)* So, baby doll, what? *Cats?* Bleah. *(Button.)* *Cats!* It's about cats. Singing cats, you'll love it. Eight o'clock, the theatre's always at eight. *(Button.)*
70 Fucking tourists. *(Button, then to* JOE.*)* Oh live a little, Joe, *eat something for Christ sake—*

JOE: Um, Roy, could you . . .

ROY: What? *(To* HARRY.*)* Hold a minute. *(Button.)* Mrs. Soffer? Mrs. . . . *(Button.)* God-fucking-dammit to hell, where
75 is . . .

JOE: (*Overlapping.*) Roy, I'd really appreciate it if . . .

ROY: (*Overlapping.*) Well she was here a minute ago, baby doll, see if . . .

(*The phone starts making three different beeping sounds, all at once.*)

80   ROY: (*Smashing buttons.*) Jesus fuck this goddam thing . . .

JOE: (*Overlapping.*) I really wish you wouldn't . . .

ROY: (*Overlapping.*) Baby doll? Ring the *Post* get me Suzy see if . . .

(*The phone starts whistling loudly.*)

ROY: CHRIST!

85   JOE: *Roy.*

ROY: (*Into receiver.*) Hold. (*Button; to* JOE.) What?

JOE: Could you please not take the Lord's name in vain?

(*Pause.*)

I'm sorry. But please. At least while I'm . . .

ROY: (*Laughs, then.*) Right. Sorry. Fuck.

90   Only in America. (*Punches a button.*) Baby doll, tell 'em all to fuck off. Tell 'em I died. You handle Mrs. Soffer. Tell her it's on the way. Tell her I'm schtupping the judge. I'll call her back. I *will* call her. I *know* how much I borrowed. She's got four hundred times that stuffed up her. . . . Yeah,

95   tell her I said that. (*Button. The phone is silent.*)

So, Joe.

JOE: I'm sorry Roy, I just . . .

ROY: No no no no, principles count, I respect principles, I'm not religious but I like God and God likes me. Baptist,

100   Catholic?

JOE: Mormon.

ROY: Mormon. Delectable. Absolutely. Only in America. So, Joe. Whattya think?

JOE: It's . . . well . . .

105   ROY: Crazy life.

JOE: Chaotic.

ROY: Well but God bless chaos. Right?

JOE: Ummm . . .

ROY: Huh. Mormons. I knew Mormons, in, um, Nevada.

110   JOE: Utah, mostly.

ROY: No, these Mormons were in Vegas.

So. So, how'd you like to go to Washington and work for the Justice Department?

JOE: Sorry?

115   ROY: How'd you like to go to Washington and work for the Justice Department? All I gotta do is pick up the phone, talk to Ed, and you're in.

JOE: In . . . what, exactly?

ROY: Associate Assistant Something Big. Internal Affairs, heart

120   of the woods, something nice with clout.

JOE: Ed . . . ?

ROY: Meese. The Attorney General.

JOE: Oh.

ROY: I just have to pick up the phone . . .

125   JOE: I have to think.

ROY: Of course.

(*Pause.*)

It's a great time to be in Washington, Joe.

JOE: Roy, it's incredibly exciting . . .

ROY: And it would mean something to me. You understand?

(*Little pause.*)

JOE: I . . . can't say how much I appreciate this Roy, I'm sort   130
of . . . well, stunned, I mean. . . . Thanks, Roy. But I have to give it some thought. I have to ask my wife.

ROY: Your wife. Of course.

JOE: But I really appreciate . . .

ROY: Of course. Talk to your wife.   135

SCENE III

Later that day. HARPER *at home, alone. She is listening to the radio and talking to herself, as she often does. She speaks to the audience.*

HARPER: People who are lonely, people left alone, sit talking nonsense to the air, imagining . . . beautiful systems dying, old fixed orders spiraling apart . . .

When you look at the ozone layer, from outside, from a spaceship, it looks like a pale blue halo, a gentle, shim-   5
mer-ing aureole encircling the atmosphere encircling the earth. Thirty miles above our heads, a thin layer of three-atom oxygen molecules, product of photosynthesis, which explains the fussy vegetable preference for visible light, its rejection of darker rays and emanations. Danger from   10
without. It's a kind of gift, from God, the crowning touch to the creation of the world: guardian angels, hands linked, make a spherical net, a blue-green nesting orb, a shell of safety for life itself. But everywhere, things are collapsing, lies surfacing, systems of defense giving way. . . . This is   15
why, Joe, this is why I shouldn't be left alone.

(*Little pause.*)

I'd like to go traveling. Leave you behind to worry. I'll send postcards with strange stamps and tantalizing messages on the back. "Later maybe." "Nevermore . . ."

(MR. LIES, *a travel agent, appears.*)

HARPER: Oh! You startled me!   20

MR. LIES: Cash, check or credit card?

HARPER: I remember you. You're from Salt Lake. You sold us the plane tickets when we flew here. What are you doing in Brooklyn?

MR. LIES: You said you wanted to travel . . .   25

HARPER: And here you are. How thoughtful.

MR. LIES: Mr. Lies. Of the International Order of Travel Agents. We mobilize the globe, we set people adrift, we stir the populace and send nomads eddying across the planet. We are adepts of motion, acolytes of the flux.   30
Cash, check or credit card. Name your destination.

HARPER: Antarctica, maybe. I want to see the hole in the ozone. I heard on the radio . . .

MR. LIES: (*He has a computer terminal in his briefcase.*) I can arrange a guided tour. Now?   35

HARPER: Soon. Maybe soon. I'm not safe here you see. Things aren't right with me. Weird stuff happens . . .

MR. LIES: Like?

HARPER: Well, like you, for instance. Just appearing. Or last
40   week . . . well never mind.
      People are like planets, you need a thick skin. Things get
      to me, Joe stays away and now. . . . Well look. My dreams
      are talking back to me.

MR. LIES: It's the price of rootlessness. Motion sickness. The
45   only cure: to keep moving.

HARPER: I'm undecided. I feel . . . that something's going to
give. It's 1985. Fifteen years till the third millennium.
Maybe Christ will come again. Maybe seeds will be
planted, maybe there'll be harvests then, maybe early figs to
50   eat, maybe new life, maybe fresh blood, maybe companionship and love and protection, safety from what's outside,
maybe the door will hold, or maybe . . . maybe the troubles
will come, and the end will come, and the sky will collapse
and there will be terrible rains and showers of poison light,
55   or maybe my life is really fine, maybe Joe loves me and I'm
only crazy thinking otherwise, or maybe not, maybe it's
even worse than I know, maybe . . . I want to know, maybe
I don't. The suspense, Mr. Lies, it's killing me.

MR. LIES: I suggest a vacation.

60   HARPER: (*Hearing something.*) That was the elevator. Oh God,
I should fix myself up, I. . . . You have to go, you shouldn't
be here . . . you aren't even real.

MR. LIES: Call me when you decide . . .

HARPER: Go!

(*The travel agent* [MR. LIES] *vanishes as* JOE *enters.*)

65   JOE: Buddy?
      Buddy? Sorry I'm late. I was just . . . out. Walking. Are
      you mad?

HARPER: I got a little anxious.

JOE: Buddy kiss.

(*They kiss.*)

70   Nothing to get anxious about.
      So. So how'd you like to move to Washington?

SCENE IV

Same day. LOUIS *and* PRIOR *outside the funeral home, sitting on a
bench, both dressed in funereal finery, talking. The funeral service for
Sarah Ironson has just concluded and* LOUIS *is about to leave for the
cemetery.*

LOUIS: My grandmother actually saw Emma Goldman speak.
In Yiddish. But all Grandma could remember was that she
spoke well and wore a hat.
      What a weird service. That rabbi . . .

5   PRIOR: A definite find. Get his number when you go to the
graveyard. I want him to bury me.

LOUIS: Better head out there. Everyone gets to put dirt on
the coffin once it's lowered in.

PRIOR: Oooh. Cemetery fun. Don't want to miss that.

10   LOUIS: It's an old Jewish custom to express love. Here,
Grandma, have a shovelful. Latecomers run the risk of
finding the grave completely filled.
      She was pretty crazy. She was up there in that home for
ten years, talking to herself. I never visited. She looked too
15   much like my mother.

PRIOR: (*Hugs him.*) Poor Louis. I'm sorry your grandma is
dead.

LOUIS: Tiny little coffin, huh?
      Sorry I didn't introduce you to. . . . I always get so clos-
ety at these family things.   20

PRIOR: Butch. You get butch. (*Imitating.*) "Hi Cousin Doris,
you don't remember me I'm Lou, Rachel's boy." Lou, not
Louis, because if you say Louis they'll hear the sibilant S.

LOUIS: I don't have a . . .

PRIOR: I don't blame you, hiding. Bloodlines. Jewish curses are   25
the worst. I personally would dissolve if anyone ever looked
me in the eye and said "Feh." Fortunately WASPs don't say
"Feh." Oh and by the way, darling, cousin Doris is a dyke.

LOUIS: No.
      Really?   30

PRIOR: You don't notice anything. If I hadn't spent the last
four years fellating you I'd swear you were straight.

LOUIS: You're in a pissy mood. Cat still missing?

(*Little pause.*)

PRIOR: Not a furball in sight. It's your fault.

LOUIS: It is?   35

PRIOR: I warned you, Louis. Names are important. Call an
animal "Little Sheba" and you can't expect it to stick
around. Besides, it's a dog's name.

LOUIS: I wanted a dog in the first place, not a cat. He sprayed
my books.   40

PRIOR: He was a female cat.

LOUIS: Cats are stupid, high-strung predators. Babylonians
sealed them up in bricks. Dogs have brains.

PRIOR: Cats have intuition.

LOUIS: A sharp dog is as smart as a really dull two-year-old   45
child.

PRIOR: Cats know when something's wrong.

LOUIS: Only if you stop feeding them.

PRIOR: They know. That's why Sheba left, because she knew.

LOUIS: Knew what?   50

(*Pause.*)

PRIOR: I did my best Shirley Booth this morning, floppy slippers, housecoat, curlers, can of Little Friskies; "Come
back, little Sheba, come back. . . ." To no avail. Le chat, elle
ne reviendra jamais, jamais . . .

(*He removes his jacket, rolls up his sleeve, shows* LOUIS *a dark purple spot on the underside of his arm near the shoulder.*)

      See.   55

LOUIS: That's just a burst blood vessel.

PRIOR: Not according to the best medical authorities.

LOUIS: What?

(*Pause.*)

      Tell me.

PRIOR: K.S., baby. Lesion number one. Lookit. The wine-   60
dark kiss of the angel of death.

LOUIS: (*Very softly, holding* PRIOR's *arm.*) Oh please . . .

PRIOR: I'm a lesionnaire. The Foreign Lesion. The American
Lesion. Lesionnaire's disease.

65 LOUIS: Stop.

PRIOR: My troubles are lesion.

LOUIS: Will you *stop*.

PRIOR: Don't you think I'm handling this well? I'm going to die.

70 LOUIS: Bullshit.

PRIOR: Let go of my arm.

LOUIS: No.

PRIOR: Let go.

LOUIS: (*Grabbing* PRIOR, *embracing him ferociously.*) No.

75 PRIOR: I can't find a way to spare you baby. No wall like the wall of hard scientific fact. K.S. Wham. Bang your head on that.

LOUIS: Fuck you. (*Letting go.*) Fuck you fuck you fuck you.

PRIOR: Now that's what I like to hear. A mature reaction.

80   Let's go see if the cat's come home.
        Louis?

LOUIS: When did you find this?

PRIOR: I couldn't tell you.

LOUIS: Why?

85 PRIOR: I was scared, Lou.

LOUIS: Of what?

PRIOR: That you'll leave me.

LOUIS: Oh.

(*Little pause.*)

PRIOR: Bad timing, funeral and all, but I figured as long as

90 we're on the subject of death . . .

LOUIS: I have to go bury my grandma.

PRIOR: Lou?

(*Pause.*)

    Then you'll come home?

LOUIS: Then I'll come home.

SCENE V

Same day, later on. Split scene: JOE *and* HARPER *at home;* LOUIS *at the cemetery with* RABBI ISIDOR CHEMELWITZ *and the little coffin.*

HARPER: Washington?

JOE: It's an incredible honor, buddy, and . . .

HARPER: I have to think.

JOE: Of course.

5 HARPER: Say no.

JOE: You said you were going to think about it.

HARPER: I don't want to move to Washington.

JOE: Well I do.

HARPER: It's a giant cemetery, huge white graves and mau-

10   soleums everywhere.

JOE: We could live in Maryland. Or Georgetown.

HARPER: We're happy here.

JOE: That's not really true, buddy, we . . .

HARPER: Well happy enough! Pretend-happy. That's better

15   than nothing.

JOE: It's time to make some changes, Harper.

HARPER: No changes. Why?

JOE: I've been chief clerk for four years. I make twenty-nine thousand dollars a year. That's ridiculous. I graduated

20   fourth in my class and I make less than anyone I know.

And I'm . . . I'm tired of being a clerk, I want to go where something good is happening.

HARPER: Nothing good happens in Washington. We'll forget church teachings and buy furniture at . . . at *Conran's* and become yuppies. I have too much to do here. 25

JOE: Like what?

HARPER: I *do* have things . . .

JOE: What things?

HARPER: I have to finish painting the bedroom.

JOE: You've been painting in there for over a year. 30

HARPER: I know, I. . . . It just isn't done because I never get time to finish it.

JOE: Oh that's . . . that doesn't make sense. You have all the time in the world. You could finish it when I'm at work.

HARPER: I'm afraid to go in there alone. 35

JOE: Afraid of what?

HARPER: I heard someone in there. Metal scraping on the wall. A man with a knife, maybe.

JOE: There's no one in the bedroom, Harper.

HARPER: Not now. 40

JOE: Not this morning either.

HARPER: How do you know? You were at work this morn-ing. There's something creepy about this place. Remem-ber *Rosemary's Baby*?

JOE: *Rosemary's Baby*? 45

HARPER: Our apartment looks like that one. Wasn't that apartment in Brooklyn?

JOE: No, it was . . .

HARPER: Well, it looked like this. It did.

JOE: Then let's move. 50

HARPER: Georgetown's worse. *The Exorcist* was in Georgetown.

JOE: The devil, everywhere you turn, huh, buddy.

HARPER: Yeah. Everywhere.

JOE: How many pills today, buddy?

HARPER: None. One. Three. Only three. 55

LOUIS: (*Pointing at the coffin.*) Why are there just two little wooden pegs holding the lid down?

RABBI ISIDOR CHEMELWITZ: So she can get out easier if she wants to.

LOUIS: I hope she stays put. 60

    I pretended for years that she was already dead. When they called to say she had died it was a surprise. I aban-doned her.

RABBI ISIDOR CHEMELWITZ: "Sharfer vi di tson fun a shlang iz an umdankbar kind!" 65

LOUIS: I don't speak Yiddish.

RABBI ISIDOR CHEMELWITZ: Sharper than the serpent's tooth is the ingratitude of children. Shakespeare. *Kenig Lear.*

LOUIS: Rabbi, what does the Holy Writ say about someone who abandons someone he loves at a time of great need? 70

RABBI ISIDOR CHEMELWITZ: Why would a person do such a thing?

LOUIS: Because he has to.

    Maybe because this person's sense of the world, that it will change for the better with struggle, maybe a person 75
who has this neo-Hegelian positivist sense of constant his-torical progress towards happiness or perfection or some-thing, who feels very powerful because he feels connected to these forces, moving uphill all the time . . . maybe that person can't, um, incorporate sickness into this sense of 80
how things are supposed to go. Maybe vomit . . . and sores

and disease . . . really frighten him, maybe . . . he isn't so good with death.

85 RABBI ISIDOR CHEMELWITZ: The Holy Scriptures have nothing to say about such a person.

LOUIS: Rabbi, I'm afraid of the crimes I may commit.

RABBI ISIDOR CHEMELWITZ: Please, mister. I'm a sick old rabbi facing a long drive home to the Bronx. You want to confess, better you should find a priest.

90 LOUIS: But I'm not a Catholic, I'm a Jew.

RABBI ISIDOR CHEMELWITZ: Worse luck for you, bubbulah. Catholics believe in forgiveness. Jews believe in Guilt. (*He pats the coffin tenderly.*)

LOUIS: You just make sure those pegs are in good and tight.

95 RABBI ISIDOR CHEMELWITZ: Don't worry, mister. The life she had, she'll stay put. She's better off.

JOE: Look, I know this is scary for you. But try to understand what it means to me. Will you try?

HARPER: Yes.

100 JOE: Good. Really try.
I think things are starting to change in the world.

HARPER: But I don't want . . .

JOE: Wait. For the good. Change for the good. America has rediscovered itself. Its sacred position among nations. And

105 people aren't ashamed of that like they used to be. This is a great thing. The truth restored. Law restored. That's what President Reagan's done, Harper. He says "Truth exists and can be spoken proudly." And the country responds to him. We become better. More good. I need to be a part of that,

110 I need something big to lift me up. I mean, six years ago the world seemed in decline, horrible, hopeless, full of unsolvable problems and crime and confusion and hunger and . . .

HARPER: But it still seems that way. More now than before. They say the ozone layer is . . .

115 JOE: Harper . . .

HARPER: And today out the window on Atlantic Avenue there was a schizophrenic traffic cop who was making these . . .

JOE: Stop it! I'm trying to make a point.

HARPER: So am I.

120 JOE: You aren't even making sense, you . . .

HARPER: My point is the world seems just as . . .

JOE: It only seems that way to you because you never go out in the world, Harper, and you have emotional problems.

HARPER: I do so get out in the world.

125 JOE: You don't. You stay in all day, fretting about imaginary . . .

HARPER: I get out. I do. You don't know what I do.

JOE: You don't stay in all day.

HARPER: No.

JOE: Well. . . . Yes you do.

130 HARPER: That's what you think.

JOE: Where do you go?

HARPER: Where do *you* go? When you walk.
(*Pause, then angrily.*) And I DO NOT have emotional problems.

135 JOE: I'm sorry.

HARPER: And if I do have emotional problems it's from living with you. Or . . .

JOE: I'm sorry buddy, I didn't mean to . . .

HARPER: Or if you do think I do then you should never have

140 married me. You have all these secrets and lies.

JOE: I want to be married to you, Harper.

HARPER: You shouldn't. You never should.

(*Pause.*)

Hey buddy. Hey buddy.

JOE: Buddy kiss . . .

(*They kiss.*)

HARPER: I heard on the radio how to give a blowjob. 145

JOE: What?

HARPER: You want to try?

JOE: You really shouldn't listen to stuff like that.

HARPER: Mormons can give blowjobs.

JOE: *Harper.* 150

HARPER: (*Imitating his tone.*) *Joe.*
It was a little Jewish lady with a German accent.
This is a good time. For me to make a baby.

(*Little pause.* JOE *turns away.*)

HARPER: Then they went on to a program about holes in the ozone layer. Over Antarctica. Skin burns, birds go blind, 155 icebergs melt. The world's coming to an end.

SCENE VI

First week of November. In the men's room of the offices of the Brooklyn Federal Court of Appeals; LOUIS *is crying over the sink;* JOE *enters.*

JOE: Oh, um. . . . Morning.

LOUIS: Good morning, counselor.

JOE: (*He watches* LOUIS *cry.*) Sorry, I . . . I don't know your name.

LOUIS: Don't bother. Word processor. The lowest of the low.

JOE: (*Holding out hand.*) Joe Pitt. I'm with Justice Wilson . . . 5

LOUIS: Oh, I know that. Counselor Pitt. Chief Clerk.

JOE: Were you . . . are you OK?

LOUIS: Oh, yeah. Thanks. What a nice man.

JOE: Not so nice.

LOUIS: What? 10

JOE: Not so nice. Nothing. You sure you're . . .

LOUIS: Life sucks shit. Life . . . just sucks shit.

JOE: What's wrong?

LOUIS: Run in my nylons.

JOE: Sorry . . . ? 15

LOUIS: Forget it. Look, thanks for asking.

JOE: Well . . .

LOUIS: I mean it really is nice of you.

(*He starts crying again.*)

Sorry, sorry, sick friend . . .

JOE: Oh, I'm sorry. 20

LOUIS: Yeah, yeah, well, that's sweet.
Three of your colleagues have preceded you to this baleful sight and you're the first one to ask. The others just opened the door, saw me, and fled. I hope they had to pee real bad. 25

JOE: (*Handing him a wad of toilet paper.*) They just didn't want to intrude.

LOUIS: Hah. Reaganite heartless macho asshole lawyers.

JOE: Oh, that's unfair.

LOUIS: What is? Heartless? Macho? Reaganite? Lawyer? 30

JOE: I voted for Reagan.

LOUIS: You did?

JOE: Twice.

LOUIS: Twice? Well, oh boy. A Gay Republican.

35 JOE: Excuse me?

LOUIS: Nothing.

JOE: I'm not . . .
    Forget it.

LOUIS: Republican? Not Republican? Or . . .

40 JOE: What?

LOUIS: What?

JOE: Not gay. I'm not gay.

LOUIS: Oh. Sorry. (*Blows his nose loudly.*) It's just . . .

JOE: Yes?

45 LOUIS: Well, sometimes you can tell from the way a person
    sounds that . . . I mean you *sound* like a . . .

JOE: No I don't. Like what?

LOUIS: Like a Republican.

(*Little pause.* JOE *knows he's being teased;* LOUIS *knows he knows.*
JOE *decides to be a little brave.*)

JOE: (*Making sure no one else is around.*) Do I? Sound like a . . .?

50 LOUIS: What? Like a . . .? Republican, or . . .? Do *I*?

JOE: Do you what?

LOUIS: Sound like a . . .?

JOE: Like a . . .?
    I'm confused.

55 LOUIS: Yes.
    My name is Louis. But all my friends call me Louise. I
    work in Word Processing. Thanks for the toilet paper.

(LOUIS *offers* JOE *his hand,* JOE *reaches,* LOUIS *feints and pecks* JOE
on the cheek, then exits.)

SCENE VII

A week later. Mutual dream scene. PRIOR *is at a fantastic makeup
table, having a dream, applying the face.* HARPER *is having a pill-
induced hallucination. She has these from time to time. For some reason,* PRIOR *has appeared in this one. Or* HARPER *has appeared in*
PRIOR's *dream. It is bewildering.*

PRIOR: (*Alone, putting on makeup, then examining the results in
    the mirror; to the audience.*) "I'm ready for my closeup, Mr.
    DeMille."
    One wants to move through life with elegance and
5   grace, blossoming infrequently but with exquisite taste,
    and perfect timing, like a rare bloom, a zebra orchid. . . .
    One wants. . . . But one so seldom gets what one wants,
    does one? No. One does not. One gets fucked. Over. One
    . . . dies at thirty, robbed of . . . decades of majesty.
10 Fuck this shit. Fuck this shit.

(*He almost crumbles; he pulls himself together; he studies his handiwork in the mirror.*)

    I look like a corpse. A corpsette. Oh my queen; you know
    you've hit rock-bottom when even drag is a drag.

(HARPER *appears.*)

HARPER: Are you. . . . Who are you?

PRIOR: Who are you?

15 HARPER: What are you doing in my hallucination?

PRIOR: I'm not in your hallucination. You're in my dream.

HARPER: You're wearing makeup.

PRIOR: So are you.

HARPER: But you're a man.

20 PRIOR: (*Feigning dismay, shock, he mimes slashing his throat with
    his lipstick and dies, fabulously tragic. Then.*) The hands and
    feet give it away.

HARPER: There must be some mistake here. I don't recognize
    you. You're not. . . . Are you my . . . some sort of imagi-
25 nary friend?

PRIOR: No. Aren't you too old to have imaginary friends?

HARPER: I have emotional problems. I took too many pills.
    Why are you wearing makeup?

PRIOR: I was in the process of applying the face, trying to
30 make myself feel better—I swiped the new fall colors at
    the Clinique counter at Macy's. (*Showing her.*)

HARPER: You stole these?

PRIOR: I was out of cash; it was an emotional emergency!

HARPER: Joe will be so angry. I promised him. No more pills.

35 PRIOR: These pills you keep alluding to?

HARPER: Valium. I take Valium. Lots of Valium.

PRIOR: And you're dancing as fast as you can.

HARPER: I'm not *addicted*. I don't believe in addiction, and I
    never . . . well, I *never* drink. And I *never* take drugs.

40 PRIOR: Well, smell *you*, Nancy Drew.

HARPER: Except Valium.

PRIOR: Except Valium; in wee fistfuls.

HARPER: It's terrible. Mormons are not supposed to be ad-
    dicted to anything. I'm a Mormon.

45 PRIOR: I'm a homosexual.

HARPER: Oh! In my church we don't believe in homosexuals.

PRIOR: In my church we don't believe in Mormons.

HARPER: What church do . . . oh! (*She laughs.*) I get it.
    I don't understand this. If I didn't ever see you before
50 and I don't think I did then I don't think you should be
    here, in this hallucination, because in my experience the
    mind, which is where hallucinations come from, shouldn't
    be able to make up anything that wasn't there to start
    with, that didn't enter it from experience, from the real
55 world. Imagination can't create anything new, can it? It
    only recycles bits and pieces from the world and reassem-
    bles them into visions. . . . Am I making sense right now?

PRIOR: Given the circumstances, yes.

HARPER: So when we think we've escaped the unbearable or-
60 dinariness and, well, untruthfulness of our lives, it's really
    only the same old ordinariness and falseness rearranged
    into the appearance of novelty and truth. Nothing un-
    known is knowable. Don't you think it's depressing?

PRIOR: The limitations of the imagination?

65 HARPER: Yes.

PRIOR: It's something you learn after your second theme
    party: It's All Been Done Before.

HARPER: The world. Finite. Terribly, terribly. . . . Well . . . This
    is the most depressing hallucination I've ever had.

70 PRIOR: Apologies. I do try to be amusing.

HARPER: Oh, well, don't apologize, you. . . . I can't expect
    someone who's really sick to entertain me.

PRIOR: How on earth did you know . . .

HARPER: Oh that happens. This is the very threshhold of rev-
75   elation sometimes. You can see things . . . how sick you
      are. Do you see anything about me?
PRIOR: Yes.
HARPER: What?
PRIOR: You are amazingly unhappy.
80 HARPER: Oh big deal. You meet a Valium addict and you fig-
      ure out she's unhappy. That doesn't count. Of course I. . . .
      Something else. Something surprising.
PRIOR: Something surprising.
HARPER: Yes.
85 PRIOR: Your husband's a homo.

(*Pause.*)

HARPER: Oh, ridiculous.

(*Pause, then very quietly.*)

      Really?
PRIOR: (*Shrugs.*) Threshhold of revelation.
HARPER: Well I don't like your revelations. I don't think you
90   intuit well at all. Joe's a very normal man, he . . .
      Oh God. Oh God. He. . . . Do homos take, like, lots of
      long walks?
PRIOR: Yes. We do. In stretch pants with lavender coifs. I just
      looked at you, and there was . . .
95 HARPER: A sort of blue streak of recognition.
PRIOR: Yes.
HARPER: Like you knew me incredibly well.
PRIOR: Yes.
HARPER: Yes.
100   I have to go now, get back, something just . . . fell apart.
      Oh God, I feel so sad . . .
PRIOR: I . . . I'm sorry. I usually say, "Fuck the truth," but
      mostly, the truth fucks you.
HARPER: I see something else about you . . .
105 PRIOR: Oh?
HARPER: Deep inside you, there's a part of you, the most in-
      ner part, entirely free of disease. I can see that.
PRIOR: Is that. . . . That isn't true.
HARPER: Threshhold of revelation.
110   Home . . .

(*She vanishes.*)

PRIOR: People come and go so quickly here . . .
      (*To himself in the mirror.*) I don't think there's any unin-
      fected part of me. My heart is pumping polluted blood. I
      feel dirty.

(*He begins to wipe makeup off with his hands, smearing it around.
A large gray feather falls from up above.* PRIOR *stops smearing the
makeup and looks at the feather. He goes to it and picks it up.*)

115 THE VOICE: (*It is an incredibly beautiful voice.*) Look up!
PRIOR: (*Looking up, not seeing anyone.*) Hello?
THE VOICE: Look up!
PRIOR: Who is that?
THE VOICE: Prepare the way!
120 PRIOR: I don't see any . . .

(*There is a dramatic change in lighting, from above.*)

A VOICE: Look up, look up,
      prepare the way
      the infinite descent
      A breath in air
      floating down   125
      Glory to . . .

(*Silence.*)

PRIOR: Hello? Is that it? Helloooo!
      What the fuck . . . ? (*He holds himself.*)
      Poor me. Poor poor me. Why me? Why poor poor
      me? Oh I don't feel good right now. I really don't.   130

SCENE VIII

That night. Split scene: HARPER *and* JOE *at home;* PRIOR *and* LOUIS
in bed.

HARPER: Where were you?
JOE: Out.
HARPER: Where?
JOE: Just out. Thinking.
HARPER: It's late.   5
JOE: I had a lot to think about.
HARPER: I burned dinner.
JOE: Sorry.
HARPER: Not my dinner. My dinner was fine. Your dinner. I
      put it back in the oven and turned everything up as high   10
      as it could go and I watched till it burned black. It's still
      hot. Very hot. Want it?
JOE: You didn't have to do that.
HARPER: I know. It just seemed like the kind of thing a mentally
      deranged sex-starved pill-popping housewife would do.   15
JOE: Uh huh.
HARPER: So I did it. Who knows anymore what I have to do?
JOE: How many pills?
HARPER: A bunch. Don't change the subject.
JOE: I won't talk to you when you . . .   20
HARPER: No. No. Don't do that! I'm . . . fine, pills are not the
      problem, not our problem, I WANT TO KNOW
      WHERE YOU'VE BEEN! I WANT TO KNOW
      WHAT'S GOING ON!
JOE: Going on with what? The job?   25
HARPER: Not the job.
JOE: I said I need more time.
HARPER: Not the job!
JOE: Mr. Cohn, I talked to him on the phone, he said I had
      to hurry . . .   30
HARPER: Not the . . .
JOE: But I can't get you to talk sensibly about anything so . . .
HARPER: SHUT UP!
JOE: Then what?
HARPER: Stick to the subject.   35
JOE: I don't know what that is. You have something you want
      to ask me? Ask me. Go.
HARPER: I . . . can't. I'm scared of you.
JOE: I'm tired, I'm going to bed.
HARPER: Tell me without making me ask. Please.   40
JOE: This is crazy, I'm not . . .
HARPER: When you come through the door at night your
      face is never exactly the way I remembered it. I get sur-

45 prised by something . . . mean and hard about the way you
look. Even the weight of you in the bed at night, the way
you breathe in your sleep seems unfamiliar.
     You terrify me.
JOE: (*Cold.*) I know who you are.
HARPER: Yes. I'm the enemy. That's easy. That doesn't change.
50   You think you're the only one who hates sex; I do; I hate
it with you; I do. I dream that you batter away at me till all
my joints come apart, like wax, and I fall into pieces. It's like
a punishment. It was wrong of me to marry you. I knew
you . . . (*She stops herself.*) It's a sin, and it's killing us both.
55 JOE: I can always tell when you've taken pills because it makes
you red-faced and sweaty and frankly that's very often
why I don't want to . . .
HARPER: Because . . .
JOE: Well, you aren't pretty. Not like this.
60 HARPER: I have something to ask you.
JOE: Then ASK! ASK! What in hell are you . . .
HARPER: Are you a homo?

(*Pause.*)

    Are you? If you try to walk out right now I'll put your
    dinner back in the oven and turn it up so high the whole
65 building will fill with smoke and everyone in it will as-
    phyxiate. So help me God I will.
        Now answer the question.
JOE: What if I . . .

(*Small pause.*)

HARPER: Then tell me, please. And we'll see.
70 JOE: No. I'm not.
        I don't see what difference it makes.

LOUIS: Jews don't have any clear textual guide to the afterlife;
    even that it exists. I don't think much about it. I see it as a
    perpetual rainy Thursday afternoon in March. Dead leaves.
75 PRIOR: Eeeugh. Very Greco-Roman.
LOUIS: Well for us it's not the verdict that counts, it's the act
    of judgment. That's why I could never be a lawyer. In
    court all that matters is the verdict.
PRIOR: You could never be a lawyer because you are over-
80 sexed. You're too distracted.
LOUIS: Not distracted, *ab*stracted. I'm trying to make a point:
PRIOR: Namely:
LOUIS: It's the judge in his or her chambers, weighing, books
    open, pondering the evidence, ranging freely over cate-
85 gories: good, evil, innocent, guilty; the judge in the cham-
    ber of circumspection, not the judge on the bench with
    the gavel. The shaping of the law, not its execution.
PRIOR: The point, dear, the point . . .
LOUIS: That it should be the questions and shape of a life, its
90 total complexity gathered, arranged and considered,
    which matters in the end, not some stamp of salvation or
    damnation which disperses all the complexity in some
    unsatisfying little decision—the balancing of the scales . . .
PRIOR: I like this; very zen; it's . . . reassuringly incompre-
95 hensible and useless. We who are about to die thank you.
LOUIS: You are not about to die.
PRIOR: It's not going well, really . . . two new lesions. My leg
    hurts. There's protein in my urine, the doctor says, but

who knows what the fuck that portends. Anyway it
shouldn't be there, the protein. My butt is chapped from   100
diarrhea and yesterday I shat blood.
LOUIS: I really hate this. You don't tell me . . .
PRIOR: You get too upset, I wind up comforting you. It's eas-
ier . . .
LOUIS: Oh thanks.   105
PRIOR: If it's bad I'll tell you.
LOUIS: Shitting blood sounds bad to me.
PRIOR: And I'm telling you.
LOUIS: And I'm handling it.
PRIOR: Tell me some more about justice.   110
LOUIS: I *am* not handling it.
PRIOR: Well Louis you win Trooper of the Month.

(LOUIS *starts to cry.*)

PRIOR: I take it back. You aren't Trooper of the Month.
    This isn't working . . .
    Tell me some more about justice.   115
LOUIS: You are not about to die.
PRIOR: Justice . . .
LOUIS: is an immensity, a confusing vastness. Justice is God.
    Prior?
PRIOR: Hmmm?   120
LOUIS: You love me.
PRIOR: Yes.
LOUIS: What if I walked out on this?
    Would you hate me forever?

(PRIOR *kisses* LOUIS *on the forehead.*)

PRIOR: Yes.   125

JOE: I think we ought to pray. Ask God for help. Ask him to-
    gether . . .
HARPER: God won't talk to me. I have to make up people to
    talk to me.
JOE: You have to keep asking.   130
HARPER: I forgot the question.
    Oh yeah. God, is my husband a . . .
JOE: (*Scary.*) Stop it. Stop it. I'm warning you.
    Does it make any difference? That I might be one
    thing deep within, no matter how wrong or ugly that   135
    thing is, so long as I have fought, with everything I have,
    to kill it. What do you want from me? What do you want
    from me, Harper? More than that? For God's sake, there's
    nothing left, I'm a shell. There's nothing left to kill.
    As long as my behavior is what I know it has to be.   140
    Decent. Correct. That alone in the eyes of God.
HARPER: No, no, not that, that's Utah talk, Mormon talk, I
    hate it, Joe, tell me, say it . . .
JOE: All I will say is that I am a very good man who has worked
    very hard to become good and you want to destroy that. You 145
    want to destroy me, but I am not going to let you do that.

(*Pause.*)

HARPER: I'm going to have a baby.
JOE: Liar.
HARPER: You liar.
    A baby born addicted to pills. A baby who does not   150
    dream but who hallucinates, who stares up at us with big
    mirror eyes and who does not know who we are.

(Pause.)

JOE: Are you really . . .

HARPER: No. Yes. No. Yes. Get away from me.

155   Now we both have a secret.

PRIOR: One of my ancestors was a ship's captain who made money bringing whale oil to Europe and returning with immigrants—Irish mostly, packed in tight, so many dollars

160   per head. The last ship he captained foundered off the coast of Nova Scotia in a winter tempest and sank to the bottom. He went down with the ship—la Grande Geste—but his crew took seventy women and kids in the ship's only long-boat, this big, open rowboat, and when the weather got too

165   rough, and they thought the boat was overcrowded, the crew started lifting people up and hurling them into the sea. Until they got the ballast right. They walked up and down the longboat, eyes to the waterline, and when the boat rode low in the water they'd grab the nearest passenger and throw them into the sea. The boat was leaky, see; seventy

170   people; they arrived in Halifax with nine people on board.

LOUIS: Jesus.

PRIOR: I think about that story a lot now. People in a boat, waiting, terrified, while implacable, unsmiling men, irre-

175   sistibly strong, seize . . . maybe the person next to you, maybe you, and with no warning at all, with time only for a quick intake of air you are pitched into freezing, turbulent water and salt and darkness to drown.

I like your cosmology, baby. While time is running out I find myself drawn to anything that's suspended, that lacks

180   an ending—but it seems to me that it lets you off scot-free.

LOUIS: What do you mean?

PRIOR: No judgment, no guilt or responsibility.

LOUIS: For me.

PRIOR: For anyone. It was an editorial "you."

185   LOUIS: Please get better. Please.

Please don't get any sicker.

SCENE IX

Third week in November. ROY and HENRY, his doctor, in HENRY's office.

HENRY: Nobody knows what causes it. And nobody knows how to cure it. The best theory is that we blame a retro-virus, the Human Immunodeficiency Virus. Its presence is made known to us by the useless antibodies which appear in

5   reaction to its entrance into the bloodstream through a cut, or an orifice. The antibodies are powerless to protect the body against it. Why, we don't know. The body's immune system ceases to function. Sometimes the body even attacks itself. At any rate it's left open to a whole horror house of

10   infections from microbes which it usually defends against.

Like Kaposi's sarcomas. These lesions. Or your throat problem. Or the glands.

We think it may also be able to slip past the blood-brain barrier into the brain. Which is of course very bad

15   news. And it's fatal in we don't know what percent of people with suppressed immune responses.

(Pause)

ROY: This is very interesting, Mr. Wizard, but why the fuck are you telling me this?

(Pause.)

HENRY: Well, I have just removed one of three lesions which biopsy results will probably tell us is a Kaposi's sarcoma le-   20 sion. And you have a pronounced swelling of glands in your neck, groin, and armpits—lymphadenopathy is another sign. And you have oral candidiasis and maybe a little more fungus under the fingernails of two digits on your right hand. So that's why . . .   25

ROY: This disease . . .

HENRY: Syndrome.

ROY: Whatever. It afflicts mostly homosexuals and drug addicts.

HENRY: Mostly. Hemophiliacs are also at risk.

ROY: Homosexuals and drug addicts. So why are you imply-   30 ing that I . . .

(Pause.)

What are you implying, Henry?

HENRY: I don't . . .

ROY: I'm not a drug addict.

HENRY: Oh come on Roy.   35

ROY: What, what, come on Roy what? Do you think I'm a junkie, Henry, do you see tracks?

HENRY: This is absurd.

ROY: Say it.

HENRY: Say what?   40

ROY: Say, "Roy Cohn, you are a . . . "

HENRY: Roy.

ROY: "You are a . . . ." Go on. Not "Roy Cohn you are a drug fiend." "Roy Marcus Cohn, you are a . . . "

Go on, Henry, it starts with an "H."   45

HENRY: Oh I'm not going to . . .

ROY: With an "H," Henry, and it isn't "Hemophiliac." Come on . . .

HENRY: What are you doing, Roy?

ROY: No, say it. I mean it. Say: "Roy Cohn, you are a homo-   50 sexual."

(Pause.)

And I will proceed, systemically, to destroy your reputation and your practice and your career in New York State, Henry. Which you know I can do.

(Pause.)

HENRY: Roy, you have been seeing me since 1958. Apart from   55 the facelifts I have treated you for everything from syphilis . . .

ROY: From a whore in Dallas.

HENRY: From syphilis to venereal warts. In your rectum. Which you may have gotten from a whore in Dallas, but it wasn't a female whore.   60

(Pause.)

ROY: So say it.

HENRY: Roy Cohn, you are . . .

You have had sex with men, many many times, Roy, and one of them, or any number of them, has made you very sick. You have AIDS.   65

ROY: AIDS.

  Your problem, Henry, is that you are hung up on words, on labels, that you believe they mean what they seem to mean. AIDS. Homosexual. Gay. Lesbian. You
70 think these are names that tell you who someone sleeps with, but they don't tell you that.

HENRY: No?

ROY: No. Like all labels they tell you one thing and one thing only: where does an individual so identified fit in the food
75 chain, in the pecking order? Not ideology, or sexual taste, but something much simpler: clout. Not who I fuck or who fucks me, but who will pick up the phone when I call, who owes me favors. This is what a label refers to. Now to someone who does not understand this, homosexual is what I am
80 because I have sex with men. But really this is wrong. Homosexuals are not men who sleep with other men. Homosexuals are men who in fifteen years of trying cannot get a pissant antidiscrimination bill through City Council. Homosexuals are men who know nobody and who nobody knows.
85 Who have zero clout. Does this sound like me, Henry?

HENRY: No.

ROY: No. I have clout. A lot. I can pick up this phone, punch fifteen numbers, and you know who will be on the other end in under five minutes, Henry?
90 HENRY: The President.

ROY: Even better, Henry. His wife.

HENRY: I'm impressed.

ROY: I don't want you to be impressed. I want you to understand. This is not sophistry. And this is not hypocrisy. This
95 is reality. I have sex with men. But unlike nearly every other man of whom this is true, I bring the guy I'm screwing to the White House and President Reagan smiles at us and shakes his hand. Because *what* I am is defined entirely by *who* I am. Roy Cohn is not a homosexual. Roy Cohn is a
100 heterosexual man, Henry, who fucks around with guys.

HENRY: OK, Roy.

ROY: And what is my diagnosis, Henry?

HENRY: You have AIDS, Roy.

ROY: No, Henry, no. AIDS is what homosexuals have. I have
105 liver cancer.

(*Pause.*)

HENRY: Well, whatever the fuck you have, Roy, it's very serious, and I haven't got a damn thing for you. The NIH in Bethesda has a new drug called AZT with a two-year waiting list that not even I can get you onto. So get on the
110 phone, Roy, and dial the fifteen numbers, and tell the First Lady you need in on an experimental treatment for liver cancer, because you can call it any damn thing you want, Roy, but what it boils down to is very bad news.

ACT TWO

In Vitro
December 1985–January 1986

SCENE I

Night, the third week in December. PRIOR *alone on the floor of his bedroom; he is much worse.*

PRIOR: Louis, Louis, please wake up, oh God.

(LOUIS *runs in.*)

PRIOR: I think something horrible is wrong with me I can't breathe . . .

LOUIS: (*Starting to exit.*) I'm calling the ambulance.

PRIOR: No, wait, I . . .   5

LOUIS: *Wait?* Are you fucking crazy? Oh God you're on fire, your head is on fire.

PRIOR: It hurts, it hurts . . .

LOUIS: I'm calling the ambulance.

PRIOR: I don't want to go to the hospital, I don't want to go   10
to the hospital please let me lie here, just . . .

LOUIS: No, no, God, Prior, stand up . . .

PRIOR: DON'T TOUCH MY LEG!

LOUIS: We have to . . . oh God this is so crazy.

PRIOR: I'll be OK if I just lie here Lou, really, if I can only   15
sleep a little . . .

(LOUIS *exits.*)

PRIOR: Louis?

  NO! NO! Don't call, you'll send me there and I won't come back, please, please Louis I'm begging, baby, please . . . (*Screams.*) LOUIS!!   20

LOUIS: (*From off; hysterical.*) WILL YOU SHUT THE FUCK UP!

PRIOR: (*Trying to stand.*) Aaaah. I have . . . to go to the bathroom. Wait. Wait, just . . . oh. Oh God. (*He shits himself.*)

LOUIS: (*Entering.*) Prior? They'll be here in . . . Oh my God.   25

PRIOR: I'm sorry, I'm sorry.

LOUIS: What did . . . ? What?

PRIOR: I had an accident.

(LOUIS *goes to him.*)

LOUIS: This is blood.

PRIOR: Maybe you shouldn't touch it . . . me. . . . I . . . (*He*   30
faints.)

LOUIS: (*Quietly.*) Oh help. Oh help. Oh God oh God oh God help me I can't I can't I can't.

SCENE II

Same night. HARPER *is sitting at home, all alone, with no lights on. We can barely see her.* JOE *enters, but he doesn't turn on the lights.*

JOE: Why are you sitting in the dark? Turn on the light.

HARPER: *No.* I heard the sounds in the bedroom again. I know someone was in there.

JOE: No one was.

HARPER: Maybe actually in the bed, under the covers with a   5
knife.

  Oh, boy. Joe. I, um, I'm thinking of going away. By which I mean: I think I'm going off again. You . . . you know what I mean?

JOE: Please don't. Stay. We can fix it. I pray for that. This is   10
my fault, but I can correct it. You have to try too . . .

(*He turns on the light. She turns it off again.*)

HARPER: When you pray, what do you pray for?

JOE: I pray for God to crush me, break me up into little pieces and start all over again.

15 HARPER: Oh. Please. Don't pray for that.

JOE: I had a book of Bible stories when I was a kid. There was a picture I'd look at twenty times every day: Jacob wrestles with the angel. I don't really remember the story,
20 or why the wrestling—just the picture. Jacob is young and very strong. The angel is . . . a beautiful man, with golden hair and wings, of course. I still dream about it. Many nights. I'm. . . . It's me. In that struggle. Fierce, and unfair. The angel is not human, and it holds nothing back, so how could anyone human win, what kind of a fight is
25 that? It's not just. Losing means your soul thrown down in the dust, your heart torn out from God's. But you can't not lose.

HARPER: In the whole entire world, you are the only person, the only person I love or have ever loved. And I love you
30 terribly. Terribly. That's what's so awfully, irreducibly real. I can make up anything but I can't dream that away.

JOE: Are you . . . are you really going to have a baby?

HARPER: It's my time and there's no blood. I don't really know. I suppose it wouldn't be a great thing. Maybe I'm
35 just not bleeding because I take too many pills. Maybe I'll give birth to a pill. That would give a new meaning to pill-popping, huh?

I think you should go to Washington. Alone. Change, like you said.

40 JOE: I'm not going to leave you, Harper.

HARPER: Well maybe not. But I'm going to leave you.

SCENE III

One A.M., the next morning. LOUIS *and a nurse,* EMILY, *are sitting in* PRIOR's *room in the hospital.*

EMILY: He'll be all right now.

LOUIS: No he won't.

EMILY: No. I guess not. I gave him something that makes him sleep.

5 LOUIS: Deep asleep?

EMILY: Orbiting the moons of Jupiter.

LOUIS: A good place to be.

EMILY: Anyplace better than here. You his . . . uh?

LOUIS: Yes. I'm his uh.

10 EMILY: This must be hell for you.

LOUIS: It is. Hell. The After Life. Which is not at all like a rainy afternoon in March, by the way, Prior. A lot more vivid than I'd expected. Dead leaves, but the crunchy
15 kind. Sharp, dry air. The kind of long, luxurious dying feeling that breaks your heart.

EMILY: Yeah, well we all get to break our hearts on this one. He seems like a nice guy. Cute.

LOUIS: Not like this.

Yes, he is. Was. Whatever.

20 EMILY: Weird name. Prior Walter. Like, "The Walter before this one."

LOUIS: Lots of Walters before this one. Prior is an old old family name in an old old family. The Walters go back to the Mayflower and beyond. Back to the Norman Conquest. He
25 says there's a Prior Walter stitched into the Bayeux tapestry.

EMILY: Is that impressive?

LOUIS: Well, it's old. Very old. Which in some circles equals impressive.

EMILY: Not in my circle. What's the name of the tapestry?

LOUIS: The Bayeux tapestry. Embroidered by La Reine Mathilde. 30

EMILY: I'll tell my mother. She embroiders. Drives me nuts.

LOUIS: Manual therapy for anxious hands.

EMILY: Maybe you should try it.

LOUIS: Mathilde stitched while William the Conqueror was off to war. She was capable of . . . more than loyalty. Devo- 35
tion. She waited for him, she stitched for years. And if he had come back broken and defeated from war, she would have loved him even more. And if he had returned mutilated, ugly, full of infection and horror, she would still have loved him; fed by pity, by a sharing of pain, she would love 40
him even more, and even more, and she would never, never have prayed to God, please let him die if he can't return to me whole and healthy and able to live a normal life. . . . If he had died, she would have buried her heart with him.

So what the fuck is the matter with me? 45

(Little pause.)

Will he sleep through the night?

EMILY: At least.

LOUIS: I'm going.

EMILY: It's one A.M. Where do you have to go at . . .

LOUIS: I know what time it is. A walk. Night air, good for 50
the. . . . The park.

EMILY: Be careful.

LOUIS: Yeah. Danger.

Tell him, if he wakes up and you're still on, tell him goodbye, tell him I had to go. 55

SCENE IV

An hour later. Split scene: JOE *and* ROY *in a fancy (straight) bar;* LOUIS *and a* MAN *in the Rambles in Central Park.* JOE *and* ROY *are sitting at the bar; the place is brightly lit.* JOE *has a plate of food in front of him but he isn't eating.* ROY *occasionally reaches over the table and forks small bites off* JOE's *plate.* ROY *is drinking heavily,* JOE *not at all.* LOUIS *and the* MAN *are eyeing each other, each al-ternating interest and indifference.*

JOE: The pills were something she started when she miscarried or . . . no, she took some before that. She had a really bad time at home, when she was a kid, her home was really bad. I think a lot of drinking and physical stuff. She doesn't talk about that, instead she talks about . . . the sky falling down, 5
people with knives hiding under sofas. Monsters. Mor-mons. Everyone thinks Mormons don't come from homes like that, we aren't supposed to behave that way, but we do. It's not lying, or being two-faced. Everyone tries very hard to live up to God's strictures, which are very . . . um . . . 10

ROY: Strict.

JOE: I shouldn't be bothering you with this.

ROY: No, please. Heart to heart. Want another. . . . What is that, seltzer?

JOE: The failure to measure up hits people very hard. From 15
such a strong desire to be good they feel very far from goodness when they fail.

What scares me is that maybe what I really love in her is the part of her that's farthest from the light, from God's love; maybe I was drawn to that in the first place. And I'm 20
keeping it alive because I need it.

ROY: Why would you need it?

JOE: There are things. . . . I don't know how well we know ourselves. I mean, what if? I know I married her because she . . . because I loved it that she was always wrong, always doing something wrong, like one step out of step. In Salt Lake City that stands out. I never stood out, on the outside, but inside, it was hard for me. To pass.

ROY: Pass?

JOE: Yeah.

ROY: Pass as what?

JOE: Oh. Well. . . . As someone cheerful and strong. Those who love God with an open heart unclouded by secrets and struggles are cheerful; God's easy simple love for them shows in how strong and happy they are. The saints.

ROY: But you had secrets? Secret struggles . . .

JOE: I wanted to be one of the elect, one of the Blessed. You feel you ought to be, that the blemishes are yours by choice, which of course they aren't. Harper's sorrow, that really deep sorrow, she didn't choose that. But it's there.

ROY: You didn't put it there.

JOE: No.

ROY: You sound like you think you did.

JOE: I am responsible for her.

ROY: Because she's your wife.

JOE: That. And I do love her.

ROY: Whatever. She's your wife. And so there are obligations. To her. But also to yourself.

JOE: She'd fall apart in Washington.

ROY: Then let her stay here.

JOE: She'll fall apart if I leave her.

ROY: Then bring her to Washington.

JOE: I just can't, Roy. She needs me.

ROY: Listen, Joe. I'm the best divorce lawyer in the business.

(*Little pause.*)

JOE: Can't Washington wait?

ROY: You do what you need to do, Joe. What you need. You. Let her life go where it wants to go. You'll both be better for that. *Somebody* should get what they want.

MAN: What do you want?

LOUIS: I want you to fuck me, hurt me, make me bleed.

MAN: I want to.

LOUIS: Yeah?

MAN: I want to hurt you.

LOUIS: Fuck me.

MAN: Yeah?

LOUIS: Hard.

MAN: Yeah? You been a bad boy?

(*Pause. LOUIS laughs, softly.*)

LOUIS: Very bad. Very bad.

MAN: You need to be punished, boy?

LOUIS: Yes. I do.

MAN: Yes what?

(*Little pause.*)

LOUIS: Um, I . . .

MAN: Yes *what,* boy?

LOUIS: Oh. Yes sir.

MAN: I want you to take me to your place, boy.

LOUIS: No, I can't do that.

MAN: No *what?*

LOUIS: No sir, I can't, I . . .
       I don't live alone, sir.

MAN: Your lover know you're out with a man tonight, boy?

LOUIS: No sir, he . . .
       My lover doesn't know.

MAN: Your lover know you . . .

LOUIS: Let's change the subject, OK? Can we go to your place?

MAN: I live with my parents.

LOUIS: Oh.

ROY: Everyone who makes it in this world makes it because somebody older and more powerful takes an interest. The most precious asset in life, I think, is the ability to be a good son. You have that, Joe. Somebody who can be a good son to a father who pushes them farther than they would otherwise go. I've had many fathers, I owe my life to them, powerful, powerful men. Walter Winchell, Edgar Hoover. Joe McCarthy most of all. He valued me because I am a good lawyer, but he loved me because I was and am a good son. He was a very difficult man, very guarded and cagey; I brought out something tender in him. He would have died for me. And me for him. Does this embarrass you?

JOE: I had a hard time with my father.

ROY: Well sometimes that's the way. Then you have to find other fathers, substitutes, I don't know. The father-son relationship is central to life. Women are for birth, beginning, but the father is continuance. The son offers the father his life as a vessel for carrying forth his father's dream. Your father's living?

JOE: Um, dead.

ROY: He was . . . what? A difficult man?

JOE: He was in the military. He could be very unfair. And cold.

ROY: But he loved you.

JOE: I don't know.

ROY: No, no, Joe, he did, I know this. Sometimes a father's love has to be very, very hard, unfair even, cold to make his son grow strong in a world like this. This isn't a good world.

MAN: Here, then.

LOUIS: I. . . . Do you have a rubber?

MAN: I don't use rubbers.

LOUIS: You should. (*He takes one from his coat pocket.*) Here.

MAN: I don't use them.

LOUIS: Forget it, then. (*He starts to leave.*)

MAN: No, wait.
       Put it on me. Boy.

LOUIS: Forget it, I have to get back. Home. I must be going crazy.

MAN: Oh come on please he won't find out.

LOUIS: It's cold. Too cold.

MAN: It's never too cold, let me warm you up. Please?

(*They begin to fuck.*)

MAN: Relax.

LOUIS: (*A small laugh.*) Not a chance.

MAN: It . . .

LOUIS: What?

MAN: I think it broke. The rubber. You want me to keep going? (*Little pause.*) Pull out? Should I . . .

LOUIS: Keep going.
    Infect me.
    I don't care. I don't care.

(*Pause. The* MAN *pulls out.*)

135   MAN: I . . . um, look, I'm sorry, but I think I want to go.
    LOUIS: Yeah.
        Give my best to mom and dad.

(*The* MAN *slaps him.*)

LOUIS: Ow!

(*They stare at each other.*)

LOUIS: It was a joke.

(*The* MAN *leaves.*)

140   ROY: How long have we known each other?
    JOE: Since 1980.
    ROY: Right. A long time. I feel close to you, Joe. Do I advise
        you well?
    JOE: You've been an incredible friend, Roy, I . . .
145   ROY: I want to be family. Familia, as my Italian friends call it.
        La Familia. A lovely word. It's important for me to help
        you, like I was helped.
    JOE: I owe practically everything to you, Roy.
    ROY: I'm dying, Joe. Cancer.
150   JOE: Oh my God.
    ROY: Please. Let me finish.
        Few people know this and I'm telling you this only
        because. . . . I'm not afraid of death. What can death bring
        that I haven't faced? I've lived; life is the worst. (*Gently
155   mocking himself.*) Listen to me, I'm a philosopher.
        Joe. You must do this. You must must must. Love; that's
        a trap. Responsibility; that's a trap too. Like a father to a
        son I tell you this: Life is full of horror; nobody escapes,
        nobody; save yourself. Whatever pulls on you, whatever
160   needs from you, threatens you. Don't be afraid; people are
        so afraid; don't be afraid to live in the raw wind, naked,
        alone. . . . Learn at least this: What you are capable of. Let
        nothing stand in your way.

SCENE V

Three days later. PRIOR *and* BELIZE *in* PRIOR'*s hospital room.*
PRIOR *is very sick but improving.* BELIZE *has just arrived.*

PRIOR: Miss Thing.
BELIZE: Ma cherie bichette.
PRIOR: Stella.
BELIZE: Stella for star. Let me see. (*Scrutinizing* PRIOR.) You
5   look like shit, why yes indeed you do, comme la merde!
PRIOR: Merci.
BELIZE: (*Taking little plastic bottles from his bag, handing them to*
    PRIOR.) Not to despair, Belle Reeve. Lookie! Magic goop!
PRIOR: (*Opening a bottle, sniffing.*) Pooh! What kinda crap is that?
10   BELIZE: Beats me. Let's rub it on your poor blistered body and
    see what it does.
PRIOR: This is not Western medicine, these bottles . . .
BELIZE: Voodoo cream. From the botanica 'round the block.

PRIOR: And you a registered nurse.
BELIZE: (*Sniffing it.*) Beeswax and cheap perfume. Cut with   15
    Jergen's Lotion. Full of good vibes and love from some lit-
    tle black Cubana witch in Miami.
PRIOR: Get that trash away from me. I am immune-suppressed.
BELIZE: I *am* a health professional. I *know* what I'm doing.
PRIOR: It stinks. Any word from Louis?   20

(*Pause.* BELIZE *starts giving* PRIOR *a gentle massage.*)

PRIOR: Gone.
BELIZE: He'll be back. I know the type. Likes to keep a girl
    on edge.
PRIOR: It's been . . .

(*Pause*)

BELIZE: (*Trying to jog his memory.*) How long?   25
PRIOR: I don't remember.
BELIZE: How long have you been here?
PRIOR: (*Getting suddenly upset.*) I don't remember, I don't give
    a fuck. I want Louis. I want my fucking boyfriend, where
    the fuck is he? I'm dying, I'm dying, where's Louis?   30
BELIZE: Shhhh, shhh . . .
PRIOR: This is a very strange drug, this drug. Emotional la-
    bility, for starters.
BELIZE: Save a tab or two for me.
PRIOR: Oh no, not this drug, ce n'est pas pour la joyeux noël   35
    et la bonne année, this drug she is serious poisonous
    chemistry, ma pauvre bichette.
        And not just disorienting. I hear things. Voices.
BELIZE: Voices.
PRIOR: A voice.   40
BELIZE: Saying what?

(*Pause.*)

PRIOR: I'm not supposed to tell.
BELIZE: You better tell the doctor. Or I will.
PRIOR: No no don't. Please. I want the voice; it's wonderful.
    It's all that's keeping me alive. I don't want to talk to some   45
    intern about it.
        You know what happens? When I hear it, I get hard.
BELIZE: Oh my.
PRIOR: Comme ça. (*He uses his arm to demonstrate.*) And you
    know I am slow to rise.   50
BELIZE: My jaw aches at the memory.
PRIOR: And would you deny me this little solace—betray my
    concupiscence to Florence Nightingale's storm troopers?
BELIZE: Perish the thought, ma bébé.
PRIOR: They'd change the drug just to spoil the fun.   55
BELIZE: You and your boner can depend on me.
PRIOR: Je t'adore, ma belle nègre.
BELIZE: All this girl-talk shit is politically incorrect, you know.
    We should have dropped it back when we gave up drag.
PRIOR: I'm sick, I get to be politically incorrect if it makes   60
    me feel better. You sound like Lou.

(*Little pause.*)

Well, at least I have the satisfaction of knowing he's in anguish somewhere. I loved his anguish. Watching him stick
his head up his asshole and eat his guts out over some rel-

65 atively minor moral conundrum—it was the best show in town. But Mother warned me; if they get overwhelmed by the little things . . .

BELIZE: They'll be belly-up bustville when something big comes along.

70 PRIOR: Mother warned me.

BELIZE: And they do come along.

PRIOR: But I didn't listen.

BELIZE: No. (*Doing Hepburn.*) Men are beasts.

PRIOR: (*Also Hepburn.*) The absolute lowest.

75 BELIZE: I have to go. If I want to spend my whole lonely life looking after white people I can get underpaid to do it.

PRIOR: You're just a Christian martyr.

BELIZE: Whatever happens, baby, I will be here for you.

PRIOR: Je t'aime.

80 BELIZE: Je t'aime. Don't go crazy on me, girlfriend, I already got enough crazy queens for one lifetime. For two. I can't be bothering with dementia.

PRIOR: I promise.

BELIZE: (*Touching him; softly.*) Ouch.

85 PRIOR: Ouch. Indeed.

BELIZE: Why'd they have to pick on you? And eat more, girlfriend, you really do look like shit.

(BELIZE *leaves.*)

PRIOR: (*After waiting a beat.*) He's gone. Are you still . . .

90 VOICE: I can't stay. I will return.

PRIOR: Are you one of those "Follow me to the other side" voices?

VOICE: No. I am no nightbird. I am a messenger . . .

PRIOR: You have a beautiful voice, it sounds . . . like a viola,

95 like a perfectly tuned, tight string, balanced, the truth. . . . Stay with me.

THE VOICE: Not now. Soon I will return, I will reveal myself to you; I am glorious, glorious; my heart, my countenance and my message. You must prepare.

100 PRIOR: For what? I don't want to . . .

THE VOICE: No death, no:

A marvelous work and a wonder we undertake, an edifice awry we sink plumb and straighten, a great Lie we abolish, a great error correct, with the rule, sword and

105 broom of Truth!

PRIOR: What are you talking about, I . . .

THE VOICE: I am on my way; when I am manifest, our Work begins;

Prepare for the parting of the air,

110 The breath, the ascent,

Glory to . . .

SCENE VI

The second week of January. MARTIN, ROY *and* JOE *in a fancy Manhattan restaurant.*

MARTIN: It's a revolution in Washington, Joe. We have a new agenda and finally a real leader. They got back the Senate but we have the courts. By the nineties the Supreme Court will be block-solid Republican appointees, and the

5 Federal bench—Republican judges like land mines, everywhere, everywhere they turn. Affirmative action? Take it to court. Boom! Land mine. And we'll get our way on just about everything: abortion, defense, Central America, family values, a live investment climate. We have the White House locked till the year 2000. And beyond. 10 A permanent fix on the Oval Office? It's possible. By '92 we'll get the Senate back, and in ten years the South is going to give us the House. It's really the end of Liberalism. The end of New Deal Socialism. The end of ipso facto secular humanism. The dawning of a genuinely American 15 political personality. Modeled on Ronald Wilson Reagan.

JOE: It sounds great, Mr. Heller.

MARTIN: Martin. And Justice is the hub. Especially since Ed Meese took over. He doesn't specialize in Fine Points of the Law. He's a flatfoot, a cop. He reminds me of Teddy 20 Roosevelt.

JOE: I can't wait to meet him.

MARTIN: Too bad, Joe, he's been dead for sixty years!

(*There is a little awkwardness.* JOE *doesn't respond.*)

MARTIN: Teddy Roosevelt. You said you wanted to. . . . Little joke. It reminds me of the story about the . . . 25

ROY: (*Smiling, but nasty.*) Aw shut the fuck up Martin.

(*To* JOE.) You see that? Mr. Heller here is one of the mighty, Joseph, in D.C. he sitteth on the right hand of the man who sitteth on the right hand of The Man. And yet I can say "shut the fuck up" and he will take no offense. 30 Loyalty. He . . . Martin?

MARTIN: Yes, Roy?

ROY: Rub my back.

MARTIN: Roy . . .

ROY: No no really, a sore spot, I get them all the time now, 35 these. . . . Rub it for me darling, would you do that for me?

(MARTIN *rubs* ROY'*s back. They both look at* JOE.)

ROY: (*To* JOE.) How do you think a handful of Bolsheviks turned St. Petersburg into Leningrad in one afternoon? *Comrades.* Who do for each other. Marx and Engels. Lenin and Trotsky. Josef Stalin and Franklin Delano Roosevelt. 40

(MARTIN *laughs.*)

ROY: *Comrades,* right Martin?

MARTIN: This man, Joe, is a Saint of the Right.

JOE: I know, Mr. Heller, I . . .

ROY: And you see what I mean, Martin? He's special, right?

MARTIN: Don't embarrass him, Roy. 45

ROY: Gravity, decency, smarts! His strength is as the strength of ten because his heart is pure! *And* he's a Royboy, one hundred percent.

MARTIN: We're on the move, Joe. On the move.

JOE: Mr. Heller, I . . . 50

MARTIN: (*Ending backrub.*) We can't wait any longer for an answer.

(*Little pause.*)

JOE: Oh. Um, I . . .

ROY: Joe's a married man, Martin.

MARTIN: Aha. 55

ROY: With a wife. She doesn't care to go to D.C., and so Joe cannot go. And keeps us dangling. We've seen that kind of thing before, haven't we? These men and their wives.

MARTIN: Oh yes. Beware.

60 JOE: I really can't discuss this under . . .

MARTIN: Then *don't* discuss. Say yes, Joe.

ROY: Now.

MARTIN: Say yes I will.

ROY: Now.

65   Now. I'll hold my breath till you do, I'm turning blue waiting. . . . *Now,* goddammit!

MARTIN: Roy, calm down, it's not . . .

ROY: Aw, fuck it. (*He takes a letter from his jacket pocket, hands it to* JOE.)

70   Read. Came today.

(JOE *reads the first paragraph, then looks up.*)

JOE: Roy. This is . . . Roy, this is terrible.

ROY: You're telling me.

    A letter from the New York State Bar Association, Martin. They're gonna try and disbar me.

75 MARTIN: Oh my.

JOE: Why?

ROY: Why, Martin?

MARTIN: Revenge.

ROY: The whole Establishment. Their little rules. Because I
80 know no rules. Because I don't see the Law as a dead and arbitrary collection of antiquated dictums, thou shall, thou shalt not, because, because I know the Law's a pliable, breathing, sweating . . . *organ,* because, because . . .

MARTIN: Because he borrowed half a million from one of his
85 clients.

ROY: Yeah, well, there's that.

MARTIN: *And* he forgot to *return* it.

JOE: Roy, that's. . . . You borrowed money from a client?

ROY: I'm deeply ashamed.

(*Little pause.*)

90 JOE: (*Very sympathetic.*) Roy, you know how much I admire you. Well I mean I know you have unorthodox ways, but I'm sure you only did what you thought at the time you needed to do. And I have faith that . . .

ROY: Not so damp, please. I'll deny it was a loan. She's got no
95 paperwork. Can't prove a fucking thing.

(*Little pause.* MARTIN *studies the menu.*)

JOE: (*Handing back the letter, more official in tone.*) Roy I really appreciate your telling me this, and I'll do whatever I can to help.

ROY: (*Holding up a hand, then, carefully.*) I'll tell you what you
100 can do.

    I'm about to be tried, Joe, by a jury that is not a jury of my peers. The disbarment committee: genteel gentleman Brahmin lawyers, country-club men. I offend them, to these men . . . I'm what, Martin, some sort of filthy lit-
105 tle Jewish troll?

MARTIN: Oh well, I wouldn't go so far as . . .

ROY: Oh well I would.

    Very fancy lawyers, these disbarment committee lawyers, fancy lawyers with fancy corporate clients and complicated cases. Antitrust suits. Deregulation. Environ- 110 mental control. Complex cases like these need Justice Department cooperation like flowers need the sun. Wouldn't you say that's an accurate assessment, Martin?

MARTIN: I'm not here, Roy. I'm not hearing any of this.

ROY: No. Of course not. 115

    Without the light of the sun, Joe, these cases, and the fancy lawyers who represent them, will wither and die.

    A well-placed friend, someone in the Justice Department, say, can turn off the sun. Cast a deep shadow on my behalf. Make them shiver in the cold. If they overstep. 120 They would fear that.

(*Pause.*)

JOE: Roy. I don't understand.

ROY: You do.

(*Pause.*)

JOE: You're not asking me to . . .

ROY: Ssshhhh. Careful. 125

JOE: (*A beat, then.*) Even if I said yes to the job, it would be illegal to interfere. With the hearings. It's unethical. No. I can't.

ROY: Un-ethical.

    Would you excuse us, Martin? 130

MARTIN: Excuse you?

ROY: Take a walk, Martin. For real.

(MARTIN *leaves.*)

ROY: Un-ethical. Are you trying to embarrass me in front of my friend?

JOE: Well it is unethical, I can't . . . 135

ROY: Boy, you are really something. What the fuck do you think this is, Sunday School?

JOE: No, but Roy this is . . .

ROY: This is . . . this is gastric juices churning, this is enzymes and acids, this is intestinal is what this is, bowel movement 140 and blood-red meat—this stinks, this is *politics,* Joe, the game of being alive. And you think you're. . . . What? Above that? Above alive is what? Dead! In the clouds! You're on earth, goddammit! Plant a foot, stay a while.

    I'm sick. They smell I'm weak. They want blood this 145 time. I must have eyes in Justice. In Justice you will protect me.

JOE: Why can't Mr. Heller . . .

ROY: Grow up, Joe. The administration can't get involved.

JOE: But I'd be part of the administration. The same as him. 150

ROY: Not the same. Martin's Ed's man. And Ed's Reagan's man. So Martin's Reagan's man.

    And you're mine.

(*Little pause. He holds up the letter.*)

    This will never be. Understand me?

(*He tears the letter up.*)

I'm gonna be a lawyer, Joe, I'm gonna be a lawyer, Joe, I'm 155 gonna be a goddam motherfucking legally licensed member of the bar lawyer, just like my daddy was, till my last bitter day on earth, Joseph, until the day I die.

(MARTIN *returns.*)

ROY: Ah, Martin's back.

160 MARTIN: So are we agreed?

ROY: Joe?

(*Little pause.*)

JOE: I will think about it.
   (*To* ROY.) I will.

ROY: Huh.

165 MARTIN: It's the fear of what comes after the doing that makes the doing hard to do.

ROY: Amen.

MARTIN: But you can almost always live with the consequences.

SCENE VII

That afternoon. On the granite steps outside the Hall of Justice, Brooklyn. It is cold and sunny. A Sabrett wagon is selling hot dogs. LOUIS, *in a shabby overcoat, is sitting on the steps contemplatively eating one.* JOE *enters with three hot dogs and a can of Coke.*

JOE: Can I . . . ?

LOUIS: Oh sure. Sure. Crazy cold sun.

JOE: (*Sitting.*) Have to make the best of it.
   How's your friend?

5 LOUIS: My . . . ? Oh. He's worse. My friend is worse.

JOE: I'm sorry.

LOUIS: Yeah, well. Thanks for asking. It's nice. You're nice. I can't believe you voted for Reagan.

JOE: I hope he gets better.

10 LOUIS: Reagan?

JOE: Your friend.

LOUIS: He won't. Neither will Reagan.

JOE: Let's not talk politics, OK?

LOUIS: (*Pointing to* JOE'*s lunch.*) You're eating three of those?

15 JOE: Well . . . I'm . . . hungry.

LOUIS: They're really terrible for you. Full of rat-poo and beetle legs and wood shavings 'n' shit.

JOE: Huh.

LOUIS: And . . . um . . . irridium, I think. Something toxic.

20 JOE: You're eating one.

LOUIS: Yeah, well, the shape, I can't help myself, plus I'm trying to commit suicide, what's your excuse?

JOE: I don't have an excuse. I just have Pepto-Bismol.

(JOE *takes a bottle of Pepto-Bismol and chugs it.* LOUIS *shudders audibly.*)

JOE: Yeah I know but then I wash it down with Coke.

(*He does this.* LOUIS *mimes barfing in* JOE'*s lap.* JOE *pushes* LOUIS'*s head away.*)

25 JOE: Are you always like this?

LOUIS: I've been worrying a lot about his kids.

JOE: Whose?

LOUIS: Reagan's. Maureen and Mike and little orphan Patti and Miss Ron Reagan Jr., the you-should-pardon-the-expression heterosexual.

30

JOE: Ron Reagan Jr. is *not* . . . You shouldn't just make these assumptions about people. How do you know? About him? What he is? You don't know.

LOUIS: (*Doing Tallulah.*) Well darling he never sucked *my* cock but . . .   35

JOE: Look, if you're going to get vulgar . . .

LOUIS: No no really I mean. . . . What's it like to be the child of the Zeitgeist? To have the American Animus as your dad? It's not really a *family,* the Reagans, I read *People,* there aren't any connections there, no love, they don't ever even   40 speak to each other except through their agents. So what's it like to be Reagan's kid? Enquiring minds want to know.

JOE: You can't believe everything you . . .

LOUIS: (*Looking away.*) But . . . I think we all know what that's like. Nowadays. No connections. No responsibilities. All   45 of us . . . falling through the cracks that separate what we owe to our selves and . . . and what we owe to love.

JOE: You just. . . . Whatever you feel like saying or doing, you don't care, you just . . . do it.

LOUIS: Do what?   50

JOE: It. Whatever. Whatever it is you want to do.

LOUIS: Are you trying to tell me something?

(*Little pause, sexual. They stare at each other.* JOE *looks away.*)

JOE: No, I'm just observing that you . . .

LOUIS: Impulsive.

JOE: Yes, I mean it must be scary, you . . .   55

LOUIS: (*Shrugs.*) Land of the free. Home of the brave. Call me irresponsible.

JOE: It's kind of terrifying.

LOUIS: Yeah, well, freedom is. Heartless, too.

JOE: Oh you're not heartless.   60

LOUIS: You don't know.
   Finish your weenie.

(*He pats* JOE *on the knee, starts to leave.*)

JOE: Um . . .

(LOUIS *turns, looks at him.* JOE *searches for something to say.*)

JOE: Yesterday was Sunday but I've been a little unfocused recently and I thought it was Monday. So I came here like   65 I was going to work. And the whole place was empty. And at first I couldn't figure out why, and I had this moment of incredible . . . fear and also. . . . It just flashed through my mind: The whole Hall of Justice, it's empty, it's deserted, it's gone out of business. Forever. The people   70 that make it run have up and abandoned it.

LOUIS: (*Looking at the building.*) Creepy.

JOE: Well yes but. I felt that I was going to scream. Not because it was creepy, but because the emptiness felt so *fast.* And . . . well, good. A . . . happy scream.   75
   I just wondered what a thing it would be . . . if overnight everything you owe anything to, justice, or love, had really gone away. Free.
   It would be . . . heartless terror. Yes. Terrible, and . . .
   Very great. To shed your skin, every old skin, one by   80 one and then walk away, unencumbered, into the morning.

(*Little pause. He looks at the building.*)

I can't go in there today.

LOUIS: Then don't.

JOE: (*Not really hearing* LOUIS.) I can't go in, I need ...

(*He looks for what he needs. He takes a swig of Pepto-Bismol.*)

85 I can't *be* this anymore. I need ... a change, I should just ...

LOUIS: (*Not a come-on, necessarily; he doesn't want to be alone.*) Want some company? For whatever?

(*Pause.* JOE *looks at* LOUIS *and looks away, afraid.* LOUIS *shrugs.*)

LOUIS: Sometimes, even if it scares you to death, you have to be willing to break the law. Know what I mean?

(*Another little pause.*)

90 JOE: Yes.

(*Another little pause.*)

LOUIS: I moved out. I moved out on my ...
I haven't been sleeping well.

JOE: Me neither.

(LOUIS *goes up to* JOE, *licks his napkin and dabs at* JOE's *mouth.*)

LOUIS: Antacid moustache.
95 (*Points to the building.*) Maybe the court won't convene. Ever again. Maybe we are free. To do whatever.
Children of the new morning, criminal minds. Selfish and greedy and loveless and blind. Reagan's children.
You're scared. So am I. Everybody is in the land of the 100 free.
God help us all.

SCENE VIII

Late that night. JOE *at a payphone phoning* HANNAH *at home in Salt Lake City.*

JOE: Mom?

HANNAH: Joe?

JOE: Hi.

HANNAH: You're calling from the street. It's ... it must be four 5 in the morning. What's happened?

JOE: Nothing, nothing, I ...

HANNAH: It's Harper. Is Harper. ... Joe? Joe?

JOE: Yeah, hi. No, Harper's fine. Well, no, she's ... not fine. How are you, Mom?

10 HANNAH: What's happened?

JOE: I just wanted to talk to you. I, uh, wanted to try something out on you.

HANNAH: Joe, you haven't ... have you been drinking, Joe?

JOE: Yes ma'am. I'm drunk.

15 HANNAH: That isn't like you.

JOE: No. I mean, who's to say?

HANNAH: Why are you out on the street at four A.M.? In that crazy city. It's dangerous.

JOE: Actually, Mom, I'm not on the street. I'm near the 20 boathouse in the park.

HANNAH: What park?

JOE: Central Park.

HANNAH: CENTRAL PARK! Oh my Lord. What on earth are you doing in Central Park at this time of night? Are you ... Joe, I think you ought to go home right now. Call 25 me from home.

(*Little pause.*)

Joe?

JOE: I come here to watch, Mom. Sometimes. Just to watch.

HANNAH: Watch what? What's there to watch at four in the ...

JOE: Mom, did Dad love me? 30

HANNAH: What?

JOE: Did he?

HANNAH: You ought to go home and call from there.

JOE: Answer.

HANNAH: Oh now really. This is maudlin. I don't like this 35 conversation.

JOE: Yeah, well, it gets worse from here on.

(*Pause.*)

HANNAH: Joe?

JOE: Mom. Momma. I'm a homosexual, Momma.
Boy, did that come out awkward. 40

(*Pause.*)

Hello? Hello?
I'm a homosexual.

(*Pause.*)

Please, Momma, Say something.

HANNAH: You're old enough to understand that your father didn't love you without being ridiculous about it. 45

JOE: What?

HANNAH: You're ridiculous. You're being ridiculous.

JOE: I'm ...
What?

HANNAH: You really ought to go home now to your wife. I 50 need to go to bed. This phone call. ... We will just forget this phone call.

JOE: Mom.

HANNAH: No more talk. Tonight. This ...
(*Suddenly very angry.*) Drinking is a sin! A sin! I raised 55 you better than that. (*She hangs up.*)

SCENE IX

The following morning, early. Split scene: HARPER *and* JOE *at home;* LOUIS *and* PRIOR *in* PRIOR's *hospital room.* JOE *and* LOUIS *have just entered. This should be fast and obviously furious; overlapping is fine; the proceedings may be a little confusing but not the final results.*

HARPER: Oh God. Home. The moment of truth has arrived.

JOE: Harper.

LOUIS: I'm going to move out.

PRIOR: The fuck you are.

JOE: Harper. Please listen. I still love you very much. You're 5 still my best buddy; I'm not going to leave you.

HARPER: No, I don't like the sound of this. I'm leaving.

LOUIS: I'm leaving.
  I already have.
10 JOE: Please listen. Stay. This is really hard. We have to talk.
HARPER: We are talking. Aren't we. Now please shut up. OK?
PRIOR: Bastard. Sneaking off while I'm flat out here, that's low. If I could get up now I'd beat the holy shit out of you.
15 JOE: Did you take pills? How many?
HARPER: No pills. Bad for the . . . (*Pats stomach.*)
JOE: You aren't pregnant. I called your gynecologist.
HARPER: I'm seeing a new gynecologist.
20 LOUIS: Oh, that's ridiculous.
PRIOR: No right. It's criminal.
JOE: Forget about that. Just listen. You want the truth. This is the truth.
  I knew this when I married you. I've known this I
25 guess for as long as I've known anything, but . . . I don't know, I thought maybe that with enough effort and will I could change myself . . . but I can't . . .
PRIOR: Criminal.
LOUIS: There oughta be a law.
30 PRIOR: There is a law. You'll see.
JOE: I'm losing ground here, I go walking, you want to know where I walk, I . . . go to the park, or up and down 53rd Street, or places where. . . . And I keep swearing I won't go walking again, but I just can't.
35 LOUIS: I need some privacy.
PRIOR: That's new.
LOUIS: Everything's new, Prior.
JOE: I try to tighten my heart into a knot, a snarl, I try to learn to live dead, just numb, but then I see someone I
40 want, and it's like a nail, like a hot spike right through my chest, and I know I'm losing.
PRIOR: Apartment too small for three? Louis and Prior comfy but not Louis and Prior and Prior's disease?
LOUIS: Something like that.
45   I won't be judged by you. This isn't a crime, just—the inevitable consequence of people who run out of—whose limitations . . .
PRIOR: Bang bang bang. The court will come to order.
LOUIS: I mean let's talk practicalities, schedules; I'll come over
50 if you want, spend nights with you when I can, I can . . .
PRIOR: Has the jury reached a verdict?
LOUIS: I'm doing the best I can.
PRIOR: Pathetic. Who cares?
JOE: My whole life has conspired to bring me to this place,
55 and I can't despise my whole life. I think I believed when I met you I could save you, you at least if not myself, but . . . I don't have any sexual feelings for you, Harper. And I don't think I ever did.

(*Little pause.*)

HARPER: I think you should go.
60 JOE: Where?
HARPER: Washington. Doesn't matter.
JOE: What are you talking about?
HARPER: Without me.
  Without me, Joe. Isn't that what you want to hear?

(*Little pause.*)

JOE: Yes.   65
LOUIS: You can love someone and fail them. You can love someone and not be able to . . .
PRIOR: You *can,* theoretically, yes. A person can, maybe an editorial "you" can love, Louis, but not *you,* specifically you, I don't know, I think you are excluded from that general 70 category.
HARPER: You were going to save me, but the whole time you were spinning a lie. I just don't understand that.
PRIOR: A person could theoretically love and maybe many do but we both know now you can't.   75
LOUIS: I do.
PRIOR: You can't even say it.
LOUIS: I love you, Prior.
PRIOR: I repeat. Who cares?
HARPER: This is so scary, I want this to stop, to go back . . .   80
PRIOR: We have reached a verdict, your honor. This man's heart is deficient. He loves, but his love is worth nothing.
JOE: Harper . . .
HARPER: Mr. Lies, I want to get away from here. Far away. Right now. Before he starts talking again. Please, please . . . 85
JOE: As long as I've known you Harper you've been afraid of . . . of men hiding under the bed, men hiding under the sofa, men with knives.
PRIOR: (*Shattered; almost pleading; trying to reach him.*) I'm dying! You stupid fuck! Do you know what that is! Love! Do 90 you know what love means? We lived together four-and-a-half years, you animal, you idiot.
LOUIS: I have to find some way to save myself.
JOE: Who are these men? I never understood it. Now I know.
HARPER: What?   95
JOE: It's me.
HARPER: It is?
PRIOR: GET OUT OF MY ROOM!
JOE: I'm the man with the knives.
HARPER: You are?   100
PRIOR: If I could get up now I'd kill you. I would. Go away. Go away or I'll scream.
HARPER: Oh God . . .
JOE: I'm sorry . . .
HARPER: It is you.   105
LOUIS: Please don't scream.
PRIOR: Go.
HARPER: I recognize you now.
LOUIS: Please . . .
JOE: Oh. Wait, I. . . . Oh!   110

(*He covers his mouth with his hand, gags, and removes his hand, red with blood.*)

  I'm bleeding.

(PRIOR *screams.*)

HARPER: Mr. Lies.
MR. LIES: (*Appearing, dressed in antarctic explorer's apparel.*) Right here.
HARPER: I want to go away. I can't see him anymore.   115
MR. LIES: Where?
HARPER: Anywhere. Far away.
MR. LIES: Absolutamento.

(HARPER *and* MR. LIES *vanish.* JOE *looks up, sees that she's gone.*)

PRIOR: (*Closing his eyes.*) When I open my eyes you'll be gone.

(LOUIS *leaves.*)

120   JOE: Harper?
PRIOR: (*Opening his eyes.*) Huh. It worked.
JOE: (*Calling.*) Harper?
PRIOR: I hurt all over. I wish I was dead.

SCENE X

The same day, sunset. HANNAH *and* SISTER ELLA CHAPTER, *a real-estate saleswoman,* HANNAH PITT's *closest friend, in front of* HANNAH's *house in Salt Lake City.*

SISTER ELLA CHAPTER: Look at that view! A view of heaven. Like the living city of heaven, isn't it, it just fairly glimmers in the sun.
HANNAH: Glimmers.
5   SISTER ELLA CHAPTER: Even the stone and brick it just glimmers and glitters like heaven in the sunshine. Such a nice view you get, perched up on a canyon rim. Some kind of beautiful place.
HANNAH: It's just Salt Lake, and you're selling the house *for*
10   me, not *to* me.
SISTER ELLA CHAPTER: I like to work up an enthusiasm for my properties.
HANNAH: Just get me a good price.
SISTER ELLA CHAPTER: Well, the market's off.
15   HANNAH: At least fifty.
SISTER ELLA CHAPTER: Forty'd be more like it.
HANNAH: Fifty.
SISTER ELLA CHAPTER: Wish you'd wait a bit.
HANNAH: Well I can't.
20   SISTER ELLA CHAPTER: Wish you would. You're about the only friend I got.
HANNAH: Oh well now.
SISTER ELLA CHAPTER: Know why I decided to like you? I decided to like you 'cause you're the only unfriendly
25   Mormon I ever met.
HANNAH: Your wig is crooked.
SISTER ELLA CHAPTER: Fix it.

(HANNAH *straightens* SISTER ELLA's *wig.*)

SISTER ELLA CHAPTER: New York City. All they got there is tiny rooms.
30   I always thought: People ought to stay put. That's why I got my license to sell real estate. It's a way of saying: Have a house! Stay put! It's a way of saying traveling's no good. Plus I needed the cash. (*She takes a pack of cigarettes out of her purse, lights one, offers pack to* HANNAH.)
35   HANNAH: Not out here, anyone could come by.
There's been days I've stood at this ledge and thought about stepping over.
It's a hard place, Salt Lake: baked dry. Abundant energy; not much intelligence. That's a combination that can
40   wear a body out. No harm looking someplace else. I don't need much room.
My sister-in-law Libby thinks there's radon gas in the basement.

SISTER ELLA CHAPTER: Is there gas in the . . .
HANNAH: Of course not. Libby's a fool.   45
SISTER ELLA CHAPTER: 'Cause I'd have to include that in the description.
HANNAH: There's no gas, Ella. (*Little pause.*) Give a puff. (*She takes a furtive drag of* ELLA's *cigarette.*) Put it away now.
SISTER ELLA CHAPTER: So I guess it's goodbye.   50
HANNAH: You'll be all right, Ella, I wasn't ever much of a friend.
SISTER ELLA CHAPTER: I'll say something but don't laugh, OK? This is the home of saints, the godliest place on earth, they say, and I think they're right. That means there's no evil here? No. Evil's everywhere. Sin's everywhere. But this   55
. . . is the spring of sweet water in the desert, the desert flower. Every step a Believer takes away from here is a step fraught with peril. I fear for you, Hannah Pitt, because you are my friend. Stay put. This is the right home of saints.
HANNAH: Latter-day saints.   60
SISTER ELLA CHAPTER: Only kind left.
HANNAH: But still. Late in the day . . . for saints and everyone. That's all. That's all.
Fifty thousand dollars for the house, Sister Ella Chapter; don't undersell. It's an impressive view.   65

ACT THREE

Not-Yet-Conscious, Forward Dawning
January 1986

SCENE I

Late night, three days after the end of Act Two. The stage is completely dark. PRIOR *is in bed in his apartment, having a nightmare. He wakes up, sits up and switches on a nightlight. He looks at his clock. Seated by the table near the bed is a man dressed in the clothing of a 13th-century British squire.*

PRIOR: (*Terrified.*) Who are you?
PRIOR 1: My name is Prior Walter.

(*Pause.*)

PRIOR: My name is Prior Walter.
PRIOR 1: I know that.
PRIOR: Explain.   5
PRIOR 1: You're alive. I'm not. We have the same name. What do you want me to explain?
PRIOR: A ghost?
PRIOR 1: An ancestor.
PRIOR: Not *the* Prior Walter? The Bayeux tapestry Prior Walter?   10
PRIOR 1: His great-great grandson. The fifth of the name.
PRIOR: I'm the thirty-fourth, I think.
PRIOR 1: Actually the thirty-second.
PRIOR: Not according to Mother.
PRIOR 1: She's including the two bastards, then; I say leave   15
them out. I say no room for bastards. The little things you swallow . . .
PRIOR: Pills.
PRIOR 1: Pills. For the pestilence. I too . . .
PRIOR: Pestilence. . . . You too what?   20
PRIOR 1: The pestilence in my time was much worse than now. Whole villages of empty houses. You could look outdoors

and see Death walking in the morning, dew dampening the ragged hem of his black robe. Plain as I see you now.

25 PRIOR: You died of the plague.

PRIOR 1: The spotty monster. Like you, alone.

PRIOR: I'm not alone.

PRIOR 1: You have no wife, no children.

PRIOR: I'm gay.

30 PRIOR 1: So? Be gay, dance in your altogether for all I care, what's that to do with not having children?

PRIOR: Gay homosexual, not bonny, blithe and . . . never mind.

PRIOR 1: I had twelve. When I died.

(The second ghost appears, this one dressed in the clothing of an elegant 17th-century Londoner.)

PRIOR 1: *(Pointing to* PRIOR 2.) And I was three years younger
35   than him.

*(*PRIOR *sees the new ghost, screams.)*

PRIOR: Oh God another one.

PRIOR 2: Prior Walter. Prior to you by some seventeen others.

PRIOR 1: He's counting the bastards.

PRIOR: Are we having a convention?

40 PRIOR 2: We've been sent to declare her fabulous incipience. They love a well-paved entrance with lots of heralds, and . . .

PRIOR 1: The messenger come. Prepare the way. The infinite descent, a breath in air . . .

45 PRIOR 2: They chose us, I suspect, because of the mortal affinities. In a family as long-descended as the Walters there are bound to be a few carried off by plague.

PRIOR 1: The spotty monster.

PRIOR 2: Black Jack. Came from a water pump, half the city
50   of London, can you imagine? His came from fleas. Yours, I understand, is the lamentable consequence of venery . . .

PRIOR 1: Fleas on rats, but who knew that?

PRIOR: Am I going to die?

PRIOR 2: We aren't allowed to discuss . . .

55 PRIOR 1: When you do, you don't get ancestors to help you through it. You may be surrounded by children but you die alone.

PRIOR: I'm afraid.

PRIOR 1: You should be. There aren't even torches, and the
60   path's rocky, dark and steep.

PRIOR 2: Don't alarm him. There's good news before there's bad.
        We two come to strew rose petal and palm leaf before the triumphal procession. Prophet. Seer. Revelator. It's a
65   great honor for the family.

PRIOR 1: He hasn't got a family.

PRIOR 2: I meant for the Walters, for the family in the larger sense.

PRIOR: *(Singing.)*

70   All I want is a room somewhere,
         Far away from the cold night air . . .

PRIOR 2: *(Putting a hand on* PRIOR'*s forehead.)* Calm, calm, this is no brain fever . . .

*(*PRIOR *calms down, but keeps his eyes closed. The lights begin to change. Distant Glorious Music.)*

PRIOR 1: *(Low chant.)* Adonai, Adonai,
    Olam ha-yichud,   75
    Zefirot, Zazahot,
    Ha-adam, ha-gadol
    Daughter of Light,
    Daughter of Splendors,
    Fluor! Phosphor!   80
    Lumen! Candle!

PRIOR 2: *(Simultaneously.)* Even now,
    From the mirror-bright halls of heaven,
    Across the cold and lifeless infinity of space,
    The Messenger comes   85
    Trailing orbs of light,
    Fabulous, incipient,
    Oh Prophet,
    To you . . .

PRIOR 1 and PRIOR 2: Prepare, prepare,   90
    The Infinite Descent,
    A breath, a feather,
    Glory to . . .

(They vanish.)

SCENE II

The next day. Split scene: LOUIS *and* BELIZE *in a coffee shop.* PRIOR *is at the outpatient clinic at the hospital with* EMILY, *the nurse; she has him on a pentamidine IV drip.*

LOUIS: Why has democracy succeeded in America? Of course by succeeded I mean comparatively, not literally, not in the present, but what makes for the prospect of some sort of radical democracy spreading outward and growing up? Why does the power that was once so carefully preserved at   5
the top of the pyramid by the original framers of the Constitution seem drawn inexorably downward and outward in spite of the best effort of the Right to stop this? I mean it's the really hard thing about being Left in this country, the American Left can't help but trip over all these petrified lit-   10
tle fetishes: freedom, that's the worst; you know, *Jeane Kirkpatrick* for God's sake will go on and on about freedom and so what does that mean, the word freedom, when she talks about it, or human rights; you have Bush talking about human rights, and so what are these people talking about, they   15
might as well be talking about the mating habits of Venusians, these people don't begin to know what, ontologically, freedom is or human rights, like they see these bourgeois property-based Rights-of-Man-type rights but that's not enfranchisement, not democracy, not what's implicit, what's   20
potential within the idea, not the idea with blood in it. That's just liberalism, the worst kind of liberalism, really, bourgeois tolerance, and what I think is that what AIDS shows us is the limits of tolerance, that it's not enough to be tolerated, because when the shit hits the fan you find out   25
how much tolerance is worth. Nothing. And underneath all the tolerance is intense, passionate hatred.

BELIZE: Uh huh.

LOUIS: Well don't you think that's true?

BELIZE: Uh huh. It is.   30

LOUIS: *Power* is the object, not being tolerated. Fuck assimilation. But I mean in spite of all this the thing about America,

I think, is that ultimately we're different from every other nation on earth, in that, with people here of every race, we can't. . . . Ultimately what defines us isn't race, but politics. Not like any European country where there's an insurmountable fact of a kind of racial, or ethnic, monopoly, or monolith, like all Dutchmen, I mean Dutch people, are well, Dutch, and the Jews of Europe were never Europeans, just a small problem. Facing the monolith. But here there are so many small problems, it's really just a collection of small problems, the monolith is missing. Oh, I mean, of course I suppose there's the monolith of White America. White Straight Male America.

BELIZE: Which is not unimpressive, even among monoliths.

LOUIS: Well, no, but when the race thing gets taken care of, and I don't mean to minimalize how major it is, I mean I know it is, this is a really, really incredibly racist country but it's like, well, the British. I mean, all these blue-eyed pink people. And it's just weird, you know, I mean I'm not all that Jewish-looking, or . . . well, maybe I am but, you know, in New York, everyone is . . . well, not everyone, but so many are but so but in England, in London I walk into bars and I feel like Sid the Yid, you know I mean like Woody Allen in *Annie Hall,* with the payess and the gabardine coat, like never, never anywhere so much—I mean, not actively despised, not like they're Germans, who I think are still terribly anti-Semitic, and racist too, I mean black-racist, they pretend otherwise but, anyway, in London, there's just . . . and at one point I met this black gay guy from Jamaica who talked with a lilt but he said his family'd been living in London since before the Civil War—the American one—and how the English never let him forget for a minute that he wasn't blue-eyed and pink and I said yeah, me too, these people are anti-Semites and he said yeah but the British Jews have the clothing business all sewed up and blacks there can't get a foothold. And it was an incredibly awkward moment of just. . . . I mean here we were, in this bar that was gay but it was a *pub,* you know, the beams and the plaster and those horrible little, like, two-day-old fish and egg sandwiches—and just so British, so *old,* and I felt, well, there's no way out of this because both of us are, right now, too much immersed in this history, hope is dissolved in the sheer age of this place, where race is what counts and there's no real hope of change—it's the racial destiny of the Brits that matters to them, not their political destiny, whereas in America . . .

BELIZE: Here in America race doesn't count.

LOUIS: No, no, that's not. . . . I mean you *can't* be hearing that . . .

BELIZE: I . . .

LOUIS: It's—look, race, yes, but ultimately race here is a political question, right? Racists just try to use race here as a tool in a political struggle. It's not really about race. Like the spiritualists try to use that stuff, are you enlightened, are you centered, channeled, whatever, this reaching out for a spiritual past in a country where no indigenous spirits exist—only the Indians, I mean Native American spirits and we killed them off so now, there are no gods here, no ghosts and spirits in America, there are no angels in America, no spiritual past, no racial past, there's only the political, and the decoys and the ploys to maneuver around the inescapable battle of politics, the shifting downwards and outwards of political power to the people . . .

BELIZE: POWER to the People! AMEN! (*Looking at his watch.*) *OH MY GOODNESS!* Will you look at the time, I gotta . . .

LOUIS: Do you. . . . You think this is, what, racist or naive or something?

BELIZE: Well it's certainly *something.* Look, I just remembered I have an appointment . . .

LOUIS: What? I mean I really don't want to, like, speak from some position of privilege and . . .

BELIZE: I'm sitting here, thinking, eventually he's *got* to run out of steam, so I let you rattle on and on saying about maybe seven or eight things I find really offensive.

LOUIS: What?

BELIZE: But I know you, Louis, and I know the guilt fueling this peculiar tirade is obviously already swollen bigger than your hemorrhoids.

LOUIS: I don't have hemorrhoids.

BELIZE: I hear different. May I finish?

LOUIS: Yes, but I don't have hemorrhoids.

BELIZE: So finally, when I . . .

LOUIS: Prior told you, he's an asshole, he shouldn't have . . .

BELIZE: You promised, Louis. Prior is not a subject.

LOUIS: You brought him up.

BELIZE: I brought up hemorrhoids.

LOUIS: So it's indirect. Passive-aggressive.

BELIZE: Unlike, I suppose, banging me over the head with your theory that America doesn't have a race problem.

LOUIS: Oh be fair I never said that.

BELIZE: Not exactly, but . . .

LOUIS: I said . . .

BELIZE: but it was close enough, because if it'd been that blunt I'd've just walked out and . . .

LOUIS: You deliberately misinterpreted! I . . .

BELIZE: Stop interrupting! I haven't been able to . . .

LOUIS: Just let me . . .

BELIZE: NO! What, *talk*? You've been running your mouth nonstop since I got here, yaddadda yaddadda blah blah blah, up the hill, down the hill, playing with your MONOLITH . . .

LOUIS: (*Overlapping*) Well, you could have joined in at any time instead of . . .

BELIZE: (*Continuing over* LOUIS.) . . . and girlfriend it is truly an awesome spectacle but I got better things to do with my time than sit here listening to this racist bullshit just because I feel sorry for you that . . .

LOUIS: I am not a racist!

BELIZE: Oh come on . . .

LOUIS: So maybe I am a racist but . . .

BELIZE: Oh I really hate that! It's no fun picking on you Louis; you're so guilty, it's like throwing darts at a glob of jello, there's no satisfying hits, just quivering, the darts just blop in and vanish.

LOUIS: I just think when you are discussing lines of oppression it gets very complicated and . . .

BELIZE: Oh is that a fact? You know, we black drag queens have a rather intimate knowledge of the complexity of the lines of . . .

LOUIS: *Ex*-black drag queen.

BELIZE: Actually ex-ex.

LOUIS: You're doing drag again?

BELIZE: I don't. . . . Maybe. I don't have to tell you. Maybe.

155   LOUIS: I think it's sexist.

BELIZE: I didn't ask you.

LOUIS: Well it is. The gay community, I think, has to adopt the same attitude towards drag as black women have to take towards black women blues singers.

160   BELIZE: Oh my we *are* walking dangerous tonight.

LOUIS: Well, it's all internalized oppression, right, I mean the masochism, the stereotypes, the . . .

BELIZE: Louis, are you deliberately trying to make me hate you?

165   LOUIS: No, I . . .

BELIZE: I mean, are you deliberately transforming yourself into an arrogant, sexual-political Stalinist-slash-racist flag-waving thug for my benefit?

(*Pause.*)

LOUIS: You know what I think?

170   BELIZE: What?

LOUIS: You hate me because I'm a Jew.

BELIZE: I'm leaving.

LOUIS: It's true.

BELIZE: You have no basis except your . . .

175   Louis, it's good to know you haven't changed; you are still an honorary citizen of the Twilight Zone, and after your pale, pale white polemics on behalf of racial insensitivity you have a flaming *fuck* of a lot of nerve calling me an anti-Semite. Now I really gotta go.

180   LOUIS: You called me Lou the Jew.

BELIZE: That was a joke.

LOUIS: I didn't think it was funny. It was hostile.

BELIZE: It was three years ago.

LOUIS: So?

185   BELIZE: You just called yourself Sid the Yid.

LOUIS: That's not the same thing.

BELIZE: Sid the Yid is different from Lou the Jew.

LOUIS: Yes.

BELIZE: Someday you'll have to explain that to me, but right now . . .

190   *You* hate me because you hate black people.

LOUIS: I do not. But I do think most black people are anti-Semitic.

BELIZE: "Most black people." *That's* racist, Louis, and *I* think most Jews . . .

195   LOUIS: Louis Farrakhan.

BELIZE: Ed Koch.

LOUIS: Jesse Jackson.

BELIZE: Jackson. Oh really, Louis, this is . . .

200   LOUIS: Hymietown! Hymietown!

BELIZE: Louis, you voted for Jesse Jackson. You send checks to the Rainbow Coalition.

LOUIS: I'm ambivalent. The checks bounced.

BELIZE: All your checks bounce, Louis; you're ambivalent about everything.

205   LOUIS: What's that supposed to mean?

BELIZE: You may be dumber than shit but I refuse to believe you can't figure it out. Try.

LOUIS: I was never ambivalent about Prior. I love him. I do. I really do.

210

BELIZE: Nobody said different.

LOUIS: Love and ambivalence are. . . . Real love isn't ambivalent.

BELIZE: "Real love isn't ambivalent." I'd swear that's a line from my favorite bestselling paperback novel, *In Love with the Night Mysterious,* except I don't think you ever read it.

215

(*Pause.*)

LOUIS: I never read it, no.

BELIZE: You ought to. Instead of spending the rest of your life trying to get through *Democracy in America.* It's about this white woman whose Daddy owns a plantation in the Deep South in the years before the Civil War—the American one—and her name is Margaret, and she's in love with her Daddy's number-one slave, and his name is Thaddeus, and she's married but her white slave-owner husband has AIDS: Antebellum Insufficiently Developed Sexorgans. And there's a lot of hot stuff going down when Margaret and Thaddeus can catch a spare torrid ten under the cottonpicking moon, and then of course the Yankees come, and they set the slaves free, and the slaves string up old Daddy, and so on. Historical fiction. Somewhere in there I recall Margaret and Thaddeus find the time to discuss the nature of love; her face is reflecting the flames of the burning plantation—you know, the way white people do—and his black face is dark in the night and she says to him, "Thaddeus, real love isn't ever ambivalent."

220

225

230

235

(*Little pause.* EMILY *enters and turns off IV drip.*)

BELIZE: Thaddeus looks at her; he's contemplating her thesis; and he isn't sure he agrees.

EMILY: (*Removing IV drip from* PRIOR'*s arm.*) Treatment number . . . (*Consulting chart.*) four.

PRIOR: Pharmaceutical miracle. Lazarus breathes again.

240

LOUIS: Is he. . . . How bad is he?

BELIZE: You want the laundry list?

EMILY: Shirt off, let's check the . . .

(PRIOR *takes his shirt off. She examines his lesions.*)

BELIZE: There's the weight problem and the shit problem and the morale problem.

245

EMILY: Only six. That's good. Pants.

(*He drops his pants. He's naked. She examines.*)

BELIZE: And. He thinks he's going crazy.

EMILY: Looking good. What else?

PRIOR: Ankles sore and swollen, but the leg's better. The nausea's mostly gone with the little orange pills. BM's pure liquid but not bloody anymore, for now, my eye doctor says everything's OK, for now, my dentist says "Yuck!" when he sees my fuzzy tongue, and now he wears little condoms on his thumb and forefinger. And a mask. So what? My dermatologist is in Hawaii and my mother . . . well leave my mother out of it. Which is usually where my mother is, out of it. My glands are like walnuts, my

250

255

weight's holding steady for week two, and a friend died two days ago of bird tuberculosis; bird tuberculosis; that
260 scared me and I didn't go to the funeral today because he was an Irish Catholic and it's probably open casket and I'm afraid of . . . something, the bird TB or seeing him or. . . . So I guess I'm doing OK. Except for of course I'm going nuts.

265 EMILY: We ran the toxoplasmosis series and there's no indication . . .

PRIOR: I know, I know, but I feel like something terrifying is on its way, you know, like a missile from outer space, and it's plummeting down towards the earth, and I'm ground
270 zero, and . . . I am generally known where I am known as one cool, collected queen. And I am ruffled.

EMILY: There's really nothing to worry about. I think that shochen bamromim hamtzeh menucho nechono al kanfey haschino.

275 PRIOR: What?

EMILY: Everything's fine. Bemaalos k'doshim ut'horim kezohar horokeea mazhirim . . .

PRIOR: Oh I don't understand what you're . . .

EMILY: Es nishmas Prior sheholoch leolomoh, baavur shen-
280 odvoo z'dokoh b'ad hazkoras nishmosoh.

PRIOR: Why are you doing that?! Stop it! Stop it!

EMILY: Stop what?

PRIOR: You were just . . . weren't you just speaking in Hebrew or something.

285 EMILY: *Hebrew?* (*Laughs.*) I'm basically Italian-American. No. I didn't speak in Hebrew.

PRIOR: Oh no, oh God please I really think I . . .

EMILY: Look, I'm sorry, I have a waiting room full of. . . . I think you're one of the lucky ones, you'll live for years,
290 probably—you're pretty healthy for someone with no immune system. Are you seeing someone? Loneliness is a danger. A therapist?

PRIOR: No, I don't need to see anyone, I just . . .

EMILY: Well think about it. You aren't going crazy. You're just
295 under a lot of stress. No wonder . . . (*She starts to write in his chart.*)

(*Suddenly there is an astonishing blaze of light, a huge chord sounded by a gigantic choir, and a great book with steel pages mounted atop a molten-red pillar pops up from the stage floor. The book opens; there is a large Aleph inscribed on its pages, which bursts into flames. Immediately the book slams shut and disappears instantly under the floor as the lights become normal again.* EMILY *notices none of this, writing.* PRIOR *is agog.*)

EMILY: (*Laughing, exiting.*) Hebrew . . .

(PRIOR *flees.*)

LOUIS: Help me.

BELIZE: I beg your pardon?

300 LOUIS: You're a nurse, give me something, I . . . don't know what to do anymore, I. . . . Last week at work I screwed up the Xerox machine like permanently and so I . . . then I tripped on the subway steps and my glasses broke and I cut my forehead, here, see, and now I can't see much and
305 my forehead . . . it's like the Mark of Cain, stupid, right, but it won't heal and every morning I see it and I think, Biblical things, Mark of Cain, Judas Iscariot and his silver

and his noose, people who . . . in betraying what they love betray what's truest in themselves, I feel . . . nothing but cold for myself, just cold, and every night I miss him,
310 I miss him so much but then . . . those sores, and the smell and . . . where I thought it was going. . . . I could be . . . I could be sick too, maybe I'm sick too. I don't know.

Belize. Tell him I love him. Can you do that?
315 BELIZE: I've thought about it for a very long time, and I still don't understand what love is. Justice is simple. Democracy is simple. Those things are unambivalent. But love is very hard. And it goes bad for you if you violate the hard
320 law of love.

LOUIS: I'm dying.

BELIZE: He's dying. You just wish you were. Oh cheer up, Louis. Look at that heavy sky out there.

LOUIS: Purple.

BELIZE: *Purple?* Boy, what kind of a homosexual are you, any-
325 way? That's not purple, Mary, that color up there is (*Very grand.*) *mauve.*

All day today it's felt like Thanksgiving. Soon, this . . . ruination will be blanketed white. You can smell it—can
330 you smell it?

LOUIS: Smell what?

BELIZE: Softness, compliance, forgiveness, grace.

LOUIS: No . . .

BELIZE: I can't help you learn that. I can't help you, Louis. You're not my business. (*He exits.*)
335

(LOUIS *puts his head in his hands, inadvertently touching his cut forehead.*)

LOUIS: Ow FUCK! (*He stands slowly, looks towards where* BELIZE *exited.*) Smell what? (*He looks both ways to be sure no one is watching, then inhales deeply, and is surprised.*) Huh. Snow.

SCENE III

Same day. HARPER *in a very white, cold place, with a brilliant blue sky above; a delicate snowfall. She is dressed in a beautiful snowsuit. The sound of the sea, faint.*

HARPER: Snow! Ice! Mountains of ice! Where am I? I . . . feel better, I do, I . . . feel better. There are ice crystals in my lungs, wonderful and sharp. And the snow smells like cold, crushed peaches. And there's something . . . some current of blood in the wind, how strange, it has that iron taste. 5

MR. LIES: Ozone.

HARPER: Ozone! Wow! Where am I?

MR. LIES: The Kingdom of Ice, the bottommost part of the world.

HARPER: (*Looking around, then realizing.*) Antarctica. This is 10 Antarctica!

MR. LIES: Cold shelter for the shattered. No sorrow here, tears freeze.

HARPER: Antarctica, Antarctica, oh boy oh boy, LOOK at this, I. . . . Wow, I must've really snapped the tether, huh? 15

MR. LIES: Apparently . . .

HARPER: That's great. I want to stay here forever. Set up camp. Build things. Build a city, an enormous city made up of

frontier forts, dark wood and green roofs and high gates
20 made of pointed logs and bonfires burning on every street
corner. I should build by a river. Where are the forests?

MR. LIES: No timber here. Too cold. Ice, no trees.

HARPER: Oh details! I'm sick of details! I'll plant them and
grow them. I'll live off caribou fat, I'll melt it over the
25 bon-fires and drink it from long, curved goat-horn cups.
It'll be great. I want to make a new world here. So that I
never have to go home again.

MR. LIES: As long as it lasts. Ice has a way of melting . . .

HARPER: No. Forever. I can have anything I want here—
30 maybe even companionship, someone who has . . . desire
for me. You, maybe.

MR. LIES: It's against the by-laws of the International Order
of Travel Agents to get involved with clients. Rules are
rules. Anyway, I'm not the one you really want.

35 HARPER: There isn't anyone . . . maybe an Eskimo. Who
could ice-fish for food. And help me build a nest for
when the baby comes.

MR. LIES: There are no Eskimo in Antarctica. And you're not
really pregnant. You made that up.

40 HARPER: Well all of this is made up. So if the snow feels cold
I'm pregnant. Right? Here, I can be pregnant. And I can
have any kind of a baby I want.

MR. LIES: This is a retreat, a vacuum, its virtue is that it lacks
everything; deep-freeze for feelings. You can be numb
45 and safe here, that's what you came for. Respect the delicate ecology of your delusions.

HARPER: You mean like no Eskimo in Antarctica. Even halluci-
MR. LIES: Correcto. Ice and snow, no Eskimo. Even hallucinations have laws.

50 HARPER: Well then who's that?

(*The* ESKIMO *appears.*)

MR. LIES: An Eskimo.

HARPER: An antarctic Eskimo. A fisher of the polar deep.

MR. LIES: There's something wrong with this picture.

(*The* ESKIMO *beckons.*)

HARPER: I'm going to like this place. It's my own National
55 Geo-graphic Special! Oh! Oh! (*She holds her stomach.*) I
think . . . I think I felt her kicking. Maybe I'll give birth
to a baby covered with thick white fur, and that way she
won't be cold. My breasts will be full of hot cocoa so she
doesn't get chilly. And if it gets really cold, she'll have a
60 pouch I can crawl into. Like a marsupial. We'll mend together. That's what we'll do; we'll mend.

SCENE IV

Same day. An abandoned lot in the South Bronx. A homeless
WOMAN *is standing near an oil drum in which a fire is burning.*
Snowfall. Trash around. HANNAH *enters dragging two heavy suit-*
cases.

HANNAH: Excuse me? I said excuse me? Can you tell me
where I am? Is this Brooklyn? Do you know a Pineapple
Street? Is there some sort of bus or train or . . . ?
I'm lost, I just arrived from Salt Lake. City. Utah? I took
5 the bus that I was told to take and I got off—well it was the

very last stop, so I had to get off, and I *asked* the driver was
this Brooklyn, and he nodded yes but he was from one of
those foreign countries where they think it's good manners
to nod at everything even if you have no idea what it is
you're nodding at, and in truth I think he spoke no English 10
at all, which I think would make him ineligible for employment on public transportation. The public being
English-speaking, mostly. Do you speak English?

(*The* WOMAN *nods.*)

HANNAH: I was supposed to be met at the airport by my son.
He didn't show and I don't wait more than three and 15
three-quarters hours for *anyone.* I should have been patient, I guess, I. . . . Is this . . .

WOMAN: Bronx.

HANNAH: Is that. . . . The *Bronx?* Well how in the name of
Heaven did I get to the Bronx when the bus driver said . . . 20

WOMAN: (*Talking to herself.*) Slurp slurp slurp will you STOP
that disgusting slurping! YOU DISGUSTING SLURP-
ING FEEDING ANIMAL! Feeding yourself, just feeding
yourself, what would it matter, to you or to ANYONE, if
you just stopped. Feeding. And DIED? 25

(*Pause.*)

HANNAH: Can you just tell me where I . . .

WOMAN: Why was the Kosciusko Bridge named after a Polack?

HANNAH: I don't know what you're . . .

WOMAN: That was a joke.

HANNAH: Well what's the punchline? 30

WOMAN: I don't know.

HANNAH: (*Looking around desperately.*) Oh for pete's sake, is
there anyone else who . . .

WOMAN: (*Again, to herself.*) Stand further off you fat loathsome whore, you can't have any more of this soup, slurp 35
slurp slurp you animal, and the—I know you'll just go pee
it all away and where will you do that? Behind what bush?
It's FUCKING COLD out here and I . . .
Oh that's right, because it was supposed to have been
a tunnel! 40
That's not very funny.
Have you read the prophecies of Nostradamus?

HANNAH: Who?

WOMAN: Some guy I went out with once somewhere, Nostradamus. Prophet, outcast, eyes like. . . . Scary shit, he . . . 45

HANNAH: Shut up. Please. Now I want you to stop jabbering
for a minute and pull your wits together and tell me how
to get to Brooklyn. Because you know! And you are going to tell me! Because there is no one else around to tell
me and I am wet and cold and I am very angry! So I am 50
sorry you're psychotic but just make the effort—take a
deep breath—DO IT!

(HANNAH *and* WOMAN *breathe together.*)

HANNAH: That's good. Now exhale.

(*They do.*)

HANNAH: Good. Now how do I get to Brooklyn?

WOMAN: Don't know. Never been. Sorry. Want some soup? 55

HANNAH: Manhattan? Maybe you know . . . I don't suppose you know the location of the Mormon Visitor's . . .

WOMAN: 65th and Broadway.

HANNAH: How do you . . .

60 WOMAN: Go there all the time. Free movies. Boring, but you can stay all day.

HANNAH: Well. . . . So how do I . . .

WOMAN: Take the D Train. Next block make a right.

HANNAH: Thank you.

65 WOMAN: Oh yeah. In the new century I think we will all be insane.

SCENE V

Same day. JOE *and* ROY *in the study of* ROY's *brownstone.* ROY *is wearing an elegant bathrobe. He has made a considerable effort to look well. He isn't well, and he hasn't succeeded much in looking it.*

JOE: I can't. The answer's no. I'm sorry.

ROY: Oh, well, apologies . . .

I can't see that there's anyone asking for apologies.

(Pause.)

JOE: I'm sorry, Roy.

5 ROY: Oh, well, apologies.

JOE: My wife is missing, Roy. My mother's coming from Salt Lake to . . . to help look, I guess. I'm supposed to be at the airport now, picking her up but. . . . I just spent two days in a hospital, Roy, with a bleeding ulcer, I was spitting up

10 blood.

ROY: Blood, huh? Look, I'm very busy here and . . .

JOE: It's just a job.

ROY: A job? A *job? Washington!* Dumb Utah Mormon hick shit!

15 JOE: Roy . . .

ROY: *WASHINGTON!* When Washington called me I was younger than you, you think I said "Aw fuck no I can't go I got two fingers up my asshole and a little moral nosebleed to boot!" When Washington calls you my pretty

20 young punk friend you go or you can go fuck yourself sideways 'cause the train has pulled out of the station, and you are *out,* nowhere, out in the cold. Fuck you, Mary Jane, get outta here.

JOE: Just let me . . .

25 ROY: Explain? Ephemera. You broke my heart. Explain that. Explain that.

JOE: I love you. Roy.

There's so much that I want, to be . . . what you see in me, I want to be a participant in the world, in your world,

30 Roy, I want to be capable of that, I've tried, really I have but . . . I can't do this. Not because I don't believe in you, but because I believe in you so much, in what you stand for, at heart, the order, the decency. I would give anything to protect you, but. . . . There are laws I can't break. It's

35 too ingrained. It's not me. There's enough damage I've already done.

Maybe you were right, maybe I'm dead.

ROY: You're not dead, boy, you're a sissy.

You love me; that's moving, I'm moved. It's nice to be

40 loved. I warned you about her, didn't I, Joe? But you don't

listen to me, why, because you say Roy is smart and Roy's a friend but Roy . . . well, he isn't nice, and you wanna be nice. Right? A nice, nice man!

(Little pause.)

You know what my greatest accomplishment was, Joe, in my life, what I am able to look back on and be proudest 45 of? And I have helped make Presidents and unmake them and mayors and more goddam judges than anyone in NYC ever—AND several million dollars, tax-free—and what do you think means the most to me?

You ever hear of Ethel Rosenberg? Huh, Joe, huh? 50

JOE: Well, yeah, I guess I. . . . Yes.

ROY: Yes. Yes. You have heard of Ethel Rosenberg. Yes. Maybe you even read about her in the history books.

If it wasn't for me, Joe, Ethel Rosenberg would be alive today, writing some personal-advice column for *Ms.* mag- 55 azine. She isn't. Because during the trial, Joe, I was on the phone every day, talking with the judge . . .

JOE: Roy . . .

ROY: Every day, doing what I do best, talking on the telephone, making sure that timid Yid nebbish on the bench 60 did his duty to America, to history. That sweet unprepossessing woman, two kids, boo-hoo-hoo, reminded us all of our little Jewish mamas—she came this close to getting life; I pleaded till I wept to put her in the chair. Me. I did that. I would have fucking pulled the switch if they'd have 65 let me. Why? Because I fucking hate traitors. Because I fucking hate communists. Was it legal? Fuck legal. Am I a nice man? Fuck nice. They say terrible things about me in the *Nation.* Fuck the *Nation.* You want to be Nice, or you want to be Effective? Make the law, or subject to it. 70 Choose. Your wife chose. A week from today, she'll be back. SHE knows how to get what SHE wants. Maybe I ought to send *her* to Washington.

JOE: I don't believe you.

ROY: Gospel. 75

JOE: You can't possibly mean what you're saying.

Roy, you were the Assistant United States Attorney on the Rosenberg case, ex-parte communication with the judge during the trial would be . . . censurable, at least, probably conspiracy and . . . in a case that resulted in exe- 80 cution, it's . . .

ROY: What? Murder?

JOE: You're not well is all.

ROY: What do you mean, not well? Who's not well?

(Pause.)

JOE: You said . . . 85

ROY: No I didn't. I said what?

JOE: Roy, you have cancer.

ROY: No I don't.

(Pause.)

JOE: You told me you were dying.

ROY: What the fuck are you talking about, Joe? I never said 90 that. I'm in perfect health. There's not a goddam thing wrong with me.

(He smiles.)

Shake?

(JOE hesitates. He holds out his hand to ROY. ROY pulls JOE into a close, strong clinch.)

95 ROY: *(More to himself than to JOE.)* It's OK that you hurt me because I love you, baby Joe. That's why I'm so rough on you.

(ROY releases JOE. JOE backs away a step or two.)

ROY: Prodigal son. The world will wipe its dirty hands all over you.
JOE: It already has, Roy.
100 ROY: Now go.

(ROY shoves JOE hard. JOE turns to leave. ROY stops him, turns him around.)

ROY: *(Smoothing JOE's lapels, tenderly.)* I'll always be here, waiting for you . . .

(Then again, with sudden violence, he pulls JOE close, violently.)

What did you want from me, what was all this, what do you want, treacherous ungrateful little . . .

(JOE, very close to belting ROY, grabs him by the front of his robe, and propels him across the length of the room. He holds ROY at arm's length, the other arm ready to hit.)

105 ROY: *(Laughing softly, almost pleading to be hit.)* Transgress a little, Joseph.

(JOE releases ROY.)

ROY: There are so many laws; find one you can break.

(JOE hesitates, then leaves, backing out. When JOE has gone, ROY doubles over in great pain, which he's been hiding throughout the scene with JOE.)

ROY: Ah, Christ . . .
Andy! Andy! Get in here! Andy!

(The door opens, but it isn't ANDY. A small Jewish Woman dressed modestly in a fifties hat and coat stands in the doorway. The room darkens.)

110 ROY: Who the fuck are you? The new nurse?

(The figure in the doorway says nothing. She stares at ROY. A pause. ROY looks at her carefully, gets up, crosses to her. He crosses back to the chair, sits heavily.)

ROY: Aw, fuck. Ethel.
ETHEL ROSENBERG: *(Her manner is friendly, her voice is ice-cold.)* You don't look good, Roy.
ROY: Well, Ethel. I don't feel good.
115 ETHEL ROSENBERG: But you lost a lot of weight. That suits you. You were heavy back then. Zaftig, mit hips.

ROY: I haven't been that heavy since 1960. We were all heavier back then, before the body thing started. Now I look like a skeleton. They stare.
ETHEL ROSENBERG: The shit's really hit the fan, huh, Roy?   120

(Little pause. ROY nods.)

ETHEL ROSENBERG: Well the fun's just started.
ROY: What is this, Ethel, Halloween? You trying to scare me?

(ETHEL says nothing.)

ROY: Well you're wasting your time! I'm scarier than you any day of the week! So beat it, Ethel! BOOO! BETTER DEAD THAN RED! Somebody trying to shake me up?   125
HAH HAH! From the throne of God in heaven to the belly of hell, you can all fuck yourselves and then go jump in the lake because I'M NOT AFRAID OF YOU OR DEATH OR HELL OR ANYTHING!
ETHEL ROSENBERG: Be seeing you soon, Roy. Julius sends his   130
regards.
ROY: Yeah, well send this to Julius!

(He flips the bird in her direction, stands and moves towards her. Half-way across the room he slumps to the floor, breathing laboriously, in pain.)

ETHEL ROSENBERG: You're a very sick man, Roy.
ROY: Oh God . . . ANDY!
ETHEL ROSENBERG: Hmmm. He doesn't hear you, I guess.   135
We should call the ambulance.

(She goes to the phone.)

Hah! Buttons! Such things they got now.
What do I dial, Roy?

(Pause. ROY looks at her, then:)

ROY: 911.
ETHEL ROSENBERG: *(Dials the phone.)* It sings!   140
(Imitating dial tones.) La la la . . .
Huh.
Yes, you should please send an ambulance to the home of Mister Roy Cohn, the famous lawyer.
What's the address, Roy?   145
ROY: *(A beat, then.)* 244 East 87th.
ETHEL ROSENBERG: 244 East 87th Street. No apartment number, he's got the whole building.
My name? *(A beat.)* Ethel Greenglass Rosenberg.
(Small smile.) Me? No I'm not related to Mr. Cohn. An   150
old friend.

(She hangs up.)

They said a minute.
ROY: I have all the time in the world.
ETHEL ROSENBERG: You're immortal.
ROY: I'm immortal. Ethel. *(He forces himself to stand.)*   155
I have *forced* my way into history. I ain't never gonna die.
ETHEL ROSENBERG: *(A little laugh, then.)* History is about to crack wide open. Millennium approaches.

SCENE VI

Late that night. PRIOR's *bedroom.* PRIOR 1 *watching* PRIOR *in bed, who is staring back at him, terrified. Tonight* PRIOR 1 *is dressed in weird alchemical robes and hat over his historical clothing and he carries a long palm-leaf bundle.*

PRIOR 1: Tonight's the night! Aren't you excited? Tonight she arrives! Right through the roof! Ha-adam, Ha-gadol . . .
PRIOR 2: (*Appearing, similarly attired.*) Lumen! Phosphor! Fluor! Candle! An unending billowing of scarlet and . . .
5 PRIOR: Look. Garlic. A mirror. Holy water. A crucifix. FUCK OFF! Get the fuck out of my room! GO!
PRIOR 1: (*To* PRIOR 2.) Hard as a hickory knob, I'll bet.
PRIOR 2: We all tumesce when they approach. We wax full, like moons.
10 PRIOR 1: Dance.
PRIOR: Dance?
PRIOR 1: Stand up, dammit, give us your hands, dance!
PRIOR 2: Listen . . .

(*A lone oboe begins to play a little dance tune.*)

PRIOR 2: Delightful sound. Care to dance?
15 PRIOR: Please leave me alone, please just let me sleep . . .
PRIOR 2: Ah, he wants someone familiar. A partner who knows his steps. (*To* PRIOR.) Close your eyes. Imagine . . .
PRIOR: I don't . . .
PRIOR 2: Hush. Close your eyes.

(PRIOR *does.*)

20 PRIOR 2: Now open them.

(PRIOR *does.* LOUIS *appears. He looks gorgeous. The music builds gradually into a full-blooded, romantic dance tune.*)

PRIOR: Lou.
LOUIS: Dance with me.
PRIOR: I can't, my leg, it hurts at night . . .
        Are you . . . a ghost, Lou?
25 LOUIS: No. Just spectral. Lost to myself. Sitting all day on cold park benches. Wishing I could be with you. Dance with me, babe . . .

(PRIOR *stands up. The leg stops hurting. They begin to dance. The music is beautiful.*)

PRIOR 1: (*To* PRIOR 2.) Hah. Now I see why he's got no children. He's a sodomite.
30 PRIOR 2: Oh be quiet, you medieval gnome, and let them dance.
PRIOR 1: I'm not interfering, I've done my bit. Hooray, hooray, the messenger's come, now I'm blowing off. I don't like it here.

(PRIOR 1 *vanishes.*)

35 PRIOR 2: The twentieth century. Oh dear, the world has gotten so terribly, terribly old.

(PRIOR 2 *vanishes.* LOUIS *and* PRIOR *waltz happily. Lights fade back to normal.* LOUIS *vanishes.*)

(PRIOR *dances alone.*)

(*Then suddenly, the sound of wings fills the room.*)

SCENE VII

Split scene: PRIOR *alone in his apartment;* LOUIS *alone in the park.*

Again, a sound of beating wings.

PRIOR: Oh don't come in here don't come in . . . LOUIS!! No. My name is Prior Walter, I am . . . the scion of an ancient line, I am . . . abandoned I . . . no, my name is . . . is . . . Prior and I live . . . *here and now,* and . . . in the dark, in the dark, the Recording Angel opens its hundred eyes and 5 snaps the spine of the Book of Life and . . . hush! Hush! I'm talking nonsense, I . . .
        No more mad scene, hush, hush . . .

(LOUIS *in the park on a bench.* JOE *approaches, stands at a distance. They stare at each other, then* LOUIS *turns away.*)

LOUIS: Do you know the story of Lazarus?
JOE: Lazarus?
10 LOUIS: Lazarus. I can't remember what happens, exactly.
JOE: I don't. . . . Well, he was dead, Lazarus, and Jesus breathed life into him. He brought him back from death.
LOUIS: Come here often?
JOE: No. Yes. Yes.
15 LOUIS: Back from the dead. You believe that really happened?
JOE: I don't know anymore what I believe.
LOUIS: This is quite a coincidence. Us meeting.
JOE: I followed you.
        From work. I . . . followed you here.   20

(*Pause.*)

LOUIS: You followed me.
        You probably saw me that day in the washroom and thought: there's a sweet guy, sensitive, cries for friends in trouble.
JOE: Yes.   25
LOUIS: You thought maybe I'll cry for you.
JOE: Yes.
LOUIS: Well I fooled you. Crocodile tears. Nothing . . . (*He touches his heart, shrugs.*)

(JOE *reaches tentatively to touch* LOUIS's *face.*)

LOUIS: (*Pulling back.*) What are you doing? Don't do that.   30
JOE: (*Withdrawing his hand.*) Sorry. I'm sorry.
LOUIS: I'm . . . just not . . . I think, if you touch me, your hand might fall off or something. Worse things have happened to people who have touched me.
JOE: Please.   35
        Oh, boy . . .
        Can I . . .
        I . . . want . . . to touch you. Can I please just touch you . . . um, here?

(*He puts his hand on one side of* LOUIS's *face. He holds it there.*)

        I'm going to hell for doing this.   40

LOUIS: Big deal. You think it could be any worse than New York City?

(*He puts his hand on* JOE'*s hand. He takes* JOE'*s hand away from his face, holds it for a moment, then.*) Come on.

45 JOE: Where?

LOUIS: Home. With me.

JOE: This makes no sense. I mean I don't know you.

LOUIS: Likewise.

JOE: And what you do know about me you don't like.

50 LOUIS: The Republican stuff?

JOE: Yeah, well for starters.

LOUIS: I don't not like that. I hate that.

JOE: So why on earth should we . . .

(LOUIS *goes to* JOE *and kisses him.*)

LOUIS: Strange bedfellows. I don't know. I never made it with
55 one of the damned before.

I would really rather not have to spend tonight alone.

JOE: I'm a pretty terrible person, Louis.

LOUIS: Lou.

JOE: No, I really really am. I don't think I deserve being loved.

60 LOUIS: There? See? We already have a lot in common.

(LOUIS *stands, begins to walk away. He turns, looks back at* JOE. JOE *follows. They exit.*)

(PRIOR *listens. At first no sound, then once again, the sound of beating wings, frighteningly near.*)

PRIOR: That sound, that sound, it. . . . What is that, like birds
or something, like a *really* big bird, I'm frightened, I . . . no,
no fear, find the anger, find the . . . anger, my blood is
clean, my brain is fine, I can handle pressure, I am a gay
65 man and I am used to pressure, to trouble, I am tough and
strong and. . . . Oh. Oh my goodness. I . . . (*He is washed*

over by an intense sexual feeling.*) Ooohhhh. . . . I'm hot, I'm
. . . so . . . aw Jeez what is going on here I . . . must have a
fever I . . .

(*The bedside lamp flickers wildly as the bed begins to roll forward
and back. There is a deep bass creaking and groaning from the bedroom ceiling, like the timbers of a ship under immense stress, and
from above a fine rain of plaster dust.*)

PRIOR: OH!   70
PLEASE, OH PLEASE! Something's coming in here, I'm
scared, I don't like this at all, something's approaching and
I. . . . OH!

(*There is a great blaze of triumphal music, heralding. The light turns
an extraordinary harsh, cold, pale blue, then a rich, brilliant warm
golden color, then a hot, bilious green, and then finally a spectacular
royal purple. Then silence.*)

PRIOR: (*An awestruck whisper.*) God almighty . . .
Very Steven Spielberg.   75

(*A sound, like a plummeting meteor, tears down from very, very far
above the earth, hurtling at an incredible velocity towards the bedroom; the light seems to be sucked out of the room as the projectile
approaches; as the room reaches darkness, we hear a terrifying
CRASH as something immense strikes earth; the whole building
shudders and a part of the bedroom ceiling, lots of plaster and lathe
and wiring, crashes to the floor. And then in a shower of unearthly
white light, spreading great opalescent gray-silver wings, the* ANGEL
descends into the room and floats above the bed.)

ANGEL: Greetings, Prophet;
The Great Work begins:
The Messenger has arrived.

(*Blackout.*)

Anna Deavere Smith

Anna Deavere Smith (b. 1950) is one of the leading performance artists working in the United States and one of the most prominent African American women working in the U.S. theater. The eldest of five children, Smith was born and raised in Baltimore; she graduated from Beaver College in 1971 and then took an M.F.A. in acting from the American Conservatory Theatre in 1976. Throughout the 1970s and 1980s, Smith pursued a dual career as a teacher of acting and as a performer. She has taught at Carnegie-Mellon University, Yale University, New York University, the American Conservatory Theatre, the University of Southern California, Stanford University, and Harvard University. Her many stage, television, and film roles include parts in *Mother Courage* (1980) and *Tartuffe* (1983), in "All My Children" (1983), and in the films *Soup for One* (1982), *Dave* (1993), and *Philadelphia* (1993). She has most recently appeared on television in "The West Wing" (2000).

As a playwright and performer, Smith is best known for a series of one-woman shows that form part of an extended series of performances collectively entitled *On the Road: A Search for American Character.* Smith began devising *On the Road* in the early 1980s. The project was inspired by acting exercises she devised for her cast while directing Adrienne Kennedy's play, *A Movie Star Has to Star in Black and White.* To wean her students away from a strictly psychological approach to acting, in which the actor's focus is on the role-as-self, Smith had them watch and then reenact celebrity television talk-show interviews as a way of building a bridge to a "character" as something other. Working with actual interview material gave Smith the working method for much of her subsequent work. For the various *On the Road* performances, Smith interviews a range of subjects who are part of a given event or situation she wants to explore. In fact, she is often invited to colleges and other organizations to use performance to help explore race, gender, and identity issues. After conducting the interviews, Smith devises a performance, using minimal props and costumes, in which she interweaves sections from the interviews, performing all of the roles herself. In 1987, she was invited by San Francisco's Eureka Theater to devise a show concerning racial attitudes in that city; it was performed under the title *From the Outside Looking In.* She also performed a piece on women in San Francisco's theater community, at the invitation of the Bay Area Women in Theater. In 1988 she was invited to conduct an oral history of the Women and Theater Program of the Association for Theatre in Higher Education; *Chlorophyll Postmodernism and the Mother Goddess / A Conversation* was performed at the Women and Theater conference in San Diego that year. She was asked to Princeton University in 1989 to conduct interviews on gender politics among students, faculty, and staff, and performed *Gender Bending;* she has conducted similar workshops and performances for the Five Colleges (Amherst, Hampshire, Mount Holyoke, and Smith colleges, and the University of Massachusetts) in Massachusetts, and for the University of Pennsylvania.

Smith is now known, though, for two performance works that confront recent urban uprisings: *Fires in the Mirror: Crown Heights, Brooklyn and Other Identities* (1992), and *Twilight: Los Angeles 1992* (1993), which concerns the unrest in Los Angeles following the acquittal of four L.A. police officers who were tried for beating an African American man, Rodney King. *Fires in the Mirror,* which earned Smith a 1992 Obie Special Citation, was shown on the Public Broadcasting Service in 1993. Both *Fires in the Mirror* and *Twilight* have been produced for television and are available from PBS. Smith's most recent play, *House Arrest,* investigates the press and the presidency; her work on the play is documented in *Talk to Me: Travels in Media and Politics,* 2000.

Fires in the Mirror concerns racial and ethnic rioting that took place in the Crown Heights neighborhood of Brooklyn, New York, in August 1991. The events that sparked three nights of rioting began on the evening of Monday, August 19, and remain in some dispute. Menachem Schneerson, the Grand Rebbe of the Lubavitcher sect of Hasidic Jews, was returning from his weekly visit to a cemetery; his car was accompanied by an unmarked police escort car and by a third car, driven by Yosef Lifsh and carrying two other Hasidic passengers. At one point Lifsh's car fell behind; apparently accelerating to catch up with the others, Lifsh's car ran a red light, glanced off another car, jumped the curb, and pinned two small African American children to a window grating. Gavin Cato was killed; his cousin Angela Cato was seriously injured.

Crown Heights has a history of racial and ethnic tension, and the accident quickly drew a large and volatile crowd. Within minutes, two ambulances arrived at the scene. The first ambulance to arrive was from a private Hasidic ambulance service; police ordered it to attend to the three Jewish men in the car and to leave the scene immediately. The police later claimed that the city ambulance was also at the scene and that they acted to protect the three men from the crowd and to reduce further confrontation. A city ambulance did attend to the children, but within minutes word that medical attention had been given first to the three white, Jewish men rather than to the two black children ignited a street riot. Three hours later, at 11:30 P.M., a group of black youths a few blocks from the accident surrounded a visiting Australian Hasidic scholar, Yankel Rosenbaum, and stabbed him to death. Lemrick Nelson, Jr., was arrested and held shortly thereafter.

FIRES IN THE MIRROR

Anna Deavere Smith as Rabbi Shea Hecht in *Fires in the Mirror: Crown Heights, Brooklyn and Other Identities*.

Over the next three days and nights both African American and Jewish groups protested the city's handling of the incident and became involved in a civil uprising. Crown Heights became the scene not only of protests and protest marches, but of widespread arson, looting, and rioting. Police, journalists, and citizens were beaten. Although the rioting broke by the end of the week, several events kept Crown Heights in the public eye: the funerals of Gavin Cato and Yankel Rosenbaum, protest marches led by the Reverend Al Sharpton and Alton Maddox, Yosef Lifsh's sudden trip to Israel, the unsuccessful effort to charge Lifsh with vehicular negligence and arrest him. Indeed, throughout the remainder of 1991 and 1992, Crown Heights remained a flashpoint: in September, the Reverend Al Sharpton flew to Israel to inform Lifsh that the Cato family had brought a civil suit against him; throughout 1992, Lubavitchers demonstrated and ran newspaper ads calling for further police investigation and judicial action in connection with Rosenbaum's death, alleging that the police had handled the riots and the subsequent investigation in a biased and unfair manner; in October 1992, Lemrick Nelson, Jr., was acquitted, provoking a Hasidic rally in protest.

In part, the Crown Heights riots reflected the tensions of an unusually diverse community. The Lubavitch is an Orthodox Jewish sect whose strict religious beliefs make them a close and easily identifiable community in the Crown Heights neighborhood. Many of the black residents of Crown Heights have recently emigrated from the Caribbean and are working to make a place for themselves in the United States. Both groups face overt and subtle discrimination in a number of ways. Moreover, before the riots, Crown Heights had been the scene of several racial incidents. In 1986, a group of young black men had beaten a Hasidic man to death in a subway station; in April 1987, four hundred African Americans marched to protest city favoritism (streets in the neighborhood are regularly closed to traffic during Jewish holidays) and harassment by a Hasidic neighborhood surveillance patrol; in 1989, a crowd of Hasidim surrounded and beat a black teenager they accused of slashing a Hasidic woman and her son.

Rather than providing a "history" of these events, Smith's *Fires in the Mirror* refracts the events through a series of monologues, some by participants—Gavin Cato's father, the Reverend Al Sharpton, Yankel Rosenbaum's brother Norman—and some by more distant observers, such as the playwrights Ntozake Shange and George C. Wolfe (who subsequently directed the television version of *Fires in the Mirror* for PBS). Performing the words of her subjects, Smith carefully weaves an elaborate texture of commentary about race and ethnicity in the United States. Beginning with topics like "identity," "hair," "race," "rhythm," Smith uses the characters' voices to frame the larger issues and attitudes surrounding black-white conflict in the United States and then moves more insistently into the specifics of the Crown Heights uprising. As with some other postmodern works—Norman Mailer's novel *The Executioner's Song,* Don De Lillo's *Libra,* or the Oliver Stone film *JFK—Fires in the Mirror* insistently blurs the boundary between the events and their retelling, presenting a kaleidoscopic re-presentation of events rather than a summary that pretends to a specious objectivity. One of the most striking features of *Fires in the Mirror* in performance is the way that Smith plays both white and black characters, men and women, Jews and non-Jews, the powerful and the oppressed, the famous and the unknown. And although Smith carefully observes the details of behavior, dress, and gesture with which her "characters" speak, her performance here is not a kind of mimicry. For instead of effacing identity, Smith's performance shows the challenges of negotiating between "identities." Smith's performance shows the difficulty of grappling with an *other's* identity, an *other's* attitudes, an *other's* orientation to the world.

FIRES IN THE MIRROR

CROWN HEIGHTS, BROOKLYN AND OTHER IDENTITIES

Anna Deavere Smith

THIS BOOK IS DEDICATED TO THE RESIDENTS OF
CROWN HEIGHTS, BROOKLYN, AND IN THE MEMORY
OF GAVIN CATO AND YANKEL ROSENBAUM

CHARACTERS

NTOZAKE SHANGE, *playwright, poet, novelist*

ANONYMOUS LUBAVITCHER WOMAN, *preschool teacher*

GEORGE C. WOLFE, *playwright, director, producing director of the New York Shakespeare Festival*

AARON M. BERNSTEIN, *physicist at Massachusetts Institute of Technology*

ANONYMOUS GIRL, *junior high school black girl of Haitian descent. Lives in Brooklyn near Crown Heights*

REVEREND AL SHARPTON, *well-known New York activist, minister*

RIVKAH SIEGAL, *Lubavitcher woman, graphic designer*

ANGELA DAVIS, *author, orator, activist, scholar. Professor in the History of Consciousness Department at the University of California, Santa Cruz*

MONIQUE "BIG MO" MATTHEWS, *Los Angeles rapper*

LEONARD JEFFRIES, *professor of African American Studies at City University of New York, former head of the department*

LETTY COTTIN POGREBIN, *author Deborah, Golda, and Me. One of the founding editors of Ms magazine*

CONRAD MOHAMMED, *New York minister for the Honorable Louis Farrakhan*

ROBERT SHERMAN, *director, Mayor of the City of New York's Increase the Peace Corps*

RABBI JOSEPH SPIELMAN, *spokesperson in the Lubavitcher community*

THE REVEREND CANON DOCTOR HERON SAM, *pastor, St. Mark's, Crown Heights Church*

ANONYMOUS YOUNG MAN #1, *Crown Heights resident*

MICHAEL S. MILLER, *executive director at the Jewish Community Relations Council*

HENRY RICE, *Crown Heights resident*

NORMAN ROSENBAUM, *brother of Yankel Rosenbaum. A barrister from Australia*

ANONYMOUS YOUNG MAN #2, *African American young man, late teens, early twenties. Resident of Crown Heights*

SONNY CARSON, *activist*

RABBI SHEA HECHT, *Lubavitcher rabbi, spokesperson*

RICHARD GREEN, *director, Crown Heights Youth Collective Codirector Project CURE, a Black-Hasidic basketball team that developed after the riots*

ROSLYN MALAMUD, *Lubavitcher resident of Crown Heights*

REUVEN OSTROV, *Lubavitcher male: at the time of the riot, was seventeen years old. Worked as assistant chaplain at Kings County Hospital*

CARMEL CATO, *father of Gavin Cato, Crown Heights resident, originally from Guyana*

IDENTITY
Ntozake Shange

THE DESERT

This interview was done on the phone at about 4:00 P.M. Philadelphia time. The only cue NTOZAKE gave about her physical appearance was that she took one earring off to talk on the phone. On stage we placed her upstage center in an arm chair, smoking. Then we placed her standing, downstage.

Hummmm.
Identity—
it, is, uh . . . in a way it's, um . . . it's sort of, it's uh . . .
it's a psychic sense of place

5   it's a way of knowing I'm not a rock or that tree?
I'm this other living creature over here?
And it's a way of knowing that no matter where I put
    myself
that I am not necessarily
what's around me.

10   I am part of my surroundings
and I become separate from them
and it's being able to make those differentiations clearly

that lets us have an identity
and what's inside our identity
is everything that's ever happened to us.   15
Everything that's ever happened
to us as well as our responses to it
'cause we might be alone in a trance state,
someplace like the desert
and we begin to feel as though   20
we are part of the desert—
which we are right at that minute—
but we are not the desert,
uh . . .
we are part of the desert,   25
and when we go home
we take with us that part of the desert that the desert
    gave us,
but we're still not the desert.
It's an important differentiation to make because you
    don't know
what you're giving if you don't know what you have   30
    and you don't
know what you're taking if you don't know what's yours
    and what's
somebody else's.

1245

Anonymous Lubavitcher Woman

STATIC

This interview was actually done on the phone. Based on what she told me she was doing, and on the three visits I had made to her home for other interviews, I devised this physical scene. A LUBA-VITCHER WOMAN, *in a wig, and loose-fitting clothes. She is in her mid-thirties. She is folding clothes. There are several children around. Three boys of different ages are lying together on the couch. The oldest is reading to the younger two. A teen-age girl with long hair, a button-down-collar shirt, and skirt is sweeping the floor.*

Well,
it was um,
35 getting toward the end of Shabbas,
like around five in the afternoon,
and it was summertime
and sunset isn't until about eight, nine o'clock,
so there were still quite a few hours left to go
40 and my baby had been playing with the knobs on the
    stereo system
then all of a sudden he pushed the button—
the *on* button—
and all of a sudden came blaring out,
at full volume,
45 sort of like a half station
of polka music.
But just like with the static,
it was blaring, blaring
and we can't turn off,
50 we can't turn off electrical,
you know electricity, on Shabbas.
So um,
uh . . .
there was—
55 we just were trying to ignore it,
but a young boy that was visiting us,
he was going nuts already, he said
it was giving him such a headache could we do
    something about it,
couldn't we get a baby
60 to turn it off;
we can't make the baby turn it off but if the baby,
but if a child under three
turns something on or turns something off it's not
    considered against the Torah,
so we put the baby by it and tried to get the baby to
    turn it off,
65 he just probably made it worse,
so the guest was so uncomfortable that I said I would go
    outside
and see if I can find someone who's not Jewish and see
    if they would
like to—
see if they could turn it off,
70 so you can have somebody who's not Jewish do a simple
    act like
turning on the light or turning off the light,
and I hope I have the law correct,
but you can't ask them to do it directly.

If they wanna do it of their own free will—
and hopefully they would get some benefit from it too,   75
so I went outside
and I saw
a little
boy in the neighborhood
who I didn't know and didn't know me—   80
not Jewish, he was black and he wasn't wearing a
    yarmulke because you can't—
so I went up to him and I said to him
that my radio is on really loud and I can't turn it off,
could he help me,
so he looked at me a little crazy like,   85
Well?
And I said I don't know what to do,
so he said okay,
so he followed me into the house
and he hears this music on so loud   90
and so unpleasant
and so
he goes over to the
stereo
and he says, "You see this little button here   95
that says on and off?
Push that in
and that turns it off."
And I just sort of stood there looking kind of dumb
and then he went and pushed it,   100
and we laughed that he probably thought:
And people say Jewish people are really smart and they
    don't know
how to turn off their radios.

George C. Wolfe

101 DALMATIANS

The Mondrian Hotel in Los Angeles. Morning, Sunny. A very nice room. GEORGE *is wearing denim jeans, a light blue denim shirt, and white leather tennis shoes. His hair is in a ponytail. He wears tortoise/ wire spectacles. He is drinking tea with milk. The tea is served on a tray, the cups and teapot are delicate porcelain.* GEORGE *is sitting on a sofa, with his feet up on the coffee table.*

I mean I grew up on a black—
a one-block street—   105
that was black.
My grandmother lived on that street
my cousins lived around the corner.
I went to this
Black—Black—   110
private Black grade school
where
I was extraordinary.
Everybody there was extraordinary.
You were told you were extraordinary.   115
It was very clear
that I could not go to see *101 Dalmatians* at the Capital
    Theatre
because it was segregated.
And at the same time

120 I was treated like I was the most extraordinary creature
     that had
been born.
So I'm on my street in my house,
at my school—
and I was very spoiled too—
125 so I was treated like I was this special special creature.
And then I would go beyond a certain point
I was treated like I was insignificant.
Nobody was
hosing me down or calling me nigger.
130 It was just that I was insignificant.

(Slight pause.)

You know what I mean so it was very clear of

(Teacup on saucer strike twice on "very clear.")

where my extraordinariness lived.
You know what I mean.
That I was extraordinary as long as I was Black.
135 But I am—not—going—to place myself

(Pause.)

in relationship to your whiteness.
I will talk about your whiteness if we want to talk
     about that.
But I,
but what,
140 that which,
what I—
what am I saying?
My blackness does not resis—ex—re—
exist in relationship to your whiteness.

(Pause.)

145 You know

(Not really a question, more like a hum.)

(Slight pause.)

it does not exist in relationship to—
it *exists*
it exists.
I come—
150 you know what I mean—
like I said, I, I, I,
I come from—
it's a very com*plex*,
con*fused*,
155 *neu*-rotic,
at times destructive
reality, but it is completely
and totally a reality
contained and, and,
160 and full unto itself.
It's complex.
It's demonic.
It's ridiculous.

It's absurd.
It's evolved.   165
It's all the stuff.
That's the way I grew up.

(Slight pause.)

So that *therefore*—
and then you're White—

(Quick beat.)

And then there's a point when,   170
and then these two things come into contact.

MIRRORS
Aaron M. Bernstein
MIRRORS AND DISTORTIONS

*Evening, Cambridge, Massachusetts. Fall. He is a man in his fifties,
wearing a sweater and a shirt with a pen guard. He is seated at a
round wooden table with a low-hanging lamp.*

Okay, so a mirror is something that reflects light.
It's the simplest instrument to understand,
okay?
So a simple mirror is just a flat   175
reflecting
substance, like,
for example,
it's a piece of glass which is silvered on the back,
okay?   180
Now the notion of distortion also goes back into
     literature,
okay?
I'm trying to remember from art—
You probably know better than I.
You know you have a pretty young woman and she   185
     looks in a mirror
and she's a witch

(He laughs.)

because she's evil on the inside.
That's not a real mirror,
as everyone knows—
you see the inner thing.   190
Now that really goes back in literature.
So everyone understood that mirrors don't distort,
so that was a play
not on words
but a concept.   195
But physicists do
talk about distortion.
It's a big
subject, distortions.
I'll give you an example—   200
if you wanna see the
stars
you make a big
reflecting mirror—

<table>
<tr><td>205</td><td>

that's one of the ways—
you make a big telescope
so you can gather in a lot of light
and then it focuses at a point
and then there's always something called the circle of
    confusion.

</td></tr>
</table>

205
   that's one of the ways—
   you make a big telescope
   so you can gather in a lot of light
   and then it focuses at a point
   and then there's always something called the circle of
      confusion.
210
   So if ya don't make the thing perfectly spherical or
      perfectly
   parabolic
   then,
   then, uh, if there are errors in the construction
   which you can see, it's easy, if it's huge,
215
   then you're gonna have a circle of confusion,
   you see?
   So that's the reason for making the
   telescope as large as you can,
   because you want that circle
220
   to seem smaller,
   and you want to easily see errors in the construction.
   So, you see, in physics it's very practical—
   you wanna look up in the heavens
   and see the stars as well as you can
225
   without distortion.
   If you're counting stars, for example,
   and two look like one,
   you've blown it.

HAIR
Anonymous Girl
LOOK IN THE MIRROR

Morning. Spring. A teen-age black GIRL *of Haitian descent. She has hair which is straightened, and is wearing a navy blue jumper and a white shirt. She is seated in a stairwell at her junior high school in Brooklyn.*

When I look in the mirror . . .
230   I don't know.
   How did I find out I was Black . . .

(*Tongue sound.*)

   When I grew up and I look in the mirror and saw I was
      Black.
   When I look at my parents,
   That's how I knew I was Black.
235   Look at my skin.
   You Black?
   Black is beautiful.
   I don't know.
   That's what I always say.
240   I think White is beautiful too.
   But I think Black is beautiful too.
   In my class nobody is White, everybody's Black,
   and some of them is Hispanic.
   In my class
245   you can't call any of them Puerto Ricans.
   They despise Puerto Ricans, I don't know why.
   They think that Puerto Ricans are stuck up and
      everything.

They say, Oh my Gosh my nail broke, look at that cute
   guy and everything.
But they act like that themselves.
They act just like White girls.   250
Black girls is not like that.
Please, you should be in my class.
Like they say that Puerto Ricans act like that
and they don't see that they act like that themselves.
Black girls, they do bite off the Spanish girls,   255
they bite off of your clothes.
You don't know what that means? biting off?
Like biting off somebody's clothes
Like cop, following,
and last year they used to have a lot of girls like that.   260
They come to school with a style, right?
And if they see another girl with that style?
Oh my gosh look at her.
What she think she is,
she tryin' to bite off of me in some way   265
no don't be bitin' off of my sneakers
or like that.
Or doin' a hairstyle
I mean Black people are into hairstyles.
So they come to school, see somebody with a certain   270
   style,
they say uh-huh I'm gonna get me one just like that uh-
   huh,
that's the way Black people are
Yea-ah!
They don't like people doing that to them
and they do that to other people,   275
so the Black girls they won't follow the Spanish girls.
The Spanish girls don't bite off of us.
Some of the Black girls follow them.
But they don't mind
They don't care.   280
They follow each other.
Like there's three girls in my class,
they from the Dominican Republic.
They all stick together like glue.
They all three best friends.   285
They don't follow nobody,
like there's none of them lead or anything.
They don't hang around us either.
They're
by themselves.   290

The Reverend Al Sharpton
ME AND JAMES'S THING

Early afternoon. Fall. A small room that is a part of a suite of of-fices in a building on West Fifty-Seventh Street and Seventh Av-enue in New York. A very large man Black man with straightened hair. REVEREND SHARPTON's *hair is in the style of James Brown's hair. He is wearing a suit, colorful tie, and a gold medallion that was given to him by Martin Luther King, Jr.* REVEREND SHARPTON *has a pinky ring, a very resonant voice even in this small room. There is a very built, very tall man who sits behind me during the interview.* REVEREND SHARPTON's *face is much younger, and more innocent than it appears to be in the media. His humor is in his face. He is very direct. The interview only lasts fifteen minutes because he had been called out of a meeting in progress to do the interview.*

James Brown raised me.
Uh . . .
I never had a father.
My father left when I was ten.

295 James Brown took me to the beauty parlor one day
and made my hair like his.
And made me promise
to wear it like that
'til I die.

300 It's a personal family thing
between me and James Brown.
I always wanted a father
and he filled that void.
And the strength that he's demonstrated—

305 I don't know anybody that reached his heights,
and then had to go as low as he did and come back.
And I think that if anybody I met in life deserved that
    type of
tribute from
somebody

310 that he wanted a kid
to look like him
and be like his son . . .
I just came home from spending a weekend with him
    now,
uh, uh,

315 I think James deserved that.
And just like
he was the father I never had,
his kids never even visited him when he went to jail.
So I was like the kid he never had.

320 And if I had to choose between arguing with people
    about my
hairstyle
or giving him that one tribute
he axed,
I'd rather give him that tribute

325 because he filled a void for me.
And I really don't give a damn
who doesn't understand it.
The press and everybody do
their thing on that.

330 It's a personal thing between me and James Brown.
And just like
in other communities
people do their cultural thing
with who they like,

335 uh,
there's nothing wrong with me doing
that with James.
It's, it's, *us.*
I mean in the fifties it was a slick.

340 It was acting like White folks.
But today
people don't wear their hair like that.
James and I the only ones out there doing that.
So it's certainlih not

a reaction to Whites.   345
It's me and James's thing.

Rivkah Siegal

WIGS

Early afternoon. Spring. The kitchen of an apartment in Crown Heights. A very pretty Lubavitcher woman, with clear eyes and a direct gaze, wearing a wig and a knit sweater, that looks as though it might be hand knit. A round wooden table. Coffee mug. Sounds of children playing in the street are outside. A neighbor, a Lubavitcher woman with light blond hair who no longer wears the wig, observes the interview at the table.

Your hair—
It only has to be—
there's different,
uhm,   350
customs in different
Hasidic groups.
Lubavitch
the system is
it should be two inches   355
long.
It's—
some groups
have
the custom   360
to shave their
heads.
There's—
the reason is,
when you go to the mikvah   365
you may, maybe,
it's better if it's short
because of what you—
the preparation   370
that's involved
and that
you have to go under the water.
The hair has a tendency to float
and you have to be completely submerged
including your hair.   375
So . . .
And I got married
when I was a little older,
and I really wanted to be married
and I really wanted to, um . . .   380
In some ways I was eager to cover my head.
Now if I had grown up in a Lubavitch household
and then had to cut it,
I don't know what that would be like.
I really don't.   385
But now that I'm wearing the wig,
you see,
with my hair I can keep it very simple
and I can change it all the time.
So with a wig you have to have like five wigs if you   390
    want to do that.
But I, uh,

I feel somehow like it's fake,
I feel like it's not me.
I try to be as much myself as I can,
395   and it just
bothers me
that I'm kind of fooling the world.
I used to go to work.
People . . .
400   and I would wear a different wig,
and they'd say I like your new haircut
and I'd say it's not mine!
You know,
and it was very hard for me to say it
405   and
it became very difficult.
I mean, I've gone through a lot with wearing wigs and
        not wearing
wigs.
It's been a big issue for me.

Angela Davis

ROPES

*Morning, Spring, Oakland, California. In reality this interview was
done on the phone, with myself and Thulani Davis. Thulani and I
were calling from an office at the Public Theatre. We do not know
exactly what* ANGELA *was doing or wearing. I believe, from things
she said, that she was sitting on her deck in her home in Oakland,
which overlooks a beautiful panorama of trees.*

410   Race, um—
of course
for many years in the history
of African Americans in this country—
was synonymous with community.
415   As a matter of fact
we were race women and race men.
Billie Holiday for example
called herself a race woman
because she supported the community
420   and as a child growing up in the South
my assumptions were
that if anybody in the race
came under attack
then I had to be there
425   to support that person,
to support the race.
I was saying to my students just the other day,
I said,
if in 1970,
430   when I was
in jail,
someone had told me
that in 1991,
a black man
435   who
said that his, um . . .
hero—

(Increased volume, speed, and energy.)

one of his heroes
was Malcolm X—
would be nominated to the Supreme Court   440
I would have celebrated
and I don't think it would have been possible at that
        time
to convince me
that I would
be absolutely opposed,   445
a black candidate—
I mean like absolutely—

(A new attack, more energy.)

or that if anyone would have told me that
a *woman* . . .
finally be elected to the Supreme Court,   450
it would have been very difficult,
as critical as I am with respect to feminism,
as critical as I have always been with what I used to call,
you know, narrow nationalism?
I don't think   455
it would have been possible to convince me that things
        would have so absolutely
shifted that
someone could have evoked
the specter of lynching
on national television   460
and that specter of lynching would be used to violate
        our history.
And I still feel that we have to point out the racism
        involved
in the razing of a Black man
and a Black woman
in that way.   465
I mean [Ted] Kennedy was sitting right there
and it had never occurred to anyone to bring him up
before
the world,
which is not to say that I don't think it should happen.   470
And it is actually a sign of how we,
in our various oppressed
marginalized communities,
have been able to turn
terrible acts of racism directed against us   475
into victory . . .
And therefore I think
Anita Hill did that,
and so it's very complicated,
but I have no problems aligning myself politically   480
against Clarence Thomas in a real passionate way,
but at the same time I can talk about the racism that led
        to the possibility
of constructing those kinds of hearings
and
the same thing with Mike Tyson.   485
So I guess that would be,
um . . .
the way in which I would begin to look at community,
and would therefore think
that race has become, uh,   490

an increasingly obsolete way
of constructing community
because it is based on unchangeable
immutable biological
495 facts
in a very pseudo-scientific way,
alright?
Now
racism is entirely different
500 because see *racism,*
uh,
actually I think
is
at the origins of this concept of race.
505 It's not—
it's not the other way around,
that there were racists,
and then the racists—
one race came to dominate
510 the others.
As a matter of fact
in order for a European colonialist
to attempt
to conquer the world,
515 to colonize the world,
they had to construct this notion
of,
uh,
the populations of the earth being divided into certain,
520 uh,
firm biological, uh,
communities,
and that's what I think we have to go back and look at.
So when I use the word race now I put it in quotations.
525 Because if we don't transform
this . . . this intransigent
rigid
notion of race,
we will be caught up in this cycle
530 of genocidal
violence
that, um,
is at the origins of our history.
So I think—
535 and I'm
I'm convinced—and this is what I'm working on in my
    political practice right now—
is that we have to find ways of coming together in a
    different way,
not the old notion of coalition in which we anchor
    ourselves very solidly
in our,
540 um,
communities,
and simply voice
our
solidarity with other people.
545 I'm not suggesting that we do not anchor ourselves in
    our communities;
I feel very anchored in,
um,

my various communities,
but I think that,
you know,   550
to use a metaphor, the rope
attached to that anchor should be long enough to allow
    us to move
into other communities
to understand and learn.
I've been thinking a lot about the need to make more   555
    intimate
these connections and associations and to really take on
    the responsibility
of learning.
So I think that we need to—
in order to find ways of working with
and understanding   560
the vastness
of our many cultural heritages
and ways of coming together without
rendering invisible all of that heterogeneity—
I don't have the answer,   565
you know
I don't know.
What I'm interested in is communities
that are not static,
that   570
can change, that can respond to new historical needs.
So I think it's a very exciting moment.

RHYTHM
Monique "Big Mo" Matthews
RHYTHM AND POETRY

*In reality this interview was done on an afternoon in the spring of
1989, while I was in residence at the University of California, Los
Angeles, as a fellow at the Center for Afro-American Studies.* MO
*was a student of mine. We were sitting in my office, which was a nar-
row office, with sunlight. I performed* MO *in many shows, and in the
course of performing her, I changed the setting to a performance setting, with microphone. I was inspired by a performance that I saw of
Queen Latifah in San Francisco, and by* MO's *behavior in my class,
which was performance behavior, to change the setting to one that was
more theatrical, since* MO's *everyday speech was as theatrical as
Latifah's performance speech. Speaking directly to the audience, pacing the stage.*

And she say, "This is for the fellas,"
and she took off all her clothes and she had on a leotard
that had all cuts and stuff in it,   575
and she started doin' it on the floor.
They were like
"Go, girl!"
People like, "That look really stink."
But that's what a lot of female rappers do—   580
like to try to get off,
they sell they body or pimp they body
to, um, get play.
And you have people like Latifah who doesn't, you know,
she talks intelligent.   585

You have Lyte who's just hard and people are scared by
    her hardness,
her strength of her words.
She encompasses that whole, New York-street sound.
It's like, you know, she'll like . . .
590   what's a line?
What's a line
like "Paper Thin,"
"IN ONE EAR AND RIGHT OUT THE OTHUH."
It's like,
595   "I don't care what you have to say,
I'm gittin' done what's gotta be done.
Man can't come across me.
A female she can't stand against me.
I'm just the toughest, I'm just the hardest/You just can't
    come up
600   against me/if you do you get waxed!"
It's like a lot of my songs,
I don't know if I'm gonna get blacklisted for it.
The image that I want is a strong strong African strong
    Black woman
and I'm not down with what's going on, like Big Daddy
    Kane had a song
605   out called "Pimpin Ain't Easy," and he sat there and he
    talk for the
whole song, and I sit there I wanna slap him, I wanna
    slap him so
hard, and he talks about, it's one point he goes, yeah
    um,
"Puerto Rican girls Puerto Rican girls call me Papi and
610   White girls say
even White girls say I'm a hunk!"
I'm like,
"What you mean 'even'?
Oh! Black girls ain't good enough for you huh?"
615   And one of my songs has a line that's like
"PIMPIN' AIN'T EASY BUT WHORIN' AIN'T
    PROPER, RESPECT AND
CHERISH THE ORIGINAL MOTHER."
And a couple of my friends were like,
"Aww, Mo, you good but I can't listen to you 'cause you
    be Men bashin'."
620   I say,
"It ain't men bashin', it's female assertin'."
Shit.
I'm tired of it.
I'm tired of my friends just acceptin'
625   that they just considered to be a ho.
You got a song,
"Everybody's a Hotty."
A "hotty" means you a freak, you a ho,
and it's like Too Short
630   gets up there and he goes,
"B I AYYYYYYYYYYYYE."
Like he stretches "bitch" out for as long as possible,
like you just a ho and you can't be saved,
and 2 Live Crew. . . . "we want some pussy," and the
    girls! "La le la le la le la,"
635   it's like my friends say,
"Mo, if you so bad how come you don't never say
    nothin about Two

Live Crew?"
When I talk about rap,
and I talk about people demeaning rap,
I don't even mention them   640
because they don't understand the fundamentals of rap.
Rap, rap
is basically
broken down
Rhythm   645
and Poetry.
And poetry is expression.
It's just like poetry; you release so much through poetry
    you get
angry, you get it?
Poetry is like   650
intelligence.
You just release it all and if you don't have a complex
    rhyme
it's like,
"I'm goin to the store."
What rhymes with store?   655
More store for more bore
"I'm going to the store I hope I don't get bored,"
it's like,
"WHAT YOU SAYIN', MAN? WHO CARES?"
You have something that flows.   660
You have to be def,
D-E-F.
I guess I have to think of something for you that ain't
    slang.
Def is dope, def is live
when you say somethin's dope   665
it means it is the epitome of the experience
and you have to be def by your very presence
because you have to make people happy.
And we are living in a society where people are not
    happy with their everyday lives.

SEVEN VERSES
Leonard Jeffries

ROOTS

3:00 P.M. Wednesday, November 20, 1991. A very large confer-
ence room in the African American Studies Department at
CUNY. Drawn venetian blinds, fluorescent lighting. DR. JEFFRIES
wears a light, multicolored African top, and a multicolored African
hat. His shoes are black functional shoes, like the shoes to a uni-
form. He sits facing the table, and often sits back with the chair
back from the table, often touches the table, and often sits back
with the chair on its back legs only. Sometimes he scratches his
head by throwing his hat forward on his head with great ease and
authority. There is a bodyguard, a large heavy-set African Amer-
ican man, present.

People are asking who is this guy Jeffries?   670
When they find out my background they're gonna be
    surprised.
They are gonna find out that I was even related to Alex
    Haley.
In fact I was a major consultant for *Roots.*

In fact there might not have been a *Roots* without me.
675 Now when I say that,
that's my own personal in-group joke wit' Alex.
He was in Philadelphia
getting his ticket to go down to Jamaica
and
680 *Roots* was lost.
He had it in a duffle bag,
a big duffle bag like this,
the whole manuscript.
It was lost in the airport of Philadelphia.
685 I got on my horse and ran around the airport of
Philadelphia
and found *Roots.*
So that's my joke.
He had this manuscript,
Alex didn't have anything else but this manuscript.
690 Now if he had lost that, that would have been it.
He didn't have any photocopies.
Alex did everything on a shoestring.
uhm
so for him to deny me now . . .
695 He never even acknowledged
Pat
Alexander
his girlfriend/secretary who he had paid with affection
and not with
resources.
700 So I didn't expect him to acknowledge me.
He called me to come down.
I called my wife who was working on her Ph.D. at Yale.
I said, "Rosalind, Alex wants us to come down to
Brunswick, Georgia,
they're filming *Roots.*"
705 She said yes she'd come down and we'd go, then she
called me back.
She said, "I got too much work," so I went down to
Brunswick, Georgia.
He introduced me to Margulies,
who was the, um, director
of *Roots,*
710 as the leading expert in America on Africa, and I said,
"Wow," to
myself, "that's kind of high."
When Margulies said,
"That makes me number two," then I realized what Alex
was doing to keep *Roots* honest.
So for two weeks I tried to change *Roots.*
715 Alex would say, "Wait a
minute, let's consult the experts."
After two weeks they got tired of me, sat me down
and said, "Dr. Jeffries," at lunch,
"we are very happy to have you here
720 but we just bought the rights to the book *Roots*
and we are under no obligation to maintain the integrity
of the book
and we certainly don't have to deal with the truth of
Black history."
Now,
this was a wipeout for me
725 I

I, there's been very few trau*matic*
moments

(*Longest pause in his text.*)

uh, just to think.
Now I wasn't even prepared for this
but Pat had called me before and said,   730
"Len, I'm looking at this document and I don't know
what to make of it."
I said, "What is it, Pat, what is it?"
and I knew she was nervous, she said,
"I'm reading a contract that says
'*Roots* has been sold to David Wolper and their heirs for   735
ever and
ever

(*He is thumping his hand on table.*)

and their heirs for ever and ever.'"
Alex had signed the contract for fifty thousand dollars.

(*He is thumping his hand on table.*)

Fifty thousand dollars for paperback *Roots.*
Something that made how much?   740
Three hundred million dollars?
He was suing them for years.
The millions he made out to TV *Roots* he spent a lot of
it to sue
Doubleday to get a better deal—I don't know if he ever
got it.
Roots was a devastation.   745
The tens of millions and hundreds of millions made on
Roots
went to produce,
not to make more Black series,
like *Roots,*
but they went to produce a *series*   750
maybe a dozen mini-series on *Jewish* history
as opposed to Black history.
You can document what was produced in terms of Black
history
compared to what was produced of Jewish history.
It's a devastation.   755
But the *one* thing that came out of this for me,
was that when these people told me, you know,
"We bought your research
We bought your history
You really have no . . ."   760
I was thrown off
I had to get out of there.
I stayed for another couple of days.
I told Alex I had to make a pilgrimage to my
grandfather's grave.
Never saw my grandfather.   765
Then I watched one more scene in the Alex Haley thing
and that finished it for me.
A cutaway of a slave ship
that was so real that they had to bring in these high
school kids,
and once these high school kids played the enslaved   770
Africans greased

down in simulated vomit
and feces
they couldn't come back,
so they had to continue to get,
775 go take these youngsters,
and some little White woman
who was there sleeping with one of those guys,
they told her, "You cannot take these kids without
    authorization."
But she would drive a bus
780 up to the schoolyard,
put the kids in it, and bring them to the set.
And it almost produced a riot
there.
But anyway this slave scene
785 was so realistic
the trainer's up on a lower deck
and Kunta Kinte's on a bottom deck
and they call down to each other,
and the trainer says,
790 "Kunta Kinte,
Be strong! Be strong!
We may have to fight.
Kill the White man and return to Mother Africa."
This was high drama.
795 All of us grown men over hiding in the shadows in
    tears.
Then
Green rushes out and said, "Break! Break!"
He said he didn't want the scene.
We said, "What?"
800 Even Lou Gossett and them were ready to *fight!*
You know 'cause they had—
a movie script is just
a skeleton,
you have to put your soul in a movie script,
805 and they put their heart and soul into what would have
    been . . .
And with the African—
because the "earth is mother" all over Africa.
So to say to go back to Mother Africa is a very
    meaningful phrase.
But this
810 Englishman refused
to accept it,
and they almost had a physical fight on the set.
They compromised and said,
"We—are—all—from—one—village,"

(*Hitting his hand rhythmically on the desk.*)

815 which is not the same thing.
After that I said, "I have to go."
I said I have to go,
and I rented a—
I flew out with Lorne Greene of all people.
820 He saw me and we had known each other for a couple
    of weeks from
the set,
and he's sitting there drinking his little drinks
talking about "Isn't *Roots* wonderful.

It's everybody's history,"
and I'm dying.   825

(*Pause.*)

Get to Atlanta.
Rent a car. Cut across the Georgia countryside.
came to a fork in the road,
made the right turn,
and there on a bluff   830
was a clapboard church
made by my grandfather
and
four
other trustees.   835
Then when
I went across the cemetery
to see, uh,
the gravesite where he was—
the tallest tombstone in the graveyard was his.   840
Uhm,
It was an obelisk.
On it was a Masonic symbol.
He was the master of the lodge.
On it was his vital statistics: 845
"*Born August the tenth 1868.*"
At the birth of the Fourteenth Amendment.
I later learned that his brother Sam was born
1865 at the birth of the Thirteenth Amendment!
And this is why people say,   850
"Who is he?
What is he?
Why is he?"
If they only know
I've had one of the best educations on the planet.   855
Yeah.
So . . .
When I went to Albany
in July,
I went knowing that you might not have   860
much time,
just like my wife said on the radio today:
"When we speak
we speak as though it is the last speech we're gonna
    make."
But I knew what was at stake   865
ever since they branded me a conspiracy theorist,
February 12, 1990,
two-column editorial in the *New York Times.*
That was,
in the concept of Jewish thinking,   870
the kiss of death.
I knew I had been targeted.
Arthur Schlesinger went and wrote a book
called *The Disuniting of America.*
He has everybody in the margin   875
except a half-page photo of myself
which said to us,
"This is the one they got to kill."
We knew that Schlesinger
and his people had sent out a thousand letters   880

to CEOs around the country
and foundation heads
not to have anything to do with
all of us involved in these studies
885 for multicultural curriculum
so, uh . . .
Knowing that I had taken this beating for two and a half
    years
it was my chance to strike out,
but people don't understand
890 that that was my way of saying,
"You bastids! . . .
for starting this process
of destroying *me*."
That was my striking out.
895 But people don't know the context.
They don't know that for two and a half years
I bore this burden
by myself
and I bore it well.
900 And now they've got a problem.
'Cause after they destroyed me,
here he is resurrected!!!!!
I spoke at Columbia, I spoke at Queens College. . . .

Letty Cottin Pogrebin
NEAR ENOUGH TO REACH

Evening. The day before Thanksgiving, 1991. On the phone. Direct, passionate, confident, lots of volume. She is in a study with a rolltop desk and a lot of books.

I think it's about rank frustration and the old story
905 that you pick a scapegoat
that's much more, I mean Jews and Blacks,
that's manageable,
because we're near,
we're still near enough to each other to reach!
910 I mean, what can you do about the people who voted
    for David Duke?
Are Blacks going to go there and deal with that?
No, it's much easier to deal with Jews who are also
    panicky.
We're the only ones that pay any attention

(Her voice makes an upward inflection.)

Do you hear?
915 Well, Jeffries did speak about the Mafia being, um,
    Mafia,
and the Jews in Hollywood.
I didn't see
this tremendous outpouring of Italian
920 reaction.
Only *Jews* listen,
only *Jews* take Blacks seriously,
only *Jews* view Blacks as full human beings that you
    should *address*
925 in their rage
and, um,
people don't seem to notice that.

But Blacks, it's like a little child kicking up against
    Arnold
Schwarzenegger
when they,   930
when they have anything to say about the dominant
    culture
nobody listens! Nobody reacts!
To get a headline,
to get on the evening news,
you have to attack a Jew.   935
Otherwise you're ignored.
And it's a shame.
We all play into it.

Minister Conrad Mohammed
SEVEN VERSES

April 1992, morning. A café/restaurant. Roosevelt Island, New York. We are sitting in the back, in an area that is surrounded by glass floor-to-ceiling windows. MR. MOHAMMED *is impeccably dressed in a suit of an elegant fabric. He wears a blue shirt and a bow tie. He has on fine shoes, designer socks, and a large fancy watch and wedding ring. His hair is closely cropped. He drinks black coffee, and uses a few packs of sugar. He is traveling with another man, also a Muslim, in the clothing of a Muslim, impeccable, who sits at another table and watches us.*

The condition of the Black man in America today is
    part and parcel,
through the devlishment   940
that permitted Caucasian people
to rob us of our humanity,
and put us in the throes of slavery . . .
The fact that our—our Black
parents   945
were actually taken
as cattle
and as, as
animals
and packed into   950
slave ships
like sardines
amid feces
and urine—
and the suffering of our people,   955
for months,
in the middle passage—
Our women,
raped
before our own eyes,   960
so that today
some look like you,
some look like me,
some look like a brother . . .
(indicating his companion)   965
This is a crime of tremendous proportion.
In fact,
no crime in the history of humanity
has before or since
equaled that crime.   970

The Holocaust did not equal it
Oh, absolutely not.
First of all,
that was a horrible crime
975   and that is something that is a disgrace in the eyes of
         civilized
people.
That, uh, crime also stinks
in the nostrils of God.
But it in no way compares with the slavery of our
         people
980   because we lost over a hundred
and some say two hundred and fifty,
million
in the middle passage
coming from Africa
985   to America.
We were so thoroughly robbed.
We didn't just lose six million.
We didn't just
endure this
990   for, for
five or six years
or from '38 to '45 or '39 to
We endured this for over three hundred years—
the total subjugation of the Black man.
995   You can go into Bangladesh today,
Calcutta,

(He strikes the table with a sugar packet three or four times.)

New Delhi,
Nigeria,
some really
1000   so-called underdeveloped nation,
and I don't care how low that person's humanity is

(He opens the sugar packet.)

whether they never
had running water,
if they'd never seen a television or anything.
1005   They are in better condition than the Black man and
         woman
in America today
right now.
Even at Harvard.
They have a contextual understanding of what their
         destiny is.

*(He strikes the table with another sugar packet three or four times
and opens it.)*

1010   But the Black man has no knowledge of that;
he's an amnesia victim

(Starts stirring his coffee.)

He has lost knowledge of himself

(Stirring his coffee.)

and he's living a beast life.

(Stirring his coffee.)

So this proves that it was the greatest
crime.   1015
Because we were cut off from our past.
Not only were we killed and murdered,
not only were our women raped
in front of their own children.
Not only did the slave master stick   1020

(The spoon drops onto saucer.)

at times,
daggers into a pregnant woman's stomach,
slice the stomach open
push the baby out on the ground and crush the head of
         the baby
to instill fear in the Massas of the plantation.   1025

(Stirring again.)

Not only were these things done,
not only were our thumbs

(Spoon drops.)

put in, in devices
that would just slowly torture the slave
and tear the thumb off from the root.   1030
Not only were we sold on the auction block
like cattle,
not permitted to marry.
See these are the crimes
of slavery that nobody wants to talk about.   1035
But the most significant crime—
because we could have recovered from all of that—
but the fact that they cut off all knowledge from us,
told us that we were animals,
told us that we were subhuman,   1040
took from us our names,
gave us names like
Smith
and Jones
and today we wear those names   1045
with dignity
and pride,
yet these were the names given to us in one of the
         greatest crimes
ever committed on the face of the earth.
So this kind of thing,   1050
Sister,
is what qualifies slavery
as the greatest
crime
ever committed.   1055
They have stolen
our garment.
Stolen our identity.
The Honorable Louis Farrakhan
teaches us   1060
that *we* are the chosen of God.
We are those people

that almighty God Allah
has selected as his chosen,
1065 and they are masquerading in our garment—
the Jews.
We don't have an identity today.
Because we are the people . . .
There are seven verses
1070 in the Bible
seven verses,
I believe it is in Deuteronomy,
that the Jews base
their chosen people, uh, uh,
1075 claim the theology,
the whole theological exegesis
with respect
of being the chosen
is based upon seven verses
1080 in the Scripture that talk
about a covenant
with Abraham.

Letty Cottin Pogrebin

ISAAC

Morning. Spring. On the phone. She is in her office in her home on West 67th Street and Central Park West in Manhattan. Her office has an old-fashioned wooden rolltop desk and bookcases filled with books. She says she was wearing leggings and a loose shirt.

Well,
it's hard for me to do that
1085 because
I think there's a tendency to make hay
with the Holocaust,
to push
all the buttons.
1090 And I mean this story about my uncle Isaac—makes *me* cry
and it's going to make your audience cry
and I'm beginning to worry
that
we're trotting out our Holocaust stories
1095 too regularly and that we're going to inure each other to the truth of
them.
But
I think
maybe if you let me read it,
1100 I would prefer to read it:

(Reading from Deborah, Golda, and Me.*)*

"I remember my mother's cousin
Isaac who came to New York
immediately after the war and lived with us for several months.
Isaac is my connection to dozens of other family members who
1105 were murdered in the concentration camps.
Because he was blond and blue-eyed he had been chosen as the designated survivor of his town.

That is the Jewish councils had instructed him to do anything
to stay alive and tell the story.
1110 For Isaac
anything turned out to mean this.
The Germans accepted his forged Aryan papers and decided that he
would have to prove by his actions that he was not a Jew.
They put him on a transport train with the Jews of his town
1115 and then gave him the task of herding into the gas chambers everyone in his train load.
After he had fulfilled that assignment
with patriotic
German efficiency,
1120 the Nazis accepted the authenticity of his identity papers and let him go.
Among those whom Isaac packed into the gas chambers that day
dispassionately as if shoving a few more items into an overstuffed
closet
1125 were his wife
and
two children.
The designated survivor
arrived in America
1130 at about age forty

(Breathes in.)

with prematurely white hair and a dead gaze within the sky blue
eyes that's helped save his life.
As promised he told his story to dozens of Jewish agencies
and community leaders and to groups of families and friends which
1135 is how I heard the account
translated from his Yiddish
by my mother.
For months he talked,
speaking the unspeakable.
1140 Describing a horror
that American Jews had suspected but could not conceive.
A monstrous tale
that dwarfed the demonology of legend
and gave me the nightmare I still dream to this day.
1145 And as he talked
Isaac seemed to grow older and older
until one night a few months later
when he finished telling everything he knew
he died."

Robert Sherman

LOUSY LANGUAGE

11:00 A.M. Wednesday, November 13, 1991. A very sunny and large, elegant living room in a large apartment near the Brooklyn Museum. MR. SHERMAN is sitting in an armchair near an enormous bouquet of flowers for the birth of his first child. He wears sweats, and a bright orange long-sleeved tee shirt. Smiles frequently, upbeat, impassioned. Fingers his wedding ring. Each phrase builds on the next, pauses are all sustained intensity, never lets up. Full. Lots of volume, clear enunciation, teeth, and tongue very involved in his speech. Good-humored, seems to like the act of speech.

1150   Do you have demographic information on Crown
              Heights?
       The important thing to remember is that—
       and I will check these numbers when I get back to the
              office—
       I think the
       Hasidim
1155   comprise only ten percent
       of the population
       of the neighborhood.
       The Crown Heights conflict has been brewing on and
              off for twenty years
       since the Hasidic community
1160   developed some serious numbers
       and some strength in Crown Heights and as African
              Americans and
       Caribbean Americans came to make up the dominant
              culture in
       Crown Heights.
       Very important to remember that
1165   those things that are expressed really as
       bias,
       those things
       that we at the Human Rights Commission
       would consider to be bias,
1170   have the same trappings of bias,
       which is complaints based on a characteristic, not on a
              knowledge of a
       specific person.
       There sort of is a soup
       of bias—prejudice, racism, and discrimination.
1175   I think bias really does relate to
       feelings with a valence,
       feelings with a, uhm,

       (Breathing in.)

       feelings that can go in a direction positive or negative
       although we usually use bias to mean a negative.
1180   What it means usually
       is negative attitudes
       that can lead to negative behaviors:
       biased
       acts, biased incidents,
1185   or biased crimes.
       Racism is hatred based on race.
       Discrimination refers to
       acts against somebody . . .
       so that the words
1190   actually tangle up.
       I think in part
       because vocabulary
       follows general awareness. . . .
       I think you know
1195   the Eskimos have seventy words for snow?

We probably have seventy different kinds of bias,
       prejudice, racism, and
discrimination,
but it's not in our mind-set to be clear about it,
so I think that we have
sort of lousy language   1200
on the subject
and that
is a reflection
of our unwillingness
to deal with it honestly   1205
and to sort it out.
I think we have very, very bad language.

CROWN HEIGHTS, BROOKLYN

AUGUST 1991

Rabbi Joseph Spielman

NO BLOOD IN HIS FEET

9:30 A.M. Tuesday, November 12, 1991. A large home on President Street in Crown Heights. Only natural light, not very much light. Dark wood. A darkish dining room with an enormous table, could seat twenty. The RABBI sits at the head of the table. Lots of stuff on the table. He wears Hasidic clothing, a black fedora, black jacket, and reading glasses. As he talks, he slightly slides around the tape-recorder microphone, which is in front of him at the table. The furniture in the dining room including his chair is, for the most part, very old, solid wood. There are children playing quietly in another room, and people come in and out frequently, but always whispering and walking carefully not to make noise, unless they speak to him directly. The children at one point came over and stared at me.

Many people were on the sidewalk,
talking, playing,
drinking
beer or whatever—   1210
being that type of neighborhood.
A car
driven by an individual—
a Hasidic individual—   1215
went through the intersection,
was hit by another car,
thereby causing it to go onto the sidewalk.
The driver on seeing
himself in such a position that he felt he was going to   1220
       definitely hit
someone,
because of the amount of people on the sidewalk,
he steered at the building,
so as to get out of the way of the people.
Obviously, for the most part,   1225
he was successful.
But regrettably,
one child was killed
and another child
was wounded.   1230
Um,
seeing what happened,
he jumped out of the car

and, realizing
1235   there may be a child under the car,
he tried to physically lift
the car
from the child.
Well, as he was doing this
1240   the Afro-Americans were beating him already.
He was beaten so much he needed stitches in the scalp
        and the face,
fifteen or sixteen stitches
and also
there were three other passengers in the car
1245   that were being beaten too.
One of the passengers was calling 911
on the cellular phone.
A Black person
pulled the phone out of his hand and ran.
1250   Just stole the—stole the telephone.
The Jewish community
has a volunteer
ambulance corps
which is funded totally from the nations—
1255   there is not one penny of government funds—
and manned by volunteers—
who many times at their expense—
supplied the equipment that they carry in order to save
        lives.
As one of the EMS ambulances were coming,
1260   one of the Hasidic ambulances or the Jewish ambulances
        came
on the scene.
The EMS responded with three ambulances on the scene.
They were there before
the Jewish ambulance came.
1265   Two or three police cars were already on the scene.
The police saw the potential for violence
and saw that the occupants of the car
were being beaten and were afraid for their safety.
At the same time the EMS asked
1270   the Hasidic ambulances for certain pieces of equipment
        that they
were out of,
that they needed to take care of the Cato kid,
and,
um,
1275   in fact, I was . . .
The Hasidic ambulance left, leaving behind one of the
        passengers.
That passenger had a walkie-talkie and he requested that I
come down to pick him up.
And at that time there was a lot of screaming and shouting
1280   and it was a mixed crowd, Hasidic and Afro-American.
The police said, "Rabbi get your people out of here."
I told them to leave and I left.
Now,
a few hours later,
1285   two and a half hours later,
in a different part of Crown Heights,
a scholar
from Australia,
Yankel Rosenbaum,

who, urr,   1290
I think he had a doctorate or he was working on his
        doctorate,
was walking on the street
on his own—
I mean he was totally oblivious—
and he was accosted by a group of young Blacks   1295
about twenty of them strong
which was being egged on by a Black
male approximately
forty years old and balding,
telling them,   1300
"Kill all Jews—
look what they did to the kid,
kill all Jews,"
and all the epithets that go along with it,
"Heil Hitler" and all of it.   1305
They stabbed him,
which later on the stab wounds were fatal
and he passed away in the hospital.
The Mayor,
hearing about the Cato kid,   1310
came to the Kings County Hospital
to give condolences to the family of the child who had
        regrettably been killed.
At the meantime they had already wheeled in
Mr. Rosenbaum.
He was in the emergency room   1315
and I was at the hospital at the same time,
and the Mayor, seeing me there,
expressed his concern
that a child,
uh, innocent child, had been killed.   1320
Where I explained to him
the fact
that,
whereas the child was killed from an unfortunate
        accident
where there was no malicious intent,   1325
here
there was an individual lying in the emergency room
who had been stabbed with malicious intent
and for the sole reason—
not that he did anything to anyone—   1330
just from the fact that he happened to be Jewish.
And the mayor went with me to the emergency room
to visit Mr. Rosenbaum.
This was approximately one and a half hours before he
        passed away.
I noticed at the time that his feet   1335
were
completely white.
And I complained to the doctor
on the scene,
"He's having a problem with blood circulation   1340
because there's no blood in his feet."
And she gave me some asinine answer.
And the mayor asked her what his condition is:
"Serious but stable."
In the meantime he was screaming and in pain   1345
and they weren't doing anything.

Subsequently they, um,
they started giving him anaesthesia in a time that
they weren't allowed to give him anaesthesia
1350   and while he was under anaesthesia,
he passed away.
So there was totally mismanagement in his case.
So whereas the Mayor,
had been fed . . .
1355   his people got
whatever information he got out of the Black community
     was
that
the driver had run a red light
and also,
1360   and that the ambulance,
the Hasidic ambulance,
refused to take care of the Black child that was dying and
rather took care of their own.
Nenh?
1365   And this is what was fed amongst the Black community.
And it was false,
it was totally false
and it was done maliciously
only with the intent to get the riots,
1370   to start up the resulting riots.

The Reverend Canon Doctor Heron Sam

MEXICAN STANDOFF

November 12, 1991, 4:00 P.M. The rectory office at St. Mark's Church in Crown Heights. A small, short office. Lived in but impeccably ordered. Some light from lamps, some from overhead. Plaques and awards everywhere. THE REVEREND is wearing a yellow shirt, priest's collar, tan summer jacket. He wears spectacles. There are clocks that make noise and sound the hour in his office and outside church bells sound during the interview, loud. Throughout the talk he is trying to get the corner of a calendar to stay down, but it continues to stick up. Finally he uses a paperweight to keep it down.

You can't have that kind of accident
if people are observing the speed limits.
People knew it was the Grand Rebbe.
People have seen the Grand Rebbe
1375   charging through the community.
He is worried
about a threat on his life
from the Satmars.
These Lubavitcher people
1380   are really very,
uh, enigmatic people.
They move so easily between
simplicity and sophistication.
Because
1385   they fear for his life,
because the Satmars
who are their sworn enemies

(He laughs/chuckles.)

have threatened to *kill*
the Rebbe.

So whenever he comes out   1390
he's gotta be *whisked!*
You know like a President
or even better than a President.
He says he's an intuhnational figuh
like a Pope!   1395
I say
then, "Why don't you get the Swiss guards
to escort you
rather than using the police
and taxpayers' money?"   1400
He's gotta be
whisked!
Quickly through the neighborhood.
Can't walk around.
He used to walk.   1405
When I first came here.
Now he doesn't walk at all.
They drive him.
And when he walked
you could tell he was in front   1410
because there was,
he was protected all around
and they spilled out onto the streets
and buses had to stop
because this BIG BAND   1415
had to escort
the Rebbe from his house over there
to the synagogue.
So the Rebbe goes to the cemetery.
Every time the Rebbe goes to the cemetery,   1420
which is once a week
to visit his dead wife
and father-in-law,
the police
lead him in escort   1425
charging down the street
at seventy miles an hour in a metropolis—
what do you want?

(Swift increase in volume and suddenly businesslike.)

It happened that on this occasion that as they were
     coming back,
uh,   1430
the police car
with its siren,
had gone over a main
intersection with the light
in favor   1435
of the police car.
The Rebbe's Cadillac had passed
when the lights had become amber
and nobody expected the bodyguard van,
uh,   1440
station wagon
to deliberately go through the red light.
So the traffic
that had the right of way kept coming and
BANG!   1445
came the collision and the careening

onto the sidewalk
had to damage whoever was there
and then, um, they were more concerned about licking
    their own
1450   wounds.
Rather than pick
the car off the boy
who died as a result.
And then the ambulance that came—
1455   the Jewish ambulance—
was concerned about the people in the van
while some boy lay dead,
a black boy lay dead on the street.
The people showed their—

(*Increase in volume.*)

1460   they burned and whatever else,
upturned
police cars
and looted,
and as a result,
1465   I think in retaliation, murdered one of the Hasidics.
But that was just the match that lit the powder keg.
It's gonna happen again and again.
There's a Mexican standoff right now
But it's gonna happen again.

Anonymous Young Man #1

WA WA WA

7:00 or 8:00 P.M. Spring. A recreation room at Ebbets Field apartments. A very handsome young Caribbean American MAN with dreadlocks, in his late teens or early twenties, wearing a bright, loose-fitting shirt. The room is ill equipped. There are a few pieces of broken furniture. It is poorly lit. A woman, Kym, with dreadlocks and shells in her hair, is at the interview. It was originally scheduled to be her interview. The ANONYMOUS YOUNG MAN #1 and the other ANONYMOUS YOUNG MAN #2 started by watching the interview from the side of the room but soon approached me and began to join in. ANONYMOUS YOUNG MAN #1 was the most vocal. ANONYMOUS YOUNG MAN #2 stood lurking in the shadows. A third young man, younger than both of them, wearing wire spectacles and a blue Wind-breaker, who looks quite like a young Spike Lee, sat silent with his hands and head on the table the entire time. There is a very bad radio or tape recorder playing music in the background.

1470   What I saw was
she was pushin'
her brother on the bike like
this,
right?
1475   She was pushin'
him
and he kept dippin' around
like he didn't know how
to ride the bike.
1480   So she kept runnin'
and pushin' him to the side.
So she was already runnin'
when the car was comin'.
So I don't know if she was runnin' toward him
because we was watchin' the car   1485
weavin',
and we was goin'
"Oh, yo
it's a Jew, man.
He broke the stop light, they never get arrested."   1490
At first we was laughin', man, we was like
you see they do anything
and get away with it,
and then
we saw that he was out of control,   1495
and den
we started regrettin' laughin',
because then
we saw where he was goin'.
First he hit a car, right,   1500
he tore a whole front fender off a car,
and then we was like
Oh
my god,
man, look at the kids,   1505
you know,
so we was already runnin' over there
by the time the accident happened.
That's how we know he was drinkin'
cause he was like   1510
Wa Wa Wa Wa
and I was like
"Yo, man, he's drunk.
Grab him,
grab him.   1515
Don't let him go anywhere."
I said,
"Grab him."
I didn't want him to limp off
in some apartment somewhere   1520
and come back in a different black jacket.
So I was like,
"Grab him,"
and then I was like, "Is the ambulance comin' for the
    kids?"
'Cause I been in a lot of confrontations with Jews   1525
    before
and I know that when they said an ambulance
is comin'
it most likely meant for them.
And they was like,
"oh, oh."   1530
Jews right?
"Ambulance comin', ambulance comin',
calm down, calm down,
God will help them,
God will help them if you believe."   1535
And he was actin' like he was dyin'.
"Wa Aww,
me too,
I'm hurt, I'm hurt, I'm hurt too."
Wan nothin wrong with him,   1540
wan nothin wrong with him.

They say that we beat up on that man
that he had to have stitches because of us.
You don't come out of an accident like that
  unmarked,
1545 without a scratch.
The most he got from us was slapped
by a little kid.
And here come the ambulance
and I was like, "That's not a city ambulance,"
1550 not like this I was upset right
and I was like,
"YO,
the man is drunk!
He ran a red light!
1555 You all ain't gonna do nothin'.'"
Everybody started comin' around, right,
'cause I was talkin' about
these kids is dyin' man!
I'm talkin' about the skull of the baby is on the ground
  man!
1560 and he's walking'!
I was like, "Don't let him get into that ambulance!"
And the Jews,
the Jews
was like private, private ambulance
1565 I was like, "Grab him,"
but my buddies was like,
"We can't touch them."
Nobody wanted to grab him,
nobody wanted to touch him,
1570 An' I was breakin' fool, man,
I was goin' mad,
I couldn't believe it.
Everybody just stood
there,
1575 and that made me cry.
I was cryin'
so I left, I went home and watched the rest of it on TV,
it was too lackadazee
so it was like me, man, instigatin' the whole thing.
1580 I got arrested for it
long after
in Queens.
Can't tell you no more about that,
you know.
1585 Hey, wait a minute,
they got eyes and ears everywhere.
What color is the Israeli flag?
And what color are the police cars?
The man was drunk,
1590 I open up his car door,
I was like, when—
I was like, he'd been drinkin'
I know our words don't have no meanin',
as Black people in Crown Heights.
1595 You realize, man,
ain't no justice,
ain't never been no justice,
ain't never gonna be no justice.

Michael S. Miller

HEIL HITLER

A large airy office in Manhattan on Lexington in the fifties. MR.
MILLER *sits behind a big desk in a high-backed swivel chair drinking coffee. He's wearing a yarmulke. Plays with the swizzle stick
throughout. There is an intercom in the office, so that when the re-
ceptionist calls him, you can hear it, and when she calls others in
other offices, you can hear it, like a page in a public place, faintly.*

I was at Gavin Cato's funeral,
at nearly every public event
that was conducted by the Lubavitcher community and   1600
  the Jewish
community as a whole.
Words of comfort
were offered to the family of Gavin Cato.
I can show you a letter that we sent   1605
to the Cato family expressing, uh,
our sorrow over the loss,
unnecessary loss, of their son.
I am not aware of a word
that was spoken at that funeral.   1610
I am not aware of a—
and I was taking notes—
of a word that was uttered
of comfort to the family of Yankel Rosenbaum.
Frankly this was a political rally rather than a funeral.   1615
The individuals you mentioned—
and again,
I am not going to participate in verbal acrimony,
not only
were there cries of, "Kill the Jews"   1620
or,
"Kill the Jew,"
there were cries of, "Heil Hitler."
There were cries of, "Hitler didn't finish the job."
There were cries of,   1625
"Throw them back into the ovens again."
To hear in *Crown Heights*
and Hitler was no lover of Blacks—
"Heil Hitler"?
"Hitler didn't finish the job"?   1630
"We should heat up the ovens"?
From *Blacks*?
Is more inexplicable
or unexplainable
or any other word that I cannot fathom.   1635
The hatred is so
deep seated
and the hatred
knows no boundaries.
There is no boundary   1640
to anti-Judaism.
The anti-*Judaism*—
if people don't want me
to use,
hear me use the word anti-Semitism.   1645

And I'll be damned if,
if preferential treatment is gonna
be the excuse
for every bottle,
1650 rock,
or pellet that's, uh, directed
toward a Jew
or the window of a Jewish home
or a Jewish store.
1655 And, frankly,
I think the response of the Lubavitcher community was
     relatively
passive.

Henry Rice

KNEW HOW TO USE CERTAIN WORDS

Thursday, November 21, 1991. The Jackson Hole restaurant on Lexington Avenue in the thirties in Manhattan. Lunchtime, dimly lit a reddish haze on everything, perhaps from a neon light. MR. RICE, *very neatly dressed, is eating a large, messy hamburger and horizontally chopped pickles. Drinking a Miller Lite. Beer is in a bottle next to a red plastic glass. He's wearing a baseball cap over very closely cut hair and a bright, multicolored, expensive-looking colored nylon jacket. Heavy new Timberland boots. Struggling to eat without making a mess of the food. At some point sits up from food and has his right hand or fist on his hip a very unaffected but truly authoritative stance. Good-natured, handsome, healthy. Patsy Cline's "Crazy" is very loud on the jukebox.*

I went back home and got my bike
because I knew I would have to be
1660 illusive.
I was there in body and in spirit
but I didn't participate in any of the violence
because basically I have a lot to lose.
But I was there
1665 and I would have defended myself if it was necessary,
most definitely.
I weaved around trouble.
When something broke out, I moved back,
when it calmed down, I would move back in on the
     front line.
1670 I was always there.
And Richard Green heard me saying something to a
     bunch of kids
about *voting*
about the power of *vote*
the power of *numbers*
1675 and he said,
uh,
I said, "Get away from me, you're an Uncle Tom,
get away from me.
Get back in your Mercedes-Benz!"
1680 No! I said that to Clarence Norman
and to Richard Green,
both of them.
I was tearing them apart.

Richard Green was very persistent.   1685
He said,
"Look, Mr. Rice,
I like the way you speak.
I need you.
Please help me.
I'm a community activist. . . .   1690
ba, ba, ba, ba, ba."

(He drops some food on his clothes, or so it seems, he looks and grins.)

It didn't get on me.
"I'm a community activist.
I need your help,
please help me,"   1695
and so forth.
Again,
I didn't pay him no mind
but we spoke
some   1600
the next day after that,
after the incidents that took place on that corner
of Albany Avenue.
A brother was beat up—
cops rushing into the Black crowd   1705
didn't rush into the Jewish crowd,
cops rushed into the Black crowd
started beatin' up
Black people.
But the next day Richard came by in a yellow van,   1710
a New York City Department of Transportation van,
with a megaphone,
yellow light flashing,

(Music segues from Patsy Cline's "Crazy" to Public Enemy's "Can't Truss It," or Naughty by Nature's "O.P.P.")

the whole works
and, um,   1715
he said,
"Henry, I need you in this van.
Drive around with me.
Let's keep some of these kids off the street tonight."
I said, "Okay."   1720
He said,
"The blood
of Black men are on your hands tonight!"
I said, "Okay."
We drive around in the van,   1725
"Young people stay in the house!
Mothers keep your children in the house,
please."
So I began fillin'
I began feeling like   1730
I had to do it
after he told me that,
"the blood of the Black man"
were on my hands,
you know.   1735
Richard Green sure know how to use certain words.

(He giggles.)

I remember reaching Albany Avenue—
kids were being chased by the police.
I jump out with a portable megaphone,
1740   I tell them, "Stop running!
The cops won't chase you!
and they won't hit you!"
The next thing I know,
cop grabs my megaphone hits me in the head with a
    stick,
1745   handcuffs me,
and takes the megaphone out of my hand.
So I'm like,
"Wait a minute
I'm doing a community service for the mayor's office."
1750   They don't want to hear it.
Matter of fact,
they still have the megaphone 'til this day.
I'm like,
"Richard Green get me
1755   out of this police car, please!"
So a Black captain came by,
thank God,
and he says, "What's goin' on?"
Richard Green explained it to him.
1760   He said, "Let him go."
Get back in the van,
there's another Brother in van,
starts saying,
"Non violence!"
1765   to the young Brothers.
They begin throwing bottles at the, uh,
at the van.
One guy got so upset
he had a nine-millimeter
1770   fully loaded.
He said, "Get the hell out of this neighborhood!"
The next day
more violence:
fires,
1775   cars being burnt,
stores being broken into,
a perception that Black youth
are going crazy in Crown Heights
like we were angry over
1780   nothing,
understand?

Norman Rosenbaum
MY BROTHER'S BLOOD

A Sunday afternoon. Spring. Crisp, clear, and windy. Across from City Hall in New York City. Crowds of people, predominantly Lubavitcher, with placards. A rally that was organized by Lubavitcher women. All of the speakers were men, but the women stand close to the stage. MR. ROSENBAUM, *an Australian, with a beard, hat, and wearing a pinstripe suit, speaks passionately and loudly from the microphone on a stage with a podium. Behind him is a man in an Australian bush hat with a very large Australian flag which*

blows dramatically in the wind. It is so windy that MR. ROSENBAUM *has to hold his hat to keep it on his head.*

Al do lay achee so achee aylay alo dalmo
My brother's blood cries out from the ground.
Let me make it clear
why I'm here.
In August of 1991,   1785
as you all have heard before today,
my brother was killed in the streets of Crown Heights
for no other reason
than that he was a Jew!   1790
The only miracle was
that my brother was the only victim
who paid for being a Jew with his life.
When my brother was surrounded,
each and every American was surrounded.   1795
When my brother was stabbed four times,
each and every American was stabbed four times
and as my brother bled to death in this city,
while the medicos stood by
and let him bleed   1800
to death, it was the gravest of indictments against this
    country.
One person out of twenty gutless individuals
who attacked my brother has been arrested.
I for one am not convinced that it is beyond the ability
    of the New York police
to arrest others.   1805
Let me tell you, Mayor Dinkins,
let me tell you, Commissioner Brown:
I'm here,
I'm not going home,
until there is justice.   1810

Norman Rosenbaum
SIXTEEN HOURS DIFFERENCE

7:00 A.M. Spring. Newark Airport, Departure Gate, Continental Airlines. MR. ROSENBAUM *is moments before his flight to L.A. and then back to Australia. Wearing a pinstripe suit with an Australian fit. Hat. Suitcase. He has sparkling blue eyes with a twinkle, rosy cheeks, and a large smile throughout the interview.*

There's sixteen hours difference between New York and
    Melbourne
and I had just gotten back to my office
and I had a phone call from my wife,
and she said she wanted me to come home straight away
and I sensed the urgency in her voice.   1815
I said, "are you all right?" She said, "Yeah."
I said, "are the children all right, you know the kids?"
    She says, "yeah."
So I'm driving home and I'm thinking, I wonder what's
    the problem now, you know?
We had some carpenters doing some work, I wonder if
    there has been a disaster,
some sort of domestic problem,   1820
and I thought, oh my God, you know, my parents,
I didn't even ask after them,
how insensitive not to even ask after my parents,

and I've got a grandmother eighty-five years old, same
    sort of thing.
1825   So I get home,
I walk in the door, and a friend of mine was standing
    there,
close friend,
does the same sort of work as me, he's a barrister and an
    academic,
and he sees me and he says,
1830   "There's got a pro—
uh,
we've got a problem. There's a problem."
I thought he was talking about a case we were working
    on together,
he says, "'Z come,
1835   come and sit down."
He goes to me,
"There's been a riot in New York,
been a riot in Crown Heights,
Yankel's been stabbed and he's dead."
1840   And
my brother was the last in the world,
I hadn't even given him a thought.
I mean the fact that my brother
could be attacked
1845   or die,
it just hadn't even entered my mind.
At first I appeared all cool, calm and collected.
I then
started asking questions
1850   like who told you,
how do you know,
are you sure?
I just asked the question,
you know,
1855   are you sure?

Anonymous Young Man #2

BAD BOY

Evening. Spring. The same recreation room as interview with
ANONYMOUS YOUNG MAN #1, YOUNG MAN #2 *is wearing a*
black jacket over his clothes. He has a gold tooth. He has some dread-
locks, and a very odd-shaped multicolored hat. He is soft-spoken, and
has a direct gaze. He seems to be very patient with his explanation.

That youth,
that sixteen-year-old
didn't murder that Jew.

(*Pause.*)

For one thing,
1860   he played baseball, right?
He was a atha-lete,
right?
A bad boy
does
1865   bad things.
Only a bad boy coulda stabbed the man.
Somebody who

does those type a things,
or who sees
those types a things.   1870
A atha-lete
sees people,
is interested in athletics,
stretchin',
exercisin',   1875
goin' to his football games,
or his baseball games.
He's not interested
in stabbin'
people.   1880
So
it's not in his mind
to stab,
to just jump into somethin',
that he has no idea about   1885
and
sta—
and kill a man.
A bad boy,
somebody who's groomed in badness,   1890
or did badness
before,
stabbed the man.
Because I used to be a atha-lete
and I used to be a bad boy,   1895
and when I was a atha-lete,
I was a atha-lete.
All I thought about was atha-lete.
I'm not gonna jeopardize my athleticism
or my career to do anything   1900
that bad people do.
And when I became a bad boy
I'm not a athalete no more.
I'm a bad boy,
and I'm groomin' myself in things that is bad.   1905
You understand, so
he's a athalete,
he's not a bad boy.
It's a big difference.
Like,   1910
mostly the Black youth in Crown Heights have two
    things to do—
either DJ or be a bad boy, right?
You either
DJ, be a MC, a rapper
or Jamaican rapper,   1915
ragamuffin,
or you be a bad boy,
you sell drugs or you rob people.
What do you do?
I sell drugs.   1920
What do you do?
I rap.
That's how it is in Crown Heights.
I been livin' in Crown Heights mosta my life.
I know for a fact that that youth, that sixteen-year-old,   1925
didn't kill that Jew.
That's between me and my Creator.

Sonny Carson

CHORDS

Lunchtime. Spring. A fancy restaurant in Brooklyn. SONNY *tells me it's where all the judges come for lunch. White linen tablecloths. Light wood walls, lamplight next to the table. Tile floor. He is eating crab cakes. He is dressed in a black turtleneck and a gray jacket. He has on a mud cloth hat. He has an authority stick with him, and it lays on the table. His bodyguard, wearing a black leather jacket, enters in the middle of the interview.* SONNY *chides him for being late.*

It's going to be a long hot summer.
I'm connected up with the young people all over the
    country
1930 and there's a thread
leading to an eruption
and Crown Heights began the whole thing.
And the Jews come second to the police
when it comes to feelings of dislike among Black folks.
1935 The police,
the police,
believe me, the police—
I know the police and the police know me
and they turn that whole place into an occupied camp
1940 with the Seventy-first Precinct as the overseers.
And don't think that everything is OK within that
    precinct among those officers
either.
Don't think that,
don't think that.
1945 You know the media has always painted me as the bad
    guy—
that's OK!
I'm a good guy to pick on.
Their viewers don't like me either,
they really don't like me because I *am* the bad guy,
1950 I am the ultimate bad guy
because of my relationship to the young people in the
    city.
I understand their language.
I respect them as the future.
I speak their language. They don't even engage in long
    dialogue
1955 anymore
just short
"words."
It always amazes me
how the city fathers,
1960 the power brokers,
just continue to deny what's happening.
And it is just getting intolerable for me to continue to
    watch
this small
arrogant
1965 group of people continue to get this kind of preferential
    treatment.
They sit on the school board.
A board of nine
and they have

four members, and their kids don't even go to public
    school.
So that's the kind of arrogance I'm talking about.   1970
I have no reason to be eagerly awaiting the coming
    together of our
people.
They owe me first.
I'm not givin' in just like that,
I don't want it.   1975
You can have it.
Like my grandmother said,
"Help the bear!
If you see me and the bear in a fight,
help the bear—   1980
don't help me,
help the bear."
I don't need any of it from them!
And I'm not gonna advocate any coming together and
    healing of
America   1985
and all that shit.
You kiddin'?
You kiddin'?
Just 'cause I can have the fortune of walking in here
and sitting and talking   1990
and having a drink,
it appear that I have all the same kinds of abilities
of other folks in here.
No, it's not that way.
'Cause tonight   1995
by nighttime it could all change for me.
So I'm always aware of that, and that's what keeps me
    goin'
today
and each day!

(He eats.)

I have   2000
this idea
about a film.
See,
these kids, they got
another kinda rhythm now,   2005
there's a whole new kinda
step that they do.
When I first heard rap
I was sittin' in a huge open kinda stadium,
boys and girls high school field,   2010
and I heard these kids come out and start rappin',
and I'm listening
but it's not really clickin',
but I was mesmerized though.
But it was simontaneouis   2015
all around the country
and I said, "Oh shit,"
and everybody I knew who was young was listenin' to it
and I said, "Wow."
Because I have always been involved with young people   2020
and all of a sudden I got it,
I really heard the rhythm,

the chords,
the discord.
2025 There's a whole new sound
that the crackers are tryin' to get, but they can't get it.
I heard it on a television commercial.
One of the most beautiful pieces of art
that I ever witnessed
2030 was a play
called
um,
um,
um,
2035 'bout, 'bout the Puerto Rican gang—
no, no, no, no, no—
the Puerto Rican gang,
the musical
that was on Broad—
2040 yeah,
West Side Story—
the answer should be
a musical.

Rabbi Shea Hecht

OVENS

*Morning. Spring. A building on Eastern Parkway. A large room
with a very long conference table. There are pictures of Lubavitcher
men on the walls.* RABBI HECHT *is wearing a shirt, open at the
neck. He has several crisp one-dollar bills in his shirt pocket. These
are, apparently, dollar bills that the Rebbe has given him. It is the
custom that the Rebbe gives out one-dollar bills on Sunday.* RABBI
HECHT *has a beard. He wears glasses, traditional Hasidic garb, including tsitses (ceremonial fringes that hang over his belt) and a red
yatmulke with gold trim which is ripped. His daughter comes in frequently to get money from him. He keeps telling her to wait until he
is finished. She becomes more and more agitated. His brother also enters frequently to ask him questions, and to tell him he's late.*

What is my goal?
2045 My goal is not
to give anybody a message
that we plan on working things out
by integrating
our two
2050 things.
By a person understanding more of their own religion
they will automatically respect another person.
The respect that my religion teaches me has nothing to
do
with understanding you.
2055 See, there's a problem.
If
the only way I'm going to respect you
is based on how much I understand you,
no matter what it is
2060 in certain circles you're gonna run into problems.
Number one,
we are different,
and we think we should and can be different.
When the Rebbe said to the Mayor
2065 that we were all

one people,
I think
what the Rebbe is talking about is that,
that common denominator that we're all children of
God, and the
respect we all have to give each other under that banner. 2070
But that does not mean that I have to invite you to my
house for
dinner,
because I cannot go back to your home for dinner,
because you're not gonna give me kosher food.
And I said, 2075
so, like one Black said,
I'll bring in kosher food.
I said eh-eh.
We can't use your ovens,
we can't use your dishes, 2080
it's, it—
it's not just a question of buying certain food,
it's buying the food,
preparing it a certain way.
We can't use your dishes, we can't use your oven. 2085
The—the higher you go
the more common denominator.
And what the Rebbe was saying,
you as the Mayor
don't get caught up in the differences, 2090
you're—
from your position is—
you have to look at it as one city
and one
human race. 2095
We are all New Yorkers
and therefore I will protect all New Yorkers.
You see
preferential treatment
suggests 2100
that you're giving the person
the police car
not because they need the police car
but because
they are who they are. 2105
You're not gonna
give them the housing
because they
need the housing—
you're giving it because of who they are. 2110
But
just because I'm a Jew
therefore I
shouldn't get the police car.
The question is 2115
a synagogue
that has five thousand Jews
leave
the synagogue
at the same time, 2120
do they have a police car to stop the traffic?
The answer is every—single—synagogue,
temple,
mosque,

2125 in
 the
 world
 stops traffic
 when five thousand people have to walk out
2130 at the same time.

Reverend Al Sharpton

RAIN

 The D.A.
 came back with no indictment.
 Uh, so then our only course
 was to ask for a special prosecutor
2135 which is appointed by the Governor,
 who's been hostile,
 and to sue civilly.
 When we went into civil court
 we went to get an order to show cause.
2140 The judge signed it and gave me a deadline of three days.
 The driver left the country. . . .
 No one even said, "Why would he run?
 If he did no wrong."
 If you and I were in an accident we'd have to go to civil
  court.
2145 Why is this man
 above the law?
 So they said, "He's in Israel."
 So I said,
 "Well, I'll go to Israel to show best effits."
2150 And the deadline
 was,
 I had to serve him by Tuesday,
 which was Yom Kippur—
 that was the judge's decision not mine.
2155 So we went.
 Alton Maddox and I
 got on a plane,
 left Monday night,
 landed Tuesday morning,
2160 went and served the American embassy, uh,
 so that
 if this man had any decency at all
 he could come to the American embassy and receive
  service,
 which he has not done to this day.
2165 Come back,
 went to court
 and showed the judge the receipts,
 and the judge said, "You made best effits,
 therefore you are now permitted,
2170 by default,
 to go ahead
 and sue the rabbi or whomever
 because you cannot do the driver."
 So it wasn't just a media grandstand.
2175 We wanted to show the world
 one, this man *ran*
 and was *allowed* to run, and, two, we wanted to be able
  to legally go

around him,
to sue the people he was working for so that we can
 bring them into
court and establish *why* and what happened. 2180
And it came out in the paper the other day
that the driver in the other car didn't even have a
 driver's license.
So we're dealing with a *complete* outrage here,
we're dealing with a double standard,
we're dealing with uh, uh, a, a 2185
situation where
Blacks do not have equal protection under the law
and the media is used to castigate us
that merely asked for justice
rather than castigate those that would hit a kid 2190
and walk away like he just stepped on a roach!
Uh,
there also is the media
contention of the young Jewish scholar
that was stabbed that night 2195
and they've even distorted
saying *my words at the funeral*
I *preached* the funeral.
Uh, [the newspaper said I]
helped to, to, uh, uh, 2200
spark or, or, or, or, or *inspire* or *incite* people to kill him
 [Yankel Rosenbaum]
when he was dead the day before
I came out there.
He was killed the night
that the young man 2205
was killed with the car accident.
I didn't even get a call
from the family
'til eighteen hours later.
So there's a whole media distortion 2210
to protect them [the Lubavitchers].
Nobody is talking about,
"Why
is this guy
in flight?" 2215
If I was a rabbi
(I am a ministuh)
and my driver hit a kid,
I would not let the driver *leave*
and I certainlih would give my condolences, 2220
or anything else I could,
to the family,
I don't care what race they are.
To this minute the Rebbe has never even uttered a word
 of
sympathy 2225
to the family,
not even sent 'em a *card*
a *flower* or *nothing!*
So it's treating us with absolute contempt
and I don't care how controversial it makes us. 2230
I *won't* tolerate being insulted.
If you piss in my face I'm gonna call it *piss*.
I'm not gonna call it rain.

Richard Green

RAGE

2:00 P.M. in a big red van. GREEN is in the front. He has a driver. I am in the back. GREEN wears a large knit hat with reggae colors over long dreadlocks. Driving from Crown Heights to Brooklyn College. He turns sideways to face me in the back, and bends down, talking with his elbow on his knee.

2235   Sharpton, Carson, and Reverend Herbert Daughtry
          didn't have any power out there really.
          The media gave them power.
          But they weren't turning those youfs on and off.
          Nobody knew who controlled the switch out there.
          Those young people had rage like an oil-well fire
2240   that has to burn out.
          All they were doin' was sort of orchestratin' it.
          Uh, they were not really the ones that were saying, "Well
          stop, go, don't go, stop, turn around, go up."
          It wasn't like that.
2245   Those young people had rage out there,
          that didn't matter who was in control of that—
          that rage had to get out
          and that rage
          has been building up.
2250   When all those guys have come and gone,
          that rage is still out here.
          I can show you that rage every day
          right up and down this avenue.
          We see, sometimes in one month, we see three bodies
2255   in one month. That's rage,
          and that's something that nobody has control of.
          And I don't know who told you that it was preferential
               treatment for
          Blacks that the Mayor kept the cops back. . . .
          If the Mayor had turned those cops on?
2260   We would still be in a middle of a battle.
          And
          I pray on both sides of the fence,
          and I tell the people in the Jewish community the same
               thing,
          "This is not something that force will hold."
2265   Those youfs were running on cops without nothing in
               their hands,
          seven- and eight- and nine- and ten-year-old boys were
               running at
          those cops
          with nothing,
          just running at 'em.
2270   That's rage.
          Those young people out there are angry
          and that anger has to be vented,
          it has to be negotiated.
          And they're not angry at the Lubavitcher community
2275   they're just as angry at you and me,
          if it comes to that.
          They have no
          role models,
          no guidance

          so they're just out there growin' up on their own,   2280
          their peers are their role models,
          their peers is who teach them how to move
          so when they see the Lubavitch
          they don't know the difference between "Heil Hitler"
          and, uh, and uh, whatever else.   2285
          They don't know the difference.
          When you ask 'em to say who Hitler was they wouldn't
               even be able
          to tell you.

(Phone rings, RICHARD picks it up, it's a mobile phone.)

          "Richard Green, can I help?
          Aw, man I tol' you I want some color   2290
          up on that wall. Give me some colors.
          Look, I'm in the middle of somethin'."

(He returns to the conversation.)

          Half them don't even know three quarters of 'em.
          Just as much as they don't know who Frederick
               Douglass was.
          They know Malcolm   2295
          because Malcolm has been played up to such an extent
               now
          that they know Malcolm.
          But ask who Nat Turner was or Mary McCleod
               Bethune or Booker T.
          Because the system has given 'em
          Malcolm is convenient and   2300
          Spike is goin' to give 'em Malcolm even more.
          It's convenient.

Roslyn Malamud

THE COUP

Spring. Midafternoon. The sunny kitchen of a huge, beautiful house on Eastern Parkway in Crown Heights. It's a large, very well-equipped kitchen. We are sitting at a table in a breakfast nook area, which is separated by shelves from the cooking area. There is a window to the side. There are newspapers on the chair at the far side of the table. MRS. MALAMUD offers me food at the beginning of the interview. We are drinking coffee. She is wearing a sweatshirt with a large sequined cat. Her tennis shoes have matching sequined cats. She has on a black skirt and is wearing a wig. Her nails are manicured. She has beautiful eyes that sparkle are very warm, and a very resonant voice. There is a lot of humor in her face.

          Do you know what happened in August here?
          You see when you read the newspapers.
          I mean my son filmed what was going on,   2305
          but when you read the newspapers . . .
          Of course I was here
          I couldn't leave my house.
          I only would go out early during the day.
          The police were barricading here.   2310
          You see,
          I wish
          I could just like

go on television.
2315 I wanna scream to the whole world.
They said
that the Blacks were rioting against the Jews in Crown
    Heights
and that the Jews were fighting back.
Do you know that the Blacks who came here to riot
    were not my
2320 neighbors?
I don't love my neighbors.
I don't know my Black neighbors.
There's one lady on President Street—
Claire—
2325 I adore her.
She's my girl friend's next-door neighbor.
I've had a manicure
done in her house and we sit and kibbitz
and stuff
2330 but I don't know them.
I told you we don't mingle socially
because of the difference
of food
and religion
2335 and what have you here.
But
the people in this community
want exactly
what I want out of life.
2340 They want to live
in nice homes.
They all go to work.
They couldn't possibly
have houses here
2345 if they didn't
generally—They have
two,
um,
incomes
2350 that come in.
They want to send their kids to college.
They wanna live a nice quiet life.
They wanna shop for their groceries and cook their
    meals and go to
their Sunday picnics!
2355 They just want to have decent homes and decent lives!
The people who came to riot here
were brought here
by this famous
Reverend Al Sharpton,
2360 which I'd like to know who ordained him?
And he brought in a bunch of kids.
I wish you could see the *New York Times,*
unfortunately it was on page twenty,
but,
2365 he brought in a bunch of kids who didn't have jobs in
    the
summertime
when you don't have a job
and you're hanging out all day.
I mean, they interviewed
2370 one of the Black girls on Utica Avenue.

She said,
"The guys will make you pregnant
at night
and in the morning not know who you are."

(*Almost whispering.*)

And if you're sitting on a front stoop and it's very, very   2375
    hot
and you have no money
and you have nothing to do with your time
and someone says, "Come on, you wanna riot?"
You know how kids are.
The fault lies with the police department.   2380
The police department did nothing to stop them.
I was sitting here in the front of the house
when bottles were being thrown
and the sergeant tells five hundred policemen
with clubs and helmets and guns   2385
to duck.
And I said to him,
"You're telling them to duck?
What should I do?
I don't have a club and a gun."
Had they put it—   2390
stopped it on the first night
this kid who came from Australia . . .

(*She sucks her teeth.*)

You know,
his parents were Holocaust survivors, he didn't have to   2395
    die.
He worked,
did a lot of research in Holocaust studies.
He didn't have to die.
What happened on Utica Avenue
was an accident.   2400
JEWISH PEOPLE
DO NOT DRIVE VANS INTO SEVEN-YEAR-OLD
    BOYS.
YOU WANT TO KNOW SOMETHING? BLACK
    PEOPLE DO NOT DRIVE
VANS INTO SEVEN-YEAR-OLD BOYS.
HISPANIC PEOPLE DON'T DRIVE VANS INTO   2405
    SEVEN-YEAR-OLD BOYS.
IT'S JUST NOT DONE.
PEOPLE LIKE JEFFREY DAHMER MAYBE THEY
    DO IT.
BUT AVERAGE CITIZENS DO NOT GO OUT
    AND TRY TO KILL

(*Sounds like a laugh but it's just a sound.*)

SEVEN-YEAR-OLD BOYS.
It was an accident!   2410
But it was allowed to fester and to steam and all that.
When you come here do you see anything that's going
    on, riots?
No.
But Al Sharpton and the likes of him like *Dowerty,*
who by the way has been in prison   2415

and all of a sudden he became Reverend *Dowerty*—
they once did an exposé on him—
but
these guys live off of this,
2420 you understand?
People are not gonna give them money,
contribute to their causes
unless they're out there rabble-rousing
My Black neighbors?
2425 I mean I spoke to them.
They were hiding in their houses just like I was.
We were scared.
I was scared!
I was really frightened.
2430 I had five hundred policemen standing in front of my
       house
every day
I had mounted police,
but I couldn't leave my block,
because when it got dark I couldn't come back in.
2435 I couldn't meet anyone for dinner.
Thank God, I told you my children were all out of
       town.
My son was in Russia.
The coup
was exactly the same day as the riot
2440 and I was very upset about it.
He was in Russia running a camp
and I was very concerned when I had heard about that.
I hadn't heard from him
that night the riot started.
2445 When I did hear from him I told him to stay in Russia,
       he'd be safer
there than here.
And he was.

Reuven Ostrov

POGROMS

*9:00 P.M. November 1991. In a basement of a Crown Heights
house. MR. OSTROV wears a yarmulke. Eating popcorn and sliced
apples. Very low, gentle-sounding nigunim music plays in the background, it almost sounds like New Age music, perhaps because traditional music is played on a modern electronic keyboard instrument.
In the show, I wore a basketball jacket with the team's insignia, and
used a basketball—which MR. OSTROV did not do at this interview,
but previously had at a basketball game. He has no beard, which is
unusual for a man his age who does have a beard if grown. He has
a very rich, deep voice.*

I was working in a hospital.
I work as an assistant chaplain at
2450 Down State Kings County Hospital.
I heard that Yankel Rosenbaum was stabbed and, um,
       they
were gonna give him an *aurtopsy*
and they asked if he had an
aurtopsy
2455 or not because in the Jewish religion a person is not
       allowed to have
an aurtopsy

and I found out later that he did have one
a few days later.
I found a Jewish man in a room,
a Russian man.   2460
His mother committed suicide
because she was, uhm, she was terrified.
She jumped out of the third floor of her apartment
       building,
committed suicide.
The mother originally came from Russia.   2465
I was speaking to her son
in one of the rooms near the morgue
trying to get his mother not to have an aurtopsy
and he was telling me that the mother
came from Russia eleven years ago   2470
and the mother left Russia eleven years ago
because of the hardships that they had over there,
and when they came to America
and when this thing started to happen in Crown
       Heights.
It became painful   2475
and it felt like, like there was no place to go.
It's like you're trapped,
everywhere you go there's Jew haters.
And then he told me she commit suicide,
told me the next morning he woke up   2480
he heard the doorbell ring.
He wasn't,
she wasn't there.
He noticed that the window was open,
which is never open   2485
because she was afraid of the cold
even in the summertime.
And he saw his mother
with blood all over her
landed head first   2490
on the concrete side of the apartment building.
After that we already knew this was getting serious,
because we had,
we had Sonny Carson come down
and we had, um,   2495
Reverend Al Sharpton come down
start making pogroms.

Carmel Cato

LINGERING

*7:00 P.M. The corner where the accident occurred in Crown Heights.
An altar to Gavin is against the wall where the car crashed. Many
pieces of cloth are draped. Some writing in color is on the wall. Candle wax is everywhere. There is a rope around the area. CATO is
wearing a trench coat, pulled around him. He stands very close to me.
Dark outside. Reggae music is in the background. Lights come from
stores on each corner. Busy intersection. Sounds from outside. Traffic.
Stores open. People in and out of shops. Sounds from inside apartments, televisions, voices, cooking, etc. He speaks in a pronounced
West Indian accent.*

In the meanwhile
it was two.
Angela was on the ground   2500

but she was trying to move. Gavin was still.
They was trying to pound him.
I was the father.
I was 'it, chucked, and pushed,
2505   and a lot of
sarcastic words were passed towards me
from the police
while I was trying to explain: It was my kid!
These are my children.
2510   The child was hit you know.
I saw everything, everything,
the guy radiator burst
all the hoses,
the steam,
2515   all the garbage buckets along the building.
And it was very loud,
everything burst.
It's like an atomic bomb,
and that's why all these people comin' round
2520   wanna know what's happening.
Oh it was very outrageous.
Numerous numbers.
All the time the police sayin'
you can't get in,
2525   you can't pass,
and the children laying on the ground.
He was hit at exactly eight-thirty.
Why?
I was standing over there.
2530   There was a little child—
a friend of mine
came up with a little child—
and I lift the child up
and she look at her watch at the same time
2535   and she say it was eight-thirty.
I gave the child back to her.
And then it happen.
Um, Um . . .
My child, these are the things I never dream about.
2540   I take care of my children.
You know it's a funny thing,
if a child get sick and he dies
it won't hurt me so bad,
or if a child run out into the street
2545   it wouldn't hurt me.
That's what's hurtin' me.
And the whole week
that Gavin died
my body was changing,
2550   I was having different feelings.
I stop eating,
I didn't et
nothin',
only drink water,
2555   for two weeks;
and I was very touchy—
any least thing that drop
or any song I hear
it would affect me.

Every time I try to do something   2560
I would have to stop.
I was
lingering, lingering, lingering, lingering,
all the time.
But I can do things,   2565
I can see things,
I know that for a fact.
I was telling myself,
"Something is wrong somewhere,"
but I didn't want to see,   2570
I didn't want to accept,
and it was inside of me,
and even when I go home I tell my friends,
"Something coming I could feel it
but I didn't want to see,"   2575
and all the time I just deny deny deny,
and I never thought it was Gavin,
but I didn't have a clue.
I thought it was one of the other children—
the bigger boys   2580
or the girl,
because she worry me,
she won't et—
but Gavin 'ee was 'ealtee,
and he don't cause no trouble.   2585
That's what's devastating me now.
Sometime it make me feel like it's no justice,
like, uh,
the Jewish people,
they are very high up,   2590
it's a very big thing,
they runnin' the whole show
from the judge right down.
And something I don't understand:
The Jewish people, they told me   2595
there are certain people I can not be seen with
and certain things I can not say
and certain people I can not talk to.
They made that very clear to me—the Jewish people—
they can throw the case out   2600
unless
I go to them with pity.
I don't know what they talkin' about.
So I don't know what kind of crap is that.
And make me say things I don't wanna say   2605
and make me do things I don't wanna do.
I am a special person.
I was born different.
I'm a man born by my foot.
I born by my foot.   2610
Anytime a baby comin' by the foot
they either cut the mother
or the baby dies.
But I was born with my foot.
I'm one of the special.   2615
There's no way they can overpower me.
No there's nothing to hide,
you can repeat every word I say.

Suzan-Lori Parks

Suzan-Lori Parks (b. 1963) is among the best known African American playwrights writing today; her work is characterized by brilliant language and elegant and powerful imagery on-stage. She is the author of *Betting on the Dust Commander* (1987), *Imperceptible Mutabilities in the Third Kingdom* (1989), *The Death of the Last Black Man in the Whole Entire World* (1990), *The America Play* (1994), *Venus* (1995), *In the Blood* (1999), *Fucking A* (2000), and *Topdog/ Underdog*, for which she won the Pulitzer Prize in Drama in 2002. She has won a range of awards for her playwriting, collaborated on the script for the Spike Lee film *Girl 6*, and currently teaches at the California School of the Arts.

TOPDOG/UNDERDOG

Topdog/Underdog is in many ways Parks's least experimental play, staging a realistic conflict between two African American brothers. At the same time, though, the realistic surface of the play is complicated by its sharp outlining of a larger historical and cultural frame of reference. For the play's two brothers—Lincoln and Booth—develop the cultural conceit of Parks's earlier *America Play*, in which a character (there called The Foundling Father) performs a "Lincoln Act" in a theme park, in which visitors pay for the pleasure of reenacting John Wilkes Booth's assassination of the president at Ford's Theater. Parks's elaborate allegory of the evacuation and persistence of history in *The America Play*—the theme park is evocatively named "The Great Hole of History"—stands behind the rivalry between Booth and Lincoln in *Topdog/Underdog*, and implies that this drama of dispossession is part of a longer historical trajectory. Here, too, Lincoln works in a seedy arcade, playing—in whiteface—the role of Lincoln as he is assassinated by paying customers. The play's murderous finale is, of course, foretold not only by the characters' names, but even in the opening moments of the play, as Booth is surprised by the entrance of Lincoln—in his full costume—and nearly shoots him.

Don Cheadle as Booth in the 2002 Joseph Papp Public Theater production of Suzan-Lori Parks's *Topdog/Underdog*.

Parks has frequently compared her dramatic writing to the "rep and rev" of jazz, the repetition and revision of a phrase of music, and "rep and rev" also provides an image of her use of history as well. While *Topdog/Underdog* is in many respects a play of fraternal rivalry not unlike Sam Shepard's *True West,* the racial and cultural specificity of the drama is deepened by Parks's deft layering of verbal and visual images of racial violence. How do we read Booth's final murder of his brother Lincoln? Is it the historical consequence of slavery, in which the only roles left for African American men are impersonating white fantasies ("dressing up like some crackerass white man," as Booth puts it) as Lincoln does, playing a petty thief (a different kind of fantasy about black men) as Booth does, or a different—though equally dubious—deception, playing the seductive patter of the three-card monte dealer? The cycles of "rep and rev" that lead to Booth's gunshot echo through personal and national history: Booth kills Lincoln, Lincoln conned Booth to bet his inheritance on the cards, Booth seduced Lincoln's wife, Lincoln was given a secret inheritance by their father Pops (with instructions to hide it from Booth), Booth was given a secret inheritance by their mother Moms (with instructions to hide it from Lincoln), Pops deserts the family, Moms deserts the family, Pops betrays Moms with his various lovers, Moms betrays Pops with her "Thursday man," Booth kills Lincoln. Parks's genius in this evocative play is, finally, the way that she honors, in the physical action of the drama, the "rep and rev" of jazz: the repetitions and revisions echo against one another, without resolving into a single, synthetic melody.

TOPDOG/UNDERDOG

Suzan-Lori Parks

THE PLAYERS

LINCOLN, *the topdog*
BOOTH *(aka 3-Card), the underdog*

I am God in nature;
I am a weed by the wall.

> Ralph Waldo Emerson
> From "Circles"
> *Essays: First Series* (1841)

AUTHOR'S NOTES: *From the "Elements of Style"*

I'm continuing the use of my slightly unconventional theatrical elements. Here's a road map.

(Rest)

Take a little time, a pause, a breather; make a transition.

A Spell

An elongated and heightened (Rest). Denoted by repetition of figures' names with no dialogue. Has sort of an architectural look:

LINCOLN
BOOTH
LINCOLN
BOOTH

This is a place where the figures experience their pure true simple state. While no action or stage business is necessary, directors should fill this moment as they best see fit.

[Brackets in the text indicate optional cuts for production.]

(Parentheses around dialogue indicate softly spoken passages (asides; sotto voce)).

SCENE ONE

Thursday evening. A seedily furnished rooming house room. A bed, a reclining chair, a small wooden chair. Some other stuff but not much else. BOOTH, *a black man in his early 30s, practices his 3-card monte scam on the classic setup: 3 playing cards and the cardboard playing board atop 2 mismatched milk crates. His moves and accompanying patter are, for the most part, studied and awkward.*

BOOTH: Watch me close watch me close now: who-see-thuh-red-card-who-see-thuh-red-card?   I-see-thuh-red-card. Thuh-red-card-is-thuh-winner. Pick-thuh-red-card-you-pick-uh-winner.   Pick-uh-black-card-you-pick-uh-loser.
5   Theres-thuh-loser, yeah, theres-thuh-black-card, theres-thuh-other-loser-and-theres-thuh-red-card, thuh-winner.

(Rest.)

Watch me close watch me close now: 3-Card-throws-thuh-cards-lightning-fast. 3-Card-that's-me-and-Ima-last. Watch-me-throw-cause-here-I-go. One-good-pickll-get-
10   you-in, 2-good-picks-and-you-gone-win. See-thuh-red-card-see-thuh-red-card-who-see-thuh-red-card?

(Rest.)

Dont touch my cards, man, just point to thuh one you want. You-pick-that-card-you-pick-a-loser, yeah, that-cards-a-loser. You-pick-that-card-that's-thuh-other-loser.
15   You-pick-that-card-you-pick-a-winner. Follow that card. You gotta chase that card. You-pick-thuh-dark-deuce-thats-a-loser-other-dark-deuces-thuh-other-loser,   red-deuce, thuh-deuce-of-heartsll-win-it-all. Follow thuh red card.

(Rest.)

20   Ima show you thuh cards: 2 black cards but only one heart. Now watch me now. Who-sees-thuh-red-card-who-knows-where-its-at? Go on, man, point to thuh card. Put yr money down cause you aint no clown. No? Ah you had thuh card, but you didnt have thuh heart.

(Rest.)

You wanna bet? 500 dollars? Shoot. You musta been   25
watching 3-Card real close. Ok. Lay the cash in my hand cause 3-Cards thuh man. Thank you, mister. This card you say?

(Rest.)

Wrong! Sucker! Fool! Asshole! Bastard! I bet yr daddy heard how stupid you was and drank himself to death just   30
cause he didnt wanna have nothing to do witchu! I bet yr mama seen you when you comed out and she walked away from you with thuh afterbirth still hanging from out twixt her legs, sucker! Ha Ha Ha! And 3-Card, once again, wins all thuh money!!   35

(Rest.)

What? Cops looking my way? Fold up thuh game, and walk away. Sneak outa sight. Set up on another corner.

(Rest.)

Yeah.

(Rest.)

Having won the imaginary loot and dodged the imaginary cops, BOOTH *sets up his equipment and starts practicing his scam all over again.* LINCOLN *comes in quietly. He is a black man in his later 30s. He is dressed in an antique frock coat and wears a top hat and fake beard, that is, he is dressed to look like Abraham Lincoln. He surreptitiously walks into the room to stand right behind* BOOTH, *who, engrossed in his cards, does not notice* LINCOLN *right away.*

BOOTH: Watch me close watch me close now; who-see-thuh-red-card-who-see-thuh-red-card?   I-see-thuh-red-card.   40

Thuh-red-card-is-thuh-winner. Pick-thuh-red-card-you-
pick-uh-winner. Pick-uh-black-card-you-pick-uh-loser.
Theres-thuh-loser-yeah-theres-thuh-black-card, theres-
thuh-other-loser-and-theres-thuh-red-card, thuh-winner.
45 Don't touch my cards, man, don't—

(*Rest.*)

Dont do that shit. Dont do that shit. Dont do that shit!

BOOTH, *sensing someone behind him, whirls around, pulling a gun
from his pants. While the presence of* LINCOLN *doesnt surprise him,
the Lincoln costume does.*

BOOTH: And woah, man dont *ever* be doing that shit! Who
thuh fuck you think you is coming in my shit all spooked
out and shit. You pull that one more time I'll shoot you!
50 LINCOLN: I only had a minute to make the bus.
BOOTH: Bullshit.
LINCOLN: Not completely. I mean, its either bull or shit, but
not a complete lie so it aint bullshit, right?

(*Rest.*)

Put yr gun away.
55 BOOTH: Take off the damn hat at least.

LINCOLN *takes off the stovepipe hat.* BOOTH *puts his gun away.*

LINCOLN: Its cold out there. This thing kept my head warm.
BOOTH: I dont like you wearing that bullshit, that shit that
bull that disguise that getup that motherdisfuckinguise
anywhere in the vicinity of my humble abode.
60 LINCOLN: Better?
BOOTH: Take off the damn coat too. Damn, man. Bad enough
you got to wear that shit all day you come up in here
wearing it. What my women gonna say?
LINCOLN: What women?
65 BOOTH: I got a date with Grace tomorrow. Shes in love with
me again but she dont now it yet. Aint no man can love
her the way I can. She sees you in that getup its gonna reflect bad on me. She coulda seen you coming down the
street. Shit. Could be standing outside right now taking
70 her ring off and throwing it on the sidewalk.

BOOTH *takes a peek out the window.*

BOOTH: I got her this ring today. Diamond. Well, diamond-
esque, but it looks just as good as the real thing. Asked her
what size she wore. She say 7 so I go boost a size 6 and a
half, right? Show it to her and she loves it and I shove it
75 on her finger and its a tight fit right, so she cant just take
it off on a whim, like she did the last one I gave her.
Smooth, right?

BOOTH *takes another peek out the window.*

LINCOLN: She out there?
BOOTH: Nope. Coast is clear.
80 LINCOLN: You boosted a ring?
BOOTH: Yeah. I thought about spending my inheritance on it
but—take off that damn coat, man, you make me nervous
standing there looking like a spook, and that damn face

paint, take it off. You should take all of it off at work and
leave it there. 85
LINCOLN: I dont bring it home someone might steal it.
BOOTH: At least *take it off* there, then.
LINCOLN: Yeah.

(*Rest.*)

LINCOLN *takes off the frock coat and applies cold cream, removing
the whiteface.*

LINCOLN: I was riding the bus. Really I only had a minute to
make my bus and I was sitting in the arcade thinking, 90
should I change into my street clothes or should I make the
bus? Nobody was in there today anyway. Middle of week
middle of winter. Not like on weekends. Weekends the
place is packed. So Im riding the bus home. And this kid
asked me for my autograph. I pretended I didnt hear him 95
at first. I'd had a long day. But he kept asking. Theyd just
done Lincoln in history class and he knew all about him,
he'd been to the arcade but, I dunno, for some reason he
was tripping cause there was Honest Abe right beside him
on the bus. I wanted to tell him to go fuck hisself. But then 100
I got a look at him. A little rich kid. Born on easy street,
you know the type. So I waited until I could tell he really
wanted it, the autograph, and I told him he could have it
for 10 bucks. I was gonna say 5, cause of the Lincoln connection but something in me made me ask for 10. 105
BOOTH: But he didnt have a 10. All he had was a penny. So
you took the penny.
LINCOLN: All he had was a *20.* So I took the 20 and told him
to meet me on the bus tomorrow and Honest Abe would
give him the change. 110
BOOTH: Shit.
LINCOLN: Shit is right.

(*Rest.*)

BOOTH: Whatd you do with thuh 20?
LINCOLN: Bought drinks at Luckys. A round for everybody.
They got a kick out of the getup. 115
BOOTH: You shoulda called me down.
LINCOLN: Next time, bro.

(*Rest.*)

You making bookshelves? With the milk crates, you making bookshelves?
BOOTH: Yeah, big bro, Im making bookshelves. 120
LINCOLN: Whats the cardboard part for.
BOOTH: Versatility.
LINCOLN: Oh.
BOOTH: I was thinking we dont got no bookshelves we dont
got no dining room table so Im making a sorta modular 125
unit you put the books in the bottom and the table top
on top. We can eat and store our books. We could put the
photo album in there.

BOOTH *gets the raggedy family photo album and puts it in the milk
crate.*

BOOTH: Youd sit there, Id sit on the edge of the bed. Gathered around the dinner table. Like old times. 130

LINCOLN: We just gotta get some books but thats great, Booth, thats real great.

BOOTH: Dont be calling me Booth no more, K?

LINCOLN: You changing yr name?

135　BOOTH: Maybe.

LINCOLN

BOOTH

LINCOLN: What to?

BOOTH: Im not ready to reveal it yet.

140　LINCOLN: You already decided on something?

BOOTH: Maybe.

LINCOLN: You gonna call yrself something african? That be cool. Only pick something thats easy to spell and pronounce, man, cause you know, some of them african

145　names, I mean, ok, Im down with the power to the peo-
ple thing, but, no ones gonna hire you if they cant say yr name. And some of them fellas who got they african names, no one can say they names and they cant say they names neither. I mean, you dont want yr new handle to

150　obstruct yr employment possibilities.

BOOTH

LINCOLN

BOOTH: You bring dinner?

LINCOLN: "Shango" would be a good name. The name of the

155　thunder god. If you aint decided already Im just throwing it in the pot. I brought chinese.

BOOTH: Lets try the table out.

LINCOLN: Cool.

They both sit at the new table. The food is far away near the door.

LINCOLN

160　BOOTH

LINCOLN: I buy it you set it up. Thats the deal. Thats the deal, right?

BOOTH: You like this place?

LINCOLN: Ssallright.

165　BOOTH: But a little cramped sometimes, right?

LINCOLN: You dont hear me complain. Although that re-
cliner sometimes Booth, man—no Booth, right—man, Im too old to be sleeping in that chair.

BOOTH: Its my place. You dont got a place. Cookie, she threw

170　you out. And you cant seem to get another woman. Yr lucky I let you stay.

LINCOLN: Every Friday you say *mi casa es su casa.*

BOOTH: Every Friday you come home with yr paycheck. Today is Thursday and I tell you brother, its a long way from

175　Friday to Friday. All kinds of things can happen. All kinds of bad feelings can surface and erupt while yr little brother waits for you to bring in yr share.

(*Rest.*)

I got my Thursday head on. Link. Go get the food.

LINCOLN *doesnt budge.*

LINCOLN: You dont got no running water in here, man.

180　BOOTH: So?

LINCOLN: You dont got no toilet you dont got no sink.

BOOTH: Bathrooms down the hall.

LINCOLN: You living in thuh Third World, fool! Hey, I'll get thuh food.

LINCOLN goes to get the food. He sees a stray card on the floor and examines it without touching it. He brings the food over, putting it nicely on the table.

LINCOLN: You been playing cards?   185

BOOTH: Yeah.

LINCOLN: Solitaire?

BOOTH: Thats right. Im getting pretty good at it.

LINCOLN: Thats soup and thats sauce. I got you the meat and I got me the skrimps.   190

BOOTH: I wanted the skrimps.

LINCOLN: You said you wanted the meat. This morning when I left you said you wanted the meat.

(*Rest.*)

Here man, take the skrimps. No sweat.

*They eat. Chinese food from syrofoam containers, cans of soda, for-
tune cookies.* LINCOLN *eats slowly and carefully.* BOOTH *eats ravenously.*

LINCOLN: Yr getting good at solitaire?   195

BOOTH: Yeah. How about we play a hand after eating.

LINCOLN: Solitaire?

BOOTH: Poker or rummy or something.

LINCOLN: You know I dont touch thuh cards, man.

BOOTH: Just for fun.   200

LINCOLN: I dont touch thuh cards.

BOOTH: How about for money?

LINCOLN: You dont got no money. All the money you got I bring in here.

BOOTH: I got my inheritance.   205

LINCOLN: Thats like saying you dont got no money cause you aint never gonna do nothing with it so its like you dont got it.

BOOTH: At least I still got mines. You blew yrs.

LINCOLN   210

BOOTH

LINCOLN: You like the skrimps?

BOOTH: Ssallright.

LINCOLN: Whats yr fortune?

BOOTH: "Waste not want not." Whats yrs?   215

LINCOLN: "Your luck will change!"

BOOTH *finishes eating. He turns his back to* LINCOLN *and fiddles around with the cards, keeping them on the bed, just out of* LIN-
COLNs *sight. He mutters the 3-card patter under his breath. His moves are still clumsy. Every once and a while he darts a look over at* LINCOLN *who does his best to ignore* BOOTH.

BOOTH: ((((Watch me close watch me close now: who-see-
thuh-red-card-who-see-thuh-red-card? I-see-thuh-red-
card. Thuh-red-card-is-thuh-winner. Pick-thuh-red-
card-you-pick-uh-winner. Pick-uh-black-card-and-you-   220
pick-uh-loser. Theres-thuh-loser, yeah, theres-thuh-
black-card, theres-thuh-other-loser-and-theres-thuh-red-
card, thuh-winner! Cop C, Stick, Cop C! Go on—))))

LINCOLN: ((Shit.))

BOOTH: (((((((One-good-pickll-get-you-in, 2-good-picks-   225
and-you-gone-win. Dont touch my cards, man, just point to thuh one you want. You-pick-that-card-you-pick-uh-

loser, yeah, that-cards-uh-loser. You-pick-that-card-thats-thuh-other-loser. You-pick-that-card-you-pick-uh-winner. Follow-that-card. You-gotta-chase-that-card!)))))))

230 LINCOLN: You wanna hustle 3-card monte, you gotta do it right, you gotta break it down. Practice it in smaller bits. Yr trying to do the whole thing at once thats why you keep fucking it up.

235 BOOTH: Show me.

LINCOLN: No. Im just saying you wanna do it you gotta do it right and if you gonna do it right you gotta work on it in smaller bits, thatsall.

BOOTH: You and me could team up and do it together. We'd
240 clean up, Link.

LINCOLN: I'll clean up—bro.

LINCOLN *cleans up. As he clears the food,* BOOTH *goes back to using the "table" for its original purpose.*

BOOTH: My new names 3-Card. 3-Card, got it? You wanted to know it so now you know it. 3-card monte by 3-Card. Call me 3-Card from here on out.

245 LINCOLN: 3-Card. Shit.

BOOTH: Im getting everybody to call me 3-Card. Grace likes 3-Card better than Booth. She says 3-Cards got something to it. Anybody not calling me 3-Card gets a bullet.

LINCOLN: Yr too much, man.

250 BOOTH: Im making a point.

LINCOLN: Point made, 3-Card. Point made.

LINCOLN *picks up his guitar. Plays at it.*

BOOTH: Oh, come on, man, we could make money you and me. Throwing down the cards. 3-Card and Link: look out! We could clean up you and me. You would throw the
255 cards and I'd be yr Stickman. The one in the crowd who looks like just an innocent passerby, who looks like just another player, like just another customer, but who gots intimate connections with you, the Dealer, the one throwing the cards, the main man. I'd be the one who
260 brings in the crowd, I'd be the one who makes them want to put they money down, you do yr moves and I do mines. You turn yr head and I turn the card—

LINCOLN: It aint as easy as all that. Theres—

BOOTH: We could be a team, man. Rake in the money! Sure
265 thered be some cats out there with fast eyes, some brothers and sisters who would watch real close and pick the right card, and so thered be some days when we would lose money, but most of the days we would come out on top! Pockets bulging, plenty of cash! And the ladies would
270 be thrilling! You could afford to get laid! Grace would be all over me again.

LINCOLN: I thought you said she was all over you.

BOOTH: She is she is. Im seeing her tomorrow but today we gotta solidify the shit twixt you and me. Big Brother Link
275 and little brother Booth—

LINCOLN: 3-Card.

BOOTH: Yeah. Scheming and dreaming. No one throws the cards like you, Link. And with yr moves and my magic, and we get Grace and a girl for you to round out the
280 posse. We'd be golden, bro! Am I right?

LINCOLN

LINCOLN

BOOTH: Am I right?

BOOTH: I dont touch thuh cards, 3-Card. I dont touch thuh cards no more.
285

LINCOLN

BOOTH

LINCOLN

BOOTH

BOOTH: You know what Mom told me when she was pack- 290
ing to leave? You was at school motherfucker you was at school. You got up that morning and sat down in yr regular place and read the cereal box while Dad read the sports section and Mom brought you yr dick toast and then you got on the damn school bus cause you didnt 295
have the sense to do nothing else you was so into yr own shit that you didnt have the sense to feel nothing else going on. I had the sense to go back cause I was feeling something going on man, I was feeling something changing. So I— 300

LINCOLN: Cut school that day like you did almost every day—

BOOTH: She was putting her stuff in bags. She had all them nice suitcases but she was putting her stuff in bags.

(Rest.)

Packing up her shit. She told me to look out for you. I 305
told her I was the little brother and the big brother should look out after the little brother. She just said it again. That I should look out for you. Yeah. So who gonna look out for me. Not like you care. Here I am interested in an economic opportunity, willing to work hard, willing to take 310
risks and all you can say you shiteating motherfucking pathetic limpdick uncle tom, all you can tell me is how you dont do no more what I be wanting to do. Here I am trying to earn a living and you standing in my way. YOU STANDING IN MY WAY, LINK! 315

LINCOLN: Im sorry.

BOOTH: Yeah, you sorry all right.

LINCOLN: I cant be hustling no more, bro.

BOOTH: What you do all day aint no hustle?

LINCOLN: Its honest work. 320

BOOTH: Dressing up like some crackerass white man, some dead president and letting people shoot at you sounds like a hustle to me.

LINCOLN: People know the real deal. When people know the real deal it aint a hustle. 325

BOOTH: We do the card game people will know the real deal. Sometimes we will win sometimes they will win. They fast they win, we faster we win.

LINCOLN: I aint going back to that, bro. I aint going back.

BOOTH: You play Honest Abe. You aint going back but you 330
going all the way back. Back to way back then when folks was slaves and shit.

LINCOLN: Dont push me.

BOOTH

LINCOLN 335

BOOTH: You gonna have to leave.

LINCOLN: I'll be gone tomorrow.

BOOTH: Good. Cause this was only supposed to be a temporary arrangement.

LINCOLN: I will be gone tomorrow. 340

BOOTH: Good.

BOOTH *sits on his bed.* LINCOLN, *sitting in his easy chair with his guitar, plays and sings.*

LINCOLN:
My dear mother left me, my fathers gone away
My dear mother left me and my fathers gone away
345   I dont got no money, I dont got no place to stay.

My best girl, she threw me out into the street
My favorite horse, they ground him into meat
Im feeling cold from my head down to my feet.

350   My luck was bad but now it turned to worse
My luck was bad but now it turned to worse
Dont call me up a doctor, just call me up a hearse.

BOOTH: You just made that up?
LINCOLN: I had it in my head a few days.
BOOTH: Sounds good.
355 LINCOLN: Thanks.

(*Rest.*)

Daddy told me once why we got the names we do.
BOOTH: Yeah?
LINCOLN: Yeah.

(*Rest.*)

He was drunk when he told me, or maybe I was drunk
360   when he told me. Anyway he told me, may not be true,
but he told me. Why he named us both. Lincoln and
Booth.
BOOTH: How come. How come, man?
LINCOLN: It was his idea of a joke.

Both men relax back as the light fades.

SCENE TWO

Friday evening. The very next day. BOOTH *comes in looking like he is bundled up against the cold. He makes sure his brother isnt home, then stands in the middle of the room. From his big coat sleeves he pulls out one new shoe then another, from another sleeve come two more shoes. He then slithers out a belt from each sleeve. He removes his coat. Underneath he wears a very nice new suit. He removes the jacket and pants revealing another new suit underneath. The suits still have the price tags on them. He takes two neckties from his pockets and two folded shirts from the back of his pants. He pulls a magazine from the front of his pants. Hes clearly had a busy day of shoplifting. He lays one suit out on* LINCOLNs *easy chair. The other he lays out on his own bed. He goes out into the hall returning with a folding screen which he sets up between the bed and the recliner creating 2 separate spaces. He takes out a bottle of whiskey and two glasses, setting them on the two stacked milk crates. He hears footsteps and sits down in the small wooden chair reading the magazine.* LINCOLN, *dressed in street clothes, comes in.*

LINCOLN: Taaaaadaaaaaaaa!
BOOTH: Lordamighty, Pa, I smells money!
LINCOLN: Sho nuff, Ma. Poppas brung home thuh bacon.
BOOTH: Bringitherebringitherebringithere.

With a series of very elaborate moves LINCOLN *brings the money over to* BOOTH.

BOOTH: Put it in my hands, Pa!   5
LINCOLN: I want ya tuh smells it first, Ma!
BOOTH: Put in neath my nose then, Pa!
LINCOLN: Take yrself a good long whiff of them greenbacks.
BOOTH: Oh lordamighty Ima faint, Pa! Get me muh med-sin!

LINCOLN *quickly pours two large glasses of whiskey.*

LINCOLN: Dont die on me, Ma!   10
BOOTH: Im fading fast, Pa!
LINCOLN: Thinka thuh children, Ma! Thinka thuh farm!
BOOTH: 1-2-3.

Both men gulp down their drinks simultaneously.

LINCOLN **and** BOOTH: AAAAAAAAAAAAAAAAAAAH!

Lots of laughing and slapping on the backs.

LINCOLN: Budget it out man budget it out.   15
BOOTH: You in a hurry?
LINCOLN: Yeah. I wanna see how much we got for the week.
BOOTH: You rush in here and dont even look around. Could
   be a fucking A-bomb in the middle of the floor you
   wouldnt notice. Yr wife, Cookie—   20
LINCOLN: X-wife—
BOOTH: —could be in my bed you wouldnt notice—
LINCOLN: She was once—
BOOTH: Look the fuck around please.

LINCOLN *looks around and sees the new suit on his chair.*

LINCOLN: Wow.   25
BOOTH: Its yrs.
LINCOLN: Shit.
BOOTH: Got myself one too.
LINCOLN: Boosted?
BOOTH: Yeah, I boosted em. Theys stole from a big-ass de-   30
   partment store. That store takes in more money in one
   day than we will in our whole life. I stole and I stole gen-
   erously. I got one for me and I got one for you. Shoes belts
   shirts ties socks in the shoes and everything. Got that
   screen too.   35
LINCOLN: You all right, man.
BOOTH: Just cause I aint good as you at cards dont mean I
   cant do nothing.
LINCOLN: Lets try em on.

They stand in their separate sleeping spaces, BOOTH *near his bed,* LINCOLN *near his recliner, and try on their new clothes.*

BOOTH: Ima wear mine tonight. Gracell see me in this and   40
   she gonna ask me tuh marry *her.*

(*Rest.*)

I got you the blue and I got me the brown. I walked in
   there and walked out and they didnt as much as bat an
   eye. Thats how smooth lil bro be, Link.
LINCOLN: You did good. You did real good, 3-Card.   45
BOOTH: All in a days work.

LINCOLN: They say the clothes make the man. All day long I wear that getup. But that dont make me who I am. Old black coat not even real old just fake old. Its got worn
50 spots on the elbows, little raggedy places thatll break through into holes before the winters out. Shiny strips around the cuffs and the collar. Dust from the cap guns on the left shoulder where they shoot him, where they shoot me I should say but I never feel like they shooting me.
55 The fella who had the gig before I had it wore the same coat. When I got the job they had the getup hanging there waiting for me. Said thuh fella before me just took it off one day and never came back.

(Rest.)

Remember how Dads clothes used to hang in the closet?
60 BOOTH: Until you took em outside and burned em.

(Rest.)

He had some nice stuff. What he didnt spend on booze he spent on women. What he didnt spend on them two he spent on clothes. He had some nice stuff. I would look at his stuff and calculate thuh how long it would take till I was
65 big enough to fit it. Then you went and burned it all up.
LINCOLN: I got tired of looking at em without him in em.

(Rest.)

They said thuh fella before me—he took off the getup one day, hung it up real nice, and never came back. And as they offered me thuh job, saying of course I would have
70 to wear a little makeup and accept less than what they would offer a—another guy—
BOOTH: Go on, say it. "White." Theyd pay you less than theyd pay a white guy.
LINCOLN: I said to myself thats exactly what I would do: wear
75 it out and then leave it hanging there and not come back. But until then, I would make a living at it. But it dont make me. Worn suit coat, not even worn by the fool that Im supposed to be playing, but making fools out of all those folks who come crowding in for they chance to play
80 at something great. Fake beard. Top hat. Dont make me into no Lincoln. I was Lincoln on my own before any of that.

The men finish dressing. They style and profile.

BOOTH: Sharp, huh?
LINCOLN: Very sharp.
85 BOOTH: You look sharp too, man. You look like the real you. Most of the time you walking around all bedraggled and shit. You look good. Like you used to look back in thuh day when you had Cookie in love with you and all the women in the world was eating out of yr hand.
90 LINCOLN: This is real nice, man. I dont know where Im gonna wear it but its real nice.
BOOTH: Just wear it around. Itll make you feel good and when you feel good yll meet someone nice. Me I aint interested in meeting no one nice, I mean, I only got eyes
95 for Grace. You think she'll go for me in this?
LINCOLN: I think thuh tie you gave me'll go better with what you got on.

BOOTH: Yeah?
LINCOLN: Grace likes bright colors dont she? My ties bright,
100 yrs is too subdued.
BOOTH: Yeah. Gimmie yr tie.
LINCOLN: You gonna take back a gift?
BOOTH: I stole the damn thing didnt I? Gimmie yrs! I'll give you mines.

They switch neckties. BOOTH *is pleased.* LINCOLN *is more* pleased.

LINCOLN: Do thuh budget.
105
BOOTH: Right. Ok lets see: we got 314 dollars. We put 100 aside for the rent. 100 a week times 4 weeks makes the rent and—
LINCOLN and BOOTH: —we dont want thuh rent spent.
BOOTH: That leaves 214. We put aside 30 for the electric
110 leaving 184. We put aside 50 for thuh phone leaving 134.
LINCOLN: We dont got a phone.
BOOTH: We pay our bill theyll turn it back on.
LINCOLN: We dont need no phone.
BOOTH: How you gonna get a woman if you dont got a
115 phone? Women these days are more cautious, more waddacallit, more circumspect. You go into a club looking like a fast daddy, you get a filly to give you her numerophono and gone is the days when she just gives you her number and dont ask for yrs.
120
LINCOLN: Like a woman is gonna call me.
BOOTH: She dont wanna call you she just doing a preliminary survey of the property. Shit, Link, you dont know nothin no more.

(Rest.)

She gives you her number and she asks for yrs. You give
125 her yr number. The phone number of yr home. Thereby telling her 3 things: 1) you got a home, that is, you aint no smooth talking smooth dressing *homeless* joe; 2) that you is in possession of a telephone and a working telephone number which is to say that you got thuh cash and thuh
130 wherewithal to acquire for yr self the worlds most revolutionary communication apparatus and you together enough to pay yr bills!
LINCOLN: Whats 3?
BOOTH: You give her yr number you telling her that its cool
135 to call if she should so please, that is, that you aint got no wife or wife approximation on the premises.

(Rest.)

50 for the phone leaving 134. We put aside 40 for "medsin."
LINCOLN: The price went up. 2 bucks more a bottle.
140
BOOTH: We'll put aside 50, then. That covers the bills. We got 84 left. 40 for meals together during the week leaving 44. 30 for me 14 for you. I got a woman I gotta impress tonight.
LINCOLN: You didnt take out for the phone last week.
145
BOOTH: Last week I was depressed. This week things is looking up. For both of us.
LINCOLN: Theyre talking about cutbacks at the arcade. I only been there 8 months, so—
BOOTH: Dont sweat it man, we'll find something else.
150

LINCOLN: Not nothing like this. I like the job. This is sit down, you know, easy work. I just gotta sit there all day. Folks come in kill phony Honest Abe with the phony pistol. I can sit there and let my mind travel.

135 BOOTH: Think of women.

LINCOLN: Sometimes.

(*Rest.*)

All around the whole arcade is buzzing and popping. Thuh whirring of thuh duckshoot, baseballs smacking the back wall when someone misses the stack of cans, some

140 woman getting happy cause her fella just won the ring toss. The Boss playing the barker talking up the fake freaks. The smell of the ocean and cotton candy and rat shit. And in thuh middle of all that, I can just sit and let my head go quiet. Make up songs, make plans. Forget.

(*Rest.*)

145 You should come down again.

BOOTH: Once was plenty, but thanks.

(*Rest.*)

Yr Best Customer, he come in today?

LINCOLN: Oh, yeah, he was there.

BOOTH: He shoot you?

150 LINCOLN: He shot Honest Abe, yeah.

BOOTH: He talk to you?

LINCOLN: In a whisper. Shoots on the left whispers on the right.

BOOTH: Whatd he say this time?

155 LINCOLN: "Does thuh show stop when no ones watching or does thuh show go on?"

BOOTH: Hes getting deep.

LINCOLN: Yeah.

BOOTH: Whatd he say, that one time? "Yr only yrself—"

160 LINCOLN: "—when no ones watching," yeah.

BOOTH: Thats deep shit.

(*Rest.*)

Hes a brother, right?

LINCOLN: I think so.

BOOTH: He know yr a brother?

165 LINCOLN: I dunno. Yesterday he had a good one. He shoots me, Im playing dead, and he leans in close then goes: "God aint nothing but a parasite."

BOOTH: Hes one *deep* black brother.

LINCOLN: Yeah. He makes the day interesting.

170 BOOTH

(*Rest.*)

Thats a fucked-up job you got.

LINCOLN: Its a living.

BOOTH: But you aint living.

LINCOLN: Im alive aint I?

(*Rest.*)

175 One day I was throwing the cards. Next day Lonny died. Somebody shot him. I knew I was next, so I quit. I saved my life.

(*Rest.*)

The arcade gig is the first lucky break Ive ever had. And Ive actually grown to like the work. And now theyre talking about cutting me.   180

BOOTH: You was lucky with thuh cards.

LINCOLN: Lucky? Aint nothing lucky about cards. Cards aint luck. Cards is work. Cards is skill. Aint never nothing lucky about cards.

(*Rest.*)

I dont wanna lose my job.   185

BOOTH: Then you gotta jazz up yr act. Elaborate yr moves, you know. You was always too stiff with it. You cant just sit there! Maybe, when they shoot you, you know, leap up flail yr arms then fall down and wiggle around and shit so they gotta shoot you more than once. Blam Blam Blam!   190 Blam!

LINCOLN: Help me practice. I'll sit here like I do at work and you be like one of the tourists.

BOOTH: No thanks.

LINCOLN: My paychecks on the line, man.   195

BOOTH: I got a date. Practice on yr own.

(*Rest.*)

I got a rendezvous with Grace. Shit she so sweet she makes my teeth hurt.

(*Rest.*)

Link, uh, howbout slipping me an extra 5 spot. Its the biggest night of my life.   200

LINCOLN

BOOTH

LINCOLN *gives* BOOTH *a 5er.*

BOOTH: Thanks.

LINCOLN: No sweat.

BOOTH: Howabout I run through it with you when I get   205 back. Put on yr getup and practice till then.

LINCOLN: Sure.

BOOTH *leaves.* LINCOLN *stands there alone. He takes off his shoes, giving them a shine. He takes off his socks and his fancy suit, hanging it neatly over the little wooden chair. He takes his getup out of his shopping bag. He puts it on, slowly, like an actor preparing for a great role: frock coat, pants, beard, top hat, necktie. He leaves his feet bare. The top hat has an elastic band which he positions securely underneath his chin. He picks up the white pancake makeup but decides against it. He sits. He pretends to get shot, flings himself on the floor and thrashes around. He gets up, considers giving the new moves another try, but instead pours himself a big glass of whiskey and sits there drinking.*

SCENE THREE

Much later that same Friday evening. The recliner is reclined to its maximum horizontal position and LINCOLN *lies there asleep. He wakes with a start. He is horrific, bleary eyed and hungover, in his full* LINCOLN *regalia. He takes a deep breath, realizes where he is and reclines again, going back to sleep.* BOOTH *comes in full of swag-*

ger. He slams the door trying to wake his brother who is dead to the world. He opens the door and slams it again. This time LINCOLN *wakes up, as hungover and horrid as before.* BOOTH *swaggers about, his moves are exaggerated, rooster-like. He walks round and round* LINCOLN *making sure his brother sees him.*

LINCOLN: You hurt yrself?

BOOTH: I had me "an evening to remember."

LINCOLN: You look like you hurt yrself.

BOOTH: Grace Grace Grace. *Grace.* She wants me back. She
5   wants me back so bad she wiped her hand over the past
where we wasn't together just so she could say we aint
never been apart. She wiped her hand over our breakup.
She wiped her hand over her childhood, her teenage
years, her first boyfriend, just so she could say that she
10   been mine since the dawn of time.

LINCOLN: Thats great, man.

BOOTH: And all the shit I put her through; she wiped it clean.
And the women I saw while I was seeing her—

LINCOLN: Wiped clean too?

15 BOOTH: Mister Clean, Mister, Mister Clean!

LINCOLN: Whered you take her?

BOOTH: We was over at her place. I brought thuh food.
Stopped at the best place I could find and stuffed my coat
with only the best. We had candlelight, we had music we
20   had—

LINCOLN: She let you do it?

BOOTH: Course she let me do it.

LINCOLN: She let you do it without a rubber?

BOOTH: —Yeah.

25 LINCOLN: Bullshit.

BOOTH: I put my foot down—and she *melted.* And she was—
huh—she was something else. I dont wanna get you jealous, though.

LINCOLN: Go head, I dont mind.

30 BOOTH

(*Rest.*)

Well, you know what she looks like.

LINCOLN: She walks on by and the emergency room fills up
cause all the guys get whiplash from lookin at her.

BOOTH: Thats right thats right. Well—she comes to the door
35   wearing nothing but her little nightie, eats up the food I'd
brought like there was no tomorrow and then goes and
eats on me.

(*Rest.*)

LINCOLN: Go on.

BOOTH: I dont wanna make you feel bad, man.

40 LINCOLN: Ssallright. Go on.

BOOTH

(*Rest.*)

Well, uh, you know what she likes. Wild. Goodlooking.
So sweet my teeth hurt.

LINCOLN: Sexmachine.

45 BOOTH: Yeah.

LINCOLN: Hotsy-Totsy.

BOOTH: Yeah.

LINCOLN: Amazing Grace.

BOOTH: Amazing Grace! Yeah. Thats right. She let me do her
how I wanted. And no rubber.   50

(*Rest.*)

LINCOLN: Go on.

BOOTH: You dont wanna hear the mushy shit.

LINCOLN: Sure I do.

BOOTH: You hate mushy shit. You always hated thuh mushy
shit.   55

LINCOLN: Ive changed. Go head. You had "an evening to remember," remember? I was just here alone sitting here.
Drinking. Go head. Tell Link thuh stink.

(*Rest.*)

Howd ya do her?

BOOTH: Dogstyle.   60

LINCOLN: Amazing Grace.

BOOTH: In front of a mirror.

LINCOLN: So you could see her. Her face her breasts her back
her ass. Graces got a great ass.

BOOTH: Its all right.   65

LINCOLN: Amazing Grace!

BOOTH *goes into his bed area and takes off his suit, tossing the clothes on the floor.*

BOOTH: She said next time Ima have to use a rubber. She let
me have my way this time but she said that next time I'd
have to put my boots on.

LINCOLN: Im sure you can talk her out of it.   70

BOOTH: Yeah.

(*Rest.*)

What kind of rubbers you use, I mean, when you was
with Cookie.

LINCOLN: We didnt use rubbers. We was married, man.

BOOTH: Right. But you had other women on the side. What 75
kind you use when you was with them?

LINCOLN: Magnums.

BOOTH: Thats thuh kind I picked up. For next time. Grace
was real strict about it.

While BOOTH *sits on his bed fiddling with his box of condoms,* LIN-
COLN *sits in his chair and resumes drinking.*

LINCOLN: Im sure you can talk her out of it. You put yr foot 80
down and she'll melt.

BOOTH: She was real strict. Sides I wouldnt wanna be taking
advantage of her or nothing. Putting my foot down and
her melting all over thuh place.

LINCOLN: Magnums then.   85

(*Rest.*)

Theyre for "the larger man."

BOOTH: Right. Right.

LINCOLN *keeps drinking as* BOOTH, *sitting in the privacy of his bedroom, fiddles with the condoms, perhaps trying to put one on.*

LINCOLN: Thats right.

BOOTH: Graces real different from them fly-by-night gals I
was making do with. Shes in school. Making something of 90

herself. Studying cosmetology. You should see what she can do with a womans hair and nails.

LINCOLN: Too bad you aint a woman.

BOOTH: What?

95 LINCOLN: You could get yrs done for free, I mean.

BOOTH: Yeah. She got this way of sitting. Of talking. Everything she does is. Shes just so hot.

(*Rest.*)

We was together 2 years. Then we broke up. I had my little employment difficulty and she needed time to think.

100 LINCOLN: And shes through thinking now.

BOOTH: Thats right.

LINCOLN

BOOTH

LINCOLN: Whatcha doing back there?

105 BOOTH: Resting. That girl wore me out.

LINCOLN: You want some med-sin?

BOOTH: No thanks.

LINCOLN: Come practice my moves with me, then.

BOOTH: Lets hit it tomorrow, K?

110 LINCOLN: I been waiting. I got all dressed up and you said if I waited up—come on, man, they gonna replace me with a wax dummy.

BOOTH: No shit.

LINCOLN: Thats what theyre talking about. Probably just talk, 115 but—come on, man, I even lent you 5 bucks.

BOOTH: Im tired.

LINCOLN: You didnt get shit tonight.

BOOTH: You jealous, man. You just jail-us.

LINCOLN: You laying over there yr balls blue as my boosted 120 suit. Laying over there waiting for me to go back to sleep or black out so I wont hear you rustling thuh pages of yr fuck book.

BOOTH: Fuck you, man.

LINCOLN: I was over there looking for something the other 125 week and theres like 100 fuck books under yr bed and theyre matted together like a bad fro, bro, cause you spunked in the pages and didnt wipe them off.

BOOTH: Im hot. I need constant sexual release. If I wasnt taking care of myself by myself I would be out there running 130 around on thuh town which costs cash that I dont have so I would be doing worse: I'd be out there doing who knows what, shooting people and shit. Out of a need for unresolved sexual release. I'm a hot man. I aint apologizing for it. When I dont got a woman, I gotta make do. Not like 135 you, Link. When you dont got a woman you just sit there. Letting yr shit fester. Yr dick, if it aint falled off yet, is hanging there between yr legs, little whiteface shriveled-up blank-shooting grub worm. As goes thuh man so goes thuh mans dick. Thats what I say. Least my shits intact.

(*Rest.*)

140 You a limp dick jealous whiteface motherfucker whose wife dumped him cause he couldnt get it up and she told me so. Came crawling to me cause she needed a man.

(*Rest.*)

I gave it to Grace good tonight. So goodnight.

LINCOLN

(*Rest.*)

Goodnight.   145

LINCOLN

BOOTH

LINCOLN

BOOTH

LINCOLN   150

BOOTH

LINCOLN *sitting in his chair.* BOOTH *lying in bed. Time passes.* BOOTH *peeks out to see if* LINCOLN *is asleep.* LINCOLN *is watching for him.*

LINCOLN: You can hustle 3-card monte without me you know.

BOOTH: Im planning to.

LINCOLN: I could contact my old crew. You could work with 155 them. Lonny aint around no more but theres the rest of them. Theyre good.

BOOTH: I can get my own crew. I dont need yr crew. Buncha hasbeens. I can get my own crew.

LINCOLN: My crews experienced. We usedta pull down a 160 thousand a day. Thats 7 G a week. That was years ago. They probably do twice, 3 times that now.

BOOTH: I got my own connections, thank you.

LINCOLN: Theyd take you on in a heartbeat. With my say. My say still counts with them. They know you from before, 165 when you tried to hang with us but—wernt ready yet. They know you from then, but I'd talk you up. I'd say yr my bro, which they know, and I'd say youd been working the west coast. Little towns. Mexican border. Taking tourists. I'd tell them you got moves like I dreamed of 170 having. Meanwhile youd be working out yr shit right here, right in this room, getting good and getting better every day so when I did do the reintroductions youd have some marketable skills. Youd be passable.

BOOTH: I'd be more than passable, I'd be the be all end all. 175

LINCOLN: Youd be the be all end all. And youd have my say. If yr interested.

BOOTH: Could do.

LINCOLN: Youd have to get a piece. They all pack pistols, bro.

BOOTH: I *got* a piece.   180

LINCOLN: Youd have to be packing something more substantial than that pop gun, 3-Card. These hustlers is upper echelon hustlers they pack upper echelon heat, not no Saturday night shit, now.

BOOTH: Whata you know of heat? You aint hung with those 185 guys for 6, 7 years. You swore off em. Threw yr heat in thuh river and you "Dont touch thuh cards." I know more about heat than you know about heat.

LINCOLN: Im around guns every day. At the arcade. Theyve all been reworked so they only fire caps but I see guns 190 every day. Lots of guns.

BOOTH: What kinds?

LINCOLN: You been there, you seen them. Shiny deadly metal each with their own deadly personality.

BOOTH: Maybe I *could* visit you over there. I'd boost one of 195 them guns and rework it to make it shoot for real again. What kind you think would best suit my personality?

LINCOLN: You aint stealing nothing from the arcade.

BOOTH: I go in there and steal if I want to go in there and
200   steal I go in there and steal.

LINCOLN: It aint worth it. They dont shoot nothing but
    blanks.

BOOTH: Yea, like you. Shooting blanks.

(*Rest.*)

(*Rest.*)

    You ever wonder if someones gonna come in there with
205   a real gun? A real gun with real slugs? Someone with uh
    axe tuh grind or something?

LINCOLN: No.

BOOTH: Someone who hates you come in there and guns
    you down and gets gone before anybody finds out.
210 LINCOLN: I dont got no enemies.

BOOTH: Yr X.

LINCOLN: Cookie dont hate me.

BOOTH: Yr Best Customer? Some miscellaneous stranger?

LINCOLN: I cant be worrying about the actions of miscella-
215   neous strangers.

BOOTH: But there they come day in day out for a chance to
    shoot Honest Abe.

(*Rest.*)

    Who are they mostly?

LINCOLN: I dont really look.
220 BOOTH: You must see something.

LINCOLN: Im supposed to be staring straight ahead. Watch-
    ing a play, like Abe was.

BOOTH: All day goes by and you never ever take a sneak peek
    at who be pulling the trigger.

Pulled in by his own curiosity, BOOTH *has come out of his bed area
to stand on the dividing line between the two spaces.*

225 LINCOLN: Its pretty dark. To keep thuh illusion of thuh
    whole thing.

(*Rest.*)

    But on thuh wall opposite where I sit theres a little elec-
    trical box, like a fuse box. Silver metal. Its got uh dent in
    it like somebody hit it with they fist. Big old dent so
230   everything reflected in it gets reflected upside down. Like
    yr looking in uh spoon. And thats where I can see em.
    The assassins.

(*Rest.*)

    Not behind me yet but I can hear him coming. Coming
    in with his gun in hand, thuh gun he already picked out
235   up front when he paid his fare. Coming on in. But not be-
    hind me yet. His dress shoes making too much noise on
    the carpet, the carpets too thin, Boss should get a new one
    but hes cheap. Not behind me yet. Not behind me yet.
    Cheap lightbulb just above my head.

(*Rest.*)

And there he is. Standing behind me. Standing in position. 240
Standing upside down. Theres some feet shapes on the
floor so he knows just where he oughta stand. So he wont
miss. Thuh gun is always cold. Winter or summer thuh
gun is always cold. And when the gun touches me he can
feel that Im warm and he knows Im alive. And if Im alive 245
then he can shoot me dead. And for a minute, with him
hanging back there behind me, its real. Me looking at him
upside down and him looking at me looking like Lincoln.
Then he shoots.

(*Rest.*)

I slump down and close my eyes. And he goes out thuh 250
other way. More come in. Uh whole day full. Bunches of
kids, little good for nothings, in they school uniforms.
Businessmen smelling like two for one martinis. Tourists
in they theme park t-shirts trying to catch it on film.
Housewives with they mouths closed tight, shooting more 255
than once.

(*Rest.*)

They all get so into it. I do my best for them. And now
they talking bout replacing me with uh wax dummy. Itll
cut costs.

BOOTH: You just gotta show yr boss that you can do things a 260
    wax dummy cant do. You too dry with it. You gotta add
    spicy shit.

LINCOLN: Like what.

BOOTH: Like when they shoot you, I dunno, scream or some-
    thing.   265

LINCOLN: Scream?

BOOTH *plays the killer without using his gun.*

BOOTH: Try it. I'll be the killer. Bang!

LINCOLN: Aaaah!

BOOTH: Thats good.

LINCOLN: A wax dummy can scream. They can put a voice- 270
    box in it and make it like its screaming.

BOOTH: You can curse. Try it. Bang!

LINCOLN: Motherfucking cocksucker!

BOOTH: That's good, man.

LINCOLN: They aint going for that, though.   275

BOOTH: You practice rolling and wiggling on the floor?

LINCOLN: A little.

BOOTH: Lemmie see. Bang!

LINCOLN *slumps down, falls on the floor and silently wiggles
around.*

BOOTH: You look more like a worm on the sidewalk. Move
    yr arms. Good. Now scream or something.   280

LINCOLN: Aaaah! Aaaaah! Aaaah!

BOOTH: A little tougher than that, you sound like yr fucking.

LINCOLN: Aaaaaah!

BOOTH: Hold yr head or something, where I shotcha. Good.
    And look at me! I am the assassin! *I am Booth!!* Come on 285
    man this is life and death! Go all out!

LINCOLN *goes all out.*

BOOTH: Cool, man thats cool. Thats enough.

LINCOLN: Whatdoyathink?

BOOTH: I dunno, man. Something about it. I dunno. It was
290   looking too real or something.

LINCOLN: They dont want it looking too real. I'd scare the
customers. Then I'd be out for sure. Yr trying to get me
fired.

BOOTH: Im trying to help. Cross my heart.

295 LINCOLN: People are funny about they Lincoln shit. Its historical. People like they historical shit in a certain way.
They like it to unfold the way they folded it up. Neatly
like a book. Not raggedy and bloody and screaming. You
trying to get me fired.

(*Rest.*)

300   I am uh brother playing Lincoln. Its uh stretch for anyones
imagination. And it aint easy for me neither. Every day I
put on that shit, I leave my own shit at the door and I put
on that shit and I go out there and I make it work. I make
it look easy but its hard. That shit is hard. But it works.
305   Cause I work it. And you trying to get me fired.

(*Rest.*)

I swore off them cards. Took nowhere jobs. Drank. Then
Cookie threw me out. What thuh fuck was I gonna do?
I seen that "Help Wanted" sign and I went up in there and
I looked good in the getup and agreed to the whiteface
310   and they really dug it that me and Honest Abe got the
same name.

(*Rest.*)

Its a sit down job. With benefits. I dont wanna get fired.
They wont give me a good reference if I get fired.

BOOTH: Iffen you was tuh get fired, then, well—then you and
315   me could—hustle the cards together. We'd have to support ourselves somehow.

(*Rest.*)

Just show me how to do the hook part of the card hustle,
man. The part where the Dealer looks away but somehow
he sees—

320 LINCOLN: I couldnt remember if I wanted to.

BOOTH: Sure you could.

LINCOLN: No.

(*Rest.*)

Night, man.

BOOTH: Yeah.

LINCOLN *stretches out in his recliner.* BOOTH *stands over him waiting for him to get up, to change his mind. But* LINCOLN *is fast asleep.*
BOOTH *covers him with a blanket then goes to his bed, turning off the
lights as he goes. He quietly rummages underneath his bed for a girlie
magazine which, as the lights fade, he reads with great interest.*

SCENE FOUR

Saturday. Just before dawn. LINCOLN *gets up. Looks around.*
BOOTH *is fast asleep, dead to the world.*

LINCOLN: No fucking running water.

*He stumbles around the room looking for something which he finally
finds: a plastic cup, which he uses as a urinal. He finishes peeing and
finds an out of the way place to stow the cup. He claws at his Lincoln getup, removing it and tearing it in the process. He strips down
to his t-shirt and shorts.*

LINCOLN: Hate falling asleep in this damn shit. Shit. Ripped
the beard. I can just hear em tomorrow. Busiest day of the
week. They looking me over to make sure Im presentable.
They got a slew of guys working but Im the only one   5
they look over every day. "Yr beards ripped, pal. Sure, we'll
getcha new one but its gonna be coming outa yr pay."
Shit. I should quit right then and there. I'd yank off the
beard, throw it on the ground and stomp it, then go strangle the fucking boss. Thatd be good. My hands around his   10
neck and his bug eyes bugging out. You been ripping me
off since I took this job and now Im gonna have to take
it outa *yr* pay, motherfucker. Shit.

(*Rest.*)

Sit down job. With benefits.

(*Rest.*)

Hustling. Shit, I was good. I was great. Hell I was the be   15
all end all. I was throwing cards like throwing cards was
made for me. Made for me and me alone. I was the best
anyone ever seen. Coast to coast. Everybody said so. And
I never lost. Not once. Not one time. Not never. Thats
how much them cards was mines. I was the be all end all.   20
I was that good.

(*Rest.*)

Then you woke up one day and you didnt have the taste
for it no more. Like something in you knew.—Like something in you knew it was time to quit. Quit while you was
still ahead. Something in you was telling you.—But hells   25
no. Not Link thuh stink. So I went out there and threw
one more time. What thuh fuck. And Lonny died.

(*Rest.*)

Got yrself a good job. And when the arcade lets you go
yll get another good job. I dont gotta spend my whole life
hustling. Theres more to Link than that. More to me than   30
some cheap hustle. More to life than cheating some idiot
out of his paycheck or his life savings.

(*Rest.*)

Like that joker and his wife from out of town. Always
wanted to see the big city. I said you could see the bigger
end of the big city with a little more cash. And if they was   35
fast enough, faster than me, and here I slowed down my
moves I slowed em way down and my Lonny, my right
hand, my Stickman, spanish guy who looked white and
could draw a customer in like nothing else, Lonny could
draw a fly from fresh shit, he could draw Adam outa Eve   40
just with that look he had, Lonny always got folks playing.

(Rest.)

Somebody shot him. They dont know who. Nobody knows nobody cares.

(Rest.)

We took that man and his wife for hundreds. No, thousands. We took them for everything they had and everything they ever wanted to have. We took a father for the money he was gonna get his kids new bike with and he cried in the street while we vanished. We took a mothers welfare check, she pulled a knife on us and we ran. She threw it but her aim werent shit. People shopping. Greedy. Thinking they could take me and they got took instead.

(Rest.)

Swore off thuh cards. Something inside me telling me—. But I was good.
LINCOLN
LINCOLN

He sees a packet of cards. He studies them like an alcoholic would study a drink. Then he reaches for them, delicately picking them up and choosing 3 cards.

LINCOLN: Still got my moves. Still got my touch. Still got my chops. Thuh feel of it. And I aint hurting no one, God. Link is just here hustling hisself.

(Rest.)

Lets see whatcha got.

He stands over the monte setup. Then he bends over it placing the cards down and moving them around. Slowly at first, aimlessly, as if hes just making little ripples in water. But then the game draws him in. Unlike BOOTH, *LINCOLNs patter and moves are deft, dangerous, electric.*

LINCOLN: (((Lean in close and watch me now: who see thuh black card who see thuh black card I see thuh black card black cards thuh winner pick thuh black card thats thuh winner pick thuh red card thats thuh loser pick thuh other red card thats thuh other loser pick thuh black card you pick thuh winner. Watch me as I throw thuh cards. Here we go.)))

(Rest.)

(((Who see thuh black card who see thuh black card? You pick thuh red card you pick a loser you pick that red card you pick a loser you pick thuh black card thuh deuce of spades you pick a winner who sees thuh deuce of spades thuh one who sees it never fades watch me now as I throw thuh cards. Red losers black winner follow thuh deuce of spaces chase thuh black deuce. Dark deuce will get you thuh win.)))

Even though LINCOLN *speaks softly,* BOOTH *wakes and, unbeknownst to* LINCOLN, *listens intently.*

(Rest.)

LINCOLN: ((10 will get you 20, 20 will get you 40.))

(Rest.)

((Ima show you thuh cards: 2 red cards but only one spade. Dark winner in thuh center and thuh red losers on thuh sides. Pick uh red card you got a loser pick thuh other red card you got a loser pick thuh black card you got a winner. One good pickll get you in, 2 good picks and you gone win. Watch me come on watch me now.))

(Rest.)

((Who sees thuh winner who knows where its at? You do? You sure? Go on then, put yr money where yr mouth is. Put yr money down you aint no clown. No? Ah, you had thuh card but you didnt have thuh heart.))

(Rest.)

((Watch me now as I throw thuh cards watch me real close. Ok, man, you know which card is the deuce of spades? Was you watching Links lighting fast express? Was you watching Link cause he the best? So you sure, huh? Point it out first, then place yr bet and Linkll show you yr winner.))

(Rest.)

((500 dollars? You thuh man of thuh hour you thuh man with thuh power. You musta been watching Link real close. You must be thuh man who know thuh most. Ok. Lay the cash in my hand cause Link the man. Thank you, mister. This card you say?))

(Rest.)

((Wrong! Ha!))

(Rest.)

((Thats thuh show. We gotta go.))

LINCOLN *puts the cards down. He moves away from the monte setup. He sits on the edge of his easy chair, but he can't take his eyes off the cards.*

Intermission

SCENE FIVE

Several days have passed. Its now Wednesday night. BOOTH *is sitting in his brand-new suit. The monte setup is nowhere in sight. In its place is a table with two nice chairs. The table is covered with a lovely tablecloth and there are nice plates, silverware, champagne glasses and candles. All the makings of a very romantic dinner for two. The whole apartment in fact takes its cue from the table. Its been cleaned up considerably. New curtains on the windows, a doily-like object on the recliner.* BOOTH *sits at the table darting his eyes around, making sure everything is looking good.*

BOOTH: Shit.

He notices some of his girlie magazines visible from underneath his bed. He goes over and nudges them out of sight. He sits back down. He notices that theyre still visible. He goes over and nudges them some more, kicking at them finally. Then he takes the spread from his bed and pulls it down, hiding them. He sits back down. He gets up. Checks the champagne on much melted ice. Checks the food.

BOOTH: Foods getting cold, Grace!! Dont worry man, she'll get here, she'll get here.

He sits back down. He goes over to the bed. Checks it for springiness. Smoothes down the bedspread. Double-checks 2 matching silk dressing gowns, very expensive, marked "His" and "Hers." Lays the dressing gowns across the bed again. He sits back down. He cant help but notice the visibility of the girlie magazines again. He goes to the bed, kicks them fiercely, then on his hands and knees shoves them. Then he begins to get under the bed to push them, but he remembers his nice clothing and takes off his jacket. After a beat he removes his pants and, in this half-dressed way, he crawls under the bed to give those telltale magazines a good and final shove. LINCOLN *comes in. At first* BOOTH, *still stripped down to his underwear, thinks its his date. When he realizes its his brother, he does his best to keep* LINCOLN *from entering the apartment.* LINCOLN *wears his frock coat and carries the rest of his getup in a plastic bag.*

LINCOLN: You in the middle of it?
BOOTH: What the hell you doing here?
5 LINCOLN: If yr in thuh middle of it I can go. Or I can just be real quiet and just—sing a song in my head or something.
BOOTH: The casas off limits to you tonight.
LINCOLN: You know when we lived in that 2-room place with the cement backyard and the frontyard with nothing
10 but trash in it, Mom and Pops would do it in the middle of the night and I would always hear them but I would sing in my head, cause, I dunno, I couldnt bear to listen.
BOOTH: You gotta get out of here.
LINCOLN: I would make up all kinds of songs. Oh, sorry, yr
15 all up in it. No sweat, bro. No sweat. Hey, Grace, howyadoing?!
BOOTH: She aint here yet, man. Shes running late. And its a good thing too cause I aint all dressed yet. Yr gonna spend thuh night with friends?
20 LINCOLN: Yeah.

BOOTH *waits for* LINCOLN *to leave.* LINCOLN *stands his ground.*

LINCOLN: I lost my job.
BOOTH: Hunh.
LINCOLN: I come in there right on time like I do every day and that motherfucker gives me some song and dance
25 about cutbacks and too many folks complaining.
BOOTH: Hunh.
LINCOLN: Showd me thuh wax dummy—hes buying it right out of a catalog.

(Rest.)

I walked out still wearing my getup.

(Rest.)

30 I could go back in tomorrow. I could tell him I'll take another pay cut. Thatll get him to take me back.

BOOTH: Link. Yr free. Dont go crawling back. Yr free at last! Now you can do anything you want. Yr not tied down by that job. You can—you can do something else. Something that pays better maybe. 35
LINCOLN: You mean Hustle.
BOOTH: Maybe. Hey, Graces on her way. You gotta go.

LINCOLN *flops into his chair.* BOOTH *is waiting for him to move.* LINCOLN *doesnt budge.*

LINCOLN: I'll stay until she gets here. I'll act nice. I wont embarrass you.
BOOTH: You gotta go. 40
LINCOLN: What time she coming?
BOOTH: Shes late. She could be here any second.
LINCOLN: I'll meet her. I met her years ago. I'll meet her again.

(Rest.)

How late is she?
BOOTH: She was supposed to be here at 8. 45
LINCOLN: Its after 2 a.m. Shes—shes late.

(Rest.)

Maybe when she comes you could put the blanket over me and I'll just pretend like Im not here.

(Rest.)

I'll wait. And when she comes I'll go. I need to sit down. I been walking around all day. 50
BOOTH
LINCOLN

BOOTH *goes to his bed and dresses hurriedly.*

BOOTH: Pretty nice, right? The china thuh silver thuh crystal.
LINCOLN: Its great.

(Rest.)

Boosted? 55
BOOTH: Yeah.
LINCOLN: Thought you went and spent yr inheritance for a minute, you had me going I was thinking shit, Booth—3-Card—that 3-Cards gone and spent his inheritance and the gal is—late. 60
BOOTH: Its boosted. Every bit of it.

(Rest.)

Fuck this waiting bullshit.
LINCOLN: She'll be here in a minute. Dont sweat it.
BOOTH: Right.

BOOTH *comes to the table. Sits. Relaxes as best he can.*

BOOTH: How come I got a hand for boosting and I dont got 65 a hand for throwing cards? Its sorta the same thing—you gotta be quick—and slick. Maybe yll show me yr moves sometime.
LINCOLN
BOOTH 70

UNIT VI · THE UNITED STATES

LINCOLN
BOOTH

LINCOLN: Look out the window. When you see Grace coming, I'll go.

75   BOOTH: Cool. Cause youd jinx it, youd really jinx it. Maybe you being here has jinxed it already. Naw. Shes just a little late. You aint jinxed nothing.

BOOTH sits by the window, glancing out, watching for his date. LINCOLN sits in his recliner. He finds the whiskey bottle, sips from it. He then rummages around, finding the raggedy photo album. He looks through it.

LINCOLN: There we are at the house. Remember when we moved in?

80   BOOTH: No.

LINCOLN: You were 2 or 3.

BOOTH: I was 5.

LINCOLN: I was 8. We all thought it was the best fucking house in the world.

85   BOOTH: Cement backyard and a frontyard full of trash, yeah, dont be going down memory lane man, yll jinx thuh vibe I got going in here. Gracell be walking in here and wrinkling up her nose cause you done jinxed up thuh joint with yr raggedy recollections.

90   LINCOLN: We had some great times in that house, bro. Selling lemonade on thuh corner, thuh treehouse out back, summers spent lying in thuh grass and looking at thuh stars.

BOOTH: We never did none of that shit.

LINCOLN: But we had us some good times. That row of nails

95   I got you to line up behind Dads car so when he backed out the driveway to work—

BOOTH: He came back that night, only time I ever seen his face go red, 4 flat tires and yelling bout how thuh white man done sabotaged him again.

100 LINCOLN: And neither of us flinched. Neither of us let on that itd been us.

BOOTH: It was at dinner, right? What were we eating?

LINCOLN: Food.

BOOTH: We was eating pork chops, mashed potatoes and

105 peas. I remember cause I had to look at them peas real hard to keep from letting on. And I would glance over at you, not really glancing not actually turning my head, but I was looking at you out thuh corner of my eye. I was sure he was gonna find us out and then he woulda whipped us

110 good. But I kept glancing at you and you was cool, man. Like nothing was going on. You was cooooool.

(Rest.)

What time is it?

LINCOLN: After 3.

(Rest.)

You should call her. Something mighta happened.

115 BOOTH: No man, Im cool. She'll be here in a minute. Patience is a virtue. She'll be here.

LINCOLN: You look sad.

BOOTH: Nope. Im just, you know, Im just—

LINCOLN: Cool.

120 BOOTH: Yeah, Cool.

BOOTH comes over, takes the bottle of whiskey and pours himself a big glassful. He returns to the window looking out and drinking.

BOOTH: They give you a severance package, at thuh job?

LINCOLN: A weeks pay.

BOOTH: Great.

LINCOLN: I blew it. Spent it all.

BOOTH: On what?   125

LINCOLN: — Just spent it.

(Rest.)

It felt good, spending it. Felt really good. Like back in thuh day when I was really making money. Throwing thuh cards all day and strutting and rutting all night. Didnt have to take no shit from no fool, didnt have to worry   130 about getting fired in favor of some damn wax dummy. I was thuh shit and they was my fools.

(Rest.)

Back in thuh day.

(Rest.)

(Rest.)

Why you think they left us, man?

BOOTH: Mom and Pops? I dont think about it too much.   135

LINCOLN: I dont think they liked us.

BOOTH: Naw. That aint it.

LINCOLN: I think there was something out there that they liked more than they liked us and for years they was struggling against moving towards that more liked something.   140 Each of them had a special something that they was struggling against. Moms had hers. Pops had his. And they was struggling. We moved out of that nasty apartment into a house. A whole house. I wernt perfect but it was a house and theyd bought it and they brought us there and every-   145 thing we owned, figuring we could be a family in that house and them things, them two separate things each of them was struggling against, would just leave them be. Them things would see thuh house and be impressed and just leave them be. Would see thuh job Pops had and how   150 he shined his shoes every night before he went to bed, shining them shoes whether they needed it or not, and thuh thing he was struggling against would see all that and just let him be, and thuh thing Moms was struggling against, it would see the food on the table every night and   155 listen to her voice when she'd read to us sometimes, the clean clothes, the buttons sewed on all right and it would just let her be. Just let us all be, just regular people living in a house. That wernt too much to ask.

BOOTH: Least we was grown when they split.   160

LINCOLN: 16 and 13 aint grown.

BOOTH: 16s grown. Almost. And I was ok cause you were there.

(Rest.)

Shit man, it aint like they both one day both, together packed all they shit up and left us so they could have fun   165 in thuh sun on some tropical island and you and me

would have to grub in thuh dirt forever. They didnt leave together. That makes it different. She left, 2 years go by. Then he left. Like neither of them couldnt handle it no
170   more. She split then he split. Like thuh whole family mortgage bills going to work thing was just too much. And I dont blame them. You dont see me holding down a steady job. Cause its bullshit and I know it. I seen how it cracked them up and I aint going there.

(Rest.)

175   It aint right me trying to make myself into a one woman man just because she wants me like that. One woman rubber-wearing motherfucker. Shit. Not me. She gonna walk in here looking all hot and shit trying to see how much she can get me to sweat, how much she can get me
180   to give her before she gives me mines. Shit.

LINCOLN
BOOTH
LINCOLN: Moms told me I shouldnt never get married.
BOOTH: She told me thuh same thing.
185 LINCOLN: They gave us each 500 bucks then they cut out.
BOOTH: Thats what Im gonna do. Give my kids 500 bucks then cut out. Thats thuh way to do it.
LINCOLN: You dont got no kids.
BOOTH: Im gonna have kids then Im gonna cut out.
190 LINCOLN: Leaving each of yr offspring 500 bucks as yr splitting.
BOOTH: Yeah.

(Rest.)

Just goes to show Mom and Pops had some agreement between them.
195 LINCOLN: How so.
BOOTH: Theyd stopped talking to eachother. Theyd stopped *screwing* eachother. But they had an agreement. Somewhere in there when it looked like all they had was hate they sat down and did thuh "split" budget.

(Rest.)

200   When Moms splits she gives me 5 hundred-dollar bills rolled up and tied up tight in one of her nylon stockings. She tells me to put it in a safe place, to spend it only in case of an emergency, and not to tell nobody I got it, not even you. 2 years later Pops splits and before
205   he goes—
LINCOLN: He slips me 10 fifties in a clean handkerchief: "Hide this somewheres good, dont go blowing it, dont tell no one you got it, especially that Booth."
BOOTH: Theyd been scheming together all along. They left
210   separately but they was in agreement. Maybe they arrived at the same place at the same time, maybe they renewed they wedding vows, maybe they got another family.
LINCOLN: Maybe they got 2 new kids. 2 boys. Different than us, though. Better.
215 BOOTH: Maybe.

Their glasses are empty. The whiskey bottle is empty too. BOOTH *takes the champagne bottle from the ice tub. He pops the cork and pours drinks for his brother and himself.*

BOOTH: I didnt mind them leaving cause you was there. Thats why Im hooked on us working together. If we could work together it would be like old times. They split and we got that room downtown. You was done with school and I stopped going. And we had to run around 220 doing odd jobs just to keep the lights on and the heat going and thuh child protection bitch off our backs. It was you and me against thuh world, Link. It could be like that again.
LINCOLN 225
BOOTH
LINCOLN
BOOTH
LINCOLN: Throwing thuh cards aint as easy as it looks.
BOOTH: I aint stupid. 230
LINCOLN: When you hung with us back then, you was just on thuh sidelines. Thuh perspective from thuh sidelines is thuh perspective of a customer. There was all kinds of things you didnt know nothing about.
BOOTH: Lonny would entice folks into thuh game as they 235 walked by. Thuh 2 folks on either side of ya looked like they was playing but they was only pretending tuh play. Just tuh generate excitement. You was moving thuh cards as fast as you could hoping that yr hands would be faster than yr customers eyes. Sometimes you won sometimes 240 you lost what else is there to know?
LINCOLN: Thuh customer is actually called the "Mark." You know why?
BOOTH: Cause hes thuh one you got yr eye on. You mark him with yr eye. 245
LINCOLN
LINCOLN
BOOTH: Im right, right?
LINCOLN: Lemmie show you a few moves. If you pick up these yll have a chance. 250
BOOTH: Yr playing.
LINCOLN: Get thuh cards and set it up.
BOOTH: No shit.
LINCOLN: Set it up set it up.

In a flash, BOOTH *clears away the romantic table setting by gathering it all up in the tablecloth and tossing it aside. As he does so he reveals the "table" underneath: the 2 stacked monte milk crates and the cardboard playing surface.* LINCOLN *lays out the cards. The brothers are ready.* LINCOLN *begins to teach* BOOTH *in earnest.*

LINCOLN: Thuh deuce of spades is thuh card tuh watch. 255
BOOTH: I work with thuh deuce of hearts. But spades is cool.
LINCOLN: Theres thuh Dealer, thuh Stickman, thuh Sides, thuh Lookout and thuh Mark. I'll be thuh Dealer.
BOOTH: I'll be thuh Lookout. Lemmie be thuh Lookout, right? I'll keep an eye for thuh cops. I got my piece on me. 260
LINCOLN: You got it on you right now?
BOOTH: I always carry it.
LINCOLN: Even on a date? In yr own home?
BOOTH: You never know, man.

(Rest.)

So Im thuh Lookout. 265
LINCOLN: Gimmie yr piece.

BOOTH *gives* LINCOLN *his gun.* LINCOLN *moves the little wooden chair to face right in front of the setup. He then puts the gun on the chair.*

LINCOLN: We dont need nobody standing on the corner watching for cops cause there aint none.

BOOTH: I'll be thuh Stickman, then.

270 LINCOLN: Stickman knows the game inside out. You aint there yet. But you will be. You wanna learn good, be my Sideman. Playing along with the Dealer, moving the Mark to lay his money down. You wanna learn, right?

BOOTH: I'll be thuh Side.

275 LINCOLN: Good.

(*Rest.*)

First thing you learn is what is. Next thing you learn is what aint. You dont know what is you dont know what aint, you dont know shit.

BOOTH: Right.

280 LINCOLN

BOOTH

BOOTH: Whatchu looking at?

LINCOLN: Im sizing you up.

BOOTH: Oh yeah?!

285 LINCOLN: Dealer always sizes up thuh crowd.

BOOTH: Im yr Side, Link, Im on yr team, you dont go sizing up yr own team. You save looks like that for yr Mark.

LINCOLN: Dealer always sizes up thuh crowd. Everybody out there is part of the crowd. His crew is part of the crowd,

290 he himself is part of the crowd. Dealer always sizes up thuh crowd.

LINCOLN *looks* BOOTH *over some more then looks around at an imaginary crowd.*

BOOTH: Then what then what?

LINCOLN: Dealer dont wanna play.

BOOTH: Bullshit man! Come on you promised!

295 LINCOLN: Thats thuh Dealers attitude. He *acts* like he dont wanna play. He holds back and thuh crowd, with their eagerness to see his skill and their willingness to take a chance, and their greediness to win his cash, the larceny in their hearts, all goad him on and push him to throw his

300 cards, although of course the Dealer has been wanting to throw his cards all along. Only he dont never show it.

BOOTH: Thats some sneaky shit, Link.

LINCOLN: It sets thuh mood. You wanna have them in yr hand before you deal a hand, K?

305 BOOTH: Cool.—K.

LINCOLN: Right.

LINCOLN

BOOTH

BOOTH: You sizing me up again?

310 LINCOLN: Theres 2 parts to throwing thuh cards. Both parts are fairly complicated. Thuh moves and thuh grooves, thuh talk and thuh walk, thuh patter and thuh pitter pat, thuh flap and thuh rap: what yr doing with yr mouth and what yr doing with yr hands.

315 BOOTH: I got thuh words down pretty good.

LINCOLN: You need to work on both.

BOOTH: K.

LINCOLN: A goodlooking walk and a dynamite talk captivates their entire attention. The Mark focuses with 2 organs primarily: his eyes and his ears. Leave one out you lose yr 320 shirt. Captivate both, yr golden.

BOOTH: So them times I seen you lose, them times I seen thuh Mark best you, that was a time when yr hands werent fast enough or yr patter werent right.

LINCOLN: You could say that. 325

BOOTH: So, there was plenty of times—

LINCOLN *moves the cards around.*

LINCOLN: You see what Im doing? Dont look at my hands, man, look at my eyes. Know what is and know what aint.

BOOTH: What is?

LINCOLN: My eyes? 330

BOOTH: What aint?

LINCOLN: My hands. Look at my eyes not my hands. And you standing there thinking how thuh fuck I gonna learn how tuh throw thuh cards if I be looking in his eyes? Look into my eyes and get yr focus. Dont think about 335 learning how tuh throw thuh cards. Dont think about nothing. Just look into my eyes. Focus.

BOOTH: Theyre red.

LINCOLN: Look into my eyes.

BOOTH: You been crying? 340

LINCOLN: Just look into my eyes, fool. Now. Look down at thuh cards. I been moving and moving and moving them around. Ready?

BOOTH: Yeah.

LINCOLN: Ok, Sideman, thuh Marks got his eye on you. Yr 345 gonna show him its easy.

BOOTH: K.

LINCOLN: Pick out thuh deuce of spades. Dont pick it up just point to it.

BOOTH: This one, right? 350

LINCOLN: Dont ask thuh Dealer if yr right, man, point to yr card with confidence.

BOOTH *points.*

BOOTH: That one.

(*Rest.*)

Flip it over, man.

LINCOLN *flips over the card. It is in fact the deuce of spades.* BOOTH *struts around gloating like a rooster.* LINCOLN *is mildly crestfallen.*

BOOTH: Am I right or am I right?! Make room for 3-Card! 355 Here comes thuh champ!

LINCOLN: Cool. Stay focused. Now we gonna add the second element. Listen.

LINCOLN *moves the cards and speaks in a low hypnotic voice.*

LINCOLN: Lean in close and watch me now: who see thuh black card who see thuh black card I see thuh black card 360 black cards thuh winner pick thuh black card thats thuh winner pick thuh red card thats thuh loser pick thuh other red card thats thuh other loser pick thuh black card you pick thuh winner. Watch me as I throw thuh cards. Here we go. 365

(*Rest.*)

    Who see thuh black card who see thuh black card? You pick thuh red card you pick a loser you pick that red card you pick a loser you pick thuh black card thuh deuce of spades you pick a winner who sees thuh deuce of spades
370   thuh one who sees it never fades watch me now as I throw thuh cards. Red losers black winner follow thuh deuce of spades chase thuh black deuce. Dark deuce will get you thuh win. One good pickll get you in 2 good picks you gone win. 10 will get you 20, 20 will get you 40.

(*Rest.*)

375   Ima show you thuh cards: 2 red cards but only one spade. Dark winner in thuh center and thuh red losers on thuh sides. Pick uh red card you got a loser pick thuh other red card you got a loser pick thuh black card you got a winner. Watch me watch me watch me now.

(*Rest.*)

380   Ok, 3-Card, you know which cards thuh deuce of spade?

BOOTH: Yeah.

LINCOLN: You sure? Yeah? You sure you sure or you just think you sure? Oh you sure you sure huh? Was you watching
385   Links lighting fast express? Was you watching Link cause he the best? So you sure, huh? Point it out. Now, place yr bet and Linkll turn over yr card.

BOOTH: What should I bet?

LINCOLN: Dont bet nothing man, we just playing. Slap me 5
390   and point out thuh deuce.

BOOTH *slaps* LINCOLN *5, then points out a card which* LINCOLN *flips over. It is in fact again the deuce of spades.*

BOOTH: Yeah, baby! 3-Card got thuh moves! You didnt know lil bro had thuh stuff, huh? Think again, Link, think again.

LINCOLN: You wanna learn or you wanna run yr mouth?

BOOTH: Thought you had fast hands. Wassup? What hap-
395   pened tuh "Links Lightning Fast Express"? Turned into uh local train looks like tuh me.

LINCOLN: Thats yr whole motherfucking problem. Yr so busy running yr mouth you aint never gonna learn noth-ing! You think you something but you aint shit.

400 BOOTH: I aint shit, I am *The* Shit. Shit. Wheres thuh dark deuce? Right there! Yes, baby!

LINCOLN: Ok, 3-Card. Cool. Lets switch. Take thuh cards and show me whatcha got. Go on. Dont touch thuh cards too heavy just—its a light touch. Like yr touching
405   Graces skin. Or, whatever, man, just a light touch. Like uh whisper.

BOOTH: Like uh whisper.

BOOTH *moves the cards around, in an awkward imitation of his brother.*

LINCOLN: Good.

BOOTH: Yeah. All right. Look into my eyes.

BOOTHs *speech is loud and his movements are jerky. He is doing worse than when he threw the cards at the top of the play.*

BOOTH: Watch-me-close-watch-me-close-now: who-see- 410
thuh-dark-card-who-see-thuh-dark-card? I-see-thuh-dark-card. Here-it-is. Thuh-dark-card-is-thuh-winner. Pick-thuh-dark-card-and-you-pick-uh-winner. Pick-uh-red-card-and-you-pick-uh-loser. Theres-thuh-loser-yeah-theres-thuh-red-card, theres-thuh-other-loser-and- 415
theres-thuh-black-card, thuh-winner. Watch-me-close-watch-me-close-now: 3-Card-throws-thuh-cards-light-ning-fast. 3-Card-thats-me-and-Ima-last. Watch-me-throw-cause-here-I-go. See thuh black card? Yeah? Who see I see you see thuh black card? 420

LINCOLN: Hahahahhahahahahahahah!

LINCOLN *doubles over laughing.* BOOTH *puts on his coat and pock-ets the gun.*

BOOTH: What?

LINCOLN: Nothing, man, nothing.

BOOTH: *What?!* 425

LINCOLN: Yr just, yr just a little wild with it. You talk like that on thuh street cards or no cards and theyll lock you up, man. Shit. Reminds me of that time when you hung with us and we let you try being thuh Stick cause you wanted to so bad. Thuh hustle was so simple. Remember? I told 430
you that when I put my hand in my left pocket you was to get thuh Mark tuh pick thuh card on that side. You got to thinking something like Links left means my left some dyslexic shit and turned thuh wrong card. There was 800 bucks on the line and you fucked it up. 435

(*Rest.*)

But it was cool, little bro, cause we made the money back. It worked out cool.

(*Rest.*)

So, yeah, I said a light touch, little bro. Throw thuh cards light. Like uh whisper.

BOOTH: Like Graces skin. 440

LINCOLN: Like Graces skin.

BOOTH: What time is it?

LINCOLN *holds up his watch.* BOOTH *takes a look.*

BOOTH: Bitch. *Bitch!* She said she was gonna show up around 8. 8-a-fucking-clock.

LINCOLN: Maybe she meant 8 *a.m.* 445

BOOTH: Yeah. She gonna come all up in my place talking bout how she *love* me. How she cant stop *thinking* bout me. Nother mans shit up in her nother mans thing in her nother mans dick on her breath.

LINCOLN: Maybe something happened to her. 450

BOOTH: Something happened to her all right. She trying to make a chump outa me. I aint her chump. I aint nobodys chump.

LINCOLN: Sit. I'll go to the payphone on the corner. I'll—

BOOTH: Thuh world puts its foot in yr face and you dont 455
move. You tell thuh world tuh keep on stepping. But Im my own man, Link. I aint you.

BOOTH *goes out, slamming the door behind him.*

LINCOLN: You got that right.

After a moment LINCOLN *picks up the cards. He moves them around fast, faster, faster.*

SCENE SIX

Thursday night. The room looks empty, as if neither brother is home. LINCOLN *comes in. Hes fairly drunk. He strides in, leaving the door slightly ajar.*

LINCOLN: Taaadaaaa!

(Rest.)

(Rest.)

Taadaa, motherfucker. Taadaa!

(Rest.)

Booth—uh, 3-Card—you here? Nope. Good. Just as well. Ha Ha *Ha Ha Ha!*

He pulls an enormous wad of money from his pocket. He counts it, slowly and luxuriously, arranging and smoothing the bills and sounding the amounts under his breath. He neatly rolls up the money, secures it with a rubber band and puts it back in his pocket. He relaxes in his chair. Then he takes the money out again, counting it all over again, but this time quickly, with the touch of an expert hustler.

LINCOLN: You didnt go back, Link, you got back, you got it back you got yr shit back in thuh saddle, man, you got back in business. Walking in Luckys and you seen how they was looking at you? Lucky starts pouring for you
5   when you walk in. And the women. You see how they was looking at you? Bought drinks for everybody. Bought drinks for Lucky. Bought drinks for Luckys damn dog. Shit. And thuh women be hanging on me and purring. And I be feeling that old call of thuh wild calling. I got
10   more phone numbers in my pockets between thuh time I walked out that door and thuh time I walked back in than I got in my whole life. Cause my shit is *back.* And back better than it was when it left too. Shoot. Who thuh man? Link. Thats right. Purrrrring all up on me and letting me
15   touch them and promise them shit. 3 of them sweethearts in thuh restroom on my dick all at once and I was *there* my shit was there. And Cookie just went out of my mind which is cool which is very cool. 3 of them. Fighting over it. Shit. Cause they knew I'd been throwing thuh cards.
20   Theyd seen me on thuh corner with thuh old crew or if they aint seed me with they own eyes theyd heard word. Links thuh stink! Theyd heard word and they seed uh sad face on some poor sucker or a tear in thuh eye of some stupid fucking tourist and they figured it was me whod
25   just took thuh suckers last dime, it was me who had all thuh suckers loot. They knew. They knew.

BOOTH *appears in the room. He is standing behind the screen, unseen all this time. He goes to the door, soundlessly, just stands there.*

LINCOLN: And they was all in Luckys. Shit. And they was waiting for me to come in from my last throw. Cant take too many fools in one day, its bad luck, Link, so they was all waiting in there for me to come in thuh door and let   30 thuh liquor start flowing and thuh music start going and let thuh boys who dont have thuh balls to get nothing but a regular job and uh weekly paycheck, let them crowd around and get in somehow on thuh excitement, and make way for thuh ladies, so they can run they hands on   35 my clothes and feel thuh magic and imagine thuh man, with plenty to go around, living and breathing underneath.

(Rest.)

They all thought I was down and out! They all thought I was some NoCount HasBeen LostCause motherfucker.   40 But I got my shit back. Thats right. They stepped on me and kept right on stepping. Not no more. Who thuh man?! Goddamnit, who thuh—

BOOTH *closes the door.*

LINCOLN
BOOTH   45

(Rest.)

LINCOLN: Another evening to remember, huh?
BOOTH

(Rest.)

Uh—yeah, man, yeah. Thats right, thats right.
LINCOLN: Had me a memorable evening myself.
BOOTH: I got news.   50

(Rest.)

What you been up to?
LINCOLN: Yr news first.
BOOTH: Its good.
LINCOLN: Yeah?
BOOTH: Yeah.   55
LINCOLN: Go head then.
BOOTH

(Rest.)

Grace got down on her knees. Down on her knees, man. Asked *me* tuh marry *her.*
LINCOLN: Shit.   60
BOOTH: Amazing Grace!
LINCOLN: Lucky you, man.
BOOTH: And guess where she was, I mean, while I was here waiting for her. She was over at her house watching tv. I'd told her come over Thursday and I got it all wrong and   65 was thinking I said Wednesday and here I was sitting waiting my ass off and all she was doing was over at her house just watching tv.
LINCOLN: Howboutthat.
BOOTH: She wants to get married right away. Shes tired of   70 waiting. Feels her clock ticking and shit. Wants to have a

baby. But dont look so glum man, we gonna have a boy
and we gonna name it after you.
LINCOLN: Thats great, man. Thats really great.
75 BOOTH
LINCOLN
BOOTH: Whats yr news?
LINCOLN

(*Rest.*)

Nothing.
80 BOOTH: Mines good news, huh?
LINCOLN: Yeah. Real good news, bro.
BOOTH: Bad news is—well, shes real set on us living together.
And she always did like this place.

(*Rest.*)

Yr gonna have to leave. Sorry.
85 LINCOLN: No sweat.
BOOTH: This was only a temporary situation anyhow.
LINCOLN: No sweat man. You got a new life opening up for
you, no sweat. Graces moving in today? I can leave right
now.
90 BOOTH: I dont mean to put you out.
LINCOLN: No sweat. I'll just pack up.

LINCOLN *rummages around finding a suitcase and begins to pack his
things.*

BOOTH: Just like that, huh? "No sweat"?! Yesterday you lost yr
damn job. You dont got no cash. You dont got no friends,
no nothing, but you clearing out just like that and its "no
95   sweat"?!
LINCOLN: Youve been real generous and you and Grace need
me gone and its time I found my own place.
BOOTH: No sweat.
LINCOLN: No sweat.

(*Rest.*)

100   K. I'll spill it. I got another job, so getting my own place
aint gonna be so bad.
BOOTH: You got a new job! Doing what?
LINCOLN: Security guard.
BOOTH

(*Rest.*)

105   Security guard. Howaboutthat.

LINCOLN *continues packing a few things he has. He picks up a
whiskey bottle.*

BOOTH: Go head, take thuh med-sin, bro. You gonna need it
more than me. I got, you know, I got my love to keep me
warm and shit.
LINCOLN: You gonna have to get some kind of work, or are
110   you gonna let Grace support you?
BOOTH: I got plans.
LINCOLN: She might want you now but she wont want you
for long if you dont get some kind of job. Shes a smart
chick. And she cares about you. But she aint gonna let you

treat her like some pack mule while shes out working her   115
ass off and yr laying up in here scheming and dreaming to
cover up thuh fact that you dont got no skills.
BOOTH: Grace is very cool with who I am and where Im at,
thank you.
LINCOLN: It was just some advice. But, hey, yr doing great just   120
like yr doing.
LINCOLN
BOOTH
LINCOLN
BOOTH   125
BOOTH: When Pops left he didnt take nothing with him. I al-
ways thought that was fucked-up.
LINCOLN: He was a drunk. Everything he did was always half
regular and half fucked-up.
BOOTH: Whyd he leave his clothes though? Even drunks   130
gotta wear clothes.
LINCOLN: Whyd he leave his clothes whyd he leave us? He
was uh drunk, bro. He—whatever, right? I mean, you aint
gonna figure it out by thinking about it. Just call it one of
thuh great unsolved mysteries of existence.   135
BOOTH: Moms had a man on thuh side.
LINCOLN: Yeah? Pops had side shit going on too. More than
one. He would take me with him when he went to visit
them. Yeah.

(*Rest.*)

Sometimes he'd let me meet the ladies. They was all very   140
nice. Very polite. Most of them real pretty. Sometimes
he'd let me watch. Most of thuh time I was just outside on
thuh porch or in thuh lobby or in thuh car waiting for
him but sometimes he'd let me watch.
BOOTH: What was it like?   145
LINCOLN: Nothing. It wasnt like nothing. He made it seem
like it was this big deal this great thing he was letting me
witness but it wasnt like nothing.

(*Rest.*)

One of his ladies liked me, so I would do her after he'd
done her. On thuh sly though. He'd be laying there, spent   150
and sleeping and snoring and her and me would be sneak-
ing it.
BOOTH: Shit.
LINCOLN: It was alright.
BOOTH   155
LINCOLN

LINCOLN *takes his crumpled Abe Lincoln getup from the closet. Isnt
sure what to do with it.*

BOOTH: Im gonna miss you coming home in that getup. I
dont even got a picture of you in it for the album.
LINCOLN

(*Rest.*)

Hell, I'll put it on. Get thuh camera get thuh camera.   160
BOOTH: Yeah?
LINCOLN: What thuh fuck, right?
BOOTH: Yeah, what thuh fuck.

BOOTH *scrambles around the apartment and finds the camera.* LIN-
COLN *quickly puts on the getup, including 2 thin smears of white
pancake makeup, more like war paint than whiteface.*

LINCOLN: They didnt fire me cause I wasnt no good. They
165   fired me cause they was cutting back. Me getting dis-
missed didnt have no reflection on my performance. And
I was a damn good Honest Abe considering.
BOOTH: Yeah. You look great man, really great. Fix yr hat.
Get in thuh light. Smile.
170   LINCOLN: Lincoln didnt never smile.
BOOTH: Sure he smiled.
LINCOLN: No he didnt, man, you seen thuh pictures of him.
In all his pictures he was real serious.
BOOTH: You got a new job, yr having a good day, right?
175   LINCOLN: Yeah.
BOOTH: So smile.
LINCOLN: Snapshots gonna look pretty stupid with me—

BOOTH *takes a picture.*

BOOTH: Thisll look great in thuh album.
LINCOLN: Lets take one together, you and me.
180   BOOTH: No thanks. Save the film for the wedding.
LINCOLN: This wasnt a bad job. I just outgrew it. I could put
in a word for you down there, maybe when business picks
up again theyd hire you.
BOOTH: No thanks. That shit aint for me. I aint into pre-
185   tending Im someone else all day.
LINCOLN: I was just sitting there in thuh getup. I wasnt pre-
tending nothing.
BOOTH: What was going on in yr head?
LINCOLN: I would make up songs and shit.
190   BOOTH: And think about women.
LINCOLN: Sometimes.
BOOTH: Cookie.
LINCOLN: Sometimes.
BOOTH: And how she came over here one night looking for
195   you.
LINCOLN: I was at Luckys.
BOOTH: She didnt know that.
LINCOLN: I was drinking.
BOOTH: All she knew was you couldnt get it up. You couldnt
200   get it up with her so in her head you was tired of her and
had gone out to screw somebody new and this time
maybe werent never coming back.

(*Rest.*)

She had me pour her a drink or 2. I didnt want to. She
wanted to get back at you by having some fun of her own
205   and when I told her to go out and have it, she said she
wanted to have her fun right here. With me.

(*Rest.*)

[And then, just like that, she changed her mind.

(*Rest.*)

But she'd hooked me. That bad part of me that I fight
down everyday. You beat yrs down and its stays there dead

but mine keeps coming up for another round. And she   210
hooked the bad part of me. And the bad part of me
opened my mouth and started promising her things.
Promising her things I knew she wanted and you couldnt
give her. And the bad part of me took her clothing off and
carried her into thuh bed and had her, Link, yr Cookie. It   215
wasnt just thuh bad part of me it was all of me, man,] I
had her. Yr damn wife. Right in that bed.
LINCOLN: I used to think about her all thuh time but I dont
think about her no more.
BOOTH: I told her if she dumped you I'd marry her but I   220
changed my mind.
LINCOLN: I dont think about her no more.
BOOTH: You dont go back.
LINCOLN: Nope.
BOOTH: Cause you cant. No matter what you do you cant get   225
back to being who you was. Best you can do is just pre-
tend to be yr old self.
LINCOLN: Yr outa yr mind.
BOOTH: Least Im still me!
LINCOLN: Least I work. You never did like to work. You bet-   230
ter come up with some kinda way to bring home the ba-
con or Gracell drop you like a hot rock.
BOOTH: I got plans!
LINCOLN: Yeah, you gonna throw thuh cards, right?
BOOTH: Thats right!   235
LINCOLN: You a double left-handed motherfucker who dont
stand a chance in all get out out there throwing no cards.
BOOTH: You scared.
LINCOLN: Im gone.

LINCOLN *goes to leave.*

BOOTH: Fuck that!   240
LINCOLN: Yr standing in my way.
BOOTH: You scared I got yr shit.
LINCOLN: The only part of my shit you got is the part of my
shit you think you got and that aint shit.
BOOTH: Did I pick right them last times? Yes. Oh, I got yr   245
shit.
LINCOLN: Set up the cards.
BOOTH: Thought you was gone.
LINCOLN: Set it up.
BOOTH: I got yr shit and Ima go out there and be thuh man   250
and you aint gonna be nothing.
LINCOLN: Set it up!

BOOTH *hurriedly sets up the milk crates and cardboard top.* LIN-
COLN *throws the cards.*

LINCOLN: Lean in close and watch me now: who see thuh
black card who see thuh black card I see thuh black card
black cards thuh winner pick thuh black card thats thuh   255
winner pick thuh red card thats thuh loser pick thuh
other red card thats thuh other loser pick thuh black card
you pick thuh winner. Who see thuh black card who see
thuh black card? You pick thuh red card you pick a loser
you pick that red card you pick a loser you pick thuh   260
black card thuh deuce of spades you pick a winner who
sees thuh deuce of spades thuh one who sees it never fades
watch me now as I throw thuh cards. Red losers black
winner follow thuh deuce of spades chase thuh black

265 deuce. Dark deuce will get you thuh win. 10 will get you
20, 20 will get you 40. One good pickll get you in 2 good
picks and you gone win.

(*Rest.*)

Ok, man, wheres thuh black deuce?

BOOTH *points to a card.* LINCOLN *flips it over. It is the deuce of
spades.*

BOOTH: Who thuh man?!

LINCOLN *turns over the other 2 cards, looking at them confusedly.*

270 LINCOLN: Hhhhh.
BOOTH: Who thuh man, Link?! Huh? Who thuh man,
Link?!?!
LINCOLN: You thuh man, man.
BOOTH: I got yr shit down.
275 LINCOLN: Right.
BOOTH: "Right"? All you saying is "right"?

(*Rest.*)

You was out on the street throwing. Just today. Werent
you? You wasnt gonna tell me.
LINCOLN: Tell you what?
280 BOOTH: That you was out throwing.
LINCOLN: I was gonna tell you, sure. Cant go and leave my
little bro out thuh loop, can I? Didnt say nothing cause I
thought you heard. Did all right today but Im still rusty, I
guess. But hey—yr getting good.
285 BOOTH: But I'll get out there on thuh street and still fuck up,
wont I?
LINCOLN: You seem pretty good, bro.
BOOTH: You gotta do it for real, man.
LINCOLN: I am doing it for real. And yr getting good.
290 BOOTH: I dunno. It didnt feel real. Kinda felt—well it didnt
feel real.
LINCOLN: We're missing the essential elements. The crowd,
the street, thuh traffic sounds, all that.
BOOTH: We missing something else too, thuh thing thatll re-
295 ally make it real.
LINCOLN: Whassat, bro?
BOOTH: Thuh cash. Its just bullshit without thuh money. Put
some money down on thuh table then itd be real, then
youd do it for real, then I'd win it for real.

(*Rest.*)

300 And dont be looking all glum like that. I know you got
money. A whole pocketful. Put it down.
LINCOLN
BOOTH
BOOTH: You scared of losing it to thuh man, chump? Put it
305 down, less you think thuh kid who got two left hands is
gonna give you uh left hook. Put it down, bro, put it down.

LINCOLN *takes the roll of bills from his pocket and places it on the
table.*

BOOTH: How much you got there?

LINCOLN: 500 bucks.
BOOTH: Cool.

(*Rest.*)

Ready?   310
LINCOLN: Does it feel real?
BOOTH: Yeah. Clean slate. Take it from the top. "One good
pickll get you in 2 good picks and you gone win."

(*Rest.*)

Go head.
LINCOLN: Watch me now: 315
BOOTH: Woah, man, woah.

(*Rest.*)

You think Ima chump.
LINCOLN: No I dont.
BOOTH: You aint going full out.
LINCOLN: I was just getting started.   320
BOOTH: But when you got good and started you wasnt
gonna go full out. You wasnt gonna go all out. You was
gonna do thuh pussy shit, not thuh real shit.
LINCOLN: I put my money down. Money makes it real.
BOOTH: But not if I dont put no money down tuh match it. 325
LINCOLN: You dont got no money.
BOOTH: I got money!
LINCOLN: You aint worked in years. You dont got shit.
BOOTH: I got money.
LINCOLN: Whatcha been doing, skimming off my weekly 330
paycheck and squirreling it away?
BOOTH: I got money.

(*Rest.*)

They stand there sizing eachother up. BOOTH *breaks away, going
over to his hiding place from which he gets an old nylon stocking
with money in the toe, a knot holding the money secure.*

LINCOLN
BOOTH
BOOTH: You know she was putting her stuff in plastic bags? 335
She was just putting her stuff in plastic bags not putting but
shoving. She was shoving her stuff in plastic bags and I was
standing in thuh doorway watching her and she was so
busy shoving thuh shit she didnt see me. "I aint made of
money," thats what he always saying. The guy she had on 340
the side. I would catch them together sometimes. Thuh
first time I cut school I got tired of hanging out so I goes
home—figured I could tell Mom I was sick and cover my
ass. Come in thuh house real slow cause Im sick and moving slow and quiet. He had her bent over. They both had 345
all they clothes on like they was about to do something like
go out dancing cause they was dressed to thuh 9s but at
thuh last minute his pants had fallen down and her dress
had flown up and theyd ended up doing something else.

(*Rest.*)

They didnt see me come in, they didnt see me watching 350
them, they didnt see me going out. That was uh Thurs-

day. Something told me tuh cut school thuh next Thursday and sure enough.—He was her Thursday man. Every Thursday. Yeah. And Thursday nights she was always all
355 cleaned up and fresh and smelling nice. Serving up dinner. And Pops would grab her cause she was all bright and she would look at me, like she didnt know that I knew but she was asking me not to tell nohow. She was asking me to— oh who knows.

(*Rest.*)

360 She was talking with him one day, her sideman, her Thursday dude, her backdoor man, she needed some money for something, thered been some kind of problem some kind of mistake had been made some kind of mistake that
365 needed cleaning up and she was asking Mr. Thursday for some money to take care of it. "I aint made of money," he says. He was putting his foot down. And then there she was 2 months later not showing yet, maybe she'd got rid of it maybe she hadnt maybe she'd stuffed it along with all her other things in them plastic bags while he waited out-
370 side in thuh car with thuh motor running. She musta known I was gonna walk in on her this time cause she had my payoff—my *inheritance*—she had it all ready for me. 500 dollars in a nylon stocking. Huh.

He places the stuffed nylon stocking on the table across from LIN-COLNs *money roll.*

BOOTH: Now its real.
375 LINCOLN: Dont put that down.
BOOTH: Throw thuh cards.
LINCOLN: I dont want to play.
BOOTH: Throw thuh fucking cards, man!!
LINCOLN

(*Rest.*)

380 2 red cards but only one black. Pick thuh black you pick thuh winner. All thuh cards are face down you point out thuh cards and then you move them around. Now watch me now, now watch me real close. Put thuh winning deuce down in the center put thuh loser reds on either
385 side then you just move thuh cards around. Move them slow or move them fast, Links thuh king he gonna last.

(*Rest.*)

Wheres thuh deuce of spades?

BOOTH *chooses a card and chooses correctly.*

BOOTH: HA!
LINCOLN: One good pickll get you in 2 good picks and you
390 gone win.
BOOTH: I know man I know.
LINCOLN: Im just doing thuh talk.
BOOTH: Throw thuh fucking cards!

LINCOLN *throws the cards.*

LINCOLN: Lean in close and watch me now: who see thuh
395 black card who see thuh black card I see thuh black card

black cards thuh winner pick thuh black card thats thuh winner pick thuh red card thats thuh loser pick thuh other red card thats thuh other loser pick thuh black card you pick thuh winner. Watch me as I throw thuh cards. Here we go.
400

(*Rest.*)

Ima show you thuh cards: 2 red cards but only one spade. Dark winner in thuh center and thuh red losers on thuh sides. Pick up red card you got a loser pick thuh other red card you got a loser pick thuh black card you got a win-
405 ner. Watch me watch me watch me now.

(*Rest.*)

Who see thuh black card who see thuh black card? You pick thuh red card you pick a loser you pick that red card you pick a loser you pick thuh black card thuh deuce of spades you pick a winner who sees thuh deuce of spades
410 thuh one who sees it never fades watch me now as I throw thuh cards. Red losers black winner follow thuh deuce of spades chase thuh black deuce. Dark deuce will get you thuh win.

(*Rest.*)

Ok, 3-Card, you know which cards thuh deuce of spades? This is for real now, man. You pick wrong Im in yr wad
415 and I keep mines.
BOOTH: I pick right I got yr shit.
LINCOLN: Yeah.
BOOTH: Plus I beat you for real.
LINCOLN: Yeah.
420

(*Rest.*)

You think we're really brothers?
BOOTH: Huh?
LINCOLN: I know we *brothers,* but is we really brothers, you know, blood brothers or not, you and me, whatduhya-
think?
425
BOOTH: I think we're brothers.
BOOTH
LINCOLN
BOOTH
LINCOLN
430
BOOTH
LINCOLN
LINCOLN: Go head man, wheres thuh deuce?

In a flash BOOTH *points out a card.*

LINCOLN: You sure?
BOOTH: Im sure!
435
LINCOLN: Yeah? Dont touch thuh cards, now.
BOOTH: Im sure.

The 2 brothers lock eyes. LINCOLN *turns over the card that* BOOTH *selected and* BOOTH, *in a desperate break of concentration, glances down to see that he has chosen the wrong card.*

LINCOLN: Deuce of hearts, bro. Im sorry. Thuh deuce of spades was this one.

(Rest.)

440   I guess all this is mines.

He slides the money toward himself.

LINCOLN: You were almost right. Better luck next time.

(Rest.)

Aint yr fault if yr eyes aint fast. And you cant help it if you got 2 left hands, right? Throwing cards aint thuh whole world. You got other shit going for you. You got Grace.

445   BOOTH: Right.
LINCOLN: Whassamatter?
BOOTH: Mm.
LINCOLN: Whatsup?
BOOTH: Nothing.
450   LINCOLN

(Rest.)

It takes a certain kind of understanding to be able to play this game.

(Rest.)

I still got thuh moves, dont I?
BOOTH: Yeah you still got thuh moves.

LINCOLN *cant help himself. He chuckles.*

455   LINCOLN: I aint laughing at you, bro, Im just laughing. Shit there is so much to this game. This game is—there is just so much to it.

LINCOLN, *still chuckling, flops down in the easy chair. He takes up the nylon stocking and fiddles with the knot.*

LINCOLN: Woah, she sure did tie this up tight, didnt she?
BOOTH: Yeah. I aint opened it since she gived it to me.
460   LINCOLN: Yr kidding. 500 and you aint never opened it? Shit. Sure is tied tight. She said heres 500 bucks and you didnt undo thuh knot to get a look at the cash? You aint needed to take a peek in all these years? Shit. I woulda opened it right away. Just a little peek.
465   BOOTH: I been saving it.

(Rest.)

Oh, dont open it, man.
LINCOLN: How come?
BOOTH: You won it man, you dont gotta go opening it.
LINCOLN: We gotta see whats in it.
470   BOOTH: We *know* whats in it. Dont open it.
LINCOLN: You are a chump, bro. There could be millions in here! There could be nothing! I'll open it.
BOOTH: Dont.
LINCOLN
475   BOOTH

(Rest.)

LINCOLN: Shit this knot aint coming out. I could cut it, but that would spoil the whole effect, wouldnt it? Shit. Sorry.

I aint laughing at you Im just laughing. Theres so much about those cards. You think you can learn them just by watching and just by playing but there is more to them 480 cards than that. And—. Tell me something, Mr. 3-Card, she handed you this stocking and she said there was money in it and then she split and you say you didnt open it. Howd you know she was for real?
BOOTH: She was for real.   485
LINCOLN: How you know. She coulda been jiving you, bro. Jiving you that there really *was* money in this thing. Jiving you big time. Its like thuh cards. And ooooh you certainly was persistent. But you was in such a hurry to learn thuh last move that you didnt bother learning thuh first one. 490 That was yr mistake. Cause its thuh first move that separates thuh Player from thuh Played. And thuh first move is to know that there aint no winning. It may look like you got a chance but the only time you pick right is when thuh man lets you. And when its thuh real deal, when its 495 thuh real fucking deal, bro, and thuh moneys on thuh line, thats when thuh man wont want you picking right. He will want you picking wrong so he will make you pick wrong. Wrong wrong wrong. Ooooh, you thought you was finally happening, didnt you? You thought yr ship had 500 come in or some shit, huh? Thought you was uh Player. But I played you, bro.
BOOTH: Fuck you. Fuck you FUCK YOU *FUCK YOU*!!
LINCOLN: Whatever, man. Damn this knot is tough. Ima cut it.

LINCOLN *reaches in his boot, pulling out a knife. He chuckles all the while.*

LINCOLN: Im not laughing at you, bro, Im just laughing.   505

BOOTH *chuckles with him.* LINCOLN *holds the knife high, ready to cut the stocking.*

LINCOLN: Turn yr head. You may not wanna look.

BOOTH *turns away slightly. They both continue laughing.* LINCOLN *brings the knife down to cut the stocking.*

BOOTH: I popped her.
LINCOLN: Huh?
BOOTH: Grace. I popped her. Grace.

(Rest.)

Who thuh fuck she think she is doing me like she done?   510
Telling me I dont got nothing going on. I showed her what I got going on. Popped her good. Twice. 3 times. Whatever.

(Rest.)

She aint dead.

(Rest.)

She werent wearing my ring I gived her. Said it was too   515
small. Fuck that. Said it hurt her. Fuck that. Said she was into bigger things. *Fuck* that. Shes alive not to worry, she aint going out that easy, shes alive shes shes—
LINCOLN: Dead. Shes—

520   BOOTH: Dead.

LINCOLN: Ima give you back yr stocking, man. Here, bro—

BOOTH: Only so long I can stand that little brother shit. Can only take it so long. Im telling you—

LINCOLN: Take it back, man—

525   BOOTH: That little bro shit had to go—

LINCOLN: Cool—

BOOTH: Like Booth went—

LINCOLN: Here, 3-Card—

BOOTH: That Booth shit is over. 3-Cards thuh man now—

530   LINCOLN: Ima give you yr stocking back, 3-Card—

BOOTH: Who thuh man now, huh? Who thuh man now?! Think you can fuck with me, motherfucker think again motherfucker think again! Think you can take me like Im just some chump some two lefthanded pussy dickbreath
535   chump who you can take and then go laugh at. Aint laughing at me you was just laughing bunch uh bullshit and you know it.

LINCOLN: Here. Take it.

BOOTH: I aint gonna be needing it. Go on. You won it you
540   open it.

LINCOLN: No thanks.

BOOTH: Open it open it open it open it. *OPEN IT!!!*

(*Rest.*)

Open it up, bro.

LINCOLN

545   BOOTH

LINCOLN *brings the knife down to cut the stocking. In a flash,* BOOTH *grabs* LINCOLN *from behind. He pulls his gun and thrusts it into the left side of* LINCOLNs *neck. They stop there poised.*

LINCOLN: Dont.

BOOTH *shoots* LINCOLN. LINCOLN *slumps forward, falling out of his chair and onto the floor. He lies there dead.* BOOTH *paces back and forth, like a panther in a cage, holding his gun.*

BOOTH: Think you can take my shit? My shit. That shit was mines. I kept it. Saved it. All this while. Through thick and through thin. Through fucking thick and through fucking thin, motherfucker. And you just gonna come up   550 in here and mock my shit and call me two lefthanded talking bout how she coulda been jiving me then go steal from me? My *inheritance.* You stole my *inheritance,* man. That aint right. That aint right and you know it. You had yr own. And you blew it. You *blew it,* motherfucker! I   555 saved mines and you blew yrs. Thinking you all that and blew yr shit. And I *saved* mines.

(*Rest.*)

You aint gonna be needing yr fucking money-roll no more, dead motherfucker, so I will pocket it thank you.

(*Rest.*)

Watch me close watch me close now: Ima go out there   560 and make a name for myself that dont have nothing to do with you. And 3-Cards gonna be in everybodys head and in everybodys mouth like Link was.

(*Rest.*)

Ima take back my inheritance too. It was mines anyhow. Even when you stole it from me it was still mines cause   565 she gave it to me. She didnt give it to you. And I been saving it all this while.

He bends to pick up the money-filled stocking. Then he just crumples. As he sits beside LINCOLNs *body, the money-stocking falls away.* BOOTH *holds* LINCOLNs *body, hugging him close. He sobs.*

BOOTH: *AAAAAAAAAAAAAAAAAAAH!*

END OF PLAY

CRITICAL CONTEXTS

ARTHUR MILLER
from "Tragedy and the Common Man" (1949)

Arthur Miller wrote this essay for the New York Times *shortly after the opening of* Death of a Salesman. *In the essay, Miller develops a reading of the tragic hero that both contests and modifies Aristotle's description of the form and style of tragic drama. He also identifies his own presiding interests in the dynamics of tragic character. How important is it to Miller to be able to retain Aristotle's categories? Why? How do the different social, political, and cultural circumstances of Greek tragedy force Miller to redefine Aristotle's understanding of the function, purpose, and meaning of tragedy, particularly his understanding of tragic "character"?*

In this age few tragedies are written. It has often been held that the lack is due to a paucity of heroes among us, or else that modern man has had the blood drawn out of his organs of belief by the skepticism of science, and the heroic attack on life cannot feed on an attitude of reserve and circumspection. For one reason or another, we are often held to be below tragedy—or tragedy above us. The inevitable conclusion is, of course, that the tragic mode is archaic, fit only for the very highly placed, the kings or the kingly, and where this admission is not made in so many words it is most often implied.

I believe that the common man is as apt a subject for tragedy in its highest sense as kings were. On the face of it this ought to be obvious in the light of modern psychiatry, which bases its analysis upon classic formulations, such as the Oedipus and Orestes complexes, for instances, which were enacted by royal beings, but which apply to everyone in similar emotional situations.

More simply, when the question of tragedy in art is not at issue, we never hesitate to attribute to the well-placed and the exalted the very same mental processes as the lowly. And finally, if the exaltation of tragic action were truly a property of the high-bred character alone, it is inconceivable that the mass of mankind should cherish tragedy above all other forms, let alone be capable of understanding it.

As a general rule, to which there may be exceptions unknown to me, I think the tragic feeling is evoked in us when we are in the presence of a character who is ready to lay down his life, if need be, to secure one thing—his sense of personal dignity. From Orestes to Hamlet, Medea to Macbeth, the underlying struggle is that of the individual attempting to gain his "rightful" position in his society.

Sometimes he is one who has been displaced from it, sometimes one who seeks to attain it for the first time, but the fateful wound from which the inevitable events spiral is the wound of indignity, and its dominant force is indignation. Tragedy, then, is the consequence of a man's total compulsion to evaluate himself justly.

In the sense of having been initiated by the hero himself, the tale always reveals what has been called his "tragic flaw," a failing that is not peculiar to grand or elevated characters. Nor is it necessarily a weakness. The flaw, or crack in the character, is really nothing—and need be nothing—but his inherent unwillingness to remain passive in the face of what he conceives to be a challenge to his dignity, his image of his rightful status. Only the passive, only those who accept their lot without active retaliation, are "flawless." Most of us are in that category.

But there are among us today, as there always have been, those who act against the scheme of things that degrades them, and in the process of action everything we have accepted out of fear or insensitivity or ignorance is shaken before us and examined, and from this total onslaught by an individual against the seemingly stable cosmos surrounding us—from this total examination of the "unchangeable" environment—comes the terror and the fear that is classically associated with tragedy.

More important, from this total questioning of what has previously been unquestioned, we learn. And such a process is not beyond the common man. In revolutions around the world, these past thirty years, he has demonstrated again and again this inner dynamic of all tragedy.

Insistence upon the rank of the tragic hero, or the so-called nobility of his character, is really but a clinging to the outward forms of tragedy. If rank or nobility of character was indispensable, then it would follow that the problems of those with rank were the particular problems of tragedy. But surely the right of one monarch to capture the domain from another no longer raises our passions, nor are our concepts of justice what they were to the mind of an Elizabethan king.

The quality in such plays that does shake us, however, derives from the underlying fear of being displaced, the disaster inherent in being torn away from our chosen image of what and who we are in this world. Among us today this fear is as strong, and perhaps stronger, than it ever was. In fact, it is the common man who knows this fear best.

Now, if it is true that tragedy is the consequence of a man's total compulsion to evaluate himself justly, his destruction in the attempt posits a wrong or an evil in his environment. And this is precisely the morality of tragedy and its lesson. The discovery of the moral law, which is what the enlightenment of tragedy consists of, is not the discovery of some abstract or metaphysical quantity.

The tragic right is a condition of life, a condition in which the human personality is able to flower and realize itself. The wrong is the condition which suppresses man, perverts the flowing out of his love and creative instinct. Tragedy enlightens—and it must, in that it points the heroic finger at the enemy of man's freedom. The thrust for freedom is the quality in tragedy which exalts. The revolutionary questioning of the stable environment is what terrifies. In no way is the common man debarred from such thoughts or such actions.

Seen in this light, our lack of tragedy may be partially accounted for by the turn which modern literature has taken toward the purely psychiatric view of life, or the purely sociological. If all our miseries, our indignities, are born and bred within our minds, then all action, let alone the heroic action, is obviously impossible.

And if society alone is responsible for the cramping of our lives, then the protagonist must needs be so pure and faultless as to force us to deny his validity as a character. From neither of these views can tragedy derive, simply because neither represents a balanced concept of life. Above all else, tragedy requires the finest appreciation by the writer of cause and effect.

No tragedy can therefore come about when its author fears to question absolutely everything, when he regards any institution, habit or custom as being either everlasting, immutable or inevitable. In the tragic view the need of man to wholly realize himself is the only fixed star, and whatever it is that hedges his nature and lowers it is ripe for attack and examination. Which is not to say that tragedy must preach revolution.

The Greeks could probe the very heavenly origin of their ways and return to confirm the rightness of laws. And Job could face God in anger, demanding his right and end in submission. But for a moment everything is in suspension, nothing is accepted, and in this stretching and tearing apart of the cosmos, in the very action of so doing, the character gains "size," the tragic stature which is spuriously attached to the royal or the highborn in our minds. The commonest of men may take on that stature to the extent of his willingness to throw all he has into the contest, the battle to secure his rightful place in his world.

There is a misconception of tragedy with which I have been struck in review after review, and in many conversations with writers and readers alike. It is the idea that tragedy is of necessity allied to pessimism. Even the dictionary says nothing more about the word than that it means a story with a sad or unhappy ending. This impression is so firmly fixed that I almost hesitate to claim that in truth tragedy implies more optimism in its author than does comedy, and that its final result ought to be the reinforcement of the onlooker's brightest opinions of the human animal.

For, if it is true to say that in essence the tragic hero is intent upon claiming his whole due as a personality, and if this struggle must be total and without reservation, then it automatically demonstrates the indestructible will of man to achieve his humanity.

The possibility of victory must be there in tragedy. Where pathos rules, where pathos is finally derived, a character has fought a battle he could not possibly have won. The pathetic is achieved when the protagonist is, by virtue of his witlessness, his insensitivity or the very air he gives off, incapable of grappling with a much superior force.

Pathos truly is the mode for the pessimist. But tragedy requires a nicer balance between what is possible and what is impossible. And it is curious, although edifying, that the plays we revere, century after century, are the tragedies. In them, and in them alone, lies the belief—optimistic, if you will, in the perfectibility of man.

It is time, I think, that we who are without kings, took up this bright thread of our history and followed it to the only place it can possibly lead in our time—the heart and spirit of the average man.

AMIRI BARAKA / LEROI JONES
from "The Revolutionary Theatre" (1966)

In "The Revolutionary Theatre," Amiri Baraka describes the challenges posed by an emerging African-American theater. How does Baraka's understanding of the necessity of "revolution"—what does Baraka mean by "revolution"—sustain his sense of what theater can and should do?

The Revolutionary Theatre should force change; it should be change. (All their faces turned into the lights and you work on them black nigger magic, and cleanse them at having seen the ugliness. And if the beautiful see themselves, they will love themselves.) We are preaching virtue again, but by that to mean NOW, toward what seems the most constructive use of the world.

The Revolutionary Theatre must EXPOSE! Show up the insides of these humans, look into black skulls. White men will cower before this theatre because it hates them. Because they themselves have been trained to hate. The Revolutionary Theatre must hate them for hating. For presuming with their technology to deny the supremacy of the Spirit. They will all die because of this.

The Revolutionary Theatre must teach them their deaths. It must crack their faces open to the mad cries of the poor. It must teach them about silence and the truths lodged there. It must kill any God anyone names except Common Sense. The Revolutionary Theatre should flush the fags and murderers out of Lincoln's face.

It should stagger through our universe correcting, insulting, preaching, spitting craziness—but a craziness taught to us in our most rational moments. People must be taught to trust true scientists (knowers, diggers, oddballs) and that the holiness of life is the constant possibility of widening the consciousness. And they must be incited to strike back against any agency that attempts to prevent this widening.

The Revolutionary Theatre must Accuse and Attack anything that can be accused and attacked. It must Accuse and Attack because it is a theatre of Victims. It looks at the sky with the victims' eyes, and moves the victims to look at the strength in their minds and their bodies.

Clay in *Dutchman,* Ray in *The Toilet,* Walker in *The Slave,* are all victims. In the Western sense they could be heroes. But the Revolutionary Theatre, even if it is Western, must be anti-Western. It must show horrible coming attractions of The Crumbling of the West. Even as Artaud designed *The Conquest of Mexico,* so we must design *The Conquest of White Eye,* and show the missionaries and wiggly liberals dying under blasts of concrete. For sound effects, wild screams of joy, from all the peoples of the world.

The Revolutionary Theatre must take dreams and give them a reality. It must isolate the ritual and historical cycles of reality. But it must be food for all those who need food, and daring propaganda for the beauty of the Human Mind. It is a political theatre, a weapon to help in the slaughter of these dimwitted fatbellied white guys who somehow believe that the rest of the world is here for them to slobber on.

This should be a theatre of World Spirit. Where the spirit can be shown to be the most competent force in the world. Force. Spirit. Feeling. The language will be anybody's, but tightened by the poet's backbone. And even the language must show what the facts are in this consciousness epic, what's happening. We will talk about the world, and the preciseness with which we are able to summon the world will be our art. Art is method. And art, "like any ashtray or senator," remains in the world. Wittgenstein said ethics and aesthetics are one. I believe this. So the Broadway theatre is a theatre of reaction whose ethics, like its aesthetics, reflect the spiritual values of this unholy society, which sends young crackers all over the world blowing off colored people's heads. (In some of these flippy Southern towns they even shoot up the immigrants' Favorite Son, be it Michael Schwerner or JFKennedy.)

The Revolutionary Theatre is shaped by the world, and moves to reshape the world, using as its force the natural force and perpetual vibrations of the mind in the world. We are history and desire, what we are, and what any experience can make us.

It is a social theatre, but all theatre is social theatre. But we will change the drawing rooms into places where real things can be said about a real world, or into smoky rooms where the destruction of Washington can be plotted. The Revolutionary Theatre must function like an incendiary pencil planted in Curtis Lemay's cap. So that when the final curtain goes down brains are splattered over the seats and the floor, and bleeding nuns must wire SOS's to Belgians with gold teeth.

Our theatre will show victims so that their brothers in the audience will be better able to understand that they are the brothers of victims, and that they themselves are victims if they are blood brothers. And what we show must cause the blood to rush, so that pre-revolutionary temperaments will be bathed in this blood, and it will cause their deepest souls to move, and they will find themselves tensed and clenched, even ready to die, at what the soul has been taught. We will scream and cry, murder, run through the streets in agony, if it means some soul will be moved, moved to actual life understanding of what the world is, and what it ought to be. We are preaching virtue and feeling, and a natural sense of the self in the world. All men live in the world, and the world ought to be a place for them to live.

What is called the imagination (from image, magi, magic, magician, etc.) is a practical vector from the soul. It stores all data, and can be called on to solve all our "problems." The imagination is the projection of ourselves past our sense of ourselves as "things." Imagination (Image) is all possibility, because from the image, the initial circumscribed energy, any use (idea) is possible. And so begins that image's use in the world. Possibility is what moves us.

The popular white man's theatre like the popular white man's novel shows tired white lives, and the problems of eating white sugar, or else it herds bigcabaroosed blondes onto huge stages in rhinestones and makes believe they are dancing or singing. WHITE BUSINESSMEN OF THE WORLD, DO YOU WANT TO SEE PEOPLE REALLY DANCING AND SINGING??? ALL OF YOU GO UP TO HARLEM AND GET YOURSELF KILLED. THERE WILL BE DANCING AND SINGING, THEN, FOR REAL!! (In *The Slave*, Walker Vessels, the black revolutionary, wears an armband, which is the insignia of the attacking army—a big red-lipped minstrel, grinning like crazy.)

The liberal white man's objection to the theatre of the revolution (if he is "hip" enough) will be on aesthetic grounds. Most white Western artists do not need to be "political," since usually, whether they know it or not, they are in complete sympathy with the most repressive social forces in the world today. There are more junior birdmen fascists running around the West today disguised as Artists than there are disguised as fascists. (But then, that word, *Fascist,* and with it, *Fascism,* has been made obsolete by the words *America,* and *Americanism.*) The American Artist usually turns out to be just a super-Bourgeois, because, finally, all he has to show for his sojourn through the world is "better taste" than the Bourgeois—many times not even that.

Americans will hate the Revolutionary Theatre because it will be out to destroy them and whatever they believe is real. American cops will try to close the theatres where such nakedness of the human spirit is paraded. American producers will say the revolutionary plays are filth, usually because they will treat human life as if it were actually happening. American directors will say that the white guys in the plays are too abstract and cowardly ("don't get me wrong . . . I mean aesthetically . . .") and they will be right.

The force we want is of twenty million spooks storming America with furious cries and unstoppable weapons. We want actual explosions and actual brutality: AN EPIC IS CRUMBLING and we must give it the space and hugeness of its actual demise. The Revolutionary Theatre, which is now peopled with victims, will soon begin to be peopled with new kinds of heroes—not the weak Hamlets debating whether or not they are ready to die for what's on their minds, but men and women (and minds) digging out from under a thousand years of "high art" and weak-faced dalliance. We must make an art that will function so as to call down the actual wrath of world spirit. We are witch doctors and assassins, but we will open a place for the true scientists to expand our consciousness. This is a theatre of assault. The play that will split the heavens for us will be called THE DESTRUCTION OF AMERICA. The heroes will be Crazy Horse, Denmark Vesey, Patrice Lumumba, and not history, not memory, not sad sentimental groping for a warmth in our despair; these will be new men, new heroes, and their enemies most of you who are reading this.

CRITICAL PERSPECTIVES

AUGUST WILSON   "The Ground on Which I Stand"
ROBERT BRUSTEIN   "Subsidized Separatism" (1996)

In 1996, the celebrated playwright August Wilson delivered an address entitled "The Ground on Which I Stand" to the Theatre Communications Group National Conference; shortly thereafter, Robert Brustein—a distinguished critic, founder of the Yale Repertory Theatre, and at the time director of the American Repertory Theatre—published a response, entitled "Subsidized Separatism." In this discussion—which was subsequently staged as a live debate between Brustein and Wilson, moderated by Anna Deavere Smith—two of the American theater's most eminent and provocative artists take on the issue that has vexed the stage since the founding of the republic: the relationship between "race" and representation.

AUGUST WILSON
The Ground on Which I Stand

I have come here today to make a testimony, to talk about the ground on which I stand and all the many grounds on which I and my ancestors have toiled, and the ground of theatre on which my fellow artists and I have labored to bring forth its fruits, its daring and its sometimes lacerating, and often healing, truths.

I wish to make it clear from the outset, however, that I do not have a mandate to speak for anyone. There are many intelligent blacks working in the American theatre who speak in loud and articulate voices. It would be the greatest of presumptions to say I speak for them. I speak only for myself and those who may think as I do.

In one guise, the ground I stand on has been pioneered by the Greek dramatists—by Euripides, Aeschylus and Sophocles—by William Shakespeare, by Shaw and Ibsen, and by the American dramatists Eugene O'Neill, Arthur Miller and Tennessee Williams. In another guise, the ground that I stand on has been pioneered by my grandfather, by Nat Turner, by Denmark Vesey, by Martin Delaney, Marcus Garvey and the Honorable Elijah Muhammad. That is the ground of the affirmation of the value of one being, an affirmation of his worth in the face of society's urgent and sometimes profound denial. It was this ground as a young man coming into manhood searching for something to which to dedicate my life that I discovered the Black Power movement of the '60s. I felt it a duty and an honor to participate in that historic moment, as the people who had arrived in America chained and malnourished in the hold of a 350-foot Portuguese, Dutch or English sailing ship, were now seeking ways to alter their relationship to the society in which they lived—and, perhaps more important, searching for ways to alter the shared expectations of themselves as a community of people.

The Black Power movement of the '60s: I find it curious but no small accident that I seldom hear those words "Black Power" spoken, and when mention is made of that part of black history in America, whether in the press or in conversation, reference is made to the Civil Rights Movement as though the Black Power movement—an important social movement by America's ex-slaves—had in fact never happened. But the Black Power movement of the '60s was a reality; it was the kiln in which I was fired, and has much to do with the person I am today and the ideas and attitudes that I carry as part of my consciousness.

I mention this because it is difficult to disassociate my concerns with theatre from the concerns of my life as a black man, and it is difficult to disassociate one part of my life from another. I have strived to live it all seamless . . . art and life together, inseparable and indistinguishable. The ideas I discovered and embraced in my youth when my idealism was full blown I have not abandoned in middle age when idealism is something less then blooming, but wisdom is starting to bud. The ideas of self-determination, self-respect and self-defense that governed my life in the '60s I find just as valid and self-urging in 1996. The need to alter our relationship to the society and to alter the shared expectations of ourselves as a racial group I find of greater urgency now than it was then.

I am what is known, at least among the followers and supporters of the ideas of Marcus Garvey, as a "race man." That is simply that I believe that race matters—that is the largest, most identifiable and most important part of our personality. It is the largest category of identification because it is the one that most influences your perception of yourself, and it is the one to which others in the world of men most respond. Race is also an important part of the American landscape, as America is made up of an amalgamation of races from all parts of the globe. Race is also the product of a shared gene pool that allows for group identification, and it is an organizing principle around which cultures are formed. When I say culture I am speaking about the behavior patterns, arts, beliefs, institutions and all other products of human work and thought as expressed in a particular community of people.

There are some people who will say that black Americans do not have a culture—that cultures are reserved for other people, most notably Europeans of various ethnic groupings, and that black Americans make up a sub-group of American culture that is derived from the European origins of its majority population. But black Americans are Africans, and there are many histories and many cultures on the African continent.

Those who would deny black Americans their culture would also deny them their history and the inherent values that are a part of all human life.

Growing up in my mother's house at 1727 Bedford Ave. in Pittsburgh, Pa., I learned the language, the eating habits, the religious beliefs, the gestures, the notions of common sense, attitudes towards sex, concepts of beauty and justice, and the responses to pleasure and pain, that my mother had learned from her mother, and which you could trace back to the first African who set foot on the continent. It is this culture that stands solidly on these shores today as a testament to the resiliency of the African-American spirit.

The term black or African-American not only denotes race, it denotes condition, and carries with it the vestige of slavery and the social segregation and abuse of opportunity so vivid in our memory. That this abuse of opportunity and truncation of possibility is continuing and is so pervasive in our society in 1996 says much about who we are and much about the work that is necessary to alter our perceptions of each other and to effect meaningful prosperity for all.

The problematic nature of the relationship between white and black for too long led us astray from the fulfillment of our possibilities as a society. We stare at each other across a divide of economics and privilege that has become an encumbrance on black Americans' ability to prosper and on the collective will and spirit of our national purpose.

In terms of economics and privilege, one significant fact affects us all in the American theatre: Of the 66 LORT theatres, there is only one that can be considered black. From this it could be falsely assumed that there aren't sufficient numbers of blacks working in the American theatre to sustain and support more theatres.

If you do not know, I will tell you that black theatre in America is alive . . . it is vibrant . . . it is vital . . . it just isn't funded. Black theatre doesn't share in the economics that would allow it to support its artists and supply them with meaningful avenues to develop their talent and broadcast and

disseminate ideas crucial to its growth. The economics are reserved as privilege to the overwhelming abundance of institutions that preserve, promote and perpetuate white culture.

That is not a complaint. That is an advertisement. Since the funding sources, both public and private, do not publicly carry avowed missions of exclusion and segregated support, this is obviously either a glaring case of oversight, or we the proponents of black theatre have not made our presence or our needs known. I hope here tonight to correct that.

I do not have the time in this short talk to reiterate the long and distinguished history of black theatre—often accomplished amid adverse and hostile conditions—but I would like to take the time to mark a few high points.

There are and have always been two distinct and parallel traditions in black art: that is, art that is conceived and designed to entertain white society, and art that feeds the spirit and celebrates the life of black America by designing its strategies for survival and prosperity.

An important part of black theatre that is often ignored but is seminal to its tradition is its origins on the slave plantations of the South. Summoned to the "big house" to entertain the slave owner and his guests, the slave began a tradition of theatre as entertainment for whites that reached its pinnacle in the heyday of the Harlem Renaissance. This entertainment for whites consisted of whatever the slave imagined or knew that his master wanted to see and hear. This tradition has its present life counterpart in the crossover artists that slant their material for white consumption.

The second tradition occurred when the African in the confines of the slave quarters sought to invest his spirit with the strength of his ancestors by conceiving in his art, in his song and dance, a world in which he was the spiritual center and his existence was a manifest act of the creator from whom life flowed. He then could create art that was functional and furnished him with a spiritual temperament necessary for his survival as property and the dehumanizing status that was attendant to that.

I stand myself and my art squarely on the self-defining ground of the slave quarters, and find the ground to be hallowed and made fertile by the blood and bones of the men and woman who can be described as warriors on the cultural battlefield that affirmed their self-worth. As there is no idea that cannot be contained by black life, these men and women found themselves to be sufficient and secure in their art and their instructions.

It was this high ground of self-definition that the black playwrights of the '60s marked out for themselves. Ron Milner, Ed Bullins, Philip Hayes Dean, Richard Wesley, Lonne Elder III, Sonia Sanchez, Barbara Ann Teer and Amiri Baraka were among those playwrights who were particularly vocal and where remain indebted to them for their brave and courageous forays into an area that is marked with land mines and the shadows of snipers—those who would reserve the territory of arts and letters and the American theatre as their own special province and point blacks toward the ball fields and the bandstands.

That black theatre today comes under such assaults should surprise no one, as we are on the verge of reclaiming and reexamining the purpose and pillars of our art and laying out new directions for its expansion. As such we make a target for cultural imperialists who seek to empower and propagate their ideas about the world as the only valid ideas, and see blacks as woefully deficient not only in arts and letters but in the abundant gifts of humanity.

In the 19th century, the lack of education, the lack of contact with different cultures, the expensive and slow methods of travel and communication fostered such ideas, and the breeding ground of ignorance and racial intolerance promoted them.

The King's English and the lexicon of a people given to such ignorance and intolerance did not do much to dispel such obvious misconceptions, but provided them with a home. I cite Webster's *Third New International Dictionary:*

"BLACK: outrageously wicked, dishonorable, connected with the devil, menacing, sullen, hostile, unqualified, illicit, illegal, violators of public regulations, affected by some undesirable condition, etc.

"WHITE: free from blemish, moral stain or impurity; outstandingly righteous, innocent, not marked by malignant influence, notably auspicious, fortunate, decent, a sterling man."

Such is the linguistic environment that informs the distance that separates blacks and whites in America and which the cultural imperialist, who cannot imagine a life existing and flourishing outside his benevolent control, embraces.

Robert Brustein, writing in an article/review titled "Unity from Diversity" [*The New Republic*, July 19–26, '93] is apparently disturbed that "there is a tremendous outpouring of work by minority artists" which he attributes to cultural diversity. He writes that the practice of extending invitations to a national banquet from which a lot of hungry people have long been excluded is a practice that can lead to confused standards. He goes on to establish a presumption of inferiority of the work of minority artists: "Funding agencies have started substituting sociological criteria for aesthetic criteria in their grant procedures, indicating that 'elitist' notions like quality and excellence are no longer functional." He goes on to say, "It's disarming in all senses of the word to say that we don't share common experiences that are measurable by common standards. But the growing number of truly talented

artists with more universal interests suggests that we may soon be in a position to return to a single value system."

Brustein's surprisingly sophomoric assumption that this tremendous outpouring of work by minority artists leads to confusing standards and that funding agencies have started substituting sociological for aesthetic criteria, leaving aside notions like quality and excellence, shows him to be a victim of 19th-century thinking and the linguistic environment that posits blacks as unqualified. Quite possibly this tremendous outpouring of works by minority artists may lead to a *raising* of standards and a *raising* of the levels of excellence, but Mr. Brustein cannot allow that possibility.

To suggest that funding agencies are rewarding inferior work by pursuing sociological criteria only serves to call into question the tremendous outpouring of plays by white playwrights who benefit from funding given to the 66 LORT theatres.

Are those theatres funded on sociological or aesthetic criteria? Do we have 66 excellent theatres? Or do those theatres benefit from the sociological advantage that they are run by whites and cater to largely white audiences?

The truth is that often where there are aesthetic criteria of excellence, there are also sociological criteria that have traditionally excluded blacks. I say raise the standards and remove the sociological consideration of race as privilege, and we will meet you at the crossroads, in equal numbers, prepared to do the work of extending and developing the common ground of the American theatre.

We are capable of work of the highest order; we can answer to the high standards of world-class art. Anyone who doubts our capabilities at this late stage is being intellectually dishonest.

We can meet on the common ground of theatre as a field of work and endeavor. But we cannot meet on the common ground of experience.

Where is the common ground in the horrifics of lynching? Where is the common ground in the maim of a policeman's bullet? Where is the common ground in the hull or the deck of a slave ship with its refreshments of air and expanse?

We will not be denied our history.

We have voice and we have temper. We are too far along this road from the loss of our political will, we are too far along the road of reassembling ourselves, too far along the road to regaining spiritual health to allow such transgression of our history to go unchallenged.

The commonalties we share are the commonalities of culture. We decorate our houses. That is something we do in common. We do it differently because we value different things. We have different manners and different values of social intercourse. We have different ideas of what a party is.

There are some commonalities to our different ideas. We both offer food and drink to our guests, but because we have different culinary values, different culinary histories, we offer different food and drink. In our culinary history, we have learned to make do with the feet and ears and tails and intestines of the pig rather than the loin and the ham and the bacon. Because of our different histories with the same animal, we have different culinary ideas. But we share a common experience with the pig as opposed to say Muslims and Jews, who do not share that experience.

We can meet on the common ground of the American theatre.

We cannot share a single value system if that value system consists of the values of white Americans based on their European ancestors. We reject that as Cultural Imperialism. We need a value system that includes our contributions as Africans in America. Our agendas are as valid as yours. We may disagree, we may forever be on opposite sides of aesthetics, but we can only share a value system that is inclusive of all Americans and recognizes their unique and valuable contributions.

The ground together. We must develop the ground together. We reject the idea of equality among equals, but we say rather the equality of all men.

The common values of the American theatre that we can share are plot . . . dialogue . . . characterization . . . design. How we both make use of them will be determined by who we are—what ground we are standing on and what our cultural values are.

Theatre is part of art history in terms of its craft and dramaturgy, but it is part of social history in terms of how it is financed and governed. By making money available to theatres willing to support colorblind casting, the financiers and governors have signaled not only their unwillingness to support black theatre but their willingness to fund dangerous and divisive assaults against it. Colorblind casting is an aberrant idea that has never had any validity other than as a tool of the Cultural Imperialists who view American culture, rooted in the icons of European culture, as beyond reproach in its perfection. It is inconceivable to them that life could be lived and enriched without knowing Shakespeare or Mozart. Their gods, their manners, their being, are the only true and correct representations of humankind. They refuse to recognize black conduct and manners as part of a system that is fueled by its own philosophy, mythology, history, creative motif, social organization and ethos. The idea that blacks have their own way of responding to the world, their own values, style, linguistics, religion and aesthetics, is unacceptable to them.

For a black actor to stand on the stage as part of a social milieu that has denied him his gods, his culture, his human-ity, his mores, his ideas of himself and the world he lives in, is to be in league with a thousand nay-sayers who wish to corrupt the vigor and spirit of his heart.

To cast us in the role of mimics is to deny us our own competence.

Our manners, our style, our approach to language, our gestures, and our bodies are not for rent. The history of our bodies—the maimings . . . the lashings . . . the lynchings . . . the body that is capable of inspiring profound rage and pungent cruelty—is not for rent.

To mount an all-black production of a *Death of a Salesman* or any other play conceived for white actors as an investigation of the human condition through the specifics of white culture is to deny us our own humanity, our own history, and the need to make our own investigations from the cultural ground on which we stand as black Americans. It is an assault on our presence, our difficult but honorable history in America; it is an insult to our intelligence, our playwrights, and our many and varied contributions to the society and the world at large.

The idea of colorblind casting is the same idea of assimilation that black Americans have been rejecting for the past 380 years. For the record, we reject it again. We reject any attempt to blot us out, to reinvent history and ignore our presence or to maim our spiritual product. We must not continue to meet on this path. We will not deny our history, and we will not allow it to be made to be of little consequence, to be ignored or misinterpreted.

In an effort to spare us the burden of being "affected by an undesirable condition" and as a gesture of benevolence, many whites (like the proponents of colorblind casting) say, "Oh, I don't see color." We want you to see us. We are black and beautiful. We are not patrons of the linguistic environment that has us as "unqualified, and violators of public regulations." We are not a menace to society. We are not ashamed. We have an honorable history in the world of men. We come from a long line of honorable people with complex codes of ethics and social discourse, people who devised myths and systems of cosmology and systems of economics. We are not ashamed, and do not need you to be ashamed for us. Nor do we need the recognition of our blackness to be couched in abstract phases like "artist of color." Who are you talking about? A Japanese artist? An Eskimo? A Filipino? A Mexican? A Cambodian? A Nigerian? An African American? Are we to suppose that if you put a white person on one side of the scale and the rest of humanity lumped together as nondescript "people of color" on the other side, that it would balance out? That whites carry that much spiritual weight? We reject that. We are unique, and we are specific.

We do not need colorblind casting; we need some theatres to develop our playwrights. We need those misguided financial resources to be put to better use. We cannot develop our playwrights with the meager resources at our disposal. Why is it difficult to imagine 9 black theatres but not 66 white ones? Without theatres we cannot develop our talents. If we cannot develop our talents, then everyone suffers: our writers; the theatre; the audience. Actors are deprived of material, and our communities are deprived of the jobs in support of the art—the company manager, the press coordinator, the electricians, the carpenters, the concessionaires, the people that work in wardrobe, the box-office staff, the ushers and the janitors. We need some theatres. We cannot continue like this. We have only one life to develop our talent, to fulfill our potential as artists. One life, and it is short, and the lack of the means to develop our talent is an encumbrance on that life.

We did not sit on the sidelines while the immigrants of Europe, through hard work, skill, cunning, guile and opportunity, built America into an industrial giant of the 20th century. It was our labor that provided the capital. It was our labor in the shipyards and the stockyards and the coal mines and the steel mills. Our labor built the roads and the railroads. And when America was challenged, we strode on the battlefield, our boots strapped on and our blood left to soak into the soil of places whose names we could not pronounce, against an enemy whose only crime was ideology. We left our blood in France and Korea and the Philippines and Vietnam, and our only reward has been the deprivation of possibility and the denial of our moral personality.

It cannot continue. The ground together: The American ground on which I stand and which my ancestors purchased with their perseverance, with their survival, with their manners and with their faith.

It cannot continue, as other assaults upon our presence and our history cannot continue: When the *New York Times* publishes an article on pop singer Michael Bolton and lists as his influences four white singers, then as an afterthought tosses in the phrase "and the great black rhythm and blues singers," it cannot be anything but purposeful with intent to maim. These great black rhythm and blues singers are reduced to an afterthought on the edge of oblivion—one stroke of the editor's pen and the history of American music is revised, and Otis Redding, Jerry Butler and Rufus Thomas are consigned to the dustbin of history while Joe Cocker, Mick Jagger and Rod Stewart are elevated to the status of the originators and creators of a vital art that is a product of our spiritual travails; the history of music becomes a fabrication, a blatant forgery which under the hallowed auspices of the *New York Times* is presented as the genuine article.

We cannot accept these assaults. We must defend and protect our spiritual fruits. To ignore these assaults would be to be derelict in our duties. We cannot accept them. Our political capital will not permit them.

So much of what makes this country rich in art and all manners of spiritual life is the contributions that we as African Americans have made. We cannot allow others to have authority over our cultural and spiritual products. We reject, without reservation, any attempts by anyone to rewrite our history so as to deny us the rewards of our spiritual labors, and to become the cultural custodians of our art, our literature and our lives. To give expression to the spirit that has been shaped and fashioned by our history is of necessity to give voice and vent to the history itself.

It must remain for us a history of triumph.

The time has come for black playwrights to confer with one another, to come together to meet each other face to face, to address questions of aesthetics and ways to defend ourselves from the nay-sayers who would trumpet our talents as insufficient to warrant the same manner of investigation and exploration as the majority. We need to develop guidelines for the protection of our cultural property, our contributions and the influence they accrue. It is time we took responsibility for our talents in our own hands. We cannot depend on others. We cannot depend on the directors, the managers or the actors to do the work we should be doing for ourselves. It is our lives and the pursuit of our fulfillment that are being encumbered by false ideas and perceptions.

It is time to embrace the political dictates of our history and answer the challenge to our duties. I further think we should confer in a city in our ancestral homeland in the southern part of the United States in 1998, so that we may enter the millennium united and prepared for a long future of prosperity.

From the hull of a ship to self-determining, self-respecting people. That is the journey we are making.

We are robust in spirit, we are bright with laughter, and we are bold in imagination. Our blood is soaked into the soil and our bones lie scattered the whole way across the Atlantic Ocean, as Hansel's crumbs, to mark the way back home.

We are no longer in the House of Bondage, and soon we will no longer be victims of the counting houses who hold from us ways to develop and support our talents and our expressions of life and its varied meanings. Assaults upon the body politic that demean and ridicule and depress the value and worth of our existence, that seek to render it immobile and to extinguish the flame of freedom lit eons ago by our ancestors upon another continent—these must be met with a fierce and uncompromising defense.

If you are willing to accept it, it is your duty to affirm and urge that defense, that respect and that determination.

I must mention here, with all due respect to W. E. B. DuBois, that the concept of a "talented tenth" creates an artificial superiority. It is a fallacy and a dangerous idea that only serves to divide us further. I am not willing to throw away as untalented 90 percent of my blood; I am not willing to dismiss the sons and daughters of those people who gave more than lip service to the will to live and made it a duty to prosper in spirit, if not in provision. All God's children got talent. It is a dangerous idea to set one part of the populace above and aside from the other. We do a grave disservice to ourselves not to seek out and embrace and enable all of our human resources as a people. All blacks in America, with very few exceptions—no matter what our status, no matter the size of our bank accounts, no matter how many and what kind of academic degrees we can place beside our names, no matter the furnishings and square footage of our homes, the length of our closets and the quality of the wool and cotton that hangs there—we all in America originated from the same place: the slave plantations of the South. We all share a common past, and despite how some us might think and how it might look, we all share a common present and will share a common future.

We can make a difference. Artists, playwrights, actors—we can be the spearhead of a movement to reignite and reunite our people's positive energy for a political and social change that is reflective of our spiritual truths rather than economic fallacies. Our talents, our truth, our belief in ourselves is all in our hands. What we make of it will emerge as a baptismal spray that names and defines. What we do now becomes history by which our grandchildren will judge us.

We are not off on a tangent. The foundation of the American theatre is the foundation of European theatre that begins with the great Greek dramatists; it is based on the proscenium stage and the poetics of Aristotle. This is the theatre that we have chosen to work in. We embrace the values of that theatre but reserve the right to amend, to explore, to add our African consciousness and our African aesthetic to the art we produce.

To pursue our cultural expression does not separate us. We are not separatists, as Mr. Brustein asserts. We are Americans trying to fulfill our talents. We are not the servants at the party. We are not apprentices in the kitchens. We are not the stableboys to the King's huntsmen. We are Africans. We are Americans. The irreversible sweep of history has decreed that. We are artists who seek to develop our talents and give expression to our personalities. We bring advantage to the common ground that is the American theatre.

All theatres depend on an audience for its dialogue. To the American theatre, subscription audiences are its life blood. But the subscription audience holds the seats of our theatres hostage to the mediocrity of its tastes, and serves to impede the further development of an audience for the work that we do. While intentional or not, it serves to keep blacks out of the theatre where they suffer no illusion of welcome anyway. A subscription thus becomes not a support system but makes the patrons members of a club to which the theatre serves as a clubhouse. It is an irony that the people who can most afford a full-price ticket get discounts for subscribing, while the single-ticket buyer who cannot afford a subscription is charged the additional burden of support to offset the subscription-buyer's discount. It is a system that is in need of overhaul to provide not only a more equitable access to tickets but access to influence as well.

I look for and challenge students of arts management to be bold in their exploration of new systems of funding theatres, including profit-making institutions and ventures, and I challenge black artists and audiences to scale the walls erected by theatre subscriptions to gain access to this vital area of spiritual enlightenment and enrichment that is the theatre.

All theatregoers have opinions about the work they witness. Critics have an informed opinion. Sometimes it may be necessary for them to gather more information to become more informed. As playwrights grow and develop, as the theatre changes, the critic has an important responsibility to guide and encourage that growth. However, in the discharge of their duties, it may be necessary for them to also grow and develop. A stagnant body of critics, operating from the critical criteria of 40 years ago, makes for a stagnant theatre without the fresh and abiding influence of contemporary ideas. It is the critics who should be in the forefront of developing new tools for analysis necessary to understand new influences.

The critic who can recognize a German neo-romantic influence should also be able to recognize an American influence from blues or black church rituals, or any other contemporary American influence.

The true critic does not sit in judgment. Rather he seeks to inform his reader, instead of adopting a posture of self-conscious importance in which he sees himself a judge and final arbiter of a work's importance or value.

We stand on the verge of an explosion of playwriting talent that will challenge our critics. As American playwrights absorb the influence of television and use new avenues of approach to the practice of their craft, they will prove to be wildly inventive and imaginative in creating dramas that will guide and influence contemporary life for years to come.

Theatre can do that. It can disseminate ideas, it can educate even the miseducated, because it is art—and all art reaches across that divide that makes order out of chaos, and embraces the truth that overwhelms with its presence, and connects man to something larger than himself and his imagination.

Theatre asserts that all of human life is universal. Love, Honor, Duty, Betrayal belong and pertain to every culture or race. The way they are acted out on the playing field may be different, but betrayal is betrayal whether you are a South Sea Islander, a Mississippi farmer or an English baron. All of human life is universal, and it is theatre that illuminates and confers upon the universal the ability to speak for all men.

The ground together: We have to do it together. We cannot permit our lives to waste away, our talents unchallenged. We cannot permit a failure to our duty. We are brave and we are boisterous, our mettle is proven, and we are dedicated.

The ground together: the ground of the American theatre on which I am proud to stand . . . the ground which our artistic ancestors purchased with their endeavors . . .with their pursuit of the American spirit and its ideals.

I believe in the American theatre. I believe in its power to inform about the human condition, its power to heal, its power to hold the mirror as 'twere up to nature, its power to uncover the truths we wrestle from uncertain and sometimes unyielding realities. All of art is a search for ways of being, of living life more fully. We who are capable of those noble pursuits should challenge the melancholy and barbaric, to bring the light of angelic grace, peace, prosperity and the unencumbered pursuit of happiness to the ground on which we all stand.

ROBERT BRUSTEIN
Subsidized Separatism

August Wilson's keynote address at the TCG (Theatre Communications Group) Conference in late June 1996, later published as "The Ground on Which I Stand," was greeted with a standing ovation by the various resident theatre people attending, though some found it divisive and disturbing. Since I was not present at the conference, I was hardly in a position to express my own reactions, though word leaked back to me that chief among the malefactors identified in Wilson's broadside—his "snipers" and "naysayers" and "cultural imperialists"—was myself.

Wilson's rambling jeremiad is essentially an effort to accentuate the achievements of black theatre, which he claims to be supreme today though "often accomplished amid adverse and hostile conditions." "Black theatre is alive, it is vibrant, it is vital," he says. But not all its practitioners are following the proper path. In the same speech Wilson manages to express his disdain for black "crossover artists" who, "like house slaves entertaining the white master and his guests," manage to "slant their material for white consumption." He rebukes white foundations for failing to create and subsidize black theatre companies. And he characterizes the idea of "color-blind casting" as "a tool of the Cultural Imperialists"—"the same idea of assimilation that black Americans have been rejecting for the past 300 years."

If you hear echoes in this of 1960s radicalism, particularly the language of black nationalism, your ears are not deceiving you. And Wilson is hardly reluctant to admit his militant inheritance. Testifying that the black power movement was "the kiln in which I was fired," he proclaims that its concern with "self-determination, self-respect and self-defense" are the values that govern his life. He claims that "I am what is known, at least among the followers and supporters of Marcus Garvey, as a 'race man.'" He announces that the ground on which he stands was pioneered "by Nat Turner, by Denmark Vesey, by Martin Delaney, Marcus Garvey and the Honorable Elijah Muhammad"—rebels or separatists all, some proponents of a return to Africa. Conspicuous by its absence is the name of Martin Luther King, among many other honored black Americans for whom the idea of integration has not been considered anathema.

The foundation of this long tirade is Wilson's insistence on black culture, particularly black theatre, not only as an unparalleled achievement but also a singular and discrete experience of life. It is an experience that cannot be fully absorbed or understood by white people, much less criticized by them: "We cannot allow others to have authority over our cultural and spiritual products," he says. "We need to develop guidelines of the protection of our cultural property, our contributions and the influence they accrue." Whites and blacks can occupy the same country, but they cannot occupy the same ground. "Where is the common ground in the horrifics of lynching? Where is the common ground in the policeman's bullet? Where is the common ground in the hull or the deck of a slave ship . . . ?" He describes "black conduct and manners as part of a system that is fueled by its own philosophy, mythology, history, creative motif, social organization and ethos." He deplores the presence of a black actor in a non-black play, standing on the stage "as part of a social milieu that has denied him his gods, his humanity, his mores, his ideas of himself and the world he lives in. . . ." Indeed, he considers the very idea of an all-black production of *Death of a Salesman* to be "an assault on our presence . . . an insult to our intelligence."

This is the language of self-segregation. At times, it is true, Wilson is willing to concede that blacks and whites breathe the same air and partake of certain "commonalities" of culture. Among these "commonalities" he mentions food, though even that admission is weirdly exclusionary. Black people have had to be satisfied with the leavings of the pig. Yet blacks and whites "share a common experience with the pig as opposed to say Muslims and Jews, who do not share that experience." (Black Muslims? Reform Jews?) It is also true that, in the rolling cadences that bring his speech to its climax, Wilson concedes the American theatre's power to "inform about the human condition, its power to heal, its power to hold the mirror as 'twere up to nature, its power to uncover the truths we wrestle from uncertain and sometimes unyielding realities." Even this boiler-plate rhetoric, however, for all its afterthought references to the unifying nature of the theatre, fails to compensate for the divisive nature of his remarks. Perhaps some future student of syntax will analyze how Wilson's vacillating use of the word "we" in the same paragraph (first inclusive: "We have to do it together," then exclusive: "We are brave and we are boisterous") betrays his ambivalent sense of American identity. This ambivalence makes for some confusing assertions. "We are black and beautiful. . . . We are not separatists. . . . We are Africans. We are Americans."

Furthermore, Wilson's insistence on the strength and uniqueness of a proud black culture is oddly inconsistent with his notion that blacks are "victims of the counting houses who hold from us ways to develop and support our talents." This inconsistency grows more glaring when Wilson directs his biblical fury toward some of these "counting houses" (his name for the funding agencies) and concludes that "the economics are reserved as privilege to the overwhelming abundance of institutions that promote and perpetrate white culture." He notes that of the sixty-six League of Resident Theatres (LORT) only one can be considered black. And in an impassioned if curious appeal for subsidized separatism, he sees no contradiction in demanding that white foundations take the responsibility for founding as well as funding black theatres, as if theatre companies were the creation of philanthropic agencies rather than the indigenous outgrowths of dedicated artists and supporting communities.

I'm not at all certain any more what constitutes a "black" or "white" theatre. Both the precarious Negro Ensemble Company and the thriving Crossroads Theater fit Wilson's exclusive definition clearly enough. But how does one describe the New York Public Theater and Atlanta Alliance Theater under their black directors George C. Wolfe and Kenneth Leon? Or the Yale Repertory Theatre and Syracuse Stage when they were led by such black directors as Lloyd Richards and Tazewell Thompson? Most American theatres today, like many American cities—indeed like many Americans—are racially mixed. Are black actors now to perform only black parts writ-

ten by black playwrights? Will James Earl Jones no longer have a chance to play Judge Brack or Darth Vader? Must we bar Andre Braugher and Denzel Washington from enacting the Shakespearean monarchs? Is Othello to be an unacceptable opportunity for Morgan Freeman or Laurence Fishburne? Will Athol Fugard be told he cannot take a colored role in his own plays? No more voodoo *Macbeths* or all-black *Godots?* No more efforts on behalf of nontraditional casting and integrated theatre companies? Must history be rolled back to the days of segregated theatres?

I fear Wilson is displaying a failure of memory—I hesitate to say a failure of gratitude—when he charges nonprofit resident theatres with using "sociological criteria" in choosing plays that "traditionally exclude blacks." All of his own plays were originated and produced by a large consortium of mainstream institutions, including the Yale Repertory Theatre, the Huntington, the American Conservatory Theater, the Goodman, the Mark Taper, and others. Wilson's pervasive tone of victimization, in fact, is oddly inappropriate for a playwright whose six LORT-generated plays, after completing the resident theatre circuit, all found their way to Broadway, where they won two Pulitzer Prizes, five New York Drama Critics Circle awards, and I don't know how many Tonys, besides generating enormous box office income for the playwright (from white and black audiences alike). Is a man who has garnered such extraordinary media attention (not to mention every conceivable playwriting fellowship) really in a position to say that blacks are being excluded from the American theatre or that these institutions only "preserve, promote, and perpetuate white culture"? Has he read any foundation reports lately? Does he have any idea of the proportion of grants, both public and private, that are exclusively reserved for inner-city audience development and multicultural activities in resident theatres?

I am the only villain identified by name in Wilson's speech. He makes reference to my article "Diversity and Unity," but there are also hidden allusions to what I wrote in "The Options of Multiculturalism," my unfavorable review of his play *The Piano Lesson,* and my *Times* op-ed piece on coercive foundation funding. Wilson specifically attacks what he calls my "surprisingly sophomoric assumption" that the present funding climate is characterized by confused standards and sociological rather than aesthetic criteria. I confess to believing that most foundations (by their own admission) no longer make artistic quality their primary consideration. But I categorically deny I ever said that "the practice of extending invitations to a national banquet from which a lot of hungry people have been excluded" (my phrase, uncredited) establishes (his phrase) "a presumption of inferiority of the work of minority artists."

Wilson's charge, with its nasty imputations of racism, is intended to characterize a review of two minority playwrights who, in my estimation, met the highest standards, and without being exclusionary. "Drenched in their own cultural juices," I wrote, "they are nevertheless capable of telling stories that include us all, thus proving again that the theatre works best as a unifying rather than a segregating medium." I was talking about transcendence, about recognizing that the greatest art embraces a common humanity. Although Wilson might dismiss such playwrights—the younger generation of black writers like Anna Deavere Smith and OyamO and Suzan-Lori Parks—as "crossover artists" entertaining the slave owner and his guests, my article was a plea to minority playwrights like himself to acknowledge, without any loss of racial consciousness, that they belong, as artists, to the same human family as everyone else.

Some people may remember that, almost alone among white critics, I have expressed reservations about Wilson's plays. This was an aesthetic judgment, not a racial one. While I admire Wilson's control of character and dialogue, a lot of his writing has seemed to me weakly structured, badly edited, prosaic, and overwritten. Consider, for instance, *Seven Guitars,* which I didn't review (I left after four guitars). I don't think it exposes "the values of white Americans based on their European ancestors" to believe that a conventionally realistic play needs an animating event, and that, however colorful its subject matter, it cannot ramble willy-nilly for one act lasting two and a half hours without establishing a line of action. My less technical objection has been that, by choosing to chronicle the oppression of black people through each of the decades, Wilson has fallen into a monotonous tone of victimization which happens to be the leitmotif of his TCG speech.

I am also disturbed by other attitudes reflected in that speech, notably that only the black experience inspires the work of black artists. In "The Options of Multiculturalism," I suggested that, while Wilson has announced he will never allow a white director to stage his plays, a backyard drama like his *Fences* shows the considerable influence of white playwrights, particularly Arthur Miller's *All My Sons.* (It may be that Wilson's anger over this conjecture ricochets into his ferocious attack on the *New York Times* for allegedly underplaying the influence of black singers on Michael Bolton—something he calls an "intent to maim.")

It is perfectly possible that I am wrong in my assessments. And I can understand how a playwright, no matter how highly praised by mainstream critics, can smart under adverse criticism, even in a relatively small-circulation periodical such as *The New Republic.* It is also no doubt painful to him that *Seven Guitars* lost the Tony this year to *Master Class.* But that is no justification for wheeling out the creaky juggernaut of black power to roll over anyone who makes a negative judgment on his plays. Indeed, Wilson seems to suggest occasionally that the only true critical function is boosterism. For at the same time Wilson is questioning the very idea of critical opinions ("The true critic does not sit in judgment . . . the critic has an important responsibility to guide and encourage . . . growth"), he is announcing that every African American, contrary to Du Bois's idea of "the talented tenth," is artistically gifted: "All God's children got talent." This is progressive-school nonsense. The greatest tribute that a critic can pay to a playwright such as Wilson is to judge and analyze his work by the same criteria as anybody else's work.

Wilson writes: "I stand myself and my art squarely on the self-defining ground of the slave quarters." Isn't it time to acknowledge that, for all the grim uncompleted racial business in this country, those quarters have long been razed to the ground? Isn't there some kind of statute of limitations on white guilt and white reparations? Isn't it possible to recognize that there is a difference between losing your freedom and losing a Tony, between toting a bale of cotton and bearing the burden of an unfavorable review? To say that whites can't understand black culture because their ancestors were not enslaved is almost as problematical as saying that Wilson can't understand the writings of a Jew because he hasn't experienced life under the pharaohs. Many brilliant black artists and intellectuals—Albert Murray, Ralph Ellison, Henry Louis Gates, Shelby Steele, and others—have repudiated the "ethnographic fallacy" that one writer's peculiar experiences can represent a whole social category. This tribalist approach, as Diane Ravitch has written, "confuses race with culture, as though everyone with the same skin color had the same culture and history."

August Wilson is more comfortable writing plays than apostolic decrees. His speech is melancholy testimony to the rabid identity politics and poisonous racial consciousness that have been infecting our country in recent years. Although Wilson would deny it, such sentiments represent a reverse form of the old politics of division, an appeal for socially approved and foundation-funded separatism. I don't think Martin Luther King ever imagined an America where playwrights such as August Wilson would be demanding, under the pretense of calling for healing and unity, an entirely separate stage for black theatre artists. What next? Separate schools? Separate washrooms? Separate drinking fountains?

The family confronts Ginni in Manjula Padmanabhan's *Harvest*.

H istoric social, political, and technological changes have reshaped the world since 1950, with a consequential impact on the theater. The aftermath of World War II has seen the remapping of the planet: the independence of India, Pakistan, and many Asian and African nations from colonial rule; the founding of Israel and the displacement of the Palestinians; and wars in Korea, Indochina, the Middle East, Africa, the Persian Gulf, Afghanistan, and Iraq. Those decades also witnessed bitter civil strife and the glimmering of peace in Northern Ireland, Argentina, Chile, the United States, Europe, and elsewhere; the Cuban missile crisis, the death of Francisco Franco in Spain, and the dismantling of the Berlin Wall; independence movements in the former Soviet Union and throughout Eastern Europe; the collapse of Yugoslavia and protracted war in Bosnia; the civil rights movement in the United States, the waning of apartheid in South Africa, the failure of peace in the Middle East.

With the rise of global communications, a global economy, and global political and military interests, such social and political revolutions immediately become the world's business. They reshape the world we live in even as we watch the changes unfold on our television screens. Fortunately, television has not really transformed the world's diverse cultures into a single "global village," but local cultures all feel the impact of events around the world. Think of the global effects of environmental disasters such as the Chernobyl nuclear power plant meltdown in 1986 and the deforestation of the rain forests of the Amazon; of medical advances such as vaccination; of epidemics like AIDS; of the international effects of social movements like nuclear disarmament, human rights, Amnesty International, feminism, and the peace movement, or, more horrifyingly, of anti-Semitism, racism, homophobia, and "ethnic cleansing."

Drama requires the collaboration of playwrights, actors, and audiences; the public structure of a theater site or building; and the social and political incentives and protections that make theatergoing attractive—it is an art deeply woven into the social fabric of a given culture and its history. Although we can still speak of the "London theater" or of "American drama," these terms have become in our era a critical convenience for reducing the dynamic variety of contemporary theater to the fictional boundaries of a single "national" culture. Although the theater still requires the support, work, and energy of its local community, today's dramatic repertoire is a global one. American playwright Sam Shepard first produced several of his plays in London. British playwright Edward Bond is more widely produced in Germany than in the United Kingdom. Many Eastern European and Latin American playwrights have been forced by censorship and political persecution to smuggle their plays to Europe or the United States to be staged. South African playwright Athol Fugard has premiered several plays in the United States. Nigerian Wole Soyinka is regularly produced throughout the world. These playwrights are deeply implicated in the working of their native cultures, but their plays have rapidly become part of the world repertoire.

Unit VII presents a different perspective on drama and theater than other units in *The Wadsworth Anthology of Drama*. Earlier units have been organized around a distinctive moment in the history of a relatively discrete culture: Athens in the fifth century BCE, Japan in the early shogunate; late medieval England and Renaissance London; late seventeenth-century London, Paris, and Madrid; and twentieth-century Europe and the United States. In many respects, this book is organized around undergraduate college teaching in the

United States today, which emphasizes the historical development of Western theater practices and dramatic literatures. This unit takes a broadly "postcolonial" perspective on contemporary drama, establishing some continuities with Western traditions while bringing other traditions of world theater and drama into view.

POSTCOLONIAL PERSPECTIVES

In the past several decades all areas of the humanities and cultural studies have come to challenge a narrowly Eurocentric vision of the contemporary world. These challenges have arisen from a wide range of causes: worldwide national independence movements, such as those in India in 1947, on the African continent throughout the 1950s and 1960s, and in Eastern Europe and the Baltic states in the 1990s; international involvement in South Africa's struggle with apartheid; global media and economic interconnections, that make business activity in Asia have an immediate impact on Wall Street; the fall of the Berlin wall in 1989, the breakup of the Soviet Union, and of the new relations between Eastern and Western Europe, and between the republics of formerly Soviet Central Asia; the return of Islam as a political, social, and military force in the West; oil crises and the war in the Persian Gulf; the challenges to "national" identity reflected in Québec's ongoing separatist movement in Canada; the various anxieties about language and immigration in the United States; racial tensions in Britain, France, Germany, and elsewhere in Europe; the ongoing political and social crisis in Northern Ireland; the emergence of Japan, South Korea, and China as economic powers; the struggles of many Latin American countries—often against both local military dictatorships and the international finance they receive—to achieve the promise of their nineteenth-century wars of liberation. In many places, these changes have not only had to overcome the military and political power of European governments—the Latin American revolutions against Spain; African and Indian independence movements—but have forced crucial challenges to the model of European culture itself, dramatizing the often oppressive entailments of the culture of "enlightenment" that was imposed on much of the world in the "civilizing" process of colonization.

In 1900, the sun never set on Britain's colonies around the world, and the legacy of three centuries of European expansion are still felt throughout the world: England, France, Spain, Portugal, the Netherlands, Italy, and Belgium all had extensive colonial holdings in Africa, Asia, and the New World. In many cases, of course, colonization was undertaken largely as a means of extracting wealth, in the form of slaves, precious metals, and/or raw materials, that could be sent back to enrich the capital: this was the model of Spanish colonization in the New World, in which Spain prevented trading between colonial cities in Mexico, Peru, Argentina, and elsewhere to have all trade proceed directly to Madrid. Even though very different patterns of colonization were practiced throughout the world, colonization always brought with it European institutions, such as Catholic and Protestant churches, legal practices and courts, schools and universities, and other aspects of European culture as well—sports and games, fashion and foods, and literature, drama, and theater. In many places, the colonial language was rapidly imposed as the language of government, education, and the law. Much as England banned Gaelic in Ireland in the eighteenth century (Gaelic is now taught in school in the Republic of Ireland, but not in state-supported schools in Northern Ireland), so in the twentieth century, postcolonial politics are often centered in the politics of language. In Latin America, for example, there has been a significant movement to reestablish various native languages—Quechua in Peru, Nahua in Mexico—as part of literary and public discourse; in Mexico, for example, many pre-Columbian architectural sites have guide materials in at least one native language, as well as in Spanish. Writers like Aimé Césaire, in French-speaking Martinique, or Wole Soyinka, growing up in preindependence Nigeria, were schooled on European writers such as Molière and Shakespeare and have used this education as part of their critical representation of the cultural politics of colonial and postcolonial rule: Césaire in his adaptation of Shakespeare's *The Tempest* to a Caribbean setting; Soyinka in the dialogue between English and Yoruba culture that informs many of his plays, including *Death and the King's Horseman.*

Language is never neutral; as Stephen Dedalus notices when talking to an English clergyman in James Joyce's *A Portrait of the Artist as a Young Man,* language encodes an entire system of social and political values—the words "Christ," "ale," and "master" mean something different to the English than they do to the Irish, much as terms like "white," "free," "citizen," or "nation" are obvious flashpoints, places where words reveal the political work that language performs. Like language itself, the values exported to the colonies often have traced within them a powerfully oppressive dynamic. For in regarding itself as bearing "civilization" into the wilderness—as though North and South America, Africa, and parts of Asia were not only uninhabited, but the highly developed cultures the Europeans found there were negligible—European culture often regards the colonized as "other" and inferior. The indigenous cultures of Africa, Latin America, and Asia were usually defined in antithesis to the values that justified the brutalities of occupation and exploitation: in opposition to the values of civilization, of a rich literary language, of an important and dynamic culture, indigenous cultures were seen as noncivil, their languages nonliterary, their cultures noncultivated, their (nonwhite) peoples nonpeople. Given this history, the cultural sphere—the sphere of theater and drama, of music and the visual arts, of literature, of film—has also been an important area of revolution as well. As the Kenyan novelist and playwright Ngũgĩ wa Thiong'o has argued, the practices of culture are in many ways more forceful than the more visible structures of the law or politics in maintaining a sense of "colonized" identity. He suggests that "decolonizing the mind" means decolonizing the tools that the mind thinks with, language, visual imagery, patterns of narrative and storytelling, everything used to make sense of the world:

> The oppressed and the exploited of the earth maintain their defiance: liberty from theft. But the biggest weapon wielded and actually daily unleashed by imperialism against that collective defiance is the cultural bomb. The effect of a cultural bomb is to annihilate a people's belief in their names, in their languages, in their environment, in their heritage of struggle, in their unity, in their capacities and ultimately in themselves. It makes them see their past as one wasteland of nonachievement and it makes them want to distance themselves from that wasteland. It makes them want to identify with that which is farthest removed from themselves; for instance, with other peoples' languages rather than their own.[1]

In their introduction to British postcolonial literatures, *The Empire Writes Back,* Bill Ashcroft, Gareth Griffiths, and Helen Tiffin "use the term 'post-colonial' . . . to cover all the culture affected by the imperial process from the moment of colonization to the present day." Although several of the playwrights and theaters presented here—Wole Soyinka from Nigeria, Maishe Maponya and Athol Fugard from South Africa, Aimé Césaire from the French island of Martinique—are readily understood within the context of national liberation movements, others point to a different, though analogous, understanding of the global politics of culture today. The Northern Irish playwright Brian Friel writes in a place where the politics of "nation"—Northern Ireland is physically part of Ireland, but politically a province of the United Kingdom—are still unresolved. Beyond that, in the twentieth century the dynamics of a kind of imperialism are not restricted to politics: a former colony— the United States—has emerged as a prodigiously powerful influence on many areas of economic and cultural life around the world, in ways that are frequently experienced as a kind of colonialism. While France, for instance, continues to struggle with the legacy of its colonization of North Africa, it also is engaged in a protracted trade controversy with the

---

[1]Ngũgĩ wa Thiong'o, *Decolonising the Mind: The Politics of Language in African Literature* (Portsmouth: Heinemann, 1986), 3.

United States, protecting the French film industry—and, by extension, "French" culture—by sharply limiting the distribution of American films. This sense that American culture, American values, American money, and American military power have become so pervasive as to threaten the political, economic, and cultural autonomy even of powerful countries—like France or Canada—informs a broader resistance to "imported" or Western or American culture. This resistance to a form of cultural imperialism animates some aspects of contemporary Asian theater, especially in plays like Manjula Padmanabhan's *Harvest;* it is also a theme in contemporary Canadian arts, in Mexico, and elsewhere. Many indigenous peoples—the aboriginal peoples of Australia, the native peoples of North and South America—were not really "colonized"; instead they were both decimated and isolated on reservations, and often stand in a quite different relationship to cultural formation in the state. Finally, it is important to understand the enormous political, economic, and cultural change sweeping the former "Second World" after the fall of the Berlin Wall in 1989—the revival of democratic republics in the eastern bloc countries, the separation of several republics from the Soviet Union, and the challenges that these changes have posed to Russian political stability—as part of a different kind of "postcolonial" lanscape, one in which the coerced protections of a fading state socialism are offset by the engulfing threat of a disorienting, often rapacious market capitalism.

POSTCOLONIAL DRAMA IN PERFORMANCE AND HISTORY

The remainder of this introduction briefly traces some connections between the dramatic, theatrical, and cultural history informing the work of playwrights presented later in the unit. This discussion—like the collection of plays assembled here—is by no means "representative": Japan's role in Asia, and the theater traditions that have developed there are very different from the energetic performance traditions of Indonesia or Malaysia, and from both the traditional and contemporary theater of India; although their histories are quite different, the energetic theatrical life of South Africa and Nigeria in the past four decades hardly spans the range of African dramatic and nondramatic performance, especially the performance traditions of North African countries like Algeria or Egypt; Argentina's orientation toward northern Europe, and the relatively sparse population of indigenous peoples in Argentina during the conquest period make its theater quite different from the flourishing theaters of Mexico and Brazil. In each of these places, however, drama and theater have come to be one of the ways in which public discourse is conducted, an esthetic engagement with the changing status of the "nation" and its peoples.

Argentina

Argentina's historical and cultural development is hardly "representative" of the diverse histories of Latin American countries. Unlike Peru or Mexico, for example, Argentina was never a source of gold or silver, and throughout the seventeenth century the vast region that comprises much of present day Argentina, Paraguay, and Uruguay was a backwater of the viceroyalty of Peru. Puerto Nuestra Señora Santa María del Buen Aire was first established by Pedro de Mendoza in 1535. But although his expedition of 1,600 men was three times the size of the contingent that accompanied Hernan Cortés in conquering Mexico, the expedition arrived late in the summer, with little time to plant crops and harvest them for winter, and in a swampy region that was not well suited to agriculture in any case. The Spaniards established bad relations with the indigenous population, who soon began to lay siege to the settlement. The settlers finally—after slaughtering their cattle—resorted to cannibalism to survive the winter. Although the original settlement of Buenos Aires held on until 1541, it was abandoned as the settlers moved north to the thriving city of Asunción.

When Buenos Aires was reestablished in 1580, the central city of Córdoba was the dominant city of the viceroyalty, but by the seventeenth century the port city of Buenos Aires—whose people still refer to themselves today as "porteños"—emerged as the center of power in the region. The economy of Argentina depended on agriculture, and plantations were run by *encomienda,* the forced servitude of the native populations, licensed by the church. Throughout the eighteenth century, Buenos Aires was the center of military development, as well as of the burgeoning cattle ranching of the *pampas* stretching to the west and south of the city. Until 1776, the region was part of the viceroyalty of Peru and ruled from Lima; when Spain reformed the trade, administrative, and legal structure of its South American colonies in 1776, Buenos Aires became the capital of the viceroyalty of the Río de la Plata. Argentina's independence was part of the continental struggle for liberation of the first decades of the nineteenth century, precipitated by Napoleon's intervention in Spain in 1808. Although the Congress declared the independence of the United Provinces of the Río de la Plata on July 9, 1816, various civil and revolutionary wars would traverse the territory for the next thirty years. Argentina lost much of its viceregal territory in the wars of independence—parts of Peru in 1814, of Bolivia in 1825, of Uruguay in 1828. Beyond that, the revolution established two patterns that would afflict Argentina for a century. First, the *caudillos*—rural ranchers and landholders, with their own private armies—wanted the new nation organized as a loose federations of provinces, not as a centralized government emanating from Buenos Aires; much of the political conflict of nineteenth-century Argentina can be understood as a struggle between the federalist and central-government forces. Second, the wars drew a generation of British traders—some of whom fought with distinction in the revolution—to Argentina; they capitalized on the rich resources and weak economy of the new country, establishing lucrative trade relations with the United States, the United Kingdom, and Europe.

In some respects, Argentina's economic growth in the early twentieth century parallels that of the United States: several waves of European immigration in the 1880s and 1890s provided the labor power to transform Argentina into a manufacturing and agricultural power (in the early decades of the twentieth century, it was a cliché to be "as rich as an Argentine"). At the same time, however, Argentina's economy was drained by outside investment: by the Bank of England in the nineteenth century, and by American and European concerns in the twentieth. This situation was exploited by the charismatic Colonel Juan Perón, who was first elected president in 1946 on the promise of better wages and social programs for workers; Perón succeeded both in reducing foreign debt and in restoring the control of major industries—railroads and communications—to Argentine corporations. But Perón's economy also produced considerable inflation, and social unrest led to a series of military *juntas,* which typically used the excuse of Communist insurgency, the familiar bogeyman of the post-Castro era in the Americas, to justify the suspension of civil law.

In 1976, General Jorge Rafael Videla led a *junta* that inaugurated seven years of state terrorism, the "Dirty War" (1976-1983) in which brutal torture was routinely practiced, and thousands of Argentine citizens (*los desaparecidos*) were made to disappear by federal, state, and local government officials. This regime and its successors frequently collaborated with European and U.S. governments—on the eve of the disastrous Falklands War, General Leopoldo Galtieri attempted to gain U.S. government investment by offering military support to the United States in its military conflicts in Central America—and received both government and private investment. The Falklands conflict proved disastrous for the *junta,* and by January 1983 General Ramón J. Camps, the Buenos Aires chief of police in the Videla government admitted that the mass graves that had been discovered were those of *desaparecidos* (the "disappeared"), and that none were alive. Dissension in the military, a more activist prosecution of military crimes by the courts, and a widening sense that the *junta* could be ousted— typified around the world by Las Madres de la Plaza de Mayo—led to the election of Raúl Alfonsín in 1983, to the promise of trials, and then to the election of Carlos Menem.

Argentina has a long and distinguished theatrical tradition; plays were performed at the Jesuit missions in Córdoba in the early 1600s, and the first theater was built in Buenos Aires in 1757; the Teatro de la Ranchería was built in 1783. Throughout the seventeenth and eighteenth centuries, most of the plays performed in Argentina—in theaters in Santiago del Estero, Catamarca, Santa Fe, Corrientes, as well as Córdoba and Buenos Aires—were either Spanish *loas* or adaptations of French and Spanish dramas. By the nineteenth century, however, Argentine theater began to develop a more local flavor: in the romanticized dramas of *gaucho* (the famous Argentine cowboy) life typified by the anonymous *El amor de la estanciera* (1814); in plays of Argentine history, such as the independence play *25 de Mayo* and the play about the Peruvian native uprising *Tupac Amaru* (1817), both written by Luis Ambrosia Morante (1775–1837); and in a variety of short, sometimes satirical plays—called *SAINETES*—on political figures, and on the typical "characters" of Argentine life. This "local color" movement—*costumbrismo*—led to several popular genres, notably the *sainete gauchesco* and the *sainete criollo.*

The magnificent Teatro Colón opera house was built in 1857, at the early edge of Buenos Aires's development as a major metropolitan area; by 1900, Buenos Aires was known as the Paris of the New World for its fashionable elegance, and supported a wide range of theaters; 1900–1910 is regarded in Buenos Aires as the "golden decade" of its theaters, and many of Argentina's best-known playwrights—such as Florencio Sánchez (1875–1910), author of *La gringa* (1904) and *Barranca abajo* ("Down the Gully," 1905)—date from this era. As in Europe and the United States, an independent theater movement—El Teatro del Pueblo (1933) and La Máscara (1939)—arose, emphasizing (on the eve of Perón's mobilization of *los descamisados,* the shirtless workers) a more political, realistic, and Marxist orientation toward the staging of social life. Given the European orientation of Buenos Aires, it's not surprising that the various modes of European theatrical experimentation of the 1950s and after—Artaud's "theater of cruelty," theater of the absurd, Brechtian epic theater—have made their impact on Argentine drama, notably in the celebrated plays of Osvaldo Dragún (1929–1999); in the turbulence of the Perón and succeeding eras, the theater has often been a place of protest, and frequently subject to implicit or explicit censorship. This is especially true of the "dirty war" period. When the Teatro Abierto was founded in 1981, its building mysteriously burned to the ground within its first week of operation. Nonetheless, although many writers and intellectuals left Argentina, many remained, and their work often traces the connections between state terrorism and the diffuse nature of cultural and economic imperialism. Though written just before the "dirty war," Griselda Gambaro's play, *Information for Foreigners,* makes a direct assault on the authoritarian state; at the same time, by treating its audience as foreign tourists, the play implicates that larger world whose social and economic support helped to maintain the terror in Argentina.

Australia   Some have argued that the American independence—British convicts were transported to the American colonies before the Revolution—played a direct role in the British settlement of Australia as a penal colony in the eighteenth century. For although Portuguese, Dutch, Spanish, and British ships had all explored the Australian coastline, European settlement of Australia dates from 1788: the First Fleet—carrying 530 male prisoners, 160 female prisoners, and 250 freemen—sailed from England on May 13, 1787, and arrived in Botany Bay in January of 1788. The settlement at Sydney was soon followed by penal colonies at Newcastle in 1804, Moreton Bay in 1824, and other colonies: by 1830, 58,000 convicts (nearly 50,000 were men) had been transported to Australia. Most were relatively petty urban criminals, and the life they found in Australia could be very hard: conditions in many of the prisons were nightmarish, and prison life was for many nearly enslavement. Yet many convicts served their time outside prison—as something like indentured servants—and many remained to settle permanently. In the early nineteenth century Australia's economy was driven by sheep ranching and mining, and by the 1860s four relatively autonomous states had been formed, which moved toward federalization in the 1880s.

Western theater was brought to Australia in much the way Timberlake Wertenbaker dramatizes it in her play *Our Country's Good:* as a performance of George Farquhar's comedy *The Recruiting Officer* in 1789, in honor of the king's birthday, one year after the establishment of the British penal colony at Sydney in 1788. Beyond the slice of theater staged in Wertenbaker's play, though, the penal colonies were in many ways responsible for stimulating the importation of theater to Australia in the eighteenth century. Robert Sideway—one of the convicts in the Farquhar production—went on to open a theater in Sydney in 1796, which was opened to convicts and freemen until he was forced to close it in 1798; theaters were also operated in the penal colonies on Norfolk Island, in the Sydney Gaol, and in the colony on the Emu Plains.

By the mid-nineteenth century, the major cities of Australia—Melbourne and Sydney—had large theaters on the model of the major London houses, theaters seating upwards of two thousand patrons offering a repertoire of classical and contemporary European plays. Given the large population of recently released convicts, censorship was widespread in Australia, though many convicts—like Robert Sideway—made their way into the theater: David Burn's play, *The Bushrangers* (1828) was based on the life of a Tasmanian convict; and Edward Geoghegan, a convict, wrote or adapted ten plays for the Sydney Royal Victoria Theater. The major theaters received international tours—by Janet Achurch in the English production of Ibsen's *A Doll House* in 1889, and by Sarah Bernhardt in 1891—and developed in many ways along the lines of commercial theaters in England or the United States. Indeed, until the 1950s, the theater scene in Australia was similar to that of Canada or the United States: large commercial theaters devoted principally to popular drama and entertainment; a small smattering of amateur or independent theaters exploring various "new" dramatic and theatrical styles.

In 1954, in commemoration of the visit of Elizabeth II to Australia, the Governors of the Commonwealth Bank established the Australian Elizabethan Theatre Trust, with the purpose of establishing a national theater. It was a propitious moment; in 1956, Ray Lawler's (b. 1921) vivid working-class play about cane cutters who take an annual visit to the city, *The Summer of the Seventeenth Doll,* opened and soon became celebrated throughout Australia and the world. In an important act of nation building, the Theatre Trust used its subsidy for a number of purposes, not only to establish a National Theatre Company (1956), an Australian Ballet (1962), and an Australian Opera (1969), but to establish and support professional theater in each of the state capital cities: companies in Melbourne and Sydney in 1960, in Adelaide in 1965, in Brisbane in 1969, in Hobart, Tasmania, 1973.

As a result, even despite a conservative sense of Australian propriety that led to the censorship of playwrights like Patrick White (1912-1990) in the 1960s, Australia today has an energetic theater scene, both in subsidized and self-sustaining companies. In 1973 the Australian National Playwrights' Conference provided a means to support emerging writers, and a range of experimental companies—The Australian Performance Group, Nimrod—stimulated a new burst of playwriting, in plays like David Williamson's (b. 1942) *The Removalists* (1971), or the plays of Louis Nowra (b. 1950), Alma De Groen (b. 1941), or Michael Gow (b. 1955).

The Black Theatre Group was also organized in the 1970s, as part of an urgent desire to sustain traditional and new performance by Australia's Aborigine peoples. The various Aborigine tribes—estimated at about 500 tribes or smaller groups, numbering about 300,000 in 1788—mainly populated the northern and eastern areas of Australia. When the British began to establish colonies, they were put under the protection of the Colonial Office in London, but to little avail: the Aborigines did not integrate well into the British colonies (as a docile labor force, for example), and most were either killed outright, died from disease, or were driven into small "mission" areas. By the 1920s and 1930s, the overwhelming majority of Aboriginal peoples were "half-caste," and many were herded into squalid settlements, such as the Moore River Settlement that provides the setting for Jack Davis's play *No Sugar.* During this period, Aborigine infants were often taken to be raised by white families, in the hope that the "Aborigine problem" would gradually disappear through intermarriage (until 1966, Australia had an unofficial "whites only" immigration policy; only "white" immigrants were allowed to settle permanently). A 1967 referendum established Aboriginal Australians as part of the national population, to be counted in the census and therefore given parliamentary representation; in 1976 the Aborigine Rights Act granted 139,000 acres in the Northern Territory to Aborigine claimants as freehold property; South Australia made a similar grant to the Pitjantjatjara people. The National Aborigine Conference was formed in 1977, elected from Aborigine and Torres Strait Islander peoples, and in the 1980s, the Aboriginal Playwright's Conference was established to further the aims of aboriginal playwrights, and to protect native traditions. Given the distinctive beliefs of the Aborigine peoples—"The Dreaming," a mythic creation time when world and its peoples were formed, and whose spirits persist in the material world—and the dance-storytelling-musical *corroboree,* it is perhaps not surprising that a number of companies devoted to developing and preserving these arts have arisen, such as the Aborigine and Islander Dance Theater Company of Sydney.

Canada

Theater in Canada, like the culture of Canada itself, has been largely defined by its two dominant European settler cultures—English and French. Until the American Revolution, much of the eastern third of North America was contested by English and French explorers and traders: Jacques Cartier sailed down the St. Lawrence River, past the sites of Québec and Montréal in the 1530s; Samuel de Champlain's extensive explorations in the first quarter of the seventeenth century helped to define important fur-trading routes. By the mid-seventeenth century, however, Louis XIV declared New France a royal province, and throughout the remainder of the seventeenth and eighteenth centuries, France and Britain vied for control of Canada. The British had several strongholds in the maritime provinces, and to the west, in present-day Ontario; the exodus of British loyalists from the American colonies during the revolution—many of whom went into French Canada—enabled Britain to gain control of Canada; the 1791 Constitutional Act recognizes British legal and civil institutions, and the increasing British dominance of the important fur trade as well. In 1841, the United Provinces of Canada, in an effort to "assimilate" French Canada more effectively, gave a plurality of seats in the parliament to the British provinces. Although Canada was united as a Dominion in 1867, and gained its autonomy in 1931, the tensions between British and French Canada remain very much alive today: the separatist Parti Québécois and its charismatic leader René Levesque came to prominence in the early 1970s, and in several recent plebiscites, the citizens of Québec have voted to remain in Canada by only a narrow margin.

Although there are records of garrison performances in English Canada—an English version of Molière's *The Misanthrope* in January of 1744, in Nova Scotia—the earliest European performances in Canada are in French Canada. At Port-Royal, in Arcadia, Marc Lescarbot's aquatic pageant *Le Théâtre de Neptune en la Nouvelle-France* was performed (in war canoes!) to honor visiting French dignitaries in November 1606, and until a production of Molière's *Tartuffe* aroused the ire of the Catholic bishop—who forbade public theater in Québec in 1694—many performances of neoclassical French playwrights, including Corneille, Racine, and Molière were given in Québec. By the early nineteenth century, however, the Amateur Canada Dramatic Society had formed in Montréal (1835), and the church came to see that modest and moral stage performance could promote Catholic values. In 1898 it sanctioned the first lay company of actors, *Les Soirées de Famille* ("Family Evenings"). By this time, however, two permanent French-speaking theaters had been built in Montréal: the Monument National (1894) and Le Théâtre des Nouveautés (1898), serving a thriving trade in both touring companies from France and in the work of French-Canadian playwrights, such as Louis-Honoré Fréchette (1839–1908), whose sensational patriotic drama *Félix Porré* opened in 1862.

Theatre in English Canada was stimulated in part by the American Revolution; many British loyalists fled the revolution to the eastern provinces of Canada. The 500–seat Grand Playhouse was built in Halifax in 1789, and by the early nineteenth century, Toronto and other cities had major theaters on the European model. Nonetheless, much of the theatrical activity in the nineteenth century was by touring companies. However, much as in Europe, several smaller amateur companies developed, both to stage the new drama, and to support Canadian playwrights. The most significant of these companies was founded in 1919 by Roy Mitchell, at the University of Toronto—the Hart House Theatre. The Hart House was responsible for importing a number of experimental European playwrights, as well as for supporting the production of Canadian playwrights, including Dora Smith Conover, and Marjorie Price; Herman Voaden's expressionistic plays of the 1930s were produced at the Play Workshop. Other art theaters were formed in other cities as well; Martha Allan returned from working at the Pasadena Playhouse to her native Montréal to found the Montréal Repertory theater in 1930; the Toronto Workers Theater was active in the 1930s as well; and the establishment of the Canadian Broadcasting Company in 1936 brought radio drama throughout the nation.

The postwar period was the first real period for the growth of Canadian drama and theater. In part spurred by the Vincent Massey Report on the Arts of 1951 and the development of the Canada Council in 1957, both English and French Canada witnessed a flowering of new theater in the 1960s and 1970s. Several institutions—notably the Dora Mavor Moore New Play Society of Toronto (1946)—worked to develop Canadian plays and playwrights, like John Coulter's epic of the Métis rebellion in western Canada, *Riel* (1950); the founding in 1960 of a National Theatre School in Montréal. Both the Stratford Festival (established in 1953) and the Shaw Festival (1962) became showcases for Canadian actors, and by the mid-1960s a range of important theaters often working with new Canadian material had been founded: the Jupiter Theatre (1951); Tarragon Theatre (1971) in Toronto; L'équipe (1943), the Rideau Vert (1948), the Théâtre du Nouveau Monde (1961), the Théâtre des Cuisines (1973) and the Théâtre Expérimental des Femmes (1979) in Montréal; the Manitoba Theatre Center (1958), the Vancouver Playhouse (1962), the Neptune Theatre in Halifax (1962).

Although Gratien Gélinas (1908–1999) is usually described as the instigator of postwar French-Canadian drama—his play *Tit-Coq* (1948) about a soldier returning to Québec after the war is a modern classic—the drama of contemporary Canada was given an important impetus by the 1967 Dominion Drama Festival. Within the year a series of important plays were produced throughout Canada as part of its Centennial celebrations—Gélinas's *Yesterday the Children Were Dancing* (in English Translation), George Ryga's (1932-1967) *The Ecstasy of Rita Joe* among them. In 1968 Michel Tremblay's (b. 1942) groundbreaking play of working-class life in Québec, *Les Belles Soeurs* was produced; the play is also notable for being written in *joual,* the characteristic dialect of the city. Many plays, such as Sharon Pollock's *Walsh* (1973) attempt to reinterpret Canadian history; this play dramatizes the relation-ship between Major James Walsh, who commanded the North West Mounted Police in the 1870s and Sitting Bull, chief of the Hunkpapa Sioux. Since throughout much of the history of Canada the French-speaking minority of Québec has been dominated by an English-speaking majority, it's not surprising that the agitation in support of Québécois independence is reflected in a variety of plays as well. Indeed, the past three decades have seen a range of plays interrogating the Québec situation—not only the well-known plays of Michel Tremblay, but plays like Jean Barbeau's *Le chemin de lacroix* (1970) about a bill permitting Anglophone Québec parents to send their children to English-language schools in violation of Québec's bilingual policy, or Jean-Claude Germain's *A Canadian Play/Une plaie canadienne* (1979) about the mythology of a unified Canada. More recently, Marianne Ackerman's *L'Affaire Tartuffe, or, The Garrison Officers Rehearse Molière* (1993) takes a production of *Tartuffe* at the moment of Québec's incorporation into English Canada in 1774 as a turning point in the imagining of a nation. Much as Canadian drama—in different ways in English and French plays, in English and French theaters—considers the dynamics of Canadian nationalism, so the more recent work of Native playwrights like Tomson Highway, Monique Mojica—author of *Princess Pocahontas and the Blue Spots* (1990)—and others engage the position and representation of Native Canadians today. In the 1990s, Canadian theater continued in a period of artistic richness characteristic of Canada's official policy of multiculturalism. Robert Lepage not only directed landmark productions of Shakespeare's *A Midsummer Night's Dream* (at Britain's Royal National Theatre, 1992) but developed a stunning series of multimedia meditations—*Needles and Opium* (1994), *Elsinore* (1995), and *The Far Side of the Moon* (2000)—at his Theater Ex Machina in Québec City. Guillermo Verdecchia's brilliant performance piece exploring *latinidad* in a wider North American context, *Fronteras Americanas* opened in 1993. Canadian drama continues to have an increasingly pronounced impact on world theater, and several plays—notably the plays of Judith Thompson, Ann-Marie MacDonald's *Good Night Desdemona, Good Morning Juliet* (1988), and several of George Walker's plays—*Zastrossi* (1981) and *Escape from Happiness* (1991)—have found mainstream audiences in the United States and in Europe.

China

The most populous country on the planet, China has a long and magnificently diverse theatrical tradition. The first records of theater in China date from the Shang Dynasty, roughly 1500 BCE, and the history of China is studded with important landmarks in the development of performance. The Han period (206 BCE–221 AD) witnessed China's first important artistic flowering, and the characteristically complex blending of spoken language, acting, music, mime, and acrobatics that distinguishes Chinese theater dates from this period as well. The first training school, "The Pear Garden," was established during the T'ang dynasty (618–904), and the earliest surviving plays date from the succeeding the Sung dynasty (960–1279), plays which only began to be rediscovered in the 1920s. Although the Mongol conquest of the later thirteenth century put China under foreign rule, in the Yuan dynasty (1279–1368), seven hundred titles survive from this period, including several plays that have had an impact on the Western theater, including Chi Chun-hsiang's *The Orphan of the House of Chao,* adapted in 1775 by Voltaire, and Li Hsing-tao's *The Story of the Chalk Circle,* which provides the foundation for Bertolt Brecht's *Caucasian Chalk Circle.* While these plays typically use music and theatrical elements, they are considerably shorter than the "southern drama" that developed in southern China after the ejection of the Mongols in the Ming dynasty (1368–1644). The "southern drama" typically has more than fifty acts; it was mastered by playwrights such as T'ang Hsien Tsu (1550–1616), whose *Peony Pavilian* (recently adapted by the American director Peter Sellars) is today perhaps the most familiar of these plays. It is only in the Ch'ing period (1644–1912) that the most familiar form of traditional theater—Beijing Opera—began to take shape. Beijing Opera is a dynamic theatrical genre, using a scenario that sets the acting, singing, acrobatic, and musical skills of the performers on a narrative framework. Although there have always been a number of regional versions of this form, in 1790 the best performers from throughout China were brought to Beijing to celebrate the eightieth birthday of the Emperor Chi'ien-lung, and Beijing Opera is conventionally dated from this event.

With the increasing opening of China to the West in the nineteenth century, and after the revolution that established the Republic of China in 1912, Western culture came to have a more direct influence on the arts in China. Usually termed "spoken drama," to distinguish it from the musical conventions of traditional Chinese theater, the first Western play—Alexandre Dumas's (*fils*) *La Dame aux camélias*—produced in China was staged by the Spring Willow Drama Society in 1907, and in the decades following, several important playwrights wrote and adapted plays in the Western style for Chinese audiences, under the rubric of the New Cultural Movement: Tian Han (1898-1968) at the Nan Guo Drama Society, Hong Shen (1894–1955) for the Theatre Association, Xia Lan (1900–1995) for the Shanghai Art and Drama Association. Perhaps the most influential playwright of the prewar period is

Ts'ao Yu (1902), whose plays *Thunderstorm* (1933) and *Sunrise* (1935) continue to be read and produced. "Spoken drama," mainly in the mode of Western realism, thrived in China, and was given additional impetus by the victory of the Communists and the founding of the People's Republic of China in 1949. The new government was at once concerned to preserve traditional Chinese theater and to promote theater that would more dynamically reflect contemporary life. The Traditional Theater Research Institute (now part of the China Arts Research Institute) was founded in 1950, and within a decade had revived hundreds of theater forms: by 1960, China had over 3,000 companies performing over 50,000 traditional plays. At the same time, companies worked to update the subject matter of traditional theater forms, using, for example, Beijing Opera to address more contemporary social issues, often in the "model plays" that trained the Beijing Opera (or related styles, such as Kun Opera or Chuan Opera) on historical subjects with a revolutionary perspective. The new government also established a National Theater Festival in 1956, which supported the work of postwar "spoken drama" playwrights, notably Lao She (1899–1966), whose play *Tea House* has become a modern Chinese classic, as well as Lao Yu (1910–1997), and the work of the Shanghai People's Art Theatre, which adapted Brecht's for Chinese audiences.

In 1966, the wife of China's leader Mao Zedong, Jiang Qing—helped by Kang Sheng and two others, becoming the notorious "Gang of Four"—instituted a decade-long Cultural Revolution. The purpose of the Cultural Revolution was at once to purge China of foreign influences, and also to institute a massive program of reeducation to the proletarian ideals of Maoist communism. The decade-long Cultural Revolution forced a generation of artists, professionals, and intellectuals—regarded by the Gang of Four as their principal political opposition—out of the major cities and into rural areas, where they would be reeducated into revolutionary culture through manual labor. Since the traditions of Chinese theater descended from aristocratic patronage, and the modern "spoken drama" theater was so clearly influenced by the West, it's perhaps not surprising that Chinese theater stagnated during the Cultural Revolution. Most theater companies disbanded during this period, and with the exception of plays specifically developed under Jiang's guidance, plays were heavily censored or prohibited altogether; only eight new "model" productions were developed, five in traditional theater forms. In 1976, however, the Gang of Four were removed from power; Deng Xiaoping inaugurated a period of new openness to the west, and allowed considerably greater latitude to artists and writers, Although previous regimes had insisted on Mao's "revolutionary realism" in the theater, in the 1980s, playwrights and performers experimented more widely: Gao Xingjian's *Absolute Signal,* a fluid hallucinatory drama, was performed briefly by the Beijing People's Art Theater in 1982, the same theater that invited Arthur Miller to direct a Chinese production of *Death of a Salesman* the following year. A Shakespeare Festival was staged in both Beijing and Shanghai in 1986, followed by Festivals of Experimental Theater in 1989 and 1993. The 1980s saw the rise of a number of important younger playwrights, including Gao Xingjian and Sha Ye Xing (b. 1939), whose satirical *Major Chen* (1980) was rivaled in controversy only by his *Confucius, Jesus Christ, and John Lennon* (1988); produced by the Shanghai People's Art Theater while he was Artistic Director. Zong Fu Xian (b. 1947) uses a rally in Tiananmen Square to indict the Gang of Four in *In the Depth of Silence* (1978).

Theater in China has a tradition of patronage, both by the aristocracy and by the state. With the rise of a market economy in the 1990s, subsidies for theaters have declined, sometimes to as little as thirty percent of operating expenses. Moreover, after the Tiananmen Square protests in 1989 theater has been subject to somewhat more censorship than in the immediately preceding decade.

Czech Republic

The contemporary Czech Republic stands at the crossroads of central Europe, and, like its political history, the history of its theater reflects the tension between native inspiration and the external influence of more powerful nations. Records of folk theater and of medieval passion plays in the Czech lands—Bohemia, Moravia, and Silesia—extend back to the thirteenth century, though religious drama was largely suspended during the Hussite religious wars of the fifteenth century. As in the rest of educated Europe, Czech schools and universities used the staging of Latin drama as a mode of instruction, particularly under the influence of the celebrated Czech teacher Comenius (Jan Komenský, 1572–1640), and playwrights such as Karel Kolčava (1656–1717) wrote important folk dramas; but it was the defeat of Czech aristocrats at the battle of Bíla Hora in 1620 by the Austrian Hapsburgs that was the most decisive factor: for the next 250 years, Czech culture would be dominated by Austria. The first purpose-built theater was constructed in Prague in 1737, exclusively for the use of foreign companies. Count Nostitz-Rieneck's Estates Theater was built in 1783, but its director, František Bulla (c.1754–1819), began to perform Czech plays there as early as 1785, an early sign of the romantic nationalism sweeping Europe and the Czech lands. By the early nineteenth century, several important dramatists were writing plays of "national awareness," including Václav Kliment Klicpera (1792–1859), Karel Hynek Thám (1763–1816) and his brother, the actor Václav Thám (1765–1816), who wrote for the Bouda ("Wooden Hut") Theater in the late 1780s, Jan Nepomuk Štěpánek (1783–1859), and most importantly, Josef Kajetán Tyl (1808–1856), who wrote both historical dramas, such as *Jan Hus* (1848), and plays of modern life ("Where Is My Home?", a song from his romantic comedy *The Fair* [1834], became the Czech national anthem in 1918). Throughout the nineteenth century, resident theater companies played both in Prague and in Brno, generating the desire for a truly native, vernacular theater.

As in Ireland and the Scandinavian countries, a desire for national independence centered on the formation of a national theater company. The first independent, Czech-speaking professional theater, the Provisional National Theater, was founded in 1862, extending the already intense discussion of the possibility of a national stage; the elegant National Theater building opened in 1881 but almost immediately burned to the ground. It was a sign of the desire for a national stage that funds were raised through subscription, and a second theater was built, opening in 1883. Although there was always concern about whether an institutional theater could be at the forefront of emerging literary movements, the National Theater saw the production of plays much in the tradition of European modernism: Ladislav Stroupeznický's (1850–1892) satiric comedies of contemporary rural life, Alois (1861–1925) and Vilém Mrstík's (1863–1912) social drama *Maryša* (1894), Gabriela Preissová's (1862–1946) *The Step Daughter*, as well as plays with expressionist elements, such as Alois Jirásek's (1851–1930) *The Lantern* (1905). The innovative director Karel Hugo Hilar (1885–1935) used expressionist techniques in the Theater of Royal Vinohrady in Prague in the 1910s, departing to lead the National Theater in 1921. Ironically, he traded places with the National Theater's master of psychological realism, the director Jaroslav Kvapil (1868–1950), who went to the Royal Vinohrady (this exchange was considerably more than a trade of artistic directors, as many of he actors traded houses as well). But modern Czech drama came to international attention with the plays of Karl Čapek (1880–1938). A well-known journalist and novelist, Čapek's first play, *The Brigand* (1920), was produced at the National Theater, and led to a string of successes. *R.U.R.* (1921)—the abbreviation is for "Rossum's Universal Robots"; the English word "robot" was coined from Čapek's play—was soon performed both in London and New York, as was *The Insect Play* (1922), which he wrote with his brother Josef (1887–1945), the famous Czech cartoonist. Čapek wrote a series of important plays, including a sequel to *R.U.R., Adam the Creator* (1927), and two plays protesting the rise of Fascism, *The White Scourge* (1937) and *The Mother* (1938). Čapek died in the year that Nazi Germany invaded Czechoslovakia, and his brother was arrested and died in the Belsen concentration camp in 1945.

With the German invasion and occupation of the Czech lands in 1938, theater in the "Protectorate of Bohemia and Moravia" was heavily censored, and the lively culture of socialist and experimental theater that had grown up in Prague and Brno in the 1920s and 1930s—

most notably Emil František Burian's (1904–1959) D-34 Theater, and the socialist Liberated Theater of Jinřich Honzl (1893–1953)—was extinguished. At the beginning of the occupation, the Nazis granted the Czechs the appearance of "cultural autonomy." The Nazis did give the Czechs a degree of cultural autonomy, so Czech theaters were able to produce plays in Czech, and some plays prohibited in Germany were produced in Czech theaters. As in the Third Reich, all plays by antifascists, Communists, pacifists, and Jewish authors were prohibited. Nonetheless, using the practice of "jinotaj"—a kind of code of theatrical communication in which subversive meanings clear to the Czech audience were "veiled" from the German authorities—some directors (including Burian, Honzl, and others) and famous performers (such as the actress Ružena Nasková [1884–1960]) risked execution. Very rapidly, however, the Czech theater was firmly policed, and many Czech artists were killed or transported to concentration camps, and with the beginning of the war most works by Allied authors were banned (by 1940 over 1300 writers had been censored in the occupied Protectorate). One of the most fascinating chapters in the history of the theater concerns the imprisonment of German and Czech Jewish artists and performers to the Terezín concentration camp outside Prague, where they performed music, classical drama, and original plays and cabaret. As the war wound to a close, and Germany's eventual defeat became clear, Hitler increased the executions at his concentration camps, and most of the inhabitants of Terezín were transported to Auschwitz and killed. On September 1, 1944, all Czech theaters were closed, and the theater workers were directed to work for the German war effort.

After the war, Czechoslovakia came under the sway of the Soviet Union, and the Communist Party took control of the government in 1948. Under the Communists, the press and artistic institutions were governed by a central office that dogmatically imposed the favored **SOCIAL REALISM** of the Soviet Union; by the mid-1950s, censorship was controlled by the Ministry of the Interior (as it had been under the Nazis), and enforced by its agency, the State Police. At the same time, the long tradition of Czech innovation in the theater managed to persist. Josef Svoboda (1920–2002) became the chief theater designer at the National Theater in 1948, leading to the preeminence of Prague as a center of theater design; his multimedia *Laterna Magica* project was first seen at the Brussels Exhibition of 1958, and now occupies its own modern theater building adjoining the National Theater. The ABC Satire Theater performed during the brief political "thaw" of the late 1950s (1955–1962), and Prague's most influential new theaters, the Theater Behind the Gate (1955–1972) and the Theater on the Balustrade (1958–1972) both date from this era as well. These theaters experimented both with plays by young Czech writers (Milan Kundera, b. 1929; Pavel Kohout, b. 1929, and Václav Havel) as well as importing the plays of Jarry, Ionesco, Beckett, and Brecht to the stage. With the Soviet invasion of Czechoslovakia in 1968, however, many artists fled the country, and many others were either forced into exile, underground, or imprisoned as the result of their resistance to the state. Newspapers were closed, and widespread purges of artistic and educational institutions were enforced. Václav Havel's involvement in the Charter 77 movement (see the Havel biography later in this Unit), for example, contributed to his imprisonment. Perhaps the most symbolic protest was that of the young philosophy student Jan Palach, who wrote a letter calling for the end of Soviet censorship; signing the note "Torch Number One," he burned himself to death in Prague's central Wenceslas Square on January 16, 1969. As was the case during the German occupation, dissident theater was pursued beyond the official stage, and many plays were copied and secretly circulated. One important form of theater available to artists in the 1970s and 1980s was "apartment theater," plays performed in the homes of actors and playwrights. Vlasta Chramostová (b. 1926) had an important apartment theater, sponsoring a famous production of *Play Macbeth* (a version of this performance is captured in Tom Stoppard's play *Cahoot's Macbeth*). With the fall of the Berlin Wall in 1989, and the Velvet Revolution that followed, the Czech Republic has witnessed an extraordinarily smooth political transition, and joined the European Union in 2004. Perhaps not surprisingly, Prague has again become an important theatrical capital, the site not only of the dynamic productions at the National Theater and Estates Theater, but of many smaller experimental companies as well. The Theater on the Balustrade is again the home of a modern repertory, and theater companies from around the world regularly come to the Czech Republic's major cities.

India   The second-most populous nation on the planet, with seventeen official languages, India has an immensely rich cultural and theatrical history. The earliest literary writing—the epic poems *Ramayana* and *Mahabharata*—date from between the tenth and fifteenth centuries BCE, and provide the narrative sources for much of the diverse range of traditional Indian performance. The oldest dramatic traditions date to the Sanskrit plays first written and performed during the Gupta empire in northern India, beginning about 100 AD; the aesthetic animating this theater is systematically explored in Bharata's *Natyasastra* (150 AD) (on Sanskrit Theater and Drama, see Unit II). Although Sanskrit has an important dramatic tradition—including King Sudraka's *The Clay Cart* and Khalidasa's *Shakuntala* (fifth century), Sanskrit—like Latin in Europe—gradually split into a range of vernacular languages; the invasion and rise of the Muslims to power after the seventh century restricted theatrical performance, and Sanskrit theater was believed until quite recently to have ceased, being replaced throughout India with an astonishingly diverse range of folk performance. As in other Asian performance forms, "theater" is not restricted to the spoken enactment of scripted plays: instead, the great majority of Indian folk theater forms use a brilliant interplay of story-telling, singing, dance, and music; there are also important forms of puppet theater as well. In the northern states of India, for instance, there is a 400-year tradition of performing the *Ramlila* and *Raslila* plays: cycle-dramas concerning events in the lives of Krishna, and Vishnu Rama. These performances often take place over three or four weeks, and involve the audiences in various kinds of religious ritual; they also mark one of the features of many Indian theater forms, the discrimination of actors from singers. In the *Ramlila,* the singer narrates the action, while the actors perform. A more recently developed form, the **JATRA,** is a staple of performance in Bengal, in eastern India. *Jatra* performances—like most Indian folk theater—do not take place in a theater, but in the open air, with the audience surrounding the performers. Unlike *Ramlila,* though, *jatra* tend to address contemporary concerns rather than the lives of mythic heroes. Indeed, the central figure of the *jatra* is always called Vivek, or "conscience": Traditionally, there is music in the *jatra,* and the actors sing; the performers are all male, and there are now professional *jatra* companies. Perhaps the most familiar form of traditional Indian performance in the West is *kathakali,* a dance-drama form from the southern state of Kerala. Performed in Malayalam—the language of Kerala—*kathakali* nonetheless preserves important elements of Sanskrit drama. In *kathakali,* the actors learn an elaborate and refined set of stylized bodily movements and detailed hand-gestures, each of which is codified as part of the *Natyasastra* tradition; having learned these techniques over many decades, the actors (all of whom are male) do not rehearse: they simply perform one of the 500 plays in the *kathakali* repertoire. Although it would be difficult to say that any form—or any three forms—can represent the range of traditional theater in India—there are literally hundreds of distinct theater and dance forms in this vast nation's rich folk and ritual traditions—what these forms share is a popular tradition of performance in village squares, at temples, or other open spaces, a complex involvement of music, acting, and dance, and a vigorously disciplined performance training.

While folk theater remains the dominant experience for the majority of Indians today, it remains in a now-productive tension with "modern" Indian theater. India has had a long history of contact with Europe: the Persians invaded northwest India in the sixth century BCE; Alexander the Great invaded again in 326 AD; the Portuguese explorer Vasco da Gama landed in India in 1498. British involvement with India was handled by the East India Company throughout the seventeenth and eighteenth centuries, but in 1858 the British government took over the Company, and in 1877 Queen Victoria became the Empress of India, and India became the "jewel" in her colonial "crown." Even before India was incorporated into the Empire, there were strong nationalist movements, and the British recognized the need for an Indian administrative class: universities were established in 1857 in the principal colonial cities, Calcutta (now Kolkata), Bombay (now Mumbai), and Madras to produce a "native" population educated to British values. In line with Thomas Babington Macaulay's infamous "Minute" to the House of Lords on Indian education, education was sustained by the teaching of English history and literature, the plays of Shakespeare and of eighteenth-century dramatists in particular. The British also produced English-language plays, and built theaters to accommodate touring companies. In the late nineteenth century, several Indian playwrights began to write plays—often in native languages such as Hindi or Urdu—in imitation of European drama; Wajid Ali Shah wrote several musical dance dramas, notably *The Tale of Radha and Krishna* (1851) and *Tale of Love* (1853); the Urdu poet Agha Hasan Amanat's *The Court of Lord Indra* (1854) was widely produced and translated. Moreover, the mid-nineteenth century also saw the rise of a new form of theater for India, profit-making companies. This kind theater, usually called Parsi Theater because these theaters were operated by Parsi businessmen (though usually employing Hindu and Muslim actors and playwrights), became the principal venue for "modern drama" in India, as the Parsi theaters often built new theater buildings on the model of Victorian proscenium theaters—such as the Victoria Theater and the Alfred Theater in 1871—and financed stage productions. Some of these plays adapted Western drama, as Agha Hashra Kashmiri (1879-1931) did in *White Blood* (1906), his adaptation of Shakespeare's *King Lear;* in the main, though, the Parsi theater was known for large-cast musical dramas, such as K.P. Khadikar's *Self Respect and Insult* (1911), a Marathi play arguing against the practice of child marriage. While the Parsi theater was extremely popular, particularly in the major urban areas, it seems finally to have been extinguished by the rise of film: indeed, many of the first Indian movie theaters were adapted from Parsi theater buildings.

While the Parsi theater represents one side of the "modernization" of Indian theater—turning it into a profit-making enterprise—there were other theater currents animating Indian theater in the later nineteenth-century. Bharatendu Harishchandra (1850–1885), for example, wrote plays in Hindi on pressing social issues—*The Sorry State of Bharat* (1880), *The Truthful King* (1875)—which were produced in public spaces. In Bengal, several playwrights used drama for specifically nationalistic purposes. Dinbandhu Mitra's *Neel Darpan* (*Indigo Mirror*) (1860) protested the plight of indigo workers, and was produced by the fledgling National Theater Company of Calcutta. When this company split into a Hindu National Theater and a Bengali National Theater, it retained this oppositional edge. The Bengali National Theater revived *Neel Darpan,* not only summoning agricultural workers to rebel against the British, but also showing the rape of a peasant woman by her British landlord. Largely due to the celebrity of this production, the government instigated the Dramatic Performances Control Act of 1876, in which local police were obliged to censor all new drama being produced in their jurisdiction. Perhaps for this reason, India's most famous poet and playwright of the colonial period—Rabindranath Tagore (1861-1941)—worked away from the realism of other playwrights, attempting to revive the mythological orientation of Sanskrit literature, and indeed to adapt it to critical purposes; Tagore won the Nobel Prize for Literature in 1913. Of course, the nationalist movement was given critical impetus by the work of Gandhi (1869–1948) and Jawaharlal Nehru (1899–1864), and "modern theater" in the twentieth century was strategically advanced by the Indian People's Theater, which opened branches in every Indian state in 1943, in many places bringing women to the stage for the first time.

India gained its independence from Britain on August 15, 1947; partition was established dividing Pakistan as an Islamic nation to the north at the same time, and in 1971 East Pakistan separated from Pakistan as Bangladesh. In the 1950s the Indian government established a range of cultural institutions, including the Cultural Academy of Performing Arts and the National School of Drama in 1959. The School's second director, Ebrahim Alkazi (b. 1925)—who had trained at the Royal Academy of Dramatic Art in London—was responsible at once for developing training in modern Western dramatic and theatrical traditions as well as for training performers in traditional Indian forms; his staging of Kalidasa's *Abhijnana Shakuntalam* (a Sanskrit play dating from 6 AD) at the Congress of Orientalists in New Delhi in 1964 is said to have inaugurated a revival of interest in exploring and preserving classical forms. In the aftermath of independence, Indian culture struggled at once to define a specifically "Indian" identity, and to modernize along the lines of Western culture: this tension governs the theater as well. The "theater of roots" movement sought to explore and experiment with traditional theater forms, sometimes using traditional tribal performers as well. One of the leading playwrights of modern India, Girish Karnad (b. 1938), writes in the Kannada language; his *Hayavadana* (1971) uses music, mime, dancing and costume of traditional theater; his *Naga Mandala* is the first modern Indian play to be produced in the U.S. (Guthrie Theater, Minneapolis, 1993). Vijay Tendulkur (b. 1928) Several other playwrights and directors have worked in traditional forms, which have also been applied to Western dramas—as in the Annette Leday/Keli Theatre Company *Kathakali King Lear* (1989). While the "theater of roots" continues to work with traditional forms, street theater has become an increasingly popular form of theater and protest; one prominent playwright, Safdar Hashimi of Delhi produced an extensive series of street production in support of the rights of the urban poor: he was murdered in 1989 during a street performance of his play *Attack!,* beaten to death by the members of a rival political organization.

The major playwrights of modern India write in a range of languages—Hindi, Kannada, Marathi, Bengali—and for a variety of theatrical traditions. There is also an emerging dramatic literature in English. Writing in the colonial language has posed a problem for writers from Joyce to Ngũgĩ, and it is controversial as well in India. At the same time, English is one of the nation's official languages; it provides the *lingua franca* for citizens from different regions, who may not speak one another's language, and when plays from one region are translated for performance in another region, they are translated into English.

Ireland and Northern Ireland

English involvement in Ireland dates to the twelfth-century "conquest" of Ireland—Henry VIII assumed the title of "King of Ireland" in 1541—and the relationship between England and Ireland has been contested ever since. In the late sixteenth and early seventeenth century, Hugh O'Neill led a series of uprisings against English immigrants, who were establishing plantations in the northern areas of Ulster; later, during the English Civil War (1641–1642), the forces that Charles I raised in Ireland were eventually defeated, and Oliver Cromwell enacted a series of brutal massacres in Ireland in retribution, confiscating lands as well. When Charles II took the English throne in 1660, the Act of Settlement confirmed the landowning claims then in place in Ireland: Catholics who had been evicted from their property were unable to regain it. In 1688 the Catholic heir, James II, ascended the English throne; when Parliament invited William of Orange (who was married to Mary Stuart, a Protestant heir) to assume the throne, James fled to Ireland: his forces were defeated at the Battle of the Boyne in 1690 and he fled to France; his Irish supporters were defeated in 1691 at Aughrim.

William's victories inaugurated a prolonged period of Irish misery: the displacement of Catholics from land and property, restrictions of their rights to education, to bear arms, to pass property to their heirs, or to vote. Although some of these laws lost force in the later eighteenth century, they provided the backdrop for political unrest in the period, particularly Wolfe Tone's mobilization of the Dublin United Irishmen in support of a French-supplied invasion. Although the French did send naval forces, and rebellions in Leinster, Ulster, and elsewhere looked promising, Tone was captured in 1798 and committed suicide in prison. In 1809, the Act of Union brought Ireland into the United Kingdom, effectively ending aspirations to nationhood. Nonetheless, throughout the nineteenth century, several movements worked for independence: Daniel O'Connell fought to repeal the Union, and Michael Davitt won security for tenants following the crop failures of 1879. Yet famine and immigration cut the Irish population in half between 1840 and 1900, and the Union's free-trade legislation turned Ireland into an impoverished supplier of raw material and labor to English factories. In the later nineteenth century, nationalism was pursued on two fronts: by the desire for "home rule" led by Charles Stewart Parnell, and by a new sense of Irish cultural identity, fostered by the Gaelic League and other cultural institutions.

Although Dublin and Ulster had supported theaters, these theaters were driven by an English repertoire: the only Irish characters to play on the stage were comic, drunken, buffoons— "Stage Irishmen." It was this sense of cultural nationalism that gave rise to the first burst of Irish theater, the founding of the Irish Literary Theater—later the Abbey Theatre— in 1899 by the poet/playwright W. B. Yeats (1865–1939), and the playwrights Lady Augusta Gregory (1852–1932) and John Millington Synge (1871–1909). The ambition of this company was to "build up a Celtic and Irish school of dramatic literature," and in the next thirty years, the Abbey succeeded not only in producing a wide range of plays on nationalsubjects—peasant dramas about rural life like Synge's *The Playboy of the Western World* (1907); plays exhuming Irish mythology, like Yeats's cycle on Cuchulain; or realistic dramas ofworking-class urban life like Sean O'Casey's *The Plough and the Stars* (1926)—but establishing both an Irish style of performance, and the materials of a national theater as well. The Abbey remains a leading theater in the Republic of Ireland, and several leading playwrights have had major productions there: Tom Murphy, Ann Devlin, and Frank McGuinness among many others.

The aborted revolution of Easter 1916 was a precursor of sweeping political change by 1917, Eamonn De Valera was elected president of Sinn Féin and campaigned for an independent Ireland rather than merely achieving Home Rule as a province of Britain; in 1919, Ireland's war of independence was under way. In 1922, Sinn Féin succeeded in negotiating a treaty with the United Kingdom for independence, but the Free State was not to include the counties of Northern Ireland, which remained a British province. There have been various periods of tension between Northern Ireland and the Republic of Ireland and between Ireland and the United Kingdom; these tensions came to a head in the late 1960s. In Northern Ireland, sharp divisions between rich and poor, the politically powerful and the oppressed have often fallen across religious divisions as well, separating Protestant Anglo-Irish from Catholics. Throughout the 1960s, Catholic and Protestant groups rioted in the Northern cities of Belfast and Derry (then, Londonderry); British soldiers were summoned to protect Protestant marchers. In 1972, the "Bloody Sunday" riots resulted in thirteen deaths, and a newly mobilized Provisional Irish Republican Army (IRA) began a series of retaliatory campaigns; the British Embassy was burned in Dublin, and the British secretary of state suspended the Northern Irish parliament and instigated direct rule.

The history of Northern Ireland for the past thirty years is the history of this conflict: the hunger strikes by Catholic prisoners in the Maze prison who claimed the right to be treated as political prisoners rather than criminals; the increasing insurgency of Protestant paramilitary forces, inspired by the nationalist rhetoric of Ian Paisley; Gerry Adams and Sinn Féin's efforts to gain and remain in a position to be part of the bargaining for peace. The IRA cease-fire of 1994 was part of that bargain, and although violence has erupted since then, the current round of peace talks seems promising.

One of the most difficult aspects of the situation in Northern Ireland is the challenge to ideas of "national identity." Although Northern Ireland is physically part of Ireland, many of its citizens—even those who do not wish to be part of the United Kingdom—feel distinct from the Republic of Ireland; similarly, the long traditions of English rule have instilled a feeling of identification with England, one strengthened (for some) by the pro-Irish violence of the IRA. In many respects the theater of Northern Ireland has had to negotiate this vexed sense of nationalism. For example, the Field Day Theatre Company was founded in

1980 by the playwright Brian Friel, the poet Tom Paulin, the actor Stephen Rea, and the poet Seamus Heaney: the purpose of the company was to develop a new theater, a new dramatic literature of the North, one that attempted to identify the distinctiveness of Northern Ireland. In plays such as Friel's *Translations* or Thomas Kilroy's (b. 1934) *The Double Cross* (1986), or even in translations like Tom Paulin's version of *Antigone, The Riot Act,* Field Day attempted to bring a specifically Northern Irish culture into dialogue with a wider world. But the work of Field Day should be seen in the context of other playwrights, some of whom, such as Christina Reid (b. 1942), see the problems of contemporary urban life in cities like Belfast to be "political" in ways that extend well beyond the problems of national identification, into areas of gender and economic exploitation. While Frank McGuinness was born in Donegal (part of the Republic of Ireland), his brilliant play *Observe the Sons of Ulster Marching Toward the Somme* (1985) uses the situation of Irish soldiers during the First World War (before the independence of the Republic and the partitioning of the northern counties) to explore the complex personal politics of Unionism. Although Field Day—which toured its productions throughout Northern Ireland—has ceased producing plays, it has published a widely read anthology of Irish writing and has sponsored a series of essays on questions of national and postcolonial art and culture.

Japan   The introductory essay of Unit II traced the development of the classical forms of Japanese theater—Noh, Kabuki, and Doll Theater—through the period of the Tokugawa shogunate (1603–1868). In 1868, the last of the Tokugawa shoguns was defeated and replaced by the Meiji Emperor, who wanted to open political, social, and cultural relations with the West, while at the same time disentangling Japan from a series of restrictive and exploitative trade relations with Europe. Indeed, throughout the 1880s and 1890s, Japan developed an aggressive military presence throughout the northern Asian Pacific, and both fought with China over the control of Korea and skirmished with Russia over the control of several of its islands. By the 1930s, Japan was a major military presence in the region. Taking advantage of political disorganization in China, Japan invaded Manchuria, and by 1938 had occupied parts of Mongolia and Kiangsu. Before drawing the United States into the Pacific theater with the bombing of its naval base at Pearl Harbor in Hawai'i, Japan had gained control of a huge territory, including all of Southeast Asia, Burma, the Philippines, and parts of New Guinea. Although the Western allies were unprepared for a Pacific war—after Pearl Harbor, the Japanese Navy greatly outnumbered the U.S. Navy—and suffered great casualties, the tide of the war was turned by one of the decisive events of the twentieth century: dropping the first atomic bombs on Hiroshima and Nagasaki. It is fair to say that life in Japan—and in different ways, in the rest of the world—was forever changed in that instant.

The new Meiji cultural connections to the West put different kinds of pressure on the traditional forms of Japanese theater. The Noh theater had been the special province of the *samurai* classes, and in the newly competitive theater marketplace was rapidly threatened with extinction. Several Noh actors—notably Umewaka Minoru (1828–1909)—worked to establish the Noh as a special part of Japan's cultural inheritance, an elite entertainment funded by the state (something like the "state opera" in many Western countries today), and today there are five Noh and two kyogen schools operating in Japan. Kabuki and Bunraku (the only form of Doll Theater still active) were more readily assimilated by the more open Japanese culture of the late nineteenth and early twentieth centuries, in large part because they had always been popular entertainments. Although there has been considerable modernization of Kabuki in the past century—contemporary Kabuki is not usually the daylong affair of the eighteenth-century theater; and to some extent Kabuki's reputation for lasciviousness has been replaced by a more "classical" orientation—the Kabuki and Bunraku theaters did not need to look for a new audience after 1868, and in many respects are a continuous performance tradition.

The history of modern Japanese theater is the history of Japan's negotiation of Western modes of playwriting and performance. The *SHIMPA* theater of the turn of the century adapted Western plays—Shakespearean tragedies and popular melodramas alike—to Japanese settings; it was a significant also for introducing actresses to the stage. Of greater consequence was the **SHINGEKI** theater. *Shingeki* ("new theater") imported both European plays in the realistic mode—Ibsen, Chekhov, Gorky, for example—and stimulated a new "realistic" style of drama among Japanese playwrights of the 1920s, 1930s, and 1940s. As it had in Europe in the 1880s, and in the United States in the 1910s and 1920s, this new dramaturgy was associated with a little theater movement. The most influential theater—the Tsukiji Little Theater of Tokyo—produced only Western playwrights in its first two years of operation, under the influence of its director Osanai Kaoru (1881–1928), who admired the work of Stanislavski and the Moscow Art Theater. Thereafter, the Tsukiji and other theaters like it tended toward social realism, plays such as Kubo Sakae's (1900–1958) splendid Marxist-inspired drama, *The Land of Volcanic Ash,* which traces the social and economic upheaval of the 1930s in a rural Japanese village on the colonial island of Hokkaido, was first performed by the Shinyo Troupe at the Tsukiji Little Theater in 1938. Although *shingeki* performance was banned during World War II, it became the predominant movement of the immediate postwar period, and Kubo's play was not only among the first plays to be staged after the war, but the play—and especially its central character, the radical agricultural scientist Kubo Amamiya—provided a model for postwar playwrights as well.

After World War II, the rebuilding of Japan was heavily financed by the United States, which also exerted considerable censorship control as well. Yet while "modern" Japanese theater had developed largely through the importation of European dramatic models, after the war, many writers worked to revive more traditional Japanese literary, dramatic, and theatrical forms. In some cases—Mishima Yukio (1925–1970) is a good example—this revival was part of an intense and conservative nationalist movement, the sense that "true" Japan was embodied in the prewar values of an imperial culture; but in other cases, it was part of a broader resistance to being culturally absorbed by the United States. A more experimental approach to blending foreign and indigenous dramatic modes arose, for instance, as part of the energetic protest against the U.S.–Japan Mutual Security Treaty in 1960. Many Japanese refused to participate in a "nuclear umbrella" agreement with the United States after the bombings of Hiroshima and Nagasaki (nearly a million demonstrated in Tokyo alone in 1959–1960), and the demonstrations around the treaty catalyzed a new introspection into the shape and meaning of Japanese culture, with its unique, deeply scarred relation to the postnuclear era. Hotta Kiyomi's (b. 1922) *The Island* (1955) was the first play about the bombings, and in the wake of the 1960 protests, a range of new kinds of theater and drama emerged: the backlash against Western dominance of Japan in the postwar period often appeared as a rejection of *shingeki* and of the Marxist politics that sustained its socialist realist esthetics. Kobo Abe's (1924–1993) plays, for example, often resonate with the **THEATER OF THE ABSURD,** but develop—as in the play *Slave Hunting* (1955)—a critique of spiritual poverty of postwar Japan. As David Goodman argues in his book *Japanese Drama and Culture in the 1960s: The Return of the Gods* (Armonk, NY: East Gate, 1988), playwrights like Fukuda Yoshiyuki (b. 1931) and Satoh Makoto (b. 1943) responded to the social and spiritual crisis of the post-1960 period in two ways: departing from *shingeki* conventions, they tend to use at least one godlike or archetypal character, and develop plays concerned "with the interrelated questions of personal redemption (salvation of the individual) and social revolution (salvation of the world)."

This new style of playwriting demanded a new style of performance, and some of the most powerful innovations of the Japanese theater in the past twenty years have involved performance style. The director Suzuki Tadashi (b. 1939) has been very influential in this regard. Suzuki's production of Satoh's play *The Black Tent* seemed to call for a "new realism"; Suzuki formed an experimental company, Suzuki Company of Toga (SCOT), in which he developed some exercises from Noh training toward a kind of performance emphasizing the actor's physicality. Suzuki's work has become well known to American audiences through his collaborations with Anne Bogart and the Saratoga International Theater Institute's productions (see Unit VI). The spiritual scars of Hiroshima and Nagasaki are perhaps more literally visible in the emergence of *BUTOH* (the word means simply "dance") performance. In *butoh,* the dancers are naked, shaven, and dusted with a white powder; their performance style demands a ferocious discipline, for their movements are exceptionally slow. Devised originally by Ohno Kazuo (b. 1966) and Tatsumi Hijikata (1928–1986), *butoh* is famous for the sense of ghostly apparitions that its dancers become onstage, enacting what Tatsumi called "the gestures of the dead."

Martinique   Christopher Columbus stopped at the island of Martinique in 1502; it was an inhospitable island, dominated by the fierce Caribs. Although both Spain and England briefly established outposts on the island, it was settled in 1658 as a French colony, soon of some six thousand settlers. As happened throughout the Caribbean, the native population was exterminated by violence and disease. But the Compagnie de Sénégal, a French slave-trading company, made frequent stops at Martinique on its way to the larger island of Guadeloupe; the French imported slaves to the island, especially after the introduction of coffee in 1723. But a series of slave uprisings (1789, 1815, 1822), and an ongoing conflict with the English over the slave trade, led France to abolish slavery in Martinique in 1848; as a result, plantation owners frequently had to import workers from India and China, and the population of Martinique today is descended from these various groups. Martinique was made a crown colony in 1674; control of the island passed briefly to the English several times in the late eighteenth and early nineteenth century. Since the 1840s, however, Martinique has been governed by France: first as a colony, then as a *département* (1946), and since 1974 as a region.

All of the colonial powers brought theaters to the Caribbean—the first theater was built in Jamaica in 1682, and a production of John Gay's *The Beggar's Opera* was staged there in 1733. Since the 1950s, Aimé Césaire—Martinique's most famous poet, playwright, and essayist—has been critical to the public life of Martinique, and indeed to the theory of postcolonial development more widely. For Césaire has played an important part in the public life of Martinique, beginning a long term of service as a deputy to the French National Assembly in 1945, and then leading his Progressive party into power in 1957, and establishing several national institutions in support of the arts and theater. In part due to his efforts and those of his followers—training performers in traditional Caribbean forms of masking, drumming, and dancing, as well as inviting celebrated playwrights and directors such as Ariane Mnouchkine and Wole Soyinka to work in Martinique—Martinique now has a thriving theater culture.

Nigeria   With ninety million people, Nigeria is Africa's most populous country; of its twenty language groups, four—Yoruba, Ibo, Hausa, and Fulani—predominate, and the histories of the Yoruba, Ibo, and Hausa peoples are entwined in Nigeria's precolonial, colonial, and postcolonial history. In the precolonial period, Nigeria was home to several rich cultures. In the northern region adjacent to Lake Chad, ninth-century Arab writers described a flourishing culture, organized around a series of walled cities along Saharan trade routes between Egypt and western Africa. With the introduction of Islam from Mali in the fourteenth century, the Hausa and Fulani peoples became Muslim; in the nineteenth century, several emirs led a massive *jihad* or holy war against religious and civil authorities, and established a new center of power in Sokoto. Yoruba culture emanated from the southwestern region of Nigeria, centered around the city of Ife (eleventh through the fifteenth centuries); this Old Oyo culture—from which contemporary Yoruba culture descends—was a complex monarchial society, spread through several important cities; this is the kingdom that the Portuguese discovered when they arrived in the city of Benin in the fifteenth century. Ibo culture was less centrally organized, and stretched in a series of villages through the southeastern part of Nigeria.

European colonization of Nigeria began around the slave trade. The Portuguese slave trade of the seventeenth and eighteenth centuries was centered in Benin; the Portuguese transported slaves to their New World colonies, and deep strains of Yoruba can be found in many New World–African cultures, particularly in Brazil. The expansion of Islamic Fulani emirates in northern Nigeria in the nineteenth century intruded into the Old Oyo empire, driving the Yoruba south, instigating a series of wars, and—by displacing a large population—stimulating the slave trade.

The British Royal Niger Company established trade with various Ibo and Yoruba leaders in the 1840s, but only established an administrative headquarters in Lagos in 1886. Although initially making contact as traders, the British presence rapidly developed from trade and missionary work into a more conventional colonial profile: consolidating territory, developing a legal apparatus, deporting local leaders who resisted, including the northern emirs, who were conquered in 1903. Originally divided into northern and southern colonies, Britain formed the Colony and Protectorate of Nigeria under a governor-general in 1914. Nigeria gained independence in 1960, but the strains between various regions and ethnic groups have not been readily resolved; in 1967 General Odumegwu Ojukwu declared a secession of the eastern states (Biafra), and despite marching successfully on Benin City, and nearly taking Lagos, surrendered in 1970. Although an initial constitution placed a legislature in each region, Nigeria has been beset by a series of brutal military regimes—the first coup in 1966 established a pattern for the 1970s, 1980s, and 1990s. In 1999, the government of Nigeria was returned to civilian control, with free elections.

The area now known as Nigeria was the home of a variety of cultures prior to becoming a British colony, and many of the performance practices of these cultures are visible in contemporary Nigerian theater and drama. Best known is the festival of *EGUNGEN;* this festival, which has been performed at least since the fourteenth century, attempts to establish a communion between the living and the dead. In it, masked and costumed celebrants proceed to a sacred grove, where the accumulated troubles of the village are removed by a "carrier." The persistence of this ritual is acknowledged by Wole Soyinka's play *Death and the King's Horseman,* which in various direct and indirect ways engages with the *egungen* narrative. Yoruba ritual is also known for the dynamic character of its gods—Obatala, the god of creation; Ogun, the god of creativity; Sango, the god of lightning—and for the use of masquerade as a central feature of ritual. One of the most popular theatrical forms in Nigeria is the Yoruba Traveling Theater; first developed by Hubert Ogunde (1916–1990), these performances generally concern a contemporary social issue, such as the exploitation of workers in his 1945 *Strike and Hunger.* Rather than a formal "drama," though, this form of theater takes the shape of a series of short skits, involving both dialogue and song, framed by a musical opening and closing number. In part because his company frequently satirized the colonial government (and was censored), Ogunde's work became widely known and imitated, and gave rise to a large number of companies practicing this narrative/dramatic/musical genre. Recently, Yoruba Traveling Theater has become almost exclusively a film genre.

In part because of the English presence—an English-language theater first opened in Lagos in 1899—in education, drama and theater played a large part in colonial Nigeria. D.A. Oloyede's play *King Elejigbo and Princess Abeje* (1904)—the first play in English by a Nigerian author—was written for a church group, and both reading and playing in the plays of the European tradition—Shakespeare, Molière, Shaw, Chekhov—formed part of the education of the generation of Nigerian writers and intellectuals who came of age with the independence. Wole Soyinka's plays often stage a rich dialogue between colonial and indigenous culture, drawing on the ritual and religious beliefs of the Yoruba. An Ibo playwright, John Pepper Clark (b. 1936) has dramatized the tales of the *ozidi* sagas—long stories that required several years to prepare and were performed by an entire village—and since the 1980s has directed his own professional theater. Femi Osofisan (b. 1946) is well known for taking a more critical, and politically engaged view of the problems of contemporary Nigerian society.

Russia   Although the Russian theater dates mainly from the eighteenth century, its impact on modern theater and drama has been profound; many of the playwrights of the nineteenth- and twentieth-century Russian theater (see Unit V) have become classics of the stage, and the theatrical innovations of the Soviet Union period (1919–1991)—SOCIAL REALISM, Vsevolod Meyerhold's (1874–1940) BIOMECHANICS, among many others—and the playwriting of contemporary Russia are part of the world theatrical repertoire today.

Theater in Russia has a long history of conflict with the Russian Orthodox Church, which was more effective than the Roman Catholic Church in its opposition to the stage. Although there are records of itinerant theater in the late middle ages, the Church's ban on theatrical performance extended well into the modern era; the first Romanov tsars erected a "house of amusement" in 1613, but Tsar Alexis (1645–1676) banned the theater with the exception of the Latin school drama until late in his reign, when he began to orient the Russian court more toward the practices of the European courts, which typically included a court stage as one of the ornaments of power. Peter the Great (1689–1725) extended the Romanov importation of European culture; he founded a theater in Moscow, and commanded attendance there for a time. Peter desired to engage Russia more directly with Europe—particularly after the wars with Sweden—founding the city of St. Petersburg on the Baltic Sea and moving his capital there from Moscow in 1712. Catherine the Great (1729–1796) ordered the founding of a professional theater; at the same time, Russia's famous "serf theaters"—theaters supported by large provincial landholders—produced generations of fine actors, many of whom followed the example of Mikhail Shchepkin (1788–1863), who came to the city (his career was pursued mainly in Moscow) to become a stage professional. As the capital, St. Petersburg saw the founding of several of Russia's preeminent theaters, including the Bolshoi, used mainly for opera and ballet, and the Maly and Alexandrinsky theaters, used as dramatic theaters in the 1750s, and important theaters were founded in the late eighteenth and early nineteenth centuries in Moscow as well; of these, Moscow's Maly Theater (1750) has had perhaps the most distinguished lineage and is today one of the world's best-known theaters. Many of Russia's greatest writers wrote for the stage, including Alexander Pushkin (1799–1837), Alexander Ostrovsky (1823–1886), and Nikolai Gogol (1809–1852), whose play *The Government Inspector* (1836) became a classic of European comedy. In the 1890s, Konstantin Stanislavsky (1863–1938) and Vladimir Nemirovich Danchenko (1858–1943) formed a literary circle experimenting with the production of new drama, founding the Moscow Art Theater in 1898; Anton Chekhov's (1860–1904) first major play, *The Seagull,* which had failed miserably in St. Petersburg, was the MAT's premiere (on Chekhov and the MAT, see Unit V).

As it was elsewhere in Europe, the period leading up to World War I was a period of intense cultural experimentation, and the success of the MAT in the realism cherished by Stanislavsky did not displace other kinds of experiment: Yevgeny Vakhtangov (1883–1922), Vsevolod Meyerhold, Alexander Tairov (1855–1950), and Mikhail Chekhov (1891–1955) all brought new styles and working methods to the MAT. With the Russian Revolution (1917–1919) and the success of the Bolshevik Party, the newly formed Union of Soviet Socialist Republics began to devise a cultural policy to form the citizens of the new soviet state. The appointment of A. V. Lunacharsky (1875–1933) as the Commissioner of Education at once ensured the survival of the Moscow Art Theater and the development of a state artistic policy; SOCIAL REALISM was confirmed as the official aesthetic policy at the first Congress of Soviet Writers in 1934. In the early phase of Soviet socialism, there was enormous excitement about the ways theater might be moved from its elitist, court-and-bourgeois past to become an instrument of revolutionary education and social change. Theaters were established throughout the USSR and supported with state funds, many of which were formed around collective purposes, such as the Trade Union Theater or the Red Army Theater. Meyerhold's efforts to locate the actor-as-worker led to a series of important collaborations, particularly with Vladimir Mayakovsky (1894–1940), whose plays *Mystery Bouffe*

(1928), *The Bed Bug* (1929), and *The Bath House* (1930) are often taken to mark the high point of Soviet drama. At the same time, Meyerhold's experiments in **CONSTRUCTIVISM**—notably his 1922 staging of Crommelynck's *The Magnanimous Cuckold*—were increasingly seen as counter to the official Soviet aesthetics, and the Meyerhold Theater was closed in 1937. Meyerhold arrived at his home to find his wife, Zinaida Raikh, murdered, and was himself arrested, tortured, and executed by the Stalin regime.

The Soviet theater system was deeply centralized; over 800 companies were supported by the state, providing lifetime stipends to playwrights, directors, actors, designers, managers, and stagehands, and keeping ticket prices very low, well within the wages of the typical worker. While this kind of support enabled theaters to support large permanent companies, the determination of the repertoire and the inability to change personnel often led to stultification. With the death of Stalin (1879–1953), however, a number of reforms were instituted that led to the founding of several new theater companies, especially the Taganka Theater (founded in 1946, but reorganized in 1964). At the same time, the theater schools associated with the MAT continued to produce well-trained and imaginative actors and directors, many of whom worked—as Yuri Lyubimov (b. 1917), director of Taganka, has done—to extend the legacy of Meyerhold, as well as exploring the once-forbidden legacy of Brecht, Beckett, and other European dramatists. Many of the theaters founded in the Soviet period have continued to flourish under the new Russian Federation: the Mayakovsky Theater, which was founded in 1922 and renamed the Theater of the Revolution in 1943, is just one example. Indeed, with the collapse of the Soviet Union and the emergence of the Russian Federation in 1991, many of Russia's chief theaters have gained a much larger international audience, both through tourism to Russia and because the companies can themselves tour more readily. The Maly Theater of St. Petersburg, under the leadership of Lev Dodin (b. 1944), has toured to Europe and the United States to considerable acclaim, praised both for the brilliance of its direction and the power of its physical performance. Although Russia no longer includes many of the republics of the former Soviet Union, it is a huge and diverse country, and continues to support theaters from the eastern border of Europe to Siberia. Many playwrights who began their careers in the Soviet era continue to write today, notably Alexander Volodin, whose important plays of the 1950s and 1960s (*The Factory Girl,* 1955; *Do Not Part with Loved Ones,* 1969) were often criticized for avoiding Communist Party themes; Mikhail Shatrov's plays are characteristic of the "socialism with a human face" ideology of the late 1960s and early 1970s. However, as the plays of Vassily Sigarev suggest, the increasingly unstable social world of contemporary Russia has led to a variety of dramatic experiments, and perhaps to a new kind of desperately ironic, absurdist drama.

Contemporary theater and drama in South Africa has been marked, as have all areas of South African life, by the imposition of racial *apartheid*—the legal separation and discrimination of various "racial" and ethnic groups—in 1948, laws which were only lifted with the election of Nelson Mandela as president in 1994. Apartheid can be seen as a politically conservative response to the social and racial situation that has developed in South Africa over the past four hundred years, in which the Portuguese, British, and Dutch vied with one another for control of the land, while at the same time being hugely outnumbered—South Africa today has about five million white inhabitants and thirty million black inhabitants—by an oppressed indigenous population.

South Africa

In 1487, Bartholomeu Dias, a Portuguese explorer, reached Mossel Bay, opening a sea route from Europe to Asia. Over the course of the next three centuries, the port at the Cape of Good Hope gained enormous strategic and military value. In 1652, the Dutch East India Company established a station there to supply water, food, and supplies to trade ships. Dutch settlers—called "Afrikaners" (or "Boers")—expanded from the immediate Cape region, conquering the Khoisan tribes, and importing slaves from Indonesia, India, Ceylon, Madagascar, and Mozambique. Throughout the eighteenth century, however, important colonies of British settlers developed in the region as well: after a series of battles and broken treaties, Britain gained control of the Cape Colony in 1806. Yet by gaining control of the region, the British were faced with two opponents: the indigenous tribes, and the Afrikaners, who resisted the imposition of British rule. The nineteenth century then witnessed two kinds of struggle. The conflict between British and Afrikaner settlers intensified when the British emancipated the colonial slaves in 1834. The years 1835-40 saw the "Great Trek," the departure of Afrikaners and their "clients"—slaves—from the Cape Colony northward, where they settled the Transvaal and Orange Free State as independent republics in 1852 and 1854 (the Trek is part of the consciousness of Afrikaner culture, and is frequently reenacted). However, the discovery of diamonds in 1867 and of gold in 1886 led to renewed conflict, as Britain attempted to annex the Afrikaner republics. The "War Between the Whites"—the Boer War of 1899–1902—led to British control of all three republics, which were united in 1910 as the Union of South Africa. The Union gained its independence from Britain in 1931, and became the Republic of South Africa in 1961, when it left the British Commonwealth.

Competing with one another for land and resources, the British and Afrikaners also had large and powerful indigenous populations to contend with, and despite the British policy against slavery, both parties systematically subjugated the black populations of South Africa. The most important of these groups were the Zulu; their leader Shaka defeated other African tribes, organized the Zulu as a kingdom in the 1820s, and was killed in 1828. In a series of conflicts—the British war with the Xhosa in 1834–1840, the Afrikaner defeat of a Zulu force at the Battle of Blood River in 1838, and the final British defeat of the Zulu in 1879—the white population gained control of the land and its people.

In many respects, the political history of modern South Africa is the history of the white minority's efforts to subordinate and control this populace. The discovery of gold and diamonds led—after the Boer War—to an increasing demand for mine laborers; although 64,000 Chinese workers were imported in 1904–1907, most of these laborers were Africans, who were increasingly segregated from the white population. When the Union of South Africa was formed in 1910, only whites were enfranchised; in 1911, the Mine and Works Act, the first of a series of laws restricting African workers to laboring work stipulated that skilled labor in the mines could only be performed by whites; in 1913, the Natives Land Act enacted the first of a series of segregation laws, by limiting African land ownership to certain reserves. Eventually, Africans were restricted to "townships," large, impoverished cities close enough to major cities to provide a constant labor supply. Moreover, the conflicts between British and Afrikaner South Africans were hardly resolved by the Union. Although South Africa participated in World War I as a dominion of the British Empire, the rise of Afrikaner nationalism in the 1930s led not only to considerable support for Germany in the country, but finally to the election of the Afrikaner National party in 1948.

The Afrikaner government installed apartheid as the law of the land in South Africa. Based on the notion that South Africa was comprised of four "racial" groups—White, Colored, Indian, and African—these laws legitimated White South Africans as the "nation," with the power to govern all other groups. Apartheid legislation was rapidly passed, and pervasive in its structuring of South African society: the Pass Laws of 1948 required one to carry a passbook at all times; the Population Registration Act of 1950 classified each person by race; the Group Areas Act forced people to live in racially segregated areas; in 1949 the Prohibition of Mixed Marriages Act passed; and in 1950 the Immorality Amendment Act prohibited sex between white and "nonwhite" persons. Property once "reserved" for ownership by Africans was claimed by whites: the segregated area of Sophiatown west of Johannesburg—where, since 1923, some African and Colored people owned land—was summarily converted into a White area, "Triomf" ("Triumph"). In the 1953 Bantu Education Act, the government assumed control of all schools—including missionary schools and colleges that had formerly educated Africans—and prohibited any instruction counter to the aims of the government; the 1959 Extension of University Education Act prohibited universities from admitting African students except with the permission of a cabinet minister.

The South African Native National Congress was founded in 1912 to advance the cause of Africans in South Africa: renamed the African National Congress, it responded swiftly to the imposition of apartheid: it organized a passive resistance campaign in 1952, and other acts of resistance throughout the 1950s. In 1959 a more radical group—the Pan African Congress, which included only Africans as members—split from the ANC; both were banned by the State of Emergency declared in 1960, after an uprising in Sharpeville when sixty Africans were shot by police during a peaceful protest. Although national and international opposition to apartheid was intense, it remained in force throughout the tumult of the 1960s, 1970s, and 1980s: the imprisonment of Nelson Mandela in 1962; the rise of the Black Consciousness Movement sponsored by Steve Biko and Barney Pityana in the late 1960s; the 1976 uprising in Soweto, a black township of one million people; the government's efforts to release the pressure on apartheid by forming black "homelands" in Transkei, Bophuthatswana, Venda, and Ciskei. By the mid-1980s, however, South Africa's isolation led to some political change: A new constitution in 1984 giving Colored, Asian, and Indian populations separate houses of parliament; the repeal of some pass laws in 1986; the release of Mandela in 1990, and the negotiations for a new constitution.

In all respects, theater in South Africa has been marked by this history. As a rough-and-tumble port, Cape Town did not support a legitimate theater until 1801, with the building of the African Theater, though performances of plays were given occasionally elsewhere (Beaumarchais's *Barber of Seville* was performed in Cape Town in 1783). By the early twentieth century, though, diamonds and gold were able to finance theater building, and every large city had several good theaters, performing European plays to white audiences. Since there was no repertory in Afrikaans, Afrikaners were particularly concerned to develop a "literary" culture: the first Afrikaans play was *Magrita Prinslo,* written by S. J. du Toit in 1897. Afrikaner theater flourished in the 1920s and 1930s, and continues today. Indeed, because the English-language theaters could rely on the traditional repertoire and touring companies, dramatic writing in English emerged much later in South Africa. Although the traditional forms of performance predate the colonial period, black theater in South Africa originates with Herbert Dhlomo (1903–1956), who studied at a mission school and became a teacher and journalist, and the author of twenty-four plays. In 1933 the Bantu Drama Society at the Bantu Men's Social Center performed his play *The Girl Who Killed to Save,* the first play by a black South African to be published in English, in 1936. Nonetheless, despite producing Dhlomo's play, the repertoire of the Bantu Drama Society was very much a European repertoire: Dhlomo himself played in Sheridan's comedy *She Stoops to Conquer.* Throughout the 1920s and 1930s, several companies—the Lucky Stars, the Syco Fans—worked to develop black drama.

The production of theater, like everything else in South African society, was segregated. In 1947 the government began funding a National Theater. Although the theater supported two companies—one in English, one in Afrikaans—they used no black actors, and included South African plays in their European repertoire only if they were written by white authors. In the 1940s, Es'kia Mphahlele and Khoti Mngoma founded the Syndicate of African Artists, but were refused government funding as long as they insisted on performing to mixed racial audiences: they were disbanded in 1956 after years of police harassment. The Union of South African Artists was organized in the 1950s to protect black artists' royalties, and engineered the production of the massively successful musical review about a boxer, *King Kong,* in 1959. Although the organization was white run, and showcased black talent to white audiences, it also performed successfully to mixed audiences, and sponsored mixed-cast shows: the Union produced Athol Fugard's *No-Good Friday* in 1958, at the Bantu Men's

Social Center in Johannesburg, with a cast including Fugard, Zakes Mokae, Bloke Modisane, and Stephen Moloi. When the show moved to the Brooke Theater, however, Fugard had to be replaced by a black actor—Lewis Nkosi—because segregated venues (the Brooke was an all-white theater) required segregated casts.

The principal challenge to resistant theater offered by the apartheid laws in the 1960s was the Group Areas Act, which prohibited the association of different races in clubs, cinemas, and restaurants; while mixed casts could perform to these segregated audiences, this loophole was closed in 1965: segregated audiences, segregated casts. In 1961, Fugard's *The Blood Knot*—about half brothers, one black (played by Mokae), one passing as white (played by Fugard)—could not be played in a legitimate theater, but gained good audiences in Dorkay House, and was shortly produced in London and New York. In 1963, Fugard began to work with the Serpent Players of Port Elizabeth, a black company, on adaptations of European playwrights—Büchner, Chekhov, Brecht, and Sophocles' *Antigone*. At the same time, however, a more improvisational, storytelling mode of theater was being developed in the townships, in plays such as Gibson Kente's *Manana, the Jazz Prophet* (1963). Kente's performances were popular and influential; in their use of narrative, mime, music, and dance to dramatize township life, they provided the form for later works like Barney Simon, Mbongeni Ngema, and Percy Mtwa's *Woza Albert!* (1981). Despite their popularity, these township playwrights had difficulty getting published; the South African Performing Arts Councils received large subsidies, but produced European plays mainly for white audiences, while the township theaters performed under poor circumstances to huge audiences, often sponsored by the Union.

The 1970s saw the real flowering of resistance theater in South Africa: Athol Fugard's collaboration with John Kani and Winston Ntshona (from the Serpent Players) led to *Sizwe Bansi Is Dead* (1972), which they performed (while the police looked on) as a mixed cast; subsequent performances were canceled. When they attempted to perform the play at the University of Witwatersrand, the security police arrested both the cast and the audience. Kente's performances became more politically inflected, in township plays like *How Long* (1973) and *Too Late* (1981), and inspired many other township works: Sol Rachilos's *The Township Wife* (1972), Sidney Sepamia's *Cry Yesterday* (1972), the Theater Workshop of Durban's *Umabatha* (the Zulu *Macbeth,* revived in London and the U.S. in 1997). The 1970s also saw the forming of several influential theater groups, including the Market Theater of Johannesburg in 1976, which produced Kente's *Mama and the Load* in 1980; Simon, Ngema, and Mtwa's *Woza Albert!* in 1981; Maishe Maponya's *Gangsters* in 1984; Ngema's *Asinamali;* and Mtwa's *Bhopa!* in 1985. The Market Theater has been influential outside South Africa as well, as many of its plays have been exported to Europe and the United States, and many of its playwrights—Fugard and Maponya, for instance—have since produced plays outside South Africa. With the lifting of apartheid, race emerges as a different kind of issue in South African drama, and has been explored by a number of playwrights, including Ismail Mahomed (b. 1959), Reza de Wet (b. 1955), Brett Bailey (b. 1967) and many others. The Grahamstown National Arts Festival continues as the premiere annual theater festival in South Africa.

ANALYZING POSTCOLONIAL THEATER AND DRAMA

In part because postcolonial drama emerges out of the complex historical dynamics of global expansion, intercultural contact, political controversy, and sometimes unfamiliar artistic traditions, analyzing and discussing this material presents unique challenges. One approach to postcolonial culture attempts to develop a "national" or "regional" model, isolating themes (apartheid in South Africa, for instance), historical questions (plays that respond to the 1960 treaty controversy in Japan), or local features of dramatic style (the prevalence of domestic realism in American drama; the use of a trickster figure by Native Canadian playwrights) to assess the relationship between theater and the place of its production. This model can also lead to productive kinds of comparative study: in what ways does it make sense to frame a dialogue, say, between the writing of Aboriginal Australian writers like Jack Davis, and Native Canadian writers like Tomson Highway?

A second model recognizes the importance that ideas of "race" have had in mapping literary study, in drawing out political affinities between African, African-American, and Caribbean writers, for example. This model interrogates the ways in which "race" informs ideas of identity across national boundaries; it might place the ideas of W.E.B. DuBois or Amiri Baraka (see Unit VI) alongside the writings of Aimé Césaire and the Senegalese poet Léopold Senghor or the black Algerian psychiatrist Frantz Fanon's incendiary and brilliant book, *The Wretched of the Earth* (1961). In these writings, "race" emerges often as a cultural construct rather than a biological "fact," though its consequences are nonetheless powerful; and theorists of the production of "race" have often found a searching model in dramatic performance, both in plays in which "race" is a conscious issue— Soyinka's *Death and the King's Horseman,* or Baraka's *Dutchman*—as well as those in which it seems to be part of the play's unconscious politics, O'Neill's *The Hairy Ape,* for example, or Pinter's *The Homecoming.* Indeed, the constructedness of "race" or "ethnicity" can be a powerful weapon for *forging* a political consciousness: while the term "Latino" or "Latina" is relatively meaningless outside the Anglo-affiliated cultures of North America (people from Latin American countries tend to identify *nationally,* much as North Americans do; they think of themselves as Mexicans, Peruvians, or Cubans), it has become an important way for people experiencing *ethnic* discrimination in the United States to organize in a common effort.

One of the most powerful ways of considering postcolonial culture—its art, music, literature, drama, and performance—is to consider the formal properties of its artworks. Postcolonial critics, however, have resisted merely imposing the critical categories of Western literary study—tragic and comic form, for example, or verbal as opposed to music drama— on postcolonial arts, largely because such works often seem designed both to resist those categories, and to dramatize their implication in a wider politics. Wole Soyinka's early play *The Lion and the Jewel,* for example, is at once a play using the familiar stereotypes of Western comedy since Plautus—a pedantic schoolteacher, a cantankerous aging king, a pretty young girl—and interrogating them as well. As the play proceeds, it seems to ask whether this way of representing African village life—comedy—is complicit with the other ways that African village life is represented in the play: in magazine pictures, as a site for a railroad station, as the "dark continent" of the schoolteacher's textbooks. In other words, the play brings about a collision between the Western dramatic traditions Soyinka learned in Lagos, Leeds, and London, and the indigenous traditions—the social routines of the village, the songs, the marriage rituals—he blends into the texture of the play. This practice of blending both "indigenous" and "colonizing" literary or performance styles is generally called **HYBRIDIZATION,** and considering plays, poems, novels, films, and music in terms of their "hybrid" blending of cultural traditions is an important way of recognizing the cultural work that artworks do. Some writers (Ngũgĩ might be an example) call for postcolonial art to resist and replace the inauthentic and oppressive means of "colonial" art—writing in the colonial language, using colonial forms, like tragedy, the novel, the pop song—as a way to locate a new and authentic space of liberation. Others (Soyinka and Homi Bhabha, for example) tend to see hybrid forms as a useful tool, an instrument for exposing the dynamics of oppression at the heart of the colonizing culture itself. Reading or listening for hybridity—the collision between the tragedy of Steve Biko and Samuel Beckett's absurdist play *Catastrophe* in Maponya's *Gangsters* for instance—involves the subtle and delicate task of putting these forms into dialogue with one another, listening for how they shape and qualify one another, open the possibility of new meanings.

READING THE MATERIAL THEATER

From the perspective of theater research, modern students of theater and drama live in an era of extraordinary privilege: generations of scholars have worked to assemble the primary and secondary materials that document earlier theaters; the amount of information available in archives, libraries, and on the internet is nearly overwhelming; and, of course, performances now can be recorded on film or videotape, or for digital media. Yet we should not be seduced into thinking that a recording of a performance is the same thing as the live performance. First, of course, the camera's perspective governs everything we see on the screen, and makes it possible to achieve effects not possible in the theater; at the same time, it also transforms the performance from an actor's medium to the camera's. Viewers of the PBS versions of Anna Deavere Smith's *Fires in the Mirror* or *Twilight* can't help noticing the role played by the camera work, which brings Smith and her characters into a sharp close-up not possible onstage, to say nothing of the many scene changes, which—while they are handled seamlessly on television—point to a distracting "realism" that betrays Smith's open theatricality in performance.

Different kinds of documents—paintings, memoirs, reviews, illustrations, promptbooks, videotapes—tell us different kinds of things about the evanescent, always-lost performance onstage. One of the most useful documents for assessing the producers' original purposes in staging a play is the program, which often contains extensive program notes. With the rise of the director since the late nineteenth-century, theater companies have often found it important to have a second "conceptual" voice in the production process: the dramaturg. Dramaturgs play a wide variety of functions. In European theater, they often have a central

role in imagining the production and work in close cooperation with the director and cast throughout the development of the play. Under these circumstances, a company might use a dramaturg not only to conduct research into the historical background of the play and its author (and even—say, in the case of Shakespeare—into the play's language), but also to help articulate a critical perspective on the play for the performance in daily dialogue with the director and actors. In other circumstances—and more commonly in the United States—the dramaturg might function both as a literary manager, helping to acquire and develop new plays, as well as a kind of researcher, providing background information to the director and to the cast, as well as playing a central part in writing program information. As theatrical production has been understood to be an art independent of the narrowly literary meanings of dramatic writing, the theatrical program has become a place to inform and educate the audience about the play, both to provide historical information and to help develop a useful perspective on the production.

In 1980, the Field Day Theatre Company premiered Brian Friel's *Translations*. In writing the play, Friel had conducted considerable research into two important events in the history of Northern Ireland in the nineteenth century: the Ordnance Survey mapping of Ireland, and the transformation of the educational system. While Friel clearly worked to incorporate the information needed to understand the play *into* the play, the Field Day Company clearly felt that a greater understanding of the historical background would help readers to understand the play, and their production of it. What follows here are extracts from the program notes of *Translations*. It's important, of course, to train a skeptical eye on such efforts to explain the work of the production: how do these notes work to structure the audience's response to the play? Do the notes provide the kinds of information you think

is needed? Do the notes tend to emphasize some elements in the play as essential for understanding the play, and overlook other, perhaps other important, elements? How do these notes provide a perspective on the playwright's work in writing the play.

FIELD DAY THEATRE COMPANY PROGRAM NOTES FOR *TRANSLATIONS*[1] (1980)

Extract from *The Hedge Schools of Ireland* by P.J. Dowling The Hedge Schools owed their origin to the suppression of all the ordinary legitimate means of education, first during the Cromwellian regime and then under the Penal Code introduced in the reign of William III and operating from that time till within less than twenty years from the opening of the nineteenth century . . .

"The Hedge Schools were clearly of peasant institution. They were maintained by the people who wanted their children educated; and they were taught by men who came from the people . . .

"The poorest and humblest of the schools gave instruction in reading, writing and arithmetic; Latin, Greek, Mathematics and other subjects were taught in a great number of schools; and in many cases the work was done entirely through the medium of the Irish language. Though the use of the vernacular was rapidly falling into decay during the eighteenth century, it was owing to the greater value of English on the fair and market rather than to any shifting of ground on the part of the schools . . .

"The Hedge Schools were the most vital force in popular education in Ireland during the eighteenth century. They emerged in the nineteenth century more vigorous still, outnumbering all other schools, and so profoundly national as to hasten the introduction of a State system of education in 1831 . . ."

Extract from *The Autobiography of William Carleton* (born in County Tyrone, 1794) "The only place for giving instruction was a barn. The barn was a loft over a cowshed and stable . . . It was one of the largest barns in the parish.

"(At the age of fourteen) I had only got as far as Ovid's *Metamorphoses*, Justin, and the first chapter of John in the Greek Testament."

Extract from the memoirs of the Reverend Mr Alexander Ross, Rector, Dungiven, County Derry. 1814 "Even in the wildest districts, it is not unusual to meet with good classical scholars; and there are several young mountaineers of the writer's acquaintance, whose knowledge and taste in the Latin poets, might put to the blush many who have all the advantages of established schools and regular instruction."

Extract from *A History of Ireland* by Edmund Curtis "In 1831 Chief Secretary Stanley introduced a system of National Education . . . The system became a great success as an educational one but it had fatal effects on the Irish language and the old Gaelic tradition. According to Thomas Davis, at this time the vast majority of the people living west of a line drawn from Derry to Cork spoke nothing but Irish daily and east of it a considerable minority. It seems certain that at least two millions used it as their fireside speech . . . But the institution of universal elementary schools where English was the sole medium of instruction, combined with the influence of O'Connell, many of the priests, and other leaders who looked on Irish as a barrier to progress, soon made rapid inroads on the native speech . . ."

Extract from *Ordnance Survey of Ireland* by Thomas Colby, Colonel, Royal Engineers (1835) "To carry on a minute Survey of all Ireland no collection of ready instructed surveyors would have sufficed. It, therefore, became indispensable to train and organise a completely new department for the purpose. Officers and men from the corps of Royal Engineers formed the basis for this new organisation, and very large numbers of other persons possessing various qualifications, were gradually added to them to expedite the great work . . .

"The mode of spelling the names of places was peculiarly vague and unsettled, but on the maps about to be constructed it was desirable to establish a standard orthography, and for future reference, to identify the several localities with the names by which they had formerly been called . . ."

Extract from the Spring Rice Report (advocating a general survey of Ireland) to the British Government; 21 June 1824 "The general tranquility of Europe, enables the state to devote the abilities and exertions of a most valuable corps of officers to an undertaking, which, though not unimportant in a military point of view, recommends itself more directly as a civil measure. Your committee trust that the survey will be carried on with energy, as well as with skill, and that it will, when completed, be creditable to the nation, and to the scientific acquirements of the present age. In that portion of the Empire to which it more particularly applies, it cannot but be received as a proof of the disposition of the legislature to adopt all measures calculated to advance the interests of Ireland."

Extracts from the letters of John O'Donovan, a civilian employee with the Ordnance Survey, later Professor of Celtic Studies, Queen's College, Belfast
Buncrana
23 August 1835
"On Friday we travelled through the Parish of Clonmany and ascended the Hill of Beinnin. Clonmany is the most Irish Parish I have yet visited; the men only, who go to markets and fairs, speak a little English, the women and children speak Irish only. This arises from their distance from Villages and Towns and from their being completely environed by mountains, which form a gigantic barrier between them and the more civilized and less civil inhabitants of the lower country." Dun Fionnchada? Dun Fionnchon?
Dunfanaghy
9 September 1835
"I am sick to death's door of the names on the coast, because the name I get from one is denied by another of

equal intelligence and authority to be correct. The only way to settle these names would be to summon a Jury and order them to say and present 'uppon ther Oathes' what these names are and ought to be. But there are several of them such trifling places that it seems to me that it matters not which of two or three appelations we give them. For example, the name Timlin's Hole is not of thirty years standing and will give way to another name as soon as that dangerous hole shall have swallowed a fisherman of more illustrious name than Tim Lyn."
Glenties
15 October 1835
"Yesterday being a fair-day at Dunglow we were obliged to leave it in consequence of the bustle and confusion. We directed our course southwards through the Parish of the Templecroan, keeping Traigh Eunach (a name which I find exceedingly difficult to Anglicise) to the right . . . On the road we met crowds of the women of the mountains who were loaded with stockings going to the stocking fair of Dunglow and who bore deep graven on their visages the effects of poverty and smoke, of their having been kept alive by the potatoe only . . . I have seen several fields of oats on this coast, some prostrated and rotting, others with the grain completely blown off the stalk—and some so green in October as to preclude the possibility of ripening at all."
Ballyshanny
1 November 1835
"I have met in this town a fine old man named Edward Quin, from whom I have received a good deal of information. He has been employed by Lieutenant Vickers to give the Irish names of places about Ballyshannon, and has saved me a good deal of trouble—I wish you could induce Mr Vickers to take him to his next district, and keep him employed writing in the Name Books, and taking down the names from the pronunciation of the country people."

[1]Courtesy Field Day Theatre Company

One of the most challenging aspects of performance today has to do with the relative ease with which cultures now come into contact with one another, use—or steal—one another's forms of art and this hybridizing tendency is often visible in the plays in Unit VII. The interpenetration of different musical idioms has become a standard aspect of contemporary pop music; for instance, reggae and ska and mambo and tango and high-life and many other musical languages once local to a given culture now filter in and out of many American pop songs. And while the music industry has worked to sell this variety by copying the restaurant industry—as "World Music"—we might wonder whether the analogy with the variety of "ethnic" or "international" cuisine in the pricey restaurant districts of major cities (or even the new interest in Asian and Mexican foods shown by McDonald's and Burger King) isn't more to the point: have the products of other cultures, their music, their food, their plays, become empty commodities, consumed by a kind of global consumer elite?

In the past two decades, this kind of controversy has animated "intercultural performance," a kind of performance that attempts to bridge the differences between two different cultures not so much by erasing or occluding them as by concocting artworks in which these boundaries become visible and meaningful. Ari-ane Mnouchkine's productions of Shakespearean or classical Greek dramas using Eastern movement and dance techniques is one well-known example; another is Peter Brook's famous staging of the Indian epic, *The Mahabharata* at the Avignon Festival in 1985, and then on tour in the following years, which used fundamentally Western theatrical techniques to stage the narrative. In 1989, David McRuvie and Annette Leday collaborated with the Kerala State Arts Academy on a production of Shakespeare's *King Lear,* adapted to the extraordinarily complex conventions of the *kathakali*—an Indian form of masked dance-drama. Unlike the hybrid works of playwrights like Maponya or Luis Valdez, this intercultural strategy does not arise from the blending of cultural materials already present in a given culture—in the way Luis Valdez's *actos* draw from both Mexican and Anglo performance traditions visible in California in the 1960s. Instead, they work to bring about a dialogue between cultures that are distant from one another in space and time.

As Marvin Carlson suggests in a careful anatomy of contemporary intercultural performances, there is not only a long tradition of intercultural performance, but a variety of ways of imagining the relationship between cultural forms that performance brings about.[1] He lists seven possibilities: a performance in a tradition foreign to the audience, such as a Noh company or the Comédie Française visiting New York; the complete assimilation of foreign elements (does anyone really hear a reggae beat as "foreign" to American pop any-more?); the assimilation of an entire foreign structure, such as Yeats's writing of Noh plays, or Maponya's work with Brechtian epic theater; making the foreign into a new blend with familiar elements (Molière's absorption of Italian *commedia dell' arte*); assimilating an entire foreign genre, such as Westerns in Japan; using some foreign elements within familiar structures, such as the dance sequences in Hwang's *M. Butterfly,* or perhaps the *egungen* costumes in Soyinka's *Death and the King's Horseman*; and importing an entire performance from another culture as something distinctly unfamiliar, such as *butoh.*

This list clarifies the extent to which intercultural performance is a highly charged, contestatory activity: Brook was widely criticized, despite the evident elegance of *The Mahabharata,* for transforming something like the national conscience of India into a piece of slick theater; similarly, while McRuvie and Leday's *Kathakali King Lear* framed an ambitious attempt to chart how far one kind of theater might be translated into the traditions of another culture, its reception was often relatively simplistic: British reviewers complained that the "true" *King Lear* was lost in the translation. As we move into the next millennium, we can certainly expect kind of theatrical and dramatic experimentation to continue, and to be challenged to think about the kind of cultural work it performs.

[1] Marvin Carlson, "Brook and Mnouchkine: Passages to India?" *The Intercultural Performance Reader,* ed. Patrice Pavis (London: Routledge, 1996), 82–83.

Aimé Césaire

Aimé Césaire, one of the most prominent and influential theorists of postcolonial culture, was born in Martinique, West Indies, in 1913; he was educated there, and in Paris at L'École Normale Supérieur, and in 1934 began *L'Étudiant Noir* with Leopold Senghor and Léon Damas. Since 1946, Césaire has served as deputy from Martinique in the French National Assembly, and was a founding member of the Parti Progressiste Martiniquais, which came to power in 1950; he served as the mayor of the capital city, Fort-de-France from 1945 to 1993. Throughout the 1950s and 1960s, Césaire laid the foundations for the theory of post-colonial culture and was closely associated with the Négritude movement—the assertion of black history, culture, and identity in the face of oppressive European culture—and he used his political influence to establish cultural institutions, such as the Service Municipale d'Action Culturelle, a school offering training in traditional Caribbean performing arts, in 1976, that would extend this understanding of Caribbean identity. Césaire's cultural criticism— *Discourse on Colonialism* (1950), *Toussaint L'Ouverture: The French Revolution and the Colonial Problem* (1960), *Culture and Colonization* (1978)—were accompanied by several volumes of poetry and four plays: *And the Dogs Were Quiet* (1956), *The Tragedy of King Christophe* (1964), *A Season in the Congo* (1966), and *A Tempest* (1969).

THE TEMPEST

Césaire's *A Tempest* is one of many works written in the past forty years taking Shakespeare's play as a site for revising colonial experience: O. Mannoni's psychoanalytic study, *Prospero and Caliban: The Psychology of Colonization* (1950); Max Dorsinville's *Caliban Without Prospero* (1974); the Cuban critic Roberto Fernández Retamar's brilliant essay, *Caliban* (1974); and David Malouf's dramatic resetting of the play to contemporary Australia, *Blood Relations* (1987), to name only a few. Shakespeare's *The Tempest* was based in part on accounts of a shipwreck in the Americas (see Unit III), and although Prospero's island seems to be at once in the Bermudas and the Mediterranean, most commentators have seen in *The Tempest* Shakespeare's representation of contact between European and New World peoples. Prospero, for example, both exploits Caliban's knowledge of the island and enslaves him and Ariel, a clear symmetry with European behavior throughout Africa and the Americas. For this reason, invoking Caliban as a kind of guiding spirit, or rewriting *The Tempest* to bring this dynamic more to the surface, has become an important strategy for evoking the relations between colonizer and colonized.

Aimé Césaire's *A Tempest* makes several uses of Shakespeare's play, taking both a more colloquial and a more clearly political perspective on the action. When Prospero is forced into exile by his brother and the Inquisition, he is trying to conceal a secret "empire" that he has discovered, ripe for conquest; when Alonso sets sail to find it, Prospero uses his magic to divert him to the island, so as to save the empire for later exploitation. We also get some idea of what kind of king Prospero might be from his treatment of Caliban and Ariel, who themselves demonstrate a range of attitudes held by colonized subjects. While Caliban refuses, like many African Americans, to continue using his "slave name" and wants to be called simply "X," like a man "whose name has been stolen," Ariel serves Prospero as a kind of overseer and identifies his interests with him.

Césaire develops a resistant reading of Shakespeare in a number of ways: showing how Prospero's power divides rather than unites Ariel and Caliban; depicting how manual labor is fit only for the indigenous Caliban, not for the European Ferdinand; summoning Eshu to invade Prospero's masque of the classical goddesses; staging Caliban's overwhelming desire for revolution. Césaire's rewriting of Shakespeare, and his critique of European colonial representation, is focused in the final scene of *A Tempest,* which enacts a striking reversal of *The*

Tempest. In Césaire's version, Prospero finds the pleasures of colonial rule so irresistible, he refuses to return to Europe.

Translator's Note

The translation of Aimé Césaire's *Une Tempête* presented more challenges than usually arise in the transfer of a play from one language into another (differences in cultural background, tone, milieu, and so on). Although Césaire has denied attempting any linguistic echo of Shakespeare, the transposition of his play into English inevitably calls up such echoes, for the literate English/American playgoer cannot help but "hear," behind the language of the play, the original text resounding in all its well-known beauty, its familiarity. For the translator, therefore, the temptation to quote the Ariel songs, for example, or to paraphrase them, was strong. When Césaire has his Ariel sing of something "proche et étrange," for example, Shakespeare's "rich and strange" must, inevitably, sound in the translator's mind.

I have attempted to avoid temptation (there is, if I recall, only one instance of direct quotation in the prose text, but it fell so aptly into place that I was unable to resist); in the main I have left the (slightly altered) song for Ariel with its Shakespearean references unchanged. In an appendix I have now added a "literal" translation of Césaire's text to give a better notion of the imagery he uses for the character. As for the other songs in the text, the options indicated are extremely free adaptations or indications of what I felt to be the substance of the originals or (as in the case of "Oh, Susannah" and "Blow the Man Down") songs familiar to an English-speaking audience that I thought reflected something of the spirit and possible familiarity of the originals.

For this revised edition, I have also included, as an appendix, a "literal" translation of these songs as they occur in French.

Then there is the question of overall tone of voice, taken for granted in *The Tempest,* where social classes, the real and the spirit worlds, are a given. In *A Tempest,* with its Caribbean (and therefore colonial) setting and its consecration to a black theater, it is essential, I feel, for the director and the actors to decide what accents, what "classes," they wish the various characters to reflect. In my own head, I have heard Ariel's song, for example, as vaguely calypso; others will have other ideas. The director may also wish to emphasize the "political" aspects of the play, in which case the accents employed by the actors would tend to serve that purpose. In any event, in translating the play I have not tried to indicate accent (other than in the Ariel song) and where slang or obscenities have been employed, the emphasis to be given will be set by the director or actor in the way that will best reflect and enhance the tone and style of the particular production.

—Richard Miller

A TEMPEST

Aimé Césaire
TRANSLATED BY RICHARD MILLER

CHARACTERS

ARIEL

TRINCULO/CAPTAIN

CALIBAN

STEPHANO

GONZALO

PROSPERO

FERDINAND

ALONSO

ESHU/MASTER OF CEREMONIES

MIRANDA

SEBASTIAN

ANTONIO

GODS *and* GODDESSES (CERES, JUNO)

BOATSWAIN

SAILORS

THE FRIAR

ELVES

NYMPHS

Ambiance of a psychodrama. The actors enter singly, at random, and each chooses for himself a mask at his leisure.

MASTER OF CEREMONIES: Come gentlemen, help yourselves. To each his character, to each character his mask. You, Prospero? Why not? He has reserves of will power he's not even aware of himself. You want Caliban? Well, that's re-
5   vealing. Ariel? Fine with me. And what about Stephano, Trinculo? No takers? Ah, just in time! It takes all kinds to make a world.

    And after all, they aren't the worst characters. No prob-lem about the juvenile leads, Miranda and Ferdinand. You,
10   okay. And there's no problem about the villains either: you, Antonio; you, Alonso, perfect! Oh, Christ! I was forgetting the Gods. Eshu will fit you like a glove. As for the other parts, just take what you want and work it out among your-selves. But make up your minds . . . Now, there's one part I
15   have to pick out myself: you! It's for the part of the Tempest, and I need a storm to end all storms . . . I need a really big guy to do the wind. Will you do that? Fine! And then some-one strong for Captain of the ship. Good, now let's go. Ready? Begin. Blow, winds! Rain and lightning *ad lib!*

ACT ONE

SCENE I

GONZALO: Of course, we're only straws tossed on the raging sea . . . but all's not lost, Gentlemen. We just have to try to get to the eye of the storm.

ANTONIO: We might have known this old fool would nag us
5   to death!

SEBASTIAN: To the bitter end!

GONZALO: Try to understand what I'm telling you: imagine a huge cylinder like the chimney of a lamp, fast as a gallop-ing horse, but in the center as still and unmoving as Cy-
10   clop's eye. That's what we're talking about when we say "the eye of the storm" and that's where we have to get.

ANTONIO: Oh, great! Do you really mean that the cyclone or Cyclops, if he can't see the beam in his own eye, will let us escape! Oh, that's very illuminating!

15 GONZALO: It's a clever way of putting it, at any rate. Literally false, but yet quite true. But what's the fuss going on up there? The Captain seems worried. (*Calling.*) Captain!

CAPTAIN: (*With a shrug.*) Boatswain!

BOATSWAIN: Aye, sir!

CAPTAIN: We're coming round windward of the island. At this 20 speed we'll run aground. We've got to turn her around. Heave to! (*Exits.*)

BOATSWAIN: Come on, men! Heave to! To the topsail; man the ropes. Pull! Heave ho, heave ho!

ALONSO: (*Approaching.*) Well, Boatswain, how are things go- 25 ing? Where are we?

BOATSWAIN: If you ask me, you'd all be better off below, in your cabins.

ANTONIO: *He* doesn't seem too happy. We'd better ask the Cap-tain. Where's the Captain, Boatswain? He was here just a 30 moment ago, and now he's gone off.

BOATSWAIN: Get back below where you belong! We've got work to do!

GONZALO: My dear fellow, I can quite understand your being nervous, but a man should be able to control himself in any 35 situation, even the most upsetting.

BOATSWAIN: Shove it! If you want to save your skins, you'd bet-ter get yourselves back down below to those first-class cab-ins of yours.

GONZALO: Now, now, my good fellow, you don't seem to know 40 to whom you're speaking. (*Making introductions.*) The King's brother, the King's son and myself, the King's counsellor.

BOATSWAIN: King! King! Well, there's someone who doesn't give a fuck more about the kind that he does about you or 45 me, and he's called the Gale. His Majesty the Gale! And right now, he's in control and we're all his subjects.

GONZALO: He might just as well be pilot on the ferry to hell . . . his mouth's foul enough!

ANTONIO: In a sense, the fellow *regales* me, as you might say. 50 We'll pull through, you'll see, because he looks to me more like someone who'll end up on the gallows, not beneath the billows.

SEBASTIAN: The end result is the same. The fish will get us and the crows will get him. 55

GONZALO: He did irritate me, rather. However, I take the at-tenuating circumstances into account . . . and, you must ad-mit, he lacks neither courage nor wit.

BOATSWAIN: (*Returning.*) Pull in the stud sails. Helmsman, into the wind! Into the wind! 60

(*Enter* SEBASTIAN, ANTONIO, GONZALO.)

BOATSWAIN: You again! If you keep bothering us and don't get below and say your prayers I'll give up and let you sail the

ship! You can't expect me to be the go-between for your
souls and Beelzebub!

65 ANTONIO: It's really too much! The fellow is taking advantage
of the situation . . .

BOATSWAIN: Windward! Windward! Heave into the wind!

(*Thunder, lightning.*)

SEBASTIAN: Ho! Ho!

GONZALO: Did you see that? There, at the top of the masts, in
70   the rigging, that glitter of blue fire, flashing, flashing?
They're right when they call these magic lands, so different
from our homes in Europe . . . Look, even the lightning is
different!

ANTONIO: Maybe its a foretaste of the hell that awaits us.

75 GONZALO: You're too pessimistic. Anyway, I've always kept
myself in a state of grace, ready to meet my maker.

(SAILORS *enter.*)

SAILORS: Shit! We're sinking!

(*The passengers can be heard singing "Nearer, my God, to Thee . . ."*)

BOATSWAIN: To leeward! To leeward!

FERDINAND: (*Entering.*) Alas! There's no one in hell . . . all the
80   devils are here!

(*The ship sinks.*)

SCENE II

MIRANDA: Oh God! Oh God! A sinking ship! Father, help!

PROSPERO: (*Enters hurriedly carrying a megaphone.*) Come daughter, calm yourself! It's only a play. There's really nothing
wrong. Anyway, everything that happens is for our own
5   good. Trust me, I won't say any more.

MIRANDA: But such a fine ship, and so many fine, brave lives
sunk, drowned, laid waste to wrack and ruin . . . A person
would have to have a heart of stone not to be moved . . .

PROSPERO: Drowned . . . hmmm. That remains to be seen. But
10   draw near, dear Princess. The time has come.

MIRANDA: You're making fun of me, father. Wild as I am, you
know I am happy—like a queen of the wildflowers, of the
streams and paths, running barefoot through thorns and
flowers, spared by one, caressed by the other.

15 PROSPERO: But you are a Princess . . . for how else does one address the daughter of a Prince? I cannot leave you in ignorance any longer. Milan is the city of your birth, and the
city where for many years I was the Duke.

MIRANDA: Then how did we come here? And tell me, too, by
20   what ill fortune did a prince turn into the reclusive hermit
you are now, here, on this desert isle? Was it because you
found the world distasteful, or through the perfidy of some
enemy? Is our island a prison or a hermitage? You've hinted
at some mystery so many times and aroused my curiosity,
25   and today you shall tell me all.

PROSPERO: In a way, it is because of all the things you mention.
First, it is because of political disagreements, because of the
intrigues of my ambitious younger brother. Antonio is his
name, your uncle, and Alonso the name of the envious King
30   of Naples. How their ambitions were joined, how my

brother became the accomplice of my rival, how the latter
promised the former his protection and my throne . . . the
devil alone knows how all that came about. In any event,
when they learned that through my studies and experiments I had managed to discover the exact location of these   35
lands for which many had sought for centuries and that I
was making preparations to set forth to take possession of
them, they hatched a scheme to steal my as-yet-unborn
empire from me. They bribed my people, they stole my
charts and documents and, to get rid of me, they denounced   40
me to the Inquisition as a magician and sorcerer. To be
brief, one day I saw arriving at the palace men to whom I
had never granted audience: the priests of the Holy Office.

(*Flashback: Standing before* PROSPERO, *who is wearing his ducal
robes, we see a* FRIAR *reading from a parchment scroll.*)

THE FRIAR: The Holy Inquisition for the preservation and integrity of the Faith and the pursuit of heretical perversion,   45
acting through the special powers entrusted to it by the
Holy Apostolic See, informed of the errors you profess, insinuate and publish against God and his Creation with regard to the shape of the Earth and the possibility of discovering other lands, notwithstanding the fact that the Prophet   50
Isaiah stated and taught that the Lord God is seated upon
the circle of the Earth and in its center is Jerusalem and that
around the world lies inaccessible Paradise, convinced that it
is through wickedness that to support your heresy you quote
Strabus, Ptolemy and the tragic author Seneca, thereby lend-   55
ing credence to the notion that profane writings can aspire
to an authority equal to that of the most profound of the
Holy Scriptures, given your notorious use by both night and
day of Arabic calculations and scribblings in Hebrew, Syrian
and other demonic tongues and, lastly, given that you have   60
hitherto escaped punishment owing to your temporal authority and have, if not usurped, then transformed that authority and made it into a tyranny, doth hereby strip you of
your titles, positions and honors in order that it may then
proceed against you according to due process through a full   65
and thorough examination, under which authority we require that you accompany us.

PROSPERO: (*Back in the present.*) And yet, the trial they said they
were going to hold never took place. Such creatures of darkness are too much afraid of the light. To be brief: instead of   70
killing me they chose—even worse—to maroon me here
with you on this desert island.

MIRANDA: How terrible, and how wicked the world is! How
you must have suffered!

PROSPERO: In all this tale of treason and felony there is but one   70
honorable name: Gonzalo, counsellor to the King of Naples
and fit to serve a better master. By furnishing me with food
and clothing, by supplying me with my books and instruments, he has done all in his power to make my exile in this
disgusting place bearable. And now, through a singular   80
turn, Fortune has brought to these shores the very men involved in the plot against me. My prophetic science had of
course already informed me that they would not be content
merely with seizing my lands in Europe and that their
greed would win out over their cowardice, that they would   85
confront the sea and set out for those lands my genius had

discovered. I couldn't let them get away with that, and
since I was able to stop them, I did so, with the help of
Ariel. We brewed up the storm you have just witnessed,
90   thereby saving my possessions overseas and bringing the
scoundrels into my power at the same time.

(*Enter* ARIEL.)

PROSPERO: Well, Ariel?
ARIEL: Mission accomplished.
PROSPERO: Bravo; good work! But what seems to be the mat-
95   ter? I give you a compliment and you don't seem pleased?
Are you tired?
ARIEL: Not tired; disgusted. I obeyed you but—well, why not
come out with it?—I did so most unwillingly. It was a real
pity to see that great ship go down, so full of life.
100 PROSPERO: Oh, so you're upset, are you! It's always like that
with you intellectuals! Who cares! What interests me is not
your moods, but your deeds. Let's split: I'll take the zeal and
you can keep your doubts. Agreed?
ARIEL: Master, I must beg you to spare me this kind of labour.
105 PROSPERO: (*Shouting.*) Listen, and listen good! There's a task to
be performed, and I don't care how it gets done!
ARIEL: You've promised me my freedom a thousand times, and
I'm still waiting.
PROSPERO: Ingrate! And who freed you from Sycorax, may I
110 ask? Who rent the pine in which you had been imprisoned
and brought you forth?
ARIEL: Sometimes I almost regret it . . . After all, I might have
turned into a real tree in the end . . . Tree: that's a word that
really gives me a thrill! It often springs to mind: palm
115 tree—springing into the sky like a fountain ending in non-
chalant, squid-like elegance. The baobab—twisted like the
soft entrails of some monster. Ask the calao bird that lives
a cloistered season in its branches. Or the Ceiba tree—
spread out beneath the proud sun. O bird, o green mansions
120 set in the living earth!
PROSPERO: Stuff it! I don't like talking trees. As for your freedom, you'll have it when I'm good and ready. In the
meanwhile, see to the ship. I'm going to have a few words
with Master Caliban. I've been keeping my eye on him,
125 and he's getting a little too emancipated. (*Calling.*) Caliban!
Caliban! (*He sighs.*)

(*Enter* CALIBAN.)

CALIBAN: Uhuru!
PROSPERO: What did you say?
CALIBAN: I said, Uhuru!
130 PROSPERO: Mumbling your native language again! I've already
told you, I don't like it. You could be polite, at least; a simple "hello" wouldn't kill you.
CALIBAN: Oh, I forgot . . . But make that as froggy, waspish,
pustular and dung-filled "hello" as possible. May today has-
135 ten by a decade the day when all the birds of the sky and
beasts of the earth will feast upon your corpse!
PROSPERO: Gracious as always, you ugly ape! How can anyone
be so ugly?
CALIBAN: You think I'm ugly . . . well, I don't think you're so
140 handsome yourself. With that big hooked nose, you look

just like some old vulture. (*Laughing.*) An old vulture with
a scrawny neck!
PROSPERO: Since you're so fond of invective, you could at least
thank me for having taught you to speak at all. You, a savage . . . a dumb animal, a beast I educated, trained, dragged 145
up from the bestiality that still clings to you.
CALIBAN: In the first place, that's not true. You didn't teach me
a thing! Except to jabber in your own language so that I
could understand your orders: chop the wood, wash the
dishes, fish for food, plant vegetables, all because you're too 150
lazy to do it yourself. And as for your learning, did you ever
impart any of *that* to me? No, you took care not to. All your
science you keep for yourself alone, shut up in those big
books.
PROSPERO: What would you be without me?   155
CALIBAN: Without you? I'd be the king, that's what I'd be, the
King of the Island. The king of the island given me by my
mother, Sycorax.
PROSPERO: There are some family trees it's better not to climb!
She's a ghoul! A witch from whom—and may God be   160
praised—death has delivered us.
CALIBAN: Dead or alive, she was my mother, and I won't deny
her! Anyhow, you only think she's dead because you
think the earth itself is dead . . . It's so much simpler that
way! Dead, you can walk on it, pollute it, you can tread   165
upon it with the steps of a conqueror. I respect the earth,
because I know that it is alive, and I know that Sycorax is
alive.
Sycorax. Mother.
Serpent, rain, lightning.   170
And I see thee everywhere!
In the eye of the stagnant pool which stares back at me,
through the rushes,
in the gesture made by twisted root and its awaiting
    thrust.
In the night, the all-seeing blinded night,   175
the nostril-less all-smelling night!
. . . Often, in my dreams, she speaks to me and warns
me . . . Yesterday, even, when I was lying by the stream
on my belly lapping at the muddy water, when the Beast
was about to spring upon me with that huge stone in his 180
hand . . .
PROSPERO: If you keep on like that even your magic won't save
you from punishment!
CALIBAN: That's right, that's right! In the beginning, the gentleman was all sweet talk: dear Caliban here, my little Cal- 185
iban there! And what do you think you'd have done without me in this strange land? Ingrate! I taught you the trees,
fruits, birds, the seasons, and now you don't give a
damn . . . Caliban the animal, Caliban the slave! I know
that story! Once you've squeezed the juice from the orange, 190
you toss the rind away!
PROSPERO: Oh!
CALIBAN: Do I lie? Isn't it true that you threw me out of your
house and made me live in a filthy cave. The ghetto!
PROSPERO: It's easy to say "ghetto"! It wouldn't be such a   195
ghetto if you took the trouble to keep it clean! And there's
something you forgot, which is that what forced me to get
rid of you was your lust. Good God, you tried to rape my
daughter!

CALIBAN: Rape! Rape! Listen, you old goat, you're the one that
put those dirty thoughts in my head. Let me tell you something: I couldn't care less about your daughter, or about
your cave, for that matter. If I gripe, it's on principle, because I didn't like living with you at all, as a matter of fact.
Your feet stink!

PROSPERO: I did not summon you here to argue. Out! Back to
work! Wood, water, and lots of both! I'm expecting company today.

CALIBAN: I've had just about enough. There's already a pile of
wood that high . . .

PROSPERO: Enough! Careful, Caliban! If you keep grumbling
you'll be whipped. And if you don't step lively, if you keep
dragging your feet or try to strike or sabotage things, I'll
beat you. Beating is the only language you really understand. So much the worse for you: I'll speak it, loud and
clear. Get a move on!

CALIBAN: All right, I'm going . . . but this is the last time. It's
the last time, do you hear me? Oh . . . I forgot: I've got
something important to tell you.

PROSPERO: Important? Well, out with it.

CALIBAN: It's this: I've decided I don't want to be called Caliban
any longer.

PROSPERO: What kind of rot is that? I don't understand.

CALIBAN: Put it this way: I'm *telling* you that from now on I
won't answer to the name Caliban.

PROSPERO: Where did you get that idea?

CALIBAN: Well, because Caliban *isn't* my name. It's as simple as
that.

PROSPERO: Oh, I suppose it's mine!

CALIBAN: It's the name given me by your hatred, and everytime
it's spoken it's an insult.

PROSPERO: My, aren't we getting sensitive! All right, suggest
something else . . . I've got to call you something. What
will it be? Cannibal would suit you, but I'm sure you
wouldn't like that, would you? Let's see . . . what about
Hannibal? That fits. And why not . . . they all seem to like
historical names.

CALIBAN: Call me X. That would be best. Like a man without
a name. Or, to be more precise, a man whose name has been
stolen. You talk about history . . . well, that's history, and
everyone knows it! Every time you summon me it reminds
me of a basic fact, the fact that you've stolen everything
from me, even my identity! Uhuru! (*He exits.*)

(*Enter* ARIEL *as a sea-nymph.*)

PROSPERO: My dear Ariel, did you see how he looked at me,
that glint in his eye? That's something new. Well, let me tell
you, Caliban is the enemy. As for those people on the boat,
I've changed my mind about them. Give them a scare,
but for God's sake don't touch a hair of their heads! You'll
answer to me if you do.

ARIEL: I've suffered too much myself for having made them suffer not to be pleased at your mercy. You can count on me,
Master.

PROSPERO: Yes, however great their crimes, if they repent you
can assure them of my forgiveness. They are men of my race,
and of high rank. As for me, at my age one must rise above
disputes and quarrels and think about the future. I have a
daughter. Alonso has a son. If they were to fall in love, I
would give my consent. Let Ferdinand marry Miranda, and
may their marriage bring us harmony and peace. That is my
plan. I want it executed. As for Caliban, does it matter what
that villain plots against me? All the nobility of Italy,
Naples and Milan henceforth combined, will protect me
bodily. Go!

ARIEL: Yes, Master. Your orders will be fully carried out.

(ARIEL *sings.*)

> Sandy seashore, deep blue sky,
> Surf is rising, sea birds fly
> Here the lover finds delight,
> Sun at noontime, moon at night.
> Join hands lovers, join the dance,
> Find contentment, find romance.
>
> Sandy seashore, deep blue sky,
> Cares will vanish . . . so can I . . .

FERDINAND: What is this music? It has led me here and now it
stops . . . No, there it is again . . .

ARIEL: (*Singing.*)

> Waters move, the ocean flows,
> Nothing comes and nothing goes . . .
> Strange days are upon us . . .
>
> Oysters stare through pearly eyes
> Heart-shaped corals gently beat
> In the crystal undersea
>
> Waters move and ocean flows,
> Nothing comes and nothing goes . . .
> Strange days are upon us . . .

FERDINAND: What is this that I see before me? A goddess? A
mortal?

MIRANDA: I know what *I'm* seeing: a flatterer. Young man, your
ability to pay compliments in the situation in which you
find yourself at least proves your courage. Who are you?

FERDINAND: As you see, a poor shipwrecked soul.

MIRANDA: But one of high degree!

FERDINAND: In other surroundings I might be called "Prince,"
"son of the King" . . . But, no, I was forgetting . . . not
"Prince" but "King," alas . . . "King" because my father has
just perished in the shipwreck.

MIRANDA: Poor young man! Here, you'll be received with hospitality and we'll support you in your misfortune.

FERDINAND: Alas, my father . . . Can it be that I am an unnatural son? Your pity would make the greatest of sorrows
seem sweet.

MIRANDA: I hope you'll like it here with us. The island is
pretty. I'll show you the beaches and the forests, I'll tell you
the names of fruits and flowers, I'll introduce you to a whole
world of insects, of lizards of every hue, of birds . . . Oh, you
cannot imagine! The birds! . . .

PROSPERO: That's enough, daughter! I find your chatter irritating . . . and let me assure you, it's not at all fitting. You are
doing too much honor to an impostor. Young man, you are
a traitor, a spy, and a woman-chaser to boot! No sooner has
he escaped the perils of the sea than he's sweet-talking the

first girl he meets! You won't get round me that way. Your arrival is convenient, because I need more manpower: you shall be my house servant.

315 FERDINAND: Seeing the young lady, more beautiful than any wood-nymph, I might have been Ulysses on Nausicaa's isle. But hearing you, Sir, I now understand my fate a little better . . . I see I have come ashore on the Barbary Coast and am in the hands of a cruel pirate. (*Drawing his sword.*) How-
320 ever, a gentleman prefers death to dishonor! I shall defend my life with my sword!

PROSPERO: Poor fool: your arm is growing weak, your knees are trembling! Traitor! I could kill you now . . . but I need the manpower. Follow me.

325 ARIEL: It's no use trying to resist, young man. My master is a sorcerer: neither your passion nor your youth can prevail against him. Your best course would be to follow and obey him.

FERDINAND: Oh God! What sorcery is this? Vanquished, a cap-
330 tive—yet far from rebelling against my fate, I am finding my servitude sweet. Oh, I would be imprisoned for life if only heaven will grant me a glimpse of my sun each day, the face of my own sun. Farewell, Nausicaa.

(*They exit.*)

ACT TWO

SCENE I

CALIBAN'*s cave.* CALIBAN *is singing as he works when* ARIEL *enters. He listens to him for a moment.*

CALIBAN: (*Singing.*)

> May he who eats his corn heedless of Shango
> Be accursed! May Shango creep beneath
> His nails and eat into his flesh!
> 5 Shango, Shango ho!
>
> Forget to give him room if you dare!
> He will make himself at home on your nose!
>
> Refuse to have him under your roof at your own risk!
> He'll tear off your roof and wear it as a hat!
> 10 Whoever tries to mislead Shango
> Will suffer for it!
> Shango, Shango ho!

ARIEL: Greetings, Caliban. I know you don't think much of me, but after all we *are* brothers, brothers in suffering and slav-
15 ery, but brothers in hope as well. We both want our freedom. We just have different methods.

CALIBAN: Greetings to you. But you didn't come to see me just to make that profession of faith. Come on, Alastor! The old man sent you, didn't he? A great job: carrying out the Mas-
20 ter's fine ideas, his great plans.

ARIEL: No, I've come on my own. I came to warn you. Prospero is planning horrible acts of revenge against you. I thought it my duty to alert you.

CALIBAN: I'm ready for him.

25 ARIEL: Poor Caliban, you're doomed. You know that you aren't the stronger, you'll never be the stronger. What good will it do you to struggle?

CALIBAN: And what about you? What good has your obedience done you, your Uncle Tom patience and your sucking up to
30 him. The man's just getting more demanding and despotic day by day.

ARIEL: Well, I've at least achieved one thing: he's promised me my freedom. In the distant future, of course, but it's the first time he's actually committed himself.

35 CALIBAN: Talk's cheap! He'll promise you a thousand times and take it back a thousand times. Anyway, tomorrow doesn't interest me. What I want is (*Shouting.*) "Freedom now!"

ARIEL: Okay. But you know you're not going to get it out of him "now," and that he's stronger than you are. I'm in a
40 good position to know just what he's got in his arsenal.

CALIBAN: The stronger? How do you know that? Weakness always has a thousand means and cowardice is all that keeps us from listing them.

ARIEL: I don't believe in violence.

45 CALIBAN: What *do* you believe in, then? In cowardice? In giving up? In kneeling and groveling? That's it, someone strikes you on the right cheek and you offer the left. Someone kicks you on the left buttock and you turn the right . . . that way there's no jealousy. Well, that's not
50 Caliban's way . . .

ARIEL: You know very well that that's not what I mean. No violence, no submission either. Listen to me: Prospero is the one we've got to change. Destroy his serenity so that he's finally forced to acknowledge his own injustice and put an
55 end to it.

CALIBAN: Oh sure . . . that's a good one! Prospero's conscience! Prospero is an old scoundrel who has no conscience.

ARIEL: Exactly—that's why it's up to us to give him one. I'm not fighting just for *my* freedom, for *our* freedom, but for
60 Prospero too, so that Prospero can acquire a conscience. Help me, Caliban.

CALIBAN: Listen, kid, sometimes I wonder if you aren't a little bit nuts. So that Prospero can acquire a conscience? You might as well ask a stone to grow flowers.

65 ARIEL: I don't know what to do with you. I've often had this inspiring, uplifting dream that one day Prospero, you, me, we would all three set out, like brothers, to build a wonderful world, each one contributing his own special thing: patience, vitality, love, will-power too, and rigor, not to men-
70 tion the dreams without which mankind would perish.

CALIBAN: You don't understand a thing about Prospero. He's not the collaborating type. He's a guy who only feels something when he's wiped someone out. A crusher, a pulveriser, that's what he is! And you talk about brotherhood!

75 ARIEL: So then what's left? War? And you know that when it comes to that, Prospero is invincible.

CALIBAN: Better death than humiliation and injustice. Anyhow, I'm going to have the last word. Unless nothingness has it. The day when I begin to feel that everything's lost, just let
80 me get hold of a few barrels of your infernal powder and as you fly around up there in your blue skies you'll see this island, my inheritance, my work, all blown to smithereens . . . and, I trust, Prospero and me with it. I hope you'll like the fireworks display—it'll be signed Caliban.

85 ARIEL: Each of us marches to his own drum. You follow yours. I follow the beat of mine. I wish you courage, brother.

CALIBAN: Farewell, Ariel, my brother, and good luck.

SCENE II

GONZALO: A magnificent country! Bread hangs from the trees and the apricots are bigger than a woman's full breast.

SEBASTIAN: A pity that it's so wild and uncultivated . . . here and there.

5 GONZALO: Oh, that's nothing. If there were anything poisonous, an antidote would never be far away, for nature is intrinsically harmonious. I've even read somewhere that guano is excellent compost for sterile ground.

SEBASTIAN: Guano? What kind of animal is that? Are you sure 10 you don't mean iguana?

GONZALO: Young man, if I say guano, I mean guano. Guano is the name for bird-droppings that build up over centuries, and it is by far the best fertilizer known. You dig it out of caves . . . If you want my opinion, I think we should inves-15 tigate all the caves on this island one by one to see if we find any, and if we do, this island, if wisely exploited, will be richer than Egypt with its Nile.

ANTONIO: Let me understand: your guano cave contains a river of dried bird-shit.

20 GONZALO: To pick up your image, all we need to do is channel that river, use it to irrigate, if I may use the term, the fields with this wonderful fecal matter, and everything will bloom.

SEBASTIAN: But we'll still need manpower to farm it. Is the is-25 land even inhabited?

GONZALO: That's the problem, of course. But if it is, it must be by wonderful people. It's obvious: a wondrous land can only contain wonderful creatures.

ANTONIO: Yes!

30 Men whose bodies are wiry and strong
And women whose eyes are open and frank . . .
creatures in it! . . .

GONZALO: Something like that! I see you know your literature. But in that case, watch out: it will all mean new responsi-35 bilities for us!

SEBASTIAN: How do you get that?

GONZALO: I mean that if the island is inhabited, as I believe, and if we colonize it, as is my hope, then we have to take every precaution not to import our shortcomings, yes, what 40 we call civilization. They must stay as they are: savages, noble and good savages, free, without any complexes or complications. Something like a pool granting eternal youth where we periodically come to restore our aging, citified souls.

45 ALONSO: Sir Gonzalo, when will you shut up?

GONZALO: Ah, Your Majesty, if I am boring you, I apologize. I was only speaking as I did to distract you and to turn our sad thoughts to something more pleasant. There, I'll be silent. Indeed, these old bones have had it. Oof! Let me sit 50 down . . . with your permission, of course.

ALONSO: Noble Old Man, even though younger than you, we are all in the same fix.

GONZALO: In other words, dead tired and dying of hunger.

ALONSO: I have never pretended to be above the human 55 condition.

(A strange, solemn music is heard.)

. . . Listen, listen! Did you hear that?

GONZALO: Yes, it's an odd melody!

(PROSPERO enters invisible. Other strange figures enter as well, bearing a laden table. They dance and graciously invite the KING and his company to eat, then they disappear.)

ALONSO: Heaven protect us! Live marionettes!

GONZALO: Such grace! Such music! Hum. The whole thing is most peculiar. 60

SEBASTIAN: Gone! Faded away! But what does that matter, since they've left their food behind! No meal was ever more welcome. Gentlemen, to table!

ALONSO: Yes, let us partake of this feast, even though it may be our last. 65

(They prepare to eat, but ELVES enter and, with much grimacing and many contortions, carry off the table.)

GONZALO: Ah! that's a fine way to behave!

ALONSO: I have the distinct feeling that we have fallen under the sway of powers that are playing at cat and mouse with us. It's a cruel way to make us aware of our dependent status.

GONZALO: The way things have been going it's not surprising, 70 and it will do us no good to protest.

(The ELVES return, bringing the food with them.)

ALONSO: Oh no, this time I won't bite!

SEBASTIAN: I'm so hungry that I don't care, I'll abandon my scruples.

GONZALO: (To ALONSO.) Why not try? Perhaps the Powers 75 controlling us saw how disappointed we were and took pity on us. After all, even though disappointed a hundred times, Tantalus still tried a hundred times.

ALONSO: That was also his torture. I won't touch that food.

PROSPERO: (Invisible.) Ariel, I don't like his refusing. Harass 80 them until they eat.

ARIEL: Why should we go to any trouble for them? If they won't eat, they can die of hunger.

PROSPERO: No, I want them to eat.

ARIEL: That's despotism. A while ago you made me snatch it 85 away just when they were about to gobble it up, and now that they don't want it you are ready to force feed them.

PROSPERO: Enough hairsplitting! My mood has changed! They insult me by not eating. They must be made to eat out of my hand like chicks. That is a sign of submission I insist 90 they give me.

ARIEL: It's evil to play with their hunger as you do with their anxieties and their hopes.

PROSPERO: That is how power is measured. I am Power.

(ALONSO and his group eat.)

ALONSO: Alas, when I think . . . 95

GONZALO: That's your trouble, Sire: you think too much.

ALONSO: And thus I should not even think of my lost son! My throne! My country!

GONZALO: (Eating.) Your son! What's to say we won't find him again! As for the rest of it . . . Look, Sire, this filthy hole is 100 now our entire world. Why seek further? If your thoughts are too vast, cut them down to size.

(*They eat.*)

ALONSO: So be it! But I would prefer to sleep. To sleep and to forget.

105 GONZALO: Good idea! Let's put up our hammocks!

(*They sleep.*)

SCENE III

ANTONIO: Look at those leeches, those slugs! Wallowing in their slime and their snot: Idiots, slime—they're like beached jellyfish.

SEBASTIAN: Shhh! It's the King. And that old graybeard is his
5   venerable counsellor.

ANTONIO: The King is he who watches over his flock when they sleep. That one isn't watching over anything. Ergo, he's not the King. (*Brusquely.*) You're really a bloodless lily-liver if you can see a king asleep without getting certain ideas . . .

10 SEBASTIAN: I mustn't have any blood, only water.

ANTONIO: Don't insult water. Every time I look at myself I think I'm more handsome, more *there*. My inner juices have always given me my greatness, my true greatness . . . not the greatness men grant me.

15 SEBASTIAN: All right, so I'm stagnant water.

ANTONIO: Water is never stagnant. It works, it works in us. It is what gives man his dimension, his true one. Believe me, you're mistaken if you don't grab the opportunity when it's offered you. It may never come again.

20 SEBASTIAN: What are you getting at? I have a feeling I can guess.

ANTONIO: Guess, guess! Look at that tree swaying in the wind. It's called a coconut palm. My dear Sebastian, in my opinion it's time to shake the coconut palm.

SEBASTIAN: Now I really don't understand.

25 ANTONIO: What a dope! Consider my position: I'm Duke of Milan. Well, I wasn't always . . . I had an older brother. That was Duke Prospero. And if I'm now Duke Antonio, it's because I knew when to shake the coconut palm.

SEBASTIAN: And Prospero?

30 ANTONIO: What do you mean by that? When you shake a tree, someone is bound to fall. And obviously it wasn't me who fell, because here I am: to assist and serve you, Majesty!

SEBASTIAN: Enough! He's my brother! My scruples won't allow me to . . . You take care of him while I deal with the old
35   Counsellor.

(*They draw their swords.*)

ARIEL: Stop, ruffians! Resistance is futile: your swords are enchanted and falling from your hands!

ANTONIO, SEBASTIAN: Alas! Alas!

ARIEL: Sleepers, awake! Awake, I say! Your life depends on it.
40   With these fine fellows with their long teeth and swords around, anyone who sleeps too soundly risks sleeping forever.

(ALONSO *and* GONZALO *awaken.*)

ALONSO: (*Rubbing his eyes.*) What's happening? I was asleep, and I was having a terrible dream!

ARIEL: No, you were not dreaming. These fine lords here are
45   criminals who were about to perpetrate the most odious of crimes upon you. Yes, Alonso, you may well marvel that a god should fly to your aid. Were to heaven you deserved it more!

ALONSO: I have never been wanting in respect for the divinity . . .

ARIEL: I don't know what effect my next piece of news will have 50 on you: The name of him who has sent me to you is Prospero.

ALONSO: Prospero! God save us! (*He falls to his knees.*)

ARIEL: I understand your feelings. He lives. It is he who reigns over this isle, as he reigns over the spirits of the air you 55 breathe . . . But rise . . . You need fear no longer. He has not saved your lives to destroy them. Your repentance will suffice, for I can see that it is deep and sincere. (*To* ANTONIO *and* SEBASTIAN.) As for you, Gentlemen, my master's pardon extends to you as well, on the condition that you renounce 60 your plans, knowing them to be vain.

SEBASTIAN: (*To* ANTONIO.) We could have got worse!

ANTONIO: If it were men we were up against, no one could make me withdraw, but when it's demons and magic there's no shame in giving in. (*To* ARIEL.) . . . We are the Duke's 65 most humble and obedient servants. Please beg him to accept our thanks.

GONZALO: Oh, how ignoble! How good of you to just wipe the slate clean! No surface repentance . . . not only do you want attrition, you want contrition as well! Why look at me as 70 though you didn't know what I was talking about? *Attrition*: A selfish regret for offending God, caused by a fear of punishment. *Contrition*: An unselfish regret growing out of sorrow at displeasing God.

ARIEL: Honest Gonzalo, thank you for your clarification. Your 75 eloquence has eased my mission and your pedagogical skill has abbreviated it, for in a few short words you have expressed my master's thought. May your words be heard! Therefore, let us turn the page. To terminate this episode, I need only convoke you all, on my master's behalf, to the cel- 80 ebrations that this very day will mark the engagement of his daughter, Miranda. Alonso, that's good news for you . . .

ALONSO: What—my son?

ARIEL: Correct. Saved by my master from the fury of the waves.

ALONSO: (*Falling to his knees.*) God be praised for this blessing 85 more than all the rest. Rank, fortune, throne, I am prepared to forgo all if my son is returned to me . . .

ARIEL: Come, Gentlemen, follow me.

ACT THREE

SCENE I

FERDINAND: (*Hoeing and singing.*)

> How life has changed
> Now, hoe in hand
> I work away all day . . .   5
>
> Hoeing all the day,
> I go my weary way . . .

CALIBAN: Poor kid! What would he say if he was Caliban! He works night and day, and when he sings, it's

> Oo–en–day, Oo–en–day, Oo–en–day, Macaya . . .   10

And no pretty girl to console him! (*Sees* MIRANDA *approaching.*) Aha! Let's listen to this!

FERDINAND: (*Singing.*)

> How life has changed
> Now, hoe in hand
> I work away all day . . .

15

MIRANDA: Poor young man! Can I help you? You don't look like you were cut out for this kind of work!

FERDINAND: One word from you would be more help to me than anything in the world.

20 MIRANDA: One word? From me? I must say, I . . .

FERDINAND: Your name—that's all: What is your name?

MIRANDA: That, I cannot do! It's impossible. My father has expressly forbidden it!

FERDINAND: It is the only thing I long for.

25 MIRANDA: But I can't, I tell you; it's forbidden!

CALIBAN: (*Taking advantage of* MIRANDA's *momentary distraction, he whispers her name to* FERDINAND.) Mi–ran–da!

FERDINAND: All right then, I shall christen you with a name of my own. I will call you Miranda.

30 MIRANDA: That's too much! What a low trick! You must have heard my father calling me . . . Unless it was that awful Caliban who keeps pursuing me and calling out my name in his stupid dreams!

FERDINAND: No, Miranda . . . I had only to allow my eyes to

35 speak, as you your face.

MIRANDA: Sssh! My father's coming! He'd better not catch you trying to sweet talk me . . .

FERDINAND: (*Goes back to work, singing.*)

> But times have changed
> Now, hoeing all the day,
> I go my weary way . . .

40

PROSPERO: That's fine, young man! You've managed to accomplish a good deal for a beginning! I see I've misjudged you. But you won't be the loser if you serve me well. Listen, my

45 young friend, there are three things in life: Work, Patience, Continence, and the world is yours . . . Hey, Caliban, I'm taking this boy away with me. He's done enough for one day. But since the job is urgent, see that it gets finished.

CALIBAN: Me?

50 PROSPERO: Yes, you! You've cheated me enough with your loafing and fiddling around, so you can work a double shift for once!

CALIBAN: I don't see why I should do someone else's job!

PROSPERO: Who's the boss here? You or me? Listen, monster: if you don't like work, I'll see to it you change your mind!

(PROSPERO *and* FERDINAND *move away.*)

55 CALIBAN: Go on, go on . . . I'll get you one day, you bastard! (*He sets to work, singing.*)

> "O–o–en–day, Oo–en–day, Oo–en–day, Macaya . . ."

Shit, now it's raining! As if things weren't bad enough . . . (*Suddenly, at the sound of a voice,* CALIBAN *stiffens.*) Do you hear

60 that, boy? That voice through the storm. Bah! It's Ariel. No, that's not his voice. Whose, then? With an old coot like Prospero . . . One of his cops, probably. Oh, fine! Now, I'm for it. Men and the elements both against me. Well, the hell with it . . . I'm used to it. Patience! I'll get them yet. In the meantime

65 better make myself scarce! Let Prospero and his storm and his cops go by . . . let the seven maws of Malediction bay!

SCENE II

Enter TRINCULO.

TRINCULO: (*Singing.*)

> Oh Susannah . . . oh don't you cry for me . . . (Etc.)

You can say that again! My dearest Susannah . . . trust Trinculo, we've had all the roaring storms we need, and more! I swear: the whole crew wiped out, liquidated . . . Nothing! 5 Nothing left . . . ! Nothing but poor wandering and wailing Trinculo! No question about it, it'll be a while before anyone persuades me to depart from affectionate women and friendly towns to go off to brave roaring storms! How it's raining! (*Notices* CALIBAN *underneath the wheelbarrow.*) Ah, an In- 10 dian! Dead or alive? You never know with these tricky races. Yukkk! Anyhow, this will do me fine. If he's dead, I can use his clothes for shelter, for a coat, a tent, a covering. If he's alive I'll make him my prisoner and take him back to Europe and then, by golly, my fortune will be made! I'll sell him to a car- 15 nival. No! I'll show him myself at fairs! What a stroke of luck! I'll just settle in here where it's warm and let the storm rage! (*He crawls under cover, back to back with* CALIBAN.)

(*Enter* STEPHANO.)

STEPHANO: (*Singing.*)

> Blow the man down, hearties, 20
> Blow the man down . . . (Etc.)

(*Takes a swig of his bottle and continues.*)

> Blow, blow, blow the man down . . . (Etc.)

Fortunately, there's still a little wine left in this bottle . . . enough to give me courage! Be of good cheer, Stephano, where there's life there's thirst . . . and vice versa! (*Suddenly* 25 *spies* CALIBAN's *head sticking out of the cover.*) My God, on Stephano's word, it looks like a Nindian! (*Comes nearer.*) And that's just what it is! A Nindian. That's neat. I really am lucky. There's money to be made from a Nindian like that. If you showed him at a carnival . . . along with the 30 bearded lady and the flea circus, a real Nindian! An authentic Nindian from the Caribbean! That means real dough, or I'm the last of the idiots! (*Touching* CALIBAN.) But he's ice cold! I don't know what the body temperature of a Nindian is, but this one seems pretty cold to me! Let's hope 35 he's not going to croak! How's that for bad luck: You find a Nindian and he dies on you! A fortune slips through your fingers! But wait, I've got an idea . . . a good swig of this booze between his lips, that'll warm him up. (*He gives* CALIBAN *a drink.*) Look . . . he's better already. The little glutton 40 even wants some more! Just a second, just a second! (*He walks around the wheelbarrow and sees* TRINCULO's *head sticking out from under the covering.*) Jeez! I must be seeing things! A Nindian with two heads! Shit! If I have to pour drink down *two* gullets I won't have much left for myself! Well, never 45 mind. It's incredible . . . your everyday Nindian is already something, but one with two heads . . . a Siamese-twin Nindian, a Nindian with two heads and eight paws, that's really something! My fortune is made. Come on, you wonderful monster, you . . . let's get a look at your other head! (*He draws* 50 *nearer to* TRINCULO.) Hello! That face reminds me of something! That nose that shines like a lighthouse . . .

TRINCULO: That gut . . .

STEPHANO: That nose looks familiar . . .

55 TRINCULO: That gut—there can't be two of them in this lousy world!

STEPHANO: Oh-my-gawd, oh-my-gawd, oh-my-gawd . . . *that's* it . . . it's that crook Trinculo!

TRINCULO: Good lord! It's Stephano!

60 STEPHANO: So, Trinculo, you were saved too . . . It almost makes you believe God looks after drunks . . .

TRINCULO: Huh! God . . . Bacchus, maybe. As a matter of fact, I reached these welcoming shores by floating on a barrel . . .

STEPHANO: And I by floating on my stomach . . . it's nearly the same thing. But what kind of creature is this? Isn't it a Nindian?

65

TRINCULO: That's just what I was thinking . . . Yes, by God, it's a Nindian. That's a piece of luck . . . he'll be our guide.

STEPHANO: Judging from the way he can swill it down, he doesn't seem to be stupid. I'll try to civilize him. Oh . . . not too much, of course. But enough so that he can be of some use.

70

TRINCULO: Civilize him! Shee-it! Does he even know how to talk?

STEPHANO: I couldn't get a word out of him, but I know a way to loosen his tongue. (*He takes a bottle from his pocket.*)

75

TRINCULO: (*Stopping him.*) Look here, you're not going to waste that nectar on the first savage that comes along, are you?

STEPHANO: Selfish! Back off! Let me perform my civilizing mission. (*Offering the bottle to* CALIBAN.) Of course, if he was cleaned up a bit he'd be worth more to both of us. Okay? We'll exploit him together? It's a deal? (*To* CALIBAN.) Drink up, pal. You. Drink . . . Yum-yum botty botty! (CALIBAN *drinks.*) You, drink more. (CALIBAN *refuses.*) You no more thirsty? (STEPHANO *drinks.*) Me always thirsty! (STEPHANO *and* TRINCULO *drink.*)

80

85

STEPHANO: Trinculo, you know I used to be prejudiced against shipwrecks, but I was wrong. They're not bad at all.

TRINCULO: That's true. It seems to make things taste better afterwards . . .

90 STEPHANO: Not to mention the fact that it's got rid of a lot of old farts that were always keeping the world down! May they rest in peace! But then, you liked them, didn't you, all those kings and dukes, all those noblemen! Oh, I served them well enough, you've got to earn your drink somehow . . . But I could never stand them, ever—understand? Never. Trinculo, my friend, I'm a long-time believer in the republic . . . you might as well say it: I'm a died-in-the-wool believer in the people first, a republican in my guts! Down with tyrants!

95

100 TRINCULO: Which reminds me . . . If, as it would seem, the King and the Duke are dead, there's a crown and a throne up for grabs around here . . .

STEPHANO: By God, you're right! Smart thinking, Trinculo! So, I appoint myself heir . . . I crown myself king of the island.

105 TRINCULO: (*Sarcastically.*) Sure you do! And why you, may I ask? I'm the one who thought of it first, that crown!

STEPHANO: Look, Trinculo, don't be silly! I mean, really: just take a look at yourself! What's the first thing a king needs? Bearing. Presence. And if I've got anything, it's that. Which isn't true for everyone. So, I am the King!

110

CALIBAN: Long live the King!

STEPHANO: It's a miracle . . . he can talk! And what's more, he talks sense! O brave savage! (*He embraces* CALIBAN.) You see, my dear Trinculo, the people has spoken! Vox populi, vox Dei . . . But please, don't be upset. Stephano is magnanimous and will never abandon his friend Trinculo, the friend who stood by him in his trials. Trinculo, we've eaten rough bread together, we've drunk rot-gut wine together. I want to do something for you. I shall appoint you Marshal. But we're forgetting our brave savage . . . It's a scientific miracle! He can talk! 120

115

CALIBAN: Yes, Sire. My enthusiasm has restored my speech. Long live the King! But beware the usurper!

STEPHANO: Usurper? Who? Trinculo?

CALIBAN: No, the other one . . . Prospero!

STEPHANO: Prospero? Don't know him. 125

CALIBAN: Well, you see, this island used to belong to me, except that a man named Prospero cheated me of it. I'm perfectly willing to give you my right to it, but the only thing is, you'll have to fight Prospero for it.

STEPHANO: That is of no matter, brave savage. It's a bargain! I'll 130 get rid of this Prospero for you in two shakes.

CALIBAN: Watch out, he's powerful.

STEPHANO: My dear savage, I eat a dozen Prosperos like that for breakfast every day. But say no more, say no more! Trinculo, take command of the troops! Let us march upon the foe! 135

TRINCULO: Yes, forward march! But first, a drink. We will need all our strength and vigor.

CALIBAN: Let's drink, my new-found friends, and let us sing. Let us sing of winning the day and of an end to tyranny.

(*Singing.*)

> Black pecking creature of the savannas 140
> The quetzal measures out the new day
>   solid and lively
>   in its haughty armor.
> Zing! the determined hummingbird
>   revels in the flower's depths, 145
>   going crazy, getting drunk,
>   a lyrebird gathers up our ravings,
> Freedom hi-day! Freedom hi-day!

STEPHANO *and* TRINCULO: (*Together.*) Freedom hi-day! Freedom hi-day! 150

CALIBAN:

> The ringdove dallies amid the trees,
> wandering the islands, here it rests—
> The white blossoms of the miconia
> Mingle with the violet blood of ripe berries 155
> And blood stains your plumage,
>   traveller!
> Lying here after a weary day
> We listen to it:
> Freedom hi-day! Freedom hi-day! 160

STEPHANO: Okay, monster . . . enough crooning. Singing makes a man thirsty. Let's drink instead. Here, have some more . . . spirits create higher spirits . . . (*Filling a glass.*) Lead the way, O bountiful wine! Soldiers, forward march! Or rather . . . no: At ease! Night is falling, the fireflies twinkle, the crickets chirp, all nature makes its brek-ke-ke-kek! 165

And since night has fallen, let us take advantage of it to
gather our forces and regain our strength, which has been
sorely tried by the unusually . . . copious emotions of the
170   day. And tomorrow, at dawn, with a new spring in our
step, we'll have the tyrant's hide. Good night, gentlemen.
(*He falls asleep and begins to snore.*)

SCENE III

PROSPER's *cave.*

PROSPERO: So then, Ariel! Where are the gods and goddesses?
They'd better get a move on! And all of them! I want all of
them to take part in the entertainment I have planned for
our dear children. Why do I say "entertainment"? Because
5   starting today I want to inculcate in them the spectacle of
tomorrow's world: logic, beauty, harmony, the foundations
for which I have laid down by my own will-power. Unfortunately, alas, at my age it's time to stop thinking of deeds
and to begin thinking of passing on . . . Enter, then!

(GODS *and* GODDESSES *enter.*)

10   JUNO: Honor and riches to you! Long continuance and increasing long life and honored issue! Juno sings to you her
blessings!
CERES: May scarcity and want shun you! That is Ceres' blessing on you.
15   IRIS: (*Beckoning to the* NYMPHS.) Nymphs, come help to celebrate here a contact of true love.

(NYMPHS *enter and dance.*)

PROSPERO: My thanks, Goddesses, and my thanks to you, Iris.
Thank you for your good wishes.

(GODS *and* GODDESSES *continue their dance.*)

FERDINAND: What a splendid and majestic vision! May I be so
20   bold to think these spirits?
PROSPERO: Yes, spirits which by my art I have from their confines called to greet you and to bless you.

(*Enter* ESHU.)

MIRANDA: But who is that? He doesn't look very benevolent!
If I weren't afraid of blaspheming, I'd say he was a devil
25   rather than a god.
ESHU: (*Laughing.*) You are not mistaken, fair lady. God to my
friends, the Devil to my enemies! And lots of laughs for all!
PROSPERO: (*Softly.*) Ariel must have made a mistake. Is my
magic getting rusty? (*Aloud.*) What are you doing here?
30   Who invited you? I don't like such loose behavior, even
from a god!
ESHU: But that's just the point . . . no one invited me . . . And
that wasn't very nice! Nobody remembered poor Eshu! So
poor Eshu came anyway. Hihihi! So how about something
35   to drink? (*Without waiting for a reply, he pours a drink.*) . . .
Your liquor's not bad. However, I must say I prefer dogs!
(*Looking at* IRIS.) I see that shocks the little lady, but to each
his own. Some prefer chickens, others prefer goats. I'm not
too fond of chickens, myself. But if you're talking about a
40   black dog . . . think of poor Eshu!

PROSPERO: Get out! Go away! We will have none of your grimaces and buffoonery in this noble assembly. (*He makes a
magic sign.*)
ESHU: I'm going, boss, I'm going . . . But not without a little   45
song in honor of the bride and the noble company, as you say.

Eshu can play many tricks,
Give him twenty dogs!
You will see his dirty tricks.

Eshu plays a trick on the Queen   50
And makes her so upset that she runs
Naked into the street

Eshu plays a trick on a bride,
And on the day of the wedding
She gets into the wrong bed!   55

Eshu can throw a stone yesterday
And kill a bird today.
He can make a mess out of order and vice-versa.
Ah, Eshu is a wonderful bad joke.
Eshu is not the man to carry a heavy load.   60
His head comes to a point. When he dances
He doesn't move his shoulders . . .
Oh, Eshu is a merry elf!

Eshu is a merry elf,
And he can whip you with his dick,   65
He can whip you,
He can whip you . . .

CERES: My dear Iris, don't you find that song quite obscene?
JUNO: It's disgusting! It's quite intolerable . . . if he keeps on,
I'm leaving!   70
IRIS: It's like Liber, or Priapus!
JUNO: Don't mention that name in my presence!
ESHU: (*Continuing to sing.*)

        . . . with his dick
        He can whip you, whip you . . .   75

JUNO: Oh! Can't someone get rid of him? I'm not staying here!
ESHU: Okay, okay . . . Eshu will go. Farewell, my dear colleagues!

(GODS *and* GODDESSES *exit.*)

PROSPERO: He's gone . . . what a relief! But alas, the harm is
done! I am perturbed . . . My old brain is confused. Power!
Power! Alas! All this will one day fade, like foam, like a   80
cloud, like all the world. And what is power, if I cannot
calm my own fears? But come! My power has gone cold.
(*Calling.*) Ariel!
ARIEL: (*Runs in.*) What is it, Sire?
PROSPERO: Caliban is alive, he is plotting, he is getting a guer-   85
rilla force together and you—you don't say a word! Well,
take care of him. Snakes, scorpions, porcupines, all stinging
poisonous creatures, he is to be spared nothing! His punishment must be exemplary. Oh, and don't forget the mud
and mosquitoes!   90
ARIEL: Master, let me intercede for him and beg your indulgence. You've got to understand: he's a rebel.
PROSPERO: By his insubordination he's calling into question the
whole order of the world. Maybe the Divinity can afford to
let him get away with it, but I have a sense of responsibility!   95

ARIEL: Very well, Master.

PROSPERO: But a thought: arrange some glass trinkets, some trumpery and some second-hand clothes too . . . but colorful ones . . . by the side of the road along which General
100 Caliban and his troops are travelling. Savages adore loud, gaudy clothes . . .

ARIEL: Master . . .

PROSPERO: You're going to make me angry. There's nothing to understand. There is a punishment to be meted out. I will
105 not compromise with evil. Hurry! Unless you want to be the next to feel my wrath.

SCENE IV

In the wild; night is drawing to a close; the murmurings of the spirits of the tropical forest are heard.

VOICE I: Fly!

VOICE II: Here!

VOICE I: Ant!

VOICE II: Here.

5 VOICE I: Vulture!

VOICE II: Here.

VOICE I: Soft-shelled crab, calao, crab, hummingbird!

VOICES: Here. Here. Here.

VOICE I: Cramp, crime, fang, opossum!

10 VOICE II: Kra. Kra. Kra.

VOICE I: Huge hedgehog, you will be our sun today. Shaggy, taloned, stubborn. May it burn! Moon, my fat spider, my big dreamcat, go to sleep, my velvet one.

VOICES: (*Singing.*)

15   King-ay
                   King-ay
                   Von-von
                   Maloto
                   Vloom-vloom!

(*The sun rises.* ARIEL's *band vanishes.* CALIBAN *stands for a moment, rubbing his eyes.*)

20 CALIBAN: (*Rises and searches the bushes.*) Have to think about getting going again. Away, snakes, scorpions, porcupines! All stinging, biting, sticking beasts! Sting, fever, venom, away! Or if you really want to lick me, do it with a gentle tongue, like the toad whose pure drool soothes me with
25 sweet dreams of the future. For it is for you, for all of us, that I go forth today to face the common enemy. Yes, hereditary and common. Look, a hedgehog! Sweet little thing . . . How can any animal—any natural animal, if I may put it that way—go against me on the day I'm setting forth to conquer
30 Prospero! Unimaginable! Prospero is the Anti-Nature! And I say, down with Anti-Nature! And does the porcupine bristle his spines at that? No, he smoothes them down! That's nature! It's kind and gentle, in a word. You've just got to know how to deal with it. So come on, the way is clear! Off
35 we go!

(*The band sets out.* CALIBAN *marches forward singing his battle song:*)

Shango carries a big stick,
He strikes and money expires!

He strikes and lies expire!
He strikes and larceny expires!
Shango, Shango ho!   40
Shango is the gatherer of the rain,
He passes, wrapped in his fiery cloak,
His horse's hoofs strike lighting
On the pavements of the sky!
Shango is a great knight!   45
Shango, Shango ho!

(*The roar of the sea can be heard.*)

STEPHANO: Tell me, brave savage, what is that noise? It sounds like the roaring of a beast at bay.

CALIBAN: Not a bay . . . more like on the prow! . . . Don't worry, it's a pal of mine.   50

STEPHANO: You are very closemouthed about the company you keep.

CALIBAN: And yet it helps me breathe. That's why I call it a pal. Sometimes it sneezes, and a drop falls on my forehead and cools me with its salt, or blesses me . . .   55

STEPHANO: I don't understand. You aren't drunk, are you?

CALIBAN: Come on! It's that howling impatient thing that suddenly appears in a clap of thunder like some God and hits you in the face, that rises up out of the very depths of the abyss and smites you with its fury! It's the sea!   60

STEPHANO: Odd country! And an odd baptism!

CALIBAN: But the best is still the wind and the songs it sings . . . its dirty sigh when it rustles through the bushes, or its triumphant chant when it passes by breaking trees, remnants of their terror in its beard.   65

STEPHANO: The savage is delirious, he's raving mad! Tough luck, Trinculo, our savage is playing without a full deck!

TRINCULO: I'm kind of shuffling myself . . . In other words, I'm exhausted. I never knew such hard going! Savage, even your mud is muddier.   70

CALIBAN: That isn't mud . . . it's something Prospero's dreamed up.

TRINCULO: There's a savage for you . . . everything's always caused by someone. The sun is Prospero's smile. The rain is the tear in Prospero's eye . . . And I suppose the mud is   75
Prospero's shit. And what about the mosquitoes? What are they, may I ask? Zzzzzz, Zzzzzz . . . do you hear them? My face is being eaten off!

CALIBAN: Those aren't mosquitoes. It's some kind of gas that stings your nose and throat and makes you itch. It's another 80
of Prospero's tricks. It's part of his arsenal.

STEPHANO: What do you mean by that?

CALIBAN: I mean his anti-riot arsenal! He's got a lot of gadgets like these . . . gadgets to make you deaf, to blind you, to make you sneeze, to make you cry . . .   85

TRINCULO: And to make you slip! Shit! This is some fix you've got us in! I can't take anymore . . . I'm going to sit down!

STEPHANO: Come on, Trinculo, show a little courage! We're engaged in a mobile ground manoeuvre here, and you know what that means: drive, initiatives, split-second decisions to 90
meet new eventualities, and—above all—mobility. Let's go! Up you get! Mobility!

TRINCULO: But my feet are bleeding!

STEPHANO: Get up or I'll knock you down! (TRINCULO *begins to walk again.*) But tell me, my good savage, this usurper of 95 yours seems very well protected. It might be dangerous to attack him!

CALIBAN: You mustn't underestimate him. You mustn't overestimate him, either . . . he's showing his power, but he's doing it mostly to impress us.

STEPHANO: No matter. Trinculo, we must take precautions. Axiom: never underestimate the enemy. Here, pass me that bottle. I can always use it as a club.

(*Highly colored clothing is seen, hanging from a rope.*)

TRINCULO: Right, Stephano. On with the battle. Victory means loot. And there's a foretaste of it . . . look at that fine wardrobe! Trinculo, my friend, methinks you are going to put on those britches . . . they'll replace your torn trousers.

STEPHANO: Look out, Trinculo . . . one move and I'll knock you down. As your lord and master I have the first pick, and with those britches I'm exercising my feudal rights . . .

TRINCULO: I saw them first!

STEPHANO: The King gets first pick in every country in the world.

TRINCULO: That's tyranny, Stephano. I'm not going to let you get away with it.

(*They fight.*)

CALIBAN: Let it alone, fool. I tell you about winning your dignity, and you start fighting over hand-me-downs! (*To himself.*) To think I'm stuck with these jokers! What an idiot I am! How could I ever have thought I could create the Revolution with swollen guts and fat faces! Oh well! History won't blame me for not having been able to win my freedom all by myself. It's you and me, Prospero! (*Weapon in hand, he advances on* PROSPERO *who has just appeared.*)

PROSPERO: (*Bares his chest to him.*) Strike! Go on, strike! Strike your Master, your benefactor! Don't tell me you're going to spare him!

(CALIBAN *raises his arm, but hesitates.*)

Go on! You don't dare! See, you're nothing but an animal . . . you don't know how to kill.

CALIBAN: Defend yourself! I'm not a murderer.

PROSPERO: (*Very calm.*) The worse for you. You've lost your chance. Stupid as a slave! And now, enough of this farce. (*Calling.*) Ariel! (*To* ARIEL.) Ariel, take charge of the prisoners!

(CALIBAN, TRINCULO, *and* STEPHANO *are taken prisoners.*)

SCENE V

PROSPERO's *cave.* MIRANDA *and* FERDINAND *are playing chess.*

MIRANDA: Sir, I think you're cheating.

FERDINAND: And what if I told you that I would not do so for twenty kingdoms?

MIRANDA: I would not believe a word of it, but I would forgive you. Now, be honest . . . you did cheat!

FERDINAND: I'm pleased that you were able to tell. (*Laughing.*) That makes me less worried at the thought that soon you will be leaving your innocent flowery kingdom for my less-innocent world of men.

MIRANDA: Oh, you know that, hitched to your star, I would brave the demons of hell!

(*The* NOBLES *enter.*)

ALONSO: My son! This marriage! The thrill of it has struck me dumb! The thrill and the joy!

GONZALO: A happy ending to a most opportune shipwreck!

ALONSO: A unique one, indeed, for it can legitimately be described as such.

GONZALO: Look at them! Isn't it wonderful! I've been too choked up to speak, or I would have already told these children all the joy my old heart feels at seeing them living love's young dream and cherishing each other so tenderly.

ALONSO: (*To* FERDINAND *and* MIRANDA.) My children, give me your hands. May the Lord bless you.

GONZALO: Amen! Amen!

(*Enter* PROSPERO.)

PROSPERO: Thank you, Gentlemen, for having agreed to join in this little family party. Your presence has brought us comfort and joy. However, you must now think of getting some rest. Tomorrow morning, you will recover your vessels—they are undamaged—and your men, who I can guarantee are safe, hale and hearty. I shall return with you to Europe, and I can promise you—I should say: promise us—a rapid sail and propitious winds.

GONZALO: God be praised! We are delighted . . . delighted and overcome! What a happy, what a memorable day! With one voyage Antonio has found a brother, his brother has found a dukedom, his daughter has found a husband, Alonso has regained his son and gained a daughter. And what else? . . . Anyway, I am the only one whose emotion prevents him from knowing what he's saying . . .

PROSPERO: The proof of that, my fine Gonzalo, is that you are forgetting someone: Ariel, my loyal servant. (*Turning to* ARIEL.) Yes, Ariel, today you will be free. Go, my sweet. I hope you will not be bored.

ARIEL: Bored! I fear that the days will seem all too short!
There, where the Cecropia gloves its impatient hands with silver,
Where the ferns free the stubborn black stumps
from their scored bodies with a green cry—
There where the intoxicating berry ripens the visit
of the wild ring-dove
through the throat of that musical bird
I shall let fall
one by one,
each more pleasing than the last
four notes so sweet that the last
will give rise to a yearning
in the heart of the most forgetful slaves
yearning for freedom!

PROSPERO: Come, come. All the same, you are not going to set my world on fire with your music, I trust!

ARIEL: (*With intoxication.*) Or on some stony plane
perched on an agave stalk
I shall be the thrush that launches
its mocking cry
to the benighted field-hand

"Dig, nigger! Dig, nigger!"
65 and the lightened agave will
straighten from my flight,
a solemn flag.
PROSPERO: That is a very unsettling agenda! Go! Scram! Before
I change my mind!

(*Enter* STEPHANO, TRINCULO, CALIBAN.)

70 GONZALO: Sire, here are your people.
PROSPERO: Oh no, not all of them! Some are yours.
ALONSO: True. There's that fool Trinculo and that unspeakable
Stephano.
STEPHANO: The very ones, Sire, in person. We throw ourselves
75 at your merciful feet.
ALONSO: What became of you?
STEPHANO: Sire, we were walking in the forest—no, it was in
the fields—when we saw some perfectly respectable clothing blowing in the wind. We thought it only right to col-
80 lect them and we were returning them to their rightful
owner when a frightful adventure befell us . . .
TRINCULO: Yes, we were mistaken for thieves and treated accordingly.
STEPHANO: Yes, Sire, it is the most dreadful thing that could
85 happen to an honest man: victims of a judicial error, a mis-
carriage of justice!
PROSPERO: Enough! Today is a day to be benevolent, and it will
do no good to try to talk sense to you in the state you're
in . . . Leave us. Go sleep it off, drunkards. We raise sail
90 tomorrow.
TRINCULO: Raise sail! But that's what we do all the time, Sire,
Stephano and I . . . at least, we raise our glasses, from dawn
till dusk till dawn. The hard part is putting them down,
landing, as you might say.
95 PROSPERO: Scoundrels! If only life could bring you to the safe
harbors of Temperance and Sobriety!
ALONSO: (*Indicating* CALIBAN.) That is the strangest creature
I've ever seen!
PROSPERO: And the most devilish too!
100 GONZALO: What's that? Devilish! You've reprimanded him,
preached at him, you've ordered and made him obey and
you say he is still indomitable!
PROSPERO: Honest Gonzalo, it is as I have said.
GONZALO: Well—and forgive me, Counsellor, if I give
105 counsel—on the basis of my long experience the only
thing left is exorcism. "Begone, unclean spirit, in the
name of the Father, of the Son and of the Holy Ghost."
That's all there is to it!

(CALIBAN *bursts out laughing.*)

GONZALO: You were absolutely right! And more so that you
110 thought . . . He's not just a rebel, he's a real tough customer! (*To* CALIBAN.) So much the worse for you, my
friend. I have tried to save you. I give up. I leave you to the
secular arm!
PROSPERO: Come here, Caliban. Have you got anything to say
115 in your own defence? Take advantage of my good humor.
I'm in a forgiving mood today.
CALIBAN: I'm not interested in defending myself. My only
regret is that I've failed.

PROSPERO: What were you hoping for?
CALIBAN: To get back my island and regain my freedom. 120
PROSPERO: And what would you do all alone here on this island, haunted by the devil, tempest tossed?
CALIBAN: First of all, I'd get rid of you! I'd spit you out, all your
works and pomps! Your "white" magic!
PROSPERO: That's a fairly negative program . . . 125
CALIBAN: You don't understand it . . . I say I'm going to spit
you out, and that's very positive . . .
PROSPERO: Well, the world is really upside down . . . We've
seen everything now: Caliban as a dialectician! However, in
spite of everything I'm fond of you, Caliban. Come, let's 130
make peace. We've lived together for ten years and worked
side by side! Ten years count for something, after all! We've
ended up by becoming compatriots!
CALIBAN: You know very well that I'm not interested in peace.
I'm interested in being free! Free, you hear? 135
PROSPERO: It's odd . . . no matter what you do, you won't suc-
ceed in making me believe that I'm a tyrant!
CALIBAN: Understand what I say, Prospero:
For years I bowed my head
for years I took it, all of it— 140
your insults, your ingratitude . . .
and worst of all, more degrading than all the rest,
your condescension.
But now, it's over!
Over, do you hear? 145
Of course, at the moment
You're still stronger than I am.
But I don't give a damn for your power
or for your dogs or your police or your inventions!
And do you know why? 150
It's because I know I'll get you.
I'll impale you! And on a stake that you've sharpened
yourself!
You'll have impaled yourself!
Prospero, you're a great magician:
you're an old hand at deception. 155
And you lied to me so much,
about the world, about myself,
that you ended up by imposing on me
an image of myself:
underdeveloped, in your words, undercompetent 160
that's how you made me see myself!
And I hate that image . . . and it's false!
But now I know you, you old cancer,
And I also know myself!
And I know that one day 165
my bare fist, just that,
will be enough to crush your world!
The old world is crumbling down!

Isn't it true? Just look!
It even bores you to death. 170

And by the way . . . you have a chance to get it over with:
You can pick up and leave.
You can go back to Europe.
But the hell you will! 175
I'm sure you won't leave.
You make me laugh with your "mission"!

Your "vocation"!
Your vocation is to hassle me.
And that's why you'll stay,
180 just like those guys who founded the colonies
and who now can't live anywhere else.
You're just an old addict, that's what you are!
PROSPERO: Poor Caliban! You know that you're headed towards
your own ruin. You're sliding towards suicide! You know I
185 will be the stronger, and stronger all the time. I pity you!
CALIBAN: And I hate you!
PROSPERO: Beware! My generosity has its limits.
CALIBAN: (*Shouting.*)

190   Shango marches with strength
along his path, the sky!
Shango is a fire-bearer,
his steps shake the heavens
and the earth
Shango, Shango, ho!

195 PROSPERO: I have uprooted the oak and raised the sea,
I have caused the mountain to tremble and have bared my
chest to adversity.
With Jove I have traded thunderbolt for thunderbolt.
Better yet—from a brutish monster I have made man!
But ah! To have failed to find the path to man's heart . . .
200 if that be where man is.
(*To* CALIBAN.) Well, I hate you as well!
For it is you who have made me
doubt myself for the first time.
(*To the* NOBLES.) . . . My friends, come near. We must say
205 farewell . . . I shall not be going with you. My fate is here:
I shall not run from it.
ANTONIO: What, Sire?
PROSPERO: Hear me well.
I am not in any ordinary sense a master,
210 as this savage thinks,
but rather the conductor of a boundless score:
this isle,
summoning voices, I alone,
and mingling them at my pleasure,
215 arranging out of confusion
one intelligible line.
Without me, who would be able to draw music from all that?
This isle is mute without me.
My duty, thus, is here,
220 and here I shall stay.

GONZALO: Oh day full rich in miracles!
PROSPERO: Do not be distressed. Antonio, be you the lieutenant
of my goods and make use of them as procurator until that
time when Ferdinand and Miranda may take effective possession of them, joining them with the Kingdom of Naples.   225
Nothing of that which has been set for them must be postponed: Let their marriage be celebrated at Naples with all
royal splendor. Honest Gonzalo, I place my trust in your word.
You shall stand as father to our princess at this ceremony.
GONZALO: Count on me, Sire.   230
PROSPERO: Gentlemen, farewell.

(*They exit.*)

And now, Caliban, it's you and me!
What I have to tell you will be brief:
Ten times, a hundred times, I've tried to save you,
above all from yourself.   235
But you have always answered me with wrath
and venom,
like the opossum that pulls itself up by its own tail
the better to bite the hand that tears it from the darkness.
Well, my boy, I shall set aside my indulgent nature   240
and henceforth I will answer your violence
with violence!

(*Time passes, symbolized by the curtain's being lowered halfway and
reraised. In semi-darkness* PROSPERO *appears, aged and weary. His
gestures are jerky and automatic, his speech weak, toneless, trite.*)

PROSPERO: Odd, but for some time now we seem to be overrun
with opossums. They're everywhere. Peccarys, wild boar, all
this unclean nature! But mainly opossums. Those eyes! The   245
vile grins they have! It's as though the jungle was laying
siege to the cave . . . But I shall stand firm . . . I shall not let
my work perish! (*Shouting.*) I shall protect civilization! (*He
fires in all directions.*) They're done for! Now, this way I'll be
able to have some peace and quiet for a while. But it's cold.   250
Odd how the climate's changed. Cold on this island . . .
Have to think about making a fire . . . Well, Caliban, old fellow, it's just us two now, here on the island . . . only you and
me. You and me. You-me . . . me-you! What in the hell is
he up to? (*Shouting.*) Caliban!   255

(*In the distance, above the sound of the surf and the chirping of birds,
we hear snatches of* CALIBAN'*s song:*)

FREEDOM HI-DAY, FREEDOM HI-DAY!

APPENDIX

LITERAL TRANSLATIONS OF SONGS
ARIEL'S SONG
(Act I, Scene 2)

Chestnut horses of the sand
They bite out the place
Where the waves expire in
Pure languor.

Where the waves die
Here come all,
Join hands
And dance.

Blond sands,
What fire!
Languorous waves,
Pure expiration.
Here lips lick and lick again
Our wounds.

The waves make a waterline . . .
Nothing is, all is becoming . . .
The season is close and strange

The eye is a fine pearl
The heart of coral, the bone of coral,
There, at the waterline
As the sea swells within us.

TRINCULO'S SONG
(Act III, Scene 2)

Virginia, with tears in my eyes
I bid you farewell.
We're off to Mexico,
Straight into the setting sun.

With sails unfurled, my dear love,

It torments me to leave you,
A tempest is brewing
Some storm is howling
That will carry off the entire crew!

STEPHANO'S SONG
(Act III, Scene 2)

(Obviously an old sea chanty or Césaire's adaptation of one.)

Bravely on, guys, step it lively,
bravely on, farewell Bordeaux,
To Cape Horn, it won't be hot,
Off to hunt the whale.

More than one of us will lose his skin
Farewell misery, farewell ship.
The ones who return with all flags flying
Will be the first-rate sailors . . .

Griselda Gambaro

Griselda Gambaro is one of the most distinguished writers of contemporary Argentina. Born in Buenos Aires in 1928, Gambaro's career as a writer has been deeply intertwined with the history and politics of her country. Argentina has a long history of repressive military rule, and Gambaro's career as a playwright began during a period of exceptional crisis, inaugurated by Juan Carlos Onganía's brutal military coup in 1966. Gambaro's plays from this period—*The Walls* (1963), *The Blunder* (1965), *The Siamese Twins* (1965), *The Camp* (1967)—concern the progressive deterioration of the fabric of society. But as the political repression of the 1960s gave way to state terrorism in the 1970s—especially the "Dirty War" (1976–1983), in which the military government systematically imprisoned and/or murdered hundreds of thousands of civilians, the "disappeared"—Gambaro's fiction and drama became increasingly engaged, making her situation in Argentina even more precarious. Her plays of the 1970s—including *Saying Yes* (1972), *Strip* (1972), *The Name* (1976), and *Information for Foreigners* (1973)—depict a world totally slipped from its moorings, in which murder, torture, and execution seem part of the horizon of everyday life.

Gambaro has written several novels as well, including *Nothing to Do with Another Story* (1972), *To Earn One's Death* (1976), *God Does Not Want Us Happy* (1979), and *Impenetrable* (1984). In 1977, *To Earn One's Death* was banned and Gambaro left Argentina to live in Spain and France. She returned to Argentina in 1980, where she continued her career as a playwright, with *Royal Gambit* (1980), *Bitter Blood* (1981), *From the Rising Sun* (1983), *Antígona Furiosa* (1986), *Fear* (1989), and *Worthless Trouble* (1990). Gambaro has lectured extensively in the United States and is currently living in Buenos Aires.

INFORMATION FOR FOREIGNERS

Griselda Gambaro's *Information for Foreigners* uses the participatory element of environmental theater to enact a sophisticated political process as theater. Ideally performed in a house, the play divides the audience into four groups, each led through the play's scenes in a different order, and then reassembled as a single audience for the final scene, scene 20.

Information for Foreigners forces its audience to engage the subtle interinvolvement between theater and the theater of state terrorism, between fiction and fact, a blurring of boundaries between the simulated and the "real" typical of postmodern art. For throughout the play, the audience is repeatedly confronted by two kinds of "performance": overtly "theatrical" or "staged" scenes—like scene 14, where the audience observes a reenactment of a scene of police violence—and "backstage" or "offstage" scenes where the "disappeared"— the man in his underwear in scene 1, the girl who is tortured with the "submarine" (held under water in a bathtub of filthy water)—accidentally come into the audience's view. The play forces its audience both to connect these two spheres of performance and to question its own role in each. The Guide repeatedly provides "Information for Foreigners" to the audience, which articulates the historical background of state violence in the 1970s, and implicitly addresses that wider, European and North American audience whose tacit or financial support kept the regime in power. The audience is, in a sense, incriminated for adopting this "tourist" role.

In many respects, *Information for Foreigners* is a play about its audience. Scene 4 reenacts the famous Milgram experiment, in which the participant's willingness to follow orders and please authority figures leads him to kill (or, in the original versions of the experiment, to believe he has killed) the "student." The Milgram experiment provides a kind of metaphor for the audience's function in *Information for Foreigners,* in that observation repeatedly involves the audience in a kind of deference to authority. The silent willingness to participate as spectators of the violence makes the audience responsible for the violence, becoming its silent authors. This implied assault on the audience's moral freedom is the point of the play's final scene, where the line between theater and torture is finally suspended, and the "stage" of torture is one the audience is explicitly shown to authorize. Having brought the audience to witness a final execution, the Guide turns to us: "Ladies and gentlemen, what are you waiting for? The show is over." As he suggests in his final, ritual chant, "Theater imitates life"; but the boundaries between theater and life, between what we see and what we know, have been forever broken:

> Who once said: here the ken
> of men and women
> here the bounds?

INFORMATION FOR FOREIGNERS

A CHRONICLE IN TWENTY SCENES

Griselda Gambaro

TRANSLATED BY MARGUERITE FEITLOWITZ

CHARACTERS

GUIDES, *number contingent on number of audience groups*

VOICES, *heard at intervals throughout*

MAN IN ROOM

GIRL, *with wet clothes*
MAN, *with pistol*

COORDINATOR
MATURE MAN/TEACHER
YOUNG MAN/PUPIL

MOTHER
FATHER

GROUP OF MEN, *attack* MAN IN AUDIENCE
MAN, *defends attacked man*

SOMEONE FROM THE AUDIENCE, *number contingent on number of audience groups*
USHERETTE

THREE MEN, *carry table*
GROUP OF MEN, *surround* GIRL
TWO WORKMEN

MOTHER (*Sara Palacio de Verdt*)
FATHER (*Marcelo Verdt*)
TWO CHILDREN (*Verdt girl and boy*)
CHIEF
TWO POLICEMEN

MAN IN LOINCLOTH

MAN (*Robert Quieto*)

NEIGHBOR #1
NEIGHBOR #2
FIRST GROUP OF MEN, *tied together*
NEIGHBOR #3
SECOND GROUP OF MEN, *tied together*
OFFICIAL
JUDGE
GUARD

GIRL, *with long hair* (HERMENEGILDA)
FOUR MEN, *on skates*
HUSBAND OF HERMENEGILDA
MOTHER OF HERMENEGILDA
NEIGHBORS

MAN (*Juan Pablo Maestre*)
WOMAN (*Miera Elena Misetich*)
TWO POLICEMEN
GROUP OF POLICEMEN, *dressed as sweepers*

GAME PLAYERS
POLICEMEN, *with clubs*

ACTOR #1
TWO MEN, *in box*

ACTRESS #1
ACTRESS #2
ACTOR #1
POLICEMAN #1
POLICEMAN #2

CHILD MONSTER

CHILDREN, *play Anton Pirulero*
FIRST MAN
SECOND MAN
THIRD MAN
YOUNG WOMAN

TWO GUARDS
PRISONERS
VISITORS TO PRISON
PRETTY GIRL

GROUP OF GUARDS, *attack* PRETTY GIRL
LITTLE OLD LADY
OUTLANDISH-LOOKING PRISONER

PROSTITUTES
MAN #1
MAN #2
MAN #3
MAN #4

The theater space can be a spacious, residential house, preferably two stories, with corridors and empty rooms, some of which interconnect. A larger space is needed for the final scene.

Situated in the passageways, propped against the walls, are two or three vertical rectangular boxes, each with a door and air holes.

In a different area, chosen by the director, sits an additional box, larger but otherwise the same as those in the passageways.

Some of the corridors are dark, while others, in obvious contrast, are crudely lit.

The audience will be divided into groups, the number and size of which will depend on the space. A particular number or color can serve to identify each group.

Group 1 will mark one possible development of the action.

Guides 1, 2, 3, 4, etc., lead their respective groups. The order in which the scenes are observed by these groups is left to the director's discretion until the last scene, scene 20, when all groups converge.

In certain scenes, actors play audience members and are actually part of the audience. Audience members, however, are never forced to participate in the action.

The groups cross in the passageways and may watch the same scene— perhaps one taking place in the passageway—when the director considers it necessary.

Excerpts introduced by the guides as "Explanation: For Foreigners" come from Argentine newspapers of the period 1971–72.

GUIDES: Organize the groups.

GUIDE: Ladies and gentlemen: Admission is ———, for adults. If you've already paid, you can't repent. The cost is already incurred. Better to enjoy yourself. No one under eighteen will be admitted. Or under thirty-five or over thirty-six. Everyone else can attend with no problem. No obscenity or strong words. The play speaks to our way of life: Argentine, Western, and Christian. We are in 1971. I ask that you stay together and remain silent. Careful on the stairs.

SCENE ONE

The GUIDE *leads the group toward one of the rooms. The room is completely in shadow. The door closes. We hear a shrill, metallic signal. Then, we hear many voices, indistinct and juxtaposed, carrying on an incomprehensible conversation.*

GUIDE: One moment . . . I don't find my flashlight. Remember, opportunity makes the thief. Watch your pocketbooks! (*Light comes up on a dark and wrinkled wall.*) Only the naked walls are left. (*The light travels. A man is seated on a chair, wearing only faded underwear. He raises his head, surprised and frightened. He covers his sex with his hands. To the audience.*) Excuse me. I've got the wrong room.

SCENE TWO

The GUIDE, *lighting the way with his flashlight, leads the group out of the room. He tries to open the door of another room. Behind the door a sweet voice sings*

VOICE:

"Carnation, sleep and dream,
the horse won't drink from the stream . . ."

GUIDE: (*Shrugging his shoulders, turns to the group.*) It's locked. (*He knocks. Nicely.*) May I? I've brought a group of spectators. And they're getting anxious.

VOICE: (*Very rudely.*) What's it to me? Beat it! I'm rehearsing.

SCENE THREE

GUIDE: (*To the group.*) Sorry. People should be brought up better, don't you think? (*Tries the latch on the next door. It gives.*) Good. Here. Go ahead. (*The group enters this other dark room. Against the wall, some chairs. The* GUIDE *shines his light on them. Then, nicely.*) You can position yourselves wherever you like. There are chairs for everyone. (*He looks.*) No, not enough to go around. (*Arranges them, offers.*) Ladies first . . . !

(*Lights on in the middle of the room. A young* GIRL *sits on a chair wearing clothes that are soaking wet. A* MAN *stands next to her, observing her with a tender smile. The* GUIDE *waits for people to get comfortable, points out places. Then, with a finger on his lips, he signals for silence and turns, like one more spectator, toward the characters who begin the action.*)

MAN: (*Always speaks softly, tenderly.*) Why didn't you dry yourself? You're getting the floor all wet. (*He bends down and dries the floor with a rag.*) Lucky it's not waxed. (*The* GIRL *shivers with cold. The* MAN *takes off his jacket, puts it on her shoulders. The* GIRL *looks at it, wraps herself in the jacket.*) Why didn't you dry yourself? Wasn't there a towel?

GIRL: No.

MAN: (*Drying the floor.*) What a mess! They fill the tub but don't put any towels. What about the water? Was it warm? (*The* GIRL *doesn't answer. He shakes her, gently.*) Was it warm?

GIRL: No.

---

ii. 2 **"Carnation, sleep and dream,"** sung by a "sweet" female Voice, the Mother in scene 5, and other voices elsewhere, is from García Lorca's *Bodas de sangre*, or *Blood Wedding*, scene 2. I use the translation by James Graham-Luján and Richard L. O'Connell in *Three Tragedies of Federico García Lorca: Blood Wedding, Yerma, Bernarda Alba* (New York: New Directions, 1955). In the original, Gambaro used only "Nana, niño, nana, del caballo grande que no quiso el agua," repeated over and over. For the English version, I chose to use many more fragments of the lullabye over the course of the play. Gambaro approved this choice in her letter to me of March 28, 1986

MAN: (*He pulls a pistol from his belt and cleans it with a rag.*) Ah! This department isn't worth shi . . . (*The* GUIDE *says something. The* MAN *shoots him a quick look.*) Right. (*He shows her his weapon.*) Do you like it? It isn't loaded. (*She looks at it but doesn't answer. The* MAN *begins loading the gun.*) Why so sad? (*Points to the group.*) Nothing will happen to you. There are lots of people. They're watching us. (*Puts the pistol back in his belt.*) You're not pretty with your hair all wet. But that's not too serious. (*He leans toward her, curious.*) Tell me, do you dye your hair? (*Still studying her.*) You're getting my jacket all wet. Sorry, it's the only one I have . . . (*He takes it gently, shakes it, and puts it on. With a shiver.*) It's damp. (*Pointing to the pistol.*) Do you want it?

GIRL: No.

MAN: I'm leaving it for you. I have another. The jacket I can't, I swear to you.

GIRL: (*Shaking her head.*) No.

MAN: (*Surreptitiously.*) Speak up! They can't hear a thing!

GUIDE: Louder! Louder!

MAN: What did I tell you? (*The* GIRL *doesn't answer.*) Look at me. (*She obeys. He holds out the gun.*) Take it!

GIRL: No . . . I don't want to.

MAN: Why are you squeezing your legs together? Do you want to go to the bathroom?

GIRL: (*Nods her head.*) Yes.

MAN: Then go!

GIRL: They're . . . watching me.

MAN: So? We're all adults, aren't we? They at least are watching. What are you doing, always looking over there? What do you see that's so pretty? (*Puts his cheek against hers. Looks in the same direction.*) Nothing! (*Separates from her.*) I like to see people's eyes when I talk to them. (*Gently, he turns her head.*) Look at me. (*He points to the pistol.*) Do you want it?

GIRL: No, no! Leave me alone!

MAN: (*Anxious.*) Would you like some stockings? (*He puts his hand on her foot.*)

GIRL: No!

MAN: Always no! Why? My intentions are good. Take it. Don't you get bored all alone? (*Insists.*) Take it, it doesn't bite. But don't squeeze the trigger. Unless . . .

GIRL: (*Barely audible.*) Unless . . .

MAN: If you squeeze, it's all over. Do you have a boyfriend?

GIRL: No.

MAN: Well then? Take it! I'm leaving it here, on the floor. All you have to do is lean down.

GIRL: For what? I don't want . . . to lean down, I don't want . . . anything.

MAN: The heart and the forehead . . . are sure. I mean, so you don't suffer . . .

GIRL: No . . .

MAN: (*Caresses her cheek.*) Of course, no. There's a sun outside. It's hot as hell. So you don't have a boyfriend? Well then . . . ? (*He goes toward the door. Turns. Smiles.*) I'm going to tell them to heat the water! (*He goes out. The* GIRL *looks at the pistol on the floor, leans down, trembling, stretches her hand. Freezes in the act.*)

GUIDE: Ladies and gentlemen, if it bothers you. (*He opens the door. Leading the group into the hallway, he explains.*) In March 1970, at the Max Planck Institute in Munich, Germany, they began an interesting experiment. Careful on the stairs.

SCENE FOUR

The group enters a white room that adjoins another, also painted white, but that may be smaller. In the first room, a small table with a cage full of white rats. On another table, a metal box outfitted with buttons and a microphone. Carefully folded on an ordinary chair, a white coat.

Through the half-open door one can see in the other room a chair whose armrests are outfitted with side straps attached to electric cables. Cables to tie down a person's legs. A microphone hangs down from the ceiling.

In the first room are the COORDINATOR, *dressed in a white coat, and two others in street clothes, a* MATURE MAN *and a* YOUNG MAN. *The* MATURE MAN *lingers in front of the cage, putting his fingers through the bars, trying to attract the rats and get them to play.*

COORDINATOR: (*To the group, in a professional tone.*) Gentlemen: The subject of our experiment is to determine the pedagogical effect of punishment. To what degree does punishment accelerate the learning process? Imagine. If with one
5   slap a child learns to behave, we waste years teaching and persuading only with nice words. We don't have time to lose. Soon he will be an adult; soon he will be molded. Molded for destruction, when one slap, two or three electrical jolts at the right moment could put things in place.
10   (*He begins observing the* MATURE MAN *playing with the rats.*) The gentlemen will help us to clarify …unclear …details … Please, sir, stop pestering those rats! Idiot! (*He goes toward him and kicks him away from the cage.*)
MATURE MAN: Okay, okay. I'm sorry. They're so cute that …
15 COORDINATOR: (*Calm.*) Of course they're cute. (*Becoming irritated.*) Shall we begin?
MATURE MAN: At your orders, sir!
COORDINATOR: (*Happy.*) One kick …and acquiescence. You, sir, emotionally more mature, will be the teacher.
20 MATURE MAN: Yes, delighted.
COORDINATOR: (*To the* YOUNG MAN.) You will be the pupil.
YOUNG MAN: (*He speaks with a metallic voice, like a parrot.*) I will be the pupil.
GUIDE: (*To the group, surreptitiously.*) Everyone's a researcher,
25   even the mule.
COORDINATOR: (*Drily.*) Silence! (*He takes money and some papers out of his pocket.*) Help yourself. Twenty-five marks, or thirty-six dollars for your trouble. If you would be so kind as to sign the receipt and the release. (*They sign, take their*
30   *money. The* COORDINATOR *hands the* TEACHER *a white coat.*) This is for you. (*Cordially, the* COORDINATOR *helps him on with the coat, adjusts the collar.*) There, now. Right this way, please. (*He leads them into the other room. The* GUIDE *follows with his group.* COORDINATOR *to the* PUPIL.) Please be seated.
35   Don't be afraid, it's an experiment, remember that.
PUPIL: Happy to please
   I sit with the greatest of ease!
COORDINATOR: I made a mistake. Take off your jacket, roll up your sleeves. (*The* PUPIL *does so.*) Thank you. We have to
40   strap you in. If you would like to resign …
PUPIL No! For the sake of science
   Let us commence!
COORDINATOR: (*Strapping him. To the* TEACHER.) Will you help me?

TEACHER: (*With dispatch.*) Yes, of course!   45
COORDINATOR: (*From a pocket of his coat, he takes a tube of cream and starts smearing the* PUPIL's *forearms.*) The cream facilitates the passage of current and prevents burns. (*Winking at him.*) It's an experiment, don't be frightened. It's like … talking to hear yourself talk.   50
PUPIL: I'm not afraid
   I'm not afraid
   I really feel I have it made.
COORDINATOR: (*Attaches electrodes to the* PUPIL's *forearms. The* TEACHER *helps diligently.*) How obliging! Thank you.   55
PUPIL: It's … very tight.
COORDINATOR: Let's loosen this a bit. (*He does.*) You—the Teacher—are going to station yourself at the microphone in the next room. (*To the* PUPIL.) You pay attention. He will read out a group of words, such as *day-sun, night-moon,*   60 *mother-love,* etc. Then he will repeat the word *day* followed by four others. You must remember which of these four words was associated with *day.* If you make a mistake, you'll receive an electric shock as punishment.
TEACHER: And then you'll learn.   65
PUPIL: Why will punishment teach me?
COORDINATOR: The shock won't be strong.
TEACHER: Never?
COORDINATOR: No! Unless he really blunders. But it's impossible. They're very obvious associations. For idiots. (*To the*   70 TEACHER.) Let's go! (*They go into the adjoining room. The* GUIDE *settles his group. The* COORDINATOR *hands the* TEACHER *a sheet of paper.*) Here is the list of words. A clean game: read slowly, with good pronunciation. Wait! Roll up your sleeve.
TEACHER: Me? What for?   75
COORDINATOR: I want to give you a charge of forty-five volts.
TEACHER: (*Surprised.*) Me? I'm the teacher!
COORDINATOR: Don't be afraid. I'm doing it so that you'll appreciate the intensity of the punishment. Otherwise, you might have a heavy hand. (*He puts an electrode on the*   80 TEACHER's *arm, pushes a button.*)
TEACHER: (*Jumps, frightened.*) That's strong!
COORDINATOR: No, no. You'll start with fifteen volts. You won't have to increase it much. Be seated. Read. Slowly, in a clear voice.   85
TEACHER: (*He sits in front of the metal box, clears his throat, reads haltingly.*) Day-sun, night-moon, mother-love, water-ship, plague-war, house-forest, child-innocence, prison-bars, window-freedom, blue-sky, bird-flight, nation-Germany, torture-dissuasion. (*He finishes, looks at the* COORDINATOR   90 *like a child awaiting instructions.*)
COORDINATOR: (*Claps him on the shoulder.*) Very good! Now you must read one word, then four more, so that the pupil will pick the correct association. If he makes a mistake, say "Error," press the first button, and tell the pupil the voltage   95 with which you're punishing him. Then read the right answer. Punishments start at 15 volts and end at 450. (*He makes a horizontal gesture with his hand.*) As you see, it couldn't be easier. Begin.
TEACHER: (*Clears his throat.*) Sun! Day, forest, mother, water.   100
VOICE OF THE PUPIL: Day!
COORDINATOR: Very good! (*Encouraging the* TEACHER.) Let's go on! Do you like it?
TEACHER: (*Like a child.*) Yes! It's terrific!

105 COORDINATOR: Continue.
     TEACHER: Night! Plague, forest, moon, child.
     VOICE OF THE PUPIL: Moon!
     TEACHER: (*Enthused.*) Correct! (*To the* COORDINATOR, *laughing.*) This is like a drug!
110 COORDINATOR: Ssshh! Go on!
     TEACHER: Mother! Day, water, child, love. (*Silence from the* PUPIL.) But this is bread in your belly! What memories do you have of your mother?
     COORDINATOR: (*With bonhomie.*) Now, don't help! It's not
115 scientific!
     VOICE OF THE PUPIL: Chi . . .
     TEACHER: (*Advises.*) No!
     COORDINATOR: (*Drily.*) Excuse me, sir. This is an experiment, not a game.
120 VOICE OF THE PUPIL: We can't repeat? (*The* TEACHER *looks at the* COORDINATOR.)
     COORDINATOR: Just this once. You've got to follow the rules.
     TEACHER: Just this once, not again. Mother: day, water, child, love. (*Silence from the* PUPIL.) Well?
125 VOICE OF THE PUPIL: Love!
     TEACHER: Very good! But faster. (*The* COORDINATOR *nods approval.*) Blue: ship, bird, sky, house. (*Silence from the* PUPIL.) I'm waiting.
     VOICE OF THE PUPIL: Want to repeat?
130 TEACHER: I won't repeat. How can you not remember? What a fool. (*Looks at the* COORDINATOR, *who assents.*) Answer, I won't wait any longer.
     VOICE OF THE PUPIL: Bird!
     TEACHER: (*Pleased.*) He made a mistake! Now what do I do?
135 COORDINATOR: (*He points to the box. The* TEACHER *vacillates in his choice among the buttons.*) The first. Fifteen volts.
     TEACHER: (*Smiles timidly. Pushes the button.*) Here we go! Take that. (*Through the door, we see that the* PUPIL *is jolted but cries out more in surprise than pain. His cries are always in a parrot-voice,*
140 *stereotyped like those of someone who, as a joke, coarsely imitates moans, groans, and pain. To the* COORDINATOR.) I didn't do anything! (*Into the microphone.*) Now remember. (*He reads.*) Plague: child, innocence, love, night.
     COORDINATOR: (*Very low.*) You forgot war.
145 TEACHER: I did?
     COORDINATOR: Plague-war. It's all right, let it go. It doesn't matter.
     TEACHER: (*Low.*) Should I repeat? (*The* COORDINATOR *shrugs.*) Well? (*The* PUPIL *is silent.*) Come on. Quick. Otherwise it's
150 boring, I get tired.
     VOICE OF THE PUPIL: Night.
     TEACHER: (*Pleased.*) He made a mistake! Thirty volts! (*Instantly presses the second button. A louder groan from the* PUPIL.) Moving right along. Child: love, mother, innocence, bird.
155 VOICE OF THE PUPIL: (*Quickly.*) Love!
     TEACHER: He made a mistake! You were dreaming! Forty-five volts! (*He pushes another button. Howling loudly, the* PUPIL *arches his back. Surprised by the howling, the* TEACHER *looks into the other room. To the* COORDINATOR, *disturbed.*) A bit strong, wasn't it?
160 COORDINATOR: (*Soothingly.*) No. This is a scientific experiment, and I am in charge. What experiment? Just as I told you: simply to determine the effectiveness of punishment in learning. If from the beginning we doubt, we'll never arrive at a conclusion.

TEACHER: Yes, that's right. The associations are easy.   165
COORDINATOR: And it's not so much. I gave you forty-five volts, remember?
TEACHER: I didn't shout. What a weakling! (*To the* PUPIL.) Listen to me. Don't scream. Pay attention. Sky: mother, child, innocence, blue.   170
VOICE OF THE PUPIL: Blue!
TEACHER: Gooooood!
COORDINATOR: Magnificent. We're already getting results.
TEACHER: It's no time to stop, then. Plague: prison, house, forest, war. Well? (*Slowly, the* COORDINATOR *closes the door con-* 175
necting the rooms.) Repeat. (*The* COORDINATOR *shakes his head.*) I can't. (*Silence from the* PUPIL.) Well? (*To the* COORDINATOR.) Can I repeat? Just this once. He's not very intelligent. (*The* COORDINATOR *snorts, accedes with a gesture.*)
TEACHER: Listen. Don't let your mind wander. Plague: prison, 180
house, forest, war.
VOICE OF THE PUPIL: Prison.
TEACHER: He's an idiot!
COORDINATOR: (*Exasperated.*) You must say, "Error," and press the button. That is your job! Save the commentary!   185
TEACHER: And now he's growling at me! (*He presses the button.*)
VOICE OF THE PUPIL: (*Screams.*) No, no! I didn't think I'd be in so much pain!
TEACHER: A smart aleck! Well, he better hold up! (*Into the microphone.*) Pupil: Pay attention. You think I like pushing 190
these little buttons? Try to remember. Blue: bird, flight, sky, freedom. (*Waits, nervous.*) Out with it!
VOICE OF THE PUPIL: I don't remember!
TEACHER: How can you not remember?
VOICE OF THE PUPIL: I don't!   195
TEACHER: (*Furious, pushes the button.*) If you don't remember, take this.
VOICE OF THE PUPIL: (*A scream.*) Sky! (*He whimpers.*)
TEACHER: Very good! (*He wipes the sweat from his face.*) You see? With a little determination, you hit it! Okay! Here we go. 200
Flight: bird, blue, forest, night. You gotta be quick. Answer.
VOICE OF THE PUPIL: I won't play!
No matter what you say!
COORDINATOR: Youth today! Now he refuses!
TEACHER: What's the matter with him? He's howling.   205
COORDINATOR: He signed the release. He can't give up. The results are important, aren't they? You're not screaming. You can be counted on.
TEACHER: Pupil? Pay attention. I am going to read you the words.
VOICE OF THE PUPIL: Go to hell! Let's change places!   210
TEACHER: Change places? That's crazy. It'll be worse for you, if you don't answer. Bird: flight, blue, plague, war. And I'm repeating the words. And it isn't allowed! Who do you think you are? Answer!
VOICE OF THE PUPIL: I'll make a mistake!   215
TEACHER: Answer! (*He pushes the button. A scream. To* COORDINATOR.) He's screaming.
COORDINATOR: He feels a bit jolted. You have just one thing to watch out for: 450 volts—kaput. Otherwise, after a week, there isn't a mark.   220
TEACHER: Listen good. Are you listening?
VOICE OF THE PUPIL: Are you listening?
TEACHER: We'll see who's listening. Bird: night, flight, house, plague.

225 VOICE OF THE PUPIL: I don't remember!

TEACHER: Don't be such an ass!

VOICE OF THE PUPIL: Don't be such an ass! Plague!

TEACHER: (*Furious.*) Imbecile! Bird-plague! (*To the* COORDINATOR.) See how he answers! (*The* COORDINATOR, *understanding, shrugs his shoulders.*) He's jerking me around! (*He pushes a button. The* PUPIL *screams, weeps. Disconcerted, to the* COORDINATOR.) And now he's crying! What do I do?

230

COORDINATOR: Keep going. Don't worry about it.

TEACHER: Listen, kid, answer right, or I'll blow you away. Window: prison, flight, torture, fr . . . freedom.

235

VOICE OF THE PUPIL: Torture! Torture!

TEACHER: What did you say? Tortoise! Idiot! You're making fun of me! (*He pushes the button. The* PUPIL *howls.*)

COORDINATOR: (*Checking.*) One hundred eighty volts. (*Smiles approvingly.*) It's moving right along.

240

VOICE OF THE PUPIL: Let me go, you're hurting me! Oh, my belly!

TEACHER: Do we stop?

COORDINATOR: No.

245 TEACHER: He doesn't remember anything!

COORDINATOR: He'll remember now.

TEACHER: You think so? He burst into tears. If he doesn't answer, this is useless.

COORDINATOR: It isn't useless! If we don't succeed in getting concrete results, all this suffering will be useless. Besides, you have to.

250

TEACHER: I do?

COORDINATOR: Of course. The tears, the screams. Think about it.

255 TEACHER: I'm not exactly sucking my thumb!

COORDINATOR: Of course not. Go ahead.

TEACHER: Nation: prison, bars, Germany, torture.

VOICE OF THE PUPIL: I don't know!

TEACHER: (*His finger on the button.*) Out with it!

260 VOICE OF THE PUPIL: Argentina!

TEACHER: (*Beside himself.*) Germany, idiot! (*He pushes the button. The* PUPIL *howls.*)

COORDINATOR: Planck Institute, Munich.

TEACHER: (*Furious.*) Prison: nation, plague, war, bars.

265 VOICE OF THE PUPIL: I don't know, let me go! I want to go home!

TEACHER: (*Screams.*) Out with it!

VOICE OF THE PUPIL: Nation!

TEACHER: You made a mistake! (*He pushes button after button. The* PUPIL *howls.*)

270

COORDINATOR: (*Stops him.*) Slow! One at a time.

TEACHER: He's fucking with me! Why doesn't he answer right?

COORDINATOR: Make him.

TEACHER: I don't like doing this to you. Is that clear? You signed. Don't count your lost sheep. Concentrate! Here's another. Do you hear me? (*Silence.*) Do you hear?

275

VOICE OF THE PUPIL: (*Lifeless.*) Vultures fly near . . .

TEACHER: Moon: night, prison, window, flight. (*To the* COORDINATOR.) He'll get this one. It's easy. (*Low.*) If he doesn't answer, what do I do?

280

COORDINATOR: (*Gently.*) I told you.

TEACHER: (*Puts his hand on the last button. Closes his eyes.*) He doesn't answer. Why doesn't he answer?

COORDINATOR: (*Softly.*) Laziness. Low level.

TEACHER: Moon.

285

VOICE OF THE PUPIL: Ni . . . Niii . . . ght . . .

TEACHER: (*Without consulting the list.*) He made a mistake. He made a mistake . . . again. (*He opens his eyes.*) It's deliberate. He can't not know. Still . . . it hurts me . . . (*He slowly pushes the last button on the box. Silence. He smiles with relief.*) He didn't scream.

290

COORDINATOR: No. (*Changes his tone. Exultantly.*) Very good! Four hundred fifty volts! Excellent! Your help has been invaluable.

TEACHER: Why didn't he help?

295

COORDINATOR: Look . . . we choose the risks we take! Sometimes we're not so lucky. (*Removes the* TEACHER'*s lab coat.*)

TEACHER: It was his fault. Wasn't it?

COORDINATOR: Yes, yes. Your work was magnificent!

TEACHER: He didn't even make an effort. A baby at the breast could have answered right. Some people like to fuck with you!

300

COORDINATOR: Yes, yes! You were splendid. (*He shakes his hand.*) Thank you ever so much. Don't worry. An unforgettable performance.

305

TEACHER: (*Flattered.*) It was nothing. I did what I could!

COORDINATOR: (*Seeing him to the door.*) No, no, you were quick, concise, sure. Thanks ever so much! (*Again he shakes his hand. The* TEACHER *exits. The* COORDINATOR *turns toward the audience, professional.*) This experiment, with recorded screams and simulated tortures, was repeated 180 times. Unfortunately, this teacher who continued his punishments to the lethal 450 volts was no exception. Eighty-five percent of the teachers proceeded in the same way. The same test was done in 1960 in the United States. The results? Sixty-six percent. They were obeying rules and weren't responsible. Curious, isn't it? Surprised?

310

315

GUIDE: Okay, enough. Don't wear out the audience. (*To his group.*) The experiment was done in Germany and the United States. Here among ourselves, it would be unthinkable, absurd. Ladies and gentlemen, let's look for something more amusing. (*He leads his group out of the room.*) This way, this way. If you would be so kind . . . Ladies and gentlemen . . .

320

SCENE FIVE

The GUIDE *leads the group to the room that in scene two was locked.*

GUIDE: (*He knocks.*) May I?

VERY SILLY VOICE: (*From inside the room.*) Yeeeess.

(*The group enters the room. Seated on a chair is a woman* [MOTHER] *made up like a doll, wearing a white dress that reaches to her feet and holding a baby in her arms. The baby, swaddled in tulle and lace, is obviously a doll. Sitting on the floor, at the woman's feet, a young man* [FATHER] *watches them with an enraptured expression. The group is enveloped in a beam of rosy light. The acting is frankly crude.*)

GUIDE: (*Pleased.*) Ah! Finally something coherent!

MOTHER: (*Rocking the child.*)

---

iv. 319 Stanley Milgram describes this experiment in his book, *Obedience to Authority* (New York: Harper & Row, 1974).

5　　　"My rose, asleep now lie
　　　　the horse is starting to cry
　　　　His poor hooves were . . ."

GUIDE: What a picture! (*To his group.*) Make yourselves com-
10　fortable. Can you see? Madam . . . (*Helps her get comfortable.
　　Then, rapidly, drily.*) Explanation: For Foreigners. Seven
　　P.M., Wednesday, December 16, 1970. Nestor Martins, at-
　　torney, defender of political prisoners and trade unions,
　　consults with his client Nildo Zenteno. They take leave of
　　one another in the street. Six men surround Martins, vio-
15　lently force him into a white Peugeot. Nildo Zenteno
　　rushes back, manages momentarily to free the lawyer. A
　　karate chop to the back of his neck brings Zenteno down as
　　well. The car speeds off. A black Chevrolet escorts it. That
　　car had pulled out of a nearby parking lot of the Federal Po-
20　lice. *Desaparecidos.* (*From newspaper.*) Nestor Martins, thirty-
　　three. Nildo Zenteno, thirty-seven.

MOTHER:

　　　" . . . bleeding,
25　　　his long mane was frozen,
　　　　and deep in his eyes
　　　　stuck a silvery dagger."

(*She suddenly stops. Distorting her voice as though she were a ven-
triloquist speaking for the little one.*) Stop it, Mama. That's old.
Daddy, tell me a story.
30　FATHER: (*Very sweet.*) Yes, darling.
MOTHER: (*Idiotic voice.*) Daddy, it has to be modern! No morals,
　　Daddy!
FATHER: Yes, darling.
MOTHER: (*Impatient.*) Come on, Daddy, start!
35　FATHER: (*Enraptured.*) Precious!
MOTHER: (*In the voice of a ferocious little child.*) I know I'm pre-
　　cious! Why do you go round and around, Daddy?
FATHER: Now, now . . . This child is in such a hurry! Daddy has
　　to think!
40　MOTHER: Enough horsing around, Daddy. Well?
FATHER: (*Laughs confusedly. Then, grossly exaggerating the tradi-
　　tional tone in which one tells a story.*) Once upon a time . . .
MOTHER: (*In the voice of a fierce, exasperated little child.*) Yeeeess . . .
FATHER: (*In the same tone.*) Once upon a time there was a tall
45　man, ugly, ugly, ugly . . . (*With disgust.*) Bolivian. (*Resum-
　　ing the story.*) He had a pile of children. (*Drily.*) They pro-
　　create a lot. Then they send the kids here.
MOTHER: What happened to the little kids?
FATHER: (*Sweetly.*) They were in the street, begging, stealing . . .
50　MOTHER: And what happened to the tall man?
FATHER: The tall man met another man. This one was a shorty.
　　They talked and talked . . .
MOTHER: (*Voice of a stupid baby.*) About what?
FATHER: Well . . . ! Ugly things! And when they were tired of
55　talking, the tall man walked him to his car.

5–7 **My rose . . . were** the Mother sings fragments from the *Blood
Wedding* lullabye　20–21 **Nestor . . . Zenteno** the disappearance
of Nestor Martins and his client Nildo Zenteno was in fact one
of the first. It happened during the term of de facto president
General Levingston, who had come to power in a coup d'état, un-
seating the previous de facto president, General Onganía

MOTHER: Who?
FATHER: The shorty. The short one was bad, bad. And then
　　some men came, and since he was bad, they put him in an-
　　other car to punish him. Because he was bad, bad. And
　　what did the tall man do?　　　　　　　　　　　　　60
MOTHER: I don't know!
FATHER: He didn't want them to punish him!
MOTHER: Stupid!
FATHER: He ran and ran and hit the good guys. And then, the
　　good guys put him into the car as well.　　　　　65
MOTHER: The good guys took them for a ride! 'Cause they're
　　so good!
FATHER: So very good!
MOTHER: And then what happened, Daddy?
FATHER: Nothing more was ever known!　　　　　70
MOTHER: Yea, yea, yea!
GUIDE: What horrible acting. So sorry. Let's look for something
　　else. (*He pushes the people toward the door.*) The whole show's
　　not like this. I hope.
MOTHER: (*Same voice of a stupid baby.*) Did they punish them a　75
　　lot, Daddy?
FATHER: Nothing more was ever known!
MOTHER and FATHER: Yea, yea, yea!
GUIDE: (*Cutting it.*) Let's go. Let's go, gentlemen. They need at
　　least another month of rehearsal. What dunces!　　80

SCENE SIX

GUIDE: Let's go upstairs, see if we have better luck. He who
　　searches finds. They say. (*The group goes up the stairs, or down,
　　if the preceding scene took place on the upper level. Natural light-
　　ing. When the group reaches the landing of the upper level.*) No, I
　　made a mistake. I had you climb to the . . . (*Stops.*) In vain.　5
　　Let's go down.

(*They go down. Suddenly, a group of men burst in, hurling themselves
at a person in the audience who is talking with someone else. This other
person is for a second paralyzed with astonishment. Then shouting, he
throws himself into the fray.*)

MAN: Let him go! Let him go!

(*He succeeds in freeing him. The two make it down a few stairs, but
the group of men rush them, surround them, and drag them down the
stairs. Over the loudspeaker a distressed voice is heard.*)

VOICE: My God, why did I run? (*Almost instantaneously, the scene
　　breaks out in another place with other characters. The groups may
　　cross at this moment. Again the voice is heard.*) My God, why　10
　　did I run? (*The scene is repeated in another spot.*) My God, why
　　did I run?
GUIDE: (*Meanwhile.*) If we search carefully, we'll find remains in
　　the catacombs. There aren't many, but we can still hope for
　　surprises. Careful please. Don't wander off now. That's it, all　15
　　together. Careful on the stairs. Look over here! (*Matter of
　　factly.*) A brutish people! Yes, we will find remains. Some-
　　times discoveries come about by chance. (*He examines the
　　door to a room. Opens it. The room is lit.*) Oh, this one has good
　　light. Imagine, ladies and gentlemen, the faith, the heroism　20
　　of the first Christians. To pray in these pigsties. It gives me
　　claustrophobia. (*He spots a form covered with canvas in a corner,*

on the floor.) Here's something. Finally! (*He draws near.*)
Stand back a little, ladies and gentlemen. (*With curiosity.*)
What is it? (*He lifts an edge of the canvas, immediately lets it
fall and steps back.*) Puah! What a shitty surprise!

VOICE: My God, why did I run?

GUIDE: Sssh! (*Turns toward the audience, with a big feigned smile,
gives the form a kick.*)

VOICE: My God, why did I run?

(*The* GUIDE *jumps on the form, tramples it, inflamed. In the doorway
to the room, another* GUIDE *appears. He claps his hands loudly.*)

GUIDE #2: Ladies and gentlemen! Please leave. Out, everyone
out! Sorry. We have a few like machines without an off button. If you would be so kind as to follow me. (*The light in
the room fades out.*)

SCENE SEVEN

GUIDE #2: What was the other one telling you?

SOMEONE FROM THE AUDIENCE: About the catacombs.

GUIDE #2: (*Glib.*) Oh, yes! The remains of the first Christians
in the catacombs . . . ! Impressive!

(*He opens a room. The* GIRL *from scene 3 is crawling on all fours toward a corner. Weak light on her. The rest of the room is in shadow.
The pistol still lies abandoned on the floor.*)

GUIDE #2: What do we have here? What is she sniffing at like
a dog? (*Goes closer. Joking, gives her a slap on the rear. Suddenly
he changes expression, helps her to get up.*) What is this? Composure. Pull yourself together.

GIRL: (*Lost.*) He told me to wait. They keep my head underwater, until . . .

GUIDE #2: (*Interrupts.*) Who threw water on you? This isn't
Carnival. Excuse me, I have to go back to work. (*Resumes his
professional tone. To the group.*) The paintings are fantastic, a
little deteriorated, but still . . . (*He shines a light on the
walls.*) Jesus, there's nothing! (*He sees a graffito in a corner,
crouches, shines a light on it.*) Gentlemen, come closer! (*Looks
more closely.*) What kind of filth is this? (*Stands.*) Please,
ladies, no! Excuse me, but the ladies may not look! (*He gestures them away.*) Gentlemen, if you like, but . . . (*To the
GIRL, very surprised.*) You did this? Your idea of fun? It was a
saint's head and they put a . . . (*He finishes with an expressive
gesture.*) Let go, let go of the pencil!

GIRL: No. It wasn't me.

GUIDE #2: (*Spots the pistol on the floor.*) What's this? Just a moment, gentlemen. (*He picks it up.*) How strange!

GIRL: He left it so that, so that . . .

GUIDE #2: So that you could bullshit me. (*He raises his arm as
though to hit her. Remembers the audience. Smiles.*) What negligence. (*Referring to the gun.*) I have to take care of everything
around here.

GIRL: I'm thirsty.

GUIDE #2: Then you'll pee and be even wetter. (*He shines his light
on the walls.*) There's nothing here either. But I swear there was.
And not this filth! (*He slaps her skirt.*) No way you're a virgin!

GIRL: I'm thirsty.

GUIDE #2: (*Looking around.*) Isn't there any water? In the other
room, there's a bathtub filled to overflowing.

GIRL: No! No, damn you!

GUIDE #2: What did I tell you? Does anyone understand
women? A difficult bunch. As you see, ladies and gentlemen, there's nothing here either. Only the walls. And this
filth. (*To the* GIRL.) You weren't getting discouraged, were
you? He left you the pistol? How strange. Who am I to . . . ?
(*He shrugs.*) But don't touch it. If you squeeze the trigger, it's
all over. The baths and . . . (*He smiles.*) I'm meddling in
something that's none of my business. This is the safety. I'm
leaving it up. Careful with the trigger. Sit down.

GIRL: (*She sits, shakes her head.*) I don't want it.

GUIDE #2: There's no danger, stupid! The slightest touch and it
goes off.

GIRL: Take it!

GUIDE #2: (*Surprised.*) Why? Soaking and thirsty, it's not a good
combination. (*He puts the pistol on her lap, takes her hand and
places it on the weapon.*) Do you have a boyfriend? Touch this
and it's all over, done with.

GIRL: I'm thirsty. (*She raises her hands.*)

GUIDE #2: Right. Sorry. I forgot: Ladies and gentlemen, forgive us for the . . . (*He points to the wall.*) How mortifying!
If you would be so kind as to follow me . . . (*He opens the
door, indicates the exit. At this moment an* USHERETTE *arrives
carrying a tray. She invites the group to have a glass of wine.*)
Help yourselves, ladies and gentlemen. It's on the house.
There's no reason to be scared: you won't have to pay for it.
It's all included. Then we'll go on with our visit. (*A scream
is heard. To the audience.*) Who screamed? Who is the imbecile who screamed?

SCENE EIGHT

The USHERETTE *steps close to the* GUIDE *and whispers a few words in
his ear.*

GUIDE: (*Making amends.*) Forgive me. In room 3 we are going
to find something interesting. "Finally!" you must be saying to yourselves. "We should have stayed home." (*He
laughs.*) Ah, theater's a risky business! What do you think?
TV's a better bet, isn't it? But no, gentlemen. All is not
lost. Please, gentlemen. I'm swallowing the "ladies" so I can
go faster. With so many "ladies and gentlemen, ladies and
gentlemen," I can't go on to anything else. (*He leads the
group through the passageway. The group is shunted aside by three
men carrying a long, half-finished table. It is missing a few strips
of wood on the surface. It is an ordinary table except that it has a
strap nailed to one end. One of the men carries a tool box.*) The
first Christians were very persecuted. They were fed to the
lions. (*The men put the table on the floor.*) Until San Martín.
What would the Spanish say about San Martín? "That son
of a bitch traitor. That black shit." (*The men start to saw and
drive nails, as though they were alone. They are blocking the passageway.*) Can't you work somewhere else? (*The men don't
answer.*) This way, gentlemen. Here's a little path. (*They*

---

vii. 1 this Guide is different from the Guide in scene 6. Since the
order of the scenes is up to the director, however, this Guide will
be called Guide #2 only in scene 7, where the shift occurs

viii. 14 **San Martín** General José de San Martín, the liberator (El
Libertador) of the southern part of South America, is an Argentine
national hero

20 *can't get through. The men move the table, forcing the group toward the* GIRL's *room.*)

WOMAN'S VOICE:

"Down he went to the river,
Oh, down he went down!"

25 GUIDE: What a pain in the ass she is with that lullabye! (*He looks at the door.*) Here we are again. We may as well … Through here. Sooner or later we'll see a whole scene. (*He opens. Joking.*) Well? Have you dried yourself? How's …(*There are some men surrounding the* GIRL. *The* GUIDE *quickly closes the door,*
30 *shoos the people away. With a false smile.*) No, I made a mistake. Room 3, they told me. Careful on the stairs. This way, ladies and gentlemen. Ladies, once again. It's nicer …

WOMAN'S VOICE:

35 "And his blood was running,
Oh, more than the water."

(*The* GUIDE *snorts. Two men have positioned the table against the wall, clearing the passage way. They are smoking cigarettes, like two workers taking a break.*)

GUIDE: (*To the* WORKMEN.) Room 3? This one here? (*The men nod yes.*) Thank you!

SCENE NINE

The room is lit with rosy light. Four chairs. There is a group comprising a man, a woman, and two other adults disguised as children, a girl and a boy. Their makeup is exaggerated, and their clothes are cheap, vulgar. The MOTHER *is sewing, the* FATHER *is seated a little apart, and the* CHILDREN *are playing at throwing a hoop.*

On the far side of the room are the CHIEF *and two* POLICEMEN. *They sit very erect with their arms crossed over their chests. The characters act very broadly, a little like marionettes. The tone is grossly exaggerated.*

GUIDE: (*In a professional tone, dry and rapid.*) Explanation: For Foreigners. July 2, 1971. Marcelo Verdt and his wife, Sara Palacio de Verdt, were kidnapped by a group of eight men. *Desaparecidos.* Both were members of RAF, Revolutionary
5 Armed Forces. According to information in the newspapers, the wife, before disappearing, brought the children to her sister for protection.

MOTHER: (*Moving her hand as though sewing.*) Children, I'm making a little outfit for the one who is best behaved!
10 CHILDREN: (*Playing.*) Thank you, Mommy!

POLICEMEN: (*Coming forward.*) Hands up, in the name of the law!

MOTHER: (*Raising her arm, protecting her face like the heroine in a silent movie.*) Oh! (*The* FATHER *doesn't move.*)

CHILDREN: Mommy, Mommy, who are they?
15 MOTHER: Don't be afraid, my darlings! No one is hurting your mother!

CHILDREN: Blessed Mommy!

POLICEMAN: (*Comes close, snatches at her clothes.*) You're disguised! (*Shoving her violently.*)

---

viii. 23–24 **Down … down** the Woman's Voice in this scene sings from the Blood Wedding lullabye   ix. 4–5 **RAF, or Revolutionary Armed Forces,** is the translation of the name of FAR, Fuerza Armada Revolucionaria, a left-wing guerilla group

CHILDREN: Mommy, Mommy, who are they? 20

POLICEMEN: Where's your husband?

MOTHER: I don't know!

CHILDREN: What do you mean, you don't know, Mommy! In the bathroom! Making caca! (*They call.*) Daddy! Daddy! They're looking for you! 25

FATHER: (*Gets up, comes forward, wide-eyed.*) Who? What's happening?

POLICEMAN: This is what's happening! It's all over! (*Screams.*) Silence everyone! Let's get out of this hole! The car's out front! 30

MOTHER: Not the children! They don't know anything about it!

POLICEMAN: Them too!

MOTHER: Have pity!

POLICEMAN: Silence! Let's go! Everyone!

(*They put the chairs together to make the car. All squeeze in. One of the* POLICEMEN *holds the hoop between his hands and handles it as though it were a steering wheel. He imitates the sound of a motor. The children wave. The* POLICEMAN *brakes suddenly. The others fall backward. They get out of the car, their gestures exaggeratedly frightened.*)

CHIEF: They fell! 35

MOTHER: (*On her knees.*) Pity!

POLICEMAN: What should we do with the kids?

CHILDREN: Daddy!

FATHER: (*Dignified.*) I'll protect you, don't be afraid. (*Puts his arms around them.*) 40

CHIEF: (*To the* POLICEMAN.) Idiot! Why did you bring the kids?

POLICEMAN: You said everyone, Chief.

MOTHER: They're innocent!

CHIEF: I'll see if they're not already lost. Kids: Who created the 45 flag?

MOTHER: (*Begging them.*) Answer right, answer right!

CHILDREN: (*In unison.*) Manuel Belgrano!

CHIEF: When?

CHILDREN: February 27, 1812. 50

CHIEF: Where?

CHILDREN: On the banks of the Paraná. He had it blessed right there, beneath a blue and white sky, blue and white sky, blue and white …

CHIEF: Exactly! Very good! (*Kisses them.*) Here's a prize. (*Gives* 55 *them each a piece of candy.*)

CHILDREN: Thank you, sir!

CHIEF: (*To the* MOTHER.) Take them home. And don't be long.

POLICEMAN: Chief, what if she doesn't return?

CHIEF: (*With an exaggeratedly sinister laugh, pointing to the* 60 FATHER.) This one stays here. It's in his interest that she return. (*To the* MOTHER.) Take my advice: be discreet. I'm doing you a favor. Don't be long. Take a taxi.

MOTHER: What are you going to do to him?

CHIEF: Nothing! From his eye to his sex. But only if I'm 65 vexed.

MOTHER: Marcelo!

FATHER: My love!

CHIEF: Take them home. We don't have any small sacks. They're only in the way. Move it. 70

MOTHER: Come, children! Give Daddy a kiss. (*The* FATHER *kisses them.*) Don't be afraid. We're going home.

CHILDREN: (*Happy.*) The men are nice, Mama!

MOTHER: (*Moves off with the* CHILDREN. *Picks up the outfit she*
75   *was sewing. To one of them.*) Tell Grandma that the hem was
turned here. Will you remember?

CHILD: Yes, Mama.

MOTHER: There's soup in the pot. Have it for supper.

CHILDREN: If you're not there, we won't eat any soup! We
80   won't eat any soup!

MOTHER: Be good!

CHILDREN: Where are you going, Mama?

MOTHER: I'm going with Daddy. You behave. (*Hugs them.*)

CHILDREN: Mommy! Mommy!

85   GUIDE: (*Choked up.*) It gets to you, doesn't it?

(*The* MOTHER *separates from the* CHILDREN *and returns toward the*
CHIEF. *During the good-bye scene the* POLICEMEN *were trying vari-*
ous sacks—as though they were items of clothing—on the FATHER.
They have found the right one. Then they take him out of the room.)

CHILDREN: (*Singing in a round.*) We won't eat any soup! We
won't eat any soup!

MOTHER: Here I am. Where's my husband?

CHIEF: Husband? What husband? Take off your clothes.

90   GUIDE: (*Quickly.*) Let's go! Let's get out of here! (*Claps his*
hands.) Out! Where's "Carnation, sleep and dream"? Who
wants more wine? (*Pushes the group toward the door.*) Follow
me! Quick! No dawdling! (*The group goes out. The* GUIDE
closes the door, leans against it.) Ouf!

SCENE TEN

GUIDE: A little wine! Careful . . . on the . . . stairs. (*The*
USHERETTE *brings him a glass of water.*) Water? For me? What
for? (*Remembers.*) Oh, right. She's waiting for water! Come,
gentlemen, this way. We're almost there. Just another little
5   minute. No reason to fret. (*Again they enter the room of the*
GIRL *from scenes 3, 7, and 8. Her clothes are drenched. The* GIRL *is*
breathing anxiously. She's seated, with the pistol, which is dry, in
her lap. To the group.) Come in. Careful on the stairs. Or
rather: fasten your seatbelts, no smoking. (*He laughs. To the*
10   GIRL, *very amiably.*) May I? (*He puts the glass and the pistol on*
the floor. Takes the chair on which she is sitting. Offers it to a
woman in the audience.) Sit, madam, sit. She may have wet it,
but she didn't piss on it! (*He dries the chair with a hankie. To*
the woman.) Please, have a seat! (*To the* GIRL.) They paid ad-
15   mission. Are you thirsty? (*The* GIRL, *lost, doesn't answer. The*
GUIDE *shakes her gently.*) Hey! Wake up. I'm asking you if
you're thirsty. (*The* GIRL, *shakes her head no.*) Oh, no? I
brought you water. Drink it. (*He takes the glass, brings it to*
her lips. The GIRL *resists.*) And now, what do I do with the
20   glass? I need my hands free. I'm working. This can't be!
Drink, little girl, drink. The water flowed . . . (*Forcing her.*)
There. There, that's good. So capricious! Well, I don't like
people pulling my leg. You're all wet. (*Puts his hand under*
her skirt.) Even your little firecracker. (*He laughs. Turns to-*
25   *ward the audience.*) Oh, excuse me. (*Takes the pistol.*) Shall I
take it? No? Freedom is within your grasp. No? (*He puts the*

---

ix. 75–76 **Tell Grandma that the hem was turned here** is
an encoded way of communicating the arrest

barrel against her breast.) How stupid. I can't. (*He cleans the*
weapon, puts it in the GIRL's *lap.*) I don't know why they trust
you so . . . It's loaded. If you had a boyfriend, old girl . . . But
like this. Idiot, why endure so much? (*Another* GUIDE *appears*   30
in the doorway.)

OTHER GUIDE: (*Shouting.*) What are you doing here? It's about to
start there! And they're giving out wine! It's not to be missed.
I saw it! Exceptional! You can understand everything!

GUIDE: Really? Step on it, fellas, let's go! Move it, girls!   35

OTHER GUIDE: (*Teases.*) Don't you mean ladies and gentlemen?

GUIDE: (*To* OTHER GUIDE.) There's wine? For sure? (OTHER
GUIDE *affirms it and leaves.*) If you would be so kind, ladies
and gentlemen . . . (*He holds open the door so the group can pass*
through. Before closing the door, in a friendly way.) Think about   40
it, little girl.

SCENE ELEVEN

In the passageway, one of the vertical wooden boxes.

GUIDE: Wait! This has always intrigued me . . . (*Tries to see*
through the peephole.) I can't see a thing. How about you, sir?
(*Someone from the audience has a look.*) It's very dark. (*He*
knocks at the door. Jokingly.) Is anyone home? *Hay alguien?*
(*Curious, he opens the door. There's a heavily madeup man inside,*   5
dressed in a loincloth, staring fixedly. Matter of factly.) Hi. (*He*
closes the door, turns toward the audience with an uncomfortable
smile. As though it were not so strange.) What a surprise! To me
this is very curious . . .

OTHER GUIDE: (*Shouts from the doorway of the other room.*) Well?   10
What are you waiting for? A carriage? If you don't get there
at the beginning, they won't understand anything!

GUIDE: (*Annoyed, referring to the vertical box.*) What about this?
Does anyone understand this? (*To the* OTHER GUIDE.) I give
the orders in my group! And if they don't get it, too bad for   15
them! This way, gentlemen! (*He leads them in the opposite di-*
rection.) Follow me! (*A panting death rattle is heard through the*
door of a room they pass.)

SCENE TWELVE

GUIDE: (*He lingers in front of the door, listening to the death rattle in-*
side.) What could this be? (*A* MAN *passes by, whistling.*)

MAN: (*To* GUIDE.) Good day!

GUIDE: Good day! (*Surprised.*) Well, he's happy! Let's follow   5
him. (*Referring to the death rattle in the room.*) Sounds like
that and we've really got a mess on our hands! We can check
it out later. (*He and the group follow the* MAN. *The* MAN *walks*
along, whistling. He meets another man who is coming from the
opposite direction.)

MAN: Good day!   10

NEIGHBOR #1: Hello! How's it going, doctor?

(*They shake hands. They continue walking together. The group fol-*
lows them. They enter a large room, where NEIGHBOR #2 *is sweeping*
the floor. Two chairs stacked in a corner, against the wall.)

NEIGHBOR #2: Hello, doctor!

GUIDE: (*To his group.*) Watch out for the cars! Stay on the sidewalk, please!

(*He situates them. He hasn't finished doing so when the* FIRST GROUP OF MEN *enters at a trot, one behind the other, tied together at their waists.*)

15 FIRST GROUP OF MEN: Let us through! Let us through!

(*They come forward, trot through the room, then suddenly halt in front of the* MAN *and surround him, forming a closed circle.*)

MAN: Excuse me.
FIRST GROUP OF MEN: Quieto! Quieto!
MAN: Are you calling me? What do you want? (*The men accelerate, tightening their circular movement, forming two closed rings.*)
20   Excuse me. Let me through.
NEIGHBOR #1: What's going on, doctor?
NEIGHBOR #2: (*Stops sweeping.*) Hey! Let him go!
NEIGHBOR #3: (*From the audience.*) What the hell is going on? (*Comes forward to help the* MAN.)
25 MAN: Let me go! Enough fooling around!

(*He pushes, tries to get through the circle. Hits, struggles. The men try to drag him toward the door.*)

NEIGHBORS: Let him go! Let him go!

(*They try to break up the group,* NEIGHBOR #2 *hitting out with his broom. The* SECOND GROUP OF MEN *enters, also at a trot and tied together at their waists. They sing.*)

SECOND GROUP OF MEN:

        Peace and security
        That is our domain
30   With a little authority
        Order will be maintained!

(*Observing the tumult, they linger.*)

OFFICIAL: (*Heading the* SECOND GROUP OF MEN.) What's going on here? This is scandalous! Halt! Separate!

(*The fight freezes.*)

NEIGHBORS: (*All at the same time.*) Sir, they were pushing him!
35   (*Alternating.*)
      —Over here.
      —Over there.
      —They tied him up.
      —They dragged him down!
40 OFFICIAL: One at a time, magpies. Who asked you anything? (*To the group in the fight.*) And you, you're prisoners in the name of the law. (*He "aims" at them, with his finger. The* SECOND GROUP OF MEN *"handcuffs" them. They're all, including the* MAN *put into a line and tied together at the wrists.*)
45 NEIGHBORS: Officer, sir:
      Why the arrest?
      He's one of the best!

_____

17 **Quieto!** Roberto Quieto, whose surname in fact means "quiet," was a prominent, highly respected liberal lawyer. Unbeknownst to most, he was also a powerful member of the Montoneros, the premier left-wing guerrilla organization

OFFICIAL: It doesn't matter, my esteemed citizens
      Have faith
      Justice is there for a reason   50
      To prevent baseness, which is treason.
NEIGHBORS: But we saw . . .
OFFICIAL: What you saw is of no consequence
      If there's offense
      Rest assured   55
      The man's secure . . .
SECOND GROUP OF MEN: Sure!

(*They "take aim" at the* NEIGHBORS.)

OFFICIAL: In my providence.

(*The* NEIGHBORS *mix in with the audience. The* OFFICIAL *moves off to the side, crosses his arms, his expression serious. The* FIRST GROUP OF MEN *and the* MAN *attacked in the first place draw near. One of the men from the second group arranges the chairs.*)

OFFICIAL: (*Seating himself. To the* MAN.) Name.
MAN: Quieto.   60
GUIDE: (*Shouts.*) Sí, Quieto! (*To his group.*) Quieto means quiet. (*Smiles.*) Stop a moment. (*Gestures toward the group.*) So they'll understand. Otherwise, they'll miss the point. (*The others stop the action. In a dry, professional tone.*) Explanation: For Foreigners. July 7, 1971. Robert Quieto, attorney, defender of politi-   65
cal prisoners, resists a kidnapping attempt. Fortunately, the neighbors intervene and call a police squad. The kidnappers turn out to be policemen. Dr. Quieto was put at the disposition of the executive power. Subsequently he was accused of having been implicated in an auto theft and of having par-   70
ticipated, after his detention, in various subversive acts. He was transferred to Rawson Prison, 730 miles from Buenos Aires. What happened then? I don't remember. Lost in the night of time. (*Smiles.*) But he wasn't so innocent. High up in the Montoneros, the son of a b——. It's not my responsibil-   75
ity. Although when you have the truth, I don't know why it should be hidden. Go on. I'm done.
OFFICIAL: (*To the* MAN.) Name.
MAN: Quieto.
OFFICIAL: Quieto! That's what I'm telling *you!* Now what is   80
      your name?
MAN: Blame.
OFFICIAL: (*Suspicious.*) Ohhhh? (*To the* FIRST GROUP OF MEN.)
      And you? What are your names?
FIRST GROUP OF MEN: (*They sing.*)   85

        Peace and security
        That is our domain
        With a little authority
        Order will be maintained!

SECOND GROUP OF MEN: 90

        If you're lying
        You'll get bruised!

OFFICIAL: Explain what happened
      I'm confused!
FIRST GROUP OF MEN: 95

        Boca will never lose!
        Boca's the team we choose!

OFFICIAL: (*Very pleased.*) For this, you are excused. But who
      began . . .

100 FIRST GROUP OF MEN: That man!

OFFICIAL: No more rhyming! (*To the* MAN.) Don't you know
      that it's a crime to incite a riot in the street? (*To the* SECOND
      GROUP OF MEN.) Did they stop traffic?

SECOND GROUP OF MEN: Yes, sir! They delayed it!

105 OFFICIAL: For how long?

SECOND GROUP OF MEN: For three minutes!

OFFICIAL: Re-create it!

SECOND GROUP OF MEN:

          In their cars the men grew irritated
110   At the office work accumulated.

OFFICIAL: (*To the first group, fiercely.*) I want a confession.
      (*Sweetly.*) What team are you from?

FIRST GROUP OF MEN:

          Boca will never lose
115   Boca . . .

OFFICIAL: Fine, fine, no need to repeat! (*The* FIRST GROUP OF
      MEN *"free" their hands, which had been "cuffed." To the* MAN.)
      What about you?

MAN: What about me?

120 OFFICIAL: What team are you from?

MAN: I nurse the same illusion.

OFFICIAL: I smell collusion. Why aren't you from San Lorenzo?

MAN: Because I'm not?

OFFICIAL: Don't be a wise guy! (*The* SECOND GROUP OF MEN
125   *hit* MAN. *To the others.*) And you, what are you waiting for?
      Get going!

MAN: You can't let them go! They attacked me! I want to see
      my attorney!

OFFICIAL: The one who gives the orders here is me. (*To the others.*)
130   And you, once again, (*Sweetly.*) why don't you do your work?

FIRST GROUP OF MEN: (*Tied together at their waists, they trot out,
      singing.*)

          For us it was a sad event
          That ended to our detriment
135   Of this our song's a testament!
          For us it was a sad event
          That ended to our detriment
          Of this our song's a testament!

OFFICIAL: (*To the* MAN.) Justice will be done.

(*One of the men in the second group puts on a judge's robe and comes
closer. Another moves in a chair and has him sit. Becoming the
GUARD, he remains standing behind the* JUDGE's *back.*)

140 JUDGE: (*To the* MAN.) You're free. Being from Boca's no crime.
      But next time . . .

114–115 **Boca** the Boca Juniors are one of the most important
Argentine soccer teams. Their home stadium is in the Buenos
Aires neighborhood of La Boca, traditionally an Italian working-
class section. San Lorenzo is another team from Greater Buenos
Aires. Soccer is by far the most passionately followed sport in
Argentina

(*The* MAN *frees his hands and stands up. The* JUDGE *turns halfway
around and grabs him from behind. No sooner has he done so when
the* GUARD *leans into the* MAN *and pushes him roughly down by
the shoulders, forcing him to sit. The* MAN *again joins his hands as
though they were handcuffed.*)

OFFICIAL: (*To the* MAN.) You stole a car. Your trial's pending.
      Your sentence could be unending!

MAN: I need defending!

OFFICIAL: Superintending! (*To the* JUDGE.) He stole a car.   145

JUDGE: He did not steal a car!

MAN: Am I absolved? Can I go?

JUDGE: Why not? Go ahead!

(*He turns so that his back is to the* MAN. *The previous scene is repeated:
the* MAN *frees his hands, the* GUARD *forces him to sit down again, etc.*)

OFFICIAL: He robbed a bank!

MAN: I was in prison!   150

JUDGE: (*It starts again.*) Absolved!

MAN: Thank you. Can I go?

JUDGE: Why not? Go ahead. (*Again. The rhythm speeds up.*)

OFFICIAL: He robbed a station!

JUDGE: (*Over his shoulder.*) What kind of station?   155

OFFICIAL: Service station. Five old wrecks.

MAN: (*Forced to sit.*) How? I was in prison!

OFFICIAL: (*With pretended fury.*) Guards, you let him go?

JUDGE: (*Turns.*) Why can't you see? There is no case. Let him
      go free! (*Turns his back.*)   160

OFFICIAL: He robbed a commissary, several stores, and several
      dairies!

MAN: (*Forced to sit.*) If I'd been seized
      How could I be eating cheese?

JUDGE: He is innocent   165
      Surely
      I declare it
      Firmly.

MAN: (*Stands up, etc.*) Thank you. Can I go?

JUDGE: Naturally. Why not. (*It starts again. The action accelerates   170
      to the point of dislocation but always remains precise. The speeches
      are transferred but not the actions, which remain a constant with
      each character.*)

OFFICIAL: Don't move. I've heard a little story!

JUDGE: He murdered a canary.   175

MAN That isn't fair!
      I love all canaries
      Everywhere!

OFFICIAL: You love them, but you kill them!

JUDGE: Guards, you let him go?   180

OFFICIAL: Your Honor, you're the witness
      Of this bad faith.

MAN: I only want to live!

JUDGE: Guards, you let him go?

OFFICIAL: If he'd been seized   185

MAN: How could I've been eating cheese?

JUDGE: Thank you.

OFFICIAL: Beat it! I can't stand you anymore!

MAN: I'm going back to my city!

JUDGE: Can I go?   190

OFFICIAL: Beat it!

MAN: (*Resisting those who are making him sit.*) No, no, I was in prison!

JUDGE: He's free! Oh, such obsession!

OFFICIAL: He's free! What fascination!

195 MAN: But I'm not!

JUDGE: Yes, you are! So you better shut up! (*Turns his back, covers his ears.*)

OFFICIAL: Enough already! He's hard to handle. All that screaming. What a scandal!

(*Gestures to the guards to take the* MAN *away. To the audience.*)

The idiots they send me, it's outrageous!
200 The courts
aren't beneficial
Unless they're
sacrificial!

(*Lights out.*)

GUIDE: Shit! What happened? They turned out the light with-
205 out telling me! Cretins! (*Take out his flashlight, switches it on.*) Where is the door? Luckily I know the house. (*Opens door. The passageway is lit.*) This way, gentlemen. There aren't any stairs. But be careful all the same. You only get to stumble once, like the tango says. Hey, hey. Everyone make it? (*He*
210 *leads the group through the passageway. They pass the door to the room where the death rattle was heard. It is heard again. The* GUIDE *puts his ear to the door. Admiringly.*) Persistent! We go in? We don't go in? What do you want to do? Free choice. At my orders! We go in!

SCENE THIRTEEN

The GUIDE *opens the door. The labored breathing stops. There is a* GIRL *with long hair laid out on a stretcher, with a sheet carefully folded under her feet.*

GUIDE: (*Advancing on tiptoe.*) Don't make any noise. She's sleep-ing. (*He approaches, looks at her. The* GIRL *smiles at him. Sweetly.*) How're you doing?

GIRL: (*Sits up, brushes her hair off her face, folds her hands in her lap.*
5   *She looks at the group with a semismile. Silence. Then, very simply, colloquially.*)
I would like to die
as softly as possible
So that my friends will think
10 she is sleeping
in the earth
become a worm
digging in the earth
so that in spring
15 the flowers blossom
After my death
I want my children
to sit at the table
and say
20 at her age
Mama
ran off with some guy
What a shame
poor old Dad

staring at the tablecloth   25
his cup of coffee
searching for her
This is how I want to die
as simply
as though I had never lived   30
What a lovely thought
to leave like that
not causing any pain
The cup of coffee
that no one drinks   35
absent . . .

(*Silently, a character mixed in with the audience goes up to the* GIRL. *He puts his hand over her mouth and nose. The* GIRL *offers desperate, mute resistance. She dies. The man gently lays her out, covers her with the sheet. Then he moves off and mixes in with the crowd, like one more spectator.*)

GUIDE: (*Amazed.*) How about that? (*Looks at the man.*) And now he's so calm! But what a feat! Phenomenal! (*He lifts the sheet. Matter of factly.*) She's dead. Poor creature! Really, with-out so much as a moan. Discreet. And in the bloom of   40
youth! (*Lets the sheet fall.*) She spoke of children, a husband. We'll have to go find them. Nice news I've got. What a bad deal. (*Hopefully.*) Anyone want to go? Of course, for this there are no volunteers. (*Furious.*) The son of a bitch. (*He goes to the door, leaving the audience.*) Excuse me. (*He opens the*   45
door, yells out.) I need someone from the family! Quick! Someone from the family! (*He comes back inside.*) She didn't move, did she? What with the advances of medicine, for a moment I thought that . . .

(FOUR MEN *enter, two-by-two, each pair moving as one. They are wearing white smocks down to their feet, very loose, belted at the waist. They come in on skates. Their faces are painted with large red smiling mouths. One pair beats pot lids; the other pair waves a white sack.*)

FOUR MEN: (*Singing.*)   50

Tachín, tachín, tachín
She died as she would have ordained
Without causing any pain.

GUIDE: What about the family? I've got to tell them . . . It's so unfortunate . . . My heartfelt sympathy. (*Extending his*   55
hand.)

FOUR MEN: (*They pay no attention to the* GUIDE. *They approach the stretcher, lift the sheet. Sing.*)

The jokester
Coaxed her   60

GUIDE: (*Very confused.*) Choked her . . . A son of a bitch who . . . (*Searches with his eyes. The* MEN *start putting the* GIRL *into the sack. Surprised.*) What are you doing? But . . .

FOUR MEN: (*Sing.*)

But nothing   65
But nothing
Just doing our bit
Ashes to ashes
Shit to shit

GUIDE: (*Indignant.*) That's gross! Don't you see there's people?   70
You must have been raised in a barn! Ladies, your forgive-

ness. I knew nothing ... The modern theater is like this. No respect for the ladies!

FOUR MEN:

(*They finish putting the* GIRL *into the sack, leaving her head out. They tie the end of the sack around her neck. It is evident that the* GIRL *is playing dead: though her head is bent over, she is able to support it. The* FOUR MEN *hold the bundle, swing it hammocklike. They sing.*)

75   If you don't like this Tin Pan band
Because it hasn't any flair
Because it just gave you a scare
Swing high, swing well
You can go to hell!

80 GUIDE: Go on!
FOUR MEN:

Tachín, tachín, tachín,
Tachín, tachín, tachín!
Pran-pran-pran!
85   Taratá-ta-ta!

(*They near the door. The* HUSBAND *and* MOTHER *enter. The* HUSBAND *is wearing threadbare clothing. His hair is long and all over the place. The* MOTHER *is the typical little old lady—black clothes, shawl over her head. Both act crudely, like prototypes of desperate people.*)

HUSBAND: What happened? I heard screams!
MOTHER: Sirs, have pity! Where is my daughter? Darling! Darling!
GUIDE: Oh my God, the family's here!
90 MOTHER and HUSBAND: (*Together.*) We've come to look for our poor Hermenegilda.
FOUR MEN:

(*They come back, set the corpse down; it supports itself against the stretcher. Horrified.*)

That name she inherited
She certainly merited!
95 MOTHER and HUSBAND: (*Together.*) We're here to find out
What she finally merited!
GUIDE: Oh no! If these two speak in verse, I'm leaving!
Although the language may be terse,
I can't bear
100   so much pain.
I'm leaving! (*He pushes away from the crowd, but upon hearing the* HUSBAND, *he stops, comes back.*)
HUSBAND: Where is she?
FOUR MEN: (*They shake the corpse in front of the* HUSBAND'*s face.*)
105   We don't know! We don't know! She was never here!
HUSBAND: What do you mean? She came here to buy wine!
FOUR MEN: (*They turn the corpse facedown on the stretcher, look underneath.*) She bought her bread and went away, evaporated ... Surely it was fated! (*They look at the ceiling. The* HUSBAND *and*
110   MOTHER *imitates them. The men point.*) Look sir. That moth ...
HUSBAND: She wasn't a moth! At dawn ...
FOUR MEN: She was a moth. At dawn
Before the sun came up full
we found her eating
115   wool

MOTHER: It's not true! She didn't like wool!
FOUR MEN: Was she a woman or a moth?
The question's far from risible.
Lady, lady don't be miserable.
Don't be upset   120
We'll give you your daughter yet.

(*They approach an interior door. They call the* HUSBAND *and* MOTHER *as one would a dog.*)

Tch, tch, tch ...

(*The* HUSBAND *and* MOTHER *advance, their smiles exaggeratedly hopeful. The others open the door. The interior is dark. The* HUSBAND *and* MOTHER *look in.*)

FOUR MEN: You'll find her here, here!
So be of good cheer, cheer!
(*Moving in unison, the* FOUR MEN *push them inside with kicks in* 125
the rump.) And stop mugging! (*They close the door. They sway.*)
Ladies, Gentlemen, dearest friends
Our show is over, Curtains!

(*They take the corpse. They lead the way to the exit, singing.*)

Tachín, tachín, tachín!
Tachín, tachín, tachín!   130
Tarará-ta-ta!
Tarará-ta-ta!

GUIDE: (*Enthused.*) Let's go, let's go! Let's follow them! See what happens! They're entertaining! (*The group follows the* FOUR MEN *and* GUIDE. *The* FOUR MEN *enter a contiguous room* 135
and close the door. An actor, pretending to be part of the audience, opens it. The interior is dark. An enormous club comes out and hits the actor over the head. He falls. The GUIDE *leans over him.*) Why did he butt in? I'm the Guide here! One to a group! (*He pokes him. The man doesn't move. He then lifts him by the armpits* 140
and puts him into one of the vertical boxes. He talks all the while, completely dissociated from his actions.) That's how it is. In they all go but ... who takes the potatoes out of the fire? The son of a bitch. If he was part of the audience, why did he make like an actor? Vanity, vanity will be the end of us all! ... 145
(*He closes the door.*) Now what were we going to see?
SOMEONE FROM THE AUDIENCE: The catacombs.
GUIDE: Right. Thank you. The first Christians really had a hard time of it. Just thinking about how the lions loved to chew them up ... Human meat, they say, is sweet. Sweet, bit- 150
ter, what could be stupider. (*They cross with another group. To the* OTHER GUIDE.) Where's there something good? We went in here, and it's all fucked up. (*Without stopping, the* OTHER GUIDE *points to a door.*)

SCENE FOURTEEN

The GUIDE *leads the group into the designated room. Inside is a group of* NEIGHBORS *all crowded together, some looking over the heads of others. On the far side, two* POLICEMEN *crouch, their expressions very attentive. In the center are the* MAN *and* WOMAN, *both heavily made-up. Their clothes are cheap, flashy; the* WOMAN *wears very high heels. All the acting is crude, infantile, and exaggerated.*

GUIDE: Attention. Ladies and gentlemen, this is the main course. So they tell me. Hope it's true. Make yourselves

comfortable. If you find a chair, be seated. Silence, please. The story of a BM, or bad marriage. (*His tone is professional,*
5 *dry and quick.*) Explanation: For Foreigners. On the afternoon of July 13, 1971, Juan Pablo Maestre and his wife, Mirta Elena Misetich, were kidnapped by a group of men. Juan Pablo Maestre managed to run a few yards but then was shot. Mirta Elena Misetich ran in the opposite direc-
10 tion, losing a shoe. She was captured and pushed into one car; her husband was thrown into another. Shortly afterward, a police squad sent to the scene recovered the shoe and ordered the doorman of an apartment building to wash the blood from the pavement. The body of Juan Pablo
15 Maestre appeared days later in Escobar. Of Mirta Elena Misetich there was no further news. Both belonged to the RAF, or Revolutionary Armed Forces. Juan Pablo Maestre, twenty-eight years old. Mirta Elena Misetich, the same age.
   MAN: (*With a conspiratorial air.*) Let's plant a bomb here
20 WOMAN: (*With a conspiratorial air.*) And a bomb over there!
   MAN: When these go off
   WOMAN: No one will be spared!
   MAN and WOMAN: (*Taking bombs with fuses out from under their clothes.*) Subversion, subversion,
      all rise up!
25   in revolution!
   MAN: (*Looking around.*) Let's go, all clear!
   WOMAN: Nothing will be left here! (*They take a few cautious steps.*)
   POLICEMAN: (*Comes forward, arm extended.*) Hands up! In the
30   name of the law!
   MAN: We're caught! Run! (*They drop their bombs and run in opposite directions.*)
   POLICEMAN: (*Aims with his finger and shoots.*) Pum!

(*The* MAN *falls. His blood is obviously fake. The other* POLICEMAN *runs after the* WOMAN.)

   WOMAN: (*Stops.*) Darling!
35 POLICEMAN: Hey, hey! Justice always triumphs! Olé!

(*The two* POLICEMEN *drag the* MAN *and* WOMAN *away. The* WOMAN *loses her shoe. They exit. Slowly, the* NEIGHBORS *untangle themselves and come forward.*)

   NEIGHBORS: The ass must be judged
   Not broken!

(*The two* POLICEMEN *reenter. The* NEIGHBORS *immediately reform their group.*)

   POLICEMEN: Of our respect
   Here's a token!

(*They're carrying the* MAN, *dragging him along. The* NEIGHBORS *watch, timidly come forward. Romantic music is heard. More* POLICEMEN *enter, smiling and wearing sweepers jackets. They swing long-handled brooms, dance as in a musical comedy.*)

---

xiv. 38–39 **"Of our respect / Here's a token"** is the couplet substituted for "violín, violón / es la mejor razón." See "Crisis, Terror, Disappearance"

GROUP OF POLICEMEN: (*They sing.*)   40

   We're here to clean!
   We're here to clean!
   The filth is gone
   Your street is clean!
   Let mothers pray   45
   let children play
   in celebration!

(*Smiling, they sweep. They lift the shoe. They sing.*)

   Little shoe, little shoe
   Whom might you belong to?
   Why, to Snow White   50
   or to her mother.

   GUIDE: What do you mean, fellas! The little lost shoe was Cinderella's!
   POLICEMAN: (*Emphatically.*) I say it's Snow White's or her mother's. (*Recovering his smile.*) Whose little shoe is this? 55
      Madam, is it yours? Say yes. A Prince Charming awaits you in the wings.
   GUIDE: No, no! Error! It's the prince, the prince who searches for the owner of the shoe, not a cop! Didn't you read the story?   60
   POLICEMAN: Calm down! It's a free interpretation. (*Smiling.*) Doesn't it belong to anyone? Neighbors? (*He shows them the shoe. The* NEIGHBORS *immediately deny ownership, shaking their heads in unison.*) So we'll look in another neighborhood. It'll belong to someone. (*He repeats, frowning in the* 65
      GUIDE'*s direction.*) It's Snow White's or her mother's.
   GUIDE: (*Servile.*) Yes, of course, her mother's. Well, let's going. We can follow you, can't we? (*To his group.*) We'll just stroll along. If you get tired, let me know.
   GROUP OF POLICEMEN: (*They go out with the shoe. Asking.*) 70
      Madam, is this yours? Is this yours? Young man? (*The group follows them. They enter another room. The* WOMAN, *wearing no makeup, is seated on a chair. Sitting nearby on the floor, with her legs crossed, is a* GIRL, *who may be the same as the one from scene 13.*)
   POLICEMAN: (*To the* WOMAN.) Madam, excuse me. We found a 75
      little shoe. Is it yours? Prince Charming will marry you. Cash in a flash! You'll live in a palace! Let's see. (*He puts the shoe on her foot.*) She's Cinderella! It fits! Perfect! What luck, old girl! You win! A royal flush! (*Bows.*) Princess! My respects! (*The* WOMAN *stares ahead, immobile. Surprised.*) Aren't 80
      you happy? What's the matter?
   WOMAN: My darling!
   POLICEMAN: Your darling was stopped by a cop. (*The* POLICEMEN *exit arm-in-arm, tap dancing.*)
   WOMAN: I was at home, eating my bread. I was   85
      making love. I was kissing my children.
   And you will be the only one who knows
   where and how my body was lost,
   how my voice became unstrung
   Only you will know   90
      how to know
   the voices of fear and the faces of
      desperation
   My God, what did the brave ones become?
   I will speak   95

Only you will know
this tongue.

(*A shot is heard.*)

100   GUIDE: What's going on? Did you hear that? It was a shot. (*Looks at the* WOMAN *and the* GIRL.) But why so quiet! It's over. Gentlemen, follow me. Did you like that? (*He leads his group out of the room.*) A bit mixed up, wasn't it? Me ... well, what do you like ... I'm old-fashioned. I prefer something else. If this was the main course, what will the others be? (*They enter the adjoining room. The* GIRL *of scenes 3, 7, and 8 lies*

105   *on the floor, shot, the pistol in her hand. The* GUIDE *looks at her, surprised. Then, matter of factly, pushing them toward the exit.*) Oh, sorry! Shall we? The jug may as well go to the fountain as ... (*Happy music is heard.*) How about that music! So there is a little happiness in this world! Enough drama!

110   Let's go. Move along. A little gaiety, dammit!

(*The poem spoken by the* WOMAN *was written by Marina, a Greek girl, who was captured and tortured.*)

SCENE FIFTEEN

As the group leaves, the music fades and after a few minutes disappears. Through the passageway comes a group holding hands. They sing.

GAME PLAYERS:
     —Martin Fisherman, will you let me pass?
     —Pass, pass, but the last one stays with me!

(*The group starts playing Martin Fisherman, a singing game somewhat like London Bridge Is Falling Down. Two children make a bridge with their arms; the others run underneath, single file, holding each other by the waist. The line of children sings for permission to pass through; the last one is taken prisoner. In another version, the children making the bridge ask questions. Those who answer correctly pass through; the others do not. Two lines form, one comprising the "free," the other "prisoners." After everyone has had a question, the longer line wins, and the game may start again.*)

GUIDE: Ladies and gentlemen, you're welcome to participate.
5   That's not coercion, only if you want to. Grotowsky used to say: The more physical distance, the more spiritual closeness. What nonsense! Don't be afraid to join in, ladies and gentlemen!

(*The game continues. Suddenly one of the men forming Martin Fisherman's bridge yells.*)

GAME PLAYERS: (*Alternately.*)
10   —I know that one! Don't let him go!
     —Me?

(*The latter tries to get off the bridge.*)

     —I know that one! Don't let him go!
     —Don't fight!
     —Just answer right!
15   —I don't have to! No!

(*He whistles over his shoulder for help. Those in his line start to push. The others shout.*)

—Don't push! Hold tight!
—Wait!

(*Nevertheless they react. The shorter line becomes crooked. A man forming the bridge yells.*)

—They're shooting! Hold tight!

(*The sound of a police whistle.* POLICEMEN *arrive, dressed like the cops in Charlie Chaplin's The Kid, with large, prehistoric-type clubs. Music is heard. Their acting is crude. They immediately start hitting those in the longer line over the head. The sound of the clubs: Plac! Plac! Plac! Those hit fall into artificially distorted poses. The men rush the bridge of Martin Fisherman, crushing the captured player, who screams.*)

GUIDE: Kids today! They don't know how to play peacefully! Let's get out of the way. I wonder if they'll tie them up. 20 (*Warns a* POLICEMAN.) Not the audience! (*The* POLICEMAN *moves his head like Harpo Marx. He spins around like an acrobat, beating on actors mixed in with the public, acting as audience members. Very confused.*) On the double, ladies and gentlemen, quickly! Let's go! No stragglers! My group this way! 25 Forward! Toward the music! (*Music floats in the air, disappears.*) Now what? (*He opens his hands in a gesture of incomprehension. Taking advantage of the* GUIDE's *position, someone comes forward and puts a tin plate full of garbage in his hands. To this person, absolutely astonished.*) What is this? (*Protests.*) Not to 30 me you don't! This is not what I get paid for! Who do they think they are?

(*Meanwhile, the game of Martin Fisherman has stopped. The* POLICEMEN *and* ACTORS *from the shorter line carry off those who were knocked unconscious and throw them into a room.*)

GUIDE: (*To the group.*) With so much confusion, I forgot about the catacombs. You'll end up leaving without seeing anything.
WOMAN'S VOICE: 35

          "The water was black there
          under the branches.
          When it reached the bridge
          it stopped and sang."

GUIDE: (*Pleased.*) Her again! What persistence! You want to 40 risk it? Sooner or later it's got to improve!

(*He opens the door. The people inside won't let him in.*)

SCENE SIXTEEN

ACTOR #1: Sorry, old man. You can't come in. Off-limits.
GUIDE: Why not? I'm bringing people.
ACTOR #1: No, old man. We're rehearsing.
GUIDE: So what? Aren't you getting tired?
ACTOR #1: No! (*He closes the door.*)   5
GUIDE: (*Outraged.*) What balls. Sorry. (*He remembers something, smiles.*) They're not gonna fuck with me. Psss! This way! There's another entrance! (*He leads them along a passageway.*)

---

xv. 36–39 "The water ... sang" the Woman's Voice sings lines from the *Blood Wedding* lullabye

They pass a vertical box like the others, only bigger. Naturally.)
10 Just a moment. (*He opens the door of the box. Inside, two men are plastered together. The* GUIDE *puts the tin plate on their shoulders. They stretch their necks desperately, trying to suck up what's on the plate. It falls. Matter of factly, to the audience.*) They let it fall! What idiots! (*He closes the door.*)

SCENE SEVENTEEN

GUIDE: Don't make a sound. Walk on tiptoe. Don't say a word. (*They enter a room. Folding screens around an illuminated central space.*) Sssh … Silence … (*The group watches the scene through the folding screens. Two* ACTORS *and two* ACTRESSES *are rehearsing* Othello, *in rehearsal clothes.* ACTRESS #1, *as Desdemona, is already dead on the floor.*)
5
ACTOR #1: (*As Iago.*) Villainous whore!
ACTRESS #2: (*As Emilia.*) She give it Cassio? No, alas, I found it, And I did give't my husband.
10 ACTOR #1: Filth, thou liest!
GUIDE: Such language!
ACTRESS #2: (*As Emilia.*) By heaven, I do not, I do not, gentlemen.
O murd'rous coxcomb! What should such a fool
15 Do with so good a wife?
ACTOR #2: (*As Othello.*) Are there no stones in heaven But what serves for the thunder?—Precious villain!

(*Othello runs at Iago. Iago strikes Emilia and leaves.* ACTOR #1 *marks his exit and sits off to one side. A* POLICEMAN *enters in Isabelesque attire.*)

POLICEMAN #1: (*To* ACTOR #2.) You killed those two women! Villain! Viper!

(*The* ACTRESSES *get up, go sit down. They watch calmly, a bit surprised.*)

20 ACTOR #1: Who told this guy to come in?
POLICEMAN #1: (*Acting, calling his men.*) Over here, men. Here!
ACTOR #1: Go act for the other side. Who called you. Get out of here!
POLICEMAN #1: Thou hast no weapon, and perforce must
25 suffer. They are dead.
ACTRESS #1: (*Joking.*) I am dead!
ACTRESS #2: (*Sings.*)

Willow, willow, willow.
Moor, she was chaste. She loved thee, cruel Moor!

30 ACTOR #1: Stop! (*To the* POLICEMAN.) Will you beat it!
POLICEMAN #1: To raise your sword against a woman!
ACTOR #2: What are you talking about?
ACTOR #1: The guy's a mental case. Beat it! (*He pushes him toward the door.*) Out! (*Returns.*) Better keep the door locked.
35 There's no telling who could walk in. Let's go, girls. That guy stank worse than a pig. (*Claps his hands.*) One more time!
POLICEMAN #1: (*Draws his sword.*) No, traitor!

---

xvii. 7 **Villainous whore!** lines from *Othello* are taken from act 5, scene 2, lines 229–235, 248–249, 256, 287, 306–307, 317, 367–371. All are found on pages 1239–1240 of *The Riverside Shakespeare* (Boston: Houghton Mifflin, 1974)

ACTOR #2: (*Returns. In spite of himself, in character.*) Wrench his sword from him.
40
POLICEMAN #1: Torments will ope your lips.
ACTOR #2: Well, thou dost best.
ACTOR #1: Cut! Right there!
POLICEMAN #1: Officers, come here! (*Another* POLICEMAN *enters, dressed in the same style.*)
45
POLICEMAN #2: What's happening, sir?
POLICEMAN #1: (*He shows him the vial he's just taken from his own pocket.*) Trotyl! And the women are dead! Oh my! O thou pernicious caitiff!
POLICEMAN #2: (*With his sword, rounds up the* ACTORS, *who move into a corner.*) Move it, or I'll take a slice! (*The* ACTRESSES *let out an inappropriate laugh.*)
50
POLICEMAN #1: Take them, too, for having laughed at the wrong time! (*In a dramatic voice.*)
To you, Lord Governor,
55
Remains the censure of this hellish villain,
The time, the place, the torture, O, enforce it!
Myself will straight aboard, and to the state
This heavy act with heavy heart relate.

(*He takes a gun from his pocket, forces the* ACTORS *to exit.*)

GUIDE: (*To his group.*) A bit confusing, the way that happened, don't you think? So you understand. (*He walks into the light. In a professional, dry and rapid voice.*) Explanation: For Foreigners. (*Fierce and rude.*) Does anyone really need an explanation? If you want to act like actors, just go into a tenement and howl like dogs, throw a good scare into people. If you don't have money, people will be even more afraid. Why scream? Why pretend? When no one can open his mouth, why would anyone scream gratuitously? (*He waits for a response, which he doesn't get.*) Okay then! (*Resumes his professional tone.*) August 6, 1971. The police burst into an old house with many rooms, like this one, in the city of Santa Fe. In one of the rooms they find eight hundred grams of trotyl. They say. One journalist and three members of the Grupo 67 theater are arrested. They're taken to Buenos Aires on suspicion of subversive actions. The district attorney recommended they be absolved on the benefit of doubt. They were absolved May 24, 1972. (*Change of tone.*) Few are called, many are chosen. Nine months in the cage. In misery. Well, that's life! (*He leaves the illuminated space, goes back to his group.*) Wait! The show goes on!
60

65

70

75

80

SCENE EIGHTEEN

A sort of deformed CHILD-MONSTER, *dressed in a floor-length white shirt with lots of lace and frills. He is heavily made-up. Others disguised as* CHILDREN *follow. The* CHILD-MONSTER *clutches a club. They sing.*

CHILDREN:

Anton, Anton Pirulero
each one, each one
attends to his game
and he who does not
he who does not
will suffer the blame.
5

(*The* CHILDREN *sit in a circle around the* CHILD-MONSTER, *who calls to one of the bigger children and gives him the club. The latter stays outside the ring. They play Anton Pirulero, in which the child playing Anton is in the center of the circle, turning around and around, his arms extended like wings. The others keep singing and pretend to play musical instruments—guitar, cornet, violin, etc. They have to be very alert, for if Anton Pirulero stops and points at one of them with his arm and that child isn't moving his own arms like Anton, then that child loses. He who loses three times is out. The game is played singing, and very fast.*)

CHILD-MONSTER: (*He is Anton Pirulero. In an out-of-tune sing-song.*)

10
> Anton, Anton Pirulero
> each one, each one
> attends to his game
> and he who does not
> he who does not
> will suffer the blame.

(*Now they play only guitar. The child with the club goes to the one who has changed places with Anton and hits him. The child falls. The game continues, faster every time. The* CHILD-MONSTER *never finishes his song, the game falls apart, and the child with the club hits out indiscriminately. Finally, the only ones left unharmed are the* CHILD-MONSTER *and the character with the club. They wave their arms and sing. The* CHILD-MONSTER *glares at the other one, more and more menacingly. He aims with his finger as though it were a revolver and kills the other child. Pum! He plays alone, his gestures increasingly spastic. The song "Anton Pirulero" becomes unintelligible. The lights go out.*)

15 GUIDE: What now? Why did they kill the lights?
VOICES: (*Singing.*)

> Anton, Anton Pirulero
> each one
20 > each one
> attends to his game.

(*Lights up. In the same space,* THREE MEN *and a* YOUNG WOMAN. *The* CHILD-MONSTER *laughs in his labored way, waves his arms, stutters.*)

CHILD-MONSTER: D-d-d-ow-ow-n-n-n! S-s-s-i-i-i-t-t-d-d-d-ow-n-n-n-n!

(*He aims his hand like a revolver. The* MEN *and* WOMAN *don't seem to notice his presence. They sit of their own volition.*)

FIRST MAN: What is your game?
SECOND MAN: Fear.
25 FIRST MAN: And yours?
THIRD MAN: Fear.
FIRST MAN: (*To the* YOUNG WOMAN.) What is your game?
YOUNG WOMAN: Fear. (*Pause.*) And the question.
FIRST MAN: What question?
30 YOUNG WOMAN: Why fear? My name is Marina. I am twenty years old. I am Greek, a prisoner, and I have been tortured. (*The* CHILD-MONSTER *stutters low, furiously. He keeps playing, getting all tangled up in his own movements.*) Time is altered, the years to come are altered

You know where you will find me 35
I, fear, I, death
I, the memory beyond reach
I, the recollection of the tenderness of your hands
I, the sadness of our broken life
I will defeat "it's not my concern" with my 40
   anguish
blast their alien sleep with fireworks,
   horrible and indecent
with countless shootings I will fall on the indifference
of those who pass by 45
until they begin to ask, to ask themselves
THREE MEN: (*In an even tone.*) Why fear?
Why torture?
Why deaths?

(*Stuttering and autistic, the* CHILD-MONSTER *plays.*)

THREE MEN: Who set limits? 50
Who once said: this much thirst
this much water?
Who once said: this much air
this much fire?
Who once said: here the ken 55
of men and women
here the bounds?
Only hope has sharp knees.
They are bleeding.

(*Darkness.*)

(*The poem spoken by the* YOUNG WOMAN *was written by Marina. The poem spoken by the* THREE MEN *is Juan Gelman's.*)

GUIDE: Now what? There they go again cutting the light 60
without warning me! I understand less and less. We're the
ones who bear the brunt of this show. I shit on poetry!
Watch your wallets! And I left my flashlight. This way,
this way. It's so dark! Don't touch each other! Whose little
ass is this? 65

(*He laughs. Opens the door. The passageway is illuminated.*)

Ah! Light, more light! What a phrase! Only a genius could
come up with that one, eh?
WOMAN'S VOICE:

> "Ay-y-y, for the big horse
> who didn't like water" 70

GUIDE: Still at it! Now that's perseverance! (*Baroque music is
heard. The* GUIDE *puts his ear to the door. Unsure.*) Do we go in
here? I don't remember. Oh well, let's do it! Come along,
gentlemen! You're almost there!

---

59 s.d. **The poem . . . Gelman's** Gelman's lines are: "Quien puso
limites? / Quien dijo alguna vez: hasta aquí la sed? hasta aquí el agua? /
Quien dijo alguna vez: hasta aquí el aire, hasta aquí el fuego? / Quien
dijo alguna vez: hasta aquí el hombre, hasta aquí, no? / Solo la es-
peranza tiene las rodillas nitidas. / Sangran." 69–70 **"Ay-y-y . . .
water"** the Woman's Voice sings from the *Blood Wedding* lullabye

SCENE NINETEEN

They enter another room. Two GUARDS *are dressing a group of squalid-looking characters who are handcuffed to the wall, heavily made-up, with false eyelashes and lots of rouge. Some are half-undressed, wearing only jackets and underwear. Others wear bras and costume jewelry. The* GUARDS *move around busily. They bring chairs. Make the prisoners sit. They arrange them artistically, crossing their legs, raising their arms as though they were holding cigarettes between their fingers. The prisoners stay in these poses. During the development of this scene, one* GUARD— *seated apart—recites with a melancholy air.*

GUARD: You, who come from the shores of the Tagus
    Every day sing of my death
    Only this do I ask
      with my dying breath
5   Every day sing of my death
    You, who come from the shores of the Tagus.

(A signal is heard. A line of frightened men and women enter. Some carry small packages in their hands, obviously clothing or food. The GUARD *watches them.)*

GUARD: No one enters without being checked. *(He turns his face away. Raises and lowers his index finger mechanically, while the people pass in front of him and go out. Recites rapidly.)*
10   With pants, no. With skirts, no. With stockings, no. With packages, no. With children, no. With faces, no. *(A* PRETTY GIRL *passes. He looks at her. His finger stops. Very nicely.)*
    Twenty little hard ones, twenty little hard ones
15   all in a roll, all in a roll
    twenty little hard ones
    in your little asshole.
    May I?
PRETTY GIRL: *(Stupidly.)* What?
20 GUARD: *(Wiggles his finger obscenely.)* May I?
PRETTY GIRL: No!
GUARD: *(Pulls himself up, undiscouraged.)* To arms! To arms against the little asshole! Right over here!

----

xix. 1 **"You, who come from the shores of the Tagus"** is from a poem of Garcilaso de la Vega. The Tagus River flows through western Spain and Portugal. In her letter to me of March 28, 1986, Gambaro brought up "substituting an English-language poem about death, provided of course it's by a Master." I decided against this option since I felt that Gambaro's appropriation of Garcilaso was important as a reference to a specific age, place, and literary tradition. One of the greatest poets of the Spanish Golden Age, Garcilaso influenced not only San Juan de la Cruz, Lope de Vega, and Cervantes but also Rafael Alberti, Pedro Salinas, Miguel Hernández, and other twentieth-century Spanish and Latin American poets. The original reads: "Vosotros, los del Tajo en su ribera / Cantáreis mi muerte cada dia / Este descanso llevaré nunque muera / Que cada día cantáreis mi muerte, / Vosotros, los del Tajo en su ribera."   13 **"Twenty little hard ones"** is from García Lorca's *Los titeres de cachiporra.* The original reads: "Veinte duritos y veinte duritos / y un rollito de veinte duritos / en el agujero del culito."

(A group of guards enters at a trot. They rush the PRETTY GIRL *and fling themselves on her as though she were the ball in a game of baseball. They roll with her out of the room.)*

GUARD: *(Moves off, uninterested. Starts again with a melancholy air.)* You, who come from the shores of the Tagus . . .   25
LITTLE OLD LADY: *(The last of the visitors. She brings a sandwich wrapped in a handkerchief.)* I've come to see my little son. He misbehaved.
GUARD: *(Deflated.)* Ah . . . Why didn't you bring him up better, madam?   30
LITTLE OLD LADY: He was always my wayward one!
GUARD: A good beating is what they need. They don't learn unless they bleed.
LITTLE OLD LADY: At ten years old, he was looking up the girls' skirts.   35
GUARD: *(Dumbfounded.)* Filthy!
LITTLE OLD LADY: *(Plaintive.)* I cut his little whistle, but it did no good!
GUARD: It's late to repent. Show me what you've brought!
LITTLE OLD LADY: *(Unwraps her handkerchief.)* A sandwich.   40
GUARD: *(Lifts the top of the bread.)* Ah! Extra testicles. No, madam! Here they only lose them. And for us that's work! Confiscated! *(He takes the sandwich.)* Out!
LITTLE OLD LADY: I want to see my son! Just once! Be generous! You have a mother too!   45
GUARD: Yeah, but she's not an old whore like you.
LITTLE OLD LADY: Why are you insulting me?
GUARD: *(With disgust.)* You're old! *(In another tone.)* All right. Go see him. I'm doing this for my mother. Sentimentality will be the end of me! *(Gestures toward one of the seated prisoners.)* There he is.   50
LITTLE OLD LADY: *(Goes toward an* OUTLANDISH-LOOKING PRISONER *and embraces him.)* Son! *(She separates, looks at him.)* No, this isn't him. *(Hugs another.)* Son! *(Looks.)* No, this one either.   55
OUTLANDISH-LOOKING PRISONER: *(Opening his arms.)* Da-da-da-da!
GUARD: Choose already. Take this one. What's the difference.
LITTLE OLD LADY: *(Leaning toward the prisoner. Timidly.)* Juan?
OUTLANDISH-LOOKING PRISONER: Da!
LITTLE OLD LADY: Son!   60
OUTLANDISH-LOOKING PRISONER: Da!
GUIDE: *(To the group.)* Pretty depressing, wouldn't you say?
GUARD: What about you all? Over here, young men!
GUIDE: *(Raises his hands.)* No! Out, quick! *(The sound of music.)* We were going to go dancing. We got the wrong room.   65 *(Very distressed.)* Let's go dancing! Dancing! Move it! Let's beat it! Let's go, gentlemen. Let's go! *(They exit.)*

SCENE TWENTY

GUIDE: Ouf! A narrow escape! *(He listens. The music gets louder. It's happy, catchy.)* That's it. Come. *(He leads his group to a large space, where at this moment all the other groups converge.)* Leave the space open, ladies and gentlemen! If you would be so kind   5 as to stand against the wall. That's it. Thank you, everyone.

(On one side of the performing space is a semitranslucent folding screen, behind which can be seen a long table. In the center, a group of women, dressed like stereotypical prostitutes, execute the gestures conventionally attributed to them: they smoke, show their legs, swing their

purses, put on makeup. A man roughly pushes in two more PROSTI-
TUTES. *They look at him with a mixture of fear and outrage. The
other women observe the new arrivals curiously, then one offers each of
the new women a cigarette. The music suddenly stops. One of the*
PROSTITUTES *starts dancing, moving slowly, singing a blues number
in a gravelly voice. A line of* FOUR MEN *enter at a trot, leading a prisoner with his eyes bandaged, to the center. They sing.*)

FOUR MEN:

> We have come, we have come
> To have some fun!

(*The* PROSTITUTES *watch them. The one dancing gradually slows
down the rhythm until she is moving in place, singing inaudibly. The
men spin the prisoner around until he becomes completely disoriented.*)

10 MAN #1: Let's play the Little Blind Cock!
MAN #2: Cockadoodledoo!

(*They play, rapidly poking and moving away from the prisoner, who
searches for them with his arms outstretched.*)

MAN #1: Play! Head down!
MAN #3: There are beams!
MAN #4: You could break your head open!

(*They play, yell "Cockadoodledoo!" One of the* PROSTITUTES *comes
forward. She first starts to join in the game, then stretches her hand toward the prisoner's bandage.*)

15 MAN #1: (*Pushes her away.*) Get out of here! This is our game!
In your place, whore!
MAN #2: (*Poking the prisoner.*) He's sweating! He's hot!
MEN #1, #3, AND #4: (*In a chorus.*) Make him strip! Make him
strip!

(*Maintaining an ambiguous air of play and violence, they take off his
jacket, his pants, his shirt; they throw his clothes, which flutter around.*)

20 MAN #1: Hard-boiled egg! Let's play hard-boiled egg!

(*They fight like children.*)

MAN #2: Me! Me!
MAN #3: Get out! Me!

(*They play. The prisoner holds his body rigid while the others rush
him, tie him up. Finally, one of the* MEN *hits him on the head. The
prisoner falls.*)

MAN #4: We warned you!
MAN #1: A beam, idiot!

MAN #2: We told you to keep your head down!   25

(*They drag the prisoner behind the screen. Through the screen, one can
see fuzzily that they are strapping him down on the table. A scream.
Instantaneously, the volume of the music shoots up; two of the men
come out from behind the screen.*)

TWO MEN: Girls, if you want to sing,
it's not prohibited!

(*They clap. The* PROSTITUTES *don't move.*)

Sing!

(*The* PROSTITUTES, *forced into it, clap and sing. Again the music gets
louder.*)

> Girls, if you want to dance,
> it's not prohibited!   30

(*The* PROSTITUTES *dance. Behind the screen, one can see the shadow
of the two* MEN *moving away from the table. The hand of the prisoner
falls softly. At the same time, the* PROSTITUTES *freeze in a musical
comedy finale. The music stops. The lights go out, then come up again.
The actors disperse, naturally. They take down the screen. The dead
man gets up from the table, gathers his clothes, and begins to dress.
Only the prisoners seated against the wall remain immobile.*)

GUIDE: (*Drily.*) Ladies and gentlemen, what are you waiting
for? The show is over. (*House lights come up.*)
GUIDE 2: (*Resentfully.*) If you clap enthusiastically in all good
haste your hands won't go to waste!

(*He claps, and the* GUIDES *and actors present imitate him.*)

GUIDE: Theater imitates life   35
If you don't clap
It means that life is rotten to the core
And we may as well just head for the door.

(*He moves the audience out toward the door. From far away can be heard
police sirens. Even when the audience is near the exit, they can hear.*)

> Who once said: here the ken
> of men and women
> here the bounds?   40

(*After a moment, repeat.*)

> Who once said: here the ken
> of men and women
> here the bounds?

Wole Soyinka

Wole Soyinka was born in 1934 in Abeokuta, Nigeria. Educated at Government College in Ibadan, Soyinka then studied at Leeds University in England, where he worked with the notable Shakespearian scholar and actor G. Wilson Knight and took his B.A. in English in 1957. He remained in England working as play reader for the Royal Court Theater before returning to Nigeria in 1959, where his first play, *The Lion and the Jewel,* was produced. In the course of the next decade, Soyinka wrote an important body of dramatic work, including the plays *The Invention* (1959), *A Dance of the Forests* (1960), *The Trials of Brother Jero* (1960), *Camwood on the Leaves* (radio play, 1960), *The Strong Breed* (1964), *Kongi's Harvest* (1964), and *The Road* (1965). He also taught at the universities of Ibadan, Ife, and Lagos, and founded two important theaters, the Orisun Theater (1964) and the Masks Theater (1960). Much of Soyinka's work is critical of authoritarian politics; he was arrested in 1967 and held as a political prisoner until 1969. Soyinka's memoir of imprisonment, *The Man Died,* was published in 1972 and was cited for excellence by Amnesty International. In the 1970s, Soyinka continued to write plays examining the tensions of tribal life in modern Africa: *Madmen and Specialists* (1970) and *Death and the King's Horseman* (1976). He also wrote plays more directly examining contemporary African politics: his rewriting of Brecht's *Threepenny Opera* as *Opera Wonyosi* (1977), and *A Play of Giants* (1985). He also wrote an adaptation of Euripides' *The Bacchae* (1973), placing the Greek narrative in a more explicitly tribal and ritualistic setting. Soyinka was awarded the Nobel Prize in 1986, the first African writer to receive the prize for literature.

Elesin faces the accusatory body of his son Olunde in Wole Soyinka's *Death and the King's Horseman* in this 1990 production at the New Rose Theatre, Portland.

DEATH AND THE KING'S HORSEMAN

Soyinka is sometimes criticized by other African writers for being too oriented toward Europe. Not only are some of his plays adaptations or imitations of European works, but Soyinka has continued to write in English—the language of the colonial power, after all—rather than writing in his native language, Yoruba. It is precisely this tension between village and metropolis, between Africa and Europe, that provides the springboard for some of Soyinka's greatest work and dramatizes the challenges of cross-cultural interaction in the complex contemporary political environment.

Death and the King's Horseman is based on events that took place in the Yoruba city of Oyo in 1946. The play opens on the day the local African king is to be buried. According to custom, his Horseman, Elesin Oba, will die on this day as well, following his master in death as he followed him in life. It is clear from the scene in the marketplace that this ritual death is, however, a celebration. The village enacts a festive and playful marriage between Elesin and a new, young bride, so that he can procreate before he dies, bringing new life into the world even as he passes out of it, but fatefully delaying his required sacrifice.

In *Death and the King's Horseman,* indigenous African culture operates within the more restricted sphere of Britain's colonial values, laws, and institutions. The region's colonial administrator, Simon Pilkings, who is on his way to a masquerade to celebrate the arrival of the Prince, acts to stop Elesin's death. However, Pilkings and his wife are wearing African ceremonial costumes of the dead to the English masquerade, a decision that is not only offensive and irreligious to the Africans they meet, but that marks their complete incomprehension of the complex situation in which they find themselves. Wearing the costume also marks the Pilkingses, and the colonial British as a whole, as figures of death, in contrast to the paradoxical life celebrated by Elesin.

Pilkings "saves" Elesin and brings about the play's tragic catastrophe. Elesin's son Olunde—studying medicine in Britain—returns to perform funeral rites for his father. However, when Elesin is prevented from dying, it becomes clear that colonial intervention has destroyed what it attempted to protect. Olunde, too, is dishonored when his father remains alive and takes the only possible course of action.

In his note to the play, Soyinka criticizes the phrase "clash of cultures" to describe his work, for it "presupposes a potential equality in *every given situation* of the alien culture and the indigenous." In *Death and the King's Horseman,* the power vested in the colonial administration signals its ability to destroy the indigenous culture it claims, ironically, to govern.

Author's Note

This play is based on events which took place in Oyo, ancient Yoruba city of Nigeria, in 1946. That year, the lives of Elesin (Olori Elesin), his son, and the Colonial District Officer intertwined, with the disastrous results set out in the play. The changes I have made are in matters of detail, sequence and of course characterisation. The action has also been set back two or three years to while the war was still on, for minor reasons of dramaturgy.

The factual account still exists in the archives of the British Colonial Administration. It has already inspired a fine play in Yoruba (Oba Wàjà) by Duro Ladipo. It has also misbegotten a film by some German television company.

The bane of themes of this genre is that they are no sooner employed creatively than they acquire the facile tag of "clash of cultures," a prejudicial label which, quite apart from its frequent misapplication, presupposes a potential equality *in every given situation* of the alien culture and the indigenous, on the actual soil of the latter. (In the area of misapplication, the overseas prize for illiteracy and mental conditioning undoubtedly goes to the blurb-writer for the American edition of my novel *Season of Anomy* who unblushingly declares that this work portrays the "clash between old values and new ways, between western methods and

African traditions"!) It is thanks to this kind of perverse mentality that I find it necessary to caution the would-be producer of this play against a sadly familiar reductionist tendency, and to direct his vision instead to the far more difficult and risky task of eliciting the play's threnodic essence.

One of the more obvious alternative structures of the play would be to make the District Officer the victim of a cruel dilemma. This is not to my taste and it is not by chance that I have avoided dialogue or situation which would encourage this. No attempt should be made in production to suggest it. The Colonial Factor is an incident, a catalytic incident merely. The confrontation in the play is largely metaphysical, contained in the human vehicle which is Elesin and the universe of the Yoruba mind—the world of the living, the dead and the unborn, and the numinous passage which links all: transition. *Death and the King's Horseman* can be fully realised only through an evocation of music from the abyss of transition.

Wole Soyinka

DEATH AND THE KING'S HORSEMAN

Wole Soyinka

CHARACTERS

PRAISE-SINGER
ELESIN, *Horseman of the King*
IYALOJA, *'Mother' of the market*
SIMON PILKINGS, *District Officer*
JANE PILKINGS, *his wife*
SERGEANT AMUSA
JOSEPH, *houseboy to the Pilkingses*
BRIDE

H.R.H. THE PRINCE
THE RESIDENT
AIDE-DE-CAMP
OLUNDE, *eldest son of Elesin*
DRUMMERS, WOMEN, YOUNG GIRLS, DANCERS AT THE BALL

The play should run without an interval. For rapid scene changes, one adjustable outline set is very appropriate.

ACT ONE

A passage through a market in its closing stages. The stalls are being emptied, mats folded. A few women pass through on their way home, loaded with baskets. On a cloth-stand, bolts of cloth are taken down, display pieces folded and piled on a tray. ELESIN OBA *enters along a passage before the market, pursued by his* DRUMMERS *and* PRAISE-SINGERS. *He is a man of enormous vitality, speaks, dances and sings with that infectious enjoyment of life which accompanies all his actions.*

PRAISE-SINGER: Elesin O! Elesin Oba! Howu! What tryst is this the cockerel goes to keep with such haste that he must leave his tail behind?

ELESIN: (*Slows down a bit, laughing.*) A tryst where the cockerel
5 needs no adornment.

PRAISE-SINGER: O-oh, you hear that my companions? That's the way the world goes. Because the man approaches a brand-new bride he forgets the long faithful mother of his children.

ELESIN: When the horse sniffs the stable does he not strain at
10 the bridle? The market is the long-suffering home of my spirit and the women are packing up to go. That Esu-harassed day slipped into the stewpot while we feasted. We ate it up with the rest of the meat. I have neglected my women.

15 PRAISE-SINGER: We know all that. Still it's no reason for shedding your tail on this day of all days. I know the women will cover you in damask and *alari* but when the wind blows cold from behind, that's when the fowl knows his true friends.

20 ELESIN: Olohun-iyo!

PRAISE-SINGER: Are you sure there will be one like me on the other side?

ELESIN: Olohun-iyo!

PRAISE-SINGER: Far be it for me to belittle the dwellers of that
25 place but, a man is either born to his art or he isn't. And I don't know for certain that you'll meet my father, so who is going to sing these deeds in accents that will pierce the deafness of the ancient ones. I have prepared my going—just tell me: Olohun-iyo, I need you on this journey and I
30 shall be behind you.

Note to this edition: Certain Yoruba words which appear in italics in the text are explained in a brief glossary at the end of the play.

ELESIN: You're like a jealous wife. Stay close to me, but only on this side. My fame, my honour are legacies to the living; stay behind and let the world sip its honey from your lips.

PRAISE-SINGER: Your name will be like the sweet berry a child places under his tongue to sweeten the passage of food. The 35 world will never spit it out.

ELESIN: Come then. This market is my roost. When I come among the women I am a chicken with a hundred mothers. I become a monarch whose palace is built with tenderness and beauty. 40

PRAISE-SINGER: They love to spoil you but beware. The hands of women also weaken the unwary.

ELESIN: This night I'll lay my head upon their lap and go to sleep. This night I'll touch feet with their feet in a dance that is no longer of this earth. But the smell of their flesh, 45 their sweat, the smell of indigo on their cloth, this is the last air I wish to breathe as I go to meet my great forebears.

PRAISE-SINGER: In their time the world was never tilted from its groove, it shall not be in yours.

ELESIN: The gods have said No. 50

PRAISE-SINGER: In their time the great wars came and went, the little wars came and went; the white slavers came and went, they took away the heart of our race, they bore away the mind and muscle of our race. The city fell and was rebuilt; the city fell and our people trudged through mountain and forest to 55 found a new home but—Elesin Oba do you hear me?

ELESIN: I hear your voice Olohun-iyo.

PRAISE-SINGER: Our world was never wrenched from its true course.

ELESIN: The gods have said No. 60

PRAISE-SINGER: There is only one home to the life of a river-mussel; there is only one home to the life of a tortoise; there is only one shell to the soul of man: there is only one world to the spirit of our race. If that world leaves its course and smashes on boulders of the great void, whose world will 65 give us shelter?

ELESIN: It did not in the time of my forebears, it shall not in mine.

PRAISE-SINGER: The cockerel must not be seen without his feathers. 70

ELESIN: Nor will the Not-I bird be much longer without his nest.

PRAISE-SINGER: (*Stopped in his lyric stride.*) The Not-I bird, Elesin?

ELESIN: I said, the Not-I bird. 75

PRAISE-SINGER: All respect to our elders but, is there really such
  a bird?
ELESIN: What! Could it be that he failed to knock on your door?
PRAISE-SINGER: (*Smiling.*) Elesin's riddles are not merely the nut
80 in the kernel that breaks human teeth; he also buries the
  kernel in hot embers and dares a man's fingers to draw it out.
ELESIN: I am sure he called on you, Olohun-iyo. Did you hide in
  the loft and push out the servant to tell him you were out?

(ELESIN *executes a brief, half-taunting dance. The* DRUMMER *moves
in and draws a rhythm out of his steps.* ELESIN *dances towards the
market-place as he chants the story of the Not-I bird, his voice changing dexterously to mimic his characters. He performs like a born raconteur, infecting his retinue with his humour and energy. More women
arrive during his recital, including* IYALOJA.)

       Death came calling.
85 Who does not know his rasp of reeds?
  A twilight whisper in the leaves before
  The great araba falls? Did you hear it?
  'Not I!' swears the farmer. He snaps
  His fingers round his head, abandons
90 A hard-won harvest and begins
  A rapid dialogue with his legs.

  'Not I,' shouts the fearless hunter, 'but—
  It's getting dark, and this night-lamp
  Has leaked out all its oil. I think
95 It's best to go home and resume my hunt
  Another day.' But now he pauses, suddenly
  Lets out a wail: 'Oh foolish mouth, calling
  Down a curse on your own head! Your lamp
  Has leaked out all its oil, has it?'
100 Forwards or backwards now he dare not move.
  To search for leaves and make *etutu*
  On that spot? Or race home to the safety
  Of his hearth? Ten market-days have passed
  My friends, and still he's rooted there
105 Rigid as the plinth of Orayan.

  The mouth of the courtesan barely
  Opened wide enough to take a ha' penny *robo*
  When she wailed: 'Not I.' All dressed she was
  To call upon my friend the Chief Tax Officer.
110 But now she sends her go-between instead:
  'Tell him I'm ill: my period has come suddenly
  But not—I hope—my time.'

  Why is the pupil crying?
  His hapless head was made to taste
115 The knuckles of my friend the Mallam:
  'If you were then reciting the Koran
  Would you have ears for idle noises
  Darkening the trees, you child of ill omen?'
  He shuts down school before its time
120 Runs home and rings himself with amulets.
  And take my good kinsman Ifawomi.
  His hands were like a carver's, strong
  And true. I saw them
  Tremble like wet wings of a fowl
125 One day he cast his time-smoothed *opele*
  Across the divination board. And all because

  The supplicant looked him in the eye and asked,
  'Did you hear that whisper in the leaves?'
  'Not I,' was his reply; 'perhaps I'm growing deaf—
  Good-day.' And Ifa spoke no more that day   130
  The priest locked fast his doors,
  Sealed up his leaking roof—but wait!
  This sudden care was not for Fawomi
  But for Osanyin, courier-bird of Ifa's
  Heart of wisdom. I did not know a kite   135
  Was hovering in the sky
  And Ifa now a twittering chicken in
  The brood of Fawomi the Mother Hen.

  Ah, but I must not forget my evening
  Courier from the abundant palm, whose groan   140
  Became 'Not I,' as he constipated down
  A wayside bush. He wonders if Elegbara
  Has tricked his buttocks to discharge
  Against a sacred grove. Hear him
  Mutter spells to ward off penalties   145
  For an abomination he did not intend.
  If any here
  Stumbles on a gourd of wine, fermenting
  Near the road, and nearby hears a stream
  Of spells issuing from a crouching form.   150
  Brother to a *sigidi,* bring home my wine,
  Tell my tapper I have ejected
  Fear from home and farm. Assure him,
  All is well.
PRAISE-SINGER: In your time we do not doubt the peace of 155
  farmstead and home, the peace of road and hearth, we do
  not doubt the peace of the forest.
ELESIN: There was fear in the forest too.
  Not-I was lately heard even in the lair
  Of beasts. The hyena cackled loud 'Not I,'   160
  The civet twitched his fiery tail and glared:
  Not I. Not-I became the answering-name
  Of the restless bird, that little one
  Whom Death found nesting in the leaves
  When whisper of his coming ran   165
  Before him on the wind. 'Not-I'
  Has long abandoned home. This same dawn
  I heard him twitter in the gods' abode.
  Ah, companions of this living world
  What a thing this is, that even those   170
  We call immortal
  Should fear to die.
IYALOJA: But you, husband of multitudes?
ELESIN: I, when that Not-I bird perched
  Upon my roof, bade him seek his nest again,   175
  Safe, without care or fear. I unrolled
  My welcome mat for him to see. Not-I
  Flew happily away, you'll hear his voice
  No more in this lifetime—You all know
  What I am.   180
PRAISE-SINGER: That rock which turns its open lodes
  Into the path of lightning. A gay
  Thoroughbred whose sudden disdains
  To falter though an adder reared
  Suddenly in his path.   185

ELESIN: My rein is loosened.
I am master of my Fate. When the hour comes
Watch me dance along the narrowing path
Glazed by the soles of my great precursors.
190   My soul is eager. I shall not turn aside.
WOMEN: You will not delay?
ELESIN: Where the storm pleases, and when, it directs
The giants of the forest. When friendship summons
Is when the true comrade goes.
195   WOMEN: Nothing will hold you back?
ELESIN: Nothing. What! Has no one told you yet?
I go to keep my friend and master company.
Who says the mouth does not believe in
'No, I have chewed all that before?' I say I have.
200   The world is not a constant honey-pot.
Where I found little I made do with little.
Where there was plenty I gorged myself.
My master's hands and mine have always
Dipped together and, home or sacred feast,
205   The bowl was beaten bronze, the meats
So succulent our teeth accused us of neglect.
We shared the choicest of the season's
Harvest of yams. How my friend would read
Desire in my eyes before I knew the cause—
210   However rare, however precious, it was mine.
WOMEN: The town, the very land was yours.
ELESIN: The world was mine. Our joint hands
Raised houseposts of trust that withstood
The siege of envy and the termites of time.
215   But the twilight hour brings bats and rodents—
Shall I yield them cause to foul the rafters?
PRAISE-SINGER: Elesin Oba! Are you not that man who
Looked out of doors that stormy day
The god of luck limped by, drenched
220   To the very lice that held
His rags together? You took pity upon
His sores and wished him fortune.
Fortune was footloose this dawn, he replied,
Till you trapped him in a heartfelt wish
225   That now returns to you. Elesin Oba!
I say you are that man who
Chanced upon the calabash of honour
You thought it was palm wine and
Drained its contents to the final drop.
230 ELESIN: Life has an end. A life that will outlive
Fame and friendship begs another name.
What elder takes his tongue to his plate,
Licks it clean of every crumb? He will encounter
Silence when he calls on children to fulfill
235   The smallest errand! Life is honour.
It ends when honour ends.
WOMEN: We know you for a man of honour.
ELESIN: Stop! Enough of that!
WOMEN: (*Puzzled, they whisper among themselves, turning mostly*
240   *to* IYALOJA.) What is it? Did we say something to give of-
fense? Have we slighted him in some way?
ELESIN: Enough of that sound I say. Let me hear no more in that
vein. I've heard enough.
IYALOJA: We must have said something wrong. (*Comes forward*
245   *a little.*) Elesin Oba, we ask forgiveness before you speak.
ELESIN: I am bitterly offended.

IYALOJA: Our unworthiness has betrayed us. All we can do is
ask your forgiveness. Correct us like a kind father.
ELESIN: This day of all days . . .
IYALOJA: It does not bear thinking. If we offend you now we   250
have mortified the gods. We offend heaven itself. Father of
us all, tell us where we went astray. (*She kneels, the other*
women follow.)
ELESIN: Are you not ashamed? Even a tear-veiled
Eye preserves its function of sight.   255
Because my mind was raised to horizons
Even the boldest man lowers his gaze
In thinking of, must my body here
Be taken for a vagrant's?
IYALOJA: Horseman of the King, I am more baffled than ever.   260
PRAISE-SINGER: The strictest father unbends his brow when
the child is penitent, Elesin. When time is short, we do not
spend it prolonging the riddle. Their shoulders are bowed
with the weight of fear lest they have marred your day be-
yond repair. Speak now in plain words and let us pursue the   265
ailment to the home of remedies.
ELESIN: Words are cheap. 'We know you for
A man of honour.' Well tell me, is this how
A man of honour should be seen?
Are these not the same clothes in which   270
I came among you a full half-hour ago?

(*He roars with laughter and the* WOMEN, *relieved, rise and rush into*
stalls to fetch rich cloths.)

WOMAN: The gods are kind. A fault soon remedied is soon for-
given. Elesin Oba, even as we match our words with deed,
let your heart forgive us completely.
ELESIN: You who are breath and giver of my being   275
How shall I dare refuse you forgiveness
Even if the offence were real.
IYALOJA: (*Dancing round him. Sings.*)
He forgives us. He forgives us.
What a fearful thing it is when   280
The voyager sets forth
But a curse remains behind.
WOMEN: For a while we truly feared
Our hands had wrenched the world adrift
In emptiness.   285
IYALOJA: Richly, richly, robe him richly
The cloth of honour is *alari*
Sanyan is the band of friendship
Boa-skin makes slippers of esteem.
WOMEN: For a while we truly feared   290
Our hands had wrenched the world adrift
In emptiness.
PRAISE-SINGER: He who must, must voyage forth
The world will not roll backwards
It is he who must, with one   295
Great gesture overtake the world.
WOMEN: For a while we truly feared
Our hands had wrenched the world
In emptiness.
PRAISE-SINGER: The gourd you bear is not for shirking.   300
The gourd is not for setting down
At the first crossroad or wayside grove.
Only one river may know its contents.

WOMEN: We shall all meet at the great market
305   We shall all meet at the great market
        He who goes early takes the best bargains
        But we shall meet, and resume our banter.

(ELESIN *stands resplendent in rich clothes, cap, shawl, etc. His sash is
of a bright red alari cloth. The* WOMEN *dance round him. Suddenly,
his attention is caught by an object off-stage.*)

ELESIN: The world I know is good.
WOMEN: We know you'll leave it so.
310 ELESIN: The world I know is the bounty
        Of hives after bees have swarmed.
        No goodness teems with such open hands
        Even in the dreams of deities.
WOMEN: And we know you'll leave it so.
315 ELESIN: I was born to keep it so. A hive
        Is never known to wander. An anthill
        Does not desert its roots. We cannot see
        The still great womb of the world—
        No man beholds his mother's womb—
320   Yet who denies it's there? Coiled
        To the navel of the world is that
        Endless cord that links us all
        To the great origin. If I lose my way
        The trailing cord will bring me to the roots.
325 WOMEN: The world is in your hands.

(*The earlier distraction, a beautiful young girl, comes along the passage through which* ELESIN *first made his entry.*)

ELESIN: I embrace it. And let me tell you, women—
        I like this farewell that the world designed,
        Unless my eyes deceive me, unless
        We are already parted, the world and I,
330   And all that breeds desire is lodged
        Among our tireless ancestors. Tell me friends,
        Am I still earthed in that beloved market
        Of my youth? Or could it be my will
        Has outleapt the conscious act and I have come
335   Among the great departed?
     PRAISE-SINGER: Elesin-Oba why do your eyes roll like a bush-
        rat who sees his fate like his father's spirit, mirrored in the
        eye of a snake? And all these questions! You're standing on
        the same earth you've always stood upon. This voice you
340   hear is mine, Oluhun-iyo, not that of an acolyte in heaven.
     ELESIN: How can that be? In all my life
        As Horseman of the King, the juiciest
        Fruit on every tree was mine. I saw,
        I touched, I wooed, rarely was the answer No.
345   The honour of my place, the veneration I
        Received in the eye of man or woman
        Prospered my suit and
        Played havoc with my sleeping hours.
        And they tell me my eyes were a hawk
350   In perpetual hunger. Split an iroko tree
        In two, hide a woman's beauty in its heartwood
        And seal it up again—Elesin, journeying by,
        Would make his camp beside that tree
        Of all the shades in the forest.

PRAISE-SINGER: Who would deny your reputation, snake-on-   355
        the-loose in dark passages of the market! Bed-bug who
        wages war on the mat and receives the thanks of the van-
        quished! When caught with his bride's own sister he
        protested—but I was only prostrating myself to her as be-
        comes a grateful in-law. Hunter who carries his powder-horn   360
        on the hips and fires crouching or standing! Warrior who
        never makes that excuse of the whining coward—but how
        can I go to battle without my trousers?—trouserless or shirt-
        less it's all one to him. Oka-rearing-from-a-camouflage-of-
        leaves, before he strikes the victim is already prone! Once   365
        they told him, Howu, a stallion does not feed on the grass
        beneath him: he replied, true, but surely he can roll on it!
WOMEN: Ba-a-a-ba O!
PRAISE-SINGER: Ah, but listen yet. You know there is the leaf-
        knibbling grub and there is the cola-chewing beetle; the   370
        leaf-nibbling grub lives on the leaf, the cola-chewing bee-
        tle lives in the colanut. Don't we know what our man feeds
        on when we find him cocooned in a woman's wrapper?
ELESIN: Enough, enough, you all have cause
        To know me well. But, if you say this earth   375
        Is still the same as gave birth to those songs,
        Tell me who was that goddess through whose lips
        I saw the ivory pebbles of Oya's river-bed.
        Iyaloja, who is she? I saw her enter
        Your stall; all your daughters I know well.   380
        No, not even Ogun-of-the-farm toiling
        Dawn till dusk on his tuber patch
        Not even Ogun with the finest hoe he ever
        Forged at the anvil could have shaped
        That rise of buttocks, not though he had   385
        The richest earth between his fingers.
        Her wrapper was no disguise
        For thighs whose ripples shamed the river's
        Coils around the hills of Ilesi. Her eyes
        Were new-laid eggs glowing in the dark.   390
        Her skin . . .
IYALOJA: Elesin Oba . . .
ELESIN: What! Where do you all say I am?
IYALOJA: Still among the living.
ELESIN: And that radiance which so suddenly   395
        Lit up this market I could boast
        I knew so well?
IYALOJA: Has one step already in her husband's home. She is
        betrothed.
ELESIN: (*Irritated.*) Why do you tell me that?   400

(IYALOJA *falls silent. The* WOMEN *shuffle uneasily.*)

IYALOJA: Not because we dare give you offence Elesin. Today
        is your day and the whole world is yours. Still, even those
        who leave town to make a new dwelling elsewhere like to
        be remembered by what they leave behind.
ELESIN: Who does not seek to be remembered?   405
        Memory is Master of Death, the chink
        In his armour of conceit. I shall leave
        That which makes my going the sheerest
        Dream of an afternoon. Should voyagers
        Not travel light? Let the considerate traveller   410
        Shed, of his excessive load, all
        That may benefit the living.

WOMEN: (*Relieved.*) Ah Elesin Oba, we knew you for a man of honour.

415 ELESIN: Then honour me. I deserve a bed of honour to lie upon.

IYALOJA: The best is yours. We know you for a man of honour. You are not one who eats and leaves nothing on his plate for children. Did you not say it yourself? Not one who blights the happiness of others for a moment's pleasure.

420 ELESIN: Who speaks of pleasure? O women, listen!
Pleasure palls. Our acts should have meaning.
The sap of the plantain never dries.
You have seen the young shoot swelling
Even as the parent stalk begins to wither.

425 Women, let my going be likened to
The twilight hour of the plantain.

WOMEN: What does he mean Iyaloja? This language is the language of our elders, we do not fully grasp it.

IYALOJA: I dare not understand you yet Elesin.

430 ELESIN: All you who stand before the spirit that dares
The opening of the last door of passage,
Dare to rid my going of regrets! My wish
Transcends the blotting out of thought
In one mere moment's tremor of the senses.

435 Do me credit. And do me honour.
I am girded for the route beyond
Burdens of waste and longing.
Then let me travel light. Let
Seed that will not serve the stomach

440 On the way remain behind. Let it take root
In the earth of my choice, in this earth
I leave behind.

IYALOJA: (*Turns to* WOMEN.) The voice I hear is already touched by the waiting fingers of our departed. I dare not refuse.

445 WOMAN: Buy Iyaloja . . .

IYALOJA: The matter is no longer in our hands.

WOMAN: But she is betrothed to your own son. Tell him.

IYALOJA: My son's wish is mine. I did the asking for him, the loss can be remedied. But who will remedy the blight of

450 closed hands on the day when all should be openness and light? Tell him, you say! You wish that I burden him with knowledge that will sour his wish and lay regrets on the last moments of his mind. You pray to him who is your intercessor to the other world—don't set this world adrift in

455 your own time; would you rather it was my hand whose sacrilege wrenched it loose?

WOMAN: Not many men will brave the curse of a dispossessed husband.

IYALOJA: Only the curses of the departed are to be feared. The

460 claims of one whose foot is on the threshold of their abode surpasses even the claims of blood. It is impiety even to place hindrances in their ways.

ELESIN: What do my mothers say? Shall I step
Burdened into the unknown?

465 IYALOJA: Not we, but the very earth says No. The sap in the plantain does not dry. Let grain that will not feed the voyager at his passage drop here and take root as he steps beyond this earth and us. Oh you who fill the home from hearth to threshold with the voices of children, you who now bestride the hidden

470 den gulf and pause to draw the right foot across and into the resting-home of the great forebears, it is good that your loins be drained into the earth we know, that your last strength be ploughed back into the womb that gave you being.

PRAISE-SINGER: Iyaloja, mother of multitudes in the teeming market of the world, how your wisdom transfigures you! 475

IYALOJA: (*Smiling broadly, completely reconciled.*) Elesin, even at the narrow end of the passage I know you will look back and sigh a last regret for the flesh that flashed past your spirit in flight. You always had a restless eye. Your choice has my blessing. (*To the* WOMEN.) Take the good news to our 480 daughter and make her ready. (*Some* WOMEN *go off.*)

ELESIN: Your eyes were clouded at first.

IYALOJA: Not for long. It is those who stand at the gateway of the great change to whose cry we must pay heed. And then, think of this—it makes the mind tremble. The fruit of such 485 a union is rare. It will be neither of this world nor of the next. Nor of the one behind us. As if the timelessness of the ancestor world and the unborn have joined spirits to wring an issue of the elusive being of passage . . . Elesin!

ELESIN: I am here. What is it? 490

IYALOJA: Did you hear all I said just now?

ELESIN: Yes.

IYALOJA: The living must eat and drink. When the moment comes, don't turn the food to rodents' droppings in their mouth. Don't let them taste the ashes of the world when 495 they step out at dawn to breathe the morning dew.

ELESIN: This doubt is unworthy of you Iyaloja.

IYALOJA: Eating the awusa nut is not so difficult as drinking water afterwards.

ELESIN: The waters of the bitter stream are honey to a man 500 Whose tongue has savoured all.

IYALOJA: No one knows when the ants desert their home; they leave the mound intact. The swallow is never seen to peck holes in its nest when it is time to move with the season. There are always throngs of humanity behind the leave- 505 taker. The rain should not come through the roof for them, the wind must not blow through the walls at night.

ELESIN: I refuse to take offence.

IYALOJA: You wish to travel light. Well, the earth is yours. But be sure the seed you leave in it attracts no curse. 510

ELESIN: You really mistake my person Iyaloja.

IYALOJA: I said nothing. Now we must go prepare your bridal chamber. Then these same hands will lay your shrouds.

ELESIN: (*Exasperated.*) Must you be so blunt? (*Recovers.*) Well, weave your shrouds, but let the fingers of my bride seal my 515 eyelids with earth and wash my body.

IYALOJA: Prepare yourself Elesin.

(*She gets up to leave. At that moment the women return, leading the* BRIDE. ELESIN'*s face glows with pleasure. He flicks the sleeves of his agbada with renewed confidence and steps forward to meet the group. As the girl kneels before* IYALOJA, *lights fade out on the scene.*)

ACT TWO

The verandah of the District Officer's bungalow. A tango is playing from an old hand-cranked gramophone and, glimpsed through the wide windows and doors which open onto the forestage verandah are the shapes of SIMON PILKINGS *and his wife,* JANE, *tangoing in and out of shadows in the living-room. They were wearing what is immediately apparent as some form of fancy-dress. The dance goes on for some moments and then the figure of a 'Native Administration' policeman emerges and climbs up the steps onto the verandah. He peeps through and observes the dancing couple, reacting with what is obviously a long-standing bewilderment. He stiffens suddenly, his expression changes to one of disbelief and horror. In his excitement he upsets a flower-pot and attracts the attention of the couple. They stop dancing.*

PILKINGS: Is there anyone out there?

JANE: I'll turn off the gramophone.

PILKINGS: (*Approaching the verandah.*) I'm sure I heard some-
    thing fall over. (*The constable retreats slowly, open-mouthed as*
5   PILKINGS *approaches the verandah.*) Oh it's you Amusa. Why
    didn't you just knock instead of knocking things over?

AMUSA: (*Stammers badly and points a shaky finger at his dress.*)
    Mista Pirinkin . . . Mista Pirinkin . . .

PILKINGS: What is the matter with you?

10 JANE: (*Emerging.*) Who is it dear? Oh, Amusa . . .

PILKINGS: Yes it's Amusa, and acting most strangely.

AMUSA: (*His attention now transferred to* MRS PILKINGS.) Mam-
    madam . . . you too!

PILKINGS: What the hell is the matter with you man!

15 JANE: Your costume darling. Our fancy dress.

PILKINGS: Oh hell, I'd forgotten all about that. (*Lifts the face
    mask over his head showing his face. His wife follows suit.*)

JANE: I think you've shocked his big pagan heart bless him.

PILKINGS: Nonsense, he's a Moslem. Come on Amusa, you
20 don't believe in all this nonsense do you? I thought you
    were a good Moslem.

AMUSA: Mista Pirinkin, I beg you sir, what you think you do
    with that dress? It belong to dead cult, not for human being.

PILKINGS: Oh Amusa, what a let down you are. I swear by you
25 at the club you know—thank God for Amusa, he doesn't
    believe in any mumbo-jumbo. And now look at you!

AMUSA: Mista Pirinkin, I beg you, take it off. Is not good for
    man like you to touch that cloth.

PILKINGS: Well, I've got it on. And what's more Jane and I have
30 bet on it we're taking first prize at the ball. Now, if you can
    just pull yourself together and tell me what you wanted to
    see me about . . .

AMUSA: Sir, I cannot talk this matter to you in that dress. I no
    fit.

35 PILKINGS: What's that rubbish again?

JANE: He is dead earnest too Simon. I think you'll have to han-
    dle this delicately.

PILKINGS: Delicately my . . . ! Look here Amusa, I think this lit-
    tle joke has gone far enough hm? Let's have some sense. You
40 seem to forget that you are a police officer in the service of
    His Majesty's Government. I order you to report your busi-
    ness at once or face disciplinary action.

AMUSA: Sir, it is a matter of death. How can man talk against
    death to person in uniform of death? Is like talking against
45 government to person in uniform of police. Please sir, I go
    and come back.

PILKINGS: (*Roars.*) Now! (AMUSA *switches his gaze to the ceiling
    suddenly, remains mute.*)

JANE: Oh Amusa, what is there to be scared of in the costume?
50 You saw it confiscated last month from those *egungun* men
    who were creating trouble in town. You helped arrest the
    cult leaders yourself—if the juju didn't harm you at the
    time how could it possibly harm you now? And merely by
    looking at it?

55 AMUSA: (*Without looking down.*) Madam, I arrest the ring-
    leaders who make trouble but me I no touch *egungun*. That

egungun itself, I no touch. And I no abuse 'am. I arrest ring-
    leader but I treat *egungun* with respect.

PILKINGS: It's hopeless. We'll merely end up missing the best
    part of the ball. When they get this way there is nothing 60
    you can do. It's simply hammering against a brick wall.
    Write your report or whatever it is on that pad Amusa and
    take yourself out of here. Come on Jane. We only upset his
    delicate sensibilities by remaining here.

(AMUSA *waits for them to leave, then writes in the notebook, somewhat
laboriously. Drumming from the direction of the town wells up.*
AMUSA *listens, makes a movement as if he wants to recall* PILKINGS
*but changes his mind. Completes his note and goes. A few moments
later* PILKINGS *emerges, picks up the pad and reads.*)

PILKINGS: Jane!   65

JANE: (*From the bedroom.*) Coming darling. Nearly ready.

PILKINGS: Never mind being ready, just listen to this.

JANE: What is it?

PILKINGS: Amusa's report. Listen. 'I have to report that it come
    to my information that one prominent chief, namely, the 70
    Elesin Oba, is to commit death tonight as a result of native
    custom. Because this is criminal offence I await further in-
    struction at charge office. Sergeant Amusa.'

(JANE *comes out onto the verandah while he is reading.*)

JANE: Did I hear you say commit death?   75

PILKINGS: Obviously he means murder.

JANE: You mean a ritual murder?

PILKINGS: Must be. You think you've stamped it all out but it's
    always lurking under the surface somewhere.

JANE: Oh. Does it mean we are not getting to the ball at all?

PILKINGS: No-o. I'll have the man arrested. Everyone remotely 80
    involved. In any case there may be nothing to it. Just rumours.

JANE: Really? I thought you found Amusa's rumours generally
    reliable.

PILKINGS: That's true enough. But who knows what may have
    been giving him the scare lately. Look at his conduct 85
    tonight.

JANE: (*Laughing.*) You have to admit he had his own peculiar
    logic. (*Deepens her voice.*) How can man talk against death
    to person in uniform of death? (*Laughs.*) Anyway, you
    can't go into the police station dressed like that.   90

PILKINGS: I'll send Joseph with instructions. Damn it, what a
    confounded nuisance!

JANE: But don't you think you should talk first to the man,
    Simon?

PILKINGS: Do you want to go to the ball or not?   95

JANE: Darling, why are you getting rattled? I was only trying
    to be intelligent. It seems hardly fair just to lock up a
    man—and a chief at that—simply on the er . . . what is that
    legal word again?—uncorroborated word of a sergeant.

PILKINGS: Well, that's easily decided. Joseph!   100

JOSEPH: (*From within.*) Yes master.

PILKINGS: You're quite right of course, I am getting rattled.
    Probably the effect of those bloody drums. Do you hear
    how they go on and on?

JANE: I wondered when you'd notice. Do you suppose it has 105
    something to do with this affair?

PILKINGS: Who knows? They always find an excuse for making a noise … (*Thoughtfully.*) Even so …

JANE: Yes Simon?

110 PILKINGS: It's different Jane. I don't think I've heard this particular—sound—before. Something unsettling about it.

JANE: I thought all bush drumming sounded the same.

PILKINGS: Don't tease me now Jane. This may be serious.

JANE: I'm sorry. (*Gets up and throws her arms around his neck.*
115 *Kisses him. The houseboy enters, retreats and knocks.*)

PILKINGS: (*Wearily.*) Oh, come in Joseph! I don't know where you pick up all these elephantine notions of tact. Come over here.

JOSEPH: Sir?

PILKINGS: Joseph, are you a christian or not?

120 JOSEPH: Yessir.

PILKINGS: Does seeing me in this outfit bother you?

JOSEPH: No sir, it has no power.

PILKINGS: Thank God for some sanity at last. Now Joseph, answer me on the honour of a christian—what is supposed to
125 be going on in town tonight?

JOSEPH: Tonight sir? You mean that chief who is going to kill himself?

PILKINGS: What?

JANE: What do you mean, kill himself?

130 PILKINGS: You do mean he is going to kill somebody don't you?

JOSEPH: No master. He will not kill anybody and no one will kill him. He will simply die.

JANE: But why Joseph?

JOSEPH: It is native law and custom. The King die last month.
135 Tonight is his burial. But before they can bury him, the Elesin must die so as to accompany him to heaven.

PILKINGS: I seem to be fated to clash more often with that man than with any of the other chiefs.

JOSEPH: He is the King's Chief Horseman.

140 PILKINGS: (*In a resigned way.*) I know.

JANE: Simon, what's the matter?

PILKINGS: It would have to be him!

JANE: Who is he?

PILKINGS: Don't you remember? He's that chief with whom I
145 had a scrap some three or four years ago. I helped his son get to a medical school in England, remember? He fought tooth and nail to prevent it.

JANE: Oh now I remember. He was that very sensitive young man. What was his name again?

150 PILKINGS: Olunde. Haven't replied to his last letter come to think of it. The old pagan wanted him to stay and carry on some family tradition or the other. Honestly I couldn't understand the fuss he made. I literally had to help the boy escape from close confinement and load him onto the next
155 boat. A most intelligent boy, really bright.

JANE: I rather thought he was much too sensitive you know. The kind of person you feel should be a poet munching rose petals in Bloomsbury.

PILKINGS: Well, he's going to make a first-class doctor. His
160 mind is set on that. And as long as he wants my help he is welcome to it.

JANE: (*After a pause.*) Simon.

PILKINGS: Yes?

JANE: This boy, he was his eldest son wasn't he?

165 PILKINGS: I'm not sure. Who could tell with that old ram?

JANE: Do you know, Joseph?

JOSEPH: Oh yes madam. He was the eldest son. That's why Elesin cursed master good and proper. The eldest son is not supposed to travel away from the land.

170 JANE: (*Giggling.*) Is that true Simon? Did he really curse you good and proper?

PILKINGS: By all accounts I should be dead by now.

JOSEPH: Oh no, master is white man. And good christian. Black man juju can't touch master.

175 JANE: If he was his eldest, it means that he would be the Elesin to the next king. It's a family thing isn't it, Joseph?

JOSEPH: Yes madam. And if this Elesin had died before the King, his eldest son must take his place.

JANE: That would explain why the old chief was so mad you
180 took the boy away.

PILKINGS: Well it makes me all the more happy I did.

JANE: I wonder if he knew.

PILKINGS: Who? Oh, you mean Olunde?

JANE: Yes. Was that why he was so determined to get away? I
185 wouldn't stay if I knew I was trapped in such a horrible custom.

PILKINGS: (*Thoughtfully.*) No, I don't think he knew. At least he gave no indication. But you couldn't really tell with him. He was rather close you know, quite unlike most of them.
190 Didn't give much away, not even to me.

JANE: Aren't they all rather close, Simon?

PILKINGS: These natives here? Good gracious. They'll open their mouths and yap with you about their family secrets before you can stop them. Only the other day …

195 JANE: But Simon, do they really give anything away? I mean, anything that really counts. This affair for instance, we didn't know they still practised that custom did we?

PILKINGS: Ye-e-es, I suppose you're right there. Sly, devious bastards.

200 JOSEPH: (*Stiffly.*) Can I go now master? I have to clean the kitchen.

PILKINGS: What? Oh, you can go. Forgot you were still here.

(JOSEPH *goes.*)

JANE: Simon, you really must watch your language. Bastard isn't just a simple swear-word in these parts, you know.

PILKINGS: Look, just when did you become a social anthropol-
205 ogist, that's what I'd like to know.

JANE: I'm not claiming to know anything. I just happen to have overheard quarrels among the servants. That's how I know they consider it a smear.

PILKINGS: I thought the extended family system took care of all
210 that. Elastic family, no bastards.

JANE: (*Shrugs.*) Have it your own way.

(*Awkward silence. The drumming increases in volume.* JANE *gets up suddenly, restless.*)

That drumming Simon, do you think it might really be connected with this ritual? It's been going on all evening.

PILKINGS: Let's ask our native guide. Joseph! Just a minute Joseph. (JOSEPH *re-enters.*) What's the drumming about?

215 JOSEPH: I don't know master.

PILKINGS: What do you mean you don't know? It's only two years since your conversion. Don't tell me all that holy water nonsense also wiped out your tribal memory.

220 JOSEPH: (*Visibly shocked.*) Master!
JANE: Now you've done it.
PILKINGS: What have I done now?
JANE: Never mind. Listen Joseph, just tell me this. Is that drum-
ming connected with dying or anything of that nature?
225 JOSEPH: Madam, this is what I am trying to say: I am not sure.
It sounds like the death of a great chief and then, it sounds
like the wedding of a great chief. It really mix me up.
PILKINGS: Oh get back to the kitchen. A fat lot of help you are.
JOSEPH: Yes master. (*Goes.*)
230 JANE: Simon . . .
PILKINGS: Alright, alright. I'm in no mood for preaching.
JANE: It isn't my preaching you have to worry about, it's the
preaching of the missionaries who preceded you here.
When they make converts they really convert them. Calling
235 holy water nonsense to our Joseph is really like insulting
the Virgin Mary before a Roman Catholic. He's going to
hand in his notice tomorrow you mark my word.
PILKINGS: Now you're being ridiculous.
JANE: Am I? What are you willing to bet that tomorrow we are
240 going to be without a steward-boy? Did you see his face?
PILKINGS: I am more concerned about whether or not we will
be one native chief short by tomorrow. Christ! Just listen to
those drums. (*He strides up and down, undecided.*)
JANE: (*Getting up.*) I'll change and make up some supper.
245 PILKINGS: What's that?
JANE: Simon, it's obvious we have to miss this ball.
PILKINGS: Nonsense. It's the first bit of real fun the European
club has managed to organise for over a year, I'm damned if
I'm going to miss it. And it is a rather special occasion.
250 Doesn't happen every day.
JANE: You know this business has to be stopped Simon. And
you are the only man who can do it.
PILKINGS: I don't have to stop anything. If they want to throw
themselves off the top of a cliff or poison themselves for the
255 sake of some barbaric custom what is that to me? If it were
ritual murder or something like that I'd be duty-bound to
do something. I can't keep an eye on all the potential suicides in this province. And as for that man—believe me it's
good riddance.
260 JANE: (*Laughs.*) I know you better than that Simon. You are going to have to do something to stop it—after you've finished blustering.
PILKINGS: (*Shouts after her.*) And suppose after all it's only a
wedding. I'd look a proper fool if I interrupted a chief on
265 his honeymoon, wouldn't I? (*Resumes his angry stride, slows
down.*) Ah well, who can tell what those chiefs actually do
on their honeymoon anyway? (*He takes up the pad and scribbles rapidly on it.*) Joseph! Joseph! Joseph! (*Some moments later
JOSEPH puts in a sulky appearance.*) Did you hear me call you?
270 Why the hell didn't you answer?
JOSEPH: I didn't hear master.
PILKINGS: You didn't hear me! How come you are here then?
JOSEPH: (*Stubbornly.*) I didn't hear master.
PILKINGS: (*Controls himself with an effort.*) We'll talk about it in
275 the morning. I want you to take this note directly to
Sergeant Amusa. You'll find him at the charge office. Get
on your bicycle and race there with it. I expect you back in
twenty minutes exactly. Twenty minutes, is that clear?
JOSEPH: Yes master. (*Going.*)

PILKINGS: Oh er . . . Joseph. 280
JOSEPH: Yes master?
PILKINGS: (*Between gritted teeth.*) Er . . . forget what I said just
now. The holy water is not nonsense. I was talking nonsense.
JOSEPH: Yes master. (*Goes.*)
JANE: (*Pokes her head round the door.*) Have you found him? 285
PILKINGS: Found who?
JANE: Joseph. Weren't you shouting for him?
PILKINGS: Oh yes, he turned up finally.
JANE: You sounded desperate. What was it all about?
PILKINGS: Oh nothing. I just wanted to apologise to him. As- 290
sure him that the holy water isn't really nonsense.
JANE: Oh? And how did he take it?
PILKINGS: Who the hell gives a damn! I had a sudden vision of
our Very Reverend Macfarlane drafting another letter of
complaint to the Resident about my unchristian language 295
towards his parishioners.
JANE: Oh I think he's given up on you by now.
PILKINGS: Don't be too sure. And anyway, I wanted to make
sure Joseph didn't 'lose' my note on the way. He looked sufficiently full of the holy crusade to do some such thing. 300
JANE: If you've finished exaggerating, come and have something to eat.
PILKINGS: No, put it all way. We can still get to the ball.
JANE: Simon . . .
PILKINGS: Get your costume back on. Nothing to worry 305
about. I've instructed Amusa to arrest the man and lock
him up.
JANE: But that station is hardly secure Simon. He'll soon get
his friends to help him escape.
PILKINGS: A-ah, that's where I have out-thought you. I'm not 310
having him put in the station cell. Amusa will bring him
right here and lock him up in my study. And he'll stay with
him till we get back. No one will dare come here to incite
him to anything.
JANE: How clever of you darling. I'll get ready. 315
PILKINGS: Hey.
JANE: Yes darling.
PILKINGS: I have a surprise for you. I was going to keep it until
we actually got to the ball.
JANE: What is it? 320
PILKINGS: You know the Prince is on a tour of the colonies
don't you? Well, he docked in the capital only this morning
but he is already at the Residency. He is going to grace the
ball with his presence later tonight.
JANE: Simon! Not really. 325
PILKINGS: Yes he is. He's been invited to give away the prizes
and he has agreed. You must admit old Engleton is the best
Club Secretary we ever had. Quick off the mark that lad.
JANE: But how thrilling.
PILKINGS: The other provincials are going to be damned envious. 330
JANE: I wonder what he'll come as.
PILKINGS: Oh I don't know. As a coat-of-arms perhaps. Any-
way it won't be anything to touch this.
JANE: Well that's lucky. If we are to be presented I won't have
to start looking for a pair of gloves. It's all sewn on. 335
PILKINGS: (*Laughing.*) Quite right. Trust a woman to think of
that. Come on, let's get going.
JANE: (*Rushing off.*) Won't be a second. (*Stops.*) Now I see
why you've been so edgy all evening. I thought you weren't

340   handling this affair with your usual brilliance—to begin
       with that is.
PILKINGS: (*His mood is much improved.*) Shut up woman and get
       your things on.
JANE: Alright boss, coming.

(PILKINGS *suddenly begins to hum the tango to which they were danc-ing before. Starts to execute a few practice steps. Lights fade.*)

ACT THREE

A swelling, agitated hum of women's voices rises immediately in the background. The lights come on and we see the frontage of a con-verted cloth stall in the market. The floor leading up to the entrance is cov-ered in rich velvets and woven cloth. The WOMEN *come on stage, borne backwards by the determined progress of Sergeant* AMUSA *and his two constables who already have their batons out and use them as a pres-sure against the* WOMEN. *At the edge of the cloth-covered floor however the* WOMEN *take a determined stand and block all further progress of the* MEN. *They begin to tease them mercilessly.*

AMUSA: I am tell you women for last time to commot my road.
       I am here on official business.
WOMAN: Official business you white man's eunuch? Official
       business is taking place where you want to go and it's a
5   business you wouldn't understand.
WOMAN: (*Makes a quick tug at the constable's baton.*) That doesn't
       fool anyone you know. It's the one you carry under your
       government knickers that counts. (*She bends low as if to peep
       under the baggy shorts. The embarrassed constable quickly puts his
10   knees together. The* WOMEN *roar.*)
WOMAN: You mean there is nothing there at all?
WOMAN: Oh there was something. You know that handbell
       which the white man uses to summon his servants . . . ?
AMUSA: (*He manages to preserve some dignity throughout.*) I hope
15   you women know that interfering with officer in execution
       of his duty is criminal offence.
WOMAN: Interfere? He says we're interfering with him. You
       foolish man we're telling you there's nothing there to inter-
       fere with.
20 AMUSA: I am order you now to clear the road.
WOMAN: What road? The one your father built?
WOMAN: You are a Policeman not so? Then you know what
       they call trespassing in court. Or—(*Pointing to the cloth-lined
       steps.*)—do you think that kind of road is built for every
25   kind of feet.
WOMAN: Go back and tell the white man who sent you to
       come himself.
AMUSA: If I go I will come back with reinforcement. And we
       will all return carrying weapons.
30 WOMAN: Oh, now I understand. Before they can put on those
       knickers the white man first cuts off their weapons.
WOMAN: What a cheek! You mean you come here to show
       power to women and you don't even have a weapon.
AMUSA: (*Shouting above the laughter.*) For the last time I warn
35   you women to clear the road.
WOMAN: To where?
AMUSA: To that hut. I know he dey dere.
WOMAN: Who?
AMUSA: The chief who call himself Elesin Oba.

WOMAN: You ignorant man. It is not he who calls himself   40
       Elesin Oba, it is his blood that says it. As it called out to his
       father before him and will to his son after him. And that
       is in spite of everything your white man can do.
WOMAN: Is it not the same ocean that washes this land and the
       white man's land? Tell your white man he can hide our son   45
       away as long as he likes. When the time comes for him, the
       same ocean will bring him back.
AMUSA: The government say dat kin' ting must stop.
WOMAN: Who will stop it? You? Tonight our husband and fa-
       ther will prove himself greater than the laws of strangers.   50
AMUSA: I tell you nobody go prove anyting tonight or anytime.
       Is ignorant and criminal to prove dat kin' prove.
IYALOJA: (*Entering, from the hut. She is accompanied by a group of*
       YOUNG GIRLS *who have been attending the* BRIDE.) What is it
       Amusa? Why do you come here to disturb the happiness of   55
       others.
AMUSA: Madame Iyaloja, I glad you come. You know me. I no
       like trouble but duty is duty. I am here to arrest Elesin for
       criminal intent. Tell these women to stop obstructing me in
       the performance of my duty.   60
IYALOJA: And you? What gives you the right to obstruct our
       leader of men in the performance of his duty.
AMUSA: What kin' duty be dat one Iyaloja.
IYALOJA: What kin' duty? What kin' duty does a man have to
       his new bride?   65
AMUSA: (*Bewildered, looks at the* WOMEN *and at the entrance to the
       hut.*) Iyaloja, is it wedding you call dis kin' ting?
IYALOJA: You have wives haven't you? Whatever the white man
       has done to you he hasn't stopped you having wives. And if
       he has, at least he is married. If you don't know what a mar-   70
       riage is, go and ask him to tell you.
AMUSA: This no to wedding.
IYALOJA: And ask him at the same time what he would have
       done if anyone had come to disturb him on his wedding
       night.   75
AMUSA: Iyaloja, I say dis no to wedding.
IYALOJA: You want to look inside the bridal chamber? You want
       to see for yourself how a man cuts the virgin knot?
AMUSA: Madam . . .
WOMAN: Perhaps his wives are still waiting for him to learn.   80
AMUSA: Iyaloja, make you tell dese women make den no insult
       me again. If I hear dat kin' insult once more . . .
GIRL: (*Pushing her way through.*) You will do what?
GIRL: He's out of his mind. It's our mothers you're talking to,
       do you know that? Not to any illiterate villager you can   85
       bully and terrorise. How dare you intrude here anyway?
GIRL: What a cheek, what impertinence!
GIRL: You've treated them too gently. Now let them see what
       it is to tamper with the mothers of this market.
GIRLS: Your betters dare not enter the market when the women   90
       say no!
GIRL: Haven't you learnt that yet, you jester in khaki and
       starch?
IYALOJA: Daughters . . .
GIRL: No no Iyaloja, leave us to deal with him. He no longer   95
       knows his mother, we'll teach him.

(*With a sudden movement they snatch the batons of the two constables.
They begin to hem them in.*)

GIRL: What next? We have your batons? What next? What are you going to do?

(*With equally swift movements they knock off their hats.*)

GIRL: Move if you dare. We have your hats, what will you do
100 about it? Didn't the white man teach you to take off your hats before women?

IYALOJA: It's a wedding night. It's a night of joy for us. Peace …

GIRL: Not for him. Who asked him here?

GIRL: Does he dare go to the Residency without an invitation?

105 GIRL: Not even where the servants eat the left-overs.

GIRLS: (*In turn. In an 'English' accent.*) Well well it's Mister Amusa. Were you invited? (*Play-acting to one another. The older* WOMEN *encourage them with their titters.*)

—Your invitation card please?

110 —Who are you? Have we been introduced?

—And who did you say you were?

—Sorry, I didn't quite catch your name.

—May I take your hat?

—If you insist. May I take yours? (*Exchanging the police-*
115 *man's hats.*)

—How very kind of you.

—Not at all. Won't you sit down?

—After you.

—Oh no.

120 —I insist.

—You're most gracious.

—And how do you find the place?

—The natives are alright.

—Friendly?

125 —Tractable.

—Not a teeny-weeny bit restless?

—Well, a teeny-weeny bit restless.

—One might even say, difficult?

—Indeed one might be tempted to say, difficult.

130 —But you do manage to cope?

—Yes indeed I do. I have a rather faithful ox called Amusa.

—He's loyal?

—Absolutely.

—Lay down his life for you what?

135 —Without a moment's thought.

—Had one like that once. Trust him with my life.

—Mostly of course they are liars.

—Never known a native tell the truth.

—Does it get rather close around here?

140 —It's mild for this time of the year.

—But the rains may still come.

—They are late this year aren't they?

—They are keeping African time.

—Ha ha ha ha

145 —Ha ha ha ha

—The humidity is what gets me.

—It used to be whisky.

—Ha ha ha ha

—Ha ha ha ha

150 —What's your handicap old chap?

—Is there racing by golly?

—Splendid golf course, you'll like it.

—I'm beginning to like it already.

—And a European club, exclusive.

—You've kept the flag flying.   155

—We do our best for the old country.

—It's a pleasure to serve.

—Another whisky old chap?

—You are indeed too too kind.

—Not at all sir. Where is that boy? (*With a sudden bellow.*) 160
Sergeant!

AMUSA: (*Snaps to attention.*) Yessir!

(*The* WOMEN *collapse with laughter.*)

GIRL: Take your men out of here.

AMUSA: (*Realising the trick, he rages from loss of face.*) I'm give you
warning …   165

GIRL: Alright then. Off with his knickers! (*They surge slowly forward.*)

IYALOJA: Daughters, please.

AMUSA: (*Squaring himself for defence.*) The first woman wey
touch me …   170

IYALOJA: My children, I beg of you …

GIRL: Then tell him to leave this market. This is the home of our mothers. We don't want the eater of white left-overs at the feast their hands have prepared.

IYALOJA: You heard them Amusa. You had better go.   175

GIRLS: Now!

AMUSA: (*Commencing his retreat.*) We dey go now, but make you no say we no warn you.

GIRL: Before we read the riot act—you should know all about that.   180

AMUSA: Make we go. (*They depart, more precipitately.*)

(*The* WOMEN *strike their palms across in the gesture of wonder.*)

WOMEN: Do they teach you all that school?

WOMAN: And to think I nearly kept Apinke away from the place.

WOMAN: Did you hear them? Did you see how they mimicked 185
the white man?

WOMAN: The voices exactly. Hey, there are wonders in this world!

IYALOJA: Well, our elders have said it: Dada may be weak, but
he has a younger sibling who is truly fearless.   190

WOMAN: The next time the white man shows his face in this market I will set Wuraola on his tail.

(*A* WOMAN *bursts into song and dance of euphoria—'Tani l'awa o
l'ogbeja? Kayi! A l'ogbeja. Omo Kekere l'ogbeja.' ['Who says we
haven't a defender? Silence! We have our defenders. Little children are
our champions.'] The rest of the* WOMEN *join in, some placing the*
GIRLS *on their back like infants, other dancing round them. The dance
becomes general, mounting in excitement.* ELESIN *appears, in wrapper
only. In his hands a white velvet cloth folded loosely as if it held some
delicate object. He cries out.*)

ELESIN: Oh you mothers of beautiful brides! (*The dancing stops.
They turn and see him, and the object in his hands.* IYALOJA *approaches and gently takes the cloth from him.*) Take it. It is no 195
mere virgin stain, but the union of life and the seeds of passage. My vital flow, the last from this flesh is intermingled
with the promise of future life. All is prepared. Listen! (*A*

steady drum-beat from the distance.) Yes. It is nearly time. The
200 King's dog has been killed. The King's favourite horse is
about to follow his master. My brother chiefs know their
task and perform it well. (*He listens again.*)

(*The* BRIDE *emerges, stands shyly by the door. He turns to her.*)

Our marriage is not yet wholly fulfilled. When earth and
passage wed, the consummation is complete only when
205 there are grains of earth on the eyelids of passage. Stay by me
till then. My faithful drummers, do me your last service.
This is where I have chosen to do my leave-taking, in this
heart of life, this hive which contains the swarm of the
world in its small compass. This is where I have known love
210 and laughter away from the palace. Even the richest food
cloys when eaten days on end; in the market, nothing ever
cloys. Listen. (*They listen to the drums.*) They have begun to
seek out the heart of the King's favourite horse. Soon it will
ride in its bolt of raffia with the dog at its feet. Together
215 they will ride on the shoulders of the King's grooms
through the pulse centres of the town. They know it is here
I shall await them. I have told them. (*His eyes appear to cloud.*
He passes his hand over them as if to clear his sight. He gives a
faint smile.) It promises well; just then I felt my spirit's ea-
220 gerness. The kite makes for wide spaces and the wind
creeps up behind its tail; can the kite say less than—thank
you, the quicker the better? But wait a while my spirit.
Wait. Wait for the coming of the courier of the King. Do
you know friends, the horse is born to this one destiny, to
225 bear the burden that is man upon its back. Except for this
night, this night alone when the spotless stallion will ride in
triumph on the back of man. In the time of my father I witnessed the strange sight. Perhaps tonight also I shall see it
for the last time. If they arrive before the drums beat for me,
230 I shall tell him to let the Alafin know I follow swiftly. If
they come after the drums have sounded, why then, all is
well for I have gone ahead. Our spirits shall fall in step
along the great passage. (*He listens to the drums. He seems*
again to be falling into a state of semi-hypnosis; his eyes scan the
235 *sky but it is in a kind of daze. His voice is a little breathless.*) The
moon has fed, a glow from its full stomach fills the sky and
air, but I cannot tell where is that gateway through which
I must pass. My faithful friends, let our feet touch together
this last time, lead me into the other market with sounds
240 that cover my skin with down yet make my limbs strike
earth like a thoroughbred. Dear mothers, let me dance into
the passage even as I have lived beneath your roofs. (*He*
comes down progressively among them. They make a way for him,
the DRUMMERS *playing. His dance is one of solemn, regal motions,*
245 *each gesture of the body is made with a solemn finality. The*
WOMEN *join him, their steps a somewhat more fluid version of his.*
Beneath the PRAISE-SINGER's *exhortations the* WOMEN *dirge*
'*Alẹ lẹ lẹ, awo mi lọ*'.)

PRAISE-SINGER: Elesin Alafin, can you hear my voice?
250 ELESIN: Faintly, my friend, faintly.
PRAISE-SINGER: Elesin Alafin, can you hear my call?
ELESIN: Faintly my king, faintly.
PRAISE-SINGER: Is your memory sound Elesin?
Shall my voice be a blade of grass and
255 Tickle the armpit of the past?

ELESIN: My memory needs no prodding but
What do you wish to say to me?
PRAISE-SINGER: Only what has been spoken. Only what concerns
The dying wish of the father of all.
ELESIN: It is buried like seed-yam in my mind   260
This is the season of quick rains, the harvest
Is this moment due for gathering.
PRAISE-SINGER: If you cannot come, I said, swear
You'll tell my favourite horse. I shall
Ride on through the gates alone.   265
ELESIN: Elesin's message will be read
Only when his loyal heart no longer beats.
PRAISE-SINGER: If you cannot come Elesin, tell my dog.
I cannot stay the keeper too long
At the gate.   270
ELESIN: A dog does not outrun the hand
That feeds it meat. A horse that throws its rider
Slows down to a stop. Elesin Alafin
Trusts no beasts with messages between
A king and his companion.   275
PRAISE-SINGER: If you get lost my dog will track
The hidden path to me.
ELESIN: The seven-way crossroads confuses
Only the stranger. The Horseman of the King
Was born in the recesses of the house.   280
PRAISE-SINGER: I know the wickedness of men. If there is
Weight on the loose end of your sash, such weight
As no mere man can shift; if your sash is earthed
By evil minds who mean to part us at the last . . .
ELESIN: My sash is of the deep purple *alari*;   285
It is no tethering-rope. The elephant
Trails no tethering-rope; that king
Is not yet crowned who will peg an elephant—
Not even you my friend and King.
PRAISE-SINGER: And yet this fear will not depart from me   290
The darkness of this new abode is deep—
Will your human eyes suffice?
ELESIN: In a night which falls before our eyes
However deep, we do not miss our way.
PRAISE-SINGER: Shall I now not acknowledge I have stood   295
Where wonders met their end? The elephant deserves
Better than that we say 'I have caught
A glimpse of something.' If we see the tamer
Of the forest let us say plainly, we have seen
An elephant.   300
ELESIN: (*His voice is drowsy.*) I have freed myself of earth and now
It's getting dark. Strange voices guide my feet.
PRAISE-SINGER: The river is never so high that the eyes
Of a fish are covered. The night is not so dark
That the albino fails to find his way. A child   305
Returning homewards craves no leading by the hand.
Gracefully does the mask regain his grove at the end of
the day . . .
Gracefully. Gracefully does the mask dance
Homeward at the end of day, gracefully . . .

(ELESIN's *trance appears to be deepening, his steps heavier.*)

IYALOJA: It is the death of war that kills the valiant,   310
Death of water is how the swimmer goes

It is the death of markets that kills the trader
And death of indecision takes the idle away
The trade of the cutlass blunts its edge
315 And the beautiful die the death of beauty.
It takes an Elesin to die the death of death ...
Only Elesin ... dies the unknowable death of death ...
Gracefully, gracefully does the horseman regain
The stables at the end of day, gracefully ...

320 PRAISE-SINGER: How shall I tell what my eyes have seen? The
Horseman gallops on before the courier, how shall I tell
what my eyes have seen? He says a dog may be confused by
new scents of beings he never dreamt of, so he must precede
the dog to heaven. He says a horse may stumble on strange
325 boulders and be lamed, so he races on before the horse to
heaven. It is best, he says, to trust no messenger who may
falter at the outer gate; oh how shall I tell what my ears
have heard? But do you hear me still Elesin, do you hear
your faithful one?

(ELESIN *in his motions appears to feel for a direction of sound, subtly,*
but he only sinks deeper into his trance-dance.)

330 Elesin Alafin, I no longer sense your flesh. The drums are
changing now but you have gone far ahead of the world. It
is not yet noon in heaven; let those who claim it is begin
their own journey home. So why must you rush like an impatient bride: why do you race to desert your Olohun-iyo?

(ELESIN *is now sunk fully deep in his trance, there is no longer sign of*
any awareness of his surroundings.)

335 Does the deep voice of *gbedu* cover you then, like the passage of royal elephants? Those drums that brook no rivals,
have they blocked the passage to your ears that my voice
passes into wind, a mere leaf floating in the night? Is your
flesh lightened Elesin, is that lump of earth I slid between
340 your slippers to keep you longer slowly sifting from your
feet? Are the drums on the other side now tuning skin to
skin with ours in *osugbo*? Are there sounds there I cannot
hear, do footsteps surround you which pound the earth like
gbedu, roll like thunder round the dome of the world? Is the
345 darkness gathering in your head Elesin? Is there now a
streak of light at the end of the passage, a light I dare not
look upon? Does it reveal whose voices we often heard,
whose touches we often felt, whose wisdoms come suddenly into the mind when the wisest have shaken their
350 heads and murmured: It cannot be done? Elesin Alafin,
don't think I do not know why your lips are heavy, why
your limbs are drowsy as palm oil in the cold of harmattan. I
would call you back but when the elephant heads for the
jungle, the tail is too small a handhold for the hunter that
355 would pull him back. The sun that heads for the sea no
longer heeds the prayers of the farmer. When the river begins to taste the salt of the ocean, we no longer know what
deity to call on, the river-god or Olokun. No arrow flies
back to the string, the child does not return through the
360 same passage that gave it birth. Elesin Oba, can you hear me
at all? Your eye-lids are glazed like a courtesan's, is it that you
see the dark groom and master of life? And will you see my
father? Will you tell him that I stayed with you to the last?
Will my voice ring in your ears awhile, will you remember
365 Olohun-iyo even if the music on the other side surpasses his

mortal craft? But will they know you over there? Have they
eyes to gauge your worth, have they the heart to love you,
will they know what thoroughbred prances towards them
in caparisons of honour? If they do not Elesin, if any there
cuts your yam with a small knife, or pours you wine in a 370
small calabash, turn back and return to welcoming hands. If
the world were not greater than the wishes of Olohun-iyo, I
would not let you go ...

(*He appears to break down.* ELESIN *dances on, completely in a trance.*
The dirge wells up louder and stronger. ELESIN's *dance does not lose its*
elasticity but his gestures become, if possible, even more weighty. Lights
fade slowly on the scene.)

ACT FOUR

A Masque. The front side of the stage is part of a wide corridor around
the great hall of the Residency extending beyond vision into the rear
and wings. It is redolent of the tawdry decadence of a far-flung but key
imperial frontier. The couples in a variety of fancy-dress are ranged
around the walls, gazing in the same direction. The guest-of-honour is
about to make an appearance. A portion of the local police brass band
with its white conductor is just visible. At last, the entrance of Roy-
alty. The band plays 'Rule Britannia', badly, beginning long before
he is visible. The couples bow and curtsey as he passes by them. Both
he and his companions are dressed in seventeenth century European
costume. Following behind are the RESIDENT *and his partner similarly*
attired. As they gain the end of the hall where the orchestra dais be-
gins the music comes to an end. The PRINCE *bows to the guests. The*
band strikes up a Viennese waltz and the PRINCE *formally opens the*
floor. Several bars later the RESIDENT *and his companion follow suit.*
Others follow in appropriate pecking order. The orchestra's waltz ren-
dition is not of the highest musical standard.

Some time later the PRINCE *dances again into view and is settled*
into a corner by the RESIDENT *who then proceeds to select couples as*
they dance past for introduction, sometimes threading his way
through the dancers to tap the lucky couple on the shoulder. Desperate
efforts from many to ensure that they are recognised in spite of, per-
haps, their costume. The ritual of introductions soon takes in PILK-
INGS *and his wife. The* PRINCE *is quite fascinated by their costume*
and they demonstrate the adaptations they have made to it, pulling
down the mask to demonstrate how the egungun *normally appears,*
then showing the various press-button controls they have innovated
for the face flaps, the sleeves, etc. They demonstrate the dance steps
and the guttural sounds made by the egungun, harass other dancers
in the hall, MRS PILKINGS *playing the 'restrainer' to* PILKINGS'
manic darts. Everyone is highly entertained, the Royal Party espe-
cially who lead the applause.

At this point a liveried footman comes in with a note on a salver and
is intercepted almost absent-mindedly by the RESIDENT *who takes*
the note and reads it. After polite coughs he succeeds in excusing the
PILKINGSES *from the* PRINCE *and takes them aside. The* PRINCE
considerately offers the RESIDENT's *wife his hand and dancing is*
resumed.

On their way out the RESIDENT *gives an order to his* AIDE-DE-CAMP.
They come into the side corridor where the RESIDENT *hands the note*
to PILKINGS.

RESIDENT: As you see it says 'emergency' on the outside. I took
the liberty of opening it because His Highness was obvi-

ously enjoying the entertainment. I didn't want to interrupt unless really necessary.

5   PILKINGS: Yes, yes of course sir.

RESIDENT: Is it really as bad as it says? What's it all about?

PILKINGS: Some strange custom they have sir. It seems because the King is dead some important chief has to commit suicide.

RESIDENT: The King? Isn't it the same one who died nearly a
10   month ago?

PILKINGS: Yes sir.

RESIDENT: Haven't they buried him yet?

PILKINGS: They take their time about these things sir. The pre-burial ceremonies last nearly thirty days. It seems tonight is
15   the final night.

RESIDENT: But what has it got to do with the market women? Why are they rioting? We've waived that troublesome tax haven't we?

PILKINGS: We don't quite know that they are exactly rioting yet
20   sir. Sergeant Amusa is sometimes prone to exaggerations.

RESIDENT: He sounds desperate enough. That comes out even in his rather quaint grammar. Where is the man anyway? I asked my aide-de-camp to bring him here.

PILKINGS: They are probably looking in the wrong verandah.
25   I'll fetch him myself.

RESIDENT: No no you stay here. Let your wife go and look for them. Do you mind my dear . . . ?

JANE: Certainly not, your Excellency. (Goes.)

RESIDENT: You should have kept me informed Pilkings. You
30   realise how disastrous it would have been if things had erupted while His Highness was here.

PILKINGS: I wasn't aware of the whole business until tonight sir.

RESIDENT: Nose to the ground Pilkings, nose to the ground. If we all let these little things slip past us where would the
35   empire be eh? Tell me that. Where would we all be?

PILKINGS: (Low voice.) Sleeping peacefully at home I bet.

RESIDENT: What did you say Pilkings?

PILKINGS: It won't happen again sir.

RESIDENT: It mustn't Pilkings. It mustn't. Where is that
40   damned sergeant? I ought to get back to His Highness as quickly as possible and offer him some plausible explanation for my rather abrupt conduct. Can you think of one Pilkings?

PILKINGS: You could tell him the truth sir.

45   RESIDENT: I could? No no no no no Pilkings, that would never do. What! Go and tell him there is a riot just two miles away from him? This is supposed to be a secure colony of His Majesty, Pilkings.

PILKINGS: Yes sir.

50   RESIDENT: Ah, there they are. No, these are not our native police. Are these the ring-leaders of the riot?

PILKINGS: Sir, these are my police officers.

RESIDENT: Oh, I beg your pardon officers. You do look a little . . . I say, isn't there something missing in their uni-
55   forms? I think they used to have some rather colourful sashes. If I remember rightly I recommended them myself in my young days in the service. A bit of colour always appeals to the natives, yes. I remember putting that in my report. Well well well, where are we? Make your report man.

60   PILKINGS: (Moves close to AMUSA, between his teeth.) And let's have no more superstitious nonsense from you Amusa or I'll throw you in the guardroom for a month and feed you pork!

RESIDENT: What's that? What has pork to do with it?

PILKINGS: Sir, I was just warning him to be brief. I'm sure you
65   are most anxious to hear his report.

RESIDENT: Yes yes yes of course. Come on man, speak up. Hey, didn't we give them some colourful fez hats with all those wavy things, yes, pink tassells . . .

PILKINGS: Sir, I think if he was permitted to make his report we
70   might find that he lost his hat in the riot.

RESIDENT: Ah yes indeed. I'd better tell His Highness that. Lost his hat in the riot, ha ha. He'll probably say well, as long as he didn't lost his head. (Chuckles to himself.) Don't forget to send me a report first thing in the morning young Pilkings.

75   PILKINGS: No sir.

RESIDENT: And whatever you do, don't let things get out of hand. Keep a cool head and—nose to the ground Pilkings. (Wanders off in the general direction of the hall.)

PILKINGS: Yes sir.

80   AIDE-DE-CAMP: Would you be needing me sir?

PILKINGS: No thanks Bob. I think His Excellency's need of you is greater than ours.

AIDE-DE-CAMP: We have a detachment of soldiers from the capital sir. They accompanied His Highness up here.

85   PILKINGS: I doubt if it will come to that but, thanks, I'll bear it in mind. Oh, could you send an orderly with my cloak.

AIDE-DE-CAMP: Very good sir. (Goes.)

PILKINGS: Now Sergeant.

AMUSA: Sir . . . (Makes an effort, stops dead. Eyes to the ceiling.)

90   PILKINGS: Oh, not again.

AMUSA: I cannot against death to dead cult. This dress get power of dead.

PILKINGS: Alright, let's go. You are relieved of all further duty Amusa. Report to me first thing in the morning.

95   JANE: Shall I come Simon?

PILKINGS: No, there's no need for that. If I can get back later I will. Otherwise get Bob to bring you home.

JANE: Be careful Simon . . . I mean, be clever.

PILKINGS: Sure I will. You two, come with me. (As he turns to go,
100   the clock in the Residency begins to chime. PILKINGS looks at his watch then turns, horror-stricken, to stare at his wife. The same thought clearly occurs to her. He swallows hard. An ORDERLY brings his cloak.) It's midnight. I had no idea it was that late.

JANE: But surely . . . they don't count the hours the way we do.
105   The moon, or something.

PILKINGS: I am . . . not so sure.

(He turns and breaks into a sudden run. The two constables follow, also at a run. AMUSA, who has kept his eyes on the ceiling throughout waits until the last of the footsteps has faded out of hearing. He salutes suddenly, but without once looking in the direction of the woman.)

AMUSA: Goodnight madam.

JANE: Oh. (She hesitates.) Amusa . . . (He goes off without seeming to have heard.) Poor Simon . . . (A figure emerges from the shad-
110   ows, a young black man dressed in a sober western suit. He peeps into the hall, trying to make out the figures of the dancers.) Who is that?

OLUNDE: (Emerging into the light.) I didn't mean to startle you madam. I am looking for the District Officer.

JANE: Wait a minute . . . don't I know you? Yes, you are
115   Olunde, the young man who . . .

OLUNDE: Mrs Pilkings! How fortunate. I came here to look for your husband.

JANE: Olunde! Let's look at you. What a fine young man
120   you've become. Grand but solemn. Good God, when did you return? Simon never said a word. But you do look well Olunde. Really!

OLUNDE: You are . . . well, you look quite well yourself Mrs Pilkings. From what little I can see of you.

125 JANE: Oh, this. It's caused quite a stir I assure you, and not all of it very pleasant. You are not shocked I hope?

OLUNDE: Why should I be? But don't you find it rather hot in there? Your skin must find it difficult to breathe.

JANE: Well, it is a little hot I must confess, but it's all in a good
130   cause.

OLUNDE: What cause Mrs Pilkings?

JANE: All this. The ball. And His Highness being here in person and all that.

OLUNDE: (*Mildly.*) And that is the good cause for which you
135   desecrate an ancestral mask?

JANE: Oh, so you are shocked after all. How disappointing.

OLUNDE: No I am not shocked Mrs Pilkings. You forget that I have now spent four years among your people. I discovered that you have no respect for what you do not understand.

140 JANE: Oh. So you've returned with a chip on your shoulder. That's a pity Olunde. I am sorry.

(*An uncomfortable silence follows.*)

I take it then that you did not find your stay in England altogether edifying.

OLUNDE: I don't say that. I found your people quite admirable
145   in many ways, their conduct and courage in this war for instance.

JANE: Ah yes the war. Here of course it is all rather remote. From time to time we have a black-out drill just to remind us that there is a war on. And the rare convoy passes
150   through on its way somewhere or on manoeuvres. Mind you there is the occasional bit of excitement like that ship that was blown up in the harbour.

OLUNDE: Here? Do you mean through enemy action?

JANE: Oh no, the war hasn't come that close. The captain did it
155   himself. I don't quite understand it really. Simon tried to explain. The ship had to be blown up because it had become dangerous to the other ships, even to the city itself. Hundreds of the coastal population would have died.

OLUNDE: Maybe it was loaded with ammunition and had
160   caught fire. Or some of those lethal gases they've been experimenting on.

JANE: Something like that. The captain blew himself up with it. Deliberately. Simon said someone had to remain on board to light the fuse.

165 OLUNDE: It must have been a very short fuse.

JANE: (*Shrugs.*) I don't know much about it. Only that there was no other way to save lives. No time to devise anything else. The captain took the decision and carried it out.

OLUNDE: Yes . . . I quite believe it. I met men like that in
170   England.

JANE: Oh just look at me! Fancy welcoming you back with such morbid news. Stale too. It was at least six months ago.

OLUNDE: I don't find it morbid at all. I find it rather inspiring. It is an affirmative commentary on life.

JANE: What is?   175

OLUNDE: That captain's self-sacrifice.

JANE: Nonsense. Life should never be thrown deliberately away.

OLUNDE: And the innocent people round the harbour?

JANE: Oh, how does one know? The whole thing was probably exaggerated anyway.   180

OLUNDE: That was a risk the captain couldn't take. But please Mrs Pilkings, do you think you could find your husband for me? I have to talk to him.

JANE: Simon? Oh. (*As she recollects for the first time the full significance of* OLUNDE'S *presence.*) Simon is . . . there is a little prob- 185
lem in town. He was sent for. But . . . when did you arrive? Does Simon know you're here?

OLUNDE: (*Suddenly earnest.*) I need your help Mrs Pilkings. I've always found you somewhat more understanding than your husband. Please find him for me and when you do, you 190
must help me talk to him.

JANE: I'm afraid I don't quite . . . follow you. Have you seen my husband already?

OLUNDE: I went to your house. Your houseboy told me you were here. (*He smiles.*) He even told me how I would recog- 195
nise you and Mr Pilkings.

JANE: Then you must know what my husband is trying to do for you.

OLUNDE: For me?

JANE: For you. For your people. And to think he didn't even 200
know you were coming back! But how do you happen to be here? Only this evening we were talking about you. We thought you were still four thousand miles away.

OLUNDE: I was sent a cable.

JANE: A cable? Who did? Simon? The business of your father 205
didn't begin till tonight.

OLUNDE: A relation sent it weeks ago, and it said nothing about my father. All it said was, Our King is dead. But I knew I had to return home at once so as to bury my father. I understood that.   210

JANE: Well, thank God you don't have to go through that agony. Simon is going to stop it.

OLUNDE: That's why I want to see him. He's wasting his time. And since he has been so helpful to me I don't want him to incur the enmity of our people. Especially over nothing.   215

JANE: (*Sits down open-mouthed.*) You . . . you Olunde!

OLUNDE: Mrs Pilkings, I came home to bury my father. As soon as I heard the news I booked my passage home. In fact we were fortunate. We travelled in the same convoy as your Prince, so we had excellent protection.   220

JANE: But you don't think your father is also entitled to whatever protection is available to him?

OLUNDE: How can I make you understand? He *has* protection. No one can undertake what he does tonight without the deepest protection the mind can conceive. What can you 225
offer him in place of his peace of mind, in place of the honour and veneration of his own people? What would you think of your Prince if he had refused to accept the risk of losing his life on this voyage? This . . . showing-the-flag tour of colonial possessions.   230

JANE: I see. So it isn't just medicine you studied in England.

OLUNDE: Yet another error into which your people fall. You believe that everything which appears to make sense was learnt from you.

235 JANE: Not so fast Olunde. You have learnt to argue I can tell that, but I never said you made sense. However cleverly you try to put it, it is still a barbaric custom. It is even worse—it's feudal! The king dies and a chieftain must be buried with him. How feudalistic can you get!

240 OLUNDE: (*Waves his hand towards the background. The* PRINCE *is dancing past again—to a different step—and all the guests are bowing and curtseying as he passes.*) And this? Even in the midst of a devastating war, look at that. What name would you give to that?

245 JANE: Therapy, British style. The preservation of sanity in the midst of chaos.

OLUNDE: Others would call it decadence. However, it doesn't really interest me. You white races know how to survive; I've seen proof of that. By all logical and natural laws this 250 war should end with all the white races wiping out one another, wiping out their so-called civilisation for all time and reverting to a state of primitivism the like of which has so far only existed in your imagination when you thought of us. I thought all that at the beginning. Then I 255 slowly realised that your greatest art is the art of survival. But at least have the humility to let others survive in their own way.

JANE: Through ritual suicide?

OLUNDE: Is that worse than mass suicide? Mrs Pilkings, what 260 do you call what those young men are sent to do by their generals in this war? Of course you have also mastered the art of calling things by names which don't remotely describe them.

JANE: You talk! You people with your long-winded, round-265 about way of making conversation.

OLUNDE: Mrs Pilkings, whatever we do, we never suggest that a thing is the opposite of what it really is. In your newsreels I heard defeats, thorough, murderous defeats described as strategic victories. No wait, it wasn't just on your news-270 reels. Don't forget I was attached to hospitals all the time. Hordes of your wounded passed through those wards. I spoke to them. I spent long evenings by their bedside while they spoke terrible truths of the realities of that war. I know now how history is made.

275 JANE: But surely, in a war of this nature, for the morale of the nation you must expect . . .

OLUNDE: That a disaster beyond human reckoning be spoken of as a triumph? No. I mean, is there no mourning in the home of the bereaved that such blasphemy is permitted?

280 JANE: (*After a moment's pause.*) Perhaps I can understand you now. The time we picked for you was not really one for seeing us at our best.

OLUNDE: Don't think it was just the war. Before that even started I had plenty of time to study your people. I saw 285 nothing, finally, that gave you the right to pass judgement on other peoples and their ways. Nothing at all.

JANE: (*Hesitantly.*) Was it the . . . colour thing? I know there is some discrimination.

OLUNDE: Don't make it so simple, Mrs Pilkings. You make it 290 sound as if when I left, I took nothing at all with me.

JANE: Yes . . . and to tell the truth, only this evening, Simon and I agreed that we never really knew what you left with.

OLUNDE: Neither did I. But I found out over there. I am grateful to your country for that. And I will never give it up.

JANE: Olunde, please . . . promise me something. Whatever 295 you do, don't throw away what you have started to do. You want to be a doctor. My husband and I believe you will make an excellent one, sympathetic and competent. Don't let anything make you throw away your training.

OLUNDE: (*Genuinely surprised.*) Of course not. What a strange 300 idea. I intend to return and complete my training. Once the burial of my father is over.

JANE: Oh, please . . . !

OLUNDE: Listen! Come outside. You can't hear anything against that music. 305

JANE: What is it?

OLUNDE: The drums. Can you hear the change? Listen.

(*The drums come over, still distant but more distinct. There is a change of rhythm, it rises to a crescendo and then, suddenly, it is cut off. After a silence, a new beat begins, slow and resonant.*)

There. It's all over.

JANE: You mean he's . . .

OLUNDE: Yes Mrs Pilkings, my father is dead. His will-power 310 has always been enormous; I know he is dead.

JANE: (*Screams.*) How can you be so callous! So unfeeling! You announce your father's own death like a surgeon looking down on some strange . . . stranger's body! You're just a savage like all the rest. 315

AIDE-DE-CAMP: (*Rushing out.*) Mrs Pilkings. Mrs Pilkings. (*She breaks down, sobbing.*) Are you alright, Mrs Pilkings?

OLUNDE: She'll be alright. (*Turns to go.*)

AIDE-DE-CAMP: Who are you? And who the hell asked your opinion? 320

OLUNDE: You're quite right, nobody. (*Going.*)

AIDE-DE-CAMP: What the hell! Did you hear me ask you who you were?

OLUNDE: I have business to attend to.

AIDE-DE-CAMP: I'll give you business in a moment you impu-325 dent nigger. Answer my question!

OLUNDE: I have a funeral to arrange. Excuse me. (*Going.*)

AIDE-DE-CAMP: I said stop! Orderly!

JANE: No no, don't do that. I'm alright. And for heaven's sake don't act so foolishly. He's a family friend. 330

AIDE-DE-CAMP: Well he'd better learn to answer civil questions when he's asked them. These natives put a suit on and they get high opinions of themselves.

OLUNDE: Can I go now?

JANE: No no don't go. I must talk to you. I'm sorry about what 335 I said.

OLUNDE: It's nothing Mrs Pilkings. And I'm really anxious to go. I couldn't see my father before, it's forbidden for me, his heir and successor to set eyes on him from the moment of the king's death. But now . . . I would like to touch his 340 body while it is still warm.

JANE: You will. I promise I shan't keep you long. Only, I couldn't possibly let you go like that. Bob, please excuse us.

AIDE-DE-CAMP: If you're sure . . .

JANE: Of course I'm sure. Something happened to upset me 345 just then, but I'm alright now. Really.

(*The* AIDE-DE-CAMP *goes, somewhat reluctantly.*)

OLUNDE: I mustn't stay long.

JANE: Please, I promise not to keep you. It's just that . . . oh you saw yourself what happens to one in this place. The Resident's man thought he was being helpful, that's the way we all react. But I can't go in among that crowd just now and if I stay by myself somebody will come looking for me. Please, just say something for a few moments and then you can go. Just so I can recover myself.

350

355 OLUNDE: What do you want me to say?

JANE: Your calm acceptance for instance, can you explain that? It was so unnatural. I don't understand that at all. I feel a need to understand all I can.

360 OLUNDE: But you explained it yourself. My medical training perhaps. I have seen death too often. And the soldiers who returned from the front, they died on our hands all the time.

JANE: No. It has to be more than that. I feel it has to do with the many things we don't really grasp about your people. At least you can explain.

365

OLUNDE: All these things are part of it. And anyway, my father has been dead in my mind for nearly a month. Ever since I learnt of the King's death. I've lived with my bereavement so long now that I cannot think of him alive. On that journey on the boat, I kept my mind on my duties as the one who must perform the rites over his body. I went through it all again and again in my mind as he himself had taught me. I didn't want to do anything wrong, something which might jeopardise the welfare of my people.

370

375 JANE: But he had disowned you. When you left he swore publicly you were no longer his son.

OLUNDE: I told you, he was a man of tremendous will. Sometimes that's another way of saying stubborn. But among our people, you don't disown a child just like that. Even if I had died before him I would still be buried like his eldest son. But it's time for me to go.

380

JANE: Thank you. I feel calmer. Don't let me keep you from your duties.

OLUNDE: Goodnight Mrs Pilkings.

385 JANE: Welcome home. (*She holds out her hand. As he takes it footsteps are heard approaching the drive. A short while later a woman's sobbing is also heard.*)

PILKINGS: (*Off.*) Keep them here till I get back. (*He strides into view, reacts at the sight of* OLUNDE *but turns to his wife.*)

390 Thank goodness you're still here.

JANE: Simon, what happened?

PILKINGS: Later Jane, please. Is Bob still here?

JANE: Yes, I think so. I'm sure he must be.

PILKINGS: Try and get him out here as quietly as you can. Tell him it's urgent.

395

JANE: Of course. Oh Simon, you remember . . .

PILKINGS: Yes yes. I can see who it is. Get Bob out here. (*She runs off.*) At first I thought I was seeing a ghost.

OLUNDE: Mr Pilkings, I appreciate what you tried to do. I want you to believe that. I can only tell you it would have been a terrible calamity if you'd succeeded.

400

PILKINGS: (*Opens his mouth several times, shuts it.*) You . . . said what?

OLUNDE: A calamity for us, the entire people.

405 PILKINGS: (*Sighs.*) I see. Hm.

OLUNDE: And now I must go. I must see him before he turns cold.

PILKINGS: Oh ah . . . em . . . but this is a shock to see you. I mean er thinking all this while you were in England and thanking God for that.

410

OLUNDE: I came on the mail boat. We travelled in the Prince's convoy.

PILKINGS: Ah yes, a-ah, hm . . . er well . . .

OLUNDE: Goodnight. I can see you are shocked by the whole business. But you must know by now there are things you cannot understand—or help.

415

PILKINGS: Yes. Just a minute. There are armed policemen that way and they have instructions to let no one pass. I suggest you wait a little. I'll er . . . yes, I'll give you an escort.

OLUNDE: That's very kind of you. But do you think it could be quickly arranged.

420

PILKINGS: Of course. In fact, yes, what I'll do is send Bob over with some men to the er . . . place. You can go with them. Here he comes now. Excuse me a minute.

AIDE-DE-CAMP: Anything wrong sir?

425

PILKINGS: (*Takes him to one side.*) Listen Bob, that cellar in the disused annexe of the Residency, you know, where the slaves were stored before being taken down to the coast . . .

AIDE-DE-CAMP: Oh yes, we use it as a storeroom for broken furniture.

430

PILKINGS: But it's still got the bars on it?

AIDE-DE-CAMP: Oh yes, they are quite intact.

PILKINGS: Get the keys please. I'll explain later. And I want a strong guard over the Residency tonight.

AIDE-DE-CAMP: We have that already. The detachment from the coast . . .

435

PILKINGS: No, I don't want them at the gates of the Residency. I want you to deploy them at the bottom of the hill, a long way from the main hall so they can deal with any situation long before the sound carries to the house.

440

AIDE-DE-CAMP: Yes of course.

PILKINGS: I don't want His Highness alarmed.

AIDE-DE-CAMP: You think the riot will spread here?

PILKINGS: It's unlikely but I don't want to take a chance. I made them believe I was going to lock the man up in my house, which was what I had planned to do in the first place. They are probably assailing it by now. I took a roundabout route here so I don't think there is any danger at all. At least not before dawn. Nobody is to leave the premises of course—the native employees I mean. They'll soon smell something is up and they can't keep their mouths shut.

445

450

AIDE-DE-CAMP: I'll give instructions at once.

PILKINGS: I'll take the prisoner down myself. Two policemen will stay with him throughout the night. Inside the cell.

AIDE-DE-CAMP: Right sir. (*Salutes and goes off at the double.*)

455

PILKINGS: Jane. Bob is coming back in a moment with a detachment. Until he gets back please stay with Olunde.

(*He makes an extra warning gesture with his eyes.*)

OLUNDE: Please Mr Pilkings . . .

PILKINGS: I hate to be stuffy old son, but we have a crisis on our hands. It has to do with your father's affair if you must know. And it happens also at a time when we have His Highness here. I am responsible for security so you'll simply have to do as I say. I hope that's understood. (*Marches off quickly, in the direction from which he made his first appearance.*)

460

465   OLUNDE: What's going on? All this can't be just because he
            failed to stop my father killing himself.
        JANE: I honestly don't know. Could it have sparked off a riot?
        OLUNDE: No. If he'd succeeded that would be more likely to
            start the riot. Perhaps there were other factors involved.
470   Was there a chieftancy dispute?
        JANE: None that I know of.
        ELESIN: (*An animal bellow from off.*) Leave me alone! Is it not
            enough that you have covered me in shame! White man,
            take your hand from my body!

        (OLUNDE *stands frozen on the spot.* JANE *understanding at last, tries
        to move him.*)

475   JANE: Let's go in. It's getting chilly out here.
        PILKINGS: (*Off.*) Carry him.
        ELESIN: Give me back the name you have taken away from me
            you ghost from the land of the nameless!
        PILKINGS: Carry him! I can't have a disturbance here. Quickly!
480   stuff up his mouth.
        JANE: Oh God! Let's go in. Please Olunde. (OLUNDE *does not move.*)
        ELESIN: Take your albino's hand from me you . . .

        (*Sounds of a struggle. His voice chokes as he is gagged.*)

        OLUNDE: (*Quietly.*) That was my father's voice.
        JANE: Oh you poor orphan, what have you come home to?

        (*There is a sudden explosion of rage from off-stage and powerful steps
        come running up the drive.*)

485   PILKINGS: You bloody fools, after him!

        (*Immediately* ELESIN, *in handcuffs, comes pounding in the direction of*
        JANE *and* OLUNDE, *followed some moments afterwards by* PILKINGS
        and the constables. ELESIN *confronted by the seeming statue of his son,
        stops dead.* OLUNDE *stares above his head into the distance. The con-
        stables try to grab him.* JANE *screams at them.*)

        JANE: Leave him alone! Simon, tell them to leave him alone.
        PILKINGS: All right, stand aside you. (*Shrugs.*) Maybe just as
            well. It might help to calm him down.

        (*For several moments they hold the same position.* ELESIN *moves a few
        steps forward, almost as if he's still in doubt.*)

        ELESIN: Olunde? (*He moves his head, inspecting him from side to
490   side.*) Olunde! (*He collapses slowly at* OLUNDE'*s feet.*) Oh son,
            don't let the sight of your father turn you blind!
        OLUNDE: (*He moves for the first time since he heard his voice, brings
            his head slowly down to look on him.*) I have no father, eater of
            left-overs.

        (*He walks slowly down the way his father had run. Light fades out
        on* ELESIN, *sobbing into the ground.*)

ACT FIVE

*A wide iron-barred gate stretches almost the whole width of the cell
in which* ELESIN *is imprisoned. His wrists are encased in thick iron
bracelets, chained together; he stands against the bars, looking out.
Seated on the ground to one side on the outside is his recent* BRIDE,
her eyes bent perpetually to the ground. Figures of the two guards

can be seen deeper inside the cell, alert to every movement ELESIN
makes. PILKINGS *now in a police officer's uniform enters noiselessly,
observes him for a while. Then he coughs ostentatiously and approaches. Leans against the bars near a corner, his back to* ELESIN.
*He is obviously trying to fall in mood with him. Some moments'
silence.*

        PILKINGS: You seem fascinated by the moon.
        ELESIN: (*After a pause.*) Yes, ghostly one. Your twin-brother up
            there engages my thoughts.
        PILKINGS: It is a beautiful night.
        ELESIN: Is that so?   5
        PILKINGS: The light on the leaves, the peace of the night . . .
        ELESIN: The night is not at peace, District Officer.
        PILKINGS: No? I would have said it was. You know, quiet . . .
        ELESIN: And does quiet mean peace for you?
        PILKINGS: Well, nearly the same thing. Naturally there is a   10
            subtle difference . . .
        ELESIN: The night is not at peace ghostly one. The world is not
            at peace. You have shattered the peace of the world for ever.
            There is no sleep in the world tonight.
        PILKINGS: It is still a good bargain if the world should lose one   15
            night's sleep as the price of saving a man's life.
        ELESIN: You did not save my life District Officer. You destroyed
            it.
        PILKINGS: Now come on . . .
        ELESIN: And not merely my life but the lives of many. The end   20
            of the night's work is not over. Neither this year nor the
            next will see it. If I wished you well, I would pray that you
            do not stay long enough on our land to see the disaster you
            have brought upon us.
        PILKINGS: Well, I did my duty as I saw it. I have no regrets.   25
        ELESIN: No. The regrets of life always come later.

        (*Some moments' pause.*)

        You are waiting for dawn white man. I hear you saying to
        yourself: only so many hours until dawn and then the danger
        is over. All I must do is keep him alive tonight. You don't
        quite understand it all but you know that tonight is when   30
        what ought to be must be brought about. I shall ease your
        mind even more, ghostly one. It is not an entire night but a
        moment of the night, and that moment is past. The moon
        was my messenger and guide. When it reached a certain
        gateway in the sky, it touched that moment for which my   35
        whole life has been spent in blessings. Even I do not know
        the gateway. I have stood here and scanned the sky for a
        glimpse of that door but, I cannot see it. Human eyes are use-
        less for a search of this nature. But in the house of *osugbo*,
        those who keep watch through the spirit recognised the   40
        moment, they sent word to me through the voice of our sa-
        cred drums to prepare myself. I heard them and I shed all
        thoughts of earth. I began to follow the moon to the abode
        of gods . . . servant of the white king, that was when you
        entered my chosen place of departure on feet of desecration. 45
        PILKINGS: I'm sorry, but we all see our duty differently.
        ELESIN: I no longer blame you. You stole from me my first-
        born, sent him to your country so you could turn him into
        something in your own image. Did you plan it all before-
        hand? There are moments when it seems part of a larger   50

plan. He who must follow my footsteps is taken from me, sent across the ocean. Then, in my turn, I am stopped from fulfilling my destiny. Did you think it all out before, this plan to push our world from its course and sever the cord
55 that links us to the great origin?

PILKINGS: You don't really believe that. Anyway, if that was my intention with your son, I appear to have failed.

ELESIN: You did not fail in the main thing ghostly one. We know the roof covers the rafters, the cloth covers blemishes;
60 who would have known that the white skin covered our future, preventing us from seeing the death our enemies had prepared for us. The world is set adrift and its inhabitants are lost. Around them, there is nothing but emptiness.

PILKINGS: Your son does not take so gloomy a view.

65 ELESIN: Are you dreaming now white man? Were you not present at my reunion of shame? Did you not see when the world reversed itself and the father fell before his son, asking forgiveness?

PILKINGS: That was in the heat of the moment. I spoke to him
70 and … if you want to know, he wishes he could cut out his tongue for uttering the words he did.

ELESIN: No. What he said must never be unsaid. The contempt of my own son rescued something of my shame at your hands. You may have stopped me in my duty but I know
75 now that I did give birth to a son. Once I mistrusted him for seeking the companionship of those my spirit knew as enemies of our race. Now I understand. One should seek to obtain the secrets of his enemies. He will avenge my shame, white one. His spirit will destroy you and yours.

80 PILKINGS: That kind of talk is hardly called for. If you don't want my consolation …

ELESIN: No white man, I do not want your consolation.

PILKINGS: As you wish. Your son anyway, sends his consolation. He asks your forgiveness. When I asked him not to despise
85 you his reply was: I cannot judge him, and if I cannot judge him, I cannot despise him. He wants to come to you to say goodbye and to receive your blessing.

ELESIN: Goodbye? Is he returning to your land?

PILKINGS: Don't you think that's the most sensible thing for
90 him to do? I advised him to leave at once, before dawn, and he agrees that is the right course of action.

ELESIN: Yes, it is best. And even if I did not think so, I have lost the father's place of honour. My voice is broken.

PILKINGS: Your son honours you. If he didn't he would not ask
95 your blessing.

ELESIN: No. Even a thoroughbred is not without pity for the turf he strikes with his hoof. When is he coming?

PILKINGS: As soon as the town is a little quieter. I advised it.

ELESIN: Yes white man, I am sure you advised it. You advise all
100 our lives although on the authority of what gods, I do not know.

PILKINGS: (Opens his mouth to reply, then appears to change his mind. Turns to go. Hesitates and stops again.) Before I leave you, may I ask just one thing of you?

105 ELESIN: I am listening.

PILKINGS: I wish to ask you to search the quiet of your heart and tell me—do you not find great contradictions in the wisdom of your own race?

ELESIN: Make yourself clear, white one.

110 PILKINGS: I have lived among you long enough to learn a saying or two. One came to my mind tonight when I stepped into the market and saw what was going on. You were surrounded by those who egged you on with song and praises. I thought, are these not the same people who say: the elder grimly approaches heaven and you ask him to bear your 115 greetings yonder; do you really think he makes the journey willingly? After that, I did not hesitate.

(A pause. ELESIN sighs. Before he can speak a sound of running feet is heard.)

JANE: (Off.) Simon! Simon!
PILKINGS: What on earth …! (Runs off.)

(ELESIN turns to his new wife, gazes on her for some moments.)

ELESIN: My young bride, did you hear the ghostly one? You sit 120 and sob in your silent heart but say nothing to all this. First I blamed the white man, then I blamed my gods for deserting me. Now I feel I want to blame you for the mystery of the sapping of my will. But blame is a strange peace offering for a man to bring a world he has deeply wronged, and to its 125 innocent dwellers. Oh little mother, I have taken countless women in my life but you were more than a desire of the flesh. I needed you as the abyss across which my body must be drawn, I filled it with earth and dropped my seed in it at the moment of preparedness for my crossing. You 130 were the final gift of the living to their emissary to the land of the ancestors, and perhaps your warmth and youth brought new insights of this world to me and turned my feet leaden on this side of the abyss. For I confess to you, daughter, my weakness came not merely from the abomination of 135 the white man who came violently into my fading presence, there was also a weight of longing on my earth-held limbs. I would have shaken it off, already my foot had begun to lift but then, the white ghost entered and all was defiled.

(Approaching voices of PILKINGS and his wife.)

JANE: Oh Simon, you will let her in won't you?   140
PILKINGS: I really wish you'd stop interfering.

(They come in view. JANE is in a dressing-gown. PILKINGS is holding a note to which he refers from time to time.)

JANE: Good gracious, I didn't initiate this. I was sleeping quietly, or trying to anyway, when the servant brought it. It's not my fault if one can't sleep undisturbed even in the Residency.   145

PILKINGS: He'd have done the same if we were sleeping at home so don't sidetrack the issue. He knows he can get round you or he wouldn't send you the petition in the first place.

JANE: Be fair Simon. After all he was thinking of your own interests. He is grateful you know, you seem to forget that. 150 He feels he owes you something.

PILKINGS: I just wish they'd leave this man alone tonight, that's all.

JANE: Trust him Simon. He's pledged his word it will all go peacefully.   155

PILKINGS: Yes, and that's the other thing. I don't like being threatened.

JANE: Threatened? (Takes the note.) I didn't spot any threat.

PILKINGS: It's there. Veiled, but it's there. The only way to prevent serious rioting tomorrow—what a cheek!   160

JANE: I don't think he's threatening you Simon.

PILKINGS: He's picked up the idiom alright. Wouldn't surprise me if he's been mixing with commies or anarchists over there. The phrasing sounds too good to be true. Damn! If only the Prince hadn't picked this time for his visit.

165

JANE: Well, even so Simon, what have you got to lose? You don't want a riot on your hands, not with the Prince here.

PILKINGS: (*Going up to* ELESIN.) Let's see what he has to say. Chief Elesin, there is yet another person who wants to see you. As she is not a next-of-kin I don't really feel obliged to let her in. But your son sent a note with her, so it's up to you.

170

ELESIN: I know who that must be. So she found out your hiding-place. Well, it was not difficult. My stench of shame is so strong, it requires no hunter's dog to follow it.

175

PILKINGS: If you don't want to see her, just say so and I'll send her packing.

ELESIN: Why should I not want to see her? Let her come. I have no more holes in my rag of shame. All is laid bare.

PILKINGS: I'll bring her in. (*Goes off.*)

180

JANE: (*Hesitates, then goes to* ELESIN.) Please, try and understand. Everything my husband did was for the best.

ELESIN: (*He gives her a long strange stare, as if he is trying to understand who she is.*) You are the wife of the District Officer?

JANE: Yes. My name, is Jane.

185

ELESIN: That is my wife sitting down there. You notice how still and silent she sits? My business is with your husband.

(PILKINGS *returns with* IYALOJA.)

PILKINGS: Here she is. Now first I want your word of honour that you will try nothing foolish.

ELESIN: Honour? White one, did you say you wanted my word of honour?

190

PILKINGS: I know you to be an honourable man. Give me your word of honour you will receive nothing from her.

ELESIN: But I am sure you have searched her clothing as you would never dare touch your own mother. And there are these two lizards of yours who roll their eyes even when I scratch.

195

PILKINGS: And I shall be sitting on that tree trunk watching even how you blink. Just the same I want your word that you will not let her pass anything to you.

200

ELESIN: You have my honour already. It is locked up in that desk in which you will put away your report of this night's events. Even the honour of my people you have taken already; it is tied together with those papers of treachery which make you masters in this land.

205

PILKINGS: Alright. I am trying to make things easy but if you must bring in politics we'll have to do it the hard way. Madam, I want you to remain along this line and move no nearer to that cell door. Guards! (*They spring to attention.*) If she moves beyond this point, blow your whistle. Come on Jane. (*They go off.*)

210

IYALOJA: How boldly the lizard struts before the pigeon when it was the eagle itself he promised us he would confront.

ELESIN: I don't ask you to take pity on me Iyaloja. You have a message for me or you would not have come. Even if it is the curses of the world, I shall listen.

215

IYALOJA: You made so bold with the servant of the white king who took your side against death. I must tell your brother chiefs when I return how bravely you waged war against him. Especially with words.

ELESIN: I more than deserve your scorn.

220

IYALOJA: (*With sudden anger.*) I warned you, if you must leave a seed behind, be sure it is not tainted with the curses of the world. Who are you to open a new life when you dared not open the door to a new existence? I say who are you to make so bold? (*The* BRIDE *sobs and* IYALOJA *notices her. Her contempt noticeably increases as she turns back to* ELESIN.) Oh you self-vaunted stem of the plantain, how hollow it all proves. The pith is gone in the parent stem, so how will it prove with the new shoot? How will it go with that earth that bears it? Who are you to bring this abomination on us!

225

230

ELESIN: My powers deserted me. My charms, my spells, even my voice lacked strength when I made to summon the powers that would lead me over the last measure of earth into the land of the fleshless. You saw it, Iyaloja. You saw me struggle to retrieve my will from the power of the stranger whose shadow fell across the doorway and left me floundering and blundering in a maze I had never before encountered. My senses were numbed when the touch of cold iron came upon my wrists. I could do nothing to save myself.

235

IYALOJA: You have betrayed us. We fed you sweetmeats such as we hoped awaited you on the other side. But you said No, I must eat the world's left-overs. We said you were the hunter who brought the quarry down; to you belonged the vital portions of the game. No, you said, I am the hunter's dog and I shall eat the entrails of the game and the faeces of the hunter. We said you were the hunter returning home in triumph, a slain buffalo pressing down on his neck, you said wait, I first must turn up this cricket hole with my toes. We said yours was the doorway at which we first spy the tapper when he comes down from the tree, yours was the blessing of the twilight wine, the purl that brings night spirits out of doors to steal their portion before the light of day. We said yours was the body of wine whose burden shakes the tapper like a sudden gust on his perch. You said, No, I am content to lick the dregs from each calabash when the drinkers are done. We said, the dew on earth's surface was for you to wash your feet along the slopes of honour. You said No, I shall step in the vomit of cats and the droppings of mice; I shall fight them for the left-overs of the world.

240

245

250

255

ELESIN: Enough Iyaloja, enough.

260

IYALOJA: We called you leader and oh, how you led us on. What we have no intention of eating should not be held to the nose.

ELESIN: Enough, enough. My shame is heavy enough.

IYALOJA: Wait. I came with a burden.

ELESIN: You have more than discharged it.

265

IYALOJA: I wish I could pity you.

ELESIN: I need neither your pity nor the pity of the world. I need understanding. Even I need to understand. You were present at my defeat. You were part of the beginnings. You brought about the renewal of my tie to earth, you helped in the binding of the cord.

270

IYALOJA: I gave you warning. The river which fills up before our eyes does not sweep us away in its flood.

ELESIN: What were warnings beside the moist contact of living earth between my fingers? What were warnings beside the renewal of famished embers lodged eternally in the heart of man. But even that, even if it overwhelmed one with a thousandfold temptations to linger a little while, a man could overcome it. It is when the alien hand pollutes the source of will, when a stranger force of violence shatters the

275

280

mind's calm resolution, this is when a man is made to commit the awful treachery of relief, commit in his thought the unspeakable blasphemy of seeing the hand of the gods in this alien rupture of his world. I know it was this thought

285   that killed me, sapped my powers and turned me into an infant in the hands of unnamable strangers. I made to utter my spells anew but my tongue merely rattled in my mouth. I fingered hidden charms and the contact was damp; there was no spark left to sever the life-strings that should stretch

290   from every finger-tip. My will was squelched in the spittle of an alien race, and all because I had committed this blasphemy of thought—that there might be the hand of the gods in a stranger's intervention.

IYALOJA: Explain it how you will, I hope it brings you peace of

295   mind. The bush-rat fled his rightful cause, reached the market and set up a lamentation. 'Please save me!'—are these fitting words to hear from an ancestral mask? 'There's a wild beast at my heels' is not becoming language from a hunter.

300   ELESIN: May the world forgive me.

IYALOJA: I came with a burden I said. It approaches the gates which are so well guarded by those jackals whose spittle will from this day on be your food and drink. But first, tell me, you who were once Elesin Oba, tell me, you who know

305   so well the cycle of the plantain: is it the parent shoot which withers to give sap to the younger or, does your wisdom see it running the other way?

ELESIN: I don't see your meaning Iyaloja?

IYALOJA: Did I ask you for a meaning? I asked a question.

310   Whose trunk withers to give sap to the other? The parent shoot or the younger?

ELESIN: The parent.

IYALOJA: Ah. So you do know that. There are sights in this world which say different Elesin. There are some who

315   choose to reverse this cycle of our being. Oh you emptied bark that the world once saluted for a pith-laden being, shall I tell you what the gods have claimed of you?

(*In her agitation she steps beyond the line indicated by* PILKINGS *and the air is rent by piercing whistles. The two* GUARDS *also leap forward and place safe-guarding hands on* ELESIN. IYALOJA *stops, astonished.* PILKINGS *comes racing, followed by* JANE.)

PILKINGS: What is it? Did they try something?

GUARD: She stepped beyond the line.

320   ELESIN: (*In a broken voice.*) Let her alone. She meant no harm.

IYALOJA: Oh Elesin, see what you've become. Once you had no need to open your mouth in explanation because evil-smelling goats, itchy of hand and foot had lost their senses. And it was a brave man indeed who dared lay hands on you

325   because Iyaloja stepped from one side of the earth onto another. Now look at the spectacle of your life. I grieve for you.

PILKINGS: I think you'd better leave. I doubt you have done him much good by coming here. I shall make sure you are not

330   allowed to see him again. In any case we are moving him to a different place before dawn, so don't bother to come back.

IYALOJA: We foresaw that. Hence the burden I trudged here to lay beside your gates.

PILKINGS: What was that you said?

IYALOJA: Didn't our son explain? Ask that one. He knows what   335 it is. At least we hope the man we once knew as Elesin remembers the lesser oaths he need not break.

PILKINGS: Do you know what she is talking about?

ELESIN: Go to the gates, ghostly one. Whatever you find there,   340 bring it to me.

IYALOJA: Not yet. It drags behind me on the slow, weary feet of women. Slow as it is Elesin, it has long overtaken you. It rides ahead of your laggard will.

PILKINGS: What is she saying now? Christ! Must your people   345 forever speak in riddles?

ELESIN: It will come white man, it will come. Tell your men at the gates to let it through.

PILKINGS: (*Dubiously.*) I'll have to see what it is.

IYALOJA: You will. (*Passionately.*) But this is one oath he cannot   350 shirk. White one, you have a king here, a visitor from your land. We know of his presence here. Tell me, were he to die would you leave his spirit roaming restlessly on the surface of earth? Would you bury him here among those you consider less than human? In your land have you no ceremonies   355 of the dead?

PILKINGS: Yes. But we don't make our chiefs commit suicide to keep him company.

IYALOJA: Child, I have not come to help your understanding. (*Points to* ELESIN.) This is the man whose weakened understanding holds us in bondage to you. But ask him if you   360 wish. He knows the meaning of a king's passage; he was not born yesterday. He knows the peril to the race when our dead father, who goes as intermediary, waits and waits and knows he is betrayed. He knows when the narrow gate was opened and he knows it will not stay for laggards who drag   365 their feet in dung and vomit, whose lips are reeking of the left-overs of lesser men. He knows he has condemned our king to wander in the void of evil with beings who are enemies of life.

PILKINGS: Yes er … but look here …   370

IYALOJA: What we ask is little enough. Let him release our King so he can ride on homewards alone. The messenger is on his way on the backs of women. Let him send word through the heart that is folded up within the bolt. It is the least of all his oaths, it is the easiest fulfilled.   375

(*The* AIDE-DE-CAMP *runs in.*)

PILKINGS: Bob?

AIDE-DE-CAMP: Sir, there's a group of women chanting up the hill.

PILKINGS: (*Rounding on* IYALOJA.) If you people want trouble …

JANE: Simon, I think that's what Olunde referred to in his letter.   380

PILKINGS: He knows damned well I can't have a crowd here! Damn it, I explained the delicacy of my position to him. I think it's about time I got him out of town. Bob, send a car and two or three soldiers to bring him in. I think the sooner he takes his leave of his father and gets out the better.   385

IYALOJA: Save your labour white one. If it is the father of your prisoner you want, Olunde, he who until this night we knew as Elesin's son, he comes soon himself to take his leave. He has sent the women ahead, so let them in.

(PILKINGS *remains undecided.*)

390   AIDE-DE-CAMP: What do we do about the invasion? We can still stop them far from here.

PILKINGS: What do they look like?

AIDE-DE-CAMP: They're not many. And they seem quite peaceful.

PILKINGS: No men?

395   AIDE-DE-CAMP: Mm, two or three at the most.

JANE: Honestly, Simon, I'd trust Olunde. I don't think he'll deceive you about their intentions.

PILKINGS: He'd better not. Alright, let them in Bob. Warn them to control themselves. Then hurry Olunde here.

400   Make sure he brings his baggage because I'm not returning him into town.

AIDE-DE-CAMP: Very good sir. (*Goes.*)

PILKINGS: (*To* IYALOJA.) I hope you understand that if anything goes wrong it will be on your head. My men have orders to

405   shoot at the first sign of trouble.

IYALOJA: To prevent one death you will actually make other deaths? Ah, great is the wisdom of the white race. But have no fear. Your Prince will sleep peacefully. So at long last will ours. We will disturb you no further, servant of the white

410   king. Just let Elesin fulfil his oath and we will retire home and pay homage to our King.

JANE: I believe her Simon, don't you?

PILKINGS: Maybe.

ELESIN: Have no fear ghostly one. I have a message to send my

415   King and then you have nothing more to fear.

IYALOJA: Olunde would have done it. The chiefs asked him to speak the words but he said no, not while you lived.

ELESIN: Even from the depths to which my spirit has sunk, I find some joy that this little has been left to me.

(*The* WOMEN *enter, intoning the dirge 'Alẹ lẹ lẹ' and swaying from side to side. On their shoulders is borne a longish object roughly like a cylindrical bolt, covered in cloth. They set it down on the spot where* IYALOJA *had stood earlier, and form a semicircle round it. The* PRAISE-SINGER *and* DRUMMER *stand on the inside of the semicircle but the drum is not used at all. The* DRUMMER *intones under the* PRAISE-SINGER'*s invocations.*)

420   PILKINGS: (*As they enter.*) What is that?

IYALOJA: The burden you have made white one, but we bring it in peace.

PILKINGS: I said *what* is it?

ELESIN: White man, you must let me out. I have a duty to per-

425   form.

PILKINGS: I most certainly will not.

ELESIN: There lies the courier of my King. Let me out so I can perform what is demanded of me.

PILKINGS: You'll do what you need to do from inside there or

430   not at all. I've gone as far as I intend to with this business.

ELESIN: The worshipper who lights a candle in your church to bear a message to his god bows his head and speaks in a whisper to the flame. Have I not seen it ghostly one? His voice does not ring out to the world. Mine are no words for any-

435   one's ears. They are not words even for the bearers of this load. They are words I must speak secretly, even as my father whispered them in my ears and I in the ears of my first-born. I cannot shout them to the wind and the open night-sky.

JANE: Simon ...

440   PILKINGS: Don't interfere. Please!

IYALOJA: They have slain the favourite horse of the king and slain his dog. They have borne them from pulse to pulse centre of the land receiving prayers for their king. But the rider has chosen to stay behind. Is it too much to ask that he speak his heart to heart of the waiting courier? (PILKINGS *turns his back*   445   *on her.*) So be it. Elesin Oba, you see how even the mere leavings are denied you. (*She gestures to the* PRAISE-SINGER.)

PRAISE-SINGER: Elesin Oba! I call you by that name only this last time. Remember when I said, if you cannot come, tell my horse. (*Pause.*) What? I cannot hear you? I said, if you   450   can-not come, whisper in the ears of my horse. Is your tongue severed from the roots Elesin? I can hear no response. I said, if there are boulders you cannot climb, mount my horse's back, this spotless black stallion, he'll bring you over them. (*Pauses.*) Elesin Oba, once you had a tongue that   455   darted like a drummer's stick. I said, if you get lost my dog will track a path to me. My memory fails me but I think you replied: My feet have found the path, Alafin.

(*The dirge rises and falls.*)

I said at the last, if evil hands hold you back, just tell my horse there is weight on the hem of your smock. I dare not   460   wait too long.

(*The dirge rises and falls.*)

There lies the swiftest ever messenger of a king, so set me free with the errand of your heart. There lie the head and heart of the favourite of the gods, whisper in his ears. Oh my companion, if you had followed when you should, we would   465   not say that the horse preceded its rider. If you had followed when it was time, we would not say the dog has raced beyond and left his master behind. If you had raised your will to cut the thread of life at the summons of the drums, we would not say your mere shadow fell across the gateway and took its   470   owner's place at the banquet. But the hunter, laden with a slain buffalo, stayed to root in the cricket's hole with his toes. What now is left? If there is a dearth of bats, the pigeon must serve us for the offering. Speak the words over your shadow which must now serve in your place.   475

ELESIN: I cannot approach. Take off the cloth. I shall speak my message from heart to heart of silence.

IYALOJA: (*Moves forward and removes the coverings.*) Your courier Elesin, cast your eyes on the favoured companion of the King.

(*Rolled up in the mat, his head and feet showing at either end is the body of* OLUNDE.)

There lies the honour of your household and of our race.   480   Because he could not bear to let honour fly out of doors, he stopped it with his life. The son has proved the father Elesin, and there is nothing left in your mouth to gnash but infant gums.

PRAISE-SINGER: Elesin, we placed the reins of the world in your   485   hands yet you watched it plunge over the edge of the bitter precipice. You sat with folded arms while evil strangers tilted the world from its course and crashed it beyond the edge of emptiness—you muttered, there is little that one man can do, you left us floundering in a blind future. Your   490   heir has taken the burden on himself. What the end will be, we are not gods to tell. But this young shoot has poured its sap into the parent stalk, and we know this is not the way of life. Our world is tumbling in the void of strangers, Elesin.

(ELESIN *has stood rock-still, his knuckles taut on the bars, his eyes glued to the body of his son. The stillness seizes and paralyses everyone, including* PILKINGS *who has turned to look. Suddenly* ELESIN *flings one arm round his neck, once, and with the loop of the chain, strangles himself in a swift, decisive pull. The guards rush forward to stop him but they are only in time to let his body down.* PILKINGS *has leapt to the door at the same time and struggles with the lock. He rushes within, fumbles with the handcuffs and unlocks them, raises the body to a sitting position while he tries to give resuscitation. The* WOMEN *continue their dirge, unmoved by the sudden event.*)

495 IYALOJA: Why do you strain yourself? Why do you labour at tasks for which no one, not even the man lying there would give you thanks? He is gone at last into the passage but oh, how late it all is. His son will feast on the meat and throw him bones. The passage is clogged with droppings from the

500 King's stallion; he will arrive all stained in dung.

PILKINGS: (*In a tired voice.*) Was this what you wanted?

IYALOJA: No child, it is what you brought to be, you who play with strangers' lives, who even usurp the vestments of our dead, yet believe that the stain of death will not cling to

505 you. The gods demanded only the old expired plantain but you cut down the sap-laden shoot to feed your pride. There is your board, filled to overflowing. Feast on it. (*She screams at him suddenly, seeing that* PILKINGS *is about to close* ELESIN's *staring eyes.*) Let him alone! However sunk he was in debt he is no pauper's carrion abandoned on the road. Since when

510 have strangers donned clothes of indigo before the bereaved cries out his loss?

(*She turns to the* BRIDE *who has remained motionless throughout.*)

Child.

(*The girl takes up a little earth, walks calmly into the cell and closes* ELESIN's *eyes. She then pours some earth over each eyelid and comes out again.*)

Now forget the dead, forget even the living. Turn your mind only to the unborn. 515

(*She goes off, accompanied by the* BRIDE. *The dirge rises in volume and the* WOMEN *continue their sway. Lights fade to a black-out.*)

GLOSSARY

alari, a rich, woven cloth, brightly coloured

egungun, ancestral masquerade

etutu, placatory rites or medicine

gbedu, a deep-timbred royal drum

opele, string of beads used in Ifa divination

osugbo, secret 'executive' cult of the Yoruba; its meeting place

robo, a delicacy made from crushed melon seeds, fried in tiny balls

sanyan, a richly valued woven cloth

sigidi, a squat, carved figure, endowed with the powers of an incubus

Brian Friel

Brian Friel (b. 1929) is perhaps the most prominent living Irish playwright, the heir of Ireland's brilliant modern dramatic tradition, the tradition of William Butler Yeats, John Millington Synge, and Sean O'Casey. Unlike these predecessors, who worked for the independence of the Republic of Ireland, Friel works in Northern Ireland, still a part of the United Kingdom. Educated in Derry and Belfast, Friel's concerns as a playwright have spanned the "troubles" of Northern Ireland, the poverty and depression of Derry in the 1930s, 1940s, and 1950s, and the installation of a British military presence and the open street warfare of the 1960s, 1970s, and 1980s. From his earliest success, *Philadelphia, Here I Come!* (1964), about a man's divided feelings concerning his emigration to the United States, Friel's drama has centered on the problems of Irish identity in the face of British rule. Many of his early plays and stories—*The Loves of Cass McGuire* (1966), *The Lovers* (1967)— are portraits of Irish life in the manner of Synge, and Friel's dramatization of the personal consequences of contemporary Irish life remains a prominent feature of fine plays like *Living Quarters* (1977) and *Faith Healer* (1979). However, Friel's drama has increasingly become more satirical—in *The Mundy Scheme* (1969) and *The Gentle Island* (1971)—and more politically concerned. In *The Freedom of the City* (1973), Friel dramatizes the fate of three people caught and killed by British soldiers in the 1972 "Bloody Sunday" riots in Derry. In *Volunteers* (1975), a crew of political prisoners are forced to work on an archaeological site, recovering the history of Celtic Ireland even as they are oppressed by British rule. In *Making History* (1988), Friel returns to the origins of Ireland's subjection to the British in the seventeenth and eighteenth centuries. In 1980, Friel and Stephen Rea founded the Field Day Theatre Company in Derry, and its first production was the play generally taken to be

The 1993 Donmar Warehouse production of Brian Friel's *Translations*.

Friel's masterpiece, *Translations*. Friel's more recent plays include *Dancing at Lughnasa* (1990), *Wonderful Tennessee* (1992), and *Give Me Your Answer, Do!* (1997). Friel has also adapted several plays—Turgenev's *A Month in the Country* (1992) and *London Vertigo*, by the eighteenth-century actor Charles Macklin (1992)—and has specialized in adapting Chekhov's drama to Irish English, in versions of *Three Sisters* (2001) and *Uncle Vanya* (1995).

TRANSLATIONS

Translations is set in early nineteenth-century Ireland and concerns the mapping—both actual and cultural—of Ireland by the British. The play takes place at a local hedge-school, a subscription school run by a local master and attended by a variety of children and adults. This Ireland is already threatened by the British culture to the east: a national school—where, presumably, English will be the required language—is about to open, and the British army surveyors have arrived to map the region, part of the 1833 Ordnance Survey of Ireland.

The play's politics are largely conveyed through the politics of language. Jimmy's Homeric Greek, for example, draws a parallel between Ireland and another lost civilization. The romance between Yolland and Maire bridges the barrier of language. They learn to communicate across this barrier, while the British army works to tear it down and destroy Irish cultural identity in the process. In mapping Ireland, the British convert local place names into English, either by translating them directly or by inventing some equivalent. As the relationship between the Irish Owen and his British officers makes clear, English is the language of power; to map the landscape with English names is a figure for rewriting Ireland and its culture into submission and, finally, into nonexistence.

Although *Translations* may seem only indirectly about contemporary Irish politics, it dramatizes a struggle for national and cultural identity that continues to embroil Northern Ireland today. Throughout the play, for example, the mysterious and unseen Donnelly twins move around the edges of the action, guerrillas hindering the British progress through the country. Finally, when Yolland is missing, we learn the true consequences of the British mapping of Ireland. Mapping the land in English is the prelude to its occupation, as the army systematically destroys the village and countryside that they have made their own. At the play's close, we scent the sickly sweet smell of blighted potatoes, the sign of the impending famine that would weaken and disperse rural Ireland.

TRANSLATIONS
Brian Friel

CHARACTERS

MANUS   BRIDGET
SARAH   HUGH
JIMMY JACK   OWEN
MAIRE   CAPTAIN LANCEY
DOALTY   LIEUTENANT YOLLAND

Act I   An afternoon in late August 1833.
Act II   A few days later.
Act III   The evening of the following day.
One interval—between the two scenes in Act Two.

The action takes place in a hedge-school in the townland of Baile Beag/Ballybeg, an Irish-speaking community in County Donegal.

ACT ONE

The hedge-school is held in a disused barn or hay-shed or byre. Along the back wall are the remains of five or six stalls—wooden posts and chains—where cows were once milked and bedded. A double door left, large enough to allow a cart to enter. A window right. A wooden stair-way without a banister leads to the upstairs living-quarters (off) of the schoolmaster and his son. Around the room are broken and forgot-ten implements: a cart-wheel, some lobster-pots, farming tools, a battle of hay, a churn, etc. There are also the stools and bench-seats which the pupils use and a table and chair for the master. At the door a pail of water and a soiled towel. The room is comfortless and dusty and func-tional—there is no trace of a woman's hand.

When the play opens, MANUS *is teaching* SARAH *to speak. He kneels beside her. She is sitting on a low stool, her head down, very tense, clutching a slate on her knees. He is coaxing her gently and firmly and—as with everything he does—with a kind of zeal.*

MANUS *is in his late twenties/early thirties; the master's older son. He is pale-faced, lightly built, intense, and works as an unpaid assis-tant—a monitor—to his father. His clothes are shabby; and when he moves we see that he is lame.*

SARAH's *speech defect is so bad that all her life she has been considered locally to be dumb and she has accepted this: when she wishes to com-municate, she grunts and makes unintelligible nasal sounds. She has a waiflike appearance and could be any age from seventeen to thirty-five.*

JIMMY JACK CASSIE—*known as the Infant Prodigy—sits by himself, contentedly reading Homer in Greek and smiling to himself. He is a bachelor in his sixties, lives alone, and comes to these evening classes partly for the company and partly for the intellectual stimulation. He is fluent in Latin and Greek but is in no way pedantic—to him it is perfectly normal to speak these tongues. He never washes. His clothes—heavy top coat, hat, mittens, which he wears now—are filthy and he lives in them summer and winter, day and night. He now reads in a quiet voice and smiles in profound satisfaction. For* JIMMY *the world of the gods and the ancient myths is as real and as immediate as everyday life in the townland of Baile Beag.*

MANUS *holds* SARAH's *hands in his and he articulates slowly and dis-tinctly into her face.*

MANUS: We're doing very well. And we're going to try it once more—just once more. Now—relax and breathe in . . . deep . . . and out . . . in . . . and out . . .

*(*SARAH *shakes her head vigorously and stubbornly.)*

MANUS: Come on, Sarah. This is our secret.

(Again vigorous and stubborn shaking of SARAH's *head.)*

MANUS: Nobody's listening. Nobody hears you.   5
JIMMY: '*Ton d'emeibet epeita thea glaukopis Athene . . .*'
MANUS: Get your tongue and your lips working. 'My name—' Come on. One more try. 'My name is—' Good girl.
SARAH: My . . .
MANUS: Great. 'My name—'   10
SARAH: My . . . my . . .
MANUS: Raise your head. Shout it out. Nobody's listening.
JIMMY: '. . . *alla hekelos estai en Atreidao domois . . .*'
MANUS: Jimmy, please! Once more—just once more—'My name—' Good girl. Come on now. Head up. Mouth open.   15
SARAH: My . . .
MANUS: Good.
SARAH: My . . .
MANUS: Great.
SARAH: My name . . .   20
MANUS: Yes?
SARAH: My name is . . .
MANUS: Yes?

*(*SARAH *pauses. Then in a rush.)*

SARAH: My name is Sarah.
MANUS: Marvellous! Bloody marvellous!   25

*(*MANUS *hugs* SARAH. *She smiles in shy, embarrassed pleasure.)*

Did you hear that, Jimmy?—'My name is Sarah'—clear as a bell. (*To* SARAH.) The Infant Prodigy doesn't know what we're at. (SARAH *laughs at this.* MANUS *hugs her again and stands up.)* Now we're really started! Nothing'll stop us now! Nothing in the wide world!   30

I. 6 **Ton . . . Athene** But the grey-eyed goddess Athene then replied to him (from Homer, *Odyssey*, 13.420)   13 **alla . . . domois** . . . but he sits at ease in the halls of the Sons of Athens . . . (from Homer, *Odyssey*, 13.423–24)

(JIMMY, *chuckling at his text, comes over to them.*)

JIMMY: Listen to this, Manus.

MANUS: Soon you'll be telling me all the secrets that have been in that head of yours all these years. Certainly, James—what is it? (*To* SARAH.) Maybe you'd set out the stools?

(MANUS *runs up the stairs.*)

35   JIMMY: Wait till you hear this, Manus.

MANUS: Go ahead. I'll be straight down.

JIMMY: '*Hos ara min phamene rabdo epemassat Athene*—' 'After Athene had said this, she touched Ulysses with her wand. She withered the fair skin of his supple limbs and destroyed
40   the flaxen hair from off his head and about his limbs she put the skin of an old man . . .'! The divil! The divil!

(MANUS *has emerged again with a bowl of milk and a piece of bread.*)

JIMMY: And wait till you hear! She's not finished with him yet!

(*As* MANUS *descends the stairs he toasts* SARAH *with his bowl.*)

JIMMY: '*Knuzosen de oi osse*—' 'She dimmed his two eyes that were so beautiful and clothed him in a vile ragged cloak be-
45   grimed with filthy smoke . . .'! D'you see! Smoke! Smoke! D'you see! Sure look at what the same turf-smoke has done to myself! (*He rapidly removes his hat to display his bald head.*) Would you call that flaxen hair?

MANUS: Of course I would.

50   JIMMY: 'And about him she cast the great skin of a filthy hind, stripped of the hair, and into his hand she thrust a staff and a wallet'! Ha-ha-ha! Athene did that to Ulysses! Made him into a tramp! Isn't she the tight one?

MANUS: You couldn't watch her, Jimmy.

55   JIMMY: You know what they call her?

MANUS: '*Glaukopis Athene.*'

JIMMY: That's it! The flashing-eyed Athene! By God, Manus, sir, if you had a woman like that about the house, it's not stripping a turf-bank you'd be thinking about—eh?

60   MANUS: She was a goddess, Jimmy.

JIMMY: Better still. Sure isn't our own Grania a class of a goddess and—

MANUS: Who?

JIMMY: Grania—Grania—Diarmuid's Grania.

65   MANUS: Ah.

JIMMY: And sure she can't get her fill of men.

MANUS: Jimmy, you're impossible.

JIMMY: I was just thinking to myself last night: if you had the choosing between Athene and Artemis and Helen of
70   Troy—all three of them Zeus's girls—imagine three powerful-looking daughters like that all in the one parish of Athens!—now, if you had the picking between them, which would you take?

MANUS: (*To* SARAH.) Which should I take, Sarah?

JIMMY: No harm to Helen; and no harm to Artemis; and indeed   75
no harm to our own Grania, Manus. But I think I've no choice but to go bull-straight for Athene. By God, sir, them flashing eyes would fair keep a man jigged up constant!

(*Suddenly and momentarily, as if in spasm,* JIMMY *stands to attention and salutes, his face raised in pained ecstasy.* MANUS *laughs. So does* SARAH. JIMMY *goes back to his seat, and his reading.*)

MANUS: You're a dangerous bloody man, Jimmy Jack.

JIMMY: 'Flashing-eyed'! Hah! Sure Homer knows it all, boy.   80
Homer knows it all.

(MANUS *goes to the window and looks out.*)

MANUS: Where the hell has he got to?

(SARAH *goes to* MANUS *and touches his elbow. She mimes rocking a baby.*)

MANUS: Yes, I know he's at the christening; but it doesn't take them all day to put a name on a baby, does it?

(SARAH *mimes pouring drinks and tossing them back quickly.*)

MANUS: You may be sure. Which pub?   85

(SARAH *indicates.*)

MANUS: Gracie's?

(*No. Further away.*)

MANUS: Con Connie Tim's?

(*No. To the right of there.*)

MANUS: Anna na mBreag's?

(*Yes. That's it.*)

MANUS: Great. She'll fill him up. I suppose I may take the class
then.   90

(MANUS *begins to distribute some books, slates and chalk, texts, etc., beside the seats.* SARAH *goes over to the straw and produces a bunch of flowers she has hidden there. During this:*)

JIMMY: '*Autar o ek limenos prosebe*—' 'But Ulysses went forth from the harbour and through the woodland to the place where Athene had shown him he could find the good swineherd who—'*o oi biotoio malista kedeto*'—what's that, Manus?

MANUS: 'Who cared most for his substance.'   95

JIMMY: That's it! 'The good swineherd who cared most for his substance above all the slaves that Ulysses possessed . . .'

---

37 **Hos . . . Athene** as she spoke Athene touched him with her wand (from Homer, *Odyssey*, 13.429)   43 **Knuzosen . . . osse** she dimmed his eyes (from Homer, *Odyssey*, 13.433)   56 **Glaukopis Athene** flashing-eyed Athene

91 **Autar . . . prosebe** but he went forth from the harbour (from Homer, *Odyssey*, 14.1)   94 **o . . . kedeto** he cared very much for his substance (from Homer, *Odyssey*, 14.3–4)

(SARAH *presents the flowers to* MANUS.)

MANUS: Those are lovely, Sarah.

(*But* SARAH *has fled in embarrassment to her seat and has her head buried in a book.* MANUS *goes to her.*)

MANUS: Flow-ers.

(*Pause.* SARAH *does not look up.*)

100 MANUS: Say the word: flow-ers. Come on—flow-ers.
SARAH: Flowers.
MANUS: You see?—you're off!

(MANUS *leans down and kisses the top of* SARAH's *head.*)

MANUS: And they're beautiful flowers. Thank you.

(MAIRE *enters, a strong-minded, strong-bodied woman in her twenties with a head of curly hair. She is carrying a small can of milk.*)

MAIRE: Is this all's here? Is there no school this evening?
105 MANUS: If my father's not back, I'll take it.

(MANUS *stands awkwardly, having been caught kissing* SARAH *and with the flowers almost formally at his chest.*)

MAIRE: Well now, isn't that a pretty sight. There's your milk. How's Sarah?

(SARAH *grunts a reply.*)

MANUS: I saw you out at the hay.

(MAIRE *ignores this and goes to* JIMMY.)

MAIRE: And how's Jimmy Jack Cassie?
110 JIMMY: Sit down beside me, Maire.
MAIRE: Would I be safe?
JIMMY: No safer man in Donegal.

(MAIRE *flops on a stool beside* JIMMY.)

MAIRE: Ooooh. The best harvest in living memory, they say; but I don't want to see another like it. (*Showing* JIMMY *her*
115 *hands.*) Look at the blisters.
JIMMY: *Esne fatigata?*
MAIRE: *Sum fatigatissima.*
JIMMY: *Bene! Optime!*
MAIRE: That's the height of my Latin. Fit me better if I had
120 even that much English.
JIMMY: English? I thought you had some English?
MAIRE: Three words. Wait—there was a spake I used to have off by heart. What's this it was? (*Her accent is strange because she is speaking a foreign language and because she does not understand*
125 *what she is saying.*) 'In Norfolk we besport ourselves around the maypoll.' What about that!

---

116 **Esne fatigata?** are you tired?   117 **Sum fatigatissima** I am very tired   118 **Bene! Optime!** good! Excellent!

MANUS: Maypole.

(*Again* MAIRE *ignores* MANUS.)

MAIRE: God have mercy on my Aunt Mary—she taught me that when I was about four, whatever it means. Do you know what it means, Jimmy? 130
JIMMY: Sure you know I have only Irish like yourself.
MAIRE: And Latin. And Greek.
JIMMY: I'm telling you a lie: I know one English word.
MAIRE: What?
JIMMY: Bo-som. 135
MAIRE: What's a bo-som?
JIMMY: You know—(*He illustrates with his hands.*)—bo-som—bo-som—you know—Diana, the huntress, she has two powerful bosom.
MAIRE: You may be sure that's the one English word you would 140 know. (*Rises.*) Is there a drop of water about?

(MANUS *gives* MAIRE *his bowl of milk.*)

MANUS: I'm sorry I couldn't get up last night.
MAIRE: Doesn't matter.
MANUS: Biddy Hanna sent for me to write a letter to her sister in Nova Scotia. All the gossip of the parish. 'I brought the 145 cow to the bull three times last week but no good. There's nothing for it now but Big Ned Frank.'
MAIRE: (*Drinking.*) That's better.
MANUS: And she got so engrossed in it that she forgot who she was dictating to: 'The aul drunken schoolmaster and that 150 lame son of his are still footering about in the hedge-school, wasting people's good time and money.'

(MAIRE *has to laugh at this.*)

MAIRE: She did not!
MANUS: And me taking it all down. 'Thank God one of them new national schools is being built above at Poll na 155 gCaorach.' It was after midnight by the time I got back.
MAIRE: Great to be a busy man.

(MAIRE *moves away.* MANUS *follows.*)

MANUS: I could hear music on my way past but I thought it was too late to call.
MAIRE: (*To* SARAH.) Wasn't your father in great voice last night? 160

(SARAH *nods and smiles.*)

MAIRE: It must have been near three o'clock by the time you got home?

(SARAH *holds up four fingers.*)

MAIRE: Was it four? No wonder we're in pieces.
MANUS: I can give you a hand at the hay tomorrow.
MAIRE: That's the name of a hornpipe, isn't it?—'The Scholar 165 In The Hayfield'—or is it a reel?
MANUS: If the day's good.
MAIRE: Suit yourself. The English soldiers below in the tents, them sapper fellas, they're coming up to give us a hand. I don't know a word they're saying, nor they me; but sure 170 that doesn't matter, does it?

MANUS: What the hell are you so crabbed about?!

(DOALTY *and* BRIDGET *enter noisily. Both are in their twenties.* DOALTY *is brandishing a surveyor's pole. He is an open-minded, open-hearted, generous and slightly thick young man.* BRIDGET *is a plump, fresh young girl, ready to laugh, vain, and with a countrywoman's instinctive cunning.* DOALTY *enters doing his imitation of the master.*)

DOALTY: Vesperal salutations to you all.

BRIDGET: He's coming down past Carraig na Ri and he's as full
175   as a pig!

DOALTY: *Ignari, stulti, rustici*—pot-boys and peasant whelps—semi-literates and illegitimates.

BRIDGET: He's been on the batter since this morning; he sent the wee ones home at eleven o'clock.

180 DOALTY: Three questions. Question A—Am I drunk? Question B—Am I sober? (*Into* MAIRE'S *face.*) *Responde—responde!*

BRIDGET: Question C, Master—When were you last sober?

MAIRE: What's the weapon, Doalty?

BRIDGET: I warned him. He'll be arrested one of these days.

185 DOALTY: Up in the bog with Bridget and her aul fella, and the Red Coats were just across at the foot of Croc na Mona, dragging them aul chains and peeping through that big machine they lug about everywhere with them—you know the name of it, Manus?

190 MAIRE: Theodolite.

BRIDGET: How do you know?

MAIRE: They leave it in our byre at night sometimes if it's raining.

JIMMY: Theodolite—what's the etymology of that word, Manus?

195 MANUS: No idea.

BRIDGET: Get on with the story.

JIMMY: *Theo—theos*—something to do with a god. Maybe *thea*—a goddess! What shape's the yoke?

DOALTY: 'Shape!' Will you shut up, you aul eejit you! Anyway,
200   every time they'd stick one of these poles into the ground and move across the bog, I'd creep up and shift it twenty or thirty paces to the side.

BRIDGET: God!

DOALTY: Then they'd come back and stare at it and look at their
205   calculations and stare at it again and scratch their heads. And cripes, d'you know what they ended up doing?

BRIDGET: Wait till you hear!

DOALTY: They took the bloody machine apart!

(*And immediately he speaks in gibberish—an imitation of two very agitated and confused sappers in rapid conversation.*)

BRIDGET: That's the image of them!

210 MAIRE: You must be proud of yourself, Doalty.

DOALTY: What d'you mean?

MAIRE: That was a very clever piece of work.

MANUS: It was a gesture.

MAIRE: What sort of gesture?

MANUS: Just to indicate . . . a presence.   215

MAIRE: Hah!

BRIDGET: I'm telling you—you'll be arrested.

(*When* DOALTY *is embarrassed—or pleased—he reacts physically. He now grabs* BRIDGET *around the waist.*)

DOALTY: What d'you make of that for an implement, Bridget? Wouldn't that make a great aul shaft for your churn?

BRIDGET: Let go of me, you dirty brute! I've a headline to do   220
before Big Hughie comes.

MANUS: I don't think we'll wait for him. Let's get started.

(*Slowly, reluctantly they begin to move to their seats and specific tasks.* DOALTY *goes to the bucket of water at the door and washes his hands.* BRIDGET *sets up a hand-mirror and combs her hair.*)

BRIDGET: Nellie Ruadh's baby was to be christened this morning. Did any of yous hear what she called it? Did you, Sarah?

(SARAH *grunts:* No.)

BRIDGET: Did you, Maire?   225

MAIRE: No.

BRIDGET: Our Seamus says she was threatening she was going to call it after its father.

DOALTY: Who's the father?

BRIDGET: That's the point, you donkey you!   230

DOALTY: Ah.

BRIDGET: So there's a lot of uneasy bucks about Baile Beag this day.

DOALTY: She told me last Sunday she was going to call it Jimmy.

BRIDGET: You're a liar, Doalty.   235

DOALTY: Would I tell you a lie? Hi, Jimmy, Nellie Ruadh's aul fella's looking for you.

JIMMY: For me?

MAIRE: Come on, Doalty.

DOALTY: Someone told him . . .   240

MAIRE: Doalty!

DOALTY: He heard you know the first book of the Satires of Horace off by heart . . .

JIMMY: That's true.

DOALTY: and he wants you to recite it for him.   245

JIMMY: I'll do that for him certainly, certainly.

DOALTY: He's busting to hear it.

(JIMMY *fumbles in his pockets.*)

JIMMY: I came across this last night—this'll interest you—in Book Two of Virgil's *Georgics*.

DOALTY: Be God, that's my territory alright.   250

BRIDGET: You clown you! (*To* SARAH.) Hold this for me, would you? (*Her mirror.*)

JIMMY: Listen to this, Manus. *'Nigra fere et presso pinguis sub vomere terra . . .'*

DOALTY: Steady on now—easy, boys, easy—don't rush me, boys— 255

---

176 *Ignari, stulti, rustici* ignoramuses, fools, peasants   181 *Responde—responde!* answer—answer   197 *theos* a god   198 *thea* a goddess

253–54 *Nigra . . . terra* land that is black and rich beneath the pressure of the plough

(He mimes great concentration.)

JIMMY: Manus?

MANUS: 'Land that is black and rich beneath the pressure of the plough ...'

DOALTY: Give *me* a chance!

260 JIMMY: 'And with *cui putre*—with crumbly soil—is in the main best for corn.' There you are!

DOALTY: There you are.

JIMMY: 'From no other land will you see more wagons wending homeward behind slow bullocks.' Virgil! There!

265 DOALTY: 'Slow bullocks'!

JIMMY: Isn't that what I'm always telling you? Black soil for corn. *That's* what you should have in that upper field of yours—corn, not spuds.

DOALTY: Would you listen to that fella! Too lazy be Jasus to
270 wash himself and he's lecturing me on agriculture! Would you go and take a running race at yourself, Jimmy Jack Cassie! *(Grabs SARAH.)* Come away out of this with me, Sarah, and we'll plant some corn together.

MANUS: All right—all right. Let's settle down and get some
275 work done. I know Sean Beag isn't coming—he's at the salmon. What about the Donnelly twins? *(To DOALTY.)* Are the Donnelly twins not coming any more?

(DOALTY shrugs and turns away.)

Did you ask them?

DOALTY: Haven't seen them. Not about these days.

(DOALTY begins whistling through his teeth. Suddenly the atmosphere is silent and alert.)

280 MANUS: Aren't they at home?

DOALTY: No.

MANUS: Where are they then?

DOALTY: How would I know?

BRIDGET: Our Seamus says two of the soldiers' horses were
285 found last night at the foot of the cliffs at Machaire Buidhe and ... *(She stops suddenly and begins writing with chalk on her slate.)* D'you hear the whistles of this aul slate? Sure nobody could write on an aul slippery thing like that.

MANUS: What headline did my father set you?

290 BRIDGET: 'It's easier to stamp out learning than to recall it.'

JIMMY: Book Three, the *Agricola* of Tacitus.

BRIDGET: God but you're a dose.

MANUS: Can you do it?

BRIDGET: There. Is it bad? Will he ate me?

295 MANUS: It's very good. Keep your elbow in closer to your side. Doalty?

DOALTY: I'm at the seven-times table. I'm perfect, skipper.

(MANUS moves to SARAH.)

MANUS: Do you understand those sums?

(SARAH nods: Yes. MANUS leans down to her ear.)

MANUS: My name is Sarah.

(MANUS goes to MAIRE. While he is talking to her the others swop books, talk quietly, etc.)

MANUS: Can I help you? What are you at?   300

MAIRE: Map of America. *(Pause.)* The passage money came last Friday.

MANUS: You never told me that.

MAIRE: Because I haven't seen you since, have I?

MANUS: You don't want to go. You said that yourself.   305

MAIRE: There's ten below me to be raised and no man in the house. What do you suggest?

MANUS: Do you want to go?

MAIRE: Did you apply for that job in the new national school?

MANUS: No.   310

MAIRE: You said you would.

MANUS: I said I might.

MAIRE: When it opens, this is finished: nobody's going to pay to go to a hedge-school.

MANUS: I know that and I ... *(He breaks off because he sees SARAH,* 315 *obviously listening, at his shoulder. She moves away again.)* I was thinking that maybe I could ...

MAIRE: It's £56 a year you're throwing away.

MANUS: I can't apply for it.

MAIRE: You *promised* me you would.   320

MANUS: My father has applied for it.

MAIRE: He has not!

MANUS: Day before yesterday.

MAIRE: For God's sake, sure you know he'd never—

MANUS: I couldn't—I can't go in against him.   325

(MAIRE looks at him for a second. Then:—)

MAIRE: Suit yourself. *(To BRIDGET.)* I saw your Seamus heading off to the Port fair early this morning.

BRIDGET: And wait till you hear this—I forgot to tell you this. He said that as soon as he crossed over the gap at Cnoc na Mona—just beyond where the soldiers are making the   330 maps—the sweet smell was everywhere.

DOALTY: You never told me that.

BRIDGET: It went out of my head.

DOALTY: He saw the crops in Port?

BRIDGET: Some.   335

MANUS: How did the tops look?

BRIDGET: Fine—I think.

DOALTY: In flower?

BRIDGET: I don't know. I think so. He didn't say.

MANUS: Just the sweet smell—that's all?   340

BRIDGET: They say that's the way it snakes in, don't they? First the smell; and then one morning the stalks are all black and limp.

DOALTY: Are you stupid? It's the rotting stalks makes the sweet smell for God's sake. That's what the smell is—rotting   345 stalks.

MAIRE: Sweet smell! Sweet smell! Every year at this time some-body comes back with stories of the sweet smell. Sweet God, did the potatoes ever fail in Baile Beag? Well, did they ever—ever? Never! There was never blight here.   350 Never. Never. But we're always sniffing about for it, aren't

we?—looking for disaster. The rents are going to go up
again—the harvest's going to be lost—the herring have
gone away for ever—there's going to be evictions. Honest
355 to God, some of you people aren't happy unless you're miserable and you'll not be right content until you're dead!

DOALTY: Bloody right, Maire. And sure St Colmcille prophesied there'd never be blight here. He said:

360   The spuds will bloom in Baile Beag
                 Till rabbits grow an extra lug.

And sure that'll never be. So we're all right. Seven threes are
twenty-one; seven fours are twenty-eight; seven fives are
forty-nine—Hi, Jimmy, do you fancy my chances as boss of
the new national school?

365 JIMMY: What's that?—what's that?

DOALTY: Agh, g'way back home to Greece, son.

MAIRE: You ought to apply, Doalty.

DOALTY: D'you think so? Cripes, maybe I will. Hah!

BRIDGET: Did you know that you start at the age of six and you
370 have to stick at it until you're twelve at least—no matter
how smart you are or how much you know.

DOALTY: Who told you that yarn?

BRIDGET: And every child from every house has to go all day,
every day, summer or winter. That's the law.

375 DOALTY: I'll tell you something—nobody's going to go near
them—they're not going to take on—law or no law.

BRIDGET: And everything's free in them. You pay for nothing
except the books you use; that's what our Seamus says.

DOALTY: 'Our Seamus.' Sure your Seamus wouldn't pay any-
380 way. She's making this all up.

BRIDGET: Isn't that right, Manus?

MANUS: I think so.

BRIDGET: And from the very first day you go, you'll not hear
one word of Irish spoken. You'll be taught to speak English
385 and every subject will be taught through English and
everyone'll end up as cute as the Buncrana people.

(SARAH *suddenly grunts and mimes a warning that the master is com-*
ing. The atmosphere changes. Sudden business. Heads down.)

DOALTY: He's here, boys. Cripes, he'll make yella meal out of
me for those bloody tables.

BRIDGET: Have you any extra chalk, Manus?

390 MAIRE: And the atlas for me.

(DOALTY *goes to* MAIRE *who is sitting on a stool at the back.*)

DOALTY: Swop you seats.

MAIRE: Why?

DOALTY: There's an empty one beside the Infant Prodigy.

MAIRE: I'm fine here.

395 DOALTY: Please, Maire. I want to jouk in the back here.

(MAIRE *rises.*)

God love you. (*Aloud.*) Anyone got a bloody table-book?
Cripes, I'm wrecked.

(SARAH *gives him one.*)

God, I'm dying about you.

(*In his haste to get to the back seat,* DOALTY *bumps into* BRIDGET *who*
is kneeling on the floor and writing laboriously on a slate resting on top
of a bench-seat.)

BRIDGET: Watch where you're going, Doalty!

(DOALTY *gooses* BRIDGET. *She squeals. Now the quiet hum of work:*
JIMMY *reading Homer in a low voice;* BRIDGET *copying her headline;*
MAIRE *studying the atlas;* DOALTY, *his eyes shut tight, mouthing his*
tables; SARAH *doing sums. After a few seconds:—*)

BRIDGET: Is this 'g' right, Manus? How do you put a tail on it? 400

DOALTY: Will you shut up! I can't concentrate!

(*A few more seconds of work. Then* DOALTY *opens his eyes and looks*
around.)

False alarm, boys. The bugger's not coming at all. Sure the
bugger's hardly fit to walk.

(*And immediately* HUGH *enters. A large man, with residual dignity,*
shabbily dressed, carrying a stick. He has, as always, a large quan-
tity of drink taken, but he is by no means drunk. He is in his early
sixties.)

HUGH: *Adsum*, Doalty, *adsum.* Perhaps not in *sobrietate perfecta*
but adequately *sobrius* to overhear your quip. Vesperal saluta- 405
tions to you all.

(*Various responses.*)

JIMMY: *Ave,* Hugh.

HUGH: James. (*He removes his hat and coat and hands them and his*
stick to MANUS, *as if to a footman.*) Apologies for my late arrival: we were celebrating the baptism of Nellie Ruadh's 410
baby.

BRIDGET: (*Innocently.*) What name did she put on it, Master?

HUGH: Was it Eamon? Yes, it was Eamon.

BRIDGET: Eamon Donal from Tor! Cripes!

HUGH: And after the *caerimonia nominationis*—Maire? 415

MAIRE: The ritual of naming.

HUGH: Indeed—we then had a few libations to mark the occasion. Altogether very pleasant. The derivation of the word
'baptize'?—where are my Greek scholars? Doalty?

DOALTY: Would it be—ah—ah— 420

HUGH: Too slow. James?

JIMMY: 'Baptizein'—to dip or immerse.

HUGH: Indeed—our friend Pliny Minor speaks of the 'baptisterium'—the cold bath.

DOALTY: Master. 425

HUGH: Doalty?

DOALTY: I suppose you could talk then about baptizing a sheep
at sheep-dipping, could you?

(*Laughter. Comments.*)

---

404 **adsum** I am present; **sobrietate perfecta** with complete sobriety 405 **sobrius** sober 407 **Ave** hail 415 **caerimonia**
nominationis ceremony of naming 422 **baptizein** to dip or immerse 423 **baptisterium** a cold bath, swimming pool

HUGH: Indeed—the precedent is there—the day you were ap-
430   propriately named Doalty—seven nines?

DOALTY: What's that, Master?

HUGH: Seven times nine?

DOALTY: Seven nines—seven nines—seven times nine—seven
times nine are—cripes, it's on the tip of my tongue, Mas-
435   ter—I knew it for sure this morning—funny that's the only
one that foxes me—

BRIDGET: (*Prompt.*) Sixty-three.

DOALTY: What's wrong with me: sure seven nines are fifty-
three, Master.

440   HUGH: Sophocles from Colonus would agree with Doalty Dan
Doalty from Tulach Alainn: 'To know nothing is the sweetest life.' Where's Sean Beag?

MANUS: He's at the salmon.

HUGH: And Nora Dan?

445   MAIRE: She says she's not coming back any more.

HUGH: Ah. Nora Dan can now write her name—Nora Dan's
education is complete. And the Donnelly twins?

(*Brief pause. Then:—*)

BRIDGET: They're probably at the turf. (*She goes to* HUGH.)
There's the one-and-eight I owe you for last quarter's arith-
450   metic and there's my one-and-six for this quarter's writing.

HUGH: *Gratias tibi ago.* (*He sits at his table.*) Before we commence our *studia* I have three items of information to impart to you—(*To* MANUS.) A bowl of tea, strong tea, black—

(MANUS *leaves.*)

Item A: on my perambulations today—Bridget? Too slow.
455   Maire?

MAIRE: *Perambulare*—to walk about.

HUGH: Indeed—I encountered Captain Lancey of the Royal
Engineers who is engaged in the ordnance survey of this
area. He tells me that in the past few days two of his horses
460   have strayed and some of his equipment seems to be mislaid.
I expressed my regret and suggested he address you himself
on these matters. He then explained that he does not speak
Irish. Latin? I asked. None. Greek? Not a syllable. He
speaks—on his own admission—only English; and to his
465   credit he seemed suitably verecund—James?

JIMMY: *Verecundus*—humble.

HUGH: Indeed—he voiced some surprise that we did not speak
his language. I explained that a few of us did, on occasion—
outside the parish of course—and then usually for the pur-
470   poses of commerce, a use to which his tongue seemed particularly suited—(*Shouts.*) and a slice of soda bread—and I
went on to propose that our own culture and the classical
tongues made a happier conjugation—Doalty?

DOALTY: *Conjugo*—I join together.

(DOALTY *is so pleased with himself that he prods and winks at*
BRIDGET.)

HUGH: Indeed—English, I suggested, couldn't really express   475
us. And again to his credit he acquiesced to my logic.
Acquiesced—Maire?

(MAIRE *turns away impatiently.* HUGH *is unaware of the gesture.*)

Too slow. Bridget?

BRIDGET: *Acquiesco.*

HUGH: *Procede.*   480

BRIDGET: *Acquiesco, acquiescere, acquievi, acquietum.*

HUGH: Indeed—and Item B . . .

MAIRE: Master.

HUGH: Yes?

(MAIRE *gets to her feet uneasily but determinedly. Pause.*)

Well, girl?   485

MAIRE: We should all be learning to speak English. That's what
my mother says. That's what I say. That's what Dan O'Connell said last month in Ennis. He said the sooner we all
learn to speak English the better.

(*Suddenly several speak together.*)

JIMMY: What's she saying? What? What?   490

DOALTY: It's Irish he uses when he's travelling around scroung-
ing votes.

BRIDGET: And sleeping with married women. Sure no
woman's safe from that fella.

JIMMY: Who-who-who? Who's this? Who's this?   495

HUGH: *Silentium!* (*Pause.*) Who is she talking about?

MAIRE: I'm talking about Daniel O'Connell.

HUGH: Does she mean that little Kerry politician?

MAIRE: I'm talking about the Liberator, Master, as you well
know. And what he said was this: 'The old language is a bar- 500
rier to modern progress.' He said that last month. And he's
right. I don't want Greek. I don't want Latin. I want English.

(MANUS *reappears on the platform above.*)

I want to be able to speak English because I'm going to
America as soon as the harvest's all saved.

(MAIRE *remains standing.* HUGH *puts his hand into his pocket and
produces a flask of whiskey. He removes the cap, pours a drink into it,
tosses it back, replaces the cap, puts the flask back into his pocket.
Then:—*)

HUGH: We have been diverted—*diverto*—*divertere*—Where   505
were we?

DOALTY: Three items of information, Master. You're at Item B.

HUGH: Indeed—Item B—Item B—yes—On my way to the
christening this morning I chanced to meet Mr George
Alexander, Justice of the Peace. We discussed the new na-   510
tional school. Mr Alexander invited me to take charge of it
when it opens. I thanked him and explained that I could do

---

451 *Gratias tibi ago* I thank you   452 *studia* studies   456 *perambulare* to walk through   466 *verecundus* shame-faced, modest
474 *conjugo* I join together

480 *Procede* proceed   481 *acquiesco, acquiescere* to rest, to find
comfort in   496 *Silentium!* silence!   505 *diverto, divertere* to
turn away

that only if I were free to run it as I have run this hedge-
school for the past thirty-five years—filling what our friend
515   Euripides calls the '*aplestos pithos*'—James?
JIMMY: 'The cask that cannot be filled.'
HUGH: Indeed—and Mr. Alexander retorted courteously and
    emphatically that he hopes that is how it will be run.

(MAIRE *now sits.*)

    Indeed. I have had a strenuous day and I am weary of you
520   all. (*He rises.*) Manus will take care of you.

(HUGH *goes towards the steps.* OWEN *enters.* OWEN *is the younger son,
a handsome, attractive young man in his twenties. He is dressed
smartly—a city man. His manner is easy and charming: everything
he does is invested with consideration and enthusiasm. He now stands
framed in the doorway, a travelling bag across his shoulder.*)

OWEN: Could anybody tell me is this where Hugh Mor
    O'Donnell holds his hedge-school?
DOALTY: It's Owen—Owen Hugh! Look, boys—it's Owen
    Hugh!

(OWEN *enters. As he crosses the room he touches and has a word for
each person.*)

525   OWEN: Doalty! (*Playful punch.*) How are you, boy? *Jacobe, quid
    agis?* Are you well?
JIMMY: Fine. Fine.
OWEN: And Bridget! Give us a kiss. Aaaaaah!
BRIDGET: You're welcome, Owen.
530   OWEN: It's not—? Yes, it *is* Maire Chatach! God! A young
    woman.
MAIRE: How are you, Owen?

(OWEN *is now in front of* HUGH. *He puts his two hands on his* FA-
THER's *shoulders.*)

OWEN: And how's the old man himself?
HUGH: Fair—fair.
535   OWEN: Fair? For God's sake you never looked better! Come
    here to me. (*He embraces* HUGH *warmly and genuinely.*) Great
    to see you, Father. Great to be back.

(HUGH's *eyes are moist—partly joy, partly the drink.*)

HUGH: I—I'm—I'm—pay no attention to—
OWEN: Come on—come on—come on—(*He gives* HUGH *his
540   handkerchief.*) Do you know what you and I are going to do
    tonight? We are going to go up to Anna na mBreag's . . .
DOALTY: Not there, Owen.
OWEN: Why not?
DOALTY: Her poteen's worse than ever.
545   BRIDGET: They say she puts frogs in it!
OWEN: All the better. (*To* HUGH.) And you and I are going to
    get footless drunk. That's arranged.

---

515 *aplestos pithos* unfillable cask   525–526 *Jacobe, quid agis?*
James, how are you?

(OWEN *sees* MANUS *coming down the steps with tea and soda bread.
They meet at the bottom.*)

    And Manus!
MANUS: You're welcome, Owen.
OWEN: I know I am. And it's great to be here. (*He turns round,* 550
    arms outstretched.) I can't believe it. I come back after six
    years and everything's just as it was! Nothing's changed!
    Not a thing! (*Sniffs.*) Even that smell—that's the same
    smell this place always had. What is it anyway? Is it the
    straw? 555
DOALTY: Jimmy Jack's feet.

(*General laughter. It opens little pockets of conversation round the
room.*)

OWEN: And Doalty Dan Doalty hasn't changed either!
DOALTY: Bloody right, Owen.
OWEN: Jimmy, are you well?
JIMMY: Dodging about. 560
OWEN: Any word of the big day?

(*This is greeted with 'ohs' and 'ahs.'*)

    Time enough, Jimmy. Homer's easier to live with, isn't he?
MAIRE: We heard stories that you own ten big shops in
    Dublin—is it true?
OWEN: Only nine. 565
BRIDGET: And you've twelve horses and six servants.
OWEN: Yes—that's true. God Almighty, would you listen to
    them—taking a hand at me!
MANUS: When did you arrive?
OWEN: We left Dublin yesterday morning, spent last night in 570
    Omagh and got here half an hour ago.
MANUS: You're hungry then.
HUGH: Indeed—get him food—get him a drink.
OWEN: Not now, thanks; later. Listen—am I interrupting you
    all? 575
HUGH: By no means. We're finished for the day.
OWEN: Wonderful. I'll tell you why. Two friends of mine are
    waiting outside the door. They'd like to meet you and I'd
    like you to meet them. May I bring them in?
HUGH: Certainly. You'll all eat and have . . . 580
OWEN: Not just yet, Father. You've seen the sappers working in
    this area for the past fortnight, haven't you? Well, the older
    man is Captain Lancey . . .
HUGH: I've met Captain Lancey.
OWEN: Great. He's the cartographer in charge of this whole 585
    area. Cartographer—James?

(OWEN *begins to play this game—his father's game—partly to involve his classroom audience, partly to show he has not forgotten it, and
indeed partly because he enjoys it.*)

JIMMY: A maker of maps.
OWEN: Indeed—and the younger man that I travelled with
    from Dublin, his name is Lieutenant Yolland and he is at-
    tached to the toponymic department—Father?—*responde*— 590
    responde!
HUGH: He gives names to places.
OWEN: Indeed—although he is in fact an orthographer—
    Doalty?—too slow—Manus?

595 MANUS: The correct spelling of those names.
OWEN: Indeed—indeed!

(OWEN *laughs and claps his hands. Some of the others join in.*)

Beautiful! Beautiful! Honest to God, it's such a delight to be back here with you all again—'civilized' people. Anyhow—may I bring them in?

600 HUGH: Your friends are our friends.
OWEN: I'll be straight back.

(*There is general talk as* OWEN *goes towards the door. He stops beside* SARAH.)

OWEN: That's a new face. Who are you?

(*A very brief hesitation. Then:—*)

SARAH: My name is Sarah.
OWEN: Sarah who?
605 SARAH: Sarah Johnny Sally.
OWEN: Of course! From Bun na hAbhann! I'm Owen—Owen Hugh Mor. From Baile Beag. Good to see you.

(*During this* OWEN—SARAH *exchange.*)

HUGH: Come on now. Let's tidy this place up. (*He rubs the top of his table with his sleeve.*) Move, Doalty—lift those books off 610 the floor.
DOALTY: Right, Master; certainly, Master; I'm doing my best, Master.

(OWEN *stops at the door.*)

OWEN: One small thing, Father.
HUGH: *Silentium!*
615 OWEN: I'm on their pay-roll.

(SARAH, *very elated at her success, is beside* MANUS.)

SARAH: I said it, Manus!

(MANUS *ignores* SARAH. *He is much more interested in* OWEN *now.*)

MANUS: You haven't enlisted, have you?!

(SARAH *moves away.*)

OWEN: Me a soldier? I'm employed as a part-time, underpaid, civilian interpreter. My job is to translate the quaint, ar-620 chaic tongue you people persist in speaking into the King's good English.

(*He goes out.*)

HUGH: Move—move—move! Put some order on things! Come on, Sarah—hide that bucket. Whose are these slates? Somebody take these dishes away. *Festinate! Festinate!*

(MANUS *goes to* MAIRE *who is busy tidying.*)

MANUS: You didn't tell me you were definitely leaving. 625
MAIRE: Not now.
HUGH: Good girl, Bridget. That's the style.
MANUS: You might at least have told me.
HUGH: Are these your books, James?
JIMMY: Thank you. 630
MANUS: Fine! Fine! Go ahead! Go ahead!
MAIRE: You talk to me about getting married—with neither a roof over your head nor a sod of ground under your foot. I suggest you go for the new school; but no—'My father's in for that.' Well now he's got it and now this is finished and 635 now you've nothing.
MANUS: I can always . . .
MAIRE: What? Teach classics to the cows? Agh—

(MAIRE *moves away from* MANUS. OWEN *enters with* LANCEY *and* YOLLAND. CAPTAIN LANCEY *is middle-aged; a small, crisp officer, expert in his field as cartographer but uneasy with people—especially civilians, especially these foreign civilians. His skill is with deeds, not words.* LIEUTENANT YOLLAND *is in his late twenties/early thirties. He is tall and thin and gangling, blond hair, a shy, awkward manner. A soldier by accident.*)

OWEN: Here we are. Captain Lancey—my father.
LANCEY: Good evening. 640

(HUGH *becomes expansive, almost courtly, with his visitors.*)

HUGH: You and I have already met, sir.
LANCEY: Yes.
OWEN: And Lieutenant Yolland—both Royal Engineers—my father.
HUGH: You're very welcome, gentlemen. 645
YOLLAND: How do you do.
HUGH: *Gaudeo vos hic adesse.*
OWEN: And I'll make no other introductions except that these are some of the people of Baile Beag and—what?—well you're among the best people in Ireland now. (*He pauses to* 650 *allow* LANCEY *to speak.* LANCEY *does not.*) Would you like to say a few words, Captain?
HUGH: What about a drop, sir?
LANCEY: A what?
HUGH: Perhaps a modest refreshment? A little sampling of our 655 *aqua vitae?*
LANCEY: No, no.
HUGH: Later perhaps when—
LANCEY: I'll say what I have to say, if I may, and as briefly as possible. Do they speak *any* English, Roland? 660
OWEN: Don't worry. I'll translate.
LANCEY: I see. (*He clears his throat. He speaks as if he were addressing children—a shade too loudly and enunciating excessively.*) You may have seen me—seen me—working in this section—section?—working. We are here—here—in this place— 665 you understand?—to make a map—a map—a map and—
JIMMY: *Nonne Latine loquitur?*

---

624 *Festinate!* hurry!

647 *Gaudeo . . . adesse* welcome   667 *Nonne Latine loquitur?* does he not speak Latin?

(HUGH *holds up a restraining hand.*)

HUGH: James.
LANCEY: (*To* JIMMY.) I do not speak Gaelic, sir.

(*He looks at* OWEN.)

670   OWEN: Carry on.
LANCEY: A map is a representation on paper—a picture—you understand picture?—a paper picture—showing, representing this country—yes?—showing your country in miniature—a scaled drawing on paper of—of—of—

(*Suddenly* DOALTY *sniggers. Then* BRIDGET. *Then* SARAH. OWEN *leaps in quickly.*)

675   OWEN: It might be better if you *assume* they understand you—
LANCEY: Yes?
OWEN: And I'll translate as you go along.
LANCEY: I see. Yes. Very well. Perhaps you're right. Well. What we are doing is this. (*He looks at* OWEN. OWEN *nods reassur-*
680   *ingly.*) His Majesty's government has ordered the first ever comprehensive survey of this entire country—a general triangulation which will embrace detailed hydrographic and topographic information and which will be executed to a scale of six inches to the English mile.
685   HUGH: (*Pouring a drink.*) Excellent—excellent.

(LANCEY *looks at* OWEN.)

OWEN: A new map is being made of the whole country.

(LANCEY *looks to* OWEN: *Is that all?* OWEN *smiles reassuringly and indicates to proceed.*)

LANCEY: This enormous task has been embarked on so that the military authorities will be equipped with up-to-date and accurate information on every corner of this part of the Empire.
690   OWEN: The job is being done by soldiers because they are skilled in this work.
LANCEY: And also so that the entire basis of land valuation can be reassessed for purposes of more equitable taxation.
OWEN: This new map will take the place of the estate agent's
695   map so that from now on you will know exactly what is yours in law.
LANCEY: In conclusion I wish to quote two brief extracts from the white paper which is our governing charter: (*Reads*) 'All former surveys of Ireland originated in forfeiture and vio-
700   lent transfer of property; the present survey has for its object the relief which can be afforded to the proprietors and occupiers of land from unequal taxation.'
OWEN: The captain hopes that the public will cooperate with the sappers and that the new map will mean that taxes are
705   reduced.
HUGH: A worthy enterprise—*opus honestum!* And Extract B?
LANCEY: 'Ireland is privileged. No such survey is being undertaken in England. So this survey cannot but be received as

---

706 ***opus bonestrum*** an honourable task

proof of the disposition of this government to advance the interests of Ireland.' My sentiments, too.   710
OWEN: This survey demonstrates the government's interest in Ireland and the captain thanks you for listening so attentively to him.
HUGH: Our pleasure, Captain.
LANCEY: Lieutenant Yolland?   715
YOLLAND: I—I—I've nothing to say—really—
OWEN: The captain is the man who actually makes the new map. George's task is to see that the place-names on this map are . . . correct. (*To* YOLLAND.) Just a few words—they'd like to hear you. (*To class.*) Don't you want to hear   720
George, too?
MAIRE: Has he anything to say?
YOLLAND: (*To* MAIRE.) Sorry—sorry?
OWEN: She says she's dying to hear you.
YOLLAND: (*To* MAIRE.) Very kind of you—thank you . . . (*To*   725
class.) I can only say that I feel—I feel very foolish to—to—to be working here and not to speak your language. But I intend to rectify that—with Roland's help—indeed I do.
OWEN: He wants me to teach him Irish!
HUGH: You are doubly welcome, sir.   730
YOLLAND: I think your countryside is—is—is—is very beautiful. I've fallen in love with it already. I hope we're not too—too crude an intrusion on your lives. And I know that I'm going to be happy, very happy, here.
OWEN: He is already a committed Hibernophile—   735
JIMMY: He loves—
OWEN: All right, Jimmy—we know—he loves Baile Beag; and he loves you all.
HUGH: Please . . . May I . . . ?

(HUGH *is now drunk. He holds on to the edge of the table.*)

OWEN: Go ahead, Father. (*Hands up for quiet.*) Please—please.   740
HUGH: And we, gentlemen, we in turn are happy to offer you our friendship, our hospitality, and every assistance that you may require. Gentlemen—welcome!

(*A few desultory claps. The formalities are over. General conversation. The soldiers meet the locals.* MANUS *and* OWEN *meet down stage.*)

OWEN: Lancey's a bloody ramrod but George's all right. How are you anyway?   745
MANUS: What sort of a translation was that, Owen?
OWEN: Did I make a mess of it?
MANUS: You weren't saying what Lancey was saying!
OWEN: 'Uncertainty in meaning is incipient poetry'—who said that?   750
MANUS: There was nothing uncertain about what Lancey said: it's a bloody military operation, Owen! And what's Yolland's function? What's 'incorrect' about the place-names we have here?
OWEN: Nothing at all. They're just going to be standardized.   755
MANUS: You mean changed into English?
OWEN: Where there's ambiguity, they'll be Anglicized.
MANUS: And they call you Roland! They both call you Roland!
OWEN: Shhhhh. Isn't it ridiculous? They seemed to get it wrong from the very beginning—or else they can't pronounce   760
Owen. I was afraid some of you bastards would laugh.

MANUS: Aren't you going to tell them?

OWEN: Yes—yes—soon—soon.

MANUS: But they . . .

765   OWEN: Easy, man, easy. Owen—Roland—what the hell. It's only a name. It's the same me, isn't it? Well, isn't it?

MANUS: Indeed it is. It's the same Owen.

OWEN: And the same Manus. And in a way we complement each other. (*He punches* MANUS *lightly, playfully and turns to* 770 *join the others. As he goes.*) All right—who has met whom? Isn't this a job for the go-between?

(MANUS *watches* OWEN *move confidently across the floor, taking* MAIRE *by the hand and introducing her to* YOLLAND. HUGH *is trying to negotiate the steps.* JIMMY *is lost in a text.* DOALTY *and* BRIDGET *are reliving their giggling.* SARAH *is staring at* MANUS.)

ACT TWO

SCENE I

The sappers have already mapped most of the area. YOLLAND'*s official task, which* OWEN *is now doing, is to take each of the Gaelic names— every hill, stream, rock, even every patch of ground which possessed its own distinctive Irish name—and Anglicize it, either by changing it into its approximate English sound or by translating it into English words. For example, a Gaelic name like Cnoc Ban could become Knockban or—directly translated—Fair Hill. These new standardized names were entered into the Name-Book, and when the new maps appeared they contained all these new Anglicized names.* OWEN'*s official function as translator is to pronounce each name in Irish and then provide the English translation.*

The hot weather continues. It is late afternoon some days later.

Stage right: an improvised clothes-line strung between the shafts of the cart and a nail in the wall; on it are some shirts and socks.

A large map—one of the new blank maps—is spread out on the floor. OWEN *is on his hands and knees, consulting it. He is totally engrossed in his task which he pursues with great energy and efficiency.*

YOLLAND'*s hesitancy has vanished—he is at home here now. He is sitting on the floor, his long legs stretched out before him, his back resting against a creel, his eyes closed. His mind is elsewhere. One of the reference books—a church registry—lies open on his lap.*

Around them are various reference books, the Name-Book, a bottle of poteen, some cups, etc.

OWEN *completes an entry in the Name-Book and returns to the map on the floor.*

OWEN: Now. Where have we got to? Yes—the point where that stream enters the sea—that tiny little beach there. George!

YOLLAND: Yes. I'm listening. What do you call it? Say the Irish name again?

5   OWEN: Bun na hAbhann.

YOLLAND: Again.

OWEN: Bun na hAbhann.

YOLLAND: Bun na hAbhann.

OWEN: That's terrible, George.

10   YOLLAND: I know. I'm sorry. Say it again.

OWEN: Bun na hAbbann.

YOLLAND: Bun na hAbbann.

OWEN: That's better. Bun is the Irish word for bottom. And Abha means river. So it's literally the mouth of the river.

YOLLAND: Let's leave it alone. There's no English equivalent 15 for a sound like that.

OWEN: What is it called in the church registry?

(*Only now does* YOLLAND *open his eyes.*)

YOLLAND: Let's see . . . Banowen.

OWEN: That's wrong. (*Consults text.*) The list of freeholders calls it Owenmore—that's completely wrong: Owenmore's the 20 big river at the west end of the parish. (*Another text.*) And in the grand jury lists it's called—God!—Binhone!—wherever they got that. I suppose we could Anglicize it to Bunowen; but somehow that's neither fish nor flesh.

(YOLLAND *closes his eyes again.*)

YOLLAND: I give up.   25

OWEN: (*At map.*) Back to first principles. What are we trying to do?

YOLLAND: Good question.

OWEN: We are trying to denominate and at the same time describe that tiny area of soggy, rocky, sandy ground where 30 that little stream enters the sea, an area known locally as Bun na hAbhann . . . Burnfoot! What about Burnfoot?

YOLLAND: (*Indifferently.*) Good, Roland, Burnfoot's good.

OWEN: George, my name isn't . . .

YOLLAND: B-u-r-n-f-o-o-t?   35

OWEN: Are you happy with that?

YOLLAND: Yes.

OWEN: Burnfoot it is then. (*He makes the entry into the Name-Book.*) Bun na hAbhann—B-u-r-n-

YOLLAND: You're becoming very skilled at this.   40

OWEN: We're not moving fast enough.

YOLLAND: (*Opens eyes again.*) Lancey lectured me again last night.

OWEN: When does he finish here?

YOLLAND: The sappers are pulling out at the end of the week. 45 The trouble is, the maps they've completed can't be printed without these names. So London screams at Lancey and Lancey screams at me. But I wasn't intimidated.

(MANUS *emerges from upstairs and descends.*)

'I'm sorry, sir,' I said, 'But certain tasks demand their own tempo. You cannot rename a whole country overnight.' 50 Your Irish air has made me bold. (*To* MANUS.) Do you want us to leave?

MANUS: Time enough. Class won't begin for another half-hour.

YOLLAND: Sorry—sorry?

OWEN: Can't you speak English?   55

(MANUS *gathers the things off the clothes-line.* OWEN *returns to the map.*)

OWEN: We now come across that beach . . .

YOLLAND: Tra—that's the Irish for beach. (*To* MANUS.) I'm picking up the odd word, Manus.

MANUS: So.

60 OWEN: . . . on past Burnfoot; and there's nothing around here that has any name that I know of until we come down here to the south end, just about here . . . and there should be a ridge of rocks there . . . Have the sappers marked it? They have. Look, George.

65 YOLLAND: Where are we?

OWEN: There.

YOLLAND: I'm lost.

OWEN: Here. And the name of that ridge is Druim Dubh. Put English on that, Lieutenant.

70 YOLLAND: Say it again.

OWEN: Druim Dubh.

YOLLAND: Dubh means black.

OWEN: Yes.

YOLLAND: And Druim means . . . what? a fort?

75 OWEN: We met it yesterday in Druim Luachra.

YOLLAND: A ridge! The Black Ridge! (*To* MANUS.) You see, Manus?

OWEN: We'll have you fluent at the Irish before the summer's over.

80 YOLLAND: Oh, I wish I were. (*To* MANUS *as he crosses to go back upstairs.*) We got a crate of oranges from Dublin today. I'll send some up to you.

MANUS: Thanks. (*To* OWEN.) Better hide that bottle. Father's just up and he'd be better without it.

85 OWEN: Can't you speak English before your man?

MANUS: Why?

OWEN: Out of courtesy.

MANUS: Doesn't he want to learn Irish? (*To* YOLLAND.) Don't you want to learn Irish?

90 YOLLAND: Sorry—sorry? I—I—

MANUS: I understand the Lanceys perfectly but people like you puzzle me.

OWEN: Manus, for God's sake!

MANUS: (*Still to* YOLLAND.) How's the work going?

95 YOLLAND: The work?—the work? Oh, it's—it's staggering along—I think—(*To* OWEN.)—isn't it? But we'd be lost without Roland.

MANUS: (*Leaving.*) I'm sure. But there are always the Rolands, aren't there?

(*He goes upstairs and exits.*)

100 YOLLAND: What was that he said?—something about Lancey, was it?

OWEN: He said we should hide that bottle before Father gets his hands on it.

YOLLAND: Ah.

105 OWEN: He's always trying to protect him.

YOLLAND: Was he lame from birth?

OWEN: An accident when he was a baby: Father fell across his cradle. That's why Manus feels so responsible for him.

YOLLAND: Why doesn't he marry?

110 OWEN: Can't afford to, I suppose.

YOLLAND: Hasn't he a salary?

OWEN: What salary? All he gets is the odd shilling Father throws him—and that's seldom enough. I got out in time, didn't I?

(YOLLAND *is pouring a drink.*)

Easy with that stuff—it'll hit you suddenly.   115

YOLLAND: I like it.

OWEN: Let's get back to the job. Druim Dubh—what's it called in the jury lists? (*Consults texts.*)

YOLLAND: Some people here resent us.

OWEN: Dramduff—wrong as usual.   120

YOLLAND: I was passing a little girl yesterday and she spat at me.

OWEN: And it's Drimdoo here. What's it called in the registry?

YOLLAND: Do you know the Donnelly twins?

OWEN: Who?   125

YOLLAND: The Donnelly twins.

OWEN: Yes. Best fishermen about here. What about them?

YOLLAND: Lancey's looking for them.

OWEN: What for?

YOLLAND: He wants them for questioning.   130

OWEN: Probably stolen somebody's nets. Dramduffy! Nobody ever called it Dramduffy. Take your pick of those three.

YOLLAND: My head's addled. Let's take a rest. Do you want a drink?

OWEN: Thanks. Now, every Dubh we've come across we've   135 changed to Duff. So if we're to be consistent, I suppose Druim Dubh has to become Dromduff.

(YOLLAND *is now looking out the window.*)

You can see the end of the ridge from where you're standing. But D-r-u-m- or D-r-o-m-? (*Name-Book.*) Do you remember—which did we agree on for Druim Luachra?   140

YOLLAND: That house immediately above where we're camped—

OWEN: Mm?

YOLLAND: The house where Maire lives.

OWEN: Maire? Oh, Maire Chatach.   145

YOLLAND: What does that mean?

OWEN: Curly-haired; the whole family are called the Chatachs. What about it?

YOLLAND: I hear music coming from that house almost every night.   150

OWEN: Why don't you drop in?

YOLLAND: Could I?

OWEN: Why not? We used D-r-o-m then. So we've got to call it D-r-o-m-d-u-f-f—all right?

YOLLAND: Go back up to where the new school is being built   155 and just say the names again for me, would you?

OWEN: That's a good idea. Poolkerry, Ballybeg—

YOLLAND: No, no; as they still are—in your own language.

OWEN: Poll na gCaorach,

(YOLLAND *repeats the names silently after him.*)

Baile Beag, Ceann Balor, Lis Maol, Machaire Buidhe, Baile   160 na gGall, Carraig na Ri, Mullach Dearg—

YOLLAND: Do you think I could live here?

OWEN: What are you talking about?

YOLLAND: Settle down here—live here.

OWEN: Come on, George.   165

YOLLAND: I mean it.

OWEN: Live on what? Potatoes? Buttermilk?

YOLLAND: It's really heavenly.

OWEN: For God's sake! The first hot summer in fifty years and you think it's Eden. Don't be such a bloody romantic. You wouldn't survive a mild winter here.

170

YOLLAND: Do you think not? Maybe you're right.

(DOALTY *enters in a rush.*)

DOALTY: Hi, boys, is Manus about?

OWEN: He's upstairs. Give him a shout.

175 DOALTY: Manus! The cattle's going mad in that heat—Cripes, running wild all over the place. (*To* YOLLAND.) How are you doing, skipper?

(MANUS *appears.*)

YOLLAND: Thank you for—I—I'm very grateful to you for—

DOALTY: Wasting your time. I don't know a word you're saying.

180   Hi, Manus, there's two bucks down the road there asking for you.

MANUS: (*Descending.*) Who are they?

DOALTY: Never clapped eyes on them. They want to talk to you.

MANUS: What about?

185 DOALTY: They wouldn't say. Come on. The bloody beasts'll end up in Loch an Iubhair if they're not capped. Good luck, boys!

(DOALTY *rushes off.* MANUS *follows him.*)

OWEN: Good luck! What were you thanking Doalty for?

YOLLAND: I was washing outside my tent this morning and he was passing with a scythe across his shoulder and he came

190   up to me and pointed to the long grass and then cut a pathway round my tent and from the tent down to the road—so that my feet won't get wet with the dew. Wasn't that kind of him? And I have no words to thank him . . . I suppose you're right: I suppose I couldn't live here . . . Just before Doalty

195   came up to me this morning, I was thinking that at that moment I might have been in Bombay instead of Ballybeg. You see, my father was at his wits end with me and finally he got me a job with the East India Company—some kind of a clerkship. That was ten, eleven months ago. So I set off for

200   London. Unfortunately I—I—I missed the boat. Literally. And since I couldn't face Father and hadn't enough money to hang about until the next sailing, I joined the army. And they stuck me into the Engineers and posted me to Dublin. And Dublin sent me here. And while I was washing this

205   morning and looking across the Tra Bhan, I was thinking how very, very lucky I am to be here and not in Bombay.

OWEN: Do you believe in fate?

YOLLAND: Lancey's so like my father. I was watching him last night. He met every group of sappers as they reported in.

210   He checked the field kitchens. He examined the horses. He inspected every single report—even examining the texture of the paper and commenting on the neatness of the handwriting. The perfect colonial servant: not only must the job be done—it must be done with excellence. Father has that

215   drive, too; that dedication; that indefatigable energy. He builds roads—hopping from one end of the Empire to the other. Can't sit still for five minutes. He says himself the longest time he ever sat still was the night before Waterloo when they were waiting for Wellington to make up his

220   mind to attack.

OWEN: What age is he?

YOLLAND: Born in 1789—the very day the Bastille fell. I've often thought maybe that gave his whole life its character. Do you think it could? He inherited a new world the day he was born—The Year One. Ancient time was at an end. The 225 world had cast off its old skin. There were no longer any frontiers to man's potential. Possibilities were endless and exciting. He still believes that. The Apocalypse is just about to happen . . . I'm afraid I'm a great disappointment to him. I've neither his energy, nor his coherence, nor his 230 belief. Do I believe in fate? The day I arrived in Ballybeg—no, Baile Beag—the moment you brought me in here, I had a curious sensation. It's difficult to describe. It was a momentary sense of discovery; no—not quite a sense of discovery—a sense of recognition, of confirmation of some- 235 thing I half knew instinctively; as if I had stepped . . .

OWEN: Back into ancient time?

YOLLAND: No, no. It wasn't an awareness of *direction* being changed but of experience being of a totally different order. I had moved into a consciousness that wasn't striving nor 240 agitated, but at its ease and with its own conviction and assurance. And when I heard Jimmy Jack and your father swapping stories about Apollo and Cuchulainn and Paris and Ferdia—as if they lived down the road—it was then that I thought—I knew—perhaps I could live here . . . 245 (*Now embarrassed.*) Where's the pot-een?

OWEN: Poteen.

YOLLAND: Poteen—poteen—poteen. Even if I did speak Irish I'd always be an outsider here, wouldn't I? I may learn the password but the language of the tribe will always elude 250 me, won't it? The private core will always be . . . hermetic, won't it?

OWEN: You can learn to decode us.

(HUGH *emerges from upstairs and descends. He is dressed for the road. Today he is physically and mentally jaunty and alert—almost self-consciously jaunty and alert. Indeed, as the scene progresses, one has the sense that he is deliberately parodying himself. The moment* HUGH *gets to the bottom of the steps* YOLLAND *leaps respectfully to his feet.*)

HUGH: (*As he descends.*)
Quantumvis cursum longum fessumque moratur   255
Sol, sacro tandem carmine vesper adest.
    I dabble in verse, Lieutenant, after the style of Ovid. (*To* OWEN.) A drop of that to fortify me.

YOLLAND: You'll have to translate it for me.

HUGH: Let's see—   260
    No matter how long the sun may linger on his long and weary journey
    At length evening comes with its sacred song.

YOLLAND: Very nice, sir.

HUGH: English succeeds in making it sound . . . plebeian.

OWEN: Where are you off to, Father?   265

II.i. 255–256 *Quantumvis . . . adest* no matter how long the sun delays on his long weary course / At length evening comes with its sacred song

HUGH: An *expeditio* with three purposes. Purpose A: to acquire a testimonial from our parish priest—(*To* YOLLAND.) a worthy man but barely literate; and since he'll ask me to write it myself, how in all modesty can I do myself justice? (*To* OWEN.) Where did this [*drink*] come from?

270 OWEN: Anna na mBreag's.

HUGH: (*To* YOLLAND.) In that case address yourself to it with circumspection. (*And* HUGH *instantly tosses the drink back in one gulp and grimaces.*) Aaaaaaagh! (*Holds out his glass for a re-*
275 *fill.*) Anna na mBreag means Anna of the Lies. And Purpose B: to talk to the builders of the new school about the kind of living accommodation I will require there. I have lived too long like a journeyman tailor.

YOLLAND: Some years ago we lived fairly close to a poet—well,
280 about three miles away.

HUGH: His name?

YOLLAND: Wordsworth—William Wordsworth.

HUGH: Did he speak of me to you?

YOLLAND: Actually I never talked to him. I just saw him out
285 walking—in the distance.

HUGH: Wordsworth? . . . No. I'm afraid we're not familiar with your literature, Lieutenant. We feel closer to the warm Mediterranean. We tend to overlook your island.

YOLLAND: I'm learning to speak Irish, sir.
290 HUGH: Good.

YOLLAND: Roland's teaching me.

HUGH: Splendid.

YOLLAND: I mean—I feel so cut off from the people here. And I was trying to explain a few minutes ago how remarkable
295 a community this is. To meet people like yourself and Jimmy Jack who actually converse in Greek and Latin. And your place names—what was the one we came across this morning?—Termon, from Terminus, the god of boundaries. It—it—it's really astonishing.

300 HUGH: We like to think we endure around truths immemorially posited.

YOLLAND: And your Gaelic literature—you're a poet yourself—

HUGH: Only in Latin, I'm afraid.

YOLLAND: I understand it's enormously rich and ornate.
305 HUGH: Indeed, Lieutenant. A rich language. A rich literature. You'll find, sir, that certain cultures expend on their vocabularies and syntax acquisitive energies and ostentations entirely lacking in their material lives. I suppose you could call us a spiritual people.

310 OWEN: (*Not unkindly; more out of embarrassment before* YOLLAND.) Will you stop that nonsense, Father.

HUGH: Nonsense? What nonsense?

OWEN: Do you know where the priest lives?

HUGH: At Lis na Muc, over near . . .
315 OWEN: No, he doesn't. Lis na Muc, the Fort of the Pigs, has become Swinefort. (*Now turning the pages of the Name-Book—a page per name.*) And to get to Swinefort you pass through Greencastle and Fair Head and Strandhill and Gort and Whiteplains. And the new school isn't at Poll na gCao-
320 rach—it's at Sheepsrock. Will you be able to find your way?

—

(HUGH *pours himself another drink. Then:—*)

HUGH: Yes, it is a rich language, Lieutenant, full of the mythologies of fantasy and hope and self-deception—a syntax opulent with tomorrows. It is our response to mud cabins and a diet of potatoes; and our only method of reply- 325 ing to . . . inevitabilities. (*To* OWEN.) Can you give me the loan of half-a-crown? I'll repay you out of the subscriptions I'm collecting for the publication of my new book. (*To* YOLLAND.) It is entitled: 'The Pentaglot Preceptor or Elementary Institute of the English, Greek, Hebrew, Latin and 330 Irish Languages; Particularly Calculated for the Instruction of Such Ladies and Gentlemen as may Wish to Learn without the Help of a Master.'

YOLLAND: (*Laughs.*) That's a wonderful title!

HUGH: Between ourselves—the best part of the enterprise. 335 Nor do I, in fact, speak Hebrew. And that last phrase— 'without the Help of a Master'—that was written before the new national school was thrust upon me—do you think I ought to drop it now? After all you don't dispose of the cow just because it has produced a magnificent calf, do you? 340

YOLLAND: You certainly do not.

HUGH: The phrase goes. And I'm interrupting work of moment. (*He goes to the door and stops there.*) To return briefly to that other matter, Lieutenant. I understand your sense of exclusion, of being cut off from a life here; and I trust you 345 will find access to us with my son's help. But remember that words are signals, counters. They are not immortal. And it can happen—to use an image you'll understand—it can happen that a civilization can be imprisoned in a linguistic contour which no longer matches the landscape 350 of . . . fact. Gentlemen. (*He leaves.*)

OWEN: 'An *expeditio* with three purposes': the children laugh at him: he always promises three points and he never gets beyond A and B.

YOLLAND: He's an astute man. 355

OWEN: He's bloody pompous.

YOLLAND: But so astute.

OWEN: And he drinks too much. Is it astute not to be able to adjust for survival? Enduring around truths immemorially posited—hah! 360

YOLLAND: He knows what's happening.

OWEN: What is happening?

YOLLAND: I'm not sure. But I'm concerned about my part in it. It's an eviction of sorts.

OWEN: We're making a six-inch map of the country. Is there 365 something sinister in that?

YOLLAND: Not in—

OWEN: And we're taking place-names that are riddled with confusion and—

YOLLAND: Who's confused? Are the people confused? 370

OWEN: —and we're standardizing those names as accurately and as sensitively as we can.

YOLLAND: Something is being eroded.

OWEN: Back to the romance again. All right! Fine! Fine! Look where we've got to. (*He drops on his hands and knees and stabs* 375 *a finger at the map.*) We've come to this crossroads. Come here and look at it, man! Look at it! And we call that crossroads Tobair Vree. And why do we call it Tobair Vree? I'll tell you why. Tobair means a well. But what does Vree

380 mean? It's a corruption of Brian—(*Gaelic pronunciation.*) Brian—an erosion of Tobair Bhriain. Because a hundred-and-fifty years ago there used to be a well there, not at the crossroads, mind you—that would be too simple—but in a field close to the crossroads. And an old man called Brian,

385 whose face was disfigured by an enormous growth, got it into his head that the water in that well was blessed; and every day for seven months he went there and bathed his face in it. But the growth didn't go away; and one morning Brian was found drowned in that well. And ever since that

390 crossroads is known as Tobair Vree—even though that well has long since dried up. I know the story because my grandfather told it to me. But ask Doalty—or Maire—or Bridget—even my father—even Manus—why it's called Tobair Vree; and do you think they'll know? I know they don't

395 know. So the question I put to you, Lieutenant, is this: what do we do with a name like that? Do we scrap Tobair Vree altogether and call it—what?—The Cross? Crossroads? Or do we keep piety with a man long dead, long forgotten, his name 'eroded' beyond recognition, whose trivial little story

400 nobody in the parish remembers?

YOLLAND: Except you.

OWEN: I've left here.

YOLLAND: You remember it.

OWEN: I'm asking you: what do we write in the Name-Book?

405 YOLLAND: Tobair Vree.

OWEN: Even though the well is a hundred yards from the actual crossroads—and there's no well anyway—and what the hell does Vree mean?

YOLLAND: Tobair Vree.

410 OWEN: That's what you want?

YOLLAND: Yes.

OWEN: You're certain?

YOLLAND: Yes.

OWEN: Fine. Fine. That's what you'll get.

415 YOLLAND: That's what you want, too, Roland.

(*Pause.*)

OWEN: (*Explodes.*) George! For God's sake! My name is not Roland!

YOLLAND: What?

OWEN: (*Softly.*) My name is Owen.

(*Pause.*)

YOLLAND: Not Roland?

420 OWEN: Owen.

YOLLAND: You mean to say—?

OWEN: Owen.

YOLLAND: But I've been—

OWEN: O-w-e-n.

425 YOLLAND: Where did Roland come from?

OWEN: I don't know.

YOLLAND: It was never Roland?

OWEN: Never.

YOLLAND: O my God!

(*Pause. They stare at one another. Then the absurdity of the situation strikes them suddenly. They explode with laughter.* OWEN *pours drinks. As they roll about, their lines overlap.*)

YOLLAND: Why didn't you tell me? 430

OWEN: Do I look like a Roland?

YOLLAND: Spell Owen again.

OWEN: I was getting fond of Roland.

YOLLAND: O my God!

OWEN: O-w-e-n. 435

YOLLAND: What'll we write—

OWEN: —in the Name-Book?!

YOLLAND: R-o-w-e-n!

OWEN: Or what about Ol-

YOLLAND: Ol-what? 440

OWEN: Oland!

(*And again they explode.* MANUS *enters. He is very elated.*)

MANUS: What's the celebration?

OWEN: A christening!

YOLLAND: A baptism!

OWEN: A hundred christenings!

YOLLAND: A thousand baptisms! Welcome to Eden! 445

OWEN: Eden's right! We name a thing and—bang!—it leaps into existence!

YOLLAND: Each name a perfect equation with its roots.

OWEN: A perfect congruence with its reality. (*To* MANUS.) Take 450 a drink.

YOLLAND: Poteen—beautiful.

OWEN: Lying Anna's poteen.

YOLLAND: Anna na mBreag's poteen.

OWEN: Excellent, George. 455

YOLLAND: I'll decode you yet.

OWEN: (*Offers drink.*) Manus?

MANUS: Not if that's what it does to you.

OWEN: You're right. Steady—steady—sober up—sober up.

YOLLAND: Sober as a judge, Owen. 460

(MANUS *moves beside* OWEN.)

MANUS: I've got good news! Where's Father?

OWEN: He's gone out. What's the good news?

MANUS: I've been offered a job.

OWEN: Where? (*Now aware of* YOLLAND.) Come on, man—speak in English. 465

MANUS: For the benefit of the colonist?

OWEN: He's a decent man.

MANUS: Aren't they all at some level?

OWEN: Please.

(MANUS *shrugs.*)

He's been offered a job. 470

YOLLAND: Where?

OWEN: Well—tell us!

MANUS: I've just had a meeting with two men from Inis Meadhon. They want me to go there and start a hedge-school. They're giving me a free house, free turf, and free milk; a 475 rood of standing corn; twelve drills of potatoes; and—

(*He stops.*)

OWEN: And what?

MANUS: A salary of £42 a year!

OWEN: Manus, that's wonderful!

480 MANUS: You're talking to a man of substance.

OWEN: I'm delighted.

YOLLAND: Where's Inis Meadhon?

OWEN: An island south of here. And they came looking for you?

485 MANUS: Well, I mean to say . . .

(OWEN *punches* MANUS.)

OWEN: Aaaaagh! This calls for a real celebration.

YOLLAND: Congratulations.

MANUS: Thank you.

OWEN: Where are you, Anna?

490 YOLLAND: When do you start?

MANUS: Next Monday.

OWEN: We'll stay with you when we're there. (*To* YOLLAND.) How long will it be before we reach Inis Meadhon?

YOLLAND: How far south is it?

495 MANUS: About fifty miles.

YOLLAND: Could we make it by December?

OWEN: We'll have Christmas together. (*Sings.*) 'Christmas Day on Inis Meadhon . . .'

YOLLAND: (*Toast.*) I hope you're very content there, Manus.

500 MANUS: Thank you.

(YOLLAND *holds out his hand.* MANUS *takes it. They shake warmly.*)

OWEN: (*Toast.*) Manus.

MANUS: (*Toast.*) To Inis Meadhon.

(*He drinks quickly and turns to leave.*)

OWEN: Hold on—hold on—refills coming up.

505 MANUS: I've got to go.

OWEN: Come on, man; this is an occasion. Where are you rushing to?

MANUS: I've got to tell Maire.

(MAIRE *enters with her can of milk.*)

MAIRE: You've got to tell Maire what?

OWEN: He's got a job!

510 MAIRE: Manus?

OWEN: He's been invited to start a hedge-school in Inis Meadhon.

MAIRE: Where?

MANUS: Inis Meadhon—the island! They're giving me £42 a

515 year and . . .

OWEN: A house, fuel, milk, potatoes, corn, pupils, what-not!

MANUS: I start on Monday.

OWEN: You'll take a drink. Isn't it great?

MANUS: I want to talk to you for—

520 MAIRE: There's your milk. I need the can back.

(MANUS *takes the can and runs up the steps.*)

MANUS: (*As he goes.*) How will you like living on an island?

OWEN: You know George, don't you?

MAIRE: We wave to each other across the fields.

YOLLAND: Sorry-sorry?

525 OWEN: She says you wave to each other across the fields.

YOLLAND: Yes, we do; oh, yes; indeed we do.

MAIRE: What's he saying?

OWEN: He says you wave to each other across the fields.

MAIRE: That's right. So we do.

YOLLAND: What's she saying?   530

OWEN: Nothing—nothing—nothing. (*To* MAIRE.) What's the news?

(MAIRE *moves away, touching the text books with her toe.*)

MAIRE: Not a thing. You're busy, the two of you.

OWEN: We think we are.

MAIRE: I hear the Fiddler O'Shea's about. There's some talk of   535
a dance tomorrow night.

OWEN: Where will it be?

MAIRE: Maybe over the road. Maybe at Tobair Vree.

YOLLAND: Tobair Vree!

MAIRE: Yes.   540

YOLLAND: Tobair Vree! Tobair Vree!

MAIRE: Does he know what I'm saying?

OWEN: Not a word.

MAIRE: Tell him then.

OWEN: Tell him what?   545

MAIRE: About the dance.

OWEN: Maire says there may be a dance tomorrow night.

YOLLAND: (*To* OWEN.) Yes? May I come? (*To* MAIRE.) Would anybody object if I came?

MAIRE: (*To* OWEN.) What's he saying?   550

OWEN: (*To* YOLLAND.) Who would object?

MAIRE: (*To* OWEN.) Did you tell him?

YOLLAND: (*To* MAIRE.) Sorry-sorry?

OWEN: (*To* MAIRE.) He says may he come?

MAIRE: (*To* YOLLAND.) That's up to you.   555

YOLLAND: (*To* OWEN.) What does she say?

OWEN: (*To* YOLLAND.) She says—

YOLLAND: (*To* MAIRE.) What-what?

MAIRE: (*To* OWEN.) Well?

YOLLAND: (*To* OWEN.) Sorry-sorry?   560

OWEN: (*To* OLLAND.) Will you go?

YOLLAND: (*To* MAIRE.) Yes, yes, if I may.

MAIRE: (*To* OWEN.) What does he say?

YOLLAND: (*To* OWEN.) What is she saying?

OWEN: Oh for God's sake! (*To* MANUS *who is descending with the* 565
empty can.) You take on this job, Manus.

MANUS: I'll walk you up to the house. Is your mother at home? I want to talk to her.

MAIRE: What's the rush? (*To* OWEN.) Didn't you offer me a drink?

OWEN: Will you risk Anna na mBreag?   570

MAIRE: Why not.

(YOLLAND *is suddenly intoxicated. He leaps up on a stool, raises his glass and shouts.*)

YOLLAND: Anna na mBreag! Baile Beag! Inis Meadhon! Bombay! Tobair Vree! Eden! And poteen—correct, Owen?

OWEN: Perfect.

YOLLAND: And bloody marvellous stuff it is, too. I love it!   575
Bloody, bloody, bloody marvellous!

(*Simultaneously with his final 'bloody marvellous' bring up very loud the introductory music of the reel. Then immediately go to black. Retain the music throughout the very brief interval.*)

SCENE II

The following night.

This scene may be played in the schoolroom, but it would be preferable to lose—by lighting—as much of the schoolroom as possible, and to play the scene down front in a vaguely 'outside' area.

The music rises to a crescendo. Then in the distance we hear MAIRE *and* YOLLAND *approach—laughing and running. They run on, hand-in-hand. They have just left the dance. Fade the music to distant background. Then after a time it is lost and replaced by guitar music.* MAIRE *and* YOLLAND *are now down front, still holding hands and excited by their sudden and impetuous escape from the dance.*

MAIRE: O my God, that leap across the ditch nearly killed me.
YOLLAND: I could scarcely keep up with you.
MAIRE: Wait till I get my breath back.
YOLLAND: We must have looked as if we were being chased.

(They now realize they are alone and holding hands—the beginnings of embarrassment. The hands disengage. They begin to drift apart. Pause.)

5 MAIRE: Manus'll wonder where I've got to.
YOLLAND: I wonder did anyone notice us leave.

(Pause. Slightly further apart.)

MAIRE: The grass must be wet. My feet are soaking.
YOLLAND: Your feet must be wet. The grass is soaking.

(Another pause. Another few paces apart. They are now a long distance from one another.)

YOLLAND: *(Indicating himself.)* George.

*(*MAIRE *nods: Yes-yes. Then:—)*

10 MAIRE: Lieutenant George.
YOLLAND: Don't call me that. I never think of myself as Lieutenant.
MAIRE: What-what?
YOLLAND: Sorry-sorry? *(He points to himself again.)* George.

*(*MAIRE *nods: Yes-yes. Then points to herself.)*

15 MAIRE: Maire.
YOLLAND: Yes, I know you're Maire. Of course I know you're Maire. I mean I've been watching you night and day for the past—
MAIRE: *(Eagerly.)* What-what?
20 YOLLAND: *(Points.)* Maire. *(Points.)* George. *(Points both.)* Maire and George.

*(*MAIRE *nods: Yes-yes-yes.)*

I—I—I—
MAIRE: Say anything at all. I love the sound of your speech.
YOLLAND: *(Eagerly.)* Sorry-sorry?

(In acute frustration he looks around, hoping for some inspiration that will provide him with communicative means. Now he has a thought:

he tries raising his voice and articulating in a staccato style and with equal and absurd emphasis on each word.)

Every-morning-I-see-you-feeding-brown-hens-and-giving- 25
meal-to-black-calf—*(The futility of it.)*—Oh my God.

*(*MAIRE *smiles. She moves towards him. She will try to communicate in Latin.)*

MAIRE: *Tu es centurio in—in—in exercitu Britannico—*
YOLLAND: Yes-yes? Go on—go on—say anything at all—I love the sound of your speech.
MAIRE: *—et es in castris quae—quae—quae sunt in agro—(The fu-* 30
tility of it.)—O my God. *(*YOLLAND *smiles. He moves towards her. Now for her English words.)* George—water.
YOLLAND: 'Water'? Water! Oh yes—water—water—very good—water—good—good.
MAIRE: Fire. 35
YOLLAND: Fire—indeed—wonderful—fire, fire, fire—splendid—splendid!
MAIRE: Ah . . . ah . . .
YOLLAND: Yes? Go on.
MAIRE: Earth. 40
YOLLAND: 'Earth'?
MAIRE: Earth. Earth. *(*YOLLAND *still does not understand.* MAIRE *stoops down and picks up a handful of clay. Holding it out.)* Earth.
YOLLAND: Earth! Of course—earth! Earth. Earth. Good Lord, 45
Maire, your English is perfect!
MAIRE: *(Eagerly.)* What-what?
YOLLAND: Perfect English. English perfect.
MAIRE: George—
YOLLAND: That's beautiful—oh, that's really beautiful. 50
MAIRE: George—
YOLLAND: Say it again—say it again—
MAIRE: Shhh. *(She holds her hand up for silence—she is trying to remember her one line of English. Now she remembers it and she de-* 55
livers the line as if English were her language—easily, fluidly, conversationally.) George, 'In Norfolk we besport ourselves around the maypoll.'
YOLLAND: Good God, do you? That's where my mother comes from—Norfolk. Norwich actually. Not exactly Norwich 60
town but a small village called Little Walsingham close beside it. But in our own village of Winfarthing we have a maypole too and every year on the first of May—*(He stops abruptly, only now realizing. He stares at her. She in turn misunderstands his excitement.)*
MAIRE: *(To herself.)* Mother of God, my Aunt Mary wouldn't 65
have taught me something dirty, would she?

(Pause. YOLLAND *extends his hand to* MAIRE. *She turns away from him and moves slowly across the stage.)*

YOLLAND: Maire.

II.ii. 27 *Tu . . . Britannico* you are a centurion in the British Army 30 *et . . . agro* and you are in the camp in the field

(She still moves away.)

Maire Chatach.

(She still moves away.)

70　Bun na hAbhann? *(He says the name softly, almost privately, very tentatively, as if he were searching for a sound she might respond to. He tries again.)* Druim Dubh?

(MAIRE stops. She is listening. YOLLAND is encouraged.)

Poll na gCaorach. Lis Maol.

(MAIRE turns towards him.)

Lis na nGall.
MAIRE: Lis na nGradh.

(They are now facing each other and begin moving—almost imperceptibly—towards one another.)

75　MAIRE: Carraig an Phoill.
YOLLAND: Carraig na Ri. Loch na nEan.
MAIRE: Loch an Iubhair. Machaire Buidhe.
YOLLAND: Machaire Mor. Cnoc na Mona.
MAIRE: Cnoc na nGabhar.
80　YOLLAND: Mullach.
MAIRE: Port.
YOLLAND: Tor.
MAIRE: Lag.

(She holds out her hands to YOLLAND. He takes them. Each now speaks almost to himself/herself.)

YOLLAND: I wish to God you could understand me.
85　MAIRE: Soft hands; a gentleman's hands.
YOLLAND: Because if you could understand me I could tell you how I spend my days either thinking of you or gazing up at your house in the hope that you'll appear even for a second.
MAIRE: Every evening you walk by yourself along the Tra Bhan
90　and every morning you wash yourself in front of your tent.
YOLLAND: I would tell you how beautiful you are, curly-headed Maire. I would so like to tell you how beautiful you are.
MAIRE: Your arms are long and thin and the skin on your shoulders is very white.
95　YOLLAND: I would tell you . . .
MAIRE: Don't stop—I know what you're saying.
YOLLAND: I would tell you how I want to be here—to live here—always—with you—always, always.
MAIRE: 'Always'? What is that word—'always'?
100　YOLLAND: Yes–yes; always.
MAIRE: You're trembling.
YOLLAND: Yes, I'm trembling because of you.
MAIRE: I'm trembling, too.

(She holds his face in her hand.)

YOLLAND: I've made up my mind . . .
105　MAIRE: Shhhh.
YOLLAND: I'm not going to leave here . . .
MAIRE: Shhhh—listen to me. I want you, too, soldier.

YOLLAND: Don't stop—I know what you're saying.
MAIRE: I want to live with you—anywhere—anywhere at all— always—always.　　　　　　　　　　　　　　　110
YOLLAND: 'Always'? What is that word—'always'?
MAIRE: Take me away with you, George.

(Pause. Suddenly they kiss. SARAH enters. She sees them. She stands shocked, staring at them. Her mouth works. Then almost to herself.)

SARAH: Manus . . . Manus!

(SARAH runs off. Music to crescendo.)

ACT THREE

The following evening. It is raining.

SARAH and OWEN alone in the schoolroom. SARAH, more waif-like than ever, is sitting very still on a stool, an open book across her knee. She is pretending to read but her eyes keep going up to the room upstairs. OWEN is working on the floor as before, surrounded by his reference books, map, Name-Book, etc. But he has neither concentration nor interest; and like SARAH he glances up at the upstairs room.

After a few seconds MANUS emerges and descends, carrying a large paper bag which already contains his clothes. His movements are determined and urgent. He moves around the classroom, picking up books, examining each title carefully, and choosing about six of them which he puts into his bag. As he selects these books:—

OWEN: You know that old limekiln beyond Con Connie Tim's pub, the place we call The Murren?—do you know why it's called The Murren?

(MANUS does not answer.)

I've only just discovered: it's a corruption of Saint Muranus. It seems Saint Muranus had a monastery somewhere about　　5
there at the beginning of the seventh century. And over the years the name became shortened to the Murren. Very unattractive name, isn't it? I think we should go back to the original—Saint Muranus. What do you think? The original's Saint Muranus. Don't you think we should go back to that?　　10

(No response. OWEN begins writing the name into the Name-Book. MANUS is now rooting about among the forgotten implements for a piece of rope. He finds a piece. He begins to tie the mouth of the flimsy, overloaded bag—and it bursts, the contents spilling out on the floor.)

MANUS: Bloody, bloody, bloody hell!

(His voice breaks in exasperation: he is about to cry. OWEN leaps to his feet.)

OWEN: Hold on. I've a bag upstairs.

(He runs upstairs. SARAH waits until OWEN is off. Then:—)

SARAH: Manus . . . Manus, I . . .

(MANUS hears SARAH but makes no acknowledgement. He gathers up his belongings. OWEN reappears with the bag he had on his arrival.)

OWEN: Take this one—I'm finished with it anyway. And it's supposed to keep out the rain.　　　　　　　　　　　15

(MANUS *transfers his few belongings.* OWEN *drifts back to his task. The packing is now complete.*)

MANUS: You'll be here for a while? For a week or two anyhow?

OWEN: Yes.

MANUS: You're not leaving with the army?

OWEN: I haven't made up my mind. Why?

20 MANUS: Those Inis Meadhon men will be back to see why I haven't turned up. Tell them—tell them I'll write to them as soon as I can. Tell them I still want the job but that it might be three or four months before I'm free to go.

OWEN: You're being damned stupid, Manus.

25 MANUS: Will you do that for me?

OWEN: Clear out now and Lancey'll think you're involved somehow.

MANUS: Will you do that for me?

OWEN: Wait a couple of days even. You know George—he's a

30 bloody romantic—maybe he's gone out to one of the islands and he'll suddenly reappear tomorrow morning. Or maybe the search party'll find him this evening lying drunk somewhere in the sandhills. You've seen him drinking that poteen—doesn't know how to handle it. Had he drink on

35 him last night at the dance?

MANUS: I had a stone in my hand when I went out looking for him—I was going to fell him. The lame scholar turned violent.

OWEN: Did anybody see you?

40 MANUS: (*Again close to tears.*) But when I saw him standing there at the side of the road—smiling—and her face buried in his shoulder—I couldn't even go close to them. I just shouted something stupid—something like, 'You're a bastard, Yolland.' If I'd even said it in English . . . 'cos he kept saying

45 'Sorry-sorry?' The wrong gesture in the wrong language.

OWEN: And you didn't see him again?

MANUS: 'Sorry?'

OWEN: Before you leave tell Lancey that—just to clear yourself.

MANUS: What have I to say to Lancey? You'll give that message

50 to the islandmen?

OWEN: I'm warning you: run away now and you're bound to be—

MANUS: (*To* SARAH.) Will you give that message to the Inis Meadhon men?

55 SARAH: I will.

(MANUS *picks up an old sack and throws it across his shoulders.*)

OWEN: Have you any idea where you're going?

MANUS: Mayo, maybe. I remember Mother saying she had cousins somewhere away out in the Erris Peninsula. (*He picks up his bag.*) Tell Father I took only the Virgil and the

60 Caesar and the Aeschylus because they're mine anyway—I bought them with the money I got for that pet lamb I reared—do you remember that pet lamb? And tell him that Nora Dan never returned the dictionary and that she still owes him two-and-six for last quarter's reading—he always

65 forgets those things.

OWEN: Yes.

MANUS: And his good shirt's ironed and hanging up in the press and his clean socks are in the butter-box under the bed.

OWEN: All right.

MANUS: And tell him I'll write.   70

OWEN: If Maire asks where you've gone . . . ?

MANUS: He'll need only half the amount of milk now, won't he? Even less than half—he usually takes his tea black. (*Pause.*) And when he comes in at night—you'll hear him; he makes a lot of noise; I usually come down and give him   75

a hand up. Those stairs are dangerous without a banister. Maybe before you leave you'd get Big Ned Frank to put up some sort of a handrail. (*Pause.*) And if you can bake, he's very fond of soda bread.

OWEN: I can give you money. I'm wealthy. Do you know what   80

they pay me? Two shillings a day for this—this—this—

(MANUS *rejects the offer by holding out his hand.*)

Goodbye, Manus.

(MANUS *and* OWEN *shake hands. Then* MANUS *picks up his bag briskly and goes towards the door. He stops a few paces beyond* SARAH, *turns, comes back to her. He addresses her as he did in Act One but now without warmth or concern for her.*)

MANUS: What is your name? (*Pause.*) Come on. What is your name?

SARAH: My name is Sarah.   85

MANUS: Just Sarah? Sarah what? (*Pause.*) Well?

SARAH: Sarah Johnny Sally.

MANUS: And where do you live? Come on.

SARAH: I live in Bun na hAbhann.

(*She is now crying quietly.*)

MANUS: Very good, Sarah Johnny Sally. There's nothing to stop   90

you now—nothing in the wide world. (*Pause. He looks down at her.*) It's all right—it's all right—you did no harm—you did no harm at all.

(*He stoops over her and kisses the top of her head—as if in absolution. Then briskly to the door and off.*)

OWEN: Good luck, Manus!

SARAH: (*Quietly.*) I'm sorry . . . I'm sorry . . . I'm so sorry,   95

Manus . . .

(OWEN *tries to work but cannot concentrate. He begins folding up the map. As he does:—*)

OWEN: Is there a class this evening?

(SARAH *nods:* Yes.)

I suppose Father knows. Where is he anyhow?

(SARAH *points.*)

Where?

(SARAH *mimes rocking a baby.*)

I don't understand—where?   100

(SARAH *repeats the mime and wipes away tears.* OWEN *is still puzzled.*)

It doesn't matter. He'll probably turn up.

(BRIDGET *and* DOALTY *enter, sacks over their heads against the rain. They are self-consciously noisier, more ebullient, more garrulous than ever—brimming over with excitement and gossip and brio.*)

DOALTY: You're missing the crack, boys! Cripes, you're missing the crack! Fifty more soldiers arrived an hour ago!

BRIDGET: And they're spread out in a big line from Sean Neal's
105 over to Lag and they're moving straight across the fields towards Cnoc na nGabhar!

DOALTY: Prodding every inch of the ground in front of them with their bayonets and scattering animals and hens in all directions!

110 BRIDGET: And tumbling everything before them—fences, ditches, haystacks, turf-stacks!

DOALTY: They came to Barney Petey's field of corn—straight through it be God as if it was heather!

BRIDGET: Not a blade of it left standing!

115 DOALTY: And Barney Petey just out of his bed and running after them in his drawers: 'You hoors you! Get out of my corn, you hoors you!'

BRIDGET: First time he ever ran in his life.

DOALTY: Too lazy, the wee get, to cut it when the weather was
120 good.

(SARAH *begins putting out the seats.*)

BRIDGET: Tell them about Big Hughie.

DOALTY: Cripes, if you'd seen your aul fella, Owen.

BRIDGET: They were all inside in Anna na mBreag's pub—all the crowd from the wake—

125 DOALTY: And they hear the commotion and they all come out to the street—

BRIDGET: Your father in front; the Infant Prodigy footless behind him!

DOALTY: And your aul fella, he sees the army stretched across
130 the countryside—

BRIDGET: O my God!

DOALTY: And Cripes he starts roaring at them!

BRIDGET: 'Visigoths! Huns! Vandals!'

DOALTY: '*Ignari! Stulti! Rustici!*'

135 BRIDGET: And wee Jimmy Jack jumping up and down and shouting, 'Thermopylae! Thermopylae!'

DOALTY: You never saw crack like it in your life, boys. Come away on out with me, Sarah, and you'll see it all.

BRIDGET: Big Hughie's fit to take no class. Is Manus about?

140 OWEN: Manus is gone.

BRIDGET: Gone where?

OWEN: He's left—gone away.

DOALTY: Where to?

OWEN: He doesn't know. Mayo, maybe.

145 DOALTY: What's on in Mayo?

OWEN: (*To* BRIDGET.) Did you see George and Maire Chatach leave the dance last night?

BRIDGET: We did. Didn't we, Doalty?

OWEN: Did you see Manus following them out?

150 BRIDGET: I didn't see him going out but I saw him coming in by himself later.

OWEN: Did George and Maire come back to the dance?

BRIDGET: No.

OWEN: Did you see them again?

BRIDGET: He left her home. We passed them going up the back 155
road—didn't we, Doalty?

OWEN: And Manus stayed till the end of the dance?

DOALTY: We know nothing. What are you asking us for?

OWEN: Because Lancey'll question me when he hears Manus's gone. (*Back to* BRIDGET.) That's the way George went 160
home? By the back road? That's where you saw him?

BRIDGET: Leave me alone, Owen. I know nothing about Yolland. If you want to know about Yolland, ask the Donnelly twins.

(*Silence.* DOALTY *moves over to the window.*)

(*To* SARAH.) He's a powerful fiddler, O'Shea, isn't he? He
told our Seamus he'll come back for a night at Hallowe'en. 165

(OWEN *goes to* DOALTY *who looks resolutely out the window.*)

OWEN: What's this about the Donnellys? (*Pause.*) Were they about last night?

DOALTY: Didn't see them if they were.

(*Begins whistling through his teeth.*)

OWEN: George is a friend of mine.

DOALTY: So. 170

OWEN: I want to know what's happened to him.

DOALTY: Couldn't tell you.

OWEN: What have the Donnelly twins to do with it? (*Pause.*) Doalty!

DOALTY: I know nothing, Owen—nothing at all—I swear to 175
God. All I know is this: on my way to the dance I saw their boat beached at Port. It wasn't there on my way home, after I left Bridget. And that's all I know. As God's my judge. The half-dozen times I met him I didn't know a word he said to me; but he seemed a right enough sort . . . (*With sud- 180
den excessive interest in the scene outside.*) Cripes, they're crawling all over the place! Cripes, there's millions of them! Cripes, they're levelling the whole land!

(OWEN *moves away.* MAIRE *enters. She is bareheaded and wet from the rain; her hair in disarray. She attempts to appear normal but she is in acute distress, on the verge of being distraught. She is carrying the milk-can.*)

MAIRE: Honest to God, I must be going off my head. I'm halfway here and I think to myself, 'Isn't this can very 185
light?' and I look into it and isn't it empty.

OWEN: It doesn't matter.

MAIRE: How will you manage for tonight?

OWEN: We have enough.

MAIRE: Are you sure? 190

OWEN: Plenty, thanks.

MAIRE: It'll take me no time at all to go back up for some.

OWEN: Honestly, Maire.

MAIRE: Sure it's better you have it than that black calf that's . . . that . . . (*She looks around.*) Have you heard anything? 195

OWEN: Nothing.

MAIRE: What does Lancey say?

OWEN: I haven't seen him since this morning.

MAIRE: What does he *think*?

200 OWEN: We really didn't talk. He was here for only a few seconds.

MAIRE: He left me home, Owen. And the last thing he said to me—he tried to speak in Irish—he said, 'I'll see you yesterday'—he meant to say 'I'll see you tomorrow.' And I laughed that much he pretended to get cross and he said

205 'Maypoll! Maypoll!' because I said that word wrong. And off he went, laughing—laughing, Owen! Do you think he's all right? What do *you* think?

OWEN: I'm sure he'll turn up, Maire.

MAIRE: He comes from a tiny wee place called Winfarthing.

210 (*She suddenly drops on her hands and knees on the floor—where* OWEN *had his map a few minutes ago—and with her finger traces out an outline map.*) Come here till you see. Look. There's Winfarthing. And there's two other wee villages right beside it; one of them's called Barton Bendish—it's there; and

215 the other's called Saxingham Nethergate—it's about there. And there's Little Walsingham—that's his mother's townland. Aren't they odd names? Sure they make no sense to me at all. And Winfarthing's near a big town called Norwich. And Norwich is in a county called Norfolk. And

220 Norfolk is in the east of England. He drew a map for me on the wet strand and wrote the names on it. I have it all in my head now: Winfarthing—Barton Bendish—Saxingham Nethergate—Little Walsingham—Norwich—Norfolk. Strange sounds, aren't they? But nice sounds; like Jimmy Jack recit-

225 ing his Homer. (*She gets to her feet and looks around; she is almost serene now. To* SARAH.) You were looking lovely last night, Sarah. Is that the dress you got from Boston? Green suits you. (*To* OWEN.) Something very bad's happened to him, I know. He wouldn't go away without telling

230 me. Where is he, Owen? You're his friend—where is he? (*Again she looks around the room; then sits on a stool.*) I didn't get a chance to do my geography last night. The master'll be angry with me. (*She rises again.*) I think I'll go home now. The wee ones have to be washed and put to bed and

235 that black calf has to be fed . . . My hands are that rough; they're still blistered from the hay. I'm ashamed of them. I hope to God there's no hay to be saved in Brooklyn. (*She stops at the door.*) Did you hear? Nellie Ruadh's baby died in the middle of the night. I must go up to the wake. It didn't

240 last long, did it?

(MAIRE *leaves. Silence. Then:*)

OWEN: I don't think there'll be any class. Maybe you should . . .

(OWEN *begins picking up his texts.* DOALTY *goes to him.*)

DOALTY: Is he long gone?—Manus?

OWEN: Half an hour.

DOALTY: Stupid bloody fool.

245 OWEN: I told him that.

DOALTY: Do they know he's gone?

OWEN: Who?

DOALTY: The army.

OWEN: Not yet.

250 DOALTY: They'll be after him like bloody beagles. Bloody, bloody fool, limping along the coast. They'll overtake him before night for Christ's sake.

(DOALTY *returns to the window.* LANCEY *enters—now the commanding officer.*)

OWEN: Any news? Any word?

(LANCEY *moves into the centre of the room, looking around as he does.*)

LANCEY: I understood there was a class. Where are the others?

OWEN: There was to be a class but my father— 255

LANCEY: This will suffice. I will address them and it will be their responsibility to pass on what I have to say to every family in this section.

(LANCEY *indicates to* OWEN *to translate.* OWEN *hesitates, trying to assess the change in* LANCEY'S *manner and attitude.*)

I'm in a hurry, O'Donnell.

OWEN: The captain has an announcement to make. 260

LANCEY: Lieutenant Yolland is missing. We are searching for him. If we don't find him, or if we receive no information as to where he is to be found, I will pursue the following course of action. (*He indicates to* OWEN *to translate.*)

OWEN: They are searching for George. If they don't find him— 265

LANCEY: Commencing twenty-four hours from now we will shoot all livestock in Ballybeg.

(OWEN *stares at* LANCEY.)

At once.

OWEN: Beginning this time tomorrow they'll kill every animal in Baile Beag—unless they're told where George is. 270

LANCEY: If that doesn't bear results, commencing forty-eight hours from now we will embark on a series of evictions and levelling of every abode in the following selected areas—

OWEN: You're not—!

LANCEY: Do your job. Translate. 275

OWEN: If they still haven't found him in two days time they'll begin evicting and levelling every house starting with these townlands.

(LANCEY *reads from his list.*)

LANCEY: Swinefort.

OWEN: Lis na Muc. 280

LANCEY: Burnfoot.

OWEN: Bun na hAbhann.

LANCEY: Dromduff.

OWEN: Druim Dubh.

LANCEY: Whiteplains. 285

OWEN: Machaire Ban.

LANCEY: Kings Head.

OWEN: Cnoc na Ri.

LANCEY: If by then the lieutenant hasn't been found, we will proceed until a complete clearance is made of this entire 290 section.

OWEN: If Yolland hasn't been got by then, they will ravish the whole parish.

LANCEY: I trust they know exactly what they've got to do. (*Pointing to* BRIDGET.) I know you. I know where you live. 295 (*Pointing to* SARAH.) Who are you? Name!

(SARAH'S *mouth opens and shuts, opens and shuts. Her face becomes contorted.*)

What's your name?

(*Again* SARAH *tries frantically.*)

OWEN: Go on, Sarah. You can tell him.

(*But* SARAH *cannot. And she knows she cannot. She closes her mouth. Her head goes down.*)

OWEN: Her name is Sarah Johnny Sally.
300 LANCEY: Where does she live?
OWEN: Bun na hAbhann.
LANCEY: Where?
OWEN: Burnfoot.
LANCEY: I want to talk to your brother—is he here?
305 OWEN: Not at the moment.
LANCEY: Where is he?
OWEN: He's at a wake.
LANCEY: What wake?

(DOALTY, *who has been looking out the window all through* LANCEY's *announcements, now speaks—calmly, almost casually.*)

DOALTY: Tell him his whole camp's on fire.
310 LANCEY: What's your name? (*To* OWEN.) Who's that lout?
OWEN: Doalty Dan Doalty.
LANCEY: Where does he live?
OWEN: Tulach Alainn.
LANCEY: What do we call it?
315 OWEN: Fair Hill. He says your whole camp is on fire.

(LANCEY *rushes to the window and looks out. Then he wheels on* DOALTY.)

LANCEY: I'll remember you, Mr Doalty. (*To* OWEN.) You carry a big responsibility in all this.

(*He goes off.*)

BRIDGET: Mother of God, does he mean it, Owen?
OWEN: Yes, he does.
320 BRIDGET: We'll have to hide the beasts somewhere—our Seamus'll know where. Maybe at the back of Lis na nGradh—or in the caves at the far end of Tra Bhan. Come on, Doalty! Come on! Don't be standing about there!

(DOALTY *does not move.* BRIDGET *runs to the door and stops suddenly. She sniffs the air. Panic.*)

The sweet smell! Smell it! It's the sweet smell! Jesus, it's the
325 potato blight!
DOALTY: It's the army tents burning, Bridget.
BRIDGET: Is it? Are you sure? Is that what it is? God, I thought we were destroyed altogether. Come on! Come on!

(*She runs off.* OWEN *goes to* SARAH *who is preparing to leave.*)

OWEN: How are you? Are you all right?

(SARAH *nods:* Yes.)

330 OWEN: Don't worry. It will come back to you again.

(SARAH *shakes her head.*)

OWEN: It will. You're upset now. He frightened you. That's all's wrong.

(*Again* SARAH *shakes her head, slowly, emphatically, and smiles at* OWEN. *Then she leaves.* OWEN *busies himself gathering his belongings.* DOALTY *leaves the window and goes to him.*)

DOALTY: He'll do it, too.
OWEN: Unless Yolland's found.
DOALTY: Hah!   335
OWEN: Then he'll certainly do it.
DOALTY: When my grandfather was a boy they did the same thing. (*Simply, altogether without irony.*) And after all the trouble you went to, mapping the place and thinking up new names for it. (OWEN *busies himself. Pause.* DOALTY *almost* 340 *dreamily.*) I've damned little to defend but he'll not put me out without a fight. And there'll be others who think the same as me.
OWEN: That's a matter for you.
DOALTY: If we'd all stick together. If we knew how to defend 345 ourselves.
OWEN: Against a trained army.
DOALTY: The Donnelly twins know how.
OWEN: If they could be found.
DOALTY: If they could be found. (*He goes to the door.*) Give me a 350 shout after you've finished with Lancey. I might know something then.

(*He leaves.*)

(OWEN *picks up the Name-Book. He looks at it momentarily, then puts it on top of the pile he is carrying. It falls to the floor. He stoops to pick it up—hesitates—leaves it. He goes upstairs. As* OWEN *ascends,* HUGH *and* JIMMY JACK *enter. Both wet and drunk.* JIMMY *is very unsteady. He is trotting behind* HUGH, *trying to break in on* HUGH's *declamation.* HUGH *is equally drunk but more experienced in drunkenness: there is a portion of his mind which retains its clarity.*)

HUGH: There I was, appropriately dispositioned to proffer my condolences to the bereaved mother . . .
JIMMY: Hugh—   355
HUGH: and about to enter the *domus lugubris*—Maire Chatach?
JIMMY: The wake house.
HUGH: Indeed—when I experience a plucking at my elbow: Mister George Alexander, Justice of the Peace. 'My tidings 360 are infelicitous,' said he—Bridget? Too slow. Doalty?
JIMMY: *Infelix*—unhappy.
HUGH: Unhappy indeed. 'Master Bartley Timlin has been appointed to the new national school.' 'Timlin? Who is Timlin?' 'A schoolmaster from Cork. And he will be a major as- 365 set to the community: he is also a very skilled bacon-curer!'
JIMMY: Hugh—
HUGH: Ha-ha-ha-ha-ha! The Cork bacon-curer! *Barbarus hic ego sum quia non intelligor ulli*—James?

III. 356 *domus lugubris* house of mourning   362 *infelix* unlucky, unhappy   368–369 *Barbarus . . . ulli* I am a barbarian here because I am not understood by anyone

370 JIMMY: Ovid.

HUGH: *Procede.*

JIMMY: 'I am a barbarian in this place because I am not understood by anyone.'

HUGH: Indeed—(*Shouts.*) Manus! Tea! I will compose a satire
375 on Master Bartley Timlin, schoolmaster and bacon-curer. But it will be too easy, won't it? (*Shouts.*) Strong tea! Black!

(*The only way* JIMMY *can get* HUGH's *attention is by standing in front of him and holding his arms.*)

JIMMY: Will you listen to me, Hugh!

HUGH: James. (*Shouts.*) And a slice of soda bread.

JIMMY: I'm going to get married.

380 HUGH: Well!

JIMMY: At Christmas.

HUGH: Splendid.

JIMMY: To Athene.

HUGH: Who?

385 JIMMY: Pallas Athene.

HUGH: *Glaukopis Athene?*

JIMMY: Flashing-eyed, Hugh, flashing-eyed!

(*He attempts the gesture he has made before: standing to attention, the momentary spasm, the salute, the face raised in pained ecstasy—but the body does not respond efficiently this time. The gesture is grotesque.*)

HUGH: The lady has assented?

JIMMY: She asked *me*—I assented.

390 HUGH: Ah. When was this?

JIMMY: Last night.

HUGH: What does her mother say?

JIMMY: Metis from Hellespont? Decent people—good stock.

HUGH: And her father?

395 JIMMY: I'm meeting Zeus tomorrow. Hugh, will you be my best man?

HUGH: Honoured, James; profoundly honoured.

JIMMY: You know what I'm looking for, Hugh, don't you? I mean to say—you know—I—I—I joke like the rest of
400 them—you know?—(*Again he attempts the pathetic routine but abandons it instantly.*) You know yourself, Hugh—don't you?—you know all that. But what I'm really looking for, Hugh—what I really want—companionship, Hugh—at my time of life, companionship, company, someone to talk
405 to. Away up in Beann na Gaoithe—you've no idea how lonely it is. Companionship—correct, Hugh? Correct?

HUGH: Correct.

JIMMY: And I always liked her, Hugh. Correct?

HUGH: Correct, James.

410 JIMMY: Someone to talk to.

HUGH: Indeed.

JIMMY: That's all, Hugh. The whole story. You know it all now, Hugh. You know it all.

(*As* JIMMY *says those last lines he is crying, shaking his head, trying to keep his balance, and holding a finger up to his lips in absurd gestures of secrecy and intimacy. Now he staggers away, tries to sit on a stool, misses it, slides to the floor, his feet in front of him, his back against the broken cart. Almost at once he is asleep.* HUGH *watches all of this. Then he produces his flask and is about to pour a drink when he sees the Name-Book on the floor. He picks it up and leafs through*

it, pronouncing the strange names as he does. Just as he begins, OWEN *emerges and descends with two bowls of tea.*)

HUGH: Ballybeg. Burnfoot. King's Head. Whiteplains. Fair Hill. Dunboy. Green Bank. 415

(OWEN *snatches the book from* HUGH.)

OWEN: I'll take that. (*In apology.*) It's only a catalogue of names.

HUGH: I know what it is.

OWEN: A mistake—my mistake—nothing to do with us. I hope that's strong enough [*tea*]. (*He throws the book on the table and crosses over to* JIMMY.) Jimmy. Wake up, Jimmy. 420 Wake up, man.

JIMMY: What—what-what?

OWEN: Here. Drink this. Then go on away home. There may be trouble. Do you hear me, Jimmy? There may be trouble.

HUGH: (*Indicating Name-Book.*) We must learn those new 425 names.

OWEN: (*Searching around.*) Did you see a sack lying about?

HUGH: We must learn where we live. We must learn to make them our own. We must make them our new home.

(OWEN *finds a sack and throws it across his shoulders.*)

OWEN: I know where I live. 430

HUGH: James thinks he knows, too. I look at James and three thoughts occur to me: A—that it is not the literal past, the 'facts' of history, that shape us, but images of the past embodied in language. James has ceased to make that discrimination. 435

OWEN: Don't lecture me, Father.

HUGH: B—we must never cease renewing those images; because once we do, we fossilize. Is there no soda bread?

OWEN: And C, Father—one single, unalterable 'fact': if Yolland is not found, we are all going to be evicted. Lancey has is- 440 sued the order.

HUGH: Ah. *Edictum imperatoris.*

OWEN: You should change out of those wet clothes. I've got to go. I've got to see Doalty Dan Doalty.

HUGH: What about? 445

OWEN: I'll be back soon.

(*As* OWEN *exits.*)

HUGH: Take care, Owen. To remember everything is a form of madness. (*He looks around the room, carefully, as if he were about to leave it forever. Then he looks at* JIMMY, *asleep again.*) The road to Sligo. A spring morning. 1798. Going into battle. 450 Do you remember, James? Two young gallants with pikes across their shoulders and the *Aeneid* in their pockets. Everything seemed to find definition that spring—a congruence, a miraculous matching of hope and past and present and possibility. Striding across the fresh, green land. 455 The rhythms of perception heightened. The whole enterprise of consciousness accelerated. We were gods that morning, James; and I had recently married *my* goddess,

---

442 *edictum imperatoris* the decree os the commander

Caitlin Dubh Nic Reactainn, may she rest in peace. And to
460   leave her and my infant son in his cradle—that was heroic,
too. By God, sir, we were magnificent. We marched as far
as—where was it?—Glenties! All of twenty-three miles in
one day. And it was there, in Phelan's pub, that we got
home-sick for Athens, just like Ulysses. The *desiderium*
465   *nostrorum*—the need for our own. Our *pietas,* James, was for
older, quieter things. And that was the longest twenty-
three miles back I ever made. (*Toasts* JIMMY.) My friend,
confusion is not an ignoble condition.

(MAIRE *enters.*)

MAIRE: I'm back again. I set out for somewhere but I couldn't
470   remember where. So I came back here.
HUGH: Yes, I will teach you English, Maire Chatach.
MAIRE: Will you, Master? I must learn it. I need to learn it.
HUGH: Indeed you may well be my only pupil.

(*He goes towards the steps and begins to ascend.*)

MAIRE: When can we start?
475   HUGH: Not today. Tomorrow, perhaps. After the funeral. We'll
begin tomorrow. (*Ascending.*) But don't expect too much. I
will provide you with the available words and the available
grammar. But will that help you to interpret between priva-
cies? I have no idea. But it's all we have. I have no idea at all.

(*He is now at the top.*)

480   MAIRE: Master, what does the English word 'always' mean?
HUGH: *Semper*—*per omnia saecula.* The Greeks called it *'aei.'* It's
not a word I'd start with. It's a silly word, girl.

(*He sits.* JIMMY *is awake. He gets to his feet.* MAIRE *sees the Name-
Book, picks it up, and sits with it on her knee.*)

MAIRE: When he comes back, this is where he'll come to. He
told me this is where he was happiest.

(JIMMY *sits beside* MAIRE.)

JIMMY: Do you know the Greek word *endogamein?* It means to   485
marry within the tribe. And the word *exogamein* means to
marry outside the tribe. And you don't cross those borders
casually—both sides get very angry. Now, the problem is
this: Is Athene sufficiently mortal or am I sufficiently god-
like for the marriage to be acceptable to her people and to   490
my people? You think about that.
HUGH: *Urbs antiqua fuit*—there was an ancient city which, 'tis
said, Juno loved above all the lands. And it was the goddess's aim and cherished hope that here should be the capital of all nations—should the fates perchance allow that.   495
Yet in truth she discovered that a race was springing from
Trojan blood to overthrow some day these Tyrian towers—a people *late regem belloque superbum*—kings of broad
realms and proud in war who would come forth for
Libya's downfall—such was—such was the course—such   500
was the course ordained—ordained by fate . . . What the
hell's wrong with me? Sure I know it backwards. I'll begin
again. *Urbs antiqua fuit*—there was an ancient city which,
'tis said, Juno loved above all the lands.

(*Begin to bring down the lights.*)

And it was the goddess's aim and cherished hope that here   505
should be the capital of all nations—should the fates perchance allow that. Yet in truth she discovered that a race was
springing from Trojan blood to overthrow some day these
Tyrian towers—a people kings of broad realms and proud
in war who would come forth for Libya's downfall . . .   510

(*Blackout.*)

464–465 *desiderium nostrorum* longing/need for our things/
people   465 *pietas* piety   481 *Semper . . . saecula* always—for
all time; *aei* always

---

485 *endogamein* to marry within the tribe   486 *exogamein* to
marry outside the tribe   492 *Urbs antiqua* **fuit** there was an ancient city   498 *late . . . superbum* kings of broad realms and
proud in war, from Virgil's *Aeneid,* book I.

Athol Fugard

Born in 1932, the South African playwright Athol Fugard left the University of Cape Town in 1953, traveled Africa, and worked as a seaman before returning to Cape Town and undertaking theater work with the Circle Players. As a mixed-race company, the Circle Players worked in violation of South Africa's apartheid laws. They brought the issue of apartheid to a head when Fugard—a white man—collaborated with the black actor Zakes Mokae in the play *The Blood Knot* (1961), a play about two brothers, one of whom is light-skinned enough to "pass" for white. The play's powerful indictment of apartheid and the fine performances of Fugard and Mokae were widely admired, and gained Fugard a reputation as a dramatist outside South Africa. Yet, despite its notoriety, the play could hardly remove apartheid itself. Fugard and Mokae were still forced to travel separately, and the government passed new laws limiting interracial theater; in addition, Fugard had his passport withdrawn for four years. In 1963, Fugard began his long association with The Serpent Players, a black company. This association was made nearly impossible, however, by the 1965 extension of the Group Areas Act, one of the principal apartheid statutes: both racially mixed casts and racially mixed audiences were forbidden. By June of 1965, Fugard was denied a permit to enter the black township of New Brighton for the dress rehearsal of Sophocles' *Antigone,* which he had adapted and produced with The Serpent Players. His passport was withdrawn again, and then again for four years, in 1967.

By the early 1970s, Fugard had written several of his best-known plays—*Hello and Goodbye* (1965), *Boesman and Lena* (1969)—when he became frustrated with his method of writing plays and decided to work more collaboratively with The Serpent Players. Fugard had worked with John Kani (b. 1944) on the 1965 *Antigone,* and Kani and Winston Ntshona (b. 1941) had performed another absurdist two-hander about convicts—Jean Genet's *Deathwatch*—with the Serpent company in 1968. Both Kani and Ntshona were recognized performers in their own right when they agreed to collaborate with Fugard in the early 1970s. These collaborations were different from Fugard's earlier adaptations of European classics for The Serpent Players, for in this work Kani and Ntshona supplied information, dialogue, and performance tropes which were scripted and shaped in dialogue with Fugard. The plays they devised—*Sizwe Bansi Is Dead* (1972) and *The Island* (1973)—are fully collaborative, for the three men improvised a variety of possible performances before setting them down in a final design; the opening monologue with the newspaper in *Sizwe Bansi Is Dead,* for instance, is based on Kani's usual stand-up performance routines. Fugard has gone on to write a number of plays about the effects of apartheid and racism on South African life, including *A Lesson from Aloes* (1980), *"Master Harold" . . . and the boys* (1982), *My Children! My Africa!* (1989), *Playland* (1993), *Valley Song* (1996), *The Captain's Tiger* (1998), and *Sorrows and Rejoicings* (2002).

"MASTER HAROLD" . . . AND THE BOYS

"Master Harold" . . . and the boys is one of Fugard's most personal and searching plays on the consequences of racial apartheid for individual human relationships. The play takes place in the St. George's Park Tea Room in Port Elizabeth, South Africa, and is set in 1950; but while the play is set during the solidification of South Africa's apartheid legislation—the Pass Laws were passed in 1948, the Prohibition of Mixed Marriages Act in 1949, and the Group Areas Act and the Immorality Amendment Act in 1950—the play has an atmosphere of hope as well, conveyed in part by the American dance music that forms the play's acoustic background. Dance is the central metaphor of the play's action, as first Sam teaches Willie, preparing him for his entry into the upcoming dance competition, and then Sam and Hally engage in a more intricate and violent emotional encounter. For Sam and Hally have a long

Willie, Hally, and Sam in the Roundabout Theater production of *"Master Harold" ... and the boys.*

history. Hally's father is an abusive, alcoholic invalid, and Sam has in many ways filled his place in Hally's life, providing both emotional and practical support. In exchange, he has had the benefit of Hally's education, learning Hally's school lessons as he helped the boy to study. Yet, while there's genuine affection between the two men, their inequality is never far from the surface, appearing even when Hally retells one of his most cherished memories, of the day Sam took him out to fly a kite: "The sheer audacity of it took my breath away. I mean, seriously, what the hell does a black man know about flying a kite?" As the play proceeds, though, Sam's efforts to calm Hally's rage against his father turns Hally against him, leading to the climactic moment in which the suppressed dynamics of racism boil to the surface. Reminding Sam that his father "is a white man and that's good enough for you," Hally then insists that Sam begin calling him "Master Harold," putting an end to their dance of emotional intimacy. Whether it will be possible for Sam and Hally to "fly another kite" remains an open question at the end of the play.

"MASTER HAROLD" . . . AND THE BOYS

Athol Fugard

CHARACTERS

HALLY
SAM
WILLIE

The St. George's Park Tea Room on a wet and windy Port Elizabeth afternoon.

Tables and chairs have been cleared and are stacked on one side except for one which stands apart with a single chair. On this table a knife, fork, spoon and side plate in anticipation of a simple meal, together with a pile of comic books.

Other elements: a serving counter with a few stale cakes under glass and a not very impressive display of sweets, cigarettes and cool drinks, etc.; a few cardboard advertising handouts—Cadbury's Chocolate, Coca-Cola—and a blackboard on which an untrained hand has chalked up the prices of Tea, Coffee, Scones, Milkshakes—all flavors—and Cool Drinks; a few sad ferns in pots; a telephone; an old-style jukebox.

There is an entrance on one side and an exit into a kitchen on the other.

Leaning on the solitary table, his head cupped in one hand as he pages through one of the comic books, is SAM. *A black man in his mid-forties. He wears the white coat of a waiter. Behind him on his knees, mopping down the floor with a bucket of water and a rag, is* WILLIE. *Also black and about the same age as* SAM. *He has his sleeves and trousers rolled up.*

The year: 1950

WILLIE: (*Singing as he works*)
"She was scandalizin' my name,
She took my money
She called me honey
5   But she was scandalizin' my name.
Called it love but was playin' a game . . ."

(*He gets up and moves the bucket. Stands thinking for a moment, then, raising his arms to hold an imaginary partner, he launches into an intricate ballroom dance step. Although a mildly comic figure, he reveals a reasonable degree of accomplishment*)

Hey, Sam.

(SAM, *absorbed in the comic book, does not respond*)

Hey, Boet Sam!

(SAM *looks up*)

I'm getting it. The quickstep. Look now and tell me.
10   (*He repeats the step*) Well?
SAM: (*Encouragingly*) Show me again.
WILLIE: Okay, count for me.
SAM: Ready?

WILLIE: Ready.
SAM: Five, six, seven, eight . . . (WILLIE *starts to dance*) A-n-d one   15
two three four . . . and one two three four. . . . (*Ad libbing as* WILLIE *dances*) Your shoulders, Willie . . . your shoulders! Don't look down! Look happy, Willie! Relax, Willie!
WILLIE: (*Desperate but still dancing*) I am relax.
SAM: No, you're not.   20
WILLIE: (*He falters*) Ag no man, Sam! Mustn't talk. You make me make mistakes.
SAM: But you're too stiff.
WILLIE: Yesterday I'm not straight . . . today I'm too stiff!
SAM: Well, you are. You asked me and I'm telling you.   25
WILLIE: Where?
SAM: Everywhere. Try to glide through it.
WILLIE: Glide?
SAM: Ja, make it smooth. And give it more style. It must look like you're enjoying yourself.   30
WILLIE: (*Emphatically*) I wasn't.
SAM: Exactly.
WILLIE: How can I enjoy myself? Not straight, too stiff and now it's also glide, give it more style, make it smooth. . . . Haai! Is hard to remember all those things, Boet Sam.   35
SAM: That's your trouble. You're trying too hard.
WILLIE: I try hard because it *is* hard.
SAM: But don't let me see it. The secret is to make it look easy. Ballroom must look happy, Willie, not like hard work. It must . . . Ja! . . . it must look like romance.   40
WILLIE: Now another one! What's romance?
SAM: Love story with happy ending. A handsome man in tails, and in his arms, smiling at him, a beautiful lady in evening dress!
WILLIE: Fred Astaire, Ginger Rogers.   45
SAM: You got it. Tapdance or ballroom, it's the same. Romance. In two weeks' time when the judges look at you and Hilda, they must see a man and a woman who are dancing their way to a happy ending. What I saw was you holding her like you were frightened she was going to run   50 away.
WILLIE: Ja! Because that is what she wants to do! I got no romance left for Hilda anymore, Boet Sam.
SAM: Then pretend. When you put your arms around Hilda, imagine she is Ginger Rogers.   55
WILLIE: With no teeth? You try.
SAM: Well, just remember, there's only two weeks left.
WILLIE: I know, I know! (*To the jukebox*) I do it better with music. You got sixpence for Sarah Vaughan?
SAM: That's a slow foxtrot. You're practicing the quick-step.   60
WILLIE: I'll practice slow foxtrot.

SAM: (*Shaking his head*) It's your turn to put money in the jukebox.

WILLIE: I only got bus fare to go home. (*He returns disconsolately to his work*) Love story and happy ending! She's doing it all right, Boet Sam, but is not me she's giving happy endings. Fuckin' whore! Three nights now she doesn't come practice. I wind up gramophone, I get record ready and I sit and wait. What happens? Nothing. Ten o'clock I start dancing with my pillow. You try and practice romance by yourself, Boet Sam. Struesgod, she doesn't come tonight I take back my dress and ballroom shoes and I find me new partner. Size twenty-six. Shoes size seven. And now she's also making trouble for me with the baby again. Reports me to Child Wellfed, that I'm not giving her money. She lies! Every week I am giving her money for milk. And how do I know is my baby? Only his hair looks like me. She's fucking around all the time I turn my back. Hilda Samuels is a bitch! (*Pause*) Hey, Sam!

SAM: Ja.

WILLIE: You listening?

SAM: Ja.

WILLIE: So what you say?

SAM: About Hilda?

WILLIE: Ja.

SAM: When did you last give her a hiding?

WILLIE: (*Reluctantly*) Sunday night.

SAM: And today is Thursday.

WILLIE: (*He knows what's coming*) Okay.

SAM: Hiding on Sunday night, then Monday, Tuesday and Wednesday she doesn't come to practice . . . and you are asking me why?

WILLIE: I said okay, Boet Sam!

SAM: You hit her too much. One day she's going to leave you for good.

WILLIE: So? She makes me the hell-in too much.

SAM: (*Emphasizing his point*) *Too* much and *too* hard. You had the same trouble with Eunice.

WILLIE: Because she also make the hell-in, Boet Sam. She never got the steps right. Even the waltz.

SAM: Beating her up every time she makes a mistake in the waltz? (*Shaking his head*) No, Willie! That takes the pleasure out of ballroom dancing.

WILLIE: Hilda is not too bad with the waltz, Boet Sam. Is the quickstep where the trouble starts.

SAM: (*Teasing him gently*) How's your pillow with the quickstep?

WILLIE: (*Ignoring the tease*) Good! And why! Because it got no legs. That's her trouble. She can't move them quick enough, Boet Sam. I start the record and before halfway Count Basie is already winning. Only time we catch up with him is when gramophone runs down.

(SAM *laughs*)

Haaikona, Boet Sam, is not funny.

SAM: (*Snapping his fingers*) I got it! Give her a handicap.

WILLIE: What's that?

SAM: Give her a ten-second start and then let Count Basie go. Then I put my money on her. Hot favorite in the Ballroom Stakes: Hilda Samuels ridden by Willie Malopo.

WILLIE: (*Turning away*) I'm not talking to you no more.

SAM: (*Relenting*) Sorry, Willie . . .

WILLIE: It's finish between us.

SAM: Okay, okay . . . I'll stop.

WILLIE: You can also fuck off.

SAM: Willie, listen! I want to help you!

WILLIE: No more jokes?

SAM: I promise.

WILLIE: Okay. Help me.

SAM: (*His turn to hold an imaginary partner*) Look and learn. Feet together. Back straight. Body relaxed. Right hand placed gently in the small of her back and wait for the music. Don't start worrying about making mistakes or the judges or the other competitors. It's just you, Hilda and the music, and you're going to have a good time. What Count Basie do you play?

WILLIE: "You the cream in my coffee, you the salt in my stew."

SAM: Right. Give it to me in strict tempo.

WILLIE: Ready?

SAM: Ready.

WILLIE: A-n-d . . . (*singing*)
"You the cream in my coffee.
You the salt in my stew.
You will always be my necessity.
I'd be lost without you. . . ." (*etc.*)

(SAM *launches into the quickstep. He is obviously a much more accomplished dancer than* WILLIE. HALLY *enters. A seventeen-year-old white boy. Wet raincoat and school case. He stops and watches* SAM. *The demonstration comes to an end with a flourish. Applause from* HALLY *and* WILLIE)

HALLY: Bravo! No question about it. First place goes to Mr. Sam Semela.

WILLIE: (*In total agreement*) You was gliding with style, Boet Sam.

HALLY: (*Cheerfully*) How's it, chaps?

SAM: Okay, Hally.

WILLIE: (*Springing to attention like a soldier and saluting*) At your service, Master Harold!

HALLY: Not long to the big event, hey!

SAM: Two weeks.

HALLY: You nervous?

SAM: No.

HALLY: Think you stand a chance?

SAM: Let's just say I'm ready to go out there and dance.

HALLY: It looked like it. What about you, Willie?

(WILLIE *groans*)

What's the matter?

SAM: He's got leg trouble.

HALLY: (*Innocently*) Oh, sorry to hear that, Willie.

SAM: Boet Sam! You promised. (WILLIE *returns to his work*)

(HALLY *deposits his school case and takes off his raincoat. His clothes are a little neglected and untidy: black blazer with school badge, gray flannel trousers in need of an ironing, khaki shirt and tie, black shoes.* SAM *has fetched a towel for* HALLY *to dry his hair*)

HALLY: God, what a lousy bloody day. It's coming down cats and dogs out there. Bad for business, chaps . . . (*Conspira-*

torial whisper) . . . but it also means we're in for a nice quiet afternoon.

165 SAM: You can speak loud. Your Mom's not here.

HALLY: Out shopping?

SAM: No, The hospital.

HALLY: But it's Thursday. There's no visiting on Thursday afternoons. Is my Dad okay?

170 SAM: Sounds like it. In fact, I think he's going home.

HALLY: *(Stopped short by SAM's remark)* What do you mean?

SAM: The hospital phoned.

HALLY: To say what?

SAM: I don't know. I just heard your Mom talking.

175 HALLY: So what makes you say he's going home?

SAM: It sounded as if they were telling her to come and fetch him.

(HALLY thinks about what SAM has said for a few seconds)

HALLY: When did she leave?

SAM: About an hour ago. She said she would phone you.
180 Want to eat?

(HALLY doesn't respond)

Hally, want your lunch?

HALLY: I suppose so. *(His mood has changed)* What's on the menu? . . . as if I don't know.

SAM: Soup, followed by meat pie and gravy.

185 HALLY: Today's?

SAM: No.

HALLY: And the soup?

SAM: Nourishing pea soup.

HALLY: Just the soup. *(The pile of comic books on the table)* And
190 these?

SAM: For your Dad. Mr. Kempston brought them.

HALLY: You haven't been reading them, have you?

SAM: Just looking.

HALLY: *(Examining the comics)* Jungle Jim . . . Batman and Robin
195 . . . Tarzan . . . God, what rubbish! Mental pollution. Take them away.

(SAM exits waltzing into the kitchen. HALLY turns to WILLIE)

HALLY: Did you hear my Mom talking on the telephone, Willie?

WILLIE: No, Master Hally. I was at the back.

HALLY: And she didn't say anything to you before she left?

200 WILLIE: She said I must clean the floors.

HALLY: I mean about my Dad.

WILLIE: She didn't say nothing to me about him, Master Hally.

HALLY: *(With conviction)* No! It can't be. They said he needed at least another three weeks of treatment. Sam's definitely
205 made a mistake. *(Rummages through his school case, finds a book and settles down at the table to read)* So, Willie!

WILLIE: Yes, Master Hally! Schooling okay today?

HALLY: Yes, okay. . . . *(He thinks about it)* . . . No, not really. Ag, what's the difference? I don't care. And Sam says you've
210 got problems.

WILLIE: Big problems.

HALLY: Which leg is sore?

(WILLIE groans)

Both legs.

WILLIE: There is nothing wrong with my legs. Sam is just making jokes. 215

HALLY: So then you *will* be in the competition.

WILLIE: Only if I can find me a partner.

HALLY: But what about Hilda?

SAM: *(Returning with a bowl of soup)* She's the one who's got trouble with her legs. 220

HALLY: What sort of trouble, Willie?

SAM: From the way he describes it, I think the lady has gone a bit lame.

HALLY: Good God! Have you taken her to see a doctor?

SAM: I think a vet would be better. 225

HALLY: What do you mean?

SAM: What do you call it again when a racehorse goes very fast?

HALLY: Gallop?

SAM: That's it! 230

WILLIE: Boet Sam!

HALLY: "A gallop down the homestretch to the winning post." But what's that got to do with Hilda?

SAM: Count Basie always gets there first.

(WILLIE lets fly with his slop rag. It misses SAM and hits HALLY)

HALLY: *(Furious)* For Christ's sake, Willie! What the hell do 235 you think you're doing!

WILLIE: Sorry, Master Hally, but it's him. . . .

HALLY: Act your bloody age! *(Hurls the rag back at WILLIE)* Cut out the nonsense now and get on with your work. And you too, Sam. Stop fooling around. 240

(SAM moves away)

No. Hang on. I haven't finished! Tell me exactly what my Mom said.

SAM: I have. "When Hally comes, tell him I've gone to the hospital and I'll phone him."

HALLY: She didn't say anything about taking my Dad home? 245

SAM: No. It's just that when she was talking on the phone . . .

HALLY: *(Interrupting him)* No, Sam. They can't be discharging him. She would have said so if they were. In any case, we saw him last night and he wasn't in good shape at all. Staff nurse even said there was talk about taking more 250 X-rays. And now suddenly today he's better? If anything, it sounds more like a bad turn to me . . . which I sincerely hope it isn't. Hang on . . . how long ago did you say she left?

SAM: Just before two . . . *(His wrist watch)* . . . hour and a 255 half.

HALLY: I know how to settle it. *(Behind the counter to the telephone. Talking as he dials)* Let's give her ten minutes to get to the hospital, ten minutes to load him up, another ten, at the most, to get home and another ten to get him in- 260 side. Forty minutes. They should have been home for at least half an hour already. *(Pause—he waits with the receiver to his ear)* No reply, chaps. And you know why? Because she's at his bedside in hospital helping him pull through a bad turn. You definitely heard wrong. 265

SAM: Okay.

(As far as HALLY is concerned, the matter is settled. He returns to his table, sits down and divides his attention between the book and his soup. SAM is at his school case and picks up a textbook)

Modern Graded Mathematics for Standards Nine and Ten. (*Opens it at random and laughs at something he sees*) Who is this supposed to be?

270 HALLY: Old fart-face Prentice.

SAM: Teacher?

HALLY: Thinks he is. And believe me, that is not a bad likeness.

SAM: Has he seen it?

275 HALLY: Yes.

SAM: What did he say?

HALLY: Tried to be clever, as usual. Said I was no Leonardo da Vinci and that bad art had to be punished. So, six of the best, and his are bloody good.

280 SAM: On your bum?

HALLY: Where else? The days when I got them on my hands are gone forever, Sam.

SAM: With your trousers down!

HALLY: No. He's not quite that barbaric.

285 SAM: That's the way they do it in jail.

HALLY: (*Flicker of morbid interest*) Really?

SAM: Ja. When the magistrate sentences you to "strokes with a light cane."

HALLY: Go on.

290 SAM: They make you lie down on a bench. One policeman pulls down your trousers and holds your ankles, another one pulls your shirt over your head and holds your arms . . .

HALLY: Thank you! That's enough.

295 SAM: . . . and the one that gives you the strokes talks to you gently and for a long time between each one. (*He laughs*)

HALLY: I've heard enough, Sam! Jesus! It's a bloody awful world when you come to think of it. People can be real bastards.

300 SAM: That's the way it is, Hally.

HALLY: It doesn't *have* to be that way. There is something called progress, you know. We don't exactly burn people at the stake anymore.

SAM: Like Joan of Arc.

305 HALLY: Correct. If she was captured today, she'd be given a fair trial.

SAM: And then the death sentence.

HALLY: (*A world-weary sigh*) I know, I know! I oscillate between hope and despair for this world as well, Sam. But
310 things will change, you wait and see. One day somebody is going to get up and give history a kick up the backside and get it going again.

SAM: Like who?

HALLY: (*After thought*) They're called social reformers. Every
315 age, Sam, has got its social reformer. My history book is full of them.

SAM: So where's ours?

HALLY: Good question. And I hate to say it, but the answer is: I don't know. Maybe he hasn't even been born yet. Or is
320 still only a babe in arms at his mother's breast. God, what a thought.

SAM: So we just go on waiting.

HALLY: Ja, looks like it. (*Back to his soup and the book*)

SAM: (*Reading from the textbook*) "Introduction: In some math-
325 ematical problems only the magnitude . . ." (*He mispronounces the word "magnitude"*)

HALLY: (*Correcting him without looking up*) Magnitude.

SAM: What's it mean?

HALLY: How big it is. The size of the thing.

330 SAM: (*Reading*) ". . . magnitude of the quantities is of importance. In other problems we need to know whether these quantities are negative or positive. For example, whether there is a debit or credit bank balance . . ."

HALLY: Whether you're broke or not.

335 SAM: ". . . whether the temperature is above or below Zero . . ."

HALLY: Naught degrees. Cheerful state of affairs! No cash and you're freezing to death. Mathematics won't get you out of that one.

340 SAM: "All these quantities are called . . ." (*Spelling the word*) . . . s-c-a-l . . .

HALLY: Scalars.

SAM: Scalars! (*Shaking his head with a laugh*) You understand all that?

345 HALLY: (*Turning a page*) No. And I don't intend to try.

SAM: So what happens when the exams come?

HALLY: Failing a maths exam isn't the end of the world, Sam. How many times have I told you that examination results don't measure intelligence?

350 SAM: I would say about as many times as you've failed one of them.

HALLY: (*Mirthlessly*) Ha, ha, ha.

SAM: (*Simultaneously*) Ha, ha, ha.

HALLY: Just remember Winston Churchill didn't do particu-
355 larly well at school.

SAM: You've also told me that one many times.

HALLY: Well, it just so happens to be the truth.

SAM: (*Enjoying the word*) Magnitude! Magnitude! Show me how to use it.

360 HALLY: (*After thought*) An intrepid social reformer will not be daunted by the magnitude of the task he has undertaken.

SAM: (*Impressed*) Couple of jaw-breakers in there!

HALLY: I gave you three for the price of one. Intrepid, daunted and magnitude. I did that once in an exam. Put
365 five of the words I had to explain in one sentence. It was half a page long.

SAM: Well, I'll put my money on you in the English exam.

HALLY: Piece of cake. Eighty percent without even trying.

SAM: (*Another textbook from* HALLY'S *case*) And history?

370 HALLY: So-so. I'll scrape through. In the fifties if I'm lucky.

SAM: You didn't do too badly last year.

HALLY: Because we had World War One. That at least had some action. You try to find that in the South African Parliamentary system.

375 SAM: (*Reading from the history textbook*) "Napoleon and the principle of equality." Hey! This sounds interesting. "After concluding peace with Britain in 1802, Napoleon used a brief period of calm to in-sti-tute . . ."

HALLY: Introduce.

380 SAM: ". . . many reforms. Napoleon regarded all people as equal before the law and wanted them to have equal opportunities for advancement. All ves-ti-ges of the feu-dal system with its oppression of the poor were abolished." Vestiges, feudal system and abolished. I'm all right on op-
385 pression.

HALLY: I'm thinking. He swept away . . . abolished . . . the last remains . . . vestiges . . . of the bad old days . . . feudal system.

SAM: Ha! There's the social reformer we're waiting for. He sounds like a man of some magnitude.
390

HALLY: I'm not so sure about that. It's a damn good title for a book, though. A man of magnitude!

SAM: He sounds pretty big to me, Hally.

395 HALLY: Don't confuse historical significance with greatness. But maybe I'm being a bit prejudiced. Have a look in there and you'll see he's two chapters long. And hell! . . . has he only got dates, Sam, all of which you've got to remember! This campaign and that campaign, and then, be-
400 cause of all the fighting, the next thing is we get Peace Treaties all over the place. And what's the end of the story? Battle of Waterloo, which he loses. Wasn't worth it. No, I don't know about him as a man of magnitude.

SAM: Then who would you say was?

405 HALLY: To answer that, we need a definition of greatness, and I suppose that would be somebody who . . . somebody who benefited all mankind.

SAM: Right. But like who?

HALLY: (He speaks with total conviction) Charles Darwin. Remember him? That big book from the library. The Origin
410 of the Species.

SAM: Him?

HALLY: Yes. For his Theory of Evolution.

SAM: You didn't finish it.

HALLY: I ran out of time. I didn't finish it because my two
415 weeks was up. But I'm going to take it out again after I've digested what I read. It's safe. I've hidden it away in the Theology section. Nobody ever goes in there. And anyway who are you to talk? You hardly even looked at it.

420 SAM: I tried. I looked at the chapters in the beginning and I saw one called "The Struggle for an Existence." Ah ha, I thought. At last! But what did I get? Something called the mistiltoe which needs the apple tree and there's too many seeds and all are going to die except one . . . ! No, Hally.

425 HALLY: (Intellectually outraged) What do you mean, No! The poor man had to start somewhere. For God's sake, Sam, he revolutionized science. Now we know.

SAM: What?

HALLY: Where we come from and what it all means.

430 SAM: And that's a benefit to mankind? Anyway, I still don't believe it.

HALLY: God, you're impossible. I showed it to you in black and white.

SAM: Doesn't mean I got to believe it.

435 HALLY: It's the likes of you that kept the Inquisition in business. It's called bigotry. Anyway, that's my man of magnitude. Charles Darwin! Who's yours?

SAM: (Without hesitation) Abraham Lincoln.

HALLY: I might have guessed as much. Don't get sentimental,
440 Sam. You've never been a slave, you know. And anyway we freed your ancestors here in South Africa long before the Americans. But if you want to thank somebody on their behalf, do it to Mr. William Wilberforce. Come on. Try again. I want a real genius. (Now enjoying himself, and so
445 is SAM. HALLY goes behind the counter and helps himself to a chocolate)

SAM: William Shakespeare.

HALLY: (No enthusiasm) Oh. So you're also one of them, are you? You're basing that opinion on only one play, you
450 know. You've only read my Julius Caesar and even I don't understand half of what they're talking about. They should do what they did with the old Bible: bring the language up to date.

SAM: That's all you've got. It's also the only one you've read.

455 HALLY: I know. I admit it. That's why I suggest we reserve our judgment until we've checked up on a few others. I've got a feeling, though, that by the end of this year one is going to be enough for me, and I can give you the names of twenty-nine other chaps in the Standard Nine class of the
460 Port Elizabeth Technical College who feel the same. But if you want him, you can have him. My turn now. (Pacing) This is a damned good exercise, you know! It started off looking like a simple question and here it's got us really probing into the intellectual heritage of our civilization.

465 SAM: So who is it going to be?

HALLY: My next man . . . and he gets the title on two scores: social reform and literary genius . . . is Leo Nikolaevich Tolstoy.

SAM: That Russian.

470 HALLY: Correct. Remember the picture of him I showed you?

SAM: With the long beard.

HALLY: (Trying to look like Tolstoy) And those burning, visionary eyes. My God, the face of a social prophet if ever I saw one! And remember my words when I showed it to you?
475 Here's a man, Sam!

SAM: Those were words, Hally.

HALLY: Not many intellectuals are prepared to shovel manure with the peasants and then go home and write a "little book" called War and Peace. Incidentally, Sam, he was
480 somebody else who, to quote, ". . . did not distinguish himself scholastically."

SAM: Meaning?

HALLY: He was also no good at school.

SAM: Like you and Winston Churchill.

485 HALLY: (Mirthlessly) Ha, ha, ha.

SAM: (Simultaneously) Ha, ha, ha.

HALLY: Don't get clever, Sam. That man freed his serfs of his own free will.

SAM: No argument. He was a somebody, all right. I accept him.

490 HALLY: I'm sure Count Tolstoy will be very pleased to hear that. Your turn. Shoot. (Another chocolate from behind the counter) I'm waiting, Sam.

SAM: I've got him.

HALLY: Good. Submit your candidate for examination.

495 SAM: Jesus.

HALLY: (Stopped dead in his tracks) Who?

SAM: Jesus Christ.

HALLY: Oh, come on, Sam!

SAM: The Messiah.

500 HALLY: Ja, but still . . . No, Sam. Don't let's get started on religion. We'll just spend the whole afternoon arguing again. Suppose I turn around and say Mohammed?

SAM: All right.

HALLY: You can't have them both on the same list!

505 SAM: Why not? You like Mohammed, I like Jesus.

HALLY: I don't like Mohammed. I never have. I was merely being hypothetical. As far as I'm concerned, the Koran is as bad as the Bible. No. Religion is out! I'm not going to waste my time again arguing with you about the existence
510 of God. You know perfectly well I'm an atheist . . . and I've got homework to do.

SAM: Okay, I take him back.

HALLY: You've got time for one more name.

515 SAM: (*After thought*) I've got one I know we'll agree on. A simple straightforward great Man of Magnitude . . . and no arguments. And *he* really *did* benefit all mankind.

HALLY: I wonder. After your last contribution I'm begin-
520 ning to doubt whether anything in the way of an intellectual agreement is possible between the two of us. Who is he?

SAM: Guess.

HALLY: Socrates? Alexandre Dumas? Karl Marx? Dostoevsky? Nietzsche?

(SAM *shakes his head after each name*)

525 Give me a clue.

SAM: The letter P is important . . .

HALLY: Plato!

SAM: . . . and his name begins with an F.

HALLY: I've got it. Freud and Psychology.

530 SAM: No. I didn't understand him.

HALLY: That makes two of us.

SAM: Think of mouldy apricot jam.

HALLY: (*After a delighted laugh*) Penicillin and Sir Alexander Fleming! And the title of the book: *The Microbe Hunters.*
535 (*Delighted*) Splendid, Sam! Splendid. For once we are in total agreement. The major breakthrough in medical science in the Twentieth Century. If it wasn't for him, we might have lost the Second World War. It's deeply gratifying, Sam, to know that I haven't been wasting my time in
540 talking to you. (*Strutting around proudly*) Tolstoy may have educated his peasants, but I've educated you.

SAM: Standard Four to Standard Nine.

HALLY: Have we been at it as long as that?

SAM: Yep. And my first lesson was geography.

545 HALLY: (*Intrigued*) Really? I don't remember.

SAM: My room there at the back of the old Jubilee Boarding House. I had just started working for your Mom. Little boy in short trousers walks in one afternoon and asks me seriously: "Sam, do you want to see South Africa?" Hey
550 man! Sure I wanted to see South Africa!

HALLY: Was that me?

SAM: . . . So the next thing I'm looking at a map you had just done for homework. It was your first one and you were very proud of yourself.

555 HALLY: Go on.

SAM: Then came my first lesson. "Repeat after me, Sam: Gold in the Transvaal, mealies in the Free State, sugar in Natal and grapes in the Cape." I still know it!

HALLY: Well, I'll be buggered. So that's how it all started.

560 SAM: And your next map was one with all the rivers and the mountains they came from. The Orange, the Vaal, the Limpopo, the Zambezi . . .

HALLY: You've got a phenomenal memory!

SAM: You should be grateful. That is why you started passing
565 your exams. You tried to be better than me. (*They laugh together.* WILLIE *is attracted by the laughter and joins them*)

HALLY: The old Jubilee Boarding House. Sixteen rooms with board and lodging, rent in advance and one week's notice. I haven't thought about it for donkey's years . . . and I
570 don't think that's an accident. God, was I glad when we

sold it and moved out. Those years are not remembered as the happiest ones of an unhappy childhood.

WILLIE: (*Knocking on the table and trying to imitate a woman's voice*) "Hally, are you there?"

HALLY: Who's that supposed to be?   575

WILLIE: "What you doing in there, Hally? Come out at once!"

HALLY: (*To* SAM) What's he talking about?

SAM: Don't you remember?

WILLIE: "Sam, Willie . . . is he in there with you boys?"   580

SAM: Hiding away in our room when your mother was looking for you.

HALLY: (*Another good laugh*) Of course! I used to crawl and hide under your bed! But finish the story, Willie. Then what used to happen? You chaps would give the game   585
away by telling her I was in there with you. So much for friendship.

SAM: We couldn't lie to her. She knew.

HALLY: Which meant I got another rowing for hanging around the "servants' quarters." I think I spent more time in there   590
with you chaps than anywhere else in that dump. And do you blame me? Nothing but bloody misery wherever you went. Somebody was always complaining about the food, or my mother was having a fight with Micky Nash because she'd caught her with a petty officer in her room. Maud   595
Meiring was another one. Remember those two? They were prostitutes, you know. Soldiers and sailors from the troopships. Bottom fell out of the business when the war ended. God, the flotsam and jetsam that life washed up on our shores! No joking, if it wasn't for your room, I would   600
have been the first certified ten-year-old in medical history. Ja, the memories are coming back now. Walking home from school and thinking: "What can I do this afternoon?" Try out a few ideas, but sooner or later I'd end up in there with you fellows. I bet you I could still find my way to your   605
room with my eyes closed. (*He does exactly that*) Down the corridor . . . telephone on the right, which my Mom keeps locked because somebody is using it on the sly and not pay-
ing . . . past the kitchen and unappetizing cooking smells . . . around the corner into the backyard, hold my   610
breath again because there are more smells coming when I pass your lavatory, then into that little passageway, first door on the right and into your room. How's that?

SAM: Good. But, as usual, you forgot to knock.

HALLY: Like that time I barged in and caught you and Cyn-   615
thia . . . at it. Remember? God, was I embarrassed! I didn't know what was going on at first.

SAM: Ja, that taught you a lesson.

HALLY: And about a lot more than knocking on doors, I'll have you know, and I don't mean geography either. Hell,   620
Sam, couldn't you have waited until it was dark?

SAM: No.

HALLY: Was it that urgent?

SAM: Yes, and if you don't believe me, wait until your time comes.   625

HALLY: No, thank you. I am not interested in girls. (*Back to his memories . . . Using a few chairs he recreates the room as he lists the items*) A gray little room with a cold cement floor. Your bed against that wall . . . and I now know why the mattress sags so much! . . . Willie's bed . . . it's propped up on   630
bricks because one leg is broken . . . that wobbly little table

with the washbasin and jug of water . . . Yes! . . . stuck to the wall above it are some pin-up pictures from magazines. Joe Louis . . .

635 WILLIE: Brown Bomber. World Title. (*Boxing pose*) Three rounds and knockout.

HALLY: Against who?

SAM: Max Schmeling.

HALLY: Correct. I can also remember Fred Astaire and Ginger
640 Rogers, and Rita Hayworth in a bathing costume which always made me hot and bothered when I looked at it. Under Willie's bed is an old suitcase with all his clothes in a mess, which is why I never hide there. Your things are neat and tidy in a trunk next to your bed, and on it there
645 is a picture of you and Cynthia in your ballroom clothes, your first silver cup for third place in a competition and an old radio which doesn't work anymore. Have I left out anything?

SAM: No.

650 HALLY: Right, so much for the stage directions. Now the characters. (SAM *and* WILLIE *move to their appropriate positions in the bedroom*) Willie is in bed, under his blankets with his clothes on, complaining nonstop about something, but we can't make out a word of what he's saying because he's got
655 his head under the blankets as well. You're on your bed trimming your toenails with a knife—not a very edifying sight—and as for me . . . What am I doing?

SAM: You're sitting on the floor giving Willie a lecture about being a good loser while you get the checker board and
660 pieces ready for a game. Then you go to Willie's bed, pull off the blankets and make him play with you first because you know you're going to win, and that gives you the second game with me.

HALLY: And you certainly were a bad loser, Willie!

665 WILLIE: Haai!

HALLY: Wasn't he, Sam? And so slow! A game with you almost took the whole afternoon. Thank God I gave up trying to teach you how to play chess.

WILLIE: You and Sam cheated.

670 HALLY: I never saw Sam cheat, and mine were mostly the mistakes of youth.

WILLIE: Then how is it you two was always winning?

HALLY: Have you ever considered the possibility, Willie, that it was because we were better than you?

675 WILLIE: Every time better?

HALLY: Not every time. There were occasions when we deliberately let you win a game so that you would stop sulking and go on playing with us. Sam used to wink at me when you weren't looking to show me it was time to let
680 you win.

WILLIE: So then you two didn't play fair.

HALLY: It was for your benefit, Mr. Malopo, which is more than being fair. (*To* SAM) But you know what my best memory is, don't you?

685 SAM: No.

HALLY: Come on, guess. If your memory is so good, you must remember it as well.

SAM: We got up to a lot of tricks in there, Hally.

HALLY: This one was special, Sam.

690 SAM: I'm listening.

HALLY: It started off looking like another of those useless nothing-to-do afternoons. I'd already been down to Main Street looking for adventure, but nothing had happened. I didn't feel like climbing trees in the Donkin Park or pretending I was a private eye and following a stranger. . . so 695 as usual: See what's cooking in Sam's room. This time it was you on the floor. You had two thin pieces of wood and you were smoothing them down with a knife. It didn't look particularly interesting, but when I asked you what you were doing, you just said, "Wait and see, Hally. 700 Wait . . . and see" . . . in that secret sort of way of yours, so I knew there was a surprise coming. You teased me, you bugger, by being deliberately slow and not answering my questions!

(SAM *laughs*)

And whistling while you worked away! God, it was infuriating! I could have brained you! It was only when you 705 tied them together in a cross and put that down on the brown paper that I realized what you were doing. "Sam is making a kite?" And when I asked you and you said "Yes" . . . ! (*Shaking his head with disbelief*) The sheer audacity of it took my breath away. I mean, seriously, what 710 the hell does a black man know about flying a kite? I'll be honest with you, Sam, I had no hopes for it. If you think I was excited and happy, you got another guess coming. In fact, I was shit-scared that we were going to make fools of ourselves. When we left the boarding house to go up onto 715 the hill, I was praying quietly that there wouldn't be any other kids around to laugh at us.

SAM: (*Enjoying the memory as much as* HALLY) Ja, I could see that.

HALLY: I made it obvious, did I? 720

SAM: Ja. You refused to carry it.

HALLY: Do you blame me? Can you remember what the poor thing looked like? Tomato-box wood and brown paper! Flour and water for glue! Two of my mother's old stockings for a tail, and then all those bits and pieces of string 725 you made me tie together so that we could fly it! Hell, no, that was now only asking for a miracle to happen.

SAM: Then the big argument when I told you to hold the string and run with it when I let go.

HALLY: I was prepared to run, all right, but straight back to 730 the boarding house.

SAM: (*Knowing what's coming*) So what happened?

HALLY: Come on, Sam, you remember as well as I do.

SAM: I want to hear it from you.

735

(HALLY *pauses. He wants to be as accurate as possible.*)

HALLY: You went a little distance from me down the hill, you held it up ready to let it go. . . . "This is it," I thought. "Like everything else in my life, here comes 740 another fiasco." Then you shouted, "Go, Hally!" and I started to run. (*Another pause*) I don't know how to describe it, Sam. Ja! The miracle happened! I was running, waiting for it to crash to the ground, but instead suddenly there was something alive behind me at the end 745 of the string, tugging at it as if it wanted to be free. I looked back . . . (*Shakes his head*) . . . I still can't believe my eyes. It was flying! Looping around and trying to climb even higher into the sky. You shouted to me to let

750 it have more string. I did, until there was none left and
I was just holding that piece of wood we had tied it to.
You came up and joined me. You were laughing.

SAM: So were you. And shouting, "It works, Sam! We've done it!"

755 HALLY: And we had! I was so proud of us! It was the most
splendid thing I had ever seen. I wished there were hundreds of kids around to watch us. The part that scared me,
though, was when you showed me how to make it dive
down to the ground and then just when it was on the
760 point of crashing, swoop up again!

SAM: You didn't want to try yourself.

HALLY: Of course not! I would have been suicidal if anything
had happened to it. Watching you do it made me nervous
enough. I was quite happy just to see it up there with its
765 tail fluttering behind it. You left me after that, didn't you?
You explained how to get it down, we tied it to the bench
so that I could sit and watch it, and you went away. I
wanted you to stay, you know. I was a little scared of having to look after it by myself.

770 SAM: (Quietly) I had work to do, Hally.

HALLY: It was sort of sad bringing it down, Sam. And it
looked sad again when it was lying there on the ground.
Like something that had lost its soul. Just tomato-box
wood, brown paper and two of my mother's old stockings!
775 But, hell, I'll never forget that first moment when I saw it
up there. I had a stiff neck the next day from looking up
so much.

(SAM *laughs.* HALLY *turns to him with a question he never thought
of asking before*)

Why did you make that kite, Sam?

SAM: (Evenly) I can't remember.

780 HALLY: Truly?

SAM: Too long ago, Hally.

HALLY: Ja, I suppose it was. It's time for another one, you
know.

SAM: Why do you say that?

785 HALLY: Because it feels like that. Wouldn't be a good day to
fly it, though.

SAM: No. You can't fly kites on rainy days.

HALLY: (*He studies* SAM. *Their memories have made him conscious
of the man's presence in his life*) How old are you, Sam?

790 SAM: Two score and five.

HALLY: Strange, isn't it?

SAM: What?

HALLY: Me and you.

SAM: What's strange about it?

795 HALLY: Little white boy in short trousers and a black man old
enough to be his father flying a kite. It's not every day you
see that.

SAM: But why strange? Because the one is white and the
other black?

800 HALLY: I don't know. Would have been just as strange, I suppose, if it had been me and my Dad . . . cripple man and
a little boy! Nope! There's no chance of me flying a kite
without it being strange. (*Simple statement of fact—no self-
pity*) There's a nice little short story there. "The Kite-
805 Flyers." But we'd have to find a twist in the ending.

SAM: Twist?

HALLY: Yes. Something unexpected. The way it ended with us
was too straightforward . . . me on the bench and you going back to work. There's no drama in that.

WILLIE: And me? 810

HALLY: You?

WILLIE: Yes me.

HALLY: You want to get into the story as well, do you? I got
it! Change the title: "Afternoons in Sam's Room" . . . expand it and tell all the stories. It's on its way to being a 815
novel. Our days in the old Jubilee. Sad in a way that they're
over. I almost wish we were still in that little room.

SAM: We're still together.

HALLY: That's true. It's just that life felt the right size in there
. . . not too big and not too small. Wasn't so hard to work 820
up a bit of courage. It's got so bloody complicated since
then.

(*The telephone rings.* SAM *answers it*)

SAM: St. George's Park Tea Room . . . Hello, Madam . . . Yes,
Madam, he's here. . . . Hally, it's your mother.

HALLY: Where is she phoning from? 825

SAM: Sounds like the hospital. It's a public telephone.

HALLY: (*Relieved*) You see! I told you. (*The telephone*) Hello,
Mom . . . Yes . . . Yes no fine. Everything's under control
here. How's things with poor old Dad? . . . Has he had a
bad turn? . . . What? . . . Oh, God! . . . Yes, Sam told me, 830
but I was sure he'd made a mistake. But what's this all
about, Mom? He didn't look at all good last night. How
can he get better so quickly? . . . Then very obviously you
must say no. Be firm with him. You're the boss. . . . You
know what it's going to be like if he comes home. . . . Well 835
then, don't blame me when I fail my exams at the end of
the year. . . . Yes! How am I expected to be fresh for school
when I spend half the night massaging his gammy leg? . . .
So am I! . . . So tell him a white lie. Say Dr. Colley wants
more X-rays of his stump. Or bribe him. We'll sneak in 840
double tots of brandy in future. . . . What? . . . Order him
to get back into bed at once! If he's going to behave like
a child, treat him like one. . . . All right, Mom! I was just
trying to . . . I'm sorry. . . . I said I'm sorry. . . . Quick, give
me your number. I'll phone you back. (*He hangs up and* 845
waits a few seconds) Here we go again! (*He dials*) I'm sorry,
Mom. . . . Okay . . . But now listen to me carefully. All it
needs is for you to put your foot down. Don't take no for
an answer. . . . Did you hear me? And whatever you do,
don't discuss it with him. . . . Because I'm frightened you'll 850
give in to him. . . . Yes, Sam gave me lunch. . . . I ate all of
it! . . . No, Mom not a soul. It's still raining here. . . . Right,
I'll tell them. I'll just do some homework and then lock
up. . . . But remember now, Mom. Don't listen to anything
he says. And phone me back and let me know what hap- 855
pens. . . . Okay. Bye, Mom. (*He hangs up. The men are staring at him*) My Mom says that when you're finished with
the floors you must do the windows. (*Pause*) Don't misunderstand me, chaps. All I want is for him to get better.
And if he was, I'd be the first person to say: "Bring him 860
home." But he's not, and we can't give him the medical
care and attention he needs at home. That's what hospitals
are there for. (*Brusquely*) So don't just stand there! Get on
with it!

(SAM *clears* HALLY*'s table*)

865   You heard right. My Dad wants to go home.

SAM: Is he better?

HALLY: (*Sharply*) No! How the hell can he be better when last night he was groaning with pain? This is not an age of miracles!

870   SAM: Then he should stay in hospital.

HALLY: (*Seething with irritation and frustration*) Tell me something I don't know, Sam. What the hell do you think I was saying to my Mom? All I can say is fuck-it-all.

SAM: I'm sure he'll listen to your Mom.

875   HALLY: You don't know what she's up against. He's already packed his shaving kit and pajamas and is sitting on his bed with his crutches, dressed and ready to go. I know him when he gets in that mood. If she tries to reason with him, we've had it. She's no match for him when it comes

880   to a battle of words. He'll tie her up in knots. (*Trying to hide his true feelings*)

SAM: I suppose it gets lonely for him in there.

HALLY: With all the patients and nurses around? Regular visits from the Salvation Army? Balls! It's ten times worse for

885   him at home. I'm at school and my mother is here in the business all day.

SAM: He's at least got you at night.

HALLY: (*Before he can stop himself*) And we've got him! Please! I don't want to talk about it anymore. (*Unpacks his school*

890   *case, slamming down books on the table*) Life is just a plain bloody mess, that's all. And people are fools.

SAM: Come on, Hally.

HALLY: Yes, they are! They bloody well deserve what they get.

SAM: Then don't complain.

895   HALLY: Don't try to be clever, Sam. It doesn't suit you. Anybody who thinks there's nothing wrong with this world needs to have his head examined. Just when things are going along all right, without fail someone or something will come along and spoil everything. Somebody should

900   write that down as a fundamental law of the Universe. The principle of perpetual disappointment. If there is a God who created this world, he should scrap it and try again.

SAM: All right, Hally, all right. What you got for homework?

905   HALLY: Bullshit, as usual. (*Opens an exercise book and reads*) "Write five hundred words describing an annual event of cultural or historical significance."

SAM: That should be easy enough for you.

HALLY: And also plain bloody boring. You know what he

910   wants, don't you? One of their useless old ceremonies. The commemoration of the landing of the 1820 Settlers, or if it's going to be culture, Carols by Candlelight every Christmas.

SAM: It's an impressive sight. Make a good description, Hally.

915   All those candles glowing in the dark and the people singing hymns.

HALLY: And it's called religious hysteria. (*Intense irritation*) Please, Sam! Just leave me alone and let me get on with it. I'm not in the mood for games this afternoon. And re-

920   member my Mom's orders . . . you're to help Willie with the windows. Come on now, I don't want any more nonsense in here.

SAM: Okay, Hally, okay.

(HALLY *settles down to his homework; determined preparations . . . pen, ruler, exercise book, dictionary, another cake . . . all of which will lead to nothing*)

(SAM *waltzes over to* WILLIE *and starts to replace tables and chairs. He practices a ballroom step while doing so.* WILLIE *watches. When* SAM *is finished,* WILLIE *tries*) Good! But just a little bit quicker on the turn and only move in to her after she's crossed over. What about this one?

(*Another step. When* SAM *is finished,* WILLIE *again has a go*)

Much better. See what happens when you just relax and   925 enjoy yourself? Remember that in two weeks' time and you'll be all right.

WILLIE: But I haven't got partner, Boet Sam.

SAM: Maybe Hilda will turn up tonight.

WILLIE: No, Boet Sam. (*Reluctantly*) I gave her a good hiding.   930

SAM: You mean a bad one.

WILLIE: Good bad one.

SAM: Then you mustn't complain either. Now you pay the price for losing your temper.

WILLIE: I also pay two pounds ten shilling entrance fee.   935

SAM: They'll refund you if you withdraw now.

WILLIE: (*Appalled*) You mean, don't dance?

SAM: Yes.

WILLIE: No! I wait too long and I practice too hard. If I find me new partner, you think I can be ready in two weeks?   940 I ask Madam for my leave now and we practice every day.

SAM: Quickstep non-stop for two weeks. World record, Willie, but you'll be mad at the end.

WILLIE: No jokes, Boet Sam.

SAM: I'm not joking.   945

WILLIE: So then what?

SAM: Find Hilda. Say you're sorry and promise you won't beat her again.

WILLIE: No.

SAM: Then withdraw. Try again next year.   950

WILLIE: No.

SAM: Then I give up.

WILLIE: Haaikona, Boet Sam, you can't.

SAM: What do you mean, I can't? I'm telling you: I give up.

WILLIE: (*Adamant*) No! (*Accusingly*) It was you who start me   955 ballroom dancing.

SAM: So?

WILLIE: Before that I use to be happy. And is you and Miriam who bring me to Hilda and say here's partner for you.

SAM: What are you saying, Willie?   960

WILLIE: You!

SAM: But me what? To blame?

WILLIE: Yes.

SAM: Willie . . . ? (*Bursts into laughter*)

WILLIE: And now all you do is make jokes at me. You wait.   965 When Miriam leaves you is my turn to laugh. Ha! Ha! Ha!

SAM: (*He can't take* WILLIE *seriously any longer*) She can leave me tonight! I know what to do. (*Bowing before an imaginary partner*) May I have the pleasure? (*He dances and sings*) "Just a fellow with his pillow . . .   970 Dancin' like a willow . . . In an autumn breeze . . ."

WILLIE: There you go again!

(SAM *goes on dancing and singing*)

Boet Sam!

975   SAM: There's the answer to your problem! Judges' announcement in two weeks' time: "Ladies and gentlemen, the winner in the open section . . . Mr. Willie Malopo and his pillow!"

(*This is too much for a now really angry* WILLIE. *He goes for* SAM, *but the latter is too quick for him and puts* HALLY'S *table between the two of them*)

HALLY: (*Exploding*) For Christ's sake, you two!

980   WILLIE: (*Still trying to get at* SAM) I donner you, Sam! Strues-god!

SAM: (*Still laughing*) Sorry, Willie . . . Sorry . . .

HALLY: Sam! Willie! (*Grabs his ruler and gives* WILLIE *a vicious whack on the bum*) How the hell am I supposed to

985   concentrate with the two of you behaving like bloody children!

WILLIE: Hit him too!

HALLY: Shut up, Willie.

WILLIE: He started jokes again.

990   HALLY: Get back to your work. You too, Sam. (*His ruler*) Do you want another one, Willie?

(SAM *and* WILLIE *return to their work.* HALLY *uses the opportunity to escape from his unsuccessful attempt at homework. He struts around like a little despot, ruler in hand, giving vent to his anger and frustration*)

Suppose a customer had walked in then? Or the Park Superintendent. And seen the two of you behaving like a pair of hooligans. That would have been the end of my

995   mother's license, you know. And your jobs! Well, this is the end of it. From now on there will be no more of your ballroom nonsense in here. This is a business establishment, not a bloody New Brighton dancing school. I've been far too lenient with the two of you. (*Behind the*

1000   *counter for a green cool drink and a dollop of ice cream. He keeps up his tirade as he prepares it*) But what really makes me bitter is that I allow you chaps a little freedom in here when business is bad and what do you do with it? The foxtrot! Specially you, Sam. There's more to life than

1005   trotting around a dance floor and I thought at least you knew it.

SAM: It's harmless pleasure, Hally. It doesn't hurt anybody.

HALLY: It's also a rather simple one, you know.

SAM: You reckon so? Have you ever tried?

1010   HALLY: Of course not.

SAM: Why don't you? Now.

HALLY: What do you mean? Me dance?

SAM: Yes. I'll show you a simple step—the waltz—then you try it.

1015   HALLY: What will that prove?

SAM: That it might not be as easy as you think.

HALLY: I didn't say it was easy. I said it was simple—like in simple-minded, meaning mentally retarded. You can't exactly say it challenges the intellect.

1020   SAM: It does other things.

HALLY: Such as?

SAM: Make people happy.

HALLY: (*The glass in his hand*) So do American cream sodas with ice cream. For God's sake, Sam, you're not asking me to take ballroom dancing serious, are you?   1025

SAM: Yes.

HALLY: (*Sigh of defeat*) Oh, well, so much for trying to give you a decent education. I've obviously achieved nothing.

SAM: You still haven't told me what's wrong with admiring something that's beautiful and then trying to do it your-   1030 self.

HALLY: Nothing. But we happen to be talking about a fox-trot, not a thing of beauty.

SAM: But that is just what I'm saying. If you were to see two champions doing, two masters of the art . . . !   1035

HALLY: Oh, God, I give up. So now it's also art!

SAM: Ja.

HALLY: There's a limit, Sam. Don't confuse art and entertainment.

SAM: So then what is art?   1040

HALLY: You want a definition?

SAM: Ja.

HALLY: (*He realizes he has got to be careful. He gives the matter a lot of thought before answering*) Philosophers have been trying to do that for centuries. What is Art? What is Life? But basi-   1045 cally I suppose it's . . . the giving of meaning to matter.

SAM: Nothing to do with beautiful?

HALLY: It goes beyond that. It's the giving of form to the formless.

SAM: Ja, well, maybe it's not art, then. But I still say it's beau-   1050 tiful.

HALLY: I'm sure the word you mean to use is entertaining.

SAM: (*Adamant*) No. Beautiful. And if you want proof, come along to the Centenary Hall in New Brighton in two weeks' time.   1055

(*The mention of the Centenary Hall draws* WILLIE *over to them*)

HALLY: What for? I've seen the two of you prancing around in here often enough.

SAM: (*He laughs*) This isn't the real thing, Hally. We're just playing around in here.

HALLY: So? I can use my imagination.   1060

SAM: And what do you get?

HALLY: A lot of people dancing around and having a so-called good time.

SAM: That all?

HALLY: Well, basically it is that, surely.   1065

SAM: No, it isn't. Your imagination hasn't helped you at all. There's a lot more to it than that. We're getting ready for the championships, Hally, not just another dance. There's going to be a lot of people, all right, and they're going to have a good time, but they'll only be spectators, sitting   1070 around and watching. It's just the competitors out there on the dance floor. Party decorations and fancy lights all around the walls! The ladies in beautiful evening dresses!

HALLY: My mother's got one of those, Sam, and, quite frankly, it's an embarrassment every time she wears it.   1075

SAM: (*Undeterred*) Your imagination left out the excitement.

(HALLY *scoffs*)

Oh, yes, the finalists are not going to be out there just to have a good time. One of those couples will be the 1950

1080 Eastern Province Champions. And your imagination left out the music.

WILLIE: Mr. Elijah Gladman Guzana and his Orchestral Jazzonions.

SAM: The sound of the big band, Hally. Trombone, trumpet, tenor and alto sax. And then, finally, your imagination also

1085 left out the climax of the evening when the dancing is finished, the judges have stopped whispering among themselves and the Master of Ceremonies collects their scorecards and goes up onto the stage to announce the winners.

1090 HALLY: All right. So you make it sound like a bit of a do. It's an occasion. Satisfied?

SAM: (*Victory*) So you admit that!

HALLY: Emotionally yes, intellectually no.

SAM: Well, I don't know what you mean by that, all I'm

1095 telling you is that it is going to be *the* event of the year in New Brighton. It's been sold out for two weeks already. There's only standing room left. We've got competitors coming from Kingwilliamstown, East London, Port Alfred.

(HALLY *starts pacing thoughtfully*)

1100 HALLY: Tell me a bit more.

SAM: I thought you weren't interested . . . intellectually.

HALLY: (*Mysteriously*) I've got my reasons.

SAM: What do you want to know?

HALLY: It takes place every year?

1105 SAM: Yes. But only every third year in New Brighton. It's East London's turn to have the championships next year.

HALLY: Which, I suppose, makes it an even more significant event.

SAM: Ah ha! We're getting somewhere. Our "occasion" is now

1110 a "significant event."

HALLY: I wonder.

SAM: What?

HALLY: I wonder if I would get away with it.

SAM: But what?

1115 HALLY: (*To the table and his exercise book*) "Write five hundred words describing an annual event of cultural or historical significance." Would I be stretching poetic license a little too far if I called your ballroom championships a cultural event?

1120 SAM: You mean . . . ?

HALLY: You think we could get five hundred words out of it, Sam?

SAM: Victor Sylvester has written a whole book on ballroom dancing.

1125 WILLIE: You going to write about it, Master Hally?

HALLY: Yes, gentlemen, that is precisely what I am considering doing. Old Doc Bromely—he's my English teacher—is going to argue with me, of course. He doesn't like natives. But I'll point out to him that in strict anthropo-

1130 logical terms the culture of a primitive black society includes its dancing and singing. To put my thesis in a nutshell: The war-dance has been replaced by the waltz. But it still amounts to the same thing: the release of primitive emotions through movement. Shall we give it a go?

1135 SAM: I'm ready.

WILLIE: Me also.

HALLY: Ha! This will teach the old bugger a lesson. (*Decision taken*) Right. Let's get ourselves organized. (*This means another cake on the table. He sits*) I think you've given me enough general atmosphere, Sam, but to build the tension 1140 and suspense I need facts. (*Pencil poised*)

WILLIE: Give him facts, Boet Sam.

HALLY: What you called the climax . . . how many finalists?

SAM: Six couples.

HALLY: (*Making notes*) Go on. Give me the picture. 1145

SAM: Spectators seated right around the hall. (WILLIE *becomes a spectator*)

HALLY: . . . and it's a full house.

SAM: At one end, on the stage, Gladman and his Orchestral Jazzonions. At the other end is a long table with the three 1150 judges. The six finalists go onto the dance floor and take up their positions. When they are ready and the spectators have settled down, the Master of Ceremonies goes to the microphone. To start with, he makes some jokes to get the people laughing . . . 1155

HALLY: Good touch! (*as he writes*) ". . . creating a relaxed atmosphere which will change to one of tension and drama as the climax is approached."

SAM: (*Onto a chair to act out the M.C.*) "Ladies and gentlemen, we come now to the great moment you have all been 1160 waiting for this evening. . . . The finals of the 1950 Eastern Province Open Ballroom Dancing Championships. But first let me introduce the finalists! Mr. and Mrs. Welcome Tchabalala from Kingwilliamstown . . ."

WILLIE: (*He applauds after every name*) Is when the people clap 1165 their hands and whistle and make a lot of noise, Master Hally.

SAM: "Mr. Mulligan Njikelane and Miss Nomhle Nkonyeni of Grahamstown; Mr. and Mrs. Norman Nchinga from Port Alfred; Mr. Fats Bokolane and Miss Dina Plaatjies 1170 from East London; Mr. Sipho Dugu and Mrs. Mable Magada from Peddie; and from New Brighton our very own Mr. Willie Malopo and Miss Hilda Samuels."

(WILLIE *can't believe his ears. He abandons his role as a spectator and scrambles into position as a finalist*)

WILLIE: Relaxed and ready to romance! 1175

SAM: The applause dies down. When everybody is silent, Gladman lifts up his sax, nods at the Orchestral Jazzonions . . .

WILLIE: Play the jukebox please, Boet Sam!

SAM: I also only got bus fare, Willie. 1180

HALLY: Hold it, everybody. (*Heads for the cash register behind the counter*) How much is in the till, Sam?

SAM: Three shillings. Hally . . . your Mom counted it before she left.

(HALLY *hesitates*)

HALLY: Sorry, Willie. You know how she carried on the last 1185 time I did it. We'll just have to pool our combined imaginations and hope for the best. (*Returns to the table*) Back to work. How are the points scored, Sam?

SAM: Maximum of ten points each for individual style, deportment, rhythm and general appearance. 1190

WILLIE: Must I start?

HALLY: Hold it for a second, Willie. And penalties?

SAM: For what?

HALLY: For doing something wrong. Say you stumble or
1195   bump into somebody . . . do they take off any points?

SAM: (*Aghast*) Hally . . . !

HALLY: When you're dancing. If you and your partner collide
into another couple.

(HALLY *can get no further.* SAM *has collapsed with laughter. He explains to* WILLIE)

SAM: If me and Miriam bump into you and Hilda . . .

(WILLIE *joins him in another good laugh*)

1200   Hally, Hally . . . !

HALLY: (*Perplexed*) Why? What did I say?

SAM: There's no collisions out there, Hally. Nobody trips or
stumbles or bumps into anybody else. That's what that
moment is all about. To be one of those finalists on that
1205   dance floor is like . . . like being in a dream about a world
in which accidents don't happen.

HALLY: (*Genuinely moved by* SAM's *image*) Jesus, Sam! That's
beautiful!

WILLIE: (*Can endure waiting no longer*) I'm starting! (WILLIE
1210   *dances while* SAM *talks*)

SAM: Of course it is. That's what I've been trying to say to you
all afternoon. And it's beautiful because that is what we
want life to be like. But instead, like you said, Hally, we're
bumping into each other all the time. Look at the three of
1215   us this afternoon: I've bumped into Willie, the two of us
have bumped into you, you've bumped into your mother,
she bumping into your Dad. . . . None of us knows the
steps and there's no music playing. And it doesn't stop
with us. The whole world is doing it all the time. Open a
1220   newspaper and what do you read? America has bumped
into Russia, England is bumping into India, rich man
bumps into poor man. Those are big collisions, Hally. They
make for a lot of bruises. People get hurt in all that bumping,
and we're sick and tired of it now. It's been going on
1225   for too long. Are we never going to get it right? . . . Learn
to dance life like champions instead of always being just a
bunch of beginners at it?

HALLY: (*Deep and sincere admiration of the man*) You've got a vision,
Sam!

1230   SAM: Not just me. What I'm saying to you is that everybody's
got it. That's why there's only standing room left for the
Centenary Hall in two weeks' time. For as long as the music
lasts, we are going to see six couples get it right, the
way we want life to be.

1235   HALLY: But is that the best we can do, Sam . . . watch six finalists
dreaming about the way it should be?

SAM: I don't know. But it starts with that. Without the dream
we won't know what we're going for. And anyway I
reckon there are a few people who have got past just
1240   dreaming about it and are trying for something real. Remember
that thing we read once in the paper about the
Mahatma Gandhi? Going without food to stop those riots
in India?

HALLY: You're right. He certainly was trying to teach people
1245   to get the steps right.

SAM: And the Pope.

HALLY: Yes, he's another one. Our old General Smuts as well,
you know. He's also out there dancing. You know, Sam,
when you come to think of it, that's what the United Nations
boils down to . . . a dancing school for politicians!   1250

SAM: And let's hope they learn.

HALLY: (*A little surge of hope*) You're right. We mustn't despair.
Maybe there's some hope for mankind after all. Keep it
up, Willie. (*Back to his table with determination*) This is a lot
bigger than I thought. So what have we got? Yes, our title: 1255
"A World Without Collisions."

SAM: That sounds good! "A World Without Collisions."

HALLY: Subtitle: "Global Politics on the Dance Floor." No. A
bit too heavy, hey? What about "Ballroom Dancing as a
Political Vision"?   1260

(*The telephone rings.* SAM *answers it*)

SAM: St. George's Park Tea Room . . . Yes, Madam . . . Hally,
it's your Mom.

HALLY: (*Back to reality*) Oh, God, yes! I'd forgotten all about
that. Shit! Remember my words, Sam? Just when you're
enjoying yourself, someone or something will come along   1265
and wreck everything.

SAM: You haven't heard what she's got to say yet.

HALLY: Public telephone?

SAM: No.

HALLY: Does she sound happy or unhappy?   1270

SAM: I couldn't tell. (*Pause*) She's waiting, Hally.

HALLY: (*To the telephone*) Hello, Mom . . . No, everything is
okay here. Just doing my homework. . . . What's your
news? . . . You've what? . . . (*Pause. He takes the receiver away
from his ear for a few seconds. In the course of* HALLY's *telephone*   1275
conversation, SAM *and* WILLIE *discretely position the stacked tables
and chairs.* HALLY *places the receiver back to his ear*) Yes, I'm
still here. Oh, well, I give up now. Why did you do it,
Mom? . . . Well, I just hope you know what you've let us
in for. . . . (*Loudly*) I said I hope you know what you've let   1280
us in for! It's the end of the peace and quiet we've been
having. (*Softly*) Where is he? (*Normal voice*) He can't hear
us from in there. But for God's sake, Mom, what happened?
I told you to be firm with him. . . . Then you and
the nurses should have held him down, taken his crutches   1285
away. . . . I know only too well he's my father! . . . I'm not
being disrespectful, but I'm sick and tired of emptying
stinking chamberpots full of phlegm and piss. . . . Yes, I do!
When you're not there, he asks *me* do it. . . . If you really
want to know the truth, that's why I've got no appetite for   1290
my food. . . . Yes! There's a lot of things you don't know
about. For your information, I still haven't got that science
textbook I need. And you know why? He borrowed the
money you gave me for it. . . . Because I didn't want to
start another fight between you two. . . . He says that every   1295
time. . . . All right, Mom! (*Viciously*) Then just remember
to start hiding your bag away again, because he'll be at
your purse before long for money for booze. And when
he's well enough to come down here, you better keep an
eye on the till as well, because that is also going to develop   1300
a leak. . . . Then don't complain to me when he starts his
old tricks. . . . Yes, you do. I get it from you on one side
and from him on the other, and it makes life hell for me.

1305 I'm not going to be the peacemaker anymore. I'm warning you now: when the two of you start fighting again, I'm leaving home. . . . Mom, if you start crying, I'm going to put down the receiver. . . . Okay . . . (*Lowering his voice to a vicious whisper*) Okay, Mom. I heard you. (*Desper-*

1310 *ate*) No. . . . Because I don't want to. I'll see him when I get home! Mom! . . . (*Pause. When he speaks again, his tone changes completely. It is not simply pretense. We sense a genuine emotional conflict*) Welcome home, chum! . . . What's that? . . . Don't be silly, Dad. You being home is just about

1315 the best news in the world. . . . I bet you are. Bloody depressing there with everybody going on about their ailments, hey! . . . How you feeling? . . . Good . . . Here as well, pal. Coming down cats and dogs. . . . That's right. Just the day for a kip and a toss in your old Uncle Ned. . . .

1320 Everything's just hunky-dory on my side, Dad. . . . Well, to start with, there's a nice pile of comics for you on the counter. . . . Yes, old Kemple brought them in. *Batman and Robin, Submariner* . . . just your cup of tea . . . I will. . . . Yes, we'll spin a few yarns tonight. . . . Okay, chum, see you in a little while. . . . No, I promise. I'll come straight

1325 home. . . . (*Pause—his mother comes back on the phone*) Mom? Okay. I'll lock up now. . . . What? . . . Oh, the brandy . . . Yes, I'll remember! . . . I'll put it in my suitcase now, for God's sake. I know well enough what will happen if he doesn't get it. . . . (*Places a bottle of brandy on the counter*) I

1330 *was* kind to him, Mom. I didn't say anything nasty! . . . All right. Bye. (*End of telephone conversation. A desolate* HALLY *doesn't move. A strained silence*)

SAM: (*Quietly*) That sounded like a bad bump, Hally.

1335 HALLY: (*Having a hard time controlling his emotions. He speaks carefully*) Mind your own business, Sam.

SAM: Sorry. I wasn't trying to interfere. Shall we carry on? Hally? (*He indicates the exercise book. No response from* HALLY)

WILLIE: (*Also trying*) Tell him about when they give out the cups, Boet Sam.

1340 SAM: Ja! That's another big moment. The presentation of the cups after the winners have been announced. You've got to put that in.

(*Still no response form* HALLY)

WILLIE: A big silver one, Master Hally, called floating trophy for the champions.

1345 SAM: We always invite some big-shot personality to hand them over. Guest of honor this year is going to be His Holiness Bishop Jabulani of the All African Free Zionist Church.

(HALLY *gets up abruptly, goes to his table and tears up the page he was writing on*)

HALLY: So much for a bloody world without collisions.

1350 SAM: Too bad. It was on its way to being a good composition.

HALLY: Let's stop bullshitting ourselves, Sam.

SAM: Have we been doing that?

HALLY: Yes! That's what all our talk about a decent world has been . . . just so much bullshit.

1355 SAM: We did say it was still only a dream.

HALLY: And a bloody useless one at that. Life's a fuck-up and it's never going to change.

SAM: Ja, maybe that's true.

HALLY: There's no maybe about it. It's a blunt and brutal fact. All we've done this afternoon is waste our time. 1360

SAM: Not if we'd got your homework done.

HALLY: I don't give a shit about my homework, so, for Christ's sake, just shut up about it. (*Slamming books viciously into his school case*) Hurry up now and finish your work. I want to lock up and get out of here. (*Pause*) And then go where? 1365 Home-sweet-fucking-home. Jesus, I hate that word.

(HALLY *goes to the counter to put the brandy bottle and comics in his school case. After a moment's hesitation, he smashes the bottle of brandy. He abandons all further attempts to hide his feelings.* SAM *and* WILLIE *work away as unobtrusively as possible*)

Do you want to know what is really wrong with your lovely little dream, Sam? It's not just that we are all bad dancers. That does happen to be perfectly true, but there's more to it than just that. You left out the cripples. 1370

SAM: Hally!

HALLY: (*Now totally reckless*) Ja! Can't leave them out, Sam. That's why we always end up on our backsides on the dance floor. They're also out there dancing . . . like a bunch of broken spiders trying to do the quick-step! 1375 (*An ugly attempt at laughter*) When you come to think of it, it's a bloody comical sight. I mean, it's bad enough on two legs . . . but one and a pair of crutches! Hell, no, Sam. That's guaranteed to turn that dance floor into a shambles. Why you shaking your head? Picture it, man. 1380 For once this afternoon let's use our imaginations sensibly.

SAM: Be careful, Hally.

HALLY: Of what? The truth? I seem to be the only one around here who is prepared to face it. We've had the 1385 pretty dream, it's time now to wake up and have a good long look at the way things really are. Nobody knows the steps, there's no music, the cripples are also out there tripping up everybody and trying to get into the act, and it's all called the All-Comers-How-to-Make-a-Fuckup-of- 1390 Life Championships. (*Another ugly laugh*) Hang on, Sam! The best bit is still coming. Do you know what the winner's trophy is? A beautiful big chamber-pot with roses on the side, and it's full to the brim with piss. And guess who I think is going to be this year's winner. 1395

SAM: (*Almost shouting*) Stop now!

HALLY: (*Suddenly appalled by how far he has gone*) Why?

SAM: Hally? It's your father you're talking about.

HALLY: So? 1400

SAM: Do you know what you've been saying?

(HALLY *can't answer. He is rigid with shame.* SAM *speaks to him sternly*)

No, Hally, you mustn't do it. Take back those words and ask for forgiveness! It's a terrible sin for a son to mock his father with jokes like that. You'll be punished if you carry on. Your father is your father, even if he is a . . . cripple 1405 man.

WILLIE: Yes, Master Hally. Is true what Sam say.

SAM: I understand how you are feeling, Hally, but even so . . .

HALLY: No, you don't!

1410 SAM: I think I do.

HALLY: And I'm telling you you don't. Nobody does. (*Speaking carefully as his shame turns to rage at* SAM) It's your turn to be careful, Sam. Very careful! You're treading on dangerous ground. Leave me and my father alone.

1415 SAM: I'm not the one who's been saying things about him.

HALLY: What goes on between me and my Dad is none of your business!

SAM: Then don't tell me about it. If that's all you've got to say about him, I don't want to hear.

(*For a moment* HALLY *is at loss for a response*)

1420 HALLY: Just get on with your bloody work and shut up.

SAM: Swearing at me won't help you.

HALLY: Yes, it does! Mind your own fucking business and shut up!

SAM: Okay. If that's the way you want it, I'll stop trying.

(*He turns away. This infuriates* HALLY *even more*)

1425 HALLY: Good. Because what you've been trying to do is meddle in something you know nothing about. All that concerns you in here, Sam, is to try and do what you get paid for—keep the place clean and serve the customers. In plain words, just get on with your job. My mother is right. 1430 She's always warning me about allowing you to get too familiar. Well, this time you've gone too far. It's going to stop right now.

(*No response from* SAM)

You're only a servant in here, and don't forget it.

(*Still no response.* HALLY *is trying hard to get one*)

And as far as my father is concerned, all you need to re-1435 member is that he is your boss.

SAM: (*Needled at last*) No, he isn't. I get paid by your mother.

HALLY: Don't argue with me, Sam!

SAM: Then don't say he's my boss.

HALLY: He's a white man and that's good enough for you.

1440 SAM: I'll try to forget you said that.

HALLY: Don't! Because you won't be doing me a favor if you do. I'm telling you to remember it.

(*A pause.* SAM *pulls himself together and makes one last effort*)

SAM: Hally, Hally . . . ! Come on now. Let's stop before it's too late. You're right. We *are* on dangerous ground. If we're not 1445 careful, somebody is going to get hurt.

HALLY: It won't be me.

SAM: Don't be so sure.

HALLY: I don't know what you're talking about, Sam.

SAM: Yes, you do.

1450 HALLY: (*Furious*) Jesus, I wish you would stop trying to tell me what I do and what I don't know.

(SAM *gives up. He turns to* WILLIE)

SAM: Let's finish up.

HALLY: Don't turn your back on me! I haven't finished talking.

(*He grabs* SAM *by the arm and tries to make him turn around.* SAM *reacts with a flash of anger*)

SAM: Don't do that, Hally! (*Facing the boy*) All right, I'm lis- 1455 tening. Well? What do you want to say to me?

HALLY: (*Pause as* HALLY *looks for something to say*) To begin with, why don't you also start calling me Master Harold, like Willie.

SAM: Do you mean that? 1460

HALLY: Why the hell do you think I said it?

SAM: And if I don't?

HALLY: You might just lose your job.

SAM: (*Quietly and very carefully*) If you make me say it once, I'll never call you anything else again. 1465

HALLY: So? (*The boy confronts the man*) Is that meant to be a threat?

SAM: Just telling you what will happen if you make me do that. You must decide what it means to you.

HALLY: Well, I have. It's good news. Because that is exactly 1470 what Mater Harold wants from now on. Think of it as a little lesson in respect, Sam, that's long overdue, and I hope you remember it as well as you do your geography. I can tell you now that somebody who will be glad to hear I've finally given it to you will be my Dad. Yes! He agrees with 1475 my Mom. He's always going on about it as well. "You must teach the boys to show you more respect, my son."

SAM: So now you can stop complaining about going home. Everybody is going to be happy tonight.

HALLY: That's perfectly correct. You see, you mustn't get the 1480 wrong idea about me and my Dad, Sam. We also have our good times together. Some bloody good laughs. He's got a marvelous sense of humor. Want to know what our favorite joke is? He gives out a big groan, you see, and says: "It's not fair, is it, Hally?" Then I have to ask: "What, 1485 chum?" And then he says: "A nigger's arse" . . . and we both have a good laugh.

(*The men stare at him with disbelief*)

What's the matter, Willie? Don't you catch the joke? You always were a bit slow on the uptake. It's what is called a pun. You see, fair means both light in color and to be just 1490 and decent. (*He turns to* SAM) I thought *you* would catch it, Sam.

SAM: Oh ja, I catch it all right.

HALLY: But it doesn't appeal to your sense of humor.

SAM: Do you really laugh? 1495

HALLY: Of course.

SAM: To please him? Make him feel good?

HALLY: No, for heaven's sake! I laugh because I think it's a bloody good joke.

SAM: You're really trying hard to be ugly, aren't you? And why 1500 drag poor old Willie into it? He's done nothing to you except show you the respect you want so badly. That's also not being fair, you know . . . and I mean just or decent.

WILLIE: It's all right, Sam. Leave it now.

SAM: It's me you're after. You should just have said "Sam's 1505 arse" . . . because that's the one you're trying to kick. Anyway, how do you know it's not fair? You've never seen it. Do you want to? (*He drops his trousers and underpants and presents his backside for* HALLY'S *inspection*) Have a good look. A real Basuto arse . . . which is about as nigger as they can 1510 come. Satisfied? (*Trousers up*) Now you can make your Dad even happier when you go home tonight. Tell him I showed you my arse and he is quite right. It's not fair. And if it will give him an even better laugh next time, I'll also

1515   let *him* have a look. Come, Willie, let's finish up and go.

(SAM *and* WILLIE *start to tidy up the tea room.* HALLY *doesn't move. He waits for a moment when* SAM *passes him*)

HALLY: (*Quietly*) Sam . . .

(SAM *stops and looks expectantly at the boy.* HALLY *spits in his face. A long and heartfelt groan from* WILLIE. *For a few seconds* SAM *doesn't move*)

SAM: (*Taking out a handkerchief and wiping his face*) It's all right, Willie.

(*To* HALLY)

Ja, well, you've done it . . . Master Harold. Yes, I'll start call-
1520   ing you that from now on. It won't be difficult anymore. You've hurt yourself, Master Harold. I saw it coming. I warned you, but you wouldn't listen. You've just hurt yourself *bad*. And you're a coward, Master Harold. The
1525   face you should be spitting in is your father's . . . but you used mine, because you think you're safe inside your fair skin . . . and this time I don't mean just or decent. (*Pause, then moving violently towards* HALLY) Should I hit him, Willie?

WILLIE: (*Stopping* SAM) No, Boet Sam.
1530   SAM: (*Violently*) Why not?

WILLIE: It won't help, Boet Sam.

SAM: I don't want to help! I want to hurt him.

WILLIE: You also hurt yourself.

SAM: And if he had done it to you, Willie?
1535   WILLIE: Me? Spit at me like I was a dog? (*A thought that had not occurred to him before. He looks at* HALLY) Ja. Then I want to hit him. I want to hit him hard!

(*A dangerous few seconds as the men stand staring at the boy.* WILLIE *turns away, shaking his head*)

But maybe all I do is go cry at the back. He's little boy, Boet Sam. Little *white* boy. Long trousers now, but he's still
1540   little boy.

SAM: (*His violence ebbing away into defeat as quickly as it flooded*) You're right. So go on, then: groan again, Willie. You do it better than me. (*To* HALLY) You don't know all of what you've just done . . . Master Harold. It's not just that you've
1545   made me feel dirtier than I've ever been in my life . . . I mean, how do I wash off yours and your father's filth? . . . I've also failed. A long time ago I promised myself I was go-ing to try and do something, but you've just shown me . . . Master Harold . . . that I've failed. (*Pause*) I've also
1550   got a memory of a little white boy when he was still wear-ing short trousers and a black man, but they're not flying a kite. It was the old Jubilee days, after dinner one night. I was in my room. You came in and just stood against the wall, looking down at the ground, and only after I'd asked
1555   you what you wanted, what was wrong, I don't know how many times, did you speak and even then so softly I almost

didn't hear you. "Sam, please help me to go and fetch my Dad." Remember? He was dead drunk on the floor of the Central Hotel Bar. They'd phoned for your Mom, but you were the only one at home. And do you remember how 1560 we did it? You went in first by yourself to ask permission for me to go into the bar. Then I loaded him onto my back like a baby and carried him back to the boarding house with you following behind carrying his crutches. (*Shaking his head as he remembers*) A crowded Main Street 1565 with all the people watching a little white boy following his drunk father on a nigger's back! I felt for that little boy . . . Master Harold. I felt for him. After that we still had to clean him up, remember? He'd messed in his trousers, so we had to clean him up and get him into bed.   1570

HALLY: (*Great pain*) I love him, Sam.

SAM: I know you do. That's why I tried to stop you from saying these things about him. It would have been so simple if you could have just despised him for being a weak man. But he's your father. You love him and you're ashamed of him. You're 1575 ashamed of so much! . . . And now that's going to include yourself. That was the promise I made to myself: to try and stop that happening. (*Pause*) After we got him to bed you came back with me to my room and sat in a corner and car-ried on just looking down at the ground. And for days after 1580 that! You hadn't done anything wrong, but you went around as if you owed the world an apology for being alive. I didn't like seeing that! That's not the way a boy grows up to be a man! . . . But the one person who should have been teach-ing you what that means was the cause of your shame. If you 1585 really want to know, that's why I made you that kite. I wanted you to look up, be proud of something, of your-self . . . (*Bitter smile at the memory*) . . . and you certainly were that when I left you with it up there on the hill. Oh, ja . . . something else! . . . If you ever do write it as a short story, 1590 there *was* a twist in our ending. I couldn't sit down there and stay with you. It was a "Whites Only" bench. You were too young, too excited to notice then. But not anymore. If you're not careful . . . Master Harold . . . you're going to be sitting up there by yourself for a long time to come, and 1595 there won't be a kite in the sky. (SAM *has got nothing more to say. He exits into the kitchen, taking off his waiter's jacket*)

WILLIE: Is bad. Is all all bad in here now.

HALLY: (*Books into his school case, raincoat on*) Willie . . . (*It is dif-ficult to speak*) Will you lock up for me and look after the 1600 keys?

WILLIE: Okay.

(SAM *returns.* HALLY *goes behind the counter and collects the few coins in the cash register. As he starts to leave . . .*)

SAM: Don't forget the comic books.

(HALLY *returns to the counter and puts them in his case. He starts to leave again*)

SAM: (*To the retreating back of the boy*) Stop . . . Hally . . .

(HALLY *stops, but doesn't turn to face him*)

Hally . . . I've got no right to tell you what being a man 1605 means if I don't behave like one myself, and I'm not doing so well at that this afternoon. Should we try again, Hally?

HALLY: Try what?

1610 SAM: Fly another kite, I suppose. It worked once, and this time I need it as much as you do.

HALLY: It's still raining, Sam. You can't fly kites on rainy days, remember.

SAM: So what do we do? Hope for better weather tomorrow?

1615 HALLY: (*Helpless gesture*) I don't know. I don't know anything anymore.

SAM: You sure of that, Hally? Because it would be pretty hopeless if that was true. It would mean nothing has been learnt in here this afternoon, and there was a hell of a lot of teach-

1620 ing going on . . . one way or the other. But anyway, I don't believe you. I reckon there's one thing you know. You don't *have* to sit up there by yourself. You know what that bench means now, and you can leave it any time you choose. All you've got to do is stand up and walk away from it.

1625

(HALLY *leaves*. WILLIE *goes up quietly to* SAM)

WILLIE: Is okay, Boet Sam. You see. Is . . . (*He can't find any bet-ter words*) . . . is going to be okay tomorrow. (*Changing his tone*) Hey, Boet Sam! (*He is trying hard*) You right. I think about it and you right. Tonight I find Hilda and say sorry. And make promise I won't beat her no more. You hear

1630 me, Boet Sam?

SAM: I hear you, Willie.

WILLIE: And when we practice I relax and romance with her from beginning to end. Non-stop! You watch! Two weeks' time: "First prize for promising newcomers: Mr. 1635 Willie Malopo and Miss Hilda Samuels." (*Sudden impulse*) To hell with it! I walk home. (*He goes to the juke-box, puts in a coin and selects a record. The machine comes to life in the gray twilight, blushing its way through a spectrum of soft, romantic colors*) How did you say it, Boet Sam? Let's 1640 dream. (WILLIE *sways with the music and gestures for* SAM *to dance*)

(*Sarah Vaughan sings*)

"Little man you're crying,
I know why you're blue,
Someone took your kiddy car away;
Better go to sleep now,   1645
Little man you've had a busy day." (*etc. etc.*)
          You lead. I follow.

(*The men dance together*)

"Johnny won your marbles,
Tell you what we'll do;
Dad will get you new ones   1650
right away;
Better go to sleep now,
Little man you've had a busy day."

Louis Nowra

Born in Melbourne in 1950, Louis Nowra studied at La Trobe University before embarking on a career as a writer. The author of 30 plays, several novels and opera libretti, and many screenplays for television and film, Nowra's work often explores the dynamics of Australian identity: the issues raised by Australia's settlement as a penal colony and the longstanding sense of dependence on European culture, by the settlers' and then the Australian government's systematic oppression of the Aboriginal peoples, and today by Australia's emergence as a deeply multicultural state. From his early plays, such as *Inside the Island* (1980), through the major dramas *The Golden Age* (1985), *Capricornia* (1988), *Summer of the Aliens* (1993), and *The Incorruptibles* (1995), Nowra has become not only one of Australia's most visible playwrights, but a major voice in the contemporary theater's engagement with the politics of national and cultural identity.

THE GOLDEN AGE

The Golden Age deftly interrogates the presiding anxieties of Australian cultural identification. Australia was founded as a British penal colony—the First Fleet brought its cargo of more than 700 British convicts to Australia in 1788—and this legacy is in many ways the subject of Nowra's play. From the opening scene, in which the Archers play a version of Euripides' *Iphigeneia in Tauris* against the backdrop of a crumbling Greek Temple, Nowra frames the white Australians' sense of their belatedness to the monuments of European culture, monuments which—like the temple itself, built by convict labor in the 1840s, but already decaying in the Australian weather—are invariably changed by their invocation in a distinctly different culture. Yet Nowra also poses a different question: are these eroded monuments degraded by their relocation to Australia, or should they be regarded as the foundations of a new and different culture? This is the question posed by Francis and Peter's discovery of "original" Australians: the descendants of escapees from the horrific Van Diemens Land (Tasmania) colony, who have managed to persist for a century or so in complete isolation. As William notes, this is the "true Australian culture": "ex-convicts, escaped convicts, failed colonists, general scum . . . even a travelling actor tired of doing bad shows for stupid colonists." While they speak a densely poetic language, and perform a superb version of Nahum Tate's adaptation of Shakespeare's *King Lear* when they meet their modern "rescuers," the consequences of their isolation are also troubling: inbreeding has resulted in a number of genetic deformities, both physical and mental. By setting the play in 1939, Nowra gives this parable additional bite. Much as the white Australians are already sensitive to their convict-lineage, the racist ideology of Hitler's Nazi Germany seems to confirm their deepest fears: Mac and Stef literalize the sense that Australians cannot escape a kind of genetic inferiority. While Peter and Francis join the fight against fascism, going to war in Europe, its racist rhetoric already inhabits the Australian homeland, as the colony are sent to a mental asylum to keep them from becoming public knowledge. Moreover, while Melorne, Queenie Ayre, Betsheb, and their tiny community represent the original white Australians, Nowra is careful to remind us that their treatment by the authorities is not unique. Arguing with William over his care of the colony, Elizabeth remarks that they are a "pathetic group," reminiscent of "those Aboriginals in shanty towns." Peter, too, at the end of the play, finding his friend Francis hiding with Betsheb, asks, "How could they have survived, anyway? They were pathetic remnants of what was probably an even more pathetic collection of people. They were like those Aboriginal tribes that withered away because their culture wasn't strong enough. It happens in nature, in human civilizations, one big animal swallows a little one." Of course, the Aborigines did not merely wither away; their culture was systematically destroyed. The Nazis systematically murdered Jews, Gypsies, and homosexuals as "inferior" peoples, but Nowra suggests that this "evil philosophy" is as much a part of Australia's incorporation of European culture as its love of Euripides and Shakespeare. Showing us how the ideology of cultural supremacy conceals the innate violence of a will to power, *The Golden Age* frames a stringent critique of an Australia blindly dependent on "European" values and culture.

THE GOLDEN AGE

Louis Nowra

THERE ARE MOMENTS WHEN SPEECH IS BUT A MOUTH PRESSED LIGHTLY AND HUMBLY AGAINST THE ANGEL'S HAND.
JAMES MERRIL
IN MEMORY OF MARVIN GAYE.

CHARACTERS

WILLIAM ARCHER, *a doctor*
ELIZABETH ARCHER, WILLIAM's *wife*
FRANCIS MORRIS, *a young engineer*
PETER ARCHER, *a young geologist*
BETSHEB, *a young woman*
STEF, *an 'autistic' child*
AYRE, *an old woman*
MELORNE, *an old man*
ANGEL, *a woman in her twenties*
MAC, *a young man*
GEORGE ROSS, M.P., *Federal Minister for Health*

MRS. WITCOMBE, *a working class woman in her fifties*
DR SIMON, *psychiatrist at the asylum*
JAMES, *a patient at the asylum*
PRIVATE CORRIS, *an Australian soldier*
A GERMAN MAN, *a man on the run*
MARY, *a maid*
A SERVANT

SETTING: *The play is set during the wartime years 1939-45, and the action moves from locations in Hobart and South-West Tasmania to Berlin in the last days of the War.*

ACT ONE

SCENE I

Hobart, 1939. A garden. It is a hot Australian night full of the sounds of cicadas and crickets. ELIZABETH ARCHER, *a middle-aged woman, stands in front of a small, crumbling Greek temple. She wears a copy of an ancient Greek dress. For a moment it seems we are in ancient Greece, but she is playing Iphigenia from* Iphigenia in Tauris.

ELIZABETH: 'I dreamed I had escaped from this island and lived at home in Argos. There I was asleep when suddenly the earth shook and tore apart. I ran outdoors and helplessly watched the whole house crumble into the earth.
5   Out of this ruin, which was my father's house, one column stood. Brown hair grew from its head and it spoke in a human voice. Weeping, I performed for it this murderous ritual for strangers, sprinkling water, as on one destined to die. I interpret this dream thus: it was my brother
10   Orestes I prepared for death and he has died. For what are pillars of a house but its sons. And those whose heads I touch with purifying water die. So now I want to pour libations for my brother.'

(WILLIAM, *about the same age as his wife, enters as Orestes. He is handcuffed, wears glasses and a dinner jacket. He stands before Iphigenia.*)

     'Do you know where you are?'
15   WILLIAM: 'Tauris, my High Priestess.'
ELIZABETH: 'And what is it known for?'
WILLIAM: 'Any Greek who lands on its shores is put to death.'
ELIZABETH: 'And yet, mysterious stranger, you are Greek and you dare to step on our island. You should have left when
20   you had the chance.'
WILLIAM: 'I was shipwrecked.'
ELIZABETH: 'I do not believe your story. Do you see the dark stain on the altar? It is the blood of previous sacrifices. Your blood will mingle with that blood to delight the
25   goddess Artemis.'

WILLIAM: 'I would not care to die if my sister were here to prepare me for my burial.'
ELIZABETH: 'A hopeless wish for a lost soul. Your sister would never be in this savage country. I gather you were captured with another man.'   25
WILLIAM: 'My friend Pylades. He is rich, his house is pure and untainted while I live nowhere and everywhere. I am an outcast, hated by the gods.'
ELIZABETH: 'I too am far from home and live only to perform these dark rites which are so savage as not to be sung. Last   30
night I dreamed my brother, whom I have not seen since we were children, was dead. Killed. His house in ruins. I now have nothing left to lose. Cruelty has overtaken me, possessed me. You are the first to sail here in a long time but you will never return home. You will die in pain and   35
lie in an unmarked grave.'

SCENE II

The same place, next morning. A servant sets up outdoor tables and chairs. Off, in the distance, FRANCIS *and* PETER *play tennis. While the servant sets up,* MR TURNER *enters. He is blind and confused. The servant doesn't see him and heads off, humming, to get another chair.* MR TURNER *hears.*

MR TURNER: Am I in the garden?

(*The servant doesn't respond.*)

     Excuse me, am I in the garden?

(*Silence. He goes a little further and finds himself on the steps of the temple. This confuses him further.*)

     Hello, is anybody here?

(*He enters the temple and disappears.*)

     (*Off*) Mrs. Archer?

(*The servant re-enters with another chair, followed by* WILLIAM.)

5 WILLIAM: I admire the boy's stamina playing in this heat.
   ELIZABETH: (*entering behind him*) His driver said he dropped
      him at the front door and now he's disappeared. Vanished!

(*She exits again. The boys appear.* PETER *looks very English in his
whites.* FRANCIS *wears tennis shoes with football socks, a T-shirt and
black football shorts.*)

   WILLIAM: Who won?
   PETER: Francis, by a whisker.
10 FRANCIS: By a mile.

(*They laugh.* PETER *pours lemonade for his friend and himself.*)

   WILLIAM: (*to* FRANCIS) You know what you two are about to
      do is quite dangerous.
   PETER: Don't nag, father.
   WILLIAM: Francis, didn't Mary lay out some tennis whites for
15   you?

(FRANCIS *is embarrassed.*)

   PETER: She did, but Francis didn't know they were for him.

(ELIZABETH *enters.*)

   ELIZABETH: I can't find him anywhere.
   WILLIAM: He'll turn up.
   ELIZABETH: I want to personally give him his cheque. I think
20   the School for the Blind should be quite pleased at how
      much was given last night. (*Glancing at* FRANCIS' *clothes*)
      Francis, didn't Mary—?
   WILLIAM: (*interrupting*) We've been through that.
   ELIZABETH: (*sitting*) The weather is exquisite! Have you been
25   to Tasmania before, Francis?
   FRANCIS: First time. Thank you for letting me stay here—
   ELIZABETH: (*waving this away*) Our pleasure. Half the time we
      think we're a separate country from the rest of Australia.

(*The boys finish their lemonade.*)

   PETER: We'll go and clean up.
30 ELIZABETH: Make it snappy. I'd like you to meet Mr Turner.

(*The boys exit.*)

      Did you speak to them about their trip?
   WILLIAM: They're determined.
   ELIZABETH: They should consider something less hazardous.
   WILLIAM: It's part of the attraction.

(MR TURNER *emerges from the temple behind them, lost and
confused.*)

35 ELIZABETH: That Francis, he's a strange boy. I watched him
      playing tennis from the balcony. He plays with such fe-
      rocity.
   WILLIAM: It's why I like him, he's had to fight so hard to get
      where he is.
40 MR TURNER: Hello?

(ELIZABETH *turns around.*)

   ELIZABETH: Mr Turner! (*Rushing to his aid*) Stay where you
      are.

   MR TURNER: Where am I?
   ELIZABETH: On the steps of the temple.
   MR TURNER: Temple?   45

(ELIZABETH *grabs him and escorts him to the chairs.*)

   ELIZABETH: I've been looking everywhere for you.
   MR TURNER: (*still confused*) I thought I was in the garden, and
      then . . .
   ELIZABETH: Sit down . . . Some lemonade? (*Pouring it without
      waiting for an answer*) You seem flustered.   50
   WILLIAM: How are you, Mr Turner?
   MR TURNER: Is that you, Mr Archer?
   WILLIAM: Yes.
   ELIZABETH: (*putting the glass in his hand*) There you are. You
      certainly won't be going home empty handed, Mr Turner.   55
      The Greek tragedy wrought a financial miracle.
   MR TURNER: I was lost.
   ELIZABETH: Excuse me?
   MR TURNER: I thought I was in the garden. I smelt roses.
      Flowers. And then I stepped into another world. I felt like 60
      Alice in Wonderland. I said 'Hello' and it echoed all about
      me. I was lost. I thought I was dead.

(*The Archers have no idea what he is talking about.*)

SCENE III

*The wilds of south-west Tasmania, evening. Two lanterns sit on the
ground.* FRANCIS, *tired and dirty, rests against his knapsack looking
at a map in the frail light cast by the lantern. He eats some biscuits.*

   FRANCIS: (*to himself*) Jesus . . .

(*Silence.*)

(*Calling*) Are you all right?

(*No answer.*)

      Peter?
   PETER: (*off*) Coming!

(FRANCIS *returns to his map.*)

   FRANCIS: Could be anywhere . . . anywhere.   5

(*A noise comes from the bush behind him.* FRANCIS *looks.*)

      Peter?

(*Silence.*)

      Is that you, Peter?

(*Silence. There is nothing.* FRANCIS *returns to his map.* PETER *enters from another direction, exhausted and dirty.*)

   PETER: Got bloody caught up in the Bauera.
   FRANCIS: The what?
   PETER: That wild rose we saw this morning. It grows around
      everything and once it's entangled all living things, it   10
      grows back on itself to form a wall. A bit like my mother.

(*He sits down and takes a stone from his pocket.*)

I found this: it was glinting in the moonlight. (*Taking a closer look at it under the lantern*) I'll have a better look at it in the morning. Once you conquered this region I'm sure you'd find huge mineral deposits.

15

FRANCIS: I'd be happy if we could conquer this map. We should go back the way we came, otherwise we'll get well and truly lost. Not that we're not anyway.

20 PETER: (*unconcerned*) We'll be fine. Do you know that this part of Tasmania is one of the most unexplored regions on earth, like the Amazon or the highlands of New Guinea? (*Standing*) It's like another world, isn't it?

FRANCIS: (*looking up at the night sky*) Can't even see the stars.

25 PETER: An underworld. (*Jumping up and down*) See how the ground springs?

FRANCIS: Soggy.

PETER: You know we're about ten foot off the ground?

(FRANCIS *laughs*.)

True. We're on the burial ground of nature. Rotten veg-
30   etable residue of centuries, ancient and petrified trees. So here we are, suspended ten foot above the true floor.

FRANCIS: That's what I love about nature; it's so treacherous.

PETER: You look at nature and your eyes glaze over.

FRANCIS: I always feel that I'm looking at a postcard.

(*Smiling*) My mother says that nature is God's Bible.

35 PETER: You know, you've never introduced me to her.

FRANCIS: Things that humans make: cars, gas works, factories: now that's something. The conquering of chaos.

PETER: You're serious?

FRANCIS: A painter does a painting and people think it's a
40   miracle. It is more wonderful to see a blueprint of a build-ing or bridge and watch it transformed into reality. The Sydney Harbour Bridge has not only conquered nature but is also beautiful. It is imagination made concrete. Mind has become matter.

(PETER *laughs*.)

45 What are you laughing at?

PETER: (*slightly bewildered*) Nothing.

FRANCIS: Take your father; he's an artist, he heals the sick. That's more important than painting. He saves lives.

(FRANCIS *notices something*.)

PETER: In a way.

50 FRANCIS: Did you see that?

PETER: Probably some animal.

(PETER *goes through his knapsack*.)

FRANCIS: I heard something over there before.

PETER: Sorry to put you through the ordeal of meeting my parents.

55 FRANCIS: It was interesting.

(PETER *laughs*.)

PETER: They have developed certain eccentricities.

FRANCIS: I heard you arguing with your dad before we left.

PETER: He doesn't want me to go to Europe; he thinks the political climate is 'unsuitable'. Since he became president of the Medical Board he taken an unnatural interest in 60 politics. Like you. At the moment he's trying to get the medical profession to protest against the deregistration of Jewish doctors in Germany. I say to him, 'Why bother? Australians don't give a damn.'

FRANCIS: (*sarcastically*) Perhaps the English will. 65

PETER: Who cares, anyway? I want to enjoy myself over there; get to know my mother's relatives, Esther's family—

FRANCIS: (*interrupting*) Esther's family?

PETER: She's partly why I'm going.

FRANCIS: You're not marrying her? 70

PETER: When I return.

FRANCIS: I thought you said you wanted to enjoy life. Think of all the women you'll never get to know.

PETER: You boys from the slums.

FRANCIS: I have my standards: I only go out with rich girls; 75 I'm trying to rise above my class.

PETER: Is that why you mix with me?

FRANCIS: Of course. You're my introductory service.

(*Suddenly a woman screams. Both men jump up. The scream goes on and on, anguished, passionate but almost ritualistic.*)

PETER: What in the hell is that?

(*It goes on, then abruptly stops. Silence. Both boys are scared.*)

That was a person, wasn't it? 80

FRANCIS: No animal could sound like that.

PETER: Maybe it was an animal in pain.

(*They take their lanterns and go to the area from which they judge the cry came.*)

FRANCIS: Here.

(PETER *comes over and shines his lantern. It reveals the corpse of a young man, his body covered in rotten flowers.*)

PETER: Christ, I'm going to be sick.

(*He moves away.* FRANCIS *holds his lantern closer and examines the body.*)

FRANCIS: He's been dead for some time. I wonder why no 85 one's buried him. They've covered him in flowers; why not bury him, then?

PETER: Perhaps someone wanted him left that way.

FRANCIS: He seems quite young.

PETER: God, he stinks. How can you be so close? 90

FRANCIS: There's something about his face . . .

PETER: It's rotten, that's all. Come on, Francis, let's get going. That screaming . . .

FRANCIS: It'll take us days to get back.

(FRANCIS *spots something*.)

Jesus . . . 95

(*He holds the lantern closer.*)

PETER: What is it?

FRANCIS: His mouth is full of gold.

(PETER *comes closer.* FRANCIS *takes out a small piece.*)

    See?

PETER: You're like my father: nothing bothers you.

95 FRANCIS: (*handing the gold piece to* PETER) See?

PETER: (*repulsed*) No thanks, not from a dead man's mouth.

(*Silence. Unnoticed, the silhouetted figure of a woman enters.*)

FRANCIS: Flowers . . . bits of gold . . .

PETER: Perhaps he was murdered.

FRANCIS: Why would a murderer do this to him? Anyway,

100   you told me nobody is supposed to be living way out
    here.

(*The woman growls softly at* FRANCIS *and* PETER. *Both boys are startled. They stand up and look at her.* BETSHEB *is young, dirty, and dressed in a nineteenth-century dress patched in various colours as if repaired over many years. She bares her teeth at them, almost like an animal, then screams violently as if cursing them. She turns and runs away. Blackout.*)

SCENE IV

A river bank, afternoon. BETSHEB *sits on the bank with* STEF, *a boy aged between fifteen and eighteen. It is hard to tell his exact age because his behaviour is so infantile. His limbs seem spastic. His gaze is distant. The woman wears the same dress as before. The boy wears only a filthy pair of long johns, years old. The woman chews up a piece of meat and passes it into the boy's mouth by placing her mouth on his, like a bird feeding its chick. He is not very hungry and protests. She gets up and goes to the river where she wets a rag. As she does so she hums to herself a tune reminiscent of a Victorian ballad. While she wets the rag the boy tries to stand, but flops down and in the process tumbles over. The woman sees him and laughs. The boy finds himself flat on his back, like a beetle that cannot right itself, as his legs and arms don't function properly. Even though he wants to get up he doesn't call out. Eventually he rights himself. The woman comes over as he begins to crawl towards something of interest, like a crippled child in a Muybridge photograph. The effort is too great and he flops down. The woman wipes his face, then her own. She then blows loudly and theatrically on his face, pretending to be the wind. The boy pathetically tries to mimic her. She stands up and spins around in her beloved dress for him. He takes no notice, his eyes looking past her. Abruptly she drops to her knees and slaps him on the face. He yelps in pain. She kisses him where she has hit him and then moves away so he can see her properly. She smiles broadly and stiffly, trying to teach him. She pushes at his mouth until it turns into a smile, but when she lets go his face returns to its expressionless mask. She is frustrated. She hums. He follows suit, but his gaze is distant. She bites his leg and he yelps in pain. As he cries out she mimics him. He looks at her for a brief moment, then beyond her. The routine is over. The woman gets up and does a whirling dervish-like dance and hums loudly to herself. Suddenly she notices something and stops. Frightened, she runs to the boy and tries to drag him off, but he is angry and fights. She drops him and heads off. She exits and moments later* FRANCIS *hurries on, followed by* PETER.

FRANCIS: (*calling after her*) Hey!

(*He runs after her.* PETER *walks over to* STEF.)

PETER: Hello!

(*The boy doesn't seem to notice him.* FRANCIS *returns.*)

FRANCIS: My God, she's quick. Lost her.

(PETER *waves his hand in front of the boy's face.*)

    Is he blind?

PETER: Maybe.   5

(*Suddenly the boy's hand snakes out and grabs* PETER*'s hand.* PETER *is startled. The boy laughs, then bites the hand.* PETER *cries out in pain.*)

FRANCIS: What happened?

PETER: He bit it.

(*Silence.*)

FRANCIS: (*to the boy*) What's your name?

(*Pause.*)

    Your name, what is it?

(*The boy rolls over, not listening, and laughs at the sky.*)

PETER: What's he laughing at?   10

(*Suddenly the boy's mood changes. He grimaces.*)

(*To the boy*) Are you all right?

(*The boy groans loudly, rising to a sharply accentuated crescendo until, abruptly, he bursts into a wide grin. Then he moves on all fours, but the effort is too much and he collapses. His face goes blank and his eyes distant.* FRANCIS *and* PETER *don't know what to make of it all.*)

PETER: (*laughing nervously*) I wouldn't mind not being here.

FRANCIS: We'd better pull him back or he might fall into the
    river.

(*They grab hold of the boy and drag him back from the river. The boy takes no notice of what is happening to him.* BETSHEB *silently enters and stands nervously nearby.* PETER *is the first to notice her.*)

PETER: (*quietly*) Francis.   15

(FRANCIS *turns and spots her. She is now extremely nervous. She sinks to her knees and dry-retches with fear. The two young men don't know what to do. The woman crawls on all fours to the boy and makes sure he is all right. She slaps him hard. He laughs. She laboriously lifts him on her back.* FRANCIS *goes to help, but* PETER *holds him back.*)

    She knows how to do it.

(*The boy clings to her back like a monkey. The woman goes off without looking at the two intruders. Silence.*)

FRANCIS: Come on.

PETER: What?

FRANCIS: Scared?

PETER: Pain in the arse.   20

(*They exit after her.*)

SCENE V

A clearing, afternoon. Four people wait: AYRE, *an old woman, sits on a homemade wooden chair; the others sit on the ground.* ANGEL *is in her late twenties. She is pale and coughs occasionally.* MELORNE, *a strong and wiry old white-haired man sits near her.* MAC, *a twenty-year-old man with blond hair sits by himself. They are dressed in old odds and ends, as though they have been to a Victorian opportunity shop. They seem expectant and their pose is like that of a Victorian photograph. On the ground are some wooden and chipped-porcelain bowls. Some pieces of meat lie near the bowls; there are also seeds, wild fruit and flowers. There is a large wash bowl in the center of this arrangement. They wait some time and then* BETSHEB *enters, half dragging, half carrying* STEF. *He grins widely as if at some private joke. She drops him down near the others. Just then* FRANCIS *and* PETER *enter. They are startled at the scene before them. All except the boy and old woman rise and bow deeply but stiffly towards the boys. Silence.*

FRANCIS: (*pointing*) We followed that girl.

(*Silence. Everyone is nervous and apprehensive. As the old woman speaks the words make little sense to the boys.*)

AYRE: To the greeny pallor o' thee kingspot; o' cunty goldy.

(PETER *smiles, amused.* FRANCIS *realizes it is a welcome.*)

FRANCIS: Thank you. My name is Francis. This is Peter. We come from Hobart.

(*Silence. They don't seem to understand.*)

5 (*Pointing to himself*) Francis. (*To* PETER) Peter.

(*The old lady nods and motions to the young woman, who goes to her.*)

AYRE: Betsheb. (*Pointing to the old man*) Melorne. (*To the woman*) Angel. (*To the autistic boy*) Stef. (*To the young man*) Mac. (*To herself*) Ayre.
PETER: Hello.
10 FRANCIS: Hello.

(*The pair are amused by the situation.* AYRE *motions to the others to find their places. There is something of an unconscious parody about the group, as if with their limited means they are giving an upper-class tea party.*)

PETER: (*to* FRANCIS) I think we're invited to a tea party.
FRANCIS: Did you understand her?
PETER: (*amused*) Not a word.

(AYRE *stays in her chair.*)

AYRE: (*smiling*) I bunter t' the windy sheet, t' the arsemine o'
15 the world. Breathe a vein, breathe a vein. (*Shaking her head*) Olcers an' 'ellpain. (*Tapping her chair*) Starry, shiny, cunty dell o' me world.

(*It is obvious she is trying to explain why she can't join the others. The visitors sit.* AYRE *claps her hands and motions to* ANGEL, *who picks up an old-fashioned porcelain doll and shows it to* FRANCIS.)

FRANCIS: It's lovely. Very old.

(ANGEL *smiles and nods.* MELORNE *walks into the center of the group, picks up a washbowl and shows it to the two men proudly.*)

PETER: (*looking into the bowl*) Gold. It must have taken a long time to collect all those tiny pieces. 20

(MELORNE *puts the bowl back in its position.*)

FRANCIS: (*to* MELORNE) We saw a dead man on the mountain. Back there. He had flowers in his hair and gold in his mouth.

(MELORNE *sits, uncomprehending.* FRANCIS *points to* BETSHEB.)

She came and cried beside him.

(STEF *lies on his back and makes wind noises at the sky.*)

PETER: He wasn't buried, but he was dead. 25

(*No one seems to understand.* BETSHEB *hands meat and fruit to* FRANCIS *and* PETER *in the only two porcelain bowls.*)

PETER: (*to* FRANCIS, *sotto voce*) I see we get the best china.

(*To* BETSHEB) Thank you.

FRANCIS: How long have you people lived here?

(*Silence.*)

Do you understand us?

(*Silence.*)

MELORNE: (*thickly*) Fer skilly we gobble in awe. 30

(BETSHEB *and* AYRE *both laugh, as at a private joke. Everyone starts to eat. They have spoons and/or battered forks. There is an embarrassing silence as people try and think of ways of bridging the gap.*)

FRANCIS: (*at last*) I come from Melbourne. Peter comes from Hobart. I'm an engineer. I design bridges. Peter is a geologist. He studies rocks. He knows all about things like that gold there.

(*No one seems to understand.* BETSHEB *feeds* STEF *by the same method she used before.* AYRE *sees the visitors' surprise.*)

AYRE: Born o' cat 'n' rack 'n' goldy sow. 35

(*They don't understand. Annoyed at being fed when he doesn't want to be,* STEF *cries out and rolls away.* ANGEL *begins to hum a tune.*)

He fed on tarse o' dark in the black quim o' a belle.

(STEF *joins* ANGEL *in humming the snatch of melody, but soon he grows very loud.*)

(*Trying to make herself understood*) Skittle. Skittle. Blackfortune.

(*The two men nod as though they can understand.* STEF's *humming is almost yelling now.* PETER *recognizes the tune and begins to sing over the top of* STEF; *he goes beyond the snatch of tune and sings the whole verse.*)

PETER: 'I finally found you', Edward said.

'I've just returned from the salt, salt sea,
40   And it is all for the love of thee.
They say you married a hanging judge,
O don't let the news, the news be true.
But a friend, he said you didn't wait for me
As I have waited on the sea for you.'

(*There is a silence, except for the quiet humming of* STEF. PETER *is embarrassed.*)

45   Those are the words of that song. My grandmother taught them to me.

(ANGEL *gives an 1850s top hat in very good condition to* MELORNE. *He makes a performing space.* BETSHEB *drags* STEF *to lie at* AYRE's *feet.* STEF *stops humming and briefly cries out in alarm.* AYRE *pats him on the head and sings a murmuring song.*)

AYRE: (*singing*)
In the night,
In the day,
50   Blue ruins, blue ruins
In Jack's Inn Bay.

(*The two young men become the audience for the others. The four bow to them. As they perform, the words sometimes seem out of keeping with their emotions, as if they, especially* MELORNE, *don't always understand what they are saying.*)

MELORNE: Bleak street o' fen 'n' bellies. Dark trees 'n' no trees betide bleak sand.

(*The scene set, he begins. He grabs* MAC *and drags him as if through terrible country. He stops.*)

(*Yelling, to* MAC) 'Toady o' the holy! Bleak King o' the dark.
55   Thou walk on loam cooked o' thou disease. Thou disease pox on the land in blood 'n' pig. (*Indicating the land and sky*) 'Rye o' the sky, rye o' the loam. Morn 'n' dark all topsy turvy.' (*Motioning to himself*) 'I, King. King o' cits.' (*Crying out*) 'Trellion! Trellion!'

(MAC *sings to entertain the tormented* MELORNE. ANGEL *plays a penny whistle to accompany him. She plays well.*)

60   MAC: (*singing*)
Up 'n' down
He go,
Up 'n' down
A-jig, jig, jig.
65   She go
Groan 'n' groan
A-jig, jig, jig.

(MELORNE *pats* MAC *on the head as one would a favourite dog.*)

MELORNE: 'A-lik a-lik a-lik a-lik a-lik . . .'

(ANGEL *enters and throws herself at* MELORNE's *feet.* ANGEL *cannot speak and* AYRE *speaks for her.* ANGEL *mimes seeking forgiveness from* MELORNE.)

AYRE: 'Poor quim me am, bleak father. Forgive me, bleak fa-
70   ther. The 'eaven is wild. Torn a-thunder so bad, so bad, we fain to live.'

MELORNE: (*yelling*) 'Ye child, dry quim. Ye rack o' truth I boil, this loam boil 'cos o' me profoundest outcastin'. (*With high emotion*) 'Outcastin'!' (*Crying at the sky*) 'Rack 'n' cat, rack 'n' cat!'   75

(*He jabs out both her eyes with a stick.*)

'Ye blind! Ye blind! Now, forsooth, ye can eye me pain o' outcastin'. Ye pain goldy sow o' me tarse!'

(*He falls to the ground and sits. Singing,* MAC *covers him with leaves and flowers.* ANGEL *plays her penny whistle.*)

MAC: (*singing*)
Up 'n' down
He go,   80
Up 'n' down
A-jig, jig, jig.
MELORNE: (*as though in his second childhood*) 'Bleak outcastin', a-blub, blub, blub.'

(BETSHEB *enters.* MELORNE *spots her. They look at one another, so ecstatic it is amusing even to the visitors, though the actors mean it seriously. Their arms out, with cries of delight they rush into one another's arms.*)

'True treasure o' quim 'n' tarse!'   85

(*They hug.*)

'Nowt more outcastin'! Nowt more!'

(*He grabs the washbasin full of gold.*)

'Joyful quim! Joyful tarse! Joyful bird! Joyful goldy sow! Joyful day!'

(*He gives the bowl to* BETSHEB.)

'Joy o' loam.' (*Quietly*) 'Nowt more outcastin! Nowt more.'

(*Everyone is happy.* MELORNE *leads as the company bows to the two young men.* AYRE *applauds and* FRANCIS *and* PETER, *who have understood very little, do likewise.* MELORNE *takes off his top hat and joyfully runs to them, holding it out, expecting a tip. Blackout.*)

SCENE VI

The same clearing, night. FRANCIS *and* PETER *lie on the ground talking softly. Not far away* AYRE *sits in her chair, half dozing, half listening to the night-birds.* STEF *lies at her feet,* MAC *nearby.*

PETER: (*to* FRANCIS, *looking at* AYRE) Is she sleeping?
FRANCIS: Listening.
PETER: To us?
FRANCIS: The owl.

(AYRE *turns in the direction of a hooting owl.*)

PETER: Did you see the huts?   5
FRANCIS: Like those old slab squatter huts. Really primitive. God knows what happens when it rains here. Maybe they go into that cave.
PETER: It's a mine. Where their gold comes from, I suppose. That young fellow, Mac; he showed me.   10

(*Silence.* AYRE *watches them, though they don't realise it.*)

FRANCIS: Well?

PETER: 'Well' what?

FRANCIS: Who do you think they are?

PETER: Maybe the play was telling us. Maybe it was their his-
15   tory.

(FRANCIS *shrugs.*)

Two timbermen were discovered up north of here. They
had been living alone for years. They had come to cut
down Huon pine. People forgot about them but they
continued to cut down the trees, though no one collected
20   them. They were still going through the motions. They
had gone mad.

(*Suddenly* AYRE *motions to the sky, quoting loudly.*)

AYRE: 'O tell me, bird, t' where is yer going'? O tell me, what
is yer want t' hear?' (*Smiling at the two men*) New chums.
25   Skittle o' chance has yer to this spot, here, down in a fine
ol' dark.

(*Pause.*)

I cup me ear t' the glommen bird. Soul o' the dead. Cryin'
out, 'Donna burst 'er 'eart, the bird is me!' No rack 'n' cat.
Heavenbirth.

(*She laughs, then sardonically motions to the hooting owl.*)

Me, moonin' in the glommen.

(*Silence.*)

30   (*With an all-encompassing motion of her hands*) Our goldy
sow, the furst t' bloodburst int' this silent sea. Past riverrun
'n' turn o' kelp int' muddy moss, seay green 'n' here. 'Ere!
Spirit eyes o' gold. In ghost time, behind us; osier 'n'
'eather 'n' 'ello, ducky. 'Oary boyos, sun-stricken girlie
35   days. Blackysmith 'n' Trunk's Tavern. I hear the goldy lifey,
the glommen lifey. Do nowt ferget dreamytime. Ferget
lifey in rattlesnake, ev'ry chum cryin' to death, 'n' into
'ere, the greeny belch o' 'eaven. Danderupping so to live
on the greasypole o' spirit friends. Spirits o' cunty dell.
40   Circle o' greeny 'ome. Stars 'n' loam, firs 'n' spermy
flower. Spirits, sprits, ghosts 'n' pitch dark, buboes o' the
face 'n' arse 'n' . . . 'n' (*motioning to* STEF *at her feet*) festerin'
lip 'n' baby birdcry. Burst mouth, hairy brain 'n' cradlepain. Goldy death, goldy backward seein'. (*Motioning to her
45   head*) Me mossy brain is the backward seein'. Pitch dark
glommen is dry sheb and rottin' tarse. The circle is burst.
(*Softly, almost to herself*) The circle is burst.

(*She looks at the men, hoping they have understood. Silence. She
shrugs.*)

(*Looking at the sky*) I cup me ear t' the glommen bird.

(MAC *arrives, lifts* AYRE *out of the chair and helps her to walk off.*
STEF, *as if startled awake, runs after them and then past them. Silence.*)

FRANCIS: Maybe she was trying to tell us what we don't
know.

50   PETER: Perhaps.

(PETER *stands.*)

Nature calls.

(*He exits.* FRANCIS *lies down, hands behind his head and thinks.
He notices a figure. It is a curious* BETSHEB *moving closer.* FRANCIS
pretends he is sleeping. She moves closer. FRANCIS *turns and faces
her. She steps back, unsure. They stare at one another. Silence.*)

FRANCIS: The man who was dead: was he your husband?

(*Pause.*)

Was he your brother?

(*Silence.*)

Do you remember my name? 'Francis'.

(*He sits up. She is frightened and hurries off into the night.*)

Come back, don't be frightened.   55

(*He jumps up and goes after her. Blackout.*)

SCENE VII

The bush, night. FRANCIS *moves out of the moonlight and into the
shadows.* BETSHEB *enters, laughing. As* MAC *enters she spins in her
dress, around and around, making herself giddy, and falls on the
ground. They both laugh as she tries to stand up, but she's still too
giddy. He approaches her and she pushes him onto the ground. She
pounces on him, growling softly like an animal. She nuzzles her face
into his neck: it tickles and he laughs.* BETSHEB *jumps on him and
straddles his chest, kissing him playfully.* MAC *grows irritated and
roughly pushes her off. He tries to jump up, but her playfulness turns
to real desperation and she grabs hold of his leg. He struggles to his
feet but she holds on to him. He tries to push her away but she won't
budge. She cries like an animal in pain and buries her face into his
crotch. He hits her away; she falls to the ground and he takes the opportunity to escape into the night.* BETSHEB, *anguished, smashes the
ground with her fists, moaning.* FRANCIS, *shocked by what he has
seen, moves into the moonlight.* BETSHEB *doesn't notice and, weeping, jumps up and runs off into the night.* FRANCIS *stands where he
is, trying to make sense of what he has seen and the extraordinary
primal agony and passion of* BETSHEB. *As he stands thinking night
gives way to dawn.* PETER *enters.*

PETER: Where did you get to last night?

(FRANCIS *starts from his preoccupation.*)

You look awful.

FRANCIS: I couldn't sleep.

PETER: The old geezer got me up. Took me into the mine. I
think he realizes I know something about rocks. I didn't   5
know if he wanted my advice or to show off. I tried to
explain that the damn thing would cave in. You should see
it, it's bloody primitive; water-logged, a few struts. We'd
better get started back soon.

(*Pause.*)

Did you hear?   10

(FRANCIS *nods.*)

What's the matter?

FRANCIS: Nothing.

PETER: Something's bothering you.

FRANCIS: I want to find out who they are.

(BETSHEB *brings in* AYRE*'s chair.* FRANCIS *catches her eye as* AYRE *comes out helped by* ANGEL. AYRE *looks more infirm than on the previous night.*)

15   (*To* BETSHEB) Last night I saw you down near the river.

(BETSHEB *doesn't understand.*)

AYRE: (*sitting in her chair and looking at the sky*) Sun, sun, sun, sun. Jack straw, barley o' life. Eh?

(*She basks her face in the morning sun and dozes.* MAC *enters and looks at* BETSHEB. *They are awkward and embarrassed about what happened the night before. Suddenly, seemingly from nowhere,* MELORNE *runs in and knocks* MAC *down.* MELORNE *circles* MAC, *smiling broadly, urging him to wrestle.* MAC *doesn't want to fight.*)

PETER: (*to* FRANCIS) He's crazy about wrestling, wants to prove himself. When we came out of the mine he jumped
20   on me, wanting to wrestle.

FRANCIS: Did you?

PETER: A bloody fit old bugger; he soon had me giving up.

FRANCIS: (*to* MELORNE, *calling*) Here!

(MELORNE *turns around.*)

PETER: What are you doing? He's crazy.

25   FRANCIS: I want to see how good he is.

(*The old man laughs. He loves wrestling.*)

(*To* MELORNE) Mad as a hatter, aren't you?

(MELORNE *nods and smiles broadly.*)

I can see it in your eyes.

PETER: Careful, he's quick.

(*But just as* PETER *warns* FRANCIS, MELORNE *leaps at him and knocks him down.* FRANCIS *quickly pushes him off and jumps up.*)

FRANCIS: (*to* PETER) He's bloody quick. Strong too. (*Smiling*
30   *at* MELORNE) Do that again.

(MELORNE *takes a step towards* FRANCIS. *The younger man jumps him. They wrestle on the ground. Everyone is enthralled by the contest. It quickly turns from a lighthearted game into something deadly serious:* FRANCIS, *like* MELORNE, *is not the type to give in. Advantage goes one way and then the other.* MELORNE *jumps up,* FRANCIS *moves towards him. The old man spits at him viciously.* FRANCIS *decides to thrash* MELORNE *now. He lunges at the old man, there is a vicious series of grabs, tackles and falls.* MELORNE *tires and pulls away.* PETER *realizes that* MELORNE *is beaten and also knows that* FRANCIS *is angry enough to do serious injury.*)

PETER: Leave him alone, Francis. You've won. You've beaten him.

FRANCIS: (*keeping his eyes on* MELORNE) No I haven't. Not yet. I'm going to crush him.

(*He moves in on* MELORNE. *They circle one another.* FRANCIS *suddenly dives on the older man, throwing him to the ground and lands on him heavily. He forces the old man into a position of defeat and pain.* MELORNE *cries out in anguish.*)

(*Yelling*) Give up!   35

PETER: (*going to him*) You've defeated him. Come on.

FRANCIS: (*to* MELORNE, *angrily*) Give up.

PETER: (*grabbing him*) Francis! (*Pulling him away*) For Christ's sake, you could kill him.

FRANCIS: That's what he wanted to do to me.   40

(MAC *and* ANGEL *go to* MELORNE *and lift him up.*)

PETER: What were you trying to prove?

FRANCIS: (*calming down*) He just seemed to be asking for it. It's the only thing he understands.

PETER: The same would apply to you, it would seem.

(MELORNE *angrily shrugs off* ANGEL *and* MAC *and walks over to* FRANCIS. *The two men stare at one another.* FRANCIS *is apprehensive.* MELORNE *abruptly thrusts out his hand.* FRANCIS *and* PETER *flinch, but he only wants to shake hands with the victor. Everyone applauds.*)

SCENE VIII

The river, twilight. BETSHEB *sits, staring out at the evening sun. Near her feet are flowers she has just picked. She hums a tune to herself. Nearby,* STEF *rolls on the ground, laughing to himself.* FRANCIS *enters and watches* BETSHEB *for some time.*

FRANCIS: Are you looking at the sunset?

(*Startled,* BETSHEB *turns around.*)

(*Smiling*) I'm not a monster . . . No more running.

(*Silence. He walks closer to the river.*)

Look at us reflected in the water, see? Upside-down.

(*He smiles and she smiles back. Silence.*)

So quiet. I'm not used to such silence. I'm a city boy, born and bred. You've never seen a city or town, have you?   5
Where I live there are dozens of factories: shoe factories, some that make gaskets, hydraulic machines, clothing. My mother works in a shoe factory. (*Pointing to his boots*) These came from my mother's factory.

(*Silence.*)

These sunsets here, I've never seen the likes of them. A bit   10
of muddy orange light in the distance, behind the chimneys, is generally all I get to see.

(*Pause.*)

You'd like the trams, especially at night. They rattle and squeak, like ghosts rattling their chains, and every so often the conducting rod hits a terminus and there is a brilliant   15

spark of electricity, like an axe striking a rock. 'Spisss!' On Saturday afternoon thousands of people go and watch the football. A huge oval of grass. (*Miming a football*) A ball like this. Someone hand passes it, 'whish', straight to me. I duck
20 one lumbering giant, spin around a nifty dwarf of a rover, then I catch sight of the goals. I boot a seventy-yard drop kick straight through the center. The crowd goes wild!

(*He cheers wildly.* BETSHEB *laughs at his actions. He is pleased to have made her laugh.*)

Not as good as your play.

(*Pause.*)

This is your home. My home is across the water, Bass Strait.

(*Silence.* STEF *rolls over and ends up near* FRANCIS' *feet.*)

25 What is it about you people? Why are you like you are?

(BETSHEB *gathers up her flowers. As she stands she drops a few.*)

Don't go.

(*He picks up the fallen flowers.*)

I was watching you pick these. My mother steals flowers from her neighbour's front garden so every morning she can have fresh flowers in her vase for Saint Teresa's por-
30 trait. She was a woman centuries ago. God fired a burning arrow of love into her. (*Smiling*) When it penetrated her, Saint Teresa could smell the burning flesh of her heart.

(BETSHEB *does a parody of the wrestling match, but to her it is so funny that she cannot go on.* FRANCIS *smiles uncertainly.* STEF *crawls across the ground, growling to himself, then sits and rocks back and forth, staring into the distance.*)

BETSHEB: (*to* FRANCIS, *with a very thick accent*) Stef 'ave cradle-pain.

(*She strokes* STEF's *head.*)

35 (*Murmuring*) Stef, Stef, Stef, Stef. (*In a sing-song voice*) Sha' it up, dee, dee, dee.
FRANCIS: You can actually talk . . . talk like the old lady. Like Ayre.

(*She looks closely at* FRANCIS.)

Talk. You can talk like Ayre.

(BETSHEB *is unsure what he's talking bout.* STEF *begins to move away;* BETSHEB *follows and helps him.* PETER *arrives unnoticed and watches* FRANCIS *watching* BETSHEB *and* STEF. *The couple leaves.* FRANCIS *picks up a few pebbles and starts to skim them across the river.*)

40 PETER: It rose last night.

(FRANCIS *turns, momentarily startled.*)

FRANCIS: Imagine how this place is in winter.
PETER: How many times can you get them to skip?

FRANCIS: Four or five.
PETER: I could never do it.
FRANCIS: Used to go down to the Yarra near Dight Falls and 45 practice.

(*Silence.*)

PETER: Is she the reason you want to stay?
FRANCIS: I want to find out about these people.
PETER: What attracts you to her?
FRANCIS: She's interesting, in a way. 50
PETER: It's because you don't know anything about her. She's probably as crazy as the rest of them.
FRANCIS: They're not crazy.
PETER: My father would certify them.

(*Pause.*)

I had a closer look at that wash basin. There's no gold in 55 it, just quartz, a bit of copper, alum, iron pyrites . . . Fool's gold. I had a look over the back there too. There used to be other houses, a long time ago. And another mine.

(*Pause.*)

FRANCIS: How's the old fellow?
PETER: Coughing up blood. 60
FRANCIS: You think he'll die?

(*Silence.*)

PETER: It wasn't your fault.

(*Silence.*)

We'll head back tomorrow morning?

(FRANCIS *nods.*)

We'll get some experts out here; they'll find out what this is all about. 65

(*Pause.*)

FRANCIS: She can't understand me, or at least I think she doesn't, but I know she's absorbing it like a sponge, soaking up what I'm saying. I see her listening to Ayre, you know, when they're together and it is as if she's soaking up all that Ayre is telling her. Remembering. Recording. 70
PETER: Check your knapsack; someone's been through it.

(*He exits.* FRANCIS *returns to skimming pebbles across the surface of the river.*)

SCENE IX

The bush, night. Clouds obscure the moon. BETSHEB *is perched on* MAC's *shoulders. They turn slowly on the spot like a ballerina on a music box. From a distance* ANGEL's *penny whistle plays a haunting tune. The whole thing has a distant dream-like feel, almost like a memory.* BETSHEB *stares up at the sky.*

BETSHEB: (*murmuring softly*)
Rain, rain, go thy way,
Come a-back ne'er a day . . .

(*She repeats this incantation over and over. The lights fade and come up again.*)

SCENE X

The bush, night. Thunder sounds. AYRE *sits in her chair, a beautiful, unworn 1850s dress on her lap. She looks up at the thunder and clouds. Something is preying on her mind. She tries to remember a song.*

AYRE: 'Little Peggy . . .' 'Peggy . . .' 'She met 'im in . . .'

(*She can't remember it. She looks down at the dress and strokes it like a lap dog.*)

'Airloomin' fer the child. Wot child? Bellsademon laughin'. Nowt need nowt Herod. We is dead. Goldy dead nowt goldy sow. Nowt tongue, nowt goldy sow, nowt 'istory.

(*Silence. She feels the beautiful material of the dress.*)

5   So fine. So fine. 'I shew yer beauty. Beauty so fine yer'll piss yerself. 'Airloomin' fer the child.'

(*Silence. She comes to a decision.*)

Nowt more outcastin'. (*Crying out to the sky*) Nowt more outcastin'!

SCENE XI

The bush, night. BETSHEB *sits alone on the ground and examines the contents of a rough cloth bag.* FRANCIS *enters and watches her surreptitiously. She takes out and examines a watch, then a book and then a small compass; finally she takes out a large lizard. She stares at it intently and hisses at it, her tongue flicking in and out at it. She seems mightily intrigued by this reptile.*

FRANCIS: (*quietly*) Betsheb.

(BETSHEB *doesn't turn around. She seems to have already known* FRANCIS *was nearby. She puts the lizard back in the cloth bag.*)

BETSHEB: (*quietly, almost to herself*) Francis.

(*He comes over and sits down beside her.*)

FRANCIS: I couldn't sleep.

(*Silence.* FRANCIS *notices the objects.*)

5   These are mine. (*Picking up the watch*) A watch. (*Winding it*) It tells the time, tells us how old we're getting.

(*He holds it to her ear.*)

See? Can you hear it? 'Tick, tick, tick', like a heartbeat.

(*He picks up the compass.*)

Compass. See the arrow? (*Indicating*) North is that way. Somewhere that way is Hobart. (*Sardonically*) Somewhere. And this . . . this is a book.

(*She nods as if she knows.*)

The Structure of Single Span Bridges.

BETSHEB: Book.   10

FRANCIS: You know it's a book?

(*She nods.*)

BETSHEB: (*pretending to read, turning the pages quickly*) Thy word.

(BETSHEB *stands and motions to the sky.*)

Rain, rain, go thy way,
Come a-back ne'er a day.   15

'Ate the olcer sky. No end. No end. Adorate the shiny brocade sky, glommen time. Queenie Ayre say in ancient glommen, King David see the brocade, King Moses see the goldy brocade, lubilashings o' shiny in ancient glommen. The sky 'e see, is me goldy brocade. See?   20

(*She stands and spins slowly, staring up at the sky as if intoxicated by it and her words. We hear distant thunder.*)

FRANCIS: The last waltz, madame.

(*He grabs her. She starts as if woken from an intense reverie.*)

Dance. Dancing. Follow me. Arm here. (*Singing a waltz melody*) Da, da, da . . . That's right, that's right, turn here, now a step here . . . Right . . .

(*She quickly picks it up.*)

My mother forced me to learn dancing so I would be able   25
to mix in the proper circles at university.

(*Suddenly he kisses her. She tries to pull away.*)

No!

(*He holds on to her roughly and kisses her again. She bites him on the lip. He grimaces in pain. She pulls away.* FRANCIS *puts a finger to his lips and spots blood on it.* BETSHEB *is apprehensive.*)

I only wanted to kiss you.

(*Pause.*)

You do it with Mac, why not with me?

(*Silence.*)

I want to break through to you and I don't know how. I   30
don't even know if you're stupid or crazy or whatever.

(*He walks towards her.*)

Don't run away. (*Smiling*) I can smell my heart burning.

(*She moves towards him and presses her forehead tightly against his.*)

BETSHEB: Me burstin' brain. Me burstin' brain. See?

(*He doesn't understand.*)

FRANCIS: You're hurting.

(*But she desperately wants him to understand.*)

35 BETSHEB: Break 'n' crack int' thee.

(*She abruptly pulls away and looks at the sky, disappointed by* FRANCIS' *lack of understanding. There is a loud roll of thunder.*)

Rain, rain, go thy way,
Come a-back ne'er a day.

(*She takes* FRANCIS' *hand and kisses it. She then takes a small cardboard-backed photograph from between her breasts and gives it to him.*)

FRANCIS: A photograph. Is this woman your mother?
BETSHEB: Ghost o' me flesh.
40 FRANCIS: Grandmother?

(BETSHEB *points to something in the photograph.*)

Painted backdrop. Photographer's studio. That's not a real mountain or waterfall.

(*She points to something else, then touches her dress.*)

Yes, it's like your dress. Well, when it was new. Is it yours?

(BETSHEB *pays no attention to his question. She takes the photograph, kisses it, then puts it inside her dress. She is ecstatic. She runs up the river bank, turns and throws herself on the ground and rolls over and over down to him like a log rolling down a hill, then jumps up, pretending to be* MELORNE *asking for his hat to take up a collection.* FRANCIS *laughs at her imitation.* BETSHEB *then squats and pretends to piss, making groaning, pissing noises; a broad grin of contentment passes over her face. She does a parody of a high-born woman. She pretends to sit and sip tea at an exclusive dinner party. She speaks as if delivering bon mots to imaginary guests.*)

BETSHEB: Shit, shit, shit, shit, shit.

(FRANCIS *laughs at her slightly bitter parody.*)

45 FRANCIS: Lady So-And-So's tea party?

(BETSHEB *is extremely happy showing off to* FRANCIS. *She prowls around him like a wild, vicious dog sniffing its prey, and then she turns into a snarling, spitting Tasmanian devil, an act which slightly unnerves* FRANCIS. *Abruptly, she changes again and begins to walk like a grande dame taking a promenade. She motions to convicts nearby and gives them orders.*)

BETSHEB: Rack 'n' cat, rack 'n' cat, rack 'n' cat, rack 'n' cat.

(*Then the grande dame farts. She discreetly waves her hand behind her to get rid of the smell.* FRANCIS *laughs at the parody.*)

FRANCIS: Where did you pick that up from? Ayre? Did Ayre teach you?

(BETSHEB *pays no attention to him. She crawls over to him, tongue flicking in and out like a lizard's. She kisses him on the mouth with her flickering tongue.*)

BETSHEB: Bellsademon kissin' 'n' spoonkissin' in the rye.
50 (*Murmuring*) The belle she lie droopin'. The gent he lie tongue out. Ho! Spoonfuckin' in the glommen.

(*She lifts her dress and sits down.*)

FRANCIS: Are you sure?

(*He sits down next to her.*)

BETSHEB: (*smiling, softly*) The belle whoopin', tongue out in the glommen.

(*They kiss.*)

FRANCIS: (*feeling her flesh*) Soft. So soft.   55

(*He kisses her on the lips again. The thunder comes closer, but they pay no attention to it. He kisses her on the inside of her legs. She ruffles his hair as if he were a dog. He takes off his shirt, then kisses her again. The whole of her body begins to tremble violently, as if possessed by involuntary muscle spasms. She lashes out and tears at her clothes. Her eyes roll, her body convulses. It is like an epileptic fit.*)

(*Concerned*) Betsheb!

(*He tries to hold her, to calm her, but her body is uncontrollable. She lashes out, without knowing what she is doing, and hits him.*)

Betsheb . . . Betsheb . . . What is it? Please . . . Do you want me to get help? (*Crying out*) Peter!

(*She begins to calm down. He strokes her as if soothing a child.*)

That's right . . . (*Soothingly*) Calm. Calm down.

(*She is still, silent.*)

I'm sorry.   60

(*Silence. He holds her in his arms. Suddenly she wakes as if from a nightmare. Horrified she realizes she has blacked out. She looks at her clothes and wipes away the saliva that has formed around the edges of her mouth. Now that she realizes what she's done she is ashamed. She jumps up and away from him.*)

BETSHEB: No, no, no . . .
FRANCIS: It's all right, it's over.

(*She is angry with her body. She starts to tear at it, then motions to her head as if to say she is stupid. She spits on her body because it has betrayed her.* FRANCIS *comes over to her, but she pushes him away, humiliated.*)

BETSHEB: Go, go!

(*Pause.*)

FRANCIS: You want me to go away? (*Motioning*) you want me to leave you? It's nothing to be ashamed of.   65
BETSHEB: (*pushing him away*) Go. Go.
FRANCIS: Will you be all right?
BETSHEB: Thee, way! Go! (*Picking up a stone and throwing it at him*) Go!

(FRANCIS *reluctantly moves away. She sinks to the ground with her back to him, exhausted.* FRANCIS *sits also, far away from her, and watches. The thunder comes closer.*)

FRANCIS: It is going to pour. You should go in.   70

(*Silence.*)

Let's go in.

(*Silence.*)

Talk to me.

(*Silence. Despondent,* BETSHEB *lies on the ground. Scattered before her are the three objects she stole from* FRANCIS' *knapsack.* FRANCIS *stares at the violent sky.* BETSHEB *stares at the objects with distant eyes. As she stares they move towards her, one by one, slowly and firmly, as though by telekinesis. The watch is first to move along the ground, then the compass, then the book. She makes no move to gather them as they stop in front of her.* FRANCIS *sees none of this.*)

BETSHEB: (*to herself, quietly*) Francis.
PETER: (*off, calling*) Francis.

(FRANCIS *stands up.* PETER *enters. Close behind him* MAC *carries* MELORNE. BETSHEB *retreats apprehensively.* MAC *puts* MELORNE *on the ground and lays him out. As he does so,* STEF *enters and sits down to play with the compass.*)

75   He's dying.
FRANCIS: Why bring him here? A storm's coming.
PETER: He wants to die outside.

(FRANCIS *is reluctant to come closer.* ANGEL *enters with a large, battered box which she puts down.*)

Come closer. He knows it wasn't your fault. He wanted to come to you.

(FRANCIS *moves closer, then drops to his knees.*)

80   FRANCIS: Sorry, old man.

(MELORNE's *hand suddenly snakes out and grabs* FRANCIS'. *He squeezes it tightly.* FRANCIS *is afraid.* MELORNE *grunts with exertion as if wrestling, then laughs triumphantly. The effort has been too much; he sinks back.* ANGEL *hurries over to him.* AYRE *enters slowly and painfully.* MELORNE *tries to cry out but cannot.* ANGEL *holds his hand. He smiles at her and dies.* ANGEL *tries to call to him, but like a baby can only get out the first part of 'Daddy'.*)

ANGEL: D-d-d-d- . . .

(*Silence.* ANGEL *silently hugs the dead* MELORNE.)

AYRE: (*to* FRANCIS *and* PETER) The circle is burst. We is burstin' int' the glommen. Outburst. Bellsademon land; cradlepain. Circle is burst. Nowt more outcastin'. Nowt
85   more sin fer bread.

(AYRE *gives* MAC *a signal and he opens the box.*)

See!

(*The two young men look inside the box.*)

Goldy sow o' the 'airloomin' pit.

(FRANCIS *takes out the doll seen before.*)

Sa, Sa.

(*He takes out the dress seen earlier.*)

Promin'. 'Airloomin'.

(*He takes out the book.*)

FRANCIS: What is it?   90
PETER: The writing's too faint to see.
AYRE: (*motioning to the distance*) Way! Way!
PETER: She's telling us to go.

(FRANCIS *suddenly realizes.*)

FRANCIS: No, this is their luggage, their belongings.
AYRE: Nowt more outcastin'. Nowt more outcastin'.   95
FRANCIS: She wants us to take them back with us. You want to go back with us, Ayre?
AYRE: Yea.

(*Silence. The storm breaks.* AYRE *looks at the grief-stricken* ANGEL *as she cradles* MELORNE.)

Nowt more outcastin'. Nowt more outcastin' . . .

SCENE XII

The Archers' garden, twilight. It is a warm evening. In the background is the Greek temple. A long table with an expensive setting is ready: porcelain crockery, silverware and crystal glasses; food is on the table. ELIZABETH *escorts* GEORGE ROSS, *Federal M.P., into the garden.*

ELIZABETH: It was such a lovely evening we decided to have it out here. We expected you later.
GEORGE: The Cabinet meeting took less time than I thought.
ELIZABETH: They won't be long.
GEORGE: I'm most intrigued to see them. Your husband's re-   5
port was extraordinary.

(*He notices the Greek temple.*)

Not many of those in Australian backyards.
ELIZABETH: It was built way back in eighteen forty—only Australians could say 'way back in eighteen forty'—by my grandfather. He loved Greece, Greek culture; a family   10
trait. So he built this little Olympus. It was said that he had a giant streak of paganism in his soul. The architect, an ex-convict, unfortunately used poor materials. It took the Parthenon two thousand years to crumble; it took our temple less than a hundred. Occasionally I let the spirits of   15
the Greeks take hold of me and I put on an ancient tragedy. Once we performed *Iphigenia in Tauris* to help a charity for unwed mothers and, do you know, some people looked down on us. But being an unwed mother is so human: one moment of passion, a lifetime of misery. Years   20
ago, William and I could have said those speeches in ancient Greek and most of the audience would have understood; many of them were academics and artists, of course. That was our greatest period of civilisation. From then on it's been all downhill. Romans conquered the world and   25
Mussolini takes years to conquer a few Ethiopian hill tribes. Ah, who are these handsome young men?

(PETER *and* FRANCIS *enter wearing tuxedos.* FRANCIS *is agitated.*)

Mr Ross, I would like to introduce my son, Peter. Peter, this is Mr George Ross, Federal Minister for Health.

30 PETER: (*shaking hands*) How do you do, sir?

ELIZABETH: And his friend, Francis Morris.

GEORGE: Very glad to meet you.

(*They shake hands.*)

ELIZABETH: Francis's fascination with these people is only matched by my husband's.

35 GEORGE: Doctor Archer's report mentioned you two found this group. I couldn't not come, my curiosity about them was too great.

ELIZABETH: This will be the first time you've seen them since you brought them back, won't it?

40 FRANCIS: Yes.

(PETER *pours* FRANCIS *a glass of wine to try and calm him.*)

GEORGE: (*looking around*) And this is where they've been staying?

ELIZABETH: William thought they would be more comfortable here and it would make studying them easier. The

45 woman, Angel, is in hospital, however. She has pulmonary tuberculosis. Her brother, Mac, is with her; it's thought he may have a touch of it too.

GEORGE: So they won't be coming tonight?

ELIZABETH: No. How was Melbourne, Francis? Francis?

(FRANCIS *sips his glass of wine. For a moment he is at a loss.*)

50 The job?

FRANCIS: I didn't get it.

ELIZABETH: Perhaps next time. Have you heard the latest about Poland, Mr Ross?

GEORGE: They say Poland is about to surrender.

55 ELIZABETH: I can feel it in my blood. Another world war. The times are definitely out of joint. And, again, we'll send our youth off to die.

GEORGE: If it's necessary to fight Nazism. Would you sign up, Francis?

60 FRANCIS: Yes. Fascism has to be destroyed; it's an evil philosophy. If I had been older I would have fought against it in Spain.

GEORGE: (*amused*) Oh, an idealist.

ELIZABETH: (*looking off*) Ah, here they are.

(*It is an extraordinary sight.* BETSHEB *and* AYRE *are dressed magnificently.* AYRE *wears the dress she held in her lap and* BETSHEB *wears a modern evening dress.* STEF *wears a dinner jacket. They are escorted by* WILLIAM, *also dressed in a dinner jacket.* STEF *shambles stiffly to the table, attracted by the glitter and the candles.* BETSHEB *guides* AYRE *in. Both women stop when they see* FRANCIS *and* PETER. *They are pleased to see both.*)

65 WILLIAM: (*to* BETSHEB) Here, I'll take Queenie Ayre.

(WILLIAM *leads* AYRE *to the central chair.* BETSHEB *and* FRANCIS *stare shyly at one another.*)

BETSHEB: 'Ello.

FRANCIS: Hello.

ELIZABETH: My, how wonderful you look.

FRANCIS: You look lovely.

(BETSHEB *spins in her dress for everyone, delighted by the praise. She stops and smiles at* FRANCIS.)

BETSHEB: (*quietly*) The belle is spoonin'. 70

(STEF *puts his hand into one of the dips. He tastes it, then spits it out in horror.*)

WILLIAM: Mr Ross, I'm Doctor Archer.

GEORGE: Of course, I remember you well; that conference last year.

(STEF *sits on the grass and rocks back and forth, humming to himself.*)

WILLIAM: Actually, in only a week Stef has improved out of sight. 75

GEORGE: Did you find out who they are?

WILLIAM: These people are the last members of a group that goes back to the eighteen fifties, during the gold rushes when everyone had the fever. Bankers, convicts, businessmen, doctors . . . but unlike in Victoria, the rush finished 80 pretty quickly here. One group moved much further into the South West looking for gold than anyone else. Most of them were ex-convicts, escaped convicts, failed colonists, general scum . . . even a traveling actor tired of doing bad shows for stupid colonists. One of the escaped convicts by 85 the name of 'Simpson' kept a notebook. Some of it is his information, but the rest of the notebook is his obsession with his dreams. He dreamed he should found his own town, independent of the rest of mankind, so he tried to. And what material did he have? Criminals, retards, the 90 lost, the desperate. (*Smiling*) So what we have before us is the true Australian culture.

GEORGE: What about the way they talk?

WILLIAM: Simpson, like his sister, had a cleft palate. Their language is a word salad made up of Cockney, Scottish, Irish 95 dialects. There must have been a thread of retardation running through the original group because some of them just didn't learn to speak.

FRANCIS: Perhaps they didn't feel the need to speak.

WILLIAM: (*amused*) Of the younger ones, only Betsheb can 100 talk. Ayre forces her to. Once Ayre dies, Betsheb will be the last repository of their culture. Stef is Angel's son; he's the final genetic mockery. Betsheb's brother died recently.

FRANCIS: The corpse?

WILLIAM: Yes. And Mac will never be able to have children 105 because his genitals are malformed. Queenie Ayre is a woman I admire more each day. It would have taken a lot of courage to come back to the world of 'rack 'n' cat'. Back to the world she had only heard about, a world of racks, whips, prison, hatred. She knows they have no fu- 110 ture in the wilderness. Inside her head she has kept everything she deems important. Dreams, memories, snatches of songs, Bible stories . . . it's had to be passed on by word of mouth.

(*Silence. The three newcomers look curiously vulnerable and* BETSHEB *and* AYRE *are embarrassed as the others stare at them.* STEF *stares at the sky.*)

115 FRANCIS: What's going to happen to them?
WILLIAM: We decided not to let the public know until we
   know a little more about them. (*Looking at* GEORGE) We
   plan to release the information on Tuesday.

(GEORGE *nods.*)

   So, ladies and gentlemen, the children of our past.

(AYRE *points to* ELIZABETH)

120 ELIZABETH: What is it, Ayre?
AYRE: (*motioning to* ELIZABETH'*s neck*) Shiny, shiny.

(ELIZABETH *takes off the necklace and gives it to her.*)

ELIZABETH: For tonight.

(*She puts it around* AYRE'*s neck.* AYRE *is very pleased.* PETER *sits
down to have a drink.* WILLIAM *pours one for* GEORGE. WILLIAM
watches as FRANCIS *approaches* BETSHEB. STEF *begins to stalk*
GEORGE.)

FRANCIS: You wear your dress with more ease than I wear
   this monkey suit.
125 BETSHEB: I look fer thee, dawnytime, day fer day.
WILLIAM: 'I looked for you every morning, day after day.'
BETSHEB: I nowt more a-feared.
WILLIAM: 'I'm not afraid any more.'
FRANCIS: (*to* WILLIAM) I know.

(*A broad smile crosses* BETSHEB'*s face as she remembers something.*)

130 BETSHEB: I see car . . .

(WILLIAM *translates, proud of his skill and also realizing that when*
BETSHEB *gets excited she is hard to understand.*)

WILLIAM: 'I was in a car.'
BETSHEB: Windwhistlin'.
WILLIAM: 'It went quickly.'
BETSHEB: 'Ome, country groan 'n' moan 'n' run.
135 WILLIAM: 'Factories and houses make noises and the land-
   scape from the car makes it look like it's running.'
BETSHEB: Voice in a stick.
WILLIAM: 'Telephone.' She loves hearing people speak on the
   telephone.
140 BETSHEB: I laugh. Let go.

(*She demonstrates listening on the telephone.*)

   Demon or 'eaven?
WILLIAM: 'The voices, are they from heaven or hell?'

(STEF *pounces on* GEORGE *and starts to chew his ankle, growling.*)

WILLIAM: Pay no attention.
GEORGE: (*thin-lipped*) I'll try.
145 ELIZABETH: Shall we sit? Francis, you escort Betsheb.

(GEORGE *pretends not to notice as* STEF *clings by his teeth to*
GEORGE'*s trousers. He makes his awkward way to the table.*
BETSHEB *is highly excited at meeting* FRANCIS *again.* WILLIAM *pulls*
STEF *free of* GEORGE'*s trousers.*)

GEORGE: Much appreciated, Doctor Archer.

(WILLIAM *sits* STEF *at the table.* BETSHEB *suddenly cries out like a
magpie. Everyone looks at her. Now that she has their attention she
decides to show off. She remembers how* FRANCIS *enjoyed her performance down by the river, so she steps away and begins to promenade like a grande dame.*)

BETSHEB: Rack 'n' cat, rack 'n' cat, rack 'n' cat . . .

(*She turns around for her return walk.* FRANCIS *realizes what will
come next.*)

FRANCIS: (*horrified*) Betsheb!

(*But* BETSHEB *doesn't hear him. She farts loudly, much to* AYRE'*s
amusement, and pretends discreetly to wave the smell away. She notices that no one else is laughing. She is suddenly worried.*)

ELIZABETH: (*to* WILLIAM) You couldn't get anything more Australian that that! (*To* BETSHEB) Bravo, Betsheb! (*Applauding*) 150
   Bravo!

(*The others applaud.* BETSHEB *is pleased.* STEF *is fascinated by the
candles, especially the one near him. He blows it out.*)

   (*To* WILLIAM) The matches.
GEORGE: Allow me, Mrs Archer.

(GEORGE *takes out his matches and relights the candle.* STEF *blows
it out again: he enjoys this game.*)

ELIZABETH: I think, Mr Ross, that shifting the candle might
   save an enormous match bill.   155
GEORGE: I think you may be right, Mrs Archer.

(GEORGE *shifts the candle.* STEF *is very annoyed and lunges across
the table at it, scattering plates and glasses everywhere. He grabs the
candle and sinks back in his chair, holding it inches from his face. He
stares at its flame as if mesmerized by it.* GEORGE *goes to take the
candle from him but the boy growls at him.*)

ELIZABETH: For your own safety, Minister, I suggest you let
   Stef keep it.

(GEORGE *does so.* WILLIAM *pours the champagne.*)

WILLIAM: I thought we might make a toast to our visitors.

(BETSHEB *goes to drink her champagne.*)

FRANCIS: Betsheb . . . not yet.   160

(AYRE *takes hers and gulps it down.* BETSHEB *sees her and follows
suit.*)

ELIZABETH: I suppose a queen is entitled to invent her own
   table manners.

(*She indicates to* William *that he should pour more champagne for the
women.*)

   (*As he sets down the bottle*) William, short and sweet before
   it's too late.

(WILLIAM *raises his glass and, with the exception of* STEF, *the others
do likewise.* AYRE *and* BETSHEB *raise their glasses, curious as to the
meaning of this ritual.*)

165 WILLIAM: To our five aliens who have landed on this strange planet, no longer called Van Diemen's Land, but Tasmania, and to their queen, Queenie Ayre.
OTHERS: Queenie Ayre.

(STEF *stares at the candle.* AYRE *downs her glass quickly. The others sip theirs,* BETSHEB *carefully imitating* FRANCIS.)

SCENE XIII

The Archer's garden, night. The meal has been eaten and only STEF *is left, lying on the grass playing with a candle.* GEORGE *and* WILLIAM *enter from the garden.* STEF *secretly stalks them.*

GEORGE: It must need a lot of gardeners.
WILLIAM: Two full-time, one part-time. It's modeled after Beckford's classical English garden, Fonthill.

(*They stop and watch* STEF, *who pretends to look at the candle.*)

GEORGE: You picked up their language very quickly. I find it
5   a real pea soup.
WILLIAM: I wouldn't leave them alone. Drove them mad, trying to understand it.
GEORGE: (*touching* STEF *with his foot*) Doesn't notice much about him, does he?
10   WILLIAM: It's hard to know.
GEORGE: Asylum patients make me feel the same way. They seem unfathomable. As if they could do anything.

(*Pause.*)

As you can well appreciate, Doctor Archer, with Australia now at war the Government has many important things
15   on its mind. Our primary aim will be to help defeat the Germans. Have you read any of the Nazi philosophy? Foul. A cesspool of human hatred.

(STEF *is intrigued by* GEORGE's *trouser legs and watches like a dog observing its prey.*)

The Cabinet decided I should take care of this matter as I have medical experience myself. You know it's going to be
20   a very popular piece in the newspapers here and overseas? That would be true to say, wouldn't it?

(STEF *pounces on* GEORGE's *leg and sinks his teeth in.*)

WILLIAM: Stef! Stef! Let go!

(WILLIAM *pulls him off.*)

GEORGE: Does he always do that?
WILLIAM: He likes to pretend he's our corgi.

(STEF *rocks back and forth and laughs at some huge private joke.*)

25   GEORGE: You realize the fuss these people are going to cause?

(WILLIAM *nods.*)

Isn't there an asylum not far from here?
WILLIAM: New Norfolk.
GEORGE: That's the one. I visited it once. Quite nice. I'll look at it again in the morning.

WILLIAM: I don't quite understand.   30
GEORGE: Do you want it plainer?
WILLIAM: These people aren't mad.
GEORGE: The Cabinet has decided that the public is not to know about these people until the war is over.
WILLIAM: But why? They're not mad!   35
GEORGE: Now listen to me. In Germany Stef would have been put to death a long time ago. The basis of Nazism is that there is a pure Aryan race and it must be kept free from impure bloodlines or genetic faults. Since they have come to power they have systematically murdered the re-   40
tarded and deformed. Imagine the glee with which the Germans would greet the news that it only took three generations to result in someone like Stef. What a coup for Nazi propaganda. They would be proved right. Once the war is over, then we'll allow the public to know about   45
them.
WILLIAM: You can't do this. They didn't come back to civilisation to be put into an asylum.
GEORGE: These people should not be seen as examples of the correctness of Nazi beliefs.   50
WILLIAM: But you'll prove it! You've demonstrated they are right by locking these people up . . .
GEORGE: This is war, Archer. I'm saying that the Nazis will bend, reshape the information for their own purposes. These people cannot be seen to be an endorsement of   55
Nazi beliefs.

(*Pause.*)

Can't you see the Government's position?
WILLIAM: I don't have much choice, do I?
GEORGE: No.

(STEF *rolls around making wind noises.* GEORGE *stares at him.*)

You know, in some ways the Nazis are right. It took only   60
three generations to get to him, only three generations to lose a language, the power to speak. They are a genetic graveyard.

(*Pause.*)

I must get back to my hotel. Tomorrow will be hectic.
WILLIAM: I'll phone for a taxi.   65

(*They walk off in silence.* BETSHEB *and* FRANCIS *enter happily from the garden.*)

FRANCIS: And is that your favourite spot?
BETSHEB: I eye the skyey blue 'n' call t' yer. Call 'n' call 'n' yer come.

(*He takes her by the waist and they dance to distant piano music.* ELIZABETH *enters.*)

ELIZABETH: There you are. Don't you want to come in and watch Mr Turner play? He came especially.   70
FRANCIS: We can hear it out here.
ELIZABETH: If Mr Turner hadn't been born blind he would have been a great pianist. She missed you. Every morning she asked William where you were. He, as you know, has become quite, quite fascinated by them.   75

(*She picks up a wine glass and sips from it.*)

Tipsy. It's as if the dead have come alive. Ghosts from the nether world of an Australian childhood.

(*The piano stops.* BETSHEB *steps away and goes into the garden near the temple steps.*)

There are rumours that William refused to allow other doctors to see them; than he kept them to himself, as if 80 they were prize exhibits that no one else could look at. For twenty-four hours a day he lives and breathes them.

(BETSHEB *squats unselfconsciously and pisses.*)

They are not children, Francis, and they are not adults; they are a poor contaminated people.

FRANCIS: I think I can look after myself, Mrs Archer.
85 ELIZABETH: Can you? I see her early in the morning, from my window, lying on the lawn, stroking herself as if she has some invisible lover; and she talks to herself or to the sky, I don't know which. At such times I doubt her sanity.

(*The piano starts again.*)

When the news of this group breaks I will lose William.
90 They will be his, he will explain them, he will make us understand them. Best I go inside. Mr Turner becomes quite put off by Queenie Ayre's snoring. (*Looking at the temple, smiling*) I remember the day before you and Peter left for your trip. I was Iphigenia bemoaning my fate. As I
95 looked down from the temple steps I saw such an expres-
 · sion of horror on your face, a look of 'What sort of world is Peter's?'

(*She laughs.* FRANCIS *smiles.*)

They'll change too. All the publicity, all the attention. Then we'll lose them.

(*She exits.* BETSHEB *shivers.*)

100 FRANCIS: Cold? You shouldn't be, it's warm.

(*He takes off his jacket and puts it over her shoulders. They dance, contented and happy. She nuzzles into him.* STEF *crawls onto the table. He steals a spoon and puts it in his jacket. Sitting on the table, he rocks back and forth, ecstatically happy.*)

ACT TWO

SCENE I

The living room of a working-class house, morning. A coffin lies on a table surrounded by flowers. FRANCIS *stands before it.* MRS WITCOMBE, *a neighbour, enters.*

MRS WITCOMBE: They'll be in in a moment.
FRANCIS: And what happens then?
MRS WITCOMBE: We follow them to the cemetery.

(*Pause.*)

So it'll be only us and her mates from work?

(FRANCIS *nods.*)

No relatives?   5
FRANCIS: I think she had relations in the country—in New South Wales, I think—but they didn't get on. Once Dad remarried, I was the only person she had.
MRS WITCOMBE: Your mum was always quiet. Kept to her-self. Lived next door for twenty-odd years and . . . When 10 I die, it'll be the same. Some distant cousins in Perth, very distant cousins in England . . . but, of course, we don't keep in touch. (*Looking at the corpse*) Never seen this dress be-fore; it's gorgeous.
FRANCIS: Her honeymoon dress.   15
MRS WITCOMBE: Looking so calm.

(*Pause.*)

At least it was quick.

(PETER *enters.* MRS WITCOMBE *doesn't notice him.*)

She was very proud of you. 'My son the engineer!' Such rotten luck. When I was young and I saw a car for the first time—I was as country girl like your mother—I was as 20 frightened of it as my horse was. I had every right to be. She gripped my hand so tightly as we waited for the am-bulance to come . . . see, its still bruised. I'll see what's hap-pening outside.

(*She exits. Silence.*)

PETER: Lots of flowers; she must have been well liked.   25
FRANCIS: Her workmates. She worked in the same shoe fac-tory for years and all her boss could give her was a brand new pair of shoes. In our neighbourhood flowers mean death. Mum said she had only ever saved money for her-self twice: the first time for her trousseau, the second for 30 her funeral, so she could go off 'like a real swell'.

(*Silence.*)

PETER: Do you still want to return to Hobart with me to-morrow?

(FRANCIS *nods.*)

But what about the house and things?
FRANCIS: It was rented. The landlord wants it cleaned up and 35 empty by Tuesday. I told Mrs Witcombe that if she cleaned it up she could have anything she wanted.
PETER: But don't you want to keep a few mementos? You can't cut loose entirely.
FRANCIS: I've got a few photographs; that's all I want. (*Look-* 40 *ing around the room*) What a life, eh? Struggle hard, marry a bastard, struggle hard, have an ungrateful son, earn enough to live in a dump. Second-hand furniture, con-crete backyard and on the walls Saint Teresa and facing her a picture of the nineteen thirty Collingwood football 45 team. If Collingwood won we had fish and chips; if they lost we didn't eat. (*Moving over to it*) Signed by all of them: Collier, Coventry . . . She plucked up all her courage to go down to training one night and got all of the team to sign it. I was with her, crimson with embarrassment. She was 50

so happy you would have thought she had had an audience with the Pope.

PETER: Why don't you take it with you?

FRANCIS: Mrs Witcombe's daughter has had her eye on it for
55   years. Mum promised it to her.

PETER: You'll regret it if you don't take a few things to remind you.

FRANCIS: One should forget the past. Do you know why I
never invited you here?

(PETER *shakes his head.*)

60   Because I was too ashamed.

SCENE II

A room in the asylum, evening. MAC *sits at a table.* WILLIAM *watches
him. There is a manual skills test on the table. A recording of* AYRE's
voice plays. MAC *doesn't really listen to it.* AYRE's *voice is slow and
deliberate, as if trying to make herself understood.*

AYRE'S VOICE: Past riverrun 'n' turn o' kelp int' muddy moss,
seay green 'n' here. There! Ghost 'n' sprit time. Goldy lifey,
glommen lifey. Thee dreamytime in greeny belch o' 'eaven.
Sprits o' cunty dell. Circle o' greeny 'ome! Nowt 'ome.
5   Burst mouth, hairy brain 'n' cradlepain. Pitch dark glommen is dry sheb and rottin' tarse. The circle is burst . . .

WILLIAM: Are you listening? That is Ayre's voice. There is
nothing wrong with your vocal cords and yet you don't
speak. Try again.

(WILLIAM *makes elementary sounds.*)

10   Copy me.

(*But* MAC *isn't interested.* WILLIAM *turns off the gramophone.*)

All right, let's get back to the test, then. Now concentrate
this time, Mac. Concentrate!

(MAC *is exhausted. He angrily throws the manual skills test on the
ground.*)

(*Angrily*) Pick it up!

(MAC, *obedient as a child, does so.* WILLIAM, *annoyed at his own
anger, stoops to help him, then sits back on the chair.*)

I know it's late. But concentrate, please. I'm just as tired as
15   you are. (*Smiling*) I'm going to conquer you. Understand
you. Now let's go through this again. We'll get it right this
time.

(*Silence.* MAC *makes no move on the manual skills test.*)

If you do it right you can go back to your ward and see
Angel. Angel. Do that test and you can go and see Angel.

(MAC *starts on his test.*)

SCENE III

The asylum gardens, afternoon. The wind sounds through the trees.
MAC *sits on a distant bench wearing an asylum uniform.* STEF *imi-*

tates the wind. His asylum jacket is very dirty. BETSHEB *stands
downstage in her beautiful bright dress. At her feet is a magazine. A
magpie sings; she imitates its call. She begins to sing much more com-
prehensibly than before.*

BETSHEB: (*singing*)
  Glow white in 'er dress,
  Gold, gold in 'er hair.
  Ruby are 'er lips,
  Love, love is e'rywhere.   5

(*The bird sings again.* BETSHEB *lies on her back and spreads out the
dress like a fan. She strokes her dress: the material feels wonderful—
so does the grass: warm and cosy. She feels her breasts and stomach:
like a child unaware of anyone else she enjoys the sensations of her
own body. A woman,* DR SIMON, *enters.*)

DR SIMON: (*to* BETSHEB) Such a dress! I would kill for one like
that. Happy?

BETSHEB: Yes.

DR SIMON: (*picking up a magazine*) Who wouldn't be on a day
like this? Been looking at the pictures? Which ones do 10
you like best? Aeroplanes? The cricketers? That's Don
Bradman. The dancers? The weddings?

(BETSHEB *laughs at a private joke. She knows which pictures she
likes best but she is not going to tell* DR SIMON.)

You're not going to tell me?

(*As* BETSHEB *continues to laugh,* DR SIMON *goes to* MAC.)

Mac, don't be so down-in-the-dumps. Come on, the man
is waiting. You'll like him. He'll take your photograph. Do 15
you want your photograph taken?

(FRANCIS *enters in army uniform with a bunch of flowers. He
watches* DR SIMON *trying to coax* MAC.)

I thought you liked seeing pictures of yourself. Come on,
for me. Come on, Mac, it won't take long.

(*She leads him off.* FRANCIS *approaches* BETSHEB, *who still laughs
to herself.*)

FRANCIS: What's so funny?

BETSHEB: Thou!   20

(*He gives her the flowers. She smells them deeply. He sits down next
to her and they kiss gently.*)

FRANCIS: (*indicating the dress*) Beautiful. The nurses wanted it
but I said it was for you. Only you. Elizabeth helped me
find it.

(*Pause.*)

Why is Mac being photographed?

(BETSHEB *takes no notice of the question as she feels* FRANCIS' *uniform.*)

He's jealous of us, you know.   25

BETSHEB: Peter?

FRANCIS: He should have reached England by now. He'll be stationed there. Live there.

(*Pause.*)

30　　The nurse said you and the others visited Angel's grave yesterday.

BETSHEB: Flowers, like this.

(*She bends down and puts her ear to the ground.*)

I ear op'n t' the Angel sprit.

FRANCIS: I spoke to Ayre before coming out here; she's looking better.

35　BETSHEB: She mus' live. She mus'! She say t' me: 'I mus' live!' (*Waving at the distance*) 'Ello!

FRANCIS: Who's that?

BETSHEB: Lorry. Gard-aner.

FRANCIS: The gardener?

40　BETSHEB: I 'elp 'im.

FRANCIS: I hope you won't help him in that dress.

BETSHEB: This dress? Nowt dirt. Me weddon dress.

FRANCIS: It's your good dress. Your best dress. You know we are not allowed. When the war is over you'll leave this

45　　place.

BETSHEB: Wid Ayre 'n' Stef 'n' Mac?

FRANCIS: (*amused*) Yes. Ayre, Stef, Mac and you.

(BETSHEB *is suddenly disturbed. She jumps up and motions to a distant building.*)

BETSHEB: There. Our bedibyes. Glommen time.

FRANCIS: You go to bed at night?

50　BETSHEB: There. Glommen time. There is a man, he listens, speakin' t' glommen demon. This girl . . .

(*She squeezes her head like a vice.*)

She bits 'er arm.

(*She demonstrates a girl biting her own arm in an obsessional, horrific way.*)

I 'ate glommen time 'ere. 'Eads burst, outburstin' wid demons.

55　FRANCIS: (*soothingly*) William can't get you out of that ward; the asylum's too crowded. Those people are mad, not you. The Government says you've got to stay here. You know that.

BETSHEB: Me quim is burnin'.

(*She touches* FRANCIS' *genitals.*)

60　FRANCIS: Betsheb!

BETSHEB: (*moving to him again*) Thou burning. Eyebright.

(*She jumps him again and he ducks out of the way. She chases after him. They both laugh, like children in a game.*)

FRANCIS: Not out here. Everyone's watching!

BETSHEB: Francis! Francis! Francis!

FRANCIS: I'll turn the hose on you.

65　BETSHEB: (*laughing*) Burnin'. Burnin'.

(*She grabs him. He falls to the ground. She kisses him.*)

FRANCIS: (*pushing her away slightly*) Betsheb, I have to tell you something.

(*She grabs him and smothers his face with quick kisses. He pushes her away, annoyed.*)

This is serious!

(BETSHEB *doesn't notice his annoyance.*)

BETSHEB: The belle she spoonin' the gent. 'E whoopin'.

(*She grabs him again.*)

FRANCIS: (*angrily*) No!　　　　　　　　　　　　　　　70

(*Almost immediately he is annoyed with himself for getting angry. She looks hurt and confused.*)

Listen. (*Touching his uniform*) You remember what I told you this uniform meant? I am in the army. Australia is at war with Germany and Italy. We have to fight to protect ourselves. To protect you, to save you from hurt, our families from hurt.　　　　　75

VOICE: (*off*) Mr Morris, the taxi's here!

FRANCIS: (*calling*) Tell him I won't be a moment. (*To* BETSHEB) I joined up to fight because we have to. And now I know I must fight for you, for Stef. The Germans are demons. Do you understand any of this?　　　　　80

(*She nods, but it's clear she doesn't.*)

I'm being shipped out tomorrow. Europe. Remember the map of the world we looked at? Well, I'm going to Europe. I won't be seeing you for some time. Goodbye.

BETSHEB: (*shocked*) 'Goodbye'?

FRANCIS: But not for long. I knew a couple of days ago but　85
couldn't tell you. Too much of a coward. This dress is my going-away present for you. And this.

(*He gives her a wrist watch.*)

You can watch the hands move, learn to tell the time. You wind it, make it go like this.

(BETSHEB *is still shocked and pays little attention.*)

BETSHEB: 'Goodbye'?　　　　　　　　　　　　　　　90

(*The taxi horn beeps.*)

FRANCIS: I must go. I'll write letter. William said he'd read them to you.

BETSHEB: Nowt 'Goodbye'.

FRANCIS: I have to; it's my duty.

BETSHEB: Nowt 'Goodbye'!　　　　　　　　　　　　　95

(*He kisses her.*)

FRANCIS: This hurts me too. I love you . . . do you understand?

BETSHEB: Nowt 'Goodbye'.

(*He begins to go, then stops briefly to pat* STEF *on the head.*)

FRANCIS: Goodbye, Stef.

(STEF *laughs and rolls over and over.* FRANCIS *pauses to look back at* BETSHEB. *She looks at him, confused and hurt. The taxi horn beeps again: he must go. He exits.*)

100 BETSHEB: (*quietly*) Nowt 'Goodbye'. (*Crying out, throwing away the watch*) Nowt 'Goodbye'!

SCENE IV

The asylum gardens, early evening. WILLIAM, *in dinner jacket, sits on the bench upstage. He watches* STEF, MAC, AYRE *and* BETSHEB *downstage. All of the group wear asylum clothes.* MAC *sleeps curled up.* STEF *examines his shoe by himself.* BETSHEB *half cradles* AYRE, *chewing bits of bread and, like a sparrow feeding its young, passing the chewed bread into* AYRE'S *mouth.* AYRE *is fading, but she is desperate to live long enough to pass on their language and memories to* BETSHEB. *It is difficult for* AYRE *to get the words out.*

AYRE: Demon 'ollarin' in glommen time.
BETSHEB: 'Demon 'ollarin' in glommen time.'

(*Silence.*)

AYRE: Sprits o' rack 'n' cat, doomtime.'
BETSHEB: 'Sprits o' rack 'n' cat, doomtime.'

(*Silence.* ELIZABETH, *wearing an expensive evening gown, enters and watches, unnoticed.*)

5 AYRE: Sprits adorate quim sold for sinbread.
BETSHEB: 'Sprits adorate quim sold for sinbread.'
AYRE: Albion is glommentime, rack 'n' cat time.
BETSHEB: 'Albion is glommentime, rack 'n' cat time.'

(*Silence.* BETSHEB *feeds* AYRE. ELIZABETH *goes towards* WILLIAM.)

ELIZABETH: The driver is waiting.

(*He looks up, puzzled.*)

10 You said we should pick you up on the way to Government House.
WILLIAM: I wanted to see if Ayre was all right.
ELIZABETH: You're always here. Why isn't Ayre inside? She looks very ill.
15 WILLIAM: She has a great fear of dying in her room. They'll go in soon for dinner.
ELIZABETH: I'm curious, William: what do you do when you come to visit them?
WILLIAM: Nothing much. Check their health. Watch.
20 ELIZABETH: You're forever here. The hospital's always ringing me. 'Where's Doctor Archer?' 'He's gone to stare at the madmen', I say.
WILLIAM: They're not mad.
ELIZABETH: They just do a very good impersonation of it.

(*Pause.*)

25 WILLIAM: Ayre is teaching Betsheb—not teaching, passing on their culture, her memories.

ELIZABETH: Do you read Francis's letters to her?
WILLIAM: Each one I have to read dozens of times. She misses him terribly.
30 AYRE: (*to* BETSHEB) Glommen sprits o' cut-throat kin.
BETSHEB: 'Glommen sprits o' cut-throat kin.'
AYRE: Pass 'elly gate t' goldy dell.'
ELIZABETH: (*to* WILLIAM) What a pathetic group they look, like those Aboriginals in shanty towns.
35 WILLIAM: She's teaching Betsheb about the night-time spirits.
ELIZABETH: Come on, the Governor is waiting.

(*He stands.*)

Your bow tie.

(*An envelope falls from his lap. As he straightens his bow tie,* ELIZABETH *picks up the envelope.*)

What's in here?
40 WILLIAM: The editor of the *Medical Journal* was going to publish them.
ELIZABETH: (*handing him the envelope*) What are they?
WILLIAM: The Chief Psychiatrist here decided she wanted photographs of Mac's interesting medical condition. 45 (*Handing the photographs to* ELIZABETH) He was always ashamed of his deformity and so that's what they photographed in brilliant close-ups. The reason why Ayre and the rest are here is because Mac couldn't have children. He knows that. And look what they go and do.
50 ELIZABETH: You would have been as callous as that.
WILLIAM: Once.
ELIZABETH: Your tie. (*Straightening his tie*) You smell like a brewery.
WILLIAM: I drink to forget what we've done to them.
55 ELIZABETH: There was nothing you could do.
AYRE: (*to* BETSHEB) Pearly dawn pass glommen time, thou pass demon time. Pass tempest 'n' temper time.
WILLIAM: (*to* ELIZABETH) It would have been nice for that to have been the Australian language.
60 ELIZABETH: When you've been drinking I can never tell when you're serious or not.
WILLIAM: Their culture is more authentic than ours. We Australians have assumed the garb of a hand-me-down culture, but at our heart is a desert. For their appalling 65 ignorance and pathetic beliefs they at least have a real core, an essence.
ELIZABETH: When you're in your cups you have a disturbing tendency to philosophise. I know this mood of yours: no sarcastic remarks about Singapore at the dinner.
70 WILLIAM: Why shouldn't I? The pompous ass said only a month ago that Singapore was impregnable. Thousands of Australians are in prison camps because of British stupidity. Betsheb.

(BETSHEB *turns to him. He motions at the sky.*)

Tempest time.

(BETSHEB *looks up at the sky.*)

75 Probably tonight.
BETSHEB: (*smiling*) Yes.

WILLIAM: You'd better get Ayre in. 'Bye, Ayre. Mac. 'Bye, Betsheb. I'll see you tomorrow.

(MAC *picks up* AYRE *and carries her inside.*)

She won't allow the nurses to touch her.

80 ELIZABETH: She's not long for this world.

WILLIAM: Probably not.

ELIZABETH: (*sarcastically*) But you've still got her voice on
record. Don't be a hypocrite. You're glad that they've been
hidden away; you've had them all to yourself. If you don't

85 recognise that, then you're blind. We had better hurry, the
Governor doesn't like to be kept waiting.

(*They exit.*)

SCENE V

On one side of the stage FRANCIS, *in army uniform with greatcoat covering his shoulders, writes by lamplight. On the other is the asylum gardens, night.* BETSHEB *washes a naked* STEF *with a bucket and sponge.*

FRANCIS: My darling Betsheb, tomorrow morning I go into
battle for the first time. The German planes have been
pounding us since we arrived.

(BETSHEB *washes* STEF'*s body as he makes wind noises. Both seem
very happy.* WILLIAM *enters and, unnoticed, watches the pair.*)

5   Crete is desolate and rocky. Why should we defend this
country? We are fighting over a place as desolate as the
moon.

(BETSHEB *washes* STEF'*s face. He laughs and then rolls away. She
catches him and continues to wash his face.*)

When we arrived we ran into a local priest who had lost
both his legs. He felt sorry for us and said: 'This is a bad
10 world and you have lost your way in it.' It was easy to see
what he meant. The paddocks were covered in burning
tanks and dying men. I imagine a battle is like being
caught in a butcher shop that is burning down.

(BETSHEB *washes* STEF'*s groin.*)

BETSHEB: (*Softly, singing*)
Hey, hey,
15   The girlie say,
Rub a dub, dub,
Spoonin' in the hay.

FRANCIS: It is said that if we win here, then we'll stop the
Germans and the war will end. There will be a peace. But
20 will I be alive to see it?

(BETSHEB *tickles* STEF'*s feet. He laughs wildly, she joins in. Their
laugher is joyous.*)

Betsheb, I am scared. I do not want to die.

SCENE VI

The asylum gardens, dusk. BETSHEB *stands on* MAC'*s shoulders.
They turn slowly, her face to the darkening sky. As if in a dream,*
ANGEL'*s penny whistle sounds.*

BETSHEB: (*singing*)
Rain, rain, go thy way,
Come a-back ne'er a day.

(*As* BETSHEB *repeats the song, unconsciously she strokes* MAC'*s face
sensuously. He is pleased to be touched by* BETSHEB.)

(*Softly*) Francis . . .

(MAC *breaks away. Astonished,* BETSHEB *tumbles to the ground.*
MAC *heads off.* BETSHEB, *perplexed by his behaviour, chases after
him. He throws her off and exits angrily.*)

SCENE VII

*The asylum gardens, late at night. Rain and hail pour down. A cry
of pain comes from the distance. Dimly, a figure hurries out into the
garden. It is* DR SIMON, *carrying an umbrella and a flashlight. The
beam darts here and there.*

DR SIMON: Betsheb! Are you out here?

(*Pause.*)

Betsheb. Bring Ayre inside.

(*Pause.*)

Betsheb! Answer me! Where are you? Come out of the rain.

(*She exits towards C Ward. Silence, Thunder.* BETSHEB *drags* AYRE
into the rain.)

BETSHEB: (*crying*) Thou mus' nowt die. Thou mus' live!   5

(*She stops to catch her breath.*)

Goldy green breathen int' thee, rain breathen int' thee.

(*She rolls* AYRE *back and forth.* AYRE *moans in agony.*)

The earth breathen int' thee. Thou mus' live!

(DR SIMON *enters again, at a distance.*)

DR SIMON: (*off*) Betsheb! Betsheb! Where are you?

(BETSHEB *huddles over* AYRE'*s body. Pause.* DR SIMON *retreats.
Once sure she has gone,* BETSHEB *turns her attention back to* AYRE.
She is barely breathing.)

BETSHEB: (*breathing into* AYRE'*s mouth*) I am in thee, thee in
me. (*Thumping* AYRE) Breathen! Breathen the tempest!   10
Breathen the rain! (*Crying out, desperately*) Breathen the
world! Thee must breathen the world!

(*But* AYRE *is dead.*)

Nowt die! Nowt die!

(*She wails in fear and horror.*)

Breathen! Breathen the world! The world is breathen
thee! Mumma! Breathen!   15

SCENE VIII

The asylum gardens, a pleasant Autumn day. MAC *lies on the ground, dead. A bloodied knife lies next to him.* DR SIMON *enters with a camera. She turns* MAC *over: his crotch is bloodied. He has castrated himself.* DR SIMON *sees someone in the distance.*

DR SIMON: Get back to your ward, Richard.

(*She watches Richard go.*)

Hurry up.

(*She turns her attention to the corpse and, taking careful aim, takes a photograph. She doesn't like the way the body is arranged, so she shifts it slightly with her foot and takes a closer picture. Silence. She stares at the corpse.*)

(*Quietly*) It's over now; you are released.

SCENE IX

The asylum gardens, a winter's day. WILLIAM *sits on the bench wearing a coat.* STEF *and* BETSHEB *sit on the grass wearing hand-me-down coats over their asylum uniforms.* BETSHEB *massages* STEF's *scalp.* WILLIAM *reads a letter to her.*

WILLIAM: 'Some people say the war will be over by Christ-mas, others say it will go on forever. There is no point to this slaughter. The Germans will lose, but they don't give
5   in; they would sooner destroy the world than surrender. My handwriting is bad. We are snowed in and my hands are shaking with the cold. The snow and the blood are endless.'

(WILLIAM *points.*)

Like the snow on Mount Wellington.

(BETSHEB *nods.*)

BETSHEB: Pass snow; nowt more outcastin'.
10 WILLIAM: Once the snow thaws, perhaps his exile will be over. Nowt more outcastin'. (*Continuing the letter*) 'I want to write about more pleasant things, Betsheb, but the war is my world at the moment. But once it is over I will re-turn. Goodbye for now, my love, Francis.'

(STEF *no longer wants his head massaged. He moves away and coughs deeply. He laughs.* BETSHEB *rises and takes the letter from* WILLIAM.)

15   You must have quite a collection now.

(*She puts it down the front of her dress. There is a blast of icy wind.* WILLIAM *shivers.*)

What a wind, eh? Straight from the South Pole.

(BETSHEB *ponders. Silence.* DR SIMON *enters and stands at a dis-tance, watching the odd trio.*)

BETSHEB: Nurse Greene got child.
WILLIAM: A baby boy.
BETSHEB: The belly o' 'er quim. Lovely.

WILLIAM: She and her husband had been trying for years to   20
have a child.
BETSHEB: Francis outcastin'; come back 'n' look at 'is belle 'n' 'e think 'the dead moon o' me cunt.'
WILLIAM: We don't know for certain.
BETSHEB: Me bod shakin' like a leaf, out o' the blue.   25
WILLIAM: Those fits you have are rare.
BETSHEB: Me bod in the toothy bite o' a bad dream.

(*Silence.*)

DR SIMON: What is Betsheb talking about?
WILLIAM: Nothing important.
DR SIMON: I'm curious.   30
WILLIAM: She just talks about things that interest her.
DR SIMON: And they don't interest you?
WILLIAM: Of course they do.
DR SIMON: Then why wouldn't I be interested?

(*Pause.* WILLIAM *turns his attention back to* BETSHEB.)

WILLIAM: (*to* BETSHEB) Don't be afraid of your body—   35
DR SIMON: (*interrupting*) If I knew the language or if you translated for me, then I would be able to help them.
WILLIAM: Like you helped Mac with the photographs?
DR SIMON: I am Chief Psychiatrist here. I have every right to have patients photographed: photographs are a legitimate   40
record of a patient's condition.
WILLIAM: You treated him as if he were a freak.
DR SIMON: That's not true. You have turned them against everyone except yourself. I have been here over four years and I still can't understand her.   45
WILLIAM: (*coldly*) Perhaps you're stupid.
DR SIMON: (*angrily*) You come here drunk. You've been re-lieved of your own post. Remember, you are only a visi-tor. You have no authority here.

(STEF *coughs.*)

If you really cared for him you wouldn't let him lie out in   50
the cold. He should be brought inside.

(*She takes a step towards* STEF. BETSHEB *moves in front of him.*)

WILLIAM: If you touch him, Betsheb will kill you.

(DR SIMON *stops.*)

(*Smiling*) Perhaps you had best get out of the cold, Doc-tor Simon.
DR SIMON: One day, Doctor Archer, you'll realise what   55
you've done to them.
WILLIAM: I know what I've done: I've protected them from the likes of you.

(DR SIMON *returns inside.* BETSHEB *sits down on the wet grass and looks at the watch* FRANCIS *gave her.*)

BETSHEB: Time is slow.

(*She looks at her watch, willing time to go faster.* STEF *lies prone on the ground, silent.* WILLIAM *puts up his collar to shield himself from the cold wind. Silence.*)

SCENE X

The asylum gardens, night. There is a moon. BETSHEB *sits on the bench staring at the night sky.*

BETSHEB: 'I cup me ear t' the glommen bird. Soul o' the dead. Cryin out "Donna burst yer 'eart, the bird is me."'

(Faint sounds of a party and dance songs of the forties come from the distance. A man in his thirties enters wearing a party hat or mask.)

JAMES: How you going? I was over there watching you talking to yourself. The New Year's party is pretty good, eh?

(BETSHEB is nervous.)

5   You've seen me around, haven't you? James, remember? I've been here almost as long as you. The nurses call me 'Jimmy'; me mum, 'Jim'. I saw you crawling out the window. I see you do that most nights. I can talk to you tonight because the ward assistant is drunk. He's not bad, Bert; keeps us up with the war news. I wanted to fight. I
10   tried to join up. I said, 'I want to murder Germans.' They refused me. They said they didn't want murderers in their army. I should have said I wanted to kill Germans. James, Jim, Jimmy, murder, kill . . . No wonder I'm at a loss in the
15   outside world; I haven't got me language skills right. Want a fuck?

(She doesn't understand.)

I can't make it plainer than that. I suppose I should ask you with words tied up with little blue bow ties but I don't know any.

(He comes closer. She stiffens.)

20   You can call me 'James', 'Jim', 'Jimmy'; I'll answer to them all.

(He makes a grab at her; she ducks away.)

(Annoyed) Why the problem? You're as fuckin' mad as me; why put up a front?
BETSHEB: *(quietly, explaining)* Francis. Francis, 'e outcastin'.
JAMES: No wonder none of us can understand you: it sounds
25   like a mouthful of marbles.

(He lunges and grabs at her. She stands still, scared.)

Others are scared of you, think you're some kind of witch. Not me. I see you pissing out here, rubbing yourself and I know. Look at you, like a bird in a trap.

(He slowly pulls her closer.)

I have dreamed of fuckin' you; now I'll make it real.
30   DR SIMON: *(off, quietly)* Jimmy.

(Pause.)

Jimmy, let her go.

(JAMES lets her go.)

JAMES: *(looking off)* Hello, Doctor Simon.
DR SIMON: Go back to the party.

JAMES: Why pick on me? She's always out, every night, yapping to herself.   35
DR SIMON: Back to your ward.

(JAMES goes. Silence. BETSHEB *lifts up her dress, offering her body in gratitude to* DR SIMON.*)*

Put down your dress, Betsheb, and go to bed. Stef needs you; he's very sick.

SCENE XI

The asylum gardens, a spring day. Birds are singing. BETSHEB *drags out the body of* STEF. *He is dead, but she tries to play with him as she once did.* DR SIMON *enters.*

DR SIMON: Let him go, Betsheb. Come on, let him go . . . He has to be examined by the coroner.

(She advances on BETSHEB, *who growls like an animal and lashes out.)*

Little bitch.

(BETSHEB growls softly.)

Like a bloody animal.

(Pause.)

(Angrily) He's dead. If you hadn't let him lie on the wet   5
grass he wouldn't be.

(WILLIAM enters. His clothes are dirty and he is very drunk.)

WILLIAM: *(to* DR SIMON, *smiling)* Fell into the flower bed. Blood and bone. Boy, do I pong! Betsheb!
DR SIMON: Doctor Archer, she won't let go of Stef.
WILLIAM: So what?   10
DR SIMON: He's been dead since early this morning.

(WILLIAM is shocked for a moment.)

WILLIAM: Stef?
BETSHEB: *(anguished)* Stef: 'e dead!
WILLIAM: No, not possible.
DR SIMON: The coroner's waiting; we have to get Stef away   15
from her.

(WILLIAM's sense of duty as a doctor returns.)

WILLIAM: Yes, yes. *(to* BETSHEB*)* You must let him go, Betsheb, there is nothing you can do. Nothing more.
BETSHEB: 'e me las' blood. Stef is me las' blood. I am cast t' the windy. 'e me las' blood, boyo.   20
WILLIAM: I know, but you must give him up.

(BETSHEB cradles STEF, focusing all her attention on him. WILLIAM *starts to walk towards her, but trips and falls. He lands and turns on his back, grinning broadly.)*

Whoops–a–daisy.

(For a moment he is bewildered, then he realises where he is.)

(To BETSHEB*)* I'm sorry.

DR SIMON: You're putrid drunk, Doctor Archer!

25 WILLIAM: God, help me, some women are observant. Yes, Doctor, I am going putrescent with alcohol.

DR SIMON: You're as crazy as she is.

WILLIAM: I'm just drunk. Get a whiff of my clothes!

(*He laughs.* DR SIMON *hurries off.*)

(*Calling after her*) Call the cops! (*Yelling*) Call anyone you 30 bloody-well please!)

(*Silence. He stares at* BETSHEB *for some time, at a loss. All her attention remains on* STEF *as she cradles him. Pause.*

(*Brushing her hair*) How I wanted to study you. To find out. I thought if I did discover everything, then I'd know. You know, of course, that this drunken old man loves you just as much as Francis does. Don't wait for him, he hasn't 35 written in a year, he's free of you. Run away, head for the hills. Nowt more outcastin'.

(*Silence.*)

I shouldn't have let you destroy me.

BETSHEB: (*looking at* WILLIAM, *quietly, almost beyond pain*) Stef . . . 'E dead.

SCENE XII

The ruins of Berlin, evening, 1945. FRANCIS, *now a lieutenant, enters carrying a pistol. He is dirty, worn and wearing a heavy army coat. He stops and looks around.* PRIVATE CORRIS *enters, also rugged up, carrying a rifle. Nearby on the ground are the remains of a huge statue: the head of Frederick the Great, its face riddled with bullet holes.*

CORRIS: I'm pretty sure I saw the bugger head this way.

FRANCIS: He's probably gone through those ruins there.

CORRIS: He wouldn't get far: there's the Americans on the other side.

(*Silence.*)

5 Sorry I fucked it up. When I turned me back he was off like a flash.

FRANCIS: (*shrugging*) It'll soon be too dark to see anything.

CORRIS: Yeah, the fires are starting up. The homeless. What a fuckin' mess, eh? They'll have to rebuild Berlin from 10 scratch. They live like rats in a tip. (*Looking at the head*) Not much bird shit.

FRANCIS: They deserved it: they started it; they were so bloody proud of their thousand-year Reich.

CORRIS: (*examining a hole in the head*) Jesus, Doctor, I've got a 15 splitting headache.

(*He laughs.*)

I once saw Mo at the Tiv; me girlfriend said I was funnier. Who do you reckon it is?

(FRANCIS *shakes his head.*)

It's not Hitler. Some old king, I guess. Wonder where the rest of him is. (*Looking around*) A leg there . . . there's some

angels. (*Sitting on the head*) Have to be careful I don't get a 20 nose up me bum. You know what I heard yesterday? After they strung up Mussolini and his mistress they pissed and shat on them. Bet you the same people who were saluting him the day before did it. Will we keep going or what?

FRANCIS: No point. Be too dark to see soon. He'll hide in the 25 ruins somewhere, find some old mate, change his identity . . . Doesn't matter.

CORRIS: Maybe the Yanks will get him.

FRANCIS: So what? You saw them with those scientists the other day putting them on the plane. Like they were 30 kings. Going to America to get well-paid jobs and yet they created the planes, the bombs, the rockets—

CORRIS: (*interrupting*) This fella was no scientist.

FRANCIS: He was Goebbels' right-hand man. He'll probably end up like the scientists: get off scot free, probably find 35 himself running a huge American publicity firm.

CORRIS: Maybe they'll go to trial.

FRANCIS: They are war criminals: who needs a trial? We should execute them straight away.

CORRIS: Got a real bee in your bonnet. 40

FRANCIS: (*coldly*) And you're a bloody idiot: you let him go.

(*Silence.*)

(*Looking around*) This is where the world ended.

CORRIS: What I wouldn't give to be back in Australia. Know what I learned in four years of fighting the Krauts? One German phrase: 'I surrender.' And to prove I was Australian 45 I'd hop about like this.

(*He starts to hop. Suddenly* FRANCIS *pulls out his revolver and fires at* CORRIS. CORRIS *ducks. There is a cry from the ruins. A figure wearing a dirty suit jumps into view and runs for* CORRIS' *gun.*)

FRANCIS: Get out of the way, Corris.

(*He fires and hits the* MAN *again.*)

Grab him.

(CORRIS *and the* MAN *struggle with the rifle, but the* MAN *is weak and bleeding badly. He falls to the ground.*)

(*To the* MAN, *pointing his revolver*) Don't move.

CORRIS: That's the bugger, Lieutenant. (*Looking closely*) Jeez, 50 he's badly hit.

FRANCIS: He must have been waiting all the time, waiting to jump you and get your rifle.

CORRIS: (*motioning with his rifle*) On your feet, Fritz. (*To* FRANCIS) I think he's hurt too bad. One in the leg isn't too 55 bad, but the chest . . .

FRANCIS: Understand English?

MAN: English? *Nein.*

FRANCIS: Get someone to help us carry him back.

CORRIS: Those Americans will help us. Be back in ten. 60

(CORRIS *heads off. Silence.*)

FRANCIS: Not such a big boy now. What's the point? You'll get off.

(*The* MAN *is dying.*)

MAN: Kill me.

(FRANCIS *is surprised.*)

Kill me. Please.

(*The* MAN *is in incredible pain.* FRANCIS *puts his gun to the* MAN's *head and calmly shoots him.*)

SCENE XIII

WILLIAM's *study, night.* WILLIAM *sits in a high-backed chair finishing the remains of a bottle of whiskey. He is drunk, but full of purpose. On his lap is an open cut-throat razor. He listens to a recording of* AYRE's *voice for the umpteenth time. As she slowly speaks he unconsciously translates.*

AYRE'S VOICE: Past riverrun 'n' turn o' kelp int' muddy moss, seay green 'n' here. There! Ghost 'n' sprit time. Goldy lifey, glommen lifey. Thee dreamytime in greeny belch o' 'eaven. Sprits o' cunty dell. Circle o' greeny 'ome! Nowt 'ome.
5   Burst mouth, 'airy brain 'n' cradlepain. Pitch dark glommen is dry sheb and rottin' tarse. The circle is burst . . .
WILLIAM: 'We came past river, past tides of kelp and mud, moss and into the sea of green and came to here. There! The time of our ancestors. A dreamtime in the green stomach of
10   heaven. All around the spirits of the fertile valley. Home. It is not home. Then something happened: there were hair lips, soft brains and children in pain. A darkness of sterile girls and boys. The circle is burst. Broken.'

(*The sound of burning wood is heard faintly. Something is burning close to* WILLIAM, *but he does not hear it, or doesn't care.*)

AYRE'S VOICE: 'Ear us, William, William. Keep us in that box.
15   We is talkin' t' thee. T' thee. The circle is burst. I ne'er more cup me ear to the glommen bird. I ne'er more helter-skelterin' wid the glommen sprits; foe 'n' friend.
WILLIAM: 'Hear us, William. Keep us in that box. We are talking to you. To *you*! The circle is broken. I'll never more lis-
20   ten to the night-birds. Never more dance with the night spirits, the good and the bad.'

(WILLIAM *finishes his drink and puts down the empty glass.*)

ELIZABETH: (*off, banging on the door, yelling*) Bill! William! Are you in there?
AYRE'S VOICE: Listen t' us, William, 'ear us words, 'member us,
25   'elp us, us who is born in card, cradlepain. Nowt more outcastin'.
WILLIAM: 'Listen to us, William. Hear our words. Remember us. Help us, who were born in pain. No more exile.'
ELIZABETH: William, answer me!
30 AYRE'S VOICE: Nowt more outcastin'.
WILLIAM: 'No more exile.'

(WILLIAM *does not hear* ELIZABETH. *He picks up the razor and calmly slits his throat. The fire grows loud.*)

SCENE XIV

The asylum gardens, late afternoon. BETSHEB *sits on the bench. Some flowers, pulled up by the roots, are scattered around her. Around*

her mouth are traces of dried blood. She wears a white hospital gown which is stained with urine and menstrual blood. She has lost control of herself. DR SIMON enters, surprised by BETSHEB's appearance.

DR SIMON: What has happened, Betsheb?

(BETSHEB *doesn't answer.*)

Larry said someone tore up all his flower beds: it was you, wasn't it?

(*Pause.*)

You must look after yourself. Come inside, let's clean you up.

(DR SIMON *grabs her. Suddenly* BETSHEB *lashes out and knocks the doctor down.*)

BETSHEB: Way! Way!   5

(BETSHEB *looks wild.* DR SIMON *gets up and moves away.*)

DR SIMON: Come on, Betsheb, come inside.
BETSHEB: (*screaming*) Nowt more!
DR SIMON: If you don't calm down I'll have to get the ward assistants to help me.
BETSHEB: (*screaming*) Nowt more!   10

(DR SIMON *hurries off for help.* BETSHEB *looks wildly about her.*)

(*screaming*) Nowt more! (*Looking up at the sky*) Nowt more!

(*Suddenly there is thunder. It is as if she cries out for the destruction of the world. The more she screams at the heavens, the louder the thunder and lightening grows.*)

SCENE XV

A prison courtyard, Berlin, afternoon. FRANCIS *sits on the ground against a wall and soaks up the last rays of sun. Silence.*

AMERICAN VOICE: (*off, crying out*) Hoy, hoy, I'm the boy! Hoy, hoy, I'm the boy!

(PETER *enters in a captain's uniform.* FRANCIS *doesn't notice him.* PETER *is shocked by* FRANCIS' *condition. He puts on a smile.*)

PETER: Long time no see, mate.
FRANCIS: Peter!

(*He stands up. They greet each other warmly.*)

So long, so bloody long!   5
PETER: Forty-two.
FRANCIS: That's right. A captain.
PETER: Didn't do so badly yourself.

(*There is an awkward pause.* FRANCIS *makes a sweeping, mocking gesture.*)

FRANCIS: My home.
PETER: (*trying to be light hearted*) Love the bluestone.   10
FRANCIS: How did you find me?
PETER: Came over from Paris a few days ago. I'm fixing up the final Australian repatriation. Heard about your case this morning. How long have you been here?

15 FRANCIS: Eight or nine weeks. This is my daily exercise. I'm like a lizard. I follow the sun around the courtyard, trying to warm my blood.

AMERICAN VOICE: (*off*) Hoy, hoy, I'm the boy! Hoy, hoy, I'm the boy!

20 FRANCIS: An American negro. Went mad and killed a whore with his bare hands 'cos she called him a nigger. (*Gesturing*) Those windows, they're black-marketeers. War criminals stare out of those windows, waiting to be sent to Nuremburg; and those windows, that's where I am: the 25 rapists and murderers section.

AMERICAN VOICE: Hoy, hoy, I'm the boy! Hoy, hoy, I'm the boy!

FRANCIS: Actually, I'm quite at home; it reminds me of Collingwood.

(*He walks a little to the left, looking up at the sun, closing his eyes.*)

30   The last bit of sun. It's freezing in the cell.

PETER: I only had time to glance at your file. The Americans think you murdered him.

FRANCIS: I did. The Kraut asked me to do it, so I obliged. Now the Australians want to show off to the Allies that 35 they can be just as tough on their men. (*Looking at the sun*) It's going.

PETER: After years in England it was the sun I missed the most and the bright blue skies.

(*Pause.*)

   Did you know my father died?

40 FRANCIS: Your mum wrote to me.

PETER: Burnt to death. Most of the rear of the house was destroyed. Mother said you stopped writing to Betsheb.

FRANCIS: What could I write to her about? How could I describe what I was seeing? Civilizations perfecting death. 45 Bombs, fighter planes, slaughtered soldiers, extermination camps, rape, blood lust. I couldn't pretend the war would end and I would return because every morning I thought I would die that day. I couldn't write any more gentle letters because I have nothing of that left inside me any 50 more. It's gone, the little I had. Once I stopped writing to her I knew I couldn't go home again. This prison perfectly suits my state of mind; I have been bred for it, just as I have been bred to kill. Do you know that people think the war will continue only it will be between the Americans and 55 Russians? It's as if this century has imagined a monster, concocted if from the deepest underworld of its brain and now it has escaped and is devouring everything. Nothing makes sense.

AMERICAN VOICE: Hoy, hoy, I'm the boy! Hoy, hoy, I'm the 60 boy!

PETER: Your bitterness will pass.

FRANCIS: I can't get rid of this dream. I have built a bridge. There is a grand opening. The ribbon is cut. Bright happy people begin to walk across the bridge. It collapses like a 65 pack of cards. I have even lost faith in my ability to build something mechanical. How I envied you with your wealth, your background, your sense of past, family, belonging. I am rootless now. It's not such a bad feeling because it's no feeling at all.

AMERICAN VOICE: Hoy, hoy, I'm the boy! (*More desperately*) 70 Hoy, hoy, I'm the boy!

FRANCIS: I wish I could go as mad as him.

PETER: You've spent too many years fighting. Everyone has.

FRANCIS: Don't you see, Peter, the war will never stop; we humans don't give up until we perfect something. Mind 75 made perfect matter.

PETER: It's over.

AMERICAN VOICE: (*desperately*) Hoy, hoy, I'm the boy!

(FRANCIS *stands on tip toe to get the last rays of the sun.*)

FRANCIS: What kept me going was my memories of that time when we found them. God, I was stricken with her. 80

(PETER *laughs.*)

   The old geezer doing Lear; I finally realized what it was: the happy version of *King Lear.*

(*The sun vanishes.*)

   Poof! Snuffed out.

(*Pause.*)

PETER: We were very innocent then.

FRANCIS: So were they. 85

AMERICAN VOICE: (*crying out*) Hoy, hoy, I'm the boy!

FRANCIS: (*calling out*) Hoy, hoy, you're the boy!

AMERICAN VOICE: (*joyfully*) Hoy, hoy, I'm the boy!

FRANCIS: Before going in I tell him that. It makes him happy. (*Holding out his hand*) I have to go in now. 90

PETER: You'd better. (*smiling*) You'll have to collect your gear. You'll be flown to England tomorrow and then . . . a slow boat to Australia.

(*Pause.*)

   They wanted a way out of it as much as you did. No one really wants to be reminded of the war any more. Con- 95 nections help, the major was a friend of my father.

(FRANCIS *is stunned.*)

AMERICAN VOICE: (*joyfully*) Hoy, hoy, I'm the boy!

PETER: The nightmare is over.

SCENE XVI

The asylum gardens, an early summer day, 1945. BETSHEB *sits, withdrawn, on the bench in a clean hospital gown. It is as if she is a doll that has had all its stuffing removed.* FRANCIS *enters in civilian clothes. He carries a large bunch of flowers. Escorting him is* DR SIMON.

DR SIMON: She always sits on that garden bench.

(*They look at her.*)

   You're the first visitor she's had in a long time.

FRANCIS: No one else?

DR SIMON: No one. Not for a year.

5 FRANCIS: She was supposed to be released once the war was over.

DR SIMON: I know nothing about that. All files about her and her group were stolen by Doctor Archer and destroyed in his house fire. Anyway, she's not in a fit condition to be re-
10 leased.

(FRANCIS *takes a step towards* BETSHEB, *but* DR SIMON *speaks again.*)

It would have been better if you had never found them. They should have remained a lost tribe.

(FRANCIS *nods.*)

She was in a terrible state. Profound depressions and re-fusing to eat, so we had to give her electric shock treat-
15 ment. Be patient with her.

(DR SIMON *exits. Silence.* FRANCIS *walks towards* BETSHEB *and stops behind her, smiling nervously.*)

FRANCIS: (*quietly*) Betsheb?

(*She doesn't hear. He walks around to face her.*)

Betsheb?

(*She doesn't seem to recognise him. He gives her the flowers: they drop from her lap onto the ground.*)

It's me. Francis. Please. Look at me.

(*She looks at him without recognition.*)

What have we done to you?

(*Silence.*)

20 I couldn't come back. I couldn't write any more. When the others died I didn't know what to write. I thought they were better off dead than living here.

(*Pause.*)

You're the last thing I ever wanted to hurt.

(*A long silence.*)

I didn't know this was going to happen. Perhaps I did, that's why I felt so guilty.

(*Silence.*)

Betsheb?

(*He kisses her. She doesn't respond. As he kisses her again, he takes out his revolver and points it at the side of her head.*)

SCENE XVII

Hobart, a summer's night, 1945. The tiny Greek temple is the same as the opening scene. ELIZABETH *stands before it in Greek costume.* PETER, *in dinner jacket, plays his father's role as Orestes.*

ELIZABETH: 'You are now ready for death, yet you seem to be facing the prospect of such a hideous fate with true calm.'

PETER: 'What else should I do? I have nothing to live for.'

ELIZABETH: 'What of your family? You were once a child: who was your mother, then? Your father? Have you a 5 sister?'

PETER: 'My sister was sacrificed for my father.'

ELIZABETH: 'I am lost too. My mother, Clytemnestra, said my brother—'

PETER: 'My darling sister! I can scarcely believe what I hear!' 10

(*He moves towards her. She steps away.*)

ELIZABETH: 'What are you doing? I am Head Priestess.'

PETER: 'Clytemnestra was my mother too! My father is the grandson of Pelops. Was yours?'

ELIZABETH: 'Yes.'

PETER: 'Iphigenia! We thought you were dead and now I have 15 found you!'

ELIZABETH: 'I am happier than words can tell.'

(*They embrace.*)

'Our strange story is beyond all dreams and thought. In-stead of killing you I must save you and so save us all. How I longed for my country and you, long before your com- 20 ing. Orestes. How my prayer joins with yours for the re-newal of our breed. We must escape.'

PETER: 'My purpose in coming here must now be revealed. I came here to steal the statue of Artemis. We shall take it back with us.' 25

ELIZABETH: 'You cannot do both; take the statue and leave me to die. If a man dies, a house, a name is lost, but if a woman dies it means nothing.'

PETER: 'No murderer of you shall I be. Either I escape to Ar-gos with you or die here with you. Now I see the plan of 30 the gods: they have intended that I should find you here. I see the strands of fate entwining themselves. Lady, I think we shall reach home!'

(MARY, *the maid, enters. Both* PETER *and* ELIZABETH *stop.*)

MARY: I'm sorry, Mrs Archer, an urgent phone call for your son. 35

PETER: Who is it, Mary?

MARY: The superintendent of New Norfolk Asylum, Mr Archer.

(PETER *heads off, followed by* MARY.)

ELIZABETH: (*exasperated*) Peter! (*To the audience*) Ladies and gentlemen, a slight pause before my son returns. In the 40 meantime the blind children would adore it if they saw you reaching even further into your pockets. Our target tonight is five hundred pounds, so dip your hands in. Go on, the heavens are clear and fortune shines on us tonight. 45

SCENE XVIII

The wilds of south-western Tasmania, day. FRANCIS *lies on the ground, dirty and sleepy. There is a sudden noise and he wakes up.*

PETER *appears wearing his old hiking gear.* FRANCIS *is surprised to see his friend. Silence.*

PETER: I knew you'd come back here.
FRANCIS: Are there any others with you?
PETER: No.

(*Pause.*)

Are you all right?
5 FRANCIS: Tired, that's all.
PETER: I'm not used to all this exercise.
FRANCIS: (*smiling*) Neither am I.

(*Silence.*)

PETER: Betsheb?
FRANCIS: Down by the river.
10 PETER: When I got to the asylum, Doctor Simon was still shaking. She said you were about to shoot Betsheb and when she called out you turned the gun on her.
FRANCIS: I wanted to put Betsheb out of her misery, but when I held it against her head I realized I should have
15 been holding it against mine. I knew what to do. I would bring Betsheb back here, bring her home. We destroyed them.
PETER: It was a combination of events. How were we to know that the Government would deal with them that
20 way?
FRANCIS: Does it bother you?
PETER: It does, but I have never been obsessed by them as you are or my father was. How could they have survived, anyway? They were pathetic remnants of what was probably
25 an even more pathetic collection of people. They were like those Aboriginal tribes that withered away because their culture wasn't strong enough. It happens in nature, in human civilisations, one big animal swallows a little one. (*Looking around*) It didn't take long for it to return to
30 the wilderness.

(BETSHEB *enters and smiles when she sees* PETER. *She hugs him.*)

BETSHEB: Peter, Peter, Peter.
PETER: Hello, Betsheb. (*To* FRANCIS) Are you going to stay here . . . with her?
FRANCIS: Why not?

(*He releases* BETSHEB, *and she lies on the ground and stares contentedly at the sky.*)

35 PETER: You're mad. How in hell will you two survive out here?
FRANCIS: They survived; why not us? It doesn't matter, anyway. Why should I go back? How can I go back after all I've seen? This is what I hate about this country: it pre-
40 tends nothing important ever happened. Everything we experienced overseas . . . we return and pretend we never experienced it. I shot that German, not out of pity, but because I was filled with hate. All right, pretend it didn't happen. You helped co-ordinate the bombing raids over
45 Germany. Forget it. We obliterated a group of people, not through deliberate cruelty, but through plain stupidity and indifference. Doesn't matter, no problems, mate. Indifference is our guiding star. We'd sooner turn our attention to making a quick quid, like children amused by shiny trin-
50 kets. We'd sooner wipe out all unpleasant memories, block our ears and pretend we can't hear the cry of pain. If we heard that cry, then our sense of ourselves would be deeper, then we shall have reached home. We are lost, rootless people: she isn't.
55 PETER: You're running away.

(*Silence.*)

FRANCIS: Will you stay with us for tonight?
PETER: If I leave now, I'll get back to the track before dark.

(*Pause.*)

I'll say I couldn't find you.

(*He looks at* BETSHEB, *who still lies on the ground staring contentedly up at the sky and trees.*)

BETSHEB: (*happily*) Rack 'n' cat o' the windy, bumpin' thru the trees.
60
PETER: She can't offer you a future.
BETSHEB: Sprits o' Melorne, Ayre, Stef, Mac, Angel. Liptalkin' softly, swirlin' in the cunty dell o' moss 'n' ferny clotty 'eart. The moon is a white 'ole, I crawl int' it t' dream. Ayre
65 liptalkin' thru me 'eart. The bird listen, he liptalk thru 'is soul. Sprits outburstin' around 'n' around, a-yellin, a-kissin'. All goldy things. All goldy sow. 'Ome. I come 'ome.

(*Silence.*)

PETER: What she's describing doesn't exist; it's a figment of her imagination.
FRANCIS: She can teach me how to see it.
70
PETER: But it's not real.
BETSHEB: (*softly, singing*)
Rain, rain, go thy way,
Come a-back ne'er a day.
PETER: Goodbye, Betsheb.
75

(*She pays no attention.*)

She lives in a world of her own. You know that. She destroyed my father just as she'll destroy you. You have done the wrong thing.
FRANCIS: Maybe I have; I don't know. But she's all I've got to believe in.
80
PETER: Goodbye.

(FRANCIS *nods a 'Goodbye.'* PETER *departs. Silence.* BETSHEB *continues to sing softly to herself.*)

FRANCIS: Betsheb? Betsheb?

(BETSHEB, *immersed in her own world, doesn't answer.* FRANCIS *sits down away from her and wonders if* PETER *is right.* BETSHEB *laughs to herself. After a time she turns around and notices* FRANCIS: *a lonely, confused figure. She stares at him and, almost as if he has heard his name, he turns and looks at her. She smiles across the gulf that separates them.*)

BETSHEB: Nowt more outcastin'.

(*The lights fade slowly to blackout.*)

THE END.

Gao Xingjian

The first Chinese writer to win the Nobel Prize for Literature, Gao Xingjian (b. 1940), was raised in provincial Ganzhou after the Communist revolution in China. His mother was an amateur actress, and when he went to Beijing in 1958 to study at the Beijing Foreign Languages Institute, he not only studied French literature, but became involved in theater as well. He was working as a translator when the Cultural Revolution (1967–1977) forced the "reeducation" of intellectuals and professionals by exiling them to rural areas to work in agriculture; he was working as a schoolteacher in southwestern China when he published his first novel, *Stars on a Cold Night* in 1980. The following year, during Deng Xiaoping's easing of cultural restrictions, he published a critical essay, "Preliminary Explorations into the Techniques of Modern Fiction," which attempted—as Brecht had done earlier in relation to Soviet realism—to articulate the purpose and power of "modernist" formal and theoretical experimentation in the face of the state-supported demands of Maoist "revolutionary realism." Though the essay proved controversial, Gao was soon appointed as playwright to the Beijing People's Art Theater; several of the plays he wrote for the company proved controversial in a climate in which formal "experimentation" signaled a departure from Party doctrines. *Bus Stop* (1981) was not produced by the company, and *Absolute Signal* was shown in a few public rehearsals before being closed after only thirteen performances: Gao was prohibited from writing for publication for a year and went into exile in southwestern China.

Returning to Beijing in 1984, he wrote *Wilderness Man,* which updates and innovates the episodic and mythological structure of traditional Chinese theater, and *The Other Shore* (1985). Insistently framing a conflict between individual characters and the Crowd, *The Other Shore* was closed during rehearsal, and Gao fled to France in 1987. In France, Gao has written a number of his most celebrated works, including *Exile* (1989)—which concerns the flight of dissidents from the Tiananmen Square uprising in 1989—and the plays *Between Life and Death* (1991), *Dialogue and Rebuttal* (1992), *Nocturnal Wanderer* (1993), *Weekend Quartet* (1995), and the novel *Spiritual Mountain* (1990). Although Gao's work is not well known in the United States, a collection of plays (to which I am indebted here) *The Other Shore: Plays by Gao Xingjian,* edited and translated by Gilbert C.F. Fong, was published in 1999. Gao's plays have, however, become part of the international theatrical repertoire, and have been produced professionally in China, Sweden, England, Austria, Germany, France, Australia, Poland, Japan, and Taiwan, as well as in the United States. Gao won the Nobel Prize for Literature in 2000.

THE OTHER SHORE

The Other Shore witnesses Gao's deep investment in theatrical experimentation, particularly his desire to investigate the means of acting in the theater. As he suggests in his notes to the play, *The Other Shore* attempts to fuse the physical elements of acting ("somatics"), language, and psychology in "a kind of emotive abstraction through performance, i.e., a non-philosophical abstraction." Noting his indebtedness to the work of Polish director Jerzy Grotowski—whose **POOR THEATER,** like Gao's, dispensed with elaborate sets, costumes, and lighting to focus attention on acting as the essence of theater—Gao also makes a significant departure: while Grotowski used physical discipline to force the actor's "sacrifice" of himself, a kind of "exposure" of his innermost identity to himself and to the audience, Gao's theater "helps the actor to ascertain his own self through the process of discovering his partners."

The tension between the demands of the self and of its relation to others animates the action of the play, which takes the shape of an allegorical journey, in the mode of plays from *Everyman* to Strindberg's *A Dream Play.* Gao suggests that the play should be performed en-

The Boston University Theater production of Gao's *The Other Shore*. Photo by Ben Sigda.

vironmentally, in an open space shared by actors and audience, and the play opens with a series of acting exercises and games, in which the performers use ropes to explore and define their group identity. This exercise demands a high level of physical training and responsiveness from the performers, as the actors work to embody the different "identities" that emerge from different relationships. The actors also use the rope exercises to begin their narrative, traveling to "the other shore," a nonexistent realm that nonetheless evokes the state of Buddhist enlightenment (sometimes called "the other shore"). But *The Other Shore* is hardly doctrine-disguised-as-allegory. Rather than a banal or a politicized vision of individual or collective peace, the play imagines a dynamic and conflictual journey, centered on a series of confrontations between individuated characters like The Woman, The Man, The Young Girl, The Card Player, The Mad Woman, and the Crowd (in a way reminiscent of the history of Greek drama, Gao's actor/protagonists emerge from and blend back into the choral Crowd). Many of the scenes revolve around The Man, who resists the Crowd's often self-deluded efforts toward conformity. Yet much of the power of this elegant play depends on the tension between Gao's lyrical language and the actors' lyrical physicality, their ability to individuate and transform the Crowd itself. Arriving at "the other shore," the actors seem both to discover and to explore their bodies, and discover and explore language as well; having discovered their instrument, the use it throughout the play to transform the Crowd—into a vengeful mob, a throng of pilgrims, a host of demented automatons, a monstrous forest. In this sense, the Crowd is not a monolithic and regimented opponent of the individual, but the network within which the individual discovers his or her identity; as Gao suggests in one of his notes, the Crowd should not be understood as a regimented entity—its "performance must be fresh, regenerating, and improvisational."

THE OTHER SHORE

Gao Xingjian

CHARACTERS

An actor playing with ropes
CARD PLAYER
"DOGSKIN" PLASTER SELLER
WOMAN
YOUNG GIRL
MAD WOMAN
MODEL
MAN
YOUNG MAN
SHADOW
HEART
MOTHER
FATHER
ZEN MASTER

OLD LADY
STABLE KEEPER
ACTORS
CROWD

TIME: *The time cannot be defined or stated precisely.*

LOCATION: *From the real world to the nonexistent other shore.*

The play can be performed in a theatre, a living room, a rehearsal room, an empty warehouse, a gymnasium, the hall of a temple, a circus tent, or any empty space as long as the necessary lighting and sound equipment can be properly installed. Lighting can be dispensed with if the play is performed during the day. The actors may be among the audience, or the audience among the actors. The two situations are the same and will not make any difference to the play.

ACTOR PLAYING WITH ROPES: Here's a rope. Let's play a game, but we've got to be serious, as if we're children playing their game. Our play starts with a game.

5   Okay, I want you to take hold of this end of the rope. You see, this way a relationship is established between us. Before that you were you and I was I, but with this rope between us we're tied to each other and it becomes you and I.

Let's try running in opposite directions. See, now you're pulling me, but then again I'm also holding you

10   back, like two locusts tied to the same string, neither of us can get away from each other. Of course, we're also like husband and wife. (*Pauses.*) But that's not a good metaphor. If I were to pull the rope real hard towards me, then we'd have to see who's stronger. The stronger one

15   pulls and the weaker is being pulled. It becomes a tug-of-war, a competition of strength, and there'll be a winner and a loser, victory and defeat.

Now if I carry this rope on my back like this and pull even harder, you'll be like a dead dog; likewise if you man-

20   age to gain control of this rope, I'll be like a horse or a cow, and you'll be able to drive me around like cattle. In other words, you'll be running the show. So you see, our relationship is not at all constant, it's not at all unchanging.

Or we can establish an even more complex relation-

25   ship. For instance if you revolve around me, I'll be the centre of your orbit, and you'll become my satellite. But if you don't wish to revolve around me, I can rotate on my own, thinking that all of you are revolving around me. Are you revolving or am I the one who's revolving? I could be

30   revolving around you or you could be revolving around me. Who knows? Perhaps we're both turning at the same time, or maybe we're both revolving around other people, or maybe those other people are revolving around us both or maybe all of us are revolving around God—maybe

35   there isn't a God after all, maybe there's only a universe rotating by itself like a millstone—now we're touching on philosophy. Never mind, we'll leave philosophy to the philosophers, let's just continue to play our game.

Everyone of you can pick up a rope and play different kinds of games, the possibilities are endless. Playing with 40   ropes is such a game, that it can be a manifestation of all kinds of interpersonal relationships.

(*The actors each choose a partner to play the game, using a piece of rope. They can switch partners or briefly make contact with other pairs of players, but the contacts are soon broken. The game becomes increasingly lively, tense, and exciting, accompanied by all kinds of salutations and screams.*)

ACTOR PLAYING WITH ROPES: Okay everybody, let's knock it off for a moment. Let's make this game bigger and more complex. Now I want all of you to hold on to one end of 45   your rope and give me the other end. This way you'll be able to establish all kinds of relationships with me, some tense, some lax, some distant, and some close, and soon your individual attitudes will have a strong impact on me. Society is complex and ever-changing, we're constantly 50   pulling and being pulled. (*Pauses.*) Just like a fly that's fallen into a spider's web. (*Pauses.*) Or just like a spider. (*Pauses.*)

The rope is like our hands. (*He lets go one rope and his partner also lets go. The rope falls on the ground.*) Or like an 55   extended antenna. (*He lets go another and his partner follows.*) Or like the language we use, for instance when we say "Good Morning" or "How are you!" (*Another rope falls to the ground.*) Or perhaps it's like looking at each other, (*Replaces another rope.*) or like the thoughts in our minds. (*His 60   back is against his current partner, but the two sides are still communicating.*) Either you're thinking of her, or she's thinking of someone else. (*He brushes past her shoulders. She and someone else are gazing into each other's eyes.*) In this way the rope is pulling all of us, binding us together. 65

We look—

(*The actors are communicating with one another through pieces of imaginary ropes.*)

We observe—
We stare—
Then there's temptation and attraction—
70 Orders and obedience—

(*In the following, the performance is accompanied by all kinds of sighs and screams but without resorting to the use of language.*)

Conflicts—
Intimacy—
Exclusion—
Entanglement—
75 Abandonment—
Emulation—
Evasion—
Repulsion—
Pursuit—
80 Encirclement—
Congregation—
Fragmentation
Dismiss!
At ease!
85 Now there is a river in front of us, not a piece of rope.
Let's cross the river and try to reach the other shore.

ACTORS: (*One after another.*) Yes, to the other shore! To the other shore!
The other shore! To the other shore! To the other shore!
90 The other shore!
Oh—Oh—Oh
The water in the river is so clear!
So cool!
Watch out, the stones are killing my feet!
95 How nice!

(*Gradually there comes the sound of running water.*)

My skirt's soaking wet!
Is the river deep?
Let's swim across to the other shore!
Don't go by yourself!
100 Look at the water spray, how it sparkles in the sunshine!
What fun, just like a waterfall.
A dam, a river flowing gently down the dam.
Form a line in the middle of the river.
Further down the water's dark blue, it's got to be really
105 deep there.
I've got some fish wriggling between my legs . . .
So exciting!
I'm going to fall.
Don't worry, hold on to me.
110 There's an eddy over there—
Look after one another, hold hands.
To the rapid waters.
To the other shore!
No one can see the other shore.
115 Cut the poetry crap! I'm falling.
Hold tight, one after another now.
Over there the water is deep blue . . .
Aahh! The water's over my waist all of a sudden!
I'm getting dizzy.
120 Close your eyes for a while.

Look in front of you, look ahead, keep your eyes open!
All looking at the other shore.
How come I can't see it?
We'll drown, all of us.
We'll all be fish food. 125
If we're going to die, let's die together.
Girls, stop blabbing, try to concentrate.
The current is very strong, tread in the shallows, try going up stream!
I can't make it across, I'm sure I can't make it. 130
Where's the other shore?
Sometimes it's dark, sometimes it's bright.
Are there lights on the other shore?
There are flowers, lots of flowers on the other shore, it's a world of flowers. 135
I'm afraid I can't make it, please don't leave me behind.

(*Sobs.*)

Can you feel it? We're drifting in the river.
Like corks on a string.
And like water weed.
Why are we going to the other shore? I really don't un- 140
derstand.
Right, why do we want to go to the other shore?
The other shore is the other shore, you'll never reach it.
But you still want to go, to see what it's like over there.
I can't see anything. 145
No oasis, and no light.
In total darkness.
It's like this . . .
No, I can't make it.
We haven't been there before. 150
We must get there.
But why?
To make a long-time wish come true, the other shore, the other shore.
No, I can't make it, I want to go home! 155
None of us can.
Can't go back at all.
O—!
Who is it?
Don't know. 160

(*Silence, only the sound of water gurgling.*)

Was somebody screaming? Did you hear it?
You must have heard it, but nobody answered.

(*Silence. Sound of sobbing.*)

This is a ditch of dead water.
There's only oblivion.

(*Bewildered, the* CROWD *slowly walk out of the dead water. Music is faintly heard. The* CROWD *gradually reach the shore and lie down totally exhausted on the ground.* WOMAN *appears in darkness. Like a strand of light mist, she walks around to inspect the people who have lost their memories. She drifts among them, touching and waking them up one by one. They lazily open their eyes and look up, turning their bodies and staring at her. They try to speak but in vain.*)

165 WOMAN: (*Raises her hand.*) Look here, this is a hand.

(*The* CROWD *utter muddled sounds from their throat.*)

WOMAN: This is a hand.
CROWD: (*Still mumbling.*) Th . . . The . . . This . . . ee . . . ha . . . han . . . hand.
WOMAN: Hand—
170 CROWD: Hand—band—sand—hand—
WOMAN: This is a foot.
CROWD: Th . . . Th . . . This . . . ee . . . fo . . . foo . . . foot.
WOMAN: (*Pointing to her eye.*) Eye.
CROWD: Ee . . . ee . . . eye . . . eye . . .
175 WOMAN: (*Gesturing.*) Your eyes are looking at your foot!
CROWD: (*Totally confused.*) Eyes . . . cook . . . cook your . . . own . . . coot . . .

(WOMAN *laughs, and the* CROWD *join in the laughter with her, giggling.*)

WOMAN: (*Stops laughing, somewhat sad.*) This is a hand—
CROWD: This is a hand, this is a band, this is a sand, this is a
180 hand . . .
WOMAN: This is a foot—
CROWD: This is a boot, this is a hoot, this is a root, this is a foot . . .
WOMAN: This is a body—your body—
185 CROWD: This is a body, this is a body, this is a body your body, this is your body is a body is a body is your body your . . .
WOMAN: (*Shakes her head, gesturing more slowly and still being patient.*) My hand—my body—my foot—this is me.
CROWD: My band, my hand, my body, my coot, my hand's
190 body's foot's my coot's hand's foot's body this is my hand's foot's body is meat!
WOMAN: Say, me—
CROWD: Say me say me say me say me say me!
WOMAN: (*Shakes her head and points to herself, from her eyes to
195 her mouth, and from her body to her feet.*) Me.
CROWD: (*Together at last.*) Me.
WOMAN: Good!
CROWD: Food! Hood! Good! Wood!
WOMAN: (*At once she waves her hand in disagreement. After
200 thinking for a moment, she points at one person among the crowd.*) You.
CROWD: (*All pointing at* THE PERSON.) You!
THE PERSON: (*He looks around him and then points at himself.*) You!
205 WOMAN: (*Shakes her head and helps him to point his finger at someone else.*) You.
CROWD: You.
WOMAN: (*Gesturing.*) Me and you.
CROWD: Me and you.
210 WOMAN: (*Laughs.*) Good!
CROWD: (*Also laugh.*) Good!

(*Music. Gradually the tempo of the music becomes faster.*)

WOMAN: Me and him!
CROWD: Me and him!
WOMAN: Them and me.
215 CROWD: Them and me.
WOMAN: Me and you.

CROWD: Me and you.
WOMAN: You and us.
CROWD: You and us.
WOMAN: Now follow me when you're seeing with your 220 eyes—
CROWD: See—
WOMAN: Tell me, who do you see?
CROWD: (*One after another.*) See him, see you, see me, see them, they see you, you see us, we see them . . . 225
WOMAN: Now say touch, give, like, and love, and you won't feel lonely any more.
CROWD: (*Becoming active.*) I touch you, you give me, I like him, he loves you, you touch me, I give him, he likes you, you love me . . . 230

(MAN *comes out from among the* CROWD.)

MAN: Who are you?
WOMAN: I'm one of you.
MAN: Where are we now?
WOMAN: The other shore, which we wanted to reach but 235 couldn't.
MAN: Are you the same person who drowned while we were crossing the river? (WOMAN *shakes her head.*) Are you her soul? (WOMAN *still shakes her head.*) Have you been hiding in our thoughts, do you appear only when we think of you? Or are you something like a kind of consciousness? 240 Did you guide us to the other shore so that we wouldn't get lost?
CROWD: (*At the same time.*) I detest you.
   You touched me!
   I'll beat you up! 245
   You hate me?
   I'll torture her.
   He cheats on me.
   You're swearing at him!
   I'll tell on you. 250
   You punish him!
   He plots against me!
   I hate you!
   You curse him!
   I'll kill you . . . 255
MAN: (*To* WOMAN.) You're so kind.
CROWD: (*Turn to face* WOMAN *one after another, playing with words.*)
   You're so generous.
   You're so lovely. 260
   You're so despicable.
   He's a bastard.
   You don't say what you mean, you're a crook.
   You're a double-dealing no-good tramp!
   She butters you up, but she's actually jealous of you. 265
   You're snaky, you teach us words so that you can talk to our men and seduce them!
   You may look so kind and gentle, but who knows if you're a whore or not?
   She's trying to seduce our husbands! 270
   Stirring up trouble among our brothers.
   A buttered bun, look, just look at her—
   Keep the girls away from her, she'll turn them into whores.

275   She may look prim and proper, but she's really more cor-
       rupt than a common whore.
       She's the one, she makes people panic, there'll be no more
       peace in this world.

(WOMAN *draws back as the* CROWD *surrounds her from all sides.*
They are excited by their own increasingly venomous language. She
cannot escape from the stares of the CROWD, *so she turns to* MAN
for help and hangs on to him.)

       CROWD: (*Getting more angry.*)
280   Whore!
       Venomous snake!
       Witch!
       Shameless slut!

(WOMAN *holds on to* MAN *and pleads for his protection. The*
CROWD *go wild.*)

       CROWD: Look, go and take a look!
285   Pooh!
       Dump her!
       Drag her away!
       Get a hold of her!
       Strip her!
290   Wring her neck! The shameless whore!

(*The* CROWD *drag her away from* MAN *and jump on her. In the con-*
fusion they strangle her to death. When MAN *pushes his way into*
the CROWD *and shakes her body, there is no response.*) (*Witnessing*
this, the CROWD *is stunned.*)

       CROWD: Dead.
       Dead?
       Dead?
       She's dead!

(*The* CROWD *disperse in a hurry.*)

295   Was she strangled to death?
       It's you—
       No, he started it.
       You shouted first!
       I was only following you, you were all shouting.
300   Who shouted first? Who?
       Who shouted first to grab her, strip her and strangle her?
       Who?
       We all shouted.
       I shouted because you did.
305   I shouted because all of you were shouting.
       But she's dead! Strangled alive!
       I didn't kill her.
       I didn't kill her.
       I didn't kill her.
310   I didn't kill her.
       I didn't kill her.
       I didn't.
       I didn't.
       Didn't.
315   Didn't.
       Didn't.

But she's dead for sure, so lovely even when she's dead.
So beautiful, nobody could help loving her.
Her skin is like jade, it's got no blemishes, it's so pure.
Look at her pretty little hands, they've got her endless ten-   320
derness in them.
My, she's like a statue of the Bodhisattva!
So pure, so prim and proper.
She gave us language, she brought us wisdom, but she was
murdered!   325
This is the greatest sin of all, you despicable lot!
Who are you talking about?
Murderers! You, all of you!
How dare you smear me? You bastard!
You're a thug!
You're a rascal!   330

(*The* CROWD *fight among themselves.*)

MAN: Are you finished? We killed her, there's no question
    about it. It's you, it's him, it's me, and it's all of us. We're
    all in it together! On this desolate other shore, she gave us
    language, but we didn't know how to cherish it; she gave   335
    us wisdom, but we didn't know how to use it! We ought
    to be shocked by what we did, but we're cowards, we're
    too spineless to feel any shame.
CROWD: What do you think we should do?
    We need a leader, a flock of sheep also needs a leader.   340
    We'll follow you.
MAN: I detest you, I detest myself. It's better for us to go our
    separate ways.
CROWD: No, don't abandon us.
    We've made up our mind to follow you, and you want to   345
    leave us?
MAN: Follow me where? Where can I lead you? (*He leaves by*
    himself. The CROWD *follow behind.*) Don't follow me! (*Trou-*
    bled.) I don't even know where I want to go myself. (*Stops*
    and tries to figure out where to go. The CROWD *still follow him* 350
    at a distance.)

(MOTHER *appears in front of him.*)

MOTHER: Do you still remember me?
MAN: Yes, mother.
MOTHER: You've almost forgotten me, haven't you?
MAN: (*On his knees.*) Yes, mother.   355
MOTHER: (*Stroking his head.*) Find yourself a girl, you really
    should start a family.
MAN: But I want to make something of myself.
MOTHER: You're too ambitious.
MAN: (*Looks down.*) I'm still your son.   360
MOTHER: Are they all following you? Where are you going to
    take them?
MAN: I don't know. I only know we should go forward, is that
    right, mother?
MOTHER: My good son. (*Embraces his head.*)   365
MAN: Your hands are cold! (*Shocked by his discovery.*) Mother,
    is this the world of the dead? Am I in another dimension?
MOTHER: There's nothing to be scared of, son. It's just a bit
    dark, a bit cold and damp, that's all.
MAN: (*Leaves her.*) How do I get out of here? Mother, I   370
    haven't lived long enough!

(MOTHER *turns and disappears. He hesitates for a moment and then follows in a hurry. A* YOUNG GIRL *blocks his way.*)

MAN: Who are you? I've seen you somewhere, but I can't re-call your name. It seems like we used to live on the same street or something, many years ago. Every day on my way
375 to school I always hoped that I could catch a glimpse of you, even if it's only your back. My heart would keep on pounding whenever I saw your long ponytail and your crimson red dress, you seemed to be wearing that crimson dress all that time. . . . I used to follow you, follow you
380 right to your doorsteps, hoping that when you turned around to close the door, you'd at least say one word to me before you went inside, or smile at me just once. But every time you'd only look at me, saying nothing. Oh, I can see those eyes of yours again . . . (*He rubs his eyes and*
385 *looks more closely, but she has disappeared into the dark shadows of the* CROWD.)

(*To the* CROWD.) We've got to get out of this ghastly place. Once we're away from this darkness we'll find light ahead of us. With the light there'll be houses, and we'll be
390 able to dry our clothes around the stove and drink some hot tea. (*Incitingly.*) We'd be able to return to our homes, see our families, our wives and husbands, our children and parents, and all our loved ones and those who love us!

(YOUNG GIRL *appears again from behind the* CROWD.)
395 Who are you?

(*Blocking her way.*) Wait, your name is on the tip of my tongue! It seems like I used to write poetry for you, that we used to go to the movies together and I held your hand in the dark, those tiny frail hands of yours . . . (*She*
400 *turns and gets away from his grasp. She is now behind him, be-coming more illusory. He turns around but cannot see her, no matter how hard he tries.*)

She always appeared in my dreams to torment me whenever I was worried and couldn't set my mind free. I
405 couldn't recall her name, I couldn't see her face clearly, I couldn't even get hold of her presence in any way, but she still kept on tormenting me.

(*Speaking to the shadowy* CROWD.) Why do you keep fol-lowing me? I need some peace and quiet, I need to be
410 alone! I don't need to be stared at by a crowd, I don't need you, just as you don't need me. What you need is someone who can guide you, to show you the way, even though once you've found a way out, or think you have, you'd put on a spurt, darting away faster than rabbits. And you'd
415 abandon your guide without even taking a second look, just like throwing away a worn-out shoe. I understand, I understand it only too well. You've all experienced loving and being loved, possessing and being possessed. I, too, have a right to be in love, to love a woman and to possess a
420 woman, and to be loved and possessed by her. I'm human just like you are, so full of desires and ambitions, I'm what you may call a career-minded man, a man who is compet-itive yet extremely weak sometimes, and a man who is righteous, compassionate, willing to sacrifice himself and
425 . . . (*He rolls on the ground and wails loudly like a fretting and self-indulgent child.*)

(*The* CROWD *is stunned. When* MAN *has had enough wailing and is totally exhausted, he settles down and gets up from the floor. He*

continues *his way forward and the* CROWD *follow silently behind him. A faint light in the dark becomes brighter. A man is seen drink-ing and playing cards alone under an oil lamp.* MAN *mimes knock-ing on the door. The* CROWD *clap their hands three times.*)

MAN: Sorry to bother you.
CARD PLAYER: (*Without lifting his head.*) Come in. Take a seat.
MAN: May I ask—
CARD PLAYER: (*Tosses a card from his hand. Looks up.*) You play 430 cards?
MAN: I've played before.

(*The* CROWD *try to squeeze in through the door.*)

CARD PLAYER: Come in, come in. Do you all want to play cards? Close the door for me. I hate draughts, they make the light flicker, which is bad for a card player's eyes. Al- 435 right, let's form a circle, I'll be the banker here. All of you will each take a card, and I'll take one myself, only one, just like you. That's only fair. The card in my hand will be the trump, there's got to be a trump, right? And it's bet-ter if I choose the trump card instead of you, it's more 440 convenient that way. (*Turns over his card.*) My card is the two of spades. I'm not trying to fly low, luck is all you need when you're playing cards. Now if you pick a spade, any spade, you'd have a higher number than mine and I'd be the loser and you'd be the winner. But if you didn't 445 pick a spade, you'd lose no matter what, it doesn't matter which card you've picked. You got me?
MAN: What happens if one wins or loses?
CARD PLAYER: The winner gets to drink the wine in this pot.
MAN: And the loser? 450
CARD PLAYER: There'll be a penalty.
MAN: I have no money, no land, no property, and no wife.
CARD PLAYER: But you do have a face, haven't you?
MAN: I don't get it.
CARD PLAYER: You'll find out soon enough. All of you, any- 455 one who loses will stick a piece of paper on his face for me.
CROWD: That's easy enough.
   How big is the paper?
   Any paper?
   The thing is, have you really got wine in your pot? 460
CARD PLAYER: Have a taste first.
CROWD: It's good.
   What aroma!
   Of course, it's the real thing.
   Let me have a sip. 465
   It's worth playing for.
CARD PLAYER: In a moment you'll pick your cards. I've shown you my card, all of you have seen it, right? Now you can only look at your own card, no ganging up, that's a no-no. 470
CROWD: (*Eager to pick their cards.*)
   That's nothing, it's fine with me.
   We should play our own games.
   Don't worry, I won't look even if you let me.
   Me, I'm honesty personified. 475
   Integrity comes first, winning and losing second.
   Hear! Hear!

(*Those who have picked their cards are silent.*)

CARD PLAYER: (*To the person who picks first.*) Show me your card. You lose.

480 THIS PERSON: (*Nods.*) What's the penalty?

(CARD PLAYER *takes a piece of paper and spits on it. He sticks the paper onto the cheek of* THIS PERSON, *who mutters something. The* CROWD *watch and laugh.* THIS PERSON *is relieved and laughs with them.*)

CARD PLAYER: (*Turns to another person.*) My friend, how about you? (THAT PERSON *shows his card.*) You lose too.

THAT PERSON: Well, give it to me.

CARD PLAYER: Stick it under your chin.

(THAT PERSON *takes a piece of paper, spits on it, and sticks it under his chin. He is somewhat embarrassed, but when he sees the* CROWD *laughing, he is himself again.*)

485 THIRD PERSON (FEMALE): It's fun.

CARD PLAYER: (*Turns towards her.*) And you? (*She shows her card and hurriedly takes it back.*)

CROWD: Did you win?
You won!

490 Did you really win?
(*She frets demurely and shakes her head.*)
Why aren't you sticking the paper on your face?
Stick the paper on, stick it on!
Come on, it's the rule, no exceptions allowed.

495 If you don't stick it on, we won't either.

THIRD PERSON (FEMALE): It's too embarrassing.

CROWD: You think we're not?
That won't do. Stick it on the ear.
Right, on the ear.

500 Stick it on the nose!
It must be different with everybody, okay? No repetitions.
Everybody gets one.

(*When the* CARD PLAYER *looks at someone, the person will show his card and then obediently stick a piece of paper on his face.*)

CROWD: (*Sticking paper to their own faces.*)
Fair and square.

505 No doubt about that.
Nobody tells you to lose, but when you do, you've got to take what comes.
Everyone gets a penalty, everyone sticks a paper on their face.

510 If you haven't got a paper on your face, you'll look odd and out of place, and people will be afraid of you.

(*The strange-looking, papered faces all turn towards* MAN.)

CARD PLAYER: My friend, it's your turn now.

MAN: I don't play.

CARD PLAYER: Everybody plays, why don't you?

515 MAN: I find the whole thing very silly. What's more, I've got to go.

CROWD: Yes, that's right. We should all be going.
Don't go by yourself.
Where are we going?

520 Right, where exactly are we going?

MAN: In any case I've got to go.

CARD PLAYER: I've got the whole place lit up and I've prepared wine. I went through all these troubles just to play

cards with you people. I've never heard of anyone who comes here and leaves without playing. You shouldn't 525 have come in the first place!

CROWD: (*Stopping Man.*) Play!
Come on, be a good sport. Don't be such a party popper.
Just play one game. Just one.
Play once and then we'll go. 530

MAN: Don't you understand? You're not really playing cards, he's playing a trick on you. You can't win. Your card, yours, and yours are all no trumps, including all the cards still in the deck. The only spade in the deck is in his hand!
(CARD PLAYER *giggles.*) Let's go! Why waste our time on 535 this guy.

CARD PLAYER: There is no such thing as time here. (*He blows on the oil lamp and the light flickers, and it gradually turns brighter again.*) There is only eternal light. (*He takes the lamp and shines on everyone from below the chin. The papered faces* 540 *look like gargoyles.*) I'm a sucker for big crowds. You're scared, aren't you?

MAN: You're a devil.

CARD PLAYER: Why don't you try feeling their arses? They've all got a bristly tail down there! (*He points to the* CROWD's 545 *bottoms and laughs out loud. Then he pushes a deck of cards in front of* MAN.) Take a card! Let everyone see if it's a spade or no trumps? (*Turns over a no trump card and flashes it in front of the* CROWD.) What is it, is it a spade or not?

PERSON A: I can't really tell. 550

CARD PLAYER: What'd you say?

PERSON B: It looked like—

CARD PLAYER: You must have seen it clearly.

PERSON C: I think I saw a—spade.

CARD PLAYER: That's right! Young lady, what do you think? 555

OBEDIENT GIRL: Spades.

CARD PLAYER: That a girl. You've made my day. Old Sir, how about you?

PERSON D: Spades, how can it not be spades?

CARD PLAYER: Bless you. (*Suddenly explodes.*) How can we let 560 him bullshit us like this and tell us that they're all no trumps? Huh?

CROWD: It's spades.
Of course it's spades. It can't be anything else.
No mistake about it. 565
We all saw it.
We're all witnesses!

CARD PLAYER: You heard what they said, didn't you? Why did you lie, why did you insist that a spade is no trump? You're scared, aren't you? Have you ever tried eating rat meat? A 570 bouncing baby rat, its hair not fully grown and its eyes unopened, the little creature still squeaking when you dip it in the sauce and put it in your mouth, ready for a bite? If you had, then you'd be brave enough to tell the truth. My friend, I'm gonna give you one more chance to tell the 575 truth. Tell me, was it spades or a no trump?

MAN: I think . . . that's still a no trump.

CARD PLAYER: You're no fun, you make people miserable. Tell me, people, is this guy bad or what?

CROWD: (*Passing the wine pot and taking sips one after another.*) 580 Bad, bad, bad, bad, bad, bad, bad, bad . . .

CARD PLAYER: (*Takes the wine from them.*) What shall we do with this bad guy?

CROWD: (*Surround* MAN.) Throw him out!

585　Tell him to get out of here!
　　　Trouble-maker.
　　　A real pest.
　　　When he's here, we've got no wine to drink.
　　　Teach him a lesson!
590　Spank him!
　　　Strip him!
　　　Take off his pants!

(*The* CROWD *try to take off* MAN's *pants.*)

CARD PLAYER: I'm gonna give you a second chance. Think
　　　clearly. Think again!
595　MAN: (*Holding up his pants.*) But I remember . . . it looked like
　　　a . . . no trump.

(CARD PLAYER *tucks the wine pot under his arm and turns away.*
The CROWD *pull at* MAN *as if they were teasing a bird.*)

CROWD: Tell him to fly!
　　　What? What did you say?
　　　Fly like a bird!
600　Men are not birds, why should they learn to fly like birds?
　　　Wow, it's so fun!
　　　Fly!
　　　Lower your head, let your arms fly!
CARD PLAYER: My friend, I refuse to believe that you're a
605　stubborn man.
OBEDIENT GIRL: (*Takes pity on* MAN.) You can't turn a spade
　　　into a no trump. What's with you? Please, try to take hold
　　　of yourself.
MAN: Maybe it was really a spade . . .
610　OBEDIENT GIRL: Then why did you say it was a no trump?
MAN: I think it should be . . .
OBEDIENT GIRL: But what should be is not necessarily the
　　　truth.
CARD PLAYER: You're a loser because you're a pighead. What
615　do you mean by "should be"? It either is or isn't. To hell
　　　with "should be."
MAN: But why can't we have "should be"?
CARD PLAYER: (*Irritated.*) Should be my foot! What do you
　　　say, should be or not should be?
620　CROWD: (*Immediately tear at* MAN.) We don't want any "should
　　　be"!
　　　We want "yes" or "no"!
　　　We want spades, not no trumps!
　　　Down with no trumps!
625　Spades are the best!
MAN: It . . . seemed . . . like a . . . sp . . .
CROWD: (*Beating their chests and stamping their feet.*) Speak up!
　　　Louder!
　　　Can't hear you!
630　You've got to clear this up!
MAN: Sp . . . Spa . . . It's spades . . . (*On his knees and collapses.*)

(*The* CROWD *surround* CARD PLAYER *and perform a strange and*
awkward dance. They exit.

A woman dressed in a white cotton skirt appears. She covers MAN
with her skirt, bends down and wraps herself in it as well. The two
form a white object which disappears with the gradually approaching
drumbeat. The drumbeat builds up into a heart-thumping bang. A

scrawny monk comes out jumping and beating a gigantic drum with
his fingers, palms, elbows, and knees as if he were bewitched. ZEN
MASTER *enters, dressed in a Buddhist robe of kasaya, his hands*
clasped together and his right shoulder bare. Other monks and nuns,
all cloaked in grey kasaya, follow ZEN MASTER *onto the stage. The*
CROWD *enter in a single file, chanting "Amitabha" as they come.*
Their chanting is not in any particular order, each singing their own
tune and at their own pitch. The chanting comes and goes, combin-
ing with the drumbeat into a cacophony of intersecting sounds. MAN
is following the CROWD; *he also chants and looks around him at*
times. The CROWD *all put down a futon, on which they sit with*
their legs crossed. MAN *does same. The drum stops, followed by the*
sound of a wooden fish★ and an inverted bell.)

ZEN MASTER: (*Recites the Vajraccedika prajna paramita sutra,*
　　　his palms clasped together and his right knee on the ground.)
　　　" . . . How much the Bodhisattvas, the great beings, have
　　　been helped with the greatest help by the Tathagata, the　635
　　　Fully Enlightened One. It is wonderful, O Lord, how
　　　much the Bodhisattvas, the great beings, have been
　　　favoured with the highest favour by the Tathagata, the
　　　Fully Enlightened One. How then, O Lord, should good
　　　men and women stand, who seek the supreme wisdom,　640
　　　how progress, how control their thoughts?"
　　　　After these words the Lord said to the Venerable Sub-
　　　huti: "Well said, well said, Subhuti! So it is, Subhuti, so it
　　　is as you say! The Tathagata has helped the Bodhisattvas,
　　　the great beings with the greatest help, and he has　645
　　　favoured them with the highest favour. Therefore, Sub-
　　　huti, listen well, and attentively! . . ."

(*Incense smoke permeates the whole place during the chanting. The*
CROWD *close their eyes in meditation, and* MAN *gradually does so*
as well. YOUNG GIRL *appears, her eyes slightly closed. She is squat-*
ting in a corner and doing her mental exercise, like a baby who is
sleeping not too tightly in a transparent egg shell, its hands and feet
pressed against the four walls of the shell. YOUNG MAN, *who has*
been hiding behind her, gets up slowly and walks towards YOUNG
GIRL *in gingerly steps. The chanting gradually fades. The* CROWD
disappear.)

ZEN MASTER: (*The sound of chanting can still be heard faintly.*)
　　　"Monks of the Buddha, nuns of the Buddha, I will teach
　　　you how they should stand, who seek the supreme wis-　650
　　　dom, how progress, how control their thoughts."
　　　　"So be it, O Lord. With a joyful heart we long to
　　　hear," the Venerable Subhuti replied to the Lord.
　　　　The Lord said: "Here, Subhuti, someone who seeks
　　　supreme wisdom should produce a thought in this man-　655
　　　ner . . ."

(YOUNG MAN *stretches his hand to touch* YOUNG GIRL's *fingers.*
Surprised, she wakes and withdraws her hand immediately.)

YOUNG GIRL: Stop it!
YOUNG MAN: Are you doing your mental exercise?
YOUNG GIRL: Yes.
YOUNG MAN: May I ask what kind of exercise are you doing?　660

★A percussion instrument made of a hollow wooden block, used
by Buddhist priests to make rhythm while chanting scriptures.

YOUNG GIRL: They say it's called Small Circular Heaven.

YOUNG MAN: Is there a Big Circular Heaven as well?

YOUNG GIRL: I don't know.

665 YOUNG MAN: You're doing something you don't know anything about?

YOUNG GIRL: (*Nervously.*) Stop interrogating me! Just stop it!

YOUNG MAN: (*Mischievously.*) Then perhaps you don't know what's the use of this exercise? (*Grabs her hand.*)

YOUNG GIRL: No, don't, you can't do that—

670 YOUNG MAN: Why not?

YOUNG GIRL: I'm scared . . .

YOUNG MAN: What's there to be scared of?

YOUNG GIRL: Don't touch me!

YOUNG MAN: What if I do?

675 YOUNG GIRL: Then I'd feel the pain.

YOUNG MAN: So you don't feel any pain right now?

YOUNG GIRL: (*Painfully.*) I can't say for sure . . .

YOUNG MAN: (*Grabs her hand by force.*) Then for once I'll let you feel the pain!

680 YOUNG GIRL: (*Begging him and trying to struggle free.*) Oh no, don't . . . (FATHER *enters carrying an umbrella. The chanting* ZEN MASTER *and the meditating* CROWD *have all disappeared. Only* MAN *is left sitting on the futon with his eyes closed.*)

YOUNG MAN: Father!

685 FATHER: Don't get into trouble. Come home with me, now!

(FATHER *drags* YOUNG MAN *along.*)

(YOUNG GIRL *disappears.*)

YOUNG MAN: (*Turns back to look. Nonchalantly.*) Why? It's not raining.

FATHER: I tell you it will.

YOUNG MAN: But it's not raining now.

690 FATHER: It'll be too late if it does.

YOUNG MAN: What if it doesn't.

FATHER: It's going to rain sooner or later! Look, what do you think I've brought my umbrella for?

YOUNG MAN: You've brought it because you have nothing

695 else to do.

FATHER: I've been carrying an umbrella all my life!

YOUNG MAN: You've brought it upon yourself.

FATHER: How dare you talk to your father like that?

YOUNG MAN: Fine, I won't say anything then.

700 FATHER: Get away from me! Go as far as you possibly can! Don't even bother coming back to see me. I don't have a son like you! (*Exits angrily.*)

(YOUNG MAN *is bewildered.* MAN *is still sitting on the futon meditating. The sound of chanting approaches, but there is no sign of* ZEN MASTER.)

CHANTING SOUND: The Buddha said: Here, subhuti, someone

705 who seeks supreme wisdom should produce a thought in this manner: "As many beings as there are in the universe of beings, comprehended under the term 'beings'—egg-born, born from a womb, moisture-born, or miraculously born; with or without form; with perception, without perception,—as far as any conceivable form of beings is

710 conceived: all these I must lead to Nirvana, into that Realm of Nirvana which leaves nothing behind. . . ."

(YOUNG MAN *turns and finds a wall of people behind him. He tries unsuccessfully to find a way to get over it.* OLD LADY *comes out from a crack in the "wall."*)

OLD LADY: Young man, do you want to go over there?

YOUNG MAN: I just want to take a look.

OLD LADY: Look, look. Everybody wants to take a look. Do you have any money?

715 YOUNG MAN: (*He searches all his pockets and finally takes out a coin.*) Here.

OLD LADY: (*Laughs out loud.*) You want to take care of me with this? Don't you have anything valuable on you at all? Something your mother gave you, for example?

720 YOUNG MAN: (*Suddenly understands.*) I've got this fountain pen, it has a gold nib, my mother gave it to me for my birthday. (*Takes the pen out and hands it over to her.*)

OLD LADY: (*Takes the pen and inspects it carefully.*) Hmm, this is quite nice. (*Stuffs the pen into her waist bag and steps aside to*

725 *reveal a crack in the "wall."*) Now you can go ahead.

YOUNG MAN: (*Hesitating.*) I'm afraid my mother might find out . . .

OLD LADY: Will she beat you?

YOUNG MAN: I . . . I can't say . . .

730 OLD LADY: You'll just have to lie to her, tell her that you've lost it. Don't you know how to lie?

YOUNG MAN: Mother wouldn't allow it.

OLD LADY: That's why you're still such a kid. I'm telling you, there's no adult who doesn't lie, and you know, without

735 lying there'd be no more happy days. All right, just go right through.

(*Crawling,* YOUNG MAN *goes through the crack of the wall of people. When he looks up he sees* YOUNG GIRL *sobbing quietly on the other side, her hands covering her face. He tries to get up, but two thugs approach and take turns beating him up.* YOUNG GIRL *and the sound of chanting disappear at the same time. Only* MAN *is left sitting on the futon and meditating with his eyes closed.*)

PLASTER SELLER: Dogskin Plasters! Dogskin Plasters! Thirteen generations in the family. Give me internal wounds,

740 external wounds, fractures, strains and contusions, give me rabies, heart-attacks, infant convulsions, geriatric strokes, lovesick young men and women, unspeakable depravity and the possessed, stick one on and you'll be as good as new. The first don't work, the second will. . . . Dogskin

745 Plasters! Dogskin Plasters! Taken junky home remedy? Swallowed the wrong drug? No problem! Infertile women, impotent men, sinners and delinquents? Sure thing! Oh yes, and the stutterers, the crooked mouthed, jealous women, avenging men, fathers who love not the

750 mothers, sons who listen not to their old men, pock-marked faces, tinea feet, one plaster cures all. The first don't work, the second will. Satisfaction guaranteed or your money gladly refunded. . . . Dogskin Plasters! Come and get the miracle Dogskin Plasters! Don't miss this

755 golden opportunity! Your chance in a life time!

(YOUNG MAN, *on the outside of the* CROWD'*s circle, finally manages to get up from his feet.* MAD WOMAN *enters.*)

MAD WOMAN: (*Approaching* YOUNG MAN.) They say I'm a whore, but they didn't say anything when they sneaked

into my bed to sleep with me. They say I'm bad as if they haven't been bad before, as if they haven't had fun with a
760   woman's body before!

(YOUNG MAN *retreats and hides himself from her. The* CROWD *turn to face them.*)

CROWD: Here comes the mad woman.
       The mad woman's here!
       The mad woman's here!
MAD WOMAN: You're mad!
765   CROWD: Look, look at her.
       She's talking crazy again.
MAD WOMAN: You're talking crazy.

(*The* CROWD *happily break out in laughter.*)

PLASTER SELLER: (*At the same time.*) If you've got money, give me money, if you don't, stay and watch the show! Dogskin
770   Plasters for sale! (*Throws a bundle of plasters on the ground.*) Big sacrifice! Everything must go! Pay what you will. Cheap! Cheap! Cheap! . . . Pooh! You stinking whore! (*Puts away plasters and exits.*)
MAD WOMAN: You're cheap! (*The* CROWD *laugh at her again.*)
775   What are you laughing at? Go laugh at yourselves! What things you wouldn't do to get into a woman's pants! You all look like you're human, but actually you're all dogs, dogs, dirty dogs.
MEN IN CROWD: (*To women in the* CROWD.) Stop her wagging
780   tongue.
       Take her away.
MAD WOMAN: Why? You're scared because I'll tell on you, right? You're hiding something, aren't you? Right, keep away from me, as far away as you can. I know exactly what's
785   going on in those shitty little heads of yours. (*Snickers.*)
MEN IN CROWD: Take her away! Take her away!

(WOMEN *in the* CROWD *come forward to drag* MAD WOMAN *away.*)

MAD WOMAN: You're afraid too, aren't you? You're afraid I'll say that all of your husbands, every single one of them, have slept with me? Afraid because you'll become like me,
790   dumped by your men after they've gotten their rocks off? Afraid your husbands will know you've screwed other men? Afraid people will find out you'd lost your cherry before you got married?
CROWD: Gag her!
795   With horse shit!
       With bull shit!
       Shut her big mouth!
MAD WOMAN: (*Grappling with* WOMEN *in the* CROWD.) Haven't you got off with a man before? You're like me,
800   you can't take your hands off your men after they've screwed you . . .

(*The* CROWD *move forward to tie up* MAD WOMAN *with ropes and gag her mouth. Crying and wailing, she becomes hysterical, but is finally dragged away by the* CROWD. YOUNG MAN *watches in astonishment and leaves with the* CROWD. MAN, *who has been sitting and meditating on the futon, also disappears at the same time. Immediately afterwards, he returns from the other side with his* SHADOW. SHADOW *is dressed in black and has on black headgear*

which covers his face. MAN and SHADOW do not look at each other. They talk only to themselves, but their steps and movements are synchronized.*)

MAN: A seed falls on to the soil—
SHADOW: A child is born onto the world—
MAN: A gust of wind blows through the forest—
SHADOW: A horse gallops on the plateau—   805
MAN: A grain of sand falls into the eye—
SHADOW: An eye is crying tears—
MAN: The tears fall on the parched desert—
SHADOW: Like entering a bustling marketplace—
MAN: People squashing people, but their eyes can't be seen—   810
SHADOW: Seeing dead fish one by one—
MAN: That's a lonely city—
SHADOW: Pop singers are yelling and screaming to exhaustion—
MAN: Only the stars can hear the wind chimes ringing—   815
SHADOW: It is not our hearts that are ringing—
MAN: It's the electric guitars picking your nerves—
SHADOW: You jump three times, nine times, eight times, seven times and you're out of breath—
MAN: Just because you're no hero—   820
SHADOW: More like a popular and low-minded farce—
MAN: An out-of-tune trumpet blows, blows, blows, blows and blows—
SHADOW: The conductor has to be right—
MAN: Everyone says he's 180% painful—   825
SHADOW: Only one minute's happiness—
MAN: It's not the time for drinking beer—
SHADOW: Chicago Nuremberg—
MAN: Once there was a war—
SHADOW: Only sparrows were killed—   830
MAN: Soldiers didn't fight, they only stood on guard—
SHADOW: And those standing on guard got to wear medals—
MAN: Who is the person speaking to me?
SHADOW: It is your shadow, your thoughts spoken out loud—
MAN: You're always following me—   835
SHADOW: When you have lost your self—
MAN: You'll come and remind me and double my trouble?
SHADOW: What are you looking for so desperately?
MAN: Now that you've reminded me! I've definitely lost something, can you tell me where to look for it?   840
SHADOW: (*Sarcastically.*) You probably do not know what you are looking for?
MAN: It appears to be . . . isn't everyone looking for it?

(*The* CROWD *enter. They form a circle and bend down to look for something in the circle, like children at play.*)

SHADOW: It would not hurt to ask them what you are looking for. (*Takes the chance to leave and disappear.*)   845
MAN: Excuse me, are you looking for—
PERSON A: A needle, they say you can lead a camel through the eye of this needle.
MAN: (*To another person.*) Excuse me, can you tell me what you're looking for?   850
PERSON B: Looking for a place where I can sit comfortably and securely. Once I'm there, I won't leave the seat ever again. (*Whispering.*) I have haemorrhoids, I can't sit on any wooden bench.

855   MAN: And, what are you looking for?

PERSON C: (*Stuttering.*) I . . . I . . . I am . . . looking for a . . . a . . . mouth . . . which can . . . s . . . s . . . peak . . . for me. I . . . I . . . have to s . . . s . . . speak a lot . . . of . . . of . . . words ev . . . every . . . every day.

860   MAN: And you, young man?

PERSON D: I'm looking for a rice bowl! You have everything, but I don't even have a rice bowl!

MAN: Of course, I know, I know it's very important to have a rice bowl. Go for it. Keep looking. (*To another person.*)

865   Excuse me, I didn't do it on purpose. (*Removes his foot.*) What are you looking for?

PERSON E: I'm looking for a pair of shoes that fits. I don't know why my shoes pinch. I want to know—

MAN: I'm also looking for—

870   PERSON E: Do your shoes pinch too?

MAN: My shoes don't pinch, but I don't know where my feet should be going.

PERSON E: You just have to follow other people's footsteps.

MAN: Are you also looking for other people's footsteps?

875   PERSON F: (*Laughing playfully.*) I'm looking for a hole I can sneak through without anyone noticing me. And then I'll come out on the other side swaggering.

MAN: How about you, my friend? You don't look like the sneaky type.

880   PERSON G: You're right.

MAN: Can you tell me what are you looking for?

PERSON G: Looking for my childhood dream.

MAN: It must be a very beautiful dream. (*To another.*) And you? Are you looking for a dream too?

885   PERSON H: No, I'm looking for a sentence.

MAN: Are you writing a poem?

PERSON H: Everybody can write poetry, just like everybody knows how to make love.

MAN: Then you're—

890   PERSON H: Thinking! Everyone's got a mind, but not everyone can think.

MAN: You're right. What you're looking for must be an epigram.

PERSON H: I'm not sure if it's an epigram. The problem is, if

895   I didn't find this sentence my thoughts would be cut off, and thoughts which have been cut off are like a cut-off kite, you'll never be able to retrieve it again. Without a sentence you just can't think, because thinking is like a chain, each ring is linked to the next one. You under-

900   stand?

MAN: Young lady, how about you? What are you looking for?

YOUNG LADY: Take a guess.

MAN: It must be something to do with love.

YOUNG LADY: You're so right! I'm waiting for a pair of eyes,

905   tender, profound, and burning with passion—

(*He avoids the young lady, but he bumps into another person.*)

PERSON I: Don't step on my toes!

MAN: Oh, I beg your pardon.

PERSON I: Never seen anyone who walks like you.

MAN: Neither have I. I'm going that way.

910   PERSON I: Everyone's looking here, what are you going to do over there?

MAN: There is nothing I want here.

PERSON I: What are you looking for?

MAN: (*Troubled.*) I don't know what I'm looking for.

PERSON I: Everybody, look! The man is a weirdo, he doesn't   915
know what he's looking for!

PERSON J: He must have found it already.

(*The* CROWD *surround* MAN.)

MAN: No, I haven't. Really I haven't. (*Walks away.*)

STABLE KEEPER: (*Coming out from the* CROWD.) Where are you going?   920

MAN: Over there.

STABLE KEEPER: You haven't found anything yet, right? How come you're going over there?

MAN: I'm not going to look for anything any more. I just want to go over there.   925

STABLE KEEPER: We're all looking here, but you insist on going there.

EVERYBODY: Shall we let him?

CROWD: No!

Absolutely not!   930

He can't go.

Just wait until we've all found it, then you can go.

MAN: Let me explain.

CROWD: There's no need, we already know.

We've been looking, you've been looking, everybody's   935
been looking, but no one's found anything. Why do you want to go there now?

It won't do.

When we say no, we mean no.

If you quit looking and we quit looking, then you can   940
go there. But everybody's still looking right now and you insist on going, of course we won't let you. How can you? If we're going to quit, we should all quit. So if we're going to look, we should all be looking, right?

MAN: I don't have anything to do with you.   945

STABLE KEEPER: My friend, we're treating you like a friend, don't you see? (*To the* CROWD.) Try again to make him understand. Okay, let's start from the beginning.

CROWD: (*One after the other.*) That's to say, yes, no, everybody looks or nobody looks, even if nobody looks or every-   950
body looks, not looking is not the same as not wanting to look, the question is whether we can look and find it—

MAN: What if I don't want to look?

CROWD: You don't want to look, sure, okay, we can't force you to if you don't want to, if you don't want to look, it   955
doesn't mean nobody should look, and if everybody looks then you can't be not looking, nobody looks you don't look no more, everybody wants to look and you don't look, everybody looks for everybody, you don't look for everybody, you don't look and everybody looks, you look   960
or not you don't look everybody looks you look or not nobody looks you look everybody looks—

MAN: (*Can't control himself.*) I'm going my way! I'm not bothering anybody, and nobody's going to bother me, okay?

STABLE KEEPER: I'll give it to you straight: No way! You've   965
found it but we haven't, it just won't wash!

MAN: But I haven't found anything!

STABLE KEEPER: Then keep looking.

MAN: I'm not looking here any more. I—want—to—go—there.   970

STABLE KEEPER: Don't you know the rules here'? We've told you over and over again, why can't you admit that you're wrong and change your ways?

CROWD: What's happening?

975   What's happening?

Son of a bitch, he's looking for trouble!

STABLE KEEPER: Wait, this is no good, it's so uncivilized. If he doesn't want to repent, let him. We won't make it difficult for him. Just tell him to crawl through here. (*Pointing to his*

980   *crotch.*) What do you say?

CROWD: (*Bursting into laughter.*) Wonderful!

(*Silence. Surprisingly,* MAN *crawls through* STABLE KEEPER*'s crotch. The* CROWD *is shocked and disappears.* MAN *picks up a key while he is crawling.* SHADOW *enters immediately.*)

SHADOW: A key? That is correct. You must have been looking for a key like this one. Yes, yes, the key is what you have been looking for!

(MAN *is on his knees, inspecting the key in his hand. He then stands up and walks to centre stage and uses the key to open an imaginary door. He pulls hard on the big and heavy door and manages to open it. He walks inside.* SHADOW *exits. Silence everywhere.*)

985 MAN: (*Inquiring.*) Hello—(*Echo: Hello—hello—hello—hello . . . hello . . .*) Ah—(*Ah—Ah—Ah—Ah . . . Ah . . . Ah . . . The echoes seem to make the room more hollow and deserted.*) Anybody home? (*Echo: Anybody home? Anybody home? Anybody home? Anybody home? Anybody home? . . .*) Nobody has ever

990   set foot in here before for sure . . . (*Echolike murmuring: so lonely, so lonely, so lonely, so lonely.*)

(MAN *looks around and finds that some objects are hidden under the cover of a piece of black cloth. He carefully pulls out a bare woman's arm from under the black cloth.*)

MAN: (*Shocked.*) O—

(*Simulated female voice sighs, echoing: O . . . O . . . O . . . O . . . O. . . . The voice seems to make him more enthusiastic. He begins to clear out what lies beneath the black cloth more diligently, and he pulls out a woman's leg.*)

MAN: (*Excited.*) Ah!

(*There is another series of simulated female voice calling urgently: Ah! Ah! Ah! Ah! Ah! Ah! . . . Finally* MAN *discovers a female mannequin hidden under the black cloth. He lifts the mannequin out and lays it down carefully. He admires it and then starts to move its hands and feet. And with increasing passion and energy, he fiddles with its shoulders, arms and the whole body, bringing it to a rather awkward forward leaning position. He turns the head around, and groping and touching, he manages to create various facial expressions. Every change he makes on the mannequin is accompanied by a simulated female voice akin to mechanical sound. The different expressions on the mannequin's face, including joy, pain, bewilderment, and peaceful staring, are also accompanied by music expressing the same sentiments in a simulated female voice. He puts the head straight so that it is staring at a not-so-distant place in front. . . . Then he stops and tries to figure out what to do next.*)

He becomes more excited now. One by one he pulls out more male and female mannequins and arranges them into a kind of pattern. After thinking for a while, he decides to put a piece of headgear on the first model. He keeps rearranging the pattern, his feet dancing to the beat of the increasingly loud music. The pattern changes according to one or more rules of his own making and at a speed which can only be observed in an instant. Gradually he finds himself hemmed in by the pattern and becomes one of its composite parts, and he crawls busily back and forth in between the mannequins. The process is a sustained and intense consumption of will power and strength.

Now the mannequins form a gigantic collective pattern using the first mannequin as its centre. As they move about, the pattern keeps changing slowly yet unstoppably. MAN runs around in a hurry, jumping, moving, and rolling among his own creations. Highly excited, he calls out and responds to the mannequins in all kinds of non-language shouts and screams. This is a process of constant discovery, renewal, rediscovery, and further renewal. But gradually the objects no longer obey his commands and the sounds they make begin to overwhelm his shouts. As he is totally drawn in among them, he gradually becomes weaker, and it becomes difficult for him to get out. After a long while he finally manages to crawl out like a worm, utterly exhausted. His creations roaringly gyrate past him and slowly disappear.)

(SHADOW *appears again, keeping a certain distance front him.*)

SHADOW: (*Narrates in a serene voice.*) Then winter came along. It was snowing hard that day, and you walked barefoot on 995 the ice to experience the bone-chilling cold. You seemed to feel that you were Jesus Christ, that you were the loneliest person, the only person who was suffering in this world. You felt that you were pervaded by the spirit of self-sacrifice, even though you were not sure for whom 1000 you would be sacrificing yourself. Yes, you did leave your footprints in the snow, and in the distance was a hazy, misty forest.

(*Totally worn out,* MAN *walks into a simulated forest made of human bodies.*)

SHADOW: (*Following him.*) You walked into the dark and shady forest. The trees, every one of them, had already 1005 shed their leaves, stretching out their shaven branches like naked women. Somberly they stood in the snow, lonely and speechless. You could not help wanting to tell them about your sorrows and torments. You recalled the time of your youth, when you waited for her on the roadside 1010 for a long long time. That day it was also snowing, and you were determined to tell her that you loved her. You want to say that at the time you were still young and innocent, but now you have sinned deeply, and you will never be able to go back to those early days any more. 1015 You have long lost your faith in people, your heart has grown old and it will not love again. Your only wish is to go walking among the trees in the forest until you are totally exhausted. Then you will collapse somewhere, hoping never to be found. 1020

(*Finally* MAN *leans against a tree to take a breath.* SHADOW *comes closer and closer, observing him.*)

SHADOW: In fact it is nothing more than a kind of self-pity.
You are unwilling to end like this, you are so vain. (*Exits.*)

(*The tree* MAN *has been leaning against bends down its trunk and speaks in a human-like voice: "Oh, here you are." Then all the trees in the forest move slowly towards him like monsters. They reveal their human forms and become the* CROWD, *all dressed in mourning clothes.*)

CROWD: (*They speak and move, but they are unfeeling and expressionless.*)
1025   We've been looking all over for you.
Come on, take us to the pub to have a drink.
You're our host, how come you're here in the snow?
You're a giant, and we have to look up to see you.
You're famous, so famous that we're scared of you.
1030   We admire you, but we don't want to idolize you.
You're no more than a crook, only we don't have your tricks.
Get up and come with us.
You should donate money to our charities for children,
1035   you must know that children need money the most.
You went through the forest alone, a forest even the devil fears to tread, you're number one.
You're a pathfinder, you've walked out a road nobody wants to walk on, you've led people astray.
1040   You're lucky, not everyone is as lucky as you are.
It's not that you're more talented than the others, it's only that they don't get the chance to show what they've got.
You're the tops, let's us give him a pat on the behind!

(*The* CROWD *laugh coldly and sinisterly. Some start to pull at him and grapple with him.*)

CROWD: (*Suddenly.*) Here he comes!
1045   Talk of the devil.
Make way.

(SHADOW *backs in as the* CROWD *step aside to make way for him.*)

MAN: (*Weakly.*) Who are you?
SHADOW: Your heart.

(*As the* CROWD *watch the drooping, blind, and deaf heart slouching past them,* SHADOW *quietly drags* MAN *away. The* CROWD *slowly follow behind the heart which is extremely old and actually invisible. All exit.*)

(*One by one the* ACTORS *enter from the other side.*)

ACTORS: We set off before dawn. The morning dew was 1050
thick, and in the dark we heard the cows breathing while they were chewing grass on a small hill nearby. In the distance, the river bend was enveloped in a shade of deep blue light brighter than the sky.
He told us a fable.
I dreamed that there's a piece of ivory in my stomach, it 1055
scared me to death!
Have you thought of becoming a bird?
Why a bird? I'm happy with the way I am, and he says he loves me.
Faulkner.   1060
I like "Roses for Emily."
I called you up many times.
Do you know how to read palms?
No need for any explanations, you don't have to explain any more!   1065
This kitten is so cute.
I think I've seen you somewhere.
I have a sweet tooth, and I'm also a sucker for sour milk.
Your hair looks so nice, is it real?

(*The sound of a baby crying.*)

Sweetie, oh, sorry, I forgot to change your diapers!   1070

(*The sound of a car engine starting.*)

How are you going to get back?
It's so bad, what kind of stupid play is this anyway?
Are you doing anything tomorrow? Shall we have dinner together?

(*Sounds of a baby crying, a car engine starting and running, bicycle bells and the trickle of running water from a tap, and in the distance, the siren of an ambulance.*)

The End

Some Suggestions on Producing *The Other Shore*

1. The so-called "spoken drama" (*huaju*) tends to emphasize and highlight the art of language; in order to free drama from its constraints and to revive drama in all its functions as a performing art, we have to provide training for a new breed of modern actors. As with the actors in traditional operas, these new actors must be versatile, and their skills should include singing, the martial arts, stylized movements and delivering dialogues. They should also be able to perform Shakespeare, Ibsen, Chekov, Aristophanes, Racine, Lao She, Cao Yu, Guo Moruo, Goethe, Brecht, Pirandello, Beckett, and even mimes and musicals. The present play is written with the intention of providing an all-around training for the actors.

2. An ideal performance should be a unity of somatics, language, and psychology. Our play is an attempt to pursue this unified artistic expression and to assist the actors to achieve this goal. In other words, we should allow the actors the chance for linguistic expression in their search for suitable somatic movements, so that language and somatics are able to evoke psychological process at the same time. For this reason, during rehearsals and actual performances, it is not advisable to separate dialogue from movement, i.e., to memorize only the dialogue, to do reading as in common practice, or to strip the language and transform the play into a mime. Certain scenes in the play do not feature dialogue, but there are still other aural expressions, which could be regarded as a kind of sound language.

3. Even though our play is abstract, the performance should not aim at sheer conceptualization in the stark fashion of the play of ideas. Our aspiration is to achieve a kind of emotive abstraction through performance, i.e., a non-philosophical abstraction. The play seeks to set up the performance on the premise of non-reality, and to fully mobilize the imagination of the actors before evoking abstraction through emotion. Therefore the performance requires not only the unity of language and somatics but also the unity of thought and psychology.

4. Except for a few simple props, the performance does not require any scenery. The characters' relationships with their surroundings and other objects are contingent upon life-like dialogue and communicative exchanges in the play. In the case of monologues or in the absence of dialogue, music, sound effects, movement, the look of the eyes and changes in posture could also take on performing roles, so that the props and surroundings will not be relegated to being inanimate objects or mere adornments.

5. The play highlights the performance's ability to ascertain in the mind of the audience the existence of non-existing objects, for instance a decrepit heart, a concrete or abstract river. We may say that this is the inherent difference between a film and a theatrical performance. Even though the play itself relies heavily upon imaginary surroundings, relationships and acting partners, real and life-like objects can be deployed as stage props at the beginning of the performance. For instance, an interpersonal relationship could be established through a piece of rope. Once an actor is equipped with the capability to relate with others, he can easily communicate with his non-existent partners anytime, anywhere. He can also materialize his non-existent partners through his power of imagination, making them come to life and communicate with them, even though they have been created through his own imagination and are actually non-existent.

6. Grotowski's training method aims at helping the actor to discover his own self and to release its potential through big-movement exercises which also relax both body and mind. Thus he calls this type of performance a form of sacrifice. Our play's performance helps the actor to ascertain his own self through the process of discover-

ing his partners. If the actor, without being obsessed with his own self, is consistently able to find a partner to communicate with him, his performance will always be positive and lively, and he will be able to gain a real sense of his own self, which has been awakened by action, and which is alert and capable of self-observation.

7. The play demands that the actors abandon completely the kind of performance dependent upon logic and semantic thinking. The liveliest performances are exactly those which are intuitive, improvisational, and on the spur of the moment. On the stage as in real life, the actor sees with his eyes, hears with his ears, and captures his partners' reactions with his free-moving body. In other words, a performance can only be lively without the use of intellect. Therefore it is best not to resort to literary analysis outside of theatrical performance or to uncover hidden meanings in the text in performing the play.

8. Our play aims at training actors who can be as versatile as the actors in Chinese traditional operas, but it is not our intention to create a new set of conventions for modern drama, because the latter aspires to the kind of acting which is non-formulaic, unregulated, and flexible. Before the actual performance, the actor should enter into a state of competitiveness similar to that of an athlete before a game, or of a cock preparing to slug it out in a cock-fight, ready to provoke as well as to receive his partners' reactions. Thus the performance must be fresh, regenerating, and improvisational, which is essentially different from gymnastic or musical performances.

9. The play's performance strives to expand and not to reduce the expressiveness of language in drama. The language in a play is voiced language, but it is not limited to beautifully written dialogue. In this play, all the sounds uttered by the actor in the prescribed circumstances are also voiced language. If an actor has learned to communicate using fragmented language which features unfinished sentences, disjointed phonetic elements, and ungrammatical constructions, he will be better able to make the unspoken words in the script come to life as voiced language.

The above suggestions are for reference only.

Václav Havel

It's not an overstatement to say that Václav Havel's life and career have been defined by the rise of state Socialism in Czechoslovakia after World War II and by the Velvet Revolution of 1989, the revolution that Havel worked to bring about, and that brought him to power as the first president of the Czech Republic in 1993. Born in 1936 into a prominent Prague business family, Havel completed secondary school in 1951 but was banned from higher education by the Communist Party officials: as a child of the pre-war privileged classes, Havel was denied the opportunity to study at the state-supported universities, and instead worked as an apprentice in a chemical laboratory, and eventually studied for two years in a technical university. He worked as a stagehand for the ABC Satire Theater in the late 1950s, and in the meantime he began his career as a writer, first writing for small literary magazines, and then joining the avant-garde Theater of the Balustrade company in 1960 (he was, eventually, also allowed to study at the Prague Academy of Performing Arts, graduating in 1967). Havel wrote a series of brilliant comedies for the theater, plays which deftly rework the arbitrary universe of the theater of the absurd as an image of contemporary Czech life in general, and of the state bureaucracy in particular: *The Garden Party* (1963), *The Memorandum* (1965), and *The Increased Difficulty of Concentration* (1968), among many others. Havel's career, like the career of the modern Czech state, pivots around the Prague Spring of 1968. In that year, fearing that the loosening of cultural and some political restrictions under the leadership of Alexander Dubček would lead Czechoslovakia away from the Eastern bloc, the Soviet Union invaded, sending tanks down the streets of Prague. The invasion galvanized intellectual and artistic opposition, and led to Havel's co-founding of the Charter 77 group, which sent an open letter to the Soviet puppet-leader Gustav Husák protesting the people's loss of freedom. In the course of the next decade, Havel was imprisoned three times, an experience that led to the writing of *The Power of the Powerless* (1978) and *Letters to Olga* (1988), as well as to several new plays, notably *Largo Desolato* (1984), which was dedicated to the playwright Tom Stoppard, who had worked to free Havel and other Czech artists from prison, *Temptation* (1986), and *Tomorrow We Begin* (1988). In 1989, shortly after the fall of the Berlin Wall, Havel founded the Civic Forum, which led the extraordinarily peaceful Velvet Revolution that transformed Czechoslovakia into a democratic state. He was elected as the president of the joint Czech and Slovak Federal Republic in 1990, and when the two countries decided to pursue independent governments, was elected as the president of the Czech Republic in 1993. Havel's complete works were published in a seven-volume edition in 1999.

TEMPTATION

The conception of *Temptation (Pokoušení)* came to Havel when he was first imprisoned in 1977; in a fitting irony, Havel was allowed to read Goethe's *Faust* and Thomas Mann's novel, *Doctor Faustus,* and began to plan a play on the Faust theme. The play was unfinished for nearly a decade, and when Havel completed a final version in the autumn of 1986, he circulated an audiotape version of the play to his friends. By the late 1980s, *Temptation* reached the stage (in a German-language production in Vienna, Austria) and immediately became one of Havel's most popular plays. We can take our bearings on the play from a speech that Havel made at Independence Hall, in Philadelphia, on July 4, 1994, "The Need for Transcendence in the Postmodern World": "Thus today we find ourselves in a paradoxical situation. We enjoy all the achievements of modern civilization that have made our physical existence on this earth easier in so many important ways. Yet we do not know what to do with ourselves, where to turn. The world of our experiences seems, chaotic, disconnected, confusing." In *Temptation,* the scientist Foustka—the spelling of his name recalls but distorts

"Faust" in just the way the play's Czech title recalls and distorts the word "temptation," and "Fistula" recalls Mephistophilis—works in a large, bureaucratic Institute; as in the other institutions that Havel anatomizes in his plays, the inhabitants of the Institute are generally more concerned with preserving the privileges of the *status quo* than in real "scientific" inquiry, and the institute is led by a Director who, throughout the play, receives messages from a Secret Messenger. As it happens, however, Foustka has assembled a library of occult books, and at the outset of the play receives a mysterious visitor—the old man with smelly feet, Fistula, becomes his Mephistophilis. But Havel's parable is not really about magic. Instead, Havel uses the Faust paradigm to consider the political potentiality of the irrational, of values, beliefs, and attitudes which cannot be reduced to their instrumental effectiveness. After all, Faustus pursued the "new knowledge" at the dawn of European scientific inquiry; Havel's Foustka is a part of the institutionalized knowledge of the modern bureaucracy. While Foustka does gain some of the magic power of his namesake (the women in the play are all suddenly attracted to him), the real impact of Fistula's seduction has to do with his effort to undermine the narrow rationalism of the scientific institute, and the ways it defends its work without recognizing more broadly humane moral imperatives. As Foustka argues, "What's even more tragic is that modern man has repressed everything that might allow him somehow to transcend himself, and he ridicules the very idea that something above him might even exist and that his life and the world might have a higher meaning of some sort." Throughout the play, Foutska struggles both with Fistula and with the Director, who brilliantly disarms Foustka's critique by absorbing the rhetoric of "magic" into the practices of "science." For while Foustka ends the play accusing the Institute of "the pride of that intolerant, all-powerful, and self-serving power that uses the sciences merely as a handy weapon for shooting down anything that threatens it," the Director closes the play with an elaborate costume party, a black mass that leaves Foustka panicked and confused. Much as the "irrational" strategies of absurdist theater provide Havel with the instrument to criticize the inhuman and "irrational" impact of state bureaucracies in his early plays, so here the "irrational," figured in Foustka's dabbling both in magic and in moral philosophy, provides leverage against a palpable, but abstract, "authority."

TEMPTATION

A Play in Ten Scenes

Václav Havel

TRANSLATED FROM THE CZECH
BY MARIE WINN
FOR ZDENEK URBANEK

CHARACTERS

DR. HENRY FOUSTKA, *scientist*
FISTULA, *a retired cripple*
DIRECTOR
VILMA, *a scientist*
DEPUTY DIRECTOR
MARKETA, *a secretary*
DR. LIBUSHE LORENCOVA, *a scientist*
DR. VILEM KOTRLY, *a scientist*
DR. ALOIS NEUWIRTH, *a scientist*
MRS. HOUBOVA, *Foustka's landlady*
DANCER
PETRUSHKA
SECRET MESSENGER
LOVER *(male)*
LOVER *(female)*

SCENES

The Institute
Foustka's apartment
The garden of the Institute
Vilma's apartment
The Institute
Intermission
Foustka's apartment
The Institute
Vilma's apartment
Foustka's apartment
The garden of the Institute

NOTE: *Before the curtain rises, during the pauses between scenes, and during the intermission, a particular piece of rock music of the "cosmic" or "astral" type may be heard. It is important that the pauses between scenes be as short as possible; consequently, the scene changes—in spite of various scenic requirements due to the alternating stage settings—should be carried out as swiftly as possible.*

SCENE 1

One of the rooms of the scientific Institute where FOUSTKA *is employed. It is something between a business office, a doctor's office, a library, a club room, and a lobby. There are three doors, one at the rear, one at the front left, one at the front right. At the right rear is a bench, a small table, and two chairs; against the rear wall is a bookcase, a narrow couch covered with oilcloth, and a white cabinet with glass windows containing various exhibits, such as embryos, models of human organs, cult objects of primitive tribes, etc. At the left is a desk with a typewriter and various papers on it, behind it is an office chair, and against the wall is a file cabinet; in the middle of the room hangs a large chandelier. There might be some additional equipment around, such as a sun lamp, a sink, or an exercise apparatus against the wall (specifically, a rypstol, a Swedish ladderlike gymnastic apparatus). The furnishings of the room are not an indication of any specific areas of interest or even of any particular personality but correspond, rather, to the indeterminate mission of the entire Institute. The combination of objects of various sorts and of various designs emphasizes the timeless anonymity of a space in which things have been brought together more by chance than for any definite purpose. As the curtain rises,* LORENCOVA, KOTRLY, *and* NEUWIRTH *are onstage.* LORENCOVA, *wearing a white doctor's coat, is seated at the desk, with a mirror propped up against the typewriter, where she is powdering her nose.* KOTRLY, *wearing a white coat, is sprawled out on the bench reading a newspaper.* NEUWIRTH, *dressed in everyday clothing, is standing in the rear by the bookcase, his back to the audience, looking at a book. There is a short pause.*

LORENCOVA *(calling)*: Marketa . . .
MARKETA *(wearing an office smock, enters through the door at left)*: Yes, Doctor?
LORENCOVA: Would you please make me a cup of coffee?
MARKETA: Certainly. 5
KOTRLY *(without glancing up)*: One for me too, please.
NEUWIRTH *(without turning around)*: And me.
MARKETA: Will that be three, then?
LORENCOVA: Right.

*(*MARKETA *exits through the left door. A short pause, after which* FOUSTKA *enters quickly through the rear door, a bit out of breath. He is wearing black trousers and a black sweater and carries a briefcase.)*

FOUSTKA: Hi. 10
KOTRLY *(putting aside the newspaper)*: Hello, Henry.
NEUWIRTH *(puts aside the book and turns around)*: Hi.

*(*LORENCOVA *tucks the compact away in the pocket of her jacket and crosses the stage to the bench where* KOTRLY *is sitting, obviously making way at the desk for* FOUSTKA. *He sets his briefcase on it and hastily takes out some papers. The others watch him with interest.)*

FOUSTKA: Were they here yet?
KOTRLY: Not yet.
LORENCOVA: What's with Vilma? 15
FOUSTKA: She just ran across the street for some oranges.

1499

(MARKETA *enters through the left door with three cups of coffee on a small tray. She puts two down on the table in front of* LORENCOVA *and* KOTRLY, *the third she hands to* NEUWIRTH, *who is standing in the rear, leaning against the bookcase.*)

LORENCOVA: Thank you.

FOUSTKA: Marketa . . .

MARKETA (*stops*): Yes, Doctor?

20 FOUSTKA: I'm sorry, but could you possibly make one more cup for me?

MARKETA: Certainly.

FOUSTKA: Thanks a lot.

(MARKETA *exits through the left door.* LORENCOVA, KOTRLY, *and* NEUWIRTH *stir their coffees, at the same time watching* FOUSTKA, *who has seated himself at the desk and is straightening out various papers and files. Finally* KOTRLY *interrupts the rather long and somewhat tense silence.*)

KOTRLY (*to* FOUSTKA): So, what?

25 FOUSTKA: What, what?

KOTRLY: How's it going?

FOUSTKA: How's what going?

(LORENCOVA, KOTRLY, *and* NEUWIRTH *exchange glances and smile. A short pause.*)

LORENCOVA: Why, your private studies.

FOUSTKA: I don't know what studies you're talking about.

(LORENCOVA, KOTRLY, *and* NEUWIRTH *exchange glances and smile. A short pause.*)

30 NEUWIRTH: Come on, Henry, even the birds and bees in the trees are buzzing about it!

FOUSTKA: I'm not interested in what the birds and bees in the trees are buzzing about, and I have no other scholarly pursuits besides those directly concerned with my work at

35 our Institute.

KOTRLY: You don't trust us, do you? I don't blame you. in certain situations caution is definitely in order.

NEUWIRTH: Especially if a person is playing both ends against the middle.

40 FOUSTKA (*quickly looks over at* NEUWIRTH): What do you mean by that?

(NEUWIRTH *moves his outstretched finger meaningfully around the room, pointing finally to the door at right, by which he means to indicate the powers that run the Institute, after which he points up and down, by which he means to indicate the power of heaven and hell.*)

You've all got overactive imaginations! Is the office party on tonight?

LORENCOVA: Of course.

(*The* DEPUTY DIRECTOR, *in everyday clothes, and* PETRUSHKA, *in a white coat, enter through the right door. They are holding hands, and will continue to hold hands during the entire play. This means that* PETRUSHKA, *who doesn't speak a word during the entire play, usually follows the* DEPUTY DIRECTOR. *He, however, doesn't pay her any special attention, creating the impression, therefore, that he is dragging her around with him as some sort of prop or mascot.* LORENCOVA, KOTRLY, *and* FOUSTKA *stand up.*)

KOTRLY: Good morning, Sir.

DEPUTY: Hello there, my friends! And please sit down. You know that neither I nor the director like to stand on ceremony here.

(LORENCOVA, KOTRLY, *and* FOUSTKA *sit down again. A short pause.*)

So what's new. Did you all get a good night's sleep? Do you have any problems? I don't see Vilma here.

FOUSTKA: She called to say that her bus broke down. But apparently she managed to get a taxi and ought to be here very soon.

(*Short pause.*)

DEPUTY: Well, are you looking forward to the party? I hope you're all coming.

KOTRLY: I'm definitely coming.

LORENCOVA: We're all coming.

DEPUTY: Wonderful! I personally consider our office parties to be a marvelous thing—mainly for their collectively psychotherapeutic effect. Just think how quickly and easily those interpersonal problems that crop up among us from time to time are resolved in that informal atmosphere! And that's entirely due to the fact that as individuals we loosen up there somehow, while as a community we somehow tighten up. Isn't that the truth?

KOTRLY: That's precisely the way I feel about it.

DEPUTY: Apart from the fact that it would be an outright sin not to use such a beautiful garden at least once in a while! (*Pause.*) I came a little early on purpose . . .

NEUWIRTH: Did something happen?

DEPUTY: The director will tell you himself. Let me just ask you to be sensible, to try to understand him, and to try not to make his already rather difficult situation even more difficult unnecessarily. After all, we know we can't knock down walls with our heads, can we—why, then, should we complicate life for others and for our own selves? I think we can be glad we have the kind of director we have, so that by helping him we'll actually be helping our own selves. We should all bear in mind that essentially he's working for a good cause, that even he is not his own master, and that therefore we have no other alternative than to exercise at least that minimal amount of self-control necessary to make sure that neither he, our Institute, nor, consequently, an of us has any unnecessary problems. Actually there's nothing unusual about any of this. After all, a certain amount of inner discipline is required of everyone everywhere in today's world! I believe that you understand what I'm saying and that you won't expect me to tell you more than I can and have already told you. We're adults, after all, aren't we?

KOTRLY: Yes.

DEPUTY: So there you are! Have you received the soap allotment yet?

FOUSTKA: I'm going to distribute it today.

DEPUTY: Splendid!

(*The* DIRECTOR, *wearing a white coat, enters through the right door.* LORENCOVA, KOTRLY, *and* FOUSTKA *stand up immediately.*)

KOTRLY: Good morning, Sir.

DIRECTOR: Hello there, my friends! And please sit down. You know that I don't like to stand on ceremony here!

DEPUTY: That's precisely what I was telling our colleagues here just a second ago, Sir!

(LORENCOVA, KOTRLY, *and* FOUSTKA *sit down again. The* DIRECTOR *looks intently at those present for a while, then steps up to* FOUSTKA *and holds out his hand.* FOUSTKA, *surprised, rises.*)

DIRECTOR (*to* FOUSTKA): Did you get a good night's sleep?

FOUSTKA: Yes, thank you.

DIRECTOR: Do you have any problems?

FOUSTKA: Not really . . .

(*The* DIRECTOR *presses Foustka's elbow in a friendly way and turns to the others.* FOUSTKA *sits down again.*)

DIRECTOR: Where's Vilma?

DEPUTY: She called to say that her bus broke down. But apparently she managed to get a taxi and ought to be here very soon.

(MARKETA *enters through the left door with a cup of coffee. She hands it to* FOUSTKA.)

FOUSTKA: Thank you.

MARKETA: Don't mention it. (*Exits through the left door.*)

DIRECTOR: Well, are you looking forward to our party?

KOTRLY: Very much, Sir.

DEPUTY: Friends, I have some very good news for you on that subject: our director has promised to drop in for a moment tonight.

LORENCOVA: Just for a moment?

DIRECTOR: That will depend on the circumstances. (*To* FOUSTKA:) I hope you're coming.

FOUSTKA: Of course, Sir.

DIRECTOR: Look, colleagues, there's no sense in my dragging this out unnecessarily—we've all got enough work of our own. So, to get to the point: as you probably know by now, there have been an increasing number of complaints lately that our Institute is not fulfilling its mission in a way that responds to the present situation . . .

NEUWIRTH: What situation?

DIRECTOR: Let's not beat around the bush, my friend! Aren't you forgetting that we're supposed to be the first to hear about certain things and also the first to react to them? Isn't that what we're paid for! But that's not the problem. We're simply beginning to feel more and more pressure to start taking the offensive, meaning that through our widely publicized, popularized, pedagogical, cultural, scholarly, and individually therapeutic scientific work we must finally start confronting—

DEPUTY: In the spirit of scientific inquiry, of course . . .

DIRECTOR: Doesn't that go without saying?

DEPUTY: Excuse me, Sir, but there does exist, unfortunately, a certain science that is not based on the spirit of scientific inquiry.

DIRECTOR: That, in my opinion, is not a science! Where was I?

KOTRLY: You were saying that somehow we're supposed to finally start confronting . . .

DIRECTOR: Certain rather isolated but nonetheless alarming manifestations of those irrational attitudes cropping up primarily among a particular segment of the younger generation, and originating in an incorrect . . .

(*The* SECRET MESSENGER *enters through the right door, steps up to the* DIRECTOR, *and whispers at length into his ear. The* DIRECTOR *nods his head gravely as he whispers. After a long while the* MESSENGER *concludes. The* DIRECTOR *nods one more time. The* MESSENGER *exits through the right door. A short pause.*)

Where was I?

KOTRLY: You were saying that those irrational attitudes we're supposed to confront originate in an incorrect . . .

DIRECTOR: Understanding of the systemic complexity of natural phenomena and the historical dynamic of civilizational processes out of which certain incomplete aspects are extracted, only to be interpreted either in the spirit of pseudoscientific theory . . .

DEPUTY: We know for a fact that a number of illegal typescripts by C. G. Jung are circulating among the youth . . .

DIRECTOR: . . . or in the spirit of an entire spectrum of mystical prejudices, superstitions, obscure doctrines, and practices disseminated by certain charlatans, psychopaths, and intelligent people . . .

(VILMA, *out of breath, rushes in through the rear door, holding a bag of oranges.*)

VILMA: Please excuse me, Sir—I'm so sorry—but can you imagine that the bus I was riding—

DIRECTOR: I know about it, sit down . . .

(VILMA *sits on the oilcloth-covered couch, waves at* FOUSTKA, *and tries to communicate something to him via gestures and mime.*)

Look, colleagues, there's no sense in my dragging this out unnecessarily—we've all got enough work of our own. I've acquainted you with the basic facts of the situation, and our consequent duties, so now everything depends entirely on you. I would only like to ask you to be sensible, to try to understand me, and to try not to make my already rather difficult situation even more difficult unnecessarily. It's all for a good cause, after all! Aren't we living in a modern day and age, for heaven's sake?

KOTRLY: We are.

DIRECTOR: So there you are! Have you received the soap allotment yet?

FOUSTKA: I'm going to distribute it today.

(*The* DIRECTOR *steps up to* FOUSTKA; FOUSTKA *stands up. The* DIRECTOR *places his hand on his shoulder and gravely looks at him for a short while.*)

DIRECTOR (*gently*): I'm counting on you, Henry.

FOUSTKA: For the soap?

DIRECTOR: The soap and everything else!

The curtain falls.

SCENE 2

Foustka's apartment. It is a smallish bachelor quarters with one door at the right rear. The walls are covered with bookshelves, which are filled with a great quantity of books. At the left is a window, in front of which is a desk covered with many papers and more books. Be-

hind it is a chair. At the right is a low sofa. Beside it is a large globe. A star chart is hanging somewhere on the bookshelves. As the curtain rises, FOUSTKA, *in a dressing gown, is kneeling in the middle of the room with four burning candles on the floor around him. He holds a fifth one in his left hand and a piece of chalk in his right hand, with which he draws a circle around himself and the four candles. A large old volume lies opened on the floor beside him. The room is dimly lit. When* FOUSTKA *completes his circle he glances at the book and studies something in it for a while. Then he shakes his head and mumbles something. At that moment someone knocks at the door.* FOUSTKA *is startled and jumps to his feet.*

FOUSTKA (*calling out*): Just a minute!

(FOUSTKA *quickly turns on the light, blows out the candles, hastily puts them away somewhere behind his desk, puts away the volume, looks around, then with his foot tries to erase the chalk circle he had drawn on the floor.*)

   (*calling:*) Who is it?
HOUBOVA (*offstage*): It's me, Professor.
FOUSTKA (*calling*): Come in, Mrs. Houbova.
185 HOUBOVA (*entering*): Boy, it's really smoky in here. You ought to air the place out.
FOUSTKA: I will, right away. Did something happen?
HOUBOVA: You have a visitor.
FOUSTKA: Me? Who?
190 HOUBOVA: I don't know. He didn't introduce himself.
FOUSTKA: So it's someone you don't know.
HOUBOVA: He hasn't been here before—at least I've never seen him.
FOUSTKA: What does he look like?
195 HOUBOVA: Well—how can I put it—a little seedy—and mainly, well . . .
FOUSTKA: What?
HOUBOVA: It's embarrassing . . .
FOUSTKA: Just say it, Mrs. Houbova!
200 HOUBOVA: Well, he simply . . . smells . . .
FOUSTKA: Really? But how?
HOUBOVA: It's hard to describe . . . sort of like Limburger cheese . . .
FOUSTKA: My word! Well, never mind, show him in.

(HOUBOVA *exits, leaving the door ajar.*)

205 HOUBOVA (*offstage*): This way, please.

(FISTULA *enters. He is a smallish person, almost a dwarf, limping, and giving off a distinctly unsavory impression. He holds a paper bag containing his slippers.* HOUBOVA *casts a final glance after him, shrugs at* FOUSTKA, *and exits, closing the door behind her.* FISTULA *is grinning stupidly.* FOUSTKA *looks at him with surprise. A pause.*)

FOUSTKA: Good evening.
FISTULA: Greetings. (*Pause. Looks around him with interest.*) What a cozy place you have here, just as I'd imagined it. Good books—a rare globe—everything somehow as it
210 ought to be—the balances don't lie.
FOUSTKA: I don't know what balances you're talking about. But first of all I don't even know who I'm speaking to . . .
FISTULA: All in good time. May I sit down?

FOUSTKA: Please. 215

(FISTULA *sits on the couch. Takes off his shoes, removes the slippers from the paper bag, puts them on, puts the shoes into the bag, and then places it on the sofa beside him. A pause.*)

FISTULA: I assume that I don't have to ask you not to mention my visit to anyone, for your sake as well as mine.
FOUSTKA: Why shouldn't I mention it?
FISTULA: You'll see why soon enough. My name is Fistula. Where I'm employed is of no importance, and in any 220 event I don't even have a permanent position, nor do I need to have one, since I'm a cripple with a pension. (*Grins stupidly as if he has made a joke.*)
FOUSTKA: I'd guess that you work in a safety-match factory.
FISTULA (*chuckles, then suddenly grows serious*): That comes from 225 a certain unidentified fungus of the foot. It makes me quite miserable and I do what I can for it, even though there's not much I can do.

(FOUSTKA *sits on the corner of the desk and looks at* FISTULA. *In his look we sense a mixture of curiosity, mistrust, and revulsion. A longer pause.*)

   Aren't you going to ask me what I want or why I've come? 230
FOUSTKA: I'm ever hopeful that you'll tell me that yourself.
FISTULA: That, of course, would be quite possible, but I had a particular reason for not doing it until now.
FOUSTKA: What was it?
FISTULA: I was interested to see whether you'd figure it out 235 for yourself.
FOUSTKA (*irately*): How could I figure it out when I've never seen you before in my life! In any case, I have neither the time nor the inclination to play guessing games with you. Unlike you, I happen to have a job and I'm leaving in a 240 few minutes . . .
FISTULA: For the office party, right? But you've got heaps of time for that!
FOUSTKA: How do you know that I'm going to the office party? 245
FISTULA: And before my arrival you weren't exactly behaving like someone in a hurry either . . .
FOUSTKA: You don't know a thing about what I was doing before your arrival.
FISTULA: I beg your pardon, but I certainly know better than 250 you do what I know and what I don't know, and how I know what I know!

(FISTULA *grins stupidly. A longer pause. Then* FOUSTKA *stands up, crosses to the other side of his desk, and turns gravely to* FISTULA.)

FOUSTKA: Look, Mister . . .
FISTULA: Fistula.
FOUSTKA: Look, Mister Fistula, I'm asking you plainly and 255 simply, in all seriousness, and I'm expecting a plain and simple, serious answer from you: What do you want?

(*A short pause.*)

FISTULA: Does the name Marbuel say anything to you? Or Loradiel? Or Lafiel?

(FOUSTKA *gives a start, quickly regains his control, gives a long shocked look at* FISTULA.)

260 FOUSTKA (*exclaiming*): Out!

FISTULA: Excuse me?

FOUSTKA: I said: Out!

FISTULA: What do you mean—out?

FOUSTKA: Leave my apartment immediately and never set
265   foot in it again!

(FISTULA *rubs his hands contentedly.*)

Did you hear me?

FISTULA: I heard you clearly and I'm delighted by this reaction of yours because it absolutely confirms that I've come
to the right place.

270 FOUSTKA: What do you mean?

FISTULA: Your fright, don't you see, makes it perfectly clear
that you're fully aware of the importance of my contacts,
which you wouldn't be if you hadn't been interested in
the aforementioned powers earlier.

275 FOUSTKA: Those names don't mean a thing to me, I haven't
the faintest idea of what you're talking about; moreover,
the suddenness of my demand that you leave merely reflected the suddenness with which I became fed up with
you. My disgust coming at the same time that you pro-
280   nounced those names was a complete coincidence! And
now, having given you this explanation, I can only repeat
what I said before, but his time without any fear that you
might mistake my meaning: Leave my apartment immediately and never set foot in it again!

285 FISTULA: Your first request for me to leave—that I'll naturally
grant, though probably not quite immediately. Your second request I will not grant, for which you will be very
grateful to me later on.

FOUSTKA: You missed my meaning. Those weren't two inde-
290   pendent requests, in fact they weren't requests at all. It was
a demand—a single and indivisible one at that!

FISTULA: I'll make a note of it. But I'd also like to point something out: the haste with which you slipped in an additional motivation for your demand, together with the
295   interesting fact that even though you claimed to be fed up
with me, you considered it important enough to slip in
this additional motivation even at the risk of delaying my
longed-for departure—that haste together with that interesting fact are proof to me of one single thing: that your
300   original fear of me as a middleman for certain contacts has
now been superseded by a fear of me as a potential informer. Let me assure you, however, that I was counting
on this phase as well. In fact had it not set in I would have
felt quite uneasy. I would have considered it peculiar and
305   would have wondered myself whether in fact *you* weren't
an informer yourself. But now let me get down to business. There's obviously no way I can prove to you that I'm
not an informer; even if I were to conjure up Ariel himself at this moment it still wouldn't eliminate the possibil-
310   ity of my being an informer. Therefore, you have only
three choices. First, to consider me an informer and to
continue to insist on my immediate departure. Second,
not to consider me an informer and to trust me. Third, not
to make up your mind for the time being as to whether
315   I'm an informer or not, but to adopt a waiting attitude,

meaning on the one hand not to kick me out immediately and on the other hand not to say anything in front
of me that might eventually be used against you if I actually *were* an informer. I'd like to recommend the third alternative.   320

(FOUSTKA *paces the room deep in thought; finally he sits down at his desk and looks over at* FISTULA.)

FOUSTKA: Very well, I'll accept that, but I'd like to point out
that there's obviously no need for me to control or restrict
my speech in any way because there's absolutely nothing
I could possibly think, much less say, that might possibly
be used against me.   325

FISTULA (*exclaiming*): Marvelous! (*Claps his hands with pleasure.*) You delight me! If I were an informer I'd have to admit that you avoided the first trap beautifully! Your
declaration is clear evidence of your absolutely solid caution, intelligence, and quick wit, qualities that I eagerly   330
welcome, since they give me hope that I'll be able to depend on you and that we'll be able to work together well.

(*Pause.*)

FOUSTKA: Listen, Mister . . .

FISTULA: Fistula.

FOUSTKA: Listen, Mister Fistula, I'd like to tell you two   335
things. First of all, your talk is a bit redundant for my taste.
You really ought to get to the point of what brought you
here more quickly. You've said virtually nothing, even
though I asked you ages ago for a serious, direct, and concise answer to the question of what you actually want.   340
And secondly, it surprises me greatly to hear that we're
supposed to be working together on something. That requires two people, after all . . .

FISTULA: Your answer had eighty-six words. Considering its
semantic value that isn't exactly a small number, and if I   345
were you I wouldn't reproach anybody too severely for
redundancy.

FOUSTKA: Bullshit is infectious, as we know.

FISTULA: I hope that as time goes by you'll adopt some of my
more important skills as well.   350

FOUSTKA: You actually want to teach me something?

FISTULA: Not only to teach . . .

FOUSTKA: What else, for God's sake?

FISTULA (*crying out*): Leave him out of this!

FOUSTKA: Well, what else are you planning to do with me?   355

FISTULA (*smiling*): To initiate you . . .

(FOUSTKA *stands up abruptly and bangs his fist on the table.*)

FOUSTKA (*shouting*): That's enough! I'm a scientist with a scientific outlook on life, holding down a responsible job at
one of our foremost scientific establishments! If anyone
were to speak in my presence in a way that's obviously in- 360
tended to spread superstition, I'd be forced to proceed in
accordance with my scientific conscience!

(*For a moment* FISTULA *stares stupidly at* FOUSTKA, *then he suddenly begins to laugh wildly and dance around the room. Just as suddenly he falls silent, comes to a stop, stoops to the ground, and with
his finger slowly traces the circle that* FOUSTKA *had drawn there ear-*

lier, after which he jumps up and begins to laugh wildly again. Then he goes over to the desk, seizes one of the hidden candlesticks, waves it in the air and, still laughing, places it on the desk. FOUSTKA watches him, goggle-eyed. Then suddenly, FISTULA becomes serious again, returns to the couch, and sits down.)

FISTULA (*matter-of-factly*): I know your views well, Doctor
Foustka. I know how much you love your work at the In-
365 stitute, and I apologize for my foolish joke. Anyhow, it's
high time for me to cut out all this preliminary joking
around. As your director emphasized again this morning,
one of your Institute's tasks is to fight against certain manifestations of irrational mysticism that keep cropping up
370 here and there as a sort of obscurely preserved residue of
the prescientific thinking of primitive tribes and the Dark
Ages of history. As a scientist you know perfectly well that
the more thoroughly you're armed with knowledge about
what you're supposed to be fighting against, that much
375 more effective your fight will be. You have at your disposal
quite a decent collection of occult literature—almost all
the basics are here, from Agrippa and Nostradamus to
Eliphas Levy and Papus—nevertheless, theory isn't everything, and I can't believe that you've never felt the need to
380 acquaint yourself with the practice of black magic directly.
I come to you as a sorcerer with several hundred successful magical and theurgical evocations under his belt who
is ready and willing to acquaint you with certain aspects
of this practice in order to give you a base for your scien-
385 tific studies. And in case you're asking yourself why in the
world a sorcerer should want to join a battle against
witchcraft, I can even give you a convincing reply to that:
I seem to be in a tricky situation in which I might come
to a bad end without cover of some sort. I am therefore
390 offering you my own self for study, and I ask nothing in
return besides your vouching for me, if the need arises,
that I turned myself over to the disposition of science, and
that therefore it would be unfair to hold me responsible
for the propagation of something which, in reality, I was
395 helping to fight against.

(FISTULA looks gravely at FOUSTKA; FOUSTKA reflects.)

FOUSTKA (*quietly*): I have a suggestion.
FISTULA: I'm listening.
FOUSTKA: To expedite our communications I'm going to
pretend that I'm not endowed with a scientific outlook
400 and that I'm interested in certain things purely out of curiosity.
FISTULA: I accept your suggestion!

(FISTULA steps up to FOUSTKA and offers him his hand; FOUSTKA hesitates a moment, then gives his hand to FISTULA, who clasps it. FOUSTKA instantly pulls his hand away in alarm.)

FOUSTKA (*crying out*): Ow! (*Gasps with pain, rubs his hand and
waves it in the air.*) Man, your temperature must be fifty be-
405 low zero.
FISTULA (*laughing*): Not quite.

(FOUSTKA finally recovers and resumes his seat at his desk. FISTULA also sits down, folds his hands in his lap, and stares with theatrically doglike resignation at FOUSTKA. A long pause.)

FOUSTKA: So?

(A long pause.)

What's going on?

(A long pause.)

What's wrong with you. Have you lost your tongue all of
a sudden? 410
FISTULA: I'm waiting.
FOUSTKA: For what?
FISTULA: For your command.
FOUSTKA: I don't understand: What command?
FISTULA: What better way for me to acquaint you with my 415
work than for you to assign me certain tasks whose ful-
fillment you can verify for yourself and whose fulfillment
matters to you for some reason?
FOUSTKA: Aha, I see. And what kind of tasks—roughly—
should they be? 420
FISTULA: That's for you to say!
FOUSTKA: All right—but still and all—it's hard to think of
anything under the circumstances . . .
FISTULA: Don't worry, I'll help you out. I think I have an idea
for an innocent little beginning of sorts. If I'm not mis- 425
taken, there's a certain young lady you admire.
FOUSTKA: I don't know what you're talking about.
FISTULA: Doctor Foustka, after everything we've said here,
you really must admit that I might occasionally know
somebody's little secret. 430
FOUSTKA: If you're talking about the secretary of our Institute, I'm not denying that she's a pretty girl, but that
doesn't necessarily mean . . .
FISTULA: What if tonight at the office party—quite unexpectedly and of course quite briefly—she were to fall in 435
love with you? How about that?

(FOUSTKA paces nervously for a short while, and then turns abruptly to FISTULA.)

FOUSTKA: Please leave!
FISTULA: Me? Why?
FOUSTKA: I repeat—go away!
FISTULA: Are you beginning that again? I thought we'd 440
reached an agreement.
FOUSTKA: You've insulted me.
FISTULA: How? In what way?
FOUSTKA: I'm not so badly off as to need magic for help in
my love life! I'm neither a weakling incapable of manfully 445
facing the facts when he doesn't manage to win by his
own efforts, nor a cad who would carry out experiments
on innocent and completely unsuspecting young girls for
his own sensual pleasure. Do you take me for some sort of
Bluebeard or what, Fistula? 450
FISTULA: Which of us knows what we really are! But that's
not the issue now. If my well-intentioned, innocent, and
quite spur-of-the-moment little idea touched a raw nerve
for some reason, I naturally apologize and withdraw it!
FOUSTKA: And I didn't even mention my main objection: I'm 455
involved in a serious relationship, and I'm faithful to my
girl friend.
FISTULA: Just as faithful as she is to you?

FOUSTKA (*startled*): What do you mean by that?

460 FISTULA: Forget it.

FOUSTKA: Wait a minute, I'm not going to let you get away with making dirty insinuations like that! I'm not interested in gossip, and I don't like impudence!

FISTULA: I'm sorry I said anything. If you've decided to be

465 blind, that's your business.

(FISTULA *removes his shoes from the paper bag and slowly begins to change footgear.* FOUSTKA *watches him uneasily. A pause.*)

FOUSTKA: You're leaving? (*Pause.*) I guess I blew up a little.

(*Pause.* FISTULA *has changed into his shoes, places his slippers in the bag, stands up, and slowly walks towards the door.*)

So what's going to happen?

FISTULA (*stops and turns around*): With what?

FOUSTKA: Well, with our agreement.

470 FISTULA: What about it?

FOUSTKA: Is it on?

FISTULA: That depends entirely on you. (*He grins.*)

The curtain falls.

SCENE 3

The garden of the Institute. It is night, and the garden is illuminated by Chinese lanterns strung along wires attached to trees. In the middle of the stage is a small bower. Beyond it in the background is a space serving as a dance floor. In the front at the left is a garden bench; at the right is an outdoor table with a variety of bottles and glasses on it. All around are trees and bushes; these, together with the darkness, make it hard to see the dancing in the background as well as the various movements of figures in the garden. Only the action in the foreground is always clearly visible. As the curtain rises, the music grows softer and its character changes; faintly audible now as if from a great distance are strains of popular dance music that will continue for the entire scene. The male and female LOVERS *are in the bower; they will remain there for the entire scene, gently embracing, caressing each other, kissing, and whispering into each other's ears, oblivious to the various goings-on around them. The* DEPUTY *with* PETRUSHKA, *and* KOTRLY *with* LORENCOVA, *are dancing as couples on the dance floor, while* VILMA *and the* DIRECTOR *are also there, each swaying separately to the music.* FOUSTKA *is standing at the table, pouring drinks into two glasses.* MARKETA *is sitting on the bench. Everyone is wearing evening clothes; the women wear long gowns. As the scene begins,* FOUSTKA *is explaining something to* MARKETA, *who is listening intently. As he is speaking* FOUSTKA *finishes pouring the drinks and slowly crosses over with them towards* MARKETA.

FOUSTKA: We must realize that out of an infinity of possible speeds, the expanding universe chose precisely the one

475 that would allow the universe itself to come into being as we know it, that is, having sufficient time and other requirements needed for the formation of solid bodies so that life would be able to begin on them—at least on one of them! Isn't that a remarkable coincidence!

480 MARKETA: That's really amazing!

(FOUSTKA *comes up to* MARKETA, *hands her a glass, sits down beside her, and both take a drink.*)

FOUSTKA: So there you are, and if you probe a bit further you'll discover that you owe your very existence to so unbelievable a multitude of similarly unbelievable coincidences that it exceeds the bounds of all probability. All those things can't exist just for themselves, can they? Don't 485 they conceal some deeper design of existence, of the world, and of nature willing you to be you, and me to be me, willing life, simply, to exist, and at its very height, as we understand it for now, the human soul, capable of fathoming it all! Or could it be, perhaps, that the cosmos 490 directly intended that one fine day it would see itself thus through our eyes and ask itself thus through our lips the very questions we're asking ourselves here and now?

MARKETA: Yes, yes, that's exactly the way I see it!

(VILMA, *who has in the interim left the dance floor, now appears at the table and pours herself a drink.*)

VILMA: Are you enjoying yourselves?   495

FOUSTKA: Marketa and I are doing a bit of philosophizing.

VILMA: Well, I seem to be in the way here. (VILMA *disappears with her glass, and after a while she can again be seen dancing alone in the background. A pause.*)

FOUSTKA: And here's another thing. Modern biology has 500 known for a long time that while the laws of survival and mutations and the like explain all sorts of things, they don't begin to explain the main thing: why does life actually exist in the first place, and above all why does it exist in that infinitely bright-colored multiplicity of its often 505 quite self-serving manifestations, which almost seem to be here only because existence wants to demonstrate its own power through them? But to demonstrate to whom? To itself? Have you ever wondered about that?

MARKETA: To tell you the truth, no, not in this way . . . but 510 from now on I'll probably think about it all the time. You know how to say things so nicely.

(NEUWIRTH *emerges from somewhere at the right. He steps up to the bench and bows to* MARKETA.)

NEUWIRTH: May I have the honor?

MARKETA (*in confusion*): Yes . . . of course.

(*She throws* FOUSTKA *a pleading, unhappy glance, and then rises.*)

FOUSTKA: You'll come back again, won't you?   515

MARKETA: Of course! Everything was so very interesting.

(NEUWIRTH *offers his arm to* MARKETA *and disappears with her. After a while they can be seen in the background dancing.* FOUSTKA *sips his drink, deep in thought. Shortly thereafter the* DIRECTOR, *who has in the interim left the dance floor, emerges from behind a bush at left, just in back of the bench.*)

DIRECTOR: A pleasant evening, isn't it?

(FOUSTKA *is a bit startled, and then quickly stands up.*)

FOUSTKA: Yes. We're in luck with the weather.

DIRECTOR: Please sit down. May I join you for a moment?

FOUSTKA: Of course.   520

(*They both sit down on the bench. An awkward pause. Then the* DIRECTOR *casually takes* FOUSTKA'S *hand and peers into his eyes.*)

DIRECTOR: Henry . . .

FOUSTKA: Yes?

DIRECTOR: What do you actually think of me?

FOUSTKA: I? Well . . . how shall I say it . . . I think that everyone
525 in our Institute is glad that you're the one in charge . . .

DIRECTOR: You don't understand. I'm interested in what you
yourself think of me—as a person—or, to be more precise, what you feel about me . . .

FOUSTKA: I respect you . . .

530 DIRECTOR: Is that all?

FOUSTKA: Well . . . how shall I say it . . . it's hard to . . . well,
it's . . .

(*At that moment the* DEPUTY, *with* PETRUSHKA, *who have in the
interim left the dance floor, appear at the right, holding hands. When
the* DIRECTOR *sees them he drops* FOUSTKA'*s hand.* FOUSTKA *is
obviously relieved.*)

DEPUTY: here you are, Sir! We've been looking high and low
for you.

535 DIRECTOR: Did something happen?

(*Making the most of the situation,* FOUSTKA *quietly stands up and
quickly disappears.*)

DEPUTY: Nothing in particular. It's only that Petrushka here
has a request to make of you, but she's just a little bashful
about coming out with it . . .

DIRECTOR: What request?

540 DEPUTY: Whether she couldn't have a dance with you.

DIRECTOR: I don't know how to lead, and I'd only step all
over her skirt. Really, there are so many better dancers
here . . .

DEPUTY: In that case would you at least accept our invitation
545 to come to the pool where our colleague Kotrly has constructed an adorable underwater light show.

(*The* DIRECTOR *peevishly gets to his feet and goes off somewhere to
the right with the* DEPUTY *and* PETRUSHKA. *Just then* KOTRLY *and*
LORENCOVA, *who have in the interim left the dance floor, appear at
the left. They go to the table.*)

KOTRLY: Have you seen my underwater light show yet?

LORENCOVA: You're doing it stupidly, Willy.

KOTRLY: What am I doing stupidly?

(*They go up to the table and* KOTRLY *pours out two drinks and
hands one to* LORENCOVA. *They sip their drinks.*)

550 LORENCOVA: You're being such an ass-kisser that even those
two idiots will get sick of you. You'll end up a total joke
and everybody will turn against you.

KOTRLY: Maybe I'm doing it stupidly, but it's still a lot better
than pretending not to be interested, and all the while
555 telling them everything!

LORENCOVA: Are you referring to Neuwirth?

KOTRLY: Who, for instance, was the first to begin talking
about Foustka's interest in black magic? If they get wind
of it, it'll be Neuwirth's doing!

560 LORENCOVA: But we all gossiped about it! You're being unfair
to him and your only excuse is that you're jealous . . .

KOTRLY: It's just like you to stick up for him!

LORENCOVA: Are you beginning that again?

KOTRLY: Libby, give me your word of honor that you never
had a thing with him! 565

LORENCOVA: Word of honor! Come on, let's dance!

(KOTRLY *and* LORENCOVA *put down their glasses on the table and
exit somewhere off to the right. After a while they can be seen in the
background, dancing. Meanwhile* NEUWIRTH *and* MARKETA *enter
from the left.* MARKETA *sits down on the bench.* NEUWIRTH *hangs
around nearby.* FOUSTKA *emerges from the bushes directly behind the
bench and sits down next to* MARKETA. *An awkward pause.*)

NEUWIRTH: Oh dear, I seem to be in the way here.

(NEUWIRTH *vanishes. After a while he can be seen in the background, dancing with* LORENCOVA; *he has evidently cut in on*
KOTRLY. *Meanwhile the* DEPUTY *and* PETRUSHKA *have appeared
on the dance floor as well, dancing together, as well as the*
DIRECTOR, *dancing alone again. A short pause.*)

MARKETA: Tell me more! Every word you say opens my eyes.
I don't understand how I could have been so blind, so superficial . . . 570

FOUSTKA: I'll begin, if you don't mind, by taking a new tack.
Has it ever occurred to you that we wouldn't be able to
understand event the simplest moral action that doesn't
serve some practical purpose? In fact, it would have to
seem quite absurd to us if we didn't recognize that hidden 575
somewhere in its deepest depths is the presumption of
something higher, some sort of absolute, omniscient, and
infinitely fair judge or moral authority through which and
within which all our activities are somehow mysteriously
appraised and validated and by means of which each one 580
of us is constantly in touch with eternity?

MARKETA: Yes, yes, that's exactly how I've felt about it all my
life! I just wasn't able to see it, let alone say it so beautifully.

FOUSTKA: So there you are! What's even more tragic is that
modern man has repressed everything that might allow 585
him somehow to transcend himself, and he ridicules the
very idea that something above him might even exist and
that his life and the world might have a higher meaning
of some sort! He has crowned himself as the highest authority, so he can then observe with horror how the world 590
is going to the dogs under that authority!

MARKETA: How clear and simple it is! I admire the way you're
able to think about everything so . . . so, well, in your own
way somehow, differently from the way most people usually talk about it, and how deeply you feel all those things! 595
I don't think I'll ever forget this evening! I have a feeling
that I'm becoming a new person every minute I'm with
you. Please forgive me for saying it so openly, but it's as if
something were radiating from inside of you that—I don't
understand how I could have walked by you so indiffer- 600
ently before—it's simply that I've never felt anything like
this before . . .

(KOTRLY *emerges from somewhere at the right, goes up to the bench,
and bows to* MARKETA.)

KOTRLY: May I have the honor?

MARKETA: I'm sorry, but I . . .

KOTRLY: Come on, Marketa, we haven't had a single dance 605
together!

(MARKETA *looks unhappily at* FOUSTKA, *who just shrugs his shoulders helplessly;* MARKETA *stands up.*)

MARKETA (*to* FOUSTKA): You'll wait here, won't you?
FOUSTKA: Of course I'll wait.

(KOTRLY *offers an arm to* MARKETA *and disappears with her. After a while they may be seen in the background, dancing.* FOUSTKA *sips his drink, deep in though. After a short while the* DIRECTOR, *who has in the interim left the dance floor, emerges from behind a bush directly in back of the bench.*)

DIRECTOR: Alone again?

(FOUSTKA *is a bit startled, then quickly stands up.*)

610   Sit down, Henry.

(FOUSTKA *sits again. The* DIRECTOR *sits down beside him. A short pause.*)

Do you smell that wonderful fragrance? Acacias . . . nasturtiums . . .
FOUSTKA: I don't know very much about fragrances.

(*An awkward pause. Then the* DIRECTOR *again casually takes Foustka's hand and gazes closely into his eyes.*)

DIRECTOR: Henry . . .
615 FOUSTKA: Yes?
DIRECTOR: Would you like to be my deputy?
FOUSTKA: Me?
DIRECTOR: I could arrange it.
FOUSTKA: But you already have a deputy.
620 DIRECTOR: If you only knew what a pain in the ass he gives me!

(*Just then the* SECRET MESSENGER *enters, goes up to the* DIRECTOR, *leans over, and whispers at length into his ear. The* DIRECTOR *gravely nods his head. After a longer time the* MESSENGER *concludes. The* DIRECTOR *nods one more time. The* MESSENGER *exits to the right. The* DIRECTOR, *who had not dropped Foustka's hand during the whispering, turns again to* FOUSTKA *and gazes closely into his eyes for a longer time.*)

Henry.
FOUSTKA: Yes?
DIRECTOR: Wouldn't you like to stop over at my place for a little while after the party? Or if you don't want to stay to
625   the end, we could both slip away without anyone noticing. I've got some homemade cherry liqueur. I could show you my collection of miniatures, we could chat in peace and quiet, and if we happened to go on too long and you didn't feel like going home that late, you could
630   easily spend the night at my place! You know that I live all alone, and what's more, it's only a hop and a skip from our Institute, so you'd have it that much easier in the morning—what do you say?
FOUSTKA: I'm very honored by your invitation, Sir, but I'm
635   afraid I've already promised that I'd go to . . .
DIRECTOR: To Vilma's?

(FOUSTKA *nods. The* DIRECTOR *gazes closely into his eyes for another moment, then, all at once, drops his hand briskly, stands up abruptly, crosses over to the table, pours himself a drink, and quickly*

drains it. FOUSTKA *remains seated on the bench, embarrassed. Then the* DEPUTY, *with* PETRUSHKA, *who have in the interim left the dance floor, emerge from the left, holding hands.*)

DEPUTY: Here you are! We've been looking all over . . .
DIRECTOR: Did something happen?
DEPUTY: Nothing in particular. Me and Petrushka here, we just wanted to ask you if you had any plans after the party. 640 We'd consider it quite an honor if you'd accept our invitation to come over for a little nightcap before bedtime. You could even spend the night at our house—if you wanted to, of course . . .
DIRECTOR: I'm tired and I have to go home. Goodbye.   645

(*The* DIRECTOR *exits quickly to the right. The* DEPUTY *looks after him in confusion, then, somewhat crestfallen, disappears with* PETRUSHKA *to the left. After a while they may be seen in the background, dancing. Just then* NEUWIRTH *and* LORENCOVA, *who have in the interim left the dance floor, appear near the table at the right.*)

NEUWIRTH: I've seen a lot of things in my day, but an educated person sucking up to his idiot bosses with ridiculous stunts like those light bulbs in the pool—that really takes the cake! (*He pours two drinks, hands one to* LORENCOVA: *they both sip.*)   650
LORENCOVA: Sucking up with the light bulbs is still a lot better than pretending not to be interested and all the while telling them everything!
NEUWIRTH: It's just like you to stick up for him!
LORENCOVA: Are you beginning that again?   655
NEUWIRTH: Libby, give me your word of honor that you never had a thing with him!
LORENCOVA: Word of honor! Come on, let's dance!

(NEUWIRTH *and* LORENCOVA *put their glasses down on the table and exit somewhere to the left. After a while they can be seen in the background, dancing. Meanwhile* KOTRLY *and* MARKETA *enter from the right.* MARKETA *sits down on the bench next to* FOUSTKA. KOTRLY *hangs around nearby. An awkward pause.*)

KOTRLY: Oh dear, I seem to be in the way here.

(KOTRLY *vanishes. After a while he can be seen in the background, dancing with* LORENCOVA. *He has evidently cut in on* NEUWIRTH.)

FOUSTKA: When a person casts God from his heart, he opens 660 a door for the devil. When you think about the increasingly stupid willfulness of the powerful and the increasingly stupid submission of the powerless, and the awful destruction committed in today's world in the name of science—and after all we *are* its somewhat grotesque 665 standard-bearers—isn't all that truly the work of the devil? We know that the devil is a master of disguises, and what more ingenious disguise could one imagine than the one offered him by the godlessness of modern times? Why, he must find the most promising base of operations in those 670 very places where people have stopped believing in him! Please forgive me for speaking so openly, Marketa, but I can't keep it stifled inside me any longer! And who else can I confide in besides you?

(MARKETA *throws her glass into the bushes and grasps Foustka's hand emotionally.*)

675 MARKETA: (*exclaiming*): I love you!

FOUSTKA: No!

MARKETA: Yes, I'll love you forever!

FOUSTKA: Oh, you poor creature! I'd be your ruin!

MARKETA: I'd rather be ruined with you and live the truth
680   than be without you and live a lie!

(MARKETA *embraces* FOUSTKA *and begins to kiss him passionately.
Just then* VILMA, *who has in the interim left the dance floor, appears
at the table. For a moment she observes the embracing couple.*)

VILMA (*icily*): Are you enjoying yourselves?

(FOUSTKA *and* MARKETA *immediately pull apart and look at* VILMA
in a state of shock.)

The curtain falls.

SCENE 4

*Vilma's apartment. It is a cozy boudoir, furnished with antiques.
There is a door at the rear. At the left is a large bed with a canopy.
At the right are two small armchairs, a large Venetian mirror, and
a vanity table with a large collection of perfumes on it. Scattered
about the room are various female odds and ends and trinkets. The
only thing folded neatly is Foustka's evening outfit next to the
bed. The colors are all feminine, predominantly pink and purple.
As the curtain rises,* FOUSTKA *is sitting in his undershorts at the
edge of the bed, and* VILMA, *in a lacy slip, is sitting at the vanity
table combing her hair, facing the mirror with her back to*
FOUSTKA. *A short pause.*

FOUSTKA: When was he here last?

VILMA: Who?

FOUSTKA: Stop asking stupid questions!

685 VILMA: You mean that dancer? About a week ago.

FOUSTKA: Did you let him in?

VILMA: He just brought me some violets. I told him I had no
time, that I was hurrying to meet you.

FOUSTKA: I asked you whether you let him in.

690 VILMA: I don't remember anymore . . . maybe he came in for
a moment.

FOUSTKA: So you kissed him!

VILMA: I kissed him on the cheek to thank him for the violets, that's all.

695 FOUSTKA: Vilma, don't treat me like a fool, for goodness sake!
I just bet you could buy him off with a mere kiss on the
cheek once you let him in! Surely he tried to dance with
you at the very least.

VILMA: Henry, drop it, for goodness sake! Can't you talk
700   about anything more interesting?

FOUSTKA: Did he try or not?

VILMA: All right, he did, if you really must know! But I won't
tell you another thing! I simply refuse to keep talking to
you on this level, because it's embarrassing, undignified,
705   insulting, and ridiculous! You know very well that I love
you, and that no dancer could possibly be a threat to you,
so stop tormenting yourself with this endless cross-exam-
ination! I don't keep pumping you for details either—and
I'd have far more reason to do so!

710 FOUSTKA: So you refuse to tell? Well in that case everything
is quite clear.

VILMA: But I've told you a hundred times that I don't go out
of my way to see him, I don't care for him, I don't dance
with him, so what else am I supposed to do, damn it!

FOUSTKA: He hangs around you, he flatters you, he wants to 715
dance with you all the time—and you enjoy it! If you
didn't enjoy it, you'd have gotten rid of him long ago.

VILMA: I won't deny that I enjoy it—any woman would enjoy it. His persistence is touching, and so is the very fact
that he never gives up, even though he knows perfectly 720
well that he doesn't have a chance. Would you, for instance, be capable of driving here at night from God
knows where for no other reason than to bring me some
violets, even though you knew the situation was hopeless?

FOUSTKA: He's persistent because you deliberately dash his 725
hopes in a way that keeps them alive and you deliberately
reject him in a way that makes him long for you more and
more! If you really slammed the door on his hopes he'd
never show up here again. But you wouldn't do that, because it amuses you to play cat and mouse with him. 730
You're a whore!

VILMA: You've decided to insult me?

FOUSTKA: How long did you dance together?

VILMA: Enough, Henry, you're beginning to be disgusting!
I've always known that you're eccentric, but I really never 735
suspected that you're capable of being this nasty! What's
suddenly brought on this pathological jealousy of yours?
This insensitivity, tactlessness, maliciousness, vengefulness?
At least if you had any objective reason for it . . .

FOUSTKA: So you're planning to keep whoring around? 740

VILMA: You have no right to talk to me like that! You kept
pawing at that girl all evening, everybody's embarrassed, I
wander around like an idiot—people feel sorry for me all
over the place—and now you have the nerve to reproach
me! Me! You do as you damn well please, I just have to 745
suffer in silence, and finally you make a scene here on account of some crazy dancer! Do you see how absurd it is?
Do you realize how terribly unfair it is? Do you have the
faintest idea of how selfish and cruel you are?

FOUSTKA: In the first place, I was certainly not pawing any- 750
one and I'd like you to please refrain from using words
like that, especially when you're referring to pure creatures like Marketa. In the second place, we're not discussing me, but you, so kindly stop changing the subject.
Sometimes I get a feeling that there's some monstrous 755
plan hidden behind all this. First, you'll resurrect feelings
within me that I'd assumed were dead long ago, and then
once you've deprived me thus of my well-known objectivity, you'll begin to tighten a web of deceit around my
heart, lightly at first, but then ever more painfully, an es- 760
pecially treacherous one because it is composed of a
multitude of delicate threads of dancerly pseudoinno-
cence! But I won't let myself be tortured on this rack
any longer! I'll do something either to myself—or to
him—or to you—or to all of us! 765

(VILMA *puts down her comb, begins to clap her hands, and walks towards* FOUSTKA *with a smile.* FOUSTKA *also begins to smile, stands
up, and walks towards* VILMA.)

VILMA: You keep getting better and better!

FOUSTKA: You weren't bad yourself.

(FOUSTKA *and* VILMA *gently embrace, kiss, and then slowly get into bed together. They settle down together comfortably, lean back against the pillows, and cover their legs with a blanket.* FOUSTKA *lights a cigarette for himself and for* VILMA. VILMA *finally ends a long pause by speaking.*)

VILMA: Henry.

FOUSTKA: Hmm . . .

770 VILMA: Isn't it beginning to get on your nerves just a bit?

FOUSTKA: What?

VILMA: You know, that I keep making you play these games.

FOUSTKA: It did bother me for quite a long time.

VILMA: And now?

775 FOUSTKA: Now just the opposite—it's beginning to scare me.

VILMA: To scare you? Why?

FOUSTKA: I have a feeling that I'm beginning to get into it too much.

VILMA (*exclaiming*): Henry! Don't tell me you're really begin-
780   ning to get jealous! Now that's fantastic! Never in my
       wildest dreams did I hope it would succeed like this! I had
       become resigned to the idea that you'd never feel any jeal-
       ousy other than the make-believe kind.

FOUSTKA: I'm sorry, but I can't share your delight.

785 VILMA: I don't understand what you're afraid of!

FOUSTKA: My own self!

VILMA: Come on!

FOUSTKA: Don't underestimate it, Vilma. Something's hap-
       pening to me. I suddenly feel capable of doing all sorts of
790   things that have always been alien to me. It's as if some-
       thing dark inside of me were suddenly beginning to flow
       out of its hiding place and into the open.

VILMA: What an alarmist you are! You're beginning to feel a
       little healthy jealousy and that throws you into a complete
795   panic! There's nothing wrong with you. Maybe you're just
       a little upset because your situation at the Institute came
       to a head this evening with that unfortunate incident with
       the director. That's obviously on your mind, and its' work-
       ing away at your unconscious, looking for some way out,
800   even though you won't admit it. That's why you're begin-
       ning to see bogeymen all over the place.

FOUSTKA: If only it were that simple.

(*Pause.*)

VILMA: Do you think he'll destroy you?

FOUSTKA: He'll certainly try. The question is whether he has
805   enough power to do it.

VILMA: But he's got all the power he wants—all the power
       there is, actually—at least as far as we're concerned.

FOUSTKA: There are other kinds of power besides the kind he
       dispenses.

(VILMA, *horrified, jumps up and kneels on the pillow opposite* FOUSTKA.)

810 VILMA: Do you mean that seriously?

FOUSTKA: Hmm . . .

VILMA: Now you're scaring me! Promise me you won't dab-
       ble in that sort of thing!

FOUSTKA: And what if I won't promise?

815 VILMA: The minute you mentioned that cripple I knew
       there'd be hell to pay! He's addled your brains! You'd ac-
       tually go so far as to get involved with him?

FOUSTKA: Why not?

VILMA: This is horrible!

FOUSTKA: At least you see that I wasn't just kidding around   820
       before.

(*Just then the doorbell rings.* VILMA *cries out in horror and quickly huddles up under the blankets.* FOUSTKA *smiles, calmly gets out of bed, and dressed just as he is—that is, in his undershorts—goes to the door and quickly opens it. There stands the* DANCER *holding a bunch of violets behind his back.*)

DANCER: Good evening. Is Vilma home?

FOUSTKA: Why?

DANCER (*points to the flowers*): I just wanted to give her a little
       something.   825

FOUSTKA (*calling to the bed*): Wilma, you have a visitor.

(VILMA *climbs out of bed, is a bit confused, can't quickly find any-thing to cover up with, and therefore goes to the door dressed only in her slip.* FOUSTKA *steps to the side, but does not go away.*)

VILMA (*to the dancer, with embarrassment*): Is that you?

DANCER: I'm sorry to disturb you at this hour—we were on
       tour—I just wanted to give you—here.

(*The* DANCER *hands* VILMA *the violets,* VILMA *takes them and sniffs them.*)

VILMA: Thank you.   830

DANCER: Well, I'll be going again. I apologize again for dis-
       turbing you.

VILMA: Bye-bye.

(*The* DANCER *exits.* VILMA *closes the door, smiles uncertainly at* FOUSTKA, *puts down the violets somewhere, steps up to him, em-braces him, and gently kisses his forehead, lips, and cheek.* FOUSTKA *stands motionless and looks coldly in front of him.*)

    I love you.

(FOUSTKA *doesn't move a hair.* VILMA *continues to kiss him. Then, suddenly,* FOUSTKA *slaps her brutally in the face.* VILMA *falls to the ground.* FOUSTKA *kicks her.*)

The curtain falls.

SCENE 5

The same room at the Institute as in Scene 1. As the curtain rises, nobody is onstage, but very soon VILMA *and* FOUSTKA *enter through the rear door.* FOUSTKA *is wearing the same evening clothes he wore at the party the previous day.* VILMA *is wearing a white coat. She has a black eye. They both seem happy.*

VILMA: We can't be the first!   835

FOUSTKA: Have you noticed that you come to work on time
       only when I stay over at your place?

VILMA: You're exaggerating.

(FOUSTKA *sits down at the desk and begins to sort out some papers.* VILMA *sits down on the oilcloth couch.*)

(*Calling.*) Marketa.

(MARKETA, *wearing an office smock, enters through the left door. When she sees* FOUSTKA *she stops abruptly and lowers her eyes.*)

840   Would you please make us two cups of coffee? A bit stronger, if possible.
MARKETA: Yes, of course.

(MARKETA *goes a bit nervously towards the left door, stealthily glancing over at* FOUSTKA, *who looks up from his papers and smiles at her jovially.*)

FOUSTKA: Well, did you get a good night's sleep?
MARKETA (*stuttering*): Thank you—yes—actually no. There
845   were so many thoughts racing through my head.
(MARKETA, *in some confusion, exits through the left door.*)
VILMA: I think you turned that poor little thing's head last night.
FOUSTKA: Oh, she'll get over it.

(*Pause.*)

850   VILMA: Henry.
FOUSTKA: Yes, darling!
VILMA: It hasn't been that good in a long time, has it?
FOUSTKA: Hmm . . .

(LORENCOVA *in a dress,* KOTRLY *also in civilian clothes, and* NEUWIRTH *in a white coat enter through the rear door.*)

KOTRLY: You're here already?
855   VILMA: Hard to believe, isn't it?

(LORENCOVA *and* KOTRLY *sit down at their places on the bench;* NEUWIRTH *leans against the bookcase.*)

LORENCOVA (*looks at Vilma's face*): My God, what's that?
VILMA: Oh you know, deathless passion.

(MARKETA *enters through the left door with two cups of coffee on a tray. She hands one to* VILMA, *and sets down the other with somewhat trembling hands in front of* FOUSTKA.)

FOUSTKA: Thanks.
LORENCOVA: Some for us too, Marketa.
860   MARKETA: Yes, Doctor Lorencova.

(MARKETA *exits quickly through the left door. The* DEPUTY, *in a white coat, and* PETRUSHKA, *in a dress, enter through the right door. They are holding hands. Everyone stands.*)

KOTRLY: Good morning, Sir.
DEPUTY: Hello there, my friends! I see we've got perfect attendance here today—that's fantastic—today of all days I would have least expected it. (*Everyone sits down again.*) I
865   think that yesterday was a real success. You all deserve thanks for that. But I must express special appreciation to our colleague Kotrly here for his underwater light effects.
KOTRLY: Please don't mention it.
DEPUTY: Well, my friends, there's no point in beating around
870   the bush any longer.
NEUWIRTH: Did something happen?
DEPUTY: The director will tell you himself. At this time I just want to implore you all to understand that certain things have to be the way they are, to meet us halfway as we meet

you halfway, and, mainly, to keep a cool head, a glowing   875
heart, and clean hands at this crucial point in time. In short, there are times when people either come through with flying colors, and then they have nothing to fear, or they don't come through, and then they have only themselves to blame for the unnecessary troubles they create as   880
a result. But you're educated people, after all—I don't have to spell it all out for you. Who'll volunteer for garden cleanup?
KOTRLY: I might as well, after all I have to go there anyhow to terminate the light bulbs.   885
DEPUTY: Splendid!

(*The* DIRECTOR, *in civilian clothes, enters through the right door. Everyone stands again.*)

KOTRLY: Good morning, Sir.
DIRECTOR: Hello there, my friends! I see we've got perfect attendance here today—that's fantastic—today of all days I would have least expected it and today of all days it's es-   890
pecially important.
DEPUTY: That's precisely what I was telling our colleagues just a second ago, Sir.

(*Everyone sits again. The* DIRECTOR *looks intently at those present for a moment and then steps up to* KOTRLY *and shakes his hand.* KOTRLY *stands up, surprised.*)

DIRECTOR: Did you get a good night's sleep?
KOTRLY: Yes, thank you.   895
DIRECTOR: Do you have any problems?
KOTRLY: Not really.

(*The* DIRECTOR *presses Kotrly's elbow in a friendly way and turns again to the others.* KOTRLY *sits again.*)

DIRECTOR: There's no point in beating around the bush, friends . . .
NEUWIRTH: Did something happen?   900
DIRECTOR: As we know, our Institute is a kind of lighthouse of truthful knowledge. I'd even go so far as to say it's something of a faithful watchdog over the scientific core of science itself—it's something like the avant-garde of progress. Therefore one might simplify it thus: We think it   905
today, they'll live it tomorrow!
DEPUTY: I've already reminded our colleagues, Sir, of the responsibility that our mission involves.
DIRECTOR: But here's why I'm saying all this: a serious thing has happened . . .   910

(*Just then the* SECRET MESSENGER *enters through the right door, steps up to the* DIRECTOR, *and whispers at length into his ear. The* DIRECTOR *gravely nods his head. After a long while the* MESSENGER *concludes. The* DIRECTOR *nods one more time and continues speaking. The* MESSENGER *exits through the right door.*)

But here's why I'm saying all this: a serious thing has happened . . .

(*Just then* MARKETA *enters through the left door carrying a tray with three cups of coffee on it. She places two on the table in front of* LORENCOVA *and* KOTRLY *and hands the third to* NEUWIRTH. *Then she heads back towards the left door.*)

But here's why I'm saying all this: a serious thing has happened . . .

(MARKETA *stops in her tracks, glances at the* DIRECTOR *and at* FOUSTKA, *then she quietly goes up to the left door and eavesdrops.*)

915 NEUWIRTH Did something happen?

DEPUTY (*to* NEUWIRTH): Please stop interrupting the director! Didn't you hear him say that he's about to tell you . . .

DIRECTOR: A serious thing has happened: a virus has lodged itself where one would have least expected it, yet in the 920 very place it can do the worst damage—that is, in the very center of antiviral battle—indeed, if I'm to stick with this metaphor, right in the central antibiotic warehouse!

(*Everyone looks at each other anxiously.* VILMA *and* FOUSTKA *exchange a glance that reveals they know there's trouble ahead.* FOUSTKA *nervously gropes for a cigarette and lights up.*)

KOTRLY: Are you saying, Sir, that right here, among us, there's someone . . .

925 DIRECTOR: Yes, with deep sorrow, bitterness, and shame I must say precisely that. We have a scientific worker here at this Institute—let me emphasize the word *scientific*—who has long and of course secretly, which only confirms his two-faced nature, been involved with various so-called 930 occult disciplines, from astrology through alchemy all the way to black magic and theurgy, in order to probe those murky waters for a would-be hidden wealth of an allegedly higher—that is prescientific—kind of learning.

KOTRLY: You mean he believes in spirits?

935 DIRECTOR: Not only that, but he is actually attempting to move from theory to practice! We have ascertained that he has established contact—

LORENCOVA: With spirits?

DEPUTY: He'd have a bit of trouble doing that, wouldn't he, 940 Sir?

DIRECTOR: That's enough! Please don't joke about things that leave a black mark on the work of our Institute, things that are a direct assault on its reputation and therefore a low blow to us all, and especially to me as the one 945 responsible for all of its scientific credibility. It is a grave and sad matter, my friends, and it's up to all of us to come to grips with it honorably! Where was I?

DEPUTY: You were discussing those contacts . . .

DIRECTOR: Ah yes. Well, then, we have learned that not long 950 ago he established direct contact with a certain element from that no-man's-land of pseudoscience, common criminality, and moral turpitude, who is suspect not only because he spreads superstition and deludes the credulous by means of various tricks, but who actually dabbles in Sa- 955 tanism, black magic, and other such poisonous practices. That's the fact of the matter, and now I'd like to open this up for discussion. Does anyone have any questions?

(*An oppressive pause.*)

KOTRLY (*quietly*): Might I ask the name of this colleague?

DIRECTOR (*to the* DEPUTY): Say it!

960 DEPUTY: I can hardly utter the words, but name him I must. We're talking about Doctor Foustka, here.

(*An oppressive pause.*)

DIRECTOR: Who else wishes to speak?

MARKETA (*timidly*): I do.

FOUSTKA (*quietly to* MARKETA): Please, I beg of you, stay out of this! 965

DIRECTOR: This concerns us all. Even the secretary here deserves a chance to speak her mind.

MARKETA: Please excuse me, Sir. I'm not a scientist and I don't know how to express myself too well, but that simply can't be true! Doctor Foustka is a wise and honor- 970 able man—I know he is—he worries about questions that we really all should be worrying about—he thinks for himself—he tries to get to the bottom of the deepest questions—the source of morality—of universal order—and all those other things—and those contacts 975 you mentioned—I simply don't believe it! Surely these are all wicked lies spread by bad people who want to harm him.

(*A deathly silence falls over the room.* FOUSTKA *is obviously in despair over Marketa's outburst. After a while the* DIRECTOR *turns matter-of-factly to the* DEPUTY.)

DIRECTOR (*to the* DEPUTY): As soon as we're finished, please arrange for her immediate dismissal! Now of all times our 980 Institute truly can't allow itself the luxury of employing a secretary who accuses the administration of lying!

DEPUTY: I'll take care of it, Sir.

DIRECTOR (*to* MARKETA): You may go get your things together. 985

FOUSTKA (*in a muffled voice to* MARKETA): You've gone mad—to ruin your life so foolishly like this—why, you won't get a job anywhere!

MARKETA: I want to suffer with you!

FOUSTKA: Excuse me, Sir, but wouldn't it be more sensible to 990 have her hospitalized? It's perfectly obvious that she doesn't know what she's saying.

DIRECTOR: Psychiatry, Doctor Foustka, is not a garbage dump for girls you've used and thrown away.

MARKETA: Henry, are you renouncing me? And everything 995 you told me last night, are you renouncing that too?

FOUSTKA (*speaking furiously through clenched teeth*): For God's sake, keep quiet!

(MARKETA *bursts into tears and runs out the left door. An awkward pause.*)

VILMA (*quietly to* FOUSTKA): If she does something rash it'll be your fault! 1000

FOUSTKA (*quietly to* VILMA): And then you'll be satisfied, won't you?

VILMA (*quietly*): Don't start that again.

FOUSTKA: I'm the one who started? Right?

DIRECTOR: Stop that! I'll ask at a higher level whether one of 1005 the local housing projects couldn't take her on as a cleaning lady.

LORENCOVA: I think that would be a very fortunate, humane, and sensible solution.

DIRECTOR (*to* FOUSTKA): Do you want to take advantage of 1010 your right to respond to the charges against you?

(FOUSTKA *stands up slowly and leans against the desk as if it were a speaker's podium.*)

FOUSTKA: Gentlemen, colleagues! I have complete faith in the objectivity and conscientiousness with which my case will be considered and I presume that at the right mo-
1015 ment I will be given the opportunity to make an extensive explanation, and that certain circumstances with which I will acquaint you on that occasion will help prove my complete innocence. For the time being, therefore, I will confine myself to expressing the hope that the pro-
1020 ceedings in this case—in keeping with our scientific approach to reality and our scientific morality—will be impartially and fully directed towards one goal alone: to discover the truth. This will further not only my own interests nor only the interests of science as such which this
1025 Institute is entrusted to guard and cultivate, but the interests of each of you as well. A different course of action, you see, might easily make my case merely the first link of a long chain of injustices the end of which I hardly dare contemplate. Thank you for your attention!

(FOUSTKA *sits down. An awkward pause. Everyone is slightly uneasy, albeit each for different reasons.*)

1030 DIRECTOR: We're living in a modern day and age, and nobody here has any intention of staging any kind of witch-hunt. That would merely resurrect the same ancient ignorance and fanaticism against which we are battling, but in a new guise. Let the manner in which our colleague
1035 Foustka's case is resolved become an inspirational model of a truly scientific approach to the facts! The truth must prevail, come what may!

(*A short pause.*)

Who volunteered for garden clean-up?
KOTRLY: I did, Sir.

(*The* DIRECTOR *steps up to* KOTRLY. KOTRLY *stands up; the* DIRECTOR *places a hand on his shoulder and looks gravely into his eyes for a while.*)

1040 DIRECTOR (*tenderly*): I'm glad you took the job, Vilem. I'll come to help you.

(MARKETA *enters through the left door, wearing a dress and carrying a small suitcase in her hand. Her face is tear-stained; she crosses the room as if sleepwalking and leaves through the rear door. Just as she closes it behind her, the chandelier crashes to the floor. It doesn't hit anyone but shatters into pieces on the floor.*)

The curtain falls.

Intermission

SCENE 6

Foustka's apartment again. As the curtain rises, FISTULA *is alone on stage. He is sitting at the desk, going through the papers lying on it. He is wearing slippers, and the paper bag with his shoes in it is lying on the desk among the papers. After a while* FOUSTKA *enters, still in evening clothes. When he spots* FISTULA *he gives a start and cries out.*

FOUSTKA: What are you doing here?

FISTULA: I'm waiting for you.
FOUSTKA: How did you get in?
FISTULA: Not through the chimney, if that's what you're won- 1045
dering. Through the door, which Mrs. Houbova kindly opened for me before she went out shopping, because I explained to her how urgently you needed to speak to me and how hard it would be for me to wait for you outside, what with my lame foot. 1050
FOUSTKA: So you tricked her—how like you!
FISTULA: You don't believe that I'm a cripple?
FOUSTKA: My having to urgently speak to you is an out-and-out lie. Quite the contrary, after everything that happened I'd hoped I'd never see you again. 1055
FISTULA: Quite the contrary, it's precisely *because* of what happened that our meeting has become many times more urgent.
FOUSTKA: And how dare you go through my papers!
FISTULA: Well, I had to do something to while away the time, 1060
didn't I?
FOUSTKA: And what about those shoes?
FISTULA: You make such a fuss about everything! (FISTULA *begins to grin stupidly, then he takes his bag, goes to the sofa, sits down, and places the bag beside him.*) Won't you sit 1065
down?

(FOUSTKA, *irritated, crosses to his desk, sits, and glares at* FISTULA.)

So what do you say to our success?
FOUSTKA: What success?
FISTULA: I never expected it to work so easily and so quickly. You're truly a gifted student. 1070
FOUSTKA: I don't know what you're talking about!
FISTULA: You know perfectly well! We had agreed to do an innocent little experiment first, hadn't we? And that turned out to surpass our fondest expectations, don't you agree? 1075
FOUSTKA: If you're referring to the fact that that unfortunate child developed a bit of a crush on me, then I'd like to say just two things. First, there was no magic involved, especially not yours; the only reason it happened was because it was the first time— 1080
FISTULA: By pure chance—
FOUSTKA: That I actually had an opportunity to have a real talk with that young woman and because I happened to be—
FISTULA: By pure chance— 1085
FOUSTKA: In pretty good form last night, so that my thoughts charmed her. Well, and as things seem to work with young girls, soon her interest was transferred—
FISTULA: By pure chance—
FOUSTKA: From what was being explained to the one who 1090
was explaining. I don't see anything about it that goes beyond the bounds of the ordinary. Second of all, seeing what happened to that poor child as a result of our conversation, my conscience is filled with heavy reproaches that it happened at all, even though I certainly never 1095
knew, and had no way of knowing, that our talk would have such consequences . . .

(FISTULA *begins to chortle and merrily slaps his thigh.*)

What's so funny about that?

FISTULA (*becomes serious*): My dear Doctor Foustka! Everybody knows that you don't believe in pure chance or coincidence. Don't you wonder how it happened that a person like you who could hardly stutter a request for a cup of coffee from that young woman until that moment suddenly found himself endowed with such impressive eloquence combined with the courage to express thoughts that are more than dangerous to express on the premises of your Institute? And doesn't it surprise you that it happened at just the very moment we had dreamed up our little idea? Honestly, aren't you a bit amazed at how your thoughts suddenly broke down that young woman's defenses—as if someone had waved a magic wand and allowed her to fall madly and indelibly in love in no time at all.

FOUSTKA: We all have moments in our lives when we seem to outdo ourselves.

FISTULA: That's just what I'm talking about!

FOUSTKA: I don't understand what you mean.

FISTULA: You didn't really expect Jeviel, the spirit of love, to arrive at our office party dressed in evening clothes all ready to fix everything up for you as if he were some sort of matchmaker? How else do you imagine he could do it than by means of your own self? He simply incorporated himself into you! Or rather, he simply awakened and liberated certain things that had always been dormant inside of you! Or to be even more precise, it was actually you yourself who decided to drop the reins restraining certain of your inner powers, and you yourself, therefore, who filled in for him, so to speak, or who fulfilled his intentions and thus won the day in his image, bearing his name!

FOUSTKA: There you are!

FISTULA: Of course a person isn't a static system of some sort—why you as a scientist must know that better than I. If a little seed is to sprout it must first be planted by someone.

FOUSTKA: If it's true that you and your . . .

FISTULA: Jeviel.

FOUSTKA: If you and your Jeviel are really responsible for planting this unfortunate seed, then I curse you from the bottom of my heart! You're a devil and I don't want to have anything to do with you.

FISTULA: You're missing the point again! If the devil exists, then above all he exists within our own selves!

FOUSTKA: Then you, needless to say, must be his favorite residence!

FISTULA: You overestimate my value at least as much as you overestimated your own just a second ago. Think of it this way: I'm only a catalyst who helps his fellow creatures awaken or accelerate things that have long existed within themselves even without his help. My help, you see, merely enables them to discover their own courage to experience and enjoy something thrilling in life and consequently to become more fulfilled themselves! We only live once; why then should we spend those precious few decades that have been allotted to us stifling under the cover of some sort of philistine scruples? Do you know why you called me a devil? In order to shift your own responsibility—purely out of fear of your own scruples and of that thing within you that breaks them down—to a place outside of your own ego, in this case onto me, and

by means of this "transference" as you scientists call it, or "projection," to ease your conscience! You hoped to fool your own scruples by using this kind of maneuver, and by assigning me that insulting name you hoped you'd actually even please them. But think of it this way, Doctor Foustka: I—a certain cripple, Fistula—wouldn't be able to move you an inch if you hadn't secretly dreamed about moving in that direction yourself long ago! Our little experiment had no other purpose than to clarify these little trivialities for you.

FOUSTKA: And what about your assurance that it was innocent? That was a dirty trick!

FISTULA: Wrong again! You're still only deceiving your own self! After all, you could have talked to the girl about the beauties of the scientific worldview and the worldwide significance of your Institute and she would have avoided any danger. But even after you did it the other way, you didn't have to abandon her so selfishly when things began to seem hopeless! But that's not the point now. There's one thing I've got to hand you, with my deepest compliments, especially since you're a beginner: your disguise—that classic tool of Jeviel's—in the pious habit of an ecstatic seeker after that one (*points his finger skyward*) as the true source of meaning of all creation and of all moral imperatives—that was truly brilliant! Congratulations!

FOUSTKA (*angrily*): What disguise? I was only saying what I believed!

FISTULA: My dear friend . . .

FOUSTKA: I'm not your friend!

FISTULA: My dear Sir, the truth isn't merely what we believe, after all, but also why and to whom and under what circumstances we say it!

(FOUSTKA *stares vacantly at* FISTULA *for a moment, then sadly nods his head, paces back and forth across the room a few times, and sits down again. After a while he begins to speak.*)

FOUSTKA (*quietly*): It's not altogether clear to me how they did it, but they sniffed out my contacts with you somehow, for which I'll most likely be fired from the Institute, punished as an example, publicly disgraced, and probably deprived of my livelihood and everything else. But certainly all this is merely superficial and immaterial, at least as far as I'm personally concerned. I see the true significance of what is in store for me as something else. It will be a deserved punishment for the unforgivable irresponsibility with which I behaved; for losing my moral vigilance and giving in to temptation, while under the poisonous influence of unjustified, malicious, and totally self-centered jealousy. I was trying to kill two birds with one stone and, in this way, hoping to win over one person and at the same time to wound another. I was truly blinded by something diabolical within me, and therefore I'm grateful to you for enabling me to have this experience, no matter how or why you did it. You simultaneously awakened both that temptation and that mean-spirited jealousy in me, and thus you made it possible for me to come to understand my own self better, especially my darkest sides. But that's not all. Your explanation has helped illuminate the true source of my doubt, which really does lie nowhere else but in my own self. Therefore I have no regrets about our meeting, if one can use that word to describe the way you forced yourself on me. It was an important lesson, and your dark designs have helped me discover a new inner light. I'm telling you this because it's my hope that we'll never see each other again, since I'm hoping that you'll leave this place immediately.

1220

(*A long pause.* FISTULA *slowly takes his shoes out of the bag, looks at them thoughtfully for a while, sniffs them, then finally places them on the ground in front of him and turns with a smile to* FOUSTKA.)

FISTULA: Each of us is master of his own fate! I really wanted to mention something else, but now I'm not sure whether it wouldn't be better to wait for a time when you'll be in more of a—please pardon the expression—hot spot and, therefore, more receptive.

1225

FOUSTKA: What did you want to mention?

FISTULA: I know that mechanism of thought rotation which you just demonstrated as well as I know these shoes of mine! We sorcerers call it the Smichovsky Compensation Syndrome.

1230

FOUSTKA: What's that?

FISTULA: When a novice first manages to break through the armor of his old defenses and opens himself up to the immense horizons of his hidden potential, after a little while something like a hangover sets in and he sinks into an almost masochistic state of self-accusation and self-punishment. Psychologically this emotional reaction is quite understandable: in an effort to mollify his betrayed scruples, almost as an afterthought, the novice mentally transforms the action through which he betrayed them into some sort of purifying lesson which he had to learn in order to become better. He makes of it, in short, a sort of small dance floor on which to perform ritual celebrations of his principles. It usually doesn't last long, and when he comes to his senses he recognizes what we, of course, knew from the start, but what we couldn't rally explain to him: that is, the grotesque discrepancy between the dubious values in whose name he called down the most frightful punishment on himself, and the fundamental, existential significance of the experience that he is trying to atone for by means of this punishment.

1235

1240

1245

1250

(FOUSTKA *jumps up and angrily smashes the table.*)

FOUSTKA: That's it—now I've really had enough! If you think that all your high-flown oratory can get me tangled up in some new pseudoadventure, you're very much mistaken!

1255

FISTULA: It's you who are very much mistaken if you think you aren't already tangled up . . .

1260

FOUSTKA (*crying out*): Get out!

FISTULA: I'd just like to warn you that when you get back in touch with reality and suddenly feel the need for a consultation, I won't necessarily be available. But that's your business, after all . . .

1265

FOUSTKA: Please—go away! I want to be alone with my Smichovsky Compensation Syndrome!

(FISTULA *slowly takes his shoes in his hands, all the while shaking his head in disbelief. Then, suddenly, he slams the shoes down on the floor, jumps up, and begins to wildly smack himself on the forehead.*)

FISTULA: I can hardly believe it! Because he dared to philosophize for a few minutes with another woman, his mistress throws a fit and denounces him for associating with a sorcerer.

1270

FOUSTKA: What? That's a dirty lie!

FISTULA: And for that he'd be willing to give up his earnings, his scientific future, and maybe everything he owns without a fight! I've seen a lot of things, but this is a first! Smichovsky himself would have had his mind blown by this one!

1275

FOUSTKA: I don't believe she'd stoop that low! After all those golden hours of sheer happiness we've had together!

FISTULA: Ah, what do you know about a woman's heart? Maybe the very memory of those hours provides the key to what she did! (FISTULA *calms down, sits down, slowly takes off his slippers, sniffs them, then carefully puts them away in his bag and begins to put on his shoes. A long pause.*)

1280

FOUSTKA (*quietly*): And what, in your opinion, could I still do?

FISTULA: Let's not get into that.

FOUSTKA: Come on, tell me.

1285

FISTULA: As you've probably realized, I don't give concrete advice and I don't make arrangements for anybody. At most I occasionally inspire . . . (*His shoes on, he grabs his bag with the slippers and heads for the door.*)

FOUSTKA (*screaming out*): Say it straight out, damn it!

1290

(FISTULA *stops, stands completely still for a moment, and then turns to* FOUSTKA.)

FISTULA: It would be enough if you mobilized, in the name of a good cause, at least one thousandth of the cunning that your director mobilizes from morning till night in the name of a bad one!

(FISTULA *begins to grin stupidly.* FOUSTKA *stares at him with amazement.*)

The curtain falls.

SCENE 7

The same room of the Institute in which Scenes 1 and 5 take place. Instead of the chandelier, a light bulb is suspended from an electrical wire. As the curtain rises, LORENCOVA, KOTRLY, *and* NEUWIRTH *are onstage.* LORENCOVA, *wearing a white coat, is sitting at the desk, a compact propped up against the typewriter, powdering her nose.* KOTRLY, *wearing a white coat, is sprawled out on the bench, reading the newspaper.* NEUWIRTH, *in civilian clothes, is standing at the rear by the bookcase, his back to the audience, examining a book. A short pause.*

LORENCOVA: What are we going to do about the coffee?

1295

KOTRLY (*without looking up*): Why don't you make it?

LORENCOVA: Why don't you?

(FOUSTKA, *wearing a black sweater and black pants, quickly enters through the rear door, a briefcase in his hand, slightly out of breath.*)

FOUSTKA: Hi.

NEUWIRTH (*without turning around*): Hi.

(*No one reacts to Foustka's entrance; all continue doing what they were doing before.* FOUSTKA *sets his briefcase down on the desk and begins to take out various papers.*)

300 FOUSTKA: Were they here yet?
NEUWIRTH (*without turning around*): Not yet.

(*When* FOUSTKA *sees that* LORENCOVA *is not going to free the desk for him he crosses over to the bench where* KOTRLY *is sitting and sits down next to him. A pause.*)

LORENCOVA: Poor Marketa.

(FOUSTKA *looks up.*)

KOTRLY (*without looking up*): What's with her?
LORENCOVA: She tried to slit her wrists.

(FOUSTKA *stands up, shaken.*)

305 KOTRLY (*without turning around*): So it's true after all?
NEUWIRTH (*without turning around*): They say she's in the psychiatric ward.
LORENCOVA: Poor thing.

(FOUSTKA *sits down again. The* DEPUTY, *in everyday clothes, and* PETRUSHKA, *in a white coat, enter through the right door, holding hands.* LORENCOVA *shoves the compact into her coat pocket.* KOTRLY *folds his newspaper.* NEUWIRTH *puts aside the book, and turns around.* LORENCOVA, KOTRLY, *and* FOUSTKA *stand up.*)

KOTRLY: Good morning, Sir.
310 DEPUTY: Hello there, my friends! And please sit down.

(LORENCOVA, KOTRLY, *and* FOUSTKA *sit down again. A short pause.*)

I don't see Vilma here.
FOUSTKA: She's at the dentist.

(*Short pause.*)

DEPUTY: As you well know, the task we're facing today is not
315 an easy one. Nobody here—as our director said so nicely—has any intention of staging a witch-hunt. The truth must prevail, come what may. But for that very reason we must remind ourselves that looking for the truth means looking for the whole, unadulterated truth. That is to say that the truth isn't only something that can be
320 demonstrated in one way or another, it is also the purpose for which the demonstrated thing is used or for which it may be misused, and who boasts about it and why, and in what context it finds itself. As scientists we know well that by tearing a certain fact out of its context we can not only
325 completely shift or change its meaning, but we can stand it right on its head and thus make a lie out of the truth or vice versa. In short, then, we shouldn't allow the living background of the acts with which we are going to concern ourselves to disappear from our field of vision, nor
330 the conclusions which we will draw about them. I hope I don't have to elaborate any further—we aren't little children, damn it! Or are we?
KOTRLY: We aren't.
DEPUTY: So there you are! Who's feeding the carrier pigeons
335 today?
NEUWIRTH: I am.
DEPUTY: Splendid!

(*The* DIRECTOR, *wearing a white coat, enters through the right door.* LORENCOVA, KOTRLY, *and* FOUSTKA *rise immediately.*)

KOTRLY: Hi.

DIRECTOR: Hello there, my friends! And please sit down.

(LORENCOVA, KOTRLY, *and* FOUSTKA *sit down. A short pause.*)

I don't see Vilma.
DEPUTY: I didn't see her either when I came. She's apparently 1340
at the dentist.

(*The* DIRECTOR *approaches* KOTRLY *and holds out his hand.* KOTRLY *rises.*)

DIRECTOR (*to* KOTRLY): Did you get a good night's sleep?
KOTRLY: Very good, thank you.

(*The* DIRECTOR *presses Kotrly's elbow in a friendly manner and turns to the others.* KOTRLY *sits down.*)

DIRECTOR: As you well know, the task we're facing today is
not an easy one.   1345
DEPUTY: That's precisely what I was telling our colleagues
just a second ago, Sir!
DIRECTOR: We all know the issue, so we can skip the preliminaries . . .

(VILMA, *out of breath, and carrying a large paper box in her hand, rushes in through the rear door.*)

VILMA: Please excuse me, Sir, I'm very sorry . . . I had an ap- 1350
pointment at the dentist this morning, and can you imagine, I—
DIRECTOR: I know about it, sit down.

(VILMA *sits on the oilcloth couch, places the box at her feet, communicates something through gestures to* FOUSTKA, *and then shows that she is crossing her fingers for him.* LORENCOVA *leans over to her.*)

LORENCOVA (*quietly*): What's this?
VILMA (*quietly*): A toaster from the repair shop.   1355
LORENCOVA (*quietly*): I thought it was a new hat.
VILMA (*quietly*): No.
DIRECTOR: Where was I?
KOTRLY: You were saying that we can skip the preliminaries . . .   1360
DIRECTOR: Ah yes. So we can skip the preliminaries and get right to the subject. Doctor Foustka, if you would kindly . . .

(*The* DIRECTOR *motions to* FOUSTKA *to come to the front.* FOUSTKA *rises, crosses to the middle of the room, and stands in the place where the* DIRECTOR *has indicated.*)

There, that's good. Shall we begin?
FOUSTKA: Certainly.
DIRECTOR: Well, then, could you tell us, my friend, whether   1365
it's true that for some time now . . .

(*At that moment the* SECRET MESSENGER *enters through the right door, steps up to the* DIRECTOR, *and whispers something at length in his ear. The* DIRECTOR *gravely nods his head. After a longer while the* SECRET MESSENGER *concludes. The* DIRECTOR *nods his head one last time. The* SECRET MESSENGER *exits through the right door.*)

Where was I?
KOTRLY: You were asking him whether it's true that for some time now . . .

1370 DIRECTOR: Ah yes. Well, then, could you tell us, Sir, whether it's true that for some time now you've been engaged in the study of what's known as occult literature?

FOUSTKA: It's true.

DIRECTOR: For how long?

1375 FOUSTKA: I don't know exactly . . .

DIRECTOR: A round number will do. A half a year? A year?

FOUSTKA: Something like that.

DIRECTOR: How many such books, in your estimation, did you read in that period?

1380 FOUSTKA: I didn't count them.

DIRECTOR: A round number will do. Five? Thirty? Fifty?

FOUSTKA: Maybe fifty.

DIRECTOR: To whom did you lend them out?

FOUSTKA: No one.

1385 DIRECTOR: Now, now, Sir, you aren't going to tell us that nobody borrowed such desirable and rare books from you, books impossible to come by these days! Your friends obviously had to see them at your place.

FOUSTKA: I don't invite friends over to my place, and I never
1390 lend books.

DIRECTOR: Very well, then. And now please concentrate—this is an important question: what led you to these studies? Why, actually, did you begin a systematic investigation of these things?

1395 FOUSTKA: I'd been uneasy for a long time about our young people's mounting interest in everything that has anything to do with the so-called supernatural. As a result of this uneasiness of mine I gradually decided to write a brochure in which I would try to demonstrate, by means
1400 of mysticism itself, how incongruous that conglomeration of twisted fragments from various cultural circles is, and how strikingly inconsistent these various idealistic and mystical theories of the past are with contemporary scientific knowledge. At the same time I especially chose
1405 mysticism as the subject for my critical attention rather than any other because of the uncritical interest it is enjoying today. My project, of course, required—

DIRECTOR (interrupting): None of us doubted, Sir, that you would answer that question precisely as you did. But in
1410 the meanwhile, none of us knows how you intend to explain the shocking fact that you allegedly practiced black magic yourself.

FOUSTKA: I didn't really practice it much; mostly I just spread the word that I did.

1415 DIRECTOR: Why?

FOUSTKA: Because that was the only way to build trust among people as mistrustful as today's sorcerers are.

DIRECTOR: So you craved their trust? Interesting, interesting! How far did you get in achieving it?

1420 FOUSTKA: So far I've been only modestly successful, my success taking the form of a certain source who visited me two times, about whom you have been informed.

DIRECTOR: Did that source tell you why it sought you out?

FOUSTKA: Apparently it knew about my interest in the prac-
1425 tice of black magic and was willing to initiate me into it.

DIRECTOR: Did you agree to that?

FOUSTKA: Not expressly, but at the same time I didn't expressly refuse. We're in a state of so-called mutual discussion.

1430 DIRECTOR: What does it want in return?

FOUSTKA: For me to testify that it put itself at the disposal of science, if the need arises.

DEPUTY: Do you hear that, Sir! What a cunning bunch they are!

DIRECTOR: It seems to me, Foustka, that it's high time to ask 1435
our pivotal question: how do you explain the fact that on the one hand you claim to have a scientific viewpoint, and consequently must know that black magic is sheer charlatanism, while on the other hand you're trying to gain the trust of sorcerers, and when one of them actually seeks 1440
you out, not only do you *not* kick him out and laugh in his face, but on the contrary, you make plans to collaborate with him, and indeed, even to cover up for him? You'll surely find it hard to explain these murky contacts and activities by invoking scientific-critical interests. 1445

FOUSTKA: It may seem foolish to you, but I simply felt from the very first that my efforts to help those seduced by charlatans and my intentions to fight effectively against such seducers must not be confined to mere theoretical-propagandistic work. I was and am to this day convinced 1450
that it wouldn't be honest to keep my hands entirely clear of living reality in an effort to keep them clean, as it were, and to lull my conscience with illusions about God knows what great practical results coming out of my theoretical struggle. I simply felt that if you start something you're 1455
obliged to finish it, and that it is my civic duty to put my theoretical knowledge in the service of the practical struggle, which means concretely searching for the hotbed of those activities, and then uncovering and convicting the perpetrators. Why, we're constantly boasting about our 1460
battle against fakery, mysticism, and superstition, but if we had to point a finger at even a single disseminator of these poisons, we couldn't do it! But not just us—it's almost unbelievable how little success anybody has had in infiltrating those areas, and thanks to that, how little is known 1465
about them! Small wonder, then, that they're spreading so rampantly. That's why I decided to win the confidence of those circles, infiltrate them, and there, in the field, to gather evidence of their guilt! Which of course I couldn't do without pretending to have at least partial belief in 1470
their spirits, initiations, evocations, magical spells, incubi, and succubi and all that other rubbish. I'd probably even be forced to swear oaths of silence or provide eventual cover-ups. In short, I decided to enlist as an inconspicuous and possibly solitary soldier in this silent war, as one 1475
might call it, because I arrived at the conclusion that my expertise put me under a direct obligation to do so. We're dealing, you see, with a sphere in which, unfortunately, a so-called broad perspective is still considered valuable, if not an actual prerequisite for any participation in its life. 1480

(*A long pause. Everyone present is stunned, each looks in confusion at the others, then finally all looks come to center on the DIRECTOR.*)

DIRECTOR: So that you actually . . . I see . . . I see . . . (*Pause.*) Well, in fact, it wouldn't be such a bad thing if our Institute could pull off a truly concrete victory like that! Our colleague Foustka is right about one thing, brochures have never won wars. 1485

DEPUTY (*to* FOUSTKA): You would therefore be willing, if I understand you correctly, to provide us with notes about

each of your encounters, whether with that source of
yours or with any others.

1490 FOUSTKA: Of course! That's exactly why I'm doing it!

DEPUTY: That wouldn't be such a bad thing, as our director
has already pointed out. But just one thing isn't clear to
me: why did we have to hear about your praiseworthy initiative only now, after certain unfair—as it turns out—ac-
1495 cusations have been leveled against you? Why didn't you
yourself keep us informed right from the start about your
decision and your first steps?

FOUSTKA: I see now that it was a mistake. But I looked at it
in a completely different way. As a researcher who is in-
1500 experienced in hands-on fieldwork, I unconsciously compared my role to the situation of an independent scientific
worker, who doesn't keep a running account of each of
his professional moves either. I thought that it would be
sufficient—just as it is in theoretical work—to write a re-
1505 port about my work only at the point where there is really something to report about, that is, when I actually had
something concretely relevant and useful in hand. It absolutely never crossed my mind that some chance information about my activities from someone uninformed
1510 about their purpose might in some way shake the confidence that I had hitherto enjoyed here.

DIRECTOR: You really can't be surprised at that, Foustka. Your
decision, however noble-minded, is unfortunately so unusual, and, truth to tell, so totally unexpected from you of
1515 all people, that logically our first conclusions were more
likely to be on the negative side.

DEPUTY: You really can't be surprised at that, Dr. Foustka.

DIRECTOR: Never mind—let's come to some sort of conclusion, then. You've convinced me that this was all a sheer
1520 misunderstanding, and I'm glad that everything was
cleared up so quickly. Needless to say, I think highly of
your brave decision and I can assure you that this work of
yours will be prized all the more for it, especially once
you get in the habit of keeping thorough records of it and
1525 simultaneously keeping us informed. Does anyone have
anything further to add? (*An awkward pause.*) Nobody
does? In that case, the time has come for a small surprise:
tomorrow's get-together at the Institute garden will be a
costume party!

1530 LORENCOVA: Bravo!

KOTRLY: A great idea!

DEPUTY: Oh, yes! I like it a lot too.

LORENCOVA: And what theme will it have?

DIRECTOR: Isn't it obvious? A witches' Sabbath!

(*A wave of commotion runs through the room.*)

1535   A gathering of devils, witches, sorcerers, and magicians.
Classy, what? Originally I only saw it as an attempt to
liven up the office party tradition with a certain parodis-
tic element. It seemed to me that if at night we made fun
of the very thing we have to fight against so seriously and
1540   soberly during the day, we could—in the spirit of modern
group-costume therapy—enhance our relationship to our
own work. Simply by treating the problem with frivolity
for a few moments we would emphasize its permanent
unfrivolity, by making light of it we would emphasize its
1545   gravity, by stepping away from it we would get closer to

it. Now, however, thanks to a timely coincidence, I think
we can see it in yet another way: as a playful tribute to the
work of our colleague Foustka here, who not only needs
to find a disguise, in the metaphorical sense of the word,
but also may face the unenviable task of finding a literal   1550
disguise soon—on that occasion when he decides to infiltrate some actual black mass or other! (*Polite laughter.*) Ah
well, let's all look at it—at least in part—as a sort of jolly
little ending to the serious transaction we just concluded!
Who's feeding the carrier pigeons today?   1555

NEUWIRTH: I am.

DIRECTOR: Splendid! (*To* KOTRLY.) Vilem, don't forget!

The curtain falls.

SCENE 8

Vilma's apartment again. As the curtain rises, FOUSTKA, *wearing
undershorts, is sitting on the bed, and* VILMA, *wearing a slip, is combing her hair at the mirror—the situation is the same as at the beginning of Scene 4.*

FOUSTKA: I just bet you could buy him off with a mere kiss
on the cheek, once he was in the house! Surely he tried
to dance with you at the very least!   1560

VILMA: Henry, drop it, for goodness sake! I don't keep pumping you for details either—and I'd have far more reason to
do so!

(*A short pause. Then* FOUSTKA *gets up and begins to walk back and
forth, deep in thought.* VILMA *stops combing her hair and looks at
him in surprise.*)

    What's wrong?

FOUSTKA: What should be wrong?   1565

VILMA: You began so well.

FOUSTKA: Somehow I'm not in the mood for it today.

VILMA: Does it arouse you too much?

FOUSTKA: It's not that.

VILMA: So what happened?   1570

FOUSTKA: You know very well.

VILMA: I don't!

FOUSTKA: You really don't know? And who denounced me
to the director about the sorcerer coming to see me, you
don't know that either?   1575

(VILMA *freezes, then throws down the comb, jumps up excitedly, and
looks at* FOUSTKA *with astonishment.*)

VILMA: For God's sake, Henry, you don't think that—

FOUSTKA: Nobody else at the Institute knew about it!

VILMA: Are you crazy? Why would I do it, for goodness sake? 1580
If you're going to insult me with the thought that I could
denounce anybody at all to that imbecile, how can you
imagine that I'd go and denounce *you*? Why, that would
be as bad as denouncing my own self! You know how
much I want you to be happy, and how I'm constantly   1585
worrying about you! How could I possibly want to destroy you all of a sudden? And my own self at the same
time—our relationship—our life together—our make-
believe jealousy games—our love—so marvelously confirmed by those flashes of true jealousy that you've begun 1590

to show in recent days, our memories of all those golden hours of sheer happiness we've had together—why, it would be pure madness!

1595 FOUSTKA: What if it were precisely the memory of those golden hours that provided the key to such an act? What do I know about a woman's heart? Maybe you wanted to get even with me over Marketa—or maybe it was just fear of that cripple and an effort to save me from what you thought were his clutches in this way.

(VILMA *runs to the bed, throws herself face down on the pillows, and begins to sob desperately.* FOUSTKA *doesn't know what to do. He looks at* VILMA *helplessly for a while, then sits down beside her cautiously and begins to stroke her hair.*)

1600 Come on, Vilma.

(*Pause.* VILMA *sobs.*)

I didn't mean it that way.

(*Pause.* VILMA *sobs.*)

I was just kidding.

(*Pause.* VILMA *sobs.*)

I just wanted to try a new game.

(*Pause.* VILMA *suddenly sits up briskly, dries her eyes with a handkerchief, and snuffles her nose to clear it. When she feels herself sufficiently calm and strong she speaks coldly.*)

VILMA: Go away!

(FOUSTKA *tries to stroke her; she pushes him away and cries out.*)

1605 Don't touch me—just go!
FOUSTKA: Vilma! I didn't say anything all that terrible! How many times did you want me to tell you far more terrible things!
VILMA: That was different. Are you even aware of what you
1610 just did? Why, you actually accused me of being a stool pigeon. I'm asking you to get dressed, to leave, and never to try to repair what you just destroyed so brutally!
FOUSTKA: Are you serious?
VILMA: At least we'll have it over with. It would have hap-
1615 pened sooner or later in any case!
FOUSTKA: Because of that dancer?
VILMA: No.
FOUSTKA: Why, then?
VILMA: I'm beginning to lose my respect for you.
1620 FOUSTKA: This is the first I've heard of it.
VILMA: It doesn't take long to happen, you know. I actually realized it only today, when I saw the way you saved your neck at the Institute. Offering the director to inform for him, and so shamelessly, in front of everybody! And now,
1625 to top it all off, you, a voluntary and self-declared stool pigeon, dare to accuse me, innocent and devoted me, of informing—and what's more, of informing on you! Do you see how absurd it is? What's happened to you? What's gotten into you? Are you actually the same person anymore?
1630 Maybe you really *are* possessed by some devil! That fellow

addled your brains. God knows what stuff he told you. God knows what spell he cast on you.

(FOUSTKA *gets up and begins to walk back and forth across the room in agitation.*)

FOUSTKA: For your information he doesn't cast spells, he only helps people understand their own selves better and face all the bad things dormant inside them! Furthermore, 1635 about my being a stool pigeon, as you put it, not only was that the only way I could save myself, it was also the only way I could help him as well! If they believe that I'm controlling him, they'll leave him alone. And the third thing, my suspecting that they found out about him from you— 1640 I simply couldn't hide it from you. What would that have done to our relationship! You might have said something unintentionally—in front of someone you trusted by mistake—or somebody could have accidentally overheard you . . . 1645
VILMA: I never said anything intentionally or not, and what bothers me about your suspicions is not your speaking up about them, or even that you spoke up so crudely, which you're now belatedly trying to make up for, but that they occurred to you at all! If you're capable of thinking some- 1650 thing like that about me for even a split second, then there's really no point in our staying together.

(*Pause.* FOUSTKA *sits down dejectedly in the armchair and stares dully into space.*)

FOUSTKA: I was a fool to say anything to you. I always spoil everything so stupidly. What am I going to do without you? I can't stand myself. 1655
VILMA: And now you're even feeling sorry for yourself!
FOUSTKA: Do you remember what we said to each other that time under the elms at the riverbank?
VILMA: Don't drag those elms into this, it won't do you any good. You've hurt me too much to talk your way out of it 1660 by manipulating our memories of the past. And besides, I asked you to do something . . .
FOUSTKA: You mean that I should leave?
VILMA: Exactly!
FOUSTKA: You're expecting the dancer, aren't you? 1665
VILMA: I'm not expecting anyone, I simply want to be alone!

(*A short pause. Then* FOUSTKA *suddenly jumps up, runs over to* VILMA, *knocks her down roughly on the bed, and grabs her wildly by the neck.*)

FOUSTKA (*in a dark voice*): You're lying, you whore!
VILMA (*crying out in terror*): Help!

(FOUSTKA *begins to strangle* VILMA. *Just then the doorbell rings.* FOUSTKA *drops* VILMA *immediately, jumps away from her in confusion, stands there for a moment helplessly, then slowly heads for the armchair and lowers himself into it heavily.* VILMA *stands up, quickly straightens herself up a bit, goes to the door, and opens it. There stands the* DANCER, *holding a bunch of violets behind his back.*)

DANCER: Excuse me for disturbing you so late, I only wanted to bring you these. (*The* DANCER *hands* VILMA *the violets.*) 1670
VILMA: Thanks! Come in, please, and stay a while . . .

(The DANCER *looks at* VILMA *in surprise, and then at* FOUSTKA *col-lapsed in the armchair staring absently into space. An awkward pause.)*

He's not feeling well, you see—I'm a little worried.

DANCER: Some sort of heart trouble?

VILMA: Probably.

675 DANCER: So in the meanwhile we could dance a little bit, what do you say? Maybe it would distract him.

The curtain falls.

SCENE 9

Foustka's apartment again. As the curtain rises, FOUSTKA *is alone onstage. Dressed in a dressing gown, he is pacing back and forth, deep in thought. After a long while someone knocks at the door.* FOUSTKA *stops in his tracks, hesitates for a moment, and then calls.*

FOUSTKA: Who is it?

HOUBOVA *(offstage)*: It's me, Doctor Foustka.

FOUSTKA *(calling)*: Come in, Mrs. Houbova.

680 HOUBOVA *(entering)*: You've got a visitor.

FOUSTKA: I do! Who?

HOUBOVA: Well, it's him again . . . you know . . . the one that . . .

FOUSTKA: That smells?

685 HOUBOVA: Yes.

FOUSTKA: Show him in.

(A short pause; HOUBOVA *stands uncertainly.)*

What's the matter?

HOUBOVA: Doctor Foustka . . .

FOUSTKA: Did something happen?

690 HOUBOVA: I'm just a stupid woman. I know it's not my place to give you advice about anything.

FOUSTKA: What's on your mind?

HOUBOVA: I'm sorry, but if I were in your place I wouldn't trust that fellow! I can't really explain it—I don't even

695 know what business he has with you—I just have a sort of strange feeling about him.

FOUSTKA: Last time you let him in yourself!

HOUBOVA: Because I was scared of him.

FOUSTKA: I'll admit he looks disreputable, but basically he's

700 harmless. Or, to be more precise, he's too insignificant to do any serious damage.

HOUBOVA: Do you have to associate with people like him? You?

FOUSTKA: Mrs. Houbova, I'm a grown-up and I know what

705 I'm doing, after all!

HOUBOVA: But I'm so worried about you! Don't you see, I remember you as a three-year-old. I don't have children of my own . . .

FOUSTKA: Of course, that's fine, I'm really grateful for your

710 concern. I understand and I appreciate it, but I think that in this case it's really unnecessary. Show him in and don't worry about it anymore.

*(*HOUBOVA *exits, leaving the door ajar.)*

HOUBOVA *(offstage)*: This way, Mister.

*(*FISTULA *enters, carrying his bag in his hand.* HOUBOVA *takes one last look after him into the room, shakes her head anxiously, and closes the door.* FISTULA, *grinning stupidly, rushes directly to the sofa, sits down, takes off his shoes, takes his slippers out of the bag and puts them on, puts the shoes into the bag, which he then places on the sofa beside him. He looks up at* FOUSTKA *and begins to grin.)*

FISTULA: So, what?

FOUSTKA: What, what?   1715

FISTULA: I'm waiting for you to begin your usual song and dance.

FOUSTKA: What song and dance?

FISTULA: That I should leave immediately and so on.

*(*FOUSTKA *walks around the room, deep in thought, then sits at his desk.)*

FOUSTKA: Listen! In the first place, I've come to understand   1720
that it's impossible simply to get rid of you and therefore it makes no sense to waste time trying to do something that's doomed to failure in advance. In the second place, without making too much of your inspirational influence, as you call it, I've come to the conclusion that time spent   1725
with you doesn't have to be a complete waste after all. If I have to be a subject for you, why, then, shouldn't you be a subject for me in turn? Or isn't that how your original proposal went: that you offer me an inside look at your practices, for which I, in exchange, guarantee you a cer-   1730
tain cover? I've decided to accept your proposal.

FISTULA: I knew you'd work yourself up to it, which was one of the reasons for my persistence. I'm glad that my persistence is finally rewarded. But not to be too humble about it, again: I don't attribute your decision to my persistence   1735
alone, but also to the obvious accomplishments our col-laboration has achieved . . .

FOUSTKA: What accomplishments are you referring to now?

FISTULA: Not only that you kept your job at the Institute, but that you actually even improved your position there.   1740
Meanwhile, it gives me great joy to state that in this par-ticular case you even managed to avoid Smichovsky's Compensatory Syndrome, which is a sign of real progress.

FOUSTKA: If you're trying to suggest that I lost all my moral values and gave in to whatever it is that you're trying to   1745
awaken inside of me, then you are very much mistaken. I'm still the same person. I'm just cooler and more in con-trol as a result of my recent experiences, which allows me to know at all times just how far and in which direction—however new it might be for me—I am able to go, with-   1750
out the risk of letting myself in for something that I might bitterly regret later on.

*(*FISTULA *grows slightly uneasy, fidgets a bit, looks around.)*

What's the matter with you?

FISTULA: Oh nothing, nothing.

FOUSTKA: You look like you're afraid, which is a condition I   1755
don't recognize in you and which would especially surprise me after the explicit promise of cover I just gave you.

*(*FISTULA *takes off his slippers and rubs the soles of his feet with both hands, sighing all the while.)*

Does it hurt?

FISTULA: It's nothing, it'll go away. (*after a while he puts on his slippers again. Then he suddenly begins to cackle.*)

FOUSTKA: What's so funny now?

FISTULA: May I be completely frank?

FOUSTKA: Suit yourself.

FISTULA: You are!

FOUSTKA: What? You find me funny? What nerve!

(FISTULA *grows serious and stares at the ground. After a while he suddenly glances up at* FOUSTKA.)

FISTULA: Look here, Doctor Foustka. The fact that you saved your neck by means of a little dirty work is quite all right. Why, Hajaha and I—

FOUSTKA: Who?

FISTULA: Hajaha, the spirit of politics—we were pointing you in that very direction! What's not quite all right is that in the process you forgot the rules of the game!

FOUSTKA: What rules? What game? What the devil are you talking about?

FISTULA: Don't you suppose that our work together has rules of its own too? Break down your own scruples as much as you want—as you know, I always welcome that sort of thing on principle. But to double-cross the very one who is leading you along this thrilling and, I might even say, revolutionary path—that, you really shouldn't do! Even a revolution has its laws! Last time you called me a devil. Imagine for a moment that I really were one! How do you suppose I'd react to your amateurish attempt to deceive me?

FOUSTKA: But I'm not trying to deceive you.

FISTULA: Look, without actually making any explicit promises, we certainly reached a sort of unspoken agreement not to talk about our work together with anyone, much less make reports on it to hostile and threatening authorities. One might even go so far as to say that we had begun—naturally with some caution—to trust each other. If you failed to understand the inner meaning of our agreement and you decided to thumb your nose at it, that was your first serious mistake. You've done enough reading, after all, to know that there are certain limits—even in my sphere—that you can't overstep; in fact, precisely here, with so much at stake, the commandment against overstepping them is especially severe. Don't you understand that if we're capable of playing around with the whole world, it is only and entirely because we depend on contacts that we're absolutely forbidden to play around with? To deceive a liar is fine, to deceive a truth teller is still allowable, but to deceive the very instrument that gives us the strength to deceive and that allows us in advance to deceive with impunity—that, you truly cannot expect to get away with! That one (*points skyward*), overwhelms Man with a multitude of unkeepable commandments, and therefore there's nothing left for him but to forgive occasionally. The others, on the other hand, liberate Man from all those unkeepable commandments, and therefore, understandably, they are totally rid of the need, opportunity, and, finally, even the capacity to forgive. But even if that weren't so, they wouldn't be able to forgive the betrayal of the very agreement releasing all that

boundless freedom. Why, such forgiveness would make their entire world collapse! But really, might not the obligation to be faithful to the authority which gives us that sort of freedom actually be the only guarantee of freedom from all obligation? Do you see what I mean?

(FOUSTKA, *who has been growing increasingly nervous during Fistula's speech, stands up and begins to pace about the room. A long pause.* FISTULA *watches him carefully. Then* FOUSTKA *suddenly comes to a stop at his desk, leans against it as if against a speaker's podium, and turns to* FISTULA.)

FOUSTKA: I see what you mean perfectly well, but I'm afraid you don't see what *I* mean!

FISTULA: Is that so?

FOUSTKA: You can look at the promise you're obviously referring to as an attempt to betray you only because you don't know why I made it and was able to make it with a clear conscience!

FISTULA: You made it in order to save your neck.

FOUSTKA: Of course, but what good would it be if the price were betrayal! I'm not that stupid! The only reason that I was able to make the promise was because I was determined right from the start not only *not* to keep it, but at the same time to cleverly use the position it gained for me—naturally in close consultation with you—for our purposes and to our advantage. In other words, to gain control over their information, while flooding them with our own disinformation; to erase the real tracks, while keeping them busy with false ones; to use their own organization to rescue those of us who are threatened, while drowning those who threaten us. And with all this, to serve our cause by being our own man hidden in the heart of the enemy, indeed, in the very heart of the enemy's division specifically designed to fight against us! I'm surprised and disappointed that you didn't understand and appreciate my plan immediately.

(FOUSTKA *sits.* FISTULA *leaps up and begins to cackle and jump around the room wildly. Then he suddenly stops and quite matter-of-factly turns to* FOUSTKA.)

FISTULA: Even if you just invented this conceit, I'll still accept it, if only to give you one last chance. Actually it *is* possible to forgive, and to give people a chance to make amends, even in our realm. If I claimed the opposite a little while ago, it was only to scare you into coming out with precisely the sort of unambiguous offer as the one you just made, thereby allowing you to save yourself at the very edge of the abyss. But obviously, and luckily for you, I'm really not the devil. He would never have let you get away with the betrayal that I just let you get away with, never!

(FOUSTKA *is visibly relieved, can't hide it, goes to* FISTULA *and embraces him.* FISTULA *jumps aside, his teeth begin to chatter, and he begins to quickly rub his arms.*)

Man, you must be a hundred below zero!

FOUSTKA (*laughing*): Not quite.

The curtain falls.

SCENE 10

The Institute garden once again. Except that the bench is now on the right and the table with drinks now on the left, everything is exactly the same as it was in Scene 3, including the lighting. As the curtain rises, the music becomes quiet and changes in style just as at the beginning of Scene 3. This time, too, it will provide a background for the entire scene unless otherwise indicated. The two LOVERS *and* FOUSTKA *are onstage. The* LOVERS *dance together in the background, where they will continue to dance without interruption for almost the entire scene, leaving their bower empty for now.* FOUSTKA *is sitting on the bench, deep in thought. All three are wearing costumes that suit the "magic" theme of the party.* FOUSTKA *is wearing the traditional theatrical costume for Faust. All characters appearing in this scene are dressed or in some cases painted in this same spirit. Some of the best-known and most common motifs traditionally used in the theater for "hellish" or "witchlike" themes should make an appearance in this scene; for instance, the colors red and black should predominate, as well as a profusion of pendants and amulets of various sorts, wildly tangled women's wigs, devils' tails, hoofs, and chains, etc. A long pause. Then, from the right,* LORENCOVA *emerges with a broom under her arm. She crosses the stage towards the table, where she pours herself a drink. Pause.*

FOUSTKA: Do you happen to know if the director is here yet?
LORENCOVA: No I don't.

(Pause. LORENCOVA *finishes her drink, puts the glass down, and vanishes to the left. After a while she can be seen in the background, dancing alone with her broom. Pause. Then the* DEPUTY *enters from the left.)*

1860 DEPUTY: Have you seen Petrushka?
FOUSTKA: She hasn't been here.

(The DEPUTY *shakes his head uncomprehendingly and vanishes to the right. After a while he may be seen in the background, swaying alone to the dance music.* FOUSTKA *gets up and goes to the table, where he pours himself a drink. The* DIRECTOR *and* KOTRLY, *holding hands, enter from the right. Unless otherwise noted, they will be holding hands for the whole scene. The* DIRECTOR, *in a particularly conspicuous devil costume, has horns on his head. The* DIRECTOR *and* KOTRLY *pay no attention to* FOUSTKA *and stop in the middle of the stage.* FOUSTKA, *at the table, watches them.)*

DIRECTOR *(to* KOTRLY): Where will you actually put it? Around here?
KOTRLY: I thought I'd put it in the bower.
1865 DIRECTOR: All right. That would be better for safety reasons too.
KOTRLY: I'll light it in the gardener's shed, then I'll secretly bring it here—it takes a few minutes to warm up. I'll set it down in the bower, and a little while later you'll see
1870 . . . (DIRECTOR *and* KOTRLY *head towards the left.)*
FOUSTKA: Excuse me, Sir . . .

(The DIRECTOR *and* KOTRLY *stop.)*

DIRECTOR: Yes, Foustka?
FOUSTKA: I wonder if you have a minute or two?
DIRECTOR: I'm sorry, Foustka, but certainly not now.

(The DIRECTOR *and* KOTRLY *disappear to the left. After a while they may be seen in the background, dancing together.* FOUSTKA, *holding his glass, crosses back to the bench, deep in thought, and sits down. The music grows noticeably louder, some well-known tango may be heard, for instance, "Tango Milonga."* VILMA *and the* DANCER *rush onstage from the left and begin to do some complicated tango figures together. These are choreographed mainly by the* DANCER, *obviously a professional, who continues to glide about the stage elaborately and skillfully with* VILMA. FOUSTKA *stares at them in astonishment. After a while the tango comes to a climax and* VILMA *and the* DANCER *do a closing figure. The music grows softer and changes its character. Out of breath but happy,* VILMA *and the* DANCER *are holding hands and smiling at each other.)*

FOUSTKA: Are you enjoying yourselves?   1875
VILMA: As you can see.

(The DEPUTY, *who has in the interim left the dance floor, enters from the left.)*

DEPUTY: Have you seen Petrushka?
VILMA: She hasn't been here.

(The DEPUTY *shakes his head impatiently and vanishes to the right. After a while he may be seen in the background, swaying alone to the dance music.* VILMA *seizes the* DANCER *by the hand and leads him away. They both disappear to the left. After a while they may be seen in the background, dancing.* FOUSTKA *stands up, crosses to the table, and pours himself a drink. The* DIRECTOR *and* KOTRLY, *who have in the interim disappeared from the dance floor, enter from the right, holding hands. They pay no attention to* FOUSTKA *but stop in the middle of the stage.* FOUSTKA, *at the table, watches them.)*

KOTRLY *(to the* DIRECTOR): How will I know when it's the right time for it?   1880
DIRECTOR: You'll figure it out somehow, or else I'll give you a signal. I'm worried about something else.
KOTRLY: What?
DIRECTOR: Can you really guarantee that nothing will go wrong?   1885
KOTRLY: What should go wrong?
DIRECTOR: Well, somebody might suffocate—or something might catch fire . . .
KOTRLY: Don't worry.

(The DIRECTOR *and* KOTRLY *head towards the left.)*

FOUSTKA: Excuse me, Sir . . .   1890
DIRECTOR: Yes, Foustka?
FOUSTKA: I realize that you have a lot of other things on your mind just now, but I won't keep you long, and I'm certain that the thing I want to talk to you about will interest you.
DIRECTOR: I'm sorry, but now it's really impossible . . .   1895

(Just then the SECRET MESSENGER *enters from the right, goes up to the* DIRECTOR, *leans over, and whispers in his ear at length. The* DIRECTOR *nods his head. While the* MESSENGER *is whispering,* LORENCOVA, *who has in the interim left the dance floor, enters from the right holding her broom in her hand. She remains standing near the bench and gazes at the* MESSENGER. *After a long while the* MESSENGER *concludes. The* DIRECTOR *nods one last time, at which*

point he disappears to the left with KOTRLY. After a while they may be seen in the background, dancing together. The MESSENGER heads towards the right, just opposite LORENCOVA. She is smiling at him. He stops directly in front of her. For a moment both of them stare at each other intently, then the MESSENGER, without taking his eyes off her, takes her broom from her hand, places it on the ground meaningfully, and commences to embrace LORENCOVA. She embraces him in return. For a moment they gaze meltingly into each other's eyes, then they begin to kiss. When they move apart after a while, they disappear together to the right, arms around each other's waists. After a while they may be seen in the background, dancing. FOUSTKA, glass in hand and deep in thought, crosses the stage to the bench and sits down. Suddenly, he becomes attentive and listens. Offstage a girl's voice may be heard, singing the melody of the music that is just playing, Ophelia's song from Hamlet.)

MARKETA (singing offstage):
    And will 'a not come again?
    And will 'a not come again?
    No, no, he is dead,
1900   Go to thy death bed,

(MARKETA emerges at left. She is barefoot, her hair is loose and flowing; on her head is a wreath made of wild flowers. She is wearing a white nightgown with the word "psychiatry" stamped at the bottom in large letters. She approaches FOUSTKA slowly, singing. He rises, aghast.)

    He never will come again.
    His beard was as white as snow
    All flaxen was his poll
    He is gone, he is gone,
1905   And we cast away moan.
    God 'a' mercy on his soul!
FOUSTKA (crying out): Marketa!
MARKETA: Oh where is that handsome Prince of Denmark?

(FOUSTKA, horrified, walks backward in front of MARKETA, she walks behind him, they slowly circle the stage.)

FOUSTKA: What are you doing here, for God's sake? Did you
1910   run away?
MARKETA: Tell him, please, when you see him, that all those things can't exist just for themselves, but that they must conceal some deeper design of existence, of the world, and of nature willing you . . .
1915 FOUSTKA: Marketa, don't you recognize me? It's Henry . . .
MARKETA: Or could it be, perhaps, that the cosmos directly intended that one fine day it would see itself thus through our eyes and ask itself thus through our lips the very questions we're asking ourselves here and now?
1920 FOUSTKA: You ought to go back—they'll help you—everything will be all right again—you'll see . . .
MARKETA (singing):
    How should I your true love know
    From another one?
1925   By his cockle hat and staff,
    And his sandal shoon.

(MARKETA vanishes to the right. Offstage the sound of her singing can still be heard, gradually fading away. FOUSTKA, upset, crosses over to the table, quickly pours himself a drink, downs it in one gulp,

and pours himself another. The DIRECTOR and KOTRLY, who have in the interim left the dance floor, appear at the right, holding hands. They pay no attention to FOUSTKA but are absorbed in their conversation.)

DIRECTOR: Surely he tried to dance with you at the very least . . .
KOTRLY: Please stop it! Can't you talk about anything more interesting?   1930
DIRECTOR: Did he try or not?
KOTRLY: All right, he did, if you really must know, then he did! But I won't tell you another thing.

(The DIRECTOR and KOTRLY slowly cross the stage and head for the exit at left.)

FOUSTKA: Excuse me, Sir . . .

(The DIRECTOR and KOTRLY stop.)

DIRECTOR: What do you want, Foustka?   1935

(Just then a cry of pain is heard from behind the bench.)

NEUWIRTH (offstage): Ow!

(The DIRECTOR, KOTRLY, and FOUSTKA look towards the bench with surprise. Out of the bushes emerges NEUWIRTH, holding his ear, obviously wounded. He is groaning.)

KOTRLY: What in the world happened to you, Louie?
NEUWIRTH: Oh, nothing.
DIRECTOR: Is something the matter with your ear?

(NEUWIRTH nods.)

KOTRLY: Did something bite you?   1940

(NEUWIRTH nods, and with his head indicates the bushes from which he had just emerged and out of which now emerges an embarrassed PETRUSHKA. She is nervously straightening her hair and her costume. The DIRECTOR and KOTRLY grin and exchange knowing looks. NEUWIRTH, groaning and holding his ear, drags himself off to the right and disappears. PETRUSHKA timidly crosses the stage to the table and with shaking hands pours herself a small drink, which she swiftly drinks. The DIRECTOR and KOTRLY try to leave.)

FOUSTKA: Excuse me, Sir . . .
DIRECTOR: What do you want, Foustka?

(Just then the DEPUTY enters from the left. At first he doesn't see PETRUSHKA, who is hidden by FOUSTKA.)

DEPUTY: Have you seen Petrushka?

(PETRUSHKA goes up to the DEPUTY, smiles at him, and takes his hand; from this moment on they will hold hands as before.)

    Where were you, sweetie pie?

(PETRUSHKA whispers something to the DEPUTY, he listens carefully, finally he nods in satisfaction. The DIRECTOR and KOTRLY try to leave.)

FOUSTKA: Excuse me, Sir . . .   1945

DIRECTOR: What do you want, Foustka?

FOUSTKA: I realize that you have a lot of other things on your mind right now, but on the other hand . . . having learned my lesson by what happened before . . I wouldn't want to neglect anything . . . You see, I have some new findings . . . I've even written them down on a piece of paper . . .

1950

(FOUSTKA beings to search, obviously looking for the paper. The DI-RECTOR and the DEPUTY exchange knowing glances and then take a few steps forward, the one leading KOTRLY by the hand, the other, PETRUSHKA, and move to the center of the stage, where all four automatically form a sort of semicircle around FOUSTKA. A short pause.)

DIRECTOR: Don't bother.

(FOUSTKA looks at the DIRECTOR in surprise, then looks around at the others. A short, suspenseful pause.)

FOUSTKA: I thought I . . .

(Again, a suspenseful pause, which is finally interrupted by the DIRECTOR.)

DIRECTOR *(sharply)*: I'm not interested in what you thought, I'm not interested in your piece of paper, I'm not interested in you. The comedy, my dear Sir, is ended!

1955

FOUSTKA: I don't understand—what comedy?

DIRECTOR: You greatly overestimated yourself and you greatly underestimated us, taking us for bigger idiots than we are.

1960

DEPUTY: You still don't understand?

FOUSTKA: No.

DIRECTOR: Very well, then, I'll give it to you straight. We knew all along what you thought of us, we knew you were merely pretending to be loyal while hiding your real interests and ideas from us. But in spite of that we decided to give you a last chance. And so while seeming to believe that cock-and-bull story about your intention to work for us out in the field, we were curious to see how you would behave after having had your lesson and your supposed narrow escape, wondering whether you might not come to your senses after all. But instead, you took the hand we offered you and spat on it in a despicable way, thus definitively sealing your own fate.

1965

1970

1975 FOUSTKA: That's not true!

DIRECTOR: You know perfectly well that it is!

FOUSTKA: Then prove it!

DIRECTOR *(to the DEPUTY)*: Shall we oblige him?

DEPUTY: I'm in favor of it.

(The DIRECTOR sharply whistles on his fingers. From the bower, where he had apparently been hidden for the entire scene, FISTULA leaps out. FOUSTKA is alarmed to see him. FISTULA quickly limps over to the DIRECTOR.)

1980 FISTULA: Did you call, Boss?

DIRECTOR: What did he tell you when you were at his house yesterday?

FISTULA: That he would pretend to be working as an informer for you, but in reality he, together with those you are fighting against, would use all their power to damage your information service. He literally said that he would

1985

be our—meaning their—man hidden in the heart of the enemy . . .

FOUSTKA *(screaming)*: He's lying!

DIRECTOR: What did you say? Would you repeat that?   1990

FOUSTKA: I said he's lying.

DIRECTOR: Man, you really have some nerve! How dare you accuse my close and faithful friend of many years and one of our best external agents of lying! Fistula never lies to us!   1995

DEPUTY: That's precisely what I wanted to say, Sir! Fistula never lies to us!

(LORENCOVA and the SECRET MESSENGER appear from the left, while at the same time the LOVERS appear from the right, all of whom have, in the interim, left the dance floor. Both pairs are holding hands. They join the others in such a way that the semicircle in the center of which FOUSTKA is standing unobtrusively widens at both sides in order to incorporate them.)

FOUSTKA: So Fistula was an informer after all, and you planted him on me to test me! What an imbecile I was not to throw him out right away! Vilma, I apologize to you for   2000
my absurd suspicions that made me lose you! Mrs. Houbova, I apologize to you—of course you knew the truth right away.

DIRECTOR: Who's he talking to?

FISTULA: His landlady, Boss.   2005

DIRECTOR: Naturally you're not the only person in the world I'm interested in. I test everybody—you'd be surprised how long it sometimes takes, compared to your trivial case—for me to get at the truth, in one way or another!

FOUSTKA *(to FISTULA)*: So I fell for your line after all!   2010

FISTULA: I beg your pardon, Doctor Foustka. *(To the DIRECTOR)* Is he still a doctor?

DIRECTOR: Who gives a shit?

FISTULA: I beg your pardon, Doctor Foustka, but there you go again, oversimplifying! Didn't I make it clear all along,   2015
by dropping hints and even spelling it out, that you had a number of alternatives, and that you alone were the master of your fate! You weren't a victim of my line, but of your own; or rather, of your pride, which made you think that you'd be able to play both ends against the middle   2020
and still get away with it! Or have you forgotten how carefully I explained to you that if a person doesn't want to come to a bad end, he must respect some form of authority, it almost doesn't matter which, and that even a revolution has its own laws? I don't see how I could have   2025
made things more obvious than that! My conscience is clear, I did what I could. Why, I couldn't have fulfilled my mission more correctly! The fact that you didn't understand anything, well, I'm afraid that's your tough luck.

DIRECTOR: Fistula is right, as ever. You cannot serve two mas-   2030
ters at once and deceive them both at the same time! You cannot take from everyone and give nothing in return! You simply must take a side!

DEPUTY: That's precisely what I just wanted to say, Sir! You simply must take a side!   2035

(The music grows noticeably louder. The tango that played earlier is heard again. At the same moment VILMA runs onstage from the left and the DANCER from the right, having in the interim left the dance floor. They run through the group of people to the center of the stage,

where they fall into each other's arms and commence to do another complicated tango figure, during which the DANCER *does a "dip" almost to the ground with* VILMA. *The music suddenly grows quiet, and* VILMA *and the* DANCER, *holding hands just as all the other couples in the room are doing, quietly join the semicircle.*)

FOUSTKA: It's paradoxical, but now that I've definitively lost and my knowledge serves no purpose to me, I'm finally beginning to understand it all! Fistula is right: I was an arrogant madman who thought he could exploit the devil without signing away his soul to him! But as everyone knows, one can't deceive the devil!

(NEUWIRTH, *with a large bandage on his ear, enters from the right, just as* MARKETA *runs in from the left. When she sees* NEUWIRTH *she calls out to him.*)

MARKETA: Papa!

(MARKETA *runs up to* NEUWIRTH *and seizes his hand. He is a little embarrassed. And even they reluctantly become part of the semicircle.*)

FISTULA: Wait a minute, now! Hold it! I never said that there is such a thing as a devil, not even while I was engaged in that provocation.

FOUSTKA: But I'm saying it! And he's actually here among us!

FISTULA: Are you referring to me?

FOUSTKA: You're just a subordinate little fiend!

DIRECTOR: I know your opinions, Foustka, and therefore I understand this metaphor of yours as well. Through me, you want to accuse modern science of being the true source of all evil. Isn't that right?

FOUSTKA: No, it isn't! Through you, I want to accuse the pride of that intolerant, all-powerful, and self-serving power that uses the sciences merely as a handy weapon for shooting down anything that threatens, it, that is, anything that doesn't derive its authority from this power or that is related to an authority deriving its powers elsewhere.

DIRECTOR: That's the legacy you wish to leave this world, Foustka?

FOUSTKA: Yes!

DIRECTOR: I find it a little banal. In countries without censorship every halfway clever little hack journalist churns out stuff like that these days! But a legacy is a legacy, so in spite of what you think of me, I'll give you an example of how tolerant I am by overlooking my reservations and applauding your last testament!

(*The* DIRECTOR *begins to clap lightly, and all the others gradually join in. At the same time the music grows louder—it is hard, wild, and aggressive rock music, a variation of the music heard before the performance and during the pauses. The clapping soon becomes rhythmic, in time with the music, which grows ever louder, slowly becoming almost deafening. Everyone onstage, with the exception of* FOUSTKA, *gradually begins to move suggestively in time with the music. At first, while clapping, they begin to wriggle gently, swaying and shaking to the music. Then this movement slowly changes into dancing. At first they each dance alone, then in couples, and finally all together. The dance is ever wilder, until it becomes a crazy, orgiastic masked ball or witches' Sabbath.* FOUSTKA *does not participate but wanders around in confusion, weaving in and out among the dancers, who variously bump into him, so that he completely loses his sense of direction and is unable to escape, though he would clearly like to.* KOTRLY, *who slipped away from the witches' Sabbath earlier, now returns, carrying a bowl with flames playing at the surface. He twists in and out among the dancers with it, trying to get to the bower, where he finally succeeds in putting the bowl down. However, on the way there he also manages to ignite Foustka's cape, so that a new chaotic element is added to the witches' Sabbath in the person of the burning* FOUSTKA, *who now, completely panicked, races around the stage. Shortly thereafter everyone is surrounded by a thick cloud of smoke streaming in from the bower where* KOTRLY *has placed his bowl. The music blasts away. Nothing can be seen onstage. Smoke penetrates the audience. Then the music suddenly stops, the house lights go on, the smoke fades, and it becomes evident that at some point during all this the curtain has fallen. After a very brief silence, music comes on again, now at a bearable level of loudness— the most banal commercial music possible. If the smoke—or the play itself—hasn't caused the audience to flee, and if there are still a few left in the audience who might even want to applaud, let the first to take a bow and thank the audience be a fireman in full uniform with a helmet on his head and a fire extinguisher in his hand.*)

Tomson Highway

Since the production of his two most celebrated plays, *The Rez Sisters* (1986) and *Dry Lips Oughta Move to Kapuskasing* (1989), Tomson Highway has become perhaps the best-known of the many Native playwrights now working in North America. Tomson Highway was born in 1951, the eleventh of twelve children, on a trapline in a Native reserve (the Canadian term for what is called a "reservation" in the United States) in northern Manitoba, Canada. Until the age of six, Highway lived a nomadic life with his family. His first language was Cree, and he did not begin to learn English until he was sent to a Roman Catholic boarding school. Like many Native children, Highway attended boarding school, visiting his family only during the summer. After graduating from high school in Winnipeg, Highway studied piano at the University of Manitoba Faculty of Music, and then studied in London before returning to Canada. He graduated with a bachelor's degree in music from the University of Western Ontario in 1975 and is an accomplished concert pianist. He remained at the university for an additional year, however, to complete a bachelor's degree in English.

After college, Highway worked at The Native Peoples' Resource Centre in London, Ontario, and at the Ontario Federation of Indian Friendship Centres in Toronto. Highway traveled to reserves across Canada, working with Native people in schools, prisons, and other institutions. He also began writing plays about Native life, many of which were performed on reserves and in Native community centers. He first worked on *The Rez Sisters* with the De-ba-jeh-mu-jig Theatre Company of Manitoulin Island, Ontario, in 1986. Like many Native theater companies, De-ba-jeh-mu-jig is devoted to the production of new plays by Native playwrights and produces an increasing number of its plays in Native languages. As artistic director of the Native Earth Performing Arts Company, Highway produced *The Rez*

Simon Starblanket and Sachary Keechigeesik in the 1989 Theater Passe Muraille production of Tomson Highway's *Dry Lips Oughta Move to Kapuskasing.*

Sisters again in Toronto in December of 1986, where it won the Dora Mavor Moore Award for the best new play of the season and was runner-up for outstanding Canadian play of the year. The play was produced in 1993 in New York by the American Indian Community House and the New York Theater Workshop.

Highway's next play, *Dry Lips Oughta Move to Kapuskasing* was first produced in Toronto in 1989 by the Native Earth Performing Arts Company. It was later moved to the Royal Alexandra Theatre in Toronto, one of the very few Canadian plays—and the first by a Native playwright—to receive a full-scale production by this commercial theater. Highway continues to work as artistic director of Native Earth Performing Arts, one of many important Native theater companies now working in Canada and the United States (others include Four Winds Theatre, Native Theatre School, Ondinnok, Takwakin Theatre, Awasikan Theatre, and A-Maize Theatre in Canada; Spiderwoman Theater, Institute of American Indian Arts, American Indian Theater Company, Minneapolis American Indian AIDS Task Force, and Off the Beaten Path in the United States). Though Highway is gay, his central aims as a playwright to date have been to make Native narrative and mythological traditions more central to contemporary Native—and non-Native—arts.

DRY LIPS OUGHTA MOVE TO KAPUSKASING

Like *The Rez Sisters*, *Dry Lips Oughta Move to Kapuskasing* concerns life on the fictional Wasaychigan Hill reserve and is written in a mixture of English, Cree, and Ojibway. However, while *The Rez Sisters* concerns a group of Native women who travel to Toronto for the "World's Biggest Bingo," *Dry Lips* is a much darker and more violent play, concerning the men of the reserve. In some respects, the poverty of life on the reserve is made evident in the play's opening scene, the run-down living room of the reserve house shared by Big Joey and Gazelle Nataways, and is developed through the men's interrupted plans to improve life on the "rez." While the women have formed a hockey team (the importance of hockey is epitomized in Pierre's mantra, "Hockey. Life. Hockey. Life."), the men squabble about their plans: Zachary Jeremiah Keechigeesik's bakery, Big Joey's radio station, and Pierre St. Pierre's new job as referee for the women's games. In some ways, the men seem threatened by the women's independence and by their brash appropriation of hockey, and this anxiety seems to imply a more generalized impotence: seedy Creature Nataways does Big Joey's bidding, even though his wife Gazelle has moved in with Big Joey; Simon Starblanket is absorbed in an endlessly aborted effort at cultural revival; Dickie Bird Halked, born with fetal alcohol syndrome, is at once shy and explosive, violently raping Patsy Pegahmagahbow with a crucifix. Even Pierre St. Pierre has a hard time finding his other skate.

Hanging around, drinking beer, complaining about the women—in many ways the Native men seem to epitomize "Canadian hoser culture," in the words of one Native critic of the play. Yet the men continually blame the women for the state of their lives, as Big Joey does in act 2: "I hate them fuckin' bitches. Because they—our own women—took the fuckin' power away from us faster than the FBI ever did." Big Joey's tirade points up the play's most controversial element, which centers on the performance of the Trickster figure Nanabush. The play begins and ends with Zachary awakening on the floor of Big Joey's house; we don't discover until the end of the play that the action has been a kind of dream, maybe a nightmare. Throughout, Nanabush occupies an elevated stage, sometimes watching the action, sometimes participating in it. In Native mythology, Nanabush is capable of changing shape and gender; neither explicitly male nor female, the Trickster uses his/her wiles in a range of legendary escapades. In *Dry Lips*, however, Nanabush takes "female" shape in a number of ways—assuming outsized breasts to play Gazelle Nataways, a large rear-end to play Patsy ("Big-Bum") Pegahmagahbow, and so on. In one reading of the play—a dream play, after all—Nanabush here enacts the men's phobias and fantasies about women, and so offers an implied critique of their sexist attitudes. From another perspective, though, one shared by many Native women who saw the play, the way Nanabush is characterized as a woman—her appearance (a version of the derogatory "squaw" stereotype), the "stripper" scene, the rape scene, the loss of the hockey puck in Gazelle/ Nanabush's enormous breasts—merely reinforces the fundamentally misogynistic attitudes of the men in the play. In this sense, *Dry Lips Oughta Move to Kapuskasing* seems poised on the razor's edge of political theater: readers, audiences, and producers of the play must consider whether it criticizes the sexist and possibly misogynist ways women are presented in the play, or whether it merely reinforces such attitudes.

Production Notes

The set for the original production of *Dry Lips Oughta Move to Kapuskasing* contained certain elements which I think are essential to the play.

First of all, it was designed on two levels, the lower of which was the domain of the "real" Wasaychigan Hill. This lower level contained, on stage-left, Big Joey's living room/ kitchen, with its kitchen counter at the back and, facing down-stage, an old brown couch with a television set a few feet in front of it. This television set could be made to double as a smaller rock for the forest scenes. Stage-right had Spooky Lacroix's kitchen, with its kitchen counter (for which Big Joey's kitchen counter could double) and its table and chairs.

In front of all this was an open area, the floor of which was covered with Teflon, a material which looks like ice and on which one can actually skate, using real ice skates; this was the rink for the hockey arena scenes. With lighting effects, this area could also be turned into "the forest" surrounding the village of Wasaychigan Hill, with its leafless winter trees. The only other essential element here was a larger jutting rock beside which, for instance, Zachary Jeremiah Keechigeesik and Simon Starblanket meet, a rock which could be made to glow at certain key points. Pierre's "little boot-leg joint" in Act Two, with its "window," was also created with lighting effects.

The upper level of the set was almost exclusively the realm of Nanabush. The principal element here was her perch, located in the very middle of this area. The perch was actually an old jukebox of a late 60's/early 70's make, but it was semi-hidden throughout most of the play, so that it was fully revealed as this fabulous jukebox only at those few times when it was needed; the effect sought after here is of this magical, mystical jukebox hanging in the night air, like a haunting and persistent memory, high up over the village of Wasaychigan Hill. Over and behind this perch was suspended a huge full moon whose glow came on, for the most part, only during the outdoor scenes, which all take place at nighttime. All other effects in this area were accomplished with lighting. The very front of this level, all along its edge, was also utilized as the "bleachers" area for the hockey arena scenes.

Easy access was provided for between the lower and the upper levels of this set.

The "sound-scape" of *Dry Lips Oughta Move to Kapuskasing* was mostly provided for by a musician playing, live, on harmonica, off to the side. It is as though the "dream-scape" of the play were laced all the way through with Zachary Jeremiah Keechigeesik's "idealized" form of harmonica playing, permeated with a definite "blues" flavor. Although Zachary ideally should play his harmonica, and not too well, in those few scenes where it is called for, the sound of this harmonica is most effectively used to underline and highlight the many magical appearances of Nanabush in her various guises.

Spooky Lacroix's baby, towards the end of act 2, can, and should, be played by a doll wrapped in a blanket. But for greatest effect, Zachary's baby, at the very end of the play, should be played by a real baby, preferably about five months of age.

Finally, both Cree and Ojibway are used freely in this text for the reasons that these two languages, belonging to the same linguistic family, are very similar and that the fictional reserve of Wasaychigan Hill has a mixture of both Cree and Ojibway residents.

A Note on Nanabush

The dream world of North American Indian mythology is inhabited by the most fantastic creatures, beings and events. Foremost among these beings is the "Trickster," as pivotal and important a figure in our world as Christ is in the realm of Christian mythology. "Weesageechak" in Cree, "Nanabush" in Ojibway, "Raven" in others, "Coyote" in still others, this Trickster goes by many names and many guises. In fact, he can assume any guise he chooses. Essentially a comic, clownish sort of character, his role is to teach us about the nature and the meaning of existence on the planet Earth; he straddles the consciousness of man and that of God, the Great Spirit.

The most explicit distinguishing feature between the North American Indian languages and the European languages is that in Indian (e.g., Cree, Ojibway), there is no gender. In Cree, Ojibway, etc., unlike English, French, German, etc., the male-female-neuter hierarchy is entirely absent. So that by this system of thought, the central hero figure from our mythology—theology, if you will—is theoretically neither exclusively male nor exclusively female, or is both simultaneously. Therefore, where in *The Rez Sisters,* Nanabush was male, in this play—"flip-side" to *The Rez Sisters*—Nanabush is female.

Some say that Nanabush left this continent when the white man came. We believe she/he is still here among us—albeit a little the worse for wear and tear—having assumed other guises. Without the continued presence of this extraordinary figure, the core of Indian culture would be gone forever.

Tomson Highway

DRY LIPS OUGHTA MOVE TO KAPUSKASING

Tomson Highway

CHARACTERS

NANABUSH *(as the spirit of Gazelle Nataways, Patsy Pegahma-*
gahbow and Black Lady Halked)
ZACHARY JEREMIAH KEECHIGEESIK—*41 years old*
BIG JOEY—*39*
CREATURE NATAWAYS—*39*
DICKIE BIRD HALKED—*17*
PIERRE ST. PIERRE—*53*

SPOOKY LACROIX—*39*
SIMON STARBLANKET—*20*
HERA KEECHIGEESIK—*39*

TIME: *Between Saturday, February 3, 1990, 11 P.M., and Satur-*
day, February 10, 1990, 11 A.M.
PLACE: *The Wasaychigan Hill Indian Reserve, Manitoulin Island,*
Ontario

ACT ONE

The set for this first scene is the rather shabby and very messy living
room/kitchen of the reserve house BIG JOEY *and* GAZELLE NATAWAYS
currently share. Prominently displayed on one wall is a life-size pin-
up poster of Marilyn Monroe. The remains of a party are obvious. On
the worn-out old brown couch, with its back towards the entrance, lies
ZACHARY JEREMIAH KEECHIGEESIK, *a very handsome Indian man.*
He is naked, passed out. The first thing we see when the light comes
up—a very small "spot," precisely focussed—is ZACHARY's *bare,*
naked bum. Then, from behind the couch, we see a woman's leg, slid-
ing languorously into a nylon stocking and right over Zachary's bum.
It is NANABUSH, *as the spirit of* GAZELLE NATAWAYS, *dressing to*
leave. She eases herself luxuriously over the couch and over Zachary's
bum and then reaches under Zachary's sleeping head, from where she
gently pulls a gigantic pair of false, rubberized breasts. She proceeds to
put these on over her own bare breasts. Then NANABUSH/GAZELLE
NATAWAYS *sashays over to the side of the couch, picks a giant hockey*
sweater up off the floor and shimmies into it. The sweater has a huge,
plunging neck-line, with the capital letter "W" and the number "1"
prominently sewn on. Then she sashays back to the couch and behind
it. Pleasurably and mischievously, she leans over and plants a kiss on
Zachary's bum, leaving behind a gorgeous, luminescent lip-stick mark.
The last thing she does before she leaves is to turn the television on.
This television sits facing the couch that ZACHARY *lies on.*
NANABUSH/GAZELLE *does not use her hand for this, though; instead,*
she turns the appliance on with one last bump of her voluptuous hips.
"Hockey Night in Canada" comes on. The sound of this hockey game
is on only slightly, so that we hear it as background "music" all the
way through the coming scene. Then NANABUSH/GAZELLE *exits, to sit*
on her perch on the upper level of the set. The only light left on stage is
that coming from the television screen, giving off its eery glow. Beat.

The kitchen door bangs open, the "kitchen light" flashes on and BIG
JOEY *and* CREATURE NATAWAYS *enter,* CREATURE *carrying a case of*
beer on his head. At first, they are oblivious to ZACHARY's *presence.*
Also at about this time, the face of DICKIE BIRD HALKED *emerges from*
the shadows at the "kitchen window." Silently, he watches the rest of
the proceedings, taking a particular interest—even fascination—in
the movements and behavior of BIG JOEY.

BIG JOEY: *(Calling out for* GAZELLE *who, of course, is not home.)*
Hey, bitch!

Keechigeesik means "heaven" or "great sky" in Cree Wasaychigan means "window" in Ojibway

CREATURE: *(As he, at regular intervals, bangs the beer case down on*
the kitchen counter, rips it open, pops bottles open, throws one to BIG
JOEY, *all noises that serve to "punctuate" the rat-a-tat rhythm of* 5
his frenetic speech.) Batman oughta move to Kapuskasing,
nah, Kap's too good for Batman, right, Big Joey? I tole you
once I tole you twice he shouldna done it he shouldna done
what he went and did goddawful Batman Manitowabi the
way he went and crossed that blue line with the puck, man, 10
he's got the flippin' puck right in the palm of his flippin'
hand and only a minute-and-a-half to go he just about gave
me the shits the way Batman Manitowabi went and crossed
that blue line right in front of that brick shithouse of a
whiteman why the hell did that brick shit-house of a white- 15
man have to be there . . .
ZACHARY: *(Talking in his sleep.)* No!
CREATURE: Hey!

*(*BIG JOEY *raises a finger signaling* CREATURE *to shut up.)*

ZACHARY: I said no!
CREATURE: *(In a hoarse whisper.)* That's not a TV kind of sound. 20
BIG JOEY: Shhh!
ZACHARY: . . . goodness sakes, Hera, you just had a baby . . .
CREATURE: That's a real life kind of sound, right, Big Joey? *(*BIG
JOEY *and* CREATURE *slowly come over to the couch.)*
ZACHARY: . . . women playing hockey . . . damn silliest thing I 25
heard in my life . . .
BIG JOEY: Well, well . . .
CREATURE: Ho-leee! *(Whispering.)* Hey, what's that on his arse
look like lips marks.
ZACHARY: . . . Simon Starblanket, that's who's gonna help me 30
with my bakery . . .
CREATURE: He's stitchless, he's nude, he's gonna pneumonia . . .
BIG JOEY: Shut up.
CREATURE: Get the camera. Chris'sakes, take a picture.

*(*CREATURE *scrambles for the Polaroid, which he finds under one end*
of the couch.)

ZACHARY: . . . Simon! *(Jumps up.)* What the?! 35
CREATURE: Surprise! *(Camera flashes.)*
ZACHARY: Put that damn thing away. What are you doing here?
Where's my wife? Hera!

(He realizes he's naked, grabs a cast iron frying pan and slaps it over
his crotch, almost castrating himself in the process.)

Ooof!

40 BIG JOEY: (*Smiling.*) Over easy or sunny side up, Zachary Jeremiah Keechigeesik?

ZACHARY: Get outa my house.

CREATURE: This ain't your house. This is Big Joey's house, right, Big Joey?

45 BIG JOEY: Shut up.

ZACHARY: Creature Nataways. Get outa here. Gimme that camera.

CREATURE: Come and geeeet it!

(*Grabs* ZACHARY's *pants from the floor.*)

ZACHARY: Cut it out. Gimme them goddamn pants.

50 CREATURE: (*Singing.*) Lipstick on your arshole, tole da tale on you-hoo.

ZACHARY: What? (*Straining to see his bum.*) Oh lordy, lordy, lordy gimme them pants.

(*As he tries to wipe the stain off.*)

CREATURE: Here doggy, doggy. Here poochie, poochie woof
55 woof! (ZACHARY *grabs the pants. They rip almost completely in half.* CREATURE *yelps.*) Yip!

(*Momentary light up on* NANABUSH/GAZELLE, *up on her perch, as she gives a throaty laugh.* BIG JOEY *echoes this,* CREATURE *tittering away in the background.*)

ZACHARY: Hey, this is not my doing, Big Joey. (*As he clumsily puts on what's left of his pants.* CREATURE *manages to get in one more shot with the camera.*) We were just having a nice quiet drink
60 over at Andy Manigitogan's when Gazelle Nataways shows up. She brought me over here to give me the recipe for her bannock apple pie cuz, goodness sakes, Simon Starblanket was saying it's the best, that pie was selling like hot cakes at the bingo and he knows I'm tryna establish this reserve's first
65 pie-making business gimme that camera.

(BIG JOEY *suddenly makes a lunge at* ZACHARY *but* ZACHARY *evades him.*)

CREATURE: (*In the background, like a little dog.*) Yah, yah.

BIG JOEY: (*Slowly stalking* ZACHARY *around the room.*) You know, Zach, there's a whole lotta guys on this rez been slippin' my old lady the goods but there ain't but a handful been stupid
70 enough to get caught by me. (*He snaps his fingers and, as always,* CREATURE *obediently scurries over. He hands* BIG JOEY *the picture of* ZACHARY *naked on the couch.* BIG JOEY *shows the picture to* ZACHARY, *right up to his face.*) Kinda em-bare-ass-in' for a hoity-toity educated community pillar like you, eh
75 Zach?

(ZACHARY *grabs for the picture but* BIG JOEY *snaps it away.*)

ZACHARY: What do you want?

BIG JOEY: What's this I hear about you tellin' the chief I can wait for my radio station?

ZACHARY: (*As he proceeds with looking around the room to collect and
80 put on what he can find of his clothes.* BIG JOEY *and* CREATURE *follow him around, obviously enjoying his predicament.*) I don't know where the hell you heard that from.

BIG JOEY: Yeah, right. Well, Lorraine Manigitogan had a word or two with Gazelle Nataways the other night. When you presented your initial proposal at the band office, you said: 85 "Joe can wait. He's only got another three months left in the hockey season."

ZACHARY: I never said no such thing.

BIG JOEY: Bullshit.

ZACHARY: W-w-w-what I said was that employment at this bak- 90 ery of mine would do nothing but add to those in such places as those down at the arena. I never mentioned your name once. And I said it only in passing reference to the fact . . .

BIG JOEY: . . . that this radio idea of mine doesn't have as much long-term significance to the future of this community as 95 this fancy bakery idea of yours, Mr. Pillsbury dough-boy, right?

ZACHARY: If that's what you heard, then you didn't hear it from Lorraine Manigitogan. You got it from Gazelle Nataways and you know yourself she's got a bone to pick with . . . 100

BIG JOEY: You know, Zach, you and me, we work for the same cause, don't we?

ZACHARY: Never said otherwise.

BIG JOEY: We work for the betterment and the advancement of this community, don't we? And seeing as we're about the 105 only two guys in this whole hell-hole who's got the get-up-and-go to do something . . .

ZACHARY: That's not exactly true, Joe. Take a look at Simon Starblanket . . .

BIG JOEY: . . . we should be working together, not against. 110 What do you say you simply postpone that proposal to the Band Council . . .

ZACHARY: I'm sorry. Can't do that.

BIG JOEY: (*Cornering* ZACHARY.) Listen here, bud. You turned your back on me when everybody said I was responsible for 115 that business in Espanola seventeen years ago and you said nothin'. I overlooked that. Never said nothin'. (ZACHARY *re-members his undershorts and proceeds, with even greater despera-tion, to look for them, zeroing in on the couch and under it.* BIG JOEY *catches the drift and snaps his fingers, signaling* CREATURE 120 *to look for the shorts under the couch. creature jumps for the couch. Without missing a beat,* BIG JOEY *continues.*) You turned your back on me when you said you didn't want nothin' to do with me from that day on. I overlooked that. Never said nothin'. You gave me one hell of a slap in the face when 125 your wife gave my Gazelle that kick in the belly. I over-looked that. Never said nothin'. (CREATURE, *having found the shorts among the junk under the couch just split seconds before* ZACHARY *does, throws them to* BIG JOEY. BIG JOEY *holds the shorts up to* ZACHARY, *smiling with satisfaction.*) That, how- 130 ever, was the last time . . .

ZACHARY: That wasn't my fault, Joe. It's that witch woman of yours Gazelle Nataways provoked that fight between her and Hera and you know yourself Hera tried to come and sew up her belly again . . . 135

BIG JOEY: Zach. I got ambition . . .

ZACHARY: Yeah, right.

BIG JOEY: I aim to get that radio station off the ground, start-ing with them games down at my arena.

ZACHARY: Phhhh! 140

BIG JOEY: I aim to get a chain of them community radio sta-tions not only on this here island but beyond as well . . .

ZACHARY: Dream on, Big Joey, dream on . . .

BIG JOEY: . . . and I aim to prove this broadcasting of games
145   among the folks is one sure way to get some pride . . .

ZACHARY: Bullshit! You're in it for yourself.

BIG JOEY: . . . some pride and dignity back so you just get your
ass on out of my house and you go tell that Chief your
Band Council Resolution can wait until next fiscal year or
150   else . . .

ZACHARY: I ain't doing no such thing, Joe, no way. Not when
I'm this close.

BIG JOEY: (*As he eases himself down onto the couch, twirling the shorts
with his fore-finger.*) . . . or else I get my Gazelle Nataways to
155   wash these skivvies of yours, put them in a box all nice and
gussied up, your picture on top, show up at your door-stop
and hand them over to your wife. (*Silence.*)

ZACHARY: (*Quietly, to* BIG JOEY.) Gimme them shorts. (*No answer. Then to* CREATURE.) Gimme them snapshots. (*Still no
160   response.*)

BIG JOEY: (*Dead calm.*) Get out.

ZACHARY: (*Seeing he can't win for the moment, prepares to exit.*) You
may have won this time, Joe, but . . .

BIG JOEY: (*Like a steel trap.*) Get out.

(*Silence. Finally* ZACHARY *exits, looking very humble. Seconds before*
ZACHARY's *exit,* DICKIE BIRD HALKED, *to avoid being seen by*
ZACHARY, *disappears from the "window." The moment* ZACHARY *is gone,*
CREATURE *scurries to the kitchen door, shaking his fist in the direction of
the already-departed* ZACHARY.)

165 CREATURE: Damn rights! (*Then strutting like a cock, he turns to* BIG
JOEY.) Zachary Jeremiah Keechigeesik never shoulda come
in your house, Big Joey. Thank god, Gazelle Nataways ain't
my wife no more . . . (BIG JOEY *merely has to throw a glance
in* CREATURE's *direction to intimidate him. At once,* CREATURE
170   *reverts back to his usual nervous self.*) . . . not really, she's yours
now, right, Big Joey? It's you she's livin' with these days,
not me.

BIG JOEY: (*As he sits on the couch with his beer, mostly ignoring* CREA-
TURE *and watching the hockey game on television.*) Don't make
175   her my wife.

CREATURE: But you live together, you sleep together, you eat
ooops!

BIG JOEY: Still don't make her my wife.

CREATURE: (*As he proceeds to try to clean up the mess around the
180   couch, mostly shoving everything back under it.*) I don't mind,
Big Joey, I really don't. I tole you once I tole you twice she's
yours now. It's like I loaned her to you, I don't mind. I can
take it. We made a deal, remember? The night she threw
the toaster at me and just about broke my skull, she tole
185   me: "I had enough, Creature Nataways, I had enough from
you. I had your kids and I had your disease and that's all I
ever want from you, I'm leavin'." And then she grabbed her
suitcase and she grabbed the kids, no, she didn't even grab
the kids, she grabbed the TV and she just sashayed herself
190   over here. She left me. It's been four years now, Big Joey, I
know, I know. Oh, it was hell, it was hell at first but you
and me we're buddies since we're babies, right? So I
thought it over for about a year . . . then one day I swallowed
my pride and I got up off that chesterfield and I walked over
195   here, I opened your door and I shook your hand and I said:

"It's okay, Big Joey, it's okay." And then we went and played
darts in Espanola except we kinda got side-tracked, remember, Big Joey, we ended up on that three-day bender?

BIG JOEY: Creature Nataways?

CREATURE: What?   200

BIG JOEY: You talk too much.

CREATURE: I tole you once I tole you twice I don't mind . . .

(*But* PIERRE ST. PIERRE *comes bursting in, in a state of great excitement.*)

PIERRE: (*Addressing the case of beer directly.*) Hallelujah! Have you
heard the news?

CREATURE: Pierre St. Pierre. Chris'sakes, knock. You're walkin'   205
into a civilized house.

PIERRE: The news. Have you heard the news?

CREATURE: I'll tell you a piece of news. Anyways, we come in
the door and guess who . . .

BIG JOEY: (*To* CREATURE.) Sit down.   210

PIERRE: Gimme a beer.

CREATURE: (*To* PIERRE.) Sit down.

PIERRE: Gimme a beer.

BIG JOEY: Give him a fuckin' beer. (*But* PIERRE *has already
grabbed, opened and is drinking a beer.*)   215

CREATURE: Have a beer.

PIERRE: (*Talking out the side of his mouth, as he continues drinking.*)
Tank you.

BIG JOEY: Talk.

PIERRE: (*Putting his emptied bottle down triumphantly and grabbing*   220
another beer.) Toast me.

BIG JOEY: Spit it out.

CREATURE: Chris'sakes.

PIERRE: Toast me.

CREATURE: Toast you? The hell for?   225

PIERRE: Shut up. Just toast me.

CREATURE/BIG JOEY: Toast.

PIERRE: Tank you. You just toasted "The Ref."

CREATURE: (*To* PIERRE.) The ref? (*To* BIG JOEY.) The what?

PIERRE: "The Ref!"   230

CREATURE: The ref of the what?

PIERRE: The ref. I'm gonna be the referee down at the arena.
Big Joey's arena. The Wasaychigan Hill Hippodrome.

CREATURE: We already got a referee.

PIERRE: Yeah, but this here's different, this here's special.   235

BIG JOEY: I'd never hire a toothless old bootlegger like you.

PIERRE: They play their first game in just a coupla days.
Against the Canoe Lake Bravettes. And I got six teeth left
so you just keep your trap shut about my teeth.

CREATURE: The Canoe Lake Bravettes?   240

BIG JOEY: Who's "they?"

PIERRE: Haven't you heard?

BIG JOEY: Who's "they?"

PIERRE: I don't believe this.

BIG JOEY: Who's "they?"   245

PIERRE: I don't believe this. (BIG JOEY *bangs* PIERRE *on the head.*)
Oww, you big bully! The Wasaychigan Hill Wailerettes, of
course. I'm talkin' about the Wasy Wailerettes, who else
geez.

CREATURE: The Wasy Wailerettes? Chris'sakes . . .   250

PIERRE: Dominique Ladouche, Black Lady Halked, that terrible Dictionary woman, Fluffy Sainte-Marie, Dry Lips

Manigitogan, Leonarda Lee Starblanket, Annie Cook, June Bug McLeod, Big Bum Pegahmagahbow, all twenty-seven
255 of 'em. Them women from right here on this reserve, a whole batch of 'em, they upped and they said: "Bullshit! Ain't nobody on the face of this earth's gonna tell us us women's got no business playin' hockey. That's bullshit!" That's what they said: "Bullshit!" So. They took matters
260 into their own hands. And, holy shit la marde, I almost forgot to tell you my wife Veronique St. Pierre, she went and made up her mind she's joinin' the Wasy Wailerettes, only the other women wouldn't let her at first on account she never had no babies—cuz, you see, you gotta be pregnant
265 or have piles and piles of babies to be a Wasy Wailerette— but my wife, she put her foot down and she says: "Zhaboonigan Peterson may be just my adopted daughter and she may be retarded as a doormat but she's still my baby." That's what she says to 'em. And she's on and they're playin'
270 hockey and the Wasy Wailerettes, they're just a-rarin' to go, who woulda thunk it, huh?

CREATURE: Ho-leee!

PIERRE: God's truth . . .

BIG JOEY: They never booked the ice.

275 PIERRE: Ha! Booked it through Gazelle Nataways. Sure as I'm alive and walkin' these treacherous icy roads . . .

BIG JOEY: Hang on.

PIERRE: . . . god's truth in all its naked splendor. (*As he pops open yet another beer.*) I kid you not, gentlemen, not for one slip-
280 pery goddamn minute. Toast!

BIG JOEY: (*Grabbing the bottle right out of* PIERRE's *mouth.*) Where'd you sniff out all this crap?

PIERRE: From my wife, who else? My wife, Veronique St. Pierre, she told me. She says to me: "Pierre St. Pierre, you'll eat your
285 shorts but I'm playin' hockey and I don't care what you say. Or think." And she left. No. First, she cleaned out my wallet, (*Grabs his beer back from* BIG JOEY's *hand.*) grabbed her big brown rosaries from off the wall. Then she left. Just slammed the door and left. Period. I just about ate my
290 shorts. Toast!

CREATURE: Shouldn't we . . . shouldn't we stop them?

PIERRE: Phhht! . . . (CREATURE *just misses getting spat on.*)

CREATURE: Ayoah!

PIERRE: . . . Haven't seen hide nor hair of 'em since. Gone to
295 Sudbury. Every single last one of 'em. Piled theirselves into seven cars and just took off. Them back wheels was squealin' and rattlin' like them little jinger bells. Just past tea-time. Shoppin'. Hockey equipment. Phhht! (*Again,* CREATURE *just misses getting spat on.*)

300 CREATURE: Ayoah! It's enough to give you the shits every time he opens his mouth.

PIERRE: And they picked me. Referee.

BIG JOEY: And why you, may I ask?

PIERRE: (*Faking humility.*) Oh, I don't know. Somethin' about
305 the referee here's too damn perschnickety. That drum-bangin' young whipperschnapper, Simon Starblanket, (*Grabbing yet another beer.*) he's got the rules all mixed up or somethin' like that, is what they says. They kinda wanna play it their own way. So they picked me. Toast me.

310 CREATURE: Toast.

PIERRE: To the ref.

CREATURE: To the ref.

PIERRE: Tank you. (*They both drink.*) Ahhh. (*Pause. To* BIG JOEY.) So. I want my skates.

315 CREATURE: Your skates?

PIERRE: My skates. I want 'em back.

CREATURE: The hell's he talkin' about now?

PIERRE: They're here. I know they're here. I loaned 'em to you, remember?

320 BIG JOEY: Run that by me again?

PIERRE: I loaned 'em to you. That Saturday night Gazelle Nataways came in that door with her TV and her suitcase and you and me we were sittin' right there on that old chesterfield with Lalala Lacroix sittin' between us and I
325 loaned you my skates in return for that forty-ouncer of rye and Gazelle Nataways plunked her TV down, marched right up to Lalala Lacroix, slapped her in the face and chased her out the door. But we still had time to make the deal whereby if I wanted my skates back you'd give 'em
330 back to me if I gave you back your forty-ouncer, right? Right. (*Produces the bottle from under his coat.*) Ta-da! Gimme my skates.

BIG JOEY: You sold them skates. They're mine.

PIERRE: Never you mind, Big Joey, never you mind. I want my
335 skates. Take this. Go on. Take it.

(BIG JOEY *fishes one skate out from under the couch.*)

CREATURE: (*To himself, as he sits on the couch.*) Women playin' hockey. Ho-leee!

(BIG JOEY *and* PIERRE *exchange bottle and skate.*)

PIERRE: Tank you. (*He makes a triumphant exit.* BIG JOEY *merely sits there and waits knowingly. Silence. Then* PIERRE *suddenly re-*
340 *enters.*) There's only one. (*Silence.*) Well, where the hell's the other one? (*Silence.* PIERRE *nearly explodes with indignation.*) Gimme back my bottle! Where's the other one?

BIG JOEY: You got your skate. I got my bottle.

PIERRE: Don't talk backwards at me. I'm your elder.

345 CREATURE: It's gone.

PIERRE: Huh?

CREATURE: Gone. The other skate's gone, right, Big Joey?

PIERRE: Gone? Where?

CREATURE: My wife Gazelle Nataways . . .

350 PIERRE: . . . your ex-wife . . .

CREATURE: . . . she threw it out the door two years ago the night Spooky Lacroix went crazy in the head and tried to come and rip Gazelle Nataways' door off for cheatin' at the bingo. Just about killed Spooky Lacroix too, right, Big
355 Joey?

PIERRE: So where's my other skate?

CREATURE: At Spooky Lacroix's, I guess.

PIERRE: Aw, shit la marde, you'se guys don't play fair.

BIG JOEY: You go over to Spooky Lacroix's and you tell him I
360 told you you could have your skate back.

PIERRE: No way, José. Spooky Lacroix's gonna preach at me.

BIG JOEY: Preach back.

PIERRE: You come with me. You used to be friends with Spooky Lacroix. You talk to Spooky Lacroix. Spooky Lacroix likes
365 you.

BIG JOEY: He likes you too.

PIERRE: Yeah, but he likes you better. Oh, shit la marde! (*As he takes another beer out of the case.*) And I almost forgot to tell you they decided to make Gazelle Nataways captain of the Wasy Wailerettes. I mean, she kind of . . . decided on her own, if you know what I mean.

BIG JOEY: Spooky Lacroix's waitin' for you.

PIERRE: How do you know?

BIG JOEY: God told me.

PIERRE: (*Pause.* PIERRE *actually wonders to himself. Then:*) Aw, bullshit.

(*Exits. Silence. Then* BIG JOEY *and* CREATURE *look at each other, break down and laugh themselves into prolonged hysterical fits. After a while, they calm down and come to a dead stop. They sit and think. They look at the hockey game on the television. Then, dead serious, they turn to each other.*)

CREATURE: Women . . . Gazelle Nataways . . . hockey? Ho-leee . . .

BIG JOEY: (*Still holding* PIERRE'*s bottle of whiskey.*) Chris'-sakes . . .

(*Fade-out.*)

(*From this darkness emerges the sound of* SPOOKY LACROIX'*s voice, singing with great emotion. As he sings, the lights fade in on his kitchen, where* DICKIE BIRD HALKED *is sitting across the table from* SPOOKY LACROIX. DICKIE BIRD *is scribbling on a piece of paper with a pencil.* SPOOKY *is knitting [pale blue baby booties]. A bible sits on the table to the left of* SPOOKY, *a knitting pattern to his right. The place is covered with knitted doodads: knitted doilies, tea cozy, a tacky picture of "The Last Supper" with knitted frame and, on the wall, as subtly conspicuous as possible, a crucifix with pale blue knitted baby booties covering each of its four extremities. Throughout this scene,* SPOOKY *periodically consults the knitting pattern, wearing tiny little reading glasses, perched "just so" on the end of his nose. He knits with great difficulty and, therefore, with great concentration, sometimes, in moments of excitement, getting the bible and the knitting pattern mixed up with each other. He has tremendous difficulty getting the "disturbed"* DICKIE BIRD *to sit still and pay attention.*)

SPOOKY: (*Singing.*) Everybody oughta know. Everybody oughta know. Who Jesus is. (*Speaking.*) This is it. This is the end. Igwani eeweepoonaskeewuk. (*"The end of the world is at hand."*) Says right here in the book. Very, very, very important to read the book. If you want the Lord to come into your life, Dickie Bird Halked, you've got to read the book. Not much time left. Yessiree. 1990. The last year. This will be the last year of our lives. Clear as a picture. The end of the world is here. At last. About time too, with the world going crazy, people shooting, killing each other left, right and center. Jet planes full of people crashing into the bushes, lakes turning black, fish choking to death. Terrible. Terrible. (DICKIE BIRD *shoves a note he's been scribbling over to* SPOOKY.) What's this? (SPOOKY *reads, with some difficulty.*) "How . . . do . . . you . . . make . . . babies?" (*Shocked.*) Dickie Bird Halked? At your age? Surely. Anyway. That young Starblanket boy who went and shot himself. Right here. Right in the einsteins. Bleeding from the belly, all this white mushy stuff come oozing out. Yuch! Brrr! I guess there's just nothing better to do for the young people on this reserve these days than go around shooting their einsteins out from inside their bellies. But the Lord has had

enough. He's sick of it. No more, he says, no more. This is it. (DICKIE BIRD *shoves another note over.* SPOOKY *pauses to read. And finishes.*) Why, me and Lalala, we're married. And we're gonna have a baby. Period. Now. When the world comes to an end? The sky will open up. The clouds will part. And the Lord will come down in a holy vapor. And only those who are born-again Christian will go with him when he goes back up. And the rest? You know what's gonna happen to the rest? They will die. Big Joey, for instance, they will go to hell and they will burn for their wicked, whorish ways. But we will be taken up into the clouds to spend eternity surrounded by the wondrous and the mystical glory of god. Clear as a picture, Dickie Bird Halked, clear as a picture. So I'm telling you right now, you've got to read the book. Very, very, very important. (DICKIE BIRD *shoves a third note over to* SPOOKY. SPOOKY *reads and finishes.*) Why, Wellington Halked's your father, Dickie Bird Halked. Don't you be asking questions like that. My sister, Black Lady Halked, that's your mother. Right? And because Wellington Halked is married to Black Lady Halked, he is your father. And don't you ever let no one tell you different.

(*Black-out. From the darkness of the theater emerges the magical flickering of a luminescent powwow dancing bustle. As it moves gradually towards the downstage area, a second—and larger—bustle appears on the upper level of the set, also flickering magically and moving about. The two bustles "play" with each other, almost affectionately, looking like two giant fire flies. The smaller bustle finally reaches the downstage area and from behind it emerges the face of* SIMON STARBLANKET. *He is dancing and chanting in a forest made of light and shadows. The larger bustle remains on the upper level; behind it is the entire person of* NANABUSH *as the spirit of* PATSY PEGAHMAGAHBOW, *a vivacious young girl of eighteen with a very big bum (i.e., an over-sized prosthetic bum). From this level,* NANABUSH/PATSY *watches and "plays" with the proceedings on the lower level. The giant full moon is in full bloom behind her. From the very beginning of all this, and in counterpoint to* SIMON'*s chanting, also emerges the sound of someone playing a harmonica, a sad, mournful tune. It is* ZACHARY JEREMIAH KEECHIGEESIK, *stuck in the bush in his embarrassing state, playing his heart out. Then the harmonica stops and, from the darkness, we hear* ZACHARY'*s voice.*)

ZACHARY: Hey. (SIMON *hears this, looks behind, but sees nothing and continues his chanting and dancing.* SIMON *chants and dances as though he were desperately trying to find the right chant and dance. Then:*) Pssst!

SIMON: Awinuk awa? (*"Who's this?"*)

ZACHARY: (*In a hoarse whisper.*) Simon Starblanket.

SIMON: Neee, Zachary Jeremiah Keechigeesik. Awus! (*"Go away!"*) Katha peeweestatooweemin. (*"Don't come bothering me [with your words]."*)

(*Finally,* ZACHARY *emerges from the shadows and from behind a large rock, carrying his harmonica in one hand and holding his torn pants together as best he can with the other.* SIMON *ignores him and continues with his chanting and dancing.*)

I. 428 **Neee** probably the most common Cree expression, meaning something like "Oh, you," or "My goodness"

ZACHARY: W-w-w-what's it cost to get one of them dough-making machines?

SIMON: (*Not quite believing his ears.*) What?

ZACHARY: Them dough-making machines. What's it cost to
435   buy one of them?

SIMON: A Hobart?

ZACHARY: A what?

SIMON: Hobart. H-O-B-A-R-T. Hobart.

ZACHARY: (*To himself.*) Hobart. Hmmm.

440   SIMON: (*Amused at the rather funny-looking* ZACHARY.) Neee, machi ma-a, ("Oh you, but naturally,") Westinghouse for refrigerators, Kellogg's for corn flakes igwa ("and") Hobart for dough-making machines. Kinsitootawin na? ("Get it?") Brand name. Except we used to call it "the pig" because it
445   had this . . . piggish kind of motion to it. But never mind. Awus. Don't bother me.

ZACHARY: What's it cost to get this . . . pig?

SIMON: (*Laughing.*) Neee, Zachary Jeremiah, here you are, one of Wasy's most respected citizens, standing in the middle of
450   the bush on a Saturday night in February freezing your buns off and you want to know how much a pig costs?

ZACHARY: (*Vehemently.*) I promised Hera I'd have all this information by tonight we were supposed to sit down and discuss the budget for this damn bakery tonight and here I went and
455   messed it all up thank god I ran into you because now you're the only person left on this whole reserve who might have the figures I need what's this damn dough-making machine cost come on now tell me!

SIMON: (*A little cowed.*) Neee, about four thousand bucks.
460   Maybe five.

ZACHARY: You don't know for sure? But you worked there.

SIMON: I was only the dishwasher, Zachary Jeremiah, I didn't own the place. Mama Louisa was a poor woman. She had really old equipment, most of which she dragged over herself
465   all the way from Italy after the Second World War. It wouldn't cost the same today.

ZACHARY: Five thousand dollars for a Mobart, hmmm . . .

SIMON: Hobart.

ZACHARY: I wish I had a piece of paper to write all this down,
470   sheesh. You got a piece of paper on you?

SIMON: No. Just . . . this. (*Holding the dancing bustle up.*) Why are you holding yourself like that?

ZACHARY: I was . . . standing on the road down by Andy Manigitogan's place when this car came by and wooof!
475   My pants ripped. Ripped right down the middle. And my shorts, well, they just . . . took off. How do you like that, eh?

SIMON: Nope. I don't like it. Neee, awus. Kigithaskin. ("You're lying to me.")

480   ZACHARY: W-w-w-why would I pull your leg for? I don't really mind it except it is damn cold out here.

(*At this point,* NANABUSH/PATSY, *on the upper level, scurries closer to get a better look, her giant powwow dancing bustle flickering magically in the half-light.* SIMON's *attention is momentarily pulled away by this fleeting vision.*)

SIMON: Hey! Did you see that?

(*But* ZACHARY, *too caught up with his own dilemma, does not notice.*)

ZACHARY: I'm very, very upset right now . . .

SIMON: . . . I thought I just saw Patsy Pegahmagahbow . . .
with this . . .   485

ZACHARY: (*As he looks, perplexed, in the direction* SIMON *indicates.*)
. . . do you think . . . my two ordinary convection ovens . . .

SIMON: (*Calling out.*) Patsy? . . . (*Pause. Then, slowly, he turns back to* ZACHARY.) . . . like . . . she made this for me, eh? (*Referring to the bustle.*) She and her step-mother, Rosie Kakapetum,   490
back in September, after my mother's funeral. Well, I was out here thinking, if this . . . like, if this . . . dance didn't come to me real natural, like from deep inside of me, then I was gonna burn it. (*Referring to the bustle.*) Right here on this spot.
Cuz then . . . it doesn't mean anything real to me, does it?   495
Like, it's false . . . it's driving me crazy, this dream where Indian people are just dropping off like flies . . .

(NANABUSH/PATSY *begins to "play" with the two men, almost as if with the help of the winter night's magic and the power of the full moon, she were weaving a spell around* SIMON *and* ZACHARY.)

ZACHARY: (*Singing softly to himself.*) Hot cross buns. Hot cross buns. One a penny, two a penny, hot cross buns . . .

SIMON: . . . something has to be done . . .   500

ZACHARY: (*Speaking.*) . . . strawberry pies . . .

SIMON: . . . in this dream . . .

ZACHARY: . . . so fresh and flakey they fairly bubble over with the cream from the very breast of Mother Nature herself . . .

SIMON: . . . the drum has to come back, mistigwuskeek ("the   505
drum") . . .

ZACHARY: . . . bran muffins, cherry tarts . . .

SIMON: . . . the medicine, the power, this . . .

(*Holding the bustle up in the air.*)

ZACHARY: . . . butter tarts . . .

SIMON: . . . has to come back. We've got to learn to dance again.   510

ZACHARY: . . . tarts tarts tarts upside-down cakes cakes cakes and not to forget, no, never, ever to forget that Black Forest Cake . . .

SIMON: . . . Patsy Pegahmagahbow . . .

ZACHARY: . . . cherries jubilee . . .   515

SIMON: . . . her step-mother, Rosie Kakapetum, the medicine woman . . .

ZACHARY: . . . lemon meringue pie . . .

SIMON: . . . the power . . .

ZACHARY: . . . baked Alaska . . .   520

SIMON: . . . Nanabush! . . .

ZACHARY: (*Then suddenly, with bitterness.*) . . . Gazelle Nataways. K'skanagoos! ("The female dog!")

(*All of a sudden, from the darkness of the winter night, emerges a strange, eery sound; whether it is wolves howling or women wailing, we are not sure at first. And whether this sound comes from somewhere deep in the forest, from the full moon or where, we are not certain. But there is definitely a "spirit" in the air. The sound of this wailing is under-cut by the sound of rocks hitting boards, or the sides of houses, echoing, as in a vast empty chamber. Gradually, as* SIMON *speaks,* ZACHARY—*filled with confusing emotion as he is—takes out his harmonica, sits down on the large rock and begins to play, a sad, mournful melody, tinged, as always, with a touch of the blues.*)

SIMON: I have my arms around this rock, this large black rock sticking out of the ground, right here on this spot. And then I hear this baby crying, from inside this rock. The baby is crying out my name. As if I am somehow responsible for it being caught inside that rock. I can't move. My arms, my whole body, stuck to this rock. Then this ... eagle ... lands beside me, right over there. But this bird has three faces, three women. And the eagle says to me: "the baby is crying, my grand-child is crying to hear the drum again." (NANABUSH/PATSY, *her face surrounded by the brilliant feathers of her bustle, so that she looks like some fantastic, mysterious bird, begins to wail, her voice weaving in and out of the other wailing voices.*) There's this noise all around us, as if rocks are hitting the sides of houses—echoing and echoing like in a vast empty room—and women are wailing. The whole world is filled with this noise. (*Then* SIMON, *too, wails, a heart-searing wail. From here on, all the wailing begins to fade.*) Then the eagle is gone and the rock cracks and this mass of flesh, covered with veins and blood, comes oozing out and a woman's voice somewhere is singing something about angels and god and angels and god ...

(*The wailing has now faded into complete silence.* ZACHARY *finally rises from his seat on the rock.*)

ZACHARY: I dreamt I woke up at Gazelle Nataways' place with no shorts on. And I got this nagging suspicion them shorts are still over there. If you could just go on over there now ... I couldn't have been over there. I mean, there's my wife Hera. And there's my bakery. And this bakery could do a lot for the Indian people. Economic development. Jobs. Bread. Apple pie. So you see, there's an awful lot that's hanging on them shorts. This is a good chance for you to do something for your people, Simon, if you know what I mean ...

SIMON: I'm the one who has to bring the drum back. And it's Patsy's medicine power, that stuff she's learning from her step-mother Rosie Kakapetum that ... helps me ...

ZACHARY: I go walking into my house with no underwear, pants ripped right down the middle, not a shred of budget in sight and wooof! ...

(PIERRE ST. PIERRE *comes bursting in on the two men with his one skate in hand, taking them completely by surprise.* NANABUSH/PATSY *disappears.*)

ZACHARY: Pierre St. Pierre! Just the man ...

PIERRE: No time. No time. Lalala Lacroix's having a baby any minute now so I gotta get over to Spook's before she pops.

SIMON: I can go get Rosie Kakapetum.

PIERRE: Too old. Too old. She can't be on the team.

SIMON: Neee, what team? Rosie Kakapetum's the last mid-wife left in Wasy, Pierre St. Pierre, of course she can't be on a team.

ZACHARY: (*To* PIERRE.) You know that greasy shit-brown chesterfield over at Gazelle Nataways?

SIMON: (*To* ZACHARY.) Mind you, if there was a team of midwives, chee-i? ("eh?") Wha!

PIERRE: Gazelle Nataways? Hallelujah, haven't you heard the news?

ZACHARY: What? ... you mean ... it's out already?

PIERRE: All up and down Wasaychigan Hill ...

ZACHARY: (*Thoughtfully, to himself, as it dawns on him.*) The whole place knows.

PIERRE: clean across Manitoulin Island and right to the outskirts of Sudbury ...

ZACHARY: Lordy, lordy, lordy ...

PIERRE: Gazelle Nataways, Dominique Ladouche, Black Lady Halked, that terrible Dictionary woman, Fluffy Sainte-Marie, Dry Lips Manigitogan, Leonarda Lee Starblanket, Annie Cook, June Bug McLeod, Big Bum Pegahmagahbow ...

SIMON: Patsy Pegahmagahbow. Get it straight ...

PIERRE: Quiet! I'm not finished ... all twenty-seven of 'em ...

SIMON: Neee, Zachary Jeremiah, your goose is cooked.

PIERRE: Phhht! Cooked and burnt right down to a nice crispy pitch black cinder because your wife Hera Keechigeesik is in on it too.

(ZACHARY, *reeling from the horror of it all, finally sits back down on the rock.*)

SIMON: Patsy Pegahmagahbow is pregnant, Pierre St. Pierre. She can't go running around all over Manitoulin Island with a belly that's getting bigger by the ...

SIMON: Aw, they're all pregnant, them women, or have piles and piles of babies and I'll be right smack dab in the middle of it all just a-blowin' my whistle and a-throwin' that dirty little black thingie around ...

ZACHARY: (*Rising from the rock.*) Now you listen here, Pierre St. Pierre. I may have lost my shorts under Gazelle Nataways' greasy shit-brown chesterfield not one hour ago and I may have lost my entire life, not to mention my bakery, as a result of that one very foolish mistake but I'll have you know that my shorts, they are clean as a whistle, I change them every day, my favorite color is light blue and black and crusted with shit my shorts most certainly are not!

SIMON: (*Surprised and thrilled at* ZACHARY's *renewed "fighting" spirit.*) Wha!

PIERRE: Whoa! Easy, Zachary Jeremiah, easy there. Not one stitch of your shorts has anything whatsoever to do with the revolution.

SIMON: Pierre St. Pierre, what revolution are you wheezing and snorting on about?

PIERRE: The puck. I'm talkin' about the puck.

ZACHARY: The puck?

SIMON: The puck?

PIERRE: Yes, the puck. The puck, the puck, the puck and nothin' but the goddam puck they're playin' hockey, them women from right here on this reserve, they're playin' hockey and nothin', includin' Zachary Jeremiah Keechigeesik's bright crispy undershorts, is gonna stop 'em.

SIMON: Women playing hockey. Neee, watstagatch! ("Good grief!")

PIERRE: "Neee, watstagatch" is right because they're in Sudbury, as I speak, shoppin' for hockey equipment, and I'm the referee! Outa my way! Or the Lacroixs will pop before I get there.

(*He begins to exit.*)

ZACHARY: Pierre St. Pierre, get me my shorts or I'll report your bootleg joint to the police.

630 PIERRE: No time. No time.

(*Exits.*)

ZACHARY: (*Calling out.*) Did Hera go to Sudbury, too? (*But* PIERRE *is gone.*)

SIMON: (*Thoughtfully to himself, as he catches another glimpse of* NANABUSH/PATSY *and her bustle.*) . . . rocks hitting boards . . .

635 ZACHARY: (*To himself.*) What in God's name is happening to Wasaychigan Hill . . .

SIMON: women wailing . . .

ZACHARY: (*With even greater urgency.*) Do you think those two ordinary convection ovens are gonna do the job or should I

640 get one of them great big pizza ovens right away?

SIMON: . . . pucks . . .

ZACHARY: Simon, I'm desperate!

SIMON: (*Finally, snapping out of his speculation and looking straight into* ZACHARY'*s face.*) Neee, Zachary Jeremiah. Okay. Goes

645 like this. (*Then, very quickly:*) It depends on what you're gonna bake, eh? Like if you're gonna bake bread and, like, lots of it, you're gonna need one of them great big ovens but if you're gonna bake just muffins . . .

ZACHARY: (*In the background.*) . . . muffins, nah, not just

650 muffins . . .

SIMON: . . . then all you need is one of them ordinary little ovens but like I say, I was only the dishwasher . . .

ZACHARY: How many employees were there in your bakery?

SIMON: . . . it depends on how big a community you're gonna

655 serve, Zachary Jeremiah . . .

ZACHARY: . . . nah, Wasy, just Wasy, to start with . . .

SIMON: . . . like, we had five, one to make the dough—like, mix the flour and the water and the yeast and all that— like, this guy had to be at work by six A.M., that's gonna

660 be hard here in Wasy, Zachary Jeremiah, I'm telling you that right now . . .

ZACHARY: . . . nah, I can do that myself, no problem . . .

SIMON: . . . then we had three others to roll the dough and knead and twist and punch and pound it on this great big

665 wooden table . . .

ZACHARY: . . . I'm gonna need a great big wooden table? . . .

SIMON: . . . hard wood, Zachary Jeremiah, not soft wood. And then one to actually bake the loaves, like, we had these long wooden paddles, eh? . . .

670 ZACHARY: . . . paddles . . .

SIMON: . . . yeah, paddles, Zachary Jeremiah, real long ones. It was kinda neat, actually . . .

ZACHARY: . . . go on, go on . . .

SIMON: Listen here, Zachary Jeremiah, I'm going to Sudbury

675 next Saturday, okay? And if you wanna come along, I can take you straight to Mama Louisa's Pasticcerria myself. I'll introduce you to the crusty old girl and you can take a good long look at her rubbery old Hobart, how's that? You can even touch it if you want, neee . . .

680 ZACHARY: . . . really? . . .

SIMON: Me? I'm asking Patsy Pegahmagahbow to marry me . . .

ZACHARY: . . . Simon, Simon . . .

SIMON: . . . and we're gonna hang two thousand of these things (*Referring to his dancing bustle.*) all over Manitoulin

685 Island, me and Patsy and our baby. And me and Patsy and our baby and this Nanabush character, we're gonna be

dancing up and down Wasaychigan Hill like nobody's business cuz I'm gonna go out there and I'm gonna bring that drum back if it kills me.

ZACHARY: (*Pause. Then, quietly.*) Get me a safety pin.   690

SIMON: (*Pause.*) Neee, okay. And you, Zachary Jeremiah Keechigeesik, you're gonna see a Hobart such as you have never seen ever before in your entire life!

SIMON/ZACHARY: (*Smiling, almost laughing, at each other.*) Neee . . .

(*Black-out.*)

(*Lights up on the upper level, where we see this bizarre vision of* NANABUSH, *now in the guise of* BLACK LADY HALKED, *nine months pregnant* [*i.e., wearing a huge, out-sized prosthetic belly*]. *Over this, she wears a maternity gown and, pacing the floor slowly, holds a huge string of rosary beads. She recites the rosary quietly to herself. She is also drinking a beer and, obviously, is a little unsteady on her feet because of this.*)

(*Fade-in on the lower level into* SPOOKY LACROIX'*s kitchen.* DICKIE BIRD HALKED *is on his knees, praying fervently to this surrealistic, miraculous vision of "the Madonna" [i.e., his own mother], which he actually sees inside his own mind. Oblivious to all this,* SPOOKY LACROIX *sits at his table, still knitting his baby booties and preaching away.*)

SPOOKY: Dickie Bird Halked? I want you to come to heaven   695
with me. I insist. But before you do that, you take one of them courses in sign language, help me prepare this reserve for the Lord. Can't you just see yourself, standing on that podium in the Wasaychigan Hill Hippodrome, talking sign language to the people? Talking about the Lord and   700
how close we are to the end? I could take a break. And these poor people with their meaningless, useless . . .

(PIERRE ST. PIERRE *comes bursting in and marches right up to* SPOOKY. *The vision of* NANABUSH/BLACK LADY HALKED *disappears.*)

PIERRE: Alright. Hand it over.

SPOOKY: (*Startled out of his wits.*) Pierre St. Pierre! You went and mixed up my booty!   705

PIERRE: I know it's here somewhere.

SPOOKY: Whatever it is you're looking for, you're not getting it until you bring the Lord into your life.

PIERRE: My skate. Gimme my skate.

SPOOKY: I don't have no skate. Now listen to me.   710

PIERRE: My skate. The skate Gazelle Nataways threw at you and just about killed you.

SPOOKY: What the hell are you gonna do with a skate at this hour of the night?

PIERRE: Haven't you heard the news?   715

SPOOKY: (*Pauses to think.*) No, I haven't heard any news.

(DICKIE BIRD *gets up and starts to wander around the kitchen. He looks around at random, first out the window, as if to see who has been chanting, then, eventually, he zeroes in on the crucifix on the wall and stands there looking at it. Finally, he takes it off the wall and plays with its cute little booties.*)

PIERRE: The women. I'm gonna be right smack dab in the middle of it all. The revolution. Right here in Wasaychigan Hill.

SPOOKY: The Chief or the priest. Which one are they gonna revolution?

PIERRE: No, no, no. Dominique Ladouche, Black Lady Halked, that terrible Dictionary woman, that witch Gazelle Nataways, Fluffy Sainte-Marie, Dry Lips Manigitogan, Leonarda Lee Starblanket, Annie Cook, June Bug McLeod, Big Bum Pegahmagahbow, all twenty-seven of 'em. Even my wife, Veronique St. Pierre, she'll be right smack dab in the middle of it all. Defense.

SPOOKY: Defense? The Americans. We're being attacked. Is the situation that serious?

PIERRE: No, no, no, for Chris'sakes. They're playin' hockey. Them women are playin' hockey. Dead serious they are too.

SPOOKY: No.

PIERRE: Yes.

SPOOKY: Thank the Lord this is the last year!

PIERRE: Don't you care to ask?

SPOOKY: Thank the Lord the end of the world is coming this year!

(*Gasping, he marches up to* DICKIE BIRD.)

PIERRE: I'm the referee, dammit.

SPOOKY: Watch your language.

(*Grabbing the crucifix from* DICKIE BIRD.)

PIERRE: That's what I mean when I say I'm gonna be right smack dab in the middle of it all. You don't listen to me.

SPOOKY: (*As he proceeds to put the little booties back on the crucifix.*) But you're not a woman.

PIERRE: You don't have to be. To be a referee these days, you can be anything, man or woman, don't matter which away. So gimme my skate.

SPOOKY: What skate?

PIERRE: The skate Gazelle Nataways just about killed you with after the bingo that time.

SPOOKY: Oh, that. I hid it in the basement. (PIERRE *opens a door, falls in and comes struggling out with a mouse trap stuck to a finger.*) Pierre St. Pierre, what the hell are you doing in Lalala's closet?

PIERRE: Well, where the hell's the basement?

(*He frees his finger.*)

SPOOKY: Pierre St. Pierre, you drink too much. You gotta have the Lord in your life.

PIERRE: I don't need the Lord in my life, for god's sake, I need my skate. I gotta practice my figure eights.

SPOOKY: (*As he begins to put the crucifix back up on the wall.*) You gotta promise me before I give you your skate.

PIERRE: I promise.

SPOOKY: (*Unaware, he threatens* PIERRE *with the crucifix, holding it up against his neck.*) You gotta have the Lord come into your life.

PIERRE: Alright, alright.

SPOOKY: For how long?

PIERRE: My whole life. I promise I'm gonna bring the Lord into my life and keep him there right up until the day I die just gimme my goddamn skate.

SPOOKY: Cross my heart.

PIERRE: Alright? Cross your heart.

(*Neither man makes a move, until* SPOOKY, *finally catching on, throws* PIERRE *a look.* PIERRE *crosses himself.*)

SPOOKY: Good.

(*Exits to the basement.*)

PIERRE: (*Now alone with* DICKIE BIRD, *half-whispering to him. As* PIERRE *speaks,* DICKIE BIRD *again takes the crucifix off the wall and returns with it to his seat and there takes the booties off in haphazard fashion.*) Has he been feedin' you this crappola, too? Don't you be startin' that foolishness. That Spooky Lacroix's so fulla shit he wouldn't know a two thousand year-old Egyptian Sphinxter if he came face to face with one. He's just preachifyin' at you because you're the one person on this reserve who can't argue back. You listen to me. I was there in the same room as your mother when she gave birth to you. So I know well who you are and where you come from. I remember the whole picture. Even though we were all in a bit of a fizzy . . . I remember. Do you know, Dickie Bird Halked, that you were named after that bar? Anyone ever tell you that? (DICKIE BIRD *starts to shake.* PIERRE *takes fright.*) Spooky Lacroix, move that holy ass of yours, for fuck's sakes! (DICKIE BIRD *laughs.* PIERRE *makes a weak attempt to laugh along.*) And I'll never forgive your father, Big Joey oops . . . (DICKIE BIRD *reacts.*) . . . I mean, Wellington Halked, for letting your mother do that to you. "It's not good for the people of this world," I says to him "it's not good for 'em to have the first thing they see when they come into the world is a goddamn jukebox." That's what I says to him. Thank god, you survived, Dickie Bird Halked, thank god, seventeen years later you're sittin' here smack-dab in front of me, hail and hearty as cake. Except for your tongue. Talk, Dickie Bird Halked, talk. Say somethin'. Come on. Try this: "Daddy, daddy, daddy." (DICKIE BIRD *shakes his head.*) Come on. Just this once. Maybe it will work. (*Takes* DICKIE BIRD *by the cheeks with one hand.*) "Daddy, daddy, daddy, daddy." (DICKIE BIRD *jumps up and attacks* PIERRE, *looking as though he were about to shove the crucifix down* PIERRE's *throat.* PIERRE *is genuinely terrified. Just then,* SPOOKY *reenters with the skate.*) Whoa, whoa. Easy. Easy now, Dickie Bird. Easy.

SPOOKY: (*Gasping again at the sight of* DICKIE BIRD *man-handling the crucifix, he makes a bee-line for the boy.*) Dickie Bird Halked? Give me that thing. (*And grabs the crucifix with a flourish. Then he turns to* PIERRE *and holds the skate out with his other hand.*) Promise.

PIERRE: Cross my heart. (*Crosses himself.*)

SPOOKY: (*Replacing the crucifix on the wall and pointing at* PIERRE.) The Lord.

PIERRE: The Lord.

(SPOOKY *hands the skate over to* PIERRE. *Just then,* CREATURE NATAWAYS *stumbles in, now visibly drunk.*)

CREATURE: The Lord!

(*Picking on the hapless* DICKIE BIRD, CREATURE *roughly shoves the boy down to a chair.*)

PIERRE: (*Holding up both his skates.*) I got 'em both. See? I got 'em.

820   CREATURE: Hallelujah! Now all you gotta do is learn how to skate.

SPOOKY: Creature Nataways, I don't want you in my house in that condition. Lalala is liable to pop any minute now and I don't want my son to see the first thing he sees when he comes into the world is a drunk.

825

PIERRE: Damn rights!

SPOOKY: . . . you too, Pierre St. Pierre.

CREATURE: Aw! William Lacroix, don't give me that holier than-me, poker-up-the-bum spiritual bull crap . . .

830   SPOOKY: . . . say wha? . . .

CREATURE: Are you preachin' to this boy, William Lacroix? Are you usin' him again to practice your preachy-preachy? Don't do that, William, the boy is helpless. If you wanna practice, go practice on your old buddy, go preach on Big Joey. He's the one who needs it.

835

SPOOKY: You're hurting again, aren't you, Creature Nataways.

CREATURE: Don't listen to Spooky Lacroix, Dickie Bird. You follow Spooky Lacroix and you go right down to the dogs, I'm tellin' you that right now. Hair spray, Lysol, vanilla ex-

840   tract, shoe polish, Xerox machine juice, he's done it all, this man. If you'd given William Lacroix the chance, he'd have sliced up the Xerox machine and ate it . . .

PIERRE: (*Mockingly, in the background.*) No!

CREATURE: . . . He once drank a Kitty Wells record. He lied

845   to his own mother and he stole her record and he boiled it and swallowed it right up . . .

PIERRE: Good heavens!

(BIG JOEY *enters and stands at the door unseen.*)

CREATURE: Made the Globe and Mail, too. He's robbed, he's cheated his best friend . . .

850   SPOOKY: Alphonse Nataways? Why are you doing this, may I ask?

CREATURE: Oh, he was bad, Dickie Bird Halked, he was bad. Fifteen years. Fifteen years of his life pukin' his guts out on sidewalks from here to Sicamous, B.C., this man . . .

SPOOKY: Shush!

855   CREATURE: and this is the same man . . .

BIG JOEY: (*Speaking suddenly and laughing, he takes everyone by surprise. They gasp. And practically freeze in their tracks.*) . . . who's yellin' and preachin' about "the Lord!" They oughta retire the beaver and put this guy on the Canadian nickel,

860   he's become a national goddamn symbol, that what you're sayin', Creature Nataways? This the kind of man you wanna become, that what you're sayin' to the boy, Creature Nataways? (*Close up to* DICKIE BIRD.) A man who couldn't get a hard-on in front of a woman if you paid him a two

865   dollar bill?

SPOOKY: (*Stung to the quick.*) And is this the kind of man you wanna become, Dickie Bird Halked, this MAN who can't take the sight of blood least of all woman's blood, this MAN who, when he sees a woman's blood, chokes up,

870   pukes and faints, how do you like that?

(PIERRE, *sensing potential violence, begins to sneak out.*)

BIG JOEY: (*Pulls a bottle out of his coat.*) Spooky Lacroix, igwani eeweepoonaskeewuk. ("The end of the world is at hand.")

(PIERRE, *seeing the bottle, retraces his steps and sits down again, grabbing a tea-cup en route, ready for a drink.*)

SPOOKY: (*Shocked.*) Get that thing out of my house!

BIG JOEY: Tonight, we're gonna celebrate my wife, Spooky Lacroix, we're gonna celebrate because my wife, the fabu-   875 lous, the incredible Gazelle Delphina Nataways has been crowned Captain of the Wasy Wailerettes. The Rez is makin' history, Spooky Lacroix. The world will never be the same. Come on, it's on me, it's on your old buddy, the old, old buddy you said you'd never, ever forget.   880

SPOOKY: I told you a long time ago, Big Joey, after what you went and done to my sister, this here boy's own mother, you're no buddy of mine. Get out of my house. Get!

BIG JOEY: (*Handing the bottle of whiskey to* CREATURE.) Creature Nataways, celebrate your wife.   885

CREATURE: (*Raising the bottle in a toast.*) To my wife!

PIERRE: (*Holding his cup out to the bottle.*) Your ex-wife.

BIG JOEY: (*Suddenly quiet and intimate.*) William. William. You and me. You and me, we used to be buddies, kigiskisin? ("Remember?") Wounded Knee. South Dakota. Spring of   890 '73. We parked my van over by that little lake, we swam across, you almost didn't make it and nothin' could get you to swim back. Kigiskisin? So here we're walkin' back through the bush, all the way around this small lake, nothin' on but bare feet and wet undershorts and this black   895 bear come up behind you, kigiskisin? And you freaked out.

(*Laughs.* PIERRE *tries, as best he can, to create a party atmosphere, to little avail.* CREATURE *nervously watches* BIG JOEY *and* SPOOKY. DICKIE BIRD *merely sits there, head down, rocking back and forth.*)

SPOOKY: (*Obviously extremely uncomfortable.*) You freaked out too, ha-ha, ha-ha.

BIG JOEY: That bear gave you a real spook, huh? (*Pause. Then, suddenly, he jumps at the other men.*) Boo! (*The other men, in-   900 cluding* SPOOKY, *jump, splashing whiskey all over the place.* BIG JOEY *laughs. The other men pretend to laugh.*) That's how you got your name, you old Spook . . .

SPOOKY: You were scared too, ha-ha, ha-ha.

BIG JOEY: . . . we get back to the camp and there's Creature   905 and Eugene and Zach and Roscoe, bacon and eggs all ready for us. Christ, I never laughed so hard in my life. But here you were, not laughin' and we'd say: "What's the matter, Spook, you don't like our jokes?" And you'd say: "That's good, yeah, that's good." I guess you were laughin' from a   910 different part of yourself, huh? You were beautiful . . .

SPOOKY: That's good, yeah, that's good.

BIG JOEY: (*Getting the bottle back from* CREATURE *and* PIERRE.) So tonight, Bear-who-went-and-gave-you-a-real-Spooky Lacroix, we're gonna celebrate another new page in our lives.   915 Wounded Knee Three! Women's version!

PIERRE: Damn rights.

BIG JOEY: (*Raising the bottle up in a toast.*) To my wife!

SPOOKY: Ha! Get that thing away from me.

PIERRE: Spooky Lacroix, co-operate. Co-operate for once. The   920 women, the women are playin' hockey.

CREATURE: To my wife!

PIERRE: Your ex-wife.

CREATURE: Shut up you toothless old bugger.

SPOOKY: Big Joey, you're not my friend no more.   925

BIG JOEY: (*Finally grabbing* SPOOKY *roughly by the throat.* CREATURE *jumps to help hold* SPOOKY *still.*) You never let a friend for life go, William Hector Lacroix, not even if you turn your back on your own father, Nicotine Lacroix's spiritual teachings and pretend like hell to be this born-again Christian.

930

SPOOKY: Let go, Creature Nataways, let go of me! (*To* BIG JOEY.) For what you did to this boy at that bar seventeen years ago, Joseph Jeremiah McLeod, you are going to hell. To hell! (BIG JOEY *baptizes* SPOOKY *with the remainder of the bottle's contents. Breaking free,* SPOOKY *grabs* DICKIE BIRD *and shoves him toward* BIG JOEY.) Look at him. He can't even talk. He hasn't talked in seventeen years! (DICKIE BIRD *cries out, breaks free, grabs the crucifix from off the wall and runs out the door, crying.* SPOOKY *breaks down, falls to the floor and weeps.* BIG JOEY *attempts to pick him up gently, but* SPOOKY *kicks him away.*) Let go of me! Let go!

935

940

CREATURE: (*Lifting the empty bottle, laughing and crying at the same time.*) To my wife, to my wife, to my wife, to my wife, to my wife . . .

(BIG JOEY *suddenly lifts* SPOOKY *off the floor by the collar and lifts a fist to punch his face. Black-out.*)

(*Out of this black-out emerges the eery, distant sound of women wailing and pucks hitting boards, echoing and echoing as in a vast empty chamber. The lights come up on* DICKIE BIRD HALKED *and* SIMON STARBLANKET, *standing beside each other in the "bleachers" of the hockey arena, watching the "ice" area (i.e., looking out over the audience). The "bleachers" area is actually on the upper level of the set, in a straight line directly in front of* NANABUSH's *perch.* DICKIE BIRD *is still holding* SPOOKY's *crucifix and* SIMON *is still holding his dancing bustle.*)

945

SIMON: Your grandpa, Nicotine Lacroix, was a medicine man. Hell of a name, but he was a medicine man. Old priest here, Father Boucher, years ago—oh, he was a terrible man—he went and convinced the people old Nicotine Lacroix talked to the devil. That's not true. Nicotine Lacroix was a good man. That's why I want you for my best man. Me and Patsy are getting married a couple of months from now. It's decided. We're gonna have a baby. Then we're going down to South Dakota and we're gonna dance with the Rosebud Sioux this summer. (*Sings as he stomps his foot in the rhythm of a powwow drum.*) " . . . and me I don't wanna go to the moon, I'm gonna leave that moon alone. I just wanna dance with the Rosebud Sioux this summer, yeah, yeah, yeah . . . "

950

955

(*And he breaks into a chant.* DICKIE BIRD *watches, fascinated, particularly by the bustle* SIMON *holds up in the air.*)

(*At this point,* ZACHARY JEREMIAH KEECHIGEESIK *approaches timidly from behind a beam, his pants held flimsily together with a huge safety pin. The sound of women wailing and pucks hitting boards now shifts into the sound of an actual hockey arena, just before a big game.*)

ZACHARY: (*To* SIMON.) Hey! (*But* SIMON *doesn't hear and continues chanting.*) Pssst!

960

SIMON: Zachary Jeremiah. Neee, watstagatch!

ZACHARY: Is Hera out there?

SIMON: (*Indicating the "ice."*) Yup. There she is.

ZACHARY: Lordy, lordy, lordy . . .

SIMON: Just kidding. She's not out there . . .

ZACHARY: Don't do that to me!

965

SIMON: . . . yet.

ZACHARY: (*Finally coming up to join the young men at the "bleachers."*) You know that Nanabush character you were telling me about a couple of nights ago? What do you say I give his name over to them little gingerbread cookie men I'm gonna be making? For starters. Think that would help any?

970

SIMON: Neee . . .

(*Just then,* big joey *enters and proceeds to get a microphone stand ready for broadcasting the game.* ZACHARY *recoils and goes to stand as far away from him as possible.*)

ZACHARY: (*Looking out over the "ice."*) It's almost noon. They're late getting started.

BIG JOEY: (*Yawning luxuriously.*) That's right. Me and Gazelle Nataways . . . slept in.

975

(CREATURE NATAWAYS *comes scurrying in.*)

CREATURE: (*Still talking to himself.*) . . . I tole you once I tole you twice . . . (*Then to the other men.*) Chris' sakes! Are they really gonna do it? Chris'sakes!

(SPOOKY LACROIX *enters wearing a woolen scarf he obviously knitted himself. He is still knitting, this time a pale blue baby sweater. He also now sports a black eye and band-aide on his face. All the men, except* PIERRE ST. PIERRE, *are now in the "bleachers," standing in a straight line facing the audience, with* DICKIE BIRD *in the center area,* SIMON *and* SPOOKY *to his immediate right and left, respectively.*)

SPOOKY: It's bad luck to start late. I know. I read the interview with Gay Lafleur in last week's Expositor. They won't get far. (*He sees* GAZELLE NATAWAYS *entering the "rink," unseen by the audience. [All the hockey players on the "ice" are unseen by the audience; it is only the men who can actually "see" them.]*) Look! Gazelle Nataways went and got her sweater trimmed in the chest area!

980

985

(*Wild cat calls from the men.*)

CREATURE: Trimmed it? She's got it plunging down to her ootsee. ("belly button.")

ZACHARY: Ahem. Smokes too much. Lung problems.

BIG JOEY: Nah. More like it's got somethin' to do with the undershorts she's wearin' today.

990

ZACHARY: (*Fast on the up-take.*) Fuck you!

BIG JOEY: (*Blowing* ZACHARY *a kiss.*) Poosees. ("Pussy cat." [*Zachary's childhood nickname.*])

SPOOKY: Terrible. Terrible. Tsk, tsk, tsk.

995

(PIERRE ST. PIERRE *enters on the lower level, teetering dangerously on his skates towards the "ice" area downstage. He wears a referee's top and a whistle around his neck.*)

PIERRE: (*Checking the names off as he reads from a clipboard.*) Dominique Ladouche, Black Lady Halked, Annie Cook, June Bug McLeod, Big Bum Pegahmagahbow . . .

SIMON: (*Calling out.*) Patsy Pegahmagahbow, turkey.

PIERRE: Shut up. I'm workin' here. . . . Leonarda Lee Starblanket, that terrible Dictionary woman, Fluffy Sainte-Marie, Chicken Lips Pegahmagahbow, Dry Lips Manigitogan, Little Hand Manigitogan, Little Girl Manitowabi, Victoria Manitowabi, Belinda Nickikoosimeenicaning, Martha Two-Axe Early-in-the-Morning, her royal highness Gazelle Delphina Nataways, Delia Opekokew, Barbra Nahwegahbow, Gloria May Eshkibok, Hera Keechigeesik, Tall Mary Ann Patchnose, Short Mary Ann Patchnose, Queen Elizabeth Patchnose, the triplets Marjorie Moose, Maggie May Moose, Mighty Moose and, of course, my wife, Veronique St. Pierre. Yup. They're all there, I hope, and the world is about to explode!

SPOOKY: That's what I've been trying to tell you!

(PIERRE ST. PIERRE, *barely able to stand on his skates, hobbles about, obviously getting almost trampled by the hockey players at various times.*)

BIG JOEY: (*Now speaking on the microphone. The other men watch the women on the "ice"; some are cheering and whistling, some calling down the game.*) Welcome, ladies igwa gentlemen, welcome one and all to the Wasaychigan Hill Hip-hip-hippodrome. This is your host for the big game, Big Joey—and they don't call me Big Joey for nothin'—Chairman, CEO and Proprietor of the Wasaychigan Hill Hippodrome, bringin' you a game such as has never been seen ever before on the ice of any hockey arena anywhere on the island of Manitoulin, anywhere on the face of this country, anywhere on the face of this planet. And there . . .

CREATURE: . . . there's Gazelle Nataways, number one . . .

BIG JOEY: . . . they are, ladies . . .

SPOOKY: . . . terrible, terrible . . .

BIG JOEY: . . . igwa gentlemen . . .

CREATURE: . . . Chris'sakes, that's my wife, Chris'sakes . . .

BIG JOEY: . . . there they are, the most beautiful . . .

SIMON: . . . give 'em hell, Patsy Pegahmagahbow, give 'em hell . . .

BIG JOEY: . . . daring, death- . . .

SIMON: (*To* ZACHARY.) . . . there's Hera Keechigeesik, number nine . . .

BIG JOEY: . . . defying Indian women . . .

SPOOKY: . . . terrible, terrible . . .

BIG JOEY: . . . in the world . . .

ZACHARY: . . . that's my wife . . .

BIG JOEY: . . . the Wasy Wailerettes . . .

(*Clears his throat and tests the microphone by tapping it gently.*)

ZACHARY: . . . lordy, lordy, lordy . . .

CREATURE: Hey, Gazelle Nataways and Hera Keechigeesik are lookin' at each other awful funny. Something bad's gonna happen, I tole you once I tole you twice, something bad's gonna happen . . .

SPOOKY: This is sign from the Lord. This is THE sign . . .

BIG JOEY: Number One Gazelle Nataways, Captain of the Wasy Wailerettes, facing off with Number Nine, Flora McDonald, Captain of the Canoe Lake Bravettes. And referee Pierre St. Pierre drops the puck and takes off like a herd of wild turtles . . .

SIMON: Aw, Spooky Lacroix, eat my shitty shorts, neee . . .

BIG JOEY: . . . Hey, aspin Number Six Dry Lips Manigitogan, right-winger for the Wasy Wailerettes . . .

ZACHARY: . . . look pretty damn stupid, if you ask me. Fifteen thousand dollars for all that new equipment . . .

BIG JOEY: . . . eemaskamat Number Thirteen of the Canoe Lake Bravettes anee-i puck . . .

CREATURE: . . . Cancel the game! Cancel the game! Cancel the game! . . .

(*Etc.*)

BIG JOEY: . . . igwa aspin sipweesinskwataygew. Hey, k'see goochin! (*Off microphone.*) Creature Nataways. Shut up. (*To the other men.*) Get this asshole out of here. . . .

SIMON: Yay, Patsy Pegahmagahbow! Pat-see! Pat-see! Pat-see! . . .

(*Etc.*)

BIG JOEY: (*Back on microphone.*) . . . How, Number Six Dry Lips Manigitogan, right-winger for the Wasy Wailerettes, soogi pugamawew igwa anee-i puck igwa aspin center-line ispathoo ana puck . . .

CREATURE: (*To* SIMON.) Shut up. Don't encourage them . . .

BIG JOEY: . . . ita Number Nine Hera Keechigeesik, left-winger for . . .

SIMON: (*To* CREATURE.) Aw, lay off! Pat-see! Pat-see! Pat-see! . . . (*Etc.*)

BIG JOEY: . . . the Wasy Wailerettes, kagatchitnat. How, Number Nine Hera Keechigeesik . . .

(*He continues uninterrupted.*)

CREATURE: . . . Stop the game! Stop the game! Stop the game! . . . (*Etc.*)

ZACHARY: Goodness sakes, there's gonna be a fight out there!

(CREATURE *continues his "stop the game,"* ZACHARY *repeats "goodness sakes, there's gonna be a fight out there,"* SIMON's *"Pat-see!" has now built up into a full chant, his foot pounding on the floor so that it sounds like a powwow drum, his dancing bustle held aloft like a shield.* SPOOKY *finally grabs the crucifix away from* DICKIE BIRD, *holds it aloft and begins to pray, loudly, as in a ceremony.* DICKIE BIRD, *caught between Simon's chanting and* SPOOKY's *praying, blocks his ears with his hands and looks with growing consternation at "the game."* PIERRE *blows his whistle and skates around like a puppet gone mad.*)

SPOOKY: The Lord is my shepherd; I shall not want. He maketh me to lie down in green pastures; he leadeth me beside the still waters. He restoreth my soul; he leadeth me in the paths of righteousness for his name's sake. Yea, though I walk through the valley of the shadow of death, I will fear no evil; for thou art with me. Yea, though I walk through the valley of the shadow of death, I will fear no evil; for thou art with me . . .

(*He repeats this last phrase over and over again. Finally,* DICKIE BIRD *freaks out, screams and runs down to the "ice" area.*)

1052 . . . **Hey,** . . . The following hockey commentary by Big Joey (pp. 1540–1541) is translated on p. 1533.

BIG JOEY: (*Continuing uninterrupted above all the other men's voices.*) …igwa ati-ooteetum blue line ita Number One Gazelle Nataways, Captain of the Wasy Wailerettes, kagagweemaskamat anee-i puck, ma-a Number Nine Hera Keechigeesik mawch weemeethew anee-i puck. Wha! "Hooking," itwew referee Pierre St. Pierre, Gazelle Nataways isa keehookiwatew her own team-mate Hera Keechigeesikwa, wha! How, Number One Gazelle Nataways, Captain of the Wasy Wailerettes, face-off igwa meena itootum asichi Number Nine Flora McDonald, Captain of the Canoe Lake Bravettes igwa Flora McDonald soogi pugamawew anee-i puck, ma-a Number Thirty-seven Big Bum Pegahmagahbow, defense-woman for the Wasy Wailerettes, stops the puck and passes it to Number Eleven Black Lady Halked, also defense-woman for the Wasy Wailerettes, but Gazelle Nataways, Captain of the Wasy Wailerettes, soogi body check meethew her own team-mate Black Lady Halked woops! She falls, ladies igwa gentlemen, Black Lady Halked hits the boards and Black Lady Halked is singin' the blues, ladies igwa gentlemen, Black Lady Halked sings the blues. (*Off microphone, to the other men.*) What the hell is goin' on down there? Dickie Bird, get off the ice! (*Back on microphone.*) Wha! Number Eleven Black Lady Halked is up in a flash igwa seemak n'taymaskamew Gazelle Nataways anee-i puck, holy shit! The ailing but very, very furious Black Lady Halked skates back, turns and takes aim, it's gonna be a slap shot, ladies igwa gentlemen, slap shot keetnatch taytootum Black Lady Halked igwa Black Lady Halked shootiwoo anee-i puck, wha! She shoots straight at her very own captain, Gazelle Nataways and holy shit, holy shit, holy fuckin' shit!

(*All hell breaks loose; it is as though some bizarre dream has entered the arena. We hear the sound of women wailing and pucks hitting boards, echoing and echoing as in a vast empty chamber. The men are all screaming at the same time, from the "bleachers," re-calling* BLACK LADY HALKED*'s legendary fall of seventeen years ago.*)

BIG JOEY: (*Dropping his microphone in horror.*) Holy Christ! If there is a devil in this world, then he has just walked into this room. Holy Christ! … (*He says this over and over again.*)

ZACHARY: Do something about her, goodness sakes, I told you guys to do something about her seventeen years ago, but you wouldn't do fuck-all. So go out there now and help her … (*Repeated.*)

CREATURE: Never mind, Chris'sakes, don't bother her. Let me out of here. Chris'sakes, let me out of here! … (*Repeated.*)

SPOOKY: Yea, though I walk through the valley of the shadow of death, I will fear no evil; for thou art with me …

(*Repeated. While* SIMON *continues chanting and stomping.*)

PIERRE: (*From the "ice" area.*) Never you mind, Zachary Jeremiah, never you mind. She'll be okay. No she won't. Zachary Jeremiah, go out there and help her. No. She'll be okay. No she won't. Yes. No. Yes. No. Help! Where's the puck? Can't do nothin' without the goddamn puck. Where's the puck?! Where's the puck? Where's the puck? …

(*He repeats this last phrase over and over again. Center- and down-stage, on the "ice" area,* DICKIE BIRD *is going into a complete "freak-out," breaking into a grotesque, fractured version of a Cree chant. Gradually,* BIG

JOEY, ZACHARY *and* CREATURE *join* PIERRE*'s refrain of "where's the puck?!", with which they all, including the chanting* SIMON *and the praying* SPOOKY*, scatter and come running down to the "ice" area. As they reach the lower level and begin to approach the audience, their movements break down into slow motion, as though they were trying to run through the sticky, gummy substance of some horrible, surrealistic nightmare.*)

PIERRE/BIG JOEY/ZACHARY/CREATURE: (*Slower and slower, as on a record that is slowing down gradually to a stop.*) Where's the puck?! Where's the puck?! Where's the puck?! … (*Etc.*)

(SIMON *continues chanting and stomping,* SPOOKY *continues intoning the last phrase of his prayer and* DICKIE BIRD *continues his fractured chant. Out of this fading "sound collage" emerges the sound of a jukebox playing the introduction to Kitty Wells' "It Wasn't God Who Made Honky Tonk Angels," as though filtered through memory. At this point, on the upper level, a giant luminescent hockey stick comes seemingly out of nowhere and, in very slow motion, shoots a giant luminescent puck. On the puck, looking like a radiant but damaged "Madonna-with-child," sits* NANABUSH, *as the spirit of* BLACK LADY HALKED, *naked, nine months pregnant, drunk almost senseless and barely able to hold a bottle of beer up to her mouth. All the men freeze in their standing positions facing the audience, except for* DICKIE BIRD *who continues his fractured chanting and whimpering, holding his arms up towards* NANABUSH/BLACK LADY HALKED. *The giant luminescent puck reaches and stops at the edge of the upper level.* NANABUSH/BLACK LADY HALKED *struggles to stand and begins staggering toward her perch. She reaches it and falls with one arm on top of it. The magical, glittering lights flare on and, for the first time, the jukebox is revealed.* NANABUSH/BLACK LADY HALKED *staggers laboriously up to the top of the jukebox and stands there in profile, one arm lifted to raise her beer as she pours it over her belly. Behind her, the full moon begins to glow, blood red. And from the jukebox, Kitty Wells sings.*)

> As I sit here tonight, the jukebox playing,
> That tune about the wild side of life;
> As I listen to the words you are saying,
> It brings memories when I was a trusting wife.
>
> It wasn't God who made honky tonk angels,
> As you said in the words of your song;
> Too many times married men think they're still single,
> That has caused many a good girl to go wrong.

(*During the "instrumental break" of the song here,* DICKIE BIRD *finally explodes and shrieks out towards the vision of* NANABUSH/BLACK LADY HALKED.)

DICKIE BIRD: Mama! Mama! Katha paksini. Katha paksini. Kanawapata wastew. Kanawapataw wastew. Michimina. Michimina. Katha pagitina. Kaweechee-ik nipapa. Kaweechee-ik nipapa. Nipapa. Papa. Papa. Papa. Papa. Papa. Papa! Mommy! Mommy! Don't fall. Don't fall. Look at the light. Look at the light. Hold on to it. Hold on to it. Don't let it go. My daddy will help you. My daddy will help you. My daddy. Daddy. Daddy. … (*Etc.*)

(*He crumples to the floor and freezes. Kitty Wells sings.*)

> It's a shame that all the blame is on us women,
> It's not true that only you men feel the same;
> From the start most every heart that's ever broken,
> Was because there always was a man to blame.

It wasn't God who made honky tonk angels;
    As you said in the words of your song;
    Too many times married men think they're still single,
    That has caused many a good girl to go wrong.

(*As the song fades, the final tableau is one of* DICKIE BIRD *collapsed on the floor between* SIMON, *who is holding aloft his bustle, and* SPOOKY, *who is holding aloft his crucifix, directly in front of and at the feet of* BIG JOEY *and, above* BIG JOEY, *the pregnant* NANABUSH/BLACK LADY HALKED, *who is standing on top of the flashing jukebox, in silhouette against the full moon, bottle held up above her mouth.* ZACHARY, CREATURE *and* PIERRE *are likewise frozen, standing off to the side of this central grouping. Slow fade-out.*)

ACT TWO

When the lights come up, DICKIE BIRD HALKED *is standing on a rock in the forest, his clothes and hair all askew. He holds* SPOOKY's *crucifix, raised with one hand up to the night sky; he is trying, as best he can, to chant, after* SIMON STARBLANKET's *fashion. As he does,* NANABUSH *appears in the shadows a distance behind him (as the spirit of* GAZELLE NATAWAYS, *minus the gigantic breasts, but dressed, this time, as a stripper). She lingers and watches with interest. Slowly,* DICKIE BIRD *climbs off the rock and walks off-stage, his quavering voice fading into the distance. The full moon glows. Fade-out.*

Fade-in on SPOOKY LACROIX's *kitchen, where* SPOOKY *is busy pinning four little pale blue baby booties on the wall where the crucifix used to be, the booties that, in Act One, covered the four extremities of the crucifix. At the table are* PIERRE ST. PIERRE *and* ZACHARY JEREMIAH KEECHIGEESIK. PIERRE *is stringing pale blue yarn around* ZACHARY's *raised, parted hands. Then* SPOOKY *joins them at the table and begins knitting again, this time, a baby bonnet, also pale blue.* ZACHARY *sits removed through most of this scene, pre-occupied with the problem of his still missing shorts, his bakery and his wife. The atmosphere is one of fear and foreboding, almost as though the men were constantly resisting the impulse to look over their shoulders. On the upper level, in a soft, dim light,* NANABUSH/GAZELLE *can be seen sitting up on her perch, waiting impatiently for "the boys" to finish their talk.*

PIERRE: (*In a quavering voice.*) The Wasy Wailerettes are dead. Gentlemen, my job is disappeared from underneath my feet.
SPOOKY: And we have only the Lord to thank for that.
5   PIERRE: Gazelle Nataways, she just sashayed herself off that ice, behind swayin' like a walrus pudding. That game, gentlemen, was what I call a real apostrophe . . .
ZACHARY: Catastrophe.
PIERRE: That's what I said, dammit. . . .
10 SPOOKY: . . . tsk . . .
PIERRE: . . . didn't even get to referee more than ten minutes. But you have to admit, gentlemen, that slap shot . . .
SPOOKY: . . . that's my sister, Black Lady Halked, that's my sister . . .
15 PIERRE: . . . did you see her slap shot? Fantastic! Like a bullet, like a killer shark. Unbelievable!
ZACHARY: (*Uncomfortable.*) Yeah, right.
PIERRE: When Black Lady Halked hit Gazelle Nataways with that puck. Them Nataways eyes. Big as plates!
20 SPOOKY: Bigger than a ditch!

PIERRE: Them mascara stretch marks alone was a perfectly frightful thing to behold. Holy shit la marde! But you know, they couldn't find that puck.
SPOOKY: (*Losing his cool and laughing, falsely and nervously.*) Did you see it? It fell . . . it fell . . . that puck went splat on her 25 chest . . . and it went . . . it went . . . plummety plop . . .
PIERRE: . . . plummety plop to be sure . . .
SPOOKY: . . . down her . . . down her . . .
PIERRE: Down the crack. Right down that horrendous, scarifyin' Nataways bosom crack.   30

(*The "kitchen lights" go out momentarily and, to the men, inexplicably. Then they come back on. The men look about them, perplexed.*)

SPOOKY: Serves . . . her . . . right for trimming her hockey sweater in the chest area, is what I say.
PIERRE: They say that puck slid somewhere deep, deep into the folds of her fleshy, womanly juices . . .
ZACHARY: . . . there's a lot of things they're saying about that 35 puck . . .
PIERRE: and it's lost. Disappeared. Gone. Phhht! Nobody can find that puck.

(*At this point,* SPOOKY *gets up to check the light switch. The lights go out.*)

ZACHARY: (*In the darkness.*) Won't let no one come near her, is what they say. Not six inches.   40
PIERRE: I gotta go look for that puck. (*Lights come back on.* PIERRE *inexplicably appears sitting in another chair.*) Gentlemen, I gotta go jiggle that woman.

(*Lights out again.*)

ZACHARY: (*From the darkness.*) What's the matter, Spook?
SPOOKY: (*Obviously quite worried.*) Oh, nothing, nothing . . . 45 (*Lights come back on.* PIERRE *appears sitting back in his original chair. The men are even more mystified, but try to brighten up anyway.*) . . . just . . . checking the lights . . . Queen of the Indians, that's what she tried to look like, walking off that ice.   50
PIERRE: Queen of the Indians, to be sure. That's when them women went and put their foot down and made up their mind, on principle, no holds barred . . .

(*A magical flash of lavender light floods the room very briefly, establishing a connection between* SPOOKY's *kitchen and* NANABUSH's *perch, where* NANABUSH/GAZELLE *is still sitting, tapping her fingers impatiently, looking over her shoulder periodically, as if to say: "come on, boys, get with it."* PIERRE's *speech momentarily goes into slow motion.*)

. . . no . . . way . . . they're . . . takin' up . . . them hockey sticks again until that particular puck is found. "The par- 55 ticular puck," that's what they call it. Gentlemen, the Wasy Wailerettes are dead. My job is disappeared. Gone. Kaput kaput. Phhht!
SPOOKY: Amen.

(*Pause. Thoughtful silence for a beat or two.*)

ZACHARY: W-w-w-where's that nephew of yours, Spook?   60
SPOOKY: Dickie Bird Halked?

PIERRE: My wife, Veronique St. Pierre, she informs me that Dickie Bird Halked, last he was seen, was pacin' the bushes in the general direction of the Pegahmagahbow acreage near Buzwah, lookin' for all the world like he had lost his mind, poor boy.

ZACHARY: Lordy, lordy, lordy, I'm telling you right now, Spooky Lacroix, if you don't do something about that nephew of yours, he's liable to go out there and kill someone next time.

SPOOKY: I'd be out there myself pacing the bushes with him except my wife Lalala's liable to pop any minute now and I gotta be ready to zip her up to Sudbury General.

PIERRE: Bah. Them folks of his, they don't care. If it's not hockey, it's bingo she's out playin' every night of the week, that Black Lady of a mother of his.

ZACHARY: Went and won the jackpot again last night, Black Lady Halked did. All fifty pounds of it . . .

PIERRE: Beat Gazelle Nataways by one number!

ZACHARY: . . . if it wasn't for her, I'd have mastered that apple pie recipe by now. I was counting on all that lard. Fifty pounds, goodness sakes.

SPOOKY: This little old kitchen? It's yours, Zachary Jeremiah, anytime, anytime. Lalala's got tons of lard.

PIERRE: Ha! She better have. Zachary Jeremiah hasn't dared go nowhere near his own kitchen in almost a week.

ZACHARY: Four nights! It's only Wednesday night, Pierre St. Pierre. Don't go stretching the truth just cuz you were too damn chicken to go get me my shorts.

PIERRE: Bah!

SPOOKY: (To ZACHARY.) Your shorts?

ZACHARY: (Evading the issue.) I just hope that Black Lady Halked's out there looking after her boy cuz if she isn't, we're all in a heap of trouble, I have a funny feeling. (Suddenly, he throws the yarn down and rises.) Achh! I've got to cook!

(He goes behind the kitchen counter, puts an apron on and begins the preparations for making pie pastry.)

SPOOKY: (To PIERRE, half-whispering.) His shorts?

(PIERRE merely shrugs, indicating ZACHARY's pants, which are still held together with a large safety pin. SPOOKY and PIERRE laugh nervously. SPOOKY looks concernedly at the four little booties on the wall where the crucifix used to be. Beat.)

(Suddenly, PIERRE slaps the table with one hand and leans over to SPOOKY, all set for an argument, an argument they've obviously had many times before. Through all this, ZACHARY is making pie pastry at the counter and SPOOKY continues knitting. The atmosphere of "faked" jocular camaraderie grows, particularly as the music gets louder later on. NANABUSH/GAZELLE is now getting ready for her strip in earnest, standing on her perch, spraying perfume on, stretching her legs, etc. The little tivoli lights in the jukebox begin to twinkle little by little.)

PIERRE: Queen of Hearts.

SPOOKY: Belvedere.

PIERRE: Queen of Hearts.

SPOOKY: The Belvedere.

PIERRE: I told you many times, Spooky Lacroix, it was the Queen of Hearts. I was there. You were there. Zachary Jeremiah, Big Joey, Creature Nataways, we were all there.

(From here on, the red/blue/purple glow of the jukebox (i.e., NANABUSH's perch) becomes more and more apparent.)

SPOOKY: And I'm telling you it was the Belvedere Hotel, before it was even called the Belvedere Hotel, when it was still called . . .

PIERRE: Spooky Lacroix, don't contribute your elder. Big Joey, may he rot in hell, he was the bouncer there that night, he was right there the night it happened.

ZACHARY: Hey, Spook. Where do you keep your rolling pin?

SPOOKY: Use my salami.

PIERRE: (To SPOOKY.) He was there.

ZACHARY: Big Joey was never the bouncer, he was the janitor.

SPOOKY: At the Belvedere Hotel.

PIERRE: Never you mind, Spooky Lacroix, never you mind. Black Lady Halked was sittin' there in her corner of the bar for three weeks . . .

SPOOKY: Three weeks?! It was more like three nights. Aw, you went and mixed up my baby's cap. (Getting all tangled up with his knitting.)

ZACHARY: Got any cinnamon?

SPOOKY: I got chili powder. Same color as cinnamon.

(Faintly, the strip music from the jukebox begins to play.)

PIERRE: . . . the place was so jam-packed with people drinkin' beer and singin' and smokin' cigarettes and watchin' the dancin' girl . . .

SPOOKY: . . . Gazelle Nataways, she was the dancing girl . . .

(The music is now on full volume and NANABUSH/GAZELLE's strip is in full swing. She dances on top of the jukebox, which is now a riot of sound and flashing lights. SPOOKY's kitchen is bathed in a gorgeous lavender light. BIG JOEY and CREATURE NATAWAYS appear at SPOOKY's table, each drinking a bottle of beer. The strip of seventeen years ago is fully recreated, the memory becoming so heated that NANABUSH/GAZELLE magically appears dancing right on top of SPOOKY's kitchen table. The men are going wild, applauding, laughing, drinking, all in slow motion and in mime. In the heat of the moment, as NANABUSH/GAZELLE strips down to silk tassels and G-string, they begin tearing their clothes off.)

(Suddenly, SIMON STARBLANKET appears at SPOOKY's door: NANABUSH/GAZELLE disappears, as do BIG JOEY and CREATURE. And SPOOKY, PIERRE and ZACHARY are caught with their pants down. The jukebox music fades.)

SIMON: Spooky Lacroix. (The lavender light snaps off, we are back to "reality" and SPOOKY, PIERRE and ZACHARY stand there, embarrassed. In a panic, they begin putting their clothes back on and reclaim the positions they had before the strip. SPOOKY motions SIMON to take a seat at the table. SIMON does so.) Spooky Lacroix. Rosie Kakapetum expresses interest in coming here to birth Lalala's baby when the time comes.

SPOOKY: Rosie Kakapetum? No way some witch is gonna come and put her witchy little fingers on my baby boy.

SIMON: Rosie Kakapetum's no witch, Spooky Lacroix. She's Patsy Pegahmagahbow's step-mother and she's Wasy's only surviving medicine woman and mid-wife . . .

SPOOKY: Hogwash!

PIERRE: Ahem. Rosie Kakapetum says it's a cryin' shame the Wasy Wailerettes is the only team that's not in the Ontario Hockey League.

ZACHARY: Ontario Hockey League?

145 PIERRE: Absolutely. The OHL. Indian women's OHL. All the Indian women in Ontario's playin' hockey now. It's like a fever out there.

ZACHARY: Shoot. (*Referring to his pastry.*) I hope this new recipe works for me.

150 PIERRE: Well, it's not exactly new without the cinnamon.

SPOOKY: (*To SIMON.*) My son will be born at Sudbury General Hospital . . .

SIMON: You know what they do to them babies in them city hospitals?

155 SPOOKY: . . . Sudbury General, Simon Starblanket, like any good Christian boy . . .

PIERRE: (*Attempting to diffuse the argument.*) Ahem. We got to get them Wasy Wailerettes back on that ice again.

SIMON: (*Refusing to let go of SPOOKY.*) They pull them away right 160 from their own mother's breast the minute they come into this world and they put them behind these glass cages together with another two hundred babies like they were some kind of scientific specimens . . .

PIERRE: . . . like two hundred of them little monsters . . .

165 ZACHARY: Hamsters!

PIERRE: . . . that's what I said dammit . . .

SPOOKY: . . . tsk . . .

PIERRE: . . . you can't even tell which hamster belongs to which mother. You take Lalala to Sudbury General, 170 Spooky Lacroix, and your hamster's liable to end up stuck to some French lady's tit.

SIMON: . . . and they'll hang Lalala up in metal stirrups and your baby's gonna be born going up instead of dropping down which is the natural way. You were born going up in-175 stead of dropping down like you should have . . .

PIERRE: Yup. You were born at Sudbury General, Spooky Lacroix, that's why you get weirder and weirder as the days get longer, that's why them white peoples is so weird they were all born going up . . .

180 SIMON: . . . instead of dropping down . . .

ZACHARY: (*Sprinkling flour in SPOOKY's face, with both hands, and laughing.*) . . . to the earth, Spooky Lacroix, to the earth . . .

SPOOKY: Pooh!

PIERRE: . . . but we got to find that puck, Simon Starblanket, 185 them Wasy Wailerettes have got to join the OHL . . .

SPOOKY: (*To SIMON.*) If Rosie Kakapetum is a medicine woman, Simon Starblanket, then how come she can't drive the madness from my nephew's brain, how come she can't make him talk, huh?

190 SIMON: Because the medical establishment and the church establishment and people like you, Spooky Lacroix, have effectively put an end to her usefulness and the usefulness of people like her everywhere, that's why Spooky Lacroix.

SPOOKY: Phooey!

195 SIMON: Do you or your sister even know that your nephew hasn't been home in two days, since that incident at the hockey game, Spooky Lacroix? Do you even care? Why can't you and that thing . . . (*Pointing at the bible that sits beside SPOOKY.*) and all it stands for cure your nephew's 200 madness, as you call it, Spooky Lacroix? What has this

thing . . . (*The bible again.*) done to cure the madness of this community and communities like it clean across this country, Spooky Lacroix? Why didn't "the Lord" as you call him, come to your sister's rescue at that bar seventeen years ago, huh, Spooky Lacroix? (*Pause. Tense silence.*) Rosie 205 Kakapetum is gonna be my mother-in-law in two months, Spooky Lacroix, and if Patsy and I are gonna do this thing right, if we're gonna work together to make my best man, Dickie Bird Halked, well again, then Rosie Kakapetum has got to birth that baby. (*He begins to exit.*)

SPOOKY: (*In hard, measured cadence.*) Rosie Kakapetum works for 210 the devil.

(*SIMON freezes in his tracks. Silence. Then he turns, grabs a chair violently, bangs it down and sits determinedly.*)

SIMON: Fine. I'll sit here and I'll wait.

SPOOKY: Fine. You sit there and you wait.

(*Silence. SIMON sits silent and motionless, his back to the other men.*)

PIERRE: Ahem. Never you mind, Spooky Lacroix, never you 215 mind. Now as I was sayin', Black Lady Halked was nine months pregnant when she was sittin' in that corner of the Queen of Hearts.

SPOOKY: The Belvedere!

PIERRE: Three weeks, Black Lady Halked was sittin' there 220 drinkin' beer. They say she got the money by winnin' the jackpot at the Espanola bingo just three blocks down the street. Three weeks, sure as I'm alive and walkin' these treacherous icy roads, three weeks she sat there in that dark corner by herself. They say the only light you could see her 225 by was the light from the jukebox playin' "Rim of Fire" by Johnny Cash . . .

ZACHARY: "Rim of Fire." Yeah, right, Pierre St. Pierre.

SPOOKY: Kitty Wells! Kitty Wells!

(*The sound of the jukebox playing "It Wasn't God Who Made Honky Tonk Angels" can be heard faintly in the background.*)

PIERRE: . . . the place was so jam-packed with people drinkin' 230 and singin' and smokin' cigarettes and watchin' the dancin' girl . . .

SPOOKY: . . . Gazelle Nataways, she was the dancing girl, Lord save her soul . . .

PIERRE: . . . until Black Lady Halked collapsed . . . 235

(*SPOOKY, PIERRE and ZACHARY freeze in their positions, looking in horror at the memory of seventeen years ago.*)

(*On the upper level, NANABUSH, back in her guise as the spirit of BLACK LADY HALKED, sits on the jukebox, facing the audience, legs out directly in front. Nine months pregnant and naked, she holds a bottle of beer up in the air and is drunk almost senseless. The song, "It Wasn't God Who Made Honky Tonk Angels," rises to full volume, the lights from the jukebox flashing riotously. The full moon glows blood red. Immediately below NANABUSH/BLACK LADY HALKED, DICKIE BIRD HALKED appears, kneeling, naked, arms raised toward his mother. NANABUSH/BLACK LADY HALKED begins to writhe and scream, laughing and crying hysterically at the same time and, as she does, her water breaks. DICKIE BIRD, drenched, rises slowly from the floor, arms still raised, and screams.*)

DICKIE BIRD: Mama! Mama!

(*And from here on, the lights and the sound on this scene begin to fade slowly, as the scene on the lower level resumes.*)

PIERRE: . . . she kind of oozed down right then and there, right down to the floor of the Queen of Hearts Tavern. And Big Joey, may he rot in hell, he was the bouncer there that
240 night, when he saw the blood, he ran away and puked over on the other side of the bar, the sight of all that woman's blood just scared the shit right out of him. And that's when Dickie Bird Halked, as we know him, came ragin' out from his mother's womb, Spooky Lacroix, in between beers, right
245 there on the floor, under a table, by the light of the juke-box, on a Saturday night, at the Queen of Hearts . . .

SPOOKY: They went and named him after the bar, you crusted old fossil! That bar, which is now called the Belvedere Hotel, used to be called the Dickie Bird Tavern . . .

250 SIMON: (*Suddenly jumping out of his chair and practically lunging at* SPOOKY.) It doesn't matter what the fuck the name of that fucking bar was! (*The lights and sound on* NANABUSH *and the jukebox have now faded completely.*) The fact of the matter is, it never should have happened, that kind of thing should
255 never be allowed to happen, not to us Indians, not to any-one living and breathing on the face of God's green earth. (*Pause. Silence. Then, dead calm.*) You guys have given up, haven't you? You and your generation. You gave up a long time ago. You'd rather turn your back on the whole thing
260 and pretend to laugh, wouldn't you? (*Silence.*) Well, not me. Not us. (*Silence.*) This is not the kind of Earth we want to inherit. (*He begins to leave, but turns once more.*) I'll be back. With Patsy. And Rosie.

(*He exits. Another embarrassed silence.*)

SPOOKY: (*Unwilling to face up to the full horror of it, he chooses, in-*
265 *stead, to do exactly what* SIMON *said: turn his back and pretend to laugh.*) That bar, which is now called the Belvedere Hotel, used to be called the Dickie Bird Tavern. That's how Dickie Bird Halked got his name. And that's why he goes hay-wire every now and again and that's why he doesn't talk. Fetal Al-
270 cohol something-something, Pierre St. Pierre . . .

ZACHARY: (*From behind the counter, where he is still busy making pie crust.*) Fetal Alcohol Syndrome.

SPOOKY: . . . that's the devil that stole the baby's tongue be-cause Dickie Bird Halked was born drunk and very, very
275 mad. At the Dickie Bird Tavern in downtown Espanola sev-enteen years ago and that's a fact.

PIERRE: Aw, shit la marde. Fuck you, Spooky Lacroix, I'm gonna go get me my rest.

(*Throws the yarn in* SPOOKY's *face, jumps up and exits.* SPOOKY *sits there with a pile of yarn stuck to his face, caught on his glasses.*)

ZACHARY: (*Proudly holding up the pie crust in its plate.*) It worked!

(*Black-out*)

(*On the upper level, in a dim light away from her perch,* NANABUSH/BLACK LADY HALKED *is getting ready to go out for the evening, combing her hair in front of a mirror, putting on her clothes, etc.* DICKIE BIRD *is*

with her, naked, getting ready to go to bed. SPOOKY's *crucifix sits on a night-table to his side. In* DICKIE BIRD's *mind, he is at home with his mother.*)

DICKIE BIRD: Mama. Mama. N'tagoosin. ("I'm sick.")   280
NANABUSH/BLACK LADY: Say your prayers.
DICKIE BIRD: Achimoostawin nimoosoom. ("Tell me about my grandpa.")
NANABUSH/BLACK LADY: Go to bed. I'm going out soon.
DICKIE BIRD: Mawch. Achimoostawin nimoosoom. ("No. Tell   285
me about my grandpa.")
NANABUSH/BLACK LADY: You shouldn't talk about him.
DICKIE BIRD: Tapweechee eegeemachipoowamit nimoosoom?
("Is it true my grandpa had bad medicine?")
NANABUSH/BLACK LADY: They say he met the devil once. Your   290
grandpa talked to the devil. Don't talk about him.
DICKIE BIRD: Eegeemithoopoowamit nimoosoom, eetweet
Simon Starblanket. ("Simon Starblanket says he had good
medicine.")
NANABUSH/BLACK LADY: Ashhh! Simon Starblanket.   295
DICKIE BIRD: Mawch eemithoosit awa aymeewatik keetnanow
kichi, eetweet Simon Starblanket. ("Simon Starblanket says
that this cross is not right for us.") (*He grabs the crucifix from
the night-table and spits on it.*)
NANABUSH/BLACK LADY: (*Grabbing the crucifix from* DICKIE BIRD,   300
she attempts to spank him but DICKIE BIRD *evades her.*) Dickie
Bird! Kipasta-oon! ("You're committing a mortal sin!") Say
ten Hail Marys and two Our Fathers.
DICKIE BIRD: Mootha apoochiga taskootch nimama keetha.
Mootha apoochiga m'tanawgatch kisagee-in. ("You're not   305
even like my mother. You don't even love me at all.")
NANABUSH/BLACK LADY: Dickie Bird. Shut up. I'll say them with
you. "Hail Mary, full of grace, the Lord is with thee . . .
"Hurry up. I have to go out. (*As* NANABUSH/BLACK LADY
HALKED *now prepares to leave.*) "Hail Mary, full of grace, the   310
Lord is with thee . . . "(*She gives up.*) Ashhh! Your father
should be home soon. (*Exits.*)
DICKIE BIRD: (*Speaking out to the now absent* NANABUSH/BLACK
LADY.) Mootha nipapa ana. ("He's not my father.") (*He grabs
his clothes and the crucifix and runs out, down to the lower level   315
and into the forest made of light and shadows.*) Tapwee anima
ka-itweechik, chee-i? Neetha ooma kimineechagan, chee-i?
("It's true what they say, isn't it? I'm a bastard, aren't I?")
(*He is now sitting on the rock, where* SIMON *and* ZACHARY *first
met in Act One.*) Nipapa ana . . . Big Joey . . . (*To himself,   320
quietly.*) . . . nipapa ana . . . Big Joey . . . ("My father is . . .
Big Joey.")

(*Silence.*)

(*A few moments later,* NANABUSH *comes bouncing into the forest, as
the spirit of the vivacious, young* PATSY PEGAHMAGAHBOW, *complete
with very large, oversized bum. The full moon glows.*)

NANABUSH/PATSY: (*To herself, as she peers into the shadows.*) Oooh,
my poor bum. I fell on the ice four days ago, eh? And it still
hurts, oooh. (*She finally sees* DICKIE BIRD *huddling on the rock,   325
barely dressed.*) There you are. I came out to look for you.
What happened to your clothes? It's freezing out here. Put
them on. Here. (*She starts to help dress him.*) What happened

330 at the arena? You were on the ice, eh? You feel like talking? In Indian? How, weetamawin. ("Come on, tell me.")

(BIG JOEY and CREATURE NATAWAYS enter a distance away. They are smoking a joint and BIG JOEY carries a gun. They stop and watch from the shadows.)

CREATURE: Check her out.

NANABUSH/PATSY: Why do you always carry that crucifix? I don't believe that stuff. I traded mine in for sweetgrass. Hey. You wanna come to Rosie's and eat fry bread with me? 335 Simon will be there, too. Simon and me, we're getting married, eh? We're gonna have a baby . . .

CREATURE: What's she trying to do?

NANABUSH/PATSY: . . . Rosie's got deer meat, too, come on, you like my Mom's cooking, eh? (She attempts to take the crucifix 340 away from DICKIE BIRD.) But you'll have to leave that here because Rosie can't stand the Pope . . .

(DICKIE BIRD grabs the crucifix back.)

CREATURE: What's he trying to do?

NANABUSH/PATSY: . . . give it to me . . . Dickie . . . come on . . .

CREATURE: He's weird, Big Joey, he's weird.

345 NANABUSH/PATSY: . . . leave it here . . . it will be safe here . . . we'll bury it in the snow . . .

(Playfully, she tries to get the crucifix away from DICKIE BIRD.)

CREATURE: Hey, don't do that, don't do that, man, he's ticklish.

NANABUSH/PATSY: (As DICKIE BIRD begins poking her playfully with the crucifix and laughing, NANABUSH/PATSY gradually 350 starts to get frightened.) . . . don't look at me that way . . . Dickie Bird, what's wrong? . . . ya, Dickie Bird, awus . . .

(DICKIE BIRD starts to grab at NANABUSH/PATSY.)

CREATURE: Hey, don't you think, don't you think . . . he's getting kind of carried away?

NANABUSH/PATSY: . . . awus . . .

355 CREATURE: We gotta do something, Big Joey, we gotta do something. (BIG JOEY stops CREATURE.) Let go! Let go!

NANABUSH/PATSY: (Now in a panic.) . . . Awus! Awus! Awus! . . .

(DICKIE BIRD grabs NANABUSH/PATSY and throws her violently to the ground, he lifts her skirt and shoves the crucifix up against her.)

BIG JOEY: (To CREATURE.) Shut up.

NANABUSH/PATSY: (Screams and goes into hysteria.) . . . Simon! . . .

(DICKIE BIRD rapes NANABUSH/PATSY with the crucifix. A heartbreaking, very slow, sensuous tango breaks out on off-stage harmonica.)

360 CREATURE: (To BIG JOEY.) No! Let me go. Big Joey, let me go, please! (BIG JOEY suddenly grabs CREATURE violently by the collar.)

BIG JOEY: Get out. Get the fuck out of here. You're nothin' but a fuckin' fruit. Fuck off. (CREATURE collapses.) I said fuck off.

(CREATURE flees. BIG JOEY just stands there, paralyzed, and watches.)

(NANABUSH/PATSY, who has gradually been moving back and back, is now standing up on her perch again (i.e., the "mound"/jukebox which no longer looks like a jukebox). She stands there, facing the

audience, and slowly gathers her skirt, in agony, until she is holding it up above her waist. A blood stain slowly spreads across her panties and flows down her leg. At the same time, Dickie Bird stands downstage beside the rock, holding the crucifix and making violent jabbing motions with it, downward. All this happens in slow motion. The crucifix starts to bleed. When DICKIE BIRD lifts the crucifix up, his arms and chest are covered with blood. Finally, NANABUSH/PATSY collapses to the floor of her platform and slowly crawls away. Lights fade on her. On the lower level, BIG JOEY, in a state of shock, staggers, almost faints and vomits violently. Then he reels over to DICKIE BIRD and, not knowing what else to do, begins collecting his clothes and calming him down.)

BIG JOEY: How, Dickie Bird, How, astum. Igwa. Mootha nantow. Mootha nantow. Shhh. Shhh. ("Come on, Dickie Bird. 365 Come. Let's go. It's okay. It's okay. Shhh. Shhh . . . ") (Barely able to bring himself to touch it, he takes the crucifix from DICKIE BIRD and drops it quickly on the rock. Then he begins wiping the blood off DICKIE BIRD.) How, mootha nantow. Mootha nantow. How, astum, keeyapitch upisees ootee. Igwani. Igwani. 370 Poonimatoo. Mootha nantow. Mootha nantow. ("Come on, it's okay. It's okay. Come on, a little more over here. That's all. That's all. Stop crying. It's okay. It's okay . . .") (DICKIE BIRD, shaking with emotion, looks questioningly into BIG JOEY's face.) Eehee. Nigoosis keetha. Mootha Wellington Halked 375 kipapa. Neetha . . . kipapa. ("Yes. You are my son. Wellington Halked is not your father. I'm . . . your father.")

(Silence. They look at each other. DICKIE BIRD grabs BIG JOEY and clings to him, BIG JOEY reacting tentatively, at first, and then passionately, with DICKIE BIRD finally bursting out into uncontrollable sobs. Fade-out.)

(Out of this darkness, gunshots explode. And we hear a man's voice wailing, in complete and utter agony. Then comes violent pounding at a door. Finally, still in the darkness, we hear SIMON STARBLANKET's speaking voice.)

SIMON: Open up! Pierre St. Pierre, open up! I know you're in there!

PIERRE: (Still in the darkness.) Whoa! Easy now. Easy on that 380 goddamn door. Must you create such a carpostrophe smack dab in the middle of my rest period? (When the lights come up, we are outside the "window" to PIERRE ST. PIERRE's little bootleg joint. PIERRE pokes his head out, wearing his night clothes, complete with pointy cap.) Go home. Go to bed. Don't be dis- 385 turbin' my rest period. My wife, Veronique St. Pierre, she tells me there's now not only a OHL but a NHL, too. Indian women's National Hockey League. All the Indian women on every reserve in Canada is playin' hockey now. It's like a fever out there. 390 That's why I gotta get my rest. First thing tomorrow mornin', I go jiggle that puck out of Gazelle Nataways. Listen to me. I'm your elder.

(SIMON shoots the gun into the house, just missing PIERRE's head.)

SIMON: (Dead calm.) One, you give me a bottle. Two, I report your joint to the Manitowaning police. Three, I shoot your 395 fucking head off.

PIERRE: Alright. Alright. (*He pops in for a bottle of whiskey and hands it out to* SIMON.) Now you go on home with this. Go have yourself a nice quiet drink. (SIMON *begins to exit.* PIERRE *calls out.*) What the hell are you gonna do with that gun?

SIMON: (*Calling back.*) I'm gonna go get that mute. Little bastard raped Patsy Pegahmagahbow. (*Exits.*)

(*Pause.*)

PIERRE: Holy shit la marde! (*Pause.*) I gotta warn him. No. I need my rest. No. I gotta warn that boy. No. I gotta find that puck. No. Dickie Bird's life. No. The puck. No. Dickie Bird. No. Hockey. No. His life. No. Hockey. No. Life. Hockey. Life. Hockey. Life. Hockey. Life. Hockey. Life ...

(*Fade-out.*)

(*Lights up on* SPOOKY LACROIX*'s kitchen.* CREATURE NATAWAYS *is sitting at the table, silent, head propped up in his hands.* SPOOKY *is knitting, with obvious haste, a white christening gown, of which a large crucifix is the center-piece.* SPOOKY*'s bible still sits on the table beside him.*)

SPOOKY: Why didn't you do something? (*Silence.*) Creature. (*Silence. Finally,* SPOOKY *stops knitting and looks up.*) Alphonse Nataways, why didn't you stop him? (*Silence.*) You're scared of him, aren't you? You're scared to death of Big Joey. Admit it.

(*Silence.*)

CREATURE: (*Quietly and calmly.*) I love him, Spooky.

SPOOKY: Say wha?!

CREATURE: I love him.

SPOOKY: You love him? What do you mean? How? How do you love him?

CREATURE: I love him.

SPOOKY: Lord have mercy on Wasaychigan Hill!

CREATURE: (*Rising suddenly.*) I love the way he stands. I love the way he walks. The way he laughs. The way he wears his cowboy boots ...

SPOOKY: You're kidding me.

CREATURE: ... the way his tight blue jeans fall over his ass. The way he talks so smart and tough. The way women fall at his feet. I wanna be like him. I always wanted to be like him, William. I always wanted to have a dick as big as his.

SPOOKY: Creature Alphonse Nataways? You know not what you say.

CREATURE: I don't care.

SPOOKY: I care.

CREATURE: I don't care. I can't stand it anymore.

SPOOKY: Shut up. You're making me nervous. Real nervous.

CREATURE: Come with me.

SPOOKY: Come with you where?

CREATURE: To his house.

SPOOKY: Whose house?

CREATURE: Big Joey.

SPOOKY: Are you crazy?

CREATURE: Come with me.

SPOOKY: No.

CREATURE: Yes.

SPOOKY: No.

CREATURE: (*Suddenly and viciously grabbing* SPOOKY *by the throat.*) Cut the goddamn bull crap, Spooky Lacroix! (SPOOKY *tries desperately to save the christening gown.*) I seen you crawl in the mud and shit so drunk you were snortin' like a pig.

SPOOKY: I changed my ways, thank you.

CREATURE: Twenty one years. Twenty one years ago. You, me, Big Joey, Eugene Starblanket, that goddamn Zachary Jeremiah Keechigeesik. We were eighteen. We cut our wrists. Your own father's huntin' knife. We mixed blood. Swore we'd be friends for life. Frontenac Hotel. Twenty one years ago. You got jumped by seven white guys. Broken beer bottle come straight at your face. If it wasn't for me, you wouldn't be here today, wavin' that stinkin' bible in my face like it was a slab of meat. I'm not a dog. I'm your buddy. Your friend.

SPOOKY: I know that.

(CREATURE *tightens his hold on* SPOOKY*'s throat. The two men are staring straight into each other's eyes, inches apart. Silence.*)

CREATURE: William. Think of your father. Remember the words of Nicotine Lacroix.

(*Finally,* SPOOKY *screams, throwing the christening gown, knitting needles and all, over the bible on the table.*)

SPOOKY: You goddamn, fucking son-of-a-bitch!

(*Black-out. Gunshots in the distance.*)

(*Lights up on* BIG JOEY*'s living room/kitchen.* BIG JOEY *is sitting, silent and motionless, on the couch, staring straight ahead, as though he were in a trance. His hunting rifle rests on his lap.* DICKIE BIRD HALKED *stands directly in front of and facing the life-size pin-up poster of Marilyn Monroe, also as though he were in a trance. Then his head drops down in remorse.* BIG JOEY *lifts the gun, loads it and aims it out directly in front. When* DICKIE BIRD *hears the snap of the gun being loaded, he turns to look. Then he slowly walks over to* BIG JOEY, *kneels down directly in front of the barrel of the gun, puts it in his mouth and then slowly reaches over and gently, almost lovingly, moves* BIG JOEY*'s hand away from the trigger, caressing the older man's hand as he does.* BIG JOEY *slowly looks up at* DICKIE BIRD*'s face, stunned.* DICKIE BIRD *puts his own thumb on the trigger and pulls. Click. Nothing. In the complete silence, the two men are looking directly into each other's eyes. Complete stillness. Fade-out. Split seconds before complete black-out, Marilyn Monroe farts, courtesy of* MS. NANABUSH: *a little flag reading "poot" pops up out of Ms. Monroe's derrier, as on a play gun. We hear a cute little "poot" sound.*)

(*Out of this black-out emerges the sound of a harmonica; it is* ZACHARY JEREMIAH KEECHIGEESIK *playing his heart out. Fade-in on* PIERRE ST. PIERRE, *still in his night-clothes but also wearing his winter coat and hat over them, rushing all over the "forest" ostensibly rushing to* BIG JOEY*'s house to warn* DICKIE BIRD HALKED *about the gun-toting* SIMON STARBLANKET. *He mutters to himself as he goes.*)

PIERRE: Hockey. Life. Hockey. Life. Hockey. Life ...

(ZACHARY *appears in the shadows and sees* PIERRE.)

ZACHARY: Hey!

PIERRE: (*Not hearing* ZACHARY.) ... Hockey. Life. Hockey. Life ...

ZACHARY: Pssst!

PIERRE: (*Still not hearing* ZACHARY.) . . . Hockey. Life. Hockey. Life. (*Pause.*) Hockey life!

ZACHARY: (*Finally yelling.*) Pierre St. Pierre!

(PIERRE *jumps.*)

470   PIERRE: Hallelujah! Have you heard the news?

ZACHARY: The Band Council went and okayed Big Joey's radio station.

PIERRE: All the Indian women in the world is playin' hockey now! World Hockey League, they call themselves. Aborigi-
475   nal Women's WHL. My wife, Veronique St. Pierre, she just got the news. Eegeeweetamagoot fax machine. ("Fax machine told her.") It's like a burnin', ragin', blindin' fever out there. Them Cree women in Saskatchewan, them Blood women in Alberta, them Yakima, them Heidis out in the
480   middle of your Specific Ocean, them Kickapoo, Chickasaw, Cherokee, Chipewyan, Choctaw, Chippewa, Wichita, Kiowa down in Oklahoma, them Seminole, Navajo, Onondaga, Tuscarora, Winnebago, Mimac-paddy-wack-why-it's-enough-to-give-your-dog-a-bone! . . .

(*As, getting completely carried away, he grabs his crotch.*)

485   ZACHARY: Pierre. Pierre.

PIERRE: . . . they're turnin' the whole world topsy-turkey right before our very eyes and the Prime Minister's a-shittin' grape juice . . . (*A gunshot explodes in the near distance.* PIERRE *suddenly lays low and changes tone completely.*) Holy shit la
490   marde! He's after Dickie Bird. There's a red-eyed, crazed devil out there and he's after Dickie Bird Halked and he's gonna kill us all if we don't stop him right this minute.

ZACHARY: Who? Who's gonna kill us?

PIERRE: Simon Starblanket. Drunk. Power mad. Half-crazed on
495   whiskey and he's got a gun.

ZACHARY: Simon?

PIERRE: He's drunk and he's mean and he's out to kill. (*Another gunshot.*) Hear that?

ZACHARY: (*To himself.*) That's Simon? I thought . . .

500   PIERRE: When he heard about the Pegahmagahbow rape . . .

ZACHARY: Pegahmagahbow what?

PIERRE: Why, haven't you heard? Dickie Bird Halked raped Patsy Pegahmagahbow in most brutal fashion and Simon Starblanket is out to kill Dickie Bird Halked so I'm on my
505   way to Big Joey's right this minute and I'm takin' that huntin' rifle of his and I'm sittin' next to that Halked boy right up until the cows come home.

(*Exits.*)

ZACHARY: (*To himself.*) Simon Starblanket. Patsy . . .

(*Black-out.*)

(*Out of this black-out come the gunshots, much louder this time, and* SIMON's *wailing voice.*)

SIMON: Aieeeeee-yip-yip! Nanabush! . . . (*Fade-in on* SIMON, *in
510   the forest close by the large rock, still carrying his hunting rifle.* SIMON *is half-crazed by this time, drunk out of his skull. The full moon glows.*) . . . Weesageechak! Come back! Rosie!

Rosie Kakapetum, tell him to come back, not to run away, cuz we need him . . .

(NANABUSH/PATSY PEGAHMAGAHBOW's *voice comes filtering out of the darkness on the upper level. It is as though* SIMON *were hearing a voice from inside his head.*)

NANABUSH/PATSY: . . . her . . .   515
SIMON: . . . him . . .
NANABUSH/PATSY: . . . her . . .

(*Slow fade-in on* NANABUSH/PATSY, *standing on the upper level, looking down at* SIMON. *She still wears her very large bum.*)

SIMON: . . . weetha ("him/her"—i.e., no gender) . . . Christ! What is it? Him? Her? Stupid fucking language, fuck you, da Englesa. Me no speakum no more da goodie Englesa, in   520
Cree we say "weetha," not "him" or "her" Nanabush, come back! (*Speaks directly to* NANABUSH, *as though he/she were there, directly in front of him; he doesn't see* NANABUSH/PATSY *standing on the upper level.*) Aw, boozhoo how are ya? Me good. Me berry, berry good. I seen you! I just seen you jumping jack-   525
ass thisa away . . .

NANABUSH/PATSY: (*As though she/he were playing games behind* SIMON's *back.*) . . . and thataway . . .

SIMON: . . . and thisaway and . . .

NANABUSH/PATSY: . . . thataway . . .   530

SIMON: . . . and thisaway and . . .

NANABUSH/PATSY: . . . thataway . . .

SIMON: . . . and thisaway and . . .

NANABUSH/PATSY: . . . thataway . . .

SIMON: . . . etcetra, etcetra, etcetra . . .   535

NANABUSH/PATSY: . . . etcetERA. (*Pause.*) She's here! She's here!

SIMON: . . . Nanabush! Weesageechak! . . . (NANABUSH/PATSY *peals out with a silvery, magical laugh that echoes and echoes.*) . . . Dey shove dis . . . whach-you-ma-call-it . . . da crucifix up your holy cunt ouch, eh? Ouch, eh? (SIMON *sees the bloody*   540
crucifix sitting on the rock and slowly approaches it. He kneels directly before it.) Nah . . . (*Laughs a long mad, hysterical laugh that ends with hysterical weeping.*) . . . yesssss . . . noooo . . . oh, noooo! Crucifix! (*Spits violently on the crucifix.*) Fucking goddamn crucifix yesssss . . . God! You're a man. You're a   545
woman. You're a man? You're a woman? You see, nineethoo-wan poogoo neetha ("I speak only Cree") . . .

NANABUSH/PATSY: . . . ohhh . . .

SIMON: . . . keetha ma-a? ("How about you?") . . . Nah. Da En-glesa him . . .   550

NANABUSH/PATSY: . . . her . . .

SIMON: . . . him . . .

NANABUSH/PATSY: . . . her . . .

SIMON: . . . him! . . .

NANABUSH/PATSY: . . . her! . . .   555

SIMON: all da time . . .

NANABUSH/PATSY: . . . all da time . . .

SIMON: . . . tsk, tsk, tsk . . .

NANABUSH/PATSY: . . . tsk, tsk, tsk.

SIMON: If God, you are a woman/man in Cree but only a man   560
in da Englesa, then how come you still got a cun . . .

NANABUSH/PATSY: . . . a womb.

(*With this,* SIMON *finally sees* NANABUSH/PATSY. *He calls out to her.*)

SIMON: Patsy! Big Bum Pegahmagahbow, you flying across da ice on world's biggest puck. Patsy, look what dey done to your

565 puss . . . (NANABUSH/PATSY *lifts her skirt and displays the blood stain on her panties. She then finally takes off the prosthetic that is her huge bum and holds it in one arm.*) Hey! (*And NANABUSH/PATSY holds an eagle feather up in the air, ready to dance.* SIMON *stomps on the ground, rhythmically, and sings.*) " . . .

570 and me I don't wanna go to the moon, I'm gonna leave that moon alone. I just wanna dance with the Rosebud Sioux this summer, yeah, yeah, yeah . . . " (SIMON *chants and he and* NANABUSH/PATSY *dance, he on the lower level with his hunting rifle in the air, she on the upper level with her eagle feather.*) How, astum,

575 Patsy, kiam. N'tayneemeetootan. ("Come on, Patsy, never mind. Let's go dance.")

(*We hear* ZACHARY JEREMIAH KEECHIGEESIK's *voice calling from the darkness a distance away.*)

ZACHARY: Hey!

(*But* SIMON *and* NANABUSH/PATSY *pay no heed.*)

NANABUSH/PATSY: n'tayneemeetootan South Dakota? . . .
SIMON: how, astum, Patsy. N'tayneemeetootan South
580 Dakota. Hey, Patsy Pegahmagahbow. . . .

(*As he finally approaches her and holds his hand out.*)

NANABUSH/PATSY: (*As she holds her hand out toward his.*) . . . Simon Starblanket . . .
SIMON/NANABUSH/PATSY: . . . eenpaysagee-itan ("I love you to death") . . .

(ZACHARY *finally emerges tentatively from the shadows. He is holding a beautiful, fresh pie.* NANABUSH/PATSY *disappears.*)

585 ZACHARY: (*Calling out over the distance.*) Hey! You want some pie?
SIMON: (*Silence. Calling back.*) What?!

(*Not seeing* ZACHARY, *he looks around cautiously.*)

ZACHARY: I said. You want some pie?
SIMON: (*Calling back, after some confused thought.*) What?
ZACHARY: (*He approaches* SIMON *slowly.*) Do you want some pie?
590 SIMON: (*Silence. Finally, he sees* ZACHARY *and points the gun at him.*) What kind?
ZACHARY: Apple. I just made some. It's still hot.
SIMON: (*Long pause.*) Okay.

(*Slowly,* NANABUSH/PATSY *enters the scene and comes up behind* SIMON, *holding* SIMON's *dancing bustle in front of her, as in a ceremony.*)

ZACHARY: Okay. But you gotta give me the gun first. (*The gun*
595 *goes off accidentally, just missing* ZACHARY's *head.*) I said, you gotta give me the gun first.

(*Gradually, the dancing bustle begins to shimmer and dance in* NANABUSH/PATSY's *hands.*)

SIMON: Patsy. I gotta go see Patsy.
ZACHARY: You and me and Patsy and Hera. We're gonna go have some pie. Fresh, hot apple pie. Then, we go to Sud-
600 bury and have a look at that Mobart, what do you say?

(*The shimmering movements of the bustle balloon out into these magical, dance-like arches, as* NANABUSH/PATSY *maneuvers it directly in front of* SIMON, *hiding him momentarily. Behind this,* SIMON *drops the base of the rifle to the ground, causing it to go off accidentally. The bullet hits* SIMON *in the stomach. He falls to the ground.* ZACHARY *lets go of his pie and runs over to him. The shimmering of the bustle dies off into the darkness of the forest and disappears,* NANABUSH/PATSY *maneuvering it.*)

ZACHARY: Simon! Simon! Oh, lordy, lordy, lordy . . . Are you alright? Are you okay? Simon. Simon. Talk to me. Goodness sakes, talk to me Simon. Ayumi-in! ("Talk to me!")
SIMON: (*Barely able to speak, as he sinks slowly to the ground beside the large rock.*) Kamoowanow . . . apple . . . pie . . . patima . . . 605 neetha . . . igwa Patsy . . . n'gapeetootanan . . . patima . . . apple . . . pie . . . neee. ("We'll eat . . . apple . . . pie . . . later . . . me . . . and Patsy . . . we'll come over . . . later . . . apple . . . pie . . . neee.")

(*He dies.*)

ZACHARY: (*As he kneels over* SIMON's *body, the full moon glowing even* 610 *redder.*) Oh, lordy, lordy . . . Holy shit! Holy shit! What's happening? What's become of this place? What's happening to this place? What's happening to these people? My people. He didn't have to die. He didn't have to die. That's the goddamn most stupid . . . no reason . . . this kind of 615 living has got to stop. It's got to stop! (*Talking and then just shrieking at the sky.*) Aieeeeeee-Lord! God! God of the Indian! God of the Whiteman! God-Al-fucking-mighty! Whatever the fuck your name is. Why are you doing this to us? Why are you doing this to us? Are you up there at all? 620 Or are you some stupid, drunken shit, out-of-your-mind-passed out under some great beer table up there in your stupid fucking clouds? Come down! Astum oota! ("Come down here!") Why don't you come down? I dare you to come down from your high-falutin' fuckin' shit-throne up 625 there, come down and show us you got the guts to stop this stupid, stupid, stupid way of living. It's got to stop. It's got to stop. It's got to stop. It's got to stop. It's got to stop. It's got to stop . . .

(*He collapses over* SIMON's *body and weeps. Fade-out. Towards the end of this speech, a light comes up on* NANABUSH. *Her perch (i.e., the jukebox) has swivelled around and she is sitting on a toilet having a good shit. He/she is dressed in an old man's white beard and wig, but also wearing sexy, elegant women's high-heeled pumps. Surrounded by white, puffy clouds, she/he sits with her legs crossed, nonchalantly filing his/her fingernails. Fade-out.*)

(*Fade-in on* BIG JOEY's *living room/kitchen.* BIG JOEY, DICKIE BIRD HALKED, CREATURE NATAWAYS, SPOOKY LACROIX *and* PIERRE ST. PIERRE *are sitting and standing in various positions, in complete silence. A hush pervades the room for about twenty beats.* DICKIE BIRD *is holding* BIG JOEY's *hunting rifle. Suddenly,* ZACHARY JEREMIAH KEECHIGEESIK *enters; in a semi-crazed state.* DICKIE BIRD *starts and points the rifle straight at* ZACHARY's *head.*)

CREATURE: Zachary Jeremiah! What are you doing here? 630
BIG JOEY: Lookin' for your shorts, Zach?

(*From his position on the couch, he motions* DICKIE BIRD *to put the gun down.* DICKIE BIRD *does so.*)

ZACHARY: (*To* BIG JOEY.) You're unbelievable. You're fucking unbelievable. You let this young man, you let your own son get away with this inconceivable act . . .

635 CREATURE: Don't say that to him, Zachary Jeremiah, don't say that . . .

ZACHARY: (*Ignoring* CREATURE.) You know he did it and you're hiding him what in God's name is wrong with you?

SPOOKY: Zachary Jeremiah, you're not yourself . . .

640 PIERRE: Nope. Not himself. Talkin' wild.

(*Sensing potential violence, he sneaks out the door.*)

BIG JOEY: (*To* ZACHARY.) He don't even know he done anything.

ZACHARY: Bull shit! They're not even sure the air ambulance will get Patsy Pegahmagahbow to Sudbury in time. Simon Starblanket just shot himself and this boy is responsible . . .

(SIMON *rises slowly from the ground and "sleep walks" right through this scene and up to the upper level, towards the full moon. The men are only vaguely aware of his passing.*)

645 BIG JOEY: He ain't responsible for nothin'.

ZACHARY: Simon Starblanket was on his way to South Dakota where he could have learned a few things and made something of himself, same place you went and made a total asshole of yourself seventeen years ago . . .

650 CREATURE: Shush, Zachary Jeremiah, that's the past . . .

SPOOKY: . . . the past . . .

CREATURE: . . . Chris'sakes . . .

ZACHARY: What happened to all those dreams you were so full of for your people, the same dreams this young man just

655 died for?

SPOOKY: (*To* BIG JOEY, *though not looking at him.*) And my sister, Black Lady Halked, seventeen years ago at that bar, Big Joey, you could have stopped her drinking, you could have sent her home and this thing never would have happened.

660 That was your son inside her belly.

CREATURE: He didn't do nothing. He wouldn't let me do nothing. He just stood there and watched the whole thing . . .

SPOOKY: Creature Nataways!

CREATURE: I don't care. I'm gonna tell. He watched this little

665 bastard do that to Patsy Pegahmagahbow . . .

BIG JOEY: (*Suddenly turning on* CREATURE.) You little cocksucker!

(DICKIE BIRD *hits* CREATURE *on the back with the butt of the rifle, knocking him unconscious.*)

SPOOKY: Why, Big Joey, why did you do that?

(*Silence.*)

ZACHARY: Yes, Joe. Why?

(*Long silence. All the men look at* BIG JOEY.)

BIG JOEY: (*Raising his arms, as for a battle cry.*) "This is the end

670 of the suffering of a great nation!" That was me. Wounded Knee, South Dakota, Spring of '73. The FBI. They beat us to the ground. Again and again and again. Ever since that spring, I've had these dreams where blood is spillin' out from my groin, nothin' there but blood and emptiness. It's

675 like . . . I lost myself. So when I saw this baby comin' out

of Caroline, Black Lady . . . Gazelle dancin' . . . all this blood . . . and I knew it was gonna come . . . I . . . I tried to stop it . . . I freaked out. I don't know what I did . . . and I knew it was mine . . .

ZACHARY: Why? Why did you let him do it? Why? Why did 680
you let him do it? Why? Why did you let him do it? Why? Why did you let him do it? (*Finally grabbing* BIG JOEY *by the collar.*) Why?! Why did you let him do it?!

BIG JOEY: (*Breaking free from* ZACHARY's *hold.*) Because I hate them! I hate them fuckin' bitches. Because they—our own 685
women—took the fuckin' power away from us faster than the FBI ever did.

SPOOKY: (*Softly, in the background.*) They always had it.

(*Silence.*)

BIG JOEY: There. I said it. I'm tired. Tired.

(*He slumps down on the couch and cries.*)

ZACHARY: (*Softly.*) Joe. Joe.   690

(*Fade-out.*)

(*Out of this darkness emerges the sound of* SIMON STARBLANKET's *chanting voice. Away up over* NANABUSH's *perch, the moon begins to glow, fully and magnificently. Against it, in silhouette, we see* SIMON *wearing his powwow bustle.* SIMON STARBLANKET *is dancing in the moon. Fade-out.*)

(*Fade-in on the "ice" at the hockey arena, where* PIERRE ST. PIERRE, *in full referee regalia, is gossiping with* CREATURE NATAWAYS *and* SPOOKY LACROIX. CREATURE *is knitting, with great difficulty, pink baby booties.* SPOOKY *is holding his new baby, wrapped in a pale blue knit blanket. We hear the sound of a hockey arena, just before a big game.*)

PIERRE: . . . she says to me: "did you know, Pierre St. Pierre, that Gazelle Nataways found Zachary Jeremiah Keechigeesik's undershorts under her chesterfield and washed them and put them in a box real nice, all folded up and even sprinkled her perfume all over them and sashayed 695
herself over to Hera Keechigeesik's house and handed the box over to her? I just about had a heart attack," she says to me. "And what's more," she says to me, "when Hera Keechigeesik opened that box, there was a picture sittin' on top of them shorts, a color picture of none other than our 700
very own Zachary Jeremiah Keechigeesik . . . (*Unseen by* PIERRE, ZACHARY *approaches the group, wearing a baker's hat and carrying a rolling pin.*) . . . wearin' nothin' but the suit God gave him. That's when Hera Keechigeesik went wild, like a banshee tigger, and she tore the hair out of Gazelle 705
Nataways which, as it turns out, was a wig . . ." Imagine. After all these years. " . . . and she beat Gazelle Nataways to a cinder, right there into the treacherous icy door-step. And that's when 'the particular puck' finally came squishin' out of them considerable Nataways bosoms." And gentle- 710
men? The Wasy Wailerettes are on again!

CREATURE: Ho-leee!

SPOOKY: Holy fuck!

PIERRE: And I say shit la ma . . . (*Finally seeing* ZACHARY, *who is standing there, listening to all this.*) . . . oh my . . . (PIERRE 715 turns quickly to SPOOKY's baby.) . . . hello there, koochie-koochie-koo, welcome to the world!

SPOOKY: It's not koochie-koochie-koo, Pierre St. Pierre. Her name's "Kichigeechacha." Rhymes with Lalala. Ain't she
720   purdy?

(Up in the "bleachers," BIG JOEY enters and prepares his microphone stand. DICKIE BIRD enters with a big sign saying: "WASY-FM" and hangs it proudly up above the microphone stand.)

PIERRE: Aw, she'll be readin' that ole holy bible before you can go: "Phhht! Phhht!"

(PIERRE accidentally spits in the baby's face. SPOOKY shoos him away.)

SPOOKY: "Phhht! Phhht!" to you too, Pierre St. Pierre.
CREATURE: Spooky Lacroix. Lalala. They never made it to
725   Sudbury General.
SPOOKY: I was busy helping Eugene Starblanket out with Simon . . .
SPOOKY/PIERRE: . . . may he rest in peace . . .
ZACHARY: Good old Rosie Kakapetum. "Stand and deliver,"
730   they said to her. And stand and deliver she did. How's the knitting going there, Creature Nataways?
CREATURE: Kichigeechacha, my god-daughter, she's wearin' all the wrong colors. I gotta work like a dog.
PIERRE: (Calling up to DICKIE BIRD HALKED.) Don't you worry a
735   wart about that court appearance, Dickie Bird Halked. I'll be right there beside you tellin' that ole judge a thing or two about that goddamn jukebox.
SPOOKY: (To CREATURE.) Come on. Let's go watch Lalala play her first game.

(He and CREATURE go up to the "bleachers" on the upper level, directly in front of NANABUSH's perch, to watch the big "game.")

740 PIERRE: (Reading from his clip-board and checking off the list.) Now then, Dominique Ladouche, Black Lady Halked, Annie Cook, June Bug Mcleod . . .

(He stops abruptly for BIG JOEY's announcement, as do the other men.)

BIG JOEY: (On the microphone.) Patsy Pegahmagahbow, who is re-cuperating at Sudbury General Hospital, sends her love and
745   requests that the first goal scored by the Wasy Wailerettes be dedicated to the memory of Simon Starblanket . . .

(CREATURE and SPOOKY, with knitting and baby, respectively, are now up in the "bleachers" with DICKIE BIRD and BIG JOEY, who are standing up beside each other at the microphone stand. PIERRE ST. PIERRE is again skating around on the "ice" in his own inimitable fashion, "warming up." ZACHARY JEREMIAH KEECHIGEESIK, meanwhile, now has his apple pie, as well as his rolling pin, in hand, still wearing his baker's hat. At this point, the hockey arena sounds shift abruptly to the sound of women wailing and pucks hitting boards, echoing and echoing as in a vast empty chamber. As this "hockey game sequence" progresses, the spectacle of the men watching, cheering, etc., becomes more and more dream-like, all the men's movements imperceptibly breaking down into slow motion, until they fade, later, into the darkness. ZACHARY "sleep walks" through the whole lower level of the set, almost as though he were retracing his steps back through the whole

play. Slowly, he takes off his clothes item by item, until, by the end, he is back lying naked on the couch where he began the play, except that, this time, it will be his own couch he is lying on. BIG JOEY continues uninterrupted.)

. . . And there they are, ladies igwa gentlemen, there they are, the most beautiful, daring, death-defying Indian women in the world, the Wasy Wailerettes! How, Number Nine Hera Keechigeesik, CAPTAIN of the Wasy Wailerettes, face-off   750
igwa itootum asichi Number Nine Flora McDonald, Captain of the Canoe Lake Bravettes. Hey, soogi pagichee-ipinew "particular puck" referee Pierre St. Pierre . . .
CREATURE: Go Hera go! Go Hera go! Go Hera go! . . .

(Repeated all the way through—and under—BIG JOEY's commentary.)

BIG JOEY: igwa seemak wathay g'waskootoo like a herd of   755
wild turtles . . .
SPOOKY: Wasy once. Wasy twice. Holy jumping Christ! Rim ram. God damn. Fuck, son-of-a-bitch, shit!

(Repeated in time to CREATURE's cheer, all the way through—and under—BIG JOEY's commentary.)

BIG JOEY: . . . Hey, aspin Number Six Dry Lips Manigitogan, right-winger for the Wasy Wailerettes, eemaskamat Num-   760
ber Thirteen of the Canoe Lake Bravettes anee-i "particular puck" . . . (DICKIE BIRD begins chanting and stomping his foot in time to CREATURE's and SPOOKY's cheers. Bits and pieces of NANABUSH/GAZELLE NATAWAYS' "strip music" and Kitty Wells' "It Wasn't God Who Made Honky Tonk Angels" begin to weave   765
in and out of this "sound collage," a collage which now has a def-inite "pounding" rhythm to it. Over it all soars the sound of ZACHARY's harmonica, swooping and diving brilliantly, recalling many of NANABUSH's appearances throughout the play. BIG JOEY continues uninterrupted.) . . . igwa aspin sipweesin-   770
skwatayew. Hey, k'seegoochin! How, Number Six Dry Lips Manigitogan igwa soogi pugamawew anee-i "particu-lar puck" ita Number Twenty-six Little Girl Manitowabi, left-winger for the Wasy Wailerettes, katee-ooteetuk blue line ita Number Eleven Black Lady Halked, wha! defense-   775
woman for the Wasy Wailerettes, kagatchitnat anee-i "particular puck" igwa seemak kapassiwatat Captain Hera Keechigeesikwa igwa Hera Keechigeesik mitooni eepimithat, hey, kwayus graceful Hera Keechigeesik, mitooni Russian ballerina eesinagoosit. Captain Hera   780
Keechigeesik bee-line igwa itootum straight for the Canoe Lake Bravettes' net igwa shootiwatew anee-i "particular puck" igwa she shoots, she scores . . . almost! Wha! Close one, ladies igwa gentlemen, kwayus close one. But Num-ber Six Dry Lips Manigitogan, right-winger for the Wasy   785
Wailerettes, accidentally tripped and blocked the shot . . .
(BIG JOEY's voice begins to trail off as, at this point, CREATURE NATAWAYS marches over and angrily grabs the microphone away from him.) . . . How, Number Nine Flora McDonald, Cap-tain of the Canoe Lake Bravettes, igwa ooteetinew anee-i   790
"particular puck" igwa skate-oo-oo behind the net igwa

---

747 . . . **And** . . . The following hockey commentary by Big Joey (pp. 1551–1552) is translated on p. 1553.

soogi heading along the right side of the rink ita Number Twenty-one Annie Cook ...

CREATURE: (*Off microphone, as he marches over to it.*) Aw shit! Aw shit! ... (*He grabs the microphone and, as he talks into it, the sound of all the other men's voices, including the entire "sound collage," begins to fade.*) ... That Dry Lips Manigitogan, she's no damn good, Spooky Lacroix, I tole you once I tole you twice she shouldna done it she shouldna done what she went and did goddawful Dry Lips Manigitogan they shouldna let her play, she's too fat, she's gotten positively blubbery lately, I tole you once I tole you twice that Dry Lips Manigitogan oughta move to Kapuskasing, she really oughta, Spooky Lacroix. I tole you once I tole you twice she oughta move to Kapuskasing, Dry Lips oughta move to Kapuskasing! Dry Lips oughta move to Kapuskasing! Dry Lips oughta move to Kapuskasing! Dry Lips oughta move to Kapuskasing Dry Lips oughta move to Kapuskasing Dry Lips oughta move to Kapuskasing Dry Lips oughta move to Kapuskasing Dry Lips oughta move to Kapuskasing ...

(*And this, too, fades into, first a whisper, magnified on tape to "otherworldly" proportions, then into a slow kind of heavy breathing. On top of this we hear* SPOOKY's *baby crying. Complete fade-out on all this [lights and sound], except for the baby's crying and the heavy breathing, which continue in the darkness. When the lights come up again, we are in* ZACHARY's *own living room [i.e., what was all along* BIG JOEY's *living room/kitchen, only much cleaner]. The couch* ZACHARY *lies on is now covered with a "starblanket" and over the pin-up poster of Marilyn Monroe now hangs what was, earlier on,* NANABUSH's *large powwow dancing bustle. The theme from "The Smurfs" television show bleeds in.* ZACHARY *is lying on the couch face down, naked, sleeping and snoring. The television in front of the couch comes on and "The Smurfs" are playing merrily away.* ZACHARY's *wife, the "real"* HERA KEECHIGEESIK, *enters carrying their baby, who is covered completely with a blanket.* HERA *is soothing the crying baby.*)

ZACHARY: (*Talking in his sleep.*) ... Dry Lips ... oughta move to ... Kapus ...

HERA: Poosees.

ZACHARY: ... kasing ... damn silliest thing I heard in my life ...

HERA: Honey.

(*Bends over the couch and kisses* ZACHARY *on the bum.*)

ZACHARY: ... goodness sakes, Hera, you just had a baby ... (*Suddenly, he jumps up and falls off the couch.*) Simon!

HERA: Yoah! Keegatch igwa kipageecheep'skawinan. ("Yoah! You almost knocked us down.")

ZACHARY: Hera! Where's my shorts?!

HERA: Neee, kigipoochimeek awus-chayees. ("Neee, just a couple of inches past the rim of your ass-hole.")

ZACHARY: Neee, chimagideedoosh. ("Neee, you unfragrant kozy": Ojibway.)

(*He struggles to a sitting position on the couch.*)

HERA: (*Correcting him and laughing.*) "ChimagideeDEESH." ("You unfragrant KOOZIE.")

ZACHARY: Alright. "ChimagideeDEESH."

HERA: And what were you dreaming abou ...

ZACHARY: (*Finally seeing the television.*) Hey, it's the Smurfs! And they're not playing hockey de Englesa.

HERA: Neee, machi ma-a tatoo-Saturday morning Smurfs. Mootha meena weegatch hockey meetaweewuk weethawow Smurfs. ("Well, of course, the Smurfs are on every Saturday morning. But they never play hockey, those Smurfs.") Here, you take her. (*She hands the baby over to* ZACHARY *and goes to sit beside him.*) Boy, that full moon last night. Ever look particularly like a giant puck, eh? Neee ...

(*Silence.* ZACHARY *plays with the baby.*)

ZACHARY: (*To* HERA.) Hey, cup-cake. You ever think of playing hockey?

HERA: Yeah, right. That's all I need is a flying puck right in the left tit, neee ... (*But she stops to speculate.*) ... hockey, hmmm ...

ZACHARY: (*To himself.*) Lordy, lordy, lordy ... (HERA *fishes* ZACHARY's *undershorts, which are pale blue in color, from under a cushion and hands them to him.* ZACHARY *gladly grabs them.*) Neee, magawa nipeetawitoos ... ("Neee, here's my sharts ... ")

HERA: (*Correcting him and laughing.*) "NipeetawiTAS." ("My SHORTS")

ZACHARY: Alright. "NipeetawiTAS." (*Dangles the shorts up to the baby's face with thumb and fore-finger and laughs. Sing-songy, bouncing the baby on his lap:*) Magawa nipeetawitas. Nipeetawitas. Nipeetawitas. Nipeetawitas ...

(*The baby finally gets "dislodged" from the blanket and emerges, naked. And the last thing we see is this beautiful naked Indian man lifting his naked baby Indian girl up in the air, his wife sitting beside them watching and laughing. Slow fade-out. Split seconds before complete black-out,* HERA *peals out with this magical, silvery* NANABUSH *laugh, which is echoed and echoed by one last magical arpeggio on the harmonica, from off-stage. Finally, in the darkness, the last sound we hear is the baby's laughing voice, magnified on tape to fill the entire theater. And this, too, fades into complete silence.*)

(*End of play.*)

TRANSLATION OF BIG JOEY'S HOCKEY COMMENTARIES

Translation from the Cree of Big Joey's hockey commentary, Act One, pages 1540–1541.

. . . Hey, and there goes Number Six Dry Lips Manigitogan, right-winger for the Wasy Wailerettes . . . and steals the puck from Number Thirteen of the Canoe Lake Bravettes . . . and skates off. Hey, is she ever flying . . . (*Off microphone.*) Creature Nataways. Shut up. (*To the other men.*) Get this asshole out of here. (*Back on microphone.*) Now, Number Six Dry Lips Manigitogan, right-winger for the Wasy Wailerettes, shoots the puck and the puck goes flying over towards the center-line . . . where Number Nine Hera Keechigeesik, left-winger for . . . the Wasy Wailerettes, catches it. Now, Number Nine Hera Keechigeesik . . . approaching the blue line where Number One Gazelle Nataways, Captain of the Wasy Wailerettes, tries to get the puck off her, but Number Nine Hera Keechigeesik won't give it to her. Wha! "Hooking," says referee Pierre St. Pierre, Gazelle Nataways has apparently hooked her own team-mate Hera Keechigeesik, wha! Now, Number One Gazelle Nataways, Captain of the Wasy Wailerettes, facing off once again with Number Nine Flora McDonald, Captain of the Canoe Lake Bravettes and Flora McDonald shoots the puck, but Number Thirty-seven Big Bum Pegahmagahbow, defense-woman for the Wasy Wailerettes, stops the puck and passes it to Number Eleven Black Lady Halked, also defense-woman for the Wasy Wailerettes, but Gazelle Nataways, Captain of the Wasy Wailerettes, gives a mean body check to her own team-mate Black Lady Halked woops! She falls, ladies and gentlemen, Black Lady Halked hits the boards and Black Lady Halked is singin' the blues, ladies and gentlemen, Black Lady sings the blues. (*Off microphone.*) What the hell is going on down there? Dickie Bird, get off the ice! (*Back on microphone.*) Wha! Number Eleven Black Lady Halked is up in a flash and grabs the puck from Gazelle Nataways, holy shit! The ailing but very, very furious Black Lady Halked skates back, turns and takes aim, it's gonna be a slap shot, ladies and gentlemen, Black Lady Halked is gonna take a slap shot for sure and Black Lady Halked shoots the puck, wha! She shoots straight at her very own captain, Gazelle Nataways and holy shit, holy shit, holy fuckin' shit!

Translation from the Cree of Big Joey's hockey commentary, Act Two, pages 1551–1552.

. . . And there they are, ladies and gentlemen, there they are, the most beautiful, daring, death-defying Indian women in the world, the Wasy Wailerettes! Now, Number Nine HeraKeechigeesik, CAPTAIN of the Wasy Wailerettes, facing off with Number Nine Flora McDonald, Captain of the Canoe Lake Bravettes. Hey, and referee Pierre St. Pierre drops the "particular puck" . . . and takes off like a herd of wild turtles . . . Hey, and there goes Dry Lips Manigitogan, right-winger for the Wasy Wailerettes, and steals the "particular puck" from Number Thirteen of the Canoe Lake Bravettes . . . and skates off. Hey, is she ever flying. Now, Number Six Dry Lips Manigitogan shoots the "particular puck" towards where Number Twenty-six Little Girl Manitowabi, left-winger for the Wasy Wailerettes, is heading straight for the blue line where Number Eleven Black Lady Halked, wha! defense-woman for the Wasy Wailerettes, catches the "particular puck" and straight-way passes it to Captain Hera Keechigeesik and Hera Keechi-geesik is just a-flyin', hey, is she graceful or what, that Hera Keechigeesik, she looks just like a Russian ballerina. Captain Hera Keechigeesik now makes a bee-line straight for the Canoe Lake Bravettes' net and shoots the "particular puck" and she shoots, she scores . . . almost! Wha! Close one, ladies and gentlemen, real close one. But Number Six Dry Lips Manitigotan, right-winger for the Wasy Wailerettes, accidentally tripped and blocked the shot . . . (CREATURE NATAWAYS *grabs the microphone away from* BIG JOEY.) . . . Now, Number Nine Flora McDonald, Captain of the Canoe Lake Bravettes, grabs the "particular puck" and skates behind the net and now heading along the right side of the rink where Number Twenty-one Annie Cook . . .

Manjula Padmanabhan

Well-known as a cartoonist in Delhi, Manjula Padmanabhan (b. 1953), has worked as a journalist and fiction writer, as well as writing for television and the stage; she has also written several children's books. After completing her university studies abroad, Padmanabhan returned to India and began a career in journalism. She wrote several plays—including *Lights Out!* (1984), *The Artist's Model* (1995), and *Sextet* (1996)—and a well-known book of short stories, *Hot Death, Cold Soup* (1995). *Harvest* won the first Onassis Prize for Theater, and premiered in Greece in 1999; it has also been produced in India. Her most recent novel is *Getting There* (2000).

HARVEST

Written in the lineage of plays like Václav Havel's *The Memorandum* or Slawomir Mrozek's *Tango,* Manjula Padmanabhan's *Harvest* develops an absurd narrative of the structure of representation and power in the contemporary globalized culture. For *Harvest* brilliantly allegorizes the relationship between the First and Third Worlds, literalizing the fundamental practices of globalization as its central dramatic situation: the Third World provides the raw materials that the First World consumes for its own survival and expansion.

In the play, Om has sold his body—through the aptly named InterPlanta Services company—to an American "Receiver." According to the terms of his contract, he and his immediate family (his wife Jaya, who is forced by the contract to pretend to be his sister, his brother Jeetu, and his mother, Ma) will enjoy a First World standard of living and lifestyle—they'll be clean, well-fed, entertained, and wealthy—until such time as his Receiver demands Om's organs for his own survival. As the play develops, however, the economic

The family confronts Ginni in Manjula Padmanabhan's *Harvest,* in the 1999 production of the play at the Teatro Texnis, Greece.

motives driving Om's sacrifice are gradually inflected by the mediatized relations of global culture. His family is consulted (on a giant-screen Contact Module that drops from the ceiling) by the Receiver, Virginia—or "Ginni," whose name recalls the demonic *djinni,* or "genies" of Indian folktales—a "blonde and white-skinned epitome of an American-style youth goddess" whose image floats above the room, and increasingly demands obedience from the family. Ma comes nearly to worship Ginni, but truly idolizes her new television, finally choosing to entomb herself inside a video sarcophagus—called the Video Paradise—where she will remain for the rest of her "life." When the InterPlanta agents come to take Om, however, they mistakenly take his wastrel brother Jeetu, removing his eyes and replacing them with a contraption that projects Ginna's sexy image directly into his brain. Although Jeetu had been the most critical of the organ-donation scheme, now that all he can see is Ginni's sultry image, he's seduced, and this virtual relationship leads him finally to "donate" his entire body.

The play's brilliant satire fully takes in First World attitudes toward India, its fear of disease, its anxiety about sanitation, its incomprehension of family and social life, its ignorance of Third World reality altogether. Replacing the family's food with "goat-shit" pellets, installing a toilet and shower in the middle of its one-room apartment, dumping the family's possessions and replacing them with Western clothes and housewares, InterPlanta at once appears to improve the family's standard of living while cutting it off from real life altogether. Yet the final scenes seem to suggest a strategy of resistance. Once Ginni has harvested Jeetu's body, she reveals that "Ginni" had only been a computer-animation after all: Jeetu had been seduced to give up his body by the empty image of youthful, sexy America, an image projected to the world to conceal that the First World paradise is aging and impotent, supporting "the poorer sections of the world, while gaining fresh bodies for ourselves." Virgil— the real Ginni—proposes that he (in the body of Jeetu) and Jaya have children to repopulate the First World; he even makes an insemination gadget appear outside the apartment while he's trying to close the deal. But if the body is, finally, what the Third World has to sell, it may still be possible to withhold it, to insist on a real rather than a mediated relationship with First World power. At the play's close, Jaya seals herself inside the apartment, with its endless food supply and television, telling Virgil that if he wants to repopulate the First World, he will have to come to her, in the flesh.

HARVEST
Manjula Padmanabhan

CHARACTERS

DONORS

OM *Twenty years old, he has been laid off from his job as a clerk and is the bread-earner of his small family. He is of medium height, nervy and thin. He would be reasonably good-looking if not for his anxious expression.*

JAYA *OM's wife. Thin and haggard at the outset, she looks older than her nineteen years, but is passionate and spirited. Her bright cotton sari has faded with repeated washing, to a meek pink. Like the others, she is barefoot at the outset. She wears glass bangles, a tiny nose-ring, ear-studs, a slender chain around her neck. No make-up aside from the kohl around her eyes and the red bindi on her forehead.*

MA *OM's mother. She is sixty years old, stooped, scrawny and crabby, wears a widow's threadbare white-on-white sari. Her hair is a straggly white.*

JEETU *OM's younger brother, seventeen and handsome. The same height as OM, he is wiry and conscious of his body. He works as a male prostitute and has a dashing, easy-going likeable personality.*

BIDYUT BAI *An elderly neighbour, very similar in appearance to MA, but timid and self-effacing.*

Also URCHINS *and the crowd outside the door. The crowd is audible rather than visible.*

GUARDS and AGENTS

GUARDS *The* GUARDS *are a group of three commando-like characters who bear the same relationship to each other whenever they appear.* GUARD 1 *is the leader of the team, a man in his mid forties, of military bearing.* GUARD 2 *is a young and attractive woman, unsmiling and efficient.* GUARD 3 *is a male clone of* GUARD 2. *Only* GUARD 1 *interacts with* DONORS.

AGENTS *The* AGENTS *are space-age delivery persons and their uniforms are fantastical verging on ludicrous, like the costumes of waiters in exotic restaurants. Their roles are interchangeable with the* GUARDS, *though it must be clear that they do not belong to the same agency.*

RECEIVERS

GINNI *We see only her face and hear her voice. She is the blonde and white-skinned epitome of an American-style youth goddess. Her voice is sweet and sexy.*

VIRGIL *He is never seen. He has an American cigarette-commercial accent—rich and smoky, attractive and rugged.*

ACT ONE

SCENE I

The sound of inner city traffic: grimy, despairing, poison-fumed. It wells up before the curtains open, then cuts out to a background rumble as . . . the lights reveal a single-room accommodation in a tenement building. It is bare but cluttered. In the foreground, stage left, is a board-bed across the tops of three steel trunks. MA *sits on the bed, her ear straining towards the wall, listening intently. Near her is the front door.* JAYA *stands by the window stage right, looking out, her face drained. To the rear is the kitchen area.*

MA: (*Grunts.*) Ho! (*Turns to look at* JAYA.) Ho—you! Come here a moment—

JAYA: (*Listlessly.*) What is it?

MA: Come here and tell me what they're saying—

5 JAYA: It's none of your business—

MA: Eh?

JAYA: What they say in their room—none of your business!

MA: The cheek of the thing! (*Turns around in indignation.*) As if she knows what my business is! Why—I'm her mother-

10 in-law! And what is she? A dry stick!

JAYA: Leave me out of it. I'm not interested.

MA: Oh of course not, your majesty! So high and mighty she is—staring out of her precious window! Stare all you like but it's useless. There's no chance he'll get the job.

15 JAYA: (*Quickly.*) I'm not the one hoping!

MA: Oh—I forgot! Missie Madam *isn't* hoping the best for her husband—like she should, like any dutiful, sane, reasonable, respectable wife—oh no! Missie Madam has her own sweet thoughts, doesn't she!

JAYA: (*Briefly enlivened.*) Oh! There—I think I see him— 20

MA: Well—well—job or not, he's not got wings, *that* I can tell you. He'll *still* have to climb four floors getting up here. But—what does he look like?

JAYA: (*Straining to see.*) He's—no—yes . . . that's him—

MA: Is his face shining? Are his footsteps sweet? A songbird 25 on his shoulder?

JAYA: It's a bit far to see such details—

MA: Pah! As if you can see them even when he's right in front of you. Now I—I can see it even without looking at him. Just from the sound of his feet. His little feet! Like flowers 30 they were—

JAYA: (*Frustrated.*) Oh—please! The way you go on—!

MA: Jealous!

JAYA: You'd like to think that—

MA: And rude, my arse. Why, you're hardly human! You must 35 have grown up in a jungle!

JAYA: Leave me alone—

MA: Alone, alone! Have you seen your neighbours? Ten in that room, twenty in the other! And harmonious, my dear! Harmonious as a TV show! But you? An empty room 40 would be too crowded for you!

JAYA: That's because I live in a room in which two people think the other two don't exist—

MA: Two and . . . two—four? Have you forgotten how to
45   count?

JAYA: Not at all! You're the one who never counts Jeetu—

MA: Huh! That pimping rascal! That soul's disgrace!

JAYA: You like to pretend he's not there—but *I'm* the one
      who has to cook for him, worry about him—

50   MA: You worry far too much about that one, if you ask me—

JAYA: Yet he's *your* son.

MA: Nah. The gods left a jackal in my belly by mistake when
      they made him—maybe that's why *you* like him—he's just
      like you, rude, insolent, ungrateful—

55   JAYA: I! *Like* him!

MA: Think I don't see the way you wet yourself when he
      walks in the door. Yes! Your brother-in-law—oh the sin
      of it, the sin! You'll suffer in your next life. See if you
      don't! You'll be made into a cockroach and I'll have to
60   smash you—(*Lifts her bare foot and stamps hard.*) just like
      this one. (*Shows* JAYA *the underside of the foot.*) See? Do you
      see your fate?

JAYA: (*Paying no attention, her ear cocked to the door.*) There!
      That's Om—

(*Goes quickly to the door, stage left. Opens it, looks out, steps out,
shutting the door behind her.*)

65   MA: (*Makes a face behind her back.*) Yah, yah! Go on—running
      out to meet him, like some idiot schoolgirl! Think I'm
      fooled by it! I'm not fooled! I see everything! Even inside
      your head! I—

(*The door opens.* OM *walks in.*)

MA: (*Half rising, her face is transformed.*) Ah, my son! My own
70   boy! What news?

(OM, *carrying a bulky parcel, his face set tight, as if too dazed to
know whether to be glad or sad.* JAYA *comes in behind him and shuts
the door.* OM *loosens the collar of his shirt.*)

MA: What? No hope? Nothing at all?

(JAYA *stands uncertainly at centre stage.*)

MA: They are fools, that's all! Don't recognize a diamond
      when they see one! It's their loss. Still . . . it would have
      been nice. A change. A godsend. How'll we manage now?

75   JAYA: (*Carefully.*) What is it? What happened?

OM: (*Looks up.*) I got it. (*Puts the package down on the bed.*)

(JAYA *stifles a sob, spins around and back to her window.*)

MA: (*As if unable to believe him.*) What? Say that again?

OM: I got it. I got the job.

MA: (*Painfully fierce intake of breath.*) Hhhhhh! Hhhhh! Oh!
80   Say it again! Say the blessed words again! (*Rises shakily to
      her feet, declaiming to the world.*) Never stop saying it! "I—
      have—got—the—job!" (*Turns to him holding out her arms.*)
      Ah my soul, my heartbeat! Come, kiss me! Let me hold
      you, fondle your ears! Why am I surprised? You deserve
85   every success.

OM: (*Starts to remove his shirt.*) Yes. It was quite easy, in the end.

MA: (*To* JAYA's *back.*) Bring him a glass of milk! Bring him two
      glasses! (*To* OM.) Come here, my darling boy! My only de-

light! Let your old mother hug you to her belly! (*She goes
to him.*)   90

OM: (*His shirt off, tucked into the waistband of his trousers.*) There
      were six thousand men—

MA: Six thousand! Waiting in the sun!

OM: No. Inside a building like a big machine. They had—like
      iron bars—snaking around and around (*His hands describe*   95
      a narrow looping channel.)—we could only stand one be-
      hind the other—like goats at the slaughterhouse—

MA: Shoo! Where has my son seen a slaughterhouse!

OM: And everywhere there were guards—

MA: Police, you mean?   100

OM: Guards in grey uniforms—you'll see them for yourself
      any minute now—they're coming—

JAYA: (*From where she stands.*) They're coming now?

OM: They have to check. They have to set it all up.

MA: What? What are you talking about?   105

JAYA: You mean it's not certain yet?

OM: They're just checking the building.

MA: For what—

JAYA: (*Bitterly.*) Better train your mother to tie her tongue
      down!   110

MA: Hear that? How your wife speaks of your mother?

OM: Ma—when the men come, you *must* keep quiet.

MA: As if I ever get a chance to speak!

JAYA: She can pretend she doesn't understand!

MA: (*Starting up indignantly.*) What—   115

OM: Yes, Ma. It's the best way. Behave as if you don't under-
      stand, when they ask.

MA: But why? What's there to hide? Have you done some-
      thing wrong?

OM: No—but—but—there's no time to explain! And you'll   120
      know for yourself any minute now—

MA: But what's the trouble! Has something gone wrong?
      What did they say to you?

OM: They have to check, you see. So that the arrangements
      are—are—all right. They're very particular—   125

JAYA: And for how long is the job?

OM: They didn't say—

MA: And what will they pay you?

OM: A lot.

MA: Huh! That's how paupers talk—"a lot". Listen to the   130
      rich? They're on first name terms with all the leading
      numbers—hundreds, thousands, hundred-thousand . . .

OM: (*His voice is hushed.*) We'll have more money than you
      and I have names for! (*Shakes his head in wonderment.*)
      Who'd believe there's so much money in the world?   135

MA: Ho!

JAYA: Can we be sure?

MA: You met with the top men? They spoke to you themselves?

OM: No . . .

MA: Pooh! Then you've got nothing!   140

OM: We were standing all together in that line. And the line
      went on—and on not just on one floor, but slanting up,
      up, forever. All in iron bars and grills. It was like being in
      a cage shaped like a tunnel. All around, up, down, side-
      ways, there were men—   145

JAYA: Doing what?

OM: Slowly moving. All the time. I couldn't understand it. . . .
      Somewhere there must be a place to stop, to write a form?
      Answer questions? But no. Just—forward, forward, for-

150   ward. One person fainted but the others pushed him on-
      ward. And at the corners, a—a sort of pipe was kept . . .
      MA: For what?
      JAYA: To make water, what else!
      MA: Even while moving?
155   OM: You had to be quick. Other men would squeeze past be-
      hind the fellow who was doing his business. Sometimes
      there was no place and he'd have to move on before he
      finished. Still dripping.
      MA: Shee!
160   OM: What could we do? As for those who had more solid de-
      posits to make—! Foo! It was terrible!
      JAYA: And then?
      OM: The stench! The heat!
      MA: But what happened?
165   OM: I don't know for how long we moved. Then there was
      a door. Inside it was dark, like being in heaven! So cool,
      so fresh! I too fainted then, with pleasure, I don't know.
      (*Stands up, reliving his movements.*) I wake up to find now
      the ground is moving under me—
170   MA: What? How's that?
      OM: I don't know. But the floor is moving. Then there's a
      sign: "REMOVE CLOTHING"—
      MA: Whaaat?
      OM: So we do that. Still moving. Then each man gets a bag.
175   To put the clothes inside.
      JAYA: . . . *naked?*
      OM: (*Nods.*) Then—a sort of—rain burst. (*He laughs shakily.*)
      I wonder if I am dreaming! The water is hot, scented.
      Then cold. Then hot air. Then again the water. It stings a
180   little, this second water. Smells like some medicine. Then
      air again. Then we pass through another place . . . I don't
      know what is happening. Ahead of me a man screams and
      cries, but we are in separate little cages now, can't move.
      At one place, something comes to cover the eyes. There's
185   no time to think, just do. Put your arm here, get one
      prick, put your arm there, get another prick—*pissshhh!*—
      pissshhh!—Sit here, stand here, take your head this side,
      look at a light that side. On and on. Finally at the end
      there's another tunnel, with pretty pictures and some mu-
190   sic. And the sign comes: RESUME CLOTHING. I just do
      what I have to do. All the time, the ground keeps mov-
      ing. Then at the end, the ground stops, we are back on
      our feet, there are steps. It must be the other side of the
      building. And as we come down, guards are standing
195   there, waiting for us. And to me they say, "You, come—"
      (*Pause.*) And that was it!
      MA: What!
      JAYA: What?
      OM: That's all. Some other men were also with me, all look-
200   ing like me, I suppose. Blank. They told us we had been
      selected. They wrote down our names, addresses . . . (*He
      hesitates.*) and . . . this-that. All details. Then they gave us
      these packets (*Indicates the package.*), told us not to open
      them and said we must go home, the guards would come
205   with us for final instructions.
      MA: But what is the work? The pay-packet? The hours?
      OM: (*Looking distracted.*) I—I'll be in the house . . .
      MA: What?! All the time?
      JAYA: (*Staring intensely at him.*) . . . you don't really know what
210   it's going to be like, do you?

MA: What kind of job pays a man to sit at home?
OM: Oh—there was some pamphlet they gave us to read,
right in the beginning. Just to tell us to be relaxed and to
do whatever we were told. In that it said that once we
were selected, each man would get special instructions. 215
That we would be monitored carefully. Not just us but
our . . . lives. To remain employed, we have to keep ourselves exactly as they tell us.
JAYA: But—but *who* will tell us—how'll we afford it—

(*There is an excited tapping on the door which was left unbolted. A
CHILD bursts in.*)

CHILD: Auntie! Auntie! They're coming to your house! Police! 220

(*From the corridor, approaching footsteps.* JAYA *shoos the child from
the door as she stands by it. The footsteps come to a halt. A small
crowd has collected out on the corridor (out of sight, but audible) to
whom* JAYA *pays no attention.*)

JAYA: Yes?
MA: (*Remaining seated.*) Let him in, let him in—
GUARD 1: (*Out of sight.*) InterPlanta Services wishes to con-
firm that this is the residence of Om Prakash?
JAYA: It is—(*And she stands aside.*)   225
GUARD 1: (*Entering officiously.*) Thank you—(*Looks around.*)
Ah. Yes. Am I addressing Mr Om Prakash?

(*As he talks, enter* GUARD 2 *and* GUARD 3. *They are both carrying equipment which they set down and immediately begin to ready
for installation.* GUARD 3 *produces collapsible cartons which he begins to set up.* GUARD 2 *starts to install a device onto the window
frame.*)

MA: Who are these people? What are they doing?
GUARD 1: (*To* OM.) Ready? We can start.
OM: What do I have to do?   230
GUARD 1: Just listen. (*He consults his clipboard and begins to read
in a loud formal voice.*) Congratulations! InterPlanta Services is proud and honoured to welcome Mr Om Prakash
to its programme! (*To* OM.) Sir, you have received the
Starter Kit? (*Doesn't wait, sights the package* OM *brought with* 235
him, nods, ticks.) Yes. There it is. Sir: you are directed to
open the kit and make it operational after our departure.
Instructions are provided within. Any questions? (OM
shakes his head. GUARD 1 *nods and ticks.*) All right.

(*In the background,* GUARD 3 *has got two cartons set up. He wears
large plastic mitts over his existing skin-tight gloves and starts dumping all the items on the kitchen counter into the cartons. Meanwhile
two or three urchins have come into the room and are goggling at the
goings-on. Just beyond the door, a crowd of onlookers is standing out
of sight, doing likewise.*)

JAYA: (*To* GUARD 1.) Hi! What're you doing! (*Turns to* OM.) 240
See—see what's happening! (*Back to* GUARD 3, *who goes
ahead.*) Who said you can touch my things? (*Tugs at his arm
but he pays her no heed.*) Hi! Stop that!
GUARD 1: (*To* OM, *who is distracted.*) Sir: we will set up the
Contact Module. It will start functioning in approxi- 245
mately two hours.
OM: I—I'm sorry, but I must—

GUARD 1: Sir: pay no attention! About the Contact Module, all details will be found in the Starter Kit.

(*Meanwhile, downstage,* JAYA *struggles with* GUARD 3.)

250 JAYA: Who told you to do that! No! (*She attempts hitting* GUARD 3, *but he continues relentlessly dumping everything into the cartons.*) You can't do this! It's my house! No! Oh! Stop it, you monster, you beast! (*She tries to return items to the counter, but he is much faster than her.*) Stop it, stop it, stop it! 255 Don't you understand what I'm saying? Are you a machine? Answer me! Oh! (*She abruptly turns in on herself and succumbs to a fit of stormy weeping.*)

(GUARD 3 *continues with his job unperturbed in the course of the other events at stage front. After removing everything but the counter top and shelf, he cleans and swabs the entire area, then sprays it with attention to corners. After that he reaches into his kit and brings out a cooking device and bottles full of multi-coloured pellets.*)

(GUARD 2 *continues her installation without interruption.*)

GUARD 1: (*Regardless of the commotion behind him.*) At the time of first contact, you and your Receiver will exchange per-260 sonal information. Your physical data has been sent for matching and we are confident that you will both be well satisfied. Any questions?

OM: Uhh uhh but what about . . . I mean, when will I actually have to—

265 GUARD 1: Sir: Any questions to the information received so far?

OM: (*Uncertainly.*) No . . . I mean—

GUARD 1: (*Nods and ticks.*) Right. When we have confirmed that the Contact Unit is functioning, you will not be re-270 sponsible for anything but the maintenance of your personal resources. Any questions?

OM: But what about

GUARD 1: Sir! Any questions?

OM: (*Subdued.*) No.

275 GUARD 1: (*Nods and ticks.*) Right. All implements of personal fuel preparation will be supplied exclusively by Inter-Planta Services. Henceforward, you and your domestic unit will consume only those fuels which will be made available to you by InterPlanta. We will provide more 280 than enough for the unit described in your data sheet, but will forbid you from sharing, selling or by any means whatsoever, commercially exploiting this facility. Any questions?

OM: No.

285 GUARD 1: (*Nods and ticks.*) We are providing a remote-source electrical connection. It will be adequate for the systems currently being used by you and your domestic unit, as well as for the equipment which we ourselves will install. But on no account must it bear any additional loads, nor 290 must it be used by any agencies other than yourselves, loaned out, rented out, sold or put to any use other than the one just described. Any questions?

OM: No.

GUARD 1: (*Nods and ticks.*) Good. Now if I can just interview 295 the members of your domestic unit—

JAYA: (*From the rear.*) I have a question!

GUARD 1: (*Doesn't acknowledge her.*)—beginning with the oldest member—

JAYA: (*Desperately.*) Your—your man has thrown my stove into his bag and broken it! Who is going to replace that? 300

OM: (*Hissed aside.*) Not now, Jaya! Just be patient—

(GUARD 1 *is shuffling papers till he gets the relevant sheet.*)

JAYA: Be patient! While my house is broken up! (*But she turns herself aside and weeps, even as she shoos the bystanders away from the door. She is not able to do this easily or efficiently be-cause she is crying too bitterly, so her actions have little impact.* 305 *The urchins who are inside wriggle aside and continue to stand where they are.*)

GUARD 1: (*Approaching* MA *and addressing her.*) Madam: Full name?

OM: (*Interceding.*) She doesn't understand your speech. Her 310 name's Indumati. Missiz Indumati Prakash.

GUARD 1: (*Continuing to address* MA *who looks genuinely bewil-dered.*) Missiz Indumati Prakash. (*Ticks.*) Relationship with Donor?

OM: Mother. 315

GUARD 1: (*Ticks.*) Have you understood all that has been said so far?

OM: Yes.

GUARD 1: (*His hand wavers. He looks up at* OM. *A flicker of nor-mal communication.*) You will explain to her? 320

OM: (*Woodenly.*) Yes.

GUARD 1: (*Ticks.*) Right. Good. Now—(*He turns.*) next rela-tive (*He sees her.*) Missiz—Missiz—(*He consults the sheet.*)

(JAYA, *who knows that it will now be her turn, shoves the children out roughly, anxiety lending determination to her movements. She slams the door shut against resistance from the other side and with some difficulty pushes the bolt home.*)

GUARD 1: —Kumar. Missiz Kumar come this way, please—

JAYA: (*Moves across to centre-stage.*) Yes—yes. 325

GUARD 1: (*Consulting his clip-board.*) Full name?

JAYA: Jaya. Mrs Jaya Kumar. (*She begins to weep anew.*)

(MA *stirs at this and looks over to where* JAYA *stands, a frown on her face.* OM *holds his head in his hands, his eyes on the floor.*)

GUARD 1: Relationship with Donor?

JAYA: (*Lifts her head. In a barely audible voice.*) Sister.

(MA *registers a shock. Her hand to her mouth, she seems to hold in her words manually. Then her hand goes to her heart.*)

GUARD 1: (*Neutral.*) Madam: please repeat response. 330

JAYA: Sister. He's my sister—I —I mean, I'm his—(*She is about to say, "brother" but succumbs to a fit of silent sobbing. Re-gains control.*) Sister. I'm . . . his . . . sister.

(MA's *face and limbs perform a dumb charade of her feelings, as she fights against the urge to react because she's not supposed to under-stand the exchange, yet she cannot make sense of what's going on.*)

GUARD 1: (*Ticks.*) Right. (*Looks around cursorily, merely to con-firm what he already knows.*) Husband? 335

JAYA: (*Nods.*) At work.

GUARD 1: (*Ticks.*) Full name?

JAYA: Jeetu—Jeeten. Jeeten Kumar.

(MA's *body jerks like a puppet. She reins in her comments with ferocious effort.*)

340 GUARD 1: (*Ticks, nods.*) Right. (*He looks up and around.*) InterPlanta recommends that those members absent at this briefing make themselves available at the nearest collection centre not later than twenty-four hours from the time of our departure, failing which such member will lose all rights to the facilities provided by us. Any ques-
345 tions? (*He does not wait for confirmation before ticking off, then looks up.*) Good. (*Turns to the other two* GUARDS.) Briefing complete, initiate departure procedure.

(*Behind him,* GUARD 2 *and* GUARD 3 *have both completed their tasks and are standing stiffly "at ease" at their stations, awaiting orders. Whatever is visible of their faces is completely blank.*)

(*Hanging from the ceiling is a white, faceted globe, at least three feet in diameter. It looks like a Japanese lantern, unlit.*)

(*In the course of the following action,* JAYA *wanders towards the window,* OM *remains seated on the bed,* MA's *physical movements subside.*)

GUARD 1: (*Moving towards them, checking off his list as he inspects and is responded to.*) Officer Contact Module Installation,
350 activity report: Installation complete?
GUARD 2: Yessir.
GUARD 1: Remote Power Reception cable in place?
GUARD 2: Yessir.
GUARD 1: Cable check complete?
355 GUARD 2: Yessir.
GUARD 1: Contact Module in operational mode?
GUARD 2: Yessir.
GUARD 1: Good. Initialize for contact.

(GUARD 2 *moves swiftly over to the* CONTACT MODULE *which is roughly at centre stage and points a remote at it. As* GUARD 2 *works, there are musical notes and clicks. The polygon stirs alight. Random facets light up. A screen-saver pattern appears. The entire polygon moves in a slow, smooth circle, then is lowered to ground level and up again.* GUARD 1 *steps back, satisfied.*)

GUARD 1: (*Paying no further attention to* GUARD 2's *activities, ad-*
360 *dresses* GUARD 3, *who is ready with two neat cartons prepared for transport.*) Officer Fuel Supplies and Installation: activity report: sanitization of supply area complete?
GUARD 3: Yessir.
GUARD 1: Installation of fuel preparation equipment com-
365 plete?
GUARD 3: Yessir.
GUARD 1: Delivery of one month's fuel supplies for family of four complete?
GUARD 3: Yessir.
370 GUARD 1: Good. Proceed with departure.

(GUARD 2 *and* GUARD 3 *station themselves by the door.*)

GUARD 1: (*Approaching* OM, *holding out his clipboard for signing with a pen offered in the same motion.*) Mr Om Prakash, I am pleased to inform you that the installation and initializa-

tion procedures have been completed satisfactorily. Thank you for your cooperation. Please sign the following activ- 375 ity report after confirming that the observations contained herein are true and accurate to the best of your knowledge. (*Hands him the clipboard.*)
OM: (*He stands up as* GUARD 1 *approaches him: Takes the clipboard, glances at it cursorily.*) Yes. I agree. (*Signs, hands the* 380 *board back.*)
JAYA: (*Over her shoulder.*) You don't need any confirmation from us?
GUARD 1: All further queries will be satisfied by the Starter Kit. (*He tucks the clipboard under his arm.*) Thank you for 385 your cooperation and valuable time! I and my colleagues deeply appreciate the contribution you are about to make towards creating a healthier, happier and longer-lived world!

(*Clicks his heels together and turns smartly towards the others.* GUARD 3 *immediately opens the latch on the door which is buffeted open by the listeners on the other side, who immediately fall back and away at the sight of* GUARD 3. GUARD 1 *exits and the other two follow suit. The door is left open and the original one or two urchins poke their noses inside, darting quick glances around.* JAYA *sees them and moves across to shoo them away again. They dart out again with no further urging from her. She shuts the door once more.*)

MA: (*To no-one in particular*) What sort of job makes a wife into 390 a sister?
OM: (*Subsides onto the bed again, head in his hands.*) Don't get confused, Ma. What they write in their reports doesn't change our lives.
MA: But what *is* she, really? A wife? Or a sister? 395
JAYA: (*Has come back and is standing at centre stage.*) How shall I cook now? They've taken all our things! Every last grain!
MA: Who is Jeetu, now? Is he a son? Or a son-in-law?
OM: Nothing's changed! The words are different, that's all.
MA: But these aren't words! They're people! 400
JAYA: Are you listening to me, (*Mocking.*) brother? (OM *looks up.*) What are we to do for food?
MA: (*Whispers.*) How can my daughter be married to my son? What will people think?
JAYA: (*Louder.*) Tell me, brother!— 405
OM: (*Stirring.*) It's in this package. Whatever we need to know.
JAYA: (*Hard.*) Even about food?
OM: (*Wearily.*) Even food.

(*Lights snap out.*)

SCENE II

The same room. OM *and* MA *are sitting upstage centre. A mat is spread on the floor and they are eating the coloured pellets of their new food.* JAYA *is leaning her head and shoulders against the side of the bed.*

The package is open. Its contents are strewn about. There are brightly coloured instruction leaflets, elaborately devised containers for pills and powders and a number of small gadgets similar in size and shape to a slide-viewing device but of obscure purpose.

MA: Tell me again: all you have to do is sit at home and stay healthy?

OM: Well—not *sit* necessarily—

MA: And they'll pay you?

5 OM: Yes.

MA: Even if you do nothing but pick your nose all day?

OM: They'll pay me.

MA: And what about off-days?

OM: (*Shrugs.*) Well. *Every* day is off, in one sense—

10 JAYA: (*Suddenly.*) Why don't you tell her the truth?

MA: Isn't this the truth?

OM: Jaya—

JAYA: (*Swinging herself around, to face them.*) Tell her. Tell your mother what you've really done—

15 MA: Shoo! Don't speak to your husband in that voice—

OM: The walls are thin. Everyone can hear. When you talk like this—

JAYA: Everyone knows already! D'you think you're the only one with this—this *job?* D'you think everyone doesn't

20 know what it means . . . when the grey guards come? (*Tears in her voice.*) All that remains to be known is which part of you's been given away!

MA: (*Mystified.*) What's this, what's this? Who's giving away parts of whom?

25 JAYA: Which goes first, the brain or the heart, that's what I want to know—

MA: (*To* OM.) I'm sorry to say, your wife has gone mad. Your sister, I mean—

OM: She's just trying to make trouble—

30 JAYA: (*Bitter laugh.*) Huh!

MA: Who cares about her? Wife or sister, Mother comes first! So tell me—these people, your employers, who exactly are they?

OM: It's—it's well, actually it's just one person.

35 MA: Just one person! With so much money to give away!

JAYA: It's a foreigner. That's why it's so much—

MA: What?

OM: (*Sighs.*) The money comes from abroad—

MA: Really! (*A sudden doubt.*) But . . . doesn't that mean you'll

40 have to go there? Abroad?

OM: Ma—no-one goes abroad these days . . .

JAYA: Not whole people, anyway!

OM: (*Warningly.*) I'm warning you now, Jaya—

MA: What's that? What's that? Knot-hole people? What d'you

45 mean—shorties?

JAYA: (*Patiently.*) Not his whole body. Just parts of it—

MA: (*To* OM.) What's your wife saying—not your body, but your what?

(JAYA *curls herself more tightly into herself.*)

OM: (*To* JAYA's *back.*) Why're you doing this? Why're you mak-

50 ing trouble?

JAYA: (*Over her shoulder.*) You said it wouldn't affect us—but see what it's done already!

OM: So *tell* me—what? In exchange for your old kitchen you have a new modern one—

55 JAYA: (*Swivelling round.*) You call this food? This—(*She indicates the pellets they have been eating.*) this—this goat-shit?

MA: It's better than what you make—

JAYA: And calling me your sister—what's that? (*Sobs.*) If I'm your sister, what does that make you? (*Hysterical edge.*) Sis-

ter, huh! My forehead burns, when I say that word, "sis- 60
ter"! (*She smears the red kumkum on her forehead in her torment and succumbs to her tears.*)

MA: Shoo! Are you a street woman? To speak in such a voice?

OM: You think I did it lightly. You think it's a heavy price. 65
But at the cost of calling you my sister . . . we'll be *rich!* Very rich! Insanely rich! What're you saying? (*He gets up to wash his hands and mouth at the kitchen sink, stopping to make his point along the way.*) But you'd rather live in this one small room, I suppose! Think it's such 70
a fine thing (*Washes his mouth, spits.*) living day in, day out, like monkeys in a hot-case—(*Washes mouth again and spits again, wipes face, mouth.*) lulled to sleep by our neighbours' rhythmic farting! Dancing to the tune of the melodious traffic! And starving. Yes—you'd prefer 75
this to being called my sister on a stupid slip of paper no-one we know will ever see!

MA: Why fight over what is finished? Tell me about this rich foreigner, your employer! Who is he? Why does he love you so much? That's what I don't understand—where did 80
he meet you?

JAYA: (*Half-sob/laugh.*) Ohh—just tell her, tell her!

OM: (*Coming back to centrestage.*) We've never met, Ma . . .

MA: What!

OM: He's rich—and old. That's all I know about him. Prob- 85
ably suffering from some illness—

MA: Then why's he paying you so much!

JAYA: Oh *Ma!*—don't you see it? Isn't it obvious?

MA: (*To* JAYA.) You're so smart that you can hear the Holy Father himself thinking but I, I need to hear with my ears— 90
(*Turns to* OM.) Tell me, my son—

OM: (*Irritated.*) Oh, you won't understand, Ma—

JAYA: I'll tell you! He's sold the rights to his organs! His skin.
His eyes. His arse. (*Sobs again.*) Sold them! (*Holds her head.*)
Oh God, oh God! What's the meaning of this nightmare! 95
(*Sobs. To* OM.) How can I hold your hand, touch your face, knowing that at any moment it might be snatched away from me and flung across the globe! (*Sobs.*) If you were dead I could shave my head and break my bangles—
but this? To be a widow by slow degrees? To mourn you 100
piece by piece? (*Sobs.*) Should I shave half my head? Break my bangles one at a time? (*Succumbs to her tears.*)

MA: (*Only half-comprehending. Turns to* OM *who stands with his back to the women.*) How is it possible?

OM: (*Looking up at* JAYA.) If you weren't so busy feeling sorry 105
for yourself, you'd have read what they say about respect-
ing the donor—

JAYA: (*Bitterly.*) Of course! They bathe him in praise while gutting him like a chicken!

MA: But why must they come to us? 110

OM: (*Holds up a pamphlet.*) Look? In this paper it says that one third of all donors are left absolutely intact!

MA: Don't they have enough of their own people?

JAYA: And where does that leave you? Two thirds a man? Half a wit? 115

OM: (*To* MA, *distractedly.*) They don't have people to spare.

JAYA: And we do, of course. Spare lives! We grow on trees, in the bushes! *What are we, teacher? Oh just some spare lives!*

120   MA: (*Uncertainly.*) Well. So long as they don't hurt you . . .

(*At this moment, a loud tone sounds. All three react, looking immediately at the globe.*)

MA: Hai! What's that sound! I must wash my hands! (*She gets up.*)

(*The polygon flickers to life. Each face displays one view of a young woman's face, unmistakably blonde and white-skinned. She is beautiful in a clear-eyed, unequivocal manner, exuding a youthful innocence and radiant purity.*)

MA: (*She sees the globe head-on.*) Ahhh! Who is this angel?

(*The room fills abruptly with the pip! of an international phone call about to commence. There is a crackling sound and an audible pause.*)

GINNI: . . . hello? Hello?

125   OM: (*Stepping forward self-consciously.*) Yes—!

GINNI: I see you!—oh, my Gad! I see you! Is that really you? Auwm? Praycash?

OM: Yes! Yes!—it's me, Om! (*He's grinning wide.* MA *looks bewildered.* JAYA *looks awe-struck.*)

130   GINNI: Well—hi! That's really great! This is Virginia—Ginni—speaking! Can you see me? How's your reception?

OM: Quite good—quite perfect, I should say! Fantastic!

GINNI: Wow! Yeah . . . well it's pretty wonderful for me too, you know! I mean, I can't tell you . . . (*Her voice grows*

135   *breathy with emotion.*) I can't *tell* you how much this means to me—

MA: (*To* JAYA.) What's it saying? I can't understand when they speak so fast—

OM: No, no, Madam! It's our pleasure! Our duty, I mean!

140   Anything we can do to help—

JAYA: (*To* MA.) She's saying that she's happy—

GINNI: It's the most beautiful day of my life! I feel I've got hope, at last! And all because of you—

OM: No, no, Madam, it is my—our—pleasure.

145   GINNI: Is it—I mean, can you see me clearly, Auwm?

OM: Perfectly clear.

GINNI: Okay—okay—now you've got to tell me—I'm just switching screens here—okay—there we are—okay! I can see . . . is that your . . . your mother? In the pink— (JAYA

150   *flinches; she is wearing a pink sari.*) whatdyacallit—sarong?

OM: We call it—sari—

GINNI: (*Sings an old tune.*) "Who's sari now? Who's sari now?!!" (*Laughs to herself.*) Hehheh—It's magical, it's wonderful! I'm really talking to India—this is really happen-

155   ing! Okay! And your sister—let's see—

JAYA: (*Stirring to life.*) No! I'm his sister!

OM: (*Flustered and confused.*) She's my wife—

GINNI: Excuse me?

JAYA: (*Hissing to* OM.) Sister. I'm your sister.

160   GINNI: You said just now—

OM: (*Still smiling woodenly.*) I mean, she is my sister, you see—

GINNI: Auwm—it says here on your form, you're not married.

OM: I'm not. She's my sister.

165   GINNI: You're sure you're not kidding me or anything?

OM: Sure, sure, of course I'm sure!

GINNI: Because it's important for us to trust one another. I mean, one little slip like that one—and I dunno. I mean, it's hard for me to tell, from so far away—

OM: No, no! I'm telling the truth! I swear on my God!   170

ginni: Okay. I mean, 'coz I've gotta know, you know. If you're married—

JAYA: (*Suddenly.*) Why?

GINNI: What's that?

JAYA: Why does it matter?   175

GINNI: Uhh—I'll get back to you on that, okay? Just now . . . lemme see . . . there's two more people in your household, am I right, Auwm? There's (*As if checking a list.*) . . . your mother and your brother-in-law. S'right?

JAYA: That is right.   180

GINNI: Just a moment—uhh—Zhaya? (*The* CONTACT MODULE *swivels towards* JAYA, *who nods.*) Is that your name? Yeah—okay, now honey: I can't handle two people at a time, okay? I mean, it's just this dumb camera, you know, can't look at two people at a time, okay? So—I'm talking   185
to Auwm, well I can't talk to you as well, okay? I mean, no offence—

JAYA: Okay.

OM: My mother is also here—

GINNI: Yes. Okay. I'm turning the scanner around (*The* CON-   190
TACT MODULE *turns.*) . . . I'm panning across the room . . . Jeeezus! It's not very much, is it? I mean—oh! Okay! I see her. Hi! Mrs Praycash? Hi! This is Ginni! Can you hear me?

MA: (*Shielding her eyes against the light.*) What?   195

GINNI: I said, this is Virginia! I'm—uh, well just look up, if you can—

OM: Ma—just take your hand down—

GINNI: Look towards the Contact Module! You know the thing hanging in the room?   200

MA: (*To* JAYA.) What's happening?

JAYA: Ma—just look at that light—

OM: The light! The light!

MA: (*Getting annoyed, straightens up to snap back at* OM.) Stop shouting!   205

GINNI: Ahhright! I see you! Mrs Praycash, glad to meet you!

MA: I can't understand a word of what that thing is saying! Is it a man or a woman?

GINNI: What do I look like to you, Mrs Praycash?

MA: (*Cupping her ear.*) Ehh?   210

JAYA: Ma—she wants to know, what she looks like—

OM: Come on, Ma! You've seen foreigners before—

GINNI: Please—Auwm—your mother can answer my questions herself—

OM: She can't understand, you see—   215

JAYA: (*To* MA.) Ma—look up at that light and say what you see—

MA: (*Looks up.*) I see an angel.

GINNI: (*Laughing.*) Ha! I look good to you?

MA: Good, bad, I don't know. All I know is I've got to take a   220
leak—(*Turns around.*)

GINNI: (*Embarrassed laugh.*) Heh! Mm. But—wait! I'm not through yet!

OM: (*As* MA *continues moving away, slowly.*) Don't go yet, Ma—she's not finished—   225

MA: Since when did I need anyone's permission to take a leak?

GINNI: I'm sorry, Mrs Praycash, this won't take a minute—

MA: Nothing doing. I'll piss myself if I don't go right away—
230 (*She moves to the door.*)

GINNI: Hey! I didn't let you go!

OM: She has some problem, you see—

MA: Wait till you're my age! (*Grunts with the effort of opening the door.*) Why they can't keep a bathroom on each floor I
235 don't know—

(*Exit* MA.)

OM: (*Apologetically.*) The toilet is two floors down, you see—

GINNI: Hmmm. Your mother's some character, Auwm. (*She doesn't sound pleased.*) I don't know if I can handle it. I mean—walking out on me like that!

240 OM: She takes a long time to get there. Old people, you know!

GINNI: Wait a minute—did you say two floors down? What about in your house? There's no toilet in your house?

JAYA: (*Bitter laugh.*) Huh!

245 OM: No-one has a toilet in the house. Forty families share one. And my mother walks so slowly—

GINNI: Forty families! (*Hushed voice.*) My Gad. Well that's—that's—(*She seems at a loss for words.*) I'm sorry, Auwm. But that's shocking. Shocking! I can't accept that!

250 OM: (*Embarrassed laugh.*) Well—I—

GINNI: No! It's wrong! It's disgusting! And I—well, I'm going to change that. I can't accept that. I mean, it's unsanitary!

OM: (*Muttering.*) Of course, of course!

GINNI: We'll just have to install one in your house.

255 JAYA: (*Startled out of her silence.*) What? In this—this room?

GINNI: Is that you again, Zhaya?

OM: (*To* JAYA.) Shh!

JAYA: I'm sorry—but we *can't!* There's no place for a toilet!

GINNI: Excuse me, but you'll have to find the space. It's inex-
260 cusable not to have your own toilet! Forty families—! It's a wonder you're all not dead of the plague years ago!

JAYA: There's only this one room!

GINNI: Look—there's enough place for a married couple and two others—you! You're married, right, Zhaya?

265 JAYA: (*Helplessly.*) Yes, but—

GINNI: (*Firmly.*) Then there's place for a toilet. I'm sorry, Zhaya, but there's no way around this one. What d'you do for baths?

JAYA: (*Close to tears.*) I—we—

270 GINNI: You—you *do* bathe, don't you? I mean, at least once a day?

JAYA: (*Overcome by the humiliation, bends her head and sobs.*)

GINNI: (*Instantly contrite.*) Hey—wait! No, please! Don't cry! I didn't mean to upset you—oh Jeez—stop, please! Look—
275 it's not your fault, okay?

OM: It's all right, she'll be all right—(*Goes over to* JAYA *and thumps her on the back.*) She's fine!

GINNI: Okay—okay—look, Zhaya—I'll make it up to you, okay? I'll send you something, okay? Just tell me what you
280 like and it's yours, okay? Jewellery, perfume, you name it—flowers?

OM: (*Bending down to speak to* JAYA.) Come on, now, come on! It'll be all right—that's enough now—

GINNI: Okay—I tell you what, I'll send you some chocolate,
285 okay? I love candy myself. Okay? I'll send you my

favourite candy and—tell you what? I'll sign off now. Okay? It's been a big day for all of us, we're all tired, aren't we? Auwm? Could you look here for a moment?

OM: (*Standing up.*) Me?

GINNI: Okay—look, I'll get back to you, okay? And I'm sorry 290 about Zhaya. Really.

OM: No, no—she's not used to this—this—

GINNI: Yeah. Well—the first contact is always a little . . . ah, intense, you know? And I meant that about . . . the toilet, okay? It'll be with you in about an hour. 295

OM: An hour—!

GINNI: Oops! Time's up—Byeeee!

(*The tone sounds again. The light fades from the* CONTACT MODULE. OM *sits down, suddenly, next to* JAYA *who is wiping her eyes.*)

OM: (*Shakily.*) My god! That was something! (*Puts his arm around* JAYA.) Imagine—a woman!

JAYA: Not old, not sick, nothing— 300

OM: Oh, she must be sick—or else why spend all this money?

JAYA: (*Tiredly.*) It's too late to ask questions now!

OM: But what can be her problem?

JAYA: Maybe there's no problem. Maybe she just likes to suck the life out of young men, like a vampire! 305

OM: Sometimes you talk rubbish—

JAYA: At least I only talk.

OM: It feels strange. To think that . . . that some part of me will be—might be, some day—inside *her*—(*Stops abruptly.*) I mean— 310

JAYA: (*Numbly.*) I know what you mean.

OM: (*Holds her a little tighter.*) I did it, all of it, for us—

JAYA: (*Moving delicately, to loosen his hold.*) Careful. I'm your sister, remember?

OM: (*Jerks his arm away.*) Oh! Sorry. 315

JAYA: (*Bitterly.*) Me too.

(*Lights fade out.*)

SCENE III

Moonlit night, on the roof of the tenement building. City skyline in the backdrop. Clotheslines, watertanks, TV antennas and water pipes snaking in all directions. There is a sense of shadowy figures, movements in the background, murmured conversations.

JAYA *appears, holding a small torch to her face.*

JAYA: (*Looking afraid but determined.*) Jeetu? Are you there? Jeetu—it's me, Jaya!

(*Quick steps, two shadows move away, one shadow materializes in front of* JAYA.)

JEETU: (*He does not look pleased to see her.*) Who told you to come? This is not the right time—

JAYA: I had to. Jeetu—you don't know what's happened— 5

JEETU: Huh! I know everything—

JAYA: So—so you've heard?

JEETU: Which part? That my brother's sold himself to the foreigners? Or that you're my wife? (*Shrugs.*) The second one is hardly . . . news! (*Looks back at her.*) Is it? (*Reaches to tweak* 10 *her plait.*) Is it?

JAYA: But you must come—they're asking for you!

JEETU: (*Frowning.*) They? Who—

JAYA: The grey guards. They came again in the evening. To
15   install the toilet—

JEETU: In the room?!

JAYA: And a bath-shower as well, imagine! We have our own
    water supply now, as much as we want—and there's no
    place to sneeze any more!

20 JEETU: (*Sardonically.*) Or . . . anything else, no doubt?

JAYA: (*Lowered tone.*) That . . . there never was.

JEETU: (*Leering.*) Didn't bother us, though, did it? (*He caresses
    her chin—but she whips her face away.*)

JAYA: And now there won't be any reason for Ma to go
25   downstairs! We'll never be alone in the room again, never!

JEETU: So what? If we can shit in public, we can just as well
    screw in public too—especially since you're now officially
    my wife!

JAYA: (*Pained*) Don't joke about it—

30 JEETU: Why not? I joke about everything else—

JAYA: My throat bulges with the lies trapped within it!

JEETU: Here—let me kiss it—

JAYA: (*Pushes him away.*) Get away! That's all finished now!

JEETU: (*He lets her go.*) As you wish.

35 JAYA: (*Gasps in indignation.*) So easy! Won't you protest a lit-
    tle at least?

JEETU: Make up your mind! D'you want me or not?

JAYA: You are all I have, now that my husband has become my
    brother . . .

40 JEETU: According to you he was never much else!

JAYA: (*Troubled.*) Still. He would come to me now and then—

JEETU: (*Shrugs.*) Maybe incest is more his style!

JAYA: No! He's too afraid! Before it was his mother. Now it's
    this . . . job.

45 JEETU: Ahh—forget him! You waste your time thinking of my
    brother!

JAYA: But what about me!

JEETU: Why? Now that you have a new . . . (*Mockingly.*) hus-
    band! (*Reaches for her shoulder.*)

50 JAYA: (*Slipping out of reach.*) Oh you—! You're a free-lancer—

JEETU: (*Laughing.*) No! My lance costs money! (*Squats down on
    a low ledge and starts to roll himself a joint.*) Had you forgotten?

JAYA: And anyway—I'm looking for a plough, not a lance—

JEETU: Oops—sorry! Wrong number! I can't afford any . . .
55   crops!

JAYA: As if I don't know that! I know that. And in any case
    . . . I feel guilty. I feel soiled—

JEETU: My, my! Such delicacy! Don't worry—I'll tell the
    world that I forced my attentions on you—routinely, in
60   phase with my mother's bowel movements!

JAYA: Oh stop—! (*Swats at him, playfully.*) You always make
    such a joke of everything!

JEETU: That's all that life is, one long joke. The only trick is
    in learning when to laugh.

65 JAYA: Easy for you to laugh! What do you care of my needs,
    my desires?

JEETU: I thought I was the *only* one who cared about your
    desires! (*Lights his joint.*)

JAYA: You care—you care—but not enough! A woman wants
70   more than just . . . (*Breaks off.*) satisfaction.

JEETU: Ah—get off my case! You women are gluttons for sat-
    isfaction—that's the bare fact of it! You cry when you

don't get it—and when you do, you cry that it's not often
    enough!

JAYA: I cry because—because you awaken one hunger while 75
    satisfying the other!

JEETU: (*Darkly.*) That other hunger is insatiable. A man has to
    protect himself against that hunger or he will find himself
    sucked dry by new little mouths, screaming "Papa!
    Papa!"—little mouths with big, big appetites—oh no! I'm 80
    afraid of that other hunger! Mortally afraid!

JAYA: (*Acidly.*) I suppose that's why so many of your "clients"
    are men!

JEETU: (*Coolly.*) Not really. It's just that there are more men
    with money to spare on services such as mine— 85

JAYA: You should be ashamed of yourself! A man—behaving
    like a vagrant bull!

JEETU: Why? I'm not fussy—cows, pigs, horses, I'll service
    all—for a price.

JAYA: You don't need to sell yourself anymore. There'll be 90
    enough money in the house now!

JEETU: But not for me—

JAYA: Yes—for all of us. For the whole building—

JEETU: No. I don't mind being bought—but I won't be *owned*!

(*There is a space of silence.*)

JAYA: (*Fidgeting.*) Well—I suppose I should go— 95

JEETU: Yes—yes—run home before the grey guards come to
    fetch you!

JAYA: Jeetu—

JEETU: (*Looking lazily up at her.*) . . . unless you had something
    else in mind. 100

JAYA: No . . . no . . . (*She can't face him.*) I mean . . . I—didn't
    bring any food.

JEETU: (*A faintly twisted smile.*) Ah . . . so we're asking for
    credit, are we?

JAYA: (*Her voice is husky.*) There's no food in the house any 105
    more! Only those goat-shit pills and some strange pow-
    ders. (*Tears in her voice.*) And—and—it's all measured out,
    you see! I couldn't take a portion without having to ex-
    plain—

JEETU: (*Looking steadily at her.*) Never mind. As a long-time 110
    client, you are permitted certain liberties. Come here—
    (*It's a short distance, barely afoot. He is seated on a step, leaning
    back against a tank. She doesn't move.*) I said, come here—

JAYA: (*As if drawn by an irresistible force.*) Jeetu—there are other
    people around! 115

JEETU: Turn the other way. (*She turns her back to him.*) Your left
    foot up on this step—(*He pats the narrow ledge on which he
    sits. She rests the heel of her left foot there. He puts his arm up
    her sari unobtrusively, barely shifting his position, looking steadily
    up at her. She looks straight ahead.*) Now tell me about this 120
    food. I'm told that it's quite tasty?

JAYA: (*Her voice is thick and strangled.*) Yes! It looks like plastic
    beads but . . . it's quite tasty!

JEETU: And filling too, they say—

JAYA: (*Gasping slightly.*) Filling, yes. It . . . is. But it's not . . . 125
    natural—it's not real food—(*She has no place to keep her
    hands and arms. She clutches her neck, her face, knotting the loose
    end of her sari around her mouth.*)

JEETU: (*Mildly.*) But it must be, don't you think? And healthy?
    I mean, isn't that the point? To keep us . . . healthy? 130

JAYA: Yes . . . yes, of course. . . . but (*She's finding it difficult to concentrate on what she says.*) . . . but . . . who knows if it's . . . *good* for us! . . . (*Gasps.*)

JEETU: Everything's good that tastes good and feels right—

135 JAYA: (*She's desperate to lean on something but the closest is a ventilation pipe. She clings to it with both hands, eyes shut tight, breathing in gasps.*) No . . . no . . . that's *not* true. . . . it's false food—uhh!—like it's a *false* marriage—Uhh!—*false—false* (*Her voice wobbles and ends on a squeak. She gasps/sobs once,*

140 *twice—*.) False. (*Breathes out, shudderingly.*) False . . . life. (*She catches her breath, wiping her face with the end of her sari-pallav.*) It's not really a life any more. We're just spare parts in someone else's garage—

JEETU: (*Removing his arm and wiping his fingers on the hem of her*

145 *sari.*) My brother, yes. But not you—

JAYA: (*Her voice is normal again.*) No! All of us. If we get sick, he might get sick too. So we all have to eat this excuse for food and live like virgin brides—

JEETU: (*Snorts.*) Good! Now there's no reason at all for me to

150 come home!

JAYA: (*Distraught.*) No! You have to, Jeetu—

JEETU: Are you mad? When they find out what I do for a living they won't be pleased! They won't be pleased with you either—

155 JAYA: (*Pleading.*) They've asked for you twice now—they'll cancel your permit if they can't confirm your presence—

JEETU: Too bad! My brother will have to find some dummy to take my place—

JAYA: Please, Jeetu! Please . . . think of me—

160 JEETU: I can't afford to think of you. Thinking of you causes too many problems for me. I'll have to go away—

JAYA: What'll I do! You can't leave me—

JEETU: I can if I must. Don't worry—your grey guards will probably have a cure for the disease of dissatisfaction as

165 well—just ask them?

JAYA: But why! Why when there's enough money for all of us, to do whatever we want!

JEETU: Because no employer pays his staff to do as they please. At least when I sell my body, I decide which part

170 of me goes into where and whom! But it's the money in the end, isn't it? I don't want to get used to the kind of money that can make stud bulls into milk cows. (*Shakes his head.*) My poor brother. Thought he was so pure. But he's like everyone else after all! Only as pure as the price of his

175 rice.

(*Lights dim out.*)

ACT TWO

SCENE I

Two months later. The same room, but transformed into a sleek residence, gleaming surfaces, chrome steel and glass. The furniture is largely of the convertible kind (Bed-cum-sofa, etc), in keeping with the restricted space. In addition, there are the gadgets—TV set, computer terminal, mini-gym, an air-conditioner, the works. To the rear and right, there are two cubicles containing the bathroom and toilet. The changes are functional rather than cosmetic. In the middle of the space is a low, Japanese-style dining table.

JAYA *is sitting on the sofa and and doing her nails. She looks over-dressed, her face is heavily made-up, jewellery winking from her ears, wrists, ankles and throat.* MA *is wearing a quilted dressing gown and is watching TV, upstage, right.* OM *is wearing a fluorescent Harlequin track-suit and sits at the computer terminal. All sport new footwear.* JAYA *in heels,* MA *in fluffy bedroom slippers,* OM *in inflatable track shoes with blinking rear lights.*

Suddenly OM *leaps up.*

OM: Look at the time!—Ma!

MA: (*Not turning around, but addressing her remark to* JAYA.) Don't call me—it's your wife's turn to do the food.

JAYA: (*Waving her hands in the air.*) Why didn't you tell me earlier? Now my nails are wet—   5

MA: And now—I'm watching my programme!

OM: (*Rushing over to dining area. He starts to set it up.*) Come on, come on! Ginni will be here with us—

MA: Better get Bidyut-bai out first—

OM: (*Stops what he's doing.*) Out? Out of where?   10

MA: (*Barely looking up.*) Out of the toilet. Didn't you see her going in? She's been there all morning!

OM: Why! Who let her use it—

MA: She can't stay away from it, she says! Gets cramps, poor thing, from waiting for the one downstairs—   15

OM: Who cares about her cramps—I want to know how she got into the habit of using our toilet at all!

MA: (*Shrugs, but aiming her rebuke in* JAYA's *direction.*) Who knows what happens when my back is turned?

JAYA: (*Aggrieved, blowing on her nails.*) Huh! Look who's talk-   20 ing! The Empress of the Bath-house herself? (*To* OM.) If your mother had her way, half this building would be bathing up here—(*Blowing on her nails.*) But how would you know? You never bother to talk to us any more!

MA: (*Placatory whine.*) We have so much! Can't we share a lit-   25 tle at least? As it is, my former friends tell me I've put on airs—

OM: (*Standing with his hands on his hips.*) Ma, I've told you. When we have our own place, that'll be another thing— but now, when we're still struggling—   30

(*At this moment there is the sound of the flush.* BIDYUT-BAI *comes out of the cubicle, trying to look inconspicuous.*)

BIDYUT-BAI: Oh . . . I hope I'm not intruding—

OM: I'm sorry, Bidyut-maasi—but who invited you to use our toilet?

BIDYUT-BAI: (*Instantly on the defensive.*) No, no! Please! I was just passing this way—   35

OM: But you used our toilet, didn't you?

BIDYUT-BAI: Toilet? What toilet? Is there a toilet in this room? My! That must be a wonder! May I see it?

OM: (*Sighing.*) Oh just go on, go on!

MA: (*Speaking up for her friend.*) How can she go on when the   40 door's been barricaded?

OM: (*Woodenly.*) She's your friend, you can let her out yourself.

MA: (*Peevishly.*) But I'm watching my programme—

JAYA: Your eyes'll be stuck to that screen from staring at it   45 twenty-four hours of the day!

MA: And why can't our busybody open it? Worn out from the tension of painting her nails, I suppose?

BIDYUT-BAI: Is anyone going to let me out?

50   JAYA: Oh! For god's sake! (*Gets up and flings herself across the room.*) I might as well apply for a job as a doorkeeper!

MA: And you'd make a bad one—

(*The warning tone sounds.*)

OM: Oh my God—Ginni's call-sound!

JAYA: (*Struggling to open the door with her nails still wet.*) Tell her

55   it's because your mother can't control her generosity—

MA: See how your sister insults me! Her own mother!

OM: (*Frantic.*) Hurry up! Hurry up!

JAYA: (*Throws the door open—*BIDYUT-BAI*wriggles past her and out.*) All right, all right—(*Slams the door shut and moves

60   quickly over to the "kitchen" to snatch up a few items from the "oven".* OM *is almost done setting the table up.*) Anyway it only takes a few minutes—

OM: (*Sitting down, as* JAYA *brings a few things from the "kitchen" area.*) You know how she hates it when we're late to eat!

65   JAYA: (*Setting things down.*) Tell your mother to come along—

MA: (*Whiningly.*) It's just about to end—

JAYA: (*Sitting down herself.*) One of these days, when this dream comes to an end, it'll be because you were too busy watching your damned TV—

70   OM: It isn't going to end—

(*The warning tone sounds a third time and the* CONTACT MODULE *springs to life.*)

OM: Ahh—

(MA *scrambles to her feet and scurries over, leaving the TV on.*)

GINNI: Hello-oo! Guess who-oo!

OM: (*He has a falsely beaming expression on his face and affects a nasal twang.*) Hello, Ginni! Hi! Howdy!

(MA *settles hurriedly into place.*)

75   GINNI: Hey—whatcha doing—eating again?

OM: No! We're just having lunch—why don't you join us?

GINNI: Lunch! Hey, that's too late—for lunch!

JAYA: No, no, Ginni! (*To* OM.) Tell her it is only ten minutes—

GINNI: I'm sorry Auwm—but I insist: you *must eat at regular*

80   *hours*—okay? We've had this problem before!

OM: Yes—yes—you see we just had some visitor—heh-heh—these people, you know! Don't understand what it means to keep to a strict schedule—

GINNI: Ah-ah! No excuses, now! That's another bad habit you

85   have, Auwm. You don't confront your booboos. Now—you've gotta learn to control it, okay? You can't help it, I know, it's a part of your culture—it's what your people do when they want to Avoid Conflict and it's even got a name: it's called "face saving". But we can't go through the

90   whole of our lives Avoiding Conflict, now can we, Auwm? You do see that?

OM: (*His smile is strained.*) Yes—yes—of course, Ginni! It is perfectly clear—

GINNI: Good! That's what I like about you, Auwm! You learn

95   real fast.

OM: (*Modestly.*) Thank you, Ginni!

GINNI: And now—let's look at how your family's doing—Mrs Praycash? I can see the food's suiting you, huh? You're putting on weight!

100   MA: (*Holding her hand to her ear, but beaming nevertheless.*) What's that? What's that?

GINNI: And Zhaya—how're you doin'? I don't see a smile on your face!

JAYA: (*Instantly pasting a smile on.*) Oh—no, no! I'm fine!

105   GINNI: It's a scientific fact that people who smile longer live longer—

JAYA: I'm smiling!

GINNI: But not enough, Zhaya. You see, it's important to smile all through the day. After all, if you're not smiling, it

110   means you're not happy. And if you're not happy, you might affect your brother's mood—and then where would we be?

JAYA: (*Grinning wide.*) I understand, Ginni.

GINNI: If I've said it once, I've said it a hundred times: The

115   Most Important Thing is to keep *Auwm* smiling. Coz if Auwm's smiling, it means his body's smiling and if his body's smiling, it means his organs are smiling. And that's the kind of organs that'll survive a transplant best, smiling organs—I mean, God forbid that it should ever come to

120   that, right? But after all, we can't let ourselves forget what this programme is about! I mean, if I'm going to need a transplant—then by God, let's make it the best damn transplant that we can manage! Are you with me?

JAYA: Yes, Ginni, of course, Ginni.

(*From the door, there is now a knocking sound.* JAYA *looks around.*)

125   GINNI: (*Reacting at once, and the* CONTACT MODULE *swivels.*) What's that? What're you looking at?

OM: (*Nervously.*) Oh nothing—just—it's nothing!

GINNI: Now—Zhaya—I saw you look—

JAYA: Really, Ginni—it's probably just the wind—

(*The knocking sound again.*)

130   MA: (*Loud whisper.*) There's someone at the door—

GINNI: What's that you said, Mrs Praycash? Someone at the door?

JAYA: (*Unable to control an exasperated sound.*) Oh—for God's sake! She treats us like children—

135   GINNI: What? Zhaya—Look! All of you—I've told you once, I've told you a zillion times! I hate it when y'all speak at once!

JAYA: (*Now faking a sneeze.*) Chhoo!—sorry, Ginni, sorry—

GINNI: (*Sounding very excited.*) That was a sneeze! Don't deny

140   it—you have a cold, Zhaya, don't you? Come on, confess—

JAYA: No, Ginni, no—it wasn't—it wasn't—

GINNI: Don't lie to me, Zhaya—I know a sneeze when I hear one—

145   JAYA: It was the—the *pepper*—

GINNI: I'll have to ask Auwm—tell me the truth, Auwm—does your sister have a cold? Does she?

OM: Cold? Oh—no, no, no! No cold, Ginni—it was only the—

150   JAYA: —pepper. It's this foreign pepper. I'm not really used to it.

GINNI: Then—why haven't you reacted before this?

(The knocking sounds again, more like a thump.)

MA: *(Looking around.)* That Bidyut-bai is really shameless—

GINNI: What? What was that?

JAYA: Nothing. She was just—

155　GINNI: You're keeping something from me! I just know it— you're all keeping something from me!

JAYA: Oh god, Ginni—we are *not!* Really!

GINNI: Yes you *are,* Zhaya! I can see it in your lying schem-

160　ing little face! You think you're such an cutie-pie, Zhaya— but you don't fool me! Not for one instant! Now *tell me*—

OM: *(Raising his voice and leaning into the viewing field of the* CONTACT MODULE.*)* No—Ginni—please! You trust me— see, look at me—are you looking? Would I tell you a lie?

GINNI: We-e-e-ell. I don't know! What was all that about?

165　Why did Zhaya sneeze? You know how terrified I am of colds, Auwm! Ever since we eradicated colds from here, where I live, it's like—like having the plague!

OM: Ginni—it's not a cold. I promise you that.

GINNI: If you get a cold, Auwm, I can't take your transplant!

170　You'll be quarantined! This whole program will go to waste!

OM: Ginni—Ginni—believe me. I will never risk your health.

GINNI: *(Calming down slightly.)* Though—I guess—they

175　screen everything that comes in. Even if you did have a cold, they'd never let your organs through—

OM: I live only for your benefit. You know that—

GINNI: All right, I believe you. I'll make myself believe you. I mean it's been hard to read your faces, you know? You

180　people don't use facial expressions, not like us, anyhow. But what *was* that your mother said just now? It sounded like . . . like . . .

JAYA: She was praying, taking the name of god—

GINNI: Oh. Yeah. Well, I don't know—sometimes I just get

185　the feeling—

OM: Please, Ginni—trust me. I would not do anything to harm our—our relationship. We have known each other only for two months, but from the first day itself, I have felt that you are just like my sister! Yes! I would not keep

190　anything from you—

GINNI: *(A touch sardonic.)* Is that right? You wouldn't keep anything from your sister—is that right, Zhaya? *(To* JAYA.*)* You're his sister, so you should know—does he keep any-thing from you?

195　OM: I mean—

JAYA: No, he doesn't. He would never tell a lie. He is pure like fresh cotton.

GINNI: *(Childlike glee.)* Pure like fresh cotton! Haha! That's

200　quaint! That's really quaint! You know what? Even if I didn't need transplants and if I wasn't so sick and all—I'd get the kick of my life from these conversations! It's like— it's like—I dunno. Human goldfish bowls, you know? I mean, I just look in on you folks every now and then and

205　it just like—blows my mind. Better than TV. Better than CyberNet. Coz this is Real Life—and don't think I don't appreciate it! You get to be my age and you really appre-ciate human companionship—

JAYA: You look very young—

210　GINNI: —what I meant, people in my country, at my age, they just don't have any worthwhile friends, you know? Noth-

ing to hold on to—nothing precious. Nothing like . . . this. I get to give you things you'd never get in your life-time and you get to give me, well . . . Maybe my life. *(Voice goes husky.)* You know? That's a special bond. Don't think I don't appreciate it.　215

OM: We know you do, Ginni—

GINNI: And now I'm feeling tired, real tired. You just don't know how tired I get sometimes—

JAYA: *(Carefully.)* Is it—is it your illness?

GINNI: I guess you could say so, Zhaya, in a manner of speak-　220 ing, yes. It's my illness. But now I've gotta go. Okay? *(The tone sounds.)* Byeeee—

OM: Good-bye, Ginni—

(Knocking sounds again.)

OM: *(Ignoring the knocking.)* See you soo-oon—

(The CONTACT MODULE *goes dead. Instantly,* JAYA *leaps up to go to the door.)*

JAYA: We've got to do something about the door! We can't 　225 have people knocking whenever they like!

MA: Oh? Now you're going to have special times for knock-ing as well?

*(*JAYA *gets to the door and opens it easily because she didn't have time to lock it completely before lunch.)*

JAYA: *(Opening the door.)* Now look—*(Stops dead and exclaims.)* Huhhhhhh!　230

*(*MA *and* OM *look up in alarm, just in time to see* JAYA *step back quickly, as* JEETU *makes a dramatic entrance—almost falling in at the door. His condition is terrible, his clothes in tatters, his hair wild, covered in solid muck and grime. Only his spirit seems undimin-ished.)*

JAYA: Oh my God—*(She bolts the door, her face grim and frowning.)*

MA: What—? *(She is momentarily speechless.)* Who is it—what is it—

JEETU: *(Staggering forward, till he can support himself on a chair* 　235 *back.)* Only . . . your beloved son, Jeetu. Yes, I can see how delighted you are to see me—*(Mock concern.)* Oh—wait! Sorry! I'm your son-in-law, now, right?

OM: *(Has risen slowly to his feet.)* My god. What have you done to yourself?　240

JEETU: Don't bother breaking coconuts at my feet! *(His tone is sarcastic but good-humoured despite all.)* Yes, yes—your arms are wide open with welcome! Thank you for inviting me to share the comforts of your modest home with me, your younger brother! *(Comes forward across to stage right. Sits on* 　245 *the silky white sofa, which receives his grimy presence with an au-dible flinch.)* And yes, I'd love to sit in this comfortable sofa—*(Succumbing to the sensuous embrace of the cushions, be-coming slighly delirious.)* Ahh! Ahhh!

JAYA: *(Concerned.)* What's the matter—are you in pain?　250

JEETU: Is it possible to know such ease? It feels so good that it hurts! Ahh! Ahh . . . ah. You know—it's a strange thing with the pavements: no matter how long you sleep on them, they never grow soft!

255 JAYA: (*Haltingly.*) You've been on the pavements!
JEETU: (*Gesturing to* JAYA.) Come, come sit by me, my darling wife! Or have you reverted to being my sister-in-law again? Come—

(JAYA *flees downstage.*)

JEETU: Well! No words to express your delight? Strange . . . at
260   one time, she used to fight for my attention—
OM: (*Trying to regain control of the situation.*) Jeetu—you owe us an explanation—
JEETU: I owe no-one anything—
OM: Where have you been these many weeks?
265 JEETU: Careful—you might go deaf to hear the things I'd tell you—
OM: But . . . are you here to stay?
JAYA: What else? You can't turn him out!
MA: (*Hard.*) Maybe we don't have a choice!
270 JEETU: Ah my loving mother speaks at last! And what does she say? What music does she pour into my parched ears?
OM: (*Sternly.*) Stop it! Things have changed around here—
JEETU: Really? I'd never have noticed—
OM: And the fact is—your permit to live with us was
275   surrendered!

(*There is a silence as* JEETU *processes this idea.*)

OM: Yes. I'm sorry—you had your chance. You chose to leave. We had to make our excuses to the guards. To explain why the fourth member of the family wasn't here. Now it's too late to take you back in—and in any case,
280   you're undoubtedly a health hazard—
JEETU: (*Getting up slowly.*) A "health hazard" did you say? (*He stands unsteadily.*) Heh! That's rich! (*Laughs.*) Me—a health "hazard"! My brother—I'm not a health hazard, I'm a walking, talking, health CATASTROPHE! (*Goes towards*
285   OM, *grinning.*) Oh, yes! I'm so unhealthy that even even my germs have germs . . . yes. My lice are dying on my skull—see? (*He offers his head for examination, to* OM, *who shrinks away.*) They're just lying in little black heaps—
JAYA: Stop! Stop it—why make things worse for yourself—
290 JEETU: Ah those honeyed words of love! How they soothe my running sores!
JAYA: What do you expect? You're the one who left. And now you come back looking like Death's first cousin—is that our fault?
295 OM: We'll have no choice—
JEETU: (*Turning towards* MA.) And you, my mother? I hear your love for me has been bought for the price of a flush toilet?
MA: When you reach my age you'll know that a peaceful shit
300   is more precious than money in the bank!
JEETU: Thank goodness I won't live long enough to be rich—
JAYA: What d'you mean—
JEETU: I'm ill. I'm going to die soon—
OM: Oh God—(*He starts to pace.*)
305 JAYA: Don't be foolish—
OM: This is serious, very serious—
MA: Of what?
JEETU: An overdose—
JAYA: Some drug?

JEETU: Called freedom. (*He sinks to the floor.*) I've been over- 310
dosing on freedom. Spent my hoard of years—splurged them all, for a few weeks of freedom on the streets. (*Lies flat.*) Freedom to lie in the filth of the open road and to drink from the open sewer! Yes. Freedom to eat the choicest servings from the garbage dump—shared only with 315
crows, flies and pigs! Ah, such freedom as you newly-rich people never know! (*He is slightly delirious. He attempts a laugh, but his voice is cracked.*) But expensive. For all that it looks so cheap, each mouthful of garbage costs a handful of years off your life. And I gorged myself! So I'm . . . 320
gone. Flat broke. Burnt out . . .

(*He turns weakly on his side and starts to throw up.*)

OM: Quick—stop him—
JAYA: (*Kneeling quickly.*) A towel—cloth, anything—

(*She uses the loose end of her sari to cover her hand as she holds his head, then wipes his face with it with the other corner—*OM *hands her disposable towels and fetches a mug of water.*)

OM: (*His face showing revulsion.*) What a mess! You'll have to incinerate your sari— 325
MA: And what about the carpet?

(JAYA *places* JEETU's *head on her lap.*)

OM: We can disinfect the whole room—and better wear the nose guard—
MA: But the lice—the lice can get into everything—then we're finished— 330
OM: Oh! (*In exasperation.*) It would have been better if—
JAYA: (*Quietly, stroking* JEETU's *dishevelled hair.*) Don't say it.
MA: What?
OM: (*Ignoring* MA.) How can we keep him! What will we tell the guards— 335
JAYA: (*With finality.*) We're not going to turn him out.
MA: There's no place for him now!
JAYA: We've managed before—
OM: (*Fretting.*) Ginni won't like it—she'll forbid it—
JAYA: (*Weakly.*) Who? 340
MA: She'll chuck him out!
OM: She'll be so angry, so angry—
JAYA: (*To* JEETU.) Shhhh, don't talk—
OM: Just think of the risk! We've gone so far—given up so much and to lose it! Just because of—of— 345
JAYA: (*Looking steadily up at him.*) Your brother. Whatever's written on paper, that's what he really is—
OM: But—(*Frets, pacing.*)
MA: What'll we do for food? There won't be enough for him— 350
JEETU: Uhhhh . . . if I could just have a little water—

(JAYA *wets one of the disposable towels, soaks it in water and drib-bles water into his mouth.*)

JAYA: Don't sit up yet.
OM: It's starting to stink! Ginni'll be furious, *furious*—
JAYA: Look, we'll wrap him up in a sheet and keep him to one side till he's better. Then when he can sit up and talk, 355
we'll just tell Ginni that's he's come back. My husband's come back from his—his business trip—

JEETU: (*Weakly, his head lolling.*) Who's this . . . Ginni . . . (*Rolls back down.*)

360 JAYA: Shhh . . . shhh—don't talk—(*She whispers to him, as if to a child.*)

MA: See how she treats him—her brother-in-law!

OM: (*Fretfully.*) How long can we keep him wrapped up! And what if Ginni finds out—

365 JAYA: (*Looking up.*) There's no point getting frantic—

OM: And who'll believe that this . . . this . . . *wreck* was away on business!

MA: (*Maliciously.*) Look how she holds him—her darling!

JAYA: We'll have to fix him up, of course. Shave his hair, give

370 him some clothes—

OM: (*Clutching his head.*) But the diseases—the diseases—

JAYA: (*Calmly.*) Clean water and strong food will cure him of whatever he has—

(*Lights dim.*)

SCENE II

The same scene, a couple of hours later. JEETU's *wasted and scab-scarred body lies in the centre. He has been shaved and visibly grows cleaner, as* JAYA *tenderly washes him and attends to the wounds puckering his skin. He is conscious and groans only occasionally.* MA *is sitting to one side, her expression blank.* OM *is at stage front right, standing, occasionally pacing. He and* JAYA *have both changed their clothes.* OM *is trying to master the emotions tearing at his face.*

OM: Any minute now—any minute!—she's going to call!

JAYA: Just try and relax—

MA: I don't understand how we plan to hide him—

JAYA: Look—look at these sores!

5 OM: (*To* JAYA.) How can you touch him with your bare hands? He must be oozing with disease—

MA: —and he! Her brother-in-law!

JAYA: (*Exasperated.*) How can I leave him to rot!

OM: Wear rubber gloves, for pity's sake!

10 JAYA: We abandoned him to the streets. The least we can do is to risk our own skin when we touch him—

OM: It's like Ginni says—the curse of the Donor World is sentimentality—

MA: (*To* JAYA.) Ginni will throw him out—just you see!

15 OM: Here I am, willing to give my whole body to improve our lives—and what're you doing? Endangering the whole project by feeling up your brother-in-law—

JAYA: (*At this she stops.*) Who switched roles with his brother? Who turned this family inside out?

20 OM: All I'm saying is—leave him till we can disinfect him at least! Show him to the guards—they'll know what to do—

JAYA: (*Resumes her task.*) What faith you have in them! They don't care about any of us, not as people, not as human beings—

25 OM: What're you saying? You don't talk enough to Ginni. If you did, you wouldn't feel this way—

MA: Oh she's jealous of our Ginni-angel! Look at her face? Pinched with envy!

OM: Ginni really cares for us—

30 JAYA: Oh yes, she *cares*—just as much as she cares about the chicken she eats for dinner—that's all you are for her, another kind of dinner—

OM: (*Contemptuously.*) How little you understand of Westerners! They are not small, petty people—like us!

MA: Oh she's just jealous, jealous! Can't bear to think of you 35 being inside that foreign angel. After all, who wouldn't want to be inside such a divine being? Why—it would be indecent to object—

OM: (*Moderately.*) Now, now, Ma—

MA: Who knows? Maybe she'll even want you for a husband 40 some day—why not? If my son's kidneys are good enough for her why not his—

OM: Ma—!

MA: Why not his children, I was going to say! Now that's what I want to know! What a miracle—grandchildren! 45 And with an angel for a daughter-in-law!

JAYA: Huh! An angel who shares her bed with her dinner—now that *would* be a miracle!

OM: Would she spend so much money on me, then? If I am just—a—a chicken to her? Answer me that! Do you know 50 how much she's spent on us? Our comfort?

JAYA: Never mind chicken—have you seen how their beef cattle live? Air-conditioned! Individual potties! Music from loudspeakers—why, they even have their own psychiatrists! All to ensure that their meat, when it finally gets 55 to Ginni's table, will be the freshest, purest, sanest, *happiest*—

OM: (*Steps towards* JAYA.) I'll slap you if you're not careful!

JAYA: (*Unimpressed.*) Mind that you wear your rubber gloves— 60

(*There's knocking at the door.*)

MA: Hear that?

OM: Who is it—who!

MA: The right-hand neighbours. Wanting to borrow a bucket of water.

OM: Well, they're not getting it— 65

MA: Yesterday they offered me money—

OM: Tell them to ask the muncipality to increase their supply.

MA: I told them—

OM: Then why don't they shut up?

MA: They told me I'd forgotten what it was like before we got 70 this external connection—they started to scream and cry—

OM: Ahh . . . ! These people! No wonder foreigners think so little of us! We have no pride, no shame!

(*Knocking increases in volume.*)

JAYA: (*To* MA.) How can you be sure that it's the neighbours? 75

OM: Who else can it be?

MA: Listen carefully. There's a code, you see—

JAYA: Supposing it's the guards?

OM: Why should they come?

(*Sustained knocking.*)

JAYA: What kind of code— 80

MA: Three knocks means it's the next-door-right-side. Two knocks means it's the next-door-left-side—

OM: There's no reason for the guards to come!

JAYA: What does loud thumping with no pattern mean?

(*Thumping on the door.*)

85   OM: (*Looking suddenly grey.*) You're right—it could be the guards!

      MA: No, no! It's the neighbours I tell you!

(*Violent thumping.*)

      JAYA: (*A touch of malice.*)—it's been two months, you know! Time to collect their fattened broiler!

90   MA: Shouldn't you just open the door and find out?

      OM: I—I—(*Looking panicked.*) What about—what about Jeetu! What'll we do about hiding him!

      JAYA: If they've come for you, they won't have eyes for anyone else—

(*Knocking, knocking, knocking.*)

95   OM: (*Sweating.*) But—Ginni looked fine at lunch-time—she looked perfectly normal—

      JAYA: Her condition is such that she can deteriorate suddenly—

      OM: But she would tell us herself! Not just send the guards—

(*Rhythmic thumping.*)

100   JAYA: Maybe she doesn't have the strength?

      OM: My god. My god—you're right! It's not happened so far, this knocking!

      JAYA: Why not just open the door and find out?

      OM: I always hoped, you see, that it would never actually
105   come to this—

      JAYA: A vain hope. Answer the door—

      OM: (*Querulous.*) A dutiful wife would open it for me!

      JAYA: You forget—I'm your sister—

      MA: That knocking's getting on my nerves now!

(*Knocking, knocking, knocking.*)

110   OM: My legs! My legs refuse to move!

      JAYA: Such a hero, my man.

(*Hammering, thumping, knocking.*)

      OM: At least she could have let us enjoy the illusion for a little longer—

      JAYA: It's in God's will, when your time is up—
115   MA: What'll they think—this delay?

      OM: Another month—another week, another day, even—

      JAYA: But in the end it would always come to this—the bill collector at the door—

      OM: Do it for me—please! I order you—you're still my wife!

(*Knock, thump, knock, thump. A pleasing rhythm.*)

120   MA: I'll be driven mad!

      OM: Would you prefer to see your son dead?

      JAYA: Maybe they just want one of your finger-nails—your hair—something unimportant—

      OM: The smallest pimple on my chin is more precious to me
125   at this moment than a diamond mine in someone else's fist! Oh—how could I have done this to myself? What sort of fool am I?

(*Knocknocknock.*)

      MA: If you don't open the door, I will—

      OM: And if you move even one muscle, I'll kill you with my bare hands—   130

      JAYA: Your mother!

      OM: Whoever opens that door is my murderer, my assassin—

      JAYA: I'm sorry, I cannot live with this—(*She's completed* JEETU*'s cleaning and starts to get up.*)

(*Thumpthumpthump.* JEETU *gingerly rolls over onto one elbow. Looks up and around him. Then collapses gently onto his belly and lies still, as if ready to sleep.*)

      OM: No!! I beg of you—please! Please! Leave that cursed   135
door alone! Seal it with cement and fire! I cannot bear to see its gape, admitting those vile, those cruel, those vicious guards! (*Groans.*) Ahhhh . . .

      JAYA: Till just a moment ago they were your dearest friends—
(*Gets up.*)   140

      OM: NO! Sit still! Don't stir! Or I'll—I'll—

(*He rushes to the door, holds himself against it.*)

      JAYA: How can I respect you? Move aside!

      OM: (*Wildly.*) I don't care! So long as you keep the guards from the door—

      JAYA: I'll offer myself in exchange—   145

      OM: They won't take you—they're very selective—

(*Knockthumpknockthump.*)

      JAYA: (*Exasperated.*) They'll break the door down in a moment!

      OM: (*Sinks to the floor. Voice barely audible.*) Yes. I never thought of that. They could do that—and then what'll happen?   150
Where'll I hide? (*Starts to crawl away from the door.*) In the fridge. That's where. I'll just crawl along here, all the way to the fridge and I'll sit there, yes—

      JAYA: (*As soon as* OM *moves away from the door,* JAYA *starts to unlock the bolts.*) Ohhh—this bravery makes my heart sick—   155

      MA: (*To* OM, *as he crawls past her.*) Why are you on the floor?

      OM: I'm hiding.

(JAYA *gets the bolts on the door open. Opens the door.*)

      JAYA: (*Off-stage.*) Yes? What d'you want?

(*There is an indistinct mumble.*)

      JAYA: (*Re-enters looking bewildered.*) Ma—it's for you—

      MA: (*Getting to her feet.*) What? Already?   160

      JAYA: There must be some mistake—

      MA: (*Coming forward briskly.*) It's very prompt, I must say!

      JAYA: (*Mystified.*) You ordered something?

      MA: (*She is already at the door.*) Yes. (*Moves out of sight, off-stage.*) Yes?—Yes! That's right! But where is it? You haven't   165
brought it? It hasn't come? You'll bring it tomorrow? When? Ah . . . Okay. No—no, I'll be at home—and—sign here? No . . . payment? Oh. Okay. Right. I'll be waiting—
(*She re-enters and shuts the door behind her.*)

      JAYA: (*She heard this exchange with no comprehension.*) Ma? What   170
was all that?

MA: (*Airily.*) Oh . . . Just something I've ordered—

JAYA: (*Astounded.*) Ordered!

MA: Something I saw on TV—

175 JAYA: But . . . how did you place the order?

MA: That thing, the remote—you press some buttons and you can buy things, do things—and they bring it right to the door! But Madam wouldn't know, would she! Too high and mighty to watch TV!

180 OM: (*He has reached as far upstage as he can comfortably go. He stops there, his hands over his head.*) I'm hiding.

JAYA: (*She locks the door.*) But what have you ordered? How much will it cost?

MA: (*Philosophically.*) You'll see, when it comes!

(*Lights dim.*)

SCENE III

OM *is lying in a foetal position on the floor, stage front right.* JEETU *is sitting at the table eating slowly, carefully. He has had a bath and is wearing* OM's *track suit.* JAYA *and* MA *are sitting beside* OM.

JAYA: He doesn't seem to hear anything I say.

MA: He's a good boy. He's just tired, that's all—

JAYA: But what'll we do! Ginni notices everything!

MA: She'll understand.

5 JAYA: Huh!

MA: You're just jealous of her. You don't see what a good, kind, generous, loving person she really is. It's a reflection on you, but of course, you're too fancy to care—

JAYA: Please! This is no time to be criticising me!

10 MA: Who's criticising? I'm just pointing out some simple truths.

JAYA: Come on, Om—get up! This'll never do—

MA: Want to watch TV? There's something good on in twenty minutes—

15 JAYA: (*Looks at* OM.) It's so typical. He can't face things. He never could.

MA: You should watch more TV. You could learn so much—

JAYA: It's amazing that he got this job at all.

MA: On *Happy Families* you can see it, the exact same situa-
20 tion. The mother has one son and one daughter—and the son gets an expensive job—

JAYA: Ma—you have two sons!

MA: But the daughter is jealous! She can't bear to see her brother succeeding, getting all the praise from the mother!
25 The poor mother was widowed in early life and has to struggle—but then one day the father comes back!

JAYA: I thought you just said he was dead?

MA: No, I never! I said the mother was widowed—meaning, she just thought the husband was dead—

30 JAYA: (*Snapping in irritation.*) Oh—it's all so pointless! Any moment now, you won't have a TV to watch!

MA: What!

JAYA: —this whole dream will come crashing down around us! The grey guards will come and take everything back!

35 MA: No!

JAYA: What d'you think—it's your birthright? To have all this water, these gadgets? The moment Ginni finds out what's happened to her little pet, she'll have the place emptied—

MA: Shoo! Such dirty lies!

40 JAYA: (*Quieter.*) And then how'll I cook without a stove?

MA: I'll slap you if you talk like that! Why, my son said so himself—we'll be rich for ever and ever—

JAYA: (*Raising her voice.*) Look at your son, Ma! Look! He's been reduced to a cabbage!

45 MA: At least a cabbage doesn't talk back!

JAYA: (*Frustrated.*) Oh! (*Angry tears.*) At least before there was nothing to lose!

JEETU: (*Suddenly.*) Why? You used to have a smile before. You've certainly lost that—

50 JAYA: Oh shut up, shut up! Who are you to talk! You're just a waster! Drifting about the streets, not caring what happened to yourself, not caring about any of us, but when you're ready to die, where d'you come? To us of course! Yes! It's so easy for you to talk—you who can't even lose yourself competently! You've come back to make sure that 55 we lose ourselves as well!

MA: Don't speak to your husband like that—

JAYA: He's *not* my husband! He's my brother-in-law!

JEETU: And your lover—

(OM *reacts to this—his limbs twitch, but he does not participate in the conversation.*)

60 MA: What's this?

JAYA: (*Broken.*) Ohh! Not now! Not this!

JEETU: How strange it is, to be here. Talking to all of you . . .

MA: (*Indifferently.*) Not that I'm surprised. Nothing from this slut surprises me. She's capable of anything—

65 JAYA: Doesn't it matter to you that you're trampling on my life? Doesn't it matter what harm you cause to others?

JEETU: When you've lost everything, when you're so weak you can't even eat the cockroaches who walk into your mouth, that's when your life's desire breathes in your 70 ear—

JAYA: And? It tells you to torment your family?

MA: She always was shameless—

JEETU: That I should see you again. You, Jaya. (*Leans back and smiles lazily, wincing slightly.* OM *listens.*) Lying there, covered in shit and dirt, ready to die—*dying* to die!—hearing the 75 engine, roaring in my ears, ready to take me away—I thought of you.

MA: I should have thrown her out from the moment she started making eyes at him—her brother-in-law!

JAYA: (*This is the closest thing to a compliment she has ever been 80 paid. She is overwhelmed with conflicting emotions, trying to cover it with sarcasm.*) And then? Some goddess picked you up?

JEETU: (*Lolling back.*) Huh! Yes. Some goddess! A dog . . .

JAYA: What? (*Uncomprehending.*) A dog?

JEETU: Came and peed on me. Straight into my mouth, 85 cheeky bastard! (JAYA *shudders in disgust and pity.*) But he revived me all right. Lucky for him he ran off—or I would have sucked him dry! Life is a strange thing. When your pockets are full with it, you throw it away like rich whores buying silk bedsheets. But the moment you've emptied 90 your purse of days, your throat begins to scream of its own accord, like a beggar in the streets—(*He imitates a beggar's cry.*) Help me, oh God!—please! Just another five min-utes—that's all I ask—just another five minutes to drink a last cup of tea—just two minutes! Just one minute, one! 95 One . . . *please* God, help this dying shithead one more time—(*Looks at her, reverts to his normal voice.*) That's when I thought of you. I knew you would revive me. (*Shuts his eyes.*) Just the smell of your hair—just the touch of your fingernails—

JAYA: (*Biting her lip.*) Hush! These are not things to be said!

MA: And it's too late, anyway. She's already married. To your elder brother—

OM: (*Suddenly.*) Who's a cabbage.

JAYA: (*Uncertainly.*) Om . . .

JEETU: That's all right. We don't need anyone. We don't need this fancy prison. We managed before. We'll manage again —

MA: (*Suddenly jumping up.*) What's the time? Look at the time! It's late—Ginni'll be angry at us—

(*From the corridor, the sound of booted steps.*)

JAYA: (*Tiredly.*) Ohh. I don't care, I don't care any more—

JEETU: That's what I say—

(*From the corridor, the sound of booted steps, closer.*)

MA: Listen! What's that sound?

(OM *hears and reacts immediately, before the others notice him, by crawling off, stage right.*)

JAYA: What's the worst they can do? Take away what was never ours to begin with—

(*From the door, a couple of sharp loud raps.*)

GUARD 1: InterPlanta Services! Open this door, please!

MA: It's the guards!

JAYA: (*Looking blankly.*) So they *have* come for him, after all.

JEETU: (*Holding out his hand.*) Come. Let me kiss your hand. Then you can go and open the door. Tell them to bugger off and take all their goodies with them.

GUARD 1: (*From outside.*) InterPlanta Services—we know you're in there! Open up!

JAYA: (*Raising her voice.*) Coming! (*She gets up.*) I might as well get it over with. (*To the door.*) Wait! It takes a while to unlock the door—

(*Works at the bolts.*)

GUARD 1: (*From outside.*) Resistance is useless! We are authorised to break down this barrier if you do not comply with our request in ten seconds exactly—(*Starts a count down.*) Ten! Nine! Eight!—

(JAYA *gets the door open.*)

GUARD 1: (*Breaking off in mid-stride.*) Sev-...ah! (*Enters, pushing* JAYA *aside as* GUARD 2 *and* GUARD 3 *take up defensive positions at the door, holding a fold-up stretcher between them.*) Right—where is the Donor? Come on, quickly now—(*He plunges straight for* JEETU.) The penalty for resistance is—

JAYA: (*In sudden alarm.*) But that's not—

(JEETU, *who has got to his feet, starts to back away*—)

MA: (*Suddenly, pointing to* JEETU.) Go on! Take him—before he runs!

(JEETU *panics and runs,* GUARD 1 *pounces for him, chasing him around the room, while the other two guards stand like goal-keepers at the door.*)

GUARD 1: Ah! He's running, is he? I'll show him—I'll show the cowardly little shit—

JAYA: (*Screaming.*) But he's not the one you want!

JEETU: (*As he runs—though he's really in no condition to make the effort and tires almost instantly.*) You fools! Can't you see I'm not your man?

GUARD 1: (*Panting in pursuit, dodging around the others, even around* OM *lying inert on the floor.*) Always the same story—no-one wants to pay their dues—come on, come on! It's hopeless to run away—

(GUARD 1 *catches him.* JAYA *screams.*)

GUARD 1: There—there—(*As* JEETU *struggles, grunting,* GUARD 1 *holds him in a cruel arm-lock.*) I've got you now—

JAYA: Don't hurt him—don't hurt him—oh he's sick! Please!

GUARD 1: Resistance is useless—(*Starts to lift/drag* JEETU *kicking and struggling, but losing strength.*) we'll have you knocked out in a second—

JEETU: (*Weakly.*) Jaya! Uhh—tell them . . . tell them—

JAYA: (*She darts forward.*) You fools! You maniacs—

MA: (*Reaches out, grabs* JAYA'*s ankle and forces her to fall.*) Let him go—slut!

JAYA: (*Paying no attention to* MA.)—He's not the one you want! My husband is there—(*She points from her ungainly position on the floor.*) There!

GUARD 1: Ohh! That's what they all say when we come to take them! (*In a falsetto, as he subdues* JEETU.) "Not me! Not me! It's my brother you want! My uncle! My son" Huh! Lying scum—(*To the other two guards.* GUARD 2 *helps him to wrestle* JEETU *to the ground, while* GUARD 3 *gets the stretcher ready.*) We have no time to spare!

(*Beyond the door interested by-standers have started to collect.*)

JAYA: How can you take the wrong man! Can't you see? Don't you have eyes in your head?

GUARD 1: —(*To the other two.*) Officer! Ready hypo!

MA: Hurry up, you fools—how long d'you think I can hold her?

GUARD 2: (*Holding a gun-shaped hypo-syringe.*) Ready, sir!

JEETU: (*Weakly.*) Jaya—Jaya—help me!

GUARD 1: Prepare to administer hypo—

JAYA: (*Struggling now with* MA *who has her ankle in a vice-like grip.*) Lemme go—lemme go! Don't you care about your own son—

MA: Your lover, you mean! Slut! Serves him right if he goes in place of my only darling—

GUARD 3: (*Holding* JEETU *in a suffocating lock.*) Yes sir—(JEETU *starts to struggle, grunting.*)

JAYA: No! (*Panicking.*) You're killing him! He's not strong enough—

GUARD 1: (*Ignoring her.*) Administer hypo—(*He aids in holding* JEETU *down.*)

(GUARD 2 *is unable to gain access to* JEETU *because he is now struggling so wildly.* JAYA *and* MA *are also struggling but* MA *is practically lying on top of* JAYA *to hold her down.*)

JAYA: They're hurting him! They'll kill him—oh! I can't bear to watch—I can't!

GUARD 1: Officer—I said, administer hypo—

190 GUARD 2: I'm trying sir—I—(*She gets in a shot.*)

JEETU: (*Howls.*) Ahhhhh! Ahhhhh!

GUARD 2: —Damn! Missed the muscle—

JEETU: Ahhhhh!

JAYA: (*In tears.*) Oh what's the use, what's the use! After all

195 we've gone through—

GUARD 1: Ready fresh hypo, officer—and hurry! He's getting out of control—

JAYA: (*No longer able to struggle.*) Oh—please, no, no! He wanted nothing—he had no part to play in this—

(GUARD 2 *fiddles with her kit, discarding one cartridge and fitting another on.*)

200 JAYA: Don't hurt him, don't hurt him—please! Oh! Oh! They'll make mincemeat out of him—

GUARD 2: (*Calmly.*) Hypo ready, sir—

GUARD 1: Administer hypo—

JEETU: (*Hollering as* GUARD 1 *and* GUARD 3 *lean with all their*

205 *weight on him.*) AHHHHHHHHHHHH! AHHHH-HHH!

GUARD 2 *holds down* JEETU's *shoulder with her knee and delivers a punch with the muzzle of the hypo.* JEETU's *body arcs up in a convulsion—he seems to hover in mid-air—*JAYA *screams—Then all is still.* JEETU *is limp and inert on the stretcher. The three guards get to their feet, returning as quickly as possible to their professional composure.* JAYA *remains clutched within* MA's *savage embrace, though she strains towards the tableau.*)

GUARD 1: Officers—initiate departure.

(GUARD 2 *and* GUARD 3 *quickly spread an opaque shield over the stretcher so that* JEETU *is completely hidden from sight.*)

JAYA: (*In a dull voice, knowing that she won't be answered.*) He's dead, isn't he? They've killed him. I feel it in my

210 bones.

GUARD 2: Donor secured for departure.

GUARD 1: Proceed with departure—

(GUARD 2 *and* GUARD 3 *hoist the stretcher up and exit. From beyond the door, the sound of the wondering crowd.* JAYA *holds out her hand helplessly in the direction of the door.*)

GUARD 1: (*Turning to* JAYA *as the other two officers vanish, removing his clipboard from his belt.*) InterPlanta Services thank

215 you for your cooperation. Your family member is about to fulfil the solemn and noble contract into which he entered. We, on our part, offer you our sincerest assurance that we will do everything in our power to ensure that he will come to no avoidable harm and will suffer no dis-

220 comforts other than what is deemed normal under the circumstances—(*He pauses.* JAYA *is looking dully at the floor, still lying half prone, though* MA *has now backed off and is straightening her clothes.*) Any questions?

JAYA: (*Not looking up.*) When will he be back?

225 GUARD 1: (*Patiently.*) Madam! Any questions?

JAYA: (*Not looking up.*) No.

GUARD 1: (*Ticking off his clipboard.*) Right. Donor will remain in our custody until such time as he is ready to be returned. This can be any period from two hours onwards

230 and upto one week—

JAYA: (*Jerks her head up.*) One week! What'll be left of him!

GUARD 1: —depending on the nature of the transplant required, the availability of artificial substitutes for the organs that the Donor has, of his own free will, made

235 available to the Receiver and the Donor's own speed of recovery. Any questions?

JAYA: (*Gets slowly to her feet.*) Yes! What part of him is going to be removed?

GUARD 1: I'm sorry, Madam, I am not free to discuss such de-

240 tails.

JAYA: You're going to cut him up and you're not even going to tell his wife what you're going to do with him?

GUARD 1: Excuse me, Madam—relationship with Donor is . . . ?

245 JAYA: (*Gives her head a guilty little shake.*) I—I meant, his family—

GUARD 1: Madam: Full details will be furnished once the formalities have been completed—

JAYA: And can I see him? In the hospital, the clinic, wherever?

250 GUARD 1: Security and health regulations prohibit any contact between Donors and their families—

JAYA: Why ask if we have questions when you don't want to answer any of them?

GUARD 1: (*Imperturbably ticking off his clipboard.*) Right. (*Hand-*

255 *ing her the clipboard.*) And now, if you would be so kind as to sign the despatch voucher—

JAYA: (*Grabs the pen and signs violently.*) There—there—your stupid forms, your—papers—your—questions . . . (*She would like to throw the pen at the floor, but it is attached to the*

260 *clip-board.*)

GUARD 1: (*Retrieving the clip-board.*) Thank you, Madam. We are grateful for your kind cooperation and assure you—

JAYA: Just get out! Take your lying, insincere face away from my door—(*Makes as if to push him.*)

265 GUARD 1: (*Moving nimbly out of her range, as he continues his spiel.*)—assure you that we will do everything in our power to return your beloved one to you in as short a time as possible—(*He leans inwards on the door handle.*) On behalf of our clients—

270 JAYA: (*Rushes at him, shouting.*) GET OUT! (*Pushes the door shut in his face.*)

GUARD 1: (*He pushes back, completing his parting message through the door.*)—we at InterPlanta Services extend our heartfelt gratitude for your family's support and compassion! (*This*

275 *last bit is shouted from behind the closed door.*)

(*Sound of boots marching away.*)

JAYA: Ahhh! (*Venting her fury against the door.*) How I hate them!

MA: (*She has been silent all along.*) Good. They've gone at last.

JAYA: (*Leaning against the door, her head against her fists.*) He's

280 gone! They've taken him—and I could do nothing to prevent it!

MA: Can I switch on my TV?

JAYA: (*Yelling at her.*) Your son goes off to the slaughterhouse and you're just worried about your TV!

285   MA: (*Mustering as much dignity as she can.*) If you watched more TV you wouldn't dare talk to your mother-in-law that way—

JAYA: (*Coming back towards her.*) Oh! So I've gone back to being your daughter-in-law, have I?

(*Stands threateningly in front of* MA, *who is facing the TV with the remote raised in readiness in her hand.*)

290   MA: I'm your mother-in-law, that's your brother-in-law on the floor there, your husband's gone to work at the spare parts factory. And you? You're just a slut who happens to be standing between me and my TV!

(*Lights dim.*)

SCENE IV

Night. The only difference between daytime and night-time is the spotlight illumination. MA *is snoring in her corner upstage and left.* JAYA *is standing uneasily in a pool of light, upstage left, near the gym equipment. She is wearing an expensive nightgown with matching robe, in satin and lace. Her face gleams with night-cream.*

OM *lies in his corner, on a sleeping pallet near the TV, apparently asleep.*

JAYA *pacing restlessly, finally comes over to where* OM *lies.*

JAYA: (*Shaking him.*) Om! Om—wake up!

(*He does not respond.*)

JAYA: Om—come on—I know you're not asleep—wake up!

OM: (*In a disembodied voice.*) Why? What's the point?

JAYA: We've got to talk. To decide what to do—

5   OM: About what?

JAYA: When they bring Jeetu back—when they realize they've got the wrong man—

OM: They've not realized that. They've used him instead of me.

10   JAYA: No! No—they *can't*—they can't be that stupid!

OM: Then why haven't they brought him back?

JAYA: Because they're . . . interrogating him. Because he collapsed, maybe, and now they're treating him—

OM: You yourself said they don't give a damn about us—why

15   should they care about him? (*He raises himself slowly.*) No. They've used him, take my word for it. Or else they'd have brought him back—

JAYA: —But—but don't they *check*? Don't they bother?

OM: (*Shrugs.*) Maybe they were in too much of a hurry?

20   JAYA: Maybe the part they've taken from him doesn't need to be so special—maybe they've just taken something small, something insignificant—

OM: Then they would have come back by now.

JAYA: It's been six hours. Six hours! They can't remove any-

25   thing of much consequence in six hours! Why—they've probably just taken his—his front teeth! His toe-nails!

OM: Then why hasn't he come back?

JAYA: (*In a small voice.*) You're right. It must be something bigger. More crucial. (*Pause.*) What d'you think it is? His stom-

30   ach? His intestines? Maybe he won't come back for a week!

OM: Or maybe they've found out he's not me and they've just done away with him!

JAYA: (*Cries out.*) No! That would be murder! They can't be allowed to murder people!

OM: (*Coldly.*) Who'd notice? We don't have the right to com- 35 plain. Technically, anyone who isn't claimed by his family within twenty-four hours of going missing can be terminated without attracting legal attention.

JAYA: All these weeks he's been away—he could've been dead! And we'd never even have known! 40

OM: It's a wonder he's alive at all. I've heard that the street gangs eat derelicts these days—

JAYA: No!

OM: Cook them and eat them. Why not? There's no law to prevent it— 45

JAYA: How did he survive!

OM: He was protected by his friends on the street. But they couldn't do it indefinitely. They forced him to come back.

JAYA: Oh. 50

OM: Whatever he says—that's the real reason he's here.

JAYA: (*Pause.*) D'you think he's really ill?

OM: Must be.

JAYA: (*With finality.*) Then it's better if he dies in their hands. They'd be humane, they wouldn't hurt him— 55

OM: Why? They could use him for research—

JAYA: No!

OM: He's not officially on their records—they can do whatever they like—

JAYA: (*Covering her ears.*) No! I don't want to think of it— 60

OM: —give him drugs and sell him to those game sanctuaries—

JAYA: Don't! Oh—please—

OM: —where the rich have licenses to hunt socially disadvantaged types—yes! That's what they've done with your 65 Jeetu! Turned him loose to become a trophy for some industrialist's daughter—

JAYA: You're—you're—(*She calms down.*) It's just your jealousy speaking, isn't it? (*She insists.*) Tell me—isn't it?

OM: What's it to you? 70

JAYA: (*Tiredly.*) I'm still your wife.

OM: Not really. On paper, you're my sister. In reality, you're nothing to me. If not for Ginni I'd throw you out like a shot. Onto the streets. To be hunted. What do I care? You betrayed me. Seduced my brother. I feel nothing but con- 75 tempt.

JAYA: You never cared for me. You never wanted me—

OM: Wanting—not wanting—what meaning do these words have in our world? What choices do we have? Was it my choice that I signed up for this programme? 80

JAYA: —Yes! You went of your own accord!

OM: No. I went because there wasn't anything left to do. I went because I lost my job in the company. And why did I lose it? Because nobody needs clerks any more! There are no new jobs now, from here till next week! It's all over! 85 The factories are all closing! There was nothing *left* for people like us! Don't you know that? There's us—and there's the street gangs—and then the rich.

JAYA: But—the village—

OM: The village is just another kind of factory now. To live 90 there you have to be born there—or you have to be an industrialist. I'm not an industrialist. I'm just a clerk. What choices do I have? I didn't even choose *this* job—I stood in queue and I was chosen! And if I hadn't got this one, there would have been other queues—but they are all just another kind of lottery in the end. It was just my fate! Like it is my fate to have a faithless tart for a wife—

JAYA: Then why didn't you go with the grey guards when they came! Why did you lie down like a corpse!

OM: I don't know what came over me. That too was my fate. It was my fate to lie down in a trance and my brother to take my place. It was his fate to face the scalpel—

JAYA: —even though he may never return?

OM: Nothing matters. Whatever happens, it's fate.

(There's a sound, indistinct.)

JAYA: Wait!—What's that?

(The sound of boots in the corridor, accompanied by a shuffling.)

JAYA: Oh! *(Turning excitedly towards the door.)* Hear that? It sounds like boots—

(She runs to the door.)

OM: It doesn't matter what they've done to him—he didn't care about his life anyway—he didn't take any responsibility for anything—

(JAYA flings the door open, leans out into the corridor—and freezes where she stands. The footsteps come to a halt. The shuffling continues. OM looks straight ahead, affecting unconcern. The shuffling draws close. JAYA stands aside, her face blank, watching as JEETU enters the room, shuffling slowly, his arms half-raised in front of him, being steered by GUARD 2, impassively. GUARD 1 enters as well.)

OM *does not look around.* JAYA *slowly re-enters, shutting the door behind her, never taking her stricken eyes off the silent, pathetic figure of* JEETU.)

(He is wearing silk pajamas white on white and a wine-red brocade robe and velvet bedroom slippers. Across his eyes, and wrapped around his head, heavy bandages.)

(JAYA remains where she is, by the door, her hands over her mouth, staring. In the foreground, MA snores lightly.)

GUARD 1: *(Clears his throat, takes out his memo pad.)* Donor Prakash, we have no words with which to express our deep and sincere appreciation of your generosity towards your Receiver . . .

(Lights fade as he drones on.)

GUARD 1: You will be glad to hear that the transplant has been a tremendous success and that henceforward you will receive every benefit and consideration due to you under the terms of your contract . . .

(Lights out and curtain.)

ACT THREE

SCENE I

Little has changed in the room. JEETU *sits on the floor with his head between his knees, facing stage front.* MA *is watching TV wearing head phones.* JAYA *and* OM *are sitting on either side of* JEETU.

JAYA: Jeetu—Jeetu speak to me—*(She tries to put her arm over his back.)*

JEETU: *(Throwing her arm off violently, not lifting up his head.)* Don't touch me!

OM: What does he care what happens to us? He's only thinking of himself.

JAYA: Jeetu, you've already paid the price—now why not live with the reward?

JEETU: *(He is silent for a beat. Then he lifts his head. In the place of his eyes are enormous goggles, created to look like a pair of imitation eyes. They fit flush with his skin, without ear pieces and cannot be removed. His voice is a hoarse whisper.)* This . . . is my *reward?*

JAYA: Jeetu—Jeetu—if you would only listen a moment—

JEETU: No! *(He gets to his feet.)* I won't listen! Because listening brings acceptance. *(He moves, but warily. He never bumps into anything but he "looks" around himself like a first-time visitor from Mars.)* And I will never accept. I will never live with this—this—

OM: Selfish, that's what he is—

JAYA: No, Jeetu, no!

JEETU: I don't need your permission to step off the bus! I make my own decisions—

OM: —only thinks of himself. Look at me?

JEETU: Yes, my brother! Look at you? Look at you with these eyes that were meant for you? *(Makes a croaking, sobbing sound, hitting his eyes with his hands.)* These eyes—these blind eyes, this sightless sight—

JAYA: But Jeetu—if they think you're Om, then we need you! Without you, they won't maintain us—

JEETU: I don't care! I'm not the one who got this job—and I'm not going to be the one to suffer the consequences—

OM: He was always selfish. Always lived just for himself—

JAYA: Jeetu—just wait till we can ask Ginni—she'll listen at least, maybe even help—

JEETU: Ginni, huh!—Ginni only helps herself—

JAYA: No, Jeetu—*(But she herself sounds uncertain.)* That's not true . . .

JEETU: You show me a rich woman who plucks a poor man's eyes out of his body and I'll show you a she-demon!

JAYA: But Jeetu, without you . . .

OM: Just wait till Ginni finds out whose eyes are in her head! Just wait!

JAYA: *(To* OM.) Why tell her? If she goes on thinking Jeetu is you then maybe—

OM: Fat chance! It's the guards who made the mistake! The moment she sees me here she'll know what happened—and she'll be mad! She'll be furious! She'll probably have the guards court-martialled—

JAYA: You heard what they said—the transplant was a success. So maybe . . . maybe it *is* all right? Maybe Jeetu's eyes are good enough?

OM: It's not so easy as you think—remember all those injections I had in the beginning? They were to prepare my

55 body, to change it so that it could match Ginni's body perfectly. But now they've taken the wrong pair of eyes—who knows what it'll do to Ginni? And what about Jeetu's infections, all the poisons and germs he's had circulating inside him—what about them? Ginni's scared about
60 catching your cold! What'll she catch from Jeetu?

JAYA: But they *said*—

OM: It takes time to know that a transplant has been a success!

JAYA: How long—

65 OM: I don't know. I'm not a doctor. Not less than a week, I think—

JEETU: Good. I'll be dead long before then—

JAYA: Jeetu—I'm not going to let you die! I don't care what she says—I'm not going to lose you again—

70 JEETU: You don't know what you're asking of me. You don't know what it's like to walk around with a nightmare wrapped around your head—

JAYA: Jeetu—

OM: (*To* JAYA.) Why waste your breath? Neither will he listen,
75 nor will it make the slightest difference to the outcome. What will be, will be, regardless of what we try to do about it—

JAYA: But *why*—when it doesn't *have* to be! Why—when all he has to do is to pretend—just for a couple of hours in a
80 day—

JEETU: Why? (*Pause.*) Because I am in place beyond death. I am in a place worse than death.

JAYA: There's no place worse than death—

JEETU: Yet I know such a place, now. (*Painfully.*) A bleached
85 and pitted place. Scars and slashes, no stillness, no dimensions. No here, no there—(*He moves his head about, "looking" at his visions.*) I see in molten bars and blinding shapes, I see symmetries and confused fragments—sparks, shadows, water on mad glass, heat dreams, trains flying on fever
90 tracks—

JAYA: But can you see me, Jeetu?

JEETU: (*Looking there.*) Yes. I see you. And through you. (*Looks around.*) And through the floor. And through all the gadgets, pulsing with electric gold, liquid atoms sizzling down
95 infinite mineshafts . . . (*He turns his gaze.*) my brother standing there, a blaze of fried nerves and straining bones, his eyes like ping-pong balls jittering in their orbits. (*Turns.*) And I can see Ma—a dim bundle of red desires bathed in a blue haze of radiation. (*Turns.*) And I can see
100 you, Jaya, my Jaya . . . I can see your purple blood, I can see your thoughts sparkling like stars through the pearly cloud of your brain, I can see your heart twitching like an epileptic kitten—yes, I can see all these things, but who would want to see them? Who can bear to see them? (*He
105 sits down, on his haunches.*) And yet . . . I can't even turn them off. I can't shut these freakish eyes of mine. I can't turn my head away, I can't end this poison-vision. I can't sleep, I can't dream, I can't even cry. (*He looks at her.*) This is what you want from me?

(*There is a silence.*)

110 JEETU: Well? You're not saying anything.

JAYA: I—(*She holds her forehead.*)

JEETU: Is it selfish to want to end this?

OM: I was willing to accept anything for my family—

JEETU: Oh yes!—And what happened when the guards came?

OM: (*Mustering what dignity he can.*) That was different. It was 115 the shock, the lack of warning—

JEETU: It was cowardice!

JAYA: (*Carefully.*) Jeetu—we've not asked anything of you so far—

JEETU: This is no time to start! 120

JAYA: Maybe you'll get used to it in time—maybe they'll be able to improve it—

JEETU: (*He clutches his head.*) Let me die before I'm too maddened by visions to make the effort!

OM: Just wait, just wait—when Ginni comes, she'll make all 125 the effort for all of us!

JAYA: Don't be so cocksure! You think she'll take your side—

OM: Of course she will. And she'll throw the two of you out, I wouldn't be surprised! For fooling her. For fooling around. For being dirty, filthy fornicators— 130

JAYA: We haven't! Not . . . not since you got the job—

OM: Ah but he hasn't been here has he! Now that he's back it'll start again, won't it? Don't think I don't know how it is with people like you! You'd do it right in front of me if you got half a chance— 135

(*The warning tone sounds.*)

JAYA: Oh my God—

OM: (*Looking relieved.*) Ah! Just let me do the talking—I'll explain everything—

JEETU: (*His whole body jerks.*) Ah! What's that? I—I—I *saw* something— 140

(*The second tone sounds.*)

JAYA: What's the matter Jeetu?

OM: You shut up, both of you! I'll explain it—and don't worry, I won't leave you two out of the picture. But if she asks me, I'll tell her—

JEETU: (*Breathlessly.*) Something's . . . happening. The blackness 145 is lifting . . . I can see . . . some sort, some sort of . . . pattern—

(*The third tone sounds.*)

GINNI: Well—hellooo-oo! Guess whoo-ooo!

JEETU: Ahh! (*He falls silent, with his mouth open in wonder, breathing heavily.*) Ahhh . . .

OM: Hello! Howdy! Hi, Ginni— 150

GINNI: Hello-ooo? Is anybody home—(*The* CONTACT MODULE *swivels.*) Auwm? (*The* CONTACT MODULE *has swivelled around to find* JEETU, *who doesn't respond.*) Isn't that you, Auwm?

OM: (*Running around to get in front of the* CONTACT MODULE.) No! No—this is me! I'm here! Here! 155

(*The* CONTACT MODULE *flips up and out of* OM's *reach.*)

GINNI: Come in, Auwm! Can you see me? Auwm?

JEETU: (*In a strange, strangled voice, not looking at the* CONTACT MODULE.) My God! My God—I can see!

GINNI: (*Sounding extremely cheerful.*) Sure you can see Auwm! 160 That's what we gave you eyes for! And I'm sure you're real glad to know that *I* can see better now! And with your eyes!

OM: (*Screaming.*) NO!! It's a mistake! There's been a terrible mistake!

(*But* JAYA *intercepts him.*)

165   JAYA: (*In a loud whisper.*) Wait—don't disturb them—
JEETU: (*Gesturing directly in front of him, in a wondering voice.*) And that . . . and you must be . . .
OM: (*He is almost in tears.*) She's wrong! She's wrong! (*But* JAYA *silences him by dragging him sharply aside.*) It's—
170   JAYA: (*Holds* OM *back.*) Shhhhh—!
GINNI: —Ginni! That's right, Auwm—it's me you're seeing 'coz I'm beaming my video image straight into your mind! So you can see me right in front of you, all of me, for once, not just my face . . . (*In a seductive voice.*) well?
175   What do you think?

(*There is a silence in the room as* JEETU *moves slowly around, looking at something that no-one else in the room with him can see. What little of his face is visible shows wonder.*)

JEETU: It's—you're—beautiful. Like . . . magic.
GINNI: You like me, Auwm? You like what you see?
JEETU: (*Shakily.*) Yes. And—and the room! What is this place?
GINNI: Oh . . . it's just where I live, Auwm, it's one of the
180   rooms in my little house—
JEETU: (*Breathing out.*) It's a palace—
GINNI: I'm glad you like it Auwm—
JEETU: I can't help but like it! Who wouldn't? (*He points around him.*) That—that—(*He has no words.*) Those . . .
185   plants! That . . . light! What are those things there? It's . . . (*Hushed.*) beautiful. Beautiful. I've never seen anything like this. Never.
OM: (*In anguish.*) But it's mine, what he's seeing—MINE!
JAYA: (*Watching carefully.*) Can't you hush?
190   OM: (*In tears.*) It's all a mistake! She'll find out and then what'll happen? What'll happen to us?
JAYA: Shhh—
JEETU: (*Wonderingly.*) And you . . . is that really . . . you?
GINNI: Yup! It's me, Ginni! You look like you're seeing me for
195   the first time, Auwm!
JEETU: I—I am! I never realized this is what you looked like—I mean, when the others talked about you—
GINNI: Well—now. I'm glad you like me so well, 'coz you know what? Now that the transplants have started, it's
200   time that we talked about the next phase—
JEETU: (*Still dazed.*) "Next phase"?
OM: (*Shouting.*) But he's the wrong man!

(JAYA *holds* OM *back.*)

(JEETU *is facing the* CONTACT MODULE, *which now rises above him and glows white as the rest of the stage lights dim.* JEETU *is bathed in the light, sealed into the vision that is projected into him.*)

GINNI: The next phase of the transplants. You see, we have to progress rapidly now and I need all your support. Until we
205   reached this platform of contact, we couldn't be sure. But now that we're sure, we've got to move really fast. Are you with me?
JEETU: (*Uncertainly.*) Yes . . .

GINNI: Because you have to be willing, for what we want to do now. You have to be really willing, Auwm—   210
JEETU: Tell me, Ginni, tell me what you want—(*He moves towards the illusion he sees.*)
GINNI: Ah-ah—can't touch me Auwm! (*He reacts by jerking his hand away.*) Well . . . you'll have to go back to the clinic and they'll prepare you—   215
JEETU: (*He continues to behave as if he is standing very close to someone, following her around as she moves out of his reach.*) You need some more parts of me?
GINNI: Well, yes—I mean, that's one way of looking at it but I—I think you should understand that time is kind of   220
short, Auwm and we really have to get a move on—
JEETU: (*He moves his body seductively, winningly.*) Just tell me what you want of me Ginni—
GINNI: The guards will come for you and they'll request you to follow them away—   225
JEETU: Anything, Ginni, anything—
GINNI: The sooner you can go the better it'll be for you—
JEETU: Whatever you say, Ginni—
GINNI: I mean, really, Auwm, if it's okay with you, I can tell the guards to come for you right now—   230
JAYA: No . . . (*But she says it softly, shaking her head, knowing that it's futile.*)
JEETU: That's fine with me, Ginni—
OM: (*Hoarsely.*) Ask her what she wants from you!
JEETU: Anything you want is fine, Ginni—   235
GINNI: Okay, Auwm, I'm turning this video session off for the moment and I'm going to ask you to wait for the guards—
JEETU: (*He holds his arms out forlornly.*) You're—you're going?
GINNI: But I'll be back, Auwm, closer than you'd ever believe . . . (*The* CONTACT MODULE *moves high, as its light starts to   240
dim.*)
JEETU: (*Stretching his arms up.*) Don't—don't—(*He drops his arms.*) Ahh—! (*Strikes his eyes.*) AHHHH!
GINNI: The guards will come, Auwm, you don't have long to wait—we'll talk again when you're in the clinic, okay?   245
JEETU: NO!! Don't leave me in this blindness—
GINNI: Remember to keep smiling Auwm—
JEETU: (*Brokenly.*) No!
GINNI: —byeeee!

(*The* CONTACT MODULE *snaps off.*)

JEETU: (*Softly.*) Ah—no! She's gone—she's gone!   250

(JAYA *and* OM *come forward around him.*)

JAYA: Jeetu—Jeetu—do you know what you've said?
JEETU: All I know is that I'm going to her—I'm going—
OM: You didn't even find out what they're going to take from you this time—
JEETU: You don't understand! I was blind! And now I have the   255
chance to see again—
JAYA: But . . . it's not *real*, what you see—I—I mean, we could watch you moving like a madman, waving your arms about, pointing to things that weren't there—

(OM, *having listened so far, begins to move away, towards the door.*)

JEETU: Ah—but they're *somewhere*, aren't they? And that's all   260
that matters to me.

JAYA: Yes—but—(*She looks dissatisfied and worried.*) she's taken your *eyes*—

JEETU: —and left me something even better! I can't tell you what things I saw—

JAYA: Really? So much?

JEETU: (*Reverentially.*) Yes—oh, yes! (*Then he pauses.*) Of course, I can't see what's directly around me. But maybe they'll find a way to change that—

JAYA: You should have asked her—

JEETU: I'd not seen her, you see, till just now! I thought she was an old woman! You never told me she was so—so *young!* (*Hushed.*) And beautiful. (*Accusingly.*) Why didn't you tell me, Jaya?

JAYA: (*Shrugs.*) You didn't seem interested—we hardly discussed Ginni at all—

JEETU: Well. It would have made all the difference if I had known. I saw all of her, you know! Standing there (*He draws her with his arms.*), all of her . . . wearing . . . almost nothing! (*JAYA bites her lip, frowning.*) And she kept . . . (*He moves his body sensuously.*) moving, like this, like that . . . wah! I could have had her, right there and then!

JAYA: (*Bitterly.*) But she wasn't real!

JEETU: She exists. That's enough for me. She's a goddess and she exists. I would do anything for her—anything!

JAYA: (*Looks depressed.*) Yes. I can see that—

JEETU: (*A touch of guilt.*) Don't hold it against me, Jaya—think of her as just another client—you were always good at that—

JAYA: Yes . . . but your other clients wanted only your services. Not your . . . body itself!

JEETU: You should be happy for me—and anyway, you've got your wish, now. I'll stay alive, and they'll go on looking after all of us—

(*There is a knocking at the door.*)

GUARD 1: (*From outside.*) InterPlanta Services!—

(*But before he can say "open up", OM has thrown the door open.*)

OM: Yes! Take me! Take me! I'm ready to go!

(*Several things happen at once. JEETU and JAYA turn towards the door, as GUARD 1 and GUARD 2 roughly shove OM aside, entering the room.*)

JEETU: Yes—

GUARD 1: Mr Om Prakash—we have been intimated of your willingness to participate in the second phase of our transplant service!

OM: (*Screaming.*) No! Not him—take ME!! I'm Om Prakash! Check your records—

(*GUARD 3 entering behind the other two, quickly grabs OM and holds him pinned to the wall, struggling.*)

JEETU: Yes—I am Om Prakash—

OM: (*From his pinned position, bellowing.*) NOOO!!! He's lying! A lying, scheming swine!!! He's my brother, I tell you— my younger brother—

GUARD 1: All right sir, if you would just follow us—we're ready to leave—

JEETU: Let's go—

(*GUARD 1 stands aside and JEETU moves towards the door.*)

JAYA: (*Darting forward.*) Jeetu—

JEETU: (*Swivelling sharply.*) Don't call me that—

JAYA: (*She is suddenly in tears.*) Don't go—just yet! Please! It's too soon, they've not explained anything—I—we—you'll never be the same again—

JEETU: (*He grabs her quickly, gives her a brief hug and pushes her away, into the waiting grasp of GUARD 2.*) You have your husband to look after—he needs you more than I—(*He turns and exits.*)

JAYA: (*Losing all restraint.*) Jeetu! JEETU!! (*GUARD 2 lets go of her and exits.*) What happened to your ideals, your freedoms! Your pride! (*She sinks to her knees.*) All gone! So easily gone—

(*GUARD 3 has a brief struggle disengaging himself from OM, but he too slips out, slamming the door behind him—then bolting it from the outside.*)

OM: (*Hollering.*) AHHHHHHHHHH! You've locked us in, you bastards! You've locked us in! (*He roars and pounds on the door.*) You can't do this to us! We've not signed any consent forms! You've not taken any permissions! AHH-HHHHHHH! You've locked us in here! AAAAAHHH-HHHH! And you've taken the wrong man—you'll regret it—you'll suffer for it—AAAAAAHHHHHHH!—

(*He subsides onto the floor, moaning. JAYA looks at the door, too shocked and defeated even to cry. She turns and walks slowly till she is near her place at the dining area. She sits, seeming distracted. Looks across at MA, who is totally absorbed by the TV programme she's watching.*)

JAYA: Ma? Ma—(*Goes across to stage right, where MA sits.*) listen to me—(*But MA can't hear her. She shakes MA by the shoulder.*) Ma! Listen to me!

MA: (*Irritated, holding one of her ear phones up from her ear.*) What is it!

JAYA: Ma—do you realize they've taken Jeetu?

MA: What?

JAYA: (*In a raised voice.*) Jeetu—they've taken him away!

MA: (*Indifferently.*) So? (*Starts to replace the ear-piece.*) He was never here to begin with—

JAYA: No! You *can't* be so indifferent—

MA: (*Shaking off her hand.*) Tch! Let me be! Why should I care what happens to Jeetu? I'm through caring about anybody—(*She replaces the ear-piece and turns back to her set.*)

JAYA: (*For a second she is nonplussed. Then she loses control.*) That's—too much! (*MA can't hear her.*) You hear me, Ma? (*She screams.*) It's just TOO MUCH! (*She darts forward and snatches the TV remote from MA's hand—.*) You can't do this—(*Smashes it on the floor, the TV abruptly goes off, as MA's reaction sets in.*) you've got be involved with what's going on around you—

MA: (*Removing headphones and getting up as fast as her old limbs will let her.*) You—GIVE THAT BACK TO ME—

(*They do not notice that OM is sitting up alertly, by the door. He is listening to something.*)

JAYA: (*Stamping on the remote.*) I won't—I won't—

MA: (*She has got up and is flailing at* JAYA *with her thin arms.*) 355 Pig-faced buffalo! Give it back or I'll—I'll shit in the water-supply!

JAYA: You wouldn't dare—(*She has not managed to break the remote yet.*)

MA: (*She has enough force to push* JAYA *off her balance.*) I'll mi- 360 crowave your entrails!—(*Pushes* JAYA *down.*) Ah! (*Snatches up the remote.*)

JAYA: (*Tackling* MA *from the ground, hanging onto her from behind and trying to claw the remote out of her hands. She is panting with the effort.*) I'm sick of being the only one to make de- 365 cisions around here! There's nothing wrong with you— you're not sick—or busy—

(*All the while* OM *has been listening, like a dog for its master, by the door. Now the sounds that he has been listening for are audible: boots in the corridor. He readies himself by flattening himself alongside the door as the footsteps come to a halt. A pause and the bolt is opened from outside.*)

MA: Let me go, you barren dog—mmmh! Mmmmh! (*She pulls her arm up so that she can gnaw at* JAYA'*s hand where it's clamped to her wrist.*) LET ME GO!

(*At this moment the door is flung open.* JAYA *and* MA *fall apart and turn to the door just as* OM *wriggles out almost the same instant.* AGENT I *enters, paying no attention to* OM.)

370 AGENT I: Madam Indumati? Who is Madam Indumati?

MA: Me! I'm Madam Indumati! (*She starts to move towards the door.*)

JAYA: (*Craning her neck.*)—Om! Om—where are you?

AGENT I: (*Salutes, announcing loudly.*) VideoCouch Enterprises, 375 Ma'm—please—(*He stands aside to open the door a little wider and leans out in anticipation. Sounds of something being wheeled along.*)

JAYA: (*Flabbergasted.*) Wh-what is this? Who're you!

MA: (*To the* AGENT.) Have you brought it?

380 AGENT I: Yes, Ma'm—

(AGENT II *and* AGENT III *wheel in a long gleaming case. It is reminiscent of Tutankhamen's sarcophagus, encrusted with electronic dials and circuitry in the place of jewels. The* AGENTS *wheel it into the centre of the room, move the dining platform aside and install the device in its place.*)

AGENT I: (*Coming forward to where* MA *stands.*) Please, Ma'm, sign here—

JAYA: (*To* MA.) Ma—who are these people—what's going on—

MA: (*Ignoring* JAYA.) What about this insti—instig—?

385 AGENT I: Installation. (*Patiently.*) Just sign this form, Ma'm, to confirm receipt of the unit—

MA: (*Taking the form and the pen.*) How do I know you won't just run away after I've signed this, eh?

AGENT I: (*Shrugs.*) As you wish, Ma'm—(*To the other two* 390 AGENTS, *expressionlessly.*) Proceed with installation.

(*The other two* AGENTS *open the case, revealing an equally ornate interior, filled with tubes, switches, circuitry. Inside are a number of containers.* AGENTS II *and* III *set about attaching the containers to various parts of the case while* AGENT I *explains to* MA.)

AGENT I: This is the SuperDeluxe VideoCouch model XL 5000! We are certain it will provide you, our valued customer, with every satisfaction! This is the nourishment panel—the hydration filter—the pangrometer! Here you see the Lexus Phantasticon which is programmed to receive 395 seven hundred and fifty video channels from all over the—

JAYA: (*Shaking him.*) Stop this at once! Explain to me what's going on!

AGENT I: (*Stops, baffled.*) Ma'm—

MA: (*To* JAYA.) Can't you shut up? It's my VideoCouch! It's 400 what I ordered the other day!

JAYA: But—

AGENT I: Ma'm—

MA: (*To the* AGENT.) Proceed!

AGENT I: (*He is off-stride.*) Uhh—This is the SuperDeluxe 405 VideoCouch model XL 5000! We are certain it will provide you, our valued customer, with every satisfaction! This is the nourishment panel—the hydration filter—the pangrometer! Here you see the Lexus Phantasticon which is programmed to receive seven hundred and fifty video 410 channels from all over the world! There are ten modes, seventeen frequencies, three sub-strate couplers, extra-sensory feedback impulses and cross-net capturing facili-ties! All media access—satellite, bio-tenna, visitelly and radiogonad. Manual control panel, neuro-stimulator and 415 full-body processing capacities—all other queries will be answered on-line from within the VideoCouch self-training program. (*He ends abruptly.*) Any questions, Ma'm?

MA: (*She has heard very little of this.*) Hanh?

AGENT I: Ma'm—if you sign the delivery voucher we can 420 complete installation—

MA: But I haven't understood a word you've said—

JAYA: (*Standing between the VideoCouch and* MA.) Ma—You MUST explain what this is about—

MA: (*To the* AGENT.) Stop her! She'll destroy it—she'll dam- 425 age it—

JAYA: (*Frustrated.*) Oh—! (*She moves away.*)

(*The* AGENT *moves to get closer to the VideoCouch.*)

JAYA: Just do it, do it! (*From stage right, watching the proceedings.*) But make sure I'm not held responsible for anything—

MA: (*To the* AGENT.) If I sign this . . . no-one can take it from 430 me, can they?

AGENT I: No, Ma'm—

MA: And your people won't go till I've got into it? (*She signs the voucher and hands it back, not glancing at the many pages of forms.*) 435

AGENT I: No, Ma'm—thank you, Ma'm—If you'll just come this way, Ma'm—

(*The other two* AGENTS *have attached a power-line to the unit and at this moment activate the system. It twinkles with small LCDs. It looks like a tiny space-module.* AGENT II *delinks the power connection and the lights continue to twinkle. She detaches the cable from the couch.*)

COUCH: (*A fruity voice issues from the VideoCouch.*) Welcome to Video Paradiso! You will not regret your choice! Please ask our authorized representative to settle you into your 440 customized, contour-gel, fully automated video-chamber! (*Appropriate music plays.*)

(*As the* COUCH *begins speaking,* MA *is helped into it by the* AGENTS. *She lies down and the* AGENTS *huddle around her, connecting her up to various pouches and tubes. They do this very quickly and she gasps and grunts once or twice. There is a breathing mask on her face. Soon they are ready to close the lid.*)

445 COUCH: Thank you for being cooperative! Your fully automatic Video Paradiso unit is now ready for operation! Just relax and let your guide show you the way to an experience of ultimate bliss—

(*The* AGENTS *gently shut the lid. There is a faint hiss, a thin vapour escapes as the two edges nest one within the other—and it is closed. The* AGENTS *secure the edges, seal them and lock them. They work extremely fast. The muted sound of the* COUCH *voice continues but becomes a constant unintelligible background hum.*)

JAYA: (*She has been craning her neck to get a view of the proceedings.*) But—how will she breathe!

450 AGENT I: (*Turning to her, as the other two* AGENTS *collapse the undercarriage and lower the unit to floor level. They replace the dining platform over the* COUCH. *It is efficiently concealed, aside from occasional blinks of light.*) Ma'm—it's a total-comfort unit Ma'm—

JAYA: Won't she have to—to—

455 AGENT I: We have a full-recycling and bio-feed-in processor! Your relative will have no further need of the outside world from now till—(*He coughs delicately.*) till she chooses to delink.

JAYA: Does she—how will she—

460 AGENT I: (*Smoothly.*) Everything is now in the customer's operation, Ma'm—the unit is fully self-sufficient—

JAYA: Won't I have to . . . switch it on or off? No . . . food? Water?

AGENT I: Total self-sufficiency, Ma'm! There is nothing to be
465 done!

(*The other two* AGENTS *are ready to leave.*)

AGENT I: Ma'm—installation is complete—

JAYA: No—wait—who's paying for this thing—

AGENT I: (*Impatient to leave, walking towards the door.*) Debited
470 from the customer's InterPlanta account Ma'm—(*As an afterthought he brings out his card.*) but in case you have any queries Ma'm, please get in touch with our local representative—

(*He hands her the card, salutes smartly but unseen, as she stares at the card. The* AGENT *turns on his heel and has left the room before she registers that he's gone.*)

JAYA: (*Startled by the sound of the door shutting.*) No—you've
475 not explained anything—(*Runs to the door.*) what happens if there's a malfunction—(*Opens the door, leans out, steps out. After a moment, comes back in, looking bewildered.*) Alone! I can't believe it—they've left me alone! Every one!

(*From the* COUCH *a friendly mumble trills out.*)

JAYA: (*Leans, exhausted, against the door.*) But not at peace.

(*Lights start to fade.*)

JAYA: (*Slides to the floor.*) Not yet at peace.

(*Lights out.*)

SCENE II

Five days later. The room is unchanged. It is night. JAYA *has fallen asleep at the table-cum-sarcophagus. There are occasional hums of sound from the VideoCouch underneath.*

She is looking worn out, unslept. With jarring suddenness the warning tone sounds. JAYA *startles awake.*

The CONTACT MODULE *is ablaze. It no longer has any face on its facets. It hovers over* JAYA.

VOICE: (*A rich, gravelly male voice.*) Zhaya . . .
JAYA: (*She is badly shocked, recoils away from the* CONTACT MODULE, *her hand to her mouth.*) Ahhh!
VOICE: Don't be frightened, Zhaya—
JAYA: (*Crawling backwards towards stage right.*) No—please—   5
VOICE: (*The* CONTACT MODULE *follows her.*) There's nothing to be afraid of, Zhaya—
JAYA: Who are you! What d'you want—
VOICE: Calm down, honey, be easy—shh, shhh—
JAYA: (*More frightened than ever, wriggling along the floor, away   10
from the light which follows her nevertheless.*) Who told you my name—how did you—
VOICE: Easy, girl, easy—don't keep moving, it's no use—

(JAYA *continues to back away.*)

JAYA: (*Almost screaming.*) NO! . . . please! Leave me alone—
I've done nothing—nothing!   15
VOICE: Zhaya—I can't harm you, honey—
JAYA: (*She is backed up against the wall stage right and can go no further.*) Please—please—(*She shields her eyes from the glare.*)
VOICE: Zhaya —Zhaya—just listen to me—
JAYA: (*Straining away from the light.*) Go away! Leave me alone!   20
VOICE: Zhaya—
JAYA: (*The accumulated tension, despair and solitude combine forces to break her. She subsides on her side in heaving sobs.*) Leave me . . . just leave me . . . please, please . . . just leave me!
VOICE: (*Abruptly the* CONTACT MODULE *moves up and away   25
from her.*) All right, Zhaya—if that's what you really want—

(*The* CONTACT MODULE *moves a comfortable distance away from her. It dims down till it looks like a Japanese paper-lantern. The rest of the stage is in darkness. Slowly, cautiously,* JAYA *raises her head, looks around herself, warily. There is a pregnant silence.*)

JAYA: Have you—gone?
VOICE: No.
JAYA: (*She is startled but waits. There's no further communication.*)   30
Hello?
VOICE: I'm here, Zhaya, if you're ready to speak to me—
JAYA: (*Warily.*) Who are you?
VOICE: Let's just say . . . I'm a friend.
JAYA: But I don't know you!   35
VOICE: Still—I'm a friend.

JAYA: How can you be—if we've never met?

VOICE: I've seen you. Heard your voice—

JAYA: How?

40 VOICE: Oh . . . we have our ways—

JAYA: (*Pause.*) You mean, you're a friend of Ginni's?

VOICE: A friend? Yeah. Sort of.

JAYA: You live where she lives?

VOICE: Sort of, yeah.

45 JAYA: How is she? Is she well?

VOICE: Oh—! (*Nonchalantly.*) Fine, she's fine—

JAYA: (*Gusts a laugh that sounds like tears.*)

VOICE: What's the matter?

JAYA: (*Parodying his tone.*) "Fine"! "Fine"!—

50 VOICE: I don't understand—

JAYA: —Ginni might be "fine, fine"—but what has happened
to my life?—She's taken Om, she's taken Jeetu! And where
is she? Now that she's "fine, fine"?

VOICE: Well, I was just getting around to that—

55 JAYA: (*Whispers.*) It's madness. Talking to a lighted ball. Sending eyes across the ocean—(*Indicates the sarcophagus.*) locking Ma into a trunk—it's all madness!

VOICE: Why don't I tell you my name?

JAYA: (*She shakes her head.*) It's not *natural*, any of it—

60 VOICE: Virgil. That's my name, Zhaya—

JAYA: I don't know you, I don't even know if you really exist, but here we are, talking! Pretending we're friends—

VIRGIL: Not pretending—

JAYA: I was pretending—with Ginni, I mean. Om said he
65 liked her, but what did he know about her, really? What
did any of us know? We saw only her face. When she
chose to show it to us. That's not a friend! That's not even
a human being!

VIRGIL: I can show you myself, Zhaya—

70 JAYA: I don't want to see you. I don't want to start thinking
of you as a real person, when all the time you're just a
voice in the air—

VIRGIL: Not just my face. All of me—

JAYA: (*She looks up suspiciously.*) You'll come *here*? In *person*?

75 VIRGIL: Sort of. A version of me—

JAYA: (*Shakes her head resolutely.*) No! I'm not interested in *versions*. I'm not like Jeetu—

VIRGIL: Tell you what. I'll show you what I look like. Then
you decide—

80 JAYA: No! I'll never pluck my eyes out or get into a box—

VIRGIL: Nothing like that. You'll see me here, with your own
eyes—

JAYA: How? (*Sarcastically.*) You'll send a statue with the
guards?

85 VIRGIL: Just come to the Module—no, wait. I'll move to you.

(*The* CONTACT MODULE *moves till it's within her reach. She
flinches back.*)

JAYA: This? You'll come from this?

VIRGIL: Don't worry! It can't harm you—

JAYA: (*Warily.*) No, but—

VIRGIL: It's very simple. Just do as I say. Reach under the
90 Module—that's right, hold the Module, it's not hot—
reach under it and push the, the uh lower panel, the flat
one right underneath—okay, gently push it—push it up—
you'll hear a click—

JAYA *follows these instructions, kneeling as she does so, touching the
glowing globe gingerly, squinting against the light. There is a click,
and she releases the* MODULE. *Falls back.*)

VIRGIL: Ah—okay! Good girl!

JAYA: Now—?   95

VIRGIL: Now . . . just wait . . . (*The* MODULE *grows bright again
and sinks to almost floor level.*) keep watching this space . . .
underneath . . . keep watching . . .

(JAYA *complies. A bright light issues from under the* CONTACT
MODULE. *Slowly it rises, creating a projection with the motion of its
ascent. A figure is revealed. A young man's bare legs, well-formed
. . . his shorts, bright and brassy . . . a bare torso*—JAYA *gasps. . . .*)

JAYA: . . . Jeetu!

(JEETU *stands there, smiling, his face no longer obscured by the goggles. He looks happy and healthy, but his expression is unfamiliar.
He looks like someone else. He seems to glow very slightly.*)

VIRGIL: (*The voice comes from the* CONTACT MODULE *though*   100
JEETU's *mouth moves.*) Well? What d'you say now?

JAYA: (*She wants to move forward.*) Jeetu . . . (*Her hand moves to
her mouth.*) Is it—you?

VIRGIL: Of course it's me, Zhaya!

JAYA: But . . . you're not—where's the (*She means the gog-*   105
gles.)—you can't be—no! It can't be—it *can't* be! (*To the*
CONTACT MODULE.) What have you done! It can't be him!

VOICE: (*Distressed.*) Oh! You're not happy? Don't you like the
way I look?

JAYA: What is this! What is this thing in front of me! What   110
have you done with—JEETU! (*She screams.*) JEETUUU-
UUU! What have they done to you! Where have you
gone!!

(*The figure walks forward.*)

VIRGIL: This *is* me, Zhaya—don't you recognize me? I'm
your Jittoo now—   115

JAYA: Oh! (*Doubles over, sinks to the ground, sobbing heartily.*)
What have you done, what have you done!

VIRGIL: (*The figure walks over to where* JAYA *kneels, kneels down
himself.*) I thought you'd be happy to see me!

JAYA: (*Refuses to look at him.*) How can I be happy with a   120
ghost!

VIRGIL: I'm not a ghost—

JAYA: You *can't* be who you look like!

VIRGIL: But I am—in one sense.

JAYA: (*She looks up.*) You can't be. It's all just another mad-   125
ness—

VIRGIL: Why, Zhaya? Trust your eyes—

JAYA: But *you're* not here! And *he's* . . . dead, isn't he? The one
to whom this . . . this . . . *body* belonged?

VIRGIL: (*Gazes meaningfully but with an entirely non-*JEETU *ex-*   130
pression on his face.) Depends. On how you define death.

JAYA: There's only one way to define death!

VIRGIL: (*Softly.*) Not where I live. (*Pause.*) We have some new
definitions. (*Pause.*) We speak of a body-death and a self-
death. (*Pause.*) The body you knew is . . . still alive. (*Waits.*)   135
Come! Doesn't that count for anything?

JAYA: (*Whispers.*) And . . . the self?

VIRGIL: (*Briskly.*) The self you knew is also alive.

JAYA: Huh—! Without his body?

140 VIRGIL: He was willing to sell, I was willing to buy—

JAYA: And you paid him in—(*She stops, realizing her mistake.*) But . . . it *wasn't* you! It was . . . Ginni! (*Staring at him.*) *Ginni?*

VIRGIL: What do *you* think, Zhaya?

145 JAYA: Ginni . . . Ginni . . . wasn't *real?*

VIRGIL: Ginni was . . . me.

JAYA: You?

VIRGIL: Me. Just a minute—(*A faint buzz, then the voice that issues is in* GINNI's *cloying tones.*) *Hello, Zhaya! Recognize me*

150 *now? This is what I sound like when my voice is a few decibels higher—*

JAYA: (*She leaps to her feet.*) But then . . . but then Jeetu was paid in phantoms!

VIRGIL: (*Standing as well.*) He sees what he wants to see. He

155 lives what he wants to live.

JAYA: And he has no body!

VIRGIL: He has a—casing.

JAYA: —but no body!

VIRGIL: He is happy, Zhaya. He made his choice—

160 JAYA: (*Shouting.*) I saw his choosing! With his mind bandaged in dreams!

VIRGIL: Was it any different than his life? Any worse? When he was lying on the streets—was that better?

JAYA: When he was lying in the streets at least he knew what

165 he was! He was—he was—(*She stops.*) But you don't know this—

VIRGIL: I do.

JAYA: You can't! We never told Ginni!

VIRGIL: But I know.

170 JAYA: He . . . told you?

VIRGIL: *You* told me—

JAYA: I? (*Frowns.*) Never!

VIRGIL: Always. I listened in to you, Zhaya. I heard every word said in the room—even when the Module was off,

175 it recorded—

JAYA: (*She is shocked.*) HHhhh! (*Starts to pace about in agitation.*)

VIRGIL: I know Jittoo's not Auwm and that Auwm's your husband.

JAYA: And about—about Jeetu being—

180 VIRGIL: Diseased. Yes—but he was more available than his brother. So we took him.

JAYA: And it doesn't matter! It makes no difference!

VIRGIL: Do I look unwell? Do I look disabled? (*Smiles ironically.*) There's no scalpel as keen as youth! His body healed

185 in hours.

JAYA: And you heard . . . every, every thing?

VIRGIL: Saw, too. I know about the toilet being loaned out to half the city! About the water being sold! About the food being shared! Every sneeze, every belch. And you

190 Zhaya—I knew when you bled and when you passed wind. I even saw you . . . pleasure yourself, Zhaya, lying there, alone. I even knew that.

JAYA: (*Humiliated.*) No! You must have slept—

VIRGIL: —and played it back when I awoke!

195 JAYA: And Ginni! Who is Ginni?

VIRGIL: Nothing. Nobody. A computer-animated wet-dream.

JAYA: What?

VIRGIL: There's a joke we have, back at the agency—well, it's not a great joke— 200

JAYA: What joke—

VIRGIL: "For every fish, a dish—"

JAYA: (*Shaking her head in despair.*) That's all we are to you—a game to play with—

VIRGIL: No, no—I just meant Ginni was something we 205 needed to bait the hook—

JAYA: Hook! Fish!

VIRGIL: You misunderstand—

JAYA: You would eat us if you could—(*Painful pause.*) Maybe you . . . do? 210

VIRGIL: Do I look like someone who would eat another human being?

JAYA: You look like Jeetu but . . . you're not him. (*Slowly.*) So I don't know what you look like. I don't know what you are. 215

VIRGIL: This is what I look like, now.

JAYA: How can I believe you?

VIRGIL: Zhaya, *you've* lied to me—but *I've* told you only the truth.

JAYA: No!—they said you'd be old! And sick! 220

VIRGIL: I am old and I was sick until I got into this young body—

JAYA: They said you were a man—

VIRGIL: And I am! Always have been—

JAYA: But then you *looked* like a woman! You *spoke* like a 225 woman—

VIRGIL: Without being one. Without ever saying I was one—

JAYA: You said you wanted Om!

VIRGIL: No, I didn't ask for Auwm. He came to us.

JAYA: You said you wanted a healthy body— 230

VIRGIL: Yes, Zhaya—yours!

JAYA: (*Stops dead.*) Mine! But it was *Om* who got the job . . .

VIRGIL: He's part of the job, but not the job itself. (*Pause.*) We're interested in women where I live, Zhaya. Child-bearing women. 235

JAYA: But . . .

VIRGIL: So we look for young couples, without children—

JAYA: . . . Om said he wasn't married!

VIRGIL: His polygraph showed he lied. All donors lie. They think we need singles. We let them think that. That way 240 only the very desperate apply. That suits us. We search for skin and blood matches. Auwm matched mine.

JAYA: Yet you've taken *Jeetu's* body!

VIRGIL: Jittoo is Auwm's brother. He was an even better match— 245

JAYA: —and now you say that all the while you've wanted me! (*Shakes her head.*) What can I believe? You sew a crooked seam and call it straight!

(*There is a silence while he looks at her.*)

VIRGIL: But this seam now is true. We look for young men's bodies to live in and young women's bodies in which to 250 sow their children—

JAYA: Why! Don't you have your own?

VIRGIL: We . . . lost the art of having children.

JAYA: How can that be?

VIRGIL: We began to live longer and longer. And healthier 255 each generation. And more demanding—soon there was competition between one generation and the next—old against young, parent against child. (*Shrugs.*) We older ones had the advantage of experience. We prevailed. But our victory was bitter. We secured Paradise—at the cost of birds and flowers, bees and snakes! We were determined to make our amends. So we designed this programme. In exchange for the life support we offer poorer sections of the world, we gain fresh bodies for ourselves.

JAYA: (*Incredulous.*) And it works? You live forever?

VIRGIL: Not all of us—every year there are fewer of us. We fixed the car, but not the driver! Time comes when the driver just wanders off and (*Shrugs.*) . . . merges with the statistics. I'm one of the stubborn ones! This is my fourth body in fifty years.

JAYA: Fourth!

VIRGIL: Two were not successful. My first wife ran away. The third one kept her child. I saw him but never held him. Still . . . I'm willing to keep trying.

JAYA: (*She stares at him.*) I have never been with child.

VIRGIL: I know I can fill your belly.

(*There is a silence.*)

JAYA: (*Drops her gaze. Hushed.*) No . . .

VIRGIL: You have longed for a child. Your arms cry out for that sweet burden. To hold it in your arms, cuddle and crush it with kisses —it is your destiny as a woman—

JAYA: (*Tormented.*) NO! (*Wrings her hands.*) It was never meant to be! Years ago a seer told me—my stars denied it—

VIRGIL: Yet I sanction it, now, I. With Jittoo's body—

JAYA: (*In panic.*) No! Jeetu's dead and you're—you're a stranger's phantom—

VIRGIL: I am real and warm and willing. (*Pats himself.*) This body is hot with life and heavy with desire! This body aches for you and to give you what you yearn for—

JAYA: (*Covers her head against his words but pleased in spite of herself.*) No! A married woman must not hear such words from a stranger's mouth—

VIRGIL: But this mouth is no stranger to you, Zhaya!

JAYA: (*Whispering.*) No, no!

VIRGIL: This voice is but the latest tenant in a house that you have known—

JAYA: No—no—

VIRGIL: You deny the truth that is humming in my newly commissioned veins—

JAYA: Please—ohh . . . it's sinful—sinful!

VIRGIL: (*Bending to look in her face.*)—but . . . echoed in your pulse?

JAYA: (*Covering her face.*) It's madness you're offering me—madness!

VIRGIL: Is it madness to offer you your heart's desire?

JAYA: I had stopped hoping—I had ceased to dream—

VIRGIL: But you can start again. I am here to make it possible.

JAYA: But (*Her voice softens.*) whose child would it be . . . Jeetu's? Or . . . yours?

VIRGIL: (*Smiles.*) This is Jittoo's body!

JAYA: Yes—but—

VIRGIL: It would belong to this body—it would belong to Jittoo's body—

JAYA: But—would it be Jeetu's *child*? Would it look like him? Have his voice?

VIRGIL: No-one can say for certain which parent a child will take after—It could look like you, after all, have your voice.

JAYA: (*Looking perplexed she extends a hand wonderingly towards the apparition.*) Yes—but—(*Her hand passes through it and she recoils in horror.*)

VIRGIL: Ah-ah! Can't touch!

JAYA: Then—how . . . how—?

(*There is a knocking at the door.*)

GUARD 1: (*Indistinctly from the door.*) InterPlanta Services! Request permission to make contact!

JAYA: Ah!

VIRGIL: Don't—don't be frightened! It's just the agency. I can tell them to wait, if you want—(*He discreetly touches a small device at his waistband.*)

JAYA: Wait! Wait for what!

VIRGIL: For you to decide if you want to proceed—

JAYA: I don't understand! What are you saying—

VIRGIL: The guards will make the child possible Zhaya. It's just a formality; a device—

JAYA: What device!

VIRGIL: —an implant. Something I sent for you, which they're ready to deliver. But you can take your time. About two or three days are still within your fertile cycle—

JAYA: (*Shouting.*) What are you talking about! I told you—no more madness! Either you are here or—

VIRGIL: (*Patiently.*) Zhaya—I'd love to travel to be with you—

JAYA: Then do it! You who are so powerful—you who can travel from body to body—

VIRGIL: —but the risks of travelling across the world are too great! The world you live in is too dangerous for me, Zhaya—

JAYA: (*Outraged.*) Then you *are* a phantom after all! (*She raises her hands to strike the figure, then whirls towards the* CONTACT MODULE.) An illusion come to mock me—again! Again!

(*The* CONTACT MODULE *flicks easily out of her reach.*)

VIRGIL: I'll show you what to do, step by step. It's simple and it's painless—

JAYA: No! (*Leaping futilely at the globe, as the figure of* JEETU *watches tranquilly, at a distance.*) The pain tells me I'm alive! I want the pain!

VIRGIL: Then you can have all the pain you want, Zhaya—just as you want. It can take the usual nine months if you want, with diet and exercise and medical personnel to monitor you—

JAYA: (*She leaps at the globe, roaring in frustration.*) AR-RRHHH!

VIRGIL: —and I'll be with you, all the way—

JAYA: I believed you! I trusted you! (*In one of her leaps she jumps from a slight height and comes fractionally closer to the globe.*) But it was just one more of your crooked truths!

VIRGIL: Nothing I have said is untrue. I can set it up so that we can be together—go places—anywhere you want—right inside your room—

370 JAYA: I don't want your make-believe travels! I don't want your tricking comforts! (*She has stopped jumping and is looking around for something with which to strike the* CONTACT MODULE.)

VIRGIL: Zhaya we can even be . . . intimate, too! Really. But
375 I thought you'd like to get to know me first—

JAYA: (*She starts to throw things up at the globe. Glasses, cushions, slippers, bottles, pill-boxes, gadgets.*) I don't want to know a ghost! (*The* CONTACT MODULE *moves, so her task isn't easy.*) I want real hands touching me! I want to feel a real weight
380 upon me! Hear your breath in my ear—feel my hair being pulled, sweat running in my mouth—

VIRGIL: And it's all possible—

JAYA: (*Sharply.*) No! Not without risking your skin! (*Shouting.*) Never! Do you hear me, whoever you are, wherever
385 you are? Never! Never! NEVER! (*With this, she strikes a direct hit.*) There is no closeness without risk!

(*There is a shower of sparks and a crack of electric light. Then the* CONTACT MODULE *goes dim. For a few seconds the lights in the whole room flicker, purple and blue. Then they stabilize.* JAYA *stands panting in the centre of the stage.* JEETU's *figure has vanished.*)

JAYA: (*Looking up, towards the darkened globe.*) You! Can you hear me?

(*From the door, a knocking.*)

GUARD 1: (*Through the door.*) InterPlanta Services! Request
390 permission to gain entry!

JAYA: (*To the* CONTACT MODULE.) Can you you hear me, You? I've forgotten your name—but it doesn't matter! You never bothered to say mine correctly anyway!

GUARD 1: (*Knocking.*) I repeat! Request permission to enter!
395 JAYA: (*To the* CONTACT MODULE.) Look: I'm not stupid, you know? I know you're stronger than me, you're richer than me. You'll get me in the end—I know you will. But I want you to risk your skin for me. Even though it's really Jeetu's skin—I want you to risk it. For me.
400 GUARD 1: (*Hammering at the door.*) Madam! Madam! We have an urgent message for you from your Receiver!

JAYA: Either that or—

GUARD 1: (*Sounds of mechanical activity at the door.*)—attaching external speaker—(*There is a scraping sound, a crackle.*)
405 JAYA: (*She grabs up a piece of broken glass.*)—you won't have me at all! In any sense!

GUARD 1: Speaker installed. Begin transmission . . .

VIRGIL: (*His voice is strained and crackled, but loud and clear enough that he is once more a presence in the room.*) Zhaya—
410 listen to me—*you can't hope to win this one!*

JAYA: I've discovered a new definition for winning. Winning by losing. I win if you lose.

VIRGIL: Zhaya, this is craziness—

JAYA: I'm sorry, you-whose-name-I-have-forgot—
415 VIRGIL: Virgil—

JAYA: It's your fault. If you want to play games with people, you should be careful not to push them off the board. You pushed me too far. Now there's nothing left for me to lose—
420 VIRGIL: —but your life, Zhaya! You still have your life ahead of you!

JAYA: What do I care about my life? You've shown me that it's not really mine any more. It's yours. I'm not willing to caretake *my* body for *your* sake! The only thing I have left which is still mine is my death. My death and my pride— 425

VIRGIL: Zhaya—Zhaya—pride is nothing. Pride is a poor man's fancy dress—

JAYA: And if I let you take it from me, I will be naked as well as poor! Do you think I haven't understood you by now? You'll never let me have what you have, you're only will- 430 ing to share your electronic shadows with me, your night-visions, your "virtual" touch! No, no—if the only clothes I can afford are these rags of pride then let me have those! Unlike Om—unlike Ma—and Jeetu—

VIRGIL: Zhaya—don't make me tell the guards to force the 435 door—if you want respect, then open the door yourself

JAYA: You can't see me, can you? I'm holding a piece of glass against my throat. If you force the door, you will push this glass into my throat.

VIRGIL: Zhaya—the food you take contains anti-suicide drugs. 440 You are physically *incapable* of taking your own life—

JAYA: Test the strength of your drugs. Force that door.

VIRGIL: Zhaya—please! We've got this far—I love your spirit—I really do. In these months and weeks, I have come to ad-mire you and care for you. Don't let me down now! 445

JAYA: Then risk your skin.

VIRGIL: (*Pause.*) You're being unreasonable—

JAYA: Is it unreasonable to ask one who has cheated death, to cross the oceans?

VIRGIL: Zhaya— 450

JAYA: I'm bored of this argument! Don't you understand? This game is over! Either you have to erase me and start again or . . . you must accept a new set of rules.

VIRGIL: (*Sulkily.*) This is ridiculous! This is blackmail—

JAYA: What use do I have for words like "blackmail" when I 455 hold my death in the palm of my hands?

VIRGIL: You're not so stupid as to think you can win against me, Zhaya—

JAYA: Stupid or not, if I lose my life, I win this game.

VIRGIL: You won't be alive to savour that victory— 460

JAYA: —but I'll die knowing that you, who live only to win, will have lost to a poor, weak and helpless woman. And I'll get more pleasure out of that first moment of death than I've had in my entire life so far!

VIRGIL: Zhaya, this is childish— 465

JAYA: You still can't see me?

VIRGIL: (*Pause.*) No—but I can get a camera—

JAYA: No, don't. I'll tell you what I'm doing (*Matches her actions to her words.*). I'm collecting all the pills and medicines I can find. I'm going to take the ones for staying awake, 470 until I run out of them. If I don't hear the sound of your own hand on my door before that time, I'll take my life. If the guards cause me any discomfort whatsoever—I'll take my life. If you do anything at all other than come here in person—I'll take my life! 475

VIRGIL: Zhaya—

JAYA: And in the meantime, I want you to practise saying my name correctly: It's Jaya—"j" as in "justice," "j" as in "jam"—

VIRGIL: Zhaya— 480

JAYA: I won't talk to you unless you say it right!

VIRGIL: (*Pause.*) Zh . . . Jaya. Jaya. Jaya—listen to me—

JAYA: No! You listen to me! I want to be left alone—truly
      alone. I don't want to hear any sounds, I don't want any
485   disturbances. I'm going to take my pills, watch TV, have a
      dozen baths a day, eat for three instead of one. For the first
      time in my life and maybe the last time of my life, I'm go-
      ing to enjoy myself, all by myself. I suggest you take some
      rest. You have a long journey ahead of you and it's sure to
490   be a hard one.

(*Lights dim out as* JAYA *settles down comfortably in front of the television, bolstered by cushions. She looks happy and relaxed. She
points the remote and turns the sound up loud. Rich, joyous music
fills the room.*)

FINAL CURTAIN

Vassily Sigarev

Vassily Sigarev was born in 1977 in the mining city of Verkhnaya Salda in the Ural mountains; his parents worked in the titanium mines, and when the mines closed with the collapse of the Russian economy after 1989, he—like many others in the city—scavenged and sold titanium from the mine's scraps. Although Sigarev remains a relatively elusive and private writer, in interviews he has revealed that he has pursued writing as a kind of escape from the violence of his family life: his brother was sentenced to a long prison sentence for killing a man in a barroom fight. His plays have been produced both in St. Petersburg and in Moscow, and with great success outside Russia: *Plasticine* (2002), *Black Milk* (2003), and *Ladybird* (2004).

BLACK MILK

The central incident of *Black Milk* may arise from an autobiographical moment. Sigarev has remarked that his mother had recently bought a toaster and paid for it to be delivered; the "delivery" charge exceeded the price of the toasters on sale in her town. The play takes place in the railway station somewhere in "the middle of My Boundless Motherland," and is typical of the landscape of Sigarev's post-Soviet drama: everything about the station is in disrepair, and even the ticket clerk is wearing only the lining of a Chinese leather coat against the cold. *Black Milk* stages the conflict between the new, capitalist Russia and the social consequences of the new economy here, well beyond the major urban centers. Poppet and Lyovchik are clearly "New Russians," lightly and fashionably clad, whose relation to the rest of the country is emblematized by their business: selling useless "wonder toasters" to people who have no cash to pay for them, and no use for them. The local townspeople are outraged when the "wonder toaster" they bought from Lyovchik for 200 roubles is selling in the village for 50, but that's hardly the real problem: as the Clerk notes, they have no need for toasters (there's no bread delivered anyway, and they all bake their own), and so have been merely seduced by the image of another kind of life. For while the railway station images the hopelessness of much of contemporary Russia—is the comatose man just drunk, or is he dying?—everyone is seduced by capitalism's chief product, the *image* of wealth. No one is immune from this seduction: after all, even the railway clerk thinks that she'll be on *Wheel of Fortune!* Yet while the dream of capitalism remains unfulfilled, the older socialist economy is no longer in place, no longer able to provide the services that once sustained their lives; when Mishanya returns with a gun to execute the Clerk as a "counter-revolutionary," it's clear what the real source of his desperation is: "So where are the pensions, the benefits, the funds?"

In Lyovchik's rapacious scams, *Black Milk* images the consequences of capitalism on contemporary Russian society, and particularly on the texture of social life: in the play, funerals go unplanned, drunkenness is rampant, and as Poppet notes, people have lost a sense of human value. In the cities, it's "trendy to be a bitch there . . . Trendy to hate and look down on everyone. You look at them and feel bitter inside. They look at you and feel bitter inside. Everyone joins in . . . it's like we're doomed. Little boy comes up to you on the street and asks for bread and you tell him to fuck off. Even if something inside you wants to give him a few kopeks." Indeed, it's this sense of the loss of human value that sustains the play's bleak finale. Poppet decides to remain here with her daughter, but Lyovchik has other plans. When Poppet refuses to let him take the daughter ("You'll turn her into a bitch. She'll only want clothes and money."), Lyovchik punches her, and the scene vertiginously wheels into a kind of expressionistic apocalypse, with magnified inhuman baby cries, the entire theater vibrating with the sound of the train, and the milk from Poppet's broken milk bottle oozing across the stage, turning black from the dirt and plaster falling from the ceiling. Despite the style of the play's finale, *Black Milk* recalls the dynamics of Chekhovian drama: outsiders arrive at a remote village and then depart, leaving everything changed and everything just the same as well. Here, though, Chekhov's gentle, misguided characters have been replaced by heartless mercenaries, and the possibility of change seems to lie frozen under the blanket of snow that ends the play.

BLACK MILK

Vassily Sigarev

CHARACTERS

NARRATOR
'POPPET', or SHURA, *twenty-five*
LYOVCHIK, *twenty-eight*
TICKET CLERK, *forty-five*
MISHANYA, *thirty-five*
AUNTIE PASHA LAVRENYOVA, *fifty*
PETROVNA, *seventy*
DRUNKEN MAN
CROWD, *carrying toasters*

NOTES

Russian names have been transcribed in order to give a sense of their sound and not according to official systems of transcription.

Poppet and Lyovchik first appear in Act One as MAN *and* WOMAN, *while in Act Two Pasha Lavrenyova first appears as* WOMAN.

ACT ONE

NARRATOR: Where should I start? I don't know . . . with the name of the town, maybe? Well, it's not exactly a town. Not even a largish village. Definitely not a village. In fact, it's not really even a populated place. It's a station. Just a
5　station. Somewhere in the middle of My Boundless Motherland. But when I say middle, I don't mean at the heart. Because My Boundless Motherland is a strange animal and its heart, as everyone knows, is located in its head. But enough of that. The head, I mean. We should
10　work out exactly where we are. I reckon that it's about in the region of the small of the back, the sacrum, or maybe even . . . No, no 'maybe' about it—that's where it is. That's where we are. Right in the centre of it. The epicentre. Things are all painfully out of step here . . . Things are re-
15　ally not right. In fact, so wrong that I want to scream, wail, yell, just so My Boundless Motherland will hear, 'You slut . . . You're not decent!' But would she hear? Would she understand? Stop to think about it? I don't know . . .
　　But this station is called Mokhovoye. As usual the name
20　isn't written on the board. And why should it be? None of the trains even stop here. Only the freight-passenger trains. The expresses, the private trains and all the other ones rush through without dropping their speed, and even sometimes speeding up so as not to catch an accidental
25　glimpse of anything untoward. Anything 'like that', if you know what I mean. Not even all the local trains stop here. The 6.37 and the 22.41 Eastbound and the 9.13 Westbound and that's it. That is it . . .
　　The station is a wooden building with a slate roof,
30　standing next to the railway track. It's November and cold. There is snow on the platform. There's a path through the snow leading right to the station doors. It's not as cold in there. You might even call it quite warm. Shall we go in? Warm up?
35　　We go in. looks alright, actually. Hardly a disgrace. The walls were painted not so long ago. Three years or so, no more. The paint's dark green, but that's a matter of taste, as they say . . . Enough of them, anyway . . . the walls, I mean. What else have we got here? Somewhere to sit? There is.
40　Two lots of station seats right in the middle. In one of the seats, closest to the iron stove, which is like a column, built

into the wall, there's a man asleep. His head is thrown back and his mouth is open wide. He's a little man, frail, but for all that he's clearly a bit the worse for wear. He's asleep. Let him sleep. We'll leave him be for the moment. Let's　45 have a look round to begin with. Right. Next to the stove is a pile of logs, a heap of rubbish and some papers or other. Going further, there's a word scratched into the wall (but a harmless one, thank God) and a plywood board with the timetable stencilled on it: Arrivals, departures,　50 waiting time at station (minutes). In the column 'waiting time at station' there are little number ones going all the way down. Well, that's logical—if you're not here, you've missed it. Anyway . . . what else? Hey! Left luggage lockers. Six of them. Out of order and filthy dirty. Shame . . .　55 we could have . . . then there's a metal door, a new one, unpainted. A metre from the door there's a window with a grille over it—the ticket office. A piece of paper is stuck to the window. It reads 'All gone', yet what is all gone, why and when is not clear. But it isn't our business any-　60 way. A woman is sitting behind the window. The ticket clerk. She's a nice, firm forty-five and she's wearing the lining from a Chinese leather coat and felt boots. Her face is smeared with a French (made in Poland) beauty mask. She is holding some knitting in her hands and she has an　65 expression of utter boredom in her eyes.
　　Silence.
　　Only the man gives out indistinct noises from time to time and there is the clicking of the knitting needles in the clerk's hands. But nothing else. It is as if it's a painted　70 scene and not a real one.
　　But no . . .
　　Can you hear? Some voices. They're coming closer. Closer. Still closer.
　　Who's this?　　　　　　　　　　　　　　　　　　　　　75
　　We're about to find out.

The door opens. A MAN *and a* WOMAN *appear. They are both young, sleek, lightly dressed. They are holding armfuls of checked canvas laundry bags—about three in each hand. And on top of all this the* WOMAN *is pregnant.*

WOMAN: (*City accent*) What a place. I almost went into labour. Why the hell did we get out at this hole.

MAN: (*City accent*) S'alright—we've made ourselves a tidy sum

80 WOMAN: (*Putting bags down*) How can they live here? It's a filthy pit. Ugh! Did you see what their nails are like?

MAN: (*Putting bags down*) Y'what?

WOMAN: Their nails . . . You wouldn't see that, not even in the Hermitage. Like black peoples', their nails . . . You see

85 them?

MAN: For the love of . . . No, I didn't see them.

WOMAN: (*Looking at the seat*) Do you reckon it's safe to sit down?

MAN: Why the hell not?

90 WOMAN: Might catch something. Bacteria. Gangrene. TB. (*She pats her tummy.*) Not recommended, apparently. I can't have any injections or antibiotics.

MAN: Put down some newspaper and you can sit there as long as you like.

95 WOMAN: Hey! That's an idea. Which one?

MAN: The furthest one.

The WOMAN *goes into her bag, gets out a pile of papers and spreads them out on two seats next to each other for her and the* MAN. *She sits down and sniffs.*

WOMAN: It smells of armpits in here a bit. Remember that old guy on the train?

MAN: (*Studying the timetable, indifferent*) Which one?

100 WOMAN: With a beard and that. Can't remember.

MAN: And?

WOMAN: The smell he was giving off. Jesus . . .

MAN: What?

WOMAN: I mean I took a sniff and phwoar . . . Started taking

105 every second breath . . . Thought I was going to die. Gas chamber, it was . . . What the fucking hell are we doing in this shithole? You've really done . . .

MAN: We've not done badly out of this, alright.

WOMAN: What's that mean?

110 MAN: Not bad.

WOMAN: Is it a fucking secret?

MAN: Would shifting five bags suit you?

WOMAN: Fucking hell. Not bad.

MAN: Well then.

Silence.

115 WOMAN: Shit, it stinks of armpits in here. What a nuisance. Fuck.

She gets out a bottle of perfume and without looking sprays all around herself. Her hand lands on the DRUNKEN MAN's *open mouth. She looks—her eyes almost fall out of her head—she screeches, jumps up and runs outside.*

MAN: What's wrong with you, Poppet? (*Looks at the man.*) What the . . . What are you doing here? (*Goes over.*) Oi! . . . you still alive? (*He nudges the old man with is foot.*)

120 What you going around scaring people for? Eh! Do you want a toaster? It's free. Hey, have you snuffed it? Eh, you going to take this toaster or what?

POPPET: (*Opening the door a crack and looking in carefully*) Lyovchik, who is it?

125 LYOVCHIK: Some old bloke.

POPPET: Is he dead?

LYOVCHIK: Pissed.

POPPET: What?

LYOVCHIK: Pissed.

POPPET: Old git! Almost gave birth 'cause of him. He's settled 130 in nicely, hasn't he?

LYOVCHIK: Weren't you looking?

POPPET: No, I wasn't looking. I only sat down. It's not like I haven't got things to worry about, without having to look out for shit everywhere. What's he doing here anyway? 135

LYOVCHIK: Sleeping, isn't he.

POPPET: He can go home and sleep.

LYOVCHIK: Tell him then.

POPPET: You tell him yourself. Like I need it. He bit me as well, the bastard! 140

LYOVCHIK: What with?

POPPET: His mouth.

LYOVCHIK: He hasn't got any teeth. And never had, I reckon.

POPPET: What do you mean?

LYOVCHIK: Just that. Have a look. 145

POPPET: You serious? (*She approaches.*)

LYOVCHIK: Have a look, go on.

POPPET: (*Holds her nose and looks in the man's mouth*). He hasn't! Where are they?

LYOVCHIK: Drunk his way through them. 150

POPPET: No. Really?

LYOVCHIK: He's probably got some disease . . .

POPPET: Yuk! I could catch something! (*She wipes her hand with a handkerchief.*)

LYOVCHIK: Forget it. It's already taken hold. 155

POPPET: What?

LYOVCHIK: Soon your teeth will start falling out and all.

POPPET: Oh, piss off, you stupid git. (*Turns away.*) What the fuck are we doing in this hole? This is a right pain in the arse. 160

LYOVCHIK: (*Creeps up behind her and jabs her in the small of the back with his index finger*) Ahhh!

POPPET: (*Jumps and squeals*) Have you fucking lost your mind! I could go into labour right now . . . And you see what sort of baby I'll give you: a spastic . . . a clown . . . 165

LYOVCHIK: Hey, Poppet . . . I didn't mean it . . . it was only . . . y'know . . . a sign of love . . .

POPPET: A sign of love . . . You're that fucking idiot from Dostoyevsky, you are. (*Pause.*) Go and get the tickets and we can get out of here. This place is winding me up. Give me 170 a fag.

LYOVCHIK: (*Gets out the packet*) Is smoking allowed here, do you reckon?

POPPET: It is for pregnant women. (*Takes a cigarette. Lights up and smokes with affected elegance.*) Will you stop standing 175 around like a Jewish mountaineer in the plains of Mongolia and go and get the fucking tickets.

LYOVCHIK: Are you in a strop then, Poppet?

POPPET: That's right.

LYOVCHIK: You've got a spot by your nose, Poppet. 180

POPPET: Very funny. Don't wet yourself laughing . . . Where? (*She gets out a little mirror and looks in it.*) It's all these infections round here—I've caught something. Where?

LYOVCHIK: Joke.

POPPET: Piss off, you useless bastard, I've had it up to here 185 with you.

LYOVCHIK: What you getting so uptight about?

POPPET: Nothing.

LYOVCHIK: Well that's alright then.

190 POPPET: Yeah.

LYOVCHIK: Yeah.

POPPET: That's alright then. (*She sits down on the windowsill and turns towards the window, smoking.*)

LYOVCHIK *stands there a bit longer and then goes over to the ticket window. The* CLERK *doesn't look at him.*

LYOVCHIK: Madam . . . (*The* CLERK *doesn't answer.*) Excuse me,
195   madam . . .

CLERK: What d'you want?

LYOVCHIK: Unit Trading, the leaders in the Russian household appliances market, have chosen you to be the lucky recipient of a super-prize . . .

200 CLERK: (*Jumps up, rubbing the mask off her face*) Bugger off!

LYOVCHIK: (*Not even faltering*). I don't think you've understood me, madam. Unit Trading, leaders in the Russian household appliances market, have chosen you to be the recipient of a super-prize, an invaluable kitchen helpmate—the wonder
205   toaster from Kanzai, a leading manufacturer of household goods and audio and video equipment.

CLERK: Bugger off . . .

LYOVCHIK: This wonder toaster has the following amazing advantages: the body of the toaster is made of high-density
210   ecological super-plastic, making it super-long lasting and unbreakable. The wonder toaster's element is made from a unique super-combination of nickel and chrome, allowing you to save between three and six times the electricity. This wonder toaster is simple to use, needs no servicing
215   and has a super contemporary design. It will save you valuable time, make you super-toast, giving you an energy burst lasting the whole day, and will generally become your best friend and a member of your family. If you are interested in this offer and you are not yet the proud
220   owner of a wonder toaster, Unit Trading will give you this one as a present. And if you aren't interested in the offer for some reason, or you already have your own wonder toaster, we suggest you order a catalogue from our company. Our internet address is www.ru.

Pause.

225 CLERK: You finished pouring out your soul? Go on then, sod off.

LYOVCHIK: You've got me wrong, madam.

CLERK: For a start, I'm not a madam. Miss.

LYOVCHIK: You've got me wrong, miss.

230 CLERK: And for a second start, I'm a trader myself with a bit of experience and your patter won't work on me. Understand?

POPPET: Lyovchik, you tell her to piss off. She's taking liberties.

235 CLERK: (*Sticks head out of window*) You can keep quiet, you silly little cow. And if you're going to smoke go outside. Smoking away in here . . .

POPPET: (*Without looking at the* CLERK) Get lost.

CLERK: What?

240 POPPET: You heard. Take a long walk to . . . Macau.

CLERK: (*Mishears*) Who did you call a cow, you little prat?

POPPET: I'm looking at her.

LYOVCHIK: So miss, are you interested in our offer?

CLERK: Move away from the window, you prat. You're stopping me working. 245

LYOVCHIK: What a shame you've chosen not to take the unique opportunity of becoming the proud owner of a wonder toaster.

CLERK: Get on with you. I've already got a couple.

LYOVCHIK: (*Leaves the window and goes across to* POPPET) What 250 you doing, frightening off the customers?

POPPET: What customers? That old battleaxe? She'll sell it back to you and buy it for a cut-down price . . . I want a Chupa.

LYOVCHIK: You can want all you like. 255

POPPET: Oh, fuck off. (*Pause.*) Have you got one then?

LYOVCHIK: I've got everything.

POPPET: Then give me one.

LYOVCHIK: Pretty please.

POPPET: Oh, piss off. (*Pause.*) Why you being such a tight bas- 260 tard?

LYOVCHIK: There you go. (*Gets out a Chupa Chups lolly.*) Stuff yourself.

POPPET: (*Grabs the Chupa Chups, unwraps it and sticks it in her mouth*) You get stuffed. Let's get out of here. It's winding 265 me up here. Bloody fleapit. Nowhere to get pissed.

LYOVCHIK: What you mean, nowhere? Bloke over there's had a few and he isn't getting in anyone's way.

POPPET: What are you suggesting? I should do the same?

LYOVCHIK: Well? You were the one who brought the bump 270 along into battle.

POPPET: Piss off. They're probably knocking back the local homemade potato-brew round here.

CLERK: (*Sticking head out of the window*) No home-brew here!

LYOVCHIK: Oh, miss! Miss, have you had a think about be- 275 coming a proud owner of the wonder toaster?

CLERK: Well, go on then, show us what you've got and I'll have a look.

LYOVCHIK: (*Reaching into bag*) It's said you shouldn't look a gift horse in the mouth. 280

CLERK: Round here we look first.

LYOVCHIK: Who's we?

CLERK: We in the trade.

LYOVCHIK: Ooh. Nice. And what do you trade, if it's not a secret? 285

CLERK: It's a secret.

LYOVCHIK: State secret, is that? (*Gets out a toaster in its box.*)

CLERK: Nearly. (*She disappears back into the hatch.*)

Sound of a bolt sliding back. The iron door opens and the CLERK 290 *comes out into the hall.*

Go on then, show us what you've got.

LYOVCHIK: (*Gets out the toaster and shows it to her*) Invaluable 295 kitchen helpmate, wonder toaster from Kanzai, the leading manufacturers of household appliances and also audio and video equipment.

CLERK: (*Looking the toaster up and down with a skeptical glance*) You telling fibs to an old woman? This is what you cook 300 bread in. My cousin has one of these.

POPPET: That's exactly what it is.

CLERK: Who asked you? Come on, give it here. (*She takes the toaster and turns it around, looking at it.*) Made in China?

305 LYOVCHIK: Come off it, miss. This is made in Malaysia.

CLERK: What are you on about? I can see it's made in China. You haven't got any winter boots?

LYOVCHIK: 'Fraid not.

CLERK: Shame. I'd have taken the boots. I'm in these felt
310 ones. No gloves?

LYOVCHIK: Only toasters.

CLERK: I'd have taken the gloves, too. But only kid gloves. 'Cause I had some, but I left them on the train. I'm not local myself, see. I just work here. I come over on the
315 train. Been doing it for two years. I've just learnt how to make vodka. I brew it up at home and then bring it down here to sell. Quite good quality actually. Keeps the locals happy. No one's been poisoned yet. Touch wood. Course, the useless bastards drink like it's going out of fashion. The
320 demand, as they say, is outrunning the supply. Where do they put it all? But I mean if you think about it, what else is there to do round here? No cinema, no TVs . . . They can't get good reception round here—'cause it's in a dip. So they drink. And that's a good thing. I've come into a
325 little bit of money at last. Bought myself a divider, an un-polished one. Unpolished is all the rage now. Walnut coloured. Not bad. Bit special. What else did I buy? Two coats from the Chinese and the Turks and a fridge. With one of those . . . what's it called . . . with two doors. There
330 was something else. Oh yeah, I had some decorating done. I'm not going to leave here now for anything. I'll work right through to my pension. And I'll keep going then, if they let me. Just now I need a downright fortune—Got to marry off my daughter. My daughter's called Varka, Var-
335 vara. Like Yakubovich's girl. I like the look of him, my goodness, that Yakubovich. Ooh, I could really go for him . . . (*Whispers.*) I'll tell you a secret—I'm going to be on that game show 'Wheel of Fortune'. That's between us, right . . . anyway Varka's my daughter and I need to get her
340 married off straightaway, she's twenty-five already and never been under a bloke. Horror to look at. Unbelievably ugly. And the main thing is she's getting uglier all the time. Spots everywhere. About seventy on each cheek. Obvious why she's got them. Not sexually mature . . . They'll go as
345 soon as she starts living a full life. But to get her started, I need some money. To hook some bloke or other. And then I'll have to slip him more to keep him there. So I'll be here until I'm pensioned off. Still, a cosy spot for it.

LYOVCHIK: Well you need the toaster then. You make him
350 toast every morning and he'll never leave.

CLERK: Just the thing. How much are you asking?

LYOVCHIK: Absolutely free of charge.

CLERK: You're having me on. Free. You can't even use the toilet for free anymore.

355 LYOVCHIK: Absolutely free of charge. You just pay delivery.

CLERK: How much?

LYOVCHIK: A mere two hundred roubles.

CLERK: What?! Did it travel in a separate compartment? Hundred and fifty.

360 LYOVCHIK: Two hundred, lady. A gift horse . . .

CLERK: We look it in the mouth round here. Hundred and fifty.

LYOVCHIK: Two hundred. For delivery.

CLERK: Hundred and seventy. That's my limit.

POPPET: Come on—that thing cost five hundred. 365

CLERK: Who asked you. Hundred and seventy. 'Cause it's made in China.

LYOVCHIK: Malaysia.

CLERK: China. Can't fool me. Hundred and eighty.

LYOVCHIK: Malaysia. It's yours. 370

CLERK: For a hundred and seventy.

LYOVCHIK: Hundred and eighty.

CLERK: But we agreed on a hundred and seventy, didn't we?

LYOVCHIK: No we didn't.

CLERK: Did. 375

LYOVCHIK: Didn't. Go on. Take it?

CLERK: Hundred and seventy?

LYOVCHIK: Hundred and seventy. A hundred and seventy.

CLERK: Yes! I love bargaining with men, oooh I do. When I go on this 'Wheel of Fortune', if I get a prize out of them, 380 well I'll do some bargaining then. Whole country will re-member, the bargaining I'll do. Being a trader is a calling, not a job to me. I'm the trader of traders, I am. Don't need to tell you—just look at how my business has grown. The sign there, that means that I'm out of vodka. There's one 385 of my usuals snoring over there. Look at him and my heart is content. You must be kidding, I wouldn't leave this place for anything. I'll leave here in a box and that's the only way. A cosy corner. As long as they don't all die on me. 'Cause recently they've been dropping like overbred dogs. 390 Dying out, once and for all. I won't have any customers soon. I've got competition now as well.

LYOVCHIK: Serious?

CLERK: Small fry. Old woman passing off her home-brew as the stuff. Early days still, but if I decide to expand the busi- 395 ness or she does, well we could have a conflict on our hands.

The door squeaks. They fall silent and look at the entrance. The door opens a crack and an old woman's head in a knitted scarf appears.

Oh! Talk of the devil. What do you want, Petrovna? What you doing on someone else's patch?

PETROVNA: (*Comes in and stands by the door. She is holding a* 400 *toaster and a bottle of home-brew vodka*). I'm . . . I'm here for them . . . I'm here to see you, my loves.

CLERK: What do you want from them? They're not going to swig your home-brew. Go on—out of here.

PETROVNA: I'm here to see you, my dears. (*She walks over* 405 *slowly.*)

LYOVCHIK: What's up, love?

PETROVNA: My old man's dead, son . . .

CLERK: Ooh, liar. What old man is that, Petrovna? He was killed back in the war. 410

PETROVNA: My old man is dead, son. I've got nothing to bury him with.

LYOVCHIK: What's that got to do with me, dear? I'm not the social services, you know.

PETROVNA: You take this thing back and the money, mine, 415 which I . . .

LYOVCHIK: What's wrong with you—banged your head, dearie? Had one too many?

CLERK: He's got a point, Petrovna.

420 LYOVCHIK: What money?

PETROVNA: Mine, which I . . .

LYOVCHIK: We haven't got your money, love. Go on. Go home. (*He turns away.*)

PETROVNA *stands there and doesn't move.*

POPPET: Go on then, old girl.

425 PETROVNA: My old man's dead, love. Got to bury him.

POPPET: Go on then, bury him.

LYOVCHIK: Or he'll go off.

PETROVNA: Wouldn't mind my money. And this is for you . . . (*She offers them the toaster.*) And this is, too. (*She shows them the bottle of vodka.*) A little gift, eh, love?

430

CLERK: What you hounding them for, Petrovna?

PETROVNA: But my old man's dead, after all . . .

CLERK: What old man? You haven't got one.

PETROVNA: I did have. And now he's died. He's lying out on the table in my room. My new old man.

435

CLERK: Lured someone into bed, did you?

PETROVNA: He turned up himself. Said he could help out. Helped out three days and then died.

CLERK: Whose old man was he?

440 PETROVNA: Mine.

CLERK: And before you, whose was he?

PETROVNA: No one's. He walked the world.

CLERK: A tramp or something?

PETROVNA: No. He was called Aleksei.

445 CLERK: And his surname?

PETROVNA: He couldn't remember.

CLERK: Well, Petrovna, you take the biscuit. Of all the odd things to do in your old age . . . And what do you want from them?

450 PETROVNA: My money. And I'll give this back to them.

CLERK: Well it's nothing to do with me. You work it out between yourselves. (*She goes over to the stove and starts throwing in firewood.*)

Silence.

PETROVNA: (*Looking at* LYOVCHIK) So what do you think, love?

LYOVCHIK: What do you want?

455 PETROVNA: I've got nothing to bury him with, eh.

LYOVCHIK: What's that got to do with me? Don't bury him then, if you haven't got the money. Take him out behind the fence and leave him there. Say you don't know who he is. What am I telling you for, anyway. You're a sensible

460 woman. You've been around.

PETROVNA: I couldn't do that, son—it would be a sin.

LYOVCHIK: One more, one less. God will forgive you.

Pause.

PETROVNA: So how about it, love? I've got nothing at all to bury him with. Take this, why don't you. And the little gift

465 here. And my money, which I . . .

POPPET: Lyovchik, send her packing, will you . . . she's driving me up the wall.

LYOVCHIK: What you being so difficult for? I won't take anything off you. You probably broke it, carrying it

470 around.

PETROVNA: I haven't used it. Cross myself, I haven't used it. (*She crosses herself.*)

LYOVCHIK: That's enough, dear. Go on. Dismissed. Get off home.

PETROVNA: How can I, son, when I've got to bury the old 475 man.

POPPET: Lyovchik, spell it out to her in four-letter words. I mean, come on . . . she's getting right up my nose.

LYOVCHIK: Did you hear that, love? They want me to send 480 you packing. With four-letter words. Shall I go ahead, or are you going to go quietly now?

The old woman stands there without moving or answering. Her eyes fill with tears. Suddenly she gets down on her knees.

PETROVNA: Don't ruin me, loves. He was a kind old man. Always pleased to see people. A wanderer. Suffered. Three times he had frostbite in his legs, and now he's dead. Ly- 485 ing on my table and we haven't washed him yet. Waiting to be buried. And will he last? Well, that's for you to decide. How you decide, that's how it'll be. And God will reward you later. He will multiply your wealth. Multiply it by ten three times, and then three times by ten. And the 490 same for your children and all your family for fifteen generations to come.

LYOVCHIK: Y' what? (*To* POPPET.) What's with her?

POPPET: Off her rocker, isn't she.

CLERK: She's a bit daft.

495

LYOVCHIK: Perhaps we should give her the money.

POPPET: Do what you like.

PETROVNA: Give it back, love, give it back.

LYOVCHIK: Alright. (*Reaches into his money belt to get out the money.*) Listen sunshine, if God doesn't multiply my wealth 500 by ten three times and then three times by ten, I'll come back and set fire to your hut.

PETROVNA: He'll multiply it by ten. By this cross, he will.

At this point the door is flung open and a procession of people begins to move into the hall slowly: men and women holding toasters. At the front is a strange-looking man with a goatee. The old woman jumps up off her knees and hides the bottle in her blouse.

VOICE IN THE CROWD: Hey, look! Petrovna's here already. Amazing—How did you manage that, Petrovna? 505

PETROVNA: (*Looking at them from under her brow*) None of your business.

ANOTHER VOICE: Your bloke is pissed again, Petrovna. He's built a bonfire in the yard and he's jumping around it.

PETROVNA: Let him. Nothing to do with you. 510

CLERK: Petrovna! Well! She's a liar, what a liar! Brilliant. We should learn from her..

General laughter. Suddenly everyone goes quiet and they look at each other.
Pause.

POPPET: Lyovchik, did you buy the tickets?

LYOVCHIK: Er . . . not yet. (*To the* CLERK.) Miss, what's-yer-name, sell us some tickets, if you wouldn't mind. 515

CLERK: Where you going?

FIRST WOMAN: (*Nudges the man with the goatee*) Mishanya, go on . . .

MISHANYA: (*Goes horribly pale*) Ahem . . . comrade visitors . . .

FIRST MAN: Mishka, don't be pathetic . . . 520

MISHANYA: (*A bit less pale*) Please don't rush off, comrade visitors . . .

LYOVCHIK: How about those tickets then, miss?

CLERK: I just asked. Where are you going?

525 MISHANYA: (*Less pale still and even slightly flushed*) I am talking to you, comrade visitors.

CLERK: They want you, I reckon.

LYOVCHIK: (*Turning around suddenly*) Me? You talking to me? (*Advances on* MISHANYA.) Hey, you talking to me?

530 MISHANYA: (*Paling again*). You.

LYOVCHIK: Out with it then. What do you want? (*Pause.*) What's wrong? You forgotten? Off you go then. (*He turns to the* CLERK.) What you got coming up?

CLERK: Stopping service at 06.37.

535 LYOVCHIK: (*Looking at his watch*) Anything before that?

CLERK: Nothing.

POPPET: What a hole. Give us a fag, Lyovchik.

LYOVCHIK: Hang on, fuck it.

POPPET: Tight bastard.

540 LYOVCHIK: I said, hang on. (*To the* CLERK.) No trains then?

CLERK: Uh-huh.

LYOVCHIK: Why's the service so shit?

MISHANYA: Sir, could I just once more . . .

CLERK: For you again.

545 POPPET: Give us a fag, Lyovchik, go on . . .

LYOVCHIK: (*Gets out the packet and throws it to* POPPET) For fuck's sake . . . here!

POPPET: Arsehole. (*Shakes out a cigarette and puts the packet in her pocket.*) I'll keep them on me then.

550 MISHANYA: Excuse me, may I have a word?

POPPET: What you going on at him for? Can't you see he's having a conversation?

MISHANYA: I just wanted . . . erm . . . well . . .

POPPET: He told you to hop it. That means cut the crap and leave the premises. Go on. Go on.

555

Pause.

Lyovchik, you tell him, eh! You've got a way with words.

LYOVCHIK: So what you come to discuss then? I don't un . . .

MISHANYA: Well . . . it's a serious thing.

LYOVCHIK: What, exactly?

560 MISHANYA: I've come for justice.

LYOVCHIK: Right. Well now you're here, you'd better take it. Where is it? Not this? (*He points at the sleeping man.*)

POPPET: (*Laughing*) Oh Lyovchik, you're a funny bastard.

Everyone laughs except MISHANYA *and sleeping 'justice'.*

CLERK: So Mishanya, you been floored? Humour from the 565 big city, eh? You'll be more careful in future.

FIRST WOMAN: Mishanya, get back at him . . .

FIRST MAN: Mishka, give them some brainy stuff.

SECOND MAN: Don't be pathetic, that's the main thing.

SECOND WOMAN: Look at him, he's finished.

570 MISHANYA: (*Reddening*) It's not me they're insulting, ladies and gentlemen. It's you they're insulting. All of you. One and all . . . And you just stand there. You've got nothing to say. It's a crying shame.

FIRST WOMAN: What d'you mean? We've got something to 575 say. You've cheated us! There.

POPPET: What?

FIRST WOMAN: You cheated us.

POPPET: (*Advances on the woman*) Say that again, sweetheart.

FIRST WOMAN: (*More subdued*) You've cheated us.

POPPET: Oh yeah?! Lyovchik, did you hear that? Did you all 580 hear? Is that an official statement then? Are you making an official statement?

FIRST WOMAN: You what?

POPPET: This is what. You've insulted the honour and worth of our company with your words. You've compromised its 585 prestige. We will be forced to demand compensation in the courts. Do you get me?

CLERK: Hey. That's serious. It'll be the bailiffs in next.

FIRST WOMAN: (*Paling*) Well, I . . . it wasn't me . . .

POPPET: Who was it then? (*To the* FIRST MAN.) Was it you? 590

FIRST MAN: What's it got to do with me all of a sudden? (*Hides toaster behind back.*) Actually I just came round to get vodka. Have you got any, Auntie Lusya?

CLERK: It's all gone.

POPPET: (*To the* SECOND MAN) You in the cap, was it you then? 595

The SECOND MAN *dives into the crowd.*

Go on then. That's it. Meeting over. Back to your houses.

THIRD MAN: Got to sort this out first.

POPPET: Sort what out, darling?

THIRD MAN: We've been told that this costs fifty roubles at the market in the town.

POPPET: Have you seen them there?   600

THIRD MAN: No, but Mishka did.

LYOVCHIK: So what? You got them for free. So be pleased.

MISHANYA: Don't cheat us—you took money from all of us.

LYOVCHIK: Drop it, eh. Anyone got complaints about the 605 quality? No. Excellent. Congratulations once again on becoming the proud owner of this kitchen helpmate, the wonder toaster from Kanzai. Right. Bye then. (*He sits down, gets out a Chupa Chups, unwraps it and puts it in his mouth.*)   610

POPPET: Lyovchik, I want one, too. (*She sits down next to him.*)

LYOVCHIK: I've already given you one.

POPPET: When? Don't lie, you bastard. You gave me a cigarette.

LYOVCHIK: And a Chupa.   615

POPPET: No you never. Come on, stop being a Jew.

LYOVCHIK: There you go. Just stop going on.

During this exchange the people in the crowd wave their arms, sigh and leave one by one. MISHANYA *tries to stop them. He talks. No one listens to him. They all leave. Then* MISHANYA *leaves as well. Only* PETROVNA *is left.*

CLERK: Bloody hell, they got themselves enough of your toasting machines. What in the world do they want with them. They don't even deliver bread round here. They all 620 bake their own rolls. Honestly, the idiots. I almost feel sorry for them. Thrown away nearly half their salary on something they can't use. Now they're going to go hungry. And they've all got kids—about half a dozen each. Breeding away 'cause they're too nice or too stupid not to. 625 Maybe they thought the state would help out. And what does the state do for them? Sod all. And then there's . . . (*Signs.*) Live to regret it, you coming here.

LYOVCHIK: We didn't do badly here.

630 CLERK: Don't doubt it for a minute. Only they won't trust you again. 'Cause they always thought that (*Makes an indistinct gesture with her hand.*) up there its all famous actors, poets and playwrights . . .

POPPET: Hey, don't go on. It's not like there's a shortage of
635 provincial holes like this, each one with its own charms.

CLERK: Not that many, after all.

POPPET: Enough for our lifetime.

CLERK: Well, you know best, I suppose.

LYOVCHIK: Do you need the toaster?

640 CLERK: What for? Sooner or later one of them will exchange theirs for a bottle. They'll admire them for a month and then start finding them homes around the place. Anyway, I'm turning in. You not going home, Petrovna?

PETROVNA: I'm here . . . to see them.

645 CLERK: Well, do your business then . . . (*She goes back to her room.*) Come up just before the train and I'll do your tickets. (*She leaves.*)

PETROVNA: What about me, love?

LYOVCHIK: What about you?

650 PETROVNA: My old man did die.

LYOVCHIK: What, seriously?

PETROVNA: By this cross (*Crosses herself.*)

LYOVCHIK: Go and take a long walk.

PETROVNA: I took one the other day.

655 LYOVCHIK: Take another one.

POPPET: To the Hermitage.

PETROVNA: Where, love?

POPPET: The Hermitage.

PETROVNA: And what's there?

660 POPPET: The Hermitage (*She bursts into laughter and looks at* LYOVCHIK. *He isn't laughing.*) Go on, go home, eh. It's late.

PETROVNA: But what about my old man?

LYOVCHIK: That's enough, alright? Enough. You'll be dead and all soon, so why go round ruining it for everyone else?

665 PETROVNA: (*Staggers back*) Dead . . .

LYOVCHIK: Dead, yeah. What difference do these two hundred roubles make to you? You're hardly going to live to enjoy them . . .

PETROVNA: You're . . . I'm off then.

670 LYOVCHIK: High time.

PETROVNA: Thank you, kind people. (*She puts the toaster on the floor.*) This is for you . . . I'm off . . . (*She starts to leave, then turns around and gets out a bottle from her bosom and places it next to the toaster.*) This is for you, too. To think of me
675 by . . . I'm off then . . . (*She leaves.*)

POPPET: What was all that for?

LYOVCHIK: Like I care. Put it in the bag.

POPPET: Why have I got to?

LYOVCHIK: Is it difficult or something?

680 POPPET: Yeah, it is. My bump gets in the way.

LYOVCHIK: You and your effing bump really get on my wick. (*He picks up the toaster and puts it in his bag.*)

POPPET: You get to me. You get right on my tits.

LYOVCHIK: Piss off.

685 POPPET: Piss off yourself. Prick with an arse for a head.

LYOVCHIK: Shut the fuck up, you four-legged sponger.

POPPET: Bastard. You got competition.

LYOVCHIK: And you think you haven't. You've got serious competition.

POPPET: (*Flushing*) Fuck off, you prick! Understand? (*Throws* 690 *her Chupa at him.*) Wanker! (*She bursts into tears.*)

LYOVCHIK: You have a cry—won't make the competition any less.

POPPET: Get out, I said! (*Stands up.*) Or I'm leaving.

LYOVCHIK: Shit, sit down. (*He sits her down.*) There she goes. 695 When we get home, you can run off where you please.

POPPET: I'll do that!

LYOVCHIK: You do it.

POPPET: I will!

The old drunk wakes up suddenly. He gets up and looks at them.

DRUNK: What's going on? 700

POPPET: (*Crying*) Nothing.

DRUNK: Someone died?

LYOVCHIK: Go back to sleep. No one's died.

DRUNK: Then you should be rejoicing. But you're . . . (*He sits down again, closes his eyes and mutters.*) If no one's 705 died you should be rejoicing. And when someone dies, then . . . 'Cause after all, life winds this way and that and it doesn't matter much which way, if someone dies . . . But people have some strange ideas . . . they're only scared of THAT SORT of death . . . and THAT SORT . . . that's 710 nothing, that's not scary. You're gone and that's it. You gotta worry about the other sort of death. That's scary, now. 'Cause that's when your spirit dies . . . And your spirit is . . . . well, that's something.

He is silent.

A train rushes through the station. There is a roaring, a clattering and everything shakes.

Silence.

LYOVCHIK *sits down next to* POPPET *and cautiously wipes away her tears with a finger.*

POPPET: When did she say the train was? 715

LYOVCHIK: A while yet.

POPPET: Give us a fag.

LYOVCHIK: (*Reaches into his pocket*) You've got them.

POPPET: Shit, I'm knackered. Like after Turkey. My back's killing me. 720

LYOVCHIK: It's alright. We've shifted almost five bags.

POPPET: Still got to give birth, haven't I?

LYOVCHIK: You'll be fine. It's only having a baby.

POPPET: Yeah. It's scary. (*She rests her head on* LYOVCHIK's *shoulder.*) Let's get some sleep, eh? 725

LYOVCHIK: Good idea.

They close their eyes. Pause.

POPPET: Lyovchik, were you winding me up about his teeth falling out 'cause of a disease?

LYOVCHIK: Why?

POPPET: Just, my teeth feel a bit wobbly. 730

LYOVCHIK: I was winding you up, wasn't I?

POPPET: It's in my mind then.

LYOVCHIK: Go to sleep, eh.

POPPET: You go to sleep. (*She opens her eyes.*) Fucking issuing
735   orders. And I threw away my Chupa 'cause of you. You're
always on my back. And those nerve cells . . . they never
come back, you know. Use them all up and we'll be like
dummies in shop windows . . . we won't give a fuck. Already I . . .
740 LYOVCHIK: I said, go to sleep.
POPPET: I'm starving. My tummy's rumbling. Can you hear it?
LYOVCHIK: (*Shifting crossly*) Fuck's sake. You're driving me
mad. Have something to eat. Who's stopping you? There's
some sandwiches in the bag.
745 POPPET: Can't be bothered to get up.
LYOVCHIK: That's your problem.
POPPET: You could get them for your pregnant wife.
LYOVCHIK: And who'd get them for me.
POPPET: You're a real git, you are.
750 LYOVCHIK: I know.
POPPET: And I'm going to give birth to another one. I can see
it now. I'll get sick all of a sudden and you'll be off straight
away. I know your lot, you bastard. Better to die now.
LYOVCHIK: (*Jumps up*) For fuck's sake, cut it out! I'm sick to
755   death of it! Just as I drop off she fucking gets going . . .
Once more and you'll get a black eye, alright?
POPPET: You wouldn't.
LYOVCHIK: I would. (*Moves further away from her, sits down and
closes his eyes.*)
760 POPPET: Off you go then. Better without you, anyway. (*She
looks around and sees the bottle of vodka.*) I'm going to get
fucking wasted, I am. Understand?

LYOVCHIK *doesn't reply.*

You'll have to drag me off when I've finished.
LYOVCHIK: (*Mutters*) Get on with it . . .
765 POPPET: You going to leave me here then?

LYOVCHIK *is silent.*

Right. I'm going to start drinking.

Pause.

Have we got a glass?

Pause.

Bastard.

She gets up to pick up the bottle.

*Suddenly the building is rocked by a tremendous blow. The door is
flung open.* LYOVCHIK *jumps up from his seat.* MISHANYA *staggers
in. He is disgustingly drunk. There is white at the corners of his
mouth and he is carrying a double-barrelled gun.*

CLERK'S VOICE: Have you lost your mind!!! Totally . . .
770 MISHANYA: I'll blow you all apart!!! Bastards!!! (*He points the
gun at* LYOVCHIK. LYOVCHIK *crouches down behind a seat.*)
Now you're scared! (*He moves the barrel so it is pointing at*
POPPET. *She pales and narrows her eyes, but doesn't move.*)
Hide, you whore! I'll blow you apart!!
775 CLERK: (*Sticking head out of window*) Mikhailo, what's going on?
MISHANYA: Ahh. You destroyed this country, eh? Bastard!
CLERK: Leave off, Mishka, what you doing?
MISHANYA: (*Aiming at her*) Answer, when Comrade Yezhov
speaks to you!

CLERK: Mishka, you've had a bit too much to drink, that's all.   780
You're confused. It happens. It's me—Auntie Lusya.
MISHANYA: Ahhh! You! You're the one I want. Bloody well
caused the genocide of the Russian people!
CLERK: By accident, Mishenka.
MISHANYA: No. It was deliberate. Ordered by the West, their   785
Secret Services. I know everything, Pani Kaplan . . . Who
shot at Lenin, eh?
CLERK: That's enough, Mishka . . .
MISHANYA: Talk! I want their names, addresses, codewords . . .
who destroyed the army? Talk!   790
CLERK: Me, probably, I . . .
MISHANYA: Correct. So where are the pensions, the benefits,
the funds? You stole them?!
CLERK: Right . . .
MISHANYA: I want bank details, account numbers . . . I'll   795
count to three and shoot . . . Talk! One . . .
CLERK: You know what? You can go to hell!
MISHANYA: . . . two . . . talk, you counter-revolutionary!
CLERK: I'll give you counter-revolutionary in the face, I will.
MISHANYA: . . . Three.   800

He presses the trigger. There is a shot. POPPET *shrieks and crouches
down.* LYOVCHIK *lies there, as if stuck to the floor.* MISHANYA *stands
there, rocking and enveloped in smoke. The gun lies at his feet. The*
CLERK *disappears. There is a second of silence, two, three seconds and
then fifteen. At last the bolt is drawn back on the iron door. The*
CLERK *charges out alive and well, although only wearing one boot—
the other is in her hand.*

CLERK: You've done it now, you waster! You blasted hitman,
you! (*She runs over to* MISHANYA *and beats him around the
head with her boot.*) I'll give you shooting with a gun, I will.
I'll give it to you till your barrel comes loose, I will.
MISHANYA: (*Covers his head with his hands.*) It did it by itself,   805
Auntie Lusya.
CLERK: I'll give you 'did it by itself'! I'll give you 'by itself'
till you can't sit down for a month. (*She grabs him by the
hair, bends him over and thrashes him on the buttocks with the
boot.*)   810
MISHANYA: I won't do it again Auntie Lusya . . . I'm
sorry . . .
CLERK: I can't hear anything—your popgun deafened me.
(*Carries on beating him.*)
MISHANYA: (*Shouts*) Ow! That hurts Auntie Lusya! Ow, Aun-   815
tie Lusya! Ouch!!! Auntie Lusya! (*He starts howling.*)
CLERK: (*Lets him go*) Get out of here!
MISHANYA: (*Stumbles, howling*) Thank you . . .
CLERK: Take your rifle, you stupid fool.
MISHANYA: Oh. (*He bends down to pick up the gun.*)   820

The CLERK *brings the boot down on his back with all her strength.*
MISHANYA *starts to screech loudly, eccentrically and rushes towards
the door.*

CLERK: Stop there!

MISHANYA *stops dead.*

Who got you drunk?
MISHANYA: C-c-can't remember.
CLERK: Tell Fedya if he gives you the gun once more he
won't see it again. Is that clear?   825

MISHANYA: Yes.

CLERK: Run along then.

MISHANYA *runs off.*

What an idiot. (*She puts on the boot.*) His brother's another strange one. What the hell's he doing, giving him a gun? Good thing he loads him up with blanks, at least. God knows what would happen if he made a mistake. That would be it. He could get into real trouble. Horrible to think about. We'd all be in for it then. You were wetting yourselves I bet, eh . . .

830

LYOVCHIK: (*Brushing himself down*) S'pose . . .

835

CLERK: How about you, girl?

POPPET *doesn't answer. She is crouching on the edge of the bench, holding her stomach with both hands.*

Course, you've got a little'un as well. Shouldn't get stressed. I remember, when I was pregnant with Varka, I was living with a right lad. Criminal type, covered in bloody tattoos he was. He was chasing after me. Oh, he was. When he was sober he was fairly quiet, wanted to settle down he kept saying, tired of roaming . . . but a bit of the hard stuff and he went off his head. Once he shouts out he wants some fun and pokes me with a knife, just here. (*She points.*) Not a real deep cut, of course—just a scratch. But all the same it was horrible. And I was really young then, as well. Didn't see them coming, as they say. I was really scared of him after that. And now I wonder if Varka isn't so ugly because all that deformed her. All that 'ecoli-gy' business was alright back then. Course, she was hideous as a kid. I used to be embarrassed going to the children's hospital with her. Little babies are supposed to be all cute, and there she was looking like a piglet. God above, she looked like a piglet. And even now I'm not sure who she takes after. There isn't an animal like her on the planet, probably.

840

845

850

855

LYOVCHIK: He lost his marbles, has he?

CLERK: Who? My fellow?

LYOVCHIK: No. The bloke just now.

CLERK: Well, who the hell knows. He seems harmless enough. Sells the Communist paper on the local trains. Stands around with a banner at the demonstrations . . . 'Proletarians of the World Unite . . .' Seen it myself. But as soon as he's had a few he starts acting up. He doesn't drink on his own, but he will if someone gives him a few. It's the second time that the useless sod has shot at me. First time was when I started selling vodka. He arrives first. Sober. Well that's it. He starts agitating to get me to shut up shop. Keeps me standing around while he gives a lecture. He got to me so much in the end that I gave him a blasting and threw him out. So what does the bastard do? Gets tanked up somewhere, takes his brother's gun and pokes it through the ticket window and gives it to me from two barrels. I was desperate for the toilet when it happened and so I shat myself. (*She laughs.*) I thought that was it and he'd killed me. Auntie Lusya Litvinenko is dead. I didn't know then that Fedya always loads it with blanks for him. He shot at Petrovna once. As an anti-social element or something. She had her head screwed on though and took his popgun off him, and then she made Fedya pay a ransom. Yeah . . . Maybe I shouldn't have slapped him. Hope I haven't disturbed things.

860

865

870

875

880

LYOVCHIK: He needs help.

CLERK: Who needs the hassle? Who's going to bother, eh? If he puts a hole in someone, then they will. But otherwise . . . (*She looks at* POPPET.) You've gone pale, love. Are you alright? Not feeling too good, eh?

885

POPPET *shakes her head.*

Mind yourself then. I've got some salts you can have.

POPPET: You don't . . . Do you know? It's all wet down there . . .

CLERK: What?

890

POPPET: All wet down there . . .

CLERK: (*Comes over*) Let's have a look . . .

POPPET: (*Presses her legs together*) What for?

CLERK: Come on then . . . What you being like a little schoolgirl for? You're a grown woman. (*She looks.*) It's your waters, love.

895

POPPET: Y'what?

CLERK: Your waters have broken.

POPPET: What for?

CLERK: Well. Going to have a baby, aren't you?

900

POPPET: I don't want to. We've got more stuff to sell. I don't want to . . .

CLERK: Well no one asked you. You're giving birth and that's it.

LYOVCHIK: But how come? It's too early.

905

CLERK: How many months?

POPPET: Eight.

CLERK: That's it then. Why did you decide to come to the middle of nowhere just when you were due?

LYOVCHIK: But people have babies after nine months . . .

910

CLERK: Who told you that?

LYOVCHIK: That's how it's always been. Says in books.

CLERK: Things are written on fences and all . . . You look like intelligent people and you go round believing what you read in books. Well, look at you two! So what are we going to do with you? A nice mess. People give birth at nine months . . . It's not like getting a passport. You give birth when you're ready to.

915

LYOVCHIK: Is the hospital far away?

POPPET: (*Stands up*) I'm not giving birth here.

920

CLERK: (*Sits her back down*) Sit down, girl. What sort of bloody hospital do you expect around here? Never even remotely been one. There was a first aid post once. But that went. But never ever a hospital. Around here people get on with it. At home. That's where they give birth and fall ill and end their days.

925

LYOVCHIK: How come?

CLERK: Like that. Simple. When you get back to your capital you can tell them how people live in Russia, 'cause they don't even have the faintest idea. Even if God was supposed to knock us out equal, we're only equal on the outside. Two arms, two legs and a head with a body. Every other way we're different. We're so different that it's frightening. Right. What are we going to do? And they want a hospital . . . probably holding out for a private room as well. We'll have to make do. One of the men round here burnt himself really badly on the stove and his wife took him into town on the stopping train. He's sitting on the train and his skin's falling off him in great big bits. Passengers were going mad. Anyway the police decide to investigate at the station. Out

930

935

940

with your papers, and all that. Course they didn't have anything with them—they hadn't exactly packed for the journey . . . So they took them in, started with the questions,
phone calls. And this bloke, he hung on and hung on and
945 then he went and died. Didn't even manage to tell them
what he thought of them properly. So there you are. And
you want hospitals on a plate. Arab sheiks or something, are
you? Had it too good, you have.
    POPPET: Lyovchik, tell her to eff off, will you?
950 CLERK: I'll tell you to eff off in a minute.
    POPPET: Lyovchik . . .
    CLERK: Keep your mouth shut!
    POPPET: Shut yours, you old bitch!
    CLERK: You say that again, eh . . .
955 POPPET: Lyovchik, let's get out of here . . .
    CLERK: I'll give you 'get out' in a minute. I'm just about ready
to take off my boot and give you a hiding like I did Mishanya. Then you'll 'get out of here' . . . You remember, I'm
running around worrying about you. But I couldn't give
960 a damn about your sort, it's the child I'm worried about.
It's not to blame is it? Even if its parents are miserable
shits.
    POPPET: (*Eyes filling with tears*) Lyovchik, tell her to go to . . .
    LYOVCHIK: Where?
965 POPPET: Anywhere . . . use the c-word . . .
    LYOVCHIK: You fucking do it. You're really winding me up.
    POPPET: Bastard. Don't you start as well.
    LYOVCHIK: Go to . . . (*He moves away and sits down next to the
man. He rubs his face.*)
970 CLERK: Right. I'm off. I'll go and see Pashka Lavrenyova.
She's got five kids. An old hand. She'll take you. Look after the office, will you. (*She goes.*) Bloody hell! Hospitals,
indeed . . . private room with a telly . . . (*She goes out.*)

Silence.

    POPPET: Give us a fag.
975 LYOVCHIK: You've got them.
    POPPET: Where? (*She rifles through her pockets.*) Which pocket?
    LYOVCHIK: How should I know, I'm not a mind reader.
    POPPET: You're a bastard. That's what you are. (*She gets out a
cigarette and tries to light it but fails.*) Help me light up.
980
    LYOVCHIK *gets up unwillingly and goes over to her and lights the
cigarette. She takes his hand in a conciliatory way.*

    What's wrong with you then?
    LYOVCHIK: (*Still angry, but softening*) What you mean?
    POPPET: Being like that.
    LYOVCHIK: Like what?
    POPPET: Like that.
985 LYOVCHIK: (*Takes back his hand*) Fucking good place to decide
to have a baby.
    POPPET: Like I did it on purpose . . .
    LYOVCHIK: (*Mocking her*). 'Like I did it on purpose.' Couldn't
you hang on or anything? Two more bloody days . . .
990 POPPET: Alright I won't then . . .
    LYOVCHIK: Don't.
    POPPET: Right. I won't. (*She gets up and throws away her ciga-
rette.*) Let's go. (*She lifts the bags.*)
    LYOVCHIK: Put them down.

    POPPET: Right. I'm off. This place is pissing me off.   995
    LYOVCHIK: I said, put them down.
    POPPET: Let's go!
    LYOVCHIK: (*Grabbing a bag*) Put them down . . . don't you get
it?
    POPPET: Let's go!   1000
    LYOVCHIK: Why are you being so bloody difficult. Sit down!
    POPPET: Get off me! I'm going!
    LYOVCHIK: Will you fucking well sit down! You're driving me
mad!
    POPPET: Get off me, you bastard! (*She tears away the bag.*) Get   1005
off me, I said! Get off! Get off, you prick! I hate you, you
bastard! I hate you! (*She throws the bags across the hall.*) Fuck
off, you cunt! Get the fuck off! Fuck off! (*She slaps him
across the face.*) Fuck off . . . (*She sits down on the floor and
starts weeping.*) I wish you'd die . . . I wouldn't even bury   1010
you, you animal. Do you understand? You'll just lie there
rotting . . . and the flies'll eat you . . . Shit on you . . . You
won't even see your bastard child . . . I'll throw it under a
train . . . myself . . . get it? D'you understand?

    LYOVCHIK *doesn't reply.*

    Get it? I said, d'you understand me? Do you? WELL, DO   1015
YOU? DO YOU? DO YOU?

*While she is talking the sound of an approaching train grows louder.
It comes closer and closer, roars louder and louder.* POPPET *shrieks
and shrieks . . . The train comes closer and closer . . . At last everything is combined into a horrible metallic gnashing, as if rusty cogs
the size of the universe were turning. The old drunk wakes up and
gets up from his place. He looks at* POPPET *and* LYOVCHIK *with an
understanding glance. He has tears in his eyes. The tears roll down
his cheeks and fall on the floor. And keep on falling . . .*

End of Act One.

ACT TWO

*Ten days have passed. It is early morning. The same station. The
same benches, the same left-luggage lockers, the same pyramid of firewood by the stove. Everything is exactly as before. The only things
that are missing are the drunk and the sign reading 'All gone'. Instead there is a board reading 'Closed temporarily' and the ticket
window has a heavy greasy blind pulled over it.*

LYOVCHIK, POPPET *and a woman, aged around fifty, enter the room.*
LYOVCHIK *pushes in a pram. The pram is antediluvian and well-
used.* POPPET *is not made-up. She has black rings under her eyes.
She is holding a half-empty checked bag. The woman is also holding
a bag.*

    LYOVCHIK: (*Looks at his watch*) Plenty of time. Almost another
whole hour. (*To* POPPET.) Are you allowed to sit down?
    WOMAN: Yes she is.

POPPET *nods.*

    Sit down, Shura.

The woman puts her bag down next to her.

    Milk. Mind you don't break the jar. I wrapped it in a   5
towel. But still . . . If something happened . . . Why don't I
wait with you . . .

POPPET: There's no need, Auntie Pasha. You go on.

AUNTIE PASHA: Well you know best.

10 LYOVCHIK: Who's the milk for? Don't you feed with these? (*He points at his chest.*)

POPPET: She won't feed from me. 'Cause I smoked . . . it's bitter, isn't it.

LYOVCHIK: Unbelievable. Has an effect, does it?

15 AUNTIE PASHA: And what did you think?

LYOVCHIK: (*Rocking the pram*) We didn't think at all . . .

AUNTIE PASHA: The nappies are all in there. Don't bother drying them out, Shura. Throw them away. They're old anyway. And when you get there you can buy some. Have
20 you forgotten anything? (*She rifles through the bag. Pause.*) Looks like you've got it all. I put some food in for you. Don't forget it or it'll go off.

POPPET: You shouldn't have. We could have bought some.

AUNTIE PASHA: Whatever next! Wasting your money. You'll be
25 needing every penny soon. Kids don't seem to eat much, but the money you'll get through—just count it and it's gone. I've brought up five myself, thank the Lord, and I know.

LYOVCHIK: No need to go and frighten us.

30 AUNTIE PASHA: Frighten you . . . I'm just telling it like it is. They're not goats, kids—you can't just send them off to graze. You need a lot of time and energy for them. Sometimes you think to yourself, what did I do that for, sometimes you stop loving them . . . when you've had it. But
35 then it all passes, passes quickly and you'll be happy again. That's how it is. (*Pause.*) Well, Shura, let's say goodbye then.

POPPET: Yeah.

AUNTIE PASHA: By the way . . . make sure that the bubbles
40 don't fill the teat when you're feeding. She'll start playing up. And for now don't wash her when she messes. Wet some cotton wool and clean her with that. Do they boil water on the train?

POPPET: (*Nods.*) Uh-huh.

45 AUNTIE PASHA: Good. That's the best. Remember to test it with your hand and wipe it dry.

POPPET: Right.

Pause.

AUNTIE PASHA: Not forgotten anything then. (*She reaches into the bag.*)
50 POPPET: You checked, Auntie Pasha.

AUNTIE PASHA: Did I? Never mind, I'll check again. (*She rummages in the bag. Pause.*) Everything's there. I didn't put in the goat's milk. She hasn't taken to it. The smell, I expect. This is cow's milk. It's a good cow, don't worry about it.
55 The main thing is not to smash the jar. Then you'd have problems. If something happens get a packet of milk at one of the stations. And just ask the attendant to boil it up for you . . . I should have put it in a tin. Maybe I've got time to run back? I should make it, I think . . .

60 POPPET: No need, Auntie Pasha.

AUNTIE PASHA: Well, I s'pose we should say goodbye then.

POPPET: Mmm.

AUNTIE PASHA: When you get back, maybe you'll drop me a line, so I don't worry, eh? We're hardly strangers now.

POPPET: Mmm. 65

LYOVCHIK: We'll send a telegram.

AUNTIE PASHA: Letter would be better. Warmer, somehow. And cheaper. And write what you decide to call her.

POPPET: OK, Auntie Pasha.

AUNTIE PASHA: Perhaps you'll invite me to the christening, if 70 you decide to christen her.

LYOVCHIK: Course we will. And we'll buy you a ticket.

AUNTIE PASHA: I'd find a way myself, for something like that.

Pause.

So, what now? Oh yes, Shurochka, I wanted to say as well, you should express so you don't lose it. 'Cause maybe 75 she'll take to it, who knows? Alright?

POPPET: Mmm.

AUNTIE PASHA: Well, that's it then, Shura . . . don't hold it against me that I shouted at you when I was doing the birth. Now I understand you were the way you were be- 80 cause you were new to it—but then I thought you were just trying it on. I thought you'd kill the kid with your trying it on. You were pushing her in and out like a lollipop. I was really worried. I've had five myself and helped out with as many, but I still can't get rid of the nerves. 85 Maybe I'll never get used to it. Like death. Doesn't matter how many you see, it's still the same . . . So, Shura, don't hold it against me, alright?

POPPET: I've forgotten it already, Auntie Pasha.

AUNTIE PASHA: You're kidding. Lusya and I swore at you so 90 much that I'm still embarrassed, even now. Where did it all come from? Probably in our blood, all those bad words. Well, never mind. (*She looks at* LYOVCHIK.) Takes after her Daddy, she does.

LYOVCHIK: What, really? (*He looks into the pram.*) You must be 95 able to tell . . . I can't see anything yet.

AUNTIE PASHA: She does, oh, she does.

LYOVCHIK: Well, you would know.

Pause.

AUNTIE PASHA: Well then Shura, good luck to you. Have a good journey. Look after your daughter. See how it's 100 turned out: born here and she'll live there. And not where she was born . . . You bring her back at some point, eh? Show her her birthplace. And don't forget us. We'll always be pleased to hear from you. (*She wipes away a tear.*) I'm old, I am, and I don't want to leave you. I've got used to 105 you. You've become like my own. Like my daughter and my granddaughter. In a minute I'll get on that train with you . . . Off you go then, take her. After all . . . well, that's enough . . . I'll be off . . . or I'll start crying properly. Goodbye Shura, my girl. (*She bends over and hug and kisses* 110 POPPET.)

POPPET: Bye bye, Auntie Pasha . . .

AUNTIE PASHA: Right . . . enough . . . I'm off.

POPPET: Auntie Pash . . .

AUNTIE PASHA: What? What do you want, Shura? 115

POPPET: No, nothing . . .

AUNTIE PASHA: Oh, I thought you said . . . right, I'm off. (*She goes over to* LYOVCHIK *and shakes his hand.*)

LYOVCHIK: How much do I owe you?

120 AUNTIE PASHA: What?

LYOVCHIK: (*Reaches into his money belt for money*) How much did you spend on her?

AUNTIE PASHA: (*Recoils*) Whatever next.

LYOVCHIK: No, really.

125 AUNTIE PASHA: Do you think I . . . Goodbye. (*She goes towards the door.*) You might move her over here as it's a bit close. Get some fresh air . . .

POPPET: Alright, Auntie Pasha.

AUNTIE PASHA *leaves.*

LYOVCHIK: (*Pushes the pram to the door and then goes over to*
130   POPPET, *laughing*) Chatty old lady.

POPPET: She's only coming up to fifty.

LYOVCHIK: Just lady then. Didn't she go on, though . . . Took her time leaving. Thought nothing would get rid of her. I can just imagine what you went through, ten days at hers.
135   Felt like shooting yourself probably.

POPPET: It was alright.

LYOVCHIK: Yeah, right. I would have killed myself.

POPPET: Well, I wouldn't.

LYOVCHIK: You're making it up. D'you know what I bought
140   you?

POPPET: What?

LYOVCHIK: (*Gets out a green packet*) Fags.

POPPET: I'm not allowed to.

LYOVCHIK: Why? She said you wouldn't be able to feed, any-
145   way.

POPPET: Maybe I will be able to. Later.

LYOVCHIK: Fuck it, eh. Let it drink cow's milk—what's the difference?

POPPET: A big difference.

150 LYOVCHIK: Well be like that then. I'm not going to force you, am I? (*Puts the packet away.*)

Pause.

Fancy a Chupa?

POPPET: No.

LYOVCHIK: Why?

155 POPPET: I just don't want one.

LYOVCHIK: Go on, take it.

POPPET: I said I didn't want one.

LYOVCHIK: What you being like that for?

POPPET: Like what?

160 LYOVCHIK: All like that . . .

POPPET: Like what?

LYOVCHIK: I don't know. All uptight or something.

POPPET. I'm not . . .

LYOVCHIK: Like you've become a mother and so straightaway
165   you're throwing your weight around. Because actually I've become a father, too—so I could start all that as well.

POPPET: I'm not throwing my weight around.

LYOVCHIK: (*Gets out a Chupa Chups*) Take the Chupa then.

POPPET: I don't want it.

170 LYOVCHIK: Well don't ask later. (*Unwraps the Chupa and sticks it in his mouth.*)

Silence.

LYOVCHIK *goes over to the ticket window and looks in.*

Where's what's-her-name? The brewer. Isn't it her shift or something?

POPPET: It's hers.

LYOVCHIK: Why isn't she here then?   175

POPPET: She's quit.

LYOVCHIK: Yeah, right. She wanted to sit it out till her pension here.

POPPET: Didn't work out.   180

LYOVCHIK: Why not?

POPPET: Someone got poisoned by her vodka.

LYOVCHIK: What? Completely?

POPPET: Completely.

LYOVCHIK: Fuck. Him, was it? The Commie with the gun?

POPPET: No.   185

LYOVCHIK: Who then? (*Pause.*) Where's that guy . . . Who was asleep . . . the one who bit you?

POPPET: He was the one who got poisoned.

LYOVCHIK: Unbelievable. Really? D'you know where I got rid of the rest of the goods?   190

POPPET: She buried him herself. Paid for it all.

LYOVCHIK: Good thing. That way no one ends up in jail . . . bought herself off. I reckon she'd have had to buy off the relatives as well.

POPPET: He didn't have any. They were all dead.   195

LYOVCHIK: She was lucky then. Hey, guess what—while you were here I went and got a new batch of stuff.

POPPET: He left a house here.

LYOVCHIK: . . . And guess what . . . Erm, so what?

POPPET: We could buy it. It'd be cheap.   200

LYOVCHIK: What the hell for?

POPPET: Well . . .

LYOVCHIK: What do you mean, 'well'?

POPPET: Well.

LYOVCHIK: Buy ourselves a little place in Magadan as well.   205
Just in case, like. Own real estate right across the country.

POPPET: There's a sawmill here. We could renovate it . . .

LYOVCHIK: What is wrong with you, Poppet?

POPPET: What?

LYOVCHIK: Are you alright in the head? You gone funny . . .   210
The things you come out with . . . Awful. I reckon you've lost it a bit. Have you?

POPPET: No.

LYOVCHIK: Watch yourself then. Have a smoke. (*He gets out the packet.*)   215

POPPET: I don't want to.

LYOVCHIK: For fuck's sake, take it. You're winding me up with this not smoking. I can see you want to.

POPPET: I don't.

LYOVCHIK: You do. (*He gets out a cigarette and sticks it in her*   220
mouth.)

POPPET *doesn't resist.* LYOVCHIK *puts it between her lips and lights it.*

Take a drag, go on. It's not lighting, fuck it. Have a drag . . .

POPPET: (*Spits out the cigarette*) I said I don't want it.

LYOVCHIK: Alright, keep your hair on . . .

POPPET: Honestly I don't want it, love.   225

LYOVCHIK: OK, OK, I'm not forcing you . . . Anyway, they took the lot. Like, when I left here, yeah, I got out at some place, worse than this, imagine . . . But more peo-ple there and even a school. So anyway I went along to this school and told them I could do a presentation there. Slipped the headteacher a hundred. All hunky-dory. Loads of people came along and they took the lot off me. So I got back on the train and went off for an-other lot. A bit less this time, 'course. You weren't with me, were you. So not bad, eh. I was happy. Covered the ticket price straightaway. You get a great audience around these places. Wow. What an audience. God, they're like kids. The money you can make around here, it's unbelievable. Just keep hauling it in . . . keep it com-ing . . . Collect it up . . . Making money . . . Hey, did that old bloke really snuff it?
POPPET: What?
LYOVCHIK: I said, was that bloke really poisoned?
POPPET: Mmm.
LYOVCHIK: Maybe he died naturally. Maybe his time was up.
POPPET: Poisoned. The spirit was bad.
LYOVCHIK: Fuck, I'm sorry for the old girl. Lost her business.
POPPET: She wanted to hang herself.
LYOVCHIK: Come on . . .
POPPET: It's true. She hanged herself right here. It was almost over. They cut her down and she survived. Afterwards she kept on howling. Kept saying there's no point in living. I came over myself to talk her out of it.
LYOVCHIK: You?
POPPET: Me.
LYOVCHIK: Well, Poppet, I can see you've been . . . enjoying yourself. So what did you say to her?
POPPET: Lots.
LYOVCHIK: Like what?
POPPET: Can't remember right now.
LYOVCHIK: Oh, come on. You remember. What did you say to her?
POPPET: I can't remember.
LYOVCHIK: Don't lie. I know what you said. (*He declaims.*) We are given but one life and we should live it so that after-wards we are not tormented by the aimlessly wasted years. Is that what you said?
POPPET: I can't remember.
LYOVCHIK: Poppet, you've gone out of your mind, I reckon . . . Christ . . . We'll have to take you along to the loony bin. The way you're talking. It isn't healthy.
POPPET: Nothing wrong with it.
LYOVCHIK: Well I can tell you how it looks from here. Any-way, we'll get back and take you for treatment. At the 'Three Fishermen' . . . will you come? We can have a ball all night. Back to civilisation.
POPPET: And what about here?
LYOVCHIK: What you on about?
POPPET: I told her that it was never too late to change your life.
LYOVCHIK: (*Not understanding*) Told who? That's enough of that crap, Poppet. It's scary talking to you. Hey, lets talk about the higher things in life, eh? D'you know how much money we've got?
POPPET: No.
LYOVCHIK: Three guesses.

POPPET: I don't know.
LYOVCHIK: Well name a figure. It's not hard.
POPPET: Hundred roubles.
LYOVCHIK: Oh come on . . . you're really pissing me off now. (*Walks around the room.*) Seven thousand dollars. Happy now?
POPPET: Happy.
LYOVCHIK: There you go, eh. And we'll make more. A load. A whole load. Fuck it, ten whole loads.
POPPET: What for?
LYOVCHIK: Eh?
POPPET: What for?
LYOVCHIK: (*Stops*) Have you got it in your head to really piss me off?
POPPET: No.
LYOVCHIK: Well sit still and shut up then.
POPPET: Alright.
LYOVCHIK: What do you mean, alright? What are you being so touchy about? I don't get it.
POPPET: I'm not . . .
LYOVCHIK: (*Mocking her*) I'm not . . . Well I am. What don't you like, eh? That I went traveling round all these holes like royalty while you were . . .
POPPET: Don't shout, you'll wake her.
LYOVCHIK: I'm not shouting. I won't wake her. Just don't get all funny with me, please. 'Cause two can play at that. I'll get so funny, that you'll fucking well end up staying here. Shit, sitting there, not interested in anything, doesn't want a Chupa, doesn't want a smoke . . . So what do you want, eh? Shall I get my arse out for you?
POPPET: Fuck off.
LYOVCHIK: (*Starts smiling*) Hey. Now I recognise you. Come on then, say something about the Hermitage . . .
POPPET: (*Also smiling, but trying to hide it. Biting her lower lip*) Well, the Hermitage . . .
LYOVCHIK: (*Suddenly roars with laugher*) Fuck, Poppet . . . Fuck it . . . you should have seen yourself just then . . . Face like the back end of a bus! (*He bends double laughing.*)
POPPET: Fuck off!
LYOVCHIK: . . . back end of a bus! (*Roars.*)
POPPET: Piss off.

Pause.

LYOVCHIK: (*Stops laughing*) Want a Chupa?
POPPET: Alright then.
LYOVCHIK: Orange flavour?
POPPET: Whatever.
LYOVCHIK: Have an orange one.
POPPET: Alright.
LYOVCHIK: (*Gets out the Chupa and unwraps it*) And that . . . chatty lady you lived with . . . did she have one of our toasters?
POPPET: Yeah.
LYOVCHIK: And?
POPPET: She has it standing out.
LYOVCHIK: Just standing there?
POPPET: Yeah.
LYOVCHIK: Right.
POPPET: She thought you bake bread in it. She stuck some dough in it and the element burnt out.

345 LYOVCHIK: Fucking aborigines. Gotta get back home. (*He looks at his watch.*) We'll get the post train as far as Chelyabinsk and then fuck it, we'll get a separate compartment. I hate those open carriages. Really gets on my tits—faces, faces, faces everywhere. Each one stupider than

350 the next. Have a Chupa. (*He gives her a Chupa Chups.*)

POPPET *take sit and holds it in her hand.* LYOVCHIK *looks in the pram.*

Why didn't you tell me we needed to buy a pram? This is a nightmare. What a total embarrassment it'll be on the train. It's a tank. Tramps push their bottles around in prams like this. Where did it come from?

355 POPPET: Auntie Pasha got it from someone.
LYOVCHIK: Probably got syphilis living in it.
POPPET: We washed it.
LYOVCHIK: What's the point. Alright. I'll get out at one of the long stops and try and buy one.

360 POPPET: Lyova, love . . .
LYOVCHIK: What?
POPPET: I probably . . .

At this moment the baby starts crying. LYOVCHIK *goes over to the pram.*

LYOVCHIK: What d'you do?
POPPET: Rock it.

365 LYOVCHIK: D'you have to sing?
POPPET: No.

LYOVCHIK *rocks the pram. The baby stops crying.*

LYOVCHIK: Is that all?
POPPET: Expect so.
LYOVCHIK: (*Leaves the pram and goes over to* POPPET) What were

370 you saying, I didn't understand?

POPPET *doesn't answer. She looks at the floor.*

Hey . . .
POPPET: Lyova, love, I don't think I'm going to go . . .
LYOVCHIK: What?

Pause.

POPPET: I don't want to go back there.

375 LYOVCHIK: I don't get it. Say that again.
POPPET: (*Louder*) I'm not going.
LYOVCHIK: You off your head or something?
POPPET: Maybe.
LYOVCHIK: Come off it. Stop going on like that.

380 POPPET: I'm not going on. I'm just not leaving, that's all . . .
LYOVCHIK: Stop it, eh? What did I do?
POPPET: It's not you. I'm just tired, Lyov.
LYOVCHIK: What you tired of? Lugging the bags around? Counting money? What are you tired of?

385 POPPET: Tired of being a bitch.
LYOVCHIK: Of being what?
POPPET: (*Gets up*) A bitch. One of many. 'Cause it's trendy to be a bitch there . . . Trendy to hate and look down on everyone. You look at them and feel bitter inside. They

390 look at you and feel bitter inside. Everyone joins in . . . it's like we're doomed. Little boy comes up to you on the street and asks for bread and you tell him to fuck off. Even

if something inside you wants to give him a few kopecks. But you tell him to fuck off. 'Cause no one else gives him any money, so why should you. Why should you, eh . . . 395 So you tell him to fuck off. And then you make it up in your head that he earns more than you do . . . When he doesn't really earn anything at all . . .
LYOVCHIK: What little boy, what you . . .
POPPET: I don't want to be like that anymore. I want to be 400 like a real person . . . like Auntie Pasha. Like them. That's how I want to be. You can be like shit to them, and they'll still be kind to you. And they'll even apologise for not giving you enough. That's how I want to be. And how I want my daughter to be. So I don't have to think 405 what a bitch I am. So I don't have that pain. Do you understand that?
LYOVCHIK: Stop screaming, you nut.
POPPET: (*Quieter*) I'm not screaming. 410
LYOVCHIK: You are.
POPPET: I'm not screaming. But the main thing is that you see it all. You see that you're not living right. But you still carry on living like that. And then you even start enjoying it, and you get a kick from it, from being a bitch. And at 415 that point your soul dies.
LYOVCHIK: And your arse? Does that die, too?
POPPET: Stop it.
LYOVCHIK: No you stop it. So you've seen the fucking light, have you? Found higher meaning? 420
POPPET: I have.
LYOVCHIK: You've just had it too good, you have. You want to stay here? Help yourself. Be my guest. Off you go. Go and live with the cows. Howl at the moon. You think there'll be tears, eh? Go to hell. No one will be shedding tears. 425 No one needs you. You stay here. Let's see how you get on here. After ten days you reckon you're one of them. Yeah right. Enjoy. You'll be washing in a tub and shitting in a ditch for a month at most before you come crying . . . You think I don't know you? 430
POPPET: You don't.
LYOVCHIK: I do. I've got you down.
POPPET: No you haven't.
LYOVCHIK: Go on then. Stay. Like I care.
POPPET: And you could stay too. 435
LYOVCHIK: Me?
POPPET: You.
LYOVCHIK: You think I'm off my head, too. I don't reckon I've lost it yet.
POPPET: No I mean it.
LYOVCHIK: What do you mean, 'mean it'? You're off your 440 head.
POPPET: There's a sawmill here. I told you.
LYOVCHIK: So what?
POPPET: We could rebuild it.
LYOVCHIK: And what? Walk around singing songs? La la 445 la . . .
POPPET: We could sell the flat. And this money. That would be enough. I went and found out.
LYOVCHIK: You went and found out just like that?
POPPET: Yeah. 450
LYOVCHIK: Well then it's all arranged. I won't argue then, keep quiet.
POPPET: And the people would have work.

LYOVCHIK: Yeah, course. And wages. And meaning in their
455   lives. All hunky-dory.

POPPET: And we could live alright.

LYOVCHIK: Wow, yeah, we'd be living the life. I can't argue.
We'd build schools all over the place, circuses, fuck it,
nursery schools . . . eh?

460   POPPET: I mean it.

LYOVCHIK: You think I'm joking? I mean it too. Your idea has
inspired me.

POPPET: Lyova . . .

LYOVCHIK: What, 'Lyova'? Lyova is already planning how he's
465   going to regenerate Russia. And how they're going to put
up a monument to him for his work, made out of pure
gold. After his death.

POPPET: Stop it.

LYOVCHIK: Hey, I've just got going. And then the grateful
470   generations to come will read about Lyova—a little paragraph in their school history books. With pictures: 'Lyova
taking the first step on the road to the regeneration of
Russia: Selling his flat.' And here he is knocking the last
nail into the rebuilt sawmill . . .

475   POPPET: Stop it.

LYOVCHIK: And here he is building the largest hydro-
electric power station in the world on the local stream
of sludge . . .

POPPET: I said, stop it!

480   LYOVCHIK: Alright, that's it then. Enough. (He looks at his
watch.) The train will be here soon. Let's go out.

POPPET: I'm not going.

LYOVCHIK: Stop it now, eh? We can finish this on the train.

POPPET: There's nothing to finish. I'm not going.

485   LYOVCHIK: I said, cut it out. Enough. This will all be desert
soon. Taiga. Forest.

POPPET: It's back there that there'll be desert. Everyone killing
each other. Ripping each other apart.

LYOVCHIK: Why are you being so difficult?

490   POPPET: 'Cause I realised . . . when I was giving birth . . . and
after, when . . .

LYOVCHIK: I'll give you a smack in a minute and then you'll
realise. Come to your senses . . .

POPPET: When I gave birth . . . I saw God.

495   LYOVCHIK: No, really? And what did he look like? Have a
beard, did he?

POPPET: No.

LYOVCHIK: Wasn't him then. God's got a beard. So what happened after that?

500   POPPET: What difference does it make?

LYOVCHIK: No go on, now you've started. I love tales about
God. Me and him are old mates.

POPPET: (After a pause) At the beginning he was standing in
the corner looking at me all the time. He was whispering
505   something . . .

LYOVCHIK: Praying was he? What else he got to do?

POPPET: And then he came over. He stroked my forehead.
And kissed me . . .

LYOVCHIK: What a bastard! Kissing other men's wives, eh?
510   Fucking Casanova.

POPPET: (Starts to cry) And then I understood that he hadn't
left me. I betrayed him and abandoned him and he didn't

betray me . . . and he'll never leave me. He'll always be
with me 'Cause he never leaves anyone. Never . . .

LYOVCHIK: Amazing guy, eh.

POPPET: And I told the ticket clerk, Auntie Lusya, about him   515
and she believed me and she said she wouldn't do anything to herself. She said that she'd live. She'd live—that's
what she said. Live. And I want to live, too. LIVE, Lyova.

LYOVCHIK: Go on then, live. Am I standing in your way? Live   520
a hundred years if you like.

POPPET: You haven't understood.

LYOVCHIK: Alright. That's enough. Are you going?

POPPET: No.

LYOVCHIK: We're off then.   525

POPPET: We?

LYOVCHIK: Us. Who else? (He nods at the pram.) With her. Did
you really think I'd leave her here? No way. It's not going
to happen. I may be a bastard, but I'm not having my offspring scattered all over the place.   530

POPPET: I won't give her to you.

LYOVCHIK: What you say, darling?

POPPET: I wont' give her to you. I gave birth to her.

LYOVCHIK: Yeah. And what came before that? Think about it?

POPPET: Nothing.   535

LYOVCHIK: Come off it! Have you conveniently forgotten
how much I spent so you could have her? Eh? Remember that? How many abortions you had when you were
screwing around. Eh? That's how I remember it . . . But
now you're a fucking saint, eh? Seen the light and visions   540
of God.

POPPET: I'll give you the money back.

LYOVCHIK: Give it back then.

POPPET: I'll pay you back.

LYOVCHIK: I need it now. Come on.   545

POPPET: You've got it. My money's in there, too.

LYOVCHIK: Yeah? How much?

POPPET: I don't know.

LYOVCHIK: Yeah, well there's nothing there, 'cause you
haven't got any. You spent all yours. You think I bought   550
you all those clothes with my own money. Fuck off, kid.

POPPET: I'll give it back to you later.

LYOVCHIK: I'm not arguing am I? You pay me back and you
can take her.

POPPET: Lyova, you're joking, aren't you . . .   555

LYOVCHIK: Course I'm joking. I'm the fucking funny man.

POPPET: You're joking . . .

LYOVCHIK: Joking. Ha. Ha. So how many abortions did you
have, little girl? Don't you remember then? D'you
know, you've got a little card . . . from the clinic. And   560
there's a box on it labeled abortions. And in the box
there's a number. Do you know what it is? Double figures. That's how it is. Twelve or fifteen. Remember that?
And now you're the fucking saint. Everyone's a bitch
and she's a saint. Bugger you. You can fuck off. God   565
doesn't come to people like you. He keeps as far away
as he can. And how many blokes did you screw? You
can't remember? Hundred? Five hundred? A million?
Why is it you didn't see God each time you got laid by
one of them? Eh? And when you had your bastards fed   570
to a vacuum cleaner. Eh?

Pause.

So what'll it be? Give us the money or we're off.

POPPET: I hate you.

LYOVCHIK: It's mutual.

575 POPPET: I HATE YOU.

LYOVCHIK: I KNOW. YOU SAID.

POPPET: I hate you!

LYOVCHIK: Shut up. Let's have the money or we're off. What's it going to be? You haven't got any money. Right. Bye

580   then.

He takes the checked bag, goes over to the pram and wheels it to the door.

POPPET: Don't touch it, you bastard! (*She runs over and grabs the pram.*)

LYOVCHIK: What's fucking wrong with you? Let go!

POPPET: You said you were joking, Lyova . . .

585 LYOVCHIK: Who? Me?

POPPET: You were joking. You don't need her.

LYOVCHIK: I do.

POPPET: You'll turn her into a bitch.

LYOVCHIK: So what?

590 POPPET: She'll only want clothes and money.

LYOVCHIK: So what? Not bad. Nice. That's how I want her to be . . .

POPPET: Lyova, please!

LYOVCHIK: What's wrong, little girl?

595 POPPET: Let us go, Lyovochka.

LYOVCHIK: Pay. Everything costs money now.

POPPET: I'll give it back later.

LYOVCHIK: You going to rebuild the sawmill, yeah?

POPPET: I'll find . . .

600 LYOVCHIK: I've had about as much as I can fucking take. Get your hands off.

POPPET: I'll find . . .

LYOVCHIK: Get your hands off, you schiz!

POPPET: No I won't.

605 LYOVCHIK: (*Looks at his watch*) What are you on? The train will be here any minute.

POPPET: I'm not letting you go.

LYOVCHIK: Right, that's enough. Come over here. (*He goes over to the ticket window*). I want to say something to

610   you . . .

POPPET: (*Follows him*) I won't let you go whatever.

LYOVCHIK: OK, so you won't let us go . . . (*He stops.*)

POPPET: (*Goes up to him*) Say it then.

LYOVCHIK: Look at this (*He points to something on the wall.*)

POPPET looks. LYOVCHIK smashes her in the stomach with his fist. POPPET's face changes. She steps back, panting, then she crouches and lays down on the ground.

615 LYOVCHIK: (*Shouting, but quietly*) You've pissed me off once and for all, you bitch! Get it? I'm sick to death of your fucking trouble-making. You're a bitch from hell. You can die down there for all I care! Die! And the flies will be all over you! Eating you! And shitting on you and not on

ME! Understand? Thinks she's a fucking crystal vase! 620 Thumbelina or something! You're a slut out of the gutter! Thinks God came to her! Kissed her! He didn't kiss you, he fucked you! Fucked you in your every hole like the scum you are! Like the cheapest whore! Understand? Understand? Right. That's enough. (*He looks at his watch.*) 625 We're off. Bye then. (*He bends down and whispers almost inaudibly.*) Fuck off. Fuck off. Fuck off . . .

He goes to the door and opens it. Then he rolls out the pram and goes out.

POPPET: (*Turns over and looks at the door, crying or maybe whispering*) I hate you! I hate you! I hate you all! All of you, you Bastards! Bitches! Bastards! Disgusting bitches! You'll 630 burn in hell! In hell! You'll go to hell! You will! Bitches! You animals! Vermin! You'll burn in hell! All of you! You left him! Betrayed him! Traitors! Traitorous bastards! You'll all burn in hell! I hate you!

The baby starts crying outside. Its wails are terrifying, not like a child's crying.

POPPET *puts her hands over her ears. She sits down and shouts up at the ceiling.*

God, give me strength! Give me strength, God. Give me 635 strength, Father! I love you, Father! I love you! I love you! I love you! Give me strength. Father . . . Father . . . My Father!

The sound of the train approaching. It sounds its horn. POPPET *looks at the door for one second and then stares back at the ceiling. She shouts out.*

I hate you! You can fuck off ! Fucking well fuck off! I don't need you! I'm not your daughter! You're nothing to 640 me! I don't want you! You're the bastard! You, not me!! Understand? Do you understand!!! UNDERSTAND!!!

The train flies into the station. The sound of a horn, everything shakes and vibrates. Plaster breaks off and drops down from the ceiling. It falls in POPPET's *eyes. The bag rolls across the seat and onto the floor. There is the sound of breaking glass. White milk, as white as snow, spreads across the floor. It spreads and mixes with the dust on the floor and becomes blacker and blacker . . . blacker and blacker. At last the train stops and everything quietens. Silence.* POPPET *stands up. She wipes the plaster out of her eyes.* LYOVCHIK *runs in.*

LYOVCHIK: Well, get a fucking move on. The pram's already in the train. It's just about to leave.

POPPET: I'm coming. Can't you see, got something in my 645 eyes.

LYOVCHIK: Get a move on . . .

POPPET: I'm coming. Stop getting at me. Give us a fag.

LYOVCHIK: You can smoke on the train.

POPPET: You scrooge.   650

LYOVCHIK: Fuck's sake, there you go then. (*He gives her the packet.*)

They go out. All that is left is the black puddle on the floor. But in it the sky, and not the ceiling, is reflected. The night sky. The moon is there. The planets and stars. Lots of stars. Millions. Billions. All the universe is reflected in this puddle. And the stars are flickering in it. Shining. Alight.

And the milk is suddenly no longer black, but white. White, like milk. White, like snow.

Darkness.

The End.

CRITICAL CONTEXTS

FRANTZ FANON (1925–1961)

"The Fact of Blackness" (1952)

Frantz Fanon was perhaps the seminal theoretician of postcolonial politics, culture, and identity; his two major books, Black Skin, White Masks *(1952) and* The Wretched of the Earth *(1961), have been widely read and have provided an important inspiration for liberation movements around the world. Born in Martinique, Fanon studied medicine in Paris and became a psychiatrist in Algeria during its wars of liberation from France. "The Fact of Blackness" is Fanon's celebrated essay describing the consciousness of "black" subjects in a world of "white" power.*

"Dirty nigger!" Or simply, "Look, a Negro!"

I came into the world imbued with the will to find a meaning in things, my spirit filled with the desire to attain to the source of the world, and then I found that I was an object in the midst of other objects.

Sealed into that crushing objecthood, I turned beseechingly to others. Their attention was a liberation, running over my body suddenly abraded into nonbeing, endowing me once more with an agility that I had thought lost, and by taking me out of the world, restoring me to it. But just as I reached the other side, I stumbled, and the movements, the attitudes, the glances of the other fixed me there, in the sense in which a chemical solution is fixed by a dye. I was indignant; I demanded an explanation. Nothing happened. I burst apart. Now the fragments have been put together again by another self.

As long as the black man is among his own, he will have no occasion, except in minor internal conflicts, to experience his being through others. There is of course the moment of "being for others," of which Hegel speaks, but every ontology is made unattainable in a colonized and civilized society. It would seem that this fact has not been given sufficient attention by those who have discussed the question. In the *Weltanschauung* of a colonized people there is an impurity, a flaw that outlaws any ontological explanation. Someone may object that this is the case with every individual, but such an objection merely conceals a basic problem. Ontology—once it is finally admitted as leaving existence by the wayside—does not permit us to understand the being of the black man. For not only must the black man be black; he must be black in relation to the white man. Some critics will take it on themselves to remind us that this proposition has a converse. I say that this is false. The black man has no ontological resistance in the eyes of the white man. Overnight the Negro has been given two frames of reference within which he has had to place himself. His metaphysics, or, less pretentiously, his customs and the sources on which they were based, were wiped out because they were in conflict with a civilization that he did not know and that imposed itself on him.

The black man among his own in the twentieth century does not know at what moment his inferiority comes into being through the other. Of course I have talked about the black problem with friends, or, more rarely, with American Negroes. Together we protested, we asserted the equality of all men in the world. In the Antilles there was also that little gulf that exists among the almost-white, the mulatto, and the nigger. But I was satisfied with an intellectual understanding of these differences. It was not really dramatic. And then. . . .

And then the occasion arose when I had to meet the white man's eyes. An unfamiliar weight burdened me. The real world challenged my claims. In the white world the man of color encounters difficulties in the development of his bodily schema. Consciousness of the body is solely a negating activity. It is a third-person consciousness. The body is surrounded by an atmosphere of certain uncertainty. I know that if I want to smoke, I shall have to reach out my right arm and take the pack of cigarettes lying at the other end of the table. The matches, however, are in the drawer on the left, and I shall have to lean back slightly. And all these movements are made not out of habit but out of implicit knowledge. A slow composition of my *self* as a body in the middle of a spatial and temporal world—such seems to be the schema. It does not impose itself on me; it is, rather, a definitive structuring of the self and of the world—definitive because it creates a real dialectic between my body and the world.

For several years certain laboratories have been trying to produce a serum for "denegrification"; with all the earnestness in the world, laboratories have sterilized their test tubes, checked their scales, and embarked on researches that might make it possible for the miserable Negro to whiten himself and thus to throw off the burden of that corporeal malediction. Below the corporeal schema I had sketched a historico-racial schema. The elements that I used had been provided for me not by "residual sensations and perceptions primarily of a tactile, vestibular, kinesthetic, and visual character,"[1] but by the other, the white man, who had woven me out of a thousand details, anecdotes, stories. I thought that what I had in hand was to construct a physiological self, to balance space, to localize sensations, and here I was called on for more.

"Look, a Negro!" It was an external stimulus that flicked over me as I passed by. I made a tight smile.

"Look, a Negro!" It was true. It amused me.

"Look, a Negro!" The circle was drawing a bit tighter. I made no secret of my amusement.

"Mama, see the Negro! I'm frightened!" Frightened! Frightened! Now they were beginning to be afraid of me. I made up my mind to laugh myself to tears, but laughter had become impossible.

I could no longer laugh, because I already knew that there were legends, stories, history, and above all *historicity*, which I had learned about from Jaspers. Then, assailed at various points, the corporeal schema crumbled, its place taken by a racial epidermal schema. In the train it was no longer a question of being aware of my body in the third person but in a triple person. In the train I was given not one but two, three places. I had already stopped being amused. It was not that I was finding febrile coordinates in the world. I existed triply: I occupied space. I moved toward the other . . . and the evanescent other, hostile but not opaque, transparent, not there, disappeared. Nausea. . . .

I was responsible at the same time for my body, for my race, for my ancestors. I subjected myself to an objective examination, I discovered my blackness, my ethnic characteristics; and I was battered down by tom-toms, cannibalism, intellectual deficiency, fetishism, racial defects, slave-ships, and above all else, above all: "Sho' good eatin'."

On that day, completely dislocated, unable to be abroad with the other, the white man, who unmercifully imprisoned me, I took myself far off from my own presence, far indeed, and made myself an object. What else could it be for me but an amputation, an excision, a hemorrhage that spattered my whole body with black blood? But I did not want this revision, this thematization. All I wanted was to be a man among other men. I wanted to come lithe and young into a world that was ours and to help to build it together.

But I rejected all immunization of the emotions. I wanted to be a man, nothing but a man. Some identified me with ancestors of mine who had been enslaved or lynched: I decided

to accept this. It was on the universal level of the intellect that I understood this inner kinship—I was the grandson of slaves in exactly the same way in which President Lebrun was the grandson of tax-paying, hard-working peasants. In the main, the panic soon vanished.

In America, Negroes are segregated. In South America, Negroes are whipped in the streets, and Negro strikers are cut down by machine-guns. In West Africa, the Negro is an animal. And there beside me, my neighbor in the university, who was born in Algeria, told me: "As long as the Arab is treated like a man, no solution is possible."

"Understand, my dear boy, color prejudice is something I find utterly foreign. . . . But of course, come in, sir, there is no color prejudice among us. . . . Quite, the Negro is a man like ourselves. . . . It is not because he is black that he is less intelligent than we are. . . . I had a Senegalese buddy in the army who was really clever. . . ."

Where am I to be classified? Or, if you prefer, tucked away?

"A Martinican, a native of 'our' old colonies."

Where shall I hide?

"Look at the nigger! . . . Mama, a Negro! . . . Hell, he's getting mad. . . . Take no notice, sir, he does not know that you are as civilized as we. . . ."

My body was given back to me sprawled out, distorted, re-colored, clad in mourning in that white winter day. The Negro is an animal, the Negro is bad, the Negro is mean, the Negro is ugly; look, a nigger, it's cold, the nigger is shivering, the nigger is shivering because he is cold, the little boy is trembling because he is afraid of the nigger, the nigger is shivering with cold, that cold that goes through your bones, the handsome little boy is trembling because he thinks that the nigger is quivering with rage, the little white boy throws himself into his mother's arms: Mama, the nigger's going to eat me up.

All round me the white man, above the sky tears at its navel, the earth rasps under my feet, and there is a white song, a white song. All this whiteness that burns me. . . .

I sit down at the fire and I become aware of my uniform. I had not seen it. It is indeed ugly. I stop there, for who can tell me what beauty is?

Where shall I find shelter from now on? I felt an easily identifiable flood mounting out of the countless facets of my being. I was about to be angry. The fire was long since out, and once more the nigger was trembling.

"Look how handsome that Negro is! . . ."

"Kiss the handsome Negro's ass, madame!"

Shame flooded her face. At last I was set free from my rumination. At the same time I accomplished two things: I identified my enemies and I made a scene. A grand slam. Now one would be able to laugh.

---

[1]Jean Lhermitte, *L'Image de notre corps* (Paris: Nouvelle Revue critique, 1939), p. 17.

The field of battle having been marked out, I entered the lists.

What? While I was forgetting, forgiving, and wanting only to love, my message was flung back in my face like a slap. The white world, the only honorable one, barred me from all participation. A man was expected to behave like a man. I was expected to behave like a black man—or at least like a nigger. I shouted a greeting to the world and the world slashed away my joy. I was told to stay within bounds, to go back where I belonged.

They would see, then! I had warned them, anyway. Slavery? It was no longer even mentioned, that unpleasant memory. My supposed inferiority? A hoax that it was better to laugh at. I forgot it all, but only on condition that the world not protect itself against me any longer. I had incisors to test. I was sure they were strong. And besides. . . .

What! When it was I who had every reason to hate, to despise, I was rejected? When I should have been begged, implored, I was denied the slightest recognition? I resolved, since it was impossible for me to get away from an *inborn complex*, to assert myself as a BLACK MAN. Since the other hesitated to recognize me, there remained only one solution: to make myself known.

In *Anti-Semite and Jew* (p. 95), Sartre says: "They [the Jews] have allowed themselves to be poisoned by the stereotype that others have of them, and they live in fear that their acts will correspond to this stereotype. . . . We may say that their conduct is perpetually overdetermined from the inside."

All the same, the Jew can be unknown in his Jewishness. He is not wholly what he is. One hopes, one waits. His actions, his behavior are the final determinant. He is a white man, and, apart from some rather debatable characteristics, he can sometimes go unnoticed. He belongs to the race of those who since the beginning of time have never known cannibalism. What an idea, to eat one's father! Simple enough, one has only not to be a nigger. Granted, the Jews are harassed—what am I thinking of? They are hunted down, exterminated, cremated. But these are little family quarrels. The Jew is disliked from the moment he is tracked down. But in my case everything takes on a *new* guise. I am given no chance. I am overdetermined from without. I am the slave not of the "idea" that others have of me but of my own appearance.

I move slowly in the world, accustomed now to seek no longer for upheaval. I progress by crawling. And already I am being dissected under white eyes, the only real eyes. I am *fixed*. Having adjusted their microtomes, they objectively cut away slices of my reality. I am laid bare. I feel, I see in those white faces that it is not a new man who has come in, but a new kind of man, a new genus. Why, it's a Negro!

I slip into corners, and my long antennae pick up the catch-phrases strewn over the surface of things—nigger underwear smells of nigger—nigger teeth are white—nigger feet are big—the nigger's barrel chest—I slip into corners, I remain silent, I strive for anonymity, for invisibility. Look, I will accept the lot, as long as no one notices me!

"Oh, I want you to meet my black friend. . . . Aimé Césaire, a black man and a university graduate. . . . Marian Anderson, the finest of Negro singers. . . . Dr. Cobb, who invented white blood, is a Negro. . . . Here, say hello to my friend from Martinique (be careful, he's extremely sensitive). . . ."

Shame. Shame and self-contempt. Nausea. When people like me, they tell me it is in spite of my color. When they dislike me, they point out that it is not because of my color. Either way, I am locked into the infernal circle.

I turn away from these inspectors of the Ark before the Flood and I attach myself to my brothers, Negroes like myself. To my horror, they too reject me. They are almost white. And besides they are about to marry white women. They will have children faintly tinged with brown. Who knows, perhaps little by little. . . .

I had been dreaming.

"I want you to understand, sir, I am one of the best friends the Negro has in Lyon."

The evidence was there, unalterable. My blackness was there, dark and unarguable. And it tormented me, pursued me, disturbed me, angered me.

Negroes are savages, brutes, illiterates. But in my own case I knew that these statements were false. There was a myth of the Negro that had to be destroyed at all costs. The time had long since passed when a Negro priest was an occasion for wonder. We had physicians, professors, statesmen. Yes, but something out of the ordinary still clung to such cases. "We have a Senegalese history teacher. He is quite bright. . . . Our doctor is colored. He is very gentle."

It was always the Negro teacher, the Negro doctor; brittle as I was becoming, I shivered at the slightest pretext. I knew, for instance, that if the physician made a mistake it would be the end of him and of all those who came after him. What could one expect, after all, from a Negro physician? As long as everything went well, he was praised to the skies, but look out, no nonsense, under any conditions! The black physician can never be sure how close he is to disgrace. I tell you, I was walled in: No exception was made for my refined manners, or my knowledge of literature, or my understanding of the quantum theory.

I requested, I demanded explanations. Gently, in the tone that one uses with a child, they introduced me to the existence of a certain view that was held by certain people, but,

I was always told, "We must hope that it will very soon disappear." What was it? Color prejudice.

> It [colour prejudice] is nothing more than the unreasoning hatred of one race for another, the contempt of the stronger and richer peoples for those whom they consider inferior to themselves and the bitter resentment of those who are kept in subjection and are so frequently insulted. As colour is the most obvious outward manifestation of race it has been made the criterion by which men are judged, irrespective of their social or educational attainments. The light-skinned races have come to despise all those of a darker colour, and the dark-skinned peoples will no longer accept without protest the inferior position to which they have been relegated.[2]

I had read it rightly. It was hate; I was hated, despised, detested, not by the neighbor across the street or my cousin on my mother's side, but by an entire race. I was up against something unreasoned. The psychoanalysts say that nothing is more traumatizing for the young child than his encounters with what is rational. I would personally say that for a man whose only weapon is reason there is nothing more neurotic than contact with unreason.

I felt knife blades open within me. I resolved to defend myself. As a good tactician, I intended to rationalize the world and to show the white man that he was mistaken.

In the Jew, Jean-Paul Sartre says, there is

> a sort of impassioned imperialism of reason: for he wishes not only to convince others that he is right; his goal is to persuade them that there is an absolute and unconditioned value to rationalism. He feels himself to be a missionary of the universal; against the universality of the Catholic religion, from which he is excluded, he asserts the "catholicity" of the rational, an instrument by which to attain to the truth and establish a spiritual bond among men.[3]

And, the author adds, though there may be Jews who have made intuition the basic category of their philosophy, their intuition

> has no resemblance to the Pascalian subtlety of spirit, and it is this latter—based on a thousand imperceptible perceptions—which to the Jew seems his worst enemy. As for Bergson, his philosophy offers the curious appearance of an anti-intellectualist doctrine constructed entirely by the most rational and most critical of intelligences. It is through argument that he establishes the existence of pure duration, of philosophic intuition; and that very intuition which discovers duration or life, is itself universal, since anyone may practice it, and it leads toward the universal, since its objects can be named and conceived.[4]

With enthusiasm I set to cataloguing and probing my surroundings. As times changed, one had seen the Catholic religion at first justify and then condemn slavery and prejudices. But by referring everything to the idea of the dignity of man, one had ripped prejudice to shreds. After much reluctance, the scientists had conceded that the Negro was a human being; *in vivo* and *in vitro* the Negro had been proved analogous to the white man: the same morphology, the same histology. Reason was confident of victory on every level. I put all the parts back together. But I had to change my tune.

That victory played cat and mouse; it made a fool of me. As the other put it, when I was present, it was not; when it was there, I was no longer. In the abstract there was agreement: The Negro is a human being. That is to say, amended the less firmly convinced, that like us he has his heart on the left side. But on certain points the white man remained intractable. Under no conditions did he wish any intimacy between the races, for it is a truism that "crossings between widely different races can lower the physical and mental level. . . . Until we have a more definite knowledge of the effect of race-crossings we shall certainly do best to avoid crossings between widely different races."[5]

For my own part, I would certainly know how to react. And in one sense, if I were asked for a definition of myself, I would say that I am one who waits; I investigate my surroundings, I interpret everything in terms of what I discover, I become sensitive.

In the first chapter of the history that the others have compiled for me, the foundation of cannibalism has been made eminently plain in order that I may not lose sight of it. My chromosomes were supposed to have a few thicker or thinner genes representing cannibalism. In addition to the *sex-linked*, the scholars had now discovered the *racial-linked*.[6] What a shameful science!

But I understand this "psychological mechanism." For it is a matter of common knowledge that the mechanism is only psychological. Two centuries ago I was lost to humanity, I was a slave forever. And then came men who said that it all had gone on far too long. My tenaciousness did the rest; I was saved from the civilizing deluge. I have gone forward.

Too late. Everything is anticipated, thought out, demonstrated, made the most of. My trembling hands take hold of nothing; the vein has been mined out. Too late! But once again I want to understand.

[2]Sir Alan Burns, *Colour Prejudice* (London: Allen and Unwin, 1948), p. 16.

[3]*Anti-Semite and Jew* (New York: Grove Press, 1960), pp. 112–13.

[4]Ibid., p. 115.

[5]Jon Alfred Mjoen, "Harmonic and Disharmonic Race-crossings," *The Second International Congress of Eugenics* (1921), *Eugenics in Race and State*, vol. 2, p. 60, quoted in Sir Alan Burns, op. cit., p. 120.

[6]In English in the original (*Translator's note*).

Since the time when someone first mourned the fact that he had arrived too late and everything had been said, a nostalgia for the past has seemed to persist. Is this that lost original paradise of which Otto Rank speaks? How many such men, apparently rooted to the womb of the world, have devoted their lives to studying the Delphic oracles or exhausted themselves in attempts to plot the wanderings of Ulysses! The pan-spiritualists seek to prove the existence of a soul in animals by using this argument: A dog lies down on the grave of his master and starves to death there. We had to wait for Janet to demonstrate that the aforesaid dog, in contrast to man, simply lacked the capacity to liquidate the past. We speak of the glory of Greece, Artaud says; but, he adds, if modern man can no longer understand the *Choephoroi* of Aeschylus, it is Aeschylus who is to blame. It is tradition to which the anti-Semites turn in order to ground the validity of their "point of view." It is tradition, it is that long historical past, it is that blood relation between Pascal and Descartes, that is invoked when the Jew is told, "There is no possibility of your finding a place in society." Not long ago, one of those good Frenchmen said in a train where I was sitting: "Just let the real French virtues keep going and the race is safe. Now more than ever, national union must be made a reality. Let's have an end of internal strife! Let's face up to the foreigners (here he turned toward my corner) no matter who they are."

It must be said in his defense that he stank of cheap wine; if he had been capable of it, he would have told me that my emancipated-slave blood could not possibly be stirred by the name of Villon or Taine.

An outrage!

The Jew and I: Since I was not satisfied to be racialized, by a lucky turn of fate I was humanized. I joined the Jew, my brother in misery.

An outrage!

At first thought it may seem strange that the anti-Semite's outlook should be related to that of the Negro-phobe. It was my philosophy professor, a native of the Antilles, who recalled the fact to me one day: "Whenever you hear anyone abuse the Jews, pay attention, because he is talking about you." And I found that he was universally right—by which I meant that I was answerable in my body and in my heart for what was done to my brother. Later I realized that he meant, quite simply, an anti-Semite is inevitably anti-Negro.

You come too late, much too late. There will always be a world—a white world—between you and us. . . . The other's total inability to liquidate the past once and for all. In the face of this affective *ankylosis* of the white man, it is understandable that I could have made up my mind to utter my Negro cry. Little by little, putting out pseudopodia here and there, I secreted a race. And that race staggered under the burden of a basic element. What was it? *Rhythm*! Listen to our singer, Léopold Senghor:

> It is the thing that is most perceptible and least material. It is the archetype of the vital element. It is the first condition and the hallmark of Art, as breath is of life: breath, which accelerates or slows, which becomes even or agitated according to the tension in the individual, the degree and the nature of his emotion. This is rhythm in its primordial purity, this is rhythm in the masterpieces of Negro art, especially sculpture. It is composed of a theme—sculptural form—which is set in opposition to a sister theme, as inhalation is to exhalation, and that is repeated. It is not the kind of symmetry that gives rise to monotony; rhythm is alive, it is free. . . . This is how rhythm affects what is least intellectual in us, tyrannically, to make us penetrate to the spirituality of the object; and that character of abandon which is ours is itself rhythmic.[7]

Had I read that right? I read it again with redoubled attention. From the opposite end of the white world a magical Negro culture was hailing me. Negro sculpture! I began to flush with pride. Was this our salvation?

I had rationalized the world and the world had rejected me on the basis of color prejudice. Since no agreement was possible on the level of reason, I threw myself back toward unreason. It was up to the white man to be more irrational than I. Out of the necessities of my struggle I had chosen the method of regression, but the fact remained that it was an unfamiliar weapon; here I am at home; I am made of the irrational; I wade in the irrational. Up to the neck in the irrational. And now how my voice vibrates!

> Those who invented neither gunpowder nor the compass
> Those who never learned to conquer steam or electricity
> Those who never explored the seas or the skies
> But they know the farthest corners of the land of anguish
> Those who never knew any journey save that of abduction
> Those who learned to kneel in docility
> Those who were domesticated and Christianized
> Those who were injected with bastardy. . . .

Yes, all those are my brothers—a "bitter brotherhood" imprisons all of us alike. Having stated the minor thesis, I went overboard after something else.

> . . . But those without whom the earth would not be the earth
> Tumescence all the more fruitful
> than
> the empty land
> still more the land
> Storehouse to guard and ripen all
> on earth that is most earth
> My blackness is no stone, its deafness
> hurled against the clamor of the day

---

[7]"Ce que l'homme noir apporte," in Claude Nordey, *L'Homme de couleur* (Paris: Plon, 1939), pp. 309–310.

My blackness is no drop of lifeless water
on the dead eye of the world
My blackness is neither a tower nor a cathedral
It thrusts into the red flesh of the sun
It thrusts into the burning flesh of the sky
It hollows through the dense dismay of its own pillar of
patience.[8]

Eyah! the tom-tom chatters out the cosmic message. Only the Negro has the capacity to convey it, to decipher its meaning, its import. Astride the world, my strong heels spurring into the flanks of the world, I stare into the shoulders of the world as the celebrant stares at the midpoint between the eyes of the sacrificial victim.

But they abandon themselves, possessed, to the essence of all things, knowing nothing of externals but possessed by the movement of all things
uncaring to subdue but playing the play of the world
truly the eldest sons of the world
open to all the breaths of the world
meeting-place of all the winds of the world
undrained bed of all the waters of the world
spark of the sacred fire of the World
flesh of the flesh of the world, throbbing with the very movement of the world.[9]

Blood! Blood! . . . Birth! Ecstasy of becoming! Three-quarters engulfed in the confusions of the day, I feel myself redden with blood. The arteries of all the world, convulsed, torn away, uprooted, have turned toward me and fed me.

"Blood! Blood! All our blood stirred by the male heart of the sun."[10]

Sacrifice was a middle point between the creation and myself—now I went back no longer to sources but to The Source. Nevertheless, one had to distrust rhythm, earth-mother love, this mystic, carnal marriage of the group and the cosmos.

In *La vie sexuelle en Afrique noire,* a work rich in perceptions, De Pédrals implies that always in Africa, no matter what field is studied, it will have a certain magico-social structure. He adds:

All these are the elements that one finds again on a still greater scale in the domain of secret societies. To the extent, moreover, to which persons of either sex, subjected to circumcision during adolescence, are bound under penalty of death not to reveal to the uninitiated what they have experienced, and to the extent to which initiation into a secret society always excites to acts of *sa-*

cred love, there is good ground to conclude by viewing both male and female circumcision and the rites that they embellish as constitutive of minor secret societies.[11]

I walk on white nails. Sheets of water threaten my soul on fire. Face to face with these rites, I am doubly alert. Black magic! Orgies, witches' sabbaths, heathen ceremonies, amulets. Coitus is an occasion to call on the gods of the clan. It is a sacred act, pure, absolute, bringing invisible forces into action. What is one to think of all these manifestations, all these initiations, all these acts? From very direction I am assaulted by the obscenity of dances and of words. Almost at my ear there is a song:

First our hearts burned hot
Now they are cold
All we think of now is Love
When we return to the village
When we see the great phallus
Ah how then we will make Love
For our parts will be dry and clean.[12]

The soil, which only a moment ago was still a tamed steed, begins to revel. Are these virgins, these nymphomaniacs? Black Magic, primitive mentality, animism, animal eroticism, it all floods over me. All of it is typical of peoples that have not kept pace with the evolution of the human race. Or, if one prefers, this is humanity at its lowest. Having reached this point, I was long reluctant to commit myself. Aggression was in the stars. I had to choose. What do I mean? I had no choice. . . .

Yes, we are—we Negroes—backward, simple, free in our behavior. That is because for us the body is not something opposed to what you call the mind. We are in the world. And long live the couple, Man and Earth! Besides, our men of letters helped me to convince you; your white civilization overlooks subtle riches and sensitivity. Listen:

Emotive sensitivity. *Emotion is completely Negro as reason is Greek*.[13] Water rippled by every breeze? Unsheltered soul blown by every wind, whose fruit often drops before it is ripe? Yes, in one way, the Negro today is richer *in gifts than in works*.[14] But the tree thrusts its roots into the earth. The river runs deep, carrying precious seeds. And, the Afro-American poet, Langston Hughes, says:
I have known rivers
ancient dark rivers

---

[8]Aimé Césaire, *Cahier d'un retour au pays natal* (Paris: Présence Africaine, 1956), pp. 77–78.

[9]Ibid., p. 78.

[10]Ibid., p. 79.

[11]De Pédrals, *La vie sexuelle en Afrique noire* (Paris: Payot), p. 83.

[12]A. M. Vergiat, *Les rites secrets des primitifs de l'Oubangui* (Paris: Payot, 1951), p. 113.

[13]My italics—F.F.

[14]My italics—F.F.

my soul has grown deep
like the deep rivers.

The very nature of the Negro's emotion, of his sensitivity, fur-thermore, explains his attitude toward the object perceived with such basic intensity. It is an abandon that becomes need, an active state of communion, indeed of identification, however negligible the action—I almost said the personality—of the object. A rhythmic attitude: The adjective should be kept in mind.[15]

So here we have the Negro rehabilitated, "standing before the bar," ruling the world with his intuition, the Negro recognized, set on his feet again, sought after, taken up, and he is a Negro—no, he is not a Negro but the Negro, exciting the fecund antennae of the world, placed in the foreground of the world, raining his poetic power on the world, "open to all the breaths of the world." I embrace the world! I am the world! The white man has never understood this magic substitution. The white man wants the world; he wants it for himself alone. He finds himself predestined master of this world. He enslaves it. An acquisitive relation is established between the world and him. But there exist other values that fit only my forms. Like a magician, I robbed the white man of "a certain world," forever after lost to him and his. When that happened, the white man must have been rocked backward by a force that he could not identify, so little used as he is to such reactions. Somewhere beyond the objective world of farms and banana trees and rubber trees, I had subtly brought the real world into being. The essence of the world was my fortune. Between the world and me a relation of coexistence was established. I had discovered the primeval One. My "speaking hands" tore at the hysterical throat of the world. The white man had the anguished feeling that I was escaping from him and that I was taking something with me. He went through my pockets. He thrust probes into the least circumvolution of my brain. Everywhere he found only the obvious. So it was obvious that I had a secret. I was interrogated; turning away with an air of mystery, I murmured:

Tokowaly, uncle, do you remember the nights gone by
When my head weighed heavy on the back of your patience or
Holding my hand your hand led me by shadows and signs
The fields are flowers of glowworms, stars hang on the bushes, on the trees
Silence is everywhere
Only the scents of the jungle hum, swarms of reddish bees that overwhelm the crickets' shrill sounds,
And covered tom-tom, breathing in the distance of the night.

You, Tokowaly, you listen to what cannot be heard, and you explain to me what the†ancestors are saying in the liquid calm of the constellations,
The bull, the scorpion, the leopard, the elephant, and the fish we know,
And the white pomp of the Spirits in the heavenly shell that has no end,
But now comes the radiance of the goddess Moon and the veils of the shadows fall.
Night of Africa, my black night, mystical and bright, black and shining.[16]

I made myself the poet of the world. The white man had found a poetry in which there was nothing poetic. The soul of the white man was corrupted, and, as I was told by a friend who was a teacher in the United States, "The presence of the Negroes beside the whites is in a way an insurance policy on humanness. When the whites feel that they have become too mechanized, they turn to the men of color and ask them for a little human sustenance." At last I had been recognized, I was no longer a zero.

I had soon to change my tune. Only momentarily at a loss, the white man explained to me that, genetically, I represented a stage of development: "Your properties have been exhausted by us. We have had earth mystics such as you will never approach. Study our history and you will see how far this fusion has gone." Then I had the feeling that I was repeating a cycle. My originality had been torn out of me. I wept a long time, and then I began to live again. But I was haunted by a galaxy of erosive stereotypes: the Negro's *sui generis* odor . . . the Negro's *sui generis* good nature . . . the Negro's *sui generis* gullibility. . . .

I had tried to flee myself through my kind, but the whites had thrown themselves on me and hamstrung me. I tested the limits of my essence; beyond all doubt there was not much of it left. It was here that I made my most remarkable discovery. Properly speaking, this discovery was a rediscovery.

I rummaged frenetically through all the antiquity of the black man. What I found there took away my breath. In his book *L'abolition de l'esclavage* Schoelcher presented us with compelling arguments. Since then, Frobenius, Westermann, Delafosse—all of them white—had joined the chorus: Ségou, Djenné, cities of more than a hundred thousand people; accounts of learned blacks (doctors of theology who went to Mecca to interpret the Koran). All of that, exhumed from the past, spread with its insides out, made it possible for me to find a valid historic place. The white man was wrong, I was not a primitive, not even a half-man, I belonged to a race

[15]Léopold Senghor, "Ce que l'homme noir apporte," in Nordey, op. cit., p. 205.

[16]Léopold Senghor, *Chants d'ombre* (Paris: Editions du Seuil, 1945).

that had already been working in gold and silver two thousand years ago. And there was something else, something else that the white man could not understand. Listen:

> What sort of men were these, then, who had been torn away from their families, their countries, their religions, with a savagery unparalleled in history?
>
> Gentle men, polite, considerate, unquestionably superior to those who tortured them—that collection of adventurers who slashed and violated and spat on Africa to make the stripping of her the easier.
>
> The men they took away knew how to build houses, govern empires, erect cities, cultivate fields, mine for metals, weave cotton, forge steel.
>
> Their religion had its own beauty, based on mystical connections with the founder of the city. Their customs were pleasing, built on unity, kindness, respect for age.
>
> No coercion, only mutual assistance, the joy of living, a free acceptance of discipline.
>
> Order—Earnestness—Poetry and Freedom.
>
> From the untroubled private citizen to the almost fabulous leader there was an unbroken chain of understanding and trust. No science? Indeed yes; but also, to protect them from fear, they possessed great myths in which 'the most subtle observation and the most daring imagination were balanced and blended. No art? They had their magnificent sculpture, in which human feeling erupted so unrestrained yet always followed the obsessive laws of rhythm in its organization of the major elements of a material called upon to capture, in order to redistribute, the most secret forces of the universe. . . .[17]
>
> Monuments in the very heart of Africa? Schools? Hospitals? Not a single good burgher of the twentieth century, no Durand, no Smith, no Brown even suspects that such things existed in Africa before the Europeans came. . . .
>
> But Schoelcher reminds us of their presence, discovered by Caillé, Mollien, the Cander brothers. And, though he nowhere reminds us that when the Portuguese landed on the banks of the Congo in 1498, they found a rich and flourishing state there and that the courtiers of Ambas were dressed in robes of silk and brocade, at least he knows that Africa had brought itself up to a juridical concept of the state, and he is aware, living in the very flood of imperialism, that European civilization, after all, is only one more civilization among many—and not the most merciful.[18]

I put the white man back into his place; growing bolder, I jostled him and told him point-blank, "Get used to me, I am not getting used to anyone." I shouted my laughter to the stars. The white man, I could see, was resentful. His reaction time lagged interminably. . . . I had won. I was jubilant.

"Lay aside your history, your investigations of the past, and try to feel yourself into our rhythm. In a society such as ours, industrialized to the highest degree, dominated by scientism, there is no longer room for your sensitivity. One must

be tough if one is to be allowed to live. What matters now is no longer playing the game of the world but subjugating it with integers and atoms. Oh, certainly, I will be told, now and then when we are worn out by our lives in big buildings, we will turn to you as we do to our children—to the innocent, the ingenuous, the spontaneous. We will turn to you as to the childhood of the world. You are so real in your life—so funny, that is. Let us run away for a little while from our ritualized, polite civilization and let us relax, bend to those heads, those adorably expressive faces. In a way, you reconcile us with ourselves."

Thus my unreason was countered with reason, my reason with "real reason." Every hand was a losing hand for me. I analyzed my heredity. I made a complete audit of my ailment. I wanted to be typically Negro—it was no longer possible. I wanted to be white—that was a joke. And, when I tried, on the level of ideas and intellectual activity, to reclaim my negritude, it was snatched away from me. Proof was presented that my effort was only a term in the dialectic:

> But there is something more important: The Negro, as we have said, creates an anti-racist racism for himself. In no sense does he wish to rule the world: He seeks the abolition of all ethnic privileges, wherever they come from; he asserts his solidarity with the oppressed of all colors. At once the subjective, existential, ethnic idea of *negritude* "passes," as Hegel puts it, into the objective, positive, exact idea of proletariat. "For Césaire," Senghor says, "the white man is the symbol of capital as the Negro is that of labor. . . . Beyond the black-skinned men of his race it is the battle of the world proletariat that is his song."
>
> That is easy to say, but less easy to think out. And undoubtedly it is no coincidence that the most ardent poets of negritude are at the same time militant Marxists.
>
> But that does not prevent the idea of race from mingling with that of class: The first is concrete and particular, the second is universal and abstract; the one stems from what Jaspers calls understanding and the other from intellection; the first is the result of a psychobiological syncretism and the second is a methodical construction based on experience. In fact, negritude appears as the minor term of a dialectical progression: The theoretical and practical assertion of the supremacy of the white man is its thesis; the position of negritude as an antithetical value is the moment of negativity. But this negative moment is insufficient by itself, and the Negroes who employ it know this very well; they know that it is intended to prepare the synthesis or realization of the human in a society without races. Thus negritude is the root of its own destruction, it is a transition and not a conclusion, a means and not an ultimate end.[19]

When I read that page, I felt that I had been robbed of my last chance. I said to my friends, "The generation of the younger black poets has just suffered a blow that can never

---

[17]Aimé Césaire, Introduction to Victor Schoelcher, *Esclavage et colonisation* (Paris: Presses Universitaires de France, 1948), p. 7.
[18]Ibid., p. 8.

[19]Jean-Paul Sartre, *Orphée Noir*, preface to *Anthologie de la nouvelle poésie nègre et malgache* (Paris: Presses Universitaires de France, 1948), pp. xl ff.

be forgiven." Help had been sought from a friend of the colored peoples, and that friend had found no better response than to point out the relativity of what they were doing. For once, that born Hegelian had forgotten that consciousness has to lose itself in the night of the absolute, the only condition to attain to consciousness of self. In opposition to rationalism, he summoned up the negative side, but he forgot that this negativity draws its worth from an almost substantive absoluteness. A consciousness committed to experience is ignorant, has to be ignorant, of the essences and the determinations of its being.

Orphée Noir is a date in the intellectualization of the *experience* of being black. And Sartre's mistake was not only to seek the source of the source but in a certain sense to block that source:

> Will the source of Poetry be dried up? Or will the great black flood, in spite of everything, color the sea into which it pours itself? It does not matter: Every age has its own poetry; in every age the circumstances of history choose a nation, a race, a class to take up the torch by creating situations that can be expressed or transcended only through Poetry; sometimes the poetic impulse coincides with the revolutionary impulse, and sometimes they take different courses. Today let us hail the turn of history that will make it possible for the black men to utter "the great Negro cry with a force that will shake the pillars of the world" (Césaire).[20]

And so it is not I who make a meaning for myself, but it is the meaning that was already there, pre-existing, waiting for me. It is not out of my bad nigger's misery, my bad nigger's teeth, my bad nigger's hunger that I will shape a torch with which to burn down the world, but it is the torch that was already there, waiting for that turn of history.

In terms of consciousness, the black consciousness is held out as an absolute density, as filled with itself, a stage preceding any invasion, any abolition of the ego by desire. Jean-Paul Sartre, in this work, has destroyed black zeal. In opposition to historical becoming, there had always been the unforeseeable. I needed to lose myself completely in negritude. One day, perhaps, in the depths of that unhappy romanticism. . . .

In any case I *needed* not to know. This struggle, this new decline had to take on an aspect of completeness. Nothing is more unwelcome than the commonplace: "You'll change, my boy; I was like that too when I was young . . . you'll see, it will all pass."

The dialectic that brings necessity into the foundation of my freedom drives me out of myself. It shatters my unreflected position. Still in terms of consciousness, black consciousness is immanent in its own eyes. I am not a potentiality of something, I am wholly what I am. I do not have to look for the universal. No probability has any place inside me. My Negro consciousness does not hold itself out as a lack. It is. It is its own follower.

But, I will be told, your statements show a misreading of the processes of history. Listen then:

> Africa I have kept your memory Africa
> you are inside me
> Like the splinter in the wound
> like a guardian fetish in the center of the village
> make me the stone in your sling
> make my mouth the lips of your wound
> make my knees the broken pillars of your abasement
> AND YET
> I want to be of your race alone
> workers peasants of all lands . . .
> . . . white worker in Detroit black peon in Alabama
> uncountable nation in capitalist slavery
> destiny ranges us shoulder to shoulder
> repudiating the ancient maledictions of blood taboos
> we roll away the ruins of our solitudes
> If the flood is a frontier
> we will strip the gully of its endless
> covering flow
> If the Sierra is a frontier
> we will smash the jaws of the volcanoes
> upholding the Cordilleras
> and the plain will be the parade ground of the dawn
> where we regroup our forces sundered
> by the deceits of our masters
> As the contradiction among the features
> creates the harmony of the face
> we proclaim the oneness of the suffering
> and the revolt
> of all the peoples on all the face of the earth
>   and we mix the mortar of the age of brotherhood
>   out of the dust of idols.[21]

Exactly, we will reply, Negro experience is not a whole, for there is not merely one Negro, there are *Negroes*. What a difference, for instance, in this other poem:

> The white man killed my father
> Because my father was proud
> The white man raped my mother
> Because my mother was beautiful
> The white man wore out my brother in the hot sun of the roads
> Because my brother was strong
> Then the white man came to me
> His hands red with blood
> Spat his contempt into my black face
> Out of his tyrant's voice:
> "Hey boy, a basin, a towel, water."[22]

---

[20]Ibid., p. xliv.

[21]Jacques Roumain, "Bois d'Ebène," *Prelude*, in *Anthologie de la nouvelle poésie nègre et malgache*, p. 113.

[22]David Diop, "Le temps du martyre," ibid., p. 174.

Or this other one:

> My brother with teeth that glisten at the compliments of
> hypocrites
> My brother with gold-rimmed spectacles
> Over eyes that turn blue at the sound of the Master's voice
> My poor brother in dinner jacket with its silk lapels
> Clucking and whispering and strutting through the drawing
> rooms of Condescension
> How pathetic you are
> The sun of your native country is nothing more now than a
> shadow
> On your composed civilized face
> And your grandmother's hut
> Brings blushes into cheeks made white by years of abasement
> and Mea culpa
> But when regurgitating the flood of lofty empty words
> Like the load that presses on your shoulders
> You walk again on the rough red earth of Africa
> These words of anguish will state the rhythm of your uneasy gait
> I feel so alone, so alone here![23]

From time to time one would like to stop. To state reality is a wearing task. But, when one has taken it into one's head to try to express existence, one runs the risk of finding only the nonexistent. What is certain is that, at the very moment when I was trying to grasp my own being, Sartre, who remained The Other, gave me a name and thus shattered my last illusion. While I was saying to him

> My negritude is neither a tower nor a cathedral,
> it thrusts into the red flesh of the sun,
> it thrusts into the burning flesh of the sky,
> it hollows through the dense dismay of its own pillar of
> patience . . .

while I was shouting that, in the paroxysm of my being and my fury, he was reminding me that my blackness was only a minor term. In all truth, in all truth I tell you, my shoulders slipped out of the framework of the world, my feet could no longer feel the touch of the ground. Without a Negro past, without a Negro future, it was impossible for me to live my Negrohood. Not yet white, no longer wholly black, I was damned. Jean-Paul Sartre had forgotten that the Negro suffers in his body quite differently from the white man.[24] Between the white man and me the connection was irrevocably one of transcendence.[25]

---

[23]David Diop, "Le Renégat."

[24]Though Sartre's speculations on the existence of The Other may be correct (to the extent, we must remember, to which *Being and Nothingness* describes an alienated consciousness), their application to a black consciousness proves fallacious. That is because the white man is not only The Other but also the master, whether real or imaginary.

[25]In the sense in which the word is used by Jean Wahl in *Existence humaine et transcendance* (Neuchâtel: La Baconnière, 1944).

But the constancy of my love had been forgotten. I defined myself as an absolute intensity of beginning. So I took up my negritude, and with tears in my eyes I put its machinery together again. What had been broken to pieces was rebuilt, reconstructed by the intuitive lianas of my hands.

My cry grew more violent: I am a Negro, I am a Negro, I am a Negro. . . .

And there was my poor brother—living out his neurosis to the extreme and finding himself paralyzed:

> THE NEGRO: I can't, ma'am.
> LIZZIE: Why not?
> THE NEGRO: I can't shoot white folks.
> LIZZIE: Really! That would bother them, wouldn't it?
> THE NEGRO: They're white folks, ma'am.
> LIZZIE: So what? Maybe they got a right to bleed you like a pig just because they're white?
> THE NEGRO: But they're white folks.

A feeling of inferiority? No, a feeling of nonexistence. Sin is Negro as virtue is white. All those white men in a group, guns in their hands, cannot be wrong. I am guilty. I do not know of what, but I know that I am no good.

> THE NEGRO: That's how it goes, ma'am. That's how it always goes with white folks.
> LIZZIE: You too? You feel guilty?
> THE NEGRO: Yes, ma'am.[26]

It is Bigger Thomas—he is afraid, he is terribly afraid. He is afraid, but of what is he afraid? Of himself. No one knows yet who he is, but he knows that fear will fill the world when the world finds out. And when the world knows, the world always expects something of the Negro. He is afraid lest the world know, he is afraid of the fear that the world would feel if the world knew. Like that old woman on her knees who begged me to tie her to her bed:

"I just know, Doctor: Any minute that thing will take hold of me."

"What thing?"

"The wanting to kill myself. Tie me down, I'm afraid."

In the end, Bigger Thomas acts. To put an end to his tension, he acts, he responds to the world's anticipation.[27]

So it is with the character in *If He Hollers Let Him Go*[28]— who does precisely what he did not want to do. That big blonde who was always in his way, weak, sensual, offered, open, fearing (desiring) rape, became his mistress in the end.

---

[26]Jean-Paul Sartre, *The Respectful Prostitute,* in *Three Plays* (New York: Knopf, 1949), pp. 189, 191. Originally, *La Putain respectueuse* (Paris: Gallimard, 1947). See also *Home of the Brave,* a film by Mark Robson.

[27]Richard Wright, *Native Son* (New York: Harper, 1940).

[28]By Chester Himes (Garden City: Doubleday, 1945).

The Negro is a toy in the white man's hands; so, in order to shatter the hellish cycle, he explodes. I cannot go to a film without seeing myself. I wait for me. In the interval, just before the film starts, I wait for me. The people in the theater are watching me, examining me, waiting for me. A Negro groom is going to appear. My heart makes my head swim.

The crippled veteran of the Pacific war says to my brother, "Resign yourself to your color the way I got used to my stump; we're both victims."[29]

---

[29]*Home of the Brave*, op. cit.

Nevertheless with all my strength I refuse to accept that amputation. I feel in myself a soul as immense as the world, truly a soul as deep as the deepest of rivers, my chest has the power to expand without limit. I am a master and I am advised to adopt the humility of the cripple. Yesterday, awakening to the world, I saw the sky turn upon itself utterly and wholly. I wanted to rise, but the disemboweled silence fell back upon me, its wings paralyzed. Without responsibility, straddling Nothingness and Infinity, I began to weep.

CRITICAL PERSPECTIVES

HOMI K. BHABHA (b. 1949)
"Of Mimicry and Man: The Ambivalence of Colonial Discourse" (1984)

Homi K. Bhabha is a leading theorist of postcolonial literature and culture, and is the author of The Location of Culture *(1994) and editor of* Nation and Narration *(1990). In "Of Mimicry and Man," Bhabha considers how notions of imitation and performance structure the relations of power and legitimation between colonized peoples and their colonizers. Although Bhabha makes a very dense argument here and uses a specialized critical vocabulary, several of his key terms and principles emerge clearly, particularly the ways in which "mimicry" can be seen to have a resistant force. How does Bhabha adapt the discourse of psychoanalysis to a critique of the formation of* political *subjects? What are the dynamics of mimicry in the colonial state? Do they operate in the same ways in the imperial metropole? Is it possible to use Bhabha's dynamic model to discuss the "interpellation" of characters in contemporary drama—Owen in Friel's* Translations, *for example, or even Om in Padmanabhan's* Harvest?

Mimicry reveals something insofar as it is distinct from what might be called an itself that is behind. The effect of mimicry is camouflage.... It is not a question of harmonizing with the background, but against a mottled background, of becoming mottled—exactly like the technique of camouflage practised in human warfare.

Jacques Lacan,
"The Line and Light," *Of the Gaze*

It is out of season to question at this time of day, the original policy of conferring on every colony of the British Empire a mimic representation of the British Constitution. But if the creature so endowed has sometimes forgotten its real insignificance and under the fancied importance of speakers and maces, and all the paraphernalia and ceremonies of the imperial legislature, has dared to defy the mother country, she has to thank herself for the folly of conferring such privileges on a condition of society that has no earthly claim to so exalted a position. A fundamental principle appears to have been forgotten or overlooked in our system of colonial policy—that of colonial dependence. To give to a colony the forms of independence is a mockery; she would not be a colony for a single hour if she could maintain an independent station.

Sir Edward Cust,
"Reflections on West African Affairs . . .
Addressed to the Colonial Office,"
Hatchard, London 1839

The discourse of post-Enlightenment English colonialism often speaks in a tongue that is forked, not false. If colonialism takes power in the name of history, it repeatedly exer-

cises its authority through the figures of farce. For the epic intention of the civilizing mission, "human and not wholly human" in the famous words of Lord Rosebery, "writ by the finger of the Divine"[1] often produces a text rich in the traditions of *trompe l'oeil,* irony, mimicry, and repetition. In this comic turn from the high ideals of the colonial imagination to its low mimetic literary effects, mimicry emerges as one of the most elusive and effective strategies of colonial power and knowledge.

Within that conflictual economy of colonial discourse which Edward Said[2] describes as the tension between the synchronic panoptical vision of domination—the demand for identity, stasis—and the counter-pressure of the diachrony of history—change, difference—mimicry represents an *ironic* compromise. If I may adapt Samuel Weber's formulation of the marginalizing vision of castration,[3] then colonial mimicry is the desire for a reformed, recognizable Other, as *a subject of a difference that is almost the same, but not quite.* Which is to say, that the discourse of mimicry is constructed around an *ambivalence:* in order to be effective, mimicry must continually produce its slippage, its excess, its difference. The authority of that mode of colonial discourse that I have called mimicry is therefore stricken by an indeterminacy: mimicry emerges as the representation of a difference that is itself a process of disavowal. Mimicry is, thus, the sign of a double articulation; a complex strategy of reform, regulation, and discipline, which "appropriates" the Other as it visualizes

This paper was first presented as a contribution to a panel on "Colonialist and Post-Colonialist Discourse," organized by Gayatri Chakravorty Spivak for the Modern Language Association Convention in New York, December 1983. I would like to thank Professor Spivak for inviting me to participate on the panel and Dr. Stephan Feuchtwang for his advice in the preparation of the paper.

[1]Cited in Eric Stokes, *The Political Ideas of English Imperialism* (Oxford: Oxford University Press, 1960), pp. 17–18.

[2]Edward Said, *Orientalism* (New York: Pantheon Books, 1978), p. 240.

[3]Samuel Weber, "The Sideshow, Or: Remarks on a Canny Moment," *Modern Languages Notes,* vol. 88, no. 6 (1973), p. 112.

power. Mimicry is also the sign of the inappropriate, however, a difference or recalcitrance which coheres the dominant strategic function of colonial power, intensifies surveillance, and poses an immanent threat to both "normalized" knowledges and disciplinary powers.

The effect of mimicry on the authority of colonial discourse is profound and disturbing. For in "normalizing" the colonial state or subject, the dream of post-Enlightenment civility alienates its own language of liberty and produces another knowledge of its norms. The ambivalence which thus informs this strategy is discernible, for example, in Locke's *Second Treatise* which *splits* to reveal the limitations of liberty in his double use of the word "slave": first simply, descriptively as the locus of a legitimate form of ownership, then as the trope for an intolerable, illegitimate exercise of power. What is articulated in that distance between the two uses is the absolute, imagined difference between the "Colonial" State of Carolina and the Original State of Nature.

It is from this area between mimicry and mockery, where the reforming, civilizing mission is threatened by the displacing gaze of its disciplinary double, that my instances of colonial imitation come. What they all share is a discursive process by which the excess or slippage produced by the *ambivalence* of mimicry (almost the same, *but not quite*) does not merely "rupture" the discourse, but becomes transformed into an uncertainty which fixes the colonial subject as a "partial" presence. By "partial" I mean both "incomplete" and "virtual." It is as if the very emergence of the "colonial" is dependent for its representation upon some strategic limitation or prohibition *within* the authoritative discourse itself. The success of colonial appropriation depends on a proliferation of inappropriate objects that ensure its strategic failure, so that mimicry is at once resemblance and menace.

A classic text of such partiality is Charles Grant's "Observations on the State of Society among the Asiatic Subjects of Great Britain" (1792)[4] which was only superseded by James Mills's *History of India* as the most influential early nineteenth-century account of Indian manners and morals. Grant's dream of an evangelical system of mission education conducted uncompromisingly in English was partly a belief in political reform along Christian lines and partly an awareness that the expansion of company rule in India required a system of "interpellation"—a reform of manners, as Grant put it, that would provide the colonial with "a sense of personal identity as we know it." Caught between the desire for religious reform

and the fear that the Indians might become turbulent for liberty, Grant implies that it is, in fact the "partial" diffusion of Christianity, and the "partial" influence of moral improvements which will construct a particularly appropriate form of colonial subjectivity. What is suggested is a process of reform through which Christian doctrines might collude with divisive caste practices to prevent dangerous political alliances. Inadvertently, Grant produces a knowledge of Christianity as a form of social control which conflicts with the enunciatory assumptions which authorize his discourse. In suggesting, finally, that "partial reform" will produce an empty form of the *imitation* of English manners which will induce them [the colonial subjects] to remain under our protection,[5] Grant mocks his moral project and violates the Evidences of Christianity—a central missionary tenet—which forbade any tolerance of heathen faiths.

The absurd extravagance of Macaulay's *Infamous Minute* (1835)—deeply influenced by Charles Grant's *Observations*—makes a mockery of Oriental learning until faced with the challenge of conceiving of a "reformed" colonial subject. Then the great tradition of European humanism seems capable only of ironizing itself. At the intersection of European learning and colonial power, Macaulay can conceive of nothing other than "a class of interpreters between us and the millions whom we govern—a class of persons Indian in blood and colour, but English in tastes, in opinions, in morals and in intellect"[6]—in other words a mimic man raised "through our English School," as a missionary educationist wrote in 1819, "to form a corps of translators and be employed in different departments of Labour."[7] The line of descent of the mimic man can be traced through the works of Kipling, Forester, Orwell, Naipaul, and to his emergence, most recently, in Benedict Anderson's excellent essay on nationalism, as the anomalous Bipin Chandra Pal.[8] He is the effect of a flawed colonial mimesis, in which to be Anglicized, is *emphatically* not to be English.

The figure of mimicry is locatable within what Anderson describes as "the inner incompatibility of empire and nation."[9] It problematizes the signs of racial and cultural

---

[4]Charles Grant, "Observations on the State of Society among the Asiatic Subjects of Great Britain," *Sessional Papers,* vol. 10, no. 282 (1812–13), East India Company.

[5]Ibid., chap. 4, p. 104.

[6]T. B. Macaulay, "Minute on Education," in *Sources of Indian Tradition,* vol. II, ed. William Theodore de Bary (New York: Columbia University Press, 1958), p. 49.

[7]Mr. Thomason's communication to the Church Missionary Society, September 5, 1819, in *The Missionary Register,* 1821, pp. 54–55.

[8]Benedict Anderson, *Imagined Communities* (London: Verso, 1983), p. 88.

[9]Ibid., pp. 88–89.

priority, so that the "national" is no longer naturalizable. What emerges between mimesis and mimicry is a *writing*, a mode of representation, that marginalizes the monumentality of history, quite simply mocks its power to be a model, that power which supposedly makes it imitable. Mimicry *repeats* rather than *re-presents* and in that diminishing perspective emerges Decoud's displaced European vision of Sulaco as:

> the endlessness of civil strife where folly seemed even harder to bear than its ignominy . . . the lawlessness of a populace of all colours and races, barbarism, irremediable tyranny. . . . America is ungovernable.[10]

Or Ralph Singh's apostasy in Naipaul's *The Mimic Men*:

> We pretended to be real, to be learning, to be preparing ourselves for life, we mimic men of the New World, one unknown corner of it, with all its reminders of the corruption that came so quickly to the new.[11]

Both Decoud and Singh, and in their different ways Grant and Macaulay, are the parodists of history. Despite their intentions and invocations they inscribe the colonial text erratically, eccentrically across a body politic that refuses to be representative, in a narrative that refuses to be representational. The desire to emerge as "authentic" through mimicry—through a process of writing and repetitio—is the final irony of partial representation.

What I have called mimicry is not the familiar exercise of *dependent* colonial relations through narcissistic identification so that, as Fanon has observed,[12] the black man stops being an actional person for only the white man can represent his self-esteem. Mimicry conceals no presence or identity behind its mask: it is not what Césaire describes as "colonialization-thingification."[13] behind which there stands the essence of the *présence Africaine*. The *menace* of mimicry is its *double* vision which in disclosing the ambivalence of colonial discourse also disrupts its authority. And it is a double-vision that is a result of what I've described as the partial representation/recognition of the colonial object. Grant's colonial as partial imitator, Macaulay's translator, Naipaul's colonial politician as play-actor, Decoud as the scene setter of the *opéra bouffe* of the New World, these are the appropriate objects of a colonialist chain of command, authorized versions of otherness. But they are also, as I

have shown, the figures of a doubling, the part-objects of a metonymy of colonial desire which alienates the modality and normality of those dominant discourses in which they emerge as "inappropriate" colonial subjects. A desire that, through the repetition of *partial presence,* which is the basis of mimicry, articulates those disturbances of cultural, racial, and historical difference that menace the narcissistic demand of colonial authority. It is a desire that reverses "in part" the colonial appropriation by now producing a partial vision of the colonizer's presence. A gaze of otherness, that shares the acuity of the genealogical gaze which, as Foucault describes it, liberates marginal elements and shatters the unity of man's being through which he extends his sovereignty.[14]

I want to turn to this process by which the look of surveillance returns as the displacing gaze of the disciplined, where the observer becomes the observed and "partial" representation rearticulates the whole notion of *identity* and alienates it from essence. But not before observing that even an exemplary history like Eric Stokes's *The English Utilitarians in India* acknowledges the anomalous gaze of otherness but finally disavows it in a contradictory utterance:

> Certainly India played *no* central part in fashioning the distinctive qualities of English civilisation. In many ways it acted as a disturbing force, a magnetic power placed at the periphery tending to distort the natural development of Britain's character. . . .[15]

What is the nature of the hidden threat of the partial gaze? How does mimicry emerge as the subject of the scopic drive and the object of colonial surveillance? How is desire disciplined, authority displaced?

If we turn to a Freudian figure to address these issues of colonial textuality, that form of difference that is mimicry— *almost the same but not quite*—will become clear. Writing of the partial nature of fantasy, caught *inappropriately,* between the unconscious and the preconscious, making problematic, like mimicry, the very notion of "origins," Freud has this to say:

> Their mixed and split origin is what decides their fate. We may compare them with individuals of mixed race who taken all round resemble white men but who betray their coloured descent by some striking feature or other and on that account are excluded from society and enjoy none of the privileges.[16]

---

[10]Joseph Conrad, *Nostromo* (London: Penguin, 1979), p. 161.

[11]V. S. Naipaul, *The Mimic Men* (London: Penguin, 1967), p. 146.

[12]Frantz Fanon, *Black Skin, White Masks* (London: Paladin, 1970), p. 109.

[13]Aimé Césaire, *Discourse on Colonialism* (New York: Monthly Review Press, 1972), p. 21.

[14]Michel Foucault, "Nietzsche, Genealogy, History," in *Language, Counter-Memory, Practice,* trans. Donald F. Bouchard and Sherry Simon (Ithaca: Cornell University Press, 1977), p. 153.

[15]Eric Stokes, *The English Utilitarians and India* (Oxford, Oxford University Press, 1959), p. xi.

[16]Sigmund Freud, "The Unconscious" (1915), SE, XIV, pp. 190–91.

Almost the same but not white: the visibility of mimicry is always produced at the site of interdiction. It is a form of colonial discourse that is uttered *inter dicta:* a discourse at the crossroads of what is known and permissible and that which though known must be kept concealed; a discourse uttered between the lines and as such both against the rules and within them. The question of the representation of difference is therefore always also a problem of authority. The "desire" of mimicry, which is Freud's *striking feature* that reveals so little but makes such a big difference, is not merely that impossibility of the Other which repeatedly resists signification. The desire of colonial mimicry—an interdictory desire—may not have an object, but it has strategic objectives which I shall call the *metonymy of presence.*

Those inappropriate signifiers of colonial discourse—the difference between being English and being Anglicized; the identity between stereotypes which, through repetition, also become different; the discriminatory identities constructed across traditional cultural norms and classifications, the Simian Black, the Lying Asiatic—all these are metonymies of presence. They are strategies of desire in discourse that make the anomalous representation of the colonized something other than a process of "the return of the repressed," what Fanon unsatisfactorily characterized as collective catharsis.[17] These instances of metonymy are the nonrepressive productions of contradictory and multiple belief. They cross the boundaries of the culture of enunciation through a strategic confusion of the metaphoric and metonymic axes of the cultural production of meaning. For each of these instances of "a difference that is almost the same but not quite" inadvertently creates a crisis for the cultural priority given to the *metaphoric* as the process of repression and substitution which negotiates the difference between paradigmatic systems and classifications. In mimicry, the representation of identity and meaning is rearticulated along the axis of metonymy. As Lacan reminds us, mimicry is like camouflage, not a harmonization or repression of difference, but a form of *resemblance* that differs/defends presence by displaying it in part, metonymically. Its threat, I would add, comes from the prodigious and strategic production of conflictual, fantastic, discriminatory "identity effects" in the play of a power that is elusive because it hides no essence, no "itself." And that form of *resemblance* is the most terrifying thing to behold, as Edward Long testifies in his *History of Jamaica* (1774). At the end of a tortured, negrophobic passage, that shifts anxiously between piety, prevarication, and perversion, the text finally

confronts its fear; nothing other than the repetition of its resemblance "in part":

> (Negroes) are represented by all authors as the vilest of human kind, to which they have little more pretension of resemblance *than what arises from their exterior forms* (my italics).[18]

From such a colonial encounter between the white presence and its black semblance, there emerges the question of the ambivalence of mimicry as a problematic of colonial subjection. For if Sade's scandalous theatricalization of language repeatedly reminds us that discourse can claim "no priority," then the work of Edward Said will not let us forget that the "ethnocentric and erratic will to power from which texts can spring"[19] is itself a theater of war. Mimicry, as the metonymy of presence is, indeed, such an erratic, eccentric strategy of authority in colonial discourse. Mimicry does not merely destroy narcissistic authority through the repetitious slippage of difference and desire. It is the process of the *fixation* of the colonial as a form of cross-classificatory, discriminatory knowledge in the defiles of an interdictory discourse, and therefore necessarily raises the question of the *authorization* of colonial representations. A question of authority that goes beyond the subject's lack of priority (castration) to a historical crisis in the conceptuality of colonial man as an *object* of regulatory power, as the subject of racial, cultural, national representation.

"This culture . . . fixed in its colonial status," Fanon suggests, "(is) both present and mummified, it testified against its members. It defines them in fact without appeal."[20] The ambivalence of mimicry—almost but not quite—suggests that the fetishized colonial culture is potentially and strategically an insurgent counter-appeal. What I have called its "identity-effects," are always crucially *split.* Under cover of camouflage, mimicry, like the fetish, is a part-object that radically revalues the normative knowledges of the priority of race, writing, history. For the fetish mimes the forms of authority at the point at which it deauthorizes them. Similarly, mimicry rearticulates presence in terms of its "otherness," that which it disavows. There is a crucial difference between this *colonial* articulation of man and his doubles and that which Foucault describes as "thinking the unthought"[21] which, for nineteenth-century Europe, is the end-

---

[17]Fanon, p. 103.

[18]Edward Long, *A History of Jamaica,* 1774, vol. 2, p. 353.

[19]Edward Said, "The Text, the World, the Critic," in *Textual Strategies,* ed. J.V. Harari (Ithaca: Cornell University Press, 1979), p. 184.

[20]Frantz Fanon, "Racism and Culture," trans. H. Chevalier, in *Toward the African Revolution* (London: Pelican, 1967), p. 44.

[21]Michel Foucault, *The Order of Things* (New York: Pantheon, 1970), part 2, chap. 9.

ing of man's alienation by reconciling him with his essence. The colonial discourse that articulates an *interdictory* "otherness" is precisely the "other scene" of this nineteenth-century European desire for an authentic historical consciousness.

The "unthought" across which colonial man is articulated is that process of classificatory confusion that I have described as the metonymy of the substitutive chain of ethical and cultural discourse. This results in the *splitting* of colonial discourse so that two attitudes towards external reality persist; one takes reality into consideration while the other disavows it and replaces it by a product of desire that repeats, rearticulates "reality" as mimicry.

So Edward Long can say with authority, quoting variously, Hume, Eastwick, and Bishop Warburton in his support, that:

> Ludicrous as the opinion may seem I do not think that an orang-utang husband would be any dishonour to a Hottentot female.[22]

Such contradictory articulations of reality and desire—seen in racist stereotypes, statements, jokes, myths—are not caught in the doubtful circle of the return of the repressed. They are the effects of a disavowal that denies the differences of the other but produces in its stead forms of authority and multiple belief that alienate the assumptions of "civil" discourse. If, for a while, the ruse of desire is calculable for the uses of discipline soon the repetition of guilt, justification, pseudoscientific theories, superstition, spurious authorities, and classifications can be seen as the desperate

effort to "normalize" *formally* the disturbance of a discourse of splitting that violates the rational, enlightened claims of its enunciatory modality. The ambivalence of colonial authority repeatedly turns from *mimicry*—a difference that is almost nothing but not quite—to *menace*—a difference that is almost total but not quite. And in that other scene of colonial power, where history turns to farce and presence to "a part," can be seen the twin figures of narcissism and paranoia that repeat furiously, uncontrollably.

In the ambivalent world of the "not quite/not white," on the margins of metropolitan desire, the *founding objects* of the Western world become the erratic, eccentric, accidental *objects trouvés* of the colonial discourse—the part-objects of presence. It is then that the body and the book lose their part-objects of presence. It is then that the body and the book lose their representational authority. Black skin splits under the racist gaze, displaced into signs of bestiality, genitalia, grotesquerie, which reveal the phobic myth of the undifferentiated whole white body. And the holiest of books—the Bible—bearing both the standard of the cross and the standard of empire finds itself strangely dismembered. In May 1817 a missionary wrote from Bengal:

> Still everyone would gladly receive a Bible. And why?—that he may lay it up as a curiosity for a few pice; or use it for waste paper. Such it is well known has been the common fate of these copies of the Bible. . . . Some have been bartered in the markets, others have been thrown in snuff shops and used as wrapping paper.[23]

---

[22]Long, p. 364.

[23]*The Missionary Register,* May 1817, p. 186.

HELEN GILBERT AND JOANNE TOMPKINS,
from *Post-Colonial Drama* (1996)

Helen Gilbert and Joanne Tompkins are both well known for their studies of postcolonial theater and drama, and teach at the University of Queensland, Australia. In this selection from their recent book Post-Colonial Drama, *Gilbert and Tompkins discuss the ways in which the body can be made to represent the impact of gender, racial, or sexualizing ideologies, and so become a site for social critique in performance. In their wide-ranging discussion of the formation of gendered and racialized bodies onstage, Gilbert and Tompkins take in many of the plays and playwrights represented in this Unit. How does this discussion of embodiment relate to the treatment of bodies in the texts of modern plays, or in the staging of bodies in the modern theater? How does the notion of "inscription"—treating the body as though it were always a signifier, already "written" with meanings—help us to understand the relationships between colonized and colonizing subjects in contemporary drama? Is it possible to use this critique of racialized and gendered bodies to read against the grain of earlier playwrights?*

The body is the inscribed surface of events (traced by language and dissolved by ideas), the locus of a dissociated self (adopting the illusion of substantial unity), and a volume of disintegration.
—Foucault (1977): 148

Foucault's definition of the body omits a crucial performative fact: the body also *moves*. In the theatre, the actor's body is the major physical symbol; it is distinguished from other such symbols by its capacity to offer a multifarious complex of meanings. The body signifies through both its appearance and its actions. As well as indicating such categories as race and gender, the performing body can also express place and narrative through skilful mime and/or movement. Moreover, it interacts with all other stage signifiers—notably costume, set, and dialogue—and, crucially, with the audience. It is not surprising, then, that the body functions as one of the most charged sites of theatrical representation.

The colonised subject's body, as Elleke Boehmer explains, has been an object of the coloniser's fascination and repulsion (and, in effect, possession) in sexual, pseudo-scientific, and political terms:

> In colonial representation, exclusion or suppression can often literally be seen as 'embodied'. From the point of view of the colonizer specifically, fears and curiosities, sublimated fascinations with the strange or the 'primitive', are expressed in concrete physical and anatomical images. . . . [T]he Other is cast as corporeal, carnal, untamed, instinctual, raw, and therefore also open to mastery, available for use, for husbandry, for numbering, branding, cataloging, description or possession.

Paying attention to the body can be a highly useful (and even essential) strategy for reconstructing post-colonial subjectivity because imperialist discourse has been both insidious and persuasive in its construction of the colonised subject as an inscribed object of knowledge. As Elizabeth Grosz argues, the body is never simply a passive object upon which regimes of power are played out:

> If the body is the strategic target of systems of codification, supervision and constraint, it is also because the body and its energies and capacities exert an uncontrollable, unpredictable threat to a regular, systematic mode of social organisation. As well as being the site of knowledge-power, the body is thus a site of *resistance*, for it exerts a recalcitrance, and always entails the possibility of a counter-strategic reinscription, for it is capable of being self-marked, self-represented in alternative ways.

The ways in which the reinscription and self-representation of colonised bodies translate into performative strategies is obviously a key issue for post-colonial theatre. Hence, current movements towards cultural decolonisation involve not just a verbal/textual counter-discourse but a reviewing of the body and its signifying practices. Whereas narrative writing tends to erase the gender and race of its authors and protagonists through its production as an artefact of predominantly western cultures, performance centralises the physical and socio-cultural specificities of its participants. It follows that post-colonial theatre (much like feminist theatre) finds in the body more than mere 'actor function' or 'actor vehicle'. The body's ability to move, cover up, reveal itself, and even 'fracture' on stage provides it with many possible sites for decolonisation.

In general, the post-colonial body disrupts the constrained space and signification left to it by the colonisers and becomes a site for resistant inscription. For instance, the Kathakali actor's stylised facial expressions signify the history of specific Indian acting traditions and communicate the carefully preserved systems of meaning through the actor's body. The colonial subject's body contests its stereotyping and representation by others to insist on self-representation by its physical presence on the stage. Corporeal signifiers quickly become politicised when a black actor appears in a traditionally 'white' role, or when a West Indian cast stages, say, a Shakespearian play; such choices, as well as colour-blind casting, contribute to the development of an identity independent from the imposed colonial one of inadequacy, subordination, and often barbarity. Because the body is open to multifarious inscriptions which produce it as a dialogic, ambivalent, and unstable signifier rather than a single, independent, and discrete entity, it is not surprising that the production of some sort of personal or cultural subjectivity via the body is complex indeed.

The post-colonial subject is often preoccupied with refusing colonially determined labels and definitions, especially those which operate in the name of race and gender. Part of the project of redefining staged identity is to affix the *colonised's* choice of signification to the body rather than to maintain the limited tropes traditionally assigned to it. This oppositional process of *embodiment* whereby the colonised creates his/her own subjectivity ascribes more flexible, culturally laden, and multivalent delineations to the body, rather than circumscribing it within an imposed, imperialist calculation of otherness. The post-colonial stage offers opportunities to recuperate the colonised subject's body—especially when it has been maimed or otherwise rendered 'incomplete'—and to transform its signification and its subjectivity. This chapter explores the process of recuperation by examining some of the basic performative elements of the post-colonial body: how it looks, what it does, how it is seen, and, most importantly, how it presents itself.

As *visual* markers of 'identity', race and gender are particularly significant in theatrical contexts even if their connotations are sometimes highly unstable. It is crucial to remember, however, that such markers are inscribed on the body through discourse—visual, verbal, or otherwise—rather than simply being unmediated or objectively given. In other words, the perceived (constructed) binary categories of male/female and white/black are never merely biologically determined but are also historically and ideologically conditioned. Moreover, as our earlier discussion of various feminisms indicates, race and gender are distinct, albeit sometimes intersecting and/or overlapping, factors which cannot be collapsed under the conceptual umbrella of marginalisation. It follows, then, that there can be neither an unproblematically essentialised 'black', 'female', or any other kind of body nor, conversely, can there be a universalised body which categorically avoids these markers of difference. If post-colonial theory has long rejected the idealised undifferentiated body of the other that is characteristic of imperialist discourse, representational practice—especially in largely iconic art-forms such as theatre—still faces the problem of how to avoid essentialist constructions of race and gender while recognising the irreducible specificity of their impact on subject formation. One possible solution is to conceptualise all markers of identity/difference as partial, provisional, and likely to change depending upon the context or the signifying system in which they operate at any particular time. This notion avoids a single (biological) origin for race or gender but leaves open the possibility of what Spivak calls 'strategic essentialism—'the foregrounding of 'pure' difference for particular political purposes.

RACE

Since one of the key features of colonialism has been the exertion of European authority over non-white peoples, it is not surprising that an emphasis on race is widespread in post-colonial drama, particularly when the projected audience includes a high proportion of white (or otherwise dominant) viewers. Two parallel, if apparently contradictory, strategies are evident: to emphasise racial difference as part of a 'scrupulously visible political interest' (Spivak) designed to recuperate marginalised subjects, or, alternatively, to dismantle all racial categories by showing their constructedness. Some plays adopt both of these approaches simultaneously, a manoeuvre which often results in a dialectical tension that further destabilises 'race' as a signifying code. A case in point is Chi and Kuckles's *Bran Nue Dae*, which highlights the presence of a large cast of Australian Aboriginal characters/ actors while at the same time insisting that race is less a colour than an attitude. In this context, it becomes artistically plausible that even several 'white' characters (played by non-Aborigines) eventually discover their Aboriginality. The play participates in current debates in Australia about the construction of Aboriginal identity and notions of authenticity based primarily on skin colour.

The physical stage presence of black, indigenous, or otherwise 'coloured' actors cannot be undervalued in discussing the counter-discursive possibilities of the body in performance, even if what constitutes race is neither fixed nor objectively measurable. On one level, staging the visibility of imperialism's racial other is in itself a subversive act since Anglo-European theatre has a long history of excluding non-

white actors while maintaining *representations* of racial difference, usually constructed through costume, make-up, and/or mask. The Othello of Shakespeare's day, for example, was played by a white actor who 'blacked up' and donned a curly-haired wig, a tradition which varied little for centuries. Not just a trope in popular entertainment (epitomised by Al Jolson's blackface performances in the early part of this century), blackface was used by Sir Laurence Olivier's version of *Othello* even as recently as the 1960s. When racially marked characters are played in this way, the resistance potential of the fictionalised black/coloured body is compromised by the 'wayward signification' of the actor's whiteness (Goldie). Matching the race (and/or gender) of the actor with that of the character does not mean, however, that the performing body completely escapes the web of imperial inscription. Rather, the body is inevitably 'read' through multiple codes and contexts and shaped not only by the narrative structures of a play itself but also by its audience. Historically, this has meant that when the nonwhite actor performed on western stages, his/her body generally carried a kind of mystique that both heightened and detracted from its significance. Another mode of *mis*representation consistent with colonial attempts to figure racial others as inferior and/or subordinate was thus conventionalised.

Whereas much western culture constructs the female body on stage as a passive to-be-looked-at object rather than as an active subject, the racially distinct body is often designed to be *overlooked* (in two senses of the word: to be examined more fully than other signifiers as an object of curiosity *and* to be rendered invisible as an object of disregard). Until quite recently, many post-colonial plays devised by whites fell into this representational trap by depicting sentimentalised or exoticised versions of racial difference. Terry Goldie's study of settler drama in Canada, Australia, and New Zealand demonstrates the ways in which images of the indigene have been circumscribed by a semiotic field that is limited to seven signifiers: orality, mysticism, violence, nature, sexuality, historicity, and an imitation of indigenous 'forms' of communication. Often moved on or off stage to create a particular atmosphere and/or elicit laughter, indigenous characters have functioned as stage properties, as fragments of the setting, and, at times, as foils against which the normative values of white society can be defined. Likewise, roles for blacks in the wider field of western drama have been constituted within racist discourses, with perhaps even more emphasis on their supposed violence and sexuality. In these prescribed spaces, imperialism's colonised subject is denied its full humanity; it performs an imposed representational function rather than being a focal point in its own right. And while some roles can be subverted in performance, there is little scope in such plays for significant interrogation of dominant assumptions about race.

When indigenous and black playwrights depict themselves on stage, the body is one of the first theatrical elements to take on new iconic possibilities. One text that manipulates the body's signification for political purposes is Monique Mojica's *Princess Pocahontas and the Blue Spots*, which deconstructs the semiotic field of 'Indianness'—to use Daniel Francis's concept of the term (1992)—by staging its common inscriptions in juxtaposition to alternative (and generally more empowering) expressions of native North American subjectivity. Conflicting images/identities are held in tension through the performing body of Contemporary Woman #1, who plays (with) the white-defined stereotypes presented, as well as transforming herself into various native characters. In this way, Mojica provides a critical rereading of the ways in which indigenous women have characteristically been coded and constrained by North and South American history, culture, and literature. The women's bodies contort to create images of imposed signifying codes; they also depict the scenery, including a volcano, thereby critiquing the conventional use of indigenous bodies to suggest the geographical landscape and/or to provide an apparently authentic atmosphere. The play employs an overabundance of clichéd Hollywood and explorer/ pioneer depictions of the 'Indian' in order to demonstrate their emptiness as representations: the sheer number of represented 'Indian' and 'native' bodies destabilises the power of the imposed depictions. Such figures as the Cigar Store Squaw, the Storybook Princess, and Princess Buttered-on-Both-Sides are effectively meaningless, having been overdetermined by and within white discourse. More specifically, Pocahontas, Christianised and re-named Lady Rebecca, is 'stuck [and] girdled' in the costume of the 'good Indian' even if it is clearly an uncomfortable fit. These 'museum exhibits' contrast sharply with the two contemporary women and with others recuperated from the margins of imperial representation: Matoaka (the younger persona of Pocahontas), Malinche, and the three Métis women who demand that their stories be told. The Storybook Princess and the Cigar Store Squaw are predictably wooden in personality and in their movements on the stage, whereas Matoaka and Malinche, in particular, embody sexualities that cannot be contained within the virgin/whore paradigm imposed upon them by the British and the Spaniards.

Mojica's interest in countering the semiotic codes of cinema and television is shared by other native Canadian writers such as Margo Kane, Daniel David Moses, and Tomson Highway, all of whom have dramatised characters/events that rework the stereotype of the Hollywood Indian. In Australia,

the project of reconstructing an indigenous subjectivity is slightly different in so far as Aborigines have been less often mythologised in/ through popular representation than simply ignored, especially in visual media. In some ways, then, the conventional Aboriginal body is underdetermined because of its systematic erasure, rather than overdetermined as a result of repeated exposure. This is not to suggest that Aborigines escape the designation of 'other', but to argue that this particular other is often less well-delineated in imperial discourse than is the 'Indian'. Nevertheless, Aboriginal inscriptions of corporeality—as opposed to European constructions of Aboriginality or a generic and even less specific otherness—function to embody in Aborigines on stage a different, more culturally accurate, subjectivity. Jack Davis's plays address the blind spots of settler history and literature on a number of levels, bringing the black body into acute visibility via individual characters (often dancers) and also through group interaction (especially across colour lines). *Kullark,* for example, inverts imperialism's racial norms in a comic depiction of first contact when Mitjitjiroo responds to Captain Stirling's proffered hand by rubbing its skin vigorously to see if the white stain can be removed. This gesture, along with the Aborigines' astonishment at the strange appearance of the Europeans, denaturalises the white body as the dominant sign of humanity. In a related manoeuvre, the play points to the *in*humanity of the invaders when they decapitate Yagan and skin him in order to remove his tribal markings for a souvenir. Here, Davis suggests that the mutilated black body functions within the colonising culture as a fetishised object. His overall project is to reinstate the corporeal presence of the Aborigines in history—and, on a metatheatrical level, in theatre—at the same time as he details the colonisers' attempts to annihilate all signs of difference. Reference to such atrocities does not mean, however, that *Kullark* simply stereotypes its characters according to race, reassigning the connotations of 'black' and 'white' in the process; rather, this play, like Davis's other works, carefully stages the misunderstandings brought about by discourses of racial otherness in a context where it is possible for conceptual gaps to be bridged. . . .

GENDER

The South African plays discussed demonstrate the constructedness of racial categories at the same time as they attempt to (re)claim strategic, if negotiable, race-inflected identities. For many post-colonial dramatists, particularly women, a parallel project is to recuperate female subjectivities while showing that gender is an ideology mapped across the body in and through representation. It seems, however, that the imperative is less to deconstruct the category of female (or male) than to intervene in the discourses that naturalise gender hierarchies. This pattern is possibly related to the perceived fixity of the gender binary. White/black classifications are quickly broken down by racial hybridity—indeed the threat of miscegenation is precisely that it produces visible signs of the permeability of racial boundaries. Gender classifications, in contrast, most often admit androgyny as merely as hypothetical category which can be dissolved into male *or* female when the biological markers of sex are known. Some writers and practitioners do share Anglo-American feminism's interest in destabilising gender binaries, whether through 'sex-radical' performance or through visually recorded (transvestite) bodies, but most are more concerned with demarcating areas of women's subjugation under imperialism. Accordingly, gender is less likely to function alone as a category of discrimination in post-colonial plays than in combination with other factors such as race, class, and/or cultural background. An additional factor complicating the delineation of a gender-specific body politics is the metaphorical link between woman and the land, a powerful trope in imperial discourse and one which is reinforced, consciously or not, in much post-colonial drama, particularly by male writers. In some instances, women's bodies are not only exploited by the colonisers but also reappropriated by the colonised patriarchy as part of a political agenda which may not fully serve the interests of the women in question.

Rape is a prominent signifier in a number of plays, particularly in countries where settlers' annexation of so-called 'unoccupied territories' disrupted not only the culture but also the livelihoods of indigenous peoples. Both native and non-native dramatists have featured inter-racial rape as an analogue for the colonisers' violation of the land, and also for related forms of economic and political exploitation. Often such representations are designed to reveal less about the experiences of the oppressed than about the rape mentality of the oppressors. In the chilling final moments of Canadian George Ryga's *The Ecstasy of Rita Joe,* for example, the rape and murder of the central protagonist by three white men provides a graphic depiction of the widespread brutality of the colonial/judicial system. This play figures Rita Joe as the site on and through which the disciplinary inscriptions of imperial patriarchy are played out as her body is progressively marked by capture, assault, and sexual penetration. Politically, she functions less as an individual than as an emblem of native cultures in Canada; hence, her death signals the grim triumph of the imperial project. As Gary Boire argues, Ryga's text can be read as a 'Foucaultian allegory' which foregrounds the sexually fragmented body of Rita Joe in order to chart the systems of power that instigate

and maintain the settler/invader society's dominance over indigenous groups.

Depending on how they are staged, theatrical images of sexual violence can have more than merely illustrative functions; in some instances, they also challenge the voyeuristic gaze of the white spectator, inviting him/her to admit complicity in that violence. Janis Balodis's *Too Young for Ghosts* critiques white invasion of indigenous land/ culture in Australia in a complex 'cross-over' scene in which the same actors play Aboriginal and Latvian women almost simultaneously. The scene collapses the rapes of two Aboriginal women with the sexual assault of their Latvian counterparts in a displaced persons camp after World War Two. This visual conflation—achieved through doubling roles and overlaying theatrical time and space—is a performative technique intended to elicit both empathy for the Aboriginal women and outrage against the colonial regime, here constructed as a more local 'war' for control over native land/bodies. Throughout the composite rape scene, the audience's perspective is further manipulated by the presence of Karl, whose position as a callous observer reminds the viewers of their own non-intervention. By collapsing chronological and spatial frameworks, Balodis is able to use the bodies of white characters/actors to stand in for black ones without appropriating Aboriginal figures in service of a narrative about migrant experience. Instead, by refusing to display the violation of the black women, the performance text frustrates the libidinal economy of inter-racial rape while still harnessing this trope's metaphorical power to express the colonisers' attitudes and actions. Using different strategies for a similar effect, Dorothy Hewett's *The Man From Mukinupin* (1979) stages the 'rape' of Aboriginal women through a savagely ironic song which details the settlers' attempts to conquer the recalcitrant landscape, a project explicitly figured as the male penetration of female space. Hewett's call for the doubling of her one Aboriginal character with the female heroine, presumably played by a white actor, effectively highlights the ways in which all women have been discursively merged with each other and with the landscape.

The treatment of rape in texts by native dramatists who recognise the significant intersections of race and gender takes on slightly different inflections, especially when local mythologies inform the wider play. Tomson Highway's *The Rez Sisters,* for example, stages rape as a violation not only of the land but also of the very spirit of native culture. In a brief but visually haunting scene, the mentally disabled Zhaboonigan reveals that a gang of white boys penetrated her vagina with a screwdriver. While she details the event with the casual disinterest of a child who has only limited understanding of what has happened, the Ojibway trickster spirit, Nanabush, *embodies* her trauma by performing the 'agonising contortions' of the rape victim. Zhaboonigan's assault thus accrues wider significance, though her own body remains relatively unmarked because the trickster absorbs and transforms her experience. Moreover, the conventional gender paradigms of such a scene are somewhat complicated by the fact that Nanabush—a spirit, who adopts the forms of either and both genders simultaneously—is played by a male dancer. In what is to some extent a mirror image of *The Rez Sisters'* rape scene, Highway's controversial companion play, *Dry Lips Oughta Move to Kapuskasing,* enacts a native youth's sexual assault of a young native woman, Patsy Pegahmagahbow. That the rape is performed with a crucifix by a victim of foetal alcohol syndrome suggests that Christian imperialism is at least partly responsible for the current schism between native men and women. On a performative level, this scene also points to the desecration of indigenous land/culture by the colonising forces, a resonance achieved in a series of stylised movements in which Dickie Bird Halked repeatedly stabs his crucifix into the earth while Nanabush, here played by a woman, lifts her skirt to reveal the blood which slowly spreads down her legs. In *Dry Lips,* Nanabush and Patsy are embodied by the same ever-transforming actor who variously functions as the *idea* of the 'real' women referred to in the play *and* as the female trickster who again absorbs Patsy's experience. Although Highway has been accused of displaying sexism and gratuitous violence, it could be argued that *Dry Lips,* like *The Rez Sisters,* actually refuses the power of rape by subsuming it within the mythological frameworks invoked, since Nanabush is, above all, the great survivor and healer. Once again, the trickster's body—operating in this text as a sign of native women/culture/land that refigures the imperial collapsing of these categories—absorbs and transforms the forces which would leave it vulnerable and degraded. After the rape, Nanabush is visibly marked but still all-powerful as she reappears in various guises throughout the rest of the dream play, and then enters the 'real' action in a final triumphant moment with the baby that foreshadows a hopeful future for the Rez.

As all these images of sexual violence suggest, women's bodies often function in post-colonial theatre as the spaces on and through which larger territorial or cultural battles are being fought. In a similar fashion, representations of fertility, pregnancy, and motherhood frequently take on political inflections, a fact which is not surprising, given that imperialism's will to power over its (female) subjects also extended to the control of many aspects of reproduction. The slave trade, in which women were bought and sold for their 'breed-ing' capacities, is the most obvious example of a political economy based on the institutionalised commodification of the female body. Dennis Scott takes up this particular subject in one of the historical scenes of *An Echo in the Bone,* foregrounding the processes by which slavery reduced the female body to its sexual and reproductive functions. The setting is an early nineteenth-century auctioneer's office where three slaves are being inspected by a regular customer while the black middleman lists their attributes in turn, lingering over the two women:

> Now this—(To BRIGIT.) please make note, the wide hips, the breasts just filling out. No offspring yet. Do you wish to see proof of virginity—perhaps you'll wish to see for yourself—indeed, that's hardly necessary, we have a long association of trust, don't we, sir. Calves well muscled, exceedingly well turned, you will notice. . . . The other. . . . Here is the doctor's certificate, equally untouched. Notice the nipples. Fire in this one sir, you'll forgive my saying so. But the clear eyes show how easily she can be taught. All kinds of things.

With their bodies anatomised by the imperial gaze, the women are positioned as merchandise and are thus denied all sense of subjectivity. At the same time, they are constructed as sex objects *and* as passive children ripe for the expert tutelage (read exploitation) of the white master. Further degradation follows when Stone puts on a glove to examine the 'goods', inspecting one of the women's teeth and then running his hand up between her thighs, as if at a livestock sale. While the male slave is also commodified, he is not described in corporeal terms; indeed, his best selling feature is that he 'can read, write and reckon like a schoolmaster'. This scene exemplifies gender's impact on slavery: women's bodies are marked for consumption within imperialism's particular brand of patriarchy. The added focus on the middleman's ingratiating 'sales talk' also gives weight to the theory that in patriarchal systems women function in a symbolic exchange which cements the relationships between men—in this case between the white slave owner and the black agent who acts as proxy for the buyer.

Whereas the bodies of black women were commandeered in some colonies to breed a slave class to fulfil the demands of imperialism's labour market, white women's bodies were often appropriated to preserve the racial (and moral) integrity of the ruling class. In Africa and India, as well as in the Caribbean, the colonial woman/wife was expected, indeed compelled, to offer her sexual, social, and reproductive labours in the service of the Empire. Where the goal was settlement rather than rule, white women were even more crucial to the imperial project because of the imperative to (re)populate newly conquered lands. Jill Shearer's quasi-historical play, *Catherine* (1978), demonstrates how the body of the

Australian settler woman functioned as part of the physical terrain upon which colonial expansion was mapped, both literally and symbolically. A large section of this metatheatrical text details the shipment of the first convict women to Botany Bay and makes abundantly clear the fact that such 'cargo' was designed to 'balance the imbalance' of the colony—that is, to prevent the male settlers' deviant sexual behaviour (with indigenous women or other men) and to provide progeny for the successful peopling of the nation. The main character, Catherine, becomes pregnant by the ship's surgeon but will not be allowed to keep her child, who has been earmarked as the first of a new generation of Australians whose ignominious heritage must be suppressed. The proposed management of Catherine's pregnancy—she will be taken care of only until she can safely deliver the baby into its father's hands—highlights the transplanted society's complete disregard for women themselves. While much of the play's narrative content critiques the convict system by exposing the ways in which it facilitated institutional control over the female body, the performance text insists on staging women's subjectivity: its structure as a play-within-a-play enables the recuperation of Catherine's body as a group of contemporary actors continually rehearse and re-interpret the fragments of her history to provide a wider comment on gender oppression.

If the settler woman's reproductive labour was harnessed in the interests of expanding the Empire, the indigenous woman's fertility presented a threat to the colonisers and was often suppressed. Eva Johnson's *Murras* (1988) addresses this issue in Australia by referring to the deliberate and systematic sterilisation of pubescent Aboriginal girls who are duped into taking medication that renders them infertile. *Murras* illustrates ways in which native women's bodies become sites of conquest in the imperial regime and how they are permanently marked by its various administrative systems, even those which purport to be benevolent. As Ruby says of her daughter in the closing scene, 'She carries the scars of the *wudjella's* [whitefellow's] medicine'. While generally much less harmful than the enforced sterilisation detailed in *Murras*, medical management of pregnancy and childbirth also has the effect, if not the intention, of bringing the bodies of indigenous women under control. Sistren Theatre Collective's *Bellywoman Bangarang* (1978) takes up the issue of western medicine as part of its focus on teenage pregnancy in Jamaica, and attempts to reclaim the birthing process through the use of African-based rituals which emphasise female power. The play's opening image features three masked interlocking figures as the mother-woman, a healer and protector who mimes a traditional labour before transforming herself into a modern-day doctor in a movement which indicates the medicalisation of childbirth. After

the stories of the four pregnant girls have been told, the mother-woman returns at the end of the play to oversee the births. She guides Marie through a difficult labour and also frees her from the ropes (symbols of fear and self-loathing) which have entangled her since her rape. Like the trickster in Highway's plays, the mother-woman is a regenerative force/spirit who disperses the effects of trauma, restoring the colonised body to physical and spiritual health.

Imperialism's attempt to exercise authority over the reproductive processes of its female subjects is sometimes paralleled with more local tendencies to reduce women to functions of gender and/or fertility. Some post-colonial drama invests female fertility with great symbolic importance but none the less subordinates women to the interests of the colonised patriarchy. In India and Africa in particular, male writers are inclined to image the land as a mother and to present the truly-fecund woman as a signifier of nationhood. Giving birth thus becomes largely metaphorical, particularly in plays concerning independence from colonial rule, where the birth of a child mirrors the birth of the new nation. This trope, also common to Caribbean drama, occurs in Michael Gilkes's *Couvade* (1972) which invokes an Amerindian birthing ritual to articulate the play's complex dream-vision of a unified post-independent Guyana. The custom of *couvade* requires the father-to-be to undertake a trial or ordeal while his wife is in labour. This tradition is designed to affirm the connection between the unborn child and its father and to ensure a successful birth. *Couvade*, recently revised for Guyana's 1993 independence anniversary celebrations, uses the ritual to chart the psychological and spiritual 'rebirth' of the protagonist, Lionel, who, along with his newborn child, becomes emblematic of the nation. While the choice of ritual is apt for Gilkes's political vision, it shifts the focus of the birth from the woman (and the child) to the man and the community. Such paradigms figure the paternal body as much more significant than the maternal counterpart; thus, possible representations of the female post-colonial subject are often limited to the merely practical.

The maternal body is also compromised by her child in several plays when, for instance, stalled or uncertain progress towards decolonisation is figured by some kind of failure in the reproductive process. The unborn, stillborn, or otherwise incomplete child has special significance in this respect and often features in several signifying capacities: as well as representing the specific and local community, this child also acts as a site of struggle between competing political groups, especially in cultures that acknowledge the presence of ancestral spirits. The *abiku* or Half-Child in Soyinka's *A Dance of the Forests* (1960), a play about and for Nigeria's independence, represents the contemporary Nigerian world of spiritual transition, matching the political and social transition of the country. *A Dance of the Forests* is a cautionary rather than a purely celebratory play in so far as it recognises the difficulties inherent in attempts to unite the variety of forces that would impact on an independent Nigeria. The uncertain location of the *abiku* in this text also points to some of the dilemmas Nigerians would face in the following decades. Just as the *abiku* is neither living nor dead, neither body nor spirit, neither recognised nor forgotten, Nigeria's independence augurs an ambivalent future. A more hopeful treatment of the spirit child occurs in Walcott's *Ti-Jean and His Brothers* where the *bolum*, a disfigured foetus who represents the Caribbean people under the tyranny of colonialism, is eventually wrested from the clutches of the devil/plantation owner and reborn into full human life. In both of these plays, the female body is once again completely removed from the (potential) birthing process: the *abiku's* 'mother', the Dead Woman, has no say in the life or role of her half-child while the *bolum* is restored to the human world as a result of Ti-Jean's victory over the devil. On a performative level, the incomplete child-figure simply transforms from the spirit state as if birthing itself independently of any mother figure. This process was imaged through costuming codes in one recent video production of *Ti-Jean* where the *bolum* was encased in a huge egg-shell which it broke upon 'hatching'.

Examples such as these suggest that male playwrights are primarily interested in childbirth as a symbolic, often unifying trope. Women, on the other hand, have a vested interest in refusing the gender-specific roles/images that circumscribe their representation. One of the most important achievements of recent women's post-colonial writing is its refusal to endorse the traditional signifiers of gender, particularly those linked to reproduction and mothering. When motherhood is invoked, it frequently becomes a very mixed 'blessing', much as it is in Buchi Emecheta's ironically titled novel, *The Joys of Motherhood*. Interestingly, with a few exceptions, post-colonial plays by women tend not to centralise birth, perhaps in an attempt to fracture the concept of 'Mother Earth', an idealistic notion that denies women full humanity and compromises their ability to change, to choose, and to be individuated. The Canadian playwright, Judith Thompson, *does* frequently foreground pregnancies—in *The Crackwalker* (1980), *Tornado* (1987), and *I Am Yours*

(1987)—but these imminent births tend not to represent a bright hope for the future. Instead, they symbolise evil or a social cancer; regardless of the baby's health, pregnancy is a metaphor for disease in Thompson's work. Likewise, Sistren's *Bellywoman Bangarang* and Shearer's *Catherine* construct the pregnant body in terms of disorder and/or pathology rather than invoking traditional images of fruition.

Our discussion of the gendered body supports Ketu Katrak's argument that 'the traditions most oppressive for women [in colonised societies] are specifically located within the arena of female sexuality: fertility/infertility, motherhood and the sexual division of labour'. While women as narrative subjects are characteristically erased in imperial and patriarchal discourses, their corporeal presence is often intensified through a focus on factors such as sexuality and reproduction. This habit can be just as limiting as the neglect of gender-specific issues. As Peggy Phelan argues, 'In excessively marking the boundaries of the woman's *body*, in order to make it thoroughly visible, patriarchal culture subjects it to legal, artistic, and psychic surveillance. This, in turn, reinforces the idea that she *is* her body'. The challenge for post-colonial dramatists—both male and female—is to refuse such body politics while re-inscribing all theatricalised bodies with more enabling markers of gender. Yet, as Monique Mojica makes clear in *Princess Pocahontas and the Blue Spots*, women as a group cannot claim a collective victim status when they have been—and continue to be—complicit in the colonisation, appropriation, and denigration of other women. In this play, Contemporary Woman #1 refuses the feminist label because its collectivity tries to override her individuality as a subject who happens to be native and who happens to be female. The contemporary characters (and actors) present to their audience transforming, individuated bodies that refuse collectivity of any type if it does not also recognise the rights of the singular subject. Contemporary Woman #1 rejects the International Women's Day march until 'feminist shoes' manage to accommodate her 'wide, square, brown feet' and so allow her to 'feel the earth through their soles'. Refusing to be both the token 'Indian' and to represent all natives, this woman demands, in Gloria Anzaldua's words, 'the freedom to carve and chisel [her] own face', thus maintaining the individuality of her body *among* groups (mis)identified solely by race or gender. . . .

Glossary

Absurd *See* **Theater of the Absurd.**

Académie Française An academy founded by Cardinal Richelieu in 1635 to resolve the critical debate surrounding Corneille's play *The Cid* and to regularize the French language.

actos Short satirical plays devised by Luis Valdez and El Teatro Campesino in the late 1960s to dramatize the conditions of farmworkers in California.

afterpiece A short play—usually a pantomime or farce—that followed the main play on the evening's bill; common in England in the eighteenth and nineteenth centuries.

agora The marketplace in ancient Greek towns; the *agora* was often used for dramatic performance.

alienation effect A stage technique developed by Bertolt Brecht in the 1920s and 1930s for "estranging" the action of the play. By making characters and their actions seem remarkable, alien, or unusual, Brecht encouraged the audience to question the social realities that produced such events, the political and ideological background of the drama and of its stage production.

allegory A literary or dramatic technique that uses actual characters, places, and actions to represent more abstract political, moral, or religious ideas. *See Everyman.*

alojería The tavern at the rear of the **patio** in a Spanish Golden Age theater, or **corral.**

amphitheater A semicircular theater design, consisting of a playing area faced by rising tiers of seats; often used outdoors, this was the design of classical Greek theaters.

anachronism Using people, places, or things that are chronologically out of keeping with the rest of the fictive world of a play or narrative; for example, using medieval English shepherds to attend the birth of Christ in medieval **cycle plays.**

anagnorisis Greek term for a character's "recognition" of something previously not known in the play. In *The Poetics,* Aristotle links *anagnorisis* with **peripeteia,** the "reversal" in the action of the play.

antagonist The force or character that opposes the main character **(protagonist)** of a play.

antimasque A scene of misrule, usually involving witches, goblins, demons, or savages, who are transformed magically into princes, gods and goddesses, or virtues in a Jacobean **masque.**

antiphonal performance Alternative or responsive singing between individuals or groups; in the Middle Ages, it commonly involved two choirs.

archon A magistrate in classical Athens; each year, an *archon* was assigned the responsibility for organizing the **City Dionysia.**

apron The section of the stage that extends toward the auditorium beyond the **proscenium.**

Atellan farce Improvised comic skits featuring stock characters performed by masked actors in ancient Rome.

atoza Upstage area in a **Noh** theater in which the musicians are seated.

auto sacramentale Elaborate Spanish religious dramas originally devised as part of the feast of Corpus Christi. *Autos* continued to be performed in Spain until 1765.

avant-garde Literally, the "advance guard"; the term usually refers to the most innovative, experimental, or unorthodox artists in a given historical period. Used almost exclusively of late nineteenth- and twentieth-century movements.

backcloth A painted cloth lowered at the rear of the stage to represent a dramatic location.

Beijing Opera   Elaborate form of Chinese theater involving an onstage orchestra, ornate costumes, music, and dance.

benefit   In the English theater of the seventeenth, eighteenth, and nineteenth centuries, a performance whose profits were assigned to a single performer or to the playwright.

biomechanics   An experimental technique for actor training and performance devised by the Russian director Vsevolod Meyerhold after the Russian Revolution (1917). The technique emphasized the actor's physical training, stressing acrobatic and choreographic elements in production.

bhava   A stageable emotion in **Sanskrit drama,** related to the play's principal *rasa,* or mood.

biwa   Four-stringed, plucked instrument used to accompany spoken narration in medieval Japan.

blank verse   An English verse meter consisting of unrhymed **iambic pentameter** lines (ten syllables with alternating stress, the first stress falling on the second syllable).

box   Box seating first appeared in theaters in the late seventeenth century; boxes were arranged around the side of the stage and the sides of the auditorium for the private accommodation of small numbers of people. Boxes were more expensive than **pit** or **gallery** seats.

box set   First devised in the 1830s, a set consisting of three practical walls enclosing the stage in a roomlike way.

bunraku   The term used for modern Japanese **doll theater,** derived from the eighteenth-century master Uemura Bunrakuken.

butai   The acting area, or stage proper, of a **Noh** theater.

butoh   A powerful form of dance developed in the post-Hiroshima era in Japan; it features nude actors, covered in white powder, whose movements are slow and ethereal.

cabaret performance   Stage performances in restaurants serving food and drink; especially popular in Europe after World War I, cabarets often were used for innovative kinds of performance.

canon   An authorized body of texts, such as the *canon* of Shakespeare's known plays; also commonly used to mean a "traditional" body of texts.

capa y espada   Literally, "cape and sword" plays, swashbuckling romances in the Spanish Golden Age theater.

Capitano   The braggart soldier of *commedia dell' arte.*

carro   Wagon used for performance of Spanish *auto sacramentale.*

catastrophe   The turning point in the plot of a classical **tragedy.**

catharsis   Literally, the "purging" that Aristotle discusses as the effect of **tragedy** in his *The Poetics.* Catharsis has been variously described as an emotional release on the part of the spectators, or as the recognition and purging of wrongdoing in the action of the play.

cazuela   The women's **gallery** above the *alojería* in a Spanish Golden Age theater, or *corral.*

character   A fictional "person" appearing in a play or other work of fiction; usually conventionalized to some degree.

chonin   Japanese term for townsmen.

choregos   An important citizen in ancient Athens given the responsibility for financing, assembling, and training the chorus of Greek **tragedy.**

chorus   A masked group of young men who sang and danced as a group in Greek **tragedy** and **comedy;** larger choruses also performed *dithyrambs.*

City Dionysia   Annual spring festival honoring the god Dionysus; one of four festivals held between December and April. Sometimes called the *Great Dionysia,* it was the site of dramatic competitions and other public displays and rituals.

comedia nueva   Mixed mode form of drama associated with Lope de Vega.

Comédie Française   The official national theater of France, devoted to the staging of the classics. Founded and chartered by Louis XIV in 1680, when Molière's company and the Marais company were united.

comedy   Traditionally a humorous literary form, comedy typically concerns the trials of love, and/or ridicules the failings of certain members of society. *See* **comedy of manners, new comedy, old comedy, romantic comedy.**

comedy of manners   Comic drama that takes the manners of high society as its subject; in comedy of manners, the dialogue is often witty or epigrammatic.

commedia dell' arte   Improvised comic plays performed by itinerant companies; it originated in Italy in the sixteenth century and then spread throughout Europe. Actors each played a stock character type and improvised the action according to a shared outline plot.

constructivist theater   A movement in the Soviet theater after World War I, and often associated with the director Vsevolod Meyerhold. Adapted from the visual arts, constructivist theater resisted the use of representational sets, using more abstract "constructions" onstage.

corral   Open-air Spanish theater of the sixteenth and seventeenth centuries, constructed within an open courtyard.

cross-dressing   One of the conventions of cross-gendered acting, in which women play male characters in male costume, and men play female characters in women's clothing.

cycle plays   A series of plays dramatizing Christian history from the Creation to the Last Judgment, devised and performed in the Middle Ages by craft guilds called *mysteries;* the cycles are sometimes also called *mystery cycles* or *mystery plays.* Performed outside the church on the Feast of Corpus Christi.

Dada   A nonsense term adopted as the name of a literary and theatrical movement in Europe after World War I; Dada developed an esthetic of random and irrational art. Dada performances became popular in cabarets of Paris, Zurich, and Berlin in the 1920s.

daimyo   Feudal lord of Japan, member of the *samurai* class of warriors, and owing duty to the *shogun.*

decorum   The concept, associated with **neoclassicism,** that the action and subject matter (idealized), language (heightened), and moral propriety (elevated), should be stylistically integrated and unified.

deme   A neighborhood in classical Athens; the root of the modern word "democracy."

demonstration   Describing the *alienation effect,* Bertolt Brecht urged his actors to "demonstrate" the roles they played, rather than identifying with them in the mode of Stanislavskian acting. Acting-as-demonstration keeps the audience aware of both the actor *and* the "character" at the same time.

dengaku-no   Form of dance, role-playing, and acrobatics popular in Japan in the eleventh and twelfth centuries; said to be one of the progenitors of **Noh** theater.

desvanes   Small open galleries on the third and fourth stories in a Spanish Golden Age theater, or *corral.*

deus ex machina   Literally, the "god from the machine"; the term refers to the practice of using a crane to lower the character of a god to the stage at the end of a classical Greek **tragedy,** usually to resolve the action of the play. In modern usage the term refers to any dramatic device that suddenly resolves the action of a play.

dithyramb   Choral hymns sung and danced to honor Dionysus as part of the **City Dionysia.** Choruses of fifty men or fifty boys drawn from each tribe performed *dithyrambs* prior to the tragedy competition; Aristotle thought **tragedy** to have originated in these dithyrambic performances.

dokekata   Comic roles in **Kabuki** theater.

doll theater   Form of Japanese theater originating in the seventeenth century; doll theater uses elaborate dolls, operated by three visible puppeteers, and combines music and narration. The most prominent form of doll theater today is called *bunraku.*

Dottore   The "doctor" or old pedant of *commedia dell' arte;* usually a friend of **Pantalone.**

drama   A literary composition, usually in dialogue form, and centering on the actions of fictional characters.

Egungen   Festival common among the Yoruba peoples of Nigeria involving masks and costumes for communication with the dead.

ekkyklema   A low platform used to roll objects or bodies from the *skene* doors onto the stage in classical Greek theater.

emotion memory   A term developed by the Russian director Constantin Stanislavski to describe an actor's "work on himself" in acting. After considering a character's circumstances in the play and his past life leading up to the action of the play, the actor tries to connect the character's situation with important events in his or her own life: this emotional or affectual connection can make the character's display of emotion onstage seem realistic and immediate.

entremeses   Short plays performed as interludes between acts of Golden Age dramas.

environmental theater   A term coined by Richard Schechner in the late 1960s to describe performances that do not distinguish between the playing area and the audience; the performance takes place throughout the theatrical environment.

epic theater   A term associated with the German director Erwin Piscator and theorized by Bertolt Brecht in the late 1920s and 1930s, epic theater uses episodic dramatic action, nonrepresentational staging, and the **alienation effect,** to demonstrate the political, social, and economic factors governing the lives of the dramatic characters. In the theater, Brecht advocated the use of placards to announce the action, visible lighting, filmscreens on the stage, and other devices to produce this epic effect.

episode   Originally, a dramatic scene in a classical Greek **tragedy,** as distinct from the choral odes; now, usually refers to any incident or event in a play. Plays that are episodic tend not to subordinate episodes to a causal plot, but simply to arrange them in a series.

exodos   The final scene and exit of the characters and chorus in a classical Greek play.

expressionist theater   An early twentieth-century movement challenging the **verisimilitude** of realistic theater by staging individual emotional, unconscious states of mind directly. In expressionist plays, the action is usually abrupt and intense; the characters are usually generalized; the plot is typically symbolic or allegorical.

extravaganza   Visual spectacle popular in nineteenth-century theater.

Fabian society   A late nineteenth-century English socialist political society; Marxist in its orientation to social change, the Fabian society advocated a policy of gradual reform rather than revolution.

farce   Usually a short comic play, often relying on a highly coincidental plot.

film noir   A **genre** of black-and-white detective films popular in the 1940s, which frequently used shadowy, nighttime settings to establish an aura of menace and foreboding.

folio   A large-format printed volume, in which only four pages (two per side) are printed on each sheet of paper; the paper is folded once to form four pages.

fourth wall   Refers to the style of realistic theater since the late nineteenth century, in which the stage is treated as a room with one wall missing. The audience is not acknowledged or addressed by the actors, but overlooks the scene as a silent, invisible observer.

fuebashira   Flute-player's pillar in a **Noh** theater, the upstage right pillar where the flute-player is positioned during the performance.

gallery In seventeenth-, eighteenth-, and nineteenth-century theaters, ascending rows of bench seating, usually located opposite the stage on the third level of the auditorium; generally the most inexpensive seats in the theater.

geisha In Japan, a hired female companion valued for artistic accomplishment; legally not classed as a prostitute.

genre Literally, "kind" or "type"; *genre* in literary and dramatic studies refers to the main types of literary form, principally tragedy and comedy. The term can also refer to forms that are more specific to a given historical era, such as **revenge tragedy** or to more specific subgenres of **tragedy** and **comedy,** such as **comedy of manners.**

given circumstances Term used by Constantin Stanislavski to describe the situation a character finds himself or herself in at the opening of the play, which the actor must construct as his first step in building the character toward performance.

gracioso The comic fool of Spanish Golden Age drama, popularized in part by Lope de Vega.

gradas The steeply raked side seats along the side of the patio in a Spanish Golden Age theater, or *corral.*

grave trap A trap door in the floor of the stage, often in the center.

hamartia A term used by Aristotle in *The Poetics* to describe the tragic hero's decisive act, the "error" or "mistake" that brings about the **tragedy.** Sometimes mistranslated as "tragic flaw," a translation that mistakenly changes the meaning of the term from the description of an action to a feature of the character's moral makeup or personality.

hanamichi Elevated gangway extending from the rear of **Kabuki** theater to the stage; major characters use this bridge for their entrances and some scenes are played here as well.

Harlequin The main character of *commedia dell' arte,* and later of English pantomime. Usually a wily schemer, Harlequin was originally played in a patched costume, which became conventionalized as the familiar diamond-covered costume. Harlequin was usually masked and carried a flat bat or paddle.

hashigakari The long bridge from the **mirror room** to the stage of a **Noh** theater.

heroic tragedy A seventeenth-century **genre,** usually on the theme of love vs. honor; associated with Dryden in England, Corneille in France, and Calderón de la Barca in Spain.

hon kyōgen The main play of a **Kabuki** performance, originally lasting from about 7 A.M. until dusk when the theater closed.

hurry door The small door leading offstage from the *atoza,* or upstage area of a **Noh** theater; used by the chorus, the stage assistants, and by dead characters.

hybridization In the theory of **postcolonial** literatures, the use of several styles—typically elements of indigenous or colonized and colonial cultures—in one work, typically to dramatize the cultural politics engrained in colonial habits of representation.

iambic pentameter English verse meter consisting of ten-syllable lines with alternating stressed and unstressed syllables, the first stress falling on the second syllable.

ideology A complex term first used in the eighteenth century to categorize political beliefs and attitudes. Used to mean (1) a body of beliefs, a doctrine; (2) a body of illusory beliefs, a false doctrine; or (3) a socially grounded system for producing beliefs and values, a way of producing meanings or doctrines.

Independent Theater Movement A late-nineteenth-century movement in Europe, in which small theaters gambled on the production of new and unconventional plays—by Ibsen, Shaw, Chekhov—to a small audience, usually outside the theatrical mainstream.

Innamorata/o The attractive young lovers of *commedia dell' arte;* played without masks.

interlude A short play, usually comic, performed during courtly feasts at the English court in the sixteenth century.

jatra   A form of Indian folk theater popular in Bengal, traditionally involving music and singing; the jatra typically centers on the adventures of a central character—Vivek, or "conscience"—and can treat contemporary social issues

jidaimono   The four- to six-act "history" section of a **Kabuki** performance.

jōruri   Performance of narrative and dialogue to the accompaniment of a samisen in Japanese theater; these elements absorbed into **doll theater.**

Kabuki   Form of Japanese popular theater originating in the early seventeenth century. Kabuki tends to encompass both comic and serious elements in elaborate and conventional performances that originally lasted from ten to twelve hours; it includes live acting, narration, music, and singing.

kamyonguk   Dance-drama form practiced in Korea, using colorful costumes, masked actors, and musical accompaniment.

katakiyaku   Villain role in **Kabuki** theater.

kathakali   An elaborate form of music and dance drama that originated in the Kerala province of southern India in the sixteenth century; kathakali uses highly conventionalized movements and hand gestures and has preserved some of the dramatic forms of classical **Sanskrit** theater.

komos   A procession and dance in ancient Greece, sometimes thought to be the origin of comic drama.

kyōgen   Brief farcical play performed as interludes between **Noh** plays.

language   One of the six constituent elements of drama defined by Aristotle in *The Poetics.*

line of business   A conventional or stock "character" type that is the specialty of a given actor; his or her "line of business" might be old men, heavy villains, comic heroines, etc.

Little Negro Theater Movement   A movement in U.S. theater in the 1920s to develop theaters owned and operated by African Americans, playing a dramatic repertory by African American writers.

Little Theater Movement   A movement in the American theater in the early twentieth century akin to the **Independent Theater Movement** in Europe. Little Theaters offered new or noncommercial plays to smaller audiences.

liturgical drama   Short dramatized sections of the Catholic Mass performed as part of the service; may have inspired the more elaborate, nonliturgical **cycle plays.**

loa   A short, typically allegorical play used to introduce a **comedy** or religious play in Spanish Golden Age theater.

machina   The Greek term for the crane used in the ancient theater to raise and lower characters, particularly the gods.

machine plays   Term used principally in seventeenth-century French theater to describe spectacular special-effects extravaganzas, in which the dramatic action—usually drawn from mythological subjects—was merely a pretext for the use of stage machinery.

magic if   Term developed by Constantin Stanislavski to describe the actor's attitude toward a role; to play "as if I were in this situation."

mansions   Structures placed at several locations inside medieval churches as settings for liturgical plays.

masque   A brief, usually symbolic, mythological, or allegorical play, with elaborate scenic effects performed at the English court during the sixteenth and seventeenth centuries; performed both by actors and by courtiers.

melodrama   First used in the late eighteenth century, the term originally referred to highly charged, popular plays using music to reinforce their clear-cut moral action; now refers more generally to plays with a schematic opposition between good and evil, in which good usually prevails.

metatheater   A term used to describe plays that self-consciously comment on the process of theater, or treat the process of theater as a metaphor for off-stage reality. Such plays sometimes use the play-within-the-play device.

Method acting   A technique of acting developed by Constantin Stanislavski at the turn of the twentieth century, which teaches actors to use **emotion memory** to enact the character's feelings persuasively and realistically in performance; method acting became especially popular in the United States in the 1930s, 1940s, and 1950s.

metsukebashira   The "gazing pillar" in a **Noh** theater, where the *shite* looks when delivering his first speech. It is the downstage right pillar.

mie   Exaggerated pose struck for expressive effect by actors in **Kabuki** theater.

mimesis   Greek word for "imitation" used by Aristotle in *The Poetics* to describe the function of art.

mirror room   The waiting room of a **Noh** theater, where actors in costume contemplate their characterization.

mise-en-scène   The "putting onstage" of a play, including the setting, scenery, direction, and action.

mitos   Lyrical plays on Mexican American life devised by Luis Valdez and El Teatro Campesino in the late 1960s and 1970s.

monopoly   The right to exclusive production of the drama.

montage   A technique used in film consisting of a rapid sequence of images.

morality drama   A late-medieval dramatic form using allegorical characters to dramatize moral and ethical problems involved in leading a Christian life.

music   A constituent element of drama as defined by Aristotle in *The Poetics;* Aristotle refers to the flute music that accompanied performance in the ancient Greek theater.

mystery cycles   *See* **cycle plays.**

naturalism   A late nineteenth-century movement that attempted to achieve an objective **verisimilitude** in art—chiefly in theater and literature—by adopting a "scientific" attitude toward its subject matter. Thematically, naturalism emphasizes the role of society, history, and personality in determining the actions of its characters, usually expressed as a conflict between the characters and their environment.

nautical shows   A type of **melodrama** popular in England in the eighteenth and nineteenth centuries on seafaring subjects; in aquatic dramas, the stage was actually flooded.

neoclassical drama   Drama written under the influence of **neoclassicism.**

neoclassicism   A movement throughout Europe in the sixteenth to eighteenth centuries to revive the forms and values of art exemplified by ancient literature; associated with the recovery of Aristotle's *The Poetics* and its translation into prescriptions for the stage.

new comedy   A form originating in the fourth and third centuries BCE, first in Greece and then in Rome. In the plays of Plautus, for instance, new comedy generally concerns a romantic plot involving a conflict between young lovers, an old man, and a tricky servant.

Noh   Japanese classical theater dating from the fourteenth century; the plays are highly poetic dramas given extremely formal production onstage. Noh drama was admired by Yeats and by other modern playwrights.

ode   In Greek drama, a song performed by the chorus while dancing.

old comedy   Satiric social comedy of fifth-century BCE Athens; Aristophanes' plays are the only surviving examples.

onnagata   Women's roles in **Kabuki** theater, all of which are played by men.

onna kabuki   Literally, "women's Kabuki," an early name for **Kabuki** companies, which were composed mainly of women.

orchestra   Literally, the "dancing place," the circular area before the **skene** where the **chorus** performed in ancient Greek theater.

pageant master   The guild officer responsible for gathering funds to finance medieval mystery pageants.

pageant wagons   Wagons carrying the sets for productions of medieval **cycle plays,** on which the plays were performed.

Pantalone   Foolish old man in *commedia dell' arte;* played masked.

pantomime   In general, silent acting using gesture and facial expression. English pantomime—or "panto"—is a spoken form, in which spectacular fairy-tale extravaganzas are performed with music and dance during the Christmas holidays.

parabasis   A choral speech in ancient Greek **comedy** in which the **chorus** comments on contemporary social issues.

parodos   The entrance song of the **chorus** in Greek tragedy.

parterre   The standing area in the auditorium of late seventeenth-century Parisian theaters; the **pit.**

pastiche   Term used by Fredric Jameson to describe the toneless quotation of earlier artistic styles in contemporary (or postmodern) works.

patents   Licenses given by the crown permitting a company to give dramatic performances; often, a patent would give a company or a small number of companies a **monopoly** on dramatic performance.

patent theaters   Theaters given **patents** (or licenses) by the crown for dramatic performance, sometimes holding a monopoly on performance. Charles II of England granted two patents and gave their owners a monopoly on dramatic performance.

patio   The flat central courtyard of a Spanish Golden Age theater, or *corral.*

peripeteia   A term used by Aristotle in *The Poetics* to describe the "reversal" in the action of a **tragedy.**

phallus   A leather phallus worn by male characters in Greek **comedy.**

pit   Floor area immediately in front of the stage in seventeenth- and eighteenth-century theaters.

plot   The sequence of events in a play or narrative; differs from the "story," which encompasses earlier events. Some works have several plots.

pointing   Common practice in the eighteenth-century theater of delivering a famous speech directly to the audience from a downstage position; to "make a point."

polis   A city-state in ancient Greece.

political theater   In conventional usage, theater that seems to question the inequities and injustices of contemporary society. Bertolt Brecht developed a more searching critique of political theater, however, in which the ideology of theatrical representation itself could be seen as the theater's "politics."

postcolonial   While referring specifically to the cultures of a nation that has gained independence, the term *postcolonial* is generally applied more broadly, referring to cultures still negotiating for political freedom, to internally colonized cultures, and to cultures that experience economic or cultural imperialism, even though they may be part of an independent nation-state.

postmodern   A term used to characterize the complex relationship between some contemporary works of art and their modernist forebears. Postmodern works are generally characterized by stylistic "quotation," an invocation and disengagement from history, and the fragmentation of artistic surface.

Prakit   The everyday, prose dialect spoken in **Sanskrit drama,** usually reserved for comic characters, women, and children.

private theaters   In Renaissance England, indoor theaters serving a more privileged audience. Often located on lands within the city limits that were not under city jurisdiction, such as Blackfriars.

prologue   In Greek **drama,** an introductory scene preceding the entrance of the **chorus.** In later usage, an introductory scene not directly part of the main action.

proscenium   An arch over the front of the stage. First used in European theaters in the Renaissance; throughout the eighteenth and nineteenth centuries, theater design gradually eliminated the **apron** that extended in front of the proscenium and decorated the proscenium arch itself, emphasizing its framelike quality.

protagonist   Literally, the "first contestant" in the ancient Greek theater, the term referred to the "first" or main actor competing for a prize. In modern usage, refers to the play's main character.

public theaters   In Renaissance England, large outdoor theaters, usually polygonal in shape, consisting of three-story galleries surrounding an open standing pit and a thrust stage.

quarto   A small-size book format, in which eight pages are printed on a single sheet of paper; the paper is folded twice to make eight pages.

raked stage   A stage that is elevated in the back and lower in the front; common in Europe after the seventeenth century. The raked stage gave rise to the terms "upstage" (toward the back, which was higher) and "downstage" (toward the front, which was lower).

Ramlila and **Raslila**   Forms of traditional found in northern India, Ramlila and Raslila performances generally last several weeks and concern events from the *Ramayana* and *Mahabharata* epic poems.

rasa   An impersonal mood or attitude of contemplation in Hindu philosophy; in **Sanskrit drama,** the play is designed to produce one of eight *rasas* in the audience: erotic, comic, pathetic, furious, heroic, terrible, odious, or marvelous. The basic *rasa* of each play is related to its bhava, or stageable emotion.

realism   A literary and theatrical practice valuing direct imitation or **verisimilitude.** Often associated with **naturalism,** modern realism is sometimes described as the inheritor of naturalism. In practice, realism is usually more concerned with psychological motives, the "inner reality," and less committed to achieving a superficial **verisimilitude** alone.

repertory   A company that performs several plays in rotation throughout a season is a repertory company; the term also refers to a set of plays.

revenge tragedy   A tragic **genre** popular in English Renaissance, usually involving a complicated intrigue plot in which the hero is force to commit murder in order to avenge himself; madness and supernatural agents (ghosts) are also a common feature. Shakespeare's *Hamlet* is the best-known example.

role-doubling   The practice of using one actor to play more than one part.

romance   A modern term used to define idealized narratives and sometimes applied to the idealized comedies written by Shakespeare late in his career, especially *The Winter's Tale* and *The Tempest.*

romantic comedy   Comic form centering on the romance between two lovers, or between several sets of lovers. Romantic comedy typically begins with some unreasonable impediment to the lovers' union, and when after a complicated series of events the obstacle is overcome, the play ends in marriage.

rōnin   *Samurai* warriors who have been disgraced and outcast from society; "men adrift."

ruido   A "noise" play or violent **comedy** in Spanish Golden Age theater.

Rupaka   The "major drama" of classical **Sanskrit** theater.

sainete   Deriving from the *genero chico* of Spain, a short, sometimes satirical play often used for interludes or *entremeses,* it was widely used for plays on regional or local-color themes in Argentina in the nineteenth century.

samisen   Three-stringed instrument that is both plucked and struck as accompaniment to narration in *jōruri.* In the late sixteenth century, became instrumental in the **doll theater.**

samurai   Warrior class of feudal Japan; *samurai* lords both patronized **Noh** playwrights and companies, and provided the code of conduct informing many **Noh, doll theater,** and **Kabuki** plays.

Sanskrit   An ancient Indo-European language; once a spoken language, by the modern era it had become mainly a written language reserved for academic and religious purposes. In **Sanskrit drama,** Sanskrit is reserved for elevated scenes and characters, while **Prakrit,** the everyday dialect, is spoken by other characters.

Sanskrit drama   The **drama** of ancient India, particularly the plays of its "Golden Age" (second to ninth centuries).

sarugaku-no   Form of dance, role-playing, and acrobatics popular in Japan in the eleventh and twelfth centuries; said to be the progenitor of **Noh** theater.

saruwaka   Comic roles in **Kabuki** theater, performed by men.

satyr play   A brief, rugged **comedy** performed by actors in satyr costumes (half-man, half-goat) after the performance of a tragic **trilogy** at the **City Dionysia;** usually on mythological subjects.

scaena   Three-story stage house behind the stage in the Roman theater, facing the audience. Elaborately decorated with columns, panels, and porticos.

scenic unity   The practice of harmonizing acting style, costumes, and sets to create the illusion of a single, unified environment on the stage.

sewamono   "Domestic plays" of the Japanese **doll theater.**

sharers   Actors and playwrights in the English Renaissance theater who, as investors in the company, took a share of the profits; they were responsible for building or leasing a theater and were legally liable for the company's actions.

shimpa   A movement in Japanese theater beginning in the late nineteenth century to adapt European **drama** to Japanese style and subject matter.

shingeki   A movement in twentieth-century Japanese theater to import the style and techniques of European realistic theater into the Japanese theater.

shite   Principal actor in **Noh** theater.

shitebashira   The upstage right pillar in a **Noh** theater, near the *hashigakari,* where the *shite* delivers his opening speech.

shogun   Hereditary military leader of Japan from the twelfth through the nineteenth centuries; the *shogun* was the most important of the *samurai* (warrior) class, composed of *daimyo* (feudal lords) and lesser *samurai.*

skene   A low building behind the **orchestra** in the Greek theater facing the audience; possibly used for changing costumes or storage.

social realism   A form of modern realistic **drama** emphasizing social messages and themes; social realism was the official **genre** approved by the Communist party in the Soviet Union after the revolution.

sociétaires   Leading actors and shareholders in the Comédie Française; upon serving twenty years, *sociétaires* were entitled to a pension.

soliloquy   A speech delivered by a character alone onstage, speaking to himself or herself, or to the audience.

soubrette   A stock character in **drama:** a young, pert female character.

spectacle   Aristotle's term for the visual element of theatrical performance in *The Poetics.*

subtext   A term first elaborated by Constantin Stanislavski, *subtext* refers to the unspoken motive for a given line or speech, what the character wants to get or to do by saying the line. It is sometimes now used more generally to suggest a text's underlying sense or meaning.

surrealist theater   A movement originating in Paris in the 1920s attempting to represent subconscious experience directly in art.

symbolist theater   A European movement of the later nineteenth and early twentieth centuries in reaction to **realism** and **naturalism.** Symbolist theater attempted to dramatize more poetic or metaphorical situations, often using unusual stage settings and ethereal dramatic action and language.

Syndicate   A group of investors who developed a massive organization for theatrical production in the United States in the late nineteenth century.

tableau/tableaux   (pl.) A motionless grouping of actors to represent a "picture" of a dramatic scene; sometimes called *tableau vivant,* a "living picture."

tableaux vivants   *See* **tableau;** *tableaux vivants* is the plural form of *tableau vivant.*

taburetes   The raised and fenced rows of benches near the stage in a Spanish Golden Age theater, or *corral.*

tachiyaku   Leading male role in **Kabuki** theater.

tertulia   An upper **gallery** occupied by church officials and intellectuals in a Spanish Golden Age theater, or *corral.*

theater   A structure built for the performance of drama; also refers to the institution of dramatic performance.

theater in the round   The presentation of a play in an arena setting, in which the audience sits on all sides of the stage area, but is separate from the playing space itself.

Theater of Cruelty   Term used by Antonin Artaud to describe his nonrepresentational, mystical, mythological theater.

Theater of the Absurd   A type of late twentieth-century **theater** and **drama,** characterized by a relatively abstract setting, and arbitrary and illogical action. It is sometimes said to express the "human condition" in a basic or "existential" way. The term was first coined by Martin Esslin.

theme   A term used to describe a consistent kind of meaning asserted by a work of literature.

tiring house   A structure at the rear of the stage in the Renaissance English **public theater,** where actors would change costumes (attire themselves), and from which they would enter the stage.

tragedy   Originating in the classical Greek theater, tragedy generally refers to serious drama, taking a central character's conflict with himself or herself, with society, or with god as its subject. Aristotle first described tragedy in his *The Poetics,* and tragedy has undergone almost continual redefinition.

tragicomedy   In the English Renaissance, a term describing a dramatic form: a play beginning like a **tragedy,** but ending happily, like a **comedy.** In modern usage, the term refers most often to a play's tone or attitude: a play that is ironic, both serious and absurd, leaning toward black comedy or tragic farce.

traveling song   Song sung in **Noh** theater by the *waki* during his first entrance; it announces who the *waki* is and where he is going.

trilogy   Three tragedies produced in sequence as part of the tragic competition in the **City Dionysia** of ancient Greece. Plays were not necessarily on the same subject.

trope   An enlargement on Catholic liturgy, through song or dramatic performance.

tsure   Followers of the *shite* and *waki* in **Noh** theater.

Upa-rupaka   The "minor drama" of classical **Sanskrit** theater.

verisimilitude   Refers to the extent to which the drama or stage setting appears to copy the superficial appearance of life offstage.

villancicos   Religious songs, like English carols, performed in Spain and its colonies.

wakashugata   Adolescent male roles in **Kabuki** theater.

wakashu kabuki   Literally, "boys' Kabuki"; the term refers to **Kabuki** companies composed mainly of adolescent boys, many of whom were prostitutes; banned by the Tokugawa shogunate in 1652.

waki   The secondary actor in **Noh** theater, who responds to the *shite*.

wakibashira   The downstage left pillar in a **Noh** theater, where the *waki* is usually positioned at the opening of the play.

waki-za   A narrow stage area along the stage-left side of a **Noh** theater stage used for seating the chorus.

wayang kulit   Shadow-puppet theater of Java concerning characters and events drawn from the *Ramayana* and *Mahabharata,* the epic poems of classical India. Performances generally begin early in the evening and last until dawn; audiences sit on both sides of a screen, against which puppeteers cast the shadows of elaborate, flat puppets, whose actions are accompanied by dialogue, narration, song, and music.

well-made play   A form of drama popularized in the nineteenth century, especially in France. The plot usually turns on the revelation of a secret and includes a character who explains and moralizes the action of the play to others; the plot is often relentlessly coincidental, often mechanically so.

wings and backdrop   Scenic practice developed in Italy and exported to France and England in the seventeenth century, using staggered painted flats in a receding series, and a painted central backcloth to depict the setting of the play.

yaro kabuki   The "adult male Kabuki" common in Japan today; the yaro kabuki replaced the boys' and women's **Kabuki** that were popular before such companies were banned in the early seventeenth century.

yugen   The Japanese term for the mysterious beauty, grace, and repose that are the goal of **Noh** performance.

yūgo   Professional prostitute in classical Japan; distinct from *geisha,* a hired companion valued for artistic accomplishment.

yūgo kabuki   Literally, "prostitutes' Kabuki," an early term for **Kabuki** companies, which were composed mainly of women.

Zanni   Wily and clever comic characters, usually clowns or servants, in *commedia dell' arte;* played masked.

zen   Term in Buddhist thought for a contemplative attitude that is disengaged from worldly desire.

Credits

Text Credits

Aeschylus, "Agamemnon" and "The Libation Bearers" from THE ORESTEIA, translated by Robert Fagles. Copyright © 1966, 1967, 1975 by Robert Fagles. Used by permission of Viking Penguin, a division of Penguin Group (USA) Inc.

Aeschylus, "The Eumenides" translated from THE COMPLETE GREEK TRAGEDIES, D. Grene & R. Lattimore, eds. Used by permission of The University of Chicago Press.

Aristophanes, "Lysistrata" trans. by Donald Sutherland. Copyright © 1959, 1961 by the Chandler Publishing Company. Used by permission of Addison-Wesley Publishers.

Aristotle, THE POETICS, trans. Gerald Else, pp. 15-47. Copyright © 1967 University of Michigan Press. Used with permission.

Antonin Artaud, excerpt from THE THEATER AND ITS DOUBLE, translated by Mary Caroline Richards. Copyright © 1958 by Grove Press, Inc. Used by permission of Grove/Atlantic, Inc.

W.H. Auden, "For the Time Being" from THE COLLECTED POEMS. Copyright 1944 and renewed © 1972 by W.H. Auden. Used by permission of Random House, Inc.

Amiri Baraka / LeRoi Jones, "Dutchman" from DUTCHMAN from SELECTED PLAYS & PROSE OF AMIRI BARAKA. Reprinted by permission of SLL/Sterling Lord Literistic, Inc. Copyright © by Amiri Baraka.

Amiri Baraka / LeRoi Jones, excerpt from THE REVOLUTIONARY THEATRE. Reprinted by permission of SLL/Sterling Lord Literistic, Inc. Copyright © by Amiri Baraka.

Samuel Beckett, ENDGAME. Copyright © 1958 by Grove Press, Inc. Renewed © 1986 by Samuel Beckett. Used by permission of Grove/Atlantic, Inc.

David Bevington, footnotes on "The Tempest" from THE COMPLETE WORKS OF WILLIAM SHAKESPEARE, ed. David Bevington. Copyright © 1980, 1973 by Scott Foresman & Company. Reprinted by permission of Pearson Educational Publishers.

Homi Bhabha, "Of Mimicry and Man: The Ambivalence of Colonial Discourse" from *October*, Vol. 28, Spring 1984, published by MIT Press. Copyright © 1984 by Homi Bhabha. Used with permission.

Augusto Boal, from THEATRE OF THE OPPRESSED, pp. 120-131, 132. Translation copyright © 1979 by Charles A. McBride & Maria-Odilia Leal McBride. Originally published in Spanish as *Teatro de Oprimido* in 1974, copyright © by Augusto Boal and in English by Urizen Books in 1979. Published by Theatre Communications Group. Used by permission of Theatre Communications Group.

Dion Boucicault, "The Octoroon" from SELECTED PLAYS OF DION BOUCICAULT. Copyright © 1987. Used with permission from The Catholic University of America Press, Washington D.C.

Photo and Illustration Credits

Index